CondorTravel
Discover
the Best Kept Secret...
Latin America
More than 33 years of experience in the industry.
One-stop-shopping with our regional netwotk.
Tailor-made Programs
Luxury Journeys
Special Interest Tours
Regional Guaranteed Departures
Community & Experiential Tours
Adventure & Multi-activity
Cruise Operations
Mlce: meetings, incentives, congresses and events
ISO
Condor Travel
info@condortravel.com
www.condortravel.com

Footprint story

It was 1921

Ireland had just been partitioned, the British miners were striking for more pay and the federation of British industry had an idea. Exports were booming in South America – how about a handbook for businessmen trading in that far away continent? The Anglo-South American Handbook was born that year, written by W Koebel, the most prolific writer on Latin America of his day.

1924

Two editions later the book was 'privatized' and in 1924, in the hands of Royal Mail, the steamship company for South America, it became The South American Handbook, subtitled 'South America in a nutshell'. This annual publication became the 'bible' for generations of travellers to South America and remains so to this day. In the early days travel was by sea and the Handbook gave all the details needed for the long voyage from Europe. What to wear for dinner; how to arrange a cricket match with the Cable & Wireless staff on the Cape Verde Islands and a full account of the journey from Liverpool up the Amazon to Manaus: 5898 miles without changing cabin!

1939

As the continent opened up, the South American Handbook reported the new Pan Am flying boat services, and the fortnightly airship service from Rio to Europe on the Graf Zeppelin. For reasons still unclear but with extraordinary determination, the annual editions continued through the Second World War.

1970s

Many more people discovered South America and the backpacking trail started to develop. All the while the Handbook was gathering fans, including literary vagabonds such as Paul Theroux and Graham Greene (who once sent some updates addressed to "The publishers of the best travel guide in the world, Bath, England").

1990s

During the 1990s the company set about developing a new travel guide series using this legendary title as the flagship. By 1997 there were over a dozen guides in the series and the Footprint imprint was launched.

2000s

The series grew quickly and there were soon Footprint travel guides covering more than 150 countries. In 2004, Footprint launched its first thematic guide: *Surfing Europe*, packed with colour photographs, maps and charts. This was followed by further thematic guides such as *Diving the World, Snowboarding the World, Body and Soul escapes, Travel with Kids and European City Breaks.*

2010

Today we continue the traditions of the last 89 years that have served legions of travellers so well. We believe that these help to make Footprint guides different. Our policy is to use authors who are genuine experts who write for independent travellers; people possessing a spirit of adventure, looking to get off the beaten track.

If your system is jaded, South America will uplift your senses with the tropical sun rising over a palm-fringed beach, or a bracing wind blowing off the southern ice fields. Light can be blinding on the high altitude salt flats, or dense and green in the rainforest. The gentle scent of ripe guava fills the countryside, but the fire of chili from that innocent-looking jar will electrify your taste buds.

As capybara wade through wetland shallows in the Pantanal, the spectacled bear struggles for survival in secret places in the Andes. Penguins congregate in the lee of glaciers, while tiny swifts dart through mighty waterfalls and their eternal rainbows. Volcanoes come to life and the earth trembles, yet elsewhere there are ancient, immovable tabletop plateaux. But surpassing all is the Amazon Basin, the earth's greatest jungle, where the immensity of the trees and the smallest details of the wildlife are truly amazing.

You can explore the cities of prehispanic civilizations and the churches of colonial times, or you can immerse yourself in the present with its celebrations and its social dilemmas. Where past and present mix, there are festivals, crafts and gastronomy, from the humble potato in its umpteen varieties to the most sophisticated of wines.

If you are looking for something more active, throw yourself off a giant sand dune into a lake, or climb the highest mountain. Walk in the treetops of the rainforest, at eye level with birds and monkeys. Help homeless street kids gain a better life, or learn the martial arts of slaves. Dance in an Andean village square to a solo violin, or in a warehouse-sized club to techno-guitarrada en Belém. Whatever South America inspires you to do, you will find that there is no limit to the passion that it fires within you.

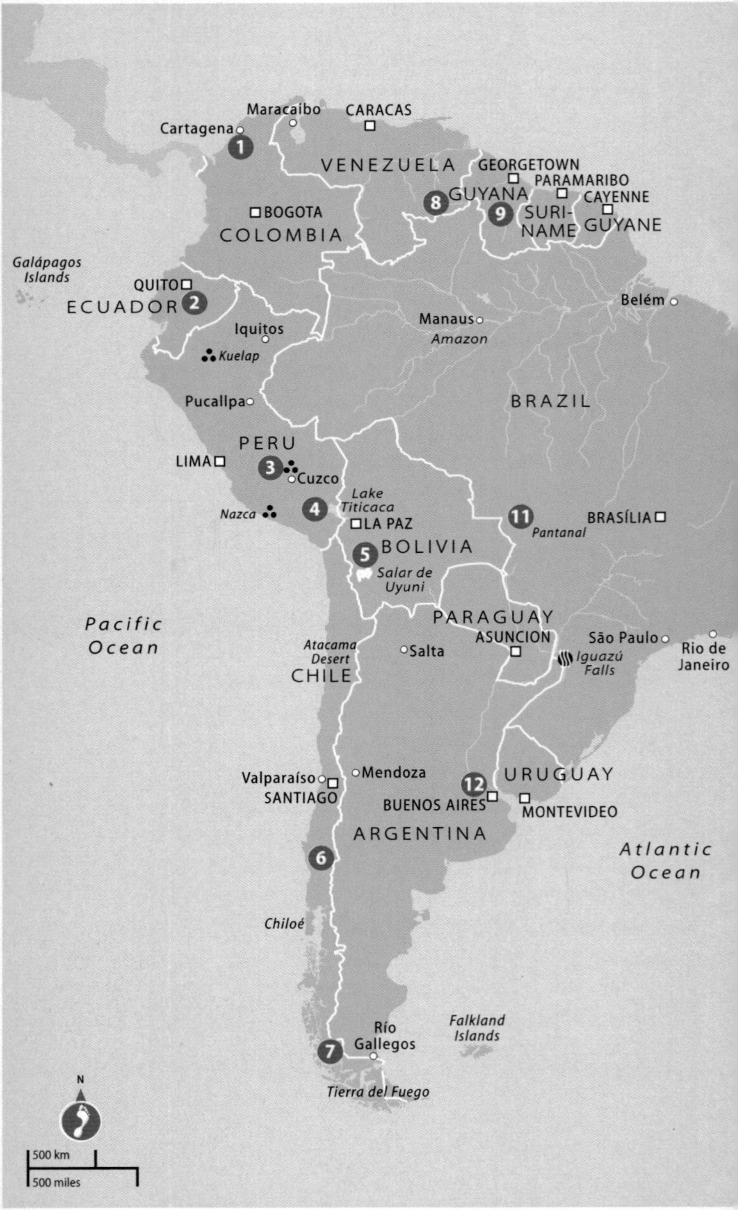
Maracaibo
CARACAS
Cartagena
1
VENEZUELA
GEORGETOWN
PARAMARIBO
CAYENNE
8
GUYANA
9
SURI-
NAME
GUYANE
BOGOTA
COLOMBIA
Galápagos
Islands
QUITO
ECUADOR
2
Belém
Manaus
Amazon
Iquitos
Kuelap
Pucallpa
BRAZIL
PERU
LIMA
3
Cuzco
Lake
Titicaca
Nazca
4
LA PAZ
11
Pantanal
BRASÍLIA
5
BOLIVIA
Salar de
Uyuni
Pacific
Ocean
PARAGUAY
ASUNCION
Atacama
Desert
Salta
São Paulo
Rio de
Janeiro
Iguazú
Falls
CHILE
Valparaíso
Mendoza
URUGUAY
SANTIAGO
12
BUENOS AIRES
MONTEVIDEO
ARGENTINA
Atlantic
Ocean
6
Chiloé
Río
Gallegos
Falkland
Islands
7
Tierra del Fuego
N
500 km
500 miles

South America highlights

See colour maps at back of book

1 Cartagena is a fine colonial city, with a history of piracy and slavery. ▸▸ page 938.

2 Herds of wild horses and llamas beneath a perfect snow-capped volcano of Cotopaxi. ▸▸ page 1091.

3 Machu Picchu is South America's premier archaeological attraction, with the gringo capital of Cuzco close by. ▸▸ page 1454.

4 Lake Titicaca is the world's highest navigable lake, with reed boats, island communities and incomparable light. ▸▸ page 1405.

5 Salar de Uyuni is the world's largest salt lake, surrounded by red and green lakes, flamingos and volcanoes. ▸▸ page 322.

6 In Chile's Lake District beautiful sheets of water are overlooked by forests and volcanoes: perfect for all

7 The Torres del Paine offer hardcor trekking at the very bottom of the Andes. ▸▸ page 865.

8 Canaima is a strange, lost world o table-top mountains, savannahs and th world's highest waterfall, Angel Falls. ▸▸ page 1660.

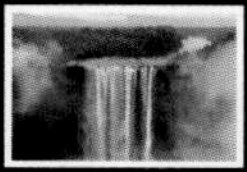

9 Kaieteur Falls, unspoilt and isolated, where the Potaro River dives 228 m off the edge of the jungle. ▸▸ page 1688.

10 Salvador, Brazil's party city, is a World Heritage Site with colonial architecture and an African soul. ▸▸ page 532.

11 Brazil's Pantanal is one of the bes places to see wildlife in South Americ ▸▸ page 665.

12 Buenos Aires is the city of tango, fashion, steak, nostalgia and wine

Top Buenos Aires.
Mid left Kaietur Falls.
Mid right Salvador.
Right Angel Falls.
Far right top Pantanal.
Far Right bottom Torres del Paine.

Far left Lake Titicaca.
Top right Salar deUyuni.
Left Cartagena.
Mid right Cuzco.
Bottom left Lake District, Chile.
Bottom right Cotopaxi.

Some 60 metres high and with a 5-km face, Perito Moreno is one of the few glaciers in the world which continues to grow. As it descends from Patagonian mountains, striking blue icebergs roar as they break off into the waters of Lago Argentino.

Best wildlife experiences

Manu Biosphere Reserve, Peru
Manu, in Peru's southeastern jungle, is one of the largest conservation units on earth, with an unsurpassed diversity of rainforest flora and fauna. Rising from 200 to 4,100 m above sea level, the reserve's oxbow lakes are home to giant otters and black caiman while in its lowland forests are jaguar, ocelot and tapir. There are 13 species of primate and almost 1,000 species of bird.

Iwokrama Rainforest Program, Guyana
Guyana is one of the final frontiers of Latin America, with few visitors. The Iwokrama Rainforest Program is a pioneering project for research and sustainable development, one of the best places to catch a glimpse of the elusive jaguar.

Galápagos Islands
The joy of the Galápagos for the visitor is the closeness of the animals. On live-aboard cruisers you travel from island to island, seeing the different birds, reptiles and marine mammals which live on or beside the waters of this volcanic archipelago. The albatross, boobies, marine iguanas and giant tortoises have no instinctive fear of humans. Add to that the chance to snorkel in the icy seas with seals, sea lions and hammerhead sharks you have an unforgettable experience.

Emas National Park, Brazil
Jewel of Brazil's endangered cerrado ecosystem, Emas National Park presents excellent wildlife-viewing opportunities and remains a stronghold of the seldom-seen

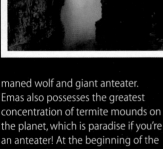

maned wolf and giant anteater. Emas also possesses the greatest concentration of termite mounds on the planet, which is paradise if you're an anteater! At the beginning of the rainy season (September- October) the termite larvae glow and the night time savanna lights up with its own bioluminescent response to the Manhattan skyline.

Noel Kempff Mercado National Park, Bolivia

In Noel Kempff Mercado National Park, Bolivia's northeastern wilderness, waterfalls cascade from the cliffs of the ancient Huanchaca Plateau. This could have been another model for Conan Doyle's Lost World and even today reaching Noel Kempff is an adventure. Inaccessibility has preserved some of South America's rarest and most impressive flora and fauna, truly, the land that time forgot.

Valdés Peninsula, Argentina

Experience a close encounter with the largest mammals on the planet, whale watching off Argentina's Valdés Peninsula. Southern right whales breed in the Patagonian waters every year, and the almost uninhabited area is home to a host of other wildlife.

Rio Carnival

A year in preparation, a multi-million dollar enterprise, the annual carnival is a lavish display of costume, music and dance. Samba schools, or blocos, proudly defend their individuality with each new song and accompanying performance. You can join a bloco (if you pay) and experience the heat of competition, or soak up the atmosphere from the sidelines.

Día de la Tradición, Argentina

10 November is the day chosen to celebrate Argentina's gaucho heritage. The home of the Día de la Tradición is San Antonio de Areco in Buenos Aires province, a town already associated with the cowboy way of life. The festival stretches for a week around the 10th with displays of horsemanship, parades, gaucho games, music and dance.

Día de Quito, Ecuador

From 1 to 6 December, the capital of Ecuador celebrates its founding with elaborate parades, bullfights, performances and music in the streets.

Semana Santa, Ayacucho, Peru

Many places in Peru make 'paintings' on the streets out of flower petals and

coloured sawdust to be trampled and destroyed by the feet of participants in religious parades. The most famous are the ones in Ayacucho. The celebrations begin on the Friday before Palm Sunday. In Semana Santa there are daily parades and nightly candlelit processions leading up to the solemn events of Good Friday.

Oruru Carnival, Bolivia

Carnival in a different style, the main feature of Oruro's pre-Lenten festival is La Diablada, the dance of the devils, performed by miners and representing the struggles between the forces of good and evil. Its most striking element is the grotesque, elaborate masks of the dancers. Celebrations take place over several days. Some are pious and private, other riotous and public, which include spectacular displays, competitions and a día del agua in which water and foam are sprayed at all and sundry.

Q'Olloriti, Peru

The 'Snow Star' festival involves a pilgrimage to a glacier 4,700 m up on Mount Ausangate, south of Cuzco. It starts 58 days after Easter Sunday and is not for the fainthearted. Nevertheless, thousands of people trek to the sacred ice, which they take home to present miniatures of the possessions and endeavours they wish to succeed in the coming year.

Elegant baroque churches with beautiful interiors dominate the cobbled streets of Ouro Preto in Brazil, the legacy of colonial riches amassed from gold and gemstones mined in the hills of Minas Gerais.

Contents

↘3 Introduction
4 Highlights map
12 Best wildlife experiences
14 Best festivals

↘19 Essentials
20 Planning your trip
23 Sport and activities
28 Responsible travel
31 Getting there
34 Getting around
38 Sleeping
39 Eating
40 Shopping
40 Essentials A-Z

↘55 Argentina
58 Planning your trip
67 Buenos Aires and the Pampas
116 West of Buenos Aires
149 Northwest Argentina
176 The Northeast
197 Lake District
224 Patagonia
254 Tierra del Fuego

↘267 Bolivia
270 Planning your trip
277 La Paz and around
301 Lake Titicaca
312 The Yungas
315 Southwest Bolivia
332 Central and Southern Highlands
357 Northern Lowlands
366 Santa Cruz and Eastern Lowlands

↘387 Brazil
390 Planning your trip
399 Rio de Janeiro
451 São Paulo
473 Minas Gerais and Espírito Santo
497 Southern Brazil
526 Foz do Iguaçu
532 Salvador de Bahia
564 Recife and northeast coast
594 Fortaleza and north coast
614 The Amazon
640 Amazon frontiers
651 Brasília and Goiás
665 The Pantanal

↘685 Chile
688 Planning your trip
696 Santiago and around
722 Valparaíso and around
736 North of Santiago
750 Far north
778 Central Valley
787 Lake District
819 Puerto Montt and Chiloé
833 Carretera Austral
852 Far south
876 Chilean Pacific Islands

↘885 Colombia
888 Planning your trip
898 Bogotá
921 Bogotá to the Venezuelan border
938 Cartagena and the north coast
976 Medellín and Chocó
988 La Zona Cafetera
998 Cali and the Cauca Valley
1005 Popayán, Tierradentro and San Agustín
1017 Southern Colombia

→

↘1025 Ecuador
1028 Planning your trip
1036 Quito
1074 Northern Ecuador
1091 Cotopaxi, Latacunga and Quilotoa
1104 Baños and Riobamba
1119 Cuenca and around
1130 Cuenca to the Peruvian border
1139 Guayaquil and south to Peru
1152 Pacific lowlands
1174 The Oriente
1190 Galápagos Islands

↘1209 Paraguay
1212 Planning your trip
1217 Asunción
1230 Región Oriental: East of Asunción
1237 Región Oriental: South of Asunción
1243 North of Asunción
1247 The Chaco

↘1253 Peru
1256 Planning your trip
1266 Lima
1297 Huaraz and the Cordilleras
1317 North coast
1350 Northern Highlands
1370 South coast
1382 Arequipa and the far south
1405 Lake Titicaca
1419 Cuzco
1446 Sacred Valley of the Incas
1464 Central Highlands
1486 Amazon Basin

↘1511 Uruguay
1514 Planning your trip
1518 Montevideo
1532 Western Uruguay
1545 Eastern Uruguay

↘1559 Venezuela
1562 Planning your trip
1570 Caracas
1588 West from Caracas
1609 Mérida and around
1626 Los Llanos and Amazonas
1631 East coast
1655 Canaima and the Orinoco Delta

↘1677 Guianas
1680 Guyana
1702 Suriname
1717 Guyane

↘1729 Falkland Islands
1730 Planning your trip
1735 Stanley and around
1744 Beyond the Falklands

↘1747 Background
1748 Pre-independence history
1754 Post-independence history
1779 Government
1781 People
1786 Land and environment
1794 Culture

↘1811 Footnotes
1812 Index
1821 Advertisers' index
1822 About the author
1822 Acknowledgements
1823 Travellers' letters
1824 Credits

Essentials

Contents

20 Planning your trip
- 20 Where to go
- 21 Itineraries
- 22 When to go

23 Sport and activities

28 Responsible travel

31 Getting there
- 31 Air
- 34 Sea

34 Getting around
- 34 Land
- 37 Boat
- 38 Maps and guidebooks

38 Sleeping

39 Eating

40 Shopping

40 Essentials A-Z

Footprint features

- 29 How big is your footprint?
- 35 Packing for South America
- 37 Carnet de passages
- 38 Sleeping price codes
- 40 Eating price codes
- 44 Second languages and anomalies

Planning your trip

South America is a magnificently varied part of the world and tremendously hospitable. It is a tantalizing mixture of enticing images and ambiguous press reports, inspiring an air of mystery and a certain amount of trepidation. In common with many other places, South America suffers from meteorological, geological and social uncertainties. Within that context you will find some of the most dramatic landscapes on earth, biological diversity in a range of habitats, historical monuments of strength and elegance and a deep cultural resilience.

Getting around

South America is a big place, so it's important not to be too ambitious on a first visit. Decide what type of holiday you want and research which countries offer what you are interested in. Then work out an itinerary in which the places you want to see and the distance between them coincides with the amount of time you have available. Over the years a Gringo Trail has become firmly established, a network of places to which foreigners tended to gravitate for reasons of shared interests, lower prices, safety in numbers and so on. Some of these places have passed into legend, others are still going strong. New places are added as fashions change or transport links are opened.

By plane you can visit many places and airpasses, both regional and domestic, will reduce the cost of flying a little, but if your travel budget (or carbon consciousness) prohibits air tickets, bus is the best alternative. Buses are rarely the stand-in-the-aisle with the chickens and the soldiers bone-shakers of lore. Many are comfortable and mechanically sound, easing the passage of long or mountainous journeys, but you should build the length of the ride into your schedule. Trains cannot be relied on as a main means of transport as most are for tourists and are highly priced at that. Car hire is also expensive and driving can be tiring, but those who enjoy the independence can do well and many bring their own cars or motorcycles. Cycling is also popular.

Where to go

The Andes

Down the length of South America runs the Andean mountain chain, which starts in the north overlooking the Caribbean and ends in the south in the fabulous towers and spires of the Chaitén Massif and the Torres del Paine National Park. Condors patrol its deep canyons and strata of rocks display colours you never knew existed in stone. Out of Lake Titicaca, the highest navigable lake in the world, strode the Inca dynasty, founding Cuzco, which has metamorphosed into the gringo capital of South America. Further south, beautiful lakes in Chile and Argentina shelter beneath snowcapped peaks. On their shores are resorts for summer watersports, fishing and winter skiing. Unlike its treeless Argentine counterpart, Chilean Patagonia is a wet and windy confusion of fjords, channels and ancient woodlands.

Forests and wetlands

In the heart of the continent, the Amazon Basin contains 20% of the world's plant and bird species, 10% of the mammals and an inestimable number of insects. In the waters live some 2,000 species of fish, plus shy giant otters, caiman and two species of freshwater dolphin. There are trees that strangle their neighbours, palms with a million thorns, plants that heal and vines that will blow your mind. Stalking in the undergrowth is the mythical jaguar, whose influence has spread through almost every religion that has come into contact with the rainforest. On its perimeter, cattle and cowboys share the land with wild birds and animals in the llanos of the

Orinoco and the wetlands of the Brazilian/Bolivian Pantanal, while mysterious ecosystems hide on table top mountains on the Venezuela/Brazil border and in Bolivia.

Islands and beaches

On the Pacific, at islands such as the Ballestas (Peru) and Isla de la Plata (Ecuador) you can see much marine life, but the destination par excellence is the Galápagos. On the peaks of massive volcanoes, which jut into the ocean, albatross, boobies, giant tortoises and iguanas have evolved with little instinctive fear of man, a paradise for naturalists. Meanwhile, the Atlantic coast of Brazil, all 7,408 km of it, is an endless succession of beaches, in wooded coves, dotted with islands in the south, palm tree- and dune-fringed in the north.

Itineraries

Three to four weeks

While three to four weeks will give plenty of time to do some exploration in any of the countries of South America, there are many itineraries covering more than one. Starting in Buenos Aires, where you will want to spend a couple of days to attune yourself, you can head west to the wine and adventure sports region of Mendoza, then cross the Andes to Valparaíso on the Pacific. Alternatively, go north to Iguazú Falls and venture into Brazil or Paraguay. Across the Río de la Plata is Uruguay, with its beaches and *estancias*. If you fly south there are many options for flitting between Argentina and Chile, in the Lake District, in the magnificent trekking territory of Torres del Paine and the Chaitén Massif and Tierra del Fuego. Northwest Argentina, with Salta as a base, opens up opportunities for crossing the Altiplano into Chile's Atacama or into southwest Bolivia with its multicoloured lakes and volcanoes. Another ideal base is Cuzco, for Machu Picchu and Peru's southeastern jungle, the circuit around Arequipa and the Nazca Lines and the route around or across Lake Titicaca to Bolivia. Further up the Andean chain, northern Peru, with its pre-Inca archaeological sites and beaches, combines well with Ecuador's avenue of volcanoes and easily reachable Amazonian jungles and Pacific beaches. Brazil, often dubbed a continent in itself, has more than enough for a month-long trip: combinations of Rio de Janeiro, Salvador, the beaches north and south, the dunes of the Lençóis Maranhenses, the Amazon, the Pantanal wetlands. But just as Iguazú fits with Argentina, so it does with southeastern Brazilian trips. At the other extreme, from Manaus on the Amazon a road heads north to the Sabana Grande of Venezuela, with its tabletop mountains and waterfalls, and on to the Caribbean. Caracas and Maracaibo are further gateways, for Venezuela's coast and the northernmost reaches of the Andean chain, leading into Colombia and its colonial jewel on the sea, Cartagena.

Six to eight weeks

To see a variety of South American destinations in less than a month, some flights will be inevitable because of the distances involved. With more time, you need not leave the ground for the above suggestions and you can add on more destinations, particularly those that require a set number of days. For instance, to appreciate fully wildlife-watching in the Iberá marshes in northeast Argentina, or staying on an *estancia* in the Pampas, Patagonia or Uruguay, allow a couple of days. Climbing in the Andes (eg Aconcagua) and long-distance trekking in the Lake District or Patagonia will take up a good four days minimum (and may require acclimatization). Likewise, the many trails in the Inca heartland. Other good trekking options include many national parks in Ecuador, the Andes in Colombia and Venezuela, and the Chapada Diamantina in Brazil. Any boat journey on the Amazon takes a few days, while trips to jungle lodges, with accompanying river journeys, also require about four days. Shorter wildlife tours can be found in the Venezuelan Llanos. The basic Salar de Uyuni tour in Bolivia is three days. From the highlands of Bolivia heading east, the steep valleys of the Yungas offer welcome warmth before the Amazonian lowlands and an array of national parks: Madidi, Amboró and Noel Kempff Mercado. From the eastern city of Santa Cruz, take the train to Brazil and the Pantanal, or the new roads across the Chaco into Paraguay. From Asunción, Iguazú and the neighbouring Jesuit missions are not too far. In the north, the Guianas have some of the least spoiled swathes of rainforest, as well as savannahs and waterfalls. On their own they can be visited in under a month, but they fit well with northern Brazil, especially Belém and the mouth of the Amazon. Don't forget that if your Spanish or Portuguese needs some encouragement, a week's intensive course is a good introduction to your trip.

Three months

In three months you can travel the length of the Andes, with plenty of side trips along the way. Some highlights might include San Agustín and Popayán in Colombia; Otavalo in northern Ecuador, with visits to birdwatching lodges; Quito and the volcanoes to the south, plus the Quilotoa circuit. Preferable crossings into Peru are at Macará for Piura and on to the fascinating archaeological and bird watching zone at Chiclayo, or south of Loja and Vilcabamba through to Chachapoyas, another area of prehispanic riches. It is simplest to take the coastal Panamerican Highway to Trujillo, then head up into the mountains and the trekking mecca of Huaraz. Spend a few days to recharging your batteries in Lima then take the train up to Huancayo and the Central Andes, or the coast road to Nazca. Either way, your goal will be Cuzco, the Sacred Valley and a rainforest trip to Manu or Tambopata, before heading into Bolivia via Lake Titicaca. An Andean journey would then pass the Salar de Uyuni before descending to Northwest Argentina or the Chilean Pacific deserts. By the time you reach the far south (time this for the warmer months) meandering through channels and fjords, boating on lakes in ancient forests, scaling mountain passes and taking remote border crossings between Chile and Argentina will easily fill the three months. You can also cross South America from east to west. The Amazon river is a major transport route as far as Iquitos in Peru, from where you can head further via Pucallpa to the Central Highlands and over to the Pacific at Pisco or Lima, or to the Cordillera Blanca via La Unión. Alternatively boats from Iquitos go to Yurimaguas for the climb up to Chachapoyas and on to Chiclayo. A more southerly route would take in some of the new Interoceánica road through the far western state of Acre, to Puerto Maldonado in Peru (for Tambopata) and then to Cuzco. If you are not so keen on being on the road for three months, a good way to break the travelling is to do a month's volunteering.

When to go

It all depends on latitude; for example, the far south of Argentina and Chile is busiest in the southern hemisphere summer, December- February; in winter, June-August, it is cold and snow and rain can disrupt transport. The further north you go the more the seasons fall into wet and dry. The Peruvian and Bolivian Andes are dry (and very cold at night) April-October, the rest of the year is rainy. The sierras of Ecuador and Colombia are wet February-May and October-November. East of the Andes is wet November-April, wettest March-May in the Amazon Basin. Each chapter details the intricacies of the weather, but changes in world climate and periodic phenomena such as El Niño can play havoc with the general rules.

Sport and activities

Climbing

ⓘ *Climbing operators are listed in the relevant places throughout the book.*

Among the most popular peaks in **Argentina** are Aconcagua, in Mendoza province, Pissis in Catamarca, and Lanín and Tronador, reached from the Lake District. The northern part of Los Glaciares National Park, around El Chaltén, has some spectacular peaks with very difficult mountaineering. There are climbing clubs in Mendoza, Bariloche, Esquel, Junín de los Andes, Ushuaia and other cities, and in some places equipment can be hired.

Some of the world's best mountaineering can be found in **Bolivia**. With a dozen peaks at or above 6,000 m and almost a thousand over 5,000 m, most levels of skill can find something to tempt them. The season is May to September, with usually stable conditions June to August. The Cordillera Real has 600 mountains over 5,000 m, including six at 6,000 m or above (Huayna Potosí is the most popular). Quimza Cruz, southeast of La Paz, is hard to get to but offers some excellent possibilities. The volcanic Cordillera Occidental contains Bolivia's highest peak, Sajama (6,542 m). The Apolobamba range, northwest of La Paz, has many peaks over 5,000 m.

The most popular form of climbing in **Brazil** is rock-face climbing *escalada*. In the heart of Rio, you can see, or join, climbers scaling the rocks at the base of Pão de Açúcar and on the Sugar Loaf itself. Not too far away, the Serra dos Órgãos provides plenty of challenges, not least the Dedo de Deus (God's Finger).

In **Chile**, some volcanoes and high mountains are difficult to get to. Others, like Villarrica and Osorno are popular excursions, although access is controlled by CONAF (see page 696) and you need permission to climb.

The best climbing in **Colombia** is in the national parks of Los Nevados (eg Nevado del Ruiz, Nevado de Tolima) and Sierra Nevada del Cocuy (check security situation and conditions before setting out). For rock and ice climbing, the Nevados and Cocuy offer some technical challenges and Suesca, north of Bogotá near Nemocón, is considered the most important centre for rock climbing in the country.

Ecuador offers some exceptional high-altitude climbing, with 10 mountains over 5,000 m – most with easy access. The four most frequently climbed are Cotopaxi , Chimborazo and Iliniza Norte. The other six, Iliniza Sur, Antisana, El Altar, Sangay, Carihuairazo and Cayambe vary in degree of difficulty and/or danger. Sangay is technically easy, but extremely dangerous from the falling rocks being ejected from the volcano. Many other mountains can be climbed and climbing clubs, guiding agencies and tour operators will give advice. There are two seasons: June to August for the western cordillera and December to February for the eastern cordillera.

In **Peru**, the Cordillera Blanca, with Huaraz as a base, is an ice climber's paradise. Over 50 summits are between 5,000 and 6,000 m and over 20 exceed 6,000 m. There is a wide range of difficulty and no peak fees are charged (although national park entrance has to paid in the Cordillera Blanca). The Cordillera Huayhuash, southeast of Huaraz, is a bit more remote, with fewer facilities, but has some of the most spectacular ice walls in Peru. In the south of the country, the Cordilleras Vilcabamba and Vilcanota are the main destinations, but Cuzco is not developed for climbing. Climbing equipment can be hired in Huaraz but the quality can be poor.

The heart of **Venezuelan** mountaineering and trekking is the Andes, with Mérida as the base. A number of important peaks can be scaled and there are some superb hikes in the highlands.

Diving

ⓘ *Dive operators are listed in the relevant places throughout the book.*

The best diving in **Brazil** is the Atol das Rocas; only available with private charter through www.dehouche.com; very expensive but completely unspoilt, with visibility up to 40 m and with one of the highest levels of biodiversity in the tropical southern Atlantic. Fernando de Noronha has coral gardens, drop-offs and wrecks which include a 50-m Brazilian navy destroyer with full armament. Visibility is up to 50 m, safe, current-free and drift diving. Amongst others, divers see at least two species of turtle, spinner dolphins, more than three species of shark, huge snapper and vast shoals of goatfish and jack. Arraial de Cabo is interesting because of the meeting of a southerly cold and northerly warm current and has the best marine life in southeast Brazil.

There are dive sites on the Caribbean and Pacific coasts of **Colombia**, but the former is more developed. Caribbean diving centres are Cartagena, Santa Marta and nearby Taganga, San Andrés and Providencia, the Islas de San Bernardo off the coast of Sucre, Isla Fuerte off Córdoba department and Capurganá, near the Panamanian border. On the Pacific, Bahía Solano and Gorgana Island offer excellent diving opportunities. Most upmarket hotels in the resorts arrange diving and snorkelling trips.

The prime spot in **Ecuador** is the Galápagos, with more than 20 dive sites: each island has its own unique underwater environment. Off the mainland, the best place to dive is the Parque Nacional Machalilla, at Isla La Plata. Colonies of sea lions can be seen here and migrating humpback whales pass this stretch of coast between late June and September.

Venezuela's waters are not as famous as those off neighbouring Bonaire, but they have excellent opportunities for seeing underwater flora, fauna and shipwrecks. The main areas are the national parks of Mochima and Islas Los Roques (more currents, so best for experienced divers), a number of sites to the east and west of Caracas, and in the waters off Isla de Margarita.

Fishing

ⓘ *Fishing operators are listed in the relevant places throughout the book.*

The main areas for fishing in **Argentina** are in the Lake District, around Junín de los Andes (south to Bariloche), and around Esquel, and further south around Río Gallegos and Río Grande. The best time for fishing is at the beginning of the season, in November and December (the season runs from early November to the end of March).

There is enormous potential for fishing in **Brazil**. Freshwater fishing can be practised in so many places that the best bet is to make local enquiries on arrival. Favoured rivers include tributaries of the Amazon, those in the Pantanal and the Rio Araguaia, but there are many others. Agencies can arrange fishing trips.

In **Chile**, the lakes and rivers of Araucanía, Los Lagos and Aisén offer great opportunities for trout and salmon fishing. The season runs from mid-November to the first Sunday in May (or from mid-September on Lago Llanquihue). Some of the world's best fishing is in the Lake District, which is a very popular region. Less heavily fished are the lakes and rivers south of Puerto Montt. Sea fishing is popular between Puerto Saavedra (Araucania) and Maullín (Los Lagos).

In **Colombia**, fishing is particularly good at Girardot, Santa Marta and Barranquilla; marlin is fished off Barranquilla. There is trout fishing, in season, in the lakes in the Bogotá area and at Lago de Tota in Boyacá. Travel agencies in Bogotá and Medellín can arrange fishing trips.

Deep-sea fishing, mainly for white and blue marlin, is exceptional in the **Venezuelan** Caribbean, but there is also good fishing closer to shore. Here again, Los Roques is a good destination, while Macuto and Río Chico on the mainland are popular. Freshwater fishing is possible in the lakes in the Andes and in the rivers in the Llanos.

Horse riding

ⓘ *Horse riding operators are listed in the relevant places throughout the book.*

In **Argentina**, many estancias offer horse riding, as well as fishing, canoeing, walking and birdwatching. Since estancias fall into four main categories, there is much variety in the type of country you can ride through. In the pampas, estancias tend to be cattle ranches extending for thousands of hectares; in the west they often have vineyards; northeastern estancias border swamps; those in Patagonia are sheep farms at the foot of the mountains or beside lakes. There is also horse riding on estancias in **Uruguay**.

In **Brazil** some of the best trails for horse riding are the routes that used to be taken by the mule trains that transported goods between the coast and the interior. A company like Tropa Serrana is an excellent place to start because their tours, including overnight horse treks, explore many aspects of the Minas Gerais countryside that visitors do not normally see.

Treks in the mountains of **Chile** can be organized in Santiago, but south of Concepción and north, the Elqui and Hurtado valleys, there are more opportunities and a number of companies organize riding holidays.

In **Ecuador** horse rentals are available in many popular resort areas including Otavalo, Baños and Vilcabamba. Throughout the country, *haciendas* also usually offer horse riding.

Mountain biking

ⓘ *Mountain biking operators are listed in the relevant places throughout the book.*

There are lots of opportunities in the mountains and Lake Districts of **Argentina** and **Chile**. The Carretera Austral is also a great ride. Bikes are manufactured locally, but quality is variable.

In **Bolivia**, hard-core, experienced, fit and acclimatized riders can choose from a huge range of possibilities. Either take a gamble and figure it out from a map, or find a guide and tackle the real adventure rides. Some popular rides in the La Paz region, achievable by all levels of riders, are La Cumbre to Coroico, down the so-called 'world's most dangerous road'; the Zongo Valley descent into the Yungas; Chacaltaya to La Paz, down from the (ex) world's highest ski-slope; Hasta Sorata, to the trekking paradise of Sorata. If you are plan on bringing your own bike and doing some hard riding, be prepared for difficult conditions, an almost complete absence of spare parts and very few good bike mechanics. There are now a number of operators offering guided mountain biking tours, but few rent good quality, safe machines. Choose a reputable company, guides who speak your language and only opt for the best, US-made bikes.

In **Colombia**, because some remote parts are unsafe, it is not wise to venture off the beaten track and you should enquire locally about the security situation before setting out. An agency like Eco-Guías in Bogotá can give details, and information may also be available at popular travellers' hotels.

Ecuador is growing in popularity as there are boundless opportunities in the Sierra, on coastal roads and in the upper Amazon basin. Agencies which offer tours, rent equipment and can help plan routes are listed under Quito and other cities.

This is a relatively new sport in **Peru**, but dedicated cyclists are beginning to open up routes which offer some magnificent possibilities. Peru has many kilometres of trails, dirt roads and single track, but very few maps to show you where to go. There is equipment for hire and tours in the Huaraz and Cuzco areas and it may be a good idea to join an organized group to get the best equipment and guiding.

Parapenting and hang-gliding

ⓘ *For Brazilian Associations, see www.abvl.com.br, the website of the Associação Brasileira de Vôo Livre, which oversees all national clubs and federations, and www.abp.esp.br, the Associação Brasileira de Parapente.*

There are state associations affiliated with ABVL and there are a number of operators offering tandem flights for those without experience. Launch sites (*rampas*) are growing in number. Among the best known is Pedra Bonita at Gávea in Rio de Janeiro, but there are others in the state. Popular *rampas* can also be found in São Paulo, Espírito Santo, Minas Gerais, Paraná, Santa Catarina, Rio Grande do Sul, Ceará, Mato Grosso do Sul and Brasília. A full list, and much else besides, can be found in the Guia 4 Ventos Brasil, www.guia4ventos.com.br, which also contains information on launch sites in other South American countries. These include sites in the Sierras de Córdoba of **Argentina**, several sites in **Peru**, including the cliffs of Miraflores (Lima) and in the Sierra Nevada de Mérida, **Venezuela**.

Skiing and snowboarding

ⓘ *Details of the major resorts and some smaller ones are given in the main text.*

In **Argentina** the season is generally from May to October. Las Leñas, south of Mendoza, is the best known, but other big resorts are at Cerro Catedral and Cerro Otto, near Bariloche and Chapelco, near San Martín de los Andes. Smaller resorts, with fewer facilities, can be found near Mendoza (Los Penitentes, Vallecitos and Manantiales), in the Lake District (Caviahue, Cerro Bayo; La Hoya – near Esquel) and near Ushuaia (Cerro Martial, Wallner). Ushuaia has a small but popular Alpine ski run and good Nordic skiing.

In **Chile** the season is from June to September. The major international ski resorts are in the Andes near Santiago: Farellones, El Colorado, La Parva, Valle Nevado, Portillo and Lagunillas. South of Santiago, skiing is mostly on the slopes of volcanoes. The larger resorts are Termas de Chillán, Villarrica/Pucón and Antillanca, but there are a great many smaller places with limited facilities which are worth the effort to get to for some adventurous fun. Details of the major resorts and some smaller ones are given in the text.

Surfing

ⓘ *Surf schools and organizations are listed in the relevant places throughout the book.*

In **Brazil** the best waves are at Cacimba do Padre beach, Fernando de Noronha (the archipelago, 345 km out in the Atlantic). International surf championships are held here annually. Other good waves are found in the south, where long stretches of the Atlantic, often facing the swell head-on, give some excellent and varied breaks. Many Brazilian mainland surf spots are firmly on the international championship circuit, including Saquarema, in Rio de Janeiro state. Best waves in Rio de Janeiro city are at Joatinga, Prainha or Grumari beaches. One of the best states for surfing is Santa Catarina (for information visit www.brazilsurftravel.com).

In **Ecuador** there are a few, select surfing spots, such as Mompiche, San Mateo, Montañita and Playas, near Guayaquil. Surf is best December to March, except at Playas where the season is June to September. In the Galápagos there is good surfing at Playa Punta Carola, outside Puerto Baquerizo Moreno on San Cristóbal.

Peru is a top international surfing destination. Its main draws are the variety of waves and the year-round action. The main seasons are September to February in the north and March to December in the south, though May is often ideal south of Lima. The biggest wave is at Pico Alto (sometimes 6 m in May), south of Lima, and the largest break is 800 m at Chicama, near Trujillo.

Trekking

South American Explorers ⓘ *www.saexplorers.org, have good information and advice on trekking and sells books.*

There is ample scope for short and long-distance trekking in **Argentina**. The best locations are in the foothills and higher up in the Andes. Some suggestions are the valleys around Salta; San Juan and La Rioja; Mendoza and Malargüe; and in the national parks of the Lake District. Around El Chaltén in Los Glaciares National Park there is some of the best trekking on the continent.

There are many opportunities for trekking in **Bolivia**, from gentle one-day hikes in foothills and valleys to challenging walks of several days from highlands to lowlands on Inca or gold-diggers trails. The best known are: the Choro, Takesi and Yunga Cruz hikes, all of whose starting points can be reached from La Paz; the Mapiri Trail and the Illampu Circuit, both approached from Sorata; and the Apolobamba treks in the northwest. Various treks are outlined in the text, especially near La Paz and from Sorata.

In **Brazil** trekking is very popular, especially in Rio de Janeiro, São Paulo, Minas Gerais, Paraná and Rio Grande do Sul. There are plenty of hiking agencies which handle tours. Trails are frequently graded according to difficulty; this is noticeably so in areas where *trilhas ecológicas* have been laid out in forests or other sites close to busy tourist areas. Many national parks and protected areas provide good opportunities for trekking (eg the Chapada Diamantina in Bahia). The latest area to come under the trekker's gaze is Jalapão in Tocantins.

In **Chile**, trekking possibilities are endless, ranging from short, signposted trails in national parks to hikes of several days, such as the circuit of the Parque Nacional Torres del Paine.

Trekking is popular in **Colombia** with walks ranging from one-day excursions out of Bogotá, or at San Agustín, to three- to four-day hikes. Good places for longer treks include the national parks of Los Nevados (from Ibagué, Manizales or Pereira), Sierra Nevada del Cocuy in the northeast, and Puracé (between Popayán and San Agustín). Well-trodden is the path to the Ciudad Perdida in the Sierra Nevada de Santa Marta, which has one of the country's main archaeological sites. In the departments of Boyacá and Santander there are many colonial *caminos reales*. Sources of information include tourist offices and Ministerio del Medio Ambiente (see Tourist information, Colombia page 897). See also Bogotá, Activities and tours (page 915).

In **Ecuador**, the varied landscape, diverse environments and friendly villages make travelling on foot a refreshing change from crowded buses. Hiking in the Sierra is mostly across high elevation *páramo*, through agricultural lands and past indigenous communities. There are outstanding views of glaciated peaks in the north and pre-Columbian ruins in the south. In the tropical rainforests of the Oriente, local guides are often required because of the difficulty in navigation and because you will be walking on land owned by local indigenous tribes. The Andean slopes are steep and often covered by virtually impenetrable cloud forests and it rains a lot. Many ancient trading routes head down the river valleys. Some of these trails are still used. Others may be overgrown and difficult to follow but offer the reward of intact ecosystems.

In **Peru** there are some fabulous circuits around the peaks of the Cordillera Blanca (eg Llanganuco to Santa Cruz, and the treks out of Caraz) and Cordillera Huayhuash. The Ausangate trek near Cuzco is also good. A second type of trek is walking among, or to, ruins. The prime example is the Inca Trail to Machu Picchu, but others include those to Vilcabamba (the Incas' last home) and Choquequirao, and the treks in the Chachapoyas region. The Colca and Cotahuasi canyons also offer superb trekking.

In **Venezuela** there are popular treks in the Sierra Nevada de Mérida, Roraima and other national parks, even in the Parque Nacional El Avila, just outside Caracas.

Whitewater rafting

ⓘ *Rafting operators are listed in the relevant places throughout the book.*

In **Argentina** there are some good whitewater rafting runs in Mendoza province, near the provincial capital, and near San Rafael and Malargüe. In the Lake District there are possibilities in the Lanín, Nahuel Huapi and Los Alerces national parks.

In **Brazil** companies offer whitewater rafting trips in São Paulo state (eg on the Rios Juquiá, Jaguarí, do Peixe, Paraibuna), in Rio de Janeiro (also on the Paraibuna, at Três Rios in the Serra dos Órgões), Paraná (Rio Ribeira), Santa Catarina (Rio Itajaí) and Rio Grande do Sul (Três Coroas). The Rio Novo, Jalapão, Tocantins, is an excellent, new destination.

In **Chile** over 20 rivers between Santiago and Tierra del Fuego are excellent for whitewater rafting. Some run through spectacular mountain scenery, such as the Río Petrohué, which flows through temperate rainforest beneath the Osorno and Calbuco volcanoes. Rafting is generally well organized and equipment is usually of a high standard. Access to headwaters of most rivers is easy. For beginners, many agencies in Santiago, Puerto Varas and Pucón offer half-day trips on grade III rivers. The best grade IV and V rafting is in Futaleufú, near Chaitén.

In **Colombia** whitewater rafting is growing in popularity and is at present based at San Gil (Santander), Villeta and Utica (Cundinamarca) and less developed in San Agustín (Huila).

Ecuador is a whitewater paradise with dozens of accessible rivers, warm waters and tropical rainforest; regional rainy seasons differ so that throughout the year there is always a river to run. The majority of Ecuador's whitewater rivers share a number of characteristics. Plunging off the Andes, the upper sections are very steep creeks offering, if they're runnable at all, serious technical grade V, suitable for experts only. As the creeks join on the lower slopes they form rivers that are less steep, with more volume. Some of these rivers offer up to 100 km of continuous grade III-IV whitewater, before flattening out to rush towards the Pacific Ocean on one side of the ranges or deep into the Amazon Basin on the other. Of the rivers descending to the Pacific coast, the Blanco and its tributaries are the most frequently run. They are within easy reach of Quito, as is the Quijos on the eastern side of the Sierra. In the Oriente, the main rivers are the Aguarico and its tributary the Dué, the Napo, Pastaza and Upano.

Peru has some of the finest whitewater rivers in the world. Availability is almost year-round and all levels of difficulty can be enjoyed. Cuzco is probably the rafting capital and the Río Urubamba has some very popular trips. Further afield is the Río Apurímac, which has some of the best whitewater rafting, including a trip at the source of the Amazon. In the southeastern jungle, a trip on the Río Tambopata to the Tambopata-Candamo Reserved Zone involves four days of white- water followed by two of drifting through virgin forest; an excellent adventure which must be booked up in advance. Around Arequipa is some first-class, technical rafting in the Cotahuasi and Colca canyons and some less-demanding trips on the Río Majes. Other destinations are the Río Santa near Huaraz and the Río Cañete, south of Lima.

Responsible travel

The benefits of international travel are self evident for both hosts and travellers: employment, understanding of different cultures and business and leisure opportunities. At the same time there is clearly a downside to the industry. Where visitor pressure is high and/or poorly regulated, there can be adverse impacts to society and the natural environment. Paradoxically, this is as true in undeveloped and pristine areas (where culture and the natural environment are less 'prepared' for even small numbers of visitors) as in major resorts.

The travel industry is growing rapidly and increasingly its impact is becoming apparent. These impacts can seem remote and unrelated to an individual trip or holiday (eg air travel is clearly implicated in global warming and damage to the ozone layer, resort location and construction can destroy natural habitats and restrict traditional rights and activities), but individual choice and awareness can make a difference in many instances and, collectively, travellers are having a significant effect in shaping a more responsible and sustainable industry.

Of course travel can have beneficial impacts and this is something to which every traveller can contribute. Many national parks are part funded by receipts from visitors. Similarly, travellers can promote patronage and protection of important archaeological sites and heritage through their interest and contributions via entrance and performance fees. They can also support small-scale enterprises by staying in locally run hotels and hostels, eating in local restaurants and by purchasing local goods, supplies and arts and crafts. In fact, since the early 1990s there has been a phenomenal growth in tourism that promotes and supports the conservation of natural environments and is also fair and equitable to local communities. This 'ecotourism' segment is probably the fastest-growing sector of the travel industry and provides a vast and growing range of destinations and activities in South America.

While the authenticity of some ecotourism operators' claims needs to be interpreted with care, there is clearly both a huge demand for this type of activity and also significant opportunities to support worthwhile conservation and social development initiatives. Organizations such as Conservation International (www.ecotour .org), the International Ecotourism Society (www.ecotourism.org), Planeta (www.planeta.com) and Tourism Concern (www.tourism concern .org.uk) are developing and/or promoting ecotourism projects and destinations (their websites are an excellent source of information for sites and initiatives throughout South America). At the same time Earthwatch (www.earthwatch.org) offers a chance to participate directly in scientific research and development projects.

How big is your footprint?

The point of a holiday is, of course, to have a good time, but if it's relatively guilt-free as well, that's even better. Perfect ecotourism would ensure a good living for local inhabitants, while not detracting from their traditional lifestyles, encroaching on their customs or spoiling their environment. Perfect ecotourism probably doesn't exist, but everyone can play their part. Here are a few points worth bearing in mind:

- Think about where your money goes and be fair and realistic about how cheaply you travel. Try to put money into local people's hands; drink local beer or fruit juice rather than imported brands and stay in locally owned accommodation wherever possible.
- Haggle with humour and appropriately. Remember that you want a fair price, not the lowest one.
- Think about what happens to your rubbish. Take biodegradable products and a water bottle filter. Be sensitive to limited resources like water, fuel and electricity.
- Help preserve local wildlife and habitats by respecting rules and regulations, such as sticking to footpaths, not standing on coral and not buying products made from endangered plants or animals.
- Don't treat people as part of the landscape; they may not want their picture taken. Ask first and respect their wishes.
- Learn the local language and be mindful of local customs and norms. It can enhance your travel experience and you'll earn respect and be more readily welcomed by local people.
- And finally, use your guidebook as a starting point, not the only source of information. Talk to local people, then discover your own adventure.

Volunteering in South America

There is some overlap between volunteering and gap-year or career-break tourism as many people who make this type of trip do some form of work. There is an increasing amount of help for students on a gap year and, in the UK at least, a well-planned and productive gap year can be an advantage when it comes to university and job application. The career-break market is growing fast and there is help online to guide you. Some organizations help from planning to finding something to do; others are quite specific in the type of project or country in which they operate: see www.gapyear.com, www.lattitude.org.uk, www.yearoutgroup.org and www.thecareerbreaksite.com. For a range of options, try www.gvi.co.uk (**Global Vision International**) or www.i-to-i.com. More specific (but not limited to South America) are www.raleigh.org.uk (**Raleigh International**), www.rainforestconcern.org (**Rainforest Concern**) www.handsupholidays.com, www.madventurer.com, www.questoverseas.com (**Quest Overseas**, which also organizes expeditions), www.thepodsite.co.uk (**Personal Overseas Development**), www.outreach international.co.uk (**Outreach**), www.projects-abroad.co.uk, located in Argentina, Bolivia, Brazil and Peru, and www.vso.org.uk (**Voluntary Service Overseas**), working in Guyana, Bolivia and Peru. An excellent place to start for low- and zero-cost volunteer programmes in South America is Steve McElhinney's website, www.volunteersouthamerica.net. See also www.volunteerlatinamerica.com.

In **Bolivia**, see www.volunteer bolivia.org.

In **Brazil**, there are two websites with information on volunteering: www.portaldo voluntario.org.br and www.voluntarios.com.br, both in Portuguese.

In **Colombia**, Peace Brigades International, www.peacebrigades.org/index.php, which protects human rights and promotes non-violent transformation of conflicts, employs foreign nationals who often work as human rights' monitors and observers. Fluent Spanish is essential. **Let's Go Volunteer**, www.letsgovolunteer.com.

In **Ecuador**, 'voluntourism' attracts many visitors. Several language schools operate volunteering schemes in conjunction with Spanish classes. **Fundación Arcoiris** (www.arcoiris.org.ec) works with a variety of nature conservation and sustainable community development projects in the far south of the country; **Fundación Jatun Sacha** (www.jatunsacha.org) has many different sites at which volunteers can work, all in exceptional natural areas; **Fundación Natura** (www.fnatura.org), a large Ecuadorean NGO, promotes environmental awareness and education.

For other options in the continent, contact, South American Explorers, see page 52.

If looking for paid work, visit the **International Career and Employment Center**, www.internationaljobs.org. To teach in international Baccalaureate (IB) schools, you need to be a qualified subject teacher (primary or secondary level) with one to two years' experience. See www.ibo.org/ for a list of bilingual schools. You don't have to speak Spanish to work in a bilingual school. Most schools offer private health care packages and annual flights home. See also www.thelajoblist.blogspot.com and http://tefltips.blogspot.com for information on teaching English in Latin America. Other resources are books by Susan Griffith, including: *Work your Way around the World*, 14th edition, 2009, and *Gap Years for Grown Ups*, 3rd edition, 2008. Other sites worth looking at for older gap years are: www.gapsforgrumpies.com, www.gapyearforgrownups.co.uk and www.goldengapyears.com.

Getting there

Air

Most South American countries have direct flights from **Europe**; only Paraguay does not. In many cases, though, the choice of departure point is limited to Madrid and one or two other cities (Paris or Amsterdam, for instance). Argentina, Brazil and Venezuela have the most options: France, Germany, Italy, Spain and the UK (although the last named not to Venezuela). Brazil also has flights from Lisbon to a number of cities. Where there are no direct flights connections can be made in the USA (Miami, or other gateways), Buenos Aires, Rio de Janeiro or São Paulo. **Main US gateways** are Miami, Houston, Dallas, Atlanta and New York. On the west coast, Los Angeles has flights to several South American cities. If buying airline tickets routed through the USA, check that US taxes are included in the price. Flights from **Canada** are mostly via the USA, although there are direct flights from Toronto to Bogotá and Santiago. Likewise, flights from **Australia** and **New Zealand** are best through Los Angeles, except for the **Qantas/LAN** route from Sydney and Auckland to Santiago, and **Qantas**' route to Buenos Aires. From **Japan** and from **South Africa** there are direct flights to Brazil. Within **Latin America** there is plenty of choice on local carriers and some connections on US or European airlines. For airpasses, see below. To Guyana, the main routes are via the Caribbean (Port of Spain, Trinidad and Barbados) or New York, Miami and Toronto. Suriname is served by flights from Amsterdam and Port of Spain, while Guyane has flights from Paris and the French-speaking Caribbean. All three have air connections with northern Brazil.

Prices and discounts

Most airlines offer discounted fares on scheduled flights through agencies who specialize in this type of fare. For a list of these agencies see page 33. If you buy discounted air tickets always check the reservation with the airline concerned to make sure the flight still exists. Also remember the IATA airlines' schedules change in March and October each year, so if you're going to be away a long time it's best to leave return flight coupons open. Peak times are 7 December-15 January and 10 July-10 September. If you intend travelling during those times, book as far ahead as possible. Between February and May and September and November special offers may be available.

Air passes

The **Mercosur Airpass** for Brazil, Argentina, Chile, Uruguay and Paraguay, using several local carriers, is available to any passenger with a return ticket to a participating country. It must be bought in conjunction with an international flight; minimum stay is seven days, maximum 45; and a minimum of two countries must be visited. Maximum number of coupons is eight, the maximum number of stops per country is four. Fares are worked out on a mileage basis and cost US$295-1,195. **TAM** also has an airpass which links Brazil with the other Mercosur countries (not valid if you arrived on **LAN**). You must include at least two of those countries with a maximum of two stops per country (four in Brazil) not including origin and destination; maximum number of countries is five; minimum stay five days, maximum 30; maximum eight coupons, which range from US$339-1,236. The **One World Visit South America** air pass links all South American countries except the Guianas for passengers arriving on airlines in the One World Alliance. Flights within South America must be made on **American Airlines** or **LAN**. Prices are mileage-based, from US$80-270; minimum three flights, maximum stay 60 days. **LAN** has an airpass valid for travel on any of its routes in South America, on any part of its network in South America (except the Falklands/Malvinas), available to anyone who has purchased an international ticket with **LAN**, or **Iberia** to Chile, from Europe. It's valid for 12 months. Coupons range from US$87-213 (250 to Easter

Island). Coupons cost more for those arriving on LAN's partners in the One World Alliance. Aerolíeas Argentinas has a South America Pass valid for 90 days on all AR and Austral routes, minimum 3 coupons, maximum 12 (US$499-1149), available to holders of an international return ticket. It must include two Argentine secotrs. The **All America Airpass**, a multi-carrier, multi-country facility from Germany's **Hahn Air**, is built up from individual sectors at specially negotiated rates that can be bought just as a single journey, or a multi-sector trip, as required and according to cost. There is no minimum or maximum stay; see *www.allairpass.com*. See the respective countries for air passes operated by national airlines.

Discount flight agents

UK and Ireland

STA Travel, T0871-230 0040, www.statravel.co.uk. 45 branches in the UK, including many university campuses. Specialists in low-cost flights and tours, good for student IDs and insurance.

Trailfinders, 194 Kensington High St, London, W8 7RG, T020-7938 3939, www.trailfinders.com. 22 branches in London and throughout the UK. Also 2 branches in Ireland (Dublin, Cork) and 2 travel centres in Australia (Brisbane, Sydney, www.trailfinders.com.au).

North America

Discount Airfares Worldwide On-Line, www.etn.nl/discount.htm. A hub of consolidator and discount agent links.

STA Travel, 1-800-781-4040, www.statravel.com. 18 branches in the USA, including university campuses.

Travel CUTS, in major Canadian cities and on university campuses, T1-866-246-9762, www.travel cuts.com. Specialist in student discount fares, IDs and other travel services.

Travelocity, www.travelocity.com. Consolidator.

South America

Despegar, www.despegar.com, www.decolar.com. Latin American online travel agency.

Australia and New Zealand

Flight Centre, with offices throughout Australia and other countries. In Australia call T133 133 or www.flightcentre.com.au.

STA Travel, T134 782, www.statravel.com.au; branches throughout Australia. In NZ: T0800-474400, www.statravel.co.nz. 130 Cuba St, Wellington, T04-385 0561. Also in major towns and university campuses.

Travel.com.au, Level 10, 17 York St, Sydney, NSW 2000, T1300 130 481, www.travel.com.au.

Note Using the internet for booking flights, hotels and other services directly is increasingly popular and you can get some good deals this way. But don't forget that a travel agent can find the best flights to suit your itinerary, as well as providing advice on documents, insurance, safety, routes, lodging and times of year to travel. A reputable agent will also be bonded to give you some protection if things go wrong.

Sea

Travelling as a passenger on a cargo ship to South America is not a cheap way to go, but if you have the time and want a bit of luxury, it makes a great alternative to flying. There are sailings from Europe to the Caribbean, east and west coasts of South America. Likewise, you can sail from US ports to east and west coast South America. In the main, passage is round trip only. Don't try to get on a non-passenger carrying cargo ship to South America from a European port; it is not possible.

Useful contacts for advice and tickets

Strand Voyages (Andy Whitehouse), The Oasis Centre, 75 Westminster Bridge Rd, London SE1 7HS, T020-7921 4340, www.strandtravelltd.co.uk. Booking agents for all routes.

Cargo Ship Voyages Ltd, 38 St Margaret's Crescent, Gravesend, Kent, DA12 4EH, T01474-333314, www.cargoshipvoyages.co.uk.

The Cruise People, 88 York St, London W1H 1QT, T020-7723 2450, and 1252 Lawrence Avenue East, Suite 210, Toronto, Canada, M3A 1C3, T416- 444 2410, www.cruisepeople.co.uk.

Globoship, Neuengasse 30, CH-3001, Bern, Switzerland, T031-313 0004, www.globoship.ch.

Travltips Cruise and Freighter Travel Association, PO Box 580188, Flushing, NY 11358, T800-872 8584, www.travltips.com.

Getting around

→ *See Getting there, above, for details of air transport including air passes.*

Land

Bus and train

The continent has an extensive road system with frequent bus services. The buses are often comfortable; the difficulties of Andean terrain affect the quality of vehicles. In mountainous country do not expect buses to get to their destination after long journeys anywhere near on time. Do not turn up for a bus at the last minute; if it is full it may depart early. Tall travellers are advised to take aisle rather than window seats on long journeys as this allows more leg room. When the journey takes more than three or four hours, meal stops at roadside restaurants (usually with toilets), good and bad, are the rule. Usually, no announcement is made on the duration of a stop; ask the driver and follow him, if he eats, eat. See what the locals are eating and buy likewise, or make sure you're stocked up well on food and drink at the start. For drinks, stick to bottled water or soft drinks or coffee (black). The food sold by vendors at bus stops may be all right; watch if locals are buying, though unpeeled fruit is, of course, reliable.

Where they still run, trains are slower than buses. They tend to provide finer scenery and you can normally see much more wildlife than from the road – it is less disturbed by one or two trains a day than by the more frequent road traffic.

Car

The car A normal car will reach most places of interest, but high ground clearance is useful for badly surfaced or unsurfaced roads and for fording rivers. For greater flexibility in mountain and jungle territory 4WD vehicles are recommended. In Patagonia, main roads are gravel rather than paved: perfectly passable without 4WD, just rough and dusty. Consider fitting wire guards for headlamps, and for windscreens too. Diesel cars are much cheaper to run than petrol ones and the fuel is easily available, although in Venezuela you may have to look hard for it outside Caracas. Standard European and Japanese cars run on fuel with a higher octane rating than is commonly available in North, South or Central America, and in Brazil petrol (*gasolina*) is in fact gasohol, with a 12% admixture of alcohol.

Packing for South America

Everybody has their own preferences, but a good principle is to take half the clothes, and twice the money, that you think you will need. Listed here are those items most often mentioned. These include an inflatable travel pillow and strong shoes (footwear over 9½ English size, or 42 European size, is difficult to find in South America). Always take out a good travel insurance policy. You should also take waterproof clothing and waterproof treatment for leather footwear and wax earplugs, vital for long bus trips or in noisy hotels. Also important are flip flops, which can be worn in showers to avoid athlete's foot, and a sheet sleeping bag to avoid sleeping on dirty sheets in cheap hotels. Other useful things include: a clothes line, a nailbrush, a vacuum flask, a water bottle, a universal sink plug of the flanged type that will fit any waste-pipe, string, a Swiss Army knife, an alarm clock, candles (for power cuts), a torch/ flashlight, pocket mirror, an adaptor, a padlock for the doors of the cheapest hotels (or for tent zip if camping), a small first-aid kit, sun hat, lip salve with sun protection, contraceptives, waterless soap, wipes and a small sewing kit. Always carry toilet paper, especially on long bus trips. The most security conscious may also wish to include a length of chain and padlock for securing luggage to bed or bus/train seat, and a lockable canvas cover for your rucksack. Contact lens wearers note that lens solution can be difficult to find in Bolivia and Peru. Ask for it in a pharmacy, rather than an opticians.

Security Spare no ingenuity in making your car secure, inside and out (even wing mirrors, spot lamps, wheels without locking nuts can be stolen). Try never to leave the car unattended except in a locked garage or guarded parking space. Lock the clutch or accelerator to the steering wheel with a heavy, obvious chain or lock. Street children will generally protect your car for a tip.

Documents To drive your own vehicle in South America, you must have an international driver's licence. You must also have the vehicle's registration document in the name of the driver, or, in the case of a car registered in someone else's name, a notarized letter of authorization. Be very careful to keep **all** the papers you are given when you enter, to produce when you leave (see box, page 37).

Insurance Insurance for the vehicle against accident, damage or theft is best arranged in the country of origin. In Latin American countries it is very expensive to insure against accident and theft, especially as you should take into account the value of the car increased by duties calculated in real (ie non-devaluing) terms. If the car is stolen or written off you will be required to pay very high import duty on its value. Third-party insurance can be very difficult to find. Some countries may insist that it be bought at the border (Venezuela seems to be the only country where it is easy to obtain). If you can get the legally required minimum cover, so much the better. If not, drive with extreme caution and very defensively. If involved in an accident and you're uninsured, your car could be confiscated. If anyone is hurt, do not pick them up (you may become liable). Try to seek assistance from the nearest police station or hospital.

Car hire The main international car hire companies operate in all countries, but they tend to be very expensive, reflecting the high costs and accident rates. Hotels and tourist agencies will tell you where to find cheaper rates, but you will need to check that you have such basics as spare wheel, toolkit and functioning lights, etc. You'll probably have more fun if you drive yourself, although it's always possible to hire a car with driver. If you plan to do a lot of driving and will have time at the end to dispose of it, investigate the possibility of buying a second-hand car locally; since hiring is so expensive it may well work out cheaper and will probably do you just as well.

Car hire insurance Check exactly what the hirer's insurance policy covers. In many cases it only protects you against minor bumps and scrapes, not major accidents, nor 'natural' damage (eg flooding). Ask if extra cover is available. Also find out, if using a credit card, whether the card automatically includes insurance. Beware of being billed for scratches which were already on the vehicle. Also check the windscreen and ask what procedures are involved if a new one is needed.

Car hire websites

Avis, www.avis.com. In all countries.
Budget, www.budget.com. In Argentina, Brazil, Chile, Ecuador, Peru, Uruguay, Suriname, Venezuela.
Hertz, www.hertz.com. All countries.
Localiza, www.localiza.com. In Argentina, Bolivia, Brazil, Chile, Colombia, Ecuador, Paraguay, Peru, Uruguay.
National, www.nationalcar.com. In Argentina, Chile, Colombia, Guyane, Paraguay, Peru.

Motorcycling

The motorcycle The bike should be off-road capable. Buying a bike in the USA and driving down works out cheaper than buying one in the UK. Get to know the bike before you go, ask the dealers in your country what goes wrong with it and arrange a link whereby you can get parts flown out to you.

Security Try not to leave a fully laden bike on its own. An Abus D or chain will keep the bike secure. A cheap alarm gives you peace of mind if you leave the bike outside a hotel at night. Most hotels will allow you to bring the bike inside. Look for hotels that have a courtyard or more secure parking and never leave luggage on the bike overnight or while it is unattended. Also take a cover for the bike.

Documents A passport, international driving licence and bike registration document are necessary. Riders fare much better with a carnet de passages (see box, opposite) than without.

Border crossings If you do not have a carnet, do not try to cross borders on a Sunday or a holiday anywhere as a charge is levied on the usually free borders in South America. South American customs and immigration inspectors are mostly friendly, polite and efficient. If in doubt ask to see the boss and/or the rule book.

Cycling

Unless you are planning a journey almost exclusively on paved roads – when a touring bike would suffice – a mountain bike is strongly recommended. The good quality ones (and the cast-iron rule is **never** to skimp on quality) are incredibly tough and rugged, with low gear ratios for difficult terrain, wide tyres with plenty of tread for good road-holding, V brakes, sealed hubs and bottom bracket and a low centre of gravity for improved stability. A chrome-alloy frame is a desirable choice over aluminium as it can be welded if necessary. Although touring bikes, and to a lesser extent mountain bikes and spares are available in the larger Latin American cities, remember that most locally manufactured goods are shoddy and rarely last. In some countries, such as Chile and Uruguay, imported components can be found but they tend to be extremely expensive. (Shimano parts are generally the easiest to find.) Buy everything you possibly can before you leave home.

Remember that you can always stick your bike on a bus, canoe or plane to get yourself nearer to where you want your wheels to take you. This is especially useful when there are long stretches of major road ahead, where all that stretches before you are hours of turbulence as the constant stream of heavy trucks and long-haul buses zoom by. In almost any country it is possible to rent a bike for a few days, or join an organized tour for riding in the mountains. You should check, however, that the machine you are hiring is up to the conditions you will be encountering, or that the tour company is not a fly-by-night outfit without back-up, good bikes or maintenance.

Visit www.warmshowers.org for a hospitality exchange for touring cyclists. A related organization is Cyclo-Camping International ⓘ *25 rue Ramus, 75020 Paris, T01-4797 6218, France, www.cci.asso.fr*.

Carnet de passages

There are two recognized documents for taking a vehicle through customs in South America: a carnet de passages issued jointly by the Fedération Internationale de l'Automobile (FIA – Paris) and the Alliance Internationale de Tourisme (AIT-Geneva), and the Libreta de Pasos por Aduana issued by the Federación Interamericana de Touring y Automóvil Clubs (FITAC). The carnet de passages is recognized by all South American customs authorities but is not required by any. The libreta, a 10-page book of three-part passes for customs, should be available from any South American automobile club member of FITAC, but in practice it is only available to non-residents from the Touring y Automóvil Club de Venezuela. At US$400, it is not worth the effort or expense, nor is it needed to enter Venezuela. If you wish to purchase one of these documents, get a carnet de passages, issued in the country where the vehicle is registered. In the UK it costs £185, £190 or £195 for 5, 10 or 25 pages respectively, available from the RAC, www.rac.co.uk. In Canada the fee is CAN$577.50 for CAA members, CAN$682.50 for non-members, CA$550 for AAA members. In all cases you have to add on administration fees, deposits and insurance premiums, which can take the cost into the thousands, depending on the value of the car. In the USA the AAA does not issue the carnet, although the HQ in Washington DC may give advice. It is available from the Canadian Automobile Association (CAA), with offices throughout Canada, www.caa.ca, who can give full details. Also from the AAA of Australia, see www.aaa.asn.au/touring/overseas.htm. Ask the motoring organization in your home country about availability of the carnet.

Boat

Because air services have captured the lucrative end of the passenger market, passenger services on the rivers are in decline. Worst hit have been the upper reaches of rivers throughout the region. The situation has been aggravated for the casual traveller by a new generation of purpose-built tugs (all engine-room and bridge), that can handle up to a dozen freight barges but have no passenger accommodation. In Peru passenger boats must now supplement incomes by carrying cargo, and this lengthens their journey cycle. In the face of long delays, travellers might consider shorter 'legs' involving more frequent changes of boat; though the more local the service, the slower and more uncomfortable it will be.

Hammocks, mosquito nets (not always good quality), plastic containers for water storage, kettles and cooking utensils can be purchased in any sizeable riverside town, as well as tinned food. Fresh bread, cake, eggs and fruit are available in most villages. Cabin bunks are provided with thin mattresses but these are often foul. Replacements can be bought locally but rolls of plastic foam that can be cut to size are also available and much cheaper. Eye-screws for securing washing lines and mosquito nets are useful, and tall passengers who are not taking a hammock and who may find insufficient headroom on some boats should consider a camp-chair.

In Venezuelan Amazonas hitching rides on boats is possible if you camp at the harbour or police post where all boats must register. Take any boat going in your direction as long as it reaches the next police post. See the special section on the Brazilian Amazon, page 614.

Sleeping price codes

LL	US$200 and over	**L**	US$151-200	**AL**	US$101-150
A	US$66-100	**B**	US$46-65	**C**	US$31-45
D	US$21-30	**E**	US$12-20	**F**	US$7-11
G	US$6 and under				

Price of a double room in high season, including taxes.

Maps and guidebooks

Those from the **Institutos Geográficos Militares or Nacionales** in the capitals are often the only good maps available in Latin America. It is therefore wise to get as many as possible in your home country before leaving, especially if travelling by land. A recommended series of general maps is that published by **International Travel Maps** (ITM) ⓘ *530 West Broadway, Vancouver BC, V5Z 1E9, Canada, T604-879 3621, www.itmb.com*, several compiled with historical notes, by the late Kevin Healey. As well as maps of South America Southern, North East and North West (1:4M), there are maps of most of the individual countries, the Amazon Basin, Easter Island, the Galápagos, the Falklands/Malvinas and several cities. Another map series that has been mentioned is that of **New World Edition** ⓘ *Bertelsmann, Neumarkter Strasse 18, 81673 München, Germany*, Mittelamerika, Südamerika Nord, Südamerika Sud, Brasilien (all 1:4M). **Stanford's** ⓘ *12-14 Long Acre, Covent Garden, London WC2E 9LP, T020-7836 1321, www.stanfords.co.uk* (other branches in Bristol and Manchester), also sells a wide variety of maps.

Sleeping

Hotels For about US$10, a cheap but not bad hotel room can be found in most countries, although in some of the Andean countries you may not have to pay that much. In some countries, it is more common for rooms to be priced per person, than per room. This is reflected in the text. For those on a really tight budget, it is a good idea to ask for a boarding house – *casa de huéspedes, hospedaje, pensión, casa familial* or *residencial* (according to country) – they are normally to be found in abundance near bus and railway stations and markets. Good-value hotels can also be found near truckers' stops/service stations; they are usually secure. There are often great seasonal variations in hotel prices in resorts. Remember, cheaper hotels don't always supply soap, towels and toilet paper; in colder (higher) regions they may not supply enough blankets, so take a sleeping bag. To avoid price hikes for gringos, ask if there is a cheaper room.

Unless otherwise stated, it is assumed that hotels listed are clean and friendly and that rooms have shower and toilet. In any class, hotel rooms facing the street may be noisy: always ask for the best, quietest room. The electric showers used in many hotels should be checked for obvious flaws in the wiring; try not to touch the rose while it is producing hot water. **Cockroaches** are ubiquitous and unpleasant, but not dangerous. Take some insecticide powder if staying in cheap hotels.

Experiment in International Living Ltd ⓘ *287 Worcester Rd, Malvern, Worcestershire WR14 1AB, T0800-018 4015 or 01684-562577, and offices worldwide, www.eiluk.org*, can arrange stays with families from one to four weeks in Argentina, Chile, Ecuador and Brazil. This has been recommended as an excellent way to meet people and learn the language. They also offer volunteering opportunities.

Travel networking is popular in South America. Visit **www.couchsurfing.com**, **www.hospitality club.org**, **www.yoursafeplanet.co.uk**, **www.stay4free.com**, or one of many similar sites. It's a great concept that works, but don't just go with a contact on the first site you look at; check the security measures and that the interests of the site's other users coincide with yours.

Toilets Many hotels, restaurants and bars have inadequate water supplies. **Almost without exception used toilet paper should not be flushed down the pan, but placed in the receptacle provided.** This applies even in quite expensive hotels. Failing to do this will block the pan or drain, a considerable health risk. It is quite common for people to stand on the toilet seat (facing the wall, easier to balance).

Youth hostels Organizations affiliated to the Youth Hostels movement exist in Argentina, Brazil, Colombia, Chile, Peru and Uruguay. There is an associate organization in Ecuador. More information in individual countries and from **Hostelling International**. Independent sites on hostelling are the **Internet Guide to Hostelling**, www.hostels.com, **www.hosteltrail.com**, geared to hostels and budget lodging in South America, **www.hostelworld.com**, **www.hostelsclub.com** and **Ho.La Hostels**, www.holahostels.com, with an extensive list of hostels in South America.

Camping Organized campsites are referred to in the text immediately below hotel lists, under each town. If there is no organized site in town, a football pitch or gravel pit might serve. Obey the following rules for 'wild' camping: (1) arrive in daylight and pitch your tent as it gets dark; (2) ask permission to camp from the parish priest, or the fire chief, or the police, or a farmer regarding his own property; (3) never ask a group of people – especially young people; (4) never camp on a beach (because of sandflies and thieves). If you can't get information from anyone, camp in a spot where you can't be seen from the nearest inhabited place, or road, and make sure no one saw you go there. In Argentina and Brazil, it is common to camp at gas/petrol stations. As Béatrice Völkle of Gampelen, Switzerland, adds, camping wild may be preferable to those organized sites which are treated as discos, with only the afternoon reserved for sleeping.

If taking a cooker, the most frequent recommendation is a multifuel stove (eg MSR International, Coleman Peak 1), which will burn unleaded petrol or, if that is not available, kerosene, benzina blanca, etc. Alcohol-burning stoves are simple, reliable, but slow and you have to carry a lot of fuel: for a methylated spirit-burning stove, the following fuels apply, *alcohol desnaturalizado*, *alcohol metílico*, *alcohol puro* (*de caña*) or *alcohol para quemar*. Ask for 95%, but 70% will suffice. In all countries fuel can usually be found in chemists/pharmacies. Gas cylinders and bottles are usually exchangeable, but if not can be recharged; specify whether you use butane or propane. Gas canisters are not always available. The Camping Clube do Brasil gives 50% discounts to holders of international campers' cards.

Eating

Food in South America is enticingly varied and regionally based. Within one country you cannot guarantee that what you enjoyed on the coast will be available in the sierras. It is impossible to list here what is on offer in each country and there is a section on food and drink in each chapter's Planning your trip section. Chinese restaurants tend to offer good value and where there are large immigrant communities you'll find excellent Japanese or Italian restaurants. Pizza is ubiquitous, sometimes genuine, sometimes anything but. Then there's fruit, fruit and more fruit in all the tropical regions, eaten fresh or as ice cream, or as a juice.

In all countries except Brazil and Chile (where cold meats, cheese, eggs, fruit, etc generally figure) breakfast usually means coffee or tea with rolls and butter, and anything more costs

Eating price codes

🍴🍴🍴 over US$12	🍴🍴 US$7-12	🍴 US$6 and under

Prices for a two-course meal for one person, excluding drinks or service charge.

extra. In Colombia and Ecuador breakfast usually means eggs, a roll, fruit juice and a mug of milk with coffee. **Vegetarians** should be able to list all the foods they cannot eat; saying "*soy vegetariano/a*" (I'm a vegetarian) or "*no como carne*" (I don't eat meat) is often not enough. Most restaurants serve a daily special meal, usually at lunchtime, which is cheap and good.

Shopping

Handicrafts, like food, enjoy regional distinctiveness, especially in items such as textiles. Each region, even every village, has its own distinct pattern or style of cloth, so the choice is enormous. In the Andes, weaving has a spiritual significance, as well as a practical one. Reproductions of pre-Columbian designs can be found in pottery and jewellery and many artisans make delightful gold and silver items. Musical instruments (eg from Bolivia), gaucho wear, the mate drinking gourd and silver straw (*bombilla*), soapstone carvings and ceramics are just some things you take home. Remember that handicrafts can almost invariably be bought more cheaply away from the capital. **Gemstones** are good in Brazil; emeralds in Colombia. Leather goods are best in Argentina, Uruguay, Brazil and Colombia, while Peru markets native cotton. Buy **beachwear** in Brazil; it is matchless. **Bargaining** seems to be the general rule in most countries' street markets, but don't make a fool of yourself by bargaining over what, to you, is a small amount of money.

Essentials A-Z

Children

→ *For health matters, see page 42.* *Visit www.babygoes2.com.*

Travel with children can bring you into closer contact with South American families and, generally, presents no special problems – in fact the path is often smoother for family groups. Officials tend to be more amenable where children are concerned and even thieves and pickpockets seem to have some traditional respect for families, and may leave you alone because of it!

Food

Food can be a problem if the children are picky eaters. It is easier to take food such as biscuits, drinks and bread with you on longer trips than to rely on meal stops. Avocados are safe and nutritious for babies as young as 6 months and most older children like them too. A small immersion heater and jug for making hot drinks is invaluable, but remember that electric current varies. Try and get a dual-voltage one (110v and 220v).

Hotels

In all hotels, try to negotiate family rates. If charges are per person, always insist that 2 children will occupy 1 bed only, therefore counting as 1 tariff. If rates are per bed, the same applies. You can often get a reduced rate at cheaper hotels. Sometimes when travelling with a child you will be refused a room in a hotel that is 'unsuitable'. On river boat trips, unless you have large hammocks, it may be more comfortable and cost effective to hire a 2-berth cabin for 2 adults and a child.

Transport

People contemplating overland travel in South America with children should remember that a lot of time can be spent waiting for public transport. Even then, buses can de delayed on the journey. Travel on trains allows more scope for moving about, but trains are few and far between these days. In many cases trains are luxurious and much more expensive than buses. If hiring a car, check that it has rear seat belts.

On all long-distance buses you pay for each seat, and there are no half-fares if the children occupy a seat each. For shorter trips it is cheaper, if less comfortable, to seat small children on your knee. There may be spare seats which children can occupy after tickets have been collected. In city and local excursion buses, small children generally do not pay a fare, but are not entitled to a seat when paying customers are standing. On sightseeing tours you should always bargain for a family rate – often children can go free. All civil airlines charge half for children under 12, but some military services don't have half-fares, or have younger age limits. Note that a child travelling free on a long excursion is not always covered by the operator's travel insurance; it is advisable to pay a small premium to arrange cover.

Disabled travellers

In most of South America, facilities for the disabled are severely lacking. For those in wheelchairs, ramps and toilet access are limited to some of the more upmarket, or most recently built hotels. Pavements are often in a poor state of repair or crowded with street vendors. Most archaeological sites, even Machu Picchu, have little or no wheelchair access. Visually or hearing-impaired travellers are also poorly catered for, but there are experienced guides in some places who can provide individual attention. There are also travel companies outside South America who specialize in holidays which are tailor-made for the individual's level of disability. Some moves are being made to improve the situation. In Chile all new public buildings are supposed to provide access for the disabled by law; PromPerú has initiated a programme to provide facilities at airports, tourist sites, etc; Quito's trolley buses are supposed to have wheelchair access, but they are often too crowded to make this practical. While disabled South Americans have to rely on others to get around, foreigners will find that people are generally very helpful. The **Global Access – Disabled Travel Network** website, www.globalaccessnews.com, is useful. Another informative site, with lots of advice on how to travel with specific disabilities, plus listings and links belongs to the **Society for Accessible Travel and Hospitality**, www.sath.org. Also see **www.access-able.com**.

LGBT (Lesbian, Gay, Bisexual, Transgendered) travellers

South America is hardly well-known for its gay-friendliness, but recent years have seen a slight shift in public opinion and attitudes. There is still a definite divide between the countryside and the city, but at least in the latter there are now more gay bars, organizations and social networks springing up. The legal framework has also been changing and homosexuality is now legal across South America, with the exception of Guyana, where male homosexuality is still a crime. Many countries have anti-discrimination laws and civil partnerships are becoming more common and recognised. There is also a slowly increasing acceptance and knowledge of transgender issues, particularly in Uruguay, Colombia and Brazil. That said, it is wise to use caution and avoid overt displays of affection in public, particularly in rural areas, where the population tends to be more conservative. In the often macho Latin culture, gay men are more likely to experience trouble or harassment than gay women, but men also have a much better developed support network of bars, clubs and organizations, while lesbian culture and communities remain more hidden.

Some of the best cities for gay life are Buenos Aires (Argentina), Santiago (Chile), Bogotá (Colombia), Rio de Janeiro and other cities in Brazil, Lima (Peru) and Quito (Ecuador). Useful websites include: **www.gaytravel.com**, **www.iglta.org** (International Gay and Lesbian Travel Association) and **www.lghei.org** (Lesbian and Gay Hospitality Exchange International). For Argentina: **www.thegay guide.com.ar**, **www.theronda.com.ar**, **http://buenosaires.queercity.info/**, **www.globalgayz.com/country/Argentina/ARG**, www.mundogay.com, www.nexo.org (both in Spanish). Brazil: **www.riogayguide.com** and **http://gayguide.net/South_America/Brazil/**. Chile: **www.santiagogay.com** and **www.opusgay.cl** (in Spanish). Colombia: **www.guiagaycolombia.com**. Ecuador: **www.gayecuador.com** and **www.quitogay.net**. Paraguay: **http://paraboi.com**. Peru: **http://lima.queercity.info/index.html**, **www.deambiente.com/web** and **www.gayperu.com** (last two in Spanish). Uruguay: **www.outinuruguay.com**.

Health → *Hospitals/medical facilities are listed in the Directory sections of each chapter.*

See your GP or travel clinic at least 6 weeks before departure for general advice on travel risks and vaccinations. Try phoning a specialist travel clinic if your own doctor is unfamiliar with health in the region. Make sure you have sufficient medical travel insurance, get a dental check, know your own blood group and, if you suffer a long-term condition such as diabetes or epilepsy, obtain a **Medic Alert** bracelet (www.medicalalert.co.uk).

Vaccinations and anti-malarials

Confirm that your primary courses and boosters are up to date. It is advisable to vaccinate against polio, tetanus, typhoid, hepatitis A and, for more remote areas, rabies. Yellow fever vaccination is obligatory for most areas. Cholera, diphtheria and hepatitis B vaccinations are sometimes advised. Specialist advice should be taken on the best antimalarials to take before you leave.

Health risks

The major risks posed in the region are those caused by insect disease carriers such as mosquitoes and sandflies. The key parasitic and viral diseases are malaria, South American trypanosomiasis (Chagas' disease) and dengue fever. Be aware that you are always at risk from these diseases. **Malaria** is a danger throughout the lowland tropics and coastal regions. **Dengue fever** (which is currently rife in Rio de Janeiro state in Brazil and in Paraguay) is particularly hard to protect against as the mosquitoes can bite throughout the day as well as night (unlike those that carry malaria); try to wear clothes that cover arms and legs and also use effective mosquito repellent. Mosquito nets dipped in permethrin provide a good physical and chemical barrier at night. **Chagas' disease** is spread by faeces of the triatomine, or assassin bugs, whereas sandflies spread a disease of the skin called **leishmaniasis**.

Some form of **diarrhoea** or intestinal upset is almost inevitable, the standard advice is always to wash your hands before eating and to be careful with drinking water and ice; if you have any doubts about the water then boil it or filter and treat it. In a restaurant buy bottled water or ask where the water has come from. Food can also pose a problem, be wary of salads if you don't know whether they have been washed or not.

There is a constant threat of **tuberculosis** (TB) and although the BCG vaccine is available, it is still not guaranteed protection. It is best to avoid unpasteurized dairy products and try not to let people cough and splutter all over you.

One of the major problems for travellers in the region is **altitude sickness**. It is essential to get acclimatized to the thin air of the Andes before undertaking long treks or arduous activities. The altitude of the Andes means that strong protection from the sun is always needed, regardless of how cool it may feel.

Another risk, especially to campers and people with small children, is that of the **hanta virus**, which is carried by some forest and riverine rodents. Epidemics have occurred in Argentina and Chile, but do occur worldwide. Symptoms are a flu-like illness which can lead to complications. Try as far as possible to avoid rodent-infested areas, especially close contact with rodent droppings.

Websites

www.cdc.gov Centres for Disease Control and Prevention (USA).

www.dh.gov.uk/en/Policyandguidance/Healthadvicefortravellers/index.htm Department of Health advice for travellers.

www.fitfortravel.scot.nhs.uk Fit for Travel (UK), a site from Scotland providing a quick A-Z of vaccine and travel health advice requirements for each country.

www.fco.gov.uk Foreign and Commonwealth Office (FCO), UK.

www.itg.be Prince Leopold Institute for Tropical Medicine.
www.nathnac.org National Travel Health Network and Centre (NaTHNaC).
www.who.int World Health Organisation.

Books

Dawood, R, editor, *Travellers' health*, 3rd ed, Oxford: Oxford University Press, 2002.
Johnson, Chris, Sarah Anderson and others, *Oxford Handbook of Expedition and Wilderness Medicine*, OUP 2008.
Wilson-Howarth, Jane. *Bugs, Bites and Bowels: the essential guide to travel health*, Cadogan 2009.

Internet

Email is common and public access to the internet is widespread. In large cities an hour in a cyber café will cost between US$0.50 and US$2, with some variation between busy and quiet times. Speed varies enormously, from city to city, café to café. Away from population centres service is slower and more expensive. Remember that for many South Americans cyber cafés provide their only access to a computer, so it can be a very busy place and providers can get overloaded.

Language

The official language of the majority of South American countries is Spanish. The exceptions are Brazil (Portuguese), Guyana and the Falklands/Malvinas (English), Suriname (Dutch) and Guyane (French). English is often spoken by wealthy and well-educated citizens, particularly in Colombia, but otherwise the use of English is generally restricted to those working in the tourism industry. The basic Spanish of Hispanic America is that of south-western Spain, with soft 'c's' and 'z's' pronounced as 's', and not as 'th' as in the other parts of Spain. There are several regional variations in pronunciation, particularly in the River Plate countries; see box, opposite. Differences in vocabulary also exist, both between peninsular Spanish and Latin American Spanish, and between the usages of the different countries.

Without some knowledge of Spanish (or Portuguese) you will become very frustrated and feel helpless in many situations. English, or any other language, is absolutely useless off the beaten track. Some initial study, to get you up to a basic vocabulary of 500 words or so, and a pocket dictionary and phrase-book, are most strongly recommended: your pleasure will be doubled if you can talk to the locals. Not all the locals speak Spanish (or Portuguese); you will find that in the more remote highland parts of Bolivia and Peru, and lowland Amazonia, some people speak only their indigenous languages, though there will usually be at least one person in each village who can speak Spanish (or Portuguese).

Language courses

If you are going to Brazil, you should learn some Portuguese. Spanish is not adequate: you may be understood but you will probably not be able to understand the answers. Language classes are available cheaply in a number of centres in South America, for instance Quito. For details, see below and also in the main text under Language courses.

Second languages and anomalies

Argentina English is the second most common language; French and Italian (especially in Patagonia) may be useful. In Spanish, the chief variant pronunciations are the replacement of the 'll' and 'y' sounds by a soft 'j' sound, as in 'azure' (though rarely in Mendoza or the northwest), the omission of the 'd' sound in words ending in '-ado', the omission of final 's' sounds, the pronunciation of 's' before a consonant as a Scottish or German 'ch', and the substitution in the north and west of the normal rolled 'r' sound by a hybrid 'rj'. In grammar the Spanish 'tú' is replaced by 'vos' and the second person singular conjugation of verbs has the accent on the last syllable eg vos tenés, podés, etc. In the north and northwest, the Spanish is closer to that spoken in the rest of Latin America.
Bolivia Outside the cities, especially in the highlands, Aymara and Quechua are spoken by much of the indigenous population. In the lowlands, some Tupi Guaraní is spoken.
Chile The local pronunciation of Spanish, very quick and lilting, with the 's' dropped and final syllables cut off, can present difficulties to the foreigner.
Colombia Colombia has arguably the best spoken Spanish in Latin America, clearly enunciated and not too fast. This is particularly true in the highlands. There are several indigenous languages in the more remote parts of the country.
Ecuador Quichua is the second official language, although it is little used outside indigenous communities in the highlands and parts of Oriente.
Paraguay Guaraní is the second official language. Most people are bilingual and, outside Asunción, speak Guaraní. Many people speak a mixture of the two languages known as *jopara*.
Peru Quechua, the Andean language that predates the Incas, has been given some official status and there is much pride in its use. It is spoken by millions of people in the Sierra who have little or no knowledge of Spanish. Aymara is used in the area around Lake Titicaca. The jungle is home to a plethora of languages but Spanish is spoken in all but the remotest areas.
Suriname The native language, called Sranan Tongo, originally the speech of the Creoles, is now a lingua franca understood by all groups, and English is widely used.
Guyane Officials do not usually (or deliberately not) speak anything other than French, but Créole is more commonly spoken.

In the **Guianas**, the Asians, Maroons and Amerindians still speak their own languages among themselves.

Academia Buenos Aires, C Hipolito Yrgoyen 571, p 4, CP 1086, T+54 11-4345 5954, www.academiabuenosaires.com
AmeriSpan, 1334 Walnut St, 6th Floor, Philadelphia, PA 19107 (PO Box 58129) T215-751 1100 (worldwide), T1-800-879-6640 (USA), SKYPE: amerispan, www.amerispan.com, offers Spanish immersion programmes, educational tours, volunteer and internship positions throughout Latin America. Language programmes are offered in Argentina, Bolivia, Brazil, Chile, Colombia, Ecuador, Peru, Uruguay and Venezuela.
Languages Abroad.com, 386 Ontario St, Toronto, Ontario, Canada, M5A 2V7, T416-925 2112, toll free T1-800-219 9924 (T0800-404 7738 – UK), www.languagesabroad.com, offers Spanish and Portuguese programmes in every South American country except Paraguay and Uruguay. They also have language immersion courses throughout the world.
Cactus, T0845-130 4775, www.cactuslanguage.com.
Spanish Abroad, 3219 East Camelback Road No 806, Phoenix, AZ 85018, USA, T1-888-722 7623, or 602-778 6791 (UK 0800-028 7706), www.spanishabroad.com, also run courses.

Local customs and laws

Appearance

There is a natural prejudice in all countries against travellers who ignore personal hygiene and have a generally dirty and unkempt appearance. Most Latin Americans, if they can afford it, devote great care to their clothes and appearance; it is appreciated if visitors do likewise. Buying clothing locally can help you to look less like a tourist. In general, clothing requirements in Brazil are less formal than in the Hispanic countries. As a general rule, it is better not to wear shorts in official buildings, upmarket restaurants or cinemas. Also in Brazil, it is normal to stare and comment on women's appearance, and if you happen to look different or to be travelling alone, you will attract attention. Single women are very unlikely to be groped or otherwise molested (except at Carnaval), but nonetheless Brazilian men can be extraordinarily persistent, and very easily encouraged.

Courtesy

Remember that politeness – even a little ceremoniousness – is much appreciated. Men should always remove any headgear and say "*con permiso*" ("*com licença*" in Brazil) when entering offices, and be prepared to shake hands (this is much more common in Latin America than in Europe or North America); always say "*Buenos días*" (until midday) or "*Buenas tardes*" ("*Bom dia*" or "*Boa tarde*" in Brazil) and wait for a reply before proceeding further. Always remember that the traveller from abroad has enjoyed greater advantages in life than most Latin American minor officials and should be friendly and courteous in consequence. Never be impatient. Do not criticize situations in public; the officials may know more English than you think and they can certainly interpret gestures and facial expressions. Be judicious about discussing politics with strangers. Politeness can be a liability, however, in some situations; most Latin Americans are disorderly queuers. In commercial transactions (eg buying goods in a shop), politeness should be accompanied by firmness, and always ask the price first (arguing about money in a foreign language can be very difficult).

Politeness should also be extended to street traders; saying "*No, gracias*" or "*Não, obrigado/a*" with a smile is better than an arrogant dismissal. Whether you give money to beggars is a personal matter, but your decision should be influenced by whether a person is begging out of need or trying to cash in on the tourist trail. In the former case, local people giving may provide an indication. On giving money to children, most agree don't do it. There are times when giving food in a restaurant may be appropriate, but find out about local practice.

Money → *See each country's Money section in Planning your trip for exchange rates.*

Cash

The main ways of keeping in funds while travelling are with cash, either US dollars or, in a growing number of places, euros; credit cards/debit cards; US dollars traveller's cheques (TCs, increasingly hard to exchange). Sterling and other currencies are not recommended. Though the risk of loss is greater, the chief benefit of US$ notes is that better rates and lower commissions can usually be obtained for them. In many countries, US$ notes are only accepted if they are in excellent, if not perfect condition (likewise, do not accept local currency notes in poor condition). Low-value US$ bills should be carried for changing into local currency if arriving in a country when banks or *casas de cambio* (exchange shops) are closed (US$5 or US$10 bills). They are very useful for shopping: shopkeepers and *casas de cambio* tend to give better exchange rates than hotels or banks (but see below). The better hotels will normally change TCs for their guests (often at a poor rate), but if you are travelling on the cheap it is essential to keep in funds. At weekends, on public holidays and when travelling off the beaten track always have plenty of local currency, preferably in small denominations. When departing by air, make sure you can pay the airport departure tax which, unless included in your ticket price, is never waived.

Approximate costs of travelling are given in the Planning your trip section of each chapter.

Plastic

Emergency contact numbers for credit card loss or theft are given in the relevant country. It is straightforward to obtain a cash advance against a credit card. Many banks are also linked to one, if not both of the main international **ATM** acceptance systems, Plus and Cirrus. Coverage is not uniform throughout the continent, though, so it may be wise to take two types of cards. Frequently, the rates of exchange on ATM withdrawals are the best available. Find out before you leave what ATM coverage there is in the countries you will visit and what international 'functionality' your card has. Check if your bank or credit card company imposes handling charges. Obviously you must ensure that the account to which your debit card refers contains sufficient funds. Before travelling, it may be worth setting up two bank accounts: one with all your funds but no debit card, the other with no funds but which does have a debit card. As you travel, use the internet to transfer money from the full account to the empty account when you need it and withdraw cash from an ATM. That way, if your debit card is stolen, you won't be at risk of losing all your capital.

By using a debit card rather than a credit card you incur fewer bank charges, although a credit card is needed as well for some purchases. With a credit card, obtain a credit limit sufficient for your needs, or pay money in to put the account in credit. If travelling for a long time, consider a direct debit to clear your account regularly. Do not rely on one card, in case of loss. If you do lose a card, immediately contact the 24-hr helpline of the issuer in your home country (keep this number in a safe place).

For purchases, credit cards of the Visa and MasterCard groups, American Express (Amex), Carte Blanche and Diners Club can be used. Transactions using credit cards are normally at an officially recognized rate of exchange; but are often subject to tax. For ATM locations, see www.visalatam.com, www.mastercard.com and www.americanexpress.com; for Western Union agents: www.westernunion.com.

Another option is to take a prepaid currency card. There are many on offer, from, for example, **Caxton**, **FairFX**, **Travelex**, banks and other organizations. It pays to check their application fees and charges carefully.

Traveller's cheques (TCs)

These are convenient but they attract thieves (though refunds can of course be arranged) and you will find that they are more difficult to change than US$ cash. Amex, Visa or Thomas Cook US$ TCs are recommended. Most banks charge a high fixed commission. *Casas de cambio* may be better for this service. Some places may ask to see the customer's record of purchase before accepting.

Exchange

When changing money on the street if possible, do not do so alone. If unsure of the currency of the country you are about to enter, check rates with more than one changer at the border, or ask locals or departing travellers. Whenever you leave a country, exchange any local currency before leaving, because the further away you get, the less the value of a country's money.

Post

→ *Local post offices are listed in the Directory sections of each chapter.*

Postal services vary in efficiency and prices are quite high; pilfering is frequent. All mail, especially packages, should be registered. Some countries have local alternatives to the post office. Check before leaving home if your embassy will hold mail, and for how long, in preference to the Poste Restante/ General Delivery (Lista de Correos) department of a country's Post Office. (Cardholders can use American Express agencies.) If there seems to be no mail at the Lista under the initial letter of your surname, ask them to look under the initial of your forename or your middle name. Remember that there is no W in Spanish; look under V, or ask. To reduce the risk of misunderstanding, use title, initial and surname only. If having items sent to you by courier (such as DHL), do not use poste restante, but an address such as a hotel: a signature is required on receipt.

Radio

World Band Radio South America has more local and community radio stations than nearly anywhere else in the world; a short wave (world band) radio offers a practical means to brush up on the language, sample popular culture and absorb some of the richly varied regional music. International broadcasters such as the BBC World Service, the Voice of America, Boston- (Mass) based Monitor Radio International (operated by Christian Science Monitor) and the Quito-based Evangelical station, HCJB, keep you abreast of news and events, in both English and Spanish.

Compact or miniature portables are recommended, with digital tuning and a full range of shortwave bands, as well as FM, long and medium wave. Detailed advice on radio models and wavelengths can be found in the annual publication, *Passport to World Band Radio* (International Broadcasting Services Ltd, USA, £17.55). Details of local stations are listed in *World Radio TV Handbook (WRTH)* (WRTH Publications, £17.50, www.amazon.co.uk).

Safety → *For specific local problems, see under the individual countries in the text.*

Drugs

Users of drugs, even of soft ones, without medical prescription should be particularly careful, as some countries impose heavy penalties – up to 10 years' imprisonment – for even possession of such substances. The planting of drugs on travellers, by traffickers or police, is not unknown. If offered drugs on the street, make no response at all and keep walking. Note that people who roll their own cigarettes are often suspected of carrying drugs and subjected to intensive searches.

Keeping safe

Generally speaking, most places in South America are no more dangerous than any major city in Europe or North America. In provincial towns, main places of interest, on daytime buses and in ordinary restaurants the visitor should be quite safe. Nevertheless, in large cities (particularly in crowded places, eg bus stations, markets), crime exists, most of which is opportunistic. If you are aware of the dangers, act confidently and use your common sense, you will lessen many of the risks. The following tips are all endorsed by travellers. Keep all documents secure; hide your main cash supply in different places or under your clothes: extra pockets sewn inside shirts and trousers, pockets closed with a zip or safety pin, moneybelts (best worn under rather than outside your clothes at the waist), neck or leg pouches, a thin chain for attaching a purse to your bag or under your clothes and elasticated support bandages for keeping money above the elbow or below the knee. Be extra vigilant when withdrawing cash from an ATM: ensure you are not being watched; never give your card to anyone, however smart he may look or plausible he may sound as a 'bank employee' wishing to swipe your card to check for problems. Keep cameras in bags; take spare spectacles (eyeglasses); don't wear expensive wristwatches or jewellery. If you wear a shoulder- bag in a market, carry it in front of you.

Ignore mustard smearers and paint or shampoo sprayers, and strangers' remarks like "what's that on your shoulder?" or "have you seen that dirt on your shoe?" Furthermore, don't bend over to pick up money or other items in the street. These are all ruses to distract your attention and make you easy prey for an accomplice. Take local advice about being out at night and, if walking after dark, walk in the road, not on the pavement/sidewalk.

It is worth knowing that genuine police officers only have the right to see your passport (not your money, tickets or hotel room). Before handing anything over, ask why they need to see it and make sure you understand the reason. Insist on seeing identification and on going to the police station by main roads. On no account take them directly back to your lodgings. Be even more suspicious if he seeks confirmation of his status from a passer-by. A related scam is for a 'tourist' to gain your confidence, then accomplices create a reason to check your documents. If someone tries to bribe you, insist on a receipt. If attacked, remember your assailants may well be armed, and try not to resist.

Leave any valuables you don't need in safe-deposit in your hotel when sightseeing locally. Always keep an inventory of what you have deposited. If there is no safe, lock your bags and secure them in your room. Hostels with shared rooms should provide secure, clean lockers for guests. If you lose valuables, always report to the police and note details of the report – for insurance purposes.

When you have all your luggage with you, be careful. From airports take official taxis or special airport buses. Take a taxi between bus station/ railway station and hotel. Keep your bags with you in the taxi and pay only when you and your luggage are safely out of the vehicle. Make sure the taxi has inner door handles and do not share the ride with a stranger. Avoid night buses; never arrive at night; and watch your belongings whether they are stowed inside or outside the cabin (roof top luggage racks create extra problems, which are sometimes unavoidable – make sure your bag is waterproof). Major bus lines often issue a luggage ticket when bags are stored in the hold of the bus. Finally, never accept food, drink, sweets or cigarettes from unknown fellow travellers on buses or trains. They may be drugged, and you would wake up hours later without your belongings.

Police

Whereas in Europe and North America we are accustomed to law enforcement on a systematic basis, in general, enforcement in Latin America is achieved by periodic campaigns. The most typical is a round-up of criminals in the cities just before Christmas. In Dec, therefore, you may well be asked for identification at any time, and if you cannot produce it, you will be jailed. If a visitor is jailed his or her friends should provide food every day. This is especially important for people on a diet, such as diabetics. In the event of a vehicle accident in which anyone is injured, all drivers involved are automatically detained until blame has been established, and this does not usually take less than 2 weeks. Never offer a bribe unless you are fully conversant with the customs of the country. (In Chile, for instance, it would land you in serious trouble if you tried to bribe a *carabinero*.) Wait until the official makes the suggestion, or offer money in some form which is apparently not bribery, for example "In our country we have a system of on-the-spot fines (*multas de inmediato*). Is there a similar system here?" Do not assume that an official who accepts a bribe is prepared to do anything else that is illegal. You bribe him to persuade him to do his job, or to persuade him not to do it, or to do it more quickly or slowly. You do not bribe him to do something which is illegal. The mere suggestion would make him very upset. If an official suggests that a bribe must be paid before you can proceed on your way, be patient (assuming you have the time) and he may relent.

Rape

This can happen anywhere. If you are the victim of a sexual assault, you are advised in the first instance to contact a doctor (this can be your home doctor if you prefer). You will need tests to determine whether you have contracted any sexually transmitted diseases; you may also need advice on post-coital contraception. You should also contact your embassy, where consular staff are very willing to help in such cases.

Student travellers

Student cards must carry a photograph if they are to be of any use in Latin America for discounts. If you are in full-time education you will be entitled to an International Student Identity Card, which is distributed by student travel offices and travel agencies in 77 countries. The ISIC gives you special prices on all forms of transport such as air, sea, rail, and access to a variety of other concessions and services. If you need to find the location of your nearest ISIC office contact the **ISIC Association**, www.istc.org, which has offices worldwide.

Telephone → *Local dialling codes are listed at the beginning of each town entry.*

The most common method of making phone calls is with a pre-paid card. These are sold in a variety of denominations in, or just outside, phone offices. Phone offices (*centros de llamadas, locutorios*) are usually private, sometimes with lots of cabins, internet and other services, at other times just a person at a table offering national and international calls, mobile phone calls through various providers and phone cards. Public phone booths are also operated with phone cards, very rarely with coins or tokens. With privatization, more and more companies are competing on the market, so you can shop around. Net2phone and SKYPE can also be used. If you want to use a mobile phone, either take your own if your provider has an agreement with a local operator (these vary from country to country), or buy a local SIM card. Phones must be tri- or quad-band; again, this varies. Rental (not cheap) and buying a pay-as-you-go phone is possible, but you will have to check the range of the phone. The area covered is often small and rates rise dramatically once you leave it.

Tour operators

4starSouthAmerica, PO Box 11552, Washington DC 20008, T1-800-747-4540 (USA/Canada), T00800-747 45400 (Europe/Australia/New Zealand/ South Africa), www.southamerica.travel. Offices also in Argentina, Brazil and Peru.

Amazing Peru, 9 Alma Rd, Manchester M19 2FG, T0800-520 0309, T1-800-216 0831 or T1-800-704 2915 or 1-800-704 2949 (USA/Canada), www.amazingperu.com. UK managed with offices in Peru, Ecuador and Chile. Wide selection of tours.

Amazing Voyages, 52 Brook St, London W1K 5DS, T020-7268 2053, www.amazingvoyages. co.uk. Luxury travel specialist.

Andean Trails, The Clockhouse, Bonnington Mill Business Centre, 72 Newhaven Rd, Edinburgh EH6 5QG, UK, T0131-467 7086, www.andeantrails.co.uk.

Audley Travel, New Mill, New Mill Lane, Witney, Oxfordshire, OX29 9SX, UK, T01993-838000, www.audleytravel.com.

Austral Tours, 20 Upper Tachbrook St, London SW1V 1SH, T020-7233 5384, www.latinamerica.co.uk. Tailor-made tours, flights and accommodation in Latin America.

Chile Tours, Suite 2, Blandel Bridge House, 56 Sloane Sq, London SW1W 8AX, T020-7730 5959, www.chiletours.org.

Chimu Adventures, www.chimuadventures. com. Web-based company providing tours, treks, active adventures and accommodation throughout South America and the Antarctic.

Condor Journeys & Adventures, 2 Ferry Bank, Colintrave, Argyll PA22 3AR, UK, T1700-841318, www.condorjourneys-adventures.com.

Condor Travel, Armando Blondet 249, San Isidro, Lima 27, T01-615 3000, www.condortravel.com. In USA T1-877-236 7199. A full range of tours, including custom-made, and services in Argentina, Bolivia, Brazil, Chile, Colombia, Ecuador and Peru (offices in each country), with a strong commitment to social responsibility.

Discover the World, Artic House, 8 Bolters Lane, Banstead, Surrey SM7 2AR, T01737-218800, www.discover-the-world.co.uk.

Dragoman, Camp Green, Debenham, Suffolk IP14 6LA, UK, T01728-861133, www.dragoman.co.uk.

eXito, 108 Rutgers Ave, Fort Collins, CO 80525, USA, T1-800-655 4053 (USA), T800-670 2605 (Canada), www.exitotravel.com.

Exodus Travels, Grange Mills, Weir Rd, London SW12 0NE, T0845-863 9600, www.exodus.co.uk.

ExpeditionTrips.com, 6553 California Av SW, Seattle, WA 98136, USA, T206-547 0700 , www.expeditiontrips.com.

Experience Chile, 13 Station Road, Beaconsfield, Bucks, HP9 1NL, UK, T020-8133 6057, www.experiencechile.org. Specialists in trips to Chile.

Explore, Nelson House, 55 Victoria Rd, Farnborough, Hampshire, GU14 7PA, UK, T0845-013 1537, www.explore.co.uk.

Galápagos Classic Cruises in conjunction with **Classic Cruises** and **World Adventures**, 6 Keyes Rd, London NW2 3XA, T020-8933 0613, www.galapagoscruises.co.uk, specialize in individual and group travel including cruises, scuba diving and land-based tours to the Galapagos, Peru, Bolivia, Brazil, Argentina, Chile, Costa Rica, Mexico, Honduras, Guatemala, Belize, Venezuela, Patagonia and Antarctica.

GAP Adventures, 19 Charlotte St, Toronto, M5V 2H5, Canada, T1-800-708 7761 (in North America), 40 Star St, London W2 1QB, T0870 999 0144, T1-416-260 0999 (outside North America & UK), www.gapadventures.com.

Geodyssey, 116 Tollington Park, London N4 3RB, UK, T020-7281 7788, www.geodyssey.co.uk.

Guerba Adventure & Discovery Holidays, Wessex House, 40 Station Rd, Westbury, Wilts BA13 3 JN, UK, T01373-828303 or 0203-147 7777 (reservations and enquiries), www.guerba.com.

Journey Latin America, 12-13 Heathfield Terrace, London W4 4JE, UK, T020-8747 8315, www.journeylatinamerica.co.uk.

Ladatco, 3006 Aviation, Suite 3A, Coconut Grove, FL 33133, USA, T1-800 327 6162, www.ladatco.com.

Last Frontiers, The Mill, Quainton Rd, Waddesdon, Bucks, HP18 0LP, UK, T01296-653000, www.lastfrontiers.com. South American specialists offering tailor-made itineraries plus family holidays, honeymoons, Galápagos and Antactic cruises.

Latin America for Less, 919 East 49 1/2 St, Austin, TX 78751, USA, T1-877-269 0309 (toll free), T0203 002 0571 (UK), www.latinamericaforless.com.

Latin American Travel Association, 46 Melbourne Rd, London SW19 3BA, www.lata.org. For useful country information and listing of all UK tour operators specializing in Latin America.

Lost World Adventures, T800-999 0558, www.lostworld.com.

Myths and Mountains, 976 Tee Court, Incline Village, NV 89451, USA, T800-670 MYTH, T775-832 5454, www.mythsandmountains.com.

Nature Expeditions International, 7860 Peters Rd, suite F-103, Plantation, FL 33324, USA, T1-800-869 0639 or 954-693 8852, www.naturexp.com.

Neblina Forest Tours, Isla Floreana E8-129 Y Av Shyris, Edif el Sol, Office 304/30, Quito, Ecuador, T0808 234 1434, www.neblinaforest.com. Birdwatching and cultural tours in Ecuador (including the Amazon and Galapagos Islands), Peru (Machu Picchu), Bolivia, Brazil, Costa Rica, Guyana and Colombia with a fully Ecuadorian/ South American staff of birding and nature guides.

Nouveaux Mondes, Rte Suisse 7, CH-1295 Mies, Switzerland, T+41-22-950 9660, info@nouveauxmondes.com.

Oasis Overland, The Marsh, Henstridge, Somerset, BA8 0TF, UK, T01963-363400, www.oasisoverland.co.uk. Small group trips to Peru and overland tours throughout South America.

Reef and Rainforest Tours Ltd, A7 Dart Marine Park, Steamer Quay, Totnes, Devon TQ9 5AL, UK,

T01803-866965, www.reefandrainforest.co.uk. Tailor-made and group wildlife tours.

Responsible Travel.com, 3rd Floor, Pavilion House, 6 Old Steine, Brighton, BN1 1EJ, UK, T01273-600030, www.responsibletravel.com.

Santours/Santini Tours & Tropical Travel, 6575 Shattuck Av, Oakland, CA 94609, USA, T001 510 652 8600, www.santours.com. International travel specialists and air consolidators.

Select Latin America, 3.51 Canterbury Court, 1-3 Brixton Rd, Kennington Park, London SW9 6DE, UK, T020-7407 1478, www.selectlatinamerica.co.uk. Tailor-made holidays and small group tours.

South America Adventure Travel, Global Encounters, JA Cabrera 4423/29, C1414BGE, Buenos Aires, Argentina, T512-592 3877, US Toll Free 877-275 4957, www.southamerica adventure.travel. Specialize in budget adventure tours, with offices throughout South America

South American Experience, Welby House, 96 Wilton Rd, London SW1V 1DW, UK, T0845-277 3366, www.southamerican experience.co.uk. Tailor-made travel throughout Latin America since 1987.

Steppes Latin America, 51 Castle St, Cirencester, Glos GL7 1QD, T01285-880980, www.steppestravel.co.uk. Tailor-made itineraries for destinations throughout Latin America.

Tambo Tours, USA, T1-888-2-GO-PERU (246-7378), www.2GOPERU.com. Long-established adventure and tour specialist with offices in Peru and the US. Customized trips to the Amazon and archaeological sites of Peru, Bolivia and Ecuador.

Travelbag, 373-375 The Strand, London WC2R OJE, and 8 other branches in the UK, T0871-703 4700 (0203-139 7427 from outside UK), www.travelbag.co.uk.

TrekAmerica Travel Ltd, TUI Travel House, Crawley Business Quarter, Fleming Way, Crawley, West Sussex, RH10 9QL, UK, T0845-313 2614, www.trekamerica.co.uk. For Peru.

Tribes Travel, 12 The Business Centre, Earl Soham, Woodbridge, Suffolk, IP13 7SA, UK, T01728-685971, www.tribes.co.uk.

Trips Worldwide, 14 Frederick Pl, Bristol BS8 1AS, UK, T0800-840 0850, www.tripsworldwide.co.uk.

Tropical Nature Travel, PO Box 5276, Gainesville, FL 32627-5276, T1-877-888-1770 or 1-877-827-8350, www.tropical naturetravel.com. Ecotour company with itineraries to Ecuador, Peru and Brazil.

Tucan, 316 Uxbridge Rd, Acton, London W3 9QP, T020-8896 1600, Avenida del Sol 616, oficina 202, AP 0637, Cuzco T51-84-241123, and 217 Alison Rd, Randwick, NSW 2031, Sydney, T02-9326 6633, www.tucantravel.com.

Veloso Tours, 34 Warple Way, London W3 0RG, UK, T020-8762 0616, www.veloso.com.

World Expeditions, 81 Craven Gardens, Wimbledon, London SW19 8LU, T020-8545 9030, UK, www.worldexpeditions.co.uk, with offices in Australia, New Zealand, USA and Canada.

Tourist information → *Local sources of information are given in the country chapters.*

South American Explorers, 126 Indian Creek Rd, Ithaca, NY, 14850, T607 277 0488, ithacaclub @saexplorers.org, www.saexplorers.org, is a non-profit educational organization staffed by volunteers, widely recognized as the best place to go for information on South America. Highly

recommended as a source for specialized information, trip reports, maps, lectures, library resources. SAE publishes a 64-page quarterly journal, helps members plan trips and expeditions, stores gear, holds post, hosts book exchanges, provides expert travel advice, etc. Annual membership fee US$60 individual (US$90 couple) includes subscription to its quarterly journal, The South American Explorer (overseas postage extra). The SAE membership card is good for many discounts throughout Ecuador, Peru, Argentina and, to a lesser extent, Bolivia and Uruguay. The Clubhouses in Quito, Lima, Cuzco and Buenos Aires are attractive and friendly. SAE will sell used equipment on consignment (donations of used equipment, unused medicines, etc are welcome).

Finding out more

It is better to seek security advice before you leave from your own consulate than from travel agencies. You can contact:

British Foreign and Commonwealth Office, Travel Advice Unit, T0845 850 2829 (travel advice), 020-7008 1500 (consular assistance from abroad). Footprint is a partner in the Foreign and Commonwealth Office's **Know before you go** campaign, www.fco.gov.uk/en/travel-and-living-abroad/.

US State Department's Bureau of Consular Affairs, Overseas Citizens Services, T1-888-407 4747 (from overseas: 202-501 4444), www.travel.state.gov. **Australian Department of Foreign Affairs**, T+61-2-6261 3305, www.smartraveller.gov.au/.

Useful websites

Website addresses for individual countries are given in the relevant chapter's Planning your trip sections and throughout the text.

www.bootsnall.com/South-America Online travel guides for South America, updated monthly.

http://gosouthamerica.about.com/ Articles and links on sights, planning, countries, culture, gay and lesbian travel.

http://lanic.utexas.edu The Latin American Network Information Center: loads of information on everything.

www.lata.org Lists tour operators, hotels, airlines, etc. Has a useful (free) guide which can also be ordered by phoning T020-8715 2913.

www.oas.org The Organization of American States site, with its magazine *Americas*.

www.planeta.com Ron Mader's website contains masses of useful information on ecotourism, conservation, travel, news, the web, language schools and articles.

www.rainforest-alliance.org Working for conservation and sustainability in Argentina, Bolivia, Brazil, Chile, Colombia, Ecuador, Peru, Uruguay and Venezuela.

www.virtualtourist.com/f/4/ South America travel forum, which can take you down some interesting alleyways, lots of links, trips, etc; good exploring here.

www.whatsonwhen.com for worldwide information on festivals and events.

Visas and documentation → *See each country's Planning your trip section for specific visa requirements.*

Passports and other important documents

You should always carry your passport in a safe place about your person, or if not going far, leave it in the hotel safe. If staying in a country for several weeks, it is worthwhile registering at your embassy or consulate. Then, if your passport is stolen, the process of replacing it is simplified and speeded up. Keep photocopies of essential documents, including your flight ticket, and some additional passport-sized photographs, or send yourself before you leave home an email with all important details, addresses, etc, which you can access in an emergency. It is your responsibility to ensure that your passport is stamped in and out when you cross borders. The absence of entry and exit stamps can cause serious difficulties; seek out the proper immigration offices if the stamping process is not carried out as you cross. Also, do not lose your entry card; replacing one causes a lot of trouble, and possibly expense. If planning to study in Latin America for a long period, get a student visa in advance.

Identity and membership cards

Membership cards of British, European and US motoring organizations can be useful for discounts off items such as hotel charges, car rentals, maps and towing charges. Business people should carry a good supply of visiting cards, which are essential for good business relations. Identity, membership or business cards in Spanish or Portuguese (or a translation) and an official letter of introduction in Spanish or Portuguese are also useful.

Women travellers

Many women travel alone or in pairs in South America without undue difficulty. Attitudes and courtesy towards western women, especially those on their own, vary from country to country. The following hints have mainly been supplied by women, but most apply to any single traveller. First-time exposure to countries where sections of the population live in extreme poverty or squalor and may even be starving can cause odd psychological reactions in visitors. So can the exceptional curiosity extended to visitors, especially women. Simply be prepared for this and try not to over-react. When you set out, err on the side of caution until your instincts have adjusted to the customs of a new culture. If, as a single woman, you can befriend a local woman, you will learn much more about the country you are visiting. Unless actively avoiding foreigners like yourself, don't go too far from the beaten track; there is a very definite 'gringo trail' which you can join, or follow, if seeking company. This can be helpful when you're looking for safe accommodation, especially if arriving after dark (which is best avoided). Remember that for a single woman a taxi at night can be as dangerous as wandering around on your own. At borders dress as smartly as possible. When travelling by bus opt for a major company as your seat is reserved and your luggage can usually be locked in the hold. It is easier for men to take the friendliness of locals at face value; women may be subject to much unwanted attention. To help minimize this, do not wear suggestive clothing and do not flirt. By wearing a wedding ring, carrying a photograph of your 'husband' and 'children', and saying that your 'husband' is close at hand, you may dissuade an aspiring suitor. When asked how long you are travelling, say only for a short time because a long journey may give the impression that you are wealthy (even if you are not). If politeness fails, do not feel bad about showing offence and departing. When accepting a social invitation, make sure that someone knows the address and the time you left. Ask if you can bring a friend (even if you do not intend to do so). A good rule is always to act with confidence, as though you know where you are going, even if you do not. Someone who looks lost is more likely to attract unwanted attention. Do not tell strangers where you are staying.

Argentina

Contents

58 Planning your trip

67 Buenos Aires and the Pampas
69 Sights
100 Around Buenos Aires
102 The Pampas
107 Atlantic Coast

116 West of Buenos Aires
116 Córdoba
121 Around Córdoba
126 Mendoza and around
133 South of Mendoza
135 Mendoza to Chile
139 San Juan and around
143 La Rioja and Catamarca

149 Northwest Argentina
149 Santiago del Estero
150 Tucumán and around
155 Cafayate
159 Salta
167 Jujuy
170 Jujuy to the Chilean and Bolivian borders

176 The Northeast
176 Up the Río Uruguay
179 Up the Río Paraná
185 The Chaco
188 Misiones
191 Iguazú Falls

197 Lake District
197 Nuequén and around
199 Parque Nacional Lanín
203 Parque Nacional Nahuel Huapi
206 Bariloche and around
215 South of Bariloche

224 Patagonia
225 Viedma, Carmen de Patagones and around
226 Puerto Madryn and around
232 Trelew and the Chubut Valley
235 Comodoro Rivadavia and inland
239 Río Gallegos and around
242 Ruta 40 to the glaciers
245 Parque Nacional Los Glaciares

254 Tierra del Fuego
255 Río Grande and around
257 Ushuaia and around

Footprint features

56 Don't miss …
60 Driving in Argentina
161 Cloud line
177 True brew
210 Walks around Bariloche
217 The Old Patagonian Express
228 Keeping up with the Joneses

At a glance

Time required 2-6 weeks.

Best time Buenos Aires, Sep-Nov, Mar-May; autumn in the Lake District. Oct-May in Patagonia; Sep-Dec for whale watching on the Atlantic coast; Jun-Aug skiing in Tierra del Fuego, but passes can be snow bound.

When not to go Holiday season, Jan-Feb, is very crowded on the beaches, in the Lake District and in Patagonia.

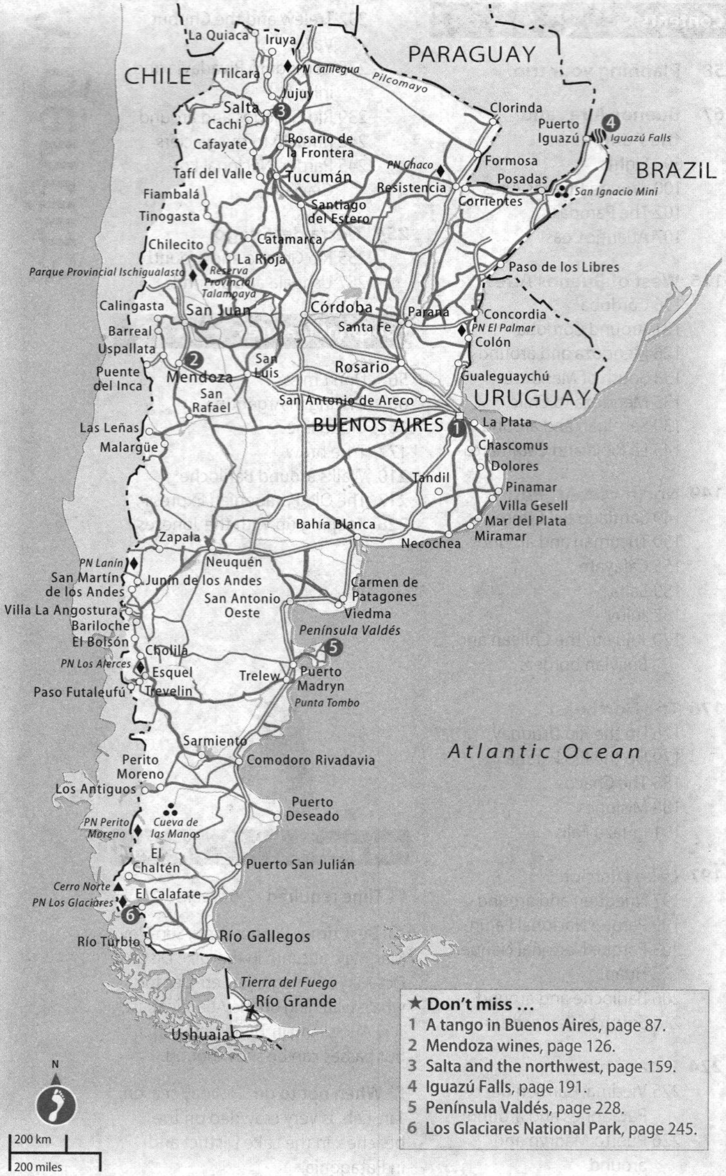

★ Don't miss …

1. A tango in Buenos Aires, page 87.
2. Mendoza wines, page 126.
3. Salta and the northwest, page 159.
4. Iguazú Falls, page 191.
5. Península Valdés, page 228.
6. Los Glaciares National Park, page 245.

Argentina is a hugely varied country, from the blistering heat of the Chaco in the north to the storms of Tierra del Fuego in the south. In between these extremes, there is so much to enjoy – from nights tangoing in the chic quarters of Buenos Aires to long days riding with gauchos in the grasslands of the pampas. You can climb to the roof of the Americas, raft Andean rivers or ski with celebrities. You can visit the birthplace of revolutionary Che Guevara and the resting place of a dinosaur known to have been bigger than T Rex. In the northwest, canyons of rocks eroded into unimaginable shapes lead to sleepy villages and staging posts on the colonial trade routes. At the northern border with Brazil, 275 waterfalls cascade into a great gorge at Iguazú. Swifts dart behind the torrents of water and birds and butterflies are easy to see in the surrounding forest. This is a must on anyone's itinerary. Endangered mammals, giant storks and anacondas live side-by-side in the Iberá marshes. In the dried-up river beds of San Juan, there are exotic rockforms at Talampaya and Ischigualasto. On the Patagonian coast, at Península Valdés, Southern right whales and elephant seals come to breed in the sheltered bays, while estuaries are home to colonies of penguins and pods of dolphin. Lonely roads cross the vast, empty plateau inland, leading to the petrified remains of giant forests and a cave with 10,000 year-old paintings of hands and animals. The Andean mountain chain ends in a jagged finale at the peaks of the Chaitén Massif, with some of the best trekking on the continent. To set the taste buds tingling, the vineyards of Mendoza and the traditional Welsh tearooms of the Chubut valley hang out the welcome sign. And (vegetarians look away), don't forget the meat, barbecued on an open wood fire at the end of the day.

Planning your trip

Where to go

The capital, **Buenos Aires**, has a distinctly European feel, its architecture mostly 20th-century, though earlier buildings can be found in San Telmo district. The central docklands have been reclaimed as an upmarket restaurant zone and the Palermo district, with its large parks and its cobbled streets, has become increasingly sought after. Across the Río de la Plata is Uruguay; just northwest is Tigre, on the Paraná delta, a popular spot for escaping the city; to the southeast are coastal resorts which lead round to the most famous, Mar del Plata. West and south of Buenos Aires stretch the grasslands of the pampas, home of the *gaucho* (cowboy) and large *estancias*.

Through **Northwest Argentina** a string of cities gives access to the Andean foothills and the higher peaks. On the way to the mountains are Córdoba, an important industrial centre close to resorts in the Sierras de Córdoba, and Santiago del Estero, Argentina's oldest city. From Tucumán, surrounded by sugar cane but in view of the Andes, there is a beautiful route through desert foothills around Cafayate and the Valles Calchaquíes to the fine city of Salta. This is the ideal centre for exploring this wonderful part of the country with its remote valleys and high-altitude mining communities. From Salta there are routes to Bolivia, through an area of isolated villages, to Chile over lonely passes and to Paraguay across the Chaco.

In the **Northeast**, the wetlands of Mesopotamia have some interesting wildlife zones, such as the Iberá Marshes, and in Misiones province, sandwiched between Brazil and Paraguay, are ruined Jesuit missions, principally San Ignacio Miní. The highlight of this region are the magnificent Iguazú Falls, usually included on any itinerary to the country.

Back in the Northwest, **Ruta 40** starts its long, frequently remote journey beside the Andes to the far south. Among the many attractions it passes are the city of Mendoza, on the main Buenos Aires-Santiago road, with its vineyards, climbing and skiing centres, and the strange lunar landscapes of San Juan province. It traverses the **Lake District**, renowned for its lovely scenery and good fishing. The main centres are San Martín de los Andes and Bariloche, but there are many smaller places to visit, like Esquel, the terminus of the Old Patagonian Express. From Bariloche and other points, there are crossings to Chile. Ruta 40 continues south to the stunning peaks and glaciers of Los Glaciares national park.

On the Atlantic side of **Patagonia**, a good place to break the journey is Puerto Madryn and the Península Valdés. Here you can see whales, elephant seals and guanaco at close quarters. Just south of here are the Welsh communities of the Chubut Valley and, south again, three areas of petrified forest. Río Gallegos is the most southerly town of any size on the mainland. One road goes west to the most visited part of Los Glaciares, El Calafate, near where the Perito Moreno glacier tumbles into Lago Argentino. Just north of here, El Chaltén at the foot of the jagged FitzRoy massif has some of the most spectacular trekking in the country. This increasingly popular area now forms part of the circuit which includes the Torres del Paine national park in Chile. Beyond Río Gallegos is the Argentine side of Tierra del Fuego. Ushuaia, on the shores of the Beagle Channel, is the best base for boat trips, hikes in the mountains and skiing in winter.

When to go

Climate ranges from sub-tropical in the north to cold temperate in Tierra del Fuego. The densely populated central zone is temperate. From mid-December to the end of February, Buenos Aires can be oppressively hot and humid, with temperatures of 27-35°C (80-95°F) and an average humidity of 70%. The city virtually shuts down in late December and early January as people escape on holiday. Autumn can be a good time to visit and spring in Buenos Aires (September-October) is often very pleasant. The Northeast is best visited in winter when it is cooler and drier. Corrientes and Misiones provinces are increasingly wet from September. The winter is also a good time to visit the Northwest, but routes to Chile across the Andes may be closed by snow at this time and spring and autumn may be better: summer rains, especially in July, can make roads impassable. In the winter (June-August) establishments may close in the far south, transport can be restricted and routes across the Andes to Chile may be blocked by snow. Spring and autumn are the best seasons for visiting the Lake District. Ideally Patagonia should be visited in December or February-April, avoiding the winter months when the weather is cold and many services are closed. There are also school holidays in July when some facilities such as youth hostels may be heavily booked. Note that Bariloche is very popular with for school groups in July and December/early January.

National parks Argentina has 38 protected areas, covering most of the country's natural environments. Best-represented are the northwestern highlands and Patagonia forests. **Administración de Parques Nacionales** (APN) ⓘ *Santa Fe 690, opposite Plaza San Martín, T4311 0303, www.parquesnacionales.gov.ar, Mon-Fri 1000-1700*, has information and advice. The APN has a library (**Biblioteca Perito Moreno**) ⓘ *public Tue-Fri 1000-1300, 1400-1730*. The website **www.patri monionatural.com** has information on Argentina's national parks, natural reserves, UN-recognized and RAMSAR sites.

Getting around

Air Internal air services are run by **Aerolíneas Argentinas** (AR), T0810-222 86527, *www.aerolineas.com.ar*, **Austral** (part of AR), LAN, T0810-999 9526, within Chile 600-526 2000, www.lan.com, and the army airline **LADE** (in Patagonia, Buenos Aires, Córdoba and Paraná), T0810-810 5233, *www.lade.com.ar*. **Sol**, T0810-444 4765, flies to cities in the centre of the country and, in summer, to coastal destinations and Uruguay, *www.sol.com.ar*. **Andes**, T0810-777-26337, based in Salta, flies between Salta, Buenos Aires and Puerto Madryn, *www.andesonline.com*. Some airlines operate during the high season, or are air taxis on a

Driving in Argentina

Roads Only 29% of Argentina's roads are paved and a further 17% improved. Most main roads are rather narrow but roadside services are good. To avoid flying stones on gravel roads (called ripio on maps) and dirt roads, don't follow trucks too closely, overtake with plenty of room, and pull over and slow down for oncoming vehicles. Most main roads have private tolls about every 100 km, US$0.20-1.50. Unprivatized secondary roads are generally poor. Internal checkpoints prevent food, vegetable and meat products entering Patagonia, Mendoza, San Juan, Catamarca, Tucumán, Salta and Jujuy provinces.

Safety All motorists are required to carry two warning triangles, a fire-extinguisher, a tow rope or chain, and a first aid kit. The handbrake must be fully operative and seat belts must be worn if fitted. Headlights must be on in the daytime on roads in Buenos Aires province.

Documents Full car documentation must be carried (including an invoice for the most recently paid insurance premium) together with international driving licence (for non-residents). For drivers of private vehicles entering Argentina from Chile, there is a special salida y admisión temporal de vehículos form.

Organizations **Automóvil Club Argentino** (ACA), Av Libertador Gen San Martín 1850, Buenos Aires, T011-4808 4000 or T0800-888 3777, www.aca.org.ar, has a travel documents service, car service facilities, and road maps (including online). Foreign automobile clubs with reciprocity with ACA are allowed to use ACA facilities and discounts (with a membership card). ACA accommodation comprises: Motel, Hostería, Hotel, Unidad Turística, and campsites. All have meal facilities.

Car hire The minimum age for renting is usually 21-25 (private arrangements may be possible). A credit card is required. Prices range from US$40-100 a day; highest prices are in Patagonia. Discounts available for weekly rental. 4WD vehicles offered in some agencies. At tourist centres such as Salta, Posadas, Bariloche or Mendoza it may be more economical to hire a taxi with driver, which includes a guide, fuel, insurance and a mechanic.

Fuel Petrol/gasoline (nafta) costs on average US$0.95 per litre and diesel US$0.85. Octane ratings: regular petrol (común) 83; super 93. Unleaded fuel is widely available in 93, 95 and 97 octane. Cars are being converted to gas natural comprimido (GNC), which costs about 25% of nafta, but filling stations are further apart. Always refuel when you can in less developed areas like Chaco and Formosa and in parts of Patagonia as even petrol stations are infrequent.

semi-regular schedule. Children under three travel free. **LADE** flights are heavily booked in advance, especially for travel during December and January. It also operates discount tickets: spouse (75%) and children (37.5%). Check in two hours before flight to avoid being 'bumped off' from over-booking. Meals are rarely served on internal flights.

Aerolíneas Argentinas has a **Visite Argentina** airpass which offers domestic flights at cheaper rates than those bought individually. You can buy from 3 to 12 coupons for a maximum of 90 days. Coupons cost from US$399 for 3 to US$1049 for 12 if purchased in conjunction with an international return ticket to Argentina with AR. With a carrier other than AR, the cost is US$499-1149. Taxes are not included. Additional sectors may not be added once the airpass has been issued. It may be bought outside or within the country on presentation of the international air ticket. Changes of route and date are permitted, at US$50 each. It is unwise to set up too tight a schedule because of delays caused by bad weather, or by AR itself (its reliability is, at the time of writing, poor). Note that AR charges foreigners more than Argentines for flight tickets. If you wish to buy a domestic flight ticket with AR outside Argentina, in only a few countries can you pay online. In most cases you have to finalise payment by phone or fax with a local AR office. This can be very frustrating. If possible use a travel agent. Flights between Buenos Aires and El Calafate are often fully booked two to three weeks ahead, and there may be similar difficulties on the routes to Bariloche and Iguazú. If you are 'wait-listed' they cannot ensure a seat. Reconfirmation at least 24 hours ahead of a flight is essential.

Bus Long-distance buses are by far the cheapest way to get around. *Coche cama* or *semi cama* buses between cities are more expensive than the *comunes*, but well worth the extra money for the comfort and fewer stops. The biggest bus companies are: **Andesmar**, T0261-405 4300, www.andesmar.com; **Chevallier**, T011-4000 5255, www.nuevachevallier.com.ar; **Flecha Bus**, T011-4000 5200, www.flechabus.com.ar; **Vía Bariloche**, T0800-333 7575, www.viabariloche.com.ar. When buying tickets at a bus office, don't assume you've been automatically allotted a seat: make sure you have one. Student discounts of 20% are sometimes available. Buses have strong a/c, even more so in summer; take a sweater for night journeys. On long-distance journeys, meals are included. They can vary from a sandwich to a full meal, so take your own food and drink for longer journeys. Note that luggage is handled by *maleteros*, who expect a tip (US$0.35 or less is acceptable) though many Argentines refuse to pay.

Taxi Licensed taxis known as *Radio Taxi* can be hired on the street, or can be called in advance and are safer. There is also a system known as *Remise*, common in smaller towns where there are no taxis, where car and driver are booked from an office and operate with a fixed fare (more than a regular taxi).

Maps Several road maps are available including those of the ACA (best and most up-to-date), **Firestone** (also accurate and detailed), and **Automapa**, www.automapa.com.ar (regional maps, Michelin-style, high quality). Topographical maps are issued by the **Instituto Geográfico Militar**

ⓘ *Av Cabildo 381, Buenos Aires, T4576 5576 (one block from Subte Ministro Carranza, Line D, or take bus 152), Mon-Fri 0800-1300, www.igm.gov.ar*. 1:500,000 sheets cost US$3 each and are 'years old'; better coverage of 1:100,000 and 1:250,000, but no city plans. Take passport if buying maps. For walkers, the **Sendas y Bosques** series is recommended: 1:200,000, laminated and easy to read, with good books containing English summaries; www.guiasendasybosques.com.ar.

Sleeping → *See page 38 for our hotel grade price guide.*

Hotels Bills in four- and five-star hotels are normally quoted without 21% VAT. It is often cheaper to book a room at reception, rather than over the internet. If you pay in cash (pesos) you may get a discount, but more expensive hotels sometimes have more expensive rates for non-Argentines. For a selection of B&Bs see www.bedandbreakfast.com/argentina.html.

Camping Camping is very popular in Argentina: there are private sites with services, or cheaper (or free) municipal sites in tourist centres (except Buenos Aires); most are very noisy and closed off-season. The average price is US$3-5 pp if you have your own tent, plus a charge for the site in some cases. Camping is allowed at the side of major highways (not recommended) and in most national parks (not at Iguazú Falls). Many ACA and YPF service stations have an area for campers (usually free) and owners are generally friendly, but ask first. Most service stations have hot showers. A list of camping sites is available from ACA (for members, but easily available) and from the national tourist office in Buenos Aires. *Guía del Acampante* is published annually, on sale at kiosks, and has a full list of campsites and discount vouchers.

If you are planning a long trip, renting a motorhome is a good idea. A recommended company is **Andean Roads Motorhome Rentals**, see www.andeanroads.com for contact details and rates (starting at US$75-165 per day for 3 weeks or more).

Estancias An *estancia* is, generally speaking, a farm, but the term covers a wide variety of establishments. Accommodation for visitors is often pricey but most *estancias* are extremely comfortable and offer an insight into traditional country life. In the pampas, they tend to be cattle ranches extending for thousands of hectares; in the west they often have vineyards; northeastern estancias border swamps; those in Patagonia are sheep farms at the foot of the mountains or beside lakes. Many also offer horse riding, fishing, canoeing or birdwatching. The national tourist board website lists all estancias: www.turismo.gov.ar. See the sites of the **Red Argentina de Turismo Rural**, www.raturestancias.com.ar, www.caminodelgaucho.com.ar (for the Pampas) and www.estanciasdesantacruz.com (for Santa Cruz province) for some suggestions.

Youth hostels **Hostelling International Argentina** ⓘ *Florida 835 pb, Buenos Aires, T011-4511 8723, www.hostels.org.ar*, offers discounts to cardholders at their 70 hostels throughout Argentina, buses and backpacker tours. An HI card in Argentina costs US$16. See www.hostelsuites.com for a chain of HI-affiliated hostels. Very few Argentine hostels have laundry facilities, which may be tricky if you have expensive trekking gear to wash carefully. HI hostels sometimes give vouchers for 10% discount on bus tickets.

Eating and drinking → *See page 40 for our Eating price guide.*

Eating out The cheapest option is always to have the set lunch as a main meal of the day and then find cheap, wholesome snacks for breakfast and supper. Also good value are *tenedor libre* restaurants – eat all you want for a fixed price. Most Argentines have lunch around 1300; restaurants open 1200-1500. Out of Buenos Aires, offices close for lunch and a siesta 1200-1700. Around 1700, many people go to a *confitería* for tea, sandwiches and cakes, but cafés are open all day except 0200-0600 and get busy from 2400. Dinner often begins at 2200 or 2230, and restaurants rarely open before 2100. Nightclubs open at 2400, but usually only get busy around 0200.

Food National dishes are based upon plentiful supplies of beef. Many dishes are distinctive and excellent; the *asado*, a roast cooked on an open fire or grill; *puchero*, a stew, very good indeed; *bife a caballo*, steak topped with a fried egg; the *carbonada* (onions, tomatoes, minced beef), particularly good in Buenos Aires; *churrasco*, a thick grilled steak; *parrillada*, a mixed grill (usually enough for two or more people), mainly roast meat, offal, and sausages; *chorizos* (including *morcilla*, blood sausage), though do not confuse this with *bife de chorizo*, which is a rump steak (*bife de lomo* is fillet steak). A *choripán* is a roll with a *chorizo* inside. *Empanada* is a tasty meat pie; *empanadas de humita* are filled with a thick paste of cooked corn/maize, onions, cheese and flour *Milanesa de pollo* (breaded, boneless chicken) is usually good value. Also popular is *milanesa*, a breaded veal cutlet. *Ñoquis* (gnocchi), potato dumplings normally served with meat and tomato sauce, are tasty and often the cheapest item on the menu; they are also a good vegetarian option when served with either *al tuco* or Argentine roquefort (note that a few places only serve them on the 29th of the month, when you should put a coin under your plate for luck). *Locro* is a thick stew made of maize, white beans, beef, sausages, pumpkin and herbs. Pizzas come in all sorts of exotic flavours, both savoury and sweet. **Note** Extras such as chips, *puré* (mashed potato) are ordered and served separately, and are not cheap. Almost uniquely in Latin America, salads are quite safe. A popular sweet is *dulce de leche* (especially from Chascomús), milk and sugar evaporated to a pale, soft fudge. Other popular desserts are *almendrado* (ice cream rolled in crushed almonds), *dulce de batata* (sweet potato preserve), *dulce de membrillo* (quince preserve), *dulce de zapallo* (pumpkin in syrup); these *dulces* are often eaten with cheese. *Postre Balcarce*, a cream and meringue cake and *alfajores*, wheat-flour biscuits filled with *dulce de leche* or apricot jam, are very popular. Note that *al natural* in reference to fruit means canned without sugar (fresh fruit is *al fresco*) Croissants (known as *media lunas*) are in two varieties: *de grasa* (dry) and *de manteca* (rich and fluffy). For local recipes (in Spanish) *Las comidas de mi pueblo*, by Margarita Palacios, is recommended. *Food and Drink in Argentina*, by Dereck Foster and Richard Tripp (Aromas y Sabores, 2003) is a pocket guide to eating customs, food terminology, wines and all things culinary.

Drink It is best not to drink tap water; in the main cities it is safe, but often heavily chlorinated. Never drink tap water in the northwest, where it is notoriously poor. It is usual to drink soda or mineral water at restaurants, and many Argentines mix it with cheap wine and with ice. Argentine wines (including champagnes, both charmat and champenoise) are sound in all price ranges. The ordinary *vinos de la casa*, or *comunes* are wholesome and relatively cheap; the reds are better than the whites. The local beers, mainly lager, are quite acceptable. In restaurants wines are quite expensive. Hard liquor is relatively cheap, except for imported whisky. *Clericó* is a white-wine *sangría* drunk in summer. **Vineyards** can be visited in Mendoza and San Juan provinces and Cafayate (in the south of Salta province). If invited to drink *mate* (pronounced 'mattay'), always accept; it's the essential Argentine drink, usually shared as a social ritual between friends or colleagues. *Mate* is a stimulating green tea made from the yerba mate plant, slightly bitter in taste, drunk from a cup or seasoned gourd through a silver, perforated straw.

Accident and emergency
Police T101. If robbed or attacked, call the tourist police, **Comisaría del Turista**, Av Corrientes 436, Buenos Aires, T011-4346 5748 (24 hrs) or T0800-999 5000, English, Italian, French, Portuguese and Ukrainian spoken. Urgent medical service T107.

Electricity
220 volts (and 110 too in some hotels), 50 cycles, AC, European Continental-type plugs in old buildings, Australian 3-pin flat-type in the new. Adaptors can be purchased locally for either type (ie from new 3-pin to old 2-pin and vice-versa).

Embassies and consulates
Visit www.mrecic.gov.ar for a full list of addresses.

Festivals and events
No work may be done on the national holidays (1 Jan, Good Fri, 1 May, 25 May, 10 Jun, 20 Jun, 9 Jul, 17 Aug, 12 Oct and 25 Dec) except where specifically established by law. There are limited bus services on 25 and 31 Dec. On Holy Thu and 8 Dec employers decide whether their employees should work, but banks and public offices are closed. Banks are also closed on 31 Dec. There are gaucho parades in San Antonio de Areco (110 km from Buenos Aires) and throughout Argentina, with fabulous displays of horsemanship and with traditional music, on the days leading up to the Día de la Tradición, 10 Nov. On 30 Dec there is a ticker-tape tradition in downtown Buenos Aires: it snows paper and the crowds stuff passing cars and buses with long streamers.

Money → *US$1 = 3.88 pesos, €1 = 5.30 pesos (Apr 2010).*
The currency is the Argentine peso (ARS or $, we use AR$), divided into 100 centavos. Peso notes I n circulation: 2, 5, 10, 20, 50 and 100. Coins in circulation: 5, 10, 25 and 50 centavos and 1 peso. Foreigners are advised to use credit cards to withdraw cash, where possible, and for making payments. If paying in cash, do so in pesos. Dollars and euros may be accepted in some tourist centres. ATMs (known as *cajeros automáticos*) can be found in every town and city. They are usually Banelco or Link, accepting international cards (check fees and transaction limits, eg about US$100 with 7.5% commission on some Visa debit cards). Changing TCs can involve lengthy bureaucracy and high commission charges, usually 10%. When crossing a land border into Argentina, make sure you have some Argentine currency as there are normally no facilities at the border. Note that fake notes circulate, mostly AR$100, 20 and 10. Check that the green numbers showing the value of the note (on the left hand top corner) shimmer; that there is a watermark; that there is a continuous line from the top of the note to the bottom about ¾ of the way along.
Credit cards Visa, MasterCard, American Express and Diners Club cards are all widely accepted in the major cities and provincial capitals, though less so outside these. There is a high surcharge on credit card transactions in many establishments; many hotels offer reductions for cash. For lost or stolen cards: **MasterCard** T0800-555 0507, **Visa** T0800-666 0171.
Cost of travelling You can find comfortable accommodation with a private bathroom and breakfast for around US$50 for 2 people, while a good dinner in the average restaurant will be around US$10-15 pp. Prices are much cheaper away from the main touristy areas: El Calafate, Ushuaia and Buenos Aires can be particularly pricey. For travellers on a budget, hostels usually cost between US$10-13 pp in a shared dorm. A cheap breakfast costs US$3 and set meals at lunchtime about US$6, US$8 in Buenos Aires. Long-distance bus travel on major routes is good value, but it's worth splashing out an extra 20% for coche cama service on overnight journeys. The average cost of internet use is US$0.80-2 per hour.

Opening hours
Business hours Banks, government offices and businesss are not open on Sat. Normal office hours are 0800-1300 in summer, 1000-1500 in winter. Some businesses open again in the evening, 1700-2000. **Banks**: opening hours vary according to city and sometimes according to the season. **Post offices**: stamps on sale during working days 0800-2000 but 0900-1300 on Sat. **Shops**: 0900-1800, many close at 1300 on Sat. Outside the main cities many close for at 1300 the daily afternoon siesta, reopening at about 1700.

Safety

Argentina is generally a safe country. You should, however, remain on your guard in big cities, especially Buenos Aires, where petty crime is a problem. Robbery, sometimes violent, and trickery do occur. Unfortunately, no respect for age applies as senior travellers are as likely to be targeted as any other tourist.

Tax

Airport taxes By law (Mar 2009) airport taxes must be included in the price of your air ticket. It was US$28 for all international flights: US$14 to Montevideo and Punta del Este from Aeroparque and US$12 on domestic flights, but rates are not now published. When in transit from one international flight to another, you may be obliged to pass through immigration and customs, have your passport stamped. You should not have to pay an airport tax on departure. There is a 5% tax on the purchase of air tickets.

VAT/IVA 21%; VAT is not levied on medicines, books and some foodstuffs.

Telephone → *Country code +54.*

Ringing: equal tones with long pauses.
Engaged: equal tones with equal pauses.
To call a **mobile phone** in Argentina, dial the city code followed by 15, then the mobile's number (eg 011-15-xxxx xxxx in Buenos Aires). To call a mobile from abroad, dial the country code, then 9, then the city code and number, ommitting 15 (eg+54-9-11-xxxx xxxx).

Time

GMT -3.

Tipping

10% in restaurants and cafés. Porters and ushers are usually tipped.

Tourist information

The national office of the Secretaría de Turismo, Av Santa Fe 883, Buenos Aires, T0800-5550016, www.turismo.gov.ar. For free tourist information anywhere in the country T0800-555 0016 (0800-2000). For tourist information abroad, contact Argentine embassies and consulates.

Tourist offices Each province has a tourist office, Casa de Provincia, in Buenos Aires, Mon-Fri 1000-1630/1730.

Buenos Aires Province, Av Callao 237, T5300 9531, www.casaprov.gba.gov.ar, www.bue.gov.ar (official site of city of Buenos Aires tourism).
Catamarca, Av Córdoba 2080, T4374 6891, www.catamarca.gov.ar.
Chaco, Av Callao 322, T4372 5209.
Chubut, Sarmiento 1172, T4381 3493, www.chubutalmundo.gov.ar.
Córdoba, Av Callao 332, T4373 4277, www.cba.gov.ar.
Corrientes, San Martín 333, p 4, T4394 2808, www.corrientes.com.ar.
Entre Ríos, Suipacha 844, T4326 2573, www.entrerios.gov.ar.
Formosa, Hipólito Yrigoyen 1429, T4381 2037, www.casadeformosa.gov.ar.
Jujuy, Av Santa Fe 967, T4393 6096, www.jujuy.gov.ar.
La Pampa, Suipacha 346, T4326 0511, www.turismolapampa.gov.ar.
La Rioja, Av Callao 745, T4815 1929, www.larioja.gov.ar/turismo.
Mar del Plata, Av Corrientes 1660, local 16, T4384 5658, www.mardelplata.gov.ar.
Mendoza, Av Callao 445, T4374 1105, www.mendoza.gov.ar.
Misiones, Santa Fe 989, T4322 1097, www.turismo.misiones.gov.ar.
Municipalidad de la Costa, B Mitre 737, T4394 2330, www.lacostaturismo.com.ar.
Neuquén, Maipú 48, T4343 2324, www.neuquen.gov.ar.
Río Negro, Tucumán 1916, T4371 7078, www.rionegro.gov.ar.
Salta, Diagonal Norte 933, p 5, T4326 2456, www.turismosalta.gov.ar.
San Juan, Sarmiento 1251, T4382 9241, http://sanjuan.cfired.org.ar.
San Luis, Azcuénaga 1087, T5778 1621, www.sanluis.gov.ar.
Santa Cruz, 25 de Mayo 279, T4325 3098, www.casadesantacruz.gov.ar.
Santa Fé, Montevideo 373, p 2, T5811 4319, www.santafe.gov.ar.
Santiago del Estero, Florida 274, p 1, T4326 9418, casasgo@casantiago.gov.ar.
Tierra del Fuego, Esmeralda 783, T4328 7040, www.tierradelfuego.org.ar.
Tucumán, Suipacha 140, T4322 0564, www.tucumanturismo.gov.ar.

For **Patagonia**, see www.patagonia.com.ar or http://patagonia-argentina.com. For youth hostels, contact **Asatej**, see Useful addresses, page 99.

Websites

http://ar.yahoo.com, www.google.com.ar Argentine search engines.
www.terra.com.ar News, entertainment, weather, tourism and Spanish phone directory.
www.mercotour.com Information on travel in Spanish, English and Portuguese.
www.guiaypf.com.ar Site of the YPF fuel company, with travel and tourist information.
www.welcomeargentina.com and **www.interpatagonia.com** Online travel guides to the whole country.
www.argentina.ar Promotional website of the various bureaux and ministries covering tourism, culture, economy, education and science.
www.argentinacontact.com Travel guide and hotel directory in English and Spanish.
www.smn.gov.ar Useful web site for forecasts and weather satellite images.
www.alojar.com.ar Accommodation search engine and tourist information in Spanish.
www.tageblatt.com.ar *Argentinisches Tageblatt*, German-language weekly, very informative.
www.buenosairesherald.com *Buenos Aires Herald*, English language daily.
www.theargentimes.com *The Argentimes*, a fortnightly publication in English aimed at the youth market, with a What's On section, available in Buenos Aires and Argentina.

Visas and immigration

Passports are not required by citizens of South American countries who hold identity cards issued by their own governments. No visa is necessary for British citizens, nationals of western European countries, Central American and some Caribbean countries, plus citizens of Australia, Canada, Croatia, Israel, Japan, Malaysia, New Zealand, Singapore, South Africa, Turkey and USA, who are given a tourist card ('tarjeta de entrada') on entry and may stay for 3 months, which can be renewed only once for another 3 months (fee US$77) at the Dirección Nacional de Migraciones, Av Antártida Argentina 1355 (Retiro), Buenos Aires, T4317 0200, open 0730-1330, or any other delegation of the Dirección Nacional de Migraciones (www.migraciones.gov.ar/accesos/delegaciones.php). For all others there are 3 forms of visa: a tourist visa (multiple entry, valid for 3 months; onward ticket and proof of adequate funds must be provided; fees vary depending on the country of origin; can be extended 90 days), a business visa and a transit visa. If leaving Argentina on a short trip, check on re-entry that border officials look at the correct expiry date on your visa, otherwise they will give only 30 days. Carry your passport at all times; backpackers are often targets for thorough searches – just stay calm; it is illegal not to have identification to hand.

At land borders if you don't need a visa, 90 days' permission to stay is usually given without proof of transportation out of Argentina. Make sure you are given a tourist card, otherwise you will have to obtain 1 before leaving the country. If you need a 90-day extension for your stay then leave the country (eg at Iguazú), and 90 further days will be given on return. Visa extensions may also be obtained from the address above, ask for 'Prorrogas de Permanencia'. No renewals are given after the expiry date. To authorize an exit stamp if your visa or tourist stamp has expired, go to Dirección Nacional de Migraciones and a 10-day authorization will be given for US$17, providing a proof of transportation out of the country. If you leave the country with a tourist card or visa that has expired, you will be fined for the number of days you have overstayed (may be as much as US$200 a day).

Reciprocal fees: in 2010 Argentina introduced entry fees for citizens of countries which require Argentines to obtain a visa and pay an entry fee, namely Australia (US$100), Canada (US$70) and the US (US$131). At the time of writing this fee was payable only at Ezeiza airport, not other airports, nor land borders, and did not apply to other nationalities. Either or both of these factors may change. For Canadians the fee is for single entry, but it is not clear if for Australians it is single entry or, as for US citizens, it is for the life of the passport, or ten years. Payment may be made in US$, pesos, by credit card or travellers' cheque. Initially, the system of collecting payments at Ezeiza was chaotic.

Weights and measures

Metric.

Buenos Aires and the Pampas

➔ *Phone code: 011. Colour map 8, B5. Pop: 2.78 million (Greater Buenos Aires 12.05 million).*

With its elegant architecture and fashion-conscious inhabitants, Buenos Aires is often seen as more European than South American. Among its fine boulevards, neat plazas, parks, museums and theatres, there are chic shops and superb restaurants. However, the enormous steaks and passionate tango are distinctly Argentine, and to really understand the country, you have to know its capital. South and west of Buenos Aires the flat, fertile lands of the pampa húmeda stretch seemingly without end, the horizon broken only by a lonely windpump or a line of poplar trees. This is home to the gaucho, whose traditions of music and craftsmanship remain alive.

Ins and outs

Getting there Buenos Aires has two **airports**, Ezeiza, for international flights, and Aeroparque, for domestic flights and most services to Uruguay. Ezeiza is 35 km southwest of the centre by a good dual carriageway which links with the General Paz highway which circles the city. The safest way between airport and city is by an airport bus service run every 30 minutes by *Manuel Tienda León*, which has convenient offices and charges US$11 one way. Radio taxis (such as *Onda Verde*, T4867 0000) charge US$32 (plus US$1.20 toll). *Remise* taxis (booked in advance) charge US$32 (including toll for a return journey) airport to town. Aeroparque is 4 km north of the city centre on the riverside; *Manuel Tienda León* has buses between the airports and also runs from Aeroparque to the centre for US$6. Remises charge US$8 and ordinary taxis US$6. As well as by air, travellers from Uruguay arrive by ferry (fast catamaran or slower vessels), docking in the port in the heart of the city, or by bus. All international and interprovincial buses use the Retiro **bus terminal** at Ramos Mejía y Antártida Argentina, which is next to the Retiro railway station. Both are served by city buses, taxis and Line C of the Subte (metro). Other train services, to the province of Buenos Aires and the suburbs use Constitución, Once and Federico Lacroze stations, all served by bus, taxi and Subte. ▸▸ *See also Transport, page 92.*

Getting around The commercial heart of the city, from Retiro station and Plaza San Martín through Plaza de Mayo to San Telmo, east of Avenida 9 de Julio, can be explored on foot, but you'll probably want to take a couple of days to explore its museums, shops and markets. Many places of interest lie outside this zone, so you will need to use public transport. City **buses** (*colectivos*) are plentiful, see below for city guides. The fare is about US$0.30 in the city, US$0.50 to the suburbs. The **metro**, or Subte, is fast and clean. It has six lines; a single fare is US$0.30. Yellow and black **taxis** can be hailed on the street, but if at all possible, book a radio taxi by phone as it is much safer s(make sure the meter is reset when you get in). *Remise* taxis, booked only through an office, cost more but are the most reliable. See Transport, below, for full details. Street numbers start from the dock side rising from east to west, but north/ south streets are numbered from Avenida Rivadavia, one block north of Avenida de Mayo rising in both directions. Calle Juan D Perón used to be called Cangallo, and Scalabrini Ortiz used to be Canning (old names are still referred to). Avenida Roque Sáenz Peña and Avenida Julio A Roca are commonly referred to as Diagonal Norte and Diagonal Sur respectively.

Tourist offices **National office** ⓘ *Av Santa Fe 883, T4312 2232, info@turismo.gov.ar, Mon-Fri 0900-1700*, maps and literature covering the whole country. There are kiosks at Aeroparque (*Aerolíneas Argentinas* section), and at **Ezeiza Airport** daily 0800-2000. **City information** ⓘ *municipal website www.bue.gov.ar, in Spanish, English and Portuguese*. There are tourist kiosks at Florida 100, at the junction of Florida and Marcelo T de Alvear (Monday-Friday 1000-1800), in Recoleta (Av Quintana 596, junction with Ortiz), in Puerto Madero (Dock 4, T4315 4265, 0930-1930, also has information on Montevideo), and at Retiro Bus Station (ground floor, T4313 0187,

0730-1430). Free guided tours are organized by the city authorities: free leaflet from city-run offices and suggested circuits on www.bue.gov.ar. Audio guided tours in several languages are available for 12 itineraries by downloading MP3 files from www.bue.gov.ar, or by dialing *8283 from a mobile phone (look for the grey plaques on the pavement showing a code in many sites around the city). **Tango information centre** ⓘ *on the first floor of Galerías Pacífico, Sarmiento 1551, T4373 2823*. Those overcharged or cheated can go to the **Tourist Ombudsman** ⓘ *Av Pedro de Mendoza 1835 (Museo Quinquela Martín, La Boca), T4302 7816, turista@defensoria.org.ar, and Defensa 1250, T4046 9682, turistasantelmo@defensoría.org.ar, both daily 1000-1800*, or to **Defensa del Consumidor** ⓘ *Venezuela 842, T4338 4900, Mon-Fri 1000-1800*.

South American Explorers has had an office in Buenos Aires for several years, a comfortable meeting place for travellers and source of knowledgeable advice. In May 2010, a new clubhouse opened at Chile 557, San Telmo. See www.saexplorers.org/clubhouses/buenosaires for latest information.

Information Good guides to bus and subway routes are **Guía T, Lumi, Peuser and Filcar** (covering the city and Greater Buenos Aires in separate editions), US$1-9 available at news stands. Also handy is Auto Mapa's pocket-size Plano of the Federal Capital, or the more detailed City Map covering La

1 Federal District of Buenos Aires

➡Buenos Aires maps
1 Federal District of Buenos Aires, page 68
2 Buenos Aires centre, page 70
3 Recoleta & Palermo, page 74
4 San Telmo, page 76

Boca to Palermo, both available at news stands, US$4.50; otherwise it is easy to get free maps of the centre from tourist kiosks and most hotels. **Buenos Aires Day & Night** is one of several free bi-monthly tourist magazines with useful information and a downtown map available at tourist kiosks and hotels. *Bainsider* (www.bainsidermag.com) is a fantastic magazine for getting to know the city. **La Nación** (www.lanacion.com.ar) has a very informative Sunday tourism section. On Friday, the youth section of **Clarín** (*Sí*) lists free entertainment; also see www.clarin.com. **Página 12** has a youth supplement on Thursday called **NO**. The **Buenos Aires Herald** publishes **Get Out** on Friday, listing entertainments. Information on what's on at www.buenosairesherald.com.

Other websites worth exploring: www.whatsupbuenosaires.com for detailed lsitings in English; the blogs, www.baexpats.com, www.baires.elsur.org, www.goodmorningba.com, and the video site www.scoopingargentina.com.

Sights

The capital has been virtually rebuilt since the beginning of the 20th-century and its oldest buildings mostly date from the early 1900s, with some elegant examples from the 1920s and 1930s. The centre has maintained the original layout since its foundation and so the streets are often narrow and mostly one way. Its original name, 'Santa María del Buen Ayre' was a recognition of the good winds which brought sailors across the ocean.

Around Plaza de Mayo

The heart of the city is the **Plaza de Mayo**. On the east side is the **Casa de Gobierno**. Called the *Casa Rosada* because it is pink, it contains the offices of the President of the Republic. It is notable for its statuary and the rich furnishing of its halls. The **Museo de los Presidentes** ⓘ *in the basement of the same building, T4344 3804, www.museo.gov.ar, closed in 2010, take passport*, has historical memorabilia. Behind the building, in the semicircular Parque Colón, is a large statue of Columbus. **Antiguo Congreso Nacional** (Old Congress Hall, 1864-1905) ⓘ *Balcarce 139, Thu, 1500-1700, closed Jan-Feb, free,* on the south of the Plaza, is a National Monument. The **Cathedral**, on the north of Plaza, stands on the site of the first church in Buenos Aires ⓘ *Rivadavia 437, T4331 2845, Mon-Fri 0800-1900, Sat-Sun 0900-1930; for guided visits, Mon-Fri 1130 (San Martín's mausoleum and Crypt), 1315 (religious art), daily 1530 (Temple and Crypt); Jan-Feb: Mon-Fri 1100 both Temple and Crypt; mass is held daily, check times*. The current structure dates from 1753-1822 (its portico built in 1827), but the 18th-century towers were never rebuilt, so that the architectural proportions have suffered. The imposing tomb (1880) of the Liberator, Gen José de San Martín, is guarded by soldiers in fancy uniforms. **Museo del Cabildo y la Revolución de Mayo** ⓘ *T4334 1782, Tue-Fri 1030-1700, Sun 1130-1800, US$1; guided visits Sun 1230, 1530, US$1.20* is in the old Cabildo where the movement for independence from Spain was first planned. It's worth a visit for the paintings of old Buenos Aires, the documents and maps recording the May 1810 revolution, and memorabilia of the 1806 British attack; also Jesuit art. In the patio is a café and stalls selling handicrafts (Thursday-Friday 1100-1800). Also on the Plaza is the Palacio de Gobierno de la Ciudad (City Hall). Within a few blocks north of the Plaza are the main banks and business houses, such as the **Banco de la Nación**, opposite the Casa Rosada, with an impressively huge main hall and topped by a massive marble dome 50 m in diameter.

On the Plaza de Mayo, the **Mothers and Grandmothers of the Plaza de Mayo** march in remembrance of their children who disappeared during the 'dirty war' of the 1970s (their addresses are H Yrigoyen 1584, T4383 0377, www.madres.org, and Piedras 153, T4343 1926, www.madresfundadoras.org.ar). The Mothers march anti-clockwise round the central monument every Thursday at 1530, with photos of their disappeared loved-ones pinned to their chests.

2 Buenos Aires centre

Sleeping

1 06 Central *D3*
2 Aspen Towers *B3*
3 BA Stop *D2*
4 Bisonte Palace *B3*
5 Castelar *E2*
6 Clan House *E3*
7 Colón *C3*
8 Dolmen *B3*
9 Dorá *B3*
10 El Conquistador *B3*
11 Faena Universe *C5*
12 Frossard *C4*
13 Goya *C3*
14 Hilton *C5*
15 Hostel Suites Obelisco *D3*
16 Kilca Hostel & Backpacker *E1*
17 La Casa de Etty *E1*
18 Limehouse *D2*
19 Marbella *E2*
20 Marriott Plaza *B4*
21 Milhouse Hostel *E3*
22 Moreno *E4*
23 NH City *E4*
24 O'Rei *C3*
25 Orly *B4*
26 Panamericano *C3*
27 Pestana *B3*
28 Plaza San Martín Suites *B3*
29 St Nicholas *D1*
30 V&S *C3*
31 Waldorf *B4*

Eating

1 Abril *B3*
2 Aroma *B4*
3 Café de la Biblioteca *B2*
4 Café Tortoni *D3*
5 Chiquilín *D1*
6 Clásica y Moderna *B1*
7 Confitería Ideal *D3*
8 Desiderio *B3*
9 El Gato Negro *C1*
10 El Palacio de la Papa Frita *C3/D1*
11 El Querandí *E4*
12 Florida Garden *B4*
13 Güerrín *D2*
14 Gianni's *B4/C3*
15 Gran Victoria *C3*
16 Il Fratello *C4*
17 La Casona del Nonno *C3*
18 La Chacra *B3*
19 La Estancia *C3*
20 La Pipeta *C4*
21 La Trastienda *E5*
22 Los Inmortales *C3*
23 Morizono *B4*
24 Palacio Español *E3*
25 Richmond *C4*
26 Saint Moritz *B3*
27 Sattva *C1*
28 Sorrento *C4*
29 Tancat *B4*
30 Tomo 1 *C3*

Bars & clubs

31 Druid In *B4*
32 El Living *B1*
33 La Cigale *C4*

Museums

1 Casa de Gobierno (Casa Rosada) & Museo de los Presidentes *D5*
2 Museo de Armas *B3*
3 Museo de Arte Hispanoamericano Isaac Fernández Blanco *A3*
4 Museo de Arte Moderno & Teatro General San Martín *D1*
5 Museo de la Ciudad *E4*
6 Museo del Cabildo y la Revolución de Mayo *E4*
7 Museo del Holocausto *B1*
8 Museo del Teatro Nacional Cervantes *B2*
9 Museo Etnográfico JB Ambrosetti *E4*
10 Museo Judío *C2*
11 Museo Nacional Ferroviario at Retiro Station *A3*
12 Museo y Biblioteca Mitre *D4*

West of Plaza de Mayo

Running west from the Plaza, the Avenida de Mayo leads 1½ km to the **Palacio del Congreso** (Congress Hall) ① *Plaza del Congreso, T4953 3081, ext 3885 for guided visits, Mon, Tue, Thu, Fri 1100, 1700, 1900, www.congreso.gov.ar; passport essential.* This huge Greco-Roman building houses the seat of the legislature. Avenida de Mayo has several examples of fine architecture of the early 20th-century, such as the sumptuous La Prensa building (No 575, free guided visits at weekends), the traditional *Café Tortoni* (No 825, www.cafetortoni.com.ar), or the eclectic Palacio Barolo (No 1370, www.pbarolo.com.ar), and many others of faded grandeur. Avenida de Mayo crosses the **Avenida 9 de Julio**, one of the widest avenues in the world, which consists of three major carriageways with heavy traffic, separated in some parts by wide grass borders. Five blocks north of Avenida de Mayo the great **Plaza de la República**, with a 67-m obelisk commemorating the 400th anniversary of the city's founding, is at the junction of Avenida 9 de Julio with Avenidas Roque Sáenz Peña and Corrientes. **Teatro Colón** ① *entrance on Libertad, between Tucumán and Viamonte, T4378 7132, www.teatrocolon.org.ar*, is one of the world's great opera houses. The interior is resplendent with red plush and gilt; the stage is huge, and salons, dressing rooms and banquet halls are equally sumptuous. A full building restoration is due to be finished in 2010. Check at the website for details of alternative venues and tickets.

Close by is the **Museo del Teatro Nacional Cervantes** ① *Córdoba 1199, T4815 8881, Mon-Fri 1000-1800, free* displays history of the theatre in Argentina and its theatre stages performances. **Museo Judío** ① *Libertad 769, T4123 0102; for visits make an appointment with the rabbi (take identification)*, has religious objects relating to Jewish presence in Argentina in a 19th-century synagogue. Close by is **Museo del Holocausto** (Shoah Museum) ① *Montevideo 919, T4811 3588, www.fmh.org.ar, Mon-Thu 1100-1900, Fri 1100-1600, US$1 (ID required)*, a permanent exhibition of pictures, personal and religious items with texts in Spanish on the Holocaust, antisemitism in Argentina and the lives of many Argentine Jews in the pre- and post-war periods. There are also seminars, temporary art exhibitions and a library (open in the afternoon). **La Chacarita** ① *Guzmán 670, daily 0700-1800, take Subte Line B to the Federico Lacroze station.* This well known cemetery has the lovingly tended tomb of Carlos Gardel, the tango singer.

North of Plaza de Mayo

The city's traditional shopping centre, Calle Florida, is reserved for pedestrians, with clothes and souvenir shops, restaurants and the elegant Galerías Pacífico. More shops are to be found on Avenida Santa Fe, which crosses Florida at Plaza San Martín. Avenida Corrientes, a street of theatres, bookshops, restaurants and cafés, and nearby Calle Lavalle (partly reserved for pedestrians), used to be the entertainment centre, but both are now regarded as faded. Recoleta, Palermo and Puerto Madero have become much more fashionable (see below). The **Basílica Nuestra Señora de La Merced** *J D Perón y Reconquista 207, Mon-Fri 0800-1800*, founded 1604, rebuilt for the third time in the 18th century, has a beautiful interior with baroque and rococo features. In 1807 it was a command post against the invading British. Next door is the **Convento de San Ramón. Museo y Biblioteca Mitre** ① *San Martín 336, T4394 8240, Mon-Fri 1300-1800, US$1*, preserves intact the household of President Bartolomé Mitre; has a coin and map collection and historical archives.

The **Plaza San Martín** has a monument to San Martín at the western corner of the main park and, at the north end, a memorial with an eternal flame to those who fell in the Falklands/ Malvinas War of 1982. On the plaza is **Palacio San Martín** ① *Arenales 761, T4819 8092, free tours in Spanish and English (check times, tours usually Thu mornings and Fri afternoons)*. Built 1905-1909, it is three houses linked together, now the Foreign Ministry. It has collections of prehispanic and 20th-century art. On the opposite side of the plaza is the opulent **Palacio Paz** (Círculo Militar), ① *Av Santa Fe 750, T4311 1071, www.circulomilitar.org, guided tours Tue-Fri 1100, 1500; Wed and Thu 1600, US$4 (in English Tue and Fri 1530, US$8.25)*. The Círculo Militar includes **Museo de Armas** ① Av *Santa Fe 702 y Maipú, Mon-Fri 1300-1900,*

US$1. It has all kinds of weaponry related to Argentine history, including the 1982 Falklands/ Malvinas War, plus Oriental weapons.

Plaza Fuerza Aérea Argentina (formerly Plaza Británica) has the clock tower presented by British and Anglo-Argentine residents, while in the **Plaza Canadá** (in front of the Retiro Station) there is a Pacific Northwest Indian totem pole, donated by the Canadian government. Behind Retiro station is **Museo Nacional Ferroviario** ⓘ *ring the bell, free, Av del Libertador 405, T4318 3343, Mon-Fri 1000-1600, free.* For railway fans: locomotives, machinery, documents of the Argentine system's history, the building is in very poor condition. In a warehouse beside is the workshop of the sculptor Carlos Regazzoni who recycles refuse material from railways.

Museo de Arte Hispanoamericano Isaac Fernández Blanco ⓘ *Suipacha 1422 (3 blocks west of Retiro), T4326 3396, Tue-Sun, 1400-1900, Thu free, US$0.35, for guided visits in English T4327 0228, tours in Spanish Sat, Sun 1500*, is one of the city's best museums. It contains a fascinating collection of colonial art, especially paintings and silver, also temporary exhibitions of Latin American art, in a beautiful neocolonial mansion (Palacio Noel, 1920s) with Spanish gardens; free concerts and tango lessons on Monday.

Recoleta and Palermo

Nuestra Señora del Pilar, Junín 1898, is a jewel of colonial architecture dating from 1732 (renovated in later centuries), facing onto the public gardens of Recoleta. A fine wooden image of San Pedro de Alcántara, attributed to the famous 17th-century Spanish sculptor Alonso Cano, is preserved in a side chapel on the left, and there are stunning gold altars. Upstairs is an interesting museum of religious art.

Next to it, the **Cemetery of the Recoleta** ⓘ *entrance at Junín 1790, near Museo de Bellas Artes (see below), T4804 7040, 0700-1800, free tours in Spanish Tue-Sun 0900, 1000, 1100, 1400, 1500, 1600 (on Tue and Thu 1100 in English)*, is one of the sights of Buenos Aires. With its streets and alleys separating family mausoleums built in every imaginable architectural style, La Recoleta is often compared to a miniature city. Among the famous names from Argentine history is Evita Perón who lies in the Duarte family mausoleum: to find it from the entrance go to the first tree-filled plaza; turn left and where this avenue meets a main avenue (go just beyond the Turriaca tomb), turn right; then take the third passage on the left. On Saturday and Sunday there is a good craft market in the park on Plaza Francia outside the cemetery (1000-2200), with street artists and performers. Next to the cemetery, the **Centro Cultural Recoleta** ⓘ *T4803 1040, www.centroculturalrecoleta.org, Tue-Fri 1400-2100, Sat, Sun, holidays 1000-2100, buses 110, 102, 17, 60 (walk from corner of Las Heras y Junín, 2 blocks) from downtown, eg Correo Central, 61/62, 93, 130 to Av del Libertador y Av Pueyrredón*, specializes in contemporary local art. Next door, the Buenos Aires Design Centre has good design and handicraft shops.

Museo de Bellas Artes (National Gallery) ⓘ *Av del Libertador 1473, T4803 0802, www.mnba.org.ar, Tue-Fri 1230-1930, Sat-Sun 0930-1930, guided tours Tue-Sun 1700, 1800, check tours available for children in summer, free.* This excellent museum gives a taste of Argentine art, as well as a fine collection of European works, particularly post-Impressionist. Superb Argentine 19th and 20th-century paintings, sculpture and wooden carvings; also films, classical music concerts and art courses. **Biblioteca Nacional** (National Library) ⓘ *Av del Libertador 1600 y Agüero 2502, T4808 6000, www.bibnal.edu.ar, Mon-Fri 0900-2000, Sat and Sun 1200-1900, closed Jan.* Housed in a modern building, only a fraction of the extensive stock can be seen. Art gallery, periodical archives; cultural events held. **Museo Nacional de Arte Decorativo** ⓘ *Av del Libertador 1902, T4802 6606, www.mnad.org, Tue-Sun 1400-1900 (Jan-Feb, closed Mon and Sun), US$0.70, guided visits 1630 (at 1430 in English).* It contains collections of painting, furniture, porcelain, crystal, sculpture exhibited in sumptuous halls, once a family residence.

Palermo Chico is a delightful residential area with several houses of once wealthy families, dating from the early 20th-century. The predominant French style of the district was broken in 1929 by the rationalist lines of the **Casa de la Cultura** ⓘ *Rufino de Elizalde 2831, T4808 0553,*

3 Recoleta & Palermo

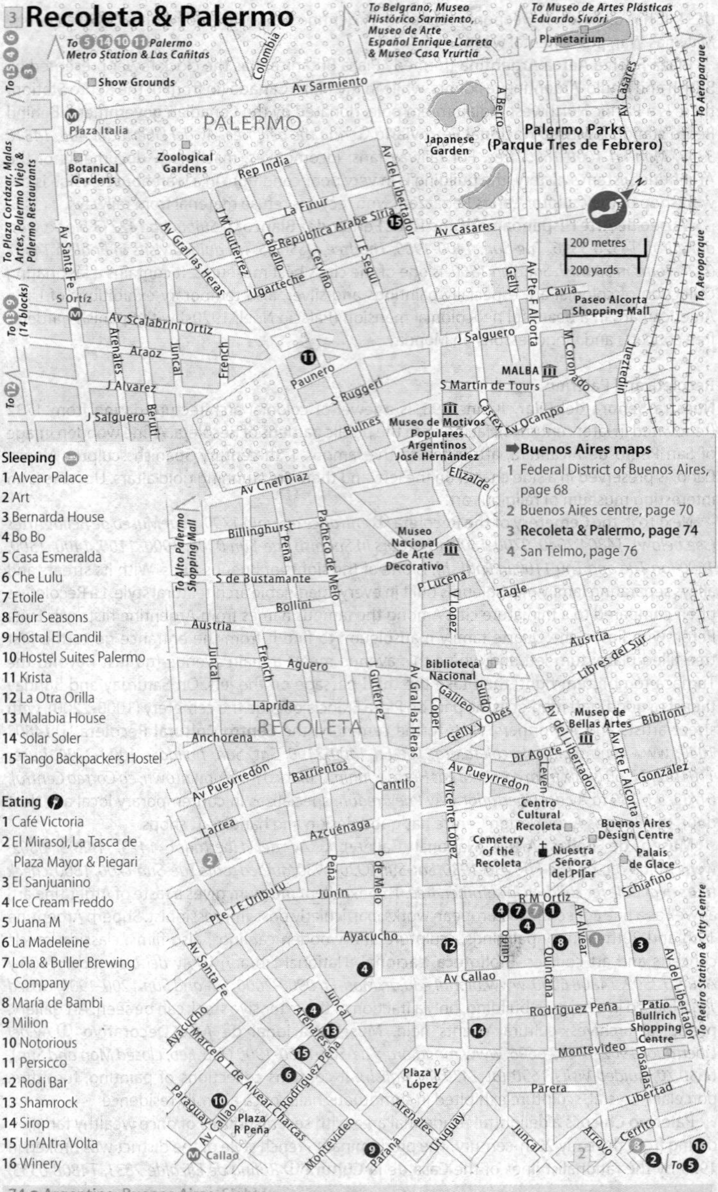

➡Buenos Aires maps

1 Federal District of Buenos Aires, page 68
2 Buenos Aires centre, page 70
3 Recoleta & Palermo, page 74
4 San Telmo, page 76

Sleeping

1 Alvear Palace
2 Art
3 Bernarda House
4 Bo Bo
5 Casa Esmeralda
6 Che Lulu
7 Etoile
8 Four Seasons
9 Hostal El Candil
10 Hostel Suites Palermo
11 Krista
12 La Otra Orilla
13 Malabia House
14 Solar Soler
15 Tango Backpackers Hostel

Eating

1 Café Victoria
2 El Mirasol, La Tasca de Plaza Mayor & Piegari
3 El Sanjuanino
4 Ice Cream Freddo
5 Juana M
6 La Madeleine
7 Lola & Buller Brewing Company
8 María de Bambi
9 Milion
10 Notorious
11 Persicco
12 Rodi Bar
13 Shamrock
14 Sirop
15 Un'Altra Volta
16 Winery

Tue-Sun 1500-2000 (Jan closed). The original residence of the writer Victoria Ocampo was a gathering place for artists and intellectuals and is now an attractive cultural centre with art exhibitions and occasional concerts.

Museo de Arte Popular José Hernández ⓘ *Av del Libertador 2373, T4803 2384, www.mujose.org.ar, Wed-Fri 1300-1900, Sat-Sun 1000-2000, US$1, free Sun; for guided tours in English T4803 2384*. The widest collection of Argentine folkloric art, with rooms dedicated to indigenous, colonial and Gaucho artefacts; handicraft shop and library. **Museo de Arte Latinoamericano (MALBA)** ⓘ *Av Figueroa Alcorta 3415, T4808 6500, www.malba.org.ar, daily 1200-1930 (Wed free, open till 2100; Tue closed), US$4 (free for ISIC holders), guided tours in Spanish or English can be booked a week in advance, T4808 6556*. One of the most important museums in the city houses renowned Latin American artists' works: powerful, moving and highly recommended. It's not a vast collection, but representative of the best from the continent. Good library, cinema (showing art house films as well as Argentine classics), seminars and shop, also has an elegant café, serving delicious food and cakes.

Of the fine **Palermo Parks**, the largest is Parque Tres de Febrero, famous for its extensive rose garden, Andalusian Patio, and delightful **Jardín Japonés** (with café) ⓘ *T4804 4922, daily 1000-1800, US$1.70, free guided visits Sat and Sun 1500*. It is a charming place for a walk, delightful for children, and with a good café serving some Japanese dishes. Close by is the **Hipódromo Argentino** (Palermo racecourse) ⓘ *T4778 2800, races 10 days per month, free*. Opposite the parks are the Botanical and Zoological Gardens. At the entrance to the **Planetarium** ⓘ *just off Belisario Roldán, in Palermo Park, T4771 9393, shows at weekends US$1.40; small museum*, are several large meteorites from Campo del Cielo. **Museo de Artes Plásticas Eduardo Sívori** ⓘ *Av Infanta Isabel 555 (Parque Tres de Febrero), T4774 9452, www.museosivori.org.ar, Tue-Fri 1200-2000, Sat and Sun 1000-2000 (1800 in winter), US$0.35 (US$1 for non-residents), Wed free, guided visits Sat and Sun 1600, 1700*. Emphasis on 19th and 20th-century Argentine art, sculpture and tapestry. The **Show Grounds** of the Argentine Rural Society, next to Palermo Park, entrance on Plaza Italia, stage the Annual Livestock Exhibition, known as Exposición Rural, in July. The **Botanical Gardens** ⓘ *Santa Fe 3951, T4831 4527, entrance from Plaza Italia (take Subte, line D) or from C República Arabe Siria, daily 0800-1800, free guided visits Sat-Sun 1030; also nocturnal tours last Fri of each month at 2100 (booking required)*, contain characteristic specimens of the world's vegetation. The trees native to the different provinces of Argentina are brought together in one section. One block beyond is **Museo Evita** ⓘ *Lafinur 2988, T4807 9433, Tue-Sun 1300-1900 (Tue-Sun 1100-1900 in summer), US$1 (US$3.40 for non-residents), Tue free for residents; guided visits in Spanish or English on request, only for groups of more than five people*. In a former women's shelter run by Fundación Eva Perón, the exhibition of dresses, paintings and other items is quite interesting though lacks the expected passion; also a library and a café.

There are three important museums in Belgrano: **Museo Histórico Sarmiento** ⓘ *Juramento 2180, T4782 2354, www.museosarmiento.gov.ar, Mon-Fri 1400-1800, Sun 1500-1830 (closed Sun Dec-Mar), US$0.35, Thu free, guided visits on second Sun of the month 1500*. The National Congress and presidential offices in 1880 now houses documents and personal effects of the former president, with a library of his work. **Museo de Arte Español Enrique Larreta** ⓘ *Juramento 2291, T4784 4040, Wed-Fri and Mon, 1500-2000, Sat-Sun 1000-1300, 1500-2000, guided visits Sat-Sun 1600, 1800, US$0.35*. The home of the writer Larreta, with paintings and religious art from the 14th to the 20th century; also has a beautiful garden ⓘ *open Mon-Fri 1000-1300 at Vuelta de Obligado 2155*. **Museo Casa Yrurtia** ⓘ *O'Higgins 2390, esq Blanco Encalada, T/F4781 0385, Tue-Fri 1300-1900, Sun 1500-1900, US$0.35*. An old house crammed with sculpture, paintings, furniture and the collections of artist Rogelio Yrurtia and his wife; peaceful garden.

South of Plaza de Mayo

The church of **San Ignacio de Loyola**, begun 1664, is the oldest colonial building in Buenos Aires (renovated in 18th and 19th centuries). It stands in a block of Jesuit origin, called the **Manzana de las Luces** (Enlightenment Square – Moreno, Alsina, Perú and Bolívar). Also in this block are the **Colegio Nacional de Buenos Aires** ⓘ *Bolivar 263, T4331 0734*, formerly the site of the Jesuits' Colegio Máximo, the Procuraduría de las Misiones (today the Mercado de las Luces, a crafts market) and 18th-century **tunnels** ⓘ *T4342 4655*. For centuries the whole block was the centre of intellectual activity, though little remains today but a small **cultural centre with art courses, concerts, plays and film shows** ⓘ *T4342 4655, www.manzanadelasluces.gov.ar, guided tours from Perú 272, Mon-Fri 1500, Sat and Sun 1500, 1630, 1800 (Mon 1300 free tour) in Spanish (in English by prior arrangement), arrive 15 mins before tour, US$1.70; the tours explore the tunnels and visit the buildings on C Perú, only some weekend tours may include San Ignacio and its cloisters, and Colegio Nacional adding an extra fee*. The **Museo de la Ciudad** ⓘ *Alsina 412, T4343 2123, Mon-Sun 1100-1900, US$0.35 (US$1 for non-residents), free on Wed.* Permanent exhibition covering social history and popular culture, special exhibitions on daily life in Buenos Aires changed every two months, and a reference library open to the public. The church of

Sleeping
1 Axel
2 Che Lagarto
3 El Hostal de Granados
4 Garden House
5 Garden House Art Factory
6 Hostel-Inn Buenos Aires
7 Hostel-Inn Tango City
8 La Casita de San Telmo
9 Lugar Gay de Buenos Aires
10 Mansión Dandi Royal
11 Ostinatto
12 Sandanzas
13 The Cocker
14 The Four

Eating
1 Dylan
2 El Desnivel
3 La Brigada
4 Lezama
5 Mi Tío

Bars & clubs
6 Boquitas Pintadas

San Francisco ⓘ *Alsina y Defensa, daily 0800-1900*, run by the Franciscan Order, was built 1730-1754 and given a new façade in 1911.

Santo Domingo ⓘ *Defensa y Belgrano, Mon-Fri 0900-1300, Sun 1000-1300*, was founded in 1751. During the British attack on Buenos Aires in 1806 some of Whitelocke's soldiers took refuge in the church. The local forces bombarded it, the British capitulated and their regimental colours were preserved in the church. General Belgrano is buried here. The church holds occasional concerts.

Museo Etnográfico JB Ambrosetti ⓘ *Moreno 350, T4345 8196, www.museoetnografico.filo.uba.ar, Tue-Fri 1300-1900, Sat-Sun 1500-1900 (closed Jan), US$0.70, guided visits Sat-Sun 1600.* Anthropological and ethnographic collections from the Mapuche and Argentina's northwest cultures (the latter a rich collection displayed on the first floor); also a small international room with a magnificent Japanese Buddhist altar.

San Telmo and La Boca

One of the few places which still has late colonial and Rosista buildings (mostly renovated in the 20th century) is the *barrio* of **San Telmo**, south of Plaza de Mayo. It's an atmospheric place, with lots of cafés, antique shops and little art galleries. On Sundays, it has a great atmosphere, with an antiques market at the Plaza Dorrego (see page 89), free tango shows (1000-1800) and live music. The 29 bus connects La Boca with San Telmo.

Parque Lezama, Defensa y Brasil, originally one of the most beautiful in the city, now rather run down and unsafe at night, has an imposing statue of Pedro de Mendoza, who (according to tradition) founded the original city in 1536 on this spot. In the park is the **Museo Histórico Nacional** ⓘ *Defensa 1600, T4307 1182, Tue-Sun 1300-1800, US$0.50, guided tours Sat-Sun 1530.* Argentine history, San Martín's uniforms and the original furniture and door of the house in which he died at Boulogne. In the park is the **Iglesia Ortodoxa Rusa** ⓘ *Brasil 315; visits on Sat afternoon (women wearing trousers will be given skirts; men in shorts will be refused entry)*, with its five blue domes and a wonderful interior.

East of the Plaza de Mayo, behind the Casa Rosada, a broad avenue, Paseo Colón, runs south towards San Telmo and as Av Almirante Brown on to the old port district of **La Boca** ⓘ *take bus 152 from Av Santa Fe, or Alem, or bus 29 from Plaza de Mayo, US$0.33*, where the Riachuelo flows into the Plata. The area's distinctive brightly painted tin and wooden houses can be seen along Caminito, the little pedestrian street used as an art market. Visit the **Museo de Bellas Artes Benito Quinquela Martín** ⓘ *Pedro de Mendoza 1835, T4301 1080, Tue-Fri 1000-1730 (in summer opens at 1100), Sat-Sun 1100-1730, closed Jan, US$0.35*, with over 1,000 works by Argentine artists, particularly Benito Quinquela Martín (1890-1977), who painted La Boca port life. Also sculptures and figureheads rescued from ships. La Boca is the poorest and roughest area within central Buenos Aires and tourists are, targets for crime. Don't go alone and stay within the cleaned-up, touristy part of Caminito and along the quay only as far as the museum. Avoid the area at night. The area is especially rowdy when the Boca Juniors football club is playing at home. At Boca Juniors stadium is **Museo de la Pasión Boquense** ⓘ *Brandsen 805, T4362 1100, www.museoboquense.com, daily 1000-1800 (opening times may change during matches), US$4.70 for non-residents. Guided tour of the stadium in Spanish or English, 1100-1700, plus ticket to the museum, US$7 for non-residents.*

Docks and Costanera Sur

Fragata Presidente Sarmiento ⓘ *dock 3, Av Dávila y Perón, Puerto Madero, T4334 9386, daily 1030-1930 (closed on rainy days), US$0.70.* A naval training ship until 1961; now a museum. Nearby, in dock 4, is the **Corbeta Uruguay** ⓘ *T4314 1090, daily 1400-1800 (closed on rainy days), 1100-1900 in summer, free,* the ship that rescued Otto Nordenskjold's Antarctic expedition in 1903. The **Puerto Madero** dock area has been renovated; the 19th-century warehouses are restaurants and bars, an attractive place for a stroll and popular nightspot. East of San Telmo on the far side of the docks, the Avenida Costanera runs as a long, spacious boulevard. A stretch of marshland reclaimed from the river forms the interesting **Costanera Sur Wildlife Reserve** ⓘ *entrances at Av Tristán Achával Rodríguez 1550 (take Estados Unidos east from San Telmo) or next to the Buquebús ferry terminal (take Av Córdoba east), T4315 4129; for pedestrians and bikers only, Tue-Sun 0800-1800 (in summer, closes at 1900), free, bus 2 passes next to the southern entrance*, where there are over 200 species of birds, including the curve-billed reed hunter. Free guided tours at weekends 1030, 1530, from the administration next to the southern entrance, but much can be seen from the road before then (binoculars useful). Also free nocturnal visits every month on the Friday closest to the full moon and the following Thursday (book Monday before, reserva_cs@buenos aires.gov.ar). It's half an hour walk from the entrance to the river shore and about three hours to walk the whole perimeter. In summer it's very hot with little shade. For details (particularly birdwatching) contact Aves Argentinas/AOP (see page 99).

Buenos Aires listings

Hotel and guesthouse prices

LL over US$200	**L** US$151-200	**AL** US$101-150
A US$66-100	**B** US$46-65	**C** US$31-45
D US$21-30	**E** US$12-20	**F** US$7-11
G US$6 and under		

Restaurant prices

ǂǂǂ over US$12	ǂǂ US$7-12	ǂ under US$6

Sleeping

Hotels in the upper ranges can often be booked more cheaply through Buenos Aires travel agencies. The tourist offices at Ezeiza and Jorge Newbery airports book rooms. If you pay in pesos in cash you may get a reduction. Room tax (VAT) is 21% and is not always included in the price. A/c is a must in high summer. Finding hotels for Fri, Sat, Sun nights can be difficult and hostels can get very busy, resulting in pressure on staff. The range of `boutique' hotels and hostels is impressive, especially in Palermo and San Telmo. The same applies to restaurants, bars and clubs. There are far more than we can list here, but between this book and Footprint's *Argentina Handbook*, we hope to have covered a good selection. There are fine examples of the **Four Seasons** (www.fourseasons.com/buenosaires), **N/A Town & Country Hotels** (www.newage-hotels.com), **Hilton** (www.hilton.com), **Marriott** (www.marriott.com) **NH** (www.nh-hoteles.com), **Pestana** (www.pestana.com), **Sofitel** (www.sofitel.com) and **Unique Hotels** (www.hotels-unique.com) chains. Hotels will store luggage, and most have English- speaking staff.

Centre *p69, map p70*

LL Alvear Palace, Av Alvear 1891, T/F4808 2100, reservations 4804 7777, www.alvearpalace.com. The height of elegance, an impeccably preserved 1920s Recoleta palace, sumptuous marble foyer, with Louis XV-style chairs, and a charming orangery where you can take tea with superb patisseries. Antique-filled bedrooms. Recommended.

LL Art, Azcuénaga 1268, T4821 6248, www.arthotel.com.ar. Charming boutique hotel on a quiet residential street, only a few blocks from Recoleta or Av Santa Fe, simply but warmly decorated, good service, solarium, compact standard rooms.

LL Aspen Towers, Paraguay 857, T5166 1900, www.aspentowers.com.ar. A modern minimalist foyer in this small hotel belies the traditional 1900 French-style bedrooms, all with jacuzzi baths, and all facilities, including a good breakfast and a pool.

LL Faena Universe, Martha Salotti 445 (Puerto Madero), T4010 9000, www.faenahotelanduniverse.com. Set in a 100-year old silo, renovated by Philippe Starck, this is not for all budgets or tastes. Eclectic decoration, staff trained to be perfect, the whole place is unique.

LL Panamericano, Carlos Pellegrini 551, T4348 5000, www.panamericano.us. Very smart and modern hotel, with luxurious and tasteful rooms, covered rooftop pool, and superb restaurant, Tomo 1. Excellent service too.

L Bisonte Palace, MT de Alvear 910, T4328 4751, www.hotelesbisonte.com. Charming, with calm entrance foyer, which remains gracious thanks to courteous staff. Plain but spacious rooms, ample breakfast, good location. Very good value.

L Colón, Carlos Pellegrini 507, T4320 3500, www.colon-hotel.com.ar. Splendid location overlooking Av 9 de Julio and Teatro Colón, extremely good value. Charming bedrooms, comfortable, pool, gym, great breakfasts, and perfect service. Highly recommended.

L El Conquistador, Suipacha 948, T4328 3012, www.elconquistador.com.ar. Stylish '70s boutique hotel, which retains the wood and chrome foyer, but has bright modern rooms, and a lovely light restaurant on the 10th floor with great views. Well situated, good value.

L Etoile, R Ortiz 1835 in Recoleta, T4805 2626, www.etoile.com.ar. Outstanding location, rooftop pool, rooms with kitchenette.

L Plaza San Martín Suites, Suipacha 1092, T5093 7000, www.plazasanmartin.com.ar. Neat modern self-contained apartments right in the city centre, comfortable and attractively decorated, with lounge and little kitchen. Sauna, gym, room service. Good value.

AL Castelar, Av de Mayo 1152, T4383 5000, www.castelarhotel.com.ar. A wonderfully elegant 1920s hotel which retains all the original features in the grand entrance and bar. Cosy bedrooms, charming staff, and excellent value. Also a spa with turkish baths and massage. Highly recommended.

AL Dolmen, Suipacha 1079, T4315 7117, www.hoteldolmen.com.ar. Good location, smart spacious entrance lobby, with a calm relaxing atmosphere, good professional service, modern, comfortable well-designed rooms, small pool.

AL Dorá, Maipú 963, T4312 7391, www.dora hotel.com.ar. Charming and old-fashioned with comfortable rooms, good service, attractive lounge with paintings. Warmly recommended.

AL Moreno, Moreno 376, T6091 2000, www.morenobuenosaires.com. 150m to Plaza de Mayo, decorated in dark, rich tones, large rooms, good value, jacuzzi, gym and chic bar. Recommended.

A Orly, Paraguay 474, T/F4312 5344, www.orly.com.ar. Good location, and comfortable plain rooms, with helpful service.

A Waldorf, Paraguay 450, T4312 2071, www.waldorf-hotel.com.ar. Welcoming staff and a comfortable mixture of traditional and modern in this centrally located hotel. Good value, with a buffet breakfast, English spoken. Recommended.

B Frossard, Tucumán 686, T4322 1811, www.hotelfrossard.com.ar. A lovely old 1940s building with high ceilings and the original doors, attractively modernized, and though the rooms are small (avoid No 11), the staff are welcoming, and this is good value, near C Florida.

B-C Goya, Suipacha 748, T4322 9269, www.goya hotel.com.ar. Welcoming and central, worth paying more for superior rooms, though all are comfortable. Good breakfast, English spoken.

C Marbella, Av de Mayo 1261, T/F4383 3573, www.hotelmarbella.com.ar. Modernized, and central, though quiet, breakfast included, multi-lingual. Recommended.

C The Clan House, Alsina 817, T4331 4448, www.bedandbreakfastclan.com.ar. Brightly-coloured, modern rooms, buffet breakfast, Wi-Fi and a small terrace, very good.

D O'Rei, Lavalle 733, T4393 7186, www.hotelorei.com.ar. Cheaper without bath, central, simple but comfortable, spotless, laundry facilities, helpful staff, no breakfast.

Youth hostels

E pp **Hostel Suites Obelisco**, Av Corrientes 830, T4328 4040, www.hostelsuites.com. Elegant hostel built in a completely restored old building in the heart of the city. Dorms, **C** doubles and private apartments, breakfast included, DVD room, free internet and Wi-Fi, laundry service. HI discount.

E pp **V&S**, Viamonte 887, T4322 0994, www.hostelclub.com. Central popular hostel (**B** in attractive double room, bath), breakfast, café, tiny kitchen, internet, lockers, tango classes, tours, warm atmosphere, welcoming. Recommended.

F pp **06 Central**, Maipú 306, T5219 0052, www.06centralhostel.com. A few metres from the Obelisco and Av Corrientes, simple, spacious dorms, nicely decorated doubles (**C**), use of kitchen, cosy communal area.

F pp **BA Stop**, Rivadavia 1194, T4382 7406, www.bastop.com. Dorms, private rooms (**C** double), breakfast included, large-screen TV, pool tables, bar, internet, English spoken, safe, very helpful staff. Repeatedly recommended.

F pp **Limehouse**, Lima 11, T4383 4561, www.limehouse.com.ar. Dorms for up to 12 and doubles with and without bath (**D-E**), popular, typical city hostel with kitchen, internet, bar, roof

terrace, "chilled", great if you like the party atmosphere, efficient staff. Recommended.
F pp **Milhouse Hostel**, Hipólito Yrigoyen 959, T4383 9383, www.milhousehostel.com. In 1890 house, lovely rooms (**C** in double) and dorms, comfortable, free breakfast, cooking facilities, laundry, internet, tango lessons, HI discounts, very popular so reconfirm bookings at all times.
F pp **St Nicholas**, B Mitre 1691 (y Rodríguez Peña), T4373 5920/8841, www.snhostel.com. Beautifully converted old house, now a party hostel with spotless rooms but beds could be better, cooking facilities, large roof terrace and a pub with daily live shows, luggage store; also **D** double rooms. Discounts for HI members.

Palermo *p73, map p74*
LL Malabia House, Malabia 1555, Palermo Viejo, T4833 2410, www.malabiahouse.com.ar. Elegant but expensive B&B with individually designed bedrooms and calm sitting rooms, great breakfast, reliable and welcoming. Recommended.
LL-L Bo Bo, Guatemala 4882, T4774 0505, www.bobo hotel.com. On a leafy street, 7 rooms decorated in contemporary style, some with private balconies, excellent restaurant.
L-C La Otra Orilla, Julián Alvarez 1779, Palermo Viejo, T4863 7426, www.otraorilla.com.ar. Homely, quiet, French-style 1930s residence with 7 very different rooms, from a great suite to a cute single. Some have a balcony or street views, others are more secluded. The patio is delightful for having breakfast in summer. Very good value.
AL Krista, Bonpland 1665, T4771 4697, www.kristahotel.com.ar. Intimate, hidden behind the plain façade of an elegant town-house, well-placed for restaurants. Good value, comfortable, individually-designed spacious rooms, Wi-Fi, wheelchair access. Recommended.
AL-B Bernarda House, Uriarte 1942, T4774 8997, www.bernardahouse.com.ar. Quiet, tastefully decorated family home for a relaxing stay, owned and run by welcoming Bernarda and Carlos. Pool, excellent food on request.
A-B Solar Soler, Soler 5676, T4776 3065, www.solarsoler.com.ar. Homely, welcoming B&B in Palermo Hollywood, excellent service, free internet. Recommended.
B-C Che Lulu, Emilio Zola 5185, T4772 0289, www.chelulu.com. Double rooms and hostel-style accommodation (**E** pp) in this rambling, laid-back house on a quiet quaint street a few blocks from Palermo subte. Not luxurious, but great value and very welcoming. Often recommended.

Youth hostels
E pp **Hostel Suites Palermo**, Charcas 4752, T4773 0806, www.suitespalermo.com. A beautiful century-old residence with the original grandeur partially preserved and a quiet atmosphere. Comfortable renovated dorms and private rooms with bath (**B** doubles), good service, small travel agency, free internet, Wi-Fi, cooking and laundry facilities, DVD room and breakfast included.
E-F pp **Hostal El Candil**, Lerma 476, T4899 1547, www.hostalelcandil.com. Argentine-Italian owned hostel with shared rooms and doubles (D pp), international atmosphere, quiet, comfortable, welcoming, with breakfast, rooftop terrace, Wi-Fi, tours arranged.
F pp **Casa Esmeralda**, Honduras 5765, T4772 2446, www.casaesmeralda.com.ar. Laid-back, dorms and **D** doubles, neat garden with hammocks and pond. Sebastián offers basic comfort with great charm.
F pp **Tango Backpackers Hostel**, Paraguay 4601, T4776 6871, www.tangobp.com. Well situated for Palermo's nightlife, lots of activities, free internet access and Wi-Fi, open terrace with outdoor showers. HI discount.

San Telmo and around *p77, maps p70 and p76*
LL Axel Hotel, Venezuela 649, T4136 9393, ww.axelhotels.com. Stunning gay hotel with 5 floors of stylishly designed rooms, each floor with a cosy living area, rooftop pool, gourmet restaurant. Recommended.
L-AL Mansión Dandi Royal, Piedras 922, T4307 7623, www.hotelmansiondandiroyal.com. A wonderfully restored 1903 residence, small upmarket hotel with an elegant tango atmosphere, small pool, good value. Daily tango lessons and *milonga* every Wed.
A La Casita de San Telmo, Cochabamba 286 T/F4307 5073, www.lacasitadesantelmo.com. 7 rooms in restored 1840's house, most open onto a garden with a beautiful fig tree, owners are tango fans; rooms rented by day, week or month.
A The Cocker, Av Garay 458, T4362 8451, ww.thecocker.com. In the heart of the antiques

district, tastefully restored art nouveau house, stylish suites, living room, roof terraces and gardens. Recommended.

B The Four, Carlos Calvo 535, T4362 1729, www.thefourhotel.com. 1930s building converted into a lovely B & B with 6 rooms, appealing terrace, welcoming staff. Recommended.

B Lugar Gay de Buenos Aires, Defensa 1120 (no sign), T4300 4747, www.lugargay.com.ar. A men-only gay B & B with 8 comfortable rooms, video room, jacuzzi, a stone's throw from Plaza Dorrego.

C Garden House Art Factory, Piedras 545, T4343 1463, www.artfactoryba.com.ar. Large, early 1900s house converted into a hotel, charming owners (see **Garden House**, below), informal atmosphere with individually designed and brightly painted private rooms (some with bath), halfway between the centre and San Telmo. Wi-Fi, free internet, breakfast included.

Youth hostels

C Ostinatto, Chile 680, T4362 9639, www.ostinatto.com. Double rooms with and without bath, shared rooms **E-F** pp, also has an apartment for rent. Minimalist contemporary design in a 1920s building, very nice, communal kitchen, free internet, Wi-Fi, promotes the arts, music, piano bar, movie room, tango lessons, arranges events, rooftop terrace.

E pp **Hostel-Inn Buenos Aires**, Humberto Primo 820, T4300 7992, www.hibuenosaires.com. An old 2-storey mansion with an outdoor terrace, dorms for up to 8 people and also private rooms, activities, loud parties, free internet and Wi-Fi, breakfast included and individual lockers in every room. HI discount.

E-F pp **Che Lagarto**, Venezuela 857, T4343 4845, www.chelagarto.com. Between Monserrat and San Telmo, large light dorms and **C** doubles with private bath, TV and fan. Attractive tango hall, the ground floor is a pub and restaurant. Price includes breakfast and free internet.

F pp **Garden House**, Av San Juan 1271, T4304 1824, www.gardenhouseba.com.ar. Small, welcoming independent hostel for those who don't want a party atmosphere; good barbecues on the terrace. Includes breakfast, free internet, some **D** doubles. Recommended.

F pp **Kilca Hostel & Backpacker**, Mexico 1545, between Saenz Peña and Virrey Cevallos, T4381 1966, www.kilcabackpacker.com. Lovingly restored 19th-century house with attractive landscaped patios. A variety of rooms from dorms to doubles; all bathrooms shared. Wi-Fi, breakfast included.

F pp **El Hostal de Granados**, Chile 374, T43625600, www.hostaldegranados.com.ar. Small, light, well-equipped rooms in an interesting building on a popular street, rooms for 2 (**C**) to 4, with bath, breakfast included, kitchen, free internet and Wi-Fi, laundry.

F pp **Hostel-Inn Tango City**, Piedras 680, T4300 5776, www.hitangocity.com. Well organized in renovated house with varied dorms and private rooms, popular, lively, parties, lots of activities, breakfast, DVD room, free internet access and Wi-Fi. HI discount.

F pp **Sandanzas**, Balcarce 1351, T4300 7375, www.sandanzas.com.ar. Arty hostel run by a group of friends. Small but with a light airy feel, **D** pp in double with bath, lounge and patio, free internet, Wi-Fi, breakfast and use of bikes, DVDs, kitchen.

Homestays and student residences

B&T Argentina, T4876 5000, www.byt argentina.com. Accommodation in student residences and host families; also furnished flats.

La Casa de Etty, Luis Sáenz Peña 617, T4384 6378, info@coret.com.ar. Run by Esther Corcias, manager of **Organización Coret**, www.angelfire.com/pq/coret. Host families.

Apartments/self catering

Bahouse, T4815 7602, www.bahouse.com.ar. Very good flats, by the week or month (from US$170 per week), all furnished and well-located in San Telmo, Retiro, Recoleta, Belgrano, Palermo and the centre.

Tu Casa Argentina, Esmeralda 980, p 2B, T4312 4127, www.tucasargentina.com. Furnished flats by the day, week, month (from US$40 per day). Credit cards not accepted, deposit and rent payable in dollars. Efficient and helpful.

Eating

Eating out in Buenos Aires is one of the city's great pleasures, with a huge variety of restaurants from the chic to the cheap. To try some of Argentina's excellent steak, choose from one of the many *parrillas*, where your huge slab of lean meat will be expertly cooked over a wood fire. If in doubt about where to eat, head for Puerto Madero, where there are lots of good places serving international as well as local cuisine. Take a taxi to Palermo or Las Cañitas for a wide range of excellent restaurants all within strolling distance. For more information on the gastronomy of Buenos Aires see: www.guiaoleo.com.ar, restaurant guide in Spanish and English; www.vidalbuzzi.com.ar, in Spanish. 2 fantastic food-oriented blogs in English are: www.saltshaker.net, chef Dan Pearlman who also runs a highly recommended private restaurant in his house, see website for details; and www.foodquests.blogspot.com, international food writer Layne Molser.

Some restaurants are *tenedor libre*: eat as much as you like for a fixed price. Most cafés serve tea or coffee plus *facturas*, or pastries, for breakfast, US$1.50-3.

Retiro, and the area between Plaza de Mayo and Plaza San Martín *p69, map p70*

TTT Chiquilín, Sarmiento 1599. *Parrilla* and pasta. Good atmosphere, though a little overpriced.

TTT El Querandí, Perú 302 y Moreno. Good food in an intimate atmosphere in this place that was opened in the 1920s and is now also a tango venue in the evening. Next door is a wine bar serving lunch and dinner at **La Cava del Querandí**, Perú 322.

TTT La Chacra, Av Córdoba 941 (just off 9 de Julio). A superb traditional *parrilla* with excellent steaks (US$24 for parrillada for 2), impeccable old-fashioned service, lively atmosphere.

TTT Morizono, Reconquista 899. Japanese dishes. Recommended for their set lunch menus.

TTT Palacio Español at the Club Español, B de Irigoyen 180 (on Av 9 de Julio, near Av de Mayo). Originally a sumptuous room in a fine building, recommended for a quiet dinner, with excellent food, basically Spanish dishes.

TTT Sorrento Corrientes 668 (just off Florida). Intimate, elegant atmosphere, one of the most traditional places in the centre for very good pastas and seafood.

TTT Tancat, Paraguay 645. Delicious Spanish food, very popular at lunchtime.

TTT Tomo 1, Panamericano Hotel, Carlos Pellegrini 521, T4326 6695. Argentine regional dishes and international cuisine of a high standard in a sophisticated atmosphere. Very expensive.

TT Abril, Suipacha y Arenales. A good small place serving a varied menu.

TT El Palacio de la Papa Frita, Lavalle 735 and 954, Corrientes 1620. Great place for a filling feed, with a large menu, and quite atmospheric, despite the bright lighting.

TT Gianni´s, Viamonte 834 and Reconquista 1028. The set menu with the meal-of-the-day makes an ideal lunch. Good risottos and salads.

TT Güerrín, Corrientes 1368. A Buenos Aires institution. Serves filling pizza and *faina* (chick pea polenta) which you eat standing up at a bar, or at tables, though you miss out on the colourful local life that way. Wonderful. For an extra service fee, upstairs room is less crowded or noisy.

TT Il Fratello, Tucumán 688. Popular for pasta at lunchtime.

TT La Casona del Nonno, Lavalle 827. Popular with tourists, for its central location and for its set price menu serving good food.

La Estancia, Lavalle 941. A slightly touristy but reliable *parrilla*, popular with business people at lunchtime, good grills, *parrillada* US$20 for 2.
La Pipeta, San Martín 498. A traditional, unpretentious place, established 40 years, for good food in a noisy atmosphere, closed Sun.
Los Inmortales, Lavalle 746. Specializes in pizza, tasty, good value, great salads, good service.
Sattva, Montevideo 446. A healthy and relaxing oasis next to the busy pizzerías district on Av Corrientes, serving vegetarian and vegan dishes. The meal of the day for lunch is always a good choice. Closed on Sun.
Gran Victoria, Suipacha 783. Good value *tenedor libre*, including parrilla, in a cheery atmosphere, also cheap set meals.

Cafés

Aroma, Florida y M T de Alvear. A great place to relax, with a huge space upstairs, comfortable chairs for watching the world go by.
Café de la Biblioteca, M T de Alvear 1155 (Asociación Biblioteca de Mujeres). Coffee and light snacks, evening shows.
Café Tortoni, Av de Mayo 825-9. This most famous Buenos Aires café has been the elegant haunt of artists and writers for over 100 years, with marble columns, stained glass ceilings, old leather chairs, and photographs of its famous clientele on the walls. Excellent coffee and cakes, good tea, excellent tango, live jazz in evenings, all rather pricey. Getting increasingly packed with tourists, but still worth a visit.
Clásica y Moderna, Callao 892, T4812 8707, www.clasicaymoderna.com. One of the city's most welcoming cafés, with a bookshop, great atmosphere, good breakfast through to drinks at night, daily live music and varied shows. Highly recommended.
Confitería Ideal, Suipacha 384. One of the most atmospheric cafés in the city. Wonderfully old-fashioned 1930s interior, serving good coffee and excellent cakes with good service. Upstairs, tango is taught and there's tango dancing at a *milonga* here. Highly recommended.
Desiderio, Av Santa Fe y Esmeralda. Good coffee and drinks, in a nice, though noisy corner on plaza San Martín.
El Gato Negro, Av Corrientes 1669. A beautiful tearoom, serving a choice of coffees and teas, and good cakes. Delightfully scented from the wide range of spices on sale.
Florida Garden, Florida y Paraguay. Another well-known café, popular for lunch, and tea.
Richmond, Florida 468, between Lavalle and Corrientes. Genteel, old fashioned and charming place for tea with cakes, and a basement where chess is played between 1200-2400 daily.
Saint Moritz, Esmeralda y Paraguay. Original late 1950s decor with a particularly calm atmosphere on a very busy corner.

The Italian ice cream tradition has been marked for decades by 'heladerías' such as **Cadore**, Av Corrientes 1695 or **El Vesuvio**, Av Corrientes 1181, the oldest of all.

West of Plaza de Mayo *p72, map p74*

3 blocks west of Plaza San Martín, under the flyover at the northern end of Av 9 de Julio, between Arroyo and Av del Libertador in La Recova, are several recommended restaurants.
El Mirasol de la Recova, Posadas 1032. Serves top-quality parrilla in an elegant atmosphere.
Piegari, Posadas 1042. Great for Italian food served in generous portions; though a bit overpriced and a noisy place.
La Tasca de Plaza Mayor, Posadas 1052. Very good Spanish tapas and attentive service.
Juana M, Carlos Pellegrini 1535 (downstairs). Excellent choice, popular with locals for its good range of dishes, and its very good salad bar.
Winery, Paseo La Recova, off Libertador 500. A chic wine bar where you can sample the best of Argentina's fine wines, light dishes such as salads and gourmet sandwiches. Also at Av Alem 880 and Juana Manso 835 (Puerto Madero).

Recoleta *p73, map p74*

Lola, Roberto M Ortiz 1805. Well known for superb pasta dishes, lamb and fish.
Sirop, Pasaje del Correo, Vte Lopez 1661, T4813 5900. Delightful chic design, delicious French-inspired food, superb patisserie too. Highly recommended.
El Sanjuanino, Posadas 1515. Atmospheric place offering typical dishes from the northwest: *humitas*, *tamales*, and *empanadas*, as well as unusual game dishes.
La Madeleine, Av Santa Fe 1726. Bright and cheerful choice open 24 hrs; quite good pastas.

María de Bambi, Ayacucho 1821. This small, quiet place is probably the best value in the area, serving very good and simple meals. Open till 2130, closed on Sun.
Rodi Bar, Vicente López 1900. Excellent *bife* and other dishes in this typical *bodegón*, welcoming and unpretentious.

Tea rooms, café-bars and ice cream

Café Victoria, Roberto M Ortiz 1865. Wonderful old-fashioned café, popular and refined, great cakes.
Ice Cream Freddo, in Recoleta at Roberto M Ortiz y Quintana, Arenales y Callao, Roberto M Ortiz y Guido, Santa Fe y Montevideo and at shopping malls. Known for the best ice cream.
Milion, Paraná 1048. Stylish bar and café in an elegant mansion with marble stairs and a garden, young and cool clientèle.
Un'Altra Volta, in Recoleta at Av Santa Fe y Av Callao, Quintana y Ayacucho, Pacheco de Melo y Av Callao. Great ice creams.

Palermo *p73, map p74*

This area of Buenos Aires is very popular, with many chic restaurants and bars in Palermo Viejo (referred to as 'Palermo Soho' for the area next to Plaza Cortázar and 'Palermo Hollywood' for the area beyond the railways and Av Juan B Justo) and the Las Cañitas district. It's a sprawling district, so you could take a taxi to one of these restaurants, and walk around before deciding where to eat. It's also a great place to stop for lunch, with cobbled streets, and 1900s buildings, now housing chic clothes shops.

The Las Cañitas area is fashionable, with a wide range of interesting restaurants mostly along CBaez, and most opening at around 2000, though only open for lunch at weekends:
Baez, Baez 240, Las Cañitas. Very trendy, with lots of orange neon, serving sophisticated Italian-style food and sushi.
Cluny, El Salvador 4618, T4831 7176. Very classy, a great place for lunch, fish and pasta with great sauces, mellow music.
Dominga, Honduras 5618, T4771 4443, www.domingarestaurant.com. Elegant, excellent food from a short but creative menu, professional service, good wine list, ideal for a romantic meal or treat, open evenings only.
Eh! Santino, Baez 194, Las Cañitas. Italian-style food in a trendy, small, if not cramped place, dark and cosy with lots of mirrors.
El Manto, Costa Rica 5801, T4774 2409. Genuine Armenian dishes, relaxed, good for a quiet evening.
Janio, Malabia 1805, T4833 6540. One of Palermo's first restaurants, open for breakfast through to the early hours, lunch US$6, sophisticated Argentine cuisine in the evening.
Novecento, Baez 199, Las Cañitas. A lively French-style bistro, stylish but unpretentious and cosy, good fish dishes among a broad menu.
Bio, Humboldt 2199, T4774 3880. Delicious gourmet organic food, on a sunny corner, open daily, but closed Mon for dinner.
Campo Bravo, Baez y Arevalo, Las Cañitas. Stylish, minimalist, superb steaks and vegetables on the *parrilla*. Popular and recommended, can be noisy.
De la Ostia, Baez 212, Las Cañitas. A small, chic bistro for tapas and Spanish-style food, good atmosphere.
El Preferido de Palermo, Borges y Guatemala, T4778 7101. Very popular *bodegón* serving both Argentine and Spanish-style dishes.
Eterna Cadencia, Honduras 5574, T4774 4100. A small bookshop with a café which is perfect for lunch, open 0900-2000.
Krishna, Malabia 1833. A small, intimate place serving very good Indian-flavoured vegetarian dishes.
La Cupertina, Cabrera y Godoy Cruz. The attention may be a bit brusque sometimes, but the northwestern Argentine dishes, plus the filling desserts are not to be missed, especially on a cold winter's day.
Morelia, Baez 260, Las Cañitas. Cooks superb pizzas on the *parrilla* or in wood ovens, and has a lovely roof terrace for summer. Also at Humboldt 2005.
Omm, Honduras 5656, T4774 4224. Cosy wine and tapas bar with good food. Also **Omm Carnes**, Costa Rica 5198, T4773 0954, for meat dishes and steak, open from 1800, closed Sun.
Social Paraíso, Honduras 5182. Simple delicious dishes in a relaxed chic atmosphere, with a lovely patio at the back. Good fish and tasty salads. Closed Sun evening and Mon.
Palermo DC, Guatemala y Carranza. Surely there is a great chef behind the excellent light

meals, sandwiches, salads and vegetable pies served at just few unpretentious tables on the pavement.

Tea rooms, café-bars and ice cream

Palermo has good cafés opposite the park on Av del Libertador, including the fabulous ice creams at **Un'Altra Volta**, Av del Libertador 3060 (another branch at Echeverría 2302, Belgrano). **Persicco**, Salguero y Cabello, Maure y Migueletes and Av Rivadavia 4933 (Caballito). The grandsons of **Freddo**'s founders also offer excellent ice cream.

Cheap eats

A few supermarkets have good, cheap restaurants: **Coto** supermarket, Viamonte y Paraná, upstairs. Many supermarkets have very good deli counters and other shops sell *fiambres* (smoked, cured meats) and cheeses for quick, cheap eating. The snack bars in underground stations are also cheap. **Delicity bakeries**, several branches, have very fresh *facturas* (pastries), cakes, breads, and American doughnuts. Another good bakery for breakfasts, sandwishes and salads is **Bonpler**, Florida 481, 0730-2300, with the daily papers, classical music. Other branches elsewhere.

San Telmo *p77, maps p70 and p76*

TTT La Brigada, Estados Unidos 461, T4361 5557. Atmospheric *parrilla*, serving excellent Argentine cuisine and wines. Very popular and compact, expensive, but recommended. Always reserve.

TT Brasserie Petanque, Defensa y Mexico. Very attractive, informal French restaurant offering a varied menu with very good, creative dishes. Excellent value for their set lunch menus. Expect slow service.

TT El Desnivel, Defensa 855. Popular parrilla, packed at weekends, good atmosphere.

TT Lezama, Brasil 359 (on Parque Lezama). Typical *bodegón*, popular with families, typical Argentine menu, huge portions, rather slow service.

TT Maraxe, Tacuarí y Chile. A reliable traditional Spanish-style place with good service, with seafood as its speciality.

T La Trastienda, Balcarce 460. Theatre café with lots of live events, also serving meals and drinks from breakfast to dinner, great music, relaxed and cool, but busy lunchtime. Recommended.

T Mi Tío, Defensa 900. A small basic place suitable for pizzas and *milanesas*, beloved by San Telmo locals.

Ice creams

Dylan, Perú 1086. Very good. **Freddo**, a few blocks away, at Defensa y Estados Unidos, has opened a new branch.

Puerto Madero *p77*

The revamped docks area is an attractive place to eat, and to stroll along the waterfront before dinner. There are good places here, generally in stylish interiors and with good service if a little overpriced: along Av Alicia Moreau de Justo (from north to south), these are recommended.

TTT El Mirasol, No 202. Very good parrilla.

TTT Katrine, No 138. Smart, with delicious fish and pasta.

TTT Cabaña Las Lilas, No 516. Excellent *parrilla*, popular with tourists.

TTT La Parolaccia, Nos 1052 and 1170. Excellent pasta and Italian-style dishes (seafood is the speciality at No 1170), executive lunch US$8 Mon-Fri, popular.

TTT-TT Fresh Market, Azucena Villaflor y Olga Cossettini. Fresh fruits and vegetables served in the most varied ways in this small, trendy restaurant and deli, from breakfasts to dinners.

Bars and clubs

Generally it is not worth going to clubs before 0230 at weekends. Dress is usually smart.

Bars

Boquitas Pintadas, Estados Unidos 1393 (Constitución), T4381 6064. Trendy pop-style bar holding art exhibitions.

Buller Brewing Company, Roberto M Ortiz 1827 (Recoleta). Brew pub. Happy hour till 2100.

La Cigale, 25 de Mayo 722, T4312 8275. Popular after office hours, good music, guest DJs on Tue.

The corner of Reconquista and Marcelo T de Alvear in Retiro is the centre of the small 'Irish' pub district, overcrowded on St Patrick's Day, 17 Mar. **Druid In**, Reconquista 1040, is by far the most attractive choice there, open for lunch and with live music weekly. **The Shamrock**, Rodríguez Peña 1220. Irish-run, popular, happy hour 1800-2400, Sat-Sun from 2000. Rock and electronic music in the basement.

There are good bars in San Telmo around Plaza Dorrego.

In Palermo Viejo, live music usually begins 2330-2400. Las Cañitas is best on Thu night; not so appealing at weekends. Good and popular are: **Bar 6**, Armenia 1676, T4833 6807, chic modern bar, good lunches, friendly atmosphere. **Mundo Bizarro**, Serrano 1222, famous for its cocktails, American-style food, electronic and pop music.

Clubs

El Living, M T de Alvear 1540, T4811 4730, www.living.com.ar. Relaxed bar, restaurant and small club, Thu-Sat.
Maluco Beleza, Sarmiento 1728. Brazilian flavour, entertaining, popular.
Niceto Club, Niceto Vega 5510, T4779 9396, www.nicetoclub.com. Early live shows and funk or electronic music for dancing afterwards.
Pacha, Av Costanera Rafael Obligado y Pampa, T4788 4280, www.pachabuenosaires.com. Electronic music on Sat.
The Roxy, Federico Lacroze y Álvarez Thomas. Rock, pop and live shows, Sat-Sun.

Gay clubs Most gay clubs charge US$10 entry. **Amerika**, Gascón 1040, www.ameri-k.com.ar. Thu-Sun. **Glam**, Cabrera 3046, www.glambsas.com.ar. Thu and Sat. **Alsina**, Alsina 940, www.alsinabuenos aires.com.ar. Fri and Sun. **Sitges**, Av Córdoba 4119, T4861 2763, www.sitges online.com.ar. Gay and lesbian bar, near Amerika.

Jazz clubs **Notorious**, Av Callao 966, T4813 6888, www.notorious.com.ar. Live jazz at a music shop. **La Revuelta**, Alvarez Thomas 1368, T4553 5530. Live jazz, bossa nova and tango. **Thelonious**, Salguero 1884, T4829 1562. Live jazz and tango.

Salsa clubs **La Salsera**, Yatay 961, T4864 1733, www.lasalsera.com. Highly regarded.

Entertainment

Details of most events are given in Espectáculos/ Entretenimientos section of main newspapers, *Buenos Aires Herald* (English) on Fri and www.whatsupbuenosaires.com.

Cinemas

The selection of films is excellent, ranging from new Hollywood releases to Argentine and world cinema; details are listed daily in main newspapers. Films are shown uncensored and most foreign films are subtitled. Tickets best booked early afternoon to ensure good seats (average price US$4, discount on Wed and for first show daily). Tickets obtainable from ticket agencies (*carteleras*), such as **Vea Más**, Paseo La Plaza, Corrientes 1660, local 2, T6320 5302 (the cheapest), **Cartelera**, Lavalle 742, T4322 1559, **Cartelera Baires**, Corrientes 1382, local 24, T4372 5058, www.cartelera-net.com.ar, and **Entradas con Descuento**, Lavalle 835, local 27, T4322 9263.

Seats can be booked by phone with credit/debit card for US$0.30 per ticket. Many cinemas in shopping malls, some on Av Corrientes and on C Lavalle, also in Puerto Madero (Dock 1) and in Belgrano (Av Cabildo). On Fri and Sat many central cinemas have *trasnoches*, late shows at 0100.
At **Village Recoleta** (Vicente López y Junín) there is a cinema complex with *trasnoche* programmes on Fri and Sat. Independent foreign and national films are shown during the **Festival de Cine Independiente**, held every Apr, more information on the festival at www.bafici.gov.ar.

Cultural events

Centro Cultural Borges, Galerías Pacífico, Viamonte y San Martín, p 1, T5555 5359, www.ccborges.org.ar. Art exhibitions, concerts, film shows and ballet; some student discounts.
Centro Cultural Recoleta, Junín 1930, by Recoleta cemetery. Many free activities (see under Sights).
Ciudad Cultural Konex, Sarmiento 3131 (Abasto), T4864 3200, www.ciudadcultural konex.org. A converted oil factory hosts this huge complex holding plays, live music shows, summer film projections under the stars, modern ballet, puppet theatre and, occasionally, massive parties.
Fundación Proa, Av Pedro de Mendoza 1929, T4303 0909, www.proa.org. Temporary exhibitions of contemporary art, photography and other cultural events in La Boca.
Luna Park stadium, Bouchard 465, near Correo Central, T5279 5279, www.lunapark.com.ar. Pop/jazz concerts, sports events, ballet and musicals.
Museo de Arte Latinoamericano, MALBA, (address and website above), is a very active

centre holding old or independent film exhibitions, seminars and conferences on arts.
Palais de Glace, Posadas 1725, T4804 1163, www.palaisdeglace.org. Temporary art and film exhibitions and other cultural events.
Teatro Gral San Martín, Corrientes 1530, T4371 0111/8, www.teatrosan martin.com.ar. Cultural activities, many free, including concerts, 50% ISIC discount for Thu, Fri and Sun (only in advance at 4th floor, Mon-Fri). The theatre's **Sala Leopoldo Lugones** shows international classic films, US$2.50.

Tango shows

Tango shows are mostly overpriced and tourist-oriented. Despite this, the music and dance are generally of a high professional standard and the shows very entertaining. Tango information office at Av Roque Sáenz Peña (Diagonal Norte) 832 p 6, T4393 4670, www.tangodata.com.ar. Also www.tangocity.com and www.todotango.com. Every year, between end Feb-Mar the city celebrates the **Festival Buenos Aires Tango**, holding tango sessions, lessons, old musical films, exhibitions and a massive open-air *milonga*, open to all, in the central avenues (www.tangodata.gov.ar for details). Every August there is a tango dancing competition open to both locals and foreigners.
Bar Sur, Estados Unidos 299, T4362 6086, www.bar-sur.com.ar. 2000-0200, US$50; plus dinner for US$70 including pizza, tapas and empanadas, drinks extra. Good fun, public sometimes join the professional dancers.
El Querandí, Perú 302, T5199 1771, www.querandi.com.ar. Tango show restaurant, daily show (2200) US$56 dinner including drink (2030), and show US$80.
El Viejo Almacén, Independencia y Balcarce, T4307 7388, www.viejoalmacen.com. Daily, dinner from 2000, show 2200, US$80 with all drinks, dinner and show; show only, US$55. Impressive dancing and singing, recommended.
Esquina Carlos Gardel, Carlos Gardel 3200 y Anchorena, T4867 6363, www.esquinacarlos gardel.com.ar. Opposite the former Mercado del Abasto, this is the most popular venue in Gardel's own neighbourhood; dinner at 2030 (dinner and show US$83), show at 2230 (US$56). Recommended.
La Ventana, Balcarce 431, T4334 1314, www.la-ventana.com.ar. Daily dinner from 2000 (dinner and show US$80) or show with 2 drinks, 2200, US$57, very touristy but very good.
Piazzolla Tango, Florida 165 (basement), Galería Güemes, T4344 8200, www.piazzollatango.com. A beautifully restored belle époque hall hosts a smart tango show; dinner at 2045 (dinner and show US$80), show at 2215 (US$60).
Señor Tango, Vieytes 1655, Barracas, T4303 0231, www.senortango.com.ar. Spectacular show with dancers, horses, etc, US$27, starts 2200 (with dinner at 2030, US$80).

Milongas are the events where locals dance tango and also *milonga* (the music that contributed to the origins of tango and is more cheerful). Tourists may join the dancers, or just watch (entry fee is much cheaper than for the shows); dancing is usually preceded by tango lessons. Milongas take place at several locations on different days; phone to confirm or check at www.tangodata.com.ar.
Centro Cultural Torquato Tasso, Defensa 1575, T4307 6506, www.torquatotasso.com.ar. Tue and Sun 2130, free (daily lessons 1700, 1830, US$5), English spoken.
Confitería Ideal, Suipacha 384, T5265 8069, www.confiteriaideal.com. Very atmospheric ballroom for daily milongas at this old central café. Most days dancing starts as early as 1500; lessons Mon-Fri start at 1200, Sat 2100. Also evening tango shows.
La Viruta (at Centro Armenio), Armenia 1366, Palermo Viejo, T4774 6357, www.lavirutatango.com. Very popular with a young and trendy crowd, Wed-Sun (check for times).
Porteño y Bailarín, Riobamba 345, T4932 5452, www.porteybailarin.com.ar. Lessons Tue, Sun at 2100, dancing at 2300.
Tango Discovery, www.tangodiscovery.com. Offers unconventional method for tango lessons developed by dancer Mauricio Castro.

Theatre

You are advised to book as early as possible for a seat at a concert, ballet, or opera. Tickets for most popular shows (including rock and pop concerts) are sold also through **Ticketek**, T5237 7200, www.ticketek.com.ar, **Entrada Plus**, T4000 1010, www.entradaplus.com.ar, or **Ticketmaster**, T4321 9700. For other ticket agencies, see Cinemas, above. The **Teatro Colón**'s opera season usually runs from Apr to Nov and there are concert performances most days. Visit www.teatro colon.org.ar for news as redevolopment of the theatre is expected to be completed in 2010. For live Argentine and Latinamerican bands, best venues are: **La Trastienda**, www.latrastienda.com, **ND Ateneo**, www.ndateneo.com.ar or **La Peña del Colorado**, www.delcolorado.com.ar.

O Shopping

Most shops outside main shopping areas and malls close lunchtime on Sat. The main, fashionable shopping streets are Florida and Santa Fe (especially between 1,000 and 2,000 blocks). Palermo is the best area for chic boutiques and well-known international fashion labels. C Defensa in San Telmo is known for its antique shops. Pasaje de la Defensa, Defensa 1179, is a beautifully restored 1880s house containing small shops.

Bookshops

You'll find most bookshops along Florida, Av Corrientes (from Av 9 de Julio to Callao) or Av Santa Fe, and in shopping malls. Second-hand and discount bookshops are mostly along Av Corrientes and Av de Mayo. Rare books are sold in several specialized stores in the Microcentro (the area enclosed by Suipacha, Esmeralda, Tucumán and Paraguay). The main chains of bookshops, usually selling a small selection of foreign books, are: **Cúspide**, with several branches on Florida, Av Corrientes and some malls, and the biggest and most interesting store at Village Recoleta, Vicente López y Junín; **Distal**, Florida 738 and more branches on Florida and Av Corrientes; **El Ateneo**, whose biggest store is on Av Santa Fe 1860, in an old theatre, there is café where the stage used to be; **Yenny** in all shopping malls, also sell music. The **Boutique del Libro** chain is also good, the nicest branch being in Palermo, Thames 1762, T4833 6637, with a café, www.boutiquedellibro.com.ar. For a larger selection of books in English: **Crack Up**, Costa Rica 4767, T4831 3502. Funky, open plan bookshop and café, open Mon-Wed till 2230, and till the early hrs the rest of the week. **Eterna Cadencia**, Honduras 5574, T4774 4100. Excellent selection of novels, classics, contemporary fiction and translations of Spanish and Argentine authors. Highly recommended for its café too. **Walrus Books**, Estados Unidos 617, San Telmo, www.walrus-books.com.ar. Second-hand books in English, including Latin American authors. Good children's section.

You can also try **ABC**, Maipú 866; **Joyce, Proust & Co**, Tucumán 1545 p 1 A, also sells books in other European languages; **Kel**, Marcelo T de Alvear 1369; **Librería Rodríguez**, Sarmiento 835; **LOLA**, Viamonte 976, Mon-Fri 1200-1830, small publishers specializing in Latin America natural history, also sell used and rare editions, most in English.

Foreign newspapers are available from news-stands on Florida, in Recoleta and the kiosk at Corrientes and Maipú.

Camping equipment

Good equipment from **Buenos Aires Sports**, Panamericana y Paraná, Martínez (Shopping Unicenter, 2nd level). **Eurocamping**, Paraná 761. **Fugate** (no sign), Gascón 238 (off Rivadavia 4000 block), T4982 0203. Also repairs equipment. **Outside Mountain Equipment**, Otero 172 (Chacarita), T4856 6204, www.outside.com.ar. Camping gas available at **Britam**, B Mitre 1111, **Todo Gas**, Sarmiento 1540, and **El Pescador**, Paraguay y Libertad. **Cacique Camping**, Esteban Echeverría 3360, Munro, T4762 1668, www.cacique.com.ar. Manufactured clothing and equipment. **Ecrin**, Av Santa Fe 2723 (Martínez), T4792 1935, www.ecrin.com.ar. Imported climbing equipment. **Montagne**, Florida 719, Paraná 772, and several others, www.montagneoutdoors.com.ar, and **Camping Center**, Esmeralda 945, www.camping-center.com.ar. Good selection of outdoor sports articles. **Costanera Uno**, at the southern end of Costanera Norte, 4312 4545, www.costanera uno.com.ar. For nautical sports, very good. GPS repair service, **Jorge Gallo**, Liniers 1522, Tigre, T4731 0323.

Handicrafts

Alhué, Juncal 1625. Very good aboriginal-style crafts. **Arte y Esperanza**, Balcarce 234, www.arteyesperanza.com.ar. Crafts made by aboriginal communities, sold by a Fair Trade organization. **Artesanías Argentinas**,

Montevideo 1386, www.artesaniasargentinas.org. Aboriginal crafts and other traditional items sold by a Fair Trade organization. **Atípica**, El Salvador 4510, Palermo Viejo, T4833 3344, www.atipicaobjetos.com.ar. Specialising in arts and crafts by local artists and designers, English, French and Portuguese spoken, see also Nancy Kulfas' trendypalermoviejo.blogspot.com. **Casa de San Antonio de los Cobres**, Pasaje de la Defensa, Defensa 1179, www.vivirenlos cobres.com.ar. Traditional Puna crafts in silver, llama or sheep wool. **El Boyero**, Florida 953, T4312 3564. High quality silver, leather, woodwork and other typical Argentine handicrafts. **Martín Fierro**, Santa Fe 992. Good handicrafts, stonework, etc. Recommended. **Plata Nativa**, Galería del Sol, Florida 860, local 41. For Latin American folk handicrafts and high quality jewellery.

Leather goods

Several shops are concentrated along Florida next to Plaza San Martín and also in Suipacha (900 block). **Aida**, Galería de la Flor, local 30, Florida 670. Quality, inexpensive leather products, can make a leather jacket to measure in the same day. **All Horses**, Suipacha 1350. Quality leather clothing. **Dalla Fontana**, Reconquista 735. Leather factory, fast, efficient and reasonably priced for made-to-measure clothes. **Casa López**, MT de Alvear 640/658; also at Patio Bullrich and Galerías Pacífico malls. The most traditional and finest leather shop, expensive but worth it. **Fortín**, Santa Fe 1245. Excellent items. **Galería del Caminante**, Florida 844. Has a variety of good shops with leather goods, arts and crafts, souvenirs, etc. **King's Game**, Maipú 984. Another good shop focusing on polo clothing. **La Curtiembre**, Juncal 1173, Paraguay 670. Affordable prices for good quality articles. **Prüne**, Florida 963 and at Florida y Av Córdoba. Fashionable designs for women, many options in leather and not very expensive. **Uma**, in shopping malls and at Honduras 5225 (Palermo Viejo). For women, the trendiest of all.

Markets

Caminito, Vuelta de Rocha (Boca), 1000-1700. Plastic arts and local crafts. **Costanera Sur**, next to the Fuente de las Nereidas. Weekends 1100-2000. Crafts, books, coins, stamps. **Feria Hippie**, in Recoleta, near cemetery. Big craft and jewellery market, Sat and Sun 1000-2200, good street atmosphere, expensive. **Feria de Mataderos**, Lisandro de la Torre y Av de los Corrales 6436, T4687 1949, subte E to end of line then taxi (US$3.50), or buses 36, 92, 97, 126, 141. Long way but few tourists, fair of Argentine handicrafts and traditions, music and dance festivals, gaucho horsemanship skills, every Sun 1200-1800 (Sat 1800-2400 in summer); nearby *Museo de los Corrales*, Av de los Corrales 6436, T4687 1949, Sun 1200-1800 (in summer, Sat 1800-2300), US$0.35. **Mercado de las Luces**, Manzana de las Luces, Perú y Alsina, Mon-Fri 1100-1900, Sun 1400-1900. Handicrafts, second-hand books, plastic arts. **Parque Centenario**, Díaz Vélez y L Marechal. Sat-Sun 1100-2000, local crafts, cheap handmade clothes, used items of all sorts. **Parque Lezama**, Brasil y Defensa, San Telmo. Handicraft market at weekends, 1100-2000. **Parque Rivadavia**, Av Rivadavia 4900. Second-hand books, records, tapes, CDs and magazines (daily); **Feria del Ombú**, for stamps, postcards and coins (Sun 0930-1430, under a big ombú tree). **Plaza Belgrano**, near Belgrano Barrancas station on Juramento, between Cuba y Obligado. Sat-Sun, 1100-2000 craft, jewellery, etc market. **Plaza Dorrego**, San Telmo. For souvenirs, antiques, etc, with free tango performances and live music, Sun 1000-1700, wonderfully atmospheric, and an array of 'antiques'. **Plaza Italia**, Santa Fe y Uriarte (Palermo). Second hand textbooks and magazines (daily), handicrafts market on Sat-Sun 1100-2000.

Music shops

Casa Piscitelli, San Martín 450. Classical, tango, folklore, jazz.
Zival's, Av Corrientes y Av Callao. Huge choice; also bookshop.

Shopping malls

Abasto de Buenos Aires, Av Corrientes 3247, T4959 3400, nearest Subte: Carlos Gardel, line B. In the city's impressive, Art Deco former fruit and vegetable market building: cheaper clothes, good choice, cinemas. **Alto Palermo**, Col Díaz y Santa Fe, T5777 8000, nearest Subte: opposite Bulnes, line D. Great for all the main clothes chain stores, and about 20 blocks' walk from

Palermo's boutiques. **Galerías Pacífico**, on Florida, between Córdoba and Viamonte, T5555 5110, nearest Subte: Plaza San Martín, line C. A beautiful mall with fine murals and architecture, many exclusive shops and good food mall with wide choice and low prices in basement. Also good set-price restaurant on 2nd floor (lunches only). Free guided visits from the fountain on lower-ground floor (Mon-Fri 1130, 1630). **Paseo Alcorta**, Salguero y Figueroa Alcorta, T5777 6500. Huge mall, spanning four levels, with cinemas, supermarket, stores, many cheap restaurants (take colectivo 130 from Retiro or Correo Central, or 67 from Constitución or Recoleta). **Patio Bullrich**, Av Del Libertador 750 and Posadas 1245, T4814 7400, nearest Subte: 8 blocks from Plaza San Martín, line C. The most upmarket mall in the city, selling chic international and Argentine fashion designer clothes, boutiques selling high-quality leather goods, and small food court in elegant surroundings.

Activities and tours

Football and rugby Football fans should see **Boca Juniors**, matches every other Sun 1500-1900 at their stadium (La Bombonera, Brandsen 805, La Boca, www.bocajuniors.com.ar, tickets for non-members only through tour operators, or the museum, T4362 1100 – see the murals; along Av Almirante Brown buses 29, 33, 53, 64, 86, 152, 168; along Av Patricios buses 10, 22, 39, 93), or their arch-rivals, **River Plate**, www.cariver plate.com.ar (to stadium take bus 29, 130 from centre going north, or bus 15 from Palermo). Football season mid-Feb to Jun, and Aug-Dec, most matches on Sun and sometimes Fri or Sat (occasionally Tue-Thu). Buy tickets (from US$8) from stadiums, sports stores near the grounds, ticket agencies such as Ticketek or hostels and hotels, which may arrange guide/transport (don't take a bus if traveling alone, phone a radio taxi; see also Tangol, below). Rugby season Apr-Oct/ Nov. For more information, **Unión Argentina de Rugby**, T4383 2211, www.uar.com.ar.

Horse racing **Hipódromo Argentino de Palermo**, a large, modern racecourse, popular year round, and at **San Isidro**. Riding schools at both.

Polo The high handicap season is Sep-Dec, but it is played all year round. Argentina has the top polo players in the world. A visit to the national finals at Palermo in Nov and Dec is recommended. For information, **Asociación Argentina de Polo**, T4777 6444, www.aapolo.com.

Swimming Public baths near Aeroparque, **Punta Carrasco** (best, most expensive, also tennis courts) and **Parque Norte**, popular. **Club de Amigos**, Av Figueroa Alcorta y Av Sarmiento, T4801 1213, www.clubdeamigos.org.ar. An indoor swimming pool is open all year round, US$6 plus US$3 for access to the club.

Tour operators and travel agents

An excellent way of seeing Buenos Aires and the surrounding area is by a 3-hr tour. Longer tours include dinner and a tango show, or a gaucho *fiesta* at a ranch (great food and dancing). Bookable through most travel agents.

4 Star Turismo, Suipacha 530, p 2, T1-888-206 9253, T5235 4549, www.4starargentina.com. Custom and group tours through Argentina and throughout the region.

Argentina Excepción, Juncal 4455, 5A, T4772 6620, www.argentina-excepcion.com. French/Argentine agency offering tailor-made, upper end tours, fly-drives, themed trips and other services. Also has a Santiago branch, www.chile-excepcion.com.

Argentina for Less, Viamonte 749, 10th floor, Office 4, T0203 006 2507 (UK), T1 887 661 6989. (USA toll free), www.argentinaforless.com. Offers price guarantee on fully customised packages.

ATI, Esmeralda 567 (and other branches), T4329 9000, www.ati viajes.com. Mainly group travel, very efficient.

Barba Charters, T4824 3366, www.barba charters.com.ar. Boat trips and fishing in the Delta and Tigre areas.

BAT, Buenos Aires Tur, Lavalle 1444 of 10, T4371 2304, www.buenosairestur.com. City tours, US$13, twice daily; Tigre and Delta, daily, 5 hrs, US$23.

Buenos Aires Vision, Esmeralda 356, p 8, T4394 4682, www.buenosaires-vision.com.ar. City tours (US$13), Tigre and Delta (from US$23), Tango (US$80-100, cheaper without dinner) and *Fiesta Gaucha* (US$55).

Cicerones de Buenos Aires, J J Biedma 883, T4330 0800, www.cicerones.org.ar. Non-profit organization offering volunteer "greeting"/ guiding service for visitors to the city; free, safe and a different experience.

Cultour, T156-365 6892 (mob), www.cultour.com.ar. A highly recommended walking tour of the city, 3-4 hrs led by a group of Argentine history/ tourism graduates, US$18. In English and Spanish.

Ecole del Sur, Av Rivadavia 1479, p 1 B, T4383 1026, www.ecoledelsur.com. Tour operator offering packages and accommodation in Buenos Aires, Argentina and Uruguay. Associated with **The Royal Family**, www.theroyalfamily.com.ar, gay and lesbian tourism and language school.

Eternautas, Av Julio A Roca 584 p 7, T5235 7295, www.eternautas.com. Historical, cultural and artistic tours of the city and Pampas guided in English, French or Spanish by academics from the University of Buenos Aires, flexible.

Eves Turismo, Tucumán 702, T4393 6151, www.eves.com. Helpful and efficient, recommended for flights.

Flyer, Reconquista 617, p 8, T4313 8224, www.flyer.com.ar. English, Dutch, German spoken, repeatedly recommended, especially for *estancias*, fishing, polo, motorhome rental.

HI Travel Argentina, Florida 835, ground floor, T4511 8723, www.hitravel.com.ar.

Hostelling International Travel, Florida 835 PB, T4511 8723, www.hostels.org.ar. Hostel network office and advisors, specialised backpacker trips.

L'Open Tour, T4116 4544, www.lopen tour.com.ar. Multilingual, 2-hr recorded tours (headphones provided) on an open bus, leaving 4 times a day, either to the south or to the north, from Plaza San Martín (opposite **Marriott Hotel**), US$20. Book in advance.

Lan&Kramer Bike Tours, T4311 5199, www.bike tours.com.ar. Daily at 0930 and 1400 next to the monument of San Martín (Plaza San Martín), 3½- 4-hr cycle tours to the south or the north of the city (US$30); they also go to San Isidro and Tigre, 4½-5 hrs, US$35, bike rental at Florida 868, p 14H.

Nomads Community Travel Agency, Lima 11, T5218 3059. Offers flight and bus tickets, specialized guides, various tours and activities and custom-made trips.

Patagonia Chopper, www.patagonia chopper.com.ar. Helicopter tours of Buenos Aires and around,15-45 mins, US$165-248 pp (min 2 people; price includes transfer in/out to/from the city centre). Flights also to Colonia and the Delta.

Pride Travel, Paraguay 523 p 2, T5218 6556, www.pride-travel.com. For gay and lesbian travellers; also rents apartments and also at Guatemala 4845, p 1 of 4, Palermo.

Say Hueque, Viamonte 749, p 6 of 1, T5199 2517/ 20, www.sayhueque.com. Recommended travel agency offering good-value tours aimed at independent travellers, friendly English-speaking staff. Specialize in tours to Patagonia, Iguazu and Mendoza.

Smile on Sea, T15-5018 8662 (mob), www.smileonsea.com. 2½-hr private boat trips off Buenos Aires coast, leaving from Puerto Madero, on 32-ft sailing boats (US$242 for up to 5 passengers). Also 8-hr trips to San Isidro and Delta (US$600 for 5).

Tangol, Florida 971, ground floor, shop 31, T4312 7276, www.tangol.com. Friendly, independent agency specializing in football and tango, plus various sports, such as polo and paragliding. Can arrange tours, plane and bus tickets, accommodation. English spoken. Discounts for students. Overland tours in Patagonia Sep-Apr.

Urban biking, Moliere 2801 (Villa Devoto), T4568 4321, www.urbanbiking.com. 4 ½-hr tours either to the south or to the north of the centre, starting daily 0900 and 1400 next to the English clock tower in Retiro, US$24. Night city tours, 3½ hrs, US$28, full day tours to San Isidro and Tigre (including kayak in the Delta), US$50, or occasionally, to the pampas. Also rents bikes.

What's Up BA, T4553 8827, http://whatsup buenosaires.com. For a wide variety of cultural experiences around the city, including finding accommodation.

Transport

Air

Ezeiza (officially Ministro Pistarini, T5480 6111, www.aa2000.com.ar), the international airport, is 35 km southwest of the centre (also handles some domestic flights to El Calafate and Ushuaia in high season). The airport has 2 terminals: 'A' for all airlines except **Aerolíneas Argentinas**, which uses 'B'. 'A' has a very modern check-in hall. There are duty free shops (expensive), exchange facilities (**Banco de la Nación**; **Banco Piano**; **Global Exchange** – rates of exchange in baggage reclaim are considerably poorer than elsewhere - only change the minimum to get you into the city) and ATMs (Visa and MasterCard), a Secretaría de Turismo desk, post office (open 0800-2000) and a left luggage office (US$3 per piece). No hotels nearby, but there is an attractive B&B 5 mins away with transfer included: **A Bernie's**, Estrada 186, Barrio Esteban Echeverría, T4480 0420, www.posada bernies.com.ar, book in advance. There is a **Devolución IVA/Tax Free** desk (return of VAT) for purchases over the value of AR$70 (ask for a Global Refund check plus the invoice from the shop when you buy). Reports of pilfering from luggage. To discourage this have your bags sealed by Secure Bag in the check-in hall. Hotel booking service at Tourist Information desk – helpful, but prices are higher if booked in this way. A display in immigration shows choices and prices of transport into the city.

Airport buses Special buses to/from the centre are run by **Manuel Tienda León** (office in front of you as you arrive), company office and terminal at Av Madero 1299 y San Martín, behind Sheraton Hotel in Retiro, T4315 5115, www.tiendaleon.com. To **Ezeiza**: 0400, 0500, then every 30 mins till 2100 and 2200, 2230, 2400 (be 15 mins early); from Ezeiza: more-or-less hourly throughout the day and night, US$11.50 (US$21.50 return), 40-min journey, pay by pesos, dollars, euros or credit card. **Manuel Tienda León** will also collect passengers from addresses in centre for US$1 extra, book the previous day. Bus from Ezeiza to Aeroparque, 1 hr, US$12. Remise taxis to town or to Aeroparque, US$38. Services on request with **Transfer Express**, T0800-444 4872, reservas@transfer-express.com.ar, airport office in front of you as you arrive, remise taxi from Ezeiza to town or to Aeroparque, US$30. **Taxi Ezeiza**, T5480 0066, www.taxiezeiza.com.ar, US$30 to the centre, US$35 to Aeroparque. Also **VIP** and **World Car** with similar prices.

Aeroparque (Jorge Newbery Airport), 4 km north of the centre, TT5480 6111, www.aa2000.com.ar, handles all internal flights, and **AR** and **Pluna** flights to Montevideo and Punta del Este. The terminal is divided into 2 sections, 'A' for all arrivals and **AR/Austral** and **LAN** check-in desks, 'B' for **Pluna**, **Andes**, **Sol** and **LADE** check-in desks. On the 1st floor there is a **patio de comidas** and many shops. At the airport also tourist information, car rental, bus companies, bank, ATMs, exchange facilities, post office, public phones, Secure Bag (US$8 per piece) and luggage deposit (between sections A-B at the information point), US$2 per piece for 12 hrs. **Manuel Tienda León** buses to Aeroparque (see above for address), 0710-0040, every hour; from Aeroparque (departs from sector B, stops at **AR**), 0900-1600 every hour, and 1800, 2000, 2130 and 2330, 20-min journey, US$4. Local buses 33 and 45 run from outside the airport to the Retiro railway station, then to **La Boca** and **Constitución** respectively. No 37 goes to **Palermo** and **Recoleta** and No 160 to **Palermo** and **Almagro**. If going to the airport, make sure it goes to Aeroparque by asking the driver, US$0.33. **Remise taxis**: are operated by

Transfer Express and **Manuel Tienda León**, US$8-9 to centre, US$38 to Ezeiza. Taxi to centre US$6. **Manuel Tienda León** operates buses between Ezeiza and Aeroparque airports, US$12, stopping in city centre, US$4. **AR/Austral** offer daily flights to the main cities; **LAN** has daily flights to some cities and tourist destinations; **Andes** flies to Salta and to Puerto Madryn, **Sol** flies to Rosario, Santa Fe and Córdoba (and in summer to Mar del Plata, Villa Gesell, Montevideo and Punta del Este), for details see text under intended destination. **LADE** offers weekly flights to **El Calafate, Ushuaia, Puerto Madryn** and **Bariloche** with several stops in Patagonia.

Bus

Local City buses are called *colectivos* and cover a very wide radius. They are clean, frequent, efficient and very fast. The basic fare is about US$0.30, US$0.50 to the suburbs. Have coins ready for ticket machine as drivers do not sell tickets, but may give change. The bus number is not always sufficient indication of destination, as each number may have a variety of routes, but bus stops display routes of buses stopping there and little plaques are displayed in the driver's window. No 86 (white and blue) runs to the centre from outside the airport terminal to the left as you leave the building, 2 hrs, US$0.50, coins only, runs all day, every 20 mins during the day. To travel to Ezeiza, catch the bus at Av de Mayo y Perú, 1 block from Plaza de Mayo (many other stops, but this is central) – make sure it has 'Aeropuerto' red sign in the window as many 86s stop short of Ezeiza. See Information in Ins and outs, above, for city guides listing bus routes.

Long distance Bus terminal at Ramos Mejía y Antártida Argentina (Subte Line C), behind Retiro station, for information and booking with credit card, T4310 0700, www.tebasa.com.ar. Information desk is at the top of long ramp to your left. All ticket offices are upstairs, even numbers to the left, foreign companies at the very end (full list at the top of the escalator). International services operate from platforms 67-75. Buenos Aires city information desk on ground floor, beside an ATM; another ATM and a bank (with exchange facilities for US$ and euros) upstairs. Locutorios with internet on ground floor. Remise taxis hiring points next to the platforms. At the basement and ground levels there are left-luggage lockers, US$1.30 for 1 day with tokens sold in kiosks; for large baggage, there's a *guarda equipaje* in the basement. Fares vary according to time of year and comfort: advance booking is essential Dec-Mar, Easter, Jul and long weekends. **Coche cama** is advisable for overnight journeys – seats fully recline and food is served. Travellers have reported getting student discounts without showing evidence of status, so it's always worth asking. For further details of bus services and fares, look under proposed destinations. There are no direct buses to either of the airports.

International buses International services are run by both local and foreign companies; heavily booked Dec-Mar (especially at weekends), when most fares usually rise sharply; fares shown here are for high season. Do not buy Uruguayan bus tickets in Buenos Aires; wait till you get to Colonia. To **Montevideo** **Bus de la Carrera**, Mon, Wed, Fri 1000, US$27, 8 hrs, with a *coche cama*, daily at 2230, via Colón and Paysandú. **CAUVI** also goes daily to Montevideo at 2130, and in summer to **Punta del Este**. Direct buses to **Santiago** (Chile), 1,400 km, **Ahumada-Fénix, CATA, Pullman del Sur**, daily, 19-21 hrs, US$60. To **Bolivia**: **Potosí Buses** goes across the border to **Villazón**, US$73, and to **Santa Cruz de la Sierra**, US$85-95. **La Preferida Bus** goes to **Yacuiba**, 34 hrs, and **Santa Cruz de la Sierra**, 36 hrs, both at US$66. **Balut** also crosses the border to **Villazón**, US$83. Most Argentine companies only reach the border, where you can change buses: to **La Quiaca** (US$48-83), to **Aguas Blancas** (US$80 with **Balut**), or to **Pocitos** (US$80 with **Balut**). Alternatively change buses at **San Salvador de Jujuy** or at **Orán**, busier transport hubs. **La Veloz del Norte** goes to **Santa Cruz de la Sierra**, US$85. To **Asunción** (Paraguay), 1,370 km via Clorinda (toll bridge): about 20 bus companies, around 18 hrs, with executive (luxury service, with **Nuestra Señora de la Asunción**, T4311 7666, US$93), *diferencial* (with food, drinks, US$80-100) and *común* or *convencional* (without food, but a/c, toilet, US$70-90). Also to **Ciudad del Este** (18-20 hrs, US$50-70), **Encarnación** (12-14 hrs, US$40-70) and minor destinations in Paraguay. To **Peru** **Ormeño** (T4313 2259) and **El Rápido Internacional** (T4315 0804), direct service to **Lima** (only stops for meals, not included in the price), Mon, Wed, Sat 1800 or Tue, Fri, Sun 1800 respectively, 3 days, US$180. **La Veloz del Norte**, T0800-444 8356, goes to **Lima** via Paso de Jama and San Pedro de Atacama, Wed, Sun 0900, 3 days, US$240 (first meal included), if you need a visa for Chile, get one before travelling. Direct buses to **Brazil** by **Pluma**, T4313 3880: **São Paulo** via Paso de los Libres, 36 hrs, US$112, **Rio de Janeiro**, 42 hrs, US$137 (via **Foz do Iguaçu**, 18 hrs, US$66), **Porto Alegre**, 20 hrs, US$86, **Florianópolis**, 26 hrs, US$100, **Curitiba**, 30 hrs, US$109. To **Rio de Janeiro**, changing buses at Posadas and Foz do Iguaçu is almost half price, 50 hrs. **Crucero del Norte** goes to **São Paulo**, 32 hrs, US$93, and **Rio de Janeiro**, 38 hrs, US$115. A third route across the Río de la Plata and through Uruguay is a bit cheaper and offers a variety of transport and journey breaks.

Driving

Driving in Buenos Aires is no problem, provided you have eyes in the back of your head and good nerves. Traffic fines are high and police increasingly on the lookout for drivers without the correct papers. Car hire is cheaper if you arrange it when you arrive rather than from home. See also Essentials, page 35, for international hire agencies. Also **Sixt**, Carlos Pellegrini 1537, T4328 8020, www.sixt.com.ar, and **Thrifty**, Carlos Pellegrini 1576, T0810-999 8500, www.thriftyar.com.ar. There are several national rental agencies, eg **Serra Lima**, Av Córdoba 3121, T4962 8508 or T0800-777 5462, or **Dietrich**, Cerrito 1575, T0810-345 3438, www.dietrich rentacar.com. **Ruta Sur**, Lavalle 482, p 5, T5238 4072, www.rutasur.com. Rents 4WDs and motorhomes. **Motoring Associations**: see ACA, page 60.

Ferry

To **Montevideo** and **Colonia** from Terminal Dársena Norte, Av Antártida Argentina 821 (2 blocks from Av Córdoba y Alem). **Buquebus**, T4316 6400, www.buquebus.com (tickets from Terminal or from offices at Av Córdoba 879 and Posadas 1452): 1) Direct to **Montevideo**, 2 a day, 3 hrs, US$69 tourist class, US$97 1st class, US$111 special class one way, vehicles US$86-112, motorcycles US$70, bus connection to Punta del Este, US$11 extra. 2) To **Colonia**, services by 2 companies: **Buquebus**: minimum 5 crossings a day, from 1 to 3 hrs, US$27 tourist class, US$37 1st class, US$44 special class one way, US$37-55 on fast vessels, with bus connection to **Montevideo** (US$11 extra). Motorcycles US$34-45, cars US$51-75 and 68-95 (depending on size of vehicle and boat). **Colonia Express**, www.coloniaexpress.com, makes 2-3 crossings a day between Buenos Aires and Colonia in a fast catamaran (no vehicles carried), 50 mins, prices start at US$6 one way if bought on the internet, or US$12 with bus connections to Montevideo; non-web prices are much higher, eg US$15-38 one way to Colonia, US$27-110 to Montevideo. Office is at Av Córdoba 753, T4313 5100; Terminal Fluvial is at Av Pedro de Mendoza 330, T4317 4100. You must go there by taxi. See under Tigre, page 101, for services to Carmelo and Nueva Palmira.

Metro (Subte)

Six lines link the outer parts of the city to the centre. **Line 'A'** runs under Av Rivadavia, from Plaza de Mayo to Primera Junta. **Line 'B'** from central Post Office, on Av L N Alem, under Av Corrientes to Federico Lacroze railway station at Chacarita, ending at Los Incas. **Line 'C'** links Plaza Constitución with the Retiro railway station, and provides connections with all the other lines but 'H'. **Line 'D'** runs from Plaza de Mayo (Catedral), under Av Roque Sáenz Peña (Diagonal Norte), Córdoba, Santa Fe and Palermo to Congreso de Tucumán (Belgrano). **Line 'E'** runs from Plaza de Mayo (Cabildo, on C Bolívar) through San Juan to Plaza de los Virreyes (connection to Premetro train service to the southwest end of the city). **Line 'H'** runs from Once to Caseros, under Av Jujuy. Note that 3 stations, 9 de Julio (Line 'D'), Diagonal Norte (Line 'C') and Carlos Pellegrini (Line 'B') are linked by pedestrian tunnels. The fare is US$0.30, the same for any direct trip or combination between lines; magnetic cards (for 1, 2, 5, 10 or 30 journeys) must be bought at the station before boarding; only pesos accepted. Trains are operated by **Metrovías**, T0800-555 1616, and run Mon-Sat 0500-2225 (Sun 0800-2200). Line A, the oldest was built in 1913, the earliest in South America; it starts running Mon-Sat at 0600. Backpacks and luggage allowed. Free map (if available) from stations and tourist office.

Taxi

Taxis are painted yellow and black, and carry Taxi flags. Fares are shown in pesos. The meter starts at US$1 when the flag goes down; make sure it isn't running when you get in. A fixed rate of US$0.10 for every 200 m or 1-min wait is charged thereafter. A charge is sometimes made for each piece of hand baggage (ask first). About 10% tip expected. Phone a radio taxi from a phone box or locutorio, giving the address of where you are, and you'll usually be collected within 5 mins. Taxis from official rank in bus terminal are registered with police and safe. For extra security, take a remise taxi booked from a booth on the bus platform itself, more expensive but very secure (to Ezeiza US$26; to Aeroparque US$9). Taxis from a registered company are safer, and some 'Radio Taxis' you see on the street are false. Check that the driver's licence is displayed. Lock doors on the inside. Worst places are the two airports and Retiro; make sure you know roughly what the fare should be before the journey: eg from Aero- parque to: Ezeiza US$21 (plus toll), Congreso US$6, Plaza de Mayo US$6, Retiro US$5, La Boca US$8. In theory fares double for journeys outside city limits (Gen Paz circular highway), but you can often negotiate. Radio Taxis (same colours and fares) are managed by several different companies (eg **Del Plata**, T4504 7776; **Pídalo**, T4956 1200; **Llámenos**, T4556 6666) and are recommended as a safer alternative; minimum fare is US$2.50.

Remise taxis operate all over the city, run from an office and have no meter. The companies are identified by signs on the pavement. Fares, which are fixed and can be cheaper than regular taxis, start at US$2.55-3 and can be verified by phoning the office, and items left in the car can easily be reclaimed. **La Terminal**, T4312 0711 is recommended, particularly from Retiro bus station.

From centre to **Ezeiza** US$26-31. Fixed-price *remise taxis* for up to 4 passengers can be booked from the **Manuel Tienda León** or **Transfer Express** counter at Ezeiza, prices above. Avoid unmarked cars at Ezeiza no matter how attractive the fare may sound; drivers are adept at separating you from far more money than you can possibly owe them. Always ask to see the taxi driver's licence. If you take an ordinary taxi the Policía de Seguridad Aeroportuaria on duty notes down the car's licence and time of departure. There have been recent reports of taxi drivers taking Ezeiza airport-bound passengers to remote places, stealing all their luggage and leaving them there. If in doubt, take a *remise* or airport bus.

Tram

Old-fashioned street cars operate Mar-Nov on Sat and holidays 1600-1930 and Sun 1000-1300, 1600-1930 and Dec-Feb on Sat and holidays 1700-2030, Sun 1000-1300, 1700-2030, free, on a circular route along the streets of Caballito district, from C Emilio Mitre 500, Subte Primera Junta (Line A) or Emilio Mitre (Line E), no stops en route. Operated by **Asociación Amigos del Tranvía**, T4431 1073, www.tranvia.org.ar. There is a new tram that runs along Av Alicia Moreau de Justo (Puerto Madero), with terminals at Av Córdoba and at Av Independencia, US$0.35.

Train

There are 4 main terminals: 1) **Retiro** (3 lines: **Mitre**, **Belgrano** and **San Martín** in separate buildings). Mitre line (run by **TBA**, T4317 4407 or T0800-333 3822, www.tbanet.com.ar). Urban and suburban services include: **Belgrano**, **Mitre** (connection to Tren de la Costa, see below), **Olivos**, **San Isidro**, and **Tigre** (see below); long distance services to **Rosario Norte**, Mon-Fri 1840, 5 hrs, US$11; to **Tucumán** via Rosario, Mon and Fri, 1040, 26 hrs, US$66 sleeper (breakfast included), US$22 pullman, US$15 1st class, US$12 turista (run by **Ferrocentral**, T4312 2989). To **Córdoba** via Rosario, Mon and Fri 2030, 14½ hrs, US$50 sleeper (breakfast included), US$15 pullman, US$12 1st class, US$8 turista (run by **Ferrocentral**). Belgrano line to northwestern suburbs, including Villa Rosa, run by **Ferrovías**, T4511 8833. San Martín line for services to Pilar and long distance services to Junín and Alberdi (see www.ferrobaires.gba.gov.ar).

2) **Constitución**, Roca line urban and suburban services to La Plata, Ezeiza, Ranelagh and Quilmes. Long distance services (run by **Ferrobaires**, T4304 0028, www.ferrobaires.gba.gov.ar): Bahía Blanca, 5 weekly, 12½ hrs, US$10-16, food mediocre; to Mar del Plata daily, 6-7 hrs, US$11-20; to Pinamar, 1-2 weekly, 6 hrs, US$11-15; to Miramar (one a day in summer only), 8 hrs, US$13-16;

to Carmen de Patagones, 20 hrs, weekly, US$18-20; also to Bolívar and Daireaux.

3) **Federico Lacroze** Urquiza line and Metro headquarters (run by **Metrovías**, T0800-555 1616, www.metrovias.com.ar). Suburban services: to General Lemos. **Trenes Especiales Argentinos**, T4554 8018, www.trenesdellitoral.com.ar, runs twice a week a train to **Posadas**, minimum 26 hrs, US$21-75, from Lacroze via the towns along Río Uruguay.

4) **Once**: Sarmiento line (run by *TBA*, see above). Urban and suburban services include **Luján** (connection at Moreno), **Mercedes** and **Lobos**. A fast service runs Mon-Fri between Puerto Madero (station at Av Alicia Moreau de Justo y Perón) and Castelar. Long distance services to Lincoln and Pehuajó (see www.ferrobaires.gba.gov.ar). Tickets checked before boarding and on train and collected at the end of the journey; urban and suburban fares are charged according different sections of each line; fares vary depending on the company, cheapest is about US$0.22.

Directory

Airline offices Aerolíneas Argentinas (AR) and **Austral**, Perú y Rivadavia, Av LN Alem 1134 and Av Cabildo 2900, T0810-2228 6527. **Aero México**, Reconquista 737 p 3, T5238 1200. **Aero Sur**, Av Santa Fe 851 p 1, T4516 0999. **Air Canada**, Av Córdoba 656, T4327 3640. **Air Europa**, MT de Alvear 925 p 1, T4322 4545. **Air France-KLM**, San Martín 344 p 23, T4317 4711. **Alitalia**, Av Santa Fe 887, T0810-777 2548. **American Airlines**, Av Santa Fe 881, T4318 1111, Av Pueyrredón 1997 and branches in Belgrano and Acassuso. **Andes**, Av Córdoba 755, 4508 6750. **Avianca**, Carlos Pellegrini 1163 p 4, T4394 5990. **British Airways**, Av del Libertador 498 p 13, T0800-222 0075. **Continental**, Carlos Pellegrini 527, T0800-333 0425. **Copa**, Carlos Pellegrini 989 p 2, T0810-222 2672. **Cubana**, Sarmiento 552 p 11, T4326 5292. **Delta**, Av Santa Fe y Suipacha, T0800-666 0133. **Gol**, T0810-266 3232. **Iberia**, Carlos Pellegrini, 1163 p 1/3, T4131 1000. **Lan**, Cerrito 866, T0810- 999 9526. **LADE**, Perú 714, T5129 9000. **Lufthansa**, M T Alvear 590, p 6, T4319 0600. **Malaysia Airlines**, Suipacha 1111 p 14, T4312 6971. Mexicana, Av Córdoba 1131, T4136 4136. **Pluna**, Florida 1, T4120 0530. **Sol**, T0810-444 4765. **South African Airways**, Av Santa Fe 846, T4319 0099. **TACA**, Carlos Pellegrini 1275, T4325 8222. **TAM**, Cerrito 1030, T4819 4800 or T0810 333 3333. **United**, Av Madero 900, T0810-777 8648. **Banks** ATMs are widespread for MasterCard or Visa (look for Link ATMs). The financial district lies within a small area north of Plaza de Mayo, between Rivadavia, 25 de Mayo, Av Corrientes and Florida. In non-central areas find banks/ATMs along the main avenues. Banks open Mon-Fri 1000-1500. Use credit or debit cards for withdrawing cash rather than carrying TCs. Most banks charge commission especially on TCs (as much as US$10). US dollar bills are often scanned electronically for forgeries, while TCs are sometimes very difficult to change and you may be asked for proof of purchase. Major credit cards usually accepted but check for surcharges. General MasterCard office at Perú 151, T4348 7000, www.mastercard.com/ar, open 0930-1800. Visa, Corrientes 1437 p 2, T4379 3400, www.visa.com.ar. **American Express** offices are at Arenales 707 y Maipú, by Plaza San Martín, T4310 3535, www.americanexpress.com.ar, where you can apply for a card, get financial services and change Amex TCs (1000-1500 only, no commission into US$ or pesos); no commission either at **Banco de la Provincia de Buenos Aires**, several branches. **Citibank**, B Mitre 502, T0810-444 2484, changes only Citicorps TCs cheques, no commission; branch at Florida 199. *Casas de cambio* include **Banco Piano**, San Martín 345, T4321 9200 (has exchange facility at Ezeiza airport, 0600-2200), www.banco piano.com.ar, changes all TCs (commission 2%). **Forex**, MT de Alvear 540, T4311 5543. **Eves**, Tucumán 702. **Banco Ciudad** at Av Córdoba 675 branch is open to tourists (with passport) for currency exchange and TCs, Mon, Sat, Sun and holidays 1000-1600. Other South American currencies can only be exchanged in *casas de cambio*. **Western Union**, branches in Correo Argentino post offices (for transfers within Argentina) and at Av Córdoba 975 (for all transfers), T0800-800 3030. **Cultural centres** **British Council**, M T de Alvear 590, p 4, T4114 8600, www.britishcouncil.org.ar (Mon-Thu 0900-1700, Fri 0900-1330). **British Arts Centre** (BAC), Suipacha 1333, T4393 6941, www.britisharts centre.org.ar. English plays and films, music concerts, photography exhibitions (closed Jan). **Goethe Institut**, Corrientes 319/43, T4311 8964, German library and newspapers (Mon, Tue, Thu 1230-1930, Fri 1230-1600, closed Jan), free German films shown, cultural programmes, German and Spanish language courses. Same building, upstairs, is the German Club, Corrientes 327. **Alliance Française**, Córdoba 946, T4322 0068, www.alianzafrancesa.org.ar. French library, film and art exhibitions. **Instituto Cultural Argentino Norteamericano (ICANA)**, Maipú 672, T5382 1500, also at 3 de Febrero 821, T4576 5970, www.icana.org.ar. **Biblioteca Centro Lincoln**, Maipú 672, T5382 1536 (also at 3 de Febrero 821, T4576 5970), www.bcl.edu.ar, Mon-Wed 1000-2000, Thu and Fri 1000-1800 (Jan and Feb Mon-Fri 1300-1900), library (members' only borrowing), English/US newspapers. **Villa Ocampo**, Elortondo 1837, Beccar, Partido de San Isidro, T4732 4988, www.villaocampo.org. Former residence of writer and founder of Revista Sur Victoria Ocampo, now owned by UNESCO, in northern suburbs, Thu-Sun 1230-1800, open for visits, courses, exhibitions, etc. **Embassies and consulates** All open Mon-Fri unless stated otherwise. **Australia**, Villanueva 1400, T4779 3500, www.argentina.embassy.gov.au. 0830-1700, ticket queuing system; take bus 29 along Av Luis María Campos to Zabala. **Austria**, French 3671, T4802 9185, www.austria. org.ar. Mon-Thu 0900-1200. **Belgium**, Defensa 113 p 8, T4331 0066, 0800-1300, www.diplobel.org/argentina. **Bolivia**, Av Corrientes 545 p 2, T4394 1463, www.embajadadebolivia.com.ar, Mon-Fri 1000-1600, with tourist information. **Brazil**, Cerrito 1350, T4515 2400, consulate at C Pellegrini 1363 p 5, www.con brasil.org.ar. 0900-1400, 1500-1700, tourist visa takes 3 working days, prices vary per nationality. **Canada**, Tagle 2828, T4808 1000, www.dfait-maeci.gc.ca/argentina. Mon-Thu 1400-1630, tourist visa Mon-Thu 0845-1130. **Chile**, Consulate, Roque Saenz Peña 547 p 2, T4331 6228, http://chileabroad.gov.cl/buenos-aires/, 0900-1400. **Denmark**, Consulate, Av LN Alem 1074 p 9, T4312 6901, www.buenosaires.um.dk. Mon-Thu 0800- 1600, Fri 0800-1300. **Finland**, Av Santa Fe 846, p 5, T4312 0600, www.finlandia.org.ar Mon-Thu 0830-1200. **France**, Santa Fe 846, p 3 y 4, T4312 2409, www.consulatfrance.int.ar, 0900-1230, 1400- 1600 (by appointment). **Germany**, Villanueva 1055, T4778 2500, www.buenos-aires.diplo.de. 0830-1100. **Ireland**, Av Del Libertador 1068 p 6, T5787 0801, www.irlanda.org.ar. 0900-1300. **Israel**, Av de Mayo 701, p 10, T4338 2500, info@buenosaires.mfa.gov.il. Mon-Thu 0900-1200, Fri 0900-1100. **Italy**, consulate at Reconquista 572, T4114 4800, www.consbuenos aires.esteri.it, Mon, Tue, Thu, Fri 0800-1100. **Japanese Consulate**, Bouchard 547 p 17, T4318 8200, www.ar.emb-japan.go.jp, 0900-1230, 1430-1700. **Netherlands**, Olga Cossettini 831 p 3, Puerto Madero, T4338 0050, www.embajadaholanda.int.ar, Mon-Thu 0900-1300, Fri 0900-1230. **New Zealand**, C Pellegrini 1427 p 5, T4328 0747, www.nzembassy.com/argentina. Mon-Thu 0900-1300, 1400-1730, Fri 0900-1300. **Norway**, Carlos Pellegrini 1427 p 2, T4328 8717, www.noruega.org.ar, 1000-1400. **Paraguay**, Av Las Heras 2545, T4802 3826, embapar@fibertel.com.ar. 0900-1400. **South Africa**, MT de Alvear 590, p 8, T4317 2900, www.embajadasudafrica.org.ar, 0830-1200. **Spain**, Av del Libertador 2075, T4802 6031, www.embajadaenargentina.es. **Sweden**, Tacuarí 147 p 6, T4329 0800, www.swedenabroad.com/buenosaires, 1000- 1200. **Switzerland**, Santa Fe 846, p10, T4311 6491, www.eda.admin.ch/buenosaires, open 0900-1200. **UK**, Luis Agote 2412 (near corner Pueyrredón y Guido), T4808 2200 (call T15-5114 1036 for emergencies only out of normal office hours), dlbairesask consularn-cleared@fco.gov.uk. Mon-Thu 1145-2030, Fri 1145-1700, Jan-Feb: Mon-Thu 1145-1730, Fri 1145-1700. **Uruguay**, Av Las Heras 1907, T4807 3040, www.embajada deluruguay.com.ar. 0930-1730, visa takes up to 15 days. **US Embassy and Consulate General**, Colombia 4300, T5777 4533 (for emergencies involving US citizens, T5777 4354 or T5777 4873 after office hours), http://buenosaires.usembassy.gov. **Internet** Prices range from US$0.40 to US$1 per hr, shop around. Most *locutorios* (phone offices) have internet access. **Language schools** Academia Buenos Aires, Hipólito Yrigoyen 571, 4th fl, T4345 5954, www.academiabuenosaires.com. **AISL**, (Argentina Improving Spanish Language), Rodríguez Peña 832, T5811 3940, www.argentin aisl.com, spanish@argentinaisl.com. **Alem**, Lavalle 166 p 5, A, T5252 0404, www.alemspanish school.com.ar. Also has internet and Wi-Fi.

All-Spanish, Talcahuano 77 p 1, T4381 3914, www.all-spanish.com.ar. One to one classes. **Amauta Spanish School**, Federizo Lacroze 2129, T4777 2130, www.amautaspanish.com. Spanish classes, one-to-one or small groups, centres in Buenos Aires and Bariloche. **Argentina I.L.E.E**, T4782 7173, info@argentinailee.com, www.argentinailee.com. Recommended by individuals and organizations alike, with schools in Córdoba and Bariloche. **Cedic**, Reconquista 715, p 11 E, T/F4315 1156, www.cedic.com.ar. Recommended. **IBL (Argentina Spanish School)**, Florida 165, 3rd floor, Office 328, T4331 4250, www.ibl.com.ar. Group and one-to-one lessons, all levels, recommended. **Bue Spanish School**, Belgrano Ave 1431, 2nd floor, appt.18, T4381 6347, www.buespanish.com.ar. Intensive and regular Spanish courses, culture programme, free materials. **Lenguas Vivas**, Carlos Pellegrini 1515, T4322 3992, cursoslv@gmail.com. Very good cheap courses. **PLS**, Carabelas 241 p 1, T4394 0543, www.pls.com.ar. Recommended for travellers and executives and their families; also translation and interpreting services. Universidad de Buenos Aires, 25 de Mayo 221, T4334 7512 or T4343 1196, www.idiomas. filo.uba.ar. Offers cheap, coherent courses, including summer intensive courses. For other schools teaching Spanish, and for private tutors look in *Buenos Aires Herald* in the classified advertisements. Enquire also at *Asatej* (see Useful addresses). For claims or suggestions on Spanish courses, contact the student ombudsman at **Defensoría del Estudiante**, defensoria@spanishinargentina.org.ar. **Medical services** Urgent medical service: for free municipal ambulance service to an emergency hospital department (day and night) **Casualty ward**, **Sala de guardia**, T107 or T4923 1051/58 (SAME). Inoculations: **Hospital Rivadavia**, Av Las Heras 2670, T4809 2000, Mon-Fri, 0700-1200 (bus 10, 37, 59, 60, 62, 92, 93 or 102 from Plaza Constitución), or **Dirección de Sanidad de Fronteras y Terminales de**

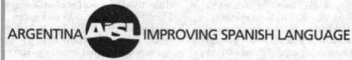

Transporte, Ing Huergo 690, T4343 1190, Mon 1400-1500, Tue-Wed 1100-1200, Thu and Fri 1500-1600, bus 20 from Retiro, no appointment required (yellow fever only; take passport). If not provided, buy the vaccines in **Laboratorio Biol**, Uriburu 153, T4953 7215, or in larger chemists. Many chemists have signs indicating that they give injections. Any hospital with an infectology department will give hepatitis A. **Travel Medicine Service (Centros Médicos Stamboulian)**, 25 de Mayo 464, T4515 3000, French 3085, T5236 7772, also in Belgrano and Flores, www.viajeros. cei.com.ar. Private health advice for travellers and inoculations centre. Public Hospitals: **Hospital Argerich**, Almte Brown esq Pi y Margall 750, T4121 0700. **Hospital Juan A Fernández**, Cerviño y Bulnes, T4808 2600/2650, probably the best free medical attention in the city. **British Hospital**, Perdriel 74, T4309 6400, www.hospital britanico.org.ar. US$24 a visit. **German Hospital**, Av Pueyrredón 1640, between Beruti and Juncal, T4827 7000, www.hospitalale man.com.ar. Both have first-aid centres (*centros asistenciales*) as do other main hospitals. Dental treatment at Solís 2180, T4305 2530/ 2110. Excellent dental treatment centre at **Carroll Forest**, Vuelta de Obligado 1551 (Belgrano), T4781 9037, www.carroll-forest. com.ar. **Post offices** **Correo Central**, **Correos Argentinos**, Sarmiento y Alem, T4891 9191, www.correoargentino. com.ar, Mon-Fri, 0800-2000, Sat 1000-1300. *Poste Restante* (only to/from national destinations) on ground floor (US$0.35 per letter). Philatelic section open Mon-Fri 1000-1800, T5550 5176. **Centro Postal Internacional**, for all parcels over 2 kg for mailing abroad, at Av Comodoro Py y Antártida Argentina, near Retiro station, helpful, many languages spoken, packing materials available, Mon-Fri 1000-1700. Post office at Montevideo 1408 near Plaza V López, friendly staff, Spanish only. Also at Santa Fe 945 and many others. **UPS**, T0800-2222 877, www.ups.com. **DHL**, T0810- 2222 345, www.dhl.com.ar. **FedEx**, T0810-3333 339, www.fedex.com. **Telephone** International and local calls, internet and fax from phone offices (*locutorios* or *telecentros*), manye city centre. **Useful addresses** **Migraciones**: (Immigration), Antártida Argentina 1355, edificio 4 (visas extended mornings only), T4317 0200, www.migraciones.gov.ar, 0730-1330 (see Visas and immigration, page 66). **Central Police Station**: Moreno 1550, Virrey Cevallos 362, T4370 5911/5800 (emergency, T101 from any phone, free). See page 64 for **Comisaría del Turista** (tourist police). **Aves Argentinas/AOP** (a BirdLife International partner), Matheu 1246, T4943 7216, www.aves argentinas.org.ar. For information on birdwatching and specialist tours, good library open Wed and Fri 1500-2000 (closed Jan). Student organizations: **Asatej**: Helpful Argentine Youth and Student Travel Organization, runs a Student Flight Centre, Florida 835, p 3, oficina 320, T4114 7611, www.asatej.com, Mon-Fri 0900-1900 (other branches in BA: Belgrano, Monserrat, Palermo, Recoleta, Caballito). Booking for flights (student discounts) including cheap 1-way flights (long waiting lists), hotels and travel; information for all South America, notice board for travellers, ISIC cards sold (giving extensive discounts; Argentine ISIC guide available here), English and French spoken; also runs: **Red Argentina de Alojamiento Para Jovenes** (affiliated to HI); **Asatej Travel Store**, at the same office, selling widerange of travel goods. **Oviajes**, Uruguay 385, p 6, T4371 6137, www.oviajes. com.ar. Tickets, information, also issues cards for Hostels of Americas, Nomads and Hostels of Europe, ISIC, ITIC and G0 25 cards, aimed at students, teachers and independent travellers. Cheap fares also at **TIJE**, San Martín 601, T5272 8453 or branches at Av Santa Fe 898, T5272 8450, Paraguay 1178, p 7, T5218 2800 and Zabala 1736, p 1, T4770 9500, www.tije.com. **YMCA**: (Central), Reconquista 439, T4311 4785, www.ymca.org.ar. **YWCA**: Tucumán 843 p 5, T4322 1550, www.acfbuenosaires.com.ar.

Tigre ➔ *Population: 31,000 (Partido de Tigre –Tigre county – 301,000).*
This touristy little town, 32 km northwest of Buenos Aires, is a popular weekend destination lying on the lush jungly banks of the Río Luján, with a fun fair and an excellent fruit and handicrafts market (Puerto de Frutos) daily 1000-1900 with access from Calles Sarmiento or Perú. There are restaurants on the waterfront in Tigre across the Río Tigre from the railway line, along Lavalle and Paseo Victorica (eg **María del Luján** is recommended); cheaper places can be found on Italia and Cazón on the near side, or at the Puerto de Frutos. North of the town is the delta of the Río Paraná: innumerable canals and rivulets, with holiday homes and restaurants on the banks and a fruit- growing centre. The fishing is excellent and the peace is only disturbed by motor-boats at weekends. Regattas are held in November. Take a trip on one of the regular launch services (*lanchas colectivas*) which run to all parts of the delta, including taxi launches – watch prices for these – from the wharf (*Estación Fluvial*). Tourist catamarans, five services daily, 1-2 hour trips, US$7-10, from Lavalle 499 on Río Tigre, T4731 0261/63, www.tigreencatamaran.com.ar, and three to eight services daily, 1½-hour trips, US$8, from Puerto de Frutos, *Río Tur* (T4731 0280, www.rioturcatamaranes.com.ar). *Sturla* (Estación Fluvial, oficina 10, T4731 1300, www.sturla viajes.com.ar) runs three 1-hour trips a day, US$6, to which can be added a lunch at Villa Julia, exclusive restaurante in Tigre (US$26) or a barbecue at an island with a daily half-day tour (US$21); also full-day tours that include lunch and kayak excursions for US$31 and 1½-hour trips to Puerto Norte (next to Aeroparque) on the Río de la Plata for US$15 pp. **Tigre tourist office** ⓘ *Lavalle y R Fernández, T4512 4497, 0900-1700, www.tigre.gov.ar*. **Centro de Guías de Tigre y Delta** ⓘ *Estación Fluvial oficina 2, T4731 3555, www.tododelta.com.ar*. For guided walks and launch trips.

Museo Naval ⓘ *Paseo Victorica 602, T4749 0608, Mon-Fri 0830-1730, Sat-Sun 1030-1830, US$1*. Worth a visit to see the displays on the Argentine navy. There are also relics of the 1982 Falklands/ Malvinas War. **Museo de Arte** ⓘ *Paseo Victoria 972, T4512 4528, Wed-Fri 0900-1900, Sat-Sun 1200-1900 (closes at 1800 in winter), US$1.70*, hosts a collection of Argentine figurative art in the former Tigre Club Casino, a beautiful belle époque building. **Museo del Mate** ⓘ *Lavalle 289, T4506 9594, www.elmuseodelmate.com, Tue-Sun 1000-1800, US$2.60*, tells the history of mate and has an interesting collection of the associated paraphernalia.

Isla Martín García
This island in the Río de la Plata (Juan Díaz de Solís' landfall in 1516) used to be a military base. Now it is an ecological/historical centre and an ideal excursion from the capital, with many trails through the cane brakes, trees and rocky outcrops – interesting birds and flowers. Boat trips: four weekly from Tigre at 0900, returning 2000, three-hour journey, US$17 return (US$32 including lunch and guide; US$73 pp including weekend overnight at inn, full board). Reservations only through *Cacciola* (address under Tigre, Transport, below), who also handle bookings for the inn and restaurant on the island. There is also a campsite.

Around Buenos Aires listings

For Sleeping and Eating price codes and other relevant information, see Essentials, pages 38-40.

Sleeping

Tigre *p100*

LL La Becasina, Arroyo Las Cañas (Delta islands second section), T4328 2687/4728 1253, www.labecasina.com . One of Argentina's most delightful places to stay, an hour by launch from Tigre, buried deep from the outside world, with 15 individual lodges on stilts in the water, connected by wooden walkways, all comforts and luxuries provided and tasteful décor, with intimate dining room, jacuzzi and pool amidst the trees. Full board, excellent food and service. Recommended.

L Villa Julia, Paseo Victorica 800, in Tigre itself, T4749 0642, www.villajulia.com.ar. Part of the New Age Town and Country group, www.newage-hotels.com. A 1913 villa converted into a chic hotel, beautifully restored fittings, comfortable, good restaurant open to non-residents.

A Los Pecanes, on Arroyo Felicaria, T4728 1932 or 156-942 7830, www.hosterialospecanes.com. On a secluded island visited regularly by hummingbirds. Ana and Richard offer a few comfortable rooms and delicious food. Ideal base for boat excursions and birdwatching.

B Casona La Ruchi, Lavalle 557, T4749 2499, www.casonalaruchi.com.ar. The Escauriza family are the hosts of this lovely 1892 villa, central, homely, cosy rooms, a garden with a pool.

B TAMET, Río Carapachay Km 24, T4728 0055, www.tamet.com.ar. For a relaxing stay on an island with sandy beaches and quite comfortable premises, with breakfast, games and canoes.

E pp **Posada de 1860**, Av Libertador 190, T4749 4034, www.tigrehostel.com.ar. A central hostel in a beautiful stylish villa with dorms for up to 6, and private rooms (**B** double); breakfast, cooking facilities and Wi-Fi. Discounts on rooms Mon-Thu, HI affiliated.

Transport

Tigre *p100*

Bus From central **Buenos Aires**: take No 60 from Constitución: the 60 'bajo' is a little longer than the 60 'alto' but is better for sightseeing.

Ferry To **Carmelo** (Uruguay) from Terminal Internacional, Lavalle 520, Tigre. **Cacciola**, T4749 0931, www.cacciolaviajes.com (in Buenos Aires at Florida 520, p 1, of 113, T4393 6100), 0830, 1630, 3½ hrs, US$18 (US$34 return). Bus/motor launch service by **Trans Uruguay/ Cacciola/Laderban** (www.transuruguay.com) to Montevideo from Tigre US$27, US$52 return. Other bus destinations in Uruguay and overnight stays in Carmelo (from US$60 pp including accommodation). Cacciola connecting bus to Tigre from Carlos Pellegrini y Av Córdoba, 0635, 1445.

To **Nueva Palmira** (Uruguay) from Terminal Internacional. **Líneas Delta Argentino**, oficina 6 at Estación Fluvial, T4731 1236, www.lineas delta.com.ar. Daily at 0730 plus 1700 on Fri, 3 hrs, US$21, US$35 return. To **Carmelo** US$23, US$37 return, and **Colonia**, 4½ hrs from Tigre, US$31, US$47 return, both daily 0730.

Note Argentine port taxes are generally included in the fares for Argentine departures.

Train From **Buenos Aires**: take train from Retiro (FC Mitre section) to Tigre, or to Bartolomé Mitre and change to the Maipú station (the stations are linked) for the **Tren de la Costa**, T4002 6000, www.trendelacosta.com.ar, US$2.70 one way, every 20 mins from Maipú Mon-Thu 0710- 2230, Fri 0710-2330, Sat-Sun 0830-2350, 25 mins. From Palermo or Recoleta, take Subte line D to Carranza, which connects with the Mitre line. (Buses to Tren de la Costa are 60 from Constitución, 19 or 71 from Once, 152 from centre.) Several stations have shopping centres (eg San Isidro), and terminus, Estación Delta, has the huge fun fair, El Parque de la Costa, and a casino. You can get off the train as many times as you want on the same ticket.

South and west of Buenos Aires the flat, fertile lands of the pampa húmeda stretch seemingly without end, the horizon broken only by a lonely windpump or a line of poplar trees. This is home to the gaucho, whose traditions of music and fine craftsmanship remain alive. Argentina's agricultural heartland is punctuated by quiet pioneer towns, like Chascomús, and the houses of grand estancias. Argentina's former wealth lay in these splendid places, where you can stay as a guest, go horse riding, and get a great insight into the country's history and gaucho culture. The mountain range at Tandil offers great walking and marvellous views.

Luján ➔ *Phone code: 02323. Population: 65,000.*

This is a place of pilgrimage for devout Catholics throughout Argentina. In 1630 an image of the Virgin brought by ship from Brazil was being transported to its new owner in Santiago del Estero by ox cart, when the cart got stuck, despite strenuous efforts by men and oxen to move it. This was taken as a sign that the Virgin willed she should stay there. A chapel was built for the image, and around it grew Luján. The chapel has long since been superseded by an impressive neo-Gothic basilica and the Virgin now stands on the High Altar. Each arch of the church is dedicated to an Argentine province, and the transepts to Uruguay, Paraguay and Ireland. Behind the Cabildo is the river, with river walks, cruises and restaurants (an excellent one is *L'Eau Vive* on the road to Buenos Aires at Constitución 2112, run by nuns, pleasant surroundings). Luján is a very popular spot at weekends, and there are huge pilgrimages on the first weekend of October, 8 May and 8 December, when the town is completely packed.

Museo Histórico Colonial ⓘ *T420245, Wed-Fri 1500-1800, Sat, Sun 1000-1800, closed Jan, US$0.70*, in the old Cabildo building, is one of the most interesting museums in the country. Exhibits illustrate its historical and political development. General Beresford, the commander of the British troops which seized Buenos Aires in 1806, was a prisoner here, as were Generals Mitre, Paz and Belgrano in later years. Next to it are museums devoted to transport and to motor vehicles and there is also a poor **Museo de Bellas Artes.**

San Antonio de Areco ➔ *Phone code: 02326. Colour map 8, B5.*

San Antonio de Areco, 113 km northwest of Buenos Aires, is a completely authentic, late 19th-century town, with single-storey buildings around a plaza filled with palms and plane trees, streets lined with orange trees, and an attractive *costanera* along the river bank. There are several *estancias* and a couple of villages with accommodation nearby and the town itself has historical *boliches* (combined bar and provisions store; eg **Los Principios**, Moreno y Mitre). The gaucho traditions are maintained in silver, textiles and leather handicrafts of the highest quality, as well as frequent gaucho activities, the most important of which is the **Day of Tradition** in the second week of November (book accommodation ahead), with traditional parades, gaucho games, events on horseback, music and dance. **Museo Gauchesco Ricardo Güiraldes** ⓘ *on Camino Güiraldes, T455839, www.museoguiraldes.com.ar, daily except Tue, 1100-1700, US$1*, is a replica of a typical *estancia* of the late 18th century, surrounded by a neat park, with impressive *gaucho* artefacts, paintings by Pedro Figari and displays on the life of Güiraldes, the writer whose best-known book, *Don Segundo Sombra*, celebrates the gaucho. He lived in the **Estancia La Porteña** ⓘ *8 km from town, www.sanantoniodeareco.com/turismo/historia/historia/laportena/ index.htm*, which dates from 1823. Superb gaucho **silverwork** for sale at the workshop and museum of **Juan José Draghi** ⓘ *Lavalle 387, T454219, www.draghiplaterosorfebres.com, 0900-1300, 1530-2000 (Sun 1000-1300 only), US$1.70 for a guided visit.* Excellent **chocolates** at **La Olla de Cobre** ⓘ *Matheu 433, T453105, www.laolladecobre.com.ar*, with a charming little café for drinking chocolate and the most amazing home-made *alfajores.* There is a large park spanning the river near the **tourist information centre**. The Centro Cultural y Museo Usina Vieja, ⓘ *Alsina 66, Tue-Sun 1100-1700,*

US$0.50, is the city museum. There are ATMs on the plaza, but nowhere to change TCs. The **tourist office** ⓘ *Zerboni y Arellano, T453165, www.san antoniodeareco.com, is by the river.* Also see www.visiteareco.com.

La Plata ➔ *Phone code: 0221. Colour map 8, B5. Population: 545,000.*
La Plata, near the shores of the Río de la Plata, was founded in 1882 as capital of Buenos Aires province and is now an important administrative centre, with an excellent university. It's a well-planned city, reminiscent of Paris in places, with the French-style **legislature** and the elegant **Casa de Gobierno** on **Plaza San Martín**, central in a series of plazas along the spine of the city. On **Plaza Moreno** to the south there's an impressive Italianate palace housing the **Municipalidad**, and the **Cathedral,** a striking neo-Gothic brick construction. North of Plaza San Martín is La Plata's splendid park, the **Paseo del Bosque**, with mature trees, a zoo and a botanical garden, a boating lake and the **Museo de La Plata** ⓘ *T425 7744, www.fcnym.unlp.edu.ar, Tue-Sun 1000-1800, closed 1 Jan, 1 May, 24, 25, 31 Dec, US$4, free guided tours, weekdays 1530, Sat-Sun 1100, 1300, 1400, 1600, in Spanish and in English (phone first), highly recommended.* This museum houses an outstanding collection of stuffed animals, wonderful dinosaur skeletons and artefacts from pre-Columbian peoples throughout the Americas. 8 km northwest of the city is the **República de los Niños** ⓘ *Camino Gral Belgrano y Calle 501, www.republica.laplata.gov.ar, daily 1000-2200, US$1, getting there: take a train from La Plata or Buenos Aires to Gonnet station, US$0.50, or bus 338 from La Plata, car park US$1.30.* This is Eva Peron's legacy, a delightful children's village with scaled-down castles, oriental palaces, a train, boat lake and restaurant. Fun for a picnic. The **Parque Ecológico** ⓘ *Camino Centenario y San Luis, Villa Elisa, T473 2449, www.parquecologico. laplata.gov.ar, 0900-1930, free, getting there: take bus 273 D or E,* is another good place for families, with native *tala* forest and plenty of birds.

The small municipal **tourist office** ⓘ *Pasaje Dardo Rocha, T427 1535, www.laplata.gov.ar, daily 1000-2000*, in an Italianate palace, also houses a gallery of contemporary **Latin American art** ⓘ *C 50 entre 6 y 7, T427 1843, www.macla.laplata.gov.ar, Tue-Fri 1000-2000, Sat-Sun 1400-2100 (1600-2200 in summer), free.*

Chascomús, Dolores and Tandil
To get to the heart of the pampas, stay in one of many estancias scattered over the plains. There are several accessible from the main roads to the coast, fast Ruta 2 (be prepared for tolls) and Ruta 11, near two well-preserved historic towns, Chascomús and Dolores. At Punta Indio, 165 km from Buenos Aires, is 1920s Tudor style **Estancia Juan Gerónimo** ⓘ *T02221-481414, 011-154 937 4326, www.juangeronimo.com.ar (L) full board, activities included, English and French spoken.* Set on the coast in a beautiful nature reserve which protects a huge variety of fauna, the estancia offers walks and horse rides in 4,000 ha. Accommodation is simple and elegant, and the food exquisite.

Chascomús is a beautifully preserved town from the 1900's, with a rather Wild West feel to it, Chascomús is a lively place built on a huge lake, perfect for fishing and water sports. There's a great little museum **Museo Pampeano** ⓘ *Av Lastra y Muñiz,T425110, Tue-Fri 0800-1400, Sat-Sun 1000-1400, 1700-1900 (Tue Fri 0900-1500, Sat-Sun 1030-1630 in winter), US$0.50*, with gaucho artefacts, old maps and fabulous antique furniture. **Tourist office** ⓘ *Av Costanera by the pier. T02241-430405, 0900-1900 daily, www.chascomus.gov.ar.* Dolores is a delightful small town, like stepping back in time to the 1900's, very tranquil. **Museo Libres del Sur** ⓘ *daily 1000-1700, US$0.30*, is an old house in Parque Libres del Sur, full of gaucho silver, plaited leather *talero*, branding irons, and a huge cart from 1868. The **Sierras de Tandil** are 2,000 million years old, among the world's oldest mountains, beautiful curved hills of granite and basalt, offering wonderful walking and riding. Tandil itself is an attractive, breezy town, a good base for exploring the sierras, with a couple of marvellous estancias close by. There's a park, **Parque Independencia**, with great views from the hill with its Moorish-style castle, and an amphitheatre, where there's a famous community theatre event throughout Easter week (book hotels ahead). The peaks nearby offer wild countryside for riding, climbing, walking, or ascent by 1.2-km cable car ride (at Cerro El Centinela, 5 km away). Very helpful **tourist information** at ⓘ *Av Espora 1120, on the way into town, T02293-432073, also at Plaza Independencia or at the bus terminal, www.turismo.tandil.gov.ar*. Look up estancias and gaucho-related activities in the region at www.caminodelgaucho.com.ar.

The Pampas listings

For Sleeping and Eating price codes and other relevant information, see Essentials, pages 38-40.

Sleeping

San Antonio de Areco *p102*
Most hotels offer discounts Mon-Thu or Fri.
AL Patio de Moreno, Moreno 251, T455197, www.patiodemoreno.com. The top hotel in town is a stylish place with spacious, minimalist rooms, a large patio with a pool and great service.
A Antigua Casona, Segundo Sombra 495, T456600, www.antiguacasona.com. Charmingly restored 1897 house with five rooms opening onto a delightful patio and exuberant garden, most relaxing and romantic. Bikes to borrow.
A Paradores Draghi, Lavalle 387, T455583, paradores@sanantoniodeareco.com. A few rooms face a manicured lawn with a pool. Just metres away Draghi family has its silversmith workshop.
B San Carlos, Zerboni y Zapiola, T453106, www.hotel-sancarlos.com.ar. On the riverside park, convenient for young families, has pool for kids, bikes to borrow (first hour free), restaurant.
C La Posada del Ceibo, Irigoyen between Ruta 8 and Smith, T454614, www.laposadadelceibo.com.ar. 1950s-style motel, family friendly, basic rooms, cable TV, small pool.
C Los Abuelos, Zerboni y Zapiola T456390. Very good, welcoming, small pool, plain but comfortable rooms with TV, facing riverside park.

Camping Two sites in the park by the river: best is **Club River Plate**, on Costanera, T454998, sports club, shady sites with all facilities, pool.

Estancias
Some of the province's finest *estancias* are within easy reach for day visits, offering horse riding, an *asado* lunch, and other activities. Stay overnight to really appreciate the peace and beauty of these historical places. Look online at: www.sanantoniodeareco.com/turismo/estancias/index.htm, or www.turismo.gov.ar/eng/menu.htm (go to Active Tourism, Rural Tourism).
LL El Ombú, T492080, T011-4737 0436 (BsAs office), www.estanciaelombu.com. Fine house with magnificent terrace dating from 1890, comfortable rooms, horse riding, English-speaking owners; price includes full board and activities but not transfer. Recommended.
LL La Bamba, T456293, T011-4444 6560 (BsAs office), www.la-bamba.com.ar. Dating from 1830, in grand parkland, charming rooms, English-speaking owners who have lived here for generations, superb meals, price is for full board. Recommended.

La Plata *p103*
A Corregidor, C 6 No 1026, T425 6800, www.hotelcorregidor.com.ar. Upmarket, modern business hotel, well furnished, pleasant public rooms, good value.
A La Plata Hotel, Av 51 No 783, T422 9090, www.weblaplatahotel.com.ar. Modern, well furnished, comfortable, spacious rooms and nice bathrooms. Price includes a dinner (drinks extra).
C Catedral, C 49 No.965, T483 0091, hotelcatedral6@hotmail.com. Modest but welcoming, modern, with fan, breakfast included.

Estancias
L Casa de Campo La China, 60 km from La Plata on Ruta 11, T0221-421 2931, www.casadecampolachina.com.ar. A charming 1930s adobe house set in eucalyptus woods, with beautifully decorated spacious rooms off an open gallery, day visits (US$45) to ride horses, or in carriages, eat *asado*, or stay the night, guests of Cecilia and Marcelo, who speak perfect English. Delicious food, meals included in price. Highly recommended.

Chascomús *p103*
L Torre Azul Spa, Mercedes y Tres Arroyos, T422984, www.torreazulspa.com.ar. Small spa with park and pool, accommodation in comfortable wooden cabins with kitchen; Wi-Fi. Price is for Mon-Thu and includes a spa session and massages, plus a dinner for 2.

B Chascomús, Av Lastra 367, T422968, www.chascomus.com.ar (under 'hoteles'). The town's most comfortable hotel, atmospheric, welcoming, with stylish turn-of-the-century public rooms and lovely terrace.
B La Posada, Costanera España 18, T423503, www.chascomus.com.ar (under 'appart cabañas'). On the laguna, delightful, very comfortable cabañas with cooking facilities.
B Laguna, Libres del Sur y Maipú, T426113, www.lgnhotel.com.ar. Traditional, old fashioned, sleepy hotel by the station. Pleasant, quiet rooms.

Estancias

Both *estancias* will collect you from Chascomús.
LL Haras La Viviana, in Castelli, 65 km from Chascomús, T011-4702 9633, http://harasla viviana.com.ar. Perfect for horse riding, since fine polo ponies are bred here. Tiny cabins in gardens by a huge laguna where you can kayak or fish, very peaceful, good service, lady novelist owner is quite a character, fluent English spoken.
AL La Horqueta, 3 km from Chascomús on Ruta 20, T011-4777 0150, www.la horqueta.com. Full board, Tudor style mansion in lovely grounds with laguna for fishing, horse riding, bikes to borrow, English-speaking hosts, safe gardens especially good for children, plain food.

Dolores *p103*
LL Dos Talas, 10 km from town, T02245-443020, www.dostalas.com.ar. The most beautiful *estancia* in the pampas, and one of the oldest. An elegant house in grand parkland designed by Charles Thays, with fascinating history, visible in all the family photos, artefacts and the vast library. This is one of the few *estancias* where you are truly the owners' guests. The rooms and the service are impeccable, regional food with traditional, family recipes; stay for days, completely relax. Pool, gaucho-style riding, English spoken.

Tandil *p103*
Many to choose from, see www.tandil.com or www.cybertandil.com.ar.
AL-A Las Acacias, Av Brasil 642, T02293-423373, www.posadalasacacias.com.ar. Attractive hostería in restored 1890s dairy farm near golf club, excellent service with good food and lovely park with pool, Italian and English spoken.
B Plaza de las Carretas, Av Santamarina 728, T447850, www.plazadelascarretas.com.ar. An early 20th-century family house, good rooms, quiet, comfy, nice garden.

Estancias

LL-L Ave María, 16 km from Tandil, past Cerro El Centinela, T02293-422843, www.avemaria tandil.com.ar. In beautiful gardens overlooking the rocky summits of the sierras. You're encouraged to feel at home and relax, swim in the pool or walk in the grounds, hills and woodland. Impeccable rooms, superb food and discreet staff who speak English. Highly recommended.
L Siempre Verde, T02292-498555, www.estanciasiempreverde.com. A 1900's house, 45 km southwest of Tandil (next to Barker) with traditional-style rooms, good views. The owners, descendants of one of Argentina's most important families, are very hospitable and helpful. Wonderful horse riding and walking among the sierras, fishing, *asados* on the hillside, camping. Highly recommended.

Eating

San Antonio de Areco *p102*
Many *parrillas* on the bank of the Río Areco.
TT **Almacén de Ramos Generales**, Zapiola 143, T456376 (best to book ahead). Perfect place, popular with locals, very atmospheric, superb meat, very good pastas and a long wine list.
TT **Café de las Artes**, Bolívar 70, T456398 (better book ahead). In a hidden spot, this cosy place serves delicious pastas with a large wine selection.
TT **La Costa Reyes**, Zerboni y Belgrano (on the riverside park). A very good traditional *parrilla* with an attractive terrace.
TT **La Ochava de Cocota**, Alsina y Alem. Relaxing, attractive, excellent service, superb *empanadas* and vegetable pies. It is also a café.
T **La Belle Epoque**, Arellano 82. This beautiful chocolate shop serves very good coffee and cakes on just a few tables on a lovely patio at the front.
T **La Esquina de Merti**, Arellano y Segundo Sombra. The ideal place for a beer on the main plaza. Go early to get a table outside.
T **La Vieja Sodería**, Bolívar y General Paz. An atmospheric and agreeable corner for varied *picadas* and sandwiches. It's also a bar and a café serving great cakes.

La Plata *p103*

🍴 **Cervecería Modelo**, C 54 y C5. Traditional German-style *cervecería*, with good menu and beer.

🍴 **Don Quijote**, Plaza Paso. Delicious food in lovely surroundings, well known.

🍴 **El Chaparral Platense**, C 60 y C 116 (Paseo del Bosque). Good *parrilla* in the park, great steaks.

🍴 **La Aguada**, C 50 entre 7 y 8. The oldest restaurant in town, good for *minutas* (light meals), famous for its *papas fritas*.

Confitería París, C 7 y 48. The best croissants, and a lovely place for coffee.

Chascomús *p103*

🍴 **Colonial**, Estados Unidos y Artigas. Great food, pastas and cakes are recommended.

🍴 **El Viejo Lobo**, Mitre y Dolores. Very good fish.

Tandil *p103*

Plenty of *pizzerías*, and good local sausages and cheeses served in *picadas* (nibbles) with drinks.

🍴🍴 **El Tronador**, San Martín 790. Wine bar and restaurant upstairs serving a menu of 5 dishes, accompanied by a choice of excellent wines.

🍴 **Carajo**, Saavedra Lamas s/n (at Club Náutico). *Parrilla* in a great location by the lake. Also tea house serving cakes in the afternoons.

🍴 **El Manco Paz**, Paz 1145. Very good and elegant *parrilla*.

🍴 **El Molino**, Juncal 936. Broad menu, meat cooked *al disco*, on an open fire, delicious.

🍴 **Epoca de Quesos**, San Martín y 14 de Julio, T448750. Atmospheric, delicious local produce, wines and *picadas*.

🍴 **La Fonda**, Yrigoyen 717. Small, attractive, home-made dishes and very good set menus which change every day.

🍴 **Taberna Pizuela**, Paz y Pinto. Attractive old place serving good simple dishes, including pizza, their speciality.

🍴 **Vieja Cantera**, Monseñor de Andrea 315 *Picadas*, simple meals and a tea room in a beautiful spote at the foot of Monte Calvario.

▲ Activities and tours

The Pampas *p102*

Horse riding All estancias offer horse riding. Other operators can be contacted from the hotels in the Pampas towns.

Trekking and mountain biking Contact an approved guide who will take you to otherwise inaccessible privately owned land for trekking. **Eco de las Sierras**, Tandil, T442741, T156 21083, www.ecodelasierras.com.ar. Lucrecia Ballesteros is a highly recommended guide, young, friendly and knowledgeable. **Horizonte Vertical**, T432762, www.horizonte- vertical.com.ar. For climbing, mountain biking, canoeing and walking. **Tierra Serrana**, T421836, trekking and mountain biking.

Transport

Luján *p102*

Bus From **Buenos Aires** Bus 57 **Empresa Atlántida** either from Plaza Once, route O (the fastest), or from Plaza Italia, routes C and D; US$2-3. To **San Antonio de Areco**, several a day, US$4, Empresa Argentina, 1 hr. Train to Once station, US$0.70 (change at Moreno).

San Antonio de Areco *p102*

Bus From **Buenos Aires** (Retiro bus terminal), 1½-2 hrs, US$7, every hour with Chevallier or Pullman General Belgrano. For connections to northern Argentina go to Pilar. **Remise** taxis **Sol**, San Martín y Alsina, T455444.

La Plata *p103*

Bus Terminal at Calle 4 and Diagonal 74, T427 3186/427 3198. To **Buenos Aires**, very frequent during the day, hourly at night, **Costera Metropolitana**, 1½ hrs either to Retiro terminal or to Centro (stops along Av 9 de Julio), via Autopista (a little shorter), US$2, or via Centenario, US$1.50. Also **Plaza** buses to Buenos Aires.

Train To/from **Buenos Aires** (Constitución), frequent, US$0.60, 1 hr 20 mins (ticket office hidden behind shops opposite platform 6).

Chascomús *p103*

Bus Frequent service, several per day to **Buenos Aires**, 2 hrs, US$5, **La Plata**, Mar del Plata, and daily to **Bahía Blanca**, **Tandil** and **Villa Gesell**; terminal T422595.

Train Station T422220. Two daily to **Buenos Aires** (Constitución), or to **Mar del Plata**, 1-2 weekly to **Pinamar** and 1 a day to **Miramar** in summer.

Tandil *p103*

Bus Frequent to **Buenos Aires** (5-6 hrs, US$15-18), **Bahía Blanca** (5-6 hrs, US$14), **Mar del Plata** (2½-3 hrs, US$8), **Necochea**. Bus terminal Av Buzón 650, T432092.

Atlantic Coast

Among the 500 km of resorts stretching from to San Clemente de Tuyú to Monte Hermoso, the most attractive is upmarket Pinamar, with the chic Cariló next door. Villa Gesell is relaxed and friendly, while, next to it are the quiet, beautiful Mar Azul and Mar de las Pampas. Mar del Plata, Argentina's most famous resort, is a huge city with packed beaches, popular for its lively nightlife and casino; much more appealing in winter. Next to it, tranquil Miramar is great for young families, and Necochea has wild expanses of dunes to explore. Near the port of Bahía Blanca is the Sierra de la Ventana, the highest range of hills in the pampas, a great place for hiking.

Partido de la Costa

San Clemente del Tuyú is closest to the capital, the first of a string of identical small resorts known as **Partido de la Costa**, not worth a detour unless you're keen on fishing. They're old-fashioned towns, cheaper than the more popular resorts further southwest, but rather run down. There's excellent sea fishing, for shark, *pejerrey* and *brotola* from pier or boats, and fish can often be bought on the beach from local fishermen, but since the Río de la Plata flows here, the water is poor for bathing. San Clemente's main attraction is **Mundo Marino** ⓘ *signposted from road into town, T430300, www.mundomarino.com.ar, US$15, children US$9*, the biggest sea life centre in South America, with performing seals and dolphins, all totally unnatural but undeniably fun for small children. Plenty of small hotels and campsites. At **Punta Rasa**, 9 km north, there is a lighthouse and a private nature reserve run by the **Fundación Vida Silvestre**, which, in summer, is home to thousands of migratory birds from the northern hemisphere, www.rpm-net.com.ar/puntarasa/. There's a beautiful stretch of empty beach 15 km south of **Mar de Ajó**, the southernmost of these resorts, which belongs to one of the few *estancias* to offer horse riding on the sands, **Palantelén** ⓘ *T02257-420983 or 011-155 3424120, www.palantelen.com.ar*. A peaceful place to walk and relax, delightful house, private tango lessons on a terrace under the stars, charming English-speaking hosts. Highly recommended. **Tourist information** ⓘ *Av Costanera 8001, Mar del Tuyú, T02246-433035, www.lacostaturismo.com.ar*.

Pinamar and Cariló → *Phone code: 02254.*

The two most desirable resorts on the coast, 340 km from Buenos Aires, via Ruta 11, are next to each other, with the quiet old fashioned Belgian pioneer town Ostende in between. **Pinamar** is one of the most attractive resorts on the whole coast, with stylish architecture and mature trees lining its avenues. It is great for young people and families, with smart *balnearios* ranging from chic, quiet places with superb restaurants, to very trendy spots with loud music, beach parties and live bands at night. There are golf courses and tennis courts, and fine hotels and smart restaurants all along the main street, Avenida Bunge, running perpendicular to the sea. It's a stylish and well-maintained resort, slightly pricey. Explore the dunes at **Reserva Dunícola**, 13 km north, by horse or 4WD. **Tourist office** ⓘ *Av Shaw 18, T491680, www.pina mar.gov.ar, www.pinamarturismo.com.ar*, English spoken, helpful, can book accommodation. **Cariló**, the most exclusive beach resort in Argentina, has a huge area of mature woodland, where its luxury apart-hotels and *cabañas* are all tastefully concealed. The *balnearios* are neat and exclusive – of which *Hemingway* is *the* place, full of wealthy Porteños – and there are good restaurants and shops around the tiny centre. The tourist office is at Boyero y Castaño, T570773.

Villa Gesell → *Phone code: 02255. Population: 24,000.*

In contrast to the rather elite Cariló, Villa Gesell, 22 km south of Pinamar, is warm, welcoming and very laid-back. Set amid thousands of trees planted by its German founder, it has grown in recent years into a thriving tourist town, but retains its village feel. The beaches are safe and there's plenty of nightlife. In January, it's overrun by Argentine youth, far quieter in late February and March. Next to it are the two of the most tranquil and charming beach retreats:

idyllic and wooded **Mar de las Pampas** and **Mar Azul** are both still underdeveloped, with fine *cabañas* to choose from. Get a map from the tourist office in Villa Gesell, or as you enter Mar de las Pampas. There's no grid system and it can be tricky finding your way around. Villa Gesell's main street is Avenida 3, pedestrianized in the evenings, full of cafés, restaurants and bars. The main **tourist office** is on the right as you drive into town ⓘ *Av de los Pioneros 1921, T458596, open 0800-2200 daily in summer, off season 0900-1900, also in bus terminal and 4 other locations, www.gesell.gov.ar*, very helpful, English spoken. See also www.mardelaspampas.com.ar.

Mar del Plata ➔ *Phone code: 0223. Colour map 8, C5. Population: 560,000.*
The oldest and most famous Argentine resort has lost much of its charm since it was built in 1874. It's now a huge city offering great nightlife in summer, but if you like some space on the beach, it's best to go elsewhere as there are plenty of better beaches on this stretch of coast. There are hundreds of hotels, all busy (and double the price) in January-February; winter can be pleasantly quiet. **Tourist offices** ⓘ *San Luis 1949, also at the airport, or, more conveniently, next to the Casino Central on Blvd Marítimo 2270, T495 1777, 0800-2000 (till 2200 in summer), www.mardelplata.gov.ar*. English spoken, good leaflets on daily events with bus routes. Also lists of hotels and apartment/chalet letting agents. For what's on, see *www.todomar delplata.com*.

The city centre is around **Playa Bristol**, with the huge casino, and **Plaza San Martín**, with pedestrian streets Rivadavia and San Martín, busy in summer with shoppers. 10 blocks south-west, the area of Los Troncos contains some remarkable mansions dating from Mar del Plata's heyday, from mock Tudor **Villa Blaquier** to **Villa Ortiz Basualdo** (1909), inspired by Loire chateaux, now the **Museo Municipal de Arte** ⓘ *Av Colón 1189, T486 1636, daily in summer 1700-2200, winter Wed-Mon 1200-1700, US$1, including guided tour*. Rooms furnished in period style. Nearby is the splendid **Museo del Mar** ⓘ *Av Colón 1114, T451 3553, www.museodelmar.org, summer 1000-2300, winter 1000-2000, US$2.70*. It has a vast collection of 30,000 sea shells, a small aquarium, café and roof terrace. The **Centro Cultural Victoria Ocampo** ⓘ *Matheu 1851, T492 2193, daily in summer, off season closed Tue and mornings, US$1*. This beautiful 1900's wooden house in lovely gardens was where the famous author entertained illustrious literary figures; concerts held in grounds in summer. Nearby is the **Villa Mitre** ⓘ *Lamadrid 3870, T495 1200, Mon-Fri 0900-2000 (0800-1700 in winter), Sat-Sun 1600-2000 (1400-1800 in winter), US$0.70*. Owned by a descendent of Bartolomé Mitre, it has a collection of old photos and artefacts. Beaches are filled with hundreds of tiny beach huts, *carpas*, rented by the day US$20-30, entitling you to use the balneario's showers, toilets, restaurants.

Beaches include fashionable **Playa Grande**, where the best hotels and shops are, as well as the famous golf course, with private *balnearios* for wealthy *porteños*, a small area open to the public; **Playa La Perla**, now packed and pretty grim, but **Playa Punta Mogotes**, further west, and beaches stretching along the road to Miramar are by far the most appealing. The **port area**, south of Playa Grande, is interesting when the old orange fishing boats come in, and at night, for its seafood restaurants. A sea lion colony basks on rusting wrecks by the Escollera Sur (southern breakwater) and fishing is good all along the coast, where *pejerrey, corvina* and *pescadilla* abound. There are one-hour boat trips along the city coast on the *Anamora*, several times daily in summer, weekends only in winter ⓘ *from Dársena B, Muelle de Guardacostas in the port, US$9, T489 0310*. Lots of theatres, cinemas, and the **Casino** ⓘ *Dec to end-Apr, 1600-0400; 1600-0500 on Sat; May-Nov, Sun-Thu 1500-0230; weekends 1500-0300; free; minimum bet US$0.70*. Lively festivals are Fiesta del Mar, in mid December, the national fishing festival in mid to late January, and the international film festival in mid-March.

Inland, 68 km west of Mar de la Plata is the town of **Balcarce** with some splendid art deco buildings and a leafy central plaza. You're most likely to visit the **Museo Juan Manuel Fangio** ⓘ *Dardo Rocha 639, T02266-425540, www.museofangio.com, daily in summer 1000-1900, winter 1000-1700, US$5, children US$2.70*. Argentina's best-loved racing driver was born here, and the Municipalidad on the plaza has been turned into a great museum, housing his trophies, and many of the racing cars he drove. There are excellent *parrillas* on the outskirts. The **Laguna La Brava**, 38 km away, at the foot of the Balcarce hills, offers *pejerrey* fishing, and plentiful birdlife in lovely wooded surroundings. Visit **Estancia Laguna Brava** ⓘ *RN 226 Km 37.5, T0223-460 8002*, for horse riding, trekking, mountain biking and water sports on the lake with fine views of Sierra Brava. Also recommended to visit is **Estancia Antiguo Casco La Brava** ⓘ *RN 226 Km 36.5, T0223-460 8062*. More information on this region at www.lagunabrava.com. **Tourist information** ⓘ *Av Suipacha entre C 27 y 29, Balcarce, T02266-422617*. For fishing, contact the **Club de Pesca Balcarce** ⓘ *Villa Laguna Brava, T0223-460 8019*. Frequent buses from Mar de la Plata.

Miramar ➔ *Phone code: 02291. Colour map 8, C5. Population: 22,000.*

Miramar, 47 km southwest of Mar del Plata, along the coast road, is a charming small resort, known as the 'city of bicycles', and orientated towards families with small children. It has a big leafy plaza at its centre, a good stretch of beach with soft sand, and a relaxed atmosphere; a quieter, low-key alternative to Mar del Plata. The most attractive area of the town is away from the high rise buildings on the sea front, at the **Vivero Dunícola Florentino Ameghino**, a 502-ha forest park on the beach, with lots of walks, restaurants and picnic places for *asado* among the mature trees. In town there are lots of restaurants along Calle 21, and good cafés at *balnearios* on the seafront. **Tourist office** ⓘ *Av Costanera y 21, T02291-420190, www.turismodemiramar.com.ar, Mon-Fri 0700-2100, Sat-Sun in summer 0900-2100*. Helpful, listings and maps.

Necochea ➔ *Phone code: 02262. Colour map 8, C5. Population: 65,000.*

Necochea is a well-established resort, famous for its long stretch of beach, and while the central area is built up and busy in the summer, further west there are beautiful empty beaches and high sand dunes. There's also a fine golf club and rafting nearby on the river Quequén. **Tourist offices** ⓘ *on the beach front at Av 79 y Av 2, T438333, www.necochea.gov.ar*, English spoken, list of apartments for rent. There are banks with ATMs and *locutorios* along the pedestrianized C 83.

The **Parque Miguel Lillo** (named after the Argentine botanist) starts three blocks west of Plaza San Martín and stretches along the seafront, a wonderful dense forest of over 600 ha. There are lovely walks along paths, many campsites and picnic spots, a swan lake with paddle boats, an amphitheatre, lots of restaurants, and places to practise various sports. West of Necochea, there's a natural arch of rock at the **Cueva del Tigre**, and beyond it stretches a vast empty beach, separated from the land by sand dunes up to 100 m high, the **Médano Blanco**. This is an exhilarating area for walking or horse riding and the dunes are popular for 4WD riding and sandboarding. Vehicles and buses stop where the road ends at Parador Médano Blanco (a good place for lunch) where you can rent 4WDs for US$50 (4 people), T155 68931. For excursions contact also **Expediciones del Este**, www.expedicionesdeleste.com.ar.

Bahía Blanca and around ➔ *Phone code: 0291. Colour map 8, C4. Pop: 300,000.*

The province's most important port and naval base, Bahía Blanca is a quiet, attractive city. It's a good starting point for exploring **Sierra de la Ventana**, 100 km north, or relaxing on beaches an hour to the east. The architecture is remarkable with many fine buildings especially around the central **Plaza Rivadavia**, notably the ornate, Italianate **Municipalidad** of 1904 and the French-style **Banco de la Nación** (1927). Three blocks north on the main shopping street, Alsina, there's the classical **Teatro Colón** (1922). Northwest of the plaza, there's the attractive **Parque de Mayo** with a fine golf course and sports centre nearby. The **Museo Histórico** ⓘ *at the side of the Teatro Municipal, Dorrego 116, T456 3117, Tue-Fri 0800-1200, 1600-2000, Sat-Sun 1600-2000* has sections on the pre-Hispanic period and interesting photos of early Bahía Blanca. Not to be missed, though, is the **Museo del Puerto** ⓘ *Torres y Cárrega, T457 3006, 7 km away in the port area at* Ingeniero White, *Mon-Fri 0830-1230, weekends 1530-1930, free; getting there: bus 500A or 504 from plaza, taxi US$5*. It houses entertaining and imaginative displays on immigrant life in the early 20th century, and a quaint *confitería* on Sunday. **Tourist office** ⓘ *in the Municipalidad* *on the main plaza, Alsina 65 (small door outside to the right), T459 4000, www.bahiablanca.gov.ar, Mon-Fri 0800-1900, Sat 0900-1900*. Very helpful.

At **Pehuén-Có**, 84 km east of Bahía Blanca, there's a long stretch of sandy beaches, with dunes, relatively empty and unspoilt (beware of jellyfish when wind is in the south), signposted from the main road 24 km from Bahía Blanca. It has a wild and untouristy feel, with very few hotels, several campsites well shaded, and a couple of places to eat. There's a more established resort at **Monte Hermoso**, 106 km east, with more hotels and a better organized campsite, but quiet, with a family feel, and wonderful beaches. One of the few places on the coast where the sun rises and sets over the sea.

Sierra de la Ventana ➔ *Phone code: 0291.*

The magnificent Sierra de la Ventana, the highest range of hills in the pampas, lies within easy reach of Bahía for a day or weekend visit (100 km north of Bahía Blanca). They hills are accessible for long hikes, with stunning views from their craggy peaks. There are daily buses and *combis* from Bahía Blanca, but you could stop at **Tornquist**, 70 km north of Bahía Blanca by Ruta 33, a quaint and attractively non-touristy place.

The sierras are reached within the **Parque Provincial Ernesto Tornquist**, 25 km northeast of Tornquist on Ruta 76. There are two main points of entry, one at the foot of Cerro Ventana and the other, further east, at the foot of Cerro Bahía Blanca. To enter the Cerro Ventana section, turn left (signposted) after the massive ornate gates from the Tornquist family home. Nearby is *Campamento Base*, T0291-156 495304, camping, basic dormitory, hot showers. At the entrance to the park itself, there's a car park and a *guardaparques* station ⓘ *Dec-Easter 0900-1700*, who can advise on walks, US$0.70-1.30 for access to paths. From here it's a two to three-hour walk to the summit of **Cerro de la Ventana**, which has fantastic views from the 'window' (which gives the range its name), in the summit ridge; clearly marked path but with no shade; ascents only permitted till 1200 and with good weather. There are also easier walks to waterfalls. To enter the Cerro Bahía Blanca section, continue 4 km further along Ruta 76. There's a car park and **interpretation centre** ⓘ *T491 0039, Dec-Easter 0900-1700*, with *guardaparques* who can advise on walks. From here you can go on a guided visit (only with own vehicle, four to five hours, access US$1.70), to natural caves, and the **Cueva de las Pinturas**, which contains petroglyphs. Also from here, an hour-long trail goes to Cerro Bahía Blanca. **Villa Ventana**, 10 km further, is a pretty, wooded settlement with excellent teashop, *Casa de Heidi*, and good food at *Las Golondrinas*. Helpful **tourist office** ⓘ *entrance to Villa Ventana, T491 0095, www.sierradelaventana.org.ar*.

The town of **Sierra de la Ventana**, further east, is a good centre for exploring the hills, with a greater choice of hotels than Villa Ventana, and wonderful open landscapes all around. There is a 18-hole golf course, and good trout fishing in the Río Sauce Grande. Excellent **tourist office** ⓘ *Av Roca, just before railway track, T491 5302 (same website as Villa Ventana).*

Atlantic Coast listings

For Sleeping and Eating price codes and other relevant information, see Essentials, pages 38-40.

Sleeping

Atlantic Coast *p107*

Since accommodation is plentiful all along the coast, only a small selection is listed here. Most resorts have *balnearios*, private beaches, where you pay US$20-50 per day for family/group use of a sunshade or beach hut, showers, toilets and restaurants. Avoid January when the whole coast is packed out.

Pinamar *p107*

There are plenty of hotels in Pinamar, of a high standard, all 4-stars have a pool. Some hotels are a long way from the beach. Book ahead in Jan and Feb. All those listed are recommended.

LL-L Del Bosque, Av Bunge 1550 y Júpiter, T482480, www.hotel-delbosque.com. Very attractive, in woods, not on the beach, a smart 4 star with pool, tennis courts, nice restaurant, good service.

LL-L Reviens, Burriquetas 79, T497010, www.hotelreviens.com. Modern, luxurious hotel, international style, right on the beach. Recommended.

AL Playas, Av Bunge 250, T482236, www.playashotel.com.ar. Lovely setting, old-fashioned large hotel with stylish rooms, comfortable lounge, small pool, good service, a couple of blocks from the beach. Recommended.

AL Viejo Hotel Ostende, Biarritz y El Cairo, T486081, www.hotelostende.com.ar. Attractive, smallish hotel, open since 1913. Although it has been renovated, it retains some historic flavour in the old wing, comfortable in a simple way, excellent service. There's a pool and private balneario. Breakfast, dinner and a beach hut are all included. Open summer only.

A La Posada, Del Tuyú y Del Odiseo, T482267, www.laposadapinamar.com.ar. Very comfortable, small, quiet, with spacious rooms, next to sea and town centre, pretty gardens where breakfast is served. An excellent choice.

A Las Araucarias, Av Bunge 1411, T480812, hotel_araucarias@hotmail.com. Attractive, small hotel with gardens.

A Soleado, Sarmiento y Nuestras Malvinas, T490304, www.pinamarsoleado.com. Large, beachfront hotel, cosy spacious rooms.

Camping Several well-equipped sites (US$15-20 per day for 4), by the beach at Ostende. One campsite, **Quimey Lemú**, www.quimeylemu.com.ar, in the woods in Pinamar, 6 blocks from bus terminal.

Villa Gesell *p107*

A De la Plaza, Av 2 entre 103 y 104, T468793, www.delaplazahotel.com. Small, spotless, with excellent service, open all year round. Rooms are plain but very comfortable, good value. Across the garden there are fully equipped apartments for 2 to 4 people and a small pool.

A Posada Piñen, Juan de Garay y R Payró (Mar de las Pampas), T479974, www.posadapinen.com. Comfortable cottage-like *hostería*, with a wonderful rustic atmosphere. Run by a welcoming couple of teachers, this is an appealing option. Breakfasts are gorgeous and include delicious homemade pies.

C Hostería Gran Chalet, Paseo 105 No 447 entre Av 4-5, T462913, www.gesell.com.ar/granchalet. Warm welcome, comfortable large rooms, good breakfast. Recommended. Closed off season.

D-E pp **Hostel El Galeón**, Av 5 No 834 (entre Paseos 108 y 109), T453785, www.elgaleon.es.tl. Popular hostel, can accommodate from singles to groups of 8 but no dorms, with bath, some rooms have kitchen, internet and Wi-Fi, cable TV, DVDs, laundry service, cooking facilities, good communal areas, convenient.

Mar del Plata *p108*

Busy traffic makes it impossible to move along the coast in summer: choose a hotel near the beach you want.

LL Costa Galana, Bv Marítimo 5725, T486 0000, www.hotelcostagalana.com. The best by far, a 5-star modern tower, all luxury facilities, at Playa Grande.

LL Hermitage, Bv Marítimo 2657 or Av Colón 1643, T451 9081, www.hermitagehotel.com.ar. Charming old-fashioned 5 star on the seafront.

AL Spa República, Córdoba 1968, T492 1142, www.hotelsparepublica.com.ar. Modern, with pool and spa, rooms with kitchen, good restaurant. Recommended.

B Los Troncos, Rodríguez Peña 1561, T451 8882, www.hotellostroncos.com.ar. Small, chalet-style

hotel in quiet residential area, handy for Güemes bars and restaurants, garden.
B Selent, Arenales 2347, T494 0878, www.hotelselent.com.ar. Quiet with neat rooms, warm welcome, great value. Open all year. Recommended.
C Costa Mogotes, Martínez de Hoz 2401, T484 3140. Tidy, with airy confitería, near Playa Punta Mogotes. Closed off season.
D Abra Marina, Alsina 2444, T486 4646. Basic clean rooms with TV and breakfast. A good budget choice open all year round.
E pp **La Casa del Balcón**, 3 de Febrero 2538, T491 5609, www.lacasadelbalcon.com.ar. Tastefully restored 1920s chalet with garden and dorms for 5 or 6, cosy private rooms (**B** double) with or without bath, breakfast, cooking facilities, fireplace, free internet and Wi-Fi. Minimum stay 4 days in summer. A very attractive choice in La Perla district.

Balcarce

B Balcarce, Balcarce y Mitre, T02266-422055, www.hotel-balcarce.com.ar. Next to the museum, on the main plaza, the most comfortable option.
Camping **Complejo Polideportivo**, Ruta 55, Km 63.5, T02266-420251, with pools and good facilities, all kinds of sports too. **Club de Pesca de Balcarce**, RN 226, Km 39.4 at Laguna Brava, T0223-460 8019, well-organized site, with all facilities, and good fishing. **Parque Idoyaga Molina**, at San Agustín, 25 km south of Balcarce, T02266-491075. A lovely park with mature trees and pond, at the edge of an old village in the hills.

Miramar *p109*

A América, Diag Rosende Mitre 1114, T420847, www.hotelamericamiramar.com.ar. One of the most attractive places in Spanish Mediterranean style, surrounded by trees, lots of games for children, bikes for hire, lovely gardens.
C Brisas del Mar, C 29 No 557, T420334. Sea front, family-run, neat rooms, cheery restaurant, attentive, good value.
Camping Lots of sites including **G** pp **El Durazno**, 2 km from town, T431984, www.campingeldurazno.com.ar, with good facilities , including shops, restaurant and cabañas. Take bus 501 marked 'Playas'.

Necochea *p109*

Most hotels are in the seafront area just north of Av 2. There are at least 100 within 700 m of the beach. Many close off season, when you can bargain with those still open.
A España, C 89 No 215, T422896 (ACA affiliated), www.hotel-espana.com.ar. Modern, well suited to families, attentive staff. Recommended.
A Ñikén, C 87 No 335, T432323, www.hotelniken.com.ar. 2 blocks from the sea. Very comfortable, 4 star, pool, good facilities, good restaurant, excellent service.
A Presidente, C 4 No 4040, T423800, www.presinec.com.ar. A 4 star large hotel recommended for excellent service, comfortable rooms and pool.
B Bahía, Diagonal San Martín 731, T423353, hotelbahia@necocheanet.com.ar. Really kind owners, comfortable rooms, pool in neat gardens. Recommended.
B Hostería del Bosque, C 89 No 350, T/F420002, www.hosteria-delbosque.com.ar. 5 blocks from beach, quiet, comfortable, lovely atmosphere in this renovated former residence of an exiled Russian princess, great restaurant. Recommended.
B San Miguel, C 85 No 301, T/F425155 (ACA). Good service and value, comfortable, open all yr.
Camping **Camping UATRE**, Av 10 y 187, T438278, the best site, a few km west of town towards Médano Blanco, great facilities, beautifully situated *cabañas*. US$2.70 pp per day. **Río Quequén**, C 22 y Ribera Río Quequén, T428068, www.cabaniasrioquequen.com.ar. Sports facilities, pool, bar, cycle hire, well-maintained in attractive setting on the river.

Bahía Blanca and around *p109*

A Austral, Colón 159, T0810-222 4683 or T456 1700, www.hoteles-austral.com.ar. Plain but spacious rooms, very good, fine views, attentive service, decent restaurant and pool.
A Argos, España 149, T455 0404, www.hotelargos.com. 3 blocks from plaza, 4-star business hotel, smart, Wi-Fi, good breakfast, restaurant.
B Bahía, Chiclana 251, T455 3050, www.bahia-hotel.com.ar. Business hotel, good value, well-equipped comfortable rooms, bright bar and *confitería*. Recommended.
C Barne, H Yrigoyen 270, T453 0294, www.barnehotel.com.ar. Family-run, low-key, good value, welcoming.
D Hospedaje Bayón, Chiclana 487, T452 2504. Quite basic but OK, cheaper without bath, no breakfast, friendly.

Camping A couple of options in town, but far better to head for Pehuen Có, see below.

Monte Hermoso

C Petit Hotel, Av Argentina 244, T02921-481818, www.petitfrentealmar.com.ar. Simple, modernized 1940s style, family-run, on the beach, restaurant, breakfast extra, cooking facilities. Recommended.

Camping There are many sites around Monte Hermoso, with good facilities, including: **Americano**, www.campingamericano.com.ar, signposted from main road 5 km before town (bus or taxi from town). Lovely shady site by beach, US$22 for 2 per day (min stay 5 days), hot showers, pool, restaurant, food shop, *locutorio*. Also various cabins for rent. Recommended. Many others, most with good facilities.

Sierra de la Ventana *p110*

Tornquist

D La Casona, Rawson 232, T0291-155 012517, http://com-tur.com.ar/lacasona/. A renovated house with plain rooms with breakfast.

D San José, Güemes 138, T0291-494 0152. Small, central, quite good plain rooms. Poor breakfast for extra US$2 pp.

Camping **Parque Norte**, just north on Ruta 76, T494 0661. Popular lakeside park to bathe/picnic.

Villa Ventana

Lots of accommodation in *cabañas*; municipal campsite by river with all facilities.

A El Mirador, on RP 76 Km 226, T0291-494 1338, www.complejoelmirador.com. Great location right at the foot of Cerro de la Ventana, comfortable rooms, some with tremendous views, very peaceful, good restaurant.

C San Hipólito, on RP 76 Km 230, T0291-156 428281, campoequino@hotmail.com. Fully furnished, comfortable, small cabins on a large ranch, welcoming owners, Polito and his wife. Ideal for families with kids. Enjoyable horse rides in the hills.

Sierra de la Ventana

L Estancia Cerro de la Cruz, just outside Sierra town (phone for directions), T011-156 1582449, www.estanciacerrodelacruz.com. Luxurious *estancia* with beautiful views, charming hosts. Price is full board. Recommended.

A Cabañas La Caledonia, Los Robles y Ombúes in **Villa Arcadia**, a couple of blocks over the railway track, T0291-4915268, www.lacaledonia.com.ar. Well-equipped, comfortable small cabins in pretty gardens with a pool. Price is for a cabin for up to 4 people.

A Las Vertientes, RP 76, Km 221, signposted just west of the turning to Villa Ventana, T491 0064, http://com-tur.com.ar/lasvertientes/. Very welcoming ranch with a house for rent (price is for 6 people; breakfast extra) in lovely surroundings, relaxing, horse riding, mountain biking, trekking, day visits, US$20pp.

B Provincial, Drago y Malvinas, T491 5025. Old 1940s place, quaint rather than comfy, fabulous views, restaurant, pool, good value.

Camping **Yamila**, access on C Tornquist, T0291-154 189266, www.campingyamila. 8m.com. Lovely shady site by river, hot showers, food shop.

❼ Eating

Mar del Plata *p108*

2 areas have become popular for smaller shops bars and restaurants: Around C Güemes:

¶¶ Almacén El Condal, Alsina y Garay. Charming old street-corner bar, serving *picadas* and drinks, popular with young crowd.

¶¶ La Bodeguita, Castelli 1252. Cuban bar with food.

¶¶ Tisiano, San Lorenzo 1332. Good pasta restaurant in leafy patio.

Around Alem, next to cemetery, lots of pubs and bars. Traditional favourites:

¶¶ Manolo, Rivadavia 2371 and on the coast at Bv Marítimo 4961. Famous for *churros* and hot chocolate in the early hours, popular with post-party people.

¶¶ Parrilla Trenque Lauquen, B de Irigoyen 2445 and Av Colón y Paunero. Traditional *parrilla*.

¶¶ Pehuén, Bernardo de Irigoyen 3666. Very good and popular parrilla.

Seafood restaurants in the Centro Comercial Puerto, many brightly lit and not atmospheric.

¶¶ El Viejo Pop. The best place, ship design, candlelit, superb paella.

¶¶ Taberna Baska, 12 de Octubre 3301. Seafood and Basque country dishes, next to the port.

Necochea *p109*

There are some excellent seafood restaurants.

¶¶¶-¶¶ La Taberna Baska, C 65 y 58. Good food and good wine list, in the Basque Centre.

Cantina Venezia, near the port at Av 59 No 259. The most famous, delicious fish, first class.
Chimichurri, C 83 No 345. Recommended for *parrilla*.
Parrilla El Loco, Av 10 y 65, T437094. A classic *parrilla*, deservedly popular for superb steaks.
Sotavento, Av Costanera y Pinolandia. On the beach, varied menu, can get very busy but good value.

Bahía Blanca and around *p109*
Lola Mora, Av Alem y Sarmiento. Elegant, delicious Mediterranean food, in a colonial-style house. Excellent and good value set meal.
Micho, Guillermo Torres 3875, T457 0346. A superb chic fish restaurant at the port (take bus 500 or 501, but go there by taxi at night, as it's in an insalubrious area).
Santino, Dorrego 38. Italian-influenced, quiet sophisticated atmosphere, good value and a welcoming glass of champagne. Recommended.
El Mundo de la Pizza, Dorrego 53. Fabulous pizzas, lots of choice, the city's favourite.
New For You, Belgrano 69. Good *tenedor libre*.

Cafés

Big Six, Belgrano 30. Burger-style take away and restaurant, good coffee and newspapers to read.
Café del Angel, Paseo del Angel, entrances at O'Higgins 71 and Drago 63. Good value lunches, friendly place.
Muñoz, O'Higgins y Drago. Sophisticated café, good for reading the papers.
Piazza, on the corner of the plaza at O'Higgins y Chiclana. Great coffee, buzzing atmosphere, good salads, and cakes too.

Monte Hermoso

Marfil, Valle Encantado 91. The smartest, delicious fish and pastas.
Pizza Jet, Valle Encantado e Int Majluf. Hugely popular for all kinds of food, arrive before 2130 to get a table.

Bars and clubs

Mar del Plata *p108*
Many bars and nightclubs are on Alem or its surroundings and start at around 0200. **Mr Jones**, Alem 3738, for the under 25s. **La Llorona**, on Olavarria, near Blvd Marítimo, for the over 25s.

Bahía Blanca *p109*
Lots of discos on **Fuerte Argentino** (along the stream leading to the park) mainly catering for under 25's: **Chocolate**, **Bahía Bonito**.

Transport

Partido de la Costa: San Clemente del Tuyú *p107*
Bus To **Mar del Plata** (and to resorts in between) are frequent, **El Rápido, El Rápido Argentino**, US$9, 3-5 hrs. To **Buenos Aires**, several companies, US$13-18, 4-5½ hrs.

Pinamar *p107*
Bus Terminal 20 mins' walk from the beach at Av Bunge e Intermédanos, T403500. To **Buenos Aires**, US$16-22, 4-5hrs, several companies.
Trains The station is a few kilometres away, free bus transfers from town.

Villa Gesell *p107*
Air Regular flights (only in summer) to **Buenos Aires** operated by **Sol**; airport 5 km away, taxi US$5.
Bus Direct to **Buenos Aires**, many companies, 5 hrs, US$20-25. To **Mar del Plata** 2 hrs, US$4.30. Terminal at Av 3 y Paseo 140.

Mar del Plata *p108*
Air Camet airport, T478 3990, 10 km north of town. Several flights daily to **Buenos Aires**, **LADE** (T491 1484), **AR/Austral** (T496 0101). In summer, **Sol** to **Buenos Aires** and **LADE** also to many Patagonian towns once a week. *Remise* taxi from airport to town, US$7-8, also bus 542 (signed Aeropuerto) US$0.40 (payable with a magnetic card).
Bus For information T451 5406. The bus terminal, in a former railway station, is central at Alberti y Las Heras, but squalid and short on services. Not a place to hang around at night. To **Buenos Aires**, 5-6 hrs, US$19-25, many companies. **El Rápido** (T494 2507) and **El Rápido Argentino** (T486 3494) run several services a day to most coastal towns: to **Villa Gesell**, 1½ hrs, US$4; to **Pinamar**, 2 hrs, US$5; to **San Clemente del Tuyú**, 3-5 hrs, US$9; to **Miramar**, 40 min, US$1.70 (also Line 212 from Terminal, US$1.10); to **Necochea**, 2 hrs, US$6; to **Bahía Blanca**, 7 hrs, US$20. The former company also goes to **Balcarce**, 1½ hrs, US$3, and to **Tandil**, 2½-3 hrs, US$8. To **Bariloche**, **Via Bariloche**, **El Rápido**

Argentino, 18-20 hrs, US$67-88. To all Patagonian towns along RN 3, ending at **Comodoro Rivadavia**, 23 hrs, US$76-88, with **Transportadora Patagónica**. To **Mendoza**, **Andesmar**, daily, 19-22 hrs, US$61-73.
Train To **Buenos Aires** (Constitución) from Estación Norte, Luro 4599, T475 6076, 13 blocks from the centre. Buses to/from centre 511, 512, 512B, 541. Also services to Miramar in summer only. See page 101 .

Miramar *p109*

Bus Terminals at C 34 y Av 23, T423359, at Fortunato de la Plaza y C 19, and a few others. **Plusmar, Micromar, La Estrella/El Cóndor** to **Buenos Aires**, 6½-7 hrs, US$21-27. To/from **Mar del Plata**, US$1.70, **El Rápido** (also Line 212, US$1.10). To **Necochea**, **El Rápido, La Estrella/El Cóndor**, 1½ hrs, US$2.30-3.
Train See page 101. Station at Av 40 y C 15, T420657.

Necochea *p109*

Bus Terminal at Av 58 y Jesuita Cardiel, T422470, 3 km from the beach area; bus 513 from outside the terminal to the beach. Taxi to beach area US$3. To **Buenos Aires**, 6½-8½ hrs, US$19-27, **La Estrella/El Cóndor**, **Plusmar** and few others. To **Mar del Plata**, **El Rápido**, US$6. To **Bahía Blanca**, **El Rápido** US$14.

Bahía Blanca and around *p109*

Air Airport Comandante Espora, lies 11 km northeast of centre, US$6 in a taxi. Airport information T486 0300. Daily flights to **Buenos Aires** with **AR/Austral** (T456 0561/ 0810-2228 6527). **LADE** (T452 1063) has weekly flights to **Buenos Aires**, **Necochea**, **Mar del Plata** and Patagonian coastal towns.
Bus Terminal in old railway station 2 km from centre, at Estados Unidos y Brown, T481 9615, connected by buses 512, 514, or taxi US$3, no hotels nearby. To **Buenos Aires** frequent, several companies, 8-10 hrs, US$30-35, shop around. Most comfortable by far is **Plusmar** suite bus, with flat beds US$41 (T456 0616). To **Mar del Plata**, **El Rápido**, US$20, 7 hrs. To **Córdoba**, 13-15 hrs, US$34-42. To **Necochea**, **El Rápido**, 5 hrs, US$14. To **Bariloche**, **El Valle, Vía Bariloche**, 11-13 hrs, US$26-45. To **Mendoza**, **Andesmar**, 16 hrs, US$50-63. To **Puerto Madryn**, **Andesmar**, **Don Otto**, **La Estrella/El Cóndor**, 8½-10½ hrs, US$30-41. To **Tornquist**, US$3.50, **Río Paraná** and **La Estrella/El Cóndor**, 1 hr 20 min; to **Sierra de la Ventana** (town) **La Estrella/El Cóndor** and **Expreso Cabildo**, 2 hr 20 min, US$5. Also minibus to Tornquist with **Cerro**, T494 1129.
Train Station at Av Gral Cerri 750, T452 9196. To/from **Buenos Aires**, see page 101.

Pehuén-Có and Monte Hermoso

Bus From Monte Hermoso either to **Buenos Aires** or **Bahía Blanca** with **La Estrella/El Cóndor**. Several combis or minibuses also to **Bahía Blanca** (eg **Ariber**, T0291-4522801, **Norte Bus**, T02921-481524). From Pehuén-Có to Bahía Blanca, with **La Patagonia**, T0291-4553215).

Sierra de la Ventana *p110*

Bus **Geotur**, San Martín 193, T491 5355. Operates a minibus a few times a day along RP 76 from Sierra de la Ventana to Tornquist, dropping off hikers at the entrance to the park. Also specializes in mountain biking, trekking and horse riding trips.

Directory

Mar del Plata *p108*

Banks Many ATMs all around the central area, along Peatonal San Martín, at Santa Fe y Rivadavia and two close together by the casino. *Casas de Cambio* **Jonestur**, San Martín 2574, and Av Luro 3185, best rates for TCs and cash. **Amex**, at *Oti Internacional*, San Luis 1630, T494 5414. **La Moneta**, Rivadavia 2615. **Cultural centres** Cultural events: reduced price tickets are often available from **Cartelera Baires**, Santa Fe 1844, local 33, or from **Galería de los Teatros**, Santa Fe 1751. **Centro Cultural Pueyrredón**, 25 de Mayo 3102, T499 7893. Every day screenings, music shows, plays or conferences, mostly free. **Internet** Broadband internet can be found everywhere. **Telephones** Many *locutorios* around the town. **Useful addresses** Immigration Office: Rivadavia 3820, T492 4271, open morning.

Bahía Blanca *p109*

Banks Many ATMs on plaza for all major cards. *Casas de Cambio*: **Pullman**, San Martín 171. **Internet** Many places along Zelarrayan and Estomba near plaza. **Post offices** Moreno 34. **Telephones** Big *locutorio* at Alsina y Chiclana, also internet.

West of Buenos Aires

Rising out of the flat arid Pampa, the Sierras of Córdoba and San Luis give a dramatic setting to popular holiday towns and mountain retreats. Beyond the plains, fertile valleys stretch along the length of the Andean precordillera and climb up to the heights of Aconcagua and its neighbours. The western provinces of Mendoza, San Juan, La Rioja and Catamarca cover extreme contrasts, but Mendoza and the surrounding area to the south is popular for its excellent wines, climbing and superb ski and adventure resorts such as Malargüe.

Córdoba

→ *Phone code: 0351. Colour map 8, A3. Population: 1.4 million. Altitude: 440 m.*

Córdoba, the second city in the country, has some fine historic buildings and a lively university population. It is also an important route centre. Córdoba the city, capital of Córdoba Province, was founded in 1573. The site of the first university in the country, established in 1613 by the Jesuits, it now has two universities. It is an important industrial centre, the home of Argentina's motor industry, and a busy modern city with a flourishing shopping centre.

Ins and outs

Getting there Pajas Blancas airport, 12 km northwest of city, T475 0392, has shops, post office, a good restaurant and a *casa de cambio* (open Monday-Friday 1000-1500). The bus service (US$0.30) can be unreliable; a regular or *remise* taxi charges around US$5. Bus terminal at Blvd Perón 250, 8 blocks east of main Plaza, T434 1700. Left luggage lockers, US$0.65 per day, *remise* taxi desk, ATM, tourist office at the lower level, where the ticket offices are. Taxi US$0.65 to Plaza San Martín. Minibuses, *diferenciales*, have better services to the sierras and depart from nearby platform; tickets on bus or from offices at terminal, first floor. ▸▸ *See also Transport, page 120.*

Tourist offices **Agencia Córdoba Turismo** ⓘ *old Cabildo, Pasaje Santa Catalina, T434 1200, www.cordoba.gov.ar*. Also at Patio Olmos Shopping, Blvd San Juan y Vélez Sársfield, T570 4100, daily 1000-2200, at the bus terminal, T433 1982, and at the airport, T434 8390. All open early morning to late at night, with useful city maps and information on guided walks and cycle tours. The municipality runs good, daily city tours leaving from the Centro Obispo Mercadillo; tourist offices have details. See also: www.cordobatrip.com, which has information in Spanish.

Sights

At the city's heart is **Plaza San Martín**, with a statue of the Liberator. On the west side is the old **Cabildo** ⓘ *Independencia 30, free, except for entry to exhibitions, 0900-2100 (Mon 1400-2100)*. Built around two internal patios, the building now houses the tourist office, a small gallery, a restaurant and a bookshop. Next to it stands the **Cathedral** ⓘ *0800-1200, 1630-2000,* the oldest in Argentina (begun 1640, consecrated 1671), with attractive stained glass windows and a richly decorated ceiling. Look out for statues of angels resembling native Americans. Behind the cathedral is the pleasant **Plaza del Fundador**, with a statue to the city founder Jerónimo Luis de Cabrera. One of the features of this part of the city is its old churches. Near Plaza San Martín at Independencia 122 is the 16th-century **Carmelo Convent** and chapel of **Santa Teresa**, whose rooms and beautiful patio form the **Museo de Arte Religioso Juan de Tejeda** ⓘ *Wed-Sat 0930-1230, US$0.65, guided visits also in English and French.* This houses one of the finest collections of religious art in the country. The **Manzana Jesuítica** ⓘ *contained within Av Vélez Sarsfield, Caseros, Duarte Quirós and Obispo Trejo, Tue-Sun 0900-1300, 1600-2000, US$1, T4332075*, has been declared a World Heritage Site by UNESCO. **La Compañía** (Obispo Trejo y Caseros, built between 1640 and 1676) has a vaulted ceiling reminiscent of a ship's hull. Behind it, on Caseros, is the beautiful **Capilla Doméstica**, a private 17th century Jesuit chapel (guided visits only). Next to it are two former Jesuit institutions: the main building of the **Universidad Nacional de Córdoba** ⓘ *T4332075, Tue-Sun 0900-1300, 1600-2000, US$1*, housing one of the most valuable libraries in the country; and the **Colegio Nacional de Montserrat**, the most traditional high school in the province. Guided tours of the church, chapel, university (called Museo Histórico) and school leave from Obispo Trejo 242 ⓘ *Tue-Sun 1000, 1100, 1700 and 1800, available in English*. The **Basílica de La Merced** ⓘ *25 de Mayo 83*, was built in the early 19th century, though its fine gilt wooden pulpit dates from the colonial period. On its exterior, overlooking Rivadavia, are fine murals in ceramic by local artist Armando Sica. Further east, at Blvd J D Perón, is the magnificent late 19th-century **Mitre railway station**, with its beautiful tiled *confitería*, still used for Sunday evening tango shows.

Museo Marqués de Sobremonte ⓘ *Rosario de Santa Fe 218, 1 block east of San Martin, T4331661,Tue-Fri 1000-1500, Sat 0900-14002, US$0.65, texts in English and German.* Formerly

Córdoba

Sleeping
1 Alex *B3*
2 Alto Paraná *B3*
3 American Córdoba Park *B1*
4 Baluch Backpackers Hostel *A2*
5 Cristal *B2*
6 Córdoba Backpackers *A1*
7 Córdoba Hostel *C2*
8 Entre Ríos *B3*
9 Heydi *B3*
10 Hostel Joven *A1*
11 NH Panorama *A1*
12 Quetzal *B3*
13 Sussex *A2*
14 Windsor *B2*

Eating
1 Alfonsina *B2*
2 Betos *B1*
3 El Anden *B2*
4 El Arrabal *C1*
5 El Ruedo *A2*
6 La Cocina de Osés & La Vieja Casa del Francés *B1*
7 L'América *B2*
8 Mandarina *A2*
9 Puerto Illia *B3*
10 Sol y Luna *A2*
11 Sorocabana *A2*
12 Upacanejo *A2*

Bars & clubs
13 Reina Alba *C1*

the house of Rafael Núñez, governor of Córdoba, and now the only surviving colonial family residence in the city, the museum displays 18th and 19th provincial history. **Museo Municipal de Bellas Artes** ⓘ *Av General Paz 33, T433 1512, Tue-Sun 0900-2100, US$0.35.* Has a permanent collection of contemporary art by celebrated Argentine artists in an early 20th-century mansion.

Córdoba listings

For Sleeping and Eating price codes and other relevant information, see Essentials, pages 38-40.

Sleeping

Córdoba *p116, map p117*

AL Windsor, Buenos Aires 214, T422 4012, www.windsortower.com. Small, smart, warm, large breakfast, sauna, gym, pool.

AL-A NH Panorama, Alvear 251, T410 3900, www.nh-hoteles.com. Comfortable, functional, small pool, gym, restaurant, views of Sierra from upper floors.

A Amerian Córdoba Park, Bv San Juan 165, T420 7000, www.amerian.com. Swish, modern hotel with marbled foyer and professional service. Comfortable, superb breakfast, convenient and reliable. Also has a business centre, spa and pool.

B Alex, Bv Illia 742, T421 4350, www.alexhotel.com.ar. Good value, modern, cosy despitre a slightly off-putting exterior. All rooms include breakfast and a mate kit, helpful staff, close to the bus station.

B Cristal, Entre Ríos 58, T424 5000, hoteles@sicordoba.com.ar. Good, comfortable, well-maintained, large breakfast, good service, a/c, welcoming.

B Heydi, Bv Illia 615, T421 8906, www.hotelheydi.com.ar. Quiet, 3 star, pleasant rooms, breakfast included.

C Quetzal, San Jerónimo 579, T/F422 9106. Refurbished, spotless, good value, breakfast is extra.

C Sussex, San Jerónimo 125, T422 9070, www.hotelsussexcba.com.ar. A/c, with breakfast, well kept, small pool, family welcome.

D Alto Paraná, Paraná 230, T428 1625, hotelaltoparana@arnet.com.ar. Close to bus terminal, hot shower, TV, breakfast, very nice, good value.

D Entre Ríos, Entre Ríos 567, T/F423 0311, hotelentrerios@yahoo.com. Basic, welcoming, some rooms a/c, 1 room has wheelchair accessbreakfast, 10% discount for ISIC members.

D-G Baluch Backpackers Hostel. San Martin 338, T422 3977, www.baluchbackpackers.com. From US$6 pp in dorm (US$7 in high season). Owned and run by backpackers, central, information and bus tickets, internet and many other services, organizes various activities.

E Córdoba Backpackers, Deán Funes 285, T422 0593, www.cordobabackpackers.com.ar. Dorms for 3 to 7 people, also doubles (**D**) with and without bath, family atmosphere, very helpful.

F pp **Córdoba Hostel**, Ituzaingó 1070, T468 7359, www.cordobahostel.com.ar. In Nueva Córdoba district, small rooms (**D** in double), cooking facilities, quite noisy, private lockers in rooms. Small discount for HI members.

F pp **Hostel Joven**, Tablada 414. Kitchen, internet, laundry, very good, helpful.

Estancias

Estancia Los Potreros, Sierras Chicas, Casilla de correo 64, 5111 Rio Ceballos, T011-6091 2692, or 011-4313 1410, www.estancialospotreros.com. An exclusive 6,000-acre working cattle farm in the wild and scenic Cordoba hills. High standard of accommodation, with warm hospitality and attention to detail in keeping with a time past. The "riders' estancia"... unrivalled in its fabulous horses (impeccably trained and calm polo horses). Even for non-equestrians you can relax by the pool, go birdwatching or just enjoy the peaceful hilltop setting and savour the delicious food and wines - all included in the price. 3 nights minimum stay. Highly recommended (either take a bus to the nearest town, Río Ceballos, or the owners will arrange a taxi from Córdoba city or airport, 1 hr).

Eating

Córdoba *p116, map p117*

¶¶ L'América, Caseros 67, T4271734. Designer restaurant with imaginative menu, traditional to sushi to French, large selection of wines, home-made bread, great service, also cheap set menus.

🍴🍴 **Betos**, San Juan 450, T469 2774. Best *lomitos* in town at this large, popular *parrilla*. Recommended.

🍴🍴 **La Cocina de Osés**, Independencia 512. Nicely decorated if rather formal, good for fish, meat dishes and homemade pastas.

🍴🍴 **Novecento**, at the Cabildo, T423 0660. Smart and lively, in an airy patio, superb Mediterranean- style cooking, excellent service. Lunch only, bar 0800-2000. Recommended.

🍴🍴 **Upacanejo**, San Jerónimo 171. Based on a popular comic character (staff dressed accordingly), *parrilla* serving excellent beef and chicken.

🍴🍴 **La Vieja Casa del Francés**, Independencia 508. Delicious grills, inviting atmosphere, expat owners happy to chat with diners. Recommended.

🍴🍴-🍴 **Sol y Luna**, Gral Paz 278, T425 1189. Mon-Sat 1200-1530. Vegetarian with a change of menu daily, fresh food, lunchtime specials, good desserts.

🍴 **Alfonsina**, Duarte Quirós 66. Rural style in an old house, simple meals, pizzas and *empanadas* or breakfasts with homemade bread, piano and guitar music, popular with the city's young crowd.

Cafés

El Anden, Buenos Aires y Entre Ríos. Tasty *facturas*, croissants and good music.

El Ruedo, Obispo Trejo y 27 de Abril. A lively *confitería*, also serving light meals.

Mandarina, Obispo Trejo 171, T0351-426 4909. Central, welcoming, leafy, lots of great breakfasts, good for lunch and dinner. Highly recommended.

Puerto Illia, Bv Illia 555. By bus terminal, and open 24 hrs for breakfasts and simple meals – great if you arrive at night or have a long wait.

Sorocabana, Buenos Aires y San Jerónimo. Great breakfasts, popular, good views of Plaza San Martín.

Bars and clubs

Cerro Las Rosas, northwest of town, locally referred just as *Cerro*, has a lively area of bars and clubs along Av Rafael Núñez, including **Arcimboldo**, No 4567. **Factory**, No 3964, popular club for all ages, playing a mix of electronic and Latin dance music. **Villa Agur**, José Roque Funes y Tristán Malbrán, is more rock and roll with food and live music.

Chateau Carreras, further northwest is another popular area. **Carreras**, on Av Ramón J Cárcano. The most popular club.

El Abasto district, on the river (about 8 blocks north of Plaza San Martín) has good places for lower budgets: **Casa Babylon**, Bv Las Heras 48, very popular disco night Fri, rock Sat. **Dvino**, Pasaje Agustín Pérez 32 (behind Puente Alvear). Before 1900, taste wines. Affordable options are around Bv San Juan and Av Vélez Sarsfield, along La Cañada or south of Bv Illia at Nueva Córdoba district. **Reina Alba**, Obispo Trejo y F Rivera, is a redesigned old house with a chic bar. **Rita**, Independencia 1162, is a refurbished old house with trendy clientele.

Studenty bars on Rondeau between Av H Yrigoyen and Chacabuco. Less noisy are: **Johnny B Good**, H Yrigoyen 320, and **Posh**, H Yrigoyen 464, for jazz, blues and bossa nova after 2400. *Cuarteto* music, a Cordobés invention, is hugely popular.

Entertainment

See free listings magazines *La Cova* and *Ocio en Córdoba*, local newspaper *La Voz del Interior*, and *www.cordoba.net*, for events.

Cinema Many cinemas including **Cineclub Municipal**, Bv Illia 49, **Teatro Córdoba**, 27 de Abril 275, both showing independent and foreign language films, and the new theatre in **Shopping Patio Olmos** (see below), with new releases.

Dance **Confitería Mitre**, Bv Perón 101 (in railway station), tango class before *milonga* (public place to dance) begins, US$1.30. The patio at the Cabildo on Fri has tango lessons and dance. **El Arrabal**, Belgrano y Fructuoso Rivera, restaurant with a tango show after 2400, Fri and Sat, US$1.70 extra.

Theatre The Festival of Latinamerican Theatre is held every Oct. **Teatro del Libertador**, Av Vélez Sarsfield 367, T433 2312, is traditional and sumptuous, with a rich history.

Shopping

Bookshops **Librería Blackpool**, Deán Funes 395, for imported English books. **Yenny-El Ateneo**, Av Gral Paz 180. Has some English titles.

Handicrafts **Mundo Aborigen**, Rivadavia 155. **Paseo de las Artes**, Achával Rodríguez y La Cañada. Handicraft market, Sat-Sun 1600-2200 (in summer 1800-2300), ceramics, leather, wood and metalware. **Unión de Artesanos**, San Martín 42 (Galería San Martín, local 22).

Shopping malls **Córdoba Shopping**, José de Goyechea 2851 (Villa Cabrera). **Nuevocentro**, Av Duarte Quirós 1400. **Patio Olmos**, Av Vélez Sarsfield y Bv San Juan. Central.

Transport

Córdoba *p116, map p117*

Air **AR/Austral** run a shuttle service several times a day to/from **Buenos Aires**, about 2 hrs. **LAN** also flies to Buenos Aires. Most major Argentine cities are served by **AR**, usually via BsAs. **Sol** flies to **Rosario** on weekdays, connexion to **Punta del Este** in summer. International flights to **Bolivia** (Santa Cruz), **Brazil** and **Chile** direct, others via BsAs.

Bus Municipal buses and electric buses (trolleys) do not accept cash. You have to buy tokens (*cospeles*) or cards from kiosks, normal US$0.30.

The terminal at Bvd Perón 250 has restaurants, supermarket, internet, left-luggage lockers. ATM and tourist office. To **Buenos Aires**, several companies, 9-11 hrs, US$28-35 *común*, US$35-40 *coche cama*. To **Salta**, 12 hrs, US$35-45. To **Jujuy**, US$41-51, 13-14 hrs. To **Mendoza**, 9-12 hrs, frequent, US$29-40. To **La Rioja**, 6-7 hrs, US$14. To **Catamarca**, 6 hrs, US$20-24. **TAC** and **Andesmar** have connecting services to several destinations in **Patagonia**. See towns below for buses to the Sierras de Córdoba. To **Santiago** (Chile), US$40, 17-19 hrs, **CATA, TAC**. To **Bolivia** take **Balut** services to the border at La Quiaca (19 hrs, US$55) or Pocitos (17 hrs, US$46).

Directory

Airline offices **Aerolíneas Argentinas/Austral**, Colón 520, T410 7676. **LADE**, 9 de Julio 1104, T423 0540. **LAN**, San Lorenzo 309 PB, esq Blvd Chacabuco, Nueva Córdoba, T0810-999-9526. **Banks** Open in the morning. There are many **Link** and **Banelco** ATMs; all accept international credit cards. **Citibank**, Ituzaingó 238, changes Citicorp and Visa TCs (no commission). **Exprinter**, Rivadavia 47. Cash and Amex TCs (low commission). **Barujel**, Rivadavia y 25 de Mayo. Cash, Amex TCs (15% commission), Visa TCs; also Western Union branch. **Cultural centres** **Asociación Argentina de Cultura Británica**, Av H Yrigoyen 496, T468 1995. Good library with books and magazines, English teaching materials, videos and a reading room, Mon-Fri 0900-2000. **Consulates** **Bolivia**, San Jeronimo 167, p 6, T424 5650. **Chile**, Crisol 280, T469 0432. **Internet** Many places, US$0.35 per hr. **Mega Cyber**, MT de Alvear 229, open til 0500. **Language schools** ILEE, T482 4829, www.ilee. com.ar. Spanish courses and lodging arranged. **Medical services** Emergencies, T107. **Hospital Córdoba**, Av Patria 656, T434 9000. **Hospital Clínicas**, Santa Rosa 1564, T433 7010. **Post offices** Colón 210, parcel service on the ground floor by the customs office. **Telephones** There are plenty of *locutorios*, many with post office and internet. **Useful addresses** **Dirección Nacional de Migraciones**, Caseros 676, T422 2740. **Police**, T101. **Fire department**, T100.

Around Córdoba

Sierras de Córdoba

The Sierras de Córdoba offer beautiful mountain landscapes with many rivers and streams, plus the advantage of good infrastructure and accessibility. Adventure tourism has really taken off here, so there's something for everyone in the hills and valleys. Popular for tourism among the upper classes in the late 19th century, the Sierras de Córdoba were opened up for mass tourism in the 1940's with the building of lots of hotels. The most visited sights lie along the valleys of **Punilla**, **Traslasierra** and **Calamuchita**, and on the east side of the **Sierra Chica**, north of Córdoba, all forming itineraries of about 70 km long each. There's a useful network of dirt roads (usually used for rally competitions!). Summer rainstorms may cause sudden floods along riversides. Beware when choosing a campsite.

Villa Carlos Paz In the Punilla Valley is this large modern town (*Phone code: 03541; Population: 56,000; Altitude: 642 m*) on an artificial lake Lago San Roque, 36 km west of Córdoba. It is the nearest resort to Córdoba and is therefore often crowded. Trips on the lake are offered in all kinds of water-vehicles, from amphibious trucks to catamarans (stalls along Avenida San Martín, opposite bus station, US$4). A chair-lift runs from the Complejo Aerosilla to the summit of the Cerro de la Cruz, which offers splendid views (US$4). North of Villa Carlos Paz, on Ruta 38, a road branches west to Tanti from where local buses go to **Los Gigantes**, a paradise for climbers, two-day treks possible (entry US$1). Club Andino has several *refugios*; contact **Club Andino Córdoba** *T0351-480 5126*. **Tourist information** ⓘ *Liniers 50, T0810-888 2729, open 0700-2100, www.villacarlospaz.gov.ar/turismo/*.

Cosquín On the banks of the Río Cosquín, 26 km north of Villa Carlos Paz, Cosquín (*Phone code: 03541; Population: 18,800; Altitude: 708 m*) is the site of the most important **folklore festival**, in the last two weeks in January. A popular rock festival is held in early February (www.cosquin rock.com) so that accommodation is almost impossible to find between 10 January and 10 February. **Museo Camín Cosquín** ⓘ *at Km 760, out of town, T451184, 0900-1230, 1400- 1800 (closes later in summer), US$0.65.* Minerals, fossils and archaeology, recommended. Take a *remise* taxi from the town centre, US$5 (or walk two hours) to the **Pan de Azúcar** hill (1,260 m), from where there is a good view over the Punilla valley. There is a chairlift to the top (all year round). **Tourist office** ⓘ *Av San Martín 560, Plaza Próspero Molino, T454644.*.

North from Córdoba

La Falda (*Phone code: 03548; Population: 16,000; Altitude: 934 m*), 82 km north of Córdoba, is a good base for walking, if not an attractive town. Visit the **Trenshow** ⓘ *Las Murallas 200, T423041, 0930-2000, US$2,* a model railway museum. **Camino de El Cuadrado** crosses the sierras eastward to Río Ceballos, passing an excellent vantage point at *Balcón de las Nubes* and the 18th-century *Estancia El Silencio*, 11 km from La Falda, where is a small museum and outdoor activities are organized.

To the west, an 80-km rough winding road goes to La Higuera, across the Cumbres de Gaspar. It crosses the vast **Pampa de Olaén**, a 1,100-m high grass- covered plateau with the tiny, 18th-century chapel of **Santa Bárbara** (20 km from La Falda) and the **Cascadas de Olaén**, with three waterfalls, 2 km south of the chapel. **Tourist office** ⓘ *Av España 50 (at the former railway station), T423007, www.lafalda.gov.ar.*

North of La Falda is **La Cumbre** (*Phone code: 03548; Population: 7,200; Altitude: 1141 m, www.alacumbre.com.ar*), at the highest point in the Punilla Valley. Founded by British engineers and workers who built the railway here in 1900, it is an attractive place with tree-lined avenues. It has classy shops, good places to eat and have tea, a golf course and, nearby, the paragliding centre of **Cuchi Corral** (see Activities and tours, below).

Capilla del Monte About 106 km north of Córdoba and set in the heart of the Sierras, Capilla del Monte (*Phone code: 03458; Altitude: 979 m*) is a good centre for trekking, paragliding and exploring this area. Excursions in the hills, particularly to Cerro Uritorco, 1,979 m, a four-hour climb (no shade, entry US$2) via La Toma where there are medicinal waters and from where there are further walking opportunities. There is horse riding and tours to meditation and 'energy' centres: the location of many sightings of UFOs, the area is popular for 'mystical tourism'. **Tourist office** ⓘ *in the old railway station, Av Pueyredón s/n, open daily 0830-2030, some English spoken, T481903, www.capilladelmonte.gov.ar and www.capilladelmonte.com.*

Jesús María (*Colour map 8, A3. Population: 27,000. Altitude: 533 m. 51 km north of Córdoba on Ruta 9*) **Estancia de Jesús María** ⓘ *T420126, Tue-Fri 0900-1900, Sat-Sun 1100-1300, 1500-1900 (in winter Mon-Fri 0900-1800, Sat-Sun 1000-1200, 1500-1800), US$0.65, easy 15-min walk from bus station: take Av Juan B Justo, north, turn left at Av Cleto Peña, cross bridge on river and follow a dirt road right about 300 m.* Dating from the 17th century, the estancia has the remains of its once famous winery, reputed to have produced the first wine in the Americas, which was served to the Spanish royal family. In the cloister is an excellent **Museo Jesuítico**, where Cuzco-style paintings, religious objects and a curious collection of plates are exhibited. **Estancia de Caroya** ⓘ *T462300, Mon-Fri 0900-1700, Sat-Sun 1000-1600, US$0.65, 20-min walk from bus station, taxi US$1.50.* A rather more humble place in the southern suburbs, this estancia also dates from the 17th century; a large white building around a lovely patio, with a quaint stone chapel beside it. **Estancia de Santa Catalina** ⓘ*T421600, winter Tue-Sun 1000-1300, 1500-1800 (summer Tue-Sun 1000-1300, 1500-1900), on weekends and holidays in Jul cloisters and novitiate are closed, US$2. From the bus station, remise taxis US$8-10 return including 2-hr stay.* Still in private hands, beautifully located in the countryside northwest of Jesús María, this is the largest of the *estancias* and has the most splendid buildings, well preserved and containing some fine religious art. Each January there is a gaucho and folklore festival, lasting 10 nights from second week; very popular. Some 4 km north of Jesús María is **Sinsacate**, a fine colonial posting inn, now a museum, with chapel attached.

At Rayo Cortado, 114 km north of Jesús María, a turning leads west to **Cerro Colorado**, 160 km north of Córdoba, the former home of the late Argentine folklore singer and composer Atahualpa Yupanqui. His house is a **museum** ⓘ *T155-198715, daily 0900-1300, 1600-2000, at the end of the winding road to Agua Escondida, also offers guided tours*, lush grounds, with chance of spotting armadillos. There are about 35,000 rock paintings by the indigenous Comechingones in the nearby **Reserva Natural y Cultural Cerro Colorado** ⓘ *at the foot of Cerro Intihuasi, daily in summer 0700-1300, 1400-2000, winter daily 0800-1900, US$1, only with guide, 1-1½ hr tour*, and a small **archaeological museum** ⓘ *T0351-4333425, daily 0700-1300, 1400-2000, tours at 0830, 1030, 1600 and 1800.* There is a cheap hostería, T03522-422180, and campsite; an unpaved road, 12 km, branches off Ruta 9 at Santa Elena, 104 km north of Jesús María. To get there: Ciudad de Córdoba bus goes to/from Córdoba 3 times weekly, 4½ hours, US$5.

Southwest of Córdoba

A scenic road southwest from Villa Carlos Paz passes **Icho Cruz**, before climbing into the Sierra Grande and crossing the Pampa de Achala, a huge granite plateau at 2,000 m. At La Pampilla, 55 km from Villa Carlos Paz, is the entrance to the **Parque Nacional Quebrada del Condorito** ⓘ *administration at Resistencia 30, T433371, Villa Carlos Paz, www.parquesnacionales.gov.ar*, covering 40,000 ha of the Pampa de Achala and surrounding slopes. This is the easternmost habitat of the condor and an ideal flying school for the younger birds. Sightings are not guaranteed (Balcón Sur is a likely spot), but there's great trekking on the *pastizal de altura* (sierran grassland). Several camping places. Tours from Villa Carlos Paz. If you have your own car, park it at the NGO Fundación Cóndor (9 km before La Pampilla), beside a handicraft shop (1 km before La Pampilla) or at El Cóndor (7 km after La Pampilla). Ciudad de Córdoba and TAC buses can stop at La Pampilla on their way to Mina Clavero (from Villa Carlos Paz: 1 hr, US$2).

Mina Clavero This is a good centre, 40 km west of Córdoba, for exploring the high *sierra* and the Traslasierra Valley (*Phone code: 03544; Colour map 8, A3; Population: 6,800; Altitude: 915 m*). There is an intriguing museum, **Museo Rocsen** ⓘ *13 km south and about 5 km east of the village of Nono, T498218, www.museorocsen.org; daily 0900 till sunset, US$1, take a taxi, US$1.50.* The personal collection of Sr Bouchón, it is a wonderfully bizarre mix of subjects, including furniture, minerals, instruments, archaeology and animals ('by far the best natural history and cultural museum, a whole day is needed to visit', Federico Kirbus). There are many hotels, *hosterías hospedajes*, campsites and restaurants around Mina Clavero; others at Cura Brochero and Nono. **Tourist office** (with ATM) ⓘ *Plazoleta Merlo, T470171, www.minaclavero.gov.ar, open 0900 till very late.*

South from Córdoba

Alta Gracia (*Colour map 8, A3; Phone code: 03547; Population: 42,600; Altitude: 580 m*). Beside Lago Tajamar, Alta Gracia, 39 km southwest of Córdoba, has an interesting **Estancia Jesuítica Alta Gracia** (a UNESCO World Heritage Site) ⓘ *T421303, www.museoliniers.org.ar, winter Tue-Fri 0900-1300, 1500-1900, Sat-Sun 0930-1230, 1530-1830 (summer Tue-Fri 0900-2000, Sat-Sun opens 30 mins later), closed 1 Jan, 1 May, 25 Dec, US$0.65, 8 guided visits a day, phone in advance for English or French tours.* If you visit only one Jesuit estancia in the Cordoba region, make it this one. The main buildings of the *estancia* are situated around the plaza. The church, completed in 1762, with a baroque façade but no tower, is open for services only. To the north of the church is the former Residence, built round a cloister and housing the **Museo Casa del Virrey Liniers**. The **Museo Manuel de Falla** ⓘ *C Pellegrini 1001, T429292, 0900-2000 (in winter 0900-1900, except Mon 1400-1900), US$0.65S,* is where the Spanish composer spent his last years, 1942-1946. Beautiful views from the Gruta de la Virgen de Lourdes, 3 km west of town. Campsite at Alta Gracia; **tourist office**, Calle del Molino esq Padre Viera, *T0810-555 2582, www.altagracia.gov.ar.*

The **Bosque Alegre and Observatory** ⓘ *21 km northwest, Fri-Sun 1000-1300, 1500-1800 (Tue-Sun 1000-1300 in summer), visits are guided by astronomers; remise taxi US$5 plus waiting time,* afford good views over Córdoba, Alta Gracia and the Sierra Grande. Che Guevara grew up in Alta Gracia after his parents left Rosario to live in the more refreshing environment in the foothills of the Andes. He had started to suffer from asthma, which would plague him for the rest of his life. See page 180. **Museo Casa de Ernesto Che Guevara** ⓘ *in Villa Nydia, Avellaneda 501, T428579, summer daily 0900-2000, winter daily 0900-1900, Mon 1400-1900, US$1, from the Sierras Hotel, go north along C Vélez Sarsfield-Quintana and turn left on C Avellaneda, take bus 'Sarmiento'.* Che lived here between 1935-1937 and 1939-1943 before going to Córdoba: plenty of personal belongings from his childhood and youth, also the letter addressed to Fidel Castro where Che resigns from his position in Cuba. Texts in Spanish and other languages.

Villa General Belgrano This completely German town (*Phone code: 03546*) 85 km south of Córdoba, was founded by the surviving interned seamen from the *Graf Spee*, some of whom still live here. It is a good centre for excursions in the surrounding mountains. Genuine German cakes and smoked sausages are sold, there is an Oktoberfest, a *Fiesta de la Masa Vienesa* in Easter week, for lovers of Viennese-style pastries, and the *Fiesta del Chocolate Alpino* during July holidays. **Tourist office** ⓘ *Av Roca 168, T461215 (or free T125 within town), www.elsitiodelavilla.com, 0830-2030, helpful German- and English-speaking staff;* climb its tower for panoramic views. **La Cumbrecita** is a charming German village 30 km west, from where Champaquí can be climbed (detailed map essential).

South of La Cumbrecita is **Villa Alpina**, a remote resort set in the forested upper valley of Río de los Reartes, 38 km west, along a poor gravel road. This is the best base for a two- or three-day trek to the **Cerro Champaquí** (2,790 m), 19 km from the village, a rewarding hike not only for the superb mountainous scenery, but also for the chance to meet local inhabitants at the several *puestos* on the way to the summit. Expect to meet many other trekkers too in high season. Go with a local guide to avoid getting lost: information at tourist offices in Villa General Belgrano (see above) or La Cumbrecita, T481088, www.lacumbrecita.gov.ar.

Around Córdoba listings

For Sleeping and Eating price codes and other relevant information, see Essentials, pages 38-40.

Sleeping

Sierras de Córdoba *p121*

Villa Carlos Paz

Plenty of hotels in all price categories, most with pools and parking.

B Florida, Belgrano 45, T421905, www.florida hotelsrl.com.ar. Opposite bus station, 3 star, comfortable, a/c, with breakfast, pool.

B Los Sauces, Av San Martín 510, T421807, www.hotellossauces.com.ar. Another good value place next to the bus, good service, pool and restaurant, breakfast included, English spoken.

Camping ACA site, Av San Martín y Nahuel Huapi, T422132. Many others.

Cosquín

B La Puerta del Sol, Perón 820, T452045, lapuertadelsol@hotmail.com. A decent choice, pool, car hire, half board available, **A**.

D Siempreverde, Santa Fe 525, behind Plaza Molina, T450093, siempreverdehosteria@ hotmail.com. Spotless, with breakfast, welcoming and informative owner María Cristina, some rooms small, comfortable, gorgeous garden.

G pp **Residencial Ale**, Tucumán 809, T450232. Simple lodging with bath, quite central, good value, helpful.

Camping Several campsites in the area, best is **San Buenaventura**, 8 km west on Río Yuspe, in shady location, beaches, good places to swim.

North from Córdoba *p121*

La Falda

All 80 hotels are full in Dec-Feb.

C La Asturiana, Av Edén 835, T422923, hotellaasturiana@yahoo.com.ar. Simple, comfortable rooms, pool, superb breakfast.

D El Colonial, 9 de Julio 491, T421831. Early 50s décor in the reception and dining room, large pool.

Camping **Balneario 7 Cascadas**, next to the dam and the seven falls (west of town), T425808. Hot showers, electricity, food shop.

La Cumbre

F pp **Hostel La Cumbre**, Av San Martín 282, T03548-451368, www.hostellacumbre.com. Dorms, rooms for up to 6 and doubles (**C**). Family-owned, HI member, historic building with garden and pool, occasional *asados*, with breakfast, hot water, internet, kitchen, laundry, information and activities. Recommended.

Capilla del Monte

B Petit Sierras, Pueyrredón y Salta, T481667, petitsierras@capilladelmonte.com. Renovated hotel with comfortable rooms. The owners run the restaurant *A Fuego Lento* (**TT**), at the access to town (discounts and free transport for guests).

Camping **G** pp **Calabalumba**, 600 m north of the centre, T489601, camping@capilladelmonte. gov.ar, municipal site, shady with pool, hot water, US$3.50 pp. Rooms and *cabañas* for 4-6 people.

Mina Clavero

E pp **Oh La La!! Hostel**, Villanueva 1192, T472634, www.ohlalahostel.com.ar. Youth hostel (double rooms **C**), shared bathrooms, tourist information, pool and gardens, a/c, heating, internet.

South from Córdoba *p123*

Alta Gracia

AL El Potrerillo de Larreta, on the road to Los Paredones, 3 km from Alta Gracia, T423804, www.potrerillodelarreta.com. Old-fashioned, fabulous 1918 resort and country club in gorgeous gardens with wonderful views. Tennis courts, 18-hole golf course, swimming pool. Great service.

C-D Hispania, Vélez Sarsfield 57, T426555. Very comfortable, breakfast, excellent tapas, fine view of the sierras, Spanish owners. Recommended.

F pp **El Portal**, San Lorenzo 589, T423616, elportalbyb@hotmail.com. Well-kept bed and breakfast hostel in a large attractive house, with and without bath, 10 mins' walk from centre.

Camping Municipal site in Parque Federico Garcia Lorca, northwest of town, T155-77786.

Villa General Belgrano
Many *cabaña* complexes, chalet-style hotels, often family-oriented. Book ahead Jan-Feb, Jul and Easter.
B Berna, Vélez Sarsfield 86, T461097, www.bernahotel.com.ar. Next to the bus station, Swiss owners, good rooms with breakfast, large garden, pool (rates 50% higher in high season), spa.
B-C La Posada de Akasha, Los Manantiales 60, T462440, http://elsitiodelavilla.com/akasha. Extremely comfortable, spotless chalet-style house, with small pool, welcoming (low season rates).
F pp **El Rincón**, T461323, www.calamuchita net.com.ar/elrincon. The only hostel in town is beautifully set in dense forests and green clearings 10-min walk from bus terminal. Dorms, doubles or singles with bath (US$9-12) and camping (US$4 pp). US$2.30 for superb breakfasts. Meals on request US$5. 20% ISIC and HI discounts, half price for children under 16. In high season rates are 25% higher and the hostel is usually full. 10 min-walk from terminal. Recommended.

La Cumbrecita
Various hotels in **B-C** range.
C El Ceibo, T481060, elceibo@lacumbrecita.info. Neat rooms for 2-4, near the entrance to the town, TV, great views, access to the river.

Eating

North from Córdoba *p121*
La Falda
El Cristal, San Lorenzo 39. Very good cooking, where the locals eat.
Pachamama, Av Edén 127. Health food shop with cheap organic vegetable pies, or wholemeal pizzas and *empanadas*.

South from Córdoba *p123*
Alta Gracia
Morena, Av Sarmiento 413. Good, imaginative contemporary Argentine cuisine, in welcoming atmosphere of nice old house.
Alta Gracia Golf Club, Av Carlos Pellegrini 1000, T422922. Superb food in elegant surroundings in this charming neighbourhood golf club. Recommended.
Hispania, Urquiza 90. Same owners as *Hotel Hispania*, an excellent and moderately priced place serving fish and seafood, delicious desserts.
Leyendas, Bv Pellegrini 797, T429042. American-style, sport-inspired bar, cosy, good hamburgers and snacks, buzzing atmosphere. Recommended.

Activities and tours

North from Córdoba *p121*
La Falda
Tour operators **Turismo Talampaya**, T470412 or T15630384, turismotalampaya@yahoo.com.ar. Local full-day trips and excursions further afield, some by 4WD.

La Cumbre
Paragliding The world-renowned paragliding site of Cuchi Corral is 9 km west of La Cumbre on an unpaved road; **Escuela de Parapentes**, Ruta 38, Km 65, T422587, www.cordoba serrana.com.ar/parapente.htm. Operators include **Fechu**, T155- 74566, and **Toti López**, T494017. The tourist office in La Falda also has a list of instructors.

Transport

Sierras de Córdoba *p121*
Villa Carlos Paz
Bus A transport hub and there are frequent buses to **Buenos Aires** and other main destinations, as well as to the towns in the Punilla and Traslasierra valleys. **Calamuchita Valley**, **Sarmiento** bus to Alta Gracia, 1 hr, US$1.50, several daily. To **Córdoba**, several companies including **Ciudad de Córdoba**, and **Car-Cor** minibus services, 45 mins, US$1.40.

Cosquín
Bus **La Calera, Lumasa** and **Ciudad de Córdoba** run frequently along the Punilla valley and to Córdoba, 1½ hrs, US$3.50.

North from Córdoba *p121*
La Falda
Bus To **Córdoba** from La Falda US$3.50, **La Calera** and **Ciudad de Córdoba**, also minibuses. Daily buses to **Buenos Aires**.

Capilla del Monte
Bus To **Córdoba**, 3 hrs, US$5; to **Buenos Aires**, many companies daily.

Southwest of Córdoba *p122*
Mina Clavero
Bus To **Córdoba**, US$5-8 depending on route 3-6 hrs; **Buenos Aires**, several lines, US$32, 12 hrs; **Mendoza**, 9 hrs, US$20.

South from Córdoba *p123*
Alta Gracia
Bus **Córdoba**, US$1.50, every 15 mins, 1 hr; **Buenos Aires**, 10-11 hrs, US$30.

Villa General Belgrano
Bus To **Córdoba**, 1½-2 hrs, US$5; **Buenos Aires**, 10-11 hrs, US$30; **La Cumbrecita** with **Pájaro Blanco**, Av San Martín 105, T461709, every 2-4 hrs, 1 hr 20 mins, US$7 return.

Mendoza and around

→ *Phone code: 0261. Colour map 8, B2. Population: city 148,000. Altitude: 756 m.*

At the foot of the Andes, Mendoza is a dynamic and attractive city, surrounded by vineyards and *bodegas*. The city was colonized from Chile in 1561 and it played an important role in gaining independence from Spain when the Liberator José de San Martín set out to cross the Andes from here, to help in the liberation of Chile. Mendoza was completely destroyed by fire and earthquake in 1861, so today it is essentially a modern city of low buildings and wide avenues (as a precaution against earthquakes), thickly planted with trees and gardens.

Ins and outs

Information Main **tourist office** ⓘ *Garibaldi y San Martín, T420 1333,* very helpful, English and French spoken, open 0900-2100. Also at Las Heras y Mitre ⓘ *T4296298, open Mon-Sat, 0900-1330,1500-1900, Sun 0900-1330*; at the Municipalidad ⓘ *9 de Julio 500, T449 5185, Mon-Fri-0800-1330*; at bus station and at airport. All hand out maps and accommodation lists, with good value apartments for short lets, private lodgings in high season, also lists of bodegas and advice on buses. It's also worth checking these useful websites: www.ciudaddemendoza.gov.ar, www.turismo.mendoza.gov.ar, www.mendoza.gov.ar and www.welcometomendoza.com.ar.

Sights

In the centre of the city is the **Plaza Independencia**, in the middle of which is the small **Museo Municipal de Arte Moderno** ⓘ *T425 7279, Mon-Sat 0900-2100, Sun 1600-2100, US$1,* with temporary exhibitions, and on the east side, leafy streets lined with cafés. Among the other pleasant squares nearby is **Plaza España**, attractively tiled and with a mural illustrating the epic gaucho poem, *Martín Fierro*. **Plaza Pellegrini** (Avenida Alem y Av San Juan) is a beautiful small square where wedding photos are taken on Friday and Saturday nights, and a small antiques market. By the Plaza San Martín is the **Basílica de San Francisco** (España y Necochea), 1880, in which is the mausoleum of the family of General San Martín.

On the west side of the city is the great **Parque San Martín** ⓘ *0900-0200 daily, the entrance is 10 blocks west of the Plaza Independencia, reached by bus 110 'Zoo' from the centre, or the trolley from Sarmiento y 9 de Julio.* It is beautifully designed, with a famous zoo ⓘ *Tue-Sun 0900-1800, US$1.50*, many areas for sports and picnics, and a large lake, where regattas are held. There is also a good restaurant. The **Museo de Ciencias Naturales y Antropológicas** ⓘ *T428 7666, Tue-Sun 0830-1300, Tue-Fri 1400-1900, weekends 1500-1900,* has an ancient female mummy among its fossils and stuffed animals. There are views of the Andes rising in a blue-black perpendicular wall, topped off in winter with dazzling snow, into a china-blue sky. On a hill in the park is the **Cerro de la Gloria**, crowned by an astonishing monument to San Martín, with bas-reliefs depicting various episodes in the equipping of the Army of the Andes and the actual crossing. An hourly bus ('Oro Negro') runs to the top of the Cerro de la Gloria from the information office at the entrance, US$1, otherwise it's a 45-minute walk.

Mendoza's interesting history can be traced in two good museums: **Museo del Pasado Cuyano** ⓘ *Montevideo 544, T423 6031, Mon-Fri 0900-1230, US$0.50,* housed in a beautiful 1873 mansion, with lots of San Martín memorabilia and an exquisite Spanish 15th-century carved altarpiece; excellent tours. Also recommended is **Museo del Area Fundacional** ⓘ *Beltrán y Videla Castillo, T425 6927, Tue-Sat 0800-2000, Sun 1500-2000 US$0.70 (interesting underground chamber with glass floor, extra US$0.20), under 6s free, getting there: buses 1 (line 13) and 3 (line 112).* It has displays of the city pre-earthquake, with original foundations revealed, and the ruins of Jesuit church **San Francisco** opposite; informative free tour. The small **Acuario Municipal** (aquarium) ⓘ *underground at Buenos Aires e Ituzaingó, daily 0900-1230, 1500-2030, US$0.50,* is fun for kids.

N

200 metres

200 yards

Sleeping
1 Campo Base *B1*
2 Chimbas Hostel *C3*
3 Confluencia *A2*
4 Damajuana *C1*
5 Dam-sire *B3*
6 Gran Hotel Mendoza *B2*
7 Hostel Alamo *B1*
8 Hostel Internacional Mendoza *C2*
9 Mendoza Inn *C1*
10 Nutibara *C1*
11 Palace *A2*
12 Park Hyatt *B1*
13 Ritz *B1*
14 Savigliano Hostel *B3*
15 Winca's San Lorenzo *C2*
16 Winca's The Apart *A2*

Eating
1 Anna *A1*
2 Boccadoro *A1*
3 Don Otto *A2*
4 Facundo *B1*
5 Ferruccio Soppelsa *A2*
6 Francesco *B1*
7 Il Dolce *B2*
8 La Sal *C1*
9 Las Tinajas *B2*
10 Mesón Español *C2*
11 Mi Tierra *C1*
12 Montecatini *A1*
13 Mr Dog *A2*
14 Por Acá & Tres con Noventa *C1*
15 Quinta Norte *B1*
16 Sr Cheff *B2*
17 Vía Civit *B1*

In the nearby suburb of Luján de Cuyo, the city's best art gallery, with a small collection of Argentine paintings, is in the house where Fernando Fader painted decorative murals, at the **Museo Provincial de Bellas Artes, Casa de Fader** ⓘ *Carril San Martín 3651, Mayor Drummond, T496 0224, Tue-Fri 0800-1800, Sat-Sun 1400-1900. US$0.50, getting there: bus 200, 40 mins, in the gardens are sculptures.*

A few other recommended trips are to the pretty village of **Cacheuta**, 29 km west, with thermal springs, to **Potrerillos**, **Puenta del Inca** and **Los Penintentes** (see Mendoza to Chile below) and to **Villavicencio**, 47 km north, good walks and a restaurant in the mountains.

Wine tours Many bodegas welcome visitors and offer tastings without pressure to buy (grape harvesting season March/April). Rent a bicycle and make a day of it. If you've only time for one, though, make it **Bodega La Rural (San Felipe)** ⓘ *at Montecaseros 2625, Coquimbito, Maipú, T497 2013, www.bodegala rural.com.ar; getting there: bus 10 (subnumbers 171, 172, 173) from La Rioja y Garibaldi.* Small, traditional with a marvellous **Museo del Vino** ⓘ *Mon-Sat 0900-1700, Sun and holidays 1000-1400.* South of Maipú is **Carinae** ⓘ *Videla Aranda 2899, Cruz de Piedra, T499 0470, www.carinaevinos.com, 1000-1800.* French owners with an interest in astronomy as well as producing fine wines. (In Maipú itself, 15 km south of Mendoza, see the lovely plaza and eat good simple food at the Club Social.) In the suburb of Godoy Cruz are the beautiful **Bodegas Escorihuela** ⓘ *Belgrano 1188, T424 2282, www.escorihuela.com.ar, tours Mon-Fri 0930, 1030, 1130, 1230, 1430, 1530, getting there: bus 'T' G Cruz from centre 9 de Julio, Godoy Cruz, or bus 10 subnumbers 174, 200, from Rioja, or 40 from the Plaza*, has an excellent restaurant run by renowned Francis Mallman (see Eating, below).

In or near **Luján de Cuyo** ⓘ *T498 1912, www.lujandecuyo.gov.ar for tourist information*, there are several bodegas. Larger ones include **Norton** ⓘ *T490 9700 ext 4, www.norton.com.ar*, hourly visits Monday-Friday, by appointment only, **Catena Zapata** ⓘ *T413 1100, www.catena wines.com,* and **Séptima** ⓘ *T498 5164, www.bodegaseptima.com.ar, Mon-Fri 1000-1700,* with sunset tastings on Tuesday and Thursday in summer. **Tapiz** ⓘ *C Pedro Molina, Russell, T496 3433, www.tapiz.com/shop/index.html or www.newage-hotels.com*, is not only a winery, but also a 1890s house converted into a superb hotel (**L**) with restaurant to match. (See also **Cavas Wine Lodge**, below.) Also with an excellent restaurant (*La Bourgogne*) and *La Posada* hotel is **Carlos Pulenta-Vistalba** ⓘ *RS Peña 3135, Vistalba, T498 9400, www.carlospulentawines.com*. Famed for its Malbec is **Renacer** ⓘ *Brandsen 1863, Perdriel, T488 1247, www.bodegarenacer.com.ar*. Also in Perdriel is **Achával Ferrer** ⓘ *C Cobos, T155- 535565, www.achaval-ferrer.com*, a boutique bodega which has won many prizes. **El Lagar de Carmelo Patti** ⓘ *Av San Martín 2614, Mayor Drummond, T498 1379*, has tours and tastings led by the owner (Spanish only). For general information on wines of the region, visit: www.turismo.mendoza.gov.ar; www.vendimia.mendoza.gov.ar on the annual wine festival; www.welcometomendoza.com.ar (expat site, more than just wine); and www.welcome argentina.com/vino/index_i.html.

Mendoza and around listings

For Sleeping and Eating price codes and other relevant information, see Essentials, pages 38-40.

Sleeping

Mendoza and around *p126, map p127*
Breakfast is included, unless specified otherwise. Hostels advertise themselves at the bus terminal, offering free transfers and lots of extras; don't be pressurized into something you don't want. The **Hyatt** (www.mendoza.park.hyatt.com) and **NH** (www.nh-hotels.com) chains have good hotels in the city. Also **Hostel Suites Mendoza**, Patricias Mendocinas 1532 (at Av Heras), T423 7018, www.hostelsuites.com.

LL Cavas Wine Lodge, Costaflores, Alto Agrelo, Luján de Cuyo, T410 6927, www.cavaswine lodge.com. A pricey but heavenly experience, ideal for a romantic and wonderfully relaxing stay. 14 spacious rooms in a beautifully restored rural mansion, with restaurant and spa. Each room has a fireplace and terrace, swimming pool, wonderful views. Highly recommended.

AL Parador del Angel, 100m from main plaza, Chacras de Coria, Luján de Cuyo, T496 2201, www.paradordelangel.com.ar. Restored 100-year old house, tastefully decorated, very relaxing, gardens, pool, owner is an experienced mountain climber.

A Gran Hotel Mendoza, España 1210 y Espejo, T405 1405, www.hotelmendoza.com. Spacious rooms, stylish decor, central, family rooms too, overpriced, but splendid views from its small restaurant.

A Nutibara, Mitre 867, T429 5428, www.nutibara.com.ar. Welcoming, eclectic decor if a bit outdated, lovely pool in a leafy patio, comfortable rooms, quiet, central. Recommended.

A Ritz, Perú 1008, T423 5115, www.ritzhotelmendoza.com.ar. Reliable, central but quiet location, excellent service. Recommended.

B Palace, Las Heras 70, T/F423 4200, hpalace@infovia.com.ar. A lovely quiet, central place, modern rooms, good value, Italian owned, popular restaurant.

C Confluencia, España 1512, T429 0430, www.hostalconfluencia.com.ar. Central, quiet, tidy, rooms for 2, 3 or 4 (**E** pp), with bath (not en suite) and breakfast, internet, cooking facilities, helpful, good choice.

C-D Hostel Alamo, Necochea 740, T429 5565, www.hostelalamo.com. Doubles rooms and shared rooms (**F** pp), easy-going hostel, helpful, safe, kitchen, internet, TV and DVDs, a good choice.

D Winca's San Lorenzo, San Lorenzo 19, sanlorenzo@wincashostel.com.ar, www.wincas hostel.com.ar. Nice, big rooms, **F** per bed, central, garden, internet, Spanish lessons, safe, pool. Also has **The Apart** apartments at Rioja 1738, T420 4066, apart@ wincashostel.com.ar, also **D**. Both recommended.

D-F Savigliano Hostel, Pedro Palacios 944, T423 7746, www.savigliano.com.ar. Rooms with bath, without (**E**) and dorms (**F**), kitchen, opposite bus station, internet, kitchen facilities, washing machine, luggage stored, helpful, tours arranged.

E pp **Damajuana**, Arístides Villanueva 282, T425 5858, www.damajuanahostel.com.ar. A great hostel, very comfortable stylish dorms also double rooms (**C**), central, pool in lovely garden, restaurant. Recommended.

F pp **Campo Base**, Mitre 946, T429 0707, www.hostelcampobase.com.ar. A lively place, discounts for HI members, cramped rooms, but lots of parties and barbecues, popular with mountain climbers, owned by expert mountain guide Roger Cangiani, who also runs a travel agency in town.

F pp **Chimbas Hostel**, Cobos 92 y Acceso Este , T431 4191, www.chimbashostel.com.ar. Rooms for 2 (**D**) to 8, shared bath, close to bus station (phone in advance for pick-up), 20 mins walk to centre, kitchen, internet and Wi-Fi, swimming pool, gym, pleasant.

F pp **Dam-sire**, Viamonte 410, San José Guaymallén, T431 5142, 5 mins from terminal. Family run, spotless, breakfast included.

F pp **Hostel Internacional Mendoza**, España 343, T424 0018, www.hostelmendoza.net. The most comfortable hostel, HI discount, part of the

Campo Base group, short walk south of the plaza, small rooms with bath, warm atmosphere, great food, barbecues on Fri, huge range of excursions. Warmly recommended.
F pp **Mendoza Inn**, Arístides Villanueva 470, T420 2486, www.mendozahostel.com. One of several hostels run by Campo Base (see below), in the lively bar area, basic, large garden that separates some rooms at the back from their bathrooms.
Camping Camping Suizo, Av Champagnat, 9½ km from city, T444 1991, modern, shady, with pool, barbecues, hot showers. Recommended. **Churrasqueras del Parque** in centre of Parque General San Martin, at Bajada del Cerro, T428 8397, 156-664859, www.complejopilmayken.com.ar. There are 2 other sites at El Challao, 6 km west of the city centre, reached by Bus 110 (El Challao) leaving hourly from C Rioja. **Saucelandia**, at Guaymallén, 9 km east, Tirasso s/n, T451 1409. Take insect repellent.

Eating

Mendoza and around *p126, map p127*
There are many open-air cafés for lunch on Peatonal Sarmiento and restaurants around Las Heras. The atmospheric indoor market on Las Heras has cheap, delicious pizza, *parrilla* and pasta. Open late.
TTT **1884 Francis Mallman**, Bodega Escorihuela, Belgrano 1188, Godoy Cruz, T424 2698. The place to go for a really special dinner. Mallman is one of the country's great chefs, exotic and imaginative menu. Open for lunch and dinner, but reservation is advisable. Highly recommended.
TT **Boccadoro**, Mitre 1976. *Parrilla*, popular, locally renowned.
TT **Casa de Campo**, Urquiza 1516, Coquimbito, T481 1605. Delicious food, with local specialities including rabbit and suckling pig (*lechón*), also good local wine. Highly recommended.
TT **Facundo**, Sarmiento 641, T420 2866. Good modern *parrilla*, lots of other choices including Italian, good salad bar.
TT **Francesco**, Chile 1268, T425 3912. Smart old town house with a wonderful garden, excellent Italian food, prepared by the Barbera family, choose from over 350 different wines.
TT **La Sal**, Belgrano 1069. Stylish, creative menu that changes with the seasons, live music, superb.
TT **Las Tinajas**, Lavalle 38, T429 1174, www.lastinajas.com. Large buffet-style/all-you-can-eat at very reasonable prices, open 1200-2400, wide selection of good quality food, pastas, grills, Chinese, desserts and so on. Cheap wine, too.
TT **Mesón Español**, Montevideo 244. Spanish food, including great paella, live music at weekends. Cheap lunch menus.
TT **Mi Tierra**, Mitre y San Lorenzo. Recommended for wine tasting with expert advice, elegantly restored 1890s house, each room devoted to a different *bodega*: Norton, Catena Zapata, Chandon and Terrazas de los Andes. Limited menu with traditionally cooked meat-based food.
TT **Montecatini**, Gral Paz 370. Good Italian food, seafood and *parrilla*, more tourist oriented, popular with families.
TT **Sr Cheff**, Primitivo de la Reta 1071. Long-established, good *parrilla* and fish.
T **Anna**, Av Juan B Justo 161, T425 1818. One of the most attractive restaurants in town, informal, French-owned, very welcoming, good food and drink, French and Italian flavours, open for lunch and dinner, excellent value, open till late. Recommended.
T **Don Otto**, Las Heras 242. Cheap and cheerful, small and central place.
T **Il Dolce**, Sarmiento 81. Good vegetarian options, inexpensive swet lunches and dinners.
T **Quinta Norte**, Mitre y Espejo. Attractively set in an old family mansion, this is a great informal place for good cheap meals that come in generous portions. Very good service.
T **Vía Civit**, Emilio Civit 277. For first-class sandwiches, tarts and pastries in a relaxed, elegant traditional bakery. Open from breakfast onwards.
Calle Arístides Villanueva, the extension of Colón heading west, has excellent restaurants and bars (as well as hostels).
TT **Por Acá**, Arístides Villanueva 557. Cosy bohemian living room for pizzas and drinks till late, popular, noisy.
T **3 90 (Tres con Noventa)**, Arístides Villanueva 451. Delicious pastas, incredibly cheap, studenty, warm cosy atmosphere. Highly recommended.
Ferruccio Soppelsa, Las Heras y España. The best place for ice cream (even wine flavours!). Recommended.

Liverpool, San Martín y Rivadavia. Pub food, sandwiches, burgers, Beatles memorabilia and a European football matches on the screen.
Mr Dog, Av Las Heras y P Mendocinas, popular fastfood chain, better than most.

❂ Festivals and events

Mendoza and around *p126, map p127*
The riotous wine harvesting festival, **Fiesta de la Vendimia**, is held in the amphitheatre of the Parque San Martín from **mid-Feb to mid-Mar**. Local wine festivals start in mid-Jan. A parallel event is the less-promoted but equally entertaining **Gay Vendimia Festival**, featuring parties, shows and the crowning of the Festival Queen. Hotels fill up fast and prices rise; also in Jul (the ski season) and around **21 Sep** (the **spring festival**).

O Shopping

Mendoza and around *p126, map p127*
Handicrafts The main shopping area is along San Martín and Las Heras, with good clothes, souvenir, leather and handicraft shops as well as vast sports emporia. **Mercado Artesanal**, San Martín 1133, 0830-1930 daily, for traditional leather, baskets, weaving; also weekend market on Plaza Independencia. Cheap shops include: **El Turista**, Las Heras 351, and **Las Viñas**, Las Heras 399. For higher quality head to **Raices**, España 1092, just off Peatonal Sarmiento. Good choice of wines at *vinotecas*, eg **Central**, Mitre y Espejo, T459 0658, www.centralvinoteca.com, English spoken; **Marcelino**, T Benegas y M Zapata, T429 3648, Mon-Fri, offers tasting courses; **Puracepa**, Av Sarmiento 644, T423 8282, English spoken, stocks a huge range; **The Vines**, Espejo 567, T438 1031, www.vinesofmendoza.com, tasteful, pricey, wine-tasting and shopping experience in a lovely restored house, presenting the best of the region's boutique bodegas, international orders only.
Supermarkets **Super Vea**, San Martín y Santiago del Estero, **Metro**, Colón 324.

▲ Activities and tours

Mendoza and around *p126, map p127*
Climbing Information from tourist office.
Club Andinista, F L Beltrán 357, Guaymallén, T431 9870, www.clubandinista.com.ar. See page 136 for Aconcagua.
Whitewater rafting Popular on the Río Mendoza; ask agencies for details, eg **Ríos Andinos**, Sarmiento 721, T429 5030, www.riosandinos.com, also offers horse riding and some rock climbing.

Tour operators

Many agencies, especially on Paseo Sarmiento, run trekking, riding and rafting expeditions, as well as traditional tours to Alta Montaña, US$25, and bodegas, US$10.
Asatej, Peatonal Sarmiento 223, T429 0029, mendoza@asatej.com.ar. Very helpful, trips, cheap travel deals.
Campo Base, Peatonal Sarmiento 231, T425 5511, www.mt-aconcagua.com. The same company that owns the youth hostels (see above) runs good expeditions, including to Aconcagua. Expert guide Roger Cangiani leads trips and gives advice on permits.
The Grapevine, Garibaldi 57, of 101, T429 7522, www.thegrapevine-winetours.com. British and Irish owned, organizes personalised tours in the wine region, including flights combined with visits and lunch. They also have their own wine club meetings and publish a very informative free magazine available everywhere.
Huentata, Las Heras 699, loc 7, T425 7444, www.huentata.com.ar. Conventional tours, plus Villavicencio, Cañon del Atuel, horse riding, Aconcagua. Recommended.
Inka Expediciones, Juan B Justo 343, T425 0871, www.inka.com.ar. Climbing expeditions, including Aconcagua, highly professional, fixed departure dates, mules for hire.
Mancagua, España 967, T429 7398, www.mancaguaviajes.com.ar. Many options in wine tours, combining different bodegas with optional lunches where wine is included. Recommended.
Mendoza Viajes Peatonal Sarmiento 129, T461 0210. Imaginative tours in comfortable coaches, professional, cheap deals available.
Postales del Plata, Tabanera s/n, Colonia Las Rosas, Tunayán (some 80 km south of Mendoza), T429 6210, www.postalesdelplata.com. Specializes in wine tours in Mendoza and Chile, cultural tours, fly fishing, has its own very good lodges at Chacras de Coria and Valle de Uco.
Trekking Travel, Adolfo Calle 4171, Villa Nueva, Guaymallén, T421 0450, www.trekking-travel.com.ar. For horse riding, mountain biking, trekking, wine tours, photographic tours and more.

Transport

Mendoza and around *p126, map p127*

Air El Plumerillo airport, 8 km north of centre, T430 7837, has a bank, tourist information, shops, restaurant and *locutorio*, but no left luggage. Reached from the centre by bus No 60 (subnumber 68) from Alem y Salta, every hour at 35 mins past the hour, 40 mins journey; make sure there is an 'Aeropuerto' sign on the front window. Taxi to/from centre US$7. Daily flights to **Buenos Aires**: 1 hr 50 mins, **AR** only. **AR/Austral** to **Córdoba**. **LAN** to **Santiago**.

Bus Most local services have 2 numbers, a general number and a 'subnumber' in brackets which indicates the specific route. Buses within and near the city are slightly cheaper with **Red Bus** cards with a magnetic strip (US$1), which are topped up, like a phone card. They are soldat designated outlets, where you can also top up; some buses have top-up machines, too. There are 2 trolley bus routes, red and blue, US$0.25.

Long distance The huge bus terminal is on the east side of Av Videla, 15 mins' walk from centre (go via Av Alem, which has pedestrian tunnel), with shops, post office, *locutorio*, tourist information and supermarket (open till 2130), a good café, left luggage lockers and toilets (between platforms 38 and 39). It's not a place to linger at night. To **Buenos Aires**, 13-17 hrs, US$43-63, many companies including **Andesmar**, **La Estrella**, **Sendas** (*coche-cama* with meals and wine). To **Bariloche**, **Andesmar** one daily, US$54-68, 19 hrs, book well ahead (alternatively **TAC** go to Neuquén and change). To **Córdoba**, 9-12 hrs, US$29-34, several companies. To **San Rafael**, many daily 3½ hrs, US$6-10. To/from **San Juan**, **Andesmar**, and others, US$7-10, 2-2½ hrs. To **Tucumán**, US$46-62, 13-14 hrs, **Andesmar**, **Autotransportes Mendoza**, **TAC**, all via San Juan, **La Rioja** (US$22-40, 6-7 hrs), and **Catamarca** 10 hrs, US$35-40. To **Salta**, via Tucumán, several companies daily, US$63, 16-18 hrs. To **Uspallata**, 5 a day with **Expreso Uspallata**, US$7, 2¼ hrs. To **Potrerillos**, 1 hr, US$2.50.

Transport to Santiago, Chile Minibuses (US$20-25, 6-7 hrs) run by **Chi-Ar**, **Nevada** and **Radio Móvil** daily leave when they have 10 passengers. When booking, ensure that the receipt states that you will be picked up and dropped at your hotel; if not you will be dropped at the bus station. Buses to Santiago daily, 10 companies, **Chile Bus**, **Cata** and **Tas Choapa** have been recommended, **Ahumada** has a *coche cama* at 0845. Most buses are comfortable, with similar rates and journey times to minibuses, those with a/c and hostess service (includes breakfast) charge more, worth it when crossing the border as waiting time can be several hours. Almost all these companies also go daily to **Viña del Mar** and **Valparaíso**. Information at Mendoza bus terminal: shop around. Book at least 1 day ahead. Passport required, tourist cards given on bus. The ride is spectacular. If you want to return, it's cheaper to buy an undated return ticket Santiago-Mendoza.

Other International buses To **La Serena**, 3 a week, 12-16 hrs, US$30, **Covalle, Cata** and others. To **Lima**, 3-4 a week, **El Rápido**, and **Ormeño**, T431 4913, 2½ days.

Directory

Mendoza and around *p126, map p127*

Airline offices Aerolíneas Argentinas/ **Austral**, Peatonal Sarmiento 82, T420 4100. **LAN**, Av España 1002, T0810-999 9526. **Banks** Many ATMs on and around Plaza San Martín taking all cards. Many *casas de cambio* along San Martín, corner of Espejo/Catamarca. Most open till 2000 Mon-Fri, and some open Sat morning. **Bike rental** **Cycles El Túnel**, at the exit of the subway coming from the bus terminal. Buys and sells cycles, also repairs. **Indiana Aventuras**, Espejo 65, T429 0002, info@indianaventuras.com.ar. **Adventure World**, Sarmiento 231, T429 0206. Winers and Bikes Rental Bikes, Urquiza 2288, Coquimbito, Maipú, T497 4067, www.delegation.ca/rentalbikes/. Good. **Cultural centres** Alianza Francesa, Chile 1754, T423 4614, www.alianzafrancesamendoza.org. **Instituto Cultural Argentino-Norteamericano**, Chile 987, T423-6271, Dirección@amicana.com. **Instituto Cuyano de Cultura Hispánica** (Spain), Villanueva 389, T423 6455. **Goethe Institut**, Av San Martín 407, T423 4990, goetheana@ speedy.com.ar, Mon-Fri, 0800-1200, 1600-2230, German newspapers, Spanish classes, very good. **Internet** Several internet cafés in the centre and some *locutorios*: a huge one on San Martín y Garibaldi, with internet. **Language schools** Intercultural –

Mendoza, República de Syria 241, T429 0269, www.spanishcourses.com.ar. **Medical facilities** Central hospital near bus terminal at Alem y Salta, T420 0600. **Lagomaggiore**, public general hospital (with good reputation) at Timoteo Gordillo s/n, T425 9700. **Hospital Materno y Infantil Humberto Notti**, Bandera de los Andes 2683, T445 0045. Medical emergencies T428 0000. **Post Office** San Martín y Colón, T429 0848, Mon-Fri 0800-2000, Sat 1000-1300. **Useful addresses** ACA, Av San Martín 985, T420 1901, and Av Bandera de los Andes y Gdor Videla, T431 3510. **Migraciones**, San Martín 1859, T424 3512.

South of Mendoza

San Rafael ➔ *Phone code: 02627. Colour map 8, B2. Population: 107,000.*

San Rafael, 236 km south of Mendoza, is a tranquil, leafy small town in the heart of fertile land which is irrigated by snow melt from the Andes to produce fine wines and fruit. A road runs west over El Pehuenche pass to Talca (Chile). Several bodegas can be visited: the impressive champagnerie at **Bianchi** ⓘ *T422 046 www.vbianchi.com*. Some 5 km west on Hpólito Yrigoyen, is the more intimate **Jean Rivier** ⓘ *H Yrigoyen 2385, T432675, bodega@jrivier.com*. Excellent wine. A small but interesting **natural history museum** ⓘ *Tue-Sun 0800-2000, free; Iselin bus along Av JA Balloffet*, is 6 km southeast of town at Isla Río Diamante. **Tourist office** ⓘ *Av H Yrigoyen y Balloffet, T437860, www.sanrafaelturismo.gov.ar*.

Southwest of San Rafael, 35 km, is the **Cañon de Atuel**, a spectacular gorge 20 km long with strange polychrome rock formations. It is famous as a rafting centre. Daily buses, *Iselin* (T435998), go to the Valle Grande dam at the near end of the canyon, returning in the evening, US$2. Here there is plenty of accommodation, campsites, river rafting and horse riding. San Rafael tour operators run day tours. **Raffeish** ⓘ *T15-409089, www.raffeish.com.ar*. Recommended as most professional rafting company. There is no public transport through the gorge to El Nihuel.

Las Leñas ➔ *Altitude: 2,250 m. Ski season: mid-Jun to end-Oct. T02627-471100, www.laslenas.com.*

At 182 km southwest of San Rafael, RN40 heads west into the Andes, and from it the road to the famous, chic (ie expensive) and internationally renowned ski resort of Las Leñas. It passes **Los Molles**, at Km 30, where there is simple accommodation: Further along the Las Leñas road is the **Pozo de las Animas**, two natural pits filled with water where the wind makes a ghostly wail, hence the name (Well of the Spirits). At the end of Valle Los Molles is Las Leñas, in a spectacular setting with excellent skiing over 64 km on 27 pistes, with a maximum drop of 1,200 m. It offers many summer adventure activities, too. Beyond Las Leñas the road continues into Valle Hermoso, accessible December to March only.

Malargüe ➔ *Phone code: 02627. Colour map 8, B2. Population: 18,100.*

Further south on Ruta 40, Malargüe is developing as a centre for hiking and horse riding in stunning open landscape nearby. Most remarkable, **La Payunia Reserve**, 208 km south, has vast grasslands and stark volcanoes where thousands of guanacos roam, best enjoyed on horseback. **Laguna Llancanelo**, 75 km southeast, is filled with a great variety of birdlife in spring, when Chilean flamingos come to nest. In addition, **Caverna de las Brujas** has extraordinary underground cave formations. Helpful **tourist office** on the main street (right hand side as you drive in from north), next to conference centre, *T471659 (open 0800-2300)*.

South of Mendoza listings

For Sleeping and Eating price codes and other relevant information, see Essentials, pages 38-40.

Sleeping

San Rafael *p133*

B Family Inn, Av Yrigoyen 5501, T431451, www.familyinnsanrafael.com.ar. Modern roadside hotel, convenient, next to the airport, spacious, functional, neat gardens, pool, restaurant and gym.

B Kalton, Yrigoyen 120, T430047, www.kalton hotel.com. Charming, long-established, excellent service, comfortable, parking. Highly recommended.

B Regine, Independencia 623, T430274, www.reginehotel.com.ar. Delightful, rustic, pool in garden, popular with older guests, relaxing, good value. Also has a *quincho* for *parrillas*.

C Rex, H Yrirgoyen 56, T422177, www.hotelrex.com.ar. Central, large comfortable rooms, heating, good value (**D** low season). Recommended.

C-D Tonin, Pellegrini 330, T422499, www.sanrafael-tour.com/tonin. A lovely quiet family-run place, modern spacious rooms, TV, next to the plaza.

E Tierrasoles Hostel, Alsina 245, T433449, www.tierrasoles.com.ar. HI member. Close to busstation, lively, welcoming, double and basic dorms, shared bath; activities organized, bikes for hire.

Camping El Parador, in the park on Isla Río Diamante, 5 km southeast, T420492. More sites at Valle Grande in the Cañón del Atuel.

Las Leñas *p133*

There are several plush hotels, all **LL-AL**, and most with pool, including **Piscis** (ask for T2700), **Aries** (T2000), **Virgo** (T2800), **Villa Capricornio** (T1380, apart-hotel), and **Geminis-Delphos** (T2400, apart-hotel), and a disco, shop renting equipment and several restaurants. For cheaper accommodation stay in Los Molles or Malargüe.

Los Molles

Cheaper options than Las Leñas, but all basic.

B Hotel Termas Lahuen-Có, T499700. The best, dating from 1930s, and now rather kitsch, with thermal baths, meals.

Malargüe *p133*

Hotels issue 50% discount for Las Leñas lift pass, minimum 2 nights' stay. Accommodation is not of a high standard, with some very poor *cabañas*.

A Microhotel Inn, Ruta 40 Norte (north of centre), T472300, www.microtelinn.com.ar. The best, with comfortable rooms and well-equipped cabins, functional, heated pool, sauna, large restaurant.

B Río Grande, Ruta 40 Norte (north of centre), T471589, hotelriogrande@infovia.com.ar. Good value, renovated rooms.

D La Posta, San Martín 646, T472079, laposta_malargue@yahoo.com.ar. Welcoming wood-lined rooms, also has *parrilla* at Roca 374.

E-F pp **Campo Base**, Telles Meneses 897, T471534, www.malarguehostel.com. Lively, basic dorms and doubles, shared bath, trips arranged.

F pp **Internacional**, Prol Constitución Nacional (Finca No65), 2 blocks from R40 Norte, south of centre, T470391, www.hostelmalargue.net. Eco-hostel in rural surroundings, on dairy farm with organic fruit and veg, good meals, basic, comfortable dorms and rooms (**D**), travel agency.

Eating

San Rafael *p133*

¶¶ La Fusta, Yrigoyen 538. Smart restaurant, serving a good value *parrilla* and delicious Italian food.

Activities and tours

Malargüe *p133*

The tourist office can arrange indepedent visits to Llancanelo and La Payunia. Good tours with **Choique**, Av San Martín y Rodríguez, T470391, www.choique.net, and **Karen Travel**, San Martín 54, T470342, www.karen travel.com.ar. Horse riding, Cueva de las Brujas, and nearby reserves.

Horse riding **Kiñe**, T02627-155 88635, www.kinie.com.ar. Horse riding in La Payunia Reserve and lodging at the **C** pp **Puesto La Agüita**, a lovely country house offering full-board. Recommended.

Rafting **Tero Aventura**, T156-00182, teroaventura@hotmail.com. Rafting and inflatable trips on Ríos Malargüe and Atuel, run by Frenchman Sylvain Maisonneuve.

Transport

San Rafael *p133*

Bus To **Mendoza**, 3-3½ hrs, US$6-10; **Neuquén**, US$26-30, 8-9 hrs.

Las Leñas *p133*

Bus From **Buenos Aires** with **Andesmar**, US$76-93, 16 hrs, not daily. From **Mendoza**, with change of bus in **San Rafael**, Tue, Thu 0600, **Iselín**, T02627-424236 (San Rafael)/471286 (Malargüe), arrives Las Leñas 1430, 1500 returns to Mendoza. From San Rafael, 1 a day with **Iselín**, US$15, and buses from **Malargüe** airport and bus station.

Malargüe *p133*

Air Regular flights **Buenos Aires** to Malargüe airport (T471600), on southern edge of town, more charter flights in the skiing season.

Bus Terminal at Aldao y Beltrán. Daily from Mendoza with **Expreso Uspallata, Iselín/CATA**, 6 hrs via **San Rafael**, minibuses direct with **Transporte Viento Sur**, 4½ hrs, U$12.

Mendoza to Chile

The route to Chile is sometimes blocked by snow in winter: if travelling by car in June-October enquire about road conditions from *ACA* in Mendoza (T431 3510). Driving without snow chains and a shovel is prohibited between Uspallata and the border, but this can be resolved in a friendly way with border police. *ACA* and Chilean Automobile Club sell, but do not rent, chains.

Potrerillos and Uspallata → *Phone code: 02624. Colour map 8, A1.*

Ruta 7 is the only route for motorists to the Chilean border, via **Potrerillos** and **Uspallata**. Leave the city south by Avenida J Vicente Zapata, Access Ruta 7, leading to Ruta 40. Follow signs to Potrerillos, Uspallata and Chile. From Mendoza to the Chilean border is 204 km. The construction of a dam has forced a detour around **Cacheuta**, though it's worth a side trip for its relaxing hot springs, and very comfortable hotel (see below).

Potrerillos is a pretty village for horse riding, walking and rafting. In summer you can hike from Potrerillos to Vallecitos over two days, passing from desert steppe to scenic peaks. **Vallecitos** (season July-September, T488810, www.skivallecitos.com) is a tiny ski resort 21 km from Potrerillos (see below) along a winding *ripio* road. It has a basic ski-lodge, ski school and snack bar. **Refugio San Bernardo** (T154-183857), cosy place run by mountain guides; the area is used as a base camp by climbers acclimatising and training before attempting Aconcagua. **Los Penitentes** is a much better ski resort, 165 km west of Mendoza, on the road to Chile, named after its majestic mass of pinnacled rocks, looking like a horde of cowled monks. Good skiing on 28 pistes, very reasonably priced, with few people on slopes. Horse treks go to Los Pentientes. In the Quebrada Vargas, south of the ski resort, is a small hut, near water, at 3,231 m, which serves as the base for the hike up Cerro Penitentes (4,351 m), the standard acclimatization climb for Aconcagua. There is a good trail to the hut; no fees charged. For **Puente del Inca** see below.

Another recommended stopping point is the picturesque village of **Uspallata**, 52 km from Potrerillos. From here you can explore the mysterious white, egg-shaped domes of Las Bóvedas (2 km on RN39 north; entry US$0.30), built by the Huarpe Indians under the Jesuits to melt silver, where there is a small, interesting museum. The RN39 leads north to Barreal and Calingasta (see page 140), unpaved for its first part, rough and tricky when the snow melts and floods it in summer. The tourist office in Uspallata keeps unreliable hours. There are two food shops, bakeries, a post office and a Shell station with motel, restaurant, shop and *locutorio* open 0900-2200.

Puente del Inca → *Colour map 8, B2. Altitude: 2,718 m.*

The road that leads from Uspallata to cross the border to Chile is one of the most dramatic in Argentina, climbing through a gorge of richly coloured rock. Surrounded by mountains of great grandeur, Puente del Inca, 72 km west of Uspallata, is a good base for trekking or exploring on horseback. The natural bridge after which the place is named is one of the wonders of South America. Bright ochre yellow, it crosses the Río Mendoza at a height of 19 m, has a span of 21 m, and is 27 m wide, and seems to have been formed by sulphur- bearing hot springs. The bridge itself cannot be crossed. There are the remains of a thermal bath complex at the river just under the bridge. Horse treks go to Los Penitentes. Los Horcones, the Argentine customs post, is 1 km west: from here you can visit the green lake of Laguna los Horcones: follow signs to Parque Provincial Aconcagua, 2 km, where there is a Ranger station, excellent views of Aconcagua, especially morning; free camping, open climbing season only. From here a trail continues to the Plaza de Mulas base camp.

Aconcagua ➔ *Colour map 8, B1. Altitude: 6,959 m.*

West of Puente del Inca on the right, there is a good view of Aconcagua, the highest peak in the Americas, sharply silhouetted against the blue sky. In 1985, a complete Inca mummy was discovered at 5,300 m on the mountain. The best time for climbing Aconcagua is from end-December to February. For camping, trekking or climbing it is first necessary to obtain a **permit**: These have five price ranges: for summer (high, mid or low season) and winter (April and May to November). Permits allow climbing, 20 days from the date it is stamped at the park entrance, long treks, 7 days, and short treks, 3 days. In summer, a permit to climb Aconcagua costs from US$155 to US$465, depending on season. In winter, climbing costs US$387 (April) and US$515 (May-November). Seven-day treks are US$67-103 (summer), US$85-155 winter; short treks cost US$46-54 (Summer), US$38-76 (winter). A day trek costs US$19 in summer and US$15.50 in winter. Treks may not go beyond base camps. Permits must be bought, in person only at **Centro de Visitantes (Subsecretaría de Turismo)** ⓘ *Av San Martín 1143, p 1, Mendoza.* A day trek permit may also be bought at the Río Horcones Visitors Centre (see next paragraph). Places selling the permits, and fees, may change, so it's vital to check the official website: www.aconcagua.mendoza.gov.ar/.

There are two access routes: Río Horcones and Río Vacas, which lead to the two main base camps, Plaza de Mulas and Plaza Argentina respectively. Río Horcones starts a few kilometres from Puente del Inca, at the Horcones ranger station. About 80% of climbers use this route. From here you can go to Plaza de Mulas (4,370 m) for the North Face, or Plaza Francia (4,200 m) for the South Face. The intermediate camp for either is Confluencia (3,300 m), four hours from Horcones. Río Vacas is the access for those wishing to climb the Polish Glacier. The Plaza Argentina base camp (200 m) is three hours from Horcones and the intermediate camps are Pampa de Leñas and Casa de Piedra. From Puente del Inca, mules are available (list at the **Dirección de Recursos Naturales Renovables** ⓘ *Parque Gral San Martín, Mendoza*, about US$120 per day for 60 kg of gear). This only takes you to Plaza de Mulas, near which is the highest hotel in the world (see below) and an accident prevention and medical assistance service (climbing season only); crowded in summer. The same service is offered at Plaza Argentina in high season (US$240 per day for mule 60 kg load). Climbers should make use of this service to check for early symptoms of mountain sickness and oedema. Take a tent able to withstand 100 mph/160 kph winds, and clothing and sleeping gear for temperatures below -40°C. Allow at least 8-10 days for acclimatization at lower altitudes before attempting the summit (four days from Plaza de Mulas). Hotel *Plaza de Mulas*, **AL** pp full board, **B** without meals, good food, information, medical treatment, recommended, also camping area; closed in winter.

In Mendoza you can book *refugio* reservations and programmes, which include trekking, or climbing to the summit, with all equipment and accommodation or camping included (see Tour operators, above). Try to agree all contract terms in advance, such as the number of members of a group, so that they aren't changed before your expedition leaves. Treks and climbs are also organized by the famous climber **Sr Fernando Grajales** ⓘ *Moreno 898, 5500 Mendoza, T1-800-516 6962, www.grajales.net (or T421 4330 and ask for Eduardo Ibarra at Hotel*

Plaza de Mulas for further information), and by **Roger Cangiani** of Campo Base (see Mendoza Activities and tours). Near the Cementerio is **Los Puquios** ⓘ *T461-317603*, camping, mules, guides. Further information from **Centro de Visitantes (Subsecretaría de Turismo)** (see also under Mendoza, www.mendoza.gov.ar).

Border with Chile

The road to the Chilean border, fully paved, goes through the 3.2-km Cristo Redentor toll road tunnel to Chile (open 24 hours; US$3 for cars, cyclists are not allowed to ride through, ask the officials to help you get a lift). The last settlement before the tunnel is tiny forlorn **Las Cuevas**, 16 km from Puente del Inca, with hostel accommodation, a basic café and a *kiosko*. In summer you can take the old road over La Cumbre pass to the statue of El Cristo Redentor (Christ the Redeemer), an 8-m statue erected jointly by Chile and Argentina in 1904 to celebrate the settlement of their boundary dispute. Take an all day excursion from Mendoza, drive in a 4WD, after snow has melted, or walk from Las Cuevas (4½ hours up, two hours down – only to be attempted by the fit, in good weather). **Expreso Uspallata** runs buses to Mendoza.

The Chilean border is beyond Las Cuevas, but all Argentine entry and exit formalities for cars and buses are dealt with at the Argentine customs post, Ingeniero Roque Carranza at Laguna Los Horcones, 2 km west of Puente del Inca. Customs are open 0900-2130. In 2010 major rebuilding work was under way on the road and border facilities. All formalities were being undertaken on the Chilean side and all farms of transport should expect delays for some time. Car drivers can undertake all formalities in advance at *migraciones* in Mendoza, or Uspallata while refuelling. You can hitchhike, or possibly bargain with bus drivers for a seat, from Los Horcones to Santiago, but if you are dropped at the entrance to the tunnel, you cannot walk through. Customs officers may help to arrange a lift through to Chile.

Mendoza to Chile listings

For Sleeping and Eating price codes and other relevant information, see Essentials, pages 38-40.

Sleeping

Potrerillos and Uspallata *p135*

Cacheuta

AL Hotel and Spa Termas Cacheuta, Ruta 82, Km 38, T490152, www.termascacheuta.com. Price is full board, warm and inviting rustic-style rooms, lovely spa for } day visits. Recommended.

Potrerillos

B Gran Hotel Potrerillos, Ruta Nacional 7, Km 50, T02624-482130. With breakfast, faded 1940s resort hotel, nice location, simple rooms, pool.

C Silver Cord B&B, Valle del Sol, T02624 481083, www.silvercordbb.com.ar. With breakfast, internet, laundry service, lots of outdoor activities and 4WD trips, guides speak English.

E pp **Campo Base Penitentes**, T0261-425 5511, www.penitentes.com.ar. A cheap ski resort option, lively, slightly cramped dorms, shared bath, restaurant, bar, minibus service to Mendoza. Hostel is open all year, offers ski programmes in season.

Camping There is also the excellent **ACA** site, T482013, shady, hot water after 1800, pool, clean.

Los Penitentes

AL Hostería Penitentes, Villa Los Penitentes T155-090432, penitentehosteria@hotmail.com. Cheery place near slopes, good café, cheaper for several nights. Recommended.

Uspallata

A Valle Andino, Ruta 7, T420095, www.hotelvalleandino.com. Modern airy place with good rooms, pool and restaurant, breakfast included.

B Hotel Uspallata, on RN 7, Km 1149, towards Chile, T420 066. Lovely location, spacious and modern in big gardens away from the centre, pool, good value, comfortable rooms, cheap restaurant.

D Los Cóndores, T420002. Great value, bright, neat rooms, good restaurant, set menus and tasty pasta dishes. Highly recommended.

D Viena, Las Heras 240, T420046. Small family-run place, good little rooms, breakfast included.

F pp **Hostel Uspallata**, RN 7, Km 1141.5, T154-667240, www.hosteluspallata.com.ar. Basic rooms sleep 2-6, some with bath, also cabins for 6-8 (**B**), discounts for HI members, bar, restaurant, tours arranged, attractive surroundings.

Puente del Inca *p135*

C Hostería Puente del Inca, RN7, Km 175, T4205304. Next to the small ski centre at Los Puquios. Doubles and rooms for 4-8, full-board option, huge cosy dining room, advice on Aconcagua, helpful owners, great atmosphere. Warmly recommended.

F pp **Hostel La Vieja Estación**, 100 m off the road, next to the Puente, T4521103. Basic but cheery hostel, 3-bunk dorms, take sleeping bag, cheap meals provided, but take own supplies and use kitchen.

Camping Possible next to the church (but windy), also at Los Puquios and Lago Horcones inside the park.

Border with Chile *p137*

F pp **Arco de las Cuevas**, Las Cuevas, T426 5273, www.arcodelascuevas.com.ar. Above the old road to Cristo Redentor. Spartan but comfortable dorms, use of kitchen US$0.65, restaurant and bar. Transfer to Aconcagua park US$5.

Eating

Potrerillos and Uspallata *p135*

Potrerillos

El Futre, opposite the ACA campsite. Typical Cuyo food, vegetarian dishes and homemade pizzas. Open all day, summer only.

Los Pinos, Av Los Cóndores, on the left hand side as you go up the hill. Recommended for trout.

Tomillo, Av Los Cóndores, El Salto. Open all day. Excellent homemade cooking, welcoming.

Uspallata

Bodega del Gato, centre. Good *parrilla*.

La Estancia de Elias, Km 1146. Opposite Shell station, good cheap food but crowded.

Pub Tibet, at the crossroads. Bar with photos from *Seven Years in Tibet*, 1997 movie which was shot here, welcoming with warm atmosphere.

Activities and tours

Potrerillos and Uspallata *p135*

Potrerillos

Argentina Rafting, T02624-482037, www.argentinarafting.com. Reliable company, organizes good trips with climbing, hiking, kayaking and other adventure sports.

Uspallata

Desnivel Turismo Aventura, C Ejército de los Andes, T420275, desnivelturismoaventura@yahoo.com.ar. Offers rafting, riding, mountain biking, trekking, climbing, skiing.

Transport

Puente del Inca *p135*

Bus Expreso Uspallata from Mendoza for **Uspallata** (6 a day) and **Puente del Inca** (3 a day) , US$7, 3½ hrs. Uspallata-Puente del Inca US$2. Local buses also go on from Puente del Inca to **Las Cuevas**, **Expreso Uspallata**, US$5 return (**Note** Take passport). Buses going to Chile do not pick up passengers on the way.

San Juan and around

→ *Phone code: 0264. Colour map 8, A2. Population: 122,000. Altitude: 650 m.*

San Juan, 177 km north of Mendoza, was founded in 1562 and is capital of its namesake province. Nearly destroyed by a 1944 earthquake, the modern centre is well laid-out, but lacks Mendoza's charm and sophistication. **Tourist office** ⓘ *Sarmiento Sur 24 y San Martín, T421 0004, turismo@sanjuan.gov.ar, daily 0730-2030 (in theory).*

Sights

You're most likely to visit on the way to the national parks further north, but there are some *bodegas* worth visiting. One of the country's largest wine producers, *Bodegas Bragagnolo*, is on the outskirts of town at Ruta 40 y Avenida Benavídez, Chimbas (bus 20 from terminal; guided tours daily 0830-1330, 1530-1930, not Sunday). West of the city, 15 km, are **Cavas de Zonda** ⓘ *R12, T494 5144, www.cavasdezonda.com*, Champagne-style and other wines cellars in tunnels in the rock, with free visit and wine tasting. **Museo Casa Natal de Sarmiento** ⓘ *Sarmiento Sur 21, summer daily 0900-1300, also Tue-Fri and Sun 1700-2000; winter Tue-Fri and Sun 0900-1900, Mon, Sat 0900-1400, US$1, free Sun.* This is the birthplace of Domingo Sarmiento (President of the Republic, 1868-1874). **Museo Histórico Celda de San Martín** ⓘ *Laprida 57 Este, Mon-Sat 0900-1400, US$1*, includes the restored cloisters and two cells of the Convent of Santo Domingo. San Martín slept in one of these cells on his way to lead the crossing of the Andes.

The **Museo Arqueológico** of the University of San Juan ⓘ *Acceso Sur entre C 5 y Progreso, Rawson, a few km south of the centre, T424 1424, Mon-Fri 0800-2000, Sat-Sun 1000-1800, US$0.70, getting there: buses 15, 49, 50 from centre*, contains an outstanding collection of prehispanic

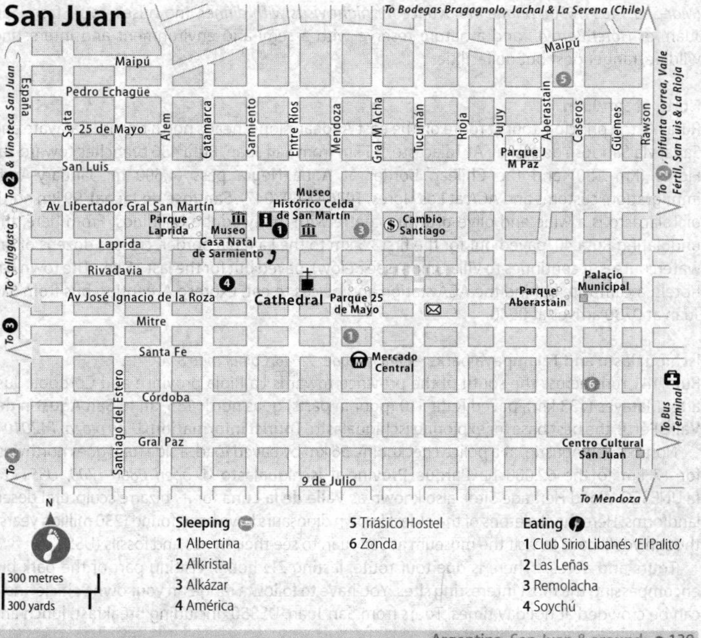

Sleeping
1 Albertina
2 Alkristal
3 Alkázar
4 América
5 Triásico Hostel
6 Zonda

Eating
1 Club Sirio Libanés 'El Palito'
2 Las Leñas
3 Remolacha
4 Soychú

indigenous artefacts, including several well-preserved mummies. **Vallecito**, 64 km east, has a famous shrine to the **Difunta Correa**, Argentina's most loved pagan saint whose infant, according to legend, survived at her breast even after the mother's death from thirst in the desert. At roadsides everywhere you'll see mounds of plastic bottles left as offerings to ask for safe journeys, and during Holy Week 100,000 pilgrims visit the site. See the remarkable collection of personal items left in tribute in several elaborate shrines, including number plates from all over the world: photographs, stuffed animals, tea sets, hair (in plaits), plastic flowers, trophies, tennis rackets and guitars. There are cafés, toilets and souvenir stalls. Buses from San Juan to La Rioja stop here for five minutes, or **Vallecitos** runs a couple of services a day.

West of San Juan → *Phone code: 02648.*

Calingasta, 135 km west of San Juan, is an idyllic, secluded village in a green valley with stunning striped rocks (cider festival in April). Ruta 12 west from San Juan along the canyon of the Río San Juan has been closed by work on two dams, so to reach Calingasta you go north of San Juan to Talacasto, then take the paved Quebrada de las Burras road to Pachaco, where a bridge crosses the Río San Juan. After the bridge, police control alternating one-way traffic to/from Calingasta for 12 km. Cyclists should note that there is no shade on these roads, fill up with water at every opportunity. Consult the police before cycling from Calingasta to San Juan. **Tourist information** ⓘ Av Argentina s/n, T421066, or *Municipalidad, Lavalle y Sarmiento, Tamberías, T492005*.

Barreal (phonce code: 02648), 40 km south of Calingasta on the road to Uspallata, is a tranquil place between the Andes and the precordillera, with great horse riding, trekking to Cerro Mercedaria, and wind-car racing (*carrovelismo*). **Tourist office** ⓘ *Calle Las Heras s/n, T441066*. At **Parque Nacional El Leoncito** (from 2,348 m), 26 km from Barreal there are two observatories ⓘ *T0264-421 3653, www.casleo.gov.ar, US$3, daily 1000-1200, 1500-1700 (Mar-Sep 1400-1630), phone in advance for night visits with dinner,* (no buses; tours from San Juan, or *Hotel Barreal*) and a nature reserve with a semi-arid environment and interesting wildlife, ranger post but no facilities.

North of San Juan

Ruta 40, the principal tourist route on the east Andean slope, heads north toward Cafayate and Salta, via San José de Jachal. At Talacasto, 55 km from San Juan, Ruta 436 branches toward Las Flores (Km 180) and the Chilean border at Agua Negra pass (4,600 m; January-April, immigration, customs and ACA at Los Flores, T02647-497047). **San José de Jachal**, 99 km north of Talacasto is a wine and olive-growing centre with many adobe buildings. From here, the undulating Ruta 40, paved but for the first 25 km to the La Rioja border, crosses dozens of dry watercourses. It continues to Villa Unión (see below), paved but for the last 15 km. The town has hotels, a campsite behind the ACA station and places to eat. Expreso Argentino bus from San Juan at 0730 arrives at 0940.

Ischigualasto and Talampaya parks → *Phone code: 02646. Colour map 8, A2.*

Ruta 141 runs across the south of the province towards La Rioja province and Córdoba. Just after Marayes (133 km), paved Ruta 510 (poor in parts) goes north 135 km to **San Agustín del Valle Fértil**, the best base for exploring Ischigualasto. **Tourist information** ⓘ *on plaza, T420104*.

North of San Agustín, at a police checkpoint, 56 km by paved road, a side road goes northwest for 17 km to the 62,000 ha **Parque Provincial Ischigualasto** ⓘ *open 0800-1700, US$11.65* (a UNESCO World Heritage Site), also known as **Valle de la Luna** for its bizarre sculptural desert landforms. Here the skeletons of the oldest known dinosaurs have been found (230 million years), though you'll have to visit the museum at San Juan to see their bones and fossils (US$2).

Tours and access There is one tour route, lasting 2½ hours, visiting part of the park but encompassing the most interesting sites. You have to follow a ranger in your own vehicle and it can be crowded at holiday times. Tours from San Juan, US$50 (including breakfast, lunch and tour), 12 hours, also full-moon tours, US$21; from San Agustín US$15-20 for a guide (in both towns, ask at tourist office). A tour is the best option if you have no car as a taxi to the park from San Agustín cannot follow the ranger. You can camp opposite the ranger station, which has a small museum, but bring all food and water; expensive confitería next to ranger station. See also Activities and tours, page 142.

Just beyond the police checkpoint, near Los Baldecitos, paved Ruta 150 heads east to Patquía and then to La Rioja or Chilecito. From the junction provincial Ruta 76 heads north to Villa Unión. 61 km north of Los Baldecitos a paved road goes 14 km east to the 215,000-ha **Parque Nacional Talampaya** ⓘ *T03825-470397, 0800-1800 (winter 0830-1730), US$6.50 for foreigners*, another collection of spectacular desert landforms and a UNESCO World Heritage Site. The park occupies the site of an ancient lake, where sediments have been eroded by water and wind for some 200 million years, forming a dramatic landscape of pale red hills. Numerous fossils have been found and some 600 year-old petroglyphs can be seen not far from the access to the gorge. Along the *cañón* of the Río Talampaya, extraordinary structures have been given popular names such as 'the balconies', 'the lift', 'the crib' or 'the owl'. At one point, the gorge narrows to 80 m and rises to 143 m. A refreshing leafy spot in the centre of the gorge, 'the botanical garden', has amazing diverse plants and trees. The end of the *cañón* is marked by the imposing cliffs of 'the cathedral' and the curious 'king on a camel'. 'The chessboard' and 'the monk', 53 m high, lie not far beyond the gorge, marking the end of the so-called **Circuito El Monje**. Only accessible with 4WD vehicles, **Circuito Los Cajones** continues in the same direction up to '*los pizarrones*', an enormous wall of rock, covered with petroglyphs, and then to '*los cajones*', a narrow pass between rock walls. **Circuito Ciudad Perdida** is another possible excursion in the park, southeast of the gorge, accessible only with 4WD vehicles, leading to an area of high cliffs and a large number of breathtaking rock formations.

Tours and access Tour operators in San Agustín combine Talampaya with Ischigualasto; some will end in La Rioja. Those from La Rioja and Chilecito sometimes combine a visit with Ischigualasto, otherwise access is difficult (check guide's fee and entrance included). Independent access is possible: buses/combis linking La Rioja and Villa Unión stop at the park entrance (a long walk to the *administración*), or better, at Pagancillo (village 30 km north), as most of the park wardens live there and offer free transfer to the park early in the morning (contact Adolfo Páez). The park itself can only be visited on tours arranged at the *administración*: guided walks to Quebrado Don Eduardo, a secondary gorge, next to the canyon (3 hours, US$10 pp); guided bike rides (3 hours, US$10 pp, cycle/helmet provided). Vehicle guided visits for Circuito Cañón de Talamapaya (US$15 pp), Circuito Los Cajones (US$20 pp); no private vehicles allowed beyond the administration; apart from the organized tours, the options are walking or cycling. Best time to visit is in the morning, for natural light and avoiding strong afternoon winds. *Administración* has small restaurant, toilets, public telephones.

San Juan and around listings

For Sleeping and Eating price codes and other relevant information, see Essentials, pages 38-40.

Sleeping

San Juan *p139, map p139*

AL-C hotels all include breakfast and parking.

AL Alkázar, Laprida 82 Este, T421 4965, www.alkazar hotel.com.ar. Comfortable rooms, pool, gym, well run, central, excellent restaurant.

B Albertina, Mitre 31 Este, T421 4222, info@hotelalbertina.com.ar. Next to cinema on plaza, welcoming, refurbished, comfortable, good service, restaurant.

B Alkristal, Av de Circunvalacíon 1055 Sur, T425 4145, alkristal@alkazarhotel.com.ar. Comfortable, well-equipped rooms, modern, on outskirts, poor breakfast, but otherwise recommended, good value. Also smart apartments, good for groups.

C América, 9 de Julio 1052 Oeste, T427 2701, www.hotel-america.com.ar. Modern, comfortable, good service, free internet, trips arranged.

F-G pp **Triásico Hostel**, Pedro Echagüe 538 Este, Rawson, T421 9528, www.triasico hostel.com.ar. Homely atmosphere, simple dorms/doubles, some with private bath (**D**), large patio with pool, tours offered. Recommended.

F-G pp **Zonda**, Caseros 486 Sur, T420 1009, www. zondahostel.com.ar. Spotless hostel, simple, light rooms, for 2-6, shared bath, hot water, breakfast at any hour, dinner available, kitchen, internet. Trips and Spanish lessons arranged. HI member discount.

West of San Juan *p140*

Calingasta

E Hotel de Campo Calingasta, T421220, restored old colonial-style building, airy rooms, colonnaded patio, pool, lovely views, very tranquil.

Barreal

A Posada de Campo La Querencia, T0264-1543 64699/504 6958, www.laquerenciaposada.com.ar. With breakfast, comfy rooms, homely, attentive owners, lots of adventure opportunities.

B Eco Posada El Mercedario, Av Roca y C de los Enamorados, T0264-1550 90907, www.elmerce dario.com.ar. On a farm, traditional adobe buildings, rooms with bath, restaurant, internet, Wi-Fi, bicycles.

C Posada San Eduardo, Av San Martín s/n, T441046. Charming colonial-style house, rooms around a courtyard, relaxing, good restaurant. There are various cabañas, eg **Kummel**, T441206, and places to stay in town.

Camping Municipal site in C Belgrano, T441241, shady, well-maintained, pool, open all year.

Ischigualasto and Talampaya parks *p140*

San Agustín del Valle Fértil

B Hostería Valle Fértil, Rivadavia s/n, T420015, www.alkazarhotel.com.ar. Good, a/c, smart, very comfortable, with fine views, also has *cabañas* and good restaurant open to non-residents.

E-F pp **Campo Base**, Tucumán entre Libertador y San Luis y, T420063, www.hostelvalledelaluna. com.ar. HI affiliated, cheerful, basic dorms, shared bath, tours.

F pp **Los Olivos**, Santa Fe y Tucumán, T420115. Welcoming and simple hostel accommodation, excellent value, with restaurant.

Camping La Majadita, lovely campsite on river 8 km west of town, hot showers, great views. **Municipal campsite**, Calle Rivadavia, 5 blocks from plaza, T420104.

Parque Nacional Talampaya

F Hotel Pagancillo, Pagancillo, T03825-156 66828. Shared bath, breakfast, comfortable.

Camping Basic site next to *administración*, US$1.

Eating

San Juan *p139, map p139*

Las Leñas, San Martín 1670 Oeste. Huge, popular *parrilla*. Vegetarian restaurant next door.

Remolacha, Santa Fe 1232 Oeste. Stylish, warm atmosphere, superb Italian-inspired menu, delicious steaks and pastas. Recommended.

Soychú, Av de la Roza 223 Oeste, T422 1939. Great value vegetarian food. Highly recommended.

Club Sirio Libanés 'El Palito', Entre Ríos 33 Sur. Pleasant, long-established, tasty food, some Middle-Eastern dishes, buffet. Recommended.

Shopping

San Juan *p139, map p139*

San Juan is known for its fine bedspreads, blankets, saddle cloths and other items made from sheep, llama and guanaco wool, fine leather, wooden plates and mortars and, of course, its wines. **Mercado Artesanal**, España y San Luis, sells woven blankets/saddlebags. For wine stores try: **La Reja**, Jujuy 424 Sur and **La Bodega**, 25 de Mayo 957 Este.

Activities and tours

San Juan *p139, map p139*

Nerja Tours, Entre Ríos 178 Sur, T421 5214, www.nerja-tours.com.ar. Good for local day trips and adventure tourism inside the national parks.

Valley Moon, Rivadavia 414 Oeste, T421 4868, www.valleymoon.com. Good local alternatives to conventional tours, also rafting, windsurfing at Rodeo, horse riding, climbing, experienced guides.

West of San Juan *p140*

Barreal

Explora Parques, C Mariano Moreno, T503 2008, www.exploraparques.com.ar. Brothers Ramón and Diego Ossa are expert guides, running 4WD expeditions and horse treks crossing the foothills of the Andes in summer, 1-15 days. Highly recommended. Also here is **Doña Pipa**, T441004,

www.cdpbarreal.com.ar, cabins, rooms, restaurant and pool.
Wind Car Barreal, T15-439647, windcarbarreal@yahoo.com.ar. For carrovelismo on the Pampa del Leoncito.

Transport

San Juan *p139, map p139*
Air Chacritas Airport, 11 km southeast on RN 20. Daily to/from **Buenos Aires**, 1½ hrs with **AR/Austral** (Av San Martín 215 Oeste, T0810-2228 6527, or 425 0487), also to Mendoza.
Bus Terminal at Estados Unidos y Santa Fe, 9 blocks east of centre (buses 33 and 35 go through the centre). T422 1604. **La Rioja**, 5-6 hrs, US$20-28, 6 companies. **Catamarca**, 6 companies, 7-8 hrs, US$27-31. **Tucumán**, 6 companies, 10-12 hrs, US$38-43. **Córdoba**, **Socasa, 20 de Julio, Autotransportes San Juan** (T422 1870), 8-9 hrs, US$20-28. **Buenos Aires**, 14-16 hrs, US$45-65. **San Agustín** with **Vallecito**, 2 a day, 4 hrs, US$10. Hrly departures to and from **Mendoza,** fares above. Also to **Barreal** and **Calingasta**, 1900, 4-5 hrs with **El Triunfo**, T421 4532, US$14.

West of San Juan *p140*
Barreal
Bus See above for San Juan; return to San Juan at 2100. Also minibus by José Luis Sosa, T441095 (434 2317 San Juan).

Ischigualasto and Talampaya parks *p140*
San Agustín del Valle Fértil
Bus **Vallecito** runs twice a day to **San Juan**, see above. 3 buses a week to **La Rioja**, 3 hrs, US$7.

Directory

San Juan *p139, map p139*
Banks Banks 0800-1300. *Banelco* and *Link* ATMs accept international credit cards. **Cambio Santiago**, Gen Acha 52 Sur, T421 2232, Mon-Fri until 2100, Sat until 1300. **Internet** Several *locutorios* have internet, those at Rivadavia y Acha, on the plaza, and Mendoza 139 Sur are open on Sun. **Useful addresses** ACA, 9 de Julio y Gral Achá, T421 4205, very helpful.

La Rioja and Catamarca

La Rioja → *Phone code: 03822. Colour map 8, A2. Population: 147,000.*
Founded 1591, at the edge of the plains, with views of Sierra de Velasco, La Rioja can be oppressively hot from November to March. But the town comes alive after the daily siesta and during the annual carnival, *Chaya* (in February), and the *Tinkunaco* festival (beginning on New Year's Eve and lasting four days). The city's main buildings and plazas date from the late 19th century, while the recent government of Carlos Menem, born in a little town 90 km north, has left a certain affluence. The **Church and Convent of San Francisco** ⓘ *25 de Mayo y Bazán y Bustos, Tue-Sun 0900-1200, 1830-2100, free,* contains the Niño Alcalde, a remarkable image of the infant Jesus. You can also see the cell (*celda*) in which San Francisco Solano lived and the orange tree, now dead, which he planted in 1592 (25 de Mayo 218). San Francisco helped to bring peace between the Spaniards and the indigenous people in 1593, an event celebrated at Tinkunaco. The **Convent of Santo Domingo** ⓘ *Luna y Lamadrid*, dates from 1623, said to be the oldest surviving church in Argentina. **Museo Arqueológico Inca Huasi** ⓘ *Alberdi 650, Tue-Fri 0900-1300, 1700-2100, Sat 0900-1300, US$0.50*, owned by the Franciscan Order, contains a huge collection of fine Diaguita Indian ceramics, considered among the most important pre-Hispanic artefacts in the country. The **Mercado Artesanal** ⓘ *Luna 790, Tue-Fri 0800-1200, 1600-2000, Sat-Sun 0900-1300,* has expensive handicrafts. The **Museo de Arte Sacro** ⓘ *in the same building Tue-Sat 0800-1200,* has 18th- and 19th-century images and Cusqueña school paintings. In a beautiful and well kept house at the opposite corner, the **Museo Folklórico** ⓘ *Luna 811, T428500, Tue-Sun 0900-1200, 1600-2000 (Tue-Sat 0900-1200 in summer), US$0.35, free guided visits,* gives a fascinating insight into traditional La Rioja life, with a superb collection of native deities, rustic wine-making machinery and delicate silver *mates*. Well worth a visit too for its

leafy patio. There are good views of La Rioja from Cerro de la Cruz (1,648 m), 23 km west, now a centre for hang-gliding. **Tourist offices**: municipal ⓘ *Av Perón 728, Mon-Fri 0800-1200, 1600-2000*; provincial ⓘ *Luna 345, T426384, daily 0800-2100, www.larioja.gov.ar/turismo*.

Chilecito → *Phone code: 03825. Colour map 8, A2. Population: 30,000.*

Chilecito, 129 km northwest of Patquía, is La Rioja province's second town. Founded in 1715, it has good views of Sierra de Famatina, especially from the top of El Portezuelo, an easy climb from the end of Calle El Maestro. The region is famous for its wines, olives and walnuts. **Finca Samay Huasi** ⓘ *3 km south, T422629, Mon-Fri 0800-1300, 1330-1930, Sat-Sun 0800-1200, 1500-1900 (closed 22 Dec-6 Jan), US$0.35*, was the house of Joaquín V González, founder of La Plata University. He designed the gardens with native trees and strange stone monoliths expressing his love of ancient cultures; there's also a small natural history museum. It's an attractive place for a relaxing day; overnight guests welcome (**F** pp, **E** pp full board, book in advance). **Molino San Francisco y Museo de Chilecito** ⓘ *J de Ocampo 50, Mon-Fri 0800-1200, 1600-2100, Sat-Sun 0830-1230, 1530-2000, US$0.35*, has archaeological, historical and artistic exhibits. At the **Cooperativa La Riojana** ⓘ *La Plata 646, T423150*, there are free guided visits (45 minutes), you can watch local grapes being processed to make a wide variety of wines, including organic products; also a smart wine shop open in the mornings. At **Santa Florentina** (8 km northwest), there are the impressive remains of a huge early 20th century foundry, linked to Chilecito and La Mejicana mine by cable car. **Tourist office** ⓘ *Castro y Bazán 52, T422688, daily 0800-1230, 1530-2100*. Also see www.chilecito tour.com and www.chilecitoturistico.com.ar.

Reserva Natural Laguna Brava

At Nonogasta 16 km south of Chilecito, the partly paved Ruta 40 heads west climbing through a deep narrow canyon in a series of hairpins to the Cuesta de Miranda (2,020 m). After the Cuesta is **Villa Unión**, 92 km from Nonogasta. From here excursions can be made by four-wheel drive vehicle to the Reserva Natural Laguna Brava, 150 km north. The road goes through **Vinchina** and Jagüe (basic facilities). Further on, as you climb the Portezuelo del Peñón, the salt lake of Laguna Brava becomes visible with some of the mightiest volcanoes on earth in the background. From the left these are the perfect cone Veladero (6,436 m), Reclus (6,335 m), Los Gemelos (6,130 m), Pissis (6,882 m) the highest volcano in the world, though inactive, and Bonete (6,759 m) which is visible from Villa Unión and Talampaya. For tours in this area see under Chilecito and La Rioja. **Access**: From Jagüe 4WD and going with two vehicles is essential; otherwise only by mountain bike. Summer rainfalls and winter snow may limit the access to only a short period in the year; usually in April or early May is best. Park entry US$2.

Catamarca → *Phone code: 03833. Colour map 8, A2. Population: 130,000. Altitude: 490 m.*

Officially San Fernando del Valle de Catamarca, the city is capital of its province, on the Río del Valle, between the Sierra de Ambato (to the west) and Ancasti (to the east), 153 km northeast of La Rioja and 240 km south of Tucumán. Now rather run-down, Catamarca is most famous for its textiles, and unless you're here for the mid-July poncho festival *(feria* with quality handicrafts, food and live music), there's little to keep you. Summers are very hot (up to 45°C). 37 km north is the much more appealing and prettier weekend retreat of **El Rodeo** with its cooler micro-climate, good walks and charming *hosterías* (tourist information T490043, helpful). In the vast open puna to the northwest, there are traces of sophisticated ancient civilizations, and the finest of the city's six museums has an outstanding collection of indigenous artefacts. **Museo Arqueológico Adán Quiroga** ⓘ *Sarmiento 446, T437413, Mon- Fri 0700-1300, 1430-2030, Sat-Sun 0830-1230, 1530-1830, US$0.50*. **Tourist office** ⓘ *Av República 446, www.catamarca.com, www.catamarca.gov.ar, 0800-2100*. Helpful leaflets with bus times and prices. **Provincial office** ⓘ *Av Gral Roca cuadra 1, T457593, www.turismocatamarca.gov.ar, Mon-Fri 0800-1300, 1500-2000*, and kiosks in airport and Terminal Shopping by bus station, Avenida Güemes.

Puna west of Catamarca

The high-altitude desert of the puna is spectacular, with a distinct culture and remote untouristy towns. It's most easily reached by the paved road to **Aimogasta** and on to the small settlements of Tinogasta and Fiambalá, useful staging posts if taking the Paso San Fransisco to Chile, or north to Andagalá, or to Belén, where the rough road to Antofagasta de la Sierra begins. The *Zonda*, a strong, dry mountain wind, can cause dramatic temperature increases.

Tinogasta (*Phone code: 03837*) is in an oasis of vineyards, olive groves, and poplars. It is the starting point for expeditions to **Pissis** the second highest mountain in South America, 6,882 m. To get there, take Ruta 60 which crosses Tinogasta in the direction of the San Francisco pass. You have to register at the police station outside Fiambalá, take passport. Expeditions organized and horse riding with Omar Monuey, La Espiga de Oro, 25 de Mayo 436 or *Varela Viajes*, T420428. At Fiambalá, contact Jonson and Ruth Reynoso, T496214.

Fiambalá is 49 km north of Tinogasta, a peaceful place in a vine-filled valley, with **Termas de Fiambalá**, hot springs, situated 14 km east (take a taxi; make sure fare includes wait and return). 4WD vehicles may be hired for approaching the Pissis-Ojos region; ask at the Intendencia.

Border with Chile – Paso San Francisco

Fiambalá is the starting-point for the crossing to Chile via Paso San Francisco (4,726 m), 203 km northwest along a paved road. In summer the border is open 24 hours, T498001. On the Chilean side roads run to El Salvador and Copiapó. This route is closed by snow June-October; take enough fuel for at least 400 km as there are no service stations from Fiambalá to just before Copiapó.

Belén → *Phone code: 03835. Colour map 6, C3. Population: 8,800. Altitude: 1,000 m.*

A quiet intimate little town, Belén is famous for its ponchos, saddlebags and rugs, which you can see being woven. The museum, **Cóndor Huasi** ⓘ *San Martín y Belgrano, 1st floor, daily*, contains fascinating Diaguita artefacts, and there is a newly constructed Virgen (the last one was struck by lightning) on the Cerro de Nuestra Señora de Belén above town; good views. Important festival: Nuestra Señora de Belén, 24 December-6 January. **Tourist information** ⓘ *bus terminal, near plaza, Rivadavia y Lavalle, T461304.*

South of Belén, Ruta 40 is paved to Chilecito via **Londres**, a quiet, pretty village. North of Belén Ruta 40 runs another 176 km, largely unpaved, to Santa María at the provincial border with Tucumán (see page 151), and on to Cafayate (page 155), or 260 km north to tiny remote **Antofagasta de la Sierra** and onwards to San Antonio de los Cobres in Salta. East of Belén, a rough and sandy road goes to **Andalgalá**, a former copper-mining town with a handicraft market, two archaeological museums and a decent hotel **D Aquasol**. For information contact **Municipalidad**, T422420, or **Andalgalá Turismo**, T03835-422405, turandalgala@cotelbelen.com.ar. Very helpful.

La Rioja and Catamarca listings

For Sleeping and Eating price codes and other relevant information, see Essentials, pages 38-40.

Sleeping

La Rioja *p143*

A/c or fan are essential for summer nights. High season is during Jul winter holidays.

A King's, Av Quiroga 1070, T422122. 4-star, buffet breakfast included, a/c gym, pool and fine rooms, also car rental.

A Plaza, San Nicolás de Bari y 9 de Julio (on Plaza 25 de Mayo), T425215, www.plazahotel-larioja.com. Functional 4-star, pool on top floor, breakfast included, a/c.

B Vincent Apart Hotel, Santiago del Estero y San Nicolás de Bari, T432326. Spotless flats for up to 4, a/c, with dining room, kitchen and fridge, breakfast included, excellent value.

D Savoy, San Nicolás de Bari y Roque A Luna, T426894, hotelsavoy@infovia.com.ar. In a quiet residential area, tidy, comfortable, with breakfast and a/c, second floor best.

Camping Several sites along Av Ramírez de Velasco, in northwest suburbs on the way to Las Padercitas and Dique Los Sauces, but the best is **Camping de la Sociedad Sirio Libanesa**, at Balneario Los Sauces, 13 km west on Ruta 75, with hot showers and pool.

Chilecito *p144*

C Chilecito (ACA), T Gordillo y A G Ocampo, T422201. A/c, comfortable, with breakfast, safe parking, pool, cheap set menus.

C Finca del Paimán, Mariano Moreno y Santa Rosa (San Miguel, 3 km southeast of town), T425102, www.fincadelpaiman.com.ar. Delightful 4½-ha farm, spacious rooms, kitchen, breakfast and transport to/from Chilecito included. You can help with fruit harvesting or jam cooking! Warmly recommended, book in advance. Also has a **hostel** in Chilecito, **Hostel del Paimán**, El Maestro 188 y A Marasso (same T), old house in town centre, with rooms **E**, or dorms **F** pp, HI affiliated, lovely garden.

D Hostal Mary Pérez, Florencio Dávila 280, T/F423156, hostal_mp@hotmail.com. Best value, comfortable, welcoming atmosphere, good breakfast. Recommended.

Camping 3 sites at Santa Florentina and Las Talas, 8 km northwest (remise taxi US$2-2.50).

Reserva Natural Laguna Brava: Villa Unión *p144*

A Hotel Pircas Negras, on Ruta 76, Villa Unión, T03825-470611, www.hotelpircasnegras.com. Large modern building, the best in the area, comfortable rooms, restaurant and pool, excursions organized.

D Hotel Noryanepat, JVGonzález 150, Villa Unión, T470133. Small rooms with a/c, good.

E Dayton, Nicolás Dávila 115, Villa Unión, T470640. Basic but decent, with breakfast.

There are several basic *hospedajes* in Vinchina.

Catamarca *p144*

Hotels are mostly unmodernized, overpriced and business oriented.

B Arenales, Sarmiento 542, T431329, www.hotel-arenales.com.ar. Comfortable plain rooms, good bathrooms, restaurant.

B Grand Hotel, Camilo Melet 41, T426715, www.grandhotelcatamarca.com.ar. Delightful, helpful owners, simple spacious rooms, a/c, TV, discounts for cash. Recommended.

B Pucará, Caseros 501, T430688. Boldly decorated entrance lounge, comfortable bedrooms with pink satin bedspreads and flamenco prints.

C Casino Catamarca, Pasaje César Carman s/n (behind the ACA service station), T432928, inforcentral@hotelcasinocatamarca.com. Smart, modern and bright, well decorated rooms, discreetly hidden casino, large pool, good value.

E pp **El Rodeo Hostel**, El Rodeo, 37 km north on RP4, T490380, www.elrodeohostel.com.ar. Daily minibus from centre. Lovely spacious rooms, **F** in dorms, great views, tours organized. Highly recommended.

E Residencial Shinkal, Vicario Segura 1120, T421083. The best and newest residencial. Not recommended for single women. No breakfast.

Puna west of Catamarca *p145*

Tinogasta

C Viñas del Sol, Perón 231, T420028.

D Hostería Novel, Córdoba 200, T420009, near airport, friendly.

E Res Don Alberto, A del Pino 419, T420323.

Fiambalá

D Hostería Municipal, Almagro s/n, T03837-496016. Good value, also restaurant.

E pp **Complejo Turístico**, at the Termas, T496016. With cabins, also camping.

Belén *p145*

AL-C Belén, Belgrano y Cubas, T461501, www.belen cat.com.ar. Comfortable, prices depend on day of arrival and excursions taken, also **Ampujaco** tour operator.

E Samay, Urquiza 349, T461320. Old fashioned but welcoming, homely little rooms with bath and fan.

Eating

La Rioja *p143*

₮₮ El Corral, Av Quiroga y Rivadavia. Traditional rustic *comidas de campo* and good local wines.

₮₮ La Vieja Casona, Rivadavia 427. Smart *parrilla*.

₮ La Aldea de la Virgen de Luján, Rivadavia 756. Lively atmosphere, cheap and popular small place, including some Middle Eastern dishes.

Chilecito *p144*
Club Arabe, 25 de Mayo entre Zelada y Dávila and Famatina. Middle Eastern food only on request, served outside under grapevines.
El Rancho de Ferrito, PB Luna 647, T422481. Popular *parrilla*, with local wines.
La Rosa, Ocampo 149, T424693. Relaxing atmosphere, huge variety of pizzas, more extensive menu Fri and Sat.

Catamarca *p144*
La Tinaja, Sarmiento 533, T435853. Delicious *parrilla* and excellent pastas, worth the price.
Salsa Criolla, República 546 on the plaza. Traditional popular *parrilla*, sloppy service, but the beef is good. **Trattoria Montecarlo**, next door, same owner, Italian style.
Richmond, the best café on the plaza, stylish.
Sociedad Española, Virgen del Valle 725, T431897. Recommended for quality and variety, paella and other Spanish specialities, friendly service; worth the 5 block walk from the plaza.

Puna west of Catamarca *p145*
Tinogasta
The water is notoriously bad in this region: avoid salads and ice, drink mineral water.
Restaurant Casa Grande, Constitución y Moreno. Good meals, try local wines.

Belén *p145*
Bar El Seminario, on the plaza. Great for beer and sandwiches, spills over onto the plaza at weekends, popular local meeting place.

Shopping

Catamarca *p144*
Local specialities Cuesta del Portezuelo, Sarmiento 571 and **Valdez**, Sarmiento 578. You can see carpets being woven at **Mercado Artesanal**, Virgen del Valle 945, wide range of handicrafts, daily 0800-1330, 1500-2100; carpet factory Mon-Fri 0800-1200, 1500-2030.

Activities and tours

La Rioja *p143*
For excursions to Talampaya, Valle de la Luna, Laguna Brava and Corona del Inca crater (high season only) and horse riding in Velasco mountains:
Aguada, D Vélez Sarsfield 742, T433695 or 15-675699, talampaya_aguada@ciudad.com.ar. Helpful agency with good tours, some English and French spoken.
Corona del Inca, PB Luna 914, T450054 or 15-663811, www.coronadelinca.com.ar. Wide range of tours, English spoken.
Néstor Pantaleo, Ecuador 813, T422103. Experienced photographer, runs 4WD trips, several languages spoken.

Chilecito *p144*
This is an excellent base for amazing treks in the Famatina mountains and 1-day trips to Talampaya and Valle de la Luna.
Alejo Piehl, T/F425102, 155-57195, www.fincadel paiman.com.ar. Experienced guide (see Sleeping, above), all inclusive 1-day tours to Talampaya and Valle de la Luna, and unforgettable 2-3 day treks to Famatina, visiting abandoned cable car stations on the way to the summit. 4WD trips. Recommended.
Inka Ñan, T423641. Leopoldo Badoul organizes excursions to the province's main attractions.

Catamarca *p144*
Mountaineering **Aníbal Vázquez**, T03835-471001, trekking in Antofagasta de la Sierra.

Transport

La Rioja *p143*
Air Airport 5 km northeast, via San Nicolás de Bari, RP5, T427239. To **Buenos Aires**, **AR**, T426307, flights often stop at Catamarca or Córdoba.
Bus New bus terminal several km from the centre; bus No 2 takes 15 mins, US$0.50, or 45 mins' walk. To **Buenos Aires**, **Gen Urquiza** and **Chevallier** from US$46, 15-17 hrs. To **Mendoza**, US$22-40, 6-7 hrs, many companies, and **San Juan** US$30-33, 5-6 hrs, same companies. To **Tucumán**, US$18-21, 5-6 hrs. To **Salta**, **Andesmar**, 10-11 hrs, US$28. Also provincial services.

Chilecito *p144*
Bus Terminal on Av Perón, on south access to town. To **San Juan** and Mendoza with **Vallecito**, US$17; to **La Rioja**, several times daily, US$6, 3 hrs. To **Córdoba**, US$20, 7 hrs, and **Buenos Aires**, US$45, 17 hrs, **El Práctico, General Urquiza** (T423279).

Catamarca *p144*
Air Airport, 20 km south, T430080. **AR/Austral** (Sarmiento 589, T424460) to/from **Buenos Aires**.
Bus Terminal 5 blocks southeast of plaza at Güemes y Tucumán T437578, with shops, café, ATM and locutorio. Taxi to/from Plaza 25 de Mayo US$0.50. **Tucumán**, several companies, 3½-4hrs, US$11-13. **Buenos Aires**, 4 companies daily, 14-18 hrs, US$45-55. **Córdoba**, 4 companies daily, 6 hrs, US$15-20. **Santiago del Estero**, 6 hrs, US$15-20. **Mendoza**, several companies daily, 10 hrs, US$35-55. **La Rioja**, several companies daily, US$7-8, 2 hrs. **Tinogasta**, see below. **Belén** via Londres, 2 companies, 5 hrs, US$10; **Marín** (via Aconquija).

Puna west of Catamarca *p145*

Tinogasta
Bus To **Tucumán**, **Empresa Gutiérrez**, 3 weekly (daily in high season). To **Catamarca Empresa Gutiérrez** (connection to Buenos Aires), **Robledo** and **Rubimar**, US$10; to/from **La Rioja**, **El Cóndor**, daily, US$8.

Fiambalá
Bus Empresa Gutiérrez to **Catamarca** via Tinogasta. For Belén, change at Aimogasta.

Belén *p145*
Bus From Belén to **Santa María**, **San Cayetano** and **Parra** (connections there to Cafayate and Salta), daily, 5 hrs, US$14. **Tinogasta**, **Robledo**, 4 weekly, 2-3 hrs, US$7. **Antofagasta de la Sierra**, **El Antofagasteño**, 2 weekly, 11 hrs, US$25. For more frequent services to **Catamarca** or **La Rioja**, take bus to Aimogasta, 1 hr, US$3.

❶ Directory

La Rioja *p143*
Banks US$ cash changed at **Banco de Galicia**, Buenos Aires y San Nicolás de Bari, and at **Daniel**, exchange facilities at Rivadavia 525.
Internet Handful of places in and around Plaza 25 de Mayo, all charge about US$0.50-1 per hr.
Post offices Av Perón 258; Western Union branch. **Telephones** Several *locutorios* in the centre and at Av Quiroga e Hipólito Yrigoyen, with internet access (US$0.60 per hr) near bus terminal.

Catamarca *p144*
Banks Many ATMs for all major cards, along Rivadavia and at bus terminal, **BBVA Banco Francés**, Rivadavia 520. **Banco de la Nación** San Martín 632. **Internet** Cedecc, Esquiú 414. **Taraj Net**, San Martín y Ayacucho. **Post offices** San Martín 753, slow, open 0800-1300, 1600-2000.
Telephones Most *telecentros* around Plaza 25 de Mayo, also at República 845 and Rivadavia 758, open 0700-2400, daily.

Northwest Argentina

Two of the oldest cities in Argentina, Santiago del Estero and Tucumán, are at the start of the route to the fascinating Northwest. Both have some good museums and other sites of interest, but the summer heat may urge you to press on to the mountains. You can break the journey between the two cities at the rather worn, but much-visited spa of Termas de Río Hondo. Of the two routes to the atmospheric city of Salta, the more beautiful is via Tafí del Valle, the wine-producing town of Cafayate and the dramatic canyon of the Quebrada de las Conchas or the equally enchanting Valles Calchaquíes. Pretty towns in arid landscapes, archaeological remains and the Andes in the distance make for a memorable journey.

Santiago del Estero → *Phone code: 0385. Colour map 6, C4. Population: 328,000.*

Founded in 1553 by conquistadores pushing south from Peru, this is the oldest Argentine city, though little of its history is visible today. It's rather run down, but the people are relaxed and welcoming (*Altitude: 200 m, 395 km north of Córdoba, 159 km southeast of Tucumán*). On the **Plaza Libertad** stand the **Municipalidad** and the **Cathedral** (the fifth on the site, dating from 1877), with the Cabildo-like Prefectura of Police. The fine **Casa de Gobierno** is on Plaza San Martín, three blocks north. In the convent of **Santo Domingo**, Urquiza y 25 de Mayo, is one of two copies of the 'Turin Shroud', given by Philip II to his 'beloved colonies of America'. On Plaza Lugones is the church of **San Francisco**, the oldest surviving church in the city, founded in 1565, with the cell of San Francisco Solano, patron saint of Tucumán, who stayed here in 1593. Beyond it is the pleasant **Parque Francisco de Aguirre**. A highly recommended museum, **Museo de Ciencias Antropológicas** ⓘ *Avellaneda 353, T421 1380, Tue-Sun 0800-2000, free,* has an eclectic collection of prehispanic artefacts, exquisitely painted funerary urns, flattened skulls, anthropomorphic ceramics and musical instruments; fascinating, if poorly presented. Also interesting is the **Museo Histórico Provincial** ⓘ *Urquiza 354, Mon-Fri 0700-1300, 1400-2000, Sat-Sun 1000-1200, free.* In a 200-year old mansion, it has 18th- and 19th-century artefacts from wealthy local families. **Carnival** is in February. **Tourist office** ⓘ *Plaza Libertad 417, T421 4243, www.turismosantiago.gov.ar.*

Some 65 km north of Santiago del Estero is **Termas de Río Hondo** (*phone code: 03858*), Argentina's most popular spa town which has its warm mineral-laden waters piped into every hotel in the city (170 of them), making it a mecca (or Lourdes?) for older visitors with arthritic or skin conditions in July and August, when you'll need to book in advance. The hotels aside, the town is mostly run down, with a cream-coloured casino dominating the scruffy plaza and scores of *alfajores* shops. **Tourist office** ⓘ *Caseros 132, T422143,* helpful accommodation advice. Go to www.turismosantiago.gov.ar and Turismo Termal.

Santiago del Estero listings

For Sleeping and Eating price codes and other relevant information, see Essentials, pages 38-40.

Sleeping

Santiago del Estero *p149*

A Carlos V, Independencia 110, T424 0303, www.carlosvhotel.com. Corner of the plaza, the city's most luxurious hotel, elegant rooms, pool, good restaurant, still good value for its range.

B Centro, 9 de Julio 131, T421 9502, www.hotelcentro.com.ar. Nice décor, very comfortable, airy restaurant, internet and Wi-Fi. Recommended.

B Libertador, Catamarca 47, T421 9252, www.hotellibertadorsrl.com.ar. Smart and relaxing, spacious lounge, plain rooms, patio with pool (summer only), elegant restaurant, 5 blocks south of plaza in the better part of town.

B Savoy, Peatonal Tucumán 39, T421 1234, www.savoysantiago.com.arS. Good budget option, characterful, faded art nouveau grandeur, swirling stairwell, large airy rooms, internet, Wi-Fi.

E Res Alaska, Santa Fe 279, T422 1360. Close to bus station, hot water, TV, fan, good value.

F pp **Res Emaus**, Av Moreno Sur 675, T421 5893. Good choice, with bath and TV, helpful. Also has another *pensión* at Granadero Saavedra 411 (basic).

Camping **Las Casuarinas**, Parque Aguirre, T421 1390. Insect repellent essential.

Eating

Santiago del Estero *p149*

Mia Mamma, on the main plaza at 24 de Septiembre 15. A cheery place for *parrilla* and tasty pastas, with good salad for starters.

Periko's on the plaza, lively, popular, for *lomitos* and pizzas.

Don Pelachi, Urquiza y Belgrano. Good value, large choice of dishes.

Transport

Santiago del Estero *p149*

Air Airport on northwest outskirts. **AR/Austral** to **Buenos Aires** and **Tucumán**.

Bus Bus information, T421 3746. Terminal, Gallo 480, has toilets, a *locutorio*, basic café and kiosks, as well as stalls selling food. Taxi US$0.80 into town, or 8 blocks' walk. **Córdoba**, 6 hrs, US$18-23; **Jujuy**, 8 hrs, US$22-28; **Salta**, 6 hrs, US$20. To **Catamarca**, 1 daily, 6 hrs, US$15. Bus Santiago-**Termas de Río Hondo** 1 hr, US$3 (bus terminal is 8 blocks north of the centre, but buses will drop you at the plaza, opposite the casino, if asked). From Termas de Río Hondo you cancontinue to **Tucumán**, 2 hrs.

Tucumán and around

➔ *Phone code: 0381. Colour map 6, C4. Population: 740,000. Altitude: 450 m.*

San Miguel de Tucumán was founded by Spaniards coming south from Peru in 1565. Capital of a province rich in sugar, tobacco and citrus fruits, it is the biggest city in the north. It stands on a plain and is sweltering hot in summer (a 1230-1630 siesta is strictly observed); so retreat to the cooler mountain town of **Tafí del Valle** in the Sierra de Aconquija. **Tourist office** ⓘ *on the plaza, 24 de Septiembre 484, T430 3644, www.turismoentucuman.com, and www.tucumanturismo.gov.ar, Mon-Fri 0800-2200, Sat-Sun 0900-2100.* Also in the bus terminal and airport.

Sights

Museo Casa Padilla ⓘ *25 de Mayo 36, on the west side of the main Plaza Independencia, Mon-Sat 0900-1230, 1600-1900,* has a small collection of art and antiques in a historical house. Also on this side of the plaza is the ornate **Casa de Gobierno** and, nearby, the church of **San Francisco**, with a picturesque façade. A block north, the **Museo de Antropología** ⓘ *25 de Mayo 265, in university building, T4311430 ext 211, Mon-Fri 0800-1200, 1700-1900, US$0.50,* has a fine small collection. On the south side of Plaza Independencia is the **Cathedral** and, two blocks south, the interesting **Casa Histórica** ⓘ *Congreso 151, T431 0826, Mon-Fri 1000-1800, Sat-Sun 1300-1900; son et lumière show in garden nightly (not Thu, not when raining) at 2130, US$1.65, tickets also from tourist office on Plaza Independencia, no seats.* Here, in 1816, the country's Declaration of Independence was drawn up.

East of the centre is the **Parque de Julio**, one of the finest urban parks in Argentina. Extending over 400 ha, it contains a wide range of sub-tropical trees as well as a lake and sports facilities. The **Museo de la Industria Azucarera** ⓘ *daily 0830-1800, free,* traces the development of the local sugar industry. There are good views over the city from **Cerro San Javier**, 27 km west of the city (*Empresa Ber Bus*, US$1.75 from bus terminal).

Tafí del Valle ➔ *Phone code: 03867. Population: 3,300. Altitude: 1,976 m.*

South of Tucumán at Acheral on RN38, Ruta 307 heads northwest out of the sugar cane fields to zigzag up through forested hills to a treeless plateau, before El Mollar and the Embalse La Angostura. Here the valley is greener and you descend gradually to Tafí del Valle, a small town and popular weekend retreat from the heat of Tucumán in the summer (106 km). It has a cool microclimate, and makes a good base for walking, with several peaks of the Sierra de Aconquija providing satisfying day-hikes. There's some excellent, if pricey, accommodation and a **cheese festival** in early February, with live music. **Tourist information** ⓘ *Peotonal Los Faroles, T421880,* *www.tafidelvalle.com, 0800-2200 daily*. Map US$1.40. Visit the **Capilla Jesuítica y Museo de La Banda**, southwest of town across bridge over Rio Tafi, 500 m on left, ⓘ *T421685, Mon-Sat 0900-1900, Sun 0900-1600 (closing early off season), US$0.75, includes a guided tour*, an 18th-century chapel and 19th-century *estancia*, with museum of archaeology and religious art. **Museo de Mitos y Leyendas Casa Duende** ⓘ *R 307, Km 58 T0381-156 408500, US$1*, is a private museum concentrating on the gods, beliefs and environment of the people of the Valles Calchaquíes. ATM at Banco de Tucumán, Miguel Critto 311, T421033. Internet on Av Perón and one on Av Critto.

Amaicha, Quilmes and Santa María

From Tafí the road runs 56 km northwest over the 3,040 m Infiernillo Pass (Km 85) with spectacular views and through grand arid landscape to sunny **Amaicha del Valle** (*Population: 5,000; Altitude: 1,997 m; tourist information T03892 421198*) with the popular **Complejo Pachamama museum** ⓘ *T421004, daily 0830-1200, 1400-1830 (closed Sun off season), US$2*, highly recommended, with overview of the Calchaquí culture, geology, tapestry for sale by Héctor Cruz, well-known Argentine sculptor and artist. From Amaicha the paved road continues north 15 km to the junction with Ruta 40.

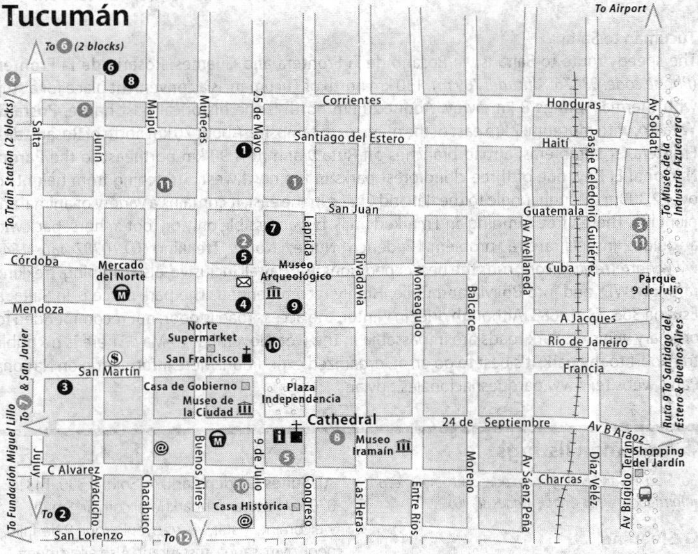

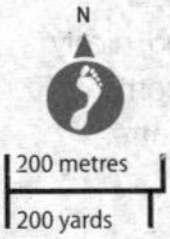

Sleeping
1 Backpacker's Tucumán
2 Carlos V
3 Catalinas Park
4 Dallas
5 Francia & Versailles
6 Hostel OH!
7 Hostería Aconquija
8 Mediterráneo
9 Miami
10 Premier
11 Suites Garden Park
12 Tucumán Hostel

Eating
1 Café de París
2 Cosas del Campo
3 El Fondo
4 Filipo
5 Il Postino
6 Klo y Klo
7 La Leñita
8 Panadería Villecco
9 Sir Harris
10 Superpanchería

Bars & clubs
11 Costumbres Argentinos

Some 35 km north, and 5 km off the main road, are the striking ruins of **Quilmes** ⓘ *0800-1800, US$1, includes guided tour and museum, with café, huge gift shop, hotel*. The setting is amazing, an intricate web of walls built into the mountain side, where 5,000 members of a Diaguita tribe lived, resisting Inca, and then Spanish domination, before being marched off to Córdoba and to the Quilmes in Buenos Aires where the beer comes from. For a day's visit take 0600 Aconquija bus from Cafayate to Santa María, alight after an hour at stop 5 km from site, or take 0700 El Indio bus (not on Thursday) from Santa María; take 1130 bus back to Cafayate, US$2; otherwise tours run from Cafayate.

Santa María (*Population: 11,000*), 22 km south of Amaicha by paved road, is a delightful, untouristy small town with an interesting archaeology museum at the **Centro Cultural Yokavil** ⓘ *corner of plaza, 0830-1300, 1700-2100, donation requested*, pleasant hotels and a municipal campsite. A helpful tourist kiosk is on the plaza, T03838-421083, with map and list of accommodation; also a *locutorio* and internet places, ATM on Mitre at Banco de la Nación (only one for miles). South of Santa María, Ruta 40 goes to Belén, see page 145. Instead of going to Amaicha to get to Quilmes, you can take the Ruta 40 up the west bank of the Río Santa María: ask for the bridge over the river and turn right. The road is paved to the Catamarca/Tucumán border, thereafter *ripio*. After 15 km, you pass **Fuerte Quemado** ⓘ *free*, an archaeological site of low-walled structures amid a variety of cactus. It's 10 km further to the Quilmes turn off.

Tucumán to Salta

The speedy route to Salta is via Rosario de la Frontera and Güemes. **Rosario de la Frontera** (*Phone code: 03876; Altitude: 769 m*), 130 km north of Tucumán, is a convenient place for a stop, with thermal springs 8 km away. About 20 km north is the historical post house, **Posta de Yatasto**, with museum, 2 km east of the main road; campsite. About 70 km north of Rosario de la Frontera, at Lumbreras, a road branches off Ruta 9 and runs 90 km northeast to the **Parque Nacional El Rey**, one of three cloudforest parks in the northwest. Stretching from heights of over 2,300m through jungle to the flat arid Chaco in the east, it contains a variety of animal and plant life. There's free camping and marked trails, but accessible only on foot or horseback with a guide; insects are a problem. Federico Norte, **Norte Trekking** ⓘ *T0387-436 1844, www.nortetrekking.com*, runs the best expeditions, full day all inclusive, also camping, trekking, rafting, 4WD, and into Bolivia and Chile. Highly recommended. The park office is in Salta, at España 366, T4312683. Although drier in winter, the access road is poor, not recommended for ordinary vehicles. Park roads are impassable in the wet, November to May. There is no public transport to the park; it's best to go on an organized expedition. More information on National Parks website: www.parquesnacionales.gov.ar.

Tucumán listings

For Sleeping and Eating price codes and other relevant information, see Essentials, pages 38-40.

Sleeping

Tucumán *p150, map p151*

All hotels include breakfast and have fans or a/c.

AL Catalinas Park, Av Soldati 380, T450 2250, www.catalinaspark.com. The city's most comfortable, good value, luxurious, minimalist hotel, overlooking Parque 9 de Julio, outstanding food and service, pool (open to non-residents), sauna, gym. Highly recommended.

AL Suites Garden Park, Av Soldati 330, T431 0700, www.gardenparkhotel.com.ar. Smart, welcoming 4-star, views over Parque 9 de Julio, pool, gym, sauna, restaurant. Also apartments.

B Carlos V, 25 de Mayo 330, T431 1666, www.hotelcarlosv.com.ar. Central, good service, with elegant restaurant.

B Dallas, Corrientes 985, T421 8500, www.dallashotel.com.ar. Welcoming, nicely furnished large rooms, good bathrooms. Recommended, though far from centre.

B Mediterráneo, 24 de Septiembre 364, T431 0025, www.hotelmediterraneo.com.ar. Good rooms, TV, a/c. 20-30% discount for *Footprint* owners.

B Premier, Crisóstomo Alvarez 510, T431 0381, info@redcarlosv.com.ar. Spacious comfortable rooms, modern bathrooms. Recommended.

B-C Francia, Crisóstomo Alvarez 467, T/F431 0781, www.franciahotel.com. Cheap apartments for 5, plain but comfortable high-ceilinged rooms, central, price depends on season.

B-C Versailles, Crisóstomo Alvarez 481, T422 9760, www.hotelversaillestuc.com.ar. A touch of class, comfortable beds though rooms a bit small, and good service, price depends on season. Recommended.

C Miami, Junín 580, 8 blocks from plaza, T431 0265, hotelmiamituc@hotmail.com. Good modern hotel, rooms with a/c and TV, though a little overpriced, discounts for HI members, pool.

E Hostería Aconquija, Av Aconquija 2530, Yerba Buena, 10 km from centre, T425 6901, www.aconquijahostel.com.ar. Youth hostel, rooms for 1-6 people, restaurant.

F pp **Backpacker's Tucumán**, Laprida 456, T430 2716, www.backpackerssalta.com/backpackers.html. Youth hostel in restored house with quiet atmosphere, lovely patio, basic dorms, well-equipped kitchen, internet, English spoken, good. Plus **D** double room with bath.

F pp **Hostel OH!**, Santa Fé 930, T430 8849, www.hosteloh.com.ar. Neat, modern hostel with shared or private rooms(D-E), quiet, kitchen and parrilla, internet, pool, games, garden and guitar lessons.

F pp **Tucumán Hostel**, Buenos Aires 669, T420 1584, www.tucumanhostel.com. The striking point of this old and quiet house is its beautiful Parador Tafinisto, at the bottom of Av Perón. Recommended for parrilla with plenty of regional dishes, and live folklore music at the weekends. Double room with bath **D**, **E** without.

Tafí del Valle *p150*

Many places, including hotels, close out of season.

AL-A Hostería Tafí del Valle, Av San Martín y Gdor Campero, T421027, www.soldelvalle.com.ar. ACA-owned, right at the top of the town, with splendid views, good restaurant, luxurious small rooms, pool.

A Lunahuana, Av Critto 540, T421330, www.luna huana.com.ar. Stylish comfortable rooms with good views, spacious duplexes for families.

A Mirador del Tafí, R 307, Km 61.2, T421219, www.mirador deltafi.com.ar. Warm attractive rooms and spacious lounge, superb restaurant, excellent views, look for midweek offers. Highly recommended.

B La Rosada, Belgrano 322, T421323, larosada@tafidelvalle.com. Spacious rooms, well decorated, plenty of hot water, comfortable, excellent breakfast included, helpful staff, lots of expeditions on offer and free use of cycles.

F pp **La Cumbre**, Av Perón 120, T421768, www.lacumbretafidelvalle.com. Basic, cramped rooms, but central, helpful owner is a tour operator with wide range of activities.

Estancias

AL Estancia Las Carreras, R 325, 13 km southwest of Tafí, T421473, www.estancialascarreras.com. A fine working estancia with lodging and a restaurant serving its own produce (including cheeses). It offers many activites such as riding, trekking, mountain biking and farm visits.

B Los Cuartos, Av Gob Critto y Av Juan Calchaquí s/n, T0381-155 874230, www.estancialoscuartos.com. Old *estancia* in town, rooms full of character, charming hosts. Recommended. Also offer a day at the *estancia*, with lunch. Delicious *té criollo*, US$5, lunch, US$8, and farm cheese can be bought here or at cheese shop on Av Miguel Critto.

Quilmes *p151*

B Parador Ruinas de Quilmes, T03892- 421075. Peaceful, very comfortable, boldly designed with weavings and ceramics, great views of Quilmes, good restaurant (residents only), free camping. Recommended.

Tucumán to Salta: Rosario de la Frontera *p152*

A Termas, Ruta 34 (6 km from bus station), T481004, www.hoteltermasalta.com.ar. Rambling place, good food, and thermal swimming pool, spa, horse riding, and golf. Baths US$2.

B ACA hostería, Ruta 34, Km 996, T481143. About 1 km from *Hotel Termas*, more comfortable, with restaurant, pool.

Eating

Tucumán *p150, map p151*
Many popular restaurants and cafés along 25 de Mayo, north from Plaza Independencia, and on Plaza Hipólito Yrigoyen.

TT El Fondo, San Martín 848, T422 2161. Superb renowned steak house.

TT Klo y Klo, Junín 657. Delightful, welcoming and charming atmosphere, good range of seafood and pastas (closed Sun evening and Mon).

TT La Leñita, 25 de Mayo 377. Recommended for *parrilla*, superb salads, live folk music at weekends.

T Sir Harris, Laprida y Mendoza. A Tucumán institution, cosy with good quality *tenedor libre*, some veggie dishes. Recommended.

T Il Postino, 25 de Mayo y Córdoba. Attractive buzzing pizza place, plus *tapas* and *tortillas* too, stylish décor. Recommended.

Cafés

Café de París, Santiago del Estero 502 y 25 de Mayo. *Tapas* bar and stylish little restaurant.

Cosas del Campo, Lavalle 857 (south of centre, next to Plaza San Martín), T420 1758. Renowned for its *empanadas*, also for take-away.

Filipo, Mendoza y 25 de Mayo. Good for a coffee or drinks, a popular smart café, good atmosphere.

Panadería Villecco, Corrientes 751. Exceptional bread, also wholemeal (*integral*) and pastries.

Superpanchería, 25 de Mayo. Bright busy hot dog place with huge range of salads and toppings.

Tafí del Valle *p150*
Many places along Av Perón.

TT-T El Portal de la Villa, Av Perón 221, T421834. Big with lots local dishes and *parrilla*, excellent *empanadas*.

Bars and clubs

Tucumán *p150, map p151*
Costumbres Argentinos, San Juan 666 y Maipú. An intimate place with a good atmosphere, for late drinks.

Festivals and events

Tucumán *p150, map p151*
9 Jul, Independence Day and **24 Sep, Battle of Tucumán**, both with huge processions/parties. **Sep, Fiesta Nacional de la Empanada**, in Famaillá, 35 km from Tucumán, 3 days of baking, eating and folk music, usually in first half of the month.

Shopping

Tucumán *p150, map p151*
Handicrafts **Mercado Artesanal**, 24 de Septiembre 565. Small, but nice selection of lace, wood and leatherwork. Daily 0800-1300, 1700-2200 (in summer, mornings only). **Norte supermarket**, Muñecas 137. **Regionales del Jardín**, Congreso 18. Good selection of local jams, *alfajores*, etc.

Activities and tours

Tafí del Valle *p150*
La Cumbre, see Sleeping, above. Energetic and helpful company, offering full day walks to nearby peaks, waterfalls and ruins, or to Cerro Muñoz, with an *asado* at the summit (4,437 m), has open-sided truck.

Transport

Tucumán *p150, map p151*
Air Airport at Benjamín Matienzo, 10 km east of town. Bus No 120 from terminal (*cospeles* required, sold in kiosks, US$0.35). Taxi US$4. **Cielos del Norte**, T426 5555, minibuses to/from airport to/from any place in town, US$1.50. To **Buenos Aires** via **Córdoba, AR/ Austral** (T431 1030). Also **LAN** (Laprida 176, T0810-999 9516), 2 flights a day.

Bus Bus terminal has 70 ticket offices, best to ask information kiosk opposite Disco T430 4696/422 2221. Local buses operate on *cospeles*, US$0.35, which you have to buy in advance in kiosks.

For long distance buses, the modern terminal is 6 blocks east of Plaza Independencia on Av Brigido Terán, with huge shopping complex, left luggage lockers (US$1), tourist information office (by *boletería* 1), lots of *locutorios*, toilets and banks (with ATM). Bus 4 from outside terminal to San Lorenzo y 9 de Julio in centre. Taxi to centre US$1. To **Buenos Aires**, many companies, 14-16 hrs,

US$45-60. To **Salta** direct (not via Cafayate), 4-4½ hrs, several companies US$15. To **Cafayate** from Tafí del Valle: see below. To **Posadas**, 17 hrs, US$40-55. To **Mendoza**, 13-14 hrs, US$46-62, via Catamarca, La Rioja, and San Juan. To **Catamarca**, **Aconquija** and other companies, 4 hrs, US$11-13. To **Andalgalá**, **Gutiérrez**, one daily, US$12. To **Córdoba**, 8 hrs, US$25-31. To/from **Santiago del Estero**, 2 hrs, US$6-7. To **La Quiaca** (border with Bolivia), **Balut** and **Andesmar**, 10 hrs, US$25-28. To **Santiago** (Chile) via Mendoza, **El Rápido Internacional**, daily, 22-24 hrs.

Tafí del Valle *p150*

Bus Smart new **Aconquija** terminal on Av Critto, with café, toilets, helpful information, T421025. To/from **Tucumán**, **Aconquija**, 8 daily, 2½ hrs (stop at El Mollar on request), US$7. To **Cafayate**, 3 a day, 2½ hrs, US$9. To **Salta**, 6 daily, 8 hrs, US$10.

Directory

Tucumán *p150, map p151*

Banks Most banks along San Martín especially 700 block between Junín and Maipú. **Maguitur**, San Martín 765, T431 0127, accepts TCs. **Maxicambio**, San Martín 779, T431 0020, currency exchange. **Car hire** Avis, at airport, T426 7777, avis@tucuman.com. **Donde Rent a Car**, Gob Gutiérrez 1384, T428 3626. **Movil Renta**, San Lorenzo 370, T431 0550, www.movilrenta.com.ar, and at airport. 20% discount for Footprint book owners. **Bicycle shop** Bike Shop, San Juan 984, T431 3121. Good. **Cultural centres** **Alliance Française**, Laprida 456, T421 9651, alianzafrancesatuc@gmail.com, free events in French. **Internet** **Cyber Noa**, 9 de Julio y San Lorenzo and **Centro Digital**, Chacabuco 32. **Cybercafé** in the *Kodak* shop at southernmost end of building that houses bus terminal, T430 6506, convenient. **Post office** Córdoba y 25 de Mayo, Mon-Fri 0800-1400, 1700-2000. **Telephone** Lots of *locutorios* including **Telecentros**, at 24 de Septiembre 612, Buenos Aires y Lavalle, San Lorenzo 704, offering broadband internet access, US$0.50-0.75 per hr.

Cafayate

→ *Phone code: 03868. Colour map 6, C3. Population: 10,700. Altitude: 1,660 m.*

Cafayate is a popular town for daytrippers and tourists, attracted by its dry sunny climate, its picturesque setting against the backdrop of the Andes and its excellent wines, of which the fruity white *Torrontés* is unique to Argentina. **Cerro San Isidro** (five hours return) gives you a view of the Aconquija chain in the south and Nevado de Cachi in the north. Six **bodegas** can be visited, including: **El Esteco** ⓘ *at the junction of Rutas 68 and 40, T155 66019, www.elesteco.com.ar*. Superb wines and a splendid setting. The oenologist Carolina Martín speaks English. **Etchart** ⓘ *2 km south on Ruta 40, T421310, www.vinosetchart.com*. More modest but also famous for good wine. Offers tours, but ring first to book. The boutique bodega, *San Pedro de Yacochuya* (T421233, www.yaco chuya.com), also has tours, beautiful hillside setting. **Vasija Secreta** ⓘ *on outskirts, next to ACA hostería, T421503*, is one of the oldest in the valley, English spoken. One block from the plaza is **Nanni** ⓘ *Chavarría 151, T421527*, very traditional, family-owned, with good tastings of organic wines. There are more vineyards at Tombolón, to the south. In all cases check visiting times as they vary and can be quite precise. The quality of tours and tastings also varies. The **tourist office** ⓘ *Nuestra Señora del Rosario 9, daily 0800-2200*. See also www.cafayate.com.

The modest **Museo de la Vid y El Vino** ⓘ *on Güemes Sur, 2 blocks south of Plaza Mon-Fri 0800-2000, Sat-Sun 0800-1300, 1400-2000,* tells the history of wine through old wine-making equipment. The tiny **Museo Arqueológico Rodolfo I Bravo** ⓘ *Calchaquí y Colón 191, T421054, Mon-Fri 1100-2100, open weekends on request, US$1,* has beautiful funerary urns, worth seeing if you haven't come across them elsewhere, and some Inca items. ATMs at *Banco de la Nación* (but no TCs), Toscano y NS del Rosario. Also at *BanSud*, Mitre y San Martín. Internet at *Sol del Valle*, Toscana 40, on Plaza, and at Güemes Norte 105 (very popular – pick your time, open late).

Ruta 68 goes northeast from Cafayate to Salta; 6 km out of town is the rather unexpected landscape of Los Médanos (dunes), whose sand is constantly moving through thickets. The road then goes through the dramatic gorge of the Río de las Conchas (also known as the **Quebrada de Cafayate**) with fascinating rock formations of differing colours, all signposted. The road goes through wild and semi-arid landscapes. The vegetation becomes gradually denser as you near Salta, a pretty river winding by your side with tempting picnic spots.

Valles Calchaquíes

A longer alternative to Salta is to take the RN40 north of Cafayate through the stunningly varied landscape of the Valles Calchaquíes to Cachi. The mainly *ripio* road (difficult after rain) winds from the spectacular rock formations of the arid **Quebrada de las Flechas** up through Andean-foothills with lush little oases and tiny unspoilt villages at **San Carlos** (helpful tourist office on plaza), **Angastaco**, a small, modern, smart town with a *Hostería*, petrol station and bus service (also with a tourist office in Municipalidad on the plaza, weekdays 0900-1300), and **Molinos** (all with limited bus services). The church of **San Pedro de Nolasco** in Molinos, mid-18th century, has a cactus-wood ceiling.

Cachi → *Phone code: 03868. Colour map 6, C3. Population: 7,200. Altitude: 2,280 m.*

Cachi is a beautiful town, in a valley made fertile by pre-Inca irrigation, set against a backdrop of arid mountains and the majestic Nevado del Cachi (6,380 m). Its rich Diaguita history, starting long before the Incas arrived in 1450, is well presented in the **Museo Arqueológico**, next to the Iglesia San José ⓘ *T491080, Mon-Fri 0830-1930, Sat-Sun 1000-1300, US$0.30,* with painted funerary urns and intriguing petroglyphs. The simple church next door has a roof and lecterns made of cactus wood. There are panoramic views from the hill-top cemetery, 20 minutes' walk from the plaza, and satisfying walks to **La Aguada** (6 km southwest), or to the ruins at **Las Pailas**, 16 km northwest, barely excavated. The view is breathtaking, with huge cacti set against snow-topped Andean peaks. It's a four-hour walk each way to Las Pailas (12-km track from the main road, the last part for a car is slow and rough; it leads to a farmstead from where it's 15 minutes on foot to the ruins; young man at the farm will offer to guide you). Cachi **tourist office** ⓘ *T491902, www.salnet.com.ar/cachi/, daily 0900-1200, 1500-2000,* and Mercado de Artesanías on the plaza. ATM at **Banco Sud**, Güemes y Ruiz de los Llanos; internet on F Suárez on corner of passage up to Plaza, 0900-1300, 1700-2130 (connection unreliable).

From Cachi to Salta follow Ruta 40 for 11 km north to Payogasta (*Hostería*), then turn right to Ruta 33. The road climbs continuously up the Cuesta del Obispo passing a dead-straight stretch of 14 km known as La Recta del Tin-Tin through the magnificent **Los Cardones National Park** ⓘ *administration office in Payogasta, 11 km from Cachi, T496005, loscardones@ apn.gov.ar,* with huge candelabra cacti, up to 6 m in height. Paving ends at the end of national park. The road reaches the summit at Piedra de Molino (3,347 m) after 43 km. Then it plunges down through the Quebrada de Escoipe, a breathtaking valley between olive green mountains, one of Argentina's great routes. The road rejoins Ruta 68 at El Carril, from where it is 37 km back to Salta.

Cafayate listings

For Sleeping and Eating price codes and other relevant information, see Essentials, pages 38-40.

Sleeping

Cafayate *p155*

Accommodation is hard to find at holiday periods (Jan, Easter, late Jul), but there are many places to stay. Off season, prices are much lower.

L Patios de Cafayate, Rutas 68 and 40, T421747, www.luxury collection.com/cafayate or www.eles teco.com.ar. A gorgeous hotel, in the converted building of the old winery (now **El Estecco**, see above), with beautifully designed rooms, sumptuous lounges, lovely gardens, with pool. There are interesting wine-oriented treatments in the spa (T421753) and the restaurant serves fine food and excellent wines. Highly recommended.

AL Viñas de Cafayate, R21, Camino al Divisadero, T422272, www.cafayatewineresort.com. On a hillside above Cafayate, colonial style, calm, welcoming with pretty, spacious bedrooms, some with views. Excellent restaurant with local delicacies, open to non-residents with reservation, full buffet breakfast. Recommended.

B Los Sauces, Calchaquí 62, T421158, lossauces@ arnet.com.ar, directly behind the cathedral. Modern, small, tasteful rooms, breakfast included, pretty garden, lovely views from upper floors.

B-C Hostería Cafayate, T421296, www.soldel valle.com.ar. Comfortable rooms around a leafy colonial-style patio, reasonably priced restaurant, pool (summer only). Highly recommended.

C Tinkunaku, Diego de Almagro 12, 1 block from plaza, T421148, www.nortevirtual.com (on Hotelería pages). Pleasant spacious rooms, with weavings on the walls. Recommended.

D Confort, Güemes Norte 232, T421091. Slightly kitsch but simple, hospitable staff. Also has well-equipped cabañas **Chalet Seis** (**A**) for up to 6, with kitchen, pool, heating.

D Hostal del Valle, San Martín 243, T421039, www.nortevirtual.com. Well kept big rooms around leafy patio, charming owner. New living room at the top has superb views over the valley (as do upper floor rooms). Highly recommended.

E pp **El Portal de las Viñas**, Nuestra Señora del Rosario 165, T421098, www.portal vinias.com.ar. Charming owner, school-teacher Mirta. Rooms for 2 to 6, all with bath (**F** pp in low season).

F pp **El Hospedaje**, Quintana de Niño y Salta, T421680, elhospedaje@nortevirtual.com. Simple but pleasant rooms in colonial-style house, wonderful pool, good value, heater in room, breakfast included, discount to HI members. Recommended.

F Hostería Docente, Güemes Norte 160, T421810. Light simple rooms, some with bath, but not breakfast, welcoming and central.

Campsite Municipal site **Lorohuasi** on RN40(S), T421051, US$2 pp plus tent. Hot water, pool, well maintained. Better still, **Luz y Fuerza**, T421568, on RN40(S), quiet, good value, US$2 pp, massive pool, information on wine tours.

Valles Calchaquíes *p156*

LL Colomé, 20 km west of Molinos, T494044, www.bodegacolome.com. Leave town via the vicuña farm and follow signs, or phone for directions from Cafayate. Recommended as one of the best places to stay in Argentina, winery in a beautiful setting with delightful rooms, horse riding, tastings of excellent wines, all food is organic, power is hydroelectric.

B Hostal Provincial de Molinos, T03868-494002, hostaldemolinos@arnet.com.ar. Huge simple rooms arranged around big courtyards, historic building, decent meals (nothing fancy, but the best you'll find in Molinos). Recommended.

Also in Molinos: **F** pp **Hospedaje San Agustín** at the Colegio Infantil, T494015. Small but spotless rooms, some with private bath, run by nuns (who don't like to advertise the place, ask around discretely for "las monjas" and someone will come and give you a key).

D pp **Hostería Angastaco**, T03868-156 39016. Price includes breakfast, basic comfy rooms, warm welcome, bar, dining room and pool (Jan-Mar).

Cachi *p156*

AL El Molino de Cachi Adentro, T491094, elmolinodecachi@salnet.com.ar. 4 km on the road to La Aguada, in restored 300-year old mill, only 5 rooms, superb food, exquisite every way, pool.

AL Finca Santana, take the road to Cachi Adentro, and ask for Camino to Finca San Miguel, on right at top, T1563 8762. 2 rooms in boutique B&B in the heart of the valley, spectacular views, and complete sense of privacy and silence. Welcoming, spacious living room, terrace and garden, gourmet breakfast, trekking can be arranged. Wonderful.

A ACA Hostería Cachi, at the top of Juan Manuel Castilla, T491904, www.soldel valle.com.ar. Smart modern rooms (with wheelchair access), great views, pool, good restaurant, non-residents can use the pool if they eat lunch.

A Casa de Campo La Paya, 12 km south of Cachi at La Paya, clearly signposted from the road, T491139, www.casadecampolapaya.com.ar. A restored 18th-century house, pool, elegant rooms, excellent dinners, hospitable, Recommended.

A El Cortijo, opposite the ACA hotel, on Av Automóvil Club s/n, T491034, www.elcortijo hotel.com. Lovely peaceful rooms, each with its own style, warm hospitality, original art works. Highly recommended.

B Llaqta Mawka, Ruiz de Los Llanos s/n, up from Plaza, T491016, www.hotelllaqtamawka. todoweb salta.com.ar. Traditional frontage hides modern block, garden/terrace, view of the Nevado de Cachi, pool. Comfy rooms, ample breakfast, internet, TV, good value, popular with tourists (street parking).

E Hospedaje Don Arturo, Bustamente s/n, T491087. Homely, small rooms, quiet street, charming owners.

F Hospedaje El Nevado de Cachi, Ruiz de los Llanos y F Suárez, T491912. Impeccable small rooms with bath around a central courtyard, hot water, *comedor*.

Camping Municipal campsite at Av Automóvil Club Argentina s/n, T491902, with pool and sports complex, also *cabañas* and *albergue*.

Eating

Cafayate *p155*

TT Baco, Güemes Norte y Rivadavia, T154-028366. Parrilla, *pasta casera*, pizzas, regional dishes, *empanadas* and *picadas*. Seating inside and on street, attractive corner, lively atmosphere. Wine a bit pricier than elsewhere, but all local, good selection, good meat dishes.

TT La Carreta de Don Olegario, Güemes, on Plaza. Huge and brightly lit, good set menus including the usual meat dishes and pastas.

TT Colorado, Belgrano 28, T421280, www.restaurantecolorado.com. Varied menu, international, local and tapas, good food and atmosphere, beer from *Imayki* micro-brewery in Salta. US-owned.

TT El Rancho, Toscano 3, T421256. On plaza, meats, regional dishes. Best mid-range option.

T El Comedor Criollo, Güemes Norte 254. A *parrilla*, also serving pasta, with *peña* at night.

T Café de las Viñas, Güemes Sur 58. Open all day, everything from breakfasts to cheap *lomitos*.

T Las Dos Marías, San Martín 27 on Plaza. Small, serves excellent food, loved by locals.

T El Rincón del Amigo, San Martín 25 on Plaza. Small place for great set menus and *empanadas*.

Cafés

Helados Miranda, Güemes Norte 170. Fabulous homemade ice cream, including wine flavour.

Cachi *p156*

T Confitería El Sol, Ruiz de Los Llanos on the plaza. Regional food, limited menu, popular with groups in summer, offers horse riding, contact via email delsol_cach i@hotmail.com or T03868-156 38690.

T Oliver Café, Ruiz de Los Llanos on the plaza. Tiny café for ice creams, coffee, breakfasts, fruit juices, sandwiches and pizza.

Shopping

Cafayate *p155*

Handicrafts Apart from the rather general souvenir shops, there are some fine handicrafts. Visit Calchaquí tapestry exhibition of **Miguel Nanni** on the main plaza, silver work at **Jorge Barraco**, Colón 157, T421244. Paintings by **Calixto Mamaní**, Rivadavia 452. Local pottery, woollen goods, etc are sold in the **Mercado de Artesanos Cafayetanos** on the plaza (small, pricey).

Activities and tours

Cafayate *p155*

Turismo Cordillerana, Quintana de Niño 59, T422137, www.turismocordillerano.com.ar. Tours, trekking, horses, bike hire.

Cycle hire Many places, ask tourist office for list. **Horse riding** Horses can be hired from **La Florida**, Bodega Etchart, 2 km south of Cafayate.

Transport

Cafayate *p155*

Bus 2 bus terminals: With **El Indio** on Belgrano, ½ block from plaza, to **Santa María** (for Quilmes) 4 daily. To **Angastaco**, **El Indio**, one daily Mon-Fri, US$4, 1½ hrs (but does not continue to Molinos and Cachi). To/from **Tucumán**, **Aconquija** (Güemes Norte y Alvarado, Cafayate, T422175/421052, open only when buses due), 3 daily, 5½ hrs, US$15; and to **Tafí del Valle**, 3 daily, US$9, 3 hrs (more via **Santa María**, 5½ hrs) with **Aconquija**.

Cachi *p156*

Bus To **Salta**, **Marcos Rueda**, T491063, daily (except Sun) at 0900, and Mon, Thu, Fri, Sun at 1500, 4½ hrs, US$11. To **Molinos** daily at 1200.

Salta → *Phone code: 0387. Colour map 6, C3. Population: 470,000. Altitude: 1,190 m.*

Founded in 1582, Salta, 1,600 km north of Buenos Aires, is an atmospheric city, with many fine colonial buildings, elegant plazas, stirring folkloric music and fabulous food. It lies in the broad Lerma valley, surrounded by steep and forested mountains, and is a good base for exploring the Andean regions, Cachi in the Calchaquí valleys to the south (described above) and the Quebrada de Humahuaca north of Jujuy (described in the next section).

Salta is a fascinating city to explore on foot; in a couple of hours you can get a feel for its wonderful architecture. Good maps are available from the **Provincial Tourist Office** ⓘ *Buenos Aires 93 (1 block from main plaza), T431 0950, www.turismosalta.gov.ar. Open weekdays 0800-2100, weekends 0900-2000*. Very helpful, gives free maps, advice on tours and arranges accommodation in private houses in high season (July), only when hotels are fully booked. The **municipal tourist office** ⓘ *Caseros 711, T0800-777 0300, Mon-Fri 0800-2100, Sat-Sun 0900-2100*, is for Salta city only, small but helpful. Other websites: www.turismoensalta.com of the Cámara de Turismo, Gral Güemes 15 y Av Virrey Toledo, T480 0719; www.saltaciudad.com.ar; www.iruya.com and www.redsalta.com. Local buses in the city charge US$0.25. A hop-on, hop-off bus called the **BTS** (Bus Turístico Salta, www.busturisticosalta.com) does a circuit of the town, US$9.

Sights

The heart of Salta, is **Plaza 9 de Julio**, planted with tall palms and surrounded by colonial buildings. On the plaza, the **Cabildo**, 1783, one of the few to be found intact in the country, houses the impressive **Museo Histórico del Norte** ⓘ *Caseros 549, Tue-Fri 0900-1800, Sat-Sun 0900-1330, US$1.50, free Wed.* The museum has displays on pre-Columbian and colonial history, independence wars, and a fine 18th-century pulpit. Opposite the Cabildo, is the 19th-century **Cathedral** (open mornings and evenings), painted pink and cream and reflected in the blue plate glass of a bank next door. It contains a huge late baroque altar (1807) and the much venerated images of the Virgin Mary and of the Cristo del Milagro, sent from Spain in 1592. The miracle was the sudden cessation of a terrifying series of earthquakes when the images were paraded through the streets on 15 September 1692. They still are, each September. Salta's newest museum, **Museo de Arqueología de Alta Montaña** (MAAM), ⓘ *Mitre 77, T437 0499, www.maam.org.ar, Tue-Sun 1100-1930, US$8*, has a superb collection of exhibits from Inca high-altitude shrines, including mummies of child sacrifices, video material in Spanish and English, also temporary exhibits. After controversy over the display of the mummies, they are exhibited with respectful sensitivity; visitors can choose whether or not to view them. A block southwest of the Plaza is the **Museo de la Ciudad 'Casa de Hernández'** ⓘ *Florida 97 y Alvarado, T4373352, Mon-Fri 0900-1300, 1600-2030, Sat 1700-2030, free.* This fine 18th-century mansion includes furniture and dull portraits, but a marvellous painting of Güemes. The magnificent façade of **San Francisco** church ⓘ *on Caseros, 0730-1200, 1700-2100*, rises above the skyline with its splendid tower, ornately decorated in plum red and gold. Further along Caseros, the Convent of **San Bernardo**, rebuilt in colonial style in the mid-19th century, has a beautifully carved wooden portal of 1762, but is not open to visitors as nuns still live there. They will open up the small shop for you, selling quaint handicrafts.

At the end of Caseros is the **Cerro San Bernardo** (1,458 m) ⓘ *accessible by cable car (teleférico from Parque San Martín), daily 1000-1900, US$5.50 return, US$3 children, fine views, 45 mins' walk to return.* At the summit are gardens, waterfalls, a café, a silver collection and playground. Further along Avenida H Yrigoyen is an impressive **statue to General Güemes**, whose *gaucho* troops repelled seven powerful Spanish invasions from Bolivia between 1814 and 1821.

Up beyond the Güemes statue is the **Museo Antropológico** ⓘ *Paseo Güemes, T422 2960, www.antropologico.gov.ar, Mon, Wed, Fri 0800-1900, Tue, Thu 0800-2100, Sat 0900-1300, 1500-1900, helpful and knowledgeable staff, US$1.50.* Fascinating displays on pre-Inca cultures include painted urns, intriguing board-flattened skulls (meant to confer superiority), a mummy discovered high in the Andes and many objects from Tastil (see below). **Museo de Ciencias Naturales** ⓘ *Parque San Martín, Tue-Sun 1530-1930, US$0.50,* displays a bewildering number of stuffed animals and birds; the armadillo collection is interesting.

Salta

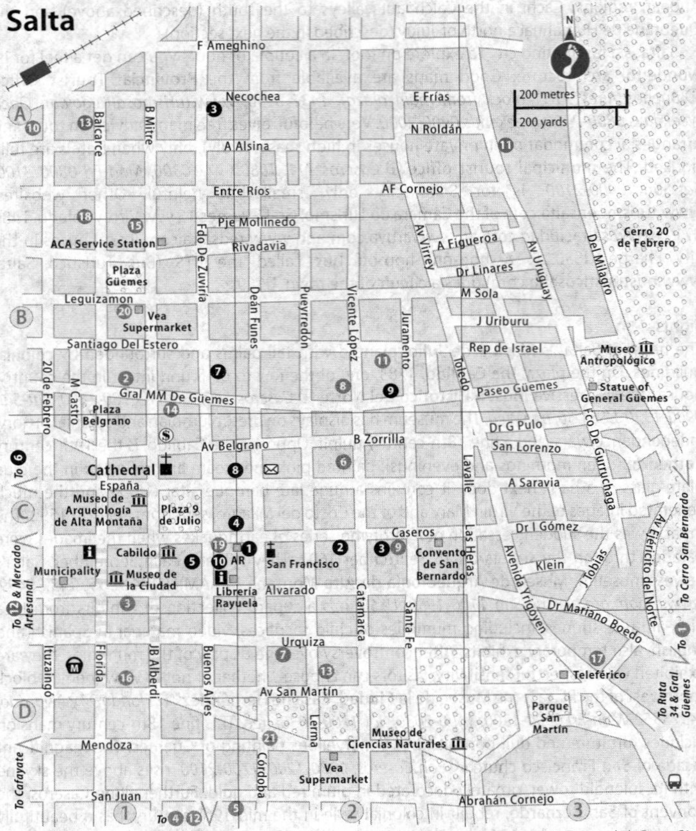

Sleeping
1 Apart Ilusión *D3*
2 Ayres de Salta *B1*
3 Backpackers City *C1*
4 Backpackers Home *D2*
5 Backpackers Soul *D1*
6 Bloomers Bed & Brunch *C2*
7 Carpe Diem *D2*
8 Correcaminos Hostel *B2*
9 Del Antiguo Convento *C2*
10 El Lagar *A1*
11 Hostal Quara *B2*
12 Hostal Sallka *D1*
13 Las Marías *D2*
14 Las Rejas *B1*
15 Legado Mítico *B1*
16 Munay *D1*
17 Petit *D3*
18 Posada de las Nubes *A1*
19 Salta *C1*
20 Solar de la Plaza *B1*
21 Terra Oculta *D2*

Eating
1 Doña Salta & Goblin *C2*
2 El Charrúa *C2*
3 El Corredor de las Empanadas *C2*
4 El Solar del Convento *C1*
5 Entre Indyas *C1*
6 La Casa de Güemes *C1*
7 La Criollita *B1*
8 La Terraza de la Posta *C1*
9 Mama Paca *B2*
10 Plaza Café *C1*

Bars & clubs
11 Gauchos de Güemes *A3*
12 La Casona del Molino *C1*
13 La Vieja Estación *A1*

Cloud line

One of the great railway journeys of South America is the Tren a las Nubes (Train to the Clouds). Engineered by Richard Maury, of Pennsylvania (who is commemorated by the station at Km 78 which bears his name) this remarkable project was built in stages between 1921 and 1948, by which time developments in road and air transport had already reduced its importance. The line includes 21 tunnels, 13 viaducts, 31 bridges, 2 loops and 2 zig-zags. From Salta the line climbs gently to Campo Quijano (Km 40, 1,520 m), where it enters the Quebrada del Toro, an impressive rock-strewn gorge. At El Alisal (Km 50) and Chorrillos (Km 66) there are zig-zags as the line climbs the side of the gorge before turning north into the valley of the Río Rosario near Puerto Tastil (Km 101, 2,675 m), missing the archaeological areas around Santa Rosa de Tastil. At Km 122 and Km 129 the line goes into 360° loops before reaching Diego de Almagro (3,304 m). At Abra Muñano (3,952 m) the road to San Antonio can be seen zig-zagging its way up the end-wall of the Quebrada del Toro below. From Muñano (3,936 m) the line drops slightly to San Antonio, Km 196. The spectacular viaduct at La Polvorilla is 21 km further at 4,190 m, just beyond the branch line to the mines at La Concordia. The highest point on the line is reached at Abra Chorrillos (4,475 m, Km 231). From here the line runs on another 335 km across a rocky barren plateau 3,500-4,300 m above sea level before reaching Socompa (3,865 m).

This is a comfortable ride, but a long day out (see page 166). The train leaves Salta to the cheerful accompaniment of musicians on the platform, then enters the Quebrada del Toro. As you climb through the gorge the landscape changes from forested mountains to farmland to arid red rock dotted with giant cactii. Eventually you reach the beautiful puna. On the seven-hour ascent there are chats from bilingual guides (English spoken, but French and Portuguese too on request), and lunch is served. If altitude sickness hits, oxygen is on hand. At La Polvorilla viaduct, you can get out briefly to admire the construction and buy locally-made llama-wool goods. Don't bother haggling: the shawls and hats are beautifully made and the people's only source of income. At San Antonio, the Argentine flag is raised to commemorate those who worked on the railway and the national anthem is sung. The descent, unfortunately, is tedious, despite more musical entertainment, so consider returning by road to see the ruins at Santa Rosa de Tastil.

San Antonio de los Cobres ➔ *Phone code: 0387, Population: 4,000, Altitude: 3,775 m.*

Sitting in the vast emptiness of the puna, San Antonio de los Cobres, 168 km by road from Salta, is a simple, remote mining town of adobe houses with a friendly Coya community. Ruta 51 leads to La Polvorilla railway viaduct (see below), 20 km, ask in town for details and beware sudden changes in the weather. Try the *quesillo de cabra* (goat's cheese) from Estancia Las Cuevas. The *Huaira Huasi* restaurant, used by tour groups, has a good menu. At **Santa Rosa de Tastil** there are important prehispanic ruins and a small **museum** ⓘ *daily 1000-1800, US$1*, recommended. Basic accommodation next door to the museum, no electricity or heating, take food, water and candles. Take El Quebradeño bus (see Transport, below), a tour from Salta, or share a taxi.

The famous **Tren a las Nubes** is a 570 km, narrow gauge railway running from Salta through the town of San Antonio de los Cobres to Socompa, on the Chilean border (see box opposite). San Antonio can also be reached by Ruta 51 from Salta. From **Campo Quijano**, the road runs along the floor of the Quebrada del Toro before climbing to Alto Blanco (paved section).

Ruta 51 from San Antonio de los Cobres to **San Pedro de Atacama**, Chile uses the **Sico** Pass (4,079 m). It's a spectacular route, crossing white salt lakes dotted with flamingos and vast expanses of desert. Most of it is unpaved and the route has been replaced by that over Jama

Pass (see page 170). There is a customs post at Paso Sico (you may be allowed to spend the night here, T498 2001), hours 0800-2000: check first in San Antonio de los Cobres if it is open. On the Chilean side continue via Mina Laco and Socaire to Toconao (road may be bad between these two points). Customs and immigration are in San Pedro de Atacama. Note that fruit, vegetables and dairy products may not be taken into Chile (search 20 km after Paso Sico). Gasoline is available in San Pedro and Calama. Obtain sufficient drinking water for the trip in San Antonio and do not underestimate the effects of altitude.

Salta listings

For Sleeping and Eating price codes and other relevant information, see Essentials, pages 38-40.

Sleeping

Salta *p159, map p160*

Book ahead in Jul holidays and around 10-16 Sep during celebrations of Cristo del Milagro. Among Salta's most desirable places to stay are its colonial-style *estancias*, known locally as *fincas*.

L Finca El Bordo de las Lanzas, 45 km east of Salta, T490 3070, www.turismoelbordo.com.ar. Formal and luxurious, a taste of aristocratic life, with splendid horse riding and charming hosts. Highly recommended.

L Legado Mítico, Mitre 647, T422 8786, www.legadomitico.com. This small, welcoming hotel is absolutely lovely, luxurious rooms each with its own personality, the personalized pre-ordered breakfasts are a fantastic way to start the day. Highly recommended.

L Solar de la Plaza, Juan M Leguizamon 669, T431 5111, www.solardelaplaza.com.ar. Elegant old former Salteño family home, faultless service, sumptuous rooms, great restaurant and a pool.

AL Finca Los Los, Chicoana, 40 km from Salta at the entrance to the Valles Calchaquíes, T0387-156 833121, www.redsalta.com/loslos. Open Mar to Dec. Great hilltop views, charming rooms, beautiful gardens, pool, unforgettable horse riding to *asados* in the mountains. Handy for the airport and Cachi. Highly recommended.

AL Finca Santa Anita, Coronel Moldes, 60 km from Salta, on the way to Cafayate T/F490 5050, www.santaanita.com.ar. Family welcome at this prize-winning organic farm on a traditional colonial-style finca: great food and all activities included in the price. Beautiful views, swimming, guided walks to prehistoric rock paintings, and horse riding. Highly recommended.

AL Hostería de Chicoana, in Chicoana, 47 km south, T490 7009, www.newsendas.com. Bohemian but faded colonial style, English and German spoken, expert guide Martín Pekarek offers adventure excursions and horses for hire. Recommended.

AL Salta, Buenos Aires 1, in main plaza, T426 7500, www.hotelsalta.com. A Salta institution with neo-colonial public rooms, refurbished bedrooms, marvellous suites overlooking plaza, *confitería* and honorary membership of the Polo and Golf Club.

AL El Lagar, 20 de Febrero 877, T431 9439, ellagar@arnet.com.ar. An intimate boutique hotel owned by wine-making Etchart family, beautifully furnished rooms full of fine paintings, excellent restaurant, gardens (guests only). Highly recommended.

AL-A Ayres de Salta, Gral Güemes 650, T422 1616, www.ayresdesalta.com.ar. Spacious, central 4-star hotel near Plaza Belgrano, everything you would expect in this price-range: spacious rooms, heated pool, great views from a roof terrace.

A Carpe Diem, Urquiza 329, T421 8736, info@carpediemsalta.com.ar. Welcoming B&B, beautifully furnished, with breakfast, convenient, internet, no children under 14. Recommended.

A pp **Finca El Manantial del Milagro**, La Silleta, 25 km from Salta, T439 5506 or T156-056860, www.hotelmanantial.com.ar. Formal style in historical estancia, beautiful views, lovely rooms, marvellous food, swimming, farming activities, riding and walking around the estate.

A Hostal Selva Montana, C Alfonsina Storni 2315, T492 1184, www.hostal-selvamontana.com.ar. At San Lorenzo, 11 km northwest of centre, extremely comfortable and relaxing modern hotel in traditional style, in forested hills, pool, horses and walks on offer. Take a taxi or bus **El Indio** interurbano from terminal.

A Bloomers Bed & Brunch, Vicente López 129, T422 7449, www.bloomerssalta.com.ar. Closed mid-May to mid-Jun. In a refurbished colonial

house, 5 spacious rooms individually decorated, and one apartment, use of kitchen, library. The brunch menu, different each day, is their speciality. Warmly recommended.
B Apart Ilusión (Sweet Dreams), José Luis Fuentes 743, Portezuelo Norte, T432 1081, www.aparthotel ilusion.com.ar. On the slopes of Cerro San Bernardo, beautiful views, new, well-equipped self-catering apartments for 2-4, decorated with local handicrafts, English-speaking owner Sonia Alvarez, welcoming, breakfast and parking available, very good value.
B Del Antiguo Convento, Caseros 113, T422 7267, www.hoteldelconvento.com.ar. Small, convenient, with old-fashioned rooms around a neat patio, very helpful, a good choice.
B Petit, H Yrigoyen 225, T421 3012, www.todoweb salta.com.ar/petithotelsalta. Handy for the bus terminal and Cerro San Bernardo, plain pleasant rooms around a patio with pool and garden.
B Posada de las Nubes, Balcarce 639, T432 1776, www.posadadelasnubes.com.ar. Charming, new, small, with simply decorated rooms around a central patio.Great location for Balcare nightlife.
C Las Marías, Lerma 255, T422 4193, www.salta guia.com/lasmarias. Central hostel, **E** pp in shared rooms, with breakfast, kitchen, close to Parque San Martín. Recommended.
C Munay, San Martín 656, T422 4936, www.munay hotel.jujuy.com. Good choice, smart rooms for 2-5 with good bathrooms, warm welcome, breakfast included. Highly recommended. Also have hotels of the same standard in Cafayate, Humahuaca Jujuy and La Quiaca.
C Las Rejas, General Güemes 569, T421 5971, www.lasrejashostel.com.ar. A lovely family house with just a few comfortable rooms, central, peaceful. Recommended.
C-D Hostal Sallka, Buenos Aires 753, T4260785, www.hostalsallka.com.ar. A little out of the centre, relaxed, with breakfast, Wi-Fi, secure parking.
E pp **Backpackers Home**, Buenos Aires 930, T423 5910, **Backpackers Soul**, San Juan 413, T431 8944, and **Backpackers City**, Alvarado 751, T431 6476, www.backpackerssalta.com. Three HI-affiliated hostels, all are well run, with dorms and private rooms (**B**, cheaper for HI members), with laundry, kitchen, Wi-Fi, and budget travel information. Crowded and popular.
E pp **Terra Oculta**, Córdoba 361, T421 8769, www.terraoculta.com. Party atmosphere, laid-back place with small dorms, homely, kitchen, TV, email, laundry, great roof terrace bar, good annex at Av San Martín y Córdoba, very popular.
F pp **Correcaminos Hostel**, Vicente López 353, T422 0731, hostelcorrecaminossalta@ hotmail.com. 4 blocks from plaza, modern dorms, 2 doubles, shared bath, laundry, kitchen, free internet, Wi-Fi, pleasant garden, good, lively.
F pp **Hostal Quara**, Santiago del Estero 137, T431 1421, www.hostalquara.com.ar. Dorms, also doubles (**D**), with breakfast, heating, use of kitchen, internet, TV room, drinks for sale, helpful staff, can organize tours. Recommended.

San Antonio de los Cobres *p161*
C Hostería de las Nubes, T490 9059, edge of San Antonio on Salta road. Smart, includes breakfast, comfortable, modern and spacious. Recommended.
F Hospedaje Belgrano, Belgrano s/n, T490 9025. Welcoming, basic, hot showers, evening meals. There are other lodgings. Ask at the Municipalidad, Belgrano s/n, T490 9045, about dorm and double room at the tourist information office (**F**) and minibus tours to salt flats and Purmamarca.

Campo Quijano
A Hostería Punta Callejas, T0387-490 4086, www.puntacallejas.com.ar. Bath, a/c, with breakfast, very clean and comfortable, pool, tennis, riding, excursions.
Camping Several sites, including municipal campsite, at entrance to Quebrada del Toro gorge, lovely spot with good facilities, hot showers, bungalows.

Eating

Salta *p159, map p160*
Salta has delicious and distinctive cuisine: try the *locro*, *humitas* and *tamales*, served in the municipal market at San Martín y Florida.
TTT **El Solar del Convento**, Caseros 444, half a block from plaza. Elegant and not expensive, champagne when you arrive, delicious steaks. Recommended.
TT **La Casa de Güemes**, España 730. Popular, local dishes and *parrilla*, traditionally cooked in the house where General Güemes lived.

Ⲯ **Doña Salta**, Córdoba 46 (opposite San Francisco convent library). Excellent regional dishes and pleasant, rustic atmosphere, good value.

Ⲯ **Entre Indyas**, Buenos Aires 44. A little hard to find as it's in an arcade, this fantastic vegetarian restaurant mixes Peruvian and Indian food. Recommended.

El Charrúa, Caseros 221, T432 1859, www.parrillaelcharrua.com.ar. A good, brightly lit family place with a reasonably priced and simple menu where *parrilla* is particularly recommended.

El Corredor de las Empanadas, Caseros 117 and Zuviría 913. Delicious *empanadas* and tasty local dishes in airy surroundings.

La Criollita, Zuviría 306. Small and unpretentious, a traditional place for tasty *empanadas*.

Ⲯ **Goblin**, Caseros 445. Over 40 artisanal beers and great pub food, popular with travellers and locals alike.

Mama Paca, Gral Güemes 118. Recommended by locals, traditional restaurant for seafood from Chile and homemade pastas.

La Terraza de la Posta, España 456. Huge menu, including steak and *empanadas*.

Cafés

Plaza Café next to *Hotel Salta* is more popular with Salteños, good for coffee or breakfast.
Rosemari, Av Belgrano y Pueyrredón. Excellent ice creams.

Bars and clubs

Salta *p159, map p160*
Visit a *peña* to hear passionate folklore music live. There are many bars, called *peñas*, with excellent live bands on Balcarce towards railway station, a great place to go at weekends (taxi US$1.50). **Balderrama**, T421 1542, is much touted but touristy (2200-0200). Head instead for: **La Casona del Molino**, Caseros 2500, T434 2835. Most authentic, in a crumbling old colonial house, good food and drink. **Gauchos de Güemes**, Uruguay 750, T421 7007, www.gauchosdesalta.com.ar, popular, delicious regional food. **La Vieja Estación**, Balcarce 885, T421 7727. Great atmosphere, good food, highly recommended.

Festivals and events

Salta *p159, map p160*
16-17 Jun, commemoration of the **death of General Martín Güemes**: folk music in evening and *gaucho* parade in morning around the Güemes statue. Salta celebrates **Carnival** with processions on the 4 weekends before Ash Wednesday at 2200 in Ciudad de Salta Stadium, 4 km south of town (US$0.50); also **Mardi Gras** (Shrove Tuesday) with a procession of floats and dancers with intricate masks of feathers and mirrors. Water is squirted at passersby and *bombas de agua* (small balloons filled with water) are sold for dropping from balconies.
15 Sep, Cristo del Milagro (see above);
24 Sep, Battles of Tucumán and Salta.

Shopping

Salta *p159, map p160*
Bookshops **Feria del Libro**, Buenos Aires 83. Huge shop, some in English. **Librería Rayuela**, Alvarado 570. Excellent, with some foreign-language books and magazines.
Handicrafts Arts and handicrafts are often cheaper in surrounding villages. **Mercado Artesanal** on the western outskirts, in the Casa El Alto Molino, San Martín 2555, T434 2808, daily 0900-2100, take bus 2, 3, or 7 from Av San Martín in centre and get off as bus crosses the railway line. Excellent range and high quality in lovely 18th-century mansion. Opposite is a cheaper tourist market for similar items, but factory-made. **Siwok Crafts**, Zuviría 30. Quality wood carvings by the Wichi indigenous people, and typical *yika* woven bags.
Markets and supermarkets **Mercado Municipal**, San Martín y Florida, for meat, fish, vegetables, *empanadas*, *humitas* and other produce and handicrafts, closed 1300-1700 and Sun. **Norte**, 20 de Febrero y Caseros. Good supermarket. **San Francisco**, Deán Funes 596, T421 2984. 24-hr pharmacy. **Vea** supermarkets at Florida y Caseros, Mitre y Leguizamon and Mendoza entre Lerma y Catamarca.

Activities and tours

Salta *p159, map p160*
There are many tour operators, mostly on Buenos Aires, offering adventure trips and excursions; staff give out flyers on the street (likewise car hire companies). Out of season,

tours often run only if there is sufficient demand; check carefully that tour will run on the day you want. At all times check that tours will go exactly where you have paid for and that they have sufficient staff and supplies. All agencies charge similar prices for tours (though some charge extra for credit card payments). City tour US$16; Valles Calchaquíes US$90; Cachi US$40; San Antonio de los Cobres US$50. The tourist office gives reports on agencies and their service.

Bici tours, T4394887, 156 838067, www.bicinorte.com.ar. Specialists in cycle tours.

Movitrack, Buenos Aires 39, T431 6749, and a desk at airport, www.movitrack.com.ar. Entertaining safaris in a 4WD truck, to San Antonio de los Cobres, Humahuaca, Cafayate and Iruya, city tours, adventure trips, German, English spoken, expensive. They also have an OxyBus for high-altitude journeys.

Norte Trekking, Av del Libertador 1151B, Barrio Grand Bourg, T436 1844, www.norte trekking.com. Excellent tours all over Salta and Jujuy, to Iruya, over Jama Pass to San Pedro de Atacama, hiking, horse riding, excursions to El Rey national park with experienced guide Federico Norte, knowledgeable, speaks English. Tailors tours to your interest and budget.

Puna Expediciones, Agustín Usandivaras 230, T434 1875 or T154-030263, www.puna expeditions .com.ar. Qualified and experienced guide Luis H Aguilar organizes treks in remote areas of Salta and Jujuy and safaris further afield. Recommended.

Ricardo Clark Expeditions, Mariano Moreno 1950, T497 1024, www.clarkexpediciones.com. Specialist birding tours, eco-safaris and treks. English spoken.

Sayta, Chicoana, 49 km from Salta, T0387-15 6836565, www.saltacabalgatas.com.ar. An estancia specializing in horse riding, for all levels of experience, good horses and attention, great *asados*, also has lodging for overnight stays, adventure and rural tourism. Recommended.

Socompa, Balcarce 998, p 1, T416 9130, www.socompa.com. Excellent company specializing in trips to the puna, 1-3-day trips to salt flats and volcanoes based at the beautiful, remote hamlet of Tolar Grande. English and Italian spoken, knowledgeable guides. Highly recommended.

Transport

Salta *p159, map p160*

Air The airport (T424 3115) is 12 km southwest, served by vans run by **Transfer del Pino**, US$3.50. Bus 22 to access to airport from San Martín, US$0.35; don't be fooled by taxi touts who tell you there is no bus. Taxi from bus station, US$5. **AR** flies to **Bs As** (2¼ hrs), and **Andes**, 1 a day. Both also to **Córdoba** and **Andes** to **Jujuy** and **Iguazú**.

Bus Terminal is 8 blocks east of the main plaza, T401 1143 for information. Taxi to centre US$2.50. Toilets, *locutorio*, café, *panadería*, kiosks. To **Buenos Aires**, several companies daily, US$60-80, 17-20 hrs (**Flecha Bus, TAC** – T431 6600). To **Córdoba**, several companies daily, 12 hrs, US$35-45. To **Santiago del Estero**, 6-7 hrs, US$20. To **Tucumán**, 4 hrs, several companies, US$15. To **Mendoza** via Tucumán, several companies daily, US$63, 16-18 hrs. To **Jujuy**, several companies hourly between 0600 and 2200, 'directo', US$8, 2 hrs. To **La Rioja**, US$28, 10-11 hrs. To **San Antonio de Los Cobres**, 5 hrs, **El Quebradeño**, daily, US$10.

To **Cachi** 1-2 daily at 0700, US$11, 4-4½ hrs, with **Marcos Rueda**, and usually continues to **Molinos**, every 2 days, US$14, 6½ hrs. To **Cafayate**, US$11, 3½ hrs, 3-4 daily with El Indio, T432 0846 (disruptions to service in late 2009). To **Belén**, US$22, Wed, via Angastaco (US$13), San Carlos, Cafayate (US$11) and Santa María (US$12).

International buses: To **Paraguay**: **Flecha Bus** (www.flechabus.com.ar) daily to Clorinda (at the border), 18 hrs, and **La Nueva Estrella**, T422 4048, 3 services weekly, US$50; buses or taxis will take you from there to Paraguay for a small fee. Alternatively travel to **Resistencia**, daily, 12 hrs, US$40 with **La Veloz del Norte, Flecha Bus, La Nueva Estrella, Autotransportes Mendoza** or to **Formosa**, with *La Nueva Estrella*, US$45, 15 hrs, changing then, to a direct bus to Asunción. To **Chile**: Services to **Calama, San Pedro de Atacama, Antofagasta, Iquique** and **Arica** with **Géminis** and **Pullman**, T422 1366, pullmansalta@yahoo.com.ar, via Jujuy and the Jama Pass, three times a week, US$45 to **San Pedro**, 11 hrs. Géminis and Pullman offices are at booths 15 and 16 in the terminal. To **Bolivia**: To **La Quiaca**, on Bolivian border, **Balut, Veloz del Norte, Flecha** and others, 7½ hrs, US$18.

To **Aguas Blancas** or **Pocitos** (both on the Bolivian border, see page 172), several companies daily, US$18, 6 hrs; for **Santa Cruz**, **La Veloz del Norte/Leal Bus**. To **Tarija** (Chifa Dragón Rojo, Sucre N-0235), minibus from **Hotel Andalucía**, Abelardi 651, T431 3259, at 0800, 8-9 hrs, US$30.

Car hire **Avis**, at the airport, Ruta 51, T424 2289, salta@avis.com.ar. Efficient and very helpful, recommended. **Europe Rent A Car**, Buenos Aires 186, T422 3609. **Ruiz Moreno**, Buenos Aires 1, T431 8049, in *Hotel Salta*, helpful. **Semisa Renta Truck 4x4**, Buenos Aires 1, Local 6, T423 6295, febearzi@salnet.com.ar. **Integral**, Buenos Aires 189, T155-016451. Many others.

Train Station at 20 de February y Ameghino, 9 blocks north of Plaza 9 de Julio, taxi US$2. The only train service is the **Tren a las Nubes** (Train to the Clouds, see page 161), which usually runs Wed, Fri, Sun between Salta and La Polvorilla viaduct departing 0705, arriving back in Salta 2348, weather permitting. Fare for foreign tourists US$120, 140 in high season (Semana Santa and 19 Jul to 2 Aug); Argentines US$100, Salteños US$60. Contact T422 3033, or Buenos Aires 011-5246 6666, www.trenalas nubes.com.ar. To **Socompa** (Chilean border): there is a cargo train with 2 passenger carriages leaving Salta once a week. You should ask at the ticket office, opens 0800, if it is running and if foreigners are allowed to travel: seats are reserved for locals. Beyond Socompa there are irregular freight trains into Chile (Augusta Victoria, Baquedano or Antofagasta), but officially the Chilean railway authorities do not permit passengers to travel on this line. To travel on by train or truck may involve a wait of several days. There are only 4 buildings in Socompa: no food or lodging, but try the Chilean customs building.

Directory

Salta *p159, map p160*

Airline offices **Andes**, España 478, T437 3516. **AR**, Caseros 475, T431 1331/1454. **LAN**, Buenos Aires 92, T0810-999-9526. **Banks** Banks, open 0900-1400, all have ATMs (many on España). **Banco de la Nación**, Mitre y Belgrano. **Banco de Salta**, España 550 on main plaza. **BMC**, España 666, changes TCs, 4.5% commission. **Dinar**, Mitre 101/109; street changers opposite. **Masventas**, España 610, T431 0298, Changes dollars, euros and Chilean pesos. You can get Chilean pesos at good rates. **Cultural centres** **Alliance Française**, Santa Fe 20, T431 2403, afsalta@ sinectis.com.ar. **Embassies and consulates** **Bolivia**, Mariano Boedo 34, T421 1040, open Mon-Fri, 0900-1400 (unhelpful, better to go to Jujuy). **Chile**, Santiago del Estero 965, T431 1857. **France**, Santa Fe 156, T431 2403. **Germany**, Las Heras 3, T422 9088, consusal@arnet.com.ar. **Italy**, Alvarado 1632, T432 1532. **Spain**, República de Israel 137, T431 2296. **Internet** Many fast and cheap places around the centre, some 24 hrs. **Medical Services** Hospital San Bernardo, Tobias 69. **Emergencies** T911. **Post offices** Deán Funes 160, between España and Belgrano. **Telephones** Several *locutorios* in town, some offer internet access. **Useful addresses** **Immigration**, Maipú 35, T421 5636, 0700-1400.

Jujuy → *Colour map 6, C4. Population: 237,000. Phone code: 0388. Altitude: 1,260 m.*

Though it lacks Salta's elegance, since there are few colonial buildings remaining, the historical city of Jujuy is the starting point for some of the country's most spectacular scenery and it has a distinctly Andean feel, evident in its food and music. With extremely varied landscapes, the area is rich in both contemporary and ancient culture, with prehispanic ruins at Tilcara, delightful villages and excursions. The **tourist office** on the plaza ⓘ *Gorriti 295, T422 1325, Mon-Fri 0700-2200, Sat-Sun 0900-2100, www.turismo.jujuy.gov.ar,* accommodation leaflet and map. Also at bus terminal, 0700-2100.

Sights

San Salvador de Jujuy (pronounced Choo-Chooey, with *ch* as in Scottish loch) often referred to by locals as San Salvador, is the capital of Jujuy province and sits in a bowl ringed by lushly wooded mountains. The city was finally established in 1593, after earlier attempts met resistance from local indigenous groups, but the city was plagued by earthquakes, sacking and the Calchaquíes Wars for the next 200 years. It struggled to prosper, then in August 1812 Gen Belgrano, commanding the republican troops, ordered the city to be evacuated and destroyed before the advancing Spanish army. This extraordinary sacrifice is marked on 23-24 August by festivities known as El Exodo Jujeño with gaucho processions and military parades.

Away from the busy shopping streets, in the eastern part of the city, is the **Plaza Belgrano**, a wide square planted with tall palms and orange trees. It's lined with impressive buildings, including the elaborate French baroque-style **Casa de Gobierno** ⓘ *daily 0900-2100,* containing the famous flag Belgrano presented to the city. On the west side is the late 19th-century **Cathedral** (the original, 1598-1653, was destroyed by earthquake in 1843) containing one of Argentina's finest colonial treasures: a gold-plated wooden pulpit, carved by *indígenas* in the Jesuit missions, depicting gilded angels mounting the stairs. The modern church of **San Francisco** ⓘ *Belgrano y Lavalle, 2 blocks west of the plaza, daily 0730-1200, 1730-2100 (Thu till 2000),* contains another fine gilded colonial pulpit, with ceramic angels around it, like that at Yavi. The **Museo Histórico Franciscano** ⓘ *daily 0900-1300, 1600-2100,* at the church, includes 17th-century paintings and other artefacts from Cuzco. There are several other museums; don't miss the **Museo Arqueológico Provincial** ⓘ *Lavalle 434, 0900-1200, 1500-2100, US$0.35,* with beautiful ceramics from the Yavi and Humahuaca cultures, haphazardly displayed, a mummified infant, and a 2500-year old sculpture of a goddess giving birth.

There are hot springs 19 km west at **Termas de Reyes** ⓘ *1 hr by bus Empresa 19 de Abril (línea 14) from bus terminal, 6 daily, last return bus 2040, US$1*, municipal baths US$0.50 and pool US$1; also cabins with thermal water. This resort (**Hotel Termas de Reyes** ⓘ *T0388-492 2522, info@termasdereyes.com.ar*) is set among magnificent mountains. Note: in January 2010 a mudslide damaged parts of Termas de Reyes; check what is open before going.

Jujuy listings

For Sleeping and Eating price codes and other relevant information, see Essentials, pages 38-40.

Sleeping

Jujuy *p167*

A Fenicia, 19 de Abril 427, T/F423 1800, www.quturismo.com.ar/fenicia/fenicia.html. A welcoming place, 1980's chic, spacious rooms (ask for the ones with swish bathrooms), some with great views. Recommended.

A Jujuy Palace, Belgrano 1060, T/F423 0433, jpalace@imagine.com.ar. Conference hotel, well-equipped rooms, also has suites, restaurant has good reputation.

B Internacional, Belgrano 501 (Plaza Belgrano), T423 1599, www.hinternacionaljujuy.com.ar. On north west corner of the Plaza, quiet, smart, good value. Great views over city.

B La Aguada, Otero 170, T423 2034, www.laaguada hosteria.com.ar. A charming family-owned hotel with 3 rooms, decorated with paintings by the owner's father, central, excellent choice.

B Panorama, Belgrano 1295, T423 2533, hotelpanorama@mail.cootepal.com.ar. Business hotel, more appealing than most, good value, stylish rooms.

C Sumay, Otero 232, T423 5065, www.sumay hotel.com.ar. Rather dark, but clean, very central, helpful staff.

D pp **Aldea Luna**, Tilquiza, 1 hr from Jujuy, 3 hrs from Salta, T0388-155 094602, www.aldea luna.com.ar. Very peaceful, set in the Yungas reserve. Dorm US$10 pp (food not included), private room US$15 pp (food not included). Restaurant with vegetarian food.

F pp **Club Hostel**, San Martín 155, 2 blocks from plaza, T423 7565, www.noroestevirtual.com.ar/ club/hostel.htm. Doubles **C**; same owners as **Yok Wahi**, larger hostel with pool, patio, free internet, lots of information, welcoming, good travel agency next door.

F pp **Yok Wahi**, Lamadrid 168, T422 9608, info@ yok-wahi.com.ar. An attractive, central hostel with tidy dorms and one double with bath (**D**), quiet atmosphere. Discounts to HI members.

There are a number of cheap places near the bus terminal, of which the following are safe and comfortable, including:

E Rany's, Dorrego 327 next to bus station, T423 0042, ranyshotel_juy@hotmail.com. Rooms for up to 6, cheaper rooms without TV, basic, but clean and the lady owner is very kind, no breakfast, but loads of cafés around.

E Res San Carlos, República de Siria 459, T422 2286, residencialsancarlos@argentina.com.ar. With bath (cheaper without) and TV, nicely maintained, comfortable, car park.

Camping E pp **El Refugio** is closest, Yala, Km 14, T490 9344, pretty spot on riverbank 14 km north of city, US$2 pp, tent US$0.65, also has youth hostel, pool, and restaurant, horse riding and treks organized. Highly recommended, great place to relax.

Eating

Jujuy *p167*

Chung King, Alvear 631. Atmospheric, regional food. Sister restaurant at No 627, '50 kinds of pizza'.

Krysys, Balcarce 272. Popular bistro-style *parrilla*, excellent steaks. Also accommodation upstairs but not recommended.

La Candelaria, Alvear 1346, some way out of town. Recommended *parrilla*, good service.

Madre Tierra, Otero y Belgrano. For vegetarians (or for a break from all the meat), delicious food (open Mon-Sat 1130-1430).

Manos Jujeños, Sen Pérez 379. Regional specialities, the best *humitas*, charming, good for the *peña* at weekends, daily 1200-1530, 2000-2400.

Ruta 9, Belgrano 75 and Costa Rica 968. Great places for regional dishes such as *locro* and *tamales*, also a few Bolivian dishes.

Following Lavalle across the bridge to the bus terminal (where it becomes Dorrego) there are lots of cheap *empanada* places.

Several good cafés, all on the same block of Belgrano between Lavalle and Necochea, including **Pingüino**, the best *heladería* in town.

Color Esperanza, Necochea 376. Bright café serving cheap *lomitos* and burgers.

Confitería La Royal Belgrano 770. A classic café, good coffee and pastries.

Sociedad Española, Belgrano y S Pérez. Good cheap set menus with a Spanish flavour.

Tía Bigote, Pérez y Belgrano. Very popular café and pizzería.

Shopping

Jujuy *p167*

Handicrafts There are stalls near the cathedral. **Centro de Arte y Artesanías**, Balcarce 427. **Paseo de las Artesanías**, on the west side of the plaza.

Maps and travel guides **Librería Belgrano**, Belgrano 602. English language magazines and some books. **Librería Rayuela**, Belgrano 636.

Markets For food, you can't beat the Municipal market at Dorrego y Alem, near the bus terminal. Outside, women sell home-baked *empanadas* and *tamales*, and delicious goat's cheese, and all kinds of herbal cures.

Supermarkets **Norte**, Belgrano 825 and a bigger branch at 19 de Abril y Necochea.

Activities and tours

Jujuy *p167*

Be Dor Turismo, Lavalle 295, T402 0241, be-dor@imagine.com.ar. 10% discount for ISIC members on local excursions.

Horus Turismo, Belgrano 722, T422 7247, horus@imgine.com.ar.

NASA, Senador Pérez 154, T422 3938, nasa@imagine.com.ar. Guided tour to Quebrada de Humahuaca (US$30 pp, min 4 people); 4WD for rent. For information on bird watching, contact Mario Daniel Cheronaza, Peatonal 38, No 848-830, Viviendas 'El Arenal', Jujuy.

Transport

Jujuy *p167*

Air Airport at El Cadillal, 32 km southeast, T491 1505, taxi US$10. **AR** (Pérez 355, T422 2575) flights to **Salta** and **Buenos Aires**.

Bus terminal at Iguazú y Dorrego, 6 blocks south of the centre, T422 2134, T491 1101.

Bus To **Buenos Aires**, 19-23 hrs, US$68-76, several daily with many companies. Via Tucumán to **Córdoba**, **Panamericano** and **La Veloz del Norte**, daily to **Tucumán**, 5¾ hrs, US$16-17, and **Córdoba**, 13-14 hrs US$51-41. To **Salta**, see above. To **La Quiaca**, 5-6 hrs, US$8, **Veloz del Norte, Balut, Flecha**. Several rigorous luggage checks en route for drugs, including coca leaves. To **Humahuaca**, **Evelia** and others, US$4.50, 3 hrs, several daily, via Tilcara 2 hrs, US$3. To **Orán** and **Aguas Blancas** (border with Bolivia), US$13, daily with **Balut** and **Brown**, via San Pedro and Ledesma. To **Purmamarca**, take buses to Susques or to Humahuaca (those calling at Purmamarca village). To **Susques**, **Purmamarca** and **Andes Bus**, US$8, 4-6½ hrs, daily (except Mon). To **Calilegua**: various companies to Libertador Gral San Martín almost every hour, eg **Balut**, US$3.65, from there take **Empresa 23 de Agosto** or **Empresa 24 de Setiembre**, leaving 0830 to **Valle Grande**, across Parque Nacional Calilegua. All Pocitos or Orán buses pass through Libertador San Martín.

To Chile: via the **Jama** pass (4,200 m), the route taken by most traffic, including trucks, crossing to northern Chile; hours 0900-1900. **Géminis** bus tickets sold at **Ortiz Viajes**, L N Alem 917, ortizviajes@latinmail.com.

Directory

Jujuy *p167*

Banks ATMs at: **Banco de Jujuy**, Balcarce y Belgrano, changes dollars. TCs can be changed at tour operators, **Be Dor** and **Horus**, Belgrano 722. **Banco Francés**, Alvear y Lamadrid; **Banco Salta**, San Martín 785. **Consulates** **Bolivia**, Independencia1098, T424 0501, colivian-jujuy@rree.gov.bo, 0900-1300. **Internet** **Cyber Explora**, Güemes 1049; **Ciber Nob**, Otero 317; **HVA**, Lavalle 390 (all US$0.50 per hr). **Telecom** centres at Alvear 870, Belgrano 730 and elsewhere. **Post offices** Independencia y Lamadrid. **Useful addresses** **Immigration**, 19 de Abril 1057, T422 2638.

Jujuy to the Chilean and Bolivian borders

Ruta 9, the Pan-American Highway, runs through the beautiful **Quebrada de Humahuaca**, a vast gorge of vividly coloured rock, with giant cacti in the higher parts, and emerald green oasis villages on the river below. (January-March ask highway police about flooding on the roads.) The whole area is very rich culturally: there are pre-Inca ruins at Tilcara (see below), and throughout the Quebrada there are fine 16th-century churches and riotous pre-Lent carnival celebrations. In Tilcara, pictures of the Passion are made of flowers and seeds at Easter and a traditional procession on Holy Wednesday at night is joined by thousands of pan-pipe musicians.

For drivers heading off main roads in this area, note that service stations are far apart: at Jujuy, Tilcara, Humahuaca, Abra Pampa and La Quiaca. Spare fuel and water must be carried.

Jujuy to Chile

Beyond Tumbaya, where there's a restored 17th-century church, Ruta 52 runs 3 km west to **Purmamarca**, a quiet, picturesque village, much visited for its spectacular mountain of seven colours, striped strata from terracotta to green (best seen in the morning), a lovely church with remarkable paintings and a good handicrafts market. (Buses to Jujuy 1½ hrs, US$2; to Tilcara US$0.75. Salta-San Pedro de Atacama buses can be boarded here, book at Hotel Manantial del Silencio a day ahead.) It's worth staying the night in Purmamarca to appreciate the town's quiet rhythm. There's a helpful, tiny tourist office on the plaza with list of accommodation, maps and bus tickets, open 0700-1800.

From Purmamarca paved Ruta 52 leads through another *quebrada* over the 4,164 m Abra Potrerillos to the **Salinas Grandes** salt flats at about 3,400 m on the Altiplano (fantastic views especially at sunset). From here roads lead southwest past spectacular rock formations along the east side of the salt flats to San Antonio de los Cobres, and west across the salt flats via Susques to the Paso de Jama (4,400 m) and Chile. The only place to stay beyond Purmamarca is at **Susques**, facing the outstanding church (see below). There are no services or money exchange at the border, which is open 0830-2200. This is the route taken by most passenger and truck traffic from Salta or Jujuy to San Pedro de Atacama.

Jujuy to Bolivia

About 7 km north of the Purmamarca turning is **La Posta de Hornillos** ⓘ *open, in theory, Wed-Mon 0830-1800, free,* a museum in a restored colonial posting house where Belgrano stayed, also the scene of several battles. About 2 km further is **Maimará** with its brightly striped rock, known as the 'Artist's Palette', and huge cemetery, decorated with flowers at Easter.

Tilcara → *Phone code: 0388. Colour map 6, C3. Population: 4,400. Altitude: 2,460 m.*

Tilcara lies 22 km north of the turn-off to Purmamarca. It's the liveliest Quebrada village, the best base for exploring the area. It has an excellent handicrafts market around its pleasant plaza and plenty of places to stay and to eat. The little tourist office on Belgrano, next to *Hotel de Turismo*. Daily 0800-2130, very helpful staff (no phone), www.tilcarajujuy.com.ar. Visit the **Pucará** ⓘ *Mon-Sat 0800-1230, 1600-2000, Sun 0900-1200, 1800-2100,* a restored prehispanic hilltop settlement, with panoramic views of the gorge, and the superb **Museo Arqueológico** ⓘ *Belgrano 445, daily 0900-1900, in Jan and Jul 0900-1230, 1400-1800, US$0.65 for both and the Jardín Botánico,* with a fine collection of pre-Columbian ceramics, masks and mummies. There are four art museums in town and good walks in all directions. Recommended guide for informative trips to the puna, Iruya, Salinas Grandes, and archaeological sites, is historian **Ariel Mosca** ⓘ *T495 5119, arielpuna@hotmail.com*. English spoken. There are fiestas throughout January, carnival and Holy Week. There's an ATM on the plaza, taking most international cards.

At **Uquía** is one of the most impressive churches in the valley (from 1691), with extraordinary Cuzqueño paintings of angels in 17th-century battle dress and other works of art.

Humahuaca ➔ *Phone code: 03887. Colour map 6, B3. Population: 8,000. Altitude: 2,940 m.*
Although Humahuaca, 129 km north of Jujuy, dates from 1591, it was almost entirely rebuilt in the mid-19th century. Now it is visited by daily coach trips. It still has a distinctive culture of its own, though, and is a useful stopping point for travelling north up to the puna, or to Iruya. On 1-2 February is *La Candelaria* festival. *Jueves de Comadres, Festival de las Coplas y de la Chicha*, at the Thursday before carnival is famously animated, lots of drinking and throwing flour and water around. Book accommodation ahead. ATM at *Banco de Jujuy* on main plaza, all major credit cards. On the little plaza is the church, **San Antonio**, originally of 1631, rebuilt 1873-80, containing a statue of the Virgen de la Candelaria, gold retables and 12 fine Cuzqueño paintings. Also on the plaza, tourists gather to watch a mechanical figure of San Francisco Solano blessing the town from **El Cabildo**, the neo-colonial town hall, at 1200 daily. Overlooking the town is the massive **Monumento a la Independencia Argentina**, commemorating the heaviest fighting in the country during the Wars of Independence. At **Coctaca**, 10 km northeast, there is an impressive and extensive (40 ha) series of pre-colonial agricultural terraces. **Humahuaca**: tourist information available from the town hall, office hours.

Iruya ➔ *Colour map 6, B3. Altitude: 2,600 m.*
A rough *ripio* road 25 km north of Humahuaca runs northeast from the Panamericana (RN9) 8 km to Iturbe (also called Hipólito Irigoyen), and then up over the 4,000 m Abra del Cóndor before dropping steeply, around many hairpin bends, into the Quebrada de Iruya. The road is very rough and unsuited to small hire cars, but is one of Argentina's most amazing drives. Iruya, 66 km from Humahuaca, is a beautiful hamlet wedged on a hillside, like a hide-away. Its warm, friendly inhabitants hold a colourful Rosario festival on first Sunday in October and at Easter. It is worth spending a few days here to go horse riding or walking: the hike (seven hours return) to the remote **San Isidro** is unforgettable. At Titiconte 4 km away, there are unrestored pre-Inca ruins (guide necessary). Iruya has no ATM or tourist information, but a public phone, post office and a few food and handicraft shops.

Tres Cruces and Abra Pampa
Some 62 km north of Humahuaca on the Panamericana is Tres Cruces, where customs searches are made on vehicles from Bolivia. **Abra Pampa** (*Population: 6,000*), 91 km north of Humahuaca, is a mining town. At 15 km southwest of Abra Pampa is the vicuña farm at **Miraflores**, the largest in Argentina. Information offered, photography permitted; buses go morning Monday-Saturday Abra Pampa-Miraflores.

Monumento Natural Laguna de los Pozuelos ⓘ *50 km northwest of Abra Pampa, park office in Abra Pampa, T03887-491048*, is a nature reserve with a lake at its centre visited by huge colonies of flamingos. There is a ranger station at the southern end of the park, with a campsite nearby. There is no bus transport, so it's best to go with a guide; the Laguna is 5 km from the road, very tough, high clearance recommended, walk last 800 m to reach the edge of the lagoon. Check with the park office before going, the lake can be dry with no birds, eg in September. (*Altitude: 3,650 m*; temperatures can drop to -25°C in winter.) *Diego Bach* leads excellent, well-informed excursions, including panning for gold as the Jesuits did. Also five-day treks on horseback to the pristine cloudforest of **Parque Nacional Baritú** ⓘ *T03885-422797, punatours@hotmail.com*, are highly recommended.

From a point 4 km north of Abra Pampa roads branch west to Cochinoca (25 km) and southwest to **Casabindo** (62 km). On 15 August at Casabindo, the local saint's day, the last and only *corrida de toros* (running with bulls) in Argentina is held, amidst a colourful popular celebration. *El Toreo de la Vincha* takes place in front of the church, where a bull defies onlookers to take a ribbon and medal which it carries. The church itself is a magnificent building, with twin bell towers, and inside a superb series of 16th century angels in armour paintings. The only place to stay is an **Albergue** at the village school, T03887-491129 (**F** per person in dorms), otherwise most visitors go on day-trips from Tilcara.

La Quiaca and Yavi ➔ *Phone code: 03885. Altitude: 3,442 m. 5,121 km from Ushuaia. Colour map 6, B3.*
On the border with Bolivia, a concrete bridge links this typical border town with Villazón on the Bolivian side. Warm clothing is essential particularly in winter when temperatures can drop to -15°C, though care should be taken against sunburn during the day. In mid-October, villagers from the far reaches of the remote *altiplano* come to exchange ceramic pots, sheepskins and vegetables, in the colourful three-day *Fiesta de la Olla*, which also involves much high-spirited dancing and drinking. Two ATMs, but no facilities for changing cash or TCs, but plenty of *cambios* in Villazón. *Farmacia Nueva*, half a block from Church, has remedies for altitude sickness. **Yavi** is 16 km east of La Quiaca. Its **church of San Francisco** (1690) ⓘ *Mon 1500-1800, Tue-Fri 0900-1200, 1500-1800, Sat-Sun 0900-1200,* is one of Argentina's treasures, with a magnificent gold retable and pulpit and windows of onyx. Caretaker Lydia lives opposite the police station and will show you round the church. Opposite the church is the 18th-century house of the Marqués Campero y Tojo, empty, but for a small selection of handicrafts.

Border with Bolivia ➔ *Do not photograph the border area.*
The border bridge is 10 blocks from La Quiaca bus terminal, 15 minutes walk (taxi US$1). Argentine office open 0700-2400; on Saturday, Sunday, and holidays there is a special fee of US$1.50 which may or may not be charged. If leaving Argentina for a short stroll into Villazón, show your passport, but do not let it be stamped by Migración, otherwise you will have to wait 24 hours before being allowed back into Argentina. Formalities on entering Argentina are usually very brief at the border but thorough customs searches are made 100 km south at Tres Cruces. Leaving Argentina is very straightforward, but travellers who need a visa to enter Bolivia are advised to get it before arriving in La Quiaca. The **Bolivian consulate** is one block south and west of the plaza, at República Arabe Siria y San Juan, open 0830-1100 and 1400-1700 weekdays, Saturday 0900-1200 (in theory). Argentine time is one hour later than Bolivia, two hours when Buenos Aires adopts daylight saving.

Parque Nacional Calilegua ➔ *Colour map 6, C3.*
ⓘ *Park office: San Lorenzo s/n, Calilegua, T03886-422046, pncalilegua@cooperlib.com.ar. Reached by Ruta 83, via Ruta 34, from just north of Libertador, the park entrance is at Aguas Negras, 12 km along the dirt road (4WD essential when wet, hitching from Libertador possible), which climbs through the park and beyond to Valle Grande (basic accommodation and shops), 90 km from Libertador.*
Libertador General San Martín, a sugar town 113 km northeast of Jujuy on Ruta 34 to south-eastern Bolivia, is the closest base for exploring the park, an area of peaks over 3,000 m and deep valleys covered in cloud forest, with a huge variety of wildlife, including 260 species of bird and 60 species of mammals (you may spot tapirs, pumas, tarucas, Andean deer and even jaguars here) There are six marked trails of various lengths (10 minutes to 5 hours). The best trek is to the summit of Cerro Amarillo (3,720 m), five days round trip from Aguas Negras, or three days from the village of San Francisco (*hospedaje* and *comedores*). There is a ranger's house at Aguas Negras, with camping; drinking water from river nearby, cooking facilities and tables. Ask rangers for directions and advice. Best time for visiting is November-March, the warmest but also the wettest. **Tourist office** ⓘ *at the bus terminal.*

Routes to Bolivia
From Libertador, Ruta 34 runs northeast 244 km, to the Bolivian border at Pocitos (also called Salvador Mazza) and Yacuiba (see Eastern Bolivia, page 375). It passes through **Embarcación** and **Tartagal** (good regional museum, director Ramón Ramos very informative). In **Pocitos**, the border town, is **Hotel Buen Gusto**, just tolerable. There are no *casas de cambio* here. The border is open 24 hours. From Yacuiba, across the border, buses go to Santa Cruz de la Sierra and Tarija. Customs at Pocitos is not to be trusted (theft reported) and overcharging for 'excess baggage' on buses occurs. Several bus companies including Atahualpa have services from the border to Salta and Tucumán.

A preferable route is via Aguas Blancas. At Pichanal, 85 km northeast of Libertador, Ruta 50 heads north via **Orán**, an uninteresting place (*Population: 60,000*).

Aguas Blancas on the border is 53 km from Orán (restaurants, shops, no accommodation, nowhere to change money and Bolivianos are not accepted south of Aguas Blancas; fill up with fuel here, or in Orán). The passport office is open from 0700 to 1200 and 1500 to 1900. Insist on an exit stamp. Buses run from Bermejo, across the river by bridge, to Tarija, 3-4 hrs, US$2.70 (US$5.50 by shared taxi). Northwest of Aguas Blancas is the **Parque Nacional Baritú**, see above, under Abra Pampa. There are no facilities.

Jujuy to the Chilean and Bolivian borders listings

For Sleeping and Eating price codes and other relevant information, see Essentials, pages 38-40.

Sleeping

Jujuy to Chile *p170*

Purmamarca

L El Manantial del Silencio, Ruta 52 Km 3.5, T0388-490 8080, www.hotelmanantial.com.ar. Signposted from the road into Purmamarca. Luxurious rooms in old estancia, wonderful views, spacious living rooms with huge fire, charming hosts, includes breakfast, heating, riding, pool, superb restaurant (guests only).

A-B La Posta, C Santa Rosa de Lima 4 blocks up from plaza, T490 8029, www.postadepurmamarca.com.ar. Breakfast, heating, helpful owner. Beautiful elevated setting by the mountain, comfortable rooms. Its restaurant at the plaza, serves delicious local fare (🍴). Highly recommended.

B El Viejo Algarrobo, C Salta behind the church, T/F490 8286, elviejoalgarrobo@hotmail.com. Small but pleasant rooms, **C** shared bath, good value and quality regional dishes in its restaurant (🍴).

D El Pequeño Inti, C Florida 10 m from plaza, T490 8099, elintidepurmamarca@hotmail.com. Small, modern rooms around a little courtyard, breakfast, hot water, good value. Recommended.

E Hospedaje Familia García, C Lavalle ½ block from Plaza, T490 8016, jhosep03@yahoo.com. ar. Family run, basic, shared bath, hot water, kitchen.

Susques

C Pastos Chicos, R52, Km 220 (at Casas Quemadas, 3 km west of Susques), T0388-423 5387, www.pastoschicos.com.ar. Rustic, comfortable, good value, internet, restaurant with regional specialities, open to non-residents. Phone for pick-up. Also has a branch in Purmamarca, T0388-490 8023, **B-C**, with breakfast.

C El Unquillar, R52, Km 219 (2 km west of Susques), T03887-490201, www.elunquillar.com.ar. Attractive, with local weavings, good rooms. Restaurant open to public. Phone for pick-up.

E Res Las Vicuñitas, San Martín, Susques, T03887-490207, opposite the church, atamabel@imagine.com.ar. Without bath, hot water, breakfast available, very basic.

Jujuy to Bolivia: Maimará *p170*

C Posta del Sol, Martín Rodríguez y San Martín, T499 7156, www.postadelsol.com. Comfortable, rooms and cabins, with good restaurant, owner is tourist guide and has helpful information.

Tilcara *p170*

Book ahead in carnival and around Easter when Tilcara is very busy.

A Posada con los Angeles, Gorriti 153 (signposted from access to town), T495 5153, www.posadaconlosangeles.com.ar. Charming individually designed rooms, garden with views of mountains, relaxed atmosphere, excursions organized. Warmly recommended.

A-B Quinta La Paceña, Padilla y Ambosetti, T495 5098, www.quintalapacena.com.ar. Peaceful, architect-designed traditional adobe house, with comfortable, stylish rooms for 2-4 (some cheaper rooms in old farmhouse), gorgeous, well-kept garden, the nicest place to stay in town.

B Hostal La Granja, at Huacalera, Km 90, T0388-426 1766, hosterialagranja@hotmail.com. A lovely rustic place with pool, outstanding food and service, a good base for exploring the region.

C Malka, San Martín s/n, 5 blocks from plaza up steep hill, T495 5197, www.malkahostel.com.ar. Beautifully located cabañas for 4-8, and an out-standing hostel (**E** pp in dorm), comfortable rustic dorms, all with kitchen and laundry facilities, HI affiliated, Wi-Fi. Owner and guide

Juan organizes a great range of trips, including several days' trek to Calilegua, horse riding, bike hire. Recommended.

D-E La Morada, Debenedetti s/n, T/F495 5118, cds.api@imagine.com.ar. Good rooms for 2-5 people with bath, cooking facilities, good option.

D-E Res El Antigal, Rivadavia s/n, ½ block from plaza, T495 5020, elantigaltilcara@yahoo.com.ar. Comfortable, good beds, sunny patio, good value, restaurant.

Camping Camping El Jardín, access on Belgrano, T495 5128, US$2 pp, hot showers, also **E** pp basic hostel accommodation.

Uquía

C Hostal de Uquía, next to the church, T03387-490523, hostaluquia@yahoo.com.ar. Comfortable place to stay, simple rooms around a courtyard, also serves dinner, very good food.

Humahuaca *p171*

A Camino del Inca, on the other side of the river, T421136, www.noroestevirtual.com.ar/camino/inca.htm. Smart, well built modern place with good restaurant, pool, excursions, a bit overpriced.

B Hostal Azul, B Medalla Milagrosa, La Banda, T421107, www.hostalazulhumahuaca.com.ar. Across the river, smart, welcoming, pleasant, simple rooms with bath, good restaurant and wine list, parking. Recommended.

E pp **Cabaña El Cardón**, T421625, www.cabanaselcardon.com.ar. Rural *cabaña* for 2-5 with all facilities, also regional foods, excursions and riding (recommended), charming family.

E pp **Res El Portillo**, Tucumán 69, T421288. Dormitories are cramped, **D** rooms, nice place, shared bath, simple bar/restaurant.

F pp **Posada El Sol**, over bridge from terminal, then 520 m, follow signs, T421466, www.posadaelsol.com.ar. Quiet rural area, shared rooms or private (**C**) in a warm welcoming place, kitchen, also laundry, horse riding, owner will collect from bus station if called in advance. HI affiliated. Recommended.

Iruya *p171*

A Hostería de Iruya, T0387-154 070909, www.hosteria deiruya.com.ar. A special place, extremely comfortable, with good food, and great views from the top of the village. Highly recommended.

D Hostal Federico Tercero, at *Café del Hostal*, bottom of the steep main street, T03887-156 29152. Owned by the delightful singer Jesús, with simple rooms, some with bath, good food from breakfast to dinner, frequent live music.

F pp **Hosp Tacacho**, on the Plaza, T03887-156 29350. Family welcome, simple rooms, great views, *comedor*.

Abra Pampa *p171*

E-F Residencial El Norte, Sarmiento 530, T491315. Private or shared room, hot water, good food. *Res y restaurante Cesarito*, 1 block from main plaza.

La Quiaca *p172*

C Hostería Munay, Belgrano 51, T423924, www.munayhotel.jujuy.com. Very pleasant, with comfortable rooms.

C-D Turismo, Siria y San Martín, T422243. Modern, comfortable rooms with TV, breakfast, pool, restaurant.

E La Frontera hotel and restaurant, Belgrano y Siria, downhill from *Atahualpa* bus stop, T422269. Good cheap food, basic but decent rooms, hospitable owner.

E-F Cristal, Sarmiento 539, T422255. Basic functional rooms, with or without bath.

Yavi *p172*

C Hostal de Yavi, Güemes 222, T03887-490523, hostaldeyavi@hotmail.com. Simple rooms but cosy sitting room, good food, relaxed atmosphere. Recommended.

D-E La Casona 'Jatum Huasi', Sen Pérez y San Martín, T03887-422316, mccailsaya@laquiaca.com.ar. Welcoming, with and without bath, breakfast.

Parque Nacional Calilegua *p172*

B Posada del Sol, Los Ceibo y Pucará, Libertador General San Martín, T03886-424900, www.posada delsoljujuy.com.ar. Comfortable, functional hotel, with gardens and pool, has advice on local trips.

C-D Finca Portal de Piedra, Villa Monte, Santa Bárbara, T03886-156 820564, portaldepiedra@yahoo.com. 17 km north of Libertador General San Martín. Eco-run finca in its own reserve

(Las Lancitas), convenient for PNs *Calilegua and El Rey*, guesthouse and cabin, simple food, horse riding, trekking, birdwatching and other excursions, from Jujuy take a bus via San Pedro and Palma Sola (which is 12 km north of the finca).

Routes to Bolivia: Orán *p173*

B Alto Verde, Pellegrini 671, T421214, hotelalto verde@arnet.com.ar. Parking, pool, a/c.
D Res Crisol, López y Planes. Hot water. Recommended.

Eating

Tilcara *p170*

Pucará, up the hill towards the Pucará, T495 5721. Exquisite, posh Andean food and hearty puddings by renowned chef Garo Jurisic, intimate, rustic atmosphere.
El Patio Comidas Lavalle 352. Great range, lovely patio at the back, popular, very good.
Música Esperanza (Bar del Centro), Belgrano 547, T495 5462. Small restaurant/café serving local dishes in the patio. Not always open. Both the restaurant and crafts shop next door sustain an NGO that organizes free art and music workshops for local children.

Cafés

El Cafecito on the plaza. For a taste of Tilcara's culture, don't miss this place, good coffee and locally grown herbal teas, peña at weekends from celebrated local musicians.
La Peña de Carlitos, on the plaza. With music from the charismatic and delightful Carlitos, also cheap *menú del día, empanadas*, and drinks.

Humahuaca *p171*

El Portillo, Tucumán 69. A simply decorated room, serving slightly more elaborate regional meals than the usual.
La Cacharpaya, Jujuy 295. Good and lively, often filled with parties at lunch time, Andean music. Recommended.

Transport

Tilcara *p170*

El Quiaqueño combines with **Andesmar/ Brown**, passes Tilcara en route to **Jujuy** 4 times a day from 1340, and en route to **La Quiaca** 6 times a day from 1110. **Jama Bus** runs between Tilcara, Humahuaca and La Quiaca.

Humahuaca *p171*

Bus Buses to all places along the Quebrada from the terminal (toilets, *confitería*, fruit and sandwich sellers outside), to **Iruya** (see below) and to **La Quiaca**, with **Balut** and **La Quiaqueña** (more comfortable), several daily, 3-3½ hrs, US$5.60. Rigorous police checks for drugs can cause delays to La Quiaca. Keep passport with you.

Iruya *p171*

Bus Daily from **Humahuaca Empresa Mendoza**, T03887-421016, 1030 daily, 3 hrs, US$6 return, returning 0600 (not on Sun) and 1515. Also trips of several days organized by tour operators.

La Quiaca *p172*

Bus Bus terminal, **España y Belgrano**, luggage storage. Several buses daily to **Salta** (US$18) with **Balut** (7½ hrs), **Atahualpa** and others. Several daily to **Humahuaca** and **Jujuy**, schedules above. Take own food, as sometimes long delays. Buses are stopped for routine border police controls and searched for coca leaves. **Note** Buses from Jujuy may arrive in the early morning when no restaurants are open and it is freezing cold outside. Nevertheless, wrap up warm and stay in the terminal until daylight as the streets are unsafe in the dark.

Yavi *p172*

No buses go to Yavi. You can hitchhike from the exit to R5 (US$1 pp is expected) or take a remise taxi for US$12 return, including ½ hr stay. **Remises La Quiaca**, Belgrano 169 (round the corner from terminal, La Quiaca), T03887-423344.

Parque Nacional Calilegua *p172*

Bus From Libertador daily at 0830 going across the park to **Valle Grande** (US$7, 5 hrs), returning the same day. Also Tue, Thu, Sat to **Santa Ana** at 0600, US$7, 5 hrs, return 1430. *Remise* charges about US$4 from Libertador to Park entrance. All Pocitos or Orán buses pass through Libertador General San Martín.

Routes to Bolivia: Aguas Blancas *p173*

Bus Between Aguas Blancas and **Orán** buses run every 45 mins, US$1, luggage checks on bus. Direct buses to **Güemes**, 8 a day, US$8; through buses to **Salta, La Veloz del Norte, Panamericano** and **Atahualpa**, several daily, US$18, 7-10 hrs. To **Tucumán**, *La Veloz del Norte, Panamericano* and **La Estrella**, 1 a day each company. To **Jujuy** with **Balut** and **Brown**, 3 daily, US$13. To **Embarcación**, US$3; some services from Salta and Jujuy call at **Orán** en route to **Tartagal** and **Pocitos**. Note that buses are subject to slow searches for drugs and contraband.

The Northeast

The river systems of the Paraná, Paraguay and Uruguay, with hundreds of minor tributaries, small lakes and marshlands, dominate the Northeast. Between the Paraná and Uruguay rivers is Argentine Mesopotamia containing the provinces of Entre Ríos, Corrientes and Misiones, this last named after Jesuit foundations, whose red stone ruins have been rescued from the jungle. The great attraction of this region is undoubtedly the Iguazú Falls, which tumble into a gorge on a tributary of the Alto Paraná on the border with Brazil. But the region offers other opportunities for wildlife watching, such as the national parks of the Wet Chaco and the amazing flooded plains of the Esteros del Iberá. This is also the region of mate tea, sentimental chamamé music and tiny chipá bread.

Up the Río Uruguay

This river forms the frontier with Uruguay and there are many crossings as you head upstream to the point where Argentina, Uruguay and Brazil meet. On the way, you'll find riverside promenades, sandy beaches and palm forests.

Gualeguaychú → *Phone code: 03446. Colour map 8, B5. Population: 74,700.*

On the Río Gualeguaychú, 19 km above its confluence with the Río Paraná and 220 km north of Buenos Aires, this is a pleasant town with a massive pre-Lenten carnival. Parades are held in the Corsódromo (see www.carnavaldelpais.com.ar or www.grancarnaval.com.ar for details of participating groups, prices of tickets, etc). Some 33 km southeast the Libertador Gral San Martín Bridge (5.4 km long) provides the most southerly route across the Río Uruguay, to Fray Bentos (vehicles US$4; pedestrians and cyclists may cross only on vehicles, officials may arrange lifts). **Tourist office** ⓘ *Plazoleta de los Artesanos, T423668, www.gualeguaychuturismo.com, 0800-2000 (2200 in summer)*. The **Uruguayan consulate** is at Rivadavia 510, T426168. **Note** This crossing is subject to unofficial border controls owing to a dispute over a paper mill across the river in Uruguay. Tourists were not being allowed to enter Uruguay here in 2010.

Nice walks can be taken along the *costanera* between the bridge and the small port, from where short boat excursions and city tours leave (also from the *balneario municipal*), T423248, high season only. **El Patio del Mate** ⓘ *G Méndez y Costanera, T424371, www.elpatiodel mate.com.ar, daily 0800-2100.* A workshop dedicated to the *mate* gourd.

Concepción del Uruguay → *Phone code: 03442. Colour map 8, B5. Population: 64,500.*

The first Argentine port of any size on the Río Uruguay was founded in 1783. Overlooking Plaza Ramírez is the church of the Immaculate Conception which contains the remains of Gen Urquiza. **Palacio San José** ⓘ *32 km west of town, T432620, www.palacios anjose.com.ar, Mon-Fri 0800-1900, , Sat-Sun 0900-1800, US$3.35, guided visits 1000, 1100, 1500, 1600, plus 1400, 1500 at weekends, US$1, and night visits in summer.* Urquiza's former mansion, set in beautiful grounds with a lake, is now a museum, with artefacts from Urquiza's life and a collection of period furniture, recommended. Take Ruta 39 west and turn right after Caseros train station. Buses to Paraná or Rosario del Tala stop at El Cruce or Caseros, 4 or 8 km away

True brew

Yerba mate (*ilex paraguayensis*) is made into a tea which is widely drunk in Argentina, Paraguay, Brazil and Uruguay. Traditionally associated with the gauchos, the modern mate paraphernalia is a common sight anywhere: the gourd (*un mate*) in which the tea leaves are steeped, the straw (usually silver) and a thermos of hot water to top up the gourd. It was the Jesuits who first grew *yerba mate* in plantations, inspiring one of the drink's names: *té de jesuitas*. Also used has been *té de Paraguay*, but now just *mate* or *yerba* will do. In southern Brazil it is called *ximarão*; in Paraguay *tereré*, when drunk cold with digestive herbs.

respectively, US$1 (take *remise* taxi from Caseros). *Remise* taxis charge about US$10 with 1½ hour wait. Tour operators run *combis* in high season US$6 including entry. **Tourist office** ⓘ *Galarza y Daniel Elía, T440812, www.concepcion entrerios.com.ar, Mon-Fri 0700-1300, 1400-2000, weekends 0700-2200 in high season*.

Colón ➔ *Phone code: 03447. Colour map 8, A5. Population: 19,200.*

Founded in 1863, Colón is 45 km north of Concepción del Uruguay. It has shady streets, an attractive *costanera* and long sandy beaches, with cliffs visible from a considerable distance. At Avenida 12 de Abril y Paso is **La Casona** (1868), with a handicraft exhibition and shop. North of the port, Calle Belgrano leads to the **Complejo Termal** ⓘ *T424717, daily 0900-2100, US$2*, with 10 thermal pools (34-40°C). **Tourist office** ⓘ *Av Costanera Quirós y Gouchón, T421233, www.colon entrerios.com.ar. Mon-Fri 0630-2100, Sat 0700-2100, Sun 0800-2100*. The **Uruguayan consulate** is at San Martín 417, T421999.

Parque Nacional El Palmar

ⓘ *51 km north of Colón, T493049. US$6.50. Buses from Colón, 1 hr, US$2, will drop you at the entrance and it is easy to hitch the last 12 km to the park administration. Remise taxis from Colón or Ubajay offer tours, 4-hr return trip, including tour or waiting time. There are camping facilities (electricity, hot water), with restaurant opposite, and a small shop.*

This park of 8,500 ha is on the Río Uruguay, entrance gates off Ruta 14, where you'll be given a map and information on walks. The park contains varied scenery with a mature palm forest, sandy beaches on the Uruguay river, indigenous tombs and the remains of an 18th-century quarry and port, a good museum and many rheas and other birds. The Yatay palms grow up to 12 m and some are hundreds of years old. It is best to stay overnight as wildlife is more easily seen in the early morning or at sunset. Very popular at weekends in summer.

Refugio de Vida Silvestre La Aurora del Palmar ⓘ *T03447-154 31689, www.auroradel palmar.com.ar, free*, is opposite the Parque Nacional El Palmar, 3 km south of Ubajay at Km 202 Ruta 14. A private reserve protecting a similar environment to that of its neighbour, La Aurora covers 1,150 ha, of which 200 are covered with a mature palm forest. There are also gallery forests along the streams and patches of *espinal* or scrub. Birds are easily seen, as are capybaras along the streams. The administration centre is only 500 m from Ruta 14 and services are well organized. There are guided excursions on horseback, on foot or canoe, two hours, US$5 per person, minimum two people. Camping US$2 is per person per day plus US$1.50 per tent, or **D** in old railway carriages. Buses from Colón or those coming from the north will drop you at the entrance. Tell the driver you are going to La Aurora del Palmar, to avoid confusion with the national park. *Remise* taxi from Ubajay costs US$3. Book in advance or check availability for excursions.

Concordia ➔ *Colour map 8, A5. Population: 93,800.*

Just downriver from Salto, Uruguay, Concordia, 104 km north of Colón, is a prosperous city. The Río Uruguay is impassable for large vessels beyond the rapids of Salto Chico near the city, and Salto Grande 32 km upriver, where there is a large international hydro electric dam, providing a crossing to Uruguay. In the streets around the main **Plaza 25 de Mayo** there are some fine public buildings. The city has a range of hotels and restaurants. **Tourist office** ⓘ *Plaza 25 de Mayo, daily 0700-2400*. The **Uruguayan consulate** is at Asunción 131, T422 1426. Above Salto Grande the river is often known as the Alto Uruguay. About 153 km upstream from Concordia is the port of **Monte Caseros**, with the Uruguayan town of Bella Unión, Brazilian border, almost opposite.

Up the Río Uruguay listings

For Sleeping and Eating price codes and other relevant information, see Essentials, pages 38-40.

Sleeping

Gualeguaychú *p176*

Accommodation is scarce during carnival. Prices double Dec-Mar, Easter and long weekends. The tourist office has a list of family accommodation.

B Puerto Sol, San Lorenzo 477, T434017, www.hotelpuertosol.com.ar. Good rooms, a/c, next to the port, has a small resort on a nearby island (transfer included) for relaxing drink.

B Tykuá, Luis N Palma 150, T422625, www.tykuahotel.com.ar. Breakfast included, 3 blocks from the bridge, a/c, internet, laundry.

Camping Several sites on riverside, including **Camping Municipal**, US$2 pp, others next to the bridge and north of it. **El Ñandubaysal**, T423298, www.nandu baysal.com.ar. The smartest, on the Río Uruguay, 15 km southeast (US$7.50 per tent).

Concepción del Uruguay *p176*

B Grand Hotel, Eva Perón 114, T422851, www.grandpalaciotexier.com.ar. Originally a French-style mansion with adjacent theatre, best rooms have a/c and TV but not much difference from standard, includes breakfast, no restaurant.

Colón *p177*

B Holimasú, Belgrano 28, T421305, www.hotel holimasu.com.ar. Nice patio, breakfast included, a/c extra, **C** in low season.

C Hostería Restaurant del Puerto, Alejo Peyret 158, T422698, www.hosteriadecolon.com.ar. Great value, lovely atmosphere in old house, breakfast included, no credit cards.

C La Posada de David, Alejo Peyret 97, T423930, www.colontrerios.com.ar/posadade david/index.htm. Nice family house, garden, welcoming, good rooms with breakfast, great value.

F pp **Sophie Hostel**, Laprida 128, T424136, sophiehostel@yahoo.com.ar. HI affiliated, renovated house with garden, cooking facilities, comfortable rooms for 2-8, welcoming owner Marcela, German and English spoken, homemade meals, great breakfast (free first morning), excellent information. Highly recommended.

Camping Several sites, some with cabins, on river bank, from US$6 daily.

Eating

Concepción del Uruguay *p176*

El Remanso, Rocamora y Eva Perón. Popular, moderately priced *parrilla*.

Colón *p177*

La Cosquilla de Angel, Alejo Peyret 180. The smartest place in town, meals include fish, set menu, live piano music in evenings.

El Viejo Almacén, Gral Urquiza y Paso. Cosy, very good cooking and excellent service.

Transport

Gualeguaychú *p176*

Bus Bus terminal at Bv Artigas y Bv Jurado, T440 688 (30-min walk to centre, *remise* taxi US$1.50). To **Concepción del Uruguay**, 1 hr, US$3. To **Fray Bentos**, 1¼ hrs, US$3.75, 2 a day (1 on Sun), arrive 30 mins before departure for immigration. To **Buenos Aires**, US$12, 3½ hrs, several daily.

Concepción del Uruguay *p176*

Bus Terminal at Rocamora y Los Constituyentes, T422352 (remise, US$0.40). To **Buenos Aires**, frequent, 4 hrs, US$15-16.65. To **Colón**, 45 mins, US$2.

Colón *p177*

Bus Terminal at Paysandú y Sourigues (10 blocks north of main plaza), T421716, left luggage at 24-hr bar. Not all long distance buses enter Colón. **Buenos Aires**, US$16.50-18, 5-6 hrs. **Mercedes** (for Iberá), several companies, 6-7 hrs, US$15. **Paraná**, 4-5 hrs, US$10. **Uruguay**: via the Artigas Bridge (US$5 toll, open 24 hrs) all formalities dealt with on Uruguayan side. *Migraciones* officials board the bus, but non-Argentines/Uruguayans should get off bus for stamp. Bus to **Paysandú**, US$3.75, 45 mins.

Concordia *p178*

Bus Terminal at Justo y Yrigoyen, 13 blocks north- west of Plaza 25 de Mayo (reached by No 2 bus). Long distance buses do not enter town; you have take a taxi from the highway. **Buenos Aires**, US$23, 6½ hrs. **Paraná** 5 a day.

To Uruguay No 4 bus from terminal, marked 'Puerto', for the **ferry** crossing to Salto, US$4, 15 mins. Get tickets at a kiosk, which shuts 15 mins before departure, outside immigration in the building marked 'Resguardo'. There are 5 departures Mon-Fri, 3 departures Sat, none on Sun, 20 mins, for passengers only.

The **bus** service via the Salto Grande dam, US$7.50, 1¼ hrs, is run by **Flecha Bus** and **Chadre**, 2 day each, not Sun (taxi only, US$25 between bus terminals); all formalities on the Argentine side, open 24 hrs. Passengers have to get off the bus to go through immigration. **Bikes** are not allowed to cross the international bridge but officials will help cyclists find a lift.

Up the Río Paraná

Several historic cities stand on the banks of the Paraná, which flows south from its confluence with the Río Paraguay. National parks protecting endangered marshes, especially at Iberá, are the highlight of the zone.

Rosario ➔ *Phone code: 0341. Colour map 8, B5. Population: 1.2 million.*

The largest city in the province of Santa Fe and the third largest city in Argentina, Rosario, 295 km northwest of Buenos Aires, is a great industrial and export centre. It has a lively cultural scene with several theatres and bars where there are daily shows. The **tourist office** ⓘ *Av Belgrano y Buenos Aires, T480 2230, www.rosario turismo.com*, is on the riverside park next to the Monumento a la Bandera. See www.viarosario.com, for the latest events information.

The old city centre is Plaza 25 de Mayo. Around it are the **cathedral** and the **Palacio Municipal**. On the north side is the **Museo de Arte Decorativo** ⓘ *Santa Fe 748, T480 2547, Thu-Sun to 1400, free.* This sumptuous former residence houses a valuable private collection of paintings, furniture, tapestries sculptures and silverwork, brought mainly from Europe. Left of the cathedral, the *Pasaje Juramento* opens the pedestrian way to the imposing **Monumento a la Bandera** ⓘ *T/F480 2238, Mon 1400-1800, Tue-Sun 0900-1800 (in summer till 1900), US$0.35 (tower), free (Salón de las Banderas).* This commemorates the site on which, in 1812, General Belgrano, on his way to fight the Spaniards in Jujuy, raised the Argentine flag for the first time. A 70 m-tower has excellent panoramic views. In the first half of November in the Parque a la Bandera (opposite the monument) *Fiesta de las Colectividades* lasts 10 nights, with stalls offering food and a stage for folk music and dances. From Plaza 25 de Mayo, Córdoba leads west towards Plaza San Martín and beyond, the Boulevard Oroño. These 14 blocks are known as the **Paseo del Siglo** and have the largest concentration of late 19th- and early 20th-century buildings in the city. **Museo de Bellas Artes J B Castagnino** ⓘ *Av Pellegrini 2202, T480 2542, www.museocastagnino.org.ar, closed Tue, open 1400-2000, Sat-Sun 1300-1900, in summer daily except Tue 1500-2100, US$0.65.* Just outside the 126-ha Parque Independencia, it has an impressive collection of French impressionist, Italian baroque and Flemish works, and one of best collections of Argentine paintings and sculpture.

Che Guevara was born here in 1928. The large white house at Entre Ríos y Urquiza where he lived for the first two years of his life before his family moved to Alta Gracia, near Córdoba (see page 123), is now an insurance company office. There are dozens of riverside resorts on the islands and sandbars opposite Rosario. Boats depart daily in summer (otherwise just at weekends) from *La Fluvial*, T447 3838, or from *Costa Alta* to the resorts.

Paraná ➔ *Phone code: 0343. Colour map 8, A5. Population: 247,600.*
About 30 km southeast of Santa Fe, the capital of Entre Ríos was, from 1854-61, capital of the Republic. The centre is on a hill offering views over the Río Paraná and beyond to Santa Fe. In the centre is the **Plaza Primero de Mayo**, around which are the **Municipalidad**, the large **Cathedral** and the **Colegio del Huerto**, seat of the Senate of the Argentine Confederation between 1854 and 1861. The **Casa de Gobierno** at Santa Fe y Laprida has a grand façade. Take pedestrianized San Martín and half block west of the corner with 25 de Junio is the fine **Teatro 3 de Febrero** (1908). Two blocks north is the **Plaza Alvear**; on the west side of which is the **Museo de Bellas Artes** ⓘ *Buenos Aires 355, T420 7868, Tue-Fri 0700-1300, 1500-1900, Sat 1000-1400, 1700-2000, Sun 1000-1300, US$0.35.* It houses a vast collection of Argentine artists' work, with many by painter Cesario Bernaldo de Quirós. The city's glory is **Parque Urquiza**, along the cliffs above the Río Paraná. It has a statue to Gen Urquiza, and a bas-relief showing the battle of Caseros, at which he finally defeated Rosas. **Tourist offices**, in the centre at ⓘ *Buenos Aires 132, T423 0183*; at Parque Urquiza ⓘ *Av Laurencena y Juan de San Martín, T420 1837*; at the bus terminal, T420 1862; and at the Hernandarias tunnel, www.turismoenparana.com. Provincial office ⓘ *Laprida 5, T422 2100, www.entrerios.gov.ar/turismo.*

Santa Fe ➔ *Phone code: 0342. Colour map 8, A4. Population: 451,600.*
From Paraná to Santa Fe, the road goes under the Río Paraná by the Herandarias tunnel, toll US$1 per car, and then crosses a number of bridges (bus service by Etacer and Fluviales, US$1, 50 minutes). Santa Fe, capital of its province, was founded by settlers from Asunción in 1573, though its present site was not occupied until 1653. The south part of the city, around the **Plaza 25 de Mayo** is the historic centre. On the Plaza itself is the majestic **Casa de Gobierno**, built in 1911-1917 in French style on the site of the historic Cabildo, in which the 1853 constitution was drafted. Opposite is the **Cathedral**, and on the east side is the **Colegio de la Inmaculada Concepción**, including the **Iglesia de Nuestra Señora de los Milagros**, dating from 1694, with an ornate dome. **Museo Histórico Provincial** ⓘ *3 de Febrero 2553, T457 3529, all year 0830-1200, afternoon hours change frequently, closed Mon, free.* The building, dating from 1690, is one of the oldest surviving civil buildings in the country. You can swim in the river at Guadalupe beach, on the Costanera Oeste. Take bus 16 from the centre to the Costanera. **Tourist offices**, at the bus terminal ⓘ *T457 4124, 0700-1300, 1500-2100*, at Paseo del Restaurador ⓘ *Bv Pellegrini y Rivadavia, T457 1881, 0700-1900* and at Boca del Tigre ⓘ *Av Paso y Zavalla, 0700-1900*, all good, www.santafeciudad.gov.ar. **Provincial office** ⓘ *San Martín 1399, T458 9475, turismo@santafe.gov.ar.*

Esteros del Iberá
The **Reserva Natural del Iberá** protects nearly 13,000 sq km of wetlands known as the **Esteros del Iberá**, similar to the Pantanal in Brazil. Over sixty small lakes, no more than a few metres deep, cover 20-30% of the protected area, which is rich in aquatic plants. Like islands in the *lagunas*, *embalsados* are floating vegetation, thick enough to support large animals and trees. Wildlife includes black caiman, marsh deer, capybara and about 300 species of bird, among them the *yabirú* or *Juan Grande*, the largest stork in the western hemisphere. More difficult to see are the endangered maned wolf, the 3-m long yellow anaconda, the *yacaré ñato* and the river otter. There is a visitors' centre by the bridge at the access to Carlos Pellegrini (see below), open 0730-1200, 1400-1800, helpful and informative park rangers. **Mercedes** (*Phone code: 03773, Population: 30,900*), 250 km southeast of Corrientes, gives the best access and is the only

point for getting regular transport to Carlos Pellegrini. There are a couple of decent places to stay, a few restaurants, ATMs and internet facilities; also a small tourist office on the plaza. The surrounding countryside is mostly grassy *pampas*, where rheas can be seen, with rocks emerging from the plains from time to time. **Carlos Pellegrini**, 120 km northeast of Mercedes (rough road), stands on beautiful *Laguna Iberá*. A one-day visit allows for a three-hour boat excursion (US$8-12 pp if not included in hotel rates), but some hotels offer more activities for longer stays, eg horse rides or guided walks. Iberá Expediciones, Yaguarté y Pindó, T154 01405, iberaexpediciones@hotmail.com, offers guided treks, horse riding and night-time 4WD trips.

Parque Nacional Mburucuyá

ⓘ *12 km east of the town of Mburucuyá, T03782-498022, free, 2 hotels. Buses San Antonio from Corrientes go daily to Mburucuyá, 2½ hrs, US$2.30; remises to the park, US$5.*

West of the Esteros del Iberá and 180 km southeast of Corrientes, this park covers 17,660 ha, stretching north from the marshes of the Río Santa Lucía. It includes savanna with *yatay* palms, 'islands' of wet Chaco forest, and *esteros*. The *mburucuyá* or passionflower gives the name to the park. Wildlife is easy to see. Formerly two *estancias*, Santa María and Santa Teresa, the land was donated by their owner, the Danish botanist Troels Pedersen, who identified 1,300 different plants here. Provincial route 86 (unpaved) crosses the park for 18 km leading to the information centre and free campsite (hot water and electricity).

Corrientes ➜ *Phone code: 03783. Colour map 6, C6. Population: 316,500.*

Corrientes, founded in 1588 is some 30 km below the confluence of the Ríos Paraguay and Alto Paraná. The 2¾ km General Belgrano bridge across the Río Paraná (toll US$1 per car) links the city with Resistencia (25 km), from where Ruta 11 goes north to Formosa and Asunción. East of Corrientes, Ruta 12 follows the Alto Paraná to Posadas and Iguazú. The river can make the air heavy, moist and oppressive, but in winter the climate is pleasant. The city is capital of Corrientes province and the setting for Graham Greene's novel, *The Honorary Consul*. **Tourist offices**, city tourist office at ⓘ *Carlos Pellegrini 542, T423779, daily 0700-2100*, good map. Provincial office ⓘ *25 de Mayo 1330, T427200, province and city information, Mon-Fri 0700-1300, and in the bus station, T414839, open 0700-2200, www.corrientes.gov.ar*.

On the **Plaza 25 de Mayo**, one of the best preserved in Argentina, the **Jefatura de Policía**, built in 19th-century French style, the Italianate **Casa de Gobierno** and the church of **La Merced**. Six blocks south is the leafy Plaza de la Cruz, on which the church of **La Cruz de los Milagros** (1897) houses a cross, the Santo Madero, placed there by the founder of the city, Juan Torres de Vera – *indígenas* who tried to burn it were killed by lightning from a cloudless sky. The **Museo de Ciencias Naturales 'Amadeo Bonpland'** ⓘ *San Martín 850, Mon-Sat 0900-1200, 1600-2000*, contains botanical, zoological, archaeological and mineralogical collections including 5,800 insects and huge wasp nest. A beautiful walk eastwards, along the Avenida Costanera, beside the Paraná river leads to **Parque Mitre**, from where there are views of sunset.

Up the Río Paraná listings

For Sleeping and Eating price codes and other relevant information, see Essentials, pages 38-40.

Sleeping

Rosario *p179*

Rosario has a good range of business hotels (eg 4 in the Solans group, www.solans.com) and, at the budget end, 15 hostels. List at www.rosario turismo.com/servicios/alojamientos.asp.

L-AL Esplendor Savoy Rosario, San Lorenzo 1022, T448 0071, www.esplendorsavoy rosario.com. Early 20th-century mansion, once Rosario's best, now completely remodelled as a luxury hotel with all modern services, Gym, business centre, Wi-Fi, etc.

AL-A Garden, Callao 45, T437 0025, www.hotel gardensa.com. Good option a little way from the centre, in the Pichincha district (next to

Blv Oroño) with superior rooms and comfortable standard rooms. Also restaurant and children's play area.

AL-A Ros Tower, Mitre 299, T529 9000, http://rostower.com.ar. New, central hotel with pool and bar on the roof, good services, spa and restaurant.

A-B Plaza del Sol, San Juan 1055, T/F421 9899, www.hotelesplaza.com. Comfortable, spacious rooms, pool on the 11th floor with splendid views, with large breakfast.

B Rosario, Cortada Ricardone 1365 (access from Entre Ríos 900 block), T/F424 2371, http://rosario.com.ar/hotelrosario/. Central, good rooms, a/c and breakfast. Larger rooms in annex.

F pp **Cool Raúl**, San Lorenzo 1670, T426 2554, www.coolraulhostel.com.ar. Good party hostel with bar, kitchen, internet, tours and other activities, cooperative owners.

F pp **Rosario Hostel**, Urquiza 1911, T440 4164, www.rosariohostels.com.ar. **D** in double room, convenient, helpful, kitchen, with breakfast, pleasant patio.

F pp **Rosario Inn**, Sgto Cabral 54, T421 0358, www.rosarioinnhostel.com.ar. **D** in double room, central, modern, with breakfast, kitchen, internet, bar, laundry, bikes and language classes.

Paraná *p180*

L Mayorazgo, Etchevehere y Miranda, Costanera Alta, T423 0333. Upmarket, overlooking Parque Urquiza, casino, pool, gym, restaurant and fine views of the river.

A Gran Hotel Paraná, Urquiza 976, T422 3900, www.hotelesparana.com.ar. Overlooking Plaza Primero de Mayo, 3 room categories (breakfast included), smart restaurant *La Fourchette*, gym.

C San Jorge, Belgrano 368, T/F422 1685, www.san jorgehotel.com.ar. Renovated house, helpful staff, older rooms are cheaper than the modern ones at the back with TV, breakfast, kitchen.

Santa Fe *p180*

C Castelar, 25 de Mayo y Peatonal Falucho, T/F456 0999. On a small plaza, 1930's hotel, good value, comfortable, breakfast included, restaurant.

C Hostal Santa Fe de la Veracruz, San Martín 2954, T/F455 1740, hostal_santafe@ciudad.com.ar. Traditional favourite, **C** superior rooms, all good value, large breakfast, restaurant, sauna (extra).

D Emperatriz, Irigoyen Freyre 2440, T/F453 0061. Attractive Hispanic-style building, plain rooms, spacious, comfortable, breakfast and a/c extra.

Esteros del Iberá *p180*

Mercedes

C La Casa de China, call for directions, T03773-156 27269. A delightful historical old house with clean rooms and a lovely patio, breakfast included. Recommended.

E World, Pujol 1162, T422508, 3 blocks from bus station. With fan and breakfast, shared bath, other meals available, Iberá information.

F pp **Delicias del Iberá**, Pujol 1162, T422508. Next to the *combis* to Pellegrini, excellent, shared bath, breakfast, good meals, garden.

Carlos Pellegrini

LL Rincón del Socorro, T03782-497161, T011-5032 6326 (in Buenos Aires), www.rincondel socorro.com. Incredibly luxurious, this estancia is part of an impressive conservation project by North American millionaire Douglas Tompkins. Beautifully set in its own 12,000 hectares 35 km south of Carlos Pellegrini, with 6 spacious bedrooms, each with bathroom and little sitting room, 3 cabañas, and elegant sitting rooms and dining rooms. Delicious home-produced organic food, hosts Leslie and Valeria speak English, excellent trips on the lagunas with bilingual guides, *asados* at lunchtime, night safaris and wonderful horse riding. Gorgeous gardens, pool with superb views all around. Highly recommended. In the same group is **Estancia San Alonso**, www.sanalonso. com, same phones, same levels of comfort and service, but deeper into the Esteros.

L pp **Posada de la Laguna**, T03773-499413, www.posadadelalaguna.com. A beautiful place run by Elsa Güiraldes (grand-daughter of famous Argentine novelist, Ricardo Güiraldes) and set on the lake, very comfortable, large neat garden and a swimming pool, full board and all excursions included, English and some French spoken, excellent country cooking. Highly recommended.

L-AL pp **Posada Aguapé**, T03773-499412, T/F011-4742 3015 (Buenos Aires), www.iberaesteros.com.ar. On a lagoon with a garden and pool, comfortable rooms, attractive dining room, rates are for full board and include 2 excursions. Recommended.

AL pp **Hostería Ñandé Retá**, T03773-499411, www.nandereta.com. Large old wooden house in a shady grove, play room, full board, home cooking, excursions.

A pp **Irupé Lodge**, T03752-438312 or 03773-154 02193, www.irupelodge.com.ar. Rustic, simple rooms, great views of the laguna from dining room, offers conventional and alternative trips, camping on islands, diving, fishing, several languages spoken.

A pp **San Juan Poriahú**, at Loreto, T03781-156 08674, T011-4791 9511 (Buenos Aires). An old estancia run by Marcos García Rams, at the northwest edge of the Esteros, full board, horse rides and boat trips to see wildlife on a property where there has been no hunting at all. Closed Jan, Feb and Jul. Access from Ruta 12. Recommended.

A pp **San Lorenzo**, at Galarza, T03756-481292. Next to 2 lakes on the northeast edge of the region, splendid for wildlife watching, full board, only 3 rooms, horse rides, walks, boat trips all included. Boat excursions by night are charged separately. Access from Gobernador Virasoro (90 km), via Rutas 37 and 41. Transfer can be arranged to/from Gobernador Virasoro or Posadas for an extra charge. Closed Jan-Feb.

E pp **Posada Ypá Sapukai**, Sarmiento 212, T03773-420155, www.argentinahostels.com. Rates include breakfast and dinner; private rooms **C** pp. Good value, nice atmosphere, excellent staff, excursion to the *laguna* is very well guided, lunch or dinner US$4. Recommended.

F pp **San Cayetano**, T03773-156 28763. Very basic, run by local guide Roque Pera, also has campsite.

Corrientes *p181*

No good value, inexpensive accommodation in the city. All those listed have a/c.

A-B Gran Hotel Guaraní, Mendoza 970, T433800, www.hguarani.com.ar. 4-star, business-oriented with restaurant, pool and gym, parking, breakfast.

B Costanera, Plácido Martínez 1098, T436100, www.hotelguia.com/hostaldelrio. In apartment tower overlooking the port, fine rooms, pleasantly decorated, pool, restaurant, breakfast.

B Turismo, Entre Ríos 650, T/F433174. Riverside location, nice style but a bit musty, smart restaurant, breakfast, large pool, adjacent casino.

Eating

Rosario *p179*

ₜₜₜ **Escauriza**, Bajada Escauriza y Paseo Ribereño, La Florida, 30 mins' drive from centre, near bridge over the Paraná, T454 1777. Said to be the "oldest and best" fish restaurant, with terrace overlooking the river.

ₜₜ **Amarra 702**, Av Belgrano 702, T447 7550. Good food, including fish and seafood, quite formal, cheap set menus Mon-Fri noon.

ₜₜ **Rich**, San Juan 1031, T411 5151. A classic, widely varied menu, superb food, reputed to be one of the best restaurants in the whole country. Set meals including pastas, meats and salads, closed Mon. Recommended.

ₜ **Hui Yang Xuan**, Laprida esq San Juan. Decent Chinese food for a change from the usual Argentine fare.

ₜ **Pampa**, Moreno 1206, T449 4303. A good *parrilla* with attractive 1940s decor.

ₜ **Patio**, at Gallega supermarkets, Pellegrini y Mitre and Pellegrini y Moreno. Cheap self-service restaurants with good range of salads.

Cafés and bars

Barra Vieja, Urquiza 1845. US$2.35 entry for men, unless bar is quiet (eg in university holdays), student bar, relaxed, friendly, open Thu-Sat night.

Café de la Opera, Mendoza y Laprida (next to *Teatro El Círculo*). Jazz, tango, Russian folk music and food, poetry or story-telling, pretty café.

La Maltería del Siglo, Roca 1601 y Santa Fé. Open every day for food, drinks and background music, livens up when major football matches are on. Food can be good, but pasta is not recommended.

Tomatte, Córdoba 1630. Trendy bar, busy after work on Wed-Fri and Fri and Sat night.

Victoria, Jujuy y Bvd Oroño. One of the oldest cafés in town and most traditional.

Santa Fe *p180*

Many good eating places, with excellent meals with wine. Many places in the centre close on Sun.

ₜ **Baviera San Martín**, San Martín 2941. Traditional, central, good varied menu.

ₜ **Club Sirio Libanés**, 25 de Mayo 2740. Very good Middle Eastern food, popular Sun lunch for families.

El Quincho de Chiquito, Av Almirante Brown y Obispo Príncipe (Costanera Oeste). Classic fish restaurant, excellent food, generous helpings and good value.

Cafés

Don Ernesto, San Martín y General López. A traditional café in the civic centre.

Las Delicias, Hipólito Yrigoyen y San Martín. Café and bakery with beautiful decor from early 20th century, good for coffees and pastries, fruit juices, sandwiches and alcohol.

Corrientes *p181*

El Solar, San Lorenzo 830. Informal, busy at lunchtime, meals by weight.

Martha de Bianchetti, 9 de Julio y Mendoza. Smart café and bakery.

Panambí, Junín near Córdoba. A traditional, central *confitería*, serving good pastries and regional breads.

Transport

Rosario *p179*

Air Airport at Fisherton, 15 km west of centre, T451 1226. *Remises* charge US$5. Daily flights to Buenos Aires with **AR** and **Sol**, 45 mins. Also **Gol** to Porto Alegre and **Lan** to santiago de Chile.

Bus Terminal at Santa Fe y Cafferata, about 30 blocks west of the *Monumento de la Bandera*, T437 3030, www.terminalrosario.gov.ar. For local buses you must buy magnetic card sold at kiosks in the centre or near bus stops (US$0.25 per journey), several bus lines to centre with stops on Córdoba (eg 101, 103, 115), US$0.25; from centre, take buses on Plaza 25 de Mayo, via C Santa Fe. *Remise* US$1.50. **Buenos Aires**, 4 hrs, US$13-18. **Córdoba**, 6 hrs, US$17.65. **Santa Fe**, 2½ hrs, US$6.50.

Train Rosario Norte station, Av del Valle y Av Ovidio Lagos. To/from Buenos Aires, operated by **TBA**, T0800-3333822, Mon-Fri 0515, return from BsAs 1815, tickets are only sold just before departures, at the station. To **Buenos Aires**, US$11. Taxis charge US$1.

Paraná *p180*

Bus Terminal at Av Ramírez 2598 (10 blocks southeast of Plaza Primero de Mayo), T422 1282. Buses 1, 6 to/from centre, US$0.75. *Remise* US$3. To **Colón** on Río Uruguay, 4-5 hrs, US$12. To **Buenos Aires**, 6-7 hrs, US$17-22.

Santa Fe *p180*

Air Airport at Sauce Viejo, 17 km south. T499 5064. Taxi US$4 from bus terminal. Daily **AR** and **Sol** to and from **Buenos Aires**.

Bus Terminal near the centre, Gen M Belgrano 2910, T457 4124. To **Córdoba**, US$8.50, 5 hrs. Many buses to **Buenos Aires** US$17-22, 6 hrs; to **Paraná** frequent service US$1.50, 50 mins; to **Rosario**, 2½ hrs, US$6.50.

Esteros del Iberá *p180*

Bus Mercedes to **Carlos Pellegrini**: **Itatí II** combis daily 1130 (schedules change frequently) from Pujol 1166, T420184, T156 29598, 3 hrs, US$6.50. Combi spends an hour picking up passengers all around Mercedes after leaving the office. Returns from Pellegrini at 0400, book by 2200 the night before at the local grocery (ask for directions). Mercedes to **Buenos Aires**, 9-10 hrs, US$27-30. Mercedes to **Corrientes**, 3 hrs, US$8. To **Puerto Iguazú**, best to go via Corrientes, otherwise via any important town along Ruta 14, eg Paso de los Libres, 130 km southeast. There is a direct bus from Carlos Pellegrini to **Posadas**.

Corrientes *p181*

Air Camba Punta Airport, 10 km east of city, T458684. (Minibus picks up passengers from hotels, T450072, US$1.50, US$3 to Resistencia airport.) **AR** (T424647) to/from Buenos Aires.

Bus Terminal: Av Maipú 2400. To **Resistencia**, **Chaco–Corrientes**, every 15 mins from Av Costanera y La Rioja at the port, 40 mins, US$1 return. Main terminal on Av Maipú, 5 km southeast of centre, bus No 103 (be sure to ask the driver if goes to terminal as same line has many different routes), 20 mins, US$0.50 To **Posadas** US$9-15, 3½-4 hrs, several companies, road paved. To **Buenos Aires**, several companies, 11-12 hrs, US$38-43. To **Asunción** (Paraguay), **Crucero del Norte**, **El Pulqui**, 5-7 hrs, US$12.

Directory

Rosario *p179*

Airline offices **Aerolíneas Argentinas**, Santa Fe 1410, T424 9517. **Gol**, T0810-266-3232.

LAN, San Luis 470 p 7, T0810-999-9526. **Sol**, T0810-444 4765. **Banks** Many banks along C Córdoba, east of plaza San Martín. Exchange at **Transatlántica**, Mitre y Rioja. TCs exchanged at **Banex**, Mitre y Santa Fe. 2% or US$10 commission. **Bike hire and repair** **Bike House**, San Juan 973, T424 5280, info@bikehouse.com.ar. **Bike Rosario**, Zeballos 327, T155 713812, www.bikerosario.com.ar, Sebastián Clérico. Bike rental (US$12 per day), bike tours, also kayak trips. **Speedway Bike Center**, Roca 1269, T426 8415, info@speedwaybikecenter.com.ar. **Internet** Several places in centre, US$0.50 per hr. **Post offices** Córdoba y Buenos Aires.

Santa Fe *p180*
Banks Banking district around San Martín y Tucumán. Exchange money and TCs at **Tourfé**, San Martín 2500, or at **Columbia**, San Martín 2275.

Corrientes *p181*
Internet Many in centre. **Post offices** San Juan y San Martín. **Telephones** Several *telecentros* in centre.

The Chaco

Much of the Chaco is inaccessible because of poor roads (many of them impassable during summer rains) and lack of public transport, but it has two attractive national parks which are reachable all year round. Resistencia and Formosa are the main cities at the eastern rim, from where Rutas 16 and 81 respectively go west almost straight across the plains to the hills in Salta province. Buses to Salta take Ruta 16, while Ruta 81 has long unpaved sections west of Las Lomitas, which make for a very hard journey after heavy rains. Presidencia Roque Sáenz Peña, 170 km northwest of Resistencia, is a reasonable place to stop over. The Chaco is one of the main centres of indigenous population in Argentina: the Toba are settled in towns by the Río Paraná and the semi-nomadic Wichi, or Mataco, live in the western region. Less numerous are the Mocoví in Chaco and the Pilagá in central Formosa. The Chaco has two distinct natural zones. The Wet Chaco spreads along the Ríos Paraná and Paraguay covered mainly by marsh-lands with savanna and groves of caranday palms, where birdwatching is excellent. Further west, as rainfall diminishes, scrubland of algarrobo, white quebracho, palo borracho and various types of cacti characterise the Dry Chaco, where South America's highest temperatures, exceeding 45°C, have been recorded. Winters are mild, with only an occasional touch of frost in the south.

Resistencia → *Phone code: 03722. Colour map 6, C6. Population: 359,100.*
The hot and energetic capital of the Province of Chaco, Resistencia is 6½ km up the Barranqueras stream on the west bank of the Paraná and 544 km north of Santa Fe. On the Paraná itself is the little port of Barranqueras. Resistencia is known as the 'city of the statues', there being over 200 of these in the streets. Four blocks from the central Plaza 25 de Mayo is the **Fogón de los Arrieros** ⓘ *Brown 350 (between López y Planes and French), T426418, open to non-members Mon-Sat 0900-1200, Mon-Fri 2100-2300, US$1.70.* This famous club and informal cultural centre deserves a visit, for its occasional exhibitions and meetings. The **Museo Del Hombre Chaqueño** ⓘ *Juan B Justo 280, Mon-Fri 0800-1200, 1600-2000, free,* is a small anthropological museum with an exhibition of handicrafts by native Wichi, Toba and Mocoví people. It has a fascinating mythology section in which small statues represent Guaraní beliefs (still found in rural areas). There are banks and *cambios* in the centre for exchange. **Tourist office** ⓘ *Plaza 25 de Mayo, T458289, Mon-Fri 0800-2000.* **Provincial tourist office** ⓘ *Santa Fe 178, T423547, Mon-Fri 0800-1300, 1400-2000, Sat 0800-1200.*

Parque Nacional Chaco

ⓘ *T03725-496166, 24 hrs, free, 115 km northwest of Resistencia, best visited between Apr-Oct to avoid intense summer heat and voracious mosquitoes.*

The park extends over 15,000 ha and protects one of the last remaining untouched areas of the Wet Chaco with exceptional *quebracho colorado* trees, *caranday* palms and dense riverine forests with orchids along the banks of the Río Negro. Some 340 species of bird have been sighted in the park. Mammals include *carayá* monkeys and, much harder to see, collared peccary, puma and jaguarundi. 300 m from the entrance is the visitors' centre and a free campsite with hot showers and electricity. There you can hire bicycles or horses for US$1.30 per hour. The paved Ruta 16 goes northwest from Resistencia and after about 60 km Ruta 9 branches off, leading north to Colonia Elisa and Capitán Solari, 5 km east of the park entrance, via a dirt road. If in a group, call the park in advance to be picked up at Capitán Solari. *La Estrella* run daily buses Resistencia-Capitán Solari, where *remise* taxis should not charge more than US$1 to the park, a short journey that can also be done on foot. Tour operators run day-long excursions to the park from Resistencia.

Formosa → *Phone code: 03717. Colour map 6, C6. Population: 198,100.*

The capital of Formosa Province, 186 km above Corrientes, is the only Argentine port of any note on the Río Paraguay. It is oppressively hot from November to March. **Tourist office** ⓘ *José M Uriburu 820 (Plaza San Martín), 1600-2000, T425192, www.formosa.gov.ar, Mon-Fri 0730-1300.* Ask about guided excursions and accommodation at *estancias.*

Border with Paraguay

The easiest crossing is by road via the Puente Loyola, 4 km north of **Clorinda** (*Phone code: 03718, Colour map 6, C6*). From Puerto Falcón, at the Paraguayan end of the bridge, the road runs 40 km northeast, crossing the Río Paraguay, before reaching Asunción. **Immigration** formalities for entering Argentina are dealt with at the Argentine end, those for leaving Argentina at the Paraguayan end. Crossing, open 24 hours. **Buses** from Puerto Falcón to Asunción run every hour, *Empresa Falcón* US$0.50, last bus to the centre of Asunción 1830.

A second route is by ferry from Puerto Pilcomayo, close to Clorinda, to Itá Enramada (Paraguay), US$0.50, five minutes, every 30 minutes. Then take bus 9 to Asunción. Argentine **immigration** is at Puerto Pilcomayo, closed at weekends for tourists. Paraguayan immigration at Itá Enramada, 24 hrs.

Parque Nacional Río Pilcomayo

ⓘ *Access to the park is free, 24 hrs, administration centre in Laguna Blanca, Av Pueyrredón y Ruta 86, T03718-470045, Mon-Fri 0700-1430.*

Some 48,000 ha, 65 km northwest of Clorinda is this national park is recognised as a natural wetland, with lakes, marshes and low-lying parts which flood during the rainy season. The remainder is grassland with caranday palm forests and Chaco woodland. Among the protected species are aguará-guazú, giant anteaters and coatis. Caimans, black howler monkeys, rheas and a variety of birds can also be seen. The park has two entrances leading to different areas. Easiest to reach on foot is Laguna Blanca, where there is an information point and a free campsite with electricity and cold water. From there, a footpath goes to the Laguna Blanca, the biggest lake in the park. A bit further is the second entrance, leading to the area of Estero Poí, with another information point and a campsite without facilities. **Godoy** buses run from Formosa or Resistencia to the small towns of Laguna Naick-Neck, 5 km from the park (for going to Laguna Blanca) and Laguna Blanca, 8 km from the park (for going to Estero Poí). **Remise** taxis from both towns should charge no more than US$3 for these short journeys. There are police controls on the way to the park because of the proximity to the Paraguay border.

The Chaco listings

For Sleeping and Eating price codes and other relevant information, see Essentials, pages 38-40.

Sleeping

Resistencia *p185*

B-C Covadonga, Güemes 200, T444444, www.hotelcovadonga.com.ar. The city's top hotel, comfortable, a/c, breakfast, swimming pool, sauna and gym.

E Bariloche, Obligado 239, T421412. Best value, welcoming, good rooms, a/c, no breakfast but there is a café at the nearby Gran Hotel Royal.

Formosa *p186*

AL Turismo, San Martín 759, T431122, hotelturismo@elpajaritosa.com.ar. Large building by the river, good views, a/c, breakfast.

B Casa Grande Apart-Hotel, Av González Lelong 185, T431573, www.casagrandeapart.com.ar. 8 blocks north of Av 25 de Mayo, by river, good 1 and 2-room apartments with kitchenette, a/c and breakfast, gym and pool.

C Plaza, José M Uriburu 920, T426767, hotelplaza@elpajaritosa.com.ar. On Plaza, good, pool, with breakfast, very helpful, some English spoken, secure parking.

E El Extranjero, Av Gutnisky 2660, T452276. Opposite bus terminal, OK, with a/c.

Eating

Resistencia *p185*

ŸŸ-Ÿ Charly, Güemes 213, T434019. *Parrilla* and international food, excellent, a/c, popular.

Ÿ San José, Roca y Av Alberdi. A popular café and *confitería* on Plaza 25 de Mayo with excellent pastries and ice creams.

Formosa *p186*

Ÿ El Fortín, Mitre 602. Traditional, good for fish.

Ÿ El Tano Marino, Av 25 de Mayo 55. Italian, pastas are the speciality.

Ÿ Yayita, Belgrano 926. Central, serves regional dishes, such as *soyo*, or *sopa paraguaya*.

Festivals and events

Resistencia *p185*

Fiesta Nacional de Pescado de los Grandes is celebrated **10-12 Oct**, Río Antequeros, 14 km away.

Formosa *p186*

The world's longest **Via Crucis** pilgrimage with 14 stops along Ruta 81 (registered in the Guinness Book of Records) takes place every Easter week, starting in Formosa and ending at the border with the province of Salta, 501 km northwest. **Festival de la caña con ruda** is held on the last night of **Jul**, when Paraguayan *caña* flavoured by the *ruda* plant is drunk as a protection against the mid-winter blues. A good chance to try regional dishes.

Transport

Resistencia *p185*

Air Airport 8 km west of town (taxi US$3), T446 009. **AR**, T445550, to/from **Buenos Aires**, 1¼ hrs.

Bus To **Corrientes**, **Chaco-Corrientes** buses stop opposite *Norte* supermarket on Av Alberdi e Illia, 40 mins, US$1 return. Modern terminal on Av Malvinas Argentinas y Av Maclean in western outskirts (bus 3 or 10 from Oro y Perón, 1 block west of plaza, 20 mins, US$0.50; *remise* US$2). To **Buenos Aires** 12-13 hrs, US$38-43 several companies. To **Formosa** 2-2½ hrs, US$5.35-7.65. To **Iguazú**, 8-10½ hrs, US$22-25, several companies, some require change of bus in **Posadas**, 5½ hrs, US$13-15. To **Salta**, **FlechaBus**, **La Nueva Estrella**, 12½ hrs, US$40. To **Asunción** several companies, 5-5½ hrs, US$10.

Formosa *p186*

Air El Pucu airport, 5 km southwest, T452490; *remise*, US$2. **AR** (T429314) to **Buenos Aires** 1½ hrs.

Bus Terminal at Av Gutnisky y Antartida, 15 blocks west of Plaza San Martín, T451766 (*remise* US$1). **Asunción**, 3 hrs, US$6. **Resistencia**, 2½ hrs, US$5.35-7.65; **Buenos Aires** 15-17 hrs, US$50-75.

Misiones

While Posadas is one of the main crossing points to Paraguay, most people will head northeast, through the province of the Jesuit Missions, towards Iguazú. This is a land of ruined religious establishments, gemstones and waterfalls.

Posadas ➔ *Phone code: 03752. Population: 280,500.*

This is the main Argentine port on the south bank of the Alto Paraná, 377 km above Corrientes, and the capital of the province of Misiones. On the opposite bank of the river lies the Paraguayan town of Encarnación, reached by the San Roque bridge. The city's centre is **Plaza 9 de Julio**, on which stand the **Cathedral** and the **Gobernación**, in imitation French style. The riverside and adjacent districts are good for a stroll. Follow Rivadavia or Buenos Aires north to Avenida Andrés Guaçurarí (referred also to as Roque Pérez), a pleasant boulevard, lively at night with several bars. Immediately north of it is the small and hilly **Bajada Vieja** or old port district. There is a good **Museo Regional Aníbal Cambas** ⓘ *Alberdi 600 in the Parque República del Paraguay, 11 blocks north of Plaza 9 de Julio, T447539, Mon-Fri 0700-1900*, its permanent exhibition of Guaraní artefacts and pieces collected from the nearby Jesuit missions is worth seeing. **Tourist office** ⓘ *Colón 1985, T447540, www.turismo. misiones.gov.ar, daily 0800-2000.*

Border with Paraguay

Argentine immigration and customs are on the Argentine side of the bridge to Encarnación. Buses across the bridge (see Transport page 191) do not stop for formalities; you must get exit stamps. Get off the bus, keep your ticket and luggage, and catch a later bus. Pedestrians and cyclists are not allowed to cross; cyclists must ask officials for assistance. Boats cross to Encarnación, 6-8 minutes, hourly Monday-Friday 0800-1800, US$1. Formalities and ticket office at main building. Port access from Av Costanera y Av Andrés Guaçurarí, T425044 (*Prefectura*).

San Ignacio Miní ➔ *Phone code: 03752. Colour map 7, C1.*

ⓘ *0700-1900, US$4 with tour (ask for English version), leaves from entrance every 20 mins. Allow 1½ hrs. Go early to avoid crowds and the best light for pictures (also late afternoon); good birdwatching. Son et lumière show at the ruins, daily after sunset, Spanish only, US$1.*

The little town of San Ignacio is the site of the most impressive Jesuit ruins in the region, 63 km northeast of Posadas. It is a good base for visiting the other Jesuit ruins and for walking. San Ignacio, together with the missions of Santa Ana and Loreto, is a UNESCO World Heritage Site. There are heavy rains in February. Mosquitoes can be a problem. The local festival is 30-31 July.

San Ignacio Miní was founded on its present site in 1696. The 100 sq-m, grass-covered plaza is flanked north, east and west by 30 parallel blocks of stone buildings with four to 10 small, one-room dwellings in each block. The roofs have gone, but the massive metre-thick walls are still standing except where they have been torn down by the *ibapoi* trees. The public buildings, some of them 10 m high, are on the south side of the plaza. In the centre are the ruins of a large church finished about 1724. The masonry, sandstone from the Río Paraná, was held together by mud. Inside the entrance, 200 m from the ruins, is the **Centro de Interpretación Jesuítico-Guaraní**, with displays on the lives of the Guaraníes before the arrival of the Spanish, the work of the Jesuits and the consequences of their expulsion, as well as a fine model of the mission. **Museo Provincial** contains a small collection of artefacts from Jesuit reducciones. For more on the Jesuits, see box, page 1753.

The ruins of two other Jesuit missions are worth visiting (US$1 each, free with ticket to San Ignacio). **Loreto** ⓘ *0700-1830*, can be reached by a 3-km dirt road (signposted) which turns off Ruta 12, 10 km south of San Ignacio. Little remains other than a few walls; excavations are in progress. There are no buses to Loreto; the bus drops you off on Ruta 12, or take a tour from Posadas or a *remise*. **Santa Ana** ⓘ *16 km south, 0700-1900, buses stop on Ruta 12,* was the site of the Jesuit iron foundry. Impressive high walls still stand and beautiful steps lead from the church to the wide open plaza The ruins are 700 m along a path from Ruta 12 (signposted).

Near San Ignacio, is the **Casa de Horacio Quiroga** ⓘ *T470124, 0800-1900, US$0.65 (includes 40-min guided tour; ask in advance for English). Take Calle San Martín (opposite direction to the ruins) to the Gendarmería HQ. Turn right and on your right are 2 attractive wood and stone houses. After 200 m the road turns left and 300 m later, a signposted narrow road branches off.* The house of this Uruguayan writer, who lived part of his tragic life here as a farmer and carpenter between 1910 and 1916 and in the 1930s, is worth a visit. Many of his short stories were inspired by the subtropical environment and its inhabitants.

San Ignacio to Puerto Iguazú

Ruta 12 continues northeast, running parallel to Río Alto Paraná, towards Puerto Iguazú. With its bright red soil and lush vegetation, this attractive route is known as the Región de las Flores. You get a good view of the local economy: plantations of *yerba mate*, manioc and citrus fruits, timber yards, manioc mills and *yerba mate* factories. The road passes through several small modern towns including Jardín America, Puerto Rico, Montecarlo and Eldorado, with accommodation, campsites, places to eat and regular bus services. Just outside Eldorado, **Estancia Las Mercedes** ⓘ *Av San Martín Km 4, T03751-431511*, is an old *yerba mate* farm with period furnishings, open for day visits with activities like riding, boating, and for overnight stays with full board (**AL**). **Wanda**, 50 km north of Eldorado, was named after a Polish princess and is famous as the site of open-cast amethyst and quartz mines which sell gems. There are guided tours to two of them, **Tierra Colorada** and **Compañía Minera Wanda** ⓘ *daily 0700-1900*.

Gran Salto del Moconá

For 3 km the waters of the Río Uruguay in a remote part of Misiones create magnificent falls (known in Brazil as Yucuma) up to 20 m high. They are surrounded by dense woodland protected by the Parque Estadual do Turvo (Brazil) and the Parque Provincial Moconá, the Reserva Provincial Esmeralda and the Reserva de la Biósfera Yabotí (Argentina). Moconá has roads and footpaths, accommodation where outdoor activities can be arranged, such as excursions to the falls, trekking in the forests, kayaking, birdwatching and 4WD trips. Alternative bases are El Soberbio (70 km southwest) or San Pedro (92 km northwest). Roads from both towns to Moconá are impassable after heavy rain. Regular bus service from Posadas to El Soberbio or San Pedro, and from Puerto Iguazú to San Pedro, but no bus all the way to the falls.

Misiones listings

For Sleeping and Eating price codes and other relevant information, see Essentials, pages 38-40.

Sleeping

Posadas *p188*

A Julio César, Entre Ríos 1951, T427930, www.juliocesarhotel.com.ar. 4-star hotel, pool and gym, spacious reasonably priced rooms, some with river views, breakfast included. Recommended.

A Posadas, Bolívar 1949, T440888, www.hotelposadas.com.ar. Business hotel with good standard rooms and bigger *especial* rooms, restaurant, free internet access for guests.

A-B Continental, Bolívar 1879 (on Plaza 9 de Julio), T440990, www.hoteleramisiones.com.ar. Standard rooms and more spacious **B** VIP rooms, some have river views, restaurant on 1st floor.

C City, Colón 1754, T433901, citysa@arnet.com.ar. Gloomy reception, but very good rooms, some overlooking plaza, with breakfast and a/c, restaurant on first floor, parking.

C Le Petit, Santiago del Estero 1630, T436031, lepetithotel@ciudad.com.ar. Good value, small, a short walk from centre on a quiet street, a/c, with breakfast.

E Residencial Misiones, Félix de Azara 1960, T430133. Dark rooms, fan, central, old house with a patio, no breakfast, poorly equipped kitchen.

San Ignacio Miní *p188*

D El Descanso, Pellegrini 270, T470207. Small detached house, 5 blocks southwest of main Av Sarmiento, Comfortable. Also with campsite.

D San Ignacio, Sarmiento 823, T470422, hotelsanignacio@arnet.com.ar. Welcoming and very informative owner Beatriz offers very good rooms with a/c and apartments for 4-5, breakfast US$2, evening meals.

D-E Res Doka, Alberdi 518, T470131, recidoka@yahoo.com.ar. Simple but comfortable rooms, handy for the ruins.

F pp **La Casa de Inés y Juan**, San Martín 1291 (no sign and no phone). Laid-back artist and writer's house, 2 rooms, small library and a backyard for pitching tents, where is also a small but delightful pool and a curious bathroom. Meals on request. Recommended.

Camping Two sites on the river splendidly set and very well-kept on a small sandy bay, reached after 45-min walk from town at the end of the road leading to Quiroga's house. **Club de Pesca y Deportes Náuticos**, on a hilly ground with lush vegetation, US$1.50 pp per day plus US$1 per tent. **Playa del Sol**, T470207, on the beach side of the bay, same prices.

Gran Salto del Moconá *p189*

A Hostería Puesta del Sol, C Suipacha, El Soberbio, T03755-495161, hostpuestadelsol@hotmail.com. Great views, pool, restaurant, comfortable, with breakfast, a/c, also has bungalows. Full board available. Boat excursions arranged to the falls, 7 to 8 hrs, US$20 pp (minimum 4 people). A less tiring journey to the falls is by an easy boat crossing to Brazil, then by vehicle to the Parque do Turvo, 7 hrs, meal included, US$20 pp. Otherwise, a 4WD journey on the Argentine side with more opportunities for trekking also takes 7 hrs, with a meal, US$20 pp. Also act as tour operators.

C pp **Refugio Moconá**, 3 km from access to the reserve, 8 km from the falls (or contact at Pasaje Dornelles 450, San Pedro), T03751-470022. Rooms for 4 to 5 people with shared bath, campsite for US$4.30 a day per tent, tents for rent, meals, boat trips and activities. Runs various boat trips and excursions, such as transfer with sightseeing to/from San Pedro, 2 hrs. Also act as tour operators.

Eating

Posadas *p188*

Most places offer *espeto corrido*, eat as much as you can *parrilla* with meat brought to the table.

ΨΨ **De La Costa**, Av Costanera. Very popular with locals, on the river bank, with great views from the upper floor, and a cheerful buzz on Sat.

ΨΨ **Diletto**, Bolívar 1729. Good for fish, such as *surubí*, and, curiously, rabbit as their speciality.

ΨΨ **El Mensú**, Fleming y Coronel Reguera (at Bajada Vieja district). Attractive house offering a varied menu with fish, pastas and a large selection of wines, closed Mon.

ΨΨ **Espeto del Rey**, Ayacucho y Tucumán. *Parrilla*, good food. Try *mandioca frita* (fried manioc).

ΨΨ **La Querencia**, on Bolívar 322 (on Plaza 9 de Julio). Traditional large restaurant offering *parrilla*, *surubí* and pastas, good service.

ΨΨ **La Rueda**, Av Costanera. A quiet smart place on the banks of the river.

San Ignacio Miní *p188*

Ψ **La Aldea**, Rivadavia y Lanusse. An attractive house serving good and cheap pizzas, *empanadas* or other simple meals.

Activities and tours

Posadas *p188*

Abra, Colón 1975, T422221, abramisiones@arnet.com.ar. Tours to San Ignacio, including Santa Ana Jesuit ruins (US$20 pp), also those in Paraguay (US$23 pp) and in Brazil (US$48 pp), plus tours to waterfalls (US$47).

Guayrá, San Lorenzo 2208, T433415, www.guayra. com.ar. Tours to Iberá (US$50-65 pp if 4 people), to Saltos del Moconá (US$80 pp if 4 people), both sites in a 5-day excursion for US$240 pp (for 4), also car rental and transfer to Carlos Pellegrini (for Iberá).

Transport

Posadas *p188*

Air Gen San Martín Airport, 12 km west, T457413, reached by Bus No 8 or 28 in 40 mins, US$0.35, *remise* US$8. To **Buenos Aires**, AR (Ayacucho 1728, T422036), direct 1 hr 25 mins, some flights call at Corrientes or Formosa, 1 hr 50 mins.

Bus Terminal about 5 km out of the city at Av Santa Catalina y Av Quaranta (T456106), on the road to Corrientes. Buses No 4, 8, 15, 21, to/from

centre, 20 mins, US$0.35, *remise* US$2. Travel agencies in the centre can book bus tickets in advance. To **Buenos Aires**, 12-13 hrs, US$40-45. Frequent services to **San Ignacio Miní**, 1 hr, US$3, and **Puerto Iguazú**, US$10, 5-6 hrs *expreso*.
International To **Encarnación** (Paraguay), **Servicio Internacional**, 50 mins, US$1, leaving at least every 30 mins from platforms 11 and 12 (lower level), tickets on bus.

To **Brazil** and the Jesuit Missions in Rio Grande do Sul, take a **Cotal**, **Aguila Dorada** or **Horianski** bus from Posadas to **San Javier**, 124 km, then a ferry, US$3.75, to Porto Xavier, from where buses run to Santo Ângelo, 4 hrs (see page 515). Immigration is at either end of the ferry crossing.

San Ignacio Miní *p188*
Bus Stop in front of the church, leaving almost hourly to **Posadas** (US$3) or to **Puerto Iguazú** (US$9). Do not rely on bus terminal at the end of Av Sarmiento, only a few stop there. More buses stop on Ruta 12 at the access road (Av Sarmiento).

❶ Directory

Posadas *p188*
Banks **Banco de La Nación**, Bolívar 1799. Round corner on Félix de Azara are **Banco Río** and **HSBC**. **Citibank**, San Martín y Colón. **Mazza**, Bolívar 1932. For money exchange, TCs accepted. **Consulates** **Paraguay**, San Lorenzo 179, T423858. Mon-Fri 0730-1400. Same-day visas. **Immigration** **Dirección Nacional de Migraciones**, Buenos Aires 1633, T427414, 0630-1330. **Internet** Many places, average US$050 per hr (usually cheaper evenings and weekends). **Medical services** **Hospital Dr Ramón Madariaga**, Av L Torres 1177, T447000. **Post offices** Bolívar y Ayacucho.

Iguazú Falls → *Colour map 7, C1.*

The mighty Iguazú Falls are the most overwhelmingly magnificent in all of South America. So impressive are they that Eleanor Roosevelt remarked "poor Niagara" on witnessing them (they are four times wider). Viewed from below, the tumbling water is majestically beautiful in its setting of begonias, orchids, ferns and palms. Toucans, flocks of parrots and cacique birds and great dusky swifts dodge in and out along with myriad butterflies (there are at least 500 different species). Above the impact of the water, upon basalt rock, hovers a perpetual 30-m high cloud of mist in which the sun creates blazing rainbows.

Ins and outs **Information** Entry is US$16, payable in pesos, reais or dollars (guests at Hotel Sheraton should pay and get tickets stamped at the hotel to avoid paying again). Argentines, Mercosur and Misiones inhabitants pay less. Entry next day is half price with same ticket. Open daily 0800-1800 (0800-1900 1 Apr-31 Aug). Visitor Centre includes information and photographs of the flora and fauna, as well as books for sale. There are places to eat, toilets, shops and a locutorio in the park. In the rainy season, when water levels are high, waterproof coats or swimming costumes are advisable for some of the lower catwalks and for boat trips. Cameras should be carried in a plastic bag. **Tourist offices** ⓘ *Aguirre 396, Puerto Iguazú, T420800*, and **Municipal office** ⓘ *Av Victoria Aguirre y Balbino Brañas, T422938, www.iguazuturismo.gov.ar, also www.iguazuargentina.com, 0900-2200*. They have a basic map of area with local information, Spanish only. National park office: ⓘ *Victoria Aguirre 66, T420722, iguazu@apn.gov.ar.*

The falls, on the Argentina-Brazil border, are 19 km upstream from the confluence of the Río Iguazú with the Río Alto Paraná. The Río Iguazú (I is Guaraní for water and guazú is Guaraní for big), which rises in the Brazilian hills near Curitiba, receives the waters of some 30 rivers as it crosses the plateau. Above the main falls, the river, sown with wooded islets, opens out to a width of 4 km. There are rapids for 3½ km above the 74 m precipice over which the water plunges in 275 falls over a frontage of 2,470 m, at a rate of 1,750 cu m a second (rising to 12,750 cu m in the rainy season).

Around the falls

➔ *In Oct-Feb (daylight saving dates change each year) Brazil is 1 hr ahead.*

On both sides of the falls there are National Parks. Transport between the two parks is via the Ponte Tancredo Neves as there is no crossing at the falls themselves. The Brazilian park offers a superb panoramic view of the whole falls and is best visited in the morning when the light is better for photography. The Argentine park (which requires a day to explore properly) offers closer views of the individual falls in their forest setting with its wildlife and butterflies, though to appreciate these properly you need to go early and get well away from the visitors areas. Busiest times are holidays and Sundays. Both parks have visitors' centres and tourist facilities on both sides are constantly being improved.

Parque Nacional Iguazú covers an area of 67,620 ha. The fauna includes jaguars, tapirs, brown capuchin monkeys, collared anteaters and coatimundis, but these are rarely seen around the falls. There is a huge variety of birds; among the butterflies are shiny blue morphos and red/black heliconius. From the Visitor Centre a small gas-run train (free), the **Tren de la Selva,** whisks visitors on a 25-minute trip through the jungle to the Estación del Diablo, where it's a 1-km walk along catwalks across the Río Iguazú to the park's centrepiece, the **Garanta del Diablo.** A visit here is particularly recommended in the evening when the light is best and the swifts are returning to roost on the cliffs, some behind the water. Trains leave on the hour and 30 minutes past the hour. However, it's best to see the falls from a distance first, with excellent

1 Around the Iguazú Falls

➔Iguazú Falls maps
1 Around the Iguazú Falls, page 192
2 Puerto Iguazú, page 195

Sleeping
1 Camping e Pousada Internacional
2 Carimã
3 Das Cataratas
4 El Viejo Americano
5 Paudimar Campestre
6 San Martin
7 Sheraton Internacional Iguazú Resort

views from the two well-organized trails along the **Circuito Superior** and **Circuito Inferior**, each taking around an hour and a half. To reach these, get off the train at the **Estación Cataratas** (after 10 minutes' journey) and walk down the **Sendero Verde**. The Circuito Superior is a level path which takes you along the easternmost line of falls, Bossetti, Bernabé Mandez, Mbiguá (Guaraní for cormorant) and San Martín, allowing you to see these falls from above. This path is safe for those with walking difficulties, wheelchairs and pushchairs, though you should wear supportive non-slippery shoes. The Circuito Inferior takes you down to the water's edge via a series of steep stairs and walkways with superb views of both San Martín falls and the Gaganta del Diablo from a distance. Wheelchair users, pram pushers, and those who aren't good with steps should go down by the exit route for a smooth and easy descent. You could then return to the Estación Cataratas to take the train to Estación Garganta, 10 and 40 minutes past the hour, and see the falls close up. Every month on the five nights of full moon, there are 1½-hour guided walks (bilingual) that may include or not a dinner afterwards or before the walk, at the Restaurant La Selva, depending on the time of departure. See www.iguazuargentina.com for dates and times. Bookings must be in person at the park, T03757-491469, or through agencies (the Park does not take reservations via email): US$30 with dinner; US$20 without.

At the very bottom of the Circuito Inferior, a free ferry crosses 0900-1600 on demand to the small, hilly **Isla San Martín** where trails lead to *miradores* with good close views of the San Martín falls. The park has two further trails: **Sendero Macuco**, 7 km return (allow 7 hours), starting from near the Visitor Centre and leading to the river via a natural pool (El Pozón) fed by a slender waterfall, **Salto Arrechea** (a good place for bathing and the only permitted place in the park). **Sendero Yacaratiá** starts from the same place, but reaches the river by a different route, and ends at Puerto Macuco, where you could take the *Jungle Explorer* boat to the see the Falls themselves (see below). This trail is really for vehicles and less pleasant to walk along; better to visit on an organized safari.

Puerto Iguazú ➔ *Phone code: 03757.*
Colour map 7, C1. Population: 19,000.

This modern town is 18 km northwest of the falls high above the river on the Argentine side near the confluence of the Ríos Iguazú and Alto Paraná. It serves mainly as a centre for visitors to the falls. The port lies to the north of the town centre at the foot of a hill: from the port you can follow the Río Iguazú downstream towards HitoTres Fronteras, a *mirador* with views over the point where the Ríos Iguazú and Alto Paraná meet and over neighbouring Brazil and Paraguay. There are souvenir shops, toilets and *La Reserva* and *La Barranca* pubs are here; bus US$0.25. **La Aripuca** ⓘ *T423488, www.aripuca.com.ar, US$1.50, turn off Ruta 12 just after Hotel Cataratas, entrance after 250 m, English and German spoken*, is a large wooden structure housing a centre for the appreciation of the native tree species and their environment. **Güira Oga** (Casa de los Pájaros) ⓘ *US$1, daily 0830-1800, turn off Ruta 12 at Hotel Orquídeas Palace, entrance is 800 m further along the road from Aripuca; T423980 (mob 156-70684)*, is a sanctuary for birds that have been injured, where they are treated and reintroduced to the wild; exquisite parrots and magnificent birds of prey. There is also a trail in the forest and a breeding centre for endangered species.

Iguazú Falls listings

For Sleeping and Eating price codes and other relevant information, see Essentials, pages 38-40.

Sleeping

Puerto Iguazú *p193, maps p192 and p195*

LL Yacutinga Lodge, 30 km from town, pick up by jeep, www.yacutinga.com. A beautiful lodge in the middle of the rainforest, with activities, learning about the bird and plant life and Guaraní culture. Accommodation is in rustic adobe houses in tropical gardens, superb food and drinks included, as well as boat trips and walks. Recommended.

LL-L Sheraton Internacional Iguazú Resort, T491800, www.sheraton.com/iguazu. Fine position overlooking the falls, excellent, good restaurant (dinner buffet US$12) and breakfast, sports facilities and bikes for hire (US$2.50 ½ day). Taxi to airport US$12. Recommended.

AL Iguazú Jungle Lodge, Hipólito Iyrigoyen y San Lorenzo, T420600, www.iguazujungle lodge.com. The most luxurious place in the town, *cabañas* and loft apartments, 7 blocks from the centre, by a river, with lovely pool. Comfortable and stylish, a/c, Wi-Fi, DVDs, great service, lofts are US$80 for 2, breakfast included. Houses sleep 7, good value if full. Warmly recommended.

AL Saint George, Córdoba 148, T420633, www.hotelsaintgeorge.com. With good breakfast, comfortable, attentive service, pool and garden, good restaurant with buffet dinner, close to bus station, parking. Recommended.

B Pirayú Resort, Av Tres Fronteras 550, on the way to the Hito, T011-4951 3001, www.pirayu.com.ar. Beautiful complex, comfortable *cabañas*, lovely river views, sports and games, pool, entertainment.

C Lilian, Beltrán 183, T420968, hotellilian@yahoo.com.ar. Bright modern rooms, quiet, 2 blocks from bus terminal, breakfast, helpful owners, a charming option.

C Res San Fernando, Córdoba y Guaraní, near terminal, T421429, hosteriasanfernando@hotmail.com. Breakfast, popular, good value.

C-D Hostería Los Helechos, Amarante 76, T420338, www.argentinahostels.com. Easy-going, popular, well maintained, a/c, with breakfast, pool, good, welcoming.

D Hostería Casa Blanca, Guaraní 121, near bus station, T421320, casablancaiguazu@arnet.com.ar. With breakfast, family run, spotless, large rooms, good showers, beautifully maintained.

D Res Paquita, Córdoba 158, opposite terminal, T420434, residencialpaquita@hotmail.com. Some rooms with balcony, a/c, a bit dated but nice setting. No breakfast but bakery next door.

D-F Hostel-inn Iguazú, Ruta 12, Km 5, T421823, www.hiiguazu.com. Great atmosphere, dorms (**F** pp with a/c or fan) and private rooms (**D**), huge outdoors recreation area and the largest pool in town, restaurant and poolside bar, internet, Wi-Fri, understaffed. Backpacker tours. HI discount.

E Noelia, Fray Luis Beltrán 119, T420729, residencialfamiliarnoelia@yahoo.com.ar. Not far from bus terminal, neat and tidy, family-run, good value, with breakfast. Recommended.

E pp **Timbó**, Misiones 147, T422698, www.timbo iguazu.com.ar. Dorms, also rooms for 2-4 (**B-D** doubles with and without bath), English spoken, welcoming, internet, garde, kitchen, weekly asado, close to bus station. Good.

F pp **Hostel Iguazú Falls**, Guaraní 70, T421295, www.hosteliguazufalls.com. 1 block from terminal, HI affiliated, cheaper for members, also double rooms (**C-D**), more expensive with breakfast and a/c, kitchen, BBQ, luggage store, laundry, internet, lovely garden, good.

F pp **El Güembé**, El Urú 120, T421035, www.elguembe.com.ar. 3 blocks from the bus station this is the nicer and quieter of 2 hostels owned by the same people, welcoming and appealing. The other, **El Güembé House**, is much noisier, but still recommended for its friendly atmosphere, parties and music. Breakfast included in both places. Double rooms **D**.

F pp **Hostel Park Iguazú**, Amarante 111, T424342, www.hostelparkiguazu.com.ar. New, 2 blocks from bus station, neat rooms for 2-4, with bath, breakfast, small pool, helpful.

Camping **El Viejo Americano**, Ruta 12, Km 3.5, T420190, www.viejoamericano.com.ar. 3 pools, wooded gardens, *cabañas* and a hostel, camping US$3 pp, food shop, electricity, barbecue.

Eating

Puerto Iguazú *p193, maps p192 and p195*

TT El Quincho del Tío Querido, Bompland 110, T420151. Recommended for *parrilla* and local fish, very popular, great value.

TT La Esquina, Córdoba 148, next to **St George**. Extensive buffet, beef, fish, salads, friendly service.

TT La Rueda, Córdoba 28. The best in town. Good food and prices, fish, steaks and pastas, often with mellow live music. Highly recommended.

T Panificadora Real, Córdoba y Guaraní. Good bread, open Sun evening; another branch at Victoria y Brasil in the centre.

T Pizza Color, Córdoba y Amarante. Popular for pizza and *parrilla*.

T Pizzería La Costa, Av Río Iguazú, on costanera. Popular, informal, high above the river on the coast road, looks basic, but the pizzas are superb.

2 Puerto Iguazú

Sleeping
1 El Güembé
2 Hostel Iguazú Falls
3 Hostel Park Iguazú
4 Hostería Casa Blanca
5 Hostería Los Helechos
6 Iguazú Jungle Lodge
7 Lilian
8 Noelia
9 Pirayú Resort
10 Res Paquita
11 Res San Fernando
12 Saint George
13 Timbó

Eating
1 El Quincho del Tío Querido
2 La Esquina
3 La Rueda
4 Panificadora Real
5 Pizza Color

Activities and tours

Iguazú Falls *p191, map p192*

Explorador Expediciones, T421632, www.hotelguia.com/turismo/explorador-expediciones, and at the Sheraton Hotel. Run by expert guide Daniel Somay, they offer two small- group tours: *Safari a la Cascada* which takes you by jeep to the Arrechea waterfall, stopping along the way to look at wildlife, with a short walk to the falls, 2 hrs, US$15. And *Safari en la Selva*, more in-depth interpretation of the wildlife all around, in open jeeps, 2 hrs, US$25. Highly recommended. There are also night walking tours to the falls when the moon is full; on clear nights the moon casts a blue halo over the falls. Explorador also run recommended 2-day expeditions in 4WDs to the Salto de Moconá. Recommended guide: Miguel Castelino, Apartado Postal 22, Puerto Iguazú (3370), Misiones, T420157, focustours@aol.com.

Jungle Explorer, T421696, www.iguazujunglexplorer.com. On *Paseo Ecológico* you float silently 3 km down the river from Estación Garganta to appreciate the wildlife on its banks, 30 mins, US$10. *Aventura Náutica* is a journey by launch to give you a soaking under the Falls, great fun, not for the faint-hearted, 12 mins, US$20. *Gran Aventura* combines the Aventura Náutica with a longer boat trip and a jeep trip along the Yacaratiá trail, 1 hr, US$40. Tickets available at all embarkation points or at Sheraton Hotel.

Puerto Iguazú *p193, maps p192 and p195*

Aguas Grandes, Mariano Moreno 58, T425500, www.aguasgrandes.com. Tours to both sides of the falls and further afield, activities in the forest, including half-day for US$20, abseiling down waterfalls, good fun.

Cabalgatas por la Selva, Ruta 12, just after the Rotonda for the road to the international bridge, T155-42180 (mob). For horse riding, 3-hr trips, US$12. Agencies arrange day tours to the Brazilian side (lunch in Foz), Itaipú and Ciudad del Este. Some include the new Duty Free mall on the Argentine side. Also to a gem mine at Wanda, US$10, and the Jesuit ruins at San Ignacio Miní, US$20 (better from Posadas, less driving time).

Transport

Iguazú Falls *p191, map p192*

Bus **Transportes El Práctico** run every 30 mins from Puerto Iguazú bus terminal, stopping at the park entrance for the purchase of entry tickets, continuing to the Visitor Centre, US$1.50. First bus 0630, last 1910, journey time 30 mins; return buses from the park: 0750-2020. You can get on or off the bus at any point en route. **Cars** are not allowed beyond visitor centre.

Puerto Iguazú *p193, maps p192 and p195*

Air Airport is 20 km southeast of Puerto Iguazú near the Falls, T420595. A bus service between airport and bus terminal connects with plane arrivals and departures, US$3, will also drop off/collect you from your hotel. **AR/Austral** and **Lan** fly direct to **Buenos Aires**, 1 hr 40 mins. **Andes** flies to **Salta** Mon-Fri.

Bus The bus terminal, at Av Córdoba y Av Misiones, T423006, has a phone office, restaurant, various tour company desks and bus offices. To **Buenos Aires**, 16-18 hrs, **Tigre Iguazú**, **Via Bariloche**, daily, US$58 *semi cama*, US$66 *cama*. To **Posadas**, stopping at San Ignacio Miní, frequent, 5-6 hrs, US$10, *expreso*; to **San Ignacio Miní**, US$9, *servicio común*. To **Salta**, US$70. **Agencia de Pasajes Noelia**, local 3, T422722, can book tickets beyond Posadas for other destinations in Argentina, ISIC discounts available.

Taxi T420973/421707.

Border with Brazil

Crossing via the Puente Tancredo Neves is straight- forward. When leaving Argentina, Argentine immigration is at the Brazilian end of the bridge. Border open 0700-2300. **Brazilian consulate**, Av Córdoba 264, T421348.

Bus Leave Puerto Iguazú terminal for Foz do Iguaçu every 20 mins, US$1.50. The bus stops at the Argentine border post, but not the Brazilian. Argentine officials stamp you in and out, but Brazilian immigration does not for a day visit (useful if otherwise you may need an expensive visa) but if you are entering Brazil for the first time, or leaving, you must insist on getting off the bus. Buses also stop at the Duty Free mall. The bus does not wait for those who need stamps, just catch the next one, of whatever company. **Taxis** Between the border and Puerto Iguazú US$5.

Border with Paraguay

Crossing to Paraguay is via Puente Tancredo Neves to Brazil and then via the Puente de la Amistad to Ciudad del Este. Brazilian entry and exit stamps are not required unless you are stopping in Brazil. US$3 charge to enter Paraguay. The **Paraguayan consulate** is at Hipólito Irigoyen y Guaraní, T424230, 0800-1500. **Bus** Direct buses (non-stop in Brazil), leave Puerto Iguazú terminal every 30 mins, US$2.75, 45 mins, liable to delays especially in crossing the bridge to Ciudad del Este. Only one bus on Sun, no schedule, better to go to Foz and change buses there.

Directory

Puerto Iguazú *p193, maps p192 and p195*

Airline offices Aerolíneas Argentinas, Brasil y Aguirre, T420168. **Andes**, Av Victoria Aguirre 283, T425566. **Lan** T0810-999 9526. **Banks** ATMs at **Macro**, Misiones y Bonpland, and **Banco de la Nación**, Av Aguirre 179. *Sheraton* has an ATM. TCs can only be changed at **Libres Cambio** in the Hito Tres Fronteras, 0800-2200. Good exchange rates at the Brazilian border. **Internet** Generally expensive, US$1-1.20 per hr. Several places in town.

Lake District

The Lake District contains a series of great lakes strung along the foot of the Andes from above 40°S to below 50°S in the Parque Nacional Los Glaciares area. This section covers the northern lakes; for convenience the southernmost lakes, including those in the Los Glaciares park area, are described under Patagonia (see page 224). The area is dramatic, beautiful and unspoilt, offering superb trekking, fishing, watersports, climbing and skiing. See the Chilean chapter, The Lake District (page 787), for map and details of the system of lakes on the far side of the Andes. These can be visited through various passes. Off season, from mid-April to June and mid-August to mid-November, many excursions, boat trips ,etc, run on a limited schedule, if at all. Public transport is also limited.

Neuquén and around

➔ *Phone code: 0299. Colour map 8, C2. Population: Greater Neuquén: 290,000.*

Founded in 1904 on the west side of the confluence of the Ríos Limay and Neuquén, Neuquén is a pleasant provincial capital and a major stop en route from the east coast to the northern lakes and Bariloche. It serves both the oilfields to the west and the surrounding fruit orchards. There are also many wine *bodegas* nearby. At the Parque Centenario (be sure *not* to take the bus to Centenario industrial suburb), is a *mirador* with good views of the city and the confluence of the rivers, where they become the Negro. Visit **Museo de la Ciudad Paraje Confluencia** ⓘ *Independencia y Córdoba,* interesting display on the Campaign of the Desert (19th-century annihilation of indigenous groups). **Tourist office** ⓘ *Félix San Martín 182, T442 4089, www.neuquentur.gov.ar. Mon-Fri 0700-2200, Sat-Sun 0800-2200* (don't confuse the streets Félix San Martín and General San Martín). **Municipal office** ⓘ *Av Argentina y Roca, T449 1200.* Also at the airport ⓘ *T444 0072, Mon-Fri 0700-2200, Sat 0730-2100, Sun 1500-2200.*

Villa El Chocón

The area around Villa El Chocón is rich in dinosaur fossils. Red sedimentary rocks have preserved, in relatively good condition, bones and footprints of the animals which lived in this region during the Cretaceous period about 100 million years ago. The **Museo Paleontológico Ernesto Bachmann** ⓘ *civic centre, T0299-4901230, daily 0800-2100, 0900-1900 in low season, US$1,* displays the fossils of a giant carnivore (*Giganotosaurus carolinii*), guides in museum give good tours. The tourist office (T490 1292, www.chocon.gov.ar) organizes guided tours to the 20-km long, 80-m high Cañón Escondido (or Coria) to see dinosaur footprints, three hours, US$5.

Zapala → *Phone code: 02942. Colour map 8, C2. Population: 35,000.*

Zapala, 185 km west of Neuquén, has an excellent geology museum, **Museo Mineralógico Dr Juan Olsacher** ⓘ *Etcheluz 52 (by bus terminal), 0900-1500, Sat-Sun 1600-2000, free*. Among the collections of minerals, fossils, shells and rocks is a complete crocodile jaw, believed to be 80 million years old, and the largest ever turtle shell found from the Jurassic. **Tourist office** ⓘ *Ruta Nacional 22, Km 1392, T02942-424296.*

Some 150 km northwest of Zapala is the **Parque Provincial Copahue-Caviahue**, protecting araucaria trees and the slopes of a gigantic volcanic crater. Caviahue is good for walking and riding and, in winter, skiing, while Copahue has thermal springs. Due west of Zapala is the beautiful **Pehuenia** region, where pehuén trees abound on the shores of lakes Aluminé and Moquehue. These two areas are just opening up to tourism; ask in the tourist office in Neuquén for transport and lodging details, and see Footprint's *Argentina Handbook*.

Neuquén and around listings

For Sleeping and Eating price codes and other relevant information, see Essentials, pages 38-40.

Sleeping

Neuquén *p197*

L Del Comahue, Av Argentina 377, T443 2040, www.hoteldelcomahue.com. 4-star, extremely comfortable, spa, pool, good service, excellent restaurant, **1900 Cuatro**.

AL Hostal del Caminante, Ruta 22, Km 1227, 13 km southwest of Neuquén, towards Zapala, T444 0118, www.hostaldelcaminante.com. A comfortable suburban place set among fruit plantations with garden, swimming pool and restaurant.

A Royal, Av Argentina 143, T448 8902, www.royalhotel.com.ar. Modern, with parking, breakfast.

B Alcorta, Alcorta 84, T442 2652. Breakfast, TV in rooms, also flats for 4, good value.

D Res Inglés, Félix San Martín 534, T442 2252. Convenient, no breakfast, good value.

Villa El Chocón *p197*

A La Posada del Dinosaurio, lakeshore, Villa El Chocón, Costa del Lago, Barrio 1, T0299-490 1200, www.posadadinosaurio.com.ar. With breakfast, comfortable, modern, all rooms have lake view.

Zapala *p198*

B Hue Melén, Brown 929, T422414. Good value, decent rooms and restaurant with best food in town.

D Coliqueo, Etcheluz 159, opposite bus terminal, T421308. Convenient and good.

D Pehuén, Elena de la Vega y Etcheluz, 1 block from bus terminal, T423135. Comfortable, recommended. There's also a municipal campsite.

Eating

Neuquén *p197*

Anónima, Av Olascoaga y Félix San Martín. Supermarket with *patio de comidas* (food hall).

El Reencuentro, Alaska 6451. Delicious *parrilla*, popular, warm atmosphere.

La Birra, Santa Fe 23. Lots of choice, welcoming, chic, modern.

Tutto al Dente, Alberdi 49. Serving delicious homemade pasta and some good value set meals.

Transport

Neuquén *p197*

Air Airport 7 km west of centre, T444 0244, www.anqn.com.ar. Bus **Centenario**, US$0.50 (with bus card), taxi US$5. **AR/Austral** flies to **Buenos Aires** and **Comodoro Rivadavia**; LADE flies to **Bariloche, Chapelco** and **Zapala**. Schedules change frequently.

Bus Terminal at Planas y Solalique, on Ruta 22, 4 km west of town. Buses US$0.45-0.75; taxi US$3. About a dozen companies to **Buenos Aires** daily, 12-16 hrs, US$33-53. To **Zapala** daily, 3 hrs, US$6.50. To **Junín de los Andes**, 5 hrs, US$12, many companies. To **San Martín de los Andes**, 6 hrs, US$15-22. To **Bariloche**, 7 companies, 5-6 hrs, US$13.50-24, sit on left. To **Mendoza**, **TAC**, daily, 12-13 hrs, US$30-35. To **Chile**: to **Temuco**, Igi-Llaima and El Valle, 12-14 hrs, US$45.

Zapala *p198*
Bus 3 companies to **San Martín de los Andes**, 3-4 hrs, US$13, via Junín de los Andes. To **Bariloche**, change at San Martín. To **Temuco** (Chile) all year, various companies, 10 hrs, daily between them, US$35. Buy Chilean pesos before leaving.

Directory

Neuquén *p197*
Airline offices AR/Austral, Santa Fe 52, T442 2409/0810-2228 6527. **LADE**, Brown 163, T443 1153. **LAN**, H Yrigoyen 347, T0810-999 9526. **Banks** Lots of ATMs on Av Argentina. *Casas de Cambio*: **Pullman**, Alcorta 144, **Exterior**, San Martín 23. **Internet and telephones** At lots of *locutorios* everywhere in centre. **Post offices** Rivadavia y Santa Fe.

Parque Nacional Lanín

ⓘ *US$7.75 to enter park (discount with student/teacher card). Helpful advice on walks from* guardaparques *at the entrance and at Puerto Canoa. Lanín National Park office, Perito Moreno y Elordi, San Martín de los Andes, T427233, Mon-Fri 0800-1300, helpful but maps poor. Bus transport into the park is tricky, with services usually running to Lago Huechulafquen from San Martín de los Andes with Ko Ko Bus, but the timetable varies from year to year.*

This beautiful, large park has sparkling lakes, wooded mountain valleys and one of Argentina's most striking peaks, the snow capped Lanín Volcano. The lakes of **Huechulafquen** and **Paimún** are unspoilt, beautiful, and easily accessible for superb walking and fishing, with three *hosterías* and blissful free camping all along the lakeside. From Puerto Canoa there is a boat excursion to **Lago Epulafquen** on the catamaran **José Julián** ⓘ *T429264, www.cata maranjosejulian.com.ar, summer only (Dec-Mar), several daily, US$8, some refreshments available on board*. Geologically, Lanín Volcano is one of the youngest of the Andes; it is extinct and one of the world's most beautiful mountains. It's a challenging and popular climb, starting near *Seccional de Guardaparques* (VHF 155675 or T491270) at Tromen pass where you must register and all climbing equipment and experience are checked. Crampons and ice-axe are essential, as is protection against strong, cold winds. There are three *refugios*, the first of which is a 5-hour walk. It's a 6-7 hour walk to the base of the volcano and back. Before setting off, seek advice from Lanín National Park office.

Border with Chile: the Tromen Pass

Formalities are carried out at the Argentine side of the Tromen Pass (Chileans call it Mamuil Malal). This route runs through glorious scenery to Pucón (135 km) on Lago Villarrica (Chile). It is less developed than the Huahum and Samoré (Puyehue) routes further south, and definitely not usable during heavy rain or snow (June to mid-November, phone to check: gendarmería, T491270, or customs, T492163). Parts are narrow and steep. (Details of the Chilean side are given under Puesco, The Lake District.) There is a campsite at Puesto Tromen (though very windy), but take food as there is only one basic shop at the pass. The international bus may not pick up passengers at Tromen or on the Chilean part of the route.

Junín de los Andes → *Phone code: 02972. Colour map 8, B4. Population: 9,000.*

Known as the trout capital of Argentina, Junín de los Andes is a relaxed, pretty town on the broad Río Chimehuín, a less touristy option than San Martín, with many trout-filled rivers and lakes nearby, and the best base for trekking in Parque Nacional Lanín. Its small **Museo Salesiano** ⓘ *Ginés Ponte y Nogueira, Mon-Fri 0900-1230, 1430-1930, Sat 0900-1230*, has a collection of items from the Mapuche culture and there are impressive sculptures at **Vía Christi** on the hill opposite ⓘ *US$0.75*. **Tourist office** ⓘ *Plaza at Col Suárez y Padre Milanesio, T02972-491160, www.junindelosandes.gov.ar. Open summer 0800-2200, Mar-Nov 0800-2100.*

San Martín de los Andes ➔ *Phone code: 02972 .Colour map 8, C1. Population: 22,000.*
This picturesque and upmarket tourist town, 40 km southwest of Junín, with its chocolate-box, chalet-style architecture, is spectacularly set at the east end of Lago Lacar. Mirador Bandurrias, 45-minute walk from the centre offers good views. There is excellent skiing on Cerro Chapelco (with varied summer activities for kids), and facilities for water skiing, windsurfing and sailing on Lago Lácar. The **tourist office** ⓘ *Av San Martín y Rosas, T427695, www.sanmartindelosandes.gov.ar or www.smandes.gov.ar, 0800-2100 all year,* has maps, accommodation lists, prices on wall board, very busy in summer, advisable to go early. Surrounded by lakes and mountains to explore, the most popular excursions are south along the **Seven Lakes Drive** (see below), north to the thermal baths at **Termas de Lahuen-Co** (also reached on foot after two days from Lagos Huechulafquen and Paimún) and to **Lagos Lolog** and **Lácar**. There's a *ripio* track along the north side of Lago Lácar with beaches and rafting at **Hua Hum**, and along the south to quieter and beautiful **Quila Quina**. Two good walks from Quila Quina: along a nature trail to a lovely waterfall, or a two-hour walk to a quiet Mapuche community in the hills above the lake. Boats from San Martín's pier, T428427, to Hua Hum three daily in season, US$36 return; to Quila Quina, hourly, 30 minutes, US$11 return. Cyclists can complete a circuit around Lago Lácar, or take the cable car up to Chapelco and come back down the paths.

Border with Chile: the Hua Hum Pass
A *ripio* road along the north shore of Lago Lácar through the Lanín National Park crosses the border to Puerto Pirihueico, where a boat crosses Lago Pirihueico; bikes can be taken (for vehicle reservations and information, www.panguipulli.cl). Border open 0800-2100 in summer, 0800-2000 winter. *Ko Ko* bus goes to the pass (usually open all year round), two hours, and *Lafit* goes up to Panguipulli (Chile), weekly off-season, US$20, check terminal for schedule. For connections from Puerto Pirihueico to Panguipulli and beyond, see Chile chapter.

Parque Nacional Lanín listings

For Sleeping and Eating price codes and other relevant information, see Essentials, pages 38-40.

Sleeping

Lago Huechulafquen *p199*
AL Huechulafquen, Ruta 61, Km 55, T02972-427598. Best, half board, comfortable cabin-like rooms, gardens, expert fishing guide, restaurant open to non-residents in high season.
Camping Several sites in beautiful surroundings on Lagos Huechulafquen and Paimún in Parque Nacional Lanín. The most recommended are: **Bahía Canicul** (48 km from Junín), **Camping Lafquen-co** (53 km from Junín) and **Piedra Mala** (65 km from Junín).

Junín de los Andes *p199*
LL Río Dorado Lodge & Fly shop, Pedro Illera 448, T491548, www.riodorado.com.ar. Comfortable rooms in log cabin-style fishing lodge, big American breakfast, pricey, great for anglers, good fly shop, lovely gardens, attentive service.
A Caleufu Travel Lodge, JA Roca 1323 (on Ruta 234), T492757, www.caleufutravellodge.com.ar. Excellent value, welcoming, very good rooms, neat garden, also comfortable apartments for up to 5 people. Owner Jorge speaks English. Recommended.
B Hostería Chimehuín, Col Suárez y 25 de Mayo, T491132, www.interpatagonia.com/hosteriachimehuin. Cosy, quaint old fishing lodge by the river, closed May. Recommended.
B Milla Piuké, Av Los Pehuenes y JA Roca (on Ruta 234), T492378, millapiuke@fronteradigital.net.ar. Most delightful and welcoming, comfortable, stylish rooms and apartments for families. Good breakfast included. Recommended.
C Posada Pehuén, Col Suárez 560, T491569, posadapehuen@fronteradigital.net.ar. A peaceful bed and breakfast with comfortable rooms, pretty garden, charming owners, good value.
C Res Marisa, JM de Rosas 360 (on Ruta 234), T491175, residencialmarisa@deandes.com.ar. A simple place with helpful owners, with bath, TV, breakfast US$1 extra, very good value.

E pp **La Casa de Marita y Aldo**, 25 de Mayo 371, T491042, casademaritayaldo@hotmail.com. A cheery and popular family house with basic accommodation.

Camping There are many sites in the area with two good ones in town, both by the river: **Mallín Laura Vicuña**, T491149, and **La Isla**, T492029, both good.

San Martín de los Andes *p200*

Single rooms are scarce. There are 2 high seasons, when rates are much higher: Jan/Feb and Jul/Aug. There are many excellent *cabañas* for families on the hill at the top of Perito Moreno. **Inmobiliaria Stordiau**, San Martín 1344, T421220, www.rohde turismo.com.ar. Recommended estate agent for renting houses, cabins and apartments per day. When everywhere else is full, Tourist Office provides a list of private addresses in high season.

LL Le Châtelet, Villegas 650, T428294/6, www.hotellechatelet.com.ar. Chic and luxurious, beautiful chalet-style hotel with excellent service to pamper you. Wood-panelled living room, gorgeous bedrooms, video library, spa and pool with massage and facial treatments. Also some suites.

L La Casa de Eugenia, Coronel Díaz, T427206, www.lacasadeeugenia.com.ar. B&B in a beautifuly renovated 1900s house, very welcoming and relaxing, cosy rooms, huge breakfast, charming hosts. Highly recommended.

AL Arco Iris, Los Cipreses 1850, T428450, www.arcoirisar.com. Comfortable, well-equipped cabañas in a quiet area of town, each has a cosy living room with TV and spacious kitchen. Own access to the river, so you can fish before breakfast or enjoy a drink on the water side in the evening. Highly recommended.

AL Hostería Walkirias, Villegas 815, T428307, www.laswalkirias.com. A lovely place, smart, tasteful rooms with big bathrooms. Breakfast and free airport transfer included. Sauna and pool room. Great value off season and for longer stays, open all year.

AL Plaza Mayor, Cnel Pérez 1199, T427302, www.hosteriaplazamayor.com.ar. A chic and homely hostería in a quiet residential area, with traditional touches in the simple elegant rooms, pool, BBQ, parking. Excellent home-made breakfast included.

A Hostería Las Lucarnas, Cnel Pérez 632, T427085, www.patagoniasuperior.com.ar/hosterialaslucarnas. Great value, centrally-located, pretty place with simple comfortable rooms, English-speaking owner. Discounts for more than five nights, open all year.

A Ojo de Agua, Pérez 1198, T427921, www.interpatagonia.com/ojodeagua. Well-equipped cabañas for 2-7, crammed next to each other in quiet part of town near the lake. Good budget option.

B Crismalú, Rudecindo Roca 975, T427283, www.interpatagonia.com/crismalu. Simple rooms in attractive chalet-style place, good value with breakfast included.

E pp **Hosteria Bärenhaus**, Los Alamos 156, Barrio Chapelco (8370), T422775. 5 km outside town, free pick-up from bus terminal and airport. Welcoming young owners, very comfortable rooms with heating, English and German spoken. Recommended.

E pp **Puma**, A Fosbery 535 (north along Rivadavia, 2 blocks beyond bridge), T422443, www.pumahostel.com.ar. Discount for HI and ISIC members, small dorms with bath and **D** double room with view, laundry, kitchen facilities, bikes for hire, very well run by mountain guide owner, good value. Recommended.

E pp **Rukalhue**, Juez del Valle 682 (3 blocks from terminal), T427431, www.rukalhue.com.ar. Large camp-style accommodation with one section full of dorm rooms and one section with doubles and triples, nice but beware fleas. Also has apartments with private bath and kitchenette.

E pp **Secuoya Hostel**, Rivadavia 411, T424485. Charming hostel, 6 blocks from the bus terminal past the river. Small rooms, welcoming common area. Closed in Jun.

Camping ACA **Camping**, Av Koessler 2195, T429430, with hot water and laundry facilities, also *cabañas*. **Camping Quila Quina**, T426919. Lovely site on a stream near Lago Lácar, 18 km from San Martín, with beaches, immaculate toilet blocks, restaurant and shop, access to boats and treks. Open only in summer and Easter.

Eating

Junín de los Andes *p199*

Ruca Hueney, Col Suárez y Milanesio, T491113. Good steak, trout and pasta dishes.

🍴 **La Posta de Junín**, JM de Rosas 160 (on Ruta 234), T492303. A recommended parrilla with good service and wine list; also trout, pizza and pastas.

San Martín de los Andes *p200*

🍴🍴🍴 **El 54**, Rivadavia y San Martín, T422564. A traditional Argentine parilla, great atmosphere. Warmly recommended.

🍴🍴🍴-🍴🍴 **El Regional**, Villegas 965, T425326. Popular for regional specialities – smoked trout, venison, wild boar, pâtés and hams, El Bolsón's homemade beer, cheerful German-style decor.

🍴🍴🍴-🍴🍴 **La Tasca**, Mariano Moreno 866, T428663. Recommended for its venison, trout and home made pastas with a varied wine list.

🍴🍴 **La Costa del Pueblo**, Costanera opposite pier, T429289. Overlooking the lake, huge range of pastas, chicken and trout dishes, generous portions, good service, cheerful. Recommended.

Cafés

Beigier, Av Costanera 814, T427037. Hidden cottage with views of the bay serving a fantastic home-made afternoon tea with home-made goodies. Only a few tables, friendly staff. Highly recommended.

Deli, Villegas y Av Costanera, T428631. Affordable place with views of the bay and nice salads, pastas and pizzas. Wi-Fi and friendly service.

O Shopping

San Martín de los Andes *p200*

Abuela Goye, San Martín 807, sells delicious chocolates and runs a good café serving gorgeous cakes and delicious ice creams.

Mamusia, San Martín 601, is also a recommended chocolate shop, also sells home-made jams.

▲ Activities and tours

San Martín de los Andes *p200*

Cycling

Many places in the centre rent mountain and normal bikes, reasonable prices, maps provided.

HG Rodados, San Martín 1061, T427345, hgrodados@smandes.com.ar. Arranges trips, rents mountain bikes, US$8 per day, also spare parts and expertise.

Fishing

Licence, US$16, plus US$3.50 extra per day for trolling and US$1.70 for fishing in Río Correntoso Boca del Chimehuin. Contact the tourist office for a list of fishing guides or the National Park office.

Jorge Cardillo Pesca, Villegas 1061, T428372. Fly shop, sells equipment, fishing licences and offers excursions.

Flotadas Chimehuin, at Junín de los Andes, T491313. Offers fully inclusive fishing packages with expert bilingual guides.

Orvis, Gral Villegas 835, T425892, www.sanmartinorvis.com.ar. Fly shop, sells equipment and offer fishing excursions.

Juan Carlos Aráuz, M Moreno 1193, T427376. Fishing guide.

Skiing

Chapelco has 29 km of pistes, many of them challenging, with an overall drop of 730 m. Very good slopes and snow conditions from Jul to Sep make this a popular resort with foreigners and wealthier Argentines. To get to the slopes, take the bus from San Martín, US$5 return. Details, passes, equipment hire from office at San Martín y Elordi, T427845. At the foot of the mountain are a restaurant and a café, with 4 more restaurants and a lodge on the mountain and a café at the top.

Tours

Prices for conventional tours are similar in most agencies. Most tours operate from 2 Jan: eg Villa la Angostura via Seven Lakes; Lakes Huechulafquen and Paimún. One day's rafting at Hua Hum, US$26-40; many other options.

El Claro, Col Díaz 751, T429363, www.elclaroturismo.com.ar. For conventional tours, horse riding, mountain biking and trekking.

El Refugio, Pérez 830, just off San Martín, upstairs, T425140, www.elrefugioturismo.com.ar. Bilingual guides, conventional tours, boat trips, also mountain bike hire, rafting, horse riding and trekking. Recommended.

Lanín Expediciones, San Martín 851, oficina 5, T429799, www.laninexpediciones.com. Adventure tourism for beginners or experts, from a 3-hr walk near San Martín, winter night walks in the forest, rafting in Aluminé, trekking in Lanín area, a 3-day ascent of the volcano, and climbs to 4,700-m Domuyo peak.

Transport

Junín de los Andes *p199*

Air Chapelco airport 19 km southwest towards San Martín, served by **AR** from Buenos Aires and **LADE** (office in bus terminal, San Martín de los Andes, T427672) from Buenos Aires, Esquel, Neuquén and Bariloche.

Bus Terminal at Olavarria y F San Martín, T492038. To **San Martín, Centenario, Castelli** and others, 30 mins, US$2.65. To **Buenos Aires**, 19-21 hrs, US$40, US$60 *cama*. To **Temuco** (5 hrs) and **Valdivia** (via Paso Tromen), 6-7 hrs, US$30, **Igi Llaima** and **Empresa San Martín**. **Castelli** goes daily in Jan-Feb (Sun, Mon, Wed, Fri in Dec) to **Lago Paimún** (Parque Nacional Lanín), 2 hrs, US$5, also **Cooperativa Litrán** daily in summer.

San Martín de los Andes *p200*

Air Chapelco airport, 23 km away. See under Junín de los Andes above.

Bus Terminal at Villegas 251 y Juez del Valle, T427044. Café, left luggage (US$0.70), toilet facilities, *kiosko, locutorio*. To **Buenos Aires**, 20 hrs, US$45, US$66 (*cama*), daily, 6 companies. To **Villa La Angostura**, **Albus** 3 a day, US$8. To **Bariloche**, 3½-4 hrs, US$13 (not via 7 Lagos), several companies. **To Chile**: **Temuco** with **Empresa San Martín**, T427294 (Mon, Wed, Fri) and **Igi Llaima**, T427750 (Tue, Thu, Sat), US$25, heavily booked in summer.

Directory

San Martín de los Andes *p200*

Banks Many ATMs on San Martín. Exchange at **Banco de la Nación**, San Martín 687, **Banco Francés**, San Martín y Sarmiento and **Andina**, Capitán Drury 876, which also changes TCs (charges 3% commission) **Banco de la Provincia de Neuquén**, Obeid y Belgrano. **Medical Services** **Hospital Ramón Carrillo**, San Martín y Coronel Rodhe, T427211. **Police station** Belgrano 635, T427300, or T101. **Post Office** Gral Roca y Pérez, Mon-Fri 0800-1300, Sat 0900-1300.

Parque Nacional Nahuel Huapi

ⓘ *US$7.75 payable at Nahuel Huapi National Park office, at San Martín 24, Bariloche, T02944-423111, daily 0900-1400, www.parquesnacionales.gov.ar.*

Covering 709,000 ha and stretching along the Chilean border, this is the oldest National Park in Argentina. With lakes, rivers, glaciers, waterfalls, torrents, rapids, valleys, forest, bare mountains and snow-clad peaks, there are many kinds of wild animals living in the region, including the pudú, the endangered huemul (both deer) as well as river otters, cougars and guanacos. Bird life, particularly swans, geese and ducks, is abundant. The outstanding feature is the splendour of the lakes. The largest is **Lago Nahuel Huapi** (*Altitude: 767 m*), 531 sq km and 460 m deep in places, particularly magnificent to explore by boat since the lake is very irregular in shape and long arms of water, or *brazos*, stretch far into the land. On a peninsula in the lake is exquisite **Parque Nacional Los Arrayanes** (see below). There are many islands: the largest is **Isla Victoria**, with its idyllic hotel. Trout and salmon have been introduced.

North of Villa La Angostura, Lagos Correntoso and Espejo both offer stunning scenery, and tranquil places to stay and walk. Navy blue Lago Traful, a short distance to the northeast, can be reached by a road which follows the Río Limay through the Valle Encantado, with its fantastic rock formations or directly from Villa La Angostura. **Villa Traful** is the perfect place to escape to, with fishing, camping, and walking. There's a tourist office at the eastern edge of town, T02944-479019, www.villatraful.info. Spectacular mountains surround the city of Bariloche, great trekking and skiing country. The most popular walks are described in the Bariloche section. South of Lago Nahuel Huapi, Lagos Mascardi, Guillelmo and Gutiérrez offer horse riding, trekking and rafting along the Río Manso. See page 218 for accommodation along their shores.

The well-maintained *ripio* road known as the '**Seven Lakes Drive**' runs south from San Martín to Bariloche via Lago Hermoso and Villa La Angostura and passes beautiful unspoilt stretches of water, framed by steep, forested mountains. There are several places to stay, open summer only. An alternative route, fully paved and faster, but less scenic is via Junín de los Andes and **Confluencia** on Ruta 40 (ACA service station and a hotel, also motel *El Rancho* just before Confluencia). Round-trip excursions along the Seven Lakes route, 5 hours, are operated by several companies, but it's better in your own transport.

Villa La Angostura → *Colour map 8, C1. Phone code: 02944. Population: 7,000.*
This pretty town, 80 km northwest of Bariloche on Lago Nahuel Huapi, is a popular holiday resort with wealthier Argentines and there are countless restaurants, hotels and *cabaña* complexes around the centre, **El Cruce** and along Ruta 231 between Correntoso and Puerto Manzano. The picturesque port, known as **La Villa**, is 3 km away at the neck of the Quetrihué Peninsula. At its end is **Parque Nacional Los Arrayanes** ⓘ *entry US$7.75*, with 300 year old specimens of the rare *arrayán* tree, whose flaky bark is cinnamon coloured. The park can be reached on foot or by bike (12 km each way; for a return walk start from 0900 to 1400), or you could take the boat back. Catamarans run at least twice daily in summer from Bahía Mansa and Bahía Brava, down at La Villa, US$8 one way (plus the National Park entry fee); tickets sold at Hotel Angostura. See also below for tours by boat from Bariloche. There is a small ski resort at **Cerro Bayo** (www.cerro bayoweb.com) with summer activities too. The **tourist office** is opposite the bus terminal ⓘ *Av Siete Lagos 93, T02944-494124, www.villalaangostura.gov.ar. Open high season 0800-2100, low season 0800-2000*. Good maps with accommodation marked.

Parque Nacional Nahuel Huapi listings

For Sleeping and Eating price codes and other relevant information, see Essentials, pages 38-40.

Sleeping

Parque Nacional Nahuel Huapi *p203*
B pp **Hostería Los Siete Lagos** (27 km north of Villa La Angostura), T02944-15497152, a charming, simple place run by very knowledgeable people about the region, on the shore of Lago Correntoso, great views and the best *tortas fritas* in the region, with the breakfast, excellent restaurant, home-made bread for sale.
Camping Several free campsites without facilities along the route, including the lovely **Lago Espejo Camping**, open all year, US$1 pp, no showers but toilets, drinking water and fireplaces. Recommended.

Villa Traful
B Cabañas Aiken, T02944-479048, www.aiken.com.ar.Well-decorated *cabañas* in beautiful surroundings near the lake (close to the tourist office), each with its own *parrillada*, also has a restaurant. Recommended.
C Hostería Villa Traful, T479005, www.hosteria villatraful.com. A cosy house with a tea room by the lake, also *cabañas* for 4-6 people, pretty gardens, good value. The owner's son, Andrés organizes fishing and boat trips.

E pp **Vulcanche Hostel**, T02944-494015, www.vulcanche.com. Chalet-style hostel in gardens with good views, with good dorms (**F** without linen) and **C** doubles, breakfast extra, large park for camping (US$6 pp). Discounts to HI members.

Villa La Angostura *p204*
Many pricey hotels and *cabañas* here; www.villalaangostura.com.ar and www.laangostura.com are two among several sites with listings.
LL La Escondida, Av Arrayanes 7014, T475313, www. hosterialaescondida.com.ar. Wonderful setting, right on the lake, 14 rooms, heated pool, offers mid-week, weekend and log-stay specials. Recommended.
L La Posada, R 231, Km 65, a few km west of town towards Chile, T494450, www.hosteriala posada.com. In a splendid elevated position off the road with clear views over the lake, welcoming, beautifully maintained hotel in lovely gardens, with pool, fine restaurant; a perfect place to relax.
AL-B Portal de Piedra, Ruta 231, Km 56 y Río Bonito (at Puerto Manzano), T494278, www.portal depiedra.com. Small, attractive *hostería* and tea room in the woods, with heated pool and a small restaurant (guests only) open in high season.

A Hostería ACA al Sur, Av Arrayanes 8 (behind the petrol station), T494168, www.acavillalaangostura.com.ar. Modern, attractive single-storey hotel with well-designed rooms in the centre of town. Recommended.

A Hostería Le Lac, Av de los 7 Lagos 2350, T488029, www.hosterialelac.com.ar. **C** in low season. 3-star, 8 rooms, some with jacuzzi and DVD, with buffet breakfast, gardens, lake view, can arrange lots of activities, several languages spoken by owner.

A Hotel Angostura, Nahuel Huapi 1911, at La Villa, T494224, www.hotelangostura.com. Built in 1938, this traditional hotel run by Familia Cilley since then has a lovely lakeside setting and a good restaurant and tea room, *Viejo Coihue*, Wi-Fi. Also has 3 cabins for 6 (**L**). Boat excursions along the nearby shore are arranged.

E pp **Bajo Cero**, Av 7 Lagos al 1200, T495454, www.bajocerohostel.com. HI affiliated, well-situated, rooms for 2-4 with bath, linen, breakfast included.

E pp **Hostel La Angostura**, Barbagelata 157, 150 m up road behind tourist office, T494834, www.hostellaangostura.com.ar. A warm, luxurious hostel, all small dorms have bathrooms, breakfast included, good **C** doubles, young welcoming owners organize trips and rent bikes for US$6 a day too. HI discounts. Recommended.

E pp **Italian Hostel**, Los Maquis 215 (5 blocks from terminal), T494376, www.italian hostel.com.ar. Welcoming, small, with dorms and **D** doubles, rustic, functional and nice, run by a biker who closes the place in Apr-Oct. Fireplace and orchard from where you can pick berries and herbs for your meals. Recommended.

Camping Osa Mayor, signposted off main road, close to town, T494304, www.campingosamayor. com.ar. Well designed leafy and level site, US$7.75-9, all facilities, also rustic *cabañas* (from **D** pp) and dorms (from **E** pp), helpful owner.

Eating

Parque Nacional Nahuel Huapi *p203*

Villa Traful

Aiken, Villa Traful. Simple meals, excellent sandwiches with home-made bread and more expensive trout dishes. Open all year round.

Ñancu Lahuen, Villa Traful. A chocolate shop, tea room, and restaurant serving local trout. Delightful and cosy, with big open fire, delicious food and reasonably priced.

Villa La Angostura *p204*

TTT Cocina Waldhaus, R 231, Puerto Manzano, T475323. Very recommended, this is 'auteur cuisine' with gorgeous local delicacies created by Chef Leo Morsea, served in a charming chalet-style building.

TTT Las Balsas, on the lake at the luxury hotel and spa of the same name, T494308, www.lasbalsas.com. The chef, Pablo Campoy, creates impressive food here, among the best in the country. The wines are superb too, and the whole atmosphere is a real treat. Dress smartly and phone in advance. Highly recommended.

TT Gran Nevada, Av Arrayanes 106, T494512. Good for cheap *parrilla* and *ñoquis* in a cheery atmosphere.

TT Los Pioneros, Av Arrayanes 267, T495525. Famous for fine local dishes in a chalet-style building and great Argentine steaks. Great pizza place next door run by the same owners. They also serve locally brewed beers.

TT Tasca Placido, Av Siete Lagos 1726, T495763. Spanish-owned, good for paella and lots of seafood.

TT T El Esquiador, Las Retamas 146 (behind the bus terminal), T494331. If on a budget, this good, popular *parrilla* has an all-you-can-eat choice of cold starters, a main meal and a dessert.

T Hora Cero, Av Arrayanes 45. Hugely popular, heaving in summer, this serves a big range of excellent pizzas and *pizza libre* (as much as you can eat for US$3.50) on Wed and Sat, a great deal.

T TemaTyCo, Ruta 231 y Mirlo, T475211. Chic tearoom with an amazing range of teas and delicious cakes.

Activities and tours

Villa La Angostura *p204*

There is lots to do here: bicycle hire and mountain biking (**Free Bikes**, Las Fucsias y Los Notros, T495047, info@free bikes.com.ar), boat trips, canopying (**Canopy Villa la Angostura**, Curruhué y Melinquina, T154-17817, www.canopyargentina.com.ar), climbing, fishing, horse riding and trekking (**Alma Sur**, T1556 4724, www.almasur.com).

Transport

Villa La Angostura *p204*

Bus Terminal at Av 7 Lagos y Av Arrayanes, opposite ACA service station. Urban buses **15 de Mayo**, US$0.50, link El Cruce (main bus stop on main road, 50 m from tourist office), La Villa, Correntoso and Puerto Manzano, and go up to Lago Espejo (US$1) and Cerro Bayo (US$1.25) in high season. To/from **Bariloche**, 1 hr, US$6, several companies. To **San Martín de los Andes**, 2½ hrs, US$8. **Via Bariloche/El Valle** goes to **Osorno**, 3½ hrs, and **Puerto Montt** (Chile), 5½ hrs, US$30; **Andesmar** and **Tas Choapa** go to **Valdivia**, US$28.

Bariloche and around → *Phone code: 02944. Colour map 8, C1. Population: 89,000.*

Beautifully situated on the south shore of Lago Nahuel Huapi, at the foot of Cerro Otto, San Carlos de Bariloche is an attractive tourist town and the best centre for exploring the National Park. There are many good hotels, restaurants and chocolate shops among its chalet-style stone and wooden buildings. Others along the lake shore have splendid views.

Ins and outs

Getting there and around The airport is 15 km east of town, the bus and train stations 3 km east. At peak holiday times (July and December-January), Bariloche is heaving with holidaymakers and students. The best times to visit are in the spring (September-November) and autumn (March-April), when the forests are in their glory, or February for camping and walking and August for skiing. ▸▸ *See also Transport, page 214.*

Tourist information **Oficina Municipal de Turismo** ⓘ *San Martín 662 (Centro Cívico), p 6, T422484, www.barilochepatagonia.info. Daily 0900-2100*. List of city buses, details of hikes and campsites and helpful in finding accommodation. **Provincial office** ⓘ *Frey y 12 de Octubre, T423188, www.rionegro tur.com.ar*. Very useful for information on hiking is *Club Andino Bariloche* (*CAB*), 20 de Febrero 30, T422266, www.clubandino.org. 0900-1300, plus 1600-2100 high season. Good *Infotrekking* maps (1:50,000, US$4.50), *Guía de Sendas y Picadas* maps (1:100,000, US$3.50 and 1:50,000, US$1.70) and a guidebook of paths, US$5, for sale. When Club Andino is closed, obtain more general information at the Nahuel Huapi National Park office (see address under Parque Nacional Nahuel Huapi, above). The *Traveller's Guru* is a free paper available throughout Patagonia, written in English by travellers with some valuable information for backpackers.

Sights

At the heart of the city is the **Centro Cívico**, built in 'Bariloche Alpine style' and separated from the lake by Avenida Rosas. It includes the **Museo de La Patagonia** which, apart from the region's fauna (stuffed), has indigenous artefacts and material from the lives of the first white settlers. ⓘ *Tue-Fri 1000-1230, 1400-1900, Mon and Sat 1000-1300, US$1*. Next to it is **Biblioteca Sarmiento** ⓘ *Mon-Fri, 0900-1900 (closed 1-15 Jan)*, a library and cultural centre. The **cathedral**, built in 1946, lies six blocks east of here, with the main commercial area on Mitre in between. Opposite the main entrance to the cathedral there is a huge rock left in this spot by a glacier during the last glacial period. On the lakeshore is the **Museo Paleontológico** ⓘ *12 de Octubre y Sarmiento, Mon-Sat 1600-1900, US$0.70*, which displays fossils mainly from Patagonia, including an ichthyosaur and replicas of a giant spider and shark's jaws.

Around Bariloche

One of South America's most important ski centres is just a few kilometres southwest from Bariloche, at **Cerro Catedral** (see Activities and tours, page 213). You can take a boat trip from Puerto Pañuelo (Km 25.5, bus 10, 20 or 21, or transfer arranged with tour operator, US$5.50) across Lago Nahuel Huapi to **Isla Victoria** and **Bosque de Arrayanes**, on the Quetrihué Peninsula; full or a half-day excursion (fewer options in low season), US$25 plus National Park entry (with **Turisur**, see address below, on the 1937 boat *Modesta Victoria*) or US$18 plus Park entry (with **Espacio**, on modern *Cau Cau*, T431372, www.islavictoriayarrayanes.com), take picnic lunch if you don't want to buy food sold on board. The all-day boat trip to **Puerto Blest**, in native Valdivian rainforest, is highly recommended. From Puerto Pañuelo, sail down to Puerto Blest (hotel, restaurant), continuing by short bus ride to Puerto Alegre and again by launch to Puerto Frías. From Puerto Blest, walk through forest to the Cascada and Laguna de los Cántaros (1½ hrs). Transfer to Puerto Pañuelo can be arranged from the agency; **Catedral Turismo** (see address below), US$18 plus Park entry and US$5 extra if going to Puerto Frías.

An old train (1912) leaves three times a week in summer from Bariloche railway station for an eight-hour excursion with two stops at Ñirihuau and Los Juncos (for birdwatching) and a walk up to **Cerro Elefante**, US$16-23 (lunch optional), T423858, www.trenhistorico avapor.com.ar. Some tour operators offer an excursion to El Maitén, from where La Trochita (the Old Patagonian Express) runs a tourist service a few days a week (see under El Bolsón and Esquel).

Avenida Bustillo runs parallel to the lakeshore west of Bariloche, with access to the mountains above. At Km 5, a cable car (teleférico) goes up to **Cerro Otto** (1,405 m) with its revolving restaurant and splendid views. Transport and other details under Activities and tours (page 213). At Km 17.7 a chairlift goes up to **Cerro Campanario** (1,049 m) ⓘ *daily 0900-1800, 7 mins, US$5*, with fine views of Isla Victoria and Puerto Pañuelo. At Km 18.3 **Circuito Chico** begins – a 60-km circular route around Lago Moreno Oeste, past Punto Panorámico and through Puerto Pañuelo to **Llao Llao**, Argentina's most famous hotel (details on this and others on Avenida Bustillo in Sleeping, below.) Take bus No 20, 45 mins, US$1, a half-day drive or tour with agency, or full day's cycle. You could also extend this circuit, returning via **Colonia Suiza** and **Cerro Catedral** (2,388 m) one of South America's most important ski centres. Whole-day trip to **Lagos Gutiérrez** and **Mascardi** and beautiful **Pampa Linda** at the base of mighty **Cerro Tronador** (3,478 m), visiting the

1 Bariloche

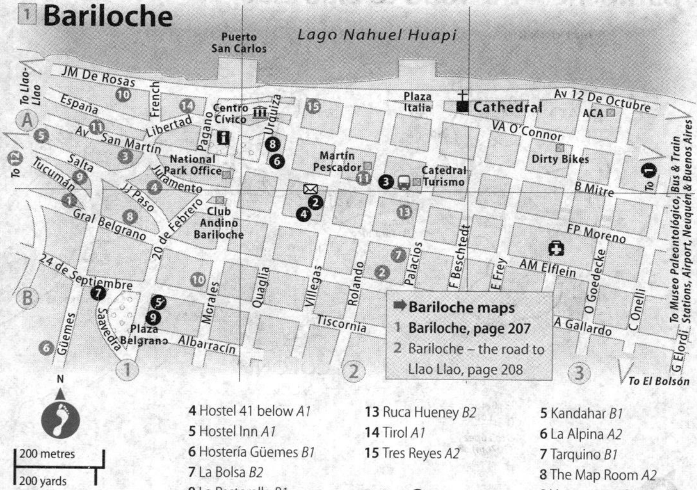

Sleeping
1 Albergue El Gaucho *B1*
2 Antiguo Solar *B2*
3 Edelweiss *A1*
4 Hostel 41 below *A1*
5 Hostel Inn *A1*
6 Hostería Güemes *B1*
7 La Bolsa *B2*
8 La Pastorella *B1*
9 Marcopolo Inn *A1*
10 Periko's *B1*
11 Premier *A2*
12 Pudu *A1*
13 Ruca Hueney *B2*
14 Tirol *A1*
15 Tres Reyes *A2*

Eating
1 Covita *A3*
2 El Boliche de Alberto *B2*
3 Huang Ji *A2*
4 Jauja *B2*
5 Kandahar *B1*
6 La Alpina *A2*
7 Tarquino *B1*
8 The Map Room *A2*
9 Vegetariano *B1*

Bars & clubs
10 Cerebro *A1*
11 Wilkenny *A1*

strange **Ventisquero Negro** (black glacier), highly recommended. Several companies run 12-hour minibus excursions to San Martín de los Andes along the famous **Seven Lakes Drive**, returning via Paso Córdoba and the Valle Encantado, but these involve few stops.

Border with Chile

The Samoré (formerly Puyehue) Pass A spectacular six-hour drive through the pass 125 km northwest of Bariloche. A good broad paved road, RN 40 then RN 231, goes around the east end of Lago Nahuel Huapi, then follows the north side of the lake through Villa La Angostura. The road is rough *ripio* from there on, with the occasional paved stretch. It passes the junction with 'Ruta de Los Siete Lagos' for San Martín at Km 90, Argentine customs (T494996) at El Rincón, Km 105, and the pass at Km 122 at an elevation of about 1,314 m. Chilean customs (T00566-4236284) is at Pajarito, Km 145, in the middle of a forest. The border is open from the second Saturday of October to 1 May, 0800-2100, winter 0900-2000 but liable to be closed after snowfalls. Chilean currency can be bought at Samoré pass customs at a reasonable rate.

Four bus companies (**El Valle, Bus Norte, Andesmar, Tas Choapa**) run daily services from Bariloche via Samoré pass to Osorno (4-6 hours, US$30) and Puerto Montt (6-7½ hours, same fare); **Andesmar** goes to Valdivia via Osorno (see Bariloche Transport below and take passport when booking). Sit on left side for best views. You can buy a ticket to the Chilean border, then another to Puerto Montt, or pay in stages in Chile, but there is little advantage in doing this.

Via Lake Todos Los Santos The route is Bariloche to Puerto Pañuelo by road (1/2 hour, departure 0700), Puerto Pañuelo to Puerto Blest by boat (1 hour), Puerto Blest to Puerto Alegre on Lago Frías by bus (15 minutes), cross the lake to Puerto Frías by boat (20 minutes), then two hours by road to

2 Bariloche – the road to Llao Llao

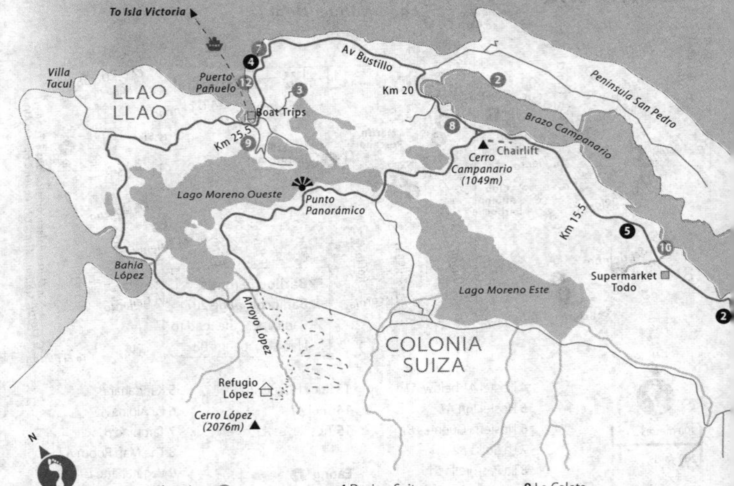

Sleeping
1 Alaska
2 Aldebaran
3 Departamentos Bellevue
4 Design Suites
5 El Yeti
6 Hostería Santa Rita
7 Katy
8 La Caleta
9 Llao-Llao
10 Petunia
11 Selva Negra

Peulla. Leave for Petrohué in the afternoon by boat (1 hour 40 minutes), cross Lago Todos Los Santos, passing the Osorno volcano, then by bus to Puerto Montt (2 hours). This route is beautiful, but the weather is often wet. The journey can be done in one day, US$170, two days with an overnight stop in Peulla (US$240 minimum, breakfast only, details of accommodation under Peulla, Chile), or longer, with other stops en route. **Cruce Andino** ⓘ *in Bariloche T425444, www.cruceandino.com*, has the monopoly on this crossing. Book in advance during the high season. The only cheaper option, recommended to cyclists, is to pay US$60 for the boat trips. The only days the trip does not run are 25 November, 25 December, 1 January and 1 May.

The Argentine and Chilean border posts are open every day. There is an absolute ban in Chile on importing any fresh food from Argentina. Further information on border crossings in the Lake District will be found in the Chile chapter. You are strongly advised to get rid of all your Argentine pesos before leaving Argentina; it is useful to have some Chilean pesos before you cross into Chile from Bariloche, though you can buy them at a reasonable rate at the Chilean border post.

Bariloche and around listings

For Sleeping and Eating price codes and other relevant information, see Essentials, pages 38-40.

Sleeping

Bariloche *p206, maps p207 and p208*

Prices rise in 2 peak seasons: Jul-Aug for skiing, and mid-Dec to Mar for summer holidays. If you arrive in the high season without a reservation, consult the listing published by the tourist office (address above). This selection gives lake-view, high-season prices where applicable. In low season you pay half of these prices in most cases. All those listed are recommended.

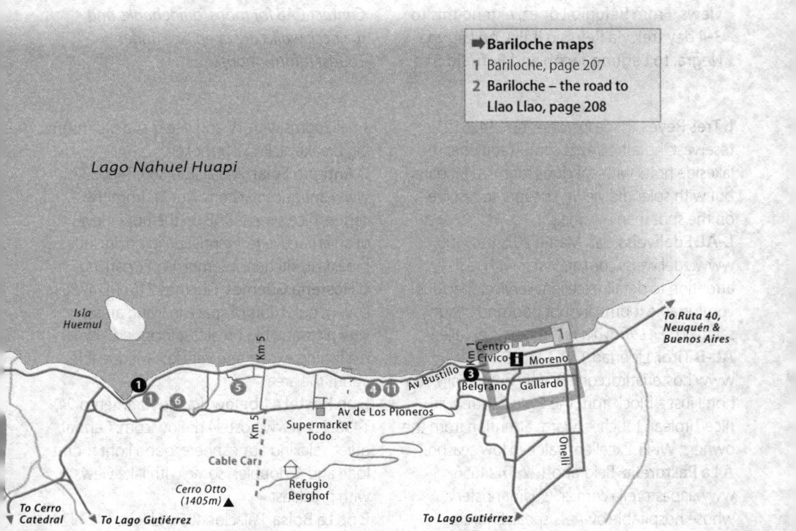

12 Tunquelén

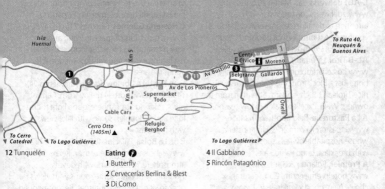

Eating
1 Butterfly
2 Cervecerías Berlina & Blest
3 Di Como
4 Il Gabbiano
5 Rincón Patagónico

Walks around Bariloche

There's a network of paths in the mountains, and several refugios allowing for treks over several days. Refugios are leased by Club Andino Bariloche. On treks to refugios remember to add costs of ski lifts, buses, food at refugios and lodging (in Club Andino refugios: US$3-7 per night, plus US$1-1.70 for cooking, or US$2-4 for breakfast, US$4-7 for dinner). Take a good sleeping bag. Horseflies (*tábanos*) infest the lake shores and lower areas in summer. Among the many great treks possible here, these are recommended: From **Llao Llao** ⓘ *getting there: bus 20 to Llao Llao*, delightful easy circuit in Valdivian (temperate) rainforest (two hours), also climb the small hill for wonderful views. Up to **Refugio López** (2,076 m) ⓘ *getting there: bus 10 to Colonia Suiza and López, US$0.75 (check return times)*, five hours return, from southeastern tip of Lago Moreno up Arroyo López, for fabulous views. From Refugio López, extend this to 3-4 day trek via Refugio Italia, on Laguna Negra, to **Laguna Jacob** and **Refugio San Martín** (poorly signposted, need experience). From Cerro Catedral to **Refugio Frey** (1,700 m, **F** pp, meals extra, camping), beautiful setting on small lake, via Arroyo Piedritas (four hours each way), or via cable car to *Refugio Lynch* and via Punta Nevada (only experienced walkers). To beautiful **Lago Gutiérrez**, 2 km downhill from Cerro Catedral, along lake shore to the road from El Bolsón and walk back to Bariloche (four hours), or Bus 50. From **Pampa Linda**, idyllic (*hosterías*, campsite), walk up to Refugio Otto Meiling (4-5 hours each way), to tranquil Laguna Ilon (5½ hours each way), or across Paso de las Nubes to **Puerto Frías**, boat back to Bariloche (two days, check if open: closed when boggy). Bus to Pampa Linda from outside Club Andino Bariloche 0830 in summer, **Expreso Meiling**, T529875, US$10 one way or from **Transitando lo Natural** ⓘ *20 de Febrero 25, T527926, 2¼ hours. Contact CAB for maps, guidebooks and to check walks are open (see under Tourist information).*

L Tres Reyes, 12 de Octubre 135, T426121, reservas@hoteltresreyes.com. Traditional lakeside hotel with spacious rooms, a bit dated, but with splendid views, cheaper to reserve on the spot than by email.

L-AL Edelweiss, San Martín 202, T445500, www.edel weiss.com.ar. 5-star with real attention to detail, excellent service, spacious comfortable rooms, indoor pool and beauty salon, Wi-Fi. *La Tavola* restaurant is excellent.

AL-B Tirol, Libertad 175, T426152, www.hosteriatirol.com.ar. Very neat family-run hotel just a block from the Civic Centre, with nice Tirolean touches, warm attention from the owners, Wi-Fi. Excellent value in low season.

A La Pastorella, Belgrano 127, T424656, www.lapastorella.com.ar. Quaint hostería, whose hospitable owners speak English, with breakfast, good value, safe.

A Premier, Rolando 263, T426168, www.hotelpremier.com. Good central choice (very good value in low season), small rooms with TV and larger superior rooms, big breakfast, English spoken.

B Antiguo Solar, A Gallardo 360, T400337, www.antiguosolar.com. Not far from the centre, nice simple B&B on the upper level of an attractive residential building, includes breakfast, kitchen, internet, Wi-Fi, parking.

C Hostería Güemes, Güemes 715, T424785. Lovely, quiet, lots of space in living areas, very pleasant, big breakfast included, owner is a fishing expert and very knowledgeable about the area.

E pp **Hostel 41 below**, Pasaje Juramento 94, T436433, www.hostel41below.com. Central, quiet, relaxing atmosphere, good light rooms for 4 and **C** doubles, some with lake views, with breakfast.

E pp **La Bolsa**, Palacios 405 y Elflein, T423529, www.labolsadeldeporte.com.ar. Relaxed atmosphere, rustic rooms with duvets, 1 double with bath, some rooms with views, deck to sit out on, free internet. Recommended.

E pp **Marcopolo Inn**, Salta 422, T400105, www.marcopoloinnbariloche.com. Central location, breakfast included, HI discount, **B** in doubles, bath, Wi-Fi, bar, restaurant, basic kitchen. In the same group is the **Hostel Inn**, Salta 308, T426084, www.hostelbariloche.com. Lake views, good public areas and kitchen, helpful staff, English spoken.

E pp **Periko's**, Morales 555, T522326, www.perikos.com. Welcoming, quiet, nice atmosphere, dorms and **B** doubles with bath (**C** without, all cheaper in low season), breakfast extra, kitchen, washing machine, *asado* every Fri, excellent service. Arranges tours, including to Ruta 40. Reserve in advance by email.

E pp **Ruca Hueney**, Elflein 396, T433986, www.rucahueney.com. Lovely, calm, comfortable beds with duvets, fabulous double room (**D**) with extra bunk beds, bathroom and great view, spotless kitchen, with breakfast, internet, Wi-Fi, very kind owners, Spanish school. Recommended.

F pp **Albergue El Gaucho**, Belgrano 209, T522464, www.hostelelgaucho.com. Welcoming, modern place in quiet part of town, some doubles with own bath (**E** pp), breakfast extra, English, Italian and German spoken.

F pp **Pudu**, Salta 459, T429738, www.hostel pudu.com. "A gem". Irish/Argentine run, dorms and doubles (**C**) with spectacular lake views, downstairs is a small garden, a bar and a huge kitchen. Long term rates available. Recommended.

Around Bariloche *p206, map p208*

LL Aldebaran, on Península San Pedro, reached from Av Bustillo Km 20.4, T448678, www.aldebaran patagonia.com. Not in chalet style, but tasteful rooms in this modern boutique hotel on the lake shore, superb views. Rustic-style restaurant, sauna and spa with outdoor pool, so you can bask under the stars. Great service from helpful bilingual staff.

LL Llao-Llao, Av Bustillo Km 25, T448530, www.llaollao.com. Deservedly famous, superb location, complete luxury, golf course, pool, spa, water sports, restaurant.

LL Pire-Hue, Cerro Catedral, T011-4807 8200 (in Buenos Aires), www.pire-hue.com.ar. Exclusive 5-star hotel in ski resort with beautiful rooms and all facilities.

L Design Suites Av Bustillo, 2½ km from Bariloche centre, T457000, www.designsuites. com. Modern, bold design in glass and wood in the stylish bar and restaurant area, huge spacious rooms with modern bathrooms, some with window side Jacuzzis, price includes breakfast, pool, gym, transfer in and out. Recommended.

L Tunquelén, Av Bustillo, Km 24.5, T448233, www.tunquelen.com. 4-star, comfortable, splendid views, feels more secluded than its neighbour *Llao-Llao*, superb restaurant, attentive service.

AL Hostería Santa Rita, Av Bustillo, Km 7.2, T461028, www.santarita.com.ar. Bus 10, 20, 21, to Km 7.5. Close to the centre, peaceful lakeside views, comfortable, lovely terrace, great service.

A Departamentos Bellevue, Av Bustillo, Km 24.6, T448389, www.bellevue.com.ar. A famous tea room with beautiful views also offers accommodation with high-quality furnishings, very comfortable, well-equipped self-catering cabañas, delicious breakfast included. Access to beaches on Lake Moreno, lovely gardens. Open year-round.

A Katy, Av Bustillo, Km 24.3, T448023, www.gringospatagonia.com. Delightful, peaceful, garden full of flowers, charming Slovenian family Kastelic, breakfast included (also half-board, **AL**). Also offers adventure tourism.

A-B La Caleta, Av Bustillo, Km 1.9, T443444, bungalows@bariloche.com.ar. *Cabañas* sleep 4, British-owned, open fire, excellent value.

F pp **Alaska**, Lilinquen 328 (buses 10, 20, 21, get off at La Florida, Av Bustillo Km 7.5), T461564, www.alaska-hostel.com. Well run, cosy with shared rustic rooms for 4, all with bath, also double without bath (**C**), nice garden, kitchen facilities, washing machine, free internet, organizes horse riding and rafting, rents mountain bikes. Recommended.

Camping List of sites from tourist office. These are recommended among the many along Bustillo. **Petunia**, Km 13.5, T461969, www.camping petunia.com. A lovely shady site going down to lakeside with all facilities. Shops and restaurants on most sites; these are closed outside Jan-Mar. **Selva Negra**, Km 2.95, T441013, camping selvanegra@infovia.com.ar. Very good, discounts for long stay. **El Yeti**, Km 5.7, T442073, gerezjc@bariloche.com.ar. All facilities, *cabañas*.

Eating

Bariloche *p206, map p207*

Bariloche is blessed with superb food, much of it locally produced, including smoked trout and salmon, wild boar and other delicacies, not least fine chocolate and, in season, delicious berries. There are many good delicatessens.

TTT Chez Philippe, Primera Junta 1080, T427291. Delicious local delicacies and fondue, fine French-influenced cuisine.

TTT Kandahar, 20 de Febrero 698, T424702. Atmospheric, warm and intimate, with exquisite food, run by ski champion Marta Peirono de Barber, superb wines and pisco sour. Dinner only, reserve in high season. Highly recommended.

TT El Boliche de Alberto, Villegas 347, T431433. Very good pasta, huge portions, popular after 2000 (queues in summer), *peña*.

TT Covita, VA O'Connor, 511, T434774. Vegetarian restaurant (also serves fish), offering curries, masalas and pastas. Open Mon-Sat for lunch, Thu-Sat for dinner.

TT Jauja, Elflein 148, T422952. Recommended for delicious local dishes, quiet and welcoming, good value.

TT Tarquino, 24 de Septiembre y Saavedra, T434774. Warm, welcoming, with trees growing through the boldly-coloured room, steaks, pasta, good wine list. Open daily for lunch and dinner.

TT Vegetariano, 20 de Febrero 730, T421820. Also fish, excellent food, beautifully served, warm atmosphere, also take-away. Highly recommended.

T Huang Ji, Rolando 268, T428168. Good Chinese, next to a bowling alley.

La Alpina, Moreno 98. Old-fashioned café serving delicious cakes, good for tea, Wi-Fi, charming.

The Map Room, Urquiza 248, T456856. Fantastic café/pub which serves large portions of interesting salads, burgers, and Bariloche's best brunch. Recommended.

Around Bariloche *p206, map p208*

TTT Il Gabbiano, Av Bustillo Km 24.3, T448346. Delicious Italian lunches and dinners. Booking essential (no credit cards), closed Tue.

TT Butterfly, Hua Huan 7831, just off Av Bustillo Km 7.9, T461441, www.butterflypatagonia.com.ar. Open from 2000. German/Argentine/Irish owned, an elite dining experience, tasting menus using only local ingredients, carefully selected wines, art exhibitions, only 6 tables. Reserve in advance and discuss the menu with the chef.

TT Di Como, Av Bustillo, Km 0.8, T522118. A 10-min walk from town. Good pizza and pasta, terrace and great views of the lake. Recommended.

TT Rincón Patagónico, Av Bustillo, Km 14.200, paraje Laguna Fantasma, T463063, www.rinconpatagonico.com.ar. Traditional *parrilla* with Patagonian lamb cooked *al palo*, huge menu but service can be minimal at busy times.

Refugio Lynch has restaurant and *confitería* up the slopes of Cerro Catedral. In **Cerro Otto** there's a revolving *confitería*, craft shop, great views. Also **Club Andino confitería**, at Refugio Berghof, 20 mins' walk from main *confitería* on summit.

Bars and clubs

Cerebro, JM de Rosas 406, www.cerebro.com.ar. The party starts at 0130, Fri best. Open Jun-Dec.

Cerveza Artesanal Gilbert, Ruta 77, Km 24, in El Establo camping area, close to Lago Moreno, Circuito Chico, T448347. Open daily 1100-2300, check ahead in off-season. Rustic, welcoming, popular beers, basic meals (TT).

Cervecería Berlina, Av Bustillo Km 11.750, T523336, www.cervezaberlina.com. Open 1200-0100 (until last person has left). Less touristy than its neighbour **Blest**, deck for watching the sunset and supping good brews. They have a diverse menu (TT). Happy hour daily 1700-1900.

Cerveceria Blest, Av Bustillo Km 11.6, T461026, www.cervezablest.com.ar. Wonderful brewery with delicious beers, serving imaginative local and German dishes and steak and kidney pie (TTT-TT). Recommended.

Wilkenny, San Martín 435, T424444. Lively Irish pub with expensive food but it really gets busy around 2400. Great place to watch televized sports.

Shopping

Bariloche *p206, map p207*

The main shopping area is on Mitre between the Centro Civíco and Beschtedt, also on San Martín.

Chocolate The local stuff is excellent: several shops on Mitre. Local wines, from the Alto Río Negro, are also good. **Abuela Goye**, Mitre 258 and Quaglia 221. First rate chocolatier, also with café in the Quaglia branch. **Fenoglio**, Mitre 301 y Rolando. Very good chocolate and superb chocolate ice cream. **Mamushka**, opposite *El Turista*. Considered the best chocolate here, also with café. **El Turista**, Mitre 231/39. Aptly named, you can watch chocolates being made here.

Outdoor gear **Arbol**, Mitre 263. Sells good-quality outdoor gear, lovely clothes and gifts. **Feria Artesanal Municipal**, Moreno y Villegas.

Supermarkets **Todo**, Mitre 281, good selection, cheap. **Uno**, Moreno 350. **La Anónima**, Quaglia 331 and a huge **Norte** at Moreno y Onelli.

▲ Activities and tours

Bariloche *p206, map p207*

Climbing

Note that at higher levels, winter snow storms can begin as early as Apr, making climbing dangerous.

Club Andino Bariloche, see Tourist information and Walks, above. The club can contact mountain guides and provide information.

Cycling

Bikes can be hired at many places in high season. **Dirty Bikes**, V O'Connor 681, T425616, www.dirtybikes.com.ar. Very helpful for repairs, but pricey.

Fishing

Martín Pescador, Rolando 257, also in Cerro Catedral in winter, at Shopping Mall Las Terrazas, T422275. Fishing, camping and skiing equipment.

Horse riding

At the **Estancia Fortín Chacabuco**, T441766, www.estanciaspatagonicas.com (also offers lodging, **A**), catering for all levels, bilingual guides. **Tom Wesley**, in country ranch by the lake at Km 15.5, office at Mitre 385, T448193, www.tom wesley.com. Tuition and full day's riding offered.

Kayaking

Patagonia Infinita, T488032, www.patagoniainfinita.com.ar. Kayaking and trekking trips in Parque Nacional Nahuel Huapi.

Pura Vida Patagonia, T448793, www.puravidapatagonia.com. Informative, attentive guides, good value, trips from 1-9 days in Nahuel Huapi and Los Alerces national parks.

Paragliding

Parapente Bariloche, T462234, parapente@bariloche.com.ar. At Cerro Otto, US$45 (transfer included).

Skiing

Cerro Catedral, T423776, www.catedralaltapatagonia.com, mid-Jun to end-Sep, busiest from mid-Jun to mid-Aug for school holidays, ski lifts: 0900-1700, ski lift pass: adults US$20 per day, ski school, US$30 per hr pp. It has 100 km of slopes of all grades, allowing a total drop of 1,010 m, and 52 km of cross country skiing routes. There are also snowboarding areas and a well-equipped base with hotels, restaurants and equipment hire, ski schools and nursery care for children. Bus are run by **3 de Mayo**, 'Catedral', leaves Moreno 480 every 90 mins (via Av Pioneros or via Av Bustillo), T425648, US$1. Cable car for Catedral T423776.

Cerro Otto, cable car passengers can take free bus leaving from huts opposite National Park office, city buses US$0.40, or at Mitre y Villegas, hourly 1030-1730 in summer, returning hourly 1115-1915. Ticket for cable car US$10 pp, T441031. Ski gear can be rented by the day from **Cebron**, Mitre 171, or **Milenium**, Mitre 125. See also **Martín Pescador**, above.

Trekking

See Walks, page 210. **Andescross**, T467502, 156 33581, www.andescross.com. Expert guides, all included. Trekking to Chile across the Andes, via Pampa Linda, Lago Frías, Peulla.

Tours

Check what your tour includes; cable cars and chair lifts usually extra. Tours get booked up in season. Most travel agencies will pick you up from your hotel, and charge roughly the same prices: Circuito Chico US$7-9, half-day; Isla Victoria and Bosque de Arrayanes US$25, full-day boat trip; Tronador, Ventisquero Negro and Pampa Linda , US$15 (US$26 plus National Park entry via Lago Mascardi by boat); Puerto Blest boat trip full-day including Cascada de los Cantaros and Lago Frías, US$22; El Bolsón US$22, full-day, including Lago Puelo.

Aguas Blancas, Morales 564, T432799, www.aguasblancas.com.ar. Rafting on the Río Manso, all grades, with expert guides, and all

equipment provided (US$37-50), also 'duckies' - inflatable kayaks for beginners, bikes and horse riding, traditional lunches included.
Catedral Turismo, Palacios 263, T425444, cattur@bariloche.com.ar. Representatives for the famous Three Lakes Crossing to Chile, boat trips to Puerto Blest and conventional tours.
Del Lago Turismo, Villegas 222, T430056, www.dellagoturismo.com.ar. Very helpful, staff speak fluent English, all conventional tours, plus horse riding, rafting. Also recommended, a combined trip by boat along Lago Mascardi to Tronador.
Diversidad, 20 de Junio 728, T428995, www.eco-family.com. Riding, walking, skiing, other adventures, based at Refugio Neumeyer (see Sleeping, above), bilingual guides. Highly recommended.
Extremo Sur, Morales 765, T427301, www.extremosur.com. Rafting and kayaking, all levels, full day all inclusive packages and longer trips to Chile.
Huala, San Martín 66, T522438, www.huala.com.ar. Offers rafting, riding, climbing, biking and more, English-speaking guides. Recommended.
Infinito Sur, T156 39624, www.infinito-sur.com. For climbing, trekking, mountain skiing, rafting, expeditions on the *estepa* in Argentine and Chilean Patagonia, highly experienced from Peru, Bolivia and all points south.
Tronador Turismo, Quaglia 283, T425644, www.tronadorturismo.com.ar. Conventional tours, trekking and rafting. Also to Refugio Neumeyer, and to Chilean border. Great adventurous wintersports options.
Turisur, Mitre 219, T426109, www.bariloche.com/turisur. Boat trips to Bosque de Arrayanes, Isla Victoria on a 1937 ship and to Tronador via Lago Mascardi. Always reserve 1 day ahead.

Guides

Martín Angaut, T156 19829, fishing_bariloche@hotmail.com. Professional fly-fishing guide, English spoken; contact at **Martín Pescador** (see above).
Daniel Feinstein, T442259, T155 05387, defeinstein@bariloche.com.ar. For trekking, biking, kayaking, natural history expeditions. Speaks English. Experienced in Argentina and Chile.
Angel Fernández, T524609, 156 09799, angel_e_fernandez@hotmail.com. For trekking, biking, kayaking, natural history expeditions. Extremely knowledgeable and charming, speaks English. Recommended.

Transport

Bariloche *p206, map p207*
Air Airport is15 km east of town, with access from Ruta 40, 7 km east of centre, T426162; bus service from town centre meets AR flights, US$2.60; also colectivos and taxis (US$6). If staying on the road to Llao Llao, west of town, expect to pay more for transport to your hotel; a taxi charges US$11 from town to Llao Llao. Car rental agencies, internet, exchange, ATM, café at the airport. Many flights a day to **Buenos Aires**, with **AR/Austral**. *AR* also flies to **Esquel, Trelew, El Calafate** (summer only) and **Ushuaia**. LADE to **Buenos Aires, Esquel** and several other destinations in Patagonia. **LAN** Chile flies to **Puerto Montt** and **Santiago**.
Bus Station 3 km east of centre; urban buses 70 and 71, to/from centre, Moreno y Rolando; also bus 10, 20, 21, 72, US$1. Taxi US$4. Bus info at terminal T432860. Toilets, small *confitería*, *kiosko*, *locutorio* with internet, tourist information desk. Left luggage US$2 per day. Bus company offices in town (purchase tickets there or at terminal): **Vía Bariloche/El Valle/Don Otto**, Mitre 321, T429012; **Chevallier/ Flechabus**, Moreno 105, T423090; **TAC**, Moreno 321, T429012; **3 de Mayo**, for local services and Viedma, Moreno 480, T425648. At terminal: **Andesmar**, T430211; **Ko Ko**, T431135. Prices rise in summer. **Buenos Aires**, 5 companies daily, 19-22 hrs, US$46, US$62 *cama* (recommended with **Via Bariloche**). To **Bahía Blanca**, **El Valle** and **El Crucero del Norte**, 14 hrs, US$26-45. To **Mendoza**, US$54-68, *Andesmar*, 19 hrs, via Piedra del Aguila, Neuquén, Cipolletti and San Rafael. To **Esquel**, via **El Bolsón**, fares and schedules given below. To **Puerto Madryn**, 13-14 hrs, US$48, with **Don Otto**. To **Viedma** (along Ruta 23), **3 de Mayo**, 14 hrs, US$28.
To **San Martín de los Andes, Ko Ko, Albus, Via Bariloche/ Turismo Algarrobal**, US$13, 3½-4 hrs. To **Villa Traful** (via Confluencia), **Via Bariloche/ Turismo Algarrobal** and **Albus**, 1½-2 hrs, US$5. To Chilean destinations, see under Border with Chile, above. To **Río Gallegos**, via Comodoro Rivadavia, eg with **Don Otto**, US$64, 14-15 hrs,

and change there. In Río Gallegos make onward connections to El Calafate and Ushuaia. **Taqsa** and **El Pingüino** a service to Río Gallegos and on to **El Calafate**, 28 hrs, US$107. To **El Calafate**, **Taqsa** daily, 36 hrs via Los Antiguos, US$120. Or take **Chaltén Travel**'s 3-day trip on Ruta 40, www.chaltentravel.com (page 252), depart 0645 on odd-numbered days from Moreno 100; or contact **Overland Patagonia** (see address under Activities and tours) for a trip along Ruta 40.

Car hire Rates are around US$40-65 per day. **Localiza**, Frey y VA O'Connor, T435374, localiza@autosurpatagonia.com.ar, reliable. **Open**, Mitre 171 local 15, T/F426325, www.opencar.com.ar, is cheaper. Likewise **Lagos**, Mitre 83, T428880, www.lagosrentacar.com.ar, and **One Way**, O'Connor 345, T436042, www.onewayrentacar.com.ar, good. To enter Chile, a permit is necessary; it's generally included in the price. State when booking car, allow 24 hrs. For international car rental agencies, see Essentials, page 36.

Train Tren Patagónico, www.trenpatagonico-sa.com.ar, to **Viedma**, Sun 1800, US$59 bed, US$30 Pullman, US$19 1st class, US$14.60 *económico*. 17-hr journey mostly at night, dusty, nice views in the first few hours. To **Jacobacci**, 4½ hrs, US$12-53. Booking office at station, 3 km east of centre (T423172), same as bus station. In Buenos Aires, Reconquista 556, T4328 1394, comercial@sefepa.com.ar.

Directory

Bariloche *p206, map p207*

Airline offices AR/Austral, Mitre 185y Villegas, T423682 (in airport, T422144). **LADE**, J O'Connor 214, T423562. **LAN**, Mitre 534, loc 1, T0810-999-9526. **Banks** Banks and exchange shops buy and sell virtually all European and South American currencies, and US dollars. Best rates from **Sudamérica**, Mitre 63, T434555; all TCs (3% commission). ATMs on Mitre at 158, 427, Moreno y Quaglia, San Martin 336. **Consulates** Chile, JM de Rosas 180, T527468, helpful. **Internet** Several cybercafés and at *locutorios* in the centre, all with similar rates. **Language schools** ILEE, www.argentinailee.com, arranges classes and home stay. **La Montaña**, Elflein 251, T524212, www.lamontana.com. Spanish courses, family lodging, activities and volunteering. **Medical facilities** **Emergencies**: Dial 107. **Clinic**: Hospital Zonal, Moreno 601, T426100. **Post offices** Moreno 175, closed Sat afternoon and Sun. **Telephones** Many *locutorios* in the centre, along Mitre and 1st block of Quaglia. **Useful addresses** **Customs**: 24 de Septiembre 12, T425216. **Immigration office**: Libertad 191, T423043. **Policía Federal** (for tourist orientation), Tiscornia y Morales, open 24 hrs, T423789/423430, English spoken.

South of Bariloche

More wild and beautiful scenery can be explored along the Andes, with a few tourist centres like El Bolsón and Esquel giving access to lakes and national parks. There is trekking, rafting, skiing and fishing on offer, a train ride on the famous La Trochita and the magnificent Los Alerces national park to explore. **Note** At the time of writing this area was badly affected by the ash fall-out from Volcán Chaitén in Chile.

Bariloche to El Bolsón

Ruta 258, the paved road from Bariloche to El Bolsón, 126 km south, passes the beautiful lakes Gutiérrez, Mascardi and Guillelmo. From the southern end of Lago Mascardi, 35 km south of Bariloche, a *ripio* road (note one-way system) runs west towards Cerro Tronador and **Pampa Linda**, the starting point for excellent trekking including the two-day walk over Paso de los Nubes to Laguna Frías (see Walks, page 210 and Sleeping, page 218). **Río Villegas**, about 70 km south of Bariloche, is very beautiful, and there's world class rafting to be done on the **Río Manso**.

El Bolsón and around ➔ *Population: 40,000. Phone code: 02944. Colour map 8, C1.*
El Bolsón is an attractive town in a broad fertile valley, surrounded by the mountains of the cordillera and dominated by the dramatic peak of Cerro Piltriquitrón 2,284 m (hence its name: the big bag). It's a magical setting which attracted thousands of hippies to create an ideological community here in the 1970's; they now produce the handicrafts, beers, fruit and jams, sold at the market on Tuesday, Thursday, Saturday, 1000-1700. There are many mountain walks and waterfalls nearby, and good fishing at Lagos Puelo (see below) and Epuyén (shops and petrol available) – both within easy access. **Tourist office** ⓘ *Av San Martín y Roca, T492604/455336, www.elbolson.gov.ar or www.bolsonturistico.com.ar. 0900-2100 all year, until 2400 in high summer.* They are extremely helpful with maps, treks to refugios and accommodation, English spoken.

There are waterfalls at **Cascada Escondida**, 10 km northwest of town (2-hour dusty walk, ask for short-cut through woods), a good place for a picnic. There are fine views from **Cerro Piltriquitrón** – drive or taxi 10 km, then walk one hour through the sculptures of the **BosqueTallado** (or 6-7 hour round trip walk), food and shelter at *refugio* (1,400 m; US$3.50), then 3-hour walk from there to the summit. Views of the valley from **Cabeza del Indio**, a good 6 km drive or bike ride from the centre, and a pleasant one hour walk up to **Cerro Amigo**: follow Gral Roca east until it becomes Islas Malvinas and continue up the hill. There is wonderful trekking in the mountains and valleys west of town on an excellent network of trails with well equipped and staffed *refugios* in superb locations; at least 8 shelters are operational, most open October-March. Most shelters offer simple accommodation (US$5 pp, sleeping bag required), some meals (US$4), basic supplies including home-baked bread and home-brewed beer, camping (US$1.50 pp), and hot showers (US$1). They have radio communication with each other and with town. Additional information and compulsory registration at the Club Andino or tourist office in El Bolsón. In high season there are minibuses to the trailheads, at other times hitch or take a remise taxi for US$5.

Cholila and around ➔ *Phone code: 02945. Population: 3,000.*
A peaceful sprawling village, 76 km south of El Bolsón, with superb views at Lago Cholila (17 km west), crowned by the Matterhorn-like mountains of Cerros Dos and Tres Picos (campsite and expensive *Hostería El Pedregoso*). Excellent fishing, canoeing and kayaking on rivers nearby. Along Valle de Cholila (Ruta 71) are several lovely old brick and wooden houses and barns. Among them are the **wooden cabins**, where Butch Cassidy, the Sundance Kid and Etta Place lived between 1901 and 1905; the cabins have been renovated, controversially (officially US$1 entry, if anyone's around to charge you). They are 13 km north, east of the road, opposite a police station. One km west of the road is the *Casa de Piedra* teahouse serving *té galés* and offering basic accommodation. **Villa Lago Rivadavia**, 15 km south of Cholila lies next to the northern gates of Parque Nacional Los Alerces, with an increasing number of *cabañas*. Tourist information hut open in summer only, opposite petrol station at El Rincón; also basic information at Municipalidad in Cholila, T498040.

At **Lago Puelo** in the **Parque Nacional Lago Puelo** there are gentle walks on marked paths, boat trips across the lake on a 1931 boat and canoes for rent. Wardens at the park entrance (US$2.55) can advise on these and a 3-day trek through magnificent scenery to Chilean border. Gorgeous homemade *alfajores* in fairy tale setting at *El Bolsonero* on the old road to Lago Puelo. Buses, US$2, from Avenida San Martín y Dorrego in El Bolsón go to the lake via Villa Lago Puelo. Boats: *Juana de Arco* ⓘ *T498946, www.interpatagonia.com/juanadearco. Information in summer from hut in Avenida San Martín y Pellegrini*, 30-minute trip, US$8.35; to the Chilean border, three hours, US$25.

Esquel ➔ *Phone code: 02945. Colour map 9, A1. Population: 30,000.*
Esquel, 293 km south of Bariloche, was originally an offshoot of the Welsh colony at Chubut, 650 km to the east, and still has a pioneer feel. A breezy open town in a fertile valley, with a backdrop

The Old Patagonian Express

Esquel is the terminus of a 402-km branch-line from Ingeniero Jacobacci, a junction on the old Buenos Aires-Bariloche mainline, 194 km east of Bariloche. This narrow-gauge line (0.75 m wide) took 23 years to build, being finally opened in 1945. It was made famous outside Argentina by Paul Theroux who described it in his book The *Old Patagonian Express*. The 1922 Henschel and Baldwin steam locomotives (from Germany and USA respectively) are powered by fuel oil and use 100 litres of water every km. Water has to be taken on at least every 40 km along the route. Most of the coaches are Belgian and also date from 1922. If you want to see the engines, go to El Maitén where the workshops are.

Until the Argentine government handed responsibility for railways over to the provincial governments in 1994, regular services ran the length of the line. Since then, services have been maintained between Esquel and El Maitén by the provincial government of Chubut.

of mountains, Esquel is the base for visiting the Parque Nacional Los Alerces and for skiing at **La Hoya** in winter (15 km, good 6½-hour trek in summer). Good walks from the town to Laguna La Zeta, 5 km, and to Cerro La Cruz, two hours (one way). It's also the departure point for the famous narrow gauge railway, **La Trochita** (see box above). **Tourist office** ⓘ *Av Alvear y Sarmiento, T451927, www.esquel.gov.ar. Daily 0800-2000, summer 0730-2200.*

Trevelin ➔ *Colour map 9, A1. Population: 5,000.*

An offshoot of the Welsh Chubut colony (see box in Patagonia section, page 228), where Welsh is still spoken, the pretty village of Trevelin, 24 km southwest of Esquel, has a Welsh chapel (built 1910, closed) and tea rooms. The **Museo Regional** ⓘ *US$1.50, 0900-2100,* in the old mill (1918) includes artefacts from the Welsh colony. The **Museo Cartref Taid** (ask for directions in the tourist office) is the house of John Evans, one of Trevelin's first pioneers, full of his belongings, another great insight into the local Welsh history. There's also a touching memorial of Evans' life at **El Tumbo del Caballo Malacara**, 200 m from the main plaza; a private garden containing the remains of Evans' horse, Malacara, who once saved his life; guided tours US$2. **Nant-y-fall Falls** ⓘ *17 km southwest on the road to the border, US$3.25 pp not including guide to 3 falls (1½-hr walk)*, are a series of impressive cascades in lovely forest. Helpful tourist office in the central plaza, *T480120*. Has maps, accommodation booking service, English spoken.

Parque Nacional Los Alerces ➔ *Colour map 9, A1.*

ⓘ *33 km west of Esquel, US$7.75, December-Easter.* One of the most appealing and untouched expanses of the Andes region, this national park has several lakes including **Lago Futalaufquen**, with some of the best fishing in the area, **Lago Menéndez** which can be crossed by boat to visit rare and impressive *alerce* trees (Fitzroya cupressoides), some of which are over 2000 years old, and the green waters of **Lago Verde**. Relatively undeveloped, access is possible only to the east side of the park, via a *ripio* road (which is an alternative way from Esquel to El Bolsón) with many camping spots and *hosterías*. Helpful *guardaparques* give out maps and advice on walks at the visitor centre (T471020 ext 23) in Villa Futalaufquen (southern end of Lago Futulaufquen); also a service station, two food shops, *locutorio* and a restaurant *El Abuelo Monje*. Fishing licences from food shops, the *kiosko* or *Hosterías Cume Hué* and *Futalaufquen*, or petrol stations in Esquel. See http://losalercesparquenacional.blogspot.com/, or T471015.

Trekking and tours The west half of the park is inaccessible, but there are splendid walks along footpaths on the southern shore of Lago Futalaufquen, with several waterfalls, and near Lago Verde further north. Treks at Los Alerces range from an hour to two or three days. All long treks require previous registration with the *guardaparques*; some paths are closed in autumn and winter. For longer options or when trails here are closed, try the El Bolsón area, Parque Nacional Nahuel Huapi or Parque Nacional Lanín. At Lago Futalaufquen's northern end, walk across the bridge over Río Arrayanes to Lago Verde. A longer more difficult trek is to **Cerro El Dedal** (1,916 m), either returning the way you came from Villa Futalaufquen, 7½ hours, or making an 8 to 10 hour loop through Puerto Limonao. Walkers must register with the *guardaparques* and you're required to start before 1000. Carry plenty of water. Also a two- to three-day hike through *coihue* forest to the tip of beautiful, secluded **Lago Krügger** ⓘ *refugio, open only Jan-Feb, campsite, US$5 pp and guardaparques' office*, where you can take a boat back to Puerto Limonao. On Lago Futalaufquen is a free campsite at Playa Blanca. **Cerros Alto El Petiso** and **La Torta** can be climbed and there is a trekkers' shelter at the base of **Cerro Cocinero. Boat trips** go to El Alerzal, from Puerto Limonao, across Lago Futalaufquen along the pea-green Río Arrayanes, lined with extraordinary cinnamon- barked trees, to Puerto Mermoud on Lago Verde. A short walk leads to Puerto Chucao, on Lago Menéndez, where another boat makes the unforgettable trip to see the majestic 2600-year old alerce trees, walking to silent Lago Cisne, past the white waters of Río Cisne. A cheaper alternative is to get to Puerto Chucao on your own and take the boat there. Boats run frequently in high season. Book through **Patagonia Verde** ⓘ *Esquel, T454396*, or **Safari Lacustre** ⓘ *T471008.*

Border with Chile: Paso Futaleufú → *Colour map 9, A1.*

There is a campsite (**Camping Puerto Ciprés**) on the Argentine side of river, 70 km southwest of Equel, via Trevelin. Cross the border river by the bridge after passing Argentine customs; Chilean customs is 1 km on the other side of river (one hour for all formalities). The Chilean town of Futaleufú is 9 km from the border. See page 223 for buses to the border.

South of Esquel, Ruta 40 is paved through the towns of **Tecka** and **Gobernador Costa** in Chubut province. At 38 km south of Gobernador Costa, gravelled Ruta 40 forks southwest through the town of Alto Río Senguer, while provincial Ruta 20 heads almost directly south for 141 km, before turning east towards Sarmiento and Comodoro Rivadavia. At La Puerta del Diablo, in the valley of the lower Río Senguer, Ruta 20 intersects provincial Ruta 22, which joins with Ruta 40 at the town of Río Mayo (see page 242). This latter route is completely paved and preferable to Ruta 40 for long-distance motorists; good informal campsites on the west side of the bridge across the Río Senguer.

South of Bariloche

For Sleeping and Eating price codes and other relevant information, see Essentials, pages 38-40.

Sleeping

Bariloche to El Bolsón *p215*

L Estancia Peuma Hue, 3 km off Ruta 40 (ex-Ruta 258 Km 25, T02944-15501030, www.peuma-hue.com. Best comfort in a homely environment, on the southern shores of Lago Gutiérrez, below Cerro Catedral Sur. Charming owner Evelyn Hoter and dedicated staff make it all work perfectly, tasty home-made food, superb horse riding and other activities, health treatments, yoga, meditation, etc, candlelit concerts. All inclusive, varied accommodation. Highly recommended.

AL El Retorno, Villa Los Coihues, on the shore of Lago Gutiérrez, T467333, www.hosteriaelretorno.com. Stunning lakeside position, comfortable hunting lodge style, family run, with a beach, tennis, very comfortable rooms (some **A**)and self-catering apartments (Bus 50, follow signs from the road to El Bolsón).

A pp **Hotel Tronador**, T441062, www.hoteltronador.com. 37 km from Bariloche, on the narrow road from Villa Mascardi to Pampa Linda (there are restricted times for going in each direction: check with tourist office), open Nov-Apr, full board, lakeside paradise, lovely rooms with lake view, beautiful gardens, charming owner, also riding, fishing and lake excursions. Also camping *La Querencia*.

AL-A Mascardi, T490518, www.mascardi.com. Luxurious hotel with a delightful setting along Lago Mascardi.

C Hostería Pampa Linda, T442038. A wonderfully comfortable, peaceful base for climbing Tronador and many other treks (plus horse riding, trekking and climbing courses), simple rooms, all with stunning views, restaurant, full board optional, packed lunches available for hikes. Charming owners, Sebastián de la Cruz is one of the area's most experienced mountaineers. Highly recommended. Nearby is **Refugio Pampa Linda** (**E** pp, T424531) and **Camping Río Manso**.

Camping **Camping Las Carpitas**, 33 km from Bariloche, T490527. Summer only, great location, all facilities, also *cabañas*. **Camping Pampa Linda**, T424531. Idyllic spacious lakeside site with trees, good meals, food shop. **Camping Los Rápidos**, after crossing the Río Manso to Pampa Linda, T461861. All facilities, attractive shaded site going down to lake, *confitería*, open all year.

El Bolsón *p216*

Difficult to find accommodation in the high season: book ahead.

A Amancay, Av San Martín 3207, T492222, www.hotelamancaybolson.com.ar. Good, comfortable and light rooms, though small and a bit old-fashioned, breakfast included.

A La Casona de Odile, Barrio Luján, T492753, www.interpatagonia.com/odile. Rustic wooden cabins with kitchen in idyllic lavender farm by stream, delicious French cooking, reserve ahead, English, French and German spoken. A special place to stay; charismatic owner. Recommended.

B La Posada de Hamelin, Int Granollers 2179, T492030, gcapece@elbolson.com. Charming rooms, welcoming atmosphere, huge breakfasts with homemade jams and cakes, German spoken. Highly recommended.

D Refugio del Lago, at Lago Epuyén, T02945-499025, a.sophie@epuyen.net.ar. Relaxed place with breakfast, also good meals, trekking, riding, canoes for hiring, also camping and *cabañas*. Recommended. Owners are mountain guides. Book in advance.

D Hostería Steiner, San Martín 670, T492224. Another peaceful place surrounded by a lovely park, wood fire, restaurant, breakfast extra, German spoken. Recommended.

D Valle Nuevo, 25 de Mayo y Belgrano, T1560 2325. Small rooms, quiet place, cooking facilities, breakfast not included, but good value. Also runs nice **Albergue Sol del Valle** next door, T492087 (**D** double, **E** pp in dorm), cooking facilities. Also rents a few good value apartments with cooking facilities.

E Altos del Sur, Villa Turismo, T498730, www.altosdelsur.bolsonweb.com. Peaceful hostel in a lovely setting, shared rooms, one double (**D**) with bath, with breakfast, dinner available, will collect from bus station if you call ahead. Recommended.

E-F pp **El Pueblito**, 4 km north in Barrio Luján, 1 km off Ruta 258 (now Ruta 40; take northbound bus along Av San Martín, US$0.50), T493560, www.elpueblitohostel.com.ar. Cosy wooden building in open country, doubles with bath (**D**), also has cabins, cooking and laundry facilities, shop, open fire. HI discounts. Recommended.

Camping **Arco Iris**, T155 58330. Blissful wooded setting near Río Azul, helpful owners. **La Chacra**, Av Belgrano 1128, T492111, campinglachacra@yahoo.com.ar, 15 mins walk from town, well shaded, good facilities, lively atmosphere in season. **Quem Quem**, on river bank Río Quemquemtreu, T493550, quemquem@elbolson.com. Lovely site, hot showers, good walks, free pickup from town. **Refugio Patagónico**, Islas Malvinas y Pastorino, T156 35463, www.refugio patagonico.com.ar. Modern, fully equipped campsite. Recommended. There are many *cabañas* in picturesque settings with lovely views in the Villa Turismo, about US$40 for up to 5 people.

Cholila and around *p216*

AL La Rinconada, Villa Lago Rivadavia, T498091. Offers tours, horse riding, kayaking, American-owned.

B El Trébol, T/F498055, eltrebol@ar.inter.net. With breakfast, comfortable rooms with stoves, meals and half board also available, family-run, large garden, popular with fishing expeditions, reservations advised, bus stops in Cholila 4 km away.

D Cumelen Huenti, in Cholila village, T496031. With bath, heating, restaurant with good home cooking, helpful.

F Cabañas Cerro La Momia, Villa Lago Rivadavia, T011-4964 2586, www.cabanascerrolamomia.com.ar. Very good *cabañas* for up to 6, picturesque setting among fruit orchards and wooded slopes. Restaurant, excursions arranged.

F pp **La Pasarela**, 2 km from town, T499061, www.lpuelo.com.ar. Dorms, camping US$5.65, shops, fuel.

Camping **Autocamping Carlos Pellegrini**, next to El Trébol, T498030. Free municipal camping in El Morro park, next to Cholila.

Camping El Abuelo, 13 km south, at Villa Lago Rivadavia, T491013.

Esquel *p216*

Hotels are often full in Jan-Feb. Ask at tourist office for lodgings in private houses.

AL-A Cumbres Blancas, Av Ameghino 1683, T/F455100, www.cumbresblancas.com.ar. Attractive modern building, a little out of centre, very comfortable, spacious rooms, sauna, gym, airy restaurant. Recommended.

A Angelina, Av Alvear 758, T452763. Good value, welcoming, big breakfast, English and Italian spoken, open high season only.

B Canela, Los Notros y Los Radales, Villa Ayelén, on road to Trevelin, T/F453890. Bed and breakfast and tea room in a lovely, quiet residential area, English spoken, owner knowledgeable about Patagonia.

C La Tour D'Argent, San Martín 1063, T454612. With breakfast, bright, comfortable, family-run, very good value, traditional restaurant.

D El Arrayán, Antártida Argentina 767, T451051. Comfortable carpeted rooms, with heating, reliable hot water, good value.

D La Chacra, Km 5 on Ruta 259 towards Trevelin, T452802, rinilachacra@ciudad.com.ar. Relaxing, spacious rooms, huge breakfast, Welsh and English spoken.

D La Posada, Chacabuco 905, T454095, laposada@art.inter.net. Tasteful B&B in quiet part of town, lovely lounge, very comfortable, breakfast included, excellent value.

D Las Mutisias, Av Alvear 1021, T452083, lasmutisias@ciudad.com.ar. Spotless place run by Emma Cleri, helpful and very hospitable, no breakfast.

E pp **Casa del Pueblo**, San Martín 661, T450581, www.epaadventure.com.ar. Smallish rooms but good atmosphere (**D** double with bath), kitchen, laundry, internet. HI discounts, organizes adventure activities.

E Lago Verde, Volta 1081, T452251, patagoniaverde@ciudad.com.ar. Breakfast extra, modern, comfortable, run by tour guides, same owners as **Patagonia Verde**, rooms for 2 and 3 with bath, near bus terminal, 2 blocks from La Trochita. Recommended.

F pp **Planeta Hostel**, Av Alvear 2833, T456846, www.planetahostel.com. 4-6 bed dorms, doubles **D**,with breakfast, internet, Wi-Fi, simple kitcehn facilities, English spoken.

E Res El Cisne, Chacabuco 778, T452256. Basic small rooms, hot water, quiet, well kept, good value, breakfast extra.

G pp **Hospedaje Rowlands**, behind Rivadavia 330, T452578. Warm family welcome, Welsh spoken, breakfast extra, basic rooms with shared bath and a double with bath (**E**), good value.

Camping **El Hogar del Mochilero**, Roca 1028 (statue of backpacker at entrance), T452166. Summer only, laundry facilities, 24-hr hot water, friendly owner, internet, free firewood for cooking. Also a basic large dorm (**F** pp).

La Rural, 1 km on road to Trevelin, T1568 1429. Well organized and shady site with facilities.

Millalen, Av Ameghino 2063 (5 blocks from bus terminal), T456164, good services and a dorm.

Trevelin *p217*

C Familia Pezzi, Sarmiento 353, T480146, hospedajepezzi@intramed.com.ar. Charming family house with a beautiful garden, open Jan-Mar only, English spoken. Recommended.

D-E pp **Casa Verde Hostal**, Los Alerces s/n, T480091, www.casaverdehostel.com.ar. 'The best hostel in Argentina', by many reckonings. Charming owners Bibiana and Charly, spacious log cabin with panoramic views of wooded mountains, comfortable dorms for 4-6 and doubles, all with bath, kitchen facilities, laundry, HI member, breakfast extra. Also a lovely rustic cabin for up to 7. English and Welsh spoken, excursions into Los Alerces, bikes for hire US$10 per day. Highly recommended.

Camping many sites, especially on the road to Futaleufú and Chile, charging about US$2-3 pp; also many *cabañas*; ask for full list at Tourist office.

Parque Nacional Los Alerces *p217*

East side of Lago Futalaufquen

LL El Aura: Lago Verde Wilderness Resort, T011-4522 7754 (Buenos Aires), www.tenrivers tenlakes.com/elaura-i.htm. Exquisite taste in these 3 stone cabins and a guest house on the shore of Lago Verde. Luxury in every respect, attention to detail, ecologically friendly. Impressive place.

A Hostería Quimé Quipan, T454134. Comfortable rooms with lake views, dinner included. Recommended.

B Motel Pucón Pai, T451425, puconpai@ ciudad.com.ar. Slightly spartan rooms, but good restaurant, recommended for fishing; campsite with hot showers, US$2 pp.

C Bahía Rosales, T471044. Comfortable *cabaña* for 6 with kitchenette and bath, **E** pp in small basic cabin without bath, and camping in open ground, hot showers, restaurant, all recommended.

C Cabañas Tejas Negras, next to Pucón Pai, T471046. Really comfortable cabañas for 4, also good camp site, and tea room.

Camping Los Maitenes, Villa Futalaufquen, excellent, US$1.50 pp, plus US$2 per tent. Several campsites at Lagos Rivadavia, Verde and Río Arrayanes, from free to US$3 depending on facilities.

Border with Chile: Gobernador Costa *p218*

E Hotels Jair, good value, and *Vega*.

Camping Municipal site, all services, US$1.

Eating

El Bolsón *p216*

TT Amancay, San Martín 3217. Good *parrilla* and homemade pastas.

TT Arcimbaldo, Av San Martin 2790, T492137. Good value *tenedor libre*, smoked fish and draft beer, open for breakfast.

TT Cerro Lindo, Av San Martín 2524, T492899. Elegant, delicious pastas, vegetarian dishes and regional specialities.

TT Jauja, Av San Martín 2867, T492448. Great meeting place, delicious fish and pasta, out-standing ice cream, English spoken. Recommended.

TT Parrilla El Quincho, 10 mins north of town, signposted from Route 258, near Cataratas del Mallín, T492870. Excellent *asado* and lamb, charming rustic parrilla with garden going down to the river, tables in the open air. Recommended.

T La Calabaza, Av San Martín y Hube. Good inexpensive food including vegetarian dishes, relaxed atmosphere.

T Morena, Av San Martín y Hube. Small and unpretentious café/restaurant; for pizzas, pastas and some very good vegetarian meals.

Cafés

Cerveza El Bolsón, RN 258, Km 123.9, T492595, www.cervezaselbolson.com. Microbrewery where you can see how the beer is made and sample the 18 varieties. *Picadas* served with beer, sitting outside in the gardens. Highly recommended.

Dulcinea, on RN 258 to El Hoyo at Km 137.5. Delightful tea room, owner Debbie speaks English, famous for cakes and rose hip tea, fondue and *asado* in the evenings in season.

La Saltenita, Av Belgrano 515. For a great selection of *empanadas*.

La Tosca, Perito Moreno y Roca (behind Tourist office). A very agreeable café, atmospheric restaurant in summer, good sandwiches.

Esquel *p216*

TT Dionisio, Av Fontana 656. Good value crêpes with the most varied fillings, *picadas* with beer or wine and meat dishes in a nice house. Also a café open in the late afternoon.

TT Don Chiquito, behind Av Ameghino 1641, T450035. Delicious pastas in a fun atmosphere with plenty of games brought to the tables by magician owner Tito. Recommended.

TT Tío Vicente, Av Ameghino y Av Fontana. Very good food; *parrilla* and pastas with varied sauces.

TT Vascongada, 9 de Julio y Mitre, T452229. Traditional style, trout and other local specialities.

T Casa Grande, Roca 441. Popular for its varied menu (such as lamb and trout), reasonable prices.

T Tío Canuto, Av Alvear 949. Restaurant/bar with live music, tango shows and lessons, Tue-Sun 1900-0300.

Cafés

María Castaña, Rivadavia y 25 de Mayo. Popular, good coffee.

Melys, Miguens 346, off Ameghino 2000. Plentiful Welsh teas and a good breakfast.

Trevelin *p217*

🍴🍴 **Patagonia Celta**, 25 de Mayo s/n, T480722. Delicious local specialities, trout and vegetarian dishes, best in town. Recommended.

🍴 **Nain Maggie**, Perito Moreno 179, T480232. Tea room, offering *té galés* and *torta negra*, expensive but good.

🍴 **Parrilla Oregon**, Av San Martín y Laprida, T480408. Large meals (particularly breakfasts), set menus based on *parrilla* and pastas.

🍴 **Parrilla del Club**, Av San Martín y Libertad. Simple, cheap, good meals.

Shopping

Esquel *p216*

Casa de Esquel (Robert Müller), 25 de Mayo 415. Wide range of new and secondhand books on Patagonia, also local crafts.

La Anónima, 9 de Julio y Belgrano. Big supermarket.

Los Vascos, 25 de Mayo y 9 de Julio. Traditional store founded in 1926, worth seeing.

Activities and tours

El Bolsón *p216*

Grado 42, Av. Belgrano 406, T493124, www.grado42.com. Tours to El Maitén to take La Trochita, 7 hrs, US$25; also short excursions in the surroundings (US$10) and day trips to Parque Nacional Los Alerces (US$32), as well as wide range of adventure activities. Sells **Chaltén Travel** bus tickets (see page 252). Recommended.

Maputur, Perito Moreno 2331, T491139, www.maputur.com.ar. Horse rides, paragliding and mountain bikes for hire (US$7 per day).

Patagonia Adventures, Hube 418, T492513, www.argentinachileflyfishing.com. Rafting, paragliding, fishing, boat trip on Lago Puelo to remote forest lodge, horse riding to Chile.

Esquel *p216*

Fishing

Tourist office has a list of guides and companies hiring out equipment.

Skiing

One of Argentina's cheapest, with laid back family atmosphere, **La Hoya**, 15 km north, has 22 km of pistes, 8 ski-lifts. For skiing information ask at **Club Andino Esquel**, Pellegrini 787, T453248; travel agencies run 3 daily minibuses to La Hoya from Esquel, US$5 return, ski pass US$15. Equipment hire from US$6 a day.

Tours

Frontera Sur, Av Alvear y Sarmiento, T450505, www.fronterasur.net. Good company offering adventure tourism of all sorts, as well as more traditional excursions, ski equipment and trekking.

Patagonia Verde, 9 de Julio 926, T454396, www.patagonia-verde.com.ar. Boat trips to El Alerzal on Lago Menéndez, rafting on Río Corcovado, tickets for 'La Trochita' and for Ruta 40 to El Calafate. Also range of adventure activities, horse riding, short local excursions and ski passes. English spoken. Excellent company, very professional.

Trevelin *p217*

Gales al Sur, Patagonia 186, T480427, www.galesalsur.com.ar. Another office in Esquel bus station, T455757. Adventure tours with mountain bikes, horses, canoes or a good pair of boots. Also bikes for rent (US$10 per day) and transfer to/from airport for all flights. English spoken.

Transport

El Bolsón *p216*

Bus Several daily from **Bariloche** and **Esquel**, with **Don Otto**, **Via Bariloche**. Check with **Vía Bariloche/El Valle**, Mitre 321, T429012, or 0800-333 7575, www.via bariloche.com, for timings. Heavily, even over-booked in high season. US$6, 2 hrs. Other destinations from these 2 towns. Buses to **Lago Puelo** with **Vía Bariloche** every 2 hrs, 4 on Sun, 45 mins, US$1.50. To **Parque Nacional Los Alerces** (highly recommended route), with **Transportes Esquel** (from ACA service station), once a day, US$7, 4-5 hrs, via Cholila and Epuyen.

Esquel *p216*

Air Airport, 20 km east of Esquel, by paved road, US$10 by taxi, US$3 by **Gales al Sur** minibus (see Activities and tours, above). To **Buenos Aires** and **Trelew** with **AR** (Av Fontana 408, T453614). **LADE** (Av Alvear 1085, T452124) to **Bariloche, Comodoro Rivadavia, El Bolsón, El Calafate, El Maitén, Mar del Plata**, **Puerto Madryn** and several other destinations in Patagonia; weekly departures.

Bus Smart terminal at Av Alvear 1871, T451584, US$1 by taxi from centre, it has toilets, *kiosko*, *locutorio* with internet, café, tourist information desk, left luggage (US$2 per day). To Buenos Aires change in Bariloche, with **Andesmar**, T450143, or **Via Bariloche**, T453528, (US$60 *cama*). To **Bariloche**, (via El Bolsón, 2½ hrs), 4-5hrs, US$8-10, **Don Otto** (T453012), **Vía Bariloche**. To **Puerto Madryn**, **Don Otto**, 9 hrs, US$27-37. To **Trelew** US$30-40, 8 hrs nightly or 0800 Tue and Sat. To **Río Gallegos** (for connections to El Calafate or Ushuaia), take **Don Otto/Transportadora Patagónica** bus to Trelew and change there. To **Trevelin**, **Vía Trevelin** (T455222) and **Jacobsen** (T453528), Mon-Fri, hourly 0600-2300, every 2 hrs weekends, 30 mins, US$2. To **Paso Futaleufú** (Chilean border) via Trevelin, **Jacobsen** 0800 daily Jan/Feb, otherwise Mon, Wed (sometimes) and Fri, US$5. Buses connect there for Chaitén.
Car hire **Los Alerces**, Sarmiento 763, T456008, www.losalercesrentacar.com.ar. Good value, good cars, top service.
Train **La Trochita** (which Paul Theroux called the Old Patagonian Express) generally runs from Esquel to **Nahuel Pan** (19 km) daily except Sun, and up to twice a day in high season (much less frequent in winter), taking 2½ hrs, US$38 return, children under 5 free. At wild and remote Nahuel Pan, there's just a small terrace of houses, home to a Mapuche community, who sell delicious cakes and display their knitwear, some of it very fine quality. Sometimes there's an extra service from **El Maitén** at the northernmost end of the line on Sat, taking 6 hrs, with a dining car. Information, in English including schedules in El Maitén, T02945-495190, and in Esquel T02945-451403, www.latrochita.org.ar. Tickets from tour operators, or from Esquel station office, Urquiza y Roggero.

Parque Nacional Los Alerces *p217*
Bus From Esquel (**Transportes Esquel**, T453529) runs daily in Jan-Feb and 2-3 weekly off season at 0800 from Esquel to Lago Puelo, 6 hrs, US$5.50 one way, along the east side of Lago Futalaufquen, passing **Villa Futalaufquen** 0915, **Lago Verde** 1030, **Lago Rivadavia** 1045 and Cholila (sit on left). On the return it passes Lago Rivadavia at 1830, Lago Verde 1845 and Villa Futalaufquen 1945, back in Esquel 2100-2130; driver will stop anywhere en route if asked, and at your hotel on return. Extra frequencies in high summer from Esquel up to Lago Verde and from Lago Puelo up to Lago Verde (**Bus La Golondrina**), US$4.50 and year round from Esquel up to Villa Futalaufquen.

Border with Chile: Paso Futaleufú *p218*
Buses from Esquel via Trevelin to **Paso Futaleufú** (La Balsa), see above. Very little traffic for hitching.

❶ Directory

Esquel *p216*
Banks **Banco de la Nación**, Av Alvear y Roca, open 0730-1300; changes US$ and euros. ATM accepts all cards. ATMs also at **Banco del Chubut**, Av Alvear 1147, **Banco Patagonia**, 25 de Mayo 739, **Bansud**, 25 de Mayo 752. Exchange also at **Finan City**, Av Fontana 673. **Internet** Many places in centre. **Post offices** Av Alvear 1192 y Fontana, Mon-Fri and Sat mornings. **Telephones** Many *locutorios* in centre, including **Cordillera**, 25 de Mayo 526. **El Alerce**, 9 de Julio y 25 de Mayo.

Patagonia

Patagonia is the vast, windy, mostly treeless plateau covering all of southern Argentina south of the Río Colorado. The Atlantic coast is rich in marine life; penguins, whales and seals can all be seen around Puerto Madryn. The far south offers spectacular scenery in the Parque Nacional Los Glaciares, with the mighty Moreno and Upsala glaciers, as well as challenging trekking around Mount Fitz Roy. The contrasts are extreme: thousands of prehistoric handprints can be found in the Cueva de las Manos, but in most of Patagonia there's less than one person to each square kilometre; far from the densely wooded Andes, there are petrified forests in the deserts; and the legacy of brave early pioneers is the over-abundance of tea and cakes served up by Argentina's Welsh community in the Chubut valley.

Patagonia's appeal lies in its emptiness. Vegetation is sparse, since a relentless dry wind blows continually from the west, raising a haze of dust in summer, which can turn to mud in winter. Rainfall is high only in the foothills of the Andes, where dense virgin beech forests run from Neuquén to Tierra del Fuego. During a brief period in spring, after the snow melt, there is grass on the plateau, but in the desert-like expanses of eastern Patagonia, water can be pumped only in the deep crevices which intersect the land from west to east. This is where the great sheep estancias lie, sheltered from the wind. There is little agriculture except in the north, in the valleys of the Colorado and Negro rivers, where alfalfa is grown and cattle are raised. Centres of population are tiny and most of the towns are small ports on the Atlantic coast. Only Comodoro Rivadavia has a population over 100,000, thanks to its oil industry. Patagonia has attracted many generations of people getting away from it all, from Welsh religious pioneers to Butch Cassidy and the Sundance Kid, and tourism is an increasingly important source of income.

Ins and outs

Getting there

Air There are daily flights from Buenos Aires to Viedma, Trelew, Comodoro Rivadavia, Río Gallegos, El Calafate's airport, Lago Argentino, and Ushuaia. It is vital that you book these flights well ahead in the summer (December to February) and the winter ski season for Ushuaia (July and August). **Aerolíneas Argentinas** (AR) and **LADE** (contact details on page 59) fly these routes and flights get booked up very quickly. At other times of the year, flights can be booked with just a few days' warning. The Chilean airline, **LAN**, flies to Ushuaia from Argentine destinations as well as Punta Arenas (for connections to Puerto Montt and Santiago) in summer.

Flying between Patagonian towns is complicated without flying all the way back to Buenos Aires, since there are only weekly fights with **LADE**, whose tickets must be booked in advance from the flight's departure point. The baggage allowance is 15 kg. Flights are often heavily booked, but check again on the day of the flight even if it is sold out. Overnight buses may be more convenient.

Road The principal roads in Patagonia are the Ruta 3, which runs down the Atlantic coast, and the Ruta 40 on the west. One of Argentina's main arteries, Ruta 3 runs from Buenos Aires to Ushuaia, interrupted by the car ferry crossing through Chilean territory across the Magellan Strait to Tierra del Fuego. It is mostly paved, except between Río Gallegos and San Sebastián (80 km north of Río Grande) and for 65 km south of Tolhuin. Regular buses run along the whole stretch, more frequently between October and April, and there are towns with services and accommodation every few hundred km. However, Ruta 40 is a wide unpaved *ripio* track which zigzags across the moors from Zapala to Lago Argentino, near El Calafate, ending at Cabo Vírgenes. It's by far the more interesting road, lonely and bleak, offering fine views of the Andes and plenty of wildlife as well as giving access to many National Parks. A number of companies run daily tourist bus services in summer between Los Antiguos and El Chaltén. The east-west road across Patagonia, from south of Esquel in the Lake District to Comodoro

Rivadavia, is paved, and there's a good paved highway running from Bariloche through Neuquén to San Antonio Oeste.

Many of the roads in southern Argentina are *ripio* – gravelled – limiting maximum speeds to 60 km per hour, or less where surfaces are poor, very hard on low-clearance vehicles. Strong winds can also be a hazard. Windscreen and headlight protection is a good idea (expensive to buy, but can be improvised with wire mesh for windscreen, strips cut from plastic bottles for lights). There are cattle grids (*guardaganados*), even on main highways, usually signposted; cross them very slowly. Always carry plenty of fuel, as service stations may be as much as 300 km apart and as a precaution in case of a breakdown, carry warm clothing and make sure your car has anti-freeze. Petrol prices in Chubut, Santa Cruz and Tierra del Fuego provinces are 40% cheaper than in the rest of the country (10-15% for diesel).

In summer hotel prices are very high, especially in El Calafate and El Chaltén. From November onwards you must reserve hotels a week or more in advance. Camping is increasingly popular and *estancias* may be hospitable to travellers who are stuck for a bed. Many *estancias*, especially in Santa Cruz province, offer transport, excursions and food as well as accommodation: see www.estanciasdesantacruz.com and www.interpatagonia.com/estancias. ACA establishments, which charge roughly the same prices all over Argentina, are good value in Patagonia. As very few hotels and restaurants have a/c or even fans, it can get uncomfortably hot in January.

Viedma, Carmen de Patagones and around

These two pleasant towns (*Phone code: 02920; Colour map 8, C4*) lie on opposite banks of the Río Negro, about 27 km from its mouth and 270 km south of Bahía Blanca. Patagones is older and charming, but most services are in Viedma (*Population: 80,000*), capital of Río Negro Province. A quiet place, its main attraction is the perfect bathing area along the shaded south bank of the river. **El Cóndor** is a beautiful beach 30 km south of Viedma, three buses a day from Viedma in summer, with hotels open January-February, restaurants and shops, free camping on beach 2 km south. And 30 km further southwest is the sealion colony, **Lobería Punta Bermeja**, daily bus in summer from Viedma; hitching easy in summer. **Provincial tourist office** ⓘ *Av Caseros 1425, T422150, www.viedma.gov.ar, 0700-1400, 1800-2000*. **Municipal tourist office** ⓘ *Av Francisco de Viedma esq Colón y Alvaro Barros, T427171, Mon-Fri 0800-2000, Sat-Sun 1100-1900*. Another office is open at weekends at El Cóndor.

Carmen de Patagones (*Population: 18,190*) was founded in 1779 and many early pioneer buildings remain in the pretty streets winding down to the river. There's a fascinating museum, **Museo Histórico Regional "Emma Nozzi"** ⓘ *JJ Biedma 64, T462729, daily 0930-1230, 1900-2100, Sun afternoon only*, with artifacts of the indigenous inhabitants, missionaries and gauchos; good guided tours. Helpful **tourist office** at ⓘ *Bynon 186, T462054* is more dynamic than Viedma's. On 7 March the Battle of Patagones (1827) is celebrated in a week-long colourful fiesta of horse displays and fine food. The two towns are linked by two bridges and a four-minute frequent ferry crossing (US$0.50).

Bahía San Blas is an attractive small resort and renowned shark fishing area, 100 km from Patagones (tourist information at www.bahiasanblas.com); plentiful accommodation. Almost due west and 180 km along the coast, on the Gulf of San Matías, is **San Antonio Oeste** (*Phone code: 02934*), and 17 km south, the popular beach resort, **Las Grutas**. The caves themselves are not really worth visiting; but the water is famously warm. Las Grutas is closed in the winter, but very crowded in the summer; accessible by bus from San Antonio hourly US$2. San Antonio is on the bus routes north to Bahía Blanca and south as far as Río Gallegos and Punta Arenas.

Viedma, Carmen de Patagones and around listings

For Sleeping and Eating price codes and other relevant information, see Essentials, pages 38-40.

Sleeping

Viedma *p225*

B Austral, 25 de Mayo y Villarino, T422615, www.hoteles-austral.com.ar. Modern, with well-equipped if rather old-fashioned rooms, Wi-Fi.

C Nijar, Mitre 490, T422833. Most comfortable, smart, modern, good service.

C Peumayen, Buenos Aires 334, T425222. Old-fashioned friendly place on the plaza.

D Iturburu Spa, 25 de Mayo 174, T430459. Good value, lovely and quiet, with steam baths, helpful staff.

Camping Good municipal site near the river, US$1.35 pp, simple; if showers not working, try Petrobras petrol station nearby.

Eating

Viedma *p225*

Parrilla Libre, Buenos Aires y Colón. Well-priced *tenedor libre* steaks in a cheerful atmosphere.

Transport

Viedma *p225*

Air Airport 5 km south. LADE (Saavedra 576, T424420) fly to **Buenos Aires**, **Mar del Plata**, **Bahía Blanca**, **Neuquén**, **San Martín de Los Andes**, **Trelew** and **Comodoro Rivadavia**.

Bus Terminal in Viedma at Av Pte Perón y Guido, 15 blocks from plaza; taxi US$2. To **Buenos Aires** 13 hrs, daily, US$35-42, **Tramat**. To **San Antonio Oeste**, 2½ hrs, several daily, US$8, **Don Otto**. To **Bahía Blanca**, 4 hrs, **Don Otto** 3 daily, US$10.

Train A comfortable sleeper train goes from Viedma to **Bariloche** overnight Fri 1800, Nov-Jan (for fares see page 215). It has a car transporter; on board there's a restaurant and a cinema car showing videos. T02944-422130, www.trenpatagonico-sa.com.ar. Book ahead.

Puerto Madryn and around

→ *Phone code: 02965. Colour map 9, A3. Population: 74,000.*

Puerto Madryn is a seaside town 250 km south of San Antonio Oeste. It stands on the wide bay of Golfo Nuevo, the perfect base for the Península Valdés and its extraordinary array of wildlife, just 70 km east. It was the site of the first Welsh landing in 1865 and is named after the Welsh home of the colonist, Jones Parry. Popular for skin diving and the nature reserves, the town's main industries are a huge aluminium plant and fish processing plants. You can often spot whales directly from the coast at the long beach of **Playa El Doradillo**, 16 km northeast (October- December). **EcoCentro** ⓘ *Julio Verne 3784, T457470, www.ecocentro.org.ar, daily 1500-1800 (usually closed Tue in winter; open longer in summer, but check with tourist office as times change), US$7.* An inspired interactive sea life information centre, art gallery, reading room and café, it is perched on a cliff at the south end of town, with fantastic views of the whole bay. **Museo de Ciencias Naturales y Oceanográfico** ⓘ *Domecq García y J Menéndez, Mon-Fri 0900-1200, 1430-1900, Sat 1430-1900, US$2.* This informative museum has displays of local flora and fauna. The **tourist office** is at ⓘ *Av Roca 223, T453504, www.madryn.gov.ar, Mon-Fri 0700-2300, Sat-Sun 0830-2300*, extremely helpful.

Around Puerto Madryn

With **elephant seal** and **sea lion** colonies at the base of chalky cliffs, breeding grounds for **Southern right whales** in the sheltered Golfo Nuevo and the Golfo San José, and **guanacos**, **rheas**, **patagonian hares** and **armadillos** everywhere on land, the area around Puerto Madryn, especially the Península Valdés, is a spectacular region for wildlife. Whales can be seen from June to mid-December, particularly interesting with their young September-October. The sea lion breeding season runs from late December to late January, but visiting is good up to late April. Bull elephant seals begin to claim their territory in the first half of August and the breeding season is late September/early October. Orcas can be seen attacking seals at Punta Norte in February/ March. Conservation officials can be found at the main viewpoints, informative but only Spanish spoken. The *EcoCentro* in Puerto Madryn, studies the marine ecosystems. **Punta Loma** ⓘ *0800-1200, 1430-1930; US$5, children US$3 (free with Península Valdés ticket), information and video, many companies offer tours, taxi US$15 ($8.30 one way, walk back)*. This is a sea lion reserve 15 km southeast of Puerto Madryn, best visited at low tide; sea lions can even be seen in Puerto Madryn harbour. See also Puerto Deseado, page 236 and Punta Tombo, page 233.

Puerto Madryn

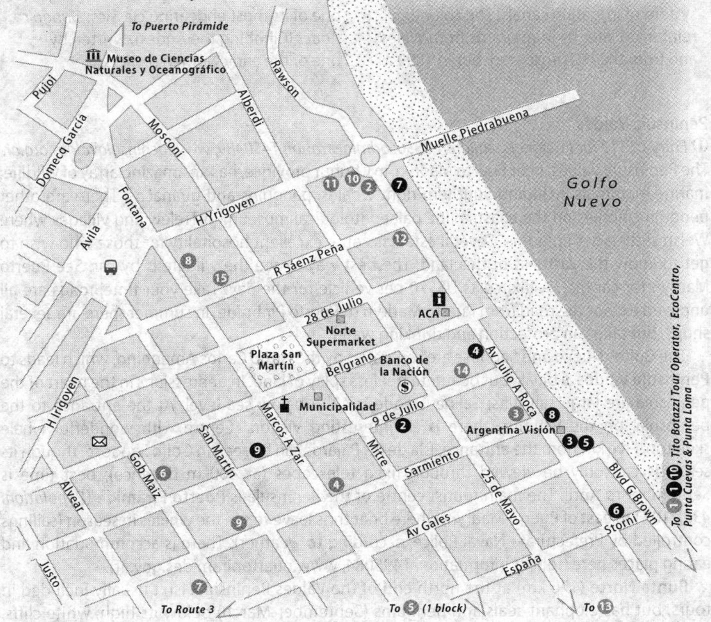

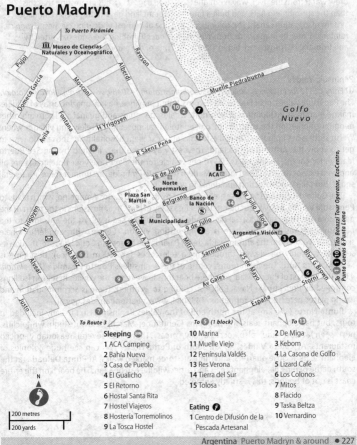

Sleeping
1 ACA Camping
2 Bahía Nueva
3 Casa de Pueblo
4 El Gualicho
5 El Retorno
6 Hostal Santa Rita
7 Hostel Viajeros
8 Hostería Torremolinos
9 La Tosca Hostel
10 Marina
11 Muelle Viejo
12 Península Valdés
13 Res Verona
14 Tierra del Sur
15 Tolosa

Eating
1 Centro de Difusión de la Pescada Artesanal
2 De Miga
3 Kebom
4 La Casona de Golfo
5 Lizard Café
6 Los Colonos
7 Mitos
8 Placido
9 Taska Beltza
10 Vernardino

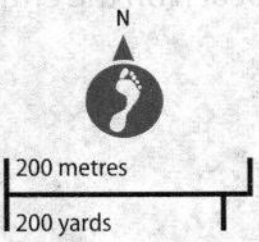

Keeping up with the Joneses

On 28 July 1865, 153 Welsh immigrants landed at Puerto Madryn, then a deserted beach deep in *indígena* country. After three weeks they pushed, on foot, across the parched pampa and into the Chubut river valley, where there is flat cultivable land along the riverside for a distance of 80 km upstream. Here, maintained in part by the Argentine government, they settled, but it was three years before they realized the land was barren unless watered. They drew water from the river, which is higher than the surrounding flats, and built a fine system of irrigation canals. The colony, reinforced later by immigrants from Wales and from the US, prospered, but in 1899 a great flood drowned the valley and some of the immigrants left for Canada. The last Welsh contingent arrived in 1911. The object of the colony had been to create a 'Little Wales beyond Wales', and for four generations they kept the Welsh language alive. The language is, however, dying out in the fifth generation. There is an offshoot of the colony of Chubut at Trevelin, at the foot of the Andes nearly 650 km to the west, settled in 1888 (see page 217). It is interesting that this distant land gave to the Welsh language one of its most endearing classics: *Dringo'r Andes* (Climbing the Andes), written by one of the early women settlers.

Península Valdés

ⓘ *Entry US$12 for foreigners, children US$6; administration T450489, www.peninsulavaldes.org.ar.* The Península Valdés, near Puerto Madryn, in Chubut province, has an amazing array of wildlife: marine mammals including Southern right whales, penguins and guanacos. There are other penguin colonies on the coast, a fine palaeontological museum in Trelew and villages where Welsh settlers set up home. Several estancias offer excellent hospitality for those who wish to get to know the vastness of this land. The best way to see the wildlife is by car. See Puerto Madryn for car hire. A taxi costs US$70 per vehicle for the day. Take your time, roads are all unpaved except the road from Puerto Madryn to Puerto Pirámide. In summer there are several shops, but take sun protection and drinking water.

The Golfos Nuevo and San José are separated by the Istmo Carlos Ameghino, which leads to **Península Valdés**, a bleak, but beautiful treeless splay of land. In depressions in the heart of the peninsula are large salt flats; Salina Grande is 42 m below sea level. At the entrance to the peninsula, on the isthmus, there is an interesting Visitors' Centre with wonderful whale skeleton. Five km from the entrance, Isla de los Pájaros can be seen in Golfo San José, though its seabirds can only be viewed through fixed telescopes (at 400 m distance); best time is September to April. The main tourist centre of the Peninsula is **Puerto Pirámide** (*Population: 430*), 107 km east of Puerto Madryn, where boat trips leave to see the whales in season (sailings controlled by Prefectura – Naval Police, according to weather). There is accommodation and eating places here (tourist information, T495084, www.puertopiramides.gov.ar).

Punta Norte (176 km) at the north end of the Valdés Peninsula, isn't usually included in tours, but has elephant seals and penguins (September-March) below its high, white cliffs, best seen at low tide, also, occasionally, orcas. There are several reasonably priced restaurants. At **Caleta Valdés**, 45 km south of Punta Norte, you can see huge colonies of elephant seals at close quarters, and there are three marked walks. At **Punta Delgada** (at the south of the peninsula) elephant seals and other wildlife can be seen. The beach on the entire coast is out of bounds; this is strictly enforced.

Puerto Madryn and around listings

For Sleeping and Eating price codes and other relevant information, see Essentials, pages 38-40.

Sleeping

Puerto Madryn *p226, map p227*
Book ahead in summer, and whale season. Note that non-Argentines will often be charged more in the pricier hotels.

AL Marina, Av Roca 7, T/F454915, teokou@infovia.com.ar. Great value little seafront apartments for up to 5 people, book ahead.

AL Península Valdés, Av Roca 155, T471292, www.hotelpeninsula.com.ar. Luxurious sea front hotel with great views. Spa, sauna, gym.

A Bahía Nueva, Av Roca 67, T451677, www.bahianueva.com.ar. One of the best sea front hotels, quite small but comfortable rooms, professional staff, cheaper in low season.

B Casa de Pueblo, Av Roca 475, T472500, www.madryncasadepueblo.com.ar. Reputed to be the first brothel in town, now a charming seafront chalet hotel with homely atmosphere, good value.

B Muelle Viejo, H Yrigoyen 38, T471284, www.muelleviejo.com. Ask for the comfortable modernized rooms in this funny old place. Rooms for 4 are excellent value, kitchen facilities.

B Tolosa, Roque Sáenz Peña 253, T471850, www.hoteltolosa.com.ar. Extremely comfortable, modern, great breakfasts. Disabled access. Recommended.

B-C Hostería Torremolinos, Marcos A Zar 64, T453215. Nice modern place, 7 simple, well decorated rooms with large beds and cable TV.

C-D Res Verona, 25 de Mayo 874, T451509, hotel_verona@hotmail.com. New, with breakfast, also has 3 apartments, excellent value.

D Hostal Santa Rita, Gob Maiz 370, T471050. Welcoming, comfy if slightly dated, dorm **E**, also kitchen facilities, breakfast extra.

E Tierra del Sur, 9 de Julio 57, T471379, tierradelsuralojamiento@yahoo.com.ar. New, good breakfast, kitchen, very helpful.

E-F pp **El Gualicho**, Marcos A Zar 480, T454163, www.elgualicho.com.ar. Best budget option, some double rooms, HI discounts, nicely designed, recently expanded, enthusiastic owner, English-speaking staff, heating, free pick up from bus terminal, Wi-Fi, *parrilla*, garden, bikes for hire, runs tours with good guides and value. Highly recommended.

E-F El Retorno, Bartomolmé Mitre 798, T456044, www.elretornohostel.com.ar. 3 blocks from beach, hot water, lockers, cosy common area, rents bikes, free bus terminal pick-up. Double rooms available (**C**).

E-F pp **Hostel Viajeros**, Gob Maíz 545, T456457, www.hostelviajeros.com. With basic breakfast, small rooms with 4 beds or doubles (**C**), big kitchen/dining room, lawn, TV, helpful.

E-F pp **La Tosca Hostel**, Sarmiento 437, Chubut, T456133, www.latoscahostel.com. Dorms have bathrooms, free pick-up from bus station if you call them, helpful. Also has small but cosy doubles (**C**).

Camping ACA, Blvd Brown 3860, 4 km south of town at Punta Cuevas, T452952. Open Sep-Apr, hot showers, café, shop, also duplexes for 4-6, no kitchen facilities, shady trees, close to the sea. Closed out of season.

Península Valdés *p228*
Puerto Pirámide

LL Las Restingas, 1ra Bajada al Mar, T495101, www.lasrestingas.com. Exclusive, sea views, very comfortable, with sophisticated regional restaurant. Good deals available in low season.

AL Del Nómade, Av de las Ballenas s/n, T495044, www.ecohosteria.com.ar. *Hostería ecológica*, uses solar power and water recycling, buffet breakfast, heating, internet, Wi-Fi, café, specializes in wildlife watching, nature and underwater photography, kayaking, adventure sports, courses offered.

A ACA Motel, T495004, aca@piramides.net. Welcoming, handy for the beach, with good seafood restaurant (you might spot whales from its terrace), camping. Jan-Feb reserved for ACA members only. There is also an ACA service station (daily) with good café and shop.

A Cabañas en el Mar, T495049, www.piramides.net. Comfortable, well-equipped 2-6 bed *cabañas* with sea view.

A The Paradise, 2da Bajada al Mar, T495030, www.hosteriaparadise.com.ar. Large comfortable rooms, suites with jacuzzis, fine seafood restaurant.

B La Nube del Angel, Segunda Baja, T495070, www.lanubedelangel.com.ar. Open all year, lovely owners, small cabañas for 2 -6 people, quiet, 5 mins walk from the beach.

Camping Municipal campsite by the black sand beach, T495084, hot showers in evening, good, get there early to secure a place. Do not camp on the beach: people have been swept away by the incoming tide.

Estancias

Several, including:

LL-L Faro Punta Delgada, Punta Delgada, T458444, www.puntadelgada.com. Next to a lighthouse, amazing setting, half and full board, excellent food, very helpful. Recommended; book in advance, no credit cards.

L Rincón Chico, near Punta Delgada, T156 88303 (T471733 in Puerto Madryn), www.rinconchico.com. A working sheep farm with luxurious accommodation, 8 rooms, walking and cycling circuits, half and full board available. Recommended.

AL La Elvira, Caleta Valdés, near Punta Cantor, T15 698709 (office in Puerto Madryn T474248), www.laelvira.com. Traditional Patagonian dishes and comfortable accommodation (B&B, half and full board available).

AL San Lorenzo, on RP3, 20 km southwest of Punta Norte, T451427 (contact through **Argentina Visión** in Puerto Madryn, see Tour operators). Great for day excursions to a beautiful stretch of coast to see penguins, fossils, bird-watching and horse treks.

Eating

Puerto Madryn *p226, map p227*

Excellent seafood restaurants, mostly charging similar prices, but quality varies. Also less-touristy take-aways, eg **Pizzería Mi Guelito**, 9 de Julio 189 and Roca 1220, **Como Su Casa**, España 187 (with vegatarian *tortas*).

TTT Placido, Av Roca 506, T455991, www.placido.com.ar. On the beach, stylish, intimate, excellent service, seafood and vegetarian options, also cheaper pasta dishes.

TTT Taska Beltza, 9 de Julio 345, T156 68085. Excellent food, chef 'El Negro' cooks superb paella, with Basque influence – book ahead, closed Mon. Highly recommended.

TT Centro de Difusión de la Pescada Artesanal, Brown, 7th roundabout, no sign, T15 538085. Authentic cantina, where the fishermen's families cook meals with their catch, very popular, go early.

TT Los Colonos, Av Roca y A Storni, T458486. Built into the wooden hull of a boat, cosy, *parrilla*, seafood and pastas. Ideal for families, with soft play area.

TT Vernardino, Blvd Brown 860, T474289, www.vernardinoclubdemar.com.ar. One of the nicest restaurants on the beach, serving great seafood,and pastas. Good choice for lunch.

T La Casona de Golfo, Av Roca 349, T455027. Good value *tenedor libre parrilla*, seafood, and 'helados libre', as much ice cream as you can eat. Great for families.

Cafés

Kebom, Av Roca 542. Popular ice cream place with big soft play area for kids.

De Miga, 9 de Julio 160. Cosy local favourite with affordably priced sandwiches and pizzas.

Lizard Café, Av Roca y Av Galés, on the seafront. Lively funky place with friendly people. Good for plentiful pizzas or for late night drinks.

Mitos, 28 de Julio 80. Stylish café with good atmosphere, televised football too. Recommended.

Activities and tours

Puerto Madryn *p226, map p227*

Diving

Puerto Madryn is a diving centre, with several shipwrecked boats in the Golfo Nuevo. A 1st dive ('bautismo') for beginners costs about US$50 pp.

Aquatours, Av Roca 550, T451954, www.aquatours.com.ar. A variety of options, including PADI courses, good value.

Lobo Larsen, Roca 885, T470277, www.lobolarsen.com. Friendly company that specializes in diving with the sea lion colony at Punta Lomas.

Puerto Madryn Buceo, Blvd Brown, 3rd roundabout in Balneario Nativo Sur, T155 13997, www.madrynbuceo.com. Courses of all kinds from beginners' dives toa week-long PADI course, around US$180, or US$50 for a day excursion.

Scuba Duba, Blvd Brown 893, T452699/452633, www.scubaduba.com.ar. Professional and good fun, instructor Javier A Crespi is very responsible.

Mountain bike hire
At **El Gualicho**, see Sleeping, or **Vernardino**, see Eating, above.

Tours
Many agencies do similar 7 and 9-hr tours to the Península Valdés, about US$42-58 pp, plus US$15 entrance to the Peninsula. They include the interpretation centre, Puerto Pirámides (the whales boat trip is US$30 extra), Punta Delgada and Caleta Valdés. Shop around to find out how long you'll spend at each place, how big the group is, and if your guide speaks English. On all excursions take binoculars. Most tour companies stay about 1 hr on location. Tours to see the penguins at Punta Tombo and Welsh villages are better from Trelew. Tours do not run after heavy rain in the low season. Recommended for Península Valdés:
Alora Viaggio, Av Roca 27, T455106, www.aloraviaggio.com. Helpful company, also has an office at the bus terminal (T456563).
Argentina Visión, Av Roca 536, T451427, www.argentinavision.com. Also 4WD adventure trips and *estancia* accommodation, English and French spoken.
Tito Botazzi, Blvd Brown y Martín Fierro, T474110, www.titobottazzi.com, and at Puerto Pirámide (T495050). Particularly recommended for small groups and well-informed bilingual guides; very popular for whale watching.

Península Valdés: Puerto Pirámide *p228*
Gato Patagonia, T15-567106, www.tourspeninsulavaldes.blogspot.com. Wildlife tours with bilingual guide Gaston Martin, also transfers.
Hydrosport, Primera Bajada,al Mar, T495065, hysport@infovia.com.ar. Rents scuba equipment and boats, and organizes land and sea wildlife tours to see whales and dolphins.
Whales Argentina, Primera Bajada al Mar, T495015. Recommended for whale watching.

Transport

Puerto Madryn *p226, map p227*
Air Airport 10 km west; LADE to **Buenos Aires**, **Bahía Blanca**, **Viedma**, **Trelew**, **Comodoro Rivadavia** and other Patagonian airports. **Andes** (T0810-7772 6337) also flies to Buenos Aires Mon, Wed, Fri. More flights to **Bariloche**, Buenos Aires, and El Calafate from Trelew. Buses to Trelew stop at entrance to airport if asked. Taxi US$45. Direct bus to Trelew airport, **Puma**, US$5, leaves 1½ hrs before flight and takes arriving passengers to Puerto Madryn.
Bus Terminal at Irigoyen y San Martín (behind old railway station), T451789, with café, clean toilets, locutorio, drinks and sweets kiosk.
To **Buenos Aires**, 18 hrs, several companies, US$58-63, *cama* US$68-72 (eg **Andesmar**). To **Bahía Blanca**, 9 ½ hrs with **Don Otto**, 2000, US$30-41. To **Comodoro Rivadavia**, 6 hrs, US$21-30. To **Río Gallegos**, 18 hrs; US$52, **TAC**. To **Trelew**, 1 hr, every hr, US$5 with **28 de Julio**, **Mar y Valle**. To **Bariloche**, 15 hrs, US$48.
Car hire Expensive, and note large excess for turning car over. Drive slowly on unpaved *ripio* roads; best to hire 4WD! **Budget**, Roca 353, T155-30723 (mob), for good value. **Madryn**, Roca 624, T452355. **Localiza** has an office (see Car Hire in Essentials). **Sigma**, T471739, or 15-699465 (24 hrs), www.sigmarentacar.com. Will deliver car to your hotel.
Taxi There are taxis outside the bus terminal, T452966/474177, and on the main plaza.

Península Valdés *p228*
28 de Julio **bus** company from Puerto Madryn to Puerto Pirámide, daily at 1000, returns 1800, US$5 each way, 1½ hrs.

Directory

Puerto Madryn *p226, map p227*
Airline offices Aerolíneas Argentinas, Roca 427, T450938. **LADE**, Roca 119, T451256. **Banks** Lots of ATMs at the following: **Banco Nación**, 9 de Julio 117. **Banco del Chubut**, 25 de Mayo 154 and **Río**, Mitre 102. **Internet and telephones** Many *locutorios* in the centre for phone and internet. **Netmadryn**, in alley off 28 de Julio 64, cheaper than most. US$0.45-0.60 per hr. **Medical services** For emergencies call 107 or 451240. Late-night pharmacy at on Belgrano y 25 de Mayo. **Post offices** Belgrano y Maiz, 0900-1200, 1500-1900.

Trelew and the Chubut Valley

→ *Phone code: 02965. Colour map 9, A3. Population: 90,000.*

Pronounced 'Trel-ay-Oo', Trelew is a busy town, with an excellent museum and a shady plaza, which hosts a small handicraft market at weekends. Visit mid-October to see the Eisteddfod (Welsh festival of arts). Evidence of Welsh settlement remains only in a few brick buildings: the 1889 **Capilla Tabernacl**, on Belgrano, between San Martín and 25 de Mayo, and the **Salón San David**, a 1913 Welsh meeting hall. On the road to Rawson, 3 km south, is one of the oldest standing Welsh chapels, **Capilla Moriah**, from 1880, with a simple interior and graves of many original settlers in the cemetery. **Museo Paleontológico Egidio Feruglio** ⓘ *Fontana 140, T420012, www.mef.org.ar, Sep-Mar daily, 0900-2000, otherwise Mon-Fri 1000-1800, Sat-Sun 1000-2000, US$6, full disabled access and guides for the blind.* This is an excellent museum, which presents the origins of life and dynamically poised dinosaur skeletons. It has good information in Spanish and free tours in English, German and Italian; also a café and shop. Also has information about **Parque Paleontológico Bryn-Gwyn**, 8 km from Gaiman (see below). **Museo Regional Pueblo de Luis** ⓘ *Fontana y Lewis Jones 9100, T424062, Mon-Fri 0800-2000, Sat-Sun 1400-2000, US$1.* In the old 1889 railway station, it has displays on indigenous societies, failed Spanish attempts at settlement and on Welsh colonization. The **Museo Municipal de Artes Visuales** ⓘ *MMAV, Mitre 350, T433774,* is in an attractive wooden building, with exhibitions of local artists. **Tourist office** on the plaza ⓘ *Mitre 387, T420139, www.trelew.gov.ar, Mon-Fri 0800-2000, Sat-Sun 0900-2100*, map available; also at the airport and bus station. See also **Entretur**, www.trelewpatagonia.gov.ar, and www.vistasdelvalle.com.ar.

Gaiman and around → *Colour map 9, A3. Population: 4,575.*

A small pretty place with old brick houses retaining the Welsh pioneer feel, Gaiman hosts the annual Eisteddfod (Welsh festival of arts) in October. It's renowned for delicious, and excessive Welsh teas and its fascinating tiny museum, **Museo Histórico Regional Galés** ⓘ *Sarmiento y 28 de Julio, T491007, US$1, Tue-Sun 1500-1900,* revealing the spartan lives of the idealistic Welsh pioneers. **Geoparque Bryn Gwyn** ⓘ *8 km south of town, T432100, www.mef.org.ar, open daily 0900-1600, closed 25 Dec and 1 Jan, US$2.50, getting there: taxi from Gaiman US$2.* Fossil beds 40 million years old are shown on a good guided tour; there is a visitor centre offering try-outs in paleontology fieldwork. **El Desafío** ⓘ *Brown 52, 2 blocks west of plaza, www.eldesafiogaiman .com.ar, US$2*, is a quaint, if weatherbeaten, theme park comprising dinosaurs made of rubbish. **Tourist office** ⓘ *Belgrano s/n, T491571, www.gaiman.gov.ar, Mon-Sat 0900-2000, Sun 1100-1800.*

Dolavon, founded in 1919, is a quiet settlement, with a few buildings reminiscent of the Welsh past. The main street, Avenida Roca, runs parallel to the irrigation canal built by the settlers, where willow trees now trail into the water, and there's a Welsh chapel, **Capilla Carmel** at one end. The old flour mill at Maipú y Roca dates from 1927 and can be visited ⓘ *T492290, Mon-Sun 1100-1900, US$3.50.* There's *Autoservicio Belgrano* at the far end of San Martin, for food supplies, one tea room, **El Molienda**, Maipú 61, but nowhere to stay. The **municipal campsite**, two blocks north of the river, is free, with good facilities.

In the irrigated valley between Dolavon and Gaiman, you'll see more Welsh chapels tucked away among fringes of tall *alamo* (poplar) trees and silver birches (best if you're in your own transport). The **San David chapel** (1917) is a beautifully preserved brick construction, with an elegant bell tower, and sturdy oak-studded door, in a quiet spot surrounded by birches.

Paved Ruta 25 runs from Dolavon west to the upper Chubut Valley, passing near the **Florentino Ameghino** dam, a good leafy spot for a picnic. From Ameghino to Tecka on Ruta 40 (south of Trevelin) is one of the most beautiful routes across Patagonia from the coast to the Andes, lots of wildlife to be seen. It goes through Las Plumas (mind the bridge if driving), Los Altares, which has an ACA motel (**C**, dep_6076@aca.org.ar), camping, fuel and some shops, and Paso Los Indios.

South of Trelew

Punta Tombo ⓘ *Park entrance US$10. Tours from Trelew and Puerto Madryn, US$50; 45 mins at the site, café and toilets, usually include a stop at Gaiman. Access from Ruta 1, a ripio road between Trelew and Camarones. Best visited Sep-Mar.* This nature reserve is 125 km south of Trelew, open from September, when huge numbers of Magellanic penguins come here to breed, the largest single penguin colony on the South American subcontinent (200,000 breeding pairs in 2009, but declining owing to changing feeding patterns). Chicks can be seen from mid- November; they take to the water January to February. It's fascinating to see these creatures up close, but noisy colonies of tourists dominate in the morning; it's quieter in the afternoon. You'll see guanacos, hares and rheas on the way. Another large **penguin colony** ⓘ *all year, US$5* – with lots of other marine life, including whales and orcas – is at Cabo Dos Bahías, easily reached from the town of **Camarones** 275 km north of Comodoro Rivadavia. The Guarda Fauna is 25 km from town.

Trelew

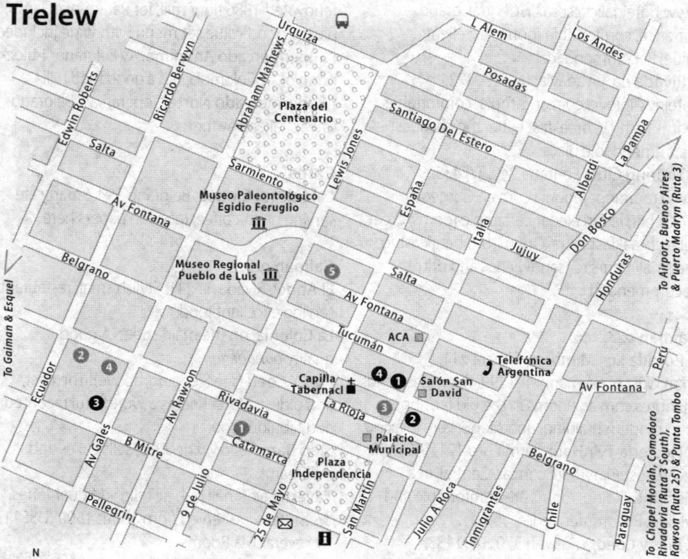

100 metres

100 yards

Sleeping
1 Galicia
2 Libertador
3 Rayentray
4 Rivadavia
5 Touring Club

Eating
1 Café de mi Ciudad
2 Delikatesse
3 El Viejo Molino
4 La Bodeguita

Trelew and the Chubut Valley listings

For Sleeping and Eating price codes and other relevant information, see Essentials, pages 38-40.

Sleeping

Trelew *p232, map p233*

AL La Casona del Río, Chacra 105, Capitán Murga, T438343, www.lacasonadelrio.com.ar.

A Feb-Jul, 5 km from town, pick-up arranged, attractive, new, family-run B&B with heating, TV, meals available, bicycles, massage, laundry, tennis and bowls, English spoken.

A Libertador, Rivadavia 31, T/F420220, www.hotellibertadortw.com. Modern hotel, highly recommended for service and comfortable bedrooms and breakfast is included.

A Rayentray, San Martín y Belgrano, T434702, www.cadenarayentray.com.ar. Large, modernized, comfortable rooms, professional staff, breakfast included, pool.

B Galicia, 9 de Julio 214, T433802, www.hotelgalicia.com.ar. Central, grand entrance, comfortable rooms, excellent value. Recommended.

C Rivadavia, Rivadavia 55, T434472, hotelriv@infovia.com.ar. Simple, comfortable rooms with TV, breakfast extra, the cheapest recommendable place.

C Touring Club, Fontana 240, T/F433997, www.touringpatagonia.com.ar. Gorgeous 1920s bar, faded elegance, simple rooms, great value, breakfast extra. Open from breakfast to the small hours for sandwiches and drinks. Recommended.

Gaiman *p232*

B Posada Los Mimbres, Chacra 211, 6 km west of Gaiman, T491299, www.posadalosmimbres.com.ar. Rooms in the old farmhouse or in modern building, good food, very relaxing.

C Hostería Ty'r Haul, Sarmiento 121, T491880, www.hosteriatyrhaul.com.ar. Central, in a historic building, rooms are comfortable and well-lit. Recommended.

C Plas y Coed, Yrigoyen 320, T491133, www.plasycoed.com.ar. Marta Rees' delightful tea shop has double and twin rooms in an annex next door, with bath and TV, includes breakfast. Highly recommended.

C Ty Gwyn, 9 de Julio 111, T491009, tygwyn@cpsarg.com. Neat, comfortable, with TV, above the tea rooms, excellent value.

Camping Los Doce Nogales is an attractive site south of the river at Chacra 202, close to **Ty Te Caerdydd** tea room, T155 18030, with showers. **Municipal site** of the Bomberos (fire brigade), US$2 pp.

Eating

Trelew *p232, map p233*

TT La Bodeguita, Belgrano 374, T437777. Delicious pastas and pizzas, with interesting art on the walls, lively atmosphere. Recommended.

T Delikatesse, Belgrano y San Martin. Best pizzas in town, cheery place, popular with families.

TT El Quijote, 25 de May 90, T434564. Recommended *parrilla*, popular with locals.

TT El Viejo Molino Gales 250, T428019. Open 1130-0030 (closed Mon), best in town, in renovated 1886 flour mill, for Patagonian lamb, pastas, good value set menu with wine included.

T Supermercado Anónima, Av Belgrano, 1 block north of Av Colombia, has a good food hall.

T Supermercado Norte, Soberanía y Belgrano. Cheap takeaway food.

Cafés

Café de mi Ciudad, Belgrano 394. Smart café serving great coffee; read the papers here.

Gaiman *p232*

El Angel, Rivadavia 241. Stylish small restaurant serving excellent food.

La Colonia, on the main street. A good quality *panadería.*

Plas Y Coed (see Sleeping, above). The best, and oldest; Marta Rees is a wonderful raconteur and fabulous cook.

Siop Bara, Tello y 9 de Julio, sells cakes and ice creams.

Tavern Las, small pub at Tello y Miguel Jones. Welsh teas are served from about 1500 (US$11) by several Tea Rooms.

Ty Gwyn, 9 de Julio 111. Larger, more modern and welcoming; generous teas.

Ty Nain, Irigoyen 283. The prettiest house and full of history, owned by the charming

Mirna Jones (her grandmother was the first woman to be born in Gaiman).

Activities and tours

Trelew *p232, map p233*
Agencies run tours to Punta Tombo, US$27.50, Chubut Valley (half-day), US$38, both as full day US$50. Tours to Península Valdés are best done from Puerto Madryn.
Nieve Mar, Italia 98, T434114, www.nievemartours.com.ar. Punta Tombo and Valdés, bilingual guides (reserve ahead), organized and efficient.
Patagonia Grandes Espacios, Belgrano 338, T435161, infopge@speedy.com.ar. Good excursions to Punta Tombo and Gaiman, but also palaeontological trips, staying in chacras, whale watching. Recommended.

Transport

Trelew *p232, map p233*
Air AR have flights to/from **Buenos Aires**, **El Calafate** and **Ushuaia**. LADE flies to Patagonian airports from **Viedma** to **Comodoro Rivadavia**, as well as **Bariloche**. Airport 5 km north of centre; taxis about US$4-6. Local buses to/from Puerto Madryn stop at the airport entrance if asked, turning is 10 mins walk, US$5; **AR** runs special bus service to connect with its flights.
Bus The terminal is on the east side of Plaza Centenario, T420121. **Local** Mar y Valle and **28 de Julio** both go frequently to **Gaiman**, 30 mins; US$1.30, and **Dolavon** 1 hr, US$1.80, to **Puerto Madryn**, 1hr, US$5. To **Puerto Pirámides**, 2½ hrs, US$7, daily, **Mar y Valle**.

Long distance **Buenos Aires**, 19-20 hrs; US$ 59-68, *cama* US$71-75, several companies go daily; to **Comodoro Rivadavia**, 5 hrs, US$15, many companies, to **Río Gallegos**, 17 hrs; US$49 (with connections to El Calafate, Puerto Natales, Punta Arenas), many companies. To **Esquel**, 9-10 hrs; US$30-40, **Mar y Valle, Empresa Chubut, Transportadora Patagónica/Don Otto**.

Bus companies Andesmar, T433535; **TUS**, T421343; **El Pingüino**, T427400; **El Cóndor**, T431675; **28 de Julio/Mar y Valle**, T432429; **Que Bus**, T422760; **El Ñandú**, T427499.
Car hire Expensive. Airport desks are staffed only at flight arrival times and cars are snapped up quickly. All have offices in town. See Essentials at the front of the book for international agencies.

South of Trelew: Camarones *233*
Bus Don Otto buses from **Trelew**, Mon and Fri, 2½ hrs, returns same day 1600. There are buses to **Reserva Natural Cabo Dos Bahías** Mon, Wed, Fri 0800 from **Trelew**, **El Nañdú**, US$5.25, 2½ hrs, returns same day 1600. **Taxi** From Camarones to Cabo Dos Bahías, US$13.50.

Directory

Trelew *p232, map p233*
Airline offices **Aerolineas Argentinas**, 25 de Mayo 33, T420222. **LADE**, Terminal de Omnibus, offices 12 /13, T435740. **Banks** Open Mon-Fri 0830-1300. **Banco de la Nación**, 25 de Mayo y Fontana. **Banco del Sud**, 9 de Julio 320, cash advance on Visa. **Internet and telephones** Several *locutorios* in centre. **Post offices** 25 de Mayo y Mitre, Mon-Fri 0900-1200. 1500-1900.

Comodoro Rivadavia and inland

→ *Phone code: 0297. Colour map 9, A2. Population: 145,000.*

The largest city in the province of Chubut, 375 km south of Trelew, oil was discovered here in 1907. It looks rather unkempt, reflecting changing fortunes in the oil industry, the history of which is described at the **Museo del Petroleo** ⓘ *3 km north, San Lorenzo 250, T455 9558, Tue-Fri 0900-1800, Sat-Sun 1500-1800, getting there: taxi US$4*. There's a beach at Rada Tilly, 8 km south (buses every 30 minutes); walk along beach at low tide to see sea lions. **Tourist office** ⓘ *Rivadavia 430 y Pellegrini, T446 2376, Mon-Fri 0900-1400*, English spoken. Also in bus terminal ⓘ *daily 0800-2100*, very helpful, English spoken.

Sarmiento ➔ *Colour map 9, A2. Population: 10,000. Phone code: 0297.*
If you're keen to explore the petrified forests south of Sarmiento and the Cueva de las Manos near Perito Moreno, take the road to Chile running west from Comodoro Rivadavia. It's 156 km to Colonia Sarmiento (known as Sarmiento), a quiet relaxed place, sitting just south of two large lakes, Musters and Colhué Huapi. This is the best base for seeing the 70 million-year old **petrified forests** of fallen araucaria trees. Most accessible is the **Bosque Petrificado José Ormachea** ⓘ *32 km south of Sarmiento on a ripio road, warden T4898047, US$3.* Less easy to reach is the bleaker **Víctor Szlapelis** petrified forest, some 40 km further southwest along the same road (follow signposts, road from Sarmiento in good condition). From December to March a *combi* service runs twice daily: contact Sarmiento tourist office. Taxi Sarmiento to forests, US$20 (three passengers), including 1 hour wait. Contact Sr Juan José Valero, the park ranger, for guided tours, Uruguay 43, T0297-489 8407 (see also the Monumento Natural Bosques Petrificados). **Tourist office** ⓘ *Pietrobelli 388, T489 8220,* is helpful, has map of town, arranges taxi to forests.

Comodoro Rivadavia to Río Gallegos
Caleta Olivia (*Population: 40,000*) lies on the Bahía San Jorge, 74 km south of Comodoro Rivadávia, with hotels (one opposite bus station, good) and a municipal campsite near beach (tourist information Av San Martín 1059). A convenient place to break long bus journeys; see the sound sculptures, **Ciudad Sonora** ⓘ *at* **Pico Truncado** *(a few simple hotels, campsite, tourist information T499 2202), daily bus service*, 58 km southwest, where the wind sings through marble and metal structures.

In a bizarre lunar landscape surrounding the Laguna Grande, **Monumento Natural Bosques Petrificados** is the country's largest area of petrified trees. The araucarias, 140 million years old, lie in a desert which was once, astonishingly, a forest. There is a museum and a well-documented 1-km trail that passes the most impressive specimens. No charge but donations accepted; please do not remove 'souvenirs'. Tours from Puerto Deseado with Los Vikingos (address on page 238). ⓘ *Access by Ruta 49 which branches off 91 km south of Fitz Roy. No facilities. Nearest campsite at Estancia La Paloma, on Ruta 49, 24 km before the entrance, T0297-443503.*

Puerto Deseado (*Colour map 9, B3; Phone code: 0297; Population: 10,000*) is a pleasant fishing port on the estuary of the Río Deseado, which drains, strangely, into the Lago Buenos Aires in the west. It's a stunning stretch of coastline and the estuary is a wonderful nature reserve, with Magellanic penguins, cormorants, and breeding grounds of the beautiful Commerson's dolphin. **Cabo Blanco**, 72 km north, is the site of the largest fur seal colony in Patagonia, breeding season December-January. **Tourist office** ⓘ *vagón histórico, San Martín 1525, T487 0220, turismo@pdeseado.com.ar.*

The quiet **Puerto San Julián** (*Colour map 9, B2; Phone code: 02962; Population: 7,150*) is the best place for breaking the 778 km run from Comodoro Rivadavia to Río Gallegos. It has a fascinating history, little of which is visible today. The first mass in Argentina was held here in 1520 after Magellan had executed a member of his mutinous crew. Francis Drake also put in here in 1578, to behead Thomas Doughty, after amiably dining with him. There is much wildlife in the area: red and grey foxes, guanacos, wildcats in the mountains, rheas and an impressive array of marine life in the coastal Reserva San Julián. Recommended zodiac boat trip run by **Excursiones Pinocho** ⓘ *T454333*, to see Magellanic penguins (September-March), cormorants and Commerson's dolphins (best in December). Ceramics are made at the **Escuela de Cerámica**; good handicraft centre at Moreno y San Martín. There is a regional museum at the end of San Martín on the waterfront. **Tourist office** ⓘ *San Martín entre Moreno y Rivadavia, T452353, www.sanjulian.gov.ar.*

Piedrabuena (*Population: 4,200*) on Ruta 3 is 125 km south of San Julián on the Río Santa Cruz. On Isla Pavón, south of town on Ruta 3 at the bridge over Río Santa Cruz, is a tourist complex, with popular wooded campsite and wildlife park, T497498, liable to get crowded in good weather. **Hostería Municipal Isla Pavón**, is a four-star catering for anglers of steelhead trout. National trout festival in March; tourist office Av G Ibáñez 388, T02962-497518. See

Transport, page 254, for Las Lengas bus Piedrabuena-El Chaltén bus service. **Santa Cruz** (turn off 9 km south of Piedrabuena) has the **Museo Regional Carlos Borgialli**, with a range of local exhibits. Ask for James Douglas Lewis, director of toruism here (Av Piedra Buena 531, T02962-498122). Municipal campsite. 24 km further south, a dirt road branches 22 km to **Parque Nacional Monte León**, which includes the Isla Monte León, an important breeding area for cormorants and terns, where there is also a penguin colony and sea lions. There are impressive rock formations and wide isolated beaches at low tide. The **Hostería Estancia Monte León** ⓘ *Ruta 3, Km 2,385, T011-4621 4780 (Buenos Aires), www.monteleon-patagonia.com*, belonging to the Argentine Patagonia Conservation Foundation owned by Mrs Kris Tompkins (see also Parque Pumalín in Chile) is a suitable base for visiting the park.

Comodoro Rivadavia and inland listings

For Sleeping and Eating price codes and other relevant information, see Essentials, pages 38-40.

Sleeping

Comodoro Rivadavia *p235*

A Lucania Palazzo, Moreno 676, T449 9300, reservas@lucania-palazzo.com. Most luxurious business hotel, superb rooms, sea views, good value, huge American breakfast, sauna and gym included. Recommended.

B Comodoro, 9 de Julio 770, T447 2300, info@comodorohotel.com.ar. Buffet breakfast included, pay extra for larger rooms.

C Azul, Sarmiento 724, T447 4628, Breakfast extra, quiet old place with lovely bright rooms, kind, great views from the *confitería*.

C Rua Marina, Belgrano 738, T447 6877. With TV and breakfast, recommended budget choice, owners are backpacker-friendly.

Sarmiento *p236*

B Chacra Labrador, 10 km from Sarmiento, T0297-489 3329, agna@coopsar.com.ar. Excellent small *estancia*, breakfast included, other meals extra and available for non-residents, English and Dutch spoken, runs tours to petrified forests at good prices, will collect guests from Sarmiento (same price as taxi).

D Hostería Los Lagos, Roca y Alberdi, T493046. Good, heating, restaurant.

E Colón, Perito Moreno 650, T489 4212. One of the better cheap places in town.

Camping **Club Deportivo Sarmiento**, 25 de Mayo y Ruta 20, T4893103. **Municipal site** near Río Senguer, 2 km north of centre on Route 243, basic, no shower, US$3 for tent, US$1 pp.

Comodoro Rivadavia to Río Gallegos *p236*

Puerto Deseado

L Estancia La Madrugada, T155 94123, lwalker@caminosturismo.com.ar, or ats@caminosturismo.com.ar. Comfortable accommodation and good Patagonian home cooking, excursions to sea lion colony and cormorant nesting area, English spoken. Highly recommended.

B Isla Chaffers, San Martín y Mariano Moreno, T4872246. Modern, central.

B Los Acantilados, Pueyrredón y España, T4872167, www.pdeseado.com.ar/acantour. Beautifully located, good breakfast.

Puerto San Julián

A Bahía, San Martín 1075, T454028, nico@sanjulian.com.ar. Modern, comfortable, good value. Recommended.

A Estancia La María, 150 km northwest of Puerto San Julián, offers transport, lodging, meals, visits to caves with paintings of human hands, guanacos, etc 4,000-12,000 years old, less visited than Cueva de las Manos. Contact Fernando Behm in San Julián, Saavedra 1163, T452328.

B Municipal, 25 de Mayo 917, T452300. Very nice, well run, good value, no restaurant.

C Res Sada, San Martín 1112, T452013. Fine, hot water, on busy main road, poor breakfast.

Camping Good municipal campsite. Magallanes 650 y M Moreno, T452806. US$2 pp plus US$1 for the use of shower, repeatedly recommended, all facilities.

Eating

Comodoro Rivadavia *p235*

ΨΨ **La Barra**, San Martín 686. Good for breakfast, coffee or lunch.

Cayo Coco, Rivadavia 102. Excellent pizzas, good service.
Dionisius, 9 de Julio y Rivadavia. Elegant *parrilla*, set menu US$5.
La Nueva Rosada, Belgrano 861. Good for beef or chicken.
Peperoni, Rivadavia 348. Cheerful, modern, pastas.
La Barca, Belgrano 935. Good *tenedor libre*.
Superquick in *La Anónima* supermarket, San Martín y Güemes. Cheap food.
Café El Sol, Av Rivadavia y 25 de Mayo. Good café to hang out in.

Comodoro Rivadavia to Río Gallegos *p236*

Puerto Deseado

La Casa de Don Ernesto, San Martín 1245. Seafood and *parrilla*.
El Pingüino, Piedrabuena 958. *Parrilla*.
El Viejo Marino, Pueyrredón 224. Considered the in town best by locals.

Puerto San Julián

Rural, Ameghino y Vieytes. Good, but not before 2100. Also bars and tearooms.
Sportsman, Mitre y 25 de Mayo. Excellent value.

Activities and tours

Comodoro Rivadavia to Río Gallegos *p236*

Puerto Deseado

Darwin Expediciones, España 2601, T156 247554, www.darwin-expeditions.com; also trips to the Monumento Natural Bosques Petrificados.
Los Vikingos, Estrada 1275, T156 245141/487 0020, www.losvikingos.com.ar. Excursions by boat to Ría Deseado reserve and Reserva Provincial Isla Pingüino, bilingual guides, customized tours.

Transport

Comodoro Rivadavia *p235*

Air Airport, 13 km north. Bus No 6 from bus terminal, hourly (45 mins), US$0.50. Taxi to airport, US$3-5. To **Buenos Aires**, **AR/Austral**. **LADE** flies to all Patagonian destinations once or twice a week, plus **Bariloche**, **El Bolsón** and **Esquel**.
Bus Terminal in centre at Pellegrini 730, T446 7305; has luggage store, *confitería*, toilets, excellent tourist information office 0800-2100, some kiosks. In summer buses usually arrive full; book ahead. Services to **Buenos Aires** 2 daily, 28 hrs, US$74-83, *cama* US$89-96. To **Bariloche**, 14½ hrs, US$27, **Don Otto**, T447 0450. To **Esquel** (paved road) 8 hrs direct with **ETAP**, T447 4841, and *Don Otto*. To **Río Gallegos**, daily, 10-12 hrs, US$33-42. To **Puerto Madryn**, US$21-30, and **Trelew**, 3 daily, 4 hrs, US$15, several companies. To/from **Sarmiento** and **Caleta Olivia**, see below. To **Coyhaique** (Chile), US$40, 12 hrs, **Giobbi** twice a week.

Sarmiento *p236*

Bus 3 daily to/from **Comodoro Rivadavia**, US$6, 2½ hrs. To **Chile** via **Río Mayo**, 0200, twice weekly; seats are scarce in Río Mayo. From Sarmiento you can reach **Esquel** (448 km north along Rutas 20 and 40); overnight buses on Sun stop at Río Mayo, take food for journey.

Comodoro Rivadavia to Río Gallegos *p236*

Caleta Olivia

Bus To **Río Gallegos**, **Andesmar**, **Sportman** (overnight) and **El Pingüino**, US$30, 9½ hrs. Many buses to/from **Comodoro Rivadavia**, 1 hr, US$3 (**La Unión** and **Sportman** at terminal, T0297-485 1134), and 3 daily to **Puerto Deseado**, **La Unión** and **Sportman**, 2½-3 hrs, US$9. To **Perito Moreno** and **Los Antiguos**, 5-6 hrs, US$15, several daily.

Puerto San Julián

Air LADE (San Martín 1552, T452137) flies weekly to **Comodoro Rivadavia**, **El Calafate**, **Gobernador Gregores**, **Puerto Deseado**, **Río Turbio** and **Río Gallegos**.
Bus **Río Gallegos**, **El Pingüino**, 6 hrs, US$15.

Directory

Comodoro Rivadavia *p235*

Airline offices Aerolineas Argentinas, 9 de Julio 870, T444 0050. **LADE**, Rivadavia 360, T447 0585. **Banks** Many ATMs and major banks along San Martín. Change money at **Thaler**, Mitre 943, Mon-Fri 0900-1300, or at weekends **ETAP** in bus terminal.
Consulates Chile, Almte Brown 456, Edif. Torraca VIII, p 1, T447 1043, conchilecomrivadavia@speedy.com.ar.
Internet Several places on San Martín, and at Rivadavia 201. **Post offices** San Martín y Moreno.

Río Gallegos and around

→ *Phone code: 02966. Colour map 9, C2. Population: 75,000.*

The capital of Santa Cruz Province, 232 km south of Piedrabuena, on the estuary of the Río Gallegos, this pleasant open town was founded in 1885 as a centre for the trade in wool and sheepskins, and boasts a few smart shops and some excellent restaurants. The delightful Plaza San Martín, 2 blocks south of the main street, Avenida Roca, has an interesting collection of trees, many planted by the early pioneers, and a tiny corrugated iron cathedral, with a wood-panelled ceiling in the chancel and stained glass windows. The small **Museo de los Pioneros** ⓘ *Elcano y Alberdi, daily 1000-1930, free,* is worth a visit. Interesting tour given by the English-speaking owner, a descendent of the Scottish pioneers; great photos of the first sheep-farming settlers, who came here in 1884 from the Malvinas/Falkland Islands. **Museo de Arte Eduardo Minichelli** ⓘ *Maipú 13, Mon-Fri 0800-1900, Sat-Sun and holidays 1400-1800 (closed Jan/Feb),* has work by local artists. **Museo Regional Padre Manuel José Molina** ⓘ *in the Complejo Cultural Santa Cruz, Av Ramón y Cajal 51, Mon-Fri 1000-1800, Sat 1500-2000,* has rather dull rocks and fossils and a couple of dusty dinosaur skeletons. **Museo Malvinas Argentinas** ⓘ *Pasteur 74, Mon and Thu 0800-1300, Tue and Fri 1300-1730, 3rd Sun of month 1530-1830.* More stimulating, it aims to inform visitors, with historical and geographical reasons, why the

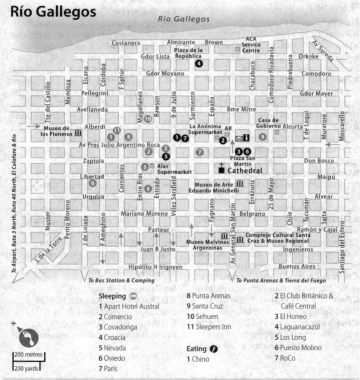

Sleeping
1 Apart Hotel Austral
2 Comercio
3 Covadonga
4 Croacia
5 Nevada
6 Oviedo
7 París
8 Punta Arenas
9 Santa Cruz
10 Sehuen
11 Sleepers Inn

Eating
1 Chino
2 El Club Británico & Café Central
3 El Horreo
4 Laguanacazul
5 Los Long
6 Puesto Molino
7 RoCo

Malvinas are Argentine. The provincial **tourist office** is at ⓘ *Roca 863, T438725, http://santacruz patagonia.gob.ar, Mon-Fri 0900-1800.* At Roca y San Martín is the **Carretón Municipal**, an information caravan open till 2100. Helpful, English spoken, has list of *estancias*, and will phone round hotels for you. At the airport, an information desk operates in high season. Small desk at bus terminal, *T442159, open till 2030 daily*.

Cabo Vírgenes ⓘ *134 km south of Río Gallegos, US$5,* is where a nature reserve protects the second largest colony of Magellanic penguins in Patagonia. There's an informative self-guided walk to see nests among the *calafate* and *mata verde* bushes. Good to visit from November, when chicks are born, to January. Great views from Cabo Vírgenes lighthouse. *Confitería* close by with snacks and souvenirs Access from *ripio* Ruta 1, 3½ hours. Tours with tour operators listed below cost US$38. About 13 km north of Cabo Vírgenes is **Estancia Monte Dinero** ⓘ *T428922, www.montedinero.com.ar,* where the English-speaking Fenton family offers accommodation(**AL** per person), food and excursions (US$90 for a day visit); excellent.

Río Gallegos and around listings

For Sleeping and Eating price codes and other relevant information, see Essentials, pages 38-40.

Sleeping

Río Gallegos *p239, map p239*

A Santa Cruz, Roca 701, T420601, http://usuarios.advance.com.ar/htlscruz/index.htm. Good value, spacious rooms with good beds, full buffet breakfast included. Recommended.

B Apart Hotel Austral, Roca 1505, T434314, apartaustral@infovia.com.ar. Modern, with bright, sunny rooms, good value, basic kitchen facilities, breakfast US$1.70 extra.

B Comercio, Roca 1302, T422458, hotelcomercio@informacionrgl.com.ar. Good value, including breakfast, nice design, comfortable, cheap *confitería*.

B Croacia, Urquiza 431, T421218, hotelcroaciarg1@yahoo.com.ar. Comfortable, spotless, huge breakfasts, helpful owners, a good choice. Recommended.

B Sehuen, Rawson 160, T425683, www.hotelsehuen.com. Good, cosy, helpful, with breakfast.

C Covadonga, Roca 1244, T420190, hotelcovadongargl@hotmail.com. Small rooms with TV, attractive old building, breakfast extra.

C Nevada, Zapiola 480, T435790. Good budget option, nice simple rooms, cable TV, no breakfast.

C París, Roca 1040, T420111. Simple rooms, shared bath, good value, with breakfast.

C Punta Arenas, F Sphur 55, T427743. Rooms with shared bath **D**. Smart and new, rooms in new wing cost more. **Something Café** attached.

D Oviedo, Libertad 746, T420118. A cheaper budget option, breakfast extra, laundry facilities, café, parking.

E pp **Sleepers Inn**, F Sphur 78, T444037, sleepersinn@gmail.com. Simple, clean rooms with one colourful wall, shared bath, warm water, TV on from early till late echoes down corridor. Breakfast is rather DIY and can't use kitchen.

Camping Camping ATSA, Ruta 3, en route to bus terminal, T422310, atsa-polid@hotmail.com. **Club Pescazaike**, Paraje Guer Aike, Ruta 3, 30 km west, T423442, info@pescazaike.com.ar, also *quincho* and restaurant, and **Chacra Daniel**, Paraje Río Chico, 3.5 km from town, T423970, ofaustral@ciudad.com.ar, *parrilla* and facilities.

Estancias

AL pp **Monte Dinero**, 120 km south of Río Gallegos, near Cabo Vírgines, T428922, www.montedinero.com.ar. Comfortable accommodation on a working sheep farm. The house is lined with wood rescued from ships wrecked off the coast, and the food is delicious and home grown. Tours of the reserve, sheepdog demonstrations. Highly recommended.

Eating

Río Gallegos *p239, map p239*

🍴 **El Club Británico**, Roca 935, T427320. Good value, excellent steaks, "magic".

🍴 **El Horreo**, Roca 863, next door to Puesto Molino. Delicious lamb dishes and good salads.

ΨΨ **Laguanacazul**, Sarmiento y Gob Lista, T444114, near the river, looking across Plaza de la República. Patagonian dishes.
ΨΨ **Puesto Molino**, Roca 862, opposite the tourist office. Inspired by *estancia* life, excellent pizzas and *parrilla* (US$15 for 2).
ΨΨ **RoCo**, Roca 1157. Large, smart restaurant, popular, with a varied menu of meat, fish, pasta and other dishes.
ΨΨ-Ψ **Los Long**, Sarsfield 90. Restaurant and salón de té.
Ψ **Chino**, 9 de Julio 29. Varied *tenedor libre*.
Café Central, Roca 900 block, next to **El Club Británico**. Smart and popular.

Activities and tours

Río Gallegos *p239, map p239*
Macatobiano Turismo, Roca 998, T422466, macatobiano@macatobiano.com. Air tickets and tours to Pingüinero Cabo Vírgenes (see above), all day trip US$38, half-day trip to Laguna Azul, a beautiful lake in a volcanic crater, US$18, and to Estancia Monte León, as well as tickets to El Calafate and Ushuaia. Recommended.

Transport

Río Gallegos *p239, map p239*
Air Airport 10 km from centre. Taxi (*remise*) to/from town US$6-8, see below). Regular flights to/from **Buenos Aires**, **Ushuaia** and **Río Grande** direct, with **AR**. **LADE** flies to**El Calafate**, **Ushuaia**, **Río Grande** and **Comodoro Rivadavia**, but not daily. Book as far in advance as possible.
Bus Terminal, T442159, at corner of Ruta 3 and Av Eva Perón, 3 km from centre (small, so can get crowded, left luggage, *confitería*, toilets, kiosk, ATM); taxi to centre US$2.75, bus Nos 1 and 12 from posted stops around town. For all long distance trips, turn up with ticket 30 mins before departure. Take passport when buying ticket; for buses to Chile some companies give out immigration and customs forms.
To **El Calafate**, 4-5 hrs, US$10, **Sportman**, **El Pingüino** (T442169, also has an office at Estrada 173, where tickets can be bought), **Interlagos**, **Taqsa** (T442194, and at airport, www.taqsa.com.ar) and **Marga**. To **Los Antiguos**, **Taqsa** and **Sportman** daily 15 hrs overnight, US$46. To **Comodoro Rivadavia**, **Andesmar**, **Don Otto/ Transportadora Patagónica** (at 1000, T442160, www.donotto.com.ar), **Sportman** and **Tecni Austral**, 10-12 hrs, US$33-42. For **Bariloche**, **Don Otto**, daily, 28 hrs, US$64 *semi cama*, US$76 *cama*, change in Comodoro Rivadavia; also **Taqsa**.
To **Buenos Aires**, 36 hrs, several daily including **El Pingüino**, **TAC**, **Andesmar**, US$116 *cama*. To **Río Grande** US$28, 9½ hrs, and **Ushuaia** US$40, **Marga**, 0900, and **Tecni Austral**, 0800.
To Chile: **Puerto Natales**, **El Pingüino**, Tue, Sat 1100, 4½ hrs, US$13. To **Punta Arenas**, **El Pingüino**, **Ghisoni** and **Pacheco**, 4½ hrs, US$10-12, El Pingüino daily, others less frequent. **By car** make sure your car papers are in order (go first to tourist office for necessary documents, then to the customs office at the port, at the end of San Martín, very uncomplicated). For road details, see Tierra del Fuego sections in Argentina and Chile.
Car hire **Localiza**, Sarmiento 237, T424417. **Cristina**, Libertad 123, T425709. **Hertz** at the airport. Essential to book rental in advance in season.
Taxi Taxi ranks plentiful, rates controlled, *remise* slightly cheaper. Note: Remise meters show metres travelled, refer to card for price; taxi meters show cost in pesos.

Directory

Río Gallegos *p239, map p239*
Airline offices **Aerolineas Argentinas**, San Martín 545, T422020. **LADE**, Fagnano 53, T422316. **Banks** Change TCs here if going to El Calafate, where it is even more difficult. 24-hr ATMs for all major international credit and debit cards all over town. **Banco Tierra del Fuego**, Roca 831, changes TCs. **Cambio El Pingüino**, Zapiola 469, and **Thaler**, San Martín 484. Both will change Chilean pesos as well as US$. **Cambio IA**, Roca 928, local 4. **Consulates** **Chile**, Mariano Moreno 148, T422364, cgrgalar@speedy.com.ar. Mon-Fri, 0900-1300. **Internet** Several on Roca; also various *locutorios* offer internet services, US$0.75 per hr. **Post office** Roca 893 y San Martin. **Telephone** *Locutorios* all over town.

Ruta 40 to the glaciers

Río Mayo (*Phone code: 02903*; tourist office Av Ejército Argentino s/n, T420400, riomayoturistico@yahoo.com.ar; fuel and hotels **C-D**) is reached by Ruta 22 (paved) which branches southwest 74 km west of Sarmiento. Every November, it holds the **Fiesta Nacional de la Esquila** (national sheep-shearing competition). From Río Mayo, a road continues west 140 km to the Chilean border at Coyhaique Alto for Coyhaique in Chile. **South of Río Mayo** Ruta 40 is unpaved as far as Perito Moreno (124 km, high-clearance advised). There is no public transport and very few other vehicles even in mid-summer. At Km 31 on this road a turning leads west to Lago Blanco, to Chile via Paso Huemules and Balmaceda (border open 0800-2000).

Perito Moreno (*Phone code: 02963; Colour map 9, B2; Population: 3,000; Altitude: 400 m*), not to be confused with the famous glacier of the same name near El Calafate, nor with nearby Parque Nacional Perito Moreno, is a provincial town with some interesting historical houses and plenty of character, 25 km east of Lago Buenos Aires, the second largest lake in South America. Southwest is Parque Laguna, with varied bird life and fishing. The town calls itself the 'archaeological capital of Santa Cruz' because of the **Cueva de las Manos** (see below). To see that you'll probably stop off here for at least one night, but if staying longer consider going the extra 56 km west to Los Antiguos (see below), especially if heading for Chile Chico. Two ATMs; traveller's cheques and US$, euros and Chilean pesos can be changed at **Banco Santa Cruz**, Av San Martín 1385, T432028. **Tourist office** ⓘ *Av San Martín y Gendarmería Nacional, low season 0800-2000, high season 0700-2300*, can advise on tours. Also has information on Patagonian *estancias*, in English.

Most of Ruta 40 is reinforced but unpaved south of Perito Moreno, but paving is complete for 50 km south of the town and around Bajo Caracoles. 124 km south, a marked road runs 46 km northeast to the famous **Cueva de las Manos** ⓘ *US$13 for foreigners, half-price for locals, under 12 free, compulsory guided tours with rangers who give information 0900-1900*. In a beautiful volcanic canyon is an intriguing series of galleries containing an exceptional assemblage of cave art, executed between 13,000 and 9,500 years ago; paintings of human hands and animals in red, orange, black, white and green. It was declared a World Heritage Site in 1999. The best time to visit is early morning or evening. Road difficult after rain.

After hours of spectacular emptiness, even tiny **Bajo Caracoles** (*Population: 100*) is a relief: a few houses with an expensive grocery store selling uninspiring *empanadas* and very expensive fuel. From here Ruta 41 goes 99 km northwest to **Paso Roballos**, continuing to Cochrane in Chile.

Parque Nacional Perito Moreno

ⓘ *Free. Park office in Gobernador Gregores, Av San Martín 409, T02962-491477. Accessible only by own transport, Nov-Mar.*

South of Bajo Caracoles, 101 km, is a crossroads. Ruta 40 heads southeast while the turning northwest goes to remote Parque Nacional Perito Moreno (free), at the end of a 90-km *ripio* track. There is trekking and abundant wildlife among the large, interconnected system of lakes below glaciated peaks, though much of the park is dedicated to scientific study only. Lago Belgrano, the biggest lake, is a vivid turquoise, its surrounding mountains streaked with a mass of differing colours. Ammonite fossils can be found. The Park ranger, 10 km beyond the park entrance, has maps and information on walks and wildlife, none in English. Camping is free: no facilities, no fires. There is no public transport into the park.

From the Parque Moreno junction to Tres Lagos, Ruta 40 improves considerably. East of the junction (7 km) is *Hotel Las Horquetas* (closed) and 15 km beyond is Tamel Aike village (police station, water). After another 34 km Ruta 40 turns sharply southwest, but if you need fuel before Tres Lagos, you must make a 72 km detour to Gobernador Gregores (always carry spare). *Estancia La Siberia*, between Ruta 40 and Lago Cardiel some 90 km from the turning, is a lunch stop on the El Calafate–Bariloche bus route, but also has rooms (**B**, open October-April, no phone). At **Tres Lagos** a road turns off northwest to Lago San Martín. From

Tres Lagos Ruta 40 deteriorates again and remains very rugged until the turnoff to the Fitz Roy sector of Parque Nacional Los Glaciares. 21 km beyond is the bridge over Río La Leona, with delightful *Hotel La Leona* whose café serves good cakes. Near here are petrified tree trunks 30 m long, protected in a natural reserve.

Border with Chile: Los Antiguos From Perito Moreno Ruta 43 (paved) runs south of Lago Buenos Aires to **Los Antiguos**, an oasis set on the lake, in the middle of a desert, 2 km from the Chilean border (*Phone code: 02963*). Blessed by a lovely climate and famous for its cherries and great views, Los Antiguos is an increasingly popular tourist town. It is developing fast, with new hotels, restaurants, bus terminal, internet and other services, ideal for a couple of days' rest and for stocking up on the basics before journeying on. **Tourist office** ⓘ *Av 11 de Julio 446, T491261, 0800-2200 in summer, morning only other times, www.losantiguos.gov.ar.*

Ruta 40 to the glaciers listings

For Sleeping and Eating price codes and other relevant information, see Essentials, pages 38-40.

Sleeping

Río Mayo *p242*

LL Estancia Don José, 2.5 km west of Río Mayo, T420015 or 0297-156 249155, www.guenguel.com.ar. Excellent *estancia*, with superb food, 2 rooms and 1 cabin. The family business involves sustainable production of guanaco fibre.

Perito Moreno

C Americano, San Martín 1327, T432538. With breakfast, has a decent restaurant.

C El Austral, San Martín 1381, T432605, hotelaustral@speedy.com.ar. Similar to others on the main street, but clean.

C Belgrano, San Martín 1001, T432019. This hotel is often booked by Ruta 40 long-distance bus companies, basic, not always clean, one key fits all rooms, helpful owner, breakfast extra, excellent restaurant.

D Alojamiento Dona María, 9 de Julio 1544, T432452. Basic but well-kept.

E pp **Santa Cruz**, Belgrano 1565. Simple rooms.

Camping Municipal site 2 km at Laguna de los Cisnes, T432072. Also 2 *cabaña* places.

Estancias 2 estancias on RN40: 28 km south:

L pp **Telken**, sheep station of the Nauta family, T02963-432079, telkenpatagonia@argentina.com or jarinauta@yahoo.com.ar. Comfortable rooms, all meals available shared with family, English and Dutch spoken, horse treks and excursions (Cueva de las Manos US$80). Highly recommended.

A Hostería Cueva de Las Manos, 20 km from the cave at Estancia Las Toldos, 60 km south, 7 km off the road to Bajo Caracoles, T02963-432856/839 (Buenos Aires 49010436, F4903 7161). Open 1 Nov-5 Apr, closed Christmas and New Year, runs tours to the caves, horse riding, meals extra and expensive.

D Estancia Turística Casa de Piedra, 75 km south of Perito Moreno on Ruta 40, in Perito Moreno ask for Sr Sabella, Av Perón 941, T02963- 432199. Price is for rooms, camping **G**, hot showers, homemade bread, use of kitchen, excursions to Cueva de las Manos and volcanoes by car or horse.

Bajo Caracoles

C Hotel Bajo Caracoles, T434963. Old-fashioned but hospitable, meals.

Parque Nacional Perito Moreno *p242*

Nearest accommodation is **A** full board **Estancia La Oriental**, T02962-452196, elada@uvc.com.ar. Splendid setting, with comfortable rooms. Nov-Mar, with horse riding, trekking. See www.cielospatagonicos.com or www.estanciasdesanta cruz.com, for other *estancias* in Santa Cruz: *Menelik* near PN Perito Moreno, and *El Cóndor*, on the southern shore of Lago San Martín, 135 km from Tres Lagos.

Tres Lagos

E Restaurant Ahoniken, Av San Martín, has rooms.

Camping At **Estancia La Lucia**, US$2.50, water, barbecue, 'a little, green paradise'; supermarket, fuel.

Border with Chile: Los Antiguos *p243*
L-A Mirador Hostería & Spa, 2 km from town, due open in 2010, until phone is installed, contact Nick van Schie at Viva el Viento (see below) for bookings. An oasis of tranquility and discreet comfort, horses, jacuzzi on the rooftop, cosy elegant rooms, Wi-Fi, restaurant and small library. Rents bicycles.
A Antigua Patagonia, Ruta 43, T491038, www.antiguapatagonia.com.ar. Luxurious rooms with beautiful views, excellent restaurant. Tours to Cueva de las Manos and nearby Monte Cevallos.
A-D Mora, Av Costanera. Contact Nick at Viva El Viento (see below). New in 2010, rooms range from dorms to 1st class with private bath. There will be coin laundry, hairdresser, as well as disabled access, restaurant, phramacy and communal kitchen.
C Argentino, Av 11 de Julio 850, T491132. Comfortable, decent restaurant.
D Albergue Padilla, San Martín 44 (just off main street), T491140. Comfortable dorms, *quincho* and garden. Also camping. El Chaltén travel tickets.
Camping An outstanding **Camping Municipal**, 2 km from centre on Ruta Provincial 43, T491265, with hot showers, **F** pp.

Eating

Border with Chile: Los Antiguos *p243*
Viva El Viento, 11 de Julio 477, T491109, or 0297-15-421 6133, www.vivaelviento.com. Dutch-owned, good atmosphere, very good food and coffee, open 0900-0100, also has Wi-Fi internet, lots of information, flights over, and boats on the lake arranged. Recommended.
Confitería y Restaurante El Tío, Av11 de Julio 508.

Transport

Río Mayo *p242*
Bus To **Sarmiento** and **Coyhaique** from bus office in the centre. Mon-Fri at 0300 **Giobbi** buses take Ruta 40 north from Río Mayo direct to Esquel.

Perito Moreno
Road distances: Bariloche 823 km, El Chaltén 582 km, El Calafate 619 km. It is nearly impossible to hitchhike between Perito Moreno and El Calafate. Hardly any traffic and few services.
Bus Terminal on edge of town next to petrol station, T432072, open only when buses arrive or depart . If crossing from Chile at Los Antiguos, 2 buses daily in summer, 1 hr, US$3.35, **La Unión** T432133. To **El Chaltén** and **El Calafate**, **Chaltén Travel**, see next paragraph, at 0800. To **Comodoro Rivadavia**, with **La Unión**, 0630, 1700 and **Sportman**, 1700, 6 hrs, US$18 (latter also to Río Gallegos US$43). **Car** Several mechanics on C Rivadavia and Av San Martín, good for repairs. **Taxi** **Parada El Turista**, Av San Martín y Rivadavia, T432592.

Border with Chile: Los Antiguos *p243*
Bus New bus terminal on Av Tehuelches with large café/restaurant, free Wi-Fi. Most bus companies will store the luggage. Minibuses from Chile arrive at this terminal. To **Comodoro Rivadavia**, US$19, **La Unión** (at Terminal, T0297-15-436 1482) and **Sportman** (at Terminal, T0297-15-405 3769), daily, 7½ hrs, via **Perito Moreno** and **Caleta Olivia**. *Albergue Padilla* sells tickets. **Sportman** and **Taqsa** (at Terminal, T0297-15-623 4882), to Río Gallegos, daily, US$46, 15 hrs. To **El Chaltén** (10 hrs) and **El Calafate** (12 hrs), via Perito Moreno, every other (even) day at 0800, US$70, also north to **Bariloche**, every odd day, US$70, **Chaltén Travel** (open only in high season, San Martín 44, T491140, www.chalten travel.com), mid-Nov-Apr, also **Ruta 40; Taqsa** all year round, about US$60. To **Chile**, **La Unión** to **Chile Chico**, 8 km west, US$3.75, 45 mins including border crossing (for routes from Chile Chico to Coyhaique, see Chile chapter).

Directory

Border with Chile: Los Antiguos *p243*
Banks ATM on Av 11 de Julio. **Internet, post and telephone** Locutorio Los Antiguos, Alameda 572, T491103. **Medical services** Hospital and medical emergency: **Patagonia**, Argentina 68, T491303. Pharmacy: **Rossi Abatedaga**, Av 11 Julio 231, T491204.

Parque Nacional Los Glaciares

This park, the second largest in Argentina, extends over 724,000 ha. It is a UNESCO World Heritage Site. 40% of it is covered by ice fields (*hielos continentales*) from which 13 major glaciers descend into two great lakes, Lago Argentino and, further north, Lago Viedma, linked by the Río La Leona, flowing south from Lago Viedma. The only accessible areas of the park are the southern area around Lago Argentino, accessible from El Calafate, and the northern area around Cerro El Chaltén (Fitz Roy). Access to the central area is difficult and there are no tourist facilities.

Ins and outs

Access to the southern part of the park is 50 km west of El Calafate, US$16 for non-Argentines. **National Park Office** in Calafate ⓘ *Av del Libertador 1302, T491005, www.losglaciares.com*, helpful, English spoken; in El Chaltén ⓘ *across the bridge at the entrance to the town, T493004, Jan-Feb 0700-2200, low season: 0900-1600*. An informative talk about the National Park and its paths is given to all incoming bus passengers. Both hand out helpful trekking maps of the area, with paths and campsites marked, distances and walking times. Note that the hotel, restaurant and transport situation in this region changes greatly from year to year.

El Calafate and around → *Phone code: 02902. Colour map 9, B1. Population: 8,000.*

This town sits on the south shore of **Lago Argentino** and exists almost entirely as a tourist centre for the **Parque Nacional los Glaciares**, 50 km away. In both El Calafate and El Chaltén most of the inhabitants came from Buenos Aires and other provincial cities. With the recent decline in tourism as a result of global recession, many people have returned north and the local population has fallen. The town has been known to get packed out in January and February, but it is empty and quiet all winter. It's neither cheap nor beautiful, but it is spotless and tidy and Lago Argentino's turquoise waters are stunning. The shallow part at Bahía Redonda is good for birdwatching in the evenings. **Tourist office** ⓘ *in the bus station, T491476, open 0800-2000 (0830-1430 May-Sep), and Rosales y Av del Libertador, T491090, open 0900-2100 (0800-2000 May-Sep), www.elcalafate.gov.ar. Helpful staff speak several languages. Provincial office: 1 de Mayo 50, T492858. See also www.calafate.com.*

For the main excursions to the glaciers, see below. At **Punta Gualicho** (or Walichu) on the shores of Lago Argentino 7 km east of town, there are cave paintings (badly deteriorated); 6-hour horse ride (US$40 pp). A recommended 15-minute walk is from the Intendencia del Parque, following Calle Bustillo up the road towards the lake through a quiet residential area to **Laguna Nímez** ⓘ *US$1, guides at the entrance in summer (likely to be closed in low season, though still a nice area away from busy centre)*, a bird reserve (fenced in), with flamingos, ducks, black-necked swans and abundant birdlife. **Centro de Interpretación Histórica** ⓘ *Av Brown y Bonarelli, US$3*, has a very informative anthropological and historical exhibition about the region, with pictures and bilingual texts, also a very relaxing café/library. There are several *estancias* within reach, offering a day on a working farm, *asado al palo,* horse riding and accommodation. **Estancia Alice 'El Galpón del Glaciar'** ⓘ *T492509, Buenos Aires T011-4311 8614, www.estanciaalice.com.ar*. **Estancia Nibepo Aike** ⓘ *on Brazo Sur of Lago Argentino in the National Park, 55 km southwest (book at Av Libertador 1215 p 1, T02966-436010, www.nibepoaike.com.ar)*, beautiful setting in a more remote area, traditional 'estancia' style with original furniture, delightful meals served and an optional boat trip on Brazo Sur. **'Cerro Frías'** ⓘ *25 km west, T492808, www.cerrofrias.com*, excursion includes one meal and an ascent of Cerro Frías (1,030 m) for great views; options are by horse, on 4WD vehicles or on foot, US$45. See also **Helsingfors**, in Sleeping below, or visit www.estanciasdesantacruz.com.

Glaciar Perito Moreno

At the western end of Lago Argentino (80 km from El Calafate) the major attraction is the Glaciar Perito Moreno, one of the few glaciers in the world that is both moving and maintaining in size, despite global warming. It descends to the surface of the water over a 5-km frontage and a height of about 60 m. Several times in the past, it advanced across the lake, cutting the Brazo Rico off from the Canal de los Témpanos; then the pressure of water in the Brazo Rico broke through the ice and reopened the channel. This spectacular rupture last occurred in March 2004. The glacier can be seen close up from a series of wooden walkways descending from the car park. Weather may be rough. The vivid blue hues of the ice floes, with the dull roar as pieces break off and float away as icebergs from the snout, are spectacular, especially at sunset. ▸▸ *See also Transport, page 253.*

Glaciar Upsala

At the northwest end of Lago Argentino, 60 km long and 4 km wide, Upsala Glacier is a stunning expanse of untouched beauty. The glacier itself, unlike its cousin Perito Moreno, is suffering badly from global warming. At the end of 2009 a huge part broke from the main mass of ice, blocking most of the lake and disrupting tourist activities. Normally it can be reached by motor-boat from Punta Bandera, 50 km west of El Calafate, on a trip that also goes to Lago Onelli and Spegazzini glaciers (with Solo Patagonia, see under Activities and tours). Small Lago

El Calafate

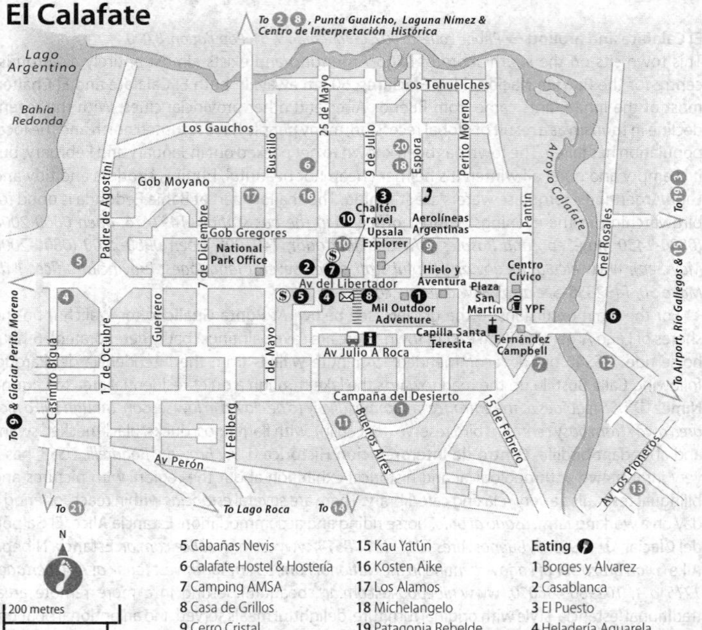

Sleeping
1 Albergue y Hostal Lago Argentino
2 Alto Verde
3 América del Sur
4 Ariel
5 Cabañas Nevis
6 Calafate Hostel & Hostería
7 Camping AMSA
8 Casa de Grillos
9 Cerro Cristal
10 El Quijote
11 Hostel Buenos Aires
12 Hostel del Glaciar 'Libertador'
13 Hostel del Glaciar 'Pioneros'
14 i Keu Ken Hostel
15 Kau Yatún
16 Kosten Aike
17 Los Alamos
18 Michelangelo
19 Patagonia Rebelde
20 Sir Thomas
21 Vientos del Sur

Eating
1 Borges y Alvarez
2 Casablanca
3 El Puesto
4 Heladería Aquarela
5 La Cocina
6 La Tablita
7 La Vaca Atada
8 Mi Viejo & Rick's Café
9 Pura Vida
10 Tierra Bendita

Onelli is quiet and very beautiful, beech trees on one side, and ice-covered mountains on the other. The lake is full of icebergs of every size and sculpted shape. **Mar Patag** runs a two-day boat trip to Upsala, Spegazzini and Moreno glaciers (see under Activities and tours).

El Chaltén and around → *Phone code: 02962.*

This small tourist town lies 217 km northwest of El Calafate in the north of the park (road paved), at the foot of the jagged peaks of the spectacular Fitz Roy massif, which soars steeply from the Patagonian steppe, its sides too steep for snow to stick. Chaltén is the Tehuelche name meaning the 'smoking mountain', and occasionally at sunrise the mountains are briefly lit up bright red for a few seconds, a phenomenon known as the 'sunrise of fire', or '*amanecer de fuego*'. The town is windy, with an Alpine feel. It's a neat place, but incredibly expensive. Nevertheless you should not let the acute commercialism detract from the fact that it offers amazing views of the nearby peaks, is the base for some of the country's finest trekking and has some very good restaurants and places to sleep. If you haven't got a tent, you can easily rent all you'll need. **Tourist office** ⓘ *Güemes 21, T493011, www.elchalten.com, excellent site with accommodation listed, Mon-Fri 0900-2000, Sat-Sun 1300-2000.*

The **Lago del Desierto**, 37 km north of El Chaltén, is surrounded by forests, a stunning virgin landscape. A short walk to a mirador at the end of the road gives fine views. Excursions from El Chaltén by **Chaltén Travel** daily in summer, and from **Restaurant Las Lengas** (see Eating, below), US$36 for 6 hours, who also runs daily transfers to connect with boats, 0830, 1500, US$21, 2-hour waiting time. Campsite at the southern end of Lago del Desierto (usually no food, although there is a kiosk that advertises *choripán*), and refugios at its northern end. To get to **Villa O'Higgins** (Chile), the southernmost town on the Carretera Austral, take the Las Lengas transfer, or JR minibus to Lago del Desierto, then a 45-minute boat trip goes to the northern end (US$28), or walk up a path alongside the east shores 4½ hours to reach the northern end. From there you can trek or go on horseback (19 km, 7 hours with guide, US$30) to Puerto Candelario Mancilla on Lago O'Higgins. A 4WD service runs from the Chilean border to Candelario Mancilla, 14 km: US$30, call Hans Silva in Villa O'Higgins T+56-67-431821 to reserve, same number for horses. Overnight at Estancia Candelario Mancilla. Next day, take a boat from Candelario Mancilla to Bahía Bahamóndez (3 hours, US$80), then a bus to Villa O'Higgins, 7 km, US$4. The border is closed from May to November (check at www.villaohiggins.com for dates, tours and boat availability and see Chile chapter, **Villa O'Higgins**, for more details).

Also daily boat trips on Lago Viedma to pass Glaciar Viedma, with ice trekking optional in the day-long tour . The *estancia* **Hostería El Pilar** (see Sleeping) is a base for trekking up Río Blanco or Río Eléctrico, or try the multi activity adventure circuit. **Las Lengas** has buses daily at 0700, 0830, 1500 to El Pilar, US$10.50, and to Río Eléctrico, US$13, for several of the hikes above and below. Highly recommended.

Trekking and climbing

Trekking The two most popular walks are to **1) Laguna Torre** (three hours each way). After 1-1½ hours you'll come to Mirador Laguna Torre with great view of Cerro Torre and Fitz Roy, and 1¼ hours more to busy Camping De Agostini near the lake, where you have fantastic views. **2) Laguna de Los Tres** (four hours each way). Walk 1¼ hours up to Camping Capri, great views of Fitz Roy, then another hour to Camping Poincenot. Just beyond it is Camping Río Blanco (only for climbers, registration at the National Park office required). From Río Blanco you can walk another hour, very steep, to Laguna de los Tres where you'll get a spectacular view (not a good walk if it's cloudy). You can connect the two paths by taking one that takes about two hours and branches off south, northwest of Laguna Capri, passes by Lagunas Madre e Hija and reaches the path to Laguna Torre, west of the Mirador. This may be too long for a day. From El Chaltén to Laguna Torre along this route takes about seven hours. **3) Loma del Pliegue Tumbado** (four hours each way). To a viewpoint where you can see both cordons and Lago Viedma: marked path from Park Ranger's office, a good day walk, best in clear weather. **4) Laguna Toro** (seven hours each way). For more experienced trekkers, to wild glacial lake across the ice cap. **5) Up Río Blanco to Piedra del Fraile** (seven hours each way, two hours each way from the road to Lago del Desierto). A beautiful walk out of the National Park to campsite with facilities, and Refugio Piedra del Fraile, neither is free. Recommended. The best day walks are Laguna Capri, Mirador Laguna Torre, both of which have great views after an hour or so. A one-hour hike is to Chorillo del Salto, a small but pristine waterfall; take the road to Lago del Desierto for about 30 minutes, then follow the marked path. No guide is necessary.

Most paths are very clear and well worn, but a map is essential, even on short walks: the park information centre gives helpful maps of treks, as do the tourist office and hotels. If you wish to buy maps, the best are by *Zagier and Urruty*, www.patagoniashop.net, 1:50,000 (US$5.95-11.95), updated quite regularly and available in shops in El Calafate and El Chaltén.

Climbing Base camp for Fitz Roy (3,405 m) is Campamento Río Blanco (see above). Other peaks include Cerro Torre (3,102 m), Torre Egger (2,900 m), Cerro Solo (2,121 m), Poincenot (3,002 m), Guillaumet (2,579 m), Saint-Exupery (2,558 m), Aguja Bífida (2,394 m) and Cordón Adela (2,938 m): most of these are for very experienced climbers. Generally the best time is mid February to end March; November-December is very windy; January is fair; winter is extremely cold, but weather is unpredictable and it all depends on the specific route being climbed. Permits for climbing are available at the national park information office. Guides are available in El Chaltén.

El Calafate to Chile

If travelling from El Calafate to Torres del Paine by car or bike, you'll cross this bleak area of steppe. About 40 km before reaching the border there are small lagoons and salt flats with flamingos (between El Calafate and Punta Arenas it is also possible to see guanacos and condors). From Calafate you can take the paved combination of Ruta 11, RN 40 and RN 5 to La Esperanza (165 km), where there's fuel, a campsite and a large but expensive *confitería* (lodging C with bath). From La Esperanza, Ruta 7 heads west (not completely paved) along the valley of the Río Coyle. A shorter route (closed in winter) missing La Esperanza, goes via El Cerrito and joins Ruta 7 at *Estancia Tapi Aike*. Ruta 7 continues to the border crossing at Cancha Carrera and then at Cerro Castillo meets the good *ripio* road between Torres del Paine (20 km north) and Puerto Natales (63 km south). For bus services along this route see under El Calafate.

Río Turbio → *Phone code: 02902. Colour map 9, C2. Population: 6,600.*

A charmless place, 267 km west of Río Gallegos, 30 km from Puerto Natales (Chile), you're most likely to visit en route to or from Torres del Paine in Chile. The site of Argentina's largest coalfield hasn't recovered from the depression hitting the industry in the 1990s. It has a cargo railway, connecting it with Punta Loyola; Mina 1 is where the first mine was opened. There is a ski centre: **Valdelén** has six pistes and is ideal for beginners, also scope for cross-country skiing between early June and late September. **Tourist information** in the municipality ⓘ *Plazoleta Castillo, T421950.*

Border with Chile

1) Paso Mina Uno/Dorotea is 5 km south of Río Turbio. Open all year, 0800-2400. On the Chilean side this runs south to join the main Puerto Natales-Punta Arenas road. **2) Paso Casas Viejas** is 33 km south of Río Turbio via 28 de Noviembre. Open all year, 0800-2400 (2200 in winter). On the Chilean side this runs west to join the main Puerto Natales-Punta Arenas road. **3) Paso Río Don Guillermo (or Cancha Carrera)** is 48 km north of Río Turbio, this is the most convenient crossing for Parque Nacional Torres del Paine. Open all year, 0800-2400 (2200 in winter). Argentine customs are fast and friendly. On the Chilean side the road continues 7 km to the border post at Cerro Castillo, where it joins the road from Puerto Natales to Torres del Paine.

Parque Nacional Los Glaciares listings

For Sleeping and Eating price codes and other relevant information, see Essentials, pages 38-40.

Sleeping

Parque Nacional Los Glaciares *p245*

LL Estancia Helsingfors, 73 km northwest of La Leona, on Lago Viedma, T/F02966-420719 (in BAs: T011-4315 1222), www.helsingfors.com.ar. Fabulous place in splendid position on Lago Viedma, stylish rooms, welcoming lounge, delicious food (full board), and excursions directly to glaciers and to Laguna Azul, by horse or trekking, plus boat trips. Open Oct-Apr.

LL Los Notros, 70 km west of Calafate on the road to the Moreno glacier, T/F499510 (in BA: T011-5277 8200), www.losnotros.com. Exclusive retreat with wonderful views of the glacier, spacious rooms, all-inclusive packages.

Camping AMSA, Olavarría 65 (50 m off the main road, turning south at the fire station), T492247. Hot water, open in summer, US$3.50 pp. **El Huala**, 42 km from El Calafate, on the road to Lago Roca. Free with basic facilities, open all year round. **Lago Roca**, 50 km from El Calafate, T499500, beautifully situated, US$4 pp, bike hire, fishing licences, restaurant/confitería, open Oct-Apr. (Ferretería Chuar, 1 block from bus terminal, sells camping gas.)

El Calafate *p245, map p246*

Prepare to pay far more for accommodation here than elsewhere in Argentina. El Calafate is very popular in Jan-Feb, so book all transport and accommodation in advance. Best months to visit are Oct, Nov and Mar, Apr when it is less crowded and less overpriced. Many hotels open only from Sep/Oct to Apr/May.

LL Kau Yatún, Estancia 25 de Mayo (10 blocks from centre, east of arroyo Calafate), T491059, www.kauyatun.com. Renovated main house of a former estancia, well-kept grounds, 2 excellent restaurants, only half board or all inclusive packages that include excursions in the National Park.

LL Kosten Aike, Gob Moyano 1243, T492424, www.kostenaike.com.ar. Relaxed yet stylish, elegant spacious rooms, jacuzzi, gym, excellent restaurant, *Ariskaiken* (open to non residents), cosy bar, garden, English spoken. Recommended.

L El Quijote, Gob Gregores 1155 , T491017, www.quijotehotel.com.ar. A very good hotel, spacious, well-designed with traditional touches, tasteful rooms with TV, restaurant *Sancho* (from US$10 for 3 courses), English and Italian spoken.

L Patagonia Rebelde, José Haro 442, T494495, www.patagonia rebelde.com. Charming new building in traditional Patagonian style, like an old inn with rustic decor, good comfort with well-heated bedrooms and comfy sitting-rooms.

AL Cabañas Nevis, Av del Libertador 1696, T493180, www.cabanasnevis.com.ar. Owner Mr Patterson offers very nice cabins for 5 and 8 (price quoted is for 5), some with lake view, great value. Recommended.

AL Los Alamos, Gob Moyano y Bustillo, T491144, www.posadalosalamos.com. **LL** in high season. Very comfortable, charming rooms, good service, lovely gardens and without doubt the best restaurant in town.

A Alto Verde, Zupic 138, T491326, www.welcomeargentina.com/altoverde. Top quality, **B** in low season, spotless, spacious, helpful, breakfast included, also with apartments for 4.

A Casa de Grillos, Pasaje Las Bandurrias, T491160, www.casadegrillos.com.ar. Welcoming B&B in the calm green area, next to Nímez nature reserve. It has all the comfort and charm of a family house, **B** low season.

A-B Ariel, Av Libertador 1693, T493131, www.hotelariel.com.ar. Modern, functional, well maintained, TV, with breakfast.

A-B Michelangelo, Espora y Gob Moyano, T491045, www.michelangelohotel.com.ar. Lovely, quiet, welcoming, TV, breakfast included, restaurant. Recommended.

B Sir Thomas, Espora 257, T492220, www.sirthomas.com.ar. Modern, comfortable wood-lined rooms, breakfast extra.

B Vientos del Sur, up the hill at Río Santa Cruz 2317, T493563, www.vientosdelsur.com. Very hospitable, calm, comfortable, TV, good views, kind family attention.

B-C Cerro Cristal, Gob Gregores 989, T491088, www.cerrocristalhotel.com.ar. Comfortable, quiet, free Wi-Fi internet and TV, breakfast included, very good value in low season.

B-C Hostel Buenos Aires, Buenos Aires 296, 200 m from terminal, T491147, www.glaciarescalafate.com. Quiet, kind owner, helpful, comfortable with doubles breakfast, cheaper without bath, good hot showers, Wi-Fi, laundry service, luggage store, bikes for hire.

B-E pp **Albergue y Hostal Lago Argentino**, Campaña del Desierto 1050-61 (near bus terminal), T491423, hostellagoargentino@cotecal.com.ar. **E** pp shared dorms with kitchen facilities, too few showers when full, nice atmosphere, good flats and **B** doubles with breakfast on a neat garden.

B-E pp **Marcopolo Calafate**, C 405, T493899, www.hostel-inn.com. Part of Hostelling International. **E** pp in dorms. Laundry facilities, breakfast included, free Wi-Fi, various activities and tours on offer.

E pp **América del Sur**, Puerto Deseado 153, T493525, www.americahostel.com.ar. Panoramic views from this comfortable, relaxed hostel, welcoming, well-heated rooms, with breakfast (**E** pp dorms for 4, **C** doubles with views, one room adapted for wheelchair users), chill-out area, fireplace, internet access, Wi-Fi, kitchen facilities. Warmly recommended, but can be noisy.

E pp **Calafate Hostel**, Gob Moyano 1226, 400 m from bus terminal, T492450, www.calafatehostels.com. A huge log cabin with good rooms: **E** pp dorms with or without bath, breakfast extra, **B** doubles with bath and breakfast. Also has **Hostería** at corner with 25 de Mayo, T491256, in **B-C** range. Kitchen facilities, internet access, lively sitting area. Book a month ahead for Jan-Feb and call ahead for free shuttle from airport, HI discounts, helpful travel agency, Chaltén Travel (see below).

E pp **Hostel del Glaciar 'Libertador'**, Av del Libertador 587 (next to the bridge), T491792, www.glaciar.com. HI discounts, open year round. Smaller and pricier than 'Pioneros', rooms are good and well-heated, all with own bath (**E** pp dorms for 4 and **A-B** doubles), breakfast extra, cooking facilities, internet access, Wi-Fi. Free transfer from bus terminal. Owners run **Patagonia Backpackers** (see below under Activities and tours).

E pp **Hostel del Glaciar 'Pioneros'**, Los Pioneros 251, T491243, www.glaciar.com. Discount for HI members, open mid Sep to mid Apr. Accommodation for all budgets: standard **C** doubles (also for 3 and 4) with bath, superior **B** doubles with bath, shared dorms up to 4 beds, **E** pp. Many languages spoken, lots of bathrooms, internet access, Wi-Fi, kitchen facilities, no breakfast, free shuttle from bus terminal. Very popular, so book well in advance and double-check. **Punto de Encuentro** restaurant with some vegetarian options. Owners run **Patagonia Backpackers** (see below under Activities and tours).

E pp **i Keu Ken Hostel**, F M Pontoriero 171, T495175, www.patagoniaikeuken.com.ar. On a hill, very helpful, flexible staff, with breakfast, hot water, heating, luggage store, good.

El Chaltén *p247*

In high season places are full: you must book ahead. Most places close in low season.

LL Los Cerros, Av San Martín, Santa Cruz, T493182, www.loscerrosdelchalten.com. Stylish but overly expensive hotel in a stunning setting with mountain views, heated swimming pool.

LL-L Hostería El Puma, Lionel Terray 212, T493095, www.hosteriaelpuma.com.ar. A little apart, splendid views, lounge with log fire, tasteful stylish furnishings, comfortable, transfers and big American breakfast included. Can also arrange tours through their excellent agency Fitz Roy Expeditions, see below. Recommended.

L-AL Senderos, Perito Moreno s/n, T493336, www.senderoshosteria.com.ar. Four types of room and suite in a new, wood-framed structure, comfortable, warm, can arrange excursions, excellent restaurant, Wi-Fi in public areas.

AL El Pilar (see above), T493002, www.hosteriaelpilar.com.ar. Country house in a spectacular setting at the meeting of Ríos Blanco and de las Vueltas, with clear views of Fitz Roy. A chance to sample the simple life with access to less-visited northern part of the park. Simple comfortable rooms, great food, very special. Owner Marcelo Pagani is an experienced mountain guide.

AL Hostería Posada Lunajuim, Trevisán s/n, T493047, www.posadalunajuim.com.ar. Stylish yet relaxed, comfortable (duvets on the beds), lounge with wood fire, with full American breakfast. Recommended.

B Nothofagus, Hensen s/n, T493087, www.nothofagusbb.com.ar. Cosy bed and breakfast, simple rooms, **C** without bath, good value (**C-D** in low season). Recommended.

C Hospedaje La Base, Lago del Desierto s/n, T493031. Good rooms for 2, 3 and 4, all with bath, tiny kitchen, self service breakfast included, great video lounge. Recommended.

C-D Ahonikenk Chaltén, Av Martín M de Güemes 23, T493070, ahonikenkchalten23@yahoo.com.ar. Nice simple rooms, some dorms, restaurant/pizzería attached, good pastas.

E pp **Albergue Rancho Grande**, San Martín s/n, T493005, chaltenrancho@yahoo.com.ar. HI-affiliated, in a great position at the end of town with good open views and attractive restaurant and lounge, accommodates huge numbers of trekkers in rooms for 4, with shared bath, breakfast extra. Also **C** doubles, breakfast extra. Helpful, internet, English spoken. Recommended. Reservations in Calafate Hostel/Chaltén Travel, Calafate.

E-F pp **Albergue Patagonia**, Av San Martín 392, T493019, www.patagoniahostel.com.ar. HI-affiliated, cheaper for members, small and cosy with rooms for 2 with own bath (**B**) or for 2 (**C-D**), 4, 5 or 6 with shared bath, kitchen, video room, bike hire, laundry, luggage store and lockers, restaurant, very welcoming. Helpful information on Chaltén, also run excursions to Lago del Desierto.

E-F pp **Cóndor de los Andes**, Av Río de las Vueltas y Halvorsen, T493101, www.condordelosandes.com. Nice little rooms for up to 6 with bath, sheets included, breakfast US$2, also doubles with bath (**B-C**), laundry service, library, kitchen, quiet, HI affiliated.

Camping del Lago, Lago del Desierto 135, T493010, centrally located with hot showers. Several others A gas/alcohol stove is essential for camping as open fires are prohibited in campsites in of the National Park. Take plenty of warm clothes and a good sleeping bag. It is possible to rent equipment in El Chaltén, ask at park office or Rancho Grande.

In the National Park Poincenot, Capri, Laguna Toro, Laguna Torre. None has services, all river water is drinkable. Pack up all rubbish and take it back to town, do not wash within 70 m of rivers. **Camping Los Troncos/Piedra del Fraile** on Río Eléctrico is behind park boundary, privately owned, has facilities.

Río Turbio *p248*

C De La Frontera, 4 km from Rio Turbio, Paraje Mina 1, T421979. The most recommendable.

D Hostería Capipe, Dufour, 9 km from town, T482935, www.hosteriacapipe.com.ar. Simple, with internet, restaurant.

Eating

El Calafate *p245, map p246*

El Puesto, Gob Moyano y 9 de Julio, T491620. Tasty thin-crust pizzas in a cosy old house. Pricier regional meals and takeaway. Recommended.

La Cocina, Av del Libertador 1245. Good pizza and pasta, including a large variety of pancakes.

La Tablita, Cnel Rosales 28 (near the bridge). Typical *parrilla*, generous portions and quality beef.

La Vaca Atada, Av del Libertador 1176. Good homemade pastas and more elaborate and expensive dishes based on trout and king crab.

Mi Viejo, Av del Libertador 1111. Popular *parrilla*, US$5.50 for grilled lamb.

Pura Vida, Av Libertador 1876, near C 17. Comfortable sofas, homemade Argentine food, vegetarian options, lovely atmosphere, lake view (reserve table). Recommended.

Rick's Café, Av del Libertador 1091. Lively *parrilla* with good atmosphere.

Tierra Bendita, Gob Gregores 1170. Popular *tenedor libre*, great food and service.

Cafés

Borges y Alvarez, Av del Libertador 1015 (Galería de los Gnomos). A lively café/bookshop, open till 0100, good place to hang out.

Casablanca, 25 de Mayo y Av del Libertador. Jolly place for omelettes, hamburgers, vegetarian, US$7 for steak and chips.

Heladería Aquarela, Av del Libertador 1177. The best ice cream – try the *calafate*.

El Chaltén *p247*

Estepa, Cerro Solo y Antonio Rojo. Small, intimate place with good, varied meals, friendly staff.

Fuegia, San Martín s/n. Pastas, trout, meat and vegetarian dishes. Dinner only, recommended.

Pangea, Lago del Desierto y San Martín. Open for lunch and dinner, drinks and coffee, calm, good music, varied menu. Recommended.

Patagonicus, Güemes y Madsen. Lovely warm place with salads, *pastas caseras* and fabulous pizzas for 2, US$3-8, open midday to midnight. Recommended.

Ruca Mahuida, Lionel Terray s/n. Widely regarded as the best restaurant with imaginative and well-prepared food.

Zaffarancho (behind Rancho Grande), bar-restaurant, good range and reasonably priced.

Josh Aike, Lago de Desierto 105. Excellent *confitería*, homemade food, beautiful building. Recommended.

Las Lengas, Viedma 95, opposite tourist office, T493023, laslengaselchalten@yahoo.com.ar. Cheaper than most. Plentiful meals, basic pastas and meat dishes. US$3 for meal of the day. Lots of information. See Lago del Desierto, above, and Transport, below, for owner's minibus services.

Domo Blanco, Costanera y De Agostini, and Güemes y Río de las Vueltas. Delicious ice cream.

Bars and clubs

El Chaltén *p247*

Cervecería Bodegón El Chaltén, San Martín 564, T493109, http://elchalten.com/cerveceria/. Brews its own excellent beer, also local dishes and pizzas, coffee and cakes, English spoken. Recommended.

Shopping

El Calafate *p245, map p246*

La Anónima. Supermarket on Av del Libertador y Perito Moreno.

El Chaltén *p247*

Several supermarkets, all expensive, and little fresh food available: **El Gringuito**, Av Antonio Rojo, has the best choice. Fuel is available next to the bridge.

Activities and tours

El Calafate *p245, map p246*

Most agencies charge the same rates and run similar excursions. Note that in winter bad weather can limit, or even cause boat trips to be cancelled.

Chaltén Travel, Av del Libertador 1174, T492212 (in Bs As T011-4326 7282), also Av Güemes y Lago del Desierto, T493092, El Chaltén, www.chalten travel.com. Huge range of tours (has a monopoly on some): glaciers, *estancias*, trekking, and bus to El Chaltén. Sell tickets along the Ruta 40 to Perito Moreno, Los Antiguos, US$70, and Bariloche, US$150, departures 0800 on odd-numbered days (0830 from El Chaltén) mid-Nov-Apr, overnight in Perito Moreno (cheaper to book your own accommodation), 36 hrs, English spoken.

Hielo y Aventura, Av del Libertador 935, T492205, www.hieloyaventura.com. Minitrekking includes walk through forests and 2-hr trek on Moreno glacier (crampons included). Also half-day boat excursion to Brazo Sur for a view of stunning glaciers, including Moreno. Recommended.

Lago San Martín, Av del Libertador 1215, p 1, T492858, lagosanmartin@cotecal.com.ar. Operates with Estancias Turísticas de Santa Cruz, specializing in arranging estancia visits, helpful.

Mar Patag, T011-4312 4427, www.cruceros marpatag.com. Exclusive 2-day boat excursion to Upsala, Spegazzini and Moreno glaciers, US$350 pp, full board.

Mil Outdoor Adventure, Av del Libertador 1029, T491437, www.miloutdoor.com. Excursions in 4WD to panoramic views, 3-6 hrs.

Mundo Austral, Av del Libertador 1114, T492365, mundoaustral@cotecal.com.ar. For all bus travel and cheaper trips to the glaciers, helpful bilingual guides.

Patagonia Backpackers, at Hosteles del Glaciar, T15-5509 5034, www.glaciar.com. Alternative Glacier tour, entertaining, informative, includes walking, US$43. Recommended constantly. Also Supertrekking en Chaltén, Oct-Apr, 2-day hiking trip, featuring the best treks in the Fitz Roy massif, including camping and ice trekking, US$200. Highly recommended. Also sells tickets for **Navimag** ferries (Puerto Natales-Puerto Montt).

Ruta 40, Libertador 1215, loc 2, T492619, www.ruta40.com.ar. Excursions in El Calafate, El Chaltén and to Perito Moreno and Los Antiguos.

Solo Patagonia, Av del Libertador 963, T491298, www.solopatagonia.com.ar. Memorable day-boat excursions to Upsala glacier and Lago Onelli (and Spegazzini glacier in summer); lunch extra in summer at restaurant on Bahía Onelli, US$60 plus transfer to Punta Bandera departure point. Recommended. Also 45-min boat trip to the front of Moreno glacier from a pier 1 km away from walkways.

El Chaltén *p247*
For **trekking on horseback** with guides: **Rodolfo Guerra**, T493020 (also hires animals to carry equipment, but can be poorly planned); **El Relincho**, T493007.
In summer **Restaurant Las Lengas**, see above, runs a regular minibus to Lago del Desierto passing by some starting points for treks and by **Hostería El Pilar**, see above.
Casa De Guías, Av Costanera Sur s/n, T493118, www.casadeguias.com.ar. Experienced climbers who lead groups to nearby peaks, to the Campo de Hielo Continental and easier treks.
Fitz Roy Expediciones, San Martín 56, T493107, www.fitzroyexpediciones.com.ar. Organizes trekking and adventure trips including on the Campo de Hielo Continental, ice climbing schools, and fabulous longer trips. Climbers must be fit, but no technical experience required; equipment provided. Email with lots of notice to reserve. Highly recommended.
Mermoz, San Martín 493, T493098, mermoz@infovia.com.ar. For trips across Lago del Desierto, with bus transfer, English spoken, helpful.
Patagonia Aventura, T493110, www.patagonia-aventura.com.ar. Has various ice trekking and other tours to Lago and Glaciar Viedma, also to Lago del Desierto.

Transport

El Calafate *p245, map p246*
Air Airport, T491230, 23 km east of town, **Transpatagonia Expeditions**, T493766, runs service from town to meet flights, US$7 open return. Taxi (T491655/492655), US$10. **AR/Austral** flies daily to/from **Buenos Aires**. Many more flights in summer to **Bariloche**, **Ushuaia** and **Trelew** (office at 9 de Julio 57, T492815). **LADE** flies to **Ushuaia**, **Comodoro Rivadavia**, **Río Gallegos** and **Esquel** (office at Julio A Roca 1004, T491262).
Bus Terminal on Roca 1004, 1 block up stairs from Av del Libertador. Some bus companies will store luggage for a fee. To **Perito Moreno** glacier see below. To **Río Gallegos** daily with 4-5 hrs, US$10, **Sportman** (T02966-15 464841), **El Pingüino**, **Interlagos** (T491179), **Taqsa** (T491843) and **Marga**. To **El Chaltén** daily with **Taqsa**, **Chaltén Travel** (T492212, at 0800, 1300, 1830), **Los Glaciares**, **Cal-Tur** (T491842), 4-5 hrs, US$35 return. To **Bariloche**, see above for **Chaltén Travel**'s buses via Los Antiguos and Perito Moreno, page 252. Also **Ruta 40** and others. **Taqsa** runs a daily bus to Bariloche via Los Antiguos at 1600, 36 hrs, US$120. A cheaper way is to take **Taqsa** or **El Pingüino** to Bariloche via Río Gallegos, 1700, 28 hrs, US$107. To **Ushuaia** take bus to Río Gallegos for connections.
Direct bus services to Chile (Take passport when booking bus tickets to Chile.) To **Puerto Natales**, daily in summer with **Cootra** (T491444), via Río Turbio, 7 hrs, or with **Turismo Zaahj** (T491631), Wed, Fri, Sun, 5 hrs, US$20 (advance booking recommended, tedious customs check at border). **Note** Argentine pesos cannot be exchanged in Torres del Paine.
Car hire Average price under US$100 per day for small car with insurance but usually only 200 free km. **Cristina**, Av del Libertador 1711, T491674, crisrenta@rnet.com.ar. **Localiza**, Av del Libertador 687, T491398, localiza calafate@hotmail.com. **ON Rent a Car**, Av del Libertador 1831, T493788 or T02966-1562 9985, onrentacar@cotecal.com.ar. All vehicles have a permit for crossing to Chile, included in the fee, but cars are poor. **Bikes for hire**, US$17 per day.

Glaciar Perito Moreno *p245*
Boat A 45-mins catamaran trip departs from near the entrance to the walkways and gets closer to the glacier's face, US$10; can be arranged independently through **Solo Patagonia** (see above) or is offered with the regular excursions. Another boat trip and a mini-trekking on the glacier are organized by **Hielo y Aventura** (see Activities and tours for both).
Bus From El Calafate with **Taqsa**, **Cal-Tur**, US$20 return; also guided excursions. Many agencies in El Calafate also run minibus tours (park entry not included). Out of season trips to the glacier may be difficult to arrange. Taxis US$77 for 4 passengers round trip including wait of 3-4 hrs at the glacier. A reliable driver is Ruben, T498707. There is small taxi stand outside the bus terminal.

El Chaltén *p247*
Bus In summer, buses fill quickly: book ahead. Fewer services off season. Daily buses to **El Calafate**, 4-5 hrs (most stop at El Calafate airtport), US$18 one way, companies given above, El Chaltén phone numbers: **Chaltén**

Travel T493005, **Cal Tur** T493062. See above for Chaltén Travel to Los Antiguos and Bariloche, page 252. To **Piedrabuena** on Ruta 3, for connections to Los Antiguos, Puerto Madryn, etc, **Las Lengas** (see Eating, above), 0530, return 1300, daily, US$28.50. **Las Lengas** also run to El Calafate airport at 0630, 1030 daily, return 1330, 1900, US$21, reserve in advance.
Taxi Servicio de Remís El Chaltén, Av San Martén 430, T493042, reliable.

Río Turbio *p248*
Bus To **Puerto Natales**, 2 hrs, US$5, hourly with **Cootra** (Tte del Castillo 01, T421448, cootra@oyikil.com.ar), and other companies. To **El Calafate**, **Cootra**, 4 hrs, US$12. **Río Gallegos**, 5 hrs, US$10 (**Taqsa**, T421422).

Directory

El Calafate *p245, map p246*
Banks Best to take cash as high commission is charged on exchange, but there are ATMs at airport, **Banco de la Provincia de Santa Cruz**, Av del Libertador 1285, and at **Banco de Tierra del Fuego**, 25 de Mayo 34. **Thaler**, Av del Libertador 1242 changes money and Tcs. **Post office** Av del Libertador 1133.
Telephone **Open Calafate**, Av del Libertador 996, huge *locutorio* for telephone and also 20 places with fast internet, central but expensive. More convenient, also big and with a café is the **Centro Integral de Comunicaciones**, Av del Libertador 1486.

El Chaltén *p247*
Banks 24-hr ATM next to the gas station at the entrance to town. Credit cards are accepted in all major hotels and restaurants.
Internet Available all over town, in restaurants, hotels and cafés.

Tierra del Fuego → *Colour map 9, C3.*

The island at the extreme south of South America is divided between Argentina and Chile, with the tail end of the Andes cordillera providing dramatic mountain scenery along the southern fringe of both countries. There are lakes and forests, mostly still wild and undeveloped, offering good trekking in summer and downhill or cross-country skiing in winter. Until a century ago, the island was inhabited by four ethnic groups, Selk'nam (or Ona), Alacaluf (Kaweskar), Haush (Manekenk) and Yámana (Yahgan). They were removed by settlers who occupied their land to introduce sheep and many died from disease. Their descendants (except for the extinct Haush) are very few in number and live on the islands. Many of the sheep farming estancias which replaced the indigenous people can be visited. Ushuaia, the island's main city, is an attractive base for exploring the southwest's small national park, and for boat trips along the Beagle channel to Harberton, a fascinating pioneer estancia. There's good trout and salmon fishing, and a tremendous variety of bird life in summer. Autumn colours are spectacular in March and April.

Ins and outs

Getting there There are no road/ferry crossings between the Argentine mainland and Argentine Tierra del Fuego. You have to go through Chilean territory. (Accommodation is sparse and planes and buses fill up quickly from Nov to Mar. Essential to book ahead.) From Río Gallegos, Ruta 3 reaches the Chilean border at Monte Aymond (67 km; open 24 hours summer, 0900-2300 April-October), passing Laguna Azul. For bus passengers the border crossing is easy, although you have about a-30-minute wait at each border post as luggage is checked and documents are stamped (it's 2 more hours to Punta Arenas). Hire cars need a document for permission to cross the border. 30 km into Chile is **Kamiri Aike**, with a dock 16 km east at **Punta Delgada** for the 20-minute Magellan Strait ferry-crossing over the Primera Angostura (First Narrows) to **Bahía Azul**. At Punta Delgada is Hostería El Faro for food and drinks. Two boats work continuously, 0700-0100 (0830-2345 April-October), US$24 per vehicle, foot passengers

US$2.80, www.tabsa.cl. The road is paved to Cerro Sombrero, from where *ripio* (unsurfaced) roads run southeast to Chilean San Sebastián (130-140 km from ferry, depending on route taken). Chilean San Sebastián is just a few houses with **Hostería La Frontera** 500 m from the border. It's 15 km east, across the border (24 hours), to Argentine San Sebastián, not much bigger, with a 7-room ACA hostería (**C**), T02964-425542; service station open 0700-2300. From here the road is paved to Río Grande (see below) and Ushuaia.

The other ferry crossing is **Punta Arenas-Porvenir**. RN255 from Kamiri Aike goes southwest 116 km to the intersection with the Punta Arenas-Puerto Natales road, from where it is 53 km to Punta Arenas. The ferry dock is 5 km north of Punta Arenas centre, at Tres Puentes. The ferry crosses to Bahía Chilota, 5 km west of Porvenir Tuesday-Sunday (subject to tides, Transportadora Austral Broom, www.tabsa.cl, publishes timetable a month in advance), 2 hours 20 minutes, US$54 per vehicle, bike US$12, foot passengers US$8.65. From Porvenir a 234 km *ripio* road runs east to Río Grande (six hours, no public transport) via San Sebastián. **Note** Fruit and meat may not be taken onto the island, nor between Argentina and Chile. ▸▸ *See also Transport, page 265. For details of transport and hotels on Chilean territory, see the Chile chapter.*

Río Grande and around → *Population: 53,000. Phone code: 02964. Colour map 9, C2.*

Río Grande is a sprawling modern town in windy, dust-laden sheep-grazing and oil-bearing plains. (The oil is refined at San Sebastián in the smallest and most southerly refinery in the world.) Government tax incentives to companies in the 1970s led to a rapid growth in population. Although incentives were withdrawn, it continues to expand, most recently into mobile phone and white goods assembly. The city was founded by Fagnano's Salesian mission in 1893; you can visit the original building **La Candelaria** ⓘ *11 km north, T430667, Mon-Sat 1000-1230, 1500-1900, Sun 1500-1900, US$1.50, afternoon teas, US$3, getting there: taxi US$6 with wait.* The museum has displays of indigenous artefacts and natural history. Río Grande's **Museo Virginia Choquintel** ⓘ *Alberdi 555, T430647, Mon-Fri 0900-1700, Sat 1500-1900* is also recommended for its history of the Selk'nam, the pioneers, missions and oil. Next door is a handicraft shop called **Kren** ("sun" in Selk'nam), which sells good local products. Nearby estancias can be visited, notably **María Behety** (15 km), with a vast sheep-shearing shed, but the area's main claim to fame is sport-fishing, especially for trout. **Local festivals**: Sheep shearing in January. Rural exhibition and handicrafts 2nd week February. Shepherd's day, with impressive sheepdog display first week March. **Tourist office** is on the plaza ⓘ *Rosales 350, T431324, rg-turismo@netcombbs.com.ar, Mon-Fri 0900-1700. Provincial office: Alberdi 131, T422887.*

Tolhuin → *Colour map 9, C2.*

About 20 km south of Río Grande, trees begin to appear on the steppe while the road, Ruta 3, runs parallel to the seashore. On Sunday people drive out to the woods for picnics, go fishing or look for shellfish on the mudflats. The road is mostly very good as it approaches the mountains to the south. **Tolhuin**, "la corazón de la isla" at the eastern tip of Lago Fagnano, is 1¼ hours from Río Grande. The small town is caters for horse riders, anglers, mountain bikers and trekkers. There are cabins, hostels and campsites. On Sunday it is crammed full of day-trippers. The **Panificadora La Unión** in the centre is renowned for its breads, pastries and chocolate and is an obligatory stop. Líder and Montiel minibuses break the Río Grande-Ushuaia journey here. **Tourist office** ⓘ *Av de los Shelknam 80, T02901-492125, tolhuinturismo@tierradelfuego.org.ar.*

The road leaves Lago Fagnano and passes *lenga* forest destroyed by fire in 1978 before climbing into healthier forests. After small Lago Verde and fjord-like Lago Escondido, the road crosses the cordillera at Paso Garibaldi. It then descends to the Cerro Castor winter sports complex and the Tierra Mayor recreation area (see Ushuaia Activities and tours, below). There is a police control just as you enter the Ushuaia city limits; passports may be checked.

Río Grande and around listings

For Sleeping and Eating price codes and other relevant information, see Essentials, pages 38-40.

Sleeping

Río Grande *p255*

Book ahead, as there are few decent choices. Several estancias offer full board and some, mainly on the northern rivers, have expensive fishing lodges, others offer horse riding.

See www.tierradelfuego.org.ar and www.estanciasfueguinas.com.

LL pp **Estancia Viamonte**, 40 km southeast on the coast, T430861, www.estanciaviamonte.com. For an authentic experience of Tierra del Fuego, built in 1902 by pioneer Lucas Bridges, writer of *Uttermost Part of the Earth*, to protect the Selk'nam/ Ona people, this working *estancia* has simple and beautifully furnished rooms in a spacious cottage. Price is for full board and all activities: riding and trekking; **AL** pp for dinner, bed and breakfast only. Delicious meals. Book a week ahead.

A Posada de los Sauces, Elcano 839, T430868, www.posadadelossauces.com.ar. Best by far, with breakfast, beautifully decorated, comfortable, good restaurant (trout recommended), cosy bar, very helpful staff.

B Isla del Mar, Güemes 963, T422883, www.hotelguia.com/hoteles/isladelmar. Pink building on river front, has seen better days, breakfast is included and staff are very friendly.

B Villa, Av San Martín 281, T424998, hotelvillarg@hotmail.com. Central, modern, restaurant/confitería, internet, TV, parking, discount given for cash.

C Argentino, San Martín 64, T422546, hotelargentino@yahoo.com. Room with bath, **E** pp without bath, camping **G** pp, oldest hotel in city, breakfast included, Wi-Fi, internet, kitchen, parking, book exchange, library, helpful owner.

Camping

Refugio Camping Club Náutico, T420536, nauticorg@speedy.com.ar, Rita and Carlos Hansen. Very helpful.

Tolhuin *p255*

AL-A Cabañas Khami, on Lago Fagnano, 8 km from Tolhuin, T422296, www.cabanaskhami.com.ar. Well-equipped, rustic cabins, good value with linen. Price given for 6 people, 3-night weekend rates available.

Eating

Río Grande *p255*

TT El Rincón de Julio, next to **Posada de los Sauces**, Elcano 800 block. For excellent *parrilla*.

TT La Nueva Colonial, Av Belgrano y Lasserre. Delicious pasta, warm family atmosphere.

TT La Rueda, Islas Malvinas 998. Excellent *parrilla*, has another branch on O'Higgins 200 block.

T La Nueva Piamontesa, Av Belgrano y Mackinlay, T426332. Cheap set menus and take away.

Cafés

El Roca (sic), Espora entre Av San Martín y Rosales, ½ block from Plaza. **Confitería** and bar in historic premises (the original cinema), good and popular.

Tío Willy, Alberdi entre Espora y 9 de Julio. Serves *cerveza artesanal* (micro brewery).

Transport

Río Grande *p255*

Air Airport 4 km west of town, T420600. Taxi US$2. To **Buenos Aires**, **AR** daily, 3½ hrs direct. LADE flies to **Río Gallegos**.

Bus To **Punta Arenas**, Chile, via Punta Delgada, 7-9 hrs, **Pacheco** (25 de Mayo 712, T425611) and **Tecni Austral** (Moyano 516, T430610), US$28.50. To **Río Gallegos**, **Tecni Austral**, Mon-Sat, 8 hrs, US$28.50; **Marga** (Mackinley 545, T434316), daily, 0900, links with **Taqsa**, connection to El Calafate and Comodoro Rivadavia.

To **Ushuaia**, 3½-4 hrs, **Montiel** (25 de Mayo 712, T420997) and **Líder** (Perito Moreno 635, T420003, www.lidertdf.com.ar), US$16.50. Both use small buses, frequent departures. They stop en route at **Tolhuin**, US$8.25. Also **Tecni Austral**, about 1600 (bus has come from Punta Arenas), and **Pacheco**.

Car hire **Europcar**, Av Belgrano 423, T430365. **Localiza**, San Martín 642, T430191.

ⓒ Directory

Río Grande *p255*

Airline offices Aerolineas Argentinas, San Martín 607,T424467, Mon-Fri 0900-1230, 1500-1900, Sat 0930-1200. **LADE**, Lasserre 445, T422968. **Banks** ATMs: several banks on San Martín by junction with Av 9 de Julio. **Link** ATM at YPF station at river end of Belgrano. **Thaler** cambio, Rosales 259, open Mon-Fri 1000-1500. **Consulates** Chile, Belgrano 369, T430523, Mon-Fri 0900-1400. **Post offices** Rivadavia 968. **Supermarkets** Norte, San Martín y Piedrabuena, good selection; also **La Anónima** on San Martín near Belgrano. **Telephone** *Locutorios* along San Martín, some with internet.

Ushuaia and around → *Phone code: 02901. Colour map 9, C2. Population: 45,000.*

Situated 212 km southwest of Río Grande, the most southerly town in Argentina and growing fast, Ushuaia is beautifully positioned on the northern shore of the Beagle Channel, named after the ship in which Darwin sailed here in 1832. Its streets climb steeply towards snow-covered Cerro Martial and there are fine views to neighbouring peaks and over the Beagle Channel to the jagged peaks of Isla Navarino (Chile). **Tourist offices** ⓘ *San Martín 674, esq Fadul, T/F424550, www.turismoushuaia.com. Mon-Fri 0800-2200, Sat-Sun 0900-2000.* 'Best in Argentina', helpful English-speaking staff, who find accommodation in summer. Information available in English, French and German. There is a tourist office at the **Muelle Turístico** ⓘ *0800-1800*, and desk at the airport. **Oficina Antártica**, at ⓘ *Muelle Turístico, T423340, antartida@tierradelfuego.org.ar, Mon-Fri 0900-1900*, has information on Antarctica and a small library with navigational charts. **Provincial tourist office** ⓘ *Maipú 505, T423340, info@tierradelfuego.org.ar.*

Time to visit March-April is a good time because of the autumn colours and the most stable weather. November, spring, has the strongest winds (not good for sailing to Antarctica). Most visitors arrive in January. Summer temperatures average at about 15°C, but exceed 20° more frequently than in the past. Likewise, there has been a reduction in snowfall in winter (average temperature 0°C). Lots of Brazilians come to ski, so a there is a mini high season in July-August. European skiers also come to train in the northern hemisphere summer.

Sights

First settled in 1884 by missionary Thomas Bridges, whose son Lucas became a great defender of the indigenous peoples here, Ushuaia's fascinating history is still visible in its old buildings and at **Estancia Harberton**, 85 km west (see below). A penal colony for many years, the old prison, **Presidio** ⓘ *Yaganes y Gob Paz, at the back of the Naval Base, Mon-Sun 0900-2000, US$11.75 for foreigners, ticket valid 48 hrs, tours in Spanish 1130, 1830, English 1400* houses the small **Museo Marítimo**, with models and artefacts from seafaring days, and, in the cells of most of the huge five wings, the **Museo Penitenciario**, which details the history of the prison and of the pioneers who came to the area. There are also temporary exhibitions, a shop and a café. Highly recommended. **Museo del Fin del Mundo** ⓘ *Maipú y Rivadavia, T421863, www.tierradel fuego.org.ar/museo, daily 0900-2000 (Mon-Sat 1200-1900 May-Oct), US$5, guided tours 1100, 1400, 1700, fewer in winter.* In the 1912 bank building, it has small displays on indigenous peoples, missionaries and first settlers, as well as nearly all the birds of Tierra del Fuego (stuffed). Recommended. The building also contains an excellent library with helpful staff. **Museo Yámana** ⓘ *Rivadavia 56, T422874, www.tierradelfuego.org.ar/mundoyamana, daily 1000-2000 high season, 1200-1900 low season, US$3.35.* Scale models depicting the geological evolution of the island and the everyday life of Yamana people, texts in English, also recommended. The **Antigua Casa de Gobierno** ⓘ *Maipú 465, Mon-Fri 1000-1200, weekends 1500-2000, free*, is another building open to the public with an exhibition on the history of the city and temporary exhibitions. Local events: second half of April, Classical Music Festival (www.festivaldeushuaia.com); winter solstice, the longest night with a torch-light procession and fireworks, 20-21 June; August, annual sled dog race and Marcha Blanca, a ski trek from Lago Escondido to Tierra Mayor valley.

Cerro Martial, about 7 km behind the town, offers fine views down the Beagle Channel and to the north. Take a chairlift (*aerosilla)*, daily first up 0930, last up 1645, last down 1730, US$8.25, tariffs change in winter, closed for repair for a time in April. To reach the chairlift, follow Magallanes out of town, allow 1½ hours. Several companies run minibus services from the corner of Maipú and Fadul, frequent departures daily in summer. Taxis charge US$5 to the base, from where you can walk down all the way back. There are several marked trails, leaflet given out at the lower platform, including to a viewpoint and to **Glaciar Martial** itself, from 600 m to 1 km. Splendid tea shop at the *Cumbres de Martial cabañas* at the base; basic *refugio* with no electricity up at the Cerro. Also by the lower platform is the **Canopy** ⓘ *USS$26, 16 for a shorter run, T02901-15510307, www.canopyushuaia.com.ar*, a series of zip lines and bridges in the trees, eight stretches of about 500 m in total (to be extended). All visitors are accompanied by staff, safe, good fun. The café at the entrance, **Refugio de Montaña**, serves hot chocolate and coffee, cakes, pizzas and has a warm stove.

Ushuaia Acuario ⓘ *Perito Moreno 2564, T422980, www.ushuaiaaquarium.com, US$8.35.* Near the shore, the aquarium exhibits only the fauna of the Beagle Channel, from the simplest anemones and bivalves, to *róbalo*, trout and *centolla*. All are in tanks filled with water direct from the Canal. It also has a small museum and video. Information signs in Spanish, some in English – don't steal them like everyone else does.

The **Estancia Harberton** ⓘ *T422742, ngoodall@tierradelfuego.org.ar, US$6.60, daily 15 Oct-15 Apr, except 25 Dec, 1 Jan and Easter, museum: US$3.30*, the oldest on the island and run by descendants of British missionary, Thomas Bridges, whose family protected the indigenous peoples here, is 85 km from Ushuaia on Ruta J. It's a beautiful place, offering guided walks

Ushuaia

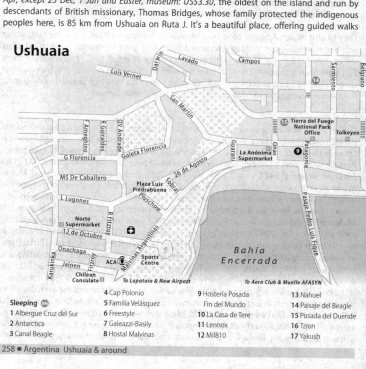

Sleeping
1 Albergue Cruz del Sur
2 Antarctica
3 Canal Beagle
4 Cap Polonio
5 Familia Velásquez
6 Freestyle
7 Galeazzi-Basily
8 Hostal Malvinas
9 Hostería Posada Fin del Mundo
10 La Casa de Tere
11 Lennox
12 Mil810
13 Nahuel
14 Paisaje del Beagle
15 Posada del Duende
16 Tzion
17 Yakush

through protected forest and delicious teas, US$6.60, or lunch, US$15 (reserve ahead), in the *Mánakatush casa de té* overlooking the bay. The impressive **Museo Acatushún** ⓘ *www.acatushun.org*, has skeletons of South American sea mammals and birds, the result of 25 years' scientific investigation in Tierra del Fuego, with excellent tours in English. You can camp free, with permission from the owners, or stay in cottages. Access is from a good unpaved road which branches off Ruta 3, 40 km east of Ushuaia and runs 45 km through forest before the open country around Harberton; marvellous views, about two hours (no petrol outside of Ushuaia and Tolhuin). The road passes Laguna Victoria, where there is a good chance of seeing condors, and the turning to Puerto Almansa fishing port.

Short boat excursions from Ushuaia are highly recommended, though the Beagle Channel can be very rough. These can be booked through most agencies. They leave from the **Muelle Turístico**, where all operators have ticket booths and representatives (**Tolkeyen and Rumbo Sur** also have offices on San Martín). All passengers must pay US$1.65 port tax; this is not included in tickets. Operators offer slight variations on a basic theme of trips to Isla de los Lobos, Isla de los Pájaros, Les Eclaireurs lighthouse and Harberton. See under Activites and tours below for details of these and of longer sea trips.

Tren del Fin del Mundo ⓘ *T431600, www.trendelfindelmundo.com.ar, 5 departures daily, US$28 tourist, US$50 1st class return, cheaper in winter, plus US$10 park entrance and cost of transport to the station, tickets at station, or travel agencies, sit on left outbound for the best views*, is the world's southernmost steam train, running new locomotives and carriages on track first laid by prisoners to carry wood to Ushuaia. A totally touristy experience with commentary in English and Spanish (written material in other languages), 50-minute ride from the Fin del Mundo station, 8 km west of Ushuaia, into Tierra del Fuego National Park (one way of starting a hike). There is one stop at Estación Macarena, 15 minutes, for a view of the river and a walk up to

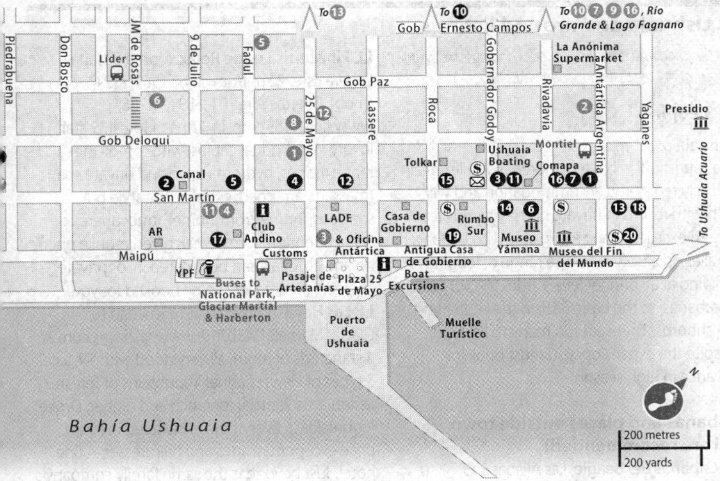

Eating
1 137 Pizzas & Pastas
2 Bodegón Fueguino
3 Café Bar Banana
4 Café de la Esquina
5 Café Tante Sara
6 Chicho's
7 Cositas Ricas
8 El Bambú
9 El Turco
10 Kaupé
11 La Estancia
12 Laguna Negra
13 Martinica
14 Moustacchio
15 Panadería Petit Real
16 Parrilla La Rueda
17 Ramos Generales
18 Sandwichería Kami
19 Tía Elvira
20 Volver

Macarena waterfall. In 1st class you can buy food and drinks at the station *confitería* to eat at your table. At the same entrance as the train station is Ushuaia's 9-hole golf course.

Parque Nacional Tierra del Fuego

ⓘ US$13. Tierra del Fuego National Park Office, San Martín 1395, Ushuaia, T421315, tierradelfuego@apn.gov.ar, Mon-Fri 0900-1600. Tourist office and National Park office have details and a map of park, with walks. For buses see Transport, page 256.

Covering 63,000 ha of mountains, lakes, rivers and deep valleys, this small but beautiful park stretches west to the Chilean border and north to Lago Fagnano, though large areas are closed to tourists. Public access is allowed from the park entrance 12 km west of Ushuaia, where you'll be given the basic map with marked walks. **1) Senda Costera**, 8 km, three hours each way. Along the shore from Ensenada. From Lago Roca, continue along to Río Lapataia, crossing the broad green river, where there are more short paths to follow. From Ensenada a boat goes to Isla Redonda, a provincial Reserva Natural, first at 1000, last back at 1700, US$23 return, US$30 to Isla Redonda and on to Lapataia. There are four trails on island, 2 hours, a refugio for sleeping, hot water, and a post office, open end-October to beginning of April. **2) Senda Hito XXIV**, along the northeast shore of Lago Roca to the Chilean frontier, 3.5 km, 90 minutes one way, lots of birdlife. **3) Cerro Guanaco** (1,106 m), 4 km, four hours one way. Challenging hike up through forest to splendid views. 4) Senda Pampa Alta, 4.9 km via a *mirador* (look out), or 3.7 km via the road, to Río Pipo. The main campsite is in a good spot at Lago Roca: see below for details of this and other sites. It's best to go in the early morning or afternoon to avoid the tour buses. You'll see geese, the torrent duck, Magellanic woodpeckers and austral parakeets. There are no legal crossing points to Chile. Helpful *guardaparque* (ranger) at Lago Roca. Remember that the weather can be cold, damp and unpredictable, even in summer; winter days are short.

Ushuaia and around listings

For Sleeping and Eating price codes and other relevant information, see Essentials, pages 38-40.

Sleeping

Ushuaia *p257, map p258*

The tourist office has a comprehensive list of all officially registered accommodation and will help with rooms in private homes, campsites, etc. An excellent choice is to stay with Ushuaia families on a B&B basis. The range of lodging is growing at all budget levels, from the very chic, to cabañas, to the basic B&B, in the centre and the suburbs. There are too many to list here. Despite the expansion, you must book in advance in high season.

Cabañas and places outside town (all are recommended)

LL Cabañas del Beagle, Las Aljabas 375, T432785/1551 1323, www.cabaniasdelbeagle.com. 3 rustic-style cabins 1.3 km above the city, fully equipped with kitchen, hydromassage, fireplace, heating, phone, self-service breakfast, very comfortable, personal attention.

LL Finisterris Lodge Relax, Monte Susana, Ladera Este, 7 km from city, T1561 2121 (mob), Buenos Aires 011-5917 8288, www.finisterris.com. In 17 ha of forest, 5-star luxury in individual cabins, with top-of-the-range fittings, hydromassage and private spa (massage arranged, extra), rustic style but spacious, 'home-from-home' atmosphere, 24-hr attention from owner, given mobile phone on arrival. Meals can be ordered in, or private chef and sommelier can be booked for you.

LL Las Hayas, Luis Martial 1650 (road to Glaciar Martial), T430710, www.lashayas.com.ar. 4 standards of room, all very good with TV, safe, 3 types of view, channel, mountains or forest. 2 restaurants: **Martial** for lunch and dinner, **Drake** for breakfast. Everything is included in room price except massages and hairdresser. A fine hotel. Just beyond is the same family company's **LL Los Cauquenes**, at Bahía Cauquen, C Reinamora 3462, T441300, www.loscauquenes.com. High quality 5-star hotel overlooking Beagle Channel, price varies according to size and view, spa, very tastefully decorated, prize-winning restaurant with US$13 lunch menu, regional food on dinner menu.

LL Cumbres del Martial, Luis F Martial 3560, 7 km from town, T424779, www.cumbresdelmartial.com.ar. At the foot of the *aerosilla* to Glaciar Martial, 4 cabañas and 6 rooms, beautifully set in the woods, charming, very comfortable, cabins have whirlpool baths. Small spa (massage extra) with saunas. The tearoom is open all year, restaurant from Dec.

LL Los Yámanas, Costa de los Yámanas 2850, western suburbs, T445960, www.hotelyamanas.com.ar. In the same group as Canoero tour operator, all rooms with Channel view, spacious, well-decorated with DirectTV, Wi-Fi, hydromassage, fitness centre, spa and conference centre outside in wooded grounds, shuttle to town. Very pleasant.

L Los Acebos, Luis F Martial 1911, T011-4393 4750, www.losacebos.com.ar. All rooms with channel view, safe, Wi-Fi, free internet, games room, **Rêve d'Orange** restaurant independent of hotel. Very comfy, as expected, but less characterful than Las Hayas.

L Tierra de Leyendas, Tierra de Vientos 2448, T443565, www.tierradeleyendas.com.ar. In the western suburbs. Five very comfortable rooms with views of the Beagle Channel, or the mountains at the back, 1 room with jacuzzi, all others with shower, excellent restaurant serving regional specialties, open only for guests for breakfast and dinner. Free internet, no cable TV, but DVDs, living room with games, library, deck overlooking Río Pipo's outflow. Only for non smokers. Recommended and award-winning.

A-B pp **Estancia Harberton**, T422742, harberton@tierradelfuego.org.ar. 2 restored buildings on the estancia (see above), very simple rooms, wonderful views, heating. Price includes breakfast, walking tour and entry to museum; 2 rooms with bath, 1 room with 2 beds, shared bath, 1 room with bunks, shared bath. Kitchenette for tea and coffee. Lunch and dinner US$30 pp without drinks. Open mid-Oct-mid-Apr.

In town

L Canal Beagle, Maipú y 25 de Mayo, T432303, www.hotelcanalbeagle.com.ar. ACA hotel (discounts for members), **AL-A** Apr-Oct, comfortable and well-attended, with a small pool, gym, sauna, clear views over the channel from some rooms (others see the container dock), good restaurant.

L Lennox, San Martín 776, T436430, www.lennoxhotel.com.ar. Boutique hotel on the main street, with breakfast, services include internet, hydromassage, TV, frigobar, restaurant and confitería on 4th floor.

L Mil810, 25 de Mayo 245, T437710, www.hotel1810.com. City hotel with 30 standard rooms, one with disabled access, no restaurant but breakfast and confitería, all rooms with flat-screen TV, minibar, safe, quite small but cosy, calm colours, good views, business centre and multiple use room where you can hang out while waiting for flight.

AL Cap Polonio, San Martín 746, T422140, www.hotelcappolonio.com.ar. Smart, central, modern, comfortable, TV, free internet, Wi-Fi, popular restaurant/café *Marcopolo*.

A-B Paisaje del Beagle, Gob Paz 1347, T421214, www.paisajedelbeagle.com. Family-run, quiet, with a cosy dining area for good breakfast (included), free internet, laundry service. Recommended.

B Hostal Malvinas, Gob Deloqui 615, T/F422626, www.hostalmalvinas.net. Comfortable but small rooms, small breakfast, free tea and coffee.

B Hostería Posada Fin del Mundo, Gob Valdez 281, T437345, www.posadafindelmundo.com.ar. Family atmosphere, comfortable rooms, good value, has character.

B Nahuel, 25 de Mayo 440, T423068, byb_nahuel@ yahoo.com.ar. Charming and talkative Sra Navarrete has a comfortable B&B with channel views from the upper rooms and the terrace, good value, but noisy street.

C Galeazzi-Basily, Gdor Valdez 323, T423213, www.avesdelsur.com.ar. Easily the best, beautiful family home, incredible welcome, in pleasant area 5 blocks from centre, breakfast included, shared bath, free internet. Also excellent *cabañas* (**A**) in the garden. Recommended.

C pp **La Casa de Tere**, Rivadavia 620, T422312, www.lacasadetere.com.ar. Shared bath, with breakfast, homemade bread and cake, use of kitchen, some rooms get lots of sun, singles, doubles and triples, hot water, helpful owner.

C Tzion, Gob Valdez 468, T432290, tzion_byb@hotmail.com. B & B with 3 rooms, 1 with bath

(**B**), high above town, 10 mins' walk from centre, nice family atmosphere (contact Daniel Pirruccio at Tolkar Turismo), cheaper low season, laundry service, English and French spoken.

C-D Familia Velásquez, Juana Fadul 361, T421719, almayo@arnet.com.ar. Cosy, welcoming house of a pioneer, with basic rooms, breakfast, cooking and laundry facilities, good.

D-E pp **Antárctica**, Antártida Argentina 270, T435774, www.antarcticahostel.com. Central, welcoming, spacious chill-out room, excellent 24-hr bar, dorms for 6 and large doubles, breakfast, free internet/Wi-Fi and kitchen facilities, bike rental (US$8.50 per day). Recommended.

E pp **Albergue Cruz del Sur**, Deloqui 636, T434099, www.xdelsur.com.ar. Welcoming Italian owner Luca, a nice, relaxed and small house with library, kitchen facilities and free tea, coffee and mate, book in advance, free internet, good for smokers. Recommended.

E pp **Freestyle**, Gob Paz 866, T432874, www.ushuaiafreestyle.com. Very busy but good, central hostel, with laundry (US$3), TV room, DVDs and pool table. Also has doubles with bath (**B**), TV and kitchenette, which will move to new **Alto Andino** hotel, which is being built in front.

E-F pp **Yakush**, Piedrabuena 118 y San Martín, T435807, www.hostelyakush.com.ar. Very-well run, central with spacious dorms, also doubles (**B** with bath, **C** without), with breakfast, free internet, book exchange and library, light kitchen and dining room and a steep garden with views. Recommended.

F pp **Posada del Duende**, Deloqui 1482, T432562, posadadelduende@hotmail.com. Also has doubles with bath (**C**), kitchen, email, hot water and heating, laundry service.

Camping In town: **La Pista del Andino**, Leandro N Alem 2873, T435890, www.lapistadelandino.com.ar. Set in the Club Andino ski premises in a woodland area, it has wonderful views over the channel. Electricity, hot showers, tea room and grocery store, US$11 per pitch, very helpful. Recommended.

Parque Nacional Tierra del Fuego *p260*

Camping

Camping Lago Roca, T433313, 21 km from Ushuaia, by forested shore of Lago Roca, a beautiful site with good facilities, reached by bus Jan-Feb. It has a backpackers' *refugio*, toilets, showers 1800-2030, restaurant and confitería, expensive small shop; camping US$4, equipment for hire with deposit, eg US$100 for tent, 40 for sleeping bag. There are also *camping agreste* sites with no facilities at **Río Pipo** 16 km from Ushuaia, **Laguna Verde**, 20 km, near Lapataia, and **Bahía Ensenada**.

Eating

Ushuaia *p257, map p258*

Lots of restaurants along San Martín and Maipú. Most open at lunchtime and again from 1900 at the earliest. Several cafés are open all the time. Ask around for currently available seafood, especially *centolla* (king crab) and *cholga* (giant mussels). Much cheaper if prepare your own meal; **Pesquera del Beagle**, Maipú 227 (closed 1600-1800 on Sun, 1300-1600 Mon), sells *centollón* (US$15 per kg ready to eat) and *centolla* (US$11 per kg; US$22.50 per kg ready to eat, just add lemon). Note *Centolla* may not be fished Nov-Dec. Beer drinkers should try the handcrafted brews of the **Cape Horn** brewery, Pilsen, Pale Ale and Stout.

TTT **Bodegón Fueguino**, San Martín 859. Tapas, homemade pastas and good roast lamb with varied sauces in a renovated 1896 *casa de pioneros*, open 1200-1500, 2000-2400, closed Mon.

TTT **Kaupé**, Roca 470 y Magallanes, T437396. Best restaurant in town, king crab, meat.

TTT **Tía Elvira**, Maipú 349. Excellent seafood, open Mon-Sat 1200-1500, 1900-2300.

TTT **Volver**, Maipú 37. Delicious seafood and fish in atmospheric 1898 house, with ancient newspaper all over the walls. Recommended.

TTT-TT **La Estancia**, San Martín 253. A cheery and good value *parrilla*. Packed in high season. All-you-can-eat for US$13.

TTT-TT **Moustacchio**, two branches 2 doors apart, San Martín 272 and at Gdor Godoy. Long established, good for seafood and meat, all-you-can-eat branch US$13.

TTT-TT **Parrilla La Rueda**, San Martín y Rivadavia. Good *tenedor libre* (US$14 with dessert) for beef, lamb and great salads. Recommended for freshness.

TT **137 Pizzas and Pastas**, San Martín 137. Tasty filling versions of exactly what the name says, plus *empanadas*, elegant decor.

¶¶ **Chicho's**, Rivadavia 72, T423469. Bright, cheerful place just off the main street, friendly staff, kitchen open to view. Fish, meat and chicken dishes, pastas, wide range of *entradas*.

¶¶ **El Turco**, San Martín 1410. A very popular place, serving generous milanesas, pastas, pizzas, seafood and meat.

¶¶-¶ **Martinica**, San Martín entre Antártida Argentina y Yaganes. Cheap, small, busy, sit at the bar facing the *parrilla* and point to your favourite beef cut. Takeaway (T432134) and good meals of the day, also pizzas and *empanadas*. Open 1130-1500, 2030-2400.

Cafés

El Bambú, Piedrabuena 276. Purely vegetarian and the only such place in town, take-away only, homemade food, delicious and good value.

Café Bar Banana, San Martín 273, T424021. Quite small, always busy, with a pool table at the back, offers good fast food, such as burgers, small pizzas, puddings, breakfasts and an all-day menú for US$7.50.

Café Chocolates, San Martín 783. Good *submarinos* (hot chocolate) and home made chocolate, also good value.

Café de la Esquina, San Martín y 25 de Mayo. Lots of lunch choices, daily specials, sandwiches, *tortas*, *picadas*, *lomitos*, café and bar. Open for 15 years, used by locals and tourists alike.

Café Tante Sara, San Martin y Fadul. Opposite the tourist office, is very good, smart, good coffee, tasty sandwiches, always busy. Also has **Cositas Ricas** at San Martín 185, a smart *confitería* and *chocolatería*, selling breads, sandwiches, chocolates, *empanadas* and snacks, coffee, lots of choice.

Laguna Negra, San Martín 513. Mainly a shop selling chocolate and other fine produce, catering to the cruise ship passengers, but has a good little café at the back for hot chocolate and coffee. Also at Libertador 1250, El Calafate. Sells postcards and stamps, too.

Panadería Petit Ideal, next to **Bar Ideal**, San Martín 393, which is a ¶¶¶ restaurant serving seafood and meat dishes in an old building at the corner of Roca. Good selection.

Ramos Generales, Maipú 749, T424317, www.ramosgeneralesushuaia.com. An old warehouse, with wooden floor and shelves and a collection of historic objects and dusty ledgers. Sells breads, pastries, wines and drinks, also cold cuts, sandwiches, salads, ice cream and coffee. Also has a dish of the day or soup for lunch, breakfasts till 1300, teas 1300-2000. Not cheap but atmospheric. Recommended.

Sandwichería Kami, San Martín 54, open 0800-2130. Friendly, simple sandwich shop, selling rolls, baguettes and *pan de miga*.

O Shopping

Ushuaia *p257, map p258*

Ushuaia's tax free status doesn't produce as many bargains as you might hope. Lots of souvenir shops on San Martín and several offering good quality leather and silver ware. In comparison, the **Pasaje de Artesanías**, by the Muelle Turístico, sells local arts and crafts.

Atlántico Sur, San Martín 627, is the (not especially cheap) duty free shop.

Boutique del Libro, San Martín y Piedrabuena and 25 de Mayo 62. A good range of books on Patagonia and Antarctica, also DVDs, English titles and guidebooks.

La Anónima, Gob Paz y Rivadavia and San Martín y Onas. Large supermarket.

Norte, 12 de Octubre y Karukinka. Supermarket, takeaway, fresh food, and fast-food diner.

▲ Activities and tours

Ushuaia *p257, map p258*

Boat trips and cruises

All short boat trips leave from the Muelle Turístico. Take your time to choose the size and style of boat you want. Representatives from the offices are polite and helpful. All have a morning and afternoon sailing and include **Isla de los Lobos, Isla de los Pájaros** and **Les Eclaireurs lighthouse**, with guides and some form of refreshment. Note that weather conditions may affect sailings, prices can change and that port tax is not included.

Barracuda, T437233, barracuda@speedy.com.ar. On a lovely old motor yacht, the first tourist boat in Ushuaia, US$32; their other boat, *Lanín*, includes Isla Bridges, US$36; all trips include a discount at the Acuario (see above).

Canoero, T433893, losyamanas@arnet.com.ar. Catamarans for 60-100 passengers, 2½ trips to the 3 main sites and Isla Bridges, US$36. They also have a 5-hr trip almost daily to the

Pingüinera on Isla Martillo near Estancia Harberton (Oct-Mar only), boats stay for 1 hr, but you cannot land on Martillo. Passengers can return to Ushuaia by bus: US$65 without stops on bus ride, US$76 with stops.

Paludine, T434865, navegandoelfindelmundo@gmail.com. omdern, fast boats with 12 passengers, US$40. Also has all-day trips on a sailing boat, 1000-1700 with lunch, prepared during a trek on Bridges, US$56 all inclusive.

Patagonia Adventure Explorer, T1546 5842, www.patagoniaadvent.com.ar. Has a sailing boat and motor boats for the standard trip, plus Isla Bridges: US$50 sailing, US$40 motoring. Good guides.

Pira-Tour, T1560 4646, piratour@gmail.com. Runs 2-3 buses a day to Harberton, from where a boat goes to the Pingüinera on Isla Martillo: 15 people allowed to land (maximum 45 per day – the only company licensed to do this). US$85 for a morning tour, including lunch at Harberton and entry to Acatushún museum; US$70 for afternoon tour.

Tres Marías, T421987, www.tresmarias web.com. The only company licensed to visit Isla H, which has archaeological sites, cormorants, other birds and plants. Also has sailing boat, no more than 10 passengers; specialist guide, café on board, US$40 on *Tres Marías*, US$50 on sailing boat.

Also **Rumbo Sur** and **Tolkeyen**; see Tours, below.

Sea trips

Ushuaia is the starting point, or the last stop, en route to Antarctica for several cruises from Oct-Mar that usually sail for 9 to 21 days along the western shores of the Antarctic peninsula and the South Shetland Islands. Other trips include stops at Falkland/Malvinas archipelago and at South Georgia. Go to **Oficina Antártica** for advice (see page 257). Agencies sell 'last minute tickets', but the price is entirely dependent on demand (available 1 week before sailing). Coordinator for trips is **Turismo Ushuaia**, Gob Paz 865, T436003, www.ushuaiaturismoevt.com.ar, which operates with IAATO members only. See the website for prices for 2010-2011 season.

To Chile Cruceros Australis, www.australis.com, operates two luxury cruise ships between Ushuaia and **Punta Arenas**, with a visit to Cabo de Hornos, frequently recommended. Full details are given under Punta Arenas, Tour operators. Check-in at **Comapa** (see below).

Ushuaia Boating, Deloqui 302 y Godoy, T436153 (or at the Muelle Turístico), T436193, ushuaiaboating@argentina.com.ar. Operates all year round a channel crossing to Puerto Navarino (Isla Navarino), 20-90 mins depending on weather, and then bus to Puerto Williams, 1 hr, US$100 one way, not including US$6.60 taxes. At **Muelle AFASYN**, near the old airport, T435805, ask about possible crossings with a club member to Puerto Williams, about 4 hrs, or if any foreign sailing boat is going to Cabo de Hornos or Antarctica. From Puerto Williams a ferry goes once a week to Punta Arenas.

Fishing

Trout season is Nov-mid Apr, licences US$13.25 per day (an extra fee is charged for some rivers and lakes). **Asociación de Caza y Pesca** at Maipú 822, T423168, cazapescush@infovia.com.ar, open Mon, Wed, Fri 1700-2100, sells licences, with list on door of other places that sell it.

Hiking and climbing

Club Andino, Fadul 50, T422335, www.clubandinoushuaia.com.ar. For advice, Mon-Fri 1000-1200, 1400-2030. Sells maps and trekking guidebooks; free guided walks once in a month in summer; also offers classes, eg yoga, dancing, karate-do and has excercise bikes. The winter sports resorts along Ruta 3 (see below) are an excellent base for summer trekking and many arrange excursions.

Nunatak, 25 de Mayo 296, T430329, www.nunatakadventure.com. Organizes treks, canoeing, mountain biking and 4WD trips to Lagos Escondido and Fagnano.

Horse riding

Centro Hípico, Ruta 3, Km 3021, T443996, 1556 9099 (mob), www.centrohipicoushuaia.com.ar. Rides through woods, on Monte Susana, along coast and through river, 2 hrs, US$35; 4-hr ride with light lunch, US$70; 7-hr ride with asado, US$105. Gentle horses, well-cared for, all guides have first-aid training. Very friendly and helpful. All rides include transfer from town and insurance. Hats provided for children; works with handicapped children. They can arrange long-distance rides of several days, eg on Península Mitre.

Winter sports

Ushuaia is becoming popular as a winter resort with 11 centres for skiing, snowboarding and husky sledging. The **Cerro Castor complex**, Ruta 3, Km 27, T499301, www.cerrocastor.com, is the only centre for Alpine skiing, with 24 km of pistes, a vertical drop of 800 m and powder snow. Attractive centre with complete equipment rental, also for snowboarding and snowshoeing. The other centres along Ruta 3 at 18-36 km east of Ushuaia offer excellent cross country skiing (and alternative activities in summer). **Tierra Mayor**, 20 km from town, T423240, or 155 13463, is the largest and recommended. In a beautiful wide valley between steep-sided mountains, offering half and full day excursions on sledges with huskies, as well as cross country skiing and snowshoeing. Equipment hire and restaurant. **Kawi Shiken** at Las Cotorras, Ruta 3, Km 26, T444152, 1551 9497 (mob), www.tierradelfuego.org.ar/hugoflores, specializes in sled dogs, with 100 Alaskan and Siberian huskies: 2 km ride on snow US$20, 2-hr trips with meal US$56. In summer offers 2-km rides in a odg cart, US$13.50.

Tours

Lots of companies offer imaginative adventure tourism expeditions. All agencies charge the same fees for excursions; ask tourist office for a complete list: Tierra del Fuego National Park, 4 hrs, US$30 (entry fee US$10 extra); Lagos Escondido and Fagnano, 7 hrs, US$45 without lunch. With 3 or 4 people it might be worth hiring a *remise* taxi.

All Patagonia, Juana Fadul 40, T433622, www.allpatagonia.com. Trekking, ice climbing, and tours; trips to Cabo de Hornos and Antarctica.

Canal, 9 de Julio 118, loc 1, T437395, www.canalfun.com. Huge range of activities, trekking, canoeing, riding, 4WD excursions. Recommended.

Comapa, San Martín 245, T430727, www.comapa.com. Conventional tours and adventure tourism, bus tickets to Punta Arenas and Puerto Natales, trips to Antarctica, agents for Curceros Australis and for Navimag ferries for Puerto Natales-Puerto Montt (10% ISIC discount for Navimag tickets). **Hertz** also at this office.

Compañía de Guías de Patagonia, San Martín 628, T437753, 1549 3288 (mob), www.compania deguias.com.ar. The best agency for walking guides, expeditions for all levels, rock and ice climbing (training provided), also diving, sailing, riding, 7-day crossing of Tierra del Fuego on foot and conventional tours. Recommended.

Límite Vertical, T1560 0868, www.limite verticaltdf.com.ar. 4WD adventures off-road to the shores of Lagos Escondido and Fagnano, taking logging trails and ripio roads, seeing beaver damage in the forests, etc. Lunch is an asado at an old saw mill; similar tours by other companies stop for lunch on shore of Fagnano. Good fun.

Rumbo Sur, San Martín 350, T422275, www.rumbosur.com.ar. Flights, buses, conventional tours on land and sea, plus Antarctic expeditions, mid-Nov to mid-Mar, English spoken.

Tolkar, Roca 157, T431412, www.tolkar turismo.com.ar. Flights, bus tickets to Argentina and Chile, conventional and adventure tourism, canoeing and mountain biking to Lago Fagnano.

Tolkeyen, San Martín 1267, T437073, www.tolkeyenpatagonia.com. Bus and flight tickets, catamaran trips (50-300 passengers), including to Harberton (Mon, Wed, Fri, US$65) and Parque Nacional, large company.

Travel Lab, San Martín 1444, T436555, travellabush@speedy.com.ar. Conventional and unconventional tours, mountain biking, trekking etc, English and French spoken, helpful.

Turismo de Campo, Fuegia Basket 414, T/F437351, www.turismodecampo.com. Adventure tourism, English/French speaking guides, boat and trekking trips in the National Park, bird watching, sailing and trips to Antarctica.

⊖ Transport

Ushuaia *p257, map p258*

Air Airport 4 km from town. Book ahead in summer; flights fill up fast. In winter flights often delayed. Taxi to airport US$4 (no bus). Schedules tend to change from season to season. Airport tourist information only at flight times, T423970. To **Buenos Aires** (Aeroparque or Ezeiza), 3½ hrs,

El Calafate, 2 hrs, and **Río Gallegos**, 1 hr, with **AR/Austral** and **LADE** (longer flights); also to **Río Grande**, 1 hr, several a week (but check with agents). In summer **LAN** flies to **Punta Arenas** twice a week. The **Aeroclub de Ushuaia** flies Mon, Wed, Fri to **Puerto Williams**, US$100 one way from the downtown airport.

Bus Urban buses from west to east across town, most stops along Maipú, US$0.45. Tourist office provides a list of minibus companies that run daily from town (stops along Maipú) to nearby attractions. To the **National Park**: in summer buses and minibuses leave from the bus stop on Maipú at the bottom of Fadul. **Pasarella**, 9 a day from 0800, last back 1900, US$11.50 return, US$13.30 to Lapataia; **Eben Ezer** 8 a day from 0830, last back 2000. From same bus stop, many other colectivos go to the Tren del Fin del Mundo, Lago Escondido, Lago Fagnano and Glaciar Martial, leave when full. For **Harberton**, check the notice boards at the station at Maipú y Fadul. The only regular bus is run by **Pira-Tur**, see Activities and tours, above. Passport needed when booking international bus tickets. Buses always booked up Nov-Mar; buy your ticket to leave as soon as you arrive. To **Río Grande**, 3½-4 hrs, combis **Líder** (Gob Paz 921, T436421), and **Montiel** (Deloqui 110, T421366), US$16.50. Also buses en route to Río Gallegos and Punta Arenas.

To **Río Gallegos**, **Tecni Austral**, 0530, 11½ hrs, US$40 (through Tolkar), and **Marga/Taqsa**, Godoy 41, daily at 0600. To **Punta Arenas**, **Tecni Austral**, 0530, 11-12 hrs (through Tolkar); **Pacheco**, 0600 and 0800 Thu, Sat, Sun, 12-13 hrs, US$53 (book through **Comapa**, address above), connect with **Bus Sur** for **Puerto Natales**, US$63; **Tolkeyen** Mon, Wed, Fri 0800 US$50, Thu, Sun 0800 US$53.

Car hire Most companies charge from about US$45 per day, including insurance and 200 km per day, special promotions available. **Localiza**, Sarmiento 81, T437780, localizaush@speedy.com.ar. Cars can be hired in Ushuaia to be driven through Chile and then left in any Localiza office in Argentina, but you must buy a one-off customs document for US$50, to use as many times as you like to cross borders. Must reserve well in advance and pay a drop-off fee. **Europcar**, Maipú 857, T430786. **Hertz**, San Martín 245. **Budget**, Godoy 45. Note that hiring a car in Tierra del Fuego is 21% cheaper than anywhere else in the current tax régime.

Taxi Cheaper than *remises*, T422007, T440225. Taxi stand by the Muelle Turístico. **Remises Carlitos**, San Martín y Don Bosco, T422222; **Bahía Hermosa**, T422233.

Directory

Ushuaia *p257, map p258*

Airline offices **Aerolíneas Argentinas**, Maipú 823, T422267, Mon-Fri 0930-1700, Sat 0930-1200, airport office opens daily 0800-2000. **LADE**, San Martín 542, shop 5, T421123. Open Mon-Fri 0800-2000, Sat-Sun 0900-1600. **Banks** Banks open 1000-1500 in summer. ATMs are plentiful all along San Martín, using credit cards is easiest (but Sat, Sun and holidays machines can be empty), changing TCs is difficult and expensive. **Banco de Tierra del Fuego**, San Martín 396 (also open on summer weekends 1000-1300 for exchange only). **Agencia de Cambio Thaler**, San Martín 788, loc 15, T421911, open Mon-Fri 1000-1500, 1700-200, Sat 1000-1300, 1700-2000, Sun 1700-2000. **Consulates** **Chile**, Jainén 50, T430909, Mon-Fri 0900-1300. **Germany**, Rosas 516, T430763, rodolfowantz@yahoo.com.ar. **Internet** Many broadband cyber cafés and *locutorios* along San Martín. Another at Paz y 25 de Mayo. **Gigabyte**, Deloqui 395, has Skype. They are often full. **Post offices** San Martín y Godoy, Mon-Fri 1000-1800, Sat 1000-1300. **Telephones** *Locutorios* all along San Martín. **Useful addresses** **Dirección Nacional de Migraciones**, Fuegia Basket 87. **Biblioteca Popular Sarmiento**, San Martín 1589, T423103. Mon-Fri 0830-2000, Sat 1000-1300, library with a good range of books about the area.

Bolivia

Contents

270 Planning your trip

277 La Paz and around
277 Ins and outs
279 Sights
284 Around La Paz

301 Lake Titicaca

312 The Yungas

315 Southwest Bolivia
315 Oruro
322 Uyuni
328 Tupiza

332 Central and Southern Highlands
332 Potosí
338 Sucre
345 Tarija
348 Cochabamba and around

357 Northern Lowlands
357 Madidi and Rurrenabaque
361 Riberalta to Brazil
364 Cochabamba to Trinidad

366 Santa Cruz and Eastern Lowlands
366 Santa Cruz
372 Southeastern Bolivia
379 Eastern Bolivia

Footprint features

268 Don't miss ...
273 Driving in Bolivia
283 Tiny treats
318 La Diablada festival
355 Fiesta de la Virgen de Urkupiña, Quillacollo

At a glance

Time required 2-4 weeks, but don't try to do too much; distances are long and land transport is slow.

Best time Altiplano: all year is good, Jun and Jul are clearest and coldest at night, and busiest. Feb/Mar and Apr good for festivals, but this is wet season. Alasitas in La Paz in late Jan should not be missed. For climbing May-Sep.

When not to go Nov-Mar is the rainy season, heaviest in lowlands but check road conditions everywhere at this time of year.

★ **Don't miss …**

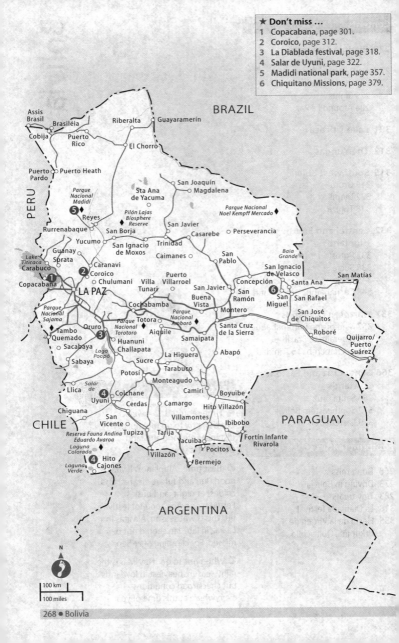

1 Copacabana, page 301.
2 Coroico, page 312.
3 La Diablada festival, page 318.
4 Salar de Uyuni, page 322.
5 Madidi national park, page 357.
6 Chiquitano Missions, page 379.

On Bolivia's Altiplano you are so far up it will make your head spin. Every day in La Paz, the highest seat of government in the world transforms itself from a melée of indigenous markets and modern business into a canyon of glittering stars as the lights come on at nightfall.

Bolivia has some of the most bio-diverse conservation areas in South America: Madidi, Amboró and Noel Kempff Mercado all have an incredible range of habitats and variety of flora and fauna, and you should visit at least one on your journey. If you fancy a trek, there are adventurous trails within a day of the capital, while anyone nostalgic for the revolutionary days of the 1960s can retrace the final steps of Che Guevara. For an exhilarating bike ride, try one of the most dangerous roads in the world, from mountain heights to the lush Yungas valleys, through waterfalls and round hairpin bends – but do go with an expert.

In Bolivia you learn to expect the unexpected. On the largest salt flat on earth, a vast blinding-white expanse, you lose track of what is land and what is sky. At Carnival in Oruro, dancers wear masks of the scariest monsters you could ever dream of. To visit the mines at Potosí, once the silver lode for the Spanish Empire, you buy dynamite and coca leaves as presents for the miners. In the surreal Reserva Eduardo Avaroa, flamingos feed from bright red and green lakes rimmed by volcanoes and Dalí-esque rock structures dot the Altiplano. In the Bolivian Amazon you can swim with pink river dolphins or fish for piranhas.

Before you go home, you can fill your bags with everything from the beautiful autumnal colours of the textiles, to packs of dried llama foetuses. The latter are said to protect homes from evil spirits but are unlikely to ingratiate you with first-world customs and agriculture officers.

Planning your trip

Where to go

La Paz is a good place to start, as many international flights land here and it is closest to the well-travelled overland routes from Peru and Chile. The city is easy to explore, but you do need to adjust to the altitude, which will leave you temporarily breathless. This is, after all, the highest seat of government in the world (Sucre, not La Paz, is Bolivia's official capital). There are some good museums and churches in La Paz, and an indigenous market area. Daytrips include the pre-Inca city of **Tiwanaku**, which is close to beautiful **Lake Titicaca**, where a night or more on its shores is recommended. Northeast of La Paz, over the cordillera, are the **Yungas**, deep subtropical valleys, rich in vegetation, where a town like **Coroico** can provide welcome relief from the chill of the Altiplano. Equally pleasant and also lower than La Paz is **Sorata**, a good base for climbing, trekking and biking.

South of La Paz is the mining city of **Oruro**, which hosts famous carnival celebrations, including the **Diablada** devil-dance, usually held in mid- to late February. Southeast are the colonial cities of **Potosí**, where Spain garnered much of its imperial wealth from abundant silver deposits and present-day miners scour the mountain for meagre pickings; and **Sucre**, one of Bolivia's finest colonial cities with dinosaur-remains nearby. **Uyuni** and **Tupiza**, further south again, are the jumping-off places for trips to high-altitude puna with salt flats, coloured lakes, flamingos and volcanoes. **Tarija**, southeast of Potosí, is best known for its fruits and wine, and delightful climate.

East of La Paz is **Cochabamba**, Bolivia's fourth largest city and centre of one of the country's main agricultural zones. **Parque Toro Toro**, with its dinosaur tracks, rock paintings, canyons and waterfalls, is a tough but stunning excursion. Further east is **Santa Cruz de la Sierra**, the country's most economically important (and largest) city, from where you can visit **Amboró**, **Noel Kempff Mercado** and other national parks, as well as follow in the footsteps of Che Guevara, take in **Samaipata**, with the country's second most important archaeological site, see the fabulous **Jesuit missions** of the Chiquitania, or ride the train to Corumbá in Brazil. Like its eastern neighbour, Bolivia has a **Pantanal** wetland, slowly opening up to tourism, with opportunities to see a magnificent range of wildlife.

From La Paz you can fly into the Beni region, in the heart of the Bolivian Amazon. **Rurrenabaque** is the chief destination and starting point for **Parque Nacional Madidi**, which claims a greater bio-diversity than anywhere else on earth. Outside of Rurrenabaque, the further north you go the fewer tourists you will meet. The dry season (May to September) is the best time to visit, although insects are present year-round.

National parks For information: **Servicio Nacional de Areas Protegidas (SERNAP)** ⓘ *Francisco Bedregal 2904 y Victor Sanjinés, Sopocachi, T242 6242*, mostly an administrative office with limited tourist information. It is best to go to Sernap's regional offices: see ⓘ *www.sernap.gov.bo*. Also **Fundación para el Desarrollo del Sistema Nacional de Areas Protegidas** ⓘ *Fundesnap, Prolongación Cordero 127, La Paz, T211 3364, www.fundesnap.org.*

When to go

The dry season is May to September, July and August see the most tourists, while some of the best festivals, eg Carnival and Holy Week, fall during the wet season – generally December to March. The country has four climatic zones: (1) The Puna and Altiplano; average temperature, 10°C, but above 4000 m may drop as low as -30°C at night from June to August. By day, the tropical sun raises temperatures to above 20°C. Rainfall on the northern Altiplano is 400-700 mm, much less further south. Little rain falls upon the western plateau between May and November, but the rest of the year can be wet. (2) The Yungas north of La Paz and Cochabamba, among the spurs of the Cordillera; altitude, 750-1500 m; average temperature 24°C. Rainfall in the Yungas is 700-800 mm a year, with high humidity.(3) The Valles, or high valleys and basins gouged out by the rivers of the Puna; average temperature 19°C. (4) The tropical lowlands; altitude 150m to 750 m; rainfall is high but seasonal (heaviest November to March, but can fall at any season); large areas suffer from alternate flooding and drought. The climate is hot, ranging from 23° to 25°C in the south and to 30°C in the north. Occasional cold winds from the south, the *surazos*, can lower the temperature suddenly and considerably.

Getting around

Air Internal air services are run by **AeroSur** *www.aerosur.com* (the principal carrier); among its international routes is a flight to Cuzco, 2-3 times a week. **TAM**, the military airline, flies to main cities as well as several smaller and more remote destinations. **Boliviana de Aviación (BoA)**, *www.boa.bo* is the new (in 2009) domestic government airline. **Aerocon** *www.aerocon.bo*, based in Trinidad, serves mostly the northen jungle. **Amaszonas** *www.amaszonas.com* flies between La Paz and Rurrenabaque. Many flights radiate from La Paz, Santa Cruz or Cochabamba. Note that a 'through' flight may require a change of plane, or be delayed waiting for a connecting flight coming from elsewhere. If your internal flight is delayed keep your baggage with you and do not check it in until the flight is definitely announced. There have been reports of theft, so make sure you have adequate baggage insurance.

Bus Buses ply most of the roads. Inter-urban buses are called *flotas*, urban ones *micros* or *minibuses* (vans); *trufis* are shared taxis. Larger bus companies run frequent services and offer a/c, TV and other mod cons, despite the generally poor state of the roads. You can usually buy tickets with reserved seats a day or two in advance. Alternatively, savings may sometimes be obtained by bargaining for fares at the last minute, although not at peak travel times like national holidays. Buses do not always leave at the scheduled time as they may wait to fill first, but you should always be at the terminal on time. A small charge is made for use of major bus terminals; payment is before departure.

In the wet season, bus travel is subject to long delays and detours, at extra cost, and cancellations are not uncommon. On all journeys, take some food, water and toilet paper. It is best to travel by day, not just so you can see the scenery and avoid arriving at your destination at night, but also for better road safety. Bus companies are responsible for any items packed in the luggage compartment or on the roof, but only if they give you a ticket for each bag.

Train The western highland railway is operated by **Ferroviaria Andina** (FCA, www.fca.com.bo). There are passenger trains to the Argentine border at Villazón from Oruro, via Uyuni and Tupiza. The eastern lowland line is run by **Ferroviaria Oriental** (www.ferroviariaoriental.com), with services from Santa Cruz to the Brazilian border. There are also several other minor but potentially interesting train routes

Maps Good maps of Bolivia are few and far between, and maps in general can be hard to find. **Instituto Geográfico Militar** (see page 294, www.igmsantacruz.com). Many IGM maps date from the 1970s and their accuracy is variable; prices also vary, US$4.50-7 a sheet. **Walter Guzmán Córdova** makes several travel and trekking maps, available from some bookshops in La Paz (see page 293). The **German Alpine Club** (**Deutscher Alpenverein**, www.alpenverein.de) produces two maps of Sorata-Ancohuma-Illampu and Illimani, but these are not usually available in La Paz.

Sleeping ➔ *See page 38 for our hotel grade price guide.*

Hotels and hostales Hotels must display prices by law. The number of stars awarded each hotel is also regulated and is fairly accurate. The following terms likewise reflect the size and quality of an establishment (from largest and best, to smallest and simplest): *hotel, hostal, residencial*, and *alojamiento*. A *pensión* is a simple restaurant, not a place to sleep.

Camping Camping is best suited to the wilderness areas of Bolivia, away from towns, villages and people. Organized campsites, car or trailer camping does not exist here. Because of the abundance of cheap hotels you should never have to camp in populated areas

Youth hostels Youth hostels or self-styled 'backpackers' are not necessarily cheaper than hotels. A number of mid-range *residenciales* are affiliated to **Hostelling International** (HI), www.hostellingbolivia.org; some others just say they are. Another website listing hostels is www.boliviahostels.com, but they are not necessarily affiliated to HI.

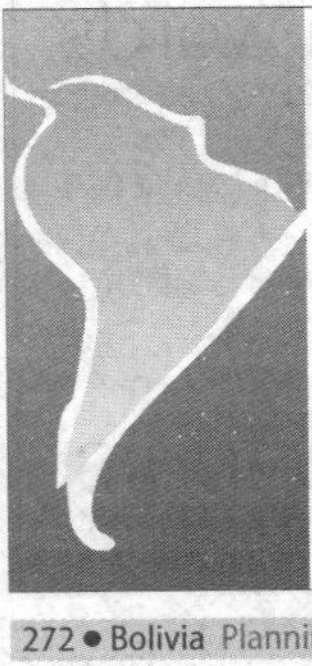

Driving in Bolivia

Road A small percentage of Bolivian roads are paved, under 25% are gravel-surfaced and the rest are earth. Any road, whatever its surface, may be closed in the rainy season (November-March). Road tolls vary from US$0.50 to US$1.50 for journeys up to 100 km. On toll roads you are given a receipt at the first toll; keep it at hand as it is asked for at subsequent toll posts. The Administradora Boliviana de Carreteras (ABC) maintains a useful website, www.abc.gov.bo, with daily updates of road conditions, including any roadblocks due to social unrest. ABC also has a toll-free phone for emergencies and to report road hazards, T800-107222.

Safety Always carry spare petrol/gas and supplies and camping equipment if going off major roads. Your car must be able to cope with altitude and freezing temperatures. Take great care on the roads, especially at night. Too many truck drivers are drunk and many vehicles drive with faulty headlights.

Documents To bring a private vehicle into Bolivia you must always have an International Driving Permit, the vehicle's registration documents and your passport. On entry you must get temporary admission from customs and surrender the document on departure (maximum 90 days; if you leave and re-enter you may – at the discretion of the customs officer – be granted an additional 90 days, up to a maximum of 180 days per year). A *carnet de passages en douane* is not required, but insurance is compulsory. It is called SOAT and can be bought locally. Generally the police are very helpful to foreign motorists.

Organizations **Automóvil Club Boliviano,** Av 6 de Agosto 2993 y Arce, La Paz, T243 2231. Check here for any special documents or permits that may be required.

Car hire The minimum age for hiring a car is 25. Rental companies may only require your licence from home, but police ask to see an international licence. Renal of a small car costs about US$350 per week; a 4WD vehicle US$600 per week or more.

Fuel 85 octane (*especial*), containing lead US$0.50 per litre (may be more when sold from a drum in remote areas). Diesel costs about the same. There may be fuel shortages, keep your tank full.

Eating and drinking → *See page 40 for our Eating price guide.*

Eating out Most restaurants do not open early but many hotels include breakfast, which is also served in markets (see below). In *pensiones* and cheaper restaurants a basic lunch (*almuerzo* – usually finished by 1300) and dinner (*cena*) are normally available. The *comida del día* is the best value in any class of restaurant. Breakfast and lunch can also be found in markets, but eat only what is cooked in front of you. Dishes cooked in the street are not safe. Llama meat contains parasites, so make sure it has been properly cooked, and be especially careful of raw salads as many tourists experience gastrointestinal upsets.

Food Bolivian highland cooking is usually tasty and *picante* (spicy). Recommended local specialities include *empanadas* (cheese pasties) and *humintas* (maize pies); *pukacapas* are *picante* cheese pies. Recommended main dishes include *sajta de pollo*, hot spicy chicken with onion, fresh potatoes and *chuño* (dehydrated potatoes), *parrillada* (mixed grill), *fricase* (juicy pork with *chuño*), *silpancho* (very thin fried breaded meat with eggs, rice and bananas), and *ají de lengua*, ox-tongue with hot peppers, potatoes and *chuño* or *tunta* (another kind of dehydrated potato). *Pique macho*, roast meat, sausage, chips, onion and pepper is especially popular with Bolivians and travellers alike. Near Lake Titicaca fish becomes an important part of the local diet and trout, though not native, is usually delicious. Bolivian soups are usually hearty and warming, including *chairo* made of meat, vegetables and *chuño*. *Salteñas* are very popular meat or chicken pasties eaten as a mid-morning snack, the trick is to avoid spilling the gravy all over yourself.

In the lowland Oriente region, the food usually comes with cooked banana, yucca and rice. The bread in this region is often sweet with cheese on top, and the rice bread is also unusual. In the north lowlands, many types of wild meat are served in tourist restaurants and on jungle tours. Bear in mind that the turtles whose eggs are eaten are endangered and that other species not yet endangered soon will be if they stay on the tourist menu.

Ají is hot pepper, frequently used in cooking. *Rocoto* is an even hotter variety (with black seeds), sometimes served as a garnish and best avoided by the uninitiated. *Llajua* is a hot pepper sauce present on every Bolivian table. It's potency varies greatly so try a little bit before applying dollops to your food.

Bolivia's temperate and tropical fruits are excellent and abundant. Don't miss the luscious grapes and peaches in season (February-April). Brazil nuts, called *almendras* or *castañas*, are produced in the northern jungle department of Pando and sold throughout the country.

The popular destinations have a profusion of cafés and restaurants catering to the gringo market. Some offer decent international cuisine at reasonable prices, but many seem convinced that tourists eat only mediocre pizza and vegetarian omelettes. There must be a hundred 'Pizzería Italianas' in Bolivia's tourist towns.

Drink The several makes of local lager-type **beer** are recommendable; *Paceña* and *Auténtica* are the best-selling brands. There are also micro-brews in La Paz (see page 287). *Singani*, the national spirit, is distilled from grapes, and is cheap and strong. *Chuflay* is *singani* and a fizzy mixer, usually 7-Up. Good **wines** are produced by La Concepción and Kolhberg vineyards, near Tarija (tours are available and both wineries have on-site shops, see page 346). *Chicha* is a fermented maize drink, popular in Cochabamba. The hot maize drink, *api* (with cloves, cinnamon, lemon and sugar), is good on cold mornings. **Bottled water** (many brands with and without gas) is readily available but make sure the seal is unbroken. Tap, stream and well water should never be drunk without first being purified. A local iodine-based water purifying product is *lugol fuerte solución*; also *tintura de iodo* (tincture of iodine), sold in pharmacies. Be sure you know how to use these, so as not to poison yourself. For **milk**, try *Leche Pil* (plain, chocolate or strawberry-flavoured).

Essentials A-Z

Accident and emergency

Police T110. Ambulance T118. Robberies should be reported to the *Policía Turística*, they will issue a report for insurance purposes but stolen goods are rarely recovered. In La Paz: Calle Hugo Estrada 1354, Plaza Tejada Sorzano frente al estadio, Miraflores, next to Love City Chinese restaurant, T222 5016. In cities which do not have a Policía Turística report robberies to the *Fuerza Especial de Lucha Contra el Crimen (FELCC)*, Departamento de Robos.

Electricity

220 volts 50 cycles AC. Sockets usually accept both continental European (round) and US-type (flat) 2-pin plugs. Also some 110 volt sockets, when in doubt, ask.

Embassies and consulates

For a full list, see www.rree.gov.bo.

Festivals and events

In Andean regions, **Carnaval Campesino** begins on **Ash Wed** and lasts for 5 days, ending with **Domingo de Tentación** in many small towns. 2 weeks before Carnaval is **Jueves de Compadres** followed by **Jueves de Comadres**. **Shrove Tue** is celebrated as **Martes de Challa**, when house owners make offerings to Pachamama and give drinks to passers-by. Carnaval is celebrated in many cities and towns usually with a **corso** parade with floats and folkloric dances, parties and water throwing. **2 Feb**: **Virgen de la Candelaria**, in rural communities, Copacabana, Santa Cruz. **Palm Sun** (Domingo de Ramos) sees parades to the church throughout Bolivia; the devout carry woven palm fronds, then hang them outside their houses. **Semana Santa** in the eastern Chiquitania is very interesting, with ancient processions, dances, and games not found outside the region. Corpus Christi is also a colourful festival. **3 May**: **Fiesta de la Invención de la Santa Cruz**, various parts. **2 Jun**: **Santísima Trinidad** in Beni Department. **24 Jun**: **San Juan**, all Bolivia. **29 Jun**: **San Pedro y San Pablo**, at Tiquina, Tihuanaco and throughout Chiquitania. **25 Jul**: **Fiesta de Santiago** (St James), Altiplano and lake region. **16 Aug**: **San Roque**, patron saint of dogs; the animals are adorned with ribbons and other decorations. **1** and **2 Nov**: **All Saints and All Souls**, any local cemetery. **18 Nov**: **Beni's Departmental anniversary**, especially in Trinidad. For other festivals on the Altiplano enquire at hotels or tourist office in La Paz. Cities are very quiet on national holidays, but celebrations will be going on in the villages. Beware of water-filled balloons thrown during carnival in even the coldest weather. Hotels are often full at the most popular places, for instance Copacabana on Good Fri; worth booking in advance.

Public holidays 1 Jan, New Year's Day; Carnival Week, Mon, Shrove Tue, Ash Wed; Holy Week: Thu, Fri and Sat; 1 May, Labour Day; Corpus Christi (movable May-Jun); 16 Jul, La Paz Municipal Holiday; 5-7 Aug, Independence; 24 Sep, Santa Cruz Municipal Holiday; 2 Nov, Day of the Dead; Christmas Day.

Money → *US$1 = Bs 6.88; €1 = Bs 9.63 (Jan 2010).*

The currency is the boliviano (Bs), divided into 100 centavos. There are notes for 200, 100, 50, 20 and 10 bolivianos, and 5, 2 and 1 boliviano coins, as well as 50, 20 and (rare) 10 centavos. Bolivianos are often referred to as pesos; expensive items, including hotel rooms, are often quoted in dollars.

Many *casas de cambio* and street changers (but not banks) accept cash euros as well as dollars. Large bills may be hard to use in small towns, always carry some 20s and 10s. Small change may be given in forms other than money: eg, sweets. ATMs (**Enlace** network T800-103060) are common in all departmental capitals and some other cities but not in small towns, including several important tourist destinations. Copacabana, Samaipata, Sorata, Rurrenabaque and Tupiza, among others, have no ATM. ATMs are not always reliable and, in addition to plastic and/or TCs, you **must** always carry some cash. Most ATMs dispense both Bs and US$. Debit cards and Amex are generally less reliable than Visa/MC credit cards at ATMs. Note that Bolivian ATMs dispense cash first and only a few moments later return your card, many tourists forget to take their card. In small towns without banks or ATMs, look for **Prodem**, which changes US$ cash at fair rates, and gives cash advances on Visa/MC for about 5% commission. **Fades** and **Fiesa** are two other institutions found throughout the country which change only US$ cash. See Ins and outs, La Paz, **Safety**, on ATM scams; these are worst in La Paz, but may occur elsewhere. For lost Visa cards T800-100188, MasterCard T800-100172.

Only US$ **Amex** TCs are accepted by most financial institutions, do not bring other brands or currencies. Most tourist establishments will not accept payment directly with TCs. They are best used by converting a larger sum to Bs at financial institutions, then paying with Bs as you travel. The best places to change TCs are: **Banco Unión**, www.bancounion.com.bo, branches in La Paz, Cochabamba and Santa Cruz, 1% commission (minimum US$5) for Bs or US$ cash; **Banco Bisa**, www.bisa.com, branches in most larger cities, approx 1% commission for Bs, US$6 flat fee for US$ cash (maximum 5 TCs); Casa de cambio **Sudamer** in La Paz, about 1% commission for Bs, 3% for US$ cash; **Banco Nacional de Bolivia** (BNB, www.bnb.com.bo) branches in departmental capitals, 3% commission for Bs. There is nowhere to change TCs on Sat afternoon and Sun.

Cost of travelling Bolivia is cheaper to visit than most neighbouring countries. Budget travellers can get by on US$15-20 per person per day for two travelling together. A basic hotel in small towns costs as little as US$4-5 per person, breakfast US$1, and a simple set lunch (*almuerzo*) around US$1.50-3. For around US$35, though, you can find much better accommodation, more comfortable transport and a wider choice in food. Prices are higher in the city of La Paz; in the east, especially Santa Cruz and Tarija; and in Pando and the upper reaches of the Beni. The average cost of using the internet is US$0.30-0.60 per hr.

Opening hours

Business hours Mon-Fri 0830-1230, 1430-1830 and Sat 0900-1200. Opening and closing in the afternoon are several hours later in the provinces. Banks normally open Mon-Fri 0900-1600, Sat 0900-1300, but may close for lunch in small towns.

Safety

Violent crime is less common in Bolivia than some other parts of South America. Tricks and scams abound however. Fake police, narcotics police and immigration officers – usually plain-clothed but carrying forged ID – have been known to take people to their 'office' and ask to see documents and money; they then rob them. Legitimate police do not ask people for documents in the street unless they are involved in an accident, fight, etc. If approached, walk away and seek assistance from as many bystanders as possible. Never get in a vehicle with the 'officer' nor follow them to their 'office'. Many of the robberies are very slick, involving taxis and various accomplices. Take only radio taxis, identified by their dome lights and phone numbers. Always lock the doors, sit in the back and never allow other passengers to share your cab. If someone else gets in, get out at once. Also if smeared or spat-on, walk away, don't let the good Samaritan clean you up, they will clean you out instead.

The countryside and small towns throughout Bolivia are generally safe. Note however that civil disturbance, although less frequent in recent years, remains part of Bolivian life. It can take the form of strikes, demonstrations in major cities and road blocks (*paros*), some lasting a few hrs, others weeks.Try to be flexible in your plans if you encounter disruptions and make the most of the attractions where you are staying if transport is not running. You can often find transport to the site of a roadblock, walk across and get onward transport on the other side. Check with locals first to find out how tense the situation is.

Road safety is an important concern for all visitors to Bolivia. Precarious roads, poorly maintained vehicles and frequently reckless drivers combine to cause many serious, if not fatal accidents. Choose your transport judiciously and don't hesitate to pay a little more to travel with a better company. Look over the vehicle before you get on; if it doesn't feel right, look for another. If a driver is drunk or reckless, demand that he stop at the nearest village and let you off. Also note that smaller buses, although less comfortable, are often safer on narrow mountain roads.

Tax

Airport tax A departure tax of US$24, payable in dollars or bolivianos, cash only, is levied on leaving by air. On internal flights an airport tax of about US$2 must be paid.

VAT/IVA 13%. Ask for an official receipt if you want it documented.

Telephone → *Country code +591.*

Equal tones with long pauses: ringing. Equal tones with equal pauses: engaged. IDD prefix: 00.

Time

GMT-4 all year.

Tipping

Up to 10% in restaurants is very generous, Bolivians seldom leave more than a few coins; otherwise give a tip for a service provided, eg, to a taxi driver who has been helpful (an extra Bs 0.50-1), to someone who has looked after a car or carried bags (usual tip Bs 0.50-1).

Tourist information

Viceministerio de Turismo, Av Camacho 1488 esquina Bueno, T02-211 9088, Mon-Fri 0830-1230, 1430-1830. Information offices at international arrivals in El Alto airport (La Paz) and Viru Viru (Santa Cruz). See under each city for addresses of tourist offices.

Useful websites

www.bolivia.com (Spanish) News, tourism, entertainment and information on regions.

www.boliviaweb.com English-language portal.

www.bolivia-online.net (Spanish, English and German) Travel information about La Paz, Cochabamba and Santa Cruz.

http://ande-mesili.com (multilingual) The site of climbing guide and author Alain Mesili, with lots of interesting links.

www.presidencia.gov.bo Presidential website.

http://lanic.utexas.edu/la/sa/bolivia Excellent database on various topics indigenous to Bolivia, maintained by the University of Texas, USA.

www.noticiasbolivianas.com All the Bolivian daily news in one place.

www.chiquitania.com Detailed information about all aspects of Chiquitanía.

Visas and immigration
A passport only, valid for 6 months beyond date of visit, is needed for citizens of almost all Western European countries, Israel, Japan, Canada, South American countries, Australia and New Zealand. Nationals of all other countries require a visa. US citizens may obtain a visa either in advance at a Bolivian consulate, or directly on entry to the country at airports and land borders. Requirements include a fee of US$135 (cash - Jan 2010; this may change), proof of sufficient funds (eg showing a credit card) and a yellow fever vaccination certificate. Only the fee is universally enforced. Some nationalities must gain authorization from the Bolivian Ministry of Foreign Affairs, which can take 6 weeks. Other countries that require a visa do not need authorisation (visas in this case take 1-2 working days). It is best to check current requirements before leaving home. Tourists are usually granted 30 days stay on entry. Some nationalities, such as Western Europeans and Israelis, can get a free extension (*ampliación*), but others must apply for a 30-day *prórroga*, at a cost of US$24. Both free and paid extensions are granted at immigration offices in all departmental capitals, up to a maximum stay of 90 days, and normally take 48 hrs to process. After 90 days you must leave the country but may, at the discretion of the immigration officer at the point of re-entry, be allowed to return after a 24-72 hr absence. If you overstay, the current fine is US$2 per day. Business visitors (unless passing through as tourists) are required to obtain a visa from a Bolivian consulate. This costs US$135 (or equivalent), applicants should confirm all details in advance.

Weights and measures
Metric, but some old Spanish measures are used for produce in markets.

Wildlife and nature
www.redesma.org Site of the Red de Desarrollo Sostenible y Medio Ambiente (in Spanish and English) has lots of links to sustainable development topics and organizations.
www.wcs.org/international/latinamerica/amazon_andes World Conservation Society site with information on the Gran Chaco and on Northwestern Bolivia.

La Paz and around → *Phone code: 02. Colour map 6, A2.*

The minute you arrive in La Paz, the highest seat of government in the world, you realize this is no ordinary place. El Alto airport is at a staggering 4,000 m above sea level. The sight of the city, lying 500 m below, at the bottom of a steep canyon and ringed by snow-peaked mountains, takes your breath away – literally. For at this altitude breathing can be a problem.

The Spaniards chose this odd place for a city on 20 October 1548, to avoid the chill winds of the plateau, and because they had found gold in the Río Choqueyapu, which runs through the canyon. The centre of the city, Plaza Murillo, is at 3,636 m, about 400 m below the level of the Altiplano and the sprawling city of El Alto, perched dramatically on the rim of the canyon.

Ins and outs → *Population: La Paz, 855,000, El Alto, 882,000.*

Getting there La Paz has the highest commercial **airport** in the world, at El Alto, high above the city at 4,058 m; T281 0240. A taxi from the airport to the centre takes about 30 minutes, US$7, to the Zona Sur US$9. There are 3 main **bus terminals**; the bus station at Plaza Antofagasta, the cemetery district for Sorata, Copacabana and Tiwanaku, and Villa Fátima for Coroico, the Yungas and northern jungle. ▸▸ *See also Transport, page 296.*

Getting around There are two types of city bus: *micros* (small, old buses), which charge US$0.20 a journey; and the faster, more plentiful minibuses (small vans), US$0.15-0.30 depending on the journey. *Trufis* are fixed route collective taxis, with a sign with their route on the windscreen, US$0.40 in the centre, US$0.50 pp outside. Taxis are often, but not always, white. There are three types: regular honest taxis which may take several passengers at once (US$0.85-1.10 for short trips), fake taxis which have been involved in robberies (see below), and radio taxis which take only one group of passengers at a time. Since it is impossible to distinguish between the first two, it is best to pay a bit more for a radio taxi which has a dome light and number and can be ordered by phone; note the number when getting in. Radio taxis charge US$1.10-1.40 in the centre, more to the suburbs.

Orientation The city's main street runs from **Plaza San Francisco** as Avenida Mcal Santa Cruz, then changes to Avenida 16 de Julio (more commonly known as El Prado) and ends at **Plaza del Estudiante**. The business quarter, government offices, central university (UMSA) and many of the main hotels and restaurants are in this area. From the Plaza del Estudiante, Avenida Villazón splits into Avenida Arce, which runs southeast towards the wealthier residential districts of **Zona Sur** and Avenida 6 de Agosto which runs through **Sopocachi**, an area full of restaurants, bars and clubs. In the valley, 15 minutes south of the centre, is Zona Sur, home to the resident foreign community. It has international shopping centres, supermarkets with imported items and some of the best restaurants and bars in La Paz (see page 292). Zona Sur begins after the bridge at La Florida beside the attractive Plaza Humboldt. The main road, Avenida Ballivián, begins at Calle 8 and continues up the hill to San Miguel on Calle 21 (about a 20-minute walk). Sprawled around the rim of the canyon is **El Alto**, now a city in its own right and, until 1996, the fastest growing in South America. Its population of almost 1 million is mostly indigenous immigrants from the countryside and its political influence has grown rapidly. El Alto is connected to La Paz by motorway (toll US$0.25, motorbikes and cycles free) and by a road to Obrajes and the Zona Sur. Minibuses from Plaza Eguino leave regularly for Plaza 16 de Julio, El Alto, more leave from Plaza Pérez Velasco for La Ceja, the edge of El Alto. Buses to and from La Paz always stop at El Alto in an area called *terminal*, off Avenida 6 de Marzo, where transport companies have small offices. If not staying in La Paz, you can change buses here and save a couple of hours. There is accommodation in the area but it is not safe at night.

Best time to visit Because of the altitude, nights are cold the year round. In the day, the sun is strong, but the moment you go into the shade or enter a building, the temperature falls. From December-March, the summer, it rains most afternoons, making it feel colder than it actually is. The two most important festivals, when the city gets particularly busy, are **Alasitas** (last week of January and first week of February) and **Festividad del Señor del Gran Poder** (end May/early June). See Festivals, page 293.

Tourist offices The **Gobierno Municipal de La Paz** has information centres at: ⓘ *Plaza del Estudiante at the lower end of El Prado between 16 de Julio and México, T237 1044, Mon-Fri 0830-1900, Sat-Sun 0930-1300*, very helpful, English and French spoken. There is an office at the bus terminal, Plaza Antofagasta, at the Casa de Cultura, Plaza Pérez Velasco (opposite San Francisco) and at Valle de la Luna, Cruce Mallasa. Tourist office for **El Alto**: **Dirección de Promoción Turística** ⓘ *C 5 y Av 6 de Marzo, Edif Vela, p 5, also at arrivals in airport, T282 9281, Mon-Fri 0800-1200, 1400-1800*; the municipality is trying to attract visitors.

Safety See also Safety, page 276. The worst areas for crime are around Plaza Murillo and the Cemetery neighbourhood where local buses serve Copacabana and Tiwanaku. Tourist police now patrol these bus stops, making them safer than in the past, but caution is still advised. Other areas, particularly Sopocachi, are generally safer.

Warning for ATM users: scams to get card numbers and PINs have flourished, especially in La Paz. The tourist police post warnings in hotels. See Essentials A-Z, page 274, for what to do in an emergency.

Sights

There are few colonial buildings left in La Paz; probably the best examples are in **Calle Jaén** (see below). Late 19th-, early 20th-century architecture, often displaying European influence, can be found in the streets around Plaza Murillo, but much of La Paz is modern. The **Plaza del Estudiante** (Plaza Franz Tamayo), or a bit above it, marks a contrast between old and new styles, between the commercial and the more elegant. The **Prado** itself is lined with high-rise blocks dating from the 1960s and 1970s.

Around Plaza Murillo

Plaza Murillo, three blocks north of the Prado, is the traditional centre. Facing its formal gardens are the Cathedral, the **Palacio Presidencial** in Italian renaissance style, known as the **Palacio Quemado** (burnt palace) twice gutted by fire in its stormy 130-year history, and, on the east side, the **Congreso Nacional.** In front of the Palacio Quemado is a statue of former President Gualberto Villarroel who was dragged into the plaza by a mob and hanged in 1946. Across from the Cathedral on Calle Socabaya is the **Palacio de los Condes de Arana** (built 1775), with beautiful exterior and patio. It houses the **Museo Nacional de Arte** ⓘ *T240 8542, www.mna.org.bo, Tue-Sat 0900-1230, 1500-1900, Sun 0900-1230, US$1.25.* It has a fine collection of colonial paintings including many works by Melchor Pérez Holguín, considered one of the masters of Andean colonial art, and which also exhibits the works of contemporary local artists. Calle Comercio, running east-west across the Plaza, has most of the stores and shops. West of Plaza Murillo, at Ingavi 916, in the palace of the Marqueses de Villaverde, and undergoing renovation since 2005, is the **Museo Nacional de Etnografía y Folklore** ⓘ *T240 8640, Mon-Sat 0900-1230, 1500-1900, Sat-Sun 0900-1230, free.* Various sections show the cultural richness of Bolivia by region through textiles and other items. It has a *videoteca*.

Northwest of Plaza Murillo is **Calle Jaén**, a picturesque colonial street with a restaurant/ peña, a café, craft shops, good views and four museums (known as Museos Municipales) housed in colonial buildings ⓘ *Tue-Fri 0900-1230, 1500-1900, Sat-Sun 1000-1300, US$0.15 each.* **Museo Costumbrista** ⓘ *on Plaza Riosinio, at the top of Jaén, T228 0758*, has miniature displays depicting incidents in the history of La Paz and well-known Paceños, as well as miniature replicas of reed rafts used by the Norwegian Thor Heyerdahl, and the Spaniard Kitin Muñoz, to prove their theories of ancient migrations. **Museo del Litoral Boliviano** (T228 0758), has artefacts of the War of the Pacific, and interesting selection of old maps. **Museo de Metales Preciosos** (T228 0329), is well set out with Inca gold artefacts in basement vaults, also ceramics and archaeological exhibits, and **Museo Casa Murillo** (T228 0553), the erstwhile home of Pedro Domingo Murillo, one of the martyrs of the La Paz independence movement of 16 July 1809, has a good collection of paintings, furniture and national costumes. In addition to the Museos Municipales is the **Museo de Instrumentos Musicales** ⓘ *Jaén 711 e Indaburo, T240 8177, Tue-Fri*

1 La Paz

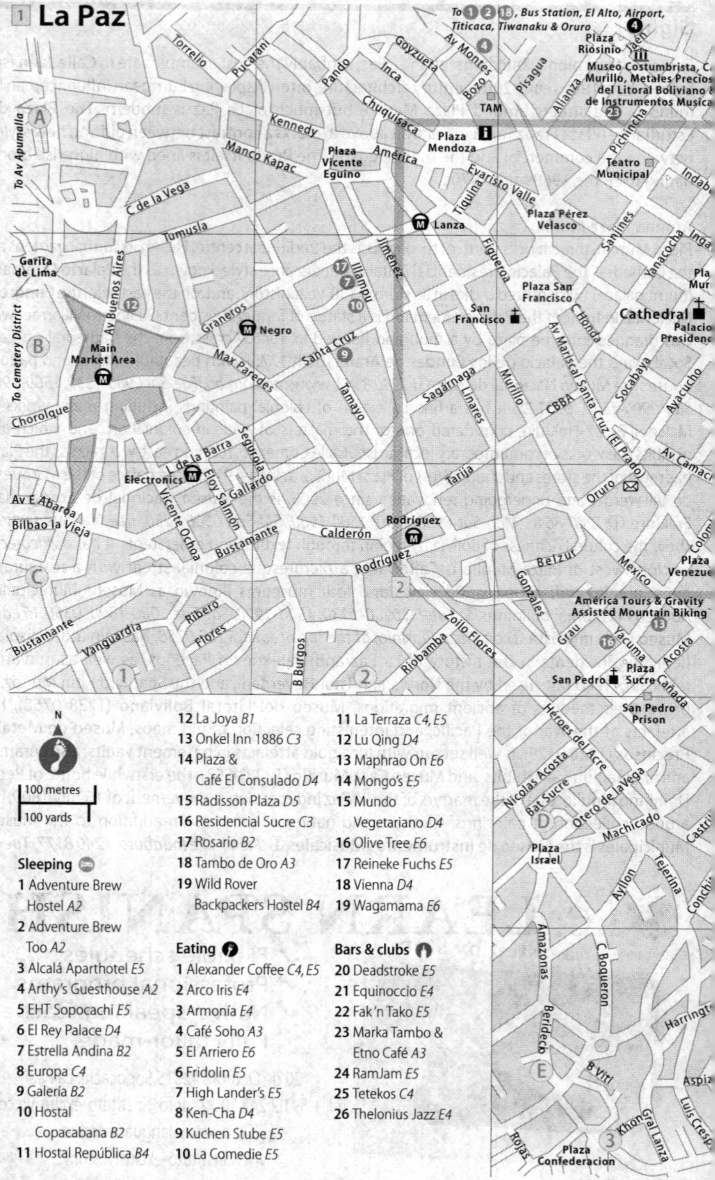

Sleeping
1 Adventure Brew Hostel *A2*
2 Adventure Brew Too *A2*
3 Alcalá Aparthotel *E5*
4 Arthy's Guesthouse *A2*
5 EHT Sopocachi *E5*
6 El Rey Palace *D4*
7 Estrella Andina *B2*
8 Europa *C4*
9 Galería *B2*
10 Hostal Copacabana *B2*
11 Hostal República *B4*
12 La Joya *B1*
13 Onkel Inn 1886 *C3*
14 Plaza & Café El Consulado *D4*
15 Radisson Plaza *D5*
16 Residencial Sucre *C3*
17 Rosario *B2*
18 Tambo de Oro *A3*
19 Wild Rover Backpackers Hostel *B4*

Eating
1 Alexander Coffee *C4, E5*
2 Arco Iris *E4*
3 Armonía *E4*
4 Café Soho *A3*
5 El Arriero *E6*
6 Fridolin *E5*
7 High Lander's *E5*
8 Ken-Cha *D4*
9 Kuchen Stube *E5*
10 La Comedie *E5*
11 La Terraza *C4, E5*
12 Lu Qing *D4*
13 Maphrao On *E6*
14 Mongo's *E5*
15 Mundo Vegetariano *D4*
16 Olive Tree *E6*
17 Reineke Fuchs *E5*
18 Vienna *D4*
19 Wagamama *E6*

Bars & clubs
20 Deadstroke *E5*
21 Equinoccio *E4*
22 Fak'n Tako *E5*
23 Marka Tambo & Etno Café *A3*
24 RamJam *E5*
25 Tetekos *C4*
26 Thelonius Jazz *E4*

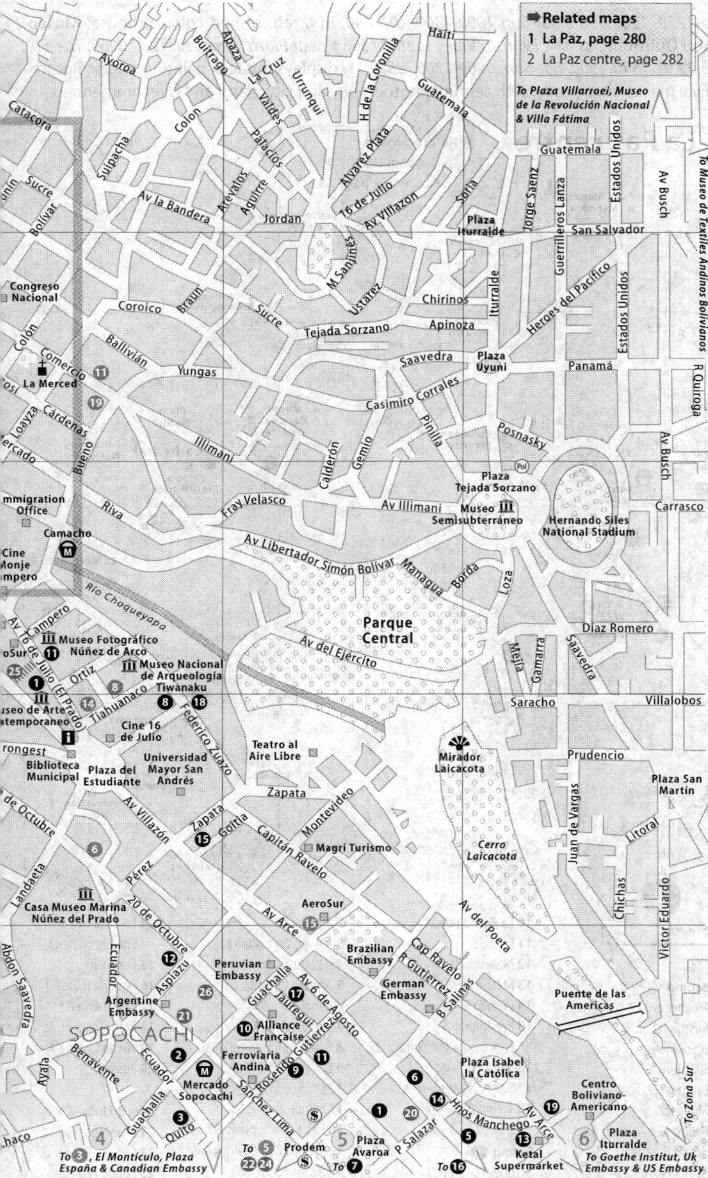
Related maps
1 La Paz, page 280
2 La Paz centre, page 282
To Plaza Villarroel, Museo de la Revolución Nacional & Villa Fátima
To Museo de Textiles Andinos Bolivianos
Haiti
Ayoroa
Buitrago
Apaza
La Cruz
Valdes
Urrunqui
H de la Coronilla
Guatemala
Catacora
Colon
Palacios
Alvarez Plata
Suipacha
Sucre
Bolívar
Av la Bandera
Arevalos
Aguirre
Jordan
16 de Julio
Av Villazon
Soria
Plaza Iturralde
Jorge Saenz
Guerrilleros Lanza
Estados Unidos
Av Busch
San Salvador
Congreso Nacional
M Sanjinés
Ustarez
Chirinos
Iturralde
Heroes del Pacifico
Coroico
Braun
Tejada Sorzano
Apinoza
Colón
Ballivián
Comercio
La Merced
Yungas
Saavedra
Plaza Uyuni
Panamá
R Quiroga
Casimiro Corrales
Pinilla
Loayza
Cárdenas
Mercado
Bueno
Illimani
Calderón
Gemio
Posnasky
Pol
Plaza Tejada Sorzano
Immigration Office
Riva
Fray Velasco
Av Illimani
Museo Semisubterráneo
Hernando Siles National Stadium
Carrasco
Camacho
Cine Monje Campero
Av Libertador Simón Bolívar
Managua
Borda
Loza
Río Choqueyapu
Campero
Av 16 de Julio (El Prado)
Museo Fotográfico Núñez de Arco
Museo Nacional de Arqueología Tiwanaku
Parque Central
Av del Ejército
Diaz Romero
Mejía
Gamarra
Saavedra
Ortiz
Tiahuanaco
Museo de Arte Contemporaneo
Saracho
Villalobos
Cine 16 de Julio
Federico Zuazo
Teatro al Aire Libre
Mirador Laicacota
Prudencio
Biblioteca Municipal
Plaza del Estudiante
Universidad Mayor San Andrés
Zapata
Plaza San Martín
20 de Octubre
Av Villazón
Zapata
Goitia
Capitán Ravelo
Montevideo
Magri Turismo
Cerro Laicacota
Juan de Vargas
Litoral
Landaeta
Pérez
Casa Museo Marina Núñez del Prado
AeroSur
Av del Poeta
Chichas
Victor Eduardo
Av Arce
Abdon Saavedra
Ecuador
Brazilian Embassy
Cap Ravelo
R Gutierrez
Peruvian Embassy
Aspiazu
Guachalla
Av 6 de Agosto
Jauregui
German Embassy
B Salinas
Puente de las Americas
Argentine Embassy
SOPOCACHI
Alliance Française
Rosendo Gutierrez
Ferroviaria Andina
Benavente
Ayala
Ecuador
Mercado Sopocachi
Sanchez Lima
Plaza Isabel la Católica
Centro Boliviano-Americano
To Zona Sur
Guachalla
Quito
Hnos Manchego
Av Arce
Chaco
Prodem
Plaza Avaroa
P Salazar
Plaza Iturralde
To 3, El Montículo, Plaza España & Canadian Embassy
To 5 22 24
To 7
To 16
Ketal Supermarket
To Goethe Institut, Uk Embassy & US Embassy

0930-1230, 1500-1900, Sat-Sun 1000-1300, US$1.40, in a refurbished colonial house. **Museo Tambo Quirquincho** ⓘ *C Evaristo Valle, south of Jaén, near Plaza Mendoza, T239 0969, Tue-Fri, 0930-1230, 1530-1900, Sat-Sun, 0900-1300, US$0.15*, displays modern painting and sculpture, carnival masks, silver, early 20th century photography and city plans, and is recommended.

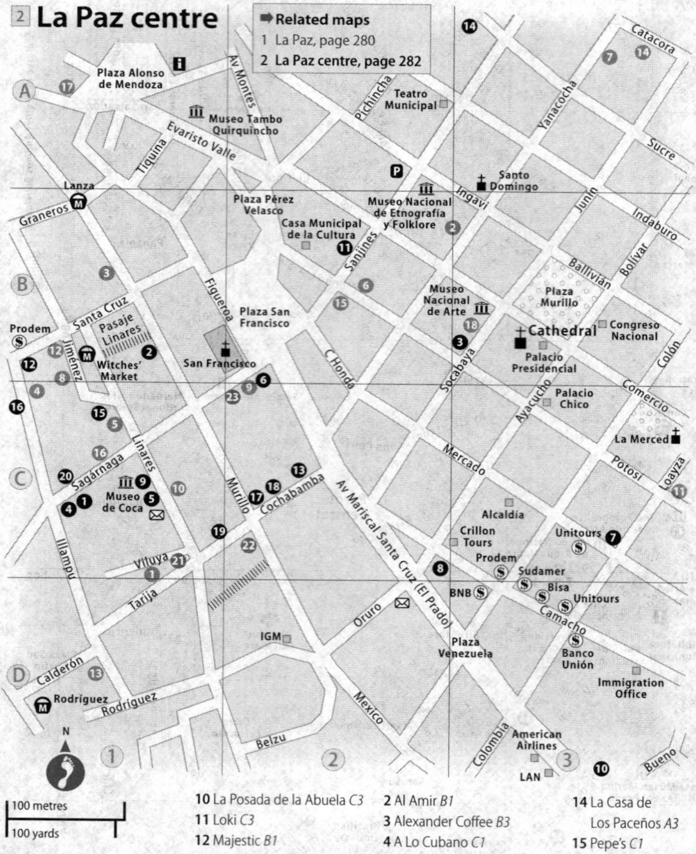

Sleeping
1 Arcabucero *C1*
2 Austria *B2*
3 El Solario *B1*
4 El Viajero *C1*
5 Fuentes *C1*
6 Gloria *B2*
7 Hospedaje Milenio *A3*
8 Hostal Cactus *B1*
9 Hostal Naira *C2*
10 La Posada de la Abuela *C3*
11 Loki *C3*
12 Majestic *B1*
13 Milton *D1*
14 Posada El Carretero *A3*
15 Presidente & La Kantuta Restaurant *B2*
16 Sagárnaga *C1*
17 Señorial Montero *A1*
18 Torino *B3*

Eating
1 100% Natural *C1*
2 Al Amir *B1*
3 Alexander Coffee *B3*
4 A Lo Cubano *C1*
5 Angelo Colonial *C1*
6 Banais *B2*
7 Café Berlin *C3*
8 Café Confitería de la Paz *C2*
9 Colonial Pot *C1*
10 Dumbos *D3*
11 El Calicanto *B2*
10 Eli's Pizza Express *D3*
12 El Lobo & Hard Rock Cafe *B1*
13 Jackie Chan *C2*
14 La Casa de Los Paceños *A3*
15 Pepe's *C1*
16 Pizzería Italia *C1*
17 Sol y Luna *C2*
18 Star of India *C2*
19 Tucan Bistro *C1*
20 Yussef *C1*

Bars & clubs
21 Blue Note Café *C1*
22 Oliver's Travels *C2*
23 Peña El Parnaso *C2*

Tiny treats

One of the most intriguing items for sale in Andean markets is Ekeko, the god of good fortune and plenty and one of the most endearing of the Aymara folk legends. He is a cheery, avuncular little chap, with a happy face, a pot belly and short legs. His image, usually in plaster of Paris, is laden with various household items, as well as sweets, confetti and streamers, food, and with a cigarette dangling cheekily from his lower lip. Believers say that these statues only bring luck if they are received as gifts. The Ekeko occupies a central role in the festival of Alacitas, the Feast of Plenty, which takes place in La Paz at the end of January. Everything under the sun can be bought in miniature: houses, trucks, buses, suitcases, university diplomas; you name it, you'll find it here. The idea is to have your mini-purchase blessed by a Yatiri, an Aymara priest, and the real thing will be yours within the year.

Plaza San Francisco up to the cemetery district

At the upper end of Avenida Mcal Santa Cruz is the **Plaza San Francisco** with the **church and monastery of San Francisco** ⓘ *open for Mass at 0700, 0900, 1100 and 1900, Mon-Sat, and also at 0800, 1000 and 1200 on Sun*. Dating from 1549, this is one of the finest examples of colonial religious architecture in South America and well worth seeing. The **Centro Cultural Museo San Francisco** ⓘ *Plaza San Francisco 503, T231 8472, Mon-Sat 0900-1800, US$2.80, students US$2.10S, allow 1½-2 hrs, guides available free but tip appreciated, some speak English and French,* offers access to various areas of the church and convent which were previously off limits, including the choir, crypt (open 1400-1730), roof, various chapels and gardens. Fine art includes religious paintings from the 17th, 18th and 19th centuries, plus visiting exhibits and a hall devoted to the works of Tito Yupanqui, the indigenous sculptor of the Virgen de Copacabana. There is a pricey but good café at entrance. Behind the San Francisco church a network of narrow cobbled streets rise steeply up the canyon walls. Much of this area is a street market. Handicraft shops, travel agencies, hotels and restaurants line the lower part of **Calle Sagárnaga** (here you find the highest concentration of tourists and pick-pockets). The **Mercado de Brujas**, 'witchcraft market', on Calles Melchor Jiménez and Linares, which cross Santa Cruz above San Francisco, sells charms, herbs and more gruesome items like llama foetuses. The excellent **Museo de la Coca** ⓘ *Linares 914, T231 1998, daily 1000-1900, US$1.20, shop with coca sweets for sale,* is devoted to the coca plant, its history, cultural significance, medical values and political implications, with explanations in Spanish and English. Nearby is the recommended **Museo de Arte Texil Andino Boliviano** ⓘ *Linares 906, T237 6396, daily 1000-1900, Sun 1000-1700, US$1.20,* a small collection of old traditional weavings (not to be confused with the larger Museo de Textiles Andinos Bolivianos in Miraflores).

Further up, from Illampu to Rodríguez and in neighbouring streets, is the produce-based **Rodríguez market** ⓘ *daily, but best on Sun morning*. Turning right on Max Paredes, heading north, is **Avenida Buenos Aires**, where small workshops turn out the costumes and masks for the Gran Poder festival, and with great views of Illimani, especially at sunset. Continuing west along Max Paredes towards the **cemetery district**, the streets are crammed with stalls selling every imaginable item. Transport converges on the cemetery district (for more information see page 296). See also Safety, page 278.

The Prado, Sopocachi, Miraflores and Zona Sur

Museo de Arte Contemporáneo Plaza ⓘ *Av 16 de Julio 1698, T233 5905, Mon-Fri 0900-2100, US$1.* In a 19th-century house which has been declared a national monument, there is a selection of contemporary art from national and international artists. The **Museo Fotográfico Nuñez de Arco** ⓘ *16 de Julio 1615, Mon-Fri 1000-1300, 1500-2000, Sat 10-1300, US$1.90* has photo collection of the early excavations of Tiawanaku and old photos of La Paz and surroundings. Just off the Prado (down the flight of stairs by the Hotel Plaza) is **Museo Nacional de Arqueología** or **Tiahuanaco** (Tiwanaku) ⓘ *Tiwanacu 93 entre Bravo y F Zuazo, T231 1621, www.bolivian.com/arqueologia, Mon- Fri 0900-1200, 1400-1800, US$1.25.* It contains good collections of the arts and crafts of ancient Tiwanaku and items from the eastern jungles. It also has an exhibition of gold statuettes and objects found in Lake Titicaca. On Avenida Libertador Simón Bolívar, from where there are views of Mt Illimani, is the **Mercado Camacho** produce market. In Sopocachi district, above Avenida 6 de Agosto, is **Casa Museo Marina Núñez del Prado** ⓘ *Ecuador 2034, T242 4175, www.bolivian.com/cmnp, daily 0930-1300, Tue-Fri 1500-1900 (may be closed afternoons and weekends), US$0.75, students US$0.30,* which houses a collection of Marina Núñez's sculptures in the family mansion. By Plaza España, is **El Montículo**, a park with great views of the city and Illimani. East of the centre, outside the Hernán Siles national football stadium, on Plaza Tejada Sorzano, is the **Museo Semisubterráneo**, a sunken garden full of replicas of statues and artefacts from Tiwanaku, refurbished in 2008, but difficult to get to because of the traffic. In the residential district of Miraflores is **Museo de Textiles Andinos Bolivianos** ⓘ *Plaza Benito Juárez 488, T224 3601, Mon-Sat 0930-1200, 1500-1800, Sun 1000-1230, US$1.25,* with displays of textiles from around the country. At the north end of Av Busch are Plaza Villarroel and **Museo del la Revolución Nacional** ⓘ *Tue-Fri 0930-1200, 1500- 1800, Sat-Sun 1000-1200, US$0.15,* a memorial of the 1952 revolution and a mausoleum with tombs of former presidents.

Around La Paz

South of La Paz

To the south of the city are dry hills of many colours, topped by the **Muela del Diablo**, a striking outcrop. Here is the **Valle de la Luna**, or 'Valley of the Moon' (US$2.10), which has a nice terraced cactus garden worth walking through; the climate in this valley is always much warmer than in the city. About 3 km from the bridge at Calacoto the road forks. For transport details see page 298. Get out of the minibus at the turning and walk a few minutes east to the Valle entrance, or get out at the football field which is by the entrance. Take good shoes and water, but do not go alone, armed robbery has occurred. Just past the Valle de la Luna is **Mallasa** where there are several small roadside restaurants and cafés and the **Hotel Oberland** (see page 289). The **zoo** ⓘ *on the road to Río Abajo, entrance just past Mallasa after Valle de la Luna, daily 0900-1700, US$0.50 adults, US$0.25 children,* in a beautiful, wide open park-like setting, conditions for the animals and birds are relatively good, but the public is allowed to feed the animals.

Tiwanaku

ⓘ *The site is open 0900-1700, US$11, including entry to museums. Allow 4 hrs to see the ruins and village. See also Transport, page 298.*

This remarkable archaeological site, 72 km west of La Paz, near the southern end of Lake Titicaca, takes its name from one of the most important pre-Columbian civilizations in South America. It is now the most popular excursion from La Paz, with facilities being improved as a result. Many archaeologists believe that Tiwanaku existed as early as 1600 BC, while the complex visible today probably dates from the eight to the 10th centuries AD. The site may have been a ceremonial complex at the centre of an empire which covered almost half Bolivia, southern Peru, northern Chile and northwest Argentina. It was also a hub of trans-Andean trade. The demise of the Tiwanaku civilization, according to studies by Alan Kolata of the University of Illinois, could have been precipitated by the flooding of the area's extensive system of raised fields (*Sukakollu*), which were capable of sustaining a population of 20,000. The Pumapunka section, 1 km south of the main complex may have been a port, as the waters of the lake used to be much higher than they are today. The raised field system is being reutilized in the Titicaca area.

One of the main structures is the **Kalasasaya**, meaning 'standing stones', referring to the statues found in that part: two of them, the Ponce monolith (centre of inner patio) and the Fraile monolith (southwest corner), have been re-erected. In the northwest corner is the Puerta del Sol, originally at Pumapunku. Its carvings, interrupted by being out of context, are thought to be either a depiction of the creator God, or a calendar. The motifs are exactly the same as those around the Ponce monolith. The **Templo Semisubterráneo** is a sunken temple whose walls are lined with faces, all different, according to some theories depicting states of health, the temple being a house of healing; another theory is that the faces display all the ethnicities of the world. The **Akapana**, originally a pyramid (said to have been the second largest in the world, covering over 28,000 sq m), still has some ruins on it. Plastering of the Akapana's walls was halted in 2009 when UNESCO, among others, declared it inappropriate. At **Pumapunku**, some of whose blocks weigh between 100 and 150 tonnes, a natural disaster may have put a sudden end to the construction before it was finished. There is a small **Museo Lítico** at the ticket office, with several large stone pieces and, at the site, the **Museo Regional Arqueológico**, containing a well-illustrated explanation of the raised field system of agriculture. Many other artefacts are in the **Museo Nacional de Arqeología** in La Paz.

Written guide material is difficult to come by; hiring a guide costs US$8 for 2 hours, some speak English but don't be bullied into taking one if you prefer to go on your own. Locals sell copies of Tiwanaku figures; cheaper here than La Paz.

The nearby **Tiwanaku village** still has remnants from the time of independence and the 16th-century church used pre-Columbian masonry. In fact, Tiwanaku for a long while was the 'quarry' for the altiplano. For the **Willkakuti**, winter solstice festival on 21 June, there is an all-night vigil and colourful dances. There is also a colourful local festival on the Sunday after Carnival.

By road to Chile

The main route to Chile is via Tambo Quemado (see page 316), but an alternative route, on which there are no trucks, is to go by good road direct from La Paz via Viacha to Santiago de Machaco (130 km, petrol); then 120 km to the border at Charaña (basic **Alojamiento Aranda**; immigration behind railway station), very bad road. In Visviri (Chile) there are no services. From Visviri a regular road runs to Putre, see Chile chapter.

Trekking and climbing near La Paz

Four so-called 'Inca Trails' link the Altiplano with the Yungas, taking you from the high Andes to the sub-tropics, with dramatic changes in weather, temperature and vegetation. Each has excellent sections of stonework and they vary in difficulty from relatively straightforward to quite hard-going. In the rainy season going can be particularly tough. For details of how to reach the starting point of each trail, see Transport sections on page 298.

Takesi Trail Start at **Ventilla** (see below), walk up the valley for about three hours passing the village of Choquekhota until the track crosses the river and to the right of the road, there is a falling-down brick wall with a map painted on it. The Takesi and Alto Takesi trails start here, following the path to the right of the wall. The road continues to Mina San Francisco. In the first hour's climb from the wall is excellent stone paving which is Inca or pre-Inca, depending on who you believe, either side of the pass at 4,630 m. There are camping possibilities at *Estancia Takesi* and in the village of Kakapi you can sleep at the **G Kakapi Tourist Lodge**, 10 beds with good mattresses, solar shower and toilet. It is run by the local community and sponsored by Fundación Pueblo. It is also possible to camp. You also have to pass the unpleasant mining settlement of Chojlla, between which and Yanakachi is a gate where it is necessary to register and often pay a small 'fee'. Yanakachi has a number of good places to stay, several good hikes and an orphanage you can help at. The Fundación Pueblo office on the plaza has information. Buy a minibus ticket on arrival in Yanakachi or walk 45 minutes down to the La Paz-Chulumani road for transport. The trek can be done in one long day, especially if you organize a jeep to the start of the trail, but is more relaxing in two or three. If you take it slowly, though, you'll have to carry camping kit. Hire mules in Choquekhota for US$8 per day plus up to US$8 for the muleteer. A 2-3 day alternative is from Mina San Francisco to El Castillo and the village of Chaco on the La Paz-Chulumani road. This trek is called La Reconquistada and has the distinction of including a 200 m disused mining tunnel.

Choro Trail (La Cumbre to Coroico) Immediately before the road drops down from La Cumbre to start the descent to Las Yungas, there is a good dirt road leading up to the *apacheta* (narrow pass) where the trail starts properly. Cloud and bad weather are normal at La Cumbre (4,660 m): you have to sign in at the Guardaparque post on the way to the pass. The trail passes Samaña Pampa (small shop, sign in again, camping US$0.60), Chucura (pay US$1.20 fee, another shop, camping), Challapampa (camping possible, US$0.60, small shop), the Choro bridge and the Río Jacun-Manini (fill up with water at both river crossings). At Sandillani it is possible to stay at the lodge or camp in the carefully tended garden of a Japanese man, Tamiji Hanamura, who keeps a book with the names of every passing traveller. He likes to see postcards and pictures from other countries. There is good paving down to Villa Esmeralda, after which is Chairo (lodging and camping), then to Yolosa. It takes three days to trek from La Cumbre to Chairo, from where you can take a truck to Puente Yolosita, the turn-off for Cocoico on the new road. From Puente Yolosita trucks run uphill to Coroico when they fill, US$0.70, 15 minutes. The Choro Trail has a reputation for unfriendliness and occasional robbery, take care.

Yunga Cruz (Chuñavi to Chulumani) The best, but hardest of the four 'Inca' trails, it has seen little use in recent years and may be badly overgrown; enquire in advance. From Chuñavi (3,710 m) follow the path left (east) and contour gently up. Camping possible after two hours. Continue along the path staying on left hand side of the ridge to reach Cerro Khala Ciudad (literally, Stone City Mountain, you'll see why). Good paving brings you round the hill to join a path coming from Quircoma (on your right); continue, heading north, to Cerro Cuchillatuca and then Cerro Yunga Cruz, where there is water and camping is possible. After this point water and camping are difficult and normally impossible until you get down to Sikilini. The last water and camping possibilities are all within the next hour, take advantage of them. Each person should have at least two litres of water in bottles. Colectivos run from Sikilini to Chulumani. Starting in Chuñavi the trek takes three days.

Huayna Potosí Huayna Potosí (6,088 m) is normally climbed in two days, with one night camped on a glacier at 5,600 m. Acclimatization and experience on ice are essential, and the mountain is dangerous out of season. There are three shelters: one by the lake, very cold; *Refugio Huayna Potosí*, near the road, US$5.60 per night, plus food; and a community-run shelter 10 minutes up from the pass (contact La Paz agencies for further information). Average cost is US$100 per person for two-day tour for 3 people (US$200 for one) including all equipment except sleeping bag. The starting point for the normal route is at Zongo, whose valley used to have a famous ice cave (now destroyed by global warming). See Climbing, hiking and trekking, page 294, for details of guides.

La Paz and around listings

Hotel and guesthouse prices
LL over US$200 **L** US$151-200 **AL** US$101-150
A US$66-100 **B** US$46-65 **C** US$31-45
G US$6 and **D** US$21-30 **E** US$12-20
F US$7-11under
Restaurant prices
TTT over US$12 TT US$7-12 T under US$6

Sleeping

Around Plaza Murillo *p279, maps p280 and p282*

L-AL Hotel Presidente, Potosí 920 y Sanjines, T240 6666, www.hotelpresidente-bo.com. The 'highest 5-star in the world'. Includes breakfast, gym and sauna, pool, all open to non-residents, internet, Wi-Fi, bar, excellent service, comfortable, heating, good food.

B Gloria, Potosí 909, T240 7070, www.hotelgloria.com.bo. Modern, central, cable TV, price includes breakfast, 2 restaurants (1 of which vegetarian), internet, good food and service, run **Gloria Tours** (www.gloriatours.com.bo). Recommended.

B Señorial Montero, Av América 120, esq Plaza Alonso de Mendoza 120, T245 7300, www.hotelsenorialmontero.com. Includes buffet breakfast, heating in rooms, cable TV, popular with tour groups; big, old-fashioned, comfortable hotel.

D Hostal República, Comercio 1455, T220 2742, www.hostalrepublica.com. **E** with shared bath, **C** in apartment, old house of former president, hot water, luggage stored, laundry service, good café, quiet garden, free internet, Wi-Fi, book ahead and ask for room on upper floor.

D The Adventure Brew Hostel, Av Montes 533, T246 1614, www.theadventurebrewhostel.com. With solar-heated showers, **F** pp in dorm, on-site microbrewery, includes breakfast and beer on arrival, rooftop terrace with great views of the city and Illimani, nightly BBQs, use of kitchen, convenient to the bus station, associated with **Gravity Assisted Mountain Biking** (see Activities and tours, below). Also has **E The Adventure Brew Too**, Av Montes 641, T228 4323. 8 or 12-bed dorms, with breakfast, internet, use of kitchen, free beer from microbrewery on arrival, garden patio with beer spa and jacuzzi, fantastic views of city, good value, popular meeting place.

E Loki, Loayza 420, T211 9024, www.lokihostel.com. Old Hotel Vienna renovated as member of this chain of popular party hostels. **E-F** in dorm (one dorm is girl-only), kitchen, free breakfast, TV room, computer room and Wi-Fi, bar (serve dinner). Has tour operator.

E Tambo de Oro, Armentia 367, T228 1565. Near bus station, private bath, hot showers, TV, good value if a bit run down, safe for luggage.

E Torino, Socabaya 457, T240 6003, www.hoteltorino.com.bo. Ask for better rooms in new section, cheaper without bath, run-down rooms in old section, popular with backpackers, free book exchange, cultural centre, travel agency, good service, internet café (pricey) and good restaurant next door for breakfast and good value lunch (weekdays 1200-1500).

F pp **Arthy's Guesthouse**, Montes 693, T228 1439, http://arthyshouse.tripod.com. Safe, helpful, popular with bikers, English spoken, use of kitchen, 2400 curfew.

F-G Austria, Yanacocha 531, T240 8540. Without bath, cheaper in shared room, basic, hot water but only three showers, safe deposit, laundry, TV lounge, use of kitchen, internet, luggage storage, no English spoken.

G pp **Hospedaje Milenio**, Yanacocha 860, T228 1263, hospedajemilenio@hotmail.com. Shared bath, electric shower, basic, family house, homely and welcoming, popular, helpful owner, quiet, kitchen, breakfast extra, security boxes, internet, laundry service, great value.

G pp **Posada El Carretero**, Catacora 1056, entre Yanacocha y Junín, T228 5271. Single and double rooms and dorms, helpful, hot showers, kitchen, laundry service, good atmosphere and value.

G pp **Wild Rover Backpackers Hostel**, Comercio 1476, T211 6903, www.wildroverhostel.com. "Party-style hostel" in renovated colonial-style house with courtyard and high-ceilings, dorms with 6-10 beds and doubles with shared bath (**F**), bar, TV room, book exchange, internet, serve dinner and breakfast, helpful staff who speak English.

Plaza San Francisco up to the cemetery district *p283, maps p280 and p282*

B Rosario, Illampu 704, T245 1658, www.hotelrosario.com. Good buffet breakfast, sauna, laundry, internet café **Jiwhaki** (free for guests, great view), Wi-Fi, good restaurant, stores luggage, very helpful staff, no smoking. Highly recommended. **Turisbus** travel agency downstairs (see Tour operators, page 296), Cultural Interpretation Centre explains items for sale in nearby 'witches' market'.

C Estrella Andina, Illampu 716, T245 6421, www.estrellaandina.com. Price includes breakfast, **D** in low season, all rooms have a safe and are decorated individually, English spoken, family run, comfortable, tidy, helpful, Wi-Fi, roof terrace, heaters on loan, cable TV, laundry service, money exchange, very nice. Also owns **D Cruz de los Andes**, Aroma 216, T245 1401, same style but shares premises with a car garage.

C Galería, Pasaje Virgen de Rosario, p 4, T246 1015. Great rooms, lots of daylight, includes breakfast, cable TV, internet, safety boxes, quiet, helpful, good value.

C Hostal Naira, Sagárnaga 161, T235 5645, www.hostalnaira.com. Hot water, comfortable but pricey, rooms around courtyard, some are dark, price includes good buffet breakfast in **Café Banais**, cable TV, safety deposit boxes, laundry service.

C La Posada de la Abuela,, C Linares 947, T233 2285. Very pleasant inn, includes continental breakfast, cable TV and Wi-Fi.

D Arcabucero, C Viluyo 307 y Linares, T/F231 3473. Price rises in high season, pleasant new rooms in converted colonial house, excellent value but check the beds, breakfast extra.

D La Joya, Max Paredes 541, T245 3841, www.hotelajoya.com. **E** without bath, breakfast included, TV, modern and comfy, lift, laundry, area unsafe at night but provides transfers.

D Milton, Illampu 1126-1130, T236 8003, www.hotelmiltonbolivia.com. Hot water, includes breakfast, psychedelic 1970s style wallpaper in many rooms, restaurant, expensive laundry, safe parking around corner, popular, will store luggage, excellent views from roof.

D Sagárnaga, Sagárnaga 326, T235 0252, www.hotel-sagarnaga.com. Cheaper in plain rooms without TV, includes breakfast, solar-powered hot water, Wi-Fi, laundry, 2 ATMs, English spoken, *peña*.

D-E Fuentes, Linares 888, T231 3966, www.hotelfuentesbolivia.com. Cheaper without bath, hot water, variety of rooms, includes breakfast, nice colonial style, comfortable, TV, internet, sauna, good value, family run, slow laundry service.

D-F Onkel Inn 1886, Colombia 257, T249 0456, www.onkel-inn-highlanders.com. Hostel in a remodelled 19th-century house, rooms with and without bath, doubles, triples and bunks, with breakfast. Jacuzzi, laundry facilities, internet, café and bar, HI affiliated.

E Hostal Copacabana, Illampu 734, T245 1626, www.hostalcopacabana.com. Hot water, good showers, soft beds, includes breakfast, internet, fading but OK.

E Majestic, Santa Cruz 359, T245 1628. Simple rooms with cable TV, breakfast included, restaurant, comfortable, laundry, safe.

E Res Sucre, Colombia 340, on Plaza San Pedro, T249 2038. **F** without bath, quiet area, hot water, big rooms, kitchen and laundry facilities, luggage stored, helpful.

F El Solario, Murillo 776, T236 7963, www.elsolario.com. Central, shared bath, luggage store, kitchen, internet, international phone calls, laundry and medical services, taxi and travel agency, good value, gets crowded.
F El Viajero, Illampu 807, T245 1640, www.lobo.co.il. **F-G** without bath, **G** pp in dorm, a reasonable hostel, decorated with plants, dorm has lockers.
F-G Hostal Cactus, Jiménez 818 y Santa Cruz, T245 1421. Shared electric showers, kitchen facilities, luggage store, poor beds and plumbing, don't leave valuables unattended, but peaceful, quiet, helpful, nice communal feel. **Coca Travels** agency downstairs, good.

The Prado, Sopocachi, Miraflores and Zona Sur *p283, map p280*
LL-L Radisson Plaza, Av Arce 2177, T244 1111, www.radisson.com/lapazbo. 5-star hotel with all facilities, includes breakfast, gym, pool and sauna (also for guests of **Plaza Hotel**), Wi-Fi, excellent buffet in restaurant (see Eating, below).
L Casa Grande, Av Ballivián 1000 y C 17, Calacoto, T279 5511, www.casa-grande.com.bo. Beautiful, top quality apartments, includes buffet breakfast, Wi-Fi, airport pickup, restaurant, very good service, US$4,200 per month.
AL Europa, Tiahuanacu 64, T231 5656, www.hoteleuropa.com.bo. Next to the Museo Nacional de Arqueología. Excellent facilities and plenty of frills, internet in rooms, health club, several restaurants,. parking. Recommended.
AL Plaza, Av 16 de Julio 1789, T237 8311. Excellent hotel with good value restaurant (see below), includes breakfast, Wi-Fi, pool.
A El Rey Palace, Av 20 de Octubre 1947, T241 8541, www.hotelreypalace.com. Includes breakfast, large suites with heating, a/c and cable TV, internet, excellent restaurant, stylish.
A-B Alcalá Aparthotel, Sanjinés 2662 at Plaza España, Sopocachi, T241 2336, www.alcalapartamentos.com. Comfortable, spacious, furnished apartments, includes breakfast, internet, 20% discount per month.
B A La Maison, Pasaje Muñoz Cornejo15, Sopocachi, T241 3704, www.alamaison-lapaz.com. Apart-hotel, brightly decorated, breakfast, laundry service, Wi-Fi, TV, kitchens in the larger flats, meals and tourist services can be arranged, daily and monthly rates available.
C EHT Sopocachi, Macario Pinilla 580 at the base of El Montículo, T241 0312. Spacious furnished apartments with kitchenette, good location and views, gym.

El Alto *p277*
D-E Alexander, Av Jorge Carrasco 61 y C 3, Ceja, Zona 12 de Octibre, T282 3376. Modern, with breakfast, **F** pp in dorm, parking, disco, cable TV.
E-F Orquídea, C Dos 22 y Av 6 de Marzo, Villa Bolívar A, near bus terminals, T282 6487. Includes breakfast, comfortable heated rooms, cheaper with shared bath, electric showers, good value. Better than others in the area.

South of La Paz *p284*
A Gloria Urmiri, Potosi 909, Urmiri, T237 0010 or 240 7070, www.hotelgloria.com.bo. At hot springs 2 hrs from La Paz, price for 2 days, 1 night (price varies according to type of room), includes entry to pools, sauna and all facilities as well as 4 meals, lunch to lunch. Transport US$6.25 pp each way. Massage available, camping US$2.80, reservations required.
A-C Allkamari, near Valle de las Animas, 30 mins from town on the road to Palca, T279 1742, www.casalunaspa.com. Reservations required, cabins for up to 8 in a lovely valley between the Palca and La Animas canyons, a retreat with nice views of Illimani and Mururata, a place to relax and star-gaze, **D** pp in dorm, solar heating, Jacuzzi included, meals on request, use of kitchen, horse and bike rentals, massage, shamanic rituals, taxi from Calacoto US$7, bus No 42 from the cemetery to Uni (7 daily weekdays, hourly weekends), get off at Iglesia de las Animas and walk 1 km.
C Oberland, Mallasa, C El Agrario 3118, entre C 2 y 3, 12 km from centre, T274 5040, www.h-oberland.com. A Swiss-owned, chalet-style restaurant (excellent, not cheap) and hotel (also good) with older resort facilities, Wi-Fi, gardens, spa, sauna, pool (open to public – US$2 – very hot water), beach volleyball, tennis. Permit camping with vehicle, US$4 pp.

Eating

Around Plaza Murillo *p279, maps p280 and p282*

¥¥ **La Casa de los Paceños**, Sucre 814, T228 0955, also at San Miguel, C Juan Capriles, T214 5903. Open 1100-1600, 1800-2200. Tourist restaurant, excellent Bolivian food, à la carte only.

¥¥ **La Kantuta**, in *Hotel Presidente*, Potosí 920, T240 6666. Excellent food, good service. **La Bella Vista** on the top floor is fancier.

¥ **El Calicanto**, Sanjinés 467, T240 8008. Great regional specialities, renovated colonial house, live music on Fri. Mon-Sat 1100-1500, Mon-Fri 1830-2200.

Cafés

Alexander Coffee, Potosí 1091. Part of a chain, sandwiches, salads, coffee, pastries.

Café Berlín, Mercado 1377 y Loayza, and at Av Montenegro 708, San Miguel, 0800-2300. Coffee, omelettes, breakfast, popular with locals and smoky.

Café Confitería de la Paz, Camacho 1202, on the corner where Ayacucho joins Av Mcal Santa Cruz. Good if expensive tea room, traditional, great coffee and cakes but very smoky.

Plaza San Francisco up to the cemetery district *p283, maps p280 and p282*

¥¥ **Pizzería Italia**, Illampu 840, T246 3152, and 809, 2nd floor, T245 0714. Thin-crust pizza, pasta and international food.

¥¥ **Star of India**, Cochabamba 170, T211 4409. British-run Indian curry house, will deliver, including to hotels. Recommended.

¥¥ **Tambo Colonial**, in *Hotel Rosario* (see above). Excellent local and international cuisine, good salad bar, buffet breakfast, peña at weekend.

¥¥-¥ **Sol y Luna**, Murillo 999 y Cochabamba, T211 5323, www.solyluna-lapaz.com. Opens Mon-Fri 0900-0100, Fri till 0200, Sat 1700-0200, Sun 1700-0100. Dutch run, breakfast, *almuerzo* and international menu, coffees and teas, full wine and cocktail list, live music Mon and Fri, movies, Wi-Fi, guide books for sale, book exchange.

¥¥-¥ **The Colonial Pot**, Linares 906, close to Sagárnaga. Bolivian and a variety of main courses including vegetarian, all-day *menú* US$3.35 and à-la-carte, pastries, snacks, hot and cold drinks, quiet, homely, music, exceptional value.

¥¥-¥ **Tucan Bistro**, Tarija 725. Open daily 1600-2400. Varied international menu, good food in laid back atmosphere, US$2 for *almuerzo* Mon-Fri; wine bar. Bolivian-Australian owned.

¥¥-¥ **Yussef**, Sagárnaga 380, second floor, T231 1167. Lebanese, mezze, good for vegetarians, good value and relaxed atmosphere.

¥ **100% Natural**, Sagárnaga 345. Range of healthy, tasty fast foods ranging from salads to burgers and llama meat, good breakfasts.

¥ **A Lo Cubano**, Sagárnaga 357, entre Linares y Illampu, T245 1797. Open Mon-Sat 1200-2200. *Almuerzo* for US$1.95, but it runs out fast, also other choices of good Cuban food, good value.

¥ **Al Amir**, Murillo 824. Middle-eastern food including falafels, hummus and mixed plate for 2 for US$5, *almuerzo* US$2.15, open daily.

¥ **Angelo Colonial**, Linares 922, T215 9633. Vegetarian options, good music, internet access, open early for breakfast, can get busy with slow service. Has a hostal at Av Santa Cruz 1058, with hot water, safe, convenient.

¥ **El Lobo**, Illampu y Santa Cruz. Israeli dishes, good meeting place, noticeboard, popular.

¥ **Jackie Chan**, Cochabamba 100 (just south of Av Mcal Santa Cruz), T233 9231. Good Chinese, excellent value, popular with locals, disco in basement at weekends.

Cafés

Banais, Sagárnaga 161, same entrance as *Hostal Naira*. Coffee, sandwiches and juices, buffet breakfast, laid-back music and computer room.

Café Soho, Jaén 747. Cosy café with small courtyard, inside and outside seating, local artwork, open Mon-Sun 0930-2300.

Hard Rock Café, Santa Cruz 399 e Illampu, T211 9318, www.hardrockcafebolivia.lobopages.com. Serves Hard Rock fair, turns into nightclub around 2400, popular with locals and tourists.

Pepe's, Pasaje Jiménez 894, off Linares. All-day breakfasts, sandwiches, omelettes, tables outside, cards and dominoes, magazines and guidebooks.

The Prado, Sopocachi, Miraflores and Zona Sur *p283, map p280*

¥¥¥ **Chalet la Suisse**, Av Muñoz Reyes 1710, Cota Cota, T279 3160, www.chaletlasuisse.com. Serves excellent fondue, steaks, booking is essential on Fri evening.

La Comedie, Pasaje Medinacelli 2234, Sopocachi, T242 3561. 'Art café restaurant', contemporary, with a French menu, good salads, wine list and cocktails, Mon-Fri 1200-2300, Sat-Sun opens at 1900.

Maphrao On, Hnos Manchego 2586, near Plaza Isabela la Católica, T243 4682. Thai and South East Asian food, warm atmosphere, good music.

El Arriero, Av 6 de Agosto 2525 (Casa Argentina), Sopocachi, T243 5060, also Av Montenegro entre C 17 y 18, San Miguel, T279 1907. The best Argentine *parrilla* in the city, also daily *almuerzo* from US$5.

El Consulado, Bravo 299 (behing Plaza Hotel), T211 7706, www.topas.bo. In gorgeous setting with outdoor seating and covered terrace, includes high-end handicraft store, book exchange, Wi-Fi, photo gallery, organic coffee and food, pricey but worth it.

High Lander's, Final Sánchez Lima 2667, Sopocachi, T243 0023. Variable Tex-Mex fare, nice atmosphere, good views from the end of the street, Mon-Fri 1200-1500, 1700-2300, Sat 1900-2330, happy hour Mon-Fri 1700-1900.

Ken-Cha, Bat Colorado 98 y F Suazo, p 2 of Japanese Cultural Center, T244 2292. Japanese restaurant with wide variety of dishes, popular.

La Tranquera, Capitán Ravelo 2123 next to Hotel Camino Real, T244 1103; also at Hotel Camino Real, Calacoto, T279 2323. International food, grill and salad bar, daily 1200-1600, 1900-2300.

Reineke Fuchs, Pje Jáuregui 2241, Sopocachi, T244 2979, and Av Montenegro y C 18, San Miguel, T277 2103, www.reinekefuchs.com. Many imported German beers and food in a German-style bar, open Mon-Fri 1200-1430 and from 1900, Sat from 1900 only.

Suma Uru, Av Arce 2177 in Radisson Plaza Hotel, T244 1111. Excellent buffet in 5-star setting, daily 1200-1500, friendly to backpackers.

Utama, in *Plaza* hotel, Av 16 de Julio 1789). 2 restaurants: **Utama** on the top floor, with the views, 1700-2300, à la carte, and **Uma**, on the ground floor, for breakfast and lunch, buffet lunch US$6.15. Recommended.

Vienna, Federico Zuazo 1905, T244 1660, www.restaurantvienna.com. Excellent German, Austrian and local food, great atmosphere and service, live piano music, popular, open Mon-Fri 1200-1400, 1830-2200, Sun 1200-1430.

Wagamama, Pasaje Pinilla 2557, T243 4911. Open Mon-Sat 1200-1400, 1900-2130 (closed Sun) serves sushi, complimentary tea, excellent service, popular with ex-pats.

Mongo's, Hnos Manchego 2444, near Plaza Isabela la Católica, T244 0714. Open 1800-0300, live music Tue, excellent Mexican fare and steaks, open fires, bar (cocktails can be pricey), club after midnight, popular with gringos and locals.

Armonía, Ecuador 2286 y Quito. Nice vegetarian buffet lunch, Mon-Sat 1200-1430.

Eli's Pizza Express, Av 16 de Julio 1400 block. English spoken, open daily including holidays (also at Comercio 914 and Av Montenegro y C 19, Zona Sur), very popular, maybe not the best pizza in La Paz, but certainly the largest omelettes.

Lu Qing, 20 de Octubre 2090 y Aspiazu, T242 4188. Chinese food, large choice of dishes, set meals on weekdays, Mon-Sat 1130-1500, 1830-2300, Sun 1100-1530.

Mundo Vegetariano, Goitia 127 entre Av Arce y Capitán Ravelo. Mon-Fri 1200-1700.

Good vegetarian set lunch including small salad bar.

The Olive Tree, Campos 334, Edificio Iturri, T243 1552. Closed Sat evening and Sun, good salads, soups and sandwiches, attentive service. Open Mon-Fri 1100-2200.

Cafés

Alexander Coffee (Café Alex), Av 16 de Julio 1832, also at 20 de Octubre 2463 Plaza Avaroa, Av Montenegro 1336, Calacoto, and the airport. Excellent coffee, smoothies, muffins, cakes and good salads and sandwiches, Wi-Fi, open 0730-2400. Recommended.

Arco Iris, F Guachalla 554 y Sánchez Lima, Sopocachi, T242 3009. Also in Achumani, C 16 by the market, T271 2577. Bakery and handicraft outlet of Fundación Arco Iris (www.arcoirisbolivia.org), which works with street children, good variety of breads, pastries, meats and cheeses.

Dumbos, Av 16 de Julio, near *Eli's* and Cinema. For meat and chicken *salteñas*, ice creams, look for the dancing furry animals outside.

Fridolin, Av 6 de Agosto 2415; and Prolongación Montenegro, San Miguel. *Empanadas*, *tamales*, savoury and sweet (Austrian) pastries, coffee, breakfast, Wi-Fi.

Kuchen Stube, Rosendo Gutiérrez 461, Sopocachi. Excellent cakes, coffee and German specialities, Mon -Fri 0800-2000, Sat-Sun 0800-1900.

La Terraza, 16 de Julio 1615, T231 0701, 0630-2400; 20 de Octubre 2171 y Gutiérrez; and Av Montenegro 1576 y C 8, Calacoto, both 0730-2400. Excellent sandwiches and coffee, pancakes, breakfasts, Wi-Fi.

Bars and clubs

The epicentre for nightlife in La Paz is currently Plaza Avaroa in Sopocachi. Clubs are clustered around here and crowds gather Fri and Sat nights.

Around Plaza Murillo *p279, maps p280 and p282*

Etno Café, Jaén 722, T228 0343. Open Mon-Sat 1930-0300. Small café/bar with cultural programmes including readings, concerts, movies, popular, serves artisanal and fair trade drinks (alcoholic or not).

San Francisco up to the cemetery district *p283, maps p280 and p282*

Blue Note Café, Viluyo esq Plaza Gaston Velasco. Open Mon-Sat 1200-2400, wine bar with light food, same owners as **Tucan Bistro**, interesting hat collection, good place to hang out for a coffee or glass of wine in relaxed atmosphere.

Oliver's Travels, Murillo y Tarija, T231 1574. Fake English pub serving breakfasts, curries, fish and chips, pasta, sports channels, music, travel agency.

The Prado, Sopocachi, Miraflores and Zona Sur *p283, map p280*

Deadstroke, Av 6 de Agosto 2460, Sopocachi, T243 3472. Bar/pool hall, café and billiards bar, food, drinks (good value for beer), billiards, pool and other games, opens 1700 (1900 on Sat).

Equinoccio, Sánchez Lima 2191, Sopocachi. Top venue for live rock music and bar, Thu-Sat, cover charge US$2.10, or more for popular bands.

Fak'n Tako, Belisario Salinas opposite Presbitero Medina. Good place to get cheap drinks before going dancing at more expensive clubs, '80s style DJ, playing lots of reggaeton and Latin music.

RamJam, C Presbitero Medina 2421, Sopocachi, T242 2295. Above Plaza Avaroa, open 1900-0400 Mon-Sat, energetic place aimed at gringos and moneyed locals, with coffee, curry, microbrewery beer and cable TV, dancing, packed Fri and Sat nights.

Tetekos, C México 1553. Loud music, cheap drinks, popular with locals and backpackers.

Theolonius Jazz Bar, 20 de Octubre 2172, Sopocachi, T242 4405. Wed-Sat shows start at 2200. Renowned for jazz (what else?), cover charge US$1.40-2.80.

Entertainment

For up-to-the-minute information on cinemas and shows, check *La Prensa* or *La Razón* on Fri, or visit www.la-razon.com. Also look for *Kaos* and *Mañana*, 2 free monthly magazines with listings of concerts, exhibits, festivals, etc.

Around Plaza Murillo *p279, maps p280 and p282*

Bocaisapo, Indaburo 654 y Jaén. Live music in a bar; no cover charge, popular, open Thu-Fri 1900-0300.

Marka Tambo, Jaén 710, T228 0041. Thu-Sat 2100-0200, also Mon-Sat 1230-1500 for lunch. US$6 for evening show, food and drinks extra, live shows with traditional dancing and music (peña), recommended.

Plaza San Francisco up to the cemetery district *p283, maps p280 and p282*

El Parnaso, Sagárnaga 189, T231 6827. Daily starting at 2030, meals available, purely for tourists but a good way to see local costumes and dancing.

Cinemas Films mainly in English with Spanish subtitles cost around US$3.50, see www.monjecampero.com and www.cineteatro16dejulio.com. **Cinemateca Boliviana**, Oscar Soria (prolong F90ederico Zuazo) y Rosendo Gutiérrez, T244 4090, info@cinematecaboliviana.org. Municipal theatre with emphasis on independent productions.

Theatre **Teatro Municipal Alberto Saavedra Pérez** has a regular schedule of plays, opera, ballet and classical concerts, at Sanjinés y Indaburo, T240 6183. The National Symphony Orchestra is very good and gives inexpensive concerts. Next door is the **Teatro Municipal de Cámara**, which shows dance, drama, music and poetry. **Casa Municipal de la Cultura 'Franz Tamayo'**, almost opposite Plaza San Francisco, hosts a variety of exhibitions, paintings, sculpture, photography, etc, mostly free. Free monthly guide to cultural events at information desk at entrance. The **Palacio Chico**, Ayacucho y Potosí, in old Correo, operated by the Secretaría Nacional de Cultura, also has exhibitions (good for modern art), concerts and ballet, Mon-Fri 0900-1230, 1500-1900, closed at weekends, free.

Festivals and events

La Paz *p277, maps p280 and p282*

Starting **24 Jan** **Alasitas**, in Parque Central up from Av del Ejército, also in Plaza Sucre/San Pedro, recommended. **Carnaval** usually in **Feb**. **End May/early Jun** **Festividad del Señor de Gran Poder**, the most important festival of the year, with a huge procession of costumed and masked dancers on the 3rd Sat after Trinity. **Jul** **Fiestas de Julio**, a month of concerts and performances at the Teatro Municipal, with a variety of music, including the University Folkloric Festival. **8 Dec**, festival around Plaza España, colourful and noisy. On **New Year's Eve** there are fireworks displays; view from higher up. See page 275 for national holidays and festivals outside La Paz.

Shopping

La Paz *p277, maps p280 and p282*

Bookshops **Los Amigos del Libro**, Av Ballivián 1273, T220 0695, also Av Montenegro 1410 (San Miguel), www.librosbolivia.com. Large stock of English, French and German books; also a few maps, expensive. **Gisbert**, Comercio 1270, and in San Miguel on a small lane opposite Café Alexander. Books, maps, stationery. **Yachaywasi**, Pasaje Trigo 447 y Av Villazón, on lane between Plaza del Estudiante and the university. Large selection, popular with students.

Camping equipment Kerosene for pressure stoves is available from a pump in Plaza Alexander, Pando e Inca. **Ayni Sport Bolivia**, Jiménez 806, open Mon-Sun 1030-2100. Rents and sometimes sells camping equipment and mountain gear (trekking shoes, fleeces, climbing equiment etc). **Caza y Pesca**, Edif Handal Center, No 9, Av Mcal Santa Cruz y Socabaya, T240 9209. English spoken. **Tatoo Bolivia**, Illampu 828, T245 1265, www.tatoo.ws. Tatoo clothing plus outdoor equipment including backpacks, shoes, etc. English and Dutch spoken.

Handicrafts Above Plaza San Francisco (see page 283), up Sagárnaga, by the side of San Francisco church (behind which are many handicraft stalls in the Mercado Artesanal), are booths and small stores with interesting local items of all sorts. The lower end of Sagárnaga is best for antiques. **Galeria Doryan**, Sagárnaga 177, is an entire gallery of handicraft shops. On Linares, between Sagárnaga and Santa Cruz, high quality alpaca goods are priced in US$. Also in this area are many places making fleece jackets, gloves and hats, but shop around for value and service. **Alpaca Style**, C 22 #14, T271 1233, Achumani, www.alpaca-style.com. Upmarket shop selling alpaca and leather clothing. **Artesanía Sorata**, Linares 900 y Sagárnaga, T245 4728, and Sagárnaga 363, T239 3041. Mon-Sat 0930-1900 (and Sun 1000-1800 high season), specializes in dolls, sweaters and weavings. **Ayni**, Illampu 704, www.aynibolivia.com. Fair trade shop in Hotel Rosario, featuring Aymara work. **Comart Tukuypaj**, Linares 958, T231 2686, and C 21, Galería Centro de Moda, Local 4B y 5B, San Miguel, Zona Sur, T 277 3049, www.comart-tukuypaj.com. High-quality textiles from an artisan community association. **Comercio Doryan**, Sagárnaga y Murillo, eg **Tejides Wari**, unit 12, Comercio Doryan, closed Sun. High-quality alpaca goods, will make to measure quickly, English spoken. **Incapallay**, Linares 958, p 2, www.incapallay.org. A weavers' cooperative from Tarabuco and Jalq'a communities, near Sucre. **Jiwitaki Art Shop**, Jaén 705, T7725 4042, jiwitakishop@yahoo.com. Run by local artists selling sketches, paintings, sculptures, literature, etc. Open Mon-Fri 1100-1300, 1500-1800. **LAM** shops on Sagárnaga. Good quality alpaca goods. **Millma**, Sagárnaga 225, T231 1338, and Claudio Aliaga 1202, Bloque L-1, San Miguel, Zona Sur, T279 2750, closed Sat afternoon and Sun. High-quality alpaca knitwear and woven items and, on the lower level of the San Miguel shop, a permanent exhibition of ceremonial 19th and 20th century Aymara and Quechua textiles (free). **Mother Earth**, Linares 870, T239 1911. 0930-1930 daily. High-quality alpaca sweaters with natural dyes. **Toshy** on Sagárnaga. Top-quality knitwear (closed Sat afternoon).

Jewellery There are good jewellery stores throughout the city: for example **Joyería King's Store**, Loayza 261, between Camacho and Mercado, T220 1331, szarf@entelnet.bo. Also Torre Ketal, C 15, Calacoto, T277 2542.

Maps IGM: head office at Estado Mayor General, Av Saavedra 2303, Miraflores, T222 0513, Mon-Thu 0900-1200, 1500-1800, Fri 0900-1200, take passport to buy maps. Also office in Edif Murillo, Juan XXIII 100 (mud track between Rodríguez y Linares), Mon-Fri 0800-1200, 1400-1800, will order maps from HQ. **Librería IMAS**, Av Mcal Santa Cruz entre Loayza y Colón, Edif Colón, T235 8234. Ask for the map collection and check what is in stock. Maps are also sold in the Post Office on the stalls opposite the Poste Restante counter.

Markets In addition to those mentioned in the Sights section (page 283), the 5-km sq **Feria 16 de Julio, El Alto** market is on Thu and Sun (the latter is bigger). Take any minibus that says La Ceja and get off at overpass after toll booth (follow crowd of people or tell driver you're going to La Feria), or take 16 de Julio minibus from Plaza Eguino. Arrive around 0900; most good items are sold by 1200. Goods are cheap, especially on Thu. Absolutely everything imaginable is sold here. Be watchful for pickpockets, just take a bin liner to carry your purchases. **Mercado Sopocachi**, Guachalla y Ecuador, a well-stocked covered market selling foodstuffs, kitchen supplies, etc.

Musical instruments Many shops on Sagárnaga/Linares, for example **Walata 855**. **Pasaje Linares**, the stairs off C Linares, has shops selling just instruments.

Shopping malls and supermarkets
Megacenter, Av Rafael Pabón, Irpavi, huge food court, 18 cinés, bowling, banks, ATMs. **Shopping Norte**, Potosí y Socabaya. Modern mall with restaurants and expensive merchandise. **Supermercado Ketal**, Av Arce y Pinillo, near Plaza Isabel la Católica, Sopocachi, Av Busch y Villalobos, Miraflores, C 21, San Miguel, and Av Ballivián y C 15, Calacoto. Well-stocked supermarket.

Activities and tours

La Paz *p277, maps p280 and p282*

City tours

Sightseeing, T279 1440, city tours on a double-decker bus, 2 circuits, downtown and Zona Sur with Valle de la Luna (1 morning and 1 afternoon departure to each), departs from Plaza Isabel la Católica and can hop on at Plaza San Francisco, tour recorded in 7 languages, US$6 for both circuits, Mon-Fri 0830 and 1430, Sat-Sun 0900 and 1430.

Climbing, hiking and trekking

Guides must be hired through a tour company. **Alberth Bolivia Tours**, Illampu 750, T245 8018, www.hikingbolivia.com. Good for climbing and trekking, helpful, equipment rental.
Andean Summits, Sotomayor, esq Muñoz Cornejo, Edif Laura, pb, T242 2106, www.andeansummits.com. For mountaineering and other trips off the beaten track; contact in advance.
Bolivian Mountains, Rigoberto Paredes 1401 y Colombia, p 3, San Pedro, T249 2775, www.bolivianmountains.com (in UK T01273-746545). High-quality mountaineering outfit with experienced guides and good equipment, not cheap.
The Adventure Climbing Company, Av Jaimes Freyre 2970, Plaza Adela Zamudio, Sopocachi, T241 4197, newhorizons20@hotmail.com. Specializes in climbing, trekking and other adventures, experienced guides.

Trek Bolivia, C Sagárnaga 392, T/F231 7106, www.trekbolivia.8k.com. Organizes expeditions in the Cordillera.

For Maps, see Essentials, page 272 and Shopping, above.

Football

Popular and played on Wed and Sun at the **Siles Stadium** in Miraflores (Micro A), which is shared by both La Paz's main teams, Bolívar and The Strongest. There are reserved seats.

Golf

Mallasilla is the world's highest golf course, at 3,318 m. Non-members can play at Mallasilla on weekdays; no need to book. Club hire, green fee, balls and a caddy also costs US$37. There is also a course at Los Pinos in the Zona Sur.

Snooker/pool/other

Picco's, Edif 16 de Julio, Av 16 de Julio 1566. Good tables and friendly atmosphere.

YMCA sportsground and gym: opposite the University of San Andrés, Av Villazón, and clubhouse open to the public (table tennis, billiards, etc).

Tour operators

America Tours SRL, Av 16 de Julio 1490 (El Prado), Edificio Avenida pb, No 9, T237 4204, www.america-ecotours.com. Cultural and ecotourism trips to many parts of the country (including Chalalán Lodge near Rurrenabaque and Parque Nacional Noel Kempff Mercado), rafting, trekking and horse-riding, English spoken. Highly professional and recommended. Basic book exchange.

Andean Base Camp, Illampu 863, T246 3782, andeanbasecamp@hotmail.com. Overland tours throughout Bolivia, Swiss staff, good reports.

Andean Secrets, no storefront, contact through quimsacruz_bolivia@hotmail.com, www.andean-secrets.com. Female mountain guide Denys Sanjines specializes in the Cordillera Quimsa Cruz.

Bolivian Journeys, Sagárnaga 363, p 2, T/F235 7848, www.bolivianjourneys.org. Camping, mountain bike tours, equipment rental, maps, English and French spoken, helpful.

B-Side Adventures, Linares 943, T211 4225, www.bside-adventures.com. Good for cycling to Coroico and other rides.

Colibrí, Alberto Ostria 1891 y J M Cáceres, Edif Isabelita p 4, Sopocachi Alto, T242 3246, www.colibri-adventures.com. Climbing, trekking, adventure tours, and more, helpful guides.

Crillon Tours, Av Camacho 1223, T233 7533, www.titicaca.com. With 24-hr ATM for cash on credit cards. A company with over 50 years experience. Joint scheduled tours with Lima arranged. Fixed departures to Salar de Uyuni, trips to Sucre, the Yungas, Beni, community tourism and much more. Recommended. Full details of their Lake Titicaca services on page 308.

Deep Rainforest, Illampu 626, T215 0385, www.deep-rainforest.com. Off the beaten track trekking, climbing, canoe trips from Guanay to Rurrenabaque, rainforest and pampas trips.

Detour, Av Mcal Santa Cruz 1392, esq Colombia, T236 1626. Good for flight tickets.

Gloria Tours/Hotel Gloria, Potosí 909, T240 7070, www.gloriatours.com.bo. Good service, see Sleeping, pages 287 and 289.

Gravity Bolivia, Av 16 de Julio 1490, Edificio Avenida, PB, No 10 (across the hall from América Tours), T241 2272, www.gravitybolivia.com. A wide variety of mountain biking tours throughout Bolivia, including the world-famous downhill ride to Coroico. Also offers rides more challenging than the Coroico ride, including single-track and high-speed dirt roads and the GhostRide, with coaching and safety equipment. Recommended. Sells guidebooks. Book on website in advance.
La Paz On Foot, C Pablo Sánchez 6981, Irpavi, T7153 9753, www.lapazonfoot.com. Walking city tours, walking and sailing trips on Titicaca and multi-day treks in the Yungas and Apolobamba. Recommended.
Lipiko Tours, Calle 7 150, Los Pinos, Zona Sur, T214 5129, www.travel-bolivia.co.uk. Tailor-made tours for all budgets, 4WD tours, trekking, climbing and adventure sport, trips to Amazon and national parks. Also cover Peru, Chile and Argentina.
Magri Turismo, Capitán Ravelo 2101, T244 2727, www.magriturismo.com. Amex representative, gives TCs against American Express card but doesn't change TCs, offers Amex emergency services and clients' mail. Recommended for tours in Bolivia, travel services. Own **La Estancia** hotel on the Isla del Sol.
Moto Andina, Urb La Colina N°6 Calle 25, Calacoto, T7129 9329, www.moto-andina.com. Motorcycle tours of varying difficulty in Bolivia, contact Maurice Manco.
Topas Travel, Carlos Bravo 299 (behind Hotel Plaza), T211 1082, www.topas.bo. Joint venture of Akhamani Trek (Bolivia), Topas (Denmark) and the Danish embassy, offering trekking, overland truck trips, jungle trips, biking and climbing, English spoken, restaurant and *pensión*.
Transturin, Av Arce 2678, Sopocachi, T242 2222, www.transturin.com. Full travel services with tours ranging from La Paz to the whole country. Details of their Lake Titicaca services on page 309.
Tupiza Tours, Villalobos 625 y Av Saavedra, Edif Girasoles, pb, Miraflores, T224 5254, www.tupizatours.com. La Paz office of the Tupiza agency. Specialize in the Salar and southwest Bolivia, but can arrange tours throughout the country.
Turisbus, Av Illampu 704, T245 1341, www.turisbus.com. Lake Titicaca and Isla del Sol, Salar de Uyuni, Rurrenbaque, trekking and Bolivian tours. Also tours and tickets to Puno and Cuzco.
Turismo Balsa, Hermanos Manchego 2526, T244 0620, www.turismobalsa.com. City and tours throughout Bolivia, see also under Puerto Pérez, page 305. Also international flight deals.

Transport

La Paz *p277, maps p280 and p282*

Air

Cotranstur minibuses, T231 2032, white with 'Cotranstur' and 'Aeropuerto' written on the side and back, go from Plaza Isabel La Católica, stopping all along the Prado and Av Mcal Santa Cruz to the airport, 0615-2300, US$0.55 (allow about 1 hr), best to buy an extra seat for your luggage, departures every 4 min. Colectivos from Plaza Isabel La Católica charge US$3.50 pp, carrying 4 passengers. Radio-taxi is US$7 to centre, US$9 to Zona Sur. Prices are displayed at the airport terminal exit. There is an **Info Tur**

office in arrivals with a *casa de cambio* next to it (dollars, euros cash and TCs, poor rates; open 0530-1300, 1700-0300, closed Sun evening - when closed try the counter where departure taxes are paid). Several ATMs in the departures hall. The international and domestic departures hall is the main concourse, with all check-in desks. There are separate domestic and international arrivals. Bar/restaurant and café upstairs in departures. For details of air services, see under destinations.

Bus

For information, T228 5858. Buses to: **Oruro**, **Potosí**, **Sucre**, **Cochabamba**, **Santa Cruz**, **Tarija** and **Villazón**, leave from the main terminal at Plaza Antofagasta (micros 2, M, CH or 130), see under each destination for details. Taxi to central hotels, US$1.10. The terminal (open 0400-2300) has a tourist booth by the main entrance, internet, a post office, **Entel**, restaurant, luggage store, near the main entrance and several private kiosks at the rear, and travel agencies. Touts find passengers the most convenient bus and are paid commission by the bus company.

To **Copacabana**, several bus companies (tourist service) pick-up travellers in their hotels (in the centre) and also stop at the main terminal, tickets from booths at the terminal (cheaper) or agencies in town. They all leave about 0800, 3½ hrs, US$3.50-4.50 one way, return from Copacabana about 1330. When there are not enough passengers for each company, they pool them. **Diana Tours** T228 2809, **Trans Titicaca**, **Turisbus** T245 1341 (more expensive), many others. You can also book this service all the way to Puno, US$7.

Public buses to **Sorata**, **Copacabana** and **Tiwanaku** leave from the Cemetery district. Companies include **Manco Capac**, **2 de Febrero**, **Trans Unificada**, **Flor de Illampu**. To get to the Cemetery district, take any bus or minibus marked 'Cementerio' going up C Santa Cruz (US$0.15-0.20). On Plaza Reyes Ortiz are **Manco Capac**, and **2 de Febrero** for **Copacabana** and **Tiquina**. From the Plaza go up Av Kollasuyo and at the 2nd street on the right (Manuel Bustillos) is the terminal for minibuses to **Achacachi**, **Huatajata** and **Huarina**, and buses for **Sorata**. Several micros (20, J, 10) and minibuses (223, 252, 270, 7) go up Kollasuyo; look for 'Kollasuyo' on the windscreen in most, but not all cases. Taxi US$1. Buses to **Coroico, the Yungas and northern jungle** leave from Villa Fátima (25 mins by micros B, V, X, K, 131, 135, or 136, or *trufis* 2 or 9, which pass Pérez Velasco coming down from Plaza Mendoza, and get off at the *ex-gasolinera* YPFB, C Yanacachi 1434). See Safety, page 278.

International buses From Plaza Antofagasta terminal: to **Buenos Aires**, US$75, 2 a week with **Ormeño**, T228 1141, 54 hrs via Santa Cruz and Yacuiba; via Villazón with **Río Paraguay**, T228 4420, 3 a week, US$75, or **Trans Americano**, US$85. Alternatively, go to Villazón and change buses in Argentina. To **Arica** via the frontier at Tambo Quemado and Chungará **Pullmanbus** at 0630 (good), **Cuevas** at 0700, **Zuleta** at 0600, **Nuevo Continente** at 1230 except Sat, **Litoral**, T228 1920, Sun-Thu 1230, US$14-18. Connecting service for Iquique or Santiago. To **Cuzco**: agencies to **Puno** where you change to a different company, most easily booked through travel agencies, US$14-22, but cheaper paying for each segment at a time. For luxury and other services to Puno see under Lake Titicaca below. Direct to Cuzco, 12 hrs with **Litoral**, US$14 via Desaguadero and Puno (5 hrs, US$8.40). To **Lima**, **Ormeño** daily at 1430, US$70, 27 hrs; **Nuevo Continente** at 0830, US$55, 26 hrs, via Desaguadero, change to **Cial** in Puno.

Car hire

Imbex, C 10 No 7812, Calacoto, T212 1010, www.imbex.com. Wide range of well-maintained vehicles; Suzuki jeeps from US$60 per day, including 200 km free for 4-person 4WD. Recommended. **Kolla Motors**, Rosendo Gutierrez 502 entre Sánchez Lima y Ecuador, T241 9141, www.kollamotors.com. 6-seater 4WD Toyota jeeps, insurance and gasoline extra. **Petita Rent-a-car**, Valentín Abecia 2031, Sopocachi Alto, T242 0329, www.rentacarpetita.com. Swiss owners Ernesto Hug and Aldo Rezzonico. Recommended for well-maintained 4WD jeeps, etc, also offer adventure tours, German, French, English spoken. Recommended. Also arranges fishing trips. Ernesto also has garage for VW and other makes, Av Jaimes Freyre 2326, T241 5264.

Highly recommended. See page 36 in Essentials for multinational car hire websites.

Taxi
Standard taxis charge US$0.85-1.70 pp for short trips within city limits. A *trufi* US$0.40-0.50 pp in the centre. Taxi drivers are not tipped. At night, for safety, only take **radio taxis** (radio móvil), which are named as such, have a unique number and radio communication (e.g. **Gold** T241 1414 in the centre, 272 2722 in Zona Sur, **Servisur** T241 9999). They charge US$0.85-2.15 in centre, more to suburbs and at night. Also good value for tours for 3 people. **Oscar Vera**, Simón Aguirre 2158, Villa Copacabana, La Paz, T223 0453, specializes in trips to the Salar de Uyuni and the Western Cordillera.

Train
Ferroviaria Andina (FCA), Sánchez Lima 2199 y Fernando Guachalla, Sopocachi, T241 9770, www.fca.com.bo, Mon-Fri 0800-1600. Sells tickets for the **Oruro-Uyunui- Tupiza-Villazón** line. Must show passport.

A **tourist train** runs from **El Alto** station, by Cuartel Ingavi, Av 6 de Marzo, every second Sun, 0800, to **Guaqui**, past Tiwanaku, returns 1330, US$5.60.

South of La Paz *p284*
Minibuses 231, 273 and 902 can be caught on C México, the Prado or Av 6 de Agosto. Alternatively take Micro 11 ('Aranjuez' large, not small bus) or ones that say 'Masalla' or 'Mallasilla' along the Prado or Av 6 de Agosto, US$0.65, and ask driver where to get off. Most of the travel agents organize tours to the Valle de la Luna. These are brief, 5 minutes stop for photos in a US$15 tour of La Paz and surroundings; taxis cost US$6, US$10 with a short wait.

Tiwanaku *p284*
To get to Tiwanaku, tours booked through agencies cost US$12 (not including entry fee or lunch). Otherwise take any **Micro** marked 'Cementerio' in La Paz, get out at Plaza Félix Reyes Ortiz, on Mariano Bautista (north side of cemetery), go north up Aliaga, 1 block east of Asín to find Tiwanaku micros, US$2, 1½ hrs, every 30 mins, 0600 to 1500. Tickets can be bought in advance. **Taxi** costs about US$25-55 return (shop around), with 2 hrs at site. Some **buses** go on from Tiwanaku to Desaguadero; virtually all Desaguadero buses stop at the access road to Tiwanaku, 2-hr walk from the site. Return buses (last back 1700) leave from south side of the Plaza in village. Minibuses (vans) to **Desaguadero**, from José María Asín y P Eyzaguirre (Cemetery district) US$2, 2 hrs, most movement on Tue and Fri when there is a market at the border.

Note When returning from Tiwanaku (ruins or village) to La Paz, do not take a minibus if it has no other passengers. We have received reports of travellers being taken to El Alto and robbed at gun point. Wait for a public bus with paying passengers in it.

Takesi Trail *p285*
Take a **Líneas Ingavi** bus from C Gral Luis Lara esq Venacio Burgoa near Plaza Líbano, San Pedro going to Pariguaya (see Yunga Cruz below), daily at 0800, US$1, 2 hrs. On Sun, also minibuses from C general Luis Lara y Boquerón,

hourly 0700-1500. To **Mina San Francisco**: hire a **jeep** from La Paz; US$85, takes about 2 hrs. **Veloz del Norte** (T02-221 8279) leaves from Ocabaya 495 in Villa Fátima, T221 8279, 0900 daily, and 1400 Thu-Sun, US$2.10, 3½ hrs, continuing to Chojlla. From Chojlla to La Paz daily at 0500, 1300 also on Thu-Sun, passing **Yanakachi** 15 mins later.

Choro Trail *p286*

To the *apacheta* pass beyond **La Cumbre**, take a **taxi** from central La Paz for US$15, 45 mins, stopping to register at the Guardaparque hut. Buses from Villa Fátima to Coroico and Chulumani pass La Cumbre. Tell driver where you are going, US$2.10. The trail is signed.

Yunga Cruz Trail *p286*

Take the **bus** to **Pariguaya** (2 hrs past Chuñavi) at 0800 Mon-Sat, 6 hrs to Chuñavi, US$2.25; 6½ hrs to Lambate (3 km further on). It's not possible to buy tickets in advance, be there at 0700. Also **Trans Río Abajo** to **Lambate** from C Gral Luis Lara y Romualdo Herrera, San Pedro, daily 0700-0800.

Huayna Potosí *p286*

The mountain can be reached by transport arranged through tourist agencies (US$100) or the refugio, **taxi** US$45. **Minibus** Trans Zongo, Av Chacaltaya y Ingavi, Ballivián, El Alto, daily 0600, 2½ hrs, US$1.80 to Zongo, check on return time. Also minibuses from the Ballivián area that leave when full; often return full (fwew on Sun). If camping in the Zongo Pass area, stay at the site near the white house above the cross.

Directory

La Paz *p277, maps p280 and p282*

Airline offices Aerolíneas Argentinas, Edif Petrolero, El Prado, Mezanine, of 13, T235 1711, www.aerolineas.com.ar. **Aerocon**, Av Arce 2549, p 1, T215 0093. **AeroSur**, Av Arce 2177, Hotel Radisson, p 5, T244 4930; also Av 16 de Julio 1616, T231 3233. **Amaszonas**, Av Saavedra 1649, Miraflores, T222 0848. **American Airlines**, Av 16 de Julio 1440, Edif Hermann, T237 2009, www.aa.com. **Boliviana de Aviación (BOA)**, Camacho 1413 y Loayza, T 211 7993, **Iberia**, Ayacucho 378, Edif Credinform p 5, T220 3911. **LAN**, Av 16 de Julio 1566, p 1, T235 8377, www.lan.com. **Lufthansa**, Av 6 de Agosto 2512 y P Salazar, T243 1717, F243 1267. **TACA**, El Prado 1479, Of 401, T231 3132, toll free T800-108222. **TAM** (Mercosur), H Gutiérrez 2323, T244 3442, www.tam.com.br. **Transportes Aéreo Militar (TAM)**, Av Montes 738 y Bozo, T268 1111. **Banks** See Money in Essentials, p 275, for exchange details. *Enlace* and *RedBank* ATMs at many sites in the city. **Bisa**, Av Gral Camacho 1333 and Av Arce 2572, Sopocachi. **BNB**, Av Camacho 1296 y Colón. **Banco Unión**, Av Camacho 1416 y Loayza. **Prodem**, Av Camacho 1277 y Colón, Illampu 784 y Santa Cruz, Sánchez Lima y Salinas and other branches. **Amex**, see *Magri Turismo* under Tour operators. **Exchange houses**: **Sudamer**, Camacho 1311 y Colón, open Mon-Fri 0830-1830, Sat 0930-1230. Good rates for currencies other than US$ including euros, 2% commission on US$ or euro TCs into dollars, frequently recommended. **Unitours**, Mercado y Loayza and Camacho y Loayza, Mon-Fri 0830-1900 or 0900-1700, Sat 0900-1230. Good rates for US$ cash. Very few deal in Argentine and Chilean pesos. Street changers on corners around Plaza del Estudiante, Camacho, Colón and Prado, OK rates. **Cultural centres Alliance Française**, Guachalla 399 esq Av 20 de Octubre T242 5005, www.afbolivia.org, French-Spanish library, videos, newspapers, and cultural gatherings information. Call for opening hours. **Centro Boliviano Americano (CBA)**, Parque Zenón Iturralde 121, T244 0650 (10 mins walk from Plaza Estudiante down Av Arce), www.cba.edu.bo. Has public library and recent US papers. **Goethe-Institut**, Av Arce 2708 esq Campos, T243 1916, www.goethe.de/lapaz. Excellent library, recent papers in German, CDs, cassettes and videos free on loan, German books for sale. **Cycle spares** See **Gravity Assisted Mountain Biking** under Tour operators, page 296, very knowledgeable, www.gravity bolivia.com. **Embassies and consulates Argentina**, Aspiazú 497, Sopocachi, T241 7737, ebolv@ mrecic.gov.ar. 24 hrs for visa, 0900-1330. **Brazil**, Av Arce 2739, Edif Multicentro, T244 2148, embajadabrasil@acelerate.com. 0900-1300, 1500-1800, Mon-Fri (visas take 2 days). **Canada**, Edif Barcelona p 2, Victor Sanjinés 2678, Plaza España, T241 5141, lapaz@international.gc.ca, Mon-Thu 0830-1700, Fri 0830-1400. **Danish Consulate**, Av Arce

2799 y Cordero, Edif Fortaleza, p 9, T243 2070, lpbamb@um.dk. Mon-Fri, 0830-1600. **France**, Av Hernando Siles 5390 y C 8, Obrajes, T214 9900, www.ambafrance-bo.org, 0900-1230. **Germany**, Av Arce 2395, T244 0066, www.la-paz.diplo.de. Mon-Fri 0900-1200. **Italy**, C 5 (Jordan Cuéllar) 458, Obrajes, T278 8506, www.amblapaz.esteri.it. Mon-Fri 0830-1300. **Netherlands Consulate**, Av 6 de Agosto 2455, Edif Hilda, p 7, T244 4040, www.mfa.nl/lap. 0900-1200. **Paraguay**, Edif Illimani, p 1, Av 6 de Agosto y P Salazar, T243 220, good visa service. Mon-Fri 0830-1300, 1500-1730. **Peruvian Consulate**, Av 6 de Agosto 2455, T244 0631, open till 1600, visa issued same day if you go early. **Spanish Consulate**, Av 6 de Agosto 2827 y Cordero, T243 0118, embespa@entelnet.bo. Mon-Fri 0830-1500. **Swedish Consulate**, Pasaje Villegas 1227, entre 20 de Octubre y 6 de Agosto, T214 6723, sweconsul@kolla.net, open 0900-1200. **Switzerland**, C 13 y 14 de Septiembre, Obrajes, T275 1225, paz.vertretung@eda.admin.ch. Mon-Fri 0900-1200. **UK**, Av Arce 2732, T243 3424, http://ukinbolivia.fco.gov.uk/en/. Mon-Thu 0830-1230, 1330-1700, Fri 0830-1330. **USA**, Av Arce 2780, T216 8000, http://bolivia.usembassy.gov, Mon-Fri 0830-1730. **Internet** There are many internet cafés in the centre of La Paz, opening and shutting all the time. Cost US$0.30-0.45 per hr, fast connections, long hours, but many closed Sun. **Language schools** Alliance Française (see also above). **Instituto Exclusivo**, Av 20 de Octubre 2315 (one block from Plaza Avaroa), Edif Mechita, T242 1072, www.instituto-exclusivo.com. Spanish lessons for individual and groups, accredited by Ministry of Education. **Instituto de La Lengua Española**, María TeresaTejada, C Aviador esq final 14, No 180, Achumani, T279 6074, T7155 6735. One-to-one lessons US$7 per hr. Recommended. **Speak Easy Institute**, Av Arce 2047, between Goitía and Montevideo, just down from Plaza del Estudiante, T/F244 1779, speakeasyinstitute@yahoo.com. US$6 for one-to-one private lessons, cheaper for groups and couples, Spanish and English taught, very good. **Private Spanish lessons** from: **Isabel Daza Vivado**, Murillo 1046, p 3, T231 1471, T7062 8016. US$4 per hr. **Enrique Eduardo Patzy**, Méndez Arcos 1060, Sopocachi, T241 5501 or 776-22210, epatzy@hotmail.com. US$6 an hr one-to-one tuition, speaks English and Japanese. Recommended. **Medical services** For hospitals, doctors and dentists, contact your consulate or the tourist office for recommendations. **Health and hygiene**: **Ministerio de Desarollo Humano, Secretaría Nacional de Salud**, Av Arce, near *Radisson Plaza*, yellow fever shot and certificate, rabies and cholera shots, malaria pills, bring own syringe. **Centro Piloto de Salva**, Av Montes y Basces, T245 0026, 10 mins walk from Plaza San Francisco, for malaria pills, helpful. **Laboratorios Illimani**, Edif Alborada p 3, of 304, Loayza y Juan de la Riva, T231 7290, open 0900-1230, 1430-1700, fast, efficient, hygienic. Tampons may be bought at most *farmacias* and supermarkets. Daily papers list pharmacies on duty (*de turno*). For contact lenses, **Optalis**, Comercio 1089. **Post offices** Correo Central, Av Mcal Santa Cruz y Oruro, Mon-Fri 0800-2000, Sat 0830-1800. Stamps are sold at post office and by some hotels. *Poste Restante* keeps letters for 2 months, no charge. Check the letters filed under all parts of your name. To collect parcels costs US$0.15. Express postal service (top floor) is expensive. **DHL**, Av Mcal Santa Cruz 1297, T278 6909, expensive and slow. **FedEx**, C 5, No 517, Achumani, T244 3537. **UPS**, Av 16 de Julio 1479, p 10, T244 5044. **Telephones** Almost every kiosk can make local calls and calls to cell-phones. Also, call centres (**Cotel**, **Entel** are the main ones) that allow for more privacy and less street noise. For international calls, lots of call centres in C Sagárnaga, usually US$0.10 per min to Europe and North America. **Useful addresses** **Immigration:** to renew a visa go to **Migración Bolivia**, Av Camacho 1468, T211 0960. Mon-Fri 0830-1230, 1430-1830, go early. Allow 48 hrs for visa extensions. **Tourist Police:** C Hugo Estrada 1354, Plaza Tejada Sorzano frente al estadio, Miraflores, next to *Love City* Chinese restaurant, T222 5016. Open 0830-1800, for insurance claims after theft.

Lake Titicaca

Lake Titicaca is two lakes joined by the Straits of Tiquina: the larger, northern lake (Lago Mayor, or Chucuito) contains the Islas del Sol and de la Luna; the smaller lake (Lago Menor, or Huiñamarca) has several small islands. The waters are a beautiful blue, reflecting the hills and the distant cordillera in the shallows of Huiñamarca, mirroring the sky in the rarified air and changing colour when it is cloudy or raining. A boat trip on the lake is a must.

Ins and outs

Getting there A paved road runs from La Paz to the Straits of Tiquina (114 km El Alto-San Pablo). ▸▸ *See also Transport, page 310.*

La Paz to Copacabana

Puerto Pérez The closest point to the capital on Lake Titicaca, Puerto Pérez, 72 km from La Paz, was the original harbour for La Paz. It was founded in the 19th century by British navigators as a harbour for the first steam boat on the lake (the vessel was assembled piece by piece in Puno). Colourful fiestas are held on New Year's Day, Carnival, 3 May and 16 July (days may change each year). There are superb views of the lake and mountains.

Huatajata Further north along the east shore of the lake is Huatajata, with *Yacht Club Boliviano* (restaurant open to non-members, Saturday, Sunday lunch only, sailing for members only) and *Crillon Tours' International Hydroharbour* and *Inca Utama Hotel* (see below). Reed boats are still built and occasionally sail here for the tourist trade. There are several small but interesting exhibits of reed boats that were used on long ocean voyages. Beyond here is **Chúa**, where there is fishing, sailing and *Transturin's* catamaran dock (see below).

Islands of Lake Huiñamarca

On **Suriqui** (1 hour from Huatajata) in Lake Huiñamarca, a southeasterly extension of Lake Titicaca, you can see reed *artesanías*. The late Thor Heyerdahl's *Ra II*, which sailed from Morocco to Barbados in 1970, his *Tigris* reed boat, and the balloon gondola for the Nasca (Peru) flight experiment (see page 1377), were also constructed by the craftsmen of Suriqui. Reed boats are still made on Suriqui, probably the last place where the art survives. On **Kalahuta** there are *chullpas* (burial towers), old buildings and the uninhabited town of Kewaya. On **Pariti** there is Inca terracing and the **Museo Señor de los Patos**, with weavings and Tiwanku-era ceramics.

From Chúa the main road reaches the east side of the Straits at **San Pablo** (clean restaurant in blue building, with good toilets). On the west side is San Pedro, the main Bolivian naval base, from where a paved road goes to Copacabana. Vehicles are transported across on barges, US$5. Passengers cross separately, US$0.20 (not included in bus fares) and passports are checked. Expect delays during rough weather, when it can get very cold.

Copacabana → *Phone code: 02. Colour map 6, A2. Population: 15,400.*

A little town on Lake Titicaca 158 km from La Paz by paved road, Copacabana has a heavily restored, Moorish-style **basilica**. ⓘ *open 0700-2030, minimum 2 people at a time to visit museum, Tue-Sun 0830-1130, 1430-1730, US$0.70.* It contains a famous 16th century miracle-working Virgen Morena (Dark Lady), also known as the Virgen de Candelaria, one of the patron saints of Bolivia. If going during Carnival or on a religious holiday, arrive early and be prepared to hold onto your place, as things tend to get very crowded. The basilica itself is notable for its spacious atrium with four small chapels; the main chapel has one of the finest gilt altars in Bolivia. The basilica is clean, white, with coloured tiles decorating the exterior arches, cupolas and chapels. Vehicles are blessed in front of the church on Saturday and Sunday. There are 17th- and

18th-century paintings and statues in the sanctuary. **Municipal tourist office** ⓘ *16 de Julio y 6 de Agosto*; also kiosk at the basilica which is rarely open. At major holidays (Holy Week, 3 May, and 6 August), the town fills with visitors, so beware of pickpockets.

On the headland which overlooks the town and port, **Cerro Calvario**, are the Stations of the Cross (a steep climb – leave plenty of time if going to see the sunset). On the hill behind the town overlooking the lake, roughly southeast of the Basilica, is the **Horca del Inca**, two pillars of rock with another laid across them (probably a sun clock, now covered in graffiti), US$3. There is a path marked by arrows. Boys will offer to guide you: fix price in advance if you want their help. There's a lovely walk along the lakeside north to Yampupata, 17 km (allow 6 hours), through unspoilt countryside. At the village, or at Sicuani ask for a rowing boat to Isla del Sol, or trip on the lake (US$8.50). Motor boats cost US$14 but are quicker. There are *alojamientos* and places to eat in Sicuani and Yumpapata.

Isla del Sol

The site of the main Inca creation myth (there are other versions) is a short distance by boat from Copacabana. Legend has it that Viracocha, the creator god, had his children, Manco Kapac and Mama Ocllo, spring from the waters of the lake to found Cuzco and the Inca dynasty. A sacred rock at the island's northwest end is worshipped as their birthplace. Near here are the impressive ruins of **Chincaca**, while 25 minutes' walk away, on the northeast side, is the village of Challapampa, with a basic **Museo de Oro** ⓘ *US$1.50, one ticket for all 3 sites, museum closed 1230-1400*. The community-run **Museo Comunitario de Etnografía** at Challa, east side ⓘ *daily 0900-1200, 1300-1800, entry by voluntary donation,* celebrates costumes used in sacred dances. On the southeast shore near Yumani and the jetty for *Crillon Tours*' hydrofoils and other craft is the **Fuente del Inca**, a pure spring, reached by Inca steps leading

Copacabana

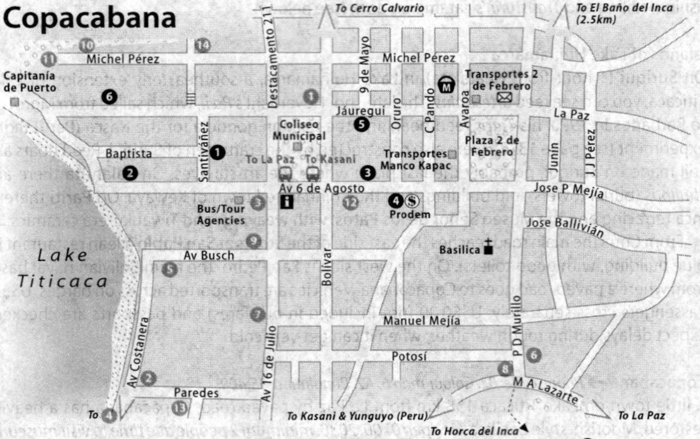

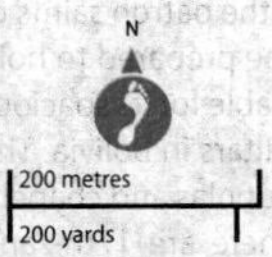

Sleeping
1 Ambassador
2 Chasqui del Sol
3 Colonial del Lago
4 Eco Lodge del Lago
5 El Mirador
6 Emperador
7 Gloria
8 Hostal Sonia
9 Kota Kahuaña
10 La Cúpula
11 Las Olas
12 Res Aransaya
13 Rosario del Lago
14 Utama

Eating
1 Café Bistrot Copacabana
2 La Orilla
3 Puerto del Sol
4 Snack 6 de Agosto
5 Sujna Wasi
6 Trattoria Sapori d'Italia

up from the water. A 2 km walk from the spring takes one to the main ruins of **Pilcocaina** ⓘ *US$0.70*, a two storey building with false domes and superb views. The island is heavily touristed and not all visitors are satisfied with their experience. Communities levy a landing fee and visitors fees at each village; vendors and beggars can be persistent. Southeast of the Isla del Sol is the Isla de la Luna (or Coati), which also may be visited – the best ruins are an Inca temple and nunnery, both sadly neglected.

Border with Peru

West side of Lake Titicaca The road goes from La Paz 91 km west to the former port of **Guaqui** (at the military checkpoint here, and other spots on the road, passports may be inspected). The road crosses the border at **Desaguadero** 22 km further west and runs along the shore of the lake to Puno. (There are three La Paz-Puno routes, see also page 1405.) Bolivian immigration is just before the bridge, open 0830-2030 (Peru is one hour earlier than Bolivia). Get exit stamp, walk 200 m across the bridge then get entrance stamp on the other side. Get Peruvian visas in La Paz. There are a few hotels and restaurants on both sides of the border; very basic in Bolivia, slightly better in Peru. Money changers on Peruvian side give reasonable rates. Market days are Friday and Tuesday: otherwise the town is dead.

Via Copacabana From Copacabana a paved road leads south to the Bolivian frontier at Kasani, then to Yunguyo. Do not photograph the border area. For La Paz tourist agency services on this route see International buses, page 297, and Activities and tours, page 308. The border is open 0830-1930 (Bolivian time); passports may be checked at Tiquina. Buses/colectivos stop here and at the Peruvian side; or you can walk, 500 m, between the two posts. If crossing into Bolivia with a motorcycle, do not be fooled into paying any unnecessary charges to police or immigration. Going to Peru, money can be changed at the border. Coming into Bolivia, the best rates are at Copacabana.

East side of Lake Titicaca

From Huarina, a road heads northwest to Achacachi (market Sunday; fiesta 14 September). Here, one road goes north across a tremendous marsh to **Warisata**, then crosses the altiplano to Sorata (see below). At Achacachi, another road runs roughly parallel to the shore of Lake Titicaca, through **Ancoraimes** (Sunday market, the church hosts a community project making dolls and alpaca sweaters, also has dorms), **Carabuco** (with colonial church), **Escoma**, which has an Aymara market every Sunday morning, to **Puerto Acosta**, 10 km from the Peruvian border. It is a pleasant, friendly town with a large plaza and several simple places to stay and eat. The area around Puerto Acosta is good walking country. From La Paz to Puerto Acosta the road is paved as far as Escoma, then good until Puerto Acosta (best in the dry season, approximately May to October). North of Puerto Acosta towards Peru the road deteriorates and should not be attempted except in the dry season. An obelisk marks the international frontier at Cerro Janko Janko, on a promontory high above the lake with magnificent views. Here are hundreds of small stone storerooms, deserted except during the busy Wednesday and Saturday smugglers' market, the only days when transport is plentiful. You should get an exit stamp in La Paz before heading to this border (only preliminary entrance stamps are given here). There is a Peruvian customs post 2 km from the border and 2 km before Tilali, but Peruvian immigration is in Puno.

Sorata → *Phone code: 02. Colour map 6, A2. Population: 8,500. Altitude: 2,695 m.*

Sorata, 163 km from La Paz (paved but for the last 15 km), is a beautiful colonial town nestled at the foot of Mount Illampu; around it are views over lush, alpine-like valleys. The climate is delightful. Nearby are some challenging long-distance hikes and, closer to the Peruvian border is more adventurous hiking and climbing country in the Cordillera de Apolobamba. The town has a charming plaza, with views of the snow-capped summit of Illampu on a clear day. The market area is near the plaza, half block down Muñecas on the right. Market day is Sunday; fiesta 14 September. There are lots of walking possibilities, including day hikes. The most popular is to **San Pedro cave** ⓘ *0800-1700, US$2, toilets at entrance*, beyond the village of San Pedro. The walk is more interesting than the cave itself, which is formed in gypsum, has an underground 'lake' and is lit (no swimming). It's best not to go alone. It is reached either by road, a 12 km walk (2½ hours) each way, or by a path along the Río San Cristóbal (about 3½ hours one way). Get clear directions before setting out. Take water, at least 1 litre per person, or else take sterilizing tablets and fill up at the tap in San Pedro. There are also drinks for sale. Taxi trucks also go there from the plaza, 0600-2200, with a 30-minute wait, for US$5, most on Sunday.

Trekking and climbing from Sorata

Sorata is the starting point for climbing **Illampu** and Ancohuma but all routes out of the town are difficult, owing to the number of paths in the area and the very steep ascent. Experience and

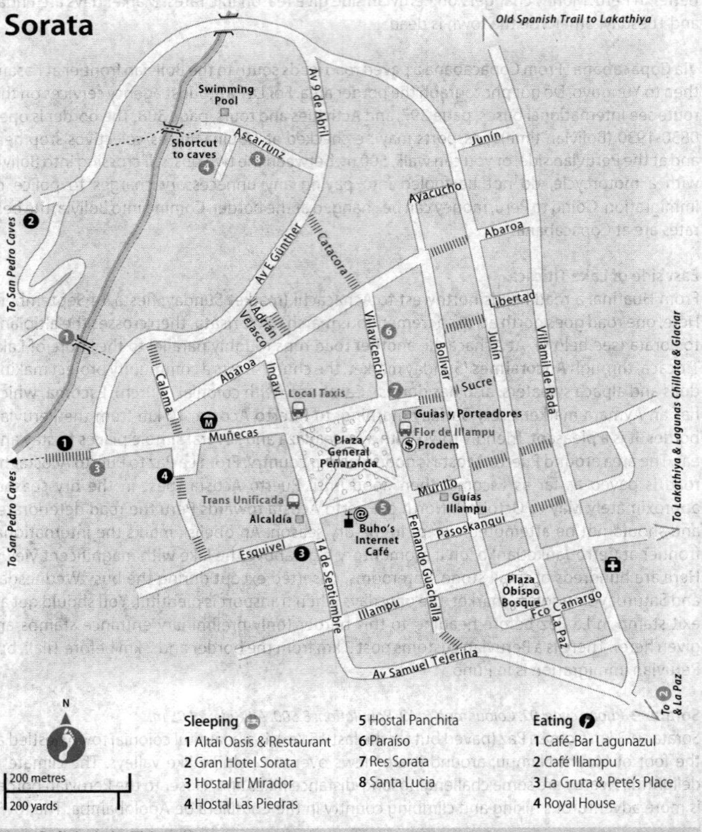

full equipment necessary and it's best to hire mules (see below). The four day trek to **Lagunas Chillata and Glaciar** is the most common route and gets busy during high season. Laguna Chillata can also be reached in a day-hike with light gear, but mind the difficult navigation and take warm clothing, food, water, sun protection, etc. Laguna Chillata has been heavily impacted by tourism (remove all trash, do not throw it in the pits around the lake) and many groups frequently camp there. The Inka Marka ruins are on the back of the rock looking towards Illampu from Laguna Chillata. The structures nearest the lake are in a sad state and unfortunately many have been converted to latrines. The **Circuito Illampu**, a 8-10 day high-altitude trek (three passes over 4,000 m, one over 5,000 m) around Illampu, is excellent. It can get very cold and it is a hard walk, though very beautiful with nice campsites on the way. Some food can be bought in Cocoyo on the third day. You must be acclimatized before setting out. Another option is the **Trans-Cordillera Trek**, 12 days from Sorata to Huayna Potosí, or 20 days all the way to Illimani at the opposite (south) end of the Cordillera Real. **Note**: Laguna San Francisco, along the Illampu Circuit, has for many years been the scene of repeated armed holdups. This is the only place in the Sorata area not considered safe and guided trekking parties were passing though in the small hours of the night to avoid contact with the local population.

Cordillera Apolobamba

The Area Protegida Apolobamba forms part of the Cordillera Apolobamba, the north extension of the Cordillera Real. The range itself has many 5,000 m-plus peaks, while the conservation area of some 483,744 ha protects herds of vicuña, huge flocks of flamingos and many condors. The area adjoins the Parque Nacional Madidi (see page 357). This is great trekking country and the 4-6-day **Charazani to Pelechuco** (or vice versa) mountain trek is one of the best in the country (see Footprint's *Bolivia Handbook* for details). It passes traditional villages and the peaks of the southern Cordillera Apolobamba.

Charazani is the biggest village in the region (3,200 m), with hot springs (US$0.75). Its three-day fiesta is around 16 July. There are some **G** *alojamientos*, restaurants and shops. **Pelechuco** (3,600 m) is a smaller village, also with **F-G** *alojamientos*, cafés and shops. The road to Pelechuco goes through the Area Protegida, passing the community of Ulla Ulla, 5 km outside of which are the reserve's HQ at La Cabaña. Visitors are welcome to see the orphaned vicuñas. There are community hostels (**F**) at the villages of Lagunillas and Agua Blanca. Basic food is available in the communities. For information, contact **Trek Apolobamba** (www.trekapolobamba.com) and SERNAP in La Paz (page 270).

Lake Titicaca listings

For Sleeping and Eating price codes and other relevant information, see Essentials, pages 38-40.

Sleeping

La Paz to Copacabana *p301*

Puerto Pérez

AL Hotel Las Balsas, run by *Turismo Balsa* (see page 296, or T02-289 5147). In beautiful lakeside setting, views of the cordillera, all rooms have balcony over the lake, negotiate out of season, fitness facilities including pool, jacuzzi, sauna. Excellent restaurant with fixed price lunch or dinner.

D Hostería Las Islas, nearby on the Plaza. Shared bath, hot water, heated rooms, comfortable but it can get crowdedat times. There's a *Blue Note* jazz bar next door.

Huatajata

C Hotel Titicaca, between Huatajata and Huarina, Km 80 from La Paz, T289 5180 (in La Paz T220 3666). This place has beautiful views, sauna, pool, good restaurant. It's very quiet during the week.

F Máximo Catari's Inti Karka hotel, on the lakeshore, T7197 8959, erikcatari@hotmail.com. **G** with shared bath. Also restaurant, full menu, open daily, average prices.

Copacabana *p301, map p302*

B-C Rosario del Lago, Rigoberto Paredes y Av Costanera, T862 2141 (reservations La Paz T244 1756), www.hotelrosario.com/lago. Includes breakfast, hot water, *Turisbus* office (see below), comfortable rooms with lake view, colonial style, beautifully furnished, internet café, handicrafts display, restaurant.

C Chasqui del Sol, Av Costanera 55, T862 2343, www.chasquidelsol.com. Includes breakfast, lakeside hotel, café/breakfast room has great views, trips organized, video room.

C Gloria Copacabana, 16 de Julio, T862 2094, www.hotel gloria.com.bo. Same group as *Gloria* in La Paz, price is full board (**B** at weekends), hot water, bar, café and restaurant with international and vegetarian food, gardens, money exchange.

C Las Olas, lake-end of Michel Pérez past La Cúpula, T862 2112, lasolascopa@hotmail.com. Tastefully decorated cabins with kitchenettes, heaters, outdoor jacuzzi, nice grounds and views. Recommended.

C-E La Cúpula, C Michel Pérez 1-3, T862 2029, www.hotelcupula.com. 5 mins' walk from centre, price depends on room (most expensive have kitchen and bath), sitting room with TV and video, fully equipped kitchen, library, hot water, book exchange, restaurant (Ⓣ with vegetarian options), great breakfast (extra), car parking, offer local tours, German owners. Recommended.

D Ecolodge del Lago, about 2 km south along the lakeshore, T862 2500 (or 245 1138 Hostal Copacabana, La Paz). Comfortable cabins in a quiet out-of-the way location, nice grounds. Includes breakfast, solar hot water, helpful owner.

E Colonial del Lago, Av 6 de Agosto y Av 16 de Julio, T862 2270. Bright rooms, some with lake view, **F** without bath, breakfast included, garden, good restaurant and *peña*.

E El Mirador, Av Costanera y Busch, T862 2289, elmiradorhotel@hotmail.com. In a pink building with lake views, breakfast included, hot water, mixed reports on service.

E Utama, Michel Pérez, T862 2013. With breakfast, hot water, good showers, comfy, book exchange.

F Ambassador, Bolívar y Jáuregui, T/F862 2216. With electric shower, upstairs rooms are a bit better than downstairs, beginning to show its age, rooftop restaurant, laundry facilities, luggage store, parking.
F Emperador, C Murillo 235, behind the Cathedral, T862 2083. Breakfast served in room for US$2, popular, laundry service and facilities, **G** with shared hot showers, helpful, tours arranged. Recommended.
F Hostal Sonia, Murillo 253, T862 2019. Some rooms with shared bath (**G**), good beds, big windows, roof terrace, laundry and kitchen facilities, breakfast in bed on request, very helpful, good value.
G pp **Kota Kahuaña**, Av Busch 15. Shared hot showers, quiet, hospitable, basic but clean.
G Res Aransaya, Av 6 de Agosto 121, T862 2229. With shared hot shower, simple but comfortable, good restaurant and café.

Isla del Sol *p302*

It is worthwhile staying overnight for the many beautiful walks through villages and Inca terraces, some still in use. Rooms are offered by many families on the island.

Yumani

Most of the *posadas* on the island are at Yumani, on the south side near the Inca steps. They take advantage of the daily arrival of tourists, but do not always provide what they advertise (hot water, clean sheets, etc). Shop araound.
D Puerta del Sol, at the peak of the hill above the village. Very popular. (**F** without bath). Nearby is the owner's father's hostel, **F Templo del Sol**, with clean rooms, comfy beds, electric showers and a good restaurant.
F Inti Kala, opposite *Templo del Sol*, T7194 4013. Shared electric showers, fantastic views, great value, serves good meals.
F Palla Khasa, T7122 7616. Book in advance. With breakfast, large rooms, good beds, restaurant with fine views.

Challa

G Posada del Inca, right on the beach. Double rooms, very basic outside toilets, no showers, contact Juan Mamani Ramos through *Entel* office, food is provided and drinks for sale.
G pp **Qhumphuri**, mid-island on the east coast, 1 hr from the Inca Steps, 1 hr from the Inca ruins in the north. Simple but comfortable rooms with bath, local furniture, great views, restaurant serves all meals (extra cost), tasty food, cooking facilities, owner Juan Ramos Ticona interested in sustainable development.

Challapampa

Several places to stay around the Plaza in Challapampa, at the north end of the island.
F-G Posada Manco Kapac. Basic but clean, hot showers, nice view, poor beds, garden for camping, can also arrange boat tickets. Price depends on whether you have a shower or a bucket.
G Hostal Don Francisco. Clean and basic, decent beds, cement floors.
La Posada del Inca, a restored colonial hacienda, owned by *Crillon Tours*, only available as part of a tour with *Crillon*, see page 308.
Magri Turismo also owns a hotel on the island, **La Estancia**, www.ecolodge-laketiticaca.com. See La Paz, Tour operators on page 295. See also *Transturin*'s overnight options on page 309.

Sorata *p303, map p304*

D Altai Oasis, T7151 9856, www.altaioasis.lobopages.com. At the bottom of the valley in a beautiful setting, with cabins (**C**), rooms with hot showers and camping (US$3 pp), transport to town US$2 for 5 people, quiet, well-designed, with good restaurant (‼-ꝉ, good breakfasts and other meals, home-gown vegetables), owners Johnny and Roxana Resnikowski, English and German spoken. Recommended.
E Hostal Las Piedras, just off Ascarrunz, T7191 6341. Well-designed and mellow, European run, **F** with shared bath, very helpful, good breakfasts. Recommended.
E-F Gran Hotel Sorata, on the outskirts immediately above the police checkpoint, T281 7378, call from Plaza for free pick-up. Spacious although bathrooms (electric showers) a bit tired, breakfast included, free filtered water, large garden with great views, swimming pool (open to non-residents for US$0.50), games room, good restaurant, internet café, accepts credit cards. Not always open.
F Hostal Panchita, on plaza, T813 5038. Shared bath, large rooms, hot water, basic but good value, sunny courtyard and good restaurant.

F Res Sorata, just off plaza, T213 6672. Administrator Louis Demers, from Quebec, and the German/Bolivian proprietors are helpful. The garden is lovely, older rooms (with shared bath) are basic, newer ones (with private bath) are adequate and good value, good showers. Restaurant with good lunch/dinner US$2.75, breakfast US$2, good service, washing machine US$1.50, DVDs to watch.

F Santa Lucía, Ascarrunz, T213 6686. Modern, carpeted rooms, comfortable, cheaper with shared bath, patio, helpful.

G Hostal El Mirador, Muñecas 400, T289 5008. With showers and toilets, kitchen, laundry facilities, sun terrace.

G pp **Paraíso**, Villavicencio 117, T213 6671. Pleasant, fairly modern, American breakfast US$1.80, hot water, restaurant.

Eating

Huatajata *p301*

ΨΨ-Ψ Inti Raymi, next to Inca Utama hotel. With fresh fish and boat trips. There are other restaurants of varying standard, most lively at weekends and in the high season.

Copacabana *p301, map p302*

ΨΨ La Orilla, Av 6 de Agosto, close to lake. Open daily 1000-2200, usually, warm, atmospheric, tasty food with local and international choices.

ΨΨ Trattoria Sapori D'Italia, Jáuregui 4, daily 1830-2200. Home-made pasta, pizza, and Italian specialties. Extensive wine-list (for Copacabana) including Italian wines.

ΨΨ-Ψ Café Bistrot Copacabana, Santiváñez y 6 de Agosto, daily 0730-2100. French and international dishes, vegetarian options, French and English spoken.

Ψ Puerto del Sol, Av 6 de Agosto. Similar to others on this avenue, good trout, eat in or takeaway.

Ψ Snack 6 de Agosto, Av 6 de Agosto, 2 branches. Good trout, big portions, some vegetarian dishes, serves breakfast.

Ψ Sujna Wasi, Jáuregui 127. Open 0730-2300, for breakfasts, vegetarian lunch, wide range of books on Bolivia, slow service.

Sorata *p303, map p304*

There are several Italian restaurants on the plaza, all quite similar (ΨΨ-Ψ), none is outstanding.

ΨΨ-Ψ Café Illampu, on the way to San Pedro cave. Swiss-run, excellent sandwiches, bread and cakes, camping US$2 pp (extra to hire tent), closed Tue and Feb-Mar.

ΨΨ-Ψ Pete's Place, Esquivel y 14 de Septiembre, 2nd floor. Vegetarian dishes and set menus, also meat, 'English tea', very good, British owner Pete is a good source of information, local maps and guide books, open Tue-Sat 0830-2200.

Ψ Café-Bar Lagunazul, on steps beyond Muñecas, in **Andean Epics Ride**. Andean specialities, coffee and various teas.

Ψ La Gruta, next to Pete's Place. Serves a cheap, large *comida del día*, fairly clean.

Ψ Royal House, off Muñecas by the market. For set meals.

Festivals and events

Copacabana *p301, map p302*

Note: At these times hotel prices quadruple.

1-3 Feb Virgen de la Candelaria, massive procession, dancing, fireworks, bullfights. **Easter**, with candlelight procession on Good Friday. **23 Jun, San Juan**, also on Isla del Sol. **4-6 Aug, La Virgen de Copacabana.**

Sorata *p303, map p304*

7 days after **Easter**, **Fiesta San Pedro**. **Jun, Feria Agro-Eco-Turística**. **14 Sep, Fiesta Patronal del Señor de la Columna**, is the main festival.

Activities and tours

Lake Titicaca *p301*

Crillon Tours (address under La Paz, Tour operators, page 295) run a hydrofoil service on Lake Titicaca with excellent bilingual guides. Tours stop at their Andean Roots "Eco Village" at Huatajata. Very experienced company. The **Inca Utama Hotel and Spa** (**AL-A**) has a health spa based on natural remedies and Kallawaya medicine; the rooms are comfortable, with heating, electric blankets, good service, bar, restaurant, reservations through *Crillon Tours* in La Paz. *Crillon* is Bolivia's oldest travel agency and is consistently recommended. Also at *Inca Utama* is an observatory (*Alajpacha*) with two telescopes and retractable roof for viewing the night sky, an Altiplano Museum, a floating restaurant and bar on the lake (*La Choza Náutica*), a 252-sq m floating island and examples of different Altiplano cultures. Health, astronomical, mystic and ecological programmes are offered. The hydrofoil trips include visits to Andean Roots complex, Copacabana, Islas del Sol and de la Luna, Straits of Tiquina and past reed fishing boats. See Isla del Sol, Sleeping, for *La Posada del Inca*. Crillon has a sustainable tourism project with Urus-Iruitos people from the Río Desaguadero area on floating islands by the Isla Quewaya. Trips can be arranged to/from Puno and Juli (bus and hydrofoil excursion to Isla del Sol) and from Copacabana via Isla del Sol to Cuzco and Machu Picchu. Other combinations of hydrofoil and land-based excursions can be arranged (also highland, Eastern lowland, jungle and adventure tours). See www.titicaca.com for full details. All facilities and modes of transport connected by radio.

Transturin (see also La Paz, Tour operators, page 295) run catamarans on Lake Titicaca, either for sightseeing or on the La Paz-Puno route. The catamarans are more leisurely than the hydrofoils of *Crillon* so there is more room and time for on-board meals and entertainment, with bar, video and sun deck. From their dock at Chúa, catamarans run day and day/night cruises starting either in La Paz or Copacabana. Puno may also be the starting point for trips. Overnight cruises involve staying in a cabin on the catamaran, moored at the Isla del Sol, with lots of activities. On the island, Transturin has the *Inti Wata* cultural complex which has restored Inca terraces, an Aymara house, the underground *Ekako* museum and cultural demonstrations and activities. There is also a 30-passenger totora reed boat for trips to the Pilcocaina Inca palace. All island-based activities are for catamaran clients only. Transturin runs through services to Puno without many of the formalities at the border.

Transturin offers last minute, half-price deals for drop-in travellers (24-48 hrs in advance, take passport): sold in Copacabana only, half-day tour on the lake, continuing to Puno by bus, or La Paz; overnight Copacabana-Isla del Sol- Copacabana with possible extension to La Paz. Sold in La Paz only: La Paz-Isla del Sol-La Paz, or with overnight stay (extension to Puno possible on request).

Turisbus (www.turisbus.com, see La Paz, Tour operators page 295 and *Hoteles Rosario*, La Paz, and *Rosario del Lago*, Copacabana) offer guided tours in the fast launches *Titicaca Explorer I*

(28 passengers) and *II* (8 passengers) to the Isla del Sol, returning to Copacabana via the Bahía de Sicuani for trips on traditional reed boats. Also La Paz-Puno, with boat excursion to Isla del Sol, boxed lunch and road transport, or with additional overnight at *Hotel Rosario del Lago*.

Sorata *p303, map p304*

Mountain biking

Andean Epics Ride, in Café-Bar Lagunazul, T7127 6685, www.andeanbiking.com. Open Apr-Nov. Good routes, innovative multi-day trips (eg to Rurrenabaque, which includes boat and 4WD combinations) with emphasis on the fairly extreme.

Trekking guides

It is much cheaper to go to Sorata and ask about trekking there than to book up a trek with an agency in La Paz. Conversely, buy all your trekking food in La Paz as Sorata shops are poorly supplied. Asociación de Guías y Porteadores, Sucre y Guachalla, T213 6698. Another guiding association is **Asociación de Guías Illampu**, Murillo entre Guachalla y Bolívar. Both offer similar services, quality and prices. Louis at *Residencial Sorata* can arrange guides and mules. Daily prices: guide prices start at US$12, porters and mules extra, remember you have to feed your guide/porter. When trekking avoid sedimented glacier melt water for drinking and treat with iodine all other water.

Transport

La Paz to Copacabana *p301*

Puerto Pérez

Bus Regular minibus service from **La Paz** Cementerio district: across from the cemetery, above the flower market, ask for buses to Batallas, US$0.75, but no public transport Batallas-Puerto Pérez.

Huatajata

Bus **La Paz**-Huatajata, US$1, frequent minibuses from Bustillos y Kollasuyo, Cementerio district, daily 0400-1800, continuing to Tiquina.

Islands of Lago Huiñamarca *p301*

Boat Máximo Catari (see Huatajata, Sleeping, above) and Paulino Esteban (east end of town, T7196 7383) arrange regular boats to the islands in Lago Huiñamarca for US$15 per hr.

Copacabana *p301, map p302*

If arriving in Bolivia at Copacabana and going to La Paz, see Safety on page 278, for scams in the Cemetery district, where public transport arrives.

Bus To/from **La Paz**, US$2 plus US$0.20 for Tiquina crossing, 4 hrs, throughout the day with **Manco Capac** and **2 de Febrero**. Both have offices on Copacabana's main plaza, but leave from Plaza Sucre, and in La Paz at Plaza Reyes Ortiz, opposite entrance to cemetery. Buy ticket in advance at weekends and on holidays. **Diana Tours**, **Combi Tours** and others daily at 1330, from 16 de Julio y 6 de Agosto, US$3.50-4.50, take you to Sagárnaga y Illampu in the tourist district, but will not drop you off at your hotel. 1-day trips from La Paz are not recommended as they allow only 1½-2 hrs in Copacabana. (See also Border with Peru via Copacabana, page 303.)

Isla del Sol *p302*

Boat **Andes Amazonía** and **Titicaca Tours** run motor boats to the island; both have offices on Av 6 de Agosto in Copacabana, by the beach. Boats leave Copacabana at 0830. Full day tours return from the island at 1600, arriving back at 1730; half-day tours return at 1100. Fare is US$2-3 if you return the same day. If you stay overnight on the island, you must buy a separate ticket back, US$3. On a full-day tour you can be dropped off at Challapampa and picked up at Yumani at 1600 (boats leave punctually, so you will have to move quickly to see the ruins in the north and then hike south to the jetty). You may also take boats to Isla del Sol from Yampupata (see page 302).

Border with Peru *p303*

Via Guaqui and Desaguadero

Bus Road paved all the way to Peru. Buses from La Paz to Guaqui and Desaguadero depart from J M Asín y P Eyzaguirre, Cementerio, from 0500, US$1.50, shared taxi US$3, 2 hrs. From Desaguadero to **La Paz** buses depart 4 blocks from bridge, last vehicle 2000.

Via Copacabana

Bus Several agencies go from La Paz to **Puno**, with a change of bus and stop for lunch at

Copacabana, or with an open ticket for continuing to Puno later. They charge US$7 and depart La Paz 0800, pick-up from hotel. They continue to the Peruvian border at Kasani and on to Puno, stopping for immigration formalities and changing money (better rates in Puno). Both **Crillon Tours** and **Transturin** have direct services to Puno without a change of bus at the border. From Copacabana to Puno, **Trans Titicaca** at 0900, 1300, and other agencies at 1330, offices on 6 de Agosto, US$3.50-4.50, 3 hrs. Also **Turisbus** at Hotel Rosario del Lago, US$7. To go direct to **Cuzco**, you will have to change in Puno where the tour company arranges connection, which may involve a wait, check details. In high season, book at least a day in advance. It is always cheaper, if less convenient, to buy only the next segment of your journey directly from local bus companies. *Colectivo* Copacabana (Plaza Sucre)-**Kasani** US$0.40 pp, 15 mins, Kasani- **Yunguyo**, where Peruvian buses start, US$0.20 pp.

East side of Lake Titicaca *p303*

Bus **La Paz** (Reyes Cardona 772, Cancha Tejar, Cementerio district, T238 2239)-**Puerto Acosta**, 5 hrs, US$4, Tue-Sun 0500. Transport past Puerto Acosta only operates on market days, Wed and Sat, and is mostly cargo trucks. Bus Puerto Acosta-La Paz at about 1500. There are frequent minivans to La Paz from **Escoma**, 25 km from Puerto Acosta; trucks from the border may take you this far.

Sorata *p303, map p304*

Bus Throughout the day from **La Paz** with **Trans Unificada** (from C Manuel Bustillos y Av Kollasuyo in the Cementerio district, T238 1693); also **Flor de Illampu** minibuses (Manuel Bustillos ½ block from Trans Unificada), US$2, 3 hrs. Booking recommended on Fri. To **Rurrenabaque**: jeeps run between Sorata and **Santa Rosa**, down the valley past Consata. From Santa Rosa transport can be arranged to Mapiri and then to Guanay, from where private boats may be arranged all the way to Rurrenabaque, or to Caranavi and thence to Coroico by road. Both are very long rough rides with interesting vegetation and stunning scenery. Sorata-Coroico by this route is excellent for offroad motorcycling. There are several camping places as well as very basic *hospedajes* in the towns. To, or from **Peru**, change buses at Huarina for Copacabana.

Cordillera Apolobamba *p305*

Charazani

Bus From Calle Reyes Cardona 732, off Av Kollasuyo, Cemetery district, La Paz, daily with **Trans Altiplano**, T283 0859, and **Trans Provincias del Norte** (No 772, T238 2239), 0600-0630, 7 hrs, US$3.50, very crowded. Return to La Paz at 1800; **Altiplano** also has 0900 on Sat and 1200 Mon, Fri.

Pelechuco

Bus From **La Paz Trans Provincias del Norte** leaves daily 0600-0700 from Ex Tranca de Río Seco in El Alto, passing through Qutapampa, Ulla Ulla and Agua Blanca to Pelechuco, between 10-12 hrs, US$5, sometimes on sale 24 hrs before departure at the booking office in Calle Reyes Cardona. Return to La Paz between 0300 and 0400 most days.

Directory

Copacabana *p301, map p302*

Banks **Prodem**, Av 6 de Agosto y Oruro, for cash advances on Visa or MasterCard only (no debit cards), 5% commission, changes US$ cash, Tue 1430-1800, Wed-Fri 0830-1230, 1430-1800, Sat-Sun 0830-1500. No ATM in town. Many *cambios* on Av 6 de Agosto change US$ cash, sometimes TCs, Euros and soles, all at poor rates. **Internet** Plenty of internet places in the centre, US$1.70 per hr. **Post offices** Plaza 2 de Febrero, open (in theory) Tue-Sat 0900- 1200, 1430-1830, Sun 0900-1500.

Sorata *p303, map p304*

Banks **Prodem**, on main plaza, T213 6679, Wed-Sun 0830-1700, Tue 1430-1700, changes US$ cash at fair rates, 5% commission on Visa/ MasterCard cash advances only (no debit cards). Nowhere in town to change TCs and no ATM. **Internet** **Buho's Internet Café**, on the plaza, 0900-1800. US$3 per hr, satellite connection but a cosy place with *artesanías* on display and for sale. **Medical services** **Hospital:** Villamil de Rada e Illampu. Has oxygen and X-ray. There is an adequately equipped **pharmacy**. **Post offices** On the plaza, 0830-1230, 1500-1800, but La Paz **Correo** is more reliable.

The Yungas

Only a few hours from La Paz are the subtropical valleys known as the Yungas. These steep, forested slopes, squeezed in between the Cordillera and the Amazon Lowlands, provide a welcome escape from the chill of the capital. The warm climate of the Yungas is also ideal for growing citrus fruit, bananas, coffee and coca leaves for the capital.

La Paz to the Yungas

All roads from La Paz to the Yungas go via **La Cumbre**, a pass at 4,725 m about one hour northeast of the city. The road out of La Paz circles cloudwards over La Cumbre; all around are towering snowcapped peaks. The first village after the peak is **Unduavi**, where there is a check point, a petrol station, and lots of roadside stalls. Here an unpaved road branches right 75 km to Chulumani. The paved road contnues to Cotapata, where it again divides: right is the old unpaved road to Yolosa, the junction 8 km from Coroico (this is the popular cycling route). To the left, the new paved road goes via Chuspipata and Puente Yolosita, where an unpaved road climbs steeply to Coroico. In addition, from Puente Villa on the Unduavi-Chulumani road, an unpaved road runs to Coripata and Coroico. For the La Cumbre-Coroico hike (Choro), see page 286.

All roads to Coroico drop some 3,500 m to the green subtropical forest in 70 km. The best views are in May-June, when there is less chance of fog and rain. The old road, the so-called "World's Most Dangerous Road", is steep, twisting, clinging to the side of sheer cliffs, and it is slippery in the wet. It is a breathtaking descent (best not to look over the edge if you don't like heights) and its reputation for danger is more than matched by the beauty of the scenery. Many tourists hire bicycles or go on a mountain-bike tour: it is your responsibility to choose top quality bikes (with hydraulic disc brakes) and a reputable company which offers bilingual guides, helmet, gloves, vehicle support throughout the day (addresses of recommended operators are given under La Paz, Tour operators). Many bike companies take riders back to La Paz the same day, but Coroico is worth more of your time. The road is especially dangerous mid-December to mid-February and many companies will not run bike tours at this time.

Coroico → *Phone code: 02. Colour map 6, A3.*

The little town of Coroico is perched on a hill at 1,760 m amid beautiful scenery. The hillside is covered with orange and banana groves and coffee plantations. Coroico is a first-class place to relax with several good walks. A colourful four-day festival is held 19-22 October. On 2 November, All Souls' Day, the cemetery is festooned with black ribbons. A good walk is up to the waterfalls, starting from **El Calvario**. Follow the stations of the cross by the cemetery, off Calle Julio Zuazo Cuenca, which leads steeply uphill from the plaza. Facing the chapel at El Calvario, with your back to the town, look for the path on your left. This leads to the falls which are the town's water supply (Toma de Agua) and, beyond, to two more falls. **Cerro Uchumachi**, the mountain behind El Calvario, can be climbed following the same stations of the cross, but then look for the faded red and white antenna behind the chapel. From there it's about 2 hours' steep walk to the top (take water). A third walk goes to the pools in the **Río Vagante**, 7 km off the road to Coripata; it takes about three hours. The **tourist information**is at the Prefectura ⓘ *Monse y Julio Zuazo Cuenca, corner of the main plaza*. There have been several incidents of young women being raped or attacked in this area; do not hike alone.

Caranavi → *Phone code: 02. Colour map 6, A2. Altitude: 600 m.*

From the junction at Puente Yolosita the paved road follows the river 11 km to Santa Bárbara, then becomes gravel for 65 km to Caranavi, an uninspiring town 156 km from La Paz. From here the road continues towards the settled area of the Alto Beni, at times following a picturesque gorge. Market days are Friday and Saturday. There is a range of hotels and *alojamientos* and buses from La Paz (Villa Fátima) to Rurrenabaque pass through. Beyond Caranavi, 70 km, is **Guanay** at the junction of the Tipuani and Mapiri rivers (basic lodging). From here there is river transport to Rurrenabaque.

Chulumani and around → *Phone code: 02. Colour map 6, A2. Altitude: 1,640 m.*
The capital of Sud Yungas, 124 km from La Paz, is a charming, relaxed little town with beautiful views and many hikes. There's a **fiesta** on 24 August (lasts 10 days) and a lively market every weekend. The road from Unduavi goes through **Puente Villa**, where a road branches north to Coroico through Coripata. The **tourist office** ⓘ *main plaza, Mon-Fri 0900-1330, 1500-2200, Sat, Sun 0700-2200, but frequently shut*, sells locally grown coffee, teas, jams and honey. **Apa Apa Ecological Park** ⓘ *8 km away, T213 6106/7254 7770 to arrange transport from town, taxi US$3 one way; or T279 0381 (La Paz), or write to Casilla 10109, Miraflores, La Paz* is the last area of original Yungas forest with lots of wildlife. The road to **Irupana**, a colonial village 1½ hours from Chulumani, passes the turn-off to the park. Ask to get off and walk 15 minutes up to the *hacienda* of Ramiro Portugal and his wife, Tildi (both speak English), who manage the park; you can use their pool after trek (3 rooms, full-board accommodation and campsite with bathrooms).

The Yungas listings

For Sleeping and Eating price codes and other relevant information, see Essentials, pages 38-40.

Sleeping

Coroico *p312*
Hotel rooms are hard to find at holiday weekends and prices are higher.

B Gloria, C Kennedy 1, T/F213 6020, www.hotelgloria.com.bo. Full board with bath (**C** bed and breakfast). Pool, breakfast extra, restaurant, internet, free transport from plaza.

B El Viejo Molino, T/F279 7329, www.hotelviejomolino.com. 2 km on road to Caranavi, Upmarket hotel and spa with pool, jacuzzi, games room etc.

C-E Esmeralda, reservations: Casilla PO Box 92 25, La Paz, www.coroico-info.com. 10 mins uphill from plaza. Bolivian-German owned, most rooms include breakfast, dorms **F** pp, hot showers, satellite TV and DVD, free pick-up (ring from bus office), English spoken, hikes arranged, and tours by open-sided truck to coca fields and waterfalls, TCs (no commission), credit cards accepted, phones, book exchange, good buffet restaurant, Finnish sauna, garden, pool, laundry, high-speed internet access US$1 per hr, Wi-Fi zone, welding facilities for overland drivers, express van to La Paz on the new road (US$50 for up to 11 passengers), book ahead. Very helpful. Recommended.

C-F Sol y Luna, 15-20 mins beyond *Hotel Esmeralda*, T7156 1626 (or Maison de la Bolivie, 6 de Agosto 2464, Ed Jardines, La Paz, T244 0588), www.solyluna-bolivia.com. 7 *cabañas*, bath and kitchen, splendid views, 2 apartments for 4 people, 2 rooms with bath, 7 rooms with shared bath for 1-4 people, meals available (vegetarian specialities), camping US$2 pp (not suitable for cars), garden, pool, laundry service, shiatsu massage (US$15-20), very good value, Sigrid, (owner) speaks English, French, German, Spanish.

D Bella Vista, C Héroes del Chaco 7 (2 blocks from main plaza), T213 6059. Beautiful rooms and views, **E** without bath, 2 racquetball courts, terrace, bike hire, restaurant, pool.

D Hostal Kory, at top of steps leading down from the plaza, T7156 4050. Huge pool, terrace, **E** without bath, electric showers, restaurant, good value, helpful.

D Matsu, 1 km from town (call for free pick-up, taxi US$2), T7069 2219. Includes breakfast, views, quiet, helpful.

E Don Quijote, 500 m out of town, on road to Coripata, T224 3354. With breakfast, electric shower, pool, quiet, nice views.

F El Cafetal, Miranda, 10-min walk from town, T7193 3979. French-run, very nice, restaurant with excellent French/Indian/ vegetarian cuisine, good value. Recommended.

F Los Silbos, Iturralde 4043, T7350 0081. Simple rooms with shared bath, electric showers, good value.
G Residencial de la Torre, Julio Zuazo Cuenca, ½ block from plaza. Welcoming place with courtyard, sparse rooms, no alcoholic drinks allowed.

Chulumani *p313*
E Hostal Familiar Dion, Alianza, just off the plaza, T213 6070. Modern, roof terrace, includes breakfast, laundry and use of kitchen, **F** without bathroom or breakfast, very good.
E Huayrani, just off Junín, T213 6351. Lovely views, includes breakfast, electric shower, garden, pool.
E **Panorama**, top of hill on Murillo, T213 6109. Some rooms with view, with breakfast, hot water, garden, pool.
F Country House, 400 m out of town. Bed and breakfast, pool, good value but rock hard beds, restaurant with home cooking. Xavier Sarabia offers a number of guided hiking tours.
G Alojamiento Danielito, Bolívar. Hot water extra, laundry facilities, good view.

Eating

Coroico *p312*
Back-stube, opposite *Hostal Kory*. German and vegetarian specialities, à la carte only, breakfasts, pastries, top quality, nice atmosphere, Mon 0830-1200, Wed-Fri 0830-1430, 1830-2200, Sat-Sun 0830-2200.
Bamboos, Iturralde y Ortiz. Good Mexican food and pleasant atmosphere, live music some nights with cover charge. Happy hour 1800-1900.
Pizzería Italia, 2 with same name on the plaza. Best in town.
Snack Hawaii, Plaza M V García Lanza. Basic snack bar on the plaza, open all day, breakfast, burgers, sandwiches, juices, also money exchange.

Chulumani *p313*
El Mesón, Plaza, 1200-1330 only. Good lunch.
La Hostería on Junín close to the *tranca*. Pizzas and hamburgers, Texan run.

Activities and tours

Coroico *p312*
Cycling
CXC, Pacheco 79, T7197 3015. Good bikes, US$20 for 6 hrs including packed lunch, a bit disorganized but good fun and helpful, English and German spoken.

Horse riding
El Relincho, Don Reynaldo, T7191 3675, 100 m past *Hotel Esmeralda* (enquire here, ask for Fernando), US$25 for 4 hrs with lunch.

Transport

Coroico *p312*
Bus From La Paz all companies are on C Yanacachi y Av Las Américas, beside the former YPFB station in Villa Fátima: buses and minibuses leave throughout the day US$4.25, 2½ hrs on the new road. **Turbus Totaí**, T221 6592, is reported reliable and there are several others. Services return to La Paz from the small terminal down the hill in Coroico, across from the fooball field. All are heavily booked at weekends and on holidays.

Pick-ups from the small mirador at Pacheco y Sagárnaga go to **Puente Yolosita**, 15 mins, US$0.70. Here you can try to catch a bus to **Rurrenabaque**, but there's more chance of getting a seat in **Caranavi**, where La Paz-Rurre buses pass through in the evening, often full. Caranavi-Rurre 12 hrs, US$6-7, **Flota Yungueña**, at 1800-1900, **Turbus Totaí** 2100-2200, and others. Alternatively, take a shared taxi from the market area in Caranavi to **Guanay**, US$3.50, 2 hrs, where you can look for a boat (no public services). Ask for Gregorio Polo, T7300 8067, who has a canoe for the trip, US$300-400. A 3-day tour will cost US$500, with meals and camping. **Bala Tours**, T03-892 2527, www.balatours.com, **Enin Tours**, T03-892 2487, enintours@yahoo.com, and others of Rurrenabaque, run tours from Rurre to Guanay and may have empty space for the trip back to Rurre. See also **Andean Epics Ride** of Sorata (p 310) and Deep Rainforest, La Paz (p 295).

Chulumani *p313*
Bus From **La Paz**, several companies from Villa Fátima,, when full 0600-1600, US$2.75, 3½ hrs: **Trans San Bartolomé**, Virgen del Carmen 1750, T221 1674; **San Cristóbal**, C 15 de Abril 408 y San Borja, T221 0607, and others.

Directory

Coroico *p312*
Banks Prodem, J Zuazo Cuenca, near main plaza, changes US$ cash, cash advance on Visa or Master Card only (no debit cards), 5% commission, closed Mon, Tue morning and Sat and Sun afternoon. **Internet** US$0.85 per hr. **Language classes** Siria León Domínguez, T7195 5431. US$5 per hr, also rents rooms and makes silver jewellery, excellent English. **Medical services** Hospital: T213 6002, the best in the Yungas, good malaria advice.

Chulumani *p313*
Banks Prodem, Plaza Villalobos y General Pando, US$ cash at fair rates, 5% commission for Visa/MasterCard cash advances. **Cooperativa San Bartolomé**, changes cash Mon-Fri 0800-1200, 1400-1700, Sat-Sun 0700-1200. **Internet** US$1 per hr.

Southwest Bolivia

The mining town of Oruro, with one of South America's greatest folkloric traditions, shimmering salt flats, coloured lakes and surrealistic rock formations combine to make this one of the most fascinating regions of Bolivia. Add some of the country's most celebrated festivals and the last hide-out of Butch Cassidy and the Sundance Kid and you have the elements for some great and varied adventures. The journey across the altiplano from Uyuni to San Pedro de Atacama is now a popular route to Chile and there are other routes south to Argentina.

Oruro → *Phone code: 02. 30 km southeast of La Paz. Colour map 6, A2. Pop: 236,110. Altitude: 3,706 m.*

The mining town of Oruro is the gateway to the altiplano of southwest Bolivia. It's a functional place which explodes into life once a year with its famous carnival, symbolized by La Diablada. Not far to the west is the national park encompassing Bolivia's highest peak, Sajama. The **tourist office** ⓘ *Montes 6072, Plaza 10 de Febrero, T/F525 0144. Mon-Fri 0800-1200, 1400-1800* is very helpful and informative. The Prefectura and the Policía de Turismo jointly run information booths at the Terminal de Buses ⓘ *T528 7774, Mon-Fri 0800-1200, 1430-1830, Sat 0830-1200; Policía de Turismo on the second floor*, and opposite the railway station ⓘ *T525 7881, same hours.*

Although Oruro became famous as a mining town, there are no longer any working mines of importance. It is, however, a major railway junction and the commercial centre for the mining communities of the altiplano, as well as hosting the country's best-known carnival (see page 318). Several buildings in the centre hint at the city's former importance, notably the baroque concert hall (now a cinema) on Plaza 10 de Febrero and the **Casa de la Cultura** (Museo Simón I Patiño) ⓘ *Soria Galvarro 5755, Mon-Fri 0900-1200, 1400-1830, US$1.35.* Built as a mansion by the tin baron Simón Patiño, it is now run by the Universidad Técnica de Oruro, and contains European furniture and temporary exhibitions. There is a view from the Cerro Corazón de Jesús, near the church of the Virgen del Socavón, five blocks west of Plaza 10 de Febrero at the end of Calle Mier.

The **Museos Sacro y Minero** ⓘ *inside the Church of the Virgen del Socavón, entry via the church 0900-1145, 1500-1730, US$1.35, guided tours every 45 mins,* contain religious art, clothing and jewellery and, after passing through old mining tunnels and displays of mining techniques, a representation of *El Tío* (the god of the underworld). **Museo Antropológico** ⓘ *south of centre on Av España y Urquidi, T526 0020, Mon-Fri 0900-1200, 1400-1800, Sat-Sun 1000-1200, 1500-1800, US$0.75, good guides, getting there: take micro A heading south or any trufi going south.* It has a unique collection of stone llama heads as well as impressive carnival masks.

The **Museo Mineralógico y Geológico** ⓘ *part of the University, Mon-Fri 0800-1200, 1430-1700, US$0.70, getting there: take micro A south to the Ciudad Universitaria,* has mineral specimens and fossils. **Casa Arte Taller Cardozo Velásquez** ⓘ *Junín 738 y Arica, east of the centre, T527 5245, Mon-Sat 1000-1200, 1500-1800, US$1.* Contemporary Bolivian painting and sculpture is displayed in the Cardozo Velásquez home, a family of artists.

Parque Nacional Sajama

A one-day drive to the west of Oruro is the **Parque Nacional Sajama** ⓘ *park headquarters in Sajama village, T0132-513 5526 (in La Paz T02-242 2272), US$3.50 payable to community of Sajama*, established in 1939 and covering 100,230 ha. The park contains the world's highest forest, consisting mainly of the rare queñual tree (Polylepis tarapacana) which grows up to an altitude of 5,500 m. The scenery is wonderful with views of sevaral volcanoes, inlcuding Sajama – Bolivia's highest peak at 6,542 m – Parinacota and Pomerape (jointly called Payachatas). The road is paved and leads across the border into the Parque Nacional Lauca in Chile. You can trek in the park, with or without porters and mules, but once you move away from the Río Sajama or its major tributaries, lack of water is a problem.

Sajama village ➔ *Population: 500. Altitude: 4,200 m.*

In Sajama village, visitors are billeted with family-run *alojamientos* (**G**) on a rotatating basis. All are basic to very basic, especially the sanitary facilities; no showers or electricity, solar power for lighting only. Alojamientos may provide limited food, so bring your own supplies. It can be very windy and cold at night; a good sleeping bag, gloves and hat are essential. Crampons, ice axe and rope are needed for climbing the volcanoes and can be hired in the village. Local guides charge US$50-70 per day. Pack animals can be hired, US$8 per day including guide. Good bathing at the Manasaya thermal complex, 6 km northwest of village; jeeps can be rented to visit, US$8-16. Many villagers sell alpaca woolen items.

By road to Chile

The shortest and most widely used route from La Paz to Chile is the road to **Arica** via the border at Tambo Quemado (Bolivia) and **Chungará** (Chile). From La Paz take the highway south towards Oruro. Immediately before Patacamaya, turn right at green road sign to Puerto Japonés on the Río Desaguadero, then on to Tambo Quemado. Take extra petrol (none available after Chilean border until Arica), food and water. The journey is worthwhile for the breathtaking views.

Bolivian **customs and immigration** are at Tambo Quemado, where there are a couple of very basic places to stay and eat. Border control is open daily 0800-2000. Shops change bolivianos, pesos chilenos and dollars. From Tambo Quemado there is a stretch of about 7 km of 'no-man's land' before you reach the Chilean frontier at Chungará. Here the border crossing, which is set against the most spectacular scenic backdrop of Lago Chungará and Volcán Parinacota, is thorough but efficient; open 0800-2000. Expect a long wait behind lines of lorries. Drivers must fill in 'Relaciones de Pasajeros', US$0.25 from kiosk at border, giving details of driver, vehicle and passengers. Do not take any livestock, plants, fruit, vegetables, or dairy products into Chile.

An alternative crossing from Oruro: several bus companies travel southwest to Iquique, via the border posts of **Pisiga** (Bolivia) and **Colchane** (Chile). The road is paved from Oruro to Toledo (32 km) and from Opoquari to Huachachalla (about 30 km). The rest of the 240 km road in Bolivia is unpaved; on the chilean side it's paved all the way to Iquique, 250 km. There is also service from Oruro to Arica via Patacamaya and Tambo Quemado.

South of Oruro

Machacamarca, about 30 minutes south of Oruro, has a good railway museum. Further south, the road runs between the flat plain of Lago Poopó and the Cordillera Azanaque, a very scenic ride. There are thermal baths at **Pazña**, 91 km from Oruro. About 65 km south is the **Santuario de Aves Lago Poopó** (a Ramsar site), an excellent bird reserve on the lake of the same name. The lake dries up completely in winter. The closest place to Oruro to see flamingos and other birds is **Lago Uru Uru** (the northern section of the Poopó lake system), go to Villa Challacollo on the road to Pisiga (minibuses 102, 10, 5 or blue micros) and walk from there. Birds start arriving with the first rains in October or November. Further along, at Km 10 is Chusakeri, where chullpas can be seen on the hillside.

Access to the lake is a little closer from **Huari**, 15 minutes south of Challapata along a paved road. Huari (124 km south of Oruro) is a pleasant little town with a large brewery; there is a small museum and Mirador Tatacuchunita, a lookout on nearby Cerro Sullka. Sunsets over the lake are superb. There are a couple of basic *alojamientos*, eg *25 de Mayo*, 2 blocks from the plaza towards Challapata, shared bath, cold water in morning only. It is about an 8 km walk from Huari to the lake, depending on the water level. Near the lake is the Uru-Muratos community of **Llapallapani** with circular adobe homes, those with straw roofs are known as *chillas* and those with conical

Oruro

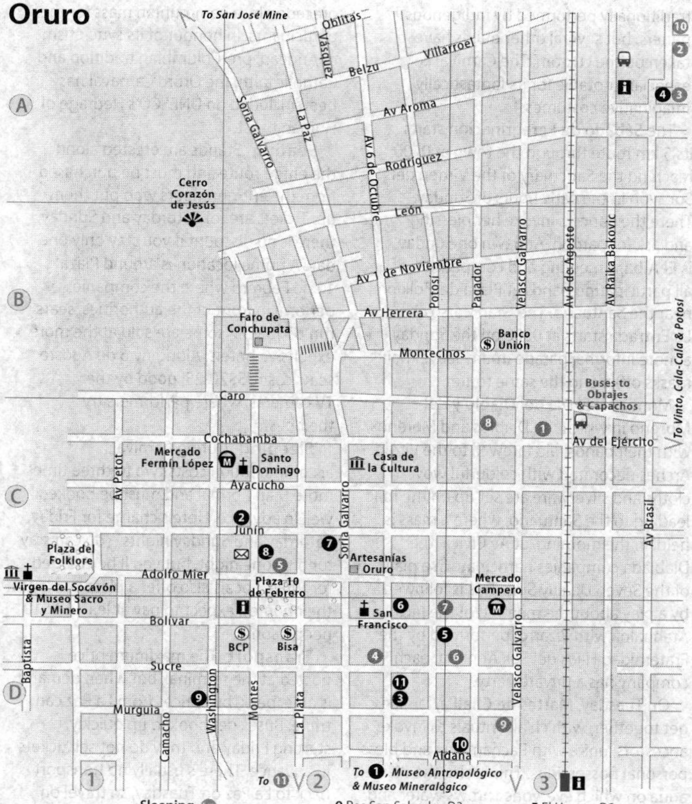

Sleeping
1 Alojamiento La Paz 1 *C3*
2 Bernal *A3*
3 El Lucero *A3*
4 Gran Sucre *D2*
5 Max Plaza *C2*
6 Repostero *D3*
7 Res Gloria *D2*
8 Res Gran Boston *C3*
9 Res San Salvador *D3*
10 Samay Wasi *A3*
11 Villa Real San Felipe *D2*

Eating
1 Café Sur *D2*
2 Caruso *C2*
3 Cocos Hard Rock *D2*
4 El Fogón *A3*
5 El Huerto *D2*
6 Govinda *D2*
7 La Cabaña *C2*
8 La Casona *C2*
9 Las Retamas *D1*
10 Nayjama *D3*
11 Panadería Doña Filo *D2*

N
200 metres
200 yards

La Diablada festival

On the Saturday before Ash Wednesday, Los Carnavales de Oruro include the famous Diablada ceremony in homage to the miraculous Virgen del Socavón, patroness of miners, and in gratitude to Pachamama, the Earth Mother. The Diablada was traditionally performed by indigenous miners, but several other guilds have taken up the custom. The Carnival is especially notable for its fantastically imaginative costumes.

The **Sábado de Peregrinación** starts its 5 km route through the town at 0700, reaching the Sanctuary of the Virgen del Socavón in the early hours of Sunday. There the dancers invoke her blessing and ask for pardon. At dawn on Sunday is **El Alba**, a meeting and competition of all participating bands at Plaza del Folklore, near the Santuario. The Gran Corso or **La Entrada** starts at 0800 on the Sunday, a more informal parade (many leave their masks off) along the same route.

Monday is **El Día del Diablo y del Moreno** in which the Diablos and Morenos, with their bands, bid farewell to the Virgin. Arches decorated with colourful woven cloths and silverware are set up on the road leading to the Santuario, where a mass is held. In the morning, at Av Cívica, the Diablada companies participate in a play of the Seven Deadly Sins. This is followed by a play about the meeting of the Inca Atahualpa with Pizarro, performed by the Fraternidad Hijos del Sol. At night, each company has a private party.

On Tuesday, **Martes de Chall'a**, families get together, with ch'alla rituals to invoke ancestors, unite with Pachamama and bless personal possessions. This is also the día del agua on which everyone throws water and sprays foam at everyone else (though this goes on throughout carnival; plastic tunics are sold for US$0.20 by street vendors).

The Friday before carnival, traditional miners' ceremonies are held at mines, including the sacrifice of a llama. Visitors may only attend with a guide and permission from Comibol, via the tourist office. Preparations begin four months before the actual event, on the first Sunday of November, and rehearsals are held every Sunday until one week before Carnival, when a plain clothes rehersal takes place, preceded by a communion mass for the participants. In honour of its syncretism of Andean, pre-Columbian tradition and Catholic faith, the Oruro Carnaval has been included on UNESCO's Heritage of Humanity list.

Seating Stands are erected along the entire route and must be purchased from the entrepreneurs who put them up. Tickets are for Saturday and Sunday, there is no discount if you stay only one day. A prime location is around Plaza 10 de Febrero where the companies perform in front of the authorities, seats run US$35-55, some are sold at the more expensive hotels. Along Av 6 de Agosto seats cost US$20-25, good by the TV cameras, where performers try their best.

Sleeping During Carnival, accommodation costs two to three times more than normal and must be booked well in advance. Hotels charge for Friday, Saturday and Sunday nights. You can stay for only one night, but you'll be charged for three. Locals also offer a place to stay in their homes, expect to pay at least US$10 per person.

Transport The maximum price is posted at the terminal, but when demand is at its peak, bus prices from La Paz can triple. Buses get booked up quickly, starting Friday and they do not sell tickets in advance. There's usually no transport back to La Paz on Tuesday, so travel on Monday or Wednesday. Many agencies organize day trips from La Paz on Saturday, depart 0430, most will pick you up from your hotel. They return late, making for a tiring day. Trips cost US$45-60, and include breakfast, a snack and sometimes a seat for the parade.

adobe roofs are *putukus*. Cabins in *putuku* style form part of a community tourism programme. Boats can be hired when the water level is high, at other times Poopó is an unattainable mirage. There is good walking in the Cordillera Azanaque behind Huari; take food, water, warm clothing and all gear. **Challapata** (*fiesta* 15-17 July) has several places to stay, eg *Res Virgen del Carmen*, by main plaza, and a gas station.

Atlantis in the Andes Jim Allen's theory of Atlantis (www.atlantisbolivia.org) is well known around Oruro. **Pampa Aullagas**, the alleged Atlantis site, is 196 km from Oruro, southwest of Lago Poopó. Access is from the town of **Quillacas** along a road that branches west from the road to Uyuni just south of Huari, or from the west through Toledo and Andamarca. A visit here can be combined with visits to the Salar de Coipasa.

Southwest of Lago Poopó, off the Oruro-Pisiga-Iquique road (turn off at **Sabaya**), is the **Salar de Coipasa**, 225 km from Oruro. It is smaller and less visited than the Salar de Uyuni, and has a turquoise lake in the middle of the salt pan surrounded by mountains with gorgeous views and large cacti. Coipasa is northwest of the Salar de Uyuni and travel from one to the other is possible with a private vehicle along the impressive **Ruta Intersalar**. Along the way are tombs, terracing and ancient irrigation canals at the archaeological site of **Alcaya** ⓘ *US$1.25*, gradually being developed by the local community (near **Salinas de Garci Mendoza**, locally known as Salinas). At the edge of the Salar de Uyuni is **Coquesa** (lodging available), which has a mirador and tombs with mummies ⓘ *US$1.25 entry to each site*. Nearby are the towering volcanic cones of Cora Cora and Tunupa. Access to the north end of the Salar de Uyuni is at **Jirira**.

Note: Getting stranded out on the altiplano or, worse yet on the salar itself, is dangerous because of extreme temperatures and total lack of drinking water. It is best to visit this area with a tour operator that can take you, for example, from Oruro through the salares to Uyuni. Travellers with their own vehicles should only attempt this route following extensive local inquiry or after taking on a guide to avoid becoming lost or bogged. The edges of the salares are soft and only established entry points or ramps should be used to cross onto or off the salt.

Oruro listings

For Sleeping and Eating price codes and other relevant information, see Essentials, pages 38-40.

Sleeping

Oruro *p315, map p317*

C Gran Sucre, Sucre 510 esq 6 de Octubre, T527 6800. Refurbished old building (faded elegance), includes buffet breakfast, cheaper rooms on the ground floor, heaters on request, friendly helpful staff. Recommended.

C Max Plaza, Adolfo Mier at Plaza 10 de Febrero, T525 2561. Includes breakfast, comfortable carpeted rooms, good central location.

C Villa Real San Felipe, San Felipe 678 y La Plata, south of the centre, T525 4993, www.villarealsanfelipe.com. Quaint hotel, nicely furnished but small rooms, heating, buffet breakfast, sauna and whirlpool, restaurant, tour operator, best hotel in town.

D Samay Wasi, Av Brasil 232 opposite the terminal, T527 6737. Modern, includes breakfast, bright rooms, hot water, internet, 30% discount for IYHF members. Recommended.

E Repostero, Sucre 370 y Pagador, T525 8001. Hot water, includes breakfast, renovated carpeted rooms are pricier but better value than the old rooms, secure parking.

F Bernal, Brasil 701, opposite bus terminal, T527 9468. Hot showers, cheaper with shared bath (no towels or toilet paper, poor value), heaters on request, restaurant, tours arranged.

F El Lucero, 21 de Enero 106 y Brasil opposite the terminal, T528 5884. Multi-storey hotel, private bath, hot water.

F Res Gran Boston, Pagador 1159 y Cochabamba, T527 4708. Refurbished house, internal rooms around a covered patio, cheaper with shared bath, good value.

F Res San Salvador, V Galvarro 6325 near train station, T527 6771. Hot water, **G** with shared bath, electric shower, best in this area.

G Res Gloria, Potosí 6059, T527 6250. 19th-century building, private toilet, shared electric shower, cheaper with shared toilet, basic, clean.

G Alojamiento La Paz, Cochabamba 180, T527 4882. Shared bath, basic, clean, hot shower extra.

Parque Nacional Sajama *p316*

B Tomarapi Ecolodge, north of Sajama in Tomarapi community, near Caripe, T02-241 4753, represented by Millenarian Tourism & Travel, Av Sánchez Lima 2193, La Paz, T02-241 4753, www.boliviamilenaria.com. Including full board (good food) and guiding service with climbing shelter at 4,900 m, helpful staff, simple but comfortable, with bath, hot water, heating.

South of Oruro *p316*

E Zuk'arani, on a hillside overlooking Salinas de Garci Mendoza and the Salar, T2513 7086, zukarani@hotmail.com. Two cabins for 4, with bath, hot water, and **F** in rooms with shared bath, hot water, meals on request.

F Posada Doña Lupe, Jirira. Hot water, cheaper without bath, use of kitchen but bring your own food, no meals available, caters to tour groups, pleasant, comfortable.

G Alojamiento Paraíso, Sabaya. Take sleeping bag, shared bath, cold water, meals on request or take own food, sells petrol.

G Doña Wadi, Salinas de Garci Mendoza, C Germán Busch, near main plaza, T513 8015. Shared bath, hot water, basic but clean, meals available.

Eating

Oruro *p315, map p317*

ΨΨ La Cabaña, Junín 609. Comfortable, smart, good international food, bar, Sun and Mon 1200-1530 only.

ΨΨ Nayjama, Aldana 1880. Good regional specialties, very popular for lunch, huge portions.

ΨΨ-Ψ El Fogón, Brasil 5021. Best of a poor lot by the bus terminal. The many greasy chicken places by the terminal are best avoided.

ΨΨ-Ψ Las Retamas, Murguía 930 esq Washington. Mon-Sat 0900-1430, 1900-2300, Sun 0900-1430. Excellent set lunches (Ψ), Bolivian and international dishes à la carte, very good pastries at **Kuchen Haus**, pleasant atmosphere, out of the way but worth the trip. Recommended.

Ψ Cocos Hard Rock, 6 de Octubre y Sucre. Mon-Sat1200-1400, 1800-2400, Sun 1200-1400. Set meals, local and international dishes.

Ψ La Casona, Pres Montes 5970, opposite Post Office. A good *pizzería*.

Ψ Govinda, 6 de Octubre 6071. Excellent vegetarian, Mon-Sat 0900-2130.

Ψ El Huerto, Bolívar 359. Good, vegetarian options, open Sun.

Cafés

Café Sur, Arce 163, near train station. Live entertainment, seminars, films, Tue-Sat, good place to meet local students.

Caruso, Junín 5898 esq Pres Montes, Mon-Sat 0800-2200, Sun 1400-2200. Breakfast, pizza, savoury and sweet snacks.

Jordan's Café Net, Bolívar 394 entre Potosí y Pagador. Coffee, breakfasts, Wi-fi.

Panadería Doña Filo, 6 de Octubre esq Sucre. Excellent savoury snacks and sweets, closed Sun, takeaway only.

Bars and clubs

Oruro *p315, map p317*

Bravo, Montesinos y Pagador. Varied music, 2100-0300.

Imagine, 6 de Octubre y Junín. Latin and other music, 2200-0400.

Shopping

Oruro *p315, map p317*

Crafts On Av La Paz the blocks between León and Belzu are largely given over to workshops producing masks and costumes for Carnival. **Artesanías Oruro**, A Mier 599, esq S Galvarro. Lovely selection of regional handicrafts produced by 6 rural community cooperatives; nice sweaters, carpets, wall-hangings.

Markets Mercado Campero, V Galvarro esq Bolívar. Sells everything, also *brujería* section for magical concoctions. **Mercado Fermín López**, C Ayacucho y Montes. Food and hardware. C Bolívar is the main shopping street. **Irupana**, S Galvarra y A Mier. Good selection of natural food and snacks.

Activities and tours

Oruro *p315, map p317*

Asociación de Guías Mineros, contact Gustavo Peña, T523 2446. Arranges visits to San José mine.

Freddy Barrón, T527 6776, lufba@hotmail.com. Custom-made tours and transport, speaks German and some English.

Santiaguito Tours, Herrera y Pagador, T528 6668. Local and regional tours, visit to San José mine costs US$15.

Transport

Oruro *p315, map p317*

Bus Bus terminal 10 blocks north of centre at Bakovic and Aroma, T525 3535, US$0.20 terminal tax to get on bus. Micro No 2 to centre, or any saying 'Plaza 10 de Febrero'. To **Challapata** and **Huari**: several companies go from the Oruro terminal to Challapata, about every hour, US$1, 1¾ hrs, and Huari, US$1.25, 2 hrs, last bus back leaves Huari about 1630. You can also take a bus to Challapata and a shared taxi from there to Huari, US$0.30. Daily services to: **La Paz** at least every hour 0400-2200, US$2-3.40, 3½ hrs;. **Cochabamba**, US$3.35-4, 4 hrs, frequent with **Copacabana**, **Azul** and **Danubio**. **Potosí**, US$2.70-4, 5 hrs, several daily, **Bustillo** and **San Miguel**. **Sucre Bustillo**, **Trans Azul** and **San José**, all around 2000, US$6.70, 9 hrs. **Tarija**, **Belgrano** at 2030, US$9.30-11.75, 16 hrs. **Uyuni**, several companies, all depart 1900-2100, US$5.35-6, 7-8 hrs. **Todo Turismo**, www.touringbolivia.com, offers a tourist bus departing from La Paz at 2100, arrange ahead for pick-up in Oruro at midnight, US$27. To **Tupiza**, via Potosí, **Boquerón** at 1230, **Illimani** at 1630 and 2030, US$9.75-11.50, 11-12 hrs, continuing to Villazón, US$10-12, 13-14 hrs. **Santa Cruz**, **Bolívar** at 2000, US$8.70, *bus cama* at 2130, US$14, 11 hrs. **Pisiga** (Chilean border), **Trans Pisiga**, Av Dehene y España, T526 2241, at 2000 and 2030, or with Iquique bound buses, US$3.75, 4-5 hrs.

International buses (US$2 to cross border): to **Iquique** via Pisiga, US$13-14, 12 hrs, buses leave around 1200 coming from Cochabamba; companies include **Trans Luján**, T02-525 8523, and **Trans Paraíso** T02-527 0765. **Arica** via Patacamaya and **Tambo Quemado**, several companies daily around 1100, US$18-25, 8 hrs, some continue to Iquique, US$21-28, 9-10 hrs.

Train The station is at Av Velasco Galvarro y Aldana, T527 4605, ticket office Mon-Fri 0800-1200, 1430-1800, Sun 0830-1120, 1530-1800. Only tickets for *ejecutivo* class are sold up to 1 week in advance, others are sold on the day before (you have to collect a number, rather than queue; touts will try to sell you a number). Tickets can also be purchased in La Paz, see page 298. **Ferroviaria Andina FCA**, www.fca.com.bo, runs services from Oruro to **Uyuni** and on to **Villazón** via Tupiza: **Expreso del Sur** runs Tue and Fri at 1530, arriving in Uyuni at 2220, and **Wara Wara** on Sun and Wed at 1900, arriving in Uyuni at 0220.

Fares: Expreso del Sur to Uyuni: *Ejecutivo* US$14, *Salón* US$7; Tupiza, 12½ hrs: US$27.50, US$12.50 respectively: Villazón, 15½ hrs: US$32, US$15. Wara Wara del Sur to Uyuni: *Ejecutivo* US$12, *Salón* US$5.50; Tupiza, 13½-14 hrs: US$21, US$9.50 respectively: Villazón, 17½ hrs: US$25, US$12. For details of trains from Uyuni to **Villazón** and for trains from Uyuni to Oruro, see Uyuni. For return times from Villazón, see page 331. Passengers with tickets Villazón-La Paz are transferred to a bus at Oruro.

Parque Nacional Sajama *p316*

To get to the park, take a La Paz-Oruro bus and change at Patacamaya. Mini-vans from Patacamaya to Sajama Sun-Fri 1200, 3 hrs, US$2.50. Sajama to **Patacamaya** Mon-Fri 0600, some days via **Tambo Quemado**, confirm details and weekend schedule locally. From Tambo Quemado to Sajama about 1530 daily, 1 hr, US$0.65. Or take a La Paz-Arica bus, ask for Sajama, try to pay half the fare, but you may be charged full fare.

South of Oruro *p316*

To **Coipasa** ask if **Trans Pisiga**, address above, is running a fortnightly service. If not, you can take one of the buses to Iquique and get off at the turnoff, but it's difficult to hire a private vehicle for onward transportation in this sparsely populated area. **Salinas de Garci Mendoza** from **Oruro**, **Trans Cabrera**, CTejerina y Caro, daily except Sat (Mon, Wed Fri, Sun 1900, Tue, Thu 0830, Sun also at 0730). Return to Oruro same days, US$3.40, 7 hrs.

Directory

Oruro *p315, map p317*

Banks Banco Bisa, Bolívar y La Plata at Plaza 10 de Febrero. **BCP**, Bolívar esq Montes at Plaza 10 de Febrero. **Banco Unión**, Pagador y Montecinos. **Casa de Cambio** at the Terminal Terrestre, US$, euros, pesos chilenos and argentinos, soles, cash only, fair rates, daily 0800-2000. **Internet** Many in town, rates US$0.35. **Post offices** Presidente Montes 1456, half block from plaza. **Telephones** Many *cabinas* in town. **Useful addresses** Immigration, S Galvarro entre Ayacucho y Cochabamba.

Uyuni → *Phone code: 02. Colour map 6, B3. Population: 18,000. Altitude: 3,665 m.*

Uyuni lies near the eastern edge of the Salar de Uyuni and is one of the jumping-off points for trips to the salt flats, volcanoes and lakes of southwest Bolivia. Still a commercial and communication centre, Uyuni was, for much of the 20th century, important as a major railway junction. Two monuments dominate Avenida Ferroviaria: one of a railway worker, erected after the 1952 Revolution, and the other commemorating those who died in the Chaco War. Most services are near the station. **Museo Arqueológico and Antropológico de los Andes Meridionales** ⓘ *Arce y Potosí, Tue-Sat 0900-1200, 1400-1800, US$0.35.* A small museum with local artefacts. Market on Avenida Potosí between the clock and Avaroa sells everything almost every day. Fiesta 11 July. There is a Railway Cemetery outside town with engines from 1907 to the 1950s, now rusting hulks.

Pulacayo, 30 minutes' ride from Uyuni, is a town at the site of a 19th-century silver mine. The train cemetery here contains the first locomotive in Bolivia and the train robbed by Butch Cassidy and the Sundance Kid.

Tourist office Dirección de Turismo Uyuni ⓘ *at the clock tower, T693 2060, open occasionally.* Subprefectura de Potosí ⓘ *Colón y Sucre, Mon-Fri 0800-1200, 1430-1830, Sat 0800-1200,* departmental information office, the place to file complaints in writing.

Salar de Uyuni

Crossing the Salar de Uyuni, the largest and highest salt lake in the world, is one of the great Bolivian trips. Driving across it is a fantastic experience, especially during June and July when the bright blue skies contrast with the blinding white salt crust. Farther south, and included on tours of the region, are the towering volcanoes, multi-coloured lakes (including Colorada and Verde) with abundant birdlife, weird rock formations, thermal activity and endless puna that make up some of most fabulous landscapes in South America.

Trips to the Salar de Uyuni enter via the *terraplén* (ramp) at **Colchani** (**Museo de la Llama y de la Sal**; see also Sleeping, below) and include stops to see traditional salt mining techniques and the Ojos del Agua, where salt water bubbles to the surface of the slat flat, perhaps a call at a salt hotel (see Sleeping, below) and a visit to the **Isla Incahuasi** ⓘ *entry US$1.40* (also known as del Pescado because of its shape). This is a coral island, raised up from the ocean bed, covered in tall cactii. There is a walking trail with superb views, a *Mongo's* café, basic lodging and toilets. If on an extended tour (see below), you may leave the Salar by another *terraplén*, eg Puerto Chupica in the southwest.

San Cristóbal

The original village of **San Cristóbal**, southwest of Uyuni, was relocated in 2002 to make way for a Canadian-owned open-pit mine, said to be one of the largest silver deposits in South America. The original church (1650) had been declared a national monument and was therefore rebuilt in its entirety. Ask at the Fundación San Cristóbal Office for the church to be opened as the interior artwork, restored by Italian techniques, is worth seeing. The fiesta is 27-28 July. San Cristóbal and other towns in the area, eg Alota (see below) and Culpina K, were offered tourism projects by the company in exchange for permission to allow the mine to proceed. Dubbed *pueblos auténticos* (authentic towns), they have yet to escape the look of the new money spent on them. The road San Cristóbal-Uyuni is paved to start with, then becomes good gravel (watch out for stones flung up by speeding trucks).

Reserva Nacional de Fauna Andina Eduardo Avaroa

ⓘ *SERNAP office at Colón y Avaroa, Uyuni, T693 2225, www.bolivia-rea.com, US$4 (due to rise substanitally in 2010; not included in tour price; pay in bolivianos). Park ranger/entry points are near Laguna Colorada, Lagunas Verde and Blanca, close to the Chilean border, and at Sol de Mañana, near Quetena Chico. See http://delipez.org/turismo.*

In the far southwest of Bolivia, in the Lípez region, is the 714,745-ha **Reserva Nacional Eduardo Avaroa** (REA). There are two access routes from Uyuni (one via the Salar) and one from Tupiza. Until recently the Reserve's wonders were quite isolated, but tours now criss-cross the puna, many on the route from Uyuni to San Pedro de Atacama. Roads are unmarked, rugged truck tracks and may be impassable in the wet season. **Laguna Colorada**, at 4,278 m, 346 km southwest of Uyuni, is just one of the highlights of the reserve, its shores and shallows encrusted with borax and salt, an arctic white counterpoint to the flaming red, algae-coloured waters in which the rare James flamingos, along with the more common Chilean and Andean flamingos, breed and live. The **Laguna Verde** (lifeless because it is laden with arsenic) and its neighbour Laguna Blanca, near the Chilean border, are at the foot of Volcán Licancábur, 5,868 m. Between Lagunas Colorada and Verde there are thermal pools at Laguna Blanca (blissful water, a challenge to get out into the bitter wind – no facilities) and at Polques, on the shores of Río Amargo/Laguna Salada by the Salar de Chalviri. A *centro comunal* has been built at Polques (with dining room, changing room and toilets). All these places are on the 'classic' tour route, across the Salar de Uyuni to **San Juan**, which has a museum of local *chullpas*, and is where most tour companies stop: plenty of lodgings. Other tours stop at **Culpina K**. Then you go to the Salar de Chiguana, Mirador del Volcán de Ollagüe, Cinco Lagunas, a chain of small, flamingo-specked lagoons, the much-photographed Arbol de Piedra in the Siloli desert, then Laguna Colorada (spend the second night here: *Hospedaje Laguna Colorada*, the newer and better D *Don Humberto* in Huayllajara, and *Campamento Ende*). From Colorada you go over the Cuesta del Pabellón, 4,850 m, to the Sol de Mañana geysers (not to be confused with the Sol de Mañana entry point), the Desierto de Dalí, a pure sandy desert as much Daliesque for the spacing of the

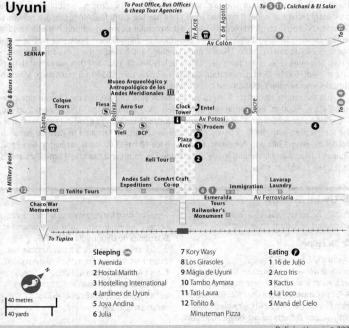

Uyuni

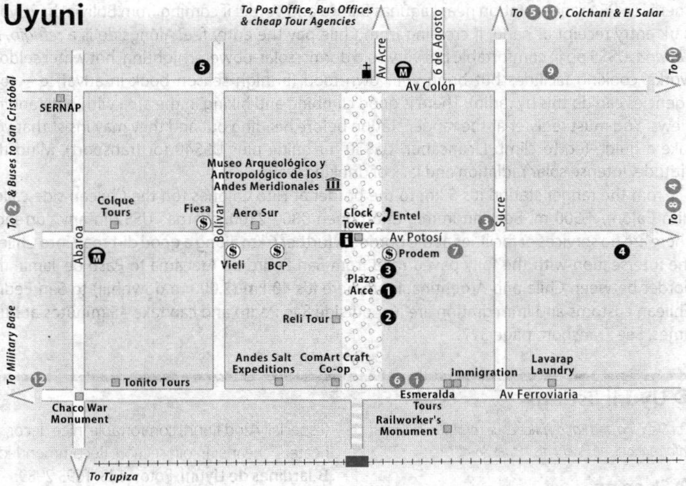

40 metres
40 yards

Sleeping
1 Avenida
2 Hostal Marith
3 Hostelling International
4 Jardines de Uyuni
5 Joya Andina
6 Julia
7 Kory Wasy
8 Los Girasoles
9 Mágia de Uyuni
10 Tambo Aymara
11 Tati-Laura
12 Toñito & Minuteman Pizza

Eating
1 16 de Julio
2 Arco Iris
3 Kactus
4 La Loco
5 Maná del Cielo

rocks, with snow-covered peaks behind, as for the shape of the rocks themselves, and Laguna Verde (4,400 m).

Jurisdiction of the reserve belongs to the villages of **Quetena Chico** and Quetena Grande (the smaller of the two), to the east of Laguna Colorada. The villagers are entitled to run lodging in the reserve: Quetena Chico runs *hospedajes* at Laguna Colorada. Quetena Grande runs *La Cabaña* at Hito Cajónes (see below). In Quetena Chico is the reserve's visitors information centre, **Centro Ecológico Ch'aska** ⓘ *daily 0730-1800*, informative displays about the region's geology, vulcanology, fauna, flora, natural and human history; a worthwhile stop. The village has two *hospedajes* (*Piedra Preciosa* and *Hostal Quetena*, both **G**, hot water extra), and places to eat.

From Tupiza Tour operators in Tupiza run trips to the REA and Salar de Uyuni and go to places not included on tours from Uyuni. These include the beautiful Lagunas Celeste and Negra below Cerro Uturunco, which is near Quetena Chico; the **Valle de las Rocas**, 4,260 m, between the villages of **Alota** and Villa Mar (a vast extension of rocks eroded into fantastic configurations, with polylepis trees in sheltered corners); and isolated communities in the puna. The high altitude scenery is out of this world. *Alojamientos* in the villages on the tour routes cannot be booked. You turn up and search for a room. All provide kitchen space for the tour's cook or independent traveller to prepare meals, take your own stove, though. See also **Tayka** in Uyuni, Activities and tours, below. There is public transport from Uyuni into the region, but rarely more than one bus a week, with several hours rough travelling. If travelling independently, note that there are countless tracks and no signposts.

Crossing into Chile

There is a REA ranger station near Lagunas Blanca and Verde: if coming from Bolivia, have your park entry receipt at hand, if crossing from Chile pay the entry fee. Alongside is a *refugio*, *La Cabaña*; US$5 pp in comfortable but very cold dorms, solar-powered lighting, hot water seldom works, cooking facilities but bring your own food (in high season book in advance – tour agencies can do this by radio). There is good climbing and hiking in the area with outstanding views. You must register at the ranger station before heading out and they may insist that you take a guide (eg to climb Licancábur, US$30 for guide plus US$40 for transport). Mind the altitude, intense solar radiation and lack of drinking water.

From the ranger station it's 5 km to the border at Hito Cajones (on the Chilean side called Hito Cajón), 4,500 m. Bolivian immigration open 0800-2100, charges US$2 in any currency. There are no services or facilities at the border. A further 6 km along a good dirt road into Chile is the intersection with the fully paved road from San Pedro de Atacama to Paso de Jama, the border between Chile and Argentina. From here it's 40 km (2,000 m downhill) to San Pedro. Chilean customs and immigration are just outside San Pedro and can take 45 minutes at busy times. See Transport, page 327.

Uyuni listings

For Sleeping and Eating price codes and other relevant information, see Essentials, pages 38-40.

Sleeping

Uyuni *p322, map p323*

Be conservative with water use, this is a very dry area, water is scarce and there may be cuts.

A-C Los Girasoles, Santa Cruz 155, 3½ blocks from clock tower, T693 2101, girasoleshotel@hotmail.com. Buffet breakfast, bright and warm (especially 2nd floor), comfortable, nice decor, heaters, cheaper in old section. Recommended.

B Jardines de Uyuni, Potosí 133, T693 2989. Includes breakfast, rustic but comfortable, hot water, heaters, open fire in the lounge, parking.

C Joya Andina, Cabrera 473 y Sucre, T693 2076, reservasjoyaandina@hotmail.com. Includes breakfast, small carpeted rooms, parking, helpful management.

C Julia, Ferroviaria 314 y Arce, T693 2134. Spacious comfortable rooms, solar heated hot water, **E** with shared bath and in low season.

C Mágia de Uyuni, Av Colón 432, T693 2541. Includes breakfast, nice ample rooms and suites upstairs with heating, cheaper in older rooms downstairs, insist on a heater, parking.

C Tambo Aymara, Camacho s/n y Colón, T693 2227, www.tamboaymara.com. Colonial-style modern hotel, inlcudes buffet breakfast, large rooms, heating, restaurant.

C-D Toñito, Av Ferroviaria 48, T693 3186, www.bolivianexpeditions.com. Includes good breakfast, spacious rooms with good beds, solar-powered showers and heating in new wing, cheaper in old section with electric showers, parking, book exchange, tours.

D Hostelling International, Potosí y Sucre, T693 2228, pucara_tours@yahoo.com. **F** with shared bath, hot water, kitchen facilities, modern and popular but poor beds, discount for IYHF.

E Avenida, Av Ferroviaria 11, near train station, T693 2078. Old but well maintained, **F** with shared bath, simple, hot water in shared showers 0700-2100, popular with travellers, laundry facilities, good value.

E Hostal Marith, Av Potosí 61, T693 2174. Good budget option, **F** with shared bath (better value), electric showers from 0830, simple, sunny cement patio with laundry facilities, tours (have own salt hotel at Atulcha near the Salar).

E Kory Wasy, Av Potosí, entre Arce y Sucre, T693 2670, kory_wasy@hotmail.com. Good fun, sunny lobby but many dark rooms, laundry facilities, tour agency.

F Tati-Laura, Cabrera 334 y Sucre, near bus terminals, T02-693 3549. Simple rooms, **G** with shared bath, electric shower, parking.

Salar de Uyuni *p322*

These *hoteles de sal* are generally visited on tours, seldom independently.

L Palacio de Sal, on the edge of the salar, near the ramp outside Colchani (book through **Jardines de Uyuni**, see above, operated by **Hidalgo Tours**, Junín esq Bolívar, T622 5186, Potosí, uyusalht@entelnet.bo). Price is half- board. Spacious, luxury salt hotel, decorated with large salt sculptures, heating, hot water, sauna, lookout on second storey with views of the salar.

L-A Luna Salada, 5 km north of Colchani near the edge of the salar, T7242 9716, 02-278 5438 (La Paz), www.lunasaladahotel.com.bo. Lovely salt hotel, with breakfast, comfortable rooms, hot water, ample common areas with lovely views of the Salar, salt floors, skylights make it warm and cozy, reserve ahead.

C Playa Blanca, on the Salar de Uyuni, about 10 km from the Colchani access and 70 km from Isla Incahuasi, T693 2772 (Uyuni). All furnishings made of salt blocks, shared bath, no showers, single beds only, all solid and liquid waste is removed in barrels. This is the only hotel left on the salar, but reports indicate that it may have been closed for environmental reasons. A stop for most tours, day visitors must consume something in order to take photos, use of toilet US$0.60. Playa Blanca has a second salt hotel in Colchani, **F**, well water is kept in buckets near the shared showers, basic. See also **Tayka** in Activities and tours, below.

G Alojamiento del Museo de Sal, on the road to the Salar from Colchani, by the *tranca*, T7272 0834. Simple salt hotel, shared bath, kitchen facilities, dining area used by groups, has a small museum with salt sculptures, reserve ahead, good value.

San Cristóbal *p322*

C Hotel San Cristóbal, T7264 2117, purpose-built, owned by the community, in centre. The bar is inside a huge oil drum, all metal furnishings. The rest is comfortable if simple, very hot water, good breakfast included, evening meal extra.

There are a couple of inexpensive *alojamientos* in town.

Eating

Uyuni *p322, map p323*

₸₸-₸ 16 de Julio, Plaza Arce y Ferroviaria, daily 0830-2230. Good value breakfast and lunch, à la carte in the evening, veggie options.

₸₸-₸ Kactus, Arce y Potosí, p 2. Daily 0730-2200. International food, homemade pasta, good pancakes, slow service.

₸₸-₸ La Loco, Av Potosí y Camacho, T693 3105. Mon-Sat 1600-0200 (food until about 2130), closes Jan-Feb. International food with a Bolivian and French touch, music and drinks till late, open fire, popular, reserve in Jul-Aug.

Arco Iris, Plaza Arce. Daily 1600-2230. Good Italian food, pizza, and atmosphere, occasional live music.

Maná del Cielo, Bolívar y Colón. Mon-Fri 0800-2000. Breafast, simple vegetarian meals and cafeteria.

Minuteman, pizza restaurant attached to *Toñito Hotel* (see above), good pizzas and soups, also breakfast.

Activities and tours

Uyuni *p322, map p323*

Organization of tours from Uyuni to the Salar is much improved, but even good companies have their off days. Travel is in 4WD Landcruisers, cramped for those on the back seat, but the staggering scenery makes up for any discomfort. Always check the itinerary, the vehicle, the menu (vegetarians should be prepared for an egg-based diet), what is included in the price and what is not (accommodation is normally not included – add US$3-4.50 pp per night). Trips are usually 3 to 4 days: Salar de Uyuni, Lagunas Colorada and Verde, back to Uyuni; Uyuni-San Pedro de Atacama, including the Salar and lakes; and Uyuni to Tupiza via all the sights. Prices range from US$70-200 pp depending on agency, departure point and season. The cheapest tours will involve insufficient staff and food, basic vehicles and accommodation. At the top end you can assemble your own tour, with driver and cook, good equipment and services. It is easy to find other people in Uyuni, especially in high season, Apr-Sep. Agencies all over Bolivia sell tours, but this may lead to misunderstandings between what is offered and what is actually delivered by the Uyuni operator. If the tour seriously fails to match the contract and the operator refuses any redress, complaints can be taken to the **Subprefectura de Potosí** in Uyuni (see above). Speak to travellers who have just returned from a tour, and try the following:

Tour operators

Andes Salt Expeditions, Av Ferroviaria 55 near Plaza Arce, T693 2116/7241 4748, www.andes-salt-uyuni.com.bo. Offers guided tours of the salar and lagunas, English and French spoken. Also have office in Potosí.

ATO Andes Travel Office, Ayacucho 222 (1 block west of Abaroa), T693 2227. Good reports, run by Belgian Isabelle and Iver, works with pre-arranged groups.

Colque Tours, Av Potosí 54, T/F693 2199, www.colquetours.com. Well-known but reports vary, has its own hostals in Uyuni (**D Kutimuy**), on the edge of the Salar and by Laguna Verde and a branch in San Pedro de Atacama.

Esmeralda, Av Ferroviaria esq Arce, T693 2130, esmeraldaivan@hotmail.com. Good tours – cheaper end of market.

Kantuta, Av Arce y Av Potosí, T693 3084, kantutatours@hotmail.com. Run by 3 eager brothers, also volcano-climbing tours, good food.

Oasis Odyssey, Av Ferroviaria, T693 3175, www.oasistours-bo.com. Good vehicles for salar tours, excellent guide (Javier Canaza and his wife, Liset, as cook; also Felipe and Emilia), they make an effort to take less used routes (eg via Cueva del Diablo). Also have office in Sucre (same prices).

Quechua Connection (José Valda), Hotel Palace, ground floor, Av Arce entre Potosí y Ferroviaria, T693 3565, 7244 0413. 1-4 day tours of the Salares, Lagunas Colorada and Verde with transfers to San Pero de Atacama, US$30-120 pp, also volcano climbing, private tours and cycling tours on the Salar.

Reli Tours, Av Arce 42, T693 3209. Reliable, good vehicles and food.

Tayka, Sucre entre Uruguay y México, T693 2987, 02-241 9252 (Fundación Prodem, La Paz), www.taykahoteles.com. Proyecto Tayka, Hoteles Ecológicos Comunitarios, a chain of upmarket hotels in Salar de Uyuni-REA area, a joint venture between Fremen Tours, Fundación Prodem and 4 local communities. Hotels have rooms with bath, hot water, heating, restaurant, price in **A** range, **B** in low season, includes breakfast.

Toñito Tours, Av Ferroviaria 152, T693 3186, www.bolivianexpeditions.com. Variety of good tours (also in La Paz, see page 295), with their own hotel at Bella Vista on the edge of the Salar. Works mostly with organized groups, no walk-ins.

San Cristóbal *p322*

Llama Mama, T7243 5983. 60 km of exclusive bicycle trails descending 2-3 or 4 hrs, depending on skill, 3 grades, US$20 pp, all inclusive, taken up by car, with guide and communication.

Transport

Uyuni *p322, map p323*

Air **Aero Sur** (Av Potosí 30, T693 3107) flies a DC-6 from Cochabamba, Tue, Thu and Sun, 0745, 1¼ hrs, returns 1600; US$100 1-way from Cochabamba, US$135 1-way from other cities, with transfer in Cochabamba. 20 kg luggage allowance from Cochabamba, 15 kg from Uyuni.

Bus Offices are on Av Arce, north of Colón. To **La Paz**, **Panasur**, Cabrera 270, www.uyunipanasur.com, daily at 2000, Wed and Sat bus cama (La Paz-Uyuni at 1900, Tue and Fri bus cama), US$12-16, 12 hrs, or transfer in Oruro. Tourist buses with **Todo Turismo**, Cabrera entre Arce y Bolívar, T693 3337, www.touringbolivia.com, daily 2000 US$27, 11 hrs (La Paz office, Plaza Antofagasta 504, Edif Paola, p1, opposite the bus terminal, T02-211 9418, daily 2100), note this service does not run if the road is poor during the rainy season. **Oruro**, several companies 2000-2130, US$6; 7 hrs. **Todo Turismo** (see above), US$20. To **Potosí** several companies 0930-1000 and 1900-2000, US$5.50, 6 hrs, spectacular scenery. To **Sucre 6 de Octubre**, 1900, or transfer in Potosí, US$8, 9 hrs. To **Tupiza** with **Quechisla**, daily 0600 (tickets on sale 1600-2000), **11 de Julio**, Wed, Fri, Sun 0900, **Trans Tupiza** bus or jeep daily 0600, 1800, US$9.50, 8 hrs. 6-8 passenger jeeps also with **12 de Octubre** daily 0600, US$11, 6 hrs or **11 de Julio**, to **Atocha** at 0530, US$4.75, 2 hrs and transfer for Tupiza at 1030, US$4, 5 hrs. For **Tarija** change in Potosí or Tupiza.

Regional services To **Vila Vila, San Cristóbal, Culpina K**, Trans Nor Lípez, Av Uruguay 240 y Av Arce, T693 2948, daily 0800, 1400, return 0700, 1600, US$2 to San Cristóbal. Same company to **Vila Vila, San Cristóbal, Culpina K, Serena, Alota, Villa Mar, Soniquera, Quetena**, Sun 1100, US$5.75 to Quetena, 10 hrs, return Wed 0300. To **Alota** and **Colcha K**, **11 de Julio**, Av Arce near México, Fri 1130, US$2.50, return Wed 1100.

Road and train A road and railway line run south from Oruro, through Río Mulato, to Uyuni (323 km, each about 7 hrs). The road is sandy and, after rain, very bad, especially south of Río Mulato. The train journey is more comfortable. Check services on arrival, T693 2320. **Expreso del Sur** leaves for **Oruro** on Thu and Sun at 0005, arriving 0700. **Wara Wara del Sur** service leaves on Tue and Fri at 0145, arriving 0910 (prices for both under Oruro). To **Atocha, Tupiza** and **Villazón** **Expreso del Sur** leaves Uyuni on Tue and Fri at 2240, arriving, respectively, at 0045, 0400 and 0705. **Wara Wara** leaves on Mon and Thu at 0250, arriving 0500, 0835 and 1205. The ticket office opens Mon-Fri 0900-1200, 1430-1800, Sat-Sun 1000-1100, and one hour before the trains leave. It closes once tickets are sold – get there early or buy through a tour agent.

Travelling to Chile Chile is 1 hr ahead of Bolivia from mid-Oct to Mar. Do not attempt to take coca leaves across the border; it is an arrestable offence. Also Chile does not allow dairy produce, tea bags, fruit or vegetables to be brought in.

The easiest way is to go to San Pedro de Atacama as part of your jeep trip to the Salar and *Lagunas* (see above). **Colque Tours**, address above, as well as running Salar and Lagunas tours that take you to **San Pedro de Atacama**, has a direct jeep leaving their office every day at 1600-1800, US$30 pp, stops overnight in Alota. They also run 2 mini-buses daily from their camp near the ranger station at Hito Cajones to San Pedro de Atacama, departing 1000 and 1700, US$6.50, 1 hr including stop at immigration. **Hostal Marith** (see Uyuni, Sleeping) also runs a US$30 service, like Colque. There is another vehicle from Hito Cajones to San Pedro de Atacama (*tránsito público*), most days at about 1000, US$6.50. At other times onward transport to San Pedro must be arranged by your agency, this can cost up to US$60 if it is not included in your tour. The ranger station may be able to assist in an emergency. The *tránsito público* leaves San Pedro for Hito Cajones at 0800 or 0830. It is usually booked through an agency in town. Sometimes it runs in the afternoon.

From Uyuni to **Avaroa** and on to **Calama**, **Centenario**, Cabrera y Arce, Mon and Thu 0330, transfer at the border to **Frontera del Norte** (from Calama Sun and Wed at 2200). With **11 de Julio**, Av Arce y Cabrera, Wed and Sun at 0600, transfer at the border to **Atacama** at 2000 (from Calama Wed, Sun 2200). To Avaroa, US$7, 4 hrs; to Calama US$18, 10 hrs allowing 2 hrs at the border.

If driving your own vehicle, from **Colchani** it is about 60 km across to the southern shore of the **Salar**. Follow the tracks made by other vehicles in the dry season. The salt is soft and wet for about 2 km around the edges so only use established ramps. It is 20 km from the southern shore to Colcha K military checkpoint. From there, a poor gravel road leads 28 km to San Juan then the road enters the Salar de Chiguana, a mix of salt and mud which is often wet and soft with deep tracks which are easy to follow; 35 km away is Chiguana, another military post, then 45 km to the end of this Salar, a few kilometres before border at Ollagüe. This latter part is the most dangerous; very slippery with little traffic. Or take the route that tours use to Laguna Colorada and continue to Hito Cajones. **Toñito Tours** of Uyuni will let you follow one of their groups and even promise help in the event of a breakdown. There is no fuel between Uyuni and Calama (Chile) if going via Ollagüe, or San Pedro de Atacama. Keep to the road at all times; the road is impassable after rain, and there are still a few unmarked sections along the border that are mined!

Directory

Uyuni *p322, map p323*

Banks BCP, Av Potosí, entre Bolívar y Arce, changes US$ cash and has the only ATM in town (doesn't always work, bring cash). **Fades**, Potosí 22, US$ cash. **Fiesa**, Potosí y Arce, US$ cash at fair rates. **Prodem**, Plaza Arce near Av Potosí, US$ cash at fair rates, Visa/Mastercard cash advances 5% comission. Several **casas de cambio** along Av Potosí, rates vary greatly, shop around. **Vieli**, Potosí 25 y Bolívar, US$ cash, 3% comission on TCs, open daily. **Internet** Many places in town, US$0.60 per hr. **Post offices** Av Arce esq C Cabrera. **Telephones** Several offices in town. **Useful addresses** Immigration: Av Ferroviaria y Sucre, T693 2062, open daily 0830-1200, 1400-1800 for visa extensions; register here before travel to Chile.

San Cristóbal *p322*

Bank Exchange Sat-Sun only. **Internet** By satellite, US$1.20 per hr. **Telephones** Public phone in entrance to **Hotel San Cristóbal**.

Tupiza → *Phone code: 02. Colour map 6, B3. Population: 37,000. Altitude: 2,990 m.*

Set in a landscape of colourful, eroded mountains and stands of huge cactii, Tupiza, 200 km south of Uyuni, is a pleasant town with a lower altitude and warmer climate than Uyuni, making it a good alternative for visits to the Reserva Nacional Eduardo Avaroa and the Salar. There are also many things to do in the area and is best known as the place from which to take **Butch Cassidy and the Sundance Kid tours**. You can take bike rides, horse and jeep tours in the surroundings, eg the Quebrada Palala with the nearby 'Stone Forest' and the Quebrada Seca. The Valle de los Machos and the Cañón del Inca together make another good excursion. Guides or detailed route descriptions are available from Tupiza Tours. Another local option is *turismo rural*, staying in nearby rural communities, arranged by local agencies usually in conjunction with horse riding tours. The statue in the main plaza is to **Victor Carlos Aramayo** (1802-1882), of the Aramayo mining dynasty, pre-eminent in the late 19th, early 20th centuries. **Chajra Huasi**, a palazzo-style, abandoned home of the Aramayo family across the Río Tupiza, may be visited (ask at Restaurant California on the Plaza). Beautiful sunsets over the fertile Tupiza valley can be seen from the foot of a statue of Christ on a hill behind the plaza. Market days are Monday, Thursday and Saturday, with local produce sold in the northern part of town; there is also a daily market at the north end of Avenida Chichas.

San Vicente → *Population: 400. Altitude: 4,500 m.*

Tupiza is the centre of Butch Cassidy and the Sundance Kid country and there are tours following their last few days. On 4 November 1908, they held up an Aramayo company payroll north of Salo. (**Aramayo hacienda** in Salo, one hour north of Tupiza, still stands. One-day tours from Tupiza go to the site of the hold-up, Huaca Huañusca.) Two days later they fought a four-man military police patrol in San Vicente, a silver and antimony mining camp. Both men are believed to have died, either at the hands of the patrol, or by Butch's own hand. But as no grave in the cemetery has yet to be identified (ask around for the keyholder), some doubt whether they were killed here at all. See *Digging Up Butch and Sundance*, by Anne Meadows (Bison Books, 2003). There is no lodging, but ask at the mine office, who may find you a room. To get to San Vicente there are tours from hotels and agencies in Tupiza (see Listings, below); there is public transport once or twice a week from Tupiza or Atocha.

South to Argentine border

Villazón (81 km south of Tupiza) The Argentine border is here at Villazón *(Phone code: 02; Population: 39,900; Altitude: 3,443 m)*. There is not much to see (good indoor market). The border area must not be photographed.

Border with Argentina Bolivian immigration office is on Avenida República de Argentina just before bridge; open daily 0500-2200. They issue entry and exit stamps. For Argentine immigration see page 172. There may be long queues on both sides. Once in Bolivia, boys offer to wheel your bags uphill to the bus stations, US$1, but they will ask for more. Change all your bolivianos into dollars or pesos, because there are no exchange facilities in La Quiaca and bolivianos are not accepted in Argentina. The Argentine consulate is at Plaza 6 de Agosto 121, T597 2011, Mon-Fri 0800-1300. **Note** Argentine time is one hour later than Bolivia, two hours when Buenos Aires adopts daylight saving.

Tupiza listings

For Sleeping and Eating price codes and other relevant information, see Essentials, pages 38-40.

Sleeping

Tupiza *p328*

D Hostal Valle Hermoso, Av Pedro Arraya 478, T694 2592, www.bolivia.freehosting.net. Good hot showers, breakfast available (**F** with shared bath), TV/breakfast room, breakfast extra, book exchange, tourist advice, firm beds, motorbike parking, surcharge on credit cards and TCs. Second location, **Valle Hermoso 2**, Av Pedro Arraya 585, T694 3441, near the bus station, 3 simple rooms with bath, several dorms for 6 or 8 with bunk beds, same prices as No 1, 10% discount for IYHF members in both locations.

D-E Mitru, Av Chichas 187, T694 3001, www.tupizatours.com. Pleasant grounds, a variety of rooms, cheaper in older rooms with bath and even cheaper with shared bath, **B-C** for suite with sitting room. All include good buffet breakfast, good hot water supply, pool, games room, cable TV, parking, kitchen, luggage store, safes, book exchange, laundry service and facilities, surcharge on credit card payments and TCs. Recommended.

E Anexo Mitru, Abaroa 20, T694 3002, www.tupizatours.com. Nicely refurbished older hotel, with buffet breakfast, shared bath cheaper, good hot showers, restaurant, kitchen, laundry facilities, use of pool and games room at **Hotel Mitru**.

E Hostal Pedro Arraya, Av P Arraya 494, T694 2734, hostalarraya@hotmail.com. Convenient to bus and train stations, **F** with shared bath, **G** in dorm, hot water, breakfast extra, use of kitchen, laundry, terrace. Check bill and confirm arrangements carefully.

E La Torre, Av Chichas 220, T694 2633, latorrehotel@yahoo.es. Lovely refurbished house, newer rooms at back, comfortable, includes breakfast, **F** shared bath and no TV, great service, use of kitchen, good value. Recommended.

E-F Renacer Chicheño, C Pinos, a few blocks from the train station, T694 2718. Cheaper with shared bath, includes basic breakfast, family home, use of kitchen.

E-F Res Centro, Av Santa Cruz 287, 2 blocks from station, T694 2705. Nice patio, motorbike and car parking, couple of rooms with bath, most shared, basic but clean, hot water some hours, parking, door closes at 2300, helpful owner, good value.

F El Refugio del Turista, Av Santa Cruz 240, T694 3155, www.tupizatours.com. Refurbished home with garden, shared bath, reliable hot water, well-equipped kitchen, laundry facilities, parking and electric outlet for camper-vans, opened in 2009, good value.

Villazón *p329*

E Center, Plaza 6 de Agosto 121, T596 5472. Pleasant rooms, electric shower, good value.

E Grand Palace, 25 de Mayo 52 esquina Potosí, 1 block southwest of bus terminal, T596 5333. Older place but adequate, **F** without bath, shower, no breakfast, helpful management.

E Hostal Plaza, Plaza 6 de Agosto 138, T597 3535. Adequate rooms, **F** without bath, electric shower, good restaurant, *La Perla*, underneath hotel, also internet below.

E Hostal Buena Vista, Av Antofogasta 508 y Santa Cruz, T596 3055. Good rooms, hot water, **F** without bath, close to the train and bus stations, above reasonable restaurant.

F Residencial El Cortijo, 20 de Mayo 338, behind post office, T596 2093. Breakfast included, basic rooms, cheaper with shared bath, intermittent hot water, parking.

Eating

Tupiza *p328*

¥¥-¥ Two places outside town serve speciality meals in rural surrounds on weekends only: **La Estancia**, 2 km north in Villa Remedios, best on Sun, *picante de cabrito* (spicy goat); **La Campiña**, in Tambillo Alto, 45 mins' walk north along the river, *cordero a la cruz* (lamb on the spit) and *lechón* (suckling pig).

¥ **Bella Nápoli**, C Florida 14, daily 0800-2300. Thin crust pizza, pasta. One of 3 pizzerías on this street, all have similar menus.

¥ **California**, Cochabamba on main plaza, daily 0800-2300. Breakfast, pizza, vegetarian and regional dishes, popular with travellers.

¥ **El Escorial**, Chichas esq Abaroa. Good value set meal at midday, à la carte in the evening.

¥ **Los Helechos**, next door to *Mitru Anexo* on Abaroa. 0800-2300, closed alternate Suns. Pasta, Bolivian dishes, breakfasts, family atmosphere.

¥ **Tu Pizza**, Sucre at Plaza Independencia, Mon-Sat 1830-2300. A variety of pizzas, slow service.

Heladería Cremalín, Cochabamba at Plaza Independencia, ice cream, juices and fruit shakes.

Villazón *p329*

Better to cross the border to La Quiaca to eat.

¥ **Las Peñas**, Plaza 6 de Agosto, next to Hostal Plaza. Good set lunch and à la carte dishes.

¥ **Los Alamos**, La Paz e Independencia, 1 block from terminal. Serves breakfasts and lunches.

Activities and tours

Tupiza *p328*

One-day jeep tours US$21-25 pp for group of 5; horse riding US$3.50-4 per hr; US$32 per day with food; 2-day San Vicente plus colonial town of Portugalete US$98 pp (plus lodging); Salar de Uyuni and Reserva Avaroa, 4 days with Spanish speaking guide, US$150-155 pp for a group of 5 (tours out of Tupiza are more expensive than those out of Uyuni because of the additional 400 km travelled). Add US$5 per day for English speaking guide. Some agencies include in their price entrance fees to Reserva Avaroa and Isla Incahuasi.

Tupiza Tours, in *Hotel Mitru* (address above), are the most experienced and are at the higher end of the market. They have additional tours: 'triathlon' of riding, biking and jeep in the surroundings, US$35 pp for group of 5 (frequently recommended), and extensions to the Uyuni tour. Also have offices in La Paz and Tarija, and offer tours in all regions of Bolivia. Highly recommended.

Valle Hermoso Tours, inside *Hostal Valle Hermoso 1*, T/F694 2592. Also recommended, offers similar tours, as do several other agencies. Most Tupiza hotels have an agency.

Transport

Tupiza *p328*

Bus There is small, well-organized, bus terminal at the south end of Av Pedro Arraya. To **Villazón** 0400, 1430, also Mon and Thu 1000, US$2.75, 2½ hrs. To **Potosí**, 1000, 2100, US$5, 7 hrs. To **Sucre**, **6 de Octubre** at 2000, **Trans Illimani** at 2030 (more comfortable, but are known to speed), US$9.50, 9 hrs, or transfer in Potosí. To **Tarija**, 1930, 2000, US$9.50, 8 hrs overnight (change here for **Santa Cruz**). To **Uyuni**, **11 de Julio**, Mon, Thu, Sat at 1000, US$9.50, 8 hrs; also 6-8 passenger jeeps daily at 0600 and 1030 (**12 de Octubre**) US$11, 6 hrs. To **Oruro**, 1200, 1700, 2000, US$11, 12 hrs. **Trans Illimani** at 1800 continues to **Cochabamba**. **Expreso Tupiza** has a direct bus to **La Paz** at 1000 (La Paz-Tupiza at 1930, 15 hrs) and **Trans Illimani** at 2100, otherwise via Potosí, 17 hrs, US$12.50. Agent for the Argentine company **Balut** at terminal sells tickets to Jujuy, Salta, Buenos Aires or Córdoba (local bus to the border at Villazón, then change to Balut), but beware overcharging.

Train Train station ticket office open Mon-Sat 0800-1100, 1530-1730, and early morning half an hour before trains arrive. To **Villazón**: **Expreso del Sur** Wed and Sat 0410; **Wara Wara** Mon and Thu at 0905. To **Atocha**, **Uyuni** and **Oruro**: *Expreso del Sur* Wed and Sat at 1825; *Wara Wara* Mon and Thu at 1905. Fares are given under Oruro.

Villazón *p329*

Bus Bus terminal is near plaza, 5 blocks from the border. Lots of company offices. Taxi to border, US$0.40 or hire porter, US$1, and walk. From **La Paz**, several companies, 18 hrs, US$16-28 (even though buses are called 'direct', you may have to change in Potosí), depart La Paz 1630, depart **Villazón** 0830-1000 and 1830-1900. To **Potosí** several between 0800-0900 and 1830-1900, 10 hrs by day, 12 hrs at night, US$6 (can take 24 hrs if wet). To **Tupiza**, several daily, US$2.75. To **Tarija**, buses overnight, daily at 1930-2030, US$5.50, 7 hrs, cold on arrival but passengers can sleep on bus until day. International buses to **Argentina**, tickets are sold in Villazón but beware scams and overcharging. Buy only from company offices, never sellers in the street. Safer still, cross to La Quiaca and buy onward tickets there.

Road A mostly unpaved but scenic road goes to Tarija. The road linking Potosí with Villazón via Camargo is in poor condition and about 100 km longer than the better road via Tupiza.

Train Station about 1 km north of border on main road, T597 2565, taxi US$2.35. To **Tupiza**, **Atocha**, **Uyuni** and **Oruro**: **Expreso del Sur** Wed, Sat, 1530, **Wara Wara del Sur** Mon, Thu 1530. Ticket office open Mon, Thu 0800-1530, Tue, Fri 0800-1200, 1430-1800, Wed 0700-1530, Sat 0700-1000, 1200-1530.

Directory

Tupiza *p328*

Banks No ATM in town. BCP, on main plaza, fair rates for cash, US$5 commission for Visa/Mastercard cash advances. **Prodem**, Cochabamba on main plaza, fair rates for cash, 5% commission for Visa/Mastercard cash advances (no debit cards). **Cooperativa El Chorolque**, Av Santa Cruz 300 y Abaroa, cash only. **Cambios Latin America**, Abaroa y Santa Cruz, open daily or knock on door (long hours), poor cash rate, 6% commission for TCs. **Internet** Many internet places, US$0.40 per hr. **Post offices** On Abaroa, northwest of plaza, Mon-Fri 0830-1800, Sat 0900-1700, Sun 0900-1200. **Telephones** Several phone offices in the centre. **Useful addresses** **Public Hospital**, on Suipacha opposite the bus terminal. **IGM** office, Bolívar y Abaroa, on the main plaza, p 2.

Villazón *p329*

Banks BCP, Oruro 111, US$ cash only. **Mercantil Santa Cruz**, Av JM Deheza 427 near main plaza, cash US$ and ATM. **Prodem**, on main plaza, cash only, on Av Argentina 326, cash and cash advances. Many *casas de cambio* on Av República de Argentina, leading to the border, change US$, pesos and euros, lower rates than the banks. **Internet** Several places, US$0.40 per hr. **Post offices** Av Antofagasta. **Telephones** Several *cabinas* in town.

Central and Southern Highlands

This region boasts two World Cultural Heritage sites, the mining city of Potosí, the source of great wealth for colonial Spain and of indescribable hardship for many Bolivians, and Sucre, the white city and Bolivia's official capital. In the south, Tarija is known for its fruit and wines and its traditions which set it apart from the rest of the country.

Potosí → *Phone code: 02. Colour map 6, B3. Population: 163,000. Altitude: 3,977 m.*

Potosí is the highest city of its size in the world. It was founded by the Spaniards on 10 April 1545, after they had discovered indigenous mine workings at Cerro Rico, which dominates the city. Immense amounts of silver were once extracted. In Spain 'es un Potosí' (it's a Potosí) is still used for anything superlatively rich.

By the early 17th century Potosí was the largest city in the Americas, but over the next two centuries, as its lodes began to deteriorate and silver was found elsewhere, Potosí became little more than a ghost town. It was the demand for tin – a metal the Spaniards ignored – that saved the city from absolute poverty in the early 20th century, until the price slumped because of over-supply. Mining continues in Cerro Rico – mainly tin, zinc, lead, antimony and wolfram.

Ins and outs

Getting there The airport, possibly the world's highest, is 5 km out of town on the Sucre road. There are no scheduled flights. A new inter-departmental terminal on Av Circunvalación, northwest of the centre, began operating in 2010. ▸▸ *See also Transport, page 337.*

Tourist office **InfoTur Potosí** ⓘ *C Ayacucho, behind the façade of Compañía de Jesús church, T623 1021, Mon-Fri 0800-1200, 1400-1800, Sat 0800-1200.* Some English spoken. Kiosk on Plaza 6 de Agosto, staffed sporadically by tourist police. The police station by the Alcaldía has a photo album showing common scams. Beware fake "plainclothes policemen", usually preceded by someone asking you for the time. The official police wear green uniforms and work in pairs. ▸▸ *See also Safety, pages 276 and 278.*

Sights

Large parts of Potosí are colonial, with twisting streets and an occasional great mansion with its coat of arms over the doorway. UNESCO has declared the city to be 'Patrimonio de la Humanidad' (World Cultural Heritage site). Some of the best buildings are grouped round the Plaza 10 de Noviembre. The old Cabildo and the Royal Treasury – Las Cajas Reales – are both here, converted to other uses. The **Cathedral** ⓘ *faces Plaza 10 de Noviembre, Mon-Fri 0930-1000, 1500-1730, Sat 0930-1000, guided tour only, US$1.*

The **Casa Nacional de Moneda**, or Mint, is nearby ⓘ *on C Ayacucho, T622 2777, Tue-Sat 0900-1200, 1430-1830, Sun 0900-1200, US$2.85, US$2.85 to take photos, US$5.70 for video, entry by regular, 2-hr guided tour only (in English at 0900, usually for 10 or more people).* Founded in 1572, rebuilt 1759-1773, it is one of the chief monuments of civil building in Hispanic America. Thirty of its 160 rooms are a museum with sections on mineralogy, silverware and an art gallery in a splendid salon on the first floor. One section is dedicated to the works of the acclaimed 17th-18th century religious painter Melchor Pérez de Holguín. Elsewhere are coin dies and huge wooden presses which made the silver strips from which coins were cut. The smelting houses have carved altar pieces from Potosí's ruined churches. You can't fail to notice the huge, grinning mask of Bacchus over an archway between two principal courtyards. Erected in 1865, its smile is said to be ironic and aimed at the departing Spanish. Wear warm clothes; it's cold inside.

Convento y Museo de Santa Teresa ⓘ *Chichas y Ayacucho, T622 3847, only by guided tour in Spanish, French or English at 0900, 1100, 1500, 1700, US$3, US$1.50 to take photos, US$25(!) for video* has an impressive amount of giltwork inside and an interesting collection of colonial and religious art. Among Potosí's baroque churches, typical of 18th-century Andean or 'mestizo' architecture, are the Jesuit **Compañía** church and bell-gable ⓘ *on Ayacucho*, whose beautiful

Potosí

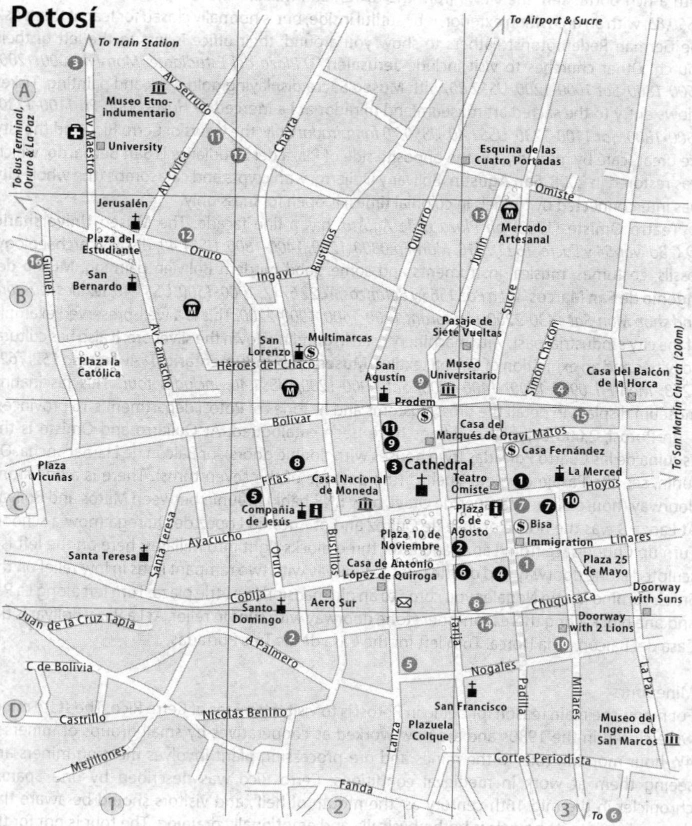

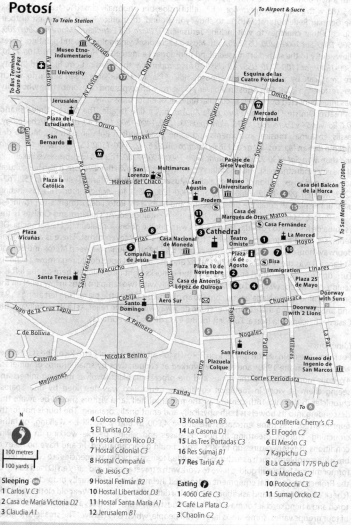

Sleeping
1 Carlos V *C3*
2 Casa de María Victoria *D2*
3 Claudia *A1*
4 Coloso Potosí *B3*
5 El Turista *D2*
6 Hostal Cerro Rico *D3*
7 Hostal Colonial *C3*
8 Hostal Compañía de Jesús *C3*
9 Hostal Felimar *B2*
10 Hostal Libertador *D3*
11 Hostal Santa María *A1*
12 Jerusalem *B1*
13 Koala Den *B3*
14 La Casona *D3*
15 Las Tres Portadas *C3*
16 Res Sumaj *B1*
17 **Res** Tarija *A2*

Eating
1 4060 Café *C3*
2 Café La Plata *C3*
3 Chaplin *C2*
4 Confitería Cherry's *C3*
5 El Fogón *C2*
6 El Mesón *C3*
7 Kaypichu *C3*
8 La Casona 1775 Pub *C2*
9 La Moneda *C2*
10 Potocchi *C3*
11 Sumaj Orcko *C2*

façade hides the modern tourist office building, and whose tower has a **mirador** ⓘ *0800-1200, 1400-1800, 30 mins later Sat-Sun, US$1.40*. **San Francisco** ⓘ *Tarija y Nogales, T622 2539, Mon-Fri 0900-1100, 1430-1700, Sat 0900-1100, US$2.15, US$1.40 to take photos, US$3 for video*, with a fine organ, worthwhile for the views from the tower and roof, museum of ecclesiastical art, underground tunnel system. Also **San Lorenzo** (1728-1744) *on Héroes del Chaco, mass 0700-1000*, with a rich portal and fine views from the tower. **San Martín** ⓘ *on Hoyos, Mon-Fri 1500-1830, US$0.85*, with an uninviting exterior, is beautiful inside, but is normally closed for fear of theft. Ask the German Redemptorist Fathers to show you around; their office is just to the left of their church. Other churches to visit include **Jerusalén** ⓘ *Plaza del Estudiante, Mon-Fri 1000-1200, 1500-1800, Sat 1000-1200, US$2.80*, with **Museo Sacro** displaying gold work and painting. Ticket allows entry to the sacred art museum and **mirador** at **La Merced** ⓘ *Hoyos, Mon-Fri 1100-1230, 1500-1800, Sat 1100-1230, US$1.40, US$0.70 for mirador only*; the views of Cerro Rico and the city are great (café by mirador). On the opposite side of Plaza del Estudiante is **San Bernardo**, which was restored in 2008. **San Agustín**, Bolívar y Quijarro, with crypts and catacombs (the whole city was interconnected by tunnels in colonial times) is open for mass only.

Teatro Omiste (1753) *on Plaza 6 de Agosto*, has a fine façade. The **Museo Universitario** ⓘ *C Bolívar 54 y Sucre, T622 7310, Mon-Fri 0800-1200, 1400-1800, US$1.40*, displays archaeology, fossils, costumes, musical instruments and some good modern Bolivian painting. **Museo del Ingenio de San Marcos** ⓘ *La Paz 1565 y Betanzos, T622 6717, 1000-1500, US$1.40; textiles museum and shop Mon-Sat 1430-2200; restaurant 1200-1500, 1900-2200*. This is a well-preserved example of the city's industrial past, with machinery used in grinding down the silver ore. It also has cultural activities and an exhibition of Calcha textiles. **Museo Etno-indumentario** ⓘ *Av Serrudo 152, T622 3258, Mon-Fri 0900-1200, 1400-1800, Sat 0900-1200, US$1.40, includes tour*. This fascinating museum displays in detail the dress, customs and histories of Potosí department's 16 provinces.

In Potosí, 2,000 colonial buildings have been catalogued. At Quijarro and Omiste is the Esquina de las Cuatro Portadas (two houses with double doors), or Balcón de Llamacancha. Off Junín, see the Pasaje de Siete Vueltas (the passage of the seven turns). There is a fine stone doorway (house of the Marqués de Otavi, now BNB bank) in Junín between Matos and Bolívar At Lanza 8 was the house of José de Quiroz and of Antonio López de Quiroga (now a school) Turn up Chuquisaca from Lanza and after three blocks right into Millares; here on the left is a sculpted stone doorway and on the right a doorway with two rampant lions in low relief on the lintel. Turning left up Nogales you come to an old mansion in a little plaza. Turn left along La Pa: and one block along there is another stone doorway with suns in relief. At La Paz y Bolívar is the Casa del Balcón de la Horca. Turn left for the Casa de las Tres Portadas.

Mine tours

For many, the main reason for being in Potosí is to visit the mines of Cerro Rico. The state mine were closed in the 1980s and are now worked as cooperatives by small groups of miners. A 4½-hour morning tour to the mines and ore-processing plant involves meeting miners an seeing them at work in medieval conditions. Cerro Rico was described by one Spanis chronicler in the mid-16th century as 'the mouth of hell', and visitors should be aware tha descending into its bowels is both physically and emotionally draining. The tour is not for th faint-hearted. The mine entrances are above 4,000 m and you will be walking, or rathe crouching, around, breathing in noxious gases and seeing people working in appallin conditions in temperatures up to 40°C. You should be acclimatized, fit and have no heart c breathing problems, such as asthma. The guided tours run by Potosí agencies are conducted b former miners; by law all guides have to work with a travel agency and carry an ID card issued b the Prefectura. Essential equipment is provided: helmet, lamp and usually protective clothir (check when booking and ask about the level of difficulty of the tour). Wear old clothes and tak torch and a handkerchief or mask to filter the dusty air, which includes asbestos fibres. The siz of tour groups varies, some are as large as 20 people, which is excessive. The smaller the grou the better. Tours cost US$15 per person for two people, US$11.50 for four, and include transport. A contribution to the miners' cooperative is appreciated, as are medicines for the health centre (*Posta Sanitaria*) on Cerro Rico. Saturday and Sunday are the quietest days (Sunday is the miners' day off).

Tarapaya

A good place to freshen up after visiting the mines (or to spend a day relaxing) is Tarapaya, 21 km on the road to Oruro, where there are thermal-bath public pools ⓘ *US$0.60, private baths US$1.20 per hr, family baths US$2.80* and cabins for rent. On the other side of the river from Tarapaya is a 60-m diameter crater lake, whose temperature is 30-34°C; take sun protection. Below the crater lake are boiling ponds but on no account swim in the lake. Several people have drowned in the boiling waters and agencies do not warn of the dangers. Camping by the lake is possible. **Balneario Miraflores** (25 km) ⓘ *pools US$0.35, private baths US$2.80* has hotter water than Tarapaya, but is not as clean. Minibuses to both balnearios go from outside Chuquimia market on Avenida Universitaria, every 30 minutes, 0600-1800, US$0.55. Taxi US$8.50 for a group. Last colectivo back to Potosí from Miraflores at 1800.

Potosí listings

For Sleeping and Eating price codes and other relevant information, see Essentials, pages 38-40.

Sleeping

Potosí *p332, map p333*

Unless otherwise stated hotels have no heating.

A Coloso Potosí, Bolívar 965, T622 2627. Comfortable modern rooms with frigo-bar, heating, bath tubs and nice views. Includes buffet breakfast, Wi-Fi, small indoor pool, parking.

B Claudia, Av Maestro 322, T622 2242, claudiahotel@yahoo.com. This modern hotel is away from the centre. Helpful staff. Recommended.

B Hostal Cerro Rico, Ramos 123 entre La Paz y Millares, T622 3539. Very good rooms upstairs, heating, hot water, cable TV, internet, helpful, parking.

B Hostal Colonial, Hoyos 8, T622 4809. A pretty colonial house near the main plaza, with heating and basic breakfast, TV, very helpful, even if you're not staying there, safe parking, best hotel in centre. Book in advance.

B Las Tres Portadas, Bolívar 1092, T623 1558. **E** pp in a large four-bed room. Old colonial house with spacious rooms, skylights, warm and nice. Includes breakfast and use of internet.

C Hostal Libertador, Millares 58, T622 7877. Colonial hotel, central heating, quiet, helpful, comfortable, restaurant, parking.

C Jerusalem, Oruro 143, T/F622 2600. Pleasant, with breakfast, helpful, laundry, good value.

E Carlos V, Linares 42 near Plaza 6 de Agosto, T622 5121. With breakfast, **F** without bath, occasional hot water 0700-1200, luggage store, 2400 curfew.

E Casa de María Victoria, Chuquisaca 148, T622 2132. Rooms open onto colonial courtyard, **F** without bath, hot water, stores luggage, popular budget choice, mine tours, owner speaks English, good breakfast, leave nothing unattended.

E El Turista, Lanza 19, T622 2492. Long established, helpful, hot showers, breakfast (US$1), great view from top rooms, good value. Recommended.

E Hostal Compañía de Jesús, Chuquisaca 445, T622 3173. Central, good value, includes breakfast, attractive but some rooms cold and dark, helpful 90% of the time.

E Hostal Felimar, Junín 14, T622 4357. Hot water, **F** without bath, includes breakfast, very good, 2 roof-top suites, basement rooms have no exterior windows but warm, quiet.

E Hostal Santa María, Av Serrudo 244, T622 3255. Hot water, cold rooms, cafeteria, popular.

E Koala Den, Junín 56, T622 6467, see *Koala Tours*, below, but book separately. Refurbished, private rooms with bath and breakfast, with heated dormitory (**G** pp) and shared showers, TV and video and use of kitchen, often full.

E La Casona, Chuquisaca 460 y Padilla, T04-623 0523, www.hotelpotosi.com. Rooms with bath, and **G** pp in dorm, a place to meet other travellers.

E Res Tarija, Av Serrudo 252, T622 2711. Poorly signed but the more expensive rooms are good, **F** without bath, helpful, large courtyard for parking.
F Res Sumaj, Gumiel 12, T622 2336, hoteljer@entelnet.bo. Small dark rooms with shared bath, kitchen, laundry, TV lounge, helpful, popular with travellers, HI discount.

Eating

Potosí *p332, map p333*
TT El Mesón, Plaza 10 de Noviembre, T622 3087. Excellent food, upmarket but good value.
TT Potocchi, Millares 24, T622 2759. International and local dishes, 0800-2230, *peña* in high season.
TT-T El Fogón, Oruro y Frías, T622 4969. Upmarket pub-restaurant, good food and atmosphere, open 1200-1500, 1800-2400.
TT-T La Casona 1775 Pub, Frías 41, T622 2954. Good food (meat fondue and trout recommended) and beer, nice atmosphere and service, open Mon-Sat 1000-1230, 1815-2400.
T Chaplin, Matos 10 y Quijarro. Pleasant, good breakfasts and fast food, vegetarian options, best *tucumanas*, Mon-Fri 0800-1200, 1600-2200, Sat 0800-1200.
T Kaypichu, Millares 16. Vegetarian, good breakfasts, open 0700-1300, 1600-2100, closed Mon.
T La Moneda, Av Quijarro 32, daily 1200-1400, 1800-2300. Good quality and value set lunch, less popular for *parrillada* in the evening.
T Sumaj Orcko, Quijarro 46. Large portions, cheap set lunch, reasonably priced, busy, popular with travellers, heating, could be cleaner, open 0900-2200, Sun 0900-1400.

Cafés

4060 Café, Hoyos entre Padilla y Millares. 'Hip' place serving interesting food, more upmarket surroundings and pricier than others, Tue-Sun 1500-2400.
Café La Plata, Plaza 10 de Noviembre at Linares. Mon-Sat 1000-2200, good for coffee, cookies and cakes, wine and beer. English and French spoken.
Confitería Cherry's, Padilla 8. Good cakes, popular, good breakfast, cheap, slow service, open 0800.

Festivals and events

Potosí *p332, map p333*
8-10 Mar is **San Juan de Dios**, with music, dancing, parades etc. In **May** there is a market on C Gumiel every Sun, with lotteries and lots of fun things for sale. **Fiesta de Manquiri**: on 3 consecutive Sat at the **end of May/ beginning of Jun** llama sacrifices are made at the cooperative mines in honour of *Pachamama*; the same occurs on **1 Aug**, the **Ritual del Espíritu**. **Carnaval Minero**, 2 weeks before carnival in Oruro, includes Tata Ckascho, when miners dance down Cerro Rico and El Tío (the *Dios Minero*) is paraded. **San Bartolomé**, or the Fiesta de Chutillos, is held from the middle of **Aug**, with the main event being processions of dancers on the weekend closest to the **24th-26th**; Sat features Potosino, and Sun national, groups. Costumes can be hired in *artesanía* market on C Sucre. Hotel and transport prices go up by 30% for the whole of that weekend. In **Oct**, **Festival Internacional de la Cultura**, in Potosí and Sucre. **10 Nov**, **Fiesta Aniversiario de Potosí**. Potosí is sometimes called the 'Ciudad de las Costumbres', especially at Corpus Cristi, Todos Santos and Carnaval, when special cakes are baked, families go visiting friends, etc.

Shopping

Potosí *p332, map p333*
Mercado Artesanal, at Sucre y Omiste, Mon-Sat 0830-1230, 1430-1830, sells handwoven cloth and regional handicrafts.
Mercado Central (see address above), sells mainly food and produce but silver is sold near the C Oruro entrance.

Activities and tours

Potosí *p332, map p333*
Trips to the Salar de Uyuni, Laguna Colorada and Laguna Verde are expensive here. See page 322 for advice on booking a trip.

The following have been recommended:
Andes Salt Expeditions, Plaza Alonso de Ibáñez 3, T622 5175, www.bolivia-travel.com.bo. Recommended guides. Run by Braulio Mamani, who speaks English. Daily city tours, bus and flight tickets, also have an office in Uyuni.

Turismo Potosí, Lanza 12 y Chuquisaca, T622 8212. Guide and owner Santos Mamani is recommended.
Greengo Tours, Quijarro 42, T623 1362, green gotours_ts@hotmail.com. Good mine tours, English spoken.
Hidalgo Tours, Junín y Bolívar 19, T622 5186, www.hidalgotours.net. Upmarket and specialized services within the city and to Salar de Uyuni. Efraín Huanca has been recommended for mine tours.
Koala Tours, Ayacucho 5, T622 2092. Run by Eduardo Garnica Fajardo (speaks English and French). Excellent mine tours by former miners have been recommended. Company donates 15% of fees to support on-site health-care facilities. Also have a hostal, *The Koala Den*, see Sleeping, and internet café.
Silver Tours, Quijarro 12, Edif Minero, T622 3600, www.silvertours.8m.com. A cheaper firm.
Sin Fronteras, Bustillos 1092, T622 4058, www.organizacionsinfronteras.com. Mine tours, Salar, trekking, transport, camping gear hire, English and French spoken, very helpful.

Transport

Potosí *p332, map p333*

Bus Buses to all destinations except Uyuni leave from the new terminal on Av Circunvalación. Daytime service only to Oruro, Sucre, Tupiza/Villazón and Camargo; all others overnight. Watch your belongings at the terminal and beware of scams. Daily services: **La Paz** 1700-2000, US$7-11, 10 hrs by paved road, *bus cama* with **Flota Copacabana** US$12-15 (all departures from La Paz 1830-2030). To travel by day, go to **Oruro**, **San Miguel** and **Bustillo** have morning departures, US$2.70-4, 5 hrs. **Cochabamba** 1830-1930, US$7-11, 11 hrs. **Sucre** frequent buses 0630-1800, US$2.50, 3 hrs. Shared taxis from behind terminal, **Cielito Lindo**, **Dino**, 2½ hrs, US$4.20 pp, drop-off at your hotel. For **Santa Cruz** change in Sucre or Cochabamba. **Tupiza** US$5, 7-8 hrs, and **Villazón**, US$6, 9-10 hrs, **Illimani** at 0700, **O'Globo** 0800, 1930, others at 1930. **Tarija** 1900-1930, US$8.30 (11.50 semi-cama), 11 hrs, spectacular journey. To go by day take a bus to **Camargo**, 6 hrs, US$4.20, then change. Buses to **Uyuni** leave from either side of the railway line at Av Toledo y Av Universitaria, 1000-1200 and 1800-1900, US$5.50, 5-6 hrs, superb scenery; book in advance.

A **taxi** in town costs US$0.60-1.

Train Station is at Av Sevilla y Villazón, between centre and Terminal de Buses, T622 3101. A 25-passenger railcar to **Sucre** Tue, Thu, Sat 0800, 6 hrs, US$3.60, tickets sold from 0700 same day.

Directory

Potosí *p332, map p333*

Airline offices Areo Sur, Cobija 25, T622 8988. **Banks** There are ATMs around the centre. BNB, Junín 6. US$ cash and 3% commission for TCs. **Prodem**, Bolívar y Junín. **Casa Fernández**, Sucre 10, for US$ and Euro cash exchange, poor rates for TCs. **Multimarcas** clothing shop, Bustillos y Héroes del Chaco. Fair rates for cash and regional currencies, 0800-2130. Many shops on Plaza Alonso de Ibáñez and on Bolívar, Sucre and Padilla display 'compro dólares' signs. **Internet** All US$0.30-0.40 per hr. **Post offices** Lanza 3, Mon-Fri 0800-2000, Sat 0800-1800, Sun 0900-1200. **Telephones** Plenty of phone offices in the centre. **Useful addresses** **Migración**: Linares y Padilla, T622 5989. Mon-Fri 0830-1230, 1430-1830, beware unnecessary charges for extensions. **Police station:** on Plaza 10 de Noviembre. Emergency T110.

Sucre → *Phone code: 04. Colour map 6, B3. Population: 272,000. Altitude: 2,790 m.*

Founded in 1538 as La Plata, it became capital of the audiencia of Charcas in 1559. Its name was later changed to Chuquisaca before the present name was adopted in 1825 in honour of the second president of the new republic. Sucre is sometimes referred to as La Ciudad Blanca, owing to the tradition that all buildings in the centre are painted in their original colonial white. This works to beautiful effect and in 1991 UNESCO declared the city a World Heritage site. There are two universities, the older dating from 1624. From 1825 to 1899 Sucre was capital of Bolivia, but lost this role in all but name to La Paz after a civil war. In 2007 Sucre demanded of the constituent assembly then sitting to return its status as true capital. When this was ignored, violent protests forced the assembly to flee the city and to rename Sucre constitutional, rather than historical capital. *La capitalidad* remains an emotionally charged issue among *sucrenses*.

Ins and outs

Getting there **Juana Azurduy de Padilla** airport is 5 km northwest of town (T645 4445); taxi to centre US$3.50. **Bus terminal** is on north outskirts of town, 3 km from centre on Ostria Gutiérrez, T644 1292; taxi US$1.10; Micro A or 3. Taxis cost US$0.60 per person within city limits. ▸▸ *See also Transport, page 343.*

Tourist office **Tourist office** ⓘ *Estudiantes 25, T644 7644, open Mon-Fri 0800-1300, 1500-1900, Sat 0900-1300*, staffed by students in unversity term only; also at the bus station, allegedly open Monday-Friday 0700-1100, 1500-1900, and at the airport, to coincide with incoming flights. **Dirección de Turismo de Alcaldía** ⓘ *Argentina 65, p 2, Casa de la Cultura, T643 5240, Mon-Fri 0800-1200, 1400-1800*, some English spoken. As in Potosí and La Paz, beware fake police and immigration officials and smearing clothes to distract and rob. Muggings have taken place in the streets leading up to La Recoleta.

Sights in the centre

Plaza 25 de Mayo is large, spacious, full of trees and surrounded by elegant buildings. Among these are the **Casa de la Libertad** ⓘ *T645 4200, www.casadelalibertad.org.bo, Tue-Sat 0915-1145, 1445-1745, Sun 0915-1145, US$2.10 with tour; US$2.80 photos, US$5.80 video.* Formerly the Assembly Hall of the Jesuit University, where the country's Declaration of Independence was signed, this house contains a famous portrait of Simón Bolívar by the Peruvian artist Gil de Castro, admired for its likeness. Also on the Plaza is the beautiful 17th century **Cathedral** ⓘ *entrance at Calle Ortiz 61 through the museum*. Worth seeing are the famous jewel-encrusted Virgin of Guadalupe, 1601, and works by Viti, the first great painter of the New World, who studied under Raphael.

San Felipe Neri ⓘ *Ortiz 165 y Azurduy, T645 4333, US$1.40 (extra charge for photos), Mon-Sat 1400-1800 with a free guide from Universidad de Turismo office on Plaza 25 de Mayo.* Visits include the neoclassical church with its courtyard, the crypt and the roof (note the penitents' benches), which offers fine views over the city. The monastery is used as a school. Diagonally opposite is the church of **La Merced**, which is notable for its gilded central and side altars. **San Miguel** ⓘ *Arenales 10, T645 1026, mass Mon-Sat 0800 and 1915, Sun 1100, no shorts, short skirts or short sleeves allowed*, completed in 1628, has been restored and is very beautiful with Moorish-style carved and painted ceilings, *alfarjes* (early 17th century), pure-white walls and gold and silver altar. In the Sacristy some early sculpture can be seen. **Santa Mónica**, Arenales y Junín, is perhaps one of the finest gems of Spanish architecture in the Americas, but has been converted into the theatre and hall for Colegio Sagrado Corazón. **San Francisco** (1581) ⓘ *Ravelo y Arce, mass daily 0700 and 1900, Sun also 1030 and 1700*, has altars coated in gold leaf and 17th century ceilings; one of its bells summoned the people of

Sucre to struggle for independence. **San Lázaro** (1538) ⓘ *Calvo y Padilla, mass daily 0700, Sun also 1000 and 1900.* This is regarded as the first cathedral of La Plata (Sucre). On the nave walls are six paintings attributed to Zurbarán; it has fine silverwork and alabaster in the Baptistery. San Miguel, San Francisco and San Lázaro are only open during mass.

Sucre

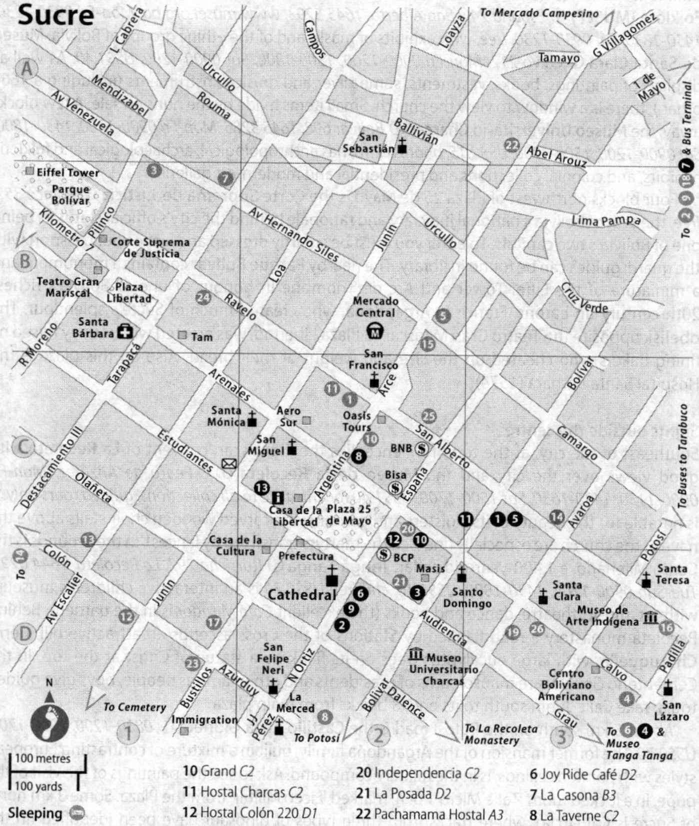

Sleeping

1 Alojamiento La Plata *C2*
2 Austria *B3*
3 Avenida *B1*
4 Casa de Huéspedes Finita *D3*
5 Casa de Huéspedes San Marcos *B2*
6 Casa Kolping *D3*
7 Cretassic Hostal *B1*
8 El Hostal de Su Merced *D2*
9 Gloria *B3*
10 Grand *C2*
11 Hostal Charcas *C2*
12 Hostal Colón 220 *D1*
13 Hostal Cruz de Popayán *C1*
14 Hostal Los Piños *D1*
15 Hostal San Francisco *B2*
16 Hostal Santa Teresa de Jesús *D3*
17 Hostal Sucre *D1*
18 Hostelling International Sucre *B3*
19 ICBA Wasi & Kultur-Café Berlin *D3*
20 Independencia *C2*
21 La Posada *D2*
22 Pachamama Hostal *A3*
23 Paola Hostal *D1*
24 Potosí *B1*
25 Res Bolivia *C2*
26 Villa Antigua *C2*

Eating

1 Amsterdam *C3*
2 Bibliocafé *D2*
3 Café Florín *D2*
4 Café Mirador *D3*
5 El Germen *C3*
6 Joy Ride Café *D2*
7 La Casona *B3*
8 La Taverne *C2*
9 La Vieja Bodega *D2*
10 Libertad *C2*
11 Locot's Café Aventura *C3*
12 Pizzería Napolitano & Plaza *C2*
13 Salon de Té Las Delicias *C2*

Bars & clubs

14 Tabaco's *C3*

Museo de Arte Indígena (Museo Téxtil Etnográfico) ⓘ *San Alberto 413 (Casa Capellánica), between San Lázaro and Plaza 25 de Mayo, T645 3841, www.asur.org.bo , Mon-Fri 0830-1200, 1430-1800, Sat opens 0930, US$2.25, English, German and French-speaking guide.* Run by *Antropólogos del Sur Andino* (ASUR), this excellent museum displays regional textiles and traditional techniques, shop sells crafts. There is also the **Museo Nacional de Etnografía y Folklore (MUSEF)** ⓘ *España 74 y San Alberto, T645 5293, www.musef.org.bo, Mon-Fri 0930-1230, 1430-1830, Sat 0930-1230, free*, with exhibits of masks and of the ethinc groups of Bolivia. **Museo de Santa Clara** ⓘ *Calvo 212, Mon-Fri 0900-1200, 1500-1800, Sat 0900-1200, US$1.40.* As well as displays of paintings, books, vestments, some silver and musical instruments (including a 1664 organ), there is a window to view the church. Small items made by the nuns on sale. A few blocks away, the **Museo Universitario Charcas** ⓘ *Bolívar 698, T645 3285, Mon-Fri 0900-1200, 1430-1800, Sat 0900-1200, 1500-1800, US$2.15, photos extra*, has anthropological, archaeological and folkloric exhibits, and colonial collections and presidential and modern-art galleries.

Four blocks northwest of Plaza 25 de Mayo is the **Corte Suprema de Justicia** ⓘ *Pilinco 352, free*, the seat of Bolivia's national judiciary and rationale behind the city's official status as being one of Bolivia's two capitals. To enter you must be smartly dressed and leave your passport with the guard; guides can be found in library. The nearby **Parque Bolívar** contains a monument and a miniature of the Eiffel Tower and Arc de Triomphe in honour of one of Bolivia's richest 20th-century tin barons, Francisco Argandoña, who created much of Sucre's splendour. The **obelisk** opposite the Teatro Gran Mariscal, in Plaza Libertad, was erected with money raised by fining bakers who cheated on the size and weight of their bread. Also on this plaza is the Hospital Santa Bárbara (1574).

Sights outside the centre

Southeast of the city, at the top of Dalence, lies the Franciscan convent of **La Recoleta** with good views over the city and the **Museo de la Recoleta** ⓘ *C Pedro de Anzúrez, Mon-Fri 0900-1130, 1430-1630, Sat 1500-1700, US$1.40 for entrance to all collections, guided tours only*. It is notable for the beauty of its cloisters and gardens; the carved wooden choir stalls above the nave of the church are especially fine (see the martyrs transfixed by lances). In the grounds is the Cedro Milenario, a 1,400-year-old cedar. **Tanga Tanga** ⓘ *Iturricha 297, La Recoleta, T644 0299, Tue-Sun 0900-1200, 1430-1800, US$1.10, children US$0.70* is an interactive children's museum with art, music, theatre, dance and books (the excellent *Café Mirador* is in the garden). Behind Recoleta monastery a road flanked by Stations of the Cross ascends an attractive hill, **Cerro Churuquella**, with large eucalyptus trees on its flank, to a statue of Christ at the top. In the Cementerio General are mausoleums of presidents and other famous people, boys give guided tours; take Calle Junín south to its end, 8 blocks from main plaza.

About 5 km south on the Potosí road is the **Castillo de la Glorieta** ⓘ *0830-1200, 1300-1700, US$0.70.* The former mansion of the Argandoña family, built in a mixture of contrasting European styles with painted ceilings, is in the military compound. Ask to see the paintings of the visit of the pope, in a locked room. Take Micro 1 or 4, marked 'Liceo Militar' from the Plaza. Some 3 km north of Sucre is **Cal Orcko**, where tracks from three types of dinosaur have been identified (in the Fancesa cement works, not open to the public). A **Parque Cretácico** ⓘ *Mon-Fri 0900-1700, Sat-Sun 1000-1700, US$4.20, crowded at weekends and holidays*, with fibreglass dinosaurs, recorded growls, a 30-minute guided tour and telescopes through which (for US$0.70) you can look at the prints on Cal Orcko off in the distance. The **Sauro Tours** bus leaves daily 0930, 1200, 1430 from corner of cathedral, US$1.40, taxi from kiosk outside the Alcaldía same price.

Tarabuco → *Colour map 6, B4. Altitude: 3,295 m.*

Tarabuco, 64 km southeast of Sucre, is best known for its colourful indigenous market on Sunday, with local people in traditional dress. It starts around 0930-1000 and is very popular with tourists, but still an enjoyable experience. Textiles are sold in a purpose-built market on C

Murillo. Next to the market is a small museum, **Incapallay** ⓘ *Murillo 25, T646 1936, www.incapallay.org, Sun 0930-1400*, run by a weavers' association. The *Pujllay* independence celebration on the third Sunday in March is very colourful and lively. No one sleeps during this fiesta. There is basic accommodation. Try the Plaza or food stalls in market offering tasty local dishes. The market is not held at Carnival (when all Tarabuco is dancing in Sucre), Pujllay, Easter Sunday or All Saints' Day.

Sucre listings

For Sleeping and Eating price codes and other relevant information, see Essentials, pages 38-40.

Sleeping

Sucre *p338, map p339*

A Refugio Andino Bramadero, 30 km from the city, details from Raul y Mabel Cagigao, Avaroa 472, T645 5592, or Restaurant Salamandra, Avaroa 510. Cabins or rooms, well-furnished, full board, drinks and transport included, excellent value, owner Raul can advises on hikes, book in advance. Recommended.

B La Posada, Audiencia 92, T646 0101. Smart, colonial-style, comfortable, W-Fi, good courtyard restaurant.

B Real Audiencia, Potosí 142, T642 5176. Modern, large rooms, restaurant, heated pool. Recommended.

B-C Villa Antigua, Calvo 237, T644 3437. Tastefully restored colonial house with garden, includes buffet breakfast, Wi-Fi, internet room, large rooftop terrace has great views, some 3-bed family rooms with kitchenette (**A**), airport transfers. Opened in 2010.

C Casa Kolping, Pasaje Iturricha 265, La Recoleta, T642 3812, www.grupo-casas-kolping.net. Pleasant, lovely location with nice views, with buffet breakfast, good **Munay Pata** restaurant (ΨΨ-Ψ), Wi-Fi and internet lounge, wheelchair access, parking.

C El Hostal de Su Merced, Azurday 16, T644 2706, www.desumerced.com. Beautifully restored colonial building, more character than any other hotel in the city, owner and staff speak French and English, good breakfast buffet, Wi-Fi, sun terrace, restaurant. Recommended.

C Independencia, Calvo 31, T644 2256. Historic colonial house, opulent salon, spiral stairs, lovely garden, comfortable, some rooms with bath, Wi-Fi, café, breakfast included.

C Paola Hostal, C Colón 138, T645 4978, paolahostal@gmail.com. Comfortable, helpful hotel, with bath and jacuzzi, laundry, cafeteria for snacks, internet, airport transfer.

C Hostal Santa Teresa de Jesús, San Alberto 431, T645 4189, www.santateresahostal.com. Refurbished colonial house, includes breakfast, comfortable, restaurant, garage.

C-D ICBA Wasi, Avaroa 326, T645 2091, www.icba-sucre.edu.bo. Part of Insituto Cultural Boliviano-Alemán, imaginatively designed, spotless rooms with solar hot water, some with kitchenette. Includes breakfast. Recommended.

D Austria, Av Ostria Gutiérrez 506, near bus station, T645 4202. Hot showers, great beds and carpeted rooms, some cable TV, cafeteria, parking, **E** with shared bath, café, parking extra.

D Grand, Arce 61, T645 2461, grandhotel_sucre @entelnet.bo. Comfortable (ask for room 18), ground floor at the back is noisy, hot showers, includes poor breakfast in room, good value lunch in *Arcos* restaurant, Wi-Fi, laundry, safe, motorcycle parking. Recommended.

D Hostal Cruz de Popayán, Loa 881 y Colón, T644 0889, www.hotelsucre.com. **F** without bath, also has dorms (**G** pp), breakfast included, free internet, in a colonial building, rooms around 3 courtyards, limited use of kitchen, coffee shop, laundry service, book exchange, internet, can arrange transport and language classes, nice courtyards but rooms are simple to basic, a bit faded, grubby and overpriced, mixed reports.

D Hostal Sucre, Bustillos 113, T645 1411, www.hostalsucre.com.bo. Comfortable if plain rooms around 2 patios, TV, Wi-Fi, room service, breakfast included, internet.

D Hostelling International Sucre, G Loayza 119 y Ostria Gutiérrez, T644 0471, www.hostelling bolivia.org. Functional hostel 1½ blocks from bus terminal, **E** without bath, **F** pp in dorms, breakfast available, kitchen, garden, WiFi, parking, discount for HI members.

E Cretassic Hostal, Av Hernando Siles 901 y Tarapacá, T645 6250. Includes breakfast, rooms

with tile floors, front rooms noisy but otherwise good value.
E Hostal Colón 220, Colón 220, T645 5823, colon220@bolivia.com. **F** with shared bath, laundry, helpful owner speaks English and German and has tourist information, breakfast included, coffee room, very nice.
E Hostal San Francisco, Av Arce 191 y Camargo, T645 2117. Colonial building, breakfast available, quiet, patio, laundry, excellent value.
E Hostal los Pinos, Colón 502, T645 5639. Comfortable, hot showers, garden, quiet, peaceful, includes breakfast, kitchen, parking.
E Potosí, Ravelo 262, T/F645 1975. Basic rooms around courtyard, popular, helpful, good value, better rooms at the front.
E Res Bolivia, San Alberto 42, T645 4346. **F** without bath, spacious rooms, fair beds, bathrooms could be cleaner, electric showers, includes good breakfast, clothes washing not allowed, safe and helpful.
E Hostal Charcas, Ravelo 62, T645 3972, hostalcharcas@yahoo.com. **F** without bath or TV, good value, huge breakfast extra, hot showers, sometimes runs bus to Tarabuco on Sun.
E-F Casa de Huéspedes Finita, Padilla 233 (no sign), T645 3220, delfi_eguez@hotmail.com. 2 rooms with bath, others without, breakfast included, hot water, heaters, full board or individual meals available on request, also apartments with fully equipped kitchens for longer stays, works with students studying Spanish. Good value, warm family atmosphere. Recommended.
F Alojamiento La Plata, Ravelo 32, T645 2102. Cheaper without bath, limited shower facilities, basic, noisy, good beds, popular with backpackers (lock rooms at all times).
F Avenida, Av H Siles 942, T645 1245. Hot showers, breakfast US$1, laundry, helpful, use of kitchen, basic but adequate.
F Casa de Huéspedes San Marcos, Arce 223, T646 2087. Cheaper without bath, flower-filled patio, use of kitchen, quiet. Recommended.
F Gloria Sur, Av Ostria Gutiérrez 438, opposite bus station, T645 2847, gloriasur@hotmail.com. Small simple rooms, cheaper with shared bath, better than it looks from the outside.
F Pachamama Hostal, Arce 450, T645 3673, hostal_pachamama@hotmail.com. Simple rooms, electric shower, kitchen facilities, pleasant patio, good value.

Eating

Sucre *p338, map p339*
The local sausages and chocolate are recommended.
TT El Huerto, Ladislao Cabrera 86, San Matías, T645 1538. International food with salad bar, good *almuerzo*, in a beautiful garden, daily 1130-1600 and Thu-Sun 1830-2100. Take a taxi there at night.
TT La Taverne of the *Alliance Française*, Aniceto Arce 35, ½ block from plaza. Mon-Sat 1800-2230, Sun 1900-2200, international food, also regular cultural events.
TT-T El Germen, San Alberto 231. Mostly vegetarian, set lunches, excellent breakfast, German pastries, open Mon-Sat 0800-2200, book exchange, German magazines. Recommended.
TT-T Pizzería Napolitano, Plaza 25 de Mayo 30. Pizzas and pasta, home-made ice cream, good lunch options till 1600, open 0830-2230, Wi-Fi.
TT-T Plaza, Plaza 25 de Mayo 33. Good food, popular with locals, set lunch with salad bar, open 1200-2400.
T La Casona, G Loayza 89 y Ostria Guitiérrez, near bus terminal. *Platos típicos*, good value, open 1200-1400, 1800-2200, closed Thu and Sun evening.
T Libertad, Calvo 43 (no sign). Daily set lunch, good, gets very busy.

Cafés

Amsterdam, Bolivar 426, Mon-Fri from 1200, Sun from 1530. Drinks, snacks and meals, book exchange, Wi-Fi, live music Wed-Thu. Dutch run, works with and supports **Centro Educativo Ñanta Sucre** (www.centro-nanta.org), for migrant children from the countryside.
Bibliocafé, N Ortiz 50, near plaza. Good pasta and light meals, *almuerzo* 1130-1600, closes 0200, Sun 1900-2400, music and drinks, Wi-Fi.
Café Florín, Bolívar 567, daily 0730 - 0200, weeknds to 0300. Breakfast, sandwiches, snacks and international meals, large portions. Sunny patio, Wi-Fi, tour bookings, cosy atmosphere in evenings. Dutch run and popular.
Café Mirador, Pasaje Iturricha 297 in Tanga Tanga museum garden, La Recoleta. Fine views, good juices, snacks and music, popular, open 0930-2000.
Joy Ride Café, N Ortiz 14. Great food and drink, good salads, open 0730-0200, weekends from

0900, Sun till 2400, very popular, upstairs lounge shows films Sun-Thu.

Kultur-Café Berlin, Avaroa 326, open 0800-2400 (except Sun). Good breakfasts, computer with internet access, German newspapers, *peña* every other Fri (in same building as *Instituto Cultural Boliviano Alemán – ICBA*), popular meeting place.

Locot's Café Aventura, Bolívar 465. Open 0800 till late, fun, bright café serving international, Mexican and Bolivian food (1200-2300), live music and theatre, Wi-Fi, European/Bolivian owned, also has agency offering 'adrenaline activities', mountain biking, hiking, riding, paragliding.

Salon de Té Las Delicias, Estudiantes 50. Great cakes and snacks, open 1600-2000.

Tertulias, Plaza 25 de Mayo 59. Italian and other dishes, breakfasts, poor service, also art gallery, 0900-2400.

La Vieja Bodega, N Ortiz 38. Good value, pasta, pizza, *pique macho*, cheapish wine.

Bars and clubs

Sucre *p338, map p339*

Mitos, Pje Tarabuco y Junín. Disco, popular with travellers, Thu-Sat 2200-0300.

Rock Bar Chatarra, Junín esq Colón. Popular bar, young crowd, open late, well-decorated.

Tabaco's, San Alberto y Avaroa. Daily 1900-2400, Sat to 0400. Small place, rock music, games.

Festivals and events

Sucre *p338, map p339*

24-26 May: **Independence** celebrations, most services, museums and restaurants closed on 25. **8 Sep: Virgen de Guadalupe**, 2-day fiesta. **21 Sep: Día del Estudiante**, music around main plaza. **Oct/Nov: Festival Internacional de la Cultura**, 2nd week, shared with Potosí.

Shopping

Sucre *p338, map p339*

Handicrafts **ASUR**, San Alberto 413 (in the *Museo de Arte Indígena*). Weavings from around Tarabuco and from the Jalq'a. Weavings are more expensive, but of higher quality than elsewhere. **Artesanías Calcha**, Arce 103, opposite San Francisco church. Recommended, knowledgeable proprietor. **Incapallay**, Audiencia 97 y Bolívar, T646 1936, www.incapallay.org. Fair trade shop selling textiles by Tarabuco and Jalq'a weavers; also in Tarabuco and La Paz. **Chocolates para Tí**, Arenales 7, Audiencia 68, at the airport and bus terminal, www.chocolates-para-ti.com. One of the best chocolate shops in Sucre. **Taboada**, Arce y Arenales, at airport and bus terminal, www.taboada.com.bo. Also very good.

Markets The central market is clean and colourful with many stalls selling *artesanía*, but beware theft.

Activities and tours

Sucre *p338, map p339*

Bolivia Specialist, N Ortiz 30, T643 7389, www.boliviaspecialist.com. Dutchman Dirk Dekker's agency for local hikes, horse riding and 4WD trips, all sorts of tours throughout Bolivia and Peru, bus and plane tickets, loads of information and connections.

Candelaria Tours, Audiencia No 1, T646 0289, catur@entelnet.bo. Hikes around Sucre, tours to weaving communities, English spoken.

Joy Ride Bolivia, N Ortiz 14, at the café, T642 5544, www.joyridebol.com. Mountain biking and hiking tours. Also rents bicycles.

L y D, final Panamá 127 y Comarapa, Barrio Petrolero, T642 0752, turismo_lyd@hotmail.com. Lucho and Dely Loredo and son Carlos (who speaks English) offer custom-made tours using private or public transport, to regional commnities and attractions, and further afield. Recommended.

Locot's Adventure, see **Locot's Café Aventura** under Eating, above. For many types of adventure sport.

Oasis Tours, Aniceto Arce 95, of 2, T643 2438, www.oasistours-bo.com. City walking tour, Chataquila, Inca Trail and indigenous communities. Have their own office in Uyuni for Salar trips. Very helpful owner.

Seatur, Plaza 25 de Mayo 24, T646 2425. Local tours, hiking trips, English, German, French spoken.

Transport

Sucre *p338, map p339*

Air Aero Sur (Arenales 31, T646 2141) flies to **La Paz** and **Santa Cruz** (via Cochabamba). TAM (Arenales 217, T646 0944) to **La Paz, Santa Cruz**, **Cochambamba**, **Tarija** and **Yacuiba**. No TAM flights are daily. Micros 1, D and F go from entrance to Av Hernando Siles, a couple of blocks from main plaza, US$0.20, 25 mins. Taxi US$3.50.

Bus Daily to/from **La Paz** at 1700-1900, 13 hrs, US$10-13 (**Trans Copacabana** and **Dorado** *bus-cama*, US$20; **Flota Copacabana** and **Trans Copacabana** *semi-cama*, US$13). To **Cochabamba**: several companies daily at 1830-1930, 8 hrs, US$7.50. To **Potosí**: 3 hrs on a paved road, frequent departures between 0630 and 1800, US$2.50, 3 hrs. Shared taxis, **Cielito Lindo**, **Dino**, 2½ hrs, US$4.20 pp. To **Oruro**: 0930 and 2000-2200, 4 companies via Potosí, 8 hrs, US$7-8.50. To **Tarija**: 4 companies, 14 hrs, US$12-14 via Potosí. To **Uyuni**: direct at 0830, **6 de Octubre**, 9 hrs, **Emperador** 0700, 1230, with change and 2-hr wait in Potosí, US$6.50-7.50. Or catch a bus to Potosí and change; try to book the connecting bus in advance. To **Villazón** via Potosí and Tupiza: at 1330, 1730, 1800, **6 de Octubre**, 12 hrs, US$11; to **Tupiza**, 9 hrs, US$9.50. To **Santa Cruz**: many companies 1600-1730, 15 hrs, US$11.50; *semi cama* US$13.

To Tarabuco Mini-vans leave when full from C Túpac Yupanqui (Parada de Tarabuco), daily starting 0630, US$1, 1¼ hrs on a good paved road. To get to the Parada take a micro "C" or "7" from the Mercado Central. Also buses to **Tarabuco** from Av de las Américas y Jaime Mendoza, same fare and times. Tourist bus from the Cathedral on Sun at 0830, US$5 round-trip, reserve at Oasis Tours (address above); also **Trans Real Audiencia**, San Alberto 73 y España, T644 3119. Return 1330; you must use the same bus you went on.

Car hire **Imbex**, Serrano 165, T646 1222, www.imbex.com. Recommended.

Road 164 km from **Potosí** (fully paved), 366 km to **Cochabamba** (for 1st hr from Sucre road is OK, terrible to **Epizana**, then paved).

Train To **Potosí**, 20-passenger railcar at 0800, Mon, Wed, Fri, US$3.60, 6 hrs. Station, El Tejar, 1 km south on Potosí road, take Micro 4, T644 0751.

Directory

Sucre *p338, map p339*

Banks There are many ATMs around town. **Bisa**, España y Calvo. **BNB**, España y San Alberto. **Casa de cambio España**, España 134, T643 2368, Mon-Fri 0830-1230, 1430-1830, Sat 0900-1200, change Amex and Visa TCs, 4% commission on US$ Tcs 6% commission on euro TCs, also changes cash. **Casa de Cambio Oasis**, Arce 95, of 2, daily 0800-2000. US$, euros, regional currencies, 4% commission for Amex, Visa US$ and euro TCs. **Cultural centres** The **Instituto Cultural Boliviano-Alemán** (Goethe Institute), Avaroa 326, T645 2091, www.icba-sucre.edu.bo. Shows films, has German newspapers and books to lend (0930-1230 and 1500-2100), runs Spanish, German, Portuguese and Quechua courses and has the *Kulturcafé Berlín* (see above). Spanish lessons cost from US$7.50 for 45 mins for 1 person, with reductions the more students there are in the class. The *ICBA* also runs a folk music *peña* on Fri. **Centro Cultural Masis**, Bolívar 561, T645 3403, www.losmasis.com. Promotes the Yampara culture through textiles, ceramics, figurines and music. Instruction in Quechua, traditional Bolivian music (3 hrs a week for US$15 a month, recommended) and handicrafts; stages musical events (daily practice 1900-2000) and exhibitions; items for sale. Open Mon-Sat 1430-2000 (knock if door closed); contact the director, Roberto Sahonero Gutierres at the centre Mon, Wed, Fri. **Alianza Francesa**, Aniceto Arce 35, T645 3599, www.afbolivia.org. Offers Spanish classes. **Centro Boliviano Americano**, Calvo 301, T644 1608. Library open Mon-Fri 0900-1200, 1500-2000 (good for reference works). Recommended for language courses. The **Casa de la Cultura**, Argentina 65, presents art exhibitions, concerts, folk dancing etc. **Internet** Many around town, average US$0.45 per hr. **Language schools** **Academia Latinoamericana de Español**, Dalence 109, T646 0537, www.latinoschool.com. Professional, good extracurricular activities, US$90 for 5 full days (US$120 for private teacher – higher prices if you book by phone or email). **Bolivian Spanish School**, C Kilómetro 7 250, T644 3841, www.bolivianspanishschool.com. Near Parque Bolívar, pleasant school, good value, excellent teachers. **Fox Academy**, San Alberto 30, T644 0688, www.foxacademysucre.com. Spanish and Quechua classes, US$5 per hr, non-profit, proceeds go to teaching English to children, volunteering arranged. **Margot Macias Machicado**, Colón 371, T642 3567, www.spanish-classes.8m.net. US$5 per hr. Recommended. **Casa Andina de Lenguas**, Loa 779, T645 1687. US$6 per hr. Several cultural centres offer language classes. **Medical services** **Hospital Santa Bárbara**, Ayacucho y

R Moreno, Plaza Libertad, T646 0133, public hospital. **Hospital Cristo de las Américas**, Av Japón s/n, T644 3269, private hospital. **Post office** Ayacucho 100 y Junín, Mon-Fri 0800-1200 and 1400-1800, Sat AM only, good service. **Useful addresses** Immigration: Bustillos 284 entre La Paz y Azurduy, T645 3647, Mon-Fri 0830-1230, 1430-1830. **Police radio patrol**: T110.

Tarija → *Phone code: 04. Colour map 6, B4. Population: 194,000. Altitude: 1,840 m.*

Tarija has a delightful climate and streets and plazas planted with flowering trees. Formerly known for its fruit, wines and traditions which set it apart from the rest of the country, it has experienced an economic boom and rapid growth since 2005 due to natural gas development in the department. It retains much of its bucolic charm for the time being, but traffic noise and fumes are becoming annoying in the city centre. The best time to visit is from January onwards, when the fruit is in season. The *indígena* strain is less evident here than elsewhere in Bolivia, but Tarija has a strong cultural heritage. Founded 4 July 1574 in the rich valley of the Río Guadalquivir, the city declared itself independent of Spain in 1807, and for a short time existed as an independent republic before joining Bolivia. In Plaza Luis de Fuentes there is a statue to the city's founder, Capitán Luis de Fuentes Vargas. The **Secretaría de Turismo y Cultura** ⓘ *Ingavi O-316 y Sucre, Edif Forti, p 1 above a store, T663 1000, Mon-Fri 0800-1200, 1500-1900*, is helpful, city and departmental map. **Dirección Municipal de Turismo** ⓘ *Bolívar y Sucre, Mercado Central, T663 3581, Mon-Fri 0800-1200, 1430-1830*, helpful, city map, SomeEnglish spoken; also have a booth at the Terminal de Buses ⓘ *T666 7701, 0700-1100, 1430-2200*.

Sights The oldest and most interesting church in the city is the **Basílica de San Francisco** ⓘ *corner of La Madrid y Daniel Campos, 0700-1000, 1800-2000, Sun 0630-1200, 1800-2000*. It is beautifully painted inside, with praying angels depicted on the ceiling and the four evangelists at the four corners below the dome. The library is divided into old and new sections, the old containing some 15,000 volumes, the new a further 5,000. To see the library, go to the door at Ingavi O-0137. Behind the church is the **Museo Fray Francisco Miguel de Mari** ⓘ *Colón y La Madrid, T664 4909, 1000-1100, 1600-1700, US$2.85*, with colonial and contemporary art collections, colonial books, the oldest of which is a 1501 *Iliad*, 19th century photograph albums and other items. Tarija's **Museo de Arqueología y Paleontología** ⓘ *Trigo y Lema, Mon-Fri 0800-1200, 1500-1800, Sat 0900-1200, 1500-1800, US$0.45*, contains a palaeontological collection (dinosaur bones, fossils, remains of several Andean elephants), as well as smaller mineralogical, ethnographic and anthropological collections. **Casa Dorada** ⓘ *Trigo e Ingavi (entrance on Ingavi), guided tours every half-hour Mon-Fri, US$0.70*. Begun in 1886 and also known as the Maison d'Or, it is now part of Casa de la Cultura. It belonged to importer/exporter Moisés Narvajas and his wife Esperanza Morales and was beautifully restored inside and out in 2009.

The outskirts of the city can be a good place to look for **fossils**: bones, teeth, parts of saurian spines, etc; things come to the surface each year after the rains. Should you find anything, leave it in situ and report it to the university. Take a micro or taxi to Morros Blancos in the direction of the airport. 5 km out of town, before the police control (*tranca*), you see lovely structures of sand looking like a small canyon (*barrancos*). Other spots are Parque Los Barrancos, 4 km north, and Padcaya, 45 km south on the doar to Bermejo. About 15 km north of the centre is the charming village of **San Lorenzo**. Just off the plaza is the **Museo Méndez** ⓘ *0900-1230, 1500-1830, minimum US$0.30 entry*, the house of the independence hero Eustaquio Méndez, 'El Moto'. The small museum exhibits his weapons, his bed, his 'testimonio'. At lunchtime on Sunday, many courtyards serve cheap meals. Minibuses from Domingo Paz y J M Saracho, every 5 mins, US$0.30. The road to San Lorenzo passes **Tomatitas** (5 km) a popular picnic and river bathing area.

Tarija produces the best wine and singani (brandy) in Bolivia and winemaking is a proud local tradition. To visit a bodega (winery) contact their shop in town beforehand to make arrangements or take a tour (see Activities and tours page 347) which provides transport and allows you to visit several different bodegas on the same day. **Wines Aranjuez** ⓘ *15 de Abril E-0241 y Suipacha, T664 2552*. **Campos de Solana** ⓘ *15 de Abril E-0259 entre Suipacha y Méndez, T664 5498*. Increasingly recognized for their selection of fine wines (the Malbec is highly regarded), as well as the popular Casa Real brand of singani. Their bodega is in El Portillo, 6 km on road to Bermejo. **Casa Vieja** ⓘ *no shop in town, T666 2605*. A traditional *bodega artesanal*, small-scale winery located in Valle de Concepción, 25 km from Tarija. Interesting and recommended. **Kohlberg** ⓘ *15 de Abril E-0275, T666 6366*. Largest and most industrialized of the wineries. **La Concepción** ⓘ *Colón y La Madrid, T665 1514*. Wines (try their Cabernet Suavignon) and Rugero singani, bodega in Valle de Concepción.

To Argentina → *Bolivia is 1 hr behind Argentina.*

The road to Villazón, 189 km, is the shortest route to Argentina, but a tiring eight hours in all (mostly unpaved but scenic). The alternative route via Bermejo is the most easily reached from Tarija, 210 km all paved, the views are spectacular (sit on right). **Bermejo** *(Population: 13,000, Altitude: 415 m)* is well supplied with places to sleep and eat, there are many casas de cambio, and this border area is considered safer than Yacuiba (see below). Note there are thorough customs searches here and it's very hot. (Expect to spend up to 4 hours at customs and immigration.) An international bridge crosses the river from Bermejo to Aguas Blancas, Argentina. From Tarija to Yacuiba/Pocitos border is 290 km (see page 375). This is the busiest of the border crossings, open 24 hours, and reported less than safe due to drug smuggling.

Tarija listings

For Sleeping and Eating price codes and other relevant information, see Essentials, pages 38-40.

Sleeping

Tarija *p345*

Blocks west of C Colón have a small O before number (oeste), and all blocks east have an E (este); blocks are numbered from Colón outwards. All streets north of Av Las Américas are preceded by N.

AL Los Parrales Resort, Urb Carmen de Aranjuez Km 3.5, T664 8444 (ask for Lic Miguel Piaggio), www.losparraleshotel.com. Only 5-star accommodation in southern Bolivia and worth it, European style amenities, can arrange city and vineyard tours and to Argentina, phone in advance for off-season discounts.

A Los Ceibos, Av Las Américas y La Madrid, T663 4430, www.hotellosceibos.com. Including excellent buffet breakfast, large rooms, mini-bar, good restaurant, pool and cocktail bar.

B La Pasarela, 10 km north of Tarija near the village of Coimata, T666 1333, www.lapasarelahotel.com. Belgian-owned hotel/restaurant/bar, includes breakfast, country views, tranquil, family atmosphere, living room, jacuzzi, swimming pool, internet, mountain bikes, laundry and camping.

C Hostal Loma de San Juan, Bolívar s/n (opposite Capilla Loma de San Juan), T663 6101. Comfortable, pool and garden, buffet breakfast included.

C Luz Palace, Sucre 921 y Domingo Paz, T663 5700, luzpalac@cosett.com.bo. Comfortable rooms, some with frigobar, includes breakfast.

D Gran Hostal Baldiviezo, La Madrid O-0443, T663 7711. Central, well-maintained, **E** with shared bath, good beds and facilities.

D Miraflores, Sucre 920, T664 3355. Includes breakfast, hot water, cheaper rooms with shared bath are simple.

D-E Hostal Carmen, Ingavi O-0784, T664 3372, vtb_hostalcarmen@hotmail.com. Older place but well maintained, includes good buffet breakfast, hot water, heating, airport transfers available. Often full, advance booking advised, very helpful, good value. Recommended.

E Hostería España, Alejandro Corrado O-0546, T664 1790. Hot showers, **F** without bath, simple rooms.

E Res Rosario, Ingavi O-0777, T664 2942. Simple rooms, **F** without bath, hot water, family atmosphere.
E Zeballos, Sucre 0966, T664 2068. Ageing hotel, some rooms small, **F** without bath, with breakfast, quiet, safe, laundry, 5 mins from plaza.
F Alojamiento Familiar, Rana S 0231 y Navajas, T664 0832. Shared hot shower, no breakfast, clean and adequate, helpful, close to bus terminal, traffic noise.

Eating

Tarija *p345*
Many restaurants (and much else in town) close between 1400 and 1600.
Cabaña Don Pepe, D Campos N-0138, near Av Las Américas. Excellent steaks and local dishes. Recommended.
La Taberna Gattopardo, on main plaza. Pizza, *parrillada* with Argentine beef, local wines, snacks, excellent salads, good value, opens 0800-2100 daily.
Mediterráneo, 15 de Abril y Colón, Plaza Sucre, T666 6083, daily 1230-1500, 1900-2400. International menu, elegant, upscale for Tarija.
Chifa New Hong Kong, Sucre O-0235. Good, smart Chinese, excellent food and good value.
Chingo's, on Plaza Sucre. Popular, serves cheap local food.
Chiqui's, Gral Trigo N-0636, Mon-Sat 0900-2200. Good value set lunch plus snacks and sweets.
El Patio, Sucre N-0458, Mon-Sat. Good set lunch with small salad bar, pleasant seating in patio, good *tucumanas al horno*.
La Fontana, La Madrid y Campos, is good for ice cream, snacks and coffee.

Festivals and events

Tarija *p345*
The city is famous for its colourful niño (child) processions on **15 Mar, Día de Tarija**. In **late Apr, Exposur** is held, approximately 20 km northwest of city; admission free; local and regional crafts, cuisine, and dances; much commercial activity as well. In the 3-day **San Roque** festival from the **1st Sun in Sep** the richly dressed saint's statue is paraded through the streets; wearing lively colours, cloth turbans and cloth veils, the people dance before it and women throw flowers from the balconies. Dogs are decorated with ribbons for the day. On **2nd Sun in Oct** the flower festival commemorates the **Virgen del Rosario** (celebrations in the surrounding towns are recommended, eg San Lorenzo and Padcaya). Another flower festival takes place in San Lorenzo in **Easter** week. Also in **Oct**, on 2 weekends mid-month, there is a **beer festival** on Av de las Américas. **La Virgen de Chaguaya, 15 Aug**, people walk from Tarija to Santuario Chaguaya, south of El Valle, 60 km south of the city. For less devoted souls, Línea P *trufi* from Plaza Sucre, Tarija, to Padcaya, US$1; bus to Chaguaya and Padcaya from terminal daily, 0700, returns 1700, US$1.35.

Activities and tours

Tarija *p345*
Internacional Tarija, Sucre 721, T664 4446. Flights and tours, helpful.
Mara Tours, Gral Trigo N-739, T664 3490. Helpful.
Sur Bike, Ballivián 601 e Ingavi, T7619 4200. Cycling trips in the countryside outside Tarija US$27-41, for a day trip including snack. Bike rentals US$16.50/day.
Tupiza Tours, Avaroa 250, entre Isaac Attie y Delgadillo, T664-3930, www.tupizatours.com. Tarija office of the Tupiza agency (due to open in early 2010). Specialize in the Salar and southwest Bolivia, but can arrange tours throughout the country.
VTB, at *Hostal Carmen* (see Sleeping above). All tours include a free city tour; 4-6 hr trips including bodegas, US$23 pp; comprehensive 10 hr "Tarija and surroundings in 1 Day", US$27; can also try your hand at excavation with palaeontology specialist! Good vehicles, recommended.
Viva Tours, 15 de Abril y Delgadillo, T663 8325, vivatour@ cosett.com.bo. Vineyard tours US$30 with lunch.

Transport

Tarija *p345*
Air Aero Sur (15 de Abril entre Daniel Campos y Colón, T663 0894) flies daily either to **La Paz**, or **Cochabamba**. **TAM** (La Madrid O-0470 entre Trigo y Campero, T662 2734), to either **La Paz, Sucre, Santa Cruz** or **Yacuiba**, depending on day of week. Shared taxi from airport to centre, US$0.75 pp, or *micro* A from Mercado Central which drops you 1 block away. Some hotels have free transport to town, you may have to call

them. On arrival at Tarija, reconfirm your return flight immediately. Airport information T664 3135. **Bus** The bus station is southeast of centre on Av de Las Américas (30 min walk from centre), T666 6701. To **La Paz** several buses at 0700-0800 and 1700 (935 km) 17 hrs, US$14, via Potosí and **Oruro** (US$12.50); check which company operates the best buses. To **Potosí**, several additional departures 1630-1800, 10 hrs, US$10. To **Sucre** at 1630 and 1800, US$12.50. To **Tupiza**, **Diamante**, 1930, and **Juárez**, 2030, US$9.50, 10 hrs. To **Santa Cruz** via Villamontes, several companies at 1830, US$14, 17 hrs. To get to Villamontes in daylight, take a **La Guadalupana** or **La Entreriana** bus from Parada del Chaco (east end of Av Las Américas) to **Entre Ríos**, US$3, 3½ hrs, some continue to Villamontes (spectacular route), mostly in daylight.

To Argentina: to **Villazón**, several companies daily, 1930-2030, 8 hrs, US$5.50, unpaved road. To **Salta**, **Dragón Rojo** (Chifa), Sucre N-0235, T666 5014, runs private vans departing daily at 0700, US$27, 8-9 hrs. To **Bermejo**, shared taxis leave when full from opposite the bus station, US$5.50, 3 hrs; bus US$3, 4 hrs. Buses to **Yacuiba** US$7, 9 hrs, most depart in the evening.

Directory

Tarija *p345*

Banks Many ATMs accept foreign cards: **BCP**, Trigo y Bolívar, ATM, US$ cash. **Bisa**, Trigo y 15 de Abril, with ATM, changes US$ cash and TCs. Dollars and Argentine pesos can be changed at a number of **casas de cambio** on Bolívar between Campos and Sucre. **Embassies and consulates** **Argentina**, Ballivián N-0699 y Bolívar, T664 4273, Mon-Fri, 0830-1230. **Germany**, Campero 321, T664 2062, tarijahk@web.de, Mon-Wed, Fri 1000-1300, helpful. **Internet** Average price US$0.25-0.55 per hr. **Language classes** Julia Gutiérrez Márquez, T663 2857. Recommended for language classes and information. **Post offices** V Lema y Sucre. Also at bus terminal. **Useful addresses** **Immigration**, Ingavi O-0789, T664 3450, Mon-Fri 0830-1230, 1430-1830. Visa renewals in 48 hrs.

Cochabamba and around

→ *Phone code: 04. Colour map 6, A3. Population: 604,000. Altitude: 2,570 m.*

Set in a bowl of rolling hills at a comfortable altitude, Cochabamba enjoys a wonderfully warm, dry and sunny climate. Its parks and plazas are a riot of colour, from the striking purple of the bougainvillaea to the subtler tones of jasmin, magnolia and jacaranda. Bolivia's fourth largest city was founded in 1574 and in colonial times it was the `breadbasket' of Bolivia, providing food for the great mining community of Potosí. Today it is an important commercial and communications centre, while retaining a small-town, rural feel.

Fertile foothills surrounding the city still provide much of the country's grain, fruit and coca. Markets, colonial towns and archaeological sites are all close by too. Further afield, the dinosaur tracks and great scenery at Torotoro National Park are worth an exhausting trip. The lowland route to Santa Cruz de la Sierra, now preferred to the old road over the mountains, has great birdwatching and the animal refuge in Villa Tunari deserves your support.

Ins and outs

Getting there and around The city is served by paved roads from La Paz and Santa Cruz. Neither airport, nor bus station are far from the centre. Buses and taxis serve both. The city is divided into four quadrants based on the intersection of Avenida Las Heroínas running west to east, and Avenida Ayacucho running north to south. In all longitudinal streets north of Heroínas the letter N precedes the four numbers. South of Heroínas the numbers are preceded by S. In all transversal streets west of Ayacucho the letter O (Oeste) precedes the numbers and all streets running east are preceded by E (Este). The first two numbers refer to the block, 01 being closest to Ayacucho or Heroínas; the last two refer to the building's number. ▸▸ *See also Transport, page 355.*

Cochabamba

100 metres

100 yards

Sleeping

1 Alojamiento Escobar *D2*
2 Americana *D2*
3 Aranjuez *A3*
4 Boston *B2*
5 Gran Hotel Cochabamba *A3*
6 Hostal Buenos Aires *A2*
7 Hostal Elisa *D1*
8 Hostal Florida *C2*
9 Hostal Versalles *D1*
10 Hostería Jardín *B1*
11 Las Vegas & Café Vivaldi *C2*
12 Monserrat *A2*
13 Regina *A2*
14 Res Concordia *D2*
15 Res Familiar *C2*
16 Res Familiar Annex *B2*
17 Res Jordán *C3*
18 Res Jordán Annex *C2*
19 Virginias *B2*

Eating

1 Brazilian Coffee Bar *A2*
2 Bufalo *A3*
3 Casablanca *A2*
4 Churasquería Tunari *A3*
5 Dumbo *B2*
6 Eli's Pizza *B2*
7 Ganesha *A2*
8 Gopal *B2*
9 La Cantonata *A2*
10 La Estancia *A3*
11 Lai-Lai *A3*
12 Paprika *A2*
13 Sole Mio *A3*
14 Suiza *A2*

Bars & clubs

15 Cocafé *A2*
16 Dalí *A2*
17 Green Pepper *A3*
18 La Tirana *A2*
19 Na Cunna *A3*

Information **Dirección de Turismo de la Alcaldía** ⓘ *Plaza Colón, east side, T425 8030, ext 4419, Mon-Fri 0800-1200, 1430-1830*. Also at bus station ⓘ *Mon-Fri 0500-1100, 1700-2300*, and Pasaje Catedral ⓘ *Mon-Fri 0800-1200, 1430-1830, Sat 0800-1200*. The departmental **tourist office** is at ⓘ *Colombia E-0340, entre 25 de Mayo y España, T422 1793, Mon-Fri 0830-1200, 1430-1630*, helpful, excellent city map and free guide. There's also an information booth at Jorge Wilstermann airport. **Tourist police** ⓘ *Plaza 14 de Septiembre, east side, T450 3880*. The unofficial web resource for the city: www.bolivia-online.net.

Safety Both Cochabamba city and department have public safety issues. Do not venture into any of the hills around town on foot (including San Pedro with the Cristo de la Concordia, San Sebastián and La Coronilla), take radio taxis (with company name, phone and identification number) at night, and mind your belongings in markets, on public transport, and other crowded places. In the main towns in the coca growing region of Chapare (Cochabamba) tourists are reasonably safe, but off the beaten track remains hazardous for outsiders. ▸▸ *See also Safety, page 276.*

Sights

At the heart of the old city is the arcaded **Plaza 14 de Septiembre** with the **Cathedral** ⓘ *Mon-Fri 0800-1200, 1700-1900, Sat-Sun 0800-1200*, dating from 1571, but much added to. Nearby are several colonial churches: **Santo Domingo**, Santiváñez y Ayacucho, begun in 1778 and still unfinished; **San Francisco**, 25 de Mayo y Bolívar, 1581, but heavily modernized in 1926; the **Convent and Museum of Santa Teresa** ⓘ *Baptista y Ecuador, T422 1252, Mon-Fri 0900-1200, 1430-1800, US$3, guides included*, original construction 1760-90, with a beautiful interior; and **La Compañía**, Baptista y Achá, whose whitewashed interior is completely devoid of the usual riot of late Baroque decoration.

Museo Arqueológico ⓘ *Aguirre y Jordán, T425 0010, Mon-Fri 0830-1730, Sat 0830-1200, US$2, free student guide (in Spanish, sometimes French or English)*. Part of the Universidad de San Simón, one of the most complete museums in Bolivia, displaying artefacts including Amerindian hieroglyphic scripts and pre-Inca textiles, through to the colonial era. **Casona Santiváñez** ⓘ *Santiváñez O-0156, Mon-Fri 0800-1200, 1430-1800, free* has a nice colonial patio, and exhibition of paintings and historic photographs.

From Plaza Colón, at the north end of the old town, the wide **Avenida Ballivián** (known as **El Prado**) runs northwest to the wealthy modern residential areas. To the north of Plaza Colón lies the Patiño family's **Palacio de Portales** ⓘ *Av Potosí 1450, T424 3137, Guided tours in Spanish Tue-Fri 1530, 1630, 1730, in English, 1600, 1700, 1800, Sat in Spanish at 0930, 1000, 1100, in English 1100, 1130, Sun Spanish 1100, English 1130, US$1.50. The gardens are open Tue-Fri 1500-1830, Sat-Sun 0930-1130*. Built in French renaissance style, furnished from Europe and set in 10 ha of gardens inspired by Versailles, the Patiño mansion was finished in 1927 but never occupied. It is now the *Centro Cultural Simón I Patiño*, with an excellent art gallery in the basement. Take micro G from Avenida San Martín.

To the south of the old town lie the bus and train stations and some of the best markets in Bolivia. These are very good for tourist items and souvenirs. The huge **La Cancha market** ⓘ *between Esteban Arze, Punata, República and Pulacayo*, is packed on Wednesday and Saturday with campesinos and well worth a visit. Woollen items are expensive but high quality (US$35-50 for an alpaca sweater). The nearby **Mercado Calatayud** is for fruit and vegetables. There is also a Saturday market at Avenida América y Villaroel, best before 0900.

Around Cochabamba

Parque Nacional Tunari, 329,183 ha, is just outside the city. Despite this proximity, it remains a beautiful unspoilt natural area and a good place for acclimatization to altitude. There are llamas and alpacas above 4000 m and even the occasional condor. The highest point in the park, Cerro

Tunari (5,035 m), offers magnificent views. There is a marked trail from the park entrance in the north of the city (micro F2 or *trufi* 35 from Av San Martín and Barrientos go to within 500 m from the entrance; but much faster by taxi, US$2 from centre) which climbs for about 20 km to Laguna Wara Wara at 3,900. Take right branches at the only two intersections and allow for three days trekking round-trip, or hire a 4WD vehicle. Another entrance can be reached from Quillacollo via the thermal springs of Liriuni. Two-day guided treks with pack animals are available from **Refugio Tunari**, see page 353.

Quillacollo, 13 km west of the city, has a Sunday market geared entirely to local produce and a famous festival (see page 355). Eight km beyond Quillacollo is a turn-off to the beautiful **Hacienda Pairumani** ⓘ *T426 0083 to check if it is open, Mon-Fri 1500-1600, Sat 0900-1130*, centre of the Patiño agricultural foundation, also known as **Villa Albina**, built in 1925-1932, furnished from Europe and inhabited by Patiño's wife, Albina. Take Trufi 211 from Plaza Bolívar in Quillacollo, or directly from Av Aroma in Cochabamba. Some 27 km west of Cochabamba are **Inka-Rakay** ruins, with fine views of the Cochabamba valley and the mountains around the ruins. A day trip to the ruins can end at the plaza in nearby Sipe Sipe or one of its local restaurants with a bowl of *guarapo* (wine-based drink) and a plate of *charque* (sun tried beef), served with potatoes, eggs and corn; best at weekends.

Tarata, 33 km southeast of Cochabamba, is a colonial town with a traditional arcaded plaza on which stand the church (daily 0800-1300) and the Casa Consistorial. In the plaza, the tower ⓘ *Mon-Fri 0800-1200, 1330-1700, Sat-Sun 0800-1200* houses a German clock with chimes. Inside the **Franciscan Convent** overlooking the town ⓘ *closed for restoration since 2007*, are the remains of the martyr, San Severino, patron saint of the town, more commonly known as the 'Saint of Rain'; festival, on the last Sunday of November, attracts thousands of people. Large procession on 3 May, day of La Santa Cruz, with fireworks and brass band. Market days Thursday and Sunday (bus US$0.65, one hour, last return 1900). For fine alpaca products, visit Doña Prima Fernández Prado ⓘ *Arce E-0115, opposite the convent*, who sells sweaters, bags and textiles from two rooms off a beautiful colonial patio. The local sausages are nationally famous.

The best way to visit surrounding villages is by **ferrobus**, a bus running on train tracks. It leaves Cochabamba's station in the middle of La Cancha market, on Tue, Thu and Sat at 0800; returning Wed, Fri and Sun at 0800. The 10-12-hour journey goes through more than 17 tunnels and over many bridges, passing through Tarata, Cliza, Mizque to Aiquile, where you can catch a bus back to Cochabamba, or less often to Santa Cruz or Sucre. Tickets are sold at the station ⓘ *La Chancha market, T455 6208, Mon-Fri 1430-1700.*

Parque Nacional Torotoro

ⓘ *Entry US$3, payable at the Oficina de Turismo de la Alcaldía in the village of Torotoro. See Transport, below.* In the province of Potosí, but best reached from Cochabamba (130 km), is **Torotoro**, a small village, set amid beautiful rocky landscape in the centre of the Parque Nacional Torotoro, covering an area of 16,570 ha and declared a National Park in 1989. Attractions include caves, a canyon, waterfalls, pictographs, ruins, fossilized dinosaur tracks and rock paintings, some of which can be seen by the Río Toro Toro just outside the village. **Umajalanta cave**, which has many stalactites and a lake with blind fish, is about 8 km northwest of Torotoro, with an hour's caving (take a head torch if possible). **El Vergel** waterfalls are fantastic and the walk along the river bed is great fun if you like rock-hopping and skipping over pools. Fossils can be seen at Siete Vueltas, 5 km from the village.

Tours or day trips can be organized by the **Asociación de Guías** in the Oficina de Turismo de la Alcaldía. Every visitor will get a map and a personal guide. Renowned guide Mario Jaldín can be reached at mariojaldin@gmail.com. The agency **Bolivia Cultura** in Cochabamba (see Activities and tours, below) offers good tours. This trip is highly recommended and tour operators now offer packages there. You should be able to speak Spanish.

Cochabamba to Santa Cruz

The lowland road from Cochabamba to Santa Cruz, fully paved, runs through Villa Tunari, Sinahota and Chimoré. **Villa Tunari** is a relaxing place and holds an annual Fish Fair 5 and 6 August, with music, dancing and food. **Parque Ecoturístico Machía**, just outside town, which offers good trails through tropical forest. The park is managed by **Inti Wara Yassi** ⓘ *Villa Tunari, T04-413 6572, www.intiwarayassi.org, entrance fee US$0.90, US$2 for camera, US$3.60 for video, donations welcome, open daily 0900-1700*, which is also an animal rescue centre. There are free-roaming monkeys and other mammals with little fear of humans. It is also a popular place for volunteering, such as building rehabilitation facilities and feeding and carrying out basic husbandry on a variety of animals and birds. The website gives full information. A new park, Parque Ambue Ari, between Santa Cruz and Trinidad, is around 600 ha of jungle teeming with wildlife, rehabilitating pumas, monkeys, birds and bears. There is much to do and few volunteers, so lots of flexibility and opportunities, and a freer routine to allow for yoga or a morning nap after the animals' breakfast! Delicious food is provided. For transport from Cochabamba see page 355.

Parque Nacional Carrasco South of Villa Tunari, this park covers 622,600 ha between 300 and 4500 m. It has 11 ecological life zones, superb birdwatching and many rivers, waterfalls, canyons and pools. Access is from Villa Tunari (by trufi), Chimoré, Totora or Puerto Villarroel. From the park entrance closest to Villa Tunari, a cable pulley takes you across the river to **Cavernas de Repechón** wildlife sanctuary. The **Kawsay Wasi** community tourism project www.tusoco.com offers two-hour guided hikes.

The mountain road The 500 km road via the mountains and Epizana to Santa Cruz is partly paved. Some sections are very poor and the new lowland route is preferred by most transport. Between Monte Puncu (Km 119) and Epizana is the turnoff to Pocona and the ruins of Incallajta. To reach the ruins follow the road for 13 km as far as the village of Collpa, then take the left fork for a further 10 km. The Inca ruins of **Inkallajta** (1463-1472, rebuilt 1525), on a flat spur of land at the mouth of a steep valley, are extensive and the main building of the fortress is said to have been the largest roofed Inca building. There are several good camping sites, but no facilities or services. Water available at nearby waterfall. The mountain road continues to Epizana, the junction for the road to Sucre, and on to Samaipata (see page 372).

Cochabamba and around listings

For Sleeping and Eating price codes and other relevant information, see Essentials, pages 38-40.

Sleeping

Cochabamba *p348, map p349*

However attractive their prices, places to stay south of Av Aroma and near the bus station are unsafe at all times.

A Aranjuez, Av Buenos Aires E-0563, T428 0076, www.aranjuezhotel.com. The most beautiful of the luxury hotels with a nice garden and lots of style, 4-star, small, good restaurant, jazz in the bar Fri-Sat night, small pool open to public (US$1). Recommended.

A Gran Hotel Cochabamba, Plaza Ubaldo Anze E-0415, T448 9520, www.granhotelcochabamba.com. One of the best hotels in Cochabamba, re-opened in 2009, pool, tennis courts, business centre, Wi-Fi, airport transfers, parking.

C Americana, Esteban Arce S-788, T425 0552. Fan, helpful, lift, laundry, parking, *Rodizio* grill next door, good service.

C Monserrat, España 0342, T452 1011, http://hotelmonserrat.com. In the bohemian zone with bars and restaurants,, internet, cable TV Cable, sauna, cafetería, buffet breakfast.

D Boston, C 25 de Mayo 0167, T422 8530, hboston@supernet.com.bo. Restaurant, luggage deposit, quiet rooms at back, safe parking. Recommended but cheaper rooms not so good.

D Regina, Reza 0359, T425 7382, www.hotelreginabolivia.com. Spacious, efficient, with breakfast, restaurant.

D Virginias, Bolívar 0553, T451 0468, virginias_hotel@hotmail.com. Quiet but central, helpful, cable TV, restaurant, parking, internet.

E Alojamiento Escobar, Aguirre S-0749, T422 5812. With bath, good value (not to be confused with *Residencial* at Uruguay E-0213).

E Hostal Buenos Aires, 25 de Mayo N-0329, T425 4005. **F** without bath, pleasant, clean communal baths, breakfast US$1.35.

E Hostal Elisa, Agustín López S-0834, T425 4404, helisa@supernet.com.bo. **F** pp without bath, good showers, hot water, good breakfast US$2.25, modern, garden, 2 blocks from bus station, laundry service, very popular with travellers, quiet, helpful owner, but small single rooms and area is unsafe.

E Hostal Florida, 25 de Mayo S-0583, T425 7911. **F** without bath or cable TV, hot water, noisy, popular, laundry service, safe deposit box, internet, breakfast.

E Hostal Versalles, Av Ayacucho S-714, T422 1096, www.hostalversalles.com. HI affiliate, 3 categories of room: carpeted, with bath and TV, cheaper without carpet, **F** with shared bath, breakfast extra, 1½ long blocks from the bus terminal.

E Hostería Jardín, Hamiraya N-0248, T424 7844. **F** without bath, garden, secure car and motorcycle parking, breakfast available, basic but in a nice area.

E Las Vegas, Esteban Arce S-0352, T422 9976. With breakfast, right next to the main plaza, cheap and convenient, safe.

F Res Concordia, Av Aroma E-437 entre 25 de Mayo y San Martín, T425 7131, concordia@boliviahostels.com. Close to bus station, with bath, hot water, a member of this network of Bolivian hostels.

F Res Familiar, Sucre E-0554, T422 7988. Very pleasant, secure, cheaper without bath, good showers, sunny courtyard. Its annex at 25 de Mayo N-0234 (entre Colombia y Ecuador), T422 7986, is also pleasant, with a big courtyard, shared bath, hot water, comfortable.

F Res Jordán, C Antesana S-0671, T422 9294. Youth hostel, *ABAJ* affiliate, modern, basic, with cable TV and small pool. Annex (**F**) at 25 de Mayo S-0651, T422 5010.

Around Cochabamba *p350*

C Refugio Tunari, Pairumani, at the foot of the Cerro Tunari, T7213 0003, www.refugiotunari.com, arranges private transport (25 mins) from Plaza Bolívar in Quillacollo. Mountain lodge with 5 comfortable rooms with private bath, restaurant, bar, living room with fireplace, sauna and large terrace. Organizes guided 2-day walking tours with tent to the Laguna Cajón (4,100 m), Cerro Tunari and other peaks in Parque Tunari. Walking trails start right from the Refugio. Scheduled to open 2010.

Parque Nactional Torotoro *p351*

E Villa Etelvina, a 15-min walk from main plaza. Offers suites with private bath and breakfast.

F Hostal Las Hermanas, T413 5736, 7221 1257, likee_daz@hotmail.com. On the main road from Cochabamba, 1 block before the main plaza on the left hand side. Basic rooms, cheaper without bath, Doña Lily serves delicious food and is very attentive.

G Alojamiento Charcas, on the main street, where the buses drop you off. Shared bath, basic.

G Tata Santiago on the main plaza. Cheaper with shared bath.

Cochabamba to Santa Cruz: Villa Tunari *p352*

B Victoria Resort, on the road to Santa Cruz, 4 km before Villa Tunari on the right, T413 6538, www.victoria-resort.com. Modern, cabaña style, 500 m from the main road in the middle of the forest, quiet, large pool, a/c, breakfast buffet.

D Los Araras, across bridge on main road to Santa Cruz, T413 6629. Cheaper midweek, large rooms, nice gardens, good breakfast. Recommended.

D Selva El Puente, Av de la Integración, 3 km from town, T7174 2596 (or book in advance at offices of *Fremen* Travel Agency). With breakfast and bath, cabins from 2 people to family-size, pool, tours to Carrasco national park, the hotel has a stream and natural pools.

E Hostal Mirador, on road to Santa Cruz, before first bridge, T448 0598. With bath, small pool and tower with views of river San Mateo.

F Res América, Santa Cruz y Av Hans Grether, T7170 7096. Excellent place owned by Sra Edilia, spacious rooms and shared bathrooms which are spotless.

G La Querencia, Beni 700, T413 6548. Pleasant terrace on river front, avoid noisy rooms at front, good cheap food, clothes-washing facilities.
G San Mateo, opposite *Baviera* restaurant, by the river. Shared bath, choice of beds (hard or soft), helpful.

Eating

Cochabamba *p348, map p349*
The restaurant and nightlife district is on España, Ecuador, Mayor Rocha and Av Ballivian (El Prado), and north of the Río Rocha on the Pasaje Boulevard de la Recoleta and Av Pando. Those on very tight budgets can find edible lunch at the **Mercado 25 de Mayo** at 25 de Mayo entre Sucre y Jordán. You'll find yummy fruit choices and salads there too.
TT **Bufalo**, Torres Sofer, p 2, Av Oquendo N-0654, T425 1597. Brazilian *rodizio* grill, all-you-can-eat buffet with salad for US$7, great service. Recommended.
TT **Churrasquería Tunari**, Pasaje Boulevard de la Recoleta, T448 8153. The most delicious meat you can find in Cochabamba.
TT **La Cantonata**, España y Mayor Rocha, T425 9222. Good Italian restaurant. Recommended.
TT **La Estancia**, Aniceto Padilla block 7, in a side street off Plaza Recoleta, T424 9262. Best steak in town, salads and international food in this traditional restaurant.
TT **Lai-Lai**, Recoleta E-0729, T424 0469. Excellent Chinese with take-away service.
TT **Sole Mio**, Av América 826 y Pando, T428 3379. A smart Neapolitan pizza restaurant, delicious, also good for desserts. Attentive service.
TT **Suiza**, Av Ballivián 820, T425 7102. International cuisine, good value. Recommended.
TT-T **Ganesha**, M Roscha E-0375. Good filling vegetarian food, buffet lunch and breakfast, mostly soy-protein based dishes, closed Sun.
TT-T **Paprika**, Av Ramón Rivero 292, T425 7035. Opens in the evening, nice atmosphere, international food, good cocktails and desserts.
T **Eli's Pizza**, 25 de Mayo N-0254 y Colombia. Son of the famous La Paz branch, great pizzas, also home delivery.
T **Gopal**, C España 250, Galería Olimpia. Bolivian Hare-krishna, US$1.50 for vegetarian lunch 1200-1500 only, open Sun for breakfast, English spoken.

Cafés

Brazilian Coffee Bar, Av Ballivián 537 just off Plaza Colón. Upmarket, tables on pavement.
Café París, Bolívar, corner of Plaza 14 de Septiembre. Serves good coffee and crêpes.
Café Vivaldi, Esteban Arce 354, next to the main plaza. Decent place to sit inside or out. Has temporary art exhibitions.
Casablanca, 25 de Mayo entre Venezuela y Ecuador. Attractive, buzzing, good food and a wide selection of coffee, popular for wine and cocktails in the evening.
Dumbo, Av Heroínas 0440. Good ice-cream parlour, popular eating and meeting spot, also does cheap meals.
Los Castores, Ballivián y Oruro. Popular, good for *salteñas*.

Parque Nacional Torotoro *p351*
Finding food is complicated in Toro Toro. You can ask for **Eucebia de Jaldín** who will cook for you in her home. **Villa Etelvina** (see Sleeping) will provide lunch and dinner for an additional US$10 pp. There are 3 stores which stock basics, best to take some food of your own.

Cochabamba to Santa Cruz: Villa Tunari *p352*
There are several eating places on both sides of the main road to Santa Cruz. The more expensive ones are on the riverside. The more popular food stalls one block from the bus terminal serve different fish dishes and have also a cheap daily menu. Upstairs at the market (breakfast and lunch) is a very cheap option.

Bars and clubs

Cochabamba *p348, map p349*
Cocafé, Mayor Rocha entre 25 de Mayo y España. Caring, family atmosphere, good place for foreigners to meet. Street musicians always pass by to show off their skills.
Dalí, Reza E-242, Plazuela Barba de Padilla acera norte, T422 8216. Famous place where the young meet for a beer before a long night's partying. Good background music.
Green Pepper, Av América casi Villarroel. Thu-Sat nights, popular dancing spot with locals and foreigners, all kinds of music.
La Tirana, Lanza y Av Ramón Rivero. Popular bar and club for a beer or to dance to mixed Latin

Fiesta de la Virgen de Urkupiña, Quillacollo

The festival lasts four days in August with much dancing and religious ceremony. Plenty of transport from Cochabamba, hotels all full. Be there before 0900 to be sure of a seat, as you are not allowed to stand in the street. The first day is the most colourful with all the groups in costumes and masks, parading and dancing in the streets till late at night. Many groups have left by the second day and dancing stops earlier. The third day is dedicated to the pilgrimage. Full details at www.urcupina.com. (Many buses, micros and *trufis* from Heroínas y Ayacucho, 20 minutes, US$0.30.)

and rock music, in a two-storey house with different spaces up and downstairs.

Na Cunna, Av Salamanca 577, T452 1982. Irish pub and restaurant, opens in the evenings, Fri live music. They also serve Guinness.

Entertainment

Cochabamba *p348, map p349*

Theatre mARTadero, Av 27 de Agosto entre Ollantay y Ladislao Cabrera, T458 8778, www.martadero.org. Cultural and artistic centre for local and international artists, exhibitions, and events, in a refurbished slaughterhouse. Daily 1500-1800. Micros/trufis P, Q, and 212 to Plaza de los Arrieros. **Teatro Achá**, España 280 y Plaza 14 de Septiembre, T425 8054. The city's oldest cultural centre, with monthly presentations. **Teatro Hecho a Mano**, Venezuela 0655 entre Lanza y Antezana, T452 9790. Theatre school.

Festivals and events

Cochabamba *p348, map p349*

Carnival is celebrated 15 days before **Lent**. Rival groups (*comparsas*) compete in music, dancing, and fancy dress, culminating in El Corso on the last Sat of the Carnival. **Mascaritas** balls also take place in the carnival season, when the young women wear long hooded satin masks. **14 Sep**: **Día de Cochabamba**.

Shopping

Cochabamba *p348, map p349*

Bookshops Los Amigos del Libro, España S-153, www.librosbolivia.com. **The Spitting Llama**, España 615 entre Plaza Barba de Padilla y La Paz, T489 4540, www.thespittingllama.com. Issue ISIC cards, sell used books, guidebooks and camping gear including GPS units, English spoken, helpful.

Handicrafts Artesanos Andinos, Pasaje Catedral, T450 8367. An artisans' association selling textiles.

Activities and tours

Cochabamba *p348, map p349*

Adventure sports

Cochabamba is growing in popularity for parapenting, with several outfits offering tamdem jumps and courses more cheaply than other places, starting at US$30-35 and US$200-250 respectively.

AndesXtremo, La Paz 138 entre Ayacucho y Junín, T452 3392, www.andesxtremo.com. Adventure sports company offering parapenting, climbing, rafting, trekking and bungee-jumps, good value, professional staff. Recommended.

Bolivia Cultura, C. Espana N-301, esquina Ecuador, T452 7272, www.boliviacultura.com. Offers the most complete service for tours to Torotoro. They run year round tours for 3 and 4 days to all the major sites and can arrange longer trips, hikes and camping. They also have reliable information on road conditions, hotels and eating.

D'Orbigny Travel, Pasaje de la Promotora 344 entre España y Heroínas, T451 1367. Run by an enthusiastic Bolivian couple, excursions in Cochabamba department and throughout Bolivia. Recommended.

Fremen, Tumusla N-0245, T425 9392, www.frementours.com. City and local tours, specialize in travel in the Bolivian Amazon. Also have offices in La Paz, Santa Cruz and Trinidad.

Transport

Cochabamba *p348, map p349*

Air Jorge Wilstermann airport, T412 0400. Airport bus is Micro B from Plaza 14 de

Septiembre, US$0.40; taxis from airport to centre US$4. Reconfirm all flights (and obtain reconfirmation number), and arrive early for international flights. Cochabamba is an air transport hub with several daily daily to/from **La Paz** (35 mins) and **Santa Cruz** (40 mins) with **Aero Sur** (Av Villarroel 105 y Av Oblitos -Pando, T440 0909), **Boliviana de Aviacion**, Jordán 202 y Nataniel Aguirre, T901-105010, and **TAM** (Av América Oeste casi George Washington, Ed Torres América, T441 1545). **Aerocon** (Av Oblitas 279 entre Villarroel y Eliodoro Camacho, T448 9177) and **TAM** have flights to **Trinidad**, with connections to other northern cities.

Bus *Micros* and *colectivos*, US$0.20; *trufis*, US$0.30. Anything marked 'San Antonio' goes to the market. *Trufis* C and 10 go from bus terminal to the city centre. The main bus terminal is on Av Aroma y Ayacucho, 600-700 m south of Plaza 14 de Septiembre (T155). To **Santa Cruz**, almost hourly 0600-2130, 12 hrs, US$7.50. (**Trans Copacabana** semi cama, 2130, US$10, **Bolívar** buscama, US$15); only minibuses take the old mountain road via Epizana, from Av República y 6 de Agosto, all day. See page 352. To/from **La Paz** almost hourly 0530-2300, 7 hrs, US$6 (**Trans Copacabana** semi cama, 2230, US$8.50, **Bolívar** buscama, 2230, 2300, US$12.50). To **Oruro**, 0600-1730 (Sun last bus at 2100), 4 hrs, US$3.35-4. To **Potosí**, departures at 2000 (US$7), 2100 (semi cama, US$11) with **Bolívar** and **Trans Copacabana**, 10 hrs. Daily to **Sucre**, 8 hrs, several companies (**Bolívar** and **Trans Copacabana** at 1930, 2000 US$7, 2030 semi cama, US$8.50). To **Sucre** by day; go to Aiquile by bus (several from Av 6 de Agosto entre Av República y Av Barrientos, none before 1200) or **ferrobus** (see page 351), then a bus at 0200-0300 passing en route to Sucre, or Fri and Sun, 2000. Local buses leave from Av Barrientos y Av 6 de Agosto, near La Coronilla for **Tarata**, **Punata** and **Cliza**. From Av 6 de Agosto y Av República to **Totora**. Av Oquendo y 9 de Abril (be careful in this area), to **Villa Tunari**, US$4.50, 4-5 hrs, several daily; **Chimoré**, US$5.75; **Puerto Villarroel**, US$7.75, 6 hrs (from 0800 when full, daily). **Taxi** About US$0.75 from anywhere to the Plaza, more expensive to cross the river; double after dark.

Parque Nacional Torotoro *p351*

Air The NGO **Mano a Mano** (www.manoamanobolivia.org) has a Cessna light aircraft and fly from Jorge Wilstermann airport, 30 mins for about US$150 one-way, up to 5 people. Reserve 7-14 days in advance. The pilot can be persuaded to fly through the canyons on the way there. Call José Luis at the hangar, T473 2819.

Bus There is public transport on Wed and Sat from the end of Av República at 1800, and Thu and Sun from Av República y Av 6 de Agosto at 0600. Buses return to Cochabamba on Mon, Tue, Fri and Sat at 0600, US$3, about 6 hrs on a recently cobbled road.

Cochabamba to Santa Cruz: Inkallajta *p352*

Take a trufi from 0500 onwards from 6 de Agosto y Manuripi (Av República) in Cochabamba (ask for the "Parada Pocona"). For 3 people the trufi will drop you off at the entrance to the Inca ruins (US$3 pp). Arrange with the driver to pick you up at a specific time to return to Cochabamba. If alone, ask to get off after arriving in Collpa at a big green sign, where the road to the ruins turns off to the right. Walk along the cobbled road for approximately 10 km to the ruins. Trufis return from Pocona to Cochabamba when full till 1600. Taxis from Pocona charge around US$14 one way to the ruins.

Directory

Cochabamba *p348, map p349*

Banks Visa and MasterCard at *Enlace* ATMs all over the town (especially on Av Ballivián) and next to the bus terminal. Cash on Visa or MasterCard from many banks; no commission on bolivianos. **Bisa**, Av Ballivián 799 y Tte Arévalo. **BNB**, Nataniel Aguirre E-198 y Jordán. **Prodem**, Calama entre Av Ayacucho y Aguirre. Money changers congregate at most major intersections, especially at Ayacucho y Achá outside *Entel*, around Plaza 14 de Septiembre and at Heroínas y 25 de Mayo. **Cultural centres** **Alianza Francesa**, La Paz 784 casi Crisóstomo Carrillo, T452 5771, www.afbolivia.org. **Instituto Cultural Boliviano-Alemán**, Lanza 727, T412 323, www.icbacbba.web.bo. Spanish classes.

Embassies and consulates Argentina, F Blanco 929, T422 9347, ccoch@mrecic.gov.ar, Mon-Fri 0830-1300, 1500-1800. **Brazil**, Plaza Quintanilla, Edif Los Tiempos II, p9, T425 5860, cchbrvc14@supernet.com.bo, 0830-1130, 1430-1730. **Germany**, Plaza Quintanilla, Edif Los Tiempos, T453 0348, gerencia.cbba@corimex.com. **Peru**, Pedro Blanco 1344 y Santa Cruz, Edif Continental, T448 6556, Mon-Fri 0800-1200, 1400-1800. **USA**, Av Oquendo, Torres Sofer p 6, T425 6714. Mon- Fri 0900-1200 (will also attend to Britons and Canadians). **Internet** Many cybercafés all over town, charging US$0.50 per hr. **Language classes** **Bolivia Sostenible**, Julio Arauco Prado 230, Zona Las Cuadras, T423 3786, www.boliviasostenible.org. Offers home stays and paid placements for volunteers. **Centro de Kori Simi Language Center**, Lanza 727, entre La Paz y Chuquisaca, T425 7248, www.korisimi.com. Spanish and Quechua school run by staff from Switzerland, Germany and Bolivia, also offers activity programme, homestays and volunteer placements. **Runawasi**, Maurice Lefebvre 0470, Villa Juan XXIII, Av Blanco Galindo Km 4.5, T424 8923, www.runawasi.org. Spanish and Quechua, also has accommodation. **Volunteer Bolivia**, Ecuador E-0342, T452 6028, www.volunteerbolivia.org. Bolivian/US-run organization which offers language classes, homestays and a recommended volunteer programme. See also Cultural centres, above. There are many qualified language teachers in the city. **Medical facilities** For hospitals, doctors and dentists, contact your consulate or the tourist office for advice. **Post offices** Av Heroínas y Ayacucho, Mon-Fri 0800-2000, Sat 0800-1800, Sun 0800-1200. **Useful addresses** **Immigration Office:** Av Ballivián y La Paz, T452 4625, Mon-Fri 0830-1630.

Northern Lowlands

Bolivia's Northern lowlands account for about 70% of national territory. Flat savannahs and dense tropical jungle stretch northwards from the great cordilleras, sparsely populated and, until recently, rarely visited by tourists. Improved roads and frequent flights, particularly to Rurrenabaque and Trinidad, are opening up the area and wildlife and rainforest expeditions are becoming increasingly popular. Most people head to Rurrenabaque. If seeking hard travel and adventure, head for Cobija or Riberalta. Beni department has 53% of the country's birds and 50% of its mammals, but destruction of forest and habitat by loggers and colonisers is proceeding at an alarming rate.

Madidi and Rurrenabaque

Caranavi to San Borja

From Caranavi, a road runs north to Sapecho, where a bridge crosses the Río Beni. Beyond Sapecho (7 km from the bridge), the road passes through Palos Blancos (several cheap lodgings). The road between Sapecho and Yucumo, three hours from Sapecho *tránsito*, is now a very good all-weather gravel surface. There are *hospedajes* (**G**) and restaurants in **Yucumo** where a road branches northwest, fording rivers several times on its way to Rurrenabaque. Taking the eastern branch from Yucumo it is 50 km (1-2 hours) to **San Borja**, a small, relatively wealthy cattle-raising centre with hotels (**E-G**) and restaurants clustered near the plaza. From San Borja the road goes east to Trinidad via **San Ignacio de Moxos**; see page 364. The road passes through part of the Pilón Lajas Reserve (see below).

Parque Nacional Madidi

ⓘ *Headquarters in San Buenaventura, about 4 blocks upriver from the plaza, T03-892 2540. US$11 entry is collected near the dock in San Buenaventura. Insect repellent and sun protection are essential.*

Parque Nacional Madidi is quite possibly the most bio-diverse of all protected areas on the planet. It is the variety of habitats, from the freezing Andean peaks of the Cordillera Apolobamba in the southwest (reaching nearly 6,000 m), through cloud, elfin and dry forest to steaming tropical jungle and pampas (neo-tropical savannah) in the north and east, that account for the array of flora and fauna within the park's boundaries. In an area roughly the size of Wales or El Salvador (1,895,750 ha) are an estimated 900 bird species, 10 species of primate, five species of cat (with healthy populations of jaguar and puma), giant anteaters and many reptiles. Madidi is at the centre of a bi-national system of parks that spans the Bolivia-Peru border. The Heath river on the park's northwestern border forms the two countries' frontier and links with the Tambopata National Reserve in Peru. To the southwest the Area Protegida Apolobamba protects extensive mountain ecosystems. It is easiest to visit the lowland areas of Madidi through Rurrenabaque; book in advance.

Pilón Lajas Biosphere Reserve and Indigenous Territory
ⓘ *HQ at Campero y Germón Busch, Rurrenabaque, T892 2246, crtmpilonlajas@yahoo.com. No entrance fee at the time of updating, but one is planned.*
Beyond the Beni River in the southeast runs the Pilón Lajas Biosphere Reserve and Indigenous Territory, home to the Tsimane and Mosetene peoples. Together with Madidi, it constitutes approximately 60,000 sq km, one of the largest systems of protected land in the neotropics. Unfortunately, much of this land is under pressure from logging interests, especially along the western border of the reserve. The Pilón Lajas Biosphere Reserve and Indigenous Territory, set up under the auspices of UNESCO, has one of the continent's most intact Amazonian rainforest ecosystems, as well as an incredible array of tropical forest animal life. NGOs have been working with the people of La Unión, Playa Ancha, Nuevos Horizontes and El Cebú to develop sustainable forestry, fish farming, cattle ranching and *artesanía*.

Rurrenabaque → *Phone code: 03. Population: 17,900.*
The charming, picturesque jungle town of Rurre (as the locals call it), on the Río Beni, is the main jumping off point for tours in the Bolivian Amazon and pampas, from 2-4 day trips through to full expeditions. Across the river is San Buenaventura (canoe US$0.15), with a **Centro Cultural Tacana** by the plaza (US$0.70). Despite its growth as a trading, transport and ecotourism centre, Rurre is a pleasant town to walk around, although the climate is usually humid. Market day is Sunday. **Dirección Regional de Turismo** ⓘ *Avaroa y Vaca Diez, Mon-Fri 0800-1200, 1430-1830, Sat 0800-1200*, has general information and a bulletin board for posting comments on tours; read this before booking a tour and write your own feedback. Bicycles rented at US$2 per hour.

Forty minutes upstream from Rurre is **San Miguel del Bala**, in a beautiful setting, 3 km from the entrance to Madidi. This community lodge gives a good taste of the jungle, offers day trips, well-laid out trails and has en suite cabins where you can stay, bar and a pool fed by a waterfall. It is owned and operated by the indigenous Tacana community.

Madidi and Rurrenabaque listings

For Sleeping and Eating price codes and other relevant information, see Essentials, pages 38-40.

Sleeping

Madidi *p357*
AL pp **Chalalán Ecolodge** is 5 hrs up-river from Rurrenabaque, at San José de Uchupiamonas, in Madidi National Park. Addresses: C Sagárnaga 189, Edif Shopping Doryan, p 2, of 22, T/F02-231 1451, or in Rurrenabaque C Comercio entre Campero y Vaca Dísez, T03-892 2419, www.chalalan.com. This is Bolivia's top ecotourism project, founded by the local Quechua-Tacana community, Conservation International and the Interamerican Development Bank, and now has a well-deserved international reputation. Accommodation is in thatched cabins,

and activities include fantastic wildlife-spotting and birdwatching, guided and self-guided trails, river and lake activities, and relaxing in pristine jungle surroundings. 3 day/2 night packages cost US$330 pp (US$300 with shared bath), plus transport to Rurre and national park fees.
A per day **San Miguel del Bala**, 40-min boat trip up river from Rurre, T/F03-892 2394, www.san migueldelbala.com. 7 cabins in delightful setting, good bathrooms, nice public areas, good restaurant, attentive staff, 3 days/ 2 nights cost US$180 pp. Advance booking required. Highly recommended.

Pilón Lajas *p358*
A per day **Mapajo**, Mapajo Ecoturismo Indígena, Santa Cruz entre Avaroa y Comercio, Rurrenabaque, T03-892 2317, www.mapajo.com. A community-run ecolodge 3 hrs by boat from Rurrenebaque has 4 *cabañas* without electricity (take a torch), shared cold showers and a dining room serving traditional meals. 3 days/2 nights cost US$220 pp. You can visit the local community, walk in the forest, go birdwatching, etc. Take insect repellent, wear long trousers and strong footwear. Recommended.

Rurrenabaque *p358*
In high season hotels fill up very quickly.
C El Ambaibo, Santa Cruz y Bolívar, T892 2107, hotel_ambaibo@hotmail.com. Includes breakfast and airport transfer, large pool (US$3 for non-guests), parking, a step up from the average in Rurre.
C Hotel Safari, Comercio on the outskirts by the river (a hot walk), T892 2410. A peaceful spot with beautiful garden and comfortable rooms, pool, terrace and a good restaurant. Recommended.
D Beni, Comercio y Arce, T892 2408. Best rooms have a/c and TV, hot showers, **F** with fan, cheaper without bath. Spacious, good service.
E Oriental, on plaza, T892 2401. Hot showers, fan, small breakfast included, quiet, hammocks in peaceful garden, family-run. A good option.
F Asaí, Vaca Díez y Busch, T7355 8946. Electric showers, quiet, laundry area, courtyard and hammocks, luggage store, breakfast extra.
F El Curichal, Comercio 1490, T892 2647, elcurichal@hotmail.com. Nice courtyard, hammocks, laundry and small kitchen facilities, helpful staff, will change TCs and money.
F Hostal Pahuichi, Comercio y Vaca Díez, T892 2558. Some big rooms with electric shower, fan, courtyard with hammocks, quite good.
F Mirador del Lobo, upstream end of Comercio, contact through El Lobo in La Paz, T02-245 1640. Large breezy building overlooking the river, some rooms with electric shower.
F Rurrenabaque, Vaca Díez y Bolívar, T892 2481. Safe, hot water, cooking and laundry facilities, adequate.
F Santa Ana, Avaroa entre Vaca Díez y Campero, T892 2399. Electric showers, thin mattresses, laundry, luggage store, pretty courtyard, basic, mixed reports.
G Hoastal El Balsero, Comercio y Pando, T892 2042. Cheaper without bath, electric shower, fan, bare but clean rooms, functional.
G Res Jislene, C Comercio, T892 2526. Erlan Caldera and family very hospitable, hot water, fan, basic, good breakfast if booked in advance, information, helpful.

Eating

Rurrenabaque *p358*
TT Camila's, Avaroa y Campero. Serves international food, parrillada on Sun, drinks, pool tables, fast service, daily 0800-0130.
TT Casa del Campo, Vaca Díez y Avaroa. Good sandwices, juices, international food, breakfast, delicious desserts, garden, hospitable staff, daily 0700-2100.
TT Stephaní y Juliano, Santa Cruz entre Bolívar y Busch. Daily 1200-1430, 1730-late. French, Italian and Arab food, good presentation and service. Recommended.
TT-T El Tacuaral, Avaroa y Santa Cruz. Daily 0700-2000. International food, breakfasts and burgers.
TT-T Luna Café, Santa Cruz entre Avaroa y Bolívar, downstairs. Open 0800-2200. International meals, pizza, snacks and drinks.
TT-T Pizzería Italia & Monkey's Bar, Avaroa entre Santa Cruz y Vaca Díez, open 0900-0100. Big pizzas, imaginative pastas, lively crowd, big screen TV, pool tables.
T La Cabaña, Santa Cruz, by the river. Mon-Sat 0800-2200, Sun 0800-1600. Good set lunch and à la carte.

La Perla de Rurre, Bolívar y Vaca Díez. Set lunch and à la carte, open 0730-2100.

Cafés

Café Piraña, Santa Cruz entre Avaroa y Bolívar, upstairs. Internet café serving coffee and snacks, small library on Amazonian topics.

French Bakery, Vaca Díez y Bolívar, run by Thierry. Delicious croissants and *pain au chocolat*, get there early.

Moskkito Bar, Vaca Díez y Avaroa. Cool bar for tall jungle tales. Burgers, pizzas, rock music and pool tables.

Pachamama, south end of Avaroa. Open 1200-2230. English/Israeli café/bar, snacks, river view, films, board games, table football and a book exchange.

Ron, an expat North American, sells banana bread, cinnamon rolls, granola bars from his kit car. Catch him at Santa Cruz y Avaroa.

Sun is the big party night in Rurre.

Activities and tours

Rurrenabaque *p358*

There are 2 types of tours, jungle or pampas. Both cost about US$40 pp per day, but prices and quality vary. It is recommended to go with an established company as competition is forcing down prices and, consequently, quality and standards of guiding. Many agencies continue to offer ecologically unsound practices such as fishing, feeding monkeys, catching caiman, handling anaconda; before signing up for a tour insist that the operator respects the environment. Some operators pool customers, so you may not go with the company you booked with and may not get the standards you might have expected. Check at the Dirección Regional de Turismo first. Jungle tours normally last 4 days and 3 nights and involve travelling by boat on the Río Beni. Lodging is either in purpose-built camps on higher-end tours, or tents at the budget end. Tours are long enough for most people to get a real sense of life in the jungle. In the rainy season the jungle is very hot and humid with many more biting insects and far fewer animals to be seen. In the more open terrain of the Pampas you will see a lot more wildlife on a 3-day tour, which involves a 4-hr jeep ride to the Río Yacuma at either end, and a series of boat trips. You see howler, squirrel and capuchin monkeys, caiman, capybara, pink dolphins, possibly anacondas and a huge variety of birds. For pampas and jungle tours, 1-day trips involve most of the time travellling, unless going to San Miguel del Bala. Pampas tours may involve wading through knee-deep water; wear appropriate shoes. It is cheaper to book tours in Rurrenabaque than La Paz.

Tour operators

Aguila Tours, Av Avaroa, T892 2478, jungle and pampas tours.

Bala Tours, Av Santa Cruz y Comercio, T3892 2527, www.balatours.com. Arranges Pampas and jungle tours, with their own lodge in each. Recommended.

Donato Tours, Santa Cruz y Comercio, T892 2571, donatotours@hotmail.com. For regular tours and A Day for the Community with trips to Pilón Lajas.

Madidi Travel, Comercio y Vaca Díez, T892 2153, in La Paz, Linares 968, T02-231 8313, www.madidi-travel.com. Specializes tours to the private Serere Sanctuary in the Madidi Mosaic (details on website), minimum 3 days/ 2 nights, good organization, food and guiding. Recommended.

Mashaquipe Tours, Comercio entre Santa Cruz y Vaca, www.mashaquipe.com. Run by an indigenous, Tacana family, with a camp in Madidi, knowledgeable guides (including women guides), mixed reports.

Turismo Ecológico Social (TES), Av Santa Cruz, T7128 9664, turismoecologicosocial@hotmail.com. Day tours to 3 local communities.

Transport

Caranavi to San Borja *p357*

Bus See page 314 for buses in Caranavi. **Yucumo** is on the La Paz-Caranavi- Rurrenabaque and San Borja bus routes. Rurrenabaque-La Paz bus passes through about 1800. If travelling to Rurrenabaque by bus take extra food in case there is a delay (anything from road blocks to flat tyres to high river levels). **Flota Yungueña** daily except Thu at 1300 from San Borja to **La Paz**, 19 hrs via Caranavi. Also San Borja to **Rurrenabaque**, **Santa Rosa**, **Riberalta**, **Guayaramerín** about 3 times a week. Minibuses and *camionetas* normally run daily between San Borja and **Trinidad** throughout the year, US$15, about 7 hrs including 20 mins crossing of Río Mamoré on ferry barge (up to 14 hrs in wet season). Gasoline available at Yolosa, Caranavi, Yucumo, San Borja and San Ignacio.

Rurrenabaque *p358*

Air Daily flights with **Amaszonas** (Comercio entre Santa Cruz y Vaca Diez, T892 2472) and **TAM** (Santa Cruz y Avaroa, T892 2398, US$63) to/from **La Paz** (US$75). Also Amaszonas daily to **Santa Cruz** (US$150). Book flights as early as possible and buy onward ticket on arrival. Check flight times in advance; they change frequently. Delays and cancellations are common. Airport taxes US$2. Airlines provide transport from town, US$0.70.

Bus To/from **La Paz** via Caranavi daily with **Flota Yungueña, Totai** and **Vaca Díez**; 18-20 hrs, US$8.50. Some continue to **Riberalta** (US$17, 13 hrs from Rurre), **Guayaramerín** (US$18, 15 hrs) or **Cobija** (US$32, 30 hrs). Rurrenebaque-**Riberalta** may take 6 days or more in the wet. Take lots of food, torch and be prepared to work. To **Trinidad**, with **Trans Guaya** (buses) or **Trans Rurrenabaque** (minibuses) daily, **Flota Yungueña** Mon, Wed, via **Yucumo** and **San Borja**, US$18, check that the road is open.

Directory

Rurrenabaque *p358*

Banks No ATMs. **Prodem**, Avaroa y Pando, Mon-Fri 0830-1800, Sat 0900-1200. Changes US$ cash at fair rates, 5.3% commission on cash advance on Visa or MasterCard. If stuck, try hotels **Beni** or **El Curichal**, 4-5% commission on TCs, but not always possible. **Immigration** Arce entre Bolívar y Busch, T892 2241, Mon-Fri 0830-1230, 1430-1830, same day for extensions. **Internet** US$1 per hr. **Post offices** On C Bolívar. Open Sat.

Riberalta to Brazil

Riberalta → *Phone code: 03. Colour map 3, B6. Population: 60,000. Altitude: 175 m.*

This town, at the confluence of the Madre de Dios and Beni rivers, is off the beaten track and a centre for brazil nut production. Change cash in shops and on street. It's very laid back, but take great care if your bus drops you in the middle of the night and everything is closed.

Guayaramerín and border with Brazil → *Phone code: 03. Colour map 4, C1.*

Guayaramerín is a cheerful, prosperous little town on the bank of the Río Mamoré, opposite the Brazilian town of Guajará-Mirim. It has an important *Zona Libre*. Passage between the two towns is unrestricted; boat trip US$1.65 (more at night).

Bolivian immigration Avenida Costanera near port; open 0800-1100, 1400-1800. Passports must be stamped here when leaving, or entering Bolivia. On entering Bolivia, passports must also be stamped at the Bolivian consulate in Guajará-Mirim. For Brazilian immigration, see page 646. The Brazilian consulate is on 24 de Septiembre, Guayaramerín, T855 3766, open 0900-1300, 1400-1700; visas for entering Brazil are given here. To enter Brazil you must have a yellow fever certificate, or be inoculated at the health ministry (free). Exchange cash at the dock on the Bolivian side where rates are written up on blackboards (no traveller's cheques), although there is an ATM at the Banco do Brasil in Guajará-Mirim; no facilities for cash.

Cobija → *Phone code: 03. Colour map 3, B5. Population: 30,000.*
The capital of the lowland Department of Pando lies on the Río Acre which forms the frontier with Brazil. A new, single-tower suspension bridge has been built across the river to Brasiléia. As a duty-free zone, shops in centre have a huge selection of imported consumer goods at bargain prices. Brazilians and Peruvians flock here to stock up. As this is a this border area, watch out for scams and cons. **Bolivian immigration** ⓘ *Av Internacional 567, T842 2081, open daily 0900-1800*. **Brazilian consulate** ⓘ *Av René Barrientos s/n, T842 2110, vcbrasco@entelnet.bo, Mon-Fri 0830-1230*.

Riberalta to Brazil listings

For Sleeping and Eating price codes and other relevant information, see Essentials, pages 38-40.

Sleeping

Riberalta *p361*
Ask for a fan and check the water supply.
C Colonial, Plácido Méndez 1, T852 3018. Charming colonial casona, large, well-furnished rooms, no singles, nice gardens and courtyard, comfortable, good beds, helpful owners.
D Lazo, NG Salvatierra. **F** without a/c, comfortable, laundry facilities, good value.
F Res El Pauro, Salvatierra 157, T852 2452. Basic, shared baths, good café.
F Res Los Reyes, near airport, T852 2628. With fan, safe, pleasant but noisy disco nearby on Sat and Sun.

Guayaramerín *p361*
C San Carlos, 6 de Agosto, 4 blocks from port, T855 3555. With a/c, hot showers, changes dollars cash, TCs and reais, swimming pool, reasonable restaurant.
F Santa Ana 25 de Mayo, close to airport, T855 3900. With bath and fan. Recommended.

Cobija *p362*
C Diana, Av 9 de Febrero 123, T842 3653. A/c, TV, safe, buffet breakfast, internet and pool.
C Nanijos, Av 9 de Febrero 147, T842 2230. Includes breakfast, a/c, TV, *comedor* does good lunch, internet, helpful.
C Triller, Av Internacional 640, T842 2024. With a/c (**E** with fan) and bath, restaurant.
D Avenida, 9 de Febrero y Tarija, T842 2108. With breakfast, a/c, fan and bath.

Eating

Riberalta *p361*
🍴 **Club Social Progreso**, on plaza. Good value *almuerzo*, excellent fish.
🍴 **Tropical**, Oruro y Juan Alberdi, near the airport. Nice atmosphere, good typical food.

Guayaramerín *p361*
🍴🍴 **Los Cocos**, at entrance to town. *Parrilla* and à la carte.
There are several places on the plaza: 🍴 **Gipssy**, good *almuerzo*; 🍴 **Los Bibosis**, popular; **Made in Brazil**, good coffee.
🍴 **Only**, 25 de Mayo y Beni, good *almuerzo*, plus Chinese.

Cobija *p362*
🍴🍴-🍴 **Las Palmas**, Av Chelio Luna Pizarro y G Fernández. Tue-Sun lunch and dinner, à la carte meals, karaoke at night.
🍴🍴-🍴 **Paladar Brasilero**, 16 de Julio y Santa Cruz. Brazilian buffet, pay by weight.
La Esquina de la Abuela, Fernández Molina y Sucre. Varied menu, good food, not cheap. *Salteñas* sold in morning.

Activities and tours

Riberalta p361

Riberalta Tours, Av Sucre 646, T852 3475, www.riberaltatours.com. Multi-day river and jungle tours, airline tickets, very helpful.

Cobija p362

Turismo Verde and **Yaminagua Tours**, Plaza del Deportista 50, T842 3456. Biking, rafting, tours to the jungle and native communities.

Transport

Riberalta p361

Air Flights to **Trinidad** with **Aerocon** (Plaza Principal near Norte 469, T852 2870). **TAM** (Av Suárez Chuquisaca, T852 3924) to **Trinidad, Santa Cruz, Cochabamba** and **La Paz**. Expect cancellations in the wet season.

Bus Roads to all destinations are appalling, even worse in the wet season. Several companies (including **Yungueña**) to **La Paz**, via **Rurrenabaque** and **Caranavi** daily, 35 hrs to 3 days or more, US$27. To **Trinidad** via Rurrenabaque and San Borja, 25-35 hrs. To **Guayaramerín** 7 daily, US$5, 2 hrs. To **Cobija** several companies, none with daily service, 10-11 hrs.

River Cargo boats carry passengers along the **Río Madre de Dios**, but they are infrequent. There are no boats to Rurrenabaque.

Guayaramerín p361

Air Daily flights to **Trinidad**, with onward connections, with **Aerocon** (25 de Mayo y 16 de Julio s/n, T855 3882). **TAM** has same services as for Riberalta.

Bus Buses leave from General Federico Román. Same long-haul services as Riberalta, above. To **Riberalta** 2 hrs, US$5, daily 0700-1730.

River Check the notice of vessels leaving port on the Port Captain's board, prominently displayed near the immigration post on the riverbank. Boats sailing up the Mamoré to **Trinidad** are not always willing to take passengers.

Cobija p362

Air Daily flights to **Trinidad**, with onward connections, with **Aerocon**, Fernández Molina y Cornejo, T842 4166. **Aero Sur**, Cornejo 123, T842 3598, flies 3 times a week to **La Paz**. **TAM** (Av 9 de Febrero 49, T842 2267), to **La Paz** or **Trinidad** on alternating days.

Bus Flota Yungueña and Flota Cobija to **La Paz** via Riberalta and Rurrenabaque, 2-3 days or more, US$30-40. To **Riberalta** with several bus companies, depart from 2 de Febrero, most on Wed, Fri, Sun at 0600; good all-weather surface; 2 river crossings on pontoon rafts, takes 10-11 hrs.

Taxi US$0.60 in centre, but more expensive beyond, charging according to time and distance, expensive over the international bridge to Brasiléia. Besides taxis there are motorbike taxis (US$0.60). **Brasiléia** can also be reached by **canoe**, US$0.35. The bridge can be crossed on foot as well, although one should be dressed neatly in any case when approaching Brazilian customs. Entry/exit stamps (free) are necessary and yellow fever vaccination certificate also (in theory), when crossing into Brazil. From Brasiléia **Real Norte**, www.realnorte.com.br, has buses to **Rio Branco**, US$7.60, and **Assis Brasil**, US$4, and **Taxis Brasileiros** run to Rio Branco, US$10.

Directory

Cobija p362

Banks Banco Unión, La Paz 48. **Prodem**, 9 de Febrero, opposite Escuela Mariano Baptista. US$ cash at fair rates, 5% for Visa/MasterCard cash advances. **Casas de cambio** on Av Internacional and Av Cornejo for exchange. Most shops will accept dollars or reais, or exchange money. **Internet** US$0.85 per hr. **Post offices** On plaza.

Cochabamba to Trinidad

Villa Tunari to the Lowlands

Another route into Beni Department is via the lowland road between Cochabamba and Santa Cruz. At Ivirgazama, east of Villa Tunari, the road passes the turn-off to **Puerto Villarroel**, 27 km further north, from where cargo boats ply irregularly to Trinidad in about four to 10 days. You can get information from the Capitanía del Puerto notice board, or ask at docks. There are only a few basic places to sleep in Villarroel and very few stores.

Trinidad → *Phone code: 03. Colour map 6, A3. Population: 96,400. Altitude: 327 m.*

The hot and humid capital of the lowland Beni Department is a dusty city in the dry season, with many streets unpaved. Primarily a service centre for the surrounding ranches and communities, most travellers find themselves in the area for boats up and down the Río Mamoré. There are two ports, Almacén and Varador, check which one your boat is docking at. Puerto Varador is 13 km from town on the Río Mamoré on the road between Trinidad and San Borja; cross the river over the main bridge by the market, walk down to the service station by the police checkpoint and take a truck, US$1.70. Almacén is 8 km from the city. The main mode of transport in Trinidad is the motorbike (even for taxis, US$0.40 in city); rental on plaza from US$2 per hour, US$8 per half day. Transport can be arranged from the airport. The **tourist office** ⓘ *in the Prefectura building at Joaquín de Sierra y La Paz, ground floor, T462 1305, ext 116*, is helpful.

About 5 km from town is the Laguna Suárez, with plenty of wildlife; swimming is safe where the locals swim, near the café with the jetty (elsewhere there are stingrays and alligators). Motorbike taxi from Trinidad, US$1.30.

San Ignacio de Moxos → *Electricity is supplied in town from 1200-2400.*

San Ignacio de Moxos, 90 km west of Trinidad, is known as the folklore capital of the Beni Department. It's a quiet town with a mainly indigenous population; 60% are *Macheteros*, who speak their own language. San Ignacio still maintains the traditions of the Jesuit missions with big *fiestas*, especially during Holy Week and the **Fiesta del Santo Patrono de Moxos**, the largest festival in the lowlands, at the end of July.

Magdalena and Bella Vista

Magdalena, northeast of Trinidad, stands on the banks of the Río Itonama. There is an abundance of wildlife and birds in the surrounding area. The city's main festival, Santa María Magdalena, is on 22 July attracting many visitors from all over. There is a Prodem office (N García entre 6 de Agosto y 18 de Noviembre, changes US$ cash). East of Magdalena, **Bella Vista** on the Río Blanco is considered by many to be one of the prettiest spots in northeast Bolivia. Lovely white sandbanks line the Río San Martín, 10 minutes' paddling by canoe from the boat moorings below town (boatmen will take you, returning later by arrangement; also accessible by motorcycle). Check that the sand is not covered by water after heavy rain. Other activities are swimming in the Río San Martín, canoeing, good country for cycling. Three well-stocked shops on plaza, but none sells mosquito repellent or spray/coils (bring your own, especially at the beginning of the wet season). There is no bank or phone office.

Cochabamba to Trinidad listings

For Sleeping and Eating price codes and other relevant information, see Essentials, pages 38-40.

Sleeping

Trinidad *p364*

C Don Bernardo, 18 de Noviembre 351 y Vaca Diez, T462 2534. A/c, with breakfast, pool.

D Gran Moxos, Av 6 de Agosto y Santa Cruz, T462 8777. Includes breakfast, a/c (**F** without), frigobar, cable TV, phone, good restaurant.

D Monteverde, 6 de Agosto 76, T462 2738. With a/c (**F** without), frigobar, includes breakfast, owner speaks English. Recommended.

D Copacabana, Tomás Villavicencio, 3 blocks from plaza, T462 2811. Good value, some beds uncomfortable, **F** without bath, helpful staff.

E Paulista, Av 6 de Agosto 36, T462 0018. **F** without bath, comfortable.

G Res 18 de Noviembre, Av 6 de Agosto 135. With bath, clean and welcoming, laundry facilities.

San Ignacio de Moxos *p364*

There are some *alojamientos* (**F**) on and around the main plaza.

Magdalena *p364*

C Internacional, near airport, T03-886 2210. With breakfast, pools and gardens, beautiful setting. Also basic hotels (**G**).

Bella Vista *p364*

G Hotel Pescador, owner Guillermo Esero Gómez very helpful and knowledgeable about the area, shared bath, provides meals for guests, offers excursions.

Eating

Trinidad *p364*

TT Club Social 18 de Noviembre, N Suárez y Vaca Díez on plaza. Good lunch for US$1.35, lively, popular with locals.

TT Pescadería El Moro, Bolívar 707 y 25 de Diciembre. Excellent fish. Also several good fish restaurants in Barrio Pompeya, south of plaza across river.

T La Casona, Plaza Ballivián. Good pizzas and set lunch, closed Tue.

T La Estancia, Barrio Pompeya, on Ibare entre Muibe y Velarde. Excellent steaks.

Heladería Oriental, on plaza. Good coffee, ice-cream, cakes, popular with locals.

Activities and tours

Trinidad *p364*

Most agents offer excursions to local *estancias* and jungle tours down river to **Amazonia**. Most *estancias* can also be reached independently in 1 hr by hiring a motorbike.

Amazonia Holiday, 6 de Agosto 680, T462 5732, F462 2806. Good service.

Fremen, Cipriano Berace 332, T462 2276, www.frementours.com. Run speed boat trips along the **Mamoré** and **Ibare** rivers and to **Parque Nacional Isiboro Sécure**; their *Flotel Reina de Enin* offers tours at US$349 pp for 4 days/3 nights, good food.

Moxos, 6 de Agosto 114, T462 1141. Multi-day river and jungle tours with camping. Recommended.

Tarope Tours, 6 de Agosto 81, T/F462 1468. For flights.

Transport

Villa Tunari to the Lowlands: Puerto Villarroel *p364*

From Cochabamba you can get a bus to **Puerto Villarroel** (see Cochabamba Transport, Bus), **Puerto San Francisco**, or **Todos Santos** on the Río Chapare.

Trinidad *p364*

Air Daily flights with **Aerocon** (Vaca Díez 26, T462 4442) and **TAM** (Bolívar 42, T462 2363) to La Paz, Santa Cruz, Cochabamba, Cobija, Riberalta and Guayaramerín. **Amaszonas** (18 de Noviembre 267, T462 2426) 2 a week to **Rurrenabaque**. Airport, T462 0678. Mototaxi to airport US$1.20.

Bus Bus station is on Rómulo Mendoza, between Beni and Pinto, 9 blocks east of main plaza. Motorbike taxis will take people with backpacks from bus station to centre for US$0.45. To **Santa Cruz** (10 hrs on a paved road, US$8-18) and **Cochabamba** (US$12-17, 20 hrs), with **Copacabana**, **Mopar** and **Bolívar** mostly overnight (*bus cama* available). To **Rurrenabaque**, US$18, 12-20 hrs. Enquire locally what services are running to San Borja and **La Paz**. Similarly to **Riberalta** and **Guayaramerín**.

River Cargo boats down the Río Mamoré to **Guayaramerín** take passengers, 3-4 days, assuming no breakdowns, best organized from Puerto Varador (speak to the Port Captain). **Argos** is recommended as friendly, US$22 pp, take water, fresh fruit, toilet paper and ear-plugs; only for the hardy traveller.

San Ignacio de Moxos *p364*

Bus The Trinidad to San Borja bus stops at the *Donchanta* restaurant for lunch, otherwise difficult to find transport to San Borja. Minibus to Trinidad daily at 0730 from plaza, also *camionetas*, check road conditions and times beforehand.

Magdalena *p364*

Road An unpaved road goes to Trinidad via San Ramón (pick-up US$10.50), passable only in the dry season. San Ramón to Magdalena takes 6 hrs on motorbike taxi, US$16.

Bella Vista *p364*

Bus There are daily buses from **Magdalena** (except in the rainy season), 2½ hrs, US$2.

Directory

Trinidad *p364*

Banks **Prodem**, Vaca Diez 31 y N Suárez, and Mercantil Santa Cruz, Joaquín de Sierra, near the plaza, both change US$ cash. Street changers on 6 de Agosto (US dollars only). **Post offices and telephones** Open daily till 1930 in same building at Av Barace, just off plaza.

Santa Cruz and Eastern Lowlands

In contrast to the highlands of the Andes and the gorges of the Yungas, eastern Bolivia is made up of vast plains stretching to the Chaco of Paraguay and the Pantanal wetlands of Brazil. Agriculture is well-developed and other natural resources are fully exploited, bringing prosperity to the region. There are a number of national parks with great biodiversity, such as Amboró and Noel Kempff Mercado. Historical interest lies in the pre-Inca ceremonial site at Samaipata, the beautiful Chiquitano Jesuit missions and, of much more recent date, the trails and villages where Che Guevara made his final attempt to bring revolution to Bolivia.

Santa Cruz → *Phone code: 03. Colour map 6, A4. Population: 1,566,000. Altitude: 416 m.*

A little over 50 years ago, what is now Bolivia's largest city was a remote backwater, but rail and road links ended its isolation. The exploitation of oil and gas in the Department of Santa Cruz and a burgeoning agribusiness sector have helped fuel the city's rapid development. Currently spearheading the eastern lowland departments' drive for greater autonomy from La Paz, Santa Cruz is far removed from most travellers' perceptions of Bolivia. The city centre still retains much of its colonial air and during the lunchtime hiatus when the locals (who like to call themselves *cambas*) take refuge from the overwhelming heat or pouring rain, it can almost seem like its original self.

Ins and outs

Getting there The international **airport** is at **Viru-Viru**, 13 km from the centre, taxi US$7, micro from Ex-Terminal (see Transport, below), or El Trompillo, US$0.70, 45 min. From airport take bus to bus terminal then taxi to centre. Regional flights operate from **El Trompillo** airport, south of the centre on the Segundo Anillo, taxi US$1.10, many micros. Long distance and local **buses** leave from the combined bus/train terminal, **Terminal Bimodal**, Avenida Montes on the Tercer Anillo, southeastern edge of the city, T348 8382. No 12 bus to/from the centre, taxi US$1.50. The city has ten ring roads, Anillos 1, 2, 3, 4 and so on. Equipetrol suburb, where many hotels and bars are situated, is northwest of the heart of the city between Anillos 2 and 3.

Tourist office In the **Prefectura** ⓘ *Junín 22 on main plaza, T334 6776, Mon-Fri 0800-1230, 1430-1800*; also desk at Viru-Viru airport, 0700-2000. The **Organización y Gestión del Destino Turístico Santa Cruz** (www.destinosantacruz.com), publishes a tourist guide (English/Spanish) entitled *Destino Turístico Santa Cruz – Bolivia* (US$10, available at most bookstores); also *Santa*

Santa Cruz

Sleeping
1 Bibosi *B1*
2 Copacabana *B1*
3 Cortez *A2*
4 Hostal Reina María *D1*
5 Hostal Río Magdalena *B3*
6 Jodanga *D3*
7 Las Américas *B2*
8 Milán *B2*
9 Res 26 de Enero *C1*
10 Res Bolívar *B2*
11 Res Cañada *D1*
12 Res Sands *B3*
13 Viru-Viru *B1*

Eating
1 Café 24, Café Lorca & Tía Lía *B2*
2 Capri *D1*
3 Fridolín *B2*
4 Fru Gelatto *B1*
5 Ken *B3*
6 La Casona *B2*
7 La Creperie *B2*
8 Los Lomitos *B3*
9 Michelangelo *D2*
10 Pizzería Marguerita *B2*
11 Rincón Brasil *B2*
12 Su Salud *B3*
13 Tapekuá *C2*
14 Vegetarian Center *B3*

Bars & clubs
15 Irlandés *B2*

Cruz y Sus Provincias, a wonderful, free little guide. APAC (see Festivals and events, below) publishes *Santa Cruz Turístico*, US$5, which covers the city and the Jesuit missions, and is very knowledgeable about the region.

Sights

The Plaza 24 de Septiembre is the city's main square with the huge **Cathedral** (now also a basilica after the late Pope John Paul II's visit) ⓘ *museum Tue, Thu, Sun 1000-1200, 1600-1800, US$1.50* and the Palacio Prefectural set around it. You can climb to a mirador in the cathedral bell tower ⓘ *Tue, Thu, Sat, Sun 1000-1200, 1600-1900, US$0.50*, nice views of the city. **Manzana Uno**, the block behind the Cathedral, has been set aside for rotating art and cultural exhibits. The heart of the city, with its arcaded streets and buildings with low, red-tiled roofs and overhanging eaves, retains a colonial feel, despite the profusion of modern, air-conditioned shops and restaurants. **Museo Histórico** ⓘ *Junín entre Libertad y 21 de Mayo, T336 5533, Mon-Fri 0800-1200, 1500-1830, free* has several displays including explorers' routes and handicrafts. Its small shop is run by La Mancomunidad and sells items made by indigenous people from sustainable sources. All proceeds are returned to the carvers, jewellers and weavers. **Museo de Historia Natural de Noel Kempff Mercado** ⓘ *Av Irala 565 entre Velasco e Independencia, T/F337 1216, www.museonoelkempff.org, Mon-Fri 0800-1200, also Mon-Tue 1500-1830, US$0.15.* It has a video library. Contact this museum for trips and information to Parque Nacional Noel Kempff Mercado (see page 381). Some 12 km on the road to Cotoca are the **Botanical Gardens** ⓘ *www.gmsantacruz.gov.bo/botanico, micro or colectivo from C Suárez Arana, 15 minutes.* **Las Lomas de Arena del Palmar** ⓘ *18 km south of the city, off the road to Palmasola, taxi (4WD required in wet season), US$30 return with 2 hours wait, hitching possible at weekends* are huge sand dunes with small lagoons for swimming (best in further lagoons which are cleaner).

Santa Cruz listings

For Sleeping and Eating price codes and other relevant information, see Essentials, pages 38-40.

Sleeping

Santa Cruz *p366, map p367*

AL Los Tajibos, Av San Martín 455, Barrio Equipetrol, T342 1000, www.lostajiboshotel.com. Set in 6 ha of lush gardens, a traditional setting for many high-end social events, luxury hotel with business centre, art gallery, restaurants, spa, etc.

A Cortez, Cristóbal de Mendoza 280 (Segundo Anillo), T333 1234, www.hotelcortez.com. Traditional tropical hotel with a/c, restaurant, pool, gardens, meeting rooms, Wi-Fi, parking, good location for dining and nightlife.

B-C Las Américas, 21 de Mayo y Seoane, T336 8778, www.lasamericas-hotel.com.bo. A/c, buffet breakfast, Wi-Fi, discount for longer stay, parking, arranges tours and car rental, restaurant, bar.

C Copacabana, Junín 217, T332 1843, hotelcopacabanascz@hotmail.com. TV, laundry service, includes breakfast, restaurant, very good, popular with European tour groups.

C Viru-Viru Junín 338, T333 5298. Includes breakfast, a/c, cheaper with fan, central.

D Bibosi, Junín 218, T334 8548, htlbibosi@hotmail.com. Cheaper with shared bath, breakfast included, fan, internet. Recommended.

D Hostal Reina María, Mons Salvatierra 466, T339 5464, www.hostalreinamaria.com. Includes breakfast, a/c and frigobar, cheaper with fan. Older house with balconies, quiet neighbourhood.

D Jodanga, C El Fuerte 1380, Zona Parque Urbano, Barrio Los Chóferes, T339 6542, www.jodanga.com. Good backpacker option 10 mins' walk from Terminal Bimodal, a/c, cheaper with fan and without bath, kitchen, bar, swimming pool, billiards, DVDs, nice communal areas, internet, laundry, helpful owner and multilingual staff.

D Milán, René Moreno 70, T339 7500. Includes breakfast, hot water, rooms small but well furnished, central location.

E Hostal Río Magdalena, Arenales 653 (no sign), T339 3011, www.hostalriomagdalena.com. Comfortable rooms, electric shower, fan, small yard and pool, good value, popular. Recommended.
E Res 26 de Enero, Camiri 32, T332 1818. **F** without bath, very clean.
E Res Bolívar, Sucre 131, T334 2500. Hot showers, some rooms with bath (**D**), others very small, lovely courtyard with hammocks, alcohol prohibited, includes good breakfast, popular. Recommended.
E Res Sands, Arenales 749, T337 7776. Most rooms with private bath (cheaper in dorm), fan, good beds, very clean, good value.
F Res Cañada, Cañada 145, near the ex-Terminal, T334 5541. **G** without bath, electric shower, fan, parking for small car, good value even though not the best location.

Eating

Santa Cruz *p366, map p367*

Santa Cruz has the best meat in Bolivia, try a local *churrasquería* (grill). Barrio Equipetrol and Av Monseñor Rivero, also known as 'El Boulevard', are the areas for the poshest restaurants and nightlife. Both are away from the centre, take a taxi. Most restaurants close Mon. The bakeries on Junín and España sell local specialities.

₸₸₸-₸₸ La Creperie, Arenales 135. Mon-Sat 1900-2400, serves good crêpes, fondues and salads.
₸₸₸-₸₸ Michelangelo, Chuquisaca 502. Excellent Italian. Mon-Fri 1200-1400, 1900-2330, Sat evenings only.
₸₸ Capri, Irala 634. "The best pizzas in town".
₸₸ La Casona, Arenales 222, T337 8495. German-run restaurant, very good food, open 1130-1500, 1900-2400.
₸₸ Pizzería Marguerita, Junín y Libertad, northwest corner of the plaza. A/c, good service, coffee, bar, also recommended, 0830-2400. Finnish owner, speaks English and German.
₸₸ Tapekuá, Ballivián y La Paz, T334 5905. French and international food, good service, live entertainment some evenings.
₸₸-₸ Ken, Uruguay 730 (1er Anillo), T333 3728, 1130-1430, 1800-2300, closed Wed. Sushi and authentic Japanese food, popular.
₸₸-₸ Los Lomitos, Uruquay 758 (1er Anillo), T332 8696. Typical *churrasquería* with local atmosphere, good meat.
₸ Rincón Brasil, Libertad 358. Brazilian-style *por kilo* place, popular, open every day 1130-1500, also (à la carte only) Tue-Sat from 1800.
₸ Su Salud, Quijarro 115. Tasty vegetarian food, filling lunches, huge portions, Sun-Fri 0800-1200. Recommended.
₸ Tía Lía, René Moreno 30. All you can eat lunch buffet with *parrillada* and salad bar, prices rise a bit at weekends, daily 1130-1500.
₸ Vegetarian Center, Aroma 64, entre Bolívar y Sucre, Mon-Sat 1200-1700. Vegetarian lunch buffet, pay by weight.

Cafés

There are lots of very pleasant a/c cafés and ice cream parlours, where you can get coffee, ice cream, drinks, snacks and reasonably priced meals.
Alexander Coffee, Junín y Libertad on the main plaza and Av Monseñor Rivero 400 in Zona El Cristo. For good coffee and people watching.
Café 24, downstairs at René Moreno y Sucre, on the main plaza, daily 0830-0200. Breakfast, juices, international meals, wine rack, nice atmosphere, Wi-Fi.
Café Lorca, upstairs at René Moreno y Sucre, on the main plaza, Mon-Sat 0900-0200, Sun 1830-0200. Meals and drinks, Spanish wines, small balcony with views over plaza, live music Tue-Sat from 2100, part of a cultural project, see www.lorcasantacruz.org.
Fridolin, 21 de Mayo 168, Pari 254, Av Cañoto y Florida and on Monseñor Rivero. Four good places for coffee and pastries.
Fru Gelatto, Ayacucho y Santa Bárbara, also on Monseñor Rivero, daily 0800-2300. Good Italian-style ice cream.

Bars and clubs

Santa Cruz *p366, map p367*

Bar Irlandés Irish Pub, 3er Anillo Interno 1216 (between Av Cristo Redentor and Zoológico), T343 0671. Irish-themed pub, food available, English-speaking owner. Also *Café Irlandés*, Plaza 24 de Septiembre, Edificio Shopping Bolívar No 157 overlooking main plaza, T333 8118, live music Wed and Sat evening. Recommended.
Kokopelli, Noel Kempff Mercado 1202 (3er Anillo Interno), bar with Mexican food and live music.

Festivals and events

Santa Cruz *p366, map p367*
Cruceños are famous as fun-lovers and their music, the *carnavalitos*, can be heard all over South America. Of the various festivals, the brightest is **Carnival**, renowned for riotous behaviour, celebrated for the **15 days before Lent**: music in the streets, dancing, fancy dress and the coronation of a queen. Beware the following day when youths run wild with buckets and balloons filled with water – no one is exempt. **24 Sep** is a holiday.

The **Festival de Música Renacentista y Barroca Americana** is held in **April** every 2 years (next in 2012) in Santa Cruz and the Jesuit mission towns of the Chiquitanía (San Javier, Concepción, among other places). It is organized by **Asociación Pro Arte y Cultura** (APAC), Beni 228, Santa Cruz, T333 2287, www.festivalesapac.com, and celebrates the wealth of sacred music written by Europeans and indigenous composers in the 17th and 18th centuries. APAC sells books, CDs, and videos of these extravaganzas and also offers – in both Santa Cruz and the mission towns – a schedule of continuous musical programmes. The festival is very popular: book hotels at least 2-3 weeks in advance. Every odd year in same locales **APAC** holds a **Festival Internacional de Teatro**, and every Aug a **Festival de la Temporada** featuring *musica misional* with local performers.

Shopping

Santa Cruz *p366, map p367*
Bookshops **Librería El Ateneo**, Independencia 365 y Mercado, T333 3338. Books in English, access to internet. **Los Amigos del Libro**, Igavi 14, T332 7937, sells foreign language books and magazines.
Handicrafts **Artebarro**, Mons Salvatierra 395, T339 0132. For ceramics. **Bolivian Souvenirs**, Shopping Bolívar, loc 10 & 11, on main plaza, T333 7805; also at Viru-Viru airport. Knitwear and crafts from all over Bolivia. See **Museo de Historia** above, for best local crafts from *La Mancomunidad*. **Paseo Artesanal Las Recova**, off Libertad, ½ block from Plaza. Many different kiosks selling crafts. **Vicuñita Handicrafts**, Ingavi e Independencia, T333 4711. Wide variety of crafts from the lowlands and the altiplano, very good.
Jewellery Carrasco, Velasco 23, T336 2841, and other branches, www.carrascojoyeros.com. For gemstones. **RC Joyas**, Bolívar 262, T333 2725. Jewellery and Bolivian gems, the manager produces and sells good maps of Santa Cruz City and department.
Markets There are many. **Bazar Siete Calles**, mainly for clothing, but food and fruit is sold outside. **Los Pozos**, Quijarro, Campero, Suárez Arana and 6 de Agosto. Open daily; in summer it's full of exotic fruits. Beware of bag-snatching. The small **Mercado Nuevo** (not new at all), for fruit and vegetables, is at Sucre y Cochabamba. **Abasto**, 3er Anillo y Av. Piraí, is the wholesale produce market, huge, frantic and colourful.

Activities and tours

Santa Cruz *p366, map p367*
The most popular tours out of Santa Cruz include: Chiquitania, 2 days/1 night, US$140; Parque Nacional Amboró, 3 days/2 nights, US$120; Parque Nacional Noel Kempff Mercado, US$430-1,100. Prices vary with group size.
Bird Bolivia, T358 2674, www.birdbolivia.com. Specializes in birding tours.
Fremen, Beni 79 y Bolívar, T333 8535, www.frementours.com. Offers tours throughout the country, including their own facilities at Villa Tunari and on the *Reina de Enín* riverboat.
Forest Tour Operator, Cuéllar 22 entre 24 de Septiembre y Libertad, T337 2042, www.forestbolivia.com. Environmentally sensitive tours to most national parks, Beni and Chiquitania. Works with local indigenous groups.
Magri Turismo, Warnes y Potosí, T334 5663, www.magriturismo.com. American Express agent, airline tickets and tours. Recommended.
Rosario Tours, Arenales 193, T336 9977, www.rosariotours.com. Highly regarded, with English-speaking staff, tours throughout Bolivia.
Ruta Verde, 21 de Mayo 318, T339 6470, www.rutaverdebolivia.com. Dutch/Bolivian owned operator running tours to national parks (Amboró, Noel Kempff Mercado), Jesuit missions, Amazonian boat trips, Pantanal tours and tailor-made tours in Bolivia; well-organized, uses local guides, English and German spoken, good value.

Transport

Santa Cruz *p366, map p367*

Air Viru-Viru, 13 km from the centre, is Bolivia's largest and most modern international airport, T181 or T383 5000 ext 272. The airport is open 24 hrs; *casa de cambio* changing cash US$ and euros at poor rates, 0630-2100; various ATMs; luggage lockers 0600-2200, US$5.50 for 24 hrs; ENTEL for phones and expensive internet, plus the usual fast food eateries. Domestic flights with **Aero Sur, Boliviana de Aviación (BoA)** and **TAM** (Bolivia), to **La Paz**, **Cochabamba**, **Sucre**, **Tarija** and **Puerto Suárez**. International flights to **Asunción**, **Buenos Aires**, **Salta**, **Tucumán**, **Lima**, **Madrid**, **Miami**, **Santiago** and **São Paulo**.

El Trompillo is the regional airport operating daily 0500-1900, T352 6600, located south of the centre on the Segundo Anillo. It has a phone office and kiosk selling drinks, but no other services. **Aero Sur** operates one daily flight from here to **Cochabamba**, continuing to either **La Paz, Sucre** or **Tarija**, and avoiding the ride out to Viru-Viru. **TAM** has flights throughout the country, different destinations on different days. **Aerocon** flies to **Trinidad** and other towns in the northern jungle.

Bus Most buses depart in the evening and travel overnight. Smaller local buses and mini-vans leave either from behind the Terminal Bimodal or from near the Ex-Terminal (the old bus station, Av Irala y Av Cañoto, which is no longer functioning). Daily buses to **Cochabamba** (US$7.50-15, 10 hrs), many *flotas* leave between 0600-0930 and 1630-2130. Direct to **Sucre** daily around 1600, 14 hrs, US$8.50-15. **Oruro** and **La Paz** 17 hrs, US$15-18, between 1630-1900 (*bus cama* US$25); change in Cochabamba for daytime travel. To **Camiri** (US$3.50, 4 hrs), **Yacuiba** (US$8-15, 8 hrs) and **Tarija**, daily, several companies; 26-32 hrs to Tarija, from US$14. To **Trinidad**, several daily after 2000, 12 hrs, US$8-18. **International**: to **Asunción** with **Yacyretá**, T362 5557, Mon, Tue, Thu, Sat, at 2000, US$55, 21 hrs via Villamontes and the Chaco. **Stel Turismo**, T349 7762, runs the same route 2000 daily; also **Pycazú** twice a week. Other companies are less reliable. See page 375 for the route to Paraguay across the Chaco. To **Buenos Aires** daily departures around 1900, US$70-90, 36 hrs, several companies.

Taxi About US$1.50 inside 1st Anillo (more at night), US$2 inside 3rd Anillo, fix fare in advance.

Train Ferroviaria Oriental, T338 7300, www.ferroviariaoriental.com. To **Quijarro** (for Brazil), see page 382, and **Yacuiba** (for Argentina), see page 375.

Directory

Santa Cruz *p366, map p367*

Airline offices **Aerolíneas Argentinas**, Edif Banco de la Nación Argentina, on main Plaza, T333 9776. **Aerocon**, Aeropuerto El Trompillo, T352 1200. **Aero Sur**, Irala 616, T336 7400, and 24 de Septiembre 46 on main plaza, T335 8413. **American Airlines**, Beni 167, T334 1314. **BoA**, Prolongación Aroma 20, Edificio Casanova, T312 1343. **GOL**, T800-100121 or 385 2200, www.voegol.com. **TAM** (Mercosur), Velasco 700 y La Riva, T337 1999, www.tam.com.br. **TAM** (Militar), El Trompillo airport, T352 9669. .

Banks ATMs in airport departure lounge and throughout the city. **Banco Unión**, Libertad 156 y Florida. **Bisa**, Beni entre Junín y Ayacucho. Two reliable *cambios* on 24 de Septiembre, on the main plaza, are **Cambio Alemán**, T332 4114; and **Casa de Cambio España**, T339 2515; both open Mon-Fri 0830-1200, 1430-1800, Sat 0900-1200, good rates for US$ cash, euros, and regional currencies, 2.5-3% commission for TCs. Many other *casas de cambio* on Libertad bewteen Junín and Florida. Street money changers on Plaza 24 de Septiembre and around bus terminal exchange guaraníes.

Car hire **Avis**, Av Cristo Redentor Km. 3.5, T343 3939, www.avis.com.bo. **Barron's**, Av Alemana 50 y Tajibos, T342 0160. Outstanding service and completely trustworthy; clean vehicles, fully equipped. **IMBEX**, C El Carmen 123, between Av Suarez Arana and Av Charcas, T311 1000, www.imbex.com. **Localiza**, Cristo Redentor entre 2do y 3er Anillo, T341 4343, www.localiza.com.

Cultural centres See **Asociación Pro Arte y Cultura** under Festivals and events, above. **Centro Boliviano Americano**, Cochabamba 66, T334 2299, www.cba.com.bo. Library with US papers and magazines, English classes, some cultural events. **Centro Cultural Franco Alemán**, 24 de Septiembre on main plaza, T335 0142, www.ccfranco aleman.org. Joint cultural institute with language courses, cultural events, library (internet access), both open Mon-Fri 0900-1200, 1530-2000. **Centro de Formación de la Cooperación Española**, Arenales 583, T335 1311, www.aecid-cf.bo (concerts, films, art exhibitions, lectures, etc), very good. **Centro Simón I Patiño**, Independencia y Suárez de Figueroa 89, T 337 2425, www.fundacionpatino.org. Exhibitions, galleries, and bookstore on Bolivian cultures. **Embassies and consulates** **Argentina**, in Edif Banco de la Nación Argentina, Plaza 24 de Septiembre, Junín 22, T334 7133, consarscruz@its.com.bo, Mon-Fri 0800-1430. **Brazil**, Av Busch 330, T333 7368, vcbrasilpsuarez@cotas.com.bo, Mon-Fri 0900-1500. It takes 24 hrs to process visa applications, reported as unhelpful. **Germany**, Libertad y Cañada Strongest, Plaza Libertad loc 201, T345 3914, mibi@cotas.com.bo, Mon-Fri 0900-1200, 1400-1700. **Israel**, Av Banzer 171, T342 4777. **Netherlands**, C Ayacucho 284, T314 0806, Mon-Fri 0900-1230. **Paraguay**, Manuel Ignacio Salvatierra 99, Edif Victoria, of 1A, T336 6113, consulpy@its.com.bo. Colour photo required for visa, Mon-Fri 0730-1400. **USA**, Av Roque Aguilera 146, 3ra Anillo, T351 3477, Mon 0900-1230, 1400-1700, Tue-Fri 0900-1230 (very limited services offered; best to go to La Paz). **Internet** Cybercafés everywhere, US$0.40 per hr. **Medical services** For hospitals, doctors and dentists, contact your consulate or the tourist office for advice. **Post office** C Junín 146. **Useful addresses** **Immigration**: Segundo Anillo y Av San Aurelio, T351 9574, Mon-Fri 0830-1200, 1430-1800, service can be very slow.

Southeastern Bolivia

The highlights of this area are southwest of Santa Cruz: the pre-Inca ruins of Samaipata, the nearby Parque Nacional Amboró and the Che Guevara Trail, on which you can follow in the final, fatal footsteps of the revolutionary.

Samaipata → *Phone code: 03. Colour map M6, A4. Altitude: 1,650 m.*

From Santa Cruz the spectacular old mountain road to Cochabamba runs along the Piray gorge and up into the highlands. Some 120 km from Santa Cruz is Samaipata, a great place to relax midweek, with good lodging, restaurants, hikes and riding, and a helpful ex-pat community. Local *artesanías* include ceramics. At weekends the town bursts into life as crowds of Cruceños come to escape the city heat and to party. See www.samaipata.info and www.guidetosamaipata.com.

The **Centro de Investigaciones Arqueológicas y Antropológicas Samaipata** has a collection of pots and vases with anthropomorphic designs, dating from 200 BC to AD 300 and, most importantly, provides information on the nearby pre-Inca ceremonial site commonly called **El Fuerte** ⓘ *daily 0900-1700, Centro 0930-1230, 1430-1830; US$7 for El Fuerte and Centro de Investigaciones, ticket valid 4 days. Guides available at El Fuerte, US$8.* This sacred structure (1,990 m) consists of a complex system of channels, basins, high-relief sculptures, etc, carved out of one vast slab of rock. Latest research on dates is conflicting. Some suggests that Amazonian people created it around 1500 BC, but it could be later. There is evidence of subsequent occupations and that it was the eastern outpost of the Incas' Kollasuyo (their Bolivian Empire). Behind the rock are poorly excavated remains of a city. It is no longer permitted to walk on the rock, so visit the museum first to see the excellent model. El Fuerte is 9 km from Samaipata; 3 km along the highway, then 6 km up a rough, signposted road (taxi US$4.50 one way, US$10 return with 2 hours wait); two to three hours' walk one way. Pleasant bathing is possible in a river on the way to El Fuerte.

In addition to tours to El Fuerte, Amboró and the Ruta del Che (see below), many other tours are offered in the Samaipata area. These include **Cuevas**, 20 km east of town, with waterfalls and pools; the beautiful **Serranía Volcanes** region (with upmarket **Laguna Volcán Gold Eco-Resort** due to open in 2010, www.lagunavolcan.com, and the **Eco-albergue Volcanes** community tourism project), further east; forest and sandstone mountains at **Bella Vista/Codo de los Andes**; the 25-m high **La Pajcha** waterfall (40 km south), which can be combined with

Postrervalle (20 km further south), which has many interesting walks and mountain bike trails. Tour operators arrange trips, often with guides who specialize in wildlife-watching.

Vallegrande and La Higuera

Some 115 km south of the Santa Cruz-Cochabamba road is La Higuera, where Che Guevara was killed. On 8 October each year, people gather there to celebrate his memory. La Higuera is reached through the colonial town of **Vallegrande** where, at **Hospital Nuestro Señor de Malta** ⓘ *no fee, but voluntary donation to the health station*, you can see the old laundry building where Che's body was shown to the international press on 9 October 1967. Near Vallegrande's air strip you can see the results of excavations carried out in 1997 which finally unearthed his physical remains (now in Cuba), ask an airport attendant to see the site. Vallegrande has a small archaeological museum *US$1.50*, above which is the **Che Guevara Room** *free*.

The schoolhouse in La Higuera (60 km south of Vallegrande) where Che was executed is now a museum. Another **museum** (T03-942 2003), owned by René Villegas, is open when he is in town. Guides, including Pedro Calzadillo, headmaster of the school, will show visitors to the ravine of El Churo (or Yuro), where Che was captured on 8 October 1967. In 2004 the **Ruta del Che** (Che Guevara Trail) was initiated, following the route of Che and his band as they fled the Bolivian army. It takes three to six days, depending on how much you do and how you travel. The trail, which is not yet fully integrated, is run by the Bolivian government, CARE International and local communities. Tour operators offer packages.

Samaipata

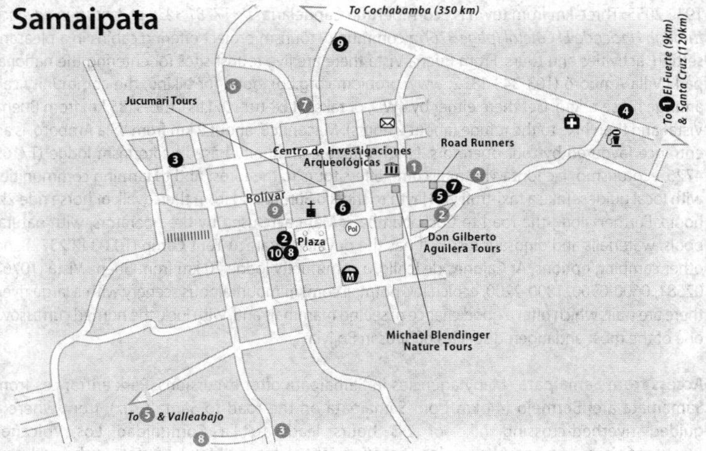

Sleeping
1 Alojamiento Vargas
2 Andoriña
3 Cabañas de Traudi
4 Don Jorge
5 El Pueblito Resort
6 Landhaus
7 La Posada del Sol
8 La Víspera
9 Res Kim & Paola

Eating
1 Café Baden
2 Chakana
3 El Descanso en Las Alturas
4 El Turista
5 La Oveja Negra
6 La Ranita
7 Latina Café
8 Media Vuelta
9 Panadería Gerlinde
10 Tierra Libre

Parque Nacional Amboró

This vast (442,500 ha) protected area lies only three hours west of Santa Cruz. Amboró encompasses four distinct major ecosystems and 11 life zones and is home to thousands of animal, plant and insect species (it is reputed to contain more butterflies than anywhere else on earth). The park is home to over 850 species of birds, including the blue-horned curassow, the very rare quetzal and cock-of-the-rock, red and chestnut-fronted macaws, hoatzin and cuvier toucans, and most mammals native to Amazonia, such as capybaras, peccaries, tapirs, several species of monkey, and jungle cats like the jaguar, ocelot and margay, and the increasingly rare spectacled bear. There are also numerous waterfalls and cool, green swimming pools, moss-ridden caves and large tracts of virgin rainforest. The park itself is largely inaccessible and much wading is required to get around, but there is good trekking in the surrounding 195,100-ha buffer zone which is where most tours operate. The best time of year to visit the park is during April to October. There are two places to base yourself: Samaipata (see also page 372) and Buena Vista. You cannot enter the park without a guide, either from a tour operator who organizes everything, or from a community-based project. The park is administered by **SERNAP**. The park's main office is in Santa Cruz ⓘ *Calle 9 Oeste 138, frente a la Plaza Italia, Barrio Equipetrol, T339 4310, Mon-Fri 0800-1200, 1400-1800*. There are subsidiary offices in Samaipata and Buena Vista. Note that there are many biting insects so take repellent, long-sleeved shirts, long trousers and good boots.

Access from Buena Vista Northwest of Santa Cruz by paved road is the sleepy town of Buena Vista (no ATM, but US$ cash can be changed). There is an interpretation office one block from the plaza, T932 2055. Three km from town is **Eco-Albergue Candelaria** ⓘ *T7781 3238 or contact in advance through Hacienda El Cafetal (page 376)*, a community tourism project offering cabins in a pleasant setting, activities and tours. From Buena Vista there are five tourist sites for entering the national park: **Villa Amboró** (T03-343 1332, www.probioma.org.bo), good for hiking; the community can arrange horse riding. Get there either by 4WD, or take a taxi-trufi to Las Cruces (35 km from Buena Vista) and then hike to the refuge (about 2 hours). **Macuñucu**, about 2 km from Villa Amboró, is an entrance favoured by tour operators. **La Chonta**, a community-based ecotourism lodge (T7169 4726, ecoturismo_lachonta@hotmail.com), offers tours to the forest and to farming communities with local guides. Take a taxi-trufi via Haytú to the Río Surutú and from there walk or horse ride 2½ hours. Further along the road to Cochabamba is **Mataracú**, used by the operators, with natural pools, waterfalls and dinosaur fossils. It has the private **Mataracú Tent Camp** (T03-342 2372) and other camping options. At **Cajones de Ichilo**, a community lodge 70 km from Buena Vista (T0763 02581, 0600-0900, 1800-2200, ecoichilo@hotmail.com) in mountainous scenery with a large river, there are trails which offer a good chance of seeing mammals and, with luck, the horned currassow, one of the most endangered species of birds in Bolivia.

Access from Samaipata Many agencies in Samaipata offer excursions. Park entrances from Samaipata are: **Bermejo** (44 km from Samaipata on the road to Santa Cruz), from where a guided riverbed-crossing hike of 2-3 hours leads to **La Comunidad Los Volcanes** (www.probioma.org.bo). **Abra de los Toros/Barrientos**, for the highest points in the park and the unexcavated Inca fortress Pucará; enter via Achira and Barrientos, which are 15 km away and reached by jeep, guide **Don Gilberto** (see Activities and tours, below). **Las Lauras**, steep hiking with giant ferns (contact **Road Runners** – see Activities and tours, below). A popular route in is via **La Yunga** (apart from the giant ferns not all that spectacular after deforestation in the 1960s, basic community-run cabins, www.fan-bo.org/layunga, **E**): drive to **Mairana** (17 km, the meal stop for long distance buses between Santa Cruz and Sucre), then it's 13-15 km by jeep. Lastly, from **Mataral** where there is a guest hut. At Mataral there is a petrol station and restaurants and a good gravel road (about to be paved) running south of the main Santa Cruz-Cochabamba road 55 km to Vallegrande (minibus service; see above).

To Paraguay

South of Santa Cruz the road passes through Abapó and Camiri. A paved road heads south from Camiri, through Boyuibe, Villamontes and Yacuiba to Argentina (see below). At Boyuibe the old road to Paraguay heads east. It is practically abandoned now that a new road has been built from Villamontes to Mariscal Estigarribia in the Paraguayan Chaco (also see below). At Boyuibe buses stop at Parador-Restaurante Yacyretá, on main road, owners are helpful, have rooms to rent. Fuel and water are available.

Villamontes → *Phone code: 04. Colour map 6, B4.*

South of Boyuibe is Villamontes (280 km east of Tarija) renowned for fishing. It holds a Fiesta del Pescado in August. It is a friendly, spread-out city on the north shore of the Río Pilcomayo, where the Chaco starts, at the base of the Cordillera de Aguaragüe, the easternmost range. The river cuts through this range (Parque Nacional Aguaragüe) forming **El Angosto**, a beautiful gorge. The road to Tarija is cut in the cliffs along this gorge. At Plaza 6 de Agosto is the **Museo Héroes del Chaco** ⓘ *Tue-Sun 0800-1200, 1400-1800, US$0.30*, with photographs, maps, artefacts, and battle models of the 1932-1935 Chaco War. There is no ATM, but banks, **Prodem** and various *cambios* change US$ cash (**Cambios San Bernardo** also changes Argentine pesos and Guaraníes). They are all on Av Méndez Arcos. There are many internet cafes and *cabinas* for phone calls in the centre.

From Villamontes, the road to Paraguay runs east to **Ibibobo** (70 km). The first 30 km is paved; thereafter it's all-weather gravel and in good condition, even after rain. Further paving is in progress. Motorists and bus travellers should carry extra water and some food, as climatic conditions are harsh and there is little traffic in case of a breakdown. Bolivian exit stamps are given at Ibibobo. If travelling by bus, passports are collected by driver and returned on arrival at Mcal Estigarribia, Paraguay, with Bolivian exit stamp. Paraguayan immigration and thorough drugs searches take place in Mcal Estigarribia. See Santa Cruz, page 371, for international bus services, and see the Chaco section of the Paraguay chapter for road conditions, etc. From Ibibobo to the Bolivian frontier post at Picada Sucre is 75 km, then it's 15 km to the actual border and another 8 km to the Paraguayan frontier post at **Fortín Infante Rivarola**. There are customs posts, but no police, immigration nor any other services at the border.

To Argentina (Yacuiba) → *Colour map 6, B4. Population: 11,000.*

From Santa Cruz a fully paved road goes through Camiri, Boyuibe and Villamontes to Yacuiba, a prosperous city (reported less-than-safe) at the crossing to Pocitos in Argentina. There is also train service from Santa Cruz to Yacuiba but this is slow and poor, road travel is a better option. In Yacuiba, there are ATMs on Campero, **Entel** and Correos. Argentine consul at Comercio y Sucre. The border crossing is straightforward. Passengers leaving Bolivia must disembark at Yacuiba, take a taxi to Pocitos on the border (US$0.40, beware unscrupulous drivers) and walk across to Argentina.

Southeastern Bolivia listings

For Sleeping and Eating price codes and other relevant information, see Essentials, pages 38-40.

Sleeping

Samaipata *p372*

Rooms may be hard to find at weekends in high season. Most of the cabins listed have kitchen, bathroom, barbecue and hammocks.

C El Pueblito Resort, camino a Valle Abajo, 20 mins' walk from town, T944 6383, www.elpueblitoresort.com. Fully-equipped cabins and rooms, restaurant and bar set around a mock colonial plaza, with shops and meditation chapel.

C-E La Víspera, 1.2 km south of town, T944 6082, www.lavispera.org. Dutch-owned organic farm with accommodation in 4 cosy cabins sleeping 3-12, camping US$4-5, delicious local produce for breakfast, in **Slow-Food Garden Café**. Very peaceful; Margarita and Pieter know pretty much everything about the local area and can arrange all excursions. They also sell medicinal and seasoning herbs, spices and maps; book exchange and horses. Highly recommended.

D-E Cabañas de Traudi, across the road from *La Víspera*, T944 6094, traudiar@cotas.com.bo. Nestled in scenic hill country, cabins for 2-8, also lovely rooms with bath, dining room, heated pool US$1.50 for non residents, sitting area with open fire, great place.

D-E Landhaus, C Murillo, T944 6033. Most central of all the *cabañas*, beautiful place with a small pool, sun loungers, garden, hammocks, parking and sauna (US$20 for up to 8 people), also rooms only with shared bathroom **F** pp; excellent restaurant and café.

E Andoriña, C Campero s/n frente *El Deber*, 2½ blocks from plaza, T944 6333. Cheaper without bath, includes breakfast with fruit and juices, tastefully decorated, kitchen, bar, public areas, garden, good views, picture library, cultural events and films. Enthusiastic owners Andrés and Doriña are very helpful and knowledgeable, English spoken, good value.

E Don Jorge, Bolívar, T944 6086. Cheaper with shared bath, hot showers, good beds, large shaded patio, good set lunch.

E La Posada del Sol, 3 blocks north of the plaza, T944 6366, www.laposadadelsol.net. Nice place, very hospitable, excellent breakfast, beautiful views, Spanish classes, good value.

E-F Alojamiento Vargas, around corner from museum. Clothes-washing facilities, use of kitchen, breakfast, owner Teresa is helpful. Recommended.

E-F Res Kim, near the plaza, T944 6161. Use of kitchen, cheaper with shared bath, family-run, spotless, good value, breakfast on request. Recommended.

F Paola, diagonal to the plaza, T944 6093. Cheaper without bath, electric shower, budget travellers' gathering place, cheap local food in restaurant.

Vallegrande and La Higuera *p373*

E La Casa del Telegrafista, La Higuera, www.lacasadeltelegrafista.com. Small, welcoming French-owned posada with restaurant, all meals extra, camping (US$2), horseback and mountain bike tours, US$15, also bikes for hire.

E Hostal Juanita, M M Caballero 123, T942 2231, Vallegrande, hostaljuanita@cotas.net. Cheaper without bath, electric shower, good value, Doña Juanita is kind.

G Res Vallegrande, on the plaza, Vallegrande. Basic accommodation.

In La Higuera you can camp in the school, but ask permission, US$0.30.

Parque Nacional Amboró *p374*

A-C Hacienda El Cafetal, 5.5 km south of town (taxi from plaza US$3), T935 2067, www.elcafetalbuenavista.com. Comfortable suites for up to 5 people, double rooms, breakfast included, restaurant, bar, birdwatching platform, on a working coffee plantation (tours available), with shade forest.

C Buenavista, 700 m out of Buena Vista, T03-932 2104, www.buenavistahotel.com.bo. Pretty place with rooms, suites and cabins with kitchen, viewing platform, pool, sauna, very good restaurant, horse riding.

D Quimori, 1 km east of Buena Vista, T03-932 2081. Includes breakfast, others meals with advance notice, pool, nice grounds, tours in dry season, family-run.

F La Casona, Av 6 de Agosto at the corner of the plaza, Buena Vista, T03-932 2083. Small simple rooms with fan, shared bath, electric shower, courtyard in hammocks, plants and birds, good value.

F Posada del Carmen, Av 6 de Agosto on the plaza, Buena Vista, T7094 4138. Cheaper without bath, a bit run down but adequate, parking.

F Res Nadia, Buena Vista, T03-932 2049. Cheaper without bath, simple, small, family run.

To Paraguay *p375*

C-E Hotel JR, Tte Coronel Sánchez 247 y Comercio, Camiri, T952 2200, jrhotelcamiri@yahoo.es. Includes buffet breakfast, a/c, parking.

D Premier, Av Busch 60, ½ block from plaza in Camiri, T952 2204. A/c, **E** with fan, spacious, comfortable, welcoming owners. Recommended.

Villamontes *p375*

C El Rancho, Av Méndez Arcos opposite the train station, 15 blocks from the centre, T672 2059, rancho@entelnet.bo. Lovely rooms, a/c, includes full breakfast, frigobar, nice grounds and pool, parking, excellent restaurant.

D Gran Hotel Avenida, Av Méndez Arcos 3 blocks east of Plaza 15 de Abril, T672 2106. A/c, includes breakfast, helpful owner, parking.
E Res Raldes, Cap Manchego 171, 1½ blocks from Plaza 15 de Abril, T672 2088, fernandoarel@gmail.com. Well maintained family run hotel, a/c, electric shower, **F** with shared bath and fan, nice courtyard, small pool, parking, good value.

To Argentina: Yacuiba *p375*
C París, Comercio 1175 y Campero, T04-682 2182. The best, with breakfast, a/c.
C Valentín, San Martín 1153, T04-682 2645, valentinhotel@hotmail.com. With breakfast, a/c (**D** with fan), restaurant, pool, sauna (extra).
E Rojas, Comercio 1025, T04-682 2883. With bath, a/c, hot water, **F** with fan.

Eating

Samaipata *p372*
TT El Descanso en Los Alturas. Wide choice including good steaks and pizzas.
TT La Oveja Negra, 3 blocks from plaza. Rustic ambience, good vegetarian dishes, nice bar.
TT Latina Café, Bolívar. A great place to hang out, laid back, there's a bar, and food (curry, chorizo, spaghetti and vegetarian: try ensalada orgásmica).
TT-T Chakana bar/restaurant/café open every day 0900-late, Dutch-owned, relaxing, *almuerzos*, good snacks and salads, cakes and ice cream, seats outside, book exchange.
TT-T Tierra Libre, 20 m from plaza, T7602 2729 (Alex and Alejandra). Good quality and sociable atmosphere, but smoky.
T El Turista, opposite the gas station on the highway. Good local dishes.
T Media Vuelta, on the plaza. Good *almuerzo*, clean kitchen.

Cafés

Café Baden, 1 km towards Santa Cruz, good for ice cream and tortes as well as steak and *schweizer würstsalat*.
La Ranita, near plaza. Tea house and bakery, French specialities.
Panadería Gerlinde, near the Santa Cruz-Cochabamba main road. Open daily 0700-2200. For superb value, tasty biscuits, bread, homemade pastas, herbs, cheese, yoghurts and cold meats; she also has a weekend stall in the market.

Parque Nacional Amboró *p374*
TT-T La Plaza, on the plaza, Buena Vista. Elegant restaurant/bar with a terrace, wide range of international dishes, good service.
T El Patujú, on the plaza, Buena Vista. The only café in town, serving excellent local coffee, teas, hot chocolate and a range of snacks. Also sells local produce and crafts.

Activities and tours

Samaipata *p372*
Those listed here are recommended. Expect to pay US$15-20 pp in a group of 4.
Gilberto Aguilera, T944 6050, considered the most knowledgeable local guide, good value tours.
Michael Blendinger, C Bolívar opposite the museum, T944 6227, www.discoveringbolivia.com. German guide raised in Argentina who speaks English, runs fully equipped 4WD tours, short and long treks, horse rides, specialist in nature and archaeology. Accommodation in cabins available, also inclusive packages.
Road Runners, Olaf and Frank, T944 6193, www.the-roadrunners.info. Speak English and German, enthusiastic, lots of information and advice, recommended tour of El Fuerte.
Ben Verhoef Tours, Campero 217, T944 6365, www.benverhoeftours.com. Owned by the Dutch couple Ben Verhoef and Susanne Lijmbach; Dutch, English, German and Spanish spoken. Offer tours along La Ruta del Che and the old Trade Route to Sucre.
See **La Víspera**, above, Margarita and Pieter, can arrange any trip, including horse riding.
Jucumari Tours, Bolívar, 1 block from the plaza, T944 6129, erwin-am@hotmail.com. Good quality and value tours run by Edwin Acuña, who has 4WD vehicle.

Parque Nacional Amboró *p374*
Amboró Travel & Adventure on the plaza, Buena Vista, T7160 0691, amborotravel@hotmail.com. Prices include transport to and from the park, guide and meals. Recommended.
Puertas del Amboró, corner of the plaza, Buena Vista, T03-932 2059, am.boro.tours@hotmail.com. They also offer full packages.

Transport

Samaipata *p372*

Bus From **Santa Cruz** to Samaipata, only Sucre-bound buses leave from the Terminal Bimodal. **Taxis Expreso Samaipata** in Santa Cruz at Av Omar Chávez 1147 y Soliz de Holguín, T333 5067 (Samaipata T944 6129), leave when full Mon-Sat 0530-2030 (for Sun book in advance), US$3.50 per person shared, or $17.50 in private vehicle, 2½ hrs. Returning to Santa Cruz, they pick you up from your hotel in Samaipata. Also various other options, all less convenient than above. Buses and micros leaving Santa Cruz for **Sucre** and other towns pass through Samaipata between 1800 and 2000; tickets can be booked with 1 days' notice through **Andoriña** hostal (see above). To get to **Samaipata** from **Sucre**, buses leave at night and arrive 0500-0600 (set your alarm in case the driver forgets to stop for you), stopping in Mairana or Mataral for breakfast, about half an hour before Samaipata.

Vallegrande and La Higuera *p373*

Bus Flota Vallegrande has 2 daily buses morning and afternoon from Santa Cruz to **Vallegrande** via **Samaipata** (at 1130 and 1630), 5 hrs, US$5. Best to book in advance. From Vallegrande market, a daily bus departs 0815 to **Pucará** (45 km), from where there is transport (12 km) to **La Higuera**. Taxi Vallegrande-La Higuera US$25-30.

Parque Nacional Amboró *p374*

Bus To **Buena Vista** **Sindicato 10 de Febrero** in Santa Cruz at Izozog 668 y Av Irala, 1er Anillo behind ex-terminal, T334 8435, 0730-1830, US$3 pp (private vehicle US$15), 2½ hrs. Also another shared taxi company nearby, and 'Linea 102' buses from regional section of Terminal Bimodal. From Buena Vista, the access to the park is by gravel road, 4WD jeep or similar recommended as rivers have to been crossed. All operators and community eco-lodge coordinators offer transport.

To **Mairana** from Samaipata, catch a Santa Cruz-Sucre bus if there are seats available. Shared taxis from Santa Cruz to Mairana with **Cotrama**, Humberto Vásquez y Primer Anillo, leave when full throughout the day, US$3.50, 3 hrs; **Señor de los Milagros**, Av Grigotá at Plaza Oruro, T357 2709, daily at 0900 and 1400, US$2. Shared taxis from Mairana to **La Yunga**, US$1.50 pp, more for an *expreso*. Taxi Samaipata-La Yunga, 30 km, US$12 one way. From Mairana there are 3 buses a week (at 1400) to **Cochabamba** on the old road, arriving at 0400: get the bus office in Cochabamba call a Radio taxi to take you to a hostal. Don't take any taxi that is waiting at the terminus.

Villamontes *p375*

Bus To **Yacuiba**, **Coop El Chaco**, Av Méndez Arcos y Ismael Montes, hourly 0630-1830, US$1.35, 1½ hrs. Cars from Av Montenegro y Cap Manchego, hourly or when full, 0630-1830, US$2, 1½ hrs. To **Camiri**, cars from Av Montenegro y Méndez Arcos, leave when full 0530-1800, US$3.50, 2 hrs. Long distance buses from terminal on Av Méndez Arcos, 13 blocks east of Plaza 15 de Abril (taxi US$0.40 pp). To **Tarija** via Entre Ríos, mostly unpaved and extremely scenic (sit on the right for best views), US$5-6, 10-11 hrs, several companies 1730-1930; for day travel, **Copacabana** may depart at 1030, 2-3 per week from the terminal; **Guadalupana**, Wed and Sat at 0930, from Coop El Chaco office. To **Santa Cruz**, several companies daily, US$4.50-8.50, some bus cama, 7-8 hrs.

To **Asunción**, buses from Santa Cruz pass through 0200-0300, reserve a day earlier, US$35, about 15 hrs. 5 companies, offices all on Av Montenegro, either side of Av Méndez Arcos. Best are **Stel**, T672 3662, or Vicky Vides T7735 0934; **Yaciretá**, T672 2812, or Betty Borda, T7740 4111.

Train Station on Av Méndez Arcos, 15 blocks east of Plaza 15 de Abril, T672 4078. The **Santa Cruz-Yacuiba tren mixto** stops here: Wed and Fri at 0505, returning to **Santa Cruz** on Wed and Fri at 1950. To Santa Cruz: Pullman US$12, 1st class US$5.30; to Yacuiba, Pullman US$6.55, 1st class US$1.50.

To Argentina: Yacuiba *p375*

Bus To **Santa Cruz**, about 20 companies run daily services, mostly at night, 14 hrs, US$8-15. To **Tarija**, daily morning and evening. To **La Paz**, via Tarija, 32 hrs, US$23. To **Sucre** with **Trans Chaqueña**, Tue, Sat 1000, US$23, 20 hrs.

Train **Santa Cruz**-Yacuiba **tren mixto** Tue and Thu, 1530, 17 hrs, returning from Yacuiba Wed and Fri, 1700, Pullman US$14, 1st class US$6.50. Since buses on the paved highway are much faster, the train is seldom used by tourists or locals.

Directory

Samaipata *p372*
Banks No ATMs or banks: take cash. Many places change US$ cash. **Internet** A couple of places with slow connection, US$1.50 per hr. **Telephone** Several cabinas around the plaza.

Eastern Bolivia

The vast and rapidly developing plains to the east of the Eastern Cordillera are Bolivia's richest area in natural resources. For the visitor, the beautiful churches and rich traditions of former Jesuit Chiquitano missions east of Santa Cruz are well worth a visit, and further east is Bolivia's portion of the Pantanal. Noel Kempff Mercado national park, meanwhile, is one of the natural wonders of South America. This combination of natural beauty, living indigenous culture and Jesuit heritage make the region one of Bolivia's hidden gems.

Chiquitano Jesuit Missions

Ten Jesuit missions survive east of Santa Cruz, six of which – San Javier, Concepción, San Rafael, Santa Ana, San Miguel and San José de Chiquitos – have churches which are UNESCO World Heritage Sites. The first three were built by the Swiss Jesuit, Padre Martin Schmidt, the other two (plus the one at San Ignacio de Velasco, demolished in 1948, see below) were built by other priests. Besides organizing *reducciones* and constructing churches, for each of which he built an organ, Padre Schmidt wrote music (some is still played today on traditional instruments) and he published a Spanish-Idioma Chiquitano dictionary based on his knowledge of all the dialects of the region. He worked in this part of the then-Viceroyalty of Peru until the expulsion of the Jesuits in 1767 by order of Charles III of Spain. One of the best ways to appreciate this region is at the bi-annual Festival de Música Renacentista y Barroca Americana, next in 2012 (see page 370).

Access to the mission area is by bus or train from **Santa Cruz**: a paved highway runs north to San Ramón (139 km) and on north, to San Javier (45 km), turning east here to Concepción (68 km), then, unpaved, to San Ignacio (171 km). One road continues east to San Matías and the Brazilian border (good gravel part of the way); others head south either through San Miguel, or Santa Ana to meet at San Rafael for the continuation south to San José de Chiquitos. By rail, leave the Santa Cruz-Quijarro train at San José and from there travel north. The most comfortable way to visit is by jeep, in five days. The route is straightforward and fuel is available. For jeep hire, see Directory, page 371. For information see **www.chiquitania.com** for extensive historical and practical information, and **www.mancochiquitana.org**, the site of the **Mancomunidad de Municipios de la Gran Chiquitania**, a non-profit organization dedicated to the economic improvement of the region; also **http://chiquitos.santacruz.gov.bo**.

San Javier (or San Xavier) The first Jesuit mission in Chiquitos (1691), its church built by Padre Schmidt between 1749 and 1752 ⓘ *US$1.15*. The original wooden structure has survived more or less intact and restoration was undertaken between 1987 and 1992 by the Swiss Hans Roth, himself a former Jesuit. Subtle designs and floral patterns cover the ceiling, walls and carved columns. One of the bas-relief paintings on the high altar depicts Martin Schmidt playing the piano for his indigenous choir. It is a fine 30 minute walk (best in the afternoon light) to **Mirador El Bibosi** and the small **Parque Piedra de Los Apóstoles**. There is also good walking or all-terrain cycling in the surrounding countryside (no maps, ask around), thermal swimming holes at **Aguas Calientes**, and horse riding from several hotels. Patron saint's *fiesta*, 3 December. Tourist guides' association has an office in the **Alcaldía** ⓘ *T7761 7902, or 7763 3203 for a guide*. Information also from the **Casa de Cultura** ⓘ *on the plaza, T963 5149*.

Concepción The village is dominated by its magnificent cathedral, completed by Padre Schmidt in 1756 and totally restored by the late Hans Roth 1975-1982 ⓘ *0700-2000, tours 1000, 1500, donation invited*. The interior of this beautiful church has an altar of laminated silver. In front of the church is a bell-cum-clock tower housing the original bells and behind it are well-restored cloisters. On the plaza, forming part of the Jesuit complex, is the **Museo Misional** ⓘ *Mon-Sat 0800-1200, 1430-1830, Sun 1000-1230, US$1.10*, which has an *artesanía* shop. The ticket also gives entry to the **Hans Roth Museum**, dedicated to the restoration process. Visit also the **Museo Antropológico de la Chiquitania** ⓘ *16 de Septiembre y Tte Capoblanco, 0800-1200, 1400-1800, free*, which explains the life of the indigenous peoples of the region. It has a café and guesthouse. Fiesta de la Inmaculada Concepción: 8 December. An orchid festival is held in the second week of October. The **Municipal tourist office** ⓘ *Lucas Caballero y Cabo Rodríguez, one block from plaza, T964 3057*, can arrange trips to nearby recreational areas, ranches and communities. An **Asociación de Guías Locales** ⓘ *south side of plaza, contact Ysabel Supepi, T7604 7085; or Hilario Orellana, T7534 3734* also offers tours to local communities many of which are developing grass-roots tourism projects: e.g. **Santa Rita**, **San Andrés** and **El Carmen**. With advance notice, they can also organize private concerts with 30 to 40 musicians. Various restaurants in town. Many places sell wood carvings and leather goods.

San Ignacio de Velasco A lack of funds for restoration led to the demolition of San Ignacio's replacement Jesuit church in 1948, the original having burnt down in 1808. A modern replica contains the elaborate high altar, pulpit and paintings and statues of saints. The **Casa de la Cultura** ⓘ *La Paz y Comercio, on the plaza, T962 2056, culturayturismo.siv@gmail.com*, has a small museum with musical instruments and can help organize local guides. The **Centro Artesanal** ⓘ *Santa Cruz entre Bolívar y Oruro* is worth a visit and there is community tourism in **San Juancito**, 18 km from town. San Ignacio is the main transport and commercial hub for the region. Laguna Guapomó on the outskirts is good for swimming, boating and fishing. Patron saint's day, preceded by a cattle fair, 31 July.

Santa Ana, San Rafael and San Miguel de Velasco The church in **Santa Ana** (founded 1755, constructed after the expulsion of the Jesuits), is a lovely wooden building. It is the most authentic of all the Jesuit *templos* and Santa Ana is a particularly authentic little village. Sr Luis Rocha or his children will show you around; ask for his house at the shop on the plaza where the bus stops. Simple accommodation and meals at **E Casa de la Comunidad Valenciana**, Bolívar y Ramanuca; and at 11 different **F Ecoalbergues Familiares**, which have been recommended. Fiesta de Santa Ana: 26 July. **San Rafael**'s church was completed by Padre Schmidt in 1748. It is one of the most beautifully restored (Concepción's also vying for this title), with mica-covered interior walls and frescoes in beige paint over the exterior. Patron saint's day, with traditional dancing, 24 October; Christmas pageant is worth seeing (*Hotel Paradita*, T962 4008, **G**, two others; four restaurants near the plaza; tourist information office T962 4022). The frescoes on the façade of the church (1766) at **San Miguel** depict St Peter and St Paul; designs in brown and yellow cover all the interior and the exterior side walls. The mission runs three schools and workshop; the sisters are very welcoming and will gladly show tourists around. There is a **Museo Etnofolclórico**, off the Plaza at C Betania; next door is the Municipalidad/Casa de la Cultura, with a tourist information office ⓘ *T962 4222*. San Miguel rivals San Ignacio for the quality of its Chiquitano art. Patron saint's day: 29 September. Some 4 km away is the **Santuario de Cotoca**, beside a lake where you can swim; ask at *La Pascana* for transport. (*Alojamiento y Restaurant La Pascana*, on plaza, T962 4220, basic, cheap meals; there are various other places to stay and eat and a public phone office.) Most traffic from San Ignacio goes via San Miguel, not Santa Ana, to San Rafael. If visiting these places from San Ignacio, it's probably better to go to San Rafael first, then go back via San Miguel. A day trip by taxi from San Ignacio to these villages costs US$35-40 (negotiate).

San José de Chiquitos ➔ *Phone code: 03. Colour map 6, B5.*
One complete side of the plaza of this dusty little town is occupied by the superb frontage of the Jesuit mission, begun in the mid-1740s. The stone buildings, in Baroque style, are connected by a wall. They are the restored 18th century chapel (the German Franciscan missionary priest may open it if asked ahead of time, T972 2156 to check which parts of the complex are open); the church (1747) with its triangular façade; the four-storey bell-tower (1748) and the mortuary (*la bóveda* – 1750), with one central window but no entrance in its severe frontage. Behind are the *colegio* and workshops, which are being transformed into study and practice rooms for the town's young musicians. The **Museo Ayoreo-Chiquitano**, ⓘ *Ovidio Barbery y Mons Gericke, 1½ blocks from plaza*, funded by Fundación para la Conversación del Bosque Chiquitano and Hombre y Naturaleza, deals with the local indigenous culture. **InfoTur** ⓘ *C Velasco, ½ block from plaza, T972 2084, www.sanjosedechiquitos.blogspot.com*, has tourist information and internet upstairs. There is an *Entel* office and a hospital. On Monday, Mennonites bring their produce to sell to shops and to buy provisions. The colonies are 50 km west and the Mennonites, who speak English, German, plattdeutsch and Spanish, are happy to talk about their way of life. Fiesta de San José is 1 May, preceded by a week of folkloric and other events.

About 2 km south from San José is the **Parque Nacional Histórico Santa Cruz la Vieja** ⓘ *daily US$3.50, pool US$1*. This includes a monument to the original site of Santa Cruz (about 1540), a *mirador* giving views over the jungle and, 5 km into the park, a religious shrine. The park's heavily forested hills contain much animal and bird life; various trails with grand views; guides available from the small village in the park (take insect repellent). It gets very hot so start early, allow over one hour on foot to walk there and take plenty of water, or hire a car and local guide.

Parque Nacional Noel Kempff Mercado
In the far northeast corner of Santa Cruz Department, **Parque Nacional Noel Kempff Mercado** (named after a pioneer of conservation in Bolivia) ⓘ *US$30 entry fee (reports vary, enquire in advance with SERNAP, see below); a guide is compulsory, US$25 per group, from the town of La Florida*, is one of the world's most diverse natural habitats. It covers 1,523,446 ha (roughly the same size as Massachusetts) and encompasses seven ecosystems, within which are 139 species of mammals (including black jaguars), 620 species of birds (including nine types of macaw), 74 species of reptiles and 110 species of orchid. Highlights include the **Huanchaca** or **Caparú Plateau**, which with its 200-500 m sheer cliffs and tumbling waterfalls is another candidate for Sir Arthur Conan Doyle's *Lost World* (Colonel Percy Fawcett, who discovered the plateau in 1910, was a friend of the writer). The three best-known waterfalls are Arco Iris and Federico Ahlfeld on the Río Paucerna (both accessible only mid-Dec to May, when water levels on the Río Puracema are sufficiently high); and the 80-m high Catarata del Encanto. For information on the park, contact **SERNAP** ⓘ *Bolívar 87, San Ignacio de Velasco, T962 2747, turismonoelkempff@gmail.com, very helpful, or in Santa Cruz (less involved) Calle 9 Oeste 138, Equipetrol, T335 2325.* Also see www.parquenoelkempff.com.

To Brazil
There are four routes from Santa Cruz: by air to Puerto Suárez, by rail to Quijarro, by road via San Matías, and via San Ignacio de Velasco to Marfil (Bolivia) and Vila Velha (Brasil). Puerto Suárez is near Quijarro and these two routes lead to Corumbá on the Brazilian side, from where there is access to the southern Pantanal. The San Matías road links to Cáceres, Cuiabá and the northern Pantanal in Brazil. The Marfil route provides an alternative access to Parque Nacional Noel Kempff Mercado from Pimenteiras do Oeste on the Brazilian side; far from the beaten path, obtain all details locally.

Puerto Suárez → *Phone code: 03. Colour map 6, B6. Population: 21,000.*
On the shore of Laguna Cáceres, this is a friendly, quiet, small town, with a shady main plaza. There is a nice view of the lake from the park at the north end of Avenida Bolívar. The area around the train station is known as *Paradero*. Do not venture into the market area unless you are looking to contract any one of innumerable intestinal illnesses, and/or have your pockets picked. Fishing and photo tours to the ecologically astonishing Pantanal can be arranged more cheaply than on the Brazilian side. You can also arrange river tours and day trips to Brazil; these are generally most easily done through a hotel, although they will add a 10-15% service charge (see below).

Quijarro → *Phone code: 03. Colour map 6, B6. Population: 17,700.*
The eastern terminus of the Bolivian railway, and the gateway to Brazil, is Quijarro. It is quite safe by day, but caution is recommended at night. The water supply is often unreliable, try the tap before checking in to a hotel. Prices are much lower than in neighbouring Brazil and there are some decent places to stay, in particular the five-star **Hotel El Pantanal** in nearby Arroyo Concepción.

Border with Brazil
The municipality by the border is known as Arroyo Concepción. You need not have your passport stamped if you visit Corumbá for the day. Otherwise get your exit stamp at Bolivian immigration (see below), formalities are straightforward. There are no formalities on the Brazilian side, you must get your entry stamp in the Corumbá bus station/*rodoviária* (see page 675). Yellow Fever vaccination is compulsory to enter Bolivia and Brazil, have your certificate at hand when you go for your entry stamp, otherwise you may be sent to get revaccinated. Bolivian immigration is at the border at Arroyo Concepción, on right just before bridge (open 0800-1200, 1400-1730 daily), or at Puerto Suárez airport, where Bolivian exit/entry stamps are issued. Money changers right at the border offer the worst rates. Ask around in the small shops past the bridge and check the rate with several of them before changing. The Brazilian consulate is in Santa Cruz, or in Puerto Suárez. See Transport, below, for taxis from the border.

Via San Matías to Cáceres
The road route from Santa Cruz is via San Ignacio de Velasco to San Matías, a busy little town with hotels and restaurants then on to Cáceres and Cuiabá. The area around San Matías is reported unsafe due to drug smuggling. From Santa Cruz it is a three-day trip, roads permitting: there are two roads: San Ignacio, Espíritu, San Vicente (with petrol station), San Matías, and the more southerly San Rafael de Velasco, Arica, Mercedes, Torno, fork left after 120 km to Cerrito, San Matías. The northerly route tends to be in better condition, but check before setting out. See under San Ignacio, page 385, for bus information. Get your passport stamped at immigration in San Matías. There are also military checks en route. It's best to cross on a weekday as the Bolivian post may not be open at the weekend. Note that immigration in San Matías will **not** extend visas. Shared taxis run from bus stop to border. Once in Brazil go to immigration in Cáceres or, on Sunday, to Polícia Federal in Cuiabá.

Eastern Bolivia listings

For Sleeping and Eating price codes and other relevant information, see Essentials, pages 38-40.

Sleeping

Chiquitano Jesuit Missions *p379*

San Javier

B Totaitú, 3 km from town, T963 5171, www.lachiquitania-bo.com. Cabins with a/c, pool and frigobar. Includes breakfast, restaurant, meeting rooms, ample grounds, horse riding and tours available.

C Momoqui, Av Santa Cruz, 1½ long blocks from plaza, T963 5095. Cabins in nice garden, buffet breakfast, Italian restaurant, pool, pleasant, horse riding available.

D Alojamiento San Xavier, C Santa Cruz, T963 5038. **F** without bath, electric shower, garden, nice sitting area. Recommended.

D El Reposo del Guerrero, C Tte Busch Becerra, T963 5022. Includes breakfast, a/c, restaurant.

E Alojamiento Ame-Tauná, on plaza opposite church, T963 5018. **F** with shared bath, showers, smart, no double beds, noisy parrot at dawn.

E-F Residencial Chiquitano, Av Santa Cruz (Av José de Arce), ½ block from plaza, T963 5072. Simple rooms with private bath, fan, large patio, friendly atmosphere, opened in 2009, good value.

F Posada El Tiluchi, on the plaza, T963 5220. Rustic rooms, hammocks on patio.

Concepción

B Gran Hotel Concepción, on plaza, T964 3031. Excellent service, including buffet breakfast, pool, gardens, bar, very comfortable. Highly recommended.

B Hotel Chiquitos, end of Av Killian, T964 3153. Colonial style construction, ample rooms, frigobar, internet, pool, gardens and sports fields, orchid nursery, parking. Includes breakfast, tours available.

D Las Misiones, C Luis Caballero, 1 block from church, T964 3021. Pleasant rooms, small pool, also has an apartment, good value.

D Oasis Chiquitano, C Germán Bush, 1½ blocks from plaza. Includes buffet breakfast, a/c, pool, nice patio with flowers.

E Colonial, Ñuflo de Chávez 7, ½ block from plaza, T964 3050. Private bath, hammocks on ample veranda, parking, breakfast extra.

E Residencial Westfalia, Saucedo 205, 2 blocks from plaza, T964 3040. **F** without bath, German-owned, nice patio, good value.

San Ignacio de Velasco

A-B La Misión, Plaza 31 de Julio, T962 2333, www.hotel-lamision.com. Luxurious, with a/c, cable TV and pool, rooms of various standards and prices, includes buffet breakfast, tours arranged.

B San Ignacio, Plaza 31 de Julio, T962 2283. In a restored former episicopal mansion, non-profit (run by diocese, funds support poor youth in the community), a/c, hot showers, breakfast. Recommended.

C Parador Santa Ana, Libertad entre Sucre y Cochabamba, T962 2075, www.paradorsantaana.blogspot.com. Small place, includes breakfast, good restaurant, rooms with a/c, internet.

E Palace, Comercio, off the plaza, T962 2063. With hot shower, includes breakfast, comfortable, good value. Other hotels (**D-G**) and places to eat near plaza.

San José de Chiquitos *p381*

E Hotel Denisse, Mons Géricke, 5 blocks east of plaza, T972 2379. With bath, a/c, cheaper with fan, nice patio, clean and comfortable, good value.

E Turubó, on the plaza, T972 2037. With a/c, **F** with fan, cheaper with shared bath, variety of different rooms, good location, laundry service.

Parque Nacional Noel Kempff Mercado *p381*

There are 2 lodges in the park: 15 beds at a renovated ranch at **Flor de Oro**, T03-313 7040 (satellite phone), about US$100 pp/day full board, book through tour agencies, with access to hikes in the pampas and forests, and river excursions to the Arco Iris and Federico Ahlfeld falls and to bays. At **Los Fierros** there are 30 beds at a more rustic facility (closed in 2009, awaiting renovation), camping possible. From here you can visit many different habitats and El Encanto falls. There are other lodging possibilities in small towns bordering the park and some camping is available. For information, contact SERNAP, or arrange through a tour operator.

Puerto Suárez *p382*

D Centro Ecológico El Tumbador, on the shores of Laguna Cáceres, 6 km, T03-339 6012 (Santa Cruz), T7268 2413, hynb_puertosuarez@yahoo.com. Cabins with bath, includes breakfast, other meals on request, part of an NGO, offers tours and volunteer opportunities.

D Sucre, Bolívar 63 on main plaza, T976 2069. A/c, with bath, pleasant, good restaurant.

F Beby, Av Bolívar 111, T976 2270. With shared bath and fan.

Quijarro *p382*

A-D Bibosi, Luis Salazar s/n, main street 3 blocks east of train station, T978 2044, www.hotelbibosi.com. Variety of rooms and prices, some with a/c, fridge and private bath, cheaper with fan and shared bath, breakfast, pool, patio, restaurant, upscale for Quijarro.

C Tamengo, Costa Rica 57, Barrio Copacabana, T978 3356, www.tamengo.com. Located by the river, all rooms with a/c (**F** pp in dorm), restaurant and bar, pool, sports fields, Wi-Fi and book exchange. Day-use of facilities by visitors US$7. Arranges tours and volunteer opportunities.

E Oasis, Av Argentina 4, T978 2159. A/c, fridge, cheaper with shared bath and a/c, **F** with fan, OK.

E Yonni, Av Brasil opposite the station, T978 2109. A/c, fridge, **F** with shared bath and fan, OK, mosquito netting on windows.

Willy Solís Cruz, Roboré 13, T978 2204, wiland_54@hotmail.com. One block from plaza, near Quijarro station, plans to offer rooms where travellers can stay (price unspecified). For years Willy has helped store luggage and assists with ticket purchases, he also has internet, laundry, cooking facilities and clothes and shoe mending. He speaks English, very helpful.

Border with Brazil *p382*

AL-A El Pantanal Resort, Arroyo Concepción, T978 2020, www.elpantanalhotel.com. With all mod cons, includes breakfast and airport transfers, gateway to the Pantanal. They arrange cruises, horse riding, expensive but worth it, discounts in dry season (very busy in Jan-Feb).

Eating

Chiquitano Jesuit Missions *p379*

San Javier

Ganadero, in Asociación de Ganaderos on plaza. Excellent steaks. Others eateries around the plaza.

Concepción

El Buen Gusto, north side of plaza. Set meals and regional specialties.

San José de Chiquitos *p381*

Sabor y Arte, Bolívar y Mons Santisteban, Tue-Sun 1800-2300. Beef and Italian dishes, coca-leaf ravioli is the specialty.

Romanazzi Pizzería, Bolívar 19. Run by elderly Italian-Bolivian who makes her own pizzas entirely from scratch. Visit at least 2 hrs before wishing to dine and describe what you'd like, very much worth the wait.

Puerto Suárez *p382*

Al Paso, Bolívar 43, near Plaza. Good value set meals and à la carte, popular.

Several small inexpensive restaurants on Bolívar 100 block, eg **El Taxista**.

Quijarro *p382*

Restaurant at **Hotel Bibosi** is the only good option, otherwise check the basic eateries along the main street but keep an eye on cleanliness. Avoid the food stalls in the street and market.

Festivals and events

The region celebrates the **Festival de Música Renacentista y Barroca Americana**. Many towns have their own orchestras, which play the Jesuit music on a regular basis.

Transport

Chiquitano Jesuit Missions *p379*

San Javier

Trans Guarayos, T346 3993, from Santa Cruz Terminal Bimodal regional departures area, 6 a day, 4 hrs, US$4, some continue to **Concepción**. Also **Jenecherú**, T348 8618, Tue, Thu, Sat 2000, with a/c and reclining seats, US$5, continuing to **Concepción, San Ignacio, San Miguel** and **San Rafael**. Several taxi-trufi companies, including **25 de Abril**, C Tundi, by Ex-Terminal in Santa Cruz, T350 4933.

Concepción

Bus **Trans Guarayos**, US$4.50, 5 hrs, and **Jenecherú**, as above, US$5.50. Many other buses between Santa Cruz and San Ignacio pass through about midnight, but drop you at the gas station on the main road, several blocks from plaza; ask around for transport to centre. To continue to **San Ignacio de Velasco**, you have to wait for these midnight buses and buy your ticket on board. Take a torch to light your way to the gas station. Alternatively take **Flota 31 del Este** (described as "rustic") from C Germán Busch in Concepción, daily at 1700, 5-6 hrs, US$4.25. Concepción to **San Javier**, 1 hr, US$1.50 .

San Ignacio de Velasco

Bus From **Santa Cruz**, **Jenecherú**, **Trans Gusmar**, T362 5540, **Expreso San Ignacio**, T364 4999, and several others from Terminal Bimodal, US$10 (bus cama US$11), 11 hrs. From **San Ignacio Trans Carretón** (Santa Cruz T349 7959) daily 0600-0700, and **Expreso San Matías** (Santa Cruz T364 8497), daily 0300-0400, go to **San Matías** for Brazil (see below), 6-7 hrs, US$7.50. **Cáceres** (Brazil) is a further 1 hr from San Matías on a paved road. To **San José de Chiquitos** via San Miguel and San Rafael, **Flota Universal**, Mon, Wed, Fri, Sat at 1400, US$5.50, 8 hrs. To **San Rafael** (1½ hrs, US$1.50) via **Santa Ana** (40 mins, US$1) with **Trans Bolivia** daily 1400 and 1700, return 0600 and 1130. Micros to **Santa Ana** (US$1.50, 1 hr), and **San Rafael** (US$2, 1½ hrs) from market area at 1430 and 1600, returning from San Rafael 1300-1400. To **San Miguel** with **Flota 31 del Este**, Chiquitos entre 24 de Septiembre y Junín, 5 daily. Tickets cannot be booked in advance.

San José de Chiquitos *p381*

Bus To **San Ignacio**, **Flota Universal** Mon, Wed, Fri, Sat 0700 from Pollos Curichi, just west of train station, US$5.50, 4-5 hrs via San Rafael and San Miguel. Seats can be reserved at their office opposite the closed petrol station. **Trans Carretón**, Av Gallardo, 1 block from train station, has buses to Santa Cruz (Mon-Sat 1930, Sun 1830, US$4.25) and Puerto Suárez. Don't try to drive the unpaved road (paving in progress, enquire locally) on this route to Brazil without 4WD, the sandy surface is hell for small cars.

Train Schedule from **Santa Cruz** as for Quijarro (see below), 8¾ hrs to San José, **Regional** and **Expreso Oriental**: Pullman US$7.50, 1st class US$3.50; **Ferrobus**: *cama* US$26, *semi-cama* US$22. To **Quijarro Regional** Mon-Sat 1843, **Expreso Oriental** Mon, Wed, Fri 2220, *Pullman* US$11, 1st class US$4.15. **Ferrobus** Wed, Fri, Mon at 0010; *cama* US$19.10, *semi-cama* US$16.30. It is possible to reserve seats on either service at the train station up to a week in advance. Trains to San José are usually delayed by an hour or 2. Always reconfirm.

Parque Nacional Noel Kempff Mercado *p381*

Air Light aircraft can be chartered from Santa Cruz to **Flor de Oro**, in the north sector of the park, usually as part of organized tours.

Road/Bus The road journey is long and arduous (often impassable Oct-Apr); eg 13-18 hrs by 4WD from Santa Cruz to **Los Fierros** in the south sector (no public transport). Further north is **Piso Firme**, where boats can be chartered to Flor de Oro, 5-9 hrs, US$250. One weekly bus **Santa Cruz-Piso Firme** with **Trans Bolivia**, 3er Anillo interno entre Av Brasil y Virgen de Cotoca, T336 3866, Thu 1100-1200, US$24, 27 hrs minimum; returns Sun morning. Journey times depend on the season, state of roads and river crossings. To reach the north sector of the park overland via Brazil take **Flota Montecristi**, next to the Club Social in San Ignacio de Velasco (get Bolivian exit stamp in San Ignacio), via **Marfil** and **Vila Velha** (Brazil border) to **Pontes e Lacerda**, Tue, Thu, Sat at 0730. In Brazil, change buses in Pontes e Lacerda for **Vilhena**, and in Vilhena for **Pimenteiras do Oeste**, from where launches cross the river to Flor de Oro; confirm all details locally. The roads are better in Brazil and prices are higher there. Tours to Noel Kempff Mercado can be arranged with operators in Santa Cruz or La Paz. A 7-day/6-night tour costs around US$1,000, not including flights, but there is a great deal of variation depending on what services you require (see operators **Ruta Verde**, Santa Cruz, p370; **América Tours**, La Paz, p295). Shorter tours are also available.

Puerto Suárez *p382*

Air The simplest way to Brazil is to fly to **Puerto Suárez**, then share a taxi to the border. The airport is 6 km north of town, T976 2347;

airport tax US$2. Flights on Mon, Wed and Fri to/from Santa Cruz with **Aero Sur**; Tue, Thr and Sat with **TAM**. Don't buy tickets for flights originating in Puerto Suárez in Corumbá, these cost more.

Taxi To **Paradero** US$1.65; to airport US$2; to **Quijarro** or the border, US$5 (day), US$6 (night) or US$0.80 pp in a colectivo.

Train The station for Puerto Suárez is about 3 km from town. It is the first station west of Quijarro.

Quijarro *p382*

Taxi To the border (**Arroyo Concepción**) US$0.50 pp; to **Puerto Suárez** US$1 pp, more at night.

If arriving from Brazil, you will be approached by Bolivian taxi drivers who offer to hold your luggage while you clear immigration. These are the most expensive cabs (US$5 to Quijarro, US$15 to Puerto Suárez) and best avoided. Instead, keep your gear with you while your passport is stamped, then walk 200 m past the bridge to a commercial area where other taxis wait (US$0.50 to Quijarro, US$1 to Puerto Suárez).

Train There is no direct service between Santa Cruz and Brazil. All trains from Santa Cruz go via San José de Chiquitos to Quijarro, from where travellers must go by *colectivo* to the border post (beware overcharging, fare should be US$0.50 pp), then by bus to Corumbá. **Regional**, 20 hrs stopping at all intermediate stations, Mon-Sat 1200 (returns at 1245), *Pullman* US$16, 1st class US$7.25. **Expreso Oriental** 16 hrs stopping at San José de Chiquitos, Roboré, Rivero Tórrez and Puerto Suárez on Mon, Wed, Fri 1630, returning Tue, Thu, Sun 1630, same fares as Regional. A **Ferrobus** runs Tue, Thu, Sun at 1900, returning Mon, Wed, Fri 1900, same stops as Expreso Oriental, 14 hrs, US$28 *semi-cama*, US$33 *cama* (not as luxurious as it claims). Take food, drinking water, insect repellent and a torch, whichever class you are travelling. From Mar-Aug take a sleeping bag for the cold; be prepared for delays. There is a computerized reservation system and tickets may be purchased several days in advance. Ticket office on ground floor of Quijarro station is open Mon-Sat 0730-1200, 1430-1800, Sun 0730-1100. There may be queues of 1-2 hrs; purchase tickets directly at the train station and avoid all touts, middlemen and agencies. Passport or some form of ID required to buy tickets but entry/exit stamps are not checked. Note that times of departure from Quijarro are approximate as they depend on when trains arrive. 500 m from station is a modern, duty-free a/c shopping complex with banks, restaurants and pool. Small **bus** terminal 3 blocks from the train station. To **Santa Cruz** several daily, 15-24 hrs, US$11. This is an arduous journey and can take several days in the rainy season; the road is poor, buses run-down, and breakdowns frequent.

Directory

Chiquitano Jesuit Missions *p379*

San Ignacio de Velasco Banks Prodem, Velasco esq Sucre, T962 2099. Cash advances on Visa and MasterCard only (no debit cards), 5% commission, also changes US$ cash. **Banco de Credito**, main plaza, ATM due to start operating in 2010.

San José de Chiquitos *p381*

Banks No ATMs, nowhere to change TCs. **Banco Unión** on main plaza, US$ cash only, fair rates. **Telephone and internet** Several *cabinas* around the plaza.

Puerto Suárez *p382*

Airline offices Aero Sur, Bolívar 100, T976 2110. **TAM**, Israel Mendias y Heroes del Chaco, T976 2205. **Banks** Bisa, Bolívar 65, ATM. **Banco Unión**, La Paz 24, **Prodem**, Bolívar 121, US$ cash only. **Supermercado Tocale**, Av Bolívar, changes Bolivianos, reais and US$, cash only. **Embassies and consulates** Brazilian Consulate, Av Raúl Otero Reich y C Suárez Abego, T976 2040, vcbrasilpsuarez@cotas.com.bo.

Quijarro *p382*

Banks Bolivianos, reais and US$ cash traded along Av Brazil opposite the station by changers with large purses sitting in lawn chairs; beware of tricks. ATMs in Arroyo Concepción (Brazilian border) and Puerto Aguirre Free Trade Zone; nowhere to change TCs. **Telephone and internet** Several phone and internet places along the main street opposite the train station.

Brazil

Contents

390 Planning your trip

399 Rio de Janeiro
435 East of Rio
442 West of Rio

451 São Paulo
468 São Paulo coast

473 Minas Gerais and Espírito Santo
473 Belo Horizonte
479 East and south of Belo Horizonte
490 Espírito Santo
494 North of Belo Horizonte

497 Southern Brazil
497 Curitiba and around
503 The Paraná coast
507 Santa Catarina
515 Rio Grande do Sul
515 Porto Alegre
521 Rio Grande do Sul state

526 Foz do Iguaçu

532 Salvador de Bahia
549 Inland from Salvador
552 South of Salvador
562 North of Salvador

564 Recife and northeast coast
564 Recife
574 Around Recife
580 South of Recife
584 João Pessoa
587 Natal

594 Fortaleza and north coast
594 Fortaleza
602 Coast east of Fortaleza
604 Coast west of Fortaleza
611 West of Fortaleza

614 The Amazon
614 Travel up the Amazon River
617 Belém and around
626 Belém to Manaus
628 Manaus

640 Amazon frontiers
640 Manaus to Colombia, Peru, Venezuela and Guyana
645 Southern Amazônia

651 Brasília and Goiás
651 Brasília
658 Goiás
664 Tocantins

665 The Pantanal
665 Ins and outs
668 Campo Grande and around
675 Corumbá
678 Cuiabá and around

Footprint features

388 Don't miss …
392 Driving in Brazil
426 Carnival in Rio
470 Rodeo Romeos
480 O Aleijadinho
544 Carnival in Bahia
615 Paradise lost?

At a glance

Time required 3-4 weeks for northeast or south, up to a year for the entire country.

Best time Feb/Mar for Carnival, also Jun and New Year's Eve. Apr-Jun and Aug-Oct are generally best.

When not to go Dec-Feb and Jul school holidays. In Amazon Mar-May are wettest, in the south it's Nov-Mar.

★ **Don't miss ...**

1 **Rio de Janeiro**, page 399.
2 **Ouro Preto**, page 480.
3 **Salvador de Bahia**, page 532.
4 **Northeastern beaches**, pages 587 and 594.
5 **The Amazon**, page 614.
6 **The Pantanal**, page 665.

Described as the sexiest nation on earth, Brazilians know how to flirt, flaunt and have fun. The Rio Carnival, with its intoxicating atmosphere and costumes to die for, is the most exuberant of a whole calendar of festivals. In this, the world's fifth largest country, football, looking good and dancing are the national passions. Everyone seems to be seduced by the sounds of samba … and by the beach.

The coast of Brazil, all 7,408 km of it, has provided a suitable stretch of sand for every volleyball champion, surfer, dune-buggy driver and party animal. Just off shore there are many islands to sail to, from the huge Marajó with its water buffalo, to highly developed Santa Catarina, to the marine paradise of Abrolhos National Park.

But Brazilians also have a spiritual side to match their hedonistic streak. Many religions flourish, most obviously the African-based candomblé, which lives happily alongside Catholicism. In the 16th to 18th centuries, when Brazil was rich in gold and diamonds, the Portuguese colonists expressed their faith in some of the most beautiful baroque buildings created anywhere at that time.

For a change from cosmopolitan life, trek through the hills of the Chapada Diamantina, take the long road into the Pantanal wetlands and watch for hyacinth macaws and capybara, sling a hammock on a river boat up the mighty Amazon, or take a walk with the wildlife in the rainforest.

Planning your trip

Where to go

Rio de Janeiro was for a long time *the* image of Brazil, with its beautiful setting – the Sugar Loaf and Corcovado overlooking the bay and beaches, its world renowned carnival, the nightlife and its *favelas* (slums – which are now being incorporated into tourism). It is still a must on many itineraries, but Rio de Janeiro state has plenty of other beaches, national parks and colonial towns (especially **Paraty**) and the imperial city of Petrópolis. **São Paulo** is the country's industrial and financial powerhouse; with some fine museums and its cultural life and restaurants are very good. All the São Paulo coast is worth visiting and inland there are hill resorts and colonial towns. The **state of Minas Gerais** contains some of the best colonial architecture in South America in cities such as Ouro Preto, Mariana, São João del Rei and Diamantina. All are within easy reach of the state capital, Belo Horizonte. Other options in Minas include national parks with good hill scenery and birdwatching and hydrothermal resorts.

The atmosphere of the South is dominated by its German and Italian immigrants. The three states, Paraná, Santa Catarina and Rio Grande do Sul have their coastal resorts, especially near Florianópolis, capital of Santa Catarina. **Rio Grande do Sul** is the land of Brazil's *gaúchos* (cowboys) and of its vineyards, but the main focus of the region is the magnificent **Iguaçu Falls** in the far west of Paraná, on the borders of Argentina and Paraguay.

The Northeast is famous for beaches and colonial history. Combining both these elements, with the addition of Brazil's liveliest African culture, is **Salvador de Bahia**, one of the country's most famous cities and a premier tourist destination. Huge sums of money have been lavished on the restoration of its colonial centre and its carnival is something special. Inland, Bahia is mostly arid sertão, in which a popular town is **Lençois**, a historical monument with a nearby national park. The highlight of the southern coast of Bahia is the beach and party zone around **Porto Seguro**, while in the north the beaches stretch up to the states of Sergipe and Alagoas and on into Pernambuco. **Recife**, capital of Pernambuco, and its neighbour, the colonial capital **Olinda**, also mix the sea, history and culture, while inland is the major handicraft centre of Caruaru. Travelling around to the north-facing coast, there are hundreds of beaches to choose from, some highly developed, others less so. You can swim, surf or ride the dunes in buggies. Last stop before the mouth of the Amazon is **São Luís**, in whose centre most of the old houses are covered in colonial tiles. East of São Luís are the extraordinary dunes and lakes of the **Lençóis Maranhenses** and the labyrinthine **Parnaíba delta**.

Through the North flows the **Amazon**, along which river boats ply between the cities of Belém, Santarém and Manaus. From **Manaus** particularly there are opportunities for exploring the jungle on adventurous expeditions or staying in lodges. North of Manaus is the overland route through Boa Vista to Venezuela. The forest stretches south to the central tableland which falls to the **Pantanal** in the far west. This seasonal wetland, the highlight of the Centre West, is one of the prime areas for seeing bird and animal life in the continent. At the eastern end of the Centre West is **Brasília**, built in the 1960s and now a World Heritage Site in recognition of its superb examples of modern architecture. Also in this region is one of the largest river islands in the world (Bananal – a mecca for fishing) and the delightful hill and river landscapes of **Bonito** in Mato Grosso do Sul.

When to go

Brazil is a tropical country, but the further south you go the more temperate the winters become and there are places in the coastal mountains which have gained a reputation for their cool climate and low humidity. The heaviest rains fall at different times in different regions: November to March in the southeast, December to March in the centre west and April to August on the northeast coast around Pernambuco (where irregular rainfall causes severe draughts). The rainy season in the north and Amazônia can begin in December and is heaviest March to May, but it is getting steadily shorter, possibly as a result of deforestation. It is only in rare cases that the rainfall can be described as either excessive or deficient. Few places get more than 2,000 mm: the coast north of Belém, some of the Amazon Basin, and a small area of the Serra do Mar between Santos and São Paulo, where the downpour has been harnessed to generate electricity.

May to September is usually referred to as winter, but this is not to suggest that this is a bad time to visit. On the contrary, April to June and August to October are recommended times to go to most parts of the country. One major consideration is that carnival falls within the hottest, wettest time of year (in February), so if you are incorporating carnival into a longer holiday, it may be wet wherever you go. Also bear in mind that mid-December to February is the national holiday season, which means that hotels, planes and buses may be full and many establishments away from the holiday areas may be shut.

The average annual temperature increases steadily from south to north, but even on the Equator, in the Amazon Basin, the average temperature is not more than 27°C. The highest recorded was 44.6°C (2006), in the dry northeastern states. From the latitude of Recife south to Rio, the mean temperature is from 23° to 27°C along the coast, and from 18° to 21°C in the Highlands. From a few degrees south of Rio to the border with Uruguay the mean temperature is from 17° to 19°C. Humidity is relatively high in Brazil, particularly along the coast.

Getting around

Air Because of the great distances, flying is often the most practical option. All state capitals and larger cities are linked several times a day and all national airlines offer excellent service. Deregulation of the airlines has reduced prices on some routes and low-cost airlines offer fares that can often be as cheap as travelling by bus (when booked through the internet). Paying with an international credit card is not always possible online; but it is usually possible to buy an online ticket through a hotel, agency or willing friend without surcharge. Most airlines' websites provide full information, including a booking service, although not all are in English. The dominant airlines are **GOL** ① *R Tamoios 246, Jardim Aeroporto, São Paulo, T0300-789 2121, www.voegol.com.br*, **TAM** ① *Av Jurandir 856, São Paulo, T011-5582 8811/4002 5700, www.tam.com.br* and **TRIP** ① *www.voetrip.com.br; T0300-789 8747*. Many other airlines operate, some regional, others nationwide. **Azul** ① *www.voeazul.com.br*, **Oceanair** (part of Avianca) ① *T011-4004 4040/T0300-789 8160, www.oceanair.com.br* and **Webjet** ① *T021-4009 0000, www.webjet.com.br*, operate the most extensive routes. **Varig**, once the national leader, is now owned by GOL, flying international routes. **Pantanal** *T0800-602 5888, www.voepantanal.com.br*, has flights mainly between São Paulo and Mato Grosso do Sul. Small scheduled domestic airlines operate Brazilian-built Bandeirante 16-seater prop-jets into virtually every city and town with any semblance of an airstrip. Internal flights often have many stops and are often quite slow. Most airports have left-luggage lockers (US$2 for 24 hrs). Seats are often unallocated on internal flights; board in good time.

TAM offers a 30-day **air pass** covering all Brazil, costing US$551-635 for four coupons (cheaper if you arrive on TAM). Additional coupons, up to a maximum of nine, may be bought. All sectors must be booked before the start of the journey. Two flights forming one connection count as two coupons. The airpass must be purchased outside Brazil, no journey may be repeated. Remember domestic airport tax has to be paid at each departure. Passengers may arrive in Brazil on any carrier except LAN. Converting the voucher can take some hours, do not plan an onward flight immediately. Cost and restrictions on the airpass are subject to change.

Gol has a similar 30-day **airpass**, from four to nine coupons, US$532-1152 (plus tax), which must be bought outside Brazil. If you have to change planes on a route, this counts as one coupon if the stop-over is less than four hours. A maximum of two connections may be made in the same city. Dates maybe changed, but routes cannot once the ticket has been bought. **Gol** also sells a **Northeast Brazil airpass**, minimum three coupons (US$390), maximum six (US$690), covering all the states between Bahia and Maranhão.

Driving in Brazil

Road Around 10% of roads are paved and several thousand more all-weather. The best highways are heavily concentrated in the southeast; those serving the interior are being improved to all-weather status and many are paved. Some main roads are narrow and therefore dangerous. Many are in poor condition.

Safety Try to never leave your car unattended except in a locked garage or guarded parking area.

Documents To drive in Brazil you need an international licence. A national driving licence is acceptable as long as your home country is a signatory to the Vienna and Geneva conventions. (See Motoring, Essentials.) There are agreements between Brazil and all South American countries (but check in the case of Bolivia) whereby a car can be taken into Brazil (or a Brazilian car out of Brazil) for a period of 90 days without any special documents. For cars registered in other countries, you need proof of ownership and/or registration in the home country and valid driving licence (as above). A 90-day permit is given by customs and procedure is very straightforward. Make sure you keep *all* the papers you are given when you enter, to produce when you leave.

Car hire Renting a car in Brazil is expensive: the cheapest rate for unlimited mileage for a small car is about US$65 per day. Minimum age for renting a car is 21 and it is essential to have a credit card. Companies operate under the terms *aluguel de automóveis* or *autolocadores*.

Fuel Fuel prices vary from week to week and according to region. *Gasolina común* costs about US$1.35 per litre with *gasolina maxi* and *maxigold* a little more. *Alcool común*; *alcool maxi* costs less. Diesel is cheap. There is no unleaded fuel. Fuel is only 85 octane. It is virtually impossible to buy premium grades of petrol anywhere. With alcohol fuel you need about 50% more than regular gasoline. Larger cars have a small extra tank for 'gasolina' to get the engine started; remember to keep this topped up.

Bus There are three standards of **bus**: *comum* or *convencional*, which are quite slow, not very comfortable and fill up quickly; *executivo* (executive), which are a few reais more expensive, comfortable, but don't stop to pick up passengers en route and are therefore safer; *semi-leito* and *leito* (literally, bed), which run at night between the main centres, offering reclining seats with foot and leg rests, toilets, and sometimes refreshments, with a higher ticket price. For journeys over 100 km, most buses have chemical toilets. A/c can make leito buses cold at night, so take a blanket or sweater (and toilet paper); on some services blankets are supplied. Some companies have hostess service. Ask for window seats (*janela*), or odd numbers if you want the view.

Buses stop frequently (every 2-4 hrs) for snacks at *postos*. Bus stations for interstate services and other long-distance routes are called . They are normally outside the city centres and offer snack bars, lavatories, left-luggage stores (*guarda volume*), local bus services and information centres. Reliable bus information is hard to come by, other than from the companies themselves at *rodoviárias* (most take credit and Visa debit cards). Buses usually arrive and depart in good time, although loading luggage, ID checks and, in some cities such as São Paulo, metal detector checks can slow things up.

Taxi Taxi meters measure distance/cost in reais. At the outset, make sure the meter is cleared and shows tariff '1', except Sunday 2300-0600, and in December when '2' is permitted. Check the meter works, if not, fix price in advance. Radio taxi service costs about 50% more but cheating is less likely. Taxis outside larger hotels usually cost more than ordinary taxis. If you are seriously cheated, note the taxi number and insist on a signed bill, threatening to go to the police; it can work. **Note** Be wary of Moto Taxis. Many are unlicensed and a number of robberies have been reported.

Hitchhiking Hitchhiking (*carona* in Portuguese) is not a safe option and is difficult everywhere; drivers are reluctant to give lifts because of fear of crime and because passengers are the driver's responsibility. Try at the highway-police check points on the main roads (but make sure your documents are in order) or at the service stations (*postos*).

Boat The main areas where boat travel is practical (and often necessary) are the Amazon region, along the São Francisco River and along the Atlantic coast. There are also some limited transport services through the Pantanal.

Train There are 30,379 km of railway track which are not combined into a unified system and most passenger services on those lines that had them have been withdrawn. Brazil has two gauges and there is little transfer between them. Two more gauges exist for the isolated Amapá Railway and the tourist-only São João del Rei line. There are suburban passenger services in Rio de Janeiro, São Paulo and other cities and long-distance services in the state of São Paulo. Several tourist trains operate, some of which are given in the text.

Maps and guides **Editora Abril** publishes *Quatro Rodas*, a motoring magazine, as well as excellent maps and guides in Portuguese and English from US$15. Its *Guia Brasil* is a type of Michelin Guide to hotels, restaurants (not the cheapest), sights, facilities and general information on hundreds of cities and towns in the country, including good street maps (we acknowledge here our debt to this publication). It also publishes a host of other books, including a *Guia das Praias*, with descriptions of all Brazil's beaches, and magazines. All are available at news stands and bookshops all over the country. For information about the *Quatro Rodas* guides, see www.abril.com.br.

Sleeping → *See page 38 for our hotel grade price guide.*

Hotels Usually hotel prices include breakfast; there is no reduction if you don't eat it. In the better hotels (category **B** and upwards) the breakfast is well worth eating: rolls, ham, eggs, cheese, cakes, fruit. Normally the apartamento is a room with bath; a quarto is a room without bath. *Pousadas* are the equivalent of bed-and-breakfast, often small and family-run, although some are very sophisticated and correspondingly priced. The type known as *hotel familiar*, to be found in the interior – large meals, communal washing, hammocks for children – is much cheaper, but only for the enterprising. The service stations (*postos*) and hostels (*dormitórios*) along the main roads provide excellent value in room and food, akin to truck-driver type accommodation in Europe, for those on a tight budget. The star rating system for hotels (five-star hotels are not price-controlled) is not the standard used in North America or Europe. Business visitors are strongly recommended to book in advance, easily done for Rio or São Paulo hotels with representation abroad. If staying more than three nights in a place in low season, ask for a discount. In hotels ask if they have a backpackers' rate for double rooms; usually better value than doubles in hostels. Motels are specifically intended for very short-stay couples: there is no stigma attached and they usually offer good value (the rate for a full night is called the *pernoite*), though the decor can be a little unsettling.

Roteiros de Charme This is a private association of hotels and *pousadas* in the southeast and northeast, which aims to give a high standard of accommodation in establishments typical of the town they are in. If you are travelling in the appropriate budget range (our **L** price range upwards), you can plan an itinerary which takes in these hotels, with a reputation for comfort and good food. Roteiros de Charme hotels are listed in the text and any one of them can provide information on the group, or visit www.roteirosdecharme.com.br.

Youth hostels For information contact **Federação Brasileira de Albergues da Juventude** ⓘ *R dos Andrades 1137, conj 214, Porto Alegre, CEP 90020-007, T0xx51-3228 3802, www.albergues.com.br.*

Its annual book and website provide a full list of good value accommodation. Also see the *Internet Guide to Hostelling*, which has list of Brazilian youth hostels: www.hostels.com/br.html. Low-budget travellers with student cards (photograph needed) can use the **Casa dos Estudantes** network.

Camping Members of the Camping Clube do Brasil or those with an international campers' card pay only half the rate of a non-member, which is US$10-15 per person. The Club has 43 sites around the country. Membership of the club itself is expensive: US$85 for six months. See **Camping Clube do Brasil**, www.campingclube.com.br. It may be difficult to get into some Clube campsites during the high season (January/February). Private campsites charge about US$8-15 per person. For those on a very low budget and in isolated areas where there is no camp site, service stations can be used as camping sites; they have shower facilities, watchmen and food; some have dormitories; truck drivers are a mine of information. There are also various municipal sites. Campsites often tend to be some distance from public transport routes and are better suited to those with their own transport. Never camp at the side of a road; wild camping is generally not possible. Good camping equipment may be purchased in Brazil and there are several rental companies. Camping gas cartridges are easy to buy in sizeable towns in the south, eg in HM shops. *Quatro Rodas' Guia Brasil* lists main campsites, see page 393. Most sizeable towns have laundromats with self service. *Lavanderias* do the washing for you but are expensive.

Eating and drinking → *See page 39 for Eating price guide.*
The main meal is usually taken in the middle of the day; cheap restaurants tend not to be open in the evening. The most common dish is *bife* (*ou frango*) *com arroz e feijão*, steak (or chicken) with rice and the excellent Brazilian black beans. The most famous dish with beans is the *feijoada completa*: several meat ingredients (jerked beef, smoked sausage, smoked tongue, salt pork, along with spices, herbs and vegetables) are cooked with the beans. Manioc flour is sprinkled over it, and it is eaten with kale (*couve*) and slices of orange, and accompanied by glasses of aguardente (unmatured rum), usually known as *cachaça* (booze), though *pinga* (drop) is a more polite term. Almost all restaurants serve the *feijoada completa* for Saturday lunch (that means up to about 1630).

Throughout Brazil, a mixed grill, including steak, served with roasted manioc flour (*farofa*; raw manioc flour is known as *farinha* goes under the name of *churrasco* (originally from the cattlemen of Rio Grande do Sul), served in specialized restaurants known as churrascarias or *rodízios*; good places for large appetites Bahia has some excellent fish dishes (see note on page 563); some restaurants in most of the big cities specialize in them. *Vatapá* is a good dish in the north; it contains shrimp or fish sauce with palm oil, or coconut milk. *Empadinhas de camarão* are worth trying; they are shrimp patties, with olives and heart of palm.

Minas Gerais has two splendid special dishes involving pork, black beans, farofa and kale; they are *tutu á mineira* and *feijão tropeiro*. A white hard cheese (*queijo prata*) or a slightly softer one (*queijo Minas*) is often served for dessert with bananas, or guava or quince paste. *Comida mineira* is quite distinctive and very wholesome and you can often find restaurants serving this type of food in other parts of Brazil.

Meals are extremely large by European standards; portions are usually for two and come with two plates. Likewise beer is brought with two glasses. If you are on your own and in a position to do so tactfully, you may choose to offer what you can't eat to a person with no food. Alternatively you could ask for an *embalagem* (doggy bag) or get a take away called *a marmita* or *quentinha*, most restaurants have this service but it is not always on the menu. Many restaurants serve *comida por kilo*, usually at lunchtime, where you serve yourself and pay for the weight of food on your plate: good for vegetarians. Unless you specify to the contrary many restaurants will lay a *coberto opcional*, olives, carrots, etc, costing US$0.65-1. **Warning** Avoid mussels, marsh crabs and other shellfish caught near large cities: they are likely to have lived in a highly polluted environment. In a restaurant, always ask the price of a dish before ordering.

For **vegetarians**, there is a growing network of restaurants in the main cities. In smaller places where food may be monotonous try vegetarian for greater variety. Most also serve fish. Alternatives in smaller towns are the Arab and Chinese restaurants.

If travelling on a tight **budget**, remember to ask in restaurants for the *prato feito* or *sortido*, a money-saving, excellent value table-d'hôte meal. The *prato comercial* is similar but rather better and a bit more expensive. *Lanchonetes* are cheap eating places where you generally sit on a stool at the counter to eat. *Salgados* (savoury pastries, also *pastel* - plural *pasteis*), *coxinha* (a pyramid of manioc filled with meat or fish and deep fried), *esfiha* (spicey hamburger inside an onion-bread envelope), *empadão* (a filling – eg chicken – in sauce in a pastry case), *empadas* and *empadinhas* (smaller fritters of the same type), are the usual fare. In Minas Gerais, *pão de queijo* is a hot roll made with cheese. A *bauru* is a toasted sandwich which, in Porto Alegre, is filled with steak, while further north it has tomato, ham and cheese filling. *Cocada* is a coconut and sugar biscuit.

Imported **drinks** are expensive, but there are some fair local wines. Chilean and Portuguese wines are sometimes available at little more than the cost of local wines. The national brands of beer, of the lager type, include Antárctica, Bohemia, Brahma, Cerpa, Itaipava and Skol. Of the black beers, Xingu is reckoned to be the best. Wine is becoming increasingly popular with some regional national table wines and good value imported bottles from Portugal and Argentina. When buying bottled drinks in supermarkets, you will pay more if you don't have empties to cash in. The local firewater, aguardente (known as cachaça or pinga), made from sugar-cane, is cheap and wholesome, but visitors should seek local advice on the best brands; São Francisco, Praianinha, Maria Fulô, '51' and Pitu are recommended makes. Mixed with fruit juices of various sorts, sugar and crushed ice, cachaça becomes the principal element in a *batida*, a delicious and powerful drink; the commonest is a lime batida or *batida de limão*; a variant of this is the *caipirinha*, a cachaça with several slices of lime in it, a *caipiroska* (or *caipirvodka*) is made with vodka, while a *saikirinha* or *caipisake* is made with sake. Cachaça with Coca-Cola is a *cuba*, while rum with Coca-Cola is a *cuba libre*. Some genuine Scotch whisky brands are bottled in Brazil; they are very popular because of the high price of Scotch imported in bottle; Teacher's is the most highly regarded brand. Locally made gin, vermouth and campari are good.

There are plenty of local soft drinks. Guaraná is a very popular carbonated fruit drink. There is an excellent range of non-alcoholic fruit juices, known as *sucos*: *caju* (cashew), *pitanga*, *goiaba* (guava), *genipapo*, *graviola* (chirimoya), *maracujá* (passion fruit), *sapoti* and *tamarindo* are recommended. Vitaminas are thick fruit or vegetable drinks with milk. *Caldo de cana* is sugar-cane juice, sometimes mixed with ice. *Agua mineral*, available in many varieties at bars and restaurants, is a cheap, safe thirst-quencher (cheaper still in supermarkets). Apart from the ubiquitous coffee, good tea is grown and sold. **Note** If you don't want sugar in your coffee or *suco*, you must ask when you order it. *Água de côco* or *côco verde* (coconut water from fresh green coconut) cannot be missed on Rio de Janeiro beaches, São Paulo and in the northeast.

Essentials A-Z

Accident and emergency

Ambulance T192. Directory enquiries T102. Police T190.

Electricity

Generally 110 V 60 cycles AV, but in some areas 220 V 60 cycles. Sockets also vary, often combination sockets for twin flat and twin round pin.

Embassies and consulates

Visit www.mre.gov.br for a full list of Brazillian embassies.

Festivals and events

See also Carnival box page 426. National holidays are **1 Jan** (New Year); 3 days up to and including Ash Wednesday (Carnival); **21 Apr** (Tiradentes); **1 May** (Labour Day); **Corpus Christi** (Jun); **7 Sep** (Independence Day); **12 Oct** (Nossa Senhora Aparecida); **2 Nov** (All Souls' Day); **15 Nov** (Day of the Republic); and **25 Dec** (Christmas). The local holidays in the main cities are given in the text. Four religious or traditional holidays (**Good Friday** must be one; other usual days are **1 Nov** All Saints' Day; **24 Dec** Christmas Eve) must be fixed by the municipalities. Other holidays are usually celebrated on the Mon prior to the date.

Money → *US$1 = R$1.77; €1 = R$2.35 (Apr 2010).* The unit of currency is the real, R$ (plural reais). It floats freely against the dollar. Any amount of foreign currency and 'a reasonable sum' in reais can be taken in; residents may only take out the equivalent of US$4000. Notes in circulation are: 100, 50, 10, 5 and 1 real; coins 1 real, 50, 25, 10, 5 and 1 centavo.

Credit cards Credit or debit cards are the most convenient way of withdrawing money. ATMs are common and frequently offer the best rate of exchange. Credit cards will be charged interest, debit cards should not, but machines that take debit cards are harder to find. The lobbies in which machines are placed usually close 2130-0400. **Bradesco** and **HSBC** are the best for this service. **Banco 24 Horas** ATMs give a long list of cards that they accept, but often do not take international cards. The same is true of **Banco do Brasil**. The foreign-owned banks tend to be good, **Santander**, **Citibank**, possibly ABN-AMRO-owned **Banco Real**. Take another credit card stowed away for emergencies in case of robbery. Emergency phone numbers: MasterCard T0800-891 3294; Visa T0800-891-3680.

Banks In major cities banks will change cash and TCs. If you keep the exchange slips, you may convert back into foreign currency up to 50% of the amount you exchanged. Take US dollars in cash, or euros, and perhaps a few TCs as a back-up. The commission on traveller's cheques can be as much as US$20 *per cheque*.

Cost of travelling Owing to the strengthening of the real against other currencies since 2006, Brazil has become expensive for the traveller. It is hard to find a room costing less than US$15 pp, although dorms are cheaper (US$10-15); in cities and holiday centres hotels cost more, about US$25. Eating out can be expensive, too, but *comida a kilo* (pay by weight) restaurants are good value. In higher class restaurants you should expect to pay around US$20 a head minimum and, in larger cities, US$40. Bus prices are good value, but because of long distances, costs can mount up. It is worth comparing bus and online air tickets. Prices are highest in Rio and São Paulo.

Opening hours
Banks: 1000-1600, but closed on Sat. Businesses: Mon-Fri 0900-1800, closing for lunch some time between 1130 and 1400. Government offices: Mon-Fri 1100-1800. Shops: open on Sat until 1230 or 1300.

Safety
Although Brazil's big cities suffer high rates of violent crime, this is mostly confined to the *favelas* (slums), which should be avoided unless accompanied by a tour leader, or NGO. If the worst does happen and you are threatened, try not to panic, but hand over your valuables. Do not resist, but report the crime to the local tourist police, who should be your first port of call in case of difficulty. The situation is much more secure in smaller towns and in the country. Also steer well clear of areas of drug cultivation and red light districts. In the latter drinks are often spiked with a drug called 'Goodnight Cinderella'. See the Safety section in Essentials at the beginning of the book for general advice.

Police There are several types of police: **Polícia Federal**, civilian dressed, who handle all federal law duties, including immigration. A subdivision is the **Polícia Federal Rodoviária**, uniformed, who are the traffic police. **Polícia Militar** are the uniformed, street police force, under the control of the state governor, handling all state laws. They are not the same as the Armed Forces' internal police. **Polícia Civil**, also state-controlled, handle local laws; usually in civilian dress, unless in the traffic division. In cities, the Prefeitura controls the **Guarda Municipal**, who handle security. **Tourist police** operate in places with a strong tourist presence.

Identification You must always carry identification when in Brazil; it is a good idea to take a photocopy of the personal details in your passport, plus that with your Brazilian immigration stamp, and leave your passport in the hotel safe deposit. Always keep an independent record of your passport details. It is a good idea to register with your consulate to expedite document replacement if yours gets lost or stolen.

Tax

Airport tax The amount of tax depends on the class of airport. The international departure tax is usually included in the ticket price. If not, you will have to pay on leaving Brazil. There are 4 categories of domestic airport for tax purposes: first-class R$19.60; second-class R$15.40; third class R$11.60; fourth class R$8. Tax must be paid on checking in, in reais or US dollars. Tax is waived if you are in Brazil less than 24 hrs.
VAT Rate varies from 7 to 25% at state and federal level; average 17-20%.

Time

Official time Brazilian standard time is GMT -3; of the major cities, only the Amazon time zone, Manaus, Cuiabá, Campo Grande and Corumbá are different (GMT -4). The state of Acre is GMT -5. Fernando do Noronha is GMT -2. Clocks go forward 1 hr in summer for approximately 5 months (usually Oct-Feb or Mar). (This does not apply to Acre.)

Telephones

International phone code +55 Ringing: equal tones with long pauses. Engaged: equal tones, equal pauses.
Dialling: When dialling from outside an area code, dial an operator code (shown by 'xx' in the book) followed by area code without the zero and then the number. To dial internationally dial 00 + operator code without the zero, then the country code and number. **Operator codes**: **Embratel**, 21 (nationwide); **Telefônica**, 15 (state of São Paulo); **Telemar**, 31 (Alagoas, Amazonas, Amapá, Bahia, Ceará, Espírito Santo, Maranhão, most of Minas Gerais, Pará, Paraíba, Pernambuco, Piauí, Rio de Janeiro, Rio Grande do Norte, Roraima, Sergipe); **Tele Centro-Sul**, 14 (Acre, Goiás, Mato Grosso, Mato Grosso do Sul, Paraná, Rondônia, Santa Catarina, Tocantins and the cities of Brasília and Pelotas); **CTBC-Telecom**, 12 (some parts of Minas Gerais, Goiás, Mato Grosso do Sul and São Paulo state); **Intelig**, 23.
Mobile phones These are widespread and coverage is excellent even in remote areas, but prices are among the highest in the world and users pay to receive calls outside the metropolitan area where their phone is registered. SIM cards are hard to come by as users require a Brazilian social security number (CPF) to buy one, similarly to buy a pay-as-you-go phone. Generally a mobile phone's 8-digit number begins with 8 or 9. When using a mobile phone you do not drop the zero from the area code as you have to when dialling from a fixed line.
NB Many hostels have internet and many hotels have free Wi-Fi. Cyber-cafés are plentiful and are usually called **Lan house**.

Tipping

Tipping is usual, but less costly than in most other countries, except for porters. Restaurants, 10% of bill if no service charge but small tip if there is; taxi drivers, none; cloakroom attendants, small tip; cinema usherettes, none; hairdressers, 10-15%; porters, fixed charges but tips as well; airport porters, about US$0.65 per item.

Tourist information

Ministério do Turismo, Esplanada dos Ministérios, Bloco U, 2nd and 3rd floors, Brasília, www.turismo.gov.br or www.braziltour.com (in many languages). **Embratur**, the Brazilian Institute of Tourism, at the same address, is in charge of promoting tourism abroad, T0xx61-3429 7777, www.embratur.gov.br. For information abroad, contact Brazil's representation overseas: France, T+33-1-5353 6962, info.fr@embratur.gov.br; Germany, T+49-69-2197 1276, info.de@embratur.gov.br; Italy, T+39-2-8633 7791, info.it@embratur.gov.br; Japan, T+81-8-5565 7591, info.jp@embratur.gov.br; Portugal, T+351-21-340 4668, info.pt@embratur.gov.br; Spain, T+34-91-503 0687, info.es@embratur.gov.br; UK, T+44-207-7399 9000, tourism@brazil.org.uk; USA, T+1-646-378 2126, info.us@embratur.gov.br, and T+1-310-341 8394, info.us2@embratur.gov.br. Tourist information bureaux are not usually helpful with information on cheap hotels and it is difficult to get information on neighbouring states. Expensive hotels provide tourist magazines for their guests. Telephone directories (not Rio) contain good street maps.

National parks are run by the **Instituto Chico Mendes de Conservação da Biodiversidade, ICMBio**, EQSW, Bloco C, Complexo Administrativo, Setor Sudoeste, Brasília, DF, T0xx61-3341 9101, www.icmbio.gov.br. National parks are open to visitors, usually with a permit issued by ICMBio.
See also the Ministério do Meio Ambiente website, www.mma.gov.br.

Useful websites

See Tourist office sites under individual cities.

www.abeta.com.br The Brazilian Association of Adventure Tourism Companies' website, with a list of memebers by state and types of activity available (in Portuguese); Abeta, R Prata 32, Cruzeiro, Belo Horizonte, T0xx31-3227 1678.

www.ipanema.com Insider's guide to Rio in English.

www.maria-brazil.org A fun site with a blog, info, tips, recommendations, mostly about Rio.

www.brasilemb.org (USA).

www.brazil.org.uk (UK).

www.brazilmax.com Bill Hinchberger's *Hip Gringo's Guide* to Brazil with loads of news, cultural articles and travel information and a strong ecological angle.

www.gringoes.com Information on all things Brazilian for visitors and ex-pats.

www.wwf.org.br World Wide Fund in Brazil.

www.socioambiental.org Accurate information on environmental and indigenous issues.

http://ran.org Accurate information on rainforest-related issues with comprehensive information on Brazil and extensive links.

www.survival-international.org The world's leading campaign organization for indigenous peoples with excellent info on various Brazilian indigenous groups.

Visas and immigration

Consular visas are not required for stays of up to 90 days by tourists from EU countries (except Cyprus, Estonia, Latvia and Malta), Israel, New Zealand, Norway, South Africa, Switzerland, South and Central American countries (except Mexico, Belize, El Salvador and Nicaragua) and some Caribbean, Asian and African countries. For them, only the following documents are required at the port of disembarkation: a passport valid for at least 6 months; and a return or onward ticket, or adequate proof that you can purchase your return fare, subject to no remuneration being received in Brazil and no legally binding or contractual documents being signed. Visas are required by US and Canadian citizens, Japanese, Australians and people of other nationalities, and those who cannot meet the requirements above, must get a visa before arrival, which may, if you ask, be granted for multiple entry. Visas are valid from date of issue. Visa fees vary from country to country, so apply to the Brazilian consulate, in the country of residence of the applicant. The consular fees range start at US$20, rising to US$35 (A$49 for Australians), US$50 (Japanese citizens), US$65 (Can$91 for Canadians), to a US$130 reciprocity fee for US citizens (the visa itself is free). In all cases there is a US$20 handling fee if you do not apply in person. Do not lose the emigration permit given to you when you enter Brazil. If you leave the country without it, you may have to pay a fine.

Foreign tourists may stay a maximum of 180 days in any one year. 90-day renewals are easily obtainable, but only at least 15 days before the expiry of your 90-day permit, from the Polícia Federal. You will have to fill out three copies of the tax form at the Polícia Federal, take them to a branch of Banco do Brasil, pay US$15 and bring 2 copies back. You will then be given the extension form to fill in and be asked for your passport to stamp in the extension. Regulations state that you should be able to show a return ticket, cash, cheques or a credit card, a personal reference and proof of an address of a person living in the same city as the office (in practice you simply write this in the space on the form). Some offices will only give you an extension within 10 days of the expiry of your permit. Some points of entry, such as the Colombian border, refuse entry for longer than 30 days, renewals are then for the same period, insist if you want 90 days. For longer stays you must leave the country and return (not the same day) to get a new 90-day permit. If your visa has expired, getting a new visa can be costly (US$35 for a consultation, US$30 for the visa) and may take up to 45 days. If you overstay your visa you will be fined US$7 per day. After paying the fine, you will be issued with an exit visa and must leave within 8 days. **Note** Officially, if you leave Brazil within the 90-day permission to stay and then re-enter the country, you should only be allowed to stay until the 90-day permit expires. If, however, you are given another 90-day permit, this may lead to charges of overstaying if you apply for an extension. For UK citizens a joint agreement allows visits for business or tourism of up to 6 months a year from the date of first entry.

Weights and measures

Metric.

Rio de Janeiro → *Phone code: 0xx21. Colour map 4, C3.*

Brazilians say: God made the world in six days; the seventh he devoted to Rio (pronounced 'Heeoo' by locals). Rio has a glorious theatrical backdrop of tumbling wooded mountains, stark expanses of bare rock and a deep blue sea studded with rocky islands. From the statue of Christ on the hunchbacked peak of Corcovado, or from the conical Pão de Açúcar (Sugar Loaf), you can experience the beauty of a bird's-eye view over the city which sweeps 220 km along a narrow alluvial strip on the southwestern shore of the Baía de Guanabara. Although best known for the curving Copacabana beach, for Ipanema – home to the Girl and beautiful sunsets, and for its swirling, reverberating, joyous Carnival, Rio also has a fine artistic, architectural and cultural heritage from its time as capital of both imperial and republican Brazil. But this is first and foremost a city dedicated to leisure: sport and music rule and a day spent hang gliding or surfing is easily followed by an evening of jazz or samba.

Ins and outs

Getting there **Aeroporto Internacional** Antônio Carlos Jobim (Galeão) is on the Ilha do Governador, about 16 km on the Petrópolis highway. Left luggage only in Terminal 1. The air bridge from São Paulo ends at Santos Dumont airport in the city centre. Taxis from here are much cheaper than from the international airport. There are also frequent buses. International

1 Rio de Janeiro

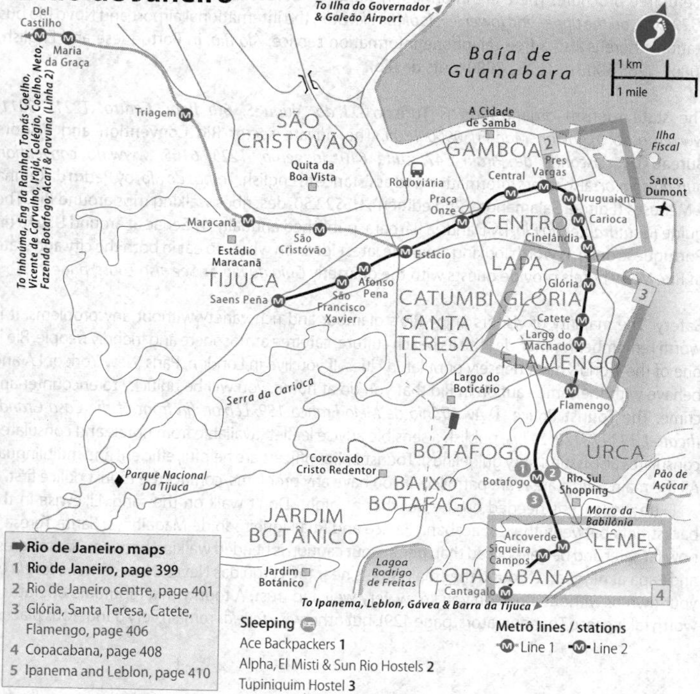

buses and those from other parts of Brazil arrive at the **Rodoviária Novo Rio** (main bus station) near the docks. » *See also Transport, page 430.*

Getting around As the city is a series of separate districts connected by urban highways and tunnels, you need to take public transport. An underground railway, the **Metrô**, runs from west and northwest under the centre to the south. Buses run to all parts, treat them with caution at night when taxis are better. Combination tickets are sold for Metrô and bus, and for Metrô and SuperVia suburban trains.

Climate Rio has one of the healthiest climates in the tropics. Trade winds cool the air. June, July and August are the coolest months with temperatures ranging from 22°C (18° in a cold spell) to 32°C on a sunny day at noon. December to March is hotter, from 32°C to 42°C. Humidity is high. It is important, especially for children, to guard against dehydration in summer by drinking as much liquid as possible. October to March is the rainy season. Annual rainfall is about 1,120 mm.

Tourist offices **Riotur** ⓘ *Praça Pio X, 119, 9th floor, Centro, T2271 7000, www.riodejaneiro-turismo.com.br and www.rio.rj.gov.br/riotur*, is the city's government tourist office. There are also booths or offices in **Copacabana** ⓘ *Av Princesa Isabel 183, T2541 7522, Mon-Fri 0900- 1800*, and **Copacabana Posto Seis** ⓘ *Av Rainha Elizabeth 36 at NS de Copacabana, T2513 0077, Mon-Fri 0900-1800*. The helpful staff speak English, French and German and have good city maps and a useful free brochure. There are information stands at **Corcovado** ⓘ *R Cosme Velho 513, T2258 1329 ext 4, on the upper and lower levels of the elevator*, the international airport and Novo Rio bus station. There is also a free telephone information service, *Alô Rio*, in Portuguese and English, T0800-2285 5000 or T2252 8080 (outside Rio).

The state tourism organization is **Turisrio** ⓘ *R da Ajuda 5, 6th floor, Centro, T2215 0011, www.turisrio .rj.gov.br, Mon-Fri 0900-1800*. The private sector **Rio Convention and Visitors Bureau** ⓘ *R Visconde de Pirajá 547, suite 610, Ipanema, T2259 6165, www.rio convention bureau.com.br*, also offers information and assistance in English. *Trilhas do Rio*, by Pedro da Cunha e Meneses (Editora Salamandra, 2nd edition), US$22.50, describes walking trips around Rio. The guide *Restaurantes do Rio*, by Danusia Bárbara, published annually by Senac at around US$10 (in Portuguese only), is worth looking at for the latest ideas on where to eat in both the city and state of Rio. Many hotels provide guests with the quarterly *Guia do Rio*. » *See also Tours, page 429.*

Safety The majority of visitors enjoy Rio's glamour and rich variety without any problems. It is worth remembering that, despite its beach culture, carefree atmosphere and friendly people, Rio is one of the world's most densely populated cities. If you live in London, Paris, New York or LA and behave with the same caution in Rio that you do at home, you will be unlucky to encounter any crime. The **Tourist Police** ⓘ *Av Afrânio de Melo Franco 159, Leblon (in front of the Casa Grande theatre), T3399 7170, 24 hrs*, publish a sensible advice leaflet (available from hotels and consulates consulates also issue safety guidelines). Tourist police officers are helpful, efficient and multilingual All the main tourist areas are patrolled. If you have any problems, contact the tourist police first.

Extra vigilance is needed on the beaches at night. Don't walk on the sand. Likewise in the backstreets between the Copacabana Palace and Rua Figueiredo de Magalhães. Santa Teresa is now far safer and better policed than before, but caution is needed walking between Santa Teresa and Lapa at night and around the small streets near the Largo das Neves. Never enter a *favela* on your own or without a person you know very well and trust. A tour with a reputable operator is worth taking (see Tour operators, page 429), but otherwise *favelas* remain very dangerous places

Background

The Portuguese navigator, Gonçalo Coelho, arrived at what is now Rio de Janeiro on 1 January 1502. Thinking that the Baía de Guanabara (the name the local *indígenas* used) was the mouth of a great river, they called the place the January River. Although the bay was almost as large

2 Rio de Janeiro centre

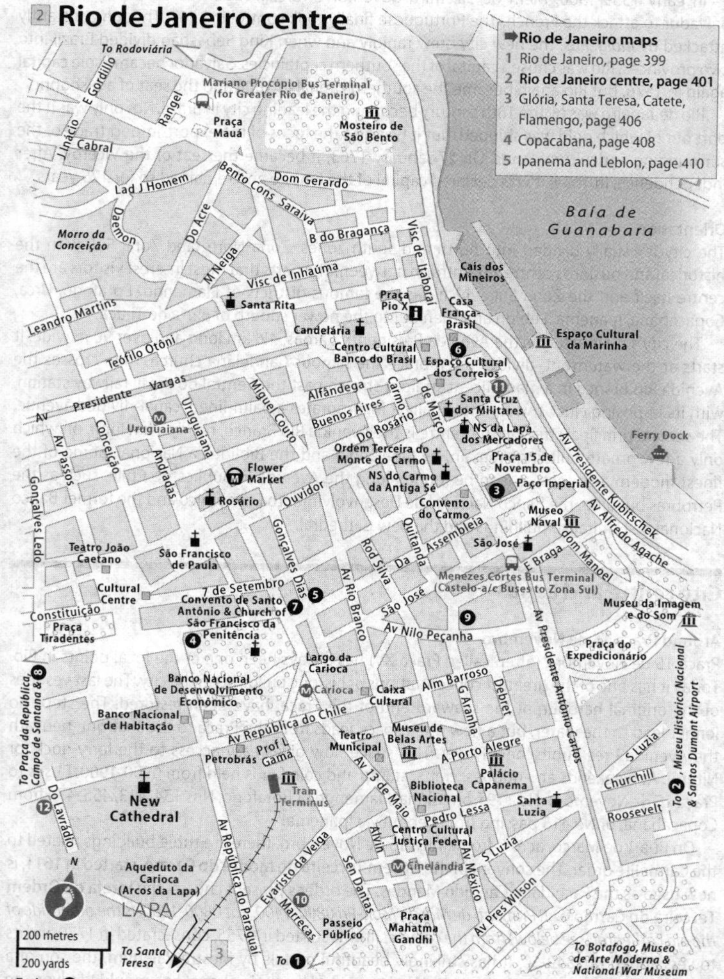

Eating

1 Adega Flor de Coimbra
2 Albamar
3 Bar das Artes
4 Bar Luiz
5 Café da Moda
6 Cais do Oriente
7 Confeitaria Colombo
8 Republique
9 Sabor Saúde

Bars & clubs

10 Club Six
11 Mercado
12 Rio Scenarium

and as safe a harbour as the Baía de Todos Os Santos to the north, the Portuguese did not take of advantage of it. In fact, it was first settled by the French, who, under the Huguenot Admiral Nicholas Durand de Villegagnon, occupied Lage Island on 10 November 1555, but later transferred to Seregipe Island (now Villegagnon), where they built the fort of Coligny.

In early 1559-1560, Mem de Sá, third governor of Brazil, mounted an expedition from Salvador to attack the French. The Portuguese finally took control in 1567. Though constantly attacked by *indígenas*, the new city grew rapidly and when King Sebastião divided Brazil into two provinces, Rio was chosen capital of the southern captaincies. Salvador became sole capital again in 1576, but Rio again became the southern capital in 1608 and the seat of a bishopric.

Rio de Janeiro was by the 18th century becoming the leading city in Brazil. Not only was it the port out of which gold was shipped, but it was also the focus of the export/import trade of the surrounding agricultural lands. On 27 January 1763, it became the seat of the Viceroy. After independence, in 1834, it was declared capital of the Empire and remained so for 125 years.

Orientation

The city is usually divided into north and south zones, Zona Norte and Zona Sul, with the historical and business centre, O Centro, in between. The parts that most interest visitors are the centre itself and the Zona Sul, which has the famous districts of Flamengo, Botafogo, Urca, Copacabana, Ipanema, Leblon and then out to the newer suburb of Barra de Tijuca.

The city's main artery is the Avenida Presidente Vargas, 4½ km long and over 90 m wide. It starts at the waterfront, divides to embrace the famous Candelária church, then crosses the Avenida Rio Branco in a magnificent straight stretch past the Central do Brasil railway station, with its imposing clock tower, until finally it incorporates a palm-lined, canal-divided avenue. The second principal street in the centre is the Avenida Rio Branco, nearly 2 km long, on which only a few ornate buildings remain, by Cinelândia and the Biblioteca Nacional. Some of the finest modern architecture is to be found along the Avenida República do Chile, such as the Petrobrás building, the Banco Nacional de Desenvolvimento Econômico and the former Banco Nacional de Habitação buildings and the new Cathedral.

City centre and Lapa

Around Praça 15 de Novembro

Praça 15 de Novembro (often called Praça XV) has always been one of the focal points in Rio. Today it has one of the greatest concentrations of historic buildings in the city. The last vestiges of the original harbour, at the seaward end of the Praça, have been restored. The steps no longer lead to the water, but a new open space leads from the Praça to the seafront, beneath the Avenida Pres Kubitschek flyover. This space now gives easy access to the ferry dock for Niterói. At weekends an antiques, crafts, stamp and coin fair is held from 0900-1900. Buses to Praça 15 de Novembro: No 119 from Glória, Flamengo or Botafogo; Nos 154, 413, 455, 474 from Copacabana, or No 415 passing from Leblon via Ipanema.

On Rua 1 de Março, across from Praça 15 de Novembro, there are three buildings related to the Carmelite order. The convent of the **Ordem Terceira do Monte do Carmo**, started in 1611, is now used as the Faculdade Cândido Mendes. The order's present church, the **Igreja da Ordem Terceira do Carmo** ⓘ *R Primeiro de Março, Mon-Fri 0800-1400, Sat 0800-1200, is the other side of the old cathedral (see below) from the convent*. It was started in 1755, consecrated in 1770 and its towers added in 1849-50. It has strikingly beautiful portals by Mestre Valentim, the son of a Portuguese nobleman and a slave girl. He also created the main altar of fine moulded silver, the throne and its chair and much else.

Between the former convent and the Igreja da Ordem Terceira do Carmo is the old cathedral, the **Igreja de Nossa Senhora do Carmo da Antiga Sé**, separated from the Carmo Church by a closed passageway. It was the chapel of Convento do Carmo from 1590 until 1754. A new church was built in 1761, which became the city's cathedral. In the crypt are the alleged remains of Pedro Alvares Cabral, the Portuguese explorer (though Santarém, Portugal, also claims to be his last resting place).

The **Paço Imperial** (former Royal Palace) ⓘ *T2533 4407, Tue-Sun 1200-1800*, is on the south-east corner of the Praça 15 de Novembro. This beautiful colonial building was built in 1743 as the residence of the governor of the Capitania. It later became the Paço Real when the Portuguese court moved to Brazil. After Independence it became the Imperial Palace. It has an exhibition space, a small display at the west end on the history of the building and the Bistro do Paço and Atrium restaurants. Recommended.

Igreja de São José ⓘ *R São José e Av Pres Antônio Carlos, Mon-Fri 0900-1200, 1400-1700, Sun 0900-1100*, is much altered since its 17th-century construction. The current building dates from 1824.

On the northwest side of Praça 15 de Novembro, you go through the Arco do Teles and the Travessa do Comércio to Rua do Ouvidor. The **Igreja Nossa Senhora da Lapa dos Mercadores** ⓘ *R do Ouvidor 35, Mon-Fri 0800-1400*, was consecrated in 1750, remodelled 1869-1872 and has been fully restored. Across the street, with its entrance at Rua 1 de Março 36, is the church of **Santa Cruz dos Militares**, built 1770-1811. It is large, stately and beautiful and has the first neoclassical façade in Brazil; the altar is by Mestre Valentim.

The Church of **Nossa Senhora da Candelária** (1775-1810) ⓘ *on Praça Pio X (Dez), at the city end of Av Pres Vargas where it meets R 1 de Março, Mon-Fri 0730-1200, 1300-1630, Sat 0800-1200, Sun 0900-1300*, has beautiful ceiling decorations and romantic paintings.

The **Centro Cultural Banco do Brasil (CCBB)** ⓘ *entrances on Av Pres Vargas and R 1 de Março 66, T3808 2089, Tue-Sun 1230-1900*, is highly recommended for good exhibitions. It has a library, multimedia facilities, a cinema, concerts (US$6 at lunchtime) and a restaurant. Opposite is the **Espaço Cultural dos Correios** ⓘ *R Visconde de Itaboraí 20, T2503 8770, Tue-Sun 1200-1900*, which holds temporary exhibitions and a postage stamp fair on Saturdays. **Casa França-Brasil** ⓘ *R Visconde de Itaboraí 253 and Av Pres Vargas, T2253 5366, Tue-Sun 1200-2000*, dates from the first French Artistic Mission to Brazil and it was the first neoclassical building in Rio. **Espaço Cultural da Marinha** ⓘ *Av Alfredo Agache at Av Pres Kubitschek, T2104 6025, Tue-Sun 1200-1700, museum, free, and 1-hr boat trip, US$4.50*, was given to the navy to become a museum containing displays on underwater archaeology and navigation and the Galeota, the boat in which the royal family was rowed around the Baía de Guanabara. Moored outside are the tug *Laurindo Pitta* ⓘ *1 hr 20 min trips Thu-Sun 1315 and 1515, US$4.50*, and the submarine *Riachuelo*, both British-built (both can be visited). Boats give access to **Ilha Fiscal** with its beautiful neo-Gothic palace ⓘ *T3870 6879, boats to Ilha Fiscal, Thu-Sun, 1300, 1430, 1600, US$4.50*. The **Museu Naval** is just south (off Praça XV) ⓘ *R Dom Manuel 15, Tue-Sun 1200-1700*, good, with English summaries to end of 19th century.

Just north of Candelária, on a promontory overlooking the bay, is the **Mosteiro** (monastery) **de São Bento** ⓘ *daily 0800-1230, 1400-1730, shorts not allowed*. Every Sunday at 1000, mass is sung with Gregorian chant and music, which is free, but arrive an hour early to get a seat. On other days, mass is at 0715. It contains much of what is best in the 17th- and 18th-century art of Brazil. São Bento is reached either by a narrow road from Rua Dom Gerardo 68, or by a lift whose entrance is at Rua Dom Gerardo 40 (taxi from centre US$5). The main body of the church is adorned in gold and red. The carving and gilding is remarkable, much of it by Frei Domingos da Conceição. The paintings, too, should be seen. The Chapels of the Immaculate Conception (Nossa Senhora da Conceição) and of the Most Holy Sacrament (Santíssimo Sacramento) are masterpieces of colonial art. The organ, dating from the end of the 18th century, is very interesting.

Around Largo da Carioca

The second oldest convent in the city is the **Convento de Santo Antônio** ⓘ *daily 0800-1800*, on a hill off the Largo da Carioca, built 1608-1615. Santo Antônio is an object of devotion for women looking for a husband and you will see them in the precincts. The church has a marvellous sacristy adorned with blue tiles and paintings illustrating the life of St Anthony. In the church itself, the baroque decoration is concentrated in the chancel, the main altar and the two lateral altars.

Separated from this church only by some iron railings is the charming church of the Ordem Terceira de **São Francisco da Penitência** ⓘ *T2262 0197, Mon-Fri 0900-1200, 1300-1600*. Its Baroque carving and gilding of walls and altar, much more than in its neighbour, is considered among the finest in Rio. There is also a Museu de Arte Sacra. Strongly recommended.

Across Ruas da Carioca and 7 de Setembro is the church of **São Francisco de Paula** ⓘ *upper end of R do Ouvidor, Mon-Fri 0900-1300*. It contains some of Mestre Valentim's work. One long block behind the Largo da Carioca and São Francisco de Paula is the **Praça Tiradentes**, old and shady, with a statue to Dom Pedro I. At the northeast corner of the praça is the **Teatro João Caetano** ⓘ *T2221 0305*. Shops nearby specialize in selling goods for umbanda, the Afro-Brazilian religion. South of the Largo da Carioca are the modern buildings on Avenida República do Chile including the new cathedral, the **Catedral Metropolitana** ⓘ *www.catedral.com.br, 0600-1900*, dedicated in November 1976. It is a cone-shaped building with capacity of 5,000 seated, 20,000 standing. The most striking feature is four enormous 60-m-high stained-glass windows – still incomplete. Crossing Avendia República do Paraguai from the cathedral are the Petrobrás building and the station, with museum, for the tram to Santa Teresa (entrance on Rua Senador Dantas – see below).

Avenida Rio Branco

Facing Praça Marechal Floriano is the **Teatro Municipal** ⓘ *T2299 1711, www.theatromunicipal.rj.gov.br, Mon-Fri 0900-1700, US$2, guided visits Mon-Fri 1300-1600, T2299 1667*. The box office is at the right-hand side of the building; ticket prices start at about US$15. One of the most magnificent buildings in Brazil in the eclectic style, it was built in 1905-1909, in imitation of the Opéra in Paris. The decorative features inside and out represent many styles, all lavishly executed. Opera and orchestral performances are given here. To book a tour of the theatre, ask for extension (ramal) 935 in advance. The **Biblioteca Nacional** ⓘ *Av Rio Branco 219, T2262 8255, Mon-Fri 0900, US$1*, dates from 1905-1910. The monumental staircase leads to a hall, off which lead the fine internal staircases of Carrara marble. It houses over nine million volumes and documents. The **Museu Nacional de Belas Artes** ⓘ *Av Rio Branco 199, T2240 0068, Tue-Fri 1000-1800, Sat, Sun and holidays 1400-1800, US$1*, was built between 1906 and 1908, in eclectic style. It has 800 original paintings and sculptures and 1,000 direct reproductions. One gallery, dedicated to works by Brazilian artists from the 17th century onwards, includes paintings by Frans Janszoon Post (Dutch 1612-1680), who painted Brazilian landscapes in classical Dutch style, and Frenchmen Debret and Taunay. It has one of the best collections of Brazilian modernism in the country, with important works by artists like Cândido Portinári and Emiliano Di Cavalcánti. The **Centro Cultural Justiça Federal**, in the former Supreme Court (1905-09) ⓘ *Av Rio Branco 241, T3261 2550, www.ccjf.trf2 .gov.br, Tue-Sun 1200-1900*, has excellent eclectic architecture; you can see the court chamber and good temporary exhibitions.

Praça Mahatma Gandhi, at the end of Avenida Rio Branco, is flanked on one side by the old cinema and amusement centre of the city, known as Cinelândia. Next to the praça is the **Passeio Público** ⓘ *daily 0900-1700*, a garden planted in 1779-1783 by the artist Mestre Valentim, whose bust is near the old gateway.

West of the Passeio and the Catedral Metropolitana is **Lapa**, an area slowly rediscovering its belle-époque, artistic past. After 40 years of neglect, streets with a reputation for extreme danger have revived; town houses have been renovated, antiques markets, cafés and music venues have opened and the area has become the heart of Bohemian Rio. You still need to be a bit vigilant here, but it's one of **the** places to go for a night out.

Praça Marechal Âncora/Praça Rui Barbosa

The **Museu Histórico Nacional** ⓘ *T2550 9224, Tue-Fri 1000-1730, Sat, Sun and holidays 1400-1800, US$2, free Sun,* has excellent displays on Brazil's history (starting with indigenous peoples), coins, a collection of beautiful carriages and temporary shows. It's a big complex, including a 16th-17th century fortress, the Caso de Trem (artillery store, 1760) and arsenal (1764). There are good English summaries and a restaurant. **Museu da Imagem e do Som** ⓘ *also on Praça Rui Barbosa, T2262 0309, Mon-Fri 1300-1800,* has photographs of Brazil and modern Brazilian paintings; also collections and recordings of Brazilian classical and popular music and a non-commercial cinema Friday-Sunday.

Zona Norte

West of the centre

About 3 km west of the public gardens of the Praça da República (beyond the Sambódromo – see box, Carnival, page 426) is the **Quinta da Boa Vista** ⓘ *daily 0700-1800,* formerly the emperor's private park, from 1809 to 1889. If you are comfortable in crowds, a good time to visit is Saturday or Sunday afternoon. It is full of locals looking for fun and relaxation and therefore more police are on hand. **Note** Beware of thieves by the park entrance and in the park itself on weekdays.

In the entrance hall of the **Museu Nacional** ⓘ *Quinta da Boa Vista, Tue-Sun 1000-1600, US$2,* is the famous Bendegó meteorite, found in the State of Bahia in 1888; its original weight, before some of it was chipped, was 5,360 kg. The museum also has important collections which are poorly displayed. The building was the principal palace of the Emperors of Brazil, but only the unfurnished Throne Room and ambassadorial reception room on the second floor reflect past glories. The museum contains collections of Brazilian indigenous weapons, dresses, utensils, etc, of minerals and of historical documents. There are also collections of birds, beasts, fishes and butterflies. Despite the need for conservation work, the museum is still worth visiting. The safest way to reach the museum is by taking a taxi to the main door. Having said that, it can be reached by Metrô to São Cristóvão, then cross the railway line and walk five minutes to the park. This is safer than taking a bus. Also in the park is the **Jardim Zoológico** ⓘ *same opening hours, US$2,* with a captive breeding programme for some endangered animals, such as golden lion tamarins.

Maracanã Stadium ⓘ *T2568 9962, 0900-1700 (0800-1100 on match days), a guided tour of the stadium (in Portuguese) from Gate 16 costs US$6 and of the museum, US$0.50.* Highly recommended for football fans. This is one of the largest sports centres in the world, with a capacity of 200,000. Matches are worth going to if only for the spectators' samba bands. There are three types of ticket, but prices vary according to the game (expect to pay US$7.50-10). Agencies charge much more for tickets than at the gate. It is cheaper to buy tickets from club sites on the day before the match. Seats in the white section have good views. Maracanã is now used only for major games; Rio teams play most matches at their home grounds (still a memorable experience, about US$2 per ticket). Maracanã can be visited most safely during a game with www.bealocal.com, T9643 0366: all is organized including transport from hotel/hostel, tickets and a safe area from which to watch the game.

Santa Teresa → *see map below.*

Known as the coolest part of Rio, this hilly inner suburb southwest of the centre, boasts many colonial and 19th-century buildings, set in narrow, curving, tree-lined streets. Today the old houses are lived in by artists, intellectuals and makers of handicrafts. As Rio's up-and-coming place to stay, it has hostels, hotels and homestays (including the upper floor of the former home

3 Glória, Santa Teresa, Catete, Flamengo

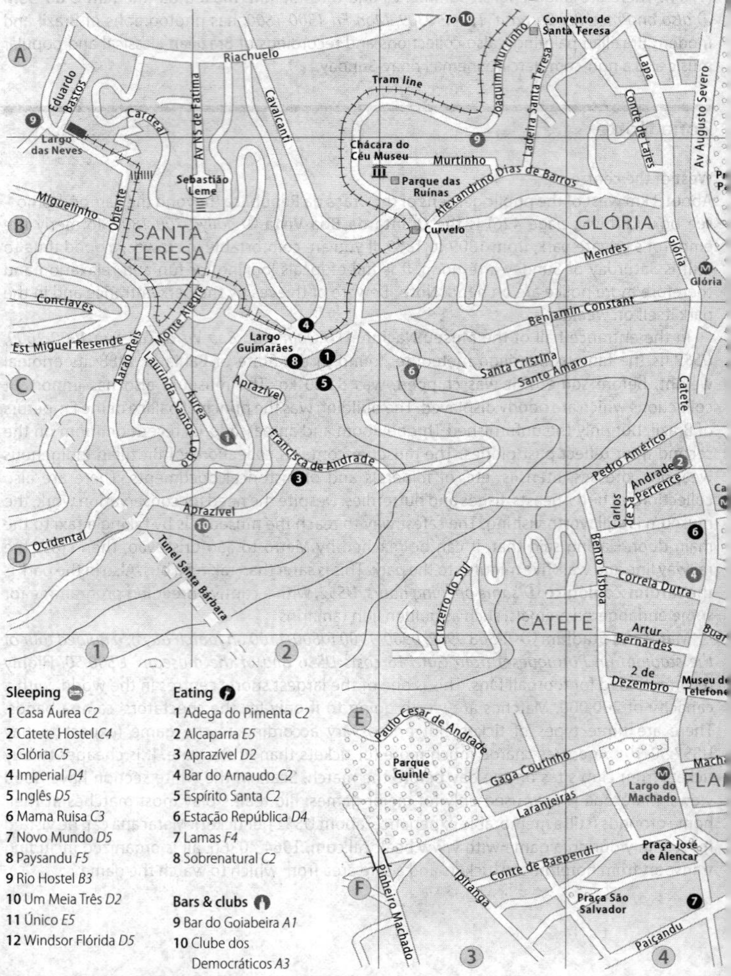

of Ronnie Biggs, the British, 1960s great train robber). Most visitors in the daytime will arrive by tram. If you stay to the end of the line, Largo das Neves, you will be able to appreciate the small-town feel of the place. There are several bars here, including Goiabeira, simple and charming with a nice view of the praça. The essential stop is the Largo do Guimarães, which has some not-to-be-missed eating places (see Eating). **Chácara do Céu** ⓘ *R Murtinho Nobre 93, T2285 0891, Tue-Sun 1200-1700, US$1, take the Santa Teresa tram to Curvelo station, walk along R Dias de Barros, following the signposts to Parque das Ruínas*. Also called Fundação Raymundo Ottoni de Castro Maia, it has a wide range of art objects and modern painters, including Brazilian; exhibitions change through the year. The **Chalé Murtinho** ⓘ *R Murtinho 41, daily 1000-1700*, was in ruins until it was partially restored and turned into a cultural centre called **Parque das Ruínas** in 1998. There are exhibitions, a snack bar and superb views.

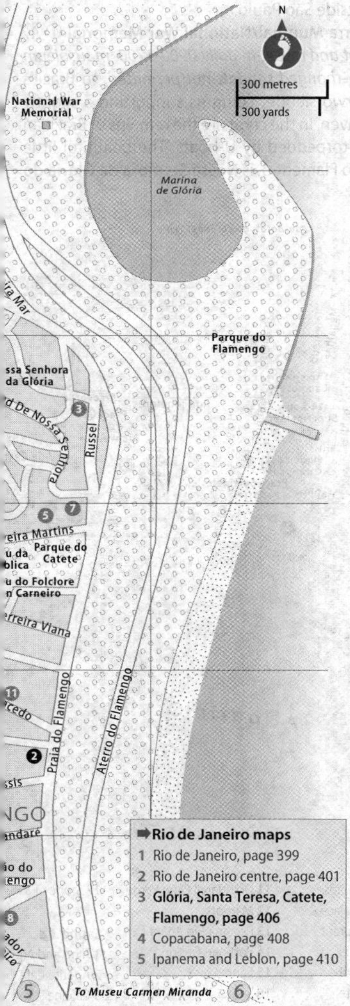

➡ **Rio de Janeiro maps**
1 Rio de Janeiro, page 399
2 Rio de Janeiro centre, page 401
3 **Glória, Santa Teresa, Catete, Flamengo, page 406**
4 Copacabana, page 408
5 Ipanema and Leblon, page 410

Santa Teresa is best visited on the traditional open-sided **tram** (US$0.30 one way), the *bondinho*. Take the Metrô to Carioca or Cinelândia, go to Rua Senador Dantas then walk along to Rua Profesor Lélio Gama (look for Banco do Brasil on the corner). The station is up this street. Take the Paula Mattos line (a second line is Dois Irmãos) and enjoy the trip as it passes over the **Arcos da Lapa** aqueduct and then winds its way up to the district's historic streets. At Largo das Neves, the tram turns round for the journey back to Rua Profesor L Gama. Normally a policeman rides each *bondinho*, but you are advised not to take valuables (see Safety, page 400). Buses Nos 206 and 214 run from Avenida Rio Branco in the centre to Santa Teresa. At night, only take a taxi, US$7.

Zona Sul → *see map opposite.*

The commercial district ends where Avenida Rio Branco meets Avenida Beira Mar. This avenue, with its royal palms and handsome buildings, coasting the Botafogo and Flamengo beaches, makes a splendid drive, Avenida Infante Dom Henrique, along the beach over re-claimed land (the Aterro), leading to Botafogo and through two tunnels to Copacabana.

Glória, Catete and Flamengo

On the Glória and Flamengo waterfront, with a view of the Pão de Açúcar and Corcovado, is the **Parque do Flamengo**, designed by Burle Marx, opened in 1965 during the 400th anniversary of the city's founding and landscaped on 100 ha reclaimed from the bay. Security in the park is in the hands of military police at the National War Memorial and it is a popular recreation area. (**Note** Beware armed robbery in Parque do Flamengo.) **Museu de Arte Moderna** ⓘ *Av Infante Dom Henrique 85, city end of Parque Flamengo, T2240 4944, www.mamrio.com.br, Tue-Sun 1200-1800, 1900 weekends and holidays, US$2.50.* This spectacular building houses works by many well-known Europeans and collections of Brazilian contemporary art, the best modern art in Brazil outside São Paulo.

The Monumento aos Mortos da Segunda Guerra Mundial/National War Memorial ⓘ *Av Infante Dom Henrique 75, opposite Praça Paris, crypt and museum daily 0900-1700, mausoleum Tue-Sun 1000-1600; free, beach clothes and rubber-thonged sandals not permitted*, to Brazil's dead in the Second World War. The Memorial is two slender columns supporting a slightly curved slab, representing two palms uplifted to heaven. In the crypt are the remains of Brazilian soldiers killed in Italy in 1944-1945 and on ships torpedoed by U-boats. The beautiful little church on the Glória Hill, overlooking the Parque do Flamengo, is **Nossa Senhora da Glória do**

4 Copacabana

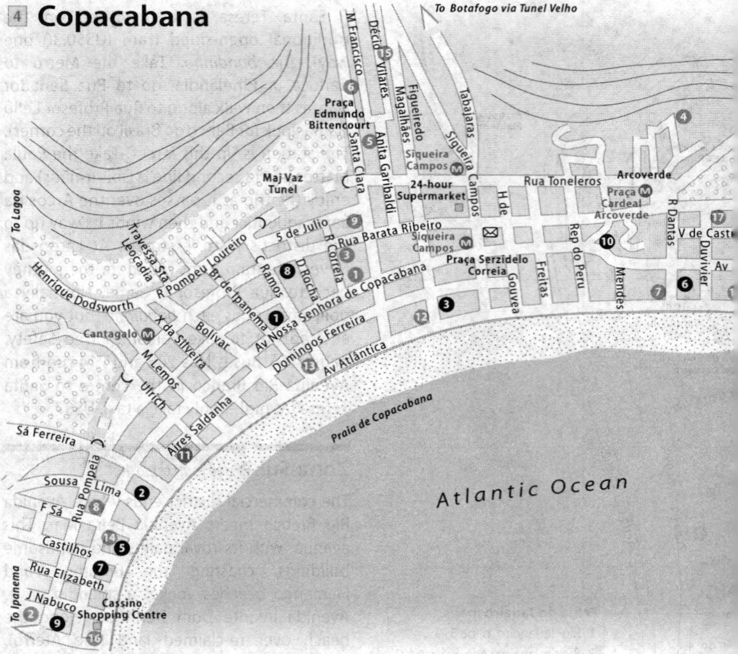

Sleeping
1 Angrense
2 Atlantis Copacabana
3 Benidorm Palace
4 CabanaCopa Hostel
5 Che Lagarto Copacabana
6 Che Lagarto Suites
7 Copacabana Palace & Cipriani Restaurant
8 Copacabana Rio
9 Copacabana Sol
10 Copinha Hostel
11 Grandarell Ouro Verde
12 Marriott
13 Pestana Rio Atlântica
14 Portinari Design
15 Santa Clara
16 Sofitel
17 Stone of a Bea

Eating
1 Aipo and Aipim
2 Apetite Café
3 Cafeina

Outeiro ⓘ *Sat-Sun 0800-1200, Mon-Fri 1300- 1700, is reached by bus 119 from the centre and 571 from Copacabana*. It was the favourite church of the imperial family; Dom Pedro II was baptized here. The building is polygonal, with a single tower. It contains excellent examples of blue-faced Brazilian tiling. Its main wooden altar, was carved by Mestre Valentim. The adjacent museum of religious art keeps the same hours, but is closed on Monday.

The charming **Parque do Catete** ⓘ *0800- 2000*, is a small park with birds and monkeys between Praia do Flamengo and the Palácio do Catete, which contains the **Museu da República** ⓘ *R do Catete 153, T3235 2650, www.museudarepublica. org.br, Tue, Thu, Fri 1200-1700, Wed 1400-1700, Sat, Sun and holidays 1400-1800, US$4, free Wed and Sun. Take bus 571 from Copacabana, or the Metrô to Catete station*. The palace was built in 1858-1866. In 1887 it was converted into the presidential seat, until the move to Brasília. The first floor is devoted to the history of the Brazilian republic. Highly recommended.

Museu do Folclore Edison Carneiro ⓘ *R do Catete 181, T2285 0441, Tue-Fri 1100-1800, Sat-Sun 1500-1800, free, signs in Portuguese, take bus 571 from Copacabana, or the Metrô to Catete station*. This museum's collection should not to be missed. There is an exhibit of small ceramic figures representing everyday life in Brazil, some very funny, some scenes animated by electric motors. There are fine Candomblé and Umbanda costumes, religious objects, ex-votos and sections on many of Brazil's festivals. It has a small, but excellent library, with helpful, friendly staff for finding books on Brazilian culture, history and anthropology.

The **Museu Carmen Miranda** ⓘ *Rui Barbosa 560, Parque do Flamengo (in front of the Morro da Viúva), T2299 5586, Tue-Fri 1100-1700, Sat-Sun 1400-1700, US$1*, houses over 3,000 items related to the famous Portuguese singer who emigrated to Brazil, then Hollywood, and is forever associated with Rio. These include her famous gowns, fruit-covered hats, jewellery and reviews, recordings and occasional showings of her films.

Botafogo

Museu Villa-Lobos ⓘ *R Sorocaba 200, T2266 3845, www.museuvillalobos.org.br, Mon-Fri 1000-1730, free*. Such was the fame and respect afforded to Latin America's most celebrated composer that Rio de Janeiro founded this museum only a year after his death in 1960. Inside the fine 19th-century building is the collection includes instruments, scores, books and recordings. The museum has occasional shows and concerts, and supports a number of classical music projects throughout Brazil. **Museu do Índio** ⓘ *R das Palmeiras 55, T2286 8899, www.museudoindio.org.br, Tue-Fri 0900-1700, Sat and Sun 1300-1700, US$1.50, Sun free. It's a 10-min walk from Botafogo Metrô; from Rodoviária, Bus 136 passes Rua São Clemente,*

➡**Rio de Janeiro maps**
1 Rio de Janeiro, page 399
2 Rio de Janeiro centre, page 401
3 Glória, Santa Teresa, Catete, Flamengo, page 406
4 Copacabana, page 408
5 Ipanema and Leblon, page 410

4 Cervantes
5 Chon Kou
6 Churrascaria Palace
7 Eclipse
8 Mala e Cuia
9 Siri Mole & Cia
10 Traiteurs de France

Bars & clubs
11 Bip Bip

also 172, 178, from Zona Sul 511, 512, 522 (to Botafogo Metrô). The museum houses 12,000 objects from many Brazilian indigenous groups. There is also a small, well-displayed handicraft shop.

Pão de Açúcar (Sugar Loaf mountain)

The Pão de Açúcar, or Sugar Loaf, is a massive volcanic cone at the entrance to Guanabara Bay that soars to 396 m. There is a restaurant (mixed reports on food, closes 1900) and a playground for children on the **Morro da Urca**, halfway up, where there are also shows at night (consult the cultural sections in the newspapers), a good video show on the history of cable-car and Abençoado bar (see page 423). You can get refreshments at the top. The sea-level cable car station is in a military area, so it is safe to visit. At Praia Vermelha, the beach to the south of the rock, is the Círculo Militar da Praia Vermelha restaurant. From here, the Pista Cláudio Coutinho runs part-way round the foot of the rock. It is a 1.2-km paved path for walking, jogging and access to climbing places. It is open 0600-1800. Here you have mountain, forest and sea side-by-side, right in the heart of the city. If you go early you may see marmosets and tanagers. You can also use the Pista Coutinho as a way of getting up the Pão de Açúcar more cheaply than the US$22 cable car ride ⓘ *www.bondinho.com.br*. About 350 m from the path entrance is a track to the left, open 0800-1800, which leads though the forest (go left at the ridge) to Morro de Urca, from where the cable car can be taken for US$10 (you can come down this way, too, but if you take the cable car from sea level you must pay full fare). You can save even more money, but use more energy, by climbing the Caminho da Costa, the continuation of the Pista Coutinho, to the summit of the Pão de Açúcar. Only one stretch, of 10 m, requires climbing gear (some say it is not necessary), but if you wait at the bottom of the path for a group going up,

5 Ipanema & Leblon

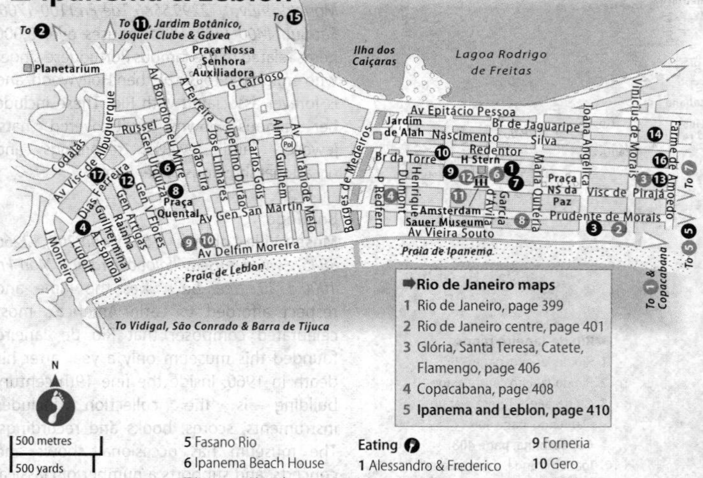

➡**Rio de Janeiro maps**
1 Rio de Janeiro, page 399
2 Rio de Janeiro centre, page 401
3 Glória, Santa Teresa, Catete, Flamengo, page 406
4 Copacabana, page 408
5 Ipanema and Leblon, page 410

Sleeping

1 Arpoador Inn
2 Best Western Sol Ipanema
3 Casa 6, Harmonia & The Lighthouse
4 Che Lagarto Ipanema
5 Fasano Rio
6 Ipanema Beach House
7 Ipanema Hostel
8 Ipanema Inn
9 Marina All Suites & Bar D'Hotel
10 Marina Palace
11 Mar Ipanema
12 San Marco

Eating

1 Alessandro & Frederico
2 Arabe de Gávea
3 Bistrô ZaZá
4 Carlota
5 Casa da Feijoada
6 Celeiro
7 Empório Saúde
8 Fellini
9 Forneria
10 Gero
11 Guimas
12 Manekineko
13 New Natural
14 Porção
15 Roberta Sudbrack
16 Satyricon
17 Zuka

they will let you tag along. This way you can descend to Morro de Urca by cable car for free and walk down from there. There are 35 rock routes up the mountain, with various degrees of difficulty. The best months for climbing are April to August. A permit to climb costs US$97; ask at the Tourist Office. See Activities and tours, page 429, for climbing clubs; there is also a book on climbing routes. ▸▸ *For getting there, see Transport, page 432.*

Corcovado

Corcovado is a hunchbacked peak, 710 m high, surmounted by a 38-m-high statue of Christ the Redeemer, O Cristo Redentor, which was completed in 1931. There is a superb view from the top (sometimes obscured by mist), to which there are a cog railway and road; taxis, cooperative minivans and train put down their passengers behind the statue. Private cars are only allowed as far as Paineiras, from where you can catch train or cabs. The 3.8 km railway itself offers fine views. Average speed is 15 kph on the way up and 12 kph on the way down. There is an exhibition of the history of the railway. From the upper terminus there is a system of escalators, one with a panoramic view, to the top, near which is a café (alternatively you can climb 220 steps up). To see the city by day and night ascend at 1500 or 1600 and descend on the last train, approximately 1815. Mass is held on Sunday in a small chapel in the statue pedestal. To reach the vast statue of Cristo Redentor at the summit of Corcovado, you have to go through Laranjeiras and Cosme Velho. The road through these districts heads west out of Catete. ▸▸ *See Transport, page 432.*

The **Museu Internacional de Arte Naif do Brasil** (MIAN) ⓘ *R Cosme Velho 561, T2205 8612, www.museunaif.com.br, Tue-Fri 1000-1800, Sat, Sun and holidays 1200-1800; closed Mon, US$3.20; discounts for groups, students and senior citizens*. This is one of the most comprehensive museums of Naive and folk paintings in the world. It is only 30 m uphill, on the same street as the station for Corcovado. There is a permanent collection of some 8,000 works by Naive artists from about 130 countries. MIAN has a good shop at Avenida Atlântica 1998.

Those who want to see what Rio was like early in the 19th century should go to the **Largo do Boticário** ⓘ *R Cosme Velho 822*, a charming small square in neo-colonial style. Much of the material used in creating the effect of the square came from old buildings demolished in the city centre. The square is close to the terminus for the Corcovado cog railway.

Copacabana ➔ *Tourist police patrol Copacabana beach until 1700. See map, page 408.*

Built on a narrow strip of land (only a little over 4 sq km) between mountain and sea, Copacabana has one of the highest population densities in the world: 62,000 per sq km, or 250,000 in all. Copacabana began to develop when the Túnel Velho (Old Tunnel) was built in 1891 and an electric tram service reached it. Weekend villas and bungalows sprang up; all have now gone. In the 1930s the Copacabana Palace Hotel was the only tall building; it is now one of the lowest on the beach. The opening of the Túnel Novo (New Tunnel) in the 1940s led to an explosion of population which shows no sign of having spent its force. Unspoilt art deco blocks towards the Leme (city) end of Copacabana are now under preservation order.

There is almost everything in this 'city within a city'. The shops, mostly in Avenida Nossa Senhora de Copacabana and the Rua Barata Ribeiro, are excellent. Even more stylish shops are to be found in Ipanema, Leblon and in the various large shopping centres in the city. The city's glamorous nightlife is beginning to move elsewhere and, after dark, Copacabana, has lost some of its former allure. At the far end of the beach, is **Museu Histórico do Exército e Forte de Copacabana** ⓘ *Av Atlântica at Francisco Otaviano, Tue-Sun 1000- 2000, US$2*, which charts the history of the army in Brazil. There are good views out over the beaches and a small restaurant. Parts of the military area are now being handed over to civilian use, including the Parque Garota de Ipanema at Arpoador, the fashionable Copacabana end of the Ipanema beach.

The world-famous beach is divided into numbered *postos*, where the lifeguards are based. Different sections attract different types of people, eg young people, artists and gays. The safest places are in front of the major hotels which have their own security, eg the Meridien on

Copacabana beach or the Caesar Park on Ipanema. The Caesar Park also has 24-hour video surveillance during the summer season, which makes it probably the safest patch of sand in Rio.
➤➤ *See also Transport, page 432.*

Ipanema and Leblon → *see map, below.*
Beyond Copacabana are the seaside suburbs of Ipanema and Leblon. The two districts are divided by a canal from the Lagoa Rodrigo de Freitas to the sea, beside which is the Jardim de Alá. Ipanema and Leblon are a little less built-up than Copacabana and their beaches tend to be cleaner. Praia de Arpoadar at the Copacabana end of Ipanema is a peaceful spot to watch surfers, with the beautiful backdrop of Morro Dois Irmãos; excellent for photography, walk on the rocks. There is now night-time illumination on these beaches. A permanent cycle track now runs all the way from the north end of Flamengo to Barra de Tijuca via Ipanema and Copacabana. On Copacabana a free bike rental scheme has been started. The seaward lane of the road running beside the beach is closed to traffic until 1800 on Sundays and holidays; this makes it popular for rollerskating and cycling.

Gávea, Lagoa and Jardim Botânico
Backing Ipanema and Leblon is the middle-class residential area of **Lagoa Rodrigo de Freitas**, by a saltwater lagoon on which Rio's rowing and small-boat sailing clubs are active. The lake is too polluted for bathing, but the road and cycling/jogging track which runs around its shores has pleasant views. Avenida Epitácio Pessoa, on the eastern shore, leads to the Túnel Rebouças which runs beneath Corcovado and Cosme Velho.

Well worth a visit is the **Jardim Botânico** (Botanical Gardens) ⓘ *T3874 1808, www.jbrj.gov.br, 0800-1700, US$2,* 8 km from the centre (see Transport, page 430). These were founded in 1808. The most striking features are the transverse avenues of 30 m high royal palms. Among the more than 7,000 varieties of plants from around the world are examples of the pau-brasil tree, now endangered, and many other threatened species. There is a herbarium, an aquarium and a library (some labels are unclear). A new pavilion contains sculptures by Mestre Valentim transferred from the centre. Many improvements were carried out before the 1992 Earth Summit, including a new Orquidário and an enlarged bookshop.

The **Planetário** ⓘ *Padre Leonel Franco 240, Gávea, T2274 0096, www.rio.rj.gov.br/planetario, observations on Tue-Thu 1830-2030, weekend shows for children; getting there: buses 125, 170, 523, 571, 750 and others.* Inaugurated in 1979, the planetarium has a sculpture of the Earth and Moon by Mario Agostinelli. There are occasional *chorinho* concerts on Thursday or Friday.

Southern suburbs

Leblon to Barra da Tijuca
The Pedra Dois Irmãos overlooks Leblon. On the slopes is Vidigal favela. From Leblon, two inland roads take traffic west to the outer seaside suburb of Barra da Tijuca: the Auto Estrada Lagoa-Barra, which tunnels under Dois Irmãos, and the Estrada da Gávea, which goes through Gávea. Beyond Leblon the coast is rocky. A third route to Barra da Tijuca is the Avenida Niemeyer, which skirts the cliffs on the journey past Vidigal, a small beach where the Sheraton is situated. Avenida Niemeyer carries on round the coast to São Conrado. On the slopes of the Pedra da Gávea, through which the Avenida Niemeyer has two tunnels, is the Rocinha favela.

The flat-topped **Pedra da Gávea** can be climbed or scrambled up for magnificent views, but beware of snakes. Behind the Pedra da Gávea is the Pedra Bonita. A road, the Estrada das Canoas, climbs up past these two rocks on its way to the Parque Nacional Tijuca. There is a spot on this road which is one of the chief hang-glider launch sites in the area (see page 429).
➤➤ *See also Transport, page 432.*

Barra da Tijuca

This rapidly developing residential area is also one of the principal recreation areas of Rio, with its 20-km sandy beach and good waves for surfing. At the westernmost end is the small beach of Recreio dos Bandeirantes, where the ocean can be very rough. The channels behind the Barra are popular with jetskiers. It gets very busy on Sundays. There are innumerable bars and restaurants, clustered at both ends, campsites (see page 418), motels and hotels: budget accommodation tends to be self-catering. Although buses do run as far as Barra, getting to and around here is best by car. A cycle way links Barra da Tijuca with the centre of the city. A bit further out is the **Museu Casa do Pontal** ⓘ *Estrada do Pontal 3295, Recreio dos Bandeirantes, Tue-Sun, 0900-1930,* a collection of Brazilian folk art. Recommended.

Parque Nacional Tijuca

ⓘ *Entry US$8.50. National park information, T2495 4863. See also Transport page 433.*

The Pico da Tijuca (1,022 m) gives a good idea of the tropical vegetation of the interior and a fine view of the bay and its shipping. A two- to three-hour walk leads to the summit: on entering the park at Alto da Boa Vista (0600-2100), follow the signposts (maps are displayed) to Bom Retiro, a good picnic place (1½ hours' walk). At Bom Retiro the road ends and there is another hour's walk up a fair footpath to the summit (take the path from the right of the Bom Retiro drinking fountain; not the more obvious steps from the left). The last part consists of steps carved out of the solid rock; look after children at the summit as there are several sheer drops, invisible because of bushes. The route is shady for almost its entire length. The main path to Bom Retiro passes the Cascatinha Taunay (a 30-m waterfall) and the Mayrink Chapel (built 1860). Beyond the Chapel is the restaurant A Floresta. Other places of interest not passed on the walk to the peak are the Paulo e Virginia Grotto, the Vista do Almirante and the Mesa do Imperador (viewpoints). Allow at least five to six hours for the excursion. Maps of the park are available; walking is safest at weekends and holidays. If hiking in the national park other than on the main paths, a guide may be useful if you do not want to get lost: for walks organized by the **Ecotourism Sector** ⓘ *T2492 2252/2492 2253, ext 217/212.*

Parque Estadual da Pedra Branca ⓘ *Núcleo Camorim, Camorim, Jacarepaguá, T3417 3642, www.inea.rj.gov.br/unidades/pqpedra_branca.asp,* the largest urban forest in the world, is also in Rio, though few Cariocas are aware of it. Pedra Branca is the city's best kept natural secret, protecting an astounding 12,500 ha of pristine rainforest, lakes and mountains, which are home to over 500 animal species. A number are threatened or critically endangered. There are many trails in the park, including one leading to the highest peak in Rio de Janeiro, the Pedra Branca (1,024 m).

Ilha de Paquetá

The island, the second largest in Guanabara Bay, is noted for its gigantic pebble shaped rocks, butterflies and orchids. At the southwest tip is the interesting Parque Darke de Mattos, with beautiful trees, lots of birds and a lookout on the Morro da Cruz. The island has several beaches, but ask about the state of the water before bathing. The only means of transport are bicycles and horse-drawn carriages (US$20 per hr, many have harnesses which cut into the horse's flesh). Neither is allowed into the Parque Darke de Mattos. A tour by trenzinho, a tractor pulling trailers, costs US$1.65, or just wander around on foot, quieter and free. Bicycles can be hired. The island is very crowded at weekends and on public holidays, but is usually quiet during the week. The prices of food and drink are reasonable. ▸▸ *See also Transport, page 433.*

Rio de Janeiro listings

Hotel and guesthouse prices
LL over US$200 **L** US$151-200 **AL** US$101-150
A US$66-100 **B** US$46-65 **C** US$31-45
D US$21-30 **E** US$12-20 **F** US$7-11
G US$6 and under
Restaurant prices
🍴🍴🍴 over US$12 🍴🍴 US$7-12 🍴 under US$6

Sleeping

All hotels **AL-A** and above in the following list are a/c. A 10% service charge is usually added to the bill and tax of 5% or 10% may be added (if not already included). Note that not all higher-class hotels include breakfast in their room rates. The best and safest places to stay in Rio are Ipanema and southern Copacabana and there are a number of decent, new budget hostels in these areas. New backpacker hostels are opening all the time and hostelling sites (www.hostels.com, www.hostelworld.com) list latest options. With a few notable exceptions, Rio's other hotels in the higher and mid-range are a mix of anonymous business chain towers and fading leftovers from the 1970s, complete with period decor. Economy hotels are found mainly in the 3 districts of Rio: Flamengo/Botafogo (best), Lapa/Fátima and Saúde/Mauá: choose with care in those districts. The city is noisy. An inside room is cheaper and much quieter. Always ask for the actual room price: it usually differs from that quoted. Also check if the quoted price is per room or per person. Prices rise considerably over New Year and Carnaval. Reserve well in advance, especially with the budget end accommodation.

Homestays
AL-B Cama e Café, R Laurinda Santos Lobo 124, T2225 4366 (9638 4850, 24 hrs), www.camaecafe.com. One of the best accommodation options in Rio with a range of some 24 homestays in Santa Teresa, from the simple to the luxurious. Very good value. They provide the opportunity to get to know locals and see Rio from the inside. Rooms can be treated as impersonally as those in a hotel, or guests can fit in as part of the household. **Cama e Café** work hard to match guests with hosts who share similar interests.

See also their sister company **www.riohomestay.com**, also T2225 4366, for more options in Leblon, Copacabana, Santa Teresa, Ipanema and other districts.

Santa Teresa *p406, map p406*
Santa Teresa is hilly and offers views out over Rio but is inconvenient for transport. New boutique hotels are opening all the time, from the **LL Hotel Santa Teresa**, R Almte Aelxandrino 660, T3380 0200, www.santateresahotel.com (French-owned, chic and exclusive 5-star, restaurant and spa behind high walls); **Mama Ruisa**, R Santa Cristina 132, T2242 1281, www.mamaruisa.com (also French-run, simple, elegant); to **L-AL Um Meia Três**, R Aprazível 163, T2232 0034, www.hotelinrio.net (small, lovely views, book online for best rates).
A Carmen e Fernando Bed and Breakfast, R Hermenegildo de Barros 172, T2507 3084, fj.simoes@uol.com.br. Discount for long stay, with bath, a/c, mosquito net, very welcoming, great breakfast, terrace with plunge pool, internet.
A Casa Áurea, R Áurea 80, Santa Teresa, T2242 5830, www.casaaurea.com.br. Small hotel in a converted colonial house. Rooms are bright and airy and service attentive. Breakfast is served in a little garden visited by marmosets in the mornings.
E pp **Rio Hostel**, R Joaquim Murtinho 361, T3852 0827, www.riohostel.com.br. Dorms (**B** in double room), with breakfast, excellent facilities include kitchen, bar, pool, internet, laundry service, hot water, airport pick-up US$17, relaxed, English spoken, events and trips organized. Owner loves all things British and Australian.

Glória, Catete and Flamengo *p407, map p406*
These are mainly residential areas between the centre and Copacabana. Catete, and Glória to the north and Flamengo to the south, lie next to a park landscaped by Burle Marx and a beautiful beach lapped by a filthy sea. They have good bus and Metrô links, but are not as safe as Ipanema.
LL Glória, R do Russel 632, Glória, www.hotelgloriario.com.br. Rio's other stylish and elegant 1920s hotel. Due to reopen in 2011 after refurbishment as a super-luxury hotel.
LL-AL Novo Mundo, Praia Flamengo 20, Catete, T2105 7000, www.hotelnovomundo-rio.com.br.

Standard 4-star rooms, suites with balcony views of the Sugar Loaf. Recommended but noisy.
L-AL Windsor Flórida, Ferreira Viana, 71/81, Catete, T2195 6800, www.windsorhoteis.com. Business-orientated hotel, bars (for private hire), restaurant, modestly decorated modern rooms.
A Paysandu, R Paissandu 23, Flamengo T2558 7270, www.paysandu hotel.com.br. Wonderful art deco tower next to the Palácio de República and Flamengo gardens, with spartan rooms but helpful staff, good location, organized tours.
B Imperial, R do Catete 186, T2556 5212, Catete, www.imperialhotel.com.br. One of the city's very first grand hotels (late 19th century). Rooms either in the grander, older main building, or the modern annexe (modern, US motel-style), better equipped but overlooking the parking lot.
B Inglês, R Silveira Martins 20, Glória, T2558 3052, www.hotelingles.com.br. Popular hotel next to the metro and in front of the Museu da República. The better rooms have a/c.
B-C Único, Ferreira Viana 54, Catete, T2205 9932, F2205 8149. Plain rooms with TV, a/c and fridge. Recommended.
C-E pp **Catete Hostel**, R do Catete 92, casa 1, Catete, T3826 0522, www.catetehostel.com.br. Dorms and doubles, all with bath, a/c and fan, breakfast included.

Botafogo *p409*
Another quiet, middle-class neighbourhood with a great beach lapped by dirty water. Convenient for public transport and Mall shopping but care should be taken at night.
A O Veleiro, T2554 8980, Praia de Botafogo, www.oveleiro.com. Address given only with reservation. B&B with a great breakfast, Canadian/ Carioca-owned, transfers to/from airport or bus station, Wi-Fi, tours, guiding, helpful staff. Recommended, but neighbourhood noisy at times.
B-E Sun Rio Hostel, R Praia de Botafogo 462, casa 5, T2226 0461, www.sunriohostel.com.br, next door to **El Misti** and **Alpha**. A/c dorms, doubles and en-suites, all very well kept. Shared kitchen, internet and Wi-Fi, bike rental and tours organized. Owner Daniela is very welcoming.
C-E pp **Alpha Hostel**, R Praia de Botafogo 462, casa 3, Botafogo, T2286 7799, www.alpha hostel.com. Normal rate. Private and dorm

rooms. Breakfast included, laundry, kitchen, internet, tours, airport and bus terminal transfer.

C-D Tupiniquim Hostel, R São Manoel 19, at R da Passagem, T021-2244 1286, www.tupiniquim hostel.com.br. Small-scale hostel in a pretty little townhouse offering interesting volunteer activities alongside the standard facilities.

D-F pp **Ace Backpackers**, R São Clemente 23, 1st floor, Botafogo, T2527 7452, www.acehostels.com.br. Popular, lively, small but spotless dorms and rooms (**C** pp), kitchen, internet, tours, laundry. Branches in Petrópolis and São Paulo.

E pp **El Misti Hostel and Pousada**, R Praia de Botafogo 462, casa 9, T2226 0991, www.elmisti hostelrio.com. Converted colonial house with dorms, shared bath, private rooms with shared bath (**B-C**), kitchen, free Wi-Fi, capoeira classes, tour service. Popular with party-goers. Convenient for public transport. Free pick-up for all bookings.

Copacabana *p411, map p408*

LL Copacabana Palace, Av Atlântica 1702, T2548 7070, www.copacabana palace.com.br. Justifiably world famous hotel with distinguished guest list, dripping in 1920s elegance. Go for cocktails and dinner if you can't afford to stay. Cipriani (🍴🍴🍴), is the best restaurant for formal evening dining in Rio with a chef from the Hotel Cipriani in Venice. Very good seafood and modern Italian fare.

LL Marriott, Av Atlântica 2600, T2545 6500, www.marriott.com. Rio's newest top end business hotel, specifically designed with a gamut of services for the business visitor.

LL Pestana Rio Atlântica, Av Atlântica 2964, T2548 6332, www.pestana.com. Part of the Portuguese Pestana group, an excellent choice, spacious bright rooms and a rooftop pool and terrace with sweeping views, very high standards. Recommended.

LL Sofitel, Av Atlântica, 4240, T2525 1232, www.sofitel.com. One of the best beachfront options, at the safer Arpoadoar end, an easy walk to Ipanema. Airy rooms (best on the upper floors), sauna, pool and **Le Pré Catelan** restaurant, with one of the best kitchens in the city.

L-AL Copacabana Rio, Av N S de Copacabana 1256, T2267 9900, www.copacabanariohotel.com.br. Quiet, efficiently run 1970s tower with simple but well-maintained 3-star rooms, small pool and generous breakfasts. Safe area at Ipanema end of beach, 1 block from the sand.

L-AL Grandarell Ouro Verde, Av Atlântica 1456, T2542 1887, www.grandarrell.com.br. The best small hotel in Copacabana with spacious, well-decorated rooms and a decent restaurant. Good for families – the hotel has a Kid's club.

L-AL Portinari Design, R Francisco Sá 17, T3222 8800, www.hotelportinari.com.br. Comfortable mock-boutique suites in a great location at the Arpoador end of Copacabana. Decent breakfast with a view on the top floor, internet and a little spa. Good service.

AL Benidorm Palace, R Barata Ribeiro 547, T2548 8880, www.benidorm.com.br. Modern rooms decked out in light wood in a tower, best and quietest at the back with small marble bathrooms. Sauna and internet in the lobby.

AL-A Copacabana Sol, R Santa Clara 141, T2549 4577, www.copacabanasolhotel.com.br. Safe, helpful, quiet, with good breakfast, Wi-Fi and cable TV.

A Angrense, Travessa Angrense 25, T021-2548 0509, www.angrensehotel.com.br. Well-kept a/c rooms in a little art deco block on a quiet street, English-speaking staff, reliable tour agency and good carnival rates.

A Atlantis Copacabana, Av Bulhões de Carvalho 61, T2521 1142, atlantishotel@uol.com.br. Fading Arpoador hotel in a quiet, safe street close to the beach. Small rooftop pool, sauna, very good value.

A Santa Clara, R Décio Vilares, 316, T2256 2650, www.hotel santaclara.com.br. Quiet, central location, a/c, TV, telephone, en suite bath, attentive service, breakfast included, tours arranged.

B-E Copinha Hostel, R Felipe de Oliveira 11, T2275 8520, www.copinhahostel.com.br. Well-run, lemon-yellow hostel with a range of a/c dorms and doubles, some with bath, kitchen, cable TV and transport services.

D pp **CabanaCopa Hostel**, Travessa Guimarães Natal 12, T3988 9912, www.cabanacopa.com.br. New hostel with dorms of various sizes, including one for women only, a/c, also private rooms (**A**), with breakfast, internet, Wi-Fi, tours, good reputation.

D-E pp **Che Lagarto Copacabana**, R Anita Garibaldi 87, T2256 2776, www.chelagarto.com. Discount for HI members. Includes breakfast and welcome drink. **A-B** in rooms with toilet and a/c. Also **B-C Che Lagarto Suites**, Santa Clara 304, T3495 3133, all double rooms, some with bath and a/c.

E pp **Stone of a Beach**, R Barata Ribeiro 111, T3209 0348, www.stoneofabeach.com.br. Several dorms and doubles (**B**). Helpful, young party atmosphere, several languages spoken, organizes tours, includes breakfast, bar.
E-F El Misti Hostel, Travessa Frederico Pamplona 20, T2547 0800, www.elmisticopacabana.com. 500 m from Copacabana beach, 200 m from metro and buses. Dorms and doubles (**B-C**). Free Wi-Fi access. Tour services, open bar, meals. Free pick-up for all bookings.

Ipanema, Leblon and further west
p412, map p410
LL Best Western Sol Ipanema, Av Vieira Souto 320, T2525 2020, www.bestwestern.com. Huge breakfast, good member of US chain, popular.
LL Fasano Rio, Av Vieira Souto 80, Ipanema, T3896 4000, www.fasano.com.br. Phillippe Starck-designed luxury hotel with rooftop terrace, fitness centre, etc, good bar and superior restaurant, **Fasano Al Mare**.
LL La Maison, R Sergio Porto 58, Gávea, T7812 5836, www.lamaisonario.com. A boutique hidden away in a converted colonial townhouse on quiet back street. Resolutely OTT decor, but rooms are more understated and views of the forest and Corcovado from the breakfast area are magnificent.
LL La Suite, R Jackson de Figueiredo 501, Joá, T2484 1962, fxdussol@hotmail.com. Versace meets Louis XIV in a riot of colour that Elton John would swoon over in this 7-room boutique between Leblon and Barra da Tijuca. Fabulous location – the pool sits eyrie-like over the exclusive beach at Joá with sweeping views out towards São Conrado. Every room has a terrace, view and a marble bathroom.
LL Marina Palace and Marina All Suites, Av Delfim Moreira 630 and 696, T2294 1794, www.hotelmarina.com.br. Two 1980s towers almost next door to each other. The former has smart, modern but standard rooms and a rooftop pool, the latter is a luxury boutique with 'designer' suites, with the excellent **Bar D'Hotel** (ΨΨΨ), light but well-flavoured fish dishes served in cool surroundings. Excellent breakfasts and cocktails.
AL-A Arpoador Inn, Francisco Otaviano 177, T2523 0060, www.arpoadorinn.com.br. Well-maintained, internet. Seafront restaurant **Azul Marinho**, off-season special offers are a good deal.
AL-A Ipanema Inn, Maria Quitéria 27, behind Caesar Park, T2523 6092, www.ipanemainn.com.br. Popular package tour and small business hotel less than 100 m from beach. Good value and location.
AL-A Mar Ipanema, R Visconde de Pirajá 539, T3875 9190, www.maripanema.com. 1 block from the beach, simple, smart, modern rooms.
B San Marco, R Visconde de Pirajá 524, T2540 5032, www.sanmarcohotel.net. Renovated 2-star 2 blocks from beach, with simple rooms and a free caipirinha for every internet booking, very helpful, internet US$2.70 per hr. Price includes breakfast. Recommended.
B-E Casa 6, R Barão da Torre 175, casa 6, T2247 1384, www.casa6ipanema.com. Charming, colourful but simple French-owned B&B in a townhouse 3 blocks from the beach. Also has doubles (**A**), good long stay rates.
B-E Ipanema Hostel, R Canning, casa 1, Ipanema, T021-2287 2928, www.riohostelipanema.com. Sister hostel to the friendly and welcoming **Rio Hostel** in Santa Teresa, range of small rooms and dorms, tour operator, internet and a lively crowd.
D pp **Harmonia**, R Barão da Torre 175, casa 18, T2523 4905, www.hostelharmonia.com. 3 blocks from beach, doubles or dorms, cheaper without breakfast, kitchen facilities, English, Spanish, German and Swedish spoken, good internet. At casa 14 in the same building is **D-E** pp **Hostel Ipanema**, T2247 7269, www.hostelipanema.com, also doubles **B**.
D pp **Ipanema Beach House**, R Barão da Torre 485, T3202 2693, www.ipanemahouse.com. Dorms and doubles (**A**) all with shared baths. Great little hostel with rooms arranged around a garden and small pool. Small bar, kitchen, internet and tours, good service.
D pp **The Lighthouse**, R Barão da Torre 175, casa 20, T2522 1353, www.thelighthouse.com.br. 1 private room for up to 4 (**B**), and a dorm for 8, kitchen, internet, very helpful.
E-F pp **Che Lagarto Ipanema**, R Paul Redfern 48, T2512 8076, www.chelagarto.com. Bright red party hostel with young staff and a terrace with views of Corcovado, dorms and doubles (**B**), cheaper with HI card.
See also under Copacabana, above.

Camping

If travelling by trailer, you can park at the **Marina Glória** car park, where there are showers and toilets, a small shop and snack bar. Pay the guards to look after your vehicle. See also **Camping Clube do Brasil**.

Self-catering apartments

Renting a small flat, or sharing a larger one, can be much better value than a hotel room. All price levels are available: eg furnished apartments for short-term let, accommodating up to 6, cost US$300 per month in Flamengo. Copacabana, Ipanema and Leblon prices range from about US$25 a day for a simple studio, starting at US$500-600 a month up to US$2,000 a month for a luxurious residence sleeping 4-6. Heading south past Barra da Tijuca, virtually all the accommodation available is self-catering. Always get a written agreement when renting and check the building's (usually excellent) security arrangements.

Private owners advertise in *Balcão*, twice weekly, *O Globo* or *Jornal do Brasil* (daily); under 'Apartamentos – Temporada'; advertisements are classified by district and size of apartment: *vagas e quartos* means shared accommodation; *conjugado* (or *conj*) is a studio with limited cooking facilities; *3 Quartos* is a 3-bedroom flat. Also see **Riotur** and **Guia 4 Rodas** for 'Apart-Hotels'.

Apartments Rio de Janeiro, www.rentinrio.com, with contact numbers in the USA and UK.

Copacabana Holiday, R Barata Ribeiro 90A, Copacabana, T2542 1525, www.copacabana holiday.com.br. Recommended, well-equipped apartments from studios to 3-bedroom, starting at US$330-833 per month, short and long-term lets, minimum 30 days.

Fantastic Rio, Av Atlântica 974, Suite 501, Copacabana, BR-22020-000, T/F2543 2667, hpcorr@hotmail.com. All types of furnished accommodation, owned by Peter Corr.

Rio Flat Rental, R Praia de Botafogo 462, casa 9, Copacabana, T2226 6368, www.rioflatrental.com. Fully furnished flats in Copacabana or Ipanema. Internet, cable TV, 24-hr security. Free pick-up from airport.

Eating

The best of Rio's many restaurants are in Copacabana, Ipanema or Leblon. Expect to pay US$30-40+ per person in the better restaurants. You can eat well for an average US$5 per person, less if you choose the prato feito at lunchtime (US$2- 7.50), or eat in a place that serves food by weight (starting at about US$10 per kg). Avoid mussels! Most restaurants are closed on 24 and 25 Dec.

Grill or barbecue houses (*churrascarias*) are relatively cheap, especially by European standards. There are many at São Conrado and Joá, on the road out to Barra da Tijuca. Look for the 'Churrascaria Rodízio', where you are served as much as you can eat. Galetos are lunch counters specializing in chicken and grilled meat, very reasonable. In the shopping centres there is usually a variety of restaurants and snack bars grouped around a central plaza where you can shop around for a good meal. Most less-expensive restaurants in Rio have basically the same type of food (based on steak, fried potatoes and rice) and serve large portions. Rio lacks that almost ubiquitous

Brazilian institution, the corner bakery, and a decent breakfast can be hard to find. But there are plenty of stand-up juice bars serving fruit juices made from as many as 25 different fruits, all of which are wonderful.

City centre and Lapa *p402, map p401*
Many restaurants in the business district are open only for weekday lunch. Many lanchonetes in this area offer good, cheap meals. **R Miguel Couto** (opposite Santa Rita church) is called the **Beco das Sardinhas** because on Wed and Fri in particular is full of people eating sardines and drinking beer. There are several Arab restaurants on Av Senhor dos Passos, which are also open Sat and Sun. In addition to those listed there are plenty of cafes, including a few new chic options on R Lavradio in Lapa; where the lively Sat antiques market is held.

TTT **Adega Flor de Coimbra**, R Teotônio Regadas 34, Lapa, T2224 4582. Founded in 1938, Portuguese food and wines, speciality *bacalhau* (salt cod). Very good.

TTT **Albamar**, Praça Marechal Âncora 184-6, T2240 8378. Populara, long-established fish and seafood, with lovely views of the bay. Open 1130-1600 Mon, 1130-2200 Tue-Sat.

TTT **Cais do Oriente**, R Visc de Itaboraí 8, T2233 2531. Wonderful restaurant with several settings; the menu is a fusion of Mediterranean, Brazilian and oriental.

TTT **Republique**, Praça da República 63 (2nd floor), T2532 9000. Designed by architect Chicô Gouveia. Chef Paulo Carvalho cooks Portuguese, Italian and French dishes.

TT **Bar Luiz**, R da Crioca 39, T2262 6900. A little bar in a colonial house in the centre, famous as much for its clientèle as its tapas and *chope* in the evening, good for a quiet snack lunch, too.

TT **Café da Moda**, R Gonçalves Dias 49, 3rd floor, Centro, T2222 0610, www.folic.com.br. An a/c café devoted to the narrow waistline, located in the **Folic** shop. Salads are named after famous models, or have more macho names for men. Light meals without hip names also available.

TT-T **Bar das Artes**, Praça 15 de Novembro 48 (Paço Imperial), T2215 5795. Salads, sandwiches and light meals in a neat, peaceful café in the former Imperial Palace.

TT-T **Confeitaria Colombo**, R Gonçalves Dias 32, near Carioca Metrô station. Recommended for atmosphere and the only one of its kind in Rio. Over 100 years old, it has the original belle époque decor, open 0900-1800, no service charge so tip the excellent waiters. More modern but similar establishments in some of the main hotels.

T **Sabor Saúde**, R da Quitanda 21, T2252 6041. Breakfast and lunch only, vegetarian and wholefood dishes and sandwiches, also light meals (not always vegetarian).

Santa Teresa *p406, map p406*

TTT **Aprazível**, R Aprazível 62, T3852 4935. Decent but unspectacular Brazilian dishes and seafood with tables outdoors in a tropical garden overlooking Guanabara Bay. This is a good Sun lunch spot when they have Choro and Samba performed by Rio's equivalent of the Buena Vista Social Club.

TT **Adega do Pimenta**, R Almte Alexandrino 296. Daily 1130-2200, Sun 1100-1800, closed Sat, Tue. A very small German restaurant in the Largo do Guimarães with excellent sausages, sauerkraut and cold beer.

TT **Bar do Arnaudo**, Largo do Guimarães, R Almte Alexandrino 316, T2252 7246. A modest-looking restaurant decorated with handicrafts but serving generous portions of wonderful Northeast Brazilian cooking. Try the *carne do sol* (sun-dried beef, or jerky) with *feijão de corda* (brown beans and herbs), or the *queijo coalho* (a country cheese, grilled).

TT **Espírito Santa**, R Almte Alexandrino 264, T2508 7095. Closed Mon, lunch only Tue, Wed, Sun. Upstairs is a chic Mediterranean restaurant with a wonderful sweeping view of the city, downstairs is a weekend basement club, good cocktails.

TT **Sobrenatural**, R Almirante Alexandrino 432, T2224 1003. Open lunch and evening, closed Mon. A charming rustic restaurant serving fish caught daily on owner's boat. For a light lunch, order a mix of excellent appetizers. Recommended.

Glória, Catete and Flamengo *p407, map p406*
There are many cheap and mid-range eating places on R do Catete; including Amazônia No 234B, and Catelândia, No 204.

TTT **Alcaparra**, Praia do Flamengo 144, Flamengo, T2557 7236. Elegant traditional Italian popular with politicians and business people. Overlooking the sea.

TT **Lamas**, Marquês de Abrantes 18A, Flamengo, T2556 0799. Steak, seafood and general Brazilian fare have been served here for over 130 years. Excellent value, great atmosphere, opens late, popular with Brazilian arts/media people. Recommended.

ꝉ **Estação República**, R do Catete 104, Catete, in the Palácio do Catete. More than 40 dishes in this per kilo restaurant, soups, sushi, salads and stews.

Botafogo *p409*

In Baixo Botafogo, those on a budget will find a number of enticing bars and restaurants on R Visconde de Caravelas.

ꝉꝉꝉ **Carême Bistrô**, R Visconde de Caravelas 113, Botafogo, T 2537 5431. An elegant and intimate little restaurant serving the best French food in Rio. Recommended.

ꝉꝉꝉ **Miam Miam**, Gen Goes Monteiro 34, T2244 0125, www.miammiam.com.br. Closed Mon. Retro chic and highly fashionable, where the alternative fashion set go for cocktails and light Mediterranean food. Chef Roberta Ciasca has launched **Oui Oui**, R Conde de Irajá 85, Botafogo, T2527-3539, for tapas-style *petiscos* and cocktails.

ꝉꝉ **Raajmahal**, R Gen Polidoro 29, Baixo Botafogo, T2542 6242. One of the few restaurants offering authentic Indian food.

ꝉꝉ **Yorubá**, R Arnaldo Quintela 94, Botafogo, T2541 9387. Evenings only except weekends, closed Mon, Tue. Award-winning Bahian cooking.

ꝉ **Aurora**, R Visconde de Caravelas corner of R Capitão Salomão 43. Varied menu and good value simple fare.

ꝉ **Botequim**, R Visconde de Caravelas No 184. Also has a varied menu and is good value.

Copacabana, Ipanema and Leblon
p411, maps p408 and p410

ꝉꝉꝉ **Alessandro & Frederico**, R Garcia D'Ávila, 134 loja D, Ipanema, T2521 0828. Upmarket café with decent café latte and breakfasts. Great juice bar next door.

ꝉꝉꝉ **Bistrô ZaZá**, R Joana Angélica 40, Ipanema. Hippy-chic, pseudo Moroccan/ French restaurant, good fish dishes and cocktails and good fun. Evenings are best for intimate dining when the tables are lit by candles.

ꝉꝉꝉ **Carlota**, R Dias Ferreira 64, Leblon, T2540 6821. The best of many on a street lined with restaurants and bars. Great unpretentious Mediterranean food in an elegant dining room.

ꝉꝉꝉ **Forneria**, R Aníbal de Mendonça 112, Ipanema, T2540 8045. Serves superior bar snacks and supreme burgers in pizza dough to the elegant, after-beach crowd.

ꝉꝉꝉ **Gero**, R Aníbal de Mendonça 157, Ipanema, T2239 8158. Light Italian fare and excellent fish in a beautiful, minimalist space.

ꝉꝉꝉ **Mala e Cuia**, R Barata Ribeiro 638, Copacabana, T2545 7566. Comida mineira at one of the restaurants in this recommended chain (also in the centre).

ꝉꝉꝉ **Manekineko**, R Dias Ferreira, 410, Leblon, T2540 7641, www.manekineko.com.br. Exquisite Japanese and Japanese fusion cooking served in an intimately designed modern dining room.

ꝉꝉꝉ **Porcão**, Barão de Torre 218, Ipanema, T2522 0999 (also on Av NS de Copacabana). One of the city's best churrascarias, serving all manner of meat in unlimited quantities for a set price.

ꝉꝉꝉ **Satyricon**, R Barão da Torre 192, Ipanema, T2521 0627. The best seafood in Rio; especially the squid. Lively crowd in a large dining room. Avoid Sat when there is a seafood buffet.

ꝉꝉꝉ **Siri Mole & Cia**, R Francisco Otaviano 42, T2233 0107. Excellent Bahian seafood and Italian coffee in elegant a/c. At the upper end of this price bracket.

ꝉꝉꝉ **Zuka**, R Dias Ferreira 233, Leblon, T3205 7154. One of the most fashionable restaurants in Rio with an eclectic fusion of everything – French and Japanese, American fast food and Italian.

ꝉꝉꝉ-ꝉꝉ **Churrascaria Palace**, R Rodolfo Dantas 16B, Copacabana. 20 different kinds of barbecued meat served on a spit at your table with buffet salads to accompany. Good value.

ꝉꝉ **Casa da Feijoada**, Prudente de Morais 10, Ipanema, T2523 4994. Serves an excellent feijoada all week. Generous portions.

ꝉꝉ **Celeiro**, R Dias Ferreira 199, Leblon. Some of the best salads in the city, and light food by weight.

ꝉꝉ **Chon Kou**, Av Atlântica 3880, T2287 3956. A traditional Chinese restaurant which also offers an extensive sushi menu, a/c; sit upstairs for good views over Copacabana beach.

ꝉꝉ **Fellini**, R General Urquiza 104, Leblon, T2511 3600, www.fellini.com.br. The best per kilo in the city with a range of delicious buffet options and plenty for vegetarians.

ꝉꝉ-ꝉ **Aipo and Aipim**, Av Nossa Senhora de Copacabana 391b and 920, Copacabana, and R Visconde de Pirajá 145, Ipanema,

T2267 8313. Popular chain, plentiful tasty food sold by weight.

₸₸-₸ **Eclipse**, Av N S de Copacabana 1309, T2287 1788, www.eclipse.com.br. Spruce, well-run and very popular 24-hr restaurant offering good value prato feito lunches and a generous range of meats, pastas, snacks and sandwiches served in the cool interior or on streetside tables.

₸₸ **New Natural**, R Barão da Torre 173, T2226 7317. One of Ipanema's most popular vegetarian and wholefood restaurants, large range of hot dishes and desserts served per kilo. Home delivery. Natural products shop next door.

₸ **Apetite Cafe**, R Souza Lima 78, T2247 3319. One of Copa's few bakery cafes. Offers a range of breakfasts, respectable coffee, snacks, options for kids and an a/c interior for when it gets too hot.

₸ **Cafeina**, C Ramos 44, T2547 8651. Very popular breakfast spot with good coffee, tasty pastries and other snacks and ice cold juices

₸ **Cervantes**, Barata Ribeiro 07-B e Prado Júnior 335B, Copacabana. Stand-up bar or sit-down, a/c restaurant, open all night, queues after 2200. Said to serve the best sandwiches in town, a local institution.

₸ **Empório Saúde**, R Visconde de Pirajá, 414, Ipanema, T2522 1494. Closed Sun and evenings. A large variety of vegetarian cooking from quiches to stews.

₸ **La Trattoria**, Av Atlântica, opposite **Hotel Excelsior**. Italian, good food and service, very reasonable. Recommended.

₸ **Traiteurs de France**, Av NS de Copacabana 386, Copacabana. Delicious tarts and pastries, not expensive.

Gávea, Lagoa and Jardim Botânico *p412*

Gávea is the heartland of trendy 20- something Rio, while Jardim Botânico and Lagoa appear, at first sight, to offer no end of exciting upmarket dining opportunities. They're mostly all show and poor value. Here are a few exceptions:

₸₸₸ **Olympe**, R Custódio Serrão 62, Lagoa, T2539 4542. Elegant French restaurant servng a mixture of traditional cuisine and Franco-Brazilian fusions. Recommended.

₸₸₸ **Roberta Sudbrack**, Av Lineu de Paula Machado 916, Jardim Botânico, T3874 0139, www.robertasudbrack.com.br. Celebrated for her European-Brazilian fusion cooking, Roberta was the private chef for President Henrique Cardoso.

₸₸ **Árabe da Gávea**, Gávea shopping mall, R Marquês de São Vicente 52, T2294 2439. By far the best Arabic restaurant in Rio.

₸₸ **Guimas**, R José Roberto Macedo Soares, Baixo Gávea, T2259 7996. One of the places where the under 30s come to be seen, especially after 2200 towards the end of the week and on Mon, before moving down the street to the two tatty bars on the corner of the street and Praça Santos Dumont. The restaurant serves simple, traditional Portuguese food, at only a handful of tables.

Bars and clubs

Rio nightlife is young and vivacious. The current hotspots are **Lapa** at weekends, with a string of clubs along Mem de Sá and Lavradio with dance steps from samba and forró to techno and hip hop. **Santa Teresa** is increasingly lively and is often used as a drinking spot before moving onto Lapa, or a night spot in its own. There is a cluster of bars around the Largo das Neves. Similarly busy, even on Sun and Mon is **Baixa Gávea**, where beautiful 20-somethings gather around Praça Santos Dumont. In **Ipanema/Leblon**, there is always activity on and around Av General San Martin and Rua Dias Ferreira. **Copacabana** nightlife is mostly seedy and tawdry. Discos like Help are sad places full of visiting males panting after the lowest common denominator. Exceptions to this rule are the clubs like Bunker, the only one to play European club music in Rio. The guidebook O Guia dos Botequins do Rio de Janeiro, describes Rio's best, most traditional bars and their history, US$20. You can find it in the **Livraria da Travessa** (see Shopping), together with similar books; some in English.

Bars Wherever you are, there's one near you. Beer costs around US$1.50 for a large bottle, but up to US$5 in the plusher bars; where you are often given an entrance card which includes 2 drinks and a token entrance fee. A cover charge of US$3-7 may be made for live music, or there might be a minimum consumption charge of around US$3, sometimes both. Snack food is always available. Copacabana, Ipanema and Leblon have many beach barracas, several open all night. The seafront bars on Av Atlántica are great for people-watching; though avoid those towards Leme as they tend to offer more than beer. The big hotels have good cocktail bars.

Clubs Clubs in Rio are either fake Europe (eg Melt and Bunker) and US (eg Nuth and 00), or samba halls undergoing a renaissance (eg Scenarium and Carioca da Gema).

Centre, Lapa and Santa Teresa

p402, maps p401 and p406

Lapa is without doubt the centre of Rio nightlife and should not be missed if you are in Rio over a weekend. Ideally come early on Sat for the afternoon market and live street tango, eat and stay for a bar and club crawl. Always be wary of pickpockets around Lapa. See also Samba schools.

Bar do Goiabeira, Largo das Neves 13, Santa Teresa, T2232 5751. One of several restaurant bars on this pretty little square, attracts an arty crowd after 2100. Decent *petiscos* and a range of aromatic vintage *cachaças*.

Bar do Mineiro, on the Largo dos Guimarães, R Pascoal Carlos Magno 99, T2221 9227. A very popular Santa Teresa bar.

Carioca da Gema, Av Mem de Sá 79, Centro, T2221 0043. Great samba club café, second only to Rio Scenarium, good food too.

Club Six, R das Marrecas 38, Lapa. Huge pounding European/NYC dance club with everything from hip-hop to ambient house. A grungy old dance hall where transvestites gossip on the stairs and bands play Gafieira or dance hall samba.

Clube dos Democráticos, R do Riachuelo 91, T2252 4611, www.clubedosdemocraticos.com.br. A grungey old dance hall where transvestites gossip on the stairs and bands play Gafieira or dance hall samba. Caetano Veloso's son Moreno – who invented the new love of dance hall samba in Rio – sometimes plays here with his band *Orquestra Imperial*. If you're 20- or 30-something at heart and a samba lover it's the place to be. Few tourists. So far…

Dama da Noite, R Gomes Freire 773, Lapa. Samba, Chorinho and crepes in the pátio.

Espírito Santa, see Santa Teresa, Eating. The basement club has great Rio funk from DJ Zod on Sat from 2200, very popular. Owner Natacha Fink has opened **Espírito Santa Emporio**, R Lavradio 34, Lapa, www.espiritosanta.com.br, a new lounge bar/restaurant next to the **Rio Scenarium** (see below). DJ Zod and DJ Mam hold weekend Carioca funk parties.

Mercado, R do Mercado 32, Centro, T2221 2327, www.mercado32.com.br. Closed weekends. In the heart of the centre in a converted 19th-century building, this little restaurant and bar offers live *MPB* on most nights during the week and live *chorinho* every Thu from 2030.

Nuth Centro, R da Quitanda 51 at 7 de Setembro, T3861 8606, www.nuthcentro.com.br. Brings Barra's cheesy take on Miami's bare-mid-riffed, buff-bodied, plastic-boobed club culture to the city centre. Wonderful for people watching. Men should wear a medallion. Take a cab. The area is nocturnally sketchy.

Rio Scenarium, R do Lavradio 20, Lapa, T3852-5516, www.rioscenarium.com.br. 3-storey Samba club in a colonial house used as a movie prop warehouse. Overflowing with Brazilian exuberance and joie de vivre, with people dancing furiously, to the bizarre backdrop of a 19th-century apothecary's shop or a line of mannequins wearing 1920s outfits. This is Rio at its Bohemian best. Buzzes with beautiful people of all ages on Fri. Arrive after 2300.

Sacrilégio, Av Mem de Sá 81, next to Carioca da Gema, Lapa, T2507 3898. Samba, Chorinho, Pagode and occasional theatre. Close to many other bars.

Semente, R Joaquim Silva 138, T2509 3591. Popular for Samba, Choro and Salsa from 2200 Mon-Sat, US$2.50 cover; minimum consumption US$2. Book a table at weekends. Great atmosphere both inside and in the streets outside. Recommended (due for a revamp in 2010).

The Week, R Sacadura Cabral 154, Zona Portuária, T2253 1020, www.theweek.com.br. The most popular dance club of choice as this book went to press. Heaving with a gay and straight crowd and with state of the art spaces, DJs and sound systems. But don't expect any Brazilian sounds, it's strictly international dance here.

Glória, Flamengo and Botafogo

p407, map p406

Look out for the frequent free live music performances at the Marina da Glória and along Flamengo beach during the summer.

Casa de Matriz, R Enrique de Novais 107, Botafogo. Great little grungey club with a bar, Atari room, small cinema and 2 dance floors. Full of Rio students.

Porão, under the Anglican church hall, R Real Grandeza 99, Botafogo. British expats meet here on Fri night.

Copacabana and Ipanema
p412, maps p408 and p410
There is frequent live music on the beaches of Copacabana and Ipanema, and along the Av Atlántica throughout the summer; especially around New Year.

A Garota de Ipanema, R Vinícius de Morais 49, Ipanema. Where the song *Girl from Ipanema* was written. Now packed with foreigners on the package Rio circuit listening to Bossa. For the real thing head up the street to Toca do Vinícius on Sun afternoon (see below).

Académia da Cachaça, R Conde de Bernadotte 26-G, Leblon; with another branch at Av Armando Lombardi 800, Barra da Tijuca. The best cachaças, great caipirinhas and traditional Brazilian dishes. Good on Fri. Owner Leo Rengel and Natacha Fink of Espírito Santa (see above) have opened **Abençoado** bar/restaurant on the summit of Morro de Urca, for Brazilian comfort snacks given a gourmet twist, caipirinhas and batidas and breathtaking views.

Barril 1800, Av Vieira Souto 110, Ipanema. Nice place to watch the sunset. Highly recommended.

Bip Bip, R Almirante Gonçalves 50, Copacabana. Botequim bar which attracts a crowd of jamming musicians every Tue, also Sun for great atmosphere.

Bom Bar, R General San Martin 1011, Leblon. A downstairs bar and an upstairs club, packed after 2300, especially Sat.

Bunker, R Raul Pompeira 94, Copacabana. European-style dance club where the likes of DJs Marky and Patife play. Busy from Wed-Sat, kicks off at about 0200. The queues have become a party in themselves – at the bar next door.

Devassa, Av General San Martin 1241, Leblon. A 2-floor pub/restaurant/bar which is always heaving. Brews its own beer.

Empório, R Maria Quitéria 37, Ipanema. Street bar which attracts hordes. Mon is busiest.

Melt, R Rita Ludolf 47, T2249 9309. Downstairs bar and upstairs sweaty club. Occasional performances by the cream of Rio's new samba funk scene, usually on Sun. Always heaving on Thu.

Shenanigans, R Visconde de Pirajá 112, Ipanema. Obligatory mock-Irish bar with Guinness and Newcastle Brown. Not a place to meet the locals.

Vinícius, R Vinícius de Morais 39, Ipanema, 2nd floor. Mirror image of the Garota de Ipanema with slightly better acts and food.

Gávea, Jardim Botânico and Lagoa *p412*

00 (Zero Zero), Av Padre Leonel Franca 240, Gávea. Mock LA bar/restaurant/club with a small outdoor area. Currently the trendiest club in Rio for Brazil's equivalent of Sloanes or Valley Girls. Gay night on Sun.

Bar Lagoa, Av Epitácio Pessoa 1674, Lagoa. Slightly older, arty crowd on weekday evenings.

Caroline Café, R JJ Seabra 10, Jardim Botânico, T2540 0705, www.carolinecafe.com. Popular bar with Rio's young and good-looking middle classes. Kicks off after 2130. Food too.

Clan Café, R Cosme Velho 564 (in front of the Corcovado train station). Great little gem of a sit down Choro and Samba club with live music every night and decent bar food.

Cozumel, Av Lineu de Paula Machado 696, Jardim Botânico. The Rio equivalent of a foam disco, with free margaritas, tacky music and a crowd most of whom are looking not to go home alone.

Mistura Fina, Av Borges de Medeiros 3207, T2537 2844, www.misturafina.com.br. Downstairs restaurant, upstairs jazz and bossa nova club. One of the few places not oriented solely to the young.

Sítio Lounge, R Marques de São Vicente 10, Gávea. The nearest thing Rio has to a lounge bar, good for a chilled out Sat night.

El Turf (aka Jockey Club), opposite the Jardim Botânico, Praça Santos Dumont 31. Opens at 2200, gets going at 2300, you may have to wait to get in if you arrive after midnight at the weekend, no T-shirts allowed, very much a Rio rich kid singles and birthday party place; another branch in Rio Sul Shopping Centre.

Barra da Tijuca *p413*

Nuth, R Armando Lombardi 999, Barra da Tijuca, www.nuth.com.br. Barra's slickest club; mock Miami with snacks. Mix of tacky Brazilian and Eurotrash music and some samba funk live acts. Expensive.

Pepe, at Posto 2, Barra da Tijuca beach. Very popular with surfers.

Entertainment

Rio de Janeiro *p399, maps p399 and p401*

Cinemas

There are cinemas serving subtitled Hollywood films and major Brazilian releases on the top floor of almost all the malls. The normal seat price is US$3, discounts on Wed and Thu (students pay half price any day of the week).

Centro Cultural do Banco do Brasil, see Sights, T2808 2020. One of Rio's better arts centres with the best art films and exhibitions from fine art to photography (Metro: Uruguaiana).

Cinemateca do MAM, Infante Dom Henrique 85, Aterro do Flamengo, T2210 2188. Cinema classics, art films and roving art exhibitions and a good café with live music. Views of Guanabara Bay from the balconies.

Estaçao Ipanema, R Visconde de Pirajá 605, Ipanema. European art cinema, less mainstream US and Brazilian releases.

Live music

Many young Cariocas congregate in Botafogo for live music. There are free concerts throughout the summer, along the Copacabana and Ipanema beaches, in Botafogo and at the parks: mostly samba, reggae, rock and MPB (Brazilian pop): there is no advance schedule, information is given in the local press (see below). Rio's famous jazz, in all its forms, is performed in lots of enjoyable venues, see the press. See www.samba-choro.com.br, for more information. Also see **Clan Café**, **Melt**, **Nuth** and **Mistura Fina** in Bars and clubs, above.

Canecão, R Venceslau Brás 215, Botafogo, T2295 3044. This big, inexpensive venue has live concerts most nights, see press for listings. For a taste of some purely local entertainment, make your way down here on Mon nights.

Centro Cultural Carioca, R do Teatro 37, T2252 6468 for advance information, www.centroculturalcarioca.com. An exciting venue that combines music (mostly samba) and dance, 1830-early morning. This restored old house with wrap-around balconies and exposed brick walls is a dance school and music venue that attracts a lovely mix of people. Professional dancers perform with musicians; after a few tunes the audience joins in. Thu is impossibly crowded; Sat is calmer. Bar food available. US$3 cover charge. Highly recommended.

Circo Voador, R dos Arcos s/n, Lapa, T2533 0354, www.circovoador.com.br. Lapa's recuperation began with this little concert hall under the arches. Some of the city's best smaller acts still play here, including Seu Jorge who first found fame playing with *Farofa Carioca* at the Circo.

Praia do Vermelha at Urca. Residents bring musical instruments and chairs onto beach for an informal night of samba from 2100-2400, free. Bus No 511 from Copacabana.

Toca do Vinícius, Vinícius de Moraes 129, Ipanema. Rio's leading Bossa Nova and Choro record shop with live concerts from some of the finest past performers every Sun lunchtime and 2000 Sun in summer.

Festivals and events

Rio de Janeiro *p399, maps p399 and p401*

Less hectic than Carnival, see box, page 426, but very atmospheric, is the festival of **Iemanjá** on the night of **31 Dec**, when devotees of the orixá of the sea dress in white and gather on Copacabana, Ipanema and Leblon beaches, singing and dancing around open fires and making offerings. The elected Queen of the Sea is rowed along the seashore. At midnight small boats are launched as offerings to Iemanjá. The religious event is dwarfed, however, by a massive New Year's Eve party, called **Reveillon** at Copacabana. The beach is packed as thousands of revellers enjoy free outdoor concerts by big-name pop stars, topped with a lavish midnight firework display. It is most crowded in front of Copacabana Palace Hotel. Another good place to see fireworks is in front of Le Meridien, famous for its fireworks waterfall at about 10 mins past midnight. **Note** Many followers of Iemanjá are now making their offerings on 29 or 30 Dec and at Barra da Tijuca or Recreio dos Bandeirantes to avoid the crowds and noise of Reveillon. The festival of **São Sebastião**, patron saint of Rio, is celebrated by an evening procession on **20 Jan**, leaving Capuchinhos Church, Tijuca, and arriving at the cathedral of São Sebastião. On the same evening, an **umbanda festival** is celebrated at the Caboclo Monument in Santa Teresa. **Carnival 5-8 Mar** 2011, **18-21 Feb** 2012 (see page 426). **Festas Juninas**: **Santo Antônio** on **13 Jun**, whose main event is a mass, followed by celebrations at the Convento do Santo Antônio and the Largo da

Carioca. Throughout the state of Rio, the festival of **São João** is a major event, marked by huge bonfires on the night of **23-24 Jun**. It is traditional to dance the quadrilha and drink quentão, cachaça and sugar, spiced with ginger and cinnamon, served hot. The Festas Juninas close with the festival of **São Pedro** on **29 Jun**. Being the patron saint of fishermen, his feast is normally accompanied by processions of boats. **Oct** is the month of the feast of **Nossa Senhora da Penha**.

O Shopping

Rio de Janeiro *p399, maps p399 and p401*

Bookshops **Da Vinci**, Av Rio Branco 185, lojas 2, 3 and 9. All types of foreign books. **Folha Seca** R do Ouvidor 37, 021-2507 7175. Next to NS de Lapa church, good range of Brazilian photography and art books difficult to find elsewhere. Ask here about **Samba do Ouvidor**, a samba show outside, or check http://sambadaouvidor.blogspot.com for dates. **Livraria da Travessa**, R Visconde de Pirajá 572, Ipanema, T021-3205 9002. Classy little bookshop, good choice of novels, magazines and guidebooks in English. Great café upstairs too. **Saraiva**, R do Ouvidor 98, T021-2507 9500. A massive (megastore) bookshop which also includes a music and video shop and a café; other branches in **Shopping Iguatemi** and **Shopping Tijuca**.

Fashion Fashion is one of the best buys in Brazil; with a wealth of Brazilian designers selling clothes of the same quality as European or US famous names at a fraction of the price. Rio is the best place in the world for buying high-fashion bikinis. The best shops in Rio are on Garcia D'Ávila and R Nascimento Silva, which runs off it, in Ipanema. This is where some of the best Brazilian designers like Andrea Saletto and Rosana Bernardes, together with international big name stalwarts like Louis Vuitton and Cartier. Most of the international names, as well as all the big Brazilian names like Lenny (Brazil's best bikinis), Alberta, Salinas, Club Chocolate and so on are housed in the **Fashion Mall** in São Conrado.

Saara is a multitude of little shops along R Alfândega and R Senhor dos Passos (between city centre and Campo Santana), where clothing bargains can be found (especially jeans, kanga beach wraps and bikinis); it is known popularly as 'Shopping a Céu Aberto'. Little shops on Aires Saldanha, Copacabana (1 block back from the beach), are good for bikinis and cheaper than in shopping centres.

Jewellery **Amsterdam Sauer**, R Garcia D'Ávila 105, with10 shops in Rio and others throughout Brazil. They offer free taxi rides to their main shop. **Antônio Bernardo**, R Garcia d'Ávila 121, Ipanema, T2512 7204, and in the Fashion Mall. Brazil's foremost jeweller who has been making beautifully understated jewellery with contemporary designs for 30 years. Internationally well known, but available only in Brazil. **H Stern**, next door to Amsterdam Sauer at R Visconde de Pirajá 490/R Garcia Dávila 113, Ipanema, has 10 outlets, plus branches in major hotels.

There are several good jewellery shops at the Leme end of Av NS de Copacabana. **Mineraux**, Av NS de Copacabana 195. For mineral specimens as against cut stones, Belgian owner.

Markets **Northeastern market** at Campo de São Cristóvão, with music and magic, on Sun 0800-2200 (bus 472 or 474 from Copacabana or centre). A recommended shop for north-eastern handicrafts is **Pé de Boi**, R Ipiranga 55, Laranjeiras, www.pedeboi.com.br. Sat antiques market on the waterfront near Praça 15 de Novembro, 1000-1700. Also in Praça 15 de Novembro is **Feirarte II**, Thu-Fri 0800-1800. **Feirarte I** is a Sun open-air handicrafts market (everyone calls it the Feira Hippy) at Praça Gen Osório, Ipanema, 0800-1800, items from all over Brazil. A **stamp, coin and postcard market** is held in the Passeio Público on Sun 0800-1300. Markets on Wed 0700-1300 on R Domingos Ferreira and on Thu, same hrs, on Praça do Lido, both Copacabana (Praça do Lido also has a Feirarte on Sat-Sun 0800-1800). **Sunday market** on R da Glória, colourful, cheap fruit, vegetables and flowers; **early-morning food market**, 0600-1100, R Min Viveiros de Castro, Ipanema. There is a **cheap market** for just about anything, especially electronic goods, outside Metro stop Uruguaiana. Excellent food and household-goods markets at various places in the city and suburbs (see newspapers for times and places). An **antiques fair** is held on the last Sat of every month on R do Lavradio in Lapa.

Music **Modern Sound Música Equipamentos**, R Barata Ribeiro 502D, Copacabana. For a large selection of Brazilian music, jazz and classical. **Toca do Vinícius**, see Live music, above.

Carnival in Rio

Carnival in Rio is spectacular. On the Friday before Shrove Tuesday, the mayor of Rio hands the keys of the city to Rei Momo, the Lord of Misrule, signifying the start of a five-day party. Imagination runs riot, social barriers are broken and the main avenues, full of people and children wearing fancy dress, are colourfully lit. Areas throughout the city such as the Terreirão de Samba in Praça Onze are used for shows, music and dancing. Bandas and blocos (organized carnival groups) seem to be everywhere, dancing, drumming and singing.

There are numerous samba schools in Rio divided into two leagues, both of which parade in the Sambódromo. The Carnival parades are the culmination of months of intense activity by community groups, mostly in the city's poorest districts. Every school presents 2,500-6,000 participants divided into alas (wings) each with a different costume and 5-9 carros alegóricos, beautifully designed floats. Each school chooses an enredo (theme) and composes a samba (song) that is a poetic, rhythmic and catchy expression of the theme. The enredo is further developed through the design of the floats and costumes. A bateria (percussion wing) maintains a reverberating beat that must keep the entire school, and the audience, dancing throughout the parade. Each procession follows a set order with the first to appear being the comissão de frente, a choreographed group that presents the school and the theme to the public. Next comes the abre alas, a magnificent float usually bearing the name or symbol of the school. Schools are given between 65 and 80 minutes and lose points for failing to keep within this time. Judges award points to each school for components of their procession, such as costume, music and design, and make deductions for lack of energy, enthusiasm or discipline.

The Sambódromo is a permanent site at R Marquês de Sapucai, Cidade Nova, is 600 m long with seating for 43,000 people. Designed by Oscar Niemeyer and built in 1983-1984, it handles sporting events, conferences and concerts during the rest of the year. A Cidade de Samba (Samba City), Rivadávia Corréa 60, Gamboa, T2213 2503, www.cidadedosambarj.com.br, Tue-Sat 1000-1900, is a theme park bringing a number of the larger schools together in one location. There is a permanent carnival production centre of 14 workshops; visitors can watch floats and costumes being prepared or watch one of the year-round carnival-themed shows.

Rio's **bailes** (fancy-dress balls) range from the sophisticated to the wild. The majority of clubs and hotels host at least one. The Copacabana Palace hotel's is elegant and expensive whilst the Scala club has licentious parties. It is not necessary to wear fancy dress; just join in, although you will feel more comfortable if you wear a minimum of clothing to the clubs. The most famous are the Red & Black Ball (Friday) and the Gay Ball (Tuesday) which are both televized.

Bandas and **blocos** can be found in all neighbourhoods and some of the most popular and entertaining are Cordão do Bola Preta (meets at 0900 on Saturday in Rua 13 de Maio 13, Centro), Simpatia é Quase Amor (meets at 1600 Sunday in Praça General Osório, Ipanema) and the transvestite Banda da Ipanema (meets at 1600 on Saturday and Tuesday in Praça General Osório, Ipanema). It is necessary to join a bloco in advance to receive their distinctive T-shirts, but anyone can join in with the bandas.

Shopping malls Rio Sul, at the Botafogo end of Túnel Novo, has almost everything the visitor may need. Some of the services in Rio Sul are: Telemar (phone office) for international calls at A10-A, Mon-Sat 1000-2200; next door is Belle Tours Câmbio, A10. There is a post office at G2. A good branch of **Livraria Sodiler** is at A03. For Eating and Entertainment, see above; live music at the **Terraço**; the **Ibeas Top Club** gym; and a cinema. A US$5 bus service runs as far as the

Tickets The Sambódromo parades start at 1900 and last about 12 hours. Gates open at 1800. There are cadeiras (seats, US$5) at ground level, arquibancadas (terraces, US$55-250) and camarotes (boxes). The best boxes are reserved for tourists and VIPs. Seats are closest to the parade, but you may have to fight your way to the front. Seats and boxes reserved for tourists have the best view, sectors 4, 7 and 11 are the best spots (they house the judging points). 6 and 13 are at the end when dancers might be tired, but have more space. The terraces, while uncomfortable, house the most fervent fans, tightly packed; this is where to soak up the atmosphere but not take pictures (too crowded). Tickets are sold at travel agencies as well as the Maracanã Stadium box office. Tickets are usually sold out before Carnaval weekend but touts outside can generally sell you tickets at inflated prices. Samba schools have an allocation of tickets which members sometimes sell, if you are offered one of these check its date. Tickets for the champions' parade at 2100 on the Saturday following Carnival are much cheaper. Taxis to the Sambódromo are negotiable and will find your gate, the nearest metrô is Praça Onze and this can be an enjoyable ride in the company of costumed samba school members. You can follow the participants to the concentração, the assembly and formation on Avenida Presidente Vargas, and mingle with them while they queue to enter the Sambódromo.

Sleeping and security Reserve accommodation well in advance. Virtually all hotels raise their prices during Carnival, although it is usually possible to find a room. Your property should be safe inside the Sambódromo, but the crowds outside can attract pickpockets; only take the money you need for fares and food.

Taking part Most samba schools accept a number of foreigners and you will be charged upwards of US$125 (+ tax) for your costume (the money helps fund poorer members of the school). You should be in Rio for at least two weeks before carnival. Attend fittings and rehearsals on time and show respect for your section leaders – enter into the competitive spirit of the event.

Rehearsals Ensaios are held at the schools' quadras from October on and are well worth seeing. (Go by taxi, as most schools are based in poorer districts.)

Samba Schools **Acadêmicos de Salgueiro**, R Silva Teles 104, Andaraí, T2238 0389, www.salgueiro.com.br. **Beija Flor de Nilópolis**, Pracinha Wallace Paes Leme 1025, Nilópolis, T2791 2866, www.beija-flor.com.br. **Imperatriz Leopoldinense**, R Prof. Lacê 235, Ramos, T2560 8037. **Mocidade Independente de Padre Miguel**, R Coronel Tamarindo 38, Padre Miguel, T3332 5823. **Portela**, R Clara Nunes 81, Madureira, T2489 6440, www.gresportela.com.br. **Primeira Estação de Mangueira**, R Visconde de Niterói 1072, Mangueira, T3872 6786, www.mangueira.com.br. **Unidos da Viradouro**, Av do Contorno 16, Niterói, T2628 7840.

Useful information Freephone T0800-701 1250 (24 hrs, English, Spanish, Portuguese). **Riotur**'s guide booklet gives information on official and unofficial events (in English). The entertainment sections of newspapers and magazines such as O Globo, Jornal do Brasil, Manchete and Veja Rio are worth checking. Liga Independente das Escolas de Samba do Rio de Janeiro, T3213 5151, http://liesa.globo.com, for schools' addresses and rehearsal times, ticket prices and lots more information.

Sheraton passing the main hotels, every 2 hrs between 1000 and 1800, then 2130.

Other shopping centres, which include a wide variety of services, include **Cassino** (Copacabana), **Norte Shopping** (Todos os Santos), **Plaza Shopping** (Niterói), **Barra** in Barra da Tijuca (see page 413) and **The Fashion Mall** in São Conrado, see above.

Activities and tours

Rio de Janeiro *p399, maps p399 and p401*

Few of the hundreds of gyms and sports clubs grant temporary (less than 1 month) membership. Big hotels may allow use of their facilities for a small deposit. As well as the sports listed below, operators also offer rafting, US$125 for a tour, and surfing lessons, US$37.

Cycling **Rio Bikers**, R Domingos Ferreira 81, room 201, T2274 5872. Tours and bike hire. **Stop Bike**, T2275 7345, Copacabana. Bike rental.

Dancing **Rio Samba Dancer**, Hélio Ricardo is a Rio native and Samba and Forró dancer. He speaks English and Spanish and teaches and accompanies individuals in dance; http://riosambadancer.com.

Diving **Squalo**, Av Armando Lombardi 949-D, Barra de Tijuca, T/F2493 3022, squalo1@hotmail.com. Offers courses at all levels, NAUI and PDIC training facilities, also snorkelling and equipment rental.

Football See Maracanã stadium, page 405.

Helicopter rides **Helisight**, R Visconde de Pirajá 580, loja 107, Térreo, Ipanema, T2259 6995, www.helisight.com.br. Prices from US$100 pp for flights from Lagoa or Pão de Açucar.

Horse racing and riding **Jockey Club Racecourse**, by Jardím Botânico and Gávea, meetings on Mon and Thu evenings and Sat and Sun 1400, US$1-2, long trousers required. Take any bus marked 'via Jóquei'. **Sociedade Hípico Brasileiro**, Av Borges de Medeiros 2448, T527 8090, Jardim Botânico. For riding.

Parapenting and hang-gliding For the Brazilian Association, see www.abvl.com.br, the website of the Associação Brasileira de Vôo Livre, which oversees all national clubs and federations. **Barra Jumping**, Aeroporto de Jacarepaguá, Av Ayrton Senna 2541, T3151 3602, www.barrajumping.com.br. Tandem jumping (Vôo duplo). **Rio Tandem Fly**, instructor Paulo Falcão T2422 6371/9966 3416, pilot Roni Falcão, T9963 6623, www.riotandemfly.com.br. Several others offer tandem jumping; check that they are accredited with the Associação Brasileira de Vôo Livre. Ask for the **Parapente Rio Clube** at São Conrado launch site. Basic cost US$120 for a tandem flight. **Delta Flight** and

Rio by Jeep, T3322 5750/9693 8800, www.deltaflight.com.br. Tandem flight tours above Rio from Pedra Bonita Mountain with instructors licensed by the Brazilian Hang-Gliding Association. Contact Ricardo Hamond. **HiltonFlyRio Hang Gliding Center**, T7840 6325/9964 2607, www.hiltonflyrio.com. DeHilton Carvalho is an ABVL certified instructor, very experienced. **Just Fly**, T/F2268 0565, T9985 7540, www.justfly.com.br. Tandem flights with Paulo Celani (licensed by Brazilian Hang Gliding Association), pick-up and drop-off at hotel included, in-flight pictures US$15 extra, flights all year, best time of day 1000-1500 (5% discount for South American and Brazil Handbook readers on presentation of book at time of reservation). **Super-fly**, T3322 2286, www.riosuperfly.com.br. Highly regarded, experienced hang-gliding operator from the Pedra Bonita. **Ultra Força Ltda**, Av Sernambetiba 8100, Barra da Tijuca, T3399 3114; 15 mins.

Rock climbing and hill walking Clube **Excursionista Carioca**, R Hilário Gouveia 71, room 206, T2255 1348. Recommended for enthusiasts, meets Wed and Fri. **ECA**, Av Erasmo Braga 217, room 305, T2242 6857. Personal guide US$100/day. **Oswaldo Mello**, T9776 2820. An experienced guide for Pão de Açúcar. **Paulo Miranda**, R Campos Sales 64/801, RJ20270-210, T/F2264 4501. **Rio Hiking**, T2552 9204/ 9721 0594, www.riohiking.com.br. Hiking tours to the top of Rio's mountains.

Tours

Most hotels offer tours but shop around for more choice. Organized trips to samba shows with dinner included, US$50, good, but it's cheaper to go independently.

4 Star Turismo do Brasil, R Senador Dantas 20, T1-800-746-4599 (USA), T3523 0379, www.4starBrazil.com. Custom and group tours in Brazil and throughout the region.

Atlantic Forest Jeep Tour, T2495 9827, T9974 0218. Jeep tours to the Parque Nacional Tijuca and trips to coffee fazendas in the Paraíba Valley, trips to Angra dos Reis and offshore islands and the Serra dos Órgãos.

Brazil Expedition, R Visconde Piraja 550 lj 201, Ipanema, T9998 2907, www.brazilexpedition.com. Backpacker bus trips south to Paraty and Ilha Grande with stops along the Costa Verde. Day trips and Rio 'starter packs', accommodation advice. Recommended.

Favela Tour, Estr das Canoas 722, Bl 2, apt 125, São Conrado, T3322 2727, T9989 0074 (mob), www.favelatour.com.br. Safe, interesting guided tours of Rio's favelas in English, Spanish, Italian, German or French, 3 hrs. Ask Marcelo Armstrong, the owner, about eco tours and river rafting. For the best price call Marcelo direct rather than through a hotel. Recommended.

Jeep Tour, T2108 5800, T9977 9610 (mob), www.jeeptour.com.br. Among their tours are escorted groups to favelas.

Madson's Private Tours, T21- 9395 3537 (mob), madson@tourguiderio.com. Madson Araújo is a Brazilian licensed tour guide offering private tours since 2004, fluent in Spanish, English, French and Italian.

Metropol, R São José 46, T2533 5010, www.metropolturismo.com.br. Eco, adventure and culture tours to all parts of Brazil.

RBW Travel, Av Rio Branco 181, suite 509, T2240-1829, www.rbwtravel.com. Travel agency, experienced staff, for all types of business and leisure travel. Owners Ricardo and Elisabeth Werwie, English spoken.

Rejane Reis Exotic Tours, T2179 6972/9222 6972 (mob), www.exotictours.com.br. Focuses on a tourism workshop in Rocinha favela. They also offer hang gliding, ultralights, paragliding, sailing, diving, voodoo, and daytime tours.

Rio G, R Teixeira de Melo, 25-A, Ipanema, T3813-0003, www.riogtravel.com. Very helpful, English spoken, specialists in the GLBT market.

Saveiros Tour, Av Infante Dom Henrique s/n, l 13/14, Marina da Glória, T2225 6064, www.saveiros.com.br. Offers tours in sailing schooners around the bay and down the coast, also 'Baía da Guanabara Histórica' historical tours.

Travel Café, R Cosme Velho 513, T2285 8302. City tours, rafting, sky diving, horse riding, tours and packages along the Costa Verde, English spoken.

Turismo Clássico, Av NS de Copacabana 1059/805, T2523 3390, comercial@turismo classico.com.br. Warmly recommended.

www.bealocal.com. Guided tours to football matches, see under Maracanã stadium, page 405, and recommended visits to favelas.

Guides

Cultural Rio, R Santa Clara 110/904, Copacabana, T3322 4872, T9911 3829 (mob), www.culturalrio. com.br. Tours escorted personally by Professor Carlos Roquette, English/French spoken, almost 200 options available, entirely flexible to your interests.

Fábio Sombra, T9729 5455, fabiosombra@ hotmail.com. Offers private and tailor-made guided tours focusing on the cultural aspects of Rio and Brazil.

Luiz Amaral Tours, R Visc de Pirajá 550, office 215, Ipanema, T2259 5532, T9637 2522, www.travelrio.com/tours.htm. Good company offering personalized tours run by Luiz Felipe Amaral who speaks good English.

⊖ Transport

Rio de Janeiro *p399, maps p399 and p401*

Air

Rio has 2 airports: **Antônio Carlos Jobim International Airport** (T3398 4527), previously called Galeão, and the **Santos Dumont** airport on Guanabara Bay (T3814 7246), for domestic flights. **Jobim international airport** is situated on Governador Island some 16 km north of the centre of Rio. It is in 2 sections: international and domestic. There is a **Pousada Galeão** (**AL**), comfortable, good value, and **Luxor Aeroporto**, in Terminal 1, T3222 9700, www.luxorhoteis. com.br, if you need an early start, follow signs in airport.

There are a/c taxis; Cootramo and Transcopass have fixed rates (US$25 Copacabana). Buy a ticket at the counter near the arrivals gate before getting into the car. Fixed-rate taxi fares from Terminal 2 are US$15 to Centro, US$20 to Copacabana/ Ipanema, US$25 to Barra da Tijuca. Credit cards accepted by some companies. The hire is for the taxi, irrespective of the number of passengers. Make sure you keep the ticket, which carries the number to phone in case of difficulty. Ordinary taxis also operate with the normal meter reading (about US$16, but some may offer cheaper rates from Copacabana to the airport, US$9-10). Do not negotiate with a driver on arrival, unless you are a frequent visitor. Beware pirate taxis which are unlicensed. It is better to pay extra for an official vehicle than risk being robbed.

The a/c 'Real' bus runs frequently from the 1st floor of the airport to Recreio dos Bandeirantes via the municipal rodoviária and city centre, Santos Dumont Airport, Flamengo, Copacabana, Ipanema and Leblon. Fares are collected during the journey, to anywhere in Rio US$4.50. The driver will stop at requested points (the bus runs along the seafront from Leme to Leblon), so it's worth checking a map so you can specify your required junction. The bus returns by the same route. Town buses M94 and M95, Bancários/ Castelo, take a circular route passing through the centre and the interstate bus station. They leave from the 2nd floor of the airport.

There are câmbios in the airport departure hall. There is also a câmbio on the 1st floor of the international arrivals area, but it gives worse rates than the Banco do Brasil, 24-hr bank, 3rd floor, which has Visa ATMs (may not accept foreign cards) and gives cash advances against Visa. Duty-free shops are well stocked, but not cheap. Duty free is open to arrivals and departures. Only US dollars or credit cards are accepted on the air-side of the departure lounge. There is a better choice of restaurants outside passport control.

The **Santos Dumont** airport on Guanabara Bay, right in the city, is used for Rio-São Paulo shuttle flights, other domestic routes, air taxis and private planes. The shuttle services operate every 30 mins from 0630 to 2230. Sit on the right-hand side for views to São Paulo, the other side coming back, book in advance for particular flights.

Bus

Local There are good services, but buses are very crowded and not for the aged or infirm during rush hours; buses have turnstiles which are awkward if you are carrying luggage. Hang on tight, drivers live out Grand Prix fantasies. At busy times allow about 45 mins to get from Copacabana to the centre by bus, less if you take a bus on the *aterro* expressway on the reclaimed waterfront. The fare on standard buses is US$1 and suburban bus fares are US$1.90. Bus stops are often not marked. The route is usually written on the front of the bus, increasingly with dot-matrix signs. Private companies operate air-conditioned (*frescão*) buses which can be flagged down practically anywhere: **Real**, **Pegaso**, **Anatur**. They run from all points in Rio Sul to the city centre, Rodoviária and the airports. Fares are US$2 (US$2.40 to the international airport). City Rio is an a/c tourist bus service with security guards which runs between all the major parts of the city. Good maps show what sites of interest are close to each bus stop, marked by grey poles and found where there are concentrations of hotels. T0800 258060.

Long distance Rodoviária Novo Rio, Av Rodrigues Alves, corner with Av Francisco Bicalho, just past the docks, T2291 5151, www.novorio.com.br. Buses run from Rio to all parts of the country. It is advisable to book tickets in advance. The rodoviária has a **Riotur** information centre, which is very helpful, T2263 4857. Left luggage costs US$4. There are ATMs and câmbios for cash only. A local bus terminal is just outside the rodoviária: turn right as you leave and run the gauntlet of taxi drivers – best ignored. The air conditioned Real bus (opposite the exit) goes along the beach to São Conrado and will secure luggage. If you need a taxi collect a ticket, which ensures against overcharging, from the office inside the entrance (to Flamengo US$10). On no account give the ticket to the taxi driver. The main bus station is reached by buses M94 and M95, Bancários/Castelo, from the centre and the airport; 136, 172, Rodoviária/ Glória/ Flamengo/Botafogo; 127, 128, 136, Rodoviária/ Copacabana; 170, Rodoviária/ Gávea/São Conrado; 128, 172, Rodoviária/ Ipanema/Leblon, 233, Tijuca.

Distances in km to some major cities with approximate journey time in brackets: Juiz de Fora, 184 (2¾ hrs); Belo Horizonte, 434 (7 hrs), São Paulo, 429 (6 hrs); Vitória, 521 (8 hrs); Curitiba, 852 (12 hrs); Brasília, 1,148 (20 hrs); Florianópolis, 1,144 (20 hrs); Foz do Iguaçu, 1,500 (21 hrs); Porto Alegre, 1,553 (26 hrs); Salvador, 1,649 (28 hrs); Recife, 2,338 (38 hrs); Fortaleza, 2,805 (48 hrs); São Luís, 3,015 (50 hrs); Belém, 3,250 (52 hrs).

International bus **Asunción**, 1,511 km via Foz do Iguaçu, 30 hrs (**Pluma**), US$80; **Buenos Aires** (**Pluma**), via Porto Alegre and Santa Fe, 48 hrs, US$100 (book 2 days in advance).

Car

Service stations are closed in many places Sat and Sun. Road signs are notoriously misleading in Rio and you can easily end up in a favela. Take care if driving along the Estr da Gávea to São Conrado as it is possible to enter unwittingly Rocinha, Rio's biggest slum.

Metro

The Metrô, www.metrorio.com.br, provides good service, clean, a/c and fast. Line 1 runs between the inner suburb of Tijuca (station Saens Peña) and Ipanema/General Osório, Line 2 from Pavuna, passing Engenho da Rainha and the Maracanã stadium, to Estácio. It operates 0500-2400 Mon-Sat, 0700- 2300 Sun and holidays. The fare is US$1.50 single; multi-tickets and integrated bus/Metrô tickets (US$2) are available. Integrated systems include Integração Expressa between certain stations (eg Estácio and Rodoviária), Metrô na Superfície from Botafogo (via Jardim Botânico) and Ipanema/General Osório to Gávea and Ipanema/ General Osório to Leblon, and Barra Expresso from Ipanema/General Osório to Barra da Tijuca.

Taxi

The fare between Copacabana and the centre is US$9.50. Between 2300 and 0600 and on Sun and holidays, 'tariff 2' is used. Official taxis are yellow with a blue stripe and have meters. Smaller ones (mostly Volkswagen) are marked TAXI on the windscreen or roof. Make sure meters are cleared and on tariff 1, except at those times mentioned above. Only use taxis with an official identification sticker on the windscreen. Don't hesitate to argue if the route is too long or the fare too much. Radio Taxis are safer but more expensive, eg **Cootramo**, T3976 9944, **Coopertramo**, T2560 2022, **Central de Táxi**, T2593 2598, **Transcoopass**, T2590 6891. Luxury cabs are allowed to charge higher rates. Inácio de Oliveira, T2225 4110, is a reliable taxi driver for excursions, he only speaks Portuguese. Recommended. **Grimalde**, T2267 9812, has been recommended for talkative daytime and evening tours, English and Italian spoken, negotiate a price. Also **Eduardo**, T3361 1315 or 9708 8542, a/c taxi.

Pão de Açúcar *p410*

Bus Bus 107 (from the centre, Catete or Flamengo) and 511 from Copacabana (512 to return) take you to the cable-car station, Av Pasteur 520, at the foot.

Cable car Praia Vermelha to Morro de Urca: first car goes up at 0800, then every 30 mins (or when full), until the last comes down at 2200 (quietest before 1000). From Urca to Sugar Loaf, the first connecting cable car goes up at 0815 then every 30 mins (or when full), until the last leaves the summit at 2200; the return trip costs US$22 (US$10 to Morro da Urca, halfway up, or from Morro da Urca to the top). Termini are ample and efficient and the present Italian cable cars carry 75 passengers. Even on the most crowded days there is little queuing.

Corcovado *p411*

Bus Take a **Cosme Velho** bus to the cog railway station at R Cosme Velho 513: from the centre or Glória/Flamengo No 180; from Copacabana take No 583, 584, from Botafogo or Ipanema/Leblon No 583 or 584; from Santa Teresa Microônibus Santa Teresa.

Car If driving to Corcovado, the entrance fee is US$5 for the vehicle, plus US$5 pp. Coach trips tend to be rather brief and special taxis, which wait in front of the station, offer tours of Corcovado and Mirante Dona Marta for US$25.

Train Every 20-30 mins between 0830 and 1830, journey time 10 mins (US$18 return; single tickets available). **Trem do Corcovado**, R Cosme Velho 513, T2558 1329, www.corcovado.com.br. Ignore touts for tours who say that the train is not running.

Taxis and minivans from Paineiras charge US$6.50 pp. Also, a 206 bus does the very attractive run from Praça Tiradentes (or a 407 from Largo do Machado) to Silvestre (the railway has no stop here now). An active walk of 9 km will take you to the top. For safety reasons go in company, or at weekends when more people are about.

Copacabana *p411, map p408*

Bus Many to and from the city centre, US$1. The buses to take are Nos 119, 154, 413, 415, 455, 474 from Av Nossa Senhora de Copacabana. If you are going to the centre from Copacabana, look for 'Castelo', 'Praça 15', 'E Ferro' or 'Praça Mauá' on the sign by the front door. From the centre to Copaca bana is easier as all buses in that direction are marked. 'Aterro' means the expressway between Botafogo and downtown Rio (closed Sun). The 'Aterro' bus does the journey in 15 mins.

Ipanema and Leblon *p412, map p410*

Bus From Botafogo Metrô terminal to Ipanema: some take integrated Metrô-Bus tickets; look for the blue signs on the windscreen. Many buses from Copacabana run to Ipanema and Leblon, plus the Metrô na Superfície from Siqueira Campos.

Jardim Botânico *p412*

Bus Take bus No 170 from the centre, or any bus to Leblon, Gávea or São Conrado marked 'via Jóquei'; from Glória, Flamengo or Botafogo take No 571, or 172 from Flamengo, or the Metrô na Superfície from Botafogo; from Copacabana, Ipanema or Leblon take No 572 (584 back to Copacabana).

Barra da Tijuca *p413*

Bus From the city centre to Barra, 1 hr, are Nos 175, 176; from Botafogo, Glória or Flamengo take No 179; Nos 591 or 592 from Leme; and from Copacabana via Leblon No 523 (45 mins-1 hr). A taxi to Zona Sul costs US$25 (US$35 after 2400).

Also the Barra Expresso from Siqueira Campos metrô station. A comfortable bus, Pegasus, goes along the coast from the Castelo bus terminal to Barra da Tijuca and continues to Campo Grande or Santa Cruz, or take the free 'Barra Shopping' bus. Bus 700 from Praça São Conrado (terminal of bus 553 from Copacabana) goes the full length of the beach to Recreio dos Bandeirantes.

Parque Nacional Tijuca *p413*

Bus Take bus No 221 from Praça 15 de Novembro, No 234 from the rodoviária or from Praça Sáens Pena, Tijuca (the city suburb, not Barra – reached by Metrô), for the park entrance, or No 454 from Copacabana to Alto da Boa Vista. Jeep tours are run by **Atlantic Forest Jeep Tour**, daily; T2495 9827, T9974 0218, or contact through travel agencies.

Ilha de Paquetá *p413*

Ferry Services leave more or less every 2 hrs from Praça 15 de Novembro, immediately north of the Niterói ferry terminal (see page 441); there are boats from 0515 (0710 on Sun and holidays) to 2300, T2533 7524, or hydrofoils between 1000 and 1600, Sat and Sun 0800-1630 hourly, T2533 4343 or Paquetá 3397 0656 (fare US$2.15 by boat, US$4.50 on Sun, 1 hr, US$5 by hydrofoil, 20 mins' journey, which more than doubles its price Sat, Sun and holidays). Other boat trips: Several agencies offer trips to Paquetá. Some also offer a day cruise, including lunch, to Jaguanum Island (see under Itacuruçá) and a sundown cruise around Guanabara Bay.

Directory

Rio de Janeiro *p399, maps p399 and p401*

Airline offices **Aerolíneas Argentinas**, Av Rio Branco, 134, 7th floor, Centro, T2103 4200. **Air France/KLM**, Av Pres Antônio Carlos 58, 9th floor, T4003 9955, www.airfrance.com.br. **American**, Av Pres Wilson 165, 5th floor, T0300-789 7778, www.aa.com.br. **Avianca**, Av Almirante Barroso 52, 34th floor, T2240 4413, www.avianca.com.br. **British Airways**, T4004-4440 toll free. **Continental**, R da Assembléia 10, sala 3711, T0800-702 7500. **Gol**, T0300-115 2121, www.voegol.com.br. **Iberia**, Av Pres Antônio Carlos 51, 9th floor, T2282 1336. **LAB**, Av Calógeras 30A, T2220 9548, www.lab airlines.com.br. **LAN**, R da Assembléia 92, office 1301, T2240 9388, www.lan.com.br. **Ocean Air**, Praça Senador Salgado Filho s/n, T0300-789 8160, www.oceanair.com.br. Offices in both airports. **TAM**, Av Rio Branco 245, T0800-570 5700, www.tam.com.br. **TAP**, Av Rio Branco 311 B, T2131 7771. **United**, Av Rio Branco 89, 17th floor, T0800-162323, www.united.com.br. **Webjet**, at Tom Jobim airport, T0300-210 1234, www.web jet.com.br. **Banks** **Citibank**, R Assembléia 100, T2291 1232, changes large US$ TCs into smaller ones, no commission, advances cash on Eurocard/ MasterCard. ATM at branch on Av NS de Copacabana at Siqueira Campos. **Banco do Brasil**, there are only 2 branches in Rio which will change US$ TCs, Praia de Botafogo, 384A, 3rd floor (minimum US$200) and the central branch at R Sen Dantas 105, 4th floor (minimum US$500 – good rates). **Banco do Brasil** at the International Airport is open 0800-2200. The international airport is probably the only place to change TCs at weekends. **Banco 24 horas** ATMs around town and in airports. Good for Visa card withdrawal. Visa cash withdrawals also at **Banco do Brasil** (many ATMs at the R Sen Dantas branch, no queues) and **Bradesco** (personal service or machines). MasterCard and Cirrus cash machines at most **HSBC** branches in Centro, Copacabana, Ipanema and other locations. Some **BBV** branches have Visa and MasterCard ATMs. Also at Santos Dumont airport. **Money changers**: Most large hotels and reputable travel agencies will change currency and TCs. Copacabana (where rates are generally worse than in the centre) abounds with câmbios and there are many also on Av Rio Branco. **Câmbio Belle Tours**, Rio Sul Shopping, ground floor, loja 101, parte A-10, Mon-Fri 1000-1800, Sat 1000- 1700, changes cash. In the gallery at Largo do Machado 29 are **Câmbio Nick** at loja 22 and, next door but one, **Casa Franca**. **Car hire** For international car rental websites, see Car hire, Essentials, page 36. **Interlocadora**, international airport T3398 3181, domestic airport T2240 0754; **Telecar**, R Figueiredo Magalhães 701, Copacabana, T2548 6778, www.telecar.com.br. Many agencies on Av Princesa Isabel, Copacabana. A credit card is essential for hiring a car. **Cultural centres** **Alliance Française**, R Duvivier 43/103, Copacabana and Rua Garcia d'Avila 72, Ipanema, T2259 4489, www.rioalianca francesa.com.br. **British Council**, R Jardim Botânico, 518R, T2105 7500, www.britishcouncil. org.br. **Caixa Cultural**, República de Chile, Av Rio

Branco, T2262 5483, www.caixacultural.com.br. Tue-Sat 1000-2200, Sun 1000-2100, a modern building with theatre, excellent free art shows and art films. **German Cultur- Institut** (Goethe), R do Passeio 62, 2nd floor, T2533 4862, www.goethe.de/br/rio. Tue-Wed 1000-1200, Thu 1530-2000, Fri 1530-1800, Sat 0900-1300. See also **Casa-França-Brasil**, page 403.

Embassies and consulates **Argentina**, Praia de Botafogo 228, T2553 1646, consar.rio@open link.com.br. Very helpful over visas, 1130-1600. **Australia**, Av Presidente Wilson 231, No 23, T3824 4624. Mon-Fri 0900-1300, 1430-1800. **Austria**, Av Atlântica 3804, T2102 0020, gkrio@gbl.com.br. **Canada**, Av Atlântica, 1130, 5th floor, T2543 3004, rio@international.gc.ca. **Finland** and **Norway**, R Lauro Müller 116/2206, Rio Sul Shopping Center, Botafogo, T2541 7732, cg.riodejaneiro@mfa.no. **France**, Av Pres Antônio Carlos 58, T3974 6699, http://riodejaneiro.ambafrance-br.org. **Germany**, R Pres Carlos de Campos 417, T2554 0004, gkrioalemao@terra.com.br (also serves Minas Gerais). **Israel**, Av NS de Copacabana 680, T2255 7599. **Italy**, Av Pres Antônio Carlos 40, T3534 1315, www.consriodejaneiro.esteri.it. **Japan**, Praia do Flemengo 200, 10th floor, T3461 9595, www.rio.br.emb-japan.go.jp. **Netherlands**, Praia de Botafogo 242, 10th floor, T2157 5400, rio@minbuza.nl. **Paraguay**, Praia de Botafogo 242, 2nd floor, T2553 2294, consulpar.rj.brasil@ hotmail.com. **Sweden**, R do Ouvidor 108, 2nd floor, Botafogo, T3852 3143, swerio.rlk@ terra.com.br. **Switzerland**, R Cândido Mendes 157, 11th floor, T2221 1867. **UK**, Praia do Flamengo 284, 2nd floor. T2555 9600, bcg.rj@fco.gov.uk, open Mon-Thu 0830-1645, Fri 0830-1630, Metrô Flamengo, or bus 170, issues a useful 'Guidance for Tourists' pamphlet. **Uruguay**, Praia de Botafogo 242, 6th floor, T2553 6030, conuruguana @consulado-uruguay.rio.org.br. **USA**, Av Pres Wilson 147, T3823 2000, www.consuladodoseua-rio.org.br. Mon-Fri 0830-1645.

Internet Throughout the city. Several places in Rio Sul Shopping, Botafogo. Many on Av NS de Copacabana and others on R Visconde de Pirajá, Ipanema. **Language courses** **Instituto Brasil-Estados Unidos**, Av Copacabana 690, 5th floor, 8-week course, 3 classes a week, US$200, 5-week intensive course US$260. Good English library at same address. **IVM Português Prático**, R do Catete 310, sala 302, US$18 per hr for individual lessons, cheaper for groups. Helpful staff. Recommended. **Cursos da UNE** (União Nacional de Estudantes), R Catete 243, include cultural studies and Portuguese classes for foreigners. Private lessons with **Camila Queiraz**, T8828 3196/3339 3485, reasonable prices. **Medical services** Vaccinations at **Saúde de Portos**, Praça Mcal Âncora, T2240 8628/8678, Mon-Fri 1000-1100, 1500-1800 (international vaccination book and ID required). **Policlínica**, Av Nilo Peçanha 38. Recommended for diagnosis and investigation. A good public hospital for minor injuries and ailments is **Hospital Municipal Rocha Maia**, R Gen Severiano 91, Botafogo, T2295 2295/2121, near Rio Sul Shopping Centre. Free, but there may be queues. **Hospital Miguel Couto**, Mário Ribeiro 117, Gávea, T2274 6050. Has a free casualty ward. **Dentist**: English-speaking, **Amílcar Werneck de Carvalho Vianna**, Av Pres Wilson 165, suite 811. **Dr Mauro Suartz**, R Visconde de Pirajá 414, room 509, T2287 6745. Speaks English and Hebrew, helpful. **Post offices** The central Post Office is on R 1 de Março 64, at the corner of R do Rosário. Av NS de Copacabana 540 and many other locations. All handle international post. There is a post office at Galeão airport. Poste Restante: Correios, Av NS de Copacabana 540 and all large post offices (letters held for a month, recommended, US$0.10 per letter). **Federal Express**, Av Calógeras 23 (near Santa Luzia church) T2262 8565, is reliable.

Telephones International calls can be made at Telemar offices: Av NS de Copacabana 540, 2nd floor; Jobim international airport (24 hrs); Novo Rio rodoviária; R Dias da Cruz 192, Méier-4, 24 hrs, 7 days a week; Praça Tiradentes 41, a few mins' walk from Metrô Carioca; R Visconde de Pirajá 111, Ipanema; R do Ouvidor 60, Centro. International telephone booths are blue. Larger Embratel offices have fax, as do many larger Correios. **Useful addresses** **Immigration:** Federal Police, Praça Mauá (passport section), Av Venezuela 2, T2291 2142. To renew a 90-day visa, US$12.50. **Student Travel Bureau**, Av Nilo Peçanha 50, sala 3103, Centro, T3526 7700, and R Visconde de Pirajá 550, lj 201, Ipanema, T2512 8577, www.stb .com.br (offices throughout Brazil) has details of discounts and cultural exchanges for ISIC holders.

East of Rio

It is not only the state capital that is blessed with beautiful beaches, forests and mountains. There are chic resorts, surfing centres and emerald green coves, national parks in rainforest-clad hills and strange rocky mountains, and fine historical towns dating from both the colonial and imperial epochs. Within easy reach of Rio are the popular coastal resorts of Cabo Frio and Búzios and the imperial city of Petrópolis.

Niterói → *Phone code: 0xx21. Colour map 7, B5. Population: 459,451.*

This city is reached across Guanabara Bay by bridge and by ferries which carry some 200,000 commuters a day. Founded in 1573, Niterói has various churches and forts, plus buildings associated with the city's period as state capital (until 1960). Many of these are grouped around the Praça da República. The **Capela da Boa Viagem** (1663) stands on an island, attached by a footbridge to the mainland. **Museu de Arte Contemporânea-Niterói** ⓘ *Mirante da Praia da Boa Viagem, T2620 2400, www.macniterio.com, Tue-Sun 1000-1800, Sat 1300-1900, US$2, Wed free; the bistro below is open Tue-Sun 0900-1800; midibus 47A or 47B*, is an Oscar Niemeyer project. It is best seen at night, especially when there is water in the pond beneath the building (which Niemeyer envisaged as a flower emerging from the water, but which is generally seen as a spaceship). There are other Niemeyer buildings near the port, when it's all done Niterói will be second to Brasília for Niemeyer buildings.

The most important historical monument is the **Fortaleza da Santa Cruz** ⓘ *T2710 7840, daily 0900-1600, US$1.50, go with guide*. Dating from the 16th century and still a military establishment, it stands on a promontory which commands a fine view of the entrance to the bay. It is about 13 km from the centre of Niterói, on the Estrada Gen Eurico Gaspar Dutra, by Adão e Eva beach (taxi 30 minutes). The **Museu de Arqueologia de Itaipu** ⓘ *20 km from the city, T2709 4079, Wed-Sun 1300- 1800*, is in the ruins of the 18th-century Santa Teresa Convent and also covers the archaeological site of Duna Grande on Itaipu beach. **Tourist office**: Neltur ⓘ *Estrada Leopoldo Fróes 773, São Francisco, T2710 2727, or 0800-282 7755, 5 km from ferry dock, www.niteroiturismo.com.br*, has a useful map. There are four cheap hotels outside the rodoviária and more upmarket places in the centre, just south of the bus terminal.

Local beaches Take bus No 33 or 49 from the dock, passing Icaraí and São Francisco, both with polluted water but good nightlife and plenty of eating places at the latter, to the fishing village of Jurujuba, with simple bars at the water's edge. About 2 km further along a narrow road are the twin beaches of Adão and Eva just before the Fortaleza da Santa Cruz (see above). To get to the ocean beaches, take a 38 or 52 bus from Praça Gen Gomes Carneiro to Piratininga, Camboinhas, Itaipu (see the archaeology museum, above) and Itacoatiara. These are fabulous stretches of sand, the best in the area, about 40 minutes' ride through picturesque countryside.

Lagos Fluminenses

To the east of Niterói lie a series of salt-water lagoons, the Lagos Fluminenses. The first major lakes, Maricá and Saquarema are muddy, but the waters are relatively unpolluted and wildlife abounds in the surrounding scrub and bush. An unmade road goes along the coast between Itacoatiara and Cabo Frio, giving access to the long, open beaches of Brazil's **Costa do Sol**.

In the holiday village of **Saquarema**, the little white church of Nossa Senhora de Nazaré (1675) is on a green promontory jutting into the ocean. Saquarema is a fishing town and one of the top spots for quality consistent pumping surf in Brazil.

The largest lake is **Araruama** (220 sq km), famous for its medicinal mud. The salinity is extremely high, the waters calm, and almost the entire lake is surrounded by sandy beaches, making it popular with families looking for safe, unpolluted bathing. The almost constant breeze makes the lake perfect for windsurfing and sailing. There are many hotels, youth hostels and campsites in the towns by the lakes and by the beaches. All around are saltpans and the wind pumps used to carry water into the pans. At the eastern end of the lake is **São Pedro de Aldeia**, which, despite intensive development, still retains some of its colonial charm.

Cabo Frio → *Phone code: 0xx22. Colour map 7, B5. Population: 140,000.*
Cabo Frio, 156 km from Rio, is a popular holiday and weekend haunt of Cariocas because of its cooler weather, white sand beaches, sailing and good underwater swimming. **Forte São Mateus** (1616) is now a ruin at the mouth of the Canal de Itajurú, which connects the Lagoa Araruama and the ocean. A small headland at its mouth protects the nearest beach to the town, Praia do Forte, which stretches south for about 7½ km to Arraial do Cabo. The canal front, Av dos Pescadores, is pretty, lined with palm trees, restaurants and schooners tied up at the dock. It leads around to the bridge, which crosses to the Gamboa district. **Convento Nossa Senhora dos Anjos** (1696), Largo de Santo Antônio in the town centre, houses the **Museu de Arte Religiosa e Tradicional** ⓘ *Wed-Fri 1400-2000, Sat-Sun 1600-2000*. Above the Largo de Santo Antônio is the **Morro da Guia**, which has a look-out and an 18th-century chapel (access on foot only). The beaches of **Peró** and **Conchas** ⓘ *'São Cristovão' (with 'Peró' on its notice board) or 'Peró' bus, US$0.65, 15-20 mins, has lots of condos, but not many places to stay*, are lovely (a headland, Ponta do Vigia, separates the two and you can walk from one to the other). **Tourist office** ⓘ *Av Américo Vespúcio s/n, Praia do Forte, at the junction of Av do Contorno and Av João Pessoa, T2647 6227/1689*. Kiosks in the centre sell maps.

Búzios → *Phone code: 0xx24. Colour map 7, B5. Population: 18,208. www.buzioschannel.com.br.*
Known as a lost paradise in the tropics, this village, 192 km from Rio, found fame in the 1964 when Brigite Bardot was photographed sauntering barefoot along the beach. The world's press descended on the sophisticated, yet informal resort, following the publicity. Originally a small fishing community, founded in 1740, Búzios remained virtually unknown until the 1950s when its natural beauty started to attract the Brazilian jet-set who turned the village into a fashionable summer resort. The city gets crowded at all main holidays, the price of food, accommodation and other services rises substantially and the traffic jams are long and stressful.

During the daytime, the best option is to head for one of the 25 beaches. The most visited are Geribá (many bars and restaurants; popular with surfers), Ferradura (blue sea and calm waters), Ossos (the most famous and close to the centre), Tartaruga and João Fernandes. Schooner trips of two to three hours pass many of the beaches: US$14-20. Escuna Queen Lory, T2623 1179. **Tourist office**: at Manguinhos, T0800-249999 (24 hours), on the western edge of the peninsula, and at Praça Santo Dumont, T2623 2099. See www.buziosonline.com.br.

Petrópolis → *Phone code: 0xx24. Post code: 25600. Colour map 7, B5. Population: 286,537.*
A steep scenic mountain road from Rio leads to this summer resort, 68 km north of Rio, known for its floral beauty and hill scenery, coupled with adventure sports. Until 1962 Petrópolis was the 'summer capital' of Brazil. Now it combines manufacturing (particularly textiles) and tourism. Whitewater rafting, hiking, climbing, riding and cycling are possible in the vicinity. Petrópolis celebrates its foundation on 16 March. Patron saint's day, São Pedro de Alcântara, 29 June. **Tourist office**: Petrotur ⓘ *Praça Liberdade, T0800-241516 or 2246 9377, www.petropolis.rj.gov.br/fctp, Mon-Tue 0900-1830, Wed-Sat 0900-2000, Sun 0900-1600*. Very helpful, good English; map not to scale. There are kiosks in the main sites of interest and the new rodoviária.

The **Museu Imperial** (Imperial Palace) ⓘ *R da Imperatriz 220, T2237 8000, Tue-Sun 1100-1800, US$4*, is Brazil's most visited museum. It is an elegant building, neoclassical in style, fully furnished and equipped. It is so well kept you might think the imperial family had left the day before, rather than in 1889. It's worth a visit just to see the Crown Jewels of both Pedro I and Pedro II. In the palace gardens is a vehicle museum and a pretty French-style tearoom, the Petit Palais. The Neo-Gothic **Catedral de São Pedro de Alcântara** ⓘ *Tue-Sat 0800-1200, 1400-1800,*

Sun 0800-1300, 1500-1930, Mon 0800-1200, completed in 1925, contains the tombs of the Emperor and Empress in the Imperial Chapel to the right of the entrance. The summer home of air pioneer **Alberto Santos Dumont** ① *R do Encanto 22, T2247 3158, Tue-Sun 0930-1700, US$2.50*, is known as 'A Encantada' and is worth a visit. The interior of the **Casa de Petrópolis** ① *R Ipiranga 716, T2231 6197, Fri-Tue 1300-1830*, is completely original and over-the-top, but has been lovingly restored. It holds art exhibitions and classical concerts. A charming restaurant in the old stables is worth a stop for coffee, if not for lunch. **Orquidário Binot** ① *R Fernandes Vieira 390, T2248 5665, Mon-Fri 0800-1100, 1300-1600, Sat 0700-1100, take bus to Vila Isabel*, has a huge collection of orchids from all over Brazil (plants may be purchased).

Serra dos Órgãos

① *0800-1700, entry US$11, best months for trekking Apr-Sep, US$17 for first day's trekking in the park, US$1.70 thereafter, but US$8.50 at weekends. For information from ICMBio, Av Rotariana s/n, Alto Teresópolis, T2152 1100, www.icmbio.gov.br/parnaso/.*

The Serra dos Órgãos, so called because their strange shapes are said to recall organ-pipes, is an 11,000-ha national park (created in 1939, the second oldest in the country). The main attraction is the precipitous Dedo de Deus ('God's Finger') Peak (1,692 m). The highest point is the 2,263 m Pedra do Sino ('Bell Rock'), up which winds a 14-km path, a climb of five to six hours (11 km). The west face of this mountain is one of the hardest climbing pitches in Brazil. Another well-known peak is the Pedra do Açu (2,245 m) and many others have names evocative of their shape. Near the Sub-Sede Guapimirim (Km 98.5, off BR-116, just outside the park) is the **Von Martius natural history museum** *0800-1700*. Near the headquarters (Sede) entrance is the Mirante do Soberbo, with views to the Baía de Guanabara. To climb the Pedra do Sino, you must sign a register (under 18s must be accompanied by an adult and have authorization from the park authorities).

Further information on the area from the **Teresópolis tourism office** ① *R Prefeito Sebastião Teixeira 20, loja 211, Shopping New Fashion, T2742 7936, www.teresopolison.com, Mon-Fri 0900-1800, Sat 0900-1700, Sun 0900-1300; also at the rodoviária; information T2742 9149, ext 4015.*

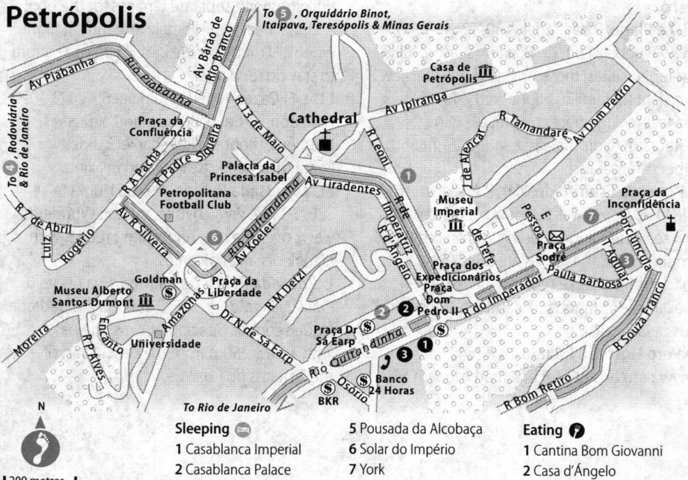

Sleeping
1 Casablanca Imperial
2 Casablanca Palace
3 Comércio
4 Geraniums
5 Pousada da Alcobaça
6 Solar do Império
7 York

Eating
1 Cantina Bom Giovanni
2 Casa d'Ángelo
3 Falconi

East of Rio listings

For Sleeping and Eating price codes and other relevant information, see Essentials, pages 38-40.

Sleeping

Cabo Frio *p436*

B Pousada Água Marinha, R Rui Barbosa 996b, Centro, T2643 8447, p.aguamarinha@uol.com.br. **C** in low season, white rooms with comfortable beds, a/c, fan, TV, frigobar, breakfast, pool and parking. About 4 blocks from Praia do Forte.

B Pousada Suzy, Av Júlia Kubitschek 48, T2643 1742. 100 m from rodoviária, **C** in low season, with a/c, cheaper with fan. Shared rooms for 8, **D**. Plain rooms but not spartan, pool, sauna, garage.

C Pousada Velas ao Vento, Av Júlia Kubitschek 5, T2644 1235. Between rodoviária and centre. Cheaper in low season, comfortable, set back from the main road but still a bit of traffic noise. Hot water, a/c, helpful owner and staff.

D Marina dos Anjos, R Bernado Lens 145, Arraial do Cabo, T2622 4060, www.marinadosanjos.com.br. Superior HI hostel with spruce dorms and doubles, facilities including a games room, sun terrace and links to tour companies and dive shops.

Peró

AL La Plage, R das Badejos 40, T2647 1746, www.redebela.com.br. **B** in low season; fully equipped suites, those upstairs have sea view, excellent for families. Right on the beach, services include pool and bar, à la carte restaurant, hydromassage, sauna, 24-hr cyber café, garage.

B Pousada Espírito do Mar, R Anequim s/n, T2644 3077, www.espiritodomar.com.br. **C** in low season. Orange building with central pool around which the rooms are built. Good, spacious but simple rooms, with extra bed available. A/c, frigobar, TV and fan. Cabo Frio bus passes outside.

D Peró Hostel, R Coutrin 13, T2647 7605, www.pero hostel.com.br. Smart modern HI hostel, doubles and dorms, many with own terraces, some with fridge, good services including tours and Tai Chi.

E pp **Albergue Internacional da Juventude de Muxarabi**, R Leonor Santa Rosa, 13, Jardim Flamboyant, T2643 0369.

Camping **Clube do Brasil**, Estrada dos Passageiros 700, 2 km from town, T2643 3124. **Camping da Estação**, on the same road, at No 370, T2643 1786.

Búzios *p436*

Prior reservations are needed in summer, at holidays such as Carnival and the New Year's Eve, and weekends. For cheaper options and better availability, try Cabo Frio.

The best rooms on the peninsula are not on the beaches, but on the Morro do Humaitá, superb views, 10 mins' walk from the town centre. Hire a beach buggy. Several private houses rent rooms, especially in summer and holidays. Look for the signs: 'Alugo Quartos'.

LL-L Casas Brancas, Alto do Humaitá 8, T2623 1458, www.casasbrancas.com.br. Far and away the best hotel in Búzios; a series of rooms perched on the hill in mock-Mykonos buildings with separate terraces for the pool and spa areas, wonderfully romantic at night when all is lit by candlelight. If you can't afford to stay go for dinner.

LL-L El Cazar, Alto do Humaitá 6, T2623 1620. Next door to Casas Brancas and almost as luxurious; though a little darker inside. Beautiful artwork, tasteful and relaxing.

LL-L Pousada Byblos, Alto do Humaitá 14, T2623 1162, www.byblos.com.br. Wonderful views over the bay, bright, light rooms with tiled floors and balconies.

L Pousada Pedra Da Laguna, Rua 6, lote 6, Praia da Ferradura, T2623 1965, www.pedradalaguna.com.br. Spacious rooms, the best with a view 150m from the beach. Part of the Roteiros do Charme.

AL Pousada Hibiscus Beach, R 1 No 22, Quadra C, Praia de João Fernandes, T2623 6221, www.hibiscusbeach.com. A peaceful spot, 15 pleasant bungalows, garden, pool, light meals available, help with car/buggy rentals and local excursions. One of the best beach hotels.

AL-A Brigitta's Guest House, R das Pedras 131, T/F2623 6157, www.buziosonline.com. brigitta. Beautifully decorated little pousada where Bardot once stayed, just 4 rooms on the main street, delightful restaurant, bar and tea house overlooking the water are worth a visit.

A Casa da Ruth, R dos Gravatás, Geribá, T2623 2242, www.buziosturismo.com/casadaruth. Simple mock-Greek rooms in lilac overlooking the beach and pool.

C-E Praia dos Amores, Av José Bento Ribeiro Dantas 92, T2623 2422. HI, not far from the bus station, next to Praia da Tartaruga and just under 1 km from the centre. The best value in Búzios. Recommended.

C-E Ville Blanche, R Turibe de Farias 222, T2623 1840. New simple pousada, central, dorms for up to 10, and bright, tiled floor doubles with balcony.

E Country Camping Park, R Maria Joaquina Justiniano 895 (off Praça da Rasa), Praia Rasa, Km 12, T2629 1155, www.buzioscamping.com.br. Chalets and a well-run, shady campsite 1 km from the beach (directions on website).

Petrópolis *p436, map p437*

LL Solar do Império, Av Koeler 276, T2103 3000, www.solardoimperio.com.br. Converted neo-classical colonial mansion set in gardens on Petrópolis's grandest street. Fittings evoke the imperial era but modern facilities include a pool, sauna and ofuro hot tub.

L Pousada da Alcobaça, R Agostinho Goulão 298, Correas, T2221 1240, www.pousadada alcobaca.com.br. Delightful, family-run country house in flower-filled gardens, pool and sauna. Worth stopping by for tea on the terrace, or dinner at the restaurant. Recommended.

AL-A Casablanca Imperial, R da Imperatriz 286, T2242 6662, www.casablancahotel.com.br. Most atmospheric in this chain, cheaper rooms in modern extension, good restaurant, pool. Also **A Casablanca Palace**, R 16 de Março 123, T2231 0818.

B York, R do Imperador 78, T2243 2662, www.hotel york.com.br. Convenient, helpful, the fruit and milk at breakfast come from the owners' farm. Recommended.

C Comércio, R Dr Porciúncula 55, T2242 3500. Some rooms with bath, simple, associated with **Trekking Petrópolis**, T2235 7607, www.rioserra.com.br/trekking, which offers trips in the surrounding mountains.

D pp **Geranium's**, R Montecaseros 237, T2242 8633. On the road to the new rodoviária, welcoming, English spoken; rooms with bathroom, breakfast included.

Serra dos Órgãos/Teresópolis *p437*

ICMBio allows camping, US$3.50 pp. There is also the **Refugio do Parque**, 2 km from park entrance of Teresópolis side, T9687 4539, refugiodoparque@bol.com.br. Rooms with bath and dormitories with shower, breakfast and soup-and-bread supper included.

L Serra dos Tucanos, Caixa Postal 98125, Cachoeiras do Macacu, T2649 1557, www.serradostucanos.com.br. British-run lodge in the Parque Estadual Três Picos near Teresópolis, with some of the very best birdwatching, guiding and facilities in the Atlantic coast forest. Cabins around a spring-water swimming pool. Airport transfers.
A Guapi Assu Bird Lodge, www.tropicalbirding.com/guapia/intro.html, c/o Regua (Reserva Ecologica de Guapi Assu), Nicholas Locke, Caixa Postal 98112, Cachoeiras de Macacu, T2745 3998, www.regua.co.uk. Private rainforest reserve with very comfortable accommodation in a spacious wooden house and guided walks through pristine forest, price is full board. Families of South America's largest and rarest primate, the woolly spider monkey live here, excellent birding.
D-E Recanto do Lord, R Luiza Pereira Soares 109, Teresópolis, T2742 5586, www.teresopolishostel.com.br. Big, well-equipped HI hostel, dorms and doubles, wonderful mountain views and 'adventure' trips in the Serra dos Órgãos.

Eating

Cabo Frio *p436*

There's a neat row of restaurants on Av dos Pescadores, mostly fish, local meats, or pasta. There is seating on the pavement under awnings, French- style. Upstairs are a number of bars and clubs.
TTT-TT Picolino, R Mcal F Peixoto 319, T2643 2436. In a nice old building, very smart, mixed menu but mostly local fish and seafood.
TT Hippocampo, R Mcal F Peixoto 283, T2645 5757. Mostly seafood.
TT "In" Sônia, Av dos Pescadores 140 loja 04. Good service and tasty fish, many dishes for 2.
TT Populeti, Av dos Pescadores e Trav Maçonica, T2645 3876. Homemade pastas, a/c, entrance in Shopping Crystal Palace. **Galeto do Zé** (below it) for snacks. Also **Do Zé** on Av dos Pescadores, T2643 4277, serving Brazilian specialities.
TT Tonto, Av dos Pescadores next to "In" Sônia. Serves pizza and local dishes (T2645 1886 for delivery), has a bar too.
TT-T Kilo-Kura, Av Teixeira e Souza 121-A. Good self-service lunches, very popular.
T Bacalhauzinho, Praça Porto Rocha. Portuguese.
T Branca, Praça Porto Rocha. Lunches à kilo 1100-1700, also fast food, pizza after 1800, coffee, pastries and cakes, good, a big, popular place.
T Chico's, Av Teixeira e Souza 30, upstairs in Centro Comercial Víctor Nunes da Rocha, T2645 7454. Smart, does breakfast, self-service.

Búzios *p436*

There are many restaurants on and around R das Pedras and one of the charms of Búzios is browsing. Cheaper options tend to be off the main drag. There are plenty of beachside barracas on the peninsula (closed out of season). A few places on Praça Santos Dumont off R das Pedras offer sandwiches and self-service food, including the homely **La Prima** on Av Manuel Turibo de Farias, which doubles as a bakery. There's a small supermarket a couple of doors away.
TTT Acquerello, R das Pedras 130, T2623 6576. Smart a/c seafood and Italian restaurant with a reasonable wine list. The best on the street.
TTT Satyricon, Av José Bento Ribeiro Dantas 500, Praia da Armação (in front of Morro da Humaitá), T2623 1595. Búzios's most illustrious restaurant specializing in Italian seafood. Decent wine list.
TT Moqueca Capixaba, R Manoel de Carvalho 116, Centro, T2623 1155. Bahian seafood with dishes cooked in coconut or dende oil.
T Banana Land, R Manoel Turíbio de Farias 50, T2623 0855. Cheap and cheerful per kilo buffet.
T Chez Michou, R das Pedras, 90, Centro, T2623 2169. An open-air bar with videos, music and dozens of choices of pancakes accompanied by ice cold beer. Always crowded.
T Fashion Cafe, R das Pedras 151, T2623 2697. Fast food and pizzas with a young crowd and a live band.

Petrópolis *p436, map p437*

TT Falconi, R do Imperador 757. Traditional Italian. Recommended.
T Cantina Bom Giovanni, R do Imperador 729 upstairs. Popular, Italian, lunch and dinner.
T Casa d'Ângelo, R do Imperador 700, by Praça Dom Pedro II. Traditional tea house with self service food that doubles as a bar at night.

Bars and clubs

Búzios *p436*

In season Búzios nightlife is young, beautiful and buzzing. Out of season it is non-existent. Most of the bars and clubs are on R das Pedras. These include **GuapoLoco**, a bizarrely shaped Mexican theme bar and restaurant with dancing. There are plenty of others including more upscale wine bar-style options like **Café Concerto**.

Privelege, Av José Bento Ribeiro Dantas 550, R Orla Bardot. One of Brazil's best European-style dance clubs with pumping techno, house and hip hop and 5 rooms including a cavernous dance floor, sushi bar and lounge.

Ta-ka-ta ka-ta, R das Pedras 256. Strewn with motorbike parts and covered with graffiti.

Transport

Niterói *p435*

Bus No 996 Gávea-Jurujuba, 998 Galeão-Charitas, 740-D and 741 Copacabana-Charitas, 730-D Castelo Jurujba, US$1.

Car The toll on the Rio-Niterói bridge is US$1.

Ferry From the 'barcas' at Praça 15 de Novembro (ferry museum at the terminal), ferry boats and launches cross every 20 mins (30 mins Sat-Sun) to Niterói (15 mins, US$1.20). Catamarans (*aerobarcas*) leave every 10 mins Mon-Fri (US$3.50). They also go to Charitas, near São Francisco beach. Of the frequent ferry and catamaran services from Praça 15 de Novembro, Rio, ferries are slower, cheaper and give better views than catamarans.

Lagos Fluminenses: Saquarema *p435*

Bus **Mil e Um (1001) Rio**-Saquarema, every 2 hrs 0730-1800, 2 hrs, US$6.50.

Cabo Frio *p436*

Air Flights from **Belo Horizonte**, **Brasília**, **Rio de Janeiro** and **São Paulo**.

Bus **Urban**: Salineira and Montes Brancos run local services. US$1.75 to **Búzios, São Pedro da Aldeia, Saquarema, Araruama** and **Arraial do Cabo**. US$1.10 for closer destinations. The urban bus terminal is near Largo de Santo Antônio, opposite the BR petrol station.

Long distance: The rodoviária is well within the city, but a fair walk from centre and beaches. City buses stop nearby. To **Belo Horizonte** US$47 (a/c). To **Petrópolis** US$24. **1001** to **Rio de Janeiro**, **Niterói** US$9, to **São Paulo** US$50 at 2100.

Búzios *p436*

Bus **Mil e Um** from Novo Rio, T0xx21-2516 1001,US$17, 2½ hrs (be at the bus terminal 20 mins before departure). Departures every 2 hrs 0700 to 1900 daily. You can also take any bus to **Cabo Frio** (many more during the day), from where it's 30 mins to Búzios. Buy tickets in advance on major holidays. Búzios' rodoviária is a few blocks' walk from centre. Some pousadas are within 10 mins on foot, eg La Coloniale, Brigitta's, while others need a local bus (US$1) or taxi. Buses from Cabo Frio run the length of the peninsula and pass several pousadas.

Car Via BR-106 takes about 2½ hrs from Rio.

Petrópolis *p436, map p437*

Bus New rodoviária 3 km north beyond Bingen by the highway; bus No 100 to centre, US$1.10. From **Rio** every 15 mins throughout the day (US$6.50) with **Única Fácil**, Sun every hr, 1 hr 10 mins, sit on the left hand side for best views. Buses leave from the Novo Rio rodoviária; also a/c buses, hourly from 1100, from Av Nilo Peçanha, US$8.25. To **Teresópolis** for the Serra dos Órgãos, **Viação Teresópolis**, 8 a day, US$6.50. **Salutário** to **São Paulo**, daily at 2330.

Serra dos Órgãos *p437*

Bus **Rio-Teresópolis**: **Viação Teresópolis** buses leave hourly from the Novo Rio rodoviária. Rodoviária at R 1 de Maio 100. Fare US$7.75.

Directory

Petrópolis *p436, map p437*

Banks **Banco do Brasil**, R Paulo Barbosa 81. A Banco 24 Horas ATM is at R Marechal Deodoro 98. Travel agencies with exchange: **BKR**, R Gen Osório 12, **Goldman**, R Barão de Amazonas 46, and **Vert Tur**, R 16 de Março 244, 1000-1630.

Post offices R do Imperador 350.

Telephone **Telerj**, R Marechal Deodoro, just above Praça Dr Sá Earp.

West of Rio

One of the main attractions near the inland highway to São Paulo is the Itatiaia National Park, a good area for climbing, trekking and birdwatching. For a really beautiful route, though, take the Rio de Janeiro-Santos section of the BR101, which hugs the forested and hilly Costa Verde southwest of Rio.

Dutra Highway

The Dutra Highway, BR-116, heads west from Rio towards São Paulo. It passes the steel town of **Volta Redonda** and some 30 km further west, the town of **Resende**. In this region, 175 km from Rio, is **Penedo** (five buses a day from Resende) which in the 1930s attracted Finnish settlers who brought the first saunas to Brazil. There is a Finnish museum, a cultural centre and Finnish dancing on Saturday. This popular weekend resort also provides horse riding, and swimming in the Portinho River. There are plenty of mid-range and cheap hotels in town. For tourist information, T0xx24-3351 1876.

Parque Nacional de Itatiaia

ⓘ *Entry per day is US$11.50 per person, half price for each succeeding day. Open 0800-1700, 0700-1400 for the higher section (you can stay till 1700). Information can be obtained from ICMBio, T0xx24-3352 1461 or 3352 7001. Avoid weekends and holidays if you want to see wildlife.*

This park, being so close to Rio and São Paulo, is a must for those with limited time who wish to see some of world's rarest birds and mammals in a whole range of different ecosystems. Trails from one hour to two days go through deep valleys shrouded in pristine rainforest, hiding icy waterfalls and clear-water rivers. The 30,000-ha mountainous park is Brazil's oldest, founded in 1937 to protect Atlantic Coast Rainforest in the Serra de Mantiqueira. It is divided into two parts, the lower, with the administration, reached from the town of Itatiaia (Km 316 on the Dutra Highway), and the upper section, reached from the Engenheiro Passos-Caxambu road (Circuito da Águas). Important species include jaguar, puma, brown capuchin and black-face titi monkeys. The park is particularly good for birds with a list of 350+, with scores of spectacular tanagers, hummingbirds, cotingas and manakins. The best trails head for Pedra de Taruga and Pedra de Maçã and the Poranga and Véu de Noiva waterfalls. The Pico das Agulhas Negras and the Serra das Prateleiras (up to 2,540 m) offer decent rock climbing. There is a **Museu de História Natural** ⓘ *Tue-Sun 1000-1600*, near the headquarters, with a depressing display of stuffed animals from the 1940s.

Information and maps can be obtained at the park office. The **Administração do Parque Nacional de Itatiaia** operates a refuge in the park, which acts as a starting point for climbs and treks. Although buses do run through the park calling at the hotels, hiring a car to visit Itatiaia is the best option.

Costa Verde (Emerald Coast)

The Rio de Janeiro-Santos section of the BR101 is one of the world's most beautiful highways, running along the aptly called Emerald Coast, which is littered with islands, beaches, colonial settlements and mountain fazendas. It is complete through to Bertioga (see page 469), which has good links with Santos and São Paulo. Buses run from Rio to Angra dos Reis, Paraty, Ubatuba, Caraguatatuba and São Sebastião, where you may have to change for Santos or São Paulo.

Itacuruçá, 91 km from Rio, is a delightful place to visit. Separated from the town by a channel is the Ilha de Itacuruçá, the largest of a string of islands stretching into the bay. Further offshore is Ilha de Jaguanum, around which there are lovely walks. Saveiros (schooners) sail around the bay and to the islands from Itacuruça (Passamar, T9979 2429). Ilha de Itacuruçá can also be reached from **Muriqui**, a popular beach resort 9 km from Itacuruçá. There are hotels on the island. **Mangaratiba**, 22 km down the coast, has muddy beaches, but the surroundings are pleasant and better beaches can be found outside town.

Angra dos Reis ➔ *Phone code: 0xx24. Post code: 23900. Colour map 7, B4. Pop: 119,247.*
Said to have been founded on 6 January 1502 (O Dia dos Reis – The Day of Kings/Epiphany), this is a small port, 151 km southwest of Rio, with an important fishing and shipbuilding industry. It has several small coves with good bathing within easy reach and is situated on an enormous bay full of islands. Of particular note are the church and convent of **Nossa Senhora do Carmo**, built in 1593 (Praça Gen Osório - closed for restoration 2009), the **Igreja Matriz de Nossa Senhora da Conceição** (1626) in the centre of town, and the church and convent of **São Bernardino de Sena** (1758-1763) on the Morro do Santo Antônio. On the Largo da Lapa is the church of **Nossa Senhora da Lapa da Boa Morte** (1752), with a sacred art museum (also closed for restoration 2009). On the Península de Angra, just west of the town, is the **Praia do Bonfim**, a popular beach, and a little way offshore the island of the same name, on which is the hermitage of Senhor do Bonfim (1780). The **TurisAngra tourist office** is at ⓘ *Av Ayrton Senna 580, T3369 7704, www.turisangra.com.br, www.angra.rj.gov.br, open 0800-2000*; also at Praça do Porto, Estação Santa Luiza, T3365 6421, and at the Rodoviária, both open 0700-1900; good information. Free Wi-Fi on the plaza near the local bus station/craft market.

Ilha Grande ➔ *Phone code: 0xx21. Colour map 7, B5.*
Ilha Grande is a mountain ridge covered in tropical forest sticking out of an emerald sea and fringed by some of the world's most beautiful beaches. As there are no cars and no roads either, just trails through the forest, the island is still relatively undeveloped. Much of it forms part of a State Park and **Biological Reserve**, and cannot even be visited (INEA visitors centre, T3361 5553, Mon-Sun 0900-1800). The island was a notorious pirate lair, then a landing port for slaves. By the 20th century it had become the site of an infamous prison for the country's most notorious criminals (closed in 1994 and now overgrown rubble). The weather is best from March to June and, like everywhere along the coast, the island is overrun during the Christmas, New Year and Carnaval period. There is a tourist office at the ferry port on arrival, T021-2220 4323, Mon-Sat 0800-1800, Sun 0900-1300, but it is best to visit **TurisAngra** (see above) first. Information at www.ilhagrande.org; also www.ilhagrande.com.br. Like several other parts of Rio de Janeiro state, Ilha Grande was affected by mudslides in early 2010.

The beach at **Vila do Abraão** may look beautiful to first arrivals but those further afield are far more spectacular. The two most famous are **Lopes Mendes**, two hours' walk from Abraão, and **Aventureiro**, six hours (you must get permission and book boat transport at **TurisAngra** in Angra dos Reis in advance; limited camping US$8.50 and rooms US$23, plus US$2.85 entry fee). Good beaches closer to Abraão include the half moon bay at **Abraãoozinho** (15 minutes' walk) and **Grande das Palmas** which has a delightful tiny whitewashed chapel (one hour 20 minutes' walk), both east of town. Lagoa Azul, Freguesia de Santana and Saco do Céu are all boat trips. Good treks include over the mountains to Dois Rios, where the old jail was situated (13 km one way, about three hours), Pico do Papagaio (980 m) through forest, a stiff, three-hour climb (guide is essential) and Pico da Pedra d'Água (1,031 m).

Paraty ➔ *Phone code: 0xx24. Post code: 23970. Colour map 7, B4. Population: 29,544.*
Paraty, 98 km from Angra dos Reis, is one of Brazil's prettiest colonial towns, whose centre has been declared a national historic monument in its entirety. It was the chief port for the export of gold in the 17th century and a coffee-exporting port in the 19th century. At the weekend Paraty buzzes with tourists who browse in the little boutiques and art galleries, or buy souvenirs from the indigenous Guaraní who sell their wares on the cobbles. Many of the numerous little bars and restaurants, like the pousadas, are owned by expat Europeans and Paulistanos, who are determined to preserve Paraty's charm. During the week, especially off season, the town is quiet and intimate. Much of the accommodation available is in colonial buildings, some sumptuously decorated, with flourishing gardens or courtyards. The town centre is out of bounds for motor vehicles; heavy chains are strung across the entrance to the streets. In spring

the roads are flooded, while the houses are above the water level. **Centro de Informações Turísticas** ⓘ *Av Roberto Silveira, near the entrance to the historical centre, T3371 1266, daily 0900-1600.* More information is available at www.paraty.com.br (Portuguese, English, Spanish), www.pmparaty.rj.gov.br and www.paraty.tur.br (Portuguese).

There are four churches: **Santa Rita** (1722), built by the 'freed coloured men' in elegant Brazilian baroque, faces the bay and the port. It houses an interesting **Museum of Sacred Art** ⓘ *Wed-Sun 0900-1200, 1300-1800, US$1.* **Nossa Senhora do Rosário e São Benedito** (1725, rebuilt 1757) ⓘ *R do Comércio, Tue 0900-1200*, built by black slaves, is small and simple. **Nossa Senhora dos Remédios** (1787-1873) ⓘ *Mon, Wed, Fri, Sat 0900-1200, Sun 0900-1500*, is the town's parish church, or Matriz, the biggest in Paraty. **Capela de Nossa Senhora das Dores** (1800) ⓘ *Thu 0900-1200*, is a small chapel facing the sea that was used mainly by the wealthy whites in the 19th century. There is a great deal of distinguished Portuguese colonial architecture in delightful settings. **Rua do Comércio** is the main street in the historical centre. The **Casa da Cadeia**, close to Santa Rita church, is the former jail and is now a public library and art gallery. The **Casa da Cultura** ⓘ *at the junction of R Samuel Costa and R Dona Geralda, Wed-Mon 1000-1930, winter to 1830, US$2.50*, houses an excellent multimedia history display (also in English, though this option can be hidden).

The town's environs are as beautiful as Paraty itself. Just a few kilometres away lie the forests of the Ponta do Juatinga peninsula, fringed by wonderful beaches, washed by little waterfalls and still home to traditional fishing communities. At **Fazenda Murycana**, an old sugar estate and 17th-century cachaça distillery, you can taste and buy the different types of cachaça. It has an excellent restaurant. Mosquitoes can be a problem, take repellent and don't wear shorts. If short of time, the one must is a boat trip round the bay; some of its islands are home to rare animals. Boats also go to wonderful beaches like **Praia da Conçeicao, Praia Vermelha** and **Praia da Lula**, all of which have simple restaurants and are backed by forest and washed by gentle waves. Further south are **Saco da Velha**, protected by an island, and **Paraty Mirim** (17 km, also reached by bus, four a day, three on Sunday). The **Gold Trail**, *www.caminhodoouro.com.br*, hiking on a road dating from the 1800s, can be done on foot or horseback. Many other adventure sports are available (see Activities and tours, page 449).

Trindade

Trindade, 27 km south of Paraty, may not be as beautiful in its own right but its setting, sandwiched between rainforested slopes and emerald sea, is spectacular. It has a long, broad beach and has long been a favourite for surf hippies from São Paulo and Rio who come in droves over Christmas and New Year. It is gradually finding its place on the international backpacker circuit as the campsites, pousadas and restaurants are cheap and cheerful.

Note If travelling along the coast into São Paulo state as far as Guarujá, do not drive or go out alone after dark.

West of Rio listings

For Sleeping and Eating price codes and other relevant information, see Essentials, pages 38-40.

Sleeping

Parque Nacional de Itatiaia *p442*

Basic accommodation in cabins and dorms in Itatiaia village, strung along the road leading to the park.

LL Simon, Km 13 on the road in the park, T3352 1122, www.hotelsimon.com.br. Price is for 3 days, full board. A 1970s concrete block at the top of the park, which marks the trailhead for the higher walks to Agulhas Negras and Três Picos. Wonderful views from fading rooms.

L-AL Hotel Donati, T3352 1110, www.hotel donati.com.br. Delightful, mock Swiss chalets and rooms, set in tropical gardens visited by animals every night and early morning. A series of trails lead off from the main building and the hotel can organize professional birding guides. Decent restaurant and 2 pools. Highly recommended. Map on web site.

B Hotel Cabanas de Itatiaia, T3352 1252. Magical views from these comfortable but ridiculously Swiss chalets on a hillside. Pool and good restaurant too.

C pp **Cabanas da Itatiaia**, T3352 1152. Simple chalets in forest in park's lower reaches. Sister hotel (Aldeia dos Pássaros) opposite has a pool. Both share facilities and are very helpful. Great breakfasts, good off season rates and riverside sauna.

C Hotel Alsene, at 2,100 m, 2 km from the side entrance to the park, take a bus to São Lourenço and Caxambu, get off at Registro, walk or hitch from there (12 km). Very popular with climbing and trekking clubs, dormitory or camping, chalets available, hot showers, fireplace, evening meal after everyone returns, drinks but no snacks.

E-F Ipê Amarelo, R João Maurício Macedo Costa 352, Campo Alegre, T/F3352 1232. HI.

Camping **Camping Clube do Brasil** site is entered at Km 148 on the Via Dutra.

Costa Verde: Itacuruçá *p442*

A-B Resort Atlântico, Praia do Axixá, T/F2680 7168, www.divingbrasil.com. Dutch/Brazilian-owned pousada, helpful, good breakfast, English spoken, meals available, diving courses (PADI).

Angra dos Reis *p443*

B Caribe, R de Conceição 255, T3365 0033, F3365 3450. Central. Recommended.

C-E Angra Hostel, Praça da Matriz 152 (at the corner of Rua do Comércio), T3364 4759. Simple hostel (HI) with reasonable breakfast and internet. A block from the quays (just on the other side of the road from the post office) and convenient if you miss a boat.

Ilha Grande *p443*

There are many pousadas in Abraão and reservations are only necessary in peak season or on holiday weekends. Ignore dockside hotel touts who lie about hotel closures and flash pictures of their lodgings to unsuspecting tourists. But if they say camping is forbidden, that is true. Numerous eating places serve the usual fish/chicken, beans and rice options.

Abraão

B Ancoradouro, R da Praia 121, T3361 5153, www.ancoradouro.ilhagrande.com. Simple rooms with en suites in a beach front building, 10 mins' walk east of the jetty.

B Farol dos Borbas, Praia do Abraão, T3361 5866, www.ilhagrandetour.com.br. A minute from the jetty. Simple, well-maintained rooms with tiled floors, fan, breakfast tables and chairs. The best rooms have balconies, the worst have no windows. Boat trips organized.

C Estalagem Costa Verde, R Amâncio Felicio de Souza 239a, T3361 5808, www.estalagem costaverde.com.br. In the town ½ a block behind the church. Bright hostel with light, well-decorated rooms, price rises in high season, rooms for 2, 3 and 4 people, great value.

C Porto Girassol, R do Praia 65, T3361 5277, portogirasol@ilhagrande.com. Simple rooms in a mock-colonial beachhouse 5 mins east of the jetty.

C-D Pousada Cachoeira, Rua do Bicão, T3361 9521, www.cachoeira.com. Lovely little pousada with a dining room palapa and living area, cabins and a terrace of rooms nestled in a forest garden next to a fast-flowing stream. Good breakfasts and boat tours. English and German spoken. **B** in high season.

C-E Aquário Hostel, Praia do Abraão, T3361 5405. Beautifully located on a spit next to the beach and with scruffy rooms and dorms, spacious, airy public areas including a bar, huge sea-water pool and wonderful ocean views.

E pp **Albergue Holdandés**, R Assembléia de Deus, T3361 5034, www.holandeshostel.com.br. Dormitories and four little chalets (**D**) lost in the forest, great atmosphere, be sure to reserve, HI affiliated.

E pp **Che Lagarto Ilha Grande**, Canto da Praia s/n, Abraão, T3361 9669, www.chelagarto.com. Includes breakfast and welcome drink. Basic dorms and doubles (**B**), some with private toilet, a/c and sea view, a loud bar, barbecue area and numerous tours and activities on offer.

Outside town

LL-L Sítio do Lobo, T2227 4138, www.sitiodo lobo.com.br. Access is only by boat. An architect commissioned house converted into a small boutique hotel, sitting on an isolated peninsula. The views are marvellous; the best room are the suites; others overlook the pool. The best food on the island.

Paraty *p443*

Over 300 hotels and pousadas; in mid-week look around and find a place that suits you best. Browse through www.paraty.com.br/ frame.htm for yet more options.

LL Pousada Picinguaba, T12-3836 9105, www.picinguaba.com. Stylish French-owned hotel in a converted convent some 30 km from Paraty; with superior service, an excellent restaurant and simple, elegant (fan-cooled) rooms. Marvellous views out over a bay of islands. Booking ahead essential.

L Bromelias Pousada & Spa, Rodovia Rio-Santos, Km 562, Graúna, T/F3371 2791, www.pousada bromelias.com.br. Asian-inspired with its own aromatherapy products and massage treatments, tastefully decorated chalets in the Atlantic coastal forest. Pool, sauna and restaurant.

L Pousada do Ouro, R Dr Pereira (or da Praia) 145, T/F3371 1311, www.pousadaouro.com.br. Near Paraty's eastern waterfront, once a private home built from a gold fortune, suites in the main building, plainer rooms in an annexe, open-air poolside pavilion in a tropical garden. Has had many famous guests.

L Pousada do Sandi, Largo do Rosário 1, T3371 2100, www.pousadadosandi.com.br. 18th-century building with a grand lobby, comfortable, adjoining restaurant and pool.

L Pousada Pardieiro, R do Comércio 74, T3371 1370, www.pousadapardieiro.com.br. Quiet, with a calm, sophisticated atmosphere, a colonial building with lovely gardens, delightful rooms facing internal patios and a small pool. Always full at weekends, no children under 15.

AL-A Hotel Coxixo, R do Comércio 362, T3371 1460, www.hotelcoxixo.com.br. Converted colonial building in the heart of the town, owned by movie-star Maria Della Costa. The best rooms in the hotel and in Paraty are the upper-floor colonial suites.

AL-A Pousada Mercado do Pouso, Largo de Santa Rita 43, T/F3371 1114, www.mercadode pouso.com.br. Historic building close to waterfront, good sea views, family atmosphere, no pool.

A Le Gite d'Indaitiba, Rodovia Rio-Santos (BR-101) Km 562, Graúna, T3371 7174, www.legitedindaiatiba.com.br. French-owned stylish chalets set in gardens on a hillside. Sweeping views of the bay, and French food to match the location.

A Morro do Forte, R Orlando Carpinelli, T/F3371 1211, www.pousadamorrodoforte.com.br. Out of the centre, lovely garden, good breakfast, pool, German owner Peter Kallert offers trips on his yacht. Recommended.

A Pousada Arte Colonial, R da Matriz 292, T3371 7231, www.paraty.com.br/artecolonial. **B** Sun-Thu, some rooms **AL** in high season. One of the best deals in Paraty: colonial building in the centre decorated with style and genuine personal touch by its French owner. Helpful, breakfast included. Highly recommended.

B Geko Hostel, Rua Orlando Carpinelli 5, Praia do Pontal, T3371 2507, www.gekohostel.com. Doubles and dorms (**E** pp), breakfast included, free pick-up from bus station, free Wi-Fi, internet café, tours arranged.

B Pousada do Corsário, Beco do Lapeiro 26, T3371 1866, www.pousadadocorsario.com.br. New building with a pool and its own gardens; next to the river and 2 blocks from the centre, simple but stylish rooms, most with hammocks outside. Highly recommended.

B-C Marendaz, R Patitiba 9, T3371 1369, www.paraty.com.br/marendaz/index.asp. Family-run, simple, charming, a block from the historical centre, cheaper with fan, also has rooms for 3-5 people.

B-F Misti Chill Hostel and Pousada, R Orlando Carplinelli 3, Praia do Pontal, T3371 2545, www.mistichill.com. Beachfront accommodation from dorms to private rooms with a/c.

C Solar dos Gerânios, Praça da Matriz, T/F33711550, www.paraty.com.br/geranio. Beautiful colonial family house on main square in traditional rustic style, excellent value, English spoken. Warmly recommended.

D Pousada do Careca, Praça Macedo Soares, T3371 1291. Very simple rooms in the historic centre, those without street windows are musty.

D Pousada Miramar, Abel de Oliveira 19, T3371 2898. One room has its own kitchen, good value. Recommended.

D-E Che Lagarto Paraty, R Dr Derly Ellena 9, T3371 1369, www.chelagarto.com. Rates include breakfast and welcome drink. Rooms with private toilet and a/c.

E pp **Casa da Aventura**, R João Luz de Rosário 176, T3371 2811, www.casadaaventura.com.br. Dorms (female, male and mixed), breakfast extra, no curtains on windows, lots of activities arranged, from simple tours to kayaking, canyoning, paragliding, diving and trekking.

E pp **Casa do Rio**, R Antônio Vidal 120, T3371 2223, www.paratyhostel.com. Peaceful little hostel with riverside courtyard and hammock, HI discount, kitchen, breakfast included. Offers jeep and horse riding trips. Recommended.

Camping **Camping Beira-Rio**, just across the bridge, before the road to the fort, T3371 1985.

Camping Club do Brasil, Av Orlando Carpinelli, Praia do Pontal, T3371 1050. Small, good, very crowded in Jan and Feb, US$8 pp. Also at Praia Jabaquara, T3371 7364.

Trindade *p444*

A Garni Cruzeiro do Sul, Rua Principal (first on the right as you enter the village), T3371 5102, www.hotelgarnicruzeirodosul.com.br. Smart little beachside pousada with duplex rooms, most of which have sea views, **AL** at Christmas.

D Pousada Marimbá, R Principal, T3371 5147. Simple colourful rooms and a little breakfast area.

D-F Ponta da Trindade Pousada & Camping, T3371 5113. Simple rooms with fan, sand-floored campsite with cold water showers and no power.

Eating

Paraty *p443*

The best restaurants in Paraty are in the historic part of town and are almost as good as any you will find in Rio or São Paulo. The less expensive restaurants, those offering *comida a quilo* (pay by weight) and the fast-food outlets are outside the historical centre, mainly on Av Roberto Silveira. Paraty has some plates unique to the region, like peixe à Parati – local fish cooked with herbs, green bananas and served with *pirão*, a mixture of manioc flour and the sauce that the fish was cooked in.

TTT **Bartolomeu**, R Samuel Costa 176, T3371 3052. Argentinian steaks, delicious salads from a chef trained in Rio's Gourmet restaurant. Good atmosphere and cocktails.

TTT **do Hiltinho**, R Mcal Deodoro 233, T3371 1432. Decent seafood, including local dishes.

TTT **Merlin O Mago**, R do Comércio 376, T3371 2157, www.paraty.com.br/merlin.htm. Franco-Brazilian cooking in an intimate dining room/bar, by a German Cordon Bleu-trained chef and illustrious photojournalist. The best in town.

TTT **Punto Di Vino**, R Mcal Deodoro 129, T3371 1348. Wood-fired pizza and calzoni served with live music and a good selection of wine.

TTT **Thai Brasil**, R Dona Geralda 345, 3371 0127, www.thaibrasil.com.br. Beautiful restaurant ornamented with handicrafts and hand-painted furniture, the cooking loosely resembles Thai, without spices.

TT **Café Paraty**, R da Lapa and Comércio. Sandwiches, appetizers, light meals, also bar with live music nightly (cover charge), a local landmark. Open 0900-2400.

TT **Dona Ondina**, R do Comércio 2, by the river. Family restaurant with well-prepared simple food (closed on Mon, Mar and Nov), good value.

T **Sabor da Terra**, Av Roberto Silveira, next to Banco do Brasil. Reliable, if not bargain-priced, self service food, closes 2200.

Bars and clubs

Paraty *p443*

Bar Coupé, Praça Matriz. A popular hang-out, outside seating, good bar snacks and breakfast.

Bar Dinho, Praça da Matriz at R da Matriz. Good bar with live music at weekends, sometimes mid-week.

Grupo Contadores, The Puppet Show, R Dona Geralda 327, T3371 1575, ecparaty@ax.apc.org. Wed, Sat 2100, US$12: a silent puppet theatre for adults only which has toured throughout the USA and Europe. Not to be missed.

Umoya, R Comendador José Luiz. Video bar and café, live music at weekends.

Festivals and events

Paraty *p443*

Feb/Mar Carnival, hundreds of people cover their bodies in black mud and run through the streets yelling like prehistoric creatures (anyone can join in). **Mar/Apr Semana Santa**, with religious processions and folk songs. **Mid-Jul Semana de Santa Rita**, traditional foods, shows, exhibitions and dances. **Aug Festival da Pinga**, the cachaça fair at which local distilleries display their products and there are plenty of opportunities to over-indulge. **Sep** (around the 8th) **Semana da Nossa Senhora dos Remédios**, processions and religious events. **Sep/Oct Spring Festival of Music**, concerts in front of Santa Rita church. The city is decorated with lights for Christmas. **31 Dec New year's**, a huge party with open-air concerts and fireworks (reserve accommodation in advance). As well as the Dança dos Velhos, another common dance in these parts is the ciranda, in which everyone, young and old, dances in a circle to songs accompanied by guitars.

The **Festa Literária Internacional de Parati** (FLIP, www.flip.org.br) occurs every northern summer and is one of the most important literary events in Latin America. It is always attended by big name writers.

Activities and tours

Parque Nacional de Itatiaia *p442*

Information on treks can be obtained from **Clube Excursionista Brasileira**, Av Almirante Barroso 2, 8th floor, Rio de Janeiro, T0xx21-2220 3695.

Wildlife guides **Edson Endrigo**, T3742 8374, www.avesfoto.com.br. Birding trips in Itatiaia and throughout Brazil. English spoken. **Ralph Salgueiro**, T3351 1823, www.ecoralph.com.

Angra dos Reis *p443*

Boat trips Trips around the bay are available, some with a stop for lunch on the island of Gipóia (5 hrs). Several boats run tours from the Cais de Santa Luzia and there are agencies for saveiros in town, boats depart between 1030-1130 daily, U$10-12 (during Jan and Feb best to reserve in advance).

Diving **Aquamaster**, Praia da Enseada, T3365 2416. US$60 for 2 dives with drinks and food, take a 'Retiro' bus from the port in Angra.

Ilha Grande *p443*

Boat trips US$13 without food or drinks, but include fruit. Ask about trips to good scuba diving sites around the coast.

Cycling Bikes can be hired and tours arranged; ask at pousadas.

Paraty *p443*

Antígona, Praça da Bandeira 2, Centro Histórico, T/F3371 2199. Daily schooner tours, 5 hrs, bar and lunch on board. Recommended.

Fausto Goyos, T9914 5506. Offers off-road tours in an ex-US military jeep to rainforest, waterfalls, historical sites, also photo safaris. He also has highly professional horse riding tours and offers lodging in youth-hostel style rooms, with or without meals.

Paraty Tours, Av Roberto Silveira 11, T/F3371 1327, www.paratytours.com.br. English and Spanish spoken.

Soberana da Costa, R Dona Geraldo 43, in Pousada Mercado do Pouso, T/F3371 1114. Also offers schooner trips in the bay. Recommended.

Transport

Parque Nacional de Itatiaia *p442*

Bus Itatiaia lies just off the main São Paulo-Rio motorway. There are connections to Itatiaia town or nearby Resende from both **Rio** and **São Paulo**. There is only 1 way into the park from Itatiaia town and 1 main road within it – which forks off to the various hotels, all of which are signposted. Four times a day (variable hours), a bus marked '504 Circular' leaves Itatiaia town for to the Park, calling at the hotels and stopping at the Simon. Coming from Resende this may be caught at the crossroads before Itatiaia. Through tickets to São Paulo are sold at a booth in the large bar in the middle of Itatiaia main street.

Costa Verde: Mangaratiba *p442*

Bus From Rio Rodoviária with **Costa Verde**, several daily, US$9.

Angra dos Reis *p443*

Bus To **Angra** at least hourly from Rio's rodoviária with **Costa Verde**, www.costaverde transportes.com.br, several direct, comfortable buses take the 'via litoral', sit on the left, US$14, 2½ hrs. From Angra to **São Paulo**, **Reunidas**, www.reunidaspaulista.com.br, 4 buses daily (3 on Sat), US$28.50, 7 hrs. To **Paraty**, many buses leave from the local bus station on Largo da Lapa near the Ilha Grande jetty, then go to the rodoviária; **Colitur** every 40 mins (Sun, holidays hourly) US$4, 2 hrs; **Costa Verde** (from Rio) roughly every 3 hrs, faster and pricier.

Ilha Grande *p443*

Ferry **Barcas SA**, T0800-704 4113, www.barcas-sa.com.br: **Angra**-Abraão Mon-Fri 1530, US$3.75, Sat-Sun 1330, US$8. Abraão-Angra: daily 1000. **Magaratiba**-Abraão daily 0800 and Fri 2200; Abraão-Mangaratiba daily 1730. US$3.65 during the week, US$8 at weekends. About 1½ hrs to both destinations. **Ilha Grande Turismo** (IGT) at Angra rodoviária, T3365 6426, www.ilhagrandeturismo.com.br, has a catamaran Angra-Abraão daily 0800, 1100, 1600, returning 0900, 1230, 1700, US$14.25 (US$11.50 in advance online) and the Resta 1 schooner, US$8.50 daily, 3 a day at weekends. Other schooners (saveiros) sail between Ilha Grande and Angra (Samurai and Rei Tomás), Mangaratiba (Acalanto II), daily, T3361 5920, and Conceição de Jacareí (Andréa), T8826 3809, 4 a day, US$8.50. There are also frequent impromptu fishing boat trips on demand between Angra and Abraão, usually before lunchtime only and most frequently in summer months. Around US$5-12.50.

Paraty *p443*

Bus To **Fazenda Murycana** take a Penha/Ponte Branca bus from the rodoviária, 4 a day; alight where it crosses a small white bridge and then walk 10 mins along a signed, unpaved road.

Rodoviária at the corner of R Jango Padua and R da Floresta. 9 buses a day go to **Rio** (241 km), 4½ hrs, US$22, **Costa Verde** – see under Angra dos Reis for details; to Angra dos Reis (98 km, 1½ hrs, US$7.50, also **Colitur** every 40 mins, US$4). 3 a day to **Ubatuba** (75 km, just over 1 hr, Colitur, US$7.50). To **São Paulo**, 5 a day, 4 on Sat (304 km via São José dos Campos, 5½ hrs, US$20, **Reunidas**, booked up quickly, very busy at weekends). To **São Sebastião**, 2 a day with **Normandy** (who also go to Rio twice a day). On holidays and in high season, the frequency of bus services increases.

Directory

Ilha Grande *p443*

No **banks** or money changing on the island. **Internet** Several places in Abraão.

Paraty *p443*

Banks **Banco do Brasil**, Av Roberto Silveira, not too far from the bus station, exchange 1000-1500, long queues and commission. 2 ATMs in town for Visa and MasterCard, 0600-2200. **Internet** Many places but connection is not cheap. **Post offices** R Mcal Deodoro e Domingos Gonçalves de Abreu, 0800-1700, Sun 0800-1200. **Telephones** **Telerj** for international calls, Praça Macedo Soares, opposite the tourist office. Local and long distance calls can be made from public phones.

São Paulo

The city of São Paulo is vast and can feel intimidating at first. But this is a city of separate neighbourhoods, only a few of which are interesting for visitors and, once you have your base, it is easy to negotiate. Those who don't flinch from the city's size and who are prepared to spend money and time here, and who get to know Paulistanos, are seldom disappointed. (The inhabitants of the city are called Paulistanos, to differentiate them from the inhabitants of the state, who are called Paulistas.) Nowhere in Brazil is better for concerts, clubs, theatre, ballet, classical music, all round nightlife, restaurants and beautifully designed hotels.

Ins and outs ➔ *Phone code: 0xx11. Colour map 7, B4.*

Getting there There are air services from all parts of Brazil, Europe, North and South America to the international **airport** at Guarulhos, also known as Cumbica, Avenida Monteiro Lobato 1985, T6445 2945 (30 km northeast of the city). The local airport of Congonhas, 14 km south of the city centre on Avenida Washington Luiz, is used for the Rio-São Paulo shuttle. It receives some flights to Belo Horizonte and Vitória and private flights only, T5090 9000. The **main rodoviária** is Tietê (T2223 7152), which is very convenient and has its own Metrô station. There are three other bus stations for inter-state bus services. ▸▸ *See also Transport, page 465.*

Getting around and orientation Much of the centre is pedestrianized, so walking is the only option if you wish to explore it. The best and cheapest way to get around São Paulo is on the Metrô system, which is clean, safe, cheap and efficient, though rather limited. Bus routes can be confusing and slow due to frequent traffic jams, but buses are safe, clean and only crowded at peak hours. All the rodoviárias (bus stations) are on the Metrô, but if travelling with luggage, take a taxi. The **Old Centre** (Praça da República, Sé, Santa Cecília) is a place to visit but not to stay. The central commercial district, containing banks, offices and shops, is known as the Triângulo, bounded by Ruas Direita, 15 (Quinze) de Novembro, São Bento and Praça Antônio Prado, but it is rapidly spreading towards the Praça da República. **Jardins**, the city's most affluent inner neighbourhood, is a good place to stay and to visit, especially if you want to shop and eat well. Elegant little streets hide hundreds of wonderful restaurants and accommodation ranges from the luxurious to the top end of the budget range. You are safe here at night. The northeastern section of Jardins, known as **Cerqueira César**, abuts one of São Paulo's grandest modern avenues, **Paulista,** lined with skyscrapers, shops and a few churches and museums including MASP (Museu de Arte de São Paulo). There are metro connections from here and a number of good hotels. **Ibirapuera Park and around**: the inner city's largest green space is home to a handful of museums, running tracks, a lake and frequent free live concerts on Sun. The adjoining neighbourhoods of Moema and Vila Mariana have a few hotels, but **Moema**¸ **Itaim** and **Vila Olimpia** are among the nightlife centres of São Paulo with a wealth of streetside bars, designer restaurants and European-style dance clubs. Hotels tend to be expensive as they are near the new business centre on Avenidas Brigadeiro Faria Lima and Luis Carlos Berrini. **Pinheiros and Vila Madalena** are less chic, but equally lively at night and with the funkiest shops.

Beware of assaults and pickpocketing in São Paulo. Thieves often use the mustard-on-the-back trick to distract you while someone else robs you. The areas around Luz station, Praça da República and Centro are not safe at night, and do not enter favelas.

Tourist offices There are tourist information booths with English speaking staff in arrivals of terminals 1 and 2 at Guarulhos airport (Cumbica, 0600-2200); and tourist booths in the Tietê bus station (0600-2200) and in the following locations throughout the city: **Olido** ⓘ *Av São João 473, daily 0900-1800*; at Parque Prefeito Mário Covas ⓘ *Av Paulista 1853, daily 0800-2000*; at ⓘ *R 15 de Novembro 347, 1st floor, T3241 5822*; and temporary booths at special events (eg at Parque

1 São Paulo

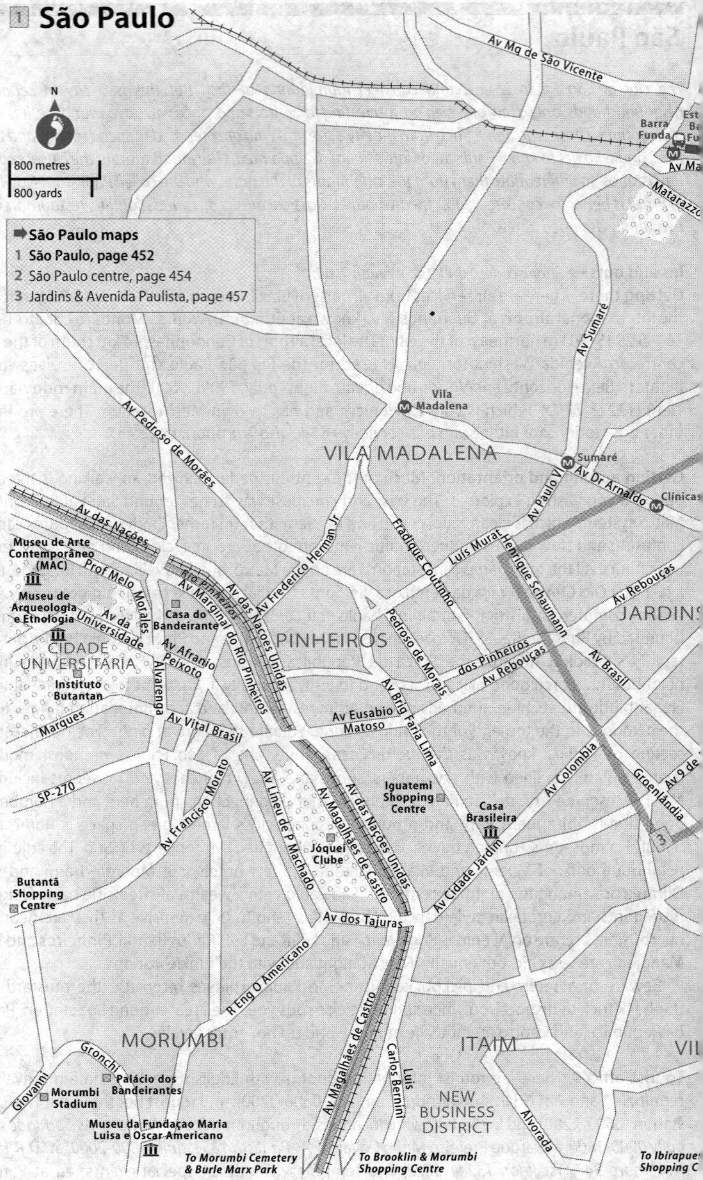

800 metres
800 yards
São Paulo maps
1 São Paulo, page 452
2 São Paulo centre, page 454
3 Jardins & Avenida Paulista, page 457
Av Mq de São Vicente
Barra Funda
Av Ma
Matarazzo
Av Sumaré
Vila Madalena
VILA MADALENA
Sumaré
Av Dr Arnaldo
Clínicas
Av Paulo VI
Av Pedroso de Moraes
Av das Nações
Museu de Arte Contemporâneo (MAC)
Prof Melo Morales
Museu de Arqueologia e Etnologia
Av da Universidade
CIDADE UNIVERSITÁRIA
Instituto Butantan
Casa do Bandeirante
Rio Pinheiros
Av Marginal do Rio Pinheiros
Av das Nações Unidas
Av Frederico Herman Jr
Fradique Coutinho
Luís Murat
Henrique Schaumann
Av Rebouças
JARDINS
PINHEIROS
Pedroso de Morais
dos Pinheiros
Av Rebouças
Av Brasil
Av Afranio Peixoto
Alvarenga
Marques
Av Vital Brasil
Av Eusabio Matoso
Av Brig Faria Lima
SP-270
Av Francisco Morato
Av Lineu de P Machado
Av Magalhães de Castro
Av das Nações Unidas
Iguatemi Shopping Centre
Casa Brasileira
Av Colombia
Groenlândia
Av 9 de
3
Jóquei Clube
Av Cidade Jardim
Butantã Shopping Centre
Av dos Tajuras
R Eng O Americano
Av Magalhães de Castro
MORUMBI
ITAIM
VI
Gronchi
Giovanni
Palácio dos Bandeirantes
Morumbi Stadium
Luis Carlos Berrini
NEW BUSINESS DISTRICT
Alvorada
Museu da Fundaçao Maria Luisa e Oscar Americano
To Morumbi Cemetery & Burle Marx Park
To Brooklin & Morumbi Shopping Centre
To Ibirapue Shopping C

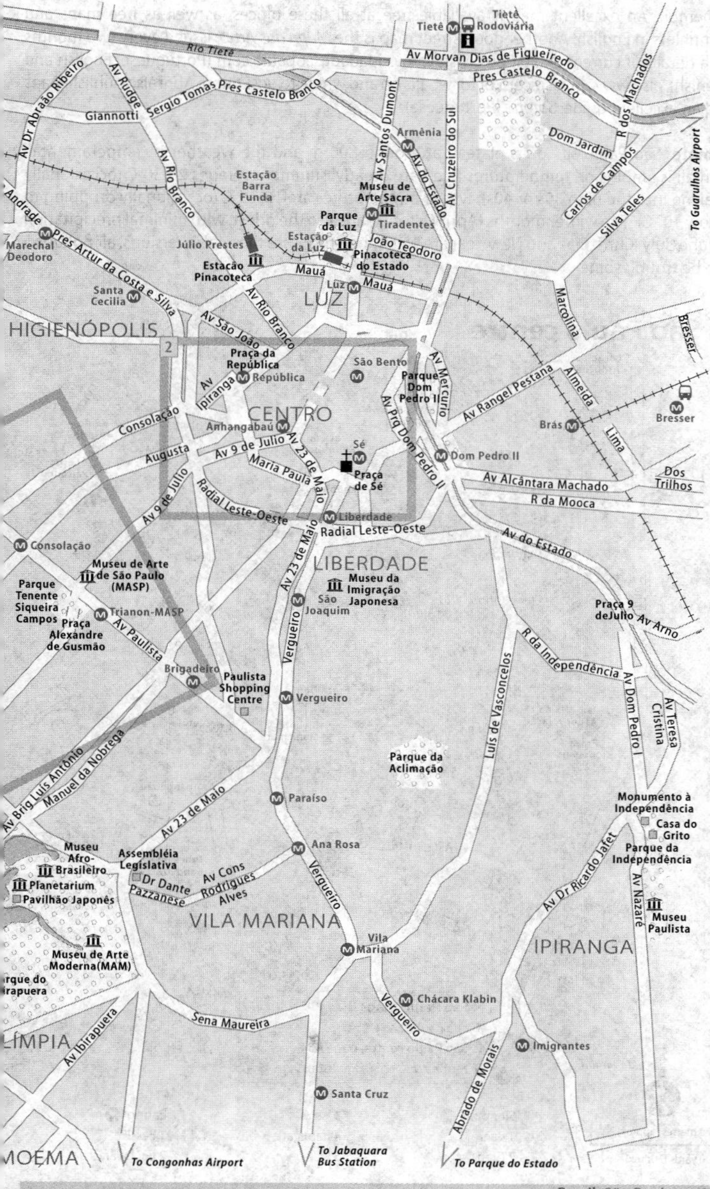

Tietê
Tietê Rodoviária
Rio Tietê
Av Morvan Dias de Figueiredo
Pres Castelo Branco
R dos Machados
Av Dr Abraão Ribeiro
Av Rudge
Giannotti
Sergio Tomas
Pres Castelo Branco
Av Santos Dumont
Armênia
Av do Estado
Av Cruzeiro do Sul
Dom Jardim
Carlos de Campos
Silva Teles
To Guarulhos Airport
Av Rio Branco
Estação Barra Funda
Museu de Arte Sacra
Parque da Luz
Tiradentes
Andrade
Marechal Deodoro
Pres Artur da Costa e Silva
Júlio Prestes
Estação da Luz
João Teodoro
Pinacoteca do Estado
Estacão Pinacoteca
Mauá
Santa Cecilia
Luz
LUZ
Marcolina
Bresser
HIGIENÓPOLIS
Av São João
Av Rio Branco
2
Praça da República
República
São Bento
Av Mercurio
Parque Dom Pedro II
Av Rangel Pestana
Almeida
Av Ipiranga
CENTRO
Consolação
Anhangabaú
Av Prq Dom Pedro II
Brás
Bresser
Lima
Augusta
Av 9 de Julio
Av 23 de Maio
Sé
Dom Pedro II
Maria Paula
Praça de Sé
Av Alcântara Machado
Dos Trilhos
R da Mooca
Av 9 de Julio
Radial Leste-Oeste
Liberdade
Radial Leste-Oeste
Av do Estado
Consolação
Av 23 de Maio
LIBERDADE
Museu de Arte de São Paulo (MASP)
Museu da Imigração Japonesa
Parque Tenente Siqueira Campos
São Joaquim
Trianon-MASP
Praça 9 deJulio
Av Arno
Praça Alexandre de Gusmão
Av Paulista
R da Independência
Luis de Vasconcelos
Brigadeiro
Paulista Shopping Centre
Vergueiro
Vergueiro
Av Dom Pedro I
Av Teresa Cristina
Manuel da Nobrega
Parque da Aclimação
Av Brig Luis Antônio
Paraíso
Av 23 de Maio
Monumento à Independência
Casa do Grito
Ana Rosa
Parque da Independência
Museu Afro-Brasileiro
Assembléia Legislativa
Av Cons Rodrigues Alves
Av Dr Ricardo Jafet
Planetarium
Dr Dante Pazzanese
Pavilhão Japonês
Vergueiro
Av Nazaré
Museu Paulista
VILA MARIANA
Museu de Arte Moderna(MAM)
Vila Mariana
IPIRANGA
rque do irapuera
Chácara Klabin
Sena Maureira
Vergueiro
LÍMPIA
Av Ibirapuera
Imigrantes
Abrado de Morais
Santa Cruz
MOEMA
To Congonhas Airport
To Jabaquara Bus Station
To Parque do Estado

Anhembi). An excellent map is available free at all these offices, as well as free maps and pamphlets in English. Another good street map is the *Mapa das Artes*, issued every two months with details of current exhibitions. Visit www.cidadedesaopaulo.com (Portuguese, English and Spanish), also www.guiasp.com.br for what's on and where to go. Editora Abril also publish maps and an excellent guide, *Sampa* (Portuguese).

Climate São Paulo sits on a plateau at around 800 m and the weather is temperamental. Rainfall is ample and temperatures fluctuate greatly: summer averages 20-30°C (occasionally peaking into the high 30s or 40s), winter temperatures are 15-25°C (occasionally dropping to below 10° C). The winter months (April-October) are also the driest, with minimal precipitation in June/July. Christmas and New Year are wet. When there are thermal inversions, air pollution can be troublesome.

2 São Paulo centre

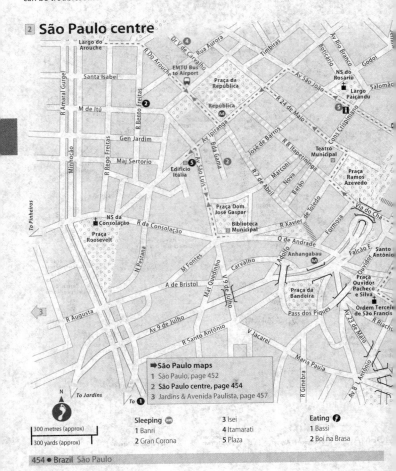

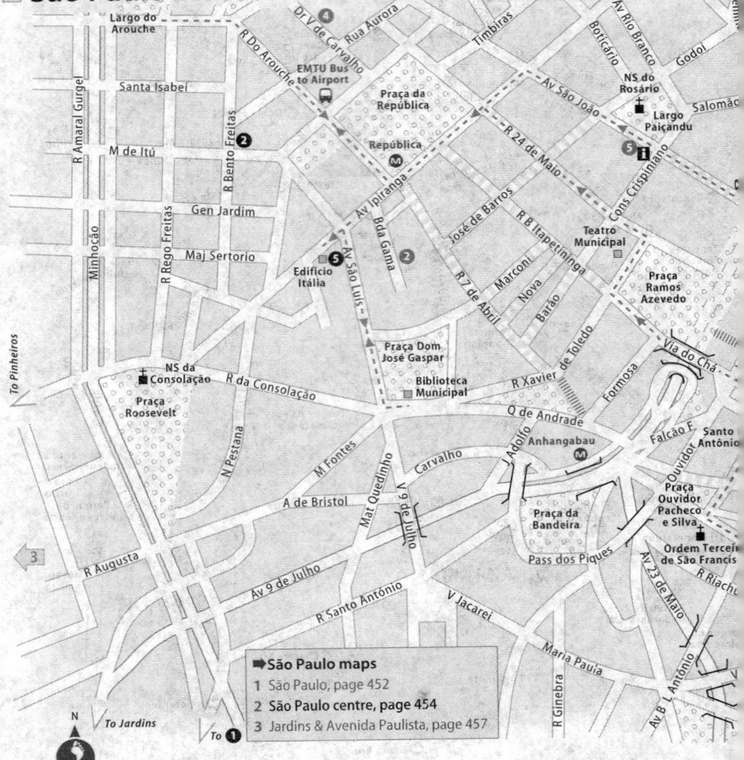

Sleeping
1 Banri
2 Gran Corona
3 Isei
4 Itamarati
5 Plaza

Eating
1 Bassi
2 Boi na Brasa

Background

Until the 1870s São Paulo was a sleepy, shabby little town known as 'a cidade de barro' (the mud city), as most buildings were made of clay and packed mud. It was transformed in the late 19th century when wealthy landowners and Santos merchants began to invest. From 1885 to 1900 the coffee boom and arrival of large numbers of Europeans transformed the state. By the late 1930s São Paulo state had one million Italians, 500,000 each of Portuguese and immigrants from the rest of Brazil, 400,000 Spaniards and 200,000 Japanese. It is the world's largest Japanese community outside Japan. Nowadays, it covers more than 1,500 sq km, three times the size of Paris.

Old Centre

A focal point of the centre is the **Parque Anhangabaú**, an open space between the Triângulo and the streets which lead to Praça da República (Metrô Anhangabaú is at its southern end). Beneath Anhangabaú, north-south traffic is carried by a tunnel. Crossing it are two viaducts: **Viaduto do Chá**, which is open to traffic and links Rua Direita and Rua Barão de Itapetininga. Along its length sellers of potions, cures, fortunes and trinkets set up their booths. The **Viaduto Santa Ifigênia**, an iron bridge for pedestrians only, connects Largo de São Bento with Largo de Santa Ifigênia.

3 Gombe
4 Sushi Yassu
5 Terraço Italia

Historic buildings walk

On **Largo de São Bento** there is the **Igreja e Mosteiro de São Bento** ⓘ *T3328 8799, www.mosteiro.org.br for details of all services, including Gregorian chant*, an early 20th-century building (1910-22) on the site of a 1598 chapel. Due south of São Bento is the **Martinelli building** ⓘ *on R Líbero Badaró at Av São João, closed*, the city's first skyscraper (1922). It was surpassed by the **Edifício Banespa** (finished 1947) ⓘ *R João Brícola 24, T3249 7180, Mon-Fri 1000-1700, US$4*, with 360° views from the top, up to 40 km, smog permitting. The newly renovated **Pateo do Collégio (Museu de Anchieta)** ⓘ *Praça Pátio do Colégio, T3105 6899, www.pateodocollegio.com.br, Metrô Sé, with a café, Tue-Sun 0900-1700, US$3*. It is an exact replica of the original Jesuit church and college but dates from 1950s. Most of the buildings are occupied by the Museu de Anchieta, named after the Jesuit captain who led the first mission. This houses, amongst other items a 17th-century font that was used to baptize *indígenas* and a collection of Guaraní art and artefacts from the colonial era and a modernist painting of the priest, by Italian Albino Menghini.

A short distance southeast of the Pateo do Collégio is the **Solar da Marquesa de Santos**, an 18th-century residential building, which now contains the **Museu da Cidade** ⓘ *R Roberto Simonsen 136, T3241 4238, Tue-Sun 0900-1700.* The **Praça da Sé** is a huge open area south of the Pateo do Collégio, dominated by the **Catedral Metropolitana** ⓘ *T3107 6832, Mon-Sat 0800-1700, Sun 0800-1830*, a massive, peaceful space. The cathedral's foundations were laid more than 40 years before its inauguration during the 1954 festivities commemorating the fourth centenary of the city. It was fully completed in 1970. This enormous building in neo-Gothic style has a capacity for 8,000 worshippers in its five naves. The interior is mostly unadorned, except for the two gilt mosaic pictures in the transepts: on the north side is the Virgin Mary and on the south Saint Paul.

West of the Praça da Sé, along Rua Benjamin Constant, is the Largo de São Francisco. Here is the **Igreja da Ordem Terceira de São Francisco** ⓘ *T3105 6899, 0730-2000*. The convent was inaugurated in 1647 and reformed in 1744. To the right is the Igreja das Chagas do Seráphico Pai São Francisco (1787), painted like its neighbour in blue and gold. Across the Viaduto do Chá is the **Teatro Municipal** ⓘ *T3223 3022*, one of the few distinguished early 20th- century survivors that São Paulo can boast. Viewing the interior may only be possible during a performance; as well as the full evening performances, look out for its midday, string quartet and 'vesperais líricas' concerts.

Praça da República

In Praça da República the trees are tall and shady. There are also lots of police. Near the Praça is the city's tallest building, the **Edifício Itália** ⓘ *Av Ipiranga 344, T2189 2929, US$5*. There is a restaurant on top and a sightseeing balcony. If you walk up Avenida São Luís, which has many airline offices and travel agencies (especially found in the Galeria Metrópole), you arrive at Praça Dom José Gaspar, in which is the **Biblioteca Municipal Mário de Andrade**, surrounded by a pleasant shady garden.

North of the centre

About 10 minutes' walk from the centre is the old **Mercado Municipal** ⓘ *R Cantareira 306, www.mercadomunicipal.com.br, Mon-Sat 0700-1800, Sun 0700-1300*, covering 27,000 sq m. **Parque da Luz** on Avenida Tiradentes (110,000 sq m) was formerly a botanical garden. It is next to the Luz railway station. There are two museums: in the park is the **Pinacoteca do Estado** (State Art Collection) ⓘ *Praça da Luz 2, T3224 1000, www.pinacoteca.org.br, Tue-Sun 1000- 1800, US$3*. It and its neighbouring sister gallery, the **Estação Pinacoteca** ⓘ *Largo General Osório 66, T3337 0185, daily 1000-1730, US$2, Sat free*, preserve the best collection of modernist Brazilian art outside the Belas Artes in Rio, together with important works by Europeans like Picasso and Chagall. Both have good cafés, the Pinacoteca has a very good art bookshop. Nearby, the **Museu de Arte Sacra** ⓘ *Av Tiradentes 676, T3326 1373, www.museuartesacra.org.br, Tue-Sun 1100-1900, US$2.25*, is modern and tasteful, housed in the serene **Igreja e Convento Nossa Senhora da Luz** (1774), still partially occupied. It has a priceless, beautifully presented collection including works by Aleijadinho, Benedito Calixto, Mestre Athayde and Francisco Xavier de Brito. The convent is one of the few colonial buildings left in São Paulo; the chapel dates from 1579.

Liberdade

Directly south of the Praça da Sé, and one stop on the Metrô, is Liberdade, the central Japanese district, now also home to large numbers of Koreans and Chinese. The Metrô station is in Praça da Liberdade, in which there is an oriental market every Sunday (see Shopping). The Praça is one of the best places in the city for Japanese food. **Museu da Imigração Japonesa** ⓘ *R São Joaquim 381, exhibition on 7th, 8th and 9th floors, T3209 5465, www.nihonsite.com.br/muse, Tue-Sun 1330-1730, US$2.50*, is excellent, with a roof garden; captions have English summaries.

Jardins and Avenida Paulista → *See map, page 457.*

Avenida Paulista has been transformed since the 1890s from the city's most fashionable promenade into six lanes of traffic lined with banks' and multibnationals' headquarters. Its highlight is undoubtedly **MASP**, the common name for the **Museu de Arte de São Paulo**

3 Jardins & Avenida Paulista

➡**São Paulo maps**
1 São Paulo, page 452
2 São Paulo centre, page 454
3 Jardins & Avenida Paulista, page 457

500 metres (approx)
500 yards (approx)

Sleeping
1 Brigadeiro *C3*
2 Dona Ziláh *A2*
3 Emiliano *B2*
4 Fasano *B2*
5 Formule 1 *C3*
6 Golden Tulip Park Plaza *C3*
7 Ibis São Paulo Paulista *A3*
8 Landmark Residence *B2*
9 Paulista Garden *C2*
10 Pousada dos Franceses *C3*
11 Renaissance *B3*
12 Transamérica Ópera *B2*
13 Unique *C2*
14 Vila Madalena Hostel *A1*

Eating
1 A Mineira *C3*
2 Baalbeck *B2*
3 Camelo *C2*
4 Charlô Bistro *B2*
5 Cheiro Verde *B2*
6 DOM *B2*
7 Figueira Rubaiyat *B1*
8 Fran's Café *B2/C3*
9 Gero *B2*
10 Jun Sakamoto *A1*
11 Kayomix *A2*
12 La Tambouille *C1*
13 Laurent *B2*
14 MASP *B3*
15 Massimo *B3*
16 Namesa *A2*
17 Paulista Grill *A1*
18 Sujinho *A3*
19 Tâmara Café *B3*
20 Vento Haragano *A2*

Bars & clubs
21 Apollinari *A2*
22 Bar Balcão *A2*
23 Finnegan's Pub *A1*

ⓘ *Av Paulista 1578 (above the 9 de Julho tunnel); T3251 5644, http://masp.uol.com.br, the nearest Metrô is Trianon-MASP; bus 805A from Praça da República goes by MASP, open 1100-1800, except Thu 1100-2000, closed Mon, US$7.50, Tue free.* The museum has the finest collection of European masters in the southern hemisphere with works by artists like Raphael, Bellini, Bosch, Rembrandt, Turner, Constable, Monet, Manet and Renoir. Also some interesting work by Brazilian artists, including Portinari. Temporary exhibitions are also held and when a popular show is on, it can take up to an hour to get in. There is a very good art shop.

Opposite MASP is **Parque Tenente Siqueira Campos** ⓘ *daily 0700-1830*, which covers two blocks on either side of Alameda Santos; a bridge links the two parts of the park. It is block of subtropical forest in the busiest part of the city. In the foyers of some of the nearby towers are various cultural centres (eg **FIESP**, Av Paulista 1313) which put on worthwhile exhibitions and are more-or-less the only sights in the city open on a Monday. The **Museu da Imagem e do Som** (**MIS**) ⓘ *Av Europa 158, T3085 1498, www.mis.sp.gov.br, Tue-Sun 1000-1800*, has photographic exhibitions, archives of Brazilian cinema and music, and a nice café. Next to MIS is the **Museu Brasiliero da Escultura** (MuBE); free to temporary exhibitions and recitals in the afternoons. Avenida Europa continues to Avenida Brigadeiro Faria Lima, on which is the **Casa Brasileira** ⓘ *Av Faria Lima 2705, T3032 3727, www.mcb.sp.gov.br, Tue-Sun 1000-1800, US$2*, a museum of Brazilian furniture. It also holds temporary exhibitions.

Cidade Universitária and Morumbi

The Cidade Universitária is on the west bank of the Rio Pinheiros, opposite the district of Pinheiros. The campus also contains the famous **Instituto Butantan** (Butantan Snake Farm and Museum) ⓘ *Av Dr Vital Brasil 1500, T3726 7222*. The insituto's collection of preserved snakes, spiders and scorpions was destroyed by fire in May 2010. Contact in advance to see if it's open to visitors. The **Museu de Arte Contemporâneo** (**MAC**) ⓘ *T3091 3538, www.mac.usp.br, Tue-Sun 1000-1900, free*, with an important collection of Brazilian and European modern art, is in the Prédio Novo da Reitoria. Also the **Museu de Arqueologia e Etnologia** (MAE) ⓘ *R Reitoria 1466, T3091 4905*, with Amazonian and ancient Mediterranean collections. Not far from the Butantã Institute, just inside Cidade Universitária, is the **Casa do Bandeirante** ⓘ *Praça Monteiro Lobato, T3031 0920*, the reconstructed home of a 17th-century pioneer.

On the west bank of the Rio Pinheiros, just southeast of the Cidade Universitária, is the palatial **Jóquei Clube/Jockey Club** ⓘ *Av Lineu de Paula Machado 1263, T2161 8300, www.jockeysp.com.br*, racecourse in the Cidade Jardim area. Take Butantã bus from República. Race meetings are held Monday and Thursday at 1930 and weekends at 1430. It has a **Museu do Turfe** ⓘ *Tue-Sun, closed Sat-Sun mornings.*

Morumbi is a smart residential district due south of the Cidade Universitária. In the area are the state government building, **Palácio dos Bandeirantes** ⓘ *Av Morumbi 4500*, the small, simple **Capela de Morumbi** ⓘ *Av Morumbi 5387*, and the Morumbi stadium of São Paulo Football Club, which holds 100,000 people. Motor racing fans might like to visit the Morumbi cemetery, last resting place of Ayrton Senna; take 6291 bus to Rua Profesor Benedito Montenegro.

Museu da Fundação Maria Luisa e Oscar Americano ⓘ *Av Morumbi 4077, Morumbi, T3742 0077, www.fundacaooscaramericano.org.br, Tue-Sun 1000-1730, US$4*, is a private collection of Brazilian and Portuguese art and furniture. The garden has fascinating paths, patios and plants; concerts are held on Sunday and courses through the week. It is close to the Palácio dos Bandeirantes.

Burle Marx Park ⓘ *Av Dona Helena Pereira de Moraes 200, Morumbi, daily 0700-1900.* Designed by famous landscape designer Burle Marx, it has trails leading through the Mata Atlântica (Atlantic rainforest).

South of the Old Centre

Ibirapuera

The **Parque do Ibirapuera** ⓘ *entrance on Av Pedro Álvares Cabral, daily 0600-1730*, was designed by Oscar Niemeyer and landscape artist Roberto Burle Marx for the city's fourth centenary in 1954. Within its 160 ha is the **Assembléia Legislativa** and a **planetarium** ⓘ *T5575 5206, shows Sat, Sun at 1500, Thu at 1930, US$5*. After many years of refurbishment it now has state-of-the-art fittings. Buy tickets 30 minutes before the show. Also in the park is the **Museu de Arte Moderna** (MAM) ⓘ *T5085 1300, www.mam.org.br, Tue-Sun 1000-1800, US$2.75, students half price, free Sun*, with art exhibitions and sculpture garden (see Nuno Ramos' Craca – Barnacle). It has a great café restaurant and art shop. **Museu Afro-Brasileiro** ⓘ *T5579 0593, Wed-Sun 1000-1800, free*: temporary exhibitions, theatre, dance and cinema spaces, photographs and panels devoted to exploring African Brazil. **Pavilhão Japonês** ⓘ *T3573 6543, Sat, Sun 1000-1700, free except for exhibitions*, exhibition space showing works from Japanese and Japanese-Brazilian artists, designed by Japanese and built exclusively with materials from Japan. It is set in Japanese gardens and has a traditional tea house upstairs. Bicycles can be hired in the park, US$3 per hour. Buses to Ibirapuera, 574R from Paraíso Metrô station; 6364 from Praça da Bandeira; to Cidade Universitária 702U or 7181 from Praça da República. Every even-numbered year the **Bienal Internacional de São Paulo** (São Paulo Biennial) at Ibirapuera has the most important show of modern art in Latin America, usually in September (next in 2010).

Parque da Independência

In the suburb of Ipiranga, 5½ km southeast of the city centre, the Parque da Independência contains the **Monumento à Independência**. Beneath the monument is the Imperial Chapel ⓘ *Tue-Sun 1300-1700*, with the tomb of the first emperor, Dom Pedro I, and Empress Leopoldina. **Casa do Grito** ⓘ *Tue-Sun 0930-1700*, the little house in which Dom Pedro I spent the night before his famous cry of Ipiranga, 'Independence or Death', is preserved in the park. The **Museu Paulista** ⓘ *T6165 8000, Tue-Sun 0900-1645, US$1*, contains old maps, traditional furniture, collections of old coins, religious art and *indígena* ethnology. Behind the Museum is the **Horto Botânico (Ipiranga Botanical Garden)** and the **Jardim Francês** ⓘ *Tue-Sun 0900-1700, getting there: take bus 478-P (Ipiranga-Pompéia for return) from Ana Rosa, or take bus 4612 from Praça da República.*

Parque do Estado (Jardim Botânico)

This large park, a long way south of the centre, at **Água Funda** ⓘ *Av Miguel Estefano 3031-3687, T5573 6300, Wed-Sun 0900-1700, getting there: take Metrô to São Judas on the Jabaquara line, then take a bus*, contains the Jardim Botânico, with lakes and trees and places for picnics, and a very fine orchid farm worth seeing during November-December (orchid exhibitions in April and November).

Excursions

Embu (M'Boy – Big Snake), 28 km from São Paulo, is a colonial town which has become a centre for artists and craftsmen. The town itself, on a hill, is surrounded by industry and modern developments and the colonial centre is quite small. Many of the old houses are painted in bright colours and most contain arts, furniture, souvenir or antiques shops. On Sunday afternoons there is a large and popular arts and crafts fair (0900-1800). On Monday almost everything is closed. In the Largo dos Jesuítas is the church of **Nossa Senhora do Rosário** (1690) and the **Museu de Arte Sacra** ⓘ *Tue-Fri 1300-1700, Sat-Sun 1000-1700*. **Paranapiaçaba** is a tiny 19th-century town in the cloudforest of the Serra do Mar, 50 km southeast of São Paulo. It was built by British railway workers. There is a small railway museum and a handful of *pousadas* and restaurants. A frequent train runs on Line 10 from Luz station to Rio Grande da Serra, US$1.50, 55 mins, from where bus No 424 runs to Paranapiaçaba in the week, every 30 minutes at weekends, about one hour. A tourist train was due to start from Luz on Sundays direct to Paranapiaçaba in 2009.

São Paulo listings

For Sleeping and Eating price codes and other relevant information, see Essentials, pages 38-40.

Sleeping

For both business and leisure, São Paulo has by far the best hotels in Brazil. The best area to stay is northeastern Jardins (also known as Cerqueria César), which is safe and well connected to the Metrô via Av Paulista. There are cheapies in the centre, but this is an undesirable area at night.

Old Centre *p455, map p454*

A Gran Corona, Basílio da Gama 101, T3214 0043, www.grancorona.com.br. In a small street. Comfortable, good services, good restaurant. Warmly recommended.

B-D Itamarati, Av Dr Vieira de Carvalho 150, T222 4133, www.hotelitamarati.com.br. Good location, safe, cheaper at weekends. Highly recommended and very popular.

D Plaza, Av São João 407, T3222 1355, reserva@plazahotel.tur.br. Budget option on this busy avenue, quieter rooms at back, breakfast included. Several other hotels on Av São João.

Liberdade *p456*

B-C Banri, R Galvão Bueno 209, T3207 8877. Good, Chinese owners, near the Metrô station. Recommended.

C Isei, R da Glória 290, T3208 6677, one block from Liberdade metro. Japanese owners, good, with cable TV, breakfast, some beds very hard.

Jardins, Avenida Paulista and around *p457, map p457*

LL Emiliano, R Oscar Freire 384, T3069 4369, www.emiliano.com.br. Bright and beautifully designed, attention to every detail and the best suites in the city. No pool but a relaxing small spa. Excellent Italian restaurant, location and service.

LL Fasano, R Vittorio Fasano 88, T3896 4077, www.fasano.com.br. One of the world's great hotels with decor like a modernist gentleman's club designed by Armani, a fabulous pool and the best formal haute cuisine restaurant in Brazil. Excellently positioned in Jardins.

LL Renaissance, Al Santos 2233 (at Haddock Lobo), T3069 2233, http://marriott.com. The best business hotel off Av Paulista with standard business rooms, a good spa, gym, pool and 2 squash courts.

LL Unique, Av Brigadeiro Luis Antônio 4700, Jardim Paulista, T3055 4700, www.hotelunique.com. The most ostentatious hotel in the country, an enormous half moon on concrete uprights with curving floors, circular windows and beautiful use of space and light. The bar on the top floor is São Paulo's answer to the LA Sky Bar and is always filled with the rich and famous after 2130.

LL-AL George V, R José Maria Lisboa 1000, T3088 9822, www.george-v.com.br. Apartments with living rooms, fully equipped kitchens, huge bathrooms and comprehensive business services. Shared facilities include sauna, indoor pool and gym. Special deals online.

AL Golden Tulip Park Plaza, Al Lorena 360, T3058 4055, www.parkplaza.com.br. Modern tower with apartments, spa and well-equipped modern gym. Good value.

AL Transamérica Ópera, Al Lorena 1748, T3062 2666, www.transamericaflats.com.br. Prices go up to **L**. Conservatively decorated but elegant and well-maintained modern flats between the heart of Jardins and Av Paulista.

A The Landmark Residence, Al Jaú 1607, T3082 8677, www.landmarkresidence.com.br. Spacious apartments, shared gym, gardens and modest business centre. Good location.

A-B Dona Ziláh, Al França 1621, Jardim Paulista, T3062 1444, www.zilah.com. Little pousada in a renovated colonial house, well maintained, decorated with a personal touch. Excellent location, bike rental and generous breakfast included.

A-B Ibis São Paulo Paulista, Av Paulista 2355, T3523 3000, www.accorhotels.com.br. Great value, modern business standard rooms with a/c, right on Paulista, cheaper at weekends.

B Formule 1, R Vergueiro 1571, T5085 5699, www.accorhotels.com.br. Another great value business-style hotel, apartments big enough for 3 make this an **E** option for those in a group. Right next to Paraíso Metro in a safe area, a/c.

B Paulista Garden, Al Lorena 21, T/F3885 8498, www.paulistagardenhotel.com.br. Small, simple rooms with a/c, cable TV and fridge, close to Ibirapuera Park.

C Pousada dos Franceses, R dos Franceses 100, Bela Vista, T3288 1592, www.pousadadosfranceses.com.br. Plain little pousada 10 mins' walk from Brigadeiro Metrô. dorms, doubles and singles, free internet, TV room, breakfast included.
C Vila Madalena Hostel, R Francisco Leitão 686, T3034 4104, www.vilamadalenahostel.com. Price for double bed, **E** in dorms for 4 or 8. 15 mins from Clínicas Metrô, well-run, popular, arty hostel with good services, bikes for rent, internet and Wi-Fi.
D Brigadeiro, Av Brig Luís Antonio 2564, T3288 3252, www.hotelbrigadeiro.com.br. Comfortable small rooms, TV, buffet breakfast, helpful.

South of the Old Centre *p459*

The area known as the New Centre, around **Av Brigadeiro Faria Lima** and **Av Luis Carlos Berrini**, has no sights of interest for the tourist, however it has the plushest, most expensive hotels.
LL Hyatt São Paulo, Av das Nações Unidas 13301, T6838 1234, http://Sãopaulo.hyatt.com. A superb business hotel, with spa, pool, state of the art business centre and marvellous views from the upper floor suites.
L-AL Blue Tree Towers, Av Brigadeiro Faria Lima 3989, Vila Olímpia, T3896 7544, www.bluetree.com.br. Modern business hotel with excellent service, ideally positioned for Faria Lima, Vila Olímpia and Itaim, pool, massage, gym, sauna and business centre.
C ACE Hostel, R Gastão da Cunha 253, Congonhas Airport, T2248 0534, www.bedandbreakfast .com.br. Pocket-sized hostel in a brightly painted house near Congonhas. Services include TV, DVD and movies, broadband, kitchen, laundry, book exchange and pick-up. Tours of São Paulo.
D-E pp **Praça da Árvore**, R Pageú 266, Saúde, T5071 5148, www.spalbergue.com.br. Well-kept pousada in a quiet street, cheaper for HI members, helpful, 2 mins from Praça do Árvore metro, kitchen, laundry and internet service (overpriced).
Associação Paulista de Albergues da Juventude, R 7 de Abril 386, Conj 22, T/F3258 0388, www.alberguesp.com.br.

Eating

Old Centre *p455, map p454*

Restaurants in the old centre tend to be lunchtime only; there are many per kg options and *padarias*.
TTT Terraço Italia, Av Ipiranga 344, T3257 6566. Average and overpriced Italian food with the best restaurant views in the city – out over an infinity of skyscrapers. Come for a coffee.
TT-T Boi na Brasa, R Bento Freitas by Praça da República. Very good meat dishes and feijoada at a reasonable price.
T Café da Pinacoteca, Pinacoteca Museum, Praça da Luz 2, T3326 0350. Portuguese-style café with marble floors and mahogany balconies. Great coffee, sandwiches and cakes.

Liberdade *p456*

TT Gombe, R Tomás Gonzaga 22, T3209 8499. Renowned for grilled tuna and noodle dishes.
TT Sushi Yassu, R Tomás Gonzaga 98, T3209 6622. The best of Liberedade's traditional Japanese restaurants. Excellent sushi/ sashimi combinations.

Jardins *p457, map p457*

Those on a budget can eat to their stomach's content in per kg places or, cheaper still, bakeries (*padarias*) There's one on almost every corner and they serve sandwiches, delicious Brazilian burgers made from decent meat and served with ham, egg, cheese or salad. They always have good coffee, juices, cakes and set lunches (*almoços*) for a very economical price. Most have a designated sitting area – either at the *padaria* bar or in an adjacent room. Juices are made from mineral or filtered water.
TTT Bassi, R 13 de Maio 668, Bela Vista, T3288 7045. Long-established meat restaurant with a fine reputation.
TTT Charlô Bistro, R Barão de Capanema 440 (next to DOM), T3088 6790 (with another branch at the Jockey Club, Av Lineu de Paula Machado 1263, Cidade Jardim, T3034 3682). One of the premier VIP and old family haunts in the city run by a scion of one of the city's establishment families. Decked out in tribute to a Paris brasserie and with food to match.

DOM, R Barão de Capanema 549, T3088 0761. Jardins' evening restaurant of the moment – Alex Attala has won the coveted Veja best chef of the year award twice. Contemporary food, fusing Brazilian ingredients with French and Italian styles and served in a large modernist dining room.

Fasano, in Hotel Fasano (see Sleeping), T3896 4077. Long regarded as the leading gourmet restaurant in São Paulo. A huge choice of modern Italian and French cooking from chef Salvatore Loi. Diners have their own lowly lit booths in a magnificent dining room, exemplary wine list, formal dress.

Figueira Rubaiyat, R Haddock Lobo 1738, T3063 3888. The most interesting of the Rubaiyat restaurant group, supervised by Argentinian chef Francis Mallman. Very lively for Sun lunch, light and airy and under a huge tropical fig tree. The best meat is served at another restaurant in the chain, Baby Beef Rubaiyat, Av Brig Faria Lima 2954, T3078 9488.

Gero, R Haddock Lobo 1629, T3064 0005. Fasano's version of a French Bistrô a Côté, but serving pasta and light Italian. Ever so casual design; be prepared for a long wait at the bar alongside people who are there principally to be seen. Reservations are not accepted.

Jun Sakamoto, R Lisboa 55, T3088 6019. Japanese with a touch of French; superb fresh ingredients (some of it flown in especially from Asia and the USA).

La Tambouille, Av 9 de Julho 5925, Jardim Europa, T3079 6276. The favourite 'old money' Franco-Italian restaurant. Excellent wine list.

Laurent, Al Lorena 1899, Cerqueira César, T3062 1452. The best French cooking in the country, French style, Brazilian ingredients.

Massimo, Al Santos 1826, Cerqueira César, T3284 0311. One of São Paulo's longest established Italian restaurants serving Northern Italian food. Credit cards are not accepted, despite the costly price.

Vento Haragano, Av Rebouças 1001, T3083 4265. One of the best rodízios in the city.

Paulista Grill, R João Moura 257, T3085 5426. Open daily from 1130 (Mon-Fri closed 1600-1800), another very good place for meat, more expensive at weekends.

A Mineira, Al Joaquim Eugénio de Lima 697, T3283 2349. Self-service Minas food by the kilo. Lots of choice. Cachaça and pudding included.

Baalbeck, Al Lorena 1330, T3088 4820. Lebanese cooking vastly superior to its luncheonette setting. Great falafel.

Camelo, R Pamplona 1873, T3887 8764. More than 40 superior pizzas with a choice of dough as well as topping.

Fran's Café, Av Paulista 358, and throughout the city. Open 24 hrs, the Brazilian equivalent of Starbuck's but with proper coffee and light meals.

Kayomix, R da Consolação 3215, T3082 2769. Brazilian Oriental fusions like salmon taratare with shimeji and shitake.

Namesa, R da Consolação 2967, T3088 7498. Great little gourmet snacky dishes, created by the chef from **DOM**.

Restaurante do MASP, Av Paulista 1578, T3253 2829. In the basement of the museum, reasonably priced standards like lasagna and stroganoff often with a garnish of live music.

Sujinho, R da Consolação 2068, Consolação, T3256 8026. South American beef in large portions, other carnivorous options also available.

Cheiro Verde, R Peixoto Gomide 1413, T289 6853 (lunch only). Hearty veggie food, like vegetable crumble in gorgonzola sauce and pasta with buffalo mozarella and sun-dried tomato.

Tâmara Cafe, Al Santos 1518, T288 1248 (lunchtimes only). Arabic cooking with good kibe, kofta and falafel.

South of the Old Centre *p459*

Vila Olímpia and Itaim

Restaurants here are ultra, ultra trendy; full of the beautiful posing in beautiful surroundings. We include only a handful of the best.

Boo, R Viradouro 132, T3078 7477. Opposite Kosushi, with a carbon copy crowd, Luso-Asian cooking and a beautiful garden setting.

Kosushi, R Viradouro 139, Itaim Bibi, T3167 7272. The first of São Paulo's chic Japanese restaurants which began life in Liberdade and is now housed in a beautifully designed Asian modernist space. Great sushi combinations.

Parigi, R Amauri 275, Itaim, T3167 1575. One of the city's premier evening places to be seen; Franco-Italian dining in a beautiful dining room.

Bars and clubs

The best places for nightlife are Itaim, Moema and Vila Olímpia, and Vila Madalena/Pinheiros. Jardins' best bars are in the top hotels. Vila Olímpia, Itaim and Moema have a series of funky, smart bars overflowing onto the street, filled with an eclectic mix of after-workers, clubbers, singles and couples; all united by being under 40 and having money. These sit alongside imitation US and European club/lounge bars playing techno, hip hop and the like. The busiest streets for a bar wander are Rua Atílio Inocenti near the junction of Av Juscelino Kubitschek and Av Brigadeiro Faria Lima, Av Hélio Pellegrino and Rua Araguari, which runs behind it. Vila Madalena is younger still, more hippy-chic, but is the best part of town to hear live, Brazilian music and uniquely Brazilian close dances like Forró, as opposed to international club sounds. The liveliest streets are Aspicuelta and Girassol.

Jardins *p457, map p457*

Apollinari, R Oscar Freire 1206, T3061 9965. Smart restaurant/bar frequented by the city's glitterati.

Bar Balcão, R Dr Melo Alves 150, T3063 6091. After work meeting place, very popular with young professionals and media types who gather on either side of the long low wooden bar which winds its way around the room like a giant snake.

Finnegan's Pub, R Cristiano Viana 358, Pinheiros. One of São Paulo's various Irish bars, this one actually run by an Irishman, popular with ex-pats.

West of the Old Centre *p457*

Vila Madalena/Pinheiros

AMP Galaxy, R Fradique Coutinho 352, T3085 7867, www.ampgalaxy.com.br. A fusion of retro 50s bar and café, boutique and, after 2300, packed dance floor with alternate live music and DJs. The crowd is 20-something and bohemian.

A Marcenaria, R Fradique Coutinho 1378, T3032 9006, www.amarcenaria.com.br. The bar of choice for the young and single who gather around 2130, until the dance floor fills up around 2300.

Bourbon Street, R dos Chanés 127, Moema, T5095 6100, www.bourbonstreet.com.br. Great little club with emerging local acts and international stars, too.

Grazie a Dio, R Girassol, 67, T3031 6568, www.grazieadio.com.br. The best bar in Vila Madalena for live music, different band every night, samba on Sun. Great for dancing, always packed.

Mood, R Teodoro Sampaio 1109, T3060 9010. European-style club with the latest sounds and DJs.

Posto 6, R Aspicuelta 644, Vila Madalena, T3812 7831. An imitation Rio de Janeiro Boteco with an attractive crowd and a backdrop of Bossa Nova and MPB. Busy from 2100 onwards.

Urbano, R Cardeal Arcoverde 614, Pinheiros, T3085 1001, www.urbano.com.br. São Paulo's premier dance club, modelled on a London club with a lounge bar area, huge dance floor and a combination of live bands and DJs. Popular with musicians and creative industry people.

South of the Old Centre *p459*

Itaim, Moema and Vila Olímpia

Liquid Lounge, Av Hélio Pellegrino 801, Vila Olímpia, T3849 5014, www.liquidlounge.com.br. Pulsing European-style dance club with a smart bar area. Always busy.

Lov.E Club & Lounge, R Pequetita 189, Vila Olímpia, T 3044 1613. Trance, house, drum 'n' bass; famous name DJs.

Na Mata Café, R da Mata 70, Itaim, T3079 0300, www.namata.com.br. Popular flirting and pick-up spot with a dark dance room, varied Brazilian and European dance tunes and select live bands.

Entertainment

São Paulo *p451, maps p454 and p457*

See the Guia da Folha section of Folha de São Paulo and Veja São Paulo of the weekly news magazine Veja for listings.

Cinema Entrance is usually half price on Wed; normal seat price is US$5 in the centre, US$7-8 in R Augusta, Av Paulista and Jardins. Cine clubs: **Cine SESC**, R Augusta 2075, and cinemas at: **Museu da Imagem e do Som**, **Centro Cultural Itaú** and **Centro Cultural São Paulo**.

Theatre The Teatro Municipal (see Sights) is used by visiting theatrical and operatic groups, as well as the City Ballet Company and the Municipal Symphony Orchestra who give regular performances. There are several other 1st-class theatres: **Aliança Francesa**, R general Jardim 182, Vila Buarque, T3017 5699, www.aliancafrancesa.com.br. **Paiol**, R Amaral Gurgel 164, Vila Buarque, T221 2462; among others. Free concerts at **Teatro Popular do Sesi**, Av Paulista 1313, T3284 9787, at midday, under MASP (Mon-Sat).

Festivals and events

São Paulo *p451, maps p454 and p457*

Foundation of the City 25 Jan. **Carnival** in **Feb** (most attractions and businesses are closed).This includes the parades of the escolas de samba in the Anhembi sambódromo – the São Paulo special group parades on the Fri and Sat and the Rio group on the Sun and Mon to maximize TV coverage. World's biggest **Gay Pride** march usually takes place in **May** on Av Paulista. In Jun there are the **Festas Juninas** and the **Festa de São Vito**, the patron saint of the Italian immigrants. **Festa da Primavera** in **Sep**. In Dec there are Christmas and New Year festivities. All year, there are countless anniversaries, religious feasts, international fairs and exhibitions, look in the press or the monthly tourist magazines to see what is on while you are in town. See Sights for the São Paulo Biennial.

Shopping

São Paulo *p451, maps p452, p454 and p457*

Bookshops **Duas Cidades**, R Bento Freitas 158, near República. Good selection of Brazilian and Spanish American literature. **La Selva**, in various shopping malls, also at airports. Sells books in English. **Letraviva**, Av Rebouças 1986. Mon-Fri 0900-1830, Sat 0900-1400, specializes in books and music in Spanish. **Librairie Française**, R Barão de Itapetininga 275, ground floor. Wide selection, also at R Professor Atilio Innocenti 920, Jardins. **Livraria Cultura**, Av Paulista 2073, loja 153, also at Shopping Villa-Lobos, Avdas Nacões Unidas 4777, Jardim Universale. New books in English, including guidebooks. **Livraria Freebook**, R da Consolação 1924, ring bell for entry. Wide collection of art books and imported books in English. **Livraria Kosmos**, Av São Luís 258, loja 6. International stock. **Livrarias Saraíva**, in various shopping malls. Sells books in English. **Livraria Triângulo**, R Barão de Itapetininga 255, loja 23, Centro, sells books in English. **Sodiler**, Shopping Market Place, Av Nações Unidas 13947, Brooklin, loja 121A, floor T.

Handicrafts **Casa dos Amazonas**, Al Jurupis 460. For souvenirs. **Ceará Meu Amor**, R Pamplona 1551, loja 7. Good quality lace from the northeast. **Galeria Arte Brasileira**, Al Lorena 2163, galeria@dialdata.com.br. Good value. **Sutaco**, handicrafts shop at República Metrô station. This promotes items from the State of São Paulo, Tue-Fri 1000-1900, Sat 1000-1500; there is a showroom at R Augusta 435, 6th floor.

Jewellery There are many other shops selling Brazilian stones, including branches of **H Stern** and **Amsterdam Sauer**.

Maps Quatro Rodas, Mapograf, Cartoplam, and the map given out by the tourist kiosks; RGN Public Ltda produces a map which is given out free in various places and which is adapted to show its sponsors' locations. A variety of maps and timetables are sold in news stands. **Editorial Abril**, Av das Nações Unidas 7221, T3037 2087, www.abril.com.br. Map, magazine and guide book publisher. **Geo Mapas**, R Gen Jardim 645, 3rd floor, Consolação. Private map publisher (40% discount for volume purchases), excellent 1988 1:5,000,000 map of Brazil, town maps. **Mapolândia**, 7 de Abril 125, 1st floor.

Open-air markets **Antiques market**, below the Museu de Arte de São Paulo. Sun, 1000-1700. **Arts and handicrafts**, are also sold in Parque Tenente Siqueira Campos/ Trianon on Sun from 0900-1700. **Flea markets**, in the main square of the Bixiga district (Praça Don Orione) and in Praça Benedito Calixto in Pinheiros. On Sun. **Ceasa flower market**, Av Doutor Gastão Vidigal 1946, Jaguaré. Tue and Fri 0700-1200, should not be missed. **'Hippy' market**, on Praça da República. Sun, reopened after temporary closure, but with stricter licensing than in the old days. **'Oriental' fair**, Praça de Liberdade. Sun 1000-1900, good for Japanese snacks, plants and some handicrafts, very picturesque, with remedies on sale, tightrope walking, gypsy fortune tellers, etc.

Shopping centres Typical of modern development are the huge **Iguatemi**, **Ibirapuera** and **Morumbi** shopping centres. They include luxurious cinemas, snack bars and most of the best shops in São Paulo. Other malls include **Paulista** and **Butantã**. On a humbler level are the big supermarkets of **El Dorado**

(Av Pamplona 1704) and **Pão de Açúcar** (Praça Roosevelt, near the Hilton); the latter is open 24 hrs a day (except Sun). São Paulo is relatively cheap for clothes (especially shoes).

Activities and tours

Football The most popular local teams are Corinthians, Palmeiras and São Paulo who play in the Morumbi and Pacaembu stadiums.

Adventure tourism **Venturas & Aventuras**, R Minerva 268, Perdizes, T3872 0362, www.venturas.com.br. Offers a wide rage of activity tours throughout the country.

Transport

São Paulo *p451, maps p452, p454 and p457*

Air From the international airport Guarulhos (also known as Cumbica), T6445 2945, there are airport taxis which charge US$45-52 on a ticket system (the taxi offices are outside Customs, 300 m down on the left; go to get your ticket then take your bags right back to the end of the taxi queue). Fares from the city to the airport are US$45-52 and vary from cab to cab. **Emtu bus service** every 30 mins from Guarulhos to Praça da República 343 (northwest side, corner of R Arouche), US$10.50, 30-45 mins, very comfortable (in the airport buy ticket at the booth in Domestic Arrivals); the same company runs services from Guarulhos to the main bus terminal, Tietê (hourly), US$10, and to Congonhas airport, T5090 9000. Buses run to Bresser bus station from Guarulhos and there are other buses to Jabaquara bus terminal, without luggage space, usually crowded. Also **Airport Bus Service**, T6221 0244, www.demanda.com.br /airbus.htm. US$14. From Congonhas airport, there are about 400 flights a week to Rio.

Airport information Money exchanges, in the arrivals hall, Guarulhos, 0800-2200 daily. Post office on the 3rd floor of Asa A. The Infraero Sala VIP has been recommended for coffee, cable TV for US$5. Mon-Fri 0800 to 1800. See Ins and outs, page 451, for the tourist office.

Bus Maps of the local bus and metro system are available at depots, for example Anhangabaú. Some city bus routes are run by trolley buses. City bus fare is US$1.25. Take an SP-Pinheiros bus from Clínicas, which takes the main highway to **Embu**; 40 mins. Get out at Largo 21 de Abril in Embu. To return to São Paulo, walk up R da Matriz from Largo 21 de Abril, turn left down Av Júnior, then left again on R Solano Trindade to a junction where the buses stop.

The main rodoviária for long distance buses is **Tietê**, which handles buses to the interior of São Paulo state, all state capitals (but see also under Barra Funda and Bresser below) and international buses. See www.passagem-em-domicilio.com.br for details of bus times and prices in Portuguese. The **left luggage** charges US$1 per day per item. You can sleep in the bus station after 2200 when the guards have gone; tepid showers cost US$2.65.

Buses from Tietê: To **Rio**, 6 hrs, every 30 mins, US$37-46 (leito, 56), special section for this route in the rodoviária, ask how to take the coastal route via Santos ('via litoral') unless you wish to go the direct route. To **Florianópolis**, 11 hrs, US$50 (leito 80). **Porto Alegre**, 18 hrs, US$75. **Curitiba**, 6 hrs, US$28-66. **Salvador**, 30 hrs, US$120 (executive, 150). **Recife**, 40 hrs, US$135. **Cuiabá**, 24 hrs, US$92. **Porto Velho**, 40 hrs, US$185. **Brasília**, 16 hrs, US$66 (leito, 132). **Foz do Iguaçu**, 16 hrs, US$50. **São Sebastião**, 4 hrs US$16.50 (say 'via Bertioga' if you want to go by the coast road, beautiful journey but few buses take this route).

International buses from Tietê: to **Montevideo**, via Porto Alegre, with **TTL**, departs Mon, Thu, Sat 2330, 31 hrs, US$134, cold a/c at night, plenty of meal stops, bus stops for border formalities, passengers disembark only to collect passport and tourist card on the Uruguayan side (also EGA, same price, US$100 to **Chuy**, Tue, Fri, Sun). To **Buenos Aires**, **Pluma**, 36 hrs. To **Santiago**, **Pluma** or **Chilebus**, 56 hrs, **Chilebus**, poor meals, but otherwise good, beware overbooking. To **Asunción** (1,044 km), US$60, 18 hrs with **Pluma**, **Brújula** or **RYSA**, all stop at Ciudad del Este. **Cometa del Amambay** runs to **Pedro Juan Caballero** and **Concepción**.

There are 3 other bus stations: **Barra Funda**, T3666 4682, with Metrô station, for buses from cities in southern São Paulo state, **Campo Grande** (14 hrs, US$74), and many places in Paraná. **Bresser**, T6692 5191, on the Metrô, is for destinations in Minas Gerais, eg **Cometa** (6967 7255) or **Transul** (T6693 8061) go to Minas Gerais: **Belo Horizonte**, 10 hrs, US$43,

11 a day (leito 71); 9 a day with **Gontijo.** **Translavras** and **Útil** also operate out of this station. Buses from Santos and the southern coast of São Paulo state arrive at **Jabaquara**, T5012 2256, at the southern end of the Metrô. Buses leave here for Santos every 15 mins, taking about 50 mins, last bus at 0100, US$7.75. Prices are given under destinations.

Car The rodízio, the restriction on car use by licence plate number, to curb traffic pollution, may be extended beyond the winter months. Check.

Metrô Two lines intersect at Praça de Sé: north-south from Tucuruvi to Jabaquara via Luz (the main interchange with CPTM suburban trains); and east-west from Corinthians-Itaquera to Palmeiras-Barra Funda (another interchange with CPTM trains and site of the rodoviária for São Paulo state and Paraná); an extension east to Guaianases is under construction. A 3rd line runs from Vila Madalena in the west, along Av Paulista, to Alto do Ipiranga in the south, meeting the Jabaquara line at Paraíso and Ana Rosa. A 4th line is being built from Vila Sônia to Luz. The system is clean, safe, cheap and efficient; the 2 main lines operate from 0500-2400, Ana Madalena to Ana Rosa 0600-2200. Fare US$1.15; backpacks are allowed. Combined bus and Metrô ticket are available, US$2, for example to Congonhas airport. Information T286 0111.

Taxi Taxis display cards of actual tariffs in the window (starting price US$4). There are ordinary taxis, which are hailed on the street, or at taxi stations such as Praça da República, radio taxis and deluxe taxis. For **Radio Taxis**, which are more expensive but involve fewer hassles, **Central Radio Táxi**, T6914 6630; **São Paulo Rádio Táxi**, T5583 2000; **Fácil**, T6258 5947; **Aero Táxi**, T6461 4090; or look in the phone book; calls are not accepted from public phones.

Train São Paulo has 3 stations: 1) **Estação da Luz** the hub for three CPTM suburban lines which operate at Metrô frequencies and with free transfers to the Metrô; 2) **Júlio Prestes station**, for commuter services to the west; 3) **Barra Funda**, services go to São José do Rio Preto (overnight), Barretos, Londrina, Maringá, Sorocaba and Ponta Grossa. There is a Metrô station and a rodoviária at Barra Funda.

Directory

São Paulo *p451, maps p452, p454 and p457*

Airline offices **Aerolíneas Argentinas**, Araújo 216, 6th floor, T259 0319 (Guarulhos airport 6445 3806). **Alitalia**, Av São Luís 50, cj 291, T3257 1922 (6445 3791). **American Airlines**, Araújo 216, 9th floor, T0800 703 4000 or 3214 4000 (6445 3808). **British Airways**, Av São Luís 50, 32nd floor, T3145 9700 (6445 2021). **Gol**, T0300-115 2121, www.voegol.com.br. **Iberia**, Araújo 216, 3rd floor, T2507 6711 (6445 2060). **JAL**, Av Paulista 542, 2nd floor, T251 5222 (6445 2040). **Lufthansa**, R Gomes de Carvalho 1356, 2nd floor, T3048 5868 (6445 2220). **OceanAir**, Av Washington Luis 7059, Av Washington Luis 7059, Santo Amaro, T2176 1000, or 4004 4040. **Rio-Sul**, R Bráulio Gomes 151, T5561 2161. **TAM**, R da Consolação 247, 3rd floor, T0300-123 1000 (24 hrs), or 3155 6700 (6445 3474). **TAP**, Av São Luís 187, T255 5366 (6445 2400). **United**, Av Paulista 777, 9-10th floor, T3145 4200/ 0800-162323 (6445 3283). **Banks** There are many national and international banks; most can be found either in the Triângulo, downtown, or on Av Paulista, or Av Brigadeiro Faria Lima. Hours 1000-1600; but some vary. All have different times for foreign exchange transactions (check at individual branches). Many **Banco 24 Horas** ATMs in the city. **Banco do Brasil** will change cash and TCs and will advance cash against Visa. All transactions are done in the foreign exchange department of any main branch (eg Av São João 32, Centro), but queues are long. **Citibank**, Av Ipiranga 855, or Av Paulista 1111 (1100-1500), cash on MasterCard. **Banespa**, for example at R Duque de Caxias 200, Centro, or Praça da República 295, accepts Visa, TCs and cash. **MasterCard**, cash against card, R Campo Verde 61, 4th floor, Jardim Paulistano. MasterCard ATMs at branches of **HSBC Bank**. Money changers: there are many câmbios on or near Praça da República. At the Tietê rodoviária there's a cambio, Mon-Fri 1000-1800, Sat 1000-1600, and Bradesco/Banco de Brasil/HSBC Visa ATMs. **Interpax**, Praça da República 177, loja 13, changes cash (many currencies) and TCs, 0930-1800, Sat 0930-1300. **Amoretur**, Praça da República 203, will change TCs. **Coraltur**, Praça da República 95. Most travel agents on Av São Luís change TCs and cash at good rates, but very few are open on Sat, let alone Sun. **Avencatur**,

Av Nações Unidas 1394, Morumbi, changes TCs, Deutschmarks, good rates. **Car hire** See Car hire, Essentials for international car rental agencies, page 36. **Interlocadora**, several branches, São Luís, T255 5604, Guarulhos T6445 3838, Congonhas T240 9287. **Cultural centres** **Centro Brasileiro Britânico**, R Ferriera de Araújo 741, Pinheiros, T3039 0508, www.cbb.org.br. Holds events, exhibitions and has a good lunch room on the top floor. **American Library**, União Cultural Brasil-Estados Unidos, R Col Oscar Porto 208. **Goethe-Instituto**, R Lisboa 974, T3088 4288 (Mon-Thu 1400-2030). **Centro Cultural Fiesp**, Av Paulista 1313, T3146 7405, 0900-1900 Tue-Sun, has foreign newspapers and magazines. See under Entertainment for Alliance Française Theatre. **Consulates** **Argentina**, Av Paulista 1106, T284 1355 (0900-1300, very easy to get a visa here). **Australia**, R Tenente Negrão 140, T3849 6281. **Bolivia**, Av Paulista 1439, conj 92, T3289 0443. 0900- 1700. **Canada**, Av Nações Unidas 12901, T5509 4343, spalo-immigration@ dfait-maeci.gc.ca. 0800-1100, 1500-1600, Fri 0800-0930, 1200-1300. **France**, Av Paulista 1842, 14th floor, T3371 5400, http://saopaulo. ambafrance-br.org. 0830-1200. **Germany**, Av Brigadeiro Faria Lima 2092, T3814 6644, info.saopaulo@alemanha.org.br. 0800-1130. **Italy**, Av Paulista 1963, T3549 5643, www.ital consul.org.br. **Israel**, Av Brig Faria Lima 1713, T3815 7788. **Japan**, Av Paulista 854, T287 0100, cgjsp@nethall.com.br. **Netherlands**, Av Brigadeiro Faria Lima 1779, T3811 3300, sao@minbuza.nl, 0900-1200. **New Zealand**, Av Campinas 579, 15th floor, T3148 0616, consuladonz@nzte.govt.nz, 0900-1300. **Norway and Sweden**, R Oscar Freire 379, 3rd floor, T883 3322 (Norway), 3061 1700 (Sweden), 0900-1300. **Paraguay**, R Bandeira Paulista 600, 15th floor, T3849 0455, 0830-1600. **Peru**, R Votuverava 350, T3819 1793, viceconsulperu@ originet.com.br. 0900-1300. **UK**, R Ferreira Araújo 741, 2nd floor, Pinheiros, T3094 2700, saopaulo@ gra-bretanha.org.br. **US**, R Henri Dunant 500, Chácara Santo Antônio, T5186 7000, www.consuladoamericanosp. org.br. 0800-1700. **Internet** Throughout the city, including in megastores. **Language courses** **Universidade de São Paulo (USP)** in the Cidade Universitária has courses available to foreigners, including a popular Portuguese course, registry is through the **Comissão de Cooperação Internacional**, R do Anfiteatro 181, Bloco das Colméias 05508, Cidade Universitária. **Medical services** **Hospital Samaritano**, R Conselheiro Brotero 1486, Higienópolis, T824 0022. Recommended. **Emergency and ambulance** T192, no charge. **Fire:** T193. **Post offices** Correio Central, Praça do Correio, corner Av São João and Prestes Máia. Booth adjoining tourist office on Praça da República, weekdays only 1000-1200, 1300-1600, for letters and small packages only. **UPS**, Brasinco, Alameda Jaú 1, 1725, 01420 São Paulo. **Federal Express**, Av São Luís 187, Galeria Metropole, loja 45, is reliable, also at Av das Nações Unidas 17891; **DHL**, Av Vereador José Diniz 2421. **Telephone** **Telefônica**, R 7 de Abril 295, near Praça da República; many other offices. **Embratel**, Av São Luís 50, and Av Ipiranga 344. For the international operator dial 000111; for international collect calls dial 000107. Red phone boxes are for national calls, blue ones for international phone calls. **Useful addresses** **Police: Deatur**, special tourist police, Av São Luís 91, T3120 3984; Guarulhos airport T6445 2686; Congonhas airport T5090 9032. **Radio Patrol**, T190. **Federal Police**, Av Prestes Maia 700, 1000-1600 for visa extensions.

São Paulo coast

On the coast there are fine beaches, although pollution is sometimes a problem. The further you go from the port of Santos, the more unspoilt the beaches become, with some areas of special natural interest.

Santos → *Phone code: 0xx13. Post code: 11000. Colour map 7, C4. Population: 417,983.*
Santos, on an island about 5 km from the open sea, is the most important Brazilian port. Over 40% by value of all Brazilian imports and about half the total exports pass through it. Santos is also a holiday resort with magnificent beaches and views. The scenery on the routes crossing the Serra do Mar is superb. The roadway includes many bridges and tunnels. From Rio the direct highway, the Linha Verde (see pages 442 and 469) is also wonderful for scenery. The port is approached by the winding Santos Channel; at its mouth is an old fort (1709). The centre of the city, on the north side of the island, is being renovated. Due south, on the Baía de Santos, is **Gonzaga**, where hotels and bars line the beachfront. Between these two areas, the eastern end of the island curves round within the Santos Channel. **Tourist offices** ⓘ *at the rodoviária, T3219 2194, Ponta da Praia, T3236 9996, and Orquidário Municipal (limited opening); information by phone T0800-173887.*

Sights The best way get around the centre of Santos is by the newly restored Victorian trams which leave on guided tours from in front of the Prefeitura Municipal on Praça Visconde de Mauá. The tram passes in front of most of the interesting sights, including the *azulejo*-covered houses on Rua do Comércio. The streets around **Praça Mauá** are very busy in the daytime. **Museu do Café** ⓘ *R 15 de Novembro 95, T3219 5585, www.museudocafe.com.br, Tue-Sat 0900-1700, Sun 1000-1700*. The old Bolsa Oficial de Café was closed to all but rich men up until the mid-20th century, but is now a delightful museum, with large wall paintings by Benedito Calixto and a very impressive art deco stained-glass ceiling. Upstairs is a small but very well-presented collection of displays. The lobby café serves some of the best coffee in Brazil. Two churches in the centre are **Santo Antônio do Valongo** (17th century, but restored), which is by the railway station on Largo Monte Alegre, and the **Capela da Ordem Terceira de Nossa Senhora do Carmo** (1760, also later restored), Praça Barão do Rio Branco. **Fundação Pinacoteca** ⓘ *Av Bartolomeu de Gusmão 15, T3288 2260, www.pinacoteca.unisanta.br, Tue-Sun 1400-1900, free*, features a large collection of ecclesiastical paintings and landscapes by one of Brazil's most distinguished early 19th-century artists.

At **Santos Football Stadium and Museum** ⓘ *Princesa Isabel 77, Vila Belmiro, T3257 4000, www.santosfc.com.br*, the ground floor houses a collection of trophies and photographs chronicling the history of Pele's club, including several cabinets devoted to him and containing his shirts, boots and other memorabilia. **Monte Serrat**, just south of the city centre, has at its summit a semaphore station and look-out post which reports the arrival of all ships in Santos harbour. There is also a church, dedicated to Nossa Senhora da Monte Serrat. The top can be reached on foot or by **funicular** (every 30 minutes, US$8). **Museu do Mar** ⓘ *R República do Equador 81*, is in the eastern part of the city; with a collection that includes several thousand shells. In the western district of José Menino is the **Orquidário Municipal** ⓘ *daily 0800-1745, bird enclosure 0800-1100, 1400-1700, US$1*, the municipal orchid gardens, in the **Praça Washington**. The flowers bloom October to February; the orchid show is in November.

The **Ilha Porchat**, a small island reached by a bridge at the far end of Santos/São Vicente bay, has beautiful views of the high seas on one side and of the city and bay on the other. The lookout was designed by Oscar Niemeyer and, in summer, there is lively nightlife here.

Itatinga, 30 km from Santos in the Serra do Mar, has remnants of Atlantic forest, mangrove and sandbanks. The area is full of wildlife. There are trails graded according to difficulty. Visitors go with one of the travel agencies officially permitted to lead groups: contact the tourism office (see above). Access is either via the village of Itatinga by boat, three hours, then by street car. Or take the BR-101 (Santos-Rio) road, a three-minute crossing by boat and then 7½ km by street car.

São Sebastião → *Phone code: 0xx12. Post code: 11600. Colour map 7, B4. Population: 58,038.*
East of Santos, a vehicle ferry (free for pedestrians) crosses from Ponta da Praia to **Guarujá**, from where a road (SP-061) runs to **Bertioga**. The coastal road beyond Bertioga is paved, and the Rio-Santos highway, 1-2 km inland, provides a good link to São Sebastião. Beyond Praia Boracéia are a number of beaches, including **Camburi**, surrounded by the Mata Atlântica, into which you can walk on the Estrada do Piavu (bathing in the streams is permitted, but use of shampoo is forbidden). There are several good hotels and restaurants in Camburi and at Praia de Boracéia. The road carries on from Camburi, past clean beach **Maresias**, a fashionable place for surfers.

From Maresias it is 21 km to São Sebastião. There are 21 good beaches and an adequate, but not overdeveloped, tourist infrastructure. The natural attractions of the area include many small islands offshore and a large portion of the **Parque Estadual da Serra do Mar** on the mainland, with other areas protected for their ecosystems. There are forest trails and old sugar plantations. In the colonial centre is **Museu de Arte Sacra** ⓘ *R Sebastião Neves 90*, in the 17th-century chapel of São Gonçalo. The town's parish church on Praça Major João Fernandes dates from the early 17th century and rebuilt in 1819. There is a **Museu do Naufrágio** near the church (free) exhibiting shipwrecks and natural history of the local area. **Tourist office** ⓘ *Av Dr Altino Arantes 174, T4522 1808.*

The beaches within 2-3 km of São Sebastião harbour are polluted; others to the south and north are clean. Ilhabela is expensive in season, when it is cheaper to stay in São Sebastião.

Ilhabela → *Phone code: 0xx12. Pop: 20,836; rising to 100,000 in high season.*
The island of São Sebastião, known popularly as Ilhabela, is of volcanic origin, roughly 390 sq km in area. The four highest peaks are Morro de São Sebastião, 1,379 m, Morro do Papagaio, 1,309 m, Ramalho, 1,205 m, and Pico Baepi, 1,025 m. All are often obscured by mist. Rainfall on the island is heavy, about 3,000 mm a year. The slopes are densely wooded and 80% of the forest is protected by the Parque Estadual de Ilhabela. The only settled district lies on the coastal strip facing the mainland, the Atlantic side being practically uninhabited except by a few fisherfolk. The island abounds with tropical plants, flowers, and wild fruits, whose juice mixed with *cachaça* and sugar makes a delicious cocktail. The terraced **Cachoeira da Toca** ⓘ *US$4, includes insect repellent*, waterfalls amid dense jungle close to the foot of the Baepi peak give cool freshwater bathing; lots of butterflies. You can walk on a signed path, or go by car; it's a few kilometres from the ferry dock. The locals claim there are over 300 waterfalls on the island, but only a few can be reached on foot. In all shady places, especially away from the sea, there thrives a species of midge known locally as *borrachudo*. A locally sold repellent (Autan) keeps them off for some time, but those allergic to insect bites should remain on the inhabited coastal strip. There is a small hospital (helpful) by the church in town. **Secretaria Municipal de Turismo** ⓘ *R Bartolomeu de Gusmão 140, Pequeá, T3896 2440, www.ilhabela.com.br.*

No alterations are allowed to the frontage of the main township, **Ilhabela**. It is very popular during summer weekends, when it is difficult to find space for a car on the ferry. It is, however, a nice place to relax on the beach, with good food and some good value accommodation.

Visit the old **Feiticeira** plantation, with underground dungeons. The road is along the coast, sometimes high above the sea, towards the south of the island (11 km from the town). You can go by bus, taxi, or horse and buggy. A trail leads down from the fazenda to the beautiful beach of the same name. Another old fazenda is **Engenho d'Água**, which is nearer to the town, which gives its name to one of the busiest beaches (the fazenda is not open to the public).

Beaches and watersports On the mainland side the beaches 3-4 km either side of the town are polluted: look out for oil, sandflies and jellyfish on the sand and in the water. There are some three dozen beaches around Ilhabela, only about 12 of them away from the coast facing the mainland. **Praia dos Castelhanos**, reached by the rough road over the island to the Atlantic side (no buses), is recommended. Several of the ocean beaches can only be reached by boat. The island is considered the **Capital da Vela** (of sailing) because its 150 km of coastline offers all types of conditions. There is also plenty of adventure for divers.

Rodeo Romeos

Some 422 km northwest of São Paulo and 115 km northwest of the city of Ribeirão Preto, is Barretos, where, in the third week in August, the Festa do Peão Boiadeiro is held. This is the biggest annual rodeo in the world. The town is taken over as 600,000 fans come to watch the horsemanship, enjoy the concerts, eat, drink and shop in what has become the epitome of Brazilian cowboy culture. Tours from the UK are run by Last Frontiers, see page 49.

Ubatuba → *Phone code: 0xx12. Post code: 11680. Colour map 7, B4. Population: 66,861.*
This is one of the most beautiful stretches of the São Paulo coast with a whole range of watersports on offer. In all, there are 72 beaches, some large, some small, some in coves, some on islands. They are spread out over a wide area, so if you are staying in Ubatuba town, you need to use the buses which go to most of them. The commercial centre of Ubatuba is at the northern end of the bay. Here are shops, banks, services, lots of restaurants (most serving pizza and fish), but few hotels. These are on the beaches north and south and can be reached from the Costamar bus terminal. **Comtur tourist office** ⓘ *Av Iperoig opposite R Profesor Thomaz Galhardo, T0800-771 7400; www.ubatuba.com.br*, is very helpful.

Saco da Ribeira, 13 km south, is a natural harbour which has been made into a yacht marina. Schooners leave from here for excursions to **Ilha Anchieta** (or dos Porcos), a popular four-hour trip. On the island are beaches, trails and a prison, which was in commission from 1908-1952. Agencies run schooner trips to Ilha Anchieta and elsewhere. Trips leave Saco da Ribeira at 1000, returning 1500, four-hour journey, US$26 per person. A six-hour trip can be made from Praia Itaguá, but in winter there is a cold wind off the sea in the afternoon, same price. The Costamar bus from Ubatuba to Saco da Ribeira (every 20 minutes, 30 minutes, US$1.50) drops you at the turn-off by the Restaurante Pizzaria Malibu.

Straddling the border of São Paulo and Rio de Janeiro states is the **Parque Nacional Serra da Bocaina** ⓘ *permission to visit must be obtained in advance from ICMBio, T0xx12-3117 2183/88 in São José do Barreiro, the nearest town*. It rises from the coast to its highest point at Pico do Tira (or Chapéu) at 2,200 m, encompassing three strata of vegetation.

Southwest from Santos → *Phone code: 0xx13.*
Itanhaém, 61 km from Santos, has a pretty colonial church of Sant'Ana (1761), Praça Narciso de Andrade, and the Convento da Nossa Senhora da Conceição (1699-1713, originally founded 1554), on a small hill. There are several good seafood restaurants along the beach, hotels and camping. There are more beaches 31 km south of Itanhaém at **Peruíbe**, where the climate is said to be unusually healthy owing to a high concentration of ozone in the air. Local rivers have water and black mud which has been proven to contain medicinal properties. There are plenty of places to stay and to eat in Peruíbe (none close to the bus station, some close out-of-season). Peruíbe marks the northernmost point of the **Estação Ecológico Juréia-Itatins** ⓘ *contact the Instituto Florestal, Estrada do Guaraú 4164, CEP 11750-000, Peruíbe, T0xx13-3457 9243, eeji@uol.com.br, for permission to visit the ecological station, www.iflorestsp.br/jureia.htm*. The station was founded in 1986 and protects 820 sq km of Mata Atlântica, "as it was when the Portuguese arrived in Brazil". The four main ecosystems are restinga, mangrove, Mata Atlântica and the vegetation at 900 m on the Juréia mountain range.

Iguape → *Phone code: 0xx13. Colour map 7, C3. Population: 27,427.*
At the southern end of Juréia-Itatins is the town of Iguape founded in 1538. Typical of Portuguese architecture, the small **Museu Histórico e Arqueológico** ⓘ *R das Neves 45, Tue-Sun 0900-1730*, is housed in the 17th-century Casa da Oficina Real de Fundição. There is also a **Museu de Arte Sacra** ⓘ *Sat-Sun 0900-1200, 1330-1700*, in the former Igreja do Rosário, Praça Rotary. **Tourist office** ⓘ *9 de Julho 63, T3841 3358.*

Opposite Iguape is the northern end of the **Ilha Comprida** with 86 km of beaches (some dirty and disappointing). This **Área de Proteção Ambiental** ⓘ *the ICMBio office of the Area de Proteção Ambiental Cananéia-Iguape-Peruíbe is at R da Saúde s/n, Canto do Morro, Iguape, T3841 2388, www.icmbio.gov.br/apacip*, is not much higher than sea level and is divided from the mainland by the Canal do Mar Pequeno. The northern end is the busiest and on the island there are good restaurants, hotels, supermarkets – fresh fish is excellent. There is also accommodation.

Cananéia and Ilha do Cardoso → *Colour map 7, C3. Population: 12,298.*
At the southern end of Ilha Comprida, across the channel, is Cananéia, 270 km from São Paulo. The colonial centre, around Praça Martim Afonso de Souza and neighbouring streets, contains the 17th-century church of **São João Batista** and the **Museu Municipal**. To the south are good beaches. For guides, contact Manoel Barroso, Avenida Independencia 65, T013-3851 1273, Portuguese only. Recommended. Cananéia has several hotels, starting in price range **B**.

For the densely wooded Ilha do Cardoso, a protected area, take a ferry from the dock at Cananéia, four hours, three daily (T3851 1268). Or drive 70 km along an unpaved road, impassable when wet, to **Ariri**, 10 minutes by boat to the island. The tiny village of Marujá, no electricity, has rustic pousadas and restaurants. There is camping and idyllic beaches; best for surfing is Moretinho.

São Paulo coast listings

For Sleeping and Eating price codes and other relevant information, see Essentials, pages 38-40.

Sleeping

Santos *p468*
Many beachfront hotels on Av Pres Wilson, cheap hotels are near the Orquidário Municipal (Praça Washington), 1-2 blocks from the beach.
AL Atlântico, No 1, T3289 4500, www.atlantico-hotel.com.br. Good, a/c, sauna, restaurant, bar.
B Hotel Natal, Av Marechal Floriano Peixoto 104, T3284 2732, www.hotelnatal.com.br. Safe, comfortable, with cable TV, fridge, full breakfast.

Ilhabela *p469*
Several in the **L-AL** range and some in the **A-B** range, mostly on the road to the left of the ferry.
AL Ilhabela, Av Pedro Paulo de Morais 151, T3896 1083, www.hotelilhabela.com.br. Family-oriented, gym, pool, good breakfast. Recommended.
A Pousada dos Hibiscos, Av Pedro Paulo de Morais 714, T3896 1375, www.pousadadoshibiscos.com.br. Good atmosphere, swimming pool. Recommended.
A Vila das Pedras, R Antenor Custódio da Silva 46, Cocaia, T3896 2433, www.viladaspedras.com.br. 11 chalets in a forest garden, tastefully decorated, nice pool.
C Estância das Bromélias Pousada, Av Col José Vicente Faria Lima 1243, Perequê, T3896 3353, www.estanciadasbromelias.com.br. Welcoming, chalets for 5, great breakfast, garden, pool, horse riding and jeep excursions, very good.
Camping Pedras do Sino, at Perequê, near ferry dock, and at Praia Grande, 11 km south.

Ubatuba *p470*
At all holiday times it is expensive, with no hotel less than US$30. On many of the beaches there are hotels and pousadas, ranging from luxury resorts to more humble establishments.
AL Saveiros, R Lucian Strass 65, Praia do Lázaro, 14 km from town, T3842 0172, www.hotelsaveiros.com.br. Pretty *pousada* with pool, restaurant, English spoken.
A São Charbel, Praça Nóbrega 280, T3832 1090, www.saocharbel.com.br. Helpful, comfortable, a/c, TV, restaurant, bar, swimming pool, etc.
A São Nicolau, R Conceição 213, T/F3832 5007. Good, TV, fridge, good breakfast.
A Xaréu, R Jordão Homem da Costa 413, T/F3832 1525. Pleasant, quiet. Recommended.
D Pousada Taiwan, R Felix Guisard Filho 60, T3832 6448. Fan or a/c, with breakfast, TV, fridge.
E-F J S Brandão, R Nestor Fonseca 173, Jardim Sumaré, CEP 11880-000, T3832 2337. 0700-2300, near the Tropic of Capricorn sign south of town.
E-F Cora Coralina, Rodovia Oswaldo Cruz, Km 89, T011-258 0388. 0800-2300, near Horto Florestal.
Camping There are about 10 sites in the vicinity, including 2 **Camping Clube do Brasil**

sites at Lagoinha (25 km from town) and Praia Perequê-Açu, 2 km north.

Iguape *p470*

B-C Solar Colonial Pousada, Praça da Basílica 30, T3841 1591. A range of rooms in a converted 19th-century house.

Camping At Praia da Barra da Ribeira, 20 km north. Wild camping is possible at Praia de Juréia, the gateway to the ecological station.

Activities and tours

Ubatuba *p470*

Companies offer trekking tours graded according to difficulty lasting from 2 hrs to 2 days. More details from the guide association, T9141 3692.

Transport

Santos *p468*

Bus In Santos US$1; to **São Vicente**, US$2. To **São Paulo** (50 mins, US$7.75) every 15 mins, from the rodoviária near the city centre, José Menino or Ponta da Praia (opposite the ferry to Guarujá). (The 2 highways between São Paulo and Santos can get very crowded, especially at rush hours and weekends.) To **Guarulhos/ Cumbica airport**, **Expresso Brasileiro** 3-4 daily, US$10, allow plenty of time as the bus goes through Guarulhos, 3 hrs. **TransLitoral** from Santos to **Congonhas airport** then to **Guarulhos/ Cumbica**, 4 daily, US$15.50, 2 hrs. To **Rio** (**Normandy** company), several daily, 7½ hrs, US$50; to Rio along the coast road is via São Sebastião (US$14.50, change buses if necessary), Caraguatatuba and Ubatuba.

Taxi All taxis have meters. The fare from Gonzaga to the bus station is about US$10.

São Sebastião *p469*

Bus 2 buses a day from **Rio** with **Normandy**, 0830 and 2300 (plus 1630 on Fri and Sun), to Rio 0600 and 2330, heavily booked in advance, US$27 (US$10 from Paraty); 4 a day from **Santos**, 4 hrs, US$14.50; 4 **Litorânea** buses a day also from **São Paulo**, US$18, which run inland via São José dos Campos, unless you ask for the service via Bertioga, only 2 a day (bus to Bertioga US$7.50). Daily buses from São Paulo to **Camburi**, 160 km, en route to São Sebastiâo/ Ilhabela, US$7.75.

Ilhabela *p469*

Bus A bus runs along the coast. **Litorânea** from **São Paulo** connects with a service right through to Ilhabela; office in Ilhabela at R Dr Carvalho 136.

Ferry At weekends and holidays the 15-20 min ferry between São Sebastião and Perequê runs non-stop day and night. During the week it does not sail 0130-0430. Free for foot passengers; cars US$15 weekdays, US$23 at weekends.

Ubatuba *p470*

Bus There are 3 bus terminals: 1) Rodoviária Costamar, R Hans Staden e R Conceição, serves all local destinations; 2) Rodoviária at R Profesor Thomaz Galhardo 513 for São José buses to Paraty, US$5, Normandy services (to Rio, US$20) and some **Itapemirim** buses; 3) Rodoviária Litorânea, the main bus station: go up Conceição for 8 blocks from Praça 13 de Maio, turn right on R Rio Grande do Sul, then left into R Dra Maria V Jean. Buses from here go to **São Paulo**, 3½ hrs, US$16.50.

Taxi In town are a rip-off, for example US$10 from the centre to the main bus terminal.

Iguape *p470*

Bus To Iguape: from **São Paulo, Santos**, or **Curitiba**, changing at Registro.

Ferry A continuous ferry service runs from Iguape to **Ilha Comprida** (free but small charge for cars); buses run until 1900 from the ferry stop to the beaches. From Iguape it is possible to take a boat trip down the coast to **Cananéia** and **Ariri**. Tickets and information from **Dpto Hidroviário do Estado**, R Major Moutinho 198, Iguape. It is a beautiful trip, passing between the island and the mainland.

Directory

Santos *p468*

Consulates **Britain**, R Tuiuti 58, 2nd floor, T3094 2700, hc.santos@fco.gov.uk. **Post office** Main post office at R Cidale de Toledo 41, Centro, also at R Tolentino Filgueiras 70, Gonzaga. **Telephone** **International calls:** can be made at R Galeão Carvalhal 45, Gonzaga.

Ubatuba *p470*

Internet **Chat and Bar**, Ubatuba Shopping, US$3 per hr. **Post office** R Dona Maria Alves between Hans Staden and R Col Dominicano. **Telephone** **Telesp**, Galhardo, close to Sérgio restaurant.

Minas Gerais and Espírito Santo

Minas Gerais was once described as having a heart of gold and a breast of iron. Half the mineral production of Brazil comes from the state, including most of the iron ore. Minas Gerais also produces 95% of all Brazil's gemstones. All this mineral wealth has left the state a legacy of sumptuous colonial cities built on gold and diamond mining. Streets of whitewashed 18th-century houses with deep blue or yellow window frames line steep and winding streets leading to lavishly decorated churches with rich gilt interiors. The colonial gold mining towns of Minas Gerais are the highlights of any visit. There are also other attractions: rugged national parks, which are great for trekking, lots of festivals and a famous cuisine, the comida mineira. The state of Minas Gerais, larger than France, is mountainous in the south, rising to the 2,787 m peak of Agulhas Negras in the Mantiqueira range, and in the east, where there is the Parque Nacional Caparaó containing the Pico da Bandeira (2,890 m). The capital, Belo Horizonte is culturally very active. From Belo Horizonte north are undulating grazing lands, the richest of which are in the extreme west: a broad wedge of country between Goiás in the north and São Paulo in the south, known as the Triângulo Mineiro. The coastal state of Espírito Santo is where mineiros head to for their seaside holidays. The most popular beaches are south of Vitória, the state capital, while north of the city are several turtle-nesting beaches. Inland are immigrant towns.

Belo Horizonte → *Phone code: 0xx31. Post code: 30000. Colour map 7, B5.*

Belo Horizonte (*Population: 4.8 million; Altitude: 800 m*) is surrounded by mountains and enjoys an excellent climate (16°-30°C) except for the rainy season (December-March). It was founded on 12 December 1897 and is one of Brazil's fastest growing cities, now suffering from atmospheric pollution. The third largest city in Brazil is a hilly city with streets that rise and fall and trees lining many of the central avenues. The large **Parque Municipal** is an oasis of green in the heart of downtown; closed at night and on Monday, except for a small section in the southwest corner (the Parque Municipal is not too safe, so it's best not to go alone). The main commercial district is around Avenida Afonso Pena; at night the movimento shifts to Savassi, southwest of the centre, where all the good eating places are.

Ins and outs

Tourist offices The municipal information is **Belotur** ⓘ *R Pernambuco 284, Funciários, T3277 9797, belotur@pbh.gov.br*. Very helpful, with lots of useful information and maps. The monthly *Guia Turístico* for events, opening times, etc, is freely available. Belotur has offices also at the southwest corner of Parque Municipal, at Confins and Pampulha airports, and at the rodoviária (particularly polyglot). See also www.guiabh.com.br. **Setur** ⓘ *Praça da Liberdade, Prédio Verde, 2 andar, T3270 8501, www.turismo. mg.gov.br*. The tourism authority for the state of Minas Gerais is helpful.

Sights

The principal building in the Parque Municipal is the **Palácio das Artes** ⓘ *Afonso Pena 1537, T3237 7234, 1000-2200, Sun 1400-2200*, which contains the **Centro de Artesanato Mineiro** (with craft shop), an exhibition of painting in Minas Gerais, a cinema, three theatres and temporary exhibitions. On the stretch of Avenida Afonso Pena outside the Parque Municipal an open-air market operates each Sunday (0800-1430). The avenue is transformed by thousands of coloured awnings covering stalls selling every conceivable type of local handicraft. Six blocks up Avenida João Pinheiro from Avenida Afonso Pena is the **Praça da Liberdade**, which is surrounded by fine public buildings, some in eclectic, fin-de-siècle-style, others more recent. At the end of the Praça is the **Palácio da Liberdade** ⓘ *Sun 0900-1800 only*. The Praça itself is very attractive, with trees, flowers, fountains which are lit at night and joggers and walkers making the most of the paths. The **railway station**, with a museum on the second floor showing a model railway, is part of a complex that includes buildings dating from the 1920s around the **Praça da Estação** (also called Praça Rui Barbosa).

Museu Mineiro ⓘ *Av João Pinheiro 342, T3269 1168, Tue-Fri 1230-1830, Sat-Sun 1000-1600, houses religious and other art. Museu Histórico Abílio Barreto i Av Prudente de Morais 202, Cidade Jardim, T3296 3896, bus 2902 from Av Afonso Pena*, in an old fazenda, is the last reminder of Belo Horizonte's predecessor, the village of **Arraial do Curral d'el Rey**. It has historical exhibits. **Jardim Botânico e Museu de História Natural** ⓘ *Instituto Agronómico, R Gustavo da Silveira 1035, Cidade Nova, T3461 7516, www.ufmg.br/mhnjb, Tue-Fri 0800-1130, 1300-1700, Sat-Sun 1000-1700 (bus 8001)*, has geological, palaeontological and archaeological displays.

About 8 km northwest from the centre is the picturesque suburb of **Pampulha**, famous for its modern buildings and the artificial lake, created in the 1930s by Brasilia architect Oscar

1 Belo Horizonte & Pampulha

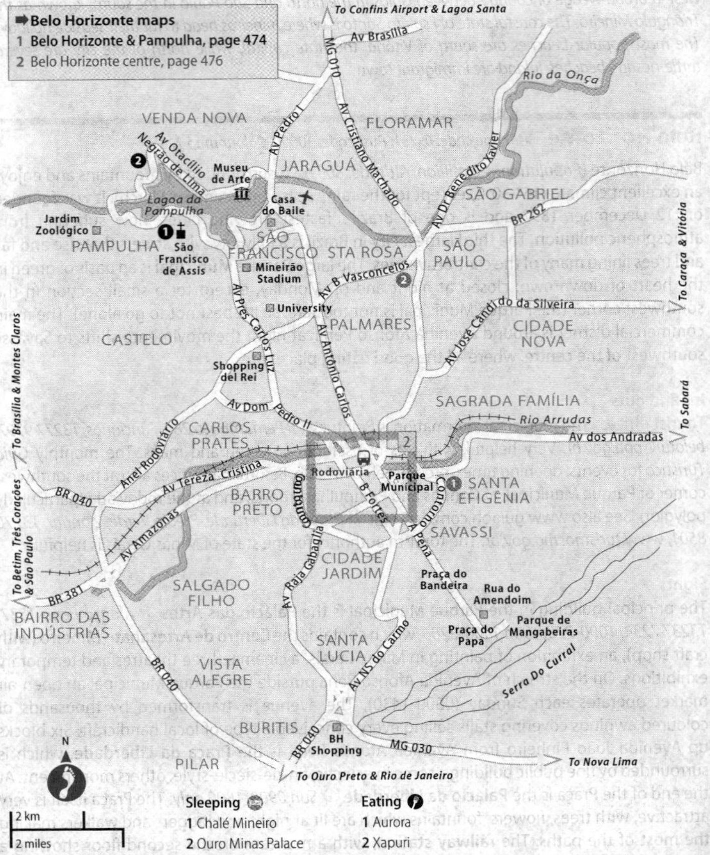

Niemeyer and landscaped by Roberto Burle Marx. The **Igreja São Francisco de Assis** ⓘ *Av Otacílio Negrão de Lima Km 12, T3441 9325*, was inaugurated in 1943. The painter Cândido Portinari installed beautiful blue and white tiles depicting Saint Francis' life on the exterior. On the wall behind the altar is a powerful composition also by Portinari. On the opposite shore is the glass and marble **Museu de Arte de Pampulha** (MAP) ⓘ *Av Octacílio Negrão de Lima 16585, T3443 4533, Tue-Sun 0900-1900, free*. It has a fine collection of modern art from Minas Gerais. The **Casa do Baile** ⓘ *Av Octacílio Negrão de Lima 751, T3277 7433, Tue-Sun 0900-1900, free*, is a perfect example of Niemeyer's fascination with the curved line. Just south of the lake is the **Mineirão** football stadium, about 750 m away. This is the second largest stadium in Brazil after the Maracanã stadium in Rio. Seats cost between US$4 and US$9.

In the southern zone of the city, just 3 km from the central area, the **Parque de Mangabeiras** ⓘ *Thu-Sun 0800-1800, is on the Serra do Curral at between 1,000 m and 1,400 m above sea level*. There are good views of the city, especially from the Mirante da Mata. Three forest trails have been laid out.

Belo Horizonte listings

For Sleeping and Eating price codes and other relevant information, see Essentials, pages 38-40.

Sleeping

Belo Horizonte *p473, maps p474 and p476*

You may spend the night in the rodoviária only if you have an onward ticket (police check at 2400). There are cheaper options near the rodoviária and in R Curitiba, but many of these hotels are not used for sleeping in. You will have a more comfortable stay in one of the youth hostels.

LL Ouro Minas Palace, Av Cristiano Machado 4001, T3429 4001 (toll free 0800-314000), www.ourominas.com.br. The most luxurious hotel in the city with palatial suites, including several for women-only on the top floors, excellent service, pool, sauna, gym, excellent business facilities, not central but within easy reach of the centre and airports.

L Grandarrell Minas, R Espírito Santo 901, T3248 0000, www.grandarrell.com.br. One of the best business hotels in the centre, full business facilities including fax and email modems in rooms, rooftop pool, not much English spoken.

L Liberty Palace, R Paraíba 1465, Savassi, T2121 0900, www.libertypalace.com.br. Business hotel in the Savassi restaurant district, standard rooms with spacious bathrooms, 24-hr room service, IDSL in all rooms and a well-appointed business centre.

L-AL Othon Palace, Av Afonso Pena 1050, T2126 0000, www.hoteis-othon.com.br. 1980s hotel, glass-fronted, excellent, safe, good restaurant, pool, helpful staff, lower floors can be noisy.

AL Le Flamboyant, R Rio Grande do Norte 1007, Savassi, T3261 7370, www.clan.com.br. Well-maintained flats with separate sitting room, TV, kitchen, pool. Some flats have two bedrooms.

A Villa Emma, R Arturo Toscanini 41, Savassi, T32823388, www.clan.com.br. The cheapest option in Savassi, spacious flats in need of a lick of paint, with 2 bedrooms, separate living area and kitchen. Internet access in some rooms.

B Esplanada, Av Santos Dumont 304, T3273 5311. An upmarket cheapie with bright rooms with en-suites, soap and towels, generous breakfasts and triples available for little more than doubles. Prices are negotiable.

D Continental, Av Paraná 241, T3201 7944. Central, quieter interior rooms. Recommended.

D São Salvador, R Espírito Santo 227, T3222 7731. Small, the best rooms are the triples with en suites, reasonable breakfast. One of many similar cheapies in the area.

D-E pp **Chalé Mineiro**, R Santa Luzia 288, Santa Efigênia, T3467 1576, www.chalemineiro hostel.com.br. Attractive, HI affiliated, with a small pool, dorms, a shared kitchen, TV lounge and telephones. Towels and bed linen are extra.

F pp **O Sorriso do Lagarto**, R Padre Severino 285, Savassi, T3283 9325, www.osorrisodo lagarto.com.br. Simple, small hostel in a converted town house with kitchen, internet, breakfast, lockers, washing machines and a living area with DVD player.

F pp **Pousadinha Mineira**, R Espírito Santo 604, Centro, T3273 8156, www.pousadinhamineira. com.br. Large central hostel with separate men's and women's wings, shared bath, breakfast extra, take your own bed linen.

Eating

Belo Horizonte *p473, maps p474 and p476*
Mineiros love their food and drink and Belo Horizonte has a lively café dining and bar scene. Savassi overflows with street cafés, bars and restaurants and is the best place in the city for a food browse. There is a lively, cheap food market on R Tomé de Souza, between Pernambuco and Alagoas, in Savassi every night between 1900 and 2300. Pampulha has the best of the fine dining restaurants; which are well worth the taxi ride. And there are plenty of cheap per kilo restaurants and *padarias* near the budget hotels in the city centre.

Aurora, R Expedicionário Mário Alves de Oliveira 421, São Luís, T3498 7567. One of the

2 Belo Horizonte centre

Belo Horizonte maps
1 Belo Horizonte & Pampulha, page 474
2 Belo Horizonte centre, page 476

Sleeping
1 Chalé Mineiro
2 Continental
3 Esplanada
4 Grandarrell Minas
5 Le Flamboyant
6 Liberty Palace
7 O Sorriso do Lagarto
8 Othon Palace
9 Pousadinha Mineira
10 São Salvador
11 Villa Emma

Eating
1 A Cafeteria
2 Café da Travessa
3 Café Tina
4 Chico Mineiro
5 Dona Derna
6 Dona Lucinha
7 Flor de Líbano
8 Kauhana
9 La Traviata
10 Sushi Beer
11 Sushi Naka
12 Taste Vin
13 Vecchio Sogno

Bars & clubs
14 de James
15 de João
16 Koyote

best restaurants in town, garden setting next to Lago da Pampulha. Imaginative menu fusing Mineira and Italian techniques and making use of unusual Brazilian fruits. Closed Mon-Tue.

𝕐𝕐𝕐 **Taste Vin**, R Curitiba 2105, Lourdes, T3292 5423. Excellent French, soufflés and provençale seafood. The wine list includes decent Brazilian options. Recommended.

𝕐𝕐𝕐 **Vecchio Sogno**, R Martim de Carvalho 75 and R Dias Adorno, Santo Agostinho, under the Assembléia Legislativo, T3292 5251. The best Italian in the city with an inventive menu fusing Italian and French cuisine with Brazilian ingredients, excellent fish. Lunch only on Sun.

𝕐𝕐𝕐-𝕐𝕐 **Xapuri**, R Mandacaru 260, Pampulha, T3496 6198. Great atmosphere, live music, very good food, a bit out of the way but recommended. Closed Mon.

𝕐𝕐 **Chico Mineiro**, R Alagoas 626, corner of Av Brasil, T3261 3237. Good local chicken specialities, lunchtime only except till 0100 at weekends.

𝕐𝕐 **Dona Derna**, R Tomé de Souza 1380, Savassi, T3223 6954. A range of restaurants in one. Upstairs is Italian fine dining with excellent dishes and a respectable wine list. Downstairs on weekdays is traditional Italian home cooking and by night a chic pizzeria called Memmo.

𝕐𝕐 **Sushi Naka**, R Gonçalves Dias 92, Funcionários, T3287 2714. Japanese, excellent sushi, sashimi and soups. Close to the centre.

𝕐𝕐-𝕐 **La Traviata**, Av Cristovão Colombo 282, Savassi, T3261 6392. A little moody Italian with terrace, strong on meat and fish, reasonable pasta and pizzas, good value house wine.

𝕐𝕐-𝕐 **Sushi Beer**, R Tomé de Souza, Savassi, T3221 1116. A large open air dining area overlooked by a long bar, superior per kilo Minas and Japanese food, plus meats and pizzas.

𝕐 **Dona Lucinha**, R Sergipe 811, Savassi, T3261 5930 and R Padre Odorico 38 (São Pedro), T3227 0562. Self service, decent meat dishes, generous portions. Lunch only on Sun. Recommended.

𝕐 **Flor de Líbano**, R Espírito Santo 234. Very cheap and good.

𝕐 **Kauhana**, R Tomé de Souza, Savassi, T3284 8714. Tasty wood-fire cooked pizzas both savoury and sweet, pleasant open-air dining area.

𝕐 **Mala e Cuia**, a chain of restaurants serving good *comida mineira* at R Gonçalves Dias 874, Savassi, T3261 3059, Av Antônio Carlos 8305, Pampulha, T3441 2993, Av Raja Gabaglia 1617, São Bento.

Cafés

A Cafeteria, Av Cristovão Colombo 152, Savassi, T3223 9901. Salads, great sandwiches in pitta bread and a range of mock-Italian standards served to a young crowd and accompanied by live music most nights. One of several such café bars on the corner of Colombo and Albuquerque.

Café da Travessa, Getúlio Vargas 1405 at Praça Savassi, T3223 8092. Great little café cum book and CD shop. Dishes range from rosti to Brazilian tapas, pasta and wraps, pizzas upstairs, great coffee. From breakfast until late.

Café Tina, Av Cristovão Colombo 336, Savassi, T3261 5068. Bohemian café serving soups, risottos and delicious puddings to an arty crowd. Closed Mon.

Bars and clubs

Belo Horizonte *p473, maps p474 and p476*

Rua Tomé de Souza in Savassi has umpteen lively bars, particularly between Paraíba and Sergipe. The beer and caipirinhas are cheap and plentiful. Try **Bar de João**, **Bar de James**, or **Bar Koyote**.

Alambique, Av Raja Gabáglia 3200, Chalé 1D, Estoril, T3296 7188. Specializes in cachaça, with mineira appetizers, designed like a country house.

Festivals and events

Belo Horizonte *p473, maps p474 and p476*

The city celebrates **Maundy Thursday**; Corpus Christi; **15 Aug**, **Assunção** (Assumption); **8 Dec**, **Conceição** (Immaculate Conception).

Shopping

Belo Horizonte *p473, maps p474 and p476*

Gemstones **Manoel Bernardes**, Av Contorno 5417, Savassi. Very reasonable.

Markets See above for the Sun **handicraft fair** on Av Afonso Pena. **Mercado Central**, Av Augusto de Lima 744. Large and clean, open every day.

Activities and tours

Belo Horizonte *p473, maps p474 and p476*

For information on the cultural and adventure tourism possibilities on the **Estrada Real**, the colonial gold and diamond roads from Minas Gerais to Paraty and Rio de Janeiro, go to the head office at R Álvares Maciel 59, 11th floor, Santa Efigênia, T3241 7166.

Ametur, R Alvarengo Peixoto 295, loja 102, Lourdes, T/F3292 2139. Open 0900-1200, 1400-1900, has information on fazendas which welcome visitors and overnight guests.
Amo-Te, Associação Mineira dos Organizadores do Turismo Ecológico, R Monte Verde 125, Alípio de Melo, T3477 5430, oversees ecotourism in Minas Gerais. For companies which arrange trekking, riding, cycling, rafting, jeep tours, canyoning, visiting national parks, or fazendas, speak to Amo-Te in the first instance.
Master Turismo (Amex representative), R da Bahia 2140, T3330 3655, www.masterturismo.com.br. At Sala VIP, Aeroporto de Confins, and Av Afonso Pena 1967, T3330 3603 (very helpful). Runs 10-day/9-night tours on the Estrada Real (see above).
Oasis Turismo, A de Lima 479/815, Centro, T3274 6422. Very helpful, manager Jacqueline.
Ouro Preto Turismo, Av Afonso Pena 4133, T3287 0505, www.ouropretotour.com.
Revetur, R Espírito Santo 1892, 1st floor, Lourdes, T3337 2500, www.revetour.com.br.
Tropa Serrana, Tullio Marques Lopes Filho, T3344 8986, http://tropaserrana.zip.net. For recommended horse riding tours.

Transport

Belo Horizonte *p473, maps p474 and p476*

Air The international airport is near Lagoa Santa, at Confins, 39 km from Belo Horizonte, T3689 2700. Taxi to centre, US$55, cooperative taxis have fixed rates to different parts of the city. Airport bus, either *executivo* from the exit, US$15, or comfortable normal bus (Unir) from the far end of the car park hourly, US$2.75, both go to/from the rodoviária.

Closer to the city is the national airport at Pampulha, which has shuttle services from several cities, including Rio and São Paulo, T3490 2001. Urban transportation to/from this airport is cheaper than from Confins. From Pampulha airport to town, take blue bus 1202, 25 mins, US$0.75, passing the rodoviária and the cheaper hotel district.

Bus The city has a good public transport system: red buses run on express routes and charge US$1.10; yellow buses have circular routes around the Contorno, US$0.75; blue buses run on diagonal routes charging US$1. There are also buses which integrate with the regional, overground Metrô.

The rodoviária is by Praça Rio Branco at the northwest end of Av Afonso Pena, T3271 3000/8933. The bus station has toilets, post office, phones, left-luggage lockers (attended service 0700-2200), shops and is clean and well organized. Buses leave from the rather gloomy platforms beneath the ticket hall. Do not leave belongings unattended.

To **Rio** with **Cometa** (T3201 5611) and **Útil** (T3201 7744), 6½ hrs, US$27 (ordinary), leito, US$56. To **Vitória** with **São Geraldo** (T3271 1911), US$35. To **Brasília** with **Itapemirim** (T3271 1019, www.itapemirim.com.br) and **Penha** (T3271 1027), 10 hrs, 6 a day including 2 leitos, only one leaves in daylight (0800), US$35-44. To **São Paulo** with **Cometa** and **Gontijo** (T3201 6130), 10 hrs, US$43. To **Foz do Iguaçu**, US$110, 22 hrs. To **Salvador** with Gontijo, US$97, 24 hrs, at 1900 daily, and São Geraldo at 1800. São Geraldo also goes to **Porto Seguro**, 17 hrs, direct, via Nanuque and Eunápolis, US$80. To **Campo Grande** with Gontijo (at 1930) and Motta (3 a day), US$70-80, a good route to Bolivia, avoiding São Paulo. All major destinations served. For buses within Minas Gerais, see under destination.
Train To **Vitória**, see page 493.

Directory

Belo Horizonte *p473, maps p474 and p476*

Airline offices **American**, Av Bernardo Monteiro 1539, Funcionários, T3274 3166. **Gol**, www.voegol.com.br. Office in the airports and bookable through most high street travel agencies. **TAM**, R Marília de Dirceu 162, Lourdes, T0300-231000/3349 5500. **United**, Av Olegário Maciel 2251, Lourdes, T3339 6060. **Webjet**, T0300-210 1234, www.webjet.com.br.
Banks **Banco do Brasil**, R Rio de Janeiro 750, Av Amazonas 303; cash is given against credit cards at **Banco Itaú**, Av João Pinheiro 195. **Citibank**, R Espírito Santo 871. Visa ATM at **Bradesco**, R da Bahia 947. **Master Turismo**, see Tour operators, above. Changing TCs is difficult, but hotels will change them for guests at a poor rate. **Embassies and consulates** **Austria**, R José Américo Cançado Bahia 199, T3333 1046, austria@planetarium.com.br. **France**, Av do Contorno 5417/2, Cruzeiro, T4501 3649, consulat.belohorizonte@yahoo.fr. **Italy**, R Inconfidentes 600, Funcionários, T3281 4211,

www.consbelo horizonte.esteri.it. **Netherlands**, R Sergipe 1167, sala 1102, T3221 7377, consulbh@gold.com.br. **Spain**, Av Raja Gabáglia 1001, sl 910, T/F3275 4480. **UK**, R dos Inconfidentes 1075, sala 1302, Savassi, T3261 2072, britcon.bhe@terra.com.br.

Internet Many places throughout the city.

Language classes Carlos Robles, T3281 1274, gatirobles@vol.com.br. Has a network of schools in Brazil, speaks good English.

Medical services Mater Dei, R Gonçalves Dias 2700, T3339 9000. Recommended.

Post offices Av Afonso Pena 1270, with fax, philatelic department and small museum, closes 1800; poste restante is behind the main office at R de Goiás 77. The branch office on R da Bahia is less busy. **Telephones** Telemig, Av Afonso Pena 1180, by the Correios, daily 0700-2200; also at the rodoviária, Confins airport, and others in the centre.

East and south of Belo Horizonte

Most of the colonial cities lie southeast and south of Belo Horizonte and many people choose to visit them on the way to or from Rio as they make for the most charming and restful of stopping places. Ouro Preto is the most famous and a much more pleasant place to stay than the state capital. Mariana is a good day trip from Ouro Preto. Further south are Congonhas, with its remarkable statuary, São João del Rei, with some beautiful colonial architecture, and Tiradentes, the most heavily visited of the Minas colonial towns after Ouro Preto. In the far south of the state, closer to the road to São Paulo, is one of Brazil's main New Age sites, São Tomé das Letras.

Sabará → *Colour map 7, B5. Population: 115,352.*

East of the state capital by 23 km is the colonial gold-mining (and steel-making) town of Sabará, strung along the narrow steep valleys of the Rio das Velhas and Rio Sabará. **Secretaria de Turismo** ⓘ *R Pedro II 223, T3672 7690.*

Rua Dom Pedro II is lined with beautiful 18th-century buildings. Among them is the **Solar do Padre Correa** (1773) at No 200, now the **Prefeitura**; the **Casa Azul** (also 1773), No 215; and the **Teatro Municipal**, former Opera House (1770 – the second oldest in Brazil). At the top of Rua Dom Pedro II is the Praça Melo Viana, in the middle of which is **Nossa Senhora do Rosário dos Pretos** ⓘ *church and museum Tue-Sun 0800-1100, 1300-1700.* The church was left unfinished at the time of the slaves' emancipation. There is a museum of religious art in the church. To the right of the church as you face it is the **Chafariz do Rosário** (the Rosário fountain). In Rua da Intendência is the museum of 18th-century gold mining in the **Museu do Ouro** ⓘ *Tue-Sun 1200-1730, US$1.30.* It contains exhibits on gold extraction, plus religious items and colonial furniture. Another fine example is the **Casa Borba Gato** ⓘ *R Borba Gato 71*; the building currently belongs to the Museu do Ouro.

The church of **Nossa Senhora do Carmo** (1763-1774) ⓘ *US$1.30 (includes a leaflet about the town)*, with doorway, pulpits and choirloft by Aleijadinho (see box, above) and paintings by Athayde, is on Rua do Carmo. **Nossa Senhora da Conceição** ⓘ *Praça Getúlio Vargas, free*, built 1701-1720, has much visible woodwork and a beautiful floor. The carvings have much gilding, there are painted panels and paintings by 23 Chinese artists brought from Macau. The clearest Chinese work is on the two red doors to the right and left of the chancel. **Nossa Senhora do Ó**, built in 1717 and showing Chinese influence, is 2 km from the centre of the town at the Largo Nossa Senhora do Ó (take local bus marked 'Esplanada' or 'Boca Grande').

If you walk up the Morra da Cruz hill from the Hotel do Ouro to a small chapel, the Capela da Cruz or Senhor Bom Jesus, you can get a wonderful view of the whole area.

Caeté → *Colour map 7, B5. Population: 36,299.*

A further 25 km is Caeté, which has several historical buildings and churches. On the Praça João Pinheiro are the **Prefeitura** and **Pelourinho** (both 1722), the **Igreja Matriz Nossa Senhora do**

O Aleijadinho

Antônio Francisco Lisboa (1738-1814), the son of a Portuguese architect and a black slave woman, was known as O Aleijadinho (the little cripple) because in later life he developed a maiming disease (possibly leprosy) which compelled him to work in a kneeling (and ultimately a recumbent) position with his hammer and chisel strapped to his wrists. His finest work, which shows a strength not usually associated with the sculpture in the 18th century, is probably the set of statues in the gardens and sanctuary of the great Bom Jesus church in Congonhas do Campo, but the main body of his work is in Ouro Preto, with some important pieces in Sabará, São João del Rei and Mariana.

Bom Sucesso (1756 rebuilt 1790) ⓘ *daily 1300-1800*, and the **Chafariz da Matriz**. Also on the Praça is the tourist information office in the Casa da Cultura (T6511855). Other churches are **Nossa Senhora do Rosário** (1750-1768), with a ceiling attributed to Mestre Athayde, and **São Francisco de Assis**. The **Museu Regional** ⓘ *R Israel Pinheiro 176, Tue-Sun 1200-1700*, in the house of the Barão de Catas Altas, or Casa Setecentista, contains 18th- and 19th-century religious art and furniture.

Parque Natural de Caraça

ⓘ *0700-2100; if staying overnight you cannot leave after 2100, US$6.50 per vehicle.*

The Parque Natural de Caraça is a remarkable reserve about 120 km east of Belo Horizonte. It has been preserved so well because the land belongs to a seminary, part of which has been converted into a hotel. The rarest mammal in the park is the maned wolf; the monks feed them on the seminary steps in the evening. Also endangered is the southern masked titi monkey. Other primates include the common marmoset and the brown capuchin monkey. Some of the bird species at Caraça are endemic, others rare and endangered. The trails for viewing the different landscapes and the wildlife are marked at their beginning and are quite easy to follow.

Ouro Preto → *Phone code: 0xx31. Post code: 35400. Colour map 7, B5. Population: 66,277.*

Founded in 1711, this famous former state capital has cobbled streets that wind up and down steep hills, crowned with 13 churches. Mansions, fountains, terraced gardens, ruins, towers shining with coloured tiles, all blend together to maintain a delightful 18th-century atmosphere. October-February is the wettest time, but the warmest month of the year is February (average 30°C). The coldest months are June-August, with the lowest temperatures in July (10°C).

Tourist office ⓘ *Praça Tiradentes 41, opens 0800, T3551 2655*, Portuguese only spoken, very helpful. The **Secretaria de Turismo** ⓘ *Casa de Gonzaga, R Cláudio Manoel 61, T3559 3200*, has lists of hotels, restaurants and local sites and a map. A local guide for a day, **Associação de Guias de Turismo (AGTOP)**, can be obtained through the tourist office, T3559 3269 at the tourist office, 3559 3252 at the rodoviária, or 3551 2655 (guide Cássio Antunes is recommended). The **Guiding Association** offers group tours of US$40 for one to 10 people. If taking a guide, check their accreditation. The tourist office and most historic buildings have several books for sale, including Lucia Machado de Almeida's *Passeio a Ouro Preto*, US$8 (in Portuguese, English and French). See also www.ouropreto.com.br (in Portuguese).

Most churches charge a conservation tax of US$1.50-5; bags and cameras are taken at the entrance and guarded in lockers (visitors keep the key). Churches are all closed Monday.

Sights In the central **Praça Tiradentes** is a statue of the leader of the **Inconfidentes**, Joaquim José da Silva Xavier. Another Inconfidente, the poet Tomás Antônio Gonzaga lived at Rua Cláudio Manoel 61, close to São Francisco de Assis church. On the north side of the praça (at No 20) is a famous **Escola de Minas** (School of Mining), founded in 1876, in the fortress-like **Palácio dos**

Governadores (1741-1748); it has the interesting **Museu de Mineralogia e das Pedras** ⓘ *1200-1700, Sat-Sun 0900-1300, US$2*, with 23,000 stones from around the world. On the side of the Praça, No 139, is the **Museu da Inconfidência** ⓘ *T3551 1121, Mon-Fri 0800-1800,* a fine historical and art museum in the former **Casa de Câmara e Cadeia**, *which has some drawings by Aleijadinho and the Sala Manoel da Costa Athayde, in an* annex. In the Casa Capitular *of NS do* Carmo is **Museu do Oratório** ⓘ *T3551 5369, daily 0930-1200, 1330-1730*, a collection of beautiful 18th- and 19th-century prayer icons and oratories including many made of egg and sea shell. **Casa dos Contos** ⓘ *R São José 12, T3551 1444, Tue-Sat 1230-1730, Sun and holidays 0900-1500, US$0.65*. Built between 1782-1784, it is the Centro de Estudos do Ciclo de Ouro (Centre for Gold Cycle Studies) and a museum of money and finance. The **Casa Guignard** ⓘ *R Conde de Bobadela 110, T3551 5155, Tue-Fri 1200-1800, Sat, Sun and holidays 0900-1500, free*, displays the paintings of Alberto da Veiga Guignard. The **Teatro Municipal** ⓘ *in R Brigadeiro Musqueiro, daily 1230-1800*, is the oldest functioning theatre in Latin America. It was built in 1769.

São Francisco de Assis (1766-1796) ⓘ *Largo de Coimbra, 0830-1145, 1330-1640, US$2.65*; the ticket also permits entry to NS da Conceição (keep your ticket for admission to the museum). This church is considered to be one of the masterpieces of Brazilian baroque. Aleijadinho worked on the general design and the sculpture of the façade, the pulpits and many other features. Mestre Athayde (1732-1827) was responsible for the painted ceiling. **Nossa Senhora da Conceição** (1722) ⓘ *0830-1130, 1330-1700, Sun 1200-1700*, is heavily gilded and contains Aleijadinho's tomb. It has a museum devoted to him. **Nossa Senhora das Mercês e Perdões** (1740-1772) ⓘ *R das Mercês, 1000-1400*, was rebuilt in the 19th century. Some sculpture by Aleijadinho can be seen in the main chapel. **Santa Efigênia** (1720-1785) ⓘ *Ladeira Santa Efigênia e Padre Faria, 0800-1200*; Manuel Francisco Lisboa (Aleijadinho's father) oversaw the construction and much of the carving is by Francisco Xavier de Brito (Aleijadinho's mentor). It has wonderful panoramic views of the city. **Nossa Senhora do Carmo** (1766-1772) ⓘ *R Brigadeiro Mosqueira, 1330-1700*, has a museum of sacred art with Aleijadinho sculptures. **Nossa Senhora do Pilar** (1733) ⓘ *Praça Mons Castilho Barbosa, 1200-1700*, also contains a religious art museum. Entry is shared with São Francisco de Paula, Ladeira de São José (1804). **Nossa Senhora do Rosário** ⓘ *Largo do Rosário*, dated from 1785, has a curved façade. The interior is much simpler than the exterior, but there are interesting side altars.

The **Mina do Chico Rei** ⓘ *R Dom Silvério, 0800-1700, US$2*, is not as impressive as some other mines in the area, but is fun to crawl about in; restaurant attached. Near the Padre Faria Church (NS do Rosário dos Brancos) is another small mine, **Mina Bem Querer** ⓘ *US$1.30*, with a pool with crystal clear water that runs through the mine. Between Ouro Preto and Mariana is the **Minas de Passagem** ⓘ *US$10, 0900-1730, last admissions at 1645*, gold mine, dating from 1719. A guided tour visits the old mine workings and underground lake (take bathing suit).

Mariana → *Phone code: 0xx31. Post code: 35420. Colour map 7, B5. Population: 46,710.*

Streets are lined with beautiful, two-storey 18th-century houses in this old mining city, which is much less hilly than Ouro Preto. Mariana's historical centre slopes gently uphill from the river and the Praça Tancredo Neves, where buses from Ouro Preto stop. **Tourist office**: Secretaria de Cultura e Turismo de Mariana ⓘ *Praça Tancredo Neves, T3557 9044*. The tourist office will help with guides and tours and offer a map and a free monthly booklet, *Mariana Agenda Cultural*, packed with local information including accommodation and eating.

Sights The first street parallel with the Praça Tancredo Neves is Rua Direita, and is home to the 300-year-old houses. At No 54 is the **Casa do Barão de Pontal** ⓘ *Tue 1400-1700*, whose balconies are carved from soapstone, unique in Minas Gerais. The ground floor of the building is a museum of furniture. At No 35 is the **Museu-Casa Afonso Guimarães** (or Alphonsus de Guimaraens) ⓘ *free*, the former home of a symbolist poet: photographs and letters. At No 7 is the **Casa Setecentista**, which now belongs to the Patrimônio Histórico e Artístico Nacional.

Rua Direita leads to the Praça da Sé, on which stands the **Cathedral** ⓘ *Basílica de Nossa Senhora da Assunção, organ concerts are given on Fri at 1100 and Sun at 1200, US$10*. The portal and the lavabo in the sacristy are by Aleijadinho. The painting in the beautiful interior and side altars is by Manoel Rabello de Sousa. Also in the cathedral is a wooden German organ (1701), a gift to the first diocese of the Capitania de Minas do Ouro in 1747. The **Museu Arquidiocesano** ⓘ *R Frei Durão, Tue-Sun 0900-1200, 1300-1700, US$2*, has fine church furniture, a gold and silver collection, Aleijadinho statues and an ivory cross. Opposite is the **Casa da Intendência/Casa de Cultura** ⓘ *R Frei Durão 84, 0800-1130, 1330-1700*, which holds exhibitions and has a museum of music. On the south side of Praça Gomes Freire is the **Palácio Arquiepiscopal**, while on the north side is the **Casa do Conde de Assumar**, who was governor of the Capitania from 1717 to 1720.

From Praça Gomes Freire, Travessa São Francisco leads to Praça Minas Gerais and one of the finest groups of colonial buildings in Brazil. In the middle of the Praça is the **Pelourinho**, the stone monument to Justice, at which slaves used to be beaten. On one side of the square is the fine **São Francisco church** (1762-1794) ⓘ *daily 0800-1700*, with pulpits designed by Aleijadinho, paintings by Mestre Athayde, who is buried in tomb No 94, a fine sacristy and one side-altar by Aleijadinho. At right angles to São Francisco is **Nossa Senhora do Carmo** (1784) *daily 1400-1700*, with steatite carvings, Athayde paintings, and chinoiserie panelling. Across Rua Dom Silvério is the **Casa da Cámara e Cadéia** (1768), at one time the Prefeitura Municipal. On Largo de São Pedro is **São Pedro dos Clérigos** (begun in 1753), one of the few elliptical churches in Minas Gerais. Restoration is under way.

Capela de Santo Antônio, on Rua Rosário Velho, is wonderfully simple and the oldest in town. It is some distance from the centre. Overlooking the city from the north, with a good viewpoint, is the church of **Nossa Senhora do Rosário**, Rua do Rosário (1752), with work by Athayde and showing Moorish influence.

Parque Nacional Caparaó

ⓘ *US$11.50. Contact R Vale Verde s/n, Alto do Caparaó, CEP 36979-000, T3747 2555, www.icmbio.gov.br/parna_caparao.*

This is one of the most popular parks in Minas (on the Espírito Santo border), with good walking through stands of Atlantic rainforest, páramo and to the summits of three of Brazil's highest peaks: Pico da Bandeira (2,890 m), Pico do Cruzeiro (2,861 m) and Pico do Cristal (2,798 m). The park, surrounded by coffee farms, features rare Atlantic rainforest in its lower altitudes and Brazilian alpine on top. Loss of forest and floral biodiversity has adversely affected wildlife, but there are nonetheless a number of Atlantic coast primates, like the brown capuchins, together with a recovering bird population. From the park entrance (where a small fee has to be paid) it is 6 km on a good unpaved road to the car park at the base of the waterfall. From the hotel (see page 486) jeeps (US$25 per jeep) run to the car park at 1,970 m (2½ hours' walk), then it's a three to four hour walk to the summit of the Pico da Bandeira, marked by yellow arrows; plenty of camping possibilities, the highest being at Terreirão (2,370 m). This is good walking country. It is best to visit during the dry season (April-October). It can be quite crowded in July and during Carnival. ⏩ *See Transport, page 488, for how to get there.*

Congonhas ➔ *Phone code: 0xx31. Post code: 36404. Colour map 7, B5. Population: 41,256.*

This hill town is connected by a paved 3½ km road with the Rio-Belo Horizonte highway. Most visitors spend little time in the town, but go straight to **O Santuário de Bom Jesus de Matosinhos** ⓘ *Tue-Sun 0700-1900, there are public toilets on the Alameda das Palmeiras, the information desk at the bus station will guard luggage and you can visit the sanctuary between bus changes*, which dominates Congonhas. The great pilgrimage church was finished in 1771; below it are six linked chapels, or pasos (1802-1818), showing scenes with life-size Passion figures carved by Aleijadinho and his pupils in cedar wood. These lead up to a terrace and courtyard. On this terrace (designed in 1777) stand 12 prophets, sculpted by Aleijadinho

a kitchen, multilingual staff, excursions. Snacks are available. Recommended (book in after 1200).
E Brumas, R Pe José Marcos Pena 68, 150 m down- hill from rodoviária, just below São Francisco de Paula church, T3551 2944, www.brumasonline .cjb.net. Hostel with dorm, kitchen, laundry and superb views. Don't walk from bus station after dark.
Camping **Camping Clube do Brasil**, Rodovia dos Inconfidentes Km 91, 2 km north, T3551 1799. Expensive but good.
Students may be able to stay, during holidays and weekends, at the self-governing student hostels, known as *repúblicas* (very welcoming, 'best if you like heavy metal music' and 'are prepared to enter into the spirit of the places'). The Prefeitura has a list of over 50 repúblicas with phone numbers, available at the Secretaria de Turismo. Many are closed Christmas to Carnival.

Mariana *p481*
A Pousada Solar dos Corrêa, R Josefá Macedo 70 and R Direita, T/F3557 2080, www.pousadasolardos correa.com.br. Central, restored 18th-century town house with spacious a/c rooms, with breakfast, TV, fridge in room, internet, parking.
B Pousada do Chafariz, R Cônego Rego 149, T3557 1492, chafariz@veloxmail.com.br. Converted colonial building, TV, fridge, parking, breakfast included.
D-E Central, R Frei Durão 8, T/F3557 1630. A charming but run-down colonial building on the attractive Praça Gomes Freire. Recommended but avoid downstairs rooms.
D-E Providência, R Dom Silvério 233, T3557 1444, www.hotelprovidencia.com.br. Along the road that leads up to the Basílica; has use of the neighbouring school's pool when classes finish at noon, small rooms, quiet.

Parque Nacional Caparaó *p482*
A Caparaó Parque, T3747 2559, 2 km from the park entrance, 15 mins' walk from the town of Alto Caparaó, nice. Ask where camping is permitted.
C São Luiz, in **Manhumirim** (Population: 20,025), good value, but **Cids Bar**, next door, Travessa 16 do Março, has better food.

São João del Rei *p483*
A Beco do Bispo, Beco do Bispo 93, 2 mins west of São Francisco de Assis, T/3371 8844, www.becodobispo.com.br. The best in town, bright a/c rooms with firm mattresses, hot showers, cable TV, pool, convenient, very helpful English speaking staff. Organizes tours. Highly recommended.
B Lenheiros Palace, Av Pres Tancredo Neves 257, T/F3371 8155, www.hotellenheiros.com.br. A modern hotel with good facilities, parking, Lenheiros Casa de Chá tea house, breakfast, no restaurant.
B Ponte Real, Av Eduardo Magalhães 254, T/F3371 7000, www.hotelpontereal.com.br. Also modern, comfortable, sizeable rooms, good restaurant.
B Pousada Casarão, opposite São Francisco church, in a converted mansion, Ribeiro Bastos 94, T3371 7447, www.pousadacasarao.com. In a delightful converted mansion house, firm beds, TV, fridge, swimming pool, games room.
C Aparecida, Praça Dr Antônio Viegas 13, T3371 2540. Central, by the bus and taxi stop, has a restaurant and lanchonete.
D Brasil, Av Presidente Tancredo Neves 395, T3371 2804. In an old house full of character and staircases, on the opposite side of the river from the railway station, cheap. Recommended but basic, no breakfast.
D Sinha Batista, R Manock Anselmo 22, T3371 5550. The best of the cheaper options, quite large rooms in a colonial building conveniently located by the central canal.

Tiradentes *p483*
LL Solar da Ponte, Praça das Mercês (proprietors John and Anna Maria Parsons), T3355 1255, www.solardaponte.com.br. Country house atmosphere, 12 rooms, price includes breakfast and afternoon tea, fresh flowers in rooms, bar, sauna, lovely gardens, swimming pool, light meals for residents only, restaurants nearby (it is in the Roteiros de Charme group, see page 393). For horse-riding treks, contact John Parsons here. Recommended.
A Pousada Mãe D'Água, Largo das Forras 50, T3355 1206, www.pousadamaedagua.com.br. Including breakfast but not tax, very nice, outdoor pool in garden.

A Pousada Três Portas, R Direita 280A, T3355 1444, www.pousadatresportas.com.br. Charming, central, in restored town house, has sauna, thermal pool, hydromassage, heating.
A Pouso das Gerais, R dos Inconfidentes 109, T3355 1234, www.pousodasgerais. com.br. Fresh fan-cooled rooms, TV, marble basins, central, quiet, pool, breakfast included. Recommended.
B-C Pousada do Arco Iris, R Frederico Ozanan 340, T3355 1167, www.arcoiristiradentesmg. com.br. The best of a string of pousadas in houses on this stretch of road just out of town. Swimming pool, popular, family-run, 5 rooms only. Price includes breakfast. Book ahead.
C Pousada do Laurito, R Direita 187, T3355 1268. Central, good value, very popular with international backpackers.

São Tomé das Letras *p484*
Streets are hard to follow because their names seem to change almost from one block to the next; numbering is also chaotic. There are lots of pousadas and rooms to let all over town.
B Pousada Arco-Iris, R João Batista Neves 19, T/F3237 1212. Rooms and chalets, sauna, swimming pool.
C dos Sonhos II (do Gê), Trav Nhá Chica 8, T3237 1235. Very nice, restaurant, swimming pool, sauna. Recommended.
D pp **Fundação Harmonia**, Estrada para Sobradinho s/n, Bairro do Canta Galo, T3237 1280. 4 km from town, but shop on the main Praça. The community emphasizes several disciplines for a healthy lifestyle, for mind and body, 'new age', workshops, massage, excursions, vegetarian food, clean accommodation.
D-E pp **Pousada Souza Reis**, Praça do Rosário 540, T3237 1264. Next to Igreja de Pedra, with bath and breakfast, TV, good value, helpful.

Eating

Ouro Preto *p480*
Try the local liquor *de jaboticaba*.
ᴛᴛ Adega, R Teixeira Amaral 24, T3551 4171. Vegetarian smorgasbord, all you can eat, 1130-1530. Highly recommended.
ᴛᴛ Casa Grande and **Forno de Barro**, both on Praça Tiradentes (Nos 84 and 54 respectively). Decent Mineira cooking.
ᴛᴛ Ouro Grill, R Sen Rocha Lagoa 61. Self-service at lunchtime, US$5, good value after 1600.

ᴛᴛᴛ Taverna ... 2828. Good loc...
ᴛ Beijinho Doce, ... pastries and cakes, ...
ᴛ Café & Cia, R São Jo... Closes 2300, very popu... at lunchtime, good salad...
ᴛ Deguste, R São José ne... Good value.
ᴛ Pasteleria Lampião, Praça ... Good views at the back (best a... lunchtime).
ᴛ Vide Gula, R Sen Rocha Lagoa 79a, T3551 4493. Food by weight, good, friendly atmosphere. Recommended.

ᴛᴛᴛ Quinto de Ouro, ... Direita ... and international dis...
ᴛᴛᴛ Theatro da ... T3355 1275 ... Brazilia...

Mariana *p481*
ᴛᴛ Engenho Nôvo, Praça da Sé 26. Bar at night, English spoken. Recommended.
ᴛᴛ Mangiare della Mamma, D Viçoso 27. Italian. Recommended.
ᴛᴛ Tambaú, R João Pinheiro 26. Regional food.
ᴛ Panela de Pedra in the Terminal Turístico serves food by weight at lunchtime.

São João del Rei *p483*
ᴛᴛᴛ Churrascaria Ramón, Praça Severiano de Resende 52. One of the better churrascarias with generous portions and plenty of side dishes.
ᴛᴛᴛ Quinto do Ouro, Praça Severiano de Rezende 04, T3371 7577. Tasty and well-prepared regional food. Said to be the best Mineira cooking in town.
ᴛᴛ Portal del Rey, Praça Severiano de Rezende 134. Comida à kilo, Minas and Arabic food; good value.
ᴛ Restaurant 611, R Tome Portes del Rei 511, Vila Santo Antônio, T3371 5590. Very cheap but great Mineira cooking. Lots of choice, popular. Also **611 Centro**, Rua Getulio Vargas 145, Centro, T3371 8793.

Tiradentes *p483*
There are many restaurants, snack bars and *lanchonetes* in town and it is a small enough place to wander around and see what takes your fancy.
ᴛᴛᴛ Estalagem, R Ministro G Passos 280. Excellent and generous traditional Mineira meat dishes.
ᴛᴛᴛ Quartier Latin, R São Francisco de Paula 46, Praça da Rodoviária, T3355 1552. French, cordon bleu chef, excellent.

is at R Padre Rolim 661, near São Francisco de Paula church, T3559 3252. A 'Circular' bus runs from the rodoviária to Praça Tiradentes, US$1. Taxi US$5. 11 buses a day from Belo Horizonte (2 hrs, **Pássaro Verde**), US$7.75. Day trips are run. Book your return journey to **Belo Horizonte** early if returning in the evening; buses get crowded. Bus to/from **Rio**, **Útil**, T3551 3166, 3 a day, US$35, 12 hrs (book in advance). Other **Útil** services to Rio go via Belo Horizonte. **Vale do Ouro** buses to **Congonhas** on the new Caminho de Ouro highway (T3551 5679 to check), otherwise take **Atual** bus, T0800- 7040560, to **Conselheiro Lafaiete**, US$8.50, 2¾ hrs, and change. Direct buses to **São Paulo**, 3 a day with **Vale do Ouro**, 11 hrs, US$41.

Mariana *p481*

Bus Mariana is only 12 km from Ouro Preto and can easily be visited as a side trip. Buses run between the Escola de Minas near Praça Tiradentes in Ouro Preto and the Secretaria de Cultura e Turismo de Mariana, Praça Tancredo Neves, every 30 mins.

Parque Nacional Caparaó *p482*

Bus The park is 49 km by paved road from Manhuaçu (about 190 km south of Governador Valadares) on the Belo Horizonte-Vitória road (BR-262). There are buses from **Belo Horizonte** (twice daily with **Pássaro Verde**), Ouro Preto or Vitória to **Manhumirim**, 15 km south of Manhuaçu. From Manhumirim, take a bus direct to Alto Caparaó, 8 a day, US$2.25. By **car** from the BR-262, go through Manhumirim, Alto Jaqutibá and Alto Caparaó, then 1 km to Hotel Caparaó Parque.

Congonhas *p482*

Bus The Rodoviária is 1½ km outside town; bus to town centre US$1; for 'Basílica', see above.

To/from **Belo Horizonte**, 1½ hrs, US$7, 8 times a day. To **São João del Rei**, 2 hrs, US$8, tickets are not sold until the bus comes in. Bus to **Ouro Preto**: direct on the new Caminho de Ouro highway, or go via Belo Horizonte or Conselheiro Lafaiete.

São João del Rei *p483*

Bus Rodoviária is 2 km west of the centre. Buses to **Rio**, 5 daily with **Paraibuna** (3 on Sat and Sun), 5 hrs, US$22. **Cristo Rei** to **São Paulo**, 8 hrs, 5 a day, and **Translavras**, 4 a day, US$27. **Belo Horizonte**, 3½ hrs, US$15. To **Tiradentes** with **Meier**, 8 a day, 7 on Sat, Sun and holidays, US$1.50.

Tiradentes *p483*

Bus Last bus back to **São João del Rei** is 1815, 2230 on Sun; fares are given above.

Taxi To **São João del Rei** costs US$25. Around town there are pony-drawn taxis; ponies can be hired for US$12.

São Tomé das Letras *p484*

Bus There are 3 daily buses (2 on Sun) to São Tomé from **Tres Corações**, the birthplace of Pelé, the legendary football star (to whom there is a statue in Praça Col José Martins), US$4, 1½ hrs (paved road). Tres Corações has hotels and regular buses to **Belo Horizonte**, US$25, 5½ hrs, and **São Paulo**, US$16.50.

Directory

Ouro Preto *p480*

Banks Banco do Brasil, R São José 189, high commission, changes TCs. **Bradesco**, corner of Senador Rocha Lagoa and Padre Rolim, opposite the Escola de Minas. **Banco 24 Horas**, Praça Alves de Brito, next to Correios. **Post offices** Praça Alves de Brito.

Espírito Santo

The coastal state of Espírito Santo is where mineiros head to for their seaside holidays. The most popular beaches are south of Vitória, the state capital, while north of the city are several turtle-nesting beaches. Inland are immigrant towns.

Vitória and around ➔ *Phone code: 0xx27. Post code: 29000. Colour map 7, B6.*
Five bridges connect the island on which Vitória stands with the mainland. The state capital is beautifully set, its entrance second only to Rio's, its beaches quite as attractive, but smaller, and the climate is less humid. Port installations at Vitória and nearby Ponta do Tubarão have led to some beach and air pollution at places nearby. It is largely a modern city: The upper, older part of town, reached by steep streets and steps, is less hectic than the lower harbour area, but both are full of cars. The car-parking boys have their work cut out to find spaces. **Tourist offices**: in the rodoviária, at the airport, T3235 6300 (helpful, with map and leaflets) and at Curva da Jurema beach, Módulo 18, T3382 3053. The **Postos de Informações Turísticas** are stafed by students. For the **Superintendência de Turismo** ⓘ *T3315 5540*. **Fala Vitória** ⓘ *T156, www.vitoria.es.gov.br.*

On Avenida República is the large **Parque Moscoso**, an oasis of quiet, with a lake and playground. Colonial buildings still to be seen in the upper city are the **Capela de Santa Luzia** (1551) ⓘ *R José Marcelino, Mon-Fri 0800-1800*. It has a painted altar, otherwise a small open space; the church of **São Gonçalo** (1766) ⓘ *R Francisco Araújo, closed to the public*, and the ruins of the **Convento São Francisco** (1591). In the **Palácio Anchieta**, or **do Governo** ⓘ *Praça João Climaco (upper city- packed with parked cars)*, is the tomb of Padre Anchieta, one of the founders of São Paulo. Praça João Climaco has some restored buildings around it, including the green Casa do Cidadão. The **Teatro Carlos Gomes** ⓘ *Praça Costa Pereira*, often presents plays, also jazz and folk festivals.

Urban beaches such as **Camburi** can be affected by pollution (about 10% according to official sources), but it is pleasant, with a fair surf. Several buses run from the centre to Camburi, but look for one with Av Beira Mar on the destination board, eg No 212. Buses pass Praia do Canto, a smart district with good restaurants and shops, then cross A Ponte de Camburi.

Vila Velha, reached by A Terceira Ponte (the Third Bridge) across the bay, is a separate municipality from Vitória. The Third Bridge, a toll road, is a sweeping structure and one of the symbols of the city. It has an excellent series of beaches: Praia da Costa is the main one, with others, including Itaparica, heading south. The second main symbol of Vila Velha is the monastery of **Nossa Senhora da Penha** (1558) ⓘ *daily 0530-1645*, on a high hill with superb views of the bay, bridge and both cities. The Dutch attacked it in 1625 and 1640. Minibuses take the infirm and not-so-devout up the hill for US$0.55 return, 0630-1715 (you have to use the phone in the upper car park if you want a ride down). A museum in the convent costs US$0.35. From here you will see that Vila Velha is neither old, nor a small town. It's a built up beachfront city, noisy at times, but the sea suffers less from pollution than Camburi. Vila Velha is the place of origin of Garoto chocolates, whose factory can be visited on weekdays (T3320 1709 for times). **Tourist information** ⓘ *T3139 9015, www.vilavelha.es.gov.br.*

Some 14 km south of Vila Velha is **Barra do Jucu**, which has bigger waves, and the **Reserva de Jacarenema**, which preserves coastal ecosystems.

Inland from Vitória
Santa Leopoldina or **Domingos Martins**, both around 45 km from Vitória, are less than an hour by bus (Pretti to Santa Leopoldina five a day, four on Sunday, Aguia Branca to Domingos Martins; Friday 1700 only). Both villages preserve the architecture and customs of the first German and Swiss settlers who arrived in the 1840s. Domingos Martins (also known as Campinho) has a Casa de Cultura with some items of German settlement. Santa Leopoldina has an interesting **museum** ⓘ *Tue-Sun 0900-1100, 1300-1800*, which covers the settlers' first years in the area.

A Pousada Três Portas, R Direita 280A,
T3355 1444, www.pousadatresportas.com.br.
Charming, central, in restored town house, has
sauna, thermal pool, hydromassage, heating.
A Pouso das Gerais, R dos Inconfidentes 109,
T3355 1234, www.pousodasgerais. com.br. Fresh
fan-cooled rooms, TV, marble basins, central,
quiet, pool, breakfast included. Recommended.
B-C Pousada do Arco Iris, R Frederico Ozanan
340, T3355 1167, www.arcoiristiradentesmg.
com.br. The best of a string of pousadas in
houses on this stretch of road just out of town.
Swimming pool, popular, family-run, 5 rooms
only. Price includes breakfast. Book ahead.
C Pousada do Laurito, R Direita 187, T3355
1268. Central, good value, very popular with
international backpackers.

São Tomé das Letras *p484*
Streets are hard to follow because their names
seem to change almost from one block to the
next; numbering is also chaotic. There are lots
of pousadas and rooms to let all over town.
B Pousada Arco-Iris, R João Batista Neves 19,
T/F3237 1212. Rooms and chalets, sauna,
swimming pool.
C dos Sonhos II (do Gê), Trav Nhá Chica 8,
T3237 1235. Very nice, restaurant, swimming
pool, sauna. Recommended.
D pp Fundação Harmonia, Estrada para
Sobradinho s/n, Bairro do Canta Galo, T3237
1280. 4 km from town, but shop on the main
Praça. The community emphasizes several
disciplines for a healthy lifestyle, for mind and
body, 'new age', workshops, massage, excursions,
vegetarian food, clean accommodation.
D-E pp Pousada Souza Reis, Praça do Rosário
540, T3237 1264. Next to Igreja de Pedra, with
bath and breakfast, TV, good value, helpful.

● Eating

Ouro Preto *p480*
Try the local liquor *de jaboticaba*.
▼▼ Adega, R Teixeira Amaral 24, T3551 4171.
Vegetarian smorgasbord, all you can eat,
1130-1530. Highly recommended.
▼▼ Casa Grande and **Forno de Barro**, both on
Praça Tiradentes (Nos 84 and 54 respectively).
Decent Mineira cooking.
▼▼ Ouro Grill, R Sen Rocha Lagoa 61. Self-service
at lunchtime, US$5, good value after 1600.

▼▼ Taverna do Chafariz, R São José 167, T3551
2828. Good local food. Recommended.
▼ Beijinho Doce, R Direita 134A. Delicious
pastries and cakes, try the truffles.
▼ Café & Cia, R São José 187, T3551 0711.
Closes 2300, very popular, *comida por kilo*
at lunchtime, good salads, juices.
▼ Deguste, R São José next to Banco Itaú.
Good value.
▼ Pasteleria Lampião, Praça Tiradentes.
Good views at the back (best at lunchtime).
▼ Vide Gula, R Sen Rocha Lagoa 79a, T3551 4493.
Food by weight, good, friendly atmosphere.
Recommended.

Mariana *p481*
▼▼ Engenho Nôvo, Praça da Sé 26. Bar at
night, English spoken. Recommended.
▼▼ Mangiare della Mamma, D Viçoso 27.
Italian. Recommended.
▼▼ Tambaú, R João Pinheiro 26. Regional food.
▼ Panela de Pedra in the Terminal Turístico
serves food by weight at lunchtime.

São João del Rei *p483*
▼▼▼ Churrascaria Ramón, Praça Severiano de
Resende 52. One of the better churrascarias with
generous portions and plenty of side dishes.
▼▼▼ Quinto do Ouro, Praça Severiano de Rezende
04, T3371 7577. Tasty and well-prepared regional
food. Said to be the best Mineira cooking in town.
▼▼ Portal del Rey, Praça Severiano de Rezende
134. Comida à kilo, Minas and Arabic food;
good value.
▼ Restaurant 611, R Tome Portes del Rei 511,
Vila Santo Antônio, T3371 5590. Very cheap
but great Mineira cooking. Lots of choice,
popular. Also **611 Centro**, Rua Getulio Vargas
145, Centro, T3371 8793.

Tiradentes *p483*
There are many restaurants, snack bars and
lanchonetes in town and it is a small enough
place to wander around and see what takes
your fancy.
▼▼▼ Estalagem, R Ministro G Passos 280. Excellent
and generous traditional Mineira meat dishes.
▼▼▼ Quartier Latin, R São Francisco de Paula 46,
Praça da Rodoviária, T3355 1552. French,
cordon bleu chef, excellent.

TTT **Quinto de Ouro**, R Direita 159. Mineira and international dishes. Recommended.
TTT **Theatro da Vila**, R Padre Toledo 157, T3355 1275. Inventive and delicious Franco-Brazilian fusion cooking served in intimate rustic-chic dining room. Views over the Serra across the garden, small theatre that holds performances in summer.
TTT **Virados do Largo**, Largo do Ó. Good Mineira food and service.
T **Maria Luisa Casa de Chá**, Largo do Ó 1, diagonally opposite Aluarte, T3355 1502. Tea, cakes and sandwiches in an arty Bohemian atmosphere. Great for breakfast.

Bars and clubs

Tiradentes *p483*

Aluarte, Largo do Ó 1, is a bar with live music in the evening, nice atmosphere, US$4 cover charge, garden, sells handicrafts.

Festivals and events

Ouro Preto *p480*

Ouro Preto is famous for its **Holy Week** processions, beginning on the Thu before Palm Sunday and continuing (but not every day) until Easter Sunday. The most famous is that commemorating Christ's removal from the Cross, late on Good Friday. Many shops close then, and on winter weekends. Attracting many Brazilians, **Carnival** here is also memorable. In **Jun**, **Corpus Christi** and the **Festas Juninas** are celebrated. Every **Jul** the city holds the **Festival do Inverno da Universidade Federal de Minas Gerais (UFMG)**, the Winter Festival, about 3 weeks of arts, courses, shows, concerts and exhibitions. Also in **Jul**, on the 8th, is the **anniversary of the city**. **15 Aug**: **Nossa Senhora do Pilar**, patron saint of Ouro Preto. **12-18 Nov**: **Semana de Aleijadinho**, a week-long arts festival.

Congonhas *p482*

Congonhas is famous for **Holy Week** processions at Bom Jesus church. The most celebrated ceremonies are the **meeting of Christ and the Virgin Mary** on the **Tue**, and the dramatized **Deposition from the Cross** late on **Good Friday**. The pilgrimage season, first half of **Sep**, draws thousands. **8 Dec**, **Nossa Senhora da Conceição**.

São João del Rei *p483*

Apr, **Semana Santa**; **15-21 Apr**, **Semana da Inconfidência**. **May or Jun**, **Corpus Christi**. **First 2 weeks of Aug**, **Nossa Senhora da Boa Morte**, with baroque music (novena barroca). Similarly, **12 Oct**, **Nossa Senhora do Pilar**, patron saint of the city. **8 Dec**, **founding of the city**. FUNREI, the university (R Padre José Maria Xavier), holds **Inverno Cultural** in **Jul**.

Shopping

Ouro Preto *p480*

Gems are not much cheaper from sellers in Praça Tiradentes than from the shops, and in the shops, the same quality of stone is offered at the same price. If buying on the street, ask for the seller's credentials. Buy soapstone carvings at roadside stalls and bus stops rather than in cities; they are much cheaper. Many artisans sell jewellery and semi-precious stones in Largo de Coimbra in front of São Francisco de Assis church. Recommended are: **Gemas de Minas**, Conde de Bobadela 63; and **Manoel Bernardis**, Conde de Bobadela 48.

Transport

Sabará *p479*

Bus **Viação Cisne** No 1059 from R Catete, **Belo Horizonte**, US$1.75, 30 mins, circular route.

Parque Natural de Caraça *p480*

Turn off the BR-262 (towards Vitória) at Km 73 and go via Barão de Cocais to Caraça (120 km). There is no public transport to the seminary. **Buses** go as far as **Barão de Cocais**, then take a taxi, US$16.50 one way. You must book the **taxi** to return for you, or else **hitch** (not easy). The park entrance is 10 km before the seminary. Or hire a **car**, or take a guide from Belo Horizonte, which will cost over US$100 (guiding, transport and meals). It is possible to stay in **Santa Bárbara** (**D Hotel Karaibe**. **D Santa Inés**), 25 km away on the road to Mariana and hitchhike to Caraça. 11 buses a day from Belo Horizonte – Santa Bárbara (fewer on Sat and Sun).

Ouro Preto *p480*

Bus Don't walk from the rodoviária to town at night; robberies have occurred. The rodoviária

East and south of Belo Horizonte listings

For Sleeping and Eating price codes and other relevant information, see Essentials, pages 38-40.

Sleeping

Sabará *p479*

B **Pousada Solar das Sepúlvedas**, R da Intendência 371, behind the Museu do Ouro, T3671 2705. Grand, rooms with TV, pool.

D **Hotel do Ouro**, R Santa Cruz 237, Morro da Cruz, T3671 5622. With bath, hot water, with breakfast, marvellous view, best value.

Parque Natural de Caraça *p480*

AL **Hospedaria do Caraça**, the seminary hotel, for reservations write to Santuário do Caraça, Caixa Postal 12, 35960-000 – Santa Bárbara, MG, T0xx31-3837 2698. It has pleasant rooms; room rates vary, price is full board. There is a restaurant serving good food which comes from farms within the seminary's lands. Lunch is served 1200-1330.

Ouro Preto *p480*

Prices indicated here are for high season; many hotels offer, or will negotiate, lower prices outside holiday times or when things are quiet.

Ask at the tourist office for accommodation in *casas de família*, reasonably priced. Avoid touts who greet you off buses and charge higher prices than those advertised in hotels; it is difficult to get hotel rooms at weekends and holiday periods.

AL **Pousada do Mondego**, Largo de Coimbra 38, T3551 2040, www.mondego.com.br. Beautifully kept colonial house in a fine location by São Francisco church, room rates vary according to view, small restaurant, Scotch bar, popular with groups. Recommended (a Roteiro de Charme hotel, see page 393), the hotel runs a jardineira bus tour of the city, 2 hrs, minimum 10 passengers, US$10 for non-guests.

AL **Pousada Solar de NS do Rosário**, Av Getúlio Vargas 270, T3551 5200, www.hotelsolardorosario.com.br. Fully restored historic building with a highly recommended restaurant, bar, sauna, pool; all facilities in rooms.

AL-B **Pousada Mirante do Café**, Fazenda Alto das Rubiáceas, Santo Antônio do Leite, 25 km west of Ouro Preto, T3335 8478, www.mirantedocafe.com.br. Price varies with season and weekend. Coffee farm with full board available, visits allowed during coffee harvest, pool, trails, horse riding and other leisure activities.

A **Luxor Pousada**, R Dr Alfredo Baeta 16, Praça Antônio Dias, T3551 2244, www.luxorhoteis.com.br. Converted colonial mansion, no twin beds, comfortable but spartan, good views, restaurant good but service slow.

B **Pousada Casa Grande**, R Conselheiro Quintiliano, 96, T/F3551 4314, www.hotelpousadacasagrande.com.br. Including breakfast, safe, good views. Recommended.

B-C **Pousada Nello Nuno**, R Camilo de Brito 59, T3551 3375, http://pousadanellonuno.com. Cheaper rooms have no bath, friendly owner Annamélia speaks some French. Highly recommended.

C **Colonial**, Trav Padre Camilo Veloso 26, close to Praça Tiradentes, T3551 3133, www.hotelc olonial.com.br. With new rooms and refurbished older rooms, pleasant.

C **Pousada Itacolomi**, R Antônio Pereira 167, T3551 2891. Next door to the Museu da Inconfidência, small but well kept with good rates for the 3-room apartments.

C **Pousada Tiradentes**, Praça Tiradentes 70, T3551 2619. Spartan rooms, but well kept and moderately comfortable, TV, fridge, conveniently located.

C **Pouso Chico Rey**, R Brig Musqueira 90, T3551 1274. Fascinating old house with Portuguese colonial furnishings, very small and utterly delightful (but plumbing unreliable), book in advance.

C **Solar das Lajes**, R Conselheiro Quintiliano 604, T/F3551 3388, www.solardaslajes.com.br. A little way from centre but with an excellent view and a pool, well run.

D **Pousada dos Bandeirantes**, R das Mercês 167, T3551 1996. Behind the São Francisco de Assis church and offering beautiful views.

D **Pousada São Francisco de Paula**, Padre JM Pen 202, next to the São Francisco de Paula church, 100 m from rodoviária, T3551 3456, pousadas@hotmail.com. One of the best views of any in the city, from the rooms or from a hammock in the garden. Rooms with and without bath or breakfast, dormitory, use of a kitchen, multilingual staff, excursions. Snacks are available. Recommended (book in after 1200).

E Brumas, R Pe José Marcos Pena 68, 150 m down- hill from rodoviária, just below São Francisco de Paula church, T3551 2944, www.brumasonline .cjb.net. Hostel with dorm, kitchen, laundry and superb views. Don't walk from bus station after dark.

Camping **Camping Clube do Brasil**, Rodovia dos Inconfidentes Km 91, 2 km north, T3551 1799. Expensive but good.

Students may be able to stay, during holidays and weekends, at the self-governing student hostels, known as *repúblicas* (very welcoming, 'best if you like heavy metal music' and 'are prepared to enter into the spirit of the places'). The Prefeitura has a list of over 50 repúblicas with phone numbers, available at the Secretaria de Turismo. Many are closed Christmas to Carnival.

Mariana *p481*

A Pousada Solar dos Corrêa, R Josefá Macedo 70 and R Direita, T/F3557 2080, www.pousadasolardos correa.com.br. Central, restored 18th-century town house with spacious a/c rooms, with breakfast, TV, fridge in room, internet, parking.

B Pousada do Chafariz, R Cônego Rego 149, T3557 1492, chafariz@veloxmail.com.br. Converted colonial building, TV, fridge, parking, breakfast included.

D-E Central, R Frei Durão 8, T/F3557 1630. A charming but run-down colonial building on the attractive Praça Gomes Freire. Recommended but avoid downstairs rooms.

D-E Providência, R Dom Silvério 233, T3557 1444, www.hotelprovidencia.com.br. Along the road that leads up to the Basílica; has use of the neighbouring school's pool when classes finish at noon, small rooms, quiet.

Parque Nacional Caparaó *p482*

A Caparaó Parque, T3747 2559, 2 km from the park entrance, 15 mins' walk from the town of Alto Caparaó, nice. Ask where camping is permitted.

C São Luiz, in **Manhumirim** (Population: 20,025), good value, but **Cids Bar**, next door, Travessa 16 do Março, has better food.

São João del Rei *p483*

A Beco do Bispo, Beco do Bispo 93, 2 mins west of São Francisco de Assis, T/3371 8844, www.becodobispo.com.br. The best in town, bright a/c rooms with firm mattresses, hot showers, cable TV, pool, convenient, very helpful English speaking staff. Organizes tours. Highly recommended.

B Lenheiros Palace, Av Pres Tancredo Neves 257, T/F3371 8155, www.hotellenheiros.com.br. A modern hotel with good facilities, parking, Lenheiros Casa de Chá tea house, breakfast, no restaurant.

B Ponte Real, Av Eduardo Magalhães 254, T/F3371 7000, www.hotelpontereal.com.br. Also modern, comfortable, sizeable rooms, good restaurant.

B Pousada Casarão, opposite São Francisco church, in a converted mansion, Ribeiro Bastos 94, T3371 7447, www.pousadacasarao.com. In a delightful converted mansion house, firm beds, TV, fridge, swimming pool, games room.

C Aparecida, Praça Dr Antônio Viegas 13, T3371 2540. Central, by the bus and taxi stop, has a restaurant and lanchonete.

D Brasil, Av Presidente Tancredo Neves 395, T3371 2804. In an old house full of character and staircases, on the opposite side of the river from the railway station, cheap. Recommended but basic, no breakfast.

D Sinha Batista, R Manock Anselmo 22, T3371 5550. The best of the cheaper options, quite large rooms in a colonial building conveniently located by the central canal.

Tiradentes *p483*

LL Solar da Ponte, Praça das Mercês (proprietors John and Anna Maria Parsons), T3355 1255, www.solardaponte.com.br. Country house atmosphere, 12 rooms, price includes breakfast and afternoon tea, fresh flowers in rooms, bar, sauna, lovely gardens, swimming pool, light meals for residents only, restaurants nearby (it is in the Roteiros de Charme group, see page 393). For horse-riding treks, contact John Parsons here. Recommended.

A Pousada Mãe D'Água, Largo das Forras 50, T3355 1206, www.pousadamaedagua.com.br. Including breakfast but not tax, very nice, outdoor pool in garden.

is at R Padre Rolim 661, near São Francisco de Paula church, T3559 3252. A 'Circular' bus runs from the rodoviária to Praça Tiradentes, US$1. Taxi US$5. 11 buses a day from Belo Horizonte (2 hrs, **Pássaro Verde**), US$7.75. Day trips are run. Book your return journey to **Belo Horizonte** early if returning in the evening; buses get crowded. Bus to/from **Rio**, **Útil**, T3551 3166, 3 a day, US$35, 12 hrs (book in advance). Other **Útil** services to Rio go via Belo Horizonte. **Vale do Ouro** buses to **Congonhas** on the new Caminho de Ouro highway (T3551 5679 to check), otherwise take **Atual** bus, T0800- 7040560, to **Conselheiro Lafaiete**, US$8.50, 2¾ hrs, and change. Direct buses to **São Paulo**, 3 a day with **Vale do Ouro**, 11 hrs, US$41.

Mariana *p481*

Bus Mariana is only 12 km from Ouro Preto and can easily be visited as a side trip. Buses run between the Escola de Minas near Praça Tiradentes in Ouro Preto and the Secretaria de Cultura e Turismo de Mariana, Praça Tancredo Neves, every 30 mins.

Parque Nacional Caparaó *p482*

Bus The park is 49 km by paved road from Manhuaçu (about 190 km south of Governador Valadares) on the Belo Horizonte-Vitória road (BR-262). There are buses from **Belo Horizonte** (twice daily with **Pássaro Verde**), Ouro Preto or Vitória to **Manhumirim**, 15 km south of Manhuaçu. From Manhumirim, take a bus direct to Alto Caparaó, 8 a day, US$2.25. By **car** from the BR-262, go through Manhumirim, Alto Jaqutibá and Alto Caparaó, then 1 km to Hotel Caparaó Parque.

Congonhas *p482*

Bus The Rodoviária is 1½ km outside town; bus to town centre US$1; for 'Basílica', see above.

To/from **Belo Horizonte**, 1½ hrs, US$7, 8 times a day. To **São João del Rei**, 2 hrs, US$8, tickets are not sold until the bus comes in. Bus to **Ouro Preto**: direct on the new Caminho de Ouro highway, or go via Belo Horizonte or Conselheiro Lafaiete.

São João del Rei *p483*

Bus Rodoviária is 2 km west of the centre. Buses to **Rio**, 5 daily with **Paraibuna** (3 on Sat and Sun), 5 hrs, US$22. **Cristo Rei** to **São Paulo**, 8 hrs, 5 a day, and **Translavras**, 4 a day, US$27. **Belo Horizonte**, 3½ hrs, US$15. To **Tiradentes** with **Meier**, 8 a day, 7 on Sat, Sun and holidays, US$1.50.

Tiradentes *p483*

Bus Last bus back to **São João del Rei** is 1815, 2230 on Sun; fares are given above.
Taxi To **São João del Rei** costs US$25. Around town there are pony-drawn taxis; ponies can be hired for US$12.

São Tomé das Letras *p484*

Bus There are 3 daily buses (2 on Sun) to São Tomé from **Tres Corações**, the birthplace of Pelé, the legendary football star (to whom there is a statue in Praça Col José Martins), US$4, 1½ hrs (paved road). Tres Corações has hotels and regular buses to **Belo Horizonte**, US$25, 5½ hrs, and **São Paulo**, US$16.50.

❶ Directory

Ouro Preto *p480*

Banks **Banco do Brasil**, R São José 189, high commission, changes TCs. **Bradesco**, corner of Senador Rocha Lagoa and Padre Rolim, opposite the Escola de Minas. **Banco 24 Horas**, Praça Alves de Brito, next to Correios. **Post offices** Praça Alves de Brito.

Espírito Santo

The coastal state of Espírito Santo is where mineiros head to for their seaside holidays. The most popular beaches are south of Vitória, the state capital, while north of the city are several turtle-nesting beaches. Inland are immigrant towns.

Vitória and around ➔ *Phone code: 0xx27. Post code: 29000. Colour map 7, B6.*
Five bridges connect the island on which Vitória stands with the mainland. The state capital is beautifully set, its entrance second only to Rio's, its beaches quite as attractive, but smaller, and the climate is less humid. Port installations at Vitória and nearby Ponta do Tubarão have led to some beach and air pollution at places nearby. It is largely a modern city: The upper, older part of town, reached by steep streets and steps, is less hectic than the lower harbour area, but both are full of cars. The car-parking boys have their work cut out to find spaces. **Tourist offices**: in the rodoviária, at the airport, T3235 6300 (helpful, with map and leaflets) and at Curva da Jurema beach, Módulo 18, T3382 3053. The **Postos de Informações Turísticas** are stafed by students. For the **Superintendência de Turismo** ⓘ *T3315 5540*. **Fala Vitória** ⓘ *T156, www.vitoria.es.gov.br.*

On Avenida República is the large **Parque Moscoso**, an oasis of quiet, with a lake and playground. Colonial buildings still to be seen in the upper city are the **Capela de Santa Luzia** (1551) ⓘ *R José Marcelino, Mon-Fri 0800-1800*. It has a painted altar, otherwise a small open space; the church of **São Gonçalo** (1766) ⓘ *R Francisco Araújo, closed to the public*, and the ruins of the **Convento São Francisco** (1591). In the **Palácio Anchieta**, or **do Governo** ⓘ *Praça João Climaco (upper city- packed with parked cars)*, is the tomb of Padre Anchieta, one of the founders of São Paulo. Praça João Climaco has some restored buildings around it, including the green Casa do Cidadão. The **Teatro Carlos Gomes** ⓘ *Praça Costa Pereira*, often presents plays, also jazz and folk festivals.

Urban beaches such as **Camburi** can be affected by pollution (about 10% according to official sources), but it is pleasant, with a fair surf. Several buses run from the centre to Camburi, but look for one with Av Beira Mar on the destination board, eg No 212. Buses pass Praia do Canto, a smart district with good restaurants and shops, then cross A Ponte de Camburi.

Vila Velha, reached by A Terceira Ponte (the Third Bridge) across the bay, is a separate municipality from Vitória. The Third Bridge, a toll road, is a sweeping structure and one of the symbols of the city. It has an excellent series of beaches: Praia da Costa is the main one, with others, including Itaparica, heading south. The second main symbol of Vila Velha is the monastery of **Nossa Senhora da Penha** (1558) ⓘ *daily 0530-1645*, on a high hill with superb views of the bay, bridge and both cities. The Dutch attacked it in 1625 and 1640. Minibuses take the infirm and not-so-devout up the hill for US$0.55 return, 0630-1715 (you have to use the phone in the upper car park if you want a ride down). A museum in the convent costs US$0.35. From here you will see that Vila Velha is neither old, nor a small town. It's a built up beachfront city, noisy at times, but the sea suffers less from pollution than Camburi. Vila Velha is the place of origin of Garoto chocolates, whose factory can be visited on weekdays (T3320 1709 for times). **Tourist information** ⓘ *T3139 9015, www.vilavelha.es.gov.br.*

Some 14 km south of Vila Velha is **Barra do Jucu**, which has bigger waves, and the **Reserva de Jacarenema**, which preserves coastal ecosystems.

Inland from Vitória

Santa Leopoldina or **Domingos Martins**, both around 45 km from Vitória, are less than an hour by bus (Pretti to Santa Leopoldina five a day, four on Sunday, Aguia Branca to Domingos Martins; Friday 1700 only). Both villages preserve the architecture and customs of the first German and Swiss settlers who arrived in the 1840s. Domingos Martins (also known as Campinho) has a Casa de Cultura with some items of German settlement. Santa Leopoldina has an interesting **museum** ⓘ *Tue-Sun 0900-1100, 1300-1800*, which covers the settlers' first years in the area.

Along the BR-262 west towards Minas Gerais, most of the hills are intensely worked, with very few patches of Mata Atlântica remaining. A significant landmark is the **Pedra Azul**, a huge granite outcrop, with a sheer face (a bit like a massive tombstone). From the side you can see a spur which looks like a finger pointing to the summit. It's a Parque Etadual, whose entrance is on the BR-262. The Pedra Azul bus stop is at the turn-off to the town of Alonso Cláudio ('region of waterfalls'). There are many pousadas around Pedra Azul and the corridor between it and the next town, **Venda Nova do Imigrante**, some 10 km, is obviously in full development. This is a pretty place to stop, with well-tended flower beds along the main street, plenty of eating places, handicrafts and local Italian produce and at least one hotel (Alpes).

Santa Teresa is a charming hill town two hours, 78 km by bus from Vitória. A brochure from the Prefeitura lists local sites of interest including waterfalls, valley views and some history. It also lists where to stay and eat. Fazendas also offer accommodation, days out and rural pursuits. See Santa Teresa's website, www.santateresa-es.com.br for more. In the Galeria de Arte, just past the rodoviária, shops sell handicrafts and lots of sweet things, honey, jams, liqueurs, sweet wines and biscuits. Stalls on the side of the main road also sell local products. There is a museum, botanical garden and small zoo for study of Mata Atlântica wildlife at the **Museu Mello Leitão** ⓘ *Av José Ruschi 4, T3259 1182, 0800-1200, 1300-1700 (closed Mon morning), US$1.* Its library includes the works of the hummingbird and orchid scientist, Augusto Ruschi. Hummingbird feeders are hung outside the administration building.

Guarapari and beaches south of Vitória → *Colour map 7, B6. Pop: 88,400.*

South of Vitória (54 km) is Guarapari, whose beaches are the closest to Minas Gerais, so they get very crowded at holiday times. The beaches also attract many people seeking cures for rheumatism, neuritis and other complaints, from the radioactive monazitic sands. Information about the sands can be found at **Setuc** ⓘ *in the Casa de Cultura, Praça Jerônimo Monteiro, T3261 3058,* and at the **Antiga Matriz** church on the hill in the town centre, built in 1585.

A little further south (20 km) is the fishing village of **Ubu**, then, 8 km down the coast, **Anchieta**. Near here are Praia de Castelhanos (5 km east, on a peninsula) and **Iriri**, a small village with two beaches, Santa Helena and Inhaúma. There is accommodation in these places. The next spot down the coast, 5 km, is **Piúma**, a calm, little-visited place, renowned for its craftwork in shells. About 3 km north of the village is Pau Grande beach, where you can surf. The resort town of **Marataízes**, with good beaches, hotels and camping, is 30 km south of Piúma. It is just north of the Rio state border. Planeta buses go to Mataraízes and Piúma from Vitória.

Turtle beaches

The **Reserva Biológica Comboios** ⓘ *open 0800-1200, 1300-1700, for information, contact Projeto Tamar, Regência, T0xx27-3274 1075, or 3274 1209, www.projetotamar.org.br,* 104 km north of Vitória via Santa Cruz, is designed to protect the marine turtles which frequent this coast. **Regência**, at the mouth of the Rio Doce, 65 km north of Santa Cruz, is part of the reserve and has a regional base for Tamar, the national marine turtle protection project.

Linhares, 143 km north of Vitória on the Rio Doce, has good hotels (**E** Modenezi, opposite bus terminal, with bath) and restaurants. It is a convenient starting place for the turtle beaches. Besides those at the mouth of the Rio Doce, there is another Tamar site at **Ipiranga** ⓘ *for information, also contact Tamar, T0xx27-9942 4754,* 40 km east of Linhares by an unmade road.

Itaúnas and around → *Colour map 7, B6.*

The most attractive beaches in the state are around **Conceição da Barra** (Population: 26,494; pleasant beach hotels). Corpus Christi (early June) is celebrated with an evening procession for which the road is decorated with coloured wood chips.

Itaúnas, 27 km north by road, or 14 km up the coast, has been swamped by sand dunes, 30 m high. From time to time, winds shift the sand dunes enough to reveal the buried church tower.

Itaúnas has been moved to the opposite river bank. The coast here, too, is a protected turtle breeding ground (Tamar, Caixa Postal 53, Conceição da Barra, T0xx27-3762 5196). There are a few pousadas and a small campsite at Itaúnas and other hotels 3 km further north at Guaxindiba. To get there take a bus from the bakery in Conceição da Barra at 0700; it returns at 1700.

Espírito Santo listings

For Sleeping and Eating price codes and other relevant information, see Essentials, pages 38-40.

Sleeping

Vitória *p490*

A **Alice Vitória**, R Cnel Vicente Peixoto 95, Praça Getúlio Vargas, T3322 1144, and round the corner,

B **São José**, Av Princesa Isabel 300, T3223 7222, www.gruponeffa.com.br. In the busy lower city, good rooms with a/c, TV, comfy beds, typical business hotels, special offers. With ¶¶-¶ **Pizza Gourmet restaurant**, which serves pizza, quick dishes and local specialities, open till 2300, modern cafeteria style, clean, clinical but OK.

C **Avenida**, Av Florentino Avidos 347, T3071 1031. With breakfast, cheaper without fridge, with TV, simple, thin mattresses, noisy avenue outside. Recommended.

C **Vitória**, R Cais de São Francisco 85, T3223 0222. Near Parque Moscoso. Comfortable rooms, some with round beds, a/c, TV, rambling building, good restaurant Mar e Sol. Quieter than Avenida.

D **Cidade Alta**, R Dionisio Rosendo 213, T3322 7188. Cheaper rooms without TV, with breakfast, hot water. Strange place on Cathedral praça, cavernous, basic, full of character.

D **Imperial**, 7 de Setembro, corner Praça Costa Pereira, T3233 5017. Noisy but cheap, cheaper without TV or bath, good value but tatty, hot water, fan, has its own à kilo restaurant (lots of other cheap eating places nearby – see below).

Adequate hotels can be found opposite the rodoviária. eg **Minas**, **Lírio**, **Spala**, **JS** and **Príncipe** nearby, which looks posher.

Camburi

A **Aruan**, Av Dante Michelini 1497, T3334 0777, www.grupohp.com.br. Good beachfront hotel with rooms with views, comfortable, free sauna, pool and internet, massage at R$15, restaurant serving wide variety of dishes, safes in rooms, helpful. In same group (same phones and www): **Porto do Sol**, Av Dante Michelini 3957, and A **Vitória Palace**, R José Texeira 323, Praia do Canto, T3325 0999.

B **Alvetur**, Av Dante Michelini 877, T3225 3911, alvetur@matrix.com.br. All the usual facilities of a beachfront hotel, outside a bit faded and plain lobby, but rooms are well furnished if unfussy, big TV. In same group are **Mata da Praia**, Av Adalberto Simão Nader 133, T3227 9422, matadapraia@matrix.com.br, and **Aeroporto**, R Ary Ferreira Chagas 35, T3325 7888, haeroporto@ebr.com.br (large rooms, well-furnished, good breakfast), both on way to airport from Camburi beach, and C **Camburi**, Av Dante Michelini 1007, T3334 0303 (rather tatty outside and in lobby).

Vila Velha

B **Itaparica Praia**, R Itapemirim 30, Coqueiral de Itaparica, Vila Velha, T3329 7385, www.hotelitaparica.com.br. More pricey in high season, rooms with sea view cost a bit more. Huge rooms with fridge and TV, pool, garage, quiet, safe and good.

C **Forte Príncipe**, R Aracruz 169, Coqueiral de Itaparica, in Vila Velha, 8 km from Vitória, T3339 1605, ask for Marcelo, www.forteprincipe.com.br. Cheaper without a/c and for HI members, all rooms with 2 floors, F pp in dorm, kitchen, TV, OK, no meals, garage. Convenient for Carone supermarket, beach and buses.

E-F **Jardim da Penha**, R Hugo Viola 135, Vitória, T3324 0738, F3325 6010, take 'Universitário' bus, get off at first University stop.

Inland from Vitória: Santa Teresa *p491*

A **Pierazzo**, Av Getúlio Vargas 115, T3259 1233, pierazzohotel@uol.com.br. Central, nice rooms with frigobar, TV, comfortable, helpful, small pool, sauna. Recommended.

Itaúnus and around: Conceição da Barra *p491*

B **Pousada Mirante**, Av Atlântica 566, T3762 1633. With a/c, completely renovated, spotless, English spoken.

B **Pousada Porto Márlin**, Praia Guaxindiba, T3762 1800, www.redemarlin.com.br. With a/c, TV, fridge, seaview, waterpark, restaurant and bar.

Camping **Camping Clube do Brasil**, full facilities, Rodovia Adolfo Serra, Km 16, T3762 1346.

Eating

Vitória *p490*

A local speciality is *Moqueca capixaba*, a seafood dish served in an earthenware pot. It is a variant of the moqueca which is typical of Bahia. Note that it's big enough for 2 people, but you can get half portions. It is served with rice and siri desfiado, crab and shrimp in a thick sauce, very tasty. Several places on R Joaquim Lírio, Praia do Canto, from breads to pastas to seafood. Lots of lanches, etc, on R G Neves at Praça Costa Pereira, in the city centre, and pizzas and others on R 7 de Setembro.

TTT **Pirão**, R Joaquim Lírio 753, Praia do Canto. Specializes in *moqueca*, also fish, seafood and a couple of meat dishes. Well-established and rightly highly regarded. Ask for a bib to keep your front clean. Closed in the evening.

T **Restaurante Expresso**, G Neves 22, T3223 1091. A better class of self-service for lunch, good choice and puddings, a/c, clean, popular.

Cafés/padarias

Cheiro Verde, R Prof Baltazar, next to Pão Gostoso. *Churrascaria* and *comida caseira*, self-service.

Expressa, as above, next door and open later in afternoon, on G Neves. For good breads, cakes, savouries and cold stuffs.

Pão Gostoso, R Prof Baltazar. Also selling breads, cakes, savouries and cold stuffs.

Inland from Vitória: Santa Teresa *p491*

T **Zitu's**, Av Getúlio Vargas 79. Self-service, good local food. There are many other eating places in the town.

Bars and clubs

Vitória *p490*

The junction of Joaquim Lírio and João da Cruz in Praia do Canto is known as O Triângulo (or Bermuda Triangle). 2 bars at the junction, **Bilac** and **Búfalo Branco** are very popular Fri and Sat with young crowd. Another bar is **Apertura**, J Lírio 811, quieter. All serve food. Many other places in the area, including The Point Plaza. From centre take any bus going to Camburi and get out opposite São José supermarket just before Ponte de Camburi.

Transport

Vitória *p490*

Air Eurico Salles airport is at Goiaberas, 11 km from the city. Several buses go there eg Nos 162, 163, 122, 212. Taxi from centre US$16.50.

Bus **City buses** are mostly green, US$1. No 212 is a good route, from rodoviária to airport, marked Aeroporto; make sure it says Via Av Beira Mar: it goes right along the waterfront, past the docks (ask to be let off for Av Princesa Isabel in centre), Shopping Vitória opposite the State Legislative Assembly, by the Third Bridge, MacDonald's near InJoy internet (look for inverted V arch on right side and immediately ring bell to get off – McDonald's is across the avenue), São José supermarket just before Ponte de Camburi, all along Camburi beach, then turns left to airport.

To Vila Velha: from Vitória take a yellow 500 bus marked 'Vilha Velha' from Praça Getúlio Vargas, or a 514 from Av Mal Mascarenhas de Moraes. No 508 connects Camburi and Vila Velha. Buses back to Vitória leave from the rodoviária, or a stop on Champagnat, almost opposite Carone supermarket, fare US$0.75. In Vila Velha, to get to Coqueiral de Itaparica (see Sleeping), go to the rodoviária and change to a blue bus, Linhas Alimentadores, No 605 or 606, marked T Ibes (ask where to get off) – you shouldn't have to pay for this connection. For NS da Penha, ask to be let off the yellow bus into Vila Velha on Av Henrique Moscoso at or near R Antônio Ataíde, which you go down (right from direction of bus) to R Vasco Coutinho then turn right.

The rodoviária is a 15-min walk west of the centre; many buses go there and there is a city bus stop just outside. It has good lanches, sweet shops and toilets (R$0.70). **Rio**, 8 hrs, US$37. **Belo Horizonte**, see above. **Ouro Preto**, **São Geraldo** US$36, 6 hrs, poor road, also **Itapemirim**, which goes to other Minas Gerais destinations. **Rio Doce** to **Juiz da Fora** and **southern Minas Gerais**. **São Paulo**, US$62, 16 hrs. **Salvador**, 18 hrs, US$120, **Aguia Branca** at 1700; **Porto Seguro** direct 11 hrs with lots of stops **Aguia Branca**, 2 a day, US$58; alternatively, take a bus to Eunápolis, then change to buses which run every hour. **Alvorada** bus from Vitória to **Guarapari**, 1½ hrs, several daily, US$5.

Train Daily passenger service to **Belo Horizonte**, departs 0700, arrives Belo Horizonte at 1940, returns 0730, arrives 2100; US$27.50 executivo (very comfortable), US$17.50 econômico. T0800 992233, CAP Centro de atendimento de pasageiros. The station is called Pedro Nolasco, Km 1 BR-262: take a yellow bus saying 'Ferroviária', best is No 515 going to Campo Grande; to the city (cross the main road outside the station), Praia do Canto and Camburi, take a 'T Laranjeiras via Beira Mar' bus.

Inland from Vitória: Santa Teresa *p491*
Bus Several buses daily from **Vitória** rodoviária with **Lirio dos Vales**, US$7, most go via Fundão on the BR-101 going north, all paved. Fewer buses via Santa Leopoldina, not all paved, a beautiful journey.

Directory

Vitória *p490*
Airline offices TAM, R Eugênio Neto 111, T3325 1222. **Banks** Banco do Brasil, Praça Pio XII, câmbio 1000-1600. ATM for Visa. Other banks close by. **HSBC**, Av Princesa Isabel 43, changes TCs, but very slow and 6% commission. **Car hire** Agencies at airport. **Telephones** Rios phone office (Telemar) on Praça Costa Pereira.

North of Belo Horizonte

Diamantina, the most remote of the colonial cities to the north of the State capital is reached from Belo Horizonte by taking the paved road to Brasília (BR-040). Turn northeast to **Curvelo**, beyond which the road passes through the impressive rocky country of the Serra do Espinhaço. Equally remote is the town of Serro, while in the Serra do Espinhaço itself is the Cipó national park, protecting high mountain grassland and rare species.

Diamantina → *Phone code: 0xx38. Post code: 39100. Colour map 7, A5. Population: 44,259.*
This centre of a once-active diamond industry Diamantina has excellent colonial buildings. Its churches are not as grand as those of Ouro Preto, but it is the least spoiled of all the colonial mining cities, with carved overhanging roofs and brackets. This very friendly, beautiful town is in the deep interior, amid barren mountains. It is lively at weekends. **President Juscelino Kubitschek**, the founder of Brasília, was born here. His **house** ⓘ *R São Francisco 241, Tue-Sun 1000-1200, 1400-1800, US$2*, is now a museum. Festivals include Carnival, 12 September, which is O Dia das Serestas, the Day of the Serenades, for which the town is famous; this is also the anniversary of Kubitschek's birth. **Departamento de Turismo** ⓘ *Casa de Cultura, Praça Antônio Eulálio 53, 3rd floor, T3531 1636*; pamphlets, reliable map, friendly and helpful, free tour of churches with guide (tip guide).

Sights The oldest church in Diamantina is **Nossa Senhora do Rosário** ⓘ *Largo Dom Joaquim, Tue-Sat 0800-1200, 1400-1800, Sun 0800-1200*, built by slaves in 1728. **Nossa Senhora do Carmo** ⓘ *R do Carmo, Tue-Sat 0800-1200, 1400-1800, Sun 0800-1200*, dates from 1760-1765 and was built for the Carmelite Third Order. It is the richest church in the town, with fine decorations and paintings and a pipe organ, covered in gold leaf, made locally.

São Francisco de Assis ⓘ *R São Francisco, just off Praça JK, Sat 0800-1200, 1400-1800, Sun 0900-1200*, was built between 1766 and the turn of the 19th century. It is notable for its paintings. Other colonial churches are the **Capela Imperial do Amparo** (1758-1776), **Nossa Senhora das Mercês** (1778-1784) and **Nossa Senhora da Luz** (early 19th century). The **Catedral Metropolitana de Santo Antônio**, on Praça Correia Rabelo, was built in the 1930s in neo-colonial style to replace the original cathedral.

After repeated thefts, the diamonds of the **Museu do Diamante** ⓘ *R Direita 14, Tue-Sat 1200-1730, Sun 0900-1200, US$1*, are now kept in the Banco do Brasil. The museum houses an important collection of materials used in the diamond industry, plus oratories and iron collars used to shackle slaves. **Casa de Chica da Silva** ⓘ *Praça Lobo Mesquita 266, Tue-Sat 1200-1730, Sun 0900-1200, free*. Chica da Silva was a slave in the house of the father of Padre Rolim (one of the Inconfidentes). She became the mistress of João Fernandes de Oliveira, a diamond contractor. Chica, who died 15 February 1796, has become a folk-heroine among Brazilian blacks.

Behind the 18th-century building which now houses the **Prefeitura Municipal** (originally the diamonds administration building, Praça Conselheiro Matta 11) is the **Mercado Municipal** or **Mercado dos Tropeiros** (muleteers) ⓘ *Praça Barão de Guaicuí*. The **Casa da Glória** ⓘ *R da Glória 297, Tue-Sun 1300-1700*, is two houses on either side of the street connected by an enclosed bridge. It contains the Instituto Eschwege de Geologia.

Walk along the **Caminho dos Escravos**, the old paved road built by slaves between the mining area on Rio Jequitinhonha and Diamantina. A guide is essential (ask at the Casa de Cultura), and beware of snakes and thunderstorms. Along the river bank it is 12 km on a dirt road to **Biribiri**, a pretty village with a well-preserved church and an abandoned textile factory. It also has a few bars and at weekends it is a popular, noisy place. About halfway, there are swimming pools in the river; opposite them, on a cliff face, are animal paintings in red. The age and origin are unknown. The plant life along the river is interesting and there are beautiful mountain views.

At **São Gonçalo do Rio das Pedras** and **Milo Verde** (35 and 42 km south of Diamantina on an unsealed road), there are trails for hiking and riding, waterfalls and some colonial buildings in the towns. Simple lodging is available.

The sleepy little town of **São Gonçalo do Rio Preto**, which sits next to a beautiful mountain river, is famous for its traditional festivals. It lies some 60 km from Diamantina on the edge of the **Parque Estadual de São Gonçalo do Rio Preto**, an area of pristine *cerrado* filled with flowering trees and particularly rich in birdlife. There are *pousadas* in São Gonçalo and cabins in the park (accessible by taxi). Guides are also available.

Serro → *Phone code: 0xx38. Post code: 39150. Colour map 7, B5. Population: 21,012.*

From Diamantina, 92 km by paved road and reached by bus from there or from Belo Horizonte, is this unspoiled colonial town on the Rio Jequitinhonha. It has six fine baroque churches, a museum and many beautiful squares. It makes queijo serrano, one of Brazil's best cheeses, being in the centre of a prosperous cattle region. The most conspicuous church is **Santa Rita** on a hill in the centre of town, reached by a long line of steps. On the main Praça João Pinheiro, by the bottom of the steps, is **Nossa Senhora do Carmo**, arcaded, with original paintings on the ceiling and in the choir. The town has two large mansions: those of the **Barão de Diamantina** ⓘ *Praça Presidente Vargas*, now in ruins, and of the **Barão do Serro** ⓘ *across the river on R da Fundição, Tue-Sat 1200-1700, Sun 0900-1200*, beautifully restored and used as the town hall and Casa de Cultura. The **Museu Regional Casa dos Ottoni** ⓘ *Praça Cristiano Ottoni 72*, is an 18th-century house with furniture and objects from the region. There are hotels in town.

Parque Nacional da Serra do Cipó

ⓘ *Entry US$7. T0xx31 3718 7228, www.guiaserradocipo.com.br, 0800-1700.*

About 105 km northeast of Belo Horizonte, **Parque Nacional da Serra do Cipó**, 33,400 sq km of the Serra do Espinhaço, covers important cerrado and gallery forest habitats, which provide a home for rare bird species like the Cipó Canastero and Grey-backed Tachuri, as well as endangered mammals such as maned wolf and monkeys such as the masked titi and brown capuchin. There are a number of carnivorous plants. The predominant habitat is high mountain grassland, with rocky outcroppings. The park can only be visited with an official guide.

North of Belo Horizonte listings

For Sleeping and Eating price codes and other relevant information, see Essentials, pages 38-40.

Sleeping

Diamantina *p494*

All are within 10 mins' walking distance of the centre unless otherwise stated.

AL Tijuco, R Macau do Melo 211, T3531 1022, www.hoteltijuco.com.br. A deliciously dated Niemeyer building with tastefully renovated plush wood interior and rooms which retain their 60s feel, great views.

A Relíquias do Tempo, R Macau de Baixo 104, T3531 1627, www.pousadareliquiasdotempo.com.br. Cosy rooms in a pretty 19th-century house just off Praça JK, decorated like a colonial family home, generous breakfasts.

A-B Pousada do Garimpo, Av da Saudade 265, T3531 1044, www.pousadadogarimpo.com.br. Plain, well-kept rooms in a smart hotel on the outskirts, pool, sauna, restaurant serving some of the city's best Minas cooking.

B-C Montanhas de Minas, R da Roman 264, T3531 3240, www.grupomontanhasdeminas.com.br. Spacious rooms with stone floors, some with balconies, decent breakfasts.

C Pousada da Seresta, R Jogo da Bola 415, T3531 2368. Rambling colonial house, quiet, good views.

C-D Pousada dos Cristais, R Joga da Bola 53, T3531 3923, www.diamantinanet.com.br/pousadadoscristais. A range of simple, large rooms in white on the edge of town, with views across the mountains.

C-D Pousada Ouro de Minas, R do Amparo 90A, T3531 2306, www.grupomontanhasdeminas.com.br. Simple well-kept rooms with tiny bathrooms in a converted colonial house. In the same group is Pousada Acaiaca, R Acaiaca 65, T3531 8383.

C-D Santiago, Largo Dom João 133, T3431 3407, hotelsantiago@jk.net. Plain, small but spruce rooms, reasonable breakfast.

C-E Pousada Dona Daizinha, R Direita 131, T3531 1351. Simple wooden-floored rooms in a colonial house; some with space for up to 5. Very good breakfast offered and friendly service.

Parque Nacional da Serra do Cipó *p495*

LL Cipó Veraneio, Rodovia MG-10, Km 95, Jaboticatubas, T3718 7000, www.cipoveraneiohotel.com.br. Comfortable a/c rooms with cable TV, fridge, in terraces of stone cabins, pool, sauna, very good tour operator and a *cachaça* distillery just up the road which produces some of Minas's finest.

LL Toucan Cipó, exclusively through www.dehouche.com as part of a tour. Luxury *fazenda* in prisitine *cerrado* forest cut by clear-water streams. Very rich in bird and mammal life.

Eating

Diamantina *p494*

TTT **Cantina do Marinho**, R Direita 113, T3531 1686. Formal, decorated with bottles of wine, black-tie waiters is celebrated for its *Salmão Provençale* and *Bacalhau*. Set lunch T.

TT **Caipirão**, R Campos Carvalho 15, T3531 1526. Minas cooking with buffet lunch cooked over a traditional wood-fired clay oven, evening à la carte.

TT **Grupiara**, R Campos Carvalho 12, T3531 3887. Decent regional cooking, convivial atmosphere, good value per kilo options at lunch.

TT **Recanto do Antônio**, Beco da Tecla 39, T3531 1147. Minas food and decent steaks, chic rustic dining room in a colonial house.

T **Sisisi**, Beco da Mota 89, T3531 3071. Pasta, Minas cooking and good value *prato feito* at lunchtime.

Bars and clubs

Diamantina *p494*

Apocalipse Point, Praça Barão de Guaicuí 78, T3531 9296. Sertaneja and Axe music. Lively.

Café a Baiuca, R da Quitanda. Coffee bar by day, funky bar by night with music DVDs and a crowd spilling out into the street.

Espaço B, R Beco da Tecla. A bookshop café serving crêpes and draught beer until late.

Festivals and events

Diamantina *p494*

Vesperatas, musicians and singers serenade from balconies along the colonial streets and drum troupes and bands parade every other Sat.

Activities and tours

Diamantina *p494*

Diamantina Tour, Praça dos Garimpeiros 616, T8801 1802. City tours, adventure activities (rappel and trekking) and trips to nearby natural attractions and Biri Biri. From US$8 pp per day.

Real Receptivo, R Campos Carvalho 19 loja 12, T3531 1636, www.realreceptivo.com.br. City tours and trips to nearby natural attractions.

Transport

Diamantina *p494*

Bus To **São Gonçalo do Rio Preto**, one bus per day. 6 buses a day to **Belo Horizonte**, via Curvelo, with **Pássaro Verde**: 2½ hrs to **Curvelo**, US$5, to **Belo Horizonte**, US$30, 5 hrs. To **Bahia**, 2 buses to **Araçuaí** per day (4 hrs); from here combis and buses run to **Itaubim** from where there are connections to Porto Seguro and other destinations in Bahia. For **Brasília**: 1 bus a day to **Montes Claros** for connections; or connect in **Curvelo**, take any Belo Horizonte bus.

Parque Nacional da Serra do Cipó *p495*

Bus Take bus to Serro (2 daily) for Santa Ana do Riacho and the Serra do Cipó.

Southern Brazil

→ *Population: 9.5 million.*

Southern Brazil comprises three states: Paraná, Santa Catarina and Rio Grande do Sul. Paraná has one of the premier tourist sites in South America, the Iguaçu Falls, described in its own section (see page 526). The Paraná coastline, albeit short, has a large area of coastal rainforest and little beach-fringed islands, like Ilha do Mel. Its main port, Paranaguá, is connected with the capital, Curitiba, by one of the most impressive railways in South America. It is the coast, however, from which Santa Catarina gains most of its reputation, with highly regarded surfing beaches and a growing interest in whale watching. Inland, the state has a distinctive European feel, including frosty and snowy winters in the highest parts. The culture of the region has been heavily influenced by large immigrant communities from Japan, Germany, Poland, Italy, Syria and Ukraine. In Rio Grande do Sul this can be seen (and tasted) in the Italian communities, well known for their wines. The southernmost state, as well as having yet more beaches, has some beautiful national parks, the remnants of Jesuit missions and the south's largest industrial centre, Porto Alegre. But above all, this is the land of the gaúcho, the Brazilian cowboy.

Curitiba and around → *Phone code: 0xx41. Post code: 80000. Colour map 7, C2.*

Situated in the Serra do Mar, Curitiba is regarded as one of Brazil's model cities for quality of life. It has something of a European feel, with leafy squares and a street that is open 24 hours. It makes a pleasant base for exploring the coast and the surrounding mountains, and is the start of one of the world's most spectacular railway journeys.

Ins and outs

Tourist offices Setu ⓘ *R Deputado Mário de Barros 1290, Centro Cívico, T3313 3500, www.pr.gov.br/turismo.* **Disque Turismo** ⓘ *T3254 1516 (state), T3352 8000 (city)*; also booths at the airport and Rodoferroviária (T3320 3121, 0700-1300). **Kiosks** ⓘ *R 24 Horas, T3324 7036, 0800-2400, 2200 at weekends, Museu Oscar Niemeyer (address below), T3350 4466*. Annual *Guía Turística de Curitiba e Paraná*, US$4, on sale at kiosks; free weekly leaflet, *Bom Programa*, available in shops, cinemas, paper stands.

Sights

One of the cleanest cities in Latin America, the capital of Paraná state has extensive open spaces and some exceptionally attractive modern architecture. The commercial centre is the busy Rua 15 de Novembro, part of which is a pedestrian area called **Rua das Flores**. The **Boca Maldita** is a particularly lively part where local artists exhibit. On Praça Tiradentes is the **Cathedral** ⓘ *R Barão do Serro Azul 31, T3324 5136*, built in neo-Gothic style and inaugurated in 1893 (restored in 1993). Behind the cathedral, near Largo da Ordem, is a pedestrian area with a flower clock and old buildings, very beautiful in the evening when the old lamps are lit, nightlife is concentrated here. The oldest church in Curitiba is the **Igreja de Ordem Terceira da São Francisco das Chagas**, built in 1737 in Largo da Ordem. Its most recent renovation was in 1978-1980. In its annex is the **Museu de Arte Sacra** ⓘ *T3321 3265*. The **Igreja de Nossa Senhora do Rosário de São Benedito** was built in the Praça Garibáldi in 1737 by slaves and was the Igreja dos Pretos de São Benedito. It was demolished in 1931 and a new church was inaugurated in 1946. A mass for tourists, Missa do Turista, is held on Sunday at 0800. An art market is held in **Praça Garibáldi** on Sunday mornings. **Museu Paranaense** ⓘ *in the Palácio São Francisco, R Kellers 289, T3304 3300, www.pr.gov.br/museupr/, Tue-Fri 0930-1730, Sat-Sun 1100-1500, US$1,*

holds permanent and temporary exhibitions, including documents, manuscripts, ethnological and historical material, stamps, works of art, photographs and archaeological pieces.

Museu de Arte Contemporânea ⓘ *R Desembargador Westphalen 16, Praça Zacarias, T3222 5172, Tue-Fri 1000-1900, Sat-Sun 1000-1600*, displays Brazilian contemporary art in its many forms, with an emphasis on artists from Paraná. All that remains of the old **Palácio Avenida** ⓘ *Travessa Oliveira Belo 11, T3321 6249*, is the façade, which was retained during remodelling works in 1991. Nowadays it has offices, an auditorium for 250 people and cultural activities. The **Rua 24 Horas**, where the whole street is protected by an arched roof, has shops, bars and restaurants that never close. On Saturday mornings there is a small fish fair at **Praça Generosa Marques**.

North of the centre, the **Solar do Barão** ⓘ *R Presidente Carlos Cavalcanti 53, T3321 3240*, built in 1880-1883, is used for concerts in the auditorium and exhibitions. The **Passeio Público**, in the heart of the city (closed Monday), inaugurated in 1886. It has three lakes, each with an island, and playground. The **Centro Cívico** is at the end of Avenida Dr Cândido de Abreu, 2 km from the centre: a monumental group of buildings dominated by the **Palácio Iguaçu**, headquarters of the state and municipal governments. In a patio behind it is a relief map to scale of Paraná. The **Bosque de João Paulo II** behind the Civic Centre on Rua Mateus Leme, was created in December 1980 after the Pope's visit to Curitiba. It also contains the **Memorial da Imigração Polonesa no Paraná** (Polish immigrants memorial). The **Museu Oscar Niemeyer** (MON) ⓘ *R Mal Hermes 999, T3350 4400, www.museuoscarniemeyer.org.br, Tue-Sun 1000-1800, US$2*, was designed by, and is devoted to the famous Brazilian modernist architect who designed Brasília and was a disciple of Le Corbusier, together with other Paranense artists. The stunning principal building is shaped like a giant eye. An underground passage, lined with exhibits and photographs, links it to a sculpture garden.

Eating
1 Bar do Victor
2 Guega
3 Ile de France
4 Madalosso
5 Porcini Trattoria
6 Salmão
7 Trattoria Barolo

Bars & clubs
8 Fire Fox
9 The Farm

About 4 km east of the rodoferroviário, the **Jardim Botânico Fanchette Rischbieter** has a fine glass house, inspired by Crystal Palace in London. The gardens are in the French style and there is also a **Museu Botánico** ⓘ *R Ostoja Roguski (Primeira Perimetral dos Bairros), T3362 1800 (museum), 0600-2000*. Take the orange Expreso buses from Praça Rui Barbosa.

Parque Nacional Vila Velha → *Colour map 7, C2.*
ⓘ *The park office (phone, toilets, lanchonete, tourist information) is 300 m from the highway and the park a further 1½ km (entrance US$3.50, 0800-1900). Allow all day if visiting all 3 sites (unless you hitch, or can time the buses well, it's a lot of walking).*
West of Curitiba on the road to Ponta Grossa is the **Museu Histórico do Mate** ⓘ *T3304 3300, free, BR 277 at Km 17*, an old water-driven mill where mate was prepared. On the same road is Vila Velha, 91 km from Curitiba: the

sandstone rocks have been weathered into most fantastic shapes. About 4 km away are the **Furnas** ⓘ *US$2*, three water holes, the deepest of which has a lift (US$1.30 – not always working) which descends almost to water level. Also in the park is the Lagoa Dourada (surrounded by forest) whose water level is the same as that in the Furnas.

Curitiba and around listings

For Sleeping and Eating price codes and other relevant information, see Essentials, pages 38-40. See also Telephone, page 397, for important phone changes.

Sleeping

Curitiba *p497, map p498*

There are some good-value hotels in the **A** and **B** categories. Some of the cheaper central hotels are seedy. There are good hotels southeast of the centre in the vicinity of the Rodoferroviária, but the cheaper ones are close to the wholesale market, which operates noisily through the night.

L Bourbon Curitiba, R Cândido Lopes 102, T3221 4600, www.bourbon.com.br. Good modern hotel in the centre with a mock old-fashioned charm, rooms have jacuzzis, business centre.

L Grand Hotel Rayon, R Visconde de Nácar 1424, T2108 1100, www.rayon.com.br. Central, much the best option for business travellers with all the expected services, pool, saunas, well-equipped gym and travel agency.

A Del Rey, R Ermelino de Leão 18, T2106 0099, www.hoteldelrey.com.br. Central, upmarket yet relaxed, large rooms, good restaurant, gym, good value. Recommended.

B Bourbon Batel Express, Av Visconde de Guarapuava 4889, T3342 7990, www.bourbon.com.br. A/c, modern and comfortable, good breakfast, wireless internet in rooms US$3/day, attentive service, good value.

B-C Deville Express, R Amintas de Barros 73, T3322 8558, www.deville.com.br. Central hotel with a bar, small modest restaurant, a/c, with fridge.

C Estação Palace, R Des Westphalen 126, T3322 9840, www.hotel-curitiba.com.br/estacao. Excellent for price, 24-hr room service, internet, rather stark but immaculate. Recommended.

C Lumini, R Gen Carneiro 1094, T/F3264 5244, www.hotellumini.com.br. Good apartment hotel in a quiet street, all rooms a/c.

C Nova Lisboa, Av 7 de Setembro 1948, T3264 1944. With breakfast, bargain for cheaper rates without breakfast. Recommended.

C O'Hara, R 15 de Novembro 770, T3232 6044, www.hotelohara.com.br. Good location, fan, excellent breakfast, parking.

D Cervantes, R Alfredo Bufrem 66, T3222 9593, www.cervanteshotel.cjb.net. Central, small but cosy.

E Casa do Estudante Luterano Universitario, R Pr Cavalcanti, T3324 3313. For those with ISIC student cards, good.

E pp **Curitiba Eco Hostel**, R Luiz Tramontin 1693, Campo Comprido, T3274 7979, www.curitibaeco hostel.com.br. Cheaper for HI members, **D** in double room, youth hostel association for Paraná is located in this suburb outside the centre – catch a bus from the Rodoviária to Praça Rui Barbosa, marked Expreso Centenário, then change to a Tramontina bus to the door.

F pp **Hostel Roma**, R Barão do Rio Branco 805, T3322 2838, www.hostelroma.com.br. Smart HI hostel with single-sex dorms, also family rooms, with bath, breakfast included, TV room, internet, members' kitchen.

Camping Camping Clube do Brasil, BR-116, Km 84, 16 km towards São Paulo, T358 6634.

Eating

Curitiba *p497, map p498*

Close to the Rodoferroviária is the market, where there are a couple of lanchonetes. The shopping malls have good food courts. Hot sweet wine sold on the streets in winter helps keep out the cold.

TTT **Bar do Victor**, R Lívio Moreira 284, São Lourenço, T3353 1920. Excellent fish restaurant, open Tue-Sat 1200-1430, 1830-2330, Sun 1130-1430.

TTT **Guega**, R Vol da Patria 539 (centre), T3023 8244. New Italian restaurant where the renowned Boulevard used to be.

TTT **Ile de France**, Praça 19 de Dexembro 538, T3223 9262, open 1900-2400, closede Sun. Top-quality French cuisine, fine wine list, reservations essential.

Madalosso, Av Manoel Ribas 5875, Santa Felicidade, T3372 2121. The largest Italian rodízio in Brazil, 4,600 seats! Closed Sun evening.

Porcini Trattoria, Rua Buenos Aires 277, Batel, T3022 5115, www.porcini.com.br. Open daily for lunch and dinner, except Mon lunch. Mainly Italian food, good salads and vegetables, superb quality, fantastic wine list. Recommended.

Trattoria Barolo, Av Silva Jardim 2487, Água Verde, T3243 3430. Closed Sun evening. Excellent Italian for fish and meat dishes and pizza, huge wine list, good prices.

Salmão, R Emiliano Perneta 924. In historic house, delicious fish and pizza, special offers, live music every night, open until 0100. Short taxi ride from centre.

Bars and clubs

Curitiba *p497, map p498*

A cluster of bars at the Largo da Ordem have tables and chairs on the pavement, music, and bar food: **Fire Fox**, Av Jaime Reis 46, flanked by **Tuba's** and **The Farm**.

Entertainment

Curitiba *p497, map p498*

Cinema There are cinemas in several shopping centres, and other places showing international films. Tickets are usually US$4-5 Mon-Thu, and US$6-8 at weekends. Best to l ook in the newspaper for music and what's on in the bars, clubs and theatres; **Gazeta do Povo** has a what's on section called *Caderno G*.

Theatres Theatre festival in Mar. **Teatro Guaíra**, R 15 de Novembro, T3304 7999, www.tguaira.pr .gov.br. For plays and revues (also has free events – get tickets early in the day). **Teatro Positivo**, R Prof Pedro Viriato Parigot de Souza 5300, Campo Comprido, T3317 3000, www.teatro positivo.com.br. An impressive theatre attracting international and Brazilian stars, on the magnificent campus of the Universidade Positivo, www.up.edu.br. Very good exhibitions are held here, too (bus lines Linha Expresso Centenário and Linha Ligeirinho Pinhais from centre).

Shopping

Curitiba *p497, map p498*

Handicrafts Feira de Arte e Artesanato, Praça Garibáldi, Sun 0900-1400. **Lojas de Artesanato**, Casa de Artesanato Centro, R Mateus Leme 22, T352 4021. **Lojas de Artesanato 'Feito Aquí'**, Dr Muricy 950, International Airport and Shopping Mueller. **Lojas Leve Curitiba**, at several locations, R 24 Horas, Afonso Pena airport, Ópera de Arame, Jardim Botánico, Memorial de Curitiba.

Shopping centres Shopping Estação, Av 7 de Setembro 2775, in the old railway station. As well as shops and restaurants, etc, has a railway museum and exhibitions on perfume and Brazil's natural environments. Others include **Shopping Crystal Plaza**, R Com Araújo, Batel, **Shopping Curitiba**, R Brig Franco at Praça Osvaldo Cruz, and largest of all, **Barigüi**, R Prof Pedro Viriato Parigot de Souza 600, Ecoville.

Activities and tours

Curitiba *p497, map p498*

Scubasul, R 13 de Maio 894, Alto São Francisco, T3232 0198, www.scubasul.com.br. Advice on diving, courses arranged, reasonable prices.

Transport

Curitiba *p497, map p498*

Air Afonso Pena (21 km away) for international and national flights, T3381 1515; good services: ATMs, left luggage, hotel booking desk, and cafés. Daily flights from Rio, São Paulo, Buenos Aires, Asunción, and cities in the interior of Paraná state. Two types of bus run from the Rodoferroviária to the airport, making several stops along the way: **Aeroporto Executivo**, www.aeroportoexecutivo.com.br, 0500-2330 daily, 20 mins, US$4; regular city bus, 40 mins, US$1.75.

Bus There are several route types on the integrated transport system and you are advised to pick up a map with details. **Express** are red and connect the transfer terminals to the city centre, pre-paid access through the silver 'tubo' bus stops; conventional orange **Feeder** buses connect the terminals to the surrounding neighbourhoods; **Interdistrict** green buses run on circular routes connecting transfer terminals and city districts without passing through the centre; **Direct or speedy** silver grey buses use the 'tubo' stations to link the main districts and connect the surrounding municipalities with Curitiba; **Conventional** yellow buses operate on the normal road network between the surrounding municipalities, the Integration

Terminals and the city centre; **City circular** white mini buses, **Linha Turismo**, circle the major transport terminals and points of interest in the traditional city centre area. US$7 (multi-ticket booklets available), every 30 mins from 0900-1700, except on Mon. First leaves from R das Flores, in front of McDonald's. Four stops allowed.

Short-distance bus services within the metropolitan region (up to 40 km) begin at Terminal Guadalupe at R João Negrão s/n. The Terminal Rodoviário/Estação Rodoferroviária is on Av Afonso Camargo s/n, T3320 3000, for other cities in Paraná and other states. Banks, restaurants, bookshops, shops, phones, post office, pharmacy, tourist agency, tourist office and public services are all here. Frequent buses to **São Paulo** (6 hrs, US$28-66) and **Rio** (12 hrs, US$55, leito US$92). To **Foz do Iguaçu**, 8 a day (**Catarinense** and others), 10 hrs, US$50. **Porto Alegre**, 10 hrs, US$45 (leito US$67). **Florianópolis**, US$27, 4½ hrs; **Blumenau** 4 hrs, US$15.50, 3 daily with **Penha/Catarinense.** Good service to most destinations in Brazil. **Pluma** bus to **Buenos Aires** (change buses at Foz do Iguaçu) and to **Asunción**, US$47. **TTL** runs to **Montevideo**, Wed, Fri, Sun 0510, 26 hrs, US$115.

Train **Rodoferroviária**, Av Afonso Camargo s/n. There are two trains running on the line from Curitiba to **Morretes** and, in the past at least, **Paranaguá**: the **Litorina**, a modern a/c railcar with on-board service with bilingual staff, which stops at Morretes, with a halt at Marumbi Park station; hand luggage only; tickets can be bought 2 days in advance; departs 0900, returns 1500, US$63 to Morretes, US$47.50 back, 3 hrs. Also the **Trem Classe Convencional**, which runs daily to Morretes, with a stop at Marumbi, buy tickets 2 days in advance, departs daily 0800, returns 1500, turístico, US$26.50 (US$18 back), executivo US$42 (US$27 back), a US$14/US$11 econômico fare is available from the ticket office only, best bought 2 weeks in advance. Schedules change frequently; check times in advance; delays to be expected. In 2009, Paranaguá station was closed and all trains were turning round at Morretes. For information and reservations, **Serra Verde Express**, T3323 4007, www.serraverde express.com.br. Tickets sold at the Rodoferro viária, Portão 8, 0700-1830 (till 1200 on Sun). Sit on the left-hand side on journey from Curitiba. On cloudy days there's little to see on the higher parts. The train is usually crowded on Sat and Sun. Serra Verde Express also gives information about trips by car on the Estrada de Graciosa and sells various packages to the coast.

Parque Nacional Vila Velha *p499*

Bus Take a bus from **Curitiba** to the park, not to the town of Ponta Grossa 26 km away. **Princesa dos Campos** bus from Curitiba 0745, 1415, 1715, 1½ hrs, US$9.40. One bus from Vila Velha between 1530-1600, US$1.10, 4½ km to turn-off to Furnas (another 15 mins' walk) and Lagoa Dourada. Bus Mon-Sat 1330 to **Furnas** – Ponta Grossa that passes the car park at the top of the park. On Sun, 1200,1620,1800. It may be advisable to go to Ponta Grossa and return to Curitiba from there (114 km, many buses a day, US$10.75, **Princesa dos Campos**, www.princesadoscampos.com.br.

Directory

Curitiba *p497, map p498*

Airline offices TAM, R Ermelino Leão 511, T3219 1200. **Trip**, at airport, T3381 1710. **Webjet**, T0300-210 1234. **Banks** Bradesco, R 15 de Novembro 155, Visa ATM. Plus or Cirrus associated credit cards can cash money at **Citibank**, R Marechal Deodoro 711 or at Buenos Aires 305 near Shopping Curitiba. **HSBC**, Travessa Oliveira Bello, 34 Sobreloja, Centro, T3777 6043, Brazilian headquarters. **Itaú** has many branches, including R 15 de Novembro 299, Centro. **Cotação**, R Marechal Deodoro 500, 2nd floor, Centro. Also **Galeria Suissa**, R Marechal Deodoro 280, open Sat when many others are closed. **Sidney**, in Shopping Mueller and on Marechal Deodoro, is a good câmbio. **Diplomata**, R Presidente Faria 145 in the arcade. **Cultural centres** British Council, R Pres Faria 51, T3232 2912, curitiba@british council.org.br. **Instituto Goethe**, R Reinaldino S de Quadros 33, T3262 8422, www.goethe.de/ ins/br/cur/deindex.htm. **Embassies and consulates** Austria, R Cândido Hartmann 570, Ed Champagnat, 28th floor, T3336 1166, cons_aus@terra.com.br, Mon-Fri 1000-1300. **Denmark**, R Prof Francisco Ribeiro 683, T3641 1112, saio@novozymes.com.

France, R Conselheiro Laurindo 490, 10th floor, 3320 5805, consulat.curitiba@yahoo.fr. **Germany**, R Emiliano Perneta 297, 2nd floor, T3222 6920, Mon-Fri 0800-1200. **Netherlands**, Av Candido de Abreu 469, conj 1606, T3353 2630, Holland@ telecorp.com.br, open 1400-1700, except emergencies. **UK**, R Pres Faria 51, 2nd floor, T3322 1202, curitiba@gra-bretanha.org.br. Mon-Fri 0830-1200, 1400-1730. **Uruguay**, Av Carlos Cavalho 417, 32 floor, T3225 5550, conurucur@ terra.com.br.

Medical services Emergency: T190 for Police and T193 for ambulance or fire. The Cajuru Hospital is at Av São José 738, T3362 1121, and the Evangélico is at Al Augusto Stellfeld 1908, T3322 4141, both of which deal with emergencies. **Post offices** Main post office is at Mal Deodoro 298; post offices also at R 15 de Novembro and R Pres Faria. **Telephones** **Tele Centro-Sul**, information, T102. **Embratel**, Galeria Minerva, R 15 de Novembro. **Useful addresses** Visa extensions: Federal police, Dr Muricy 814, 1000-1600.

The Paraná coast

The railway to the coast winds its way around the slopes of the Marumbi mountain range, across rushing rivers and through the forest to the sea. There are pretty colonial towns en route. The coast itself only has a few beaches, but in compensation has some of the richest biodiversity in Brazil.

Curitiba to Paranaguá

Two roads and a railway run from Curitiba to Paranaguá. The railway journey is the most spectacular in Brazil. There are 13 tunnels and sudden views of deep gorges and high peaks and waterfalls as the train rumbles over dizzy bridges and viaducts. Near Banhado station (Km 66) is the waterfall of Véu da Noiva; from the station at Km 59, the mountain range of **Marumbi** can be reached. See page 502 for schedules and fares. Of the roads, the older, cobbled Estrada da Graçiosa, with numerous viewpoints and tourist kiosks along the way, is much more scenic than the paved BR277.

Parque Nacional Marumbi

Marumbi Park is a large area of preserved Atlantic rainforest and is a UNESCO World Heritage Site and Biosphere Reserve. The forest in the 2,343-ha park is covered in banana trees, palmito and orchids. There are rivers and waterfalls and among the fauna are monkeys, snakes and toucans. A climbing trail reaches 625 m to Rochedinho (two hours). Hands need to be free to grasp trees, especially during the rainy season (December to March), when trails are muddy. The last five minutes of the trail is a dangerous walk along a narrow rock trail. At the park entrance, notify administration of your arrival and departure. There is a small museum, video, left luggage and the base for a search and rescue unit at weekends. Volunteer guides are available at weekends. Wooden houses can be rented for US$55 a night; take torch. Camping is free. To get there take the train from Curitiba at 0815, arriving Marumbi at 1020. Return at 1540 to Curitiba. If continuing the next day to Morretes your Curitiba-Marumbi ticket is valid for the onward journey.

Morretes → *Colour map 7, C3. www.morretes.com.br.*

Morretes, founded in 1721, is one of the prettiest colonial towns in southern Brazil. Whitewashed colonial buildings with painted window frames straddle the pebbly river and church spires stick up from a sea of red tiled roofs against the backdrop of forested hills. The Estrada da Graciosa road passes through Morretes and the train stops here too. Most of the numerous restaurants serve the local speciality, Barreado, a meat stew cooked in a clay pot – originally a day in advance of Carnaval in order to allow women to escape from their domestic chores and enjoy the party. There are a handful of pousadas too and a series of walks into the mountains. **Antonina**, 14 km from Morretes is as picturesque, less touristy, and sits on the Baía do Paranaguá. It can be reached by local bus from Morretes.

Paranaguá ➔ *Phone code: 0xx41. Colour map 7, C3. Population: 128,000.*

In the centre of Paranaguá colonial buildings decay in the heat and humidity; some are just façades encrusted with bromeliads. The **Museu de Arqueologia e Etnologia** ⓘ *R General Carneiro 66, T3423 2511, www.proec.ufpr.br, temporarily closed 2009*, is housed in a formidable 18th-century Jesuit convent. Other attractions are a 17th-century fountain, the church of **São Benedito**, and the shrine of **Nossa Senhora do Rocio**, 2 km from town. **Tourist information** ⓘ *R General Carneiro 258, Setor Histórico, T3420 2940, www.fumtur.com.br*. Boat schedules, toilet, and left-luggage available.

The Paranaguá region was an important centre of indigenous life. Colossal shell middens, called **Sambaquis**, some as high as a two-storey building, protecting regally adorned corpses, have been found on the surrounding estuaries. They date from between 7,000 (possibly earlier) and 2,000 years ago, built by the ancestors of the Tupinguin and Carijo people who encountered the first Europeans to arrive here. The Spanish and Portuguese disputed the bay and islands when gold was found in the late 16th century. More important is the area's claim to be one of Latin America's biodiversity hotspots and the best place on the Brazilian coast to see rare rainforest flora and fauna. Mangrove and lowland subtropical forests, islands, rivers and rivulets here form the largest stretch of Atlantic coast rainforest in the country and protect critically endangered species (see below). Most of the bay is protected by a series of national and state parks, but it is possible to visit on an organized tour from Paranaguá. The **Barcopar** cooperative ⓘ *access from Praça 29 de Julho (Palco Tutóia), T3422 8159*, offers a range of excellent trips in large and small vessels ranging from two hours to two days, US$10 per person to US$100.

At the mouth of the Baia de Guaratuba are two towns connected by ferry, **Caiobá** on the north shore (50 km from Paranaguá) and **Guaratuba** on the south. A few km north of Caiobá is **Matinhos**, a popular beach resort, especially in October when Paraná's surf championships are held here. A recommended restaurant here is **La Bodeguita**, Av Paranaguá, Betaras, T3452 6606, mainly fish, huge helpings.

Ilha do Mel

ⓘ *Entrance fee US$15; foreigners must show passport and fill in a form before boarding the boat. Limit of 5,000 visitors a day.*

Ilha do Mel sits in the mouth of the Baía de Paranaguá and was of strategic use in the 18th century. On this popular weekend escape and holiday island there are no roads, no vehicles and limited electricity. Outside of Carnaval and New Year it is a laid back little place. Bars pump out Bob Marley and Maranhão reggae; surfers lounge around in hammocks and barefooted couples dance forró on the wooden floors of simple beachside shacks. Much of the island is forested, its coastline is fringed with broad beaches, broken in the south by rocky headlands.

The rugged eastern half, where most of the facilities are to be found is fringed with curving beaches and capped with a lighthouse, Farol das Conchas, built in 1872 to guide shipping into the bay. The flat, scrub forest-covered western half is predominantly an ecological protection area, its northern side watched over by the Fortaleza Nossa Senhora dos Prazeres, built in 1767 on the orders of King José I of Portugal, to defend what was one of the principal ports in the country. The best surf beaches are Praia Grande and Praia de Fora. Both are about 20 minutes' walk from the Nova Brasilia jetty. Fortaleza and Ponta do Bicho on the north shore are more tranquil and are safe for swimming. They are about 45 minutes' walk from the jetty or five minutes by boat. Farol and Encantadas are the liveliest and have the bulk of the accommodation, restaurants and nightlife. A series of well-signposted trails, from 20 minutes to three hours, cover the island and its coast. It is also possible to take a long day walking around the entire island, but the stretch along the southern shore between Encantadas and Nova Brasilia has to be done by boat. **Information**: www.pousadasilhadomel.com.br.

Superagüi National Park

The island of Superagüi and its neighbour, Peças, the focus for the Guaraqueçaba Environmental Protection Area which is part of the Nature Conservancy's parks in peril programme (http://parks inperil.org). They also form a national park and UNESCO World Heritage Site. Access to the park and accommodation can be arranged through the village on Superagüi beach, just north of Ilha do Mel. Many endangered endemic plants and animals live in the park, including hundreds of endemic orchids, Atlantic rainforest specific animals like brown howler monkeys and large colonies of red-tailed Amazons (a parrot on the red list of critically endangered species and which can be seen nowhere else). There are also jaguarundi, puma and jaguar. The *indígena* village is one of several Guarani villages in the area; other inhabitants are mostly of European descent, living off fishing. There is superb swimming from deserted beaches, but watch out for stinging jelly fish. Contact ICMBio on the island, 2 km out of the village, for information.

The Paraná coast listings

For Sleeping and Eating price codes and other relevant information, see Essentials, pages 38-40. See also Telephone, page 397, for important phone changes.

Sleeping

Morretes *p503*

A-B Pousada Graciosa, Estrada da Graciosa Km 8 (Porto da Cima village), T3462 1807, www.morretes.com.br/pousadagraciosa. Much the best in the area; some 10 km north of Morretes with simple but comfortable wooden chalets set in rainforest. Promotes cycling tours.

B-C Pousada Cidreira, R Romulo Pereira 61, T3462 1604, loizetycidreira@uol.com.br. Central, plain tiled rooms, TV, most with balcony. Breakfast.

D Hotel Nhundiaquara, R General Carneiro 13, T3462 1228, F3462 1267. Smart, beautifully set on the river, but service, public areas and rooms do not match up to the exterior, with breakfast.

Paranaguá *p504*

AL Camboa, R João Estevão (Ponta do Caju), T3420 5200, www.hotelcamboa.com.br. Full- or half -board available. Family resort, tennis courts, large pool, saunas, trampolines, a restaurant and a/c rooms, out of town near the port. Book ahead. Also has **A Camboa Capela**, in an 18th-century house in Antonina, same phone and website.

AL San Rafael, R Julia Costa 185, T3423 2123, www.sanrafaelhotel.com.br. Business hotel with plain rooms, restaurants, pool and jacuzzis.

D Ponderosa, R Pricilenco Corea 68 at 15 Novembro, T3423 2464. A block east and north of the boat dock, some rooms with a view.

D Pousada Itiberê, R Princesa Isabel 24, T3423 2485. Very smart spartan rooms, some with sea views, helpful service from the elderly Portuguese owner, shared bath, 3 blocks east of the boat dock.

Camping Arco Iris, Praia de Leste, on the beach, 29 km south of Paranaguá, T458 2001.

Ilha do Mel *p504*

All rooms are fan cooled unless otherwise stated.

A-B Long Beach, Praia Grande, T9944 9204, www.lbeach.cjb.net. Best on the beach, chalets for up to 6, very popular with surfers. Book ahead.

B Caraguatá, Encantadas, T3426 9097, pousada caraguata@uol.com.br. A/c, fridge, close to jetty.

B Pôr do Sol, Nova Brasilia, T3426 8009, www.pousadapordosol.com.br. Simple, elegant rooms around a shady garden, large deck with cabins and hammocks by the beach. Breakfast.

C Enseada, Farol, T9978-1200, pousadaenseada@uol.com.br. 4 en suite rooms with TVs and fridges, charmingly decorated. Lots of rescued cats.

C Dona Quinota, Fortaleza, T3426 8171/9978 3495, http://donaquinota.zeta.8x.com.br. Little blue and cream cottages right on the beach, 3 km from Nova Brasilia. Includes breakfast and supper. **Dona Clara** next door is very similar.

C Recanto do Frances, Encantadas, T3426 9105, www.recantodofrances.com.br. Full of character, with each chalet built in a different style to represent a different French city. 5 mins from Prainha or Encantadas. Good crêpe restaurant.

D pp **Aconchego**, Nova Brasilia, T3426 8030, www.cwb.matrix.com.br/daconchego. Very clean, beachside deck with hammocks, TV and breakfast area, charming. Includes breakfast.
D D'Lua, Farol, T3426 8031, daluapousada_ilhadomel@hotmail.com. Basic and hippy with a friendly new-age owner, Jô (closed low season).
D Farol da Ilha, Farol, T3426 8017/9136 2138. Dorms and double rooms in a garden, surf boards for rent. Price includes generous breakfast.
D Girassol, Farol, T3426 8006, heliodasilva@onda.com.br. Wooden rooms in a little fruit tree and bougainvillea garden, close to jetty. Breakfast.
D Plâncton, Farol at Fora, T3426 8061. A range of wooden buildings in a hummingbird-filled garden, fresh atmosphere, Italian food in high season.
D Recanto da Fortaleza, Ponta do Bicho, T3426 8000, www.ilhadomelpousada.com.br. The best of the 2 next to the Fort, basic cabins, free pick-up by boat from Nova Brasilia (ring ahead), bike rental. Price includes breakfast and dinner.
D pp **Recanto Tropical**, Farol, opposite D'Lua, T3426 8054. Open out of season, good breakfast.

You can rent a fisherman's house on Encantadas, ask for **Valentim's Bar**, or for Luchiano. Behind the bar is **Cabanas Dona Maria**, shared showers, cold water; food available if you ask in advance. Many pousadas and houses with rooms to rent (shared kitchen and living room). Shop around, prices from US$10 double, low season, mid-week.

Camping There are mini campsites with facilities at Encantadas, Farol and Brasília. Camping is possible on the more deserted beaches (good for surfing). If camping, watch out for the tide, watch possessions and beware of the bicho de pé which burrows into feet (remove with a needle and alcohol) and the borrachudos (discourage with Autan repellent).

Eating

Morretes *p503*

TTT Armazém Romanus R Visc Do Rio Branco 141. Family-run restaurant with the best menu and wine list in the region, dishes from home-grown ingredients, including barreado and desserts.
TT Terra Nossa R 15 de Novembro 109. Barreado, pasta, pizzas and fish, generous portions.
T Madalozo R Alm Frederico de Oliveira 16, overlooking the river. Good *barreado* and generous salads.

Ilha do Mel *p504*

Many pousadas serve food, some only in season (Christmas-Carnaval). Many have live music or dancing (especially in high season) after 2200.
TT Fim da trilha, Prainha (Fora de Encantadas), T3426 9017. Spanish seafood restaurant, one of the best on the island. Also has a *pousada*.
T Colmeia, Farol. Snacks, crêpes and good cakes and puddings.
T Mar e Sol, Farol. Huge portions of fish, chicken with chips and rice and a small selection of more adventurous dishes like bass in shrimp sauce.
T Toca do Abutre, Farol. Live music and huge plates of fish or chicken with rice, beans and chips.
T Zorro, Encantadas. One of many cheap seafront restaurants, forró dancing in the evenings.

Transport

Ilha do Mel *p504*

Ferry By ferry from Paranaguá to Encantadas and Nova Brasilia, at 0930 and 1500, 1 hr 40 mins, US$7.50, boats leave from R Gen Carneiro (R da Praia) in front of the Tourist Information kiosk. Also ferry from **Pontal do Paraná** (Pontal do Sul), daily from 0800 to 1800 (last boat from island to mainland) every hr at weekends, less frequently in the week. From **Paranaguá**, take the **bus** to Pontal do Sul (many daily, 1½ hrs, US$1), then wait for the ferry, US$5. There are handicraft stalls at the ferry point. The last bus back to Paranaguá leaves at 2200. Alternatively, go to the small harbour in Paranaguá and ask for a boat to Ilha do Mel, US$30 one-way (no shade). Make sure the ferry goes to your chosen destination (Nova Brasília or Encantadas are the most developed areas).

Superagüi National Park *p505*

Ferry From Paranaguá Sat 1000 arriving 1400, return Sun 1530 (2 stops en route), US$11 one way. Private boats from Praia da Fortaleza on Ilha do Mel run if the weather is good. Commercially organized tours are available through ICMBio, or Barcopar, T3422 8159.

Santa Catarina

Famous for its beaches and popular with Argentine and Paraguayan holidaymakers in high summer, this is one of the best stretches of Brazilian coast for surfing, attracting 1½ million visitors to the 170 beaches just in the summer months of January and February. For the rest of the year they are pleasant and uncrowded. Immigrant communities, such as the German, give a unique personality to many towns and districts with the familiar European pattern of mixed farming. Rural tourism is important and the highlands, 100 km from the coast, are among the coldest in Brazil, giving winter landscapes reminiscent of Europe, or Brazil's southern neighbours.

Florianópolis ➔ *Phone code: 0xx48. Colour map 5, B5. Population: 342,315.*

Halfway along the coast of Santa Catarina is the state capital and port of Florianópolis, founded in 1726 on the Ilha de Santa Catarina. The island is joined to the mainland by two bridges, one of which is Ponte Hercílio Luz, the longest steel suspension bridge in Brazil (closed for repairs). The newer Colombo Machado Salles bridge has a pedestrian and cycle way beneath the roadway. The natural beauty of the island, beaches and bays make Florianópolis a magnet for holidaymakers in summer. The southern beaches are usually good for swimming, the east for surfing, but be careful of the undertow. **Tourist office**: Setur, head office at ⓘ *Portal Turístico de Florianópolis, mainland end of the bridge, Av Eng Max de Souza 236, Coqueiros, T3952 7000, open 0800-2000 (Sat-Sun 1800)*. **Tourist information line** ⓘ *T0800-644300*. Office in the **Largo da Alfândega** ⓘ *Mon-Fri 0800-1830, Sat-Sun 0800-1800*. At Rodoviária, Avenida Paulo Fontes, *T3228 1095*, free maps; www.guiafloripa.com.br, and for the state www.sc.gov.br.

In the 1960s Florianópolis port was closed and the aspect of the city's southern shoreline was fundamentally changed, with land reclaimed from the bay. The two main remnants of the old port area are the late 19th-century **Alfândega** and **Mercado Público**, both on Rua Conselheiro Mafra, fully restored and painted ochre. In the Alfândega is a **handicraft market** ⓘ *Mon-Fri 0900-1900, Sat 0900-1200*. The market is divided into boxes, some are bars and restaurants, others **shops** ⓘ *T3224 0189, Mon-Fri 0600-1830, Sat 0600-1300*, a few fish stalls open on Sun. The **Cathedral** *on Praça 15 de Novembro*, was completed in 1773. **Forte Sant'ana** (1763), beneath the Ponte Hercílio Luz, houses a **Museu de Armas Major Lara Ribas** ⓘ *daily 0900-1700, free*, with a collection of guns and other items, mostly from the 19th and 20th centuries. **Museu Histórico** ⓘ *in the 18th-century Palácio Cruz e Souza, Praça 15 de Novembre, Tue-Fri 1000-1800, Sat-Sun 1000-1600, US$1*, has a beautiful Art Nouveau interior, a display on the poet Cruz e Sousa and other documents and objects. **Museu de Antropologia** ⓘ *Trindade University Campus, Mon-Fri 0900-1200, 1300-1700*, has a collection of stone and other archaeological remains from the cultures of the coastal *indígenas*. **Museu do Homem Sambaqui** ⓘ *at the Colégio Catarinense, R Esteves Júnior 711, Mon-Fri 1330-1630, closed Jan*, exhibits pieces from the sambaqui culture and fossils. There is a look-out point at **Morro da Cruz**; take *Empresa Trindadense* bus, US$0.80, waits 15 minutes, or walk. **Boat trips** from US$15, can be made in the bay with **Scuna Sul** ⓘ *T3225 1806, www.scunasul.com.br*.

Ilha de Santa Catarina ➔ *Colour map 7, C3.*

There are 42 beaches around the island. The most popular are the surfers' beaches such as Praia Moçambique; for peace and quiet try Campeche or the southern beaches; for sport, the Lagoa de Conceição has jet skis and windsurfing. You can walk in the forest reserves, hang glide or paraglide from the Morro da Lagoa, sandboard in the dunes of Joaquina. Surfing is prohibited 30 April-30 July because of the migration of the island's largest fish, the tainha.

Lagoa da Conceição has beaches, dunes, fishing, church of NS da Conceição (1730), market every Wednesday and Saturday, post office. From the Centro da Lagoa on the bridge there are daily boat trips to Costa da Lagoa which run until 1830, check when you buy your ticket, US$5 return.

Across the island at **Barra da Lagoa** ⓘ *take 'Barra da Lagoa' bus, Transol No 403, every 15 mins from Terminal Urbano, 55 mins, US$1.25*, is a pleasant fishing village and surf beach, lively in the summer, with lots of good restaurants. The same bus goes to beaches at **Mole** (good walking, sand beach, surfing, lively at night) and at **Joaquina** (surfing championships in January).

Florianópolis

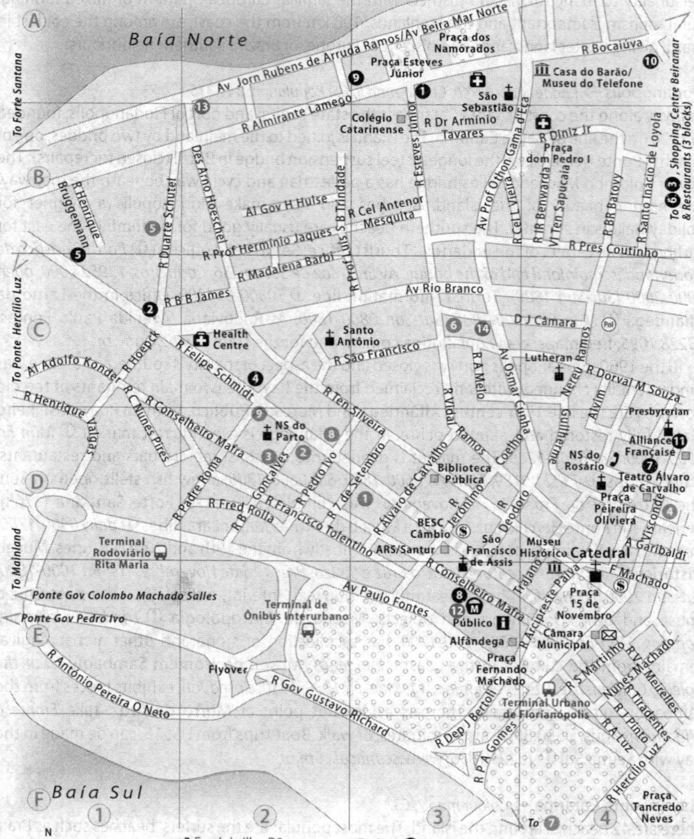

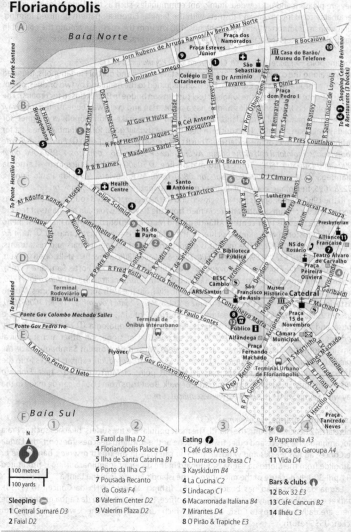

Sleeping
1 Central Sumaré *D3*
2 Faial *D2*
3 Farol da Ilha *D2*
4 Florianópolis Palace *D4*
5 Ilha de Santa Catarina *B1*
6 Porto da Ilha *C3*
7 Pousada Recanto da Costa *F4*
8 Valerim Center *D2*
9 Valerim Plaza *D2*

Eating
1 Café das Artes *A3*
2 Churrasco na Brasa *C1*
3 Kayskidum *B4*
4 La Cucina *C2*
5 Lindacap *C1*
6 Macarronada Italiana *B4*
7 Mirantes *D4*
8 O Pirão & Trapiche *E3*
9 Papparella *A3*
10 Toca da Garoupa *A4*
11 Vida *D4*

Bars & clubs
12 Box 32 *E3*
13 Café Cancun *B2*
14 Ilhéu *C3*

There is a pleasant fishing village at **Ponta das Canas**, walk 1 km to Praia Brava for good surfing, and the beach at **Canasvieiras** is good. Also in the north of the island, is **Praia dos Ingleses** (bus 602), very built up, but popular with families. **Forte São José da Ponta Grossa** is beautifully restored with a small **museum** ⓘ *US$2*. To get there take a bus to Jureré and Daniela beaches go there.

In the south of the island are **Praia do Campeche** ⓘ *getting there: 30 mins by bus (Pantano do Sul or Costa de Dentro) from Florianópolis*, **Praia da Armação** with, just inland, **Lagoa do Peri** (a protected area). Further south is **Pântano do Sul**, an unspoilt fishing village with a long, curved beach, lovely views, several pousadas, bars and restaurants, though not much nightlife. From here it's a good 4-km walk over rocks and a headland to beautiful **Lagoinha do Leste. Praia dos Naufragados**: take bus to Caieira da Barra do Sul and then a one hour walk through fine forests. **Forte Nossa Senhora da Conceição** is on a small island just offshore. It can be seen from the lighthouse near Praia dos Naufragados or take a boat trip with Scuna Sul from Florianópolis.

Porto Belo Beaches ➔ *Phone code: 0xx47. Population: 10,704.*

On the coast north of Florianópolis there are many resorts. They include Porto Belo, a fishing village on the north side of a peninsula settled in 1750 by Azores islanders, with a calm beach and a number of hotels and restaurants. Around the peninsula are wilder beaches reached by rough roads: Bombas, Bombinhas, Quatro Ilhas (quieter, 15 minutes' walk from Bombinhas), Mariscal, and, on the southern side, Zimbros (or Cantinho). Many of the stunning beaches around **Bombinhas** are untouched, accessible only on foot or by boat. The clear waters are good for diving.

Blumenau ➔ *Phone code: 0xx47. Post code: 89100. Colour map 7, C3. Pop: 261,808.*

The BR-101 heads north, parallel to the coast, passing **Camboriú** (Phone code: 0xx47. Colour map 7, C3. Population: 41,445), the most concentrated beach development on Brazil's southern coast. From 15 December to February it is very crowded and expensive. A little further north is the port of Itajaí.

Some 47 km up the Rio Itajaí-Açu (61 km by paved road from Itajaí) is the prosperous city of **Blumenau**, where high-tech and electronics industries are replacing textiles as the economic mainstay. The surrounding district was settled mostly by Germans and this is reflected in the clean, orderly street scene and some almost caricatured Germanic architecturecture. See the **Museu da Família Colonial** ⓘ *Av Duque de Caxias 78, Tue-Fri 0900-1700, Sat 0900-1200, 1400-1630, Sun 0900-1200*, the **German Evangelical Church**, and the houses, now **museums** *0800-1800*, of **Dr Bruno Otto Blumenau** and of **Fritz Müller** (a collaborator of Darwin), who bought the Blumenau estate in 1897 and founded the town. **Tourist office** ⓘ *T3222 3176, www.blumenau.sc.gov.br.*

Oktoberfest, second largest street party in Brazil, is usually held in the first half of October, with hundreds of thousands packing into the Vila Germanica Park for live music, draught beer and events such as drinking competitions and the 'sausage Olympics'. There is also a fun fair and folk dancing shows. Weekends can be very crowded. It is repeated, but called a 'summer festival', in the three weeks preceding Carnival.

At **Pomerode**, 33 km west of Blumenau, the north German dialect of Plattdeutsch is still spoken and there are several folkloric groups keeping alive the music and dance of their ancestors. There is an excellent zoo ⓘ *R Herman Weege 180, daily 0800-1800, US$5*. Next door, **Cevejaria Schornstein** ⓘ *R Herman Weege 60* serves beers from its own onsite microbrewery, with German-influenced snacks and main meals, huge portions, high quality ingredients. The **Museu Pomerano** ⓘ *Rodovia SC 418, Km 3*, tells the story of the colonial family. **Museu Ervin Kurt Theichmann** ⓘ *R 15 de Novembro 791*, has sculptures. *Festa do Pomerania* is in January. www.pomerode.sc.gov.br.

São Francisco do Sul

➔ *Phone code: 0xx47. Colour map 7, C3. Population: 32300. www.saofranciscodosul.com.br.*

Some 80 km up the coast at the mouth of the Baia de Babitonga, São Francisco do Sul is the port for the town of Joinville, 45 km inland at the head of the Rio Cachoeira. There is an interesting **Museu Nacional do Mar** reflecting Brazil's seafaring history. The centre has over 150 historical sites and has been protected since 1987. There are some excellent **beaches** nearby.

Joinville itself is the state's largest city. It lies 2 km from the main coastal highway, BR-101, by which Curitiba and Florianópolis are less than three hours away. The industry does not spoil the considerable charm of the city. The **Alameda Brustlein**, better known as the **Rua das Palmeiras**, is an impressive avenue of palm trees leading to the **Palácio dos Príncipes**. The trees have been protected since 1982. The futuristic **cathedral** ⓘ *on Av Juscelino Kubitscheck with R do Príncipe*, has spectacular windows recounting the story of man. The **Casa da Cultura** (Galeria Municipal de Artes 'Victor Kursansew') ⓘ *R Dona Fransisca 800, Mon-Fri 0900-1800, Sat 0900-1300*, also contains the School of Art 'Fritz Alt', the School of Music 'Vila Lobos' and the School of Ballet. A number of museums and exhibition centres reflect the history of the area and the city's artistic achievements. In July, Joinville hosts the largest dance festival in the world, attracting around 4,000 dancers over 12 days. Styles include jazz, folklore and classical ballet. There is also an annual beer festival, Fenachopp, in October. There are many good restaurants and good air and road links to other parts of Brazil. **Tourist office** ⓘ *at the corner of Praça Nereu Ramos with R do Príncipe*. **Promotur** ⓘ *R 15 de Novembro 4543, Glória, T3453 2663, or 0800-643 5015, www.promotur.com.br; also www.joinville.sc.gov.br.*

Southern Santa Catarina

At **Praia do Rosa**, 101 km south of Florianópolis, is the headquarters of the **Right Whale Institute** ⓘ *Instituto Baleia Franca, www.baleiafranca.org* ⓘ *R Manoel Álvaro de Araújo 200, Centro, Garopaba, Santa Catarina, CEP 88495-000, T3254 4198*. This is one of Brazil's prime **whale-watching** sites. The southern right whales come to the bay to calve from May to November and trips can be arranged to see them. The institute's base is **Turismo Vida, Sol e Mar** ⓘ *Praia do Rosa, Imbituba, Santa Catarina, CEP 88780-000, T3355 6111, www.vidasolemar.com.br*, which has over ten years' experience in right whale watching and dolphin watching. There is also **L-AL Pousada Vida, Sol e Mar**, same phone and web address, an 'eco-resort' with plush cabins, pool, restaurant, horse riding, snorkelling, surf school and other activities. There are many other pousadas in the town, and a good youth hostel ⓘ *Albergue de Juventude Dinda Rosa, Estrada Geral do Rosa s/n, T3355 6614*. The hostel has its own (expensive) convenience store. Book in advance, as the unspoilt beach is very popular with surfers and is listed as one of the 29 most beautiful bays in the world by the French-based organisation Les Plus Belles Baies du Monde. If lodging is hard to find, try 14 km north in **Garopaba**, where there are many more places to stay and other beaches to visit (www.guiagaropaba.com.br). Whales can also be seen here.

Laguna ➔ *Phone code: 0xx48. Colour map 7, C3. Population: 47,568.*

Some 27 km from Tubarão is the fishing port of Laguna. The town, founded in 1676, was the capital of the Juliana Republic in 1839, a short-lived separatist movement led by Italian idealist Guiseppe Garibáldi. The town's historic centre has a couple of basic lodgings, while resort-style hotels can be found over the hill at Mar Grosso.

About 16 km away (by ferry and road) are beaches and dunes at **Cavo de Santa Marta**. Also from Laguna, take a Lagunatur or Auto Viação São José bus to **Farol**: eight buses a day Monday-Friday, US$2.20, including 10-minute ferry crossing over the mouth of the Lagoa Santo Antônio. Look out for dolphins (botos). Here is a fishing village with many excellent beaches and the largest **lighthouse** in South America, built by the French in 1890, guided tours available. There are countless pousadas in the village, along with sevaral campsites; the one by the lighthouse at Santa Marta Pequena is popular with surfers.

São Joaquim and around → *Colour map 7, C2. Population: 22,836. Altitude: 1,360 m.*
Buses from the coalfield town of Tubarão (27 km from Laguna) go inland to Lauro Müller, then over the Serra do Rio do Rastro (beautiful views of the coast in clear weather) to **Bom Jardim da Serra**. The road continues to **São Joaquim**. The highest town in southern Brazil, it regularly has snow in winter. Eleven km outside the town on the way to Bom Jardim da Serra is the **Parque Ecológico Vale da Neve** (Snow Valley). Forty km away by bus is the town of **Urubici**. Surrounded by natural beauty spots and with an excellent tourist infrastructure, Urubici (www.urubici-sc.com.br) is very popular with Brazilian adventure tourists but largely undiscovered by foreign travellers. English speaking guides can be arranged. The **Parque Nacional de São Joaquim** in the Serra Geral (33,500 ha, T3278 4002) has canyons containing sub-tropical vegetation, and araucaria forest at higher levels. There is no bus (Secretaria de Turismo de São Joaquim, T049-3233 2790, www.serracatarinense.com).

Santa Catarina listings

For Sleeping and Eating price codes and other relevant information, see Essentials, pages 38-40. See also Telephone, page 397, for important phone changes.

Sleeping

Florianópolis *p507, map p508*
AL-A Porto da Ilha, R Dom Jaime Câmara 43, T3322 0007, hotel@portodailha.com.br. Central, comfortable, **A-B** at weekends. Recommended.
A Faial, R Felipe Schmidt 603, T3225 2766, www.hotelfaial.com.br. Comfortable and traditional hotel with good restaurant. Also owns the **Farol da Ilha**, R Bento Gonçalves 163, T3225 3030, www.hotelfaroldailha.com.br, which is good too, convenient for the bus station.
A Florianópolis Palace, R Artista Bittencourt 14, T3224 9633, www.floph.com.br. Large a/c rooms, pool, sauna, 1970s hotel.
A Valerim Plaza, R Felipe Schmidt 705, T0800- 702 3000, www.hotelvalerim.com.br. More modern than Valerim Center, buffet restaurant open till 2300.
B Valerim Center, R Felipe Schmidt 554, T0800-702 3000. Large rooms, hot water, hard beds.
C Pousada Recanto da Costa, R 13 de Maio 41. With breakfast, hot water, laundry facilities, parking, 15 mins' walk from centre.
C-E Central Sumaré, R Felipe Schmidt 423, T222 5359. With breakfast, basic.
F pp **Ilha de Santa Catarina**, R Duarte Schutel 227, T3225 3781, alberguesfloripa@uol.com.br. HI, good breakfast included, cooking facilities, clean, free Wi-Fi, some traffic noise, luggage store. Prices rise in Dec-Feb; more expensive for non-members.
Camping Camping Clube do Brasil, São João do Rio Vermelho, north of Lagoa da Conceição, 21 km out of town; also at Barra da Lagoa, Lagoa da Conceição, Praia da Armação, Praia dos Ingleses, Praia Canasvieiras. Wild camping allowed at Ponta de Sambaqui and Praias Brava, Aranhas, Galheta, Mole, Campeche, Campanhas and Naufragados; 4 km south of Florianópolis, campsite with bar at Praia do Sonho on the mainland, beautiful, deserted beach with island fort nearby. 'Camping Gaz' cartridges from **Riachuelo Supermercado**, on R Alvim and R São Jorge.

Ilha de Santa Catarina *p507*
There are many pousadas and apartments to rent on on the island. Agencies have offices in Florianópolis rodoviária, where you can shop around for what suits you best.

Lagoa da Conceição
D pp **Tucano House**, R das Araras 229 (on many hostel websites, eg hostelworld.com). Backpacker hostel with dorms and 1 double, with breakfast, hot water, local information, kitchen, internet, bar.

Barra da Lagoa
C Pousada Floripaz, Servidão da Prainha 20 (across hanging bridge at bus station, take bus 403 from terminal municipal), T3232 3193, www.qlitoral.com.br/floripaz. Book in advance, tours by boat and car on island. Recommended.
E pp **The Backpackers**, opposite **Pousada Floripaz**. Good hostel, including free surf board hire, cable TV, English spoken. Recommended.
Camping Fortaleza da Barra, T3232 3199. Basic facilities, helpful owner. Looks after valuables.

Joaquina

A Joaquina Beach, R A Garibaldi Santiago, T3232 5059, reservas@joaquinabeachhotel.com.br. Pleasant hotel with a/c. Safes, sea views more expensive, buffet breakfast.

D Pousada Dona Zilma, R Geral da Praia da Joaquina 279, T3232 5161. Quiet, safe. Recommended.

Praia dos Ingleses

C Companhia Inglesa, R Dom João Becker 276, T3269 1350, www.hotelciainglesa.com.br. Little beach hotel with pool and helpful staff. Recommended for families.

C Marcos Barroso, T9983 4472. Good-value apartments.

Praia do Campeche

L-AL Pousada Natur Campeche, Servidão Família Nunes 59, T3237 4011, www.naturcampeche.com.br. Also has hotel at Av Pequeno Príncipe 2196, a little cheaper, both with gardens, quiet, pousada has pool and is closer to the beach.

L-A Pousada Vila Tamarindo, Av Campeche 1836, T3237 3464, www.tamarindo.com.br. Tranquil setting with lovely views, gardens, helpful staff, good buffet breakfast.

AL Hotel São Sebastião da Praia, Av Campeche 1373, T/F3338 2020, www.hotelsao sebastiao.com.br. Resort hotel on splendid beach, special monthly rate Apr-Oct, excellent value.

Near Pântano do Sul

B Pousada Sítio dos Tucanos, Estrada Geral da Costa de Dentro 2776, T3237 5084, www.pousadasitiodostucanos.com. **AL** in high season. English, French, Spanish spoken, spacious bungalows in garden setting, excellent organic food. Very highly recommended. Take bus to Pântano do Sul, walk 6 km or telephone and arrange to be picked up by German owner.

D Albergue do Pirata, R Rosalia P Ferreira 4973, Pântano do Sul, T9960 1344. HI. With breakfast, natural surroundings, lots of trails.

Blumenau *p509*

Reservations are essential during Oktoberfest.

A-B Glória, R 7 de Setembro 954, T3326 1988, hotelgloria@hotelgloria.com.br. German-run, excellent coffee shop.

C Herrmann, Floriano Peixoto 213, T3322 4370. One of the oldest houses in Blumenau, rooms with or without bath, excellent big breakfast, German spoken.

F pp **Grün Garten Pousada**, R São Paulo 2457, T3339 6529, www.grungarten.com.br. Youth hostel with dorms, 15 mins' walk from rodoviária. **C** for a double room.

Camping Municipal campsite, 3 km out on R Pastor Osvaldo Hesse; Paraíso dos Poneis, 9 km out on the Itajaí road, also Motel; **Refúgio Gaspar Alto**, 12 km out on R da Glória.

Pomerode

There are a couple of good mid-range hotels: **B-C Schroeder**, R 15 de Novembro 514, T3387 0933, hotel.schroeder@terra.com.br, and **Pousada Max**, R 15 de Novembro 257, T3387 3070, www.pousadamax.com.br.

São Francisco do Sul *p510*

A Zibamba, R Fernandes Dias 27, T/F3444 2077. Central, good restaurant.

Joinville

AL Tannenhof, Visconde de Taunay 340, T/F3433 8011, www.tannenhof.com.br. 4-star, pool, gym, traffic noise, excellent breakfast, restaurant.

A-B Anthurium Parque, São José 226, T/F4009 6299, anthurium@anthurium.com.br. Colonial building, once home to a bishop, good value, English spoken, pool, sauna.

C-D Mattes, 15 de Novembro 801, T3422 3582, www.hotelmattes.com.br. Good facilities, big breakfast, German spoken. Recommended.

D Pousada Flor do Brasil, R Paraíba 764. Opposite bus station, clean rooms with fan, TV, private bath.

Laguna *p510*

C Turismar, Av Rio Grande do Sul 207, Mar Grosso, T3647 0024, F3647 0279. 2-star, view over Mar Grosso beach, TV.

D Beiramar, R 3 de Maio 92, Mar Grosso, T3644 0260. No breakfast, TV, rooms with view over lagoon.

D Recanto, Av Eng Machado Salles 108, T3644 0902. With breakfast, central, basic but modern and clean. Also own snackbar next door.

São Joaquim and around *p511*

D Maristela, R Manoel Joaquim Pinto 220, T3233 0007. No heating so can be cold, helpful, good breakfast; 5 mins' walk from rodoviária.

Bom Jardim da Serra

C Moretti, Rua Antão de Paula Velho, T3232 0106. Owner is helpful.

Urubici

A Urubici Park, Av Adolfo Konder 2278, T3278 5300. Cosy and attractive mountain lodge hotel with pool and excellent breakfast, helpful staff, good value. Highly recommended.

Eating

Florianópolis *p507, map p508*

On Rua Bocaiúva, east of R Almte Lamego, there are several Italian restaurants, barbecue places and a fish restaurant, **Toca da Garoupa** (turn on to R Alves de Brito 178). **Don Pepé Forno a Lenha** is a romantic spot with a serenador (cover charge applies).

TT Lindacap, R Felipe Schmidt 1132 (closed Mon). Recommended, good views.

TT Macarronada Italiana, Av Beira Mar Norte 2458. Good Italian food.

TT O Pirão overlooks the market square in Mercado Público. Elegant, self-service, open 1100-1430.

TT Papparella, Almte Lamego 1416. Excellent giant pizzas.

TT Trapiche, Box 31 in the Mercado Público. Also self-service fish and seafood (see also Bars, below).

T Churrasco na Brasa, R Felipe Schmidt 860, Mon-Sat. Good value per kilo lunch spot serving fish, meat, chicken and salads.

T Kayskidum, Av Beira Mar Norte 2566. Lanchonete and crêperie, very popular.

T La Cucina, R Padre Roma 291. Mainly vegetarian buffet lunch, Mon-Sat, pay by weight, good, fresh ingredients.

T Mirantes, R Alvaro de Carvalho 246, Centro. Self-service buffet, good value.

T Vida, R Visc de Ouro Preto 298, next to Alliance Française. Excellent value vegetarian lunches served in an attractive colonial building.

T Café das Artes, R Esteves Junior 734 at north end. Nice café with excellent cakes.

Ilha de Santa Catarina *p507*

Lagoa da Conceição

TT-T Bodeguita, Av das Rendeiras 1878. Very good value and atmosphere.

TT-T Oliveira, R Henrique Veras. Excellent seafood.

Barra da Lagoa

On R Altimiro Barcelos Dutra there are several snackbars selling excellent wholemeal pastries stuffed with tasty, fresh ingredients. Good vegetarian options.

TT-T Meu Cantinha, R Orlando Shaplin 89. Excellent seafood.

TT Ponta das Caranhas, R Jornalista M de Menezes 2377, T232 3076. Excellent seafood, lovely location on the lake.

Blumenau *p509*

TT Cavalinho Branco, Av Rio Branco 165. Good German food and huge meals.

TT Deutsches Eck, R 7 de Septembro 432. Recommended, especially carne pizzaiola.

TT Frohsinn, Morro Aipim (panoramic view). Good German food.

T Amigo, Peixoto 213. Huge cheap meals.

T Internacional, Nereu Ramos 61. Chinese, very good, moderate prices.

Patisseria Bavaria, Av 7 Septembro y Zimmerman. Very good cakes and fruit juices.

Bars and clubs

Florianópolis *p507, map p508*

Free open air concert every Sat morning at the market place near the bus terminal.

To find out about events and theme nights check the Beiramar centre for notices in shop windows, ask in surf shops or check notice-boards in the University in Trindade. The newspaper Diário Catarinense details bigger events. The Mercado Público in the centre, which is alive with fish sellers and stalls during the day, has a different atmosphere at night; the stall, **Box 32**, serves good, if expensive, seafood, and at night becomes a busy bar specializing in cachaça, including its own brand.

Café Cancun, Av Beira Mar Norte, T225 1029. Wed-Sat from 2000, bars, restaurant, dancing, sophisticated.

Empórium, Bocaiúva 79. A shop by day and popular bar at night.

Ilhéu, Av Prof Gama d'Eça e R Jaime Câmara. Bar and club open until early hrs, tables spill outside, very popular with locals, fills up quickly, music a mixture of 1980s and 1990s hits, small dance floor.

Ilha de Santa Catarina *p507*
Throughout high summer the beaches open their bars day and night. The beach huts of Praia Mole invite people to party all night (bring a blanket). Any bars are worth visiting in the Lagoa area (around the Boulevard and Barra da Lagoa), especially the **Confraria das Artes**.

Festivals and events

Florianópolis *p507, map p508*
In **Dec** and **Jan** the whole island dances to the sound of the Boi-de-Mamão, a dance which incorporates the puppets of Bernunça, Maricota (the Goddess of Love, a puppet with long arms to embrace everyone) and Tião, the monkey. Around **Easter** is the Festival of the Bull, **Farra de Boi**. It is only in the south that, controversially nowadays, the bull is killed on Easter Sunday. The festival arouses fierce local pride.

Activities and tours

Brazil Ecojourneys, Estrada Rozália Paulina Ferreira, 1132 Armação Florianópolis, T3389 5619, http://brazilecojourneys.com. Tours in Southern Brazil, adventure, wildlife, GLBT and volunteering.

Transport

Florianópolis *p507, map p508*
Air International and domestic flights arrive at Hercílio Luz airport, Av Deomício Freitas, 12 km south of town, on the island. Take 'Corredor Sudoeste' bus No 186 from Terminal Urbano.
Bus There are 3 bus stations for routes on the island, or close by on the mainland: Terminal de Ônibus Interurbano (TICEN), Av Paulo Fontes, immediately east of the rodoviária Rita Maia; Terminal Urbano between Av Paulo Fontes and R Antônio Luz, east of Praça Fernando Machado; and a terminal at R Silva Jardim and R José da Costa. Yellow micro buses (Transporte Ejecutivo), starting from the south end of Praça 15 de Novembro and other stops, charge US$2. Normal bus fares to any point on the island are US$2.20.

International and buses from other Brazilian cities arrive at the rodoviária Rita Maia, at the east (island) end of the Ponte Colombo Machado Salles.

Several buses daily with **Catarinense** to **Porto Alegre** (US$30-60, 7 hrs, road being made into a dual carriageway), **São Paulo**, 10 hrs (US$50, leito US$80), **Rio**, 20 hrs (US$75 convencional, US$120 leito); to **Foz do Iguaçu** (US$60), to **Curitiba** US$27. To **Blumenau** US$14, 3 hrs. To **Laguna** US$11. To **São Joaquim** at 1145, 1830 with **Reunidos**, T3224 3727, 5 hrs, US$20.
International buses **Montevideo**, US$98, daily, by **TTL**. **Buenos Aires**, US$75, **Pluma**, buses very full in summer, book 1 week in advance. **Asunción**, US$60-112.

Porto Belo Beaches *p509*
Bus **Florianópolis** to Porto Belo, several daily with **Rainha**, fewer at weekends, more frequent buses to **Tijuca**, **Itapema** and **Itajaí**, all on the BR-101 with connections. Buses from Porto Belo to the beaches on the peninsula.

Blumenau *p509*
Bus Rodoviária is 7 km from town (get off at the bridge over the river and walk 1 km to centre). Bus to the rodoviária from Av Presidente Castelo-Branco (Beira Rio). There are connections in all directions from Blumenau. To **Curitiba**, US$15.50, 4 hrs, frequent buses with **Penha** and **Catarinense**. To **Pomerode Coletivos Volkmann** (T387 1321) daily US$1.50, 1 hr; also several daily with **Reunidas** and **Catarinense** (US$2.50); check schedules at tourist offices.

São Francisco do Sul *p510*
Bus Terminal is 1½ km from centre. Three buses daily with **Catarinense** to **Curitiba**, US$12, 3½ hrs.

Laguna *p510*
Bus To/from **Porto Alegre**, 5½ hrs, with **Santo Anjo**; same company goes to **Florianópolis**, 2 hrs, US$10, 6 daily.

São Joaquim *p511*
Bus To **Florianópolis** 1145 and 1830 with **Reunidos** and 0800 via Tubarão (Nevatur), 5½ hrs, US$20. Florianópolis-Bom Jardim da Serra, US$1.

Directory

Florianópolis *p507, map p508*
Airline offices TAM, T0800 570 5700.
Banks Banco do Brasil, Praça 15 de Novembro, exchange upstairs, 1000-1 500, huge commission on cash or TCs. ATMs downstairs. Banco Estado de Santa Catarina (BESC), câmbio, R Felipe Schmidt e Jerônimo Coelho, also Praça 15 de Novembro 341, 1000-1600, no commission on TCs. Money changers on R Felipe Schmidt outside BESC. **Car hire** Auto Locadora Veleiros, R Silva Jardim 1050, T3225 8207, hotel_veleiros@ uol.com.br. **Locarauto**, Silva Jardim 816, T3225 9000. **Post offices** Praça 15 de Novembro 5. **Telephones** Praça Pereira Oliveira 20.

Blumenau *p509*
Banks **Câmbios/travel agencies: Vale do Itajaí Turismo e Cambio**, Av Beira Rio 167, very helpful, German spoken.

Rio Grande do Sul → *Population: 10.2 million.*

Rio Grande do Sul is gaúcho country; it is also Brazil's chief wine producer. The capital, Porto Alegre, is the most industrialized city in the south, but in the surroundings are good beaches, interesting coastal national parks and the fine scenery of the Serra Gaúcha. On the border with Santa Catarina is the remarkable Aparados da Serra National Park. In the far west are the remains of Jesuit missions. In southern Rio Grande do Sul there are great grasslands stretching as far as Uruguay to the south and Argentina to the west. In this distinctive land of the gaúcho, or cowboy (pronounced ga-oo-shoo in Brazil), people feel closer to Uruguay and Argentina than Brazil (except where football is concerned).

The gaúcho culture has developed a sense of distance from the African-influenced society of further north. This separationist strain was most marked in the 1820s and 1830s when the Farroupilha movement, led by Bento Gonçalves, proclaimed the República Riograndense in 1835.

Porto Alegre → *Phone code: 0xx51. Colour map 7, inset. Population: 1,360,590.*

The capital of Rio Grande do Sul is where cowboy culture meets the bright lights. It lies at the confluence of five rivers (called Rio Guaíba, although it is not a river in its own right) and thence into the great freshwater lagoon, the Lagoa dos Patos, which runs into the sea. The freshwater port is one of the most up-to-date in the country and Porto Alegre is the biggest commercial centre south of São Paulo. It is also one of the richest and best-educated parts of Brazil and held the first three World Social Forums (2001-2003), putting the city in a global spotlight. Standing on a series of hills and valleys on the banks of the Guaíba, it has a temperate climate through most of the year, though the temperature at the height of summer can often exceed 40°C and drop below 10°C in winter. The city has a good tourist infrastructure, interesting cultural centres and lively nightlife. Football is also a great source of local pride, with Porto Alegre's two major sides, Grêmio and Internacional, both making the spurious claim to be 'world champions'.

Ins and outs

Tourist offices T0800-517686, www2.porto alegre rs.gov.br/turismo. Porto Alegre Turismo ⓘ *Travessa do Carmo 84, Cidade Baixa, T3212 3464, daily 0830-1800; also at airport; Usina do Gasômetro, Tue-Sun 0900-2100; Mercado Público, Mon-Fri 0900-1900, Sat 0900-1800; Mercado do Bom Fim, Loja 12, T3333 1873, daily 0900-1830, the airport and various shopping centres*. For the state: SETUR ⓘ *Av Borges de Medeiros 1501, 10th floor, T3288 5400, www.turismo.rs.gov.br*. The market area in Praça 15 de Novembro and the bus terminal are dangerous at night. Thefts have been reported in Voluntários da Pátria and Praça Parcão.

Sights

The older residential part of the town is on a promontory, dominated previously by the **Palácio Piratini** (Governor's Palace) and the imposing **cathedral** (1921-45 and 1972, but very neoclassical) on the **Praça Marechal Deodoro** (or da Matriz). Also on, or near this square, are the neoclassical **Theatro São Pedro** (1858), the **Solar dos Câmara** (1818, now a historical and cultural centre), the **Biblioteca Pública** – all dwarfed by the skyscraper of the **Assembléia Legislativa** – and the **Museu Júlio de Castilhos** ⓘ *Duque de Caxias 1231, T3221 3959, Tue-Sun 1000-1800*, which has an interesting collection on the history of the state. Down Rua General Câmara from Praça Marechal Deodoro is the **Praça da Alfândega**, with the old customs house and the Museu de Arte de Rio Grande do Sul (see below). A short walk east of this group, up Rua 7 de Setembro, is Praça 15 de Novembro, on which is the neoclassical **Mercado Público**, selling everything from religious artefacts to spices and meat. There are some good cafés and bars here. For art from the state, visit the **Museu de Arte do Rio Grande do Sul** ⓘ *Praça Senador Florêncio (Praça da Alfândega), T3227 2311, www.margs.org.br, Tue-Sun 1000-1900, free.*

Porto Alegre

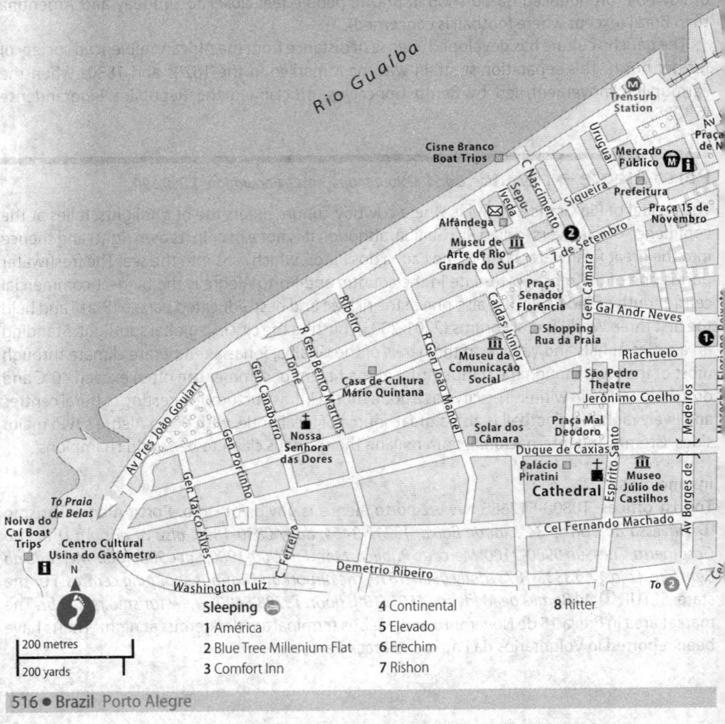

Museu de Comunicação Social ⓘ *R dos Andradas 959, T3224 4252, Mon-Fri 0900-1800, Sat 0900-1200, free*, in the former A Federação newspaper building (1922), deals with the development of the media in Brazil since the 1920s.

A large part of **Rua dos Andradas** (Rua da Praia) has been pedestrianised and gets very busy in the afternoons. Going west along Rua dos Andradas, you pass the wide stairway that leads up to the two high white towers of the church of **Nossa Senhora das Dores**, the oldest in the city. At the end of the promontory, the **Usina do Gasômetro** has been converted from a thermoelectric station into a cultural centre and good café. Its enormous chimney is a city landmark and there is a stunning view of sunset from the balcony. In the **Cidade Baixa** quarter are the colonial **Travessa dos Venezianos** (between Ruas Lopo Gonçalves and Joaquim Nabuco) and the **house of Lopo Gonçalves**, which houses the **Museu de Porto Alegre Joaquim José Felizardo** ⓘ *R João Alfredo 582, T3226 7570, Tue-Sun 0900-1200, 1330-1800, free*, a collection on the history of the city.

The central **Parque Farroupilha** (called Parque Redenção) has many attractions and on Sundays there is an antiques and handicrafts fair at the José Bonifácio end. The **Jardim Botânico** (Bairro Jardim Botânico, bus 40 from Praça 15 de Novembro), is on Rua Salvador França 1427, Zona Leste.

Eating

1 Atelier de Massas
2 Café do Cofre & Santander Cultural
3 Chopp Stübel
4 Koh Pee Pee
5 Wunderbar

On the 5-km wide **Rio Guaíba** there are several sailing clubs (see Activities and tours, page 519). You can see a good view of the city, with glorious sunsets, from the **Morro de Santa Teresa** (take bus 95 from the top end of Rua Salgado Filho, marked 'Morro de Santa Teresa TV' or just 'TV').

Porto Alegre beach resorts

The main beach resorts of the area are to the east and north of the city. Heading east along the BR-290, 112 km from Porto Alegre is **Osório**, a pleasant lakeside town with a few hotels. From here it is 18 km southeast to the rather polluted and crowded beach resort of **Tramandaí** (five buses daily from Porto Alegre, US$3.50). The beaches here are very popular, with lots of hotels, bars, restaurants, and other standard seaside amenities. Extensive dunes and lakes in the region provide an interesting variety of wildlife and sporting opportunities. The beach resorts become less polluted the further north you travel, and the water is clean by the time you reach Torres (see below). Among the resorts between the two towns is **Capão da Canoa**, with surfing at Atlântida beach. The Lagoa dos Quadros, inland, is used for windsurfing, sailing, water-skiing and jet-skiing.

Torres ➔ *Phone code: 0xx51. Colour map 7, inset. Population: 30,880.*

Torres is a well developed resort, with a number of beaches, several high class, expensive hotels, a wide range of restaurants, professional surfing competitions and entertainment. Torres holds a ballooning festival in April. There is an annual independence day celebration on 16 September. Torres gets its name from the three huge rocks, or towers, on the town beach, Praia Grande. Fishing boats can be hired for a trip to **Ilha dos Lobos**, a rocky island 2 km out to sea, where sea lions spend the winter months. Dolphins visit Praia dos Molhes, north of the town, the year round and whales can occasionally be seen in July. The **tourist office** ⓘ *Estrada do Mar, Km 89, Auto Posto Mirim, Sala 02, T3605 2284, www.clictorres.com.br.*

There is a paved road running south from Tramandaí along the coast to **Quintão**, giving access to many beaches. Of note is **Cidreira**, with Hotel Farol on the main street (**D** with bath). Bus from Porto Alegre US$8.

Porto Alegre listings

For Sleeping and Eating price codes and other relevant information, see Essentials, pages 38-40. See Telephone, page 397, for important phone changes.

Sleeping

Porto Alegre *p515, map p516*

Hotels in the area around R Garibáldi and Voluntários da Patria between Av Farrapos and rodoviária are overpriced and used for short stays.

L-AL Blue Tree Millenium Flat, Av Borges de Medeiros 3120, Praia de Belas, T3026 2200, www.bluetree.com.br. Smart mini-apartments with microwave, study and breakfast bar. The rooftop pool, gym and bar have stunning sunset views. Recommended.

AL-A Continental, Lg Vespasiano Júlio Veppo 77, T3027 1900, www.hoteiscontinental.com.br. High standards, cheaper at weekends, pool, gym.

A Ritter, Lg Vespasiano Júlio Veppo 55, opposite rodoviária, T3228 4044, www.ritterhoteis.com.br. Four-star and 3-star wings, English, French, German spoken, bar, small pool, sauna.

B Comfort Inn, R Loureiro da Silva 1660, Cidade Baixa, T2117 9000, www.atlanticahotels.com.br. Good value 3-star with gym, Wi-Fi, breakfast. Handy for Cidade Baixa nightlife.

B Rishon, R Dr Flores 27, Centro, T3228 1387, www.hoteisrishon.com.br. Rooms with cable TV, fridge, microwave, breakfast included, central.

C-D Elevado, Av Farrapos 65, T/F3224 5250, www.hotelelevado.com.br. Youth hostel association member, big rooms, microwave and coffee, good value.

C-D Erechim, Av Júlio de Castilhos 341, near rodoviária, T3228 7044, www.hotelerechim.com.br. A good option among several cheap places in this area, 2 standards of room, accredited by Brazilian youth hostel association.

D-E América, Av Farrapos 119, T/F3226 0062, www.hotelamerica.com.br. Bright, large rooms with sofas, garage, HI-affiliated. Recommended.

Camping Praia do Guarujá, 16 km out on Av Guaíba.

Eating

Porto Alegre *p515, map p516*

The Central Market along the Praça is lined with lancherias. Vegetarians might try some of the campeiro soups and casseroles or visit one of the many health food lunch buffet spots.

TTT **Al Dente**, R Mata Bacelar 210, Auxiliadora, T3342 8534. Good, if expensive northern Italian cuisine. Closed Sun, reservations needed Fri-Sat.

TTT **Chopp Stübel**, R Quintino Bocaiúva 940, Moinhos de Vento, T3332 8895. Open 1800-0030, closed Sun, German food and good beers. Recommended.

TTT **Koh Pee Pee**, R Schiller 83, T3333 5150. Pricey but very good Thai food.

TTT **Wunderbar**, R Marquês do Herval 598, Moinhos de Vento, T3222 4967. German cooking, very busy 1830 till last diner leaves. Recommended.

TT **Atelier de Massas**, R Riachuelo 1482, T3225 1125. Lunch and dinner, Italian, closed Sun, fantastic pastas and steaks, excellent value.

TT **Chalé da Praça 15**, Praça 15 de Novembro. Nice spot, good for early evening drinks and snacks.

TT **Coqueiros,** R João Alfredo 208, T3227 1833. 1130-1430, 1930-2400, closed Sun and Mon evening. Cheap and cheerful churrasco.

TT **Komka**, Av Bahia 1275, San Geraldo, T3222 1881. Open 1130-1430, 1900-2300, closed Sun, also do churrasco. Recommended.

Ilha Natural, R Gen Câmara 60, T3224 4738. Self-service vegetarian, lunch only Mon-Fri.
Nova Vida, R Demétrio Ribeiro 1182, T3226 8876.1100-1500, closed Sun, vegetarian, good lasagne.
Spaguetti Express, Centro Comercial Nova Olária, Lima e Silva 776. Good Italian.

Cafés

Café do Cofre, 7 de Setembro 1028 (below Santander Cultural), T3227 8322. Lunch only. Good light meals, including salads and sushi.
Café Dos Cataventos, in Casa de Cultura Mário Quintana, R dos Andrades 736, in courtyard. Also **Restaurant Majestic** on roof, T3226 0153. Both serve good drinks, snacks and meals. Fantastic rooftop sunsets. 1200-2300.

The café in **Usina do Gasômetro** is very good for sandwiches and speciality coffee. Cheap.

Bars and clubs

Porto Alegre *p515, map p516*

Bars

On weekend nights, thousands head for the Cidade Baixa and spill out of the bars and clubs along Rua da República and José do Patrimônio.
Bar do Goethe, R 24 de Outubro 112, Moinhos de Vento, T3222 2043. Reunion each Tue, 2030, for foreign language speakers.
Bar Perimetral, Av Loureiro da Silva 1696, Cidade Baixa, T3211 2422. Hugely popular beer and snack bar, packed at weekends. Mon-Thu 1800-1200, Fri-Sun 1800 until last customer.
Sargeant Peppers, Dona Laura 329, T3331 3258. Live music Thu-Sat, closed Mon.

Clubs

Ossip, Av República 677 e João Afredo, T3224 2422. Pleasant wine bar.
Wanda Bar, R Comendador Coruja 169, Floresta. T3224 4755. Gay club, open from 2030.
Zelig, R Sarmento Leite 1086, Cidade Baixa, T3286 5612, www.zelig.com.br. Off-beat restaurant, bar and exhibition space. Good, diverse menu and DJs covering a broad musical spectrum. Very busy Sun (2000-late).

Entertainment

Porto Alegre *p515, map p516*

Art galleries **Casa de Cultura Mário Quintana**, R dos Andradas 736, T3221 7147. A lively centre for the arts, with exhibitions, theatre, pleasant bar, etc, open 0900-2100, 1200-2100 Sat-Sun.
Santander Cultural, R 7 de Setembro 1028, T3287 5718. Cultural centre with a beautiful interior (a former bank), good value art house cinema and a café, holds some interesting exhibitions. Mon-Fri 1000-1900, Sat-Sun 1100-1900.
Theatre **São Pedro**, Praça Mal Deodoro, T3227 5100. Free noon and late afternoon concerts Sat, Sun, art gallery, café.

Festivals and events

Porto Alegre *p515, map p516*

On **2 Feb** (a local holiday) is the festival of **Nossa Senhora dos Navegantes** (Iemanjá), whose image is taken by boat from the central quay in the port to the industrial district of Navegantes. **Semana Farroupilha** celebrates gaúcho traditions with parades in traditional style, its main day being **20 Sep**. The Carnival parade takes place in Av A do Carvalho, renamed Av Carlos Alberto Barcelos (or Roxo) for these 3 days only, after a famous Carnival designer. **Feira do Livro** in Praça da Alfândega, **Oct-Nov**.

Shopping

Porto Alegre *p515, map p516*

Bookshops **Livraria Londres**, Av Osvaldo Aranha 1182. Used books in English, French and Spanish and old Life magazines.
Markets Street market (leather goods, basketware, etc) in area around the central Post Office. Good leather goods are sold on the streets. Sun morning handicraft and bric-a-brac market (plus sideshows) Av José Bonifácio (next to Parque Farroupilha). There is a very good food market.
Shopping centres The **Praia de Belas** shopping centre, among the largest in Latin America, is a US$5 taxi ride from town.

Activities and tours

Porto Alegre *p515, map p516*

Popular open-top **tourist bus** around the city from Travessa do Carmo 84, Cidade Baixa, T3212 3464, portoalegre@turismo.prefpoa.com.br. US$5, reservations necessary.
Two **boats trips** around islands in estuary: **Cisne Branco**, from Cais do Porto, near Museu de Arte de Rio Grande do Sul, T3224 5222,

www.barcocisnebranco.com.br. Several sailings on Sun, fewer mid-week, 1 hr, US$10. **Noiva do Caí**, from the Usina do Gasômetro, T3211 7662. Several on Sun, fewer mid-week, one hr, US$3 (check winter schedules).

Transport

Porto Alegre *p515, map p516*

Air The international airport is on Av dos Estados, 8 km from the city, T3358 2000.

Bus 1st-class local minibuses (*Lotação*), painted in a distinctive red, blue and white pattern, stop on request, fares about US$1.70. Safer and more pleasant than normal buses (US$1). There are regular buses to the rodoviária. **Torres**, 9 a day, US$12.

International and interstate buses arrive at the rodoviária at Largo Vespasiano Júlio Veppo, on Av Mauá with Garibáldi, T3210 0101, www.rodoviaria-poa.com.br. Facilities include a post office and long-distance telephone service until 2100. There are 2 sections to the terminal; the ticket offices for interstate and international destinations are together in 1 block, beside the municipal tourist office (very helpful). The intermunicipal (state) ticket offices are in another block; for travel information within the state, ask at the very helpful booth on the station concourse.

To **Rio**, US$121, 26 hrs with **Penha**; **São Paulo**, US$75, 18 hrs; **Florianópolis**, US$30-60, 7 hrs with **Santo Anjo** (take an executivo rather than a convencional, which is much slower); **Curitiba**, from US$45 convencional to US$67 leito, coastal and Serra routes, 11 hrs; **Rio Grande**, US$24, every 2 hrs from 0600, 4½ hrs. **Foz do Iguaçu**, US$58-66, 13 hrs. To **Jaguarão** on Uruguayan border at 2400, 6 hrs, US$20. **Uruguaiana**, US$37, 8 hrs. Many other destinations.

International buses Note Take your passport and tourist card when purchasing international bus tickets. To **Montevideo**, with TTL executivo daily 2030 US$70 (leito Fri only at 2100, www.ttl.com.br), or take an ordinary bus to border town of Chuí, 7 hrs, US$33-40, walk or taxi across the border, then bus to Montevideo (US$16). To **Asunción** with **Unesul** at 1900, Tue, Fri, 18 hrs via **Foz do Iguaçu**, US$56. There are bus services to **Buenos Aires**, 19 hrs with **Pluma**, 1805 daily, route is Uruguaiana, Paso de los Libres, Entre Ríos and Zárate. For **Misiones** (Argentina), take 2100 bus (not Sat) to Porto Xavier on the Río Uruguay, 11 hrs, US$30, get exit stamp at police station, take a boat to San Javier, US$2.50, go to Argentine immigration at the port, then take a bus to Posadas (may have to change in Leandro N Além).

Metrô Trensurb, to the Mercado Público, one stop from the rodoviária, US$1.

Road Good roads radiate from Porto Alegre, and Highway BR-116 is paved to Curitiba (746 km). To the south it is paved (mostly in good condition), to Chuí on the Uruguayan border, 512 km, and to Rio Branco, also on the border. In summer visibility can be very poor at night owing to mist, unfenced cows are a further hazard. The paved coastal road to Curitiba via Itajaí (BR-101), of which the first 100 km is the 4-lane Estrada General Osório highway, is being dualled to Florianópolis, so a rough ride while work progresses. Nevertherless it's a better journey than the BR-116 via Caxias and Lajes. The road to Uruguaiana is entirely paved but bumpy.

Directory

Porto Alegre *p515, map p516*

Banks Banco do Brasil, Av dos Estados 1515, T371 1955 (also has Visa/Plus ATM), and Av Assis Brasil 2487, T341 2466. 1000-1500, good rates for TCs. Branch at Uruguai 185 has Visa/Plus ATM. Many branches of **Bradesco** have Visa ATMs, also **Banco 24 Horas** for Visa ATMs. **Citibank**, R7 de Setembro 722, T3220 8619. MasterCard ATMs at any **HSBC** branch. **MasterCard**, cash against card, R 7 de Setembro 722, 8th floor, Centro. **Exprinter**, R Hilário Ribeiro 292 (best for cash). For other addresses consult tourist bureau brochure. **Cultural centres Instituto Goethe**, 24 de Outubro 122, T3222 7832, www.goethe.de/br/ poa/demail.htm. Mon-Fri, 0930-1230, 1430-2100, occasional concerts, bar recommended for German Apfelkuchen. **Embassies and consulates Argentina**, R Coronel Bordini 1033, Moinhos de Vento, T/F3321 1360, caleg@zaz.com.br. 1000-1600. **France**, R Dr Timóteo 752, sala 8, Bairro Moinhos de Vento, T3222 6467, consulat.portoalegre@yahoo.fr. **Germany**, R Prof Annes Dias 112, 11th floor, Centro, T3224 9592. 0830-1130. **Italy**, R José de Alencar 313, T3230 8200, www.consportoalegre.esteri.it. 0900-1200. **Japan**, Av João Obino 467, Alto Petrópolis,

T3334 1299, cjpoa@terra.com.br. 0900-1130, 1400-1700. **Spain**, R Ildefonso Simões Lopes 85, Três Figueiras, T3338 1300, consuladoesp@terra.com.br. 0900-1430. **UK**, R Antenor Lemos 57 cj. 303, Menino Deus, T3232 1414, portoalegre@ gra-bretanha.org.br. 0830-1230, 1330-1630. **Uruguay**, Av Cristóvão Colombo 2999, Higienópolis, T3325 6200, conurugran@ terra.com.br, 0900-1500.

Language courses Portuguese and Spanish, **Matilde Dias**, R Pedro Chaves Barcelos 37, Apdo 104, T3331 8235, malilde@ estadao.com.br.
Post offices R Siqueira Campos 1100, Centro, Mon-Fri 0900-1800, Sat 0900-1230.
Telephones R Borges de Medeiros 475, and upstairs at rodoviária.

Rio Grande do Sul state

Mountains, vineyards, cowboys, waterfowl and ruined Jesuit missions are all part of the mix that makes up Brazil's southernmost state.

Serra Gaúcha ➔ *Population: Canela, 33,625; Gramado, 29,593.*

The Serra Gaúcha boasts stunningly beautiful scenery, some of the best being around the towns of Gramado and Canela, about 130 km north of Porto Alegre. There is a distinctly Swiss/Bavarian flavour to many of the buildings in both towns. In December the Christmas displays are genuinely impressive, and in winter it can snow. This is excellent walking and climbing country among hills, woods, lakes and waterfalls. For canoeists, the Rio Paranhana at Três Coroas is renowned, especially for slalom (**A-C** pp **Refúgio do Pomar**, Estrada do Laticínio 1330, Rodeio Bonito, T0xx51-9668 6463, http://pousada-refugiodopomar.blogspot.com, is recommended for peace and quiet, Buddhist temple nearby, good food and rafting and walking options, HI affiliated). Local crafts include knitted woollens, leather, wickerwork, and chocolate.

Gramado, at 850 m on the edge of a plateau with views, provides a summer escape from the 40°C heat of the plains. It lives almost entirely by tourism and the main street, Avenida Borges de Medeiros, is full of kitsch artisan shops and fashion boutiques. In December the Christmas displays draw hordes of visitors, and throughout the summer, thousands of hydrangeas (hortênsias) bloom. About 1.5 km along Avenida das Hortênsias towards Canela is the **Prawer Chocolate Factory** ⓘ *Av das Hortênsias 4100. T3286 1580, www.prawer.com.br, free tours of the truffle-making process and free tasting. 0830-1130, 1330-1700, closed weekends.* Opposite is the **Hollywood Dream Car Automobile Museum** ⓘ *Av das Hortênsias 4151, T3286 4515, 0900-1900, US$8*, with a collection of dating back to a 1929 Ford Model A and Harley Davidson motorbikes from 1926. For a good walk/bike ride into the valley, take the dirt road Turismo Rural 28, Um Mergulho no Vale (A Dive into the Valley), which starts at Avenida das Hortênsias immediately before Prawer. **Tourist office** ⓘ *Av das Hortênsias 2029, T3286 0200, www.gramadosite.com.br.* Internet at **Cyber** ⓘ *Av Borges de Medeiros 2016, 1300-2300, US$2.80 per hr.*

A few kilometres along the plateau rim, **Canela** is less tourism and shopping-oriented than its neighbour (frequent bus service from Gramado, 10 minutes). **Tourist office** ⓘ *R Dona Carlinda 455, T3282 1510, www.canelaturismo.com.br.* The **Mundo a Vapor** museum ⓘ *RS 235 Rodovia Canela-Gramado, T3282 1115, daily 0915-1700, US$5, children US$2.50*, is an interesting museum dedicated to steam power. The main attraction is the dramatic reconstruction of the famous 1895 rail disaster in Montparnasse, Paris. Kids and adults clamour to have their picture taken alongside a giant steam train that appears to have burst through the front of the building.

About 7 km away is the **Parque Estadual do Caracol** ⓘ *T3278 3035, 0830-1800, US$4*, with a spectacular 130-m high waterfall where the Rio Caracol tumbles out of thick forest. A 927-step metal staircase leads to the plunge pool. There is an 18-km circular bike route continuing on to **Parque Ferradura** (US$4), with good views into the canyon of the Rio Cai. From the Ferradura junction, take the right to continue to the **Floresta Nacional** ⓘ *T3282 2608, 0800-1700, US$17 to visit and stay overnight.* From here, the dirt road continues round to Canela. Another good hike or bike option is the 4-km track southeast of Canela past Parque das Sequóias (www.sequoias.com.br) to **Morro Pelado**. At over 600 m, there are spectacular views from the rim edge.

Parque Nacional de Aparados da Serra → *Colour map 7, inset.*
ⓘ *Wed-Sat 0900-1800, US$11.50, T3251 1262, parnaaparadosdaserra@icmbio.gov.br.*
The major attraction at the Parque Nacional de Aparados da Serra is a canyon, 7.8 km long and 720 m deep, known locally as the Itaimbezinho. Here, two waterfalls cascade 350 m into a stone circle at the bottom. For experienced hikers (and with a guide) there is a difficult path to the bottom of Itaimbezinho. One can then hike 20 km to Praia Grande in Santa Catarina state. The park is 80 km from São Francisco de Paula (18 km east of Canela, 117 km north of Porto Alegre). With similar scenery but no tourist infrastructure is the neighbouring **Parque Nacional da Serra Geral** ⓘ *open daily 0800-1700, US$11.50, T3251 1277, same email as above.*

Tourist excursions, mostly at weekends, from **São Francisco de Paula** (a few hotels and *pousadas*; tourist information at southern entrance to town, T3244 1602). At other times, take a bus to Cambará do Sul (0945, 1700, 1¼ hours, US$4): several pousadas (see www.cambaraonline.com.br for a list) Also near Cambará is **Campofora** ⓘ *T3244 2993, www.campofora.com.br*, for riding expeditions in national park.

Caxias do Sul and around
→ *Phone code: 0xx54. Post code: 95000. Colour map 7, inset. Population: 360,419.*
This expanding modern city's population is principally of Italian descent and it is the centre of the Brazilian wine industry. The church of **São Pelegrino** has paintings by Aldo Locatelli and 5 m-high bronze doors sculptured by Augusto Murer. There is a good **Museu Municipal** ⓘ *R Visconde de Pelotas 586, T3221 2423, Tue-Sat 0830-1130, 1330-1700, Sun 1400-1700*, with displays of artefacts of the Italian immigration. Italian roots are again on display in the **Parque de Exposições Centenário**, 5 km out on Rua Ludovico Cavinato. January-February is the best time to visit. There is a tourist information kiosk in Praça Rui Barbosa and another at the **rodoviária** ⓘ *R Ernesto Alves 1341, T3218 3000*, a 15-minute walk from the main praça (but many buses pass through the centre). **Tourist office** ⓘ *R Ludovico Cavinatto, 1431, T0800-541 1875, www.caxias.tur.br.*

Caxias do Sul's festival of grapes is held February to March. Good tour and tasting (six wines) at **Adega Granja União**, R Os 18 de Forte 2346. Visit also the neighbouring towns and sample their wines: **Farroupilha** 20 km from Caxias do Sul. **Nova Milano**, 6 km away (bus to Farroupilha, then change – day trip). **Bento Gonçalves**, 40 km from Caxias do Sul, www.bentogoncalves.rs.gov.br. **Garibáldi**, which has a dry ski slope and toboggan slope – equipment hire, US$5 per hr. A restored steam train leaves Bento Gonçalves for a 2-hour trip to **Carlos Barbosa**; called 'a rota do vinho' (the wine run), it goes through vineyards in the hills. US$31-34, including wines, with live band; reserve in advance through **Giordani Turismo** ⓘ *R 13 de Maio 581, Loja 109, Bento Gonçalves, T3455 2788, www.mfumaca.com.br*. Another worthwhile trip is to **Antônio Prado**, 1½ hours by Caxiense Bus. The town is now a World Heritage Site because of the large number of original buildings built by immigrants in the Italian style.

Jesuit Missions → *Colour map 7, C1. Colour map 8, A6.*
West of **Passo Fundo**, 'the most gaúcho city in Rio Grande do Sul', are the **Sete Povos das Missões Orientais**. The only considerable Jesuit remains in Brazilian territory (very dramatic) are at **São Miguel das Missões** (*www.saomiguel-rs.com.br/turismo*), some 50 km from **Santo Ângelo**. At São Miguel, now a World Heritage Site, there is a church, 1735-1745, and small **museum** ⓘ *0900-1800, US$2.50*. The ruins are not well signposted, it is best to ask for directions at the rodoviária. A son et lumière show in Portuguese is held daily, in winter at 2000, and later in summer, although times depend on how many people there are. The show ends too late to return to Santo Ângelo but is worth sticking around for; book a room at the lovely hostel next to the ruins. Gaúcho festivals are held on some Sunday afternoons, in a field near the Mission.

Border with Argentina → *Colour map 7, C1.*
From Santo Ângelo it is a four-hour bus ride to the border town of **Porto Xavier** and an easy crossing (short ferry ride across the Río Uruguay) into Argentina. For exit and entry stamps, visit the federal police at the ferry stations on either side. The five-minute crossing (US$3.75) takes passengers to San Javier, from where there are regular buses, via Posadas, to Iguazú. From the Argentine ferry station it is a short bus or taxi ride to the town centre, with cashpoints, shops, and the bus station.

South of Porto Alegre → *Colour map 7, inset.*
South of Quintão a track runs to the charming town of **Mostardas** (www.mostardas.rs.gov.br; **E Hotel Mostardense** ⓘ *R Bento Conçalves 203, T3673 1368*, good, helpful, cold water), thence along the peninsula on the seaward side of the Lagoa dos Patos to São José do Norte, opposite Rio Grande (see below). Mostardas, famous for its woollen goods, is a good base for visiting the national park **Lagoa do Peixe** ⓘ *information: Praça Luís Martins 30, Mostardas, T3673 1464, free,* park has no infrastructure. This is one of South America's top spots for migrating birds: flamingos and albatross are among the visitors. The main lake (which has highest bird concentration) is about 20 km from Mostardas and the town of **Tavares**. The park is, however, under threat from invasive planting of trees.

São Lourenço do Sul About 40 km to the south (towards Rio Grande) begins the Costa Doce of the Lagoa dos Patos. São Lourenço (*Phone code: 0xx53; Population: 43,691; www.saolourenco.net*) is a good place to enjoy the lake, the beaches, fish restaurants and watersports. The town hosts a popular four-day festival in March. On the BR-116, **Pelotas** is the second largest city in the State of Rio Grande do Sul, 271 km south of Porto Alegre, on the Rio São Gonçalo which connects the shallow Lagoa dos Patos with the Lagoa Mirim. There are many good hotels and transport links to all of the state and the Uruguay border at Chuí.

South of Pelotas is the **Taim** water reserve on the Lagoa Mirim ⓘ *T3503 3151, esec_taim.rs@icmbio.gov.br, Estação Ecológica do Taim, BR-471, Km 492, a permit from ICMBio is needed to visit.* Many protected species, including black swans and the quero-quero (the Brazilian lapwing). There are trails outside the reserve.

Rio Grande Some 59 km south of Pelotas, at the entrance to the Lagoa dos Patos, is the city Rio Grande (*Phone code: 0xx53; Population: 186,544; www.riogrande.rs.gov.br*). It is the distribution centre for the southern part of Rio Grande do Sul, with significant cattle and meat industries. During the latter half of the 19th century Rio Grande was an important centre, but today it is a rather poor town, notable for the charm of its old buildings. The **Catedral de São Pedro** dates from 1755-1775. **Museu Oceanográfico** ⓘ *2 km from centre on Av Perimetral, T3232 9107, daily 0900-1100, 1400-1700, bus 59 or walk along waterfront*, has an interesting collection of 125,000 molluscs. The tourist kiosk is at junction of Rua Duque de Caxias and Rua General Becaleron.

Excursions To **Cassino**, a popular seaside town on the ocean, 24 km, over a good road. Travelling south, beaches are Querência (5 km), Stela Maris (9 km), Netuno (10 km), all with surf. The breakwater (the Barra), 5 km south of Cassino, no bus connection, through which all vessels entering and leaving Rio Grande must pass, is a tourist attraction. Barra-Rio Grande buses, from the east side of Praça Ferreira pass the Superporto. Across the inlet from Rio Grande is the settlement of **São José do Norte**, founded in 1725. There are ferries every half hour, 30 minutes, São José to Rio Grande; there are also three car ferries daily. A poor road runs north to Mostardas. **Tourist information** from Rua General Osório 127.

Border with Uruguay: coastal route → *Colour map 7, inset. Population: 5,167.*
The Brazilian border town is **Chuí**. The BR-471 from Porto Alegre and Pelotas skirts the town and carries straight through to Uruguay, where it becomes Ruta 9. The main street crossing west to

east, Avenida Internacional (Avenida Uruguaí on the Brazilian side, Avenida Brasil in Uruguay) is lined with clothes and household shops in Brazil, duty free shops and a casino in Uruguay. São Miguel fort, built by the Portuguese in 1737, now reconstructed with period artefacts, is worth a visit. A lighthouse 10 km west marks the Barro do Chuí inlet, which has uncrowded beaches and is visited by sea lions. Brazilian immigration is about 2½ km from the border, on BR-471, road to Pelotas. Buses stop at customs on both sides of the border, except those from Pelotas, on which you must ask the bus to stop for exit formalities. International buses make the crossing straightforward: the company holds passports; hand over your visitor's card on leaving Brazil and get a Uruguayan one on entry. Have luggage available for inspection. Make sure you get your stamp, or you will have trouble leaving Brazil.

Entering Brazil From Uruguay, on the Uruguayan side, the bus will stop if asked, and wait while you get your exit stamp (with bus conductor's help); on the Brazilian side, the appropriate form is completed by the rodoviária staff when you purchase your ticket into Brazil. The bus stops at Polícia Federal (BR-471) and the conductor completes formalities while you sit on the bus.

Border with Uruguay: inland routes → *Colour map 8, A6.*

At **Aceguá**, 60 km south of Bagé, where Brazilian immigration is located, there is a crossing to the Uruguayan town of Melo, and further east, **Jaguarão** with the Uruguayan town of **Rio Branco**, linked by the 1½ km long Mauá bridge and approach road across the Rio Jaguarão.

Entering Uruguay Before crossing into Uruguay, you must visit Brazilian Polícia Federal in Bagé to get an exit stamp; if not, the Uruguayan authorities will send you back. The crossing furthest west is **Barra do Quaraí** to Bella Unión, via the Barra del Cuaraim bridge. This is near the confluence of the Rios Uruguai and Quaraí. Thirty kilometres east is another crossing from **Quaraí** to **Artigas** in a cattle-raising and agricultural area.

The southern interior of the state is the region of the real gaúcho. Principal towns of this area include **Santana do Livramento**. Its twin Uruguayan city is Rivera. All one need do is cross the main street to Rivera, but by public transport this is not a straightforward border. The town has hotels and a youth hostel.

Rio Grande do Sul state listings

For Sleeping and Eating price codes and other relevant information, see Essentials, pages 38-40. See Telephone, page 397, for important phone changes.

Sleeping

Serra Gaúcha *p521*

Gramado

Plenty of hotels and restaurants (mostly pricey).

A Chalets do Vale, R Arthur Reinheimer 161 (off Av das Hortênsias at about 4700), T3286 4151, chaletsdovale@via-rs.net. 3 homely chalets in lovely setting, kitchen, TV, good deal for groups of 4/families.

E pp **Albergue Internacional de Gramado**, Av das Hortênsias 3880, T3295 1020, www.gramadohostel.com.br. Cosy and new, dorms, also has doubles, cheaper for HI members.

Camping Camping Gramado, R Venerável 877, T3286 2615.

Canela

AL Serra Verde, Av Osvaldo Aranha 610, T3278 9700, www.serraverdehotel.com.br. Thermal pools, sauna, massage, TV, internet, parking, very good.

A Bela Vista, R Osvaldo Aranha 160, T/F3282 1327, hrabal@pdh.com.br, near rodoviária. Rooms and cabins, good breakfasts.

D pp **Pousada do Viajante**, R Ernesto Urbani 132, T3282 2017. Kitchen facilities, dormitories and double rooms.

Camping Camping Clube do Brasil, 1 km from waterfall in Parque do Caracol, 1 km off main road, signposted (8 km from Canela), T3282 4321. Sell excellent honey and chocolate. **Sesi**, camping or cabins, R Francisco Bertolucci 504, 2½ km outside Canela, T/F3282 1311. Lovely parkland setting, good facilities. Recommended.

Caxias do Sul *p522*
Hotels fill up early in the afternoon.
AL Mabu Personal Royal, R Garibáldi 153, T3289 2000, www.hoteismabu.com.br. Smart business hotel with Wi-Fi, rooms and suites, some with mini kitchen.
C Pérola, Marquês de Herval 237, T3223 6080. Good value.
C Somensi, R Siba Paes 367, Bento Gonçalves, T3453 3111, hotelsomensi@ibest.com.br, near the Pipa Pórtico and Cristo Rei church in the upper town. And there are others.
D Pousada Casa Mia, Trav Niterói 71, Bento Gonçalves, T3451 1215, www.pousada casamia.com.br. HI youth hostel with 2 branches (Av Osvaldo Aranha 381, T3454 4936).

Jesuit Missions *p522*

São Miguel

There is a pizza restaurant next to the rodoviária and several snack bars selling decent burgers.
B Hotel Barichello, Av Borges do Canto 1567, T3381 1272. Nice and quiet, restaurant with churrasco for lunch.
C-D Pousada das Missões, São Nicolau 601, next to the ruins, T3381 1202, www.pousada tematica.com.br. Private rooms with or without a/c and TV, youth hostel, lovely site with swimming pool, cheaper for HI members. Highly recommended.

Santo Ângelo

AL-B Maerkli, Av Brasil 1000, T/F3313 2127. Recommended.
C Turis, R Antônio Manoel 726, T3313 5255. Good value rooms with a/c and fridge, good breakfast, internet access.
D Hotel Nova Esperança, Trav Centenário 463, T3312 1173. Behind bus station.

Rio Grande *p523*
A Atlântico Rio Grande, R Duque de Caxias 55, T3231 3833. Recommended, good value.
C-D Paris, R Mal F Peixoto 112, T3231 3866. Old, charming and recommended, but cold in winter.

Border with Uruguay: coastal route *p523*

Chuí

B Bertelli Chuí, BR-471, Km 648, 2 km from town, T3265 1266, www.bertellichuihotel.com.br. Comfortable, with pool.
D Rivero, Colômbia 163-A, T3265 1271. With bath, without breakfast.
D San Francisco, Av Colombia e R Chile. Shower, restaurant.

Eating

Serra Gaúcha *p521*

Gramado

TTT Bella du Valais, Av das Hortênsias 1432, T3286 1744. Expensive but very good Swiss cuisine.
T Hakone, R Garibáldi 271, T3286 1403. One of very few moderately priced places to eat in Gramado. Good fixed price lunchtime buffet and evening *rodizio* of pizza, pasta, salad and soup.

Canela

TT Bifão e Cia, Av Osvaldo Aranha 301. Good meat dishes.

South of Porto Alegre: Rio Grande *p523*
TT Blue Café, R Luis Loréa 314. Expresso machine and good cake. 0830-1930 (2300 Fri when jazz/blues music).
TT Parrillada Don Lauro, R Luís Loréa 369. Uruguayan steak in pleasant restaurant, fairly cheap.
T Rio's, R Val Porto 393. Vast but good churrascaria.
T Tia Laura, 29 km from town on BR-392 north to Pelotas. Excellent, specializes in home cooking and café colonial.

Transport

Jesuit Missions *p522*
Bus from **Porto Alegre** to **São Miguel das Missões** daily at 0645 with **Ouro e Prata**, 9½ hrs, US$24. Same company runs many more buses a day to **Santo Ângelo** (T3313 2618), 6½-8 hrs, US$23-27, also *leito*, except Sat, US$35. Buses between São Miguel and Santo Ângelo with **Antonello**, 4 a day.

South of Porto Alegre: Lagoa do Peixe *p523*
Bus Porto Alegre-Mostardas 4½ hrs, US$13 with **Palmares**. From Mostardas you can hop off the 1045 bus which passes through the northern end of the park on its way to the beach (basic hotels and restaurants). Three buses a week between Mostardas/Tavares and São José do Norte (130 km, terrible in the wet), via Bojuru, US$12.50, 5 hrs in theory.

São Lourenço do Sul *p523*
Bus From **Porto Alegre** US$14, 6 a day.

Rio Grande *p523*
Bus Frequent daily to and from **Pelotas** (56 km), 1 hr, US$3, **Bagé** (280 km), **Santa Vitória** (220 km), and **Porto Alegre** (5 a day, US$24, 4 hrs). All buses to these destinations go through Pelotas. Road to Uruguayan border at **Chuí** is paved, but the surface is poor (5 hrs by bus, at 0700 and 1430). Bus tickets to Punta del Este or Montevideo at 2330 from rodoviária.

Border with Uruguay: coastal route *p523*
Chuí
Bus Rodoviária on R Venezuela. Buses run from Chuí to **Pelotas** (6-7 daily, US$15, 4 hrs), **Rio Grande** (0700, 1400, 5 hrs, US$12) and **Porto Alegre** (1200, 2330, 7¾ hrs, US$33-40).

Border with Uruguay: inland route *p524*
Santana do Livramento
Bus Rodoviária at Gen Salgado Filho e general Vasco Alves. Bus to **Porto Alegre**, 2 daily, 7 hrs, US$35; services also to **São Paulo** and other destinations.

Foz do Iguaçu

The Iguaçu Falls are the most stunning waterfalls in South America. Their magnitude, and the volume of water that thunders over the edge, has to be seen to be believed. They are 32 km from the city of Foz do Iguaçu. For a description of the falls, maps and an account of road links between Argentina, Brazil and Paraguay, see the Argentina chapter.

Ins and outs

Tourist offices **Foz do Iguaçu**: Secretaria Municipal de Turismo ⓘ *Praça Getúlio Vargas 69, T3521 1455, 0700-2300, www.fozdoiguacu.pr.gov.br.* Very helpful, English spoken. There is a 24-hour tourist help line number, T0800-451516. Very helpful. Airport tourist information is also good, open for all arriving flights, gives map and bus information, English spoken. Helpful office, free map, at the rodoviária, English spoken.

Parque Nacional Foz do Iguaçu → *Colour map 7, C1.*
ⓘ *US$21, payable in reais, Argentine pesos or dollars, includes obligatory transport within the park (discounts for Mercosur, Brazilian and local residents). The park is open daily, 0900-1700 in winter, and to 1800 in summer (check if the park is closed until 1300 on Mon); T3521 4400, www.cataratasdoiguacu.com.br.*
The Brazilian national park was founded in 1939 and the area was designated a World Heritage Site by UNESCO in 1986. Fauna most frequently encountered are little and red brocket deer, South American coati, white-eared opossum, and a sub-species of the brown capuchin monkey. The endangered tegu lizard is common. Over 100 species of butterflies have been identified, among them the electric blue Morpho, the poisonous red and black heliconius and species of Papilionidae and Pieridae. The bird life is rewarding for bird- watchers. Five members of the toucan family can be seen.

Take a bus or taxi to the park's entrance, Km 21 from Foz. There's a smart modern **visitor centre** here, with toilets, ATM, a small café, a large souvenir shop and a Banco do Brasil câmbio (0800-1900). An **Exposição Ecològica** has information about the natural history of the falls and surrounding park (included in entry fee; English texts poor). Nature lovers are advised to visit first thing in the morning or late in the afternoon, preferably in low season, as crowds can significantly detract from the experience of the falls and surrounding park (at peak times like Semana Santa up to 10,000 visitors a day arrive). From the entrance, shuttle buses leave every 10-15 minutes for the 10 km to the start of the Cascades Trail, another 1 km to the end of the road at Porta Canoas. There are Portuguese, Spanish and English announcements of the stops (each bus will carry three bikes).

The bus stops first at the start of the **Macuco Safari** (see page 530). From there it continues to the Hotel das Cataratas and the start of a 1.2 km paved walk to the falls. This is an easy walk, taking you high above the Rio Iguaçu, giving splendid views of all the falls on the Argentine side from a series of galleries. At the end of the path, you can walk down to a boardwalk at the foot of the Floriano Falls which goes almost to the middle of the river to give a good view of and a light spraying from the Garganta del Diablo. There is also a viewing point almost under the powerful Floriano Falls, a dramatic view. From here, there are 150 steps up to the **Porto Canoas** complex (there is a lift for those who find stairs difficult); you can also return the way you came, and walk a little further along the road. The Porto Canoas complex consists of a big souvenir shop, toilets, a café, a fast food place (mixed reports) and smart **restaurant** ⓘ *buffet lunch, 1200-1600, good value*, all with good view of the river above the falls. Return to the visitor centre and entrance either by the free shuttle bus, or by walking back as far as Hotel das Cataratas (good lunch with a view of the falls) and taking the bus from there. The whole visit will take around two hours, plus time for lunch. Never feed wild animals and keep your distance when taking photos; coatis have been known to attack visitors with food.

Foz do Iguaçu

Sleeping
1 Arterial
2 Baviera
3 Del Rey
4 Foz do Iguaçu
5 Foz Plaza
6 Foz Presidente
7 Luz
8 Pousada da Laura
9 Rafain Centro
10 San Juan Centro
11 San Remo
12 Suiça
13 Tarobá

Eating
1 Atos
2 Bier Garten
3 Búfalo Branco
4 City Caffé
5 Marias e Maria
6 Oficina do Sorvete
7 Rafain
8 Tropicana
9 Zaragoza

Bars & clubs
10 Alquimia
11 Armazém
12 BR3
13 Capitão
14 Oba! Oba!

Foz do Iguaçu and around ➔ *Phone code: 0xx45. Population: 301,400.*

A small, modern city, 28 km from the falls, with a wide range of accommodation and good communications by air and road with the main cities of southern Brazil and Asunción in Paraguay. The **Parque das Aves bird zoo** ⓘ *Rodovia das Cataratas Km 16, 100 m before the entrance to the park, T3529 8282, www.parquedasaves.com.br, 0830-1730, US$12*, has received frequent good reports. It contains Brazilian and foreign birds, many species of parrot and beautiful toucans, in huge aviaries through which you can walk, with the birds flying and hopping around you. There are other birds in cages and a butterfly and hummingbird house.

The **Itaipu dam** ⓘ *on the Río Paraná 12 km north, a short film is shown at the visitor centre 10 mins before each guided visit, 8 departures daily between 0800 and 1600, US$11-29, children and seniors half price for all visits, check times with tourist office, take passport and wear long trousers and sensible shoes, T0800-645 4645, www.itaipu.gov.br*, is the site of the largest single power station in the world, built jointly by Brazil and Paraguay. Construction of this massive scheme began in 1975 and it became operational in 1984. The main dam is 8 km long, creating a lake which covers 1,400 sq km. The 18 turbines have an installed capacity of 12,600,000 Kw and produce about 75 bn Kwh a year, providing 80% of Paraguay's electricity and 25% of Brazil's. The Paraguayan side may be visited from Ciudad del Este. There is also the **Ecomuseu de Itaipu** ⓘ *Av Tancredo Neves, Km 11, T0800-645 4645, Tue-Sun 0830-1730, US$4.50 (US$13 for combined Ecomuseu and dam visit)*, and **Refúgio Bela Vista** *closed Tue, 4 visits a day from the visitor centre, 5 at weekends, US$10, or US$17 for visit combined with the dam*, animal rescue centre, both geared to educate about the preservation of the local culture and environment, or that part which isn't underwater. Recommended.

Border with Argentina

If entering Argentina only for the day, there is no need to obtain a Brazilan exit stamp but you must get Argentine stamps for any visit. The city bus between Foz do Iguaçu and Puerto Iguazú therefore only stops and waits at the Argentine border post, not the Brazilian one. If you are crossing from one country to the other for an extended period and need stamps from both, then you can ask the bus driver for a transfer, get off at the Brazilian border post and get on the next bus through without paying again. If entering Brazil only for the day, in principle a stamp is required, especially if you need a visa. In practice it is not asked for, but confirm this before crossing as practices change. Note that the bus will not wait for you at the Brazilian border post.

Between October-February Brazil is one hour ahead of Argentina. It takes about two hours to get from Foz to the Argentine falls, very tiring when the weather is hot.

Border with Paraguay ➔ *Brazil is 1 hr ahead of Paraguay.*

The Ponte de Amizade/Puente de Amistad (Friendship Bridge) over the Río Paraná, 6 km north of Foz, leads straight into the heart of Ciudad del Este. Paraguayan and Brazilian immigration formalities are dealt with at opposite ends of the bridge. Ask for relevant stamps if you need them. A large new customs complex has been built at the Brazilian end of the bridge.

Foz do Iguaçu listings

For Sleeping and Eating price codes and other relevant information, see Essentials, pages 38-40. See Telephone, page 397, for important phone changes.

Sleeping

Foz do Iguaçu *p528, map p527*

Note Check hotels' websites for internet prices and special offers. Av Juscelino Kubitschek and the streets south of it, towards the river, are unsafe at night. Many prostitutes around R Rebouças and Almirante Barroso. Taxis are only good value for short distances when you are carrying all your luggage.

L Rafain Centro, Mal Deodoro 984, T3521 3500, www.rafaincentro.com.br. Smart, comfortable, attractive pool area, good restaurant, Wi-Fi.

L Suíça, Av Felipe Wandscheer 3580, T3025 3232, www.hotelsuica.com.br. Some way out of the city, but charming, comfortable, Swiss manager, helpful with tourist information, attractive pool.

AL Foz do Iguaçu, Av Brasil 97, T3521 4455, www.hotelfozdoiguacu.com.br. Smart, attractive pool and terrace, well-designed rooms, good value.

AL Foz Plaza, R Marechal Deodoro 1819, T3521 5500, www.fozplazahotel.com.br. Serene and very nice, Wi-Fi.

AL San Juan Centro, R Marechal Deodoro 1349, T2105 9100, www.sanjuan hoteis.com.br. **A** if booked on-line. A/c, comfortable, excellent buffet breakfast, popular, good value. Recommended.

A Del Rey, R Tarobá 1020, T2105 7500, www.hoteldelreyfoz.com.br. Nothing fancy, but perennially popular, little pool, great breakfasts, Wi-Fi. Recommended.

A Foz Presidente, R Xavier da Silva 1000, T3572 4450, www.fozpresidentehoteis.com.br. Good value, decent rooms, restaurant, pool, with breakfast, convenient for buses, Wi-Fi.

A Tarobá, R Tarobá 1048, T2102 7770, www.hotel taroba.com.br. Bright and welcoming, small pool, nice rooms, helpful, a/c, good breakfast (extra), free Wi-Fi. Recommended.

A-B Luz, Av Costa e Silva Km 5, near Rodoviária, T3522 3535, www.luzhotel.com.br. A/c, TV, pool. Recommended.

B Baviera, Av Jorge Schimmelpfeng 697, T3523 5995, www.hotelbavieraiguassu.com.br. Chalet-style exterior, on main road, central for bars and restaurants, comfortable, if rather gloomy rooms.

C Pousada da Laura, R Naipi 671, T3572 3374. **E** pp in shared dorm with good breakfast. Secure, kitchen, laundry facilities, internet, Wi-Fi, a popular place to meet other travellers.

C San Remo, Xavier da Silva 563 at Tarobá, T3523 1619, roberto_171@hotmail.com. Scrupulously clean though small rooms with TV, all you can eat breakfast, English, Spanish and Hebrew spoken. In-house travel agency.

D Arterial, Av José Maria de Brito 2661, T3573 1859, hotelarterial@hotmail.com. Near rodoviária. Good value, huge breakfast, cable TV, a/c, opposite is a 24-hr buffet restaurant.

D Pousada Evelina, R Irlan Kalichewski 171, Vila Yolanda, T3574 3817, www.pousada evelina.com.br. Lots of tourist information, English, French, Italian, Polish and Spanish spoken, internet, good breakfast and location, near Chemin Supermarket, near Av Cataratas on the way to the falls. Recommended.

Camping Camping e Pousada Internacional, R Manêncio Martins 21, 1½ km from town, T3529 8183, www.campinginternacional.com.br. For vehicles and tents, US$10 pp (half with International Camping Card), also basic cabins (**E**), helpful staff, English, German and Spanish spoken, pool, restaurant. **Note** Camping is not permitted by the Hotel das Cataratas and falls.

Outside Foz do Iguaçu

LL Hotel das Cataratas, directly overlooking the Falls, Km 32 from Foz, T2102 7000, www.hotel dascataratas.com. Generally recommended but caters for lots of groups, attractive colonial-style building with pleasant gardens (where wildlife can be seen at night and early morning) and pool. Non-residents can eat here, midday and evening buffets; also à-la-carte dishes and dinner with show. Member of the Orient Express group.

On the road to the falls (Rodovia das Cataratas) are:

LL-L San Martin, Km 17, T3521 8088, www.hotelsanmartin.com.br. Attractive 4-star, a/c, TV, Wi-Fi, pool, sports, nightclub, several eating options, luxury, comfortable, lots of packages offered. Recommended.

L Carimã, Km 10, T3521 3000, www.hotel carima.com.br. 4-star, popular with groups, well laid out, lots of facilities, good restaurant, pool, bars, good value.

C-E Paudimar Campestre, Av das Cataratas Km 12.5, Remanso Grande, near airport, T3529 6061, www.paudimar.com.br. In high season HI members only. From airport or town take Parque Nacional bus (0525-0040) and get out at Remanso Grande bus stop, by Hotel San Juan, then take the free shuttle (0700-1900) to the hostel, or 1.2 km walk from main road. Camping as well (**F**), pool, soccer pitch, quiet, kitchen and communal meals, breakfast. Highly recommended. For assistance, ask for owner, Gladis. The hostel has telephone, fax and internet for guests' use. Tours run to either side of the falls (good value). Paudimar desk at rodoviária.

C-F Hostel Natura, Rodovia das Cataratas Km 12.5, Remanso Grande, T3529 6949, www.hostelnatura.com (near the Paudimar). Rustic hostel with a small pool set in fields, public areas include a pool table, TV lounge and a small kitchen. Rooms with fan. Hostel can arrange visits to the falls; website has detailed instructions for how to reach them.

Eating

Foz do Iguaçu *p528, map p527*

Plenty of places here serve Middle Eastern food.

TTT Búfalo Branco, R Rebouças 530, T3523 9744. Superb all you can eat churrasco, includes filet mignon, bull's testicles, salad bar and desert. Sophisticated surroundings and attentive service. Highly recommended.

TTT Cabeça de Boi, Av Felipe Wandscheer, Km 6, T3525 3358. Live music, buffet, churrasco, but coffee and pastries also.

TTT Rafain, Av das Cataratas, Km 6.5, T3523 1177, closed Sun. Out of town, take a taxi or arrange with travel agency. Set price for excellent buffet with folkloric music and dancing (2100-2300), touristy but very entertaining. Recommended.

TTT Zaragoza, R Quintino Bocaiúva 882, T3574 3084. Large and upmarket, for Spanish dishes and seafood. Recommended.

TT Atos, Av Juscelino Kubitschek 865, T3572 2785. Per kilo buffet with various meats, salads, sushi and puddings. Lunch only.

TT Bier Garten, Av Jorge Schimmelpfeng 550, T3523 3700. Pizzeria and choparia, beer garden in name only but some trees.

TT Tropicana, Av Juscelino Kubitschek 228, T3574 1701. All-you-can-eat pizza or churrascaria with salad bar, good value.

Cafés

City Caffé, Av Jorge Schimmelpfeng 898. Stylish café open daily 0800-2330 for sandwiches, Arabic snacks and pastries.

Marias e Maria, Av Brasil 505. Good confeitaria.

Oficina do Sorvete, Av Jorge Schimmelpfeng 244. Daily 1100-0100. Excellent ice creams, a popular local hang-out.

Bars and clubs

Foz do Iguaçu *p528, map p527*

Bars, all doubling as restaurants, concentrated on Av Jorge Schimmelpfeng for 2 blocks from Av Brasil to R Mal Floriano Peixoto. Wed to Sun are best nights; crowd tends to be young.

Alquimia, Av Jorge Schimmelpfeng 334, T3572 3154. Popular nightclub, open 2400-0500.

Armazém, R Edmundo de Barros 446, T3572 7422. Intimate and sophisticated, attracts discerning locals, good atmosphere, mellow live music, US$1 cover. Recommended.

BR3, Av Jorge Schimmelpfeng corner with Av Brasil. Modern, open till 2400.

Capitão Bar, Av Jorge Schimmelpfeng 288 and Almte Barroso, T3572 1512. Large, loud and popular, nightclub attached.

Oba! Oba!, Av das Cataratas 3700, T529 6596 (Antigo Castelinho). Live samba show Mon-Sat 2315-0015, very popular, US$12 including drink.

Activities and tours

Parque Nacional Foz do Iguaçu *p526*

Tours

Macuco Safari, T3529 6262, or 9963.3857, www.macuco safari.com.br, 1 hr 45 mins, US$45, involves a ride down a 1½-km path through the forest in open jeeps. Then a fast motor boat whisks you close to the falls themselves (similar to Jungle Explorer on the Argentine side, but more expensive and the guides aren't as good). Portuguese, English and Spanish spoken, take insect repellent. Helicopter tours over the falls leave from near the entrance, US$30 pp, 8 mins. Apart from disturbing visitors, they disturb bird life and so the altitude has been increased, making the flight less attractive. Lots of companies on both sides organize conventional tours to the falls, useful more for convenience rather than information, since they collect you from your hotel. Half day, US$13, plus park entrance price.

Foz do Iguaçu *p528, map p527*

Tours

There are many travel agents on Av Brasil. Beware of overcharging by touts at the bus terminal.

Caribe Tur at the airport, Hotel das Cataratas and other branches, T3529 7505, www.grupo caribe.com.br, runs tours from the airport to the Argentine side and Hotel das Cataratas (book hotel direct, not at the airport).

STTC Turismo, Ruth Campo Silva (recommended guide), Hotel Bourbon, Av das Cataratas, T/F3529 8580. Several branches.

Transport

Parque Nacional Foz do Iguaçu *p526*

Bus Leave from the Terminal Urbana in Foz, Av Juscelino Kubitschek and República Argentina, every 40 mins from 0730-1800, and are clearly marked 'Parque Nacional'. You can get on or off at any point on the route past the airport and Hotel das Cataratas, 40 mins, US$1.50 one way, payable in reais or pesos (bus route ends at the Park entrance where you purchase entry tickets and change to a park bus). Taxi US$11, US$45 return including waiting (negotiate in advance).

Foz do Iguaçu *p528, map p527*
Air Iguaçu international airport, Km 19.5, south of town near the falls. In Arrivals is **Banco do Brasil** and **Caribe Tours e Câmbio**, car rental offices, tourist office and an official taxi stand, US$16.50 to town centre. All buses marked Parque Nacional pass the airport in each direction, US$1.50, 0525-0040, does not permit large amounts of luggage but backpacks OK. Many hotels run minibus services for a small charge. Daily flights to **Rio, São Paulo, Curitiba** and other Brazilian cities.
Bus For transport to the falls see above under Parque Nacional Foz do Iguaçu. Long distance terminal (Rodoviária), Av Costa e Silva, 4 km from centre on road to Curitiba; bus to centre from next to the taxis, US$1.05. Taxi US$8. Book departures as soon as possible. As well as the tourist office, there is a Cetreme desk for tourists who have lost their documents, Guarda Municipal (police), Visa ATM, and luggage store. To **Curitiba**, **Catarinense, Pluma**, 9-10 hrs, paved road, US$50. To **Guaíra** via Cascavel only, 5 hrs, US$20. To **Florianópolis**, **Catarinense** (www.catarinense.net) and **Reunidas**, US$55, 14 hrs. **Reunidas** to **Porto Alegre**, US$58-66. To **São Paulo**, 16 hrs, **Pluma** US$50, 1 *convencional*, 1 *leito*; also has 2 daily to **Rio** 22 hrs, US$83. To **Campo Grande**, US$59.

Foz do Iguaçu and around: Itaipu dam *p528*
Bus Runs from outside the Terminal Urbano to the visitor centre, US$1.50, marked 'Usina Itaipu'. The Noelia company in Puerto Iguazú includes Itaipu in its tours of the the falls, T422722.

Border with Argentina: Foz do Iguaçu/ Puerto Iguazú *p528*
Bus Marked 'Puerto Iguazú' run every 20 mins from the Terminal Urbana, crossing the border bridge; 30 mins' journey, 3 companies, US$2.50. See above for procedures regarding entry stamps. **Note** Be sure you know when the last bus departs from Puerto Iguazú for Foz (usually 1900); last bus from Foz 1950. If visiting the Brazilian side for a day, get off the bus at the Hotel Bourbon, cross the road and catch the bus to the Falls, rather than going into Foz and out again. Combined tickets to Puerto Iguazú and the falls cost more than paying separately. For buses to **Buenos Aires**, see Puerto Iguazú, Transport for the options. There is a Pluma bus direct from Foz, 1830 Tue, Thu, Sat, and you can also go to Posadas via Paraguay.

Border with Paraguay: Foz do Iguaçu/ Ciudad del Este *p528*
Bus (Marked Cidade-Ponte) leave from the Terminal Urbana, Av Juscelino Kubitschek, for the Ponte de Amizade (Friendship Bridge), US$0.75. To **Asunción, Pluma** (0700), RYSA (direct at 1430, 1830), from Rodoviária, US$16.50-20 (cheaper from Ciudad del Este).
Car If crossing by private vehicle and only intending to visit the national parks, this presents no problems. Another crossing to Paraguay is at **Guaíra**, at the northern end of the Itaipu lake. It is 5 hrs north of Iguaçu by road and can be reached by bus from Campo Grande and São Paulo. Ferries cross to Saltos del Guaira on the Paraguayan side.

Directory

Foz do Iguaçu *p528, map p527*
Airline offices **Gol**, at airport, T3521 4230, or 0300-115 2121. **Ocean Air**, at airport, T3521 4256. **TAM**, R Rio Branco 640, T3523 8500 (offers free transport to Ciudad del Este for its flights, all cross-border documentation dealt with).
Banks It is difficult to exchange on Sun but quite possible in Paraguay where US dollars can be obtained on credit cards. There are plenty of banks and travel agents on Av Brasil. **Banco do Brasil**, Av Brasil 1377. ATM, high commission for TCs. **Bradesco**, Av Brasil 1202. Cash advance on Visa. **HSBC**, Av Brasil 1151, for MasterCard ATM. **Banco 24 Horas** at Oklahoma petrol station. Câmbio at **Vento Sul**, Av Brasil 1162, no TCs, good rates for cash. Also **Corimeira**, Av Brasil 148.
Embassies and consulates **Argentina**, Travessa Eduardo Bianchi 26, T3574 2969. Mon-Fri 1000-1500. **France**, R Ernesto Keller 995, Jardim Eliza II, T3529 6850, 0900-1230. **Paraguay**, R Marechal Deodoro 901, T3523 2898, Mon-Thu 0830-1530, Fri 0830-1500. **Medical services** Free 24-hr clinic, Av Paraná 1525, opposite Lions Club, T3521 1850. Few buses: take taxi or walk (about 25 mins). **Post offices** Praça Getúlio Vargas 72. **Telephones** Several call centres.

Salvador de Bahia

➔ *Phone code: 0xx71. Post code: 40000. Colour map 5, C5. Population: 3.2 million.*

Salvador, the third largest city in Brazil, is capital of the state of Bahia, dubbed 'Africa in exile' for its mixture of African and European which finds its most powerful expression in Carnival. Often referred to as Bahia, rather than Salvador, the city is home to a heady mix of colonial buildings, beautiful beaches, African culture and pulsating musical rhythms. It stands on the magnificent Baía de Todos os Santos, a sparkling bay dotted with 38 islands. The bay is the largest on the Brazilian coast covering an area of 1,100 sq km. Rising above the bay on its eastern side is a cliff which dominates the landscape and, perched on top, 71 m above sea level, are the older districts with buildings dating back to the 17th and 18th centuries. Beyond the state capital are many fine beaches, particularly in the south around Porto Seguro, while inland is the harsh sertão, traversed by the Rio São Francisco.

Ins and outs

Getting there Luis Eduardo Magalhães airport is 32 km from city centre. The **Rodoviária** is 5 km from the city with regular bus services to the centre and Campo Grande; the journey can take up to one hour especially at peak periods. ▸▸ *See also Transport, page 547.*

Getting around The broad peninsula on which the city of Salvador is built is at the mouth of the Baía de Todos Os Santos. On the opposite side of the bay's entrance is the Ilha de Itaparica. The commercial district of the city and its port are on the sheltered, western side of the peninsula; residential districts and beaches are on the open Atlantic side. The point of the peninsula is called Barra, which is itself an important area. The centre of the city is divided into two levels, the Upper City (or Cidade Alta) where the Historical Centre lies, and the Lower City (Cidade Baixa) which is the commercial and docks district. The two levels are connected by a series of steep hills called *ladeiras*. The easiest way to go from one level to the other is by the 74-m-high **Lacerda** lift which connects Praça Cairu in the lower city with Praça Municipal in the upper, US$0.05. There is also the Plano Inclinado Gonçalves, a funicular railway which leaves from behind the Cathedral going down to Comércio, the commercial district (US$0.05, closes 1300 on Saturday and all Sunday). Most visitors limit themselves to the Pelourinho and historical centre, Barra, the Atlantic suburbs (notably Rio Vermelho which has lively nightlife) and the Itapagipe peninsula, which is north of the centre. The roads and avenues between these areas are straightforward to follow and are well served by public transport. Other parts of the city are not as easy to get around, but have less of a tourist interest. If going to these areas a taxi may be advisable until you know your way around. ▸▸ *See also Transport, page 547.*

Climate Temperatures range from 25°C to 32°C, never falling below 19°C in winter. Humidity can be high, which may make the heat oppressive. It rains somewhat all the year but the main rainy season is between May and September. Nevertheless, the sun is never far away.

Tourist offices **Bahiatursa** ⓘ *Av Simon Bolivar s/n, Centro de Convenções da Bahia, 1st floor, T3117 3000, www.bahiatursa.ba.gov.br*, has lists of hotels and accommodation in private homes. Other offices at: **Pelourinho** ⓘ *R das Laranjeiras 12, T3321 2133, daily 0830-2100*, English and German spoken; **Instituto Mauá** ⓘ *Praça Azevedo Fernandes 01, Porto da Barra, T3264 4671, Mon-Fri 0900-1800, Sat 1000-1500*; **Rodoviária** ⓘ *T3450 3871, daily 0730-2100*, good, English spoken; **airport** ⓘ *T3204 1244, daily 0730-2300*; in the **Mercado Modelo** ⓘ *T3241 0242, Mon-Sat 0900-1800, Sun 0900-1330*; **Sac Shopping Barra** ⓘ *Av Centenario 2992, T3264 4566, Mon-Fri 0900-1900, Sat 0900-1400*, and **Sac Shopping Iguatemi** ⓘ *Av Tancredo Neves 148, Pituba, T480 5511, Mon-Fri 0900-2100, Sat 0900-1300*. Offices have noticeboards for messages and details of travel throughout the State of Bahia. See also www.bahia.com.br, www.cultura.ba.gov.br, and www.setur. ba.gov.br, the Secretaria de Turismo's site. **Maps:** from **Departamento de Geografia e Estadística** ⓘ *Av Estados Unidos (opposite Banco do Brasil, Lower City*, and from newsstands or airport book shop, US$1.50.

Security The authorities have made efforts to police the old part of the city and Barra, which are now well lit at night. The civil police are reported to be very sympathetic and helpful. Police are little in evidence after 2300, however, and at night you should leave valuables securely in your hotel. Also at night, the areas around and in the lifts and buses are unsafe. Do not walk down any of the links between the old and new city, especially the Ladeira de Misericórdia, which links the Belvedere, near the Lacerda Lifts, with the lower city. Nor should you walk around the forts in Porto da Barra at night. As in all large cities, use your common sense and be careful of your possessions at all times and in all districts. There have been reports of armed muggings on the sand dunes surrounding Lagoa do Abaeté. Do not visit them alone. Should a local join you on the street or at your table for a chat, leave at once if drugs are mentioned and beware other scams.

Background

On 1 November 1501, All Saints' Day, the navigator Amérigo Vespucci sailed into the bay. As the first European to see it, he named it after the day of his arrival. The first Governor General, Tomé de Sousa, arrived on 23 March 1549 to build a fortified city to protect Portugal's interest from constant threats of Dutch and French invasion. Salvador was formally founded on 1 November 1549 and remained the capital of Brazil until 1763. By the 18th century, it was the most important city in the Portuguese Empire after Lisbon, ideally situated in a safe, sheltered harbour along the trade routes of the 'New World'.

The city's first wealth came from the cultivation of sugar cane and tobacco, the plantations' workforce coming from the West coast of Africa. For three centuries Salvador was the site of a thriving slave trade. Even today, Salvador is described as the most African city in the Western Hemisphere and the University of Bahia boasts the only chair in the Yoruba language in the Americas. The influence permeates the city: food sold on the street is the same as in Senegal and Nigeria, Bahian music is fused with pulsating African polyrhythms, men and women nonchalantly carry enormous loads on their heads, fishermen paddle dug-out canoes in the bay, the pace of life is a little slower than elsewhere. The pulse of the city is candomblé, an Afro-Brazilian religion in which the African deities of Nature, the Goddess of the sea and the God of creation are worshipped. These deities (or orixás) are worshipped in temples (terreiros) which can be elaborate, decorated halls, or simply someone's front room with tiny altars to the orixá. Candomblé ceremonies may be seen by tourists – but not photographed – on Sunday and religious holidays. Contact the tourist office, Bahiatursa, or see their twice-monthly calendar of events. Salvador today is a city of 15 forts, 166 Catholic churches, 1,000 candomblé temples and a fascinating mixture of old and modern, rich and poor, African and European, religious and profane. It is still a major port exporting tropical fruit, cocoa, sisal, soya beans and petrochemical products. Its most important industry, though, is tourism. Local government has done much to improve the fortunes of this once rundown, poor and dirty city and most visitors feel that the richness of its culture is compensation enough for any problems they may encounter. The Bahianas (black women who dress in traditional 18th-century costumes) are street vendors who sit behind their trays of delicacies, savoury and seasoned, made from the great variety of local fish, vegetables and fruits. Their street food is one of the musts for visitors.

Sights

Centro Histórico

There is much more of interest in the Upper than in the Lower City. From Praça Municipal to the Carmo area 2 km north along the cliff is the Centro Histórico (Historical Centre), now a national monument and also protected by UNESCO. It was in this area that the Portuguese built their fortified city and where today stand some of the most important examples of colonial architecture in the Americas. This area is undergoing a massive restoration programme funded by the Bahian state government and UNESCO. Colonial houses have been painted in pastel colours. Many of the bars have live music which spills out onto the street on every corner. Patios have been created in the open areas behind the houses with open air cafés and bars. Artist ateliers, antique and handicraft stores have brought new artistic blood to what was once the

1 Salvador centre

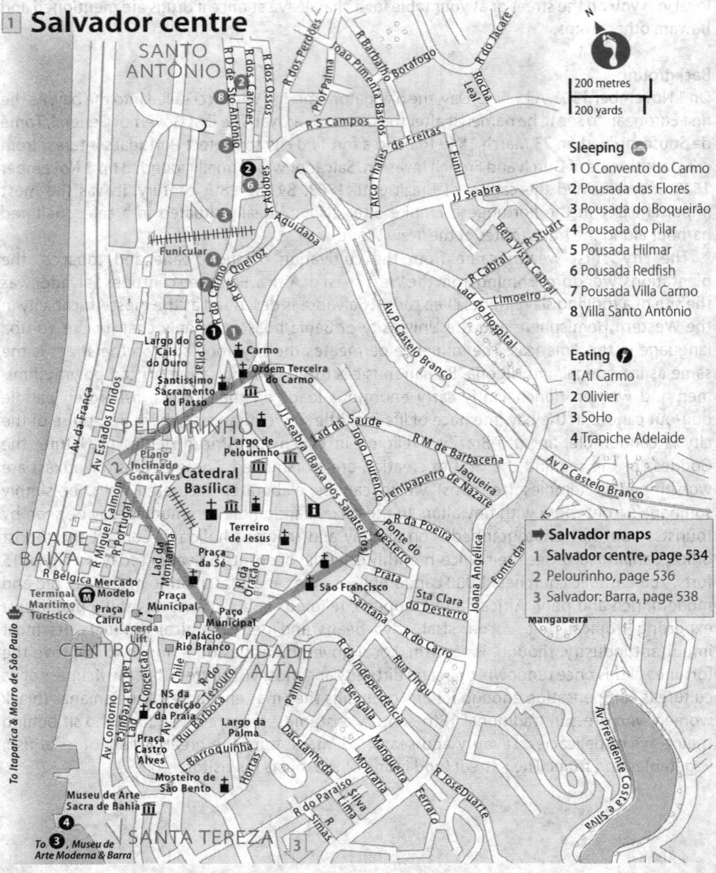

Salvador maps
1 Salvador centre, page 534
2 Pelourinho, page 536
3 Salvador: Barra, page 538

bohemian part of the city. Many popular traditional restaurants and bars from other parts of Salvador have opened new branches here. Its transformation has also attracted many tourist shops and the area can get crowded.

Praça Municipal, Praça de Sé and Terreiro de Jesus

Dominating the Praça Municipal is the old Casa de Câmara e Cadeia or **Paço Municipal** (Council Chamber – 1660), while alongside is the **Palácio Rio Branco** (1918), once the Governor's Palace. Leaving it with its panoramic view of the bay, Rua da Misericórdia goes north passing the **Santa Casa Misericórdia** ⓘ *Rua da Misericórdia 6, T3322 7355, Mon-Fri 1000-1730, Sun 1300-1700* (1695 – see the high altar and painted tiles), to Praça da Sé. This praça with its mimosa and flamboyant trees leads into Terreiro de Jesus, a picturesque praça named after the church which dominates it. Built in 1692, the **church of the Jesuits** became the property of the Holy See in 1759 when the Jesuits were expelled from all Portuguese territories. The façade is one of the earliest examples of baroque in Brazil, an architectural style which was to dominate the churches built in the 17th and 18th centuries. Inside, the vast vaulted ceiling and 12 side altars in baroque and rococo frame the main altar completely leafed in gold. The tiles in blue, white and yellow in a tapestry pattern are also from Portugal. It houses the tomb of Mem de Sá. The church is now the city Cathedral (**Catedral Basílica**) ⓘ *0900-1100, 1400-1700*. On the eastern side of the square is the church of **São Pedro dos Clérigos** ⓘ *Mon-Fri 1300-1700*, which is beautifully renovated, while close by, on the south-side, is the church of the **Ordem Terceira de São Domingos** (Dominican Third Order) ⓘ *T3242 4185, Mon-Fri, 0800-1200, 1400-1700*, which has a beautiful painted wooden ceiling and fine tiles. Nearby is **Museu Afro-Brasileiro** ⓘ *in the former Faculty of Medicine building, Terreiro de Jesus, T3321 2013, Mon-Fri 0900-1700, US$1.65, students US$0.85*, compares African and Bahian Orixás (deities) celebrations, beautiful murals and carvings, all in Portuguese. **Museu Arqueológico e Etnográfico** ⓘ *in the basement of the same building, Mon-Fri 0900-1700, US$0.55*, houses archaeological discoveries from Bahia (stone tools, clay urns, etc), an exhibition on *indígenas* from the Alto Rio Xingu area (artefacts, tools, photos), recommended. There is a museum of medicine located in the same complex.

Facing Terreiro de Jesus is Praça Anchieta and the church of **São Francisco** ⓘ *T3322 6430, Mon-Sat 0700-1830, cloisters US$1, church free*. Its simple façade belies the treasure inside. The entrance leads to a sanctuary with a spectacular painting on the wooden ceiling, by local artist José Joaquim da Rocha (1777). The main body of the church is the most exuberant example of baroque in the country. The cedar wood carving and later gold leaf was completed after 28 years in 1748. The cloisters of the monastery are surrounded by a series of blue and white tiles from Portugal. Next door is the church of the **Ordem Terceira de São Francisco** (Franciscan Third Order – 1703) ⓘ *T3321 6968, daily 0800-1700, US$2, students US$1*. It has a façade intricately carved in sandstone. Inside is a quite remarkable Chapter House with striking images of the Order's most celebrated saints.

Largo do Pelourinho

Leading off the Terreiro de Jesus is Rua Portas do Carmo (formerly Alfredo Brito), a charming, narrow cobbled street lined with fine colonial houses painted in different pastel shades. This street leads into the Largo do Pelourinho (Praça José Alencar), which was completely renovated in 1993. Considered the finest complex of colonial architecture in Latin America, it was once the site of a pillory where unscrupulous tradesmen were publicly punished and ridiculed. After the cleaning of the area, new galleries, boutiques and restaurants are opening, and at night the Largo is lively, especially on Tuesday (see Bars and clubs, page 543) . **Nosso Senhor Do Rosário Dos Pretos church** ⓘ *T3241 5781, Mon-Fri 0900-1730, small entry fee*, the so-called Slave Church, dominates the square. It was built by former slaves over a period of 100 years. The side altars honour black saints. The painted ceiling is very impressive, the overall effect being one of tranquillity in contrast to the complexity of the Cathedral and São Francisco.

At the corner of Portas do Carmo and Largo do Pelourinho is a small museum to the work of Jorge Amado, who died in 2002, **Casa da Cultura Jorge Amado** ⓘ *Mon-Sat 0900-1900, free.* Information is in Portuguese only, but the café walls are covered with colourful copies of his book jackets. The Carmo Hill is at the top of the street leading out of Largo do Pelourinho.

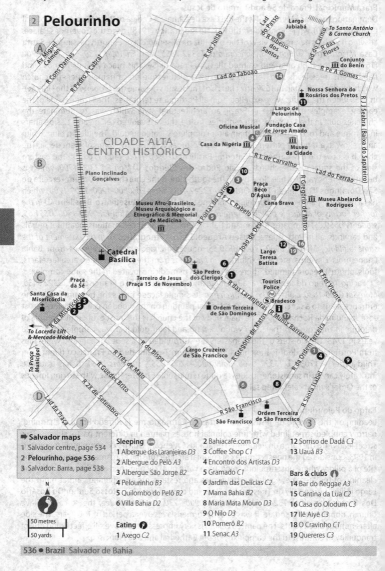

2 Pelourinho

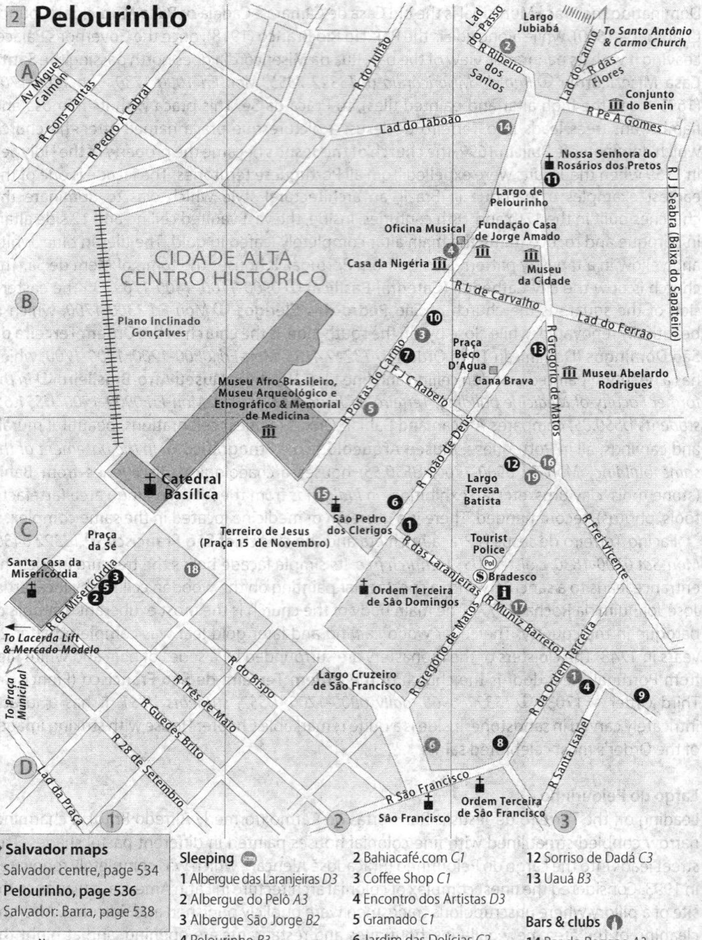

➡ Salvador maps
1 Salvador centre, page 534
2 Pelourinho, page 536
3 Salvador: Barra, page 538

Sleeping
1 Albergue das Laranjeiras *D3*
2 Albergue do Pelô *A3*
3 Albergue São Jorge *B2*
4 Pelourinho *B3*
5 Quilombo do Pelô *B2*
6 Villa Bahia *D2*

Eating
1 Axego *C2*
2 Bahiacafé.com *C1*
3 Coffee Shop *C1*
4 Encontro dos Artistas *D3*
5 Gramado *C1*
6 Jardim das Delícias *C2*
7 Mama Bahia *B2*
8 Maria Mata Mouro *D3*
9 O Nilo *D3*
10 Pomerô *B2*
11 Senac *A3*
12 Sorriso de Dadá *C3*
13 Uauá *B3*

Bars & clubs
14 Bar do Reggae *A3*
15 Cantina da Lua *C2*
16 Casa do Olodum *C3*
17 Ilê Aiyê *C3*
18 O Cravinho *C1*
19 Quereres *C3*

Museu Abelardo Rodrigues ⓘ *Solar Ferrão, Pelourinho, R Gregório de Mattos 45, 1300-1900 except Mon, US$0.55*, is a religious art museum, with objects from the 17th, 18th and 19th centuries, mainly from Bahia, Pernambuco and Maranhão. **Museu da Cidade** ⓘ *Largo do Pelourinho, Mon and Wed-Fri 0930-1800, Sat 1300-1700, Sun 0930-1300, US$0.50*, has exhibitions of arts and crafts and old photographs. From the higher floors of the museum you can get a good view of the Pelourinho. The newly restored **Conjunto do Benin** ⓘ *R Padre Agostinho Gomes 17, Pelourinho, T3241 5679, Mon-Fri 1200-1800, below NS do Rosario dos Pretos*, has diverse exhibitions and shows African crafts, photos and videos on Benin and Angola. The **Casa da Nigéria** ⓘ *R Portas do Carmo 26, Pelourinho, T3328 3782*, offers a similar programme orientated more to Yoruba culture and has showcases of African and African Brazilian arts and crafts, photographs and a library.

The **Carmo church** (Carmelite Third Order, 1709) ⓘ *Mon-Sat 0800-1130, 1330-1730, Sun 1000-1200, US$1*, houses one of the sacred art treasures of the city, a sculpture of Christ made in 1730 by a slave who had no formal training, Francisco Xavier das Chagas, known as O Cabra. One of the features of the piece is the blood made from whale oil, ox blood, banana resin and 2,000 rubies to represent the drops of blood. **Museu do Carmo** ⓘ *in the Convento do Carmo, Mon-Sat 0800-1200, 1400-1800, Sun 0800-1200, US$0.15*, has a collection of icons and colonial furniture.

South of the Praça Municipal

Rua Chile leads to **Praça Castro Alves**, with its monument to Castro Alves, who started the campaign which finally led to the Abolition of Slavery in 1888. Two streets lead out of this square, Avenida 7 de Setembro, busy with shops and street vendors selling everything imaginable, and, parallel to it, Rua Carlos Gomes. **Museu de Arte Sacra** ⓘ *R do Sodré 276 (off R Carlos Gomes), Mon-Fri 1130-1730, US$2*, is in the 17th-century convent and church of Santa Teresa, at the bottom of the steep Ladeira de Santa Teresa. Many of the 400 carvings are from Europe, but some are local. Among the reliquaries of silver and gold is one of gilded wood by Aleijadinho (see box, page 480). **São Bento church** ⓘ *Av 7 de Setembro, Mon-Sat 0630-1230, 1600-1900, Sun 0700-1130, 1700-1900*, was rebuilt after 1624, but it has fine 17th-century furniture.

Both streets eventually come to **Campo Grande** (also known as Praça Dois de Julho). In the centre of the praça is the monument to Bahian Independence, 2 July 1823. Avenida 7 de Setembro continues out of the square towards the Vitória area. There are some fine 19th-century homes along this stretch, known as Corredor da Vitória. The **Museu de Arte Moderna** ⓘ *off Av Contorno, T3329 0660, Tue-Fri 1300-2100, Sat 1500-2100 and Sun 1400-1900, free*, converted from an old sugar estate house and outbuildings, is open for special exhibitions. The restaurant (Solar do Unhão) is still there and the buildings are worth seeing for themselves (best to take a taxi as access can be dangerous). **Museu Costa Pinto** ⓘ *Av 7 de Setembro 2490, weekdays 1430-1900, but closed Tue, Sat-Sun 1500-1800, US$2.50*, is a modern house with collections of crystal, porcelain, silver, furniture, etc. It also has the only collection of balangandãs (slave charms and jewellery), highly recommended. **Museu de Arte da Bahia** ⓘ *Av 7 de Setembro 2340, Vitória, Tue-Fri 1400-1900, Sat-Sun 1430-1900, US$1.60*, has interesting paintings of Brazilian artists from the 18th to the early 20th century.

Barra

From Praça Vitória, the avenue continues down Ladeira da Barra (Barra Hill) to Porto da Barra. The best city beaches are in this area. Also in this district are the best bars, restaurants and nightlife. The Barra section of town has received a facelift with a new lighting system. The pavements fill with people day and night and many sidewalk restaurants and bars are open along the strip from Porto da Barra as far as the Cristo at the end of the Farol da Barra beach. Great attention to security is given. A little further along is the **Forte de Santo Antônio da Barra** and **lighthouse**, 1580, built on the spot where Amérigo Vespucci landed in 1501. It is right at the mouth of the bay where Baía de Todos Os Santos and the South Atlantic Ocean meet and is the site of the first lighthouse built in the Americas. The interesting **Museu Hidrográfico** ⓘ *Tue-Sat 1300-1800, US$1.30*, which has a good café for watching the sunset, is housed in the upper section of the Forte de Santo Antônio; fine views of the bay and coast, recommended.

Atlantic beach suburbs

The promenade leading away from the fort and its famous lighthouse is called Avenida Oceânica, which follows the coast to the beach suburbs of **Ondina**, Amaralina and Pituba. The road is also called Avenida Presidente Vargas, but the numbering is different. Beyond Pituba are the **best ocean beaches** at Jaguaripe, **Piatã** and Itapoã. En route the bus passes small fishing colonies at Amaralina and Pituba where jangadas can be seen. A jangada is a small raft peculiar to the northeastern region of Brazil used extensively as well as dug-out canoes. Near Itapoã is the **Lagoa do Abaeté**, surrounded by brilliant, white sands. This is a deep, freshwater lake where local women traditionally come to wash their clothes and then lay them out to dry in the sun. The road leading up from the lake offers a panoramic view of the city in the distance, the coast, and the contrast of the white sands and fresh water less than 1 km from the sea and its golden beaches. **Note** See Security, page 533. Near the lighthouse at **Itapoã** there are two campsites on the beach. A little beyond the campsites are the magnificent ocean beaches of Stella Maris and Flamengo, both quiet during the week but very busy at the weekends. Beware of strong undertow at these beaches. Apart from Porto da Barra, all the beaches before Itapoã are polluted with sewage (a new system is under construction). The Sunday paper, *A Tarde*, publishes the condition of the beaches.

Bonfim and Itapagipe

See also the famous church of **Nosso Senhor do Bonfim** on the Itapagipe peninsula in the suburbs north of the centre, whose construction began in 1745. It draws endless supplicants

Salvador: Barra

3

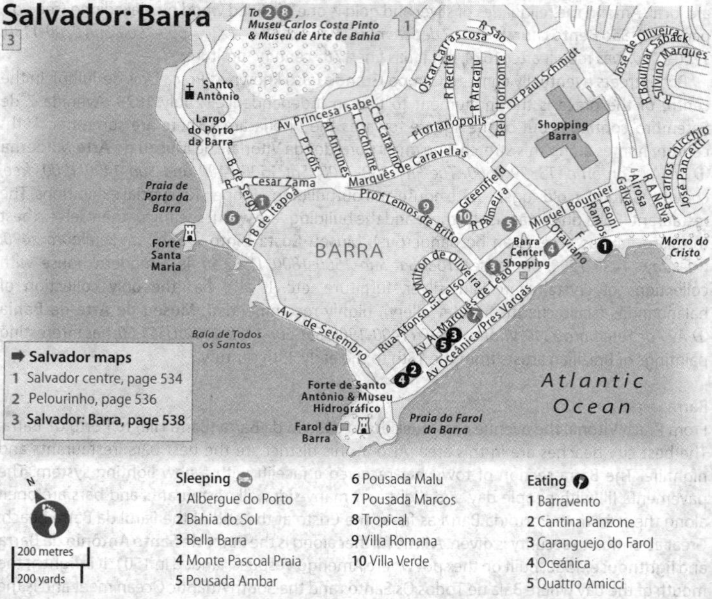

➡ Salvador maps

1 Salvador centre, page 534

2 Pelourinho, page 536

3 Salvador: Barra, page 538

Sleeping

1 Albergue do Porto
2 Bahia do Sol
3 Bella Barra
4 Monte Pascoal Praia
5 Pousada Ambar
6 Pousada Malu
7 Pousada Marcos
8 Tropical
9 Villa Romana
10 Villa Verde

Eating

1 Barravento
2 Cantina Panzone
3 Caranguejo do Farol
4 Oceânica
5 Quattro Amicci

(particularly on Friday and Sunday) offering favours to the image of the Crucified Lord set over the high altar; the number and variety of ex-voto offerings is extraordinary. The processions over the water to the church on the third Sunday in January are particularly interesting. Also on the Itapagipe peninsula is a colonial fort on **Monte Serrat** point, and at Ribeira the church of **Nossa Senhora da Penha** (1743). The beach here has many restaurants, but the sea is polluted (bus from Praça da Sé or Avenida França).

Itaparica

Across the bay from Salvador lies the island of Itaparica, 29 km long and 12 km wide. The town of Itaparica is very picturesque, with a fair beach in the town, and well worth a visit. Take a bus or kombi by the coast road (Beira Mar) which passes through the villages of Manguinhos, Amoureiras and Ponta de Areia. The beach at Ponta de Areia is one of the best on the island and is very popular. There are many barracas on the beach, the best and busiest is Barraca Pai Xango, always very lively.

In Itaparica there are many fine residential buildings from the 19th century, plus the church of **São Lourenço**, one of the oldest in Brazil, and there are delightful walks through the old town. During the summer months the streets are ablaze with the blossoms of the beautiful flamboyant trees. The beaches at **Mar Grande** are fair but can be dirty at times. There are many pousadas in Mar Grande and at the nearby beaches of Ilhota and Gamboa (both to the left as you disembark from the ferry).

From Bom Despacho there are many buses, kombis and taxis to all parts of the island, including beaches at Ponta de Areia, Mar Grande, Berlinque, **Aratuba** and **Cacha Pregos**. Kombis and taxis can be rented for trips but be prepared to bargain. There are also buses to other towns such as Nazaré das Farinhas, Valença (see page 552) and also **Jaguaribe**, a small, picturesque colonial port. Both of these towns are on the mainland connected by a bridge on the southwest side of the island, turn off between Mar Grande and Cacha Pregos (bus company, **Viazul**). There are good beaches across the bay on the mainland, but a boat is needed to reach these (US$16).

Salvador de Bahia listings

For Sleeping and Eating price codes and other relevant information, see Essentials, pages 38-40. See Telephone, page 397, for important phone changes.

Sleeping

The Centro Histórico is the ideal place to stay; the Pelourinho if you're on a tight budget and Santo Antônio if you are looking for reasonably priced hotels with real charm and character. Barra also has some cheap options but is increasingly seedy. Business visitors will find the best hotels in Rio Vermelho, overlooking the ocean and a 10-min taxi ride from the centre. Self-contained a/c apartments with kitchens and hotel services can be rented by the day. Standards are generally high.

Centro Histórico *p534, maps p534 & p536*

LL O Convento do Carmo, R do Carmo 1, T3327 8400, www.pestana.com. Outstanding historical hotel in the centre with a range of suites in a beautifully converted baroque convent, excellent restaurant, spa, small pool, business services.

LL-L Villa Bahia, Largo do Cruzeiro de São Francisco 16-18, T3322 4271, www.villabahia.com. Boutique hotel in a renovated 18th-century town house, themed rooms, the airiest and brightest of which is the Goa room. Small pool, hot tub on the roof.

A Pelourinho, R das Portas do Carmo 20, T3322 3939, www.hotelpelourinho.com. Refurbished 1960s hotel with bright decorations, some rooms with great views over the bay, some special offers.

B-D Quilombo do Pelô, R das Portas do Carmo 13, T3322 4371. A Jamaican hotel and restaurant in the Pelourinho, with dorms and rooms ranging to a top-floor suite with jacuzzi.

C Pousada da Praça, Rui Barbosa, 5, T3321 0642, www.pousadadapracahotel.com.br. Simple, pretty, old colonial house, quiet, secure, big breakfast, rooms with and without bath, **E** pp in shared room. Insist on a receipt; streets around can be noisy.

E pp **Albergue das Laranjeiras**, R Inácio Acciolli 13, Pelourinho, T/F3321 1366, www.laranjeiras hostel.com.br. In beautiful colonial building in heart of the historical district, can be noisy, café and crêperie downstairs, English spoken. **B** double, **C** with shared bath, cheaper for HI members and in low season. Good for meeting other travellers. Warmly recommended.

E pp **Albergue do Pelô**, R do Passo 5, T3242 8061, www.alberguedopelo.com.br. Bright reception area, simple freshly painted dorms for 4-12. All are single sex. Breakfast included.

E-F pp **Albergue São Jorge**, R das Portas do Carmo 25, Pelourinho, T3266 7092, www.saojorgehostel.com. Dorms and shared rooms, with breakfast, kitchen and laundry facilities, lockers, internet access, helpful owner speaks English, lots of activity.

Santo Antônio

AL Pousada das Flores, R Direita de Santo Antônio 442, near Santo Antônio fort, T/F3243 1836, www.pflores.com.br. Brazilian/French owners, excellent breakfast, beautiful old house.

AL-A Pousada do Pilar, R Direita do Santo Antônio 24, T3241 6278, www.pousadadopilar.com. Run by the owners of Morro do São Paulo's **Vila Guaiamu**, functional a/c rooms, international cable TV, verandas with excellent Baía de Todos os Santos views, good breakfast, helpful manager, Filipe, pleasant roof terrace bar.

AL-A Pousada Redfish, Ladeira do Boqueirão 1, T3243 8473, www.hotelredfish.com. English-owned stylish little boutique with plain, large rooms, some with terraces and open-air showers.

AL-A Villa Santo Antônio, R Direita de Santo Antônio 130, T3326 1270, www.hotel-santoantonio.com. Bright and comfortable converted colonial house, best rooms with views over the bay, a/c, all rooms different, good service and breakfast.

A Pousada do Boqueirão, R Direita do Santo Antônio 48, T3241 2262, www.pousada boqueirao.com.br. Family-run, beautiful house overlooking bay, remodelled, relaxed atmosphere, most European languages spoken, great food, first class in all respects. Highly recommended.

B Pousada Villa Carmo, R do Carmo 58, T/F3241 3924, www.pousadavillacarmo.com.br. Italian/Brazilian owned, many European languages spoken, very comfortable, rooms with fan or a/c.

B-C Pousada Baluarte, R Baluarte, 13, T3327 0367, www.pousadabaluarte.com. Bohemian household, lovely owners, 5 rooms, cheaper without bath, excellent home made breakfasts.

C-D Pousada Hilmar, R Direita de Santo Antônio 136, T3243 4959, www.pousada hilmar.com.br. Several types of room with and without a/c and TV, with breakfast, a good option in a quiet street.

Campo Grande/Vitória

Upmarket residential area, between Barra and city centre, convenient for museums.

L Tropical Hotel da Bahia, Av 7 de Setembro 1537, Campo Grande, T2105 2000, www.tropical hotel.com.br. Well run, convenient for city centre, very much a business hotel.

A Bahia do Sol, Av 7 de Setembro 2009, T3338 8800, www.bahiadosol.com.br. Comfortable, safe and frigobar in room, family run, good breakfast and restaurant, bureau de change. Ask for a room onthe upper floors.

Barra *p537, map p538*

A Monte Pascoal Praia, Av Oceânica 176, Farol beach, T3203 4000, www.montepascoal.com.br. Renovated 1970s hotel in garish colours but well-kept and well-run. With pool, sauna, gym, restaurant and decent service.

B-C Villa Verde, R da Palmeira 190, T3489 1978, www.pousadavillaverde.com. Cheaper longer stays, a/c studios with kitchen and double room with fan, garden, terrace, hammocks, internet, safe, very good. Recommended.

C Bella Barra, R Afonso Celso 439, T3264 3260, www.hotelbellabarra.com.br. Simple, a/c rooms, internet, plenty of services, safe, English spoken, tours, car hire arranged.

C Villa Romana, R Lemos Brito 14, T3264 6522, www.villaromana.com.br. 1960s hotel with basic a/c rooms and a pool, good location.

C-D Pousada Ambar, R Afonso Celso 485, T3264 6956, www.ambarpousada.com.br. Also has albergue at **E-F**. Good service, breakfast, internet, convenient, French owner also speaks English.

C-D Pousada Malu, 7 de Setembro 3801, T3264 4461. Small rooms along an external corridor in a hotel overlooking the sea. With breakfast, cooking and laundry facilities.

E pp **Albergue do Porto**, R Barão de Sergy 197, T3264 6600, www.alberguedoporto.com.br. One block from beach, short bus ride or 20 mins on foot from historical centre. IYHA hostel in beautiful turn-of-the-century house, cheaper for members, breakfast, convenient, English spoken, double rooms with a/c and bath available (**B-C**, depending on season), kitchen, laundry facilities, safe, TV lounge, games room, internet, courtyard. Highly recommended.

E-F Pousada Marcos, Av Oceânica 281, T3264 5117, www.pousadamarcos.com.br. Youth hostel-style, great location near the lighthouse, very busy, notices in Hebrew for potential travelling companions, kitchen, efficient.

Atlantic beach suburbs *p538*

LL Pestana Bahia, R Fonte de Boi 216, Rio Vermelho, T/F2103 8000, www.pestana.com. One of the best in Salvador, all comfort and facilities including for the disabled. No access to the sea.

A-B Catharina Paraguaçu, R João Gomes 128, Rio Vermelho, T3334 0089, www.hotelcatharina paraguacu.com.br. Charming, small, colonial-style, tastefully decorated.

B Ibis, R Fonte do Boi 215, T3330 8300, www.accorhotels.com.br. Large hotel in this budget business chain, safe, a/c and with sea views from the upper floors. Great value.

Camping Note that sea bathing is dangerous off shore near the campsites. **Camping Clube do Brasil**, R Visconde do Rosário 409, Rosário, T3242 0482. **Ecológica**, R Alameida da Praia, near the lighthouse at Itapoã, take bus from Praça da Sé direct to Itapoã, or to Campo Grande or Barra, change there for Itapoã, about 1 hr, then 30 mins' walk, T3374 3506. Bar, restaurant, hot showers. Highly recommended.

Pensionatos These are places to stay in shared rooms (up to 4 per room); part or full board available. **Pierre Marbacher**, R Carlos Coqueijo 68A, Itapoã, T3249 5754 (Caixa Postal 7458, 41600 Salvador). He is Swiss, owns a beach bar at Rua K, speaks English and rents houses or rooms.

At Carnival it's worth renting a flat; the tourist office has a list of agents. They can also arrange rooms in private houses; however, caution is advised as not all householders are honest.

Itaparica *p539*

A Pousada Arco Iris, Estrada da Gamboa 102, Mar Grande, T3633 1316. Magnificent building and setting in mango orchard, expensive, good if slow restaurant, Manga Rosa. They have camping facilities next door, shady, not always clean.

A Quinta Pitanga, R da Alegria 10, in Itaparica town, T3631 1834. Beautifully decorated by the owner Jim Valkus, 3 suites and 2 singles, beachfront property, a retreat, excellent restaurant. Expensive but highly recommended, accepts day visitors and offers artists' residencies (www.sacatar.org).

C Pousada Um Canto do Mar, Av Beira Mar s/n, Praia de Aratuba, T3638 2244, www.pousadaum cantodomar.com.br. Bright, simple cabins overlooking beach, lively in summer, quiet the rest of the year, helpful staff, decent breakfast.

C Sonho do Verão, R São Bento 2, opposite Pousada Arco Iris, Mar Grande, T3633 1316, sonhodeverao@internet.com.br. Chalets and apartments, cooking facilities, French and English spoken. Like other pousadas they rent bicycles (US$3 per hr); they also rent horses (US$5 per hr).

C-D Pousada Icaraí, Praça da Piedade, Itaparica town, T3631 1110, hicarai@ hotmail.com. Charming, good location.

C-D Pousada Zimbo Tropical, Estrada de Cacha Pregos, Km 3, Rua Yemanjá, Aratuba, T/F3638 1148. French/Brazilian-run, good breakfast, evening meals available. Recommended.

Eating

Local specialities

The main dish is *moqueca*, seafood cooked in a sauce made from coconut milk, tomatoes, red and green peppers, fresh coriander and *dendê* (palm oil). It is traditionally cooked in a wok-like earthen- ware dish and served piping hot at the table. Served with moqueca is *farofa* (manioc flour) and a hot pepper sauce which you add at your discretion, it's usually extremely hot so try a few drops before venturing further. The dendê is somewhat heavy and those with delicate stomachs are advised to try the *ensopado*, a sauce with the same ingredients as the moqueca, but without the palm oil.

Nearly every street corner has a Bahiana selling a wide variety of local snacks, the most famous of which is the *acarajé*, a kidney bean dumpling fried in palm oil which has its origins in West Africa. To this the Bahiana adds *vatapá*, a dried shrimp and coconut milk pâté (also delicious on its own), fresh salad and hot sauce (*pimenta*). For those who prefer not to eat the palm oil, the *abará* is a good substitute. Abará is steamed, wrapped in banana leaves. Seek local advice on which are most hygienic stalls to eat from. Two good Bahianas are Chica, at Ondina beach (on the street to the left of Mar A Vista Hotel) and Dinha at Largo da Santana (very lively in the late afternoon), who serves acarajé until midnight, extremely popular. Bahians usually eat *acarajé* or *abará* with a chilled beer on the way home from work or on the beach at sunset. Another popular dish with African origins is *Xin-Xin de Galinha*, chicken on the bone cooked in dendê, with dried shrimp, garlic and squash.

Centro Histórico *p534, maps p534 & p536*

TTT Mama Bahia, R das Portas do Carmo 21, T3322 4397, Pelourinho, www.mamabahia.com.br. Steaks and northeastern meat dishes, good but modest South American wine list. Look out for extras, such as "music fee".

TTT Maria Mata Mouro, R da Ordem Terceira 8, Pelourinho, T3321 3929. International menu, excellent service, relaxing atmosphere, closed Sun night.

TTT O Nilo, R das Laranjeiras 44, T9159 0937. Superior Lebanese food in an intimate restaurant.

TTT Sorriso da Dadá, R Frei Vicente 5, T3321 9642, www.dada.com.br. Bahia's most famous chef has had many illustrious clients, but her once excellent *moquecas* and *vatapas* are not what they were.

TTT Uauá, R Gregório de Matos 36, Pelourinho, T3321 3089. Elegant, colonial restaurant and bar, typical Bahian cuisine.

TTT-TT Axego, R João de Deus1, T3242 7481. Celebrated for its seafood, *feijoada* at Sun lunch.

TTT-TT Encontro dos Artistas, R das Laranjeiras 15, T3321 1721. Very good seafood and *moquecas* served in a little street-side restaurant.

TTT-TT Jardim das Delícias, R João de Deus 12, Pelourinho, T3321 1449. Elegant restaurant and antiques shop with tropical garden, very reasonable for its setting, classical or live music.

TT Quilombo do Pelô, R das Portas do Carmo 13, see Sleeping. Rustic Jamaican restaurant, open daily from 1100, good food with relaxed, if erratic service, vegetarian options.

TT Senac, Praça José Alencar 13-15, Largo do Pelourinho, T3324 4557. State-run catering school, with typical Bahian cooking upstairs and per kilo lunches downstairs, both a/c. Upstairs is better but lots of choice, including vegetarian, downstairs.

TT-T Pomerô, R Portas do Carmo 33, Pelourinho, T3321 5556, www.pomero.com.br. Closed Mon. Good value, simple grilled meats, fish steaks, bar snacks, *moquecas*, popular.

T Bahiacafé.com, Praça da Sé 20, T3322 1266. Smart, Belgian-run internet café, good breakfasts, excellent food, English spoken.

T Coffee Shop, Praça da Sé 5, T3322 7817. Cuban-style café serving sandwiches; main attraction is excellent coffee, and tea served in china cups, doubles as cigar shop.

T Gramado, Praça da Sé. One of few food-by-weight restaurants in area, basic, lunch only.

Santo Antônio

TTT-TT Al Carmo, R Rua do Carmo 66, Santo Antônio, T3242 0283. A favourite spot to watch the sun sink over the bay, caipirinha or chilled wine in hand. Italian food is average, the music has an optional cover charge.

TTT-TT Olivier, R Direita de Santo Antônio 61, T3241 3829. Cosy French restaurant with live light jazz and MPB most weekend nights in season, decent caipirinhas.

Between Historical Centre and Barra

TTT SoHo, on Av Contorno 1010, Píer D, Bahia Marina, T3322 4554. One of the city's most fashionable restaurants. Excellent Japanese food. Great cocktails and sea views, dinner only. Bus connections poor, go by taxi.

TTT Trapiche Adelaide, Praça Tupinmabas 2, Av Contorno, T3326 2211, www.trapichea delaide.com.br. Very chic, mood-lit glass-walled rectangle built out over the water, stunning views. Excellent seafood. Dress well and take a taxi.

Barra *p537, map p538*

TTT Barravento, Av Oceânica 814, T3247 2577. Popular, upmarket beach bar restaurant, seafood, steaks, cocktails and *chope*.

TT Cantina Panzone, Av Oceânica 114, T3264 3644. Pizza and pasta, lively in season.

ΨΨ Oceánica, Pres Vargas 1, T3264 3561. Long-established, popular seafood restaurant, open till late.

ΨΨ Quatro Amicci, R Dom Marcos Teixeira 35. Excellent pizzas from wood-fired oven, bright, lively at weekends.

Ψ Caranguejo do Farol, Av Oceânica 235, above the road, T3264 7061. Specializing in crab, extremely busy, also a buzzing bar.

Many medium-priced a/c restaurants in **Shopping Barra** and **Barra Center Shopping**.

Itparica *p539*

ΨΨ Philippe's Bar and Restaurant, Largo de São Bento, Mar Grande. French and local cuisine, information in English and French.

Ψ Restaurant Rafael in the main praça, Mar Grande. For pizzas and snacks.

There are many Bahianas selling *acarajé* in the late afternoon and early evening in the main praça by the pier at Mar Grande.

Bars and clubs

Nightlife is concentrated on and around the Pelourinho where there is always a free live street band on Tue and at weekends. The Pelourinho area is also good for a bar browse; though be wary after 2300. There are many bars on the Largo de Quincas Berro d'Água, especially along R Portas do Carmo. R João de Deus and its environs are dotted with simple pavement bars with plastic tables. The most famous Salvador musicians are the *maracatú* drum orchestras like **Olodum** and **Ilê Aiyê** (see below). There is live music all year round but the best time to hear the most frenetic performers, particularly the *axê* stars, is during Carnaval.

Largo do Pelourinho *p535, map p536*

Bar do Reggae and **Praça do Reggae**, Ladeiro do Pelourinho, by Nossa Senhora dos Rosarios dos Pretos. Live reggae bands every Tue and more frequently closer to carnival.

Cantina da Lua, Praça 15 de Novembro 2, Terreiro de Jesus, T3322 4041. Daily, popular, good place to meet, outdoor seating, but the food isn't great.

Casa do Olodum, R Gregório de Mattos 22, T3321 5010, http://olodum.uol.com.br. Olodum's headquarters where they perform live every Tue and Sun at 1930 to packed crowds.

Ilê Aiyê, R do Curuzu 197, Liberdade, T3256 8800, www.ileaiye.com.br. Ilê Aiyê's headquarters. Details of live performances throughout Salvador are published here.

O Cravinho, Praça 15 de Novembro 3, T3322 6759. Dark little ba with occasional live music, cachaça made on the premises and bar food. Take care in this area after 2300.

Quereres, R Frei Vicente 7, T3321 1616. Lively little club in a colonial house playing Brazilian samba funk, hip hop and *axê*, busy Tue and Fri.

Barra *p537, map p538*

Most Barra nightlife happens at the Farol da Barra (lighthouse). R Marquês de Leão is very busy, with lots of bars with tables on the pavement. Like the Pelourinho, the whole area is good for a browse, but be wary of pickpockets.

Habeas Copos, R Marquês de Leão 172. Famous and traditional street side bar, very popular.

Atlantic beach suburbs *p538*

Once the bohemian section of town the nightlife in **Rio Vermelho** rivals Pelourinho. There are a number of lively bars around the Largo de Santana, a block west of the Hotel Catharina Paraguaçu.

Café Calypso, Trav Prudente Moraes 59, Rio Vermelho. Live Brazilian rock on Tue and Fri.

Havana Music Bar, R Cardeal da Silva 117, Rio Vermelho. Live bands Wed-Sat, best after 2230.

Pimentinha, Boca do Rio. One of the few clubs to be lively on Mon.

Teatro Sesi Rio Vermelho, R Borges dos Reis 9, Rio Vermelho, T334 0668. The best place in the city to see contemporary Salvador bands live.

Entertainment

Salvador de Bahia *p532, maps p534, 536 & p538*

The **Fundação Cultural do Estado da Bahia** edits *Bahia Cultural*, a monthly brochure listing monthly cultural events. These can be found in most hotels and Bahiatursa information centres. Local newspapers *A Tarde* and *Correio da Bahia* have good cultural sections listing all events in the city.

Cinema The main shopping malls at Barra, Iguatemi, Itaigara and Brotas, and **Cineart** in Politeama (Centro), run more mainstream movies. The impressive Casa do Comércio building near Iguatemi houses the **Teatro do SESC** with a mixed programme of theatre,

Carnival in Bahia

Carnival officially starts on Thursday night at 2000 when the keys of the city are given to the Carnival King 'Rei Momo'. The unofficial opening though is on Wednesday with the Lavagem do Porto da Barra, when throngs of people dance on the beach. Later on in the evening is the Baile dos Atrizes, starting at around 2300 and going on until dawn, very bohemian, good fun. Check with Bahiatursa for details, also http://home.centraldo carnaval.com.br and www.carnaval.salvado r.ba.gov.br (see under Rio for carnival dates).

Carnival in Bahia is the largest in the world and it encourages active participation. It is said that there are 1½ million people dancing on the streets at any one time.

There are two distinct musical formats. The Afro Blocos are large drum-based troupes (some with up to 200 drummers) who play on the streets accompanied by singers atop mobile sound trucks. The first of these groups was the Filhos de Gandhi (founded in 1949), whose participation is one of the highlights of Carnival. Their 6,000 members dance through the streets on the Sunday and Tuesday of Carnival dressed in their traditional costumes, a river of white and blue in an ocean of multicoloured carnival revellers. The best known of the recent Afro Blocos are Ilê Aiye, Olodum, Muzenza and Malê Debalê. They all operate throughout the year in cultural, social and political areas. Not all of them are receptive to foreigners among their numbers for Carnival. The basis of the rhythm is the enormous surdo (deaf) drum with its bumbum bumbum bum anchorbeat, while the smaller repique, played with light twigs, provides a crack-like overlay. Ilê Aiye take to the streets around 2100 on Saturday night and their departure from their headquarters at Ladeira do Curuzu in the Liberdade district is not to be missed. The best way to get there is to take a taxi to Curuzu via Largo do Tanque thereby avoiding traffic jams. The ride is a little longer in distance but much

cinema and music Wed-Sun. **Teatro da Barra**, Av Marquês de Caravelas 50, Barra, small independent cinema with foreigh films, US$2.50.

Music

During the winter (Jul-Sep) ring the blocos to confirm that free rehearsals will take place.

Ara Ketu, T3264 8800 www.araketu.com, hails from the sprawling Periperi suburb in the Lower City. Once a purely percussion band Ara Ketu has travelled widely and borrowed on various musical forms (samba, candomblé, soukous, etc) to become a major carnival attraction and one of the most successful bands in Bahia. Rehearsals take place on Thu nights at 1930 on Trapiche Barnabé, Comércio. As these get very full, buy tickets in advance from Pida kiosks, the Central do Carnaval, Ticketmix and at the bloco's HQ, R Afonso Celso, 161, Barra.

Banda Olodum (address above) drumming troupe made famous by their innovative powerhouse percussion and involvement with Paul Simon, Michael Jackson and Branford Marsalis, their weekly rehearsals take place in front of packed crowds.

Didá Neguinho do Samba was the musical director of Olodum until he founded Didá, an all-woman drumming group based along similar lines to Olodum. They rehearse on Fri nights in the Praça Teresa Batista, Pelourinho. Starts 2000, US$10.

Filhos de Gandhi, the original and largest African drumming group, formed by striking stevedores during the 1949 carnival. The hypnotic shuffling cadence of Filhos de Gandhi's afoxé rhythm is one of the most emotive of Bahia's carnival.

Ilê Aiyê, address above. Established in Liberdade, the largest suburb of the city, Ilê Aiyê is a thriving cultural group dedicated to preserving African traditions which under the guidance of its president Vovô is deeply committed to the fight against racism. Rehearsals take place mid week at Boca do Rio and on Sat nights in front of their headquarters at Ladeira do Curuzu in Liberdade.

Timbalada, T3355 0680, www.timbalada.com. Carlinhos Brown is a local hero. He has become one of the most influential musical composers in Brazil today, mixing great lyrics, innovative rhythms and a powerful stage presence. He quicker in time. A good landmark is the Paes Mendonça supermarket on the corner of the street from where the bloco leaves. From there it's a short walk to the departure point.

The enormous trios eléctricos 12 m sound trucks, with powerful sound systems that defy most decibel counters, are the second format. These trucks, each with its own band of up to 10 musicians, play songs influenced by the afro blocos and move at a snail's pace through the streets, drawing huge crowds. Each Afro Bloco and bloco de trio has its own costume and its own security personnel who cordon off the area around the sound truck. The bloco members can thus dance in comfort and safety.

There are three official Carnival routes. The oldest is Osmar, from Campo Grande to Praça Castro Alves near the old town. The blocos go along Avenue 7 de Setembro and return to Campo Grande via the parallel R Carlos Gomes. The best night at Praça Castro Alves is Tuesday (the last night of Carnival) when the famous 'Encontro dos trios' (Meeting of the Trios) takes place. Trios jostle for position in the square and play in rotation until dawn (or later!) on Ash Wednesday. It is not uncommon for major stars from the Bahian (and Brazilian) music world to make surprise appearances.

The second route is Dodô, from Farol da Barra to Ondina. The blocos alternativos ply this route. These are nearly always trios eléctricos connected with the more traditional blocos who have expanded to this now popular district. The third and newest route is Batatinha, in the historic centre and the streets of Pelourinho. No trios eléctricos take part on this route, but marching bands, folkloric groups and fancy-dress parades.

Day tickets for these are available the week leading up to Carnival. Check with Bahiatursa on where the tickets are sold for the stands. There is little or no shade from the sun so bring a hat and lots of water. Best days are Sunday to Tuesday. Or just go it alone; find a barraca in the shade and watch the blocos go by.

played percussion with many Bahian musicians, until he formed his own percussion group, Timbalada. He has invested heavily in his native Candeal neighbourhood: the Candy All Square, a centre for popular culture, is where the Timbalada rehearsals take place every Sun night. 1830, US$20 from Sep to Mar. Not to be missed.

Artists and bands using electronic instruments and who tend to play in the *trios eléctricos* draw heavily on the rich rhythms of the drumming groups creating a new musical genre known as **Axé**. The most popular of such acts are **Chiclete com Banana**, www.chicletecombanana.com.br, and **Ivete Sangalo**. Also look out for the internationally famous **Daniela Mercury**. **Gerónimo** was one of the first singer/song- writers to use the wealth of rhythms of the Candomblé in his music and his song *E d'Oxum* is something of an anthem for the city. **Mariene de Castro** is Bahia's most exciting new artist and one of the few singing traditional Bahian samba.

All the above have albums released and you can find their records easily in most record stores. See Shopping in the Pelourinho. Also try Flashpoint in Shopping Iguatemi.

Theatre

Castro Alves, at Campo Grande (Largo 2 de Julho), T3339 8000, www.tca.ba.gov.br, seats 1400 and is considered one of the best in Latin America. It also has its own repertory theatre, the **Sala de Coro**, for more experimental productions. The theatre's Concha Acústica is an open-air venue used frequently in the summer, attracting the big names in Brazilian music.

Theatro XVIII, R Frei Vicente, T3332 0018, www.theatroxviii.com.br, an experimental theatre in the Pelourinho.

Teatro Gregório de Matos in Praça Castro Alves, T3322 2646, offers space to new productions and writers.

Vila Velha, Passéio Público, Gamboa da Cima, T3336 1384. A historically important venue where many of the *tropicalistas* first played. Nowadays it has an eclectic programme of modern dance, theatre and live music. **Grupo Teatro Olodum** often works here.

❂ Festivals and events

Salvador de Bahia *p534, maps p534, 536 & p538*
6 Jan (Epiphany); **Ash Wednesday** and **Maundy Thursday**, half-days; **2 Jul** (Independence of Bahia); **30 Oct**; **Christmas Eve**, half-day. An important local holiday is **Festa do Nosso Senhor do Bonfim**; it takes place on the 2nd Sun after Epiphany, but the washing or *lavagem* of the Bonfim church, with its colourful parade, takes place on the preceding Thu (usually mid-Jan). The **Festa da Ribeirav** is on the following Mon. Another colourful festival is that of the **fishermen of Rio Vermelho** on **2 Feb**; gifts for Yemanjá, Goddess of the Sea, are taken to sea in a procession of sailing boats to an accompaniment of candomblé instruments. The Holy Week processions among the old churches of the upper city are also interesting. For **Carnival**, see box, above.

O Shopping

Largo do Pelourinho *p535, map p536*
Bookshops Graúna, Av 7 de Setembro 1448, and R Barão de Itapoã 175, Porto da Barra, many English titles. **Livraria Brandão**, R Ruy Barbosa 104, Centre. Secondhand English, French, Spanish and German books. **Livraria Planeta**, Carlos Gomes 42, loja 1, sells used English books.
Handicrafts **Artesanato Santa Bárbara**, R Portas do Carmo 7. Excellent handmade lace products. **Atelier Portal da Cor**, Ladeira do Carmo 31. Run by a co-operative of local artists, Totonho, Calixto, Raimundo Santos, Jô, good prices. Recommended. **Instituto Mauá**, R Gregório de Matos 27. Open Tue-Sat 0900-1800, Sun 1000-1600, good-quality Bahian handicrafts at fair prices, better value and quality for crafts than the Mercado Modelo. **Loja de Artesanato do SESC**, Largo Pelourinho. Mon-Fri 0900-1800 (closed for lunch), Sat 0900-1300, similar store to Instituto Mauá. **Rosa do Prado**, R Inacio Aciolly 5. Cigar shop packed with Brazilian 'charutos'.
Jewellery In the Pelourinho are: **Casa Moreira**, Ladeira da Praça, just south of Praça da Sé. Exquisite jewellery and antiques, most very expensive, but some affordable charms. **Scala**, Praça da Sé. Handmade jewellery using locally mined gems (eg. Acquamarine, amethyst and emerald), workshop at back.

Markets Mercado Modelo, at Praça Cairu, lower city, offers many tourist items such as wood carvings, silver-plated fruit, leather goods, local musical instruments. Lace items for sale are often not handmade (despite labels), are heavily marked up and are much better bought at their place of origin (for example Ilha de Maré, Pontal da Barra and Marechal Deodoro). Bands and dancing, especially Sat (but for money from tourists taking photos), closed at 1200 Sun. The largest and most authentic market is the **Feira de São Joaquim**, 5 km from Mercado Modelo along the sea front: trucks, burros, horses, boats, people, mud, very smelly, every day (Sun till 1200 only), busiest on Sat morning; interesting African-style pottery and basketwork; very cheap. (The car ferry terminal for Itaparica is nearby.) Every Wed from 1700-2100 is a **handicrafts fair** in the 17th- century fort of Santa Maria at opposite end of Porto da Barra beach.
Music in the Pelourinho The major carnival afro blocos have boutiques selling T-shirts, etc: **Boutique Olodum**, on Praça José Alencar, **Ilê Aiyê**, on R Francisco Muniz Barreto 16. **Cana Brava**, R João de Deus 22, T3321 0536. CD shop with knowledgeable American owner. **Oficina de Investigação Musical**, R das Portas do Carmo 24, T3322 2386. Handmade traditional percussion instruments (and lessons, US$15 per hr), Mon-Fri 0800-1200 and 1300-1600. Best place to buy berimbaus in Bahia.
Shopping centres **Barra** and **Iguatemi** are the largest and best stocked. They are the most comfortable places to shop – havens of a/c cool in the heat of summer.

▲ Activities and tours

Salvador de Bahia *p534, maps p534, 536 & p538*
Boat and bus tours Available from several companies. All-day boat trip on Baía de Todos Os Santos last from 0800-1700 including a visit to Ilha dos Frades, lunch on Itaparica (not included), US$20 pp. City tours also cost US$20 pp
Capoeira A martial art, often said to have developed from the traditional foot-fighting technique introduced from Angola by African slaves, but latterly claimed to be have originated with the indigenous people of Brazil and then modified by slaves. The music is by drum, tambourine and berimbau; there are several different kinds of the sport. If you want to

attempt Capoeira, the best school is **Mestre Bimba**, R das Laranjeiras, T3322 0639, open 0900-1200, 1500-2100, basic course in Capoeira regional, US$32 for 20 hrs. Another Capoeira regional school is **Filhos de Bimba**, R Durval Fraga, 6, Nordeste, T3345 7329. Exhibitions take place in the Largo do Pelourinho every Friday evening around 2000, very authentic, in the upper city. You can also see capoeiristas in public spaces like the Pelourinho, outside the Mercado Modelo and at Campo Grande. Genuine capoeiristas do not expect a contribution, but if you wish to take pictures ask first. At the Casa da Cultura at Forte de Santo Antônio there is also free live music on Sat night.

Tour operators and guides

Cultour, R João Gomes 88, Sala 8, Sobrado da Praça, Rio Vermelho, T3335 1062, www.cultour.it. Offers some of the best cultural tours in the city. Less 'touristy' than operators in the Pelourinho area.
Dieter Herzberg, T3334 1200. A recommended guide who speaks German,
Tatur Turismo, Av Tancredo Neves 274, Centro Empresarial Iguatemi, Sala 228, Bloco B, T3450 7216, www.tatur.com.br. Run by Irishman, Conor O'Sullivan. English spoken. Specializes in Bahia, arranges private guided tours and can make any necessary travel, hotel and accommodation arrangements. Highly recommended.

Transport

Salvador de Bahia *p534, maps p534, 536 & p538*
Air An a/c bus service every 30-40 mins between the new Luis Eduardo Magalhães Airport and the centre, a distance of 32 km, costs US$4. It takes the coast road to the city, stopping at hotels en route. Service runs 0500-2200 (0600 at weekends) and 0630-2100 from the Praça da Sé to the airport. Also ordinary buses, US$0.90. 'Special' taxis to both Barra and centre (buy ticket at the airport desk next to tourist information booth), US$35; normal taxis (from outside airport), US$30. Allow plenty of time for travel to the airport and for check-in. ATMs are in a special area to the extreme right as you arrive, a good place to get money. **Banco do Brasil** is to the extreme left, open Mon-Fri 0900-1500. **Jacarandá** exchange house is in front of international arrivals, open 24 hrs a day, but poor rates and only good for changing a small amount (count your money carefully). Tourist information booth open 24 hrs, English spoken, has list of hotels and useful map.

Daily flights to all the main cities.

Bus Local buses US$0.90, executivos, a/c, US$1.80, US$2 or US$4 depending on the route. On buses and at the ticket-sellers' booths, watch your change and beware pickpockets (one scam used by thieves is to descend from the bus while you are climbing aboard). To get from the old city to the ocean beaches, take a 'Barra' bus from Praça da Sé to the Barra point and walk to the nearer ones; the Aeroporto executivo leaves Praça da Sé, passing Barra, Ondina, Rio Vermelho, Amaralina, Pituba, Costa Azul, Armação, Boca do Rio, Jaguaripe, Patamares, Piatã and Itapoã, before turning inland to the airport. The glass-sided Jardineira bus goes to Flamengo beach (30 km from the city) following the coastal route; it passes all the best beaches; sit on the right hand side for best views. It leaves from the Praça da Sé daily 0730-1930, every 40 mins, US$2. For beaches beyond Itapoã, take the executivo to Stella Maris and Flamengo beaches. These follow the same route as the Jardineira.

Long distance buses leave from the Rodoviária, near Shopping Iguatemi, T3460 8300. Bus RI or RII, 'Centro-Rodoviária-Circular'; in the centre, get on in the Lower City at the foot of the Lacerda lift; buses also go to Campo Grande (US$0.90). A quicker executive bus from Praça da Sé or Praça da Inglaterra (in front of McDonald's), Comércio, run to Iguatemi Shopping Centre, US$2, weekdays only, from where there is a walkway to the rodoviária (take care in the dark, or a taxi, US$15). To **Belém**, 33 hrs, US$148 comercial with **Itapemirim**, T3358 0037, www.itapemirim.com.br. To **Recife**, US$70, 13 hrs, 2 a day and 1 leito, **Itapemirim**. To **Rio**, 23-28 hrs, US$90-109, **Itapemirim**, good stops, clean toilets, recommended. **São Paulo**, 30 hrs, US$120, leito US$150 (0815 with **Viação Nacional**, 2 in afternoon with São Geraldo). To **Fortaleza**, 19 hrs, US$77 at 0900 with Itapemerim. **Ilhéus**, 7 hrs, **Aguia Branca**, www.vab.com.br, *double plus* US$42, several. **Porto Seguro**, overnight at 2000, US$64. To **Lençóis** 3 a day, 8 hrs, US$24 with **Real Expresso**, www.realexpresso.com.br, quickest and safest is early morning bus. **Belo Horizonte**, 22 hrs, **Gontijo**, T3358 7448, www.gontijo.com.br, at 1700, US$97, São Geraldo at 1800. There are daily bus services to **Brasília** along the fully paved BR-242, via Barreiras, 3 daily, 23 hrs, **Paraíso**, US$90. Frequent services to the majority of destinations; a large panel in the main hall lists destinations and the relevant ticket office. **Taxi** Taxi meters start at US$0.75 for the 'flagdown' and US$0.20 per 100 m. They charge US$30 per hr within city limits, and 'agreed' rates outside. Taxi Barra-Centro US$10 daytime; US$15 at night. Watch the meter, especially at night; the night-time charge should be 30 higher than daytime charges.

Itaparica *p539*
Ferry The main passenger ferry leaves for Bom Despacho from São Joaquim (buses for Calçada, Ribeira stop across the road from the ferry terminal; the 'Sabino Silva – Ribeira' bus passes in front of the Shopping Barra). First ferry from Salvador at 0540 and, depending on demand, at intervals of 45 mins thereafter; last ferry from Salvador at 2230. Returning to Salvador the 1st ferry is at 0515 and the last at 2300. In summer ferries are much more frequent. Information from **COMAB/Ferry Fácil**, open 0700-2300 at terminal. A one way ticket for foot passengers Mon-Fri is US$1.75, Sat-Sun US$2. Catamarans depart for Bom Despacho twice daily, US$3 (US$3.75 at weekends). **Mar Grande** can be reached by a smaller ferry (**Lancha**) from the Terminal Marítimo in front of the Mercado Modelo in Salvador. The ferries leave every 45 mins and the crossing takes 50 mins, US$2.40 return.

Directory

Salvador de Bahia *p534, maps p534, 536 & p538*
Airline offices **Gol**, T3204 1608. **Ocean Air**, T3204 1502. **TAM**, Praça Gago Coutinho, T0800-570 5700. **TAP**, Av Tancredo Neves 1632, salas 1206/7, T0800-707 7787. **Webjet**, at airport, T0300-210 1234. **Banks** Banks are open 1000-1600. Selected branches of major banks have ATMs for Visa, eg **Bradesco**, also **Banco 24 Horas**. Don't change money on the street especially in the Upper City where higher rates are usually offered. Changing at banks can be bureaucratic and time-consuming. **Citibank**, R Miguel Calmon 555, Comércio, centre, changes TCs. Branch at R Almte Marquês de Leão 71, Barra, has ATM. MasterCard ATMs at branches of **HSBC**. Also at **Credicard**, 1st floor, Citibank building, R Miguel Calmon 555, Comércio. **Figueiredo**, opposite Grande Hotel da Barra on Ladeira da Barra will exchange cash at good rates. **Shopping Tour** in Barra Shopping centre changes dollars, as will other tour agencies. If stuck, all the big hotels will exchange, but at poor rates. **Car hire** If renting a car check whether credit card or cash is cheapest. See page 35, for multinational car rental agencies. **Embassies and consulates** **France**, Pierre Sabate, T9987 0673, consulat.salvador@yahoo.fr. **Germany**, R Jogo do Carneiro 49, Saúde, T3242 2670, Mon-Fri 0900-1200. **Netherlands**, R Largo do Carmo 04, Sl 101, Santo Antônio, T3241 3001, hleusen@dannemann-sa.com.br, Mon-Fri 0900-1100. **Spain**, R Mcal Floriano 21, Canela, T3336 9055. Mon-Fri 0900-1400. **Switzerland**, Av Tancredo Neves 3343, 5th floor, sala 506b, T3341 5827. **UK**, R Caetano Moura 35, T3247 8216, lhanson@uol.com.br. **USA**, http://virtual.embaixada-americana.org.br/salvador/. **Internet** There are numerous internet cafés throughout the touristy parts of the city. **Language classes** **Casa do Brasil**, R Milton de Oliveira 231, Barra, www.casadobrazil.com.br. **Diálogo**, R Dr João Pondé 240, Barra, T3264 0007, www.dialogo-brazilstudy.com. Accommodation with host families, optional dance, *capoeira* and cookery classes. **Medical services** **Clinic**: Barão de Loreto 21, Graça. **Medical**: yellow fever vaccinations free at **Delegação Federal de Saúde**, R Padre Feijó, Canela. **Post offices** Main post office and poste restante is in Praça Inglaterra, in the Lower City, Mon-Fri 0800-1700, Sat 0800-1200. Several other offices, including R Portas do Carmo 43, rodoviária, airport, Barra and Iguatemi Shopping Malls. **Useful addresses** **Immigration**: (for extensions of entry permits), **Policia Federal**, Av O Pontes 339, Aterro de Água de Meninos, Lower City, T3319 6082, open 1000-1600. Show an outward ticket or sufficient funds for your stay, visa extension US$17.50. **Tourist Police**: R Gregório de Matos 16, T3321 1092. **Delegacia de Proteção ao Turista**, Praça José de Anchieta 14, T3322 7155.

Inland from Salvador

There are strong historical associations inland from Salvador, seen in the colonial exploitation of sugar and diamonds. Lençóis, famous for the latter, also has some beautiful countryside, which is ideal for trekking. On the coast south of Salvador, there is a whole string of popular resorts. It was on this part of what is now Brazil that the Portuguese first made landfall. Bahia's north coast runs from the Coconut Highway onto the Green Line, just to give of an idea of how the shore looks – and don't forget the beaches there, too.

The Recôncavo

The area around Salvador, known as the Recôncavo Baiano, was one of the chief centres of sugar and tobacco cultivation in the 16th century. Some 73 km from Salvador is **Santo Amaro da Purificação**, an old sugar centre sadly decaying, noted for its churches (often closed because of robberies), municipal palace (1769), fine main praça, birthplace of the singers Caetano Veloso and his sister Maria Bethania and ruined mansions including Araújo Pinto, former residence of the Barão de Cotegipe. Other attractions include the splendid beaches of the bay, the falls of Vitória and the grotto of Bom Jesus dos Pobres. The festivals of **Santo Amaro**, 24 January-2 February, and **Nossa Senhora da Purificação** on 2 February itself are interesting. There is also the **Bembé do Mercado** festival on 13 May. Craftwork is sold on the town's main bridge. There are no good hotels or restaurants.

Cachoeira and São Félix

At 116 km from Salvador and only 4 km from the BR-101 coastal road are the towns of Cachoeira (Bahia's 'Ouro Preto', *Population: 30,416*) and São Félix (*Population: 13,699*), on either side of the Rio Paraguaçu below the Cachoeira dam. Cachoeira was twice capital of Bahia: once in 1624-1625 during the Dutch invasion, and once in 1822-1823 while Salvador was still held by the Portuguese. There are beautiful views from above São Félix.

Cachoeira's main buildings are the **Casa da Câmara e Cadeia** (1698-1712), the **Santa Casa de Misericórdia** (1734 – the hospital, someone may let you see the church), the 16th-century **Ajuda** chapel (now containing a fine collection of vestments), and the Convent of the **Ordem Terceira do Carmo**, whose church has a heavily gilded interior. Other churches are the **Matriz** with 5-m-high azulejos, and **Nossa Senhora da Conceição do Monte**. There are beautiful lace cloths on the church altars. All churches are either restored or in the process of restoration. The **Museu Hansen Bahia** ⓘ *R Ana Néri*, houses fine engravings by the German artist who made the Recôncavo his home in the 1950s. There is a great wood-carving tradition in Cachoeira. The artists can be seen at work in their studios. Best are Louco Filho, Fory, both in Rua Ana Néri, Doidão, in front of the Igreja Matriz and J Gonçalves on the main praça. A 300 m railway bridge built by the British in the 19th century spans the Rio Paraguaçu to São Felix where the Danneman cigar factory can be visited to see hand-rolling. **Tourist office** ⓘ *R Ana Néri 4, Cachoeira, T3425 1123.*

Lençóis ➔ *Phone code: 0xx75. Colour map 5, C4. Population: 8,910.*

This historical monument and colonial gem was founded in 1844 to exploit the diamonds in the region. While there are still some *garimpeiros* (gold prospectors), it is not precious metals that draw most visitors, but the climate, which is cooler than the coast, the relaxed atmosphere and the wonderful trekking and horse riding in the hills of the Chapada Diamantina. A few of the options are given below under Excursions, and pousadas and tour operators offer guiding services to point you in the right direction. This is also a good place for buying handicrafts. **Tourist office** in the market next to the river.

Parque Nacional da Chapada Diamantina → *Colour map 5, C4.*

Palmeiras, 50 km from Lençóis, is the headquarters of the Parque Nacional da Chapada Diamantina (founded 1985), which contains 1,500 sq km of mountainous country. There is an abundance of endemic plants, waterfalls, large caves (almost all of which can only be visited with a guide), rivers with natural swimming pools and good walking tours. **Parque Nacional da Chapada Diamantina** Information, ICMBio ⓘ *R Barão do Rio Branco 7, Palmeiras, T0xx75-3332 2229; entry US$2.75*. See also www.infochapada.com.

Excursions near Lençóis and in the Chapada Diamantina

There are more than 24 tour operators in Lençóis and visiting even the most distant sights on a tour (or an extended hike) is straightforward. Most tours tend to be car-based and rather sedentary as these are more profitable. As there are plenty of great sights and hikes around Lençóis, be sure to take a good look at all the options before making a choice. The most impressive sights in the Chapada are included in the standard packages. Most have an entrance fee. These include the extensive **Gruta do Lapa Doce**, US$5, and **Pratinha** caves, US$5 (the latter are cut through by glassy blue water). The table-top mountains at the **Morro de Pai Inácio**, US$2, 30 km from Lençóis, offer the best view of the Chapada, especially at sunset. The 384-m high **Cachoeira da Fumaça** (Smoke Waterfall, also called **Glass**) is the second highest in Brazil and lies deeper within the park, 2½ hours hike from the village of **Capão**. The view is astonishing; the updraft of the air currents often makes the water flow back up creating the 'smoke' effect. The **Rio Marimbus** flows through an area of semi-swamp reminiscent of the Pantanal and very rich in birdlife while the **Rio Mucugezinho** plunges over the blood-red **Cachoeira do Diabo** in an extensive area of *cerrado* just below the craggy **Roncador** (snorer) waterfall. Near Lençóis, visit the **Serrano** with its wonderful natural pools in the river bed, which give a great hydromassage, or the **Salão de Areia**, where the coloured sands for the bottle paintings come from. **Ribeirão do Meio** is a 45-minute walk from town; here locals slide down a long natural water chute into a big pool (it is best to be shown the way it is done and to take something to slide in). Also near Lençóis are two very pretty waterfalls, the **Cachoeira da Primavera** and the **Cachoeira Sossego**, a 'picture postcard' cascade plunging into a swimming pool.

Inland from Salvador listings

For Sleeping and Eating price codes and other relevant information, see Essentials, pages 38-40. See Telephone, page 397, for important phone changes.

Sleeping

Cachoeira *p549*

B Pousada do Convento de Cachoeira, Praça da Aclamação, T3425 1716. In a restored 16th-century convent, good restaurant.

D Pousada Labarca, R Inocêncio Boaventura 37, T3425 1070, http://labarca.zip.net. Nice *pousada* with art gallery, paintings by Argentine owner, organizes local trips and to candomblé ceremonies.

D-F Pousada d'Ajuda, R Largo d'Ajuda s/n, next to Igreja da Boa Morte, T3425 5278. Spacious rooms with little corners cordoned off for showers, and dorms for up to 4. .

Lençóis *p549*

LL-AL Canto das Águas, Av Senhor dos Passos, T/F3334 1154, www.lencois.com.br. Riverside hotel with a/c or fan, pool, efficient, best rooms are in the new wing. A Roteiro de Charme hotel.

AL Hotel de Lençóis, R Altinha Alves 747, T3369 5000, www.hoteldelencois.com.br. Rooms organized in terraces set in a grassy garden on the edge of the park. Good breakfast, pool and restaurant.

A Pousada Vila Serrano, R Alto do Bonfim 8, T3334 1486, www.vilaserrano.com.br. Great little mock-colonial pousada in a small garden 5 mins from town centre. Excellent service, welcoming, breakfast and excursions organized.

C Casa da Geleia, R Gen Viveiros 187, T3334 1151, casadageleia@hotmail.com. 6 smart chalets set in a huge garden at the entrance to the town, English spoken, good breakfast

(Ze Carlos is a keen birdwatcher and an authority on the region, Lia makes excellent jams).

C-D Estalagem de Alcino, R Gen Viveiros 139, T3334 1171. An enchanting, beautifully restored house furnished with 19th-century antiques. Most have shared bathrooms. Superb breakfast served in hummingbird-filled garden. Highly recommended.

D Casa de Hélia, R da Muritiba 3, T3334 1143, www.casadehelia.com.br. Attractive little guest-house, English and some Hebrew spoken, good facilities, legendary breakfast. Recommended.

D Pousada Violeiro, R Prof Assis 70, T3534 1259, www.pousadavioleiro.com.br. Very simple rooms with room for up to 4 (**E**) just behind the bus stop near the river. Quiet and conservative.

D-E Pousada dos Duendes, R do Pires, T/F3334 1229, www.pousadadosduendes.com. English-run *pousada*, shared hot showers, breakfast (vegetarians and vegans catered for), welcoming, comfortable. Their tour agency (**H2O Expeditions**) arranges tours and treks from 1 to 11 days and more, Olivia Taylor is very helpful.

D-E IYHA Lençóis, R Boa Vista 121, T3334 1497, www.hostelchapada.com.br. A large, well-run hostel with an adventure sports agency in one of the town's grand old houses. Singles, en suite doubles and single-sex 4-6 room dorms; shared kitchen and a large garden with hammocks.

Camping **Camping Lumiar**, near Rosário church in centre, T3334 1241, with popular restaurant. Recommended.

House rental

Destino Chapada, Praça Horácio de Matos 3, Centro, T/F3334 1395, www.destino chapada.com.br. All manner of accommodation throughout Lençóis and the Chapada.

Eating

Cachoeira*p549*

Café com Arte Sebo Ana Néri, R 13 de Maio 16. *Petiscos*, good coffee, beer and art from local and international artists.

Casa Comercial NS Rosário o Recanto do Misticismo, Praça da Aclamação s/n. Typically 'Cachoeira', pizza café and restaurant with 2 candomblé-inspired shrines, occasional live music.

Pouso da Palavra, Praça da Aclamação s/n. Arty little café in a cosy period house, owned by poet Damário Da Cruz, exhibitions of local artists' work, CDs, souvenirs and beautiful mandala candle shades for sale.

Lençóis *p549*

Cozinha Aberta, Rui Barbosa 42, T3334 1309, www.cozinhaaberta.com.br. The best in town with organic and slow food from Paulistana chef Deborah Doitschinoff. Just east of main praça.

Artistas da Massa, R Miguel Calmon. Italian dishes, mainly pasta and pizza.

Neco's, Praça Maestro Clarindo Pachêco 15, T3334 1179. Neco and his wife offer a set meal of local dishes of the kind once eaten by the *garimpeiro* miners, like saffron-stewed mutton accompanied by prickly pear cactus, crisp, tart *batata da terra* and fried green banana.

Gaya, Praça Horáçio Matos s/n, T3334 1167. Organic and wholefood with large and unseasoned salads, generous juices and sandwiches. The owners organize trips into the Chapada.

Bars and clubs

Lençóis *p549*

Fazendinha e Tal, Rua das Pedras 125. Very popular bar with rustic garimpeiro decoration serving hundreds of different cachacas and with occasional live music.

Festivals and events

Cachoeira *p549*

São João (**24 Jun**), 'Carnival of the Interior' celebrations include dangerous games with fireworks. **Nossa Sehora da Boa Morte** (**early Aug**) is also a major festival. A famous candomblé ceremony at the Fonte de Santa Bárbara is held on **4 Dec**.

Shopping

Lençóis *p549*

The Mon morning market is recommended. There is a local craft market just off the main praça every night.

Instrumentos, R das Pedras 78, T3334 1334. Unusual faux-Brazilian and African musical instruments by quirky ex-pat Argentine Jorge Fernando.

Zambumbeira, R das Pedras at Tamandare, T3334 1207. Beautiful ceramics by renowned artisans like Zé Caboclo, jewellery, walking sticks and arty bric-a-brac.

Activities and tours

Lençóis *p549*

Chapada Adventure, Av 7 de Setembro 7, T3334 2037, www.chapadaadventure.com.br. A small operator offering good value car-based tours and light hiking throughout the Chapada.

Fora da Trilha, R das Pedras 202, www.foradatrilha.com.br. Longer hikes and light adventures, from canyoning to rapelling.

Venturas e Aventuras, Praça Horácio de Matos 20, T3334 1304. Excellent trekking expeditions, up to 6 days.

Guides

Each pousada generally has a guide attached to it to take residents on tours, about US$20-30. The following are recommended:

Edmilson (known locally as Mil), R Domingos B Souza 70, T3334 1319. Knows the region extremely well, knowledgeable and reliable.

Roy Funch, T/F3334 1305, funchroy@yahoo.com, www.fcd.org.br. The ex-director of the Chapada Diamantina National Park is an excellent guide and has written a visitor guide to the park in English. (Recommended as the best information on history, geography and trails of the Chapada.) Highly recommended. He can be booked through www.elabrasil.com from the USA or UK.

Luiz Krug, contact via **Vila Serrano**, T3334 1102. An independent, English-speaking guide specializing in geology and caving.

Trajano, contact via **Vila Serrano** or **Casa da Hélia**, T3334 1143, Speaks English and some Hebrew and is a good-humoured guide for treks to the bottom of the Cachoeira da Fumaça.

Zé Carlos, T3334 1151, through **Casa da Geleia** or **Vila Serrano**. The best guide for birding.

Body and soul

The Chapada is a centre for alternative treatments. All the practitioners listed come highly recommended.

Anita Marti, T9989 8328. Healing and therapeutic massage and treatments.

Dieter Herzberg, T9984 2720, dieterherzberg@yahoo.com.br. All manner of therapeutic and healing massage.

Jaques Gagnon, T3334 1281, www.janeladaalma.com. Neuro-structural therapy and healing massage.

Transport

Cachoeira *p549*

Bus From **Salvador** (**Camurjipe**) every hr or so from 0530; **Feira Santana**, 2 hrs, US$6.

Lençóis *p549*

Air Airport, Km 209, BR-242, 20 km from town T3625 8100. **Trip** (T0300-789 8747, www.voetrip.com.br) flies from Salvador on Sat, otherwise air taxi only.

Bus Terminal, T3334 1112. **Real Expresso** from **Salvador** 3 a day, US$24, *comercial* via Feira de Santana. Book in advance, especially at weekends and holidays. For the rest of Bahia state change at Feira de Santana; it is not necessary to go via Salvador. Buses also from **Recife**, **Ibotirama**, **Barreiras** or **Palmas** (for Jalapão), **Chapada dos Veadeiros** and **Brasília**, 16 hrs, US$60 (all with transfer in Seabra, several buses daily).

Directory

Lençóis *p549*

Banks There is a **Bradesco** with an ATM, and a **post office** (Mon-Fri 0900-1700) on the main square.

South of Salvador

On the coast south of Salvador is a whole string of popular resorts. It was on this part of what is now Brazil that the Portuguese first made landfall. Bahia's north coast runs from the Coconut Highway onto the Green Line, to give of an idea of how the shore looks, and don't forget the beaches there.

Valença → *Phone code: 0xx75. Colour map 7, A6. Population: 77,509.*

In this small, attractive town, 271 km south of Salvador via a paved road, two old churches stand on rising ground; the views from Nossa Senhora do Amparo are recommended. It is at the mouth of the Rio Una, which enters an enormous region of mangrove swamps. The main attraction is the beaches on the mainland (Guabim, 14 km north) and on the island of Tinharé. **Secretaria de Turismo**, T3641 8610. Avoid touts at the rodoviária.

Tinharé, Boipeba and Morro de São Paulo ➔ *Phone code: 0xx75.*

Tinharé is a large island (1½ hours south of Valença by boat) separated from the mainland by the estuary of the Rio Una and mangrove swamps, so that it is hard to tell which is land and which is water. The most popular beaches and pousadas are at Morro de São Paulo. Immediately south is the island of **Boipeba**, separated from Tinharé by the Rio do Inferno. Accommodation is split between Velha Boipeba, the little town where the riverboat ferry arrives, the adjacent beach, Boca da Barra, which is more idyllic and the fishing village Moreré. This is a one-hour walk or half an hour's boat ride south, US$20 (high tide only). You may get a ride on school 'bus' (a trailer pulled by a tractor, US$2.50) or Moreré's donkey owner will accompany you on foot. Boipeba's community tourism association is at www.ilhaboipeba.org.br.

Morro de São Paulo is on the headland at the northernmost tip of Tinharé, lush with ferns, palms and birds of paradise. The village is dominated by the lighthouse and the ruins of a colonial fort (1630), built as a defence against European raiders. It has a landing place on the sheltered landward side, dominated by the old gateway of the fortress. From the lighthouse a path leads to a ruined look out with cannon, which has panoramic views. The fort is a good point to watch the sunset from. Dolphins can be seen in August. Fonte de Ceu waterfall is reached by walking along the beach to **Gamboa** then inland. Watch the tide; it's best to take a guide, or take a boat back to Morro (US$0.50-1). No motor vehicles are allowed on the island. On 7 September there's a big festival with live music on the beach. **Tourist office** ⓘ *Praça Aureliano Lima, T3652 1083, www.morrosp.com.br*, or visit *www.morrodesaopaulo.com.br*. **Note** There is a port tax of US$3.25 payable at the prefeitura on leaving the island.

Itacaré ➔ *Phone code: 0xx73.*

This picturesque fishing village sits in the midst of remnant Atlantic Coast rainforest at the mouth of the Rio de Contas. Some of Bahia's best beaches stretch north and south. A few are calm and crystal clear, the majority are great for surfing. There are plenty of beaches within walking distance of town. Itacaré is rapidly becoming a sophisticated surf resort for the São Paulo middle classes and is very busy with Brazilian tourists in high season. Much of the accommodation here is tasteful, blending in with the natural landscape and there are many excellent restaurants and lively if still low key nightlife. Pousadas are concentrated in town and around the Praias da Coroinha and Concha, the first beaches to the north and south of the town centre. Besides surfing, operators are now offering trekking and mountain biking trips in the Mata Atlântica, off-roading, rafting, waterfall-climbing and other adrenalin activities. North of Itacaré is the **Peninsula de Maraú**, fringed with beautiful beaches to its tip at **Barra Grande**. To explore the area fully you will need a car or to take a tour. **Secretaria Municipal de Turismo de Itacaré** ⓘ *R João de Souza, T3251 2940, sec.turismo@itacare.ba.gov.br, prefeitura 3251 2130, www.itacare.com.br.*

Ilhéus ➔ *Phone code: 0xx73. Post code: 45650. Colour map 7, A6. Population: 222,127.*

At the mouth of the Rio Cachoeira, 462 km south of Salvador, the port serves a district which produces 65% of all Brazilian cocoa. A bridge links the north bank of the river with Pontal, where the airport is located. Ilhéus is the birthplace of Jorge Amado (1912-2002) and the setting of one of his most famous novels, *Gabriela, cravo e canela* (Gabriela, Clove and Cinnamon). The church of **São Jorge** (1556), the city's oldest, is on the Praça Rui Barbosa; it has a small museum. In Alto da Vitória is the 17th-century **Nossa Senhora da Vitória**, built to celebrate a victory over the Dutch. The **Secretária de Turismo** is at ⓘ *R Santos Dumont s/n, anexo da Prefeitura, 5th floor, T2101-5500.*

North of Ilhéus, two good beaches are Marciano, with reefs offshore and good surfing, and Barra, 1 km further north at the mouth of the Rio Almada. South of the river, Pontal beaches can be reached by 'Barreira' bus; alight just after Hotel Jardim Atlântico. Between Ilhéus and **Olivença** are more fine beaches. At nearby **Una** there is an important wildlife sanctuary and ecopark devoted to protecting the Golden-face Tamarin, the **Reserva Biológica de Una** ⓘ *www.ecoparque.org.br*.

Porto Seguro and the Discovery Coast

➔ Phone code: 0xx73. Post code: 45810. Colour map 7, A6. Population: 95,721.

About 400 km south of Ilhéus on the coast is the old town of Porto Seguro. In 1500, Pedro Álvares Cabral sighted land at Monte Pascoal south of Porto Seguro. As the sea here was too open, he sailed north in search of a secure protected harbour, entering the mouth of the Rio Burnahém to find the harbour he later called Porto Seguro (safe port). Where the first mass was celebrated, a cross marks the spot on the road between Porto Seguro and Santa Cruz Cabrália. A rather uncoordinated tourist village, **Coroa Vermelha**, has sprouted at the site of Cabral's first landfall, 20 minutes by bus to the north of Porto Seguro.

Porto Seguro itself is Bahia's second most popular tourist destination, with charter flights from Rio and São Paulo and plenty of hustle and bustle. Contact the **Secretária de Turismo de Porto Seguro** ⓘ *Praça dos Pataxós, T3288 3708, turismo@portonet.com.br. Information desk at Praça Manoel Ribeiro Coelho 10*. A website for the entire coast is www.portonet.com.br.

To its historical quarter, **Cidade Histórica**, take a wide, steep, unmarked path uphill from the roundabout at the entrance to town. Three churches (Nossa Senhora da Misericórdia (1530), Nossa Senhora do Rosário (1534), and Nossa Senhora da Pena (1718), the former jail and the monument marking the landfall of Gonçalo Coelho comprise a small, peaceful place with lovely gardens and panoramic views.

Only 10 minutes north of Coroa Vermelha, **Santa Cruz Cabrália** is a delightful small town at the mouth of the Rio João de Tiba, with a splendid beach, river port, and a 450-year-old church with a fine view. A good trip from here is to Coroa Alta, a reef 50 minutes away by boat, passing along the tranquil river to the reef and its crystal waters and good snorkelling. A 15-minute river crossing by ferry to a new road on the opposite bank gives easy access to the deserted beaches of **Santo André** and **Santo Antônio**. The beautiful and inspiring Pataxó indigenous reserve of **Juqueira**, a Pataxó project that is rejuvenating traditional ways of life, language and culture, lies just north of Porto Seguro and is well worth a half-day visit (with **Portomondo**, see Porto Seguro Tour operators).

Arraial da Ajuda ➔ *Colour map 7, A6.*

Immediately across the Rio Buranhém south from Porto Seguro is the village of Arraial da Ajuda, the gateway to the idyllic beaches of the south coast. Set high on a cliff, there are great views of the coastline from behind the church of Nossa Senhora da Ajuda in the main praça. Each August there is a pilgrimage to the shrine of Nossa Senhora da Ajuda. Ajuda has become more popular than Porto Seguro with younger tourists and independent travellers and there are many pousadas, from the very simple to the very sophisticated, restaurants, bars and small shops. In high season there are frequent parties on the beach or in the main street, called the Broadway. At Brazilian holiday times it is very crowded. The town has a famous Capoeira school (with classes for foreigners).

The **beaches**, several protected by a coral reef, are splendid. The nearest is 15 minutes' walk away. During daylight hours those closest to town (take 'R da Praia' out of town to the south) are extremely busy; excellent barracas sell good seafood, drinks, and play music. The best beaches are Mucugê, Pitinga ('bronzeamento irrestrito' or nude sunbathing) and Taipé.

Trancoso ➔ *Phone code: 0xx73.*

Some 15 km from Ajuda, 25 km south of Porto Seguro by paved road, is Trancoso. This pretty, peaceful town, with its beautiful beaches (Praia dos Nativos is the most famous), has become very chic, with the rich and famous from home and abroad buying properties and shopping in the little boutiques. In summer it can get packed. Trancoso has an historic church, São João

Batista (1656). From the end of Praça São João there is a fine coastal panorama. It is possible to walk along the beach to Ajuda via the village of Rio da Barra; allow three hours.

Caraíva and around → *Phone code: 0xx73. www.caraiva.com.br.*
This atmospheric, peaceful fishing village on the banks of the Rio Caraíva, 65 km south of Porto Seguro, and near the Pataxó Indian Reserve has no wheeled vehicles or nighttime electricity, but has marvellous beaches and is a real escape from the more developed Trancoso and Porto Seguro. Despite the difficulty of getting there, it is becoming increasingly popular. Good walks are north to Praia do Satu (Sr Satu provides an endless supply of coconut milk), or 6 km south to a rather sad Pataxó Indian village (watch the tides). Horses can be hired from Pousada Lagoa or Pizzaria Barra Velha. Boats can be hired for US$40 per day from Zé Pará to Caruípe beach, or snorkelling at Pedra de Tatuaçu reef. Prainha river beach, about 30 minutes away, and mangrove swamps can also be visited by canoe or launch. The high season is December- February and July; the wettest months are April-June and November. Use flip-flops for walking the sand streets and take a torch. There are no medical facilities and only rudimentary policing. There are a series of super-luxurious isolated resorts 10 km south of Caraíva at the Ponta do Corumbau.

Parque Nacional de Monte Pascoal → *Colour map 7, A6.*
South of Porto Seguro,via a 14 km paved access road at Km 796 of the BR-101, the Parque Nacional de Monte Pascoal was set up in 1961 to preserve the flora and fauna of the coastal area in which Europeans made landfall in Brazil (Caixa Postal 24, CEP 45836-000 Itamaraju, T0xx73-3294 1110).

Caravelas and around → *Colour map 7, A6. Population: 20,103.*
Further south still, 107 km from Itamaruju (93 km south of Eunápolis), is this charming town, rapidly developing for tourism, but a major trading town in 17th and 18th centuries. Caravelas is in the mangroves; the beaches are about 10 km away at Barra de Caravelas (hourly buses), a fishing village. There are food shops, restaurants and bars.

The **Parque Nacional Marinho dos Abrolhos** is 70 km east of Caravelas. Day trips leave from Caravelas and take about 2½ hours to reach the archipelago. Humpback whales are invariably seen between July and November. Abrolhos is an abbreviation of Abre os olhos: 'Open your eyes' from Américo Vespucci's exclamation when he first sighted the reef in 1503. Established in 1983, the park consists of five small islands (Redonda, Siriba, Guarita, Sueste, Santa Bárbara), which are volcanic in origin, and several coral reefs. The warm current and shallow waters (8-15 m deep) make for a rich undersea life (about 160 species of fish) and good snorkelling. The park is best visited in October-March, entry is US$28.50. Diving is best December to February. The archipelago is administered by ICMBio and a navy detachment mans a lighthouse on Santa Bárbara, which is the only island that may be visited. Permission from **Parque Nacional Marinho dos Abrolhos** ⓘ *Praia do Kitomgo s/n, Caravelas, Bahia 45900, T0xx73-3297 1111, www.ibama.gov.br/parna_abrolhos/*. Visitors can't stay on the islands, but may stay overnight on schooners. Visits and permits can be organized through **Portomondo** in Porto Seguro, or in Caravelas (see page 560).

South of Salvador listings

For Sleeping and Eating price codes and other relevant information, see Essentials, pages 38-40. See Telephone, page 397, for important phone changes.

Sleeping

Valença *p552*

B Guabim, Praça da Independência 74, T3641 4114, guaibimhotel@ig.com.br. Modest with bath and buffet breakast, good **Akuarius** restaurant.

B do Porto, Av Maçônica 50, T3641 5226, hdoporto@vca.mma.com.br. Helpful, safe, good breakfast, good restaurant.

C Galeão, R Barão de Jequiriça 191, T3641 3066. With balcony, TV, a/c, safe.

D Valença, R Dr H Guedes Melo 15, T3641 2383. Comfortable, good breakfast. Recommended.

Tinharé, Boipeba and Morro de São Paulo *p553*

Morro de São Paulo

There are many cheap pousadas and rooms to rent near the fountain (Fonte Grande) but this part of town is very hot at night. A number of beach hotels are at the bottom of the main street where you turn right on to Primeira Praia (first beach).

L-A Pousada Farol do Morro, Primeira Praia, T3652 1036, www.faroldomorro.com.br. Little huts running up the hill all with a sea view and served by a private funicular railway, pool.

AL-B Pousada Vista Bela, R da Biquinha 15, T3652 1001, www.vistabelapousada.com. Owner Petruska is extremely welcoming, good rooms, those to the front have good views and are cooler, all have fans, hammocks. Price depends on season and type of room.

B Pousada Colibri, R do Porto de Cima 5, T3652 1056, pousadacolibri@svn.com.br. 6 apartments up some steep steps. Cool, always a breeze blowing, excellent views, Helmut, the owner, speaks English and German.

C Pousada Gaúcho, R da Prainha 79, T3652 1243. On same street as the steps to Pousada Colibri. Huge breakfast, shared bath.

C Pousada Ilha do Sol, Primeira Praia, T3652 1576. Modest but scrupulously clean, good views.

Terceira Praia (3rd beach)

AL-A Pousada Fazenda Caeira, T3652 1042, www.fazendacaeira.com.br. Spacious, airy chalets in a coconut grove overlooking the sea, good breakfasts, library, games room.

AL-B Fazenda Vila Guaiamú, T3652 1035, www.vilaguaiamu.com.br. 7 tastefully decorated chalets set in tropical gardens visited by marmosets, tanagers and rare cotingas, excellent food. The hotel has a spa and the Italian photographer-owner runs an eco-tourism project protecting a rare species of crab which lives in the fazenda's river. Guided walks available. Highly recommended.

C Pousada Aradhia, T3652 1239. Balconies with ocean view, very good facilities.

Boipeba

A Pousada Tassimirim, ½-hr walk south of town, T3653 6030, or 9981 2378 (R Com Madureira 40, 45400-000 Valença), www.ilhaboipeba.org.br/pousadas.html. Bungalows, bar, restaurant, including breakfast and dinner.

A-C Santa Clara, Boca da Barra, T3653 6085, www.santaclaraboipeba.com. Californian- owned, with the island's best restaurant, large, tasteful cabins and a good-value room for 4 at **D** pp. Therapeutic massages available. Recommended.

B-C Horizonte Azul, Boca da Barra, T3653 6080, www.ilhaboipeba.org.br/pousadas.html. Next to Santa Clara, a range of chalets in a hillside garden visited by hundreds of rare birds. Owners speak English and French. Lunch available. Recommended.

C Pousada Moreré, Moreré town, T9981 1303. Simple rooms with fan. Good restaurant and bar.

D Pousada do Canto, Moreré, T3653 6131, morerecantosul@yahoo.com.br. A variety of rooms and cabins, some thatched, prices rise in high season, lovely surroundings.

Itacaré *p553*

LL Txai Resort, Praia de Itacarezinho, T2101 5000, www.txai.com.br. The most self-consciously exclusive resort in Bahia; on a deserted beach with very tasteful bungalows overlooking a deep blue pool shaded by its own stand of palms. Excellent spa and a full range of activities including diving and horse riding.

LL-AL Villa de Ocaporan, Rua C between the town and Praia da Concha, T3251 2470, www.villadeocaporan.com.br. Brightly coloured, spacious chalets around a charming little pool, good Bahian restaurant.

A-B Art Jungle, T9975 1083, www.artjungle.org. 6 tree houses in a modern sculpture garden in the middle of forest, great views. A favourite with celebrities, yet relatively unpretentious.

A-B Pousada da Lua, Praia da Concha, T3251 2209, www.pousadadalua.com. A handful of little chalets in forest filled with marmosets and parakeets. Great breakfast.

C-D Pedra Bonita, R Lodônio Almeida 120, T9141 4372, www.itacarehostel.com.br. Pleasant little HI hostel with small doubles and dorms (**E** pp) in an annexe, small pool, internet and TV area.

C-D Pousada Estrela, R Pedro Longo 34, T3251 2006, pousadaestrela@backpacker.com.br. Well-maintained, simple rooms, homemade breakfast with lots of choice, very helpful.

Ilhéus *p553*
Plenty of cheap hotels near the municipal rodoviária in centre and *pousadas* along the coast to Olivença.
C Britânia, R Jorge Amado 16, T3634 1722. The best value in the town centre with large rooms in an early 20th-century wooden hotel just west of the Cathedral square.

Porto Seguro *p554*
Prices rise steeply Dec-Feb and Jul. Off-season rates can drop by 50%, for stays of more than 3 nights negotiate. Outside Dec-Feb rooms with bath and hot water can be rented for US$150 per month.
AL Estalagem Porto Seguro, R Marechal Deodoro 66, T3288 2095, hotelestalagem@hotelestalagem.com.br. In an old colonial house, relaxing atmosphere, a/c, TV, pool, good breakfast. Highly recommended.
AL Pousada Casa Azul, 15 de Novembro 11, T/F3288 2180, p.casazul@uol.com.br. TV, a/c, good pool and garden, quiet part of town.
AL Vela Branca, R Dr Antonio Ricaldi (Cidade Alta), T3288 2318, www.velabranca.com.br. Luxury resort with a wonderful view out over the water. Beautiful pool, tennis courts, sauna and spacious a/c rooms.
B Pousada Jandaias, R das Jandaias 112, T3288 2611, www.jandaias.com.br. Fan, great breakfast.
B Pousada dos Navegantes, Av 22 de Abril 212, T3288 2390, www.portonet.com.br/navegantes. A/c, TV, pool, conveniently located. Recommended.
C-D Porto Seguro Hostel, R Cova da Moça 720, T3288 1742. Large, modern HI hostel with a pool, games room and a range of dorms (**E** pp), doubles and family rooms.
Camping **Camping Mundaí Praia**, US$10 per night, T3679 2287. **Tabapiri Country**, BR-367, Km 61.5, next to the rodoviária on the road leading to the Cidade Histórica, T3288 2269.

Santa Cruz Cabrália
B Victor Hugo, Villa de Santo Antônio, Km 3, T3671 4064, www.portonet.com.br/victorhugo. Smart, tasteful, right on the beach.
E pp **Maracaia**, Coroa Vermelha on road to Porto Seguro, Km 77.5, T3672 1155, www.maracaia hostel.com.br. Low season price, HI affiliated.

Arraial da Ajuda *p554*
At busy times, don't expect to find anything under US$15 pp in a shared room for a minimum stay of 5-7 days. Camping is best at these times.
LL-L Pousada Pitinga, Praia Pitinga, T3575 1067, www.pousadapitinga.com.br. Bold architecture amid Atlantic forest, a hideaway, great food and pool, a Roteiros de Charme hotel.
AL Pousada Canto d'Alvorada, Esterada d' Ajuda 1993, T3575 1218. **B** out of season, Swiss run, 7 cabins, restaurant, laundry facilities.
A Pousada Erva Doce, Estrada do Mucugê 200, T3575 1113, www.ervadoce.com.br. Good restaurant, well-appointed chalets (**AL** in high season).
B Pousada Flamboyant, Estrada do Mucugê 89, T3575 1025, www.flamboyant.tur.br. Pleasant courtyard, pool, good breakfast.
B Pousada Tubarão, R Bela Vista 74, beyond the church on the right, T3575 1086, tubarao@arraial.com.br. Good view of the coastline, cool, good restaurant.
B-C O Cantinho, Praça São Bras, T3575 1131, www.pousadacantinho.com.br. Terraces of smart rooms, a/c or fan, nice courtyard, excellent breakfast, discounts off season.
B-C Pousada do Roballo, T3575 1053, www.pousadadoroballo.com.br. Welcoming with a tiny pool and rooms with little verandas in gardens.
D-E pp **Hostel Arraial**, R do Campo 94, T3575 1192, www.arraialdajudahostel.com.br. Backpacker hostel with HI discounts, more expensive in Jan, with breakfast, snack bar, pool, good location at the top of town.
Camping Generally, Arraial da Ajuda is better for camping than Porto Seguro. **Chão do Arraial**, 5 mins from Mucugê beach, shady, good snack bar, also hire tents. Recommended. **Praia**, T3575 1020, on Mucugê Beach, good position and facilities.

Trancoso *p554*
There are many houses to rent, very good ones are rented by Clea who can be contacted at **Restaurant Abacaxi**.
LL Etnia, Estrada Velha do Arraial (just west of the Quadrado), T3668 1137, www.etniabrasil. com.br. Very chic, well-run and beautifully kept pousada set in shady, hilly lawned gardens. Fashionable.

L-A Mata N'ativa, Estrada Velha do Arraial (next to the river on the way to the beach), T3668 1830, www.matanativapousada.com.br. The best in town, a series of elegant cabins in a lovingly maintained garden by the riverside, cheaper in low season. Owners Daniel and Daniela are very hospitable and run one of the few hotels to adopt environmental best practice. Good English, Spanish and Italian. Recommended.
A Caipim Santo, T3668 1122, to the left of the main praça, www.capimsanto.com.br. With breakfast and the best restaurant in Trancoso. Recommended.
D-E pp **Condominio dos Nativos**, Praia dos Nativos, T3668 1641, www.condominiodos nativos.com. Owned by Gustavo and Ana, excellent double-bedroom villas (1, 2 and 4 rooms) with kitchen and patio, also double a/c rooms, 150 m from beach, lots of local information, free internet, breakfast extra, gardens, very welcoming. Prices are for low season.

About 500 m inland away from main praça (known as the 'quadrado') lies the newer part of Trancoso (known as the 'invasão') with some good value *pousadas*.

Caraíva *p555*

AL-A Vila do Mar, R 12 de Outubro s/n, T3668 5111, www.pousadaviladomar.com.br. The plushest hotel in town, with spacious, stylish airy, wooden cabanas overlooking the beach set on a lawn around an adult and children's pool.
B-C Bar Pousada Varandão, on the ridge above the hill on the northern bank of the river, T9199 4563, varandao@yahoo.com.br, Rooms in a big house for up to 10 people (E pp) and a suite for a couple. Superb views With B&B.
C Pousada Flor do Mar, R 12 de Outubro s/n, on the beach, T9985 1608, www.caraiva.tur.br/ flordomar. Charming beach front pousada with airy rooms – the best right at the beachfront.

Corumbau and Caravelas *p555*

LL Tauana, T3668 5172, www.tauana.com. Perhaps the finest luxury beach resort in Brazil, with a series of huge and beautifully appointed mock indigenous cabins overlooking a secluded beach. Perfect for a honeymoon.
B Pousada Caravelense, Praça Teófilo Otoni 2, T3297 1182. TV, fridge, good breakfast, excellent restaurant. Recommended.
D Beco Shangri-lá, Sete de Setembro 219, T3297 1059. Simple rooms with bath, breakfast.
D Pousada Juquita, Praia do Grauçá, Barra de Caravelas, T3674 1038. Use of kitchen, big breakfast, bath, airy rooms, the owner is Secka who speaks English.

Eating

Tinharé, Boipeba and Morro de São Paulo *p553*

There are plenty of restaurants in Morro de São Paulo town and on the 2nd and 3rd beaches. Most are OK though somewhat overpriced. For cheap eats stay in a *pousada* which includes breakfast, stock up at the supermarket and buy seafood snacks at the *barracas* on the 2nd beach.
TT Belladonna on the main street. Good Italian restaurant with great music, a good meeting point, owner Guido speaks Italian, English and French, open evenings only.
TT Bianco e Nero, Morro town. Reasonably good pizza, pasta and grilled food.
TT Chez Max, 3rd beach. Simple but decent seafood in a pretty restaurant overlooking the sea.
T Comida Natural, on the main street. Good breakfasts, *comida a kilo*, good juices.

Itacaré *p553*

There are plenty of restaurants in Itacaré, mostly on R Lodônio Almeida. Menus here are increasingly chic and often include a respectable wine list.
TTT Casa Sapucaia, R Lodônio Almeida, T251 3091. Sophisticated Bahian food with an international twist.
TTT Dedo de Moça, R Plínio Soares (next to the São Miguel Church), T3251 3391. One of Bahia's best restaurants, with dishes which combine Brazilian ingredients with French and Oriental techniques. Lovely little bar.
TT Boca de Forno, R Lodônio Almeida 134, T3251 2174. The busiest restaurant in Itacaré, serving good wood-fired pizzas in tastefully decorated surroundings.
TT La In, R Lodônio Almeida 116, T3251 3054. Great little Bahian and seafood restaurant, colourful, very good value lunches and dinners. Right next to the youth hostel.
T O Restaurante, Rua Pedro Longo 150, T3251 2012. One of the few restaurants with a *prato feto*, and a mixed seafood menu.

Ilhéus *p553*

Try the local drink, *coquinho*, coconut filled with cachaça. Also try *suco de cacau* at juice stands.

TTT Vesúvio, Praça Dom Eduardo, next to the cathedral, made famous by Amado's novel (see above). Good but pricey.

TT Os Velhos Marinheiros, Av 2 de Julho. A recommended eating place on the waterfront.

T Nogar, Av Bahia 377, near sea. Pizzas and pasta.

Porto Seguro *p554*

There are numerous restaurants on the town's streets and many snack bars along the waterfront and river.

TT da Japonêsa, Praça Pataxós 38. Excellent value with varied menu, open 0800-2300. Recommended.

TT-T Portinha, R Saldanha Marinho 33, T3288 2743. Lively little self-service restaurant in a square near the river. Good variety and great puddings.

Arraial da Ajuda *p554*

TTT Don Fabrizio, Estrada do Mucugê 402, T575 1123. The best Italian in town, in an upmarket open air restaurant with live music and reasonable wine.

TTT Manguti, Estrada do Mucugê, T575 2270, www.manguti.com.br. Reputed by some to be the best in town, meat, pasta, fish alongside other Brazilian dishes. Very popular and informal.

TT Nipo, Estrada do Mucugê 250, T575 3033. Reasonably priced but decent Japanese with hotel delivery.

TT Pizzaria do Arraial, Praça São Bras 28. Basic pizzeria and pay by weight restaurant.

T Mineirissima, Estrada do Mucugê, T575 3790. Good value pay by weight with very filling Minas Gerais food and moquecas. Opens until late but menu service only after 1800.

T Paulinho Pescador, Praca São Bras 116. Open 1200-2200, closed Mon, excellent seafood, also chicken and meat, one price (US$5), English spoken, good service, popular, there are often queues for tables.

Recommended barracas are **Tem Q Dá** and **Agito** on Mucugê beach and **Barraca de Pitinga** and **Barraca do Genésio** on Pitinga.

Trancoso *p554*

Food in Trancoso is expensive. Those on a tight budget should shop at the supermarket between the main square and the new part of town. There are numerous fish restaurants in the *barracas* on the beach. None is cheap.

TTT Cacau, Praca São João, Quadrado, T3668 1266. One of the best in town with a varied international and Brazilian menu. Pleasant surrounds.

TTT Capim Santo, Praca São João, Quadrado, T3668 1122. Wonderful Brazilian-European fusion cooking in intimate garden surroundings. Great caipirinhas.

TTT Japaiano, Praca São João, Quadrado, T3668 2121. Japanese-Brazilian fusion cooking from acclaimed Carioca and ex-Nobu chef Felipe Bronze.

T Portinha, on the main square. The only place serving food at a reasonable price. Excellent pay by weight options and good if overpriced juices.

Caraíva *p555*

There is forró dancing 0100-0600 at **Pelé** and **Ouriços** on alternate nights in season.

TT Boteco do Pará, by the river, just east of the 'port'. Serves the best fish in the village, US$7-8 (try sashimi or moqueca). Also has simple lodging, **Pousada da Canoa**.

Bars and clubs

Tinharé, Boipeba and Morro de São Paulo *p553*

Morro de São Paulo

There is always plenty going on in Morro. The liveliest bars are **87** and **Jamaica**, both on the 2nd beach. These tend to get going after 2300 when the restaurants in town empty.

Itacaré *p553*

There is frequent extemporaneous forró and other live music all over the city and most restaurants and bars have some kind of music between Oct and Apr.

Porto Seguro *p554*

Porto Seguro is famous for the lambada. There are lots of bars and street cafés on Av Portugal. **Pronto Socorro do Choppe, Doce Letal 50** and **Studio Video Bar** are all lively places.

Porto Prego on R Pedro Álvares Cabral. A good bar for live music, small cover charge. **Sotton Bar**, Praça de Bandeira. Lively.

Arraial da Ajuda *p554*
The lambada is danced at the **Jatobar** bar (summer only), by the church on the main square (opens 2300 – pensão at the back is cheap, clean and friendly). **Limelight** has raves all year round. Many top Brazilian bands play at the beach clubs at Praia do Parracho during the summer, entry is about US$20. Entry to other beach parties is about US$10. There is also a capoeira institute; ask for directions.

Festivals and events

Ilhéus *p553*
Festa de São Sebastião, **17-20 Jan**, **Carnival**, **Festa de São Jorge**, **23 Apr**, **Foundation day**, **28 Jun**, and **Festa do Cacau** throughout **Oct**.

Activities and tours

Porto Seguro *p554*
Tour operators
Portomondo, Ponta do Apaga Fogo 1, Marina Quinta do Porto Hotel, T3575 3686, www.portomondo.com. The best operator in southern Bahia with tours around Trancoso, Caraíva and Corumbau and to Monte Pascoal and Abrolhos. Excellent diving and ecotourism itineraries and car or helicopter transfers to hotels in Trancoso and further south.

Transport

Valença *p552*
Bus Long-distance buses from new rodoviária, Av Abel de Aguiar Queirós, Aguazinha, T3641 4805. Local buses from the old rodoviaria. Many buses a day to/from **Salvador**, 5 hrs, US$13, several companies including **Águia Branca**.
Ferry For the shortest route to Valença, take the ferry from São Joaquim to Bom Despacho on Itaparica island, from where it is 130 km to Valença via Nazaré das Farinhas. To/from **Bom Despacho** on Itaparica, **Camarujipe** and **Águia Branca**, 16 a day, 2 hrs, US$7.

Tinharé, Boipeba and Morro de São Paulo *p553*
Air Air taxi from Salvador airport US$75 1-way, 20 mins, **Addey** T3377 1993, www.addey.com.br.
Ferry From Salvador, several companies operate a catamaran (1½ hrs) service from the Terminal Marítimo in front of the Mercado Modelo to Morro de São Paulo. Times vary according to the weather and season. **Catamara Gamboa do Morro**, T9975 6395. Part of the trip is on the open sea, which can be rough. Boats leave every day from **Valença** for Gamboa (1½ hrs) and Morro de São Paulo (1½ hrs) from the main bridge in Valença 5 times a day (signalled by a loud whistle). The fare is US$4.50. A *lancha rápida* taking 25 mins travels the route between Valença and Morro, US$12. Only buses between 0530-1100 from Salvador to Valença connect with ferries. If not stopping in Valença, get out of the bus by the main bridge in town, don't wait till you get to the rodoviária, which is a long way from the ferry. Private boat hire can be arranged if you miss the ferry schedule. A responsible local boatman is **Jario**. He also offers excursions to other islands, especially **Boipeba**. There is a regular boat from Valença to Boipeba Mon-Sat 1230 (check tide), return 1500-1700, 4 hrs, US$5. Also, Mon-Sat bus Valença-Torrinha at 1100 (plus 1400 in summer) connectsw with a boat to Boipeba, 2½ hrs.

Itacaré *p553*
Bus The rodoviária is a few mins' walk from town. Porters are on hand with barrows to help with luggage. Frequent buses 0700-1900 to **Ilhéus** (the nearest town with an airport), 45 mins, US$7 along the paved road. To **Salvador**, change at **Ubaitaba** (3 hrs, US$5) or Ilhéus; Ubaitaba-Salvador, 6 hrs, US$16, several daily.

Ilhéus *p553*
Air Daily flights to **Salvador** in high season with **Gol** (www.voegol.com.br) and **TAM** (www.tam.com.br).
Bus Rodoviária is 4 km from the centre on Itabuna road. Several daily to **Salvador**, 8 hrs, US$40 *leito*, **Expresso São Jorge**; 0620 bus goes via Itaparica, leaving passengers at Bom Despacho ferry station on the island – thence 50-mins ferry to Salvador. To **Eunápolis**, 5 hrs, US$10, this bus also leaves from the central bus terminal. Other destinations include **Porto Seguro** (one per day), US$20, slow bus. Local buses leave from Praça Cairu. Insist that taxi drivers have meters and price charts.

Porto Seguro *p554*

Air Airport T3288 1880. Regular flights from **Rio**, **São Paulo**, **Salvador** and **Belo Horizonte**. Taxi airport-Porto Seguro, US$15. Also buses.

Bus From Porto Seguro: **Salvador** (**Águia Branca**), daily, 12 hrs, US$80. **Vitória**, daily, 11 hrs, US$60. **Ilhéus**, daily 0730, 5½ hrs, US$20-50. **Eunápolis**, 1 hr, US$6. For **Rio** direct buses (**São Geraldo**), leaving at 1745, US$70, 18 hrs, from Rio direct at 1600 (very cold a/c, take warm clothes), or take 1800 for Ilhéus and change at Eunápolis. To **Belo Horizonte** daily, direct, US$80 (São Geraldo). Other services via Eunápolis (those going north avoid Salvador) or Itabuna (5 hrs, US$25).

The rodoviária has reliable luggage store and lounge on the 3rd floor, on the road to Eunápolis, 2 km from the centre, regular bus service (30 mins) through the city to the old rodoviária near the port. Local buses US$0.45. Taxis charge US$7 from the rodoviária to the town or ferry (negotiate at quiet times).

Arraial da Ajuda *p554*

Ferry Across the Rio Buranhém from Porto Seguro take 15 mins to the south bank, US$1 for foot passengers, US$6 for cars, every 30 mins day and night. It is then a further 5 km to Arraial da Ajuda, US$1 by bus; kombis charge US$1.50 pp; taxis US$10.

Trancoso *p554*

Bus Buses run regularly on the newly paved road between Porto Seguro, Ajuda and Trancoso, at least every hour in high season: US$4 Porto Seguro-Trancoso, US$2.40 Ajuda-Trancoso. Arriving from the south, change buses at Eunápolis from where the newly paved Linha Verde road runs.

Caraíva and around *p555*

Caraíva can only be reached by **canoe** across the river. Access roads are poor and almost impossible after heavy rain. There are services several times a day from Trancoso, which is the easiest point of access. **Aguia Azul** bus company takes this route from Porto Seguro at 0700 and 1500, via Trancoso. If arriving by bus from the south, change to **Aguia Azul** bus in Itabela, departs at 1500, or take a taxi, about 50 km. Heading south take the bus to Eunápolis at 0600, 3 hrs.

Corumbau

Beach buggy taxis take you to the river crossing (US$40). It's about a 10 km walk from Caraíva.

Parque Nacional de Monte Pascoal *p555*

From Caraíva there is a river crossing by **boats** which are always on hand. **Buses** run from **Itamaraju** 16 km to the south, at 0600 Fri-Mon.

Caravelas *p555*

Bus To **Texeira de Freitas** (4 a day), **Salvador**, **Nanuque** and **Prado**. **Flights** from **Belo Horizonte, São Paulo** and **Salvador** to Caravelas; otherwise fly to Porto Seguro.

Parque Nacional Marinho dos Abrolhos

The journey to the islands takes about 3-4 hrs depending on the sea conditions. Between Jul and early Dec humpback whale sightings are almost guaranteed. Boats leave at 0700 from the Marina Porto Abrolhos just north of Caravelas town centre (around US$50 depending on numbers) and they return at dusk. It is possible to dive or snorkel at Abrolhos. If you are coming from Porto Seguro everything including transfers can be arranged by Portomondo (see above). In Caravelas, book with **Abrolhos Turismo**, Praça Dr Emílio Imbassay 8, T3297 1149, www.abrolhosturismo.com.br, or **Catamarã Veleiro Sanuk**, T3297 1344, www.catamarasanuk.cjb.net.

Directory

Porto Seguro *p554*

Banks **Banco do Brasil**, Av Beira Mar, open 1000-1500, changes TCs and US$ cash, also Visa ATM. Also at airport. **Bradesco**, Av Getúlio Vargas, Visa ATM. **Bicycle hire** **Oficina de Bicicleta**, Av Getúlio Vargas e R São Pedro, about US$13 for 24 hrs. Also at Praça de Bandeira and at 2 de Julho 242. **Car hire** Several companies at the airport. **Post offices** In the mini-shopping centre on the corner of R das Jandaias and Av dos Navegantes.

Arraial da Ajuda *p554*

Banks Mobile **Banco do Brazil** in the main square during high season. **Internet** Various places in town.

North of Salvador

The paved BA-099 coast road from near Salvador airport is known as the Estrada do Coco (Coconut Highway, because of the many plantations) and for 50 km passes some beautiful beaches. The best known from south to north are Ipitanga (with its reefs), Buraquinho, **Jauá** (with reefs, surfing, pools at low tide, clean water), Arembepe (famous hippy village in 1960s with a Tamar turtle protection project, T0xx71-3624 1049, arembepe@tamar.org.br), Guarajuba, Itacimirim, Castelo Garcia D'Ávila (with its 16th-century fort) and Forte. Regular buses serve most of these destinations.

Praia do Forte

The former fishing village, 80 km north of Salvador, takes its name from the castle built by a Portuguese settler, Garcia D'Ávila, in 1556 to warn the city to the south of enemy invasion. Praia do Forte is now a pleasant resort town with all but one of the streets of sand and lovely beaches. Inland from the coast is a restinga forest, which grows on sandy soil with a very delicate ecosystem. Near the village is a small *pantanal* (marshy area), which is host to a large number of birds, caimans and other animals. Birdwatching trips on the pantanal are rewarding. The **Tamar Project** ⓘ *Av Farol Garcia D'Ávila s/n, T0xx71-3676 0321, www.projetotamar.org.br,* preserves the sea turtles which lay their eggs in the area. Praia do Forte is now the headquarters of the national turtle preservation programme and is funded by the Worldwide Fund for Nature.

The coast road north

The Linha Verde (the extension of the Estrada do Coco) runs for 142 km to the border of Sergipe, the next state north; the road is more scenic than the BR-101, especially near Conde. There are very few hotels or pousadas in the more remote villages. The most picturesque are **Imbassaí**, **Subaúma**, **Baixio** (very beautiful, where the Rio Inhambupe meets the sea) and **Conde**. Sítio do Conde on the coast, 6 km from Conde, has many pousadas, but the beaches are not very good. Sítio do Conde is an ideal base to explore other beaches at Barra do Itariri, 12 km south, at the mouth of a river (fine sunsets). The last stop on the Linha Verde is **Mangue Seco**. A steep hill rising behind the village to tall white sand dunes offers superb view of the coastline. There are plenty of small cheap places to stay along the seafront from the jetty, none with addresses or phone numbers (the village is tiny). There are simple restaurants around the main square next to the church. The beach has a handful of *barracas* serving cheap fish. Access from Sergipe is by boat on the Rio Real from Pontal (10-minute crossing). Buses run between Pontal and Estância twice a day. The ferry across the river usually leaves before 1000 in the morning. A private launch will cost US$10, but it usually possible to find someone to share the ride.

North of Salvador listings

For Sleeping and Eating price codes and other relevant information, see Essentials, pages 38-40. See Telephone, page 397, for important phone changes.

Sleeping

North of Salvador: Jauá *p562*

B Lagoa e Mar, Praia de Jauá, T/F3672 1573, www.hotellagoaemar.com.br. Very good breakfast, spacious bungalows, swimming pool, 350 m to beach, restaurant, helpful, transport to airport, 10% discount to Footprint owners.

Praia do Forte *p562*

The town's main street had its name changed from Alameda do Sol to Av ACM. This street doesn't have numbers marked, so you just have to walk along to find the place you want. Prices rise steeply in the summer season. It may be difficult to find cheap places to stay.

LL-AL Praia do Forte EcoResort, Av do Farol, T3676 4000, www.praiadoforte.com. Large scale family resort set in tropical gardens on the beach and with programmes to visit the nearby protected areas. Room are spacious, well appointed and comfortable. Service, which includes a spa and entertainment, is excellent. Beautiful pool.

L-AL Aloha Brasil Pousada, R da Aurora, T3676 0279, www.pousadaalohabrasil.com.br. Relaxing tropical garden and pool, charming rooms with king size beds and verandas.

L-AL Porto Zarpa, R da Aurora, T3676 1414, www.portozarpa.com.br. Large, 2-storey building in gardens, close to beach, cable TV, parking, pool, good for families.

AL-A Sobrado da Vila, Av ACM, T3676 1088, www.sobradodavila.com.br. Best in the village itself with a range of individually decorated rooms with balconies and a good-value restaurant, convenient for restaurants.

A Ogum Marinho, Av ACM, T3676 1165, www.ogummarinho.com.br. A/c, cheaper with fan, nice little courtyard garden, good restaurant and service. It has an art gallery with work by Brazilian artists.

A-B Pousada Casa de Praia, Praça dos Artistas 08-09, T3676 1362, www.casadepraia.tur.br. Good value and location rooms, with and without a/c, popular.

B-C Pousada João Sol, R da Corvina, T3676 1054, www.pousadajoaosol.com.br. 6 well-appointed chalets. The owner speaks English, Spanish and German. Great breakfast.

C Pousada Tatuapara, Praça dos Artistas 1, T3676 1466, www.tatuapara.com.br. Spacious and well-maintained, fan, fridge, good breakfast, pool.

D Pousada Tia Helena, Alameda das Estrelas, just east of the Praça dos Artistas, T3676 1198, 9901 2894, www.tiahelenapraiadoforte.com.br. Helena, the motherly proprietor provides an enormous breakfast, simple rooms. Reductions for 3-day stays.

E pp **Albergue da Juventude**, Praia do Forte, R da Aurora 3, T3676 1094, www.albergue.com.br. Smart youth hostel with decent shared rooms and rooms with en suites (**B-C**), a large breakfast, fan, kitchen and shop, cheaper for HI members.

Eating

Praia do Forte *p562*

ΨΨ Bar Do Souza, Av ACM, on the right as you enter the village. Best seafood in town, open daily, live music at weekends. Recommended.

ΨΨ O Europeu, Av ACM, T3676 0232. Anglo-Brazilian owned, with the most adventurous menu in town with well-prepared dishes. The owners, William and Vera, are very knowledgeable about the area. Recommended.

Ψ Cafe Tango, Av ACM, T3676 1637. Pleasant open-air tea and coffee bar with great pastries and cakes.

Ψ Casa da Nati, Av ACM, T3676 1239. Per kilo and Bahian food from a Praia do Forte native.

Ψ Point do Ivan, Av ACM. T99971711. Bahian food, good *moqueca, bobo de camarão* and cheap *prato feito.*

Shopping

Galeria de Arte Claudia Ferraris, Alameda das Estrelas, T9125 1191 or T9165 8325, www.claudiaferraris.com. European artist who produces Brazilian-themed art, eg tile-sized capoeira canvases that beautifully reproduce the movement of the martial art. Recommended.

Joia Rara, Av ACM, T3676 1503. Tailor-made jewellery using Brazilian precious stones set in white gold, gold or silver. The client chooses the stone which is then polished. These include Bahian emeralds, aquamarines, tourmalines and amethysts, The shop doubles up as the artist's studio. Authentic and good value.

Nativa, Av ACM, T3676 0437. Artisan clothing from Brazil's northeast region. Beautiful hand-embroidered shirts, skirts, and bags. Quite chic and unusual.

Activities and tours

Praia do Forte *p562*

Praia do Forte is ideal for windsurfing and sailing owing to constant fresh Atlantic breezes.

Odara Turismo, in the EcoResort Hotel, T3676 1080. Imaginative tours to surrounding areas and outlying villages and beaches using 4WD vehicles. They are very friendly and informative. Recommended. The owners, Norbert and Papy, speak English and German.

Transport

Praia do Forte *p562*

Bus To **Salvador** (US$4): **Linha Verde** from 0530 to 1800 daily, 1½ hrs.

Recife and the northeast coast

The eight states north of Bahia are historically and culturally rich, but generally poor economically. Steeped in history are, for instance, Recife, Olinda, or São Luís and cultural heritage abounds (eg 'Forró' and other musical styles, many good museums, lacework, ceramics). There is a multitude of beaches: if established resorts aren't your thing, you don't have to travel far for somewhere more peaceful, while off the beaten track are some which have hardly been discovered.

Pernambuco was the seat of Dutch Brazil in the 17th century. Its capital, Recife, and close neighbour, Olinda, have the most creative music scene in the northeast and their famous wild carnival draws thousands of visitors.

Recife → *Phone code: 0xx81. Post code: 50000. Colour map 5, B6. Population: 1.42 million.*

The capital of Pernambuco State, 285 km north of Maceió and 839 km north of Salvador, was founded on reclaimed land by the Dutch prince Maurice of Nassau in 1637 after his troops had burnt Olinda, the original capital. The city centre consists of three portions, always very busy by day; the crowds and the narrow streets, especially in the Santo Antônio district, can make it a confusing city to walk around. Recife has the main dock area, with commercial buildings associated with it. South of the centre is the residential and beach district of Boa Viagem, reached by bridge across the Bacia do Pina. Olinda, the old capital, is 7 km to the north (see page 574).

Ins and outs

Tourist offices Empetur (for the State of Pernambuco), **main office** ⓘ *Complexo Viário Vice-Governador Barreto Guimarães s/n, Salgadinho, T3427 8000, between Recife and Olinda, www.empetur.com.br*. Branches at **airport** ⓘ *T3341 6090, 24 hours*, helpful but few leaflets, English spoken, and **Praça of Boa Viagem** ⓘ *T3463 3621*, English spoken, helpful. Maps are available, or can be bought at newspaper stands in city; also sketch maps in monthly guides Itinerário Pernambuco and Guia do Turista. For the **Secretaria de Turismo da Prefeitura do Recife** ⓘ *T3224 7198*. Hours of opening of museums, art galleries, churches, etc are published in the *Diário de Pernambuco* and *Jornal do Comércio*. The former's website has lots of tourist information, www.dpnet.com.br/turismo/ or via www.pernambuco.com.

Opportunistic theft is unfortunately common in the streets of Recife and Olinda (especially on the streets up to Alto da Sé, Olinda). Prostitution is reportedly common in Boa Viagem – choose nightclubs with care.

Sights

The best sights are the churches of **Santo Antônio do Convento de São Francisco** (1606) *in the R do Imperador*, which has beautiful Portuguese tiles, and adjoining it the finest sight of all, the **Capela Dourada** (Golden Chapel, 1697) ⓘ *Mon-Fri 0800-1130, 1400-1700, Sat morning only, US$1, no flash photography*; it is through the Museu Franciscano de Arte Sacra. **São Pedro dos Clérigos** (1782) ⓘ *in São José district, daily 0800-1130, 1400-1600*, should be seen for its façade, its fine wood sculpture and a splendid trompe-l'oeil ceiling. **Nossa Senhora da Conceição dos Militares** (1771) ⓘ *R Nova 309, Mon-Fri 0800-1700*, has a grand ceiling and a large 18th-century primitive mural of the battle of Guararapes (museum next door). Other important churches are **Santo Antônio** (1753-1791) ⓘ *Praça da Independência, Mon-Fri 0800-1200, 1400-1800, Sun 1700-1900*, rebuilt in 1864. **Nossa Senhora do Carmo** (1663) ⓘ *Praça do Carmo, Mon-Fri 0800-1200, 1400-1900, Sat-Sun 0700-1200*. **Madre de Deus** (1715) ⓘ *in R Madre de Deus in the district of Recife, Tue-Fri 0800-1200, 1400-1600*, with a splendid high altar, and sacristy. The **Divino Espírito Santo** (1689) ⓘ *Praça 17 in Santo Antônio district, Mon-Fri 0800-1630, Sat 0800-1400, Sun 1000-1200*, the original church of the Jesuits. There are many others.

1 Recife orientation

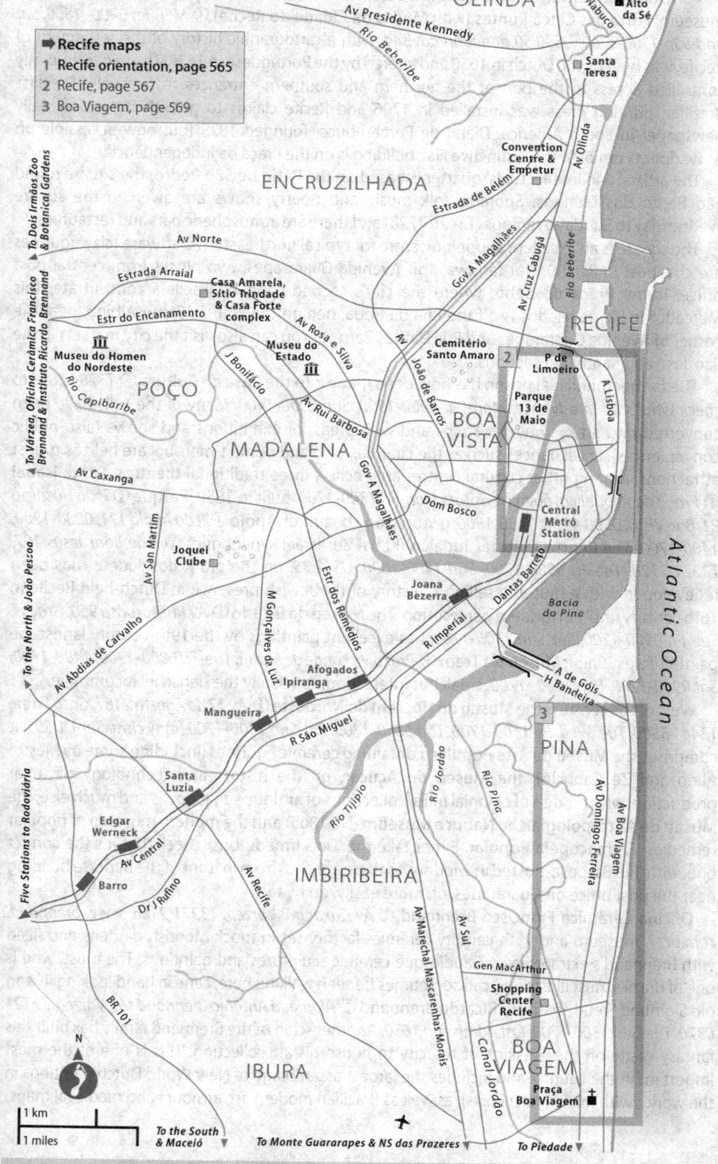

Recife maps
1 Recife orientation, page 565
2 Recife, page 567
3 Boa Viagem, page 569
To Northern Beaches
OLINDA
J Nabuco
Alto da Sé
Av Presidente Kennedy
Rio Beberibe
Santa Teresa
Convention Centre & Empetur
Av Olinda
ENCRUZILHADA
Estrada de Belém
To Dois Irmãos Zoo & Botanical Gardens
Av Norte
Estrada Arraial
Casa Amarela, Sítio Trindade & Casa Forte complex
Estr do Encanamento
Gov A Magalhães
Av Cruz Cabugá
Rio Beberibe
RECIFE
To Várzea, Oficina Cerâmica Francisco Brennand & Instituto Ricardo Brennand
Museu do Homen do Nordeste
Av Rosa e Silva
Museu do Estado
J Bonifácio
Av João de Barros
Cemitério Santo Amaro
2
P de Limoeiro
POÇO
Rio Capibaribe
Av Rui Barbosa
Parque 13 de Maio
A Lisboa
BOA VISTA
MADALENA
Av Caxangá
Gov A Magalhães
Dom Bosco
Central Metrô Station
Av San Martim
Joquei Clube
To the North & João Pessoa
Atlantic Ocean
Estr dos Remédios
M Gonçalves da Luz
Joana Bezerra
Dantas Barreto
Bacia do Pina
Av Abdias de Carvalho
R Imperial
A de Góis
H Bandeira
Afogados
Ipiranga
Mangueira
3
R São Miguel
PINA
Santa Luzia
Rio Jordão
Rio Pina
Rio Tijipio
Av Domingos Ferreira
Av Boa Viagem
Edgar Werneck
Av Central
Five Stations to Rodoviária
Barro
Dr J Rufino
Av Recife
IMBIRIBEIRA
Av Sul
Av Marechal Mascarenhas Morais
Gen MacArthur
Shopping Center Recife
BR 101
N
BOA VIAGEM
IBURA
Canal Jordão
Praça Boa Viagem
1 km
1 miles
To the South & Maceió
To Monte Guararapes & NS das Prazeres
To Piedade

Forte do Brum ⓘ *Tue-Fri 0900-1600, Sat-Sun 1400-1600* (built by the Dutch in 1629) is an army museum. **Forte das Cinco Pontas** (with **Museu da Cidade do Recife**) ⓘ *Mon-Fri 0900- 1800, Sat and Sun 1300-1700, US$0.50 donation advised*, with a cartographic history of the settlement of Recife, was built by the Dutch in 1630 and altered by the Portuguese in 1677. The two forts jointly controlled access to the port at the northern and southern entrances respectively. The first Brazilian printing press was installed in 1706 and Recife claims to publish the oldest daily newspaper in South America, Diário de Pernambuco, founded 1825 (but now accessible on www.dpnet.com.br/). The distinctive lilac building is on the Praça da Independência.

The artists' and intellectuals' quarter is based on the **Pátio de São Pedro**, the square round São Pedro dos Clérigos. Sporadic folk music and poetry shows are given in the square Wednesday to Sunday evenings (T3426 2728) and there are atmospheric bars and restaurants.

The square is an excellent shopping centre for typical northeastern craftware (clay figurines are cheapest in Recife). Not far away, off Avenida Guararapes, two blocks from central post office, is the **Praça do Sebo**, where the city's second-hand booksellers concentrate; this Mercado de Livros Usados is off the Rua da Roda, behind the Edifício Santo Albino, near the corner of Avenida Guararapes and Rua Dantas Barreto. You can also visit the city markets in the São José and Santa Rita sections.

The former municipal prison has now been made into the **Casa da Cultura** ⓘ *T3284 2850 to check what's on in advance, Mon-Sat 0900-1900, Sun 0900-1400*. Many of the cells have been converted into art or souvenir shops and with areas for exhibitions and shows (also public conveniences). Local dances such as the ciranda, forró and bumba-meu-boi are held as tourist attractions. Among other cultural centres are Recife's three traditional **theatres, Santa Isabel** ⓘ *Praça da República, open to visitors Mon-Fri 1300-1700*, built in 1850. **Parque** ⓘ *R do Hospício 81, Boa Vista, 0800-1200, 1400-1800*, restored and beautiful. **Apolo** ⓘ *R do Apolo 121, 0800-1200, 1400-1700*. The **Centro Cultural Judaico** (Kahal Zur Israel synagogue) ⓘ *R de Bom Jesus 197, T3224 2128, Tue-Fri 0900-1700, Sun 1400-1800, US$2.25*, on the old R dos Judeus, has been redeveloped with a museum telling the story of the Jewish presence in Dutch-held Recife in 16th century until Portuguese persecution. The **Museu do Estado** ⓘ *Av Rui Barbosa 960, Graças, Tue-Fri 0900-1700, Sat-Sun 1400-1700*, has excellent paintings by the 19th-century landscape painter, Teles Júnior. **Museu do Trem** ⓘ *Praça Visconde de Mauá, Tue-Fri 0800-1200, 1400-1700, Sat 0900-1200, Sun 1400- 1700*, small but interesting, especially the Henschel locomotive.

West of the centre is the **Museu do Homem do Nordeste** ⓘ *Av 17 de Agosto 2187, Casa Forte, T3441 5500, Tue, Wed, Fri 1100-1700, Thu 0800-1700, Sat-Sun 1300-1700 (may close Sun), US$1*. It comprises the **Museu de Arte Popular**, containing ceramic figurines (including some by Mestre Alino and Zé Caboclo); the **Museu do Açúcar**, on the history and technology of sugar production, with models of colonial mills, collections of antique sugar bowls and much else; the **Museu de Antropologia**, the **Nabuco Museum** (No 1865) and the modern museum of popular remedies, **Farmacopéia Popular**. Either take the 'Dois Irmãos' bus (check that it's the correct one, with 'Rui Barbosa' posted in window, as there are two) from in front of the Banorte building near the post office on Guararapes, or, more easily, go by taxi.

Oficina Cerâmica Francisco Brennand ⓘ *Av Caxangá, Várzea, T3271 2466, www.brennand.com.br*. A museum and 19th-century ceramics factory set in mock-Moorish gardens and filled with Brennand's extraordinary Gaudiesque ceramic sculptures and paintings. The artist, who is one of Brazil's most illustrious, can sometimes be seen walking here, cane in hand looking like an old Sigmund Freud. **Instituto Ricardo Brennand** ⓘ *Alameda Antônio Brennand s/n, Várzea, T2121 0370, Tue-Sun 1300-1700, last admission 1630*. Another scion of the Brennand family has built this fantasy castle on the outskirts of the city to house his art collection. This is one of the most important in the country and includes the largest assemblage of New World Dutch paintings in the world (with many Franz Posts), as well as Brazilian modern art, armoury and medieval maps.

2 Recife

➡Recife maps
1 Recife orientation, page 565
2 Recife, page 567
3 Boa Viagem, page 569

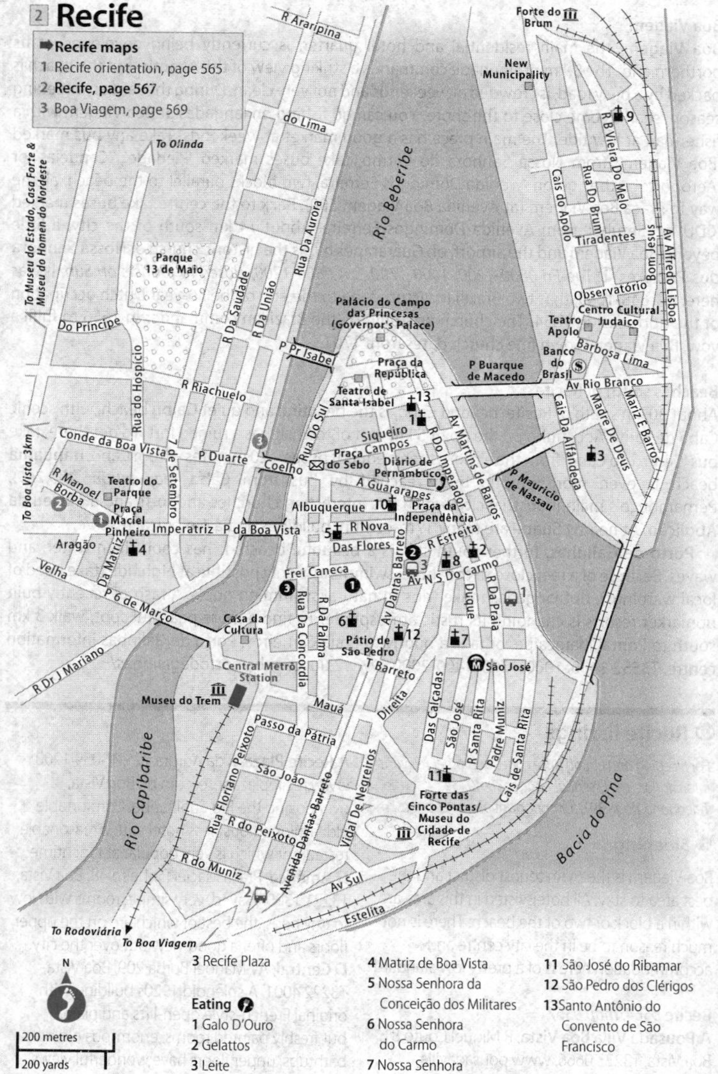

Sleeping
1 América
2 Central
3 Recife Plaza

Eating
1 Galo D'Ouro
2 Gelattos
3 Leite

Churches
1 Capela Dourada
2 Espírito Santo
3 Madre de Deus
4 Matriz de Boa Vista
5 Nossa Senhora da Conceição dos Militares
6 Nossa Senhora do Carmo
7 Nossa Senhora do Livramento
8 Nossa Senhora do Rosário dos Pretos
9 Pilar
10 Santo Antônio
11 São José do Ribamar
12 São Pedro dos Clérigos
13 Santo Antônio do Convento de São Francisco

Buses
1 To Itamaracá & Igarassu
2 To Porto da Galinhas
3 To Boa Viagem

Boa Viagem

Boa Viagem, the main residential and hotel quarter, is currently being developed at its northern end. The 8-km promenade commands a striking view of the Atlantic, but the beach is backed by a busy road, is crowded at weekends and not very clean. During the January breeding season, sharks come close to the shore. You can go fishing on jangadas at Boa Viagem with a fisherman at low tide. The main praça has a good market at weekends. Take any bus marked 'Boa Viagem'; from Nossa Senhora do Carmo, take buses marked 'Piedade', 'Candeias' or 'Aeroporto' – they go on Avenida Domingos Ferreira, two blocks parallel to the beach, all the way to Praça Boa Viagem (at Avenida Boa Viagem 500). Back to the centre take buses marked 'CDU' or 'Setubal' from Avenida Domingos Ferreira. About 14 km south of the city, a little beyond Boa Viagem and the airport, on Guararapes hill, is the historic church of **Nossa Senhora dos Prazeres** ⓘ *Tue-Fri 0800-1200, 1400-1700, Sat 0800-1200, closed to tourists on Sun*. It was here, in 1648-1649, that two Brazilian victories led to the end of the 30-year Dutch occupation of the northeast in 1654. The church was built by the Brazilian commander in 1656 to fulfil a vow. Boa Viagem's own fine church dates from 1707.

Beaches south of Recife

About 30 km south of Recife, beyond Cabo, is the beautiful and quiet **Gaibu** beach, with scenic Cabo de Santo Agostinho on the point 5 km east of town. It has a ruined fort. To get there, take bus 'Centro do Cabo' from the airport, then frequent buses – 20 minutes – from Cabo. **Itapuama** beach is even more empty, both reached by bus from **Cabo** (*Population: 140,765*), Pernambuco's main industrial city, which has interesting churches and forts and a **Museu da Abolição.** At nearby **Suape** are many 17th-century buildings and a biological reserve.

Porto de Galinhas, further south still, is a beautiful beach. It has cool, clean water, and waves. Because of a reef close to the shore, swimming is only possible at high tide (take heed of local warnings), but jangadas make trips to natural swimming pools. A rash of recently built upmarket resorts is changing its rustic atmosphere. To find a more peaceful spot, walk 3 km south to Pontal Maracaipe, or take a buggy to Praia Carneiros. Porto de Galinhas information centre, T3552 1480, 1000-1200, 1400-2000, www2.uol.com.br/portodegalinhas/.

Recife listings

For Sleeping and Eating price codes and other relevant information, see Essentials, pages 38-40. See Telephone, page 397, for important phone changes.

Sleeping

Boa Viagem is the main tourist district and the best area to stay. All hotels listed in this area are within a block or two of the beach. There is not much reason to be in the city centre and accommodation here is of a pretty low standard.

Recife *p564, map p567*

A Pousada Villa Boa Vista, R Miguel Couto 81, Boa Vista, T3223 0666, www.pousadavilla boavista .com.br. Only modern hotel in town, 5-min cab ride from centre, plain, comfortable a/c rooms (with powerful showers), around a courtyard. Quiet, safe.

A Recife Plaza, R da Aurora 225, T3059 1200, www.recifeplazahotel.com.br, Boa Vista, overlooking the Rio Capibaribe. Comfortable old fashioned business hotel with a reasonable restaurant which is very popular at lunchtime.

D América, Praça Maciel Pinheiro 48, Boa Vista, T3221 1300. Frayed, very simple rooms with low foamy beds, the best of which are on the upper floors and offer a good view out over the city.

D Central, Av Manoel Borba 209, Boa Vista, T3222 4001. A splendid 1920s building with original French-style open-lifts and plain, but freshly painted rooms, enormous old iron bathtubs, upper floors have wonderful views.

Boa Viagem *p568, map p569*

AL-B Recife Monte, R Petrolina e R dos Navegantes 363, T2121 0909, www.recife montehotel.com.br. Very smart and good value

Boa Viagem

Boa Viagem detail

➡ Recife maps

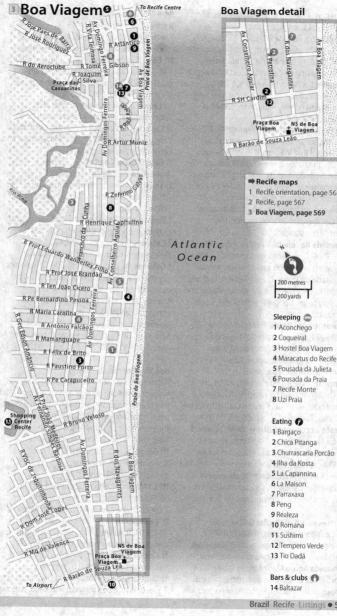

1 Recife orientation, page 565
2 Recife, page 567
3 Boa Viagem, page 569

Sleeping

1 Aconchego
2 Coqueiral
3 Hostel Boa Viagem
4 Maracatus do Recife
5 Pousada da Julieta
6 Pousada da Praia
7 Recife Monte
8 Uzi Praia

Eating

1 Bargaço
2 Chica Pitanga
3 Churrascaria Porcão
4 Ilha da Kosta
5 La Capannina
6 La Maison
7 Parraxaxa
8 Peng
9 Realeza
10 Romana
11 Sushimi
12 Tempero Verde
13 Tio Dadá

Bars & clubs

14 Baltazar

for category, caters to business travellers, also has suites in **LL** range.
B Aconchego, Félix de Brito 382, T3326 2989, aconchego@novaera.com.br. Motel style rooms around pleasant pool area, a/c, sitting room, English-speaking owner, will collect from airport.
C Coqueiral, R Petrolina, 43, T3326 5881. Dutch-owned (Dutch, English, French spoken), a/c, small and homely with pretty breakfast room. Recommended.
C Uzi Praia, Av Conselheiro Aguiar 942, T/F3466 9662. A/c, cosy, sister hotel across the road.
D pp **Hostel Boa Viagem**, R Aviador Severiano Lins 455, T3326 9572, www.hostelboaviagem.com.br. From doubles (**B**) and singles with a/c to dormitories, well-located HI hostel, excellent value, good bathrooms, pool, owners speak French and are from Caruaru so can arrange trips. Call ahead to arrange transport from airport or bus station.
D Pousada da Julieta, R Prof Jose Brandão 135, T3326 7860, hjulieta@elogica.com.br. 1 block from beach, very good value. Recommended.
D Pousada da Praia, Alcides Carneiro Leal 66, T3326 7085. A/c, TV, safe, a/c, rooms vary (some tiny), very helpful, popular with Israelis. Roof-top breakfast room.
E Maracatus do Recife, R Maria Carolina 185, T3326 1221, alberguemaracatus@yahoo.com. Hostel with good breakfast, no hot water, simple, cooking facilities, pool, safe, mosquitoes can be a problem.
Camping There is no camping within the city. For information on camping throughout Pernambuco state, call **Paraíso Camping Clube**, Av Dantas Barreto 512, loja 503, T3224 3094.
Private accommodation During Carnival and for longer stays at other times, private individuals rent rooms and houses in Recife and Olinda; listings can be found in the classified ads in *Diário de Pernambuco*, or ask around the streets of Olinda. This accommodation is generally cheaper, safer and quieter than hotels.

Beaches south of Recife: Gaibu *p568*
L-E Casa dos Golfinhos, T081-8861 4707, www.gaibu-bedandbreakfast.com. B&B close to the beach, under German management.
C Pousada Aguas Marinhas, Av Beira Mar 56, Gaibu, T3522 6346. A/c, comfortable, fridge, **E** without bath, breakfast, French spoken, very nice.

Eating

Recife *p564, map p567*
Lanchonetes abound in the city, catering to office workers, but tend to close in evening.
TTT Leite (lunches only), Praça Joaquim Nabuco 147/53 near Casa de Cultura. Old and famous, good service, smart (another branch in Boa Viagem, at Prof José Brandão 409).
TTT Lisboa á Noite, R Geraldo Pires 503. Good, reasonable, open Sun evenings.
TT Casa de Tia, Gamboa do Carmo 136. Lunch only, must arrive by 1215, try cosido, a meat and vegetable stew, enough for 2.
TT Galo D'Ouro, Gamboa do Carmo 83. Well-established, international food.
TT Tivoli, R Matias de Albuquerque, Santo Antônio. Lunches downstairs, a/c restaurant upstairs, good value.
T Buraquinho, Pátio de São Pedro. Lunch only, generous servings of caipirinha, friendly.
T Casa dos Frios, da Palma 57, loja 5. Delicatessen/sandwich bar, salads, pastries.
T Gelattos, Av Dantas Barreto, 230. Great sucos (try the delicious guarana do amazonas with nuts), hamburgers and sandwiches.
T Savoy Bar, Av Guararapes. The haunt of Pernambucan intellectuals since 1944, with poetry all over the walls and the legend that Sartre and De Beauvoir once ate there, buffet Mon-Sat 1100-1500, US$2, also lunch by weight.

Boa Viagem *p568, map p569*
Restaurants on the main beach road of Av Boa Viagem are pricey; venture a block or two inland for cheaper deals. Be careful of eating the local small crabs, known as *guaiamum*; they live in the mangrove swamps which take the drainage from Recife's mocambos (shanty towns).
TTT Bargaço, Av Boa Viagem 670. Typical northeastern menu specializing in seafood, sophisticated with small bar.
TTT La Maison, Av Boa Viagem, 618, T3325 1158. Fondue restaurant in low-lit basement, with rosé wine and peach melba on menu.
TT La Capannina, Av Cons Aguiar 538, T3465 9420. Italian, pizzas, salad, pasta and sweet and savoury crêpes, delivery service.
TT Chica Pitanga, R Petrolina, 19, T3465 2224. Upmarket, excellent food by weight.
TT Churrascaria Porcão, Av Eng Domingos Ferreira 4215. Good for meat and salad, popular.

Ilha da Kosta, R Pe Bernardino Pessoa, 50, T3466 2222. Self-service seafood, sushi, pizza and Brazilian cuisine, open 1100 to last client and all afternoon.

Parraxaxa, R Baltazar Pereira, 32, T9108 0242. Rustic-style, award-winning, northeastern buffet, including breakfast. Recommended.

Sushimi, T3463 6500. Classic, Japanese fast-food in suitably sterile surroundings. One of a range of options in Shopping Center Recife (open 1000-2200, T3464 6000) in Boa Viagem.

Peng, Av Domingos Ferreira, 1957. Self-service, some Chinese dishes, bargain, rather than gourmet food, in area with few other restaurants.

Realeza, Av Boa Viagem, on corner with Av Atlântico. Beachfront location, hamburgers, snacks and pizza.

Romana, R Setubal 225. Deli/bakery with a few tables and chairs, pastries, coffee, yoghurt.

Tempero Verde, R S H Cardim, opposite Chica Pitanga. Where the locals go, bargain meal of beans, meat and salad, US$1.50, simple, self-service, pavement tables.

TioDadá, R Baltazar Pereira 100. Loud, TV screens, good value portions of beef.

Bars and clubs

Recife centre *p564, map p567*

Most bars (often called 'pubs', but nothing like the English version) stay open until dawn. The historic centre of Recife Antigo has been restored and is now an excellent spot for nightlife. Bars around R do Bom Jesus such as **London Pub**, No 207, are the result of a scheme to renovate the dock area. The Graças district, west of Boa Vista, on the Rio Capibaribe, is popular for bars and evening entertainment. Discos tend to be expensive and sophisticated. Best times are around 2400 on Fri or Sat, take a taxi. The Pina zone, north of the beginning of Boa Viagem, is one of the city's major hang-out areas with lively bars, music and dancing. Try to visit a northeastern Forró where couples dance to typical music, very lively especially Fri and Sat, several good ones at Candeias.

Calypso Club, R do Bom Jesus. US$5, live local bands playing traditional music to rock.

The 2 most popular nightclubs (both huge, 2300 to dawn) are **Downtown Pub**, R Vigário Tenório, disco, live music, US$5, and **Fashion Club**, Av Fernando Simões Barbosa 266, Boa Viagem in front of Shopping Centre Recife, T3327 4040, US$8. Techno and rock bands.

Boa Viagem *p568, map p569*

Baltazar, R Baltazar Pereira 130, T3327 0475. Live music nightly, bar snacks, large and popular. Open 1600 to early hours.

Papillon Bar, Av Beira Mar 20, Piedade, T3341 7298. Forró Wed-Sat.

Entertainment

Recife *p564, map p567*

Theatre **Agenda Cultural** details the cultural events for the month, free booklet from tourist offices. Shows in the **Recife/Olinda Convention Center**, US$10, traditional dances in full costume.

Festivals and events

Recife *p564, maps p567 and p569*

1 Jan, Universal Brotherhood. Carnival in Recife features a pre-carnavalesca week of shows, processions and balls, before the Galo da Madrugada, with up to a million participants officially opens Carnaval on the Sat morning. The festival continues until Tue with trios elétricos, samba and the distinctive local maracatu and frevo dances and rhythms. **12-15 Mar**, parades to mark the city's foundation. **Mid-Apr**, **Pro- Rock Festival**, a week-long celebration of rock, hip-hop and manguebeat at Centro de Convenções, Complexo de Salgadinho and other venues. Check Diário de Pernambuco or Jornal do Comércio for details. **Jun, Festejos Juninos.** The days of Santo Antônio (13 Jun), São João (24 Jun), São Pedro and São Paulo (29 Jun), form the nuclei of a month-long celebration whose roots go back to the Portuguese colony. Intermingled with the Catholic tradition are Indian and African elements. The annual cycle begins on **São José's day**, **19 Mar**, historically the 1st day of planting maize; the harvest in Jun then forms a central part of the festejos juninos. During the festivals the forró is danced. This dance, now popular throughout the Northeast, is believed to have originated when the British builders of the local railways held parties that were 'for all'. **11-16 Jul**, **Nossa Senhora do Carmo**, patron saint of the city. **Aug** is the **Mes do Folclore. Oct**, **Recifolia**, a repetition of carnival over a whole weekend; dates differ each year. **1-8 Dec** is the festival of **Iemanjá**, with typical foods and drinks, celebrations and offerings to the goddess; also **8 Dec**, **Nossa Senhora da Conceição**.

Shopping

Recife *p564, maps p567 and p569*

Bookshops **Almanque Livros**, Largo do Varadouro 418, loja 58. Bohemian atmosphere, sells food and drink. **Livraria Brandão**, R da Matriz 22 (used English books and some French and German), and bookstalls on the R do Infante Dom Henrique. **Livraria Saraiva**, Rua 7 de Setembro 280. The best selection of Brazilian literature in the city. **Livro 7**, R do Riachuelo 267. An emporium with an impressive stock.

Melquísidec Pastor de Nascimento, a local character, has a second- hand stall at Praça do Sebo. **Sodiler** at Guararapes airport has books in English, newspapers, magazines; also in the Shopping Center Recife.

Markets **Afogados market**. For herbal remedies and spices. **Cais de alfandega**, Recife Barrio, market of local work, 1st weekend of every month. **Casa da Cultura**; the permanent craft market. Prices for ceramic figurines are lower than Caruaru. **Domingo na Rua**, Sun market in Recife Barrio, with stalls of local artesanato and performances. **Hippy fair** at Praça Boa Viagem, on the sea front, wooden statues of saints, weekend only. **Mercado São José** (1875) for local products and handicrafts. **Sítio Trindade**, Casa Amarela. Sat craft fair. On 23 Apr, here and in the Pátio de São Pedro, you can see the *xangô* dance.

Shopping malls **Shopping Center Recife** between Boa Viagem and the airport. **Shopping Tacaruna**, Santo Amaro, buses to Olinda pass it.

Activities and tours

Recife *p564, maps p567 and p569*

Diving Offshore are some 20 wrecks, including the remains of Portuguese galleons, with diverse marine life.

Mergulhe Coma, T3552 2355, T9102 6809, atlanticdivingasr@hotmail.com. English speaking instructors for PADI courses.

Seagate, T3426 1657/9972 9662, www.seagate recife.com.br. Daily departures and night dives.

Transport

Recife *p564, maps p565, p567 and p569*

Air The Gilberto Freyre international airport, 12 km from the city in Boa Viagem, is the best and most modern in Brazil; with plenty of places for coffees and magazines and boutiques of elegant little tourist shops. T3464 4188. Internal flights to all major cities. Bus to airport, No 52, US$0.75. Airport taxis cost US$10 to the seafront. There is a bank desk before customs which gives much the same rate for dollars as the moneychangers in the lobby.

Bus City buses cost US$0.55-1.10; they are clearly marked and run frequently until about 2300 weekdays, 0100 weekends. Many central bus stops have boards showing routes. CID/SUB or SUB/CID signs on the front tell you whether buses are going to or from the suburbs from/to the city centre (cidade). On buses, especially at night, look out for landmarks as street names are written small and are hard to see. Integrated bus-**metrô** (see Train, below) routes and tickets (US$1.50) are available. Urban transport information, T158. See below for buses to Olinda and other destinations outside the city. Taxis are plentiful; fares double on Sun, after 2100 and on holidays; number shown on meter is the fare; don't take the taxi if a driver tells you it is km.

Porto de Galinhas can be reached by bus from the southern end of Av Dantas Barreto, 8 a day, 7 on Sun, 0700-1700, US$2.25. Buses leave for **Igarassu** from Av Martins de Barros, in front of Grande Hotel, Recife, 45 mins, US$1.65.

The rodoviária, mainly for long-distance buses, is 12 km outside the city at São Lourenço da Mata (it is called Terminal Integrado dos Passageiros, or TIP, pronounced 'chippy'). T3452 1999. There is a 30-min metrô connection to the central railway station, entrance through Museu do Trem, opposite the Casa da Cultura, 2 lines leave the city, take train marked 'Rodoviária'. From Boa Viagem a taxi all the way costs US$30, or go to Central Metrô station and change there. Bus US$1.65, 1 hr, from the centre or from Boa Viagem. The train to the centre is much quicker than the bus. Bus tickets are sold at Cais de Santa Rita (opposite EMTU) and **Fruir Tur**, at Praça do Carmo, Olinda.

To **Salvador**, daily 1930, 12 hrs, US$70. To **Rio**, daily 2100, 44 hrs, US$118-155. To **São Paulo**, 1630 daily, 50 hrs, US$136-148. To **Foz**

do Iguaçu, Fri and Sun 1030, 55 hrs, US$182. To **Brasília**, daily 2130, 39 hrs, US$136. To **Belo Horizonte**, daily 2115, 34 hrs, US$114. To **João Pessoa**, every 20-30 mins, 2 hrs, US$12. To **Carauru**, see below. Buses to Olinda, see below; to beaches beyond Olinda from Av Dantas behind the post office. To **Cabo** (every 20 mins) and beaches south of Recife from Cais de Santa Rita.

Train Commuter services, known as the **Metrô** (but not underground), leave from the central station; they serve the rodoviária (frequent trains, 0500-2300, US$0.75 single). To reach the airport, get off the Metrô at Central station (not Joana Bezerra, which is unsafe) and take a bus or taxi (US$16.50) to Boa Viagem.

Directory

Recife *p564, maps p567 and p569*

Airline offices **Gol**, T3464 4793 or T0300-115 2121. **TAM**, airport T3462 6799/0800-123100. **TAP**, Praça Min Salgado Filho, Imbiribeira, T3465 0300. **Trip**, at airport, T3464 4610. **Webjet**, T0300-210 1234, www.webjet.com.br.
Banks Banks open 1000-1600, hours for exchange vary 1000-1400, sometimes later. **Banco do Brasil**, Shopping Centre Boa Viagem (Visa), helpful. **MasterCard**, cash against card, Av Conselheiro Aguiar 3924, Boa Viagem. **Citibank**, Av Marques de Olinda 126 and Av Cons Aguiar 2024, MasterCard with ATM. Also at branches of **HSBC**, eg Av Conde de Boa Vista 454 and Av Cons Aguiar 4452, Boa Viagem, and at **Banco 24 Horas. Bradesco**, at: Av Cons Aguiar 3236, Boa Viagem; Av Conde de Boa Vista; Rua da Concórdia 148; Getúlio Vargas 729; all have credit card facility, 24-hr ATMs but no exchange. **Exchange**: **Anacor**, Shopping Center Recife, loja 52, also at Shopping Tacaruna, loja 173. **Norte Câmbio Turismo**, Av Boa Viagem 5000, and at Shopping Guararapes, Av Barreto de Menezes.
Cultural centres **British Council**, Domingos Ferreira 4150, Boa Viagem, T2101 7500, recife@britishcouncil.org.br. 0800-1500, reading room with current English newspapers, very helpful. **Alliance Française**, R Amaro Bezerra 466, Derby, T3222 0918, www.af.rec.br. **Embassies and consulates** **Denmark**, Ed Empresarial Center II, R Antônio Lumack do Monte 96, conj 303, Boa Viagem, T3466 6466, frederico2005@gmail.com, open 0800-1200, 1400-1800. **France**, Av Conselheiro Aguiar 2333, 6th floor, T3117 3290, http://recife.ambafrance-br.org. **Germany**, R Antônio Lumack do Monte 128, 16th floor, Boa Viagem, T3463 5350, info.recife@alemanha.org.br, Mon-Fri 0900-1200, serving the Northeast. **Italy**, Av Domingos Ferreira 2222, 2nd floor, T3466 4200, www.consrecife.esteri.it. Mon, Wed, Fri 0930-1200, serving the Northeast. **Japan**, R Padre Carapuceiro 733, 14th floor, Boa Viagem, T3327 7264. **Netherlands**, Av Conselheiro Aguiar 1472, Sala 142, T3465 6704, consuladoholandes.rec@uol.com.br. **Sweden**, R Ernesto de Paula Santos, Boa Viagem, T3465 2940. **Switzerland**, Av Conselheiro Aguiar 4880, loja 32, Boa Viagem, T3326 3144. **UK**, Av Cons Aguiar 2941, 3rd floor, Boa Viagem, T2127 0230, recife@british consulate.org.br. 0800-1130. **US**, Gonçalves Maia 163, Boa Vista, T3416 3050.
Internet In Shopping Centre Recife in Boa Viagem, Shopping Boa Vista, city centre, and many otherss. **Medical services** **Unimed**, Av Bernardo Vieira de Melo 1496, Guararapes, T3462 1955/3461 1530, general medical treatment. **Unicordis**, Av Conselheiro Aguiar 1980, Boa Viagem, T3326 5237, equipped for cardiac emergencies; also at Av Conselheiro Roas e Silva 258, Aflitos, T421 1000. **Note** Dengue fever has been resurgent in Recife.
Post offices Including poste restante, Central Correios, 50001, Av Guararapes 250. In Boa Viagern, Av Cons Aguiar e R Col Sérgio Cardim. **Telephones** **Embratel**, Av Agamenon Magalhães, 1114, Parque Amorim district; also Praça da Independência. **International telephones**: **Telemar**, Av Conselheiro Aguiar, Av Herculano Bandeira 231, and Av Conde da Boa Vista, all open 0800-1800. **Useful addresses** **Tourist Police**, T3326 9603/3464 4088.

Around Recife

'Around Recife' is a bit of literary licence because this section deals with not only fine colonial towns not far from the state capital, but also the Fernando de Noronha archipelago, way out in the Atlantic. Of the former, Olinda is one of the best examples in Brazil and only minutes from Recife. In the drier interior is Caruaru, a fascinating market town. Fernando de Noronha, best reached from Recife (hence its inclusion here), has a wonderful marine environment and is ideal for those who are seeking a remote destination.

Olinda ➔ *Phone code: 0xx81. Post code: 53000. Colour map 5, B6. Population: 367,902.*

The old capital of Brazil founded in 1537 and named a World Heritage Site by UNESCO in 1982 is about 7 km north of Recife. A programme of restoration, partly financed by the Netherlands government, was initiated in order to comply with the recently conferred title of National Monument, but many of the buildings are still in desperate need of repair. The compact

Sleeping
1 7 Colinas
2 Albergue do Fortim
3 Olinda Hostel
4 Pousada Alquimia
5 Pousada do Amparo
6 Pousada d'Olinda
7 Pousada d'Olinda no Varadouro
8 Pousada dos Quatro Cantos
9 Pousada Peter
10 Pousada São Francisco
11 São Pedro

Eating
1 Goya
2 Maison do Bonfim
3 Mourisco
4 Oficina do Sabor

Bars & clubs
5 Farandola
6 Marola

network of cobbled streets is steeped in history and invites wandering. This is a charming spot to spend a few relaxing days and a much more appealing base than Recife.

Many of the historic buildings have irregular opening hours, but can be viewed from the outside. The **Tourist office** ⓘ *Praça do Carmo, T3429 9279, daily 0900-2100*, provides a complete list of all historic sites with a useful map, Sítio Histórico. Guides with identification cards wait in Praça do Carmo. They are former street children and half the fee for a full tour of the city (about US$15) goes to a home for street children. If you take a guide you will be safe from mugging which, unfortunately, occurs.

The **Basílica e Mosterio de São Bento** ⓘ *R São Bento, Mon-Fri 0830-1130, 1430-1700, Mass Sat 0630 and 1800; Sun 1000*, with Gregorian chant. Monastery closed except with written permission. Founded 1582 by the Benedictine monks, burnt by the Dutch in 1631 and restored in 1761, this is the site of Brazil's first law school and the first abolition of slavery. The magnificent gold altar was on loan to New York's Guggenheim Museum at the time of writing. Despite its weathered exterior, the **Convento de São Francisco** (1585) ⓘ *Ladeira de São Francisco, Tue-Fri 0700-1130, 1400-1700, Sat 0700-1200, US$0.40, mass Tue 1900, Sat 1700 and Sun 0800*, has splendid woodcarving and paintings, superb gilded stucco, and azulejos in the Capela de São Roque within the church of **Nossa Senhora das Neves** in the same building. Make the short, but very steep, climb up to the **Alto da Sé** for memorable views of the city and the coastline stretching all the way to Recife. Here, the simple **Igreja da Sé** (1537) ⓘ *Mon-Fri 0800-1200, 1400-1700*, a cathedral since 1677, was the first church to be built in the city. Nearby, the **Igreja da Misericórdia** (1540) ⓘ *R Bispo Coutinho, daily 1145-1230, 1800-1830*, has fine tiling and gold work. On a small hill overlooking Praça do Carmo, the **Igreja do Carmo** church (1581) has been closed for some years, with restoration planned.

There are some houses of the 17th century with latticed balconies, heavy doors and brightly painted stucco walls, including a house in Moorish style at **Praça João Alfredo 7**, housing the Mourisco restaurant and a handicrafts shop, Sobrado 7. The local colony of artists means excellent examples of regional art, mainly woodcarving and terracotta figurines, may be bought in the Alto da Sé, or in the handicraft shops at the **Mercado da Ribeira** ⓘ *R Bernardo Vieira de Melo* (Vieira de Melo gave the first recorded call for independence from Portugal, in Olinda in 1710). Handicrafts are also sold at good prices in the Mercado Eufrásio Barbosa, by the junction of Av Segismundo Gonçalves and Santos Dumont, Varadouro. There is a **Museo de Arte Sacra** ⓘ *R Bispo Coutínho, Tue-Fri 0900-1300*, in the former Palacío Episcopal (1696). At R 13 de Maio 157, in the 18th-century jail of the Inquisition, is the **Museu de Arte Contemporânea** ⓘ *same hours as Museu Regional*. The **Museu Regional** ⓘ *R do Amparo 128, Tue-Fri 0900-1700, Sat and Sun 1000-1800*, is excellent. **Museu do Mamulengo** ⓘ *Amparo 59, Mon-Fri 0900-1430*, has Pernambucan folk puppetry.

The **beaches** close to Olinda are reported to be seriously polluted. Those further north from Olinda, beyond Casa Caiada, are beautiful, usually deserted, palm-fringed; at **Janga**, and **Pau Amarelo**, the latter can be dirty at low tide (take either a 'Janga' or 'Pau Amarela' bus, Varodouro bus to return). At many simple cafés you can eat sururu (clam stew in coconut sauce), agulha frita (fried needle-fish), miúdo de galinha (chicken giblets in gravy) and casquinha de carangueijo (seasoned crabmeat). Visit the Dutch fort on Pau Amarelo beach; small craft fair here on Saturday nights.

Igarassu → *Colour map 5, B6. Population: 82,277.*

Igarassu, 39 km north of Recife on the road to João Pessoa, has the first church ever built in Brazil (SS Cosme e Damião, built in 1535), the Livramento church nearby, and the convent of Santo Antônio with a small museum next door. The church of Sagrado Coração is said to have housed Brazil's first orphanage. Much of the town (founded in 1535) is a National Monument.

Caruaru ➔ *Colour map 5, C6. Population: 253,634. Altitude: 554 m.*

The paved road from Recife passes through rolling hills, with sugar cane and large cattle fazendas, before climbing an escarpment. As the road gets higher, the countryside becomes drier, browner and rockier. Caruaru, 134 km west of Recife, is a busy, modern town, one of the most prosperous in the agreste in Pernambuco. It is also culturally very lively, with excellent local and theatre and folklore groups.

Caruaru is most famous for its markets. The Feira da Sulanca is basically a clothes market supplied mostly by local manufacture, but also on sale are jewellery, souvenirs, food, flowers and anything else that can go for a good price. The most important day is Monday. There is also the Feira Livre or do Troca-Troca (free, or barter market). On the same site, Parque 18 de Maio, is the Feira do Artesanato, leather goods, ceramics, hammocks and basketware, all the popular crafts of the region. It is tourist-oriented but it is on a grand scale and is open daily 0800-1800.

The little clay figures (figurinhas or bonecas de barro) originated by Mestre Vitalino (1909-1963), and very typical of the Nordeste, are the local speciality; most of the local potters live at **Alto da Moura**, 6 km away (a bumpy 30-minute bus ride, US$0.65), where a house once owned by Vitalino is open (the **Casa Museu Mestre Vitalino**), with personal objects and photographs, but no examples of his work.

Fernando de Noronha ➔ *1 hr behind Brazilian Standard Time.*

This small archipelago 345 km off the northeast coast was declared a Marine National Park in 1988. There are many unspoilt beaches and interesting wildlife and excellent scuba-diving and snorkelling. Only one island is inhabited and is dominated by a 321 m peak. It is part of the state of Pernambuco administered from Recife. The islands were discovered in 1503 by Amérigo Vespucci and were for a time a pirate lair. In 1738 the Portuguese built the Forte dos Remédios (begun by the Dutch), later used as a prison in this century, and a church to strengthen their claim to the islands. Remains of the early fortifications still exist.

Vila dos Remédios, near the north coast, is where most people live and socialize. At Baía dos Golfinhos is a lookout point for watching the spinner dolphins in the bay. On the south side there are fewer beaches, higher cliffs and the coastline and islands are part of the marine park.

All development is rigorously controlled by ICMBio, to prevent damage to the nature reserve. Many locals are dependent on tourism and most food is brought from the mainland; prices are about double. Entry to the island is limited to two plane-loads per day. There is a daily tax of US$68, valid for 10 days. Take sufficient reais as dollars are heavily discounted. For information, contact the national park office and Tamar information centre (open 0900-2200), Al do Boldró s/n, Fernando de Noronha, T0xx81-3619 1171, infonoronha@tamar.org.br. The rains are from February-July; the island turns green and the sea water becomes lovely and clear. The dry season is August-March, but the sun shines all year round. No repellent available for the many mosquitoes.

Around Recife listings

For Sleeping and Eating price codes and other relevant information, see Essentials, pages 38-40. See Telephone, page 397, for important phone changes.

Sleeping

Olinda *p574, map p574*

Prices at least triple during Carnival when 5-night packages are sold. Rooms at regular prices can often be found in Boa Viagem during this time. All of the following, and even most of the cheaper hotels outside the old city, have a pool.

Historic centre

If you can afford it, staying in a beautiful converted mansion (pousada) is the ideal way to absorb the colonial charm of Olinda.

AL 7 Colinas, Ladeira de São Francisco 307, T/F3439 6055, www.hotel7 colinas.com.br. Spacious, new hotel with all mod cons in private gated grounds with a large swimming pool.

AL Pousada do Amparo, R do Amparo 199, T3439 1749, www.pousadoamparo.com.br. Olinda's best hotel is a gorgeous, 18th-century house, full of antiques and atmosphere in the Roteiros do Charme group. Rooms have 4-poster beds and each is decorated differently. The public areas include a spacious, art-filled foyer, a pool and sauna area surrounded by a little garden and an excellent, delightfully romantic restaurant.

AL-B Cama e Café, T021-2225 4366, www.camaecafe.com.br. The Rio-based homestay company (see p 414) has 5 *casas* in Olinda on its books: **Alma, Dani, Ede, Janete** and **Juvino**.

B Pousada dos Quatro Cantos, R Prudente de Morais 441, T3429 0220, www.pousada4cantos.com.br. A large converted town house with a little walled garden and terraces, bright rooms and suites decorated with Pernambuco arts and crafts, furnished mostly with antiques, welcoming and full of character.

B Pousada São Francisco, R do Sol 127, T3429 2109, www.pousadasaofrancisco.com.br. Well-kept and airy a/c rooms with terraces and pokey bathrooms. Pool and bar in pleasant gardens visited by hummingbirds in the early morning, restaurant, parking. Outside the historic centre but within walking distance.

B-C Pousada Peter, R do Amparo 215, T/F3439 2171, www.pousadapeter.com.br. Wide range of prices per season. Rather small a/c rooms in converted town house, spacious lobby decorated with Pernambuco arts and crafts and colourful art work by the cantankerous German owner. Breakfast is served on the terrace overlooking distant Recife and the modest pool.

C-E Pousada d'Olinda, P João Alfredo 178, T/F3494 2559, www.pousadadolinda.com.br. Basic but well-kept dorms and doubles around a pool, garden, communal breakfast area, good breakfast, lunchtime restaurant, 10% off for owners of Footprint Handbooks in low season, English, French, German, Arabic and Spanish spoken.

C-E Pousada d'Olinda no Varadouro, R 15 de Novembro 98, T3439 1163, www.pousadadolinda varadouro.com.br. Little suites in a converted town house and cheaper communal rooms, best are on upper floors, spacious open air dining area/restaurant and a small pool.

D São Pedro, R 27 Janeiro 95, T3439 9546, www.pousadapedro.com. Quiet, walled garden, small shaded pool, delightful breakfast area and lobby decorated with art and antiques. Rustic rooms are tiny but tasteful, a/c, best are on the upper floor.

D-E Albergue do Fortim, R do Sol 151, T3429 1939, www.pousadadofortim.com.br. Simple but clean rooms with a/c at the cheapest rates in Olinda. Some are big enough for 4. Breakfast US$2 extra.

E Olinda Hostel, R do Sol 233, T3429 1592, www.alberguedeolinda.com.br. HI hostel, 8-bed rooms with fan and shared bath, tropical garden, TV room, hammocks, small pool.

Outside the historic centre

Hotels on R do Sol and in Bairro Novo are below the old city and on the roads heading north.

C Cinco Sóis, Av Ministro Marcos Freire 633, Bairro Novo, T/F3429 1347. A/c, fridge, hot water, parking.

D Pousada Alquimia, R Prudente de Morais 292, T3429 1457. Simple, lovely house, good breakfast, caring owners whose son is a painter with a workshop at the front.

D Cheiro do Mar, Av Ministro Marcos Freire 95, T3429 0101. Very good small hostel with some doubles (room No 1 is noisy), cooking facilities, ask driver of 'Rio Doce/Piedade' or 'Bairra de Jangada/ Casa Caiada' bus (see Transport, below) to drop you at Albergue de Juventude on the sea front.

Camping Olinda Camping, R Bom Sucesso 262, Amparo, T3429 1365. US$5 pp, space for 30 tents, 5 trailers, small huts for rent, quiet, well-shaded, on bus route, recommended.

Caruaru *p576*

Cheap hospedarias are around the central Praça Getúlio Vargas. Lots of cheap lunch restaurants.

A Grande Hotel São Vicente de Paulo, Av Rio Branco 365, T3721 5011, F3721 5290. Good, a/c, central, laundry, garage, bar, restaurant, pool, TV.

C Centenário, 7 de Setembro 84, T3722 4011, F3721 1033. Also suites, good breakfast, pool, central, can be noisy, otherwise recommended.

C Central, R Vigário Freire 71, T3721 5880. Suites or rooms, all with a/c, TV, good breakfast, in the centre. Recommended.

Fernando de Noronha *p576*

LL Pousada Maravilha, T3619 1290. One of the finest beach hotels in South America. Luxurious bungalows (and smaller annex rooms on a hill overlooking the Bahia do Sueste. Understated good taste in the public areas which overlook an infinity pool and the Atlantic. Excellent restaurant, gym, sauna, massage and help with tours and services on the island. Transfer from Rio, São Paulo or Recife can be arranged.

LL Pousada do Vale, T3619 1293, www.pousadadovale.com. Well-run pousada, comfortable rooms, best are the duplex wooden bungalows. 300 m from Vila dos Remedios town centre.

LL Zé Maria, R Eunice Cordeiro 1, T3619 1258, www.pousadazemaria.com.br. Spacious bungalows with generous beds, verandas with hammocks and views to the Morro do Pico, small deep-blue half-moon pool.

L-AL Solar dos Ventos, T3619 1347, www.pousada solardosventos.com.br. Next to the Maravilha, shares the same spectacular view, but not in the sameleague, well-appointed bungalows, no pool.

A Pousada dos Corais, Residencial Floresta Nova, Quadra "D" Casa 07, T3619 1147, www.pousadacorais.com.br. 8 small, plain a/c rooms around a little pool. Good breakfast.

C Verde Livre, Vila Remédios, T3619 1312. With a/c, TV, fridge and breakfast, simple but good.

Eating

Olinda *p574, map p574*

Several lanchonetes and fast-food options along the seafront. The traditional Olinda drinks, **Pau do Índio** (contains 32 herbs) and **Retetel**, are both made on the R do Amparo. Also try tapioca, a local dish made of manioc with coconut or cheese.

TTT **Goya**, R do Amparo, 157. Regional food, particularly seafood, beautifully presented.

TTT **Oficina do Sabor**, R do Amparo, 355, T3429 3331, www.oficinadosabor.com. Consistently wins awards, pleasant terrace overlooking city, food served in hollowed-out pumpkins and lots of vegetarian options.

TT **Maison do Bomfim**, R do Bonfim, 115. Serene, fan-cooled, rustic-style restaurant, French cuisine, as well as Brazilian and Italian.

TT **Samburá**, Av Min Marcos Freire 1551. With terrace, try caldeirada and pitu (crayfish), lobster in coconut sauce or daily fish dishes, very good.

T **Mourisco**, Praça João Alfredo 7. Excellent, good value food by weight in lovely, part-covered, garden, delicious deserts. Warmly recommended.

Fernando de Noronha *p576*

TTT **Ecologiku's**, Estr Velha do Sueste, T3619 1807. Opened sided restaurant with a little garden, great Bahian food, delicious *moqueca*. Good *caipirinhas*.

TTT **Porto Marlin**, Porto de Santo Antônio, T3619 1452. Good Japanese food à la carte with an all you can eat buffet on Thu and Sat from 1800.

T **Jacaré**, Praça Pres Eurico Dutra (next to the Banco Real), T3619 1947. Best value on the island with lunchtime seafood and general Brazilian buffet.

T **Açai e Raizes**, BR363, Floresta Velha, T3619 0058. Roadside sandwich bar with good snacks, puddings and delicious cream of *cupuaçu* and *açai*.

T **Cia da Lua**, Bosque dos Flamboyantes, T3619 1631. Decent coffee, snacks, sandwiches, internet access and car and buggy rental.

Bars and clubs

Olinda *p574, map p574*

Every Fri night bands of wandering musicians walk the streets serenading passers-by. Each Sun from 1 Jan to Carnival there is a mini Carnival in the streets.

Beginning at dusk, but best after 2100, the Alto da Sé becomes the scene of a street fair, with arts, crafts, makeshift bars and barbecue stands, and impromptu traditional music; even more animated at Carnival. Plenty of funky bars on R do Sol.

Cantinho da Sé, Ladeira da Sé 305. Lively, good view of Recife, food served.

Farandola, R Dom Pedro Roeser 190, behind Carmo church. Mellow bar with festival theme and 'big-top' style roof. Warmly recommended.

Marola, Trav. Dantas Barreto 66. Funky wooden barraca on rocky shoreline specializing in seafood, great caiprifrutas (frozen fruit drink with vodka – try the cashew), can get crowded. Recommended.

Pernambucanamente, Av Min Marcos Freire 734, Bairro Novo. Live, local music every night.

Fernando de Noronha *p576*
Vila dos Remédios town has several bars; including a pizzeria with lively weekend forró from 2200 on weekends, and a bar with live reggae nightly in high season.

Festivals and events

Olinda *p574, map p574*
At Olinda's **carnival** thousands of people dance through the narrow streets of the old city to the sound of the frevo, the brash energetic music which normally accompanies a lively dance performed with umbrellas. The local people decorate them with streamers and straw dolls, and form themselves into costumed groups to parade down the R do Amparo; **Pitombeira** and **Elefantes** are the best known of these groups. **Foundation Day** is celebrated with 3 days of music and dancing, **12-15 Mar**, night time only.

Caruaru *p576*
17 Dec-2 Jan, **Festas Natalinas**; Semana Santa, Holy Week, with lots of folklore and handicraft events; **18-22 May**, city's anniversary. **13 Jun Santo Antônio** and **24 Jun São João**, the latter a huge forró festival, are part of Caruaru's Festas Juninas. **Sep**, **Micaru**, a street carnival; also in **Sep**, **Vaquejada** (a Brazilian cross between rodeo and bull fighting), biggest in the northeast.

Activities and tours

Olinda *p574, map p574*
Viagens Sob O Sol, Prudente de Moraes 424, T3429 3303, transport offered to all parts, any type of trip arranged, also car hire.
Victor Turismo, Av Santos Domont 20, Loja 06, T3494 1467. Day and night trips to Recife.

Fernando de Noronha *p576*
Boat trips and jeep tours are available; it is also possible to hire a beach buggy.
Locadora Ilha do Sol, T3619 1132, or 9985 4051, for buggy rental and guided tours of the island. You can hitch everywhere as everyone stops. There are good hiking, horse riding and mountain biking possibilities, but you must either go with a guide or ranger in many parts.
Diving Diving is organized by **Atlantis Divers**, T0xx81-3619 1371, **Águas Claras**, T3619 1225, in the hotel grounds, and **Noronha Divers**, T3619 1112. Diving costs between US$65-100 and equipment rental from US$65. This is the diving mecca for Brazilian divers with a great variety of sites to explore and fish to see.
Surfing Iaponã, T3619 1947, or 9635 7176, iapadosurf@hotmail.com. Classes from one of the island's best; US$25 per class including equipment.

Transport

Olinda *p574, map p574*
Bus From **Recife**: take any bus marked 'Rio Doce', No 981 which has a circular route around the city and beaches, or No 33 from Av Nossa Senhora do Carmo, US$1 or 'Jardim Atlântico' from the central post office at Siqueira Campos; from Boa Viagem, take bus marked 'Piedade/Rio Doce' or 'Bairra de Jangada/Casa Caiada' (US$1, 30 mins). Change to either of these buses from the airport to Olinda: take 'Aeroporto' bus to Av Domingos Ferreira, Boa Viagem, and ask to be let off; and from the Recife Rodoviária: take the metrô to Central station and then change. In all cases, alight in Praça do Carmo. Taxi drivers between Olinda and Recife try to put meters onto rate 2 at the Convention Centre (between the 2 cities), but should change it back to 1 when queried (taxi to Recife US$12, US$18 to Boa Viagem at night).

Caruaru *p576*
Bus The rodoviária is 4 km from the town; buses from Recife stop in the centre. Bus from centre, at the same place as Recife bus stop, to rodoviária, US$0.65. Many buses from TIP in **Recife**, 2 hrs, US$6.75.

Fernando de Noronha *p576*
Air Daily flights from **Recife** with **Trip**, 1 hr 20 mins, US$400 return. From Natal **Trip**, 1 hr, US$300 return.

Directory

Olinda *p574, map p574*
Banks There are no facilities to change TCs, or ATMs in the old city. **Banco do Brasil**, R Getúlio Vargas 1470. **Bradesco**, R Getúlio Vargas 729, Visa ATM. **Bandepe** on the same Av has MasterCard ATM. **Post offices** Praça do Carmo, open 0900-1700. **Telephones** International calls can be made at **Telemar** office on Praça do Carmo, Mon-Sat 0900-1800.

South of Recife

Two small states, Alagoas and Sergipe, are wedged between Pernambuco and Bahia. For no good reason, most people pass through, but there are some good examples of colonial architecture and, like the entire northeast coast, some fine beaches.

South to Alagoas

There are many interesting stopping points along the coast between Recife and Maceió. The main highway, BR-101, heads a little inland from the coast, crossing the state border near Palmares. It then continues to Maceió. On the coast the Pernambuco-Alagoas border is by São José da Coroa Grande, after which a coastal road, unpaved in parts, runs to Barra do Camaragibe. Just after the mouth of the Rio Camaragibe is Praia do Morro, Pedra do Cebola and Carro Quebrado, where beach buggies can be hired for trips up the coast. Further south is **Barra de Santo Antônio**, a busy fishing village, with a palm fringed beach on a narrow peninsula, a canoe-ride away. The beaches nearby are beautiful: to the south, near the village of Santa Luzia, are Tabuba and Sonho Verde. Two unspoilt fishing villages, which have good places to stay and are pretty much close to paradise are **Japaratinga** and **Maragogi**, www.maragogionline.com.br; try **Pousada Mariluz** (**A**), T0xx82-3296 1511, www.pousada mariluz.com.br. The natural pools at the reef of As Galés are beautiful; trips can be arranged at the Frutos do Mar restaurant.

Maceió and around → *Phone code: 0xx82. Post code: 57000. Colour map 5, C6.*

The capital of Alagoas state (*Population: 797,759*) is mainly a sugar port, but for tourism it's friendly, safe and good value. Two of its old buildings, the **Palácio do Governo**, which also houses the **Fundação Pierre Chalita** (Alagoan painting and religious art) and the church of **Bom Jesus dos Mártires** (1870, covered in tiles), are particularly interesting. Both are on the Praça dos Martírios (or Floriano Peixoto). The **cathedral**, Nossa Senhora dos Prazeres (1840), is on Praça Dom Pedro II. The helpful **tourist office** is at Setur ⓘ *R Boa Vista 453, Centro, T3315 5700* (also at airport and rodoviária). The municipal tourist authority is **Seturma** ⓘ *R Sá e Albuquerque 310, T3336 4409*; information post on Pajuçara beach, by Hotel Solara. Also visit www.turismomaceio.com.br.

Lagoa do Mundaú, a lagoon whose entrance is 2 km south at **Pontal da Barra**, limits the city to the south and west: excellent shrimp and fish are sold at its small restaurants and handicraft stalls; a nice place for a drink at sundown. Boats make excursions in the lagoon's channels. Beyond the city's main dock the beachfront districts begin; within the city, the beaches are smarter the further from the centre you go. The first, going north, is **Pajuçara** where there is a nightly craft market. At weekends there are wandering musicians and entertainers. Further out, **Jatiúca**, **Cruz das Almas** and **Jacarecica** (9 km from centre) are all good for surfing. The beaches, some of the finest and most popular in Brazil, have a protecting coral reef a kilometre or so out. Bathing is much better three days before and after full or new moon, because tides are higher and the water is more spectacular. Jangadas take passengers to a natural swimming pool 2 km off Pajuçara beach (**Piscina Natural de Pajuçara**), at low tide you can stand on the sand and rock reef (beware of sunburn). You must check the tides, there is no point going at high tide. Jangadas cost US$5 per person per day (or about US$20 to have a jangada to yourself). On Sunday or local holidays in the high season it is overcrowded (at weekends lots of jangadas anchor at the reef selling food and drink).

By bus (22 km south), past Praia do Francês, the attractive colonial town and former capital of Alagoas, **Marechal Deodoro**, overlooks the Lagoa Manguaba. The 17th-century **Convento de São Francisco**, Praça João XXIII, has a fine church (Santa Maria Magdalena) with a superb baroque wooden altarpiece, badly damaged by termites. You can climb the church's tower for views. Adjoining it is the **Museu de Arte Sacra** ⓘ *Mon-Fri 0900-1300, US$0.40, guided tours available, payment at your discretion*. Also open to visitors is the **Igreja Matriz de Nossa Senhora da Conceição** (1783). The town is the birthplace of Marechal Deodoro da Fonseca, founder of the Republic; the modest **house** ⓘ *Mon-Sat 0800-1700, Sun 0800-1200, free*, where he was born is on the Rua Marechal Deodoro, close to the waterfront. On a day's excursion, it is easy to visit the town, then spend some time at beautiful **Praia do Francês**. The northern half of the beach is protected by a reef, the southern half is open to the surf. Along the beach there are many barracas and bars selling drinks and seafood; also several pousadas.

Penedo → *Phone code: 0xx82. Post code: 57200. Colour map 5, C6. Population: 56,993.*
This charming town, some 35 km from the mouth of the Rio São Francisco, with a nice waterfront park, Praça 12 de Abril, was originally the site of the Dutch Fort Maurits (built 1637, razed to the ground by the Portuguese). The colonial town stands on a promontory above the river. Among the colonial architecture, modern buildings on Av Floriano Peixoto do not sit easily. On the Praça Barão de Penedo is the neoclassical **Igreja Matriz** (closed to visitors) and the 18th-century **Casa da Aposentadoria** (1782). East and a little below this square is the Praça Rui Barbosa, on which are the **Convento de São Francisco** (1783 and later) and the church of **Santa Maria dos Anjos** (1660). As you enter, the altar on the right depicts God's eyes on the world, surrounded by the three races, one Indian, two negroes and the whites at the bottom. The church has fine trompe-l'oeil ceilings (1784). The convent is still in use. Guided tours are free. The church of **Rosário dos Pretos** (1775-1816), on Praça Marechal Deodoro, is open to visitors. **Nossa Senhora da Corrente** (1764), on Praça 12 de Abril, and **São Gonçalo Garcia** (1758-1770) ⓘ *Av Floriano Peixoto, Mon-Fri 0800-1200, 1400-1700*. Also on Avenida Floriano Peixoto is the pink **Teatro 7 de Setembro** (No 81) of 1884. The **Casa de Penedo** ⓘ *R João Pessoa 126 (signs point the way up the hill from F Peixoto), Tue-Sun 0800-1800*, displays photographs and books on, or by, local figures. **Tourist information**: in the Casa da Aposentadoria.

An interesting crossing into Sergipe can be made by frequent ferry (car and foot passengers) from Penedo to **Neópolis**.

Aracaju → *Phone code: 0xx79. Post code: 49000. Colour map 5, C5. Population: 461,534.*
Capital of Sergipe founded 1855, it stands on the south bank of the Rio Sergipe, about 10 km from its mouth, 327 km north of Salvador. In the centre is a group of linked, beautiful parks: **Praça Olímpio Campos**, in which stands the cathedral, **Praça Almirante Barroso**, with the Palácio do Governo, and **Praças Fausto Cardoso** and **Camerino**. Across Av Rio Branco from these two is the river. There is a handicraft centre, the **Centro do Turismo** ⓘ *in the restored Escola Normal, on Praça Olímpio Campos, Rua 24 Horas, 0900-1300, 1400-1900*; the stalls are arranged by type (wood, leather, etc). The city's beaches are at **Atalaia**, 16-km by road, and the 30-km long **Nova Atalaia**, on Ilha de Santa Luzia across the river. It is easily reached by boat from the Hidroviária (ferry station), which is across Avenida Rio Branco from Praça Gen Valadão. For tourist information, try **Turismo Sergipe**, Travessa Baltazar Góes 86, Edificio Estado, T3179 1937, www.setur.se.gov.br.

São Cristóvão is the old state capital, 17 km southwest of Aracaju on the road to Salvador. It was founded in 1590 by Cristóvão de Barros. It is the fourth oldest town in Brazil. Built on top of a hill, its colonial centre is unspoiled: the **Museu de Arte Sacra e Histórico de Sergipe** contains religious and other objects from the 17th to the 19th centuries; it is in the **Convento de São Francisco** ⓘ *Tue-Fri 1000-1700, Sat-Sun 1300-1700*. Also worth visiting (and keeping the same hours) is the **Museu de Sergipe** in the former **Palácio do Governo** both are on Praça de São Francisco. Also on this square are the churches of **Misericórdia** (1627) and the **Orfanato Imaculada Conceição** (1646, permission to visit required from the Sisters), and the **Convento de São Francisco**. On Praça Senhor dos Passos are the churches **Senhor dos Passos** and **Terceira Ordem do Carmo** (both 1739), while on the Praça Getúlio Vargas (formerly Praça Matriz) is the 17th-century **Igreja Matriz Nossa Senhora da Vitória** ⓘ *Tue-Fri 1000-1700, Sat-Sun 1500-1700*.

Estância ➔ *Colour map 5, C5*
On the BR-101, almost midway between Aracaju and the Sergipe-Bahia border, and 247 km north of Salvador, is Estância, one of the oldest towns in Brazil. Its colonial buildings are decorated with Portuguese tiles. The month-long festival of **São João** in June is a major event. There are pleasant hotels, but most buses stop at the Rodoviária, which is on the main road (four hours from Salvador).

South of Recife listings

For Sleeping and Eating price codes and other relevant information, see Essentials, pages 38-40. See Telephone, page 397, for important phone changes.

Sleeping

Maceió *p580*
It can be hard to find a room during the Dec-Mar holiday season, when prices go up. There are many hotels on Praia Pajuçara, mostly along Av Dr Antônio Gouveia and R Jangadeiros Alagoanos.
L Enseada, Av A Gouveia 171, T3214 3700, www.hotelenseada.com.br. 1980s business hotel on the waterfront, pool restaurant. Recommended.
AL Sete Coqueiros, Av A Gouveia 1335, T2126 7777, www.setecoqueiros.com.br. 3-star, a/c, TV, phone, good restaurant, pool.
A Velamar, Av A Gouveia 1359, T3327 5488, atendimento@hotelvelamar.com.br. A/c, TV, fridge, safes in rooms.
B Buongiorno, R Jangadeiros Alagoanos 1437, T3327 4447, vapini@ig.com.br. A/c, fridge, English-speaking owner, helpful.
B Casa Grande da Praia, R Jangadeiros Alagoanos 1528, T3231 3332, hcgpraia@matrix.com.br. A/c and TV, cheaper without. Recommended.
B Costa Verde, R Jangadeiros Alagoanos 429, T3231 4745. Bath, fan, good family atmosphere, English, German spoken.
B-D Pousada Cavalo Marinho, R da Praia 55, Riacho Doce (15 km from the centre), facing the sea, T3355 1247, www.pousadacavalomarinho.com. Use of bicycle, canoes and body boards including, hot showers, German and English spoken, tropical breakfasts, Swiss owner. Very highly recommended (nearby is **Lua Cheia**, good food and live music at night).
C Sol de Verão, R Eng Mário do Gusmão 153, Ponta Verde beach, T/F3231 6657. Small rooms without baths and some larger and pricier a/c options with en suites.
D Alagamar, R Prefeito Abdon Arroxelas 327, T3231 2246, alag@superig.com.br. Excellent hostel, good location and value. IH affiliated, requires reservations Dec-Feb, Jul and Aug.
Camping **Camping Pajuçara**, at Largo da Vitória 211, T3231 7561, clean, safe, food for sale.

Penedo *p581*
A São Francisco, Av Floriano Peixoto 237, T3551 2273, www.hotelsaofrancisco.tur.br. Standard rooms have no a/c, TV, fridge. Recommended except for poor restaurant.
B Pousada Colonial, Praça 12 de Abril 21, T3551 2355, F3551 3737. Luxo and suite have phone, TV and fridge, suites have a/c, spacious, good cheap restaurant, front rooms with view of the river.
C Pousada Estilo, Praça Jacome Calheiros 79, T3551 2465. Cheaper without TV, quiet, river views, very nice.
C Turista, R Siqueira Campos 143, T3551 2237. With bath, fan, hot water. Recommended.

Aracaju *p581*
A range of hotels in the centre, including:
A Grande, R Itabaianinha 371, T3211 1383, F3211 1388. A/c, TV, fridge, central, **Quartier Latin** restaurant.
B Brasília, R Laranjeiras 580, T3214 2964, F3214 1023. Good value, good breakfasts. Recommended.

Eating

Maceió *p580*
Local specialities include oysters, *pitu*, a crayfish (now becoming scarce), and *sururu*, a kind of cockle. Local ice cream, Shups, recommended. Many good bars and restaurants in Pajuçara, eg on Av Antônio Gouveia. The beaches for 5 km from the beginning of Pajuçara to Cruz das Almas in the north are lined with barracas (thatched bars), providing music, snacks and meals until 2400 (later at weekends). Vendors

on the beach sell beer and food during the day: clean and safe. There are many other bars and barracas at Ponto da Barra, on the lagoon side of the city. Most hotels offer free transport to restaurants; ask at reception.

TTT Spettus, Av Silvio Carlos Viana 1911, Ponta Verde. Excellent churrascaria, fine service and worth the expense.

TT Divina Gula, R Eng Paulo Brandão Nogueira 85, Jatiúca. Minas specialities, very good, huge helpings, also *cachaçaria*.

TT New Hakata, R Eng Paulo Brandão Nogueira 95, Jatiúca. Good Japanese with *rodizios* on Tue.

T Nativa, Osvaldo Sarmento 56. Vegetarian, good views.

T O Natural, R Libertadora Alagoana (R da Praia) 112. Vegetarian.

Aracaju *p581*

T Gonzaga, Rua Santo Amaro 181. Lunch only, good value, popular, excellent traditional dishes.

Festivals and events

Maceió *p580*

27 Aug: **Nossa Senhora dos Prazeres; 16 Sep**: **Freedom of Alagoas; 8 Dec**: **Nossa Senhora da Conceição; 15 Dec**: **Maceiofest**, 'a great street party with trios elêctricos'; **Christmas Eve; New Year's Eve**, half-day.

Transport

Maceió *p580*

Air 20 km from centre, taxi about US$33. Buses to airport from near Hotel Beiriz, R João Pessoa 290 or in front of the Ferroviária, signed 'Rio Largo'; alight at Tabuleiro dos Martins, then 7-8 mins' walk to the airport, bus fare US$1.15.

Bus Frequent local buses, confusingly marked, serve all parts of the city. Bus stops are not marked: it is best to ask where people look as if they are waiting. The 'Ponte Verde/Jacintinho' bus runs via Pajuçara from the centre to the rodoviária, also take 'Circular' bus (25 mins Pajuçara to rodoviária); Taxis from town go to all the northern beaches, but buses run as far as Ipioca (23 km). The Jangadeiras bus marked 'Jacarecica- Center, via Praias' runs past all the beaches as far as Jacarecica. From there you can change to 'Riacho Doce-Trapiche', 'Ipioca' or 'Mirante' buses for Riacho Doce and Ipioca. To return take any of these options, or take a bus marked 'Shopping Center' and change there for 'Jardim Vaticana' bus, which goes through Pajuçara. Buses and kombis to Marechal Deodoro, Praia do Francês and Barra de São Miguel leave from R Zacarias Azevedo, near the ferroviária: bus US$1.15, kombi US$1.45 to Marechal Deodoro, 30 mins, calling at Praia do Francês in each direction. Last bus back from Praia do Francês to Maceió at 1800.

The rodoviária is 5 km from centre, on a hill with good views and cool breezes. Taxi, US$13.25 to Pajuçara. Bus to **Recife**, 10 a day, 3½ hrs express (more scenic coastal route, 5 hrs) US$14. **Maceió-Aracaju**, 5 hrs, US$14 with **Bonfim**. To **Salvador**, 10 hrs, 4 a day, US$44.

Penedo *p581*

Bus 451 km from **Salvador** (US$25, 6 hrs, daily bus 0600, book in advance), at same time for **Aracaju** (US$14). Buses south are more frequent from **Neópolis**, 6 a day (0630-1800) to Aracaju, 2 hrs, US$8. 115 km from **Maceió**, 5 buses a day in either direction, US$12, 3-4 hrs. **Rodoviária**: Av Duque de Caxias, behind Bompreço supermarket.

Aracaju *p581*

Bus Interstate rodoviária is 4 km from centre, linked by local buses from adjacent terminal (buy a ticket before going on the platform). To **Salvador**, 6-7 hrs, 11 a day with **Bonfim**, US$25.

João Pessoa → *Phone code: 0xx83. Post code: 58000. Colour map 5, B6. Pop: 597,934.*

It is a bus ride of two hours through sugar plantations over a good road from Recife (126 km) to João Pessoa, capital of the State of Paraíba on the Rio Paraíba. It's a pleasant, historical town with a rich cultural heritage. The beaches, beside the turquoise waters of the Atlantic, are wonderful. At Ponta do Seixas is the most easterly point in Brazil; near here the Trans- amazônica highway begins its immense, if not controversial, route west into the heart of the country. The city tourist office is **SETUR**, ⓘ *Praça Pedro Américo 70, T3218 9852, and Parque Solon de Lucena 216, Centro, T3218-9852, www.joaopessoa.pb.gov.br/secretarias/setur/* and there is a **Centro Turístico** at ⓘ *Av Almte Tamandaré 100, Tambaú, T3214-8270*. The **Secretaria de Turismo** (Setde) is at Jaguaribe ⓘ *Av João da Mata s/n, Bloco 2, 1st floor, T3218 4400, www.setde.pb.gov.br.*

Sights

João Pessoa is a capital that retains a small town atmosphere. In the **Centro Histórico** is the São Francisco Cultural Centre (Praça São Francisco 221), one of the most important baroque structures in Brazil, with the beautiful church of **São Francisco** which houses the **Museu Sacro e de Arte Popular** ⓘ *Tue-Sun 0800-1200, 1400-1700*. Other tourist points include the **Casa da Pólvora**, now the **Museu Fotográfico Walfredo Rodríguez** (Ladeira de São Francisco) ⓘ *Tue-Sun 0800-1200, 1400-1700*. Also the **Teatro Santa Roza** (1886) ⓘ *Praça Pedro Américo, Varadouro, 1400-1700*. **Casa do Artesão** ⓘ *Praça da Independência 56, Centro, Tue-Fri 0900-1700, Sat-Sun 1000-1800*, where popular artists exhibit their work, with more than a thousand items on display, has been nominated as the best popular museum in Brazil.

João Pessoa's parks include the 17-ha **Parque Arruda Câmara**, north of the centre, and **Parque Solon de Lucena** or **Lagoa**, a lake surrounded by impressive palms in the centre of town, the city's main avenues and bus lines go around it.

The beachfront stretches for some 30 km from Ponta do Seixas (south) to the port of **Cabedelo** (north), on a peninsula between the Rio Paraíba and the Atlantic Ocean. This is Km 0 of the Transamazônica highway. The ocean is turquoise green and there is a backdrop of lush coastal vegetation. About 7 km from the city centre, following Avenida Presidente Epitáceo Pessoa is the beach of **Tambaú** (take bus No 510 'Tambaú' from outside the rodoviária or the city centre, alight at Hotel Tropical Tambaú), which has many hotels and restaurants. Regional crafts, including lace-work, embroidery and ceramics are available at Mercado de Artesanato, Centro de Turismo, Almte Tamandaré 100. The town's main attractions are its beaches, where most tourists stay. About 14 km south of the centre is the Cabo Branco lighthouse at Ponta do Seixas, the most easterly point of continental Brazil and South America; there is a panoramic view from the cliff top. **Cabo Branco** is much better for swimming than **Tambaú**. Take bus 507 'Cabo Branco' from outside the rodoviária to the end of the line; hike up to the lighthouse.

The best known beach of the state is **Tambaba**, the only official nudist beach of the Northeast, 49 km south of João Pessoa in a lovely setting. Two coves make up this famous beach: in the first bathing-suits are optional, while the second one is only for nudists. Strict rules of conduct are enforced. Between Jacumã (many hotels, restaurants) and Tambaba are several nice beaches such as **Tabatinga** which has summer homes on the cliffs and **Coqueirinho**, surrounded by coconut palms, good for bathing, surfing and exploring caves.

João Pessoa listings

For Sleeping and Eating price codes and other relevant information, see Essentials, pages 38-40. See Telephone, page 397, for important phone changes.

Sleeping

João Pessoa *p584*

All those listed are at Tambaú, unless indicated otherwise:

L Tropical Tambaú, Av Alm Tamandaré 229, T3218 1919, www.tropicalhotel.com.br. An enormous round building on the seafront which looks like a military bunker and has motel-style rooms around its perimeter. Comfortable and with good service. Recommended.

L-AL Caiçara, Av Olinda 235, T/F2106 1000, www.hotelcaicara.com.br. A slick, business orientated place (Best Western) with a pleasant restaurant attached.

AL Xênius, Av Cabo Branco 1262, T3226 3535, www.xeniushotel.com.br. Popular standard 4-star with a pool, good restaurant and well kept but standard a/c rooms (low-season reductions).

A Royal Praia, Coração de Jesus, T2106 3000, www.royalhotel.com.br. Comfortable a/c rooms with fridges around a pool.

C-D Solar Filipéia, R Isidro Gomes 44, behind Centro de Turismo, T3247 3744, www.solarfilipeia.com.br. Very smart hotel with large, bright rooms with bathrooms in tile and black marble and excellent service. A real bargain.

C-D Teiú Hotel Pousada, R Carlos Alverga 36, T3247 5475. Centrally located and 1 block from the beach. Intimate, with balconies and sea view. Recommended.

C-D Villa Mare Apartment Hotel, Av Négo 707, T3226 2142, www.pbnet.com.br/openline/george. Comfortable apartments for 2 or 3 people with full amenities per night or from US$400-500 per month. Helpful staff. Recommended.

D Pousada Mar Azul, Av João Maurício 315, T3226 2660. Very clean large rooms, the best are on the upper level, right on the oceanfront road. Some have a/c and private bathrooms, others have fans. Well kept, safe and a real bargain.

D-E Hostel Manaíra, R Major Ciraulo 380, Manaíra, T3247 1962, www.manairahostel.br2.net. Friendly, brand new hostel close to the beach, with a pool, internet, barbecue, cable TV and breakfast. A real bargain.

Eating

João Pessoa *p584*

There are few options in the centre, other than the stalls in Parque Solon de Lucena next to the lake, beside which are some simple restaurants. Every evening on the beachfront, stalls are set up selling all kinds of snacks and barbecued meats. At Cabo Branco there are many straw huts on the beach serving cheap eats and seafood.

TTT Adega do Alfredo, Coração de Jesus. Very popular traditional Portuguese restaurant in the heart of the club and bar area.

TTT Gulliver, Av Olinda 590, Tambaú. Fashionable French/Brazilian restaurant frequented by João Pessoa's upper middle classes.

TT Mangaí, Av General Édson Ramalho 696, Manaíra. This is one of the best restaurants in the northeast to sample the region's cooking, with almost 100 different hot dishes to choose from, sitting in copper tureens over a traditional wood-fired stove some 20 m long.

TT Cheiro Verde, R Carlos Alverga 43. Self service, well established, regional food.

TT Sapore d'Italia, Av Cabo Branco 1584, Standard Italian fare including pizza.

TT Toca do Caju, Av N S dos Navegantes 750. Self service, price by kilo, good value. international food and barbecue.

Bars and clubs

João Pessoa *p584*

There are many open bars on and across from the beach in Tambaú and Cabo Branco. The area known as Feirinha de Tambaú, on Av Tamandaré by the *Tambaú Hotel* and nearby streets, is very lively, with R Coração do Jesus being the centre. There are numerous little bars and *forró* places here.

Festivals and events

João Pessoa *p584*

Pre-carnival celebrations are renowned: the bloco Acorde Miramar opens the celebrations the Tue before Carnival and on Wed, known as **Quarta Feira de Fogo**, thousands join the

Muriçocas de Miramar. Celebrations for the patroness of the city, **Nossa Senhora das Neves**, take place for 10 days around **5 Aug**.

Shopping

João Pessoa *p584*

Mercado Central, Centro. Bus 513, 511. Basic, big, dirty, but interesting. All fruit and spices of the region are sold there. **Supermercado Pão de Açúcar**, Av Epitácio Pessoa 1200-1400. Also good value lunches. Minimarket **O Canto do Galeto**, Av Ruy Carneiro 183, next to **fruit market**, serves take-away grilled chicken.

Activities and tours

João Pessoa *p584*

Half-day city tours (US$15), day trips to Tambaba (US$23) and Recife/Olinda (US$42). For nighttime folklore dances, ask at **Tropical Tambaú** for details. Buggy tours go to places where buses do not go. Check prices with **Lula-Lula Turismo** outside Tropical Tambaú. US$100 per car for day trips to Tambaba. English speaking driver **Orlando**, T9984 8010, has car f or sightseeing, very helpful, takes 3.

Cliotur, in Centro de Turismo,Tambaú (see Ins and outs, above). Air tickets, information about international airlines, tours around the city, buggy rides, serious people.

Luck Turismo, Av Tamandaré 229, in **Tropical Tambaú**, T3247 1856, www.luckreceptivo.com.br. A range of tours, some English-speaking guides.

Transport

João Pessoa *p584*

Air Aeroporto Presidente Castro Pinto, Bayeux, 11 km from centre, T3232 1200; national flights. Taxi to centre costs US$22, to Tambaú US$31.

Bus Most city buses stop at the rodoviária and go by the Lagoa (Parque Solon de Lucena). Take No 510 for Tambaú, No 507 for Cabo Branco.

Rodoviária is at R Francisco Londres, Varadouro, 10 mins from the centre, T3221 9611; luggage store; PBTUR information booth is helpful. Taxi to the centre US$3, to Tambaú US$13. To **Recife** with Boa Vista or Bonfim, every 30 mins, US$12, 2 hrs. To **Natal** with **Nordeste**, every 2 hrs, US$17 convencional, 3 hrs. To **Fortaleza** with **Nordeste**, at 2000, 10 hrs, US$45, convencional, US$82 executivo. To **Salvador** with **Progresso**, 3 weekly, US$60, 14 hrs. To **Belém** with **Guanabara**, T3221 7255, daily at 1000, US$135, convencional, 36-39 hrs.

Directory

João Pessoa *p584*

Airline offices GOL, at airport, T0300-115 2121. **TAM**, Av Senador Rui Carneiro 512, T3247 2400. **Banks** MasterCard Cirrus and Amex cashpoints at **Banco 24 Horas**, at gas station, **Posto Select**, Av Nego 196, Tambaú, not on line all the time, and **HSBC**, R Peregrino de Carvalho 162, Centro, also at Av Epitácio Pessoa 1797, 0600-2300, and a cashpoint outside **Mag Shopping**, Manaíra. Câmbios at **Action Câmbio**, Manaíra Shopping, cash and TCs. **Mondeo Tour**, Av Nego 46, near Posto Select, no TCs. **Internet** Many cybercafés in Tambaú: at telephone office in Centro de Turismo, Almte Tamandaré 100, loja 15. **Post offices** Main office is at Praça Pedro Américo, Varadouro; also at Parque Solon de Lucena 375; and by the beach at Av Rui Carneiro 195, inside small gallery, behind the Centro de Turismo. **Telephones** Calling stations at: Centro de Turismo, Tambaú, loja 15, sells international call cards; rodoviária and airport. **Useful numbers** Car accidents T194. **Tourist police**, Delegacia de policia ao turista, Centro de Turismo, Tambaú, T3214 8022, open 0800-1800.

Natal → *Phone code: 084. Colour map 2, B6. Population: 713,000.*

Natal, capital of Rio Grande do Norte, located on a peninsula between the Rio Potengi and the Atlantic Ocean, is one of the most attractive cities of Brazil's northeast coast, as well as a popular destination for those seeking sun and good beaches. The air is said by NASA to be the second purest in the world, after Antarctica. The inventors of the beach-buggy must have had Rio Grande do Norte in mind as the dunes and strand that surround the city are ideal for daredevil stunts and whizzing along the open sands.

Ins and outs

Tourist offices Secretaria de Turismo do Estado (SETUR) ⓘ *R Mossoró 359, Petrópolis, T232 2500, www.setur.rn.gov.br.* Information booths at **Centro de Turismo** ⓘ *T211 6149 (see Shopping, page 592)*, **Avenida Pres Café Filho s/n** ⓘ *Praia dos Artistas daily 0800-2100*, **Central do Cidadão** ⓘ *Praia Shopping, T232 7234 (see Shopping, below, there is also a Policia Federal office here)*, **Cajueiro de Pirangi** ⓘ *Parnamirim, T238 2347 (see Around Natal, below)*, **rodoviária** ⓘ *T232 7310*, and **airport** ⓘ *T643 1043*. For information T0800-841516, or, for the Policia Federal T205 2080, and for the Tourist Police T232 7404 (Delegacia do Turista).

Sights

The oldest part is the **Ribeira** along the renovated riverfront. The **Cidade Alta**, or Centro, is the main centre and Avenida Rio Branco its principal artery. The main square is made up by the adjoining **praças: João Maria, André de Albuquerque, João Tibúrcio** and **7 de Setembro**. At Praça André de Albuquerque is the old cathedral (inaugurated 1599, restored 1996). The small church of **Santo Antônio** ⓘ *R Santo Antônio 683, Cidade Alta, Tue-Fri 0800-1700, Sat 0800-1400*, dates from 1766. It has a blue and white façade, a fine, carved wooden altar and a sacred art museum.

On a hill overlooking Ribeira is the **Centro do Turismo** ⓘ *R Aderbal de Figueiredo 980, off R Gen Gustavo C Farias*, Petrópolis (see Bars and clubs, and Shopping, page 592). A converted prison with a wide variety of handicraft shops, art gallery, antique shop and tourist information booth, it offers good view of the Rio Potengi and the sea. At Praia do Forte, the tip of Natal's peninsula, is the **Forte dos Reis Magos** ⓘ *T221 0342, 0800-1630 daily except Christmas Day, New Year and Carnaval, US$1*. The star-shaped fort was begun in 1598 and is now the city's main historical monument. Its blinding white walls contrast with the blue of sea and sky. You can wander round the interior rooms, mostly empty although the former military prison now houses a lanchonete, and there are guides. The easiest way to get there is by taxi or on a tour; no buses go to the entrance, from where you have to walk along a causeway to the fort. Between it and the city is a military installation.

The **Museu Câmara Cascudo** ⓘ *Av Hermes de Fonseca 1440, Tirol, T211 8404, Tue-Fri 0800-1700, US$1*, has exhibits on archaeological digs, Umbanda rituals and the sugar, leather and petroleum industries. **Museu do Mar** ⓘ *Av Dinarte Mariz (Via Costeira), Praia de Mãe Luiza, T215 4433, Mon-Fri 0800-1130, 1400-1700, free*. It has aquariums with regional sea life and exhibits with preserved specimens. At Mãe Luiza is a lighthouse with beautiful views of Natal and surrounding beaches (take a city bus marked 'Mãe Luiza'). It is only open on Sunday, until 1700; at other times T221 2631.

A large ecological zone, the **Parque das Dunas**, separates the commercial centre from Ponta Negra, 12.5 km away, the beach and nightlife spot where most visitors stay.

Beaches

Natal has excellent beaches, some of which are also the scene of the city's nightlife. East of the centre, from north to south are: **Praia do Forte, do Meio, dos Artistas, de Areia Preta** and **Mãe Luzia**. The first two have reefs offshore, therefore little surf, and are appropriate for windsurfing.

The others are urban beaches and local enquiries regarding pollution are recommended before bathing. Mãe Luzia marks the start of the **Via Costeira**, which runs south along the ocean beneath the towering sand dunes of **Parque das Dunas** (access restricted to protect the 9 km of dunes), joining the city to the neighbourhood and popular beach of Ponta Negra. A cycle path parallels this road and provides great views of the coastline. Lining Mãe Luzia and Barreira d'Água (the beach across from Parque das Dunas) are the city's four and five-star hotels.

Furthest south is vibrant and pretty **Ponta Negra**, justifiably the most popular beach. The seafront, Avenida Erivan França, is a car-free promenade for much of its length; the remainder is the busiest part of town. It has many hotels, from albergues up to three- and four-star, restaurants and bars (see Listings, page 592). The northern end of the beach is good for surfing, while the southern end is calmer and suitable for swimming. At the south end of the beach is **Morro do Careca**, a 120-m high dune with a sand-skiing slope surrounded by vegetation. Although no longer used for sand-skiing, it remains one of the 'postcards' of the city.

Around Natal

The coast south ofthe city is referred to as **Litoral Sul**, to the north as **Litoral Norte**. Dune buggies are the only way to travel here. Tours are available through travel agencies (see page 592).

Pirangi do Norte, 25 km from Natal, has calm waters, is popular for watersports and offshore bathing (500 m out) when natural pools form between the reefs. In the town is the world's largest cashew-nut tree (cajueiro maior do mundo, entry US$0.75); branches springing from a single trunk cover an area of some 8,400 sq m, a whole city block. A guide on site offers a brief explanation and there is a look-out for seeing the tree from above. Outside are handicraft stalls, tourist information and musicians.

Beyond Barreta is the long, pristine beach of **Malembar**, access on foot or by a five-minute boat ride across the mouth of the **Lagoa Guaraíra** from Tibau do Sul at the south end. The ferries to/from Tibau do Sul costs US$7 return; buggy drivers should not add this fee to a day tour. Crossings are determined by the state of the tide (times are critical and you should follow the buggy driver's instructions regarding departure times). Around **Tibau do Sul** the lovely beaches circled by high cliffs, the lagoons, Atlantic forest and the dolphins are some of the attractions that make this one of the most visited stretches of the southern coast (it can get crowded during holiday periods and weekends). South of town there are fine, wide, white-sand beaches, separated by rocky headlands, set against high cliffs and coconut groves.

Ponta Negra

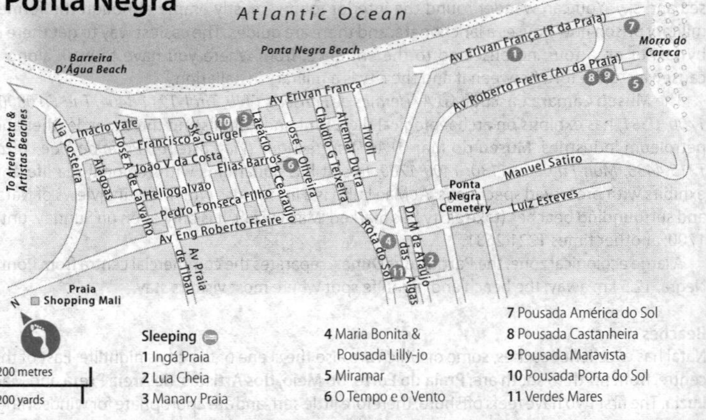

At Praia do Madeiro and neighbouring **Baía dos Golfinhos**, the ocean is calm and clear and dolphins can often be seen (ask locally for the best time and swim from Madeiro beach to see them, rather than take an expensive tour from Pipa). Between Praia do Madeiro and Pipa, on a 70-m high dune, is the **Santuário Ecológico de Pipa** ⓘ *0800-1600, US$4*. This 60-ha park was created in 1986 to conserve the mata atlântica forest; there are 17 trails and lookouts over the cliffs which afford an excellent view of the ocean and dolphins.

Praia da Pipa, 3 km further south (85 km from Natal), is popular with Brazilians and foreigners alike, for its beautiful beaches and charming restaurants. The town is expanding rapidly and its nightlife is the talk of the area.

The coast **north of Natal** is known for its many impressive, light-coloured sand dunes, some reaching a staggering 50 m in height. A 25-minute ferry crossing on the Rio Potengi takes you from Natal to **Redinha**, an urban beach, with ocean and river bathing, and buggies to hire.

The best-known beach in the state, **Genipabu** is 30 km north of the city. Its major attractions are very scenic dunes and the Lagoa de Genipabu, a lake surrounded by cashew trees and dunes where tables are set up on a shoal in the water and drinks served. There are also many bars and restaurants on the sea shore. The dunes are a protected **Parque Ecológico** ⓘ *T9974 8265*, and only authorized buggy drivers are allowed to enter. All buggy tours go through the dunes and make the most of the vehicles' manoeuvrability on the fantastic slopes and hollows: prepare yourself for 'emoção'. At the top of a dune overlooking the lake and coast are lots of colourful umbrellas and handicraft stalls. **Camel rides** ⓘ *dromedários, T225 2053, www.dromedunas.com.br, US$19 for 2 people, 12-14 mins*, start from here. Less exotic are **donkey rides** ⓘ *starting at US$0.65 per person*.

North of Genipabu is **Jacumã**, 49 km from Natal. At Lagoa de Jacumã, a lake surrounded by dunes, you can aerobunda, sit in a sling and fly on a cable into the water. Really refreshing. To get back up to the top of the dune you take the fusca funicular, a 'cable car' made from a trolley on a rail, powered by a wheel-less VW Beetle. All this for only US$1.75. Lovely beaches continue along the state's coastline; as you get further away from Natal the beaches are more distant from the main highways and access is more difficult. At **Maracajaú**, 63 km from Natal, low tide reveals an extensive area of shallow water where you can snorkel (US$15 including equipment), or dive (US$30); contact **Maracajaú Diver** ⓘ *T261 6200, 9983 4264, www.maracajaudiver.com.br*. It's 7 km out to sea and launches (15 minutes) or catamarans (30 minutes) take tourists out to rafts anchored on the reef. You must check tide times before going here.

Natal listings

For Sleeping and Eating price codes and other relevant information, see Essentials, pages 38-40. See Telephone, page 397, for important phone changes.

Sleeping

Natal *p587*

The **Via Costeira** is a strip of enormous, upmarket beachfront hotels, which are very isolated, with no restaurants or shops within easy walking distance. **Ponta Negra** is the ideal place to stay, with its attractive beach and concentration of restaurants. Economical hotels are easier to find in the city proper but there is otherwise not much reason to stay there (no nightlife and a long way from the action). Prices of beach hotels below are for the high season (Dec-Feb and Jul), unless otherwise stated.

In the centre

LL Maine, Av Salgado Filho 1791, Lagoa Nova, T4005 5774, www.hotelmaine.com.br. On the principal avenue leading from the centre to Ponta Negra. Full service in this 4-star hotel, including free internet service, restaurant with panoramic views.

B Natal Center, R Santo Antônio 665, T3221 2355, natalcenterhotel@samnet.com.br. Business hotel in the city centre, rooms with a/c, fridge and TV, restaurant and pool.

C Casa Grande, R Princesa Isabel 529, T211 0555. 'Big house' built around family home, popular with business visitors. A/c, cheaper without bath (also low season discounts), good breakfast, pleasant, excellent value. Recommended.

D Natal, Av Rio Branco 740, Centro, T3222 2792, www.hotelnatal.com. On a busy part of the main street, well-established, a/c, cheaper with fan, popular with local guests.

Near rodoviária

There are several in the area, but the only reason to stay here is if arriving very late or departing very early.

B Pousada Esperança, Av Capt Mor Gouveia 418, T205 1955. With bath, a/c, cheaper with fan or without bath.

Beaches *p587, map p588*

Praia do Meio, Praia dos Artistas and Praia de Areia Preta

The distinction between these first 2 beaches is often blurred. Most hotels here are on the beachfront Av Pres Café Filho, the numbering of which is illogical. Many pousadas open for just 1 season, then close for good.

A Bruma, Av Pres Café Filho 1176, Praia dos Artistas, T/F2202 4303, hotelbruma@zaz.com.br. Slick, intimate, beachfront balconies, also has more expensive suites, pool, terrace. Recommended.

D Pousada do Paxá, Av Pres Café Filho 11, T202 2848. Clean, beachfront, breakfast extra, real bargain, but also has more expensive rooms. Recommended.

Ponta Negra

Here, too, the street numbering is pretty chaotic.

LL-L Manary Praia, R Francisco Gurgel 9067, T/F3204 2900, www.manary.com.br. Price depends on view from room; phone in advance as prices vary greatly according to month. This is a very stylish hotel on a quiet corner, some rooms overlook the pool/terrace and beach, all are very comfortable, 'neocolonial' design using local materials, member of the Roteiro de Charme group, see page 393. Recommended.

AL Hotel e Pousada O Tempo e o Vento, R Elias Barros 66, T/F3219 2526, www.otempoeovento.com.br. **C** in low season, a/c, fridge, safe in room, pool and wet bar, clean, luxo rooms are very comfortable, good breakfast. Recommended.

A Ingá Praia, Av Erivan França 17, T3219 3436, www.ingapraiahotel.com.br. **B** without sea view, **C** in low season (service tax not included). Very comfortable, clean and cosy, rooms have all the expected facilities. Recommended.

A Miramar, Av da Praia 3398, T3219 2131. Price reduced by half in low season. Quite high up with good views, family-run, very clean, internet for guests 0800-1800, restaurant, 2 pools, games room, English spoken.

A-B Pousada Castanheira, Rua da Praia 221, T3236 2918, www.pousadacastanheira.com.br. English/Brazilian owners, **C** in low season, comfortable spacious rooms with TV, fridge and safe, small pool, breakfast room with sea view, room service, parking, very helpful staff. Recommended.

B Maria Bonita 2, Estrela do Mar 2143, T3236 2941, www.mariabonita2.com.br. With a/c, **C** with fan, not as close to the beach as most, but near the Broadway and its nightlife.

B-C Pousada Lilly-jo, Estrela do Mar 2183, T3236 2278, www.pousadalillyjo.com. Nice place, with pool, helpful, owner speaks English, good breakfast.

C Pousada Maravista, R da Praia 223, T3236 4677, www.pousadamaravista.com. One of the cheaper options, next to Pousada Castanheira, high-ceilinged rooms, hot showers, TV, fan, good breakfast, simple, English spoken, Marilyn is very welcoming. Recommended.

C Pousada Porta do Sol, R Francisco Gurgel 9057, T3236 2555, www.pousadaportadosol.com.br. Clean and tidy, good seafront location, TV, fridge, a/c except in rooms with sea breeze, some fans, good mattresses, excellent breakfast, pool, good value, English and French spoken (ask for Patrick or Suerda). Recommended.

D pp **Lua Cheia**, R Dr Manoel Augusto Bezerra de Araújo 500, Ponta Negra, T3236 3696, www.luacheia.com.br. HI hostel in 'castle' with 'medieval' **Taverna Pub** in basement (see Bars and clubs below). Includes breakfast. Highly recommended.

D Pousada América do Sol, R Erivan França 35, T3219 2245, www.pousadaamericadosol.com.br. Price per person in albergue-style rooms with bath, hot water, lockers, cheaper without a/c, popular, simple, use of kitchen, breakfast included. Also has pousada rooms at **B** (half-price in low season), a/c, TV, frigobar, includes breakfast, parking.

E pp **Verdes Mares**, R das Algas 2166, Conj Algamar, Ponta Negra, T236 2872, www.hostelverdesmares.com.br. HI hostel, **C-D** in double room, includes breakfast, discount in low season, quiet, comfortable. Also recommended.

Around Natal: Praia da Pipa *p589*
In Pipa more than 30 pousadas and many private homes offer accommodation. See www.pipa.com.br for some listings.

LL Toca da Coruja, Av Baía dos Golfinhos, T3246 2226, www.tocadacoruja.com.br. Comfortable chalets and rooms (cheaper in low season), with all facilities including safe in room, in gardens with lots of trees, quiet, member of the Roteiros de Charme group, see page 393.

AL Ponta do Madeiro, Rota do Sol, Km 3, Tibaú do Sul, T3246 4220, www.pontado madeiro.com.br. Beautifully set in Mata atlântica with access to Madeiro beach, between Pipa and Tibaú, 3 types of chalet in gardens, pool, restaurant, trips on land and sea.

AL Sombra e Água Fresca, Praia do Amor, Km 1, T3246 2258, www.sombraeaguafresca.com.br. A/c, fridge, pools, restaurant with beautiful view especially at sunset. **A** in low season.

A Pousada da Bárbara, 1st right after church in centre, T3246 2351, pousadadabarbara@ yahoo .com.br. **B** in low season, 20 m from town beach, a/c, TV, hot shower and veranda, pool, very good.

A Pousada Bicho Preguiça, R Praia do Amor 15, T3246 2128, www.pipabicho preguica.com.br. A variety of rooms with cable TV, a/c, frigobar, internet for guests, 24-hr restaurant and bars.

C Pousada Pomar da Pipa, R da Mata, T3246 2256, www.pomardapipa.com. 150 m from praça, quiet, beautiful garden, very helpful, good value.

C-D Vera-My house,T9988 5154, veramyhouse @uol.com.br. With bath, **E** pp in dormitory, use of kitchen, no breakfast. Good value, friendly. Recommended.

Eating

Natal *p587*
Prawns feature heavily on menus here as Natal is the largest exporter in Brazil.

TTT **Raro Sabor**, R Seridó 722, Petrópolis. Exclusive bistro serving international dishes, emphasis on French cuisine. Closed Mon.

TT **Bella Napoli**, Av Hermes da Fonseca 960, Tirol. Good Italian food.

TT **Camarões Express**, Av Sen Salgado Filho 2234, Natal Shopping. Express prawns in 15 styles. Open for lunch only at weekends.

TT **Mangaí**, Av Amintos Barros 3300, Lagoa Nova. Very good regional food (carne do sol, tapioca and many other sertaneja dishes) in rustic atmosphere, open 0600-2200, closed Mon. Recommended.

TT **Marenosso**, in the Centro do Turismo. Specializes in seafood and local dishes like carne do sol, sweets, expresso coffee.

TT **Thin-San**, Av Hermes da Fonseca 890, Tirol. Good Chinese food, popular.

T **China Palace**, Av Afonso Pena 554, Petrópolis. For cheap lunches, a mixture of Chinese and Brazilian dishes, self-service.

T **Habib's**, also in Natal Shopping. A branch of the cheap Middle Eastern food chain.

T **A Macrobiótica**, Princesa Isabel 524, vegetarian, shop, lunch only. Next door is **Neide**, at No 530, for coffee and sweets.

Beaches *p588, map p588*

Ponta Negra

TTT **Sobre Ondas**, Av Erivan França 14. Seafood and international dishes, average food, underwater theme, internet.

TTT **Tereré**, Rota do Sol 2316. All-you-can-eat barbecue, including Argentinian beef, ribs, as well as fish and salad.

TT **Barraca do Caranguejo**, Av Erivan França 1180. Live music nightly from 2100. 12 different types of prawn dish for US$6.75, rodízio style.

TT **Beterraba**, Av Erivan França 108, Santa Fe Mall. Upstairs, overlooking street and sea, specializes in grills and salads, fruit salads and juices.

TT **Camarões**, Av Eng Roberto Freire 2610. Also at Natal Shopping Centre. Touristy, but very good seafood.

TT **Cipó Brasil**, Av Erivan França 3 and Rua Aristides Porpinho Filho 3111 (behind Lua Cheia youth hostel). Jungle theme, 4 levels, sand floors, lantern-lit, dishes and rinks well-presented. Serves pizzas and crêpes (house speciality), good for cocktails, live music nightly after 2100. In the same group is **Casa de Taipa**, R Dr Manoel E B de Araújo 130A, next to Taverna Pub (see below), serving tapioca, salads, juices and coffee.

TT **Ponta Negra Grill**, Av Erivan França 22. Large, several terraces, popular for steaks, seafood and cocktails, lively.

T **Grande Muralha**, Av Erivan França 12, Casa Branca Center. Upstairs, Chinese, Japanese and Brazilian food with executive meals at good prices.

Cafés

Dulce France, Av Afonso Pena 628, Vila Colonial Shopping, corner of R Mossoró. Café selling crêpes, salads and coffee.

The malls in Ponta Negra have a variety of cafés and bars:

Ponta Negra Mall, Av Erivan França 24. Smart stalls sell sandwiches and snacks, also shops and Fellini restaurant. It can be accessed from Av Roberto Freire.

Santa Fe Mall, Av Erivan França 108. With Beach Café, Blackout Beer (popular in early evening), *Beterraba* restaurant (see above) and Bistro de Suisse for pizzas, pastas, meats and drinks.

Bars and clubs

Natal *p587*

Ponta Negra beach is lively at night and the venue for a full-moon party, when there is live music all night.

Aquamarina Praia, Av Roberto Freire 22a, Ponta Negra. Pavement beachfront bar, attached to restaurant/hotel, large TV screen, open 24 hrs. Also has internet.

Blackout B52, Rua Chile 25. 1940s theme, best night is 'Black Monday'.

Centro de Turismo (see Shopping, below) has Forró com Turista, a chance for visitors to learn this fun dance, Thu at 2200; many other enjoyable venues where visitors are encouraged to join in.

Downtown Pub, Rua Chile 11. Four bars, dancefloor, games area, cybercafé, live bands, open Thu-Sat. Both popular bar/nightclubs are in the Ribeira district, in restored historic buildings.

Taverna Pub, R Dr Maneol, A B de Araújo, 500, Ponta Negra. Medieval-style pub in youth hostel basement. Eclectic (rock, Brazilian pop, jazz, etc.) live music Tue-Sun from 2200, best night Wed. Recommended. This street and the one that joins it by Taverna/Lua Cheia is known as 'Broadway', with lots of bars and cafés.

Zás-Trás, Rua Apodi 500, Tirol. Daily shows, except Sun, with a variety of local dances and presentations and a comedy act. Also has handicraft shops and a restaurant.

Festivals and events

Natal *p587*

In **Jan** is the **Festa de Nossa Senhora dos Navegantes** when numerous vessels go to sea from Praia da Redinha, north of town.

Mid-Dec sees **Carnatal**, the Salvador-style out of season carnival, a lively 4-day music festival with dancing in the streets.

Shopping

Natal *p587*

Handicrafts **Centro Municipal de Artesanato**, Av Pres Café Filho, Praia do Meio. Daily 1000-2200. Sand-in-bottle pictures are very common in Natal.

Centro de Turismo, R Aderbal de Figueiredo, 980, off R Gen Gustavo C Farias, Petrópolis. A converted prison with a wide variety of handicraft shops, art gallery, antique shop, café, restaurant and tourist information booth, offers good view of the Rio Potengi and the sea, daily 0900-1900, Thu at 2200 is Forró com Turista (see above).

Shopping centres **Natal Shopping**, Av Senador Salgado Filho 2234, Candelária, between Ponta Negra and the centre. Large mall with restaurants, ATMs, cinemas and 140 shops. Free shuttle bus service to major hotels.

Praia Shopping, Av Eng Roberto Freire 8790, Ponta Negra. Smart shops, including **AS Livros** book and coffee shop (lojas 505-506); food hall with lots of options and a **Habib's**. There are more restaurants outside, mostly fast food, on R Praia de Genipabu. It also has internet, exchange (see Directory, below) and the **Central do Cidadão**. This facility has a tourist office (see above), post office, federal police office and Banco do Brasil with ATM; open Tue-Fri 1000-2200, Sat 1000-1800.

Activities and tours

Natal *p587*

Boat tours To natural swimming pools at Pirangi do Norte, 25 km south of Natal, and to the nearby beaches of the Litoral Sul are available from **Marina Badauê**, Pirangi do Norte. A 2-hr tour includes hotel pick-up, a snack (or breakfast if you take an early tour), and allows time for a swim, US$15 per person. The company has a restaurant and bar at the seashore. Boat trips to Barra do Cunhaú, 86 km south of Natal, go through mangroves, visit an island and a salt mine with **Passeio Ecológico Cunhaú**.

Diving **Miami Dive**, T202 4727, natalnautica @natal.digi.com.br. For groups of up to 10, beginners' courses, dives up to 20 m. Associated with Império do Sol chalets in Pipa, T3246 2381, www.imperiodosol.com.br. See also Maracajaú, page 589.

Tour operators
A city tour costs US$20; if it includes the northern beaches US$25-30, including southern beaches US$40-45. Buggy tours are by far the most popular, US$100 for a full day in high season, US$85 in low season (shorter options are available). If you book direct with the buggy owner, rather than through a hotel or agency, there will be a discount. The price should include all commissions and ferry crossings. Buggy drivers (bugueiros) have an association (APCBA, R Projetada 405, Praia de Genipabu, Extremoz, T225 2061) and all members must be approved by Setur and Detran. Look for the sign 'Autorizado Setur' plus a number on the buggy. **Cariri Ecotours**, T3234 4068, www.caririecotours.com.br. Mainly 4WD tours throughout Ceará, the Sertão, Paraíba and Pernambuco, to natural monuments and archaeological sites, with a strong ecological emphasis. Also works with **Aventura** (www.aventuraturismo.com.br) for coastal Land Rover trips. Trustworthy, excellent guides.

Transport

Natal *p587*
Air **Aeroporto Augusto Severo**, Parnamirim, T3644 1041. The airport has a tourist office, VIP Câmbio, ATMs, car hire, restaurants and shops.
Bus **Rodoviária**, Av Capitão Mor Gouveia 1237, Cidade da Esperança. Regional tickets are sold on street level, interstate on the 2nd floor. To **Recife**, 5 daily, US$21 convencional, US$34 executivo, 4 hrs. With **Nordeste** to **Mossoró**, US$21 convencional, US$34 executivo, 4 hrs. To **Aracati**, US$27, 5½ hrs. To **Fortaleza**, US$39, US$82 leito, 7½ hrs. To **João Pessoa**, see page 586. With **São Geraldo** to **Maceió**, buses both direct and via Recife, US$50 convencional, 10 hrs. To **Salvador**, US$105 executivo, 20 hrs. With **Boa Esperança** to **Teresina**, US$105 executivo, 17-20 hrs. To **Belém**, US$135, 32 hrs.
Taxi Taxis are expensive compared to other cities; US$12 for 10-min journey.

Around Natal *p588*
Pirangi do Norte
Bus From Natal, new rodoviária, **Viação Campos**, many daily, US$1.40 to Pirangi, 1 hr.

Tibau do Sul and Pipa
Bus From Natal **Transul**, 6 a day to Tibau do Sul and on to Pipa, and **Oceano** buses, T3203 2440, from the new rodoviária, several daily, US$5.25. **Oceano** and VW combis go to **Goianinha** from where buses run south to João Pessoa.
Buggy tours **Rivatur**, Tibau do Sul, T9982 8331, ask for Rivaldo, rivatur@uol.com.br. Tours south and north of Natal and to the interior and Paraíba; US$100 for 5 hrs, US$175 for 8 hrs, US$27 to Natal, with sightseeing. Also arranges boat (US$15) and horse rides (US$18).

Redinha
Bus Regular **Oceano** (address above), from the old rodoviária to Redinha.
Ferry Frequent ferry service for Redinha from **Cais Tavares de Lira**, **Ribeira** (Natal), weekdays 0530-1900, weekend and holidays 0800-1830, US$1 per person, US$6 for car. If on a buggy tour, the fare is included in the cost.

Genipabu
Bus **Guanabara** from the old rodoviária every 30 mins from 0530, till 2030.

Jacumã
Bus **Riograndense**, from **Natal**, 1100 and 1800 to **Jacumã** (0730 and 1800, Sun).

Directory

Natal *p587*
Airline offices **TAM**, Av Afonso Pena 844, Tirol, T3201 2020, at airport, T3087 1458, freephone 0800-570 5700. **Trip**, Av Prudente de Morais 4283, sala2, T3643 1450. **Webjet**, T0300-210 1234, www.webjet.com.br.
Banks **Banco 24 horas**, Natal Shopping, Cirrus, Visa, MasterCard and Plus. **Banco do Brasil**, Seafront ATM, Ponta Negra for Cirrus, Visa, MasterCard and Plus. Also, Av Rio Branco 510, Cidade Alta, US$ cash and TCs at poor rates, cash advances against Visa, Mon-Fri 1000-1600.

Dunas Câmbio, Av Roberto Freire 1776, Loja B-11, Capim Macio (east of Parque das Dunas), cash and TCs, 0900-1700. **Natal Câmbio**, in Natal Shopping, open Mon-Sat 1000-2200. **Ponta Negra Câmbio**, Av Erivan França 91, cash and TCs, Mon-Fri 0900-2200, Sat 1000-2100, Sun 0900-2000. **Praia Câmbio** in Praia Shopping, open Mon-Sat 0900-2200, Sun 0900-1700. **Sunset Câmbio**, Av Hermes da Fonseca 628, Tirol, cash and TCs, 0900-1700. **Car hire** **BR Rede Brasil**, Av Eng Roberto Freire 9100, Ponta Negra, T3236 3344, www.redebrasil natal.com.br. **Dudu Locadora**, Av Rio Branco 420, Centro. There are many other rental agencies on Av Eng Roberto Freire for cars and buggies. Buggy rental about US$45 a day, price depends on make. **Post offices** R Princesa Isabel 711, Centro; Av Rio Branco 538, Centro, Av Engenheiro Hildegrando de Góis 22, Ribeira, Av Praia de Ponta Negra 8920, Ponta Negra. **Telephone** R Princesa Isabel 687 and R João Pessoa, Centro; Av Roberto Freire 3100, Ponta Negra, Shopping Cidade Jardim, Av Roberto Freire, Ponta Negra; and rodoviária.

Fortaleza and the north coast

➔ Phone code: 0xx88 outside metropolitan Fortaleza, but prefix numbers beginning with 3 with 0xx85. The state of Ceará has been dubbed A Terra da Luz, Land of Light. It has some of the finest beaches in Brazil, scenic dunes and almost constant sunshine. The sophisticated capital, Fortaleza, is still home to jangadas (traditional fishing boats), while its nightlife is famous throughout the country. As well as the mysterious Parque Nacional de Sete Cidades, Piauí shares with Maranhão the remarkable Parnaíba delta, which is beginning to be recognized as a major ecological site with great tourist potential. The Parque Nacional Lençóis Maranhenses, across the delta, is a landscape of fabulous sand dunes and crystal lakes. Maranhão's capital, São Luis, is one of Brazil's UNESCO sites of worldwide cultural importance, because of its colonial centre.

Fortaleza

➔ Phone code: 0xx85. Post code: 60000. Colour map 5, B5. Population: 2.1 million.

Fortaleza, the fifth largest city in Brazil, is a busy metropolis with many highrise buildings, an important clothes manufacturing industry, many hotels and restaurants and a lively nightlife. Fishermen's *jangadas* still dot the turquoise ocean across from the beach and transatlantic cruise ships call in for refuelling. The mid-day sun is oppressive, tempered somewhat by a constant breeze; evening temperatures can be more pleasant, especially by the sea. The wettest months are March to July, known locally as 'winter'.

Ins and outs

Tourist offices Setur, state tourism agency ⓘ *Centro Administrativo Virgílio Távora, Cambeba, T3101 4639, www.setur.ce.gov.br*. Information booths at Centro de Turismo, has maps, information about beach tours (0700-1800, Sunday 0700-1200); rodoviária (0600-1800 daily), airport (24 hours) and Farol de Mucuripe (0700-1730). **Disque Turismo** ⓘ *T0800-991516, 24-hr*. Posta Telefônica Beira Mar, on Beira Mar almost opposite Praiano Palace, information, sells Redenção tickets to Jericoacoara, good range of postcards and clothes, papers and magazines.

Safety In Fortaleza avoid the Serviluz favela between the old lighthouse (Avenida Vicente de Castro), the favela behind the railway station, the Passeio Público at night, Avenida Abolição at its eastern (Nossa Senhora da Saúde church) and western ends. Also be careful at Mucuripe and Praia do Futuro. Generally, though, the city is safe for visitors.

Sights

Praça do Ferreira, from which pedestrian walkways radiate, is the heart of the commercial centre. The whole area is dotted with shady squares. **Fortaleza Nossa Senhora da Assunção** ⓘ *Av Alberto Nepomuceno, daily 0800-1100, 1400-1700*, originally built in 1649 by the Dutch, gave the city its name. Near the fort, on Rua Dr João Moreira, is the 19th-century **Passeio Público** or Praça dos Mártires, a park with old trees and statues of Greek deities. West of here, a neoclassical former prison (1866) houses the **Centro de Turismo do Estado** (Emcetur) ⓘ *Av Senador Pompeu 350, near the waterfront, T0800-991516, closed Sun*, with museums, theatre and high-quality craft shops (bargaining expected). It houses the **Museu de Arte e Cultura Populares** and the **Museu de Minerais**. Further west along Rua Dr João Moreira, at **Praça Castro Carreira** (commonly known as Praça da Estação), is the nicely refurbished train station **Estação João Felipe** (1880).

The **Teatro José de Alencar** ⓘ *on praça of the same name, T229 1989, Mon-Fri 0800-1700, hourly tours, English speaking guides, US$1, Wed free*, was inaugurated in 1910. This magnificent iron structure was imported from Scotland and is decorated in neo-classical and art nouveau styles. It also houses a library and art gallery. The new **cathedral**, completed in 1978, in gothic style but concrete, stands beside the new, **Mercado Central** with beautiful stained glass windows. Both are on Praça da Sé, at Avenida Alberto Nepomuceno. The **Museu do Maracatu** ⓘ *Rufino de Alencar 231, at Teatro São José*, houses costumes of this ritual dance of African origin.

The **Centro Dragão do Mar de Arte e Cultura** ⓘ *R Dragão do Mar 81, Praia de Iracema*, hosts music concerts, dance, and art and photography exhibitions. It has various entrances, from Ruas Almirante Barroso, Boris and from junction of Monsenhor Tabosa, Dom Manuel and Castelo Branco. This last one leads directly to three museums: on street level, the **Memorial da Cultura Cearense**, with changing exhibitions; on the next floor down is an art and cultural exhibit; in the basement is an excellent audio-visual museum of **El Vaqueiro**. Also at street level is the Livraria Livro Técnico. There is a planetarium with a whispering gallery underneath. The centre also houses a contemporary art museum (**Museu de Arte Contemporânea do Ceará**) ⓘ *T3488 8600, www.dragaodomar.org.br, Tue-Fri 0830-2130, Sat and Sun 1430-2130, US$1 for entry to each museum/gallery, free on Sun*. This area is very lively at night.

Fortaleza has 25 km of beaches, many of which are the scene of the city's nightlife; those between **Barra do Ceará** (west) and **Ponta do Mucuripe** (east) are polluted. **Praia de Iracema** is one of the older beach suburbs with some original turn-of-the-century houses. East of Iracema, the **Avenida Beira Mar** (Avenida Presidente Kennedy) connects **Praia do Meireles** with Volta da Jurema and **Praia do Mucuripe**, 5 km from the centre. Fortaleza's main fishing centre, jangadas, bring in the catch here. **Praia do Futuro**, 8 km southeast of the centre, is the most popular bathing beach, 8 km long, unpolluted, with strong waves, sand dunes and fresh-water showers, but no natural shade; there are many vendors and barracas serving local dishes. Thursday night, Saturday and Sunday are very busy. A city bus marked 'P Futuro' from Praça Castro Carreira, 'Praia Circular', does a circular route to Praia do Futuro; a bus marked 'Caça e Pesca' passes all southeast beaches on its route. Praia do Futuro has few hotels or buildings because the salt-spray corrosion is among the strongest in the world. About 29 km southeast of the centre is **Praia Porto das Dunas**, popular for watersports including surfing; the main attraction is **Beach Park** ⓘ *US$25*, a water park.

Northwest of the centre is **Praia Barra do Ceará**, 8 km, where the Rio Ceará flows into the sea. Here are the ruins of the 1603 Forte de Nossa Senhora dos Prazeres, the first Portuguese settlement in the area. The beaches west of the Rio Ceará are cleaner, lined with palms and have strong waves. A new bridge across this river gives better access to this area, for example, **Praia de Icaraí**, 22 km, and **Tabuba**, 5 km further north. Beyond Tabuba, 37 km from Fortaleza, is **Cumbuco**, a lively beach, dirty in high season, chaotic bars, horse riding, dunes which you can sandboard down into a rainwater lake, palm trees.

Fortaleza listings

For Sleeping and Eating price codes and other relevant information, see Essentials, pages 38-40. See Telephone, page 397, for important phone changes.

Sleeping

Fortaleza *p594, map p596*
Almost all hotels offer reduced prices in the low season. There are many pousadas in the Iracema/Meireles area, but they change frequently.

Centre

D Passeio, R Dr João Moreira 221, Centro, T/F3226 9640. Opposite Passeio Público (which is not so enticing when the prostitutes are about) and near Centro Turismo, homely, rooms with high ceilings, a/c or fan, gloomy passages, good value.

E Big, Gen Sampaio 485, on Praça da Estação in centre, T3212 2066. All rooms with fan, cheaper without TV, even cheaper without bath, simple breakfast, OK, but caution needed at night, right in thick of the central scrum.

By the beach

LL-L Imperial Othon Palace, Av Beira Mar 3470, Meireles, T3466 5500, www.hoteis-othon.com.br. Beach front location, large hotel with all facilities common to this group, business and tourists catered for, pool, sauna, massage (recommended feijoada on Sat).

Fortaleza

Sleeping

1 Abrolhos Praia & Villamaris *B6*
2 Agua Marinha *A3*
3 Albergue Praia de Iracema *A3*
4 Alfa Residence *B5*
5 Beira Mar *B6*
6 Best Western Colonial Praia *A4*
7 Big *A1*
8 Ibis *A4*
9 Imperial Othon Palace *B6*
10 Jardim *B4*
11 Ondas Verdes *A4*
12 Passeio *A1*
13 Ponta Mar *B6*
14 Pousada Atalaia *A4*

LL-L Seara Praia, Av Beira Mar 3080, Meireles, T4011 2200, www.hotel seara.com.br. 30% cheaper in low season, smart, comfortable luxury hotel with pool, gym, cyber café, French cuisine.

L Beira Mar, Av Beira Mar 3130, T3242 5000, Meireles, www.hotelbeiramar.com.br. Some rooms seafront, others side view, comfortable rooms, safe, pool, 24-hr business centre (internet), parking, good value, especially in low season.

L Praiano Palace, Av Beira Mar 2800, Meireles, T4008 2200, www.praiano.com.br. Much the same services and standards, but not quite as luxurious, opposite the craft fair. And **Ponta Mar**, Av BM 2200, Meireles, T4006 2200, www.ponta mar.com.br. Aimed more at the business market, but still a good location and similar facilities.

AL Best Western Colonial Praia, R Barão de Aracati 145, Iracema, T4005 4644, www.colonial praiahotel.com.br. 4-star, **B** in low season, pleasant grounds and big pool, low-rise, which is unusual, popular with families, laundry service.

AL-A Agua Marinha, Av Almte Barroso 701, Iracema, T3219 0303, www.aguamarinha hotel.com.br. Less 10% in low season, a/c, TV, room safe, fridge and generally comfortable, pool, internet.

A-C Alfa Residence, Av Mons Tabosa 1320, Meireles, T3248 2020. Associated with Coimbra Residence Flat, Prime Plus car hire, all in same block. Apartments with a/c, TV, fridge, unfussy but welcoming, use of pool and sauna at Coimbra.

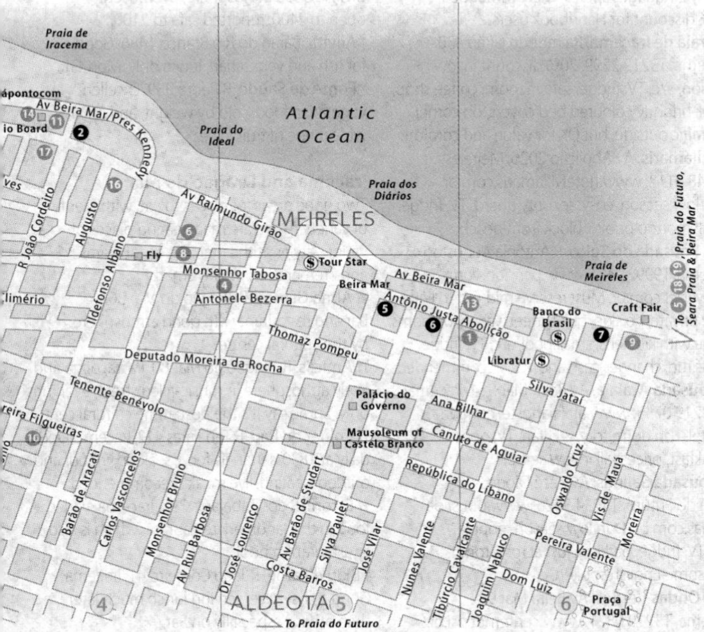

15 Pousada Beleza Tropical *B3*
16 Pousada do Suiço *A4*
17 Praia de Iracema *A4*
18 Praiano Palace *B6*
19 Seara Praia *B6*

Eating
1 Alma Gêmea, Amici's & Santa Clara Café Orgânico *A2*
2 Blau d'Fame & Brazão *A4*
3 Colher do Pau *A3*
4 Estoril *A3*
5 Habib *B5*
6 Ideal *B5*
7 La Fiorentina *B6*
8 La Habanera *A3*
9 Le Sandras *C3*
10 Xadrez *A1*

A Ibis, Atualpa Barbosa de Lima 660, Iracema, T3219 2121, www.accorhotels.com.br. Breakfast extra, in Accor style, with usual facilities, pool.

B Abrolhos Praia, Av Abolição 2030, Meireles, T/F3248 1217. Pleasant, TV, fridge, hot shower, a/c, rooms a bit spare but no different from others in this category, soft beds, discount in low season, 1 block from beach, internet.

B Pousada Icaraí, Praia Icaraí, just before town on curve in road, T0xx85-3318 2000. English/Brazilian owners, ask for Fiona. A good out-of-town base with beautiful gardens, lots of budgerigars flying free, pools, restaurant, near beach and bus to Fortaleza.

B Jardim, Idelfonso Albano 950, Aldeota, T3226 9711, www.hoteljardim.com.br. No sign outside, nice garden, excursions arranged, many languages spoken. Recommended, 20% discount for Handbook users.

B Praia de Iracema, Raimundo Girão 430, Iracema, T3219 2299. 20% discount in low season, a/c, TV, fridge, safe in room, coffee shop, pool, brightly coloured bed covers, on corner so traffic outside, but OK for value and comfort.

B Villamaris, Av Abolição 2026, Meireles, T3248 0112, www.hotelvillamaris.com.br. **C** in low season, cosy, security guard, TV, fridge, small rooftop pool, 1 block from beach.

B-C Pousada do Suiço, R Antônia Augusto 141, Iracema, T9992 9481, www.pension-vom-schweizer.com.br. Must reserve mid-Oct to Feb. Very private, no sign, quiet street, variety of rooms, some with kitchens, small pool, a/c, TV, fridge, Swiss run, changes cash and TCs. Recommended.

C Pousada Atalaia, Av Beira Mar 814, Iracema, T/F3219 0755, www.atalaiahostel.com.br. Hostel, **E** in dormitory, a/c, fan, TV, good breakfast, prices fall in low season.

C Pousada Salinas, Av Zezé Diogo 3300, Praia do Futuro, T3234 3626, www.pousada salinas.com.br. **D** in low season, popular, a/c, TV, fridge, parking, just across from sea, some English spoken.

C-D Ondas Verdes, Av Beira Mar 934, Iracema, T3219 0871, www.centernet.psi.br/ hotelondasverdes. Fan, TV, very good value for location, convenient for just about everything, French owner. Recommended.

C-D Pousada Beleza Tropical, R Dom Joaquim 132, Iracema, T3219 0515. A/c, hot water, TV, fridge, breakfast by the pool, good.

D Albergue Praia de Iracema, Av Almte Barroso 998, T3219 3267, www.aldeota.com/ albergue. Basic hostel but busy, helpful staff.

Camping **Barra Encantada**, Praia do Barro Preto, Iguape, 42 km southeast, T3361 6047, US$10 pp, Camping Club members US$5 pp, see Eastern Coast, page 602.

Fortaleza Camping Club, R Pedro Paulo Moreira 505, Parque Manibura, Água Fria, 12 km, T3273 2544, many trees for shade, US$7 pp.

Eating

Fortaleza *p594, map p596*

Centre

There are several options around and in the railway station.

TTT Xadrez, Emcetur restaurant, in the old prison. Good atmosphere, overpriced, open to 2400, reported safe to 2100.

T Alivita, Barão do Rio Branco 1486. Good for fish and vegetarian, lunch only, Mon-Fri.

T Fonte de Saúde, R Pedro 339. Excellent vegetarian food, sold by weight, and a wide range of fruit juices.

Iracema and Dragão do Mar

Two good areas for places to eat, with plenty of variety. There are many eating places of various styles at the junction of Tabajaras and Tremembés, mostly smart.

TT Alma Gêmea, R Dragão do Mar 30. Bar and restaurant with good atmosphere by the cultural centre.

TT Amici's, R Dragão do Mar 80. Pasta, pizza and lively atmosphere in music-filled street, evenings only. Some say it's the best at the cultural centre.

TT Colher do Pau, R Tabajaras 412, Iracema. Opens daily at 1830, sertaneja food, seafood, indoor and outdoor seating, live music. Recommended.

TT Estoril, R dos Tabajaras 397, Iracema. Varied food in this landmark restaurant, which is also a restaurant school.

T Blau d'Fame, R João Cordeiro 41, Iracema. Good self-service, serving lunch much later than others, especially on Sat.

T Brazão, R João Cordeiro corner of Av R Girão, Iracema, next to Blau d'Fame. The only place open 24 hrs, but the food is not that special.

Urban beaches

Several good fish restaurants at Praia de Mucuripe, where the boats come ashore between 1300 and 1500. R J Ibiapina, at the Mucuripe end of Meireles, 1 block behind beach, has pizzerias, fast food restaurants and sushi bars.

TTT-TT La Fiorentina, Osvaldo Cruz 8, corner of Av Beira Mar, Meireles. Some seafood expensive, but fish, meats, pasta, unpretentious, attentive waiters, good food, frequented by tourists and locals alike.

TTT-TT Le Sandras, Av Santos Dumont 938, Aldeota. Successor to Sandras of Praia do Futuro. Brightly painted old building, cool yellow inside, tasteful, elegant with outdoor, indoor and a/c seating, garden, French-trained owner, novo cearanse and Mediterranean cooking, lobster still a speciality, good food.

T Churrascaria Picanha de Veras, R Carlos Vasconcelos 660, Aldeota. Good for chicken.

T Dom Pastel, R Carlos Vasconcelos 996, Aldeota. Pay-by-weight.

T Habib, Av Abolição, corner with Av Barão de Studart, Meireles (and other branches). Modern middle-eastern fast-food restaurant, excellent service, set menus are a bargain, good deserts. Recommended.

T Ideal, Av Abolição e José Vilar, Meireles. Open 0530-2030, bakery serving lunches, small supermarket and deli, good, handy.

Out of town

TTT-TT Lá na Roça, opposite the church, in the district of Eusêbio. Excellent *sertaneja* restaurant, very popular on Sun, pay by weight, go early to be sure of a table – all local dishes and sweets. Eusêbio is reached from the CE 040, the road to Iguape and Aquiraz. On this road out of the city is the best place for tapioca shacks. As well as the rough traditional shacks, there is a whole complex for tapioca sellers at the Estrada do Fio.

TT Carneiro de Ordones, R Azevedo Bolão 571, Parquelândia, near North Shopping. Crowded with locals Sat-Sun for every kind of lamb dish.

T Casa de Farinha, CE 040 Km 13. Mon-Fri 1100-1500 à la carte only, Sat, Sun and holidays 1100-1800 self-service *sertaneja* food, very good. It is also a working cassava/manioc mill and museum so you can see the whole process of making tapioca. A good place to take kids, plenty of games for them.

T Delicias de Cana, Km 18. A working sugar mill, selling rapa dura flavoured with fruits and nuts (cashew – of course, sesame).

T La Habanera, Praça da Igreja in Iracema, Av Beira Mar e Ararius. Café, wicker chairs, marble tables, old photos of Fidel, Che, et al, coffee and cigars.

T Santa Clara Café Orgânico, R Dragão do Mar 81, at end of red girder walkway (or upstairs depending which way you go), www.santaclara.com.br. Café, delicious organic coffees, juices, cold drinks, plus sandwiches and desserts.

Bars and clubs

Fortaleza *p594, map p596*

Fortaleza is renowned for its nightlife and prides itself with having the liveliest Mon night in the country. *Forró* is the most popular dance and there is a tradition to visit certain establishments on specific nights. **Mon** Forró is danced at the **Pirata Bar**, Iracema, US$5, open-air theme bar, from 2300, and other establishments along R dos Tabajaras and its surroundings. **Tue** Live golden oldies at **Boate Oásis**, Av Santos Dumont 6061, Aldeota. **Wed** Regional music and samba-reggae at **Clube do Vaqueiro**, city bypass, Km 14, by BR-116 south and E-020, at 2230. **Thu** Live music, shows and crab specialities at the beach shacks in Praia do Futuro, **Chico do Caranguejo**, lively bar with some sex tourism. Also recommended for crab is **Atlântico**. For music, Rebu (traditional) and Vila Galé (for tourists). **Fri** Singers and bands play regional music at **Parque do Vaqueiro**, BR-020, Km 10, past city bypass. **Sat** Forró at **Parque Valeu Boi**, R Trezópolis, Cajueiro Torto, **Forró Três Amores**, Estrado Tapuio, Eusêbio and **Cantinho do Céu**, CE-04, Km 8. **Sun** Forró and música sertaneja at **Cajueiro Drinks**, BR-116, Km 20, Eusêbio.

Some of the best areas for entertainment, with many bars and restaurants are: the Av Beira Mar, Praia de Iracema, the hill above Praia de Mucuripe and Av Dom Luís. The streets around Centro Cultural Dragão do Mar on R Dragão do Mar are lively every night of the week. Brightly painted, historic buildings house restaurants where musicians play to customers and the pavements are dotted with cocktail carts.

Caros Amigos, R Dragão do Mar, 22. Live music at 2030: Tue, Brazilian instrumental;

Wed, jazz; Thu, samba; Sun, Beatles covers, US$1 (also shows music on the big screen). **Restaurant e Crêperie Café Crème**, R Dragão do Mar 92, live music on Tue.

Festivals and events

Fortaleza *p594, map p596*

6 Jan, **Epiphany**; **Ash Wednesday**. **19 Mar**, **São José**; **Christmas Eve**; **New Year's Eve**, half-day. The **Festas Juninas** in Ceará are much livelier than carnival. A festival, the **Regata Dragão do Mar**, takes place at Praia de Mucuripe on the last Sun in **Jul**, during which the traditional jangada (raft) races take place. Also during the last week of Jul, the out-of-season Salvador-style carnival, **Fortal**, takes place along Avs Almte Barroso, Raimundo Giro and Beira Mar. On **15 Aug**, the local Umbanda terreiros (churches) celebrate the **Festival of Iemanjá** on Praia do Futuro, taking over the entire beach from noon till dusk, when offerings are cast into the surf. Well worth attending (members of the public may 'pegar um passo' – enter into an inspired religious trance – at the hands of a pai-de-santo). For 4 days in **mid-Oct** Ceará Music, a festival of Brazilian music, rock and pop, is held Marina Park.

Shopping

Fortaleza *p594, map p596*

Bookshops **Livraria Livro Técnico**, see Dragão do Mar, above, has several branches, on Dom Luis, Praça Ferreira, Shopping Norte and at UFC university. **Livraria Nobel** bookstore and coffee shop in Del Paseo shopping centre in Aldeota. **Siciliano**, bookstore and coffee shop in new part of Iguatemi shopping mall, with just a bookstore in the old part.

Handicrafts Fortaleza has an excellent selection of locally manufactured textiles, which are among the cheapest in Brazil, and a wide selection of regional handicrafts. The local craft specialities are lace and embroidered textile goods; also hammocks (US$15 to over US$100), fine alto-relievo wood carvings of northeast scenes, basket ware, leatherwork and clay figures (*bonecas de barro*). Bargaining is OK at the **Mercado Central**, Av Alberto Nepomuceno (closed Sun), and the **Emcetur Centro de Turismo** in the old prison (see above). Crafts also available in shops near the market, while shops on R Dr João Moreira 400 block sell clothes. Every night (1800-2300) there are stalls along the beach at Praia Meireiles. Crafts also available in the commercial area along Av Monsenhor Tabosa.

Shopping centres The biggest is **Iguatemi**, south of Meireles on way to Centro de Convenções; it also has modern cinemas. Others are **Aldeota** and **Del Paseo** in Aldeota, near Praça Portugal.

Activities and tours

Fortaleza *p594, map p596*

Diving **Projeto Netuno/Manta Diving Center**, R Oswaldo Cruz 2453, Dionísio Torres, T3224 4114, www.pnetuno.com.br.

Surfing Surfing is popular on a number of Ceará beaches. Kite surfing also catching on.

Windsurfing A number of Ceará beaches are excellent for windsurfing. Equipment can be rented in some of the popular beaches such as Porto das Dunas and in the city. **Bio Board**, Av Beira Mar 914, T3242 1642, www.bio board.com.br. Looks after equipment for you, windsurf school, Açaizeiro Café with açai, juices, sandwiches upstairs (opens 1000 till 2000, 1900 Sat, 1800 Sun), also travel agency. **Windclub**, Av Beira Mar 2120, Praia dos Diários, T9982 5449. Equipment rental, lessons also available.

Tour operators

Many operators offer city and beach tours. Others offer adventure trips further afield, most common being off-road trips along beaches from Natal in the east to the Lençois Maranhenses in the west.

Dunnas Expedições, T3264 2514, contact by email: comercial@dunnas.com.br; www.dunnas.com.br. Off-road tours with a fleet of white Land Rover Defenders, experienced, environmentally and culturally aware, very helpful and professional staff. Recommended.

Sunny Tour, Av Prof A Nunes Freire 4097, Dionísio Torres, T0xx85-9986 5689, also has a bus-cum-stand on Av Beira Mar near the craft fair. Offers beach tours (eg 3 in 1 day, 6 in 4 days, trips to Jericoacoara).

Transport

Fortaleza *p594, map p596*

Air Aeroporto Pinto Martins, Praça Eduardo Gomes, 6 km south of centre, T3477 1200.

Airport has a tourist office, car hire, food hall upstairs, internet, Laselva bookstore and Banco do Brasil (changes cash, US$20 commission on TCs, open 1100-1500). Direct flights to major cities. Bus 404 from airport to Praça José de Alencar in the centre, US$1, also 066 Papicu to Parangaba and 027 Papicu to Siqueira, or luxury Guanabara service from Beira Mar via Iracema, a/c, US$1.20; taxis US$14 to centre, Av Beira Mar or Praia do Futuro, more at night depending on destination. Use Cooperativa Taxi Comum or Taxi Especial Credenciado.

Bus Rodoviária at Av Borges de Melo 1630, Fátima, 6 km south from centre. Many city buses (US$1.20) including 'Aguanambi' 1 or 2 which go from Av Gen Sampaio, 'Barra de Fátima-Rodoviária' from Praça Coração de Jesus, 'Circular' for Av Beira Mar and the beaches, and 'Siqueira Mucuripe' from Av Abolição. Taxi to Praia de Iracema, or Av Abolição US$11. There is a luggage store. Opposite the rodoviária is Hotel Amuarama, which has a bar and restaurant; there's also a lanchonete.

Nordeste: To **Mossoró**, 10 a day, US$16.50, **Natal**, 8 daily, US$39 executivo, US$82 leito, 7½ hrs. **João Pessoa**, 2 daily, US$45 semi-leito, 10 hrs. **Boa Esperança**, stops at Fortaleza on its Belém-Natal route only. **Itapemirim** to **Salvador**, US$82, 1900, 23 hrs. **Guanabara**, T256 0214, to **Recife**, 5 daily, US$65, 12 hrs, book early for weekend travel. **Guanabara** to **Teresina**, several daily, US$44, 10 hrs; to **Parnaíba** US$38; to **Belém**, 2 daily, US$94 executivo, 23 hrs. **Piripiri**, for **Parque Nacional de Sete Cidades**, US$33, 9 hrs, a good stop en route to Belém, also **Guanabara**, who go to **São Luís**, 3 daily, US$73, 18 hrs.

In **Ceará**: Guanabara to **Sobral** US$11, **Ubajara** 0800, 1800, return 0800, 1600, 6 hrs, US$16.50. Also **Ipu Brasília** to **Sobral** and to **Camocim** 1120, 1530. To **Majorlândia**, US$8.25.

Directory

Fortaleza *p594, map p596*

Airline offices TAM, Av Santos Dumont 2849, Aldeota, T261 0916, T0800-570 5700. **Trip**, at airport T3477 1747. **Webjet**, T0300-210 1234, www.webjet.com.br. **Banks** Banco do **Nordeste**, R Major Facundo 372, a/c, helpful, open 0900-1630. Recommended. TCs exchanged and cash with Visa at **Banco do Brasil**, R Barão do Rio Branco 1500, also on Av Abolição (high commission on TCs). **Banco Mercantil do Brasil**, Rua Major Facundo 484, Centro, Praca do Ferreira: cash against MasterCard. Cirrus/MasterCard ATM at international airport; others at **HSBC** and **Banco 24 Horas** throughout the city. ATM for Cirrus/ MasterCard and Visa outside cinema at Centro Cultural Dragão do Mar. Also at Av Antonio Sales and Iguatemi Shopping. Exchange at **Tropical Viagens**, R Barão do Rio Branco 1233, **Libratur**, Av Abolição 2194, open 0900-1800 Mon-Fri, 0800-1200 Sat; also has kiosk outside Othon hotel on Av Beira Mar which is open every day till 2300. Recommended. More câmbios on Av Mons Tabosa: eg **TourStar**, No 1587, **Sdoc**, No 1073. **Car hire** Many car hire places on Av Monsenhor Taboso, and at its junction with Ildefonso Albano. **Brasil Rent a Car**, Av Abolição 2300, T0xx85-3242 0868. There are also many buggy rental shops. **Note** When driving outside the city, have a good map and be prepared to ask directions frequently as road signs are non-existent, or placed after junctions. **Embassies and consulates** **Belgium**, R Eduardo Garcia 909, Aldeota, T3091 5185, consulbelce@ig.com.br. **France**, R João Cordeiro 831, Iracema, T3226 3470, consulat.fortaleza@ yahoo.fr. **Germany**, R Dr Lourenço 2244, Meireles, T3246 2833, DghonkonsulBRD@ aol.com. **Netherlands**, R Dom Luis 880, T3268 2700, consuladoholanda@tradetec.com.br. **Sweden** and **Norway**, R Leonardo Mota 501, Aldeota, T3242 0888, marcos@emitrade.com.br. **Switzerland**, R Dona Leopoldina 697, Centro. **UK**, R Leonardo Mota, 501, Meireles, T3242 0888, annette@edsonqueiroz.com.br. **US**, http://virtual .embaixada-americana.org.br/fortaleza/. **Internet** Many internet cafés around the city. **Medical services** Instituto Dr José **Frota** (IJF), R Barão do Rio Branco 1618, T255 5000. Recommended public hospital. **Post offices** Main branch at R Senador Alencar 38, Centro; Av Monsenhor Tabosa 1109 and 1581, Iracema; at train station; opposite rodoviária. Parcels must be taken to Receita Federal office at Barão de Aracati 909, Aldeota (take 'Dom Luiz' bus). **Telephones** International calls from **Emcetur** hut on Iracema beach and from offices of **Telemar**; at rodoviária and airport.

Coast east of Fortaleza

Aquiraz, 31 km east of Fortaleza, first capital of Ceará which conserves several colonial buildings and has a religious art museum, is the access point for the following beaches: **Prainha**, 6 km east, a fishing village and 10 km long beach with dunes, clean and largely empty. You can see jangadas coming in daily in the late afternoon. The village is known for its lacework: you can see the women using the bilro and labirinto techniques at the **Centro de Rendeiras**. 18 km southeast of Aquiraz is **Praia Iguape**, another fishing and lacework village, 3 km south of which is **Praia Barro Preto**, wide, tranquil, with sand dunes, palms and lagoons. All these beaches have accommodation.

Cascavel, 62 km southeast of Fortaleza (Saturday crafts fair), is the access point for the beaches of **Caponga** and **Águas Belas**, where traditional fishing villages coexist with fancy weekend homes and hotels.

Some 4 km from **Beberibe**, 78 km from Fortaleza, is **Morro Branco**, with a spectacular beach, coloured craggy cliffs and beautiful views. Jangadas leave the beach at 0500, returning at 1400-1500, lobster is the main catch in this area. The coloured sands of the dunes are bottled into beautiful designs and sold along with other crafts such as lacework, embroidery and straw goods. Jangadas may be hired for sailing (one hour for up to six people US$30). Beach buggies (full day US$100) and taxis are also for hire. The beach can get very crowded at holiday times. There are pousadas, or you can rent fishermen's houses. Meals can also be arranged at beach-front bars. South of Morro Branco and 6 km from Beberibe is **Praia das Fontes**, which also has coloured cliffs with sweet-water springs; there is a fishing village and a lagoon. South of Praia das Fontes are several less developed beaches including **Praia Uruaú** or **Marambaia**. The beach is at the base of coloured dunes, there is a fishing village with some accommodation. Just inland is Lagoa do Uruaú, the largest in the state and a popular place for watersports. Buggy from Morro Branco US$45 for four.

Canoa Quebrada ➔ *Colour map 5, B5. Visit www.canoa-quebrada.com.*

On the shores of the Rio Jaguaribe, **Aracati** is the access point to the southeastern-most beaches of Ceará; it is along the main BR-304. The city is best known for its Carnival and for its colonial architecture.

About 10 km from Aracati is Canoa Quebrada on a sand dune, famous for its labirinto lacework and coloured sand sculpture, for sand-skiing on the dunes, for the sunsets, and for the beaches. There are many bars, restaurants and forró establishments. Canoa Quebrada is beginning to suffer from unplanned development. To avoid biting insects (bicho do pé), wear shoes. There is nowhere to change money except Banco do Brasil in Aracati. In the second half of July the Canoarte Festival takes place, it includes a jangada regatta and music festival.

South of Canoa Quebrada and 13 km from Aracati is **Majorlândia**, an attractive village, with many-coloured sand dunes and a wide beach with strong waves, good for surfing; the arrival of the fishing fleet in the evening is an important daily event; lobster is the main catch. It is a popular weekend destination with beach homes for rent and Carnaval here is lively.

Community tourism Some 120 km east of Fortaleza, in the district of Beberibe, is **Prainha do Canto Verde**, a small fishing village on the vast beach, which has an award-winning community tourism project. There are guesthouses (eg **E Dona Mirtes**, with breakfast, will negotiate other meals), houses for rent (US$30/month in community house; **Casa Cangulo**, or **Chalé Marésia**), restaurants (good food at Sol e Mar), a handicraft cooperative, jangada and catamaran cruises, fishing and walking trails. Each November there is a Regata Ecológica, with jangadas from up and down the coast competing. (For the regatta, Christmas and Semana Santa, add 30% to prices.) This is a simple place, which lives by artesanal fishing (ie no big boats or industrial techniques) and has built up its tourism infrastructure without any help from outside investors (they have been fighting the speculators since 1979). It's a very friendly place and foreigners are welcome to get to know how the fisher folk live; knowledge of Portuguese is essential. To get to Prainha do Canto Verde, take a São Benedito bus to Aracati or Canoa Quebrada, buy a ticket to Quatro Bocas and ask to be let off at Lagoa da Poeira, two hours from Fortaleza. If you haven't booked a transfer in advance, Márcio at the Pantanal restaurant at the bus stop will take you, US$4. A truck from the village goes to Aracati for US$5 return.

Ponta Grossa is near Icapuí, the last municipality before Rio Grande do Norte (access from Mossoró), from where you then head to Redonda. Ponta Grossa is down a sand road just before Redonda. Both Ponta Grossa and Redonda are very pretty places, nestled at the foot of the cliffs, but Ponta Grossa has its own community tourism development. One of the main attractions of Ponta Grossa is that, offshore, is one of the few places where manatees (*peixe boi marinho*) visit. You can try to spot them from the cliffs. Beach trips go from Canoa Quebrada to Ponta Grossa for lunch, but if you want to stay here, you need to speak Portuguese. Cabins for rent are under construction and there are restaurants/bars. The tourism coordinator is **Eliabe** ⓘ *T0xx88-9964 5846*.

For further information on community tourism and the preservation of traditional ways of life in Ceará, contact **Instituto Terramar** ⓘ *R Pinho Pessoa 86, Joaquim Távora, Fortaleza, T0xx85-3226 4154, www.terramar.org.br.*

Coast east of Fortaleza listings

For Sleeping and Eating price codes and other relevant information, see Essentials, pages 38-40. See Telephone, page 397, for important phone changes.

Sleeping

Canoa Quebrada *p602*

There are several pousadas in town. Villagers will let you sling your hammock or put you up cheaply (Verónica recommended, European books exchanged; Sr Miguel rents good clean houses for US$10 a day).

B Pousada Sete Mares, R Quatro Ventos 400, T3368 2247, www.pousada7mares hpg.com.br. A recommended pousada with a/c chalets, pool.

C Pousada California, R Nascer do Sol 136, T3421 7039, www.californiacanoa.com. Prices vary according to room and season, a/c, **E** pp in dorm, TV, pool, bar, internet, buggy tours, horse riding, kite surfing, book exchange, several languages spoken, use of kitchen.

C Pousada Lua Morena, R Principal, T3421 7030, www.canoaquebrada.com. Chalets with direct access to beach, with a/c, fridge, TV, hot water, pool, good value, English, Dutch and German spoken.

D-E Pousada Alternativa, R Francisco Caraço, T3421 7276, www.geocities.com/pousadaalternativa. Rooms with a/c and bath, cheaper with fan and without fridge, central, safe.

Transport

Coast east of Fortaleza *p602*

Bus Daily bus service from Fortaleza rodoviária to **Prainha**, 11 daily, US$1.85; **Iguape**, hourly between 0600 and 1900, US$2.20. To **Caponga**: direct bus from Fortaleza rodoviária (4 a day, US$2.75) or take a bus from Fortaleza to Cascavel (80 mins) then a bus from Cascavel (20 mins). **São Benedito**, at Fortaleza rodoviária: to **Beberibe**, 10 a day, US$4.50; **Cascavel**, US$2.50; **Morro Branco**, 4 a day, US$5; **Canoa Quebrada**, 4 a day (5 on Sun), US$9; **Aracati**, 6 a day, US$8.50. **Natal**-Aracati bus via Mossoró, 6 hrs, US$16.50; from Mossoró (90 km) US$5.20, 2 hrs; **Fortaleza**-Aracati (142 km), besides São Benedito, Guanabara or Nordeste many daily, US$8.20, 2 hrs; Aracati-**Canoa Quebrada** from Gen Pompeu e João Paulo, US$1; taxi US$8.

Coast west of Fortaleza

Paracuru, a fishing port which has the most important Carnaval on the northwest coast, is two hours by bus from Fortaleza (**D Villa Verde**, near the main square, is a good place to stay). West of Paracuru, about 120 km from Fortaleza and 12 km from the town of Paraipaba, is **Lagoinha**, a very scenic beach, with cliffs, dunes and palms by the shore; a fishing village is on one of the hills.

Some seven hours by bus and 230 km from Fortaleza is the sleepy fishing village of **Almofala**, home of the Tremembés Indians who live off the sea and some agriculture. There is electricity, but no hotels or restaurants, although locals rent hammock space and cook meals. Bathing is better elsewhere, but the area is surrounded by dunes and is excellent for hiking along the coast to explore beaches and lobster-fishing communities. In Almofala, the church with much of the town was covered by shifting sands and remained covered for 50 years, reappearing in the 1940s; it has since been restored. There is also a highly praised turtle project.

Jijoca de Jericoacoara (Gijoca) is near the south shore of scenic Lagoa Paraíso (or Lagoa Jijoca), the second largest in the state. There are pousadas on its shore. It is excellent for windsurfing as it has a 'comfortable' wind, very good for beginners and those gaining experience (Jericoacoara is for 'professionals'). There is also good for kite surfing. **Note** The low season, August to November, is the windy season.

Jijoca is one of the access points for **Jericoacoara**, or 'Jeri' (*Phone code*: 0xx88, www.portaljericoacoara.com, http://jericoacoara.jeri.com). One of the most famous beaches of Ceará and all Brazil (if not the world), it has towering sand dunes, deserted beaches with little shade, cactus-covered cliffs rising from the sea and interesting rock formations. The most famous is the **Pedra Furada**, a rock arch by the sea. Its atmosphere has made it popular with Brazilian and international travellers, with crowds at weekends mid-December to mid-February, in July and during Brazilian holidays. Many places full in low season, too. Jericoacoara is part of an environmental protection area which includes a large coconut grove, lakes, dunes and hills covered in caatinga vegetation (ICMBio, R Praia da Malhada s/n, Jericoacoara, T3669 2140, parnajericoacoara.ce@ibama.gov.br). The village east of Jeri, **Preá**, is much quieter, with simple fish restaurants.

Parnaíba → *Phone code: 0xx86. Post code: 64200. Colour map 5, A4. Population: 132,282.*

Parnaíba makes a good break in the journey north or south. It's a relaxed, friendly place, with a pretty colonial centre by the river and connections to Jericoacoarara and Tutóia (and onward to São Luís and the Lençóis Maranhenses). Tours into the Delta do Parnaíba can be arranged from here (see page 611). They leave from Porto das Barcas (Tatus), a pleasant shopping and entertainment complex, with several good restaurants and a large open-air bar on the riverside. Buses between Parnaíba and Porto das Barcas leave every hour and take 10 minutes.The tourist office, **Piemtur**, is at Terminal Turístico Porto das Barcas, T3321 1532, piemtur-parnaiba@ig.com.br.

Delta do Parnaíba and the Parque Nacional Lençóis Maranhenses → *Colour map 5, A3.*

These twin parks comprise two of Brazil's most extraordinary landscapes. The **Delta do Parnaíba** is one of the largest river deltas in the world, a labyrinth of mangroves, rivers and unspoilt tropical islands with largely unstudied wildlife and traditional Caiçara fishing communities. The adjacent **Lençóis Maranhenses** (ICMBio contact T0xx98-3349 1155) is a 155,000-ha coastal desert of vast shifting dunes and isolated communities cut by broad rivers and, in the rainy season (June-September), pocked with lakes, whose clear reflective waters are a vivid sky blue against brilliant white sand. Crossing the Parnaíba delta, which separates Piauí from Maranhão, can only be done by chartered boat for up to 12 people from either **Tutóia** or Porto das Barcas. It is also possible to take a cheap though infrequent public boat from Parnaíba to various of the islands (see page 611). Trips into the Lençóis Maranhenses all the way from São

Luís to Jericoacoara are easy to organize from São Luís or **Barreirinhas** with **EcoDunas** (see page 610). As well as Barreirinhas – the main centre – there is accommodation in the little beach towns of Caburé, Atins and Vassouras up the Rio Preguiças. Rural Maranhão and Piauí have a big problem with wind- and ocean-borne plastic waste.

São Luís ➔ *Phone code: 0xx98. Post code: 65000. Colour map 5, A3. Population: 870,028.*
The capital of Maranhão state, 1,070 km west of Fortaleza, founded in 1612 by the French and named after St Louis of France, is in a region of heavy tropical rains, but the surrounding deep forest has been cut down to be replaced by babaçu palms. It stands upon São Luís island between the bays of São Marcos and São José. The urban area extends to São Francisco island, connected with São Luís by three bridges. An old slaving port, the city has a large black population, and has retained much African culture with, these days, lots of music including good reggae. São Luís tourist offices, **Central de Serviços Turísticos** ⓘ *Praça Benedito Leite, T098-3212 6211, www.turismo.ma.gov.br,* and **São Luís Turismo** ⓘ *www.saoluisturismo.com.br,* have useful websites. Also see http://saoluis-ma.com.br.

The old part, on very hilly ground with many steep streets, is still almost pure colonial. The historical centre is being restored with UNESCO support and the splendid results (eg the part

São Luís historic centre

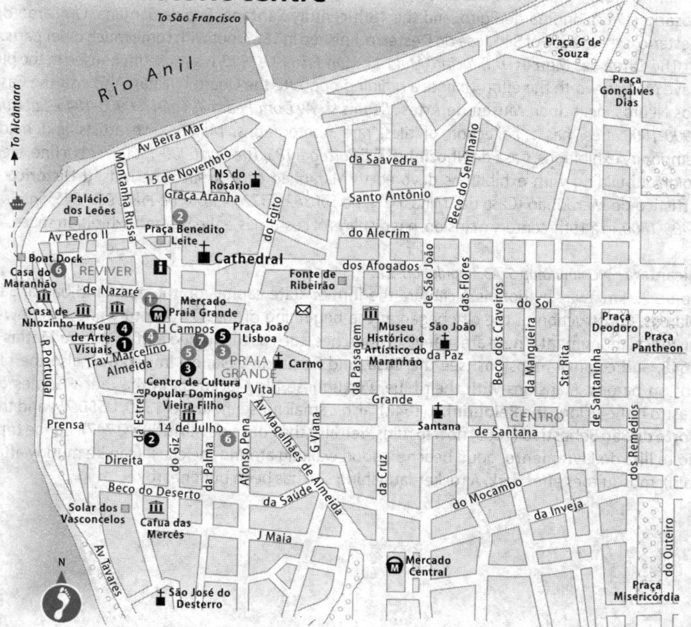

200 metres
200 yards

Sleeping
1 Cantaria
2 Grand São Luís
3 HI Solar das Pedras
4 Internacional
5 Portas da Amazônia
6 Pousada Colonial

Eating
1 Antigamente
2 Armazen Estrela
3 Dom Francisco
4 Papagaio Amarelo
5 Scorpions

Bars & clubs
6 Reggae Bar do Porto
7 Reggae (Roots)

known as Reviver) rival the Pelourinho of Salvador. The damp climate stimulated the use of ceramic tiles for exterior walls, and São Luís shows a greater variety of such tiles than anywhere else in Brazil, in Portuguese, French and Dutch styles. The commercial quarter (R Portugal, also called Rua Trapiche) is still much as it was in the 17th century. One house on this street has been renovated as the **Casa do Maranhão** ⓘ *Tue-Fri 0900-1900, Sat-Sun 0900-1800, free*, a showcase for the natural and cultural riches of the state, with displays of costumes and video presentations. The progress of the renewal of the historical centre can be seen in the 19th-century **Solar dos Vasconcelos** ⓘ *R da Estrela 462, Mon-Fri 0800-1900, Sat-Sun 0900-1900.*

The **Palácio dos Leões** (Governor's Palace) ⓘ *Av Dom Pedro II, T3214 8638, Mon, Wed, Fri 1500-1800, US$3*, has beautiful floors of dark wood (jacarandá) and light (cerejeira), French furniture and great views from terrace. The restored **Fortaleza de Santo Antônio**, built originally by the French in 1614, is on the bank of the Rio Anil at Ponta d'Areia. The **Fábrica Canhamo (CEPRAMA)** ⓘ *R São Pantaleão 1232, Madre de Deus, near Praia Grande, T3232 2187, Mon-Fri 0900-1900, Sat 0900-2000, Sun 0900-1300*, a restored factory, houses an arts and crafts centre. The **Centro de Cultura Popular Domingos Vieira Filho** (**Casa da Festa**) ⓘ *R do Giz 225, T3218 9924, Tue-Sun 0900-1900*, has exhibitions on the **Festa do Divino**, the African-Brazilian *Tambor- de-Mina* spirit religion (similar to *candomblé*) and Christmas festivities.

The best colonial churches are the **Cathedral** (1629), on Praça Dom Pedro II, and the churches of **Carmo** (1627), Praça João Lisboa, **São João Batista** (1665), Largo São João, **Nossa Senhora do Rosário** (1717), on Rua do Egito, and the 18th-century **Santana**, Rua de Santana. On Largo do Desterro is the church of **São José do Desterro**, finished in 1863, but with some much older parts.

The **Cafua das Mercês** ⓘ *R Jacinto Maia 43, Mon-Fri 0900-1800*, is a museum housed in the old slave market, worth the effort to find: a building opposite the Quartel Militar. Also visit the Casa dos Negros, next door. **Museu de Artes Visuais** ⓘ *Av Dom Pedro II, Tue-Fri 0900-1840, Sat-Sun 0900-1800, free*, has a collection of tiles, rare photographs, Marahnense artists and holds temporary exhibitions. **Casa de Nhozinho** ⓘ *R Portugal 185, Tue-Sun 0900-1900, free* is a fine, tiled colonial building with exhibitions devoted to Maranhão *caboclo* life. The **Museu Histórico e Artístico do Maranhão** (Casa das Minas) ⓘ *R do Sol 302, T3221 4537, Tue-Fri 0900-1845, Sat-Sun 1400-1800*, in a 19th-century mansion, has displays of costumes, a theatre and exhibition space.

Alcântara → *Colour map 5, A3. Population: 21,291.*

Some 22 km away by boat is Alcântara the former state capital, on the mainland bay of São Marcos. Construction of the city began at the beginning of the 17th century and it is now a historical monument. There are many old churches, such as the ruined **Matriz de São Matias** – 1648, and colonial mansions (see the **Casa**, and **Segunda Casa, do Imperador**, also the old cotton barons' mansions with their blue, Portuguese tiled façades). In the Praça Gomes de Castro is the pillory, the **Pelourinho** (1648), also a small museum (0900-1330, US$0.75) and the **Forte de São Sebastião** (1663) now in ruins. See also the **Fonte de Miritituia** (1747). Canoe trips go to **Ilha do Livramento**, good beaches, good walking around the coast (can be muddy after rain), mosquitoes after dark. A rocket-launching site has been built nearby.

Coast west of Fortaleza

For Sleeping and Eating price codes and other relevant information, see Essentials, pages 38-40. See Telephone, page 397, for important phone changes.

Sleeping

Coast west of Fortaleza *p604*

Jijoca de Jericoacoara

A-B Pousada do Paulo, Córrego do Urubu s/n, T0xx88-3669 1181. Has a windsurf school, US$18.50 for beginner's course, US$20 equipment hire per hr, US$50 per day, longer rates negotiable. It's also a good place to stay (prices depends on season and cabin, lovely location with lake views, garden, beach, hammocks and various sizes of cabin, all very nice, some with TV and a/c; excellent restaurant, bar.

Jericoacoara

4-5-day packages for Reveillon are available, but prices rise steeply. Many pousadas can be found on www.portaljericoacoara.com. Ask around for families who take in guests.

LL-L Recanto do Barão, R do Forró 433, T3242 0685, www.recantodobarao.com. 21 rooms mostly for 3 to 5 (ie families, groups), nicely decorated with hibiscus theme, lots of hammocks, a/c, TV, fridge, hot shower, big rooms, upper balcony for sunset, pool, Land Rover tours. Good reputation.

A-B Casa do Turismo, R das Dunas, T669 2000, www.casado turismo.com. Nice rooms, all a/c, hot shower, TV, some with upper floor with mattress. Information, tours, horse rental, Redenção bus tickets (only place selling them, 1030-1400 and 1730-2200), windsurf school, kite surf, sandboard rental, telephone calls, post office, exchange.

A-C Por do Sol, R das Dunas 50, T3669 2099, pordosoljeri@yahoo.com.br. Family atmosphere, lovely place to stay, with a/c or fan, buggy trips arranged. Recommended.

B Casa Nostra, R das Dunas, T3669 2035, www.portaljericoacoara.com/casanostra.htm. Nice rooms, good breakfast, money exchange, Italian spoken. Recommended.

B Isalana Praia, R Principal, T3660 2009. A/c, minibar, TV, very helpful, ask for Will Louzada.

B Pousada Papagaio, Beco do Forró, T3669 2142. With bath, recommended, tours.

B Pousada da Renata, T3669 2061. Owned by the sister of Fernanda at Pousada do Paulo at Jijoca. Patio with hammocks, breakfast, English, Italian and German spoken. Renata also has **Pousada do Serrote**, 100 m from Praia da Malhada, same phone, and 9961 5522.

B-C Pousada Azul, R das Dunas, T3669 2182, www.portaljericoacoara.com/pousada_azul_em_jericoacoara.htm. Under new ownership, redecorated, variety of rooms and suites.

C Calanda, R das Dunas (across from Casa do Turismo, by setting sun dune), T3669 2285. With solar energy, Swiss run, good rooms, good breakfast, restaurant with varied menu, good views, helpful, German, English and Spanish spoken, full moon party every month. Warmly recommended.

C Chalé dos Ventos, R São Francisco 50, T3669 2023, www.portaljericoacoara.com/pousada_chale_dos_ventos_jericoacoara.htm. Price depends on room, chalet on 2 floors, good views, great breakfast, nice atmosphere.

C Pousada do Véio, T3669 2015. All rooms with a/c, bath, hot water and fan, some have a/c and fridge.

D Pousada Tirol, R São Francisco 202, T3669 2006. HI-affiliated, non-members pay more, also has double rooms at **B** (**C** in low season), with breakfast, hot water, safe, helpful, great fun. Recommended. Also has very busy cyber café, US$3 per hr – 10 mins free use for all guests.

Parnaíba *p604*

AL-B Pousada dos Ventos, Av São Sebastião 2586, Universidade, T/F3323 2555, www.pousada dosventos.com.br. The best business hotel in town, 10 minutes taxi ride from the centre, spacious, simple rooms and an attractive breakfast area next to the pool.

B-C Pousada das Barcas, R do Comércio 100, T3321 2718, joaopaulo.pousada@yahoo.com.br. The best pousada in town, with rooms arranged in a charming 17th-century building in the old colonial centre right next to the river.

B-D Pousada Chalé Suiço, Av Padre R J Vieira 448, Fátima, T3321 3026, www.chalesuico.com.br. Cheaper without a/c or breakfast, bar, laundry, pool, tours arranged, wind-surfing, sandboarding, buggies and bikes.

D Residencial, R Almirante Gervásio Sampaio 375, T3322 2931, www.residencialpousada.com.br. Very plain, simple doubles, dorms and plusher en-suites with cold water showers gathered around a plant-filled courtyard. There are many other basic hotels nearby.

Delta do Parnaíba and Parque Nacional Lençóis Maranhenses *p604*

Delta do Parnaíba

E pp **Ilha das Canarias**, Morro do Meio Caiçara Comunidade. Bring a hammock and ask at **Raimundo Aires** restaurant (good for fish), idyllic beaches nearby. Simple, no showers, just the river.

Barreirinhas

Most hotels can organize tours.

C Belo Horizonte, R Joaquim Soeiro de Carvalho 245, T3499 0054, www.bhmirante.com.br. Near the central square, well-kept tiled and whitewash rooms, quietest at the front, welcoming owner, pleasant rooftop breakfast area. Also owns **Pousada do Mirante** in Caburé, with restaurant.

C-D Pousada Igarapé, R Coronel Godinho 320, Centro, T0xx98-9111 0461. Small, boxy rooms, a/c or fan, opposite the Assembleia de Deus church (noisy hellfire sermons at weekends).

D-E Tia Cota, R Coronel Godinho 204, T3349 1237. Simple rooms, fan or a/c, decent beds and mattresses, ranging from phone box-sized with shared baths to more spacious en-suite doubles.

Caburé

Pousada do Paulo, T9143 4668. Rooms for up to 4, well-kept. The owner was the first to settle here and named the town after a local bird. Best food in the village. Watch out for glass on the vast, sweeping Atlantic beach

São Luís *p605, map p605*

Many cheap hotels can be found in R da Palma, very central (eg **G Pousada Ilha Bela**, safe), and R Formosa.

A Grand São Luís, Praça Dom Pedro II 299, T2109 3500, www.grandsaoluis.com.br. 1960s 'grand dame' with plainly decorated rooms, the best of which have sweeping sea views. Business facilities, pool and gym.

A-B Portas da Amazônia, R do Giz 129, T3222 9937, www.portasdaamazonia.com.br. Tastefully converted rooms in a colonial building in the heart of the centre. Smart and well run.

B-C Pousada Colonial, R Afonso Pena 112, T3232 2834, www.clickcolonial.com.br. Well kept rooms in a beautiful restored, tiled house, a/c, comfortable, quiet. Recommended.

D Cantaria, R da Estrela 115, T3221 3390. Spartan but bright rooms, a/c or fan, good views out over Rua da Estrela

D-E HI Solar das Pedras, R da Palma 127, T3232 6694, www.ajsolardaspedras.com.br. By far the best backpacker option in town. Well-run with a range of tidy 4-6 person dorms (**E** pp) and doubles, internet, large lockers and a little garden at the back.

D-E Internacional, R da Estrela 175, T3231 5154. Very scruffy, tiny hot boxes with button-sized windows and fan, in a dilapidated house reached by rickety wooden stairs. Inexplicably popular with backpackers but definitely only for the desperate. There are other options nearby.

Alcântara *p606*

B Pousada dos Guarás, Praia da Baronesa, T3337 1339. A beach front *pousada* with bungalows, good restaurant, canoe hire and advice on excursions around the town.

D Pousada Bela Vista, Vila Jerico s/n, Cema, T3337 1569, danniloalcantara@ ig.com.br. Cabins and pretty suites with great views out over the bay and a good restaurant.

D-E Sítio Tijupá, R de Baixo s/n at the Post Office, T3337 1291. Tiny simple *pousada* with small but well-kept rooms, with fan.

E Pousada da Josefa, R Direita, T3337 1109. A family-run restaurant and pousada right in the centre with a range of very simple, plain rooms. Look at several.

Eating

Coast west of Fortaleza *p604*

Jericoacoara

There are several restaurants serving vegetarian and fish dishes.

Carcará, R do Forró. Restaurant and bar, northeastern specialities, seafood and pastas, said to be "o mais fino" in town.

Espaço Aberto, R Principal. Meat dishes, delicious seafood, salads, pleasant atmosphere. Recommended.

Naturalmente On the beach. Nice atmosphere, wonderful crêpes. Recommended.

¶¶ **Pizzaria Banana**, R Principal 26. Many choices of pizza, salads, sandwiches, good.

¶¶ **Pizzaria Dellacasa**, R Principal, next to phone office. Good variety of pizza, pasta, salads, art gallery.

¶¶ **Pizzaria Reggae**, R Principal. Another pizza place, with a Caribbean theme.

¶¶ **Taverna**, R Principal. Cantina and restaurant, lovely pasta and pizza, crêpes, expresso coffee. Drinks.

¶¶ **Tudo na Brasa**, R Principal. Particularly recommended for the churrascaria.

¶ **A Casa da Tia Angelita**, for tortas, tapiocas and other local fare.

¶ **Tempero da Terra**, R São Francisco. Restaurant and lanchonete, comida caseira, meat and fish dishes, nothing fancy, but well cooked and tasty.

São Luís *p605, map p605*

R da Estrela has many eating places with good food and outdoor terraces (eg **Antigamente**, No 220, T3232 3964, which has live music Thu-Sat, and adjacent **Papagaio Amarelo**, both of which have live music). Good food also in the Mercado Praia Grande. R dos Afogados has many places for lunch. There is further choice in the São Francisco district, just across bridge. The centre is very lively on Fri and Sat. On Sun it is largely closed and most people go to Praia Calhau to eat and relax.

¶¶¶-¶¶ **Dom Francisco**, Rua do Giz 155, T8137 3010. Good local food in a local setting, per kg at lunchtime (1100-1600), à la carte at night.

¶¶ **Armazen Estrela**, R da Estrela 401, T3254 1274. Great little *botequin* in a cool room with Romanesque brick arches. Good food and live music at weekends.

¶ **Scorpions**, R da Palma 83, T3221 8078. Great value per kilo with a good choice of filling stews, salads and *pratos feitos*.

Alcântara *p606*

¶¶-¶ **Bar do Lobato**, on the praça. Pleasant, with good, simple food, fried shrimps highly recommended.

Bars and clubs

Coast west of Fortaleza *p604*

Jericoacoara

Forró nightly in high season at R do Forró, Wed and Sat in low season, 2200. Action moves to bars when forró has stopped about 0200. There are also frequent parties to which visitors are welcome. Once a week in high season there is a folk dance show which includes capoeira. After forró, **Padaria Santo Antônio** opens, selling special breads, coconut, banana, cheese, 0230-0700. There is a free open-air cinema at Club Ventos, Wed, Sat 1800.

São Luís *p605, map p605*

There is *cacuriá* dancing, drum parades and buzzing nightlife every Fri and Sat along the north end of **R do Giz** and along **R João Gualberto**.

Reggae Bar do Porto, R do Portugal 49, T3232 1115. One of the best reggae bars in the city with a broad range of live acts and DJs.

Reggae (Roots) Bar, R da Palma 86, T3221 7580. Live reggae and Maranhão roots music most nights. Especially lively at weekends.

Festivals and events

São Luís *p605, map p605*

On **24 Jun** (São João) is the **Bumba-Meu-Boi**. For several days before the festival street bands parade, particularly in front of the São João and São Benedito churches. There are dances somewhere in the city almost every night in Jun. In **Aug**, **São Benedito**, at the Rosário church.

Alcântara *p606*

Principal festivals: **Festa do Divino**, at **Pentecost** (Whitsun); **29 Jun**, **São Pedro; early Aug**, **São Benedito**.

Activities and tours

Coast west of Fortaleza *p604*

Jericoacoara

Clube dos Ventos, R das Dunas, T3669 2288, www.clubedosventos.com. With restaurant and bar, windsurf equipment hire from US$80 per day, US$250 deposit. Windsurf courses from US$67 for beginners. Kitesurf courses start at US$200 for 2 hrs, through to 5-days. Kite surfing at Preá and Lagoa Jijoca.

Jeri Off Road, T0xx88-3669 2268, 9958 5457, www.jeri.tur.br. Adventure trips in the area, transfers, buggy rides and kitesurf. Recommended, but popular.

Buggy tours Cost US$45 for a buggy to all the sites. **Associação de Bugueiros**, ABJ, R Principal.

Delta do Parnaíba and Parque Nacional Lençóis Maranhenses *p604*
Eco Dunas, R Inácio Lins 164, Barreirinhas, T098-3349 0545, also at São Luís airport, www.ecodunas.com.br. The best option for tours of Lençóis Maranhenses, the Delta and options all the way from São Luís to Jericoacoara, or vice versa. Excellent guides, infrastructure and organization. Some English spoken and flights arranged.

São Luís *p605*
Phylipi, T8118 1710, phylipi@hotmail.com. Knowledgeable city guide, reliable, personable and good value at US$30 for a 3-hr tour of the city centre for up to 10 people. Speaks English and French.

Transport

Coast west of Fortaleza *p604*
Paracuru and Lagoinha
Bus from **Fortaleza**, **Brasileiro** to Paracuru, 2 hrs, US$2.25, to Lagoinha, 3 hrs, US$3.50.

Almofala
Bus From **Fortaleza Redenção** to Almofala 0700, 1730, US$10.

Jijoca and Jericoacoara
Bus **Redenção** buses, T0xx85-3256 2728/1973, www.redencaoonline.com.br, from Fortaleza to **Jijoca** and **Jericoacoara** from the rodoviária 1030, 1530 (VIP) and 1830 and the Av Beira Mar at the Posta Telefônica opposite Praiano Palace Hotel 30 mins later. The journey takes 6 hrs and costs US$20.50 one way (VIP US$24). Always check times of the Redenção buses from Fortaleza as they change with the season. A jardineira (open-sided 4WD truck) meets the Redenção bus from Fortaleza, at Jijoca (included in the Redenção price). Buses return from Jeri at 0730 (VIP), 1400 and 2230; the jardineira leaves from Casa do Turismo (see above for ticket sale times). Hotels and tour operators run 2 or 3-day tours to Jeri from Fortaleza. If not on Redenção or a tour, 'guides' will besiege new arrivals in Jijoca with offers of buggies, or guiding cars through the tracks and dunes to Jeri for US$10. If you don't want to do this, ask if a pick-up is going: US$5 pp up front, 22 km, 30 mins. In a buggy it's US$25 per buggy.

If coming from Belém or other points north and west, go via Sobral (from Belém US$60, 20 hrs), where you change for Cruz, 40 km east of Jijoca, a small pleasant town with basic hotels (there is only one bus a day Sobral-Cruz, US$16.50, 3-4 hrs, but **Redenção** runs to **Cruz** from Fortaleza 4 times a day, US$15.50. Either continue to Jijoca the next day (Cruz-Jijoca, daily about 1400, US$2.20, meets jardineira for Jeri, Cruz-Jericoacoara, US$4.50) or take an horário pick-up Cruz-Jijoca.

An alternative from the west, especially if going through Parnaíba, is by buggy or jardineira from **Camocim** (a pleasant town at the mouth of the Rio Coreaú separating Piauí and Ceará, facing the dunes on the eastern shore), which is 1½-2 hrs by road from Parnaíba. 2 buses a day, US$12, with **Guanabara**. It has several hotels and eating places. You take a ferry across the river, US$1 per passenger, then the vehicle. To avoid getting stuck in Camocim, take the early bus at around 0700. This connects with the 1100 vehicle to Jericoacoara (2 hrs, US$10).
You can break the journey from Camocim to Jericoacoara at villages such as **Nova Tatajuba** (on the west margin of the outflow of Lagoa Grande; the beach is wide, dunes follow the shore, the ocean is clear and calm and there is a fishing village with a few basic pousadas), or **Guriú** where hammock space can be found. There is good bird watching here. Walk 4 hrs, or take a boat across the bay to Jericoacoara. The journey along the beach has beautiful scenery. In Jericoacoara ask around for buggy or jardineira rides to Camocim, about US$20 pp.

Parnaíba *p604*
Bus To **Fortaleza**, 10 hrs, US$50; **São Luís**, 12 hrs, US$48, very bad road, better to go via Tutóia; **Teresina**, 6 hrs, US$50.

Delta do Parnaíba and Lençóis Maranhenses *p604*
Bus **Parnaíba-Tutóia**: bus, 2½ hrs, US$8, with **Nazaré** at 0700, 1200 and 1400. Tutóia-**Barreirinhas** by Toyota pick-up, leave when full from the dock area for **Paulinho Neves** (1 hr, US$6); pick-ups leave from here to Barreirinhas (2 hrs, US$10). Frequent buses from Tutóia to São Luís. **São Luis-Barreirinhas**,

with **Cisne Branco**, 3-3½ hrs on a new road, US$20, 4 a day. Hotels in São Luís can book minivan trips, same price as bus.

Ferry Up the Parnaíba delta to the crab-fishing village of **Morro do Meio** on Ilha das Canarias, boats on Mon at high tide (usually in the small hours) from Porto das Barcas (Tatus). It is sometimes possible to hitch a lift from Ilha das Canarias to Tutóia with a crab fisherman. Charter boat to Tutóia from Parnaíba, Porto das Barcas, for 12 people for about US$175 (eg **Capitão Báu**, T086-3323 0145, 8831 9581 mob), or contact **Clip Turismo** (Av Presidente Vargas 274, Parnaíba, T3323 9838, and at Porto das Barcas, T3322 2072, www.clipecoturismo.com.br) for boat trips at US$30-50 pp, minimum 4 people. To **Caburé**, **Mandacuru** (with a lighthouse offering sweeping views) and **Atins**: daily boat service from end of the Orla in Barreirinhas (US$5 pp, 3-4 hrs). There is accommodation in Caburé and Atins and in the tiny riverside dune community at Vassouras (bring hammock).

São Luís *p605, map p605*

Air Internal flights with **Gol** and **TAM** to Fortaleza, Salvador, Teresina, São Paulo, Rio, Belém. Airport 15 km from centre, T3217 6133; buses ('São Cristovão') to city until midnight, US$1. Minivans every 40 mins until 2200 stop at Praça Deodoro (1 hr). Taxi US$30.

Bus Rodoviária is 12 km from the centre on the airport road, 'Rodoviária via Alemanha' bus to centre (Praça João Lisboa), US$1. Bus to **Fortaleza**, US$66, 4 a day, 18 hrs. To **Belém**, 13 hrs, US$40, **Transbrasiliana**. Also to **Recife**, 25 hrs, and all other major cities and local towns.

Alcântara *p606*

Ferry

Ferries cross the bay daily, leaving São Luís dock (Terminal Hidroviário Campos Melo, west end of R Portugal, T3232 0692) or from São Francisco district at about 0700 and 0930, returning from Alcântara about 0830 and 1600: check time and buy the ticket the day before as departure depends on the tides. The journey takes 60 mins, return US$20, worth paying extra for 'panorámica' seat. The sea can be very rough between Sep and Dec. Sometimes catamaran tours can be booked through tour operators in São Luís, meals are not included.

Directory

São Luís *p605, map p605*

Banks TCs at **Banco do Brasil**, Praça Deodoro. **HSBC**, off Praça João Lisboa. Accepts Master Card/Maestro. **Agetur**, R do Sol 33-A, T3231 2377. **Language courses** Portuguese lessons: Sra Amin Castro, T3227 1527. Recommended. **Medical services** **Clínica São Marcelo**, R do Passeio 546, English speaking doctor.

West of Fortaleza

Western Ceará

At 340 km from Fortaleza and at 840 m is **Ubajara** ⓘ *T3634 1300 ext 231 for tourist information; www.portalubajara.com.br*, with an interesting Sunday morning market selling produce of the sertão.

About 3 km from town is **Parque Nacional Ubajara** ⓘ *US$11.50, the ICMBio office is at the park entrance, 5 km from the caves, T0xx85-3634 1388, guide US$2.25, there is bar by the entrance serving juices, snacks, refrigerantes, etc*, with 563 ha of native highland and caatinga brush. The park's main attraction is the Ubajara cave on the side of an escarpment. Fifteen chambers totalling 1,120 m have been mapped, of which 360 are open to visitors. Access is along a 6-km footpath and steps (2-3 hours, take water) or with a **cablecar** ⓘ *T3634 1219, 0900-1430, last up at 1500, US$2.25*, which descends the cliff to the cave entrance. Lighting has been installed in nine caverns of the complex. A guide leads visitors in the cave, which is completely dry and home to 14 types of bat. At one point the lights are turned out to appreciate total blackness. Several rock formations look like animals: horse's head, jacaré, snake. The views of the sertão from the upper cablecar platform are superb. In the national park there is a new easy walkway through the woods with stunning views at the end. Start either to the left of the Park entrance, or opposite the snack bar near the cable car platform. The locals' route, and another good trail through caatinga, is from Araticum, 8 km, which is 7 km by bus from Ubajara.

Teresina ➔ *Phone code: 0xx86. Post code: 64000. Colour map 5, B3. Population: 715,360.*
About 435 km up the Rio Parnaíba is the state capital. The city is reputed to be the hottest after Cuiabá (temperatures rise to 42°C). The **Palácio de Karnak** (the old governor's palace) ⓘ *just west of Praça Frei Serafim, Mon-Fri 1530-1730*, contains lithographs of the Middle East in 1839 by David Roberts RA. Also see the **Museu do Piauí** ⓘ *Praça Marechal Deodoro, Tue-Fri 0800-1730, Sat-Sun 0800-1200, US$1*. There is an interesting **open market** by the Praça Marechal Deodoro and the river is picturesque, with washing laid out to dry along its banks. The market is a good place to buy hammocks, but remember to bargain hard. Every morning along the river bank there is the **troca-troca** where people buy, sell and swap. An undercover complex (**Mercado Central do Artesanato**) ⓘ *Mon-Fri 0800-2200*, has been built at Rua Paissandu 1276 (Praça Dom Pedro II). Most of the year the river is low, leaving sandbanks known as coroas (crowns). There is a good, clean supermarket on Praça Marechal Deodoro 937 with fresh food. Local handicrafts include leather and clothes. **Teresina: Setur** ⓘ *Av Antonino Freire 1473, T3216 6000*. **Piemtur** ⓘ *at the same address, T3221 5511, www.piemtur.pi.gov.br for both.*

Parque Nacional de Sete Cidades ➔ *Colour map 5, B4.*
ⓘ *0800-1700, US$7 plus US$17-22 for compulsory guide, prices vary for group size and if on foot or in car.*
Unusual eroded rock formations decorated with mysterious inscriptions are to be found in the Parque Nacional de Sete Cidades, 12 km from Piracuruca, 190 km northeast of Teresina. The rock structures are just off the Fortaleza-Teresina road. From the ground it looks like a medley of weird monuments. The inscriptions on some of the rocks have never been deciphered; one theory suggests links with the Phoenicians, and the Argentine Professor Jacques de Mahieu considers them to be Nordic runes left by the Vikings. There is plenty of birdlife, and iguanas, descending from their trees in the afternoon. Just inside the park is **B Parque Hotel Sete Cidades**, T3223 3366, www.hotelsetecidades.com.br, pleasant, good restaurant, natural pool nearby, camping (US$5.75). Local food is limited and monotonous: bring a few delicacies, and especially fruit. Piripiri is a cheap place to break the Belém-Fortaleza journey; several good hotels. **Parque Nacional de Sete Cidades**: For park information, contact ICMBio ⓘ *Rod Min Vicente Fialho, Piripiri, CEP 64260-000, T3343 1342*. Colourful brochures with good map.

West of Fortaleza listings

For Sleeping and Eating price codes and other relevant information, see Essentials, pages 38-40. See Telephone, page 397, for important phone changes.

Sleeping

Western Ceará: Ubajara *p611*

A Pousada da Neblina, Estrada do Teleférico, 2 km from town, near the park, T3634 1270. In beautiful cloud forest, swimming pool, with breakfast and private shower (**C** without breakfast) restaurant open 1100-2000. Meals recommended. Campground (US$15 per tent).

C Marina Camping, on Ibiapina road 4 km south from Ubajara town, T3634 1364. Restaurant, pool, sauna, good value.

D Hotel Churrascaria Ubajara, R Juvêncio Luís Pereira 370, Ubajara town, T3634 1261. Small restaurant.

D Paraíso, in the centre of Ubajara town, T3634 1728. Reckoned to be the best in town.

D Sítio do Alemão, take Estrada do Teleférico 2 km from town, after the Pousada da Neblina turn right, signposted, 1 km to Sítio Santana, in the coffee plantation of Herbert Klein, T0xx88-9961 4645, www.sitio-do-alemao.20fr.com. Here, down a path, there are 3 small chalets, with full facilities, and 2 older ones with shared bath, **E**, view from breakfast/hammock area to Sertão, excursions, bicycle hire offered, if chalets are full Mr Klein may accommodate visitors at the house (Caixa Postal 33, Ubajara, CE, CEP 62350-000). No meals other than breakfast but Casa das Delícias in Ubajara will send lasagne if necessary. Warmly recommended.

Note Camping not allowed in the national park.

Teresina *p612*
Many cheap hotels and dormitórios around Praça Saraiva. Many other cheap ones in R São Pedro and in R Alvaro Mendes.

A-B Sambaíba, R Gabriel Ferreira 230-N, T3222 6712, hotelsambaiba@bol.com.br. 2-star, central, good.

C-D Fortaleza, Felix Pacheco 1101, Praça Saraiva, T3221 2984. Fan, basic. Recommended.

C-D Grande, R Alvaro Mendes 906, T3221 2713. Very friendly and clean.

C-D Teresinha, Av Getúlio Vargas 2885, opposite rodoviária, T3221 0919. A/c, cheaper with fan.

Eating

Teresina *p612*
Many places for all pockets in Praça Dom Pedro II.

TT Camarão do Elias, Av Pedro Almeida 457, T232 5025. Good seafood.

TT Pesqueirinho, R Domingos Jorge Velho 6889, in Poty Velho district. For fish dishes.

T Sabores Rotisserie, R Simplício Mendes 78, Centro. By kg, good quality and variety.

Festivals and events

Teresina *p612*
Teresina is proud of its **Carnival**, which is then followed by **Micarina**, a local carnival in **Mar**. There is much music and dancing in **Jul** and **Aug**, when there is a **Bumba-meu-Boi**, the Teresina dance festival, **Festidanças**, and a convention of itinerant guitarists.

Transport

Western Ceará: Ubajara *p611*
Guanabara **bus** from **Fortaleza**, 0800, 1800, return 0800, 1600, 6 hrs, US$12.

Teresina *p612*
Air Flights to **Fortaleza, Brasília, Rio, São Paulo, São Luís, Belém, Manaus**. Buses from outside the airport run straight to town a nd to the rodoviária.

Bus Rodoviária, T3218 1514. The bus trip from **Fortaleza** is scenic and takes 9 hrs (US$44). There are direct buses to **Belém** (13 hrs, US$50), **Recife** (16 hrs, US$60) and to **São Luís** (6 hrs, US$24) and **Salvador** (18 hrs).

Parque Nacional de Sete Cidades and Piripiri *p612*
Bus ICMBio staff bus leaves the Praça da Bandeira in Piripiri (26 km away, rodoviária T3276 2333), at 0700, ask for a lift. It passes *Hotel Fazenda Sete Cidades* at 0800 (**A-B**, at Km 63 on BR-222, T0xx86-3276 2222, camping US$5; also has a free pick-up to the park), reaching the park 10 mins later. If you miss the bus, take a mototaxi. Return at 1630, or hitchhike (to walk takes all day, very hot, start early). Taxi from Piripiri, US$33, or from Piracuruca, US$46. Bus Teresina-Piripiri and return, throughout the day 2½ hrs, US$8.25. Bus São Luís-Piripiri, 3 a day, 10 hrs, US$33. Several daily buses Piripiri-**Fortaleza**, 9 hrs, US$33. Bus Piripiri-**Ubajara**, marked 'São Benedito', or 'Crateús', 2½ hrs; US$8.25, first at 0700 (a beautiful trip).

Directory

Teresina *p612*
Banks There are ATMs for both Visa and MasterCard, eg **Banco 24 Horas – TecBan**, Av João XXIII 2220.

The Amazon

The area is drained by the mighty Amazon, which in size, volume of water – 12 times that of the Mississippi – and number of tributaries has no equal in the world. At the base of the Andes, far to the west, the Amazonian plain is 1,300 km wide, but east of the confluences of the Madeira and Negro rivers with the Amazon, the highlands close in upon it until there is no more than 80 km of floodplain between them. Towards the river's mouth – about 320 km wide – the plain widens once more and extends along the coast southeastwards into the state of Maranhão and northwards into the Guianas.

Brazilian Amazônia, much of it still covered with tropical forest, is 56% of the national area. Its jungle is the world's largest and densest rain forest, with more diverse plants and animals than any other jungle in the world. It has only 8% of Brazil's population, and most of this is concentrated around Belém (in Pará), and in Manaus, 1,600 km up the river. The population is sparse because other areas are easier to develop.

Northern Brazil consists of the states of Pará, Amazonas, Amapá and Roraima. The states of Rondônia and Acre are dealt with under Southern Amazônia, *see page 645.*

Ins and outs

Climate The rainfall is heavy, but varies throughout the region; close to the Andes, up to 4,000 mm annually, under 2,000 at Manaus. Rains occur throughout the year but the wettest season is between December and May, the driest month is October. The humidity can be extremely high and the temperature averages 26°C. There can be cold snaps in December in the western reaches of the Amazon basin. The soil, as in all tropical forest, is poor.

Travel up the Amazon River

Rivers are the arteries of Amazônia for the transport of both passengers and merchandise. The two great ports of the region are Belém, at the mouth of the Amazon, and Manaus at the confluence of the Rio Negro and Rio Solimões. Manaus is the hub of river transport, with regular shipping services east to Santarém and Belém along the lower Amazon, south to Porto Velho along the Rio Madeira, west to Tabatinga (the border with Colombia and Peru) along the Rio Solimões and northwest to São Gabriel da Cachoeira along the Rio Negro. There is also a regular service connecting Belém and Macapá, on the northern shore of the Amazon Delta, and Santarém and Macapá.

The size and quality of vessels varies greatly, with the largest and most comfortable ships generally operating on the Manaus-Belém route. Hygiene, food and service are reasonable on most vessels but **overcrowding** is a common problem. Many of the larger ships offer air-conditioned berths with bunkbeds and, for a higher price, 'suites', with a private bathroom (in some cases, this may also mean a double bed instead of the standard bunkbed). The cheapest way to travel is 'hammock class'; on some routes first class (upper deck) and second class (lower deck) hammock space is available, but on many routes this distinction does not apply. Some new boats have air-conditioned hammock space. Although the idea of swinging in a hammock may sound romantic, the reality is you will probably be squeezed in with other passengers, possibly next to the toilets, and have difficulty sleeping because of **noise** and an aching back. Most boats have some sort of rooftop bar serving expensive drinks and snacks.

Riverboat travel is no substitute for visiting the jungle. Except for a few birds and the occasional dolphin, little wildlife is seen. However, it does offer an insight into the vastness of Amazônia and a chance to meet some of its people. Extensive local inquiry and some flexibility in one's schedule are indispensable for river travel. **Agencies** on shore can inform you of the arrival and departure dates for several different ships, as well as the official (highest) prices for each, and they are sometimes amenable to bargaining. Whenever possible, **see the vessel** yourself (it may mean a journey out of town) and have a chat with the captain or business

Paradise lost?

Successive modern Brazilian governments have made strenuous efforts to develop Amazônia. Roads have been built parallel to the Amazon to the south (the Transamazônica), from Cuiabá (Mato Grosso) northwards to Santarém (Pará), and northeast from Porto Velho through Humaitá to the river bank opposite Manaus. Unsuccessful attempts were made to establish agricultural settlements along these roads; major energy and mining projects for bauxite and iron ore are bringing rapid change. More environmental damage has been caused to the region by gold prospectors (garimpeiros), especially by their indiscriminate use of mercury, than by organized mining carried out by large state and private companies using modern extraction methods. The most important cause of destruction, however, has been large scale deforestation to make way for cattle ranching, with logging for hardwoods for the Asian markets coming a close second.

There is a gradually growing awareness among many Brazilians that their northern hinterland is a unique treasure and requires some form of protection and recently some encouraging moves have been made. On the other hand, government is still intent upon some form of development in the region, as its seven-year Avança Brasil programme demonstrated. Scientists argued in 2001 that if the plan went ahead, its road improvement and other elements would lead to a loss of between 28% and 42% of Amazon rainforest by 2020, with only about 5% of the region untouched. This report led to a reassessment of the plan.

manager to confirm departure time, length of voyage, ports of call, price, etc. Inspect cleanliness in the kitchen, toilets and showers. All boats are cleaned up when in port, but if a vessel is reasonably clean upon arrival then chances are that it has been kept that way throughout the voyage. You can generally arrange to sleep on board a day or two before departure and after arrival, but be sure to secure carefully your belongings when in port. If you take a berth, lock it and keep the key even if you will not be moving in right away. If you are travelling hammock class, board ship at least 6-8 hours before sailing in order to secure a good spot (away from the toilets, tables where people eat and the engine and check for leaks in the deck above you). Be firm but considerate of your neighbours as they will be your intimate companions for the duration of the voyage. Always keep your gear locked. Take some light warm clothing, it can get very chilly at night.

Compare fares for different ships and remember that prices may fluctuate with supply and demand. Most ships sail in the evening and the first night's supper is not provided. Empty cabins are sometimes offered to foreigners at reduced rates once boats have embarked. **Payment** is usually in advance. Insist on a signed ticket indicating date, vessel, class of passage, and berth number if applicable.

All ships carry cargo as well as passengers and the amount of cargo will affect the length of the voyage because of weight (especially when travelling upstream) and loading/unloading at intermediate ports. All but the smallest boats will transport vehicles, but these are often damaged by rough handling. Insist on the use of proper ramps and check for adequate clearance. Vehicles can also be transported aboard cargo barges. These are usually cheaper and passengers may be allowed to accompany their car, but check about food, sanitation, where you will sleep (usually in a hammock slung beneath a truck), and adequate shade.

The following are the **major shipping routes** in Amazônia, indicating main intermediate ports, average trip durations, and basic fares. Facilities in the main ports are described in the appropriate city sections, see below. There are many other routes and vessels providing extensive local service. All **fares shown are one-way only** and include all meals unless otherwise stated.

The Amazon system is 6,577 km long, of which 3,165 km are in Brazilian territory. Ships of up to 4-5,000 tonnes regularly negotiate the Amazon for a distance of about 3,646 km up to Iquitos, Peru.

Boat services

Belém–Manaus Via Santarém, Óbidos and Parintins on the lower Amazon. Five to six days upriver, four days downriver, including 18-hour stop in Santarém, US$180 upriver, US$150 down; suites also available, US$350-250, hammock space US$75-US$65. Vehicles are also carried. The Belém–Manaus route is very busy. Try to get a cabin.

Belém–Santarém 2½ days upriver, 1½ days downriver, berth US$135, suite US$150, hammock space US$45 up, US$38 downriver. All vessels sailing Belém–Manaus will call in Santarém.

Santarém–Manaus Same intermediate stops as above. Two days upriver, 1½ days downriver, US$85 berth, US$30 hammock. All vessels sailing Belém–Manaus will call in Santarém and there are many others operating only the Santarém–Manaus. Speedboats (lanchas) on this route take 11 hours sitting, US$79 (US$55, 9 hours, to Parintins).

Belém–Macapá (Porto Santana) Non-stop, 24 hours on large ships, double berth US$130, hammock space US$36 pp, meals not included but can be purchased onboard (expensive). Also non-stop fast catamaran *Atlântica*, eight hours, three a week, US$36. Same voyage via Breves, 36-48 hours on smaller riverboats, hammock space US$30 pp including meals. See page 624.

Macapá (Porto Santana)–Santarém Via Boca do Jari, Prainha, and Monte Alegre on the lower Amazon, two days upriver, 1½ days downriver, berth US$155, hammock US$48.

Manaus-Porto Velho Via Humaitá on the Rio Madeira (from where there are buses to Porto Velho, saving about 24 hours). Tuesday and Friday, five days upriver, 3½ days downriver (up to seven days when the river is low), US$180, hammock space US$60.

Manaus–Tefé 36 hours, US$70 double berth, US$20 hammock space. Jet boats US$55, 7 hours, continuing to Tabatinga (flights Manaus–Tefé–Tabatinga).

Manaus–Tabatinga Via Fonte Boa (three days), Tonantins (four days), São Paulo de Olivença (five days) and Benjamin Constant along the Rio Solimões. Six days upriver (depending on cargo), three days downriver, US$220 upriver, hammock space US$65, cheaper downriver (the *Voyager* fleet is recommended).

Manaus–São Gabriel da Cachoeira Leaving from Porto Raimundo in Manaus not the main boat port, six days along the Rio Negro, US$180, hammock space US$60.

What to take

A hammock is essential on all but the most expensive boats; it is often too hot to lie down in a cabin during day. Light cotton hammocks seem to be the best solution. Buy a wide one on which you can lie diagonally; lying straight along it leaves you hump-backed. A climbing carabiner clip is useful for fastening hammocks to runner bars of boats. It is also useful for securing baggage, making it harder to steal.

Health → *See also Health, Essentials, page 42.*

There is a danger of malaria in Amazônia. Mosquito nets are not required when in motion as boats travel away from the banks and too fast for mosquitoes to settle, though repellent is a boon for night stops. From April to October, when the river is high, the mosquitoes can be repelled by Super Repelex spray or K13. A yellow-fever inoculation is strongly advised; it is compulsory in some areas and may be administered on the spot with a pressurized needle gun. The larger ships must have an infirmary and carry a health officer. Drinking water is generally taken on in port (ie city tap water), but taking your own mineral water is a good idea.

Food
Ample but monotonous, better food is sometimes available to cabin passengers. Meal times can be chaotic. Fresh fruit is a welcome addition; also take plain biscuits, tea bags, seasonings, sauces and jam. Non-meat eaters should take vegetables and tinned fish. Fresh coffee is available; most boats have a bar of sorts. Plates and cutlery may not be provided. Bring your own plastic mug as drinks are served in plastic beakers which are jettisoned into the river.

In Amazônia Inevitably fish dishes are very common, including many fish with indengous names, eg matrinchã, jaraqui, pacu, tucunaré, and tambaqui, which are worth trying. Pirarucu is another delicacy of Amazonian cuisine, but because of overfishing it is in danger of becoming extinct. Also shrimp and crab dishes (more expensive). Specialities of Pará include duck, often served in a yellow soup made from the juice of the root of the manioc (tucupi) with a green vegetable (jambu); this dish is the famous pato no tucupi, highly recommended. Also tacaca (shrimps served in tucupi), vatapá (shrimps served in a thick sauce, highly filling, simpler than the variety found in Salvador), maniçoba (made with the poisonous leaves of the bitter cassava, simmered for eight days to render it safe – tasty). Caldeirada, a fish and vegetable soup, served with pirão (manioc puree) is a speciality of Amazonas. There is also an enormous variety of tropical and jungle fruits, many unique to the region. Try them fresh, or in ice creams or juices. Avoid food from street vendors.

Belém and around

From Belém, the great city near the mouth of the Amazon, to Parintins, site of a renowned annual festival, on the border with Amazonas state, it is 60 hours by boat. This section deals with the first few stops on the river, plus the route through Amapá state to the frontier with French Guiane.

Belém → *Phone code: 0xx91. Post code: 66000. Colour map 5, A1. Population: 1.3 million.*

Belém (do Pará) is the great port of the Amazon. It is hot (mean temperature, 26°C), but frequent showers freshen the streets. There are fine squares and restored historic buildings set along broad avenues. Belém used to be called the 'City of Mango Trees' and there are many such trees remaining.

Tourist offices **Belém Paratur** ⓘ *Praça Maestro Waldemar Henrique s/n, T3212 0575, www.paratur.pa.gov.br.* Helpful, some staff speak English.

Belém has its share of crime and is prone to gang violence. Take sensible precautions especially at night. Police for reporting crimes, Rua Santo Antônio e Trav Frei Gil de Vila Nova.

Sights The largest square is the **Praça da República** where there are free afternoon concerts; the main business and shopping area is along the wide Av Presidente Vargas leading to the river and the narrow streets which parallel it. The neoclassical **Teatro da Paz** (1868-1874) ⓘ *Tue-Fri 0900-1800, tours at set times US$2,* is one of the largest theatres in the country. It stages performances by national and international stars and also gives free concert and theatre shows; worth visiting, recently restored. Visit the **Cathedral** (1748) ⓘ *Mon 1500-1800, Tue-Fri 0800-1100, 1530-1800,* another neoclassical building which contains several remarkable paintings. It stands on Praça Frei Caetano Brandão, opposite the 18th-century **Santo Aleixandre** church, which is noted for its wood carving. The 17th-century **Mercês** church (1640), near the market, is the oldest church in Belém; it forms part of an architectural group known as the Mercedário, the rest of which was heavily damaged by fire in 1978 and is being restored.

The **Basílica of Nossa Senhora de Nazaré** (1909) ⓘ *Praça Julho Chermont on Av Magalhães Barata, Mon-Sat 0500-1130, 1400-2000, Sun 0545-1130, 1430-2000*, built from rubber wealth in romanesque style, is an absolute must for its stained-glass windows and beautiful marble. A museum at the basilica describes the Círio de Nazaré religious festival. The **Palácio Lauro Sodré** or **Museu do Estado do Pará** ⓘ *Praça Dom Pedro II, T3225 3853, Mon-Fri 0900-1800, Sat-Sun 1900-1200*, a gracious 18th-century Italianate building, contains Brazil's largest framed painting, 'The Conquest of Amazônia', by Domenico de Angelis. The **Palácio Antônio Lemos, Museu da Cidade** ⓘ *Tue-Fri 0900-1200, 1400-1800, Sat-Sun 0900-1300*, which houses the **Museu de Arte de Belém** and is now the **Prefeitura**, was originally built as the Palácio Municipal between 1868 and 1883. In the downstairs rooms there are old views of Belém; upstairs the historic rooms, beautifully renovated, contain furniture, paintings etc, all well explained.

The Belém market, known as **'Ver-o-Peso'** was the Portuguese Posto Fiscal, where goods were weighed to gauge taxes due (hence the name: 'see the weight'). It now has lots of gift shops selling charms for the local African-derived religion, umbanda; the medicinal herb and natural perfume stalls are also interesting. It is one of the most varied and colourful markets in South America; you can see giant river fish being unloaded around 0530, with frenzied wholesale buying for the next hour; a new dock for the fishing boats was built just upriver from the market in 1997. The area around the market swarms with people, including many armed thieves and pickpockets.

In the old town, too, is the **Forte do Castelo** ⓘ *Praça Frei Caetano Brandão 117, T3223 0041, daily 0800-2300*. The fort overlooks the confluence of the Rio Guamá and the Baía do Guajara

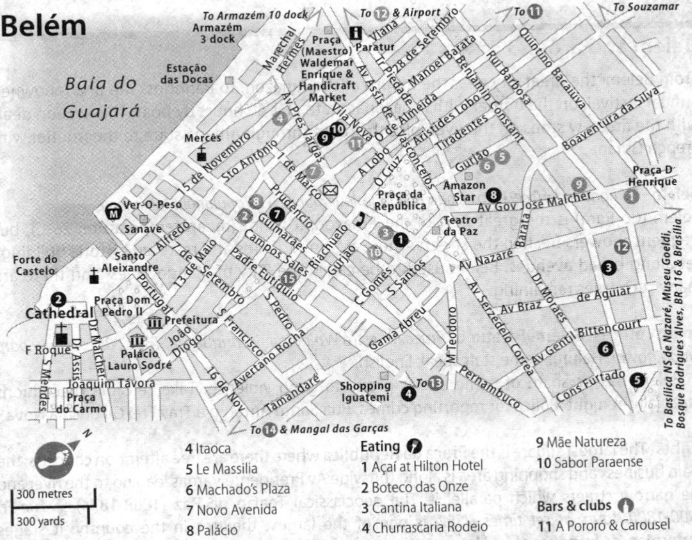

Sleeping
1 Amazônia Hostel
2 Fortaleza
3 Grão Pará
4 Itaoca
5 Le Massilia
6 Machado's Plaza
7 Novo Avenida
8 Palácio
9 Regente
10 Sete Sete
11 Unidos
12 Vila Rica

Eating
1 Açaí at Hilton Hotel
2 Boteco das Onze
3 Cantina Italiana
4 Churrascaria Rodeio
5 Churrascaria Tucuruvi
6 Doces Bárbaros
7 Govinda
8 Lá em Casa
9 Mãe Natureza
10 Sabor Paraense

Bars & clubs
11 A Pororó & Carousel
12 Café Com Arte
13 do Gilson
14 Mormoço
15 São Mateus

and was where the Portuguese first set up their defences. It was rebuilt in 1878. The site also contains the Círculo Militar restaurant (entry US$1.30; drinks and salgadinhos served on the ramparts from 1800 to watch the sunset; the restaurant serves Belém's best Brazilian food). At the square on the waterfront below the fort the açaí berries are landed nightly at 2300, after picking in the jungle (açaí berries ground up with sugar and mixed with manioc are a staple food in the region).

At the **Estação das Docas**, the abandoned warehouses of the port have been restored into a complex with an air-conditioned interior and restaurants outside. The Terminal Marítimo has an office of Valverde Tours, which offers sunset and nighttime boat trips. The Boulevard das Artes contains the **Cervejaria Amazon** brewery, with good beer and simple meals, an archaeological museum and arts and crafts shops. The Boulevard de Gastronomia has smart restaurants and the 5-star Cairu ice cream parlour (try açaí or the Pavê de Capuaçu). Also in the complex are ATMs, internet café, phones and good toilets.

The **Mangal das Garças** ⓘ *end of Av Tamandaré, on the waterfront, 10 mins' walk east of cathedral* is a good new park with flora of the state, including mangroves, a butterful and hummingbird house, colourful birds, a museum, viewing tower and the **Manjar das Garças** restaurant (good for all-you-can-eat meals).

The **Bosque Rodrigues Alves** ⓘ *Av Almte Barroso 2305, T3226 2308, 0900-1700, closed Mon*, is a 16-ha public garden (really a preserved area of original flora), with a small animal collection; yellow bus marked 'Souza' or 'Cidade Nova' (any number) 30 minutes from 'Ver-o-Peso' market, also the bus from the Cathedral. The **Museu Emílio Goeldi** ⓘ *Av Magalhães Barata 376, www.museu-goeldi.br, Tue-Thu 0900-1200, 1400-1700, Fri 0900-1200, Sat-Sun 0900-1700, US$1.30, additional charges for specialist area*, takes up a city block and consists of the museum proper (with a fine collection of Marajó Indian pottery, an excellent exhibition of Mebengokre Indian lifestyle) and botanical exhibits including Victoria Régia lilies. Take a bus from the Cathedral.

A return trip on the ferry from Ver-o-Peso to **Icaoraci** provides a good view of the river. Several restaurants here serve excellent seafood; you can eat shrimp and drink coconut water and appreciate the breeze coming off the river. Icaoraci is 20 km east of the city and is well-known as a centre of ceramic production. The pottery is in Marajoara and Tapajonica style. Take the bus from Av Presidente Vargas to Icoaraci (one hr). Open all week but best on Tuesday to Friday. Artisans are friendly and helpful, will accept commissions and send purchases overseas.

The nearest beach is at **Outeiro** (35 km) on an island near Icoaraci, about an hour by bus and ferry (the bus may be caught near the Maloca, an *indígena*-style hut near the docks which serves as a nightclub). A bus from Icoaraci to Outeiro takes 30 minutes. Further north is the island of **Mosqueiro** (86 km) ⓘ *buses Belém-Mosqueiro every hr from rodoviária, US$2, 80 mins*, accessible by an excellent highway. It has many beautiful sandy beaches and jungle inland. It is popular at weekends when traffic can be heavy (also July) and the beaches can get crowded and polluted. Many hotels and weekend villas are at the villages of Mosqueiro and Vila; recommended (may be full weekends and July). Camping is easy and there are plenty of good places to eat.

Ilha do Marajó → *Colour map 5, A1.*

At almost 50,000 sq km, the world's largest island formed by fluvial processes is flooded in rainy December to June and provides a suitable habitat for water buffalo, introduced from India in the late 19th century. They are now farmed in large numbers (try the cheese and milk). It is also home to many birds, crocodiles and other wildlife, and has several good beaches. It is crowded at weekends and in the July holiday season. The island was the site of the pre-Columbian Marajoaras culture.

Ponta de Pedras

Boats leave Belém (near Porto do Sal, seat US$4.35, cabin US$47 for two, five hours) most days for Ponta de Pedras (**D Hotel Ponta de Pedras**, good meals, buses for Soure or Salvaterra meet the boat). Bicycles for hire (US$1 per hour) to explore beaches and the interior of the island. Fishing boats make the eight-hour trip to Cachoeira do Arari (one pousada, **D**) where there is a Marajó museum. A 10-hour boat trip from Ponta de Pedras goes to the Arari lake where there are two villages, Jenipapo built on stilts, forró dancing at weekends, and Santa Cruz which is less primitive, but less interesting (a hammock and a mosquito net are essential). There is a direct boat service to Belém twice a week.

Soure ➔ *Colour map 5, A1. Population: 20,000.*
The 'capital' of the island has fine beaches: Araruna (2 km – take supplies and supplement with coconuts and crabs, beautiful walks along the shore), do Pesqueiro (bus from Praça da Matriz, 1030, returns 1600, eat at Maloca, good, cheap, big, deserted beach, 13 km away) and Caju-Una (15 km). Small craft await passengers from the Enasa boats, for Salvaterra village (good beaches and bars: seafood), 10 minutes, or trips are bookable in Belém from Mururé, T3241 0891. There are also 17th-century Jesuit ruins at Joanes as well as a virgin beach. Changing money is only possible at very poor rates. Take plenty of insect repellent.

Macapá ➔ *Phone code: 0xx96. Post code: 68900. Colour map 2, C6. Population: 283,308.*
The capital of Amapá State is situated on the northern channel of the Amazon Delta and is linked to Belém by boat and daily flights. Along with Porto Santana it was declared a Zona Franca in 1993 and visitors flock to buy cheap imported electrical and other goods. Each brick of the **Fortaleza de São José do Macapá**, built between 1764 and 1782, was brought from Portugal as ballast; 50 iron cannons remain. Today it is used for concerts, exhibits, and colourful festivities on the anniversary of the city's founding, 4 February. In the handicraft complex (**Casa do Artesão**) ⓘ *Av Azárias Neto, Mon-Sat 0800-1900*, craftsmen produce their wares onsite. A feature is pottery decorated with local manganese ore, also woodcarvings, leatherwork and indigenous crafts. **São José Cathedral**, inaugurated by the Jesuits in 1761, is the city's oldest landmark.

The riverfront is a very pleasant place for an evening stroll. The **Complexo Beira-Rio** has food and drink kiosks, and a nice lively atmosphere. The pier (trapiche) has been rebuilt and is a lovely spot for savouring the cool of the evening breeze, or watching sunrise over the Amazon. There is a monument to the equator, **Marco Zero** (take Fazendinha bus). The equator also divides the nearby enormous football stadium in half, aptly named O Zerão. South of here, at Km 12 on Rodovia Juscelinho Kubitschek, are the **botanical gardens**. **Fazendinha** (16 km from the centre) is a popular local beach, very busy on Sunday. **Curiarú**, 8 km from Macapá, was founded by escaped slaves, and is popular at weekends for dancing and swimming.

Tourist offices: Detur ⓘ *Av Raimundo Álvares da Costa 18, Centro, T3223 0627. Branch at airport.*

Border with Guyane ➔ *Colour map 2, B6.*
The main road crosses the Rio Caciporé and continues to the border with Guyane at **Oiapoque** (*Population: 13,000*), on the river of the same name. It is 90 km inland from the Parque Nacional Cabo Orange (ICMBio contact T0xx96-3521 2706), Brazil's northernmost point on the Atlantic coast. About 7 km to the west is Clevelândia do Norte, a military outpost and the end of the road in Brazil. Oiapoque is remote, with its share of contraband, illegal migration, and drug trafficking. It is also the gateway to gold fields in the interior of both Brazil and Guyane. Visitors should take care late at night; the town is popular with French Guiana weekenders, most of them single men in search of the town's numerous women of ill repute. Prices here are high, but lower than in neighbouring Guyane. The **Cachoeira Grande Roche** rapids can be visited, upstream along the Oiapoque River, where it is possible to swim, US$30 per motor boat. The road north to the Guyane border (BR-156) is unpaved from Tatarugalzinho and is difficult in parts, especially during the wet season (but open throughout the year). It is advisable to carry extra fuel, food and water from Macapá onwards. Immigration officers will stamp you out the

day before if you want to make an early start to Guyane. A bridge linking Guyane and Amapá is under construction and the road is asphalted all the way to Cayenne. As combis to Cayenne leave before lunch it is best to get to St-Georges before 1000. There is already much deforestation along the Brazilian side of the road and many Brazilian *garimpeiros* and hunters are causing havoc in Guyane.

Belém and around listings

For Sleeping and Eating price codes and other relevant information, see Essentials, pages 38-40. See Telephone, page 397, for important phone changes.

Sleeping

Belém *p617, map p618*

There are now a few decent mid-range hotels in the city and a few clean, well-kept bargains in the upper budget category. The cheapest rooms are still very scruffy in Belém: consider an upgrade, this is a place where US$3-4 can make an enormous difference.

L Machado's Plaza, R Henrique Gurjão 200, T4008 9800, www.machadosplazahotel.com.br. Bright, brand new hotel with smart and tastefully decorated a/c rooms, a small business centre, plunge pool and a pleasant a/c breakfast area. Good value.

AL Itaoca, Av Pres Vargas 132, T4009 2400, itaoca@canal13.com.br. Well kept, bright a/c rooms, the best are on the upper floors away from the street noise, and with river views. Decent breakfast.

AL Regente, Av Gov José Malcher 485, T3181 5000, www.hotelregente.com.br. Small, a/c rooms with standard 3 star fittings above a noisy street. Popular with US tour groups.

AL Vila Rica, Av Júlio César 1777, T3210 2000, www.hotelvilarica.com.br/hotel_belem.htm. 5 mins from airport, helpful with transfers, very good.

A Le Massilia, R Henrique Gurjão 236, T3224 2834, www.massilia.com.br. Intimate, French owned boutique hotel with chic little duplexes and more ordinary doubles. Excellent French restaurant (🍴) and a tasty French breakfast.

B-C Grão Pará, Av Pres Vargas 718, T3224 9600. A/c rooms with contemporary fittings, smart, hot water, the best have superb river views, excellent breakfast, great value.

C Sete Sete, Trav 1 de Março 673, T3222 7730. Clean but still gloomy little rooms, good breakfast, convenient location, but be careful after dark.

C Unidos, Ó de Almeida 545, T3229 0600. Simple, spacious a/c rooms with cable TV and clean en suites.

C-D Novo Avenida, Av Pres.Vargas 404, T3242 9953, www.hotelnovoavenida.com.br. Slightly frayed but spruce rooms with decent breakfast. Groups of can sleep in large rooms for **E** pp. Very good value.

D pp **Amazônia Hostel**, Av Gov José Malcher 592, Nazaré (between Quintino Bocaiúva and Rui Barbosa), T4008 4800, www.amazonia hostel.com.br. Good hostel. (Don't confuse with **Amazônia**, R Ó de Almeida 548, which is not recommended.)

D-E Fortaleza, Trav Frutuoso Guimarães 276, T3212 1055. Unkempt hotel with a range of basic wood-floor rooms and dorms around a communal sitting area. Popular with backpackers. Careful in this area after dark.

D-E Palácio, Trav Frutuoso Guimarães, T3212 8422. Opposite and almost identical to the *Fortaleza*, though with scruffier communal areas and slightly cleaner rooms, and a restaurant/snack bar.

Ilha do Marajó *p619*

Soure

B Ilha do Marajó, 2a Travessa 10, 15 mins' walk from centre, T/F3741 1315, himarajo@inter conect.com.br. A/c, bath, pool, popular with package tours.

B Marajó, Praça Inhangaíba 351, Centro, T3741 1396. A/c, bath, clean, helpful owner.

D Pousada Asa Branca, Rua 4, T3741 1414. A/c, **E** with fan, breakfast, dirty, poor food.

Salvaterra

A Pousada das Guarãs, Av Beira Mar, Salvaterra, T/F4005 5656, www.pousadadosguaras.com.br. Well-equipped, tour programme, on beach.

Joanes

C Pousada Ventania do Rio-Mar, take bus, US$1.20 from Foz do Cámara, T3646 2067, 9992 5716, www.pousadaventania.com. Near the beach, with bath and breakfast, fan, hammocks, laundry service, arranges tours on horseback or canoe, Belgian and Brazilian owners. Ask about their social integration projects with locals.

Macapá *p620*

AL Ceta Ecotel, R do Matodouro 640, Fazendinha, T3227 3396, www.ecotel.com.br. 20 mins from town centre by taxi. All furniture made on site, a/c, sports facilities, gardens with sloths and monkeys, ecological trails. Highly recommended.

AL-A Atalanta, Av Coracy Nunes 1148, T3223 1612. 10 mins' walk from the river. The best business-style hotel in town with a rooftop pool and comfortable, modern a/c rooms, includes generous breakfast.

A Pousada Ekinox, R Jovino Dinoá 1693, T3223 0086, www.ekinox.com.br. Nice atmosphere, a/c, book and video library, excellent meals and service, riverboat tours available. Recommended.

C Glória, Leopoldo Machado 2085, T3222 0984. A/c, minibar, TV.

D-E Santo Antônio, Av Coriolano Jucá 485, T3222 0226, 1 block south and half a block east of Praça da Bandeira. Best rooms are on upper floors, cheaper with fan, good breakfast extra; **E** in dorm.

Border with Guyane: Oiapoque *p620*

Plenty of cheap, poorly maintained hotels along the waterfront.

D Kayaman, Av Joaquim Caetano da Silva 760, T3521 1256. A/c and bath, **E** with fan, poor showers, basic, international calls.

D Pousada Central, Av Coracy Nunes 209, one block from the river, T3521 1466. A/c, bath, **E** with fan and shared bath.

Eating

Belém *p617, map p618*

All the major hotels have good restaurants.

TTT Açaí Hilton Hotel, Av Pres Vargas 882, T3242 6500. Recommended for regional dishes and others, Sun brunch or daily lunch and dinner.

TTT Boteco das Onze, Praça F C Brandão s/n, T3224 8599. The best regional cooking in Belem with live music every night and river views.

TTT Churrascaria Rodeio, Trav Padre Eutíquio 1308 and Rodovia Augusto Montenegro Km 4, T3248 2004. A choice of 20 cuts of meat and 30 buffet dishes for a set price. Well worth the short taxi ride to eat all you can.

TTT Churrascaria Tucuruvi, Trav Benjamin Constant 1843, Nazaré, T3235 0341. Good value.

TTT Lá em Casa, Av Governador José Malcher 247 (also in Estação das Docas). Try menu paraense, good cooking, fashionable.

TT Cantina Italiana, Trav Benjamin Constant 1401. Very good Italian, also delivers.

TT Mãe Natureza, Manoel Barata 889, T3212 8032. Vegetarian and wholefood dishes in a bright clean dining room. Lunch only.

TT Sabor Paraense, R Sen Manoel Barata 897, T3241 4391. A variety of fish and meat dishes served in a bright, light dining room.

T Doces Bárbaros, Benjamin Constant 1658, T3224 0576. Cakes, snacks, sandwiches and decent coffee. Lunch only.

T Govinda, Ó de Almeida 198. Basic but tasty vegetarian food. Lunch only.

T Good snack bars serving *vatapá* (Bahian dish), tapioca rolls, etc, are on Assis de Vasconcelos on the eastern side of the Praça da Republica.

Macapá *p620*

TTT Chalé, Av Pres Vargas 499. Nice atmosphere and good food.

TT Cantinho Baiano, Av Beira-Rio 1, Santa Inês. Good seafood. 10 mins' walk south of the fort. Many other restaurants along this stretch about 1½ km beyond the Cantino Baiano including the **Vista Amazônica**, see Sleeping, above.

TT Martinho's Peixaria, Av Beira-Rio 810. Another good fish restaurant.

T Bom Paladar Kilo's, Av Pres Vargas 456. Good pay-by-weight buffet.

T Sorveteria Macapá, R São José 1676, close to centre. Excellent ice cream made from local fruit.

Bars and clubs

Belém *p617, map p618*

Belém has some of the best and most distinctive live music and nightlife in northern Brazil.

A Pororó. Vast warehouse jam packed with techno *brega* acts playing a kind of up tempo disco driven 2/4 dance to thousands of people every Fri and Sat.

Bar do Gilson, Travessa Padre Eutíquio 3172, T3272 1306. A covered courtyard decorated with black and white photography, live samba and *choro* at weekends.

Café com Arte, Av Rui Barbosa 1436. Good after 2300. A colonial house with 3 floors devoted to live rock and DJs.

Carousel, Av Almte Barroso at Antônio Baena. Live *aparelhagem* – a kind of up-tempo techno with twanging guitars played by DJs on a sound stage that looks like the flight control gallery for a 1970s starship. Has to be seen to be believed. Every Fri.

Mormoço, Praça do Arsenal s/n, Mangal das Garças. A warehouse-sized building on the waterfront, some of the best live bands in Belém at weekends, playing local rhythms like *carimbó* and Brazilianized reggae and rock.

São Mateus, Travessa Padre Eutíquio 606. A mock Carioca *boteco* street bar, Belém rock and Brazilian soul most nights.

Festivals and events

Belém *p617, map p618*

Círio (Festival of Candles) in **Oct**, is based on the legend of the Nossa Senhora de Nazaré, whose image was found on the site of her Basílica around 1700. On the 2nd Sun in Oct, a procession carries a copy of the Virgin's image from the Basílica to the cathedral. On the Mon, 2 weeks later, the image is returned to its usual place. There is a Círio museum in the Basílica crypt, enter at the right side of the church; free. (Hotels are fully booked during Círio.)

Macapá *p620*

Marabaixo is the traditional music and dance of the state of Amapá; a festival held 40 days after Easter. The sambódromo, near Marco Zero, is used by Escolas de Samba during Carnaval and by Quadrilhas during the São João festivities.

Shopping

Belém *p617, map p618*

A good place to buy hammocks is the street parallel to the river, 1 block inland from Ver-o-Peso, starting at US$5-7.50.

Arts and crafts market, Praça da República every weekend. Seed and bead jewellery, whicker, hammocks and raw cotton weave work, toys and knic-knacs. Mostly predictable but the odd gem.

Complexo São Brás, Praça Lauro Sodré. Handicraft market and folkloric shows in a building dating from 1911.

Parfumaria Orion, Trav Frutuoso Guimarães 268. Sells a variety of perfumes from Amazonian plants, much cheaper than tourist shops.

Activities and tours

Belém *p617, map p618*

Larger hotels organize city and 1-day boat tours.

Amazon Star, R Henrique Gurjão 236, T/F3241 8624, amazonstar@amazonstar.com.br. City and river tours, Ilha de Marajó hotel bookings and tours, very professional, good guides, jungle tours, books flight tickets. Repeatedly recommended.

Amazônia Sport & Ação, Av 25 de Setembro 2345, T3226 8442. Extreme sports, diving and climbing.

Macapá *p620*

Awara, Av Presidente Vargas 2396-B, T/F3222 0970. Recommended for city and river tours.

Marco Zero, R São José 2048, T3223 1922. Recommended for flights.

Transport

Belém *p617, map p618*

Air Bus 'Perpétuo Socorro-Telégrafo' or 'Icoaraci', every 15 mins from the Prefeitura, Praça Felipe Patroni, to the airport, 40 mins, US$0.65. Taxi to airport, US$15 (ordinary taxis are cheaper than Co-op taxis, buy ticket in advance in Departures side of airport). ATMs for credit cards in the terminal. Airport T3210 6272.

Daily flights south to **Brasília** and other Brazilian cities, and west to **Santarém** and **Manaus**. To **Paramaribo** and **Cayenne**, 2 a week with Surinam Airways. Travellers entering Brazil from Guyane may need a 60-day visa (takes 2 days) before airlines will confirm their tickets. Internal flights also offered by TAM.

Bus The rodoviária is at the end of Av Governador José Malcher 5 km from the centre (T3246 8178). Take Aeroclube, Cidade Novo, No 20 bus, or Arsenal or Canudos buses, US$1, or taxi, US$10 (day), US$12 (night) (at rodoviária you are given a ticket with the taxi's number on it, threaten to go to the authorities if the driver tries to overcharge). Good snack bar, showers (US$0.15) and 2 agencies with information and tickets for riverboats. Regular bus services to all major cities. To **Santarém**, via Marabá (on the Trans- amazônica) once a week (US$100, can take longer than boat, goes only in dry season). **Transbrasiliana** go direct to Marabá, 16 hrs, US$44. To **São Luís**, 2 a day, US$40, 13 hrs, interesting journey through marshlands. To **Fortaleza**, US$94 (24 hrs), many companies. To **Recife**, US$115, 34 hrs.

Ferry To **Santarém, Manaus**, and intermediate ports (see River Transport, Amazônia, page 616). All larger ships berth at Portobrás/Docas do Pará (the main commercial port) at Armazém (ware- house) No 10 (entrance on Av Marechal Hermes, corner of Av Visconde de Souza Franco). The guards will sometimes ask to see your ticket before letting you into the port area, but tell them you are going to speak with a ship's captain. Ignore the touts who approach you and avoid a boat called *Amazon Star*: it has a deservedly bad reputation. **Macamazónia**, R Castilho Franca, sells tickets for most boats, open Sun. There are 2 desks selling tickets for private boats in the rodoviária; some hotels recommend agents for tickets. Purchase tickets from offices 2 days in advance. Smaller vessels (sometimes cheaper, usually not as clean, comfortable or safe) sail from small docks along Estrada Nova (not a safe part of town). Take a Cremação bus from Ver-o-Peso.

To **Macapá (Porto Santana)**, the quickest (12 hrs) are the catamaran Atlântico I or the launches Lívia Marília and Atlântico II (slightly slower), all leaving at 0700 on alternate days. Other boats take 24 hrs: **Silja e Souza** (Wed) of Souzamar, Trav Dom Romualdo Seixas corner R Jerônimo Pimentel, T3222 0719, and **Almirante Solon** (Sat) of Sanave (Serviço Amapaense de Navegação, Castilho Franca 234, opposite Ver-o- Peso, T3222 7810), slightly cheaper, crowded, not as nice. Via Breves, ENAL, T3224 5210 (see River Transport in Amazônia, page 616). Smaller boats to Macapá also sail from Estrada Nova.

Ilha do Marajó *p619*

Ferry From Belém docks the Enasa ferry sails to Soure on Fri at 2000 (4 hrs, US$10). There are daily boats to Foz do Cámara at 0630, 0700 and 1300 (1½-3 hrs US$7.50). Then take a bus to Salvaterra and a ferry to Soure. Boats return from Foz do Cámara at 0800 and 1100. There is a 'taxi-plane' service to Soure leaving Belém at 0630 returning 1600, US$60.

Macapá *p620*

Air TAM (T223 2688), fly to Belém and other Brazilian cities. **Gol** fly to Belém (at night), Brasília and São Paulo.

Bus Rodoviária on BR-156, north of Macapá. To **Amapá**, **Calçoene** and **Oiapoque** (15-17 hrs, US$33), at least 2 daily. The road is from Amapá to the border is due to be paved; before then you may have to get out and walk up hills, bus has no a/c.

Ferry Ships dock at Porto Santana, 30 km from Macapá (frequent buses US$2.50, or share a taxi US$30). To **Belém**, **Silja e Souza** of Souzamar, Cláudio Lúcio Monteiro 1375, Santana, and **Almirante Solon** of Sanave, Av Mendonça Furtado 1766. See under Belém, River Services, for other boats. Purchase tickets from offices 2 days in advance. Also smaller and cheaper boats. The faster (12 hr) catamaran Atlântico I or launches leave for Belém most days. **São Francisco de Paula I** sails to **Santarém** and **Manaus**, not going via Belém.

Border with Guyane: Oiapoque *p620*

Air Flights to **Macapá** Mon-Fri with **Penta**, office on the waterfront, T/F3521 1117. While waiting for flights to Cayenne from St-Georges, it is much cheaper to stay on the Brazilian side.

Bus At least 2 a day for **Macapá**, 12-15 hrs (dry season), 14-24 hrs (wet season), US$33. Also shared jeeps, US$22.50 in the back, or US$55 in the cabin. You may be asked to show your Polícia Federal entry stamp and Yellow Fever vaccination certificate either when buying a ticket from the offices on the waterfront or at the bus station when boarding for Macapá.

Ferry **Crossing to Guyane**: motorized canoes cross to St-Georges de L'Oyapock, 10 mins down-stream, US$5 pp, bargain for return fare. A vehicle ferry will operate until the bridge is completed.

Directory

Belém *p617, map p618*

Airline offices Penta, Av Sen Lemos 4700, T3244 7777. **Rico**, Av Assis de Vasconcelos 207, Campinas, T3241 4433. **Surinam Airways**, R Gaspar Viana 488, T3212 7144, airport 211 6038, English spoken, helpful with information and documentation. **Banks** Banco do Brasil, Av Pres Vargas (near Hotel Central), good rates but US$20 commission and slow, Visa ATMs, and other Brazilian banks (open 0900-1630, but foreign exchange only until 1300). **HSBC**, Av Pres Vargas near Praça da República has MasterCard Cirrus and Amex ATMs. **Banco de Amazônia** (Basa), on Pres Vargas, gives good rates for TCs (Amex or Citicorp only), but does not change cash. **Itaú**, R Boaventura 580, good TCs and cash rates. Money can only be changed at banks during the week. At weekends hotels will only exchange for their guests, while restaurants may change money, but at poor rates. Exchange rates are generally the best in the north of the country. **Embassies and consulates** **Denmark**, Nordisk Timber Ltda, Rod Augusto Montenegro Km 11, Icoaraci, T4006 7700, fls.br@dlh-group.com. **Finland/Sweden**, Av Senador Lemos 529, Umarizal, T3222 0148. **Germany**, R Tiradentes 67, sala 204, T3212 8366, hsteffen.bel@orm.com.br. **UK**, Av Governador Magalhães Barata 651, Sala 610, T4009 0050, chris.mayhew@wilsonsons.com.br. **Venezuela**, opposite French Consulate, Av Pres Pernambuco 270, T3222 6396 (Venezuelan visa for those entering overland takes 3 hrs, costs US$30 for most nationalities, but we are told that it is better to get a visa at Manaus, Boa Vista or before you leave home. **Medical services** Health: a yellow fever certificate or inoculation is mandatory. It is best to get a yellow fever vaccination at home (always have your certificate handy) and avoid the risk of recycled needles. Medications for malaria prophylaxis are not sold in Belém pharmacies. Bring an adequate supply from home. **Clínica de Medicina Preventativa**, Av Bras de Aguiar 410 (T3222 1434), will give injections, English spoken, open 0730-1200, 1430-1900 (Sat 0800-1100). **Hospital Ordem Terceira**, Trav Frei Gil de Vila Nova 2, doctors speak some English, free consultation but it's a bit primitive. Surgery open Mon 1300-1900, Tue-Thu 0700-1100, 24 hrs for emergencies. The British consul has a list of English-speaking doctors. **Post offices** Av Pres Vargas 498, but international parcels are only accepted at the Post Office on the praça at the corner of Trav Frutuoso Guimarães e R 15 de Novembro, next door to NS das Mercês (hard to find). **Telephones** For phone calls: **Telemar**, Av Pres Vargas. Fax at the Post Office, Av Pres Vargas.

Macapá *p620*

Banks Banco do Brasil, R Independência 250, cash, Visa, ATM and TCs. Visa ATM also at **Bradesco**, Cândido Mendes 1316. MasterCard and Amex ATM at **HSBC**, Av Pres Vargas. **Casa Francesa**, Independência 232, changes euros (euros can be bought in Macapá and Belém). **Embassies and consulates** For the French honorary consul, ask at Pousada Ekinox, visas for Guyane have to be obtained from Brasília which can take a while. **Post offices** Av Coriolano Jucá. International calls can be made at São José 2050, 0730-1000.

Border with Guyane: Oiapoque *p620*

Banks Exchange: It is possible to exchange US$ and reais to euros, but dollar rates are low and TCs are not accepted anywhere. **Banco do Brasil**, Av Barão do Rio Branco, open 1000-1500, and **Bradesco**, have Visa facilities to withdraw reais which can be changed into euros. **Casa Francesa**, on the riverfront, and one câmbio in the market sell reais for US$ or euros. Rates are worse in St-Georges. Best to buy euros in Belém, or abroad. **Post offices** Av Barão do Rio Branco, open 0900-1200, 1400-1700. **Useful addresses** Immigration: **Polícia Federal**, for Brazilian exit and entry stamps, is on the road behind the church about 500 m from the river.

Belém to Manaus

A few hours up the broad river from Belém, the region of the thousand islands is entered. The passage through this maze of islets is known as 'The Narrows' and is perhaps the nicest part of the journey. The ship winds through 150 km of lanes of yellow flood with equatorial forest within 20 m or 30 m on both sides. On one of the curious flat-topped hills after the Narrows stands the little stucco town of **Monte Alegre**, an oasis in mid-forest (airport; some simple hotels, **D-E**). There are lagoon cruises to see lilies, birds, pink dolphins; also village visits (US$25-40 per day).

Santarém → *Phone code: 0xx93. Post code: 68000. Colour map 4, A5. Population: 262,538.*

The third largest city on the Brazilian Amazon is small enough to walk around. It was founded in 1661 as the Jesuit mission of Tapajós; the name was changed to Santarém in 1758. There was once a fort here and attractive colonial squares overlooking the waterfront remain. Standing at the confluence of the Rio Tapajós with the Amazon, on the southern bank, Santarém is halfway (two or three days by boat) between Belém and Manaus. Most visitors breeze in and out on a stopover by boat or air. **Tourist office: SANTUR** ⓘ *Tv Inácio Corrêa 22, T/F3523 2434*, has good information available in English.

The yellow Amazon water swirls alongside the green-blue Tapajós; the **meeting of the waters**, in front of the market square, is nearly as impressive as that of the Negro and Solimões near Manaus. A small **Museu dos Tapajós** in the old city hall on the waterfront, now the **Centro Cultural João Fora** ⓘ *open 0900, closed weekend, free*, downriver from where the boats dock, has a collection of ancient Tapajós ceramics, as well as various 19th-century artefacts. The unloading of the fish catch between 0500 and 0700 on the waterfront is interesting. There are good beaches nearby on the Rio Tapajós.

Alter do Chão

Some 34 km west of Santarém is this friendly village on the Rio Tapajós, at the outlet of Lago Verde. Of particular interest is the **Centro do Preservação de Arte Indígena** ⓘ *R Dom Macedo Costa, T527 1110, 0800-1200, 1300-1700*, which has a varied collection of artefacts from tribes of Amazônia and Mato Grosso. Good swimming in the Tapajós from the beautiful, clean beach.

Óbidos and around → *Phone code: 0xx93. Population: 46,500.*

At 110 km up-river from Santarém (five hours by boat), Óbidos is located at the narrowest and deepest point on the river. It is a picturesque and clean city with many beautiful, tiled buildings and some nice parks. Worth seeing are the **Prefeitura Municipal** ⓘ *T547 1194*, the cuartel and the **Museu Integrado de Óbidus** ⓘ *R Justo Chermont 607, Mon-Fri 0700-1100, 1330-1730*. There is also a **Museu Contextual**, a system of plaques with detailed explanations of historical buildings throughout town. The airport has flights to Manaus, Santarém and Parintins.

Just across the Pará-Amazonas border, between Santarém and Manaus, is **Parintins** (*Phone code: 0xx92. Post code: 69150-000*), 15 hours by boat upriver from Óbidos. Here, on the last three days of June each year, the **Festa do Boi** draws over 50,000 visitors. Since the town has only two small hotels, everyone sleeps in hammocks on the boats that bring them to the festival from Manaus and Santarém. The festival consists of lots of folkloric dancing, but its main element is the competition between two rival groups, the Caprichoso and the Garantido, in the bumbódromo, built in 1988 to hold 35,000 spectators.

Belém to Manaus listings

For Sleeping and Eating price codes and other relevant information, see Essentials, pages 38-40. See Telephone, page 397, for important phone changes.

Sleeping

Santarém *p626*

AL Amazon Park I, Av Mendonça Furtado 4120, T3523 2800, amazon@ netsan.com.br. Swimming pool, 4 km from centre, taxi US$4.

A-B Mirante, Trav Francisco Correa, 115, T3067 7100, www.mirantehotel.com. Homely, a/c, fridge, TV, some rooms with balcony, individual safes, internet, good value. Recommended.

B-C Brasil Grande Hotel, Trav 15 de Agosto 213, T3522 5660. Family-run, with restaurant.

B-C New City, Trav Francisco Correia 200, T3523 2351. A/c, frigobar, good, will collect from airport.

B-C Santarém Palace, Rui Barbosa 726, T3523 2820. A/c, TV, fridge, comfortable.

C Brasil, Trav dos Mártires 30, T3523 6665. Nice, family-run, includes good breakfast, communal bath, good food, good service.

C Horizonte, Trav Senador Lemos 737, T522 5437, horizontehotel@bol.com.br. With a/c, **F** with fan, modern.

C-D Rios, R Floriano Peixoto 720, T522 5701. Large rooms, comfortable, a/c, fridge and TV.

Alter do Chão *p626*

A Pousada Tupaiulândia, Pedro Teixeira 300, T0xx93-3527 1157. A/c, unimpressive but OK, very helpful, good breakfast for US$5, next to telephone office opposite bus stop.

D Pousada Villa Praia, first on the right as you enter the village, T3527 1130. Large rooms, a/c, very helpful staff, good value.

Óbidos *p626*

Several in our **C** price range.

C Braz Bello, R Corrêia Pinto, on top of the hill. Shared bath, full board available.

C Pousada Brasil, R Correia Pinto. Basic, with bath, cheaper without.

Eating

Santarém *p626*

TT Mascote, Praça do Pescador 10. Open 1000-2330, restaurant, bar and ice cream parlour.

TT Mascotinho, Praça Manoel de Jesus Moraes, on riverfront. Bar/pizzeria, popular, outside seating, good view.

TT Santa Antônio, Av Tapajós 2061. Churrasco and fish.

T Lucy, Praça do Pescador. Good juices and pastries. Recommended.

Alter do Chão *p626*

Lago Verde, Praça 7 de Setembro. Good fresh fish, try caldeirada de tucunaré, huge portions.

Festivals and events

Santarém *p626*

29 Jun, **São Pedro**, with processions of boats on the river and boi-bumbá dance dramas.

Alter do Chão *p626*

2nd week in Sep, **Festa do Çairé**, religious processions and folkloric events.

Activities and tours

Santarém *p626*

Amazon Jungle Tours, R Galdino Veloso 200, T3529 0146, 9903 7320, radarfinder@ hotmail.com. Tours from 1 to 7 days by boat, English, French and Spanish spoken.

Amazon Tours, Trav Turiano Meira 1084, www.amazonriver.com. Owner Steve Alexander is a very friendly, helpful man who can give you lots of hints on what to do. He also organizes excursions for groups to remote areas which are quite expensive. Recommended. **Santarém Tur**, in Amazon Park, and at R Adriano Pimental 44, T3522 4847, www.santaremtur.com.br. Owned by Perpétua and Jean-Pierre Schwarz (speaks French), friendly, helpful, also group tours (group of 5, US$65 per day pp). Recommended.

Gil Serique, Av Adriano Pimentel 80, T3522 5174, 9654 3702, www.youramazon.org. English-speaking guide. Recommended.

Transport

Santarém *p626*

Air 15 km from town, T523 1021. Internal flights only. Buses run to the centre or waterfront. From the centre the bus leaves in front of the cinema in Rui Barbosa every 80 mins from 0550 to 1910, or taxis (US$15 to waterfront). The hotels Amazon Park and New City have free buses for guests; you may be able to take these.

Bus Rodoviária is on the outskirts, take 'Rodagem' bus from the waterfront near the market, US$0.35. Santarém to **Marabá** on the Rio Tocantins with Transbrasiliana. From Marabá there are buses east and west on the Transamazônica. Enquire at the rodoviária for other destinations. Road travel during rainy season is always difficult, often impossible.

Ferry To **Manaus**, **Belém**, **Macapá**, **Itaituba**, and intermediate ports (see River transport, page 616). Boats to Belém and Manaus dock at the Cais do Porto, 1 km west, take 'Floresta-Prainha', 'Circular' or 'Circular Externo' bus; taxi US$7.50. Boats to other destinations, including Macapá, dock by the waterfront by the centre of town. Local service to **Óbidos**, US$18, 4 hrs, **Oriximiná** US$20, **Alenquer**, and **Monte Alegre** (US$18, 5-8 hrs).

Alter do Chão *p626*

Bus Tickets and information from the bus company kiosk opposite Pousada Tupaiulândia. From Santarém: bus stop on Av São Sebastião, in front of Colégio Santa Clara, US$2, about 1 hr.

Óbidos and around: Parintins *p626*

Ferry Apart from boats that call on the **Belém-Manaus** route, there are irregular sailings from **Óbidos** (ask at the port). Journey times are about 12-15 hrs from **Manaus** and 20 from **Santarém**. There is also a small airport with **flights** to **Manaus**, **Óbidos** and **Santarém**.

Directory

Santarém *p626*

Airline offices Penta, Trav 15 de Novembro 183, T523 2532. **Banks** Cash withdrawals on Visa at Banco do Brasil, Av Rui Barbosa 794. It is very difficult to change dollars (impossible to change TCs anywhere), try travel agencies. **Post office** Praça da Bandeira 81. **Telephones** Posto Trin, R Siquiera Campos 511. 0700-1900 Mon-Sat, 0700-2100 Sun.

Manaus → *Phone code: 0xx92. Post code: 69000. Colour map 4, A3. Population: 1.7 million.*

The next city upriver is Manaus, capital of Amazonas State – the largest in Brazil. Once an isolated urban island in the jungle, it now sprawls over a series of eroded and gently sloping hills divided by numerous creeks (igarapés). The city is growing fast and 20-storey modern buildings are rising above the traditional flat, red-tiled roofs. An initiative in 2001 saw the start of a restoration programme in which historic buildings have been given a new lease of life and theatres, cultural spaces and libraries created. Manaus is an excellent port of entry for visiting the Amazon. Less than a day away are river islands and tranquil waterways. The opportunities for trekking in the forest, canoeing and meeting local people should not be missed and, once you are out of reach of the urban influence, there are plenty of animals to see. There is superb swimming in the natural pools and under falls of clear water in the little streams which rush through the woods, but take locals' advice on swimming in the river (both for nature's animal hazards and man's pollution).

Ins and outs → *Manaus is 1 hr behind Brazilian standard time (2 hrs Oct-Feb, Brazil's summer time).*

Getting there Boats dock at different locations depending on where they have come from. The **docks** are quite central. The **airport** is 18 km from the centre, the **bus terminal** 9 km. Both are served by local buses and taxis.

Getting around All city bus routes start below the cathedral in front of the port entrance; just ask someone for the destination you want. The city centre is easily explored on foot (although bear in mind an average temp of 27°C). ▸▸ *See Transport, page 638, for further details.*

Tourist office AmazonasTur (state tourism office) ⓘ *R Saldanha Marinho 321, T2123 3800, www.visitamazonas.am.gov.br, open 0800-1700. Offices at Avenida Eduardo Ribeiro 666, near Teatro Amazonas, T3182 6250, Mon-Fri 0800-1700, Sat 0800-1200.* Limited English and information. At the airport ⓘ *T3182 9850, daily 24 hrs.* Also in Amazonas Shopping Center ⓘ *Av Djalma Batista 482, Chapada, T3648 1396, Mon-Sat 0900-2200, Sun and holidays 0300-2100,* in the new cruise ship terminal at the docks (open when a ship is in town). ManausTur (Fundação Municipal de Turismo) ⓘ *Av 7 de Setembro 384, T3215 3447, www.manaus.am.gov.br.* Weekend editions of *A Crítica*, newspaper, list local entertainment and events. See also www.culturamazonas.am.gov.br and www.manausonline.com.

Security Manaus is a friendly, if busy city and a good deal safer than the big cities of southern Brazil. As in any city, the usual precautions against opportunist crime should be taken, especially

Manaus

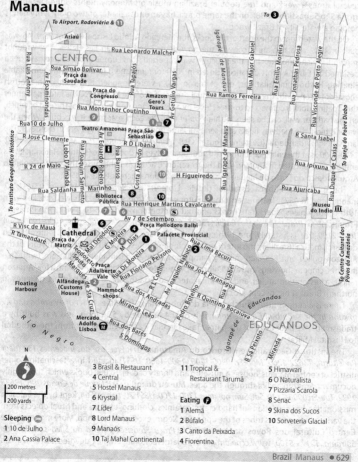

Sleeping
1 10 de Julho
2 Ana Cassia Palace
3 Brasil & Restaurant
4 Central
5 Hostel Manaus
6 Krystal
7 Lider
8 Lord Manaus
9 Manaós
10 Taj Mahal Continental
11 Tropical & Restaurant Tarumã

Eating
1 Alemã
2 Búfalo
3 Canto da Peixada
4 Fiorentina
5 Himawari
6 O Naturalista
7 Pizzaria Scarola
8 Senac
9 Skina dos Sucos
10 Sorveteria Glacial

when arriving at night (see River transport in Amazônia on staying on boats in port). Bars and streets in the working heart of port area, south of Rua Quintino, are not places to hang around after dark. ▸▸ *See page 632 for advice on choosing a jungle tour.*

Sights

Dominating the centre is a **Cathedral** built in simple Jesuit style on a hillock; very plain inside or out. Nearby is the main shopping and business area, the tree-lined Avenida Eduardo Ribeiro; crossing it is Av 7 de Setembro, bordered by ficus trees. **Teatro Amazonas** ⓘ *Praça São Sebastião, T3622 1880 for information on programmes, Mon-Sat 0900-1600, 20-min tour US$5.70. Recommended.* About same price for a concert. This opulent theatre was completed in 1896 during the great rubber boom following 15 years of construction. It has been restored four times and should not be missed. There are ballet, theatre and opera performances several times a week and free popular Brazilian music on Monday nights, June-December. **Igreja São Sebastião** (1888), on the same praça, has an unusual altar of two giant ivory hands holding a water lily of Brazil wood.

On the waterfront in the heart of the docks, the **Mercado Adolfo Lisboa**, Rua dos Barés 46, was built in 1902 as a miniature copy of the now demolished Parisian Les Halles. The wrought ironwork which forms much of the structure was imported from Europe and is said to have been designed by Eiffel. A short distance (closed in 2010 for renovation) to the west the remarkable **Floating Harbour installations**, completed in 1902, were designed and built by a Scottish engineer to cope with the up to 14 m annual rise and fall of the Rio Negro. The large passenger ship floating dock is connected to street level by a 150 m-long floating ramp, at the end of which, on the harbour wall, can be seen the high water mark for each year since it was built. When the water is high, the roadway floats on a series of large iron tanks measuring 2½m in diameter. The large beige **Alfândega** (Customs House) ⓘ *R Marquês de Santa Cruz, Mon-Fri 0800-1200, 1400-1600*, is at the entrance to the city if your boat arrives to dock at the Floating Harbour. It was entirely prefabricated in England, and the tower once acted as lighthouse. The entire **Conjunto Arquitetônico do Porto de Manaus** was declared a national heritage site in 1987.

The **Biblioteca Pública Estadual** (Public Library) ⓘ *R Barroso 57, Mon-Fri 0730-1730*, inaugurated in 1871, features an ornate European cast iron staircase. It is well stocked with 19th-century newspapers, rare books and old photographs, and worth a visit. The **Palacete Provincial** ⓘ *Praça Heliodoro Balbi, T3635 5832, Tue-Fri 0900-1700, Sat 1000-1900, Sun 1600-2100, free*, is a stately, late 19th-century civic palace, housing six small museums: Museu de Numismática (Brazilian and international coins and notes), Museu Tiradentes (history of the Amazon police and Brazilian military campaigns), Museu da Imagem e do Som (with free internet, cinema showings and a DVD library), Museu de Arqueologia (preserving a few Amazon relics), a restoration atelier and the Pinacoteca do Estado, one of the best art galleries in northern Brazil. It has decent a/c café.

There is a curious little church, **Igreja do Pobre Diabo** ⓘ *at the corner of Av Borba and Av Ipixuna in the suburb of Cachoeirinha*; it is only 4 m wide by 5 m long, and was built by a tradesman, the 'poor devil' of the name. Take Circular 7 Cachoeirinha bus from the cathedral to Hospital Militar.

The **Instituto Geográfico e Histórico do Amazonas** ⓘ *R Frei José dos Inocentes 132 (near Prefeitura), T3622 1260, Mon-Fri 0900-1200, 1300-1600, US$1*, located in a fascinating older district of central Manaus, houses a museum and library of over 10,000 books which thoroughly document Amazonian life through the ages. **Museu do Índio** ⓘ *R Duque de Caxias 296, T3635 1922, Tue-Fri 0900-1730, Sat, Sun, holidays 1300-1700, US$1.70, free on Sun*, kept by the Salesian missionaries, has collections of handicrafts, ceramics, clothing, utensils and ritual objects from the various indiegenous tribes of the upper Rio Negro; excellent craft shop. More modern is the **Centro Cultural dos Povos da Amazônia** ⓘ *Praça Francisco Pereira da Silva s/n, Bola da Suframa, T2125 5300, www.ccpa.am.gov.br*, a large cultural complex devoted to Amazonian indigenous peoples, with a large, well-curated museum whose artefacts including splendid headdresses, ritual clothing and weapons; explanatory displays in Portuguese and passable English. There are also play areas for the kids, a library and internet.

Botanic Gardens, **Instituto Nacional de Pesquisas Amazonas** (INPA) ⓘ *Estrada do Aleixo, at Km 3, not far from the Museu de Ciências Naturais da Amazônia, T3643 3377, www.inpa.gov.br, Mon-Fri 0900-1100, 1400-1630, Sat-Sun 0900-1600, US$2, take any bus to Aleixo.* At the centre for scientific research in the Amazon, labs (not open to the public) investigate farming, medicines and tropical diseases in the area. There is a small museum and restaurant, lots of birds, named trees and manatees (best seen Wednesday and Friday mornings when the water is changed), caimans and giant otters; worth a visit. INPA also manages what is probably the largest urban rainforest reserves in the world, on the northeastern edge of Manaus. The **zoo** ⓘ *Estrada Ponta Negra 750 (look for the life-size model jaguar), T3625 2044, Tue-Sun 0900-1630, US$0.65, plus US$1 for trail, getting there: take bus 120 or 207, 'Ponta Negra', from R Tamandaré, US$1.* It is run by CIGS, the army jungle-survival unit. It has been expanded and improved and has a 800-m trail which leads into the zoo itself.

Excursions About 15 km from Manaus is the confluence of the yellow-brown Solimões (Amazon) and the blue-black Rio Negro, which is itself some 8 km wide, commonly known as the **'meeting of the waters'**. The two rivers run side by side for about 18 km (says one traveller) without their waters mingling. You can see this natural phenomenon in a range of ways depending on time and budget. Tourist agencies run boat trips to this spot (US$60-160) from town, or take you down to the CEASA ferry dock and make a trip from there. The simplest route is to take a taxi or No 713 'Vila Buriti' bus to the CEASA ferry dock, and take the car ferry across. The ferry (very basic, with no shelter on deck and no cabins) runs all day until 1800 (approximately). Passenger ferries commute the crossing and you'll skim over the meeting of the waters for US$2 each way. Small private launches cross, 40 minutes' journey, US$15-20 per seat, ask for the engine to be shut off at the confluence, you should see dolphins especially in the early morning. Alternatively, hire a motor boat from near the market (US$17 per person, US$95 per boat, up to eight people), or take a boat from the **Hotel Tropical** (US$100 for 5 people); allow three to four hours to experience the meeting properly). A 2-km walk along the Porto Velho road from the CEASA ferry terminal will lead to a point from which Victoria Regia water lilies can be seen in April/May-September in ponds, some way from the road. Agencies can arrange tours.

A new 3.5-km road bridge is being built over the Rio Negro connecting Manaus with Iranduba. It will be completed in late 2010.

Museu Seringal ⓘ *Igarapé São João, 15 km north of Manaus up the Rio Negro, Tue-Sun 0800-1600, T3234 8755, US$3, US$15 round trip on a private launch from the Hotel Tropical,* is a full-scale reproduction of an early 20th-century rubber-tapping mansion house, serf quarters, factory and shop complete with authentic products. A guided tour, especially from one of the former rubber tappers, brings home the full horror of the system of debt peonage which enslaved Brazilians up until the 1970s. The museum can be visited with **Amazon Flower** or **Amazon Gero's Tours**.

The small town of **Presidente Figueiredo** is set in forest and savannah rich in waterfalls and cut by many clear-water rivers. Numerous threatened and endangered bird species live here, including Guianan Cock of the Rock. Presidente Figueiredo can easily be visited in a day trip from Manaus.

Arquipélago de Anavilhanas, the largest archipelago in a river in the world, is in the Rio Negro, some 100 km upstream from Manaus, near the town of Novo Airão. There are hundreds of islands, covered in thick vegetation. When the river is low, white sand beaches are revealed, as well as the roots and trunks of the trees. Tour companies arrange visits to the archipelago (see page 636).

Mamirauá ⓘ *4-day, 3-night package US$360 all inclusive ("worth every penny"). Reservations through T0xx97-3343 4672, www.mamiraua.org.br, or Amazon Gero's Tours. Book well in advance. All profits go to local projects and research. Daily flights Manaus-Tefé, then 1½ hours by boat to* *lodge.* This sustainable development reserve, at the confluence of the Rios Solimões, Japurá and Auti-Paraná, is one of the best places to see the Amazon. It protects flooded forest (várzea) and is listed under the Ramsar Convention as an internationally important wetland. In the reserve **Uakari** (www.uakarilodge.com.br) is a floating lodge with 10 suites. Lots of mammals and birds to see, including cayman, dolphin and harpy eagles, also the endangered piraracu fish. Visitors are accompanied by guides the whole time.

Tours from Manaus

There are two types of tours: those based at **jungle lodges** and **river boat trips**. Most tours, whether luxury or budget, combine river outings on motorized canoes with piranha fishing, caiman spotting, visiting local families and short treks in the jungle. Specialist tours include fishing trips and those aimed specifically at seeing how the people in the jungle, caboclos, live. Booking in advance on the internet is likely to secure you a good guide (who usually works for several companies and may get booked up). Be sure to ascertain in advance the exact itinerary of the tour, that the price includes everything (even drink and tips), that guides are knowledgeable and will accompany you themselves and that there will be no killing of anything rare. Ensure that others in your party share your expectations and are going for the same length of time. Choose a guide who speaks a language you understand. A shorter tour may be better than a long, poor one. Packaged tours, booked overseas, are usually of the same price and quality as those negotiated locally.

Note There are many hustlers at the airport and on the street (particularly around the hotels and bars on Joaquim Nabuco and Miranda Leão), and even at the hotels. Don't go with the first friendly face you meet. Investigate a few operators, make enquiries and check for official and ABAV (Brazilian Association of Travel Agents) credentials personally. Secretaria de Estado da Cultura e Turismo is not allowed by law to recommend guides, but can provide you with a list of legally registered companies. Unfortunately, disreputable operations are rarely dealt with in any satisfactory manner and most continue to operate. When you are satisfied that you have found a reputable company, book direct with the company itself and ask for a detailed, written contract if you have any doubts.

Flights over the jungle give a spectacular impression of the extent of the forest. Bill Potter, resident in Manaus, writes: "opposite Manaus, near the junction of the Rio Negro and the Rio Solimões, lies the **Lago de Janauri**, a small nature reserve. This is where all the day or half-day trippers are taken, usually combined with a visit to the 'meeting of the waters'. Although many people express disappointment with this area because so little is seen and/or there are so many 'tourist-trash' shops, for those with only a short time it is worth a visit. You will see some birds and with luck dolphins. In the shops and bars there are often captive parrots and snakes. The area is set up to receive large numbers of tourists, which ecologists agree relieves pressure on other parts of the river. Boats for day trippers leave the harbour constantly throughout the day, but are best booked at one of the larger operators. Remember that in the dry season, one-day tours may not offer much to see if the river is low."

Those with more time can take the longer cruises and will see various ecological environments. To see virgin rainforest, a five-day trip by boat is needed. Most tour operators operate on both the Rio Solimões and the Rio Negro. The Rio Negro is considered easier to navigate, generally calmer and with fewer biting insects, but as it is a black water river with forest growing on poor soil and the tannin-filled waters are acidic, there are fewer frutiferous trees and fish and therefore fewer animals. The tributaries of the Solimões have higher concentrations of wildlife; including biting insects. Currently most Solimões tours go to the Rio Mamori area via the Port Velho highway and the Mamori river. There is plenty of deforestation along the initial stages of this river. The best lodges for wildlife are the furthest from Manaus but don't expect to see lots of animals. This is difficult anywhere in the Amazon, but you should see caiman, macaws, boa constrictors and river dolphins. It is the immensity of the forest and rivers and the seemingly limitless horizons, as well as a glimpse of the extraordinary way of life of the Amazon people, which make these tours exciting. For the best wildlife options in the Brazilian Amazon head for Alta Floresta, the Mamirauá reserve near Tefé (see above), or the little visited forests of northern Roraima.

Generally, between April and September excursions are only by boat; in the period October to March the Victoria Regia lilies virtually disappear. If using a camera, do remember to bring a fast film as light is dim.

Prices vary, but usually include lodging, guide, transport, meals and activities. The recommended companies charge within the following ranges (per person): one day, US$50-100; three days, eg to Anavilhanas Archipelago, US$195-285. Longer, specialized, or more luxurious excursions will cost significantly more. Most river trips incorporate the meeting of the waters on the first day, so there is no need to make a separate excursion. For Lodges, see under Sleeping, below.

What to take Leave luggage with your tour operator or hotel in Manaus and only take what is necessary for your trip. Long sleeves, long trousers, shoes and insect repellent are advisable for treks where insects are voracious. Take a mosquito net (and a hammock mosquito net if going on a cheaper tour) for trips in February-June. A hat offers protection from the sun on boat trips. Bottled water and other drinks are expensive in the jungle, so you may want to take your own supplies.

Manaus listings

For Sleeping and Eating price codes and other relevant information, see Essentials, pages 38-40. See Telephone, page 397, for important phone changes.

Sleeping

Manaus *p628, map p629*

10% tax and service must be added to bills. Hotel booking service at airport (see Transport, below, on taxi drivers' ruses). The best option is the area around the Teatro Amazonas, where the Italianate colonial houses and cobbled squares have been refurbished. A less good alternative is the Zona Franca, which is convenient for shops, banks, restaurants and the port area, but is not very safe at night. Av Joaquim Nabuco and R dos Andradas have many cheap hotels (**E**), most of which charge by the hour and all of which are in an area which is undesirable after dark.

LL-L Taj Mahal Continental, Av Getúlio Vargas 741, T3627 3737, www.grupotajmahal.com.br. Large, impressive, best of the central hotels, popular, tour agency for flights, revolving restaurant, massage and high level of service. Recommended.

LL-AL Tropical, Av Coronel Teixeira 1320, Ponta Negra, T2123 5000, www.tropicalhotel.com.br. A lavish, 5-star hotel 20 km outside the city (taxi to centre, US$25). All imaginable comforts and services, departure point for river cruises and agency which arranges them, churrascaria, pool, 24-hr coffee shop, open to well-dressed non-residents. Take minibus from R José Paranaguá in front of Petrobras building at the corner of Dr Moreira, US$6.50 return, 0830, 0930, 1130 to hotel, 1200, 1400, 1500, 1800 to town, or take Ponta Negra bus, US$1, then walk. It is rarely full, except in Jan-Feb. Companion hotel with more modern rooms, **Tropical Business**, same price and web address, T2123 3000, is in a large tower block in same grounds. Superb views from upper floors, beautiful infinty pool in gardens.

L-AL Lord Manaus, R Marcílio Dias 217, T3622 2844, www.lordmanaus.com.br. Pleasant, spacious a/c lobby and standard, though well-presented rooms.

AL-A Lider, Av 7 de Setembro 827, T3621 9700, www.liderhotelmanaus.com.br. Small, modern a/c rooms with little breakfast tables. The best are at the front on the upper floors. Very well kept.

A Ana Cassia Palace, R dos Andradas 14, T3303 3637, www.hotelanacassia.com.br. Gloriously faded, large rooms, some with great views of port, restaurant, pool. **Agenciatur Ana Cassia** is a decent tour agency selling a wide variety of river trips.

A Manaós, Av Eduardo Ribeiro 881, T3633 5744, www.hotelmanaos.brasilcomercial.com. Smart a/c rooms with marble floors, decent breakfast, internet, next to Teatro Amazonas.

B Krystal, R Barroso 54, T3233 7535, www.kystal lidermanaus.com.br. A range of small though business-like, well-maintained modern a/c rooms.

B-C Brasil, Av Getúlio Vargas 657, T3233 7271, www.hotelbrasil.tur.br. Mid-market option close to centre, faded rooms and tiny bathrooms and balconies, small pool.

B-C Central, R Dr Moreira 202, T3622 2600, www.hotelcentralmanaus.com.br. A business hotel in the Zona Franca, check rooms thoroughly as many are very scruffy, but a few are good, excellent breakfast.

C-D 10 de Julho, R Dez de Julio 679, T3232 6280, www.hoteldezdejulho.com. Near opera house, a/c, much the best cheap option, English speaking, clean though simple rooms (some with a/c and hot water), efficient, but poor laundry, good tour operator (with different owner).

E pp **Hostel Manaus**, R Lauro Cavalcante 231, Centro, T3233 4545, www.hostelmanaus.com. **F** for HI members. Fine restored old house, with excellent value dorms and private rooms, best to confirm bookings. Good location 1 block from Museu do Homem do Norte, reasonably central and quiet. Australian- run. (Not to be confused with non-HI hostel in the city now using a similar name.)

Camping There are no campsites near Manuas; it is difficult to find a good, safe place to camp wild.

Lodges near Manaus

There are several lodges within a few hrs boat or car journey from Manaus. Most emphasize comfort (although electricity and hot water is limited) rather than a real jungle experience, but they are good if your time is limited and you want to have a brief taste of the Amazon rainforest. It is not possible just to turn up at a jungle lodge, you will need the lodge to bring you there through its own designated transport, or to arrive with a tour company. Agencies for reservations are also listed. Very few of the lodges are locally owned and only a small percentage of labour is drawn from local communities. Only a handful of people have benefited from a boom which has seen the total number of beds rise from just 6 in 1979 to over 1000 today. See www.viverde.com.br for general information on lodges.

LL Anavilhanas Jungle Lodge, Edif Manaus Shopping Center, Av Eduardo Ribeiro 520, sala 304, T3622 8996, www.anavilhanaslodge.com. Small, elegant lodge on the Anavilhanas Archipelago, 3 to 6-day packages, comfortable, trips to see river dolphins included. In the Roteiros do Charme group.

LL Ariaú Amazon Towers, Rio Ariaú, 2 km from Archipélago de Anavilhanas, Manaus office at R Leonardo Malcher 699, T2121 5000, www.ariau towers.com.br. 60 km and 2 hrs by boat from Manaus on a side channel of the Rio Negro. Complex of towers connected by walkways, beach (Sep-Mar), trips to the Anavilhanas islands in groups of 10-20. Highly recommended.

LL Pousada dos Guanavenas on Ilha de Silves, T3656 1500, www.guanavenas.net. 300 km from Manaus on the road to Itacoatiara then by boat along the Rio Urubu, views of Lago Canacari. Comfortable rooms with a/c and hot water and a good restaurant on a black water lake some 4-5 hrs from Manaus, but in an area with abundant wildlife.

L Acajatuba Jungle Lodge, office at Av 7 de Setembro 1899, Manaus, T3084 3461, www.acajatuba.com.br. A 40- apartment lodge in a beautiful area on lake Acajatuba just below the Anavilhanas islands, 70 km from Manaus. Packages from 2 to 6 days. Good piranha fishing, plenty of caiman and lots of várzea forest. It's close to Ariaú. Service can be patchy.

L Amazon Ecopark Lodge, Igarapé do Tarumã, 20 km from Manaus, 15 mins by boat, jungle trails; 60 apartments with shower, bar, restaurant, T9146 0594, www.amazoneco park.com.br. Comfortable lodge with 60 apartments and a decent restaurant only 15 mins from Hotel Tropical and used by them for many of their day trips. 1 to 4-day packages. Pleasant guided walks but poor for wildlife.

L Juma Lodge, T3232 2707, www.jumahotel. com.br. Small lodge on the Rio Juma, idyllic location near the Rio Mamori, 2½ hrs south of Manaus by road and boat, all-inclusive 3 to 6-day packages. One of best options for wildlife and birdwatching.

AL Aldeia dos Lagos Lodge, Silves Project, T3248 9988, www.viverde.com.br/aldeia. Simple floating lodge on a lake, run in conjunction with the local community and WWF. Good for birds and caiman.

AL Amazon Antônio Lodge, through **Antônio Jungle Tours**, www.antonio-jungletours.com. A thatched roof wooden lodge, rooms with fan, observation tower. In a beautiful location overlooking a broad curve in the river Urubu some 200 km from Manaus.

AL Mamori Jungle Lodge, through **Amazon Gero's Tours**, www.amazongerotours.com. One of the more comfortable lodges in Paraná do Araça on the Lago Mamori. Smart wooden chalets with suites of individual rooms, beds with mosquito nets. The best deals are with a designated tour.

AL Rainforest Lodge, contact **MS Empreendimentos**, T3233 9182, rflodge@n3.com.br. On the banks of Lago Januacá, 4 hrs from Manaus, 14 bungalows with fans, pool, restaurant, snack bar.

C-F Cabana Tachi, www.amazongerotours.com. Rustic, community-owned lodge run in partnership with **Amazon Gero's Tours**, profits and resources return to the community. In one of the most pristine stretches of forest in the region. Good for wildlife.

C-F Zequinha, also through **Amazon Gero's Tours**, www.amazongerotours.com. Simple, wooden, fan-cooled rooms and one a/c suite in a round maloca building 100 m from a bluff overlooking the Lago Mamori.

Eating

Manaus *p628, map p629*

Many restaurants close on Sun nights and Mon. City authorities grade restaurants for cleanliness: look for A and B.

TTT **Banzeiro**, R Libertador, 102, Nossa Senhora das Graças, T3234 1621, www.restaurantebanzeiro.com.br. 20 mins cab ride from the centre. One of the best restaurants in the city, beautifully presented regional cooking with a gourmet twist.

TTT **Himawari**, R 10 de Julho 618. Swish, sushi and Japanese food, attentive service, opposite Teatro Amazonas, open Sun night, when many restaurants close. Recommended.

TTT-TT **Restaurant Tarumã** in Tropical Hotel (see above). Dinner only.

TT **Búfalo**, churrascaria, Av Joaquim Nabuco 628. Best in town, US$7, all-you-can-eat Brazilian barbecue.

TT **Canto da Peixada**, R Emílio Moreira 1677 (Praça 14 de Janeiro). Superb fish dishes, lively atmosphere, unpretentious, close to centre, take a taxi.

TT **Fiorentina**, R José Paranaguá 44, Praça Heliodoro Balbi. Fan-cooled, traditional Italian, including vegetarian dishes, average food but one of best options in centre, watch out for the mugs of wine! Great feijoada on Sat, half-price on Sun.

TT **Pizzaria Scarola**, R 10 de Julho 739, corner with Av Getúlio Vargas. Standard Brazilian menu, pizza delivery, popular.

T **Alemã**, R José Paranaguá, Praça Heliodoro Balbi. Food by weight, great pastries, hamburgers, juices, sandwiches.

T **Brasil**, Av Getúlio Vargas next to hotel of same name. Food by weight, juice and sandwich kiosk outside hotel.

T **O Naturalista**, R 7 de Setembro 752, 2nd floor. Vegetarian pay-by-weight, lunch only, good.

T **Senac**, R Saldanha Marinho, 644. Cookery school, self-service, open daily, lunch only. Highly recommended.

T **Skina dos Sucos**, Eduardo Ribeiro e 24 de Maio. Regional fruit juices and snacks.

T **Sorveteria Glacial**, Av Getúlio Vargas 161 and other locations. Recommended for ice cream.

Bars and clubs

Manaus *p628, map p629*

The city has very lively nightlife – especially live forró and pagodé.

Bar do Armando, 10 de Julho e Tapajós, behind the Teatro. Bohemian atmosphere, good place for drinking outside.

Djalma Oliveira, R 10 de Julho 679, T9112 3942, djalmatour@hotmail.com. Nightlife tours throughout Manaus and private car hire. Manaus clubs are often far from the centre. Djalma is far better value for a night out than a taxi.

Entertainment

Manaus *p628, map p629*

Performing arts For Teatro Amazonas and Centro Cultural Pálacio Rio Negro, see above.

Teatro da Instalação, R Frei José dos Inocentes, T/F3622 2840. Performance space in recently restored historic buildings with free music and dance (everything from ballet to jazz), Mon-Fri May-Dec at 1800. Charge for performances Sat and Sun. Recommended.

Funfair In Praça da Saudade, R Ramos Ferreira, there is a Sun funfair from 1700; try prawns and calaloo dipped in tacaca sauce.

❂ Festivals and events

Manaus *p628, map p629*

6 Jan: **Epiphany**; **Ash Wednesday**, half-day; **Maundy Thursday**; **24 Jun**: **São João**; **14 Jul**; **5 Sep**; **30 Oct**; **1 Nov**, **All Saints' Day**, half-day; **Christmas Eve**; **New Year's Eve**, half-day.
Feb: **Carnival** dates vary – 5 days of Carnival, culminating in the parade of the Samba Schools. 3rd week in **Apr**: **Week of the Indians**, indigenous handicraft. In **Jun**: **Festival do Amazonas**; a celebration of all the cultural aspects of Amazonas life, indigenous, Portuguese and from the northeast, especially dancing; **29 Jun**: **São Pedro**, boat processions on the Rio Negro. In **Sep**: **Festival da Bondade**, last week, stalls from neighbouring states and countries offering food, handicrafts, music and dancing, SESI, Estrada do Aleixo Km 5. **Oct**: **Festival Universitário de Música – FUM**, the most traditional festival of music in Amazonas, organized by the university students, on the University Campus. **8 Dec**: **Processão de Nossa Senhora da Conceicão**, from the Igreja Matriz through the city centre and returning to Igreja Matriz for a solemn mass.

O Shopping

Manaus *p628, map p629*

Since Manaus is a free port, the whole area a few blocks off the river front is full of electronics shops. All shops close at 1400 on Sat and all day Sun.
Bookshops **Livraria Nacional**, R 24 de Maio 415. Stocks some French books. **Usados CDs e Livros**, Av Getúlio Vargas 766. Good selection of used books, English, German, French and Spanish. **Valer**, R Ramos Ferreira 1195. A few English classics stocked, best bookshop in city.
Handicrafts There are many handicrafts shops in the area around the Teatro Amazonas. **Galeria Amazônica**, R Costa Azevedo 272, Largo do Teatro, T3233 4521, www.galeriamazonica.org.br. A large, modern space filled with Waimiri Atroari indigenous arts and crafts, one of the best places for buying indigenous art in Brazil. In the Praça do Congresso, Av E Ribeiro, there is a very good Sun craftmarket. **Ecoshop**, Largo de São Sebastião, T3234 8870, and Amazonas Shopping, T3642 2026, www.ecoshop.com.br. Indigenous arts and crafts from all over the Amazon, including Yanomami and Tikuna baskets, Wai Wai necklaces and Baniwa palm work. The souvenir shop at the INPA has some interesting Amazonian products on sale. For hammocks go to R dos Andradas, many shops. **Central de Artesanato Branco e Silva**, R Recife 1999, T3642 5458. A gallery of arts and crafts shops and artists studios selling everything from indigenous art to wooden carvings by renowned Manaus sculptor Joe Alcantara.
Markets and supermarkets The **Mercado Adolfo Lisboa** (see above) was closed temporarily in 2010. There is a good supermarket at the corner of Av Joaquin Nabuco and Av Sete de Setembro. **Shopping Amazonas**, outside the city, is a mall with cinema, supermarket, fast food.

▲ Activities and tours

Manaus *p628, map p629*

Check agencies' licences from tourist office and ABAV. If in the least doubt, use only a registered company.
Swimming For swimming, go to Ponta Negra beach by Soltur bus, US$1, though the beach virtually disappears beneath the water in Apr-Aug; popular by day and at night with outdoor concerts and samba in the summer season. Boats to nearby beaches from **Hotel Tropical** cost US$2.25 pp. Every Sun, boats leave from the port in front of the market to beaches along Rio Negro, US$2.65, leaving when full and returning at end of the day. This is a real locals' day out, with loud music and foodstalls on the sand. Good swimming at waterfalls on the Rio Tarumã, lunch is available, shade, crowded at weekends. Take Tarumã bus from R Tamandaré or R Frei J dos Inocentes, 30 mins, US$1.10 (very few on weekdays), getting off at the police checkpoint on the road to Itacoatiara.

Tour operators

Amazing Tours Agency, Leopoldo Carpinteiro Peres 1570, T8165 1118, UK contact: T07726 115298, www.amazingtours.com.br. Leonardo is a local guide who grew up in the jungle and has a good knowledge of flora and fauna. English spoken, and some Dutch. Also trips to Jau National Park.

Amazon Antônio Tours, Hostel Manaus, R Lauro Cavalcante 231, T3234 1294, www.antonio-jungletours.com. Jungle tours on the Rio Urubu, a black water river 200 km northeast of Manaus. Good prices for backpackers.

Amazon Clipper Cruises, R Sucupira 249, Conj Kissia, Planalto, www.amazonclipper.com.br. Informed guides, well-planned activities, comfortable cabins and good food.

Amazon Gero's Tours, R 10 de Julho 679, T9983 6273, www.amazongerotours.com. Backpacker-oriented tours south of the Solimões and bookings made for lodges everywhere. Gero, the owner is very friendly and dedicated.

Amazon Jungle Tours, R Dr Moreira 163, 1st floor, T3231 1067, www.arquipelagotours.com.br. A range of tours throughout the region with special emphasis on supporting local communities and environmentally responsible practice. Packages include rainforest camping, jungle lodge tours, riverboat cruises and the chance to live with riverine families from a few days to a few weeks and work with and for the community.

Amazon Nature Tours, Av 7 de Setembro 188, Manaus, www.amazon-nature-tours.com (in USA T401-423 3377). Well-regarded expedition cruises on the live-aboard motor yacht *Tucano*, all cabins with a/c and bath, small groups, experienced guides for trips into the forest, 8 days on the rivers Negro and Amazon, US$2,650.

Amazonatours, T3232 8271/9624 2419 or in Spain 34-61-521 9070, www.amazonatours.com. Spanish/Brazilian run agency offering trips further afield and to their small lodge in the Tupana Natural Reserve. Recommended.

Community Houseboat tours, through **Geraldo Mesquita**, T3232 4755, kelly_kardoso@hotmail.com. River tours on traditional wooden Amazon river boats, some of which are over 40 years old, sleeping in cabins or hammocks on board and the option of nights camping in the forest or spent in traditional riverine communities. Proceeds from the trips revert to the local people.

Heliconia, R Col Salgado 63, Aparecida, T3234 5915, www.heliconia-amazon.com. Run by French researcher Thérèse Aubreton.

Iguana Tour, R 10 de Julho 679, T3633 6507, or 9627 4151 (24 hrs), www.amazonbrasil.com.br. Short and long tours, plenty of activities, many languages spoken.

Jaguar Adventure Tours R Marciano Armond, Vila Operária 23A, Cachoeirinha, T9156 7185, www.amazontoursbrazil.com. Carlos Jorge Damasceno, multilingual, deep jungle exploration with an ecological slant and visits to remote historical and indigenous settlements.

Swallows and Amazons, R Ramos Ferreira 922, T3622 1246, www.swallowsandamazonstours.com. Mark and Tania Aitchison offer a wide range of riverboat tours and accommodation (up to 16 days); they have their own houseboat, river boat and 15-room private jungle lodge. They also sell tours to other lodges, offer trips to other parts of the Amazon (including outside Brazil), fishing trips, bird-watching tours and short tours around the city. Very comprehensive service, with full assistance for travellers (reservations, email, transfers, medical, etc), English-, French- and Spanish-speaking guides.

Tucunaré Turismo, R Miranda Leão 194, T3234 5017, www.tucunareturismo.com.br.

Branch at the airport and a few blocks east of the docks. Good for internal flights.

Guides

Guides are licensed to work only through tour agencies, so it is safest to book guides through approved agencies. Advance notice and a minimum of 3 people for all trips offered by these guides:

Cristina de Assis, T9114 2556, amazonflower@bol.com.br. Offers tours telling the story of the city and the rubber boom with visits to historic buildings and the Museu Seringal, trips to the Rio Negro to swim with pink dolphins (these need to be organized at least a week in advance), to Presidente Figueiredo, the Boi Bumba party in Parintins and the forest. Cristina speaks good English.

Mathias Raimundo, T8142-2321, junglespecialist.mathias@gmail.com. Guiding through the jungle on the Rio Negro and Lago Tracaja (between Juma and Mamori lakes), tracking for 3 or more days, sleeping in hammocks, survival techniques, bird watching, from US$85 pp per day. Can arrange lodges on request.

Pedro Fernandes Neto, T8831 1011, pedroffneto@hotmail.com. Adventure tour specialist offering light adventure trips to the large INPA rainforest reserve, the forest around Manaus and the waterfalls and rivers of Presidente Figueiredo (see above).

⊖ Transport

Manaus *p628, map p629*

Air Airport T3652 1212. **International flights**: **Copa** and **TAM** have flights to **Miami**. **Internal flights**: **Trip** has the most extensive network (www.voetrip.com.br), and there are frequent internal flights with **TAM** and **Gol**. **Rico Airlines** fly to Porto Velho and other Amazon destinations. Domestic airport tax US$7. The taxi fare to or from the airport is US$28, with meter (check the driver uses it). Bus to town leaves from stop outside terminal on the right. Bus No 306 'Aeroporto Internacional' (or from R Tamandaré near the cathedral), US$1.25. Buses are 24 hr, but less reliable in the night so get a taxi if time is critical. It is sometimes possible to use the more regular, faster service run by the Tropical Hotel; many tour agencies offer free transfers without obligation. Check all connections on arrival. Local flights leave from airport terminal 2: make sure in advance of your terminal. **Note** Check in time is 2 hrs in advance. Allow plenty of time at Manaus airport, formalities are very slow especially if you have purchased duty-free goods. The restaurant serves good à la carte and buffet food through the day. Many flights depart in the middle of the night and while there are many snack bars there is nowhere to rest.

Bus Manaus rodoviária is 9 km out of town at the intersection of Av Constantino Nery and R Recife, T3642 5805. Take a local bus from centre, US$0.70, marked 'Aeroporto Internacional' or 'Cidade Nova' (or taxi, US$6.50) and ask the driver to tell you where to get off. Local buses to Praça 14 or the airport leave from Praça Adalberto Vale (take airport bus and alight just after Antárctica factory) or take local bus to Ajuricaba.

Ferry To **Santarém**, **Belém**, **Porto Velho**, **Tefé**, **Tabatinga** (for Colombia and Peru), **São Gabriel da Cachoeira**, and intermediate ports (see Boat services, page 616). Almost all passenger vessels now berth at the first (downstream) of the floating docks which is open to the public 24 hrs a day. Tickets are sold at booths at the boat terminal in front of the docks. A tourist office in a purpose-built shopping complex on the dockside will help travellers buy tickets (avoiding touts) and will translate for you as you look over the boats. The names and itineraries of departing vessels are displayed here as well as on the docked boats themselves. The port is relatively clean, well organized, and has a pleasant atmosphere.

ENASA (the state shipping company) sells tickets for private boats at its office in town (prices tend to be high here), R Mcal Deodoro 61, T3633 3280. Local boats and some cargo barges still berth by the concrete retaining wall between the market and Montecristi. Boats for São Gabriel da Cachoeira and Novo Airão go from São Raimundo, up river from the main port. Take bus 101 'São Raimundo', or 112 'Santo Antônio', 40 mins; there are 2 docking areas separated by a hill, the São Raimundo balsa, where the ferry to Novo Airão, on the Rio Negro, leaves every afternoon (US$13); and the Porto Beira Mar de São Raimundo, where the São Gabriel da Cachoeira boats dock (most departures Fri). **Note** Departures to the less important destinations are not always known at the **Capitânia do Porto**, Av Santa Cruz 265, Manaus. Be careful of people who wander around boats after they've arrived at a port: they are almost certainly looking for something to steal.

Immigration For those arriving by boat who have not already had their passports stamped (eg from Leticia), the immigration office is on the first of the floating docks. Take the dock entrance opposite the cathedral, bear right, after 50 m left, pass through a warehouse to a group of buildings on a T section.

Road The Catire Highway (BR 319) from Manaus to Porto Velho (868 km), has been officially closed since 1990. Enquire locally if the road is passable for light vehicles; some bridges are flimsy. The alternative for drivers is to ship a car down river on a barge, others have to travel by boat.

Directory

Manaus *p628, map p629*

Airline offices Meta, Av Santos Dumont 1350, T3652 1105. **Rico**, R 24 de Maio 60-B and at airport, T4009 8333, www.voerico.com.br. **TAM**, Av Joaquim Nabuco 1846 Sl-2, T3233 7744. **Trip**, Av Boulevard Álvaro Maia 2166, Adrianópolis, T3652 1243. **Banks** Banco do **Brasil**, G Moreira, and airport, changes US$ cash, 8% commission, both with ATMs for Visa/Plus, Cirrus/MasterCard. Most offices shut at 1500; foreign exchange operations 0900-1200 only, or even as early as 1100. **Bradesco**, Av 7 de Setembro 895/293, for Visa ATM. **HSBC**, R Dr Moreira 226. ATM for Visa, Cirrus, MasterCard and Plus. **Credicard**, Av Getúlio Vargas 222 for Diner's cash advances. Cash at main hotels; **Câmbio Cortez**, 7 de Setembro 1199, converts TCs into US$ cash, good rates, no commission. Also in Amazonas Shopping Center, end of Av Djalma Batista. Do not change money on the streets. **Embassies and consulates** **Austria**, Rua 5, 4, QE, Jardim Primavera T3642 1939, argro@oi.com.br. **Belgium**, 13 qd D conj Murici, T3236 1452. **Colombia**, R 24 de Maio 220, Rio Negro Center, T3622 6078, double check whether a Colombian tourist card can be obtained at the border. **Denmark**, R Timbiras 306, T3649 3050, bsb@argo.com.br, also handles Norway. **Finland**, R Marcílio Dias 131, T3622 6276. **France**, Av João Valério 209, S/H Vieiralves, T3877 0754, consulado.manaus@gmail.com. Mon, Wed 0830-1130, Tue, Thu, Fri 1500-1800. **Germany**, Av 24 Maio 220, Ed Rio Negro Centre, sala 812, T3622 8800, 1000-1200. **Japan**, R Fortaleza 416, T3232 2000. **Netherlands**, R M Leão 41, T3622 1366, ilko@bemol.com.br. **Peru**, Rua H, 12, Morada do Sol, Aleixo, T3642 1203. **Portugal**, R Ferreira Pena 37, T3633 1235. **Spain**, Al Cosme Ferreira 1225, Aleixo, T3644 3800. **Sweden**, R Rio Quixito 86, T3616 9043. **UK**, R Poraquê 240, Distrito Industrial, T3613 1819, vincent@internext.com.br. **US**, http://virtual.embaixada-americana.org.br/manaus/. **Venezuela**, R Rio Jataí 839, T3233 6006, convemao@vivax.com.br, 0800-1200. Some nationalities entering Venezuela overland need a visa (check in advance with a Venezuelan consulate); all need a yellow fever certificate. **Internet** Many around the Teatro. **Medical services** **Clínica São Lucas**, R Alexandre Amorin 470, T3622 3678, reasonably priced, some English spoken, good service, take a taxi. **Hospital Tropical**, Av Pedro Teixeira (D Pedro I) 25, T3238 1711. Centre for tropical medicine, not for general complaints, treatment free, some doctors speak a little English. Take buses 201 or 214 from Av Sete de Setembro in the city centre. **Pronto Soccoro 28 de Agosto**, R Recife 1581, T3642 4272, free for emergencies. **Post offices** Main office including poste restante on Marechal Deodoro. On the 1st floor is the philatelic counter where stamps are sold, avoiding the long queues downstairs. Staff don't speak English but are used to dealing with tourists. For airfreight and shipping, Alfândega, Av Marquês Santa Cruz (corner of Marechal Deodoro), Sala 106. For airfreight and seamail, Correio Internacional, R Monsenhor Coutinho e Av Eduardo Ribeiro (bring your own packaging). **Telephone** International calls can be made from local call boxes with an international card. Also **Telemar**, Av Getúlio Vargas 950 e R Leo Malcher. **Useful addresses** **Police:** to extend or replace a Brazilian visa, take bus from Praça Adalberto Vale to Kissia Dom Pedro for Polícia Federal post, people in shorts not admitted, T3655 1517.

Amazon frontiers

To get to the border with Colombia and Peru, a river boat is the only alternative to flying and this, of course, is the true way to experience the Amazon. On the route to Venezuela, buses and trucks have almost entirely replaced river traffic to Boa Vista, from where roads go to Santa Elena de Uairén and Lethem in Guyana.

Rondônia and Acre, lands which mark not just the political boundaries between Brazil and Peru and Bolivia, but also developmental frontiers between the forest and colonization. Much of Rondônia has been deforested. Acre is still frontier country with great expanses of forest in danger of destruction.

Manaus to Colombia, Peru, Venezuela and Guyana

Benjamin Constant and around → *Phone code: 0xx97. Colour map 3, A5.*

Benjamin Constant is on the border with Peru, with Colombian territory on the opposite bank of the river. The **Ticuna Indian Museum** ⓘ *Av Castelo Branco 396*, display photographs, costumes, traditional art and music. **Tabatinga** (*Phone code: 0xx97*) is 4 km from Leticia (Colombia). The Port Captain in Tabatinga is reported as very helpful and speaks good English. The port area of Tabatinga is called **Marco**. A good hammock will cost US$20 in Tabatinga (try Esplanada Teocides) or Benjamin Constant. A mosquito net for a hammock is essential if sailing upstream from Tabatinga; much less so downstream. **Note** In this area, carry your passport at all times.

Up the Rio Javari

West of Benjamin Constant, one of the Amazon's main tributaries, the Rio Javari, forms the border between Peru and Brazil. This is one of the best places to observe wildlife on this section of the Amazon. There are several privately owned reserves here, with comfortable accommodation and excellent facilities for birdwatching, and dolphin and caiman spotting. We list two below.

Border with Colombia and Peru

Check all requirements and procedures before arriving at this multiple border. Enquire carefully about embarkation/disembarkation points and where to go through immigration formalities. If waiting for transport, Tabatinga has convenient hotels for early morning departures, but Leticia has the best money changing facilities and more internet facilities (try the bookshop next to the church). **Note** When crossing these borders, check if there is a time difference (for example, Brazilian summer time, usually mid-October to mid-February). **Consulates** Brazilian ⓘ *Cra 9, No 13-84, Leticia, T08-592 7530, brvcleticia@yahoo.com.br, 1000-1600, Mon-Fri, onward ticket and 2 black-and-white photos needed for visa (photographer nearby); allow 36 hrs*, efficient, helpful. **Peruvian** ⓘ *Cra 11, No 5-32, Leticia, T08-592 7204, 0900-1300; note that no entry or exit permits are given here.*

Brazilian immigration Entry and exit stamps are given at the Polícia Federal, 2 km from the Tabatinga docks, best to take a taxi, 24 hours. Proof of US$500 or an onward ticket may be asked for. There are no facilities in Benjamin Constant. One-week transit in Tabatinga is permitted. The Colombian consulate is at ⓘ *R Gen Sampaio 623, T3412 2104, ctabatin@minrelext.gov.co, 0800-1600*. Tourist cards are issued on presentation of two passport photos. **Note** If coming from Peru, you must have a Peruvian exit stamp and a yellow fever certificate.

Colombian immigration DAS ⓘ *C9, No 9-62, T59-24878, secamaadm@das.gov.co, Leticia, and at the airport*. Exit stamps to leave Colombia by air or overland are given by DAS no more than 1 day before you leave. If flying into Leticia prior to leaving for Brazil or Peru, get an exit stamp while at the airport. Check both offices for entry stamps before flying into Colombia. To enter Colombia you must have a tourist card to obtain an entry stamp, even if you are passing through Leticia en route between Brazil and Peru (the Colombian consul in Manaus may tell you otherwise; try to get a tourist card elsewhere). The Colombian Consular Office in Tabatinga issues tourist cards; 24-hour transit stamps can be obtained at the DAS office. If visiting Leticia without intending to go anywhere else in Colombia, you may be allowed to enter without immigration or customs formalities (but traveller's cheques cannot be changed without an entry stamp). Travel between Colombia and Brazil and Peru is given below. Travel from/into Colombia is given under Leticia. **Note** There are no customs formalities for everyday travel between Leticia and Tabatinga.

Peruvian immigration Entry/exit formalities take place at Santa Rosa. Every boat leaving and entering Peru stops here. There is also an immigration office in Iquitos (Mcal Cáceres 18th block, T235371), where procedures for leaving can be checked. There is no Brazilian consulate in Iquitos No exchange facilities in Santa Rosa; reais and dollars are accepted, but soles are not accepted in Leticia and only occasionally in Tabatinga.

Manaus to Venezuela and Guyana

The road which connects Manaus and Boa Vista (BR-174 to Novo Paraíso, then the Perimetral, BR-210, rejoining the BR174 after crossing the Rio Branco at Caracaraí) can get badly potholed. There are service stations with toilets, camping, etc, every 150-180 km, but all petrol is low octane. Drivers should take a tow cable and spares, and bus passengers should prepare for delays in the rainy season. At Km 100 is Presidente Figueiredo, with many waterfalls and a famous cave with bats, shops and a restaurant. About 100 km further on is a service station at the entrance to the **Uaimiri Atroari Indian Reserve**, which straddles the road for about 120 km. Private cars and trucks are not allowed to enter the Indian Reserve between sunset and sunrise, but buses are exempt from this regulation. Nobody is allowed to stop within the reserve at any time. At the northern entrance to the reserve there are toilets and a spot to hang your hammock (usually crowded with truckers overnight). At Km 327 is the village of Vila Colina with Restaurante Paulista, good food, clean, you can use the shower and hang your hammock. At Km 359 there is a monument to mark the equator. At Km 434 is the clean and pleasant Restaurant Goaio. Just south of Km 500 is Bar Restaurante D'Jonas, a clean, pleasant place to eat, you can also camp or sling a hammock. Beyond here, large tracts of forest have been destroyed for settlement, but already many homes have been abandoned.

At **Caracaraí**, a busy port with modern installations on the Rio Branco, a bridge crosses the river for traffic on the Manaus-Boa Vista road. It has hotels in our **D-E** range. Boa Vista has road connections with the Venezuelan frontier at Santa Elena de Uairén (237 km, paved, the only gasoline 110 km south of Santa Elena) and Bonfim for the Guyanese border at Lethem. Both roads are open all year.

Boa Vista → *Phone code: 0xx95. Post code: 69300. Colour map 2, B2. Population: 200,568.*

The capital of the extreme northern State of Roraima, 785 km north of Manaus, is a pleasant, clean, laid-back little town on the Rio Branco. Tourism is beginning here and there are a number interesting new destinations opening up, many offering a chance to explore far wilder and fauna-rich country than that around Manaus. The landscape is more diverse, too, with a mix of tropical forest, savannah and highlands dotted with waterfalls. The area immediately around the city has been heavily deforested. It has an interesting modern cathedral; also a museum of local indigenous culture (poorly kept). There is swimming in the Rio Branco, 15 minutes from the town centre (too polluted in Boa Vista), reachable by bus only when the river is low. **Tourist office**: **Detur** ⓘ *R Coronel Pinto 267, T3623 2365, www.portal.rr.gov.br*. Information is available at the rodoviária, T3623 1238; also in the **Prefeitura's tourist office** ⓘ *R Floriano Peixoto, Centro, beside the Orla Tuamanan, Tue-Sun 1600-2200.*

Border with Venezuela

Border searches are thorough and frequent at this border crossing. If entering Brazil, ensure in advance that you have the right papers, including yellow fever certificate, before arriving at this border. Officials may give only two months' stay and car drivers may be asked to purchase an unnecessary permit. Ask to see the legal documentation. Everyone who crosses this border to Venezuela must also have a yellow fever certificate. Check requirements for visas beforehand (some nationalities need one, but not, for example, Western Europeans). See the Directory, below, for the Venezuelan consulate. There is another Venezuelan consulate in Manaus (see above). On the Brazilian side there is a basic hotel, Pacaraima Palace, a guest house, camping and a bank.

Border with Guyana → *Colour map 2, B3. Population: 9,326.*

The main border crossing between Brazil and Guyana is from **Bonfim**, 125 km (all paved) northeast of Boa Vista, to Lethem. The towns are separated by the Rio Takutu, which is crossed by a new bridge (no toll to cross). The river crossing is 2.5 km from Bonfim, 1.6 km north of Lethem. Formalities are strict on both sides of the border: it is essential to have a yellow fever vaccination both to leave Brazil and to enter Guyana The bus passes through Brazilian Immigration where you receive your exit stamp. After the bridge, there are taxis to the Guyana Immigration office (US$3-5). You are given a visa for the exact amount of time you stipulate staying. The border is open 24 hours, but officials tend to leave immigration after 1800.

There is no Guayanese consul in Boa Vista, so if you need a visa for Guyana, you must get it in São Paulo or Brasília (see Guyana Documents in Essentials). Reais can be changed into Guyanese dollars in Boa Vista. There are no exchange facilities in Lethem, but reais are accepted in town.

Manaus to Colombia, Peru, Venezuela and Guyana listings

For Sleeping and Eating price codes and other relevant information, see Essentials, pages 38-40. See Teiephone, page 397, for important phone changes.

Sleeping

Benjamin Constant and around *p640*

There are a number of very cheap, simple *pousadas* in town.

B Benjamin Constant, R Getulio Vargas 36, beside ferry, T3415 5638. A/c, some rooms with hot water and TV, good restaurant, arranges tours, postal address Apto Aéreo 219, Leticia, Colombia. Recommended.

Tabatinga

B Takana, R Osvaldo Cruz, 970, T3412 3557, takanahotel@hotmail.com. Comfortable and clean, hot water, a/c. Recommended.

C Vitoria Regia, R da Patria, 820, T3412 2668. Basic rooms, cable TV and bath. Prices negotiable.

E Santiago, R Pedro Teixeira, 49, T3412 4680. Very basic but large rooms with bath.

F Pajé, R Pedro Teixeira 367, T3412 2774. Next to the Santiago, a little cheaper and a little cleaner.

Up the Rio Javari *p640*

LL pp **Reserva Natural Heliconia**, T+57-8-592 5773 (Leticia), www.amazon heliconia.com. Price, based on 2 people, includes transport from Leticia and all food and activities (except canopy and massage treatments). Up a small tributary of the Yavarí, about 1 hr by peque peque from Palmarí, isolated, comfortable cabins (with bathrooms open to the forest behind) set around a jungle garden. Night-time caiman-spotting excursions as well as trips to visit local indigenous communities, excellent walks, birdwatching and fishing tours.

A pp **Reserva Naturai Palmarí**, T+57-1-482 7148 (Bogotá), www.palmari.org. Includes all food and alcohol, activities (except jungle walks greater than 24 hrs, sport fishing and canopy), and Wi-Fi and internet access. Within a 10-min walk of all three types of Amazon forest, accommodation is in simple cabins or a large communal maloca. Guides from local communities, bird watching, fishing and kayaking. Colombian-German owner Axel Antoine-Feill has set up the Instituto de Desenvolvimiento Socioambiental do Vale do Javarí, www.idsavj.org, to work with local indigenous communities. Getting there: arrange transport from Leticia (not included), or catch a river taxi from Tabatinga to Benjamin Constant, 15 mins, US$8, then a colectivo on the road to Atalaia do Norte, 40 mins, US$5.50, where the reserve will arrange a pick-up for the final hour's journey by boat, US$25.

Boa Vista *p641*

Accommodation is generally expensive. Economic hardship has caused an increase in crime, sometimes violent.

AL Aipana Plaza, Joaquim Nabuco 53, T3224 4116, aipana@technet.com.br. Best in town with plain rooms decorated with photos of Roraima, hot water, a/c, cable TV, attractive pool area with a shady little bar.

A Uiramutam Palace, Av Capt Ene Garcez 427, T3224 9757, uiramutam@technet.com.br. Business hotel with modest rooms, a/c, cable TV and large bathrooms. Decent pool.

B Barrudada, R Araújo Filho 228, T3623 1378. Simple a/c rooms in a modern tower block very close to the centre. The best on the upper floors have views out to the river. Breakfast and lunch included.

C Eusêbio's, R Cecília Brasil 1107, T3623 0300. Spruce, modest rooms with a/c and en suites with c/w showers. The best are airy and on the upper floors. Pleasant pool and a laundry service. Has a good a/c restaurant (🍴🍴) serving fish, *feijoada* and meat dishes and a generous breakfast.

D-E Ideal, R Araújo Filho 481, T3224 6342. Simple but well-kept rooms, some have a/c, generous breakfast and convenient for the centre.

Camping Rio Caaumé, 3 km north of town (unofficial site, small bar, clean river, pleasant).

Border with Guyana: Bonfim *p642*

D Bonfim, owned by Mr Myers, who speaks English and is very helpful, fan, shower.

Eating

Benjamin Constant and around *p640*

In Benjamin Constant eat at **Pensão Cecília**, or **Bar-21 de Abril**, which is cheaper.

🍴 **Te Contei?**, Av da Amizade 1813, Tabatimga. Pay-by-the-kilo barbecued meats, salads. At night excellent pizzas served.

🍴 **Tres Fronteras Do Amzonas**, R Rui Barbosa, Barrio San Francisco, Tabatinga. Excellent mix of Brazilian, Peruvian and Colombian dishes.

Boa Vista *p641*

There are several restaurants serving snacks and juices on the riverside along R Floriano Peixoto.

🍴🍴 **Peixada Tropical**, R Pedro Rodrigues at Ajuricaba. A range of river fish dishes in various styles from Bahian sauces to Milanesa.

🍴 **1000 Sabores**, R Araújo Filho e Benjamin Constant. Pizzas, snacks and juices. Open early and closing late.

🍴 **Café com Leite Suiço**, at Santa Cecilia, 15 mins by car on road to Bom Fim. Open 0630-1300 for regional food, US$4, good.

🍴 **Catequeiro**, Araújo Filho e Benjamin Constant. Recommended *prato feito*.

🍴 **Frangão**, R Homen de Melo e Cecília Brasil. Barbecued chicken, fish accompanied by salads, rice, beans, etc.

🍴 **La Góndola**, Benjamin Constant e Av Amazonas. Good.

Border with Guyana: Bonfim *p642*

There is a café at the rodoviária, opposite the church, whose owner speaks English and gives information. **Restaurante Internacional**, opposite the rodoviária, on other side from church; another restaurant a bit further from the rodoviária serves good food. Local speciality, fried cashew nuts.

Bars and clubs

Boa Vista *p641*

R Floriano Peixoto is lively after dark at weekends when there is live music in and around the **Orla Taumanan**; a complex of little bars and restaurants.

Toca, Orla Taumanan, T9971 5454. River cruises and parties with live music and dancing.

Activities and tours

Benjamin Constant and around: Tabatinga *p640*

Travellers Jungle Home, R Marechal Rondon, 86. English and French owners, budget prices.

Boa Vista *p641*

Aguia Tours, Av Benjamin Constant 1683A, T3624 1516. Can book buses and flights and the owner speaks some English

Roraima Adventures, R Sebastião Diniz 787, T3624 9611, 9115 4171, www.roraima-brasil.com.br. A range of interesting trips to little known and little visited parts of Roraima including the spectacular Tepequem and Serra Grande mountains and the Rio Uraricoera, which is replete with wildlife. Pre-formed groups get the best prices, which are competitive with Manaus. Helpful with visas for Venezuela.

Transport

Border with Colombia and Peru *p640*

Brazil to Colombia

Air Local airlines provide flights in the region. From the airport at Tabatinga to town by mini-bus, US$1. See also under Leticia (Colombia). Regular minibus from airport to Leticia, US$0.90.

Ferry From Manaus to Benjamin Constant boats normally go on to Tabatinga, and start from there when going to Manaus. Boat services from Manaus to Benjamin Constant, 7 days, or more; to Manaus, 4 days, or more. They usually wait 1-2 days in both Tabatinga and Benjamin Constant before returning to Manaus; you can stay on board. It's quicker to get off the river boat in Benjamin Constant and take a fast ferry, US$3, 2 hrs, to Tabatinga, than stay on the river boat for the crossing from Benjamin Constant. Boats arrive in Benjamin Constant at 0600, so you can take the 0700 ferry and have a enough time in Tabatinga to get exit stamps and book the launch to Iquitos for the next day. For information on boats to/from Manaus, see Manaus Shipping and River Transport in Amazônia.

Taxi Travel between Tabatinga and Leticia is very informal; taxis between the 2 towns charge US$5.50 (more if you want to stop at immigration offices, exchange houses, etc; beware of taxi drivers who want to rush you expensively over the border before it 'closes'), or US$1 in a colectivo (more after 1800).

Brazil to Peru

Ferry Santa Rosa-Tabatinga or Leticia, US$2.50 (in reais, soles or pesos). Between Tabatinga and Iquitos in Peru there are 3 companies with 20-seater speedboats, US$60 one way, buy ticket 1 day in advance (**River Fox** not recommended, unsafe). They take 11-12 hrs. Luggage limit is 15 kg. Departure from Tabatinga is 0530 (be there 0500). In Tabatinga ask for Fábio Dickinson and Leo who sell tickets for the fast boats, both speak Spanish and Fábio speaks English, very helpful. There are also cheaper, slower lanchas, which 2 days (US$15-17.50 hammock, US$25-30 cabin). Boat services are given under **Iquitos** in the Peru chapter. Passengers leaving and entering Peru must visit immigration at Santa Rosa when the boat stops there. For entry into Brazil, formalities are done in Tabatinga; for Colombia, in Leticia.

Boa Vista *p641*

Air Flights to **Manaus** with **Meta**, and to **Georgetown**. Also flights to São Paulo, Rio de Janeiro, Belém, etc. Book through **Aguia**, R Benjamin Constant 1683B, T3624 1516 (owner speaks some English). No left luggage, information or exchange facilities at the airport, which is 4 km from the centre. Bus 'Aeroporto' from the centre is US$0.50. Taxi to rodoviária, US$10, to centre US$13, 45 mins' walk.

Bus (See also Border Crossings, page 647.) Rodoviária is 3 km at the end of Av Ville Roy; taxi to centre, US$10, bus US$0.90, 10 mins (marked '13 de Setembro' or 'Joquey Clube' to centre). The local bus terminal is on Av Amazonas, by R Cecília Brasil, near central praça. It is difficult to get a taxi or bus to the rodoviária in time for early morning departures; as it's a 25-min walk, book a taxi the previous evening. To **Manaus**, US$60, several companies including **Eucatur**, 12 hrs, at least 6 daily, executivo service at 1800/1900 with meal stop. Advisable to book. Buses between Boa Vista and **Caracaraí** take 8 hrs.

Border with Venezuela *p642*

Bus One bus a day goes from Boa Vista rodoviária to **Santa Elena de Uairén**, stopping at all checkpoints, US$20, 4 hrs, take water. Or share a taxi, US$10 pp. Through buses to **Ciudad Guayana, Ciudad Bolívar** (eg **Caribe**), US$40.

Border with Guyana: Bonfim *p642*

Bus Boa Vista-Bonfim 6 a day US$11, 2½ hrs; colectivos charge US$25.

Directory

Benjamin Constant and around: Tabatinga *p640*

Banks **Banco do Brasil**, Av da Amizade. Has a Visa cash point and changes TCs at poor rate. Best to change money in Leticia. Dollars are accepted everywhere; Colombian pesos are accepted in Tabatinga, Peruvian soles are rarely accepted. **Internet** Infocenter, Av da Amizade 1581.

Boa Vista *p641*

Airline offices Gol, Praça Santos Dumont 100, T3224 5824/0300-115 2121. **Meta**, Praça Santos Dumont 100, T3224 7490. **Banks** US$ and Guyanese notes can be changed in Boa Vista. TCs and cash in **Banco do Brasil**, Av Glaycon de Paiva 56, 1000-1300 (minimum US$200), has Visa/Plus ATM. There is no official exchange agency and the local rates for bolívares are low: the Banco do Brasil will not change bolívares. **HSBC**, Av Ville Roy 392, MasterCard ATM. **Bradesco**, Av Jaime Brasil 441, Visa ATM. Best rate for dollars, **Casa PedroJosé**, R Araújo Filho 287, also changes TCs and bolívares; **Timbo's** (gold and jewellery shop), Av B Constant 170, will change money. **Embassies and consulates** Guyana, Av Benjamin Constant 1020 E, T3224 2674, mcabral19@hotmail.com, open mornings only. **Venezuela**, Av Benjamin Constant 968, T3623 9285, venezubv@technet.com.br, Mon-Fri 0830-1300. Visas available, relaxed service, allow 24-48 hrs. **Medical services** Yellow fever inoculations are free at a clinic near the hospital.

Southern Amazônia

Porto Velho → *Phone code: 0xx69. Post code: 78900. Colour map 4, B1. Population: 450,000.*

This city stands on a high bluff overlooking a curve of the Rio Madeira. It first prospered during the local gold and timber rush and now is booming as the result of the Madeira Hydroelectric Complex, the first two dams are currently one of the largest civil engineering projects in the world. 80% of sewage will be treated by 2011, one of the first Brazilian cities to achieve this. Buildings in the centre are being renovated and by 2012 the city will be very attractive. But it is less of a tourist city than Rio Branco, a far more interesting access point to Brazil from Peru or Bolivia.

At the top of the hill, on Praça João Nicoletti, is the **Cathedral**, built in 1930, with beautiful stained glass windows; the **Prefeitura** is across the street. The principal commercial street is Avenida 7 de Setembro, which runs from the railway station and market hall to the upper level of the city, near the rodoviária. The centre is hot, noisy and sprawls from the river to the bus station (1½ km). In the old railway yards known as Praça Madeira-Mamoré are the **Museus Ferroviário** (see below) and **Geológico** ⓘ *both 0800-1800* and a promenade with bars by the river, a wonderful place to watch the sunset. A neoclassical **Casa do Governo** faces Praça Getúlio Vargas, while Praça Marechal Rondon is spacious and modern. There are several viewpoints over the river and railway yards: **Mirante I** (with restaurant) is at the end of Rua Carlos Gomes; **Mirante II** (with a bar and ice cream parlour), at the end of Rua Dom Pedro II, is the best place to watch the sunset over the river. There is a clean fruit and vegetable market at the corner of Rua Henrique Dias and Avenida Farquhar and a dry goods market three blocks to the south, near the port. **Tourist office**: Setur/Ro ⓘ *www.setur.ro.gov.br. See also www.portovelho.ro.gov.br and www.rondonia.ro.gov.br.* Tourist office at the airport opens when flights arrive. Malaria is common in the area.

About 5 km northeast of the city is the **Parque Nacional Municipal**, a small collection of flora in a preserved area of jungle and one of very few parks in the city.

The Madeira–Mamoré Railway → *See www.efmm.net.*

Porto Velho was the terminus of the Madeira-Mamoré railway. It was supposed to go as far as Riberalta, on the Rio Beni, above that river's rapids, but stopped short at Guajará Mirim. Over 6,000 workers died during its construction (1872-1913). The BR-364 took over many of the railway bridges, leaving what remained of the track to enthusiasts to salvage what they could. The museum ⓘ *Praça Madeira-Mamoré, T3901 3186, free*is open to visitors. The railway itself is undergoing refurbishment and will reopen, to run some 10 km through Porto Velho and its suburbs, in 2011 to coincide with the inauguration of a large riverside park dotted with Vitória Régia lily ponds and a new museum devoted to the history of the city.

The BR-364 ➔ *Colour map 4, C2.*

The Marechal Rondon Highway, BR-364, is fully paved to Cuiabá, 1,550 km. A result of the paving of BR-364 is the development of farms and towns along it; least population density is in the south between Pimenta Bueno and Vilhena. From Porto Velho south, the towns include **Ariquemes** (202 km from Porto Velho). (*Phone code: 0xx69)*, buses hourly from 0600, three to four hours, hotels, bank); **Ji Paraná** (*376 km, phone code: 0xx69*), on the shores of the Rio Machado, a pleasant town with a small riverside promenade, which has several bars, lively at night; several hotels. **Note** At the Mato Grosso state border, proof of yellow-fever inoculation is required: if no proof is presented, a new shot is given.

Parque Nacional Pacaás Novos ➔ *765,800 ha.*

The Parque Nacional Pacaás Novos, lies west of the BR-364; it is a transitional zone between open plain and Amazonian forest. The majority of its surface is covered with cerrado vegetation and the fauna includes jaguar, brocket deer, puma, tapir and peccary. The average annual temperature is 23°C, but this can fall as low as 5°C when the cold front known as the friagem blows up from the South Pole. Details from **ICMBio** ⓘ *Av Tancredo Neves s/n, Campo Novo, T3239 2031; entry US$3.*

Guajará Mirim ➔ *Phone code: 0xx69. Colour map 4, B1. Population: 38,045.*

From Porto Velho, the paved BR-364 continues 220 km southwest to Abunã (hotels **E**), where the BR-425 branches south to Guajará Mirim. The BR-425 is a fair road, partly paved, which uses the former rail bridges (poor condition). It may be closed March-May. Across the Mamoré from Guajará Mirim is the Bolivian town of Guayaramerín, which is connected by road to Riberalta, from where there are air services to other Bolivian cities. Guajará Mirim is a charming town. The **Museu Municipal** ⓘ *T541 3362, 0500-1200, 1400-1800*, is at the old Guajará Mirim railway station beside the ferry landing; highly recommended. Banco do Brasil only changes money in the morning.

Border with Bolivia

Get Brazilian exit and entry stamps from **Polícia Federal** ⓘ *Av Presidente Dutra 70, corner of Av Quintino Bocaiúva, T3541 4021*. The Bolivian consulate is at Avenida Beira Rio 505, 1st floor, T3541 8620, consuladodabolivia@brturbo.com.br, Guajará Mirim; visas are given here.

Rio Branco ➔ *Phone code: 0xx68. Post code: 69900. Colour map 3, B6. Population: 253,059.*

The BR-364 runs west from Porto Velho to Abunã (239 km), then in excellent condition, 315 km to Rio Branco the capital of the State of Acre. This intriguing state is rich in natural beauty, history and the seringueiro culture. During the rubber boom of the late 19th century, many Nordestinos migrated to the western frontier in search of fortune. As a result, the unpopulated Bolivian territory of Acre was gradually taken over by Brazil and formally annexed in the first decade of the 20th century. In compensation, Bolivia received the Madeira–Mamoré railroad, as described above. The chief industries are rubber and castanho-de-pará (Brazil nut) extraction and, now that ranching has slowed down, ecotourism. While Rondônia has lost well over 50% of its forest, Acre retains 82% primary forest. It has some of the most exciting ethno-tourism projects in South America.

Rio Branco is clean, well-maintained and orderly with the highest percentage of cycle ways of any city in Brazil. There are attractive green spaces and a lively waterfront promenade, the **Mercado Velho**, which buzzes with bar life in the evenings, especially at weekends. The Rio Acre, navigable upstream as far as the Peru and Bolivia borders, divides the city into two districts, Primeiro (west) and Segundo (east), on either side of the river. In the central, Primeiro district are **Praça Plácido de Castro**, the shady main square; the **Cathedral**, Nossa Senhora de Nazaré, along Avenida Brasil; the neo-classical **Palácio Rio Branco** on Rua Benjamin Constant, across from Praça Eurico Gaspar Dutra. Two bridges link the districts. In the Segundo district is the **Calçadão da Gameleira**, a pleasant promenade along the shore, with plaques and an old tree marking the location of the original settlement. The **Horto Forestal**, in Vila Ivonete (1° distrito), 3 km north of the centre ('Conjunto Procon' or 'Vila Ivonete' city-buses), has native Amazonian trees, a small lake, paths and picnic areas.

Museu da Borracha (Rubber Museum) ⓘ *Av Ceará 1144, T3223 1202, Tue-Fri 0800-1800, Sat-Sun 1600-2100*, in a lovely old house with a tiled façade, has information about the rubber boom, archaeological artefacts, a section about Acreano Indians, memorabilia from the annexation and a display about the Santo Daime doctrine. Recommended. **Casa Povos da Floresta** ⓘ *Parque da Maternidade, Centro, T3224 5667, Wed-Fri 0800-1800, Sat-Sun 1600-2100, free* has displays and artefacts devoted to the forest people of Acre, including various of the indigenous peoples and the *seringueiro* rubber tappers who colonised the state. **Tourist office**: For Acre: CAT ⓘ *Av Getúlio Vargas 91, Praça dos Povos da Floresta, Centro (Antigo Bar Municipal), T3223 3998, cat.turismo@ac.gov.br*; **Secretária de Turismo** at the Estádio ⓘ *Av Chico Mendes, T3901 3024, www.ac.gov.br.*

Xapuri → *Phone code: 0xx68. Colour map 3, B5.*

Xapuri is where **Chico Mendes** lived and worked. Mendes, leader of the rubber tappers and opponent of deforestation, was murdered by landowners in 1988. His legacy is increased awareness of sustainability in the state and his colleague, Marina Silva, was appointed Environment Minister by President Lula da Silva. Both the rubber-tappers' community and the forest Mendes sought to protect survive. Jaguar, harpy eagle and tapir are still abundant here, as are towering Brazil nut and kapok trees. Besides the functioning rubber tapping community, Xapuri is now an ecotourism venture (see Sleeping, below). Chico Mendes' cousin works as a guide. A stay here for one or two nights is a magical experience, well worth undertaking if en route between Brazil and Peru/Bolivia. Book through **Maanaim**, see Tour operators, below.

Rio Branco time is one hour behind Porto Velho and Manaus time; this means two hours behind Brazilian Standard Time.

Border with Bolivia and Peru

The BR-317 from Rio Branco heads south and later southwest, parallel to the Rio Acre; it runs to **Brasiléia** (three hotels, two basic lodgings, several restaurants – La Felicitá is good, Polícia Federal give entry/exit stamps), opposite the Bolivian town of Cobija on the Rio Acre. A striking, single-tower suspension bridge crosses the river. It is possible to stay in Epitaciolândia (**C Hotel Kanda**, five minutes' walk from the police post) and cross into Bolivia early in the morning. Ask the bus driver to let you off near Polícia Federal, open 0700-2200, to get passport stamped. Cobija is opposite. The border is open 24 hours on the Brazilian side, 0800-1800 in Cobija. **Bolivian consulate** ⓘ *R Hilário Meireles 236, Brasiléia, T3546 5760, colivianbrasileia@yahoo.es*. If going to Peru, a taxi from Polícia Federal to the Rodoviária costs US$2.

The road ends at Assis Brasil (120 km) where the Peruvian, Bolivian and Brazilian frontiers meet. Across the Rio Acre are Iñapari (Peru) and Bolpebra, Bolivia. In **Assis Brasil**, there are three hotels, two restaurants (including a good churrascaria on the main street), some shops, a bank which does not change US dollars (the hotel owner may be persuaded to oblige). Cross to Iñapari from Assis Brasil by another distinctive suspension bridge. The Brazilian border is open 0830-1200, 1400-1830 daily, the Peruvian side 0930-1300, 1500-1930 daily. There are waits of 20-30 minutes at each border post when taking the international bus. **Note** There is no Polícia Federal in the village, get entry/exit stamps in Brasiléia. Take small denomination dollar bills or Peruvian soles as there is nowhere to change money on the Peruvian side.

Southern Amazônia listings

For Sleeping and Eating price codes and other relevant information, see Essentials, pages 38-40. See Telephone, page 397, for important phone changes.

Sleeping

Porto Velho *p645*

Cheap rooms are hard to come by as many are taken by migrant workers on the twin dams project. From the rodoviária, take bus No 301 'Presidente Roosevelt' (outside Hotel Pontes), which goes to railway station at riverside, then along Av 7 de Setembro as far as Av Marechal Deodoro. It passes several hotels.

AL Vila Rica, Av Carlos Gomes 1616, T3224 3433, www.hotelvilarica.com.br. Tower block with restaurant, pool and sauna.

A Central, Tenreiro Aranha 2472, T2181 2500, www.enter-net.com.br/hcentral. A/c, TV, fridge, Wi-Fi, reliable and remodelled. Recommended.

B Samauma, R Dom Pedro II 1038, T3224 5300, hotelsamauma@hotmail.com. Best mid-range option in the centre, comfortable rooms with a/c, international TV, popular restaurant, WiFi, breakfast, welcoming staff.

C Líder, R Carlos Gomes 3189, immediately behind the rodoviária to northeast, T3225 2727. Boxy but bright rooms, with bath, solar-heated water, breakfast included.

C Por do Sol, R Carlos Gomes 3168, behind the rodoviária to the northeast, T3222 9161, hotelpordosol@yahoo.com.br. A/c rooms off a corridor, the best are in the middle. Free Wi-Fi, breakfast included.

C-D Tía Carmen, Av Campos Sales 2995, T3221 7910. Very good, honest, Wi-Fi, good cakes in lanche in front of hotel, refurbished 2009. Recommended.

Guajará Mirim *p646*

AL Pakaas Palafitas Lodge, Estrada do Palheta Km 18, T/F3541 3058, www.pakaas.com.br. 28 bungalows in a beautiful natural setting, price is per person per day.

C Jamaica, Av Leopoldo de Mato 755, T/F3541 3721. A/c, fridge, parking.

C Lima Palace, Av 15 de Novembro 1613, T3541 3421. A/c, fridge, parking.

D Fénix Palace, Av 15 de Novembro 459, T3541 2326. Recommended.

D Mamoré, R M Moraes, T3541 3753. Clean, friendly.

Centro Deportivo Afonso Rodrigues, Av 15 de Novembro, T541 3732. There's a basic dorm, **E**, opposite the rodoviária.

Rio Branco *p646*

AL-A Terra Verde, R Marechal Deodoro 221, T3213 6000, www.terraverdehotel.com.br. One of the best in the city, well appointed a/c rooms and more luxurious suites, pool, breakfast and free Wi-Fi.

AL-A Imperador Galvez, R Santa Inés 401, T3223 7027, www.hotelimperador.com.br. Comfortable, quiet, modern rooms with TV and free Wi-Fi, large pool, huge breakfasts.

A Irmãos, R Rui Barbosa 450-69, T3214 7100, www.irmaospinheiro.com.br. Bright, spacious rooms, refurbished in 2010, pool, free Wi-Fi, generous breakfast, some English-speaking staff. There's a *churrascaria* next door.

A Loureiro, R Marechal Deodoro 304, T3224 3110. A/c, spotless rooms, TV. Close to the river with many shops and restaurants a stroll away.

B-C Afa, R Franco Ribeiro 108, T3224 1396. Simple rooms, quiet and well-kept but small windows, good breakfast.

C Papai, R Floriano Peixoto 849, T3223 6868. Central, simple but garish pink and lime green a/c rooms, best on the upper floors, free Wi-Fi.

D Ouro Verde, R Uirapuru 326, next to rodoviária, T3223 2378. No frills option, rooms only a little larger than the beds they contain, but with bath, clean and tidy, on a sunny terrace. With breakfast.

Xapuri *p647*

B-D Pousada Ecologica Serengal Cachoeira, Ramal do Cachoeira, Xapuri, T9984 4738 through Maanaim, see below. In the Chico Mendes reserve, a series of comfortable wooden cabanas, with a/c, suites and dorms, open-sided public dining and lounge area, overlooking a small river. Day and night safari walks are US$15.

Eating

Porto Velho *p645*

TTT Caravela do Madeira, R José Camacho 104, T3221 6641. The city's business lunch venue, a/c, international menu.

ŸŸŸ Myoshi, Av Amazonas 1280, Bairro NS das Graças, T3224 4600, www.myoshi.com.br, a 15 cab ride from the centre. Large, a/c, open plan dining room serving the best Japanese foodt in the city, evening sushi and sashimi buffet, also Brazilian fusion options. Also delivers.

ŸŸ Café Madeira, Majo Amarantes at Carlos Gomes on the riverfront, T3229 1193. Overlooking the Madeira, *petisco* bar snack, a favourite spot for a sunset beer.

ŸŸ Emporium, Av Presidente Dutra 3366, T3221 2665. Nice atmosphere, good meats and salads, expensive drinks, open 1800-2400. The street behind Emporium is known as the **Calçada da Fama** and is replete with bars and restaurants. It's very busy at weekends.

Guajará Mirim *p646*

Oasis, Av 15 de Novembro 460. The best place to eat. Recommended (closed Mon).

Rio Branco *p646*

Local specialities *Tacacá*; a soup served piping hot in a gourd (*cuia*) combines manioc starch (*goma*), cooked jambu leaves which numb mouth and tongue, shrimp, spices and hot pepper sauce; recommendation from Sra Diamor, Boulevar Augusto Monteiro 1046, Bairro 15 in the 2° distrito (bus Norte-Sul from the centre), other kiosks. Also a delicious Amazonian take on Espírito Santo or Bahia's *moqueca*.

ŸŸŸ-ŸŸ Mata Nativa, Estrada Via Verde Km 2 1971, T3221 3004. Regional food served in an open-sided maloca set in a garden on the road to Sena Madureira, 6 km from the centre. Plates are big enough for 4 people, very popular on weekends.

ŸŸ Afa, R Franco Ribeiro 108, T3224 1396, www.afabistro.com.br. The best-value per kilo restaurant in the city, with a wide choice of dishes. Plenty of veggie options.

ŸŸ Elcio, Av Ceará 2513. Superb fish moquecas (rich coconut sauce flavoured with an Amazon leaf, xicoria, and fresh coriander and accompanied with rice, pirão, farofa and delicious chilli and tucupi sauce). Serves 2-3 people.

Shopping

Porto Velho *p645*

Porto Velho Shopping, 2½ km east of the rodoviária, www.pvshopping.com.br. With many a/c boutiques, travel agencies and restaurants in the food emporium and a 6 screen multiplex cinema with films in English.

Indian handicrafts **Artesanato Indígena Karitiana**, R Rui Barbosa 1407 between José Camacho and Calama, T3229 7591, daily 0800-1200, 1400-1700. An indigenous-run cooperative selling art including beads, earrings and necklaces, ritual items and weapons.

Activities and tours

Rio Branco *p646*

Tour operators **Maanaim Amazônia**, Hotel Imperador Galvez, R Santa Inés 401, T3223 3232, www.maanaim.amazonia.com. Trips to the Chico Mendes reserve in Xapuri and and other good ethno-tourism projects in the Amazon, staying in remote indigenous villages in the Vale do Jurua in the far west of the state.

Transport

Porto Velho *p645*

Air Airport 8 km west of town. Take bus marked 'Aeroporto' (last one between 2400-0100). Daily flights to many Brazilian cities.

Bus Rodoviária is on Jorge Teixeira between Carlos Gomes and Dom Pedro II. It has restaurants, snack bars and 24-hr ATM. From town take bus No 407 'Norte Azul', or any 'Esperança da Communidade' or 'Presidente Roosevelt' bus from the cathedral in the centre to the rodoviária, 1½ km. Health and other controls at the Rondônia-Mato Grosso border are strict. To break up a long trip is much more expensive than doing it all in one stretch.

To **São Paulo**, 1000, 40 hrs, US$185. To **Cuiabá**, 24 hrs, US$75. To **Guajará-Mirim**, see below. To **Rio Branco**, **Viação Rondônia**, 5 daily, 8 hrs, US$32. To **Campo Grande** 27 hrs, US$155. To **Cáceres** for the Pantanal, 18 hrs, US$66.

Ferry See River Transport, page 616. Passenger service from **Porto Cai N'Água** (which means 'fall in the water', watch out or you might!), for best prices buy directly at the boat, avoid touts on the shore. Boat tickets for Manaus are also sold in the rodoviária. The Rio Madeira is fairly narrow so the banks can be seen and there are several 'meetings of waters'. Shipping a car: São Matheus Ltda, Av Terminal dos Milagros 400, Balsa, takes vehicles on pontoons, meals, showers, toilets, cooking and sleeping in your car is permitted.

Road Road journeys are best done in the dry season, the 2nd half of the year.

The BR-364: Ji Paraná *p646*
Bus To **Porto Velho**, US$34, 16 hrs; to **Cuiabá**, 15 hrs, US$60.

Guajará Mirim *p646*
Bus From **Porto Velho** to Guajará Mirim, 5-6 hrs, 6 daily from 0630, fastest at midday, US$22.

Guajará Mirim/Guayaramerín *p646*
Speedboat across the Rio Mamoré (border with Bolivia), US$1.65 (more at night), 5-min crossing, operates all day, tickets at the waterside; **ferry** crossing for vehicles, T3541 3811, Mon-Sat 0800-1200, Mon-Fri 1400-1600, 20-min crossing.

Rio Branco *p646*
Air Plácido de Castro, BR-364, Km 18 Sena Madureira, T3211 1003; taxi to centre US$28, or take any bus marked 'Custódio Freire' (US$1) to the urban bus terminal in the city centre. Buses also run to the rodoviária. **Gol**, **TAM** and **TRIP** fly to Rio Branco: daily flights to **Campo Grande** and **Cuiabá** (with immediate onward connections to São Paulo, Foz do Iguaçu), to **Cruzeiro do Sul**, **Manaus**, **Porto Velho** and **Tabatinga**. International flights to **Cuzco** with **Star Perú** Mon and Thu. It is also possible to reach Peru through Cruzeiro do Sul where a weekly flight to **Pucallpa** and on to Lima with Star Peru was scheduled for July 2010.
Bus Rodoviária on Av Uirapuru, Cidade Nova, 2° distrito (east bank), T3224 6984, 5 km from centre; city bus 'Norte-Sul' to the centre. Taxi drivers will change money, poor rates. To **Porto Velho**, **Viação Rondônia**, see above. To **Guajará Mirim**, daily with **Rondônia** at 1130 and 2200, 5-6 hrs, US$20; or take Inácio's Tur shopping trip, 3 per week. From Rio Branco the BR-364 continues west (in principle) to Cruzeiro do Sul and Japim, with a view to reaching the Peruvian frontier further west when completed.
Car Prices for car rentals with the nationwide agencies are higher in Acre than in other states.

Border with Bolivia and Peru *p647*
At least 4 buses daily with **Real Norte** (US$15) and numerous combi vans (taxi lotação from Calçadão da Gameleira, Segundo district, Rio Branco) to **Brasiléia** and **Epitaciolândia**, whose rodoviária is 100 m from the Brazilian border post. Onward transport from Cobija to La Paz (1490 km) only May-Nov, but daily flights with **Aerosur** (www.aerosur.com), direct or via Cochabamba, and 3 a week with **BOA** (www.boa.com.bo) via Cochabamba. Three daily buses and numerous shared combi vans (also from Calçadão da Gameleira) to **Assis Brasil** with **Real Norte** (4-5 hrs), and one daily direct bus to **Puerto Maldonado** (8-10 hrs) with **Móvil Tours** (US$40), for direct connections to Cuzco.

Directory

Porto Velho *p645*
Airline offices Rico, Av Pinheiro Machado 744, T3222 2105. **TAM**, RJ Castilho 530, T0800-570 5700. **Trip**, T3222 0879. **Banks** Morning only; **Banco do Brasil**, Dom Pedro II 607, cash and TCs (2% commission, minimum commission US$15), minimum exchange US$200. **Marco Aurélio Câmbio**, R José de Alencar 3353, T9984 0025, efficient, good rates, Mon-Fri 0900-1500. **Parmetal**, R Joaquim Nabuco 2265, cash only, good rates, Mon-Fri 0730-1800, Sat 0730-1300. Exchange available at airport (ask tourist office if no one about). It is difficult elsewhere in Rondônia. **Medical services** Hospital Central, R Júlio de Castilho 149, 24 hr emergencies. **Dentist**: at Carlos Gomes 2577; 24-hr clinic opposite. **Post offices** Av Pres Dutra 2701, corner of Av 7 de Setembro. **Telephones** Tele Centro Sul, Av Pres Dutra 3023 e Dom Pedro II, 0600-2300 daily.

Rio Branco *p646*
Post offices Corner of R Epaminondas Jácome and Av Getúlio Vargas. **Telephones** On Av Brasil between Marechal Deodoro and Av Getúlio Vargas, long delays for international calls.

Brasília and Goiás

The Centre West is the frontier where the Amazon meets the central plateau. It is also Brazil's frontier with its Spanish American neighbours. Lastly, it contains the border between the expansion of agriculture and the untouched forests and savannahs. On this region's eastern edge is Brasília, the symbol of the nation's commitment to its empty centre. Although not generally viewed as a tourist attraction, Brasília is interesting as a city of pure invention along the lines of Australia's Canberra and Washington in the United States. Its central position makes it a natural crossroads for visiting the north and interior of Brazil and, when passing through, it is well worth undertaking a city tour to view its innovative modern design.

Goiás is quite a mixture: colonial mining towns, a modern, planned state capital and centres which owe their existence to rapidly expanding agriculture. There are two fine national parks, Emas and Chapada dos Veadeiros. An interesting festival, with processions on horseback, is held in Pirenópolis during May/June. In Tocantins, Brazil's newest state, Jalapão is a fantastic landscape, fast-becoming a desirable destination.

Brasília → *Phone code: 0xx61. Post code: 7000. Colour map 7, A3. Population: 2.1 million (2000).*

Ins and outs

Orientation The Eixo Monumental divides the city into Asa Sul and Asa Norte (north and south wings) and the Eixo Rodoviário divides it east and west. Buildings are numbered according to their relation to them. For example, 116 Sul and 116 Norte are at the extreme opposite ends of the city. The 100s and 300s lie west of the Eixo and the 200s and 400s to the east; Quadras 302, 102, 202 and 402 are nearest the centre and 316, 116, 216 and 416 mark the end of the Plano Piloto. Residential areas are made up of six-storey apartment blocks, called 'Super-Quadras'. All Quadras are separated by feeder roads, along which are the local shops. There are also schools, parks and cinemas in the spaces between the Quadras (especially in Asa Sul). The main shopping areas, with more cinemas, restaurants, etc, are situated on either side of the city bus station (rodoviária). The private residential areas are west of the Super-Quadras, and on the other side of the lake. At right angles to these residential areas is the 'arrow', the 8-km-long, 250-m-wide **Eixo Monumental**. The main north-south road (Eixo Rodoviário), in which fast-moving traffic is segregated, follows the curve of the bow; the radial road is along the line of the arrow – intersections are avoided by means of underpasses and cloverleaves. Motor and pedestrian traffic is segregated in residential areas. A limited Metrô has been built to the southwestern suburbs. It is worth telephoning addresses away from the centre to ask how to get there. ▸▸ *See also Transport, page 664.*

Climate The climate is mild and the humidity refreshingly low, but overpowering in dry weather. The noonday sun beats hard, but summer brings heavy rains and the air is usually cool by night. Altitude: 1,171 m.

Tourist offices **Setur** ⓘ *Centro de Convenções, 3rd floor, T3429 7600*, helpful, English-speaking staff, good map of the city. There is a **branch** ⓘ *at rodoferroviária, daily 0800-2000*, at the **TV Tower** ⓘ *0900-1800*, and at the **airport** ⓘ *T3033 9488, daily 0730-2230*; they will book hotels and have maps of the city, but have more limited information. The **Ministério do Turismo** is at Esplanada dos Ministérios, Bloco U, 2nd and 3rd floors, www.turismo.gov.br (in many languages). See also www.infobrasilia.com.br, www.aboutbrasilia.com. **Maps** Detailed street maps of the city are impossible to find. Newsagents and the airport sell a map showing the *quadras*. Otherwise, see **Adetur**'s map.

Background

The purpose-built federal capital of Brazil succeeded Rio de Janeiro (as required by the Constitution) on 21 April 1960. The creation of an inland capital had been urged since the beginning of the 19th century, but it was finally brought into being after President Kubitschek came to power in 1956, when a competition for the best general plan was won by Professor Lúcio Costa, who laid out the city in the shape of a bent bow and arrow. (It is also described as a bird, or aeroplane in flight.) Only light industry is allowed in the city and its population was limited to 500,000; this has been exceeded and more people live in a number of shanty towns, with minimal services, located well away from the main city, which is now a UNESCO World Heritage Site. Brasília is on undulating ground in the unpopulated uplands of Goiás, in the heart of the undeveloped Sertão. The official name for central Brasília is the Plano Piloto.

Sights

At the tip of the arrow is the **Praça dos Três Poderes**, with the Congress buildings, the Palácio do Planalto (the President's office), the Supremo Tribunal Federal opposite it and the Ministério da Justiça and Palácio Itamaraty respectively below them. Nineteen tall Ministry buildings line the Esplanada dos Ministérios, west of the Praça, culminating in two towers linked by a walkway to form the letter H, representing Humanity. They are 28 storeys high: no taller buildings are allowed in Brasília. Where the bow and arrow intersect is the city bus terminal (rodoviária), with the cultural and recreational centres and commercial and financial areas on either side. There is a sequence of zones westward along the shaft of the arrow; a hotel centre, a radio city, an area for fairs and circuses, a centre for sports, the **Praça Municipal** (with the municipal offices in the Palácio do Buriti) and, lastly (where the nock of the arrow would be), the combined bus and railway station (rodoferroviária) with the industrial area nearby. Other than the Santuário Dom Bosco and the JK bridge, the most impressive buildings are all by Oscar Niemeyer, Brazil's leading architect.

Brasília: Plano Piloto

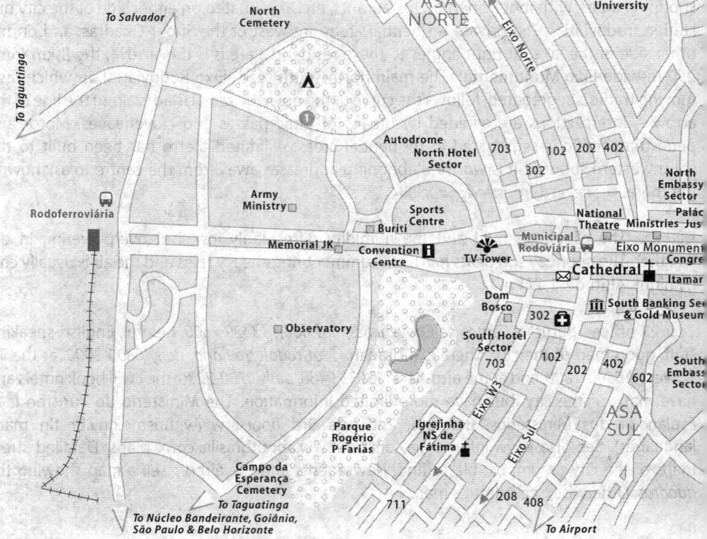

The **Palácio da Alvorada**, the President's official residence (not open to visitors), is on the lakeshore. The 80-km drive along the road round the lake to the dam is attractive. There are spectacular falls below the dam in the rainy season. Between the Praça dos Três Poderes and the lake are sites for various recreations, including golf, fishing and yacht clubs, and an acoustic shell for shows in the open air. The airport is at the eastern end of the lake. Some 395 ha between the lake and the northern residential area (Asa Norte) are reserved for the Universidade de Brasília, founded in 1961. South of the university area, the Av das Nações runs from the Palácio da Alvorada along the lake to join the road from the airport to the centre. Along it are found all the principal embassies. Also in this area is the attractive vice-presidential residence, the **Palácio do Jaburu** (not open to visitors). This area is very scenic.

A fine initial view of the city may be had from the **television tower** ⓘ *West Eixo Monumental, Mon 1400-2000, Tue-Sun 0800-2000*, which has a free observation platform at 75 m; also bar and souvenir shop. If the TV tower is closed, the nearby Alvorada hotel has a panoramic terrace on the 12th floor (lift to 11th only): ask at reception. A good and cheap way of seeing Brasília is by taking a bus from the municipal rodoviária at the centre: the destinations are clearly marked. The circular bus routes 106, 108 and 131 go round the city's perimeter. If you go around the lake by bus, you must change at the Paranoá dam; to or from Paranoá Norte take bus 101, 'Rodoviária', and to and from Sul, bus 100, bypassing the airport. Tours 1300-1700, start from the downtown hotel area and municipal rodoviária (US$12-20). Many hotels arrange city tours (see also Tour operators). Some buildings are open 1000-1400 Saturday-Sunday, with guided tours in English, well worth it.

Praça dos Três Poderes: **Congress** ⓘ *Mon-Fri 0930-1200, 1430-1630 (take your passport), guides free of charge (in English 1400-1700)*. Visitors may attend debates when Congress is in session (Friday morning). Excellent city views from the 10th floor in Annex 3. The **Palácio do Planalto** ⓘ *Sun 0930-1330, 30-min tours,* may also be visited. The guard is changed ceremonially at the Palácio do Planalto on Friday at 1730. The President attends if he is available. Opposite the Planalto is the Supreme Court building, **Supremo Tribunal Federal**. **Espaço Lúcio Costa** ⓘ *Tue-Sun 0900-1800, free,* contains a model of Plano Piloto, sketches and autographs of the designer's concepts and gives the ideological background to the planning of Brasília. (Town clothes (not shorts or minis) should be worn when visiting all these buildings.) The **Museu Histórico de Brasília** ⓘ *Tue-Sun and holidays 0900-1800*, is really a hollow monument, with tablets, photos and videos telling the story of the city. The sculpture 'Os Candangos' in front of the Planalto is a symbol of the city. By Bruno Giorgi, it pays homage to the candangos, or pioneer workers who built Brasília on empty ground. The marvellous building of the Ministry of Foreign Affairs, the **Itamarati** ⓘ *guided visits Mon, Wed, Fri 1500-1700, free,* has modern paintings and furniture and beautiful water gardens. Opposite the Itamarati is the **Palácio da Justiça** ⓘ *Mon-Fri 0900-1200, 1500-1700*, with artificial cascades between its concrete columns. The **Panteão**

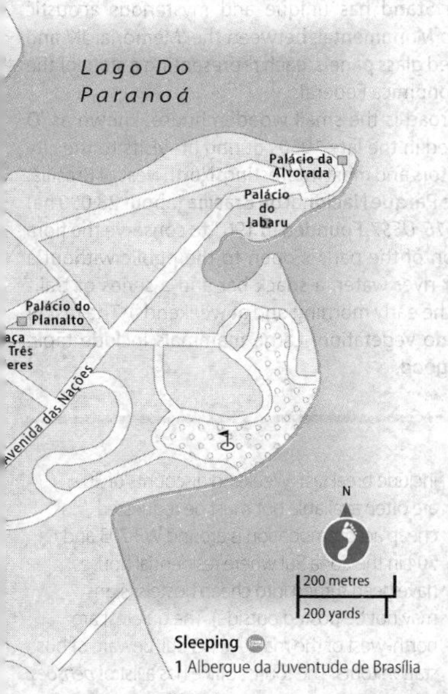

Tancredo Neves is a 'temple of freedom and democracy', built 1985-1986 by Niemeyer. It includes an impressive homage to Tiradentes, the precursor of Brazilian independence.

Niemeyer is well into his nineties but still working. His **Procuradaria Geral da República**, comprising two glass cylinders, one suspended from a concrete cog, opened in 2002. The **Museu Nacional de Brasília**, on the Conjunto Cultural da República (next to the cathedral), and the adjacent **Biblioteca Nacional** are the last grand projects Niemeyer designed for the capital. The former is particularly impressive, a huge dome of white concrete, blank but for a door halfway up, sitting in a shallow pool of water which reflects it like a mirror. This door is reached by a long sinuous ramp. Inside is a 700-seat auditorium and state-of-the-art galleries.

The **Catedral Metropolitana** ⓘ *0800-1930, T3224 4073*, on the Esplanada dos Ministérios, is a spectacular circular building in the shape of the crown of thorns. Three aluminium angels, suspended from the airy, domed, stained-glass ceiling, are by the sculptor Alfredo Ceschiatti, who also made the five life-sized bronze apostles outside. The baptistery, a concrete representation of the Host beside the cathedral, is connected to the main building by a tunnel (open Sundays only). The outdoor carillon was a gift from the Spanish government: the bells are named after Columbus's ships.

South of the TV tower on Avenida W3 Sul, at Quadra 702, is the Sanctuary of **Dom Bosco** ⓘ *T3223 6542, 0800-1800*, a modernist cube with tall gothic arches filled with stained glass that shades light to dark blue and indigo as it ascends. It is especially striking in late afternoon when shafts of light penetrate the building.

The **Templo da Boa Vontade** ⓘ *Setor Garagem Sul 915, lotes 75/76, T3245 1070, www.tbv.com.br, 24 hrs, getting there: take bus 151 from outside the Centro do Convenções or on Eixo Sul to Centro Médico*. This is a seven-faced pyramid topped by one of the world's largest crystals, a peaceful place dedicated to all philosophies and religions.

A permanent memorial to Juscelino Kubitschek, the '**Memorial JK**' ⓘ *daily 0900-1800, US$1.50*, contains his tomb and his car, together with a lecture hall and exhibits. It has toilets and a lanchonete. The **Monumental Parade Stand** has unique and mysterious acoustic characteristics (the complex is north of the Eixo Monumental, between the 'Memorial JK' and the rodoferroviária). There are remarkable stained glass panels, each representing a state of the Federation, on the ground floor of the Caixa Econômica Federal.

Some 15 km out along the Belo Horizonte road is the small wooden house, known as '**O Catetinho**', in which President Kubitschek stayed in the late 1950s during his visits to the city when it was under construction; it is open to visitors and most interesting. Northwest of Brasília, but only 15 minutes by car from the centre, is the **Parque Nacional de Brasília** (about 28,000 ha) ⓘ *contact the park's office, BR 040 SMU, T3465 2016, US$7*. Founded in 1961 to conserve the flora and fauna of the Federal Capital, only a portion of the park is open to the public without a permit. There is a swimming pool fed by clear river water, a snack bar and a series of trails through gallery forest (popular with joggers in the early morning and at weekends). The rest of the park is grassland, gallery forest and cerrado vegetation. Large mammals include tapir, maned wolf and pampas deer; birdwatching is good.

Brasilia listings

For Sleeping and Eating price codes and other relevant information, see Essentials, pages 38-40. See Telephone, page 397, for important phone changes.

Sleeping

Brasília *p651*

The best area is the northern hotel zone which has shops and restaurants nearby. Prices usually include breakfast. Weekend discounts of 30% are often available but must be requested. Most cheap accommodation is around W3 703 and 704 in the Zona Sul where residential houses have been turned into cheap hostels (signs may not be posted outside). The quietest are north-west of the main Av W3 Sul. Beware of bus station touts. The tourist office has a list of *pensões*.

Asa Norte

Moderately priced hotels are mostly found in this sector only.

LL Blue Tree Park, Trecho 1, lt1-B, Bl C (Lagoa Norte), T3424 7000, www.bluetree.com.br. The city's, newest, most luxurious business hotel, with rooms in a giant red horseshoe overlooking the lake, an enormous pool and excellent, comprehensive business facilities.

LL-L Kubitschek Plaza, Qd 2, bloco E, T3319 3543, www.kubitschek.com.br. Popular business hotel with modern rooms and excellent facilties; broadband in rooms, pool, sauna and gym. Sister hotel, the Manhattan Plaza (www.manhattan.com.br) next door is very similar.

AL Bittar Inn, Qd 2 bloco N, T3328 7150, www.hoteisbittar.com.br. Simple rooms, a bit cramped, at the cheaper end of this chain's hotels, good value for the area.

AL-A Aristus, Qd 2 bloco O, T3328 8675, www.aristushotel.com.br. Newly painted and delightfully dated seventies block with simple a/c rooms and breakfast.

A Casablanca, Qd 3 bloco A, T3328 8586, www.casablancabrasilia.com.br. Another 1970s delight; more intimate than most in the area, but some noisy rooms.

B El Pilar, Qd 3 bloco F, T3328 5915, www.elpilar.com.br. Plain, freshly painted, with fan. Avoid rooms below street level as they collect car fumes.

D pp **Albergue da Juventude de Brasília**, Setor Recreativo Parque Norte (SRPN), Quadra 02, Lote 02, T3343 0531, www.brasiliahostel.com.br. Cheaper for HI members, also has double rooms (**B**), also cheaper Jan-Feb. Kitchen, laundry, cyber-café, in same grounds as Camping de Brasília. Take bus 143 from municipal rodoviária.

Asa Sul

Until Nov 2009, there were several small *pousadas* in the Asa Sul (703 Sul), but all were closed by a judge for being in a residential zone. At the time of writing it is not known if any has reopened.

L Nacional, Qd 1 bloco A, T3321 7575, www.hotelnacional.com.br. Cavernous, frayed old-fashioned and a city landmark with many tour agencies outside.

A Alvorada, Qd 4 bloco A, T2195 1122, www.alvoradahotel.com.br. Another relic with good view from roof terrace, some special offers.

Eating

Brasília *p651*

At weekends, few restaurants in central Brasília are open. Plenty of choice of restaurants in all brackets in the Pier 21 entertainment mall on the lake shore. Other cheaper options along R 405/406.

Asa Norte

All of the large hotels in this area have upmarket restaurants, most catering to business visitors.

TTT Trattoria da Rosario, SHIS Ql 17, Bloco H, Loja 215, Lago Sul, Fashion Park, T3248 1672, www.trattoriadarosario.com.br, closed Mon, lunch only on Sun. Northern Italian food from chef Rosario Tessier. Excellent Uruguayan lamb.

TTT Universal Diner, SCLS 210, Bloco B, loja 30, T3443 2089 (lunch only on Sun), www.universaldiner.com.br. One of the city's best contemporary restaurants with cooking strongly Asian influences from New York trained chef Mara Alcamim.

TT Boa Saúde, Av W3 Norte Quadra 702, Edif Brasília Rádio Center. Sun-Fri 0800-2000. Respectable vegetarian with a range of salads, quiches and pies.

TT Bom Demais, Av W3 Norte, Qd 706. Comfortable, serving fish, beef and rice, etc, live music at weekends (cover charge US$1).

T Conjunto Nacional, SDN, Cj A, enormous mall and food court with 50 restaurants.

The municipal rodoviária provides the best coffee and pasties in town (bottom departure level).

Asa Sul

There are many cheap places on Av W3 Sul, eg at Blocos 502 and 506.

TTT La Chaumière, Av W3 Sul, Qd 408, bloco A, loja 13, T3242 7599, www.lachaumiere.com.br; lunch only Sun. The city's favourite French cooking in classical surroundings.

TTT Le Français, Av W3 Sul, Qd 404, bloco B, loja 27, T3225 4583. French food served in bistro atmosphere, classic and modern dishes.

TTT O Convento, SHIS, QI 9, conjunto 9, casa 4, T3248 1211, www.oconvento.com.br. The best for regional and Brazilian cuisine in a mock farmhouse dining room decorated with antiques and arts and crafts.

TTT Piantella, SCLS 202, bloco A, loja 34, T3224 9408, www.piantella.com.br. A favourite of senior politicians, vast menu combining *feijoada*, Italian food, steaks and seafood, good wines, too.

ŸŸŸ **Porcãoc**, Sector de Clubes Sul, Trecho 2, cj 35, rest 3, T3223 2002, www.porcao.com.br. Upmarket chain restaurant specializing in churrasco, piano bar, large veranda.

ŸŸŸ **Zuu**, 210 Sul, Bloco C, loja 38, T3244 1039. Open-plan dining room popular with society couples, Brazilian menu strong on meat and poultry.

ŸŸ **O Espanhol**, Av W3 Sul, Qd 404, bloco C, loja 07, T3224 2002. Open daily. Host to the city's annual Spanish festival and serving respectable seafood.

ŸŸ **Oca da Tribo**, SCES Trecho 2m opposite Agenpol, T3226 9880, www.ocadatribo.com.br. Wholefood restaurnat with vegetarian options and others, good buffet lunch, Dutch chef.

ŸŸ **Vercelli**, SCLS 410, bloco D, loja 34, T3443 0100. Lunch only. Pizzas, pastas and a great deal more on a huge menu.

Ÿ **Naturama**, SCLS 102, bloco B, loja 9, T3225 5125. Vegetarian and wholefood dishes, lunchtime.

Other districts

ŸŸŸ **Alice**, SHIS QI 17, Comércio Local, T3248 7743, www.restaurantealice.com.br. French home cooking in a faux-Provençale dining room in Brasília's plushest district, Lago Sul.

ŸŸŸ **Aquavit**, Mansões do Lago Norte, ML 12, conj 01, casa 05, 55, T3369 2301, www.restaurante aquavit.com. Run by Danish architect-turned-chef Simon Lau Cederholm, stunning location, glass-walled and floored rectangle suspended over a tropical garden with views of the lake and city skyline. The meal to enjoy is Cederholm's *Babette's Feast* Banquet, an ingredient-by-ingredient reproduction of the meal in Gabriel Axel's Academy Award-winning film.

ŸŸŸ **Patu Anu**, SMLN Trecho 12, Cj 01, Cs 07, S de Mansões do Lago, T3369 2788, www.patuanu.com.br. Without doubt **the** fine dining location in the city, tucked away in the forest with sweeping views. The kitchen is headed by Michelin-starred Lucas Arteaga, formerly of San Sebastian in the Basque Country. The menu is Franco-Latin fusion.

Places serving prato feito or comercial (cheap set meals) can be found all over the city, especially on Av W3 and in the Setor Comercial Sul. Other good bets are the Conjunto Nacional and the Conjunto Venâncio, 2 shopping/office complexes on either side of the municipal rodoviária. Tropical fruit flavour ice cream can be found in various parlours, eg Av W3 Norte 302. Freshly made fruit juices in all bars.

Bars and clubs

Brasília *p651*

Arena Café, CA 7, bloco F1, loja 33, T3468 1141. Popular gay bar with DJs from Thu to Sat.

Bar Brasília, SHC/S CR, quadra 506, bloco A, loja 15, parte A, T3443 4323. Little boteco with 1950s decor, draught beer and wooden tables. Lively after 1900, especially Fri.

Bier Fass, SHIS Q 5, bloco E, loja 52/53, T3248 1519. Cavernous bar/restaurant with live music Tue-Sun and 20/30s crowd. Happy hour from 1800.

Café Cancun, Shopping Liberty Mall, SCN, cuadra 3, bloco D, loja 52, T3327 1566. Tacky Mexican restaurant by day and teen and 20-something beautiful people club alter dark.

Clube de Choro, SDC, quadra 3, bloco G, T3327 0494. Wed-Sat, one of the best clubs in the country devoted to the music which gave rise to samba. Top names from all over Brazil as well as the city itself. Great atmosphere. Tickets sold 9 days in advance.

Frei Caneca, Brasília Shopping, SCN, quadra 5, bloco A, lojas 82s/94s, T3327 0202. Similar to Café Cancun. Dreadful 'flashback' night on Thu, most interesting at weekends.

Gates Pub, Av W3 Sul 403, T3225 4576, www.gatespub.com.br. Great for forró dancing and live music with a young, middle class crowd.

UK Brasil Pub, SCLS 411, bloco B, loja 28, T3346 5214. Some of the best live bands in the city play here. Guinness, sandwiches, all ages.

Entertainment

Brasília *p651*

Information about entertainment, etc is available in 2 daily papers, *Jornal de Brasília* and *Correio Brasiliense*. Any student card (provided it has a photograph) will get you into the cinema/ theatre/concert hall for half price.

Cinema **Pier 21**, SCSS, Trecho 2, Cj 32/33, is an enormous complex with 13 cinema screens, nightclubs, restaurants, video bars and children's theme park.

Theatre There are 3 auditoria of the **Teatro Nacional**, Setor Cultural Norte, Via N 2, next to the bus station, T3325 6239, foyer open

0900-2000, box office open at 1400; the building is in the shape of an Aztec pyramid. The Federal District authorities have 2 theatres, the **Galpão** and **Galpãozinho**, between Quadra 308 Sul and Av W3 Sul. There are several other concert halls.

Shopping

Brasília *p651*

Bookshops Livraria Sodiler in Conjunto Nacional and at the airport. English books (good selection).

Handicrafts Artíndia, SRTVS, Qd 702, also in the rodoviária and at the airport. For Amerindian handicrafts. **Feira hippy** at the base of the TV tower Sat, Sun and holidays. Leather goods, wood carvings, jewellery, bronzes. **Galeria dos Estados**, which runs underneath the eixo from Setor Comercial Sul to Setor Bancário Sul, 10 mins' walk from municipal rodoviária, south along Eixo Rodoviário Sul. For handicrafts from all the Brazilian states.

Shopping malls The best shopping centres are Shopping Brasília below the southern hotel zone and Patio Brasília below the northern. Both have a wide range of boutiques and fast food restaurants. There are many others.

Activities and tours

Brasília *p651*

Many tour operators have their offices in the shopping arcade of the Hotel Nacional.

City tours (3-4 hrs) with English commentary can also be booked at the airport by arriving air passengers – a convenient way of getting to your hotel if you have heavy baggage. Some tours have been criticized as too short, others that the guides speak poor English, and for night-time tours, the flood lighting is inadequate on many buildings.

Presmic Turismo, SIA trecho 03, lotes 625/695, Shopping SIA, sala 208C, T3225 0155, www.presmic.com.br. Full-, half-day and night-time city tours (0845, 1400 and 1930 respectively).

Toscana SCLS 413, Bloco D, loja 22/24, T242 9233. Recommended as cheap and good.

Transport

Brasília *p651*

Air Airport, 12 km from centre, T3364 9000. Frequent daily flights to **Rio** and **São Paulo** (1½ hrs in both cases) and to main cities. Bus 102 or 118 to airport, regular, US$1, 30 mins. Taxi US$13 (meter rate 2 used to airport), worth it. Left luggage at airport (tokens for lockers, US$0.65).

Bus The terminal (rodoferroviária, T3363 2281) beside the railway station, from which long-distance buses leave, has post office (0800-1700, Sat 0800-1200) and telephone. Bus 131 between rodoviária, the municipal terminal, and rodoferroviária, US$1.65; taxi rodoferroviária to Setor Hoteleiro Norte, US$12. There are showers (US$0.65). Both bus stations have large luggage lockers. To **Rio:** 17 hrs, 6 comuns (US$70) and 3 leitos (about US$115) daily. To **São Paulo:** 16 hrs, 7 comuns (about US$66) and 2 leitos (US$132) daily (**Rápido Federal** recommended). To **Belo Horizonte:** 12 hrs, US$35-44, also 2 leitos daily. To **Belém:** 36 hrs, 4 daily (US$74, **Trans Brasília**). To **Salvador:** 24 hrs, 3 daily (US$90). To **Cuiabá:** 17½ hrs (US$66) daily at 1200 with **São Luis**. For **Mato Grosso:** generally **Goiânia** seems to be the better place for buses. **Barra do Garças:** 0830 and 2000, takes 9 hrs with **Araguarina**, T3233 7598, US$27 return. All major destinations served. Bus tickets for major companies sold at the city rodoviária.

Directory

Brasília *p651*

Airline offices GOL, premium rate number, T0300-115 2121, airport 3364 9370. **TAM**, SHN Hotel Nacional, Gallery Store, 36/37, T3325 1300, or 4002 5700. **Webjet**, T0300-210 1234. **Banks** Foreign currency (but not always Amex cheques) exchanged at branches of: **Banco Regional de Brasília**, SBS Q 1, Bl E, and **Banco do Brasil**, Setor Bancário Sul, latter also at airport (ATM, bank open weekends and holidays), US$20 commission for TCs. **MasterCard** office, SCRN 502, Bl B, loja 31-32, T225 5550, for cash against card; ATMs at Citibank, SCS Quadra 06, bloco A, loja 186, T215 8000, **HSBC**, SCRS 502, bloco A, lojas 7/12, and **Banco 24 Horas** at airport, and all over the city, including the Rodoferroviária. Good exchange rates at Hotel Nacional and hotels with 'exchange-turismo' sign. **Car hire** All large companies at the airport and the Car Rental Sector. Multinational agencies and **Interlocadora**, airport, T0800-138000. **Unidas**, T2365 2266 at airport, Mon-Fri 0800-1800. **Cultural centres** British Council,

Ed Centro Empresarial Varig, SCN Q 04 bloco B, Torre Oeste Conjunto 202, T2106 7500, brasilia@britishcouncil .org.br. **Cultura Inglesa**, SCLRN 704 Bloco B/Loja Térrea 57, T3327 5400, gerente.asa.norte2@cultura inglesa.net. **American Library**, Casa Thomas Jefferson, SEPS 706/906, Conj B, T3443 6588, www.thomas.org.br. **Aliança Francesa**, SEPS EQ 708/907 Lote A, T3242 7500, www.afbrasilia.org.br. **Instituto Cultural Goethe**, Av W5 Sul, SEPS-EQS 707/907, bloco F, salas 103-137, T3244 6776, www.goethe.de/brasilia. **Embassies and consulates** **Australia**, SES Av das Nações, Qd 801, conjunto K, lote 7, T3226 3111, www.brazil.embassy.gov.au. **Austria**: SES, Av das Nações Q811, lote 40, T3443 3111, www.aussenministerium.at/brasilia. **Bolivia**, SHIS QI 19 Conj 13 Casa 19, Lago Sul, T3366 3432, www.embolivia.org.br. **Canada**: SES, Av das Nações Q 803 lote 16, T3424 5400, www.dfait-maeci.gc.ca/ brazil. **Finland**: SES, Av das Nações Q 807, lote 27, T3443 7151, brasilia@finlandia.org.br. **France**: SES, Av das Nações Q801, L04, T3222 3999, http://brasilia.ambafrance-br.org. **Germany**: SES, Av das Nações Q807, L25, T3442 7000, www.brasilia.diplo.de/pt/Start seite.htm. **Guyana**: SHIS QI 05, conj 19, casa 24, Lago Sul, T3248 0874, embguyana@apis.com.br. **Israel**: SES, Av das Nações, Q 809, lote 38, T2105 0500, info@brasilia.mfa.gov.il. **Netherlands**: SES, Av das Nações Q 801, lote 5, T3961 3200, www.mfa.nl/ brazilie. **New Zealand**: SHIS Q1 09, conj 16, casa 01, Lgo Sul, T3248 9900, zelandia@nwi.com.br. **South Africa**: SES, Av das Nações Q 801, lote 06, T3312 9500, www.africa dosul.org.br. **Suriname**: SHIS Q19 Conj 8 casa 24, T3248 3595. **Sweden**: Av das Nações Q 807, lote 29, T3443 1444, swebra@open gate.com.br. **Switzerland**: SES, Av das Nações Q 811, lote 41, T3443 5500, www.eda. admin.ch/brasilia. **UK**: SES, Quadra 801, Conjunto K lote 8 (British Commonwealth Chamber of Commerce), Av das Nações, T3329 2300, contato@reinounido.org.br. **US**: SES, Av das Nações Q801, L03, T3312 7000, www.embaixada-americana.org.br. **Venezuela**: SES, Av das Nações Q803, lote 13, T2101 1011, www.emb venezuela.org.br. **Post offices** **Poste restante**, Central Correio, 70001; SBN-Cj 03, BL-A, Ed Sede da ECT, central office is in the Setor Hoteleiro Sul, between Hotels Nacional and St Paul. Another post office is in Ed Brasília Rádio, Av 3 Norte.

Goiás

Goiânia → *Phone code: 062. Colour map 4, A1. Population: 1.1 million.*

The state capital is famous for its street cafés and is a good place to stop between Brasília and the rest of the Cent West. It is a spacious city, founded in 1933, with well-lit main avenues radiating out from the central **Praça Cívica**, on which stand the Government Palace and main Post office. Goiânia has more parks and gardens than any other of Brazil's large cities and many are filled with interesting forest and cerrado plants, as well as marmosets and remarkably large numbers of birds. **Tourist office**: Semtur ⓘ *R 32 esq Rua 15, No 394, Setor Marista, T3524 1010, atendimento@turismogoiania.com.br*, and the Prefietura's website: www4.goiania.go.gov.br. **Agetur** (state tourism association) ⓘ *R 30 corner of Rua 4, Centro de Convenções, T3201 8122.* Tourist office at the Rodoviária, T3224 8466. Extensive information, maps and bus routes in Novo Guia Turístico de Goiás, available at news stands, US$2.25.

The **Museu Zoroastro Artiaga** ⓘ *Praça Cívica 13, T3223 1763, 0900-1700 (1600 Sat-Sun)*, has a small but interesting collection of indigenous and historical objects, fossils and religious items as well as cases depicting indigenous and early settler life in Goiás. **Museu Antropológico do UFG** ⓘ *Praça Universitária, 1 km east of Praça Cívica, T3209 6010, Tue-Fri 0900-1700*, houses wide-ranging ethnographic displays on the *indígenas* of the Centre West. The **Museu de Artes de Goiânia** ⓘ *Rua 6 605, T3524 1190, Mon-Fri 0800-2100, Sat-Sun 0900-1600, free*, in the Bosque dos Buritis gardens has a room showcasing the work of a number of local artists including Siron Franco, who is nationally renowned. The **Casa do Indio** is a centre for indigenous arts and craft production and an important meeting place for indigenous peoples like the Xavantes. The shop there sells a variety of handicrafts. The **Memorial do Cerrado Museum** ⓘ *Av Bela Vista Km 2, Jd*

Olímpico, T3227 1723, Tue-Sat 0900-1200, 1400-1700, US$4.55, just outside the city, provides an interesting introduction to Cerrado life, with reconstructions of indigenous villages, quilombos and colonial streets as well as planted cerrado vegetation.

Cidade de Goiás (Goiás Velho) ➔ *Phone code: 062. Colour map 1, C5.*

This delightful town (*Population: 30,000*) nestled amid cerrado-covered ridges is one of Central Brazil's hidden gems. Its cobbled streets lined with Portuguese whitewash and brilliant yellow and blue façades and elegantly simple baroque churches have been awarded UNESCO World Heritage status. The town was founded in 1727 as Vila Boa and like its Minas counterparts became rich on gold, before becoming the capital of Goiás state, which it remained until just before the Second World War. The **tourist office** ⓘ *T371 3047, daily 0900-1700*, is housed in the Quintal do Vinte, a beautiful 18th-century former barracks on Praça Brasil Caiado. No English is spoken. The Museu Casa de Cora Coralina is a better source of information. Churches are usually open in the mornings and closed on Monday.

The most interesting streets in the colonial part of town spread out from the two principal plazas, Praça Brasil Caiado and, immediately below it towards the river, Praça do Coreto. The former is dominated by a lavish baroque fountain which once supplied all the town's water. The oldest church, **São Francisco de Paula** (1763) ⓘ *Praça Zacheu Alves de Castro*, sits on a platform overlooking the market and the Rio Vermelho. It has a beautiful 19th-century painted ceiling by André Antônio da Conceição, depicting the life of St Francis. **Nossa Senhora da Abadiá** ⓘ *R Abadia s/n*, has a similarly understated but impressive painted ceiling, whilst the other 18th-century churches like **Nossa Senhora do Carmo** ⓘ *R do Carmo – on the riverside*, and **Santa Bárbara** ⓘ *R Passo da Pátria*, are even simpler. The latter sits on a hill a kilometre or so east of the town affords wonderful sunset views. The **Museu das Bandeiras** ⓘ *Praça Brasil Caiado/Largo do Chafariz, T3371 1087, Tue-Fri 0900-1700, Sat 1200-1700, Sun 0900-1300, US$1.30*, was once the centre of local government. Its rooms, furnished with period pieces, sit over a small but forbidding dungeon. The old governor's palace, the **Palacio Conde dos Arcos** ⓘ *Praça do Coreto, T3371 1200, Tue-Sat 0800-1700, Sun 0900-1300, US$1.30*, has a display of 19th-century furniture and plaques describing the town's life in colonial times. The **Museu de Artes Sacras** ⓘ *Praça do Coreto, T3371 1200, Tue-Sat 0800-1700, Sun 0900-1300, US$1.30*, houses some 18th-century church silverware and a series of painted wooden statues by one of Brazil's most important religious sculptors, José Joaquim da Veiga Valle. A stroll from the Praça do Coreto, downhill and across the river will bring you to the **Museu Casa de Cora Coralina** ⓘ *R do Cândido 20, T3371 1990, Tue-Sun 0900-1700, US$1.30*, the former home of Goiás's most respected writer, with a collection of her belongings and a restful walled riverside garden at the back. The staff here are extremely helpful and knowledgeable about the city, though they speak no English. The 18th-century **Mercado Municipal**, next to the old rodoviária, 500 m west of the central Praça do Coreto, is a wonderful spot for cheap lunches, breakfasts and photography. Little artisan shops are springing up all over the town.

Pirenópolis ➔ *Colour map 1, C5. Phone code: 062. Population: 23,000. Altitude: 770 m.*

This lovely colonial silver mining town, 165 km due west of Brasília, has a well-preserved centre. It's almost as pretty as Cidade de Goiás and is National Heritage Site. The city is the nation's unofficial silver capital and is a good place to stock up on presents. It's also a favourite weekend haunt for the capital's middle classes who congregate in the lively restaurants and bars which line the northern end of Rua do Rosário. One of Brazil's most unusual and vibrant festivals takes place here every May/June (see page 663) and at weekends the Praça Central fills with country folk in stetsons and spurs, blasting out Sertanejo music from their souped-up cars. **Tourist office**: Centro de Atendimento ao Turista ⓘ *R do Bonfim 14, Centro Histórico, T3331 2729, www.pirenopolis.tur.br*. Poor English.

The **Igreja Matriz Nossa Senhora do Rosário**, which has been restored after being gutted by a fire in 2002, is the oldest church in the state (1728). It is open to the public, but its lavish interior is sadly no more. **Nosso Senhor de Bonfim** (1750-1754), which houses an impressive lifesize crucifix from Bahia, was transported here on the backs of 260 slaves. **Nossa Senhora do Carmo** ⓘ *daily 1300-1700*, serves as a museum of religious art. **Museu Família Pompeu** ⓘ *R Nova 33, Tue-Fri 1300-1700, Sat 1300-1500, Sun 0900-1200*, displays the best collection of pictures and documents devoted to the history of the city (in Portuguese only). The tiny, private **Museu das Cavalhadas** ⓘ *R Direita 37, officially Fri and Sat 0800-1700, but sporadic, US$1.30*, has a collection of masks and costumes from the Festa do Divino. **Fazenda Babilônia** ⓘ *25 km southwest by paved road, Sat and Sun 0800-1700, US$2.65*, is a fine example of an 18th-century sugar fazenda, now a small museum, original mill, no public transport.

Chapada dos Veadeiros

ⓘ *Entry US$11.50. ICMBio, R GO 239 Km 36, Vila São Jorge, Alto Paraíso, T3455 1116, www.icmbio.gov.br/parna_veadeiros. Visitors centre open 0800-1200 for entry to trails which are open till 1800, Tue-Sun.*

These table top mountains, drained by countless fast-flowing rivers which rush through deep gorges and plummet over spectacular waterfalls are less famous, but much bigger than Diamantina or Guimarães. And unlike both those areas its forests have never been felled (it was designated a World Heritage Site by UNESCO in 2001). The Chapada is covered in cerrado forest – a habitat of such floral diversity that it has recently been declared a biological hotspot by Conservation International. Rare mammals including jaguar, maned wolf, puma, tapir, ocelot and giant anteater are abundant and although no one has yet compiled a serious bird list spectaculars and rarities include red shouldered macaw, coal crested finch, helmeted manakin and various key indicator species like rusty margined guan and bare face currasow. King vultures are abundant. At present trips within the park itself are limited to day visits only; but there are plans to change this as walks of as long as nine days can be easily organized at a good price. Visits to the surrounding countryside without one not recommended – it is easy to get lost and guides are not expensive. The park is reached by paved state highway 118 to **Alto Paraíso de Goiás**, then a paved road around 40 km west to **São Jorge** (1 km from park entrance). Alto Paraiso is best for visits to the eastern sections of the Chapada, São Jorge for the park itself.

Parque Nacional Emas

ⓘ *US$7. Permission to visit from ICMBio, T0xx64-3929 6000. Day trips are not recommended, but 4-day, 3-night visits to the Park can be arranged through agencies (eg Focus Tours, www.focustours.com).*

In the far southwest of the state, covering the watershed of the Araguaia, Taquari and Formoso rivers, is the small **Parque Nacional Emas**, 98 km south of Mineiros just off the main BR-364 route between Brasília and Cuiabá (112 km beyond Jataí). Almost 132,868 ha of undulating grasslands and cerrado contain the **world's largest concentration of termite mounds**. Pampas deer, giant anteater, greater rhea, or 'ema' in Portuguese, and maned wolf are frequently seen roaming the grasses. The park holds the greatest concentration of blue-and-yellow macaws outside Amazônia, and blue-winged, red-shouldered and red-bellied macaws can also be seen. (There are many other animals and birds.) Along with the grasslands, the park supports a vast marsh on one side and rich gallery forests on the other. As many of the interesting mammals are nocturnal, a spotlight is a must.

Goiás listings

For Sleeping and Eating price codes and other relevant information, see Essentials, pages 38-40. See Telephone, page 397, for important phone changes.

Sleeping

Goiânia *p658*

The best hotels are 1 km from the centre in the Setor Oeste which has many restaurants and bars. Most hotels in the centre are frayed 1970s blocks.

L Castro's Park, Av República do Líbano 1520, Setor Oeste, T3096 2000, www.castrospark.com.br. 5-star tower a few blocks from the centre, gym, pool, best for business. Plenty of restaurants and bars nearby.

L Papillon, Av Republica do Libano 1824, T3219 1500, www.papillonhotel.com.br. Modern rooms and suites, pool, gym, sauna, business facilities, very popular, book ahead.

AL Address, Av República do Líbano 2526, T3257 1000, www.addresshotel.com.br. Well-equipped business hotel, the best in the city, modern rooms with separate living areas, broadband access, gym, pool, restaurant, bar, good views from the upper floors.

A-B Rio Vermelho, R 4 No26, T3227 2500, www.hotelriovermelho.com.br. Simple, in a quiet street with lots of cheap restaurants, cheapest with fan, close to the centre.

B Oeste Plaza, 389 Rua 2, Setor Oeste, T3224 5012. Well-maintained, modern, small a/c rooms, those on higher floors have good views, small pool and gym.

C Karajás, Av Goiás and R 3 No 860, T3224 9666. Good value in a once luxury hotel now fallen somewhat from grace, convenient.

C-D Goiânia Palace, Av Anhangüera 5195, T3224 4874, Goiâniapalace@terra.com.br. Art deco building with a range of rooms from simple doubles with fan to suites, good breakfast, well located.

E Antoninho's, R 68 No 41, T3223 1815. Very basic but well looked after, only a few rooms have windows, safe, good breakfast.

E Paissandú, Av Goiás 1290 at R 55, T3224 4925. Very simple, fan or a/c, 8 blocks north of the centre.

Camping Itanhangá municipal site, Av Princesa Carolina, 13 km, T292 1145. Attractive wooded location, reasonable facilities.

Cidade de Goiás *p659*

AL-A Vila Boa, Morro Chapéu do Padre s/n, 1 km southeast of the centre, T3371 1000, www.hotelvilaboa.com.br. The best in town, though inconvenient for the centre, pool, bar, restaurant and good views.

A Casa da Ponte, R Moretti Foggia s/n, T3371 4467. Art deco building next to bridge across Rio Vermelho, a/c rooms, the best overlook the river.

C Pousada do Ipê, R Cel Guedes de Amorim 22, T3371 2065. Rooms around a courtyard dominated by a huge mango tree. The annexe has a pool and bar.

C-D Pousada do Vovô Jura, R Sta Barbara 38, T3371 1746. Colonial house set in a little garden with views out over the river and Serra.

D Pousada do Sol, R Americano do Brasil, T3371 1717. Well maintained, fans, friendly and central.

D-E Pousada dos Sonhos, R 15 Novembro 22, T3372 1224. Simple and convenient, plain rooms with shared bath, good breakfast.

D-E Pousada Reis, R 15 Novembro 41, T3371 1565. A simple cheapie next to the Sonhos offering similar rooms but shoddier service.

Camping Cachoeira Grande campground, 7 km along the BR-070 to Jussara (near the tiny airport). Attractive, well-run, with bathing place and snack bar. More basic site (**Chafariz da Carioca**) in town by the river.

Pirenópolis *p659*

At Festa do Divino (see page 663) it's essential to book ahead or visit from Brasília.

A Casa Grande, R Aurora 41, T3331 1758, www.casagrandepousada.com.br. Chalets in a tropical garden with a pool gathered around a large colonial house on the edge of town.

A Casarão, R Direita 79, T3331 2662, www.ocasarao.pirenopolis.tur.br. A converted colonial town house decorated with antiques, garden and small pool, a/c rooms with 4-poster beds, mosquito nets.

A-B Arvoredo, R Direita s/n, T3331 3479, www.arvoredo.tur.br. Peaceful, small pool, views over the town. Simple rooms with large beds and excellent special rates during the week.

C Pouso do Sô Vigario, R Nova 25, T3331 1206, www.pousadaspirenopolis.com.br. Small rooms but pleasant public areas, good location, decent breakfast in a little garden next to the pool.

D Rex, Praça da Matriz, T331 1121. Five rooms, all with fridge and TV, arranged around a courtyard. Good breakfast and location.
E-F Arco Iris, R dos Pireneus s/n, T3331 1686. Very simple but well-kept, fan, shared bath, no breakfast.
Camping Roots, R dos Pireneus 96, camproots@yahoo.com. In easy reach of the centre with power, hot water and some English-speaking staff.

Chapada dos Veadeiros *p660*

Alto Paraiso

AL-A Camelot, on the main road just north of town, T3446 1581, www.pousadacamelot.com.br. Delightfully kitsch, mock-Arthurian castle with proper hot showers and comfortable a/c rooms with satellite TV.
AL-A Portal da Chapada, 9km along the road to São Jorge, T3446 1820, www.portaldachapada.com.br. The best choice for birdwatchers, with cabins in the cerrado. Comfortable with a/c.
A Casa Rosa, R Gumersindo 233, T3446 1319, www.pousadacasarosa.com.br. Good a/c rooms, the best in chalets near the pool.
C-D Pousada do Sol, R Gumersindo 2911, T3446 1201. Small and simple, with a range of rooms, the best with balconies and fridges.

São Jorge

Prices often go up 30% at weekends.
AL Casa das Flores, T9976 0603, www.pousadacasadasflores.com.br. Elegant, tastefully decorated rooms (candle-lit), sauna, pool and great breakfast.
AL-A Áquas de Março, T3347 2082, www.chapadadosveadeiros.com.br. A range of simple rooms decorated by local artists' work, pleasant garden, saunas, good breakfast.
AL-A Trilha Violeta, T3455 1088, www.trilhavioleta.com.br. Fan, rooms around a bougainvillea filled garden. Reasonable restaurant.
D Casa Grande, T9623 5515/446 1388, www.pousadacasagrande.com.br. Simple but well looked after, good breakfast.
Camping Tatoo, at the top of town, tattoo@travessia.tur.br, or tattoosj@yahoo.com.br. Powered sites from only US$3. Pizzas from wood oven, small bar, English spoken, very helpful.

Parque Nacional Emas *p660*

Mineiros

B Pilões Palace, Praça Alves de Assis, T3661 1547. Restaurant, comfortable.
C 14 de Maio, R Onze 11, T3661 1532. No a/c, good churrasco restaurant attached.

Dorm accommodation at the park headquarters; kitchen and cook available but bring own food.

Eating

Goiânia *p658*

Gioanian cooking is like that of neighbouring Minas – meat heavy, with huge portions of accompanying vegetable dishes and of course beans and rice. The city has a good range of restaurants and bars, especially around Praça Tamandaré and Av Rep de Líbano in the Setor Oeste. Other mid-range options exist on and around Av Anhaguera between Tocantins and Goiás. Street stands (pamonharías) sell pamonha snacks, tasty pastries made with green corn, sweet, savoury, or picante/spicy; all are served hot and have cheese in the middle, some include sausage.
TTT **Bella Luna**, R 10 704 (Praça Tamandaré). Excellent pizza, pasta and northern Italian dishes.
TTT **Celson & Cia**, R 15 539 at C 22. Very popular Goiás and Mineira meat restaurant with a good cold buffet. Evenings only except at weekends.
TTT **Chão Nativo**, Av Rep Líbano 1809. The city's most famous Goiânian restaurant also serving local and Mineira food. Lively after 2000 and lunchtime on weekends.
TT **China**, R 7 623 (Praça Tamandaré). Chinese and Japanese food in a/c surroundings.
TT **Floresta**, R 2 at R 9. Lively corner bar with grilled steaks, Brazilian standards and snacks (T). Open until late.
TT **Tribo do Açai**, R 36 590. Buzzing little fruit juice bar with excellent buffet salads and health food.
TT **Walmor**, R 3 1062 at R 25-B. Large portions of some of Brazil's best steaks, attractive open-air dining area, best after 2000.
T **Buffalo's Grill**, Praça Tamandaré. Pizzas, grilled meat, sandwiches and crêpes. Open 24 hrs.
T **Giraffa**, Av Rep Líbano 1592. Fast food with some more sumptuous set plates.
T **Mineiro**, R 4 No 53. Good Mineira per kilo buffet with lots of choice and some veggie options. One of several on this block.
T **Primo Patio**, Av Rep Líbano (opposite Castro's Plaza). Pizza, pasta and grilled steak and chicken.

Cidade de Goiás *p659*

🍴🍴 **Dali**, R 13 de Maio 26, T3372 1640. Riverside restaurant offering a broad range of international and local dishes.

🍴🍴 **Flor do Ipê**, Praça da Boa Vista 32 (end of the road leading from the centre across the bridge, T3372 1133. The best Goiânian food, enormous variety, lovely garden setting. Highly recommended.

🍴 **Degus't Fun Pizzaria**, R Quinta Bocaiuva (next to Praça do Coreto), T3371 2800. Pizza, casseroles, soups and very friendly service from a mother and daughter team.

Pirenópolis *p659*

There are plenty of options along R do Rosário, serving a surprising range of international food including some vegetarian and Asian options. Many have live music at night (and an undisclosed cover charge – be sure to ask). There are cheaper options near the Igreja Bonfim in the upper part of town.

🍴🍴 **Caffe e Tarsia**, R do Rosário 34, T3331 1274, www.caffetarsia.com.br. One of the best in town with rich Goiás cooking, a decent wine list and live music at the weekends.

🍴 **Chiquinha**, R do Rosário 19. Serves local cuisine (heavy on meat).

Bars and clubs

Goiânia *p658*

Goiânia is surprisingly lively, with some of the best nightlife in central Brazil. This is especially true around the various festivals and carnival. There is an active gay scene and plenty of choices of clubs and bars. Most locals tend to drink in the restaurants, many of which double up as bars (see above) before heading to a club at around 2300.

Festivals and events

Cidade de Goiás *p659*

Many festivals here and a very lively arts scene. The streets blaze with torches during the solemn Fogaréu processions of Holy Week, when hooded figures re-enact Christ's descent from the cross and burial. Carnaval is a good deal more joyous and still little known to outsiders. Plans are to make carnival a series of traditional masked balls, as it was at the turn of the 20th century.

Pirenópolis *p659*

Festa do Divino Espírito Santo, 45 days after Easter (Pentecost-**May/Jun**), is one of Brazil's most famous and extraordinary folkloric/religious celebrations. It lasts 3 days, with medieval costumes, tournaments, dances and mock battles between Moors and Christians, a tradition held annually since 1819. The city throbs with life over this period.

Shopping

Pirenópolis *p659*

Two of the best jewellers are **Cristiano**, who has travelled extensively in South America as is reflected in his designs, and **Rodrigo Edson Santos**, R do Rosário 3, T3331 3804.

Activities and tours

Goiânia *p658*

Travel agents in town can arrange day tours. **Turisplan Turismo**, R 8 No 388, T3224 7076. Also sells regular bus tickets.

Cidade de Goiás *p659*

Frans and Susana Leeuweenberg (through Serra Dourada). Birding and wildlife trips in the surrounding area (or anywhere in Goiás – with advanced notice) from a husband and wife team of biologists who have been working hard to protect the cerrado for many years. English, French and Dutch spoken.

Serra Dourada Aventura, no fixed office, reachable on T3371 4277 or 9238 5195, through www.vilaboadegoias.com.br or orlei@vilaboadegoias.com.br. Hiking in the Serra Dourada and bespoke trips to the wilds of the Rio Araguaia (with notice). Very good value.

Pirenópolis *p659*

There are plenty of walks and adventure activities in the cerrado and hills, birding is good and there is a reasonably healthy population of maned wolf and the various South American cats, including jaguar. The landscape is rugged, with many waterfalls and canyons. Guides are essential as many attractions are well off the beaten track.

Drena, R do Carmo 11 (across the bridge and up the hill, on the left), T3331 3336. A range of walks and adventure activities, good value, well run, English spoken. They organize trips to **Santuário de Vida Silvestre Vagafogo**, T3335

8490, the private reserve of Evandro Engel Ayer: good birding (species list and library) and many interesting animals. Evandro is very knowledgeable and helpful, speaks good English and serves one of the best light lunches in Goiás. **Mosterio Buddhisto**, a simple Zen monastery near a series of beautiful cascades in the heart of pristine cerrado forest. Day visits with light walks or longer term retreats. Particularly magical at sunset.

Chapada dos Veadeiros *p660*

By far the easiest way to visit is with one of the tour operators in Alto Paraiso. Prices vary according to season and group number.

Alternativas, T3446 1000, www.alternativas.tur.br. Light adventure activities and treks, run by locals, excellent and really go out of the way to help. Sasa speaks good English. Recommended.

Chapada Ecotours, T3446 1345, www.transchapada.com.br. Light adventure and visits to the major sights.

EcoRotas, R dos Nascentes 129, T3446 1820, www.altoparaiso.com. Van-based tours to the principal sights. Suitable for all ages.

Travessia, T3446 1595, www.travessia.tur.br. Treks of several days to over a week and rappelling and canyoning from one of the country's most respected instructors, ion David. Little English.

⊖ Transport

Goiânia *p658*

Air Santa Genoveva, 6 km northeast off Rua 57, T3265 1500. Flights to **Brasília**, **São Paulo** and other cities. Taxi from centre US$9.

Bus Rodoviária on Rua 44 No 399 in the Norte Ferroviário sector, about a 40-min walk to downtown (T3229 0070). Buses 'Rodoviária-Centro' (No 404) and 'Vila União-Centro' (No 163) leave from stop on city side of terminal, US$1; No 163 goes on to the Praça Tamandaré.

To **Brasília**, 207 km, at least 15 departures a day, 2½ hrs, US$11, and **São Paulo**, 900 km via Barretos, US$53, 14½ hrs, leito services at night. To **Cidade de Goiás**, 136 km, hourly from 0500, 2½ hrs, US$11. **Pirenópolis** 0700 and 1700, 2 hrs, US$11. **Campo Grande**, 935 km, 4 services daily, 18 hrs, US$66. To **Cuiabá** (Mato Grosso), 916 km on BR-158/070 via Barra do Garças, or 928 km on BR-060/364 via Jataí (both routes paved, most buses use the latter route), 4 buses a day, US$42, 15-16 hrs, continuing to Porto Velho (Rondônia) and Rio Branco (Acre) – a very trying journey indeed.

Cidade de Goiás *p659*

Bus The rodoviária is 2 km out of town. Regular services to Goiânia (2½ hrs), Aruanã, Barra do Garças and Jussara. All buses stop at the old bus station (rodoviária velha) next to the Mercado Municipal. Ask to get out here.

Pirenópolis *p659*

Bus 2 a day to **Brasília** (2-4 hrs) and 2 per day to **Goiânia** (3 hrs).

Chapada dos Veadeiros *p660*

Bus At least 2 per day Brasília-Alto Paraiso (3-4 hrs) and on to São Jorge. One a day to **Palmas** in Tocantins.

Parque Nacional Emas *p660*

Bus Twice weekly from **Mineiros**. **Car** 6 hrs' drive from **Campo Grande**, 20 hrs from Goiânia, paved road poor. The road to the park is unpaved.

Tocantins

To the north of Goiás, and extracted from that state in 1988, is Tocantins, dominated by vast rivers, cerrado forests and, increasingly soya plantations. The state was formed largely at the whim of one powerful landowner, José Wilson Siqueira Campos; who for the first decade of its existence ran the state like a personal fiefdom. Although new to tourism Tocantins has some stunning scenery and is the only state in the country to have Amazonian forest, Pantanal, cerrado forest and sertão. The greatest draw is **Jalapão**, a region of sweeping yellow sand- dunes, vast plains cut by fast-flowing clear-water rivers and dotted with table top mountains eroded into bizarre shapes. The air is so clear that it is possible to see for hundreds of kilometres to every horizon; and the landscape so empty that cars can be heard from miles away. There is plentiful wildlife too – including maned wolf, puma and some of the world's rarest birds including Brazilian merganser and Spix's macaw.

The capital of Tocantins is **Palmas** (*Phone code: 0xx63; Colour map 5, C1; www.palmas.to.gov.br*), a modern planned city laid out in an incomprehensible mathematical plan and on the edge of the dammed and flooded Tocantins river. Brazil's newest city is an interesting detour on the highway between Belém (1,282 km away) and Brasília (973 km). There are waterfalls in the surrounding mountains and beaches on the River Tocantins, which make for a relaxing stop on an otherwise long drive. The BR-153 is close to the city and provides a good road connection, both north to Maranhão, Pará, and south to Goiás. **Tourist offices** airport ⓘ *T3219 3760*, and Parque Cesamar ⓘ *506 Sul, Av NS–04, LO 11, Área Verde, T3218 5570*.

Tocantins listings

For Sleeping and Eating price codes and other relevant information, see Essentials, pages 38-40. See Telephone, page 397, for important phone changes.

Sleeping

Tocantins *p664*

There are numerous hotels in Palmas.

A Pousada dos Girassóis, 103-C. cj 3, lt 44, T3219 4500, www.pousadadosgirassois.com.br. The best in town with standard 3 star rooms with fitted furniture and a/c and the best restaurant in town. Jalapão tours leave from here.

B Roma, Av L02-104 Norte, lote 23, T3215 3033, www.hotelroma-to.com.br. Pleasant, bright, airy rooms, internet access.

D-E Alfredo's, Av JK 103 Sul, Qd 101, lotes 23/24, T3215 3036. Simple rooms around a garden courtyard, with a/c or fan. Trips arranged.

Activities and tours

Tocantins *p664*

Korubo Expedicoes, T011-3582 6968, www.korubo.com.br. Excellent tours to Jalapão staying in their luxurious purpose-built safari camp, modelled on those in Botswana; whitewater rafting, trekking, jeep trips and wildlife tours included in the price.

Transport

Tocantins *p664*

Air Airport, Av NS 5, 2 km from centre, T3216 1237. Flights to Belém, Brasília, Goiânia and São Paulo.

Bus City buses are plentiful and cheap. Rodoviária, Acsuso 40, T3216 1603.

The Pantanal

This vast wetland, which covers a staggering 21,000 sq km (the size of Belgium, Portugal, Switzerland and Holland combined), between Cuiabá, Campo Grande and the Bolivian frontier, is one of the world's great wildlife preserves. Parts spill over into Bolivia, Paraguay and Argentina to form an area totalling some 100,000 sq km. Partly flooded in the rainy season (see below), the Pantanal is a mecca for wildlife tourism or fishing. Whether land or river-based, seasonal variations make a great difference to the practicalities of getting there and what you will experience. A road runs across Mato Grosso do Sul via Campo Grande to Porto Esperança and Corumbá, both on the Rio Paraguai; much of the road is across the wetland, offering many sights of birds and other wildlife.

Ins and outs

The Pantanal plain slopes some 1 cm in every kilometre north to south and west to east to the basin of the Rio Paraguai and is rimmed by low mountains. One hundred and seventy five rivers flow from these into the Pantanal and after the heavy summer rains they burst their banks, as does the Paraguai itself; to create vast shallow lakes broken by patches of high ground and stands of *cerrado* forest. Plankton then swarm to form a biological soup that contains as many as 500 million microalgae per litre. Millions of amphibians and fish spawn or migrate to consume them. And these in turn are preyed upon by waterbirds and reptiles. Herbivorous mammals graze on the stands of water hyacinth, sedge and savanna grass and at the top of the food chain lie South America's great predators – the jaguar, ocelot, maned wolf and yellow anaconda. In June at the end of the wet when the sheets of water have reduced to small lakes or canals wildlife concentrates and then there is nowhere on earth where you will see such vast quantities of birds or such enormous numbers of crocodilians. Only the plains of Africa can compete for mammals and your chances of seeing a jaguar or one of Brazil's seven other species of wild cat are greater here than anywhere else on the continent. There are over 700 resident and migratory bird species in the Pantanal and birding along the Transpantaneira road in the north or in one of the fazendas in the south can yield as many as 100 species a day; especially between late June and early October. Many species overlap with the Amazon region, the Cerrado and Chaco and the area is particularly rich in waterbirds. Although the Pantanal is often described as an ecosystem in its own right, it is in reality made up of many distinct habitats which in turn have their own, often distinct biological communities. Botanically it is a mosaic, a mixture of elements from the Amazon region including *várzea* and gallery forests and tropical savanna, the *cerrado* of central Brazil and the dry *chaco* of Paraguay.

Only one area is officially a national park, the **Parque Nacional do Pantanal Matogrossense** in the municipality of Poconé, 135,000 ha of land and water, only accessible by air or river. Obtain permission to visit the park at ICMBio ⓘ *R Rubens de Mendonça, Cuiabá, CEP 78008, T0xx65-3345 1187*. Hunting in any form is strictly forbidden throughout the Pantanal and is punishable by four years imprisonment. Fishing is allowed with a licence (enquire at travel agents for latest details); it is not permitted in the spawning season or piracema (1 October-1 February in Mato Grosso do Sul, 1 November-1 March in Mato Grosso). Like other wilderness areas, the Pantanal faces important threats to its integrity. Agro-chemicals and garimpo mercury washed down from the neighbouring planalto are a hazard to wildlife. Visitors must share the responsibility of protecting the Pantanal and you can make an important contribution by acting responsibly and choosing your guides accordingly: take your rubbish, don't fish out of season, don't let guides kill or disturb fauna, don't buy products made from endangered species and report any violation to the authorities.

When to go

The Pantanal is good for seeing wildlife year-round. However, the dry season between July and October is the ideal time as animals and birds congregate at the few remaining areas of water. During these months you are very likely to see jaguars. This is the nesting and breeding season, when birds form vast nesting areas, with thousands crowding the trees, creating an almost insupportable cacophony of sounds. The white sand river beaches are exposed, caiman bask in the sun, and capybaras frolic amid the grass. July sees lots of Brazilian visitors who tend to be noisy, decreasing the chances of sightings. From the end of November to the end of March (wettest in February), most of the area, which is crossed by many rivers, floods. At this time mosquitoes abound and cattle crowd on to the few islands remaining above water. In the southern part, many wild animals leave the area, but in the north, which is slightly higher, the animals do not leave.

What to take

Most tours arrange for you to leave your baggage in town, so you need only bring what is necessary for the duration of the tour with you. In winter (June-August), temperatures fall to 10° C, warm clothing and covers or sleeping bag are needed at night. It's very hot and humid during summer and a hat and sun protection, factor 30 or above, is vital. Wear long sleeves and long trousers and spray clothes as well as skin with insect repellent. Insects are less of a problem July-August. Take insect repellent from home as mosquitoes, especially in the North Pantanal, are becoming immune to local brands. Drinks are not included in the price of packages and tend to be over-priced, so if you are on a tight budget bring your own. Most importantly, make sure you take a pair of binoculars.

Getting there

There are three options for visiting the Pantanal: by tour, through a working ranch (*fazenda*) or by self-drive. Entry into the northern Pantanal comes either via the Transpantaneira road in the north, reached from the city of Cuiabá, which cuts through the wetland and is lined with fazendas, or the town of Barão do Melgaço which is surrounded by large lakes and rivers and is not as good for wildlife. In the south the access points are Campo Grande, Corumbá and Miranda, which offers access to many of the *fazendas*. *Fazendas* in the northern or southern Pantanal can also be booked directly; most now have websites and a tour of them can be taken with a hire car.

Types of tour

Tourist facilities in the Pantanal currently cater to four main categories of visitors. **Sport fishermen** usually stay at one of the numerous speciality lodges scattered throughout the region, which provide guides, boats, bait, ice and other related amenities. Bookings can be made locally or in any of Brazil's major cities. **All-inclusive tours** combining air and ground transportation, accommodation at the most elaborate fazendas, meals, guided river and land tours, can be arranged from abroad or through Brazilian travel agencies. This is the most expensive option. **Moderately priced tours** using private guides, camping or staying at more modest fazendas can be arranged locally in Cuiabá (where guides await arrivals at the airport) or through the more reputable agencies in Corumbá. **The lowest priced tours** are offered by independent guides in Corumbá, some of whom are unreliable and travellers have reported at times serious problems here (see below). For those with the minimum of funds, a glimpse of the Pantanal and its wildlife can be had on the bus ride from Campo Grande to Corumbá, by lodging or camping near the ferry crossing over the Rio Paraguai (Porto Esperança), and by staying in Poconé and day-walking or hitching south along the Transpantaneira. **Note** Whatever your budget, take binoculars!

Choosing a tour

Most tours combine 'safari' jeep trips, river-boat trips, piranha fishing and horse riding with accommodation in lodges. Excursions often take place at sunset and sunrise as these are the best times for spotting bird and wildlife. A two-day trip, with a full day taken up with travel each way, allows you to experience most of what is on offer. Longer tours tend to have the same activities spread out over a longer period of time. The best way to enjoy a tour is not to have fixed expectations about what you will see, but to take in the whole experience that is the Pantanal.

Many budget travellers en route to or from Bolivia make Corumbá their base for visiting the Pantanal. Such tourists are often approached, in the streets and at the cheaper hotels, by salesmen who speak foreign languages and promise complete tours for low prices. They then hand their clients over to agencies and/or guides, who often speak only Portuguese, and may deliver something quite different. Some travellers have reported very unpleasant experiences and it is important to select a guide with great care anywhere. By far the best way is to speak with other travellers who have just returned from a Pantanal tour. Most guides also have a book containing comments from their former clients. Do not rush to sign up when first approached, always compare several available alternatives. Discuss the planned itinerary carefully and try to get it in writing (although this is seldom possible – threaten to go to someone else if necessary). Try to deal directly with agencies or guides, not salesmen (it can be difficult to tell who is who). Always get an itemized receipt. Bear in mind that a well-organized three-day tour can be more rewarding than four days with an ill-prepared guide. There is fierce competition between guides who provide similar services, but with very different styles. Although we list a few of the most reputable guides below, there are other good ones and most economy travellers enjoy a pleasant if spartan experience. Remember that travellers must shoulder part of the responsibility for the current chaotic guiding situation in Corumbá. Act responsibly and don't expect to get something for nothing.

It appears to be the case that once a guide is recommended by a guidebook, he ceases to guide and sets up his own business working in promoting and public relations, using other guides to work under his name. Guides at the airport give the impression that they will lead the tour, but they won't. Always ask who will lead the party and how big it will be. Less than four is not economically viable and he will make cuts in boats or guides.

Campo Grande and around

Campo Grande → *Phone code: 0xx67. Post code: 79000. Colour map 7, 1. Pop: 663,621.*

Capital of the State of Mato Grosso do Sul. It was founded in 1899. It is a pleasant, modern city. Because of the terra roxa (red earth), it is called the 'Cidade Morena'. In the centre is a shady park, the **Praça República**, commonly called the Praça do Rádio after the Rádio Clube on one of its corners. Three blocks west is **Praça Ari Coelho**. Linking the two squares, and running through the city east to west, is Av Afonso Pena; much of its central reservation is planted with yellow ypé trees. Their blossom covers the avenue, and much of the city besides, in spring. The municipal **Centro de Informação Turística e Cultural** ⓘ *Av Noroeste 5140 corner Afonso Pena, T3324 5830, Tue-Sat 0800-1900, Sun 0900-1200*, sells maps and books. Housed in Pensão Pimentel, a beautiful mansion built in 1913, it also has a database about services in the city and cultural information.

Some distance from the centre is the large **Parque dos Poderes**, which contains the Palácio do Governo and other secretariats, paths and lovely trees. Even larger is the 119-ha **Parque das Nações Indígenas**. Despite its name this is almost completely covered with grassy areas and ornamental trees. But it's a pleasant place for a stroll or quiet read and has good birdlife and a couple of museums: **Museu de Arte Contemporânea** ⓘ *R Antônio Maria*

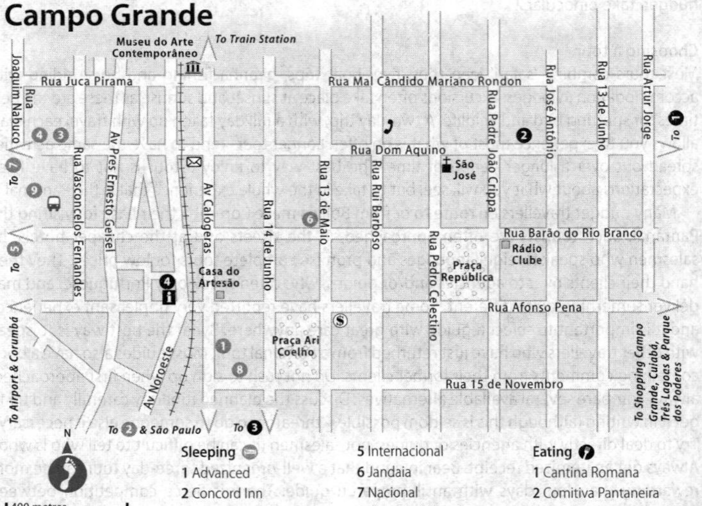

Sleeping		Eating
1 Advanced	5 Internacional	1 Cantina Romana
2 Concord Inn	6 Jandaia	2 Comitiva Pantaneira
3 Cosmos	7 Nacional	3 Gaúcho Gastão
4 Iguaçu	8 Pousada LM	4 Morada dos Bais
	9 Youth Hostel	

Coelho 6000, T3326 7449, Tue-Fri 1200-1800, Sat-Sun 1400-1800, US$2. This preserves the largest collection of modern art in the state; permanent and temporary exhibitions. **Museu Dom Bosco (Indian Museum)** ⓘ *Av Afonso Pena, Parque das Nações Indígenas, T3326 2254/9788, temporarily closed 2009-2010*, contains relics from the various tribes who were the recipients of the Salesians aggressive missionary tactics in the early and mid-20th century. The largest collections are from the Tukano and Bororo people from the Upper Rio Negro and Mato Grosso respectively, both of whose cultures the Salesians were responsible for almost completely wiping out. There is also a rather depressing display of stuffed endangered species (mostly from the Pantanal, though some are from other areas of Brazil or other countries), two-headed calves and seashells from around the world.

Bonito → *Phone code: 0xx67. Post code: 79290. Colour map 6, B6. Population: 17,000.*

The municipality of Bonito, 248 km from Campo Grande, is in the Serra do Bodoquena. It is surrounded by beautiful *cerrado* forest cut by clear-water rivers rich with fish and dotted with plunging waterfalls and deep caves. It has become Brazil's foremost ecotourism destination; which in Brazilian terms means that families come here to romp around in Nature: from light adventure activities like caving to gentle rafting and snorkelling, all with proper safety measures and great even for small children. Despite the heavy influx of visitors plenty of wildlife appears around the trails when it's quiet. The wet season is January to February; December to February is hottest, July to August coolest. **Tourist office Comtur** ⓘ *Av Cel Pilad Rebuá 1250, T3255 2160 (no English spoken), www.bonito-ms.com.br*. Bonito is prohibitively expensive for those on a budget. All the attractions in the area can only be visited with prior booking through a travel agent. As taxis are exorbitant, it is best to book with one of the few agencies that offers tours and transport. Owners also enforce limits on the number of daily visitors so, at busy times, pre-booking is essential. Bonito is very popular, especially during December to January, Carnival, Easter, and July (advance booking is essential).

Some 26 km from Bonito is **Lagoa Azul**. The cave is named after a lake 50 m long and 110 m wide, 75 m below ground level. The water, 20°C, is a jewel-like blue as light from the opening is refracted through limestone and magnesium. Prehistoric animal bones have been found in the lake. The light is at its best January-February, 0700-0900, but is fine at other times. A 25-ha park surrounds the cave. You must pay a municipal tax, US$10; if not using your own transport, a car for four costs US$20. Also open is **Nossa Senhora Aparecida cave**, which has superb stalactites and stalagmites; no tourism infrastructure.

The **Balneário Municipal** ⓘ *7 km on road to Jardim, US$4*, on the Rio Formoso, with changing rooms, toilets, camping, swimming in clear water, plenty of fish to see (strenuous efforts are made to keep the water and shore clean). **Hormínio waterfalls** ⓘ *13 km, US$1*, eight falls on the Rio Formoso, suitable for swimming; bar and camping. **Rafting** on the Rio Formoso: 2½ hours, minimum four people, US$15 per person, a mixture of floating peacefully downriver, swimming and shooting four waterfalls, lifejackets available; arranged by many agencies. The **Aquário Natural** ⓘ *US$25*, is one of the springs of the Rio Formoso. To visit you must have authorization from the owners; you can swim and snorkel with five types of fish. Do not swim with suntan oil on. Other tours are: from the **springs of the Rio Sucuri** to its meeting with the Formoso (permission required to visit), about 2 km of crystal-clear water, with swimming or snorkelling, birdwatching, very peaceful; **Aquidaban**, a series of limestone/ marble waterfalls in dense forest; **Rio da Prata** ⓘ *US$24*, a spring with underground snorkelling for 2 km, stalactites, bats, very beautiful, also parrots and other animals can be seen on the trip, The **fishing** season is from 1 March-31 October. In late October, early November is the piracema (fish run), when the fish return to their spawning grounds. Hundreds can be seen jumping the falls. **Note** Bonito's attractions are nearly all on private land and must by visited with a guide. Owners also enforce limits on the number of daily visitors so, at busy times, pre-booking is essential.

Ponta Porã ➔ *Phone code: 0xx67. Post code: 79900. Population: 67,000*

There is a paved road from Campo Grande to the Paraguayan border to Ponta Porã, separated from Pedro Juan Caballero in Paraguay only by a broad avenue. With paved streets, good public transport and smart shops, Ponta Porã is more prosperous than its neighbour, although Brazilians cross the border to play the casino and visit the cheaper shops. In addition to the free movement of people and goods, the blending of cultures here is impressive. There are many *Brasiguayos* with one parent of each nationality and *Portoñol* is the common tongue. There are many banks on Av Brasil (one block back from the border) with ATMs but no exchange facilities; many cambios on the Paraguayan side.

Border with Paraguay ➔ *Colour map 7, B2.*

There are no border posts between the two towns. The **Brazilian Polícia Federal** ⓘ *Av Pres Vargas 70, ½ block back from the border street, T3431 1428, Mon-Fri 0730-1130, 1330-1730*, is closed weekends but officers on duty might provide an entry stamp if you are on a bus that is passing through. The Paraguayan consulate in Ponta Porã (Av Pres Vargas 130, T3431 6312) does not issue visas, the nearest ones that do are in São Paulo, Curitiba and Foz do Iguaçu. **Check requirements carefully**, and ensure your documents are in order: without the proper stamps you will inevitably be sent back somewhere later on in your travels. Taking a taxi between offices can speed things up if pressed for time; drivers know border crossing requirements; US$10.

Campo Grande to Corumbá

BR-262 is paved from Campo Grande to Corumbá and the Bolivian border. The scenery is marvellous. Some 200 km west of Campo Grande is **Miranda**, where a road heads south to Bodoquena and Bonito. As a gateway to the Pantanal and Bonito, it is far closer to both than either Corumbá or Campo Grande. Many of the best of the southern Pantanal fazendas lie here, too. Every October Miranda throws the spectacular **Festa do Homen Pantaneiro**, four days of rodeos, lassoing and general revelry (dates vary each year). There is a tourist booth just outside the bus station, opposite the **Zero Hora** bakery and supermarket. Internet at **Star Informática**, Rua Francisco Rebúa 149. The town has both a **Bradesco** and a **Banco do Brasil**.

To the southern Pantanal

Many tours out of Campo Grande and Miranda take a dirt road running off the BR 262 Campo Grande–Corumbá highway called the **Estrada Parque**. It begins halfway between Miranda and Corumbá at a turn off called **Buraco da Piranha** (Piranha hole), heads north into the Pantanal and then, after 51 km, turns west to Corumbá at a point called the **Curva do Leque**. This is the overland access point to **Nhecolândia**, a region rich in wildlife. There are excellent fazendas off the Estrada Parque road and an increasing number opening up to tourism around Miranda.

Campo Grande and around listings

For Sleeping and Eating price codes and other relevant information, see Essentials, pages 38-40. See Telephone, page 397, for important phone changes.

Sleeping

Campo Grande *p668, map p668*

The better hotels are in the centre. There are lots of cheap hotels near the rodoviária so it is easy to leave bags in the *guarda volumes* and shop around. This area is not safe at night.

L Jandaia, R Barão do Rio Branco 1271, T3316 7700, www.jandaia.com.br. The city's best hotel, aimed at a business market. Modern well-appointed rooms (with IDSL) in a tower, pool, gym and some English spoken.

A Advanced, Av Calógeras 1909, T3321 5000, www.hoteladvanced.com.br. Spacious if spartan rooms with hot showers, in an 80s block, very small pool, cheaper with fan.

A Internacional, Allan Kardec 223, T3384 4677. Quiet street near rodoviária. Modern, comfortable with a/c or fan and some renovated suites, small pool, restaurant.

B Concord Inn, Av Calógeras 1624, T3321 2999. A standard town hotel with a small pool and recently renovated a/c rooms with modern fittings.

B Iguaçu, R Dom Aquino 761, T3322 4621, www.hoteliguacu.com.br. **D** with fan. Very popular well-kept hotel next to the rodovíaria with smart, simple a/c rooms with cable TV. Good breakfast.

C-D Pousada LM, R 15 de Novembro 201, T3321 5207, www.lmhotel.com.br. Tiny, basic en suites around a courtyard, all with a TV, fridge and some with terraces. Cheaper with fan.

D Cosmos, R Dom Aquino 771, near the rodoviária, T3384 4270. Simple but bright and well-kept 1980s rooms with decent mattresses and en suites.

D Nacional, R Dom Aquino, 610, T3383 2561, hotelnacional@ig.com.br. Simple, quiet rooms with fans, some rooms with bath, proper mattresses in a well-kept hotel with a TV room and internet, good value.

D Youth hostel, R Joaquim Nabuco 185, opposite rodoviária, T3321 0505, ajcampogrande@hotmail.com. Simple, musty little rooms with saggy foam mattresses and frayed bathrooms. Laundry, kitchen, internet; reception open 24 hrs. **Ecological Expeditions** offer Pantanal trips from their office next door. Their other branch at R Barão Rio Branco 343, T3325 6874, has marginally better rooms for 10% more; but the mattresses are still hot and foamy.

Bonito *p669*

AL Pira Miuna, R Luis da Costa Leite 1792, T3255 1058, www.piramiunahotel.com.br. Ugly building with the most comfortable a/c rooms in the centre and a large pool area with jacuzzis and a bar.

AL Pousada Olho d'Água, Rod Três Morros, Km 1, T3255 1430, olhodagua@vip2000.net. Comfortable cabins with fan, set in a garden next to a small lake. Horse riding, bike rental, solar-powered hot water and great food from the vegetable garden. Recommended.

A Tapera, Estrada Ilha do Padre, Km 10, on hill above Shell station on road to Jardim, T3255 1700. Fine views, cool breezes, peaceful, a/c, very comfortable, own transport an advantage.

C Canaã, R Col Pilad Rebuá 1376, T3255 1282. A scruffy lobby leads to gloomy though well-maintained motel-style rooms with a/c and bath.

C-E Pousada São Jorge, Av Col Pilad Rebuá 1605, T3255 4046, www.pousadasaojorge.com.br. Clean dorms with bunks and en suites (the best with 2 bathrooms) and a pleasant public dining area with snack bar. Price per person for dorms.

D pp **Pousada Muito Bonito**, Pilad Rebuá 1448, T/F3255 1645. With bath, or rooms with bunkbeds, nice patio, excellent, helpful owners, including breakfast, also with tour company (Mario Doblack speaks English, French and Spanish). Warmly recommended.

D pp **Pousada Rio do Peixe**, R 29 de Maio 820, T3255 2212, pousadariodopeixe@viabonito.com.br. More expensive with TV, Italian-owned, very helpful, excellent breakfast, tours arranged.

E pp **Albergue do Bonito**, R Lúcio Borralho 716, T/F3255 1462, www.ajbonito.com.br. Price pp in dorm, HI affiliated hostel, cheaper for members, English spoken, pool, laundry facilities, use of kitchen, hot showers, secure parking, rents bicycles.

Camping At **Ilha do Padre**, 12 km north of Bonito, T/F255 1430. On island with natural pools, very pleasant, no regular transport. 4 rustic cabins with 4 bunk beds, or 2 bunks and a double, US$10 pp. Youth hostel with dorms, US$6 pp, same price for camping. Toilets, showers, clothes washing, meals, bar, electricity, lots of trees. You can swim anywhere, to enter the island for a day US$3. Camping also at **Poliana** on Rio Formosa, 100 m past Ilha do Padre, T255 1267. Very pleasant.

Ponta Porã *p670*

AL-A Barcelona, R Guia Lopes 45, T3431 3061, www.hotelbarcelonapp.com.br. Maze-like building, a/c, restaurant, indoor pool, parking.

A Pousada do Bosque, Av Pres Vargas 1151, T3431 1181, www.hotelpousadadobosque.com.br. 'Fazenda style' with lovely grounds and pool, sports fields, restaurant, parking, comfortable rooms with a/c and fridge.

B Interpark, Av Brasil 3684, T3431 1209, www.grupointerhoteis.com.br. Comfortable modern rooms with a/c and fridge, small pool, restaurant.

D Guarujá, R Guia Lopes 63, T3431 1619. With a/c and fridge, cheaper with fan, parking, faded but functional.
D Vila Velha, Av Marechal Floreano 2916, T3431 2760. Private bath, electric shower, fan, basic.

Campo Grande to Corumbá: Miranda *p670*
A-D Águas do Pantanal, Av Afonso Pena 367, T3242 1242, www.aguasdopantanal.com.br. Much the best in town, comfortable a/c rooms and cheaper backpacker accommodation, attractive pool surrounded by tropical flowers, helpful travel agency. Usually have a rep waiting at the rodoviária.
C Pantanal, Av Barão do Rio Branco 609, T3242 1068. Well-maintained a/c rooms with en suites along a gloomy corridor, pool.
D-E Diogo, Av Barão do Rio Branco s/n, T3242 1468. Very simple but well-kept doubles, triples and quadruples, some with a/c.

To the southern Pantanal *p670*
LL Refúgio Ecológico Caiman, 36 km from Miranda, T011-3706 1800 (São Paulo), www.caiman.com.br. The most comfortable, stylish accommodation in the Pantanal. Tours and guiding are excellent.
LL-L Fazenda Xaraés, Estrada Parque, www.xaraes.com.br. One of the most luxurious fazendas, with a pool, tennis court, sauna, air strip and surprisingly plain but well-appointed a/c rooms. The immediate environs have been extensively cleared, but there are some wild areas of savanna and *cerrado* nearby and there are giant otter in the neighbouring Rio Abodrai.
L-AL Fazenda Bela Vista, Estrada Parque, www.pousadabelavista.com.br. On the banks of the Rio Papagaio in the foothills of the Serra do Urucum hills in a transition zone between Pantanal and higher ground. Bird and primate life is very rich. Guiding is good, but express your interest in wildlife beforehand.
L-AL Fazenda Rio Negro, Estrada Parque, T3326 0002, www.fazendarionegro.com.br. A Conservation International project based at a 13,000-ha farm on the shores of the Rio Negro; the main aim is the protection of jaguars. One of the oldest fazendas in the Pantanal (1920s). Guiding is good, but express your interest in wildlife beforehand.
AL Cacimba de Pedra, Estr Agachi, T9957 5814, www.cacimbadepedra.com.br. A Jacaré caiman farm and pousada in beautiful dry deciduous forest with abundant wildlife. A/c rooms sit in front of an inviting pool.
AL Fazenda San Francisco, turn off BR 262 30 km west of Miranda, T3242 3333, www.fazendasanfrancisco.tur.br. One of the best places in the Pantanal for wild cats, preserved through Roberto Coelho's pioneering Gadonça project (www.pro carnivoros.org.br), a great success here. Birdwatching is also excellent. Simple rustic a/c cabins around a pool in a garden filled with rheas. Food and guides are excellent.
AL Fazenda Santa Inés, Estr. La Lima Km 19, T3326 6062, www.fazendasantaines.com.br. A very comfortable family-oriented fazenda overlooking an artificial lake. Tours are aimed firmly at the Campo Grande weekend market and although there is little wildlife here, food is excellent and there is a range of light adventure activities for kids.
AL Pousada Rio Vermelho, off Estrada Parque, T3321 4737, www.pousadariovermelho.com.br. A rustic fazenda in a wild area on the banks of a river famous for its population of jaguars. Simple, well-kept a/c rooms. Coordinate with other visitors through the fazenda in advance as the fazenda lies well off the Estrada Parque.
AL-A Fazenda Meia Lua, BR-262 Km 551, 10 mins from Miranda, T9988 2284, www.fazenda meialua.com.br. Charming newly opened fazenda with a pool, lovely garden filled with hummingbirds and accommodation in a/c cabins or simple a/c rooms, attentive owners.
AL-A Fazenda Baia Grande, Estr La Lima Km 19, T3382 4223, www.fazendabaiagrande.com.br. Very comfortable a/c rooms around a pool in a garden. The fazenda is surrounded by savanna and stands of cerrado. The owner, Alex is very eager to please and enthusiastic.
A Fazenda 23 de Março, T3321 4737, www.fazenda23demarco.com.br. Simple, rustic fazenda with 4 rooms and programmes oriented to budget travellers. Visitors can learn to lasso, ride a bronco and turn their hand to other Pantanal cowboy activities.

Eating

Campo Grande p668, map p668

Local specialities *Caldo de piranha* (soup), *chipa* (Paraguayan cheese bread), sold on streets, delicious when hot, and local liqueur, *pequi com caju*, which contains *cachaça*. There are many cheap restaurants around the rodoviária and many other in a/c surrounds in the Shopping Campo Grande mall (R Afonso Pena 4909).

Comitiva Pantaneira, R Dom Aquino 2221, T3383 8799. Hearty, tasty and very meaty regional dishes served by waiters in cowboy gear, or as a buffet, lunchtime only.

Gaúcho Gastão, R 14 de Julho 775, T3384 4326. The best churrascaria in a town, famous for its beef, comfortable, a/c, lunch only.

Cantina Romana, R da Paz, 237, T3324 9777. Over 20 years serving Italian dishes, salads and a lunchtime buffet, good atmosphere.

Sabor en Quilo, R Barão do Rio Branco 1118 and R Dom Aquino 1786, T3383 3911/3325 5102. Self-service per kilo restaurants with plenty of choice including sushi on Sat, lunchtime only.

Morada dos Bais, Av Noroeste, 5140, corner with Afonso Pena, behind tourist office. Brazilian and Italian dishes, snacks and coffee served in a pretty courtyard, lunchtime only.

Bonito p669

Santa Esmeralda, R Cel Pilad Rebuá 1831. Respectable Italian food in one of the few a/c dining rooms.

Cantinho do Peixe, R 31 de Março 1918, T3255 3381. A la carte Pantanal fish dishes including good *pintado na telha* (grilled surubim).

Tapera, R Cel Pilad Rebuá 480, T3255 1110. Good, home-grown vegetables, breakfast, lunch, pizzas, meat and fish dishes, opens 1900 for evening meal.

Da Vovó, R Sen F Muller 570, T3255 2723. A great per kilo serving Minas and local food all cooked in a traditional wood-burning aga. Plenty of vegetables and salads.

Mercado da Praça, R 15 Novembro 376, T3255 2317. The cheapest in town, a snack bar in the local supermarket offering sandwiches, juices, etc, open 0600-2400.

Campo Grande to Corumbá: Miranda p670

Cantina Dell'Amore, Av Barão do Rio Branco 515, T3242 2826. The best in town with fish, passable pasta and jacaré steak.

Zero Jora, Av Barão do Rio Branco at the rodoviária, T3242 1330. 24 hour snack bar, provision shop and out the back, with its own private waterfall, a passable, good value per kilo restaurant.

Shopping

Campo Grande p668, map p668

Arts and crafts There is a market (Feira Livre) on Wed and Sat. Local native crafts, including ceramics, tapestry and jewellery, are good quality. A local speciality is Os Bugres da Conceição, squat wooden statues covered in moulded wax. **Arte do Pantanal**, Av Afonso Pena 1743. **Barroarte**, Av Afonso Pena 4329. Very good selections. **Casa do Artesão**, Av Calógeras 2050, on corner with Av Afonso Pena. Housed in an historic building, Mon-Fri 0800-2000, Sat 0800-1200.

Shopping centre Shopping Campo Grande, Av Afonso Pena 4909, www.shoppingcampogrande.com.br, is the largest shopping mall in the city.

Activities and tours

Campo Grande p668, map p668

City Tour, T3321 0800 or through larger hotels. Half day tours of the city's sights including the Museu Dom Bosco and the Parque das Nações Indígenas.

Ecological Expeditions, R Joaquim Nabuco 185, T3382 3505, www.pantanaltrekking.com and in Corumbá. Attached to the youth hostel at the bus station. Budget camping trips and lodge-based trips in Nhecolândia (sleeping bag needed) for 3, 4 or 5 days ending in Corumbá.

Impacto, R Padre João Crippa 686, T3325 1333, www.impactotour.com.br. Very helpful, Pantanal and Bonito tours. Prices vary according to accommodation; wide range offered. 2-day packages for 2 from US$190-600. English spoken.

Open Door Tour, R Alan Kardec 87, Galeria Maria Auxiliadora, Sala 4, T3321 8303, www.opendoortur.com.br. Specialists in the Pantanal region and Amazon and booking agents for flights and buses.

Bonito *p669*
There is very little to choose between agencies in Bonito, who offer the same packages for the same price, so shop around to see which you like the feel of best. English speakers are hard to come by. We list only those who also offer transport or a specialist service such as cave diving.
Impacto, R Cel Pilad Rebuá 1515, T3255 1414, see above under Campo Grande. English speaking staff and the possibility of organized transport. These can be pre-booked through their efficient head office in Campo Grande or through Águas do Pantanal tours in Miranda.
Ygarapé, R Cel Pilad Rebuá 1956, T3255 1733, www.ygarape.com.br. One of the few to speak even basic English and to offer transport to the sights. Also PDSE accredited cave diving.

Campo Grande to Corumbá: Miranda *p670*
Both of the operators below can organize lodging during the Festa do Homen Pantaneiro.
Águas do Pantanal Tours, Águas do Pantanal hotel, Av Afonso Pena 367, T3242 1242, www.aguasdopantanal.com.br. Well-organized tours to the fazendas around Miranda, to those on the Estrada Parque, to the sights around Bonito. They also run exclusive 1 or 2-day trips on the Rio Salobrinha to the Sanctuario Baía Negra, a little-visited river which is great for snorkelling and teeming with wildlife.
Marcello Yndio, lives in Bonito, contact him via T9638 3520, yndian@hotmail.com, marcelloyndio@gmail.com or marcelloyndio@yahoo.com.br. Kadiweu indigenous guide with many years experience. Very good English, French, Spanish and Italian and decent Hebrew. Great for small groups who want to get off the beaten track. Prices are competitive with budget operators in Campo Grande and Corumbá.

Transport

Campo Grande *p668, map p668*
Air Daily flights to most major cities. Airport T3368 6000. City bus No 158, 'Popular' stops outside airport. Taxi to airport, US$8. **Banco do Brasil** at airport exchanges dollars; **Bradesco** just outside has a Visa ATM. Airport also has tourist information booths, car rental and airline offices. It is safe to spend the night at the airport.

Bus Rodoviária is in the block bounded by Ruas Barão do Rio Branco, Vasconcelos Fernandes, Dom Aquino and Joaquim Nabuco, T3321 8797, all offices on 2nd floor. At V Fernandes end are town buses, at the J Nabuco end state and interstate buses. In between are shops and lanchonetes, 1 km walk from Praça República. Taxi to rodoviária, US$4.80.

São Paulo, US$66, 14 hrs, 9 buses daily, 1st at 0800, last at 2400. **Cuiabá**, US$46, 10 hrs, 12 buses daily, leito at 2100 and 2200. To **Porto Velho**, 27 hrs, US$155, 2 daily. To **Brasília**, US$70, 23 hrs at 1000 and 2000. To **Goiânia**, **São Luís** 1100, 2000, 15 hrs on 1900 service, US$66, others 24 hrs. **Corumbá**, with **Andorinha**, 8 daily from 0600, 6 hrs, US$28. Campo Grande-Corumbá buses connect with those from Rio and São Paulo, similarly those from Corumbá through to Rio and São Paulo. Twice daily direct service to **Foz do Iguaçu** (17 hrs) with **Integração**, US$58.50. To **Ponta Porã** for Paraguay, see below.

Bonito *p669*
Bus Rodoviária is on the edge of town. From **Campo Grande**, US$25, 5½-6 hrs, 1500, returns at 0530. Bus uses MS-345, with a stop at Autoposto Santa Cruz, Km 60, all types of fuel, food and drinks available.

Ponta Porã *p670*
Bus The rodoviária is 3 km out on the Dourados road (Brazilian city buses from the *ponto* in the centre to Rodoviaria, **São Domingos** or **Sanga Puitã**, 20 mins, US$1.50; taxi US$10. To/from **Campo Grande**, **Expresso Queiroz**, 11 daily, 5 hrs, US$27.50; From Ponta Porã to **Bonito** or **Corumbá**, change at **Jardim** (a friendly little town with a good services, offering access to various natural attractions similar to those of Bonito at more modest prices): Ponta Porã-Jardim, **Cruzeiro do Sul** (www.cruzeirodosulms.com.br) at 0600 and 1530 Mon-Sat, 4 hrs, US$22; connect the following day at 0500 from Jardim to Corumbá (Corumbá to Jardim at 1400) via Bonito, 7 hrs, US$26. Also Jardim to Miranda, 1430 daily, 4 hrs, US$20. To **São Paulo**, **Motta** at 3 a day, 14 hrs, US$100, US$132 *leito*.

Campo Grande to Corumbá: Miranda *p670*
Bus **Campo Grande**-Miranda, 12 a day, 2-3 hrs, US$20.To **Corumbá**; 10 daily, 3-4 hrs, US$20. To **Bonito**, 1 daily, 2-3 hrs, US$13.50 at 1630.

Directory

Campo Grande *p668, map p668*
Airline offices **Trip**, T3368 6137. **TAM**, office at airport, T0800-570 5700. **Banks** ATMs at **Banco do Brasil**, 13 de Maio e Av Afonso Pena, open 1000-1500, commission US$10 for cash, US$20 for TCs, regardless of amount exchanged. Visa ATM at **Bradesco**, 13 de Maio e Av Afonso Pena. **HSBC**, R 13 de Maio 2837, ATM. **Banco 24 horas**, R Maracaju, on corner with 13 de Junho. Also at R Dom Aquino e Joaquim Nabuco. **Overcash Câmbio**, R Rui Barbosa 2750, open Mon-Fri 1000-1600. **Car hire** Agencies on Av Afonso Pena and at airport. **Embassies and consulates** **Bolivia**, R Spipe Calarge 99, T3342 6933, consulado_cgms04@ yahoo.com. **Medical services** Yellow and Dengue fevers are both present in Mato Grosso do Sul. Get your immunizations at home. **Post offices** On corner of R Dom Aquino e Calógeras 2309 and Barão do Rio Branco corner Ernesto Geisel. **Telephones** **Telems**, R 13 de Maio e R 15 de Novembro, daily 0600-2200.

Bonito *p669*
Banks **Banco do Brasil**, R Luiz da Costa Leite 2279, for Visa. Hoteliers and taxi drivers may change money. **Post offices** R Col Pilad Rebuá. **Telephones** Santana do Paraíso.

Corumbá→ *Phone code: 0xx67. Post code: 79300. Pop: 95,701.*

Situated on the south bank by a broad bend in the Rio Paraguai, 15 minutes from the Bolivian border, Corumbá offers beautiful views of the river, especially at sunset. It is hot and humid (70%); cooler in June to July, very hot from September to January. It has millions of mosquitoes in December to February. The municipal tourist office, **Sematur** ⓘ *R América 969, T231 6996,* provides general information and city maps.

There is a spacious shady **Praça da Independência** and the port area is worth a visit. Av Gen Rondon between Frei Mariano and 7 de September has a pleasant palm lined promenade which comes to life in the evenings. The **Forte Junqueira**, the city's most historic building, which may be visited only through a travel agency, was built in 1772. In the Serra do Urucum to the south is the world's greatest reserve of manganese, now being worked. Corumbá has long been considered the best starting point for the southern part of the Pantanal and although many operators have shifted base to Campo Grande or Miranda, the town still offers various boat and jeep trips and access to the major hotel and farm accommodation. Almost all of the Campo Grande agencies have offices here and there are still a number of upmarket cruise companies along the water front.

Border with Bolivia

Over the border from Corumbá are Arroyo Concepción, Puerto Quijarro and Puerto Suárez. From Puerto Quijaro a 650-km railway runs to Santa Cruz de la Sierra. There is a road of sorts. There are flights into Bolivia from Puerto Suárez.

Brazilian immigration Formalities are constantly changing so check procedures in advance. Brazilian Polícia Federal stamp passports only at their office in the rodoviária ⓘ *Mon-Fri 0800-1100, 1400-1600, Sat-Sun 1400-1700*, long queues for entry stamps but much quicker for exit. If leaving Brazil merely to obtain a new visa, remember that exit and entry must not be on the same day. Money changers at the border and in Quijarro offer the same rates as in Corumbá. **Bolivian consulate** ⓘ *R Porto Carrero 1651 esq Firmo de Matos, Corumbá, T3231 5605, consuladobol@ hotmail.com, Mon-Fri 0800-1600.* A fee is charged to citizens of those countries which require a visa. A yellow fever vaccination certificate is required; go to Rua 7 de Setembro, Corumbá, for an inoculation (preferably get one at home).

Corumbá listings

For Sleeping and Eating price codes and other relevant information, see Essentials, pages 38-40. See Telephone, page 397, for important phone changes.

Sleeping

Corumbá *p675*

Although there are hostels around the bus station, this is a 10-min walk to the centre of town on the river bank where most of the hotels, restaurants and tour operators lie.

A-B Águas do Pantanal, R Dom Aquino Corrêa 1457, T3231 6582, www.aguasdopantanal hotel.com.br. The smartest in town together with the Nacional Palace, a/c rooms in a 1980s tower, pool and sauna.

A-B Nacional Palace, R América 936, T3234 6000, www.hnacional.com.br. Smart, modern a/c rooms, a decent pool and parking.

C-D Angola, R Antônio Maria 124, T3231 7727. Huge, scruffy, a/c and with fan. Internet via shared terminals. Safe as it is in front of the Polícia Federal.

C-E Salette, R Delamaré 893, T3231 6246. Cheap and cheerful with a range of rooms, the cheapest with fans and shared bathrooms. Recommended.

D Premier, R Antônio Maria Coelho 389, T3231 4937. Basic, small a/c rooms without windows. Prices are negotiable.

D Santa Rita, R Dom Aquino 860, T3231 5453. Modern, well-kept, a/c, all rooms TV and bath.

D-E Corumbá IYHA, R Colombo 1419, T3231 1005, www.corumbahostel.com.br. New, well-equipped modern hostel with helpful staff and a pool. Fan or a/c rooms and dorms.

Eating

Corumbá *p675*

Local specialities These include *peixadas corumbaenses*, a variety of fish dishes prepared with the catch of the day; as well as ice cream, liquor and sweets made of *bocaiúva*, a small yellow palm fruit, in season Sep-Feb. There are several good restaurants in R Frei Mariano. Lots of open-air bars on the river front.

TTT-TT Avalom, R Frei Mariano 499, T3231 4430. Chic little restaurant bar with streetside tables and decent pasta, pizza and fish. Especially busy after 2100 on Fri.

TT Almanara, R América 961. Arabic and Turkish.

TT Laço de Ouro, R Frei Mariano 556, T3231 7371. Popular fish restaurant with a lively atmosphere and tables spilling out onto the street.

TT-T Peixeria de Lulú, R Dom Aquino 700, T3232 2142. A local institution, good river fishes.

T Panela Velha, R 15 de Novembro 156, T3232 5650. Popular lunchtime restaurant with a decent, cheap all you can eat buffet.

T Verde Frutti, R Delamare 1164, T3231 3032. A snack bar with a wide variety of juices and great, ice-cold *acai na tigela*.

Festivals and events

Corumbá *p675*

2 Feb, **Festa de Nossa Senhora da Candelária**, Corumbá's patron saint, all offices and shops are closed. **24 Jun**, **Festa do Arraial do Banho de São João**, fireworks, parades, traditional food stands, processions and the main event, the bathing of the image of the saint in the Rio Paraguai.

21 Sep, Corumbá's anniversary, includes a Pantanal fishing festival held on the eve.

Early-mid Oct, **Festival Pantanal das Águas**, with street parades featuring giant puppets, dancing in the street and occasional water fights.

Shopping

Corumbá *p675*

Shops tend to open early and close by 1700.

Casa do Artesão, R Dom Aquino Correia 405. Open Mon-Fri 0800-1200, 1400-1800, Sat 0800-1200, good selection of handicrafts, small bookshop, friendly staff but high prices.

CorumbArte, Av Gen Rondon 1011. For good silk-screen T-shirts with Pantanal motifs.

Livraria Corumbaense, R Delamaré 1080. For state maps.

Supermarkets **Frutal**, R 13 de Junho 538, open 0800-2000. **Ohara**, Dom Aquino 621.

Activities and tours

Corumbá *p675*

Ecological Expeditions, R Antônio Maria 78 (see under Campo Grande, above, for details).

Green Track, R Antônio João, Corumbá, T3231 2258, with representatives in Campo Grande at their bus station office. One of the longest established budget operators offering camping and lodge based trips to Nhecolândia starting in

Campo Grande or Corumbá, where they have a budget hostel. Basic, but good value tours.

Mutum Turismo, R Frei Mariano 17, T3231 1818, www.mutumturismo.com.br. Cruises and upmarket tours (mostly aimed at the Brazilian market) and airline, train and bus reservations.

Pantur, R América 969, T3231 2000, www.pantur.com.br. Packages to Bonito and the fazendas on the Estrada Parque, including some of the less visited like Bela Vista and Xaraes. Flights and bus tickets can be booked here too.

Fishing and river cruises

These all leave from Corumbá.

Pérola do Pantanal, in Hotel Nacional (see above), T3231 1470, www.peroladopantanal.com.br. Fishing and 'eco' tours on their large river boat the *Kalypso* with jeep trip option on the Estrada Parque.

O Pantaneiro, R Manoel Cavassa 225, quays, T3231 3372, www.opantaneirotur.com.br. Cruises on by far the most comfortable modern boat sailing out of Corumbá, day trips in small launches.

Transport

Corumbá *p675*

Air Airport, R Santos Dumont, 3 km. Daily flights to **Campo Grande**, **Cuiabá** and **São Paulo**. No public transport from airport to town, you have to take a taxi. Car hire at the airport.

Bus The rodoviária is on R Porto Carreiro at the south end of R Tiradentes, next to the railway station. City bus to rodoviária from Praça da República, US$1.50; taxis are extortionate but mototaxis charge US$1. **Andorinha** services to all points east. To **Campo Grande**, 7 hrs, US$27.50, 13 buses daily, between 0630 and midnight, interesting journey ('an excursion in itself'), take an early bus to see plentiful wildlife, connections from Campo Grande to all parts of Brazil.

Border with Bolivia: Corumbá/Arroyo Concepción *p675*

Bus Leaving Brazil, take Canarinho city bus marked Fronteira from the port end of R Antônio Maria Coelho to the Bolivian border (15 mins, US$1), walk over the bridge to Bolivian immigration, then take a colectivo to Quijarro or Puerto Suárez. Taxi from Corumbá rodoviaria to Bolivian border US$16.50, negotiable. Ask to be taken directly to Bolivian immigration, not to a Bolivian cab who will hold your luggage while your passport is stamped. Overcharging and sharp practices are common. Touts at the Corumbá rodoviária offer hotels, Pantanal tours and railway tickets to Santa Cruz. The latter cost double the actual fare and are not recommended.

When travelling from Quijarro, take a taxi or walk to the Bolivian border to go through formalities. Just past the bridge, on a small side street to the right, is the bus stop for Corumbá, take a bus to the rodoviária for Polícia Federal, US$1, don't believe taxi drivers who say there is no bus.

Train Timetables for trains from Puerto Quijarro to Santa Cruz change frequently, so check on arrival in Corumbá. It may be best to stay in Quijarro to get a good place in the queue for tickets.

Directory

Corumbá *p675*

Banks Banco do Brasil, R 13 de Junho 914, ATM. **HSBC**, R Delamare 1068, ATM. **Car hire** **Unidas**, R Frei Mariano 633, T/F231 3124. **Post offices** main at R Delamaré 708; branch at R 15 de Novembro 229. **Telephones** R Dom Aquino 951, near Praça da Independência, 0700-2200 daily. To phone Quijarro/Puerto Suárez, Bolivia, costs slightly more than a local call, dial 214 + the Bolivian number.

Cuiabá

➔ *Phone code: 0xx65. Post code: 78000. Colour map 7, A1. Pop: 483,346. Altitude: 176 m.*

The capital of Mato Grosso state on the Rio Cuiabá, an upper tributary of the Rio Paraguai, is in fact two cities: Cuiabá on the east bank of the river and Várzea Grande, where the airport is, on the west. It is very hot; coolest months for a visit are June, July and August, in the dry season.

Cuiabá has an imposing government palace and other fine buildings round the green **Praça da República.** On the square is the **Cathedral**, with a plain, imposing exterior, two clock- towers and, inside, coloured-glass mosaic windows and doors. Behind the altar is a huge mosaic of Christ in majesty, with smaller mosaics in side chapels. Beside the Cathedral is the leafy **Praça Alencastro**. On **Praça Ipiranga**, at the junction of Avs Isaac Póvoas and Tenente Col Duarte, a few blocks west of the central squares, there are market stalls and an iron bandstand from Huddersfield, UK. On a hill beyond the praça is the church of **Bom Despacho**, built in the style of Notre Dame de Paris (in poor condition, closed to visitors). In front of the Assembléia Legislativa, Praça Moreira Cabral, is a point marking the **Geogedesic Centre of South America** (see also under Chapada dos Guimarães). **Museus de Antropologia, História Natural e Cultura Popular** ⓘ *in the Fundação Cultural de Mato Grosso, Praça da República 151, Mon-Fri 0800-1730, US$0.50,* displays historical photos, a contemporary art gallery, stuffed Pantanal fauna, indigenous, archaeological finds and pottery. At the entrance to Universidade de Mato Grosso, 10 minutes by bus from the centre (by pool), is the small **Museu do Índio/Museu Rondon** ⓘ *T3615 8489, Tue- Sun 0800-1100, 1330-1700, US$1,* with artefacts from tribes mostly from the state of Mato Grosso. Particularly beautiful are the Bororo and Rikbaktsa headdresses made from macaw and currasow feathers and also the Kadiwéu pottery. **Tourist information** at Secretaria de Desenvolvimento do Turismo ⓘ *Sedtur, in the Centro Político Administrativo, T3613 9300, www.sedtur.mt.gov.br, Mon-Fri 0700-1800.* Good maps, helpful, contact them if you have any problems with travel agencies; also book hotels and car hire, some English and Spanish spoken. Also at the airport, T3692 6204. **Ramis Bucair** ⓘ *R Pedro Celestino 280,* is good for detailed maps of the region.

Cuiabá

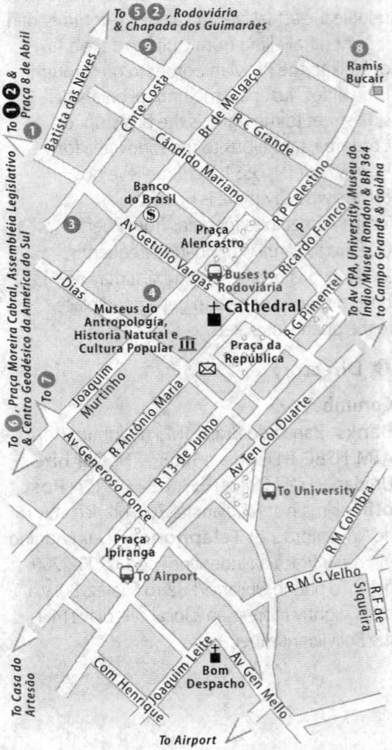

Sleeping
1 Amazon Plaza
2 Ipanema
3 Mato Grosso
4 Mato Grosso Pálace
5 Nacional
6 Panorama
7 Portal do Pantanal
8 Pousada Ecoverde
9 Ramos

Eating
1 Choppão
2 Getúlio

N
200 metres
200 yards

Cuiabá to Pantanal ➔ *Colour map 6, A6.*

A paved road turns south off the main Cuiabá-Cáceres road to **Poconé** (102 km from Cuiabá, hotels, 24-hour gas station – closed

Sunday). From here, the Transpantaneira runs 146 km south to Porto Jofre (just a petrol station, petrol and diesel, but no alcohol available). The road is of earth, in poor condition, with ruts, holes and many bridges that need care in crossing. Easiest access is in the dry season (July-September), which is also the best time for seeing birds and, in September, the trees are in bloom. In the wet, especially January to February, there is no guarantee that the Transpantaneira will be passable. The wet season, however, is a good time to see many of the shyer animals because more fruit, new growth and other high calorie foods are available, and there are fewer people.

Campos de Jofre, about 20 km north of Porto Jofre, is said to be magnificent between August and October. In Poconé one can hitch to Porto Jofre, or hire a vehicle in Cuiabá. You will get more out of this part of the Pantanal by going with a guide; a lot can be seen from the Transpantaneira in a hired car, but guides can take you into fazendas some 7 km from the Transpantaneira and will point out wildlife. Recommended guides in Cuiabá are under Tour operators. Although there are gas stations in **Pixaim** (a bridge across the Rio Pixaim, two hotels and a tyre repair shop) and Porto Jofre, they are not always well stocked, best to carry extra fuel.

Barão de Melgaço ➔ *Colour map 7, A1.*

On Rio Cuiabá, 130 km from Cuiabá (TUT bus at 0730 and 1500, US$8.50), Barão de Melgaço is reached by two roads: the shorter, via Santo Antônio de Leverger, unpaved from Santo Antônio to Barão (closed in the wet season), or via São Vicente, longer, but more pavement. The way to see the Pantanal from here is by boat down the Rio Cuiabá. Boat hire, for example from Restaurant Peixe Vivo on waterfront, up to US$100 for a full day; or enquire with travel agencies in Cuiabá. The best time of day would be sunset, but this may mean returning after dark. Initially the river banks are farms and small habitations, but they become more forested, with lovely combinations of flowering trees (best seen September-October). After a while, a small river to the left leads to Chacororé and Sia Mariana lakes, which join each other via an artificial canal which has led the larger of the two lakes to drain into the smaller and begin to dry out. Boats can continue beyond the lakes to the Rio Mutum, but a guide is essential because there are many dead ends. The area is rich in birdlife and the waterscapes are beautiful.

Cáceres ➔ *Phone code: 065. Post code: 78200. Colour map 6, A6. Population: 85,857.*

On the banks of the Rio Paraguai, 200 km west of Cuiabá, Cáceres is very hot but clean and hospitable. It has a number of well preserved 19th-century buildings, painted in pastel colours.

The **Museu Histórico de Cáceres** ⓘ *R Antônio Maria by Praça Major João Carlos*, is a small local history museum. The main square, Praça Barão de Rio Branco, has one of the original border markers from the Treaty of Tordesillas, which divided South America between Spain and Portugal; it is pleasant and shady during the day. In the evenings, between November and March, the trees are packed with thousands of chirping swallows (andorinhas). The praça is surrounded by bars, restaurants and ice cream parlours and comes to life at night. The city is known for its many bicycles as most people seem to get around on two wheels. Until 1960, Cáceres had regular boat traffic, today it is limited to a few tour boats and pleasure craft. The town is at the edge of the Pantanal. Vitória Regia lilies can be seen north of town, just across the bridge over the Rio Paraguai along the BR-174. Local festivals are the Piranha Festival, mid-March; International Fishing Festival in mid-September; annual cattle fair.

Border with Bolivia

An unpaved road runs from Cáceres to the Bolivian border at San Matías. Brazilian immigration is at Polícia Federal, Av Getúlio Vargas. Ask here for Fiscales Federales, which is the customs point for those entering or leaving by private vehicle. Leaving Bolivia, get your passport stamped at Bolivian immigration (1000-1200, 1500-1700), then get your passport stamped at Cáceres, nowhere in between, but there are luggage checks for drugs.

Chapadа dos Guimarães

→ *Phone code: 065. Post code: 78195. Population: 15,755. Colour map 7, A1.*

Some 68 km northeast of Cuiabá lies one of the oldest plateaux on earth. It is one of the most scenic areas of Brazil and visitors describe it as an energizing place. The pleasant town of Chapada dos Guimarães, the main centre, is a base for many beautiful excursions in this area; it has the oldest church in the Mato Grosso, **Nossa Senhora de Santana** (1779), a bizarre blending of Portuguese and French baroque styles, and a huge spring-water public swimming pool (on Rua Dr Pem Gomes, behind the town). Formerly the centre of an important diamond prospecting region, today Chapada is a very popular destination for Cuiabanos to escape the heat of the city at weekends and on holidays. It is a full day excursion from Cuiabá through lovely scenery with many birds, butterflies and flora. There is a post office at Rua Fernando Corrêa 848. The Festival de Inverno is held in last week of July, and Carnival is very busy. Accommodation is scarce and expensive at these times. The **Secretaria de Turismo e Meio Ambiente** office, Rua Quinco Caldas 100, near the praça, provides a useful map of the region and organizes tours. Weekdays 0800-1100, 1300-1800.

The Chapada is an immense geological formation rising to 700 m, with rich forests, curiously eroded rocks and many lovely grottoes, peaks and waterfalls. A **national park** (T3301 1133, entry US$11.50) has been established in the area just west of the town, where the **Salgadeira** tourist centre offers bathing, camping and a restaurant close to the Salgadeira waterfall.

The beautiful 85 m **Véu da Noiva** waterfall (Bridal Veil), 12 km before the town near Buriti (well-signposted, ask bus from Cuiabá to let you off), is reached by a short route, or a long route through forest. Other sights include the **Mutuca** beauty spot, **Rio Claro**, the viewpoint over the breathtaking 80 m-deep **Portão do Inferno** (Hell's Gate), and the falls of **Cachoeirinha** (small restaurant) and **Andorinhas**.

About 8 km east of town is the **Mirante do Ponto Geodésico**, a monument officially marking the Geodesic Centre of South America, which overlooks a great canyon with views of the surrounding plains, the Pantanal and Cuiabá's skyline on the horizon; to reach it take Rua Fernando Corrêa east. Continuing east, the road goes through agricultural land and later by interesting rock formations including a stone bridge and stone cross. Some 45 km from Chapada you reach the access for **Caverna do Francês** or Caverna Aroe Jari ('the dwelling of the souls' in the Bororo language), a sandstone cave over 1 km long, the second largest in Brazil; it is a 1-km walk to the cave, in it is Lagoa Azul, a lake with crystalline blue water. Take your own torch/flashlight (guides' lamps are sometimes weak). A guide is necessary to get through fazenda property to the cave, but not really needed thereafter.

Other excursions are to the **Cidade de Pedra** rock formations, 25 km from town along the road to the diamond prospecting town of Água Fria. Nearby is a 300 m wall formed by the Rio Claro and 60 km from town are the **Pingador** and **Bom Jardim** archaeological sites, caverns with petroglyphs dating back some 4,000 years.

Cuiabá and around listings

For Sleeping and Eating price codes and other relevant information, see Essentials, pages 38-40. See Telephone, page 397, for important phone changes.

Sleeping

Cuiabá *p678, map p678*

L Amazon Plaza, Av Getúlio Vargas 600, T2121 2000, www.hotelamazon.com.br. By far the best in the centre with very smart modern rooms, good views over the city, shady pool area, excellent service includes broadband in all rooms.

AL Mato Grosso Pálace, Joaquim Murtinho 170, T3614 7000, www.hotelmt.com.br. Conveniently located behind the Praça República, standard 3-star rooms with cable TV, fridge, hot showers, Wi-Fi.

B-C Mato Grosso, R Comandante Costa 252, T3614 7777, www.hotelmt.com.br. The best value mid-range option in the centre with

renovated a/c or fan-cooled rooms, the brightest of which are on the 2nd floor or above, good breakfast, Wi-Fi, very helpful. Recommended.
B-C Panorama, Praça Moreira Cabral 286, T3322 0072. Very simple, plain rooms, a/c or fan, some rooms with good views.
C Pousada Ecoverde, R Pedro Celestino 391, T3624 1386, www.ecoverdetours.com. The best value, if idiosyncratic option, rooms with spacious bathrooms in a converted town house. Facilities include excellent tour agency, laundry service, internet and free airport/bus station pick-up (with 12 hrs notice).
C Ramos, R Campo Grande 487, T3624 7472, www.hotelramos.com.br. A variety of simple a/c and fan-cooled rooms, also has dorms, all bath, free Wi-Fi, laundry service. **Pantanal Nature** travel agency is in reception.

By the rodoviária

B Nacional, Jules Rimet 22, T3621 3277. Right opposite the front of the bus station and convenient for those who don't need to go into town. Plain a/c rooms with renovated en suites.
C Ipanema, Jules Rimet 12, T3621 3069. Opposite the front of the bus station and with very well kept rooms, a/c or fan, cable TV, internet access, huge lobby TV for films or football. Many other options between here and the **Nacional**.
C pp **Portal do Pantanal**, Av Isaac Povoas 655, T/F3624 8999, www.portaldopantanal.com.br. HI hostel, with breakfast, cheaper with fan, internet access US$3 per hr, laundry, use of kitchen.

Cuiabá to Pantanal *p678*

LL Araras Eco Lodge, Km 32, T3682 2800, www.araraslodge.com.br. Book direct or through Pantanal Explorer. One of the most comfortable with 14 a/c rooms; pool, excellent tours and food, homemade *cachaça* and a walkway over a private patch of wetland filled with capybara and cayman. Very popular with small tour groups from Europe. Book ahead.
L Pousada Rio Clarinho, Km 42, book through Pantanal Nature. Charming budget option on the Rio Clarinho which makes up in wildlife what it lacks in infrastructure. The river has rare water birds, as well as river and giant otters and occasionally tapir.
L Pousada Rio Claro, Km 42, book through Natureco. Comfortable fazenda with a pool and simple a/c rooms on the banks of the Rio Claro which has a resident colony of giant otters.
L Pouso Alegre, Km 36, T626 1545, 9968 6101. Rustic pousada, simple accommodation, a/c or fan. One of the largest fazendas and overflowing with wildlife and particularly good for birds (especially on the morning horseriding trail). Many species not yet seen elsewhere in the northern Pantanal have been catalogued here. Their remote oxbow lake is particularly good for water birds. Birding guides provided with advance notice. Best at weekends when the very knowledgeable owner Luís Vicente is there.
A Fazenda Piuval, Km 10, T3345 1338, www.pousadapiuval.com.br.The first fazenda on the Transpantaneira and one of the most touristy, with scores of day visitors at weekends. Rustic farmhouse accommodation, pool, excellent horse and walking trails and boat trips on their vast lake.
C Caranda Fundo, Transpantaneira Km 43, book through Pantanal Nature, T3322 0203. One of the best option for budget travellers. Visitors sleep in hammocks in a large room (bring a hammock mosquito net). Tours include horse rides, treks and night safaris; hyacinth macaws nest on the fazenda and there are many mammals, including howler monkeys, peccaries and huge herds of capybara.

Barão de Melgaço *p679*

L Pousada Passárgada, Sia Mariana, Barão de Melgaço, T3713 1128, in Barão de Melgaço on riverside, through **Nature Safaris**, Av Marechal Rondon, Barão de Melgaço, or agencies in Cuiabá. Much cheaper if booked direct with the owner, Maré Sigaud, Mato Grosso, CEP 786807, Pousada Passárgada, Barão de Melgaço. Programmes from 3 days up, full board, boat, Land Rover and trekking expeditions, transport from Barão de Melgaço either by boat or 4WD can be arranged with the owner who speaks English, French and German. Closed Dec-Feb.
C Barão Tour Hotel, in Barão de Melgaço town. Apartments with a/c, restaurant, boat trips and excursions (Cuiabá T322 1568). There are a handful of cheaper options near the waterfront.

Cáceres *p679*

A Caiçaras, R dos Operários 745, corner R Gen Osório, T3223 3187, F3223 2692. Modern, with a/c rooms and cheaper options without a fridge.

A-B Ipanema, R Gen Osório 540, T3223 1177. Simple town hotel with a/c rooms, a pool and a restaurant.

C-D Charm, Col José Dulce 405, T/F3223 4949. A/c and fan-cooled rooms, with or without a shared bath.

D-E União, R 7 de Setembro 340. Near the rodoviária. Fan, cheaper with shared bath, basic but good value.

Chapada dos Guimarães *p680*

AL-A Solar do Inglês, R Cipriano Curvo 142, T3301 1389, www.chapadadosguimaraes.com.br. In an old converted house near town centre with 7 rooms each with bath, TV and frigobar. Garden, swimming pool and sauna. Breakfast and afternoon tea included.

A Turismo, R Fernando Corrêa 1065, a block from rodoviária, T3791 1176 (or 3301 1639), hotelturismo@chapadadosguimaraes.com.br. A/c rooms with a fridge, cheaper with fan, restaurant, breakfast and lunch excellent, very popular, German-run; Ralf Goebel, the owner, is very helpful in arranging excursions.

C-D Rio's Hotel, R Tiradentes 333, T3791 1126 (or 3301 1636), rios@chapadadosguimaraes.com.br. A/c rooms with a fridge, cheaper with fan, cheaper with shared bath, good breakfast.

B Pousada Bom Jardim, Praça Bispo Som Wunibaldo 461, T3301 2668, bomjardim@chapadadosguimaraes.com. Fan, comfortable, parking, good breakfast. Recommended.

D São José, R Vereador José de Souza 50, T3301 1574, www.pousadasaojose.tur.br. Fan, cheaper with shared bath and no fan, hot showers, basic, no breakfast, good, owner Mário sometimes runs excursions.

Camping Aldeia Velha, in the Aldeia Velha neighbourhood at the entrance to town from Cuiabá, T322 7178 (Cuiabá). Fenced area with bath, hot shower, some shade, guard.

Eating

Cuiabá *p678, map p678*

City centre restaurants only open for lunch. On Av CPA are many restaurants and snack bars. There are several cheap restaurants and lanchonetes on R Jules Rimet across from the rodoviária.

TTT Getúlio, Av Getúlio Vargas 1147, T3264 9992. An a/c haven from the heat with black tie waiters, excellent food, with meat specialities, pizza, good buffet lunch on Sun. Live music upstairs on Fri and Sat from significant cult Brazilian acts.

TTT-TT Choppão, Praça 8 de Abril, T3623 9101. A local institution, buzzing at any time of the day or night. Go for huge portions of delicious food or just for *chopp* served by fatherly waiters. The house dish of chicken soup promises to give diners drinking strength in the early hours and is a meal in itself. Warmly recommended.

TT Panela de Barro, R Cmdte Costa 543. Self-service, a/c lunchtime restaurant with a choice of tasty regional dishes.

TT-T Miranda's, R Cmdte Costa 716. Decent self-service per kilo lunchtime restaurant with good value specials.

Cáceres *p679*

TT Corimbá, R 15 de Novembro s/n, on riverfront. Fish specialities, and general Brazilian food.

T Gulla's, R Cel José Dulce 250. Buffet by kilo, good quality and variety. Recommended.

T Panela de Barro, R Frei Ambrósio 34, near rodoviária. *Comida caseira* with the usual gamut of meat dishes with squash, rice, black beans and salads.

Chapada dos Guimarães *p680*

TT Nivios, Praça Dom Wunibaldo 631. The best place for good regional food.

TT-T Fellipe 1, R Cipriano Curvo 596, T3301 1793. One of the few per kilo restaurants in the village, on the south western corner of the praç next to the church, mostly meat options, beans, rice, unseasoned salads and sticky puddings. Also has à la carte.

Bars and clubs

Cuiabá *p678, map p678*

Cuiabá is quite lively at night, bars with live music and dance on Av CPA. Av Mato Grosso also has many bars and restaurants. 4 cinemas in town.

Café Cancun, R Candido Mariano at São Sebastião. One of a chain of popular Brazilian club bars attracting a mid-20s to 40s crowd.

Shopping

Cuiabá *p678, map p678*

Handicrafts in wood, straw, netting, leather, skins, Pequi liquor, crystallized caju fruit, compressed guaraná fruit (for making the drink), indigenous objects on sale at the airport, rodoviária, craft shops in centre, and daily market, Praça da República, interesting. Fish and vegetable market, picturesque, at the riverside.
Casa de Artesão, Praça do Expedicionário 315, T321 0603. Sells all types of local crafts in a restored building. Recommended.

Chapada dos Guimarães *p680*

Crafts, indigenous artefacts, sweets and locally made honey from **Casa de Artes e Artesanato Mato Grossense**, Praça Dom Wunibaldo. Regional sweets from **Doceria Olho de Sogra**, Praça Dom Wunibaldo 21. **João Eloy de Souza Neves** is a local artist, his paintings, music and history about Chapada (*Chapada dos Guimarães da descoberta aos dias atuais*) are on sale at **Pousada Bom Jardim**.

Activities and tours

Cuiabá *p678, map p678*

You should expect to pay US$60-90 per person per day for tours in the Pantanal. All these agencies arrange trips to the Pantanal. Budget trips are marginally more expensive than those in the Southern Pantanal (around US$10 per day), but accommodation based in fazendas is more comfortable. For longer or special programmes, book in advance.
Natureco, R Benedito Leite 570, T3321 1001, www.pantanaltour.net. Fazenda-based Pantanal tours, trips to the Chapada dos Guimarães and to Nobres – the Bonito of Mato Grosso. Specialist birding and wildlife guides available with advance notice. Some English spoken.
Pantanal Explorer, R Gov Ponce de Arruda 670, Várzea Grande, T3682 2800, www.pantanal explorer.com.br. Works with lodges/pousadas in the Pantanal (eg **Araras Eco Lodge**), Amazon, Cerrado and Chapada dos Guimarães. Various packages, birdwatching, riding available.

Wildlife guides for the Pantanal and Mato Grosso

Recommended birding and wildlife guides for the northern Pantanal and Mato Grosso are listed below. All guides work freelance for other companies as well as employing other guides for trips when busy. Most guides await incoming flights at the airport; compare prices and services in town if you don't wish to commit yourself at the airport. The tourist office recommends guides; this is not normal practice and their advice is not necessarily impartial.
Giuliano Bernardon, T8115 6189, giubernardon @gmail.com. Young birding guide from the Chapada dos Guimarães, with a good depth of knowledge and experience in the Chapada, Pantanal, Mato Grosso Amazon and Atlantic coastal forest.
Boute Expeditions, R Getúlio Vargas 64, Várzea Grande, near airport, T3686 2231, www.boute-expeditions.com. Paulo Boute, one of the most experienced birding guides in the Pantanal; works from home and speaks good English and French.
Fabricio Dorileo, fabriciodorileo18@ yahoo.com.br or through Eduardo Falcão, rejaguar@bol.com.br. Excellent birding guide with good equipment, good English and many years experience in the Pantanal and Chapada dos Guimarães.
Pantanal Bird Club, T3624 1930, 9981 1236, www.pantanalbirdclub.org. Good for even the most exacting clients, PBC are the most illustrious birders in Brazil with many years experience, owner Braulio Carlos. Tours throughout the area and to various parts of Brazil.
Pantanal Nature, R Campo Grande 487, T3322 0203, or 9955 2632, www.pantanalnature. com.br. Embratur licensed guide, Ailton Lara, expert wildlife and birding knowledge, frequent jaguar sitings, works with small groups and will customize tours, well organized agency. He also goes to the Chapada dos Guimarães, Nobres (with crystal clear rivers filled with dourado) and Jardim da Amazônia in the north of Mato Grosso. Speaks English. Recommended.
Joel Souza, owner of Pousada Ecoverde, see Sleeping, above, T9638 1614, www.eco verdetours.com. Speaks English, German and Italian, knowledgeable and very helpful, checklists for flora and fauna provided, will arrange all transport, accommodation and activities, tends to employ guides rather than guiding himself.

Chapada dos Guimarães *p680*
4-hr tours are about US$26 pp, minimum 5 persons; 7-8 hr tours, US$32 pp, minimum 5; horseback day tour, US$32 pp, minimum 2; an 8-10 km hike with a guide, US$26 pp, minimum 2; bicycle tour with guide, US$26 pp, minimum 2. Tours from Cuiabá cost US$45-52 pp, but a one-day tour is insufficient for a full appreciation of what the area has to offer.
Guides **Ecoturismo Cultural**, Av Cipriano Curvo 655, T3301 1393, 9952 1989, www.chapadadosguimaraes.com.br/ ecoturis.htm. Recommended tours, with bilingual guides who know the area well; tours from 1 to 8 days.
Cássio Martins of **AC Tour**, R Tiradentes 28, T3791 1122, often waits at the rodoviária.
José Paulino dos Santos is a guide working with the **Secretaria de Turismo e Meio Ambiente**, T3791 1245.

Transport

Cuiabá *p678, map p678*
Air Airport in Várzea Grande. By air to most major cities. ATMs outside include **Banco do Brasil** and **Bradesco** for Visa, MasterCard/Cirrus; there is a post office and a **Sedtur** office (not always open). Taxi to centre US$15, 'Aeroporto' bus from Praça Ipiranga US$0.50. There is a direct Airport-Rodoviária bus; bus stop is by the farmacia outside airport.
Bus Many bus routes have stops in the vicinity of Praça Ipiranga. Rodoviária is on R Jules Rimet, Bairro Alvorada, north of the centre; town buses stop at the entrance. Bus No 202 from R Joaquim Murtinho behind the cathedral, 20 mins. Comfortable buses (toilets) to **Campo Grande**, 10 hrs, US$46, 12 buses daily, leito at 2000 and 2100. **Goiânia**, 14 hrs, US$52; direct to **Brasília**, 24 hrs, US$50, leito US$100. To **Porto Velho**, 6 buses a day, US$75, 24 hrs, 21 hrs. **Andorinha** 1700 bus São Paulo-Cuiabá connects with Porto Velho service. Several to **São Paulo**, eg **Motta**, US$84. Connections to all major cities.

Cáceres *p679*
Bus Rodoviária, Terminal da Japonesa. **Colibri/União Cascavel** buses Cuiabá-Cáceres, US$20, many daily between 0630-2400 (book in advance), 3½ hrs.
Ferry For information on sailings, ask at the **Capitânia dos Portos**, on the corner of the main square at waterfront. At the waterfront you can hire a boat, US$10 per hr pp, minimum 3.

Border with Bolivia: Cáceres/San Matías *p679*
Bus The bus fare Cáceres-San Matías is US$20 with **Transical-Velásquez**, Mon-Sat at 0630 and 1500, Sun 1500 only (return at same times), 3 hrs.

Chapada dos Guimarães *p680*
Bus 7 daily to and from **Cuiabá** (Rubi 0700-1900, last back to Cuiabá 1800), 1½ hrs, US$5.50.
Car Hiring a car in Cuiabá is the most convenient way to see many of the scattered attractions, although access to several of them is via rough dirt roads which may deteriorate in the rainy season; drive carefully as the area is prone to dense fog.

Directory

Cuiabá *p678, map p678*
Airline offices TAM, T0800-570 5700. **Trip**, T3682 2555. **Banks** **Banco do Brasil**, Av Getúlio Vargas e R Barão de Melgaço, commission US$10 for cash, US$20 per transaction for TCs, very slow for TCs, but best rates, also has ATM; **Incomep Câmbio**, R Gen Neves 155, good rates. It is difficult to get cash advances on credit cards especially MasterCard, for Visa try Banco do Brasil.
Car hire Agencies have offices at the airport.
Embassies and consulates **Bolivia:** R Paramaribo 174, Qd 08 Lote 06, Jardim das Américas, T3627 1343, colivian_cuiaba@brturbo.com, open Mon-Fri 0900-1700. **Post offices** Main branch at Praça da República, fax service. **Telephones** R Barão de Melgaço 3209, 0700-2200, also at rodoviária, 0600-2130, international service.

Cáceres *p679*
Banks **Banco do Brasil**, R Cel José Dulce 234. HSBC, R Cel José Dulce 145. **Casa de Câmbio Mattos**, Comandante Bauduino 180, next to main praça, changes cash and TCs at good rates.
Telephones Praça Barão de Rio Branco s/n.

Chile

Contents

688 Planning your trip

696 Santiago and around
719 Around Santiago

722 Valparaíso and around
722 Valparaíso
731 Viña del Mar and around

736 North of Santiago
736 Ovalle to La Serena
745 North of La Serena

750 Far north
750 Antofagasta and around
754 North of Antofagasta
758 San Pedro de Atacama
763 Iquique and around
769 Arica and Lauca

778 Central Valley
778 Rancagua to Chillán
783 Concepción and around

787 Lake District
787 Temuco and around
794 Lagos Villarrica, Calafquén and Panguipulli
805 Valdivia and Osorno
812 Southern lakes

819 Puerto Montt and Chiloé
819 Puerto Montt
825 Chiloé

833 Carretera Austral
834 Puerto Montt to Chaitén
836 Chaitén to Coyhaique
846 Lago General Carrera and around

852 Far south
852 Punta Arenas and around
859 Puerto Natales and around
865 Parque Nacional Torres del Paine
871 Tierra del Fuego

876 Chilean Pacific Islands
876 Juan Fernández Islands
877 Rapa Nui/Easter Island

Footprint features

686 Don't miss …
690 Driving in Chile
879 The cultural development of Easter Island

At a glance

Time required 2-4 weeks.

Best time Oct-Dec and Mar-Apr are best; Jun-Aug good for the north. Jan/Feb are busiest holiday months and south can be very crowded. Independence celebrations 18-19 Sep is a busy time.

When not to go Jun-Aug in the south. Dec-Feb in Santiago when pollution is highest.

★ **Don't miss …**

1 **Valparaíso**, page 722.
2 **Lauca National Park**, page 772.
3 **Lake District**, page 787.
4 **Chiloé**, page 825.
5 **Carretera Austral**, page 833.
6 **Torres del Paine**, page 865.

Chile is a ribbon of land squashed between the Pacific and the Andes. Its landscape embraces glacial wilderness and moonscapes, lakes and volcanoes, beaches and salt flats. The north is characterized by the burnt colours of the driest desert in the world. Should rain fall in this barren land, flower seeds that have lain in wait seize the moment to bloom, bringing brilliant colours where no life seemed possible. Snow-capped volcanoes in the Lauca National Park appear close enough to touch in the rarefied air. In one day it is possible to scale a mountain with ice axe and crampons, soak off the exhaustion in a thermal bath and rest beneath the stars of the Southern Cross. Real stargazers will want to visit the astronomical observatories near La Serena, while lovers of mystery will head south for the folklore of Chiloé, Land of Seagulls. The Chilean Lake District is the homeland of the Mapuche, the people who resisted the Spaniards and who proudly maintain their culture and traditions. The lakes themselves are beautiful, set in farmland, overlooked by yet more snow-capped volcanoes. Before the road peters out, blocked by fjords and icefields, the Carretera Austral reveals ancient woodlands, hot springs beside the sea, mountains like castles and raging, emerald rivers – a paradise for fishing and cycling. To reach the ultimate goal of trekkers and birdwatchers, the fabulous granite towers and spires of the Torres del Paine National Park, you have to take a boat, or fly, or make the long haul through Argentina. There are seaports of every size, with their fishing boats, pelicans and sea lions. The most romantic is Valparaíso, described by one observer as "a Venice waiting to be discovered", with its warren of streets and brightly painted houses, its singular lifts up to the clifftops and its old bars.

Note On 27 February 2010 an earthquake of 8.8 on the Richter Scale hit south-central Chile. Regions VII and VIII suffered the heaviest damage, less so Regions VI and IX; more details are given in the text .

Planning your trip

Where to go

A great many of Chile's attractions are outdoors, in the national parks, adventure sports, etc, but the capital, **Santiago**, has a rich cultural life (museums, handicrafts shopping) and is a good base for visiting nearby areas. These include the vineyards of the Maipo Valley, the Andean foothills in the Cajón del Maipo and the ski resorts. The port of Valparaíso and the beach resorts to north and south, principally Viña del Mar, are only a couple of hours away.

North of Santiago is La Serena, a popular seaside resort, from which can be reached the Elqui Valley, where Chilean pisco is made, and three major astronomical observatories. Heading north, the land becomes more barren, but every few years after rain, usually September to October, the flowers that have lain dormant in the desert burst into bloom; if you are in the area, a sight not to be missed. Inland from Antofagasta, the next main city, a road goes to Calama, the huge copper mine at Chuquicamata and the isolated Andean town and popular tourist resort of San Pedro de Atacama. Its attractions are lunar landscapes, hot geysers, salt flats and the way of life at high altitude. Alternatively, from Antofagasta you can take the spectacular coast road to the **Far North** and the ports of Iquique, near which are several archaeological sites, thermal springs and abandoned nitrate mines, and Arica, the last main town before Peru. The road route into Bolivia from Arica passes through the magnificent Parque Nacional Lauca, with its wealth of Andean bird and animal life, high lakes and remote volcanoes.

South of Santiago, the longitudinal highway runs south through the Central Valley passing through or near a number of cities, such as Rancagua, Talca, Chillán and Concepción (the country's second city). There are national parks which deserve a visit in both the Andean foothills and the coastal range of mountains. You can visit vineyards, thermal springs, unspoilt beaches or simply enjoy real Chilean rural life.

The **Lake District** is home to the popular lakes of Villarrica and Llanquihue, but many others are far less developed. Protected areas of great beauty and first-class opportunities for adventure sports and fishing abound. Temuco, at the northern end of this region, is the centre of Mapuche culture and has a huge produce market. Wooded Valdivia, near the coast, is worth a detour for the trip to the rivermouth to see the ruined Spanish forts that protected this outpost of the empire. The southern gateway to the Lake District is Puerto Montt, the starting point for the long haul south. The city's fishing harbour, Angelmó, with its market and food stalls, is not to be missed. From Puerto Montt you can cross to Argentina by road and ferries on Lago Todos los Santos and neighbouring Lagos Frías and Nahuel Huapi on the way to Bariloche.

The island of **Chiloé**, a short bus and ferry ride from Puerto Montt, has a distinctive culture and a green landscape which is the result of its Pacific coastal climate. On the mainland, running south from Puerto Montt, the Carretera Austral has opened up an area of forests, lakes and rivers, linking small communities of settlers. The biggest town is Coyhaique and there are regular excursions by sea and air to the stunning glacier at the Laguna San Rafael. A four-day sea voyage from Puerto Montt takes you to Puerto Natales in **Chilean Patagonia**, near Chile's most dramatic national park, the Torres del Paine. Hiking around the vertical mountains with their forested slopes, past lakes and glaciers, in the presence of a multitude of southern Andean wildlife is an unforgettable experience (but do allow for the unpredictability of the weather). If you prefer not to venture this far south by ship, there are regular flights to the main city of Chilean Patagonia, Punta Arenas, and there is no problem crossing from Argentina by road or by ferry from **Tierra del Fuego**. The contrast between this southernmost part of the country with the dry, desert north could not be greater.

When to go

The best times to visit vary according to geographical location. For the heartland, any time between October and April is good, but the most pleasant seasons are spring (September to

November) and autumn (March-April). In Santiago itself, summers (December to February) are roasting hot and winters (June-August) polluted. The heat of the north is less intense from June to September. In the south December to March, summer, is the best time to visit. Along the Carretera Austral this is the only realistic time to travel because at other times ferry schedules are restricted and in mid-winter many transport services do not run at all. Further south, there is more leeway. The Torrres del Paine park is open year round, though snow, fewer hours of daylight and reduced accommodation mean that only day hikes are feasible in winter. Also bear in mind that January to February in the Lake District and further south are the busiest months, with raised prices, hotels and buses full, lots of backpackers on the road and advance booking often essential. In this holiday season business visitors may find making appointments difficult, but otherwise any time of year is good for working in Santiago.

Getting around

Air Most flights of **LAN**, *www.lan.com* (under the banner **Lan Express**), between Santiago and major towns and cities, are given in the text. LAN has a modern fleet and good service, but allow plenty of time when checking in. If you didn't print your boarding pass from the internet, you must check in electronically at a booth before you are allowed to the counter to drop luggage. **Sky** *www.skyairline.cl* has a less extensive network than LAN. In the north flights are offered by **Principal** (PAL), *www.aerolineaprincipal.cl*. Try to sit on the left flying south, on the right flying north to get the best views of the Andes. On long routes with stops, check if it is cheaper to buy each sector separately. LAN's 'South America Air Pass' can be used on all LAN routes within South America, including the 16 Chilean cities it serves. It must be purchased abroad in conjunction with an international ticket on a LAN flight (or Iberia from Europe) and reservations made well ahead. Domestic single flights cost between US$92 and US$136 each, while flights to Easter Island cost US$250 each way (prices are higher for those arriving on other airlines). Air taxes must be paid on each flight. Route changes and cancellations may be made prior to the flight date on payment of a penalty. Confirm domestic flights at least 24 hours before departure.

Bus Buses are frequent and on the whole good. Apart from holiday times, there is little problem getting a seat on a long-distance bus. Salón-cama services run between main cities on overnight services. **Tur-Bus** (www.turbus.cl), and **Pullman** (www.pullman.cl), each covering the whole country as far south as Puerto Montt, are among the best companies. Standards on routes vary. Tur-bus itineraries can be checked and tickets bought online. Prémium buses have six fully reclining seats. Salón-cama means 25 seats, semi-cama means 34 and salón-ejecutivo or clásico means 44 seats. Price ranges in the text below indicate the cheapest to the most expensive on that route. Stops are infrequent. Since there is lots of competition between bus companies, fares may be bargained lower with smaller operators, particularly just before departure. Prices are highest between December and March, and during the Independence celebrations in September.

Driving in Chile

Road Most roads are in good condition and many are paved. The main road is the Panamericana (Ruta 5) from La Serena to Puerto Montt. A coastal route running much of the length of Chile is being paved. Motorways tolls are very expensive, but the charge includes towing to the next city and free ambulance in case of accident.
Safety In the south (particularly on the Carretera Austral), and in the desert north, always top up your fuel tank and carry spare fuel (you may have to buy a can if renting a car). *Carabineros* (national police) are strict about speed limits (100-120 kph on motorways): Turistel maps mark police posts. Car drivers should have all their papers in order and to hand as there are occasional checks. In suburban areas headlights should be switched on, day and night.
Documents For drivers of private vehicles entering Chile from Argentina, there is a special *salida y admisión temporal de vehículos* form. From Peru or Bolivia, customs type out a *título de importación temporal de vehículos* (temporary admission), valid for the length of stay granted by immigration. Your immigration entry/exit card is stamped *'entrada con vehículo'* so you must leave the country with your vehicle (so you cannot go to Bariloche, for example, without your car). Foreigners must have an international driving licence. Insurance is obligatory and can be bought at borders. A *carnet de passages* is not officially required for foreign-owned motorcycles: a temporary import paper is given at the border.
Organizations **Automóvil Club de Chile**, Av Andrés Bello 1863, Providencia, Santiago, T02-431 1313, www.automovil club.cl. It publishes a *Guía Caminera* and has a country-wide network. It has a car hire agency (with discounts for members or affiliates).
Car hire Shop around as there is a lot of competition. Reputable Chilean companies offer much better value than the well- known international ones, although rates may not always include insurance or 19% VAT. In northern Chile, where mountain roads are bad, check rental vehicles very carefully before setting out. Hire companies charge a large premium to collect the car from another city, so unless making a round-trip it makes economic sense to travel by public transport, then rent a car locally. If intending to leave the country in a hired car, you must obtain authorization from the hire company.
Fuel Gasoline becomes more expensive the further north and further south you go. Unleaded fuel, 93, 95 and 97 octane, US$0.66-0.80, is available in all main cities. Diesel is widely available, US$0.60 a litre. Larger service stations usually accept credit cards, but check before filling up.

Students with ISIC cards may get discounts, except in high season; discounts are also often available for return journeys. Most bus companies will carry bicycles, but may ask for payment.

Pachamama by Bus ⓘ *Agustinas 2113, Santiago, T02-688 8018, www.pachamamabybus.com* is a backpackers' hop-on, hop-off bus service running from Santiago to the north and south weekly, taking scenic routes with frequent stops, with camping where hostel accommodation is not available. English speaking guides.

Hitchhiking Hitchhiking is generally easy and safe throughout Chile, although you may find that in some regions traffic is sparse, so you are less likely to catch a lift (drivers will sometimes make hand signals if they are only going a short distance beyond – this is not a rude gesture!).

Taxis Taxis have meters, but agree beforehand on fares for long journeys out of city centres or special excursions. In some places a surcharge is applied late at night. Taxi drivers may not know the location of streets away from the centre. There is no need to tip unless some extra service, like the carrying of luggage, is given. Black colectivos in urban areas (collective taxis) operate on fixed routes identified by numbers and destinations. They have fixed charges, often little more expensive than buses, which increase at night and which are usually advertised in the front windscreen. They are flagged down on the street corner (in some cities such as Puerto Montt there are signs). Take small change as the driver takes money and offers change while driving. Yellow colectivos also operate on some inter-urban routes, leaving from a set point when full.

Train There are 4,470 km of line, of which most are state owned. Passenger services in the south go from Santiago to Chillán (plans to recommence services to Puerto Montt remain unrealised). Passenger services north of the Valparaíso area have ceased, though there are regional train lines in the Valparaíso and Concepción areas. There is a scenic line from Talca along the valley of the Río Maule to Constitución and a tourist steam train inland from Valdivia on Sundays in summer. In the far north, only the line from Arica to Tacna (Peru) carries passengers. Trains in Chile are moderately priced. See Santiago, Transport, page 716, rail company offices. See www.efe.cl, Chilean Railway Company, with useful information on timetables and fares.

Sleeping ➔ *See page 38 for our hotel grade price guide.*

Chile is still relatively behind the times with accommodation, so the posher hotels are often uninspiring international chains, while the 'historic' hotels are often run down. Some characterful B&Bs are cropping up and in most parts of Chile accommodation is plentiful. Finding a room to suit your budget should be easy. In popular tourist destinations, especially in the south in high season, many families offer rooms: these are advertised by a sign in the window. People often meet buses to offer rooms, which vary greatly in quality and cleanliness; have a look before committing. In summer especially, single rooms can be hard to find.

On hotel bills IVA (VAT) is charged at 19%. The government waives VAT on hotel bills paid in dollars or Euros at authorized hotels only. As a result, larger hotels (but few other establishments) can offer you much lower tariffs if you pay in dollars or Euros than those advertised in pesos. But check the exchange rate: it may be so poor that you end up paying more in dollars than in pesos. Establish clearly in advance what is included in the room price.

Camping Camping is easy but not always cheap at official sites. A common practice is to charge US$18 for up to five people, but if a site is not full, owners will often give a pitch to a single camper for around US$8. A few hostels allow camping in their garden and offer good value rates. Cheap gas stoves can be bought in camping shops in Santiago and popular trekking areas and green replaceable cylinders are available throughout the country. Campsites are very busy in January and February.

Wild camping is easy and safe in remote areas of the far south and in the *cordillera* north of Santiago. In Mapuche and Aymará communities it is courteous and advisable to go to the primary school or some other focal point to meet prominent members of the community first. Camping wild in the north is difficult, because of the lack of water. In much of central and central-southern Chile the land is fenced off and as it is officially illegal to camp on private land without permission, it may be necessary to ask first. Also note that in the Lake District and Chiloé, between mid-December and mid-January, huge horseflies (*tábanos*) can be a real problem when camping, hiking and fishing: do not wear dark clothing.

Youth hostels Backpackers should consult **www.backpackerschile.com** and **www.backpackers best.cl**. The former focuses on hostels charging around US$15-25 pp and are all of a good standard, while the latter features lots of hostels in a broad price range. There are youth hostels (*albergues*) throughout Chile; average cost about US$12-24 pp. Although some hostels are open only from January to the end of February, many operate all year round. The IH card is usually readily accepted, but YHA affiliated hostels are not necessarily the best. A Hostelling International card costs US$26. These can be obtained from **Asociación Chilena de Albergues Turísticos Juveniles** ⓘ *Hernando de Aguirre 201, of 602, Providencia, Santiago, T411 2050, www.hostelling.cl.* In summer there are makeshift hostels in many Chilean towns, usually in the main schools; they charge up to US$7 per person and are good meeting places. Don't expect much sleep or privacy, though.

Eating and drinking → *See page 40 for our restaurant price guide.*

Eating out Breakfast is usually instant coffee or tea with bread, butter and jam. Lunch, served from 1300 to 1530, tends to be the main meal of the day and many restaurants serve a cheaper fixed-price meal at lunch time. When this consists of a single dish it is known as *la colación*, when there is more than one course it is called *el menú*. In more expensive places, this may not be referred to on the menu. Dinner is between 2000 and 2230. *Las onces* (literally elevenses) is the name given to a snack usually including tea, bread, cheese, etc, eaten by many Chileans as their evening meal. The cheapest restaurants in urban areas tend to be by the transport terminals and markets or, in coastal areas, by the port. Also try the *casinos de bomberos* (firemen's canteens) in most towns.

Food A very typical Chilean dish is *cazuela de ave* (or *de vacuno*), a nutritious stew containing large pieces of chicken (or beef), pumpkin potatoes, rice, and maybe onions, and green peppers. *Valdiviano* is another stew, common in the south, consisting of beef, onion, sliced potatoes and eggs. *Empanadas de pino* are turnovers filled with meat, onions, raisins, olives and egg chopped up together. *Pastel de choclo* is a casserole of meat and onions with olives, topped with a maize-meal mash, baked in an earthenware bowl. *Humitas* are mashed sweetcorn mixed with butter and spices and baked in sweetcorn leaves. *Prieta* is a blood sausage stuffed with cabbage leaves. A normal *parrillada* or *asado* is a giant mixed grill served from a charcoal brazier. *Bife/lomo a lo pobre* (a poor man's steak) can be just the opposite: it is a steak topped by two fried eggs, chips and fried onions. The Valparaíso speciality is the *chorrillana*, chips topped with fried sliced steak, fried onions and scrambled eggs, while in Chiloé you can enjoy a *curanto*, a meat, shellfish and potato stew traditionally cooked in a hole in the ground.

What gives Chilean food its personality is the **seafood**. The delicious congrio fish is a national dish, and *caldillo de congrio* (a soup served with a massive piece of kingclip/ling, onions and potatoes) is excellent. A *paila* can take many forms (the paila is simply a kind of dish), but the commonest are made of eggs or seafood. *Paila Chonchi* is a kind of bouillabaisse, but has more flavour, more body, more ingredients. *Parrillada de mariscos* is a dish of grilled mixed seafood, brought to the table piping hot on a charcoal brazier. Other excellent local fish are the *cojinova*, the *albacora* (swordfish) and the *corvina* (bass). A range of mussels (*choritos/ cholgas*) is available, as are abalone (*locos*), clams (*almejas*) and razor clams (*machas*). Some bivalve shellfish may be periodically banned because they carry the disease **marea roja** (which is fatal in humans). *Cochayuyo* is seaweed, bound into bundles, described as 'hard, leathery thongs'. The *erizo*, or sea-urchin, is also commonly eaten as are *picorocos* (sea barnacles) and the strong flavoured *piure*. *Luche* is dried seaweed, sold as a black cake, like 'flakey bread pudding' to be added to soups and stews. **Avocado** pears (*paltas*) are excellent, and play an important role in recipes. Make sure that vegetables are included in the price for the main dish; menus often don't make this clear. Local **fast food** is excellent. *Completos* are hot dogs with a huge variety of fillings. A *barros jarpa* is a grilled cheese and ham sandwich and a *barras luco* is a grilled cheese and beef sandwich. *Sopaipillas* are cakes made of a mixture including pumpkin, served in syrup. Ice cream is very good; try *lúcuma* and *chirimoya* (custard apple) flavours.

Drink Tap **water** is safe to drink in main cities but bottled water is safer for the north. The local **wines** are very good; the best are from the central areas. The bottled wines cost from US$3 upwards; the very best wines will cost about US$50 in a smart restaurant. The *Guía de vinos de Chile*, published every year in January (English edition available) has ratings and tasting notes for all Chilean wines on the market. **Beer** is quite good and cheap (about US$1.50 for a litre bottle, plus US$0.50 deposit in shops). Draught lager is known as Schop. Chilean brewed beers include

Cristal, Escudo and Royal Guard, Austral (good in the far south), Báltica, Brahma and Heineken. Malta, a brown ale, is recommended for those wanting a British-type beer. There are good local breweries in Valparaíso, Punta Arenas and Llanquihue near Puerto Varas and several good microbreweries around the country.

Pisco, made from grapes, is the most famous spirit. It is best drunk as a 'Pisco Sour' with lime or lemon juice and sugar. Two popular drinks are **vaina**, a mixture of brandy, egg and sugar and **cola de mono**, a mixture of aguardiente, coffee, milk and vanilla served very cold at Christmas. **Chicha** is any form of alcoholic drink made from fruit, usually grapes. **Cider** (*chicha de manzana*) is popular in the south. **Mote con huesillo**, made from wheat hominy and dried peaches, is a soft drink, refreshing in summer. A *vitamina* is a 100% pure fruit juice drink.

Coffee is generally instant except in espresso bars in major cities. Elsewhere specify *café-café* or *expresso*. A *cortado* is an expresso with hot frothed milk served in a glass. Tea is widely available. If you order *café*, or *té*, *con leche*, it will come with all milk; if you want just a little milk, you must specify that. After a meal, try an *agüita* (infusion) – hot water in which herbs such as mint or aromatics such as lemon peel, have been steeped. There is a wide variety, very refreshing.

Essentials A-Z

Accident and emergency

Emergency (*carabineros*) T133.
Police (detectives, *investigaciones*) T134.
Ambulance (*ambulancia*) T132. **Fire brigade** (*bomberos*) T131. **Forest fires** (*incendios forestales*) T130. **Policía Internacional**, head office Gral Borgoña 1052, Santiago, T02-737 1292, Mon-Fri 0900-1700, handle immigration, lost tourist cards.

Electricity

Chile's supply is 220 volts AC, 50 cycles. Sockets are 3 round pins in a line, which will accept 2-pin plugs.

Embassies and consulates

Visit http://chileabroad.gov.cl for a complete list.

Festivals and events

Public holidays 1 Jan, New Year's Day; Semana Santa (Fri and Sat); 1 May, Labour Day; 21 May, Glorias Navales/Navy Day; 29 Jun, San Pedro y San Pablo; 16 Jul, Virgen del Carmen; 15 Aug, Asunción de la Virgen; 18, 19 Sep, Independence Days; 12 Oct, Día de la Raza; 31 Oct, Día Nacional de las Iglesias Evangélicas y Protestantes; 1 Nov, Todos los Santos; 8 Dec, Inmaculada Concepción; 25 Dec, Christmas.

Maps

The **Instituto Geográfico Militar**, Dieciocho 369, Santiago, T02-410 9463, www.igm.cl, Mon-Fri 0830-1730, has detailed geophysical and topographical maps of the whole of Chile, useful for climbing; expensive, but the Biblioteca Nacional, Alameda 651 (T360 5200) will allow you to photocopy. Matassi maps (JLM Mapas), F02-236 4808, jmatassi@interactiva.cl, US$6-8, usually with a red cover, are good value but often contain errors. The *Copec Guides* (see Tourist information, below) are useful for roads and towns, but not all distances are exact. Good road maps are also published by Tur-Bus. Good trekking maps for Central Chile can be ordered from www.trekkingchile.com.

Money → *US$1= 521 pesos, €1= 708 pesos (Feb 2010).*

The unit of currency is the peso, its sign is $. Notes are for 1,000, 2,000, 5,000, 10,000 and 20,000 pesos and coins for 1, 5, 10, 50, 100 and 500 pesos. Small shops and bus drivers do not look kindly upon being presented with large notes, especially in the morning and in rural areas. The best exchange rates offered are in Santiago. MasterCard emergency T1230-020-2012; Visa T1230-020-2136; Amex emergency call collect (USA) 336-393-1111.

Plastic/TCs/banks (ATMs)

The easiest way to obtain cash is by using ATMs which operate under the sign Redbanc (www.redbanc.cl, for a full list); they take Cirrus (MasterCard), Maestro and Plus (Visa) and permit transactions up to 200,000 pesos chilenos per day. Commission may be charged. Instructions are available in English. Note that **Banco del Estado Redbanc** ATMs take only MasterCard. Visa and MasterCard are common in Chile. American Express and Diner's Club are less useful. TCs are most easily exchanged in Santiago. US dollars cash and euros can be exchanged. Even slightly damaged or marked foreign notes may be rejected for exchange. Exchange shops (*casas de cambio*) are open longer hours and often give slightly better rates than banks, including for TCs. It is always worth shopping around. Rates get worse as you go north from Santiago. Official rates are quoted in daily newspapers.

Cost of travelling

The average cost for a traveller on an economical budget is about US$40-45 per day for food, accommodation and land transportation (more for flights, tours, car hire, etc). Breakfast in hotels, if not included in the price, is about US$2.50 (instant coffee, roll with ham or cheese, and jam). *Alojamiento* in private houses and hostels (bed, breakfast and often use of kitchen) starts at about US$12. Internet costs US$0.60-1 per hr. Southern Chile is much more expensive between 15 Dec and 15 Mar. Santiago tends to be more expensive for food and accommodation than other parts of Chile.

Opening hours

Banks : 0900-1400, closed Sat. Government offices : 1000-1230 (the public is admitted for a few hours only). Other offices : Mon-Fri 0830-1230, 1400-1800. Shops (Santiago) : 1030-1930, Sat 0930-1330.

Safety

Chile is one of the safest countries in South America for the visitor. Like all major cities around the world, though, Santiago and Valparaíso do have crime problems. Law enforcement officers are *carabineros* (green military uniforms), who handle all tasks except immigration. *Investigaciones*, in civilian dress, are detective police who deal with everything except traffic.

Taxes

Airport taxes

Airport tax is US$30 for international flights (should be included in flight ticket price); US$9.55 for international flights under 500 km and domestic flights over 270 km; US$3.75 for domestic flights under 270 km.

VAT

VAT/IVA is 19%.

Telephone → *Country code T+56.*

Ringing: a double ring repeated regularly. Engaged: equal tones with equal pauses. International roaming is becoming more common, but buying a local pay- as-you-go may be a cheaper option. Major airports and hotels often have rental desks, can advise on local outlets and how to use mobiles. Mobile numbers are preceded by 08 or 09.

Time

Official time is 4 hrs behind GMT, 3 hrs behind in summer. Clocks change from mid-Sep or Oct to early Mar.

Tipping

10% in restaurants, if service is not included in the bill; tip about 100 pesos in bars/soda fountains. Porters: US$1 or US$0.15 a piece of luggage. Taxi-drivers are not tipped.

Tourist information

The national secretariat of tourism, **Sernatur**, www.sernatur.cl, has offices throughout the country (addresses given in the text). City offices provide town maps and other information. A recommended series of books is published by **Copec** (in Spanish), notably a 4-part guide to the country, Norte, Centro, Sur and a camping guide with road map, with information and a wealth of maps including neighbouring tourist centres in Argentina, in Spanish only. There are also associated titles. The price of each volume depends where you buy it; they can be found in bookshops, Copec filling stations and news stands in most city centres. **CONAF** (the Corporacíon Nacional Forestal), Presidente Bulnes 285, Santiago, T663 0000, www.conaf.cl, publishes a number of leaflets (in Spanish and English) and has documents and maps about the national park system. **CODEFF** (Comité Nacional Pro-Defensa de la Fauna y Flora), Ernesto Reyes 035, Providencia, Santiago, T02-777 2534, www.codeff.cl, can also provide information on environmental questions. For regulations on sport fishing, see www.sernapesca.cl.

Useful websites

www.chile.cl (Spanish and English), and **www.visit-chile.org** (English, Spanish), both have information on Chile.

www.dibam.cl Official site for museums, libraries and galleries.

www.senderodechile.cl Information on the project to build a trekking/mountain biking path running the whole length of Chile.

www.trekkingchile.com Information site on hiking, trekking, mountaineering, culture and travelling in Chile.

www.chip.cl Chile Information Project, Av Santa María 227, of 12, Recoleta, Santiago, gives access to *The Santiago Times* English-language daily, www.santiagotimes.cl, travel information, hotels (with commission), history, wine and more. Its related sites are the *Valparaíso Times*, www.valparaisotimes.cl, and the *Patagonia Times*, http://patagoniatimes.cl/.

www.ancientforests.org/chile.htm Site of Ancient Forest International, Box 1850, Redway, CA 95560, T/F707-923 4475, USA. Information regarding Chilean forests.

www.chile-hotels.com Reservations for many hotels in Chile (particularly upmarket ones); prices may be cheaper booking direct.

www.surfchile.cl For surfers.

www.welcomechile.com Interpatagonia's Chile site with tourist information.

Visas and immigration

Passport (valid for at least 6 months) and tourist card only are required for entry by all foreigners except citizens of Kuwait, Egypt, Saudi Arabia and UAE, most African countries, Guyana, Cuba, Russian Federation and former Soviet bloc countries not now in the EU, who require visas. It is imperative to check tourist card and visa requirements before travel. National identity cards are sufficient for entry by citizens of all South American countries. Tourist cards are valid in most cases for 90 days, but some are for 60 and others 30 days. Tourist cards can be obtained from immigration offices at major land borders and Chilean airports; you must surrender your tourist card on departure (if you lose it ask immigration for a replacement). If you wish to stay longer than 90 days (as a tourist), you must buy a 90-day extension from the Departamento de Extranjería (head office San Antonio 580, Santiago, www.extranjeria.gob.cl, address for extensions in Santiago under Useful addresses, page 718), or any local *gobernación* office. It costs US$100. To avoid the long queue and long-winded bureaucracy, make a day-trip to Argentina, Bolivia or Peru and return with a new tourist card (the authorities don't like it if you do this more than 3-4 times). An onward ticket is required. Tourist card holders may changetheir status to enable them to stay on in employment if they have a contract; they need to contact the Extranjería in whichever province they will be working. On arrival you will be asked where you are staying in Chile. **Note** On arrival by air, US citizens will be charged an administration fee of US$131, Canadians US$125, Australians US$56 and Mexicans US$23 (this is a reciprocal tax payable because Chileans have to pay the equivalent amount when applying for visas to enter these countries; rates are posted at arrivals and they do change). This tax is not charged at land borders. The permission is valid for multiple entry and for the life of the passport. The tax should be paid in cash. For some nationalities a visa will be granted within 24 hrs upon production of an onward ticket, for others, authorization must be obtained from Chile. For other nationalities who need a visa, a charge is made. To travel overland to or from Tierra del Fuego a multiple entry visa is essential since the Argentine-Chilean border is crossed more than once (it is advisable to get a multiple entry visa before arriving, rather than trying to change a single entry visa once in Chile). A student card is useful for getting discounts on transport and access to various concessions and services. They can be obtained from Hernando de Aguirre 201, of 602, Providencia, T411 2050, and cost US$16, photo and proof of status required; www.isic.cl.

Weights and measures

The metric system is obligatory but the quintal of 46 (101.4 lbs) is used.

Santiago and around

➔ *Phone code: 02. Colour map 8, B1. Population: 6 million. Altitude: 600 m.*

Santiago, the political, economic and financial capital of Chile, is one of the most beautifully set of any South American city, standing in a wide plain with the magnificent chain of the Andes in full view – rain and pollution permitting. Nearly 40% of Chileans live in and around Santiago, which is now the sixth largest city in South America. It's a modern industrial capital, full of skyscrapers, bustle, noise and traffic, and smog is a problem especially between April and September. Santiago bursts with possibilities, with its parks, museums, shops and hectic nightlife, and is also within easy reach of vineyards, beaches and Andean ski resorts.

Ins and outs

Getting there The airport is 26 km northwest of the centre. **Tur-Bus**, US$3, and **Centropuerto**, US$2.50, run from airport to city centre. There are also shuttle services to/from hotels and private addresses (US$8-10 shared, depending on zone) and taxis (US$18-30). The railway station, Estacíon Central, which only serves the south of the country, is on the Alameda, as are the four main bus terminals. All can be reached by buses, taxi or the Metro. The bus terminals are Alameda, for Pullman Bus and Tur-Bus services; next door is Terminal Santiago, for the south of the country, and some international destinations (metro Universidad de Santiago); San Borja, for regional and northern destinations (metro Estación Central); Los Héroes (nearest the centre, metro Los Héroes) for some southern, northern and international routes. Another terminal at Metro Pajaritos (Line 1) serves Valparaíso, Viña del Mar and the coast (airport buses stop here). ▸▸ *See also Transport, page 714.*

1 Santiago orientation

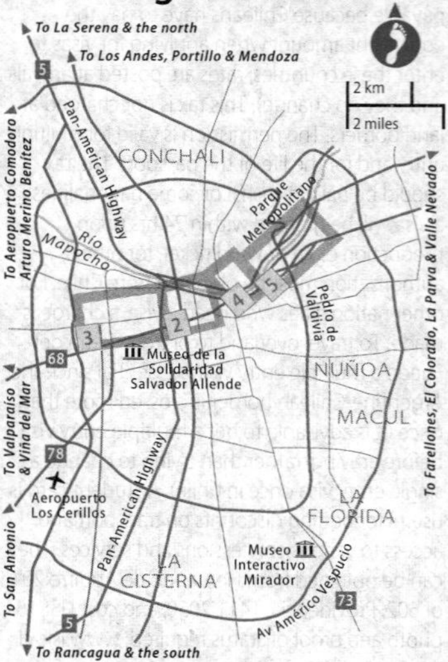

➡ Santiago maps

1 Santiago orientation, page 696
2 Santiago centre, page 697
3 Santiago west of centre, page 698
4 Bellavista & Lastarria, page 700
5 **Providencia, page 702**

Getting around The Metro (underground railway) has four lines: Line 1 runs west-east between Escuela Militar and San Pablo, under the Alameda. Line 2 runs north-south from Vespucio Norte to La Cisterna. Line 4 runs north-south from Tobalaba to Plaza de Puente Alto, with a branch from V Mackenna to La Cisterna. Line 5 runs northwest-southeast from Quinta Normal to Vicente Valdés. The east-west Line 1 follows the main axis, linking the bus and train stations, the centre, Providencia and beyond. Trains run daily from 0600 (Monday-Saturday), 0800 (Sunday and holidays) to about 2300. Fares cost US$0.65-0.80 depending on time of day. City buses: the old system of yellow *micros* is being replaced by *Transantiago* (2005-2010); details under Transport, below. You pay by *Bip* card (purchased in advance), US$3 for a rechargeable card. Taxis are abundant, but Radio Taxis, called in advance, are safer. Colectivos (collective taxis) run on fixed routes to the suburbs.

Tourist offices **Servicio Nacional de Turismo Sernatur** ⓘ *Av Providencia 1550, metro Manuel Montt, next to Providencia Municipal Library, T731 8336/8337, info@sernatur.cl, Mon-Fri 0845-1830, Sat 0900-1400*, maps, brochures and posters. Good notice board. **Information office also at the airport** daily 0900-2100, T601 9320. **Municipal Tourist Board** ⓘ *Casa Colorada, Merced 860, metro Plaza de Armas, T632 7783, and at Cerro Santa Lucía, T664 4216, www.municipalidaddesantiago.cl, Mon-Thu 1000-1800, Fri 1000-1700*, good free booklet: *Historical Heritage of Santiago: A Guide for visitors in English and Spanish*, on historic buildings. Almost all museums are closed on Monday and on 1 November.

2 Santiago centre

➡ Santiago maps
1 Santiago orientation, page 696
2 Santiago centre, page 697
3 Santiago west of centre, page 698
4 Bellavista & Lastarria, page 700
5 Providencia, page 702

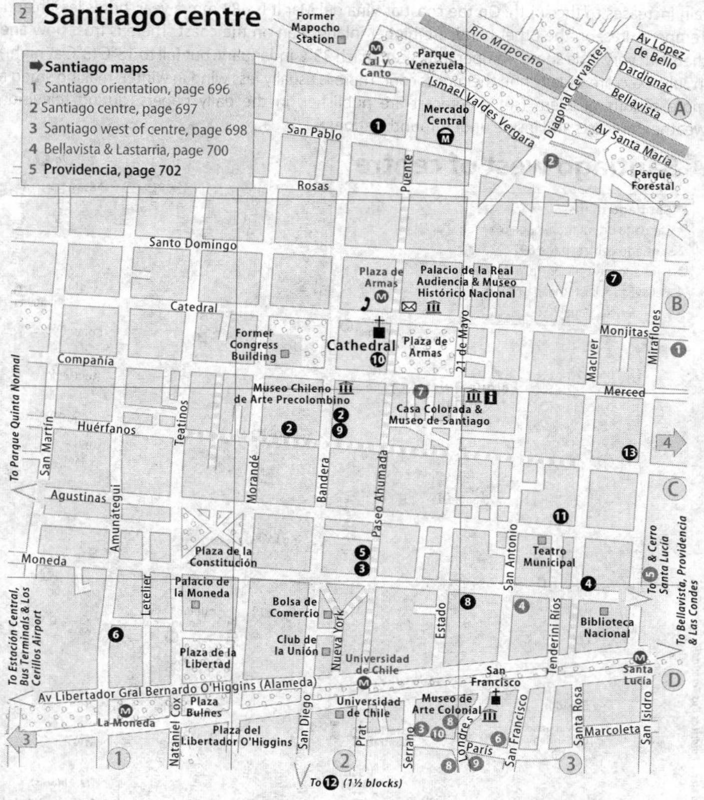

Sleeping
1 Andes Hostel *B3*
2 Casaltura *A3*
3 Fundador *D2*
4 Galerías *D3*
5 Hostal Santa Lucía *B3*
6 París *D3*
7 Plaza de Armas Hostel *B2*
8 Plaza Londres *D2*
9 Res Londres *D3*
10 Vegas *D2*

Eating
1 Bar Central *A2*
2 Bar Nacional No 2 *C2*
3 Café Caribe *C2*
4 Café Colonia *C3*
5 Café Haití *C2*
6 Círculo de Periodistas *D1*
7 Da Carla *B3*
8 El Naturista *D3*
9 El Rápido *C2*
10 Faisán d'Or *B2*
11 Lung Fung *C3*
12 Masticón *D2*
13 Topanco *C3*

Orientation The centre of the old city lies between the Mapocho and the Avenida O'Higgins, which is usually known as the Alameda. From the Plaza Baquedano (usually called Plaza Italia), in the east of the city's central area, the Mapocho flows to the northwest and the Alameda runs to the southwest. From Plaza Italia the C Merced runs due west to the Plaza de Armas, the heart of the city, five blocks south of the Mapocho. An urban motorway runs the length of Santiago from east to west under the course of the Río Mapocho.

Best time to visit There is rain during the winter (May-August), but the summers are dry. The rain increases to the south. On the coast at Viña del Mar it is 483 mm a year, but is less inland. Temperatures, on the other hand, are higher inland than on the coast. There is frost now and then, but very little snow. Temperatures can reach 33°C in January, but fall to 13°C (3°C at night) in July. Days are usually hot, the nights cool. There is usually less wind in winter, making smog a more serious problem (smog forecast are published in the daily papers, during television weather forecasts and inside underground stations).

3 Santiago west of centre

Sleeping
1 Che Lagarto
2 Conde de Ansúrez
3 Happy House Hostel
4 Hostal de Sammy
5 Hostal Río Amazonas Barrio Brasil
6 Hostelling Internacional Santiago
7 La Casa Amarilla
8 La Casa Roja
9 Luz Azul
10 Moai Hostel
11 Res Mery
12 Tur Hotel Express

Security Like all large cities, Santiago has problems of theft. Pickpockets and bag- snatchers, who are often well-dressed, operate especially on the Metro and around the Plaza de Armas. Avoid the *poblaciones* (shanty towns), notably Pudahuel and parts of the north (such as Conchalí), especially if you are travelling alone or have only recently arrived.

Sights

Around the Plaza de Armas On the eastern and southern sides of the Plaza de Armas there are arcades with shops; on the northern side is the post office and the Municipalidad; and on the western side the Cathedral and the archbishop's palace. The **Cathedral**, much rebuilt, contains a recumbent statue in wood of San Francisco Javier, and the chandelier which lit the first meetings of Congress after independence; it also houses an interesting museum of religious art and historical pieces (0930-1230, 1530-1830, free). In the Palacio de la Real Audiencia on the Plaza de Armas is the **Museo Histórico Nacional** ⓘ *No 951, T411 7000, www.dibam.cl/historico_nacional, Tue- Sun 1000-1730, US$1.15, free on Sun, signs in Spanish*, covering the period from the Conquest until 1925.

Eating
1 Confitería Torres
2 El Hoyo
3 Las Vacas Gordas
4 Los Buenos Muchachos
5 Los Chinos Ricos
6 Majestic
7 Ostras Azócar

Just west of the Plaza is the **Museo Chileno de Arte Precolombino** ⓘ *in the former Real Aduana, Bandera 361, www.pre colombino.cl, Tue-Sun 1000-1800, US$6.35, students and children free, displays in English*. Its collection of objects from the pre-Columbian cultures of Central America and the Andean region is highly recommended for the quality of the objects and their presentation. At Calle Merced 864, close to the Plaza de Armas, is the **Casa Colorada** (1769), home of the Governor in colonial days and then of Mateo de Toro, first president of Chile. It is now the **Museo de Santiago** ⓘ *T633 0723, Tue-Sat 1000-1800, Sun and holidays, 1100-1400, US$3, students free*. It covers the history of Santiago from the Conquest to modern times, with excellent displays and models, some signs in English, guided tours. From the Plaza de Armas Paseo Ahumada, a pedestrianized street lined with cafés runs south to the Alameda four blocks away, crossing Huérfanos.

Four blocks north of the Plaza de Armas is the interesting **Mercado Central** ⓘ *21 de Mayo y San Pablo*, the best place in Santiago for seafood. The building faces the Parque Venezuela, on which is the Cal y Canto metro station and, at its western end, the former **Mapocho Railway Station** ⓘ *www.estacion mapocho.cl*, now a major cultural centre and concert venue. If you head east from Mapocho station, by the river, you pass through the Parque Forestal (see below), before coming back to Plaza Italia.

Along the Alameda The Alameda runs through the heart of the city for over 3 km. It is 100 m wide, and ornamented with gardens and statuary: the most notable are the equestrian statues of Generals O'Higgins and San Martín; the statue of the Chilean historian Benjamín Vicuña MacKenna who, as mayor of Santiago, beautified Cerro Santa Lucía (see below); and the great monument in honour of the battle of Concepción in 1879.

From the Plaza Italia, where there is a statue of Gen Baquedano and the Tomb of the Unknown Soldier, the Alameda skirts, on the right, Cerro Santa Lucía, and on the left, the Catholic University. Beyond the hill the Alameda passes the neoclassical **Biblioteca Nacional** ⓘ *Av O'Higgins 651, Santa Lucia metro, www.dibam.cl/ biblioteca_nacional, Mon-Fri 0900-1900, Sat 0910-1400 (Dec-Mar 0900-1800, closed Sat), free*, good concerts, temporary exhibitions. Beyond, on the left, between calles San Francisco and Londres, is the oldest church in Santiago:

4 Bellavista & Lastarria

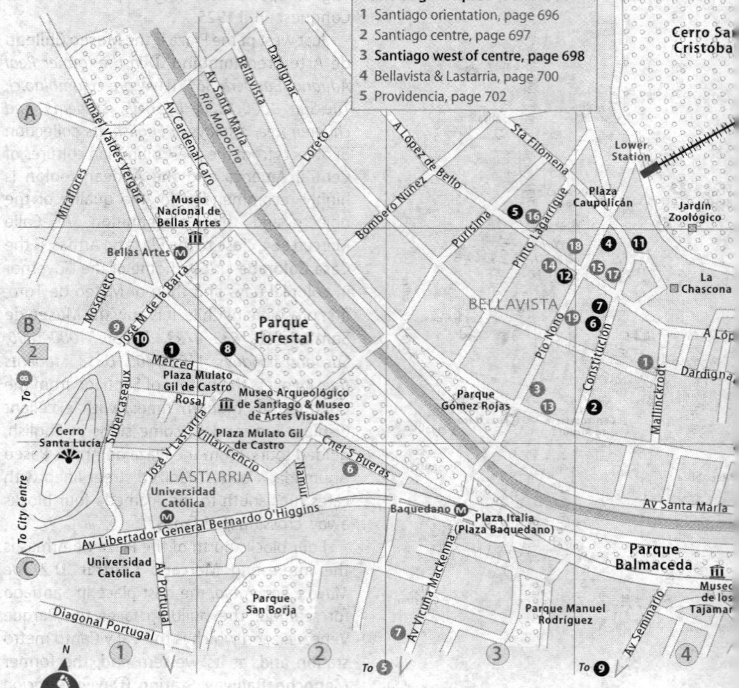

Sleeping
1 Bellavista Hostel *B4*
2 Casa Condell *C4*
3 Del Patio *B3*
4 El Patio Suizo *C4*
5 Hostal Casa Grande *C3*
6 Hostal Forestal *C2*
7 Hostal Río Amazonas Plaza Italia *C3*
8 Hostal Santa Lucía *B1*
9 Kapital *B1*
10 Marilú's B&B *C6*

Eating
1 Bombón Oriental *B1*
2 Cienfuegos *B4*
3 De Cangrejo a Conejo *B5*
4 Eladio *B4*
5 El Otro Sitio *A3*
6 El Tablao *B4*
7 Etniko *B4*
8 Les Assassins *B2*
9 Olan *B4*
10 Opera Catedral *B1*
11 Pasta e Vino *B4*
12 Venezia *B3*

the red-walled church and monastery of **San Francisco** (1618). Inside is the small statue of the Virgin that Valdivia carried on his saddlebow when he rode from Peru to Chile. The **Museo Colonial San Francisco** ⓘ *by Iglesia San Francisco, Londres 4, T639 8737, www.museosanfrancisco.cl, Tue-Sat 1000-1300, 1500-1800, Sun 1000-1400, US$1.50*, houses religious art, including 54 paintings of the life of St Francis; in the cloisters is a room containing Gabriela Mistral's Nobel medal. South of San Francisco is the Barrio París-Londres, built 1923-1929, now restored. Two blocks north of the Alameda is **Teatro Municipal** ⓘ *C Agustinas 794, www.municipal.cl, tours Tue 1300-1500, Sun 1100-1400, US$4.*

A little further west along the Alameda, is the Universidad de Chile; the Club de la Unión is almost opposite. Nearby, on Calle Nueva York is the **Bolsa de Comercio**; the public may view the trading; passport required. One block further west is Plaza de la Libertad. North of the plaza, hemmed in by the skyscrapers of the Centro Cívico, is the **Palacio de la Moneda** ⓘ *guided tours of the palace 0900-1300 final Sun of every month, courtyards are open to the public (access from north side) Mon-Fri 1000-1800 unless important state business is being carried out*, the Presidential Palace (1805) containing historic relics, paintings and sculpture, and the elaborate 'Salón Rojo' used for official receptions. Although the Moneda was damaged by air attacks during the military coup of 11 September 1973 it has been fully restored. Ceremonial changing of the guard every other day, 1000, never on Sunday. The large new **Centro Cultural Palacio La Moneda** ⓘ *T355 6500, www.ccplm.cl, 0900-2100, exhibitions 1000-1930 daily, US$1.15, films US$2.30-3.75*, houses temporary exhibitions as well as an arts cinema and an interesting gallery of Chilean handicrafts (both closed Monday).

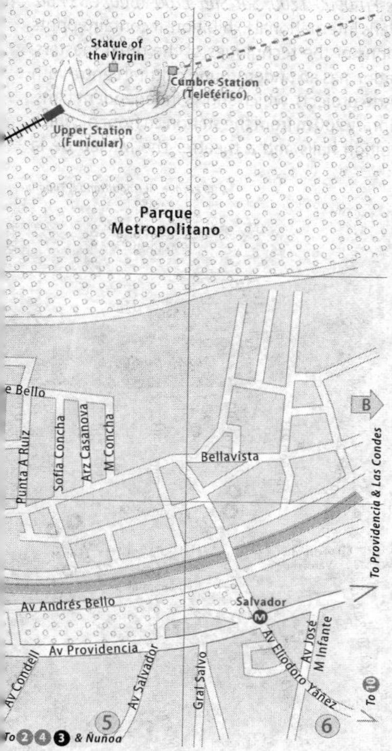

Bars & clubs

13 Back Stage & La Casa en el Aire *B4*
14 Bogart *B3*
15 Disco Salsa *B4*
16 Jammin' Club *A3*
17 La Bodeguita de Julio *B4*
18 La Otra Puerta *B3*
19 Tu Tu Tanga *B3*

West of the centre **Barrio Brasil**, with Plaza Brasil at its heart and the Basílica del Salvador two blocks from the plaza, is one of the earliest parts of the city. It has some fine old buildings, especially around Calle Concha y Toro, but now it's a more bohemian, studenty area with lots of places to stay as well as numerous bars, clubs, cafés and lively restaurants (Metro República). Five blocks south of the Alameda is the **Palacio Cousiño** ⓘ *C Dieciocho 438, www.palaciocousino.cl, Metro Toesca, Tue-Fri 0930-1330, 1430-1700, Sat-Sun 0930-1330, US$3, guided tour only (Spanish/English), cloth bootees provided to protect floors.* This large mansion in French rococo style has a superb Italian marble staircase and other opulent items. Recommended.

Parque O'Higgins ⓘ *10 blocks south of Alameda; take Metro Line 2 to Parque O'Higgins station, bus from Parque Baquedano via Avs MacKenna and Matta*. It has a small lake, tennis courts, swimming pool (open from 5 December), an open-air stage, a club, the racecourse of the Club Hípico and an amusement park, **Fantasilandia** ⓘ *daily in summer, winter weekends only till 2000, US$10, US$7.50 children, unlimited rides*. There are kite-flying contests on Sunday, basic restaurants, craft shops, an aquarium, an insect, reptile and shellfish museum and the **Museo del Huaso** ⓘ *T556 1927, Mon-Fri 1000-1700, Sun 1000-1400, free*, a collection of criollo clothing and tools. During the Independence celebrations around 18 September, there are many good *peñas*.

The Alameda continues west to the **Planetarium** ⓘ *Alameda 3349, T718 2900, www.planetariochile.cl, US$6*. Opposite it on the southern side is the railway station (Estación Central or Alameda). On Avenida Matucana, running north from here, is the popular Parque Quinta Normal (at Avenida D Portales). It was founded as a botanical garden in 1830. Near the park is **Museo Artequín** ⓘ *Av Portales 3530, Tue-Fri 0900-1700, Sat-Sun 1100-1800, US$1.60*. Housed in the Chilean pavilion built for the 1889 Paris International Exhibition, it contains prints of famous paintings and activities and explanations of the techniques of the great masters. Recommended. The new Quinta Normal metro station has an underground cultural centre with theatres and a free art cinema (part of the Metro Arte project), which shows independent films. The government is building an enormous public library 200 m from the station, in front of which is **Centro Cultural Matucana**, with several exhibition halls and a theatre. The **Museo de la**

5 Providencia

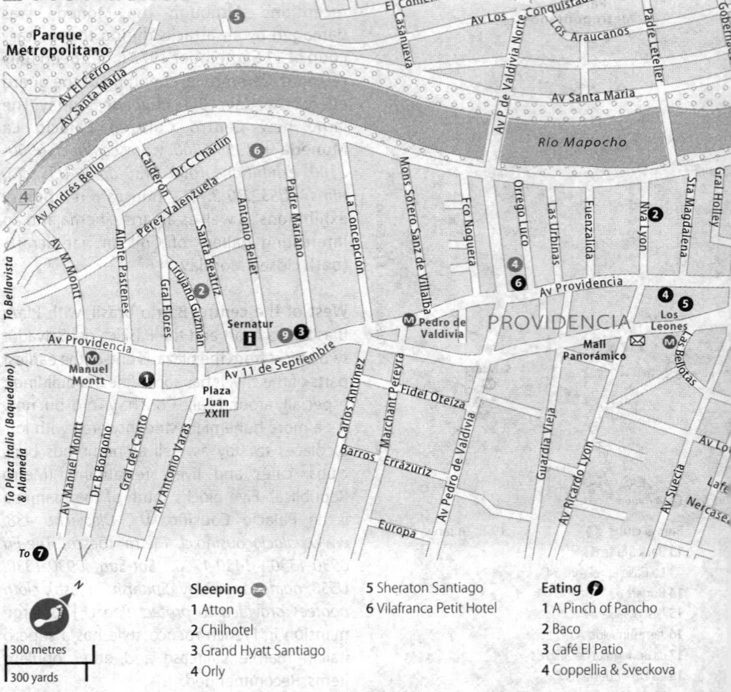

Sleeping
1 Atton
2 Chilhotel
3 Grand Hyatt Santiago
4 Orly
5 Sheraton Santiago
6 Vilafranca Petit Hotel

Eating
1 A Pinch of Pancho
2 Baco
3 Café El Patio
4 Coppellia & Sveckova

Solidaridad Salvador Allende ⓘ *Av República 475, T689 8761, www.mssa.cl, Tue-Sun 1000-1900, US$1.20, Sun free*, houses a highly regarded collection of 20th-century works donated by Chilean and other artists (Picasso, Miró, Matta and many more) who sympathized with the Allende government, plus some personal items of the president himself. The contents were hidden during the Pinochet years.

East of the centre **Cerro Santa Lucía** ⓘ *closes at 2100; visitors must sign a register at the entrance, giving their ID card number*, bounded by Calle Merced to the north, Alameda to the south, Calles Santa Lucía and Subercaseaux, is a cone of rock rising steeply to a height of 70 m (reached by stairs and a lift from the Alameda). It can be climbed from the Caupolicán esplanade, on which stands a statue of that Mapuche leader, but the ascent from the northern side, with a statue of Diego de Almagro, is easier. There are striking views of the city from the top, where there is a fortress, the Batería Hidalgo (no public access). It is best to descend the eastern side, to see the small Plaza Pedro Valdivia with its waterfalls and statue of Valdivia. The area is not safe after dark.

Parque Forestal lies due north of Santa Lucía hill and immediately south of the Mapocho. **Museo Nacional de Bellas Artes** ⓘ *www.mnba.cl (Spanish only), Tue-Sun 1000-1850, US$1, free Sun, café*, is in an extraordinary example of neoclassical architecture. It has a large display of Chilean and foreign painting and sculpture; contemporary art exhibitions are held several times a year. In the west wing is the **Museo de Arte Contemporáneo** ⓘ *www.mac.uchile.cl, closed 2009.*

Parque Balmaceda (Parque Gran Bretaña), east of Plaza Italia, is perhaps the most beautiful in Santiago (the Museo de los Tajamares, which holds monthly exhibitions, is here).

Between the Parque Forestal, Plaza Italia and the Alameda is the **Lastarria** neighbourhood (Universidad Católica Metro). Calle José Victorino Lastarria itself has a number of popular, smart restaurants, while the **Plaza Mulato Gil de Castro** ⓘ *C Lastarria 307* has a mural by Roberto Matta and the **Museo Arqueológico de Santiago** and the **Museo de Artes Visuales** ⓘ *T638 3502, Tue-Sun 1030-1830, US$2 for both, free on Sun.* The former exhibits Chilean archaeology, anthropology and pre-Columbian art and the latter modern art. Occasional shows are put on in the square. On the street outside the Plaza are stalls selling objets d'art and old books.

The **Bellavista district**, on the north bank of the Mapocho from Plaza Italia at the foot of Cerro San Cristóbal, is the main focus of nightlife in the old city. Around Calle Pío Nono are restaurants and cafés, theatres, galleries and craft shops (most selling lapis lazuli). **La Chascona** ⓘ *F Márquez de la Plata 0192, Bellavista, T777 8741, www.fundacionneruda.org, Tue- Sun 1000-1800, US$4.65 guided visits only (available in English and French US$6.50).* This was the house of the poet Pablo Neruda and now houses the Fundación Pablo Neruda (see page 733).

➡Santiago maps
1 Santiago orientation, page 696
2 Santiago centre, page 697
3 Santiago west of centre, page 698
4 Bellavista & Lastarria, page 700
5 Providencia, page 702

5 El Giratorio
6 El Huerto
7 Oriental

Bars & clubs
8 Brannigan Pub
9 Phone Box Pub

The sharp, conical hill of **San Cristóbal**, to the northeast of the city, forms the **Parque Metropolitano** ⓘ *open daily 0900-2100, there are 2 entrances: from Pío Nono in Bellavista and further east from Pedro de Valdivia Norte. Getting there: by funicular: every few minutes from Plaza Caupolicán at the northern end of C Pío Nono (it stops on its way at the Jardín Zoológico, www.zoologico.cl, near the Bellavista entrance), US$3 return, Mon 1300-2000, Tue-Sun 1000-2000. By teleférico from Estación Oasis, Av Pedro de Valdivia Norte via Tupahue to San Cristóbal, the funicular's upper station, summer only, Mon 1430-1900, Tue-Fri 1230-1900, Sat-Sun 1030- 1930, US$3.50; combined funicular/teleférico ticket: US$5.25. A minibus service runs within the Parque Metropolitano from the Bellavista entrance, US$1, and taxi-colectivos run from here to the summit and, in summer, to the swimming pools (see Sports below). To get to Tupahue om foot from Pedro de Valdivia Metro station is about 1 km. Vehicle entry costs US$3.75.* It is the largest and most interesting of the city's parks. On the summit (300 m) stands a colossal statue of the Virgin, which is floodlit at night; beside it is the astronomical observatory of the Catholic University which can be visited on application to the observatory's director. Further east in the Tupahue sector there are terraces, gardens, and paths; in one building there is a good, expensive restaurant Camino Real (T232 1758, www.eventoscaminoreal.cl) with a splendid view from the terrace, and an Enoteca (exhibition of Chilean wines: you can taste one of the three 'wines of the day', US$3 per glass, and buy if you like, at bodega prices). Nearby is the Casa de la Cultura which has art exhibitions and free concerts at midday on Sunday. There are two good swimming pools at Tupahue and Antilén. East of Tupahue are the Botanical Gardens ⓘ *daily 0900-1800, guided tours available*, with a collection of Chilean native plants.

Providencia East of Plaza Italia, the main east-west axis of the city becomes **Avenida Providencia** which heads out towards the residential areas, such as **Las Condes**, at the eastern and upper levels of the city. It passes through the neighbourhood of Providencia, a modern area of shops, offices, bars and restaurants around Pedro de Valdivia and Los Leones metro stations (particularly Calle Suecia), which also contains the offices of Sernatur, the national tourist board. At Metro Tobalaba it becomes Avenida Apoquindo. Here, in **El Bosque Norte**, there are lots more good, mid-range and expensive restaurants.

Museo Ralli ⓘ *Sotomayor 4110, Vitacura (further east still), Tue-Sun 1100-1700, closed in summer, free*, has an excellent collection of works by modern European and Latin American artists, including Dali, Chagall, Bacon and Miró. **Museo de la Moda** ⓘ *Vitacura 4562, metro Escuela Militar, www.museodelamoda.cl, Tue-Sun 1000-1830, US$6.50 including optional guided tour, El Garage café open Mon-Fri 1000-1800*, is South Americas only fashion museum.

Southeast of the centre, in La Florida district, is the excellent **Museo Interactivo Mirador** (MIM) ⓘ *Punta Arenas 6711, Mirador metro (Line 5), T280 7800, www.mim.cl, Mon 0930-1330, Tue-Sun 0930-1830, US$6, concessions US$4*, a fun, interactive science and technology museum, perfect for a family outing. There is also an aquarium in the grounds.

Cementerio General ⓘ *www.cementeriogeneral.cl, to get there take any Recoleta bus from C Miraflores*. In the barrio of Recoleta, just north of the city centre, this cemetery contains the mausoleums of most of the great figures in Chilean history and the arts, including Violeta Parra, Víctor Jara and Salvador Allende. There is also an impressive monument to the victims, known as "*desaparecidos*" (disappeared) of the 1973-1990 military government.

Another memorial to the troubled Pinochet era is in the southeastern suburb of Peñalolén, the **Parque por la Paz** ⓘ *Av Arrieta 8401, www.villagrimaldicorp.cl; from Tobalaba metro take any bus marked Peñalolén heading south down Tobalaba, get off at Tobalaba y José Arrieta and catch a bus, or walk 15-20 mins, up Arrieta towards the mountains*. It stands on the site of **Villa Grimaldi**, the most notorious torture centre.

Santiago and around listings

Hotel and guesthouse prices

LL over US$200	**L** US$151-200	**AL** US$101-150
A US$66-100	**B** US$46-65	**C** US$31-45
D US$21-30	**E** US$12-20	**F** US$7-11
G US$6 and under		

Restaurant prices

TTT over US$12	TT US$7-12	T under US$6

Sleeping

Santiago centre *p699, map p697*

Note Check if breakfast and 19% tax are included in the price quoted.

LL-AL Fundador, Paseo Serrano 34, T387 1200, www.hotelfundador.cl. Helpful, charming, good location, pool, spa, bar, restaurant, internet.

LL-AL Galerías, San Antonio 65, T470 7400, www.hotelgalerias.cl. Excellent, large rooms, generous breakfast, good location, welcoming, check web page for special rates.

A-B Vegas, Londres 49, T632 2514, www.hotelvegas.net. Standard 3 star, convenient for centre in Barrio París Londres. Also rents apartments.

B Kapital, Merced 433, T638 1624. Small hotel with decent-sized rooms, quieter on upper floors. Some rooms with jacuzzis, good value.

B Plaza Londres, Londres 77, T633 3320, and at No 35, T638 3939, www.hotelplazalondres.cl. In the convenient París Londres district, a/c, internet, TV, good, but breakfast could be better.

C-D París, París 813, T664 0921, carbott@latinmail.com. Great location, good meeting place, luggage store, good breakfast extra. Phone in advance in summer.

C Res Londres, Londres 54, T638 2215, www.londres.cl. Old mansion with original features in perfect location near San Francisco church, without breakfast, cheaper without bath, pleasant common rooms, good, safe, laundry service, usually full, advance bookings in high season, arrive early. Recommended.

E pp **Andes Hostel**, Monjitas 506, T632 9990, www.andeshostel.com. In Bellas Artes neighbourhoods, dorm accommodation, **B-C** rooms with bath, bar downstairs with pool table, barbeque nights on roof terrace, kitchen facilities, well run.

E pp **Che Lagarto Santiago**, Tucapel Jiménez 24, T699 1493, www.chelagarto.com. Metro Los Héroes. HI hostel, part of South American chain. Free breakfast and internet. Shared rooms for 2 to 6; rooms with private toilet and fan, **C**. Comfortable common areas, excellent kitchen facilities, satellite TV, no laundry.

F pp **Plaza de Armas Hostel**, Compañía 960, Apt 607, T671 4562, www.plazadearmashostel.com. In dorms. **B-C** rooms with bath, bright with fantastic views over the Plaza, pleasant terrace, kitchen facilities, quieter rooms in an annex. A good choice.

West of the centre *p701, map p698*

A-B Happy House Hostel, Catedral 2207, T688 4849, www.happyhousehostel.cl. Also dorms **D** pp. One of the best hostels in the city, in a restored mansion with all mod-cons, spacious kitchen and common areas, internet, pool table, bar, sauna, jacuzzi, roof terrace, breakfast, free tea and real coffee all day, book exchange, English and French spoken, lots of information. Highly recommended.

C Hostal Río Amazonas, Rosas 2234, Barrio Brasil, T671 9013, www.hostalrioamazonas.cl.

Convenient, central, good, charming hosts, internet access, helpful.

C La Casa Roja, Agustinas 2113, Barrio Brasil, T696 4241, www.lacasaroja.cl. Doubles with and without bath (**D**), **F** pp in dormitory, huge mansion restored over 7 years, good kitchen, 2 bars, swimming pool, cricket net, lots of activities and tours, Spanish classes. Lively (use earplugs if you want a good night's sleep) and rooms may vary. Often recommended.

D La Casa Amarilla, Santo Domingo 2433-2445, T696 4070, www.casaamarillasantiago.com. Close to metro Cumming, 2 houses in nice neighbourhood with rooms for overnight and long-stay lets, spacious, use of kitchen, Wi-Fi, washing machine, large garden. Recommended.

D Moai Hostel, Riquelme 536, www.moaiviajero hostel.cl. With breakfast, shared bath, **E** in dorm, 3 rooms with bath (**C**), internet/Wi-Fi, airport transfer, kitchen, laundry service, book exchange, film library, Spanish classes, popular. Close to Santa Ana metro.

E pp **Hostelling Internacional Santiago**, Cienfuegos 151, T671 8532, www.hisantiago.cl (5 mins from Metro Los Héroes). **B** pp with bath, also rooms with shared bath (**C**). Modern, satellite TV, no cooking facilities, sterile, cafeteria, parking. See page 691 for **Asociación Chilena de Albergues Turísticos Juveniles**, www.hostelling.cl.

E pp **Luz Azul**, Santa Mónica 1924, T696 4856, www.luzazulhostel.com. Dorms for up to 10 and one double at **B**, Wi-Fi, mountain bike rental, book and music exchange, bar. Breakfast included.

Near bus terminals and Estación Central

A Tur Hotel Express, O'Higgins 3750, p 3, in the Turbus Terminal, T800-200350, www.turbus.cl. Comfortable business standard with breakfast, cable TV, a/c, free internet. Useful if you need to take an early flight as buses leave for the airport from here.

A Conde de Ansúrez, Av República 25, T696 0807, República metro, www.ansurez.cl. Convenient for airport bus, central station and bus terminals, helpful, safe, luggage stored.

C Res Mery, Pasaje República 36, off 0-100 block of República, T696 8883, www.residencialmery.virtuabyte.cl. Big green art deco building down an alley, most rooms without bath, all with single beds, quiet, helpful owners. Recommended.

South of the Alameda

C Hostal de Sammy, Toesca 2335, T689 8772, www.hostaldesammy.com. **F** pp in dorms. Good-value US-run hostel with decent common areas, table tennis, pool table, big-screen TV with hundreds of films, hearty breakfast included. Good info, fast internet, Wi-Fi, kitchen facilities, helpful. Recommended.

East of the centre and Bellavista

p703, map p700

A-B Del Patio, Pío Nono 61, Bellavista, T732 7571, www.hoteldelpatio.cl, a boutique design hotel in a 19th-century mansion, with breakfast, Wi-Fi. New boutique hotel in a refurbished old wooden building overlooking the lively Patio Bellavista. The location is great for bars, restaurants and nightlife, but at weekends it can be seriously noisy until late at night.

C Hostal Casa Grande, Vicuña MacKenna 90, T222 7347, Baquedano metro, www.hostal casagrande.cl. Cheaper without bath, labyrinthine, old high-ceilinged building, quiet, good value.

B Hostal Río Amazonas, Plaza Italia, Vicuña Mackenna 47, T635 1631, www.hostalrioamazonas.cl. In a restored mansion, with breakfast, Wi-Fi, good value, helpful (same owners as hostel at Rosas 2234, see above).

B El Patio Suizo, Condell 847, T474 0634, www.patiosuizo.com. Metro Parque Bustamante. Comfortable Swiss-run B&B in a quiet residential part of Providencia, TV, patio, internet, English, German spoken; Spanish classes. Recommended.

B-C Hostal Santa Lucía, Santa Lucía 168, T664 8478, www.hostalsantalucia.cl, opposite Cerro Santa Lucía. **E-F** pp in dorms. With breakfast, some rooms with bath, fine views from upstairs rooms and the roof terrace, Wi-Fi, some English spoken.

C Casa Condell, Condell 114, T209 2343, www.casacondell.cl, Salvador metro. Also 4-bed dorms, **D-E** pp. Pleasant old house, central, quiet, nice roof-terrace, with or without breakfast, kitchen facilities, free local phone calls, English spoken, good but baths shared between rooms can be a problem.

C Bellavista Hostel, Dardignac 0184, T732 8737, www.bellavistahostel.com. Breakfast included, European-style, **E** pp in dorms, sheets provided but make your own bed, kitchen facilities, free internet, good fun hostel in the heart of this lively area. Recommended.

C Hostal Forestal, Cnel Santiago Bueras 120, T638 1347, www.hostalforestal.cl. Doubles (some with bath) and dorms (**E-F** pp), with breakfast, on a quiet side street near the Plaza Italia. Comfy lounge with internet and big screen TV, barbeque area, kitchen facilities, information, English spoken.

E pp **La Chimba Hostel**, Ernesto Pinto Lagarrigue 262, Bellavista, T735 8978, www.lachimba.com. Popular backpacker place to stay with good facilities.

Providencia and Las Condes *p704, map p702*

LL Grand Hyatt Santiago, Av Kennedy 4601, Las Condes, T950 1234, http://santiago.grand.hyatt.com. Superb, beautifully decorated, large outdoor pool, gym, Thai restaurant.

LL Sheraton Santiago, Santa María 1742, T233 5000, www.sheraton.cl. One of the best, good restaurant, good buffet lunch, and all facilities. Note: another member of the Starwood brand, **W Hotels**, is to open a property in Las Condes (Isidora Goyenechea 3000, T947 2043) in 2009.
AL Atton, Alonso de Córdova 5199, Las Condes, T422 7979, www.atton.cl. Good value, comfortable, very helpful, internet in rooms, full disabled access. Recommended.
AL-A Orly, Pedro de Valdivia 027, Metro Pedro de Valdivia, T231 8947, www.orly hotel.com. Small, comfortable, convenient, Cafetto café attached with good value meals. Recommended.
A Vilafranca Petit Hotel, Pérez Valenzuela 1650, T235 1413, www.vilafranca.cl. Manuel Montt metro. High end B&B, small but impeccable rooms, quiet, cosy, pleasant garden, English spoken, Wi-Fi. Recommended.

A-B Chilhotel, Cirujano Guzmán 103, T264 0643, metro Manuel Montt, www.chilhotel.cl. Small, comfortable, family-run, includes breakfast, luggage store, airport transfer US$19.
B Marilú's Bed and Breakfast, Rafael Cañas 246 C, T235 5302, www.bedandbreakfast.cl. Comfortable, shared bath, good beds, English and French spoken, secure. recommended.

Longer stay accommodation

See the classified ads in *El Mercurio*; flats, homes and family pensiones are listed by district, or in *www.elRastro.cl*, or try the notice board at the tourist office. Rates for 2-bed furnished apartments in a reasonable neighbourhood start at around US$250 per month. A month's rent and a month's deposit are normally required. Estate agents handle apartments. Recommended apartments are **Santa Magdalena**, Helvecia 244, Las Condes, T374 6875, www.santamagdalena.cl. Well serviced.

Eating

Some of the best seafood restaurants are to be found in the Mercado Central (by Cal y Canto Metro, lunches only), or in the Vega Central market on the opposite bank of the Mapocho and on Av Cumming and C Reyes in Barrio Brasil. It is difficult to eat cheaply in the evening apart from fast food, so if you're on a tight budget, make the lunchtime *almuerzo* your main meal.

Santiago centre *p699, map p697*
ΨΨΨ-ΨΨ Da Carla, MacIver 577, T633 3739. Traditional Italian food, good.
ΨΨΨ-ΨΨ Majestic, Santo Domingo 1526, T695 8366, in hotel of same name (**AL-A**, www.hotelmajestic.cl). Excellent Indian restaurant, with a good range of vegetarian dishes.
ΨΨΨ-ΨΨ Opera Catedral, Jose Miguel de la Barra 407, Bellas Artes metro, T664 5491, www.opera catedral.cl. Very good, if expensive, French restaurant on the ground floor. Upstairs is a minimalist pub-restaurant, usually packed at night, serving fusion food at reasonable prices.
ΨΨ Faisán d'Or, Plaza de Armas. Good *pastel de choclo*, pleasant place to watch the world go by.
ΨΨ Lung Fung, Agustinas 715. Delicious oriental food, the oldest Chinese restaurant in Santiago, large cage in the centre with noisy parrots.
Ψ Bar Central, San Pablo 1063. Typical food.

¥ Bar Nacional No 2, Bandera 317. Popular, local specialities, big portions; also at Huérfanos 1151.
¥ Círculo de Periodistas, Amunátegui 31, p 2. Unwelcoming entrance, good value lunches.
¥ Confitería Torres, Alameda 1570. Traditional bar/restaurant, good ambience, live music Fri-Sat.
¥ Masticón, San Diego 152. Good service, excellent value, popular, wide range of fast food and traditional Chilean food.
¥ El Naturista, Moneda 846. Excellent vegetarian, "healthy portions", wide-ranging menu, as well as juices, beer and wine, closes 2100.
¥ El Rápido, Bandera, next to Bar Nacional No 2. Specializes in *empanadas* and *completos*, good food, good fun.

Cafés

Café Caribe and **Café Haití**, both on Paseo Ahumada and elsewhere in centre and Providencia. Good coffee, institutions for the Santiago business community.
Café Colonia, MacIver 133. Splendid variety of cakes, pastries and pies, fashionable and pricey.
Topanco, Huérfanos 609, T633 2635. Mexican style café-bar serving good coffee, homemade *media lunas*, English spoken, helpful owner.

West of the centre *p701, map p698*

¥¥¥-¥¥ Las Vacas Gordas, Cienfuegos 280, Barrio Brasil, T697 1066. Good value grilled steaks, nice wine selection, very popular so book in advance.
¥¥ El Hoyo, San Vicente 375, T689 0339. Closed Sun. Celebrated 100-yr-old *chichería* serving hearty Chilean fare.
¥¥ Los Buenos Muchachos, Cumming 1031, T698 0112, www.losbuenosmuchachos.cl. Cavernous hall seating over 400 serving plentiful traditional Chilean food, traditional Chilean dance shows at night. Very popular.
¥¥ Los Chinos Ricos, Brasil 373, on the Plaza, T696 3778. Good Chinese, popular with families on Sun lunchtime.
¥¥ Ostras Azócar, Gral Bulnes 37. Reasonable prices for oysters. Several other seafood restaurants in same street.

East of the centre: Bellavista and Lastarria *p703, map p700*

On C Lastarria are the busy, smart eateries: **Patagonia, Victorino, El Callejón de Mesas, Café El Observatorio, R** and **Zabo**.
¥¥¥ Cienfuegos, Constitución 67, Bellavista, T248 9080. Tue-Sat evenings. Reputedly one of the best restaurants in town serving Chilean/European fusion. Excellent food, but portions are small given the price. Service can be slow at weekends.
¥¥¥ El Otro Sitio, López de Bello 53. Peruvian, excellent food, elegant, good service.
¥¥¥ Les Assassins, Merced 297, T638 4280. Good French cuisine in small, family-run bistro, with decent wine list; good-value set lunches.
¥¥¥ Pasta e Vino, Constitución 299-317, Bellavista, T940 2800. New Santiago branch of renowned Valparaíso Italian restaurant in new boutique hotel, **LL The Aubrey**, www.theaubrey.com.
¥¥¥-¥¥ Los Adobes del Argomedo, Argomedo 411 y Lira, 10 blocks south of the Alameda, T222 2104, www.losadobesde argomedo.cl. Long-established traditional restaurant. Good Chilean food, floor show (Mon-Sat) includes *cueca* dancing, salsa and folk.
¥¥¥-¥¥ De Cangrejo a Conejo, Italia 805 y Bilbao, T634 4041, www.decangrejoaconejo.cl. Metro Parque, Bustamante or Salvador. Small but varied menu, ranging from crab to rabbit. The food is invariably excellent. Lovely garden. Deservedly popular. No sign outside.
¥¥¥-¥¥ Etniko, Constitición 172, Bellavista, T732 0119. Sushi and Thai restaurant that also functions as a lively bar later in the night. No sign, just knock.
¥¥ El Tablao, Constitución 110, T737 8648. Traditional Spanish restaurant. The food is reasonable but the main attraction is the live flamenco show on Fri-Sat nights.
¥¥ Eladio, Pío Nono 251. Good steaks, Argentine cuisine, excellent value, also has bingo.
¥¥ Venezia, Pío Nono, corner of López de Bello. Huge servings of traditional Chilean home-cooked fare (allegedly one of Neruda's favourite haunts), good value.
¥¥-¥ Olan, Seminario 96A-B. Excellent value, tasty Peruvian food in unpretentious surroundings. Another branch opposite at No 67, slightly higher prices.
Bombón Oriental, Merced 345, Lastarria, T639 1069. Superb Turkish coffee, arabic snacks and sweets.

Providencia *p704, map p702*

¥¥¥ El Giratorio, 11 de Septiembre 2250, p16, T232 1827. Revolving French restaurant offering great views and good food.

¥¥¥-¥¥ **A Pinch of Pancho**, Gral del Canto 45, T235 1700. Very good fish and seafood.
¥¥¥-¥¥ **Baco**, Nueva de Lyon 113, T231 4444. Metro Los Leones. Sophisticated French restaurant, good food, extensive wine list with many quality wines available by the glass.
¥¥¥-¥¥ **Oriental**, Manuel Montt 584. Excellent Chinese, one of the best in Santiago. Highly recommended.
¥¥ **El Huerto**, Orrego Luco 054, Providencia, T233 2690. Vegetarian. Open daily, varied menu, very good, popular. Recommended.
¥¥ **Café El Patio**, 2 branches in Providencia 1652 precinct, by **Phone Box Pub**. Tofu and pasta as well as fish dishes, pizza, tasty sandwiches, popular, good drinks, internet access, "centro artístico y artesanal". Very pleasant.

Cafés

For snacks and ice cream there are several good places on Av Providencia including **Coppellia**, No 2211, **Bravissimo**, No 1406, **El Toldo Azul**, No 1936, **Sveckova**, No 1652 precinct. Also **Salón de Té Tavelli**, drugstore precinct, Av Providencia 2124. Also **Sebastián**, Fuenzalida 26, Los Leones Metro, very good.

Providencia: Las Condes *p704*

This area has many 1st-class restaurants, including grills, serving Chilean (often with music), French and Chinese cuisine. They tend to be more expensive than central restaurants. Many are located on El Bosque Norte, near Tobalaba metro stop.
¥¥¥-¥¥ **Miguel Torres**, Isidora Goyenechea 2874, T242 9360. Tapas bar owned by the well-known Spanish winery.
¥¥¥-¥¥ **Puerto Marisko**, Isidora Goyenechea 2918, T251 9542. Renowned for seafood but also serves pasta and meat dishes, over 20 years of experience.
¥¥ **Le Fournil**, Vitacura 3841, T228 0219. Excellent French bakery and restaurant, popular at lunchtime.

Bars and clubs

For all entertainments, nightclubs, cinemas, theatres, restaurants, concerts, *El Mercurio* Online website has all listings and a good search feature, www.emol.com. Listings in weekend newspapers, particularly *El Mercurio* and *La Tercera*. Also *Santiago What's On*. Lively areas to head for are: **Barrio Brasil**, a number of bars and restaurants dotted around the Plaza Brasil and on Avs Brasil and Cumming. Popular with Chilean students (Metro República). **Bellavista**, good selection of varied restaurants, bars, clubs and salsotecas. Reasonable prices (Metro Baquedano). Avs Suecia and Gral Holley in **Providencia**, muchof it pedestrianized. Lots of bars and some restaurants, clubs and salsotecas (Metro Los Leones). **Plaza Ñuñoa**, a number of good bars dotted around the Plaza in the middle-class suburb of Ñuñoa. From Av Providencia Condell leads to Ñuñoa, 18 blocks, passing various small bars and restaurants on the way, eg at junctions with Rancagua and Santa Isabel, or take metro to Irrarrázaval. **El Bosque Norte**, chic bars and expensive restaurants for the Chilean jetset (Metro Tobalaba).

East of the centre: Bellavista *p703, map p700*

Back Stage, Patio Bellavista. Good-quality live jazz and blues.
Bogart, Av López de Bello 34. Disco-rock bar. 2 other similar bar son the same block.
Disco Salsa, Pío Nono 223. Good atmosphere, salsa and dance classes.
Jammin' Club, Antonia López de Bello 49. Reggae.
La Bodeguita de Julio, Constitución 256. Cuban staff and Cuban cocktails, excellent live music and dancing possible, very popular, free entry before 2300, very good value.
La Casa en el Aire, Patio Bellavista. Pleasant atmosphere, live music. Recommended.
La Otra Puerta, Pío Nono 348. Lively salsoteca with live music.
Tu Tu Tanga, Pío Nono 127. Busy at night, cheap beer, good value. Similar next door.

Providencia *p704, map p702*

Clubs in Providencia can be expensive; up to US$20 or more to get in.
Brannigan's Pub, Suecia 35, T232 7869. Good beer, live jazz, lively.
Golden Bell Inn, Hernando de Aguirre 27. Popular with expats.
Ilé Habana, Bucaré just off Suecia. Bar with salsa music, often live, and a good dance floor.
Phone Box Pub, Providencia 1670, T235 0303. Very popular with expats, serves numerous European beers. A good place to go if you are missing home.

Providencia: Las Condes *p704*
Country Village, Av Las Condes 10680. Mon-Sat from 2000, Sun from lunch onwards, live music Fri and Sat.
Flannery's Irish Geo Pub, Encomenderos 83, T233 6675, www.flannerys.cl. Irish pub, serving Guinness on draft, good lunches including vegetarian options, popular among gringos and Chileans alike.
Las Urracas, Vitacura 9254. US$20, free before 2300 if you eat there. Variety of cocktails.
Morena Pizza and Dance Bar, Av Las Condes 10120. Good sound system, live music at weekends, happy hour before 2200.
Tequila, Av Las Condes at Paseo San Damián. One of a few popular bar-restaurants in the area.

Ñuñoa
Basic Bar & Restaurant, Av Irarrázaval 667, www.basicbar.net. Mon-Fri opens 1730, Sat 1830, Sun 1600 till midnight or later. Drinks, Californian, Mexican and Italian food, music, events and sports on the big screen (nearest metro Irarrázaval, 3 blocks).
Club de Jazz de Santiago, José Pedro Alessandri 85, T326 5065, www.clubdejazz.cl. Regular live jazz in candle-lit bar, pleasant.

Entertainment

Santiago *p696, maps p697, p698, p700, p702*
There's a good guide to cinema in the free newspaper *publimetro*, given out at metro stations on weekday mornings.
Cinemas 'Ciné Arte' (quality foreign films) is popular. Cinemas specializing in this type of film include: **El Biógrafo**, Lastarria 181, T633 4435. **Casa de Extensión UC**, Alameda 390, T635 1994. **Centro Arte Alameda**, Av Bernado O'Higgins 139, T664 8821, www.centroartealameda.cl. **Cine Arte Normandie**, Tarapacá 1181, T697 2979. **Tobalaba**, Av Providencia 2563, T231 6630.
Many multiplex cinemas across the city show mainstream releases, nearly always in the original English with subtitles. Seats cost US$4-7 with reductions on Mon, Tue and Wed (elsewhere in the country the day varies). Some cinemas offer discounts to students and over 60s (proof required).
Classical concerts Free concerts are sometimes given in San Francisco church in summer. Arrive early for a seat.
Theatres **Teatro Municipal**, Agustinas y San Antonio, www.municipal.cl. Stages international opera, concerts by the Orquesta Filarmónica de Santiago, and the Ballet de Santiago, throughout the year. On Tue at 2100 there are free operatic concerts in the Salón Claudio Arrau; tickets range from US$10 for a very large choral group with a symphony orchestra, and US$12 for the cheapest seats at the ballet, to US$100 for the most expensive opera seats. Some cheap seats are often sold on the day of concerts.
Teatro Municipal de Nuñoa, Av Irarrázaval 1564, T277 7903, www.ccn.cl. Dance, art exhibitions, cinema, children's theatre. **Teatro Universidad de Chile**, Plaza Baquedano, T978 2203, www.teatro.uchile.cl, is the home of the Orquesta y Coro Sinfónica de Chile and the Ballet Nacional de Chile. There are a great number of theatres which stage plays in Spanish, either in the original language or translations.

Festivals and events

Santiago *p696, maps p697, p698, p700, p702*
Religious festivals and ceremonies continue throughout **Holy Week**, when a priest washes the feet of 12 men. The image of the Virgen del Carmen (patron of the Armed Forces) is carried through the streets by cadets on **16 Jul**.
On **Independence Day**, **18 Sep**, many families get together or celebrate in *fondas* (small temporary constructions made of wood and straw where people eat traditional dishes, drink *chicha* and dance *cueca*). During **Nov** there is a **free art fair** in the Parque Forestal on the banks of the Río Mapocho, lasting a fortnight.

Shopping

Santiago *p696, maps p697, p698, p700, p702*
Antique stores in Plaza Mulato Gil de Castro and elsewhere on Lastarria (Merced end).
Bookshops Book prices are high compared with neighbouring countries and Europe.
Apostrophes, Merced 324, www.apostrophes.cl, specializes in foreign-language publications.
In the precinct at Av Providencia 1652, Metro Pedro de Valdivia, are **Books**, No 5, T235 1205, second-hand English books, exchange for best deal; **Chile Ilustrado**, next door, No 6, T235 8145, chileil@tnet.cl, specializes in books relating to Chile, flora, fauna, history and anthropology (mostly in Spanish); **Librería Australis**, No 5,

travel books, maps, books on Chile (plus other books, New Age and handicraft shops).
Feria Chilena del Libro, Huérfanos 623. Largest bookstore in Santiago, good for travel books and maps; also at Nueva York 3, Agustinas 859, Mall Parque Arauco and Providencia 2124.
Le Comptoir, Shopping los Cobres local F3, Av Vitacura 6780, T218 7368, www.comptoir.cl. French books, good selection of literature, books ordered on request. **Librería Albers**, Vitacura 5648, Las Condes, T218 5371, www.texto.cl. Spanish, English and German, good selection, cheaper than most, helpful, also German and Swiss newspapers. **Librería Inglesa**, Huérfanos 669, local 11, Pedro de Valdivia 47, Providencia 2653, Vitacura 5950. Good selection of English books. **Librería Lila**, Providencia 1652, local 3. Mind/body/spirit specialists, best in Santiago in this field. **Librería Universitaria**, Alameda 1050, T695 1529, in unmistakable yellow building next to Universidad de Chile metro. Good selection of books in Spanish. **LOM Ediciones**, Estación Mapocho, Mon-Fri 1000-2000, Sat 1000-1400. Very good, large stock from its own publishing house (literature, history, sociology, art, politics), also bar and reading room with recent Chilean papers and magazines.

For cheap English books, try the second-hand book kiosks on San Diego between Eleuterio Ramírez and Cóndor, 4 blocks south of Plaza Bulnes.

Camping and outdoor equipment There are a number of 'hunting' shops on Bulnes 1-2 blocks south of the Alameda, with a basic range of outdoor equipment. Also try the **Mall Sport**, Av Las Condes 13451. **Andes Gear**, Helvecia 210, Las Condes, T245 7076, www.andesgear.cl. Good range of good-quality clothes and equipment. Imported camping goods from **Club Andino** and **Federación de Andinismo** (see below). **La Cumbre**, Av Apoquindo 5258, T220 9907, www.lacumbreonline.cl. Mon-Fri 1100-2000, Sat 1100-1600, Dutch run, very helpful, good climbing and trekking equipment. **Lippi**, Av Italia 1586, Nuñoa, T225 6803, www.lippi.cl. Santa Isabel Metro. Chile's premier outdoor equipment maker. Excellent-quality clothes, boots, tents, etc. **Mountain Service**, Santa Magdalena 75, T234 3439, Providencia, www.mountain service.cl. English spoken, tents, stoves, clothing, equipment rental. Recommended. **Parafernalia**, Huérfanos 1973 y Brasil. Second-hand gear. Recommended. **Peregrin**, del Arzobispo 0607, Bellavista, T02-735 1587. Salvador metro. Decent-quality locally made outdoor clothes. **Tatoo Adventure Gear**, Av Los Leones 81 and Dr Torres Boonen 686, Providencia, www.tatoo.ws, has all the best brands of outdoor gear. Also has shops in Ecuador, Peru, Colombia and Bolivia.

Those wishing to spend a reasonable amount of money on good-quality crafts can go to Pomaire (see page 719), where items from all over Chile are for sale at competitive prices. The gemstone, lapis lazuli, can be found in a few expensive shops in Bellavista but is cheaper in the arcades on the south side of the Plaza de Armas. Other craft stalls can be found in an alleyway 1 block south of Av O'Higgins between A Prat and San Diego; on the 600 to 800 blocks of Santo Domingo and at Pío Nono y Av Santa María in Bellavista.

Aldea de Vitacura, Vitacura 6838, T735 3959. Open 1000-2000. **Centro Artesanal Santa Lucía**, Santa Lucía metro, south exit. This is the best place to buy generic *artesanía* in central Santiago. Lapis lazuli can be bought here cheaply. Also has a wide variety of woollen goods, jewellery, etc. **Dauvin Artesanía Fina**, Providencia 2169, local 69, www.artesaniasvdauvin.cl. Los Leones metro. **Morita Gil**, Los Misioneros 1991, Pedro de Valdivia Norte, T232 6853. **Pueblito Artesanal Los Domínicos**, Apoquindo 9805, Las Condes, www.pueblito losdominicos.com. Metro Los Domínicos. The best upmarket craft fair in Chile. A good range of modern and traditional Chilean crafts from ceramics to textiles, a pleasant central piazza, and places where the artisans can be seen working on wood, silver, glass and so on. Although more expensive than, for instance, the market in Santa Lucía, this is a good and attractive option.
Maps See Driving in Chile box, page 690 and also page 693. **Librería Australis**, Av Providencia 1670, local 5. Local, regional and trekking maps.
Markets For food: **Mercado Central**, between Puente y 21 de Mayo by the Río Mapocho (Cal y Canto Metro) is excellent but quite expensive. There is a cheaper market, the **Vega Central**, on the opposite bank of the river. The **Bío Bío** flea market on C Bío Bío, Metro Franklin (follow crowds), on Sat and Sun morning is huge;

everything under the sun, lots of it having fallen off the back of a lorry.

Music **Billboard**, Providencia 2314 and at La Bolsa 75 (downtown). Good source for rock, jazz and alternative music. **Feria de Disco**, Paseo Ahumada and in numerous malls. The biggest chain, often sell tickets for rock concerts.

Shopping malls Numerous; generally open daily 1000-2100. **Alto Las Condes**, Av Kennedy 9001; **Apumanque**, Manquehue y Apoquindo; **Mall del Centro**, Rosas 900 block, just north of the Plaza de Armas. The most central. **Parque Arauco**, Av Kennedy 5413, north of Metro Escuela Militar; **Plaza Vespucio** at terminus of Línea 5, Bellavista de La Florida.

Wine **El Mundo del Vino**, Isidora Goyenechea 2931, T584 1173, www.elmundodelvino.cl. For all types of Chilean wines, good selection across the price range; also in the Alto Las Condes and Parque Arauco malls. **Vinopolis**, El Bosque Norte 038 and Pedro de Valdivia 036. Mon-Fri 0900-2300, Sat 1000-2300, Sun 1000-2200. Also at airport. Sells all types of Chilean wines, good selection across the price range.

▲ Activities and tours

Santiago *p696; maps p697, p698, p700, p702*

Cricket There is a burgeoning cricket league based around Santiago, see www.cricketchile.cl for more information. **La Casa Roja** hostel, see Sleeping, above, has a cricket net in its grounds.

Cycling For parts and repairs the only place to go is C San Diego, south of the Alameda. The 800 and 900 blocks have scores of bicycle shops with spare parts, new models and repairs much cheaper than you will find in Providencia or Las Condes.

Football Main teams including Colo Colo who play at the **Estadio Monumental** (reached by any bus to Puente Alto; tickets from Av Monumental 5300, Macul, T294 7300), **Universidad de Chile**, play at Estadio Nacional, Av Grecia 2001, Ñuñoa, Ñuble metro, line 5 (tickets from Av General Miranda 2094, Ñuñoa), and **Universidad Católica** who play at San Carlos de Apoquindo, reached by bus from Metro Escuela Militar, tickets from Andrés Bello 2782, Providencia, T231 2777.

Horse racing **Club Hípico**, Blanco Encalada 2540, highly recommended, entry to main stand US$5, every Sun and every other Wed afternoon. **Hipódromo Chile**, Av Hipódromo Chile 1715, Independencia, T270 9237, every Sat.

Skiing and climbing **Club Alemán Andino**, El Arrayán 2735, T232 4338, www.dav.cl. Open Tue and Fri, 1800-2000, May-Jun. **Club Andino de Chile**, Av Lib O'Higgins 108, T274 9252, clubandino@skilagunillas.cl, ski club (open 1900-2100 on Mon and Fri). **Federación de Andinismo de Chile**, Almte Simpson 77A (T222 0888, www.feach.cl). Open daily (frequently closed Jan/Feb), has the addresses of all the mountaineering clubs in the country and runs a mountaineering school. **Skitotal**, Apoquindo 4900, of 40-42, T246 0156, www.skitotal.cl, for 1-day excursions and good value ski hire. Equipment hire is much cheaper in Santiago than in ski resorts. Sunglasses are essential. For ski resorts in the Santiago area see below.

Swimming In Parque Metropolitano, Cerro San Cristóbal: **Antilén**, open in summer Wed-Mon 1000-1900, US$11, fine views, and **Tupahue**, large pool with cafés, Tue-Sun 1000-1900, entry US$9 but worth it (check if they are open in winter, one usually is). In **Parque O'Higgins**, T556 9612, 1330-1830 summer only, US$4. Olympic pool in **Parque Araucano** (near Parque Arauco Shopping Centre, Metro Escuela Militar), open Nov-Mar Tue-Sat 0900-1900.

Tennis Municipal courts in Parque O'Higgins. Estadio Nacional, Av Grecia y Av Marathon, has a tennis club which offers classes.

Tours A number of agencies offer day trips from Santiago. Typical excursions are to the Wine Valleys, Isla Negra (Pablo Neruda's seaside villa), visits to nearby haciendas and adventure tours such as whitewater rafting, rock climbing or trekking in the Cajón del Maipo, southeast of the city. Many agencies advertise in the **Sernatur** tourist office (see above).

Turismo Cocha, El Bosque Norte 0430, Providencia, Metro Tobalaba, T600-464 1000, www.cocha.com.

Adventure tours and trekking

Altue Expediciones, General Salvo 159, Providencia, T02-235 1519, www.altue.com. For wilderness trips including tour of Patagonia. Recommended.

Antarctic Expeditions, Ebro 2740, of 602, T481 6910, www.antarctic.cl. Expeditions to Patagonia and Antarctica from Punta Arenas on board their *'Antarctic Dream'*.

Azimut 360, General Salvo 159, Providencia, T235 1519, www.azimut360.com. Adventure and ecotourism including mountaineering all over Chile, low prices. Highly recommended.
Bikes and Wine, Pucara 4313A, Nuñoa, T209 1342, www.bikesandwine.cl. Interesting trips around the wineries of the Acongagua vally by bike.
Cascada Expediciones, Camino al Volcán 17710, San José de Maipo,T232 9878, www.cascada-expe diciones.cl. Specialize in activity tours in remote areas.
Catamaranes del Sur, Pedro de Valdivia Norte 0210, Providencia, T231 1902, tours of Chilean Patagonia. In Puerto Chacabuco: José Miguel Carrera 50, T351112, www.catamaranesdelsur.cl.
ChileAltitudes°, T9022 9522, www.chile altitudes.com. Affordable eco tours, from horse riding to skiing.
La Bicicleta Verde, Santa María 277, T570 9338, www.labicicletaverde.com. Sightseeing tours around the capital by bike. Also rents bicycles.
Patagonia Connection SA, Fidel Oteíza 1921, of 1006, Providencia (Metro Pedro de Valdivia), T225 6489, www.patagonia-connection.com. For excursion by boat Puerto Montt–Coyhaique/ Puerto Chacabuco–Laguna San Rafael. Also run Puyuhuapi Lodge & Spa, see page 841.
Reto Stöckli, T212 4665, www.swisschile tours.com. Good independent English- speaking guide offering tours around the Santiago area.
Santiago Adventures, Guardia Vieja 255, of 403, Providencia, T244 2750, www.santiago adventures.com. US-run, offering adventure day tours, wine tours, city tours, skiing and Patagonia.
Travel Art, Europa 2081, T378 3440, www.travelart.cl. Biking, hiking and multi-active tours throughout Chile.
Valle Nevado, Av Vitacura 5250, No 304, Vitacura, T477 7000, www.vallenevado.com. Skiing, snowboarding, trekking and mountain biking.

Transport

Santiago *p696, maps p697, p698, p700, p702*

Air

International and domestic flights leave from **Arturo Merino Benítez Airport** at Pudahuel, 26 km northwest of Santiago, off Ruta 68, the motorway to Viña del Mar and Valparaíso. The terminal has most facilities, including Afex cambio, ATMs, tourist offices which will book accommodation and a fast-food plaza. Left luggage US$9 per bag per day. Airport information T690 1752, www.aeropuertosantiago.cl.

Airport taxi: drivers offer rides to the city outside Arrivals, but the official taxi service is more reliable, if a little more expensive: US$18 to Pajaritos or Quinta Normal, US$22 to the centre, US$24 to Providencia, up to US$30 to Las Condes. Radio Taxi to airport is cheaper, eg US$20 from Providencia. Many hotels run a transfer service. Frequent bus services to/from city centre by 2 companies: **Tur-Bus**, from Terminal Alameda 0615-2400, US$3, every 30 mins; and **Centropuerto** (T601 9883, from Metro Los Héroes), US$2.50, 0640, 2330, every 15 mins. Buses leave from outside airport terminal and, in Santiago, call at Metro Pajaritos (not 0645-0815), Estación Central, Terminal Santiago and most other regular bus stops.

From airport you can take Tur-Bus to Pajaritos, US$2.80, and take metro from there. Companies that run a good shuttle service are: **Tur Transfer** (T677 3600, www.turtransfer.cl), **Delfos** (T601 0590, www.transferdelfos.cl) and **Transvip** (T677 3000, www.transvip.cl), US$10-12 shared vehicle, US$20-28 exclusive, depending on zone, 10% discount if you book return to airport with same company. Otherwise, to go to the airport, book the previous day.

Bus

Local The *Transantiago* (www.tran santiago.cl) system is designed to reduce congestion and pollution, but as yet (2009) has failed to do so. The city is divided into 10 zones lettered A to J. Within each zone, buses (known as *micros*) are the same colour as that given to the zone (eg white for zone A: central Santiago). Zones are linked by trunk lines, run by white *micros* with a green stripe. The system integrates with the metro. Buses display the number and direction of the route within the system. Payment is by prepaid *Bip* card only. A card costs US$3, to which you add however much you want to pay in advance. They are most conveniently bought at Metro stations. For a day or so it's probably not worth investing in a Bip card (just use the Metro), but for a few days it's good value. Long-term visitors can buy personalized cards, to prevent theft, etc. There are also *colectivos* (collective taxis) on fixed routes to the suburbs. Routes are displayed with route numbers. Fares vary, depending on the length of the journey, but are usually between US$1.50-2.50 (higher fares at night). **Taxis** (black with yellow roofs) are abundant and fairly cheap: minimum charge of US$0.35, plus US$0.15 per 200 m. Taxi drivers are permitted to charge more at night, but in the daytime check that the meter is set to day rates. At bus terminals, drivers will charge more – best to walk a block and flag down a cruising taxi. Avoid taxis with more than one person in them especially at night. Various Radio Taxi services operate (eg **Radio Taxis Andes Pacífico**, T912 6000, www.andespacifico.cl); rates are above those of city taxis but they are more reliable.

Long distance There are frequent, and good, interurban buses to all parts of Chile. Take a look at the buses before buying the tickets (there are big differences in quality among bus companies); ask about the on-board services, many companies offer drinks for sale, or free, and luxury buses have meals, videos, headphones. Reclining seats are standard and there are also salón cama sleeper buses. Fares from/to the capital are given in the text. On Fri evening, when night departures are getting ready to go, the terminals can be chaotic. There are 5 bus terminals: 1) **Terminal Alameda**, which has a modern extension called Mall Parque Estación (don't confuse with Mall Paseo Estación, see below) with good left luggage (US$3.40 per day), ATMs and internet, O'Higgins 3712, Metro Universidad de Santiago, T776 2424. All **Pullman-Bus** and **Tur-Bus** services go from here, they serve almost every destination in Chile, good quality but prices a little higher than others. **Tur-Bus** also has booking offices at Universidad de Chile and Tobalaba metro stations, at Av Apoquindo 6421, T212 6435, and in the Parque Arauco and Alto Las Condes malls for those beginning their journeys in Las Condes. 2) **Terminal Santiago**, O'Higgins 3878, 1 block west of Terminal Alameda, T376 1755, www.terminaldebusessantiago.cl, Metro Universidad de Santiago. Services to all parts of southern Chile, including the only service to Punta Arenas (48 hrs). Also international departures. Has a Redbanc ATM. 3) **Terminal San Borja**, O'Higgins y San Borja, 1 block west of Estación Central, 3 blocks east of Terminal Alameda, Metro Estación Central (entrance is, inconveniently, via a busy shopping centre, Mall Paseo Estación), T776 0645. Mainly departures to the Central Valley area, but also to northern Chile. Booking offices and departures organized according to destination. 4) **Terminal Los Héroes on Tucapel Jiménez**, just north of the Alameda, Metro Los Héroes, T420 0099. A smaller terminal with booking offices of 8 companies, to the north, the south and Lake District and some international services (Lima, Asunción, Montevideo, Buenos Aires, Bariloche, Mendoza). 5) **Metro Pajaritos** (Metro Línea 1), to Valaparaíso, Viña del Mar and places on the central coast; airport shuttle buses call here. It can be more convenient to take a bus from here than from the central terminals. Some long-distance buses call at Las Torres de Tajamar, Providencia 1108, which is more convenient if you are planning to stay in Providencia.

Note See the note under Taxis about not taking expensive taxis parked outside bus terminals, but note that official Tur-Bus taxis are good and reliable. Also check if student rates are available (even for non-students), or reductions for travelling same day as purchase of ticket; it is worth bargaining over prices, especially shortly before departure and out of summer season.
International buses Most services leave from Terminal Santiago, though there are also departures from Terminal Los Héroes. There are frequent services from Terminal Santiago through the Cristo Redentor tunnel to **Mendoza** in Argentina, 6-7 hrs, US$15, many companies, departures around 0800, 1200 and 1600, touts approach you in Terminal Santiago. Many of these services continue to **Buenos Aires**, 24 hrs, US$50, and many companies in Terminal Santiago have connections to other Argentine cities (eg **Bahía Blanca**, **Córdoba** and **San Juan**). For destinations like **Bariloche** or **Neuquén**, it is better make connections in Temuco or Osorno. There are also minibuses to Mendoza from the Terminal Santiago, US$20-25, 6 hrs, shorter waiting time at customs. To **Lima**, **Ormeño** (Terminal Santiago), Tue and Fri 0900, 51 hrs; it is cheaper to take a bus to Arica, a colectivo to Tacna, then bus to Lima.

Car

Car hire Prices vary a lot so shop around first. Tax of 19% is charged, usually included in price quoted. If possible book a car in advance. Information boards full of flyers from companies at airport and tourist office. A credit card is usually asked for when renting a vehicle. Many companies will not hire a car to holders of drivers licences in left hand drive countries unless they have an international licence. Remember that in the capital driving is restricted according to licence plate numbers; look for notices in the street and newspapers. Main international agencies and others are available at the airport (see Essentials, page 36, for web addresses).
Automóvil Club de Chile car rental from head office (see Maps), discount for members and members of associated motoring organizations.
Alameda, Av Bernado O'Higgins 4332, T779 0609, www.alameda rentacar.cl, San Alberto Hurtado metro, line 1, also in the airport, good value.
Rosselot, Francisco Bilbao 2032, Providencia, T381 2200, www.rosselot.cl. Also at airport, T690 1374. Reputable Chilean firm with national coverage.
Verschae, José Domingo Cañas 3018, Ñuñoa, T269 9437, www.verschae.com. Good value, branches throughout country.

Ferry and cruise operators

Navimag, Naviera Magallanes SA, Av El Bosque Norte 0440, p 11, Las Condes, T442 3120, www.navimag.com. For services from **Puerto Montt** to **Puerto Chacabuco, Puerto Natales** and **Laguna San Rafael**. M/n **Skorpios**: Augusto Leguía Norte 118, Las Condes, T477 1900, www.skorpios.cl. For luxury cruise out of Puerto Montt to **Laguna San Rafael** and adventure strips from Puerto Natales to Puerto Edén and the Campo Hielo del Sur.

Metro

See www.metrosantiago.cl. Line 1 runs west-east between **San Pablo** and **Escuela Militar**, under the Alameda (an extension is being built eastwards to Los Domínicos); Line 2 runs north-south from **Vesupcio Norte** to **La Cisterna**; Line 4 runs from **Tobalaba** on Line 1 south to **Plaza de Puente Alto**, with a branch (4a) from **V Mackenna** to **La Cisterna**; Line 5 runs northwest-southeast from **Quinta Normal** via **Baquedano** to **Vicente Valdés** on Line 4 (an extension being built westwards to Maipú). The trains are modern, fast, quiet, and very full at peak times. The first train is at 0600 (Mon-Sat), 0800 (Sun and holidays), the last about 2300 (2330 on Fri-Sat, 2230 on Sun). Fares vary according to time of journey; there are 3 charging periods, according to demand: the peak rate is US$0.80, the general rate US$0.70 and there is a cheaper rate at unsociable hours, US$0.65. The simplest solution is to buy a *tarjeta Bip* (see Local Buses, above), the charge card from which the appropriate fare is deducted. Transantiago bus services connect with the metro.

Train

All trains leave from **Estación Central (Alameda)** at O'Higgins 3322. The line runs south to **Rancagua**, **Talca**, **Chillán**, **Concepción** and **Temuco**. There are several trains a day as far as Chillán, but at the time of writing trains were not running beyond Chillán. Check at the time of travel for resumption of services, or take a bus from Chillán. There are frequent local Metrotren services to Rancagua and San Fernando. For reservations: T600-585 5000, open till 2230, www.terra-sur.cl. **Booking offices** Alameda O'Higgins 3170, Mon-Fri 0600-2205, Sat-Sun 0730-2205; Universidad de Chile metro, loc 10, Mon-Fri 0900-2000, Sat 0900-1400; Av M Montt 037, loc 14, Providencia, T346 7480; **Turismo Cocha**, Av Kennedy 5413, loc 150, Las Condes, T464 2209. Left luggage office at Estación Central, open till 2300. **Note** Schedules change with the seasons, so check timetables in advance. Summer services are booked up a week in advance.

Directory

Santiago *p696, maps p697, p698, p700, p702*

Airline offices **Aerolíneas Argentinas**, Roger de Flor 2921, Las Condes, T210 9300. **Air France**, Nueva Costanera 3420, Vitacura, T290 9330, www.airfrance.cl; **American Airlines**, Huérfanos 1199, T679 0000. **Continental**, Fidel Oteiza 1921, Suite 703, T200 2100. **Delta**, Isadora Goyenechea 2939, of 601, Las Condes, T280 1600. **Iberia**, Bandera 206, p 8, T870 1050. **LAN**, Huérfanos 926, T600-526 2000, Universidad de Chile metro, and Av Providencia 2006, p 1, Mon-Fri 0900-1810, Sat 1000-1245 (to avoid queues, buy tickets at the office in the airport). **Lufthansa**, Av El Bosque Norte 500, p 16, Las Condes, T630 1655. **Principal** (PAL), Huérfanos 811, T481 4307. **Sky Airline**, Fuenzalida 55, Providencia, and Huérfanos 815, T600-600 2828. **Banks** (Banks, open 0900-1400, closed on Sat. Exchange rates are published in El Mercurio and La Nación.) For Cirrus/MasterCard and Visa ATMs just look for the Redbanc sign, most commonly in banks, pharmacies or Copec petrol stations. **Banco de Chile**, Ahumada 251 and other branches, www.bancodechile.cl, minimum of formalities. **Casas de Cambio** (exchange houses) in the centre are mainly situated on Paseo Ahumada and Huérfanos (metro Universidad de Chile or Plaza de Armas). In Providencia several on Av Pedro de Valdivia. Use them, not banks, for changing TCs. Some casas de cambio in the centre open Sat morning (but check first). Most cambios charge 3% commission to change US$ TCs into US$ cash; check beforehand. **Exprinter**, Bombero Ossa 1053, good rates, low commission. **Afex**, Moneda 1148 (and 19 other branches), good rates for TCs. Avoid street money changers (particularly common on Ahumada, Bandera, Moneda and Agustinas): they pull any number of tricks, or will usually ask you to accompany them to somewhere obscure. The passing of forged notes and muggings are reported. **Cultural centres** **Centro Cultural Matucana**, Av Matucana 100 y Moneda, T682 4502, www.m100.cl. Art exhibitions, cheap films, sculpture workshop, café. **Instituto Chileno Británico de Cultura**, Huérfanos 554, T413 2350, www.britanico.cl. 0930-1900, except 1330-1900 Mon, and 0930-1600 Fri, has British papers and library (also in Providencia, Darío Urzúa 1933, Ñuñoa, Campo de Deportes 181, and Las Condes, Av Américo Vespucio Sur 631), runs language courses. **British Council**, Eliodoro Yáñez 832, near Providencia, T410 6900, www.britishcouncil.org/ chile.htm. **Instituto Chileno Francés de Cultura**, Francisco Noguera 176, Providencia, T470 8060, www.icf.cl. **Instituto Chileno Alemán de Cultura**, Goethe-Institut, Esmeralda 650, T571 1950, www.goethe.de/ins/cl/sao/deindex.htm. **Instituto Chileno Norteamericano de Cultura**, Moneda 1467, T677 7070, www.norte americano.cl. Good for US periodicals, cheap films on Fri. Also runs language courses and free Spanish/English language exchange hours (known as Happy Hours) which are a good way of meeting people. **Embassies and consulates** **Argentina**, Miraflores 285, T582 2500, www.embargentina.cl/. Consulate Vicuña MacKenna 41, T582 2608. Australians need letter from their embassy to get visa here, open 0900-1400 (visa US$25, free for US citizens), if you need a visa for Argentina, get it here or in the consulates in Concepción, Puerto Montt or Punta Arenas, there are no facilities at the borders. **Australia**, Isidora Goyenechea 3621, T550 3500, www.chile.embassy.gov.au, 0900-1200. **Austria**, Barros Errázuriz 1968, p 3, T223 4774. **Belgium**, Av Providencia 2653, depto 1103, T232 1070. **Bolivia**, Santa María 2796, T232 8180 (Metro Los Leones). 0930-1400. **Canada**, Nueva Tajamar 481, Torre Norte, p 12, T652 3800, www.dfait-maeci.gc.ca/latin-america/chile/embassy/embassy-en.asp (good information book). **France**, Condell 65, T470 8000, www.france.cl. **Germany**, Las Hualtatas 5677, T463 2500, www.santiago.diplo.de. **Israel**, San Sebastián 2812, p 5, T750 0500, http://santiago.mfa.gov.il. **Italy**, Clemente Fabres 1050, Providencia, T470 8400, www.ambsantiago.esteri.it. **Japan**, Av Ricardo Lyon 520, p 1, T232 1807, www.cl.emb-japan.go.jp. **Netherlands**, Apoquindo 3500, piso 13, Las Condes, El Golf metro, T756 9200, www.embajadadeholanda.cl. **New Zealand**, Av El Golf 99, of 703, Las Condes, T290 9802, www.nzembassy.cl. **Norway**, San Sebastián 2839, T234 2888, www.noruega.cl/info/embassy.htm. **Peru**, Bucarest 162, Providencia, T231 8020, www.conpersantiago.cl. **South Africa**, Av 11 de Septiembre 2353, p 17, Providencia, T231 2862, www.embajada-sudafrica.cl. **Spain**, 11 de Septiembre 2353, p 9, Providencia, T233 4070. **Sweden**, 11 de Septiembre 2353, p 4, Providencia, T940 1700, www.embajadasuecia.cl. **Switzerland**, Av Americo Vespucio Sur 100, p 14, T263 4211, metro Escuela Militar, www.eda.admin.ch/santiago. Open 1000- 1200. **United Kingdom**, El Bosque Norte 0125 (Metro Tobalaba), T370 4100, www.britemb.cl. Will hold letters, consular section (F370 4180, in emergency T9-233 3285) open 0930-1230. **United States**, Andrés Bello 2800, T330 3000, www.embajadaeeuu.cl.

Hospitals Emergency hospital at Marcoleta 377, T633 2051 (emergency), T354 3266 (general enquiries). **Hospital del Salvador**, Av Salvador 334 or J M Infante 551, T274 0093 emergency, T340 4000 general, Mon-Thu 0800-1300 and 1330-1645, Fri 0800-1300 and 1330-1545 (has **Vacunatoria Internacional** at Salvador 467, 4 blocks south of Salvador metro). Also **Vacunatoria Internacional**, Hospital Luis Calvo, MacKenna, Antonio Varas 360. **Clínica Central**, San Isidro 231-243, Santa Lucia metro, T463 1400, open 24 hrs, German spoken. **Emergency pharmacy**, Portugal 155, Universidad Católica metro, T631 3005. Consult www.farmaciasahumada.cl for other emergency pharmacies. **Note** If you need to get to a hospital, it is better to take a taxi than wait for an ambulance.

Internet Internet cafés are everywhere; usual price US$0.60-1 per hr. **Language schools** **Bellavista**, Calle del Arzobispado 0609, Providencia, T732 3443, www.escuelabellavista.cl. Group and individual classes, lodging with families, free activities. **Escuela de Idiomas Violeta Parra**, Triana 853, Providencia, T236 4241, www.tandemsantiago.cl. Courses aimed at budget travellers, information programme on social issues, arranges accommodation and visits to local organizations and national parks. **ILEE**, www.argentinailee.com, see Buenos Aires, Language schools, has a branch in Providencia. **Natalislang Language Centre**, Vicuña Mackenna 6, p 7, T222 8721, www.natalislang.com. Also has a branch in Valparaíso: Plaza Justicia 45, of 602, T032-246 9936. Many private teachers, including **Lucía Araya Arévalo**, T749 0706 (home), 731 8325 (office), 09-480 3727, lusara5@hotmail.com. Speaks German and English. **Carolina Carvajal**, Av El Bosque Sur 151, dpto Q, Las Condes, T734 7646, ccarvajal@interactiva.cl. Exchange library, internet access. Highly recommended. **Patricio Ríos**, Tobalaba 7505, La Reina, T226 6926. Speaks English. Recommended. **Patricia Vargas Vives**, JM Infante 100, of 308, T/F244 2283, www.escueladeespanol.cl. Qualified and experienced (US$14 per hr). Recommended. **Post offices** Plaza de Armas and Moneda between Morandé and Bandera. Also sub offices in Providencia at Av 11 de Septiembre 2092, Pedro de Valdivia 1781, Providencia 1466, Luis Thayer Ojeda 0146 and in Estación Central shopping mall. These open Mon-Fri 0900-1800, Sat 0900-1230. Poste restante well organized (though only kept for 30 days), passport essential, list of letters and parcels received in the hall of central Post Office (one list for men, another for women, indicate Sr or Sra/Srta on envelope); Plaza de Armas office also has philatelic section, 0900-1630, and small stamp museum (ask to see it). If sending a parcel, the contents must first be checked at the Post Office. Paper, tape, etc on sale. **Telephones** The cheapest call centres are on Calles Bandera, Catedral and Santo Domingo, all near the Plaza de Armas. International calls from here are ½ the price of main company offices. **Useful addresses** **Immigration** To extend tourist visa, or any enquiries regarding legal status, go to **Departamento de Extranjería**, Agustinas 1235, 1 block north of the Moneda, T550 2454, www.extranjeria. gob.cl. Mon-Fri 0900-1330. Visit for an extension of tourist visa or any enquiries regarding legal status. Expect long queues. Note that this can also be done at any provincial *extranjería* office. **Policia Internacional**: For lost tourist cards, see Accident and emergency, page 693.

Around Santiago

Pomaire

In this little town 65 km west of Santiago, good-quality handicrafts from all over Chile are for sale at prices cheaper than those in Santiago. The area is rich in clay and pottery can be bought and the artists can sometimes be seen at work. The town is famous for its *chicha de uva* and for its Chilean dishes, recommended.

Vineyards

Several vineyards in the Santiago area can be visited. The following are easily accessible and tours should be booked in advance. **Aquitania** ⓘ *Av Consistoral 5100, Peñalolen, T791 4500, www.aquitania.cl, bus D17 or taxi from metro Quilín*. Small vineyard making high-end wines, interesting tours in Spanish and English, with good tastings. **Cousiño-Macul** ⓘ *Av Quilín 7100, Peñalolén, east outskirts of the city, tours Mon-Fri, T351 4175, www.cousinomacul.cl, US$10*. **Concha y Toro** ⓘ *Virginia Subercaseaux 210, Pirque, near Puente Alto, 25 km south of Santiago, T476 5269, www.conchaytoro.cl, US$12, metro to Las Mercedes, then taxi or colectivo*. Short tours (three a day in Spanish, four daily in English). Professional but highly commercial. **De Martino** ⓘ *Manuel Rodríguez 229, Isla de Maipo, 40 km southwest of Santiago, T819 2062, www.demartino.cl, direct bus to Isla de Maipo from Terminal San Borja*. Quality tours in this high-end winery with an excellent reputation. **Undurraga** ⓘ *Santa Ana, 34 km southwest of Santiago, T372 2850, www.und urraga.cl, US$12, getting there: take a Talagante bus from the Terminal San Borja to the entrance*. Three tours daily. **Viña Santa Rita** ⓘ *Padre Hurtado 0695, Alto Jahuel, Buin, 45 km south, T362 2520, www.santarita.cl, US$10, getting there: take a bus from Terminal San Borja to Alto Jahuel*. Good tours in English and Spanish. The vineyard has a good restaurant and a private museum. Weekend tours only available to those with restaurant reservations (lunch US$40 per head).

Upper Maipo Valley

Southeast of Santiago is the rugged, green valley of the **Cajón del Maipo**. A road runs through the villages of San José de Maipo, Melocotón and San Alfonso, near which is the Cascada de Animas waterfall (a pleasant walk). At **El Volcán** (1,400 m), 21 km beyond San Alfonso, there are astounding views, but little else. From El Volcán the road (very poor condition) runs 14 km east to Lo Valdés and the nearby warm natural baths at **Baños Morales** ⓘ *from Oct, US$4*. About 12 km further east up the mountain are **Baños Colina**, hot thermal springs (free, horses for hire). This area is popular at weekends and holiday times, but is otherwise deserted. If visiting this area or continuing further up the mountain, be prepared for military checks. There are no shops, so take food (local goat's cheese may be sold at the roadside, or at farmhouses). North of Baños Morales, **Parque Nacional El Morado** ⓘ *Oct-Apr, US$4, administration near the entrance*, covers an area of 3000 ha including several high peaks, an exceptionally secluded and beautiful place with wonderful views.

Ski resorts

There are six main ski resorts near Santiago, four of them around the mountain village of **Farellones**. Farellones, on the slopes of Cerro Colorado at 2,470 m, only 32 km from the capital and reached by road in under 90 minutes, was the first ski resort built in Chile. Now it is a service centre for the three other resorts, but it provides accommodation, has a good beginners area with fairly basic equipment for hire and is connected by lift to El Colorado. Popular at weekends, it has several large restaurants. It offers beautiful views for 30 km across 10 Andean peaks and incredible sunsets. Daily ski-lift ticket, US$42, allows access to El Colorado; combined tickets for all four resorts and group tickets available. One-day return shuttles are available from Santiago, US$15; enquire **Ski Club Chile** ⓘ *Goyenechea Candelaria 4750, Vitacura (north of Los Leones Golf Club), T211 7341*.

El Colorado ⓘ *www.elcolorado.cl*, is 8 km further up Cerro Colorado and has a large ski lodge at the base, offering all facilities, and a restaurant higher up. There are 16 lifts giving access to a large intermediate ski area with some steeper slopes. Daily lift ticket US$42 (including Farellones ski-lifts); equipment rental, eg US$30 for full ski gear, US$34 for snowboard kit. **La Parva**, nearby at 2,816 m, is the upper class Santiago weekend resort with 30 pistes and 14 lifts, 0900-1730. Accommodation is in a chalet village and there are some good bars in high season. Good intermediate to advanced skiing, not suitable for beginners. Lift ticket, US$40-55.

Valle Nevado ⓘ *T02-477 7000, www.vallenevado.com*, is 16 km from Farellones. It offers the most modern ski facilities in Chile with 34 runs, 40 km of slopes and 41 lifts. The runs are well prepared and are suitable for intermediate level and beginners. There is a ski school and heli-skiing. Lift ticket US$44-59, equipment rental starts at US$39. In summer, this is a good walking area, but altitude sickness can be a problem.

Portillo ⓘ *www.skiportillo.cl*, 2,855 m, is 145 km north of Santiago and 62 km east of Los Andes near the customs post on the route to Argentina. One of Chile's best-known resorts, Portillo is on the Laguna del Inca, 5½ km long and 1½ km wide; this lake, at an altitude of 2,835 m, has no outlet, is frozen over in winter, and its depth is not known. It is surrounded on three sides by accessible mountain slopes. The 23 runs are varied and well prepared, connected by 12 lifts, two of which open up the off-piste areas. This is an excellent family resort, with a highly regarded ski school. Cheap packages can be arranged at the beginning of and out of season. Lift ticket US$40, equipment hire from US$32. There are boats for fishing in the lake (afternoon winds can make the homeward pull much longer than the outward pull). Out of season this is another good area for walking, but get detailed maps before setting out.

Lagunillas is 67 km southeast of Santiago in the Cajón del Maipo ⓘ *www.skilagunillas.cl*. Accommodation is in the lodges of the **Club Andino de Chile** (see Skiing page 713). Lift ticket US$30. It is more basic than the other ski centres in the region, with less infrastructure, but the skiing is good. Being lower than the other resorts, its season is shorter, but it is also cheaper.

Santiago to Argentina

The route across the Andes via the Cristo Redentor tunnel is one of the major crossings to Argentina. Before travelling check on weather and road conditions beyond Los Andes. See International Buses, page 716. Some 77 km north of Santiago is the farming town of **Los Andes**. There is a monument to the Clark brothers, who built the Transandine Railway to Mendoza (now disused). The town has several hotels. The road to Argentina follows the Aconcagua valley for 34 km until it reaches the village of **Río Blanco** (1,370 m). East of Río Blanco the road climbs until Juncal where it zig-zags steeply through a series of 29 hairpin bends at the top of which is Portillo (see above).

Border with Argentina Los Libertadores The old pass, with the statue of Christ the Redeemer (**Cristo Redentor**), is above the tunnel on the Argentine side. On the far side of the Andes the road descends 203 km to Mendoza. The 4 km long tunnel is open 24 hours September-May, 0700-2300 Chilean time June-August, toll US$5. Note that this pass is closed after heavy snowfall, when travellers may be trapped at the customs complex on either side of the border. The Chilean border post of Los Libertadores is at Portillo, 2 km from the tunnel. Bus and car passengers are dealt with separately. Bicycles must be taken through on a pick-up. There may be long delays during searches for fruit, meat and vegetables, which may not be imported into Chile. A Casa de Cambio is in the customs building in Portillo. Note that in 2010 major rebuilding works were taking place at this border, to both the road and facilities. Delays can be expected and, at the time of writing, all formalities were being undertaken on the Chilean side.

Around Santiago listings

For Sleeping and Eating price codes and other relevant information, see Essentials, pages 38-40.

Sleeping

Upper Maipo Valley *p719*

A Refugio Alemán Lo Valdés, 14 km east of El Volcán, Lo Valdés, T220 7610, 09-9-220 8525, www.refugiolovaldes.com. **E** per person in dorm. Stone-built chalet accommodation. Good restaurant. Lots of trekking and climbing information. Recommended.

A-B Cabañas Corre Caminos, Estero Morales 57402, Baños Morales, T269 2283, www.loscorrecaminos.com. Cabins sleeping 2-5 people. Food available, activities including horse riding and massages.

C Pensión Díaz, Manzana C, sitio 10, Lo Valdés, T861 1496. Basic, **F** for singles.

C Res Los Chicos Malos, Baños Morales, T624 1887, T09-9323 6424, www.banos morales.cl. Comfortable, fresh bread, good meals. There are also *cabañas* and a campsite.

Ski resorts *p719*

Farellones

LL Posada de Farellones, T201 3704, www.skifarellones.com. Cosy and warm, Swiss style, transport service to slopes, decent restaurant. Price for half board. Also **Farellones**, www.hotelfarellones.cl, and **La Cornisa**, www.lacornisa.cl, both **LL**.

B pp **Refugio Alemán**, Camino La Capilla 662, www.refugioaleman.cl. Shared rooms with shared bathrooms, rate includes half board. English spoken. Good value.

C pp **Refugio Universidad de Chile**, Los Cóndores 879, T321 1595, www.dta.cl/ refugio-u.htm. Shared rooms with half board. Standard *refugio*, often fills up with university students at weekends.

El Colorado and Valle Nevado

Apartment accommodation for daily and weekly rental in El Colorado. Also apartment and resort hotel facilities in **Valle Nevado**, where the 5-star resort has been completely renovated, boutique shops, gourmet dining, also has backpacker facilities, www.vallenevado.com.

La Parva

LL-L Condominio Nueva La Parva, reser-vations in Santiago, El Bosque Norte 0177, piso 2, T339 8482, www.skilaparva.cl. Good hotel and restaurant. 3 other restaurants.

Portillo

LL-AL Hotel Portillo, Renato Sánchez 4270, Las Condes, T263 0606, www.skiportillo.com. On the shore of Laguna del Inca. From lakeside suites with full board and fabulous views, to bunk rooms without bath. Self-service lunch, open all year, minibus to Santiago US$70. Cinema, nightclub, swimming pool, sauna and medical service.

Lagunillas

B pp **Refugio Club Andino**, T07-600 8057, or gmosulz@gmail.com, www.skilagunillas.cl. Cabins with full board.

Santiago to Argentina *p720*

LL Baños El Corazón, at San Esteban, 2 km north of Los Andes, T034-482852, www.termasel cora zon.cl. Full board, swimming pool; thermal baths extra, take bus San Esteban/El Cariño (US$0.50).

Transport

Pomaire *p719*

Bus From Santiago take the Melipilla bus from Terminal San Borja, every few mins, US$2 each way, 1 hr; alight at side road to Pomaire, 2-3 km from town, colectivos every 10-15 mins. It's easier to visit on a tour, often combined with Isla Negra, see page 733, or by car.

Upper Maipo Valley *p719*

Take line 4 metro to Floridazas Mercedes, from where there are regular bus and colectivo services as far as San Gabriel. Negotiate with the colectivo driver if you wish to go further.

Ski resorts *p719*

Bus From Santiago leave from Av Apoquindo 4900 (Escuela Militar Metro), daily from 0800-1000 in season, essential to book in advance, **Ski Total**, T246 6881, www.skitotal.cl (also runs ski programmes, lots of information), US$18 return to El Colorado and La Parva, US$16 to Valle Nevado, US$33 to Portillo (Wed, Sat).

Also **Ski Van**, 0830 from the Telefónica building, Plaza Italia, Baquedano metro, or McDonalds Canta Gallo, Av Las Condes 12107, T219 2672, www.skivan.cl, US$16.50 to El Colorado, La Parva, Farellones, US$18.50 to Valle Nevado. Reserve in advance; also for hotel or airport pick-up and minibuses to Portillo. It is easy to hitch from the junction of Av Las Condes/El Camino Farellones (YPF petrol station in the middle), reached by a Barnechea bus. Portillo is easily reached by any bus from Los Héroes terminal, Santiago, to **Mendoza**; US$10 to the resort. You may have to hitch back.

Santiago to Argentina *p720*

Bus Los Andes terminal is 1 block from the plaza. To **Santiago** US$3. Also to **Mendoza** (Argentina); will drop you off at **Portillo**.

Valparaíso and around

Sprawling over a crescent of forty-two hills (cerros) that rear up from the sea, Valparaíso, the capital of V Región, is unlike any other Chilean city. The main residential areas obey little order in their layout and the cerros have a bohemian, slightly anarchic atmosphere. Here you will find mansions mingling with some of Chile's worst slums and many legends of ghosts and spirits. It is an important naval base and, with the new Congress building, it is also the seat of the Chilean parliament. Pacific beaches close to the capital include the international resort of Viña del Mar, Reñaca, Concón and several others. On the same stretch of coast is the port of San Antonio. This coastline enjoys a Mediterranean climate; the cold sea currents and coastal winds produce much more moderate temperatures than in Santiago and the central valley. Rainfall is moderate in winter and the summers are dry and sunny.

Valparaíso → *Phone code: 032. Colour map 8, B1. Population: 300,000.*

First settled in 1542 (but not officially 'founded' until the end of the 20th century), Valparaíso became a small port used for trade with Peru. It was raided by pirates, including Sir Francis Drake, at least seven times in the colonial period. The city prospered from independence more than any other Chilean town. It was used in the 19th century by commercial agents from Europe and the US as their trading base in the southern Pacific and became a major international banking centre as well as the key port for US shipping between the East Coast and California (especially during the gold rush). Its decline was the result of the development of steam ships which refuelled instead at the coal mines around Concepción and the opening of the trans-continental railway in the United States and then the Panama Canal in 1914. It then declined further owing to the development of a container port in San Antonio, the shift of banks to Santiago and the move of the middle-classes to nearby Viña del Mar, but Valparaíso is now reviving. It is officially the Cultural Capital of Chile and much work is being done to renovate the historical centre and museums and to build new galleries. The historic centre and Cerros Alegre and Concepción are a UNESCO World Cultural Heritage site.

Ins and outs

Getting there To Valparaíso from the international airport at Pudahuel: take a bus to Pajaritos, US$3, cross the platform and take a bus to Valparaíso. To return to the airport, catch any Santiago bus and ask to be let off at the 'paradero de taxis' before the Cruce de Pudahuel. Taxis wait here to go to the airport for US$7 (about 7 minutes' ride, compared with an hour if you go into Santiago). Taxis run 0700-2000 (2300 in summer). Only take a taxi with an official Airport Taxi sticker (pirates overcharge). The long distance bus terminal is on Pedro Montt 2800 block, corner of Rawson, 1 block from Av Argentina. ➤➤ *See also Transport, page 730.*

Getting around Buses are frequent in El Plan, which is also served by a trolley bus (see below). Ascensores connect the lower and upper cities, as do taxis, colectivos and certain bus routes (fares and some routes are given under Transport, page 730).

Tourist offices Offices are located in the **Municipalidad** ⓘ *Av Argentina 864, Mon-Fri 0830-1400, www.ciudaddevalparaiso.cl*, but are not keen on attending to the public. Your best bet are the kiosks by the Plaza Sotomayor and the Plaza Aníbal Pinto, although these are also a bit of a mixed bag. There are also two information offices in the bus terminal, but these are privately run on a commission basis and hence do not give impartial advice. Don't be fooled by the old municipal tourist office sign. See also www.capitalcultural.cl.

Safety Robbery is an occasional problem in El Puerto and around the ascensores on Av Argentina. The upper outskirts of town, while offering amazing views, are not the safest places, particularly after dark. The poorer and rougher districts tend to be those furthest from the centre. Also, be aware that Calle Chacabuco (on which some hotels are located) is the pick-up point for local rent-boys.

Sights

Little of the city's colonial past survived the pirates, tempests, fires and earthquakes of the period. Most of the principal buildings date from after the devastating earthquake of 1906 (further serious earthquakes occurred in July 1971 and in March 1985) though some impression of its 19th century glory can be gained from the banking area of the lower town which is known as **El Plan**. This is the business centre, with once fine office buildings on narrow streets strung along the edge of the bay. Above, covering the hills ('cerros'), is a fantastic, multicoloured agglomeration of fine mansions, tattered houses and shacks, scrambled in oriental confusion along the narrow back streets. Superb views over the bay are offered from most of the 'cerros'. The lower and upper cities are connected by steep winding roads, flights of steps and 15 ascensores or funicular railways dating from the period 1883-1914. The most unusual of these is **Ascensor Polanco** (entrance from Calle Simpson, off Avenida Argentina, a few blocks from the bus station), which is in two parts, the first of which is a 160 m horizontal tunnel through the rock, the second a vertical lift to the summit on which there is a *mirador*. One of the best ways to see the lower city is on the historic **trolley bus**, which takes a circular route from the Congress to the port (US$0.50). Some of the cars, imported from Switzerland and the US, date from the 1930s. Another good viewpoint is from top of Ascensor Barón, near the bus terminal.

The old heart of the city is the **Plaza Sotomayor**, dominated by the former Intendencia (Government House), now used as the seat of the admiralty. Opposite is a fine monument to the 'Heroes of Iquique' (see page 763). Bronze plaques on the Plaza illustrate the movement of the shoreline over the centuries and an opening, protected by a glass panel, shows parts of the original quay, uncovered when a car park was being excavated. The modern passenger quay is one block away (with poor quality, expensive handicraft shops) and nearby is the railway station for trains to Viña del Mar and Limache. The streets of El Puerto run on either side from Plaza Sotomayor. Serrano runs northwest for two blocks to the Plaza Echaurren, the oldest plaza in Valparaíso, once the height of elegance, today the home of sleeping drunks. Nearby stands the stucco church of **La Matriz**, built in 1842 on the site of the first church in the city. Remnants of the old colonial city can be found in the hollow known as El Puerto, grouped round La Matriz. **Museo del Mar Almirante Cochrane** ⓘ *Merlet 195, Tue-Sun 1000-1800, free*, has temporary exhibitions and has good views over the port. Take Ascensor Cordillera from C Serrano, off Plaza Sotomayor, to Cerro Cordillera; at the top, on Plazuela Eleuterio Ramírez, take C Merlet to the left (a slightly dodgy area).

Further northwest, along Bustamante lies the Plaza Aduana from where Ascensor Artillería rises to the bold hill of **Cerro Artillería**, crowned by a park, the huge Naval Academy and the **Museo Naval** ⓘ *www.museonaval.cl, Tue-Sun 1000-1730, US$1.30*, with naval history 1810-1880 and exhibitions on Chile's two naval heroes: Lord Cochrane and Arturo Prat. Avenida

Altamirano runs along the coast at the foot of Cerro Playa Ancha to **Las Torpederas**, a small bathing beach. The **Faro de Punta Angeles**, on a promontory just beyond Las Torpederas, was the first lighthouse on the West Coast (30-40 minutes' walk from Cerro Artillería).

Both **Cerro Concepción** and **Cerro Alegre** have fine architecture and scenic beauty. Artists and students have long lived there, lending them a slightly bohemian feel, and the cerros are becoming deservedly very popular with visitors. A signed, 2-km walk starts at the top of Ascensor Turri (Cerro Concepción), leading to Paseo Mirador Gervasoni and Calle Pupudo through a labyrinth of narrow streets and stairs (the municipal tourist office has a good map). Two museums on these hills are: **Museo Municipal de Bellas Artes** ⓘ *Paseo Yugoslavo, Cerro Alegre; take Ascensor El Peral from Plaza de la Justicia, off Plaza Sotomayor. Tue-Sun 1000-1800, free*. Housed in the impressive Palacio Baburizza, it displays Chilean landscapes and seascapes and some modern paintings by Chilean and contemporary artists. **Casa de Lukas** ⓘ *Paseo Mirador Gervasoni 448, Cerro Concepción, www.lukas.cl, US$2, Tue-Sun 1100-1900*, is a beautiful villa dedicated to the work of one of Chile's most famous caricaturists; recommended.

1 Valparaíso

➡ Valparaíso maps
1 **Valparaíso, page 724**
2 El Puerto, Cerros Alegre & Concepción, page 726

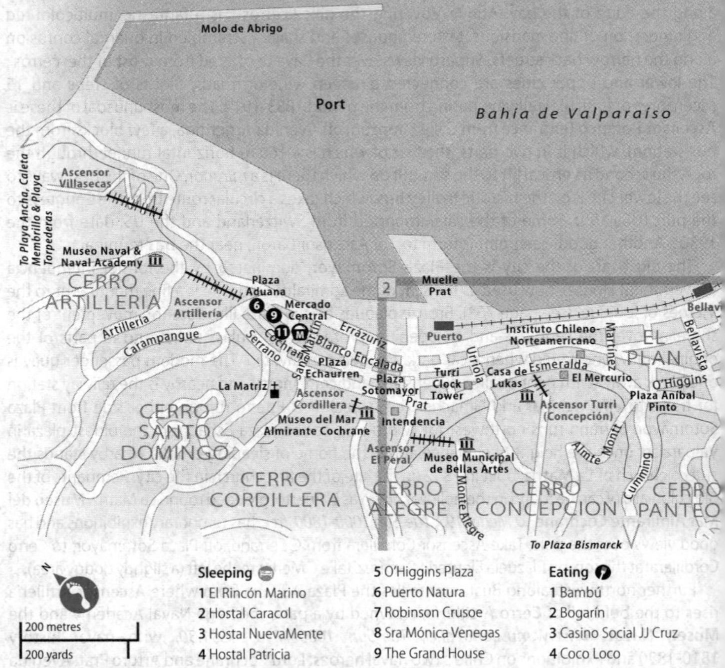

Sleeping
1 El Rincón Marino
2 Hostal Caracol
3 Hostal NuevaMente
4 Hostal Patricia
5 O'Higgins Plaza
6 Puerto Natura
7 Robinson Crusoe
8 Sra Mónica Venegas
9 The Grand House

Eating
1 Bambú
2 Bogarín
3 Casino Social JJ Cruz
4 Coco Loco

Southeast of Plaza Sotomayor Calles Prat, Cochrane and Esmeralda run through the old banking and commercial centre to Plaza Aníbal Pinto, around which are several of the city's oldest bars and cafés. On Esmeralda, just past the Turri Clock Tower and Ascensor is the building of **El Mercurio de Valparaíso**, the world's oldest Spanish-language newspaper still in publication, first published in 1827. Further east is the Plaza Victoria with the Cathedral. Near Plaza Victoria is the **Museo de Historia Natural**ⓘ *Condell 1546, T225 7441, www.dibam.cl/sdm_mhn_valpo, Tue-Fri 1000-1300, 1400-1800, Sat-Sun 1000-1400* and **Galería Municipal de Arte** ⓘ *Condell 1550, T222 0062, Mon-Sat 1000-1900, free*both in 19th century Palacio Lyon. Above Plaza Victoria on Cerro Bellavista is the **Museo al Cielo Abierto**, a collection of 20 street murals on the exteriors of buildings, designed by 17 of Chile's most distinguished contemporary artists. It is reached by the Ascensor Espíritu Santo at the end of Calle Huito, or by walking downhill from Casa "La Sebastiana", former house of **Pablo Neruda** ⓘ *Ferrari 692, Av Alemania, Altura 6900 on Cerro Florida, T225 6606, www.fundacionneruda.org/informaciones_sebastiana.htm, Tue-Sun 1010-1800, Jan-Feb 1030-1850, US$5; getting there: bus 612 (O) from Av*

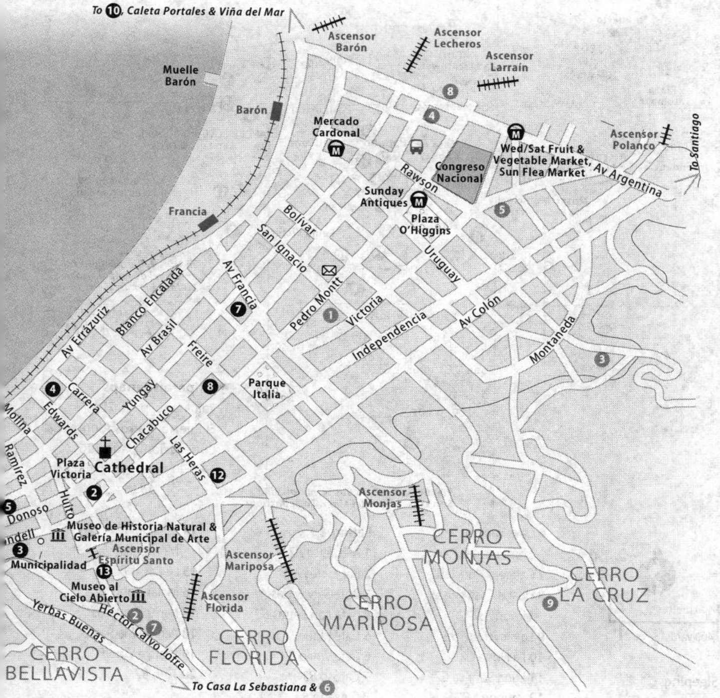

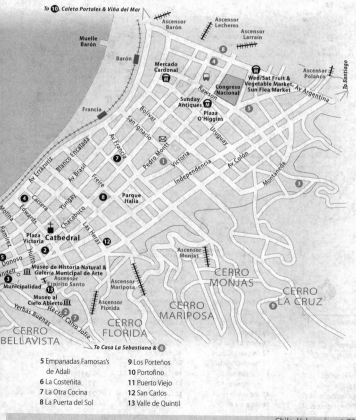

5 Empanadas Famosas's de Adali
6 La Costeñita
7 La Otra Cocina
8 La Puerta del Sol
9 Los Porteños
10 Portofino
11 Puerto Viejo
12 San Carlos
13 Valle de Quintil

Argentina, US$0.65, or colectivo from Plazuela Ecuador, US$0.65. This has interesting displays, guides in English and German, wonderful views and is worth a visit (see also his house at Isla Negra, below). It has an art gallery and a small café. East of Plaza Victoria, reached by following Calle Pedro Montt is Plaza O'Higgins (antiques market on Sunday mornings – see Shopping), which is dominated by the huge square arch of the imposing new Congreso Nacional. Opposite is the bus terminal, while four blocks north on Errázuriz is the Barón train station and the **Muelle Barón**, the new terminal for cruise ships. The end of this pier gives a good view of Valparaíso's amphitheatre-like setting. Just off the pier is a small colony of sea-lions and at the pier's base kayaks can be hired (www.puertodeportivo.cl). A new coastal

2 El Puerto, Cerros Alegre & Concepción

Sleeping
1 Acontraluz *C2*
2 Backpackers House El Yoyo *B3*
3 Brighton *B2*
4 Casa Aventura *B2*
5 Casa Higueras *B1*
6 Casa Thomas Somerscales *C2*
7 Catalejo House *B2*
8 Hostal Casa Verde Limón *B3*
9 La Bicyclette *B2*
10 La Nona *C2*
11 Luna Sonrisa *C2*
12 Patiperro *B2*
13 Puerta de Alcalá *B3*
14 Templeman Apartments *B2*
15 The Yellow House *B2*
16 Ultramar *B3*

Eating
1 Alegretto *B2*
2 Bar Inglés *A2*
3 Bote Salvavidas *A1*
4 Café con Letras *B2*
5 Café Riquet *A3*
6 Café Vinilo *B2*
7 Caruso *B3*
8 Cinzano *B3*
9 Color Café *B2*
10 El Desayunador *B2*
11 El Dominó *B3*
12 La Colombina *B1*
13 La Concepción *B2*
14 Le Filou de Montpellier *B2*
15 Le Pastis *B2*
16 Malandrino *C2*
17 Mastodonte *A2*
18 Pan de Magia *C2*
19 Pasta e Vino *B2*
20 Turri *B2*

Bars & clubs
21 El Irlandés *A3*
22 La Piedra Feliz *A2*
23 La Playa *B1*

walkway runs northeast from here past several small beaches as far as **Caleta Portales**, a small fishing harbour with several seafood restaurants almost at the edge of Viña del Mar.

Small boats make 30-minute tours of the harbour from Muelle Prat, near Plaza Sotomayor (Spanish only). US$3 pp, wait for boat to fill up or pay US$18 to hire a whole boat, recommended if sunny.

Valparaíso listings

For Sleeping and Eating price codes and other relevant information, see Essentials, pages 38-40.

Sleeping

Valparaíso *p722, maps p724 and p726*

El Plan

A Puerta de Alcalá, Pirámide 524, T222 7478, www.hotelpuertadealcala.cl. Good 3-star standard of facilities, reasonable restaurant.

Cerros Alegre and Concepción

The best option is to stay on one of the Cerros, eg Alegre or Concepción. There are new hostels opening all the time. Those in the following list are recommended.

LL-L Acontraluz, San Enrique 473, Cerro Alegre, T211 1320, www.hotel acontraluz.cl. Probably the best of the new boutique hotels here. Rooms facing the sea have balconies with tremendous views. Buffet breakfast. Bright, Victorian house fully restored with attention to detail and no expense spared. English, French, Russian spoken.

LL-L Casa Higueras, Higuera 133, Cerro Alegre, T249 7900, www.hotelcasahigueras.cl. Small, elegant hotel on 5 levels, a variety of rooms, good views, fine restaurant, spa, sauna, pool and gardens.

L-AL Casa Thomas Somerscales, San Enrique 446, Cerro Alegre, T233 1006, www.hotels omerscales.cl. Spacious rooms in a restored mansion with period furniture. Basic English spoken, Wi-Fi, top-floor rooms lovely views.

AL-A Brighton, Paseo Atkinson 151, Co Concepción, T222 3513, www.brighton.cl. New building in traditional style, good views, small rooms beautifully furnished, live tango and bolero music in the bar at weekends, good restaurant (not cheap).

A Templeman Apartments, Pierre Loti 65B, Co Concepción, T225 7067, www.derementeria.cl/apart. Stylish self-contained apartments, peaceful.

B La Nona, Galos 660, Cerro Alegre, T249 5706, www.bblanona.com. Comfortable, welcoming B&B, some rooms with bath, plenty of information and activities, English spoken, Wi-Fi, use of kitchen. Recommended.

B-C Luna Sonrisa, Templeman 833, Cerro Alegre, T273 4117, www.lunasonrisa.cl. **D** singles, **E** pp in shared rooms. Some rooms with bath. Newly restored, bright, comfortable, large kitchen, lots of information, excellent breakfast including wholemeal bread and real coffee, Wi-Fi, tours arranged, English and French spoken, friendly and helpful, and run by the author of the *Chile Handbook*.

C Casa Aventura, Pasaje Gálvez 11, off C Urriola, Cerro Concepción, T275 5963, www.casaventura .cl. Dorms **F** pp. One of Valparaíso's longest established backpackers' hostels, in a restored traditional house, with good breakfast, German and English spoken, tours, helpful, deservedly popular, informative, kitchen facilities.

C La Bicyclette, Almte Montt 213, Cerro Alegre, T222 2215, www.bicyclette.cl. Basic, bright rooms, **E** pp in shared rooms, shared bath, book exchange, lovely patio, French run, rents bicycles.

C Patiperro, Templeman 657, T317 3153, www.patiperrohostel.cl/. Family-run, doubles and big dorms, shared facilities, use of kitchen, lots of movies, Wi-Fi, lockers, also in **HoLa** group, good choice.

D Hostal Casa Verde Limón, Subida Cumming, El Descanso 196, Cerro Cárcel, T212 1699, http://casaverdelimon.blogspot.com/. Double rooms and a dorm, shared bath, use of kitchen, TV, Wi-Fi, in **HoLa** group.

Other Cerros

L-B Ultramar, Pérez 173, Cerro Cárcel, T221 0000, www.hotelultramar.cl. Boutique hotel in a converted Italianate building (1907), modern design, buffet breakfast, free internet, café, attentive staff. Rooms are spacious with great views but may get stuffy in summer.

AL-A Puerto Natura, Héctor Calvo 850, Cerro Bellavista, T222 4405, www.puertonatura.cl. In a restored mansion set in large grounds with fruit trees and small swimming pool, excellent views. There is also a holistic centre with sauna, massages and yoga classes. Recommended.

LL-AL Robinson Crusoe, Héctor Calvo Jofre 389, Co Bellavista, T249 5499, www.hotels.tk/robinson. Boutique hotel with beautiful rooms, some with shared bath, spectacular views from lovely roof terrace, peaceful, restaurant.

A The Grand House, Federico Varela 25, Cerro La Cruz, T221 2376, www.thegrandhouse.cl. Charming house, almost Victorian decor, excellent breakfast, "a true gem".

B-C Hostal Caracol, Héctor Calvo 371, Cerro Bellavista, T239 5817, www.hostal caracol.cl. **E** pp in dorms. On a quiet residential hill. Pleasant patio and barbeque area, heating. English spoken. A good choice.

C Catalejo House, Bernardo Vero 870, Cerro San Juan de Dios, T225 9150, www.catalejohouse.com. Cheaper with shared bath, breakfast, internet, cable TV, good view, good reports.

B The Yellow House, Capitán Muñoz Gamero 91, Cerro Artillería, T233 9435, www.theyellowhouse.cl. One of several hostels and B&Bs in this area, tucked away on a cobbled side street. Quiet, Australian-run, some rooms with extensive views, good showers. Recommended.

E Backpackers House El Yoyo, Subida Ecuador 355, Co Yungay, T259 1087, ktyoyo@hotmail.com. **F** pp in dorms, a bit cramped, with breakfast, kitchen facilities, new bar area, a friendly and fun place for younger crowd, English spoken.

Near the terminal

A O'Higgins Plaza, Retamo 517, T223 5616, www.restaurantohiggins.cl. A good business standard, next to the Congress building but not the most interesting part of town.

C-D El Rincón Marino, San Ignacio 454, T222 5815, www.rinconmarino.cl. Uninspiring location, but good value and only 4 blocks from the bus terminal.

C-D Hostal Patricia,12 de Febrero 315, T222 0290, http://hostalpatricia.cl/. **F** pp in dorms, shared hot showers, family accommodation, use of kitchen, good local knowledge, internet, Wi-Fi, closed off season.

D Hostal NuevaMente, Pocuro 1088, T317 6125, www.hostalnuevamente.cl. Beautiful old hostel with big, light rooms, about 15 mins' walk from centre. Run by a helpful young couple, good local information, some English spoken, use of kitchens, good breakfast included, Wi-Fi, movies, tours, bike hire.

F pp **Sra Mónica Venegas**, Av Argentina 322, casa B, T221 5673, 2 blocks from bus terminal. Popular, French spoken, welcoming, helpful, Wi-Fi.

Eating

Valparaíso *p722, maps p724 and p726*

El Plan

TTT-TT Bote Salvavidas, by Muelle Prat. Elegant fish restaurant overlooking the port.

TTT Coco Loco, Blanco 1781 pisos 21 y 22, T222 7614. Plush revolving restaurant 70 m above the bay, extensive menu.

TT Bar Inglés, Cochrane 851 (entrance also on Blanco Encalada), T221 4625. Historic bar dating from the early 1900s, a chart shows the ships due in port. Good food and drink. Recommended.

TT La Costeñita, Blanco 86. Good seafood, with incredibly kitsch décor.

TT La Otra Cocina, Yungay 2250, near Francia. Good seafood, cosy, good service.

TT Los Porteños, Valdivia 169 and Cochrane 102. A seafood favourite, terse service but good food.

TT At Caleta Membrillo, 2 km northwest of Plaza Sotomayor (take any Playa Ancha bus), there are several good fish restaurants including **Club Social de Pescadores**, Altamirano 1480, good, and **El Membrillo**.

TT Cinzano, Plaza Aníbal Pinto 1182, T221 3043. The oldest bar in Valparaíso, also serving food. Flamboyant live music at weekends, noted for tango (no dancing by guests allowed). Service can be awful.

T Bambú, Independencia 1790, T223 4216. Closed Sun. Vegetarian lunches only.

T Casino Social JJ Cruz, Condell 1466, T225 0319. Valparaíso's most traditional restaurant/museum, famous for its chorillanas, open all night, very popular.

T El Dominó, Cumming 67. Traditional, serves empanadas, chorillanas, etc.

T Empanadas Famosas's de Adali, S Donoso 1381. Some of the best empanadas in Valparaíso with a wide range of fillings.

¥ **La Puerta del Sol**, Montt 2033, T223 5158. Traditional Chilean dishes, great chips served outside.

¥ **Mastodonte**, Esmeralda 1139. No nonsense, very good value, traditional food in incredibly kitsch surroundings. Excellent service and cheap locally brewed draft beer.

¥ **Puerto Viejo**, Cochrane y Valdivia. Very good-value set lunch fish dishes.

¥ **San Carlos**, Las Heras y Independencia. Traditional family-run restaurant with lots of character that hasn't changed in years. Lunch only. Good food guaranteed, always full of locals. Recommended.

There are good cheap seafood lunches upstairs at both main markets, Mercado Central by Plaza Echaurren and Mercado Cardonal behind the bus terminal.

Bogarín, Plaza Victoria 1670. Great juices and snacks.

Café Riquet, Plaza Aníbal Pinto. One of the oldest cafés in Valparaíso, good coffee and breakfast.

Cerros Alegre and Concepción

¥¥¥ **La Concepción**, Papudo 541, Cerro Concepción, T2498192. Creative food, beautifully presented and well served, magnificient views.

¥¥¥ **Le Pastis**, Concepción 280, Cerro Concepción, T249 3319. New bistro serving exquisite, if expensive French classics.

¥¥¥-¥¥ **La Colombina**, Paseo Yugoeslavo 15, Cerro Alegre, T223 6254. The most traditional of the area's restaurants. Good food, wide range of wines, fine views, especially from the top floor.

¥¥¥-¥¥ **Pasta e Vino**, Templeman 352, Cerro Concepción, T249 6187. Wonderfully inventive, tasty pasta dishes, haughty service. Advance booking essential, closed Mon.

¥¥¥-¥¥ **Turri**, Templeman 147, Cerro Concepción, T225 9198. Reasonable food, wonderful views, a bit of a tourist trap.

¥¥ **Alegretto**, Pilcomayo 529, Cerro Concepción. Lively British owned pizzería, exotic but very tasty toppings, can get busy.

¥¥ **Caruso**, Cumming 201, Cerro Cárcel, T259 4039, www.caruso.cl. Mostly seafood and fish with a Peruvian touch. Uses inshore fish not found in other restaurants. Good wine list and regular tastings.

¥¥ **Café Vinilo**, Almte Montt 448, T223 0665. Inventive lunchtime menus with gourmet interpretations of traditional Chilean dishes. Also a lively bar at night.

¥¥ **Le Filou de Montpellier**, Almte Montt 382, T222 4663. French-run, set lunch menu deservedly popular, also open weekday evenings.

¥¥ **Malandrino**, Almirante Montt 532, Cerro Alegre. Traditional pizzas baked in a clay oven using mostly organic ingredients. Cosy atmosphere. Popular with locals as well as tourists.

Café con Letras, Almte Montt 316, Co Concepción. Intimate café serving good coffee and snacks, soup in winter, lots of reading material available.

Color Café, Papudo 526, Co Concepción. Cosy arty café serving tea and real coffee, fresh juice, good cakes, snacks and all-day breakfasts, regular live music, art exhibits, local art and craft for sale.

El Desayunador, Almte Montt 399, Cerro Alegre T275 5735. Breakfast bar open early. Wide range of teas, real coffee, cakes, also serves vegetarian lunches.

Pan de Magia, Almte Montt 738 y Templemann, Co Alegre. Cakes, cookies and by far the best wholemeal bread in town, all take away.

Other Cerros

¥¥¥ **Portofino**, Bellamar 301, Co Esperanza, T262 9939. Great views, classiest restaurant serving some of the best food in Valparaíso.

¥¥ **Valle de Quintil**, Rodolfo 254, Cerro Bellavista, T246 9631. At the top of the ascensor Espíritu Santo. Good fish dishes, extensive views.

Bars and clubs

Valparaíso *p722, maps p724 and p726*

El Plan

The Plaza Sotomayor/El Puerto area can be dangerous at night. There are many bars on Subida Ecuador, but be careful which ones you go into, as in some of them you risk being eaten alive (**El Muro**, for example, is rough and sordid). **El Coyote Quemado** is by far the best.

El Huevo, Blanco 1386. One of Valparaíso's most popular nightspots with 3 levels of dancing and drinking.

El Irlandés, Blanco 1279. Decent and good fun Irish-run Irish bar with bitter on tap and a good selection of beer, live music at weekends.

Pagano, Blanco 236, El Puerto. 80s music and 'anything-goes' atmosphere.

La Piedra Feliz, Errázuriz 1054. Every type of music depending on the evening, large pub, live music area, and dance floor, entrance US$9.
La Playa, Serrano 567, near Plaza Sotomayor. Old English-style bar, live music, student crowd.
Proa Al Cañaveral, Errázuriz 304. Seafood restaurant downstairs, bar upstairs with dancing from 0100, poetry reading on Thu, Latin pop music, mostly students.

Cerros Alegre and Concepción

Brighton (see Sleeping), great views at night, and **Café Vinilo** (see Eating, above), good place to meet locals and travellers.
Poblenou, Urriola 476, Cerro Alegre, T032-2495245. Open Sun. Intimate wine bar serving tapas and other snacks.

Festivals and events

Valparaíso *p722, maps p724 and p726*
New Year is celebrated by a 3-day festival, culminating in a spectacular, 40-minute firework display launched from the harbour and naval ships, which is best seen from the Cerros. The display is televised nationally and about a million visitors come to the city at this time. Book well in advance; accommodation doubles or trebles in price at this time, but it's well worth it.

Shopping

Valparaíso *p722, maps p724 and p726*
Bookshops CRISIS, on Pedro Montt by the bus terminal. Excellent new and second-hand bookshop, small selection in English. **Cummings 1**, just off Plaza Aníbal Pinto. Wide selection of new and used books in English and other languages. **Librería Ivens**, on Plaza Aníbal Pinto. Good general bookshop, the oldest in Valparaíso.
Department stores **Ripley**and **Falabella**, both on Plaza Victoria. **Almacenes París** on Av Argentina.
Markets Large antiques market on Plaza O'Higgins every Sun. Very good selection, especially old shipping items. Along Av Argentina there is a huge, colourful fruit and vegetable market on Wed and Sat and a crowded flea market on Sun. Good locally made handicrafts on Cerros Alegre and Concepción.

Activities and tours

Valparaíso *p722, maps p724 and p726*
Turismo Nuevo Mundo, Edif Turismo Nuevo Mundo, Muelle Prat, T225 3817, www.turismonuevomundo.cl. Local tours, English spoken, has offices in Argentina, Brazil and US.

Horse riding

Ritoque Expediciones, north of Concón, T281 6344, www.ritoqueexpediciones.cl. Excellent day trips over a variety of terrain. Galloping encouraged. Also full moon rides. Recommended. Pickup service from Valparaíso and Viña del Mar.

Skiing

Valposki, T09-842 83502, www.valposki.cl. Regular day-trips to El Colorado, Farellones and La Parva ski resorts.

Wine tours

Wine Tours Valparaíso, T273 4659, www.winetoursvalparaiso.cl. Small-group tours to the Casablanca valley with an English-speaking guide.

Transport

Valparaíso *p722, maps p724 and p726*
Ascensores ½ the ascensores are municipal (US$0.20). Private ones charge up to 3 times more. Sometimes you pay on entrance, sometimes on exit.
Bus US$0.50 within El Plan, US$0.65 to Cerros, US$0.80 to Viña del Mar from C Errázuriz. Bus 612, known as the 'O', from Av Argentina near the bus terminal to Plaza Aduana gives fine panoramic views of the city and bay.

Long distance terminal is on Pedro Montt 2800 block, corner of Rawson, 1 block from Av Argentina; plenty of buses between terminal and Plaza Sotomayor. To **Santiago**, 1¾ hrs, US$6-8, frequent (book return in advance on long weekends and public holidays).

To **Chillán**, 7 hrs, US$16; to **Concepción**, 8 hrs, US$17; to **Pucón**, 12 hrs, US$22-35; to **Puerto Varas** and **Puerto Montt**, 14 hrs, US$25-44; to **La Serena**, 7 hrs, US$14-28; to **Antofagasta**, 17 hrs, US$40-60; to **San Pedro de Atacama**, 24 hrs, US$50-75.
To **Mendoza** (Argentina) 5 companies, 8 hrs, early morning, from US$17.

Taxi More expensive than Santiago: a short run under 1 km costs US$2. Taxi colectivos, slightly more expensive than buses, carry sign on roof indicating route, very convenient.
Train Regular service on **Merval**, www.merval.cl, the Valparaíso metropolitan line between Valparaíso, **Viña del Mar**, **Quilpué** and **Limache**; services every 10 mins. A modern system with a similar card system to Santiago. Cards cost US$1.70; 3 levels of fare depending on time of day, US$0.70 to Viña.

Directory

Valparaíso *p722, maps p724 and p726*
Airline offices LAN, Esmeralda 1048, T600-562 2000. **Banks** Banks open 0900 to 1400, closed Sat. Many Redbanc ATMs on Prat, and one at the bus terminal. Casas de Cambio: best exchange rates from **Marin Orrego**, 3rd floor of the stock exchange building, Prat y Urriola, only changes US$ and euro cash; for other currencies, there are several *casas de cambio* along Prat and Esmeralda. **Cultural centres** Parque Cultural ex-Cárcel de Valparaíso, C Castro s/n, Cerro Cárcel, T221 9179, www.culturart.cl, or see www.redcultural.cl for programmes. The converted former prison has guided tours, exhibitions, shows, lecturers, etc. Opposite is the Disidentes cemetery, worth a visit, good views. **Instituto Chileno-Norteamericano**, Esmeralda 1069, T245 0400, www.chilenonorteamericano.cl. Library, free internet for members, regular cinema nights. **Embassies and consulates** Argentina, Blanco 625, p 5, T221 3691, cvalparaiso@embargentina.cl. **Peru**, Errázuriz 1178, of 71, T225 3403, www.conpervalparaiso.cl. **Sweden**, Almte Señoret 70, p 10, T225 0305, nberrios@ajbroom.clS. **UK**, Blanco 1199, p 5, T221 3063. **Internet** Average price US$0.75 per hr. Many places in El Plan. On Cerro Alegre, at Templeman y Urriola. **Post offices** North side of Pedro Montt between San Ignacio and Bolívar. Also on C Prat. **Telephones** Cheap call centres all over El Plan and a couple on Cerros Alegre and Concepción.

Viña del Mar and around

→ *Phone code: 032. Colour map 8, B1. Population: 304,203.*

Northeast of Valparaíso via Avenida España which runs along a narrow belt between the shore and precipitous cliffs is one of South America's leading seaside resorts, Viña del Mar. A mixture of fashionable seaside destinations and fishing communities lines the coast to the north, while south of Valparaíso are more popular resorts at the mouth of the Río Maipo. Pablo Neruda's famous seaside home at Isla Negra is also found here. For a change from the sea visit La Campana national park with its native woodlands, panoramic views and Darwinian associations (some parts were closed after the February 2010 earthquake). For **tourist information** in Viña del Mar try **Sernatur** ⓘ *Quillota 72 esq 2 Norte, T268 3355, infovalparaiso@sernatur.cl.* Municipal office on Plaza Vergara. See www.vinadelmarchile.cl and www.vinadelmar.cl.

The older part of Viña del Mar is situated on the banks of a dried-up estuary, the Marga Marga, which is crossed by bridges. Around Plaza Vergara and the smaller Plaza Sucre to its south are the **Teatro Municipal** (1930) and the exclusive **Club de Viña**, built in 1910. The municipally owned Quinta Vergara, formerly the residence of the shipping entrepreneur Francisco Alvarez, lies two blocks south. The **Palacio Vergara**, in the gardens, houses the **Museo de Bellas Artes** and the **Academia de Bellas Artes** ⓘ *T268 0618, museum Tue-Sun 1000-1400, 1500-1800, US$1.* Part of the grounds is a playground, and there is a modern outdoor auditorium where concerts and events are held throughout the year and, in February, an international music festival.

Calle Libertad runs north from the plaza, lined with banks, offices and shops. At the junction with 4 Norte is the **Palacio Carrasco**, now a cultural centre. In the same grounds is **Museo Fonk** ⓘ *C 4 Norte 784, www.museofonck.cl, Mon-Fri 1000-1800, Sat and Sun 1000-1400, US$3,* is an archaeological and natural history museum, with objects from Easter Island and the Chilean mainland, including Mapuche silver. East of this is **Palacio Rioja** ⓘ *Quillota 214, Tue-Sun*

1000-1400, 1500-1800, was built in 1906 by a prominent local family and now used for official municipal receptions, ground floor preserved in its original state. Four blocks further east is the **Valparaíso Sporting Club** with a racecourse and playing fields, while to the north, in the hills is the **Estadio Sausalito**, home to Everton football club.

On a headland overlooking the sea is **Cerro Castillo**, the summer palace of the President of the Republic. Just north, on the other side of the lagoon is the Casino, built in the 1930s and set in beautiful gardens, US$5 (open all year). It now includes the five-star *Hotel del Mar* complex, see www.hoteldelmar.cl.

Museo de la Cultura del Mar ⓘ *in the Castillo Wulff, on the coast near Cerro Castillo, T262 5427, Tue-Sat 1000-1300, 1430-1800, Sun 1000-1400*, contains a collection on the life and work of the novelist and maritime historian, Salvador Reyes.

The main beaches, Acapulco and Mirasol are located to the north, but south of Cerro Castillo is Caleta Abarca, also popular. The coastal route north to Reñaca provides lovely views over the sea.

Jardín Botánico Nacional ⓘ *8 km southeast of the city, www.jardin-botanico.cl, US$2, getting there: take bus 203 from Calle Alvarez, get off at the puente El Olivar, cross the bridge and walk 15 minutes.* Formerly the estate of the nitrate baron Pascual Baburizza, this is now administered by CONAF (3 Norte 541, T232 0272). Covering 405 ha, it contains over 3,000 species from all over the world and a collection of Chilean cacti, but the species are not labelled. It's a good place for a picnic; there's also a canopy adventure trail, with ziplines linking trees within the park.

Viña del Mar

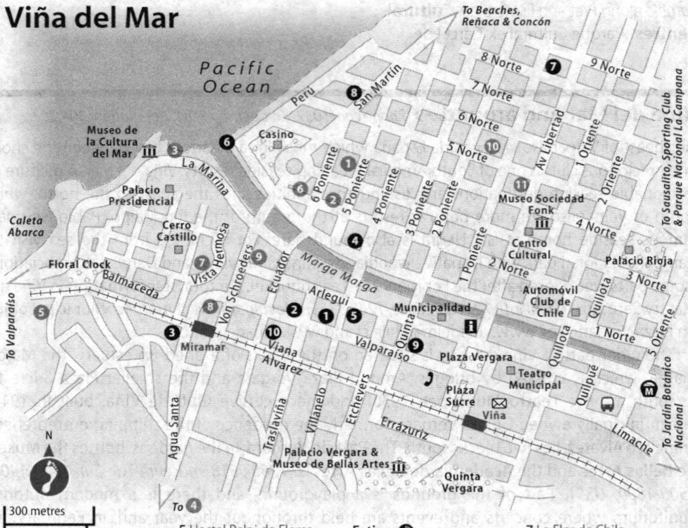

Sleeping
1 Agora
2 Andalué
3 Cap Ducal
4 Genross
5 Hostal Reloj de Flores
6 Monterilla
7 Offenbacher Hof
8 Res Blanchait
9 Res Capric
10 Residencia 555
11 Vancouver Viña

Eating
1 Africa
2 Alster
3 Café Journal
4 Ciboulette
5 Club Giacomo
6 Enjoy del Mar
7 La Flor de Chile
8 Las Delicias del Mar
9 Samoiedo
10 Shawarma Kabab

Resorts north of Viña del Mar

North of Viña del Mar the coast road runs through **Las Salinas**, a popular beach between two towering crags, **Reñaca** (long beach, upmarket, good restaurants) and **Cochoa**, where there is a sealion colony 100 m offshore, to **Concón** (18 km). Famous for its restaurants. Concón has six beaches stretching along the bay between Caleta Higuerilla in the west end and, in the east, La Boca (the largest of the six, excellent for beach sports, horses and kayaks for hire). Tourist office: Maroto 1030, www.concon.cl. **Quintero**, 23 km north of Concón, is a slightly dilapidated fishing town on a rocky peninsula with lots of small beaches (hotels and residenciales).

Horcón (also known locally as Horcones) is set back in a cove surrounded by cliffs, a pleasant small village, mainly of wooden houses. Packed out in January-February, the rest of the year it is a charming place, populated by fishermen and artistsut of season, with a tumbledown feel unlike the more well-to-do resorts to north and south. Horses still drag the small fishing boats out of the sea. Vegetation is tropical with many cacti on the cliff tops. Across the headland to the south is **Playa Cau Cau**, a cove now dominated by a condominium. Further north is **Maitencillo** with a wonderful long beach, heaving in high summer but a ghost town off season. Some 14 km beyond is **Zapallar**, a fashionable resort with a lovely beach. A hint of its former glory is given by a number of fine mansions along Avenida Zapallar. At **Cachagua**, 3 km south, a colony of penguins on an offshore island may be viewed from the northern end of the beach; take binoculars. **Papudo** (*Phone code: 033*), 10 km further north, was the site of a naval battle in November 1865 in which the Chilean vessel Esmeralda captured the Spanish ship Covadonga. Following the arrival of the railway Papudo rivalled Viña del Mar as a fashionable resort in the 1920s but it has long since declined. With its lovely beach and fishing port, it is an idyllic spot (except in high summer).

Resorts south near the mouth of the Río Maipo

San Antonio is a commercial centre for this part of the coast. It is a container and fishing port and is the terminal for the export of copper brought by rail from El Teniente mine, near Rancagua. To the south are the resorts of Llolleo and Rocas de Santo Domingo. **Cartagena**, 8 km north of San Antonio, is the most popular resort on this part of the coast. The centre is around the hilltop Plaza de Armas. To the south is the picturesque Playa Chica, overlooked by many of the older hotels and restaurants; to the north is the Playa Larga. Between the two a promenade runs below the cliffs; high above hang old houses, some in disrepair but offering spectacular views. Cartagena is packed in summer, but out of season it is a good centre for visiting nearby resorts of Las Cruces, El Tabo and El Quisco. There are many hotels and bus connections are good.

North of Cartagena in the village of **Isla Negra** is the beautifully restored **Museo-Casa Pablo Neruda** ⓘ *T035-461284, must book in advance, US$5.50, guided tour in Spanish, US$6.50 in English, Jan-Feb Tue-Sun 1000-2000, rest of year Tue-Sun 1000-1800, www.fundacionneruda.org/home_islanegra.htm.* Bought by Neruda in 1939, and constantly added to over time, this house, overlooking the sea, was his writing retreat in his later years. It contains artefacts gathered by Neruda from all over the world. Neruda and his last wife, Mathilde, are buried here; the touching gravestone is beside the house. The house has a good café specializing in Neruda's own recipes.

Parque Nacional La Campana

This 8,000-ha park ⓘ *US$3*, includes Cerro La Campana (1,828 m) which Darwin climbed in 1834 and Cerro El Roble (2,200 m). Some of the best views in Chile can be seen from the top. Near Ocoa there are areas of Chilean palms (*kankán* – which give edible, walnut-sized coconuts in March-April), now found in its natural state in only two locations in Chile. There are three entrances: at Granizo (from which the hill is climbed), reached by paved road from Limache, 4 km west, via Olmué; at Cajón Grande (with natural bathing pools), reached by unpaved road which turns off the Olmué-Granizo road; at Palmar de Ocoa to the north reached by unpaved road (10 km) leading off the Pan-American Highway at Km 100 between Hijuelas and Llaillay.

Viña del Mar and around listings

For Sleeping and Eating price codes and other relevant information, see Essentials, pages 38-40.

Sleeping

Viña del Mar *p731, map p732*
There are lots of places to stay, mostly **AL-A**, although many are in the business district and not convenient for the beaches. Out of season agencies rent furnished apartments. In season it's cheaper to stay in Valparaíso.

L-AL Cap Ducal, Marina 51, T262 6655, www.capducal.cl. Old-mansion charm – a ship-shaped building literally overhanging the ocean, with an elegant restaurant, serving good seafood.

AL Monterilla, 2 Norte 65, T297 6950, www.monterilla.cl. Unpretentious carpetted rooms with flat-screen TV and Wi-Fi, some have king-size beds. Some English spoken.

A Agora, 5½ Poniente 253, T269 4669, www.hotel agora.cl. On a quiet side street, brightly coloured rooms, most with full-size bathtub. Wi-fi zones, English spoken, helpful staff (on 4 floors but no lift).

A Andalué, 6 Poniente 124, T268 4147, www.hotelandalue.cl. Good location, decent rooms, restaurant downstairs and heated pool on the roof. Good value.

A-B Genross, Paseo Monterrey 18, T266 1711, genrosshotel@hotmail.com. Beautiful mansion, airy rooms, garden patio and sitting room, informative, English spoken. Closed in winter.

A-B Offenbacher Hof, Balmaceda 102, T262 1483, www.offenbacher-hof.cl. Large wooden house in a quiet residential street overlooking the city centre, peaceful, helpful. The best rooms are spacious with cable TV. Recommended.

B Residencia 555, 5 Norte 555, T297 2240, residencial555@vtr.net. **C** for singles. Characterful wooden house with antique furniture. Rooms range widely in size and have cable TV, good value, though advance reservations difficult as deposit required and credit cards not accepted.

B Vancouver Viña, 5 Norte 650, T248 2983, www.hotelvancouvervina.cl. Carpeted modest rooms with cable TV, good value, café downstairs.

B-C Hostal Reloj de Flores, Los Baños 70, Caleta Abarca, www.hostalrelojdefloresbb.com. In restored building, cheaper with shared bath and in low season, breakfast, film and book library, kitchen, laundry service, babysitters.

There are lots of cheap *residenciales* around Von Schroeders y Valparaíso, but this is the red-light district and is unpleasant at night. The best options here are probably:

C Res Blanchait, Valparaíso 82A, T297 4949, www.blanchait.cl.**D-E** singles. Some rooms with bath, good service, breakfast extra.

C Res Capric, von Schroeders 39, T297 8295, hcapricvina@hostelling.cl. **E-F** pp in shared rooms. Run-down rooms with bath and TV, breakfast included, special rates for IH members.

Resorts north of Viña del Mar *p733*

Reñaca

AL Oceanic, Av Borgoño 12925, T283 0006, www.hoteloceanic.cl. Comfortable, spacious rooms dramatically set on the ocean front; pay the extra for an ocean view and to escape the street noise. Good restaurant (mostly seafood).

Quintero

C Res Brazilian, 21 de Mayo 1336, T293 0590, anasatt@yahoo.com. With breakfast, large windows but no view, well maintained, warm sea-water baths for US$6.

Horcón

Lots of cabañas in Horcón, shop around, especially off season.

C Arancibia, T279 6169. With or without bath, pleasant gardens, good food.

C Juan Esteban, Pasaje Miramar, Casa 2, T279 6056, www.juanesteban.cl. **E** singles. English, Portuguese and Italian spoken, nice terrace with view. Recommended. Also fully equipped *cabañas* (**A**) for 4 people.

Resorts south near the mouth of the Río Maipo *p733*

AL Rocas de Santo Domingo, La Ronda 130, San Antonio, T035-444356, www.hotelrocas.cl. Good, including decent breakfast, helpful staff, restaurant, 20 minutes to sea.

D Violeta, Condell 140, Cartagena, T035-450 372. Swimming pool, good views.

C pp **Hostal Casa Azul**, Av Santa Luisa s/n, Isla Negra, T035-461154. Shared bath, hot showers, garden (camping available), kitchen and laundry, breakfast included, helpful. Recommended.

D Res Carmona, Playa Chica, Cartagena, T035-450485. Small rooms, basic but clean, good value.
D Res Paty's, Alacalde Cartagena 295, Cartagena, T035-450469. Nice spot, good value.

Eating

Viña del Mar *p731, map p732*
Many good bars and restaurants on and around San Martín between 2 and 8 Norte; cuisine including Austrian, Mexican, Chinese and Italian. Cheap bars and restaurants around Calle Valparaíso and Von Schroeders. Not too safe at night.
TTT Ciboulette, 1 Norte 191, T269 0084. Intimate Belgian-owned and run bistro serving traditional French cuisine. Good wine list.
TTT-TT Enjoy del Mar, Av Perú s/n, T250 0785. Modern restaurant serving everything from gourmet dishes to barbecues and fast food, all on an open terrace on the seafront.
TTT-TT Fellini, 3 Norte 88, T297 5742. Wide range of fresh pasta dishes in delicious sauces, good.
TTT-TT Las Delicias del Mar, San Martín 459. Award-winning Basque seafood restaurant, "brilliant food, wine and service".
T Africa, Valparaíso 324. Extraordinarily kitsch façade, pasta and fast food.
T Café Journal, Agua Santa y Alvarez. Excellent-value set lunch. Recommended.
T Club Giacomo, Villanelo 131. A Viña institution, traditional set lunches with a pool hall annex.
T La Flor de Chile, 8 Norte 607 y 1 Poniente. Good, typical Chilean food.
T Shawarma kabab, Ecuador 255. Authentic middle-eastern fare, including kebabs and stuffed vine leaves.

Cafés

Alster, Valparaíso 225. Elegant but pricey.
Samoiedo, Valparaíso 637. Confitería, old-time café.

Bars and clubs

Viña del Mar *p731, map p732*
Barlovento, 2 Norte y 5 Poniente. The designer bar in Viña, on 3 floors with a lovely roof terrace, serves great pizzas and good beer.

Activities and tours

Resorts north of Viña del Mar *p733*
Ritoque Expediciones, just north of Concón, T032-281 6344/09-730 5212 , www.ritoque expediciones.cl. Horse riding, full- or ½-day trips to lakes, sand dunes, scrubland, beaches, you can help herd cows or just gallop, also full moon rides, can collect from Valaparaíso or Viña, English spoken. Highly recommended.

Transport

Viña del Mar *p731, map p732*
Bus 2 blocks east of Plaza Vergara at Av Valparaíso y Quilpué. To **Santiago**, US6-8, 1¾ hrs, frequent, same companies as for Valparaíso from Pajaritos in Santiago, heavily booked in advance for travel on Sun afternoons. Long distance services: prices and itineraries similar to Valparaíso.
Train Services on the Valparaíso Metropolitan line (Merval) stop at Viña (see under Valparaíso).

Resorts north of Viña del Mar *p733*
Bus From Valparaíso and Viña del Mar: to **Concón** frequent, bus 601, US$1, frequent; to **Quintero** and **Horcón**, **Sol del Pacífico**, every 30 mins, US$3, 2 hrs; to **Zapallar** and **Papudo**, **Sol del Pacífico**, 4 a day (2 before 0800, 2 after 1600), US$6. All of these from Av Libertad in Viña, or Errázuriz in Valparaíso.

Resorts south near the mouth of the Río Maipo *p733*
Bus From San Antonio: buses to **Valparaíso**, **Pullman Lago Peñuelas**, every 30 mins until 2000, US$6; to **Santiago**, Pullman Bus, every 30 mins in summer, US$7. Regular bus services to **Isla Negra** from Santiago (**Pullman Bus**) and Valparaíso (**Pullman Lago Peñuelas**), 1½ hrs, US$6.

Parque Nacional La Campana *p733*
The entrances at **Granizo** (paradero 45) and **Cajón Grande** (paradero 41) are reached by local bus/colectivo from outside Limache train station. No public transport to Ocoa. Get a bus to La Calera and bargain with a taxi or colectivo driver. Expect to pay US$20-25.

Directory

Viña del Mar *p731, map p732*
Banks Many Redbanc ATMs on Libertad and on Arlegui; also on C Valparaíso (but this is not a safe area at night). Many casas de cambio on Arlegui and Valparaíso; shop around for best rates and avoid changing money on the street, especially if alone. **Internet** Several the length of Calle Valparaíso, also telephone offices.

North of Santiago

Along the coast is a mixture of fishing villages, deserted beaches and popular resorts, while inland the scenery is wonderfully dramatic but little visited. The land becomes less fertile as you go further north. Ovalle is a good centre for trips to see petroglyphs and the coastal forests at the Parque Nacional Fray Jorge. The largest resort is La Serena, from where access can be made to the Elqui Valley, one of Chile's major pisco-producing regions and one of the world's major astronomical centres.

From the Río Aconcagua to the Río Elqui is a transitional zone between the fertile heartland and the northern deserts. The first stretch of the Pan-American Highway from Santiago is inland through green valleys with rich blue clover and wild artichokes. North of La Ligua, the Highway mainly follows the coastline, passing many beautiful coves, alternately rocky and sandy, with good surf, though the water is very cold. The valleys of the main rivers, the Choapa, Limarí and Elqui, are intensively farmed using irrigation to produce fruit and vegetables. There is a striking contrast between these lush valley floors and the arid mountains with their dry scrub and cactus. In some areas, condensation off the sea provides sufficient moisture for woods to grow. Rainfall is rare and occurs only in winter. On the coast the average temperature is 15°C in winter, 23°C in summer; the interior is dry, with temperatures reaching 33°C in summer, but it is cooler in winter and very cold at night.

Ovalle to La Serena

Ovalle and around ➔ *Phone code: 053. Colour map 8, A1. Population: 53,000.*
This town lies inland, 412 km north of Santiago, in the valley of the Río Limarí, a fruit-growing and mining district. Market days are Monday, Wednesday, Friday and Saturday, till 1600; the market (*feria modelo*) is off Benavente (east of the centre). The town is famous for its *talabarterías* (saddleries), products made of locally mined lapis lazuli, goats cheese and dried fruits. Wine is produced in the Limarí Valley and tours to *bodegas* such as Tamaya (www.tamaya.cl) and Tabalí (www.tabali.cl) are arranged under the Ruta del Vino heading. **Museo del Limarí** ⓘ *in the old railway station, Covarrubias y Antofagasta, Tue-Fri 0900-1300, 1500-1900, Sat-Sun 1000-1300, US$1, free on Sun*, has displays of petroglyphs and a good collection of Diaguita ceramics and other artefacts. Unofficial tourist information kiosk on the Plaza de Armas.

Monumento Nacional Valle del Encanto ⓘ *about 22 km southwest of Ovalle, open all year, 0800-1800, US$2, getting there: no local bus service; you must take a southbound long distance bus and ask to be dropped off – 5 km walk to the valley; flag down a bus to return; alternatively, use a tour operator*. This is a most important archaeological site. Artefacts from hunting peoples from over 2,000 years ago have been found but the most visible remains date from the Molle culture (AD 700). There are over 30 petroglyphs as well as great boulders, distributed in six sites. There are camping facilities.

Termas de Socos ⓘ *35 km southwest of Ovalle on the Pan-American Highway, www.termasocos.cl, US$9, bus US$2*, has a swimming pool and individual tubs fed by thermal springs, as well as sauna, jacuzzi and water massage (very popular). It also boasts a reasonable hotel (see Sleeping, below) and a campsite (**G** per tent) nearby.

Monumento Natural Pichasca ⓘ *47 km northeast of Ovalle, 0800-1800, US$4, getting there: daily buses from Ovalle to Hurtado the turn off about 42 km from the city, from here it is 3 km to the park and about 2 km more to sites of interest*. An unpaved and largely winding road leads to the park, which contains petrified tree trunks, archaeological remains, including a vast cave with vestiges of ancient roof paintings, and views of rock formations on the surrounding mountains.

Beyond the village of Pichasca it is 32 km to Hurtado. The road winds along the side of the valley, with the Andes easily visible at its head. Near **Vado Morrillos**, 4 km before Hurtado, is the **Corral Los Andes** (see Sleeping, below). The road continues to **Hurtado** village at 1300 m, near which are the only petroglyph in Chile depicting the sun, hinting at possible links to the Incas, **Cerro Gigante** (2825 m) and a Diaguita cemetery. From Hurtado a road runs north to Vicuña in the Elqui Valley (see below) only 46 km away. This is a desolate but beautiful road, very poor in places with very little traffic and no public transport. Pickups can be hired in Hurtado for US$35-40.

Parque Nacional Fray Jorge ⓘ *90 km west of Ovalle and 110 km south of La Serena at the mouth of the Río Limarí, T620058, Sat, Sun and holidays 0900-1700, last car admitted 1600, US$5; no public transport, take a tour.* Visits closely controlled owing to risk of fire. The Park is reached by a dirt road leading off the Pan-American Highway. It contains original forests which contrast with the otherwise barren surroundings. Receiving less than 113 mm of rain a year, the forests survive because of the almost constant covering of fog. Waterproof clothing is essential when you visit.

The good inland road between Ovalle and La Serena makes an interesting contrast to Ruta 5 (Panamericana), with a fine pass and occasional views of the Andes across cacti-covered plains and semi-desert mountain ranges. North of Ovalle 61 km a side road runs 44 km southeast (last 20 km very bad) to **Andacollo** (*Population: 10,216; Altitude: 1,050 m*). This old town, in an area of alluvial gold washing and manganese and copper mining, is one of the great pilgrimage sites in Chile. In the enormous **Basilica** (1893), 45 m high and with a capacity of 10,000, is the Virgen del Rosario de Andacollo. The **Fiesta Grande** from 23-27 December attracts 150,000 pilgrims. The ritual dances date from a pre-Spanish past. Colectivos run to the festival from Benavente, near Colocolo, in La Serena, but 'purists' walk (torch and good walking shoes essential). There is also a smaller festival, the Fiesta Chica on the first Sunday of October. The tourist office on the Plaza arranges tours to the Basilica and to mining operations.

Coquimbo → *Phone code: 051. Colour map 8, A1. Population: 106,000.*

On the same bay as La Serena, 84 km north of Ovalle, is this important port, with one of the best harbours on the coast and major fish-processing plants. The city is strung along the north shore of a peninsula. On the south shore lies the suburb of Guayacán, with an iron-ore loading port, a steel church designed by Eiffel, an English cemetery and a 83-m high cross to mark the Millennium (US$2 to climb it). In 1981 heavy rain uncovered 39 ancient burials of humans and llamas which had been sacrificed; they are exhibited in a small **Museo del Sitio** ⓘ *in the Plaza Gabriela Mistral, open Jan-Feb only, Mon-Sat 0930-2030, Sun 0930-1400, free, tourist information.* The **municipal tourist office** is at Las Heras 220, T313971. Summer boat trips of the harbour and nearby Punta Lobos cost US$5. Nearby is **La Herradura**, 2½ km from Coquimbo, slightly more upmarket and with the best beaches. Resorts further south, **Totoralillo** (12 km), **Guanaqueros** (37 km) and **Tongoy** (50 km), have good beaches and can be reached by rural buses or colectivos.

La Serena → *Phone code: 051. Colour map 8, A1. Population: 120,000.*

La Serena, built on a hillside 2 km inland from Bahía de Coquimbo, is an attractive city and tourist centre, 11 km north of Coquimbo (473 km north of Santiago) and is the capital of IV Región (Coquimbo). The city was founded by Juan de Bohón, aide to Pedro de Valdivia, in 1544, destroyed by the Diaguita in 1546 and rebuilt by Francisco de Aguirre in 1549. The city was sacked by the English pirate Sharpe in 1680. In the colonial period the city was the main staging-post on the route north to Peru. In the 19th century the city grew prosperous from copper-mining. While retaining colonial architecture and churches, the present-day layout and style have their origins in the 'Plan Serena' drawn up in 1948 on the orders of President Gabriel González Videla, a native of the city. **Sernatur** ⓘ *Matta 461, p 1, in Edificio de Servicios Públicos (next to post office on the Plaza de Armas), T225199, infocoquimbo@sernatur.cl, Mon-Fri 0845-1830 (2030 in summer), Sat-Sun 1000-1400, plus 1600-2000 in summer. Kiosk at bus terminal (summer only).* See www.laserena.cl.

Around the attractive Plaza de Armas are most of the official buildings, including the Post Office, the **Cathedral** (built in 1844 and featuring a carillon which plays every hour) and the **Museo Histórico Regional** at the Casa González Videla ⓘ *www.dibam.cl/subdirec_museos/*

mhr_videla/home.asp, Mon-Fri 1000-1800, Sat 1000-1300, US$1 (ticket also valid for Museo Arqueológico), which includes several rooms on the man's life. Ticket are also valid for **Museo Arqueológico** ⓘ *Cordovez y Cienfuegos, T224492, www.dibam.cl/sdm_m_laserena/index.asp, Tue-Fri 0930-1750, Sat 1000- 1300, 1600-1900, US$1, students free, Sun 1000-1300, free*. It has an outstanding collection of Diaguita and Molle exhibits, especially of attractively decorated pottery, also Easter Island exhibits. There are 29 other churches, several of which have unusual towers. **La Recova**, the craft market, at Cienfuegos y Cantournet, includes a large display of handicrafts (some imported) and, upstairs, several good restaurants. One block west of the Plaza de Armas is the **Parque Pedro de Valdivia** ⓘ *daily 1000-2000, US$1.50*. One block south is the delightful **Parque Japonés**.

Avenida Francisco de Aguirre, a pleasant boulevard lined with statues and known as the Alameda, runs from the centre to the coast, terminating at the **Faro Monumental**, a small, neo-colonial mock-castle and lighthouse, now a pub. A series of beaches stretch from here to

La Serena

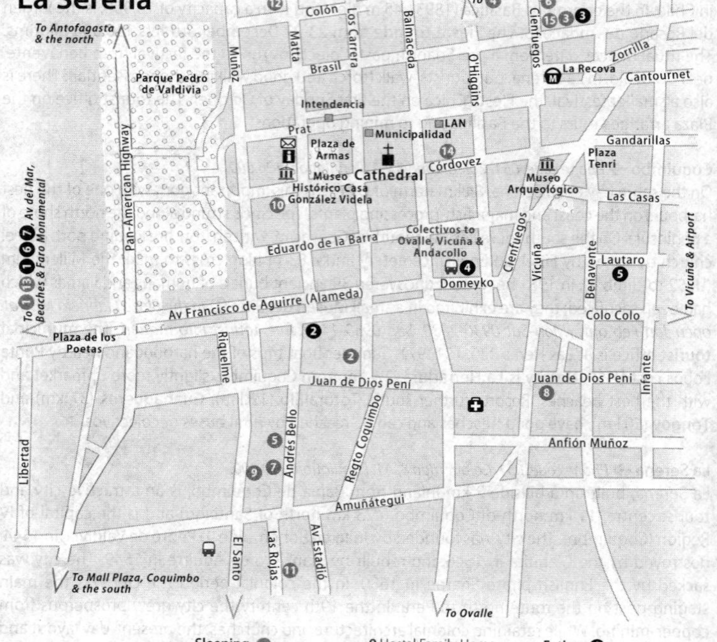

Sleeping
1 Cabañas Bahía Drake
2 Camino de Luna
3 Casa Alejandro Muñoz
4 Del Cid
5 El Punto
6 Hostal Croata
7 Hostal D'Gregoria
8 Hostal El Hibisco
9 Hostal Family Home
10 Hostal Gladys
11 Hostal María Casa
12 Hostal Villanueva de la Serena
13 La Serena Plaza
14 Londres
15 Res Suiza

Eating
1 Costa Inca
2 Daniela 2
3 Donde El Guatón
4 El Callejón
5 Govindas
6 La Mía Pizza
7 Porotos

Coquimbo, 11 km south, linked by the Av del Mar. Many apartment blocks, hotels, cabañas and restaurants line this part of the bay. The sectors between 4 Esquinas and Peñuelas are probably the best bet for sunbathing or dipping a toe in the water.

Elqui Valley

The valley of the Río Elqui is one of the most attractive oases in this part of northern Chile. There are orchards, orange groves, vineyards and mines set against the imposing, arid mountains. The Elqui Valley is the centre of pisco production with nine distilleries, the largest being Capel in Vicuña. Elqui is also well-known as a centre of mystical energy and is one of the main astronomical centres of the world, with three important observatories. Tour operators in La Serena and Coquimbo arrange tours to the smaller municipal observatory at Mamalluca near Vicuña.

At 2,200 m, 89 km southeast of La Serena in the Elqui Valley, 51 km south of Vicuña, **El Tololo** ⓘ *www.ctio.noao.edu, visitors by permit only every Sat 0900-1300; for permits (free) write to Casilla 603, La Serena, T051-205200, then pick your permit up before 1200 on the day before (the office is at Colina Los Pinos, on a hill behind the new University – personal applications can be made here for all three observatories), they will insist that you have private transport; you can hire a taxi, US$75 for the whole day, but you will require the registration number when you book* belongs to Aura, an association of US and Chilean universities. It possesses one of the largest telescopes in the southern hemisphere (4-m diameter), six others and a radio telescope. At 2,240 m, 150 km northeast of La Serena **La Silla** ⓘ *www.ls.eso.org, registration in advance in Santiago essential (Alonso de Córdoba 3107, Santiago, T02-463 3280) or write to recepstg@eso.org, every Sat, 1330-1700, except Jul-Aug* belongs to ESO (European Southern Observatory), and comprises 14 telescopes. From La Serena it is 120 km north along Route 5 to the turn-off, then another 36 km. At 2,510 m, 162 km northeast of La Serena, 30 km north of La Silla **Las Campanas** ⓘ *T207301, or write to Casilla 601, La Serena, www.lco.cl, open with permission every Sat 1430-1730* belongs to the Carnegie Institute, has five telescopes and is a smaller facility than the other two. To get there, follow Route 5 to the same junction as for La Silla, take the turning for La Silla and then turn north after 14 km. La Silla and Las Campanas can be reached without private transport by taking any bus towards Vallenar two hours, US$4, getting out at the junction (*desvío*) and hitch from there.

The road up the valley is paved as far as Pisco Elqui, 37 km beyond **Vicuña**, the valley's capital. This small, friendly town, 66 km east of La Serena, was founded in 1821. On the west side of the plaza are the municipal chambers, built in 1826 and topped in 1905 by a medieval-German-style tower, the Torre Bauer, imported by the German-born mayor of the time. The tourist office is on Plaza de Armas. There is an ATM. There are good views from Cerro La Virgen, north of town. **Capel Pisco distillery** ⓘ *1½ km east of Vicuña, to the right of the main road, guided tours (in Spanish) are offered Dec-May Mon-Sat 1000-1800, free, no booking required.* **Museo Gabriela Mistral** ⓘ *Gabriela Mistral 759, www.dibam.cl/sdm_mgm_vicuna, Jan-Feb Mon-Sat 1000-1900, Sun 1000-1800, rest of year Mon-Fri 1000-1745, Sat 1030-1800, Sun 1000-1300, US$1.20, free Mon Mar-Dec, students ½ price*, contains manuscripts, books, awards and many other details of the poet's life. Next door is the house where the poet was born. There are two observatories near the town which give the public the chance to see the stars: **Observatorio Astronómico Comunal de Vicuña** ⓘ *Gabriela Mistral 260, Vicuña, T411352, www.mamalluca.org, on Cerro Mamalluca, 6 km north of Vicuña, 1,500 m above sea level, visits daily at 2100, 2300, 0100 in summer, 1800, 2000, 2200 in winter, US$10 plus optional transport (US$4) per person, guides in Spanish and English for groups of 5 or more, book in advance.* **Observatorio del Pangue** ⓘ *,16 km south of Vicuña on the road to Hurtado, bookings through agencies in La Serena as part of a tour or directly from San Martín 233, Vicuña, T412584, www.observatoriodelpangue.blogspot.com, 2 or 3 visits nightly, US$23 including transport*. Groups are limited to 12 people; tours are informative and in good English and French as well as Spanish, and the telescopes are more powerful than those at Mamalluca. Always book in advance.

From Vicuña the road runs through Paihuano (camping) to **Monte Grande**, where the schoolhouse where Gabriela Mistral lived and was educated by her sister is now a **museum**

ⓘ *C Principal s/n, T415015, Tue-Sun 1000-1300, 1500-1800 (till 1900 in Jan-Feb), US$0.80.* The poet's tomb is at the edge of town, opposite the Artesanos de Cochiguaz pisco distillery, which is open to the public. (Buses from the plaza in Vicuña.) Here the road forks, one branch leading to the Cochiguaz valley. There is no public transport. Along this road are several new age settlements; it is said that the valley is an important energy centre. There are several campsites. At night, there is no better place on earth to star gaze. When the moon is new, or below the horizon, the stars seem to be hanging in the air; spectacular shooting stars can be seen every couple of seconds, as can satellites crossing the night sky. Back on the main road, just south of Monte Grande, is the **Cavas del Valle** organic winery with free tastings. The other branch road leads to **Pisco Elqui**, an attractive village with the newly restored church of Nuestra Señora del Rosario on a shady plaza. It's also famous for its night skies and beautiful scenery. At the Hotel Elqui, the **Astropub** has telescopes for stargazing. Horses can be hired, with or without guide (Ramón Luis, T451168, is recommended). Its new-age attractions include alternative therapies and massages. More traditional is the **Tres Erres** pisco plant, which is open to the public and gives guided tours in Spanish, US$4. Some 4 km further up the valley at **Los Nichos**, a small *pisco* distillery is open for visits (closed lunchtime) and sells dried fruit and other local products.

Border Paso Agua Negra Paso Agua Negra (4,775 m) is reached by partly-paved road from Guanta, 30 km past Rivadavia. Chilean immigration and customs at Juntas, 84 km west of the border, 88 km east of Vicuña. Border open 0800-1700; January-April only, check rest of year. No public transport beyond Rivadavia. Tell officials if you intend to camp between border posts.

Ovalle to La Serena listings

For Sleeping and Eating price codes and other relevant information, see Essentials, pages 38-40.

Sleeping

Ovalle and around *p736*

AL Termas de Socos, Panamericana Norte Km 370, 35 km southwest of Ovalle, T053-198 2505, www.termasocos.cl. Reasonable hotel offering full board and access to thermal pools.

AL-A Hacienda Juntas, near Monte Patria, Km 38, T711290, www.haciendajuntas.cl. In 90 ha of vineyards, with pleasant gardens, spectacular views and pool. Restaurant open in high season only.

AL-A PlazaTurismo, Victoria 295, T623258, www.plazaturismo.cl. Spacious rooms with Wi-Fi, some overlooking the plaza.

B-C Gran Hotel, Vicuña Mackenna 210 (entrance through Galería Yagnam), T621084. Decent rooms with Wi-Fi, good value and service.

C Roxy, Libertad 155, T620080. Big basic rooms, large colonial-style patio covered in vines in summer, a bit run-down, but a reasonable choice.

E Jaime's Crazy House, Tocopilla 92, T626761, www.jaimecrazyhouse.com. Breakfast extra, dorms (**F** pp)and private rooms, convenient, family atmosphere, lots of information, tours arranged, cyber café. Recommended.

Camping G pp **Camping y Piscina Los Pumas del Encanto**, 10 mins' walk from Valle del Encanto, T623667, www.campingpiscina pumasencanto.tk. Nice place with lots of trees and plants, owner Adrián Tello is very knowledgeable.

Río Hurtado

A-C pp **Hacienda Los Andes**, Vado Morillos, T691822, www.haciendalos andes.com. German-Austrian management at this highly regarded colonial style hacienda, all meals use organic local produce, expert horse riding tours, from US$585 pp for 4 days/3 nights.

C Tambo de Limarí, Caupolicán 27, Hurtado, T053-1982121. **F** singles. Excellent *hospedaje* with wonderful breakfast. Owner Señora Orieta is very friendly. There is an interesting collection of ancient riding spurs, stirrups and Spanish padlocks. Recommended.

Parque Nacional Fray Jorge

One *cabaña* for hire (**A**) sleeping 5. Basic accommodation (**C**) in an old hacienda and 2 campsites in the national park; 1 at the administration centre, the other 3 km away at El Arrayancito.

Coquimbo *p737*

Generally accommodation is cheaper than in La Serena. Several hotels in La Herradura.

B Lig, Aldunate 1577, T311171. Comfortable, with breakfast, overpriced, near bus terminal.

C Hostal Nomade, Regimento Coquimbo 5, T315665, www.hostalnomade.cl. **E** singles, **F** pp in dorms. HI-affiliated, kitchen and laundry facilities, internet, tours arranged, also camping. English spoken.

C-D Iberia, Lastra 400, T312141. Cheaper without bath, pleasant and recommended.

La Serena *p737, map p738*

Route 5 from La Serena to Coquimbo is lined with cheap accommodation; Av del Mar, 500 m off the highway, also hotels and other accommodation (buses run along Route 5, not Av del Mar). The tourist office in the bus terminal is helpful. Do not be pressurized by touts at the bus station into choosing rooms. Similarly, do not be pressurized to buy tours in hotels: established agencies may give better service and deals.

AL-A La Serena Plaza, Francisco de Aguirre 0660, T225745, www.hotelserenaplaza.cl. Upmarket hotel by the beach with spacious rooms, swimming pool, gym and restaurant. Good value.

A-B Cabañas Bahia Drake, Av del Mar 1300, T223367, www.cabanasbahiadrake.cl. Pleasant, fully equipped *cabañas* for 2 to 6, on the seafront, with swimming pool.

A-B Del Cid, O'Higgins 138, T212692, www.hoteldelcid.cl. Characterful, central, with smallish but spotless rooms around a courtyard. Parking available, English spoken. Recommended.

A-B Londres, Cordovez 550, T219066, www.hotellondres.cl. Simple, bright rooms with good beds, cable TV, Wi-Fi and decent bathrooms.

B-C El Punto, Andrés Bello 979, T228474, www.hostalelpunto.cl. **D** without bath, with breakfast, tasteful, comfortable, café, laundry, parking, book exchange, English and German spoken, Wi-Fi, arranges tours to Elqui Valley. Highly recommended.

B-C Hostal Villanueva de La Serena, Colón 290, T550268, www.hostalvillanueva.cl. Large rooms, clean with hot water, TV and breakfast.

C Casa Alejandro Muñoz, Brasil 720, T484013, alejandrocasavictoriana@hotmail.com. Rooms in family home in old part of town, hot showers, good breakfast, garden, kitchen and laundry facilities, tours, English and French spoken, nice atmosphere.

C Hostal D' Gregoria, Andrés Bello 1067, T224400. Very helpful, good beds, some with bath, close to terminal, excellent breakfast, garden, good local information; if full she will divert you to her mother's house, also good but less convenient for the bus station. Highly recommended.

C-D Camino de Luna, Los Carrera 861, T051-486037, hostalcaminodeluna@gmail.com. Nice rooms with cable TV, some with bath. Bright patio. Owner from Valdivia keen to practice English.

C-D Hostal Croata, Cienfuegos 248, T224997, www.hostalcroata.cl. With breakfast, kitchen and laundry facilities, cable TV, patio, hospitable. Recommended.

C-D Hostal Family Home, Av Santo 1056, T224059, www.familyhome.cl. Some rooms with bath, kitchen facilities, thin walls and slightly tatty, but it has a 24-hr reception and is close to the bus terminal so useful if you are arriving at night.

C-D Res Suiza, Cienfuegos 250, T216092, residencial.suiza@terra.cl. With breakfast, good beds, excellent value. Recommended.

D Hostal Gladys, Gregorio Cordovez 247 (by the Plaza de Armas), T09 540 3636, www.hostalgladys.cl. Cheaper without breakfast and with shared bath, digital TV, hot water, free internet, Wi-Fi, kitchen facilities and laundry service, helpful, Gladys works at tourist information in bus terminal (15 mins away).

E Hostal El Hibisco, Juan de Dios Peni 636, T211407, mauricioberrios2002@yahoo.es. Delightful hosts, welcome drink, good breakfast included, hot water, lots of information. Recommended.

E pp **Hostal María Casa**, Las Rojas 18, T229282, www.hostalmariacasa.cl. Very welcoming and helpful, near bus terminal, laundry facilities, garden, camping, book in advance, excellent value. Highly recommended.

Elqui Valley *p739*

Vicuña

AL Hostería Vicuña, Sgto Aldea 101, T411301, www.valledeelqui.cl/hosteriavicuna.html. In spacious grounds, pool, tennis court, poor restaurant, parking. Has seen better days.

B Halley, Gabriela Mistral 542, T412070, turismohalley@yahoo.es. Pleasantly old-fashioned hotel with high-ceilinged rooms, colonial- style courtyard, and a pleasant pool.

C Hosp Sundari, C Principal 3, San Isidro (15 mins walk from Vicuña), T412072, www.manos.cl/sundari/. Delightful bungalows, with breakfast, spotless, TV, internet, bicycles, pool in lovely gardens, aloe and other herbal therapies.

C La Elquina, O' Higgins 65, T411317, anamorainostroza@terra.cl. Includes breakfast, **E** without bath, relaxed, quiet, lovely garden, laundry and kitchen facilities. Highly recommended.

C Rita Klamt, Condell 443, T419611, rita_klamt@yahoo.es. **D-E** single. Impeccably kept bed and breakfast. Excellent breakfast, ample kitchen facilities, pleasant garden with pool, helpful, German and some English spoken. Highly recommended.

C Sol del Valle, Gabriela Mistral 743, T411078, elquisoldelvalle@hotmail.com. Including breakfast, swimming pool, vineyard, restaurant.

C Valle Hermoso, Gabriela Mistral 706, T411206, nury_alvarez@hotmail.com. Comfortable, parking. Recommended.

Camping Camping y Piscina Las Tinajas, east end of Chacabuco. Swimming pool, restaurant.

Pisco Elqui

Prices are much lower outside Jan-Feb; if you're heading for Argentina, there is basic, clean accommodation at Huanta (Guanta on many maps), 46 km from Vicuña. *Cabañas* include **L-AL Los Misterios de Elqui**, A Prat, T051-1982544, www.misteriosdeelqui.cl, and **A-B Los Dátiles**, A Prat s/n, T451226, www.losdatileselqui.cl.

AL Elqui Domos, Sector los Nichos s/n, T09-7709 2879, www.elquidomos.cl. Accommodation in geodesic domes with roofs that open for a direct view of the night sky, English spoken.

A El Tesoro del Elqui, T051-451069, www.tesoro-elqui.cl. *Cabañas* for up to 4, shared room for up to 4 with shared bath (**D**), café, pool, pleasant gardens, German and English spoken.

B Refugio La Isla, Sector La Isla, T09-7476 9924, refugiolaisla@gmail.com. Idyllic retreat on a hillside overlooking the village. Simple, rustic, some rooms with bath. Kitchen facilities, pool, meditation room. Access difficult without transport. Recommended.

C Elqui, O'Higgins s/n by the plaza, T451130. Hot shower, central, good restaurant and bar. Recommended.

C Hostal Triskel, Callejón Baquedano, T09-9419 8680, www.hostaltriskel.cl. Cheaper in low season, **E** singles, shared bath, with breakfast, kitchen, attractive, bike rental, activities and tours arranged, therapies.

Camping G Campsite behind Camping El Olivo (which is closed). Excellent facilities, cold water, lots of trees by river, helpful owner, laundry facilities, very nice.

Eating

Ovalle *p736*

TT Club Social Arabe, Arauco 255. Spacious glass-domed premises, limited selection of Arab dishes.

T Casino La Bomba, Aguirre 364. Run by fire brigade, good value almuerzos.

T El Calamar, in the middle of the Feria Modelo. Good-value lunches – fish and meat. There are many more cheap eateries at the entrance to the market.

El Quijote, Arauco 294. Intimate bar, old-timers' haunt full of socialist posters and memorabilia.

Coquimbo *p737*

Seafood tends to be better here than La Serena.

¥¥¥-¥¥ Sal y Pimienta del Capitán Denny, Aldunate 769. Mainly fish cooked Chilean style, one of the best in town, pleasant, old fashioned.

¥¥ La Picada, Costanera near statue of O'Higgins. Excellent, try the tasty *pebre*.

¥ La Bahía, Pinto 1465. Good food and value.

¥ La Barca, Ríos y Varela. Modest, but good food.

La Serena *p737, map p738*

Most restaurants close off season on Sun; generally more expensive here than in Coquimbo. The best place for seafood is the Sector de Pescadores (¥¥) at **Peñuelas**, on the coast halfway between La Serena and Coquimbo. Take any bus to Coquimbo and get out at the junction with Los Pescadores; walk 300 m to the coast.

¥¥¥-¥¥ Donde El Guatón, Brasil 750. Parrillada, also good seafood, one of the better places in the town centre.

¥¥¥-¥¥ Porotos, Av del Mar 900-B, Sector El Faro, T051-210937. Wide variety of well presented dishes (fish, meat and pasta), decent portions and attentive service.

¥¥ Costa Inca, Av del Mar 2500, T212802. Good value and a range of delicious Peruvian dishes.

¥¥ La Mía Pizza, Av del Mar 2100, T212232. Italian, good-value pizzas and also fish dishes, good wine list.

¥ Daniela 2, F de Aguirre 335. Good-quality Chilean home cooking. Recommended.

¥ Govindas, Lautaro 841, T224289. Open Mon-Fri lunchtime, cheap vege- tarian food served in a Hari Krishna yoga centre.

Diavoletto, Prat 565 and O'Higgins 531. Fast food and ice cream, popular. Other cafés on Prat 500 block and Balmaceda 400 block.

Elqui Valley: Vicuña *p739*

¥¥ Club Social de Elqui, Gabriela Mistral 435. Attractive patio, good value *almuerzo*, real coffee.

¥¥ Halley, Gabriela Mistral 404. Good meat, with local specialities, goat (huge portion) and rabbit.

¥ Michel, Gabriela Mistral 180. Popular, good value almuerzo.

¥ Yo Y Soledad, Gabriela Mistral 364. Inexpensive, hearty Chilean food, good value.

Bars and clubs

La Serena *p737, map p738*

Most of the clubs are on Av del Mar and in Peñuelas, but in town you could try the following:

El Callejón, O'Higgins 635. Lounge bar and patio, with a relaxed atmosphere, young crowd. Also serves cheap food. Fills up with students at weekends.

El Nuevo Peregrino, Peni y Andrés Bello. Intimate bar with live music at weekends.

Festivals and events

Coquimbo *p737*

Coquimbo hosts **La Pampilla**, by far the biggest independence day celebrations in Chile. Between 200-300,000 people come from all over the country for the fiesta, which lasts for a week from **14-21 Sep**. It costs a nominal US$1.50 to enter the main dancing area (peñas cost extra); plenty of typical Chilean food and drink.

Activities and tours

La Serena *p737, map p738*

Valle del Elqui US$30, Parque Nacional Fray Jorge US$50, Tongoy US$40, Reserva Nacional Los Pingüinos and the Isla Damas US$50. Some also run tours to Valle del Encanto, Andacolla and Isla Chañaral. Responsible operators will not run tours to Mamalluca or Las Damas in bad weather.

Chile Safari, Matta 367, T09-8769 7686, www.chilesafari.com. Biking, surfing.

Delfines, Matta 591A, T223624, www.turismoaventuradelfines.cl. Traditional and adventure tours, bike rental, birdwatching and full tourist service.

Elqui Total, Parcela 17, El Arrayan at Km 27 along the road from La Serena to Vicuña, T09-9219 7872, www.elquitotal.cl. Offer short horse-riding trips from their base.

Elqui Valley Tours, Los Carrera 515, T215057, www.elquivalleytour.cl. Good for local tours, enthusiastic guides.

Jeep Tour La Serena, T09-9291 8105, www.jeeptour-laserena.cl. Private and small group tours (max 6 people) of the area led by Swiss Guide Daniel Russ. Apart from the usual tours he also offers trips to the

Paso Agua Negra and also a transfer service to San Juan in Argentina (summer only).
Talinay Adventure Expeditions, Prat 470, in the courtyard, T218658, www.talinay chile.com. Offers a range of local tours, also trekking and climbing.

Transport

Ovalle and around *p736*
Bus Most of the many rural buses leave from either of 2 terminals outside the Feria Modelo. The main bus terminal is the Terminal Media Luna (by the rodeo ring on Ariztía Oriente) just south of the city centre. Buses to **Santiago**, several, 6½ hrs, US$11; to **Valparaíso**, 6 hrs, US$11; to **Antofagasta**, 14 hrs, US$28; to **La Serena**, 1½ hrs, US$3.50. To **Hurtado**, **Buses M&R**, T691866, T09-9822 0320, has buses on Mon, Wed, Fri at 1200, 1230 and 1500, Sat 1400, Tue and Thu at 1615 and 1645, and Sun 1700 and 1730, US$3.

Taxi
Abel Olivares Rivera, T620352. Recommended. The round trip to **Parque Nacional Fray Jorge** costs US$75.

Andacollo
Colectivo from Ovalle, US$4; **bus**, US$3.

Coquimbo *p737*
Bus Terminal at Varela y Garriga. To **La Serena**, US$1.

La Serena *p737, map p738*
Air Aeropuerto La Florida, 5 km east of the city, T271812. To **Santiago** and **Copiapó**, with **LAN**.
Bus City buses US$0.75. Bus terminal, El Santo y Amunátegui (about 8 blocks south of the centre). **Tur-Bus** office, Balmaceda entre Prat y Cordovez. Buses daily to **Santiago**, several companies, 7-8 hrs, US$15-25. To **Valparaíso**, 7 hrs, US$15-25. To **Caldera**, 6 hrs, US$14. To **Calama**, US$30-65, 16 hrs. To **Antofagasta**, 12-13 hrs, several companies, US$28-43, and to **Iquique**, 17 hrs, US$35-69, and **Arica**, 20 hrs, US$43-55. To **Vicuña** and **Pisco Elqui**, see below. To **Coquimbo**, bus No 8 from Av Aguirre y Cienfuegos, US$1, every few mins.
Car hire **Daire**, Balmaceda 3812, T226933, recommended, good service; **Flota Verschae**, Av Balmaceda 3856, T241685, good value, recommended; **La Florida** at airport, T271947.
Taxi US$0.75 + US$0.25 per every 200 m. Colectivos with fixed rates, destination on roof; also to Coquimbo from Aguirre y Balmaceda.

Elqui Valley: Vicuña *p739*
Bus To **La Serena**, about 10 a day (more in summer), most by **Via Elqui/Megal Bus**, first 0800, last 1930, 1 hr, US$3, colectivo from bus terminal US$4. To **Pisco Elqui**, 10 a day with Vía Elqui, 1 hr, US$3.25. Buses from Pisco Elqui to La Serena go via Vicuña, US$3.25.

Directory

La Serena *p737, map p738*
Airline offices LAN, Balmaceda 406, T600-526 2000, also an office in the Mall Plaza.
Banks ATMs at most banks and in the bus terminal. Casas de cambio: **Inter**, Balmaceda 431; **Cambio Fides**, Caracol Colonial, Balmaceda 460, good rates, changes TCs; also **Cambio Caracol** in the same building. If heading north note that La Serena is the last place to change TCs before Antofagasta. **Cultural centres** **Alianza Francesa**, Matta 665, T211005, laserena@alliancesfrancaises.net. Library, films, etc.
Internet Cybercafés in the city centre.
Telephones Lots of call centres in the town centre.

North of La Serena

North of the Río Elqui, the transitional zone continues to the mining and agro-industrial centre of Copiapó. Thereafter begins the desert, which is of little interest, except after rain. Then it is covered with a succession of flowers, insects and frogs, in one of the world's most spectacular wildlife events. Rain, however, is rare: there is none in summer; in winter it is light and lasts only a short time. Annual precipitation at Copiapó is about 115 mm. Drivers must beware of high winds and blowing sand north of Copiapó.

The Huasco valley is an oasis of olive groves and vineyards. It is rugged and spectacular, dividing at Alto del Carmen, 30 km east of Vallenar, into the Carmen and Tránsito valleys. There are pisco distilleries at Alto del Carmen and San Félix. A sweet wine, Pajarete, is also produced.

Reserva Nacional Pingüino de Humboldt

Some 72 km north of La Serena, a road branches west off the Panamericana to **Punta de Choros**. This is the departure point for the Humboldt Penguin Natural Reserve, on Islas Chañaral, Choros and Damas. Besides penguins, there are seals, sea lions, a great variety of seabirds and, offshore, a colony of grey dolphin. Isla Damas has interesting flora, too. To visit the reserve, tours are available from La Serena and Vallenar or you can hire a boat with local fishermen (around US$80 for up to 10 people). Isla Damas is the only island at which it is possible to disembark (entrance US$5) and camping is allowed, but you must first seek permission from **CONAF** in Punta de Choros, T051-272798; toilet but no drinking water.

Vallenar → *Phone code: 051. Colour map 8, A1. Population: 47,000. Altitude: 380 m.*

This is the chief town of the Huasco valley, 194 km north of La Serena. It has a pleasant Plaza de Armas, with marble benches. About seven blocks southeast is the **Museo del Huasco** ⓘ *Sgto Aldea 742, Tue-Fri 1500-1800, US$1*. It contains historic photos and artefacts from the valley. At the mouth of the river, 56 km west, is the pleasant port of Huasco (cheap seafood restaurants near the harbour). The staff at the Municipalidad on Plaza de Armas are helpful and there is a tourist kiosk on the plaza in summer.

Copiapó → *Phone code: 052. Colour map 6, C2. Population: 127,000. Altitude: 400 m.*

The valley of the Río Copiapó, generally regarded as the southern limit of the Atacama desert, is an oasis of farms, vineyards and orchards about 150 km long. Copiapó is an important mining centre. Founded in 1744, Copiapó became a prosperous town after the discovery in 1832 of the third largest silver deposits in South America at Chañarcillo (the mine was closed in 1875). The discoverer, Juan Godoy, a mule-driver, is commemorated at Matta y O'Higgins. Opposite is the **Museo Regional del Atacama** ⓘ *Mon 1400-1745, Tue-Fri 0900-1745, Sat 1000-1245, 1500-1745, Sun 1000-1245, US$1 (free Sun)*, with collections on local history, especially the Huentelauquén people, thought to have flourished 10,000 years ago, and the 19th century. **Museo Mineralógico** ⓘ *Colipí y Rodríguez, 1 block east from Plaza Prat, Mon-Fri 1000-1300, 1530-1900, Sat 1000-1300, US$1*. This is the best museum of its type in Chile, with a collection of weird and wonderful minerals and fossils from Chile and around the world. Many ores shown are found only in the Atacama desert. The Museo Ferroviario at the old railway station on Calle Martínez opens irregularly, but the Norris Brothers steam locomotive and carriages used in the inaugural journey between Copiapó and Caldera in 1851 (the first railway in South America) can be seen at the Universidad de Atacama about 2 km north of the centre on Avenida R Freire. Helpful **tourist office** ⓘ *Los Carrera 691, north side of Plaza Prat, T212838, infoatacama@sernatur.cl, Mon-Fri 0830-1930, Sat 1030-1430, 1630-1930, Sun 1030-1430; out of season Mon-Fri 0830-1730 only.*

Border with Argentina: Paso San Francisco

Paso San Francisco is reached either by the unpaved Camino Internacional northeast from Copiapó, or by an unpaved road southeast from El Salvador: both routes join near the Salar de Maricunga in the **Parque Nacional Tres Cruces**, 96 km west of Paso San Francisco. Two alternative routes from Copiapó run through the park. The road then passes Laguna Verde before entering Argentina, where a paved road continues to Tinogasta. The border post is at Fiambalá, 210 km beyond the border, open 0700-1900, but there is also a police post at La Gruta, 24 km beyond the border. Chilean immigration and customs are near the Salar de Maricunga, 100 km west of the border, open 0900-1900 (24 hours in summer); US$2 per vehicle charge for crossing Saturday, Sunday and holidays. This crossing is liable to closure after snow: T052-198 1009 for road reports. Always take spare fuel. Paving of the Chilean side started in 2009.

Caldera and around → *Phone code: 052. Colour map 6, C2. Population: 12,000.*

This is a port and terminal for the loading of iron ore, 73 km northwest of Copiapó. **Iglesia de San Vicente de Paul** (1862) on the Plaza de Armas was built by English carpenters working for the railway company. The restored train station houses a cultural centre and tourist office (summer only). **Bahía Inglesa**, 6 km south of Caldera, 6 km west of the Highway, is popular for its beautiful white sandy beaches and unpolluted sea. It's rather expensive and can get crowded in summer and at weekends, but off season makes a perfect, deserted retreat. It was originally known as Puerto del Inglés after the visit in 1687 of the English 'corsario', Edward Davis.

Chañaral → *Phone code: 052. Colour map 6, C2. Population: 12,000.*

The valley of the Río Salado, 130 km in length, less fertile or prosperous than the Copiapó or Huasco valleys, is the last oasis south of Antofagasta. Chañaral, a town with old wooden houses perched on the hillside at the mouth of the Salado, is 93 km north of Caldera. In its heyday it was the processing centre for ore from the nearby copper mines of El Salado and Las Animas. Now it is a base for visits to beaches and the Parque Nacional Pan de Azúcar. There's a tourist information kiosk on the Pan-American Highway at the south end of Chañaral (closed winter). If it is closed, go to the Municipalidad.

Parque Nacional Pan de Azúcar

ⓘ *US$6 (US$3 for Chileans). CONAF office in Caleta Pan de Azúcar, 0830-1230, 1400-1800 daily, maps available. There are heavy fines for driving in 'restricted areas' of the park.*

The park, north of Chañaral, consists of the Isla Pan de Azúcar on which Humboldt penguins and other sea-birds live, and some 43,769 ha of coastal hills rising to 800 m. There are fine beaches (popular at weekends in summer). Fishermen near the CONAF office offer boat trips round Isla Pan de Azúcar to see the penguins, US$8.50 per person (minimum total US$85). Alternatively, a 2½-hour walk goes from the office to a mirador with extensive views over the south of the park. Vegetation is mainly cacti, of which there are 26 species, nourished by frequent sea mists (*camanchaca*). The park is home to 103 species of birds as well as guanaco and foxes. Pollution from nearby copper mining is a threat. There are two entrances: north by good secondary road from Chañaral, 28 km to Caleta Pan de Azúcar; from the Pan-American Highway 45 km north of Chañaral, along a side road 20 km.

Taltal → *Phone code: 055. Colour map 6, C2. Population: 9,000.*

This is the only town between Chañaral and Antofagasta, a distance of 420 km. Along Avenida Prat are several wooden buildings dating from the late 19th century, when Taltal prospered as a mineral port of 20,000 people. It is now a fishing port with a mineral processing plant. North 72 km is the Quebrada El Médano, a gorge with ancient rock-paintings along the upper valley walls.

North of La Serena listings

For Sleeping and Eating price codes and other relevant information, see Essentials, pages 38-40.

Sleeping

Reserva Nacional Pingüino de Humboldt: Punta de Choros *p745*

C Cabañas Los Delfines, Pilpilen s/n, sitio 33, T09-9639 6678. Cabins for up to 6. There are other sleeping and eating options in the area.

Vallenar *p745*

Listed hotels and restaurants all recommended.

A Hostería de Vallenar, Ercilla 848, T614379, http://hotelesatacama.cl. Good, pool, parking, with breakfast and restaurant, Hertz car hire office.

A Puerto de Vega, Ramírez 201, T618534, www.puertodevega.cl. Probably the best in town, 12 individually-decorated rooms, pleasant patio and pool.

B Cecil, Prat 1059, T614071. A good modern hotel with hot water and a swimming pool.

C Hostal Camino del Rey, Merced 943, T613184. Cheaper without bath, good value.

D Vall, Aconcagua 455, T613380, hostal_vall@yahoo.es. With breakfast, parking, good value.

D Viña del Mar, Serrano 611, T611478. Nice rooms, clean *comedor*, a good choice.

Copiapó *p745*

A Chagall, O'Higgins 760, T213775, www.chagall.cl. The best of the executive hotels, central, some rooms with king-size beds and desk, modern fittings, internet, spacious lounge and bar open to public.

B La Casona, O'Higgins 150, T217278, www.lacasonahotel.cl. More like a home than a hostel, desert colours, good beds, cable TV, pleasant garden, restaurant, bar, internet access, English spoken.

B Rocca D'Argento, Maipú 580, T218744, www.atacamachile.com/ hotelrocca. Ugly exterior and mixed standard of rooms, some are spacious and good value, cable TV, heating, tours and car hire arranged.

B-C Corona del Inca, Las Heras 54, T363489, sanval@tie.cl. With breakfast, big rooms, quiet, good value. No restaurant.

B-C Montecatini I, Infante 766, T211363, h.montecatini@terra.cl. Large rooms around beautiful courtyard, swimming pool. Some smaller rooms without TV are cheaper. Helpful, best value in this price bracket. **Montecatini II**, Atacama 374, T211516, is **A-B**.

C Palace, Atacama 741, T212852. Comfortable, breakfast extra, parking, central, nice patio. Good value.

D Res Benbow, Rodríguez 541, T217634. Basic rooms, some with bath, but the best value of the many *residenciales* on this part of Rodríguez. Usually full of mine workers. Excellent value full-board deals.

D Res Eli, Maipú 739, T219650. **F-G** singles. Simple rooms, good beds, decent choice.

D Res Rocío, Yerbas Buenas 581, T215360. **F** singles. Some rooms with bath and cable TV, patio. Good budget option.

D pp **Res Torres**, Atacama 230, T240 727. **F** singles. Without bath, hot water, quiet.

Caldera *p746*

Caldera is cheaper than Bahía Inglesa in summer.

A Hostería Puerta del Sol, Wheelwright 750, T315205, www.hosteriapuertadelsol.com. Cabins with good beds, all mod cons, kitchen, swimming pool, view over bay.

A Portal del Inca, Carvallo 945, T315252, www.portaldelinca.cl. Cabins with kitchen, English spoken, restaurant not bad, order breakfast on previous night.

B Costanera, Wheelwright 543, T316007. Takes credit cards, simple rooms.

D pp **Res Millaray**, Cousiño 331, Plaza de Armas, T315528. Good value, basic.

Bahía Inglesa

A Los Jardines de Bahía Inglesa, Av Copiapó, T315359, www.jardinesbahia.cl. Open all year, *cabañas* from 2 to 11 people, good beds, comfortable.

B Cabañas Playa Paraíso, Av Costanera 6000, T09-886 7666, www.cabanasparaiso.cl. Idyllic spot on the beach, 6 km south of town. Cosy cabins for up to 6, BBQs, kitchen, solar-powered, Reiki and massages available. Recommended.

B El Coral, Av El Morro, T315331. Restaurant overlooking sea, has some cabins, good seafood, groups welcome, open all year.

B-C Camping Bahía Inglesa, Playa Las Machas, T315424. Fully equipped *cabañas* for up to 5 persons, **C** tent site.
B-C Domo Chango Chile, Av El Morro 610, T316168, www.changochile.cl. Lodging in domes, sleeping up to 5, by the beach, comfortable, with excellent restaurant, also called **Domo**, specialising in fish, seafood, meats, salads and desserts.

Chañaral *p746*
B Hostería Chañaral, Müller 268, T48050. Slightly dated, but spacious rooms and attentive service, the food is good in the beautiful dining room. With pool room and parking.
C Jiménez, Merino Jarpa 551, T480328.
D without bath, modern, patio with lots of birds, restaurant good value, convenient for Pullman Bus. Recommended.
C-D Hostal Sutivan, Comercio 365, T489123, hostalsutivan@terra.cl. **E-F** singles. Nice rooms with or without bath, good beds, excellent value. Also arranges tours to Pan de Azúcar. Highly recommended.
E Res Molina, Pinto 583, T480075. Shared bath, kitchen and laundry facilities, nice family (owner runs good tours of the Pan de Azúcar park, see Activities and tours). Recommended.
F pp **Hostal Playa Mar**, Av Merino Jarpa y Zuleta, T489039. Next to TurBus, small rooms, shared bath, with breakfast, kitchen, Wi-Fi.

Parque Nacional Pan de Azúcar *p746*
AL-A There are a dozen or so *cabañas* in the park run by **Gran Atacama** in Copiapó (Mall Plaza Real, T219271, www.granatacama.cl). Reservations and advance payment are essential in high season. Perfectly placed on a deserted beach behind the *caleta*, sleep 6. Discounts may be possible off season.

E-F pp. Some fishermen in the *caleta* let out rooms; quite basic.
Camping Three campsites in the park, one in the Caleta, run by the fishermen, and **Camping El Piquero** and **El Soldado** run by **Gran Atacama** in Copiapó (see above).

Taltal *p746*
B Mi Tampi, O'Higgins 138, T055-613605, www.hotelmitampi.cl. Best hotel in town, comfortable spacious rooms, good service, Wi-Fi. Advance booking essential. Recommended.
C-D Hostal de Mar, Carrera 250, T613539. Simple rooms, cable TV, only the front 2 rooms have external windows. Breakfast extra.
D Hostería Taltal, Esmeralda 671, T611173, btay@entelchile.net. Passable restaurant, Wi-Fi zone, cheaper rooms without bath. Decent enough but doesn't do justice to its seafront location.
E San Martín, Martínez 279, T611088. Without bath, good *almuerzo*.

Eating

Vallenar *p745*
Cheap eating places along south end of Av Brasil.
TT Bavaria, Serrano 802. Chain restaurant, good.
TT Pizza Il Boccato, Plaza O'Higgins y Prat. Good coffee, good food, popular.
T La Pica, Brasil y Faez. Good for cheap meals, seafood, cocktails.

Copiapó *p745*
TT Bavaria, Chacabuco 487 (Plaza Prat) and on Los Carrera. Good variety, restaurant and cafe.
TT Chifa Hao Hwa, Colipí 340 and Yerbas Buenas 334. Good Chinese, one of several in town.
TT Entre Yuntas, Vallejos 226. Rustic but cosy, Peruvian/Chilean food, live music Fri and Sat.
TT-T La Vitrola, Cosmocentro Plaza Real, p 2. Self-service lunch buffet, good range, reasonably priced, good views.
T Benbow, Rodríguez 543. Good value *almuerzo*, extensive menu.
T Don Elias, Los Carrera e Yerbas Buenas. Excellent seafood, popular.

Caldera *p746*
El Teatro, Gana 12, T316768. Generally considered to be the best restaurant in town.
T Miramar, Gana 090. At pier, good seafood.

Bahía Inglesa
See **Domo Hostel**, above.
TT El Plateao, El Morro 756-B on the Costanera. Seafood with Peruvian and Oriental influences, first class.

extra fee, taxis from the airport will drive past La Portada). Hitching is easy. From the main road it is 2 km to the beach which, though beautiful, is too dangerous for swimming; there is a seafood restaurant (La Portada) and café (open lunch-time only). A number of bathing beaches are also within easy reach.

Juan López, 38 km north of Antofagasta, is a windsurfers' paradise. The sea is alive with birds, including Humboldt penguins, especially opposite Isla Santa María. For those with their own transport, follow the road out of Juan López to the beautiful cove at Conchilla. Keep on the

Antofagasta

N

200 metres
200 yards

Sleeping
1 Ancla Inn *C2*
2 Casa El Mosaico *C1*
3 Ciudad de Avila *B3*
4 Colón *B2*
5 Dakota *B2*
6 Florencia Suites *C1*
7 Hostal del Norte *A3*
8 Hostal Frontera *B3*
9 Marsal *C3*
10 Res El Cobre *C3*
11 Res La Riojanita *B2*

Eating
1 Aromas y Sabores de la India *C3*
2 Café del Centro *B2*
3 Club de la Unión & Café Bahía *B2*
4 El Arriero *B2*
5 El Chico Jaime *C2*
6 El Curicano *B3*
7 Hotel Antofagasta *B1*
8 Panda *C2*
9 Picadillo *C1*
10 Pizzante *C2*
11 Rincón Oriental *A2*
12 Spell café *B1*
13 Tomodachi *C1*
14 Tío Jacinto *C2*

Bars & clubs
15 Wally's Pub *C2*

track to the end at Bolsico. **Mejillones** (*Population: 5,500*), a little fishing port 60 km north of Antofagasta, stands on a good natural harbour protected from westerly gales by high hills. Until 1948 it was a major terminal for the export of tin and other metals from Bolivia: remnants of that past include a number of fine wooden buildings: the Intendencia Municipal, the Casa Cultural (built in 1866) and the church (1906), as well as the Capitanía del Puerto. The town has been transformed in recent years by the building of the largest port in South America, which links Argentina, southern Brazil and Paraguay with the lucrative markets of the Asian Pacific Rim.

Antofagasta and around listings

For Sleeping and Eating price codes and other relevant information, see Essentials, pages 38-40.

Sleeping

Antofagasta and around *p750, map p751*
L Florencia Suites, Croacia 0126, T789221, www.florenciasuites.cl. Luxury suites on the coast south of the city centre with lovely sea views. Also restaurant and pool. Recommended.
AL Marsal, Prat 867, T268063, www.marsal hotel.cl. Modern, very comfortable, bright and spacious rooms, internet, Catalan owner. Recommended.
A Ancla Inn, Baquedano 516, T224814, www.ancla inn.cl. One of the city's larger hotels with restaurant, car park, pool and sauna. Reasonably good value but avoid the interior rooms.
B Colón, San Martín 2434, T261851, hotel. colon@terra.com. Comfortable, with breakfast, hot water, quiet, cash only, reasonable value
B-C Dakota, Latorre 2425, T251749, floreria magnolia@hotmail.com. With breakfast and cable TV, popular, good value. Recommended.
C Casa El Mosaico, Playa El Huáscar (south of town), Casa 18, behind Kamikaze Disco, T9-938 0743, www.chilegreentours.com. Private and shared rooms (**E** pp) in new guesthouse associated with **Chile Green Tours**, lots of activities and tours, information and the hostel itself is recommended. The perfect place to relax for a few days after spending time in the desert.
C Ciudad de Avila, Condell 2840, T/F221 040, hotelciudaddeavila@yahoo.es. Spotless, good value, TV, basic restaurant. Recommended.
C-D Hostal Frontera, Bolívar 558, T281219. Basic but with good hot showers and decent beds, TV, convenient for Tur-Bus and Pullman.
C-D Res El Cobre, Prat 749, T225162. Some rooms with bath, set around a central courtyard, bright and clean, but tatty.
E Hostal del Norte, Latorre 3162, T251265, hostaldelnorte_aft@hotmail.com. Some rooms with bath, comfortable, quiet, brighter annex at the back.
D-E Res La Riojanita, Baquedano 464, T381056. Basic, very helpful, Older rooms have high ceilings but are run- down, newer rooms with bath are smaller. Not a bad budget option.

Camping To the south on the road to Coloso are: **Las Garumas**, Km 6, T247763 ext 42, **E** per site (ask for lower price out of season), **C** for cabins, cold showers and beach (reservations Av Angamos 601, casilla 606).

Juan López
C Hostería Sandokan, Juan López, T223022. Standard facilities, nice location.

Eating

Antofagasta and around *p750, map p751*
Many bars and restaurants are closed on Sun.
ΨΨΨ Club de la Unión, Prat 474, p 2, T268371. Open to non-members, traditional atmosphere, excellent almuerzo and service.
ΨΨΨ-ΨΨ Picadillo, Av Grecia 1000. Lively atmosphere, serves a wide range of dishes. Good music. Recommended.
ΨΨΨ-ΨΨ Tomodachi, Grecia 1730, T376552. The best of the city's sushi restaurants.
ΨΨ Aromas y Sabores de la India, Copiapó 1294. Indian restaurant and takeaway, the only one of its kind in northern Chile.
ΨΨ El Arriero, Condell 2644, T264371. Grills and traditional hearty criollo food. Good service, cheap set lunch, popular, live music.
ΨΨ Panda, Condell 2505. Self-service, Chinese and Chilean, eat all you can for US$9.
ΨΨ Pizzante, Carrera 1857, T223344. Good pasta, seafood and vegetarian options.

🍴🍴 **Rincón Oriental**, Washington 2432. Excellent Cantonese, 'over the top' décor. Recommended.
🍴🍴 **Spell café**, outdoor food court in the mall. Varied menu including catch of the day. Good service. Wide range of drinks, fresh juices.
🍴🍴 **Tío Jacinto**, Uribe 922. Friendly atmosphere, serves good seafood.
🍴🍴-🍴 **El Chico Jaime**, Mercado Central 2nd floor, local 115, T227401. Best of the restaurants in the central market, good food and friendly service.
🍴 **El Curicano**, Simón Bolívar 607. Good value, basic set menu lunches and dinners.

Above the market are several good places selling cheap seafood *almuerzos* and super-cheap set lunches, including **El Mariscal** and **Toledo**. Good fish restaurants in Terminal Pesquero Centro and at Caleta Coloso, 18 km south.

Cafés

Hotel Antofagasta, Balmaceda 2575 (T228811, www.hotelantofagasta.cl, 4-star, **AL** range), offers an all-you-can-eat buffet breakfast for US$8. The only place open early for breakfast.
Café Bahía, Prat 474. Open at 0900 for for real coffee.
Café del Centro, Galería, Prat 482. Real coffee.

Bars and clubs

Antofagasta and around *p750, map p751*

Thanks to Antofagasta's student population, the city's nightlife is buzzing. The most popular bars and clubs are 16 km south of the town in Balneario El Huáscar. Take micro 103 from C Matta to get there. There is also a wide choice on O'Higgins.
Wally's Pub, Toro 982. British expat-style with darts, pool and beer, closed Sun.
X3, probably the best of the clubs at El Huáscar.

Entertainment

Antofagasta and around *p750, map p751*

Teatro Municipal, Sucre y San Martín, T264919. Modern, state-of-the art theatre.
Teatro Pedro de la Barra, Condell 2495. Theatre run by University of Antofagasta, regular programme of plays, reviews, concerts, etc, high standard, details in press.

Festivals and events

Antofagasta and around *p750, map p751*

29 Jun, San Pedro, the image of the patron saint of the fishermen is taken out by launch to the breakwater to bless the first catch of the day. On the last weekend of **Oct**, the city's immigrant communities put on a joint festival on the seafront, with national foods, dancing and music.

Shopping

Antofagasta and around *p750, map p751*

The new **Mall Plaza Antofagasta**, Balmaceda y Maipú has a wide variety of shops and a pleasant promenade on the roof, with colourful flowers and views out to the ocean.
Bookshops Antartica, in the mall. Best selection in town.
Food shops and supermarkets Bótica, Latorre 2410. **Korlaert**, on Ossa 2400-2500 block. **Líder**, A Pinto, north of the port. **Tottus**, Balmaceda, south side of the mall. Huge supermarket.
Markets Feria Modelo O'Higgins (next to fish market on Av Pinto). Excellent fruit and veg, also restaurants. The municipal market is at Matta y Uribe.

Activities and tours

Antofagasta and around *p750, map p751*

Many tour companies offer packages to the Atacama, but it is generally better to book tours in San Pedro de Atacama.
Buceo Magallanes, Balmaceda 2615, T244873, www.buceomagallanes.cl. Regular diving trips and courses.
Chile Green Tours, see **Casa El Mosaico**, under Sleeping, above.
Soul Surf, Ejercito 155, local 15, near the Balneario Municipal, www.soulsurf.cl. Gives classes and rents and sells surfing equipment. See www.surfantofagasta.cl for more information on surfing in the area.

Transport

Antofagasta and around *p750, map p751*

Air Cerro Moreno Airport, 22 km north. Taxi to airport US$23, but cheaper if ordered from hotel. For airport transfers, **Aerobus**, T262727, US$6. **LAN**, **Principal** and **Sky** fly daily to **Santiago**, **Copiapó**, **Iquique** and **Arica**. **LAN** also daily to La Serena.
Bus No main terminal; each company has its own office in town (some quite a distance from the centre). Buses for **Mejillones**, 1 hr, US$2, from Corsal terminal, Condell y Sucre; also

minibuses Latorre 2730. To **Tocopilla**, 2½ hrs, US$6, many daily. Bus company offices: **Flota Barrios**, Condell 2682, T268559; **Géminis** and **Romani**, Latorre 3055, T251796; **Pullman Bus**, Latorre 2805, T262591; **Tur-Bus**, Latorre 2751, T264487. To **Santiago**, many companies: 18 hrs, US$39-70; book in advance in high season. If all seats to the capital are booked, catch a bus to **La Serena** (12 hrs, US$26-42), or **Ovalle**, 14 hrs, and re-book. To **Valparaíso**, US$39. To **Copiapó**, 7 hrs, US$18-32. Frequent buses to **Iquique**, US$16-21, 6 hrs. To **Arica**, US$20-37, 11 hrs. To **Calama**, several companies, US$7, 3 hrs; to **San Pedro de Atacama**, **Tur-Bus** 6 daily, 5 hrs, US$8, or via Calama.

To **Salta, Argentina** **Géminis**, Tue, Fri, Sun 0700, via Calama, San Pedro de Atacama, Paso de Jama and Jujuy, US$70, 18 hrs. Also **Pullman Bus**, US$77. Book in advance, take food and as much warm clothing as possible; also small denomination US dollars, as nowhere to change Chilean pesos en route.

Juan López

Bus At weekends in summer only, also mini-buses daily in summer from Latorre y Sucre, Antofagasta.

Directory

Antofagasta and around *p750, map p751*

Airline offices LAN, Paseo Prat, T265151, or 600-526 2000. **Principal**, Sucre 375, T569758, or 600-425 3510. **Sky**, Velásquez 890, T459090, or 600-600 2828. **Banks** It's difficult to change TCs south of Antofagasta until you reach La Serena. Several with ATMs around the plaza and the rest of the centre. **Casas de Cambio** are mainly on Baquedano, such as **Ancla**, No 524, Mon-Fri 0900-1400, 1600-1900 (at weekends try ice cream shop next door) and shopping centre at No 482-98. **Afex**, Latorre 2572. **Car hire** First, Bolívar 623, T225777. Plus international agencies. **Andrés Ljubetic Romo**, Atacama 2657, T268851, is a recommended mechanic. **Consulates** **Argentina**, Blanco Encalada 1933, T220440. **Belgium**, Baquedano 299, T268669. **Bolivia**, Washington 2675, p 13, T225010. **France**, Esmeralda 2286; **Germany**, Pérez Zujovic 4940, T556387, hans.schaefer@reptal.cl. **Italy**, Matta 1945, of 808, T227791. **Netherlands**, Washington 2675, of 902, T266252, juromu@gmail.com. **Spain**, Rendic 4946, T269596. **Cultural centres** Instituto **Chileno Norteamericano**, Carrera 1445, T262731. **Centro Cultural Nueva Acrópolis**, Uribe 786, T493885, www.antofagasta.nueva-acropolis.cl, lots of activities, including tai chi and yoga, talks and discussions. **Internet and telephone** Lots in the centre, especially around the bus terminals. **Post offices** on Plaza Colón. 0830-1900, Sat 0900-1300. Also at Washington 2613.

North of Antofagasta

To Iquique

Two routes go north towards Iquique: the Pan-American Highway and the coastal route. At Km 101 on the Pan-American, Carmen Alto (98 km north of Antofagasta, petrol, food), a paved road leads to Calama. To the west of the Highway are the remains of several nitrate towns. 107 km north of Carmen Alto is the crossroads to Tocopilla (72 km west) and Chuquicamata (east) and, 81 km beyond, **Quillagua**, officially the driest place in the world (customs post, all southbound vehicles and buses are searched). 111 km further is the first of three sections of the Reserva Nacional del Tamarugal. In this part are the **Geoglyphs of Cerro Pintados**, some 400 figures (humans, animals, geometric shapes) on the hillside (3 km west of the highway). The second part of Tamarugal is near La Tirana (see page 765), the third 60 km north of Pozo Almonte.

The coastal route is more picturesque than the Pan-American Highway. On this road, 187 km north of Antofagasta, is **Tocopilla** (Phone code: 055; Colour map 6, B2; Population: 24,600), a useful place to stop. It has one of the most dramatic settings of any Chilean town, sheltering at the foot of 500-m high mountains that loom inland. A thermal power station and the port facilities used to unload coal and to export nitrates and iodine from María Elena and Pedro de

Valdivia dominate the town. There are some interesting early 20th century buildings with wooden balustrades and façades, but it was heavily damaged by an earthquake on 14 November 2007 and it's generally a rundown, slightly menacing place. There are two good beaches: Punta Blanca (12 km south) and Caleta Covadonga, 3 km south with a swimming pool.

The coast road from Tocopilla north to Iquique is paved, 244 km, with fantastic views of the rugged coastline and tiny fishing communities. The customs post at **Chipana-Río Loa** (90 km north) searches all southbound vehicles for duty-free goods; 30 minutes delay. Basic accommodation is available at **San Marcos**, a fishing village, 131 km north. At **Chanaballita**, 184 km north there is a hotel, *cabañas*, camping, restaurant, shops. There are also campsites at **Guanillos**, Km 126, **Playa Peruana**, Km 129 and **Playa El Aguila**, Km 160.

Calama → *Phone code: 055. Colour map 6, B2. Population: 106,970. Altitude: 2,265 m.*

Calama lies in the oasis of the Río Loa, 202 km north of Antofagasta. Initially a staging post on the silver route between Potosí and Cobija, it is now an expensive, unprepossessing modern city, serving the nearby mines of Chuquicamata and Radomiro Tomic. Calama can be reached from the south by the paved road from Carmen Alto (see above), or from the north by Route 24 via Chuquicamata. The road passes many abandoned nitrate mines, *oficinas*. **Tourist office** ⓘ *Latorre 1689, T531707, www.cala macultural.cl, Mon-Fri 0800-1300, 1400-1800*. Map, tours, helpful staff, English spoken.

Two kilometres from the centre on Avenida B O'Higgins is the **Parque El Loa** ⓘ *daily 1000-1800*, which contains a reconstruction of a typical colonial village built around a reduced-scale reproduction of Chiu Chiu church. Nearby in the park is the **Museo Arqueológico y Etnológico** ⓘ *Tue-Fri 1000-1300, 1400-1800, Sat-Sun 1400-1830, US$0.75*, with an exhibition of prehispanic cultural history. Also the **Museo de Historia Natural** ⓘ *Wed-Sun, 1000-1300, 1500-1830, US$1*, with an interesting collection on the oficinas and on the region's ecology and palaeontology.

Chuquicamata → *Phone code: 055. Colour map 6, B2. Altitude: 2,800 m.*

North of Calama 16 km is the site of the world's largest open-cast copper mine, employing 8,000 workers and operated by Codelco (the state copper corporation). The visual spectacle of the site makes for a memorable visit. Everything about Chuquicamata is huge: the pit from which the ore is extracted is four km long, two km wide and 730 m deep; the giant trucks, with wheels over 3½ m high, carry 310 ton loads and work 24 hours a day; in other parts of the plant 60,000 tons of ore are processed a day. Guided tours, by bus, in Spanish (although guides usually speak reasonable English) leave from the ex-Colegio Chuquicamata ⓘ *Mon-Fri 1330 (less frequent in low season, tourist office in Calama has details), 1 hr, US$2 donation to the charity. Advance booking is needed for tours (up to a week in high season), English spoken; either call the office in Chuquicamata (T322122, visitas@codelco.cl) or from the tourist office in Calama; passport number essential*. Wear covered shoes, long trousers and long sleeves; filming is permitted in certain areas. Tours may be canceled without notice if there are high winds. Chuquicamata town has been closed off and much of it destroyed. Now that no one lives there, colectivos from Calama are scarce (ask the tourist office where you might catch one). For tours it is better to drive yourself or take a taxi (US$13) and arrive in Chuquicamata at 1300 at the latest.

From Calama it is 273 km north to Ollagüe, on the Bolivian border. (There is no petrol between Calama and Uyuni in Bolivia. If really short try buying from the carabineros at Ollagüe or Ascotán, the military at Conchi or the mining camp at Buenaventura, 5 km from Ollagüe.) The road follows the Río Loa, passing Chiu Chiu (33 km), one of the earliest Spanish settlements in the area. Just beyond this oasis, a small turning branches off the main road to the hamlet of **Lasana**, 8 km north of Chiu Chiu. Petroglyphs are clearly visible on the right-hand side of the road. There are striking ruins of a pre-Inca pukará, a national monument; drinks are on sale. If arranged in advance, Línea 80 colectivos will continue to Lasana for an extra charge. Pre-book the return trip, or walk back to Chiu Chiu. At **Conchi**, 25 km north of Lasana, the road crosses the

Río Loa via a bridge dating from 1890 (it's a military zone, so no photographs of the view are allowed). Beyond Chiu Chiu the road deteriorates, with deep potholes, but, north of Ascotán (carabinero checkpoint at 3,900 m), it improves as it crosses the Salares de Ascotán and de Carcote and Ollagüe (ask about the conditions on the Salares at Ascotán or Ollagüe before setting out, especially in December/January or August). There are many llama flocks along this road and flamingos on the salares.

Ollagüe ➔ *Colour map 6, B2. Altitude: 3,690 m.*

This village, on the dry floor of the Salar de Ollagüe, is surrounded by a dozen volcanic peaks of over 5,000 m. The border with Bolivia is open 0800-2000; US$2 per person charge for entry to Bolivia. A bad unmade road from Ollagüe runs into Bolivia and it is on the new Ruta Altiplanica, or "Inca Road" which runs from San Pedro de Atacama via El Tatio, Ascotán and Colchane to Visviri, with a planned continuation to Cuzco. There is a municipal hostel and food and drink is available in town. At this altitude the days are warm and sunny, nights cold (minimum -20° C). There are only 50 mm of rain a year, and water is very scarce.

Between Chiu Chiu and El Tatio (see below), **Caspana** (*Population: 400; Altitude: 3,305 m*) is beautifully set among hills with a tiny church dating from 1641 and a **museum** ⓘ *Tue-Sun 1000-1300, 1500-1730*, with interesting displays on Atacameño culture. Basic accommodation is available (the nearest to El Tatio). A poor road runs north and east through valleys of pampas grass with llama herds to **Toconce**, which has extensive prehispanic terraces set among interesting rock formations. There are archaeological sites nearby and the area is ideal for hiking. Further information from the tourist office in Calama, who may also help with arranging transport.

North of Antafagasta listings

For Sleeping and Eating price codes and other relevant information, see Essentials, pages 38-40.

Sleeping

To Iquique: Tocopilla *p754*

B-C Atenas, 21 de Mayo 1448, T813651. Characterless but comfortable. With bath and cable TV. Restaurant.

B-C Hostal Puerto Caliche, J Montt Salamanca 1040, T816286, www.hostalpuertocaliche.cl. Rooms with TV, breakfast, Wi-Fi, parking, restaurant.

C Croacia, Bolívar 1332, T810332. Modern, helpful, cheaper without bath. Opposite on Bolívar is the **Sucre**, same ownership, same price.

C Vucina, 21 de Mayo 2069, T813088. Safe parking.

Calama *p755*

L Park, Camino Aeropuerto 1392, T319900, www.parkplaza.cl/calama. On the edge of town by the airport. First class, pool, bar and restaurant.

A El Mirador, Sotomayor 2064, T340329, www.hotelmirador.cl. Price includes bath, internet, parking, TV and breakfast, good atmosphere and services, pleasant rooms, helpful.

A Hostería Calama, Latorre 1521, T341511, www.hosteriacalama.cl. Comfortable heated rooms, good food, buffet breakfast and service; gym and small pool. Airport transfer.

A LyS, Vicuña MacKenna 1819, T361113, www.lyshotel.cl. Business hotel, upstairs rooms more spacious, Wi-Fi. Often full Mon-Wed with mining engineers. A good choice.

B Res Alecris, Félix Hoyos 2143, T341616. **C** without bath, single, double and triple rooms, well-maintained, very clean, family atmosphere, often fully booked with miners, safe (CCTV, near police station), no breakfast, sunny courtyard. Chatty owner Alejandro.

B Universo, Sotomayor 1822, T361640, hoteluniverso@gmail.com. Decent rooms with bath, most face onto a corridor, but those with windows onto the street are much better and good value.

C-D Cavour, Sotomayor 1841, T314718, residencialcavour@hotmail.com. Hot water, TV, no breakfast, rooms off an open-air corridor, simple, hospitable but a bit run-down.

D San Sebastián, Pinto 1902, T343810. Meals available, family run, rooms with bath and TV in annex across the street.

Eating

Calama *p755*

On pedestrian part of C Eleuterio Ramírez, several cafés, juice bars, heladerías and fast food places.

🍴🍴 **Bavaria**, Sotomayor 2095. Good restaurant with cafetería downstairs, real coffee, open 0800, very popular, not quiet, also cheaper café at Latorre 1935, upstairs.

🍴🍴 **Mariscal JP**, Félix Hoyos 2127. Closed Mon. Best seafood in town, worth that bit extra (has another branch in the Mercado Central at Latorre 1974).

🍴🍴 **Mexicano**, Latorre 1986A. Genuine Mexican cuisine, live music at weekends.

🍴🍴-🍴 **Club Croata**, on Abaroa, Plaza 23 de Marzo. Excellent value 4-course almuerzo, good service.

🍴 **Don Elias**, Antofagasta 2029, opposite the Frontera bus station (no sign). Open 0800 for breakfast. Cheap, hearty, no-frills Peruvian home-cooking. Packed at lunchtime.

Shopping

Calama *p755*

Craft stalls On Latorre 1600 block.

Market Feria El Loa on Antofagasta between Latorre and Vivar, selling fruit juices and crafts.

Supermarkets El Cobre, Vargas 2148. **Económico**, Grecia 2314.

Activities and tours

Calama *p755*

Several agencies run 1-day and longer tours to the Atacama region, including San Pedro; these are usually more expensive than tours from San Pedro and require a minimum number for the tour to go ahead. Be wary of agencies with poorly maintained vehicles and poor guides; standards here not generally very high. Operators with positive recommendations include: **Sol del Desierto**, Grau 723, loc 7A, T330428, www.soldeldesierto.cl. A variety of day tours around Chiu Chiu and San Pedro. Also operators listed under San Pedro de Atacama, below.

Transport

To Iquique: Tocopilla *p754*

Bus Bus companies' offices are on 21 de Mayo. Buses to **Antofagasta** many daily, US$6, 2½ hrs. To **Iquique**, along coastal road, 3 hrs, US$7, frequent. To **Calama**, **Tur-Bus** 3 a day, 3 hrs, US$7.

Calama *p755*

Air Airport is modern and efficient with Redbanc ATM, restaurant upstairs, shop with internet. **LAN** (Latorre 1726, T600-526 2000), daily, to **Santiago**, via Antofagasta; also **Sky** (Latorre 1499, T310190, or 600-600 2828). LAN also flies to **Iquique** and **Arica** twice a week. Transfer services from the airport are offered by **Transfer City Express**, T341022, US$9.

Bus No main terminal, buses leave from company offices: **Flota Barrios**, Ramírez 2298; **Frontera**, Antofagasta 2041, T318543; **Géminis**, Antofagasta 2239, T341993; **Kenny Bus**, Vivar 1954; **Pullman**, Balmaceda 1802, T311410; **Tur-Bus**, Granaderos, about 12 blocks north of centre, tickets from Ramírez y Balmaceda, T316699. To **Santiago** 23 hrs, US$50-95. To **La Serena**, usually with delay in Antofagasta, 16 hrs, US$35-65. To **Antofagasta**, 3 hrs, several companies, US$8. To **Iquique**, 6 hrs, via Tocopilla, US$20, 3 daily with **Tur-Bus**. To **Arica**, usually overnight, US$28, 9 hrs, or change in Antofagasta. To **Chuquicamata** (see above). To **San Pedro de Atacama**, **Tur-Bus** several daily, 1½ hrs, US$4, **Frontera**, 6 a day. To Toconao, see below. To **Ollagüe** for Bolivia: **Frontera del Norte** (Wed, Sun at 2200) and **Atacama** (Thu, Mon 2000), US$12, 5 hrs. For Uyuni, cross the border, then board bus to Uyuni. To **Salta**, Argentina, early morning on Tue, Fri and Sun, 15 hrs, **Géminis** US$70; **Pullman Bus**, US$77.

Local transport Public transport runs on a *colectivo* system, black cabs with a number on the roof. Just ask which number goes where you want to and flag it down. US$0.75 by day, US$0.85 after 2100. **Taxis**, basic fare US$4.

Car hire A hired car shared between several people is an economic alternative for visiting the Atacama region. A 4WD jeep (necessary for the desert) costs US$100 a day, a car US$70. Hire companies include **Alamo**, T364543 (good), **Avis**, T319757, **Budget**, T341076, **Hertz**, T341380 and **IQSA**, T310281. All offices close Sat 1300 till Mon morning. Airport offices only open when flights arrive. If intending to drive in the border area, visit the police in San Pedro to get maps of which areas may have landmines. See Essentials for agency web addresses.

Train Station on Av Balmaceda opposite Sotomayor, T348900. The train from Calama to **Uyuni** (Bolivia) was cancelled in 2007.

Directory

Calama *p755*

Banks Exchange rates are generally poor especially for TCs. Many Redbanc ATMs on Latorre and Sotomayor. Several **cambios**, eg **Marbumor**, 2 branches on Sotomayor (at Latorre and Av Balmaceda), changes US$, TCs, Argentine pesos and bolivianos, **Moon Valley**, Vivar 1818, and **Parina**, Sotomayor 1984, US$ only. **Consulates** **Bolivia**, León Gallo 1985A, open (in theory) Mon-Fri 0900-1230, helpful. **Internet** Many places in the centre, usually about US$1 per hr. **Post office** Granaderos y V Mackenna. 0830-1300, 1530-1830, Sat 0900-1230, will not send parcels over 1 kg. **Telephones** Lots of phone offices. **Entel**, Sotomayor 2027, is good for phone, fax and internet.

San Pedro de Atacama → *Phone code: 055. Colour map 6, B2. Population: 2,824.*

San Pedro de Atacama (*Altitude: 2,436 m*), 103 km southeast of Calama (paved, no fuel, food or water along the way) is a small town, more Spanish-Indian looking than is usual in Chile. Long before the arrival of the Spanish, the area was the centre of the Atacameño culture. There is a definite sense of history in the shady streets and the crumbling ancient walls, which drift away from the town into the fields, and then into the dust. Owing to the clear atmosphere and isolation, there are wonderful views of the night sky. Lunar landscapes, blistering geysers and salt flats are all close by. Now famous among visitors as the centre for excursions in this part of the Atacama, San Pedro can be overrun with visitors in summer. The **tourist office** on the plaza ⓘ *Toconao y Gustavo Le Paige, T851420, sanpedrodeatacama@gmail.com, open Mon-Wed and Fri 1000-1330, 1500-1930, Sat 1000-1400*. Helpful, has a useful suggestions book, with feedback from other visitors about agencies' tours. See also www.sanpedroatacama.com and www.sanpedrodeatacama.net. **Note** The main tourist season October-end February is accompanied by high prices and pressure on resources. ATMs come and go and are out of comission as often as they are working. If coming from inside Chile stock up on pesos before arriving. Dollars, Argentine pesos and bolivianos can be exchanged at bad rates and most companies accept credit cards, but with high charges.

The **Iglesia de San Pedro**, dating from the 17th century, is supposedly the second oldest church in the country. It has been heavily restored (the tower was added in 1964). The roof is made of cactus. Nearby, on the Plaza, is the **Casa Incaica**, the oldest building in San Pedro. **Museo Arqueológico** ⓘ *www.ucn.cl/museo, Mon-Fri, 0900-1200, 1400-1800 (Sat-Sun opens at 1000), US$3.50*. The collection of Padre Gustave Paige, a Belgian missionary who lived in San Pedro between 1955 and 1980, is now under the care of the Universidad Católica del Norte. It is a fascinating repository of artefacts, well organized to trace the development of prehispanic Atacameño society. Labels on displays (in Spanish and English) are good, and there is a comprehensive booklet in Spanish and English.

Around San Pedro de Atacama

The **Valle de la Luna** ⓘ *US$4* with fantastic landscapes caused by the erosion of salt mountains, is a nature reserve 12 km west of San Pedro. It is crossed by the old San Pedro-Calama road. Although buses on the new Calama-San Pedro road will stop to let you off where the old road branches off 13 km northwest of San Pedro (signposted to Peine), it is far better to travel from San Pedro on the old road, either by bicycle (but difficult after sunset) or by car (a 20-km round trip is possible). The Valle is best seen at sunset (if the sky is clear), although this is also the most crowded time. Do not leave any rubbish behind on desert excursions – the dry climate preserves it perfectly. Take water, hat, camera and torch. Camping is forbidden.

The **Pukará de Quitor** ⓘ *3 km north of San Pedro along the river, US$4*, is a pre-Inca fortress restored in 1981. The fortress, which stands on the west bank, was stormed by the Spanish under Pedro de Valdivia. A further 4 km up the river there are Inca ruins at Catarpe. At **Tulor** ⓘ *12 km southwest of San Pedro, US$4*, there is an archaeological site where parts of a stone-age village (dated 800 BC-AD 500) have been excavated; can be visited on foot, or take a tour. Nearby are the ruins of a 17th century village, abandoned in the 18th century because of lack of water.

El Tatio ⓘ *Altitude: 4,321 m; entry US$6*, the site of geysers, is a popular attraction. From San Pedro it is reached by a maintained road which runs northeast past the thermal pools at **Puritama** (28 km, US$9, worth a visit). The geysers are at their best 0600-0800, though the spectacle varies: locals say the performance is best when weather conditions are stable. Following recent accidents a series of stone walls and wooden walkways has been built around the geysers, which some say has taken away from the spectacle. A swimming pool has been built nearby (take costume and towel). There is no public transport and hitching is impossible. If going in a hired car, make sure the engine is suitable for very high altitudes and is protected with antifreeze. If driving in the dark it is almost impossible to find your way: the sign for El Tatio is north of the turn off (follow a tour bus). Tours arranged by agencies in San Pedro and Calama; nearest *hospedaje* in Caspana (see above).

Toconao ⓘ *Population: 500*, 37 km south of San Pedro de Atacama, is on the eastern shore of the Salar de Atacama. All houses are built of bricks of white volcanic stone, *sillar*, which gives the

San Pedro de Atacama

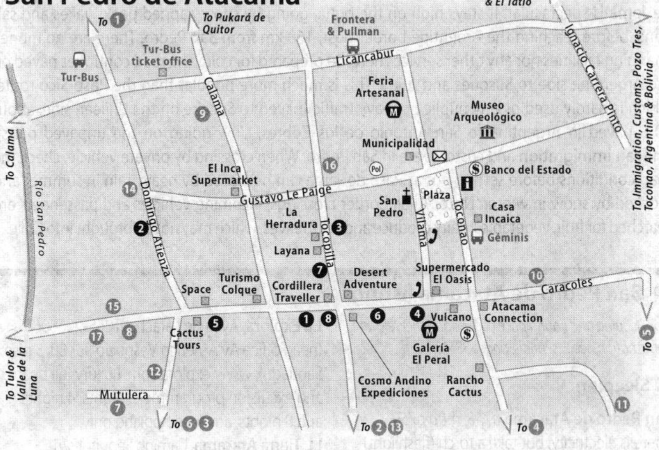

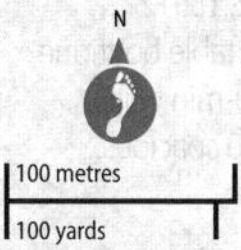

Sleeping
1 Altiplánico
2 Awasi
3 Elim
4 Hostal Edén Atacameño
5 Hostal Mamatierra
6 Hostal Martita
7 Hostal Miskanty
8 Hostal Puritama
9 Hostal Sonchek
10 Hostelling International
11 Hostería San Pedro
12 Kimal
13 La Casa de Don Tomás
14 Res Chiloé
15 Res Don Raul
16 Res Vilacoyo
17 Takha-Takha

Eating
1 Adobe & Casa Piedra
2 Bendito Desierto
3 Café Etnico
4 Café Tierra Todo Natural
5 La Casona
6 La Estaka
7 Les Copains
8 Milagro

village a very characteristic appearance totally different from San Pedro. The 18th-century church and bell tower are also built of volcanic stone. East of the village is a beautifully green gorge called the Quebrada de Jere, filled with fruit trees and grazing cattle (entry US$2). Worth visiting are the vineyards which produce a sweet wine. The quarry where the *sillar* is worked can be visited, about 1½ km east (the stones sound like bells when struck).

South of Toconao is one of the main entrances to the **Salar de Atacama** ⓘ *entry is controlled by CONAF in Toconao, US$4*. This vast 300,000-ha salt lake (the third largest expanse of salt flats in the world) is home to three of the world's five species of flamingo – the Andean, Chilean and James – and other birds (although some can only be seen when lakes form in winter). The air is so dry that you can usually see right across the Salar. A huge lake half a metre below the surface contributes to a slight haze in the air. The area is also rich in minerals. Three areas of the Salar form part of the **Reserva Nacional de los Flamencos**, which is in seven sectors totalling 73,986 ha and administered by CONAF in San Pedro.

From Toconao the road heads south through scenic villages to the mine at Laco (one poor stretch below the mine), before proceeding to Laguna Sico (4,079 m), and Paso Sico to Argentina.

Border with Bolivia and Argentina ➔ *Between Oct and Mar, Chilean time is 1 hr later than Bolivian.* **Hito Cajón** for the border with Bolivia is reached by road 47 km east of San Pedro. The first 35 km are the paved road to Paso de Jama (see below), then it's unpaved to Hito Cajón. From the border it is 7 km north to Laguna Verde. Chilean immigration and customs are in San Pedro, open 0800-2300 (maybe closed lunchtimes). For the Bolivian consulate, see under Calama. Bolivian immigration only gives 1 month entry here.

The ride from San Pedro de Atacama to Salta on a fully paved road through the 4,400-m **Paso de Jama** is spectacular. It stays high on the puna, going by snow-capped peaks, lakes and salt pans, before reaching the Argentine border post, 160 km from San Pedro. There are no money changing facilities nor any other services here. Be prepared for cold. The road continues paved on the Argentine side to Susques and Jujuy. This is much more popular than the **Paso Sico** route, which is hardly used by any public or heavy traffic (paved to Socaire on the Chilean side, about 40% paved in Argentina to San Antonio de los Cobres, slow going on the unpaved parts). **Chilean immigration** and customs are in San Pedro. When crossing by private vehicle, check the road conditions before setting out as Paso de Jama can be closed by heavy rain in summer and blocked by snow in winter. **Note** At all border crossings, incoming vehicles and passengers are searched for fruit, vegetables, dairy produce and coca leaves, which may not be brought into Chile.

San Pedro de Atacama listings

For Sleeping and Eating price codes and other relevant information, see Essentials, pages 38-40.

Sleeping

San Pedro de Atacama *p758, map p759*
There is electricity, but take a torch (flashlight) for walking at night. Rooms are scarce in Jan/Feb, and expensive all year round. There are a number of unregistered hostels, usually **F-G** pp, but security is often lax.

LL Awasi, Tocopilla 4,T851460, www.awasi.cl. One of several new 5-star resorts in the area. All-inclusive packages. Just 8 cabins, all built with traditional materials, fine food, excellent customer service, professional tours. Recommended.

LL Explora, Ayllú de Larache, T055-2066060 (head office Av Américo Vespucio Sur 80, 5 piso, Santiago), www.explora.com. Luxury full board and excursion programme, 3 nights, 4 nights and 8 nights, advance booking only.

LL Tierra Atacama, Camino Séquitor s/n, Allyu de Yaye, T555977, www.tierra atacama.com. The new competition to the Explora, somewhat removed from the village itself. Very good reports.

LL-L Altiplánico, Atienza 282, T851212, www.altiplanico.com. Comfortable boutique hotel on the edge of town (20-min walk), adobe huts, well designed and spacious.

LL-L Alto Atacama, Camino Pucara Suchor, T056-912 3900 (reservations), www.altoatacama.com. In the Catarpe valley, spacious rooms, all with terrace, with breakfast, spa, observatory, packages and excursions offered.

L Hostería San Pedro, Toconao 460, T851011, hsanpedro@chilesat.net. The town's oldest luxury hotel. Pool (residents only), petrol station, cabins, some rooms with satellite TV, quite comfortable.

L Kimal, Atienza 452 y Caracoles, T851030, www.kimal.cl. Small, intimate, near the centre, room size varies, swimming pool with jacuzzi and spa. Good restaurant (open to the public) and buffet breakfast. Recommended.

AL La Casa de Don Tomás, Tocopilla s/n, T851176, www.dontomas.cl. Good accommodation, bright and spacious lounge, quiet, good sized swimming pool, snacks served. Late check out/and check in. Decent value.

A-B Elim, Palpana 6, T851567, www.hostalelim.cl. Run by its owners, good breakfast, laundry service, nice hot showers. Recommended.

A-C Takha-Takha, Caracoles s/n, T851038, www.takhatakha.com. Pretty, lovely garden and shady patiorooms with bath are nicer than those without. Also camping (US$9 pp). Laundry facilities. Recommended.

B Hostal Sonchek, Le Paige 170, T851112, soncheksp@hotmail.com. **E** pp in dorms. Decent value hostel, some rooms with bath, kitchen and laundry facilities, café, English and French spoken.

B Res Don Raul, Caracoles 130-B, T851138, www.donraul.cl. Pleasant rooms, good value, kitchen facilities, Wi-Fi. Breakfast extra.

B-C Haramaksi, Coya, near Tulor, 10 km southwest of San Pedro, T09-9595 7567, www.haramaksi.cl. Simple accommodation in traditional Atacameño surroundings. An escape from the hubbub of San Pedro.

B-C Hostal Mamatierra, Pachamama 615, T851418, hostalmamatierra@sanpedrodeatacama.com. **E** pp in shared rooms. 5 mins' walk from the centre, will pick you up from the bus terminals. Some rooms with bath, kitchen facilities, peaceful.

B-C Hostal Martita, Palpana 4, T851394. 5 mins' walk from centre, some rooms with bath, good beds, reasonable value.

B-C Hostal Miskanty, Pasaje Mutulera 141, T851430, miskanty@hotmail.com. Simple but pleasant rooms with bath, laundry service.

B-C Hostal Puritama, Caracoles 113, T851540, hostalpuritama@sanpedrodeata cama.com. Some rooms with bath, simple, comfortable, large patio, kitchen facilities, good showers, camping available.

B-C Res Chiloé, Atienza 404, T851017. Rooms with bath much nicer than those without, good clean bathrooms, good beds, breakfast extra, no singles. Sunny veranda, laundry facilities, luggage store.

B-D Hostal Edén Atacameño, Toconao 592, T851154. Rooms without bath are basic, internet facilities, unkempt kitchen. Also camping.

C Hostelling International, Caracoles 360, T851426, www.hostellingatacama.com. **E** pp in dorms. Lively hostel, cramped shared rooms with lockers. Bicycle rental.

C-D Res Vilacoyo, Tocopilla 387, T851006. Without bath, good kitchen facilities, hammock in courtyard, laundry service. One of few good budget options in the centre. Recommended.

Camping Alberto Terrazas Oasis Camping at Pozo 3, 5 km east of town, has the best facilities including a swimming pool.

Camping Los Perales, Tocopilla 481.

Toconao *p759*

There are basic residenciales.

F pp, **Res Valle deToconao**, on Láscar. Nice and quiet, also serving good, simple meals.

Eating

San Pedro de Atacama *p758, map p759*

Few places are open before 1000. Drink bottled water as the local supply has a high mineral content, which may not agree with some.

TTT-TT Bendito Desierto, Atienza 426. Inventive food served in a kind of grotto.

TTT-TT La Estaka, Caracoles 259, T851201. Wood fire, cane roof, jazz music, pizzería and other dishes, good food, bar and book exchange, lively after 2300, favoured spot of the local New Age crowd.

TT Adobe, Caracoles. Open fire, internet, good atmosphere and meeting place, loud music. Described as "like Greenwich Village/Islington in the Atacama".

Casa Piedra, Caracoles. Open fire, also has a cheap menu, many of the waiters are musicians who sometimes play live folk music, good food and cocktails. Recommended.

La Casona, Caracoles. Good food, vegetarian options, cheap almuerzo, large portions. Interesting "Cubist-style" desert paintings. Popular and recommended.

Milagro, Caracoles. Good food, vegetarian options, attentive service. Recommended.

Café Etnico, Tocopilla 423, T851377. Good food, juices and sandwiches, cosy, book exchange, internet (free for diners).

Les Copains, Tocopilla 442, T09-8210 4379. Good sandwiches, juices and pizzas.

Empanadium, Galería El Peral, Caracoles 317, loc 5. Over 100 varieties of *empanada* with unusual local fillings.

Café Tierra Todo Natural, Caracoles. Excellent fruit juices, "the best bread in the Atacama", real coffee, yoghurt, best for breakfast, opens earliest.

Shopping

San Pedro de Atacama *p758, map p759*

Handicrafts There are a couple of craft markets, one near the plaza, and the other in the **Galería el Peral**, Caracoles 317. Very little *artesanía* is produced in San Pedro itself, most comes from Bolivia.

Activities and tours

San Pedro de Atacama *p758, map p759*

Mountain biking Bicycles for hire all over town, by the hour or full day: US$10 for 'professional' model, cheaper for 'amateur'. Tracks in the desert can be really rough, so check the bike's condition and carry a torch if riding after dark.

Swimming pools Piscina Oasis, at Pozo Tres, only 3 km southeast but walking there is tough and not recommended. Open all year daily (except Mon) 0500-1730, US$2 to swim, sometimes empty. Camping US$4, good showers and picnic facilities, very popular at weekends.

Tour operators

Usual tour rates, not including entry fees: to Valle de la Luna, US$13. To the Salar de Atacama, US$20 pp. To Altiplano lakes (including Toconao and Salar de Atacama), US$60. To El Tatio (begin at 0400) with trekking, US$35 pp (take swimming costume and warm clothing). Beware of tours to Valle de la Luna leaving too late to catch sunset – leave before 1600.

Before taking a tour, check that the agency has dependable vehicles, suitable equipment (eg oxygen for El Tatio), experienced drivers, a guide who speaks English if so advertised, and that the company is well-established. Always get a receipt. Report any complaints to the municipality or Sernatur. There are about 25 agencies, but some are temporary and/or open for only part of the year. Some operators will offer a reduction if you book a series of tours with them.

Atacama Connection, Caracoles y Toconao, T851421, www.atacamaconnection.com. For local tours, trekking, private tours.

Cactus Tours, Atienza 419, T851534, www.cactustour.cl. Good tours to local sites, good vehicles, most guides speak English. Recommended.

Cordillera Traveller, Caracoles, T851291, www.cordilleratraveller.com. Specialises in tours to Salar de Uyuni.

Cosmo Andino Expediciones, Caracoles s/n, T/F851069, http://cosmoandino-expediciones.cl/. Very professional and experienced, English, French, German, Dutch spoken, good vehicles, drivers and guides, owner Martin Beeris (Martín El Holandés). Recommended.

Desert Adventure, Caracoles s/n, T/F851067, www.desertadventure.cl. Good guides and range of trips, English spoken, modern fleet of vehicles, mostly good reports.

La Herradura, Tocopilla s/n, T851087, laherradura atacama@yahoo.es. Horseback tours with good local guides, mountain bike hire. Recommended.

Layana, Tocopilla 418, T851308, www.turismo layana.cl. Offer the usual range of tours. Fun, but not necessarily the most responsible.

Rancho Cactus, Toconao, T851506, www.rancho-cactus.cl. Offers horse riding with good guides to Valle de la Luna and other sites (Farolo and Valerie – speaks French and English), not for experienced riders.

Space, Caracoles 166, T851935/09-817 8354, www.spaceobs.com. Run by French astronomer Alain, who speaks 3 languages and has set up a small observatory in the village of Solor, south of San Pedro; gives tours 2000-2330 to study the night sky, hot drink included but wear all your warmest clothes.

Turismo Colque, Caracoles, T851109, www.colquetours.com. Specialists for tours to Bolivia, including 1-day tour to Laguna Verde and 3-day tours to Laguna Colorado and the Salar de Uyuni; Visa and Mastercard accepted, hires sleeping bags, sometimes recommended but more often receives critical reports. Has agencies in Uyuni and La Paz.
Vulcano, Caracoles 317, T851023, www.vulcanochile.cl. Mountain climbs, sandboarding and other adventure tours to infrequently visited areas, mountain bike hire, English-speaking guides. Recommended.

Transport

San Pedro de Atacama *p758, map p759*
Bus Most buses leave from Licancábur opposite the football field. **Tur-Bus** terminal on Atienza, north of the centre. To **Calama**: US$4, **Frontera** (7 daily), 1½ hrs, **Tur-Bus**, T851549, several daily. Frequencies vary with more departures in Jan-Feb and some weekends. Book in advance to return from San Pedro on Sun afternoon. Tur-Bus to **Arica**, 2030, US$32. **Tur-Bus** to **Santiago**, several daily, 23 hrs, US$60-100. **Frontera** to **Socaire**, Mon, Thu, Fri 1930, Sun 1230, 2200, US$3; to **Toconao**, 4 a day (3 on Sun), US$1.50. **To Argentina**: **Géminis**, on Toconao (changes bolivianos), Tue, Fri, Sun 1130, to **Salta**, US$45, 9 hrs, reserve in advance and book Salta hotel as bus arrives 0100-0200 (schedules change often). **Pullman** (Frontera office), Tue, Fri, Sun 1045, US$45.

Border with Bolivia
Tránsito público leaves San Pedro for **Hito Cajón** at 0800 or 0830 and costs US$6.50, return about 1000 Chilean time. It is usually booked through an agency in town. Occasionally it runs in the afternoon. **Tránsito público** from the border to San Pedro takes passengers to their hotels after passing through immigration. There is no other public transport to Hito Cajón: do not be tempted to hitch to the border and beyond as you risk being stranded without water or shelter at sub-zero temperatures.

Directory

San Pedro de Atacama *p758, map p759*
Banks See above for ATMs. **Cambio Atacama** on Toconao, casi Caracoles, changes TCs, good rates for cash, 1030-1800 daily. Some places change euros; ask around. **Internet and telephone** Several places in town. **Inti Sol**, Tocopilla s/n. Opens 0900, also serves good coffee and juices. **Post offices** in the Casa Parroquial on the Plaza, open 0900-1230, 1430-1800.

Iquique and around

The Cordillera de la Costa slowly loses height north of Iquique, terminating at the Morro at Arica (see page 769): from Iquique north it drops directly to the sea and as a result there are few beaches along this coast. Inland, the central depression (pampa) 1,000-1,200 m is arid and punctuated by salt-flats south of Iquique. Between Iquique and Arica it is crossed from east to west by four gorges. East of this depression lies the sierra, the western branch of the Andes, beyond which is a high plateau, the altiplano (3,500-4,500 m) from which rise volcanic peaks. In the altiplano there are a number of lakes, the largest of which, Lago Chungará (see page 772), is one of the highest in the world. The coastal strip and the pampa are rainless; on the coast temperatures are moderated by the Pacific, but in the pampa variations of temperature between day and night are extreme, ranging from 30°C to 0°C. The altiplano is much colder.

Iquique → *Phone code: 057. Colour map 6, B2. Population: 200,000.*
Iquique is an attractive port and city with well-preserved historical buildings. Around it the desert pampa stretches north, south and to the mountains. Several oases also have strong historical associations, either in the form of geoglyphs, the last evidence of peoples long vanished, or the ghost towns of nitrate operations. Mamiña and Pica are thermal resorts within easy reach of Iquique; both are beautiful, tranquil places.

The name of the capital of I Región (Tarapacá) and one of the main northern ports, is derived from the Aymara word *ique-ique*, meaning place of 'rest and tranquillity'. The city, 492 km north of Antofagasta and 47 km west of the Pan-American Highway, is situated on a rocky peninsula at the foot of the high Atacama pampa, sheltered by the headlands of Punta Gruesa and Cavancha. The city, which was partly destroyed by earthquake in 1877, became the centre of the nitrate trade after its transfer from Peru to Chile at the end of the War of the Pacific. A short distance north of town along Amunátegui is the **Free Zone (Zofri)** ⓘ *Mon-Sat 1100-2100, limit on tax free purchases US$1,000 for foreigners, getting there: colectivo from the centre US$0.80*. It is worth visiting this giant shopping centre, which sells all manner of imported items, including electronic goods. It is much better value than its equivalent in Punta Arenas. **Tourist office** ⓘ *Sernatur, Serrano 145, of 303, T312238, infoiquiqe@sernatur.cl, Mon-Fri, 0830-1630*. Masses of information, very helpful. See also www.iquique.cl and www.iquique.travel.

In the centre of the old town is the **Plaza Prat**. On the northeast corner of the Plaza is the Centro Español, built in extravagant Moorish style by the local Spanish community in 1904; the ground floor is a restaurant, on the upper floors are paintings of scenes from Don Quijote and from Spanish history. Three blocks north of the Plaza is the old Aduana (customs house) built in 1871; in 1891 it was the scene of an important battle in the Civil War between supporters of President Balmaceda and congressional forces. Part of it is now the **Museo Naval** ⓘ *Esmeralda 250, Tue-Fri 1000-1300, 1600-1900, Sat 1000-1400, US$0.60*, focusing on the Battle of Iquique, 1879. Along Calle Baquedano, which runs south from Plaza Prat, are the attractive former mansions of the 'nitrate barons', dating from between 1880 and 1903. The finest of these is the **Palacio Astoreca** ⓘ *O'Higgins 350, Tue-Fri 1000-1300, Sat 1000-1330, Sun 1100-1400, US$1*. Built in 1903, it was subsequently the Intendencia and now a museum of fine late 19th century furniture and shells. **Museo Regional** ⓘ *Baquedano 951, Mon-Fri 0830-1300, 1530-1830, Sat 1030-1300, Sun (in summer) 1000-1300, 1600-2000, free*, contains an archaeological section tracing the development of prehispanic civilizations in the region; an ethnographical collection of the Isluga culture of the Altiplano (AD 400), and of contemporary Aymara culture; also a section devoted to the nitrate era which includes a model of a nitrate office and the collection of the nitrate entrepreneur, Santiago Humberstone. Sea lions and pelicans can be seen from the harbour. There are **cruises** ⓘ *US$5, 45 mins, minimum 10 people*, from the passenger pier.

The **beaches** at Cavancha just south of the town centre are good; those at Huaiquique are reasonable, November-March. There are restaurants at Cavancha. For surfers, etc, the better bet is the pounding surf of Playa Brava, further to the south. Piscina Godoy is a fresh water swimming pool on Av Costanera at Aníbal Pinto and Riquelme, open in the afternoon, US$1. Cerro Dragón, the large sand dune behind Iquique, is the place for sandboarding; great for views too. There are several hills where you can paraglide, good for beginners.

Around Iquique

Humberstone, a large nitrate town, is now abandoned. It is at the junction of the Pan-American Highway and the road to Iquique. Entry by 'donation', US$3, guided tours Saturday-Sunday, leaflets available, T751213. Colectivo from Iquique US$3; phone near site for booking return. Though closed since 1961, you can see the church, theatre, pulpería (company stores) and the swimming pool (built of metal plating from ships' hulls). Nearby are the ruins of other mining towns including Santa Laura. Local tour companies run trips to the area, including Humberstone, Santa Laura, Pisagua and **Pozo Almonte**, 52 km east (*Population: c. 5,400*). This town was the chief service provider of the nitrate companies until their closure in 1960. The **Museo Histórico Salitrero** ⓘ *on the tree-shaded plaza, Mon-Fri 0830-1300, 1600-1900*, displays artefacts and photographs of the nitrate era.

To Cerro Pintados (see page 754) take any bus south, US$4, and walk from the Pan-American Highway then hitch back or flag down a bus. From Pozo Almonte 74 km (paved), **Mamiña** (*Population: c. 600; Altitude: 2,750 m*) has abundant thermal springs and a mud spring (**Baño Los Chinos** ⓘ *0930-1300*). The therapeutic properties of the waters and mud are Mamiña's main claim to fame. Mineral water from the spring is sold throughout northern Chile. There are ruins of a prehispanic pukará (fortress) and a church, built in 1632, the only colonial Andean church in Chile with two towers. An Aymara cultural centre, Kaspi-kala, has an artesanía workshop and outlet.

La Tirana (*Population: 550; Altitude: 995 m*) is famous for a religious festival to the Virgen del Carmen, held from 10 to 16 July, which attracts some 150,000 pilgrims. Over 100 groups dance night and day, decked out in spectacular colourful masks, starting on 12 July. All the dances take place in the main plaza in front of the church; no alcohol is served. Accommodation is impossible to find, other than in organized camp sites (take tent) which have basic toilets and

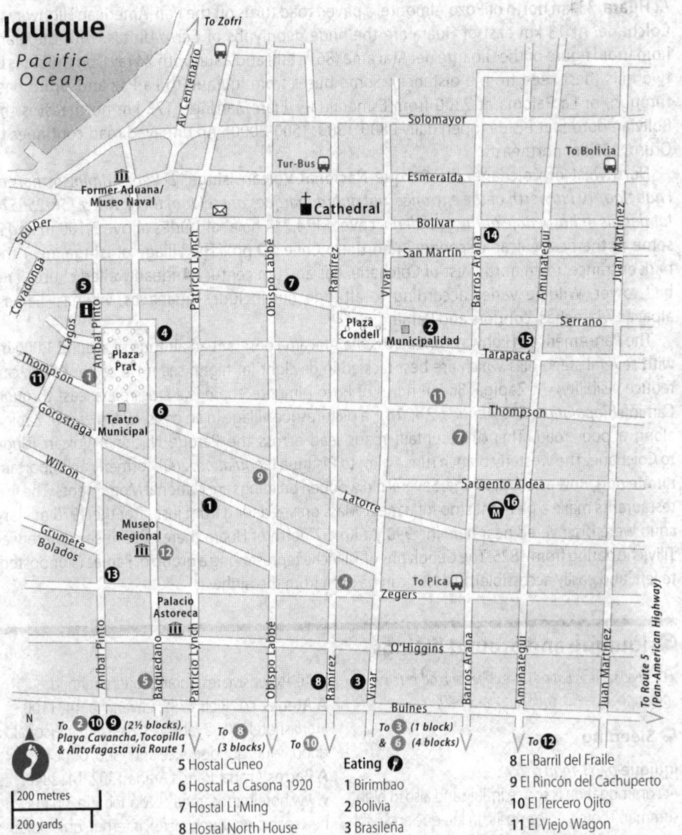

Sleeping
1 Arturo Prat
2 Atenas
3 Barros Arana
4 Cano
5 Hostal Cuneo
6 Hostal La Casona 1920
7 Hostal Li Ming
8 Hostal North House
9 Inti-Llanka
10 Manuel Rodríguez Express
11 Res Nan-King
12 YMCA

Eating
1 Birimbao
2 Bolivia
3 Brasileña
4 Casino Español
5 Cioccolata
6 Colonial
7 Compañía Italiana de Bomberos
8 El Barril del Fraile
9 El Rincón del Cachuperto
10 El Tercero Ojito
11 El Viejo Wagon
12 Kiru
13 La Picada Curicana
14 mi Perú
15 Nan King
16 Sciaraffia

showers. It is 10 km east of the Pan-American Highway (70 km east of Iquique), turn-off 9 km south of Pozo Almonte. **Pica** (*Population: 1,767; Altitude: 1,325 m*), 42 km from La Tirana, was the most important centre of early Spanish settlement in the area. Most older buildings date from the nitrate period when it became a popular resort. The town is famous for its pleasant climate, citrus groves and two natural springs, the best of which is **Cocha Resbaladero** ⓘ *0700-2000 all year, US$4, snack bar, changing rooms, beautiful pool, tourist office opposite.*

Many other sites around Iquique, including the Giant of the Atacama (see below) and places to see fossilized dinosaur footprints, are difficult to visit without a car; tours available though from Pica.

From Iquique to the Bolivian Border

At **Huara**, 33 km north of Pozo Almonte, a paved road turns off the Pan-American Highway to **Colchane**. At 13 km east of Huara are the huge geoglyphs of Cerro Unitas, with the giant humanoid figure of the Gigante del Atacama (86 m tall) and a sun with 24 rays, on the sides of two hills (best seen from a distance). Some buses from Iquique to La Paz and Oruro pass through, or La Paloma at 2300 from Esmeralda y Juan Martínez. 173 km northeast is the Bolivian border at Pisiga (open daily 0800-1300, 1500-2000). An unpaved road continues to Oruro, 233 km northeast.

Northwest of Colchane, the **Parque Nacional Volcán Isluga** ⓘ *Park Administration at Enquelga, 10 km north of the entrance, but guardaparques are seldom there, Arica T58-250570 for details of hospedaje at the guardería*, covers 174,744 ha at altitudes above 2,100 m and is some of the best volcanic scenery in northern Chile. (**D** pp). The village of **Isluga**, near the park entrance, 6 km northwest of Colchane, has an 18th century Andean walled church and bell tower. Wildlife varies according to altitude but includes guanacos, vicuñas, llamas, alpacas, vizcachas, condors and flamingos.

The Pan-American Highway runs across the Atacama desert at an altitude of around 1,000 m, with several steep hills which are best tackled in daylight (at night, sea mist, camanchaca, can reduce visibility). At **Zapiga**, 80 km north of Pozo Almonte, there is a crossroads: east through Camiña (*Population: 500; Altitude: 2,400 m*), a picturesque village in an oasis, 67 km east of Zapiga along a poor road. Thence mountain roads lead across the Parque Nacional Volcán Isluga to Colchane. The westerly branch runs 41 km to **Pisagua** (*Population: 200*), formerly an important nitrate port, now a fishing village. Several old wooden buildings are National Monuments. The fish restaurants make a pleasant stop for a meal. Mass graves dating from just after the 1973 military coup were discovered near here in 1990. At Km 57 north of Huara there is a British cemetery at Tiliviche dating from 1825. The Geoglyphs of Tiliviche representing a group of llamas (signposted, to left, and easily accessible), Km 127, can be seen from the highway.

Iquique and around listings

For Sleeping and Eating price codes and other relevant information, see Essentials, pages 38-40.

Sleeping

Iquique *p763, map p765*

Accommodation is scarce in July and also in high summer. There's no campsite in Iquique and wild camping is forbidden on Playa Brava and Playa Cavancha. All hotels in the list are recommended.

AL-A Arturo Prat, Aníbal Pinto 695, Plaza Prat, T520000, www.hotelarturoprat.cl. 4-star, attentive service, good value, pool, games room, health suite, expensive restaurant, tours arranged.

A Atenas, Los Rieles 738, Cavancha, T431100, atenashotel2002@yahoo.es. Pleasant, personal, good value, good service and food, pool.

A Barros Arana, Barros Arana 1302, T412840, www.hotelbarrosarana.cl. Modern (in 2 parts – newer section much nicer), internet, quiet area, pool, good value.

B Manuel Rodríguez Express, Rodríguez 550, T427524, www.hotelmanuel rodriguez.cl. Small standard 3 star. Decent rooms with big TVs, bright common areas and Wi-Fi. Near the beach.

B-C Cano, Ramírez 996, T315580, www.hotelcano.cl. Big rooms, nice atmosphere, good value.
C Hostal La Casona 1920, Barros Arana 1585, T413000, www.casonahosteliquique.cl. **E** pp in shared rooms. Recently opened, fun, in a quiet area of town not far from the beach, English spoken.
C Hostal North House, Labbé 1518, T427008, miguel.flyiquique@gmail.com. Simple rooms, cable TV, foam mattresses, good location, English spoken, kitchen facilities. The owner is a paragliding instructor.
C Hostal Cuneo, Baquedano 1175, T428654, hostalcuneo@hotmail.com. With or without bath, helpful, piano in the living room, good value.
C Inti-Llanka, Obispo Labbé 825, T311104, www.inti-llanka.cl. Spacious rooms with good beds, helpful, good value.
C-D Hostal Li Ming, Barros Arana 705, T421912, www.hostal.cl. Simple, good value, small rooms, some with bath, cable TV.
C-D Res Nan-King, Thompson 752, T330691. Small but nice rooms, well-kept, cable TV, no breakfast.
D YMCA, Baquedano 964, T573596, www.ymcaiquique.com. **F** pp in shared rooms. Impressive façade, modern interior, most rooms are dorm-style with their own bathroom. Basic, but clean and central.

Around Iquique *p764*

Mamiña

It is extremely difficult to find lodging in Mamiña as hotels generally have exclusive contracts with the nearby mine.

Pica

Hotels fill up at weekends, holiday times and during La Tirana's festival 10-16 Jul: book ahead.
C Camino del Inca, Esmeralda 14, T/F057-741008, hotelcaminodelinca@hotmail.com. With breakfast, shady patio, table football, good value. Recommended.
C Los Emilios, Cochrane 201, T741126. With breakfast, interesting old building with nice lounge and patio, small pool. Recommended.
C O'Higgins, Balmaceda 6, T741524, hohiggins@123mail.cl. Modern, well furnished, **E-F** for singles.
D San Andrés, Balmaceda 197, T741319, gringa733@hotmail.com. **F** singles. With breakfast, basic, excellent restaurant, serves good value 4-course *almuerzos*. Safe parking.

Eating

Iquique *p763, map p765*

The restaurants on the wharf on the opposite side of Av Costanera from the bus terminal are poor value. There are several good, cheap seafood restaurants on the 2nd floor of the central market, Barros Arana y Latorre. Also many restaurants on the Península Cavancha.
TTT-TT Casino Español, Plaza Prat, T423284. Good meals well served in beautiful Moorish-style 1904 building.
TTT-TT El Tercer Ojito, P Lynch 1420, T471448. Well-presented fish, sushi, pasta and vegetarian options with a Peruvian twist, served in a pleasant courtyard, deservedly popular.
TTT-TT El Viejo Wagon, Thompson 85, T341428. Fish and seafood cooked according to traditional northern recipes. Regarded by many as the best restaurant in the town centre.
TTT-TT Kiru, Amunátegui 1912, Cavancha. Half elegant restaurant, half sports bar, Peruvian influenced food, fish and good pasta. Huge *pisco sours*. Recommended.
TT Brasileña, Vivar 1143, T423236. Brazilian run, serves seafood in the week, Brazilian food on Sat.
TT Colonial, Plaza Prat. Fish and seafood, popular, good value.
TT El Barril del Fraile, Ramírez 1181, T390334. Good seafood, nice atmosphere.
TT Nan King, Amunátegui 533, T420434. Large portions, good value, renowned as best Chinese in town.
TT La Picada Curicana, Pinto y Zegers. Good hearty Central Chilean country cooking (such as oven-roasted game, served in clay pots), large portions, good value *menú de la casa*.
TT Sciaraffia, Sgto Aldea 803 (Mercado Centenario). Open 24 hrs, good value, large choice.
TT-T Compañía Italiana de Bomberos, Serrano 520, T527520. Authentic Italian cuisine, excellent value *almuerzo*, otherwise more expensive, but recommended.
T Bolivia, Serrano 751. *Humitas* and *salteñas*. Recommended.
T El Rincón del Cachuperto, Valenzuela 125, Peninsula Cavancha. Famed as having the best seafood *empanadas* in Iquique.
T Peña mi Perú, Bolívar 711. Open 24 hrs. Cheap Chilean and Peruvian staples.

Birimbao, Gorostiaga 419. Opens early for breakfast (0800). Fresh juices.
Cioccolata, Pinto 487, T427478 (another branch in the Zofri). Very good coffee and cakes.
Salon de Té Don Luis, Latorre y Vivar. Very popular for *onces*, quite expensive.

Around Iquique: Pica *p766*
Try the local *alfajores*, delicious cakes filled with cream and mango honey.
₸₸ **El Edén**, Riquelme 12. 1st class local food in delightful surroundings, fine ice cream, best restaurant in town.
₸ **La Mía Pappa**, Balmaceda, near plaza. Good selection of meat and juices, attractive location.
₸ **La Palmera**, Balmaceda 115. Excellent *almuerzo*, popular with locals, near plaza.
₸ **La Viña**, Ibáñez 70, by Cocha de Resbaladero. Good cheap *almuerzo*.

Bars and clubs

Iquique *p763, map p765*
Most discos are out of town on the road south to the airport.
Siddharta, Mall Las Américas, locales 10-11-193. Sushi.
Taberna Barracuda, Gorostiaga 601, T427969. For late night food, drink, nice decor, nice atmosphere.

Activities and tours

Iquique *p763, map p765*
The tourist office maintains a full list of operators. Iquique is a good place for **paragliding**: several agencies offer 30- to 40-min tandem flights from around US$60. It also offers some of the best **surfing** in Chile with numerous reef breaks on **Playa Brava**, south of the city. Surfboard rental and surf classes are available from a number of agencies. Lessons cost roughly US$11 per hr.
Altazor, Flight Park, Vía 6, manzana A, sitio 3, Bajo Molle, T380110, www.altazor.cl. Recommended for parapenting; will pick you up from wherever you are staying. Also offers week-long courses including accommodation, as do many other operators.
Avitours, Baquedano 997, T527692, www.avitours.cl. Tour to Pintados, La Tirana, Humberstone, Pica, etc, some bilingual guides, day tours start at US$30.
Civet Adventure, Bolivar 684, T428483, civetcor@vtr.net. Adventure tourism in the desert and the High Andes, photo adventure, mountainbike tours, landsailing, trekking, English, German and Spanish spoken, contact Sergio Cortez. Recommended.
Extremonorte expeditions, www.extremonorte.cl. Good tours to the Altiplano and desert, responsible. Also run the **Tren Pampino**, www.trenpampino.cl, a project to link various ghost towns and saltpeter plants by train.
Paraventura, T315780/09-874 1334, paraventura@entelchile.net. Frank Valenzuela, qualified tandem pilot, professional and helpful, great 40-min flights. Recommended.

Transport

Iquique *p763, map p765*
Air Diego Aracena international airport, 35 km south at Chucumata. Taxi US$16; airport transfer, T310800, US$7 for 3 or more passengers, unreliable. **LAN**, **Principal** and **Sky** fly to **Arica, Antofagasta** and **Santiago**.
Bus Terminal at north end of Patricio Lynch (not all buses leave from here); bus company offices are near the market on Sgto Aldea and B Arana. **Tur-Bus**, Ramírez y Esmeralda, T472987 (420634 at terminal), with Redbanc ATM and luggage store. **Pullman**, in terminal T426522. Southbound buses are searched for duty-free goods, at Quillagua on the Pan-American Highway and at Chipana on the coastal Route 1. To **Arica**, buses and colectivos, US$11, 4½ hrs. To **Antofagasta**, US$14, 6 hrs. To **Calama**, 6 hrs, US$16-23. To **Tocopilla** along the coastal road, buses and minibuses, several companies, 3 hrs, US$10. To **La Serena**, 18 hrs, US$35-70. To **Santiago**, 25 hrs, several companies, US$50-75.
International buses To **Bolivia Litoral**, T423670, 2200 daily to **Oruro** and **La Paz**, US$30. **Salvador** and others from Esmeralda near Juan Martínez around 2100-2300, same price (passengers may have a cold wait for customs to open at 0800).
Car hire **Econorent**, Labbé y O'Higgins, T600-200 0000, weekend specials; **IQSA**, Labbé 1089, T/F417068. **Procar**, Serrano 796, T/F413470 (airport T410920).

Around Iquique *p764*
Mamiña
Bus **Transportes Tamarugal**, Barros Arana 897, Iquique, daily 0800, 1600, return 1800, 0800,

2½ hrs, US$7, good service. Also with **Turismo Mamiña**, Latorre 779, daily, more-or-less same prices and frequency.

Pica

Bus Minibus **Iquique**-Pica: **San Andrés**, Sgto Aldea y B Arana, Iquique, daily 0930, return 1800; **Pullman Chacón**, Barros Arana y Latorre, many daily; **Santa Rosa**, Barros Arana 777, daily 0830, 0930, return 1700, 1800. US$4 one-way, 2 hrs.

Directory

Iquique *p763, map p765*
Airline offices LAN, Tarapacá 465, and in Mall Las Américas, T600-526 2000. **Principal**, Paseo Prat 570, T576678, or 600-425 3510. **Sky**, Tarapacá 530, T415013/600-600 2828.

Banks Numerous Redbanc ATMs in the centre and the Zofri. Cambios: **Afex**, Lynch 467A, for TCs. **Money Exchange**, Lynch 548, loc 1-2. Best rates for TCs and cash at casas de cambio in the Zofri, eg **Wall Street** (sells and cashes Amex TCs). **Consulates** **Bolivia**, Gorostiaga 215, Departamento E, T527472, colivian-iquique@entelchile.net. Mon-Fri 0930-1200. **Peru**, Zegers 570, T411466, consulperu-iquique @rree.gob.pe. **Internet and telephone** Several in and around the centre. **Language schools** Academia de Idiomas del Norte, Ramírez 1345, T411827, www.languages.cl. Swiss run, Spanish classes and accommodation for students. **Post offices** In the Zofri, there is another branch in the **Mall de las Américas**.

Arica and Lauca

The Lauca national park, the most northerly in Chile, has some of the country's most stunning scenery: high lakes, snow-capped volcanoes, lava fields and varied bird life. Small Andean villages near the park retain their Aymara culture. Lauca is easily reached from Arica, Chile's northernmost city and capital of the new Arica-Parinacota Region (Región XV). It is the main outlet for Bolivian trade and is even closer to Peru. It's a busy place, dominated by the rocky headland of El Morro.

Arica → *Phone code: 058. Colour map 6, A1. Population: 174,064.*

Arica, 20 km south of the Peruvian border, is built at the foot of the Morro headland and is fringed by sand dunes. The Andes can be clearly seen from the anchorage. Arica used to be the principal route for travellers going overland to Bolivia, via the Parque Nacional Lauca. Now there is competition from the San Pedro de Atacama-Uyuni route, so new routes are being considered to link this part of the coast with San Pedro, via the high altitude national parks. This is an important port and route-centre. The road route to La Paz via Tambo Colorado is now paved and Arica is a popular seaside destination for landlocked Bolivians, as well as Chileans. A 63-km railway runs north to Tacna in Peru. Regrettably, Arica is also becoming a key link in the international drugs trade. The **Sernatur tourist office** ⓘ *San Marcos 101, T252054, infoarica@sernatur.cl, in a kiosk next to the Casa de la Cultura, Mon-Fri 0830-1300, 1500-1830*, is very helpful, English spoken, good map, list of tour companies. Municipal kiosk also on San Marcos, opposite Sernatur, opens at 0830. See www.arica.cl.

The **Morro**, with a good view from the park on top, was the scene of a great victory by Chile over Peru in the War of the Pacific on 7 June 1880. Walk to the southernmost end of Calle Colón, past a small museum displaying a number of Chinchorro mummies, and then follow the pedestrian walkway up to the summit. Here the **Museo Histórico y de Armas** ⓘ *www.museomorro arica.cl, daily, 0830-2000, US$1*, contains weapons and uniforms from the War of the Pacific.

At the foot of the Morro is the **Plaza Colón** with the cathedral of San Marcos, built in iron by Eiffel. Though small it is beautifully proportioned and attractively painted. It was brought to Arica from Ilo (Peru) in the 19th century, before Peru lost Arica to Chile, as an emergency measure after a tidal wave swept over Arica and destroyed all its churches. Eiffel also designed the nearby Aduana (customs house) which is now the **Casa de la Cultura** ⓘ *Mon-Fri 0830-2000*. Just north of the Aduana is the La Paz railway station; outside is an old steam locomotive (made in Germany in 1924) once used on this line. In the station is a memorial to John Roberts Jones, builder of the Arica portion of the railway. The **Casa Bolognesi**, Colón y Yungay, is a fine old

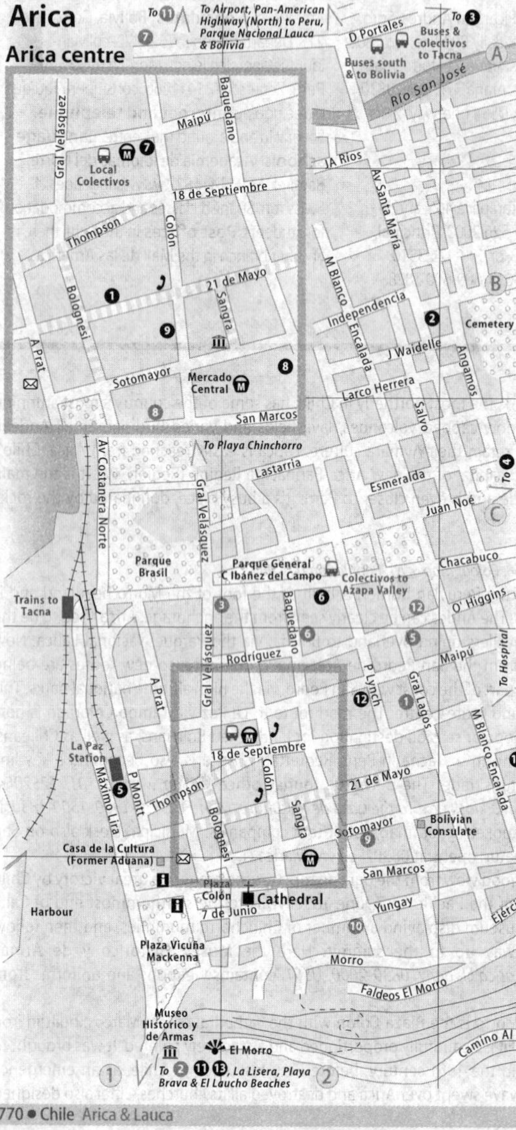

Sleeping
1 Americano *D2*
2 Arica *E1*
3 D'Marie-Jeanne y David *C1*
4 Hostal Jardín del Sol *D3*
5 Hostal Pacífico *D2*
6 Hostal Venecia *D2*
7 Maison de France *A1*
8 Plaza Colón *Detail*
9 Res América *D2*
10 Savona *E2*
11 Sunny Days *A1*
12 Surf House *C2*

Eating
1 Café-Restaurant B *Detail*
2 Chifa El Mesón *B2*
3 Cyclo Public *A3*
4 Don Floro *C3*
5 El Andén *D1*
6 El Congrio con Agallas *C2*
7 El Rey del Marisco *Detail*
8 Jalapeño Bar *Detail*
9 La Bomba *Detail*
10 Los Aleros del 21 *D3*
11 Maracuyá *E1*
12 Open Bar *D2*
13 Ostión Dorado *E1*

building painted blue and white. It holds temporary exhibitions. Hidden away on a small side street behind the cathedral is the private **Museo del Mar** ⓘ *Pasaje Sangra 315, www.museodelmardearica.cl, Mon-Sat 1100-1900, US$2* has over 1,000 exhibits from around the world, well-displayed.

Worthwhile sights outside Arica include the **Museo Arqueológico de San Miguel de Azapa** ⓘ *at Km 13 on the road east to the Azapa valley, T205555, www.uta.cl/masma, daily Jan-Feb 0900-2000, Mar-Dec 1000-1800, US$5, getting there: take a yellow colectivo from P Lynch y Chacabuco and 600 block of P Lynch, US$1.50*. Built around an olive press, it contains a fine collection of pre-Columbian weaving, pottery, wood carving and basketwork from the coast and valleys, and also seven mummified humans from the Chinchorro culture (8000-2000 BC), the most ancient mummies yet discovered. Explanations in several languages are loaned free at the entrance. In the forecourt of the museum are several boulders with pre-Columbian petroglyphs. In San Miguel itself is an old cemetery and several typical restaurants (eg **La Picada del Muertito**, at entrance to cemetery, Km 13, T264189). On the road between Arica and San Miguel there are several groups of geoglyphs of humans and llamas ('stone mosaics') south of the road (signed to Cerro Sagrado, Cerro Sombrero an Azapa Archaeological Circuit is advertised). North of Arica along Route 11, between Km 14 and Km 16, is the **Lluta valley** where you can see along the hillsides four groups of geoglyphs, representing llamas, and eagle and human giants. The road continues through the Parque Nacional Lauca and on to Bolivia. Take a bus from Mackenna y Chacabuco.

By road to Bolivia

1) Via **Chungará** (Chile) and **Tambo Quemado** (Bolivia). This, the most widely used route, begins by heading north from Arica on the Pan-American Highway (Route 5) for 12 km before turning right (east towards the cordillera) on Route 11 towards Chungará via Putre and Parque Nacional Lauca. The road passes **Termas de Juasi** ⓘ *just after Km 130, look for sign, US$2*, rustic thermal baths, with mud baths and a small swimming pool. This road is now paved to La Paz, estimated driving time six hours. 2) Via **Visviri** (Chile) and **Charaña** (Bolivia), following the La Paz-Arica railway line. This route should not be attempted in wet weather.

Border with Bolivia: Chungará Immigration is open 0800-2000; US$2 per vehicle crossing 1300-1500, 1850-2100 and Saturday, Sunday and holidays. For details of through buses between Arica and La Paz see below under Transport, Arica.

Border with Bolivia: Visviri Immigration is open 0800-2000. Chilean formalities at Visviri, 7 km west of the border, Bolivian formalities at Charaña, just over the border (local barter market every other Friday). When crossing with a private vehicle, US$2 per vehicle is charged between 1300-1500, 1850-2000 and Saturday, Sunday and holidays.

Border with Peru: Chacalluta-Tacna ➔ *Between Oct-Mar Chilean time is 1 hr ahead of Peruvian, 2 hrs.* Immigration is open Sunday-Thursday 0800-2400, Friday-Saturday 24 hours; it's a fairly uncomplicated crossing. For Peruvian immigration. When crossing by private vehicle, US$2 per vehicle is charged between 1300-1500, 1850-2400 and on Saturday, Sunday, holidays. Drivers entering Chile are required to file a form, Relaciones de Pasajeros, giving details of passengers, obtained from a stationery store in Tacna, or at the border in a booth near Customs. You must also present the original registration document for your car from its country of registration. The first checkpoints outside Arica on the road to Santiago also require the Relaciones de Pasajeros form. If you can't buy the form, details on a piece of paper will suffice or you can get them at service stations. The form is not required for travel south of Antofagasta. Money exchange facilities at the bus terminal in Tacna.

Parque Nacional Lauca

The Parque Nacional Lauca, stretching to the border with Bolivia, is one of the most spectacular national parks in Chile. It is 176 km east of Arica and access is easy as the main Arica-La Paz road runs through the park and is paved. On the way is a zone of giant candelabra cactus, between 2,300-2,800 m. At Km 90 there is a pre-Inca pukará (fortress) above the village of Copaquilla and, a few kilometres further, there is an Inca tambo (inn) at Zapahuira. Situated at elevations from 3,200 m to 6,340 m (beware of soroche unless you are coming from Bolivia), the park covers 137,883 ha and includes numerous snowy volcanoes including three peaks of over 6,000 m. At the foot of Volcán Parinacota and its twin, Pomerape (in Bolivia – they are known collectively as Payachatas), is a series of lakes among a jumble of rocks, called Cotacotani. Black lava flows can be seen above Cotacotani. **Lago Chungará** (4,517 m, 7 km by 3 km) is southeast of Payachatas, a must for its views of the Parinacota, Sajama and Guallatire volcanoes and for its varied wildlife. At the far end of the lake is the Chile/Bolivia border. The park contains over 120 species of bird, resident or migrant, as well as camelids, vizcacha and puma. A good base for exploring the park and for acclimatization is **Putre** (*Population: 4,400; Altitude: 3,500 m*), a scenic village, 15 km before the entrance with a church dating from 1670 and surrounded by terracing dating from pre-Inca times, now used for cultivating alfalfa and oregano. From here paths provide easy walking and great views. Festivals: Pacahayame, last Sunday in October, festival of the potato: religious celebration and traditional dancing. Feria de la Voz Andina, November (check dates and reserve room and transport in advance), with dancing, foods, handicrafts, very popular. **Tourist office** on main plaza, helpful, some English spoken, organizes tours. CONAF subadministration office in town, Teniente del Campo 301, T585704, is open 0900-1230, 1300-1730.

At **Parinacota** (*Altitude: 4,392 m*), at the foot of Payachatas, there is an interesting 17th century church – rebuilt 1789 – with 18th-century frescoes and the skulls of past priests (ask at the stalls outside the church for Señor Sipriani with the key, donations appreciated). Local residents knit alpaca sweaters, US$26 approximately; weavings of wildlife scenes also available. Weavings are sold from stalls outside the church. CONAF office, which administers the national park, and visitors centre is also here, open 0900-1230, 1300-1730. It's a walk of about one hour from the village to Cotacotani. From here an unpaved road runs north to the Bolivian border at Visviri (see above). You can climb Guane Guane, 5,097 m, in two to three hours, ask at the **CONAF refugio**. Lago Chungará is 20 km southeast of Parinacota.

During the rainy season (January-February), roads in the park may be impassable; check in advance with CONAF in Arica (see Useful addresses, Arica, below). It can be foggy as well as wet in January-March. A map of the park is available from Sernatur in Arica. Maps are also available from the Instituto Geográfico Militar. If driving off the main road, 4WD is necessary.

Reserva Nacional Las Vicuñas → *Altitude: 4,300-6,060 m.*

South of Lauca is the beautiful Reserva Nacional Las Vicuñas, covering 209,131 ha of altiplano. Many of these beautiful creatures can be seen as well as, with luck, condors, rheas and other birds. Administration is at Guallatiri, reached by turning off the Arica-La Paz road onto the A147 2 km after Las Cuevas, where there is also a CONAF *refugio* (see Sleeping, below). The same road leads into the **Monumento Natural Salar de Surire**, for which the same weather and road conditions apply. The Salar, also at 4,300 m, is a drying salt lake of 17,500 ha. It has a year-round population of 12,000-15,000 flamingos (Chilean, Andean and James). Administration is in **Surire**, 48 km south of Guallatiri and 129 km south of Putre. A normal car can reach Surire in the dry season, but a high clearance vehicle is essential for all other roads and, in the summer wet season (January to March, also August), 4WD vehicle: take extra fuel. In the wet, roads may be impassable. There is no public transport to these wildlife reserves, but tours can be arranged in Putre or Arica. See Footprint's *Chile Handbook*, or ask tour operators such as Latinorizons about routes through these parks from Arica to San Pedro de Atacama. Also check with CONAF in Arica about road conditions and whether the parks are closed at any time.

Arica and Lauca listings

For Sleeping and Eating price codes and other relevant information, see Essentials, pages 38-40.

Sleeping

Arica *p769, map p770*

For apartment rental on the beach, see local newspapers.

L Arica, San Martín 599, about 2 km along shore (frequent micros and colectivos), T254540, www.panamericanahoteles.cl. 4-star, best, price depends on season, decent restaurant, tennis court, pool, lava beach (not safe for swimming), American breakfast.

A Americano, General Lagos 571, T257752, www.hotelamericano.cl. Airy, spacious rooms, pleasant patio, rooms on upper floor have views to the Morro and are recommended. Also gym and sauna (extra charge).

B Plaza Colón, San Marcos 261, T/F254424, www.hotelplazacolon.cl. With breakfast, comfortable (but avoid basement rooms), convenient location opposite the cathedral.

B Savona, Yungay 380, T231000, www.hotel savona.cl. Recently refurbished but with many original features. Rooms on upper floors are bigger, a/c, airport transfer, internet access, Wi-Fi, terrace, pool, bike rental, attentive service, English spoken. Highly recommended.

C D'Marie-Jeanne y David, Velásquez 792, T258231, http://hoteldmariejeanney david.cl. With breakfast, TV, laundry, parking, snacks in café, French spoken, quite comfy, ask for courtyard room as rooms by main road noisy.

C Hostal Jardín del Sol, Sotomayor 848, T232795, www.hostaljardindelsol.cl. With breakfast, comfortable, beds with duvets, good value, free internet, stores luggage, some info, bike hire. Large kitchen area (US$1 charge). Highly recommended.

C Sunny Days, Tomás Aravena 161 (a little over halfway along P de Valdivia, 800 m from bus terminal, transport to hotel), T241038, www.sunny-days-arica.cl. **F** pp in shared rooms. Run by a New Zealander and his Chilean wife. Laundry facilities, some rooms with bath, English spoken, cosy atmosphere, lots of info, book exchange, bike rental, will pick you up from the terminal. Convenient for the beach. One of the best hostels in the north of Chile. Recommended.

C-D Maison de France, Aurelio Valdivieso 152, pob Chinchorro, T223463, atchumturist@hotmail.com. Owned by Frenchman Cristian, breakfast US$2, good meals, kitchen facilities, information on tours and self-guided trips, convenient for beach and nightlife. Recommended.

C-D Surf House, O'Higgins 661, T312213, www.aricasurfhouse.cl. Surfers' hostel (the owner also runs a surf school), decent beds and showers, large common areas, kitchen facilities. Tours, jet-ski rental. Good value.

D-E Hostal Pacífico, Gen Lagos 672, T251616, hostalpacifico672@hotmail.com. Good option in the city centre, some rooms with bath and cable TV.

D-E Hostal Venecia, Baquedano 741, T252877, hostalvenecia@gmail.com. Spotless, small rooms, hot water. Recommended.

D-E Res América, Sotomayor 430, T254148, www. residencialamerica.com. Recently refurbished, hot water, some rooms with bath, hospitable, good value.

Parque Nacional Lauca *p772*

There are 2 CONAF refuges in the park: at **Lago Chungará**, and **Las Cuevas** (by the Arica-Tambo Quemado road, 5 km from park entrance, not open to the general public, study and other groups only). Chungará has 6 beds, a campsite for 3 tents, cooking facilities, hot showers, **F** pp, sleeping bag essential, take your own food, candles and matches. Advance booking in Arica essential, or ask at the Parinacota or Putre offices.

Putre

If arriving from Bolivia, remember that no fresh produce may be brought across the border into Chile, so plan accordingly if using a CONAF refugio.

AL Hostería Las Vicuñas, Baquedano 80, T231028, www.chileanaltiplano.cl. Bungalow-style, with half-board, helpful, heating, internet, restaurant, does not accept credit cards. In the same group are **E** pp **Hostal Pachamama**, C 2 No 10, shared rooms for 4, shared bath, and **A Cabañas Tuto**, cabins for 5-6.

A-B Chakana Mountain Lodge, Cochrane s/n, T09-9745 9519, www.la-chakana.com. Also shared rooms, **E** pp. Modest cabins on the edge of town with pleasant views, English spoken, good breakfast, lots of hiking info. A good choice if you don´t mind the walk.

B-C Kukulí, Canto y Baquedano, T09-9161 4709. 10 decent rooms with bath and breakfast, in town.

C-D Hostal Cali, Baquedano 399, T09-8536 1242, krlos_team@hotmail.com. **E-F** with shared bath or single, pleasant, no heating, hot water, good restaurant, supermarket.

C-D Res La Paloma, O'Higgins 353, T09-9197 9319, lapalomaputre@hotmail.com. Some rooms with bath, hot showers after 0800 unless requested, no heating but lots of blankets, good food in large, warm restaurant, indoor parking; supermarket opposite.

F Hostal Chez Charlie, contact through *Latinorizons* (see Activities and tours, below). Comfortable, shared bath, hot water, good value, French and English spoken.

Camping **Sra Clementina Cáceres**, blue door on C Lynch, allows camping in her garden and offers lunch.

Parinacota

Accommodation is available with various families, ask at food and artesanía stands. You can camp behind the CONAF office for free, great site.

Reserva Nacional Las Vicuñas: Salar de Surire *p772*

At Surire, the CONAF office has 4 beds available, prior application to CONAF in Arica essential.

Eating

Arica *p769, map p770*

Many good places on 21 de Mayo and offering meals, drinks, real coffee, juices and outdoor seating.

TTT **Maracuyá**, San Martín 0321, at the northern end of Playa El Laucho south of the centre, T227600. Arica's premier restaurant specializing in fish and seafood. Expensive, but worth it.

TT **Chifa El Mesón**, Santa María 1364. One of several good-value Chinese restaurants in the area. Generous portions and clean kitchen in view of the diners.

TT **Cyclo Public**, Diego Portales 1364 T262098. Open from 2030. Fashionable seafood and pasta restaurant, vegetarian options, reasonably priced. Recommended.

TT **El Rey del Marisco**, Colón 565, p 2, T229232. Seafood specialities. A timeless sort of place, in business for 35 years, very good.

TT **Jalapeño Bar**, Baquedano 369, Tex-Mex specialities, relaxed atmosphere. Good value.

TT **El Congrio con Agallas**, O'Higgins 478-A, T232805, www.elcongrioconagallas.cl. Good fish and seafood restaurant.

TT **Los Aleros del 21**, 21 de Mayo 736, T254641. One of the city's longest-established restaurants, specializing in southern Chilean cuisine, large portions, lots of pork dishes; recommended also for seafood and service.

TT **Mata Rangi**, on the pier. Good food in fishy environment, good-value *menú de casa*.

TT-T **Café-Restaurante B**, 21 de Mayo 233. Very good, extensive menu including seafood.

TT-T **Don Floro**, V MacKenna 847, T231481. Good seafood, steaks and Peruvian specialities, good service, popular little place. Recommended.

TT-T **El Andén**, in former La Paz railway station. Good value, inventive menu, Mon-Fri, à la carte at weekends. An old train carriage is one of the dining areas.

TT-T **Ostión Dorado**, Playa Corazones. A small shack selling fabulous *empanadas* and other super-fresh seafood.

T **La Bomba**, Colón 357, at fire station, T255626. Good value *almuerzo*, friendly service.

T **Mercado Colón**, Maipú y Colón. Several stalls offering tasty good value lunches and fresh juices. Recommended.

T **Open Bar**, Maipú 500 y Lynch. Fantastically good-value lunches. Tapas served in the evening. There is an antique snooker table in the corner.

Parque Nacional Lauca: Putre *p772*

T **Kuchamarka**, Baquedano between La Paloma supermarket and Hostal Cali. Popular, good value, specializes in local dishes, including alpaca, as well as vegetarian options.

T **Rosamel**, Latorre y Carrera, on plaza. Pleasant, good restaurant. Also has rooms to let, **C-D**.

Bars and clubs

Arica *p769, map p770*

Chill Out, 21 Sep y Lynch. Open till 0400, but doesn't get going until 2400, popular bar. Also **Bar Central**, next door.

Soho, Playa Chinchorro. Disco.

Tunic On the coast past Playa Brava, south of Arica. Popular with the gay/alternative crowd.

Entertainment

Arica *p769, map p770*

Teatro Municipal de Arica, Baquedano 234. Wide variety of theatrical and musical events, exhibitions. Recommended.

Festivals and events

Arica *p769, map p770*

End-Jan/Feb, **Fiesta del Sol**, a festival of Andean dance and music, a slightly more debauched version of the festival at La Tirana. **June**, **Festival of Arica** and the national *cueca* dance championships. **7 Jun**, anniversary of the Chilean victory in the **Battle of the Morro**, with parties and fireworks. **29 Jun**, **San Pedro**, religious service at fishing wharf and boat parades. First weekend of **Oct**, **Virgen de las Peñas**, pilgrimage to the site of the Virgin, some 90 km inland near Livilcar.

Shopping

Arica *p769, map p770*

Many shopping galerías in the centre, also pharmacies, electrical appliances and clothes shops. Ferias for clothes on Velázquez.

Calle 21 de Mayo is pedestrianized, with many shops, restaurants and internet cafés.

Crafts **Poblado Artesanal**, Plaza Las Gredas, Hualles 2825 (take bus 2, 3 or 7). Expensive but especially good for musical instruments, open Tue-Sun 0930-1300, 1530-1930, *peña* Fri and Sat 2130; shop not always open out of season.

Markets **Feria Turística Dominical**, Sun market, along Chacabuco between Valásquez and Mackenna, mostly bric a brac. **Mercado Central**, Sotomayor y Sangra, between Colón and Baquedano. Mostly fruit and vegetables, mornings only. Smaller fruit and veg market, with food stalls, on Colón between 18 de Septiembre and Maipú.

Parque Nacional Lauca: Putre *p772*

Buy all food for the park in Putre, which has markets where bottled water, fresh bread, vegetables, meat, cheese and canned foods can be obtained. The **Cooperativo** on the plaza is usually cheapest. Fuel (both petrol and diesel) is available from the **Cali** and **Paloma** supermarkets; expect to pay a premium. **Sra Daria Condori**'s shop on C O'Higgins sells locally made *artesanía* and naturally coloured alpaca wool. Other than a small shop with limited supplies in Parinacota, no food is available outside Putre. Take drinking water with you as water in the park is not safe.

Activities and tours

Arica *p769, map p770*

Surfing There's good surfing at **Playa Las Machas** and **Playa Chinchorro**, north of the city (good for beginners), and at **La Ex Isla Alacrán**. For surfing lessons and equipment rental, try **Yoyo Surf School**, T311120, www.surfschool.cl. English spoken, best to call before 0900.

Swimming Olympic pool in **Parque Centenario**, Tue-Sat. Take No 5A bus from 18 de Septiembre. The best beach for swimming is **Playa Chinchorro**, north of town (bus 24). Buses 7 and 8 run to beaches south of town – the first 2 beaches, La Lisera and El Laucho, are both small and mainly for sun- bathing. Playa Brava is popular for sunbathing but not swimming (dangerous currents).

Tours operators

All charge similar prices for tours: Valle de Azapa US$20; city tour US$16; Parque Nacional Lauca, see page 772.

Andean Duncan Tours, Yungay 343, Dept 13, T314829, www.andeanduncantour.blogspot.com. Interesting day tours geared towards the cruise ship market, including archeological tours, birdwatching, traditional villages and the altiplano. English spoken. Recommended.

Clinamen Safaris y Expediciones, Sotomayor 361, piso 2, T313289, www.clinamen.cl. Bespoke small-group expeditions (maximum 3 people) to the Altiplano. Guide Christian Rolf speaks fluent English, German and French.

Latinorizons, Bolognesi 449, T/F250007, www.latinorizons.com. Specializes in tours to Parque Nacional Lauca and the Altiplano, small

groups in four-wheel drive Landcruiser; also tourist train rides from Arica, bike rental, not cheap, but good. Recommended.
Parinacota Expeditions, Thompson y Bolognesi, T256227, www.parinacota expediciones.cl. One of the oldest operators in Arica for altiplano tours.
Raices Andinas, Paseo Thompson, Feria 3 Esquinas, loc 21, T233305, www.raices andinas.com. Specializes in Altiplano trips, English spoken. Often recommended.
Suma Inti, Gonzalo Cerda 1366, T225685, www.sumainti.cl. Tours to the altiplano. Recommended guide Freddy Torrejón Aravire.
Vientos del Norte, Prat 430, of 1, T231331, www.vientosdelnorteadventure.cl. Another small operator offering trips to the Altiplano, English spoken. Good reports.

Parque Nacional Lauca *p772*
One-day tours are offered by most tour operators and some hotels in Arica, daily in season, according to demand at other times, US$35 pp with breakfast and light lunch; but some find the minibuses cramped and dusty. You spend all day in the bus (0730-2030) and you will almost certainly suffer from soroche. You can leave the tour and continue on another day as long as you ensure that the company will collect you when you want (tour companies try to charge double for this). Much better are 1½-day tours, 1400-1800 next day (eg Latinorizons), which include overnight in Putre and a stop on the ascent at the Aymara village of Socorama, US$65. Two-day tours, including food and accommodation, start at US$100 pp in group of 5. For 5 or more, the most economical proposition is to hire a vehicle. Full-day tours of the National Park starting at 0830, arranged in Putre, cost US$45, covering all aspects of Lauca.
Alto Andino Nature Tours, Baquedano 299, Putre (Correo Putre) T09-9890 7291, www.birdingaltoandino.com. Specialist birdwatching tours of the area and also walking tours along the Camino del Inca. All tours personalized and customized, English spoken, owner is an Alaskan biologist/naturalist. Recommended.
Tour Andino, C Baquedano 340, Putre, T09- 011 0702, www.tourandino.com. Comfortable 4WD tours from 1 to 4 days with Justino Jirón (owner) to Lauca and other areas, excellent, knowledgeable, flexible. Recommended.
Turismo Taki, is located in Copaquila, about 45 km west of Putre, 100 km east of Arica. Restaurant, camping site and excursions to nearby pucarás, Inca tambo and cemetery, good local food, English and Italian spoken.

Transport

Arica *p769, map p770*
Air Airport 18 km north of city at Chacalluta, T211116. Taxi to town US$10, colectivo US$5 per person. Flights to **Santiago**, LAN and **Sky** via Iquique and, less frequently, **Antofagasta.**
To **Lima**, **LanPerú** and others from Tacna (Peru), enquire at travel agencies in Arica.
Bus Local buses run from Maipú, US$0.60. Long distance buses leave from 2 adjacent terminals, both northeast of the centre at Av Portales y Santa María, T241390, many buses and colectivos (eg Nos 8, 18) pass (US$0.80), taxi US$2; terminal tax US$0.40. All luggage is carefully searched for fruit 30 mins prior to boarding and at 2 stops heading south. Bus company offices at bus terminal: **Pullman**, T223837; **Tur-Bus**, T241059.

To **Iquique**, frequent, US$10, 4½ hrs, also collective taxis, several companies, all in the terminal. To **Antofagasta**, US$20-32, 11 hrs. To **Calama**, 10 hrs, US$21, several companies, all between 2000 and 2200. To **San Pedro de Atacama**, 2200, 11½ hrs, US$25. To **La Serena**, 23 hrs, US$40-75. To **Santiago**, 30 hrs, a number of companies, US$50-85 (most serve meals of a kind, somewhat better on the more expensive services; student discounts available). To **Viña del Mar** and **Valparaíso**, 29 hrs, US$55.
International buses See below for transport to Bolivia and Peru.
Car hire **American**, Gen Lagos 559, T257752, servturi@entelchile.net. **Cactus**, Baquedano 635, T257430, cactusrent@ latinmail.com. **Hertz**, Baquedano 999, T231487, and at airport, has been recommended for good service. **Klasse**, Velásquez 760, piso 2, Loc 25, T058-254498. good deals. Several others and at Chacalluta airport. Antifreeze is essential for Parque Nacional Lauca, 4WD if going off paved roads.
Taxi Colectivos on fixed routes within city limit line up on Maipú entre Velásquez y Colón (all are numbered), US$2 pp (more after 2000). Taxis are

black and yellow and are scarce; hire a colectivo instead, US$2-3.

Border with Bolivia *p771*

Bus To **La Paz**, Bolivia, at least 4 companies from terminal, US$23, most via Chungará (some daily). Buses from Arica to Visviri, **Humire**, T220198/260164, Tue and Fri, 1030, US$12, also Sun 0830 en route to La Paz; **Martínez**, Tue and Fri 2230 en route to La Paz, both from terminal. Colectivos from Arica US$15. In Visviri take a jeep across the border to Charaña. Buses from Charaña to La Paz, leave before 1000, US$6, 6 hrs.

Border with Peru *p771*

Colectivos Run from the international bus terminal on Diego Portales to **Tacna**, US$4 pp, 1½ hrs. There are many companies and you will be besieged by drivers. For quickest service take a Peruvian colectivo heading back to Peru. Give your passport to the colectivo office where your papers will be filled. After that, drivers take care of all the paperwork. Also buses from the same terminal, US$2, 1 hr longer than journey by colectivo. For Arequipa it is best to go to Tacna and catch an onward bus there.

Train Station at Máximo Lira, by the port, to **Tacna** Mon-Sat 0900 and 2000, 1½ hrs, US$2, return Mon-Sat 0600, 1600. Buy ticket at least a day in advance and arrive early.

Parque Nacional Lauca *p772*

Bus **La Paloma** (Flota Paco) buses leave Germán Riesco 2071, Arica (bus U from centre) for **Putre** daily at 0700, 4 hrs, US$6, returning from La Paloma supermarket 1330 (book in advance – beware overcharging, overworked drivers); also **Guttiérez**, Wed, Fri 0630, Sun 2000, from Esteban Ríos 2140, T229338, but in theory passing outside the international bus terminal. **Jurasi** collective taxi leaves Arica daily at 0700, picks up at hotels, T222813, US$12. If you take an Arica-La Paz bus for Putre, it is 3 km from the crossroads to the town at some 4,000 m, tough if you've come straight up from sea level. **Humire** buses run to **Parinacota** 1030, Tue and Fri, US$8. Hostal Cali runs buses to Bolivia. Bus to La Paz from Putre crossroads or Lago Chungará can be arranged in Arica (same fare as from Arica).

Hitchhiking Hitching back to Arica is not difficult, with lots of carabineros coming and going; you may be able to bargain on one of the tour buses. Trucks from Arica to La Paz sometimes give lifts, a good place to try is at the Poconchile control point, 37 km from Arica.

Directory

Arica *p769, map p770*

Airline offices LAN, A Prat 391, T600-526 2000 (closes 1330 on Sat). **Sky**, 21 de Mayo 356, T251816/600-600 2828. **Banks** Many Redbanc ATMs on 21 de Mayo and by Plaza Colón. Money changers on 21 de Mayo and its junction with Colón, some accept TCs. **Cambio**, in Cosmo Center, Colón 600, cash and TCs, reasonable rates. **Consulates Bolivia**, P Lynch 298, T583390, colivian-arica@yahoo.com. **Peru**, Av 18 de Setiembre 1554, T231020, conperarica@terra.cl. **Cultural centres** Alianza Francesa, 18 de Septiembre 399, loc 295, T231130, arica@alliancesfrancaises.net. **Internet and telephones** Plenty of locutorios in the centre. **Language classes** SW Academia de Artes y **Lenguas**, 21 de Mayo 483, p 3, T258645, www.spanishinchile.blog spot.com. Chilean/British school, US$10 per hr. **Post offices** Prat 375, down pedestrian walkway. Mon-Fri 0830-1330, 1500-1900, Sat 0900-1230. To send parcels abroad, contents must be shown to Aduana (1st floor of post office) on Mon-Fri 0800-1200. Your parcel will be wrapped, but take your own carton. **Useful addresses** **CONAF**, Av Vicuña MacKenna 820, T201200, aricayparinacota.oirs@conaf.cl. Mon-Fri 0830-1300, 1430-1630 (take Colectivo 1). Aug-Nov is best season for mountain climbing; permits needed for summits near borders. Either go to the governor's office in Putre, or contact **Dirección Nacional de Fronteras y Límites del Estado** (DIFROL) Bandera 52, p 5, Santiago, T02-679 4200, in advance, listing the mountains you wish to climb.

Parque Nacional Lauca: Putre *p772*

Banks Bank in Putre changes dollars but commission on TCs is very high. The ATM does not take international cards. Internet on the plaza.

Central Valley

One of the world's most fecund and beautiful landscapes, with snowclad peaks of the Andes to the east and the Cordillera de la Costa to the west, the Central Valley contains most of Chile's population. A region of small towns, farms and vineyards, it has several protected areas of natural beauty. Five major rivers cross the Central Valley, cutting through the Coastal Range to the Pacific: from north to south these are the Rapel, Mataquito, Maule, Itata and Biobío. Some of the river valleys provide ideal conditions for growing grapes and making wine and you can wander between vineyards. This is also Chilean cowboy country and at rural shows you can see displays of horsemanship.

On 27 February 2010 an earthquake of strength 8.8 on the Richter Scale struck south-central Chile. Its epicentre was 150 km north of Concepción, 32 km below the surface of the Pacific Ocean. The O'Higgins, Maule and Biobío regions were worst hit. From Santiago north and from the Lake District south all tourist services were operating normally. The cities of Curicó, Talca, Chillán, Concepción and Talcahuano were very badly damaged, as were many other towns, villages and vineyards. Worst affected was the coast where tsunamis almost obliterated the resorts of Constitución, Pichilemu, Iloca and others. At least 600 people were killed, but exact numbers will perhaps never be known, and many thousands were left homeless. At the time of going to press rebuilding was well underway and there is no reason to remove Chile from your travel plans. The Panamerican Highway was open, with a few detours between Santiago and Puerto Montt, and many services were getting back to normal, even if under difficult conditions. Rail services from Santiago to Chillán were expected to be running by end-2010. It is impossible to say which businesses, national parks and other attractions will be open by the start of the 2010-2011 summer season. We advise you to contact the local offices of Sernatur, or Sernatur in Santiago (www.sernatur.cl), Conaf (www.conaf.cl) and http://mopinforma.blogspot.com/ (Ministry of Public Works) for up-to-date information and means of offering support.

Rancagua to Chillán

Rancagua → *Phone code: 072. Colour map 8, B1. Population: 167,000.*
The capital of VI Región (Libertador Gen Bernardo O'Higgins) lies on the Río Cachapoal, 82 km south of Santiago. Founded in 1743, it is a service and market centre. At the heart of the city is an attractive tree-lined plaza, the Plaza de los Héroes, and several streets of single-storey colonial-style houses. In the centre of the plaza is an equestrian statue of O'Higgins. The main commercial area lies along Avenida Independencia, which runs west from the plaza towards the bus and rail terminals. The National Rodeo Championships are held at the end of March in the Complejo Deportivo, north of the centre (US$18 per day; plenty of opportunities for purchasing cowboy items). **Tourist office** ⓘ *Germán Riesco 277, T230413, inforancagua@sernatur.cl (this office could not be contacted in Mar 2010).*

Around Santa Cruz and **San Fernando** (51 km south of Rancagua) is the Colchagua Valley, another wine-producing zone. For the Ruta del Vino here ⓘ *Plaza de Armas 298, Santa Cruz, T072-823199, www.rutadelvino.cl (calling for donations Apr 2010 - the musuem was destroyed).* Among vineyards that can be visited is **Viña La Playa** ⓘ *Camino a Calleuque, Peralillo, Sant Cruz, T02-657 9990, www.hotelvinalaplaya.cl, Wed-Sat 1200-1600, open Apr 2010,* which also has its own "fabulous" boutique hotel (**LL-L**) with massage, therapies, riding and cycling. For information on the Cachapoal wine producing zone, with details on tours and vineyard visits, enquire at the **Ruta del Vino Cachapoal** ⓘ *T08-232 1399.*

Curicó → *Phone code: 075. Colour map 8, B1. Population: 103,919. Altitude: 200 m.*
Between the Ríos Lontué and Teno, 192 km from Santiago, Curicó is the only town of any size in the Mataquito Valley. It was founded in 1744. Most of the historic centre was destroyed in the

February 2010 earthquake. In mid-March is the Fiesta de la Vendimia with displays on traditional wine-making (cancelled in 2010). Overlooking the city, the surrounding countryside and with views to the distant Andean peaks is Cerro Condell (100 m); it is an easy climb to the summit from where there are a number of walks. One of the largest bodegas in Chile, **Miguel Torres**, is worth a visit ⓘ *5 km south of the city, T564100, www.migueltorres.cl, daily 1000-1700 in autumn and winter, daily 1000-1900 in spring and summer, tours in Spanish only. Open in Apr 2010. Getting there: take a bus for Molina from the local terminal or outside the railway station and get off at Km 195 on the Pan- American Highway.* For information on the vineyards of Curicó, see the **Ruta del Vino del Valle de Curicó** ⓘ *Prat 301-A, Curicó, T328972, http://rutadelvinocurico.cl.* All municipal offices were operating out of a large tent after the earthquake.

Parque Nacional Radal Siete Tazas

ⓘ *Closed March 2010.*

The park is in two parts, one at Radal, 65 km east of Curicó, the other at Parque Inglés, 9 km further east. At Radal, the Río Claro flows through a series of seven rock cups (*siete tazas*) each with a pool emptying into the next by a waterfall. The river goes through a canyon, 15 m deep but only 1½ m wide, ending abruptly in a cliff and a beautiful waterfall. There is excellent trekking in the park, through beautiful woods and scenery, similar to what can be found further south, but with a better climate.

Talca ➔ *Phone code: 071. Colour map 8, B1. Population: 175,000.*

At 56 km south of Curicó (258 km from Santiago via dual carriageway) this is the most important city between Santiago and Concepción. It is a major manufacturing centre and the capital of VII Región (Maule). Founded in 1692, Talca was destroyed by earthquakes in 1742 and 1928 and was again heavily damaged in Februry 2010. **Museo O'Higginiano** ⓘ *just off the Plaza de Armas at 1 Norte 875, T615880, www.dibam.cl/sdm_moba_talca; not known if this museum is open.* This museum is in a colonial mansion in which Bernardo O'Higgins lived as a child. The house was later the headquarters of O'Higgins' Patriot Government in 1813-14 (before his defeat at Rancagua). In 1818 O'Higgins signed the declaration of Chilean independence here. The **Maule Valley** ⓘ *information from the Villa Cultural Huilquilemu, 7 km southeast of Talca, T071-246460, www.valledelmaule.cl - under reconstruction Apr 2010*, is another wine producing region, with vineyards that can be visited. The **tourist office** is at ⓘ *1 Oriente 1150, p 4, T233669, infomaule@sernatur.cl, this office could not be contacted Mar 2010. See www.talca.cl.*

Constitución and the coast

At the mouth of the Río Maule, 89 km from San Javier on the Pan-American Highway (south of Talca), **Constitución** is an important port and seaside resort. The town and coast were almost completely destroyed in February 2010. Expect new services to be open in the 2010-2011 summer season.

Vilches

ⓘ *Several buses a day from Talca to Alto Vilches, US$2-3, 2½ hrs.*

This is the starting point for the climb to the volcanoes **Quizapu** (3,050 m) and **Descabezado** (3,850 m), both of which are in the **Reserva Nacional Altos del Lircay** ⓘ *US$5.50, entrance 2 km from Alto Vilches bus stop, partially closed after the February 2010 earthquake, http://altosdelircay.cl*, which covers 12,163 ha. There are good hikes, including in the Area de Protección Alto Vilches, which has the Piedras Tacitas, a stone construction supposedly made by the aboriginal inhabitants of the region. A longer trek is to Laguna del Alto, eight hours. For walks on Descabezado Grande and Cerro Azul (ice axe, crampons and guide needed) and for riding in the area, contact **Casa Chueca** in Talca. Administration and Antahuara campsite are near the entrance.

To the border with Argentina: Paso Pehuenche

A road south of Talca, paved for the first 65 km, runs southeast from the Panamericana along **Lago Colbún** and up the broad valley of the Río Maule to reach the Argentine border at Paso Pehuenche. At the western end of the lake is the town of Colbún, from where a road goes to Linares on the Panamericana. Thermal springs 5 km south of Colbún at Panimávida, and 12 km, Quinamávida. Campsites on south shore. While in Panimávida, try the local *Bebida Panimávida*, made from spring water, sparkling or still, flavoured with lemon or raspberry. Paso Pehuenche (2,553 m) is reached by poor unpaved road southeast from Lago Colbún. Chilean customs is at La Mina, 106 km from Talca, 60 km from the border (Camping La Querencia, 4 km west of La Mina). On the Argentine side the road continues to Malargüe and San Rafael. The border is normally open December-March 0800-2100, April-November 0800-1900.

Chillán ➔ *Phone code: 042. Colour map 8, B1. Population: 146,000. Altitude: 118 m.*

Chillán, 150 km south of Talca, is capital of Ñuble province. Following an earthquake in 1833, the site was moved slightly to the northwest, though the older site, Chillán Viejo, is still occupied. Further earthquakes in 1939 and 1960, and again in February 2010, ensured that few old buildings have survived. Chillán was the birthplace of Bernardo O'Higgins and of the world-famous pianist, Claudio Arrau (interactive museum at Arrau 568, T433390, www.museoarrau.cl). The Fiesta de la Vendimia is an annual wine festival held in the third week in March. **Tourist office** ⓘ *18 de Septiembre 455, at the side of Gobernación, T223272, infochillan@sernatur.cl - this office cold not be contacted Mar 2010. See www.municipalidadchillan.cl.*

The centre of the city is **Plaza O'Higgins**, on which stands the modern **Cathedral** designed to resist earthquakes. **San Francisco** church, three blocks northeast, has a museum of religious and historical artefacts. Above the main entrance is a mural by Luis Guzmán Molina, a local artist, an interpretation of the life of San Francisco in a Chilean context. Northwest of the Plaza O'Higgins, on the Plaza Héroes de Iquique, is the **Escuela México**. It was donated to the city after the 1939 earthquake. In its library are murals by the great Mexican artists David Alvaro Siqueiros and Xavier Guerrero which present allegories of Chilean and Mexican history. The **Mercado y Feria Municipal** (covered and open markets at Riquelme y Maipón) sell regional arts and crafts and have many cheap, good restaurants, serving regional dishes; open daily, Sunday until 1300. Three blocks further south is the **Museo Naval El Chinchorro** ⓘ *Collin y I Riquelme*, containing naval artefacts and models of Chilean vessels. In Chillán Viejo (southwest of the centre) there is a monument and park at **O'Higgins' birthplace** ⓘ *park 0830-2000*. It has a 60 m long mural depicting his life (an impressive, but sadly faded, mosaic of various native stones), and a **Centro Histórico y Cultural**, with a gallery of contemporary paintings by regional artists.

Quinchamalí is 27 km southwest of Chillán, a little village famous for the originality of its craftsmen in textiles, basketwork, black ceramics, guitars and primitive paintings (all on sale in Chillán market). Handicraft fair, second week of February.

Termas de Chillán

East of Chillán 82 km by good road (paved for the first 50 km), 1,850 m up in the Cordillera, are thermal baths and, above, the largest ski resort in southern Chile. There are two open-air thermal pools (officially for hotel guests only) and a health spa with jacuzzis, sauna, mud baths, etc. Suitable for families and beginners and cheaper than centres nearer Santiago, the ski resort has 32 runs (the longest is 13 km), 11 lifts, snowboarding and other activities. It also has two hotels (the 5-star Gran Termas de Chillán Hotel, and the 3-star Pirigallo) and condominium apartments. Season: middle June to the end of September. Information and reservations from **Chillán Ski Centre** ⓘ *Barros Arana 261, T042-434200, www.termaschillan.cl, lift pass US$40 per day, US$30 per ½-day, equipment hire about US$30 pp.*

Rancagua to Chillán listings

For Sleeping and Eating price codes and other relevant information, see Essentials, pages 38-40.

Sleeping

Rancagua *p778*

AL Mar Andino, Bulnes 370, T645400, www.hotelmarandino.cl. New, modern, comfortable, decent restaurant, business centre, pool.

A-B Aguila Real, Brasil 1045, T222047, hotel aguilareal@terra.cl. Modern 3-star, with breakfast, cable TV, laundry, restaurant. Some English spoken.

B España, San Martín 367, T230141, noraberriosf@latinmail.com. Cheaper without bath, central, hot water, pleasant, laundry, food served.

B-C Hostal El Parrón, San Martín 135, T758550, www.hostalelparron.cl. New hostel in a 2-storey art-deco-style house in the centre, cable TV, internet, patio.

Curicó *p778*

At the time of writing it is not known which hotels are operating here.

Parque Nacional Radal Siete Tazas *p779*

At the time of writing it is not known which hotels or campsites are operating here.

Talca *p779*

Check in advance if hotels are open.

A-B Casa Chueca, Camino Las Rastras, 4 km from Talca by the Río Lircay, T071-197 0096, T09-9419 0625, www.trekkingchile.com. Phone hostal from bus terminal for directions on how to get there. **E** pp in rooms with shared bath. With breakfast, good dinner on request, Austrian and German owners, many languages spoken, lovely setting, swimming pool, mountain bikes, good trekking, riding and climbing tours arranged. Also Spanish classes. Enthusiastically recommended. Closed Jun-Aug.

B Terranova, 1 Sur 1026, T239603, www.hotelterranova.cl. A decent business standard with treatment room, sauna, Wi-fi and internet, buffet breakfast.

B-C Cordillera, 2 Sur 1360, T221817, www.cordillerahotel.cl. Decent standard, no frills, serves a good breakfast.

B-C Hostal del Puente, 1 Sur 407, T220930, www.hostaldelpuente.cl. Large breakfast extra, cable TV, family-owned, parking in central courtyard, lovely gardens, English spoken. Recommended for atmosphere, price and surroundings.

C Hostal del Río, 1 Sur 411, T225448, www.hostaldelrio.cl. Rival to Del Puente next door (run by owner's brother), a little cheaper, also good.

Vilches *p779*

C-D Refugio del Tricahue, in Maule Valley, south of Vilches (take Armerillo bus from Talca, 1½ hrs, US$1.60), refugio.tricahue@yahoo.fr, no phone or internet at refuge, for details www.refugio-tricahue.cl. Small hostel, French/Begian run, **E** pp in bunk room, **G** camping, hot water, breakfast extra, no other meals provided but use of kitchen, hot springs, fishing gear, horses for rent, guides to private reserve, very pleasant. Open Apr 2010.

Camping **Antahuara** 500 m from Reserva Altos de Lircay administration, at 1,300 m, hot showers, light at each site, beautiful location, US$16.

Chillán *p780*

Check in advance if hotels are open.

AL Gran Hotel Isabel Riquelme, Constitución 576, T434400, www.hotelisabelriquelme.cl. Central business hotel, with cable TV, internet, restaurant, laundry, parking.

A-B Cordillera, Arauco 619, on Plaza de Armas, T215211, www.hotelcordillera.cl. 3-star, small, all rooms with heating, good.

B-C Libertador, Libertad 85, T223255, www.hlbo.cl. Reasonably spacious rooms, cable TV, Wi-Fi. Recently refurbished.

Other good hotels whose condition is not known include: **Ventura**, O'Higgins 638, T227588. 3 star, pleasant garden, good home cooked food (restaurant open to non-residents). **Hostal Marbella**, Libertad 336B, T09-8949 0641. Airy but basic rooms with TV, shared bath and parking.

Termas de Chillán *p780*

A Cabañas La Piedra, Los Coihues 1143, Km 48 on road to Termas de Chillán, Recinto, T08-415 7735, www.cabanaslapiedra.cl. Price is for cabaña for 2, also cabins for 4, 5, 6 and 8, nestled in forest, "tranquil and rejuvenating", pool, Wi-Fi, hiking trips to the mountains, music performances outdoors around the pool under stars, good restaurants closeby. Manager Jacqueline van Nunen speaks English, German, Dutch, Spanish.

AL-A pp **Robledal**, at Las Trancas on the road to the Termas, Km 70-76 from Chillán, T432030, www.hotelrobledal.cl. Pleasant rooms, bar, restaurant, sauna and jacuzzi, tours offered.

A-B MI Lodge, T09-321 7567, www.milodge.com. Small lodge with fine views, hot tub and good restaurant. Price depends on season.

There are many *cabañas* in Las Trancas, usually **A** pp for up to 6, see www.vallelastrancas.cl. Also **D-E Hostelling International**, Km 73.5, T423718, hostellinglastrancas@gmail.com. Camping available 2 km from the slopes.

Eating

Rancagua *p778*

There are eating places west of Plaza de los Héroes, eg on Independencia and Astorga.

La Cocina Artesanal, O'Carroll 60. Traditional meat and seafood dishes.

Transport

Rancagua *p778*

Bus The terminal for regional buses is at Doctor Salinas y Calvo, just north of the market. Frequent services to **Santiago** from **Tur-Bus** terminal at Calvo y O'Carroll, T241117, US$5, 1¼ hrs.

Train Train station on Av La Marina, T230361, T0600-585 5000 for tickets. Main line services between Santiago and Chillán stop here. Also regular services to/from **Santiago** on Metrotren, 1¼ hrs. Services were due to resume in mid to late-2010.

Curicó *p778*

Bus Long distance terminal at Prat y Maipú. Local buses, as well as some long distance services, from Terminal Plaza, Prat y Maipú. **Tur-Bus** stop and office, M de Velasco, 1 block south. **Pullman del Sur** terminal, Henríquez y Carmen. Many south- bound buses bypass Curicó, but can be caught by waiting outside town. To **Santiago** US$6, 2½ hrs, several companies, frequent. To **Talca** every 15 mins, US$3.40, 1 hr. To **Temuco**, **Alsa** and **Tur-Bus**, US$16-24, 7 hrs.

Train Station is at the west end of Prat, 4 blocks west of Plaza de Armas, T310028, tickets from Maipú 657, T0600-585 5000. Services were due to resume in mid to late-2010.

Parque Nacional Radal Siete Tazas *p779*

Take a **minibus** from Terminal Plaza, Curicó, to **Molina**, 26 km south, US$1; from Molina bus at 1700 weekdays, 0800 Sun, to **Radal** village in summer, return 0730 (1800 Sun), 3 hrs, US$5. It's a further 6.5 km to Siete Tazas and 11 km to Parque Inglés. Access by car is best as the road through the park is paved.

Talca *p779*

Bus Terminal at 12 Oriente y 2 Sur. From **Santiago**, US$6.60. To **Chillán**, frequent, US$5.40. To **Temuco**, US$13.50, 6 hrs. To **Puerto Montt**, US$22-37, 10½ hrs. **Train**: station at 11 Oriente 1000, T0600-585 5000. Services were due to resume in mid to late-2010.

Car hire **Trekker Ltda**, Casilla 143, Talca, T197 2757, 09-8501 6211, www.trekkerchile.com. Has camper vans, trucks and 4WD vehicles available for routes throughout Chile and into Argentina.

Chillán *p780*

Bus Two long-distance terminals: Central, Brasil y Constitución (**Tur-Bus, Línea Azul, Tas Choapa, Alsa-LIT**); Northern, Ecuador y O'Higgins for other companies. Local buses leave from Maipón y Sgto Aldea. To **Santiago**, 5½ hrs, US$10-11.50. To **Concepción**, every 30 mins, 1½ hrs, US$4. To **Temuco**, 3½ hrs, US$9-12.

Train Station, 5 blocks west of Plaza de Armas on Brasil, T0600-585 5000 (tickets also from **Centrotour**, 18 de Septiembre 486, loc 201, T221306). Services were due to resume in mid to late-2010. **Note** No trains between Chillán and Temuco; no date set for resumption.

Termas de Chillán *p780*

Ski **buses** run Jun-Sep from **Libertador** 1042 at 0800 and from Chillán Ski Centre, subject to demand, US$50 (includes lift pass). Summer bus service (Jan-mid-Mar), from **Anja**, 5 de Abril 594, Thu, Sat, Sun only, 0730, US$12 return, book in advance. At busy periods hitching may be possible from Chillán Ski Centre.

Directory

At the time of writing, it was not known which public services were operating in Talca *p779* or Chillán *p780*.

Concepción and around

→ *Phone code: 041. Colour map 8, B1. Population: almost 250,000.*

The third biggest city in Chile (516 km from Santiago) and the most important city in southern Chile, is also a major industrial centre. Capital of VIII Región (Biobío), Concepción is 15 km up the Biobío River. Founded in 1550, Concepción became a frontier stronghold in the war against the Mapuche after 1600. Destroyed by an earthquake in 1751, it was moved to its present site in 1764. It was severely damaged again by the February 2010 earthquake. In late March 2010 Sr Nelson Oyarzo of the Sernatur office in Concepción wrote: "we are not yet in a position to give information. Museums are slowly remounting their exhibits. In Parque Lota all the sculptures were toppled and the ground opened up in various places. Talcahuano is in ruins. Hotels are gradually having water restored, but there is no gas connection. In a couple of months things should be back to normal. In the Cordillera, reserves and national parks were unaffected."

The climate is very agreeable in summer, but from April to September the rains are heavy; the annual average rainfall, nearly all of which falls in those six months, is from 1,250 mm to 1,500 mm. **Tourist office**: Sernatur ⓘ *Aníbal Pinto 460, T274 1337, infobiobio@sernatur.cl.* CONAF, Barros Arana 215, p 2, T624000, biobio@conaf.cl.

Sights

In the attractive **Plaza de Armas**, or de la Independencia, at the centre are the **Intendencia** and the **Cathedral**. It was here that Bernardo O'Higgins proclaimed the independence of Chile on 1 January 1818. **Cerro Caracol** can easily be reached on foot starting from the statue of Don Juan Martínez de Rozas in the Parque Ecuador, arriving at the Mirador Chileno after 15 minutes. From here it is another 20 minutes' climb to **Cerro Alemán**. The **Biobío** and its valley running down to the sea lie below.

The **Galería de la Historia** ⓘ *Lincoyán y V Lamas by Parque Ecuador*, is a depiction of the history of Concepción and the region; upstairs is a collection of Chilean painting. The **Casa del Arte** ⓘ *Chacabuco y Paicaví, near Plaza Perú, T220 4290*, contains the University art collection; the entrance hall is dominated by La Presencia de América Latina, by the Mexican Jorge González Camerena (1965), a mural depicting Latin American history. Free explanations are given by University Art students.

The **Museo y Parque Hualpen** ⓘ *16 km from Concepción*, is a house built around 1885 (a national monument) and its gardens. It contains beautiful pieces from all over the world, two hour visit, recommended. The park also contains Playa Rocoto, at the mouth of the Río Biobío. Take a city bus to Hualpencillo from Freire, ask the driver to let you out then walk 40 minutes, or hitch. Go along Avenida Las Golondrinas to the Enap oil refinery, turn left, then right (it is signed).

Talcahuano → *Population: 244,000.*

At the neck of the Península de Tumbes, Talcahuano has the best harbour in Chile. It is Chile's main naval station and an important commercial and fishing port. As said above, it was wrecked by the February 2010 earthquake.

Costa del Carbón

South of the Biobío is the Costa del Carbón, until recently the main coal producing area of Chile, linked with Concepción by road and two bridges over the Biobío. **Lota** (*Population: 52,000; 42 km south of Concepción*) was, until its closure in 1997, the site of the most important **coalmine** in Chile. It, and the **Parque de Lota Isadora Cousiño**, covering 14 ha on a promontory to the west of the town, were heavily damaged in Febraury 2010. The park was the life's work of Isadora Cousiño, whose family owned the mine. Laid out by English landscape architects in the last century, it contains plants from all over the world, ornaments imported from Europe, romantic paths and shady nooks offering views over the sea, and peafowl and pheasants roaming freely. South of Lota the road runs past the seaside resort of **Laraquete** where there are miles of golden sand, very popular in summer.

Cañete ➔ *Phone code: 041. Colour map 8, C1. Population: 15,642.*

A small town, 130 km south of Concepción, on the site of Fort Tucapel where Pedro de Valdivia and 52 of his men were killed by Mapuche warriors in 1553. **Museo Mapuche** ⓘ *Juan Antonio Ríos, T261 1093, www.dibam.cl/sdm_mm_canete, 1 km south on the road to Contulmo, website closed Apr 2010*, is housed in a modern building inspired by the traditional Mapuche ruca; includes Mapuche ceramics and textiles. There is nowhere to change dollars in town.

Contulmo ➔ *Population: 2,000.*

A road runs south from Cañete along the north side of **Lago Lanalhue** to Contulmo, a sleepy village at the foot of the Cordillera. It hosts a Semana Musical (music week) in January. The wooden Grollmus House and Mill are 3 km northwest along the south side of the lake. The house, dating from 1918, has a fine collection of every colour of copihue (the national flower) in a splendid garden. The mill, built in 1928, contains the original wooden machinery. From here the track runs a further 9 km north to the Posada Campesina Alemana, an old German-style hotel in a fantastic spot at the water's edge. The Monumento Natural Contulmo, 8 km south and administered by CONAF (Av Pdte Frei 288, Cañete, T611241), covers 82 ha of native forest.

Los Angeles and around ➔ *Phone code: 043. Colour map 8, C1. Population: 114,000.*

On the Pan-American Highway, Los Angeles is 110 km south of Chillán. It is the capital of Biobío province. Founded in 1739 as a fort, it was destroyed several times by the Mapuche. Here, too, sever damage was recorded in February 2010 (www.8va.cl). It has a large Plaza de Armas and a good daily market. **Tourist office**: ⓘ *Caupolicán p 3, of 6, T317107*; CONAF: ⓘ *J Manzo de Velasco 275, T321086.* Some 25 km north of Los Angeles is the spectacular **Salto El Laja** where the Río Laja plunges 47 m over the rocks. Numerous tour groups stop here and the place is filled with tourist kiosks.

Parque Nacional Laguna de Laja ➔ *CONAF had not announced the reopening of this park in Mar 2010.*

East of Los Angeles via a 93-km road which runs past the impressive rapids of the Río Laja, this park is dominated by the active Antuco volcano (2,985 m) and the glacier-covered Sierra Velluda. The Laguna is surrounded by stark scenery of scrub and lava. There are 46 species of birds including condors and the rare Andean gull. There are several trails. Nearby is the Club de Esquí de Los Angeles with two ski-lifts, giving a combined run of 4 km on the Antuco volcano (season, May-August).

Angol ➔ *Phone code: 045. Colour map 8, C1. Population: 39,000.*

Capital of the Province of Malleco, Angol is reached from Collipulli and Los Angeles. Founded by Valdivia in 1552, it was seven times destroyed by the *indígenas* and rebuilt. The church and convent of San Beneventura, northwest of the attractive Plaza de Armas, built in 1863, became the centre for missionary work among the Mapuche. El Vergel, founded in 1880 as an experimental fruit-growing nursery, now includes an attractive park and the **Museo Dillman Bullock** ⓘ *Mon-Fri 0900-1900, Sat-Sun 1000-1900, US$1, 5 km from town, colectivo No 2*, with pre-Columbian indigenous artefacts. There is a **Tourist Office** ⓘ *O'Higgins s/n, T045-711255*, across bridge from the bus terminal. Ask here about lodging in Vegas Blancas for Nahuelbuta (see below). CONAF, Prat 191, p 2, T711870.

Parque Nacional Nahuelbuta

ⓘ *CONAF had not announced the reopening of this park in March 2010.*

Situated in the coastal mountain range at an altitude of 800-1,550 m, this beautiful park covers 6,832 ha of forest and offers views over both the sea and the Andes. Although the forest includes many species of trees, the monkey puzzle araucaria) is most striking; some are over 2,000 years old, 50 m high and 3 m in diameter. There are also 16 species of orchids as well as pudu deer, Chiloé foxes, pumas, black woodpeckers and parrots. There is a **Visitors' Centre** ⓘ *at Pehuenco, 5 km from the entrance, camping is near the Visitors' Centre; there are many other campsites along the road from El Cruce to the entrance, at Kms 20 and 21.*

Concepción listings

For Sleeping and Eating price codes and other relevant information, see Essentials, pages 38-40.

Sleeping

Concepción *p783*

As said above, hotels were slowly returning to service in Mar 2010, but it has not been possible to confirm which will be back to normal by end-2010. Check before arrival.

AL Alborada, Barros Arana 457, T291 1121, www.hotelalborada.cl. Good 4-star with all mod cons, disabled-friendly, tours offered.

AL-A El Dorado, Barros Arana 348, T222 9400, www.hoteleldorado.co.cl. Comfortable, spacious rooms, central, bar, cafeteria, parking.

B Concepción, Serrano 512, T222 8851, hotelconcepcion@entelchile.net. Central, comfortable, heating, English spoken. Recommended.

B Hostal Bianca, Salas 643-C, T225 2103, www.hostalbianca.cl. **C** with shared bath, with breakfast, Wi-Fi and internet, food available, parking, student discounts.

C Hostal Antuco, Barros Arana 741, flats 31-33, T223 5485, hostalantuco@hotmail.com. Entry via Galería Martínez. Some rooms with bath. Simple and spartan, but clean and reasonable value.

C Maquehue, Barros Arana 786, p 8, T221 0261, www.hotelmaquehue.cl. Good services, with restaurant, laundry. Highly recommended.

Other places in our **C** range: **Cecil**, Barros Arana 9, T273 9981, near railway station (formerly recommended). **Res Colo Colo**, Colo Colo 743, T222 7118. Meals available. **Silvia Uslar**, Edmundo Larenas 202, T222 7449 (not signed). Previously recommended as excellent.

Cañete *p784*

B-C Nahuelbuta, Villagrán 644, T261 1073, hotelnahuelbuta@lanalhueturismo.cl. Cheaper without bath, pleasant, parking.

C-D Derby, Mariñán y Condell, T261 1960. Without bath, basic, restaurant.

C-D Gajardo, 7° de la Línea 817 (1 block from plaza). Without bath, old fashioned, pleasant rooms.

Contulmo *p784*

D Central, Millaray 131, T261 8089, hotelcentral@lanalhueturismo.cl. Without bath, no sign, very hospitable.

Lago Lanalhue

A Hostal Licahue, 4 km north of Contulmo towards Cañete, T09-9779 7188, www.licahue.cl. **B** in low season. With breakfast, also full board and cabins, attractively set overlooking lake, pool. Open Apr 2010. Highly recommended.

Camping Camping **Huilquehue**, 15 km south of Cañete on lakeside. **Elicura**, Contulmo. Clean. Recommended. **Playa Blanca**, Playa Blanca, 10 km north of Contulmo. Clean.

Los Angeles *p784*

It is not known which hotels in town are open after the February 2010 earthquake.

Outside town

AL-A Salto del Laja, Salto El Laja, T321706, www.saltodellaja.cl. Good rooms, fine restaurant, 2 swimming pools, on an island overlooking the falls.

A-B El Rincón, Panamericana Sur Km 494 (20 km north of Los Angeles), exit Perales/El Olivo, 2 km east, T09-9441 5019, www.elrinconchile.cl. **C** with shared bath. Beautiful property beside a small river, restful, Chilean and European cuisine, includes vegetarian, Spanish classes, horse riding and rafting tours arranged, free internet, English, French, German and Spanish spoken. Recommended.

B Complejo Turístico Los Manantiales, Salto El Laja, T/F314275, losmanantialesdelsaltodellaja@hotmail.com, with camping.

Parque Nacional Laguna de Laja *p784*

B Cabañas Lagunillas, T321086, 2 km from park entrance. Open all year, cabins sleep 6, lovely spot close to the river among pine woods, restaurant, also camping US$5 pp.

E 2 other refugíos: **Digeder**, 11 km from the park entrance, and **Universidad de Concepción**, both on slopes of Volcán Antuco, for both T041-229054, office O'Higgins 740.

Eating

Concepción *p783*

At the time of writing it was not known which restaurants and cafés survived the Feb 2010 earthquake.

Shopping

Concepción *p783*

The main shopping area is north of Plaza de Armas.

Handicrafts Feria Artesanal, Freire 777. **Mercado Municipal,** 1 block west of the Plaza de Armas. Seafood, fruit and veg.

Transport

Concepción *p783*

Air Airport north of the city, off the main road to Talcahuano. In summer flights daily to and from **Santiago** (**LAN** and **Sky**), fewer in winter; connections to **Temuco**, **Puerto Montt** and **Punta Arenas**..

Bus Terminal Collao, for long distance services (also for **Lota**, **Cañete** and **Contulmo**), is 2 km east, on Av Gral Bonilla, next to football and athletics stadium. (Several buses to city centre, US$0.75, taxi US$5.) **Tur-Bus**, **Línea Azul** and **Buses Bío Bío** services leave from Terminal Camilo Henríquez 2 km northeast of main terminal on J M García, reached by buses from Av Maipú in centre, via Terminal Collao. To **Santiago**, 6½ hrs, US$15-30. To **Los Angeles**, US$4. To **Loncoche**, 5½ hrs, US$12. To **Pucón**, direct in summer only, 7 hrs, US$18. To **Valdivia**, 7 hrs, US$16-34. To **Puerto Montt** several companies, US$17-30, about 9 hrs. Best direct bus to **Chillán** is **Línea Azul**, 2 hrs, US$3.

Train Station at Prat y Barros Arana, **Efe** ticket office, Av Padre Hurtado 570, T0600-585 5000. Direct long-distance services to Santiago are currently suspended.

Costa del Carbón: Lota *p783*

Bus Concepción-Lota, 1½ hrs, US$2. Many buses bypass the centre: catch them from the main road.

Cañete *p784*

Bus Leave from 2 different terminals: J Ewert, **Inter Sur** and **Thiele** from Riquelme y 7° de la Línea, **Jeldres**, **Erbuc** and other companies from the Terminal Municipal, Serrano y Villagrán. To **Santiago**, 9 hrs, US$18. To **Concepción**, 3 hrs, US$6. To **Angol** US$6.

Contulmo *p784*

Bus To **Cañete**, frequent, US$2. To **Concepción**, US$7, 4 hrs; to **Temuco**, **Thiele** and **Erbuc**, US$8.

Los Angeles *p784*

Bus Long distance bus terminal on northeast outskirts of town, local terminal at Villagrán y Rengo in centre, by market. To **Salto de Laja**, every 30 mins with **Bus Bío Bio**, US$2 return. To **Santiago**, 6½ hrs, US$15-24. To **Viña del Mar** and **Valparaíso**, 8 hrs, US$17. Every 30 mins to **Concepción**, US$4, 2 hrs. To **Temuco**, US$7, hourly. To **Curacautín**, daily at 0945, 1600, 3 hrs, US$9 (otherwise change in Victoria).

Parque Nacional Laguna de Laja *p784*

Bus ERS Bus from Los Angeles (Villagrán 507, by market) to **Abanico**, 20 km past Antuco (6 a day, US$2), then 2 hrs/4 km walk to park entrance (hitching possible). Or bus to **Antuco**, 2 hrs, weekdays 5 daily, 2 on Sun and festivals, last return 1730, US$3, then hitch last 24 km. Details from CONAF in Los Angeles.

Angol *p784*

Bus To **Santiago** US$16-38, **Los Angeles**, US$3. To **Temuco**, Trans **Bío-Bío**, frequent, US$5.

Parque Nacional Nahuelbuta *p784*

Bus In Dec-Feb there is a direct bus from **Angol**, Sun 0800, return 1700. Otherwise, take the bus to **Vegas Blancas** (27 km west of Angol) 0700 and 1600 daily, return 0900 and 1600, 1½ hrs, US$2, get off at El Cruce, from where it is a steep 7 km walk to park entrance. Sometimes the bus goes to the park entrance, ask first.

Directory

Concepción *p783*

At the time of writing, it was not known which public services were operating in this city.

Airline offices LAN, O'Higgins 648, T600-526 2000. **Consulates** **Argentina**, O'Higgins 420, of 82, T223 0257.

Lake District

The Lake District, stretching southwards from Temuco to Puerto Montt, is one of Chile's most beautiful regions. There are some 12 great lakes of varying sizes, as well as imposing waterfalls and snowcapped volcanoes. There are a number of good bases for exploring. Out of season many facilities are closed, in season (from mid-December to mid-March), prices are higher and it is best to book well in advance, particularly for transport. About 20,000 Mapuches live in the area, particularly around Temuco. Although Mapudungun is becoming less prevalent, there are possibly 100,000 more of mixed descent who speak the native tongue, nearly all of them bilingual.

Temuco and around

→ *Phone code: 045. Colour map 8, C1. Population: 227,000. Altitude: 107 m.*

Although at first sight rather grey and imposing, Temuco is a lively university city and one of the fastest growing commercial centres in the south. Founded in 1881 after the final treaty with the Mapuches and the arrival of the railway, this city is the capital of IX Región (Araucanía), 677 km south of Santiago. Temuco is proud of its Mapuche heritage and it is this that gives it its distinctive character, especially around the outdoor market. The **Sernatur office** is at ⓘ *Bulnes 586, on main plaza, T211969, infoaraucania@sernatur.cl. Mon-Thu 0900-1400, 1500-1730, Fri 0900-1400, 1500-1630.* It has good leaflets in English. Also in the municipal market. See also www.temucochile.com. CONAF is at Bilbao 931, p 2, T298114, temuco@conaf.cl. Sernap for fishing permits, Miraflores 965. North and east of the city are five national parks and reserves, notably Conguillio with its araucaria forests, and flora and fauna found nowhere else. It is great for hiking, or touring by car or even mountain bike. There are also various skiing opportunities.

Sights

The centre is the Plaza Aníbal Pinto, around which are the main public buildings including the cathedral and the Municipalidad. Very little of the old city remains; practically every wooden building burned down following the 1960 earthquake. Temuco is the Mapuches' market town and you may see some, particularly women, in their typical costumes in the huge produce market, the **Feria** ⓘ *Lautaro y Pinto*, one of the most fascinating markets in Chile. Mapuche textiles, pottery, woodcarving, jewellery, etc are also sold inside and around the municipal market, Aldunate y Diego Portales (it also sells fish, meat and dairy produce), but these are increasingly touristy and poor quality. There is a handicraft fair every February in the main plaza. The **Casa de la Mujer Mapuche** ⓘ *in the Gymnasium, between Corvalín and Almte Barroso, Padre las Casas suburb, T233886/09-9169 4682, Mon-Fri 0930-1300, 1500-1830, take bus 8a or 10, colectivo 13a*, sells many crafts, including textiles made by a Mapuche weavers' co-operative, all with traditional designs. A couple of km northwest of the centre is the **Museo de la Araucanía** ⓘ *Alemania 84, Mon-Fri 0900-1700, Sat 1100-1700, Sun 1100-1400, US$1.50 (free Sun), take bus 1 from the centre*. It is devoted to the history and traditions of the Mapuche nation, with a section on German settlement. For information on visits to Mapuche settlements, eg Chol Chol, go to the Sernatur office in the Plaza. There are views of **Temuco from Cerro Ñielol** ⓘ *US$1.50, 0830-2030*. This park has a fine collection of native plants in the natural state, including the national flower, the copihue rojo. This is a good site for a picnic with an excellent visitors' centre run by CONAF. A tree marks the spot where peace was made with the Mapuche. Bicycles are only allowed in before 1100. At the top of the hill there is a restaurant, which also has dancing (not always open).

Northeast of the centre, 2 km, is the **Museo Nacional Ferroviario Pablo Neruda** ⓘ *Barros Arana 0565, T227613, Tue-Sun 0900-1800, US$2, concessions US$0.75, take micro 1 Variante, 9 Directo, 4b, taxi from centre US$2.50*, the newly restored national railway museum. Exhibits include over 20 engines and carriages (including the former presidential carriage) dating from 1908 to 1953. The grounds contain rusting hulks and machinery. Temporary exhibitions in the annex.

Curacautín and around → *Population: 12,500. Altitude: 400 m.*
Curacautín is a small town 84 km northeast of Temuco (road paved) and 56 km southeast of Victoria by paved road. Deprived by new, stricter controls of its traditional forestry industry (there were several sawmills), Curacautín is trying to recreate itself as a centre for tourism. It is a useful base for visiting the nearby national parks and hot springs (CONAF office, Yungay 240, T881184).

Termas de Manzanar, are indoor hot springs, 17 km east of Curacautín (US$14, open all year, www.termasdemanzanar.cl), reached by bus from Temuco and Victoria. The building dates from 1954. The road passes the Salto del Indio , where there are 30-m high falls, US$1.60 (Km 71 from Victoria) and *cabañas*, and Salto de la Princesa, an even more impressive 50-m waterfall, 3 km beyond Manzanar, with a hostería and camping.

The beautiful pine-surrounded **Termas de Tolhuaca** ⓘ *all year, US$16, taxi from Curacautín US$25, www.termastolhuaca.cl*, are 35 km to the northeast of Curacautín by unpaved road, or 82 km by rough, unpaved road from just north of Victoria (high clearance four-wheel drive vehicle essential). Just 2 km north of the Termas is the **Parque Nacional Tolhuaca** ⓘ *Dec-Apr, taxi from Curacautín US$17*, including waterfalls, two lakes, superb scenery and good views of volcanoes from Cerro Amarillo. Park administration is near Laguna Malleco, with a campsite nearby. Much of the park, together with the neighbouring Reserva Nacional Malleco, was severely damaged by forest fires in early 2002. It will take several decades fully to recover, but some half-day trails are open.

Reserva Nacional Nalcas Malalcahuello .
Northeast of Curacautín, this 31,305 ha park is on the slopes of the **Lonquimay** volcano (2,865 m). It is much less crowded than nearby Parque Nacional Conguillio. The volcano began erupting on Christmas Day 1988; the new crater is called Navidad. To see it, access is made from Malalcahuello, 15 km south and halfway between Curacautín and Lonquimay town. In the park, which is one of the best areas for seeing unspoilt araucaria forest, CONAF has opened several marked trails, from one hour to two days in length. There is a municipal refugio at the foot of the volcano. From Malalcahuello it is a one-day hike to the Sierra Nevada mountain, or a two-day hike to Conguillio national park (with equipment and experience, otherwise use a guide). CONAF office on main road in Malalcahuello gives information, as does **La Suizandina**, which gives good access to treks and the ascent of the volcano. Sra Naomi Saavedra at **Res Los Sauces** arranges transport; see Sleeping, below.

Los Arenales ski resort ⓘ *T045-463027 – Lonquimay tourist office, or 08-901 8810, season Jun-Sep, taxi from Curacautín US$17, in winter access from Lonquimay town side only*, is at Las Raices Pass on the road from Malalcahuello to Lonquimay town. Four lifts go up to 2,500 m with great views, ski pass US$25, equipment hire US$23. It is a good, small resort with a nice restaurant. Also in winter, the main route from Malalcahuello to Lonquimay town, goes through the ex-railway tunnel of **Las Raices** ⓘ *toll US$2.50*. At 4.8 km it was, until recently, the longest tunnel in South America. Now it's in poor condition, unlit and has constant filtration. There is talk of repair, but it's unwise to go through by bicycle.

Parque Nacional Conguillio
East of Temuco by 80 km, this is one of the most popular parks in Chile ⓘ *US$6, visitor centre (open Dec-Mar) at the park administration by Lago Conguillio*, but is deserted outside January/February and weekends. In the centre is the 3,125 m **Llaima volcano**, which is active (eruptions in 2008 and 2009 led to partial closure of the park). There are two large lakes, **Laguna Verde** and **Laguna Conguillio**, and two smaller ones, **Laguna Arco Iris** and **Laguna Captrén**. North of Laguna Conguillio rises the snow covered **Sierra Nevada**, the highest peak of which

Lake District

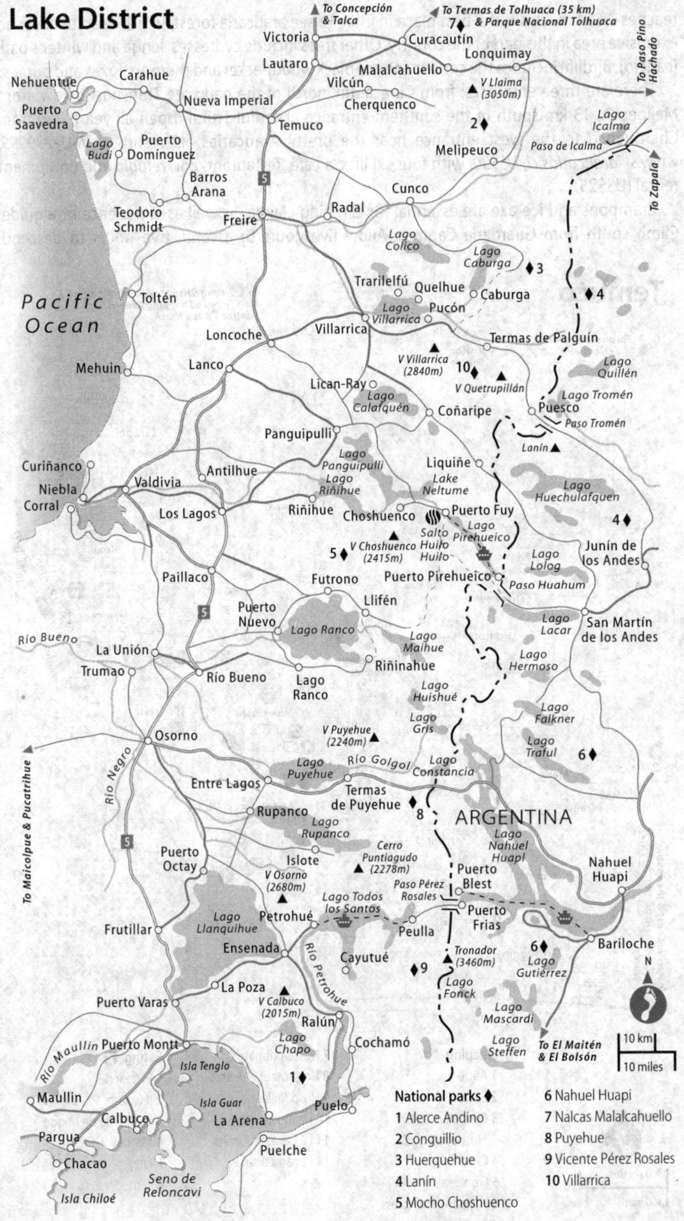

reaches 2,554 m. This is the best place in Chile to see araucaria forest, which used to cover an extensive area in this part of the country. Other trees include cypresses, lenga and winter's bark (canelo). Birdlife includes the condor and the black woodpecker and there are foxes and pumas.

There are three entrances: from Curacautín, north of the park: see Transport below; from Melipeuco, 13 km south of the southern entrance at Truful-Truful (open all year); and from Cherquenco to the west entrance near the pretty **Araucarias** ski resort ① *T045-239999, www.skiaraucarias.cl, US$30*, with four ski lifts, a café, restaurant, bar, *refugio* and equipment rental (US$25).

Crampons and ice-axe are essential for climbing Llaima, as well as experience or a guide. Climb south from Guardería Captrén. Allow five hours to ascend, two hours to descend.

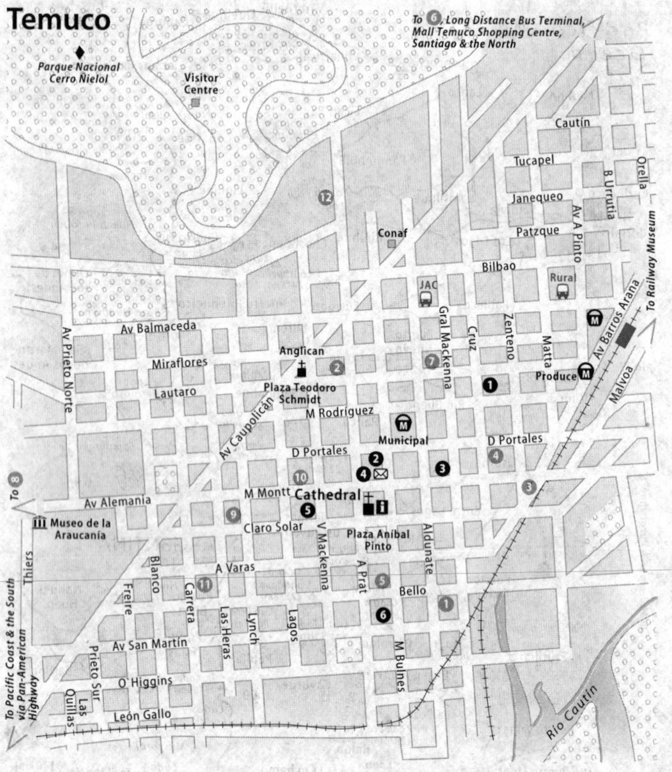

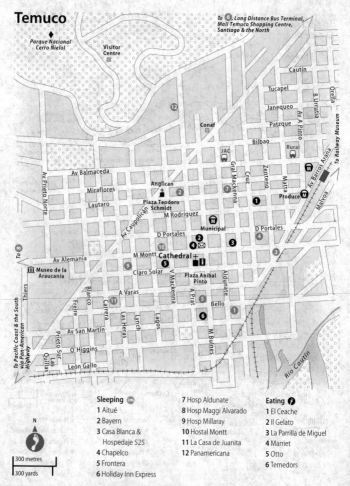

Sleeping
1 Aitué
2 Bayern
3 Casa Blanca & Hospedaje 525
4 Chapelco
5 Frontera
6 Holiday Inn Express
7 Hosp Aldunate
8 Hosp Maggi Alvarado
9 Hosp Millaray
10 Hostal Montt
11 La Casa de Juanita
12 Panamericana

Eating
1 El Ceache
2 Il Gelato
3 La Parrilla de Miguel
4 Marriet
5 Otto
6 Temedors

N
300 metres
300 yards

Information on the climb is available from **Guardería Captrén**. There is a range of walking trails, from 1 km to 22 km in length. One is a two or three day hike around Volcán Llaima to Laguna Conguillio, which is dusty, but with beautiful views of Laguna Quepe, then on to the Laguna Captrén guardería. Information on access and trails from **CONAF** in Temuco or administration by Lago Conguillio.

Border with Argentina

Paso Pino Hachado (1,884 m) can be reached either by paved road, 73 km southeast from Lonquimay, or by unpaved road 129 east from Melipeuco. On the Argentine side this road continues to Zapala. Chilean immigration and customs are in Liucura, 22 km west of the border, open September-mid-May 0800-2000, winter 0800-1900. Very thorough searches and 2-3 hour delays reported, especially when entering Chile. Buses from Temuco to Zapala and Neuquén use this crossing: see under Temuco. **Paso de Icalma** (1,298 m) is reached by unpaved road, 53 km from Melipeuco, a good crossing for those with their own transport, although it maybe impassable in winter (phone Policía Internacional in Temuco, Prat 19, to check: T293890). On the Argentine side this road continues to Zapala. Chilean immigration is open mid-October to mid-March 0800-2000, winter 0800-1900.

Temuco and around listings

For Sleeping and Eating price codes and other relevant information, see Essentials, pages 38-40.

Sleeping

Temuco *p787, map p790*

Accommodation in private houses, category **F** minimum, can be arranged by tourist office.

L-AL Panamericana, Prat 0220, T239999, www.pan americanahoteles.cl. 5-star, the best hotel in town, weekend promotions.

AL Frontera, Bulnes 726, T200400, www.hotelfrontera.cl. With breakfast, good business standard, large conference room.

A Aitué, A Varas 1048, T212512, www.hotelaitue.cl. Business standard, central, bar, English spoken, comfortable, Wi-Fi.

A Bayern, Prat 146, T276000, www.hotel bayern.cl. Standard 3-star. Small rooms, helpful, buffet breakfast, Wi-Fi, parking, cheaper in dollars than pesos.

A Holiday Inn Express, Av R Ortega 01800, T223300, www.holidayinnexpress.cl. A member of the Chileanized version of this chain, good value, with breakfast, a/c, heating, free internet, pool, out of town but convenient for the bus terminal, worth considering if driving.

B-C Chapelco, Cruz 401, T749393, www.hotel chapelco.cl. Airy, cable TV, laundry, internet in lobby, comfortable, good service. Recommended.

B-C Hostal Montt, M Montt 637, T982488, www.hostalmontt.cl. Comfortable if overpriced, some rooms with bath, parking, cable TV, breakfast included, gym.

B-C La Casa de Juanita, Carrera 735, T213203, juany362@hotmail.com. Cheaper without bath, quiet, breakfast, hot water, laundry, heating, parking. Many others in this range on Bello, west of plaza.

C Hosp Maggi Alvarado, Recreo 209, off Av Alemania, T409804, cppacl@gmail.com. Small rooms (**E** singles), helpful, nice atmosphere. Also has a good-value *cabaña* sleeping 4.

C-D Casa Blanca, Montt 1306 y Zenteno, T277799, hostalcasablancatemuco@ gmail.com. **F** singles. With breakfast, slightly run-down, but good value for rooms with bath.

C-D Hospedaje 525, Zenteno 525, T233982. Without breakfast, some rooms with bath, good value, older part has poor beds but also good value.

C-D Hosp Aldunate, Aldunate 187, T270057, cristorresvalenzuela@hotmail.com. **E** singles, cooking facilities, some rooms with TV and bath.

C-D Hosp Millaray, Claro Solar 471, T645720, hostalmillaray_tco@yahoo.es. Simple, basic, but unfriendly. Other private houses on this street in same price range.

Curacautín and around *p788*

B-C Hostal Las Espigas, Miraflores 315, T881138, rivaseugenia@hotmail.com. Good rooms, kitchen, breakfast, dinner available on request.

B-C Plaza, Yungay 157 (main plaza), T881256, www.rotondadelcautin.cl. With **La Cabaña** restaurant, pricey. Also has **C Hostería La Rotunda del Cautín**, Termas de Manzanar, T881569. Rooms and good mid-range restaurant.
D Turismo, Tarapacá 140, T881116, hotelturismocuracautin@ gmail.com. Good food, hot shower, comfortable, good value if old-fashioned (singles **E-F**).

Termas de Manzanar

L-AL Termas de Manzanar, T045-881200, www.termasdemanzanar.cl. Overpriced, cheaper rooms do not include access to thermal baths, also has suites with thermal jacuzzi.
B Anden Rose, 5 km west of Manzanar, Casilla 123, Curacautín, T09-9869 1700, www.andenrose.com. Cosy rooms, cheaper without bath, with breakfast, restaurant serving international and Bavarian food, bike, horse, kayak rental, jeep tours arranged, German/Chilean run.
D Hostería Abarzúa, Km 18, T045-870011. Simple, cheaper rooms without bath, full board available (good food), also campsite.

Termas de Tolhuaca

L Termas de Tolhuaca, T045-881211, www.termastolhuaca.cl. With full board, including use of baths and horse riding, very good; jacuzzi and massage also available. Camping US$16.
D Res Roja, **F** singles, hot water, food, camping near the river.

Reserva Nacional Nalcas Malalcahuello *p788*

Lonquimay

AL-A La Suizandina, Km 83 Carretera Internacional a Argentina, T045-1973725 or 09-884 9541, www.suizandina.com. Hostel 3 km before Malalcahuello Erbuc bus from Temuco 2½ hrs), with a range of rooms from private room with heating and large Swiss breakfast with home-baked bread (cheaper in low season), to shared rooms **D**, camping US$10, half board available, credit cards accepted, laundry, book exchange, bike and ski rental, horse riding, travel and trekking information, German and English spoken. "Like being in Switzerland". Recommended.
C Res Los Sauces, Estación 510, in Malalcahuello village, T09-7497 8706. **F** singles with shared bath and use of kitchen, hot water. Also good-value *cabañas*. Full board available.
C-D Hostal Lonquimay, Pinto 555, Lonquimay, T891324. **E-F** singles. Basic rooms with shared bath and breakfast.

Parque Nacional Conguillio *p788*

A La Baita, in the park, 3 km south of Laguna Verde, T581253/09-9733 2442, www.labaita conguillio.cl. Cabins with electricity, hot water, kitchen and wood stoves, charming, lots of information, Italian/ Chilean owned. Recommended.
A-B Cabañas Vista Hermosa, 10 km from the southern entrance, T09-9444 1630. Clean but spartan wooden cabins, each with a wood stove and fantastic views to the volcano. Electricity in afternoon only. Run by a horse-riding guide (he's a former champion equestrianist). Good food. Recommended.
A-B Adela y Helmut, Faja 16000, Km 5 Norte, Cunco (on the way to Melipeuco, 16 km from Cunco, website has directions, phone for pick-up from bus stop; Nar-Bus, Cruzmar and Inter-Sur buses from Santiago and Temuco pass the Faja and will drop passengers who phone the guesthouse for pick-up), T09-8258 2230 , www.adelay helmut.com. Guesthouse and restaurant on a Mapuche/ German owned farm, English spoken, room for families and for backpackers in 6-bed dorm (**E** pp), meals extra, kitchens, hot showers, solar heating, mountain bike rental, good reports. Pick-up from Temuco US$44. They run year-round tours to Conguillio National Park, hot springs, Mapuche and other sites, also for non-residents, from 3 days/2 nights to 7 days/6 nights. They can also arrange fly fishing packages and golf.
E Hosp Icalma, Aguirre Cerda 729, Melipeuco, T581108. Spacious, basic rooms, with shower and breakfast. Recommended.
Camping Camping Los Pioneros, 2 km out of Melipeuco on road to the park, also Centro Turístico with cabañas, T581005, turismo pioneros @araucaniaandina.cl. Hot water, full board available, tours to the park. Various other sites dotted around the park, by Lakes Conguillio and Captrén, all administered by CONAF, T298213.

Eating

Temuco *p787, map p790*

Many good restaurants around Av Alemania and Mall Mirage, about 10 blocks west of centre. Make for the Mercado Municipal on Aldunate y Portales, or the rural bus terminal, where there are countless restaurants serving very cheap set meals at lunch.

La Caleta, Mercado Municipal, Aldunate y Portales. One of the better choices in the covered market serving fish and seafood.

La Parrilla de Miguel, Montt 1095, T275182. Good for meat, large portions, and wine; one of the better restaurants.

Otto, V MacKenna 530. German food, cakes, etc.

El Ceache, Cruz 231. Simple food such as chicken and fries, good value set lunch.

Temedors, San Martín 827. Good value lunch.

Cafés

Il Gelato, Bulnes 420. Delicicious ice cream.

Marriet, Prat 451, loc 9. Excellent coffee.

Parque Nacional Conguillio *p788*

Buy supplies in Temuco, Curacautín or Melipeuco: much cheaper than the shop in the park.

Shopping

Temuco *p787, map p790*

Crafts Best choice in the indoor municipal market at Aldunate y Portales, and in the **Casa de la Mujer Mapuche** (see Sights, above). **Fundación Chol-Chol**, Sector Rengalil, Camino Temuco–Nueva Imperial Km 16, T614007, www.chol chol.org. Contact Johanna Pérez (speaks English), or Esteban Bastias. This non-profit organization sells traditional Mapuche textiles, naturally dyed and hand woven by local women.

Market **Temuco Feria**, Lautaro y Aníbal Pinto. This is one of the most fascinating markets in Chile, with people bringing excellent fruit and vegetables from the surrounding countryside, including spices, fish, grains, cheese and honey. Also many inexpensive bars and restaurants nearby.

Supermarket **Santa Isabel**, Caupolicán y Montt, and Rodríguez 1100 block. There is a modern shopping mall north of city; buses 2 or 7. **Frutería Las Vegas**, Matta 274, dried fruit (useful for climbing/trekking).

Activities and tours

Temuco *p787, map p790*

Tours to Parque Nacional Conguillio cost generally US$60 for 1 day; to Villarrica volcano US$90.

Transport

Temuco *p787, map p790*

Air Manquehue Airport 6 km southwest of the city. There is an airport transfer service to the city and to hotels in Villarrica and Pucón, US$15 (may not run out of season). Taxis charge US$8. There is no public bus. **LAN** to **Santiago, Concepción, Osorno, Puerto Montt** and **Balmaceda**. **Sky** to **Santiago, Concepción, Osorno** and **Puerto Montt**.

Bus Long-distance bus terminal north of city at Pérez Rosales y Caupolicán, city bus 2, 7 or 10; colectivo 11P; taxi US$2.50. **JAC** has its own efficient terminal at Balmaceda y Aldunate, 7 blocks north of the Plaza, which also serves neighbouring towns. **NarBus** and **Igi-Llaima** are opposite. Buses to **Santiago**, many overnight, 8-9 hrs, US$18-48. To **Concepción**, **Bío Bío** (Lautaro entre Prat y Bulnes), US$11, 4 hrs. To **Chillán**, 3½ hrs, US$9-12. **Cruz del Sur**, 3 a day to **Castro**, 10 a day to **Puerto Montt** (US$10-18, 5-6 hrs). To **Valdivia**, **JAC**, several daily, US$10, 2½ hrs. To **Osorno** US$8, 4¼ hrs. To **Villarrica** and **Pucón**, **JAC**, many between 0705 and 2045, 1½ hrs, and 2 hrs, US$6. Buses to neighbouring towns leave from Terminal Rural, Pinto y Balmaceda, or from bus company offices nearby. To **Coñaripe**, 3 hrs, and **Lican Ray**, 2 hrs. To **Panguipulli**, Power and Pangui Sur 3 hrs, US$6. Pangui Sur to **Loncoche**, US$3, **Los Lagos**, US$5, **Mehuin** in summer only. To **Curacautín** via Lautaro, **Erbuc**, US$5, 4 daily, 2½ hrs. To **Lonquimay**, Erbuc, 4 daily, 3½ hrs, US$6. To **Contulmo**, US$11, and **Cañete**, US$11, **Erbuc** and **Thiele**.

Buses to Argentina: **Igi Llaima** and **Narbus** to **Junín de los Andes**, early morning but not daily, US$30, advance booking required. **Ruta Sur** (Miraflores 1151) to **Zapala**, 10-12 hrs (US$35), 3 a week. To **Neuquén**, 7 companies, 16 hrs (US$45), via Paso Pino Hachado. To **Bariloche** you have to change bus in Osorno, **Tas- Choapa** US$40.

Car hire **Automóvil Club de Chile**, San Martín 278, T910522. **Christopher Car**, Varas 522, T215988, recommended. **Euro**, MacKenna 426,

T210311, helpful, good value. **Full Famas**, at airport and in centre T215420, highly recommended.

Train Ticket office at Barros Arana 191, T600-585 5000, open Mon-Fri 0930-1300, 1430-2000, www.efe.cl. At the time of writing, services north to Santiago and south to Puerto Montt are suspended.

Curacautín *p788*

Bus Terminal on the main road, by the plaza. Buses to/from **Temuco**, **Los Angeles** and **Santiago**.

Lonquimay

Bus Bus Erbuc from **Temuco** via Lautaro, US$6 to **Malalcahuello**, 4 a day, 2½ hrs, 3½ to Lonquimay town, US$6.

Parque Nacional Conguillio *p788*

For touring, hire a 4WD vehicle in Temuco. See also **Adela y Helmut**, under Sleeping, above.

To the northern entrance: **taxi** from Curacautín to Laguna Captrén, US$40 one way. To **Melipeuco** (stops at Hospedaje Icalma), buses every hour from Balmaceda bus terminal, Temuco (or flag down at Mackenna y Varas), 2½ hrs, US$5, and once a day to **Icalma** when no snow on road. Transport can be arranged from Melipeuco into the park (ask in grocery stores and hospedajes, US$40 one way). To **Cunco**, every 20 mins from same terminal. To the western entrance: daily **buses** from Temuco to Cherquenco, from where there is no public transport to the park. Private transport is the best way to see the area.

Directory

Temuco *p787, map p790*

Airline offices LAN, Bulnes 687, T600-526 2000. **Sky**, Bulnes 655, loc 4, T747300, or 600-600 2828 for information. **Banks** Many ATMs at banks on Plaza Aníbal Pinto. Also at the JAC bus terminal (Visa). Many cambios around the plaza, all deal in dollars and Argentine pesos. **Bicycle repairs** On Balmaceda, **Don Cheyo**, No 1266, another at No 1294, **Monsalves**, No 1448, opposite rural bus terminal. Also **Oxford**, Andrés Bello 1040, T211869. **Consulates** **Netherlands**, Bulnes 815, of 302, T592622, german.nicklas@gmail.com, Honorary Consul, Germán Nicklas, is friendly and helpful. **Internet** Many on Prat and Mackenna, south of the Plaza, up to US$1 per hr. **Hospitals** Manuel Montt 115. **Motor mechanic** **ServiTren**, Edgardo Schneider Reinike and Peter Fischer (peocito@yahoo.de), Matta 0545 y Ruta 5, T/F212775, for cars and motorcycles, German spoken. **Post offices** Portales 839.

Lagos Villarrica, Calafquén and Panguipulli

Wooded Lago Villarrica, 21 km long and about 7 km wide, is one of the most beautiful in the region, with the active, snow-capped Villarrica volcano (2,840 m) to the southeast. Villarrica and Pucón, resorts at the lake's southwest and southeast corners, are among the more expensive in the region, but are definitely worth a visit. South of Lago Villarrica, a necklace of six lakes with snowy peaks behind, form picture-postcard views. Calafquén and Panguipulli are the most visited, but there are also hot springs, national parks and interesting routes to Argentina.

Villarrica → *Phone code: 045. Colour map 8, C1. Population: 27,000. Altitude: 227 m.*

The quiet town of Villarrica, pleasantly set at the extreme southwest corner of the lake, can be reached by a 63-km paved road southeast from Freire (24 km south of Temuco on the Pan-American Highway), or from Loncoche, 54 km south of Freire, also paved. Founded in 1552, the town was besieged by the Mapuche in the uprising of 1599: after three years the surviving Spanish settlers, 11 men and 13 women, surrendered. The town was refounded in 1882. The **Muestra Cultural Mapuche** ⓘ *Pedro de Valdivia y Zegers, open all summer*, features a Mapuche ruca and stalls selling good handicraft. There is a livestock market every Monday about 1400; riding equipment for sale. In January and February Villarrica has a summer programme with many cultural and sporting events (including the Semana de Chilenidad) and on 18-19 September the Gran Fiesta Campestre de Villarrica is held in the indoor riding arena of the Parque Natural Dos Ríos (see Sleeping), with typical foods, music, dancing, competitions and shows. **Tourist office** ⓘ *Valdivia 1070, T411162, open daily in summer, Mon-Fri off season; information and maps.*

Pucón ➔ *Phone code: 045. Colour map 8, C1. Population: 13,000. Altitude: 227 m.*
Pucón, on the southeastern shore of Lago Villarrica, 26 km east of Villarrica, is the major tourist centre on the lake. The black sand beach is very popular for swimming and watersports. Between New Year to end-February it is very crowded and expensive; off season it is very pleasant. Apart from the lake, other attractions nearby include whitewater rafting, winter sports (see Skiing below) and several **canopy** (see Ziplining under Activities and tours) sites. **Tourist office** in the municipal building ⓘ *O'Higgins 483, T293002, ofturismo@municipalidadpucon.cl,* sells fishing licences (US$1 per month). There is also the **Chamber of Tourism** at the entrance to Pucón from Villarrica ⓘ *T441671, www.puconturismo.cl.* See also **www.pucononline.cl.**

There is a pleasant *paseo*, the **Costanera Otto Gudenschwager**, which starts at the lake end of Ansorena (beside Gran Hotel Pucón, Holzapfel 190, T441001) and goes along the shore. Walk 2 km north along the beach to the mouth of the Río Trancura (also called Río Pucón), with views of the volcanoes Villarrica, Quetrupillán and Lanín. To cross the Río Pucón: head east out of Pucón along the main road, then turn north on an unmade road leading to a new bridge; from here there are pleasant walks along the north shore of the lake to Quelhue and Trarilelfú, or northeast towards Caburga, or up into the hills through farms and agricultural land, with views of three volcanoes and, higher up, of the lake. The journey to Caburga (see below) is a perfect mountain bike day trip.

Boat trips ⓘ *daily 1500 and 1900, summer only, 2 hrs, US$9,* on the lake leave from the landing stage at La Poza at the western end of O'Higgins. Or take a boat ⓘ *summer only, US$15,* to the mouth of the river from near the **Gran Hotel.**

Parque Nacional Villarrica
The park has three sectors: **Volcán Villarrica** ⓘ *US$6.15,* **Volcán Quetrupillán** and the **Puesco sector** which includes the slopes of the Volcán Lanín on the Argentine border. Each sector has its own entrance and ranger station. A campsite with drinking water and toilets is below the refuge, 4 km inside the park. The Villarrica volcano, 2,840 m, 8 km south of Pucón, can be climbed up and down in seven to eight hours, good boots, ice axe and crampons, sunglasses, plenty of water, chocolate and sun block essential. Beware of sulphur fumes at the top – occasionally agencies provide gas masks, otherwise take a cloth mask moistened with lemon juice – but on good days you can see into the crater with lava bubbling at 1,250°C. On the descent you toboggan down the snow rather than walk, good fun.

Entry to Volcán Villarrica is permitted only to groups with a guide and to individuals who can show proof of membership of a mountaineering club in their own country. Several agencies take excursions, US$65-85, including park entry, guide, transport to park entrance and hire of equipment (no reduction for those with their own equipment); at the park entrance equipment is checked – good boots, crampons and ice-axe essential. Entry is refused if the weather is poor. Reputable travel agencies will not start out if the weather is bad: establish in advance what terms apply in the event of cancellation and be prepared to wait a few days. Many guides, all with equipment; ask for recommendations at the tourist office. For US$10 you can take the ski lift for the first part of the ascent; this is recommended as it saves 400 m climbing on scree.

Skiing ⓘ *Lift pass US$28-40 full day, depending on the season; ski season is Jul-Sep, occasionally longer. Equipment rental US$23 per day. Information on snow and ski-lifts (and, perhaps, transport) from tourist office or Gran Hotel Pucón.* The Pucón resort, *T441901, www.skipucon.cl,* owned by the Gran Hotel Pucón, is on the eastern slopes of the volcano, reached by a track, 35 minutes. The centre offers equipment rental, ski instruction, first aid, restaurant and bar as well as wonderful views from the terrace. The centre is good for beginners; more advanced skiers can try the steeper areas. (Skiing trips to the summit are very tough going and only for the fit.)

Lagos Caburga and Colico

Lago Caburga (spelt locally Caburgua), a very pretty lake in a wild setting 25 km northeast of Pucón, is unusual for its beautiful white sand beach (it also has a black sand beach – other beaches in the area are of black volcanic sand) and has supposedly the warmest water of all the lakes here. The west and much of the shores of the lake are inaccessible to vehicles. The north shore can be reached by a road from Cunco via the north shore of Lago Colico, a more remote lake north of Lago Villarrica. The village of Caburga, at the southern end is reached by a turning off the main road 8 km east of Pucón. The southern end of the lake and around Caburga is lined with campsites. There is a supermarket in Caburga. Rowing boats may be hired US$3 per hour. Just off the road from Pucón, Km 15, are the Ojos de Caburga, beautiful pools fed from underground, particularly attractive after rain (entry US$1; ask bus driver to let you off). Alternatively, take a mountain bike from Pucón via the Puente Quelhue.

Parque Nacional Huerquehue

ⓘ *The park is open 0830-1800, US$8 (children and seniors ½-price), the warden is very helpful; parking 1½ km along the track, US$1.*

East of Lago Caburga, the park includes steep hills and at least 20 lakes, some of them very small. Entrance and administration are near Lago Tinquilco, the largest lake, on the western edge of the park. The park entrance is 7 km (3 km uphill, 3 km down, one along Lago Tinquilco) from Paillaco, which is reached by an all-weather road which turns off 3 km before Caburga. From the entrance there is a well-signed track north to three beautiful lakes, Lagos Verde, Chico and Toro. The track zig-zags up (sign says 5 km, but worth it) to Lago Chico, then splits left to Verde, right to Toro. From Toro you can continue to Lago Huerquehue and Laguna los Patos (camping). People in the park rent horses and boats. There is a restaurant at Tinquilco. Otherwise take your own food.

South of the Huerquehue Park on a turning from the Pucón-Caburga road there are **Termas de Quimey-Co**, about 29 km from Pucón, campsite, two cabins and hotel **Termas de Quimey-Co** ⓘ *T08-775 2113, www.termasquimeyco.com, US$12.25-14.25*, new, less ostentatious or expensive than **Termas de Huife Hostería** ⓘ *T441222, www.termashuife.cl, Pucón, Km 33*, US$22.50 high season (US$17.50 low), including use of pool, modern, pleasant (hotel in **LL** range offers daily shuttle from/to Pucón, or taxi from Pucón, US$32.50 high season, US$28.50 low season). Beyond Huife are the hot springs of **Los Pozones**, Km 35, set in natural rock pools, US$8, US$19 at night (a good time to go), basic but popular with travellers. The road there is rough.

Cañi Forest Sanctuary, south of Parque Nacional Huerquehue and covering 500 ha, was the first private forest reserve established in Chile, owned by the non-proft Fundación Lahuén ⓘ *US$5*. It contains 17 small lakes and is covered by ancient native forests of coihue, lenga and some of the oldest araucaria trees in the country. From its highest peak, **El Mirador**, five volcanoes can be seen. There is a self-guided trail, US$8 plus transport; for tours with English-speaking guide, contact **the Cañi Guides Program** ⓘ *see www.ecole.cl.*

Route to Argentina

From Pucón a road runs southeast via Curarrehue to the Argentine border. At Km 18 there is a turning south to the **Termas de Palguín** ⓘ *T441968, http://termasdepalguin.blogspot.com, US$9-10*, with a hotel (**AL-C** depending on meal plan and season). There are many beautiful waterfalls within hiking distance: for example, Salto China (entry US$1.50, restaurant, camping); Salto del Puma and Salto del León, both 800 m from the Termas (entry US$2 for both). From Pucón take Bus Regional Villarrica from Palguín y O'Higgins at 1100 to the junction (10 km from Termas); last bus from junction to the Termas at 1500, so you may have to hitch back. Taxi from Pucón, US$20.

Near Palguín is the entrance to the Quetrupillán section of the Parque Nacional Villarrica (high clearance vehicle necessary, horses best), free camping, wonderful views over Villarrica Volcano and six other peaks. Ask rangers for the route to the other entrance.

The road from Pucón to Argentina passes turnings north at Km 23 to **Termas de San Luis** ⓘ *T045-412880, www.termasdesanluis.cl, US$18*, and Km 35 to **Termas de Pangui** (15 km from main road, US$10), both with hotels, the latter with teepees (T045-442039). It continues to Curarrehue, from where it turns south to Puesco and climbs via **Lago Quellelhue**, a tiny gem set between mountains at 1,196 m to reach the border at the **Mamuil Malal** or **Tromén Pass**. To the south of the pass rises the graceful cone of Lanín volcano. On the Argentine side the road runs south to Junín de los Andes, San Martín de los Andes and Bariloche.

Chilean immigration and customs

Chilean immigration and customs at Puesco, open 0800-1900 (to 2100 December-March), US$2 per vehicle at other times. There are free CONAF campsites with no facilities at Puesco and 5 km from the border near Lago Tromén. Daily bus from Pucón, 1800, two hours, US$3. It's a hard road for cyclists, but not impossible.

Lago Calafquén → *Colour map 8, C1. Population: 1,700. Altitude: 207 m.*

Dotted with small islands, Lago Calafquén is a popular tourist destination. **Lican-Ray** 30 km south of Villarrica on a peninsula on the north shore, is the major resort on the lake. There are two fine beaches each side of the rocky peninsula. Boats can be hired and there are catamaran trips. Although very crowded in season, most facilities close by the end of March and, out of season, Lican-Ray feels like a ghost town. 6 km to the east is the river of lava formed when the Villarrica volcano erupted in 1971. The **tourist office** ⓘ *open daily in summer, Mon-Fri off season*, is on the plaza.

Coñaripe (*Population: 1,253*), 21 km southeast of Lican-Ray at the eastern end of Lago Calafquén, is another popular tourist spot. Its setting, with a 3-km black sand beach surrounded by mountains, is very beautiful. From here a road (mostly ripio) around the lake's southern shore leads to Lago Panguipulli (see below) and offers superb views over Villarrica volcano, which can be climbed from here. Most services are on the Calle Principal. The **tourist office**, on the plaza, T063-317378, is open 15 November-15 April daily, otherwise weekends only.

Termas Vergara are 14 km northeast of Coñaripe by a steep ripio road which continues to Palguín. There are nice open-air pools here. **Termas Geométricas** ⓘ *3 km beyond Termas Vergara, T09-7477 1708, www.termasgeometricas.cl, US$28, US$12 in low season*. There are 17 good new pools, geometrically shaped and linked by wooden walkways. There is a small café.

From Coñaripe a road runs southeast over the steep **Cuesta Los Añiques** offering views of tiny Lago Pellaifa. The **Termas de Coñaripe** are at Km 16 ⓘ *T045-411111, www.termasconaripe.cl, US$14.50-16.50*. Further south at Km 32 are the **Termas de Liquiñe** ⓘ *T063-317377, 8 different thermal centres, from US$6 to US$10 pp*. Opposite Liquiñe are the new Termas Río de Liquiñe, good heated cabañas, good food, personal spa bath, large outdoor thermal pool. From there you can walk up to the thermal source, US$0.40 to cross river by boat, one hour excursion. There is a road north to Pucón through Villarrica National Park, high-clearance and 4WD vehicle essential.

The border with Argentina, **Paso Carirriñe**, is reached by unpaved road from Termas de Liquiñe. It is open 15 October-31 August. On the Argentine side the road continues to San Martín de los Andes.

Lago Panguipulli and around

→ *Phone code: 063. Colour map 8, C1. Population: 8,000. Altitude: 136 m.*

The lake is reached by paved roads from Lanco and Los Lagos on the Pan-American Highway or unpaved roads from Lago Calafquén. A road leads along the beautiful north shore, wooded with sandy beaches and cliffs. Most of the south shore is inaccessible by road. **Panguipulli**, at the northwest corner of the lake in a beautiful setting, is the largest town in the area. The Iglesia San Sebastián is in Swiss style, with twin towers; its belltower contains three bells from Germany. In summer, catamaran trips are offered on the lake and excursions can be made to Lagos Calafquén, Neltume, Pirehueico and to the northern tip of Lago Riñihue. In the last week of January is Semana de Rosas, with dancing and sports competitions. **Tourist office** by the plaza ⓘ *T310435, www.sietelagos.cl, also www.municipalidadpanguipulli.cl*, is open daily December-February, otherwise weekdays only.

Choshuenco (*Population: 622; tourist information T063-318305*) lies 45 km east of Panguipulli at the eastern tip of the lake. To the south is the Reserva Nacional Mocho Choshuenco (7,536 ha) which includes two volcanoes: Choshuenco (2,415 m) and Mocho (2,422 m). On the slopes of Choshuenco the Club Andino de Valdivia has ski-slopes and three refugios. This can be reached by a turning from the road which goes south from Choshuenco to Enco at the east end of Lago Riñihue (the lake southwest of Lago Panguipulli). East of Choshuenco a road leads to Lago Pirehueico, via the impressive waterfalls of Huilo Huilo, where the river channels its way through volcanic rock before thundering down into a natural basin. The falls are three hours' walk from Choshuenco, or take the Puerto Fuy bus and get off at Alojamiento Huilo Huilo (see Sleeping, below), from where it is a five-minute walk to the falls.

East of Choshuenco is **Lago Pirehueico**, a long, narrow and deep lake, surrounded by virgin lingüe forest. It is largely unspoilt, although there are plans to build a huge tourist complex in Puerto Pirehueico. There are no roads along the shores of the lake, but two ports. **Puerto Fuy** (*Population: 300*) is at the north end 21 km from Choshuenco, 7 km from Neltume. **Puerto Pirehueico** is at the south end. A ferry runs between the two ports, then a road to the Argentine border crossing at Paso Hua-Hum.

The border with Argentina, **Paso Hua-Hum** (659 m), is 11 km from Puerto Pirehueico (very hard for cyclists with steep climbs, no public transport to border). On the Argentine side the road leads alongside Lago Lacar to San Martín de los Andes and Junín de los Andes. Chilean immigration is open summer 0800-2100, winter 0800-2000.

Lagos Villarrica, Calafquén and Panguipulli listings

For Sleeping and Eating price codes and other relevant information, see Essentials, pages 38-40.

Sleeping

Villarrica *p794*

Lodging in private homes in our **C-D** range can be found on Muñoz blocks 400 and 500, Koerner 300 and O'Higgins 700 and 800. More upmarket accommodation is on the lakefront.

LL Villarrica Park Lake, Km 13 on the road to Pucón, T450000, www.villarricaparklakehotel.cl. 5-star, all rooms with balconies overlooking the lake, spa with pools, sauna, solarium, fishing trips.

AL El Ciervo, Koerner 241, T411215, www.hotelelciervo.cl. Comfortable rooms, pleasant grounds, German-style breakfasts, German and some English spoken, pool, terrace, Wi-Fi. Recommended.

AL Parque Natural Dos Ríos, 13 km west of Villarrica, T09-9419 8064, www.dosrios.de. With full board. Tranquil 40-ha nature park with *cabañas* on the banks of the Río Toltén (white-sand beach), horse riding, birdwatching, children-friendly, German and English spoken.

AL-A Hostería de la Colina, Las Colinas 115, overlooking town, T411503, www.hosteriadelacolina.com. With breakfast, large gardens, good service, Wi-Fi, good restaurant (the owner makes fresh ice cream every day), fine views, English spoken, very attentive service. Highly recommended.

AL-A Hotel y Cabañas El Parque, 3 km east on Pucón road, T411120, www.hotelelparque.cl. Lakeside with beach, tennis courts, with breakfast, good restaurant set meals. Recommended.

B Bungalowlandia, Prat 749, T/F411635, www.bungalowlandia.cl. Cabañas for 2, dining room, good facilities, pool.

B Hostería Bilbao, Henríquez 43, T411186, www.interpatagonia.com/bilbao. Small rooms, pretty patio, good restaurant.

B Hotel Yachting Kiel, Koerner 153, T411631, www.yachtingkiel.cl. Small 6-room hotel, 3 with views across the lake to the volcano. The others are smaller and much cheaper. Spacious bathrooms, cable TV and heating. German and some English spoken. Good restaurant.
C La Torre Suiza, Bilbao 969, T/F411213, www.torresuiza.com. Some rooms with bath, **E** pp in dorms, kitchen facilities, camping, cycle rental, book exchange, lots of info, good breakfast included, internet and W-Fi, reserve in advance. German and English spoken. Recommended.
C-D Hosp Nicolás, Anfion Muñoz 477, T410 232. **F** singles. Simple rooms with bath, cable TV. Breakfast included. Good value, but thin walls.
D Chito Fuentes, Vicente Reyes 665, T045-411595. **F** singles. Basic rooms above a restaurant.
Camping Many sites east of town on Pucón road, open in season only and expensive.

Pucón *p795*
In summer (Dec-Feb) rooms may be hard to find. Plenty of alternatives (usually cheaper) in Villarrica. Prices below are Jan-Feb. Off-season rates are 20-40% lower and it is often possible to negotiate. Many families offer rooms, look for the signs or ask in bars/restaurants. Touts offer rooms to new arrivals; check that they are not way out of town.
LL Antumalal, 2 km west of Pucón, T441011, www.antumalal.com. Luxury class, very small, picturesque chalet-type, magnificent views of the lake (breakfast and lunch on terrace), gardens, with meals, open year round, pool, hot tub, sauna and private beaches.
L Interlaken, Caupolicán 720, T441276, www.hotelinterlaken.cl. Chalets with full facilities, water skiing, pool, no restaurant. Recommended.
AL Malalhue, Camino Internacional 1615, T443130, www.malalhue.cl. One of the better hotels, about 15 mins' walk from the centre, helpful, most staff speak English. Rooms at the back are quieter and have views of the volcano.
AL-A Gudenschwager, Pedro de Valdivia 12, T442025, www.hogu.cl. Refurbished 1920s hotel. 20 simple centrally heated rooms (thin walls), some with lake and volcano view. Cheaper rooms with shared bath. Reasonable rates off season. Living room with big screen TV and Wi-Fi area. English spoken.

AL-A La Posada Plaza-Pucón, Valdivia 191, T441088, www.plazapucon.cl. Pleasant rooms if a bit dated, also a spacious cabin, gardens and pool.

A Cabañas Ruca Malal, O'Higgins 770, T442297, www.rucamalal.cl. Lovely cabins in a pretty garden, spacious, well-equipped and decorated, various sizes, pool.

A La Tetera, Urrutia 580, T/F464126, www.tetera.cl. 6 rooms, some with bath, with good breakfast, fresh coffee, English spoken, book swap, information centre, good Spanish classes, car rental, Wi-Fi, book in advance. Recommended.

A-B Hostal Gerónimo, Alderete 665, T443762, www.geronimo.cl. Recently refurbished, rooms with cable TV, quiet, smart, bar, restaurant, open all year. Recommended.

A-C Hostería ¡école!, General Urrutia 592, T441675, www.ecole.cl. **E** pp dorms without breakfast, some rooms with bath, shop, vegetarian and fish restaurant, forest treks (departure for Lahuén Foundation's Cani Forest Sanctuary), rafting and biking, information, language classes, massage, Wi-Fi.

B Rumbo Sur, Colo Colo 361, T443840, http://hostalrumbosur.blogspot.com/. **D-E** in dorms and shared rooms, with and without bath, use of kitchen, Wi-Fi, associated with **Rumbo Sur 360** climbing agency.

C Donde Germán, Brasil 640, T442444, www.dondegerman.cl. Rooms or dorms **F**. Fun, organizes tours, internet, book in advance. Recommended.

C Hosp Víctor, Palguín 705, T443525, www.pucon.com/victor. **E-F** pp in 4-bed dorms. Some rooms with bath, kitchen facilities, TV, laundry. A decent choice.

C Hostal Backpackers, Palguín 695, T441417, www.backpackerspucon.com. With or without bath, quiet, next to JAC buses, good kitchen, internet, 10% discount on Politur activities, Navimag reservations, tourist information.

C Res Lincoyán, Av Lincoyán 323, T441144, www.lincoyan.cl. Cheaper in low season, meals extra, comfortable.

C-D Hosp Graciela, Pasaje Rolando Matus 521 (off Av Brasil), 443294. Comfortable, good food.

C-D Hosp Irma Torres, Lincoyán 545, T442226, www.hospedajeirmapucon.es.tl. With and without bath, cooking facilities, laundry service, tourist information, bicycle hire and internet.

C-D Hosp Lucía, Lincoyán 565, T441721, lucia hostal@hotmail.com. Safe, quiet, cooking facilities.

C-D Hosp Sonia, Lincoyán 485, T045- 441269, www. pucon.com/sonia. **F** singles. Basic but clean rooms, some with bath. Use of kitchen, can be crowded, basic English spoken.

D-E pp **The Tree House**, Urrutia 660, T444679, www.treehousechile.cl. British/Chilean-owned, both are tour leaders so lots of information, work with local community, shared rooms with and without bath, 1 private room (**B**), homemade breakfast extra, safe, Wi-Fi, use of kitchen.

E pp **El Refugio**, Palguín 540, T441596, www.hostalelrefugio.cl. Dorm or private room, sahred bath, small, convenient, cosy, Dutch/Chilean owned, kitchen facilities, internet, Wi-Fi, laundry service. Recommended.

E pp **Etnico Hostel and Adventures**, Ansorena 160, p 2, T441426, www.holahostels.com. Owner is mountain guide. Hot showers, dorms, TV room, DVDs, kitchen, sushi restaurant across the street, car and bike parking, lots of activities.

E pp **Tr@vel Pucón**, Blanco Encalada 190, T444093, pucontravel@terra.cl. Garden, tours, kitchen, Spanish classes, near Tur-Bus terminal.

Camping There are many camping and cabin establishments. Those close to Pucón include: **La Poza**, Costanera Geis 769, T441435, campinglapoza@hotmail.com, hot showers, good kitchen. Recommended. **Saint John**, Km 7, T441165, www.saintjohnpucon.cl, open Dec-Mar, also cabañas. Several sites en route to volcano, including: **L'Etoile**, Km 2, T442188, in attractive forest.

Lago Caburga *p796*

L-AL Trailanqui, 20 km west of Lago Colico (35 km north of Villarrica), T578218, www.trailanqui.com. Luxurious hotel on the river-bank, with suites and restaurant, also equipped *cabañas*, Wi-Fi, campsite, horse riding, pool.

AL-A Landhaus San Sebastián, east of Lago Caburga, T045-1972360, www.landhaus.cl. With bath and breakfast, good meals, laundry facilities, English and German spoken, Spanish classes, good base for nearby walks.

Parque Nacional Huerquehue *p796*
B-C Refugio Tinquilco, 3½ km from park entrance, where forest trail leads to lakes Verde and Toro, T02-777 7673, T09-9539 2728, www.tinquilco.cl. Rooms with bath, **E** for bunk bed, cheaper without sheets, no breakfast, meals available, heating, hot water, 24-hr electricity, sauna, cooking facilities. Recommended. There is also the **B Puerto Parque Tinquilco**, with hotel and cabins, T441480, www.parquehuerquehue.cl.
C Braatz and **Soldans**, 2 German speaking families, offer accommodation, no electricity, food and camping (US$6); they also rent rowing boats on the lake. **E** pp Nidia Carrasco Godoy runs a hospedaje in the park, T09-9443 2725. With breakfast, hot water, camping.
Camping only at the park entrance, 2 sites, US$10. 1½ km before the park entrance.

Route to Argentina *p796*
C Rancho de Caballos, 36 km southeast of Pucón on the dirt road to Coñaripe, T09-8346 1764 (limited signal), www.rancho-de-caballos.com. Restaurant with vegetarian dishes, laundry and kitchen facilities; also *cabañas* and camping, self-guided trails, horse-riding trips US$70 per day, English and German spoken, recommended.
C Ruca Rayen, T09-9711 8064. Idyllic spot on the banks of the Río Palguín, 15 mins' walk from the main road (regular buses to Pucón). Some rooms with bath. Good breakfast included. English-speaking Austrian-Mapuche hosts (Margot's parents own Kila Leufu, below). The perfect choice if you want to avoid the hustle and bustle of Pucón. Meals served, horse-riding. Offers trekking information and mountain-bike hire, camping possible. Recommended.
C-D Kila-Leufu, 23 km east on road to Curarrehue, T09-876 4576 , www.kilaleufu.cl. **E** pp in shared room. Rooms on the Martínez family farm, contact Irma or Margot (see Ruca Rayen, above) in advance, price includes breakfast, home-grown food served, horse riding, boat tours, treks, camping facilities. Recommended.

Lago Calafquén and around *p797*
Lican-Ray
B Cabañas Los Nietos, Manquel 125, Playa Chica, T431078. Self-catering cabins.
B Hostería Inaltulafquen, on Playa Grande, Punulef 510, T431115, www.hotel-refugio .com. With breakfast, English spoken, comfortable, trips to thermal springs.
E Res Temuco, G Mistral 515, Playa Grande, T431130. Without bath, with breakfast, good.
Camping **Floresta**, T211954, **C** for 6 people, 500 m east of town. 6 sites to west and many along north shore towards Coñaripe.

Coñaripe
C-D Hosp Chumay, Las Tepas 201, on Plaza, T317287, turismochumay@hotmail.com. **F** singles. With restaurant, internet, tours, some English spoken, good.
Camping Sites on beach charge US$20, but if you walk ½-¾ km from town you can camp on the beach free. Cold municipal showers on beach, US$0.35. **Isla Llancahue**, 5 km east, T317360. Campsite with *cabañas* on an island in Río Llancahue.

Termas de Coñaripe
L Termas de Coñaripe, T411111, www.termasconaripe.cl. Excellent hotel with 4 pools, good restaurant, spa with a variety of treatments, cycles and horses for hire. Full board available.

Termas de Liquiñe
AL Termas de Liquiñe, T063-317377. Full board, cabins, restaurant, hot pool, small native forest. **D** for accommodation in private houses.
F pp **Hosp La Casona**, Camino Internacional, T063-197 1633. Hot shower, good food, comfortable; tours from Lican-Ray in summer, 0830-1830 with lunch.

Panguipulli *p797*
B Hostal España, O'Higgins 790, T063-311166, www.hostalespana.cl.kz. Rooms with breakfast, central.
C Central, Valdivia 115, T09-9882 3955. Good breakfast, **F** singles. Recommended.
D Hosp Familiar, Los Ulmos 62, T311483. **F** singles, English and German spoken, kitchen facilities, helpful, good breakfast.
F pp **Hostal Orillas del Lago**, M de Rosas 265, T311710 (or 312499 if no reply, friends have key). From plaza walk towards lake, last house on left, 8 blocks from terminal. Good views, kitchen, backpacker place.
Camping **El Bosque**, P Sigifredo 241, T311489. Small, good, but not suitable for vehicle

camping, hot water. Also 3 sites at Chauquén, 6 km southeast on lakeside.

Choshuenco

B-C Hostería Ruca Pillán, San Martín 85, T318220, www.rucapillan.cl. Also cabins, **A**. Family-run hotel overlooking the lake. English spoken, tours.

C-D Hostal Choshuenco, Bernabé s/n, T318214, jcarrilloh@telsur.com. A little run-down but clean, good meals, breakfast included. Also *cabañas*.

D pp **Alojamiento Huilo Huilo**, Km 9 east from Choshuenco (1 km before Neltume). Basic but comfortable and well situated for walks, good food.

Lago Pirehueico

C Hospedaje y Cabañas Puerto Fuy, Puerto Fuy. Hot water, good food in restaurant.

D Hostal Kay Kaen, Puerto Fuy, T063-167 1632. Meals, use of kitchen, bike rental. One of several private houses offering accommodation.

E pp **Restaurant San Giovani**, Puerto Fuy. Family atmosphere, good rooms, breakfast and other meals. There is also accommodation in private houses.

Camping On the beach (take own food).

Eating

Villarrica *p794*

ΨΨΨ El Tabor, S Epulef 1187, T411901. Fish and seafood specialities, excellent but pricey.

ΨΨΨ La Cava del Roble, Valentín Letelier 658, p 2, T416446. Excellent grill, specialises in exotic meat and game, extensive wine list. Recommended.

ΨΨ La Vecchia Cucina, Pedro de Valdivia 1011, T411798. Good Italian serving a range of pizzas and pastas.

ΨΨ The Travellers, Letelier 753, T413617. Varied menu including vegetarian and Asian food, bar, English spoken.

ΨΨ-Ψ Juanito, Vicente Reyes 678. Closed Sun. Good, and cheap end of the range.

Ψ Casa Vieja, Letelier y Muñoz. Good-value set lunch, family-run.

Ψ El Marítimo, Alderete 769, T412034. Generally first-rate, unpretentious, serving traditional fish and seafood.

Ψ El Turismo, Epulef 1201 y Rodriguez. No frills, good Chilean dishes. Recommended.

Café 2001, Henríquez 379. Best coffee in town. Also good cakes and friendly service at a reasonable price. For ice cream, try the stall next door.

Pucón *p795*

See Sleeping for other recommendations.

ΨΨΨ Puerto Pucón, Fresia 251. One of Pucón's older restaurants, Spanish, stylish.

ΨΨΨ-ΨΨ La Maga, Alderete 276 y Fresia, T444277. Uruguayan *parrillada* serving excellent steak. So good that several imitations have opened up nearby to take the overspill.

ΨΨΨ-ΨΨ Senzo, Fresia 284, T449005. Fresh pasta and risotto prepared by a Swiss chef.

ΨΨ Arabian, Fresia 354-B, T443469. Arab specialities – stuffed vine leaves, falafel, etc.

ΨΨ ¡école!, in Hostería of same name, General Urrutia 592. Good vegetarian restaurant.

ΨΨ Il Baretto, Fresia 124, T443515. Stone-baked pizzas. Better value than Buonatesta across the road.

Ψ Rap Hamburguesa, O'Higgins 625. Open late. Freshly made hamburgers, chips and Chilean fast food.

Cafés

Café de la P, O'Higgins y Lincoyán. Real coffee.

Cassis, Fresia 223. Chocolates, ice creams, pancakes and snacks as well as coffee.

Mamas and Tapas, O'Higgins y Arauco. Drink and snacks. There are several others on O'Higgins.

Lago Calafquén: Lican-Ray *p797*

ΨΨ-Ψ Café Ñaños, Urrutia 105. Very good, reasonable prices, helpful owner.

ΨΨ-Ψ Restaurant-Bar Guido's, Urrutia 405. Good value.

Panguipulli *p797*

ΨΨ-Ψ Café Central, M de Rosas 750. Fixed menu, good and cheap at lunchtimes, expensive in evenings.

ΨΨ-Ψ El Chapulín, M de Rosas 639. Good food and value. Several cheap restaurants in O'Higgins 700 block.

Shopping

Pucón *p795*

Camping equipment **Eltit supermarket**, O'Higgins y Fresia. **Outdoors & Travel**, Lincoyán 36, clothing, equipment, maps.

Handicrafts market Just south of O'Higgins on Ansorena; local specialities are painted wooden flowers.

▲ Activities and tours

Villarrica *p794*

Fundo Huifquenco, just south of town (500 m) along Av Matta, T415040, www.fundohuifquen co.cl. Working farm, trails, horseriding, carriage tours, bicycle hire, meals (book in advance).

Novena Región, Parque Ecológico 3 Esteros, 20 km from Villarrica towards Panguipulli, T09-8901 2574, www.novena-region.com. Mushing and husky trekking on the winter snow with Siberian Huskies. Also igloo building. Unique in Chile.

Politur, Anfión Muñoz 647, T414547, www.politur.com. Villarrica branch of the Pucón agency (see below), with a recommendable *hostal* on the premises, convenient, good tours and service.

Rodrigo Puelma, T09-9625 1345. Private guide, speaks basic English. Recommended.

Ríos Family, T412408. Birdwatching and fishing trips.

Pucón *p795*

Climbing **Sierra Nevada**, O'Higgins 524-A, T444210, www.sierranevadapucon.cl. Offers *Via Ferrata*, a kind of climbing up sheer rock faces for beginners using metal hand-and-foot- holds embedded in the rock.

Fishing Pucón and Villarrica are celebrated as centres for fishing on Lake Villarrica and in the beautiful Lincura, Trancura and Toltén rivers. Local tourist office will supply details on licences and open seasons, etc. Two fishing specialists are **Mario's Fishing Zone**, O'Higgins 580, T444259, www.flyfishingpucon.com (expensive but good), and **Off Limits**, O'Higgins 560, T442681, www.offlimits.cl (English and Italian spoken).

Horse riding **Rancho de Caballos**, see Sleeping, above. Average hire costs about US$30 ½ day, US$70 full day (transfer from Pucón extra). **Centro de Turismo Ecuestre Huepilmalal**, Camino a Termas de Huife, Km 25, T09-9643 2673, www.huepil-malal.cl. Rodolfo Coombs and Carolina Pumpin, 40 mins from town, also with lodging; from riding lessons (US$30) to 10-day treks. Highly recommended.

Mountain biking Bike hire from US$2.50 per hr to US$20 per day from several travel agencies on O'Higgins.

Thermal springs Dozens of thermal springs in the area, ranging from the upmarket to the natural. Transport is provided by tour operators.

Watersports Water-skiing, sailing, windsurfing at Playa Grande beach by Gran Hotel and La Poza beach end of O'Higgins (more expensive than Playa Grande, not recommended). Playa Grande: waterskiing US$16 for 15 mins, Laser sailing US$16 per hr, sailboards US$16 per hr, rowing boats US$8 per hr.

Whitewater rafting Very popular on the Río Trancura. Many agencies offer trips (see below), Trancura Bajo (grade III), US$30; Trancura Alto (grades 3 and 4), US$45.

Ziplining Called **Canopy** (sliding from platform to platform along a metal cord). Several agencies can arrange this. The best (and most safety conscious) is **Bosque Aventura**, Arauca 611 y O'Higgins, T444030, www.canopypucon.cl.

Tour operators

Tour operators arrange trips to thermal baths, trekking to volcanoes, whitewater rafting, etc. For falls, lakes and termas it's cheaper, if in a group, to flag down a taxi and bargain. Many agencies, so shop around: prices vary at times, quality of guides and equipment variable. In high season, when lots of groups go together, individual attention may be lacking. Prices for climbing Villarrica are given below.

Aguaventura, Palguín 336, T444246, www.aguaventura.com. French-run, in summer kayaking and rafting specialities, in winter "snowshop" for ski and snowboard rental, volcano climbing, trekking.

Kayak Chile, O'Higgins, T09-8837 3253, www.kayakchile.net. Day trips and classes for all levels, all guides are UK or US trained, maximum of 2 students per instructor, responsible. Recommended. Also sells used equipment.

Mountain Life Adventure, Palguín 360, T444564, www.mountainlife- adventure.com. Villarrica hike plus treks and climbs up other volcanoes in the region.

Paredón, T444663, www.paredon expeditions.com. Specializes in small-group excursions to Volcán Villarrica. English spoken, good equipment. Recommended.

Politur, O'Higgins 635, T441373, www.politur.com. Well-established and responsible, good for volcano trek and rafting; a little pricier than others.
Roncotrack, O'Higgins y Arauco, T449597, www.roncotrack.cl. Small group quad-bike excursions from 1½ hrs to 1½ days, good fun. Also hires out good quality bicycles and offers a wide range of other tours.
Sur Expediciones, O'Higgins 615, T444030, www.surexpediciones.com. One of the better agencies for the volcano trip, offers many other activities.
Trancura, several offices on O´Higgins, T441189, www.trancura.com. The biggest and cheapest of the agencies. They have their own **termas** for thermal springs trips, they offer many other activities, including rafting and climbing. For these last two, their safety standards have not met municipal standards, leading to accidents, some fatal.
Travel Aid, Ansorena 425, loc 4, T444040, www.travelaid.cl. Helpful general travel agency, sells trekking maps, guidebooks, lots of information, agents for **Navimag** and other boat trips, English and German spoken.

Transport

Villarrica *p794*

Bus Terminal at Pedro de Valdivia y Muñoz. JAC at Bilbao 610, T411447, and opposite for Pucón and Lican-Ray. Terminal Rural for other local services at Matta y Vicente Reyes. To **Santiago**, 10 hrs, US$20-55, several companies. To **Pucón**, with **Vipu-Ray** (main terminal) and JAC, in summer every 15 mins, 40 mins' journey, US$1.50; same companies to **Lican-Ray**, US$2. To **Valdivia**, JAC, US$7, 5 a day, 2½ hrs. To **Coñaripe** (US$3) and **Liquiñe** at 1600 Mon-Sat, 1000 Sun. To **Temuco**, JAC, US$4-6.40. To **Loncoche** (Ruta 5 junction for hitching), US$3. To **Panguipulli**, go via Lican-Ray, occasional direct buses. Buses to Argentina: buses from Temuco to **Junín de los Andes** pass through Villarrica, fares are the same as from Temuco, T412733, book in advance. Note that if the Tromén pass is blocked by snow buses go via Panguipulli instead of Villarrica and Pucón.

Pucón *p795*

Air Airport 2 km on Caburga road. Check with airlines for summer flights from **Santiago** via Temuco.
Bus No municipal terminal: each company has its own terminal: **JAC**, Uruguay y Palguín; **Tur-Bus**, O'Higgins 910, east of town; **Igi Llaima** and **Cóndor**, Colo Colo y O'Higgins. JAC to **Villarrica** (very frequent, US$1.50), **Temuco** (frequent, US$4-6.40, 2 hrs, rápido US$5, 1¾ hr) and **Valdivia** (US$9, 3 hrs). Tur-Bus direct to **Valdivia, Osorno** and **Puerto Montt**, 6 hrs, US$16, daily. To **Santiago**, 10 hrs, US$20-60, many companies, early morning and late evening. Colectivos to **Villarrica** from O'Higgins y Palguín. Buses to Argentina: Buses from Temuco to **Junín** pass through Pucón, fares are the same as from Temuco.
Car hire Hire prices start at US$32 per day; **Avis**, Arauco 302, T465328, www.avischile.cl; **Hertz**, in the Gran Hotel, T441664; **Kilometro Libre**, Alderete 480, T444399, www.rentacarkilometrolibre.com; **Pucón Rent A Car**, Colo Colo 340, T443052, www.puconrentacar.cl.
Taxi Araucaria, T442323.

Lago Caburga *p796*

Bus Buses **Caburgua** run minibuses every 30 mins from Pucón to **Caburga**, US$1.50; there are colectivos from Ansorena y Uruguay. If walking or cycling, turn left 3 km east of Pucón (sign to Puente Quelhue) and follow the track (very rough) for 18 km through beautiful scenery. Recommended.

Parque Nacional Huerquehue *p796*

Buses **Caburgua** from **Pucón**, 3 daily, 1½ hrs, US$3.

Lago Calafquén and around *p797*

Lican-Ray

Bus Leave from offices around plaza. To **Villarrica**, 1 hr, US$2, **JAC** frequent in summer. In summer, there are direct buses from **Santiago** (**Tur-Bus** US$20, 10 hrs, salón cama US$50) and **Temuco** (2½ hrs, US$7). To **Panguipulli**, Mon-Sat 0730.

Coñaripe

Bus To **Panguipulli**, 7 a day (4 off season), US$3 and 16 daily to **Villarrica**, US$3.

Nightly bus direct to **Santiago**, **Tur-Bus** and **JAC**, 11½ hrs, US$25, salón cama in summer, US$50.

Panguipulli *p797*
Bus Terminal at Gabriela Mistral y Portales. To **Santiago** daily, US$21-50. To **Valdivia**, frequent (Sun only 4), several companies, 2 hrs, US$5. To **Temuco** frequent, **Power** and **Pangui Sur**, US$6, 3 hrs. To **Puerto Montt**, US$12. To **Choshuenco**, Neltume and Puerto Fuy, 3 daily, 3 hrs, US$7. To **Coñaripe** (with connections for Lican-Ray and Villarrica), 7 daily, 4 off season, 1½ hrs, US$3.

Lago Pirehueico
Bus Daily **Puerto Fuy** to **Panguipulli**, 3 daily, 3 hrs, US$7.
Ferry The **Hua Hum** sails from Puerto Fuy to Puerto Pirehueico at 0800, 1300, 1800 (Jan-Feb), 1400 (rest of year), returns 2 hrs later, foot passengers US$1.75, cars US$31, motorbikes US$9.50. A beautiful crossing, comparable to the lakes crossing from Puerto Montt to Bariloche, but at a fraction the price (to take vehicles reserve in advance on T063-197 1871, see **Somarco**'s website, www.barcazas.cl). In summer there are buses to **Argentina** at 1100 (does not wait for passengers on 0800 ferry) and 1900. If you can't wait till then it's a 50-km walk to San Martín de los Andes.

❶ Directory

Villarrica *p794*
Banks ATMs at banks on Pedro de Valdivia between Montt and Alderete. **Carlos Huerta**, A Muñoz 417, **Central de Repuestos**, A Muñoz 415 (good rates), **Turcamb**, Henríquez 576, and **Cristopher Exchange**, Valdivia 1061, all change TCs and cash. **Bicycle shops** Mora Bicicletas, G Körner 760, helpful. **Internet** At the **Central de Llamadas**, Henríquez 567, 2nd floor. **Cybercafé Salmon**, Letelier y Henríquez. **Post offices** A Muñoz 315. Open 0900-1300, 1430-1800 (Mon-Fri), 0900-1300 (Sat).

Pucón *p795*
Airline offices **Lan**, Urrutia y Costanera, daily 1000-1400, 1800-2200. **Banks** There are 3 or 4 banks with ATMs and several *casas de cambio* on O'Higgins, although *cambio* rates are universally poor. Much better to change money in Temuco. **Internet** Several sites on O'Higgins, US$2 per hr. **Post offices** Fresia 183.

Valdivia and Osorno

Valdivia is a very pleasant city at the confluence of the Ríos Calle Calle and Cruces, which form the Río Valdivia. It is set in rich agricultural land receiving some 2,300 mm of rain a year. To the north of the city is a large island, Isla Teja, where the Universidad Austral de Chile is situated. The student population adds zest to the nightlife. At the mouth of the Rio Valdivia are a group of historic forts which make a good day's outing from the city. Osorno, further south, is not such a tourist city, but it is a base for visiting the attractive southern lakes.

Valdivia ➔ *Phone code: 063. Colour map 8, C1. Population: 127,000. 839 km south of Santiago.*
Valdivia was one of the most important centres of Spanish colonial control over Chile. Founded in 1552 by Pedro de Valdivia, it was abandoned as a result of the Mapuche insurrection of 1599 and the area was briefly occupied by Dutch pirates. In 1645 it was refounded as a walled city, the only Spanish mainland settlement south of the Río Biobío. The coastal fortifications at the mouth of the river also date from the 17th century. They were greatly strengthened after 1760 owing to fears that Valdivia might be seized by the British, but were of little avail during the Wars of Independence: overnight on 2 February 1820 the Chilean naval squadron under Lord Cochrane seized San Carlos, Amargos and Corral and turned their guns on Niebla and Mancera, which surrendered the following morning. From independence until the 1880s Valdivia was an outpost of Chilean rule, reached only by sea or by a coastal route through Mapuche territory. From 1849 to 1875 Valdivia was a centre for German colonization of the Lake District. In 2007 it became capital of the newly created Región XIV, Los Ríos. **Tourist offices** ⓘ *Av Prat 555, by the dock, T239060, infovaldivia@sernatur.cl.* Good map of region and local rivers, list of hotel prices

and examples of local crafts with artisans' addresses. Open daily in summer, weekdays only off season. See www.valdiviaonline.cl and www.munivaldivia.cl, the municipal website.

Sights The city centre is the tree-lined, shady **Plaza de la República**. A pleasant walk is along **Avenida Prat** (or **Costanera**), which follows the bend in the river, from the bus station to the bridge to **Isla Teja**, the **Muelle Fluvial** (boat dock) and the riverside market. Boats can be hired at the bend for US$6 per hour. Sealions lounge around the dock. On Isla Teja, near the library in the University, are a **botanic garden** and **arboretum** with trees from all over the world. West of the botanical gardens is the 30-ha **Parque Saval**, with areas of native forest, as well as the **Lago de los Lotos** (beautiful blooms in spring) ⓘ *all open during daylight hours, US$0.80*. On boat trips round the island you can see lots of waterfowl. Also on Isla Teja is the **Museo Histórico y Antropológico** ⓘ *T212872, museohistorico@uach.cl, Tue-Sun, 1000-1300, 1400-1800, daily 1000-2000 in summer, US$2.50*. Run by the University, it contains exhibits on archaeology, ethnography and the history of German settlement, beautifully housed in the former mansion of Carlos Anwandter, a prominent German immigrant. Next door is the **Museo de Arte Moderno** ⓘ *Jan-Feb Tue-Sun, 1000-1300, 1400-1800, off season only open for temporary exhibitions, US$2*.

The surrounding district has lovely countryside of woods, beaches, lakes and rivers. The various rivers are navigable and there are pleasant journeys by rented motor boat on the **Ríos Futa** and **Tornagaleanes** around the **Isla del Rey**. Boat tours go to the **Santuario de la Naturaleza Carlos Anwandter** ⓘ *Boat Isla del Río, daily 1415, 6 hrs, US$22 pp*. The Refuge is an area on the Río Cruces which flooded as result of the 1960 earthquake; lots of bird species are visible. In summer there is a regular steam train service to **Antilhue** (20 km) ⓘ *tickets at station, Ecuador 2000, T214978, and Independencia 540,T219225, and at Muelle Fluvial, www.ecovaldivia.com/ruta-tren-antilhue.htm, every Sun Jan-Feb, other weekends and holidays throughout the year, US$8 return, 1½-hr trip, return 2 hrs later*, where the train is met by locals selling all sorts of local culinary specialities. This is the only steam train in Chile (the engine dates from 1913), good; book in advance and ask about additional trips on public holidays.

Parque Oncol ⓘ *27km northwest of Valdivia, park entry US$3.15, students, children and seniors US$1, T800-370222, www.parque oncol.cl, buses Jan-Feb daily 1000 from tourist office at the dock, return 1800, US$21 with park entry*, 754 ha of Valdivian native forest, with several trails and lookouts, zipline (*canopy*) site, US$20 (US$24 in January-February), picnic area and campsite, US$15.50.

Coastal resorts near Valdivia

At the mouth of the Río Valdivia there are attractive villages which can be visited by land or river boat. The two main centres are Niebla on the north bank and Corral opposite on the south bank. **Niebla**, 18 km from Valdivia, is a spread-out resort with seafood restaurants and accommodation (also plenty of cabañas and campsites on the road from Valdivia). To the west of the resort is the **Fuerte de la Pura y Limpia Concepción de Monfort de Lemus** ⓘ *daily in summer 1000-1900, closed Mon in winter, US$1, Sun free, tourist information and telephone office nearby*, on a promontory. Partially restored in 1992, it has an interesting museum on Chilean naval history.

Corral, quieter than Niebla, is a fishing port with several good restaurants 62 km from Valdivia by road (unsuitable for cars without four-wheel drive or high clearance). The dilapidated but atmospheric Castillo de San Sebastián, with 3 m wide walls, was defended by a battery of 21 guns. It has a museum and offers a view upriver. In summer there are re-enactments of the 1820 storming of the Spanish fort by the Chileans (daily, 1200 and 1800). ⓘ *Entry US$5 Jan-Feb, US$1.50 off season*. North along the coast are the remains of Castillo San Luis de Alba de Amargos (3 km) and Castillo de San Carlos, with pleasant beaches (4 km). The coastal walks west and south of Corral are splendid. The helpful tourist office on Corral's pier can provide some trekking tips.

In midstream, between Niebla and Corral is **Isla Mancera** a small island, fortified by the Castillo de San Pedro de Alcántara, which has the most standing buildings. The island is a pleasant place to stop, but it can get crowded when an excursion boat arrives.

Osorno and around ➔ *Phone code: 064. Colour map 8, C1. Population: 132,000.*

Founded in 1553, abandoned in 1604 and refounded in 1796, Osorno later became one of the centres of German immigration. On the large Plaza de Armas stands the modern cathedral, while to the east of the plaza along MacKenna are a number of late 19th-century mansions built by German immigrants, now National Monuments. **Museo Histórico Municipal** ⓘ *Matta 809, entrance in Casa de Cultura, daily 1100-1900 in summer; winter Mon-Fri 0930-1730, Sat 1500-1800, US$1.50*, includes displays on natural history, Mapuche culture, refounding of the city and German colonization. The **Museo Interactivo de Osorno** (MIO) ⓘ *in the former train station, 3 blocks southwest of the plaza, T212996, www.municipalidadosorno.cl/, Mon-Thu 0815-1300, 1445-1815, Fri closes 1715, Sat pm only*, is an interactive science museum designed for both children and adults. **Tourist offices:** Sernatur in provincial government office ⓘ *Plaza de Armas, O'Higgins 667, p 1, T237575, infosorno@sernatur.cl*. Municipal office in the bus terminal and kiosk on the Plaza de Armas. Both open December-February. Contact **Skiing Club Andino**, see page 857, for advice on skiing. **Automóvil Club de Chile**, Manuel Bulnes 463, T540080.

About 47 km east of Osorno, **Lago Puyehue** (*Colour map 8, C1; Altitude: 207 m; www.puyehuechile.cl*) is surrounded by relatively flat countryside. At the western end is **Entre Lagos** (*Population: 4,000*) and the **Termas de Puyehue** ⓘ *0830-2000, outdoor pools till 1900, US$52-80 for a day pass including meals, drinks and access to all facilities, price depends on day and season, www.puyehue.cl*, is at the eastern end.

The **Parque Nacional Puyehue**, east of Lago Puyehue, stretches to the Argentine border. On the east side are several lakes and two volcanic peaks: **Volcán Puyehue** (2,240 m) in the north (access via private track US$14 belonging to El Caulle restaurant, with camping,

Valdivia

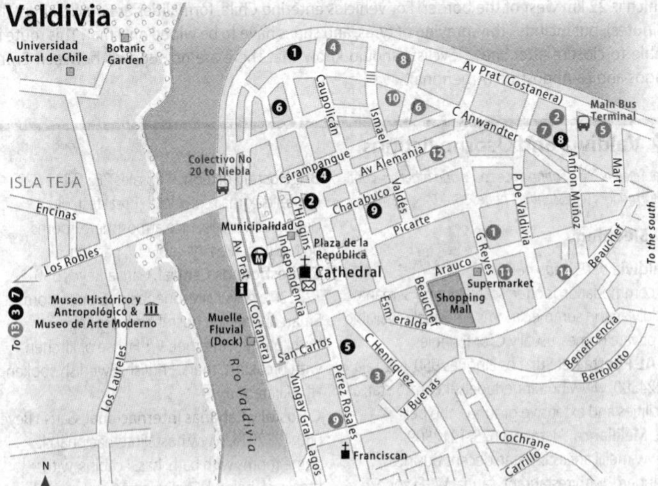

100 metres
100 yards

Sleeping
1 Airesbuenos Central
2 A Muñoz 345
3 Camilo Henríquez 749
4 Encanto del Río
5 Hostal Ana María
6 Hostal Anwandter
7 Hostal Casagrande
8 Hostal Prat
9 Hostal Torreón
10 Hostal Totem
11 Hostal y Cabañas Internacional
12 Melillanca
13 Puerta del Sur
14 Villa Beauchef

Eating
1 Agridulce
2 Café Haussmann
3 Cervecería Kunstmann
4 Chester's
5 Entrelagos
6 La Calesa
7 Lomodetoro
8 Shanghai
9 Volcán

www.elcaulle.com) and **Volcán Casablanca** (also called Antillanca, 1,900 m). Park administration is at Aguas Calientes, 4 km south of the Termas de Puyehue. There is a ranger station at Anticura. Leaflets on attractions are available.

At **Aguas Calientes** there is an open-air pool (dirty) ⓘ *www.termasaguascalientes.cl, 0830-1900*, with very hot thermal water beside the Río Chanleufú, and a very hot indoor pool ⓘ *0830-2000, US$26-41 for a day pass including use of pool and all meals, reductions for children, price depends on day and season*. There are also cabins for 4-10 people, a campsite, US$20-30 up to 4 people, and varous therapies and massages.

From Aguas Calientes the road continues 18 km southeast to Antillanca on the slopes of **Volcán Casablanca**, past three small lakes and through forests. This is particularly beautiful, especially at sunrise, with the snow-clad cones of Osorno, Puntiagudo and Puyehue forming a semicircle. The tree-line on Casablanca is one of the few in the world made up of deciduous trees (nothofagus or southern beech). From Antillanca it is possible to climb Casablanca for even better views of the surrounding volcanoes and lakes, no path, seven hours return journey, information from Club Andino in Osorno. Attached to the Hotel Antillanca is one of the smallest ski resorts in Chile; there are three lifts, ski instruction and first aid available. Skiing quality depends on the weather: though rain is common it often does not turn to snow. See under Osorno for buses. No public transport from Aguas Calientes to Antillanca; try hitching – always difficult, but it is not a hard walk.

Border with Argentina: Paso Puyehue

Chilean immigration Open the second Saturday in October to the second Saturday in March 0800-2100, otherwise 0800-1900. The Chilean border post is at Pajaritos, 4 km east of **Anticura**, which is 22 km west of the border. For vehicles entering Chile, formalities are quick (about 15 minutes), but includes the spraying of tyres, and shoes have to be wiped on a mat. This route is liable to closure after snow. Cyclists should know that there are no supplies between Entre Lagos and La Angostura (Argentina).

Valdivia and Osorno listings

For Sleeping and Eating price codes and other relevant information, see Essentials, pages 38-40.

Sleeping

Valdivia *p805, map p807*

Accommodation is often scarce during Semana Valdiviana. In summer, rooms are widely available in private homes, usually **C**, or **F** singles.

L-AL Puerta del Sur, Los Lingües 950, Isla Teja, T224500, www.hotelpuertadelsur.com. 5 star, all facilities and extensive grounds, the best.

AL Melillanca, Alemania 675, T212509, www.melill anca.cl. 4-star, decent business standard, with restaurant, sauna, Wi-Fi zones. Recommended.

A Encanto del Río, Prat 415, T225740, www.hotel encantodelrio.cl. Small, new, comfortable, rooms on the middle floor have balconies and river views, disabled access, Wi-Fi, central heating.

B-C Hostal Prat, Prat 595, T222020. TV, good breakfast, views to industrial zone over the river.

B-C Hostal Torreón, P Rosales 783, T212 622, mrprelle@gmail.com. With breakfast, old German-style villa, nice atmosphere, rooms on top floor are airy, cable TV, parking.

C Airesbuenos Central, García Reyes 550, T222202, www.airesbuenos.cl. **E** pp in dorms. Smart and bright hostel, some rooms with bath, garden, internet, Wi-Fi, use of kitchen, with breakfast, tours, English, Swedish spoken, HI affiliated.

C Hostal y Cabañas Internacional, García Reyes 660, T212015, www.hostalinternacional.cl. Some rooms with bath, has 4 cabins, with breakfast, helpful, English and German spoken, use of kitchen, barbecue area, book exchange, tours. Recommended.

C Hostal Totem, Anwandter 425, T292849, www.turismototem.cl. Simple rooms, French and basic English spoken, tours arranged. Recommended.

C Villa Beauchef, Beauchef 844, T216044, hbeauchef@gmail.com. With or without bath, with breakfast, cable TV, Wi-Fi, thin walls.
D Camilo Henríquez 749, Casa 6, T431494/520836, arlene_ola@hotmail.com. **E** pp singles. Charming tumbledown mansion, wildly sloping floors (after-effect of 1960 earthquake), large rooms, some with bath, kitchen, laundry, internet, Wi-Fi, some English spoken. Recommended.

Around the bus terminal

B Hostal Anwandter, Anwandter 601, T218587, http://www.valdiviachile.cl/ anwandter.php. Cheaper without bath and in low season, with breakfast, other meals extra, use of kitchen, internet, Wi-Fi, TV, hot water.
B Hostal Casagrande, Anwandter 880, T202035, www.hotelcasagrande.cl. Heated but small rooms in attractive old house, buffet breakfast, convenient, cable TV, internet, Wi-Fi, laundry, great views. Recommended.
D pp **Hostal Ana María**, José Martí 11, 3 mins from terminal, T222468, anamsandovalf@hotmail.com. With breakfast, Wi-Fi, use of kitchen, good value, also cabañas.
E-F pp **A Muñoz 345**, outside terminal. Breakfast, very basic.
Camping Camping Centenario, in Rowing Club on España. **F** per tent, overlooking river.
Isla Teja, T213584, lovely views over river.

Coastal resorts near Valdivia *p806*

B Cabañas Fischer, Del Castillo 1115, Niebla, T282007, rosemarief24@gmail.com. Cabins and 2 campsites, Wi-Fi. Worth bargaining out of season.
B El Castillo, Antonio Ducce 750, Niebla, T282061, hotelelcastillo@hotmail.com. With breakfast, heating, TV, internet and pool.

Osorno *p807*

AL Waeger, Cochrane 816, T233721, www.hotelwaeger.cl. 4-star, restaurant, comfortable but room sizes vary greatly.
A-B Eduviges, Eduviges 856, T/F235023, www.hoteleduviges.cl. Cheaper without bath. Spacious, quiet, attractive, gardens, laundry, internet, also cabañas. Recommended.
C-D Hostal Riga, Amthauer 1058, T232945, resiriga@surnet.cl. Pleasant. Highly recommended but heavily booked in season.
D Res Hein's, Errázuriz 1757, T234116. **E** without bath, old-fashioned, spacious, family atmosphere.
E There are pleanty of cheap options near the bus terminal, for instance on Los Carrera.
Camping Municipal site off Ruta 5 near south entrance to city, open Jan-Feb only, poor facilities, US$9 per site, swimming pool.

Around Osorno *p807*

Lago Puyehue

LL Hotel Termas de Puyehue, at the Termas de Puyehue, T064-331400 or T600-293 6000, www.puyehue.cl. All inclusive: meals, drinks, use of thermal pools and all activities (Spa extra), well maintained, meals expensive, in beautiful scenery, heavily booked Jan-Feb, cheaper May to mid-Dec.
B Hosp Millarey, Ramírez 333, Entre Lagos, T09-761 6625. With breakfast, **E** singles, excellent.
B Hostal y Cabañas Miraflores, Ramírez 480, Entre Lagos, T371275, http://hostalmiraflores.blogspot.com. Pleasant rooms and cabins (**A-B**), with Wi-Fi.
D Ruta Gasthaus 215, Osvaldo Muñoz 148, Entre Lagos, T371357. **F** singles, with bath and good breakfast, German spoken, good value.
Camping **Camping No Me Olvides**, Km 56, on south shore of Lake Puyehue, T371633, www.nomeolvides.cl. US$15 pp, also cabañas.
Playa Los Copihues, Km 56.5, on south shore of Lake Puyehue, T371645. Hot showers, good.

Aguas Calientes and Antillanca

A Hotel Antillanca, T235114, www.skiantillanca.cl. More expensive with full board. Includes free mountain biking and parapenting, at foot of Volcán Casablanca, restaurant/café, with pool, sauna, friendly club-like atmosphere; also has a *refugio*.
Camping See Aguas Calientes, above. **CONAF refugio** on Volcán Puyehue, but check with CONAF in Anticura whether it is open.
Los Derrumbes, 1 km from Aguas Calientes, no electricity, US$25 per site.

Eating

Valdivia *p805, map p807*

Several fish restaurants on the Costanera facing the boat dock serve cheap, tasty food and have nice atmosphere. There are others upstairs in the municipal market.

𝕋𝕋𝕋-𝕋𝕋 **Agridulce**, Prat 327, T433435, www.agridulcevaldivia.cl. Perfect mix of sophisticated dishes using local produce, tapas and generous sandwiches. Good service and good value. Recommended.
𝕋𝕋𝕋-𝕋𝕋 **Lomodetoro**, Los Robles 170, Isla Teja, T346423. Probably the best steak in town. Good wine list.
𝕋𝕋 **Cervecería Kunstmann**, Ruta T350, No 950, T222570, www.cerveza-kunstmann.cl. On road to Niebla. Restaurant serving German/Chilean food, brewery with 5 types of beer, beautiful interior, museum. Recommended.
𝕋𝕋 **La Calesa**, O'Higgins 160, T225467. Elegant, intimate, Peruvian and international cuisine. Good *pisco sours*. Recommended.
𝕋𝕋 **Shanghai**, Andwandter y Muñoz. Pleasant Chinese.
𝕋 **Chester's**, Henríquez 314. Good-value pizzas and fast food. Open late.
𝕋 **Volcán**, Caupolicán y Chacabuco. *Pichangas*, *cazuelas*, great food at a good price.

Cafés

Café Haussmann, O'Higgins 394. A Valdivia institution. Good tea, cakes and *crudos*.
Café Moro, Independencia y Libertad. Airy café with a mezzanine art gallery. Good for breakfast, good value lunches, popular bar at night.
Entrelagos, Pérez Rosales 622. Ice cream and chocolates.
La Baguette, Libertad y Yungay. Panadería with French-style cakes, brown bread. Repeatedly recommended.
Mi Pueblito, San Carlos 190. Wholemeal bread and vegetarian snacks to take away.

Coastal resorts near Valdivia *p806*

𝕋𝕋 **Las Delicias**, Ducce 583, Niebla, T213566. With restaurant with 'a view that would be worth the money even if the food wasn't good'. Also *cabañas* and camping.

Osorno *p807*

Good cheap restaurants in the municipal market.
𝕋𝕋𝕋 **Atelier**, Freire 468. Fresh pasta and other Italian delights, good.
𝕋𝕋 **Dino's**, Ramírez 898, on the plaza. Restaurant upstairs, bar/cafeteria downstairs, good.
𝕋𝕋 **Wufehr**, Ramirez 959, loc 2. Local raw meat specialities and sandwiches. Popular with locals.
𝕋𝕋-𝕋 **Club de Artesanos**, MacKenna 634. Decent and hearty traditional Chilean fare.
𝕋 **Café Literario Hojas del Sur**, MacKenna 1011 y Cochrane. More like a living room than a café, cosy, Wi-Fi.
𝕋 **La Cabaña**, Ramirez 774, T272479. Wide variety of cheap lunches ranging from Chinese to home-cooked Chilean. Excellent value.
𝕋 **Panadería**, at Ramírez 977. Bakery with good wholemeal bread.

Around Osorno: Lago Puyehue *p807*

𝕋𝕋𝕋-𝕋𝕋 **Jardín del Turista**, Ruta 215, Km 46, T371214, Entre Lagos, www.interpatagonia.com/jardindelturista. Very good, also has *cabañas* and suites.
𝕋𝕋 **Pub del Campo**, Entre Lagos, T371220. Reasonable prices. Highly recommended.

Festivals and events

Valdivia *p805, map p807*

Semana Valdiviana, in **mid-Feb**, culminates in Noche Valdiviana on the Sat with a procession of elaborately decorated boats which sail past the Muelle Fluvial. Accommodation is scarce during festival. In **Sep** there is a film festival.

Shopping

Valdivia *p805, map p807*

Bookshops Librería de Valdivia, Lautaro 177. Excellent bookshop with a small selection of maps, literature in English and French. Sunday book and antiques fair at the Torreón del Barro.
Supermarket Hiper-Unico, Arauco 697 (4-screen cinema at Plaza Dos Ríos next door). Colourful riverside market with livestock, fish, etc.

Activities and tours

Valdivia *p805, map p807*

To Corral and Niebla and other boat trips along the river, many the kiosks along the Muelle Fluvial. Boats will only leave with a minimum of 10 passengers, so off-season organize in advance. Full list of operators in tourist information office.
Tourist House, Camilo Henríquez 266, T433115, www.casadelturista.com. Offer a range of excursions and give good advice.

Sea kayaking

Pueblito Expediciones, San Carlos 188, T245055, www.pueblitoexpediciones.cl. Offer classes and trips in sea kayaks in the waters around Valdivia, courses from US$40.

Transport

Valdivia *p805, map p807*

Air LAN to/from **Santiago** every day via Temuco, or Concepción.

Bus Terminal at Muñoz y Prat, by the river. To **Santiago**: several companies, 10 hrs, most services overnight, US$25-65; ½-hourly buses to/from **Osorno**, 2 hrs, several companies, US$5. To **Panguipulli**, **Empresa Pirehueico**, about every 30 mins, US$5. Many daily to **Puerto Montt**, US$7.50, 3 hrs. To **Puerto Varas**, 3 hrs, US$7. To **Frutillar**, US$6, 2½ hrs. To **Villarrica**, by **JAC**, 6 a day, 2½ hrs, US$7, continuing to **Pucón**, US$9, 3 hrs. Frequent daily service to Riñihue via Paillaco and Los Lagos. To Argentina: to **Bariloche** via Osorno, 7 hrs, **Bus Norte**; to **Zapala**, **Igi-Llaima**, Mon, Thur, Sat, 2300, change in Temuco at 0200, arrive Zapala 1200-1500, depending on border crossing, US$45.

Coastal resorts near Valdivia *p806*

Ferry The tourist boats to **Isla Mancera** and **Corral** offer a guided ½-day tour (US$25-40, some with meals) from the Muelle Fluvial, Valdivia (behind the tourist office on Av Prat 555). The river trip is beautiful, but you can also take a **bus** (orange No 20) to Niebla from outside bus station or along Calles Andwandter and Carampangue in Valdivia, regular service between 0730 and 2100, 30 mins, US$1.20 (bus continues to Los Molinos), then cross to Corral by **Somarco** vehicle ferry, every 2 hrs, US$1.25. There are occasional buses from Valdivia to Corral.

Osorno *p807*

Air LAN, E Ramírez 802, T600-526 2000, daily Osorno- **Santiago**, via Concepción and/or Temuco.

Bus Main terminal 4 blocks from Plaza de Armas at Errázuriz 1400. Left luggage open 0730-2030. Bus from centre, US$0.50. To **Santiago**, frequent, US$22.50, salón cama US$44, 11 hrs. To **Concepción**, US$16-34. To **Temuco**, US$10. To **Pucón** and **Villarrica**, frequent, US$15. To **Frutillar**, US$3, **Llanquihue**, **Puerto Varas** (US$4) and **Puerto Montt** (US$6) services every 30 mins. To **Puerto Octay**, US$3, every 20 mins. Local buses to **Entre Lagos**, **Puyehue** and **Aguas Calientes** leave from the Mercado Municipal terminal, 1 block west of main terminal.

Around Osorno: Lago Puyehue *p807*

Bus To **Entre Lagos** from Osorno, frequent services in summer, **Expreso Lago Puyehue** and **Buses Barria**, 1 hr, US$2, reduced service off-season. Some buses by both companies continue to **Aguas Calientes** (off-season according to demand) 2 hrs, US$5. Buses that continue to Aguas Calientes do not stop at the lake (unless you want to get off at Hotel Termas de Puyehue and clamber down).

Border with Argentina: Anticura *p808*

Bus To Anticura, 2-3 buses daily from **Osorno**, 3 hrs, US$8. Several bus companies run daily services from **Puerto Montt** via Osorno to Bariloche along this route (see under Puerto Montt for details). Although less scenic than the ferry journey across Lake Todos Los Santos and Laguna Verde (see page 813) this crossing is far cheaper, more reliable and still a beautiful trip (best views from the right hand side of the bus).

Directory

Valdivia *p805, map p807*

Airline offices LAN, Maipú 271, T600-5262000. **Banks** Redbanc ATM at Supermercado Hiper-Unico (see above) and at several banks in the centre. Casa de Cambio at Carampangue 325, T213305. **Turismo Austral**, Arauco y Henríquez, Galería Arauco, accepts TCs. **Internet** Several in the centre, average charge US$0.80 per hr. **Post offices** O'Higgins y Maipú.

Osorno *p807*

Banks Several banks with ATMs around the plaza. Casas de cambio at **Cambio Tur**, MacKenna 1004, T234846. **Turismo Frontera**, Ramírez 949, local 11 (Galería Catedral). **Internet** Several places in the centre.

Southern lakes

This is one of the most beautiful areas in a part of Chile which already has plenty to boast about. Lago Llanquihue, with its views to volcanoes and German-influenced towns, adjoins the Parque Nacional Vicente Pérez Rosales. The oldest national park in the country, this contains another beautiful lake, Todos los Santos, three major volcanoes, waterfalls and a memorable lakes route to Argentina. The region ends at the Seno de Reloncaví, a peaceful glacial inlet, often shrouded in soft rain.

Lago Llanquihue

The lake, covering 56,000 ha, is the second largest in Chile. Across the great blue sheet of water can be seen two snowcapped volcanoes: the perfect cone of Osorno (2,680 m) and the shattered cone of Calbuco (2,015 m), and, when the air is clear, the distant Tronador (3,460 m). The largest towns, Puerto Varas, Llanquihue and Frutillar are on the western shore, linked by the Pan-American Highway. There are roads around the rest of the lake: that from Puerto Octay east to Ensenada is very beautiful, but is narrow with lots of blind corners, necessitating speeds of 20-30 kph at best in places (see below).

Puerto Octay → *Phone code: 064. Colour map 8, C1. Population: 2,500.*

A peaceful, picturesque small town at the north tip of the lake with a backdrop of rolling hills, Puerto Octay was founded by German settlers in 1852. The town enjoyed a boom in the late 19th century when it was the northern port for steamships on the lake. The church and the enormous German-style former convent survive from that period. **Museo el Colono** ⓘ *Independencia 591, Tue-Sun 1015-1300, 1500-1700, US$2, www.museopuertooctay.cl*, has displays on German colonization. Another part of the museum, housing agricultural implements and machinery for making chicha, is just outside town on the road to Centinela. 3 km south along an unpaved road is the Peninsula of Centinela, a beautiful spot with a launch dock and watersports. From the headland are fine views of the volcanoes and the Cordillera of the Andes; a very popular spot in good weather, good for picnics (taxi US$2 one way). Rowing boats and pedalos can be hired.

Frutillar Bajo → *Phone code: 065. Colour map 8, C1. Population: 9,000. Altitude: 70 m.*

About halfway along the west side of the lake, Frutillar is divided into Frutillar Alto, just off the main highway, and Frutillar Bajo beautifully situated on the lake, 4 km away. (Colectivos run between the two towns, five minutes, US$0.50.) Frutillar Bajo is possibly the most attractive – and expensive – town on the lake. At the north end of the town is the Reserva Forestal Edmundo Winckler, run by the Universidad de Chile, 33 ha, with a guided trail through native woods. **Museo Colonial Alemán** ⓘ *T421142, museofrutillar@uach.cl, daily 1000-1930 summer, Tue-Sun 1000-1730, winter, US$3.50*, includes a watermill, replicas of two German colonial houses with furnishings and utensils of the period, a blacksmith's shop (personal engravings for US$9), a campanario (circular barn with agricultural machinery and carriages inside), gardens and handicraft shop. In late January to early February there is a highly regarded classical music festival (www.semanasmusicales.cl) and a new, state-of-the-art concert hall on the lakefront, **Teatro del Lago** (www.teatrodellago.cl), due to open fully in 2010. Accommodation must be booked well in advance. New tourist office on the Costanera (www.munifrutillar.cl and www.frutillar.com), helpful.

Puerto Varas and around → *Phone code: 065. Colour map 8, C1. Population: 22,000.*

This beauty spot was the southern port for shipping on the lake in the 19th century. It is infinitely preferable as a centre for visiting the southern lakes to Puerto Montt, 20 km to the south. The Catholic church, built by German Jesuits in 1918, is a copy of the church in Marieenkirche in the Black Forest. North and east of the **Gran Hotel Puerto Varas** (1934) are German style mansions dating from the early 20th century. **Parque Philippi**, on top of the hill, is pleasant; walk up to Hotel Cabañas del Lago on Klenner, cross the railway and the gate is on the right. Puerto Varas is a good base for trips around the lake. On the south shore two of the best beaches are **Playa Hermosa** (Km 7) and **Playa Niklitschek** (Km 8, entry fee charged). **La Poza**, at Km 16, is a little lake to the south of Lago Llanquihue reached through narrow channels overhung with vegetation. **Isla Loreley**, an island on La Poza, is very beautiful (frequent boat trips, US$5); a concealed channel leads to yet another lake, the Laguna Encantada. The **tourist office** is in the Municipalidad ⓘ *San Francisco 413, T361330, turismo@ptovaras.cl, see http://turismopuertovaras.blogspot.com and www.puertovaras.org*. Many places close in the off-season.

Ensenada

East of Puerto Varas by 47 km, Ensenada is at the southeast corner of Lake Llanquihue, which is the town's main attraction. Minibuses run from Puerto Varas, frequent in summer (see below).

Volcán Osorno

North of Ensenada, Osorno volcano can be reached from Ensenada, or from a road branching off the Puerto Octay-Ensenada road at Puerto Klocker, 20 km southeast of Puerto Octay. Guided ascents (organized by agencies in Puerto Varas) set out from the *refugio* at **La Burbuja** where there is a small ski centre in winter ⓘ *usually open Jun-Sep, ski ticket US$30, equipment rental US$30, ski school, see www.volcan osorno.com for conditions* and pleasant short walks with great views in summer. From here it is six hours to the summit. The volcano can also be climbed from the north (La Picada); this route is easier and may be attempted without a guide, although only experienced climbers should attempt to climb right to the top as ice climbing equipment is essential and there are many craters hidden below thin crusts of ice.

Parque Nacional Vicente Pérez Rosales

ⓘ *Open 0900-1800 (1730 in winter). The park is infested by horseflies in Dec-Feb: cover up as much as possible with light-coloured clothes which may help a bit.*

Lago Todos los Santos The most beautiful of all the lakes in southern Chile, this long, irregularly shaped sheet of emerald-green water has deeply wooded shores and several small islands rising from its surface. In the waters are reflected the slopes of Volcán Osorno. Beyond the hilly shores to the east are several graceful snow-capped mountains, with the mighty Tronador in the distance. To the north is the sharp point of Cerro Puntiagudo, and at the northeastern end Cerro Techado rises cliff-like out of the water. The ports of **Petrohué** at its western and **Peulla** at its eastern ends are connected by boat. Trout and salmon fishing are excellent in several parts including Petrohué. CONAF has an office in Petrohué with a visitors' centre, small museum and 3D model of the park. There is a *guardaparque* office in Puella. There are no roads round the lake and the only scheduled vessel is the **Cruce Andino** service with connections to Bariloche (Argentina), but private launches can be hired for trips.

Petrohué Petrohué, 16 km northwest of Ensenada, is a good base for walking. The **Salto de Petrohué** *US$2.50*, is 6 km from Petrohué (unpaved, dusty, lots of traffic; bus US$1), 10 km (paved) from Ensenada. Near the falls is a snackbar; there are also two short trails, the Senderos de los Enamorados and Carileufú. **Peulla**, is a good starting point for hikes in the mountains. The Cascadas Los Novios, signposted above the Hotel Peulla, are stunning.

For crossing the border with Argentina, **Paso Pérez Rosales**. Chilean immigration is in Peulla, 30 km west of the border, open daily, summer 0800-2100, winter 0800-2000.

Seno de Reloncaví and Cochamó

The Reloncaví estuary, the northernmost of Chile's glacial inlets, is recommended for its local colour, its wildlife (including sealions and dolphins) and its peace. **Ralún**, a small village at the northern end of the estuary, is 31 km southeast from Ensenada by a poorly paved road along the wooded lower Petrohué valley. Roads continue, unpaved, along the east side of the estuary to Cochamó and Puelo and on the west side to Canutillar. In Ralún there is a village shop and post office. Just outside the village there are thermal springs with baths, US$2, reached by boat across Río Petrohué, US$3.50 pp.

Cochamó, 17 km south of Ralún on the east shore of the estuary, is a pretty village, with a fine wooden church similar to those on Chiloé, in a striking setting, with the estuary and volcano behind. It is becoming a popular new centre for many outdoor activities in the alerce forests and among the granite peaks (trekking, climbing, kayaking, riding, birdwatching and fishing). **Puelo**, further south, on the south bank of the Río Puelo, is a most peaceful place. From here the road (very rough) continues to Puelche on the Carretera Austral.

The **Gaucho Trail** east from Cochamó to **Paso León** on the Argentine border dates from the colonial period and runs along Río Cochamó to La Junta, then along the north side of Lago Vidal, passing waterfalls and the oldest surviving *alerce* trees in Chile at El Arco. The route takes 3-4 days by horse, 5-6 days on foot, depending on conditions, which are best December to March. A road is due to be built which will allow access by jeep. From Paso León it is a three-hour walk to the main road to Bariloche.

Southern lakes listings

For Sleeping and Eating price codes and other relevant information, see Essentials, pages 38-40.

Sleeping

Puerto Octay *p812*

Camping wild and barbecues are forbidden on the lakeshore.

B-C Zapato Amarillo, 35 mins' walk north of town, T210787, www.zapatoamarillo.cl. **E** pp in dorms. Book in advance in high season, spotless kitchen, great breakfasts, homemade bread, meals, German/English spoken, mountain bikes, canoes, tours, house has a grass roof. Highly recommended.

Camping El Molino, beside lake, US$20 for up to 5 people. Recommended.

Centinela

L-AL Hotel Centinela, T 391326, www.hotelcentinela.cl. Built in 1914 as a summer mansion, Edward VIII once stayed here. Newly restored, idyllic location with superb views, also has *cabañas*, excellent restaurant, bar, open all year.

C-D Hostería La Baja, Centinela, T391269. With breakfast and bath, beautifully situated at the neck of the peninsula. Good value.

Camping Municipal site on lakeside, T391326. US$18 per site. *Cabañas* on the peninsula.

East of Puerto Octay

C Hostería Irma, 2 km south of Las Cascadas, T396227. Very pleasant, good food; also farmhouse accommodation and camping.

Frutillar Bajo *p812*

AL-A Ayacara, Av Philippi 1215, T421550, www.hotelayacara.cl. Beautiful rooms with lake view, welcoming, have a pisco sour in the library in the evening.

AL-A Hostal Cinco Robles, 1 km north of Frutillar Bajo, T421351, www.cinco-robles.com. Small, pleasant large grounds with views and private beach. With breakfast, restaurant, parking, Wi-Fi.

A Residenz/Café am See, Av Philippi 539, T421539, www.hotelamsee.cl. Good breakfast, café has German specialities.

A Winkler, Av Philippi 1155, T421388. Much cheaper in low season. Recommended. Also sells cakes from the garage, **Kuchen Laden**.

A-B Casona del 32, Caupolicán 28, T421369. With breakfast, comfortable old house, central heating, English and German spoken, excellent.

A-B Lagune Club, 3 km north of Frutillar Bajo, T330033, www.interpatagonia.com/laguneclub. In an old country house in 16 ha of land, private beach, fishing trips, free pickup from terminal. Disabled-visitor friendly. Also *cabañas*. Good value in dollars.

B Apart Hotel Frutillar, Philippi 1175, T421515, www.aparthotel frutillar.cl. Rooms with views, cable TV, Wi-Fi, good breakfasts, meals available.

B Hostería Trayén, Av Philippi 963, T421346, tttrayen33@hotmail.com. With bath, nice rooms, good breakfast.
B Hosp Vivaldi, Av Philippi 851, T421382. Quiet, comfortable, excellent breakfast and lodging, also family accommodation. Recommended.
C Hosp Angélica, Pérez Rosales 590. *Cabañas* and excellent breakfast.
C Hosp Tía Clarita, Pérez Rosales 648, T421806, hospedaje tiaclarit@hotmail.com. Kitchen facilities, very welcoming, good value.

North of Frutillar Bajo

AL Salzburg, Camino Playa Maqui, T421589, www.salzburg.cl. Excellent, spa, sauna, restaurant, mountain bikes, arranges tours and fishing.

Frutillar Alto

Several good-value places to stay along Carlos Richter (main street). Cheap accommodation in the school, sleeping bag required.
Camping Los Ciruelillos, 2 km south, T339123. Most services. **Playa Maqui**, 7 km north of Frutillar, T339139. Fancy, expensive.

Puerto Varas *p812*

L Bellavista, Pérez Rosales 60, T232011, www.hotelbellavista.cl. 4-star hotel with king-size beds; cheerful, restaurant and bar, overlooking lake and main road, sauna and parking.
L Cabañas del Lago, Klenner 195, T232291, www.cabanasdellago.chi.cl. On Philippi hill overlooking lake, 4-star hotel, good breakfast, bar and restaurant. Also self-catering cabins sleeping 5 (good value for groups), heating, sauna, swimming pools and games room. Often full with package groups.
L-AL Licarayén, San José 114, T232305, www.hotelicarayen.cl. Overlooking lake, comfortable, with gym and sauna, book in season. Recommended.
AL Colonos del Sur Mirador, Estación 505, T235555, www.colonosdelsur.cl. Good views, good restaurant, tea room, decent rooms, but a bit dated compared to its new branch, the 5-star, **LL Gran Colonos del Sur** at Del Salvador 24.
AL Los Alerces, Pérez Rosales 1281, T232060, www.cabanaslosalerces.cl. 4-star hotel, breakfast, cabin complex (price depends on season when rest of hotel is closed), attractive, helpful.
AL-A El Greco, Mirador 134, T233880, www.hotelelgreco.cl. Beautifully refurbished old German mansion, wooden interior and full of artworks, stylish boutique hotel with simple rooms with cable TV. A good choice.
A Weisserhaus, San Pedro 252, T346479, www.weisserhaus.cl. Central, cosy, family-run, with German-style breakfast, good facilities, comfortable, very helpful, internet and Wi-Fi, TV, central heating, very pleasant.
A-B Hostería Outsider, San Bernardo 318, T232910, www.turout.com. With breakfast, some rooms with internet, real coffee, meals, horse riding, rafting, sea kayaking, climbing, German and English spoken. Book ahead in season.
B Amancay, Walker Martínez 564, T232201, cabamancay@chile.com. Also has cabañas for 4, includes breakfast, good, German spoken. Recommended.
B Canales del Sur, Pérez Rosales 1631A, 1km east of town, T717618, www.canalesdelsur.cl. Pleasantly set on the lakeside. Very helpful, family-run, tours arranged, good breakfast, garden, laundry, internet and car hire. Recommended.
B-C Casa Azul, Manzanal 66 y Rosario, T232904, www.casa azul.net. **E** pp in dorms. Lovely building, some rooms with bath, good buffet breakfast with home-made muesli (US$5), kitchen facilities, heating, garden, book exchange, German and English spoken. Reserve in advance in high season. Recommended.
B-C Compass del Sur, Klenner 467, T232044, www.compassdelsur.cl. **E** pp in shared rooms, Chilean-Swedish run, kitchen facilities, internet, breakfast included, cable TV in comfy lounge, helpful, German, English, Swedish spoken. Highly recommended, but reserve in advance in high season.
C Casa Margouya, Santa Rosa 318, T237640, www.margouya.com. **E** in shared rooms, with breakfast. Bright, colourful, kitchen facilities, lots of information, French run, English spoken.
C Ellenhaus, San Pedro 325, T233577, www.ellenhaus.cl. More expensive with bath, **E** pp in dorms, kitchen and laundry facilities, lounge, hospitable, tours, German spoken. Recommended.
C Hosp Carla Minte, Maipo 1010, T232880, www.interpatagonia.com/carlaminte/. Rooms with bath and breakfast in a family home,

excellent breakfast, cable TV, charming, very comfortable, "top class".

C Las Dalias, Santa Rosa 707, T233277, las_dalias@hotmail.com. Quiet family home, cheaper with shared bath, central, good breakfast, parking, German spoken.

C Pathfinder Inn, Walker Martínez 561, T312515, www.pathfinderinn.com. **E** pp in dorms. New small HI-affilliated hostel, with bunkbeds only. Good location, internet.

D Hosp Don Raúl, Salvador 928, T310897, www.informatur.com/hospedajes. Laundry and cooking facilities, spotless, helpful, camping **F** pp. Recommended.

E pp **Patiperros**, Mirador 135, T235050, www.jardinsa.cl. Comfortable hostel, with breakfast.

Camping Wild camping and use of barbecues is not allowed on the lake shore.

Casa Tronador, Tronador y Manzanal, T09-9078 9631. Expensive but central. **CONAF**, Km 49, site at Puerto Oscuro, beneath road to volcano, very good. **Playa Hermosa**, Km 7, T252223, fancy, US$22 per site (negotiate in low season), take own supplies, recommended. **Playa Niklitschek**, Km 8, T338352. Full facilities.

Ensenada *p813*

L Hotel Ensenada, Km 45, T212028, www.hotelensenada.cl. Olde-worlde, price is for ½-board, good food, good view of lake and Osorno Volcano, runs tours, mountain bikes and tennis for guests only, internet.

AL-A Cabañas Brisas del Lago, Km 42, T212 012, www.brisasdellago.cl. Chalets for up to 6 and rooms for up to 3 on beach, good restaurant nearby, supermarket next door. Highly recommended for self-catering.

B Hosp Ensenada, Km 43, T212050, www.hospedajensenada.blogspot.com. Very clean, most rooms with bath, excellent breakfast.

B-C Casa Ko', Km 37, T09-7703 6477, www.casako.com. 3 km off Puerto Varas-Ensenada road, ask bus to drop you at sign or phone in advance for pick-up. Camping **G**, tents for hire. Traditional house, helpful owners, lovely surroundings and views, with breakfast, restaurant, internet, book exchange, laundry service. Plenty of activities plus programme for artists, potographers, musicians, etc.

Camping **Montaña**, central Ensenada. Fully equipped, nice beach sites. Also at Playa Larga, 1 km further east, and at Puerto Oscuro, 2 km north. **Trauco**, 4 km west, T236262. Large site with shops, fully equipped.

Volcán Osorno *p813*

There are 2 *refugios* (**E**), both of them south of the summit and reached from the southern access road: **La Burbuja**, the former ski-club centre, 14 km north of Ensenada at 1250 m) and **Refugio Teski Ski Club**, www.teskiclub.cl, just below the snowline. Price per person, meals served.

Parque Nacional Vicente Pérez Rosales *p813*

Petrohué

LL Hotel Petrohué, Ruta 225, Km 60, T065-212025, www.petrohue.com. Excellent views, ½-board available, also has cabins, pool, cosy, restaurant, log fires, sauna and heated swimming pool; organizes hiking, fishing and other activities. Albergue in the school in summer. CONAF office can help find cheaper family accommodation.

Peulla

L Natura, T367094, www.hotelnatura.cl. Rooms and suites, disabled facilities, lots of activities offered, breakfast, restaurant.

AL Hotel Peulla, T367094, www.hotel peulla.cl. Including dinner and breakfast, cheaper out of season. Beautiful setting by the lake and mountains, restaurant and bar, expensive meals, cold in winter, often full of tour groups (older partner of Natura).

D pp **Res Palomita**, 50 m west of Hotel Peulla. ½-board, family-run, simple, comfortable but small, shared rooms, separate shower, book ahead in season, lunches, expensive tours.

Camping Camping wild and picnicking in the national park is forbidden. At Petrohué on far side beside the lake, no services, cold showers, locals around the site sell fresh bread (local fishermen will ferry you across). At Peulla, opposite CONAF office. Good campsite 1½ hrs' walk east of Peulla, take food. A small shop in Peulla sells basic goods, including fruit and veg.

Seno de Reloncaví *p813*

Ralún

Lodging is available with families and at restaurant **Navarrito** (**D**, basic) and **E** pp **Posada Campesino** (very friendly, clean and simple, without breakfast).

Cochamó

A Campo Aventura (San Bernadino 318, Puerto Varas) T/F065-232910, www.campo-aventura.com. 4 km south of Cochamó in Valle Rio Cochamó, full board available (great breakfast), local food, and very fresh milk from their own cow, camping **F**. Kitchen, sauna, book exchange. Also a renovated mountain house at their other base in the valley of La Junta. They specialize in horseback and trekking between the Reloncaví Estuary and the Argentine border, 2-10 days.

C-D Cochamó, T216212. Basic but friendly and clean, often full with salmon farm workers, good meals. Next door is **D Mercado Particular Sabin**, one of several other *pensiones*.

D Edicar, on seafront by the dock/ramp. With breakfast, hot shower, good value. Recommended.

D Hosp Maura, JJ Molina 12. Beautiful location overlooking the estuary, excellent food, good for kids, highly recommended.

Also a large number of *cabañas*, a campsite and a few eating places.

Puelo

Basic lodging is available at the restaurant or with families – try Roberto and Olivia Telles, no bath/shower, meals on request, or Ema Hernández Maldona; 2 restaurants.

Eating

Puerto Octay *p812*

ΨΨ El Rancho del Espanta-Pajaros, 6 km south on the road to Frutillar, T339141. In a converted barn with wonderful views over the lake, serves all kind of spit roasted meat. All-you-can-eat, with salad bar and drinks included. Also arranges horse riding trips. Recommended.

ΨΨ Fogón de Anita, 1 km out of town, T391455. Mid-priced grill. Also German cakes and pastries.

Ψ Restaurante Baviera, Germán Wulf 582. Cheap and good, salmon and *cazuelas*.

Frutillar Bajo *p812*

ΨΨ Andes, Philippi 1057. Good set menus and à la carte.

Ψ Casino de Bomberos, Philippi 1060. Upstairs bar/restaurant, memorable painting caricaturing the firemen in action (worth studying while awaiting your meal), good value.

Cafés

Many German-style cafés and tea-rooms on C Philippi (the lakefront) eg the **Salón de Te Trayén**, see Sleeping.

Puerto Varas *p812*

ΨΨΨ-ΨΨ Mediterráneo, Santa Rosa 068, T237268. On the lakefront, international and local food, interesting varied menu, often full and pricier than of late.

ΨΨ Di Carusso, San Bernardo 318. Italian trattoria, good fresh pasta dishes on Fri. Recommended.

ΨΨ Dominga Patagonia, Walker Martínez 551, T238981. Interesting fusion cuisine with Peruvian elements, cosy, generous *pisco sours*. Recommended.

ΨΨ La Olla, Ruta 225, 4 east of town towards Ensenada, T234605. Good, popular for seafood, fish and meat, traditional Chilean cuisine. Recommended.

ΨΨ-Ψ Donde El Gordito, downstairs in market. Good range of meat dishes, no set menu.

Cafés

Café Danés, Del Salvador 441. Coffee and cakes.

Punto Café, Del Salvador 348. Cybercafé, bar and art gallery.

Ensenada *p813*

Most eating places close off season. There are a few pricey shops. Take your own provisions.

ΨΨΨ Latitude 42, **Yan Kee Way** resort, T212030. Expensive, excellent and varied cuisine, very good quality wine list. Lake views.

Ψ Canta Rana is recommended for bread and küchen.

Activities and tours

Puerto Varas *p812*

Horse riding **Quinta del Lago**, Km 25 on road to Ensenada, T330193, www.quintadellago.com. All levels catered for, US$35-85 for 2-5 hrs, also has accommodation. See also **Campo Aventura**, below.

Kayak **Al Sur**, Del Salvador 100, T232300, www.alsurexpeditions.com. Sea-kayak, rafting and trekking tours, good camping equipment, English spoken, official tour operators to Parque Pumalín.

Ko'kayak, San Bernardo 318 and Ruta 225, Km 40, T09-9310 5272, www.kokayak.com.

Kayaking and rafting trips, good equipment and after-trip lunch, French/Chilean-run.
Miralejos, San Pedro 311, T234892, www.miralejos.cl. Kayaking in northern Patagonia, also trekking, horse riding and mountaineering. Associated is **Trekking Cochamó**, same address, www.trekkingcochamo.cl, which concentrates on adventure sports in Cochamó.
Yak Expediciones, owner Juan Federico Zuazo (Juanfe), T971623/09-8332 0574, www.yak expediciones.cl. Experienced and safe kayaking trips on lakes and sea, especially recommended for trips in the fjords of Pumalín, small groups, also runs courses. Frequent good reports.
Ziplining (*canopy*), offered by several operators.

Tour operators
Most tours operate in season only (1 Sep-15 Apr).
Aqua Motion, San Pedro 422, T232747, www.aquamotion.cl. Agency for trekking, rafting, climbing, birdwatching and other activities in Chile , German and English spoken.
Campo Aventura Travel Agency, San Bernando 318, T232910, www.campo-aventura.com. Specializes in tailor-made tours and excursions in Chile, Argentina, Bolivia and Peru, including 1-, 3- and 10-day trips on horseback (see above under Cochamó, Sleeping).

Seno de Reloncaví: Cochamó *p814*
See **www.secretpatagonia.cl** for a group of operators who specialise in the area.
Sebastián Contreras C Morales, T216220, is a recommended independent guide who offers tours on horseback and hires out horses.

Transport

Puerto Octay *p812*
Bus To **Osorno** every 20 mins, US$3; to **Frutillar** (1 hr, US$1.50), **Puerto Varas** (2 hrs) and **Puerto Montt** (3 hrs, US$5) **Thaebus**, 5 a day. Around the east shore: to **Las Cascadas** (34 km), Mon-Fri 1730, returns next day 0700.

Frutillar Bajo *p812*
Bus Most leave from the small bus terminal at Alessandri y Richter in Frutillar Alto. To **Puerto Varas** (US$1.50) and **Puerto Montt** (US$2), frequent, **Full Express**. To **Osorno**, **Turismosur** 1½ hrs, US$3. To **Puerto Octay**, **Thaebus**, 6 a day, US$1.50.

Puerto Varas *p812*
Bus The bus terminal is on the northern outskirts of town, take a colectivo or taxi to the centre. To **Santiago**, US$30-75, several companies, 12 hrs. To **Puerto Montt**, 30 mins, **Thaebus** and **Full Express** every 15 mins, US$1.50, 30 mins. Same frequency to **Frutillar** (US$1.50, 30 mins) and **Osorno** (US$4, 1 hr). To **Valdivia** US$7, 3 hrs. To **Bariloche**, by lakes route, see above. Minibuses to **Ensenada** leave from San Bernardo y Martínez, hourly.

Parque Nacional Vicente Pérez Rosales *p813*
Minibuses Every 30 mins to Petrohué from Puerto Montt and Puerto Varas in summer (US$4, 1¼ hrs from Puerto Varas), much less frequent off season. Last bus to Ensenada at 1800.
Ferry See page 819 for **Cruce Andino** crossing.

Seno de Reloncaví *p814*
Bus From Puerto Montt to **Ralún**, **Cochamó** and **Puelo**, 5 a day via Puerto Varas and Ensenada, with **Bohle** and **Fierro**: US$4.50 to Ralún, US$7 to Cochamó (2½ hrs). **Boats** In summer boats sail up the Estuary from Angelmó. The **Sernatur** office in Puerto Montt has details of scheduled trips.

Directory

Frutillar Bajo *p812*
Useful services **Banco Santander**, on the lakeside, has Redbanc ATM.

Puerto Varas *p812*
Banks Redbanc ATMs at several banks. **Turismo Los Lagos**, Del Salvador 257 (Galería Real, local 11). Daily 0830-1330, 1500-2100, Sun 0930-1330, accepts TCs, good rates.
Internet and telephone Several places in the centre. **Post offices** San José y San Pedro; Del Salvador y Santa Rosa.

Puerto Montt and Chiloé

➔ *Phone code: 065. Colour map 8, C1. Population: 160,000.*

Just 20 minutes south of Puerto Varas, and 1,016 km south of Santiago, Puerto Montt is the gateway to the shipping lanes to the south, namely the island of Chiloé and the wilds of Patagonia. It's a rapidly growing, disordered modern city, developing in line with a boom in salmon fishing. Angelmó, a fishing port 2 km west, is most popular with visitors for its seafood restaurants and handicraft shops, but is not worth a visit of more than a day or two.

Puerto Montt

Ins and outs

Tourist offices **Puerto Montt**: For information and town maps, go to the kiosk just southeast of the Plaza de Armas run by the municipality ⓘ *T261823 (open till 1800 on Sat), or the bus station, T261848.* See www.puerto monttchile.cl for information on the web. **Sernatur** is in the Intendencia Regional ⓘ *Av Décima Región 480 (p 2), T256999, infoloslagos@sernatur.cl, 0830-1300, 1430-1730, Mon-Thu, 0830-1630 Fri*, for regional information. CONAF is at Ochogavia 458, T486102, loslagos@conaf.cl, but cannot supply information on national parks. Provincial office: Urmeneta 977, p 5 (Edif Isla del Rey), T486400. **Automóvil Club de Chile** ⓘ *Esmeralda 70, T350390, gpuertomontt@automovilclub.cl*, includes car rental.

Sights

The capital of X Región (Los Lagos) was founded in 1853 as part of the German colonization of the area. Good views over the city and bay are offered from outside the Intendencia Regional on Avenida X Region. The port is used by fishing boats and coastal vessels, and is the departure point for vessels to Puerto Chacabuco, Laguna San Rafael and for the long haul south to Puerto Natales. A paved road runs 55 km southwest to Pargua, where there is a ferry service to Chiloé.

The **Iglesia de los Jesuitas** on Gallardo, dating from 1872, has a fine blue-domed ceiling; behind it on a hill is the campanario (clock tower). **Museo Regional Juan Pablo II** ⓘ *Portales 997 near the bus terminal, daily 1030-1800, US$1*, documents local history and has a fine collection of historic photos of the city; also memorabilia of the Pope John Paul II's visit in 1988. The fishing port of **Angelmó**, 2 km west, has become a tourist centre with seafood restaurants and handicraft shops (reached by Costanera bus along Portales and by colectivos Nos 2, 3, 20 from the centre, US$0.30).

The wooded **Isla Tenglo**, reached by launch from Angelmó (US$2 each way), is a favourite place for picnics. Magnificent view from the summit. The island is famous for its curantos, served by restaurants in summer. Boat trips round the island from Angelmó last 30 minutes, US$9. **Parque Provincial Lahuen Nadi** (US$3) contains some ancient trees in swampland, more accessible than some of the remoter forests. Take the main road to the airport, which leads off Ruta 5. After 5 km, turn right (north) and follow the signs. West of Puerto Montt the Río Maullin, which drains Lago Llanquihue, has some attractive waterfalls and good fishing (salmon). At the mouth of the river is the little fishing village of **Maullin**, founded in 1602.

To Argentina via Lago Todos Los Santos

This popular but ever more expensive route to Bariloche, involving ferries across Lago Todos Los Santos, Lago Frías and Lago Nahuel Huapi is outstandingly beautiful whatever the season, though the mountains are often obscured by rain and heavy cloud. The route is via Puerto Varas, Ensenada and Petrohué falls (20 minutes stop) to Petrohué, where it connects with catamaran service across Lago Todos Los Santos to Peulla. Lunch stop in Peulla two hours (lunch not included in fare: Hotels Natura and Peulla are expensive, see page 816 for alternatives). Chilean customs in Peulla, followed by a 2-hour bus ride through the Paso Pérez Rosales to Argentine customs in Puerto Frías, 20 minute boat trip across Lago Frías to Puerto Alegre and 15-minute bus from Puerto Alegre to Puerto Blest, where there is a long wait (and poor food). From Puerto Blest it is a beautiful one hour catamaran trip along Lago Nahuel Huapi to Puerto Pañuelo (Llao Llao), from where there is a 30-minute bus journey to Bariloche (bus drops passengers at hotels, camping sites or in town centre). From 1 May to 30 August this trip is done over two days with overnight stay in Peulla at Hotel Peulla or Hotel Natura. (You may break the journey at any point and continue next day.) The route is operated by **Cruce Andino**, Puerto Varas, T065-236150, www.cruceandino.com. Fares are given under Transport, below.

Sea routes south of Puerto Montt

To Puerto Natales The dramatic 1,460 km journey first goes through Seno Reloncaví and Canal Moraleda. From Bahía Anna Pink along the coast and then across the Golfo de Penas to Bahía Tarn it is a 12-17 hours sea crossing, usually rough. The journey continues through Canal Messier, Angostura Inglesa and the Concepción, Sarmiento and White channels. It takes just under 4 days. Navimag's vessel *Evangelistas*, a functional but comfortable 123-m-long freight and passenger roll-on roll-off ferry, makes the journey. It may call at Puerto Chacabuco en route south and north, and stops off Puerto Edén on Isla Wellington (one hour south of Angostura Inglesa). This is a fishing village with one hospedaje (20 beds), three shops, scant provisions, one off-licence, one café, and a *hospedaje* for up to 20 people (open intermittantly). Population is 180, including five carabineros and the few remaining Alacaluf. It is the drop-off point for exploring Isla Wellington, which is largely untouched, with stunning mountains. If stopping,

Puerto Montt

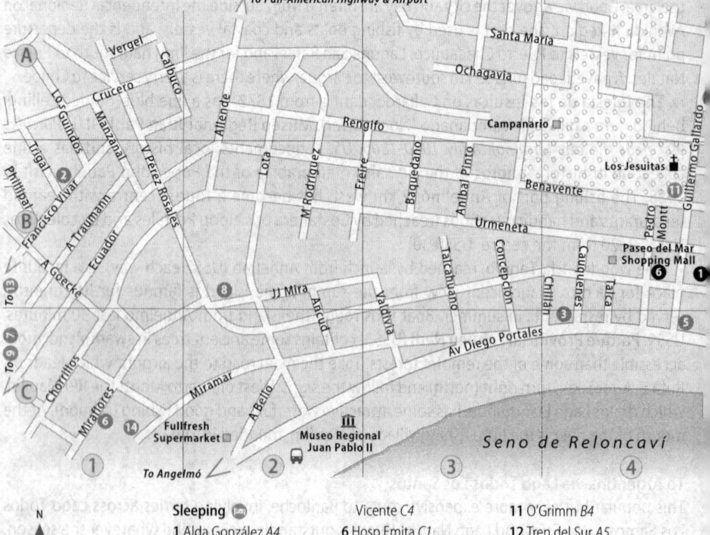

Sleeping
1 Alda González *A4*
2 Casa Perla *B1*
3 Club Presidente *C4*
4 Gran Hotel Don Luis *B5*
5 Gran Hotel Don Vicente *C4*
6 Hosp Emita *C1*
7 Hosp Rocco *C1*
8 Hostal Pacífico *B2*
9 Hostal Suizo *C1*
10 Millahue *C6*
11 O'Grimm *B4*
12 Tren del Sur *A5*
13 Vista al Mar *B1*
14 Vista Hermosa *C1*

200 metres
200 yards

take food; maps (not very accurate) available in Santiago. Passengers on the *Evangelistas* may disembark for 2½ hours on the third morning to walk around the village. Between November and March, the *Evangelistas* also visits the Pío XI, or Bruggen Glacier, the largest in South America, for an hour on the southward journey. Going north it stops at the Amalia or Brujo Glacier (depending on weather conditions) on the second evening. The service is not very reliable so always check that it is running.

Puerto Montt listings

For Sleeping and Eating price codes and other relevant information, see Essentials, pages 38-40.

Sleeping

Puerto Montt *p819, map p820*
Accommodation is expensive in season, much cheaper off season. Check with the tourist office.

L Gran Hotel Don Vicente, Av Portales 450, T432900, www.granhoteldonvicente.cl. With breakfast, business class, excellent restaurant, seafood. Recommended.

L-AL Gran Hotel Don Luis, Urmeneta y Quillota, T259001, www.hoteldonluis.cl.

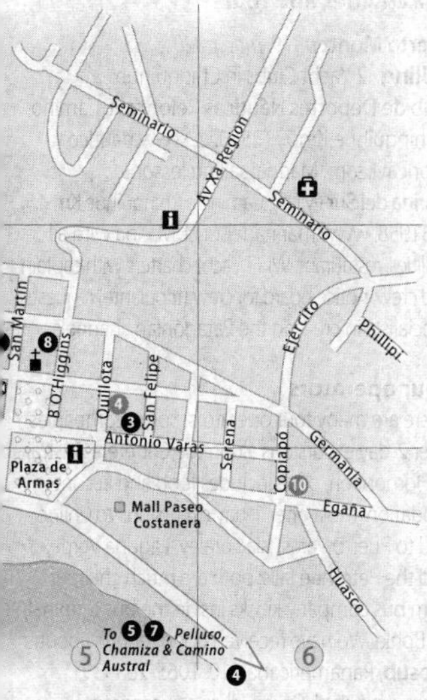

Eating
1 Cafés Central and Real *B4*
2 Café Haussman *B5*
3 Club Alemán *B5*
4 Club de Yates *C5*
5 Cotele *C5*
6 Dino *B4*
7 Pazos *C5*
8 Polo Sur *B5*

Comfortable 4-star, gym, sauna, business centre, etc.

AL Club Presidente, Av Portales 664, T251666, www.presidente.cl. 4-star, with breakfast, very comfortable, also suites. Recommended.

AL O'Grimm, Gallardo 211, T252845, www.ogrimm.com. With breakfast, cosy, pleasant rooms with lounge area, central, restaurant with occasional live music.

A-B Tren del Sur, Santa Teresa 643, T343939, www.trendelsur.cl. "Boutique" *hostal* with pleasant public areas, objects recycled from the old railway, some rooms without windows, buffet breakfast, café, heating, Wi-Fi, very helpful English-speaking owner.

B Hostal Pacífico, J J Mira 1088, T256229, www.hostalpacifico.cl. Breakfast included, cable TV, parking, comfortable, some rooms a bit cramped. Discounts for foreign tourists.

B Millahue, Copiapó 64, T253829, www.hotelmillahue.cl. With breakfast, modern but slightly run down, good restaurant.

B-C Hostal Suizo, Independencia 231, T/F252640, rossyoelckers@yahoo.es. **E** pp in shared rooms, some rooms with bath. With small breakfast, painting and Spanish classes, German and Italian spoken, Spanish classes. Convenient for Navimag ferry.

C Alda González, Gallardo 552, T253334. With or without bath, with breakfast, cooking facilities, popular, German and English spoken, near the Plaza de Armas. Recommended.

C Hosp Emita, Miraflores 1281, T250 725, hospedaje_emita@hotmail.com. Some rooms with bath, includes breakfast with homemade bread, safe, near the bus terminal.

C Hosp Rocco, Pudeto 233, T272897, www.hospedajerocco.cl. **D-E** in dorms. Renovated, breakfast, real coffee, English spoken, laundry, quiet residential area, convenient for Navimag. Recommended.

C Vista al Mar, Vivar 1337, T255625, www.hospedajevistaalmar.unlugar.com. Helpful, welcoming, good breakfast, phone for a lift from bus station.
C Vista Hermosa, Miramar 1486, T319600, http://hostalvistahermosa.cl/. With breakfast, very good, ask for front room for best views (10 mins' walk uphill from terminal), use of kitchen, Wi-Fi, also has a fully equipped cabin.
C-D Casa Perla, Trigal 312, T262104, www.casaperla.com. **F** pp in shared rooms. With breakfast, French, English spoken, helpful, use of kitchen, meals, Spanish classes offered off season, laundry, internet, pleasant garden, good meeting place. Recommended.
Camping **Camping Municipal** at Chinquihue, 10 km west (bus service), Oct-Apr, fully equipped with tables, seats, barbecue, toilets and showers; small shop, no kerosene. Others on this road: **Los Alamos**, Km 15, T256067.

Eating

Puerto Montt *p819, map p820*
Local specialities include *picoroco al vapor*, a giant barnacle whose flesh looks and tastes like crab, and curanto. Cheap food in Puerto Montt bus terminal.

In Angelmó, there are several dozen small, seafood restaurants in the old fishing port, past the fish market, very popular, lunches only; ask for *té blanco* (white wine – they are not legally allowed to serve wine).

Other seafood restaurants in Chinquihue, west of Angelmó.
TTT Club de Yates, Juna Soler s/n, Costanera east of centre, T284000. Excellent seafood, fine views from a pier.
TTT-TT Cotele, Juan Soler s/n, Pelluco, 4 km east, T278000. Only serves beef, but serves it as well as anywhere in southern Chile. Recommended. Reservations advised.
TTT Club Alemán, Varas 264, T252551. Old fashioned, good food and wine.
TTT-TT Pazos, Pelluco, T252552. Serves the best *curanto* in the Puerto Montt area.
TT Café Haussman, San Martín y Urmeneta. German cakes, beer and *crudos*. Recommended.
TT Dino, Varas 550. Restaurant upstairs, snacks downstairs (try the lemon juice), often has an all-you-can-eat buffet.
TT Polo Sur (Centro Español), O'Higgins 233. Nice airy upstairs room, good food, good service.
T Café Central, Rancagua 117. Spartan décor, generous portions (sandwiches and *pichangas* – savoury salad snack). Giant TV screen.
T Café Real, Rancagua 137. For *empanadas*, *pichangas*, *congrío frito*, and lunches.

Cafés

Asturias, Angelmó 2448. Often recommended.
Café Plaza, Urmeneta 326. Good location, pool table, nice atmosphere.

Shopping

Puerto Montt *p819, map p820*
Woollen goods and Mapuche-designed rugs can be bought at roadside stalls in Angelmó and on Portales opposite the bus terminal. Prices much the same as on Chiloé, but quality often lower.
Supermarkets **Fullfresh**, opposite bus terminal, open 0900-2200 daily. Also in the **Paseo del Mar** shopping mall, Talca y A Varas, and in the old railway station. **Paseo Costanera**, is a mall on the seafront.

Activities and tours

Puerto Montt *p819, map p820*
Sailing 2 Yacht Clubs in Chinquihue:
Club de Deportes Náuticas Reloncaví, Camino a Chinquihue Km 7, T255022, www.nauticoreloncavi.com. Marina, sailing lessons.
Marina del Sur (MDS), Camino a Chinquihue Km 4.5, T251958, www.marinadelsur.cl. Marina with all facilities, restaurant, Wi-Fi, yacht charters with captain and crew, notice board for crew (tripulante) requests, specialists in cruising the Patagonian channels.

Tour operators

There are many tour operators. Some companies offer 2-day excursions along the Carretera Austral to Hornopirén, price includes food and accommodation. Most offer 1-day excursions to Chiloé and to Puerto Varas, Isla Loreley, Laguna Verde, and the Petrohué falls: both are much cheaper from bus company kiosks inside the bus terminal, eg Bohle. We have received good reports about:
Ecosub, Panamericana 510, T065-263939, www.ecosub.cl. Scuba-diving excursions.
Eureka Turismo, Gallardo 65, T065-250412, www.chile-travel.com/eureka.htm. Helpful, German and English spoken.
Travellers, Gral Bulnes 1009, T262099, www.travellers.cl. Open Mon-Fri 0900-1330,

1500-1830, Sat 0900-1400 for booking for Navimag ferry Puerto Edén to Puerto Natales and other cruises and packages country-wide, bespoke incoming tours, car hire, English-run.

Transport

Puerto Montt *p819, map p820*

Air El Tepual Airport is 13 km northwest of town, T486200. **ETM** bus from terminal (T294294, www.busesetm.cl) 1½ hrs before departure, US$3; also meets incoming flights. **ETM** minibus service to/from hotels, US$7. Taxi US$12. **LAN** and **Sky** have several flights daily to **Santiago**, **Balmaceda** (for Coihaique) and **Punta Arenas**. In Jan, Feb and Mar you may well be told that flights are booked up, but cancellations may be available from the airport. To Chaitén, see page 836.

Bus Terminal (very crowded, disorganized, beware hotel touts and thieves) on sea front at Portales y Lota, has telephone, restaurants, casa de cambio (left luggage, US$2.50 per item for 24 hrs). To **Puerto Varas** (US$1.50), **Llanquihue**, **Frutillar** (US$2), **Puerto Octay** (US$5) and **Osorno** (US$6) minibuses every few mins, **Expreso Puerto Varas**, **Thaebus** and **Full Express**. To **Ensenada** and **Petrohué**, **Buses JM** several daily. To **Pucón**, US$16, 6 hrs. To **Temuco** US$10-18, to **Valdivia**, US$7.50, 3½ hrs. **Concepción**, US$17-30. To **Santiago**, *clásico* 12 hrs, US$30-75, several companies including **Tur-Bus**, very good, and **Tas Choapa Royal Class**. To **Punta Arenas**, **Pacheco**, **Turibus** and others, 1-3 a week, about US$80 depending on company (bus goes through Argentina via Bariloche, take US$ cash for Argentina expenses en route), 32-38 hrs. Also take plenty of food for this "nightmare" trip. Book well in advance in Jan-Feb and check if you need a multiple-entry Chilean visa. Also book any return journey before setting out. For services to **Chiloé**, see page 825.

To Argentina via Lago Todos Los Santos The route is operated only by **Cruce Andino**, www.cruceandino.com. Bus from Puerto Montt daily at 0745; the fare is a hefty US$230 for the one-day trip. From 1 May to 31 Aug the trip takes 2 days, with overnight in Peulla (Hotels **Natura** or **Peulla**, not included). Note that the trip may be cancelled if the weather is poor; difficulty in obtaining a refunds or assistance have been reported. If you take the boat from Petrohué to Peulla, you can cross to Argentina and carry on to Bariloche (check on the availability of public transport, bus and boat, across the border). In high season you must book ahead.

Buses to Argentina via Osorno and the Puyehue pass Daily services to Bariloche on this route via Osorno, 7 hrs, are run by **Cruz del Sur, Río de la Plata, Tas Choapa** and **Bus Norte**, US$26. Out of season, services are reduced. Buy tickets for international buses from the bus terminal. Book well in advance in Jan and Feb; ask for a seat on the right hand side for the best views.

Car hire **Automóvil Club de Chile**, address above, and at airport. **Autovald**, Sector Cardenal, Pasaje San Andrés 60, T256043, www.autovald.cl, cheap rates. **Egartur**, Benavente 575, loc. 3, T257336, www.egartur.cl, good service, recommended, will deliver your car to your hotel for free. **Full Famas**, Portales 506, T258060 and at airport, T263750. Helpful, good value, has vehicles that can be taken to Argentina. **Salfa Sur**, Pilpilco 800, also at Airport, T065-290224, www.salfasur.cl. Good value. See Essentials for international agencies.

Ferry To **Puerto Natales**: The **Evangelistas** or **Puerto Edén** of **Navimag** (Naviera Magallanes SA), Terminal Transbordadores, Angelmó 2187, T432300, sail to Puerto Natales throughout the year on Fri at 1600, taking about 3 days, arriving Mon. It returns on Tue 0600, arriving Puerto Montt Fri morning. Check-in in Puerto Montt must be done 5 hrs before departure. In Puerto Natales check-in is 1300 to 2100 on Mon; dinner is not included. Confirm times and booking 48 hrs in advance. The fare, including meals, ranges from US$420 pp in C berth (sheets are extra, take your own or a sleeping bag), to US$1,100-1,250 pp in double cabin (high season prices, Nov-Mar; fares 10-20% lower Apr-Oct). First class is recommended, but hardly luxurious. Check the website, www.navimag.cl, for discounts and special offers. Cars are carried for US$435, motor-cycles for US$132. Payment by credit card or foreign currency is accepted in all Navimag offices. The vessel is a mixed cargo/ passenger ferry which includes live animals in the cargo. On board is a book exchange, video films are shown, there are guided talks and information sessions and you can play bingo. Food is good and plentiful and includes vegetarian options at lunch and dinner. Passengers tend to take their own food and alcohol. Standards of service and comfort vary, depending on the number of passengers and weather conditions. Take sea-sickness tablets, or buy them on board (you'll be advised when to take them!). **Booking** Tickets can be booked through many travel agencies, **Navimag** offices throughout the country, or direct from www.navimag.com. Book well in advance for departures between mid-Dec and mid-Mar especially for the voyage south (Puerto Natales to Puerto Montt is less heavily booked). It is well worth going to the port on the day of departure if you have no ticket. Departures are frequently delayed by weather conditions – or even advanced. For details and next season's fares see Navimag's website. **Note** It is cheaper to fly and quicker to go by bus via Argentina. The route does not pass Laguna San Rafael.

To **Puerto Chacabuco**: **Navimag**'s ferries **Evangelistas** or **Puerto Edén** sail twice a week to Puerto Chacabuco (80 km west of Coyhaique). The cruise to Puerto Chacabuco lasts about 24 hrs. The high-season fares are from US$78-118 for bunks, US$178 pp in most expensive double cabin, cars US$260, motorcycles US$113, bicycles US$57. There is a canteen; long queues if the boat is full. Food is expensive so take your own. The same vessels go to Laguna San Rafael from Puerto Montt, on specific dates depending on the time of year. It is a 5-day, 4-night trip, with activities, all meals and a boat trip to the glacier. Accommodation ranges from US$578 to US$1,178 pp (in double cabin). You can also do the return trip from Puerto Chacabuco, or Puerto Montt-Laguna San Rafael-Puerto Chacabuco (www.navimag.com, for schedules, fares and dates).

To **Laguna San Rafael**: The m/n *Skorpios 2* of **Skorpios Cruises**, Augusto Leguía Norte 118, Santiago, www.skorpios.cl, T02-477 1900, leaves Puerto Montt for a luxury cruise to San Rafael, via Chiloé and Puerto Aguirre. The fare varies according to season, type of cabin and number of occupants: double cabin from US$1,400 pp. Generally service is excellent, the food superb, and at the glacier, you can chip ice off the face for your whisky. After the visit to San Rafael the ship visits Quitralco Fjord where there are thermal pools and boat trips on the fjord, and Chiloé. From Puerto Montt it's a 7-day/6-night cruise. The *Skorpios 3* sails from Puerto Natales to Glaciar Pío XI in the Campo de Hielo Sur and Puerto Edén, 5 days, fares from US$2,000 pp, double cabin. An optional first day includes a visit to Torres del Paine. **Patagonia Connection SA**, Fidel Oteíza 1921, of 1006, Providencia, Santiago, T02-225 6489, www.patagonia-connection.com. Operates Patagonia Express, a catamaran which runs from Puerto Chacabuco to Laguna San Rafael via Termas de Puyuhuapi, see page 837. Tours lasting 3 to 5 days start at Balmaceda airport and go to Puyuhuapi via Queulat by bus. Longer tours include the catamaran service from the Termas de Puyuhuapi to Laguna San Rafael, returning via Puerto Aisén. High season mid Nov-18 Mar, low season mid-Oct-mid Nov and 19 Mar-end Apr. High season price for a double cabin on the San Rafael trip: US$1,760 pp. Highly recommended.

To **Chaitén**, via Ayacara, **Naviera Austral** runs this service, as well as Hornopirén-Chaitén, but check with the company first to see if it is running: Angelmó 2187, T270430, www.navieraustral.cl.

Directory

Puerto Montt *p819, map p820*

Airline offices Aerotaxis del Sur, A Varas 70, T252523, www.aerotaxisdelsur.cl. **Cielo Mar**, Quillota 245 loc 1, T266666. **LAN**, O'Higgins 167, T600-526 2000. **Sky**, Benavente 405, T437 557, or 600-600 2828 for information. **Banks** Many ATMS in the city. Commission charges vary widely. **Afex**, Portales 516 and at airport. **Inter**, Talca 84. For cash, TCs, no commission on Amex. **Note** The last city on the mainland with Visa ATM before Coyhaique. Obtain Argentine pesos before leaving Chile. There is a cambio at the bus terminal. **Consulates** **Argentina**, Pedro Montt 160, p 6, T253996, cpmontt@ embargentina.cl, quick visa service. **Germany**, Varas 525, of 306, T252828, c.aleman_ptomontt@surnet.cl. Tue-Wed 0930-1200. **Netherlands**, Isla Tenglo 206, Terrazas De Angelmó, T257728, e.hoelck@ entelchile.net. **Spain**, O'Higgins 233, p 3, T252855, v.consuladopmontt@gmail.com. **UK**, Dione 1030, Lomas de Reloncaví, T282676. **Cycle repairs** Kiefer, Pedro Montt 129, T253079. 3 shops on Urmeneta, none very well stocked. **Internet and telephones** City centre and Av Angelmó. **Motorcycle repairs** Miguel Schmuch, Urmeneta 985, T258877. **Post offices** Rancagua 126. 0830-1830 (Mon-Fri), 0830-1300 (Sat).

Chiloé → *Colour map 9, A1.*

The island of Chiloé is 250 km long, 50 km wide and covers 9,613 sq km. Thick forests cover most of its western side. The hillsides in summer are a patchwork quilt of wheat fields and dark green plots of potatoes. The population is 116,000 and most live on the sheltered eastern side. The west coast, exposed to strong Pacific winds, is wet for most of the year. The east coast and the offshore islands are drier, though frequently cloudy. The culture of Chiloé has been strongly influenced by isolation from Spanish colonial currents, the mixture of early Spanish settlers and indigenous people and a dependence on the sea. Religious and secular architecture, customs and crafts, combined with delightful landscapes, all contribute to Chiloé's uniqueness.

Ins and outs

Getting there Regular ferries cross the straits of Pargua between Pargua, 55 km southwest of Puerto Montt on the mainland, and Chacao on Chiloé. Seals, birds and occasionally dolphins can be seen. **Buses**: Puerto Montt to Pargua, frequent, US$3, one hour, though most buses go through to Ancud (3½-4 hours) and Castro. Transport to the island is dominated by **Cruz del Sur**, who also own Trans Chiloé and have their own ferries. Cruz del Sur run frequent services from Puerto Montt to Ancud and Castro, six a day to Chonchi and Quellón; their fares are highest but they are faster (their buses have priority over cars on Cruz del Sur ferries). **Fares from Puerto Montt**: to Ancud, **Cruz del Sur** US$7, **Queilén Bus** (independent company), US$6; to Castro, Cruz del Sur US$9, Trans Chiloé US$9 and Queilén Bus, US$6; to Chonchi, US$7, Quellón, US$12. There are direct bus services from Santiago, Valdivia and Temuco to Chiloé. Buses drive on to the ferry (passengers may leave the bus). **Ferries** About 24 crossings daily, 30-minute crossing, operated by several companies including Transmarchilay and Cruz del Sur; all ferries carry buses, private vehicles (cars US$16 one way, motorcycles US$11, bicycles US$3, more expensive at night) and foot passengers (US$1). ▸▸ *See also Transport, page 832.*

Background

The original inhabitants of Chiloé were the Chonos, who were pushed south by the Huilliches invading from the north. The first Spanish sighting was by Francisco de Ulloa in 1553 and in 1567 Martín Ruiz de Gamboa took possession of the islands on behalf of Spain. The small Spanish settler population divided the indigenous population and their lands between them. The rising of the Mapuche after 1598 which drove the Spanish out of the mainland south of the Río Biobío left the Spanish community on Chiloé (some 200 settlers in 1600) isolated. During the 17th century, for instance, it was served by a single annual ship from Lima.

The islanders were the last supporters of the Spanish Crown in South America. When Chile rebelled the last of the Spanish Governors fled to the island and, in despair, offered it to Britain. Canning, the British Foreign Secretary, turned the offer down. The island finally surrendered in 1826.

The availability of wood and the lack of metals have left their mark on the island. Some of the earliest churches were built entirely of wood, using wooden pegs instead of nails. These early churches often displayed some German influence as a result of the missionary work of Bavarian Jesuits. Two features of local architecture often thought to be traditional are in fact late 19th century in origin. The replacement of thatch with thin tiles (*tejuelas*) made from alerce (larch) wood, which are nailed to the frame and roof in several distinctive patterns, and *palafitos* or wooden houses built on stilts over the water.

The island is also famous for its traditional handicrafts, notably woollens and basketware, which can be bought in the main towns and on some of the off-shore islands, as well as in Puerto Montt.

Although the traditional mainstays of the economy, fishing and agriculture, are still important, salmon farming has become a major source of employment. Seaweed is harvested for export to Japan. Tourism provides a seasonal income for a growing number of people. Nevertheless, the relatively high birth rate and the shortage of employment in Chiloé have led to regular emigration. See www.chiloe.cl.

Ancud and around → *Phone code: 065. Colour map 9, A1. Population: 30,000.*
Ancud lies on the north coast of Chiloé 34 km west of the Straits of Chacao at the mouth of a great bay, the Golfo de Quetalmahue. Founded in 1767 to guard the shipping route around Cape Horn, it was defended by two fortresses, the Fuerte San Antonio and Fuerte Ahui on the opposite side of the bay. The port is dominated by the **Fuerte San Antonio**, built in 1770, the site of the Spanish surrender of Chiloé to Chilean troops in 1826. Close to it are the ruins of the **Polvorín del Fuerte** (a couple of cannon and a few walls). A lovely 1 km walk north of the fort leads to the secluded beach, **Arena Gruesa**, where public concerts are held in summer. 2 km east is a **mirador** offering good views of the island and across to the mainland, even to the Andes on a clear day. Near the Plaza de Armas is the **Museo Regional** ⓘ *Libertad 370, T622413, www.dibam.cl/sdm_mr_ancud, Tue-Fri 1000-1730, Sat-Sun 1000-1400, US$1.25, reductions for seniors and students*. As well as an interesting collection on the early history of Chiloé, it has good shops and café. **Tourist office**: Sernatur ⓘ *Libertad 665, T622665, infochiloe@sernatur.cl. Mon-Thu 0830-1730, Fri 0830-1630, Sat-Sun (summer only) 0900-1800*. Ask here about the Agro Turismo programme, staying with farming families.

To **Faro Corona**, the lighthouse on Punta Corona, 34 km west, along the beach, offers good views with birdlife and dolphins (2-3 buses daily, though none is the right time for seeing birds). The best time of day to see birds is early morning or late afternoon/evening. The duty officer may give a tour, recommended. To **Pumillahue** ⓘ *27 km southwest, 2-3 buses daily, or take a tour, taxi, or or hitch*, where nearby there is a Humboldt and Magellanic penguin colony from October to late March (the birds are seen early morning or late afternoon). Hire a fishing boat to see it, US$10 per person for a guided tour.

Chepu (*Population: 230*, www.chepu.cl) on the coast southwest of Ancud (38 km) is famed for its sea-fishing and the drowned forest (Valley of Dead Trees, devastated by a tsunami in 1960) and environment of its river. There is a wide range of birdlife and good opportunites for horseriding and boat trips here. The **Mirador de Chepu** information centre gives views of the wetlands, information about the flora, fauna and tourist options, has a café and rents kayaks. Chepu is also the northern entry for the Parque Nacional Chiloé, see page 828.

Ancud to Castro
There are two routes: direct along Route 5, the Pan-American Highway, crossing rolling hills, forest and agricultural land, or via the east coast along unpaved roads passing through small farming and fishing communities. The two main towns along the coastal route, **Quemchi** (*Population: 1,700; basic accommodation, small tourist office in the plaza*) and Dalcahue, can also be reached by roads branching off Route 5.

Dalcahue (*Population: 5,000*), 74 km south of Ancud, is more easily reached from Castro, 30 km further south. It is one of the main ports for boats to the offshore islands, including Quinchao and Mechuque. The wooden church on the main plaza dates from the 19th century and, like all the Chilote churches, is a UNESCO World Heritage Site. The market is on Sunday, from 0700 to 1300; good quality. Tourist kiosk in season. There are various basic hotels (**F** pp) and a restaurant. Buses to Castro, hourly, 40 minutes, US$2. Also colectivos to Castro and Achao, US$3.

Quinchao Island
The main settlement on this island is **Achao**, a quiet, pretty fishing village with a market. Its wooden church, built in 1730 and saved by a change of wind from a fire which destroyed much of the town in 1784, is a fine example of Chilote Jesuit architecture. The original construction

was without use of nails. It now contains a small museum, US$1. The tourist office at Serrano y Progreso is open between December and March only (www.islaquinchao.com). There are various hotels (**C-D**) and restaurants.

Chiloé

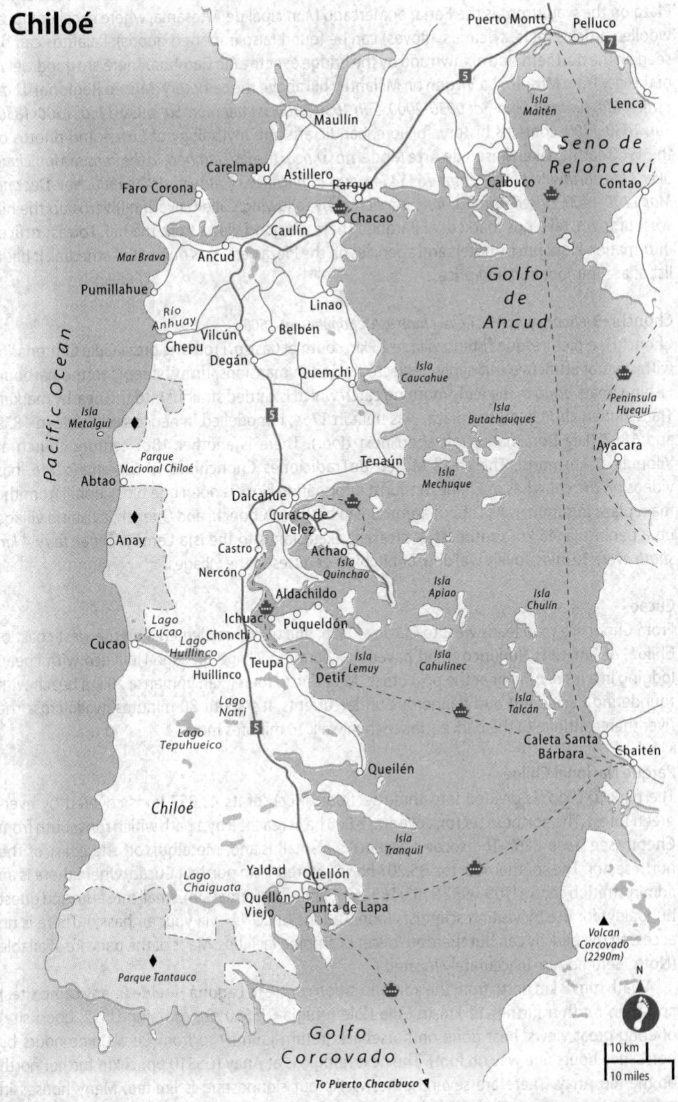

Castro ➔ *Phone code: 065. Colour map 9, A1. Population: 29,000.*
The capital of Chiloé lies on a fjord on the east coast, 88 km south of Ancud. Founded in 1567, the centre is situated on a promontory, from which there is a steep drop to the port. On the Plaza de Armas is the large **Cathedral**, strikingly decorated in lilac and orange, with a splendid wood panelled interior, built by the Italian architect, Eduardo Provosoli in 1906. South of the Plaza on the waterfront is the **Feria**, or Mercado Municipal de Artesanía, where excellent local woollen articles (hats, sweaters, gloves) can be found (also imported goods). Palafitos can be seen on the northern side of town and by the bridge over the Río Gamboa. There are good views of the city from **Mirador La Virgen** on Millantuy hill above the cemetery. **Museo Regional** ⓘ *on Esmeralda, summer Mon-Sat 0930-2000, Sun 1030-1300; winter Mon-Sat 0930-1300, 1500-1830, Sun 1030-1300*, contains history, folklore, handicrafts and mythology of Chiloé and photos of the 1960 earthquake. **Museo de Arte Moderno** ⓘ *near the Río Gamboa, in the Parque Municipal, over 3 km northwest of the centre, T635454, www.mamchiloe.cl, Jan-Feb 1000-1800, Nov-Dec and Mar 1100-1400, closed Apr-Oct, free*, is reached by following Calle Galvarino Riveros up the hill west of town, take bus marked 'Al Parque'. There are good views from the hill. **Tourist office**: Information kiosk run by hotels and agencies on the Plaza de Armas opposite Cathedral. It has a list of accommodation and prices.

Chonchi ➔ *Phone code: 065. Colour map 9, A1. Population: 4,500.*
Chonchi is a picturesque fishing village 25 km south of Castro. From the plaza Calle Centenario, with several attractive but sadly neglected wooden mansions, drops steeply to the harbour. Fishing boats bring in the early morning catch which is carried straight into the nearby market. The wooden church, on the plaza, was built in 1754, remodelled in neoclassical style in 1859 and 1897 (key from handicraft shop next door). There is another 18th century church at Vilopulli, 5 km north. The small **Museo deTradiciones Chonchinas** ⓘ *Centenario 116*, has videos on the churches of Chiloé. A tourist information kiosk is open one block uphill from the main plaza in summer. Ask about agrotourism between Chonchi and Queilén, a fishing village on a peninsula, 46 km southeast. A pleasant excursion is to the **Isla Lemuy** ⓘ *free ferry 4 km south every 30 mins*; lovely walking, or hitching or buses to the villages.

Cucao
From Chonchi a road leads west to Cucao, 40 km, one of two settlements on the west coast of Chiloé. At Km 12 is **Huillinco** (road paved), a charming village on Lago Huillinco with cheap lodging in a *residencial* or at the post office. Near Cucao there is an immense 20 km beach with thundering Pacific surf and dangerous undercurrents. It's about 30 minutes' walk: cross the river then continue to the park entrance then walk 10 minutes more.

Parque Nacional Chiloé
The park ⓘ *US$3*, is divided into three sections. Much of its 43,057 ha is covered by evergreen forest. The northern sector, covering 7,800 ha, is reached by a path which runs south from **Chepu** (see page 826). The second section is a small island, **Metalqui**, off the coast of the north sector. The southern sector, 35,207 ha, is entered 1 km north of Cucao, where there is an administration centre (T09-9932 9193/T532501, limited information), small museum and guest bungalow for use by visiting scientists (applications to CONAF via your embassy). There is no access to the park by car, but there are decent camping facilities. Maps of the park are available (**Note** Refugios are inaccurately located.)

A path runs 3 km north from the administration centre to **Laguna Huelde** (many camp sites) and then north a further 12 km to Cole Cole refugio (US$10 pp, camping US$2, good site) offering great views, best done on horseback (return journey to/from Cucao nine hours by horse, five hours one way on foot). The next refugio is at **Anay** (US$10 pp), 5 km further north on the Río Anay. There are several other walks but signposting is limited. Many houses in

Cucao rent horses (check horses and equipment carefully). **Miguelangelo Allende** has been recommended. If you hire a guide you pay for his horse too. Horseflies are bad in summer (wear light coloured clothing).

Quellón → *Phone code: 065. Colour map 9, A1. Population: 13,500. 92 km south of Castro.*
There are pleasant beaches nearby at Quellón Viejo (with an old wooden church), Punta de Lapa and Yaldad. The launch *Puerto Bonito* sails three times daily in summer from the pier, US$16 to tour the bay passing Punta de Lapa, Isla Laitec and Quellón Viejo. A trip can also be made to Chaiguao, 11 km east, where there is a small Sunday morning market. Horses can be hired, also kayaks with a guide. There is a campsite. **Museo Amador Cardenas Paredes** ⓘ *Pedro Montt 309*, has an odd collection of antique typewriters and sewing machines. There are amazing views of the mainland on a clear day. **Tourist office** ⓘ *Vargas y García*, is often closed, even in summer. See also **Cámara de Turismo Quellón** ⓘ *T09-191 2150, www.turismoquellon.cl*. Note that the street numbering system in Quellón is unfathomable.

From Quellón you can go to **Parque Tantauco**, still under development. It covers 120,000 ha of woods and wetlands at the southernmost part of the Island, with many endangered endemic species of mammal. It's a private park, with two camping areas and 7 walking trails. Access is by road or by a 5-hour boat trip from Quellón. Information from **Oficina Parque Tantauco** ⓘ *Av La Paz 068, Quellón, T680066, www.parquetantauco.cl*, or **Fundación Futuro** ⓘ *Av Apoquindo 3000, p 19, Las Condes, Santiago, www.fundacionfuturo.cl*.

Chiloé listings

For Sleeping and Eating price codes and other relevant information, see Essentials, pages 38-40.

Sleeping

Ancud *p826*

AL Panamericana, San Antonio 30, T622340, www.panamericanahoteles.cl. Nice views of the bay, attractive, very comfortable, helpful, restaurant, tours offered, English spoken.

A Galeón Azul, Libertad 751, T622567, www.hotelgaleonazul.cl. Small heated rooms with cable TV, rather basic for the price but excellent views. Bright restaurant.

A-B Don Lucas, Costanera 906, T620950, www.hoteldonlucas.cl. Renovated with nice rooms, some with sea view, disabled access, Wi-Fi. A good choice.

B Hostal Vista al Mar, Costanera 918, T622 617, www.vistaalmar.cl. Close to buses, **E** pp in dorms, also self-catering apartments. Views over the bay heating, internet, meals in restaurant **El Rincón**.

B-C Balai, Pudeto 169, T622541, www.hotelbalai.cl. With heating, laundry, parking, restaurant, cable TV, interesting local paintings, models and artefacts on display. Tours arranged.

B-C Mundo Nuevo, Costanera 748, T628383, www.newworld.cl. **E** pp in dorms. With breakfast, comfortable, one room has a boat-bed, great views over the bay, lots of info, heating, good showers, kitchen facilities, car and bicycle hire, English and German spoken. Highly recommended.

C Hostal Chiloé, O'Higgins 274, T622869, hchiloe@yahoo.es. With bath, food served, laundry service, Wi-Fi.

C Hostal Lluhay, Cochrane 458, T622656, www.hostal-lluhay.cl. Meals served. Attentive, heating, Wi-Fi, nice lounge. Recommended.

C Madryn, Bellavista 491, T622128, www.hotelmadryn.cl. With cable TV, breakfast, also meals, laundry, internet, tours arranged.

C-D Hosp Alto Bellavista, Bellavista 449, T622384. Very helpful, good breakfast, some rooms with bath, **F** pp shared rooms.

C-D Hosp San José, Las Américas 661, T629944, hostalsanjose6@hotmail.com. **D-E** with shared bath. With breakfast, good family atmosphere, nice views from lounge, hot water, use of kitchen, internet, tours offered, bicycle hire. Recommended.

D Hosp Ancud, Los Carrera 821, T622296, macriser@latinmail.com. Nice house, welcoming, kitchen facilities.

D Hosp Austral, A Pinto 1318, T624847, hospedajeaustral@hotmail.com. Cosy wooden house, near long-distance bus station, with breakfast, shared bath, family of Mirta Ruiz, very welcoming, dinner extra, kitchen facilities extra. Frequently recommended.

D Hosp O'Higgins 6, O'Higgins 06, T622266. With breakfast, spacious, interesting objets d'art, near sea, nice views. Recommended

E pp **Hosp Don Luis**, Av Almte Latorre 1225, T620325. With basic breakfast, private and shared rooms, good shared hot showers, friendly family, lots of information (Don Luis works at the bus station), use of kitchen.

Camping Arena Gruesa, Av Costanera Norte 290, T623428, arenagruesa@yahoo.com.

Playa Gaviotas, 5 km north, T09-9653 8096, also has *cabañas*. **Playa Larga Huicha**, 9 km north, **E** per site, bath, hot water, electricity.

Castro *p828*

Hotels on San Martín are convenient for the bus terminals. Several lodgings on Los Carrera 500-700 blocks, in our **E** pp range.

AL-A Cabañas Trayen, 5 km south of Castro, T633633, www.trayenchiloe.cl. Cheaper off season, lovely views, cabins for 4 to 6.

AL-A Hostería de Castro, Chacabuco 202, T632301, www.hosteriadecastro.cl. Recently expanded, the new section is spacious and comfortable, with wonderful views and nice suites. The old section is less good. Good restaurant.

AL-A Unicornio Azul, Pedro Montt 228, T632359, www.hotelgaleonazul.cl/unicornio/. Good views over bay, comfortable, restaurant.

A Casita Española, Los Carrera 359, T635186, www.hosteriadecastro.cl. Heating, TV, parking, good, in same group as **Hostería de Castro**.

B Alerce Nativo, O'Higgins 808, T632267, www.hotelalercenativo.cl. Heating, helpful, breakfast, also has *cabañas* (4 km south of Castro) and restaurant.

B Palafito Hostel, Riquelme 1210, T531008, www.palafitohostel.com. In a restored traditional *palafito* building over the water. Helpful staff, good breakfast, Wi-Fi, tours arranged. Recommended.

B-C Casa Blanca, Los Carrera 308, T632726, nelysald@surnet.cl. With breakfast, cheaper rooms with shared bath, modern, warm, also *cabañas*, sleep 6.

C Hosp Don Miguel, Barros Arana, T634748. With breakfast, welcoming, one double with bath and rooms with shared bath, communal eating, good views, very helpful.

D Hosp El Mirador, Barros Arana 127, T633795, maboly@yahoo.com. With breakfast, some rooms with bath, cosy, relaxing, kitchen, internet, popular. Warmly recommended.

C Hosp Sotomayor, Sotomayor 452, T632464. **F** singles. With breakfast, TV, quiet, small beds.

C-D Hosp América, Chacabuco 215, T634364. With breakfast, shared bath, very good food, cable TV.

C-D Hosp El Molo, Barros Arana 140, T635026, elmolochiloe@gmail.com. Comfortable, safe, welcoming, internet, cable TV, cooking facilities. Recommended.

D-E Hosp Teresita, Juan Williams 839, Villa Guarello, T638540, hospedajeteresita@hotmail.com. Not central but owner meets buses, good view, comfortable, nice atmosphere.

C-D Res Capullito, San Martín 709, T635262. A quiet, clean and friendly place to stay.

Camping Camping Pudú, Ruta 5, 10 km north of Castro, T632286, cabins, showers with hot water, sites with light, water, kids' games. Several sites on road to Chonchi, including **Llicaldad**, Esmeralda 269, T638188, also has cabañas.

Chonchi *p828*

AL-A Cabañas Treng Treng, José Pinto Pérez 420, T672532, www.trengtreng.cl. Impeccable fully furnished cabins sleeping 2-7. Splendid views, some English spoken. Recommended.

A Posada El Antiguo Chalet, Irrarázavel s/n, T671221, fco_barrientos@hotmail.com. **B** in winter, charming, beautiful location.

B-C Cabañas Amankay, Centenario 410, T671367. Cosy, kitchen facilities, sleeps 4-10.

C Esmeralda By The Sea, 100 m east of the new market on waterfront , T671328, www.esmeraldabythesea.cl. Main building has comfortable rooms with bath; annexe cheaper but with shared bath (**E** pp). With breakfast, dinner available (salmon, vegetarian), attractive, English spoken, knowledgeable owner, internet, cooking and laundry facilities, book exchange, rents bicycles, camping equipment, tours arranged.

C Hostería Mirador, Alvarez 198, T671351. With breakfast, good value. Recommended.

D Huildín, Centenario 102, T671388. Some rooms with bath, old fashioned, decent rooms with good beds but windows are onto an interior passages, also cabañas **A**, garden with superb views.

Camping Los Manzanos, Aguirre Cerda y Juan Guillermo, T671263. **E** per site.

Cucao *p828*

C Parador Darwin, at park entrance, Cucao sector, T09-9799 9923. With breakfast, good food with vegetarian options, real coffee. Recommended camping also available.

C Posada Cucao, T633040/09-9896 9855. With breakfast, meals available, hot water, pleasant.

E pp **Provisiones Pacífico**, with full board or demi-pension, friendly, good, home-made bread, candles provided, no hot water.

Camping Several campsites (check prices first), including **Lago Mar**, 2 km east of Cucao, T635552, US$15 per site.

Quellón *p829*

Cámara de Turismo Quellón lists various hotels and *cabañas*.

B El Chico Leo, P Montt 325, T681567, elchicoleo@turismoquellon.cl. With TV, heating and breakfast, **D** with shared bath, also has restaurant. Same familiy has **Rancho Leo Man**, Balneario Punta de Lapa 3332, T546340, rancholeoman@gmail.com, tourist complex with small wood, trails, restaurant, cabins (**B**) and rooms (**C** with jacuzzi, **D** without).

Eating

Ancud *p826*

ŸŸ Quetalmahue, 12 km west of Ancud on the road to Faro Corona and Fuerte Ahui, T09-9033 3930. The best place for traditional *curantos al hoyo* (cooked in the ground, daily in summer).

ŸŸ-Ÿ Sacho, Mercado Municipal, local 7, T622918. Renowned for its *curantos*, not fancy but huge portions and very reasonable. Several similar places in the same arcade.

Ÿ El Cangrejo, Dieciocho 155. Seafood. Highly recommended.

Ÿ Hamburguería, Av Prat. Much better than name suggests, good seafood.

ŸŸ La Pincoya, Prat 61, on waterfront. Good seafood, service and views.

Ÿ El Pingüinito, in an alley behind the market. Very cheap, decent lunches. Look for other cheap places in the market area, good food.

Castro *p828*

Breakfast before 0900 is difficult to find. By the market many places offer set lunch, usually fish dishes. In the market, try *milcaos*, fried potato cakes with meat stuffing. Also *licor de oro*, like Galliano.

ŸŸ Donde Eladio, Lillo 97. Meat and seafood specialities on offer.

ŸŸ Don Octavio, Pedro Montt 261. Good food and nice views over bay, specializes in seafood.

ŸŸ La Playa, Lillo 93. Good seafood.

Ÿ Don Camilo, Ramírez 566. Average food, also has pleasant accommodation.

Ÿ Palafito restaurants near the Feria Artesanía on the waterfront offer good food and good value, including **Rapa Nui**, **Brisas del Mar** and **La Amistad**.

Ÿ Sacho, Thompson 213. Good sea views, clean.

Cafés **Años Luz**, San Martín on corner of Plaza. Good café/bar/restaurant, live music at weekends, great cocktails.

La Brújula del Cuerpo, Plaza de Armas. Fast food, good coffee, snacks.

Stop Inn Café, Martín Ruiz shopping centre, Gamboa. Good coffee.

Chonchi *p828*

ŸŸ-Ÿ There are 6 *cocinarías* on the top floor of the new market serving traditional seafood.

Ÿ El Alerce, Candelaria 308. Excellent value, seafood.

Ÿ El Trébol, Irarrázabal 187, T671203. Good views over the harbour.

Quellón *p829*

ŸŸ Los Suizos, Ladrilleros 399. Swiss cuisine, good, slow service, internet.

ŸŸ Tierra del Fuego, P Montt 445, T682079. For fish, seafood and other local dishes. In hotel of same name.

Ÿ Fogón Onde Agüero, La Paz 307. Good cheep traditional food. Popular at lunchtime.

Shopping

Castro *p828*

Bookshops **Annay Libros**, Serrano 357, and **El Tren**, Thompson 229 for books on Chiloé. CDs of typical Chilote music are widely available.

Handicrafts Mercado Artesanal, Lillo on the wharf, good value woollens at reasonable prices.
Market The municipal market is on Yumbel, off Ulloa, uphill northwest of town: fish and vegetables.
Supermarket Beckna, O'Higgins y Aldea. Bakes good bread.

Chonchi *p828*
Handicrafts From **Feria artesanal**, on the waterfront, and from the parroquia, next to the church (open Oct-Mar only).

Activities and tours

Ancud *p826*
Aki Turismo, patio of Mercado Municipal, T545253, www.akiturismochiloe.cl. Good value trips to the penguin colony and other tours.
Austral Adventures, Costanera 904, T/F625977, www.austral-adventures.com. Bespoke small group tours of the archipelago and northern Patagonia (including Parque Pumalín) on land and sea. Good English speaking guides, lots of interesting choices; director Britt Lewis.
Carlos Oyarzún, T09-9657 4021.
An independent guide based in Ancud offering sit-on-top kayak tours.
Patagón Chiloé, Bellavista 491, T622128, www.patagonchiloe.cl. Tours to the penguin colony, Chepu and other parts of Chiloé.

Castro *p828*
Tours to Parque Nacional Chiloé US$33, to Isla Mechuque (east of Dalcahue) US$45.
Costa Sur, O'Higgins 670, of 11, T632788, www.turismocostasur.cl. Offers a variety of tours on the island. Also trekking.
Turismo Pehuén, Esmeralda 198, T635254, www.turismopehuen.cl. Naviera Austral agency, kayak and boat trips, trips to national park, penguin colony, around the island and car rental.
Sergio Márquez, local guide, Felipe Moniel 565, T632617, very knowledgeable, has transport.

Transport

Ancud *p826*
Bus Terminal on the east outskirts at Av Prat y Marcos Vera, reached by bus 1, or Pudeto colectivos. **Cruz del Sur** has its own station in centre. Local buses also central at Pedro Montt 538. To **Castro**, US$3-4, frequent (see below), 1½ hrs. To **Puerto Montt**, frequent services, see Ins and outs, above. To **Quemchi** via the coast, 2 hrs, US$3.

Quinchao Island *p826*
Ferry From **Dalcahue**, frequent, free for pedestrians and cyclists. Arriagada **buses** from **Ancud**, 5 a day. Frequent to **Castro**, US$3, Achao Express.

Castro *p828*
Bus Frequent services to **Chonchi**, choose between buses **Cruz del Sur, Queilén Bus** and others, minibuses and colectivos (from Esmeralda y Chacabuco). **Arroyo** and **Ocean Bus** both run to **Cucao**, 6 a day in season, first 0930, last back 1600 1½ hrs, US$4 (1200 and 1600 off season, avoid Fri when school children are going home – much slower, lots of stops). To **Dalcahue** frequent services by **Gallardo** and **Arriagada**, also colectivos from San Martín 815. To **Achao** via Dalcahue and Curaco de Vélez, Arriagada, several daily, last return from Achao 1730, US$4. To **Puqueldón** on the island of Lemuy, **Gallardo**, 4 daily Mon-Sat, US$3.50. To **Quemchi**, daily with **Queilén Bus**, 1½ hrs, US$4. To **Quellón**, **Regional Sur** and **Trans Chiloé**, frequent. To **Queilén**, **Queilén Bus** and others, 6 a day, US$4.

Long distance buses leave from 2 terminals: **Cruz del Sur**, T632389, **Trans Chiloé** and Arriagada from Cruz del Sur terminal on San Martín 500 block behind the cathedral. Other services leave from the Municipal Terminal, San Martín, 600 block (2 blocks further north). Frequent services to **Ancud** and **Puerto Montt** by Cruz del Sur, Trans Chiloé and Queilén Bus. Cruz del Sur also run to **Osorno**, **Valdivia**, **Temuco**, **Concepción** and **Santiago**. **Bus Norte** to Ancud, Puerto Montt, Osorno and Santiago daily. There are also services to Coyhaique.

Chonchi *p828*
Buses and **taxis** to **Castro**, frequent, US$1.15, from main plaza. Services to **Quellón** (US$1.90), Cucao (US$2.50) and **Queilén** from Castro and Puerto Montt also call here.

Cucao *p828*
Bus From Castro see above; in season as many as 4 buses a day, last departure 1600, reduced service off-season; hitching is very difficult. From **Chonchi** daily bus at 0930, returning 1700, more in summer.

Quellón *p829*

Bus To **Castro**, 2 hrs, frequent, **Cruz del Sur**, US$4; also to **Ancud** and **Puerto Montt**, US$12. **Ferries Naviera Austral**, Pedro Montt 457, Quellón, T682207, www.navieraustral.cl. They run ferries from Quellón to Chaitén once a week (more in high season, also from Castro), US$38-50 passengers, US$14 bicycle, US$33 motorbike, US$135 car. To Puerto Chacabuco (via Melinka, Raul Marin Balmaceda, Santo Domingo, Melimoyu, Puerto Gala (Isla Toto), Puerto Cisnes, Puerto Gaviota (Caleta Amparo) and Puerto Aguirre) weekly, 24 hrs, reclining seat US$43, bunk US$72, cars US$230, bicycles US$16. All services leave from Castro when Quellón's port is out of commission and schedules are subject to last-minute changes due to inclement weather. Check with the company for schedules and fares for 2010.

Directory

Ancud *p826*

Banks ATMs at **BCI**, Ramírez, 1 block from plaza. **Post offices** On corner of Plaza de Armas at Pudeto y Blanco Encalada. **Telephones** Plaza de Armas. Mon-Sat 0700-2200; ENTEL, Pudeto 219, with internet; Los Carrera 823.

Castro *p828*

Banks **Banco de Chile** with ATM at Plaza de Armas, accepts TCs (at a poor rate). **BCI**, Plaza de Armas, MasterCard and Visa ATM. Better rates from **Julio Barrientos**, Chacabuco 286, cash and TCs. **Post offices** On west side of Plaza de Armas. **Telephones** Latorre 289. **Entel**: O'Higgins entre Gamboa y Sotomayor.

Quellón *p829*

Banks **Banco del Estado**, Ladrilleros. MasterCard only, no commission on US$ cash. **Banco de Chile**, Ladrilleros 315, Visa ATM.

Carretera Austral

A third of Chile lies to the south of Puerto Montt, but until recently its inaccessible land and rainy climate meant that it was only sparsely populated and unvisited by tourism. The Carretera Austral, or Southern Highway, has now been extended south from Puerto Montt to Villa O'Higgins, giving access to the spectacular virgin landscapes of this wet and wild region, with its mountains, fjords and islands, hitherto isolated communities, and picturesque ports. Ships were the only means of access and remain important for exporting the timber grown here, and for bringing visitors; see page 820. The unexpected eruption of Chaitén volcano in 2008 has caused major disruption to the northern part of the Carretera, not least to services in the town of Chaitén. Make enquiries before going to this area.

The only settlement of any size is Coyhaique and its nearby airport at Balmaceda and the equally nearby Puerto Chacabuco are the principal entry points. Coyhaique is a good starting point for exploring the Carretera, north to the thermal springs at Puyuhuapi and the unspoilt national park of Queulat, for trekking expeditions and for fishing. Coyhaique is also a good place for booking Parque Nacional Laguna San Rafael glacier trips, for which boats leave from Puerto Chacabuco.

The Carretera extends 575 km from Coyhaique to Villa O'Higgins, beyond which the southern icefields and their glaciers bring the roadway to a halt. This southernmost section of the Carretera is the wildest and most dramatic, with beautiful unspoilt landscapes around Lago General Carrera. The fairy tale peaks of Cerro Castillo offer challenging trekking, and there's world class fishing in the turquoise waters of Río Baker. A road runs off to Puerto Ibáñez for lake crossings to Chile Chico, a convenient border crossing to Argentina, while a more adventurous cross-border route involves road, lake and foot or horseback travel to El Chaltén.

Ins and outs

Getting there and around This road can be divided into three major sections: **Puerto Montt-Chaitén** (or however much of it is open), **Chaitén-Coyhaique**, and **Coyhaique-Villa O'Higgins**. The road is paved just south of Chaitén and around Coyhaique, from just north of Villa Amengual to Villa Cerro Castillo and Puerto Ibáñez. Currently, the rest is 'ripio' (loose stones) and many sections are extremely rough and difficult after rain. The Carretera is very popular with cyclists, even though they can't expect to make fast progress. Motorists need to carry sufficient fuel and spares, especially if intending to detour along any of the highway's many side roads, and protect windscreens and headlamps from stones. Unleaded fuel is available all the way to Villa O'Higgins. There is now a road between Puerto El Vagabundo and Caleta Tortel, and the Carretera Austral is connected by a free ferry between Puerto Yungay and Río Bravo, where it continues to Villa O'Higgins. So far, there is little infrastructure for transport or accommodation among the rural hamlets, so allow plenty of time for bus connections, and bring cash, as there are few banking facilities along the whole route. Camping will give you more freedom for accommodation and there are many beautiful sites. Having your own transport here is definitely preferable. If you intend to hitchhike, **note** that it is essential to take up to three days' worth of supplies as you can be stuck for that long, especially in the far south. At the same time (for campers too), food supplies are limited and tend to be expensive. ▸▸ *See also Transport, pages 835, 844 and 851.*

Best time to visit The landscape throughout the region is lushly green because there is no real dry season. On the offshore islands and the western side of the Andes annual rainfall is over 2,000 mm, though inland on the steppe the climate is drier and colder. Westerly winds are strong, especially in summer, but there's plenty of sunshine too, especially around Lago General Carrera (described in the Southern Section), which has a warm microclimate. January and February are probably the best months for a trip to this region.

Puerto Montt to Chaitén

This section of the Carretera Austral, 205 km, should include two ferry crossings. Before setting out, it is imperative to check which ferries are running and when and, if driving, make a reservation: do this in Puerto Montt (not Santiago), at the Naviera Austral and Transmarchilay offices, both at Angelmó 2187, T065-270430/270000, www.navieraustral.cl, www.transmarchilay.cl (Spanish only). An alternative route to Chaitén is by ferry from Puerto Montt or Quellón/Castro.

The road (Ruta 7) heads east out of Puerto Montt, through Pelluco, and follows the shore of the beautiful Seno Reloncaví. It passes the southern entrance of the **Parque Nacional Alerce Andino** ⓘ *US$8, no camping within park boundaries*, which contains one of the best surviving areas of alerce trees, some over 1,000 years old (the oldest is estimated at 4,200 years old). Wildlife includes pudú, pumas, vizcachas, condors and black woodpeckers. There are two entrances: 2½ km from Correntoso (35 km east of Puerto Montt) at the northern end of the park (with ranger station and campsite) and 7 km east of Lenca (40 km south of Puerto Montt) at the southern end. There are three other ranger posts, at Río Chaicas, Lago Chapo and Sargazo. Ranger posts have little information; map is available from CONAF in Puerto Montt.

At 46 km from Puerto Montt (allow one hour), is the first ferry at **La Arena**, across the Reloncaví Estuary to **Puelche**. See Transport, page 835, for Ferry details. **Río Negro** is now called **Hornopirén** after the volcano above it. From here south, access is determined by the volcanic activity. In normal times a second ferry sails to Caleta Gonzalo, one of the centres for the Parque Pumalín (see below). At the mouth of the fjord is the small Isla Llancahué, with a hotel and thermal springs (day entry US$14), good for hiking in the forests amid beautiful scenery. Boat to the island 50 minutes, US$60 one-way shared between passengers, T09-9642 4857; look out for dolphins and fur seals en route.

Parque Pumalín

Caleta Gonzalo is the entry point for Parque Pumalín for visitors from the north. Owing to the **Chaitén volcano** the southern part of the park and all the park's lodgings were closed in 2009. The park, created by the US billionaire Douglas Tompkins, is a private reserve of 700,000 ha in two sections which has been given Nature Sanctuary status. Covering large areas of the western Andes, with virgin temperate rainforest, the park is spectacularly beautiful, and is seen by many as one of the most important conservation projects in the world. **Information centres** ⓘ *Klenner 299, Puerto Varas, T065-250079; Fiordo Reñihué, Caleta Gonzalo (not always open). In USA T415-229-9339, www.pumalinpark.org (Spanish and English).*

South of Caleta Gonzalo the Carretera Austral winds through the park's beautiful unspoilt scenery, and there is a steep climb on the ripio road to two lakes, Lago Río Blanco and Lago Río Negro, with panoramic views. After the eruption of Volcán Chaitén, the government decided to abandon Chaitén, cutting off utilities, rebuilding the town 10 km north at Santa Barbara and moving the seat of provincial government to Futaleufú, taking with it the bank. Chaitén, however, survives with running water, generators and fuel. There are shops, *hospedajes* and *cabañas* and all transport links: ferries to Puerto Montt and Chiloé, flights and buses.

Puerto Montt to Chaitén listings

For Sleeping and Eating price codes and other relevant information, see Essentials, pages 38-40.

Sleeping

Puerto Montt to Chaitén *p834*

LL Alerce Mountain Lodge, Km 36 Carretera Austral, T253044, www.mountainlodge.cl. In Los Alerces de Lenca private reserve, beside Parque Nacional Alerce Andino, beautiful lodge with rooms and cabins, offering packages from 2 to 4 nights, with trekking, riding, fishing, guides speak English, good food, all-inclusive except drinks.

Hornopirén

A-B Hotel Termas de Llancahué, Isla Llancahué. To get there, make arrangements by phoning T09-9642 4857, www.termasdellancahue.cl. Price is per person for full board (excellent food), hot spring at the hotel, cheaper with shared bath.

B-C Hostería Catalina, Ingenieros Militares s/n, T217359, www.hosteriacatalina.cl. Comfortable rooms with breakfast and bath, a good place to stay.

C Hornopirén, Carrera Pinto 388, T217256. Rooms with shared bath, also *cabañas* and restaurant at the water's edge. Recommended.

Chaitén *p835*

The following are open, all welcoming travellers, with hot water and meals: **Cabañas Brisas del Mar** (Corcovado 278), **Cabañas Pudú**, **Casa de Rita** (Riveros y Pratt), **El Refugio** (Corcovado y Juan Todesco), **Hosp y Restaurante Corcovado** (Corcovado 410), **Hosp Don Carlos** (Almte Riveros y Pratt), **Hosp Llanos** (Corcovado 378), and **Shilling** (Corcovado 258). .

Activities and tours

Chaitén *p835*

Chaitur, O'Higgins 67, T09-7468 5608, www.chaitur.com. General travel agent making bus, boat, plane and hotel reservations. Also offers tours to hot springs, galciers, beaches, Carretera Austral, photography trips. Still **the** place to find about local conditions. English and French spoken, helpful, book exchange, internet when the phone lines are reconnected. Highly recommended.

Transport

Puerto Montt to Chaitén *p834*

Parque Nacional Alerce Andino

Bus To the north entrance: take a **Fierro** or **Río Pato** bus to **Correntoso** (or **Lago Chapo** bus which passes through Correntoso), several daily except Sun, then walk. To the south entrance: take any **Fierro** bus to **Chaicas, La Arena, Contau** and **Hornopirén**, US$2.50, getting off at Lenca sawmill, then walk (signposted).

La Arena to Puelche

Ferry The *Trauco*, across the Reloncaví Estuary, 30 mins, every 1½ hrs, US$19.75 for a car, US$14 for motorcycle, US$5.50 for bicycle, US$1 for foot passengers, 0715-2000 daily. Arrive at least 30 mins early to guarantee a place; buses have priority. Roll-on roll-off type operating all year. See www.transmarchilay.cl for more details.

Hornopirén

Bus Fierro (T253022) and **Jordán** (T254938) run Mon-Sat 0800 and 1330 (Sun 1500, 1730) from **Puerto Montt**, US$7.50; return 0530, 1330 Mon-Sat, 1245, 1500 Sun.

Ferry Hornopirén to **Chaitén** via Ayacara: in Jan-Feb 2010 the *Mailén* sailed Mon, Wed, Sat at 0900. Check with **Naviera Austral**, www.navieraustral.cl, to see if this service is running: in Hornopirén T07-968 1646, in Ayacara T07-475 1168, in Chaitén T07-976 0342.

Chaitén *p835*

Air Emergency airstrip on the road at Santa Bárbara. Daily flights to **Puerto Montt** with **Aerocord** (19 pasengers) and **Patagonia Airlines** (9 passengers), US$75.

Bus Terminal at **Chaitur**, O'Higgins 67. To **Coyhaique**, Thu 1000, direct in summer, 12 hrs, otherwise overnight stop in La Junta, to which buses depart Mon, Tue, Fri, Sat 0930. Connections to Puyuhuapi and Coyhaique 0600 next day. Minibuses usually travel full, so can't pick up passengers en route. Buses to **Futaleufú**, daily except Thu, 0930; change here for buses to the Argentine border.

Ferry

The ferry port is about 1 km north of town. Schedules change frequently and ferries are infrequent off season. **Naviera Austral**, Corcovado 266, T07-976 0342, www.navieraustral.cl.

To **Chiloé**, **Naviera Austral** operates ferry services to **Quellón** or **Castro**, once a week, more in summer (Dec-Mar); fares given under Quellón, above.

To **Puerto Montt**, **Naviera Austral**, 5 weekly in summer 2010 via Ayacara, 10 hrs, passengers US$42, US$55 with bunk, car US$166, bike US$19.

Chaitén to Coyhaique

This section of the Carretera Austral, runs 422 km through breathtaking and varied scenery, passing tiny villages, most notably the idyllic Puyuhuapi, where there are thermal pools, and good trekking in Parque Nacional Queulat. While the northern part of the Carretera is disrupted, access is from the south. Roads which branch off east to the Argentine border at the picturesque Futaleufú and at Palena are subject to period closures because of volcanic ash, see page 835. Consequently, there may be disruption to services so before going to, or before crossing from Argentina in this region, check if there are travel restrictions.

Puerto Cárdenas, 44 km south of Chaitén, is on the northern tip of **Lago Yelcho**, a beautiful lake on Río Futaleufú surrounded by hills, much loved by anglers for its salmon and trout. Further south at Km 60, a path leads to **Ventisquero Yelcho** (two hours' walk there), a dramatic glacier with high waterfalls. Note that the path passes a campsite whose administrator charges walkers US$3.50 to go to the glacier. Whether he is legally entitled to do this is a contentious issue.

At **Villa Santa Lucía**, an uninspiring modern settlement 76 km south of Chaitén, with basic food and accommodation, a road branches east to the Argentine border. There are two crossings: Futaleufú and Palena, both reached from **Puerto Ramírez** past the southern end of Lago Yelcho, 24 km east of Santa Lucia. Here the road divides: the north branch runs along the valley of the Río Futaleufú to Futaleufú and the southern one to Palena. The scenery is spectacular, but the road is hard going: single track ripio, climbing steeply in places (tough for bikes; allow plenty of time).

Futaleufú → *Phone code: 065.*

The new provincial capital, 8 km west of the border, nestles in a bowl amid steep mountains on the Río Espolón. Its houses are neatly slatted with alerce wood and the wide streets are lined with shrubs and roses. Access to challenging whitewater rafting on the Río Futaleufú has made it into one of the southern hemisphere's prime centres for the sport, but with kayaking, riding, trekking, mountain biking and canyoning on offer Futaleufú now calls itself the capital of adventure tourism. **Lago Espolón**, west of Futaleufú, reached by a turning 41 km northeast of Villa Santa Lucía, is a beautiful lake in an area enjoying a warm microclimate: 30°C in the day in summer, 5°C at night, with excellent fishing at the lake's mouth. The lake is even warm enough for a quick dip, but beware of the currents. Banco del Estado on the plaza has a MasterCard ATM. **Tourist office** ⓘ *on the plaza at O'Higgins and Prat, T721241, www.futaleufu.cl, daily in summer, 0900-2100*, for accommodation, maps and fishing licences.

Border with Argentina

Chilean immigration is at the border, 8 km east of Futaleufú. The border is just west of the bridge over the Río Grande: straightforward crossing, open 0800-2000. For Argentinian immigration, see page 218. Change money in Futaleufú; nowhere to change at the border but you can pay the bus fare to Esquel (Argentina) in US dollars. Alternatively, cross into Argentina further south near **Palena**, which is 8 km west of the border and has a Chilean immigration office. **Note** If entering from Argentina, no fresh produce may be brought into Chile. There may be some disruption to services due to the recent eruption of the Chaitén volcano, see page 835. Check locally before going.

XI Región

La Junta in the XI (eleventh) Region is a village 151 km south of Chaitén. La Junta has a service station, where there's a minimarket. From the village you can visit **Lago Rosselot**, surrounded by forest in the **Reserva Nacional Lago Rosselot**, 9 km east of La Junta. The same road continues east, 74 km, to Lago Verde and the Argentine border: open summer 0800-2200, winter 0800-2000. Another road leads northwest, with a ferry crossing over the Río Palena (four daily), to the fishing village of **Puerto Raúl Marín Balmaceda** (hostels and camping). Different species of dolphin can be seen and Raúl Marín forms one apex of the blue whale triangle: the giant cetacean may be sighted on the ferry to Quellón in the summer. On clear days there are wonderful views of Volcán Melimoyu from the beach.

Puyuhuapi → *Phone code: 067. Population: 500.*

With the most idyllic setting along the whole Carretera Austral, Puyuhuapi lies in a tranquil bay at the northern end of the Puyuhuapi fjord, 46 km south of La Junta. The blissful thermal pools at Termas de Puyuhuapi are nearby. The village was founded by four German-speaking Sudeten families in 1935, and handwoven carpets are still made here, now to world renown. **Alfombras de Puyuhuapi** ⓘ *T325131, www.puyuhuapi.com, daily in summer 0830-1930, closed lunch, English spoken*. This is the best stopping point between Chaitén and Coyhaique with phone, fuel, shops, but no banks: hotels may change dollars. **Tourist office** ⓘ *by the Municipalidad, main street, Mon-Sat in season, 1000-1400, 1600-1900*, helpful.

Termas del Ventisqero ⓘ *6 km south of Puyuhuapi beside the Carretera overlooking the fjord, T325228, www.termasventisqueropuyuhuapi.cl*. In season the baths are open until 2300 and during the day there is a café. See Sleeping below for the Termas de Puyuhuapi at the Puyuhuapi Lodge and Spa.

South of Puyuguapi, 24 km, is the 154,093-ha **Parque Nacional Queulat** ⓘ *CONAF, La Junta, T314128, eladio.pinto@conaf.cl, daily Dec-Mar 0830-2100, rest of year 0830-1830, US$5, camping US$15 per site, CONAF campsite with cold showers*. It is most visited for the spectacular hanging glacier, **Ventisquero Colgante**. 2.5 km off the road passing the guardeparques' house, you'll find parking and camping areas. Three walks begin from here: a short stroll through the woodland to a viewpoint of the Ventisquero, or cross the river where the path begins to Laguna Tempanos, where boats cross the lake in summer. The third trail, 3.25 km, takes 2½ hours to climb to a panoramic viewpoint of the Ventisquero, where you can watch the ice fall into huge waterfalls like sifted sugar.

Puerto Cisnes

At 59 km south of Puyuhuapi, a winding road branches west and follows the Río Cisnes 33 km to Puerto Cisnes (*Population :1,784*), a fishing village and salmon-farming centre at the mouth of the river on Puyuhuapi fjord, set amongst steep mountains. The Río Cisnes, 160 km in length, is recommended for rafting or canoeing, with grand scenery and modest rapids except for the horrendous drop at Piedra del Gato. Good camping in the forest, and fuel is available in the village.

At 89 km south of Puyuhuapi is **Villa Amengual** and, at Km 92, a road branches east, 104 km to La Tapera and to the Argentine border. Chilean immigration is 12 km west of the border, open summer 0800-2200, winter 0800-2000. On the Argentine side the road continues to meet up with Ruta 40, a section with few services for fuel or food.

Coyhaique → *Phone code: 067. Colour map 9, A1. Population: 43,297.*

A growing centre for tourism, Coyhaique, 420 km south of Chaitén, is a busy small town perched on a hill between the Ríos Simpson and Coyhaique. It has a cinema and all main services, including stores selling hiking gear and warm clothes. It's a good idea to get cash here as there are no banks along the Carretera Austral. The **Museo Regional de la Patagonia Central** ⓘ *Lillo 23, Tue-Sun winter 0830-1730, summer 0900-2000, US$1 is in the Casa de Cultura*. It traces local history through photos of the first pioneers, as well as sections on archaeology, mineralogy and zoology. From the bridge over the Río Simpson look for the **Piedra del Indio**, a rock outcrop which looks like a face in profile. **Tourist offices:** Sernatur office (very helpful, English spoken) ⓘ *Bulnes 35, T231752,*

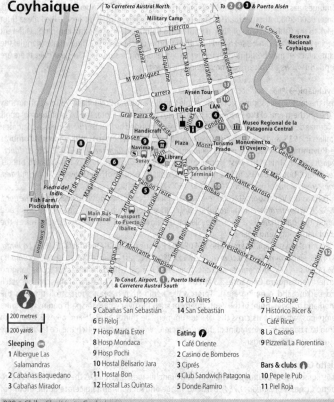

Coyhaique

200 metres

200 yards

Sleeping

1 Albergue Las Salamandras

2 Cabañas Baquedano

3 Cabañas Mirador

4 Cabañas Río Simpson

5 Cabañas San Sebastián

6 El Reloj

7 Hosp María Ester

8 Hosp Mondaca

9 Hosp Pochi

10 Hostal Belisario Jara

11 Hostal Bon

12 Hostal Las Quintas

13 Los Ñires

14 San Sebastián

Eating

1 Café Oriente

2 Casino de Bomberos

3 Ciprés

4 Club Sandwich Patagonia

5 Donde Ramiro

6 El Mastique

7 Histórico Ricer & Café Ricer

8 La Casona

9 Pizzería La Fiorentina

Bars & clubs

10 Pepe le Pub

11 Piel Roja

infoaisen@sernatur.cl. Mon-Fri 0830-1730, high season Mon-Fri 0830-2000, Sat-Sun 1000-1800. See www.patagoniachile.cl. CONAF, Av Ogana 1060, T212109, aysen@conaf.cl.

Just outside the town, the **Reserva Nacional Coihaique** ⓘ *0830-1700 Oct-Apr, US$1.75, information from CONAF*, has some trails for walking or biking, with picnic grounds, campsites and a *refugio*. A satisfying walk is up to Cerro Cinchao, and great views from Sendero Los Leñeros to Laguna Verde. Walk to Laguna Verde and Laguna Venus particularly recommended. Follow Baquedano to the end, over bridge, and past the guardeparque's hut where all the trails begin. There are well-marked walks of between 20 minutes and five hours. Ski centre **El Fraile**, 29 km from Coyhaique, is 1,599 m above sea level, with five pistes, powder snow, in the middle of ñire (Antarctic beech) and lenga forests (1,000 people capacity).

Border with Argentina: Coyhaique Alto

A 43-km road runs east to this crossing. On the Argentine side the road leads through Río Mayo and Sarmiento to Comodoro Rivadavia. **Chilean immigration** is at Coyhaique Alto, 6 km west of the border, open summer 0800-2200, winter 0800-2000.

Puerto Aisén and Puerto Chacabuco → *Phone code: 067. Colour map 9, A1. Population: 13,050.*

The paved road between Coyhaique and Puerto Aisén passes through **Reserva Nacional Río Simpson**, with beautiful waterfalls, lovely views of the river and excellent fly-fishing. Administration/museum is at the entrance, 32 km west of Coyhaique, no marked trails; campsite opposite turning to Santuario San Sebastián, US$7.

Puerto Aisén is 67 km west of Coyhaique at the meeting of the rivers Aisén and Palos. Formerly the region's major port, it has been replaced by Puerto Chacabuco, 15 km to the west, and though it remains an important centre for services, there's little of interest for the visitor. It's also very wet. In summer, the *Apulcheu* sails regularly down the northern shore of the Aisén Fjord to Termas de Chiconal, a spectacular one hour trip by boat, US$50 (take your own food) – book in the tourist office or **Turismo Rucaray**, on the plaza, rucaray@entelchile.net. **Tourist office** ⓘ *in the Municipalidad, Prat y Sgto Aldea, www.portchacabuco.cl, Dec-Feb only*, gives information on shipping movements.

The Puente President Ibáñez, once the longest suspension bridge in Chile, and a paved road lead to **Puerto Chacabuco** 15 km away; a regular bus service runs between the two. The harbour, rather a charmless place, is a short way from the town.

Balmaceda

From Coyhaique, the Carretera Austral heads south past huge bluffs, through deforested pasture (most dramatically on the slopes of Cerro Galera near El Blanco) and farmsteads edged with alamo (poplar) trees, before entering flatter plains and rolling hills. At around Km 41, a paved road runs east past the airport at Balmaceda to the Argentine border at Paso Huemules (no accommodation). Chilean immigration is open winter 0800-2000, summer 0800-2200.

Puerto Ibáñez

The Carretera Austral starts to climb again, past the entrance to the Reserva Nacional Cerro Castillo (see below). It winds up through the attractive narrow gorge of Río Horqueta, to a pass between Cerro Castillo and its neighbours, before dropping down a 6-km slalom into the breathtaking valley of Rio Ibáñez. (This is currently the most southerly paved section and the road is safe and wide here). Here the road forks east to Puerto Ibáñez, a further 31 km away, for the ferry crossing of vast Lago General Carrera.

Puerto Ibáñez (*Population: 828*) is the principal port on the Chilean section of the lake. As such you'll probably just pass through to reach the ferry. It is, however, a centre for distinctive pottery, leather production and vegetable growing (you can buy salad from greenhouses and visit potters). Local archaeology includes rock art and the largest Tehuelche cemetery in Patagonia.

There are various hotels, but no other services. Fuel (sold in 5-litre containers) is available at Luis A Bolados 461 (house with five laburnum trees outside). Most shops and restaurants are closed Sunday. There are some fine waterfalls, including the Salto Río Ibáñez, 6 km north.

Villa Cerro Castillo

From the turning to Puerto Ibáñez the Carretera Austral goes through Villa Cerro Castillo (Km 8), a quiet village in a spectacular setting beneath the striking, jagged peaks of **Cerro Castillo**, overlooking the broad valley below. There's a petrol station, public phone, several food shops and a tiny tourist information kiosk by the road side (January-February only), with details of guides offering trekking and horse rides.

The village is a good place to stop for a few days with two appealing attractions. There are truly spectacular treks from one to four or five days in the **Reserva Nacional Cerro Castillo** (179,550 ha, US$1.60), whose entrance is 64 km south of Coyhaique.One goes around the fairytale castle peaks of Cerro Castillo, starting at Las Horquetas Grandes, a bend in the river Río Ibáñez, 8 km south of the park entrance, where any bus driver will let you off. It follows Río La Lima to the gorgeous Laguna Cerro Castillo, then animal trails around the peak itself, returning to the village (accommodation or bus back to Coyhaique). Another equally spectacular five-day trek goes around Lago Monreal. These are challenging walks: attempt only if fit, and ideally, take a guide, as trails are poorly marked (IGM map essential, purchase in advance in Coyhaique).The guardería is on the Senda Ibáñez, 50 m to the left of the main road (as you head south), opposite Laguna Chinguay to the right, with access to walks and campsite (US$7, take equipment – there are no refugios). The picnic ground is open summer 0830-2100, winter to 1830. Ask in Villa Cerro Castillo for details.

A few kilometres south of the village is the **Monumento Nacional Alero Las Manos de Cerro Castillo** ⓘ *US$1 charged Dec-Apr*. In a shallow cave, a few handprints have been made on the side of vertical rocks high above the Río Ibáñez. There's no clue to their significance, but they're in a beautiful place with panoramic views. This makes a delightful two hours' walk. The site is accessible all year, signposted clearly from the road. There is also a small local museum, 2 km south of Villa Cerro Castillo ⓘ *open Dec-Mar 0900-1200*.

Chaitén to Coyhaique listings

For Sleeping and Eating price codes and other relevant information, see Essentials, pages 38-40.

Services in Futaleufú may be suspended due the eruption of the Chaitén volcano. Check the situation before going.

Sleeping

Chaitén to Coyhaique *p836*

Villa Santa Lucía

D pp Several places on main street: ask at **Nachito**, the café where the bus stops, which serves good breakfasts.

Futaleufú *p836*

L El Barranco, O'Higgins 172, T721314, www.elbarrancochile.cl. Elegant rustic rooms, luxurious, pool, good restaurant, and expert fishing guides, horses and bikes for hire, half and full board available.

AL Río Grande, O'Higgins y Aldea, T721320, www.pachile.com. Also upmarket but not such good value, spacious attractive rooms, internet, international restaurant, popular with rafting groups.

B Cabañas Río Espolón, Río Espolón, T9645 4172, follow Cerda to the end, www.futaleufu.cl/locales/crioespolon.htm. Cosy *cabañas* in secluded riverside setting, also recommended parrilla, bar. Popular with river-rafting groups, book ahead.

B Cabañas Veranada, Sargento Aldea 480, T721266, www.turismofutaleufu.cl. Well-equipped cabins with excellent beds and good kitchens. All have slow-burning wood stoves except one with an open fireplace. Recommended.

C-D Adolfo B&B, O'Higgins 302, T721256, lodeva@surnet.cl. Best value in this range, comfortable rooms in family home, shared hot showers, kitchen, with breakfast. Warmly recommended.

E pp **Continental**, Balmaceda 595, T721222. **F** singles. Oldest in town, no breakfast, basic, but clean and welcoming.

Camping Aldea Puerto Espolón, Sector La Puntilla, 400m from town, T09-94477448, www.aldeapuertoespolon.blogspot.com. Accommodation in pre-erected teepees and dome-tents. Several other campsites.

XI Región: La Junta *p837*

AL Espacio y Tiempo, T314141, www.espacioytiempo.cl. Spacious rooms, warm and cosy atmosphere, restaurant, attractive gardens, fishing expeditions. Recommended.

C Res Copihue, Varas 611, T09-9501 8874. Some rooms with bath, with breakfast, good meals, changes money at poor rates.

C-D Res Patagonia, Lynch 331, T09-7702 8181. Good meals, small rooms, limited bathrooms.

C-D Hostería Valdera, Varas s/n, T314105, luslagos@hotmail.com. Breakfast and bath, meals served. Excellent value.

Puyuhuapi *p837*

LL-L Puyuhuapi Lodge and Spa. Reservations: Patagonia Connection, Santiago, T02-225 6489, www.patagonia-connection.com, or directly at the hotel, T/F325103. Splendidly isolated on a nook in the sea fjord, the hotel owns the thermal baths: outdoors by the fjord so that you can dive in for a refreshing swim afterwards, or in the lovely indoor spa complex where there are jacuzzis of sea water, good for sufferers of arthritic and skin conditions, expert massage facilities. Good packages for de-stressing with all activities from riding, trekking, mountain biking, yoga and the thermals included. Price includes use of baths, boat transfer, full board US$50 extra, excellent restaurant. Guests met at Balmaceda airport, or arrive by boat from Puerto Chacabuco, taking in the San Rafael lake and glaciers (from US$1170 for 2 for 3 nights, all included, depending on season and room category). Highly recommended. Boats leave frequently from a 2 hrs' walk from town, US$5 each way, 10 mins' crossing.

L El Pangue, 18 km north, Km 240 at end of Lago Risopatrón, Parque Nacional Quelat, T325128, www.elpangue.com. Rooms and luxurious *cabañas* for 4 to 7 in splendid rural setting, with hot water and heating, horseriding, all meals extra, restaurant, trekking, mountain bikes, pool, great views, restful. Recommended.

B Aonikenk, Hamburgo 16, T325208, aonikenkturismo@yahoo.com. Pleasant heated *cabañas* (not sound-proofed), good beds, helpful, informative, bike hire.

B Casa Ludwig, Otto Uebel s/n, T325220, www.casaludwig.cl. Cheaper with shared bath. Open Nov-Mar; enquire in advance at other times. In a beautiful 4-storey house built by first German settlers, wonderful views, a range of rooms, good breakfast, comfortable; charming owner Luisa is knowledgeable about the area, speaks German and English. Highly recommended.

B-C Hostería Alemana, Otto Uebel 450, T325118, www.hosteríaalemana.cl. A large traditional wooden house on the main road by the water, very comfortable, lovely lake views and garden. Warmly recommended.

D Sra Leontina Fuentes, Llantureo y Circunvalación, T325106. Clean, hot water, good breakfast for US$3.

Camping Campsite behind the general store.

Puerto Cisnes *p837*

AL-B Cabañas Río Cisnes, Costanera 101, T346404. Cabins sleep 4 to 8. Owner, Juan Suazo, offers sea fishing trips in his boat.

C Hostería El Gaucho, Holmberg 140, T346514. With bath and breakfast, dinner available.

Also various cabañas and *residenciales*.

Villa Amengual

E pp **Res El Encanto**, Fca Castro 33-A, T188-2-1964517. With restaurant and café, one of several cheap options in town, including **Res Bienvenido** and **Villa Mañihuales** (T234803), both **E**, on Ibar.

Coyhaique *p838, map p827*

Plentiful accommodation. The tourist office has a list.

L-AL El Reloj, Baquedano 828, T231108, www.elrelojhotel.cl. Tasteful, quiet place in a former sawmill, with a good restaurant, charming, comfortable wood panelled rooms, some with wonderful views, nice lounge, Wi-Fi. Recommended as the best in town.

A Cabañas Mirador, Baquedano 848, T233191. Attractive, well-equipped *cabañas*, also rooms, in lovely gardens with panoramic views of the Reserva Forestal, and Río Coyhaique below, book in advance. Recommended.

A Hostal Belisario Jara, Bilbao 662, T/F23 4150. Most distinctive and delightful, an elegant and welcoming small place, with TV and excellent breakfast. Recommended.

A Los Ñires, Baquedano 315, T232261, www.doncarlos.cl. Small rooms showing their age, but excellent gourmet restaurant, also serves breakfast, parking, free Wi-Fi.

A San Sebastián, Baquedano 496, T233427. Modern, spacious rooms with great views over the Reserva, with breakfast, good value. Recommended. Also **Cabañas San Sebastián**, Freire 554, T231762. Central, very good.

A-B Cabañas Río Simpson, 3 km north on road to Pto Aisén, T/F232183, www.cabanasrio simpson.cl. Fully equipped cabins for 2-6 people plus 1 luxury cabin, **L** sleeping 7. Horse riding, fishing and tours Tame alpacas in grounds.

B Hostal Bon, Serrano 91, T231189, hostal_bon@hotmail.com. Simple but very welcoming place, with multilingual owner. They also have cabañas near Reserva Forestal 1km away.

C Albergue Las Salamandras, Sector Los Pinos, 2 km south in attractive forest, T/F211865, www.salamandras.cl. Double rooms, dorms (**E** pp) and 1 cabin (**A-C**), kitchen facilities, winter sports and trekking (Jun-Oct), cycling information. Highly recommended.

C Cabañas Baquedano, Baquedano 20, T232520, Patricio y Gedra Guzmán, http://balasch.cl/cabanas/. Welcoming, well-maintained, lovely place, 7 cabañas of varying standards, with splendid views over the Reserva Forestal, very helpful hosts who speak English, access to river, great value. Recommended.

C Hostal Las Quintas, Bilbao 1208, T231173. Spartan, but clean and very spacious rooms (some in very bizarre design) with bath and breakfast.

C-D Hosp Pochi, Freire 342, T256968. Rooms in a family home with bath and cable TV, breakfast included, very pleasant owners, good value. Recommended.

D Hosp María Ester, Lautaro 544, T233023. With breakfast (extra), some rooms with bath and TV, use of kitchen (extra charge), laundry facilities, also has *cabañas* (**C**) with bath, hot water and kitchenette, local information.

D Hosp Mondaca, Av Simpson 571, T254676. Small (only 3 rooms) but spotless family home, hospitable, breakfast extra.

Many more hospedajes and private houses with rooms; ask tourist office for a list.

Camping Tourist office on plaza or Sernatur in Coyhaique has a full list of all sites in XI Región. There are many camping sites in Coyhaique and on the road between Coyhaique and Puerto Aisén, eg **Camping Alborada**,at Km 2, T238868, US$14 per site, hot shower, and **Camping Río Correntoso**, Km 42, T232005, US$20 per site, showers, fishing. Camping in Reserva Nacional Río Simpson, US$7.

Puerto Aisén and Puerto Chacabuco *p839*

Accommodation is hard to find, most is taken up by fishing companies in both ports. There are several places to eat along Tte Merino and Aldea in Puerto Aisén.

LL-L Loberías del Sur, José Miguel Carrera 50, Puerto Chacabuco, T351112, www.loberias delsur.cl. Rebuilt 5-star hotel, the best around here and whose restaurant serves the best food in the area (handy for meal or a drink before boarding ferry – climb up steps direct from port). Same owner as Catamaranes del Sur (see Shipping, below), which also has a nearby nature reserve, Parque Aiken del Sur.

A Patagonia Green, 400 m from bridge (on Pto Chacabuco side), T336796, www.patagoniagreen.cl. Nice cabins for up to 5, kitchen, heating, TV, gardens, arranges tours to Laguna San Rafael, fishing, mountain biking, riding, trekking, etc, English spoken.

A-B Caicahues, Michimalonco 660, Puerto Aisén, T336633. The most recommended in this port, with heating and internet, book ahead.

C Hosp Mar Clara, Carrera 970, Puerto Aisén, T330945. More expensive with bath. Basic, clean, thin walls, looks nicer from outside than within.

Puerto Ibáñez *p839*

Various hotels in our **D-F** range, also a campsite.

B Cabañas Shehen Aike, Luis Risopatrón 55, T423284, www.aike.cl. Swiss-Chilean owned, large cabins, lots of ideas for trips, bike rental, organizes tours, fine food, welcoming, English spoken, best to phone in advance.

D Vientos del Sur, Bertrán Dixon 282, T423208. Good, nice family, dormitories, check the bill, cheap meals (restaurant open till late) but not as good as the lodging; also adventure activities.

E Hosp Don Francisco, San Salvador y Lautaro. Very hospitable, good food round the clock.

Villa Cerro Castillo *p840*

D Cabañas Don Niba, Los Pioneros 872, T419920. Friendly but basic *hospedaje*, good value. Recommended.

D Hostería Villarrica, O'Higgins 59, next to Supermercado Villarrica, T419500. Welcoming, basic, hot showers, and meals too, kind owners can arrange trekking guides and horse riding.

D Res María, Padre O Ronchi, near the office of Mar del Sur and Fantasía supermarket.

Eating

Futaleufú *p836*

ŸŸ Futaleufú, Cerda 407, T721295. Serves typical Chilean meat dishes and local foods.

ŸŸ Martín Pescador, Balmaceda y Rodríguez, T721279. For fish and meat dishes, rustic.

ŸŸ-Ÿ Sur Andes, Cerda 308, T721405. Café serving cakes, sweets, light meals and real coffee. Also sells handicrafts.

Puyuhuapi *p837*

ŸŸ Café Rossbach, Costanera. Run by the descendants of the original German settlers, an attractive place by the water for delicious salmon, tea and *küchen*.

ŸŸ Lluvia Marina, next to Casa Ludwig, veronet@entelchile.net. The best café, also selling handicrafts. Superb food in relaxed atmosphere, a great place to just hang out, owner Veronica is very helpful.

Coyhaique *p838, map p827*

ŸŸŸ Histórico Ricer, Horn 48 y 40, p 2, T232920. Central, warm and cosy, serving breakfast to dinner, regional specialities, with good vegetarian options, historical exhibits. Also has **Café Ricer** at No 48, serving light food.

ŸŸŸ-ŸŸ Ciprés, Baquedano 022, yelisa@patagoniachile.cl. Entrance through a private house. Fabulous view, Patagonian/Mediterranean cuisine, large portions, good, wine by the glass.

ŸŸ La Casona, Obispo Vielmo 77, T238894. Justly reputed as best in town, charming family restaurant serves excellent fish, congrio especially, but best known for grilled lamb.

ŸŸ-Ÿ Casino de Bomberos next to the fire station, Gral Parra 365, T231437. For great atmosphere and a filling lunch, can be slow when serving groups. Recommended.

ŸŸ-Ÿ Donde Ramiro, Freire 319, T256885. Good set lunches, big screen TV (watch football here).

Ÿ Club Sandwich Patagonia, Moraleda 433. 24-hr fast food and huge Chilean sandwiches, a local institution.

Ÿ El Mastique, Bilbao 141. Cheap but good pasta and Chilean food.

Ÿ Pizzería La Fiorentina, Prat 230. Tasty pizzas, good service. Recommended.

Cafés

Cafe Oriente, Condell 201. Serves a good lunch and tasty cakes.

Bars and clubs

Coyhaique *p838, map p827*

El Boliche, Moraleda 380. A beer- drinkers' bar. Many bars on the same street.

Pepe le Pub, Parra 72. Good cocktails and snacks, relaxed, live music at weekends.

Piel Roja, Moraleda y Condell. Good music, laid back, open Wed, Fri, Sat 1000-0500 for dancing, pub other nights. Recommended, but not cheap.

Shopping

Coyhaique *p838, map p827*

Camping equipment Condor Explorer, Dussen 357, T670349. Decent stock.

Bookshop Librería Rincón de Poeta, Moraleda y Parra. Good little place with some English books, maps and art books.

Handicrafts Artesanía Manos Azules, Riquelme 435. Sells fine handicrafts. **Feria de Artesanía** on the plaza. **Kaienk**, Plaza 219-A, T02245216, www.telaresdelapatagonia.cl, sells good-quality locally produced knitware.

Activities and tours

Futaleufú *p836*

Tour operators arrange whitewater rafting trips, prices starting from US$75 pp. Local fishing guides can also be found in the village.

Expediciones Chile, Mistral 296, T721386, www.exchile.com. Whitewater rafting, kayaking, etc. Offers the best multi-day trips, book in advance. Day trips can be booked at office.

Futaleufú Explore, O'Higgins 772, T721527, www.futaleufuexplore.com. A respected rafting company.

Rancho Las Ruedas, Pilota Carmona s/n, T8856 6339, rancholasruedas@hotmail.com. The best horseriding in the area.

Coyhaique *p838, map p827*

Many tours operate Sep to Apr, some Dec-Mar only. The surrounding area is famous for trout fishing with several *estancias* offering luxury accommodation and bilingual guides. Most general tour operators also offer specialist fishing trips.

Andes Patagónicos, Horn 48 y 40, loc 11, T216711, www.ap.cl. Trips to local lakes, Tortel, historically based tours and bespoke trips all year round. Good, but not cheap.

Aysen Tour, Gral Parra 97, T237070, www.aysentour.cl. Tours along the Carretera Austral, also car rental.

Cabot, Lautaro 339, T230101, www.cabot.cl. Horse-riding excursions to Cerro Castillo and other tours.

Camello Patagón, Moraleda 463, T244327, www.camellopatagon.cl. Trips to Capilla de Marmol in Río Tranquilo, also has a cosy café with good coffees. Closes 2000.

Casa del Turismo Rural, Dussen 357-B, T214031, www.casaturismorural.cl, Mon-Fri 1000-1330, 1530-2000 (also weekends in high season). An association of 40 families, mostly in the countryside, who offer activities such as horseriding and fishing. Many do not have telephones or internet, make reservations here.

Cóndor Explorer, Dussen 357, T573634, www.condorexplorer.com. Good small-scale agency specializing in trekking, but also Carretera tours, English spoken. Recommended.

Expediciones Coyhaique, Portales 195, T231783, www.coyhaiqueflyfishing.com. Fly-fishing experts.

Geo Turismo, Balmaceda 334, T573460, www.geoturismopatagonia.cl. Offers wide range of tours, English spoken, professional. Recommended.

Turismo Prado, 21 de Mayo 417, T231271, www.turismoprado.cl. Tours of local lakes and other sights, Laguna San Rafael trips and historical tours. Also offers general tourist information and accepts TCs.

Transport

Futaleufú *p836*

Bus Bus to **Chaitén** 6 days a week, information from **Chaitur** in Chaitén. To **Puerto Montt** via Argentina, Mon 0630, 13 hrs, US$38, with **Transporte Patagonia Norte**.

Border with Argentina *p837*

Bus From west side of plaza in Futaleufú, a **Jacobsen** bus runs to the border, 3 times a week, and Mon-Fri in Jan-Feb, US$4, 30 mins, connecting with services to Trevelin and Esquel.

La Junta

Bus To **Chaitén** 4 a week, information from **Chaitur**. To **Coyhaique**, with **Daniela** (T09-9512 3500), **M&C** (T242626), and **Lagunas**, 7 hrs, US$20. To **Puerto Cisnes**, with **Empresa Entre Verde** (T314275), US$10.

Puyuhuapi *p837*

Bus Daily to **Coyhaique**, US$18, 6 hrs, plus 2 weekly to **Lago Verde**.

Puerto Cisnes *p837*

Bus To **Coyhaique**, **Transportes Terra Austral**, T254335, **Bus Alegría**, T231350, run a daily (not Sun) service, US$15.

Coyhaique *p838, map p827*

Air Most flights from Balmaceda (see page 839), although Coyhaique has its own airport, Tte Vidal, about 5 km southwest of town. **Don Carlos** (www.doncarlos.cl), to **Chile Chico** (Mon-Sat), **Cochrane** (Mon, Thu) and **Villa O'Higgins** (Mon, Thu, recommended only for those who like flying, with strong stomachs, or in a hurry).

Bus Full list of buses from tourist information. Terminal at Lautaro y Magallanes, but most buses leave from their own offices.

To **Puerto Aisén**, minibuses run every 45 mins, 1 hr **Suray** (A Prat 265, T238387) and **São Paulo** (at terminal, T255726), US$3. Change here for **Puerto Chacabuco**, 20 mins, US$1. To **Puerto Ibáñez** on Lago Gral Carrera, several minibus companies (connect with ferry to Chile Chico) pick up 0530-0600 from your hotel, 1½ hrs, book the day before (eg **Yamil Ali**, Prat y Errázuriz, T219009, **Miguel Acuña**, M Moraleda 304, T251579 or 8900 4590, recommended).

Buses on the **Carretera Austral** vary according to demand, and they are always full so book early. Bikes can be taken by arrangement. North towards **Chaitén**: in summer 2010 one service direct a week, US$34-40, otherwise change in La Junta: **Becker** (Parra 335, T232167) and **Queulat** (Parra 329, T242626); in winter these stop overnight in La Junta. These two companies also continue to **Futaleufú**, US$34. To **Puerto Cisnes**, **Terra Austral** (at terminal, T232067), Mon-Sat, **Don Oscar** (T254335), less frequent, US$14. South to **Cochrane** daily in summer with either **Don Carlos** (Subteniente Cruz 63, T231981, www.doncarlos.cl), **Sao Paulo**, or **Acuario 13** (at terminal), US$20. All buses stop at **Cerro Castillo**. (US$8), **Bahía Murta** (US$12), **Puerto Tranquilo** (US$14) and **Puerto Bertrand** (US$16).

To Argentina: **Giobbi/Trans Austral**, T232067, at Terminal Municipal, run buses **Comodoro Rivadavia**, via Sarmiento, US$40. Daily buses from Com Rivadavia to Bariloche. Other options are given under Balmaceda and Chile Chico.

Car hire If renting a car, a high 4WD vehicle is recommended for Carretera Austral. Buy fuel in Coyhaique, several stations. There are several rental agencies in town, charging at least US$150 a day, including insurance, for 4WD or pick-up. Add another US$50 for paperwork to take a vehicle into Argentina. **Automóvil Club de Chile**, Simón Bolívar 194, T231649.

Ferry office **Navimag**, Paseo Horn 47 D, T233306, www.navimag.com.

Taxi US$7.50 to **Tte Vidal airport** (US$2 if sharing). Fares in town US$3, 50% extra after 2100. Taxi colectivos (shared taxis) congregate at Prat y Bilbao, average fare US$1.

Puerto Aisén and Puerto Chacabuco *p839*

Bus See under **Coyhaique**, above.

Ferry **Navimag's** *Puerto Edén* and *Evangelistas* sail each Fri from Puerto Chacabuco to Puerto Montt, taking about 24 hrs (for details, see Sea routes south of Puerto Montt, page 823). They divert from their schedule in summer to run a 5-day trip from Puerto Montt to Laguna San Rafael, calling at Puerto Chacabuco.

Catamaranes del Sur also have sailings to Laguna San Rafael, US$1,080 for a 3-day trip (pp, double cabin), US$1,610 for 5 days, all-inclusive. Shipping Offices: **Agemar**, Tte Merino 909, T332716, Puerto Aisén. **Catamaranes del Sur**, J M Carrera 50, T351115, www.catamaranesdelsur.cl. **Naviera Austral**, Terminal de Transbordadores, T351493, www.navieraustral.cl. **Navimag**, Terminal de Transbordadores, Puerto Chacabuco, T351111, www.navimag.com. It is best to make reservations in these companies' offices in Puerto Montt, Coyhaique or Santiago. For trips to Laguna San Rafael, see page 824.

Balmaceda *p839*

Air Balmaceda airport is used for daily flights to **Santiago** with **LAN**, via **Puerto Montt**, and **Sky**, which sometimes makes several stops. Landing can be dramatic owing to strong winds. **Sky** also flies to **Punta Arenas**, 3 flights weekly. Minibuses to/from hotels in Coyhaique (56 km) US$8, 3 companies who all sell tickets at baggage carousel. Taxi from airport to Coyhaique, 1 hr, US$30. Car rental agencies at the airport; very expensive.

Puerto Ibáñez *p839*

Bus Minibus to **Coyhaique**, 1½ hrs, US$7.55. There is a road to **Perito Moreno**, Argentina, but no public transport.

Ferry Two ferries, **Pilchero** and **Chelenco** sail between Puerto Ibañez and **Chile Chico**, daily except Saturday in summer, less often otherwise. Both take passengers and vehicles, fares about US$6.75 per adult (combined minivan/ferry ticket from Coyhaique US$11, with Miguel Acuña, see page 845), US$3.15 for bikes, motorbikes US$8, cars US$40, uncomfortable but beautiful 2½ hr crossing, take food and warm clothing as the ferries are completely open, but for a small cabin where coffee is served and one can warm up. Passports required, reservations essential: **Chelenco**, in Coyhaique, Mar del Sur, Av Baquedano 146-A, T231255/233367; in Puerto Ibáñez, Padre O Ronchi 166, T423239; in Chile Chico T411864. Write to msur@patagoniachile.cl for sailings; they change frequently. **Pilchero** in Coyhaique, Simón Bolivar 254, T234240. At the quay, Café El Refugio has toilets and sells sandwiches and snacks. Minibuses meet the ferry in Puerto Ibáñez for Coyhaique.

Villa Cerro Castillo *p840*
Bus 6 a week in summer to both **Coyhaique** and **Cochrane**, companies as above under Coyhaique. To **Río Tranquilo**, US$7.

Directory

Coyhaique *p838, map p827*
Airline offices **Don Carlos**, address under Bus, above. **LAN**, Moraleda 402 , T600-526 2000. **Sky**, Prat 203, T240827 or 600-600 2828. **Banks** Several **Redbanc** ATMs in centre. Casas de cambio: **Turismo Prado**, see Tour operators. **Emperador**, Bilbao 222, T233727. **Bicycle rental** **Manuel Iduarte**, Parra y Bulnes, check condition first. **Bicycle repairs** **Tomás Madrid Urrea**, Pasaje Foitzich y Libertad, T252132. Recommended. **Internet** **Cyber Patagonia**, 21 de Mayo 525. Good value. **Trapananda**, on Moraleda next to LAN, T210525, open until late, serves basic food, has scanners, printers and CD/DVD burners. Others in centre. **Language schools** **Baquedano International Language School**, Baquedano 20, at Cabañas of Sr Guzmán (see Sleeping), T232520, www.balasch .cl. US$400 per week course including lodging and all meals, 4 hrs a day one-to-one tuition, other activities organized at discount rates. **Post offices** Cochrane 202. **Telephones** Several call centres; shop around.

Puerto Aisén *p839*
Banks **BCI**, Prat, for Visa. **Banco de Chile**, Plaza de Armas, cash only. **Redbanc** ATM in Puerto Chacabuco. **Post offices** south side of bridge. **Telephones** On south side of Plaza de Armas, next to Turismo Rucaray, which posts boat information and has internet. **Entel**, Libertad 408. Internet access.

Lago General Carrera and around

Southwest of Villa Cerro Castillo, the Carretera continues to afford stunning views, for instance minty-green Lago Verde and the meandering Río Manso, with swampy vegetation punctuated by the silver stumps of thousands of burnt trees, huge mountains behind. Lago General Carrera (Lago Buenos Aires in Argentina) straddles the border and, at 2,240 sq km, is the second largest lake in South America. It's an area of outstanding beauty. Sheltered from the icy west winds by the Campo de Hielo Norte, the region also has the best climate in Southern Chile, with little rain, some 300 days of sunshine and a microclimate at Chile Chico that allows the cultivation of the same crops and fruit as in the Central Valley. Ferries cross the lake (see above), but it is worth taking time to follow the Carretera Austral around the lake's western shores.

Bahía Murta (*Km 198; Population: 586*), 5 km off the Camino, lies at the northern tip of the central 'arm' of the lake. There is a tiny tourist information hut, which opens summer 1000-1430, 1500-1930. Petrol is available from a house with a sign just before Puerto Murta. There's a public phone in the village.

Back on the Carretera Austral, **Puerto Río Tranquilo**, Km 223, is a slightly larger hamlet where the buses stop for lunch: fuel is available. Capilla del Marmol, in fact a limestone cliff vaguely resembling sculpted caves, is reached by a wonderful boat ride (ask at petrol station, to hire a boat US$45 with guide).

El Maitén, Km 277 south of Coihaique, an idyllic spot at the southwest tip of Lago General Carrera, is where a road branches off east along the south shore of the lake towards Chile Chico, while the Carretera Austral continues south to Puerto Bertand.

South of El Maitén the Carretera Austral becomes steeper and more winding (in winter this stretch, all the way to Cochrane, is icy and dangerous). At Km 294, is the hamlet of **Puerto Bertrand**, lying by the dazzling turquoise waters of Río Baker. As this river is world renowned for fly fishing, good accommodation in Puerto Bertrand is either in one of the luxury cabañas that cater for wealthy anglers, or in a simple room in the village.

At **Puerto Guadal**, 13 km east of El Maitén, there are shops, accommodation, restaurants, a post office, petrol and a lovely stretch of lakeside beach. Further east is the villages of Mallín Grande (Km 40), **Paso de las Llaves**, a 30-km stretch carved out of the rock face on the edge of the lake, and Fachinal (turn off at Km 74). A further 5 km east is the **Garganta del Diablo**, a narrow gorge of 120 m with a fast-flowing stream below.

Chile Chico ➔ *Population: 4,500.*

This is a quiet town in a fruit-growing region, 125 km east of El Maitén. It has an annual fruit festival at end-January and a small museum (open summer only). There are fine views from Cerro de las Banderas. It's 7 km to Los Antiguos, Argentina, where food and accommodation are preferable. **Laguna Jeinimeni**, 52 km from Chile Chico, is a beautiful place with excellent fishing, where you can also see flamingos and black necked swans. The **tourist office** (helpful but usually closed) is in the Casa de la Cultura on O'Higgins. An unofficial purple tourist kiosk on the quay where the ferry arrives, sells bus tickets for Ruta 40 (Argentina), but has some accommodation information. Municipal website: www.chilechico.cl.

Border with Argentina

Chilean immigration 2 km east of Chile Chico. Open summer 0730-2200, winter 0800-2000. Argentine side closes for lunch 1300-1400. Remember that you can't take fresh food across in either direction, and you'll need ownership papers if crossing with a car. If entering Argentina here you will not have to fill in an immigration form (ask if you need entry papers).

Cochrane ➔ *Population: 2,996.*

From Puerto Bertand heading south, the road climbs up to high moorland, passing the confluence of the Ríos Neff and Baker (there is a mirador – lookout – here), before winding into Cochrane, 343 km south of Coyhaique. The scenery is splendid all the way; the road is generally rough but not treacherous. Watch out for cattle on the road and take blind corners slowly. Sitting in a hollow on the Río Cochrane, Cochrane is a simple place, sunny in summer, good for walking and fishing. The **Reserva Nacional Lago Cochrane**, 12 km east, surrounds Lago Cochrane. Campsite at Playa Vidal. Boat hire on the lake costs US$15 per person. Northeast of Cochrane is the beautiful **Reserva Nacional Tamango** ⓘ *Dec-Mar 0830-2100, Apr-Nov 0830-1830. Ask in the CONAF office (Río Neff 417, T522164) about visiting because some access is through private land and tourist facilities are rudimentary, US$6, plus guided visits to see the huemules, Tue, Thu, Sat, US$80 for up to 6 people*. It has lenga forest, a few surviving huemul deer as well as guanaco, foxes and lots of birds including woodpeckers and hummingbirds. Access 9 km northeast of Cochrane, along Río Cochrane. There are marked paths for walks between 45 minutes and five hours, up to Cerro Tamango (1,722 m) and Cerro Temanguito (1,485 m). Take water and food, and windproof clothing if climbing the Cerros. The views from the reserve are superb, over the town, the nearby lakes and to the Campo de Hielo Norte to the west. It is inaccessible in the four winter months. **Tourist office** ⓘ *on corner of plaza on Dr Steffen, T522115, www.cochranepatagonia.cl, summer Mon-Fri 0830-2000, Sat-Sun 1100-2000, off season Mon-Fri 0830-1730*. ATM for Mastercard only.

Caleta Tortel ➔ *Population: 448.*

The Carretera Austral runs south of Cochrane and, after 105km, at the rather bleak looking Puerto Vagabundo, the road branches west to Caleta Tortel (see Transport, below). This quiet village at the mouth of the river, was until very recently accessible only by water and has no streets, only

7 km of walkways of cypress wood. Surrounded by mountainous land with abundant vegetation, it has a cool, rainy climate, and its main trade is logging, though this is declining as the town looks towards tourism. Located between the Northern and Southern Ice Fields, Tortel is within reach of two glaciers: **Glaciar Steffens** is to the north, a 2½-hour boat journey and three-hour walk, crossing a glacial river in a rowing boat. A boat for 10 people costs US$190. **Glaciar Jorge Montt** is to the southwest, five hours by boat, through landscapes of pure ice and water, US$300 for 10 people. Another boat trip is to the Isla de los Muertos, which has an interesting history, US$70 for 10. At the entrance to the village is a small tourist information office with information on lodging and a useful map. There is a post office, open Monday-Friday 0830-1330. The phone office number is T211876. **CONAF**, T211876, orlando.beltran@conaf.cl.

Villa O'Higgins

The Carretera Austral runs to Puerto Yungay (122 km from Cochrane), then another 110 km to **Villa O'Higgins**. There is one free ferry (*Padre Antonio Ronchi*) crossing between Yungay (military base) and Río Bravo (1000, 1200, 1800, return to Yungay an hour later, 45 minutes, capacity 4-5 cars). The road beyond Río Bravo is very beautiful, but often closed by bad weather (take food – no shops or fuel on the entire route, few people and few vehicles for hitching). Tourist information is available from the Municipalidad, Lago Christie 121, T/F067-211849. See www.villaohiggins.cl.

It is possible to go from Villa O'Higgins to El Chaltén, Argentina. The road continues 7 km south to Bahía Bahamóndez on Lago O'Higgins (bus US$4), from where a boat leaves for Chilean immigration at Candelario Mancilla ⓘ *open Nov-Apr 0800-2200, 2¾ hours, US$80; departures one Wed and every Sat in Nov, Wed, Sat in Dec, Mon, Wed, Sat in Jan and Feb, Sat in Mar. There are other departures, including two in Apr and one in mid Nov, but exact dates should be checked as the schedule alters yearly*. A detour to Glaciar O'Higgins costs US$40 on the regular crossing or between US$90-150 for a day-long special trip, depending from which side of the lake you start (cheaper from Candelario Mancilla). Sailings may be cancelled if the weather is bad. Then it's 14 km to the Argentine border and a further 5 km to Argentine immigration at Punta Norte on Lago del Desierto. The first part can be done on foot, on horseback, or by 4WD service for US$30 (takes 4 passengers and luggage, call Hans Silva in Villa O'Higgins, T431821, to reserve car or horses). The next 5 km is a demanding hike, or you can take a horse for US$30, with an extra horse to carry bags (Ricardo is great horseman with an excellent sense of humor).

The route descends sharply towards Lago de Desierto. Bridges were washed away in 2009/2010 and you will have to balance on boulders and tree trunks over the streams. Make sure to wear good boots for crossing wetland. Panoramas on the descent are breathtaking, including of Cerro Fritz Roy. A short detour to Laguna Larga (on the right as you walk from the border) is worth it if you have the energy. The 40-minute boat crossing of the lake passes glaciers and ice fields on your right ⓘ *daily except Mon, US$20 if bought in Argentina, more if prepaid in Chile*. Finally it takes over an hour by bus or minivan on a gravel road to El Chaltén (37 km). Several companies including Transporte Las Lengas and JR Turismo Alternativo await the boat ⓘ *from US$13 if bought by the jetty, up to US$30 if prepaid*. There is no food available on either side of the lake, but Argentine immigration at Punta Norte are friendly and, if you are cold, may offer you coffee.

The best combination is to take 4WD from Candelario Mancilla to the border and then continue on horseback. This ensures that the trip can be done in a day (depart Villa O'Higgins 0800, arrive El Chaltén 2130; full details on www.villaohiggins.cl, T067-431821). Allow for delays, though, especially if horses aren't available for hire. It's a good option to pay for each portion of the route separately. The route closes in late April. With the opening of this route it is possible to do the Carretera Austral and go on to Argentina's Parque Nacional Los Glaciares and Chile's Torres del Paine without doubling back on yourself.

Parque Nacional Laguna San Rafael

ⓘ *US$6, at the glacier there is a small ranger station which gives information; a pier and 2 paths have been built, one of which leads to the glacier.*

Some 150 nautical miles south of Puerto Aisén is the **Laguna San Rafael**, into which flows a glacier, 30 m above sea level and 45 km in length. The glacier has a deep blue colour, shimmering and reflecting the light. It calves small icebergs, which seem an unreal, translucent blue, and which are carried out to sea by wind and tide. The glacier is very noisy; there are frequent cracking and banging sounds, resembling a mixture of gunshots and thunder. When a hunk of ice breaks loose, a huge swell is created and the icebergs start rocking in the water. The glacier is disintegrating and is predicted to disappear entirely by 2013. Some suggest that the wake from tour boats is contributing to the erosion.

The thick vegetation on the shores, with snowy peaks above, is typical of Aisén. The only access is by plane or by boat. The glacier is equally spectacular from the air or the sea. The glacier is one of a group of four that flow in all directions from Monte San Valentín. This icefield is part of the Parque Nacional Laguna San Rafael (1,740,000 ha), regulated by CONAF. In the national park are puma, pudú (miniature deer), foxes, dolphins, occasional sealions and sea otters, and many species of bird. Walking trails are limited (about 10 km in all) but a lookout platform has been constructed, with fine views of the glacier.

Lago General Carrera and around listings

For Sleeping and Eating price codes and other relevant information, see Essentials, pages 38-40.

Sleeping

Lago General Carrera *p846*

Bahía Murta

E **Res Patagonia**, Pje España 64, Bahía Murta, T419600. Comfortable, serves food. Free camping by lake at Bahía Murta.

Puerto Río Tranquilo

AL **Hostal el Puesto**, Pedro Lagos 258, T02-1964555, www.elpuesto.cl. No doubt the most comfortable place in Río Tranquilo, with breakfast, also organizes tours.

A **Hostal Los Pinos**, Godoy 51, Puerto Río Tranquilo, T411576. Family run, well maintained, good mid-price meals. Recommended.

B **Campo Alacaluf**, Km 44 on the Río Tranquilo-Bahía Exploradores side road, T419500. Wonderful guesthouse hidden away from civilization. Run by very friendly German family. Recommended.

C **Cabañas Jacricalor**, Carretera Austral 245, Puerto Río Tranquilo, T419500 (public phone). Tent-sized *cabañas*, hot shower, good meals, good information for climbers.

C **Hostal Carretera Austral**, 1 Sur 223, Río Tranquilo, T419500. Also serves mid-range/ cheap meals.

El Maitén

LL **Mallín Colorado Ecolodge**, Carretera Austral Km 273, 2 km west of El Maitén, T02-919 6112/ 02-360 9742, www.mallincolorado.cl. Comfortable *cabañas* in sweeping gardens, complete tranquillity, charming owners, 4-10 day packages available, including transfers from Balmaceda, horseriding, estancia trip, superb meals, open Oct-Apr. Highly recommended.

L **Hacienda Tres Lagos**, Carretera Austral Km 274, just west of cruce Maitén, T067-411323, T02-3334 4122 (Santiago), www.haciendatres lagos.com. Set in spacious grounds on the lake-shore. Small, boutique resort with bungalows, suites and less luxurious standard cabins. Good restaurant, wide range of excursions offered, sauna, jacuzzi, good service. English spoken. Recommended.

Puerto Bertrand

AL **Lodge Río Baker**, Puerto Bertrand, T411499, riobaker@hotmail.com. Full board, warmly recommended fishing lodge, also all-inclusive fishing packages.

AL **Patagonia Baker Lodge and Restaurant**, Puerto Bertrand, towards the south side of the lake, T411903, www.pbl.cl. Stylish cabañas in woodland, fishing lodge, birdwatching, fabulous views upriver towards rapids and the mountains beyond.

C Hostería Puerto Bertrand, Puerto Bertrand, T419900. With breakfast, other meals available, also *cabañas*, activities.
D Hosp Doña Ester, Casa No 8, Puerto Bertrand, T09-9990 8541. Rooms in a pink house, good.
D Turismo Hospedaje Campo de Hielo Norte, Ventisquero Neff s/n. Owned by Anselmo Soto, open in tourist season only, very hospitable and helpful.

Puerto Guadal
AL Terra Luna Lodge, on lakeside, 2 km from Puerto Guadal, T431263, www.terra-luna.cl. Welcoming well-run place with lodge, bungalows and camping huts (**B**), also has restaurant, many activities offered.
A El Mirador Playa Guadal, 2 km from Puerto Guadal towards Chile Chico, T09-9234 9130, www.patagoniaplayaguadal.cl. Cabañas near beach, fishing, walks to nearby waterfalls, meals extra, restaurant with fixed rate menus Sep-Nov, Mar-May, à la carte Jan-Feb. Recommended.
D Hostería Huemules, Las Magnolias 382, Puerto Guadal, T431212. Breakfast, good views.
Camping Site at east end of village.

Chile Chico *p847*
C Casa Quinta No me Olvides/Manor House Don't Forget Me, Sector Chacras, Camino Internacional s/n, T09-9833 8006. Hospedaje and camping, cooking facilities, shared bathrooms, hot showers, honey, eggs, fruit and vegetables for sale, tours arranged to Lago Jeinimeni and Cueva de las Manos. Recommended.
C Hostería de la Patagonia, Camino Internacional s/n, Casilla 91, T411337.
Also camping; full-board available. Good food, English, French and Italian spoken, trekking, horse riding, white-water rafting. Recommended.
C Hosp Don Luis, Balmaceda 175, T411384. Meals available, laundry, helpful.
E pp **Hospedaje** at Tel Sur phone centre, in the middle of O'Higgins. Use of kitchen, helpful owners also sell bus tickets for La Unión buses to Los Antiguos and Comodoro Rivadavia.
Camping Free site at Bahía Jara, 5 km west of Chile Chico, then turn north for 12 km.

Cochrane *p847*
In summer it is best to book rooms in advance.
A Wellmann, Las Golondrinas 36, T/F522171. Comfortable, warm, hot water, good meals. Recommended.
C Cabañas Rogeri, Río Maitén 80, T522264, rogeri3@hotmail.cl. Cabañas for 4, with kitchen facilities, price includes breakfast.
C Res Cero a Cero, Lago Brown 464, T522158, ceroacero@hotmail.com. With breakfast, welcoming. Recommended.
C Res Rubio, Tte Merino 871, T522173. Very nice, breakfast included, lunch and dinner extra.
C Res Sur Austral, Prat 334, T522150. Breakfast included, with bath, **E** pp shared bath, hot water, also very nice.
D Res El Fogón, San Valentín 65, T522240. Its pub is the only eating place open in low season, it's the best restaurant at any time of year.
D-E Res Cochrane, Dr Steffens 451, T522370. Also serves good meals, laundry, hot shower, breakfast. Recommended. Also camping.

Caleta Tortel *p847*
There are several *hospedajes*. All prices are cheaper in the low season. For all T067-234815 (public phone) or 211876 (municipality).
AL Entre Hielos lodge, sector centro, Tortel. T02-196 0271, www.entrehielostortel.cl. Newly built, the only upmarket accommodation in town.
C Estilo, Sector Centro, Tortel, tortelhospedajeestilo@yahoo.es. Warm and comfortable, good food. Entertaining, talkative host (if your Spanish is up to it). Recommended.
C Hosp Costanera, Sra Luisa Escobar Sanhueza. Cosy, warm, lovely garden, full board available, breakfast included (also open to non-guests).
Camping There is camping at sector Junquillo at the far end of town.

Villa O'Higgins *p848*
B El Mosco, at the northern entrance to the town, T431819, patagoniaelmosco@yahoo.es. **E-F** pp in dorms. Spanish run, kitchen facilities, games, laundry facilities, trekking maps and information. Can help with bike repairs. Camping available, English spoken. More expensive than the rest, but nothing else competes in terms of infrastructure. Recommended.

C Cabañas San Gabriel, Lago O'Higgins 310. Nice cabins. A good choice for small groups.
D Res Campanario, Lago O'Higgins 72. Opposite El Mosco, friendly, kitchen facilities, camping.
E Los Nirres, Lago O'Higgins 72, **F** singles. Basic accommodation, goods meals. Several other similar places in town.

Eating

Chile Chico *p847*
Café Refer, O'Higgins 416. Good, despite exterior.
Cafetería Loly y Elizabeth, PA González 25, on Plaza. Coffee, delicious ice cream and cakes.

Caleta Tortel *p847*
Café Celes Salom, bar/restaurant serving basic, cheap meals, disco on Sat, occasional live bands.

Lago General Carrera and around *p846*
Patagonia Adventure Expeditions, T411330, www.adventurepatagonia. com. Professional outfit running exclusive fully-supported treks to the Campo de Hielo Norte and the eastern side of Parque Nacional Laguna San Rafael. Expensive but a unique experience and recommended. Also organize rafting on the Río Baker and provide general help organizing tours, treks and expeditions.

Transport

Chile Chico *p847*
Bus Several minibuses daily to **Cochrane**, US$22, 5 hrs. See above for ferry to Puerto Ibáñez and connecting minibus to Coyhaique. Ferry and minibus tickets from **Miguel Acuña**, Refugio Muelle Local, T411804 (for urgent enquiries call mobiles 9217 3520 or 8900 4590).

Border with Argentina: Chile Chico–Los Antiguos *p847*
Bus In summer, irregular minibuses from Chile Chico ferry to Los Antiguos on the Argentine side 0800-2200, US$3.75 (in Chilean pesos), ½-1 hr including formalities: ask on quayside. **Minibus Jaime Acuña**, T411553.

Cochrane *p847*
Air Don Carlos to **Coyhaique**, Mon, Thu, US$75.
Bus Company agencies: **Don Carlos**, Prat 344, T522150; **Acuario 13** and **Sao Paulo**, Río Baker 349, T522143. There are 6 buses a week between Coyhaique and Cochrane, check with companies for current timetables, US$20. To **Río Tranquilo**, US$11. To **Villa O'Higgins**, **Acuario 13** (T067-255726), Sun, Thu 0730, return Mon, Fri 0830, 6-7 hrs, US$19. To **Tortel**, **Gabriel Becerra** and **Buses Aldeas**, daily between them, US$10. Minibuses, including **Bus Ale**, Las Golondrinas 399, T522448, daily to **Chile Chico**, US$22. Petrol is available at the **Esso** and **Copec** servicentros.

Caleta Tortel *p847*
Bus From **Cochrane**, see above. On Sun Dec-Mar a bus runs between Tortel and **Villa O'Higgins**, 4 hrs, US$30, 0830 to Tortel, 1630 back to O'Higgins, T067-431821.

Parque Nacional Laguna San Rafael *p849*
Ferry Cruises are run by : **Skorpios** (see under Puerto Montt); **Catamaranes del Sur**, **Compañía Naviera Puerto Montt** and **Navimag**. **Patagonia Express** runs catamaran trips from Puerto Chacabuco to Laguna San Rafael via Termas de Puyuhuapi, in tours lasting 4-6 days, from Puerto Montt via Coyhaique including the catamaran service, the hotel stay at Termas de Puyuhuapi and the day excursion to Laguna San Rafael (see page 824). Other charters available. Private yachts can be chartered in Puerto Montt.

Directory

Chile Chico *p847*
Banks It's best to change money in Coyhaique. ATM in the middle of O'Higgins for Mastercard and Cirrus, not Visa. Dollars and Argentine pesos can be changed in small amounts in shops and cafés, including Loly y Elizabeth, at poor rates. **Hospital** Lautaro s/n, T411334. **Post offices** On the plaza.

Far south

This wild and wind-blown area, covering the glacial regions of southern Patagonia and Chilean Tierra del Fuego, is beautiful and bleak, with stark mountains and open steppe. Little vegetation survives here and few people; though it represents 17.5% of Chile's total area, it is inhabited by under 1% of the population. The southernmost city of Punta Arenas and the attractive, quiet port of Puerto Natales are the two main centres, the latter being the gateway to the Torres del Paine and Balmaceda national parks. In summer it is a wonderful region for climbing, hiking, boat trips and the southernmost crossings to Argentina.

Summers are sunny and very variable, with highs of 15° C. In winter snow covers the country, except those parts near the sea, making many roads more or less impassable, except on horseback. Cold, piercing winds blow, particularly in spring, when they may exceed 100 kph. Despite chilly temperatures, protection against the sun's ultraviolet rays is essential here and in summer, too, windproof clothing is a must.

Punta Arenas and around

➔ *Phone code: 061. Colour map 9, C2. Population: Punta Arenas 150,000, Puerto Natales 20,500.*

About 2,140 km south of Santiago, Punta Arenas lies on the eastern shore of the Brunswick Peninsula facing the Straits of Magellan at almost equal distance from the Pacific and Atlantic oceans. Founded in 1843, it has grand neoclassical buildings and an opulent cemetery, testimony to its wealthy past as a major port and centre for exporting wool. In the late 19th century, Salesian Missions were established to control the indigenous population so sheep farming could flourish. The city's fortunes slumped when the Panama Canal opened in 1914, but it remains a pleasant place, with attractive, painted wooden buildings away from the centre and superb fish restaurants. Good roads connect the city with Puerto Natales, 247 km north, and with Río Gallegos in Argentina.

Ins and outs

Tourist office Sernatur ⓘ *Lautaro Navarro 999 y Pedro Montt, T225385, infomagallanes@sernatur.cl, open Mon-Thu 0815-1800, Fri 0815-1700. See www.patagonia-chile.com*. There is also the tourist information **kiosk** in the plaza ⓘ *opposite Centro Español, T200610, Mon-Thu 0800-1730, Fri 0800-1630, informacionturistica@puntaarenas.cl*. Experienced staff, good town map with all hotels and internet places marked, English spoken, can book hotels. See www.chileaustral.com. **CONAF** ⓘ *Av Bulnes 0309, p 4, T238554, magallanes.oirs@conaf.cl.*

Sights

In the centre of the **Plaza Muñoz Gamero** is a striking statue of Magellan with a mermaid and two indigenous Fuegians at his feet. Around the plaza are a number of impressive neo-classical buildings, the former mansions of the great sheep ranching families of the late 19th century. **Palacio Sara Braun** (1895), now the Hotel José Nogueira, has several elegant rooms which are open to the public ⓘ *1000-1300, 1800-2030, US$2*. Around the corner, on Magallanes is the **Teatro Cervantes** (now a cinema with beautifully decorated interior). The fascinating **Museo de Historia Regional Braun Menéndez** ⓘ *Magallanes 949, T244216, www.dibam.cl/sdm_mr_magallanes, Mon-Sat 1030-1700, 1030-1400 Sun (1030-1400 daily May-Sep), US$2, guided tours in Spanish, information in English*, was once the mansion of Mauricio Braun, built in 1905. It has fabulously decorated rooms, with ornate furniture, paintings and marble and crystal imported from Europe. Highly recommended. Further north, is the impressive **Cemetery** ⓘ *Av Bulnes 929, daily, 0800-1800, later in summer*, charting a history of European immigration and shipping disasters through the huge mausoleums, divided by avenues of huge trees.

Punta Arenas

Sleeping
1 Backpackers' Paradise *B3*
2 Cabo de Hornos *C2*
3 Chalet Capital *C1*
4 Cóndor de Plata *C2*
5 Diego de Almagro *C3*
6 Ely House *A3*
7 Finis Terrae *C2*
8 Hosp Independencia *D1*
9 Hosp Miramar *D1*
10 Hostal Al Fin del Mundo *C3*
11 Hostal Ayelen *B3*
12 Hostal de la Avenida *B2*
13 Hostal de la Patagonia *B3*
14 Hostal del Sur *B1*
15 Hostal Dinka's House *A3*
16 Hostal El Conventillo *C3*
17 Hostal Hain *D2*
18 Hostal La Estancia *B3*
19 Hostal Paredişo *A3*
20 Hostal Sonia Kuscevic *A2*
21 Hostal Taty's House *A3*
22 José Nogueira (Palacio Sara Braun) *C2*
23 Luna Hostal *B3*
24 Monterrey *B2*
25 The Pink House *A3*
26 Tierra del Fuego *C2*

Eating
1 Café Cyrano *A2*
2 Café Montt *C3*
3 Club Croata *D2*
4 Coffee Net *C2*
5 Damiana Elena *A2*
6 Dino's Pizza *B2*
7 El Asador Patagónico *B3*
8 El Quijote *C3*
9 History Coffee *C3*
10 La Luna & Jekus *C3*
11 La Marmita *B3*
12 La Tasca *D2*
13 Lomit's *C2*
14 O' Sole Mío *C3*
15 Remezón *D2*
16 Sabores *B2*
17 Santino *C2*
18 Sotitos *D3*

Bars & clubs
19 La Taberna del Club de la Unión *C2*
20 Pub Olijoe *D3*

The perfect compliment to this is **Museo Regional Salesiano Mayorino Borgatello** ⓘ *in the Colegio Salesiano, Av Bulnes 336 (entrance next to church), T221001, www.museomaggiorinoborgatello.cl, Tue-Sun 1000-1230, 1500-1800 (hours change frequently), US$4*. It covers the fascinating history of the indigenous peoples and their education by the Salesian missions, beside an array of stuffed birds and gas extraction machinery. The Italian priest, Alberto D'Agostini, who arrived in 1909 and presided over the missions, took wonderful photographs of the region and his 70-minute film can be seen on video (ask). Highly recommended. The **Instituto de la Patagonia** ⓘ *Av Bulnes Km 4 north (opposite the University), T244216, outdoor exhibits Mon-Fri 0830-1130, 1430-1830, Sat 0830-1230, US$2*, has an open-air museum with artefacts used by the early settlers, pioneer homes, library and botanical gardens.

Museo Naval y Marítimo ⓘ *Pedro Montt 981, T205479, Jan-Feb Tue-Sun 0930-1700; Mar-Dec Tue-Sun 0930- 1230, 1400-1700, US$1.50*, has shipping instruments, maps, photos and relics from the Chilean navy and famous navigators. Recommended. West of the Plaza Muñoz Gamero on Calle Fagnano is the Mirador Cerro de La Cruz offering a view over the city and the Magellan Straits. The **Parque María Behety**, south of town along 21 de Mayo, features a scale model of Fuerte Bulnes and a campsite, popular for Sunday picnics; ice rink here in winter.

The city's waterfront is undergoing an extensive face-lift (2009-2010), with public boardwalks and outdoor spaces under special shelters giving protection from the sun's strong ultraviolet rays. It's an impressive construction project that will beautify the city centre.

Around Punta Arenas

West of town (7 km) is the **Reserva Forestal Magallanes** ⓘ *US$5, taxi US$7.50*, with nature trails from 45 minutes to 2 days, camping and refugios, and several places to visit, including a hill with beautiful views over town and the surroundings. Some 56 km south, **Fuerte Bulnes** is a replica of the wooden fort erected in 1843 by the crew of the Chilean vessel *Ancud* to secure Chile's southernmost territories after Independence. Little to see but an interesting story. Nearby is **Puerto de Hambre**, a beautiful, panoramic spot where there are ruins of the church built in 1584 by Sarmiento de Gamboa's colonists. Tours by several agencies. Some 195 km to the northeast on Ruta 255, towards Argentina, is **Parque Nacional Pali Aike** ⓘ *US$2, refugio for 4*, near Punta Delgada. One of the oldest archaeological sites in Patagonia (Pali Aike means 'desolate place of bad spirits' in Tehuelche). Evidence of aborigines from 10,000-12,000 years ago, in an extraordinary place with volcanic rock of different colours. Tour operators offer a full day trip, US$70; for more details, ask at CONAF, who manage the park.

Isla Magdalena, a small island 30 km northeast, is the location of the **Monumento Natural Los Pingüinos**, a spectacular colony of 60,000 pairs of Magellanic penguins, who come here to breed between November and January (also skuas, kelp gulls and other marine wildlife). Magdalena is one of a group of three islands (the others are Marta and Isabel), visited by Drake, whose men killed 3,000 penguins for food. Boat trips to the island are run by **Comapa** and **Cruceros Australis** call here (see Activities and tours, below). Some 70 km north of Punta Arenas, **Otway Sound** ⓘ *Oct-mid Mar, US$5*, has a colony of Magellanic penguins, viewed from walkways and bird hides, best seen in the morning. Rheas can also be seen. It is becoming a popular area for sea-kayaking and other adventure sports.

Punta Arenas listings

For Sleeping and Eating price codes and other relevant information, see Essentials, pages 38-40.

Sleeping

Punta Arenas *p852, map p853*
Hotel prices are lower during winter months (Apr-Sep). For accommodation in private houses, usually **E** pp, ask at the tourist office. No campsites in or near the city.

LL Cabo de Hornos, Muñoz Gamero 1039, on the plaza, T715000, www.hoteles-australis.com. 4-star, newly refurbished, comfy, bright and spacious rooms, with good views from 4th floor up.

LL-L Finis Terrae, Colón 766, T228200, www.hotelf inisterrae.com. Modern, international style, comfortable, great views from rooftop café/bar, English spoken. Recommended.

LL-L José Nogueira, Plaza de Armas, Bories 959 y P Montt, in former Palacio Sara Braun, T711000, www.hotelnogueira.com. Best in town, stylish rooms, warm atmosphere, excellent service. Smart restaurant in the beautiful loggia. A few original rooms now a 'small museum', with a portrait of Sara Braun.

L Tierra del Fuego, Colón 716, T226200, www.puntaarenas.com. Spacious, tasteful, TV, 2nd floor rooms have kitchenette. Popular Café 1900 downstairs, excellent restaurant open to non residents. Recommended.

AL Diego de Almagro, Colón 1290, T208800, www.dahoteles.com. Very modern, good international standard, on waterfront, heated pool, gym, big bright rooms. Highly recommended.

A Chalet Chapital, Sanhueza 974, T730100, www.hotelchaletchapital.cl. Small well-run hotel, smallish rooms, helpful staff, a good choice in this price range. Recommended.

A Cóndor de Plata, Av Colón 556, T247987, www.condordeplata.cl. Named after the aeroplane of German aviator and explorer Günther Plüschow, with relics, modern, hot water, full-size bathtubs, TV, café, laundry service, internet.

A Hostal de la Avenida, Colón 534, T247532. Attractive rooms, central heating, cable TV, pretty courtyard with plants and apple tree, breakfasts.

A Hostal de la Patagonia, O'Higgins 730, T249970, www.ecotourpatagonia.com. **B** in low season, heating, TV, Wi-Fi, buffet breakfast, afternoon tea/onces, smart, comfy, well-appointed.

B Hostal Sonia Kuscevic, Pasaje Darwin 175, T248543, www.hostalsk.cl. One of the city's oldest guesthouses, with breakfast, kitchen facilities, hot water, heating, parking. Better value for longer than short stays, good discount with Hostelling International card.

B Hostal del Sur, Mejicana 151, T227249, hostaldelsur@hotmail.com. Impeccable old house with modern rooms in residential area, welcoming, excellent breakfast, advance booking in summer. Recommended.

B-C Hostal Ayelen, Lautarro Navarro 763, T242413, www.ayelenresidencial.com. Family atmosphere, very helpful, 120-year old house with some new rooms at the back, bathroom a bit small but super clean, comfy, hot water, TV, heating, breakfast at any hour, Wi-Fi.

B-C Hostal La Estancia, O'Higgins 765, T249130, www. estancia.cl. Simple but comfortable rooms, some with bath. Heating in passageways but not in rooms. Very good kitchen facilities, internet, lots of information, English spoken. Excellent breakfast with real coffee. Recommended.

B-C The Pink House, Caupolicán 99, T222436, www.chileanpatagonia.com/pink house. Impeccable rooms with or without bath, breakfast, internet. Pickup from bus station, English spoken. Recommended.

C Hostal Al Fin del Mundo, O'Higgins 1026, T710185, www.alfindelmundo.cl. **F** pp in dorms. With breakfast, bright, cosy, shared baths, central, helpful, laundry service, book exchange, internet, cooking facilities, English spoken. Recommended.

C Hostal Dinka's House, Caupolicán 169, T244292, www.dinkashouse.cl. With breakfast, use of kitchen, laundry, internet, very colourful, painted deep red with lots of real and imitation flowers, gnomes, etc, attended by Dinka herself.

C Hostal Parediso, Angamos 1073A, T224212, hostalparediso@hotmail.com. Nice simple place, breakfast, parking, decent rooms with heating and cable TV, use of kitchen, great value, welcoming. Recommended.

C Luna Hostal, O'Higgins 424, T221764, hostalluna@hotmail.com. Quiet house with delightful rooms with or without bath, comfy beds with duvets, or F in dorms, use of kitchen, laundry facilities.

C **Hostal Taty's House**, Maipu 1070, T241525, www.hostaltatyshouse.cl. Decent rooms with cable TV. Good beds, good choice in this price bracket, basic English spoken.

D-E pp **Ely House**, Caupolicán 75, T226660, ely@chileanpatagonia.com. Cheaper without bath, lovely, with breakfast, comfortable, heating and hot water, kitchen, collect from airport.

D **Hosp Miramar**, Almte Señoret 1190, T215446. Rooms and dorms (F pp), helpful staff, good breakfast, good views over the bay, though on the edge of the red-light district.

D pp **Monterrey**, Bories 621, T220636, monterrey@turismoaventura.net. Cheaper without breakfast (which is good), tiny rooms with TV, heating, clothes washing, use of kitchen, comfortable but a bit tatty in public areas, discounts for long stay, charming people.

D **Backpackers' Paradise**, Carrera Pinto 1022, T240104, backpackersparadise@hotmail.com. Popular, limited bathroom facilities, only curtains dividing the large dorms, not exactly comfortable, cooking and laundry facilities, internet, luggage store.

E **Hosp Independencia**, Independencia 374, T227572, www.chileaustral.com/independencia. F pp in shared rooms. Use of kitchen, laundry, bike rental, internet, good value. Highly recommended. Also good value cabañas away from the centre.

C-D **Hostal El Conventillo**, Pasaje Korner 1034, T242311, www.hostalelconventillo.com. With breakfast, 'hip' hostel with rooms for 2-6 with shared bath, cheerful, good value, free internet.

E **Hostal Hain**, José Nogueira 1600, remezona@hotmail.com. Convenient, secure, helpful, English spoken, kitchen facilities and internet, good.

Eating

Punta Arenas *p852, map p853*

Many eating places close Sun. **Note** *Centolla* (king crab) is caught illegally by some fishermen using dolphin, porpoise and penguin as live bait. There are seasonal bans on *centolla* fishing to protect dwindling stocks; out of season *centolla* served in restaurants will probably be frozen. If there is an infestation of red tide (*marea roja*), a disease which is fatal to humans, bivalve shellfish must not be eaten. Mussels should not be picked along the shore because of pollution and the *marea roja*. Sernatur and the Centros de Salud have leaflets.

TTT **Remezón**, 21 de Mayo 1469, T241029. Regional specialities such as krill. Very good, but should be, given sky-high prices.

TTT-TT **El Asador Patagónico**, O'Higgins 694, T222463. New branch of the well-regarded Puerto Natales restaurant specializing in spit-roasted lamb.

TT-TT **Damiana Elena**, Magallanes 341. Stylish restaurant serving Mediterranean food with a Patagonian touch, popular with locals, book ahead at weekends, open Mon-Sat from 2000.

TTT-TT **Sabores**, Mejicana y Bories. Upstairs, pleasant, quite traditional, comfy, varied menu of well-cooked seafood, fish, pastas, meats, etc.

TTT-TT **Sotitos**, O'Higgins 1138. An institution, famous for seafood in elegant surroundings, excellent. Book ahead in season.

TTT-TT **La Tasca**, Plaza Muñoz Gamero 771, above Teatro Cervantes in Casa Español. Large helpings, limited selection, decent set lunch.

TT **La Luna**, O'Higgins 1017, T228555. Fish, shellfish and local specialities, huge pisco sours, popular, reasonable. Under same ownership is **O' Sole Mío**, O'Higgins 974, T242026, for cheap pasta dishes.

TT **La Marmita**, Plaza Sampiao. Intimate, "mestizo" restaurant decorated in pastel shades, regional dishes with international twist, vegetarian options, food prettily presented, open 1230-1500, 1830-2330, very good.

TT **Santino**, Colón 657, T710882. Good pizzas, large bar, good service, open Mon-Sat till 0300.

TT-T **Club Croata**, Errázuriz 812, p 2. Good value lunch menu on weekdays, nice dining room, quick service, good food. À la carte at weekends.

TT-T **El Quijote**, Lautaro Navarro 1087, T241225. Meat dishes, fish, soups, salads, good burgers and sandwiches, daily lunch specials, bright atmosphere, happy hour 1900-2100. Recommended.

T **Dino's Pizza**, Bories 557. Good value pizza in a cheerful fast food atmosphere, lots of choice, irregular opening hours.

T **Lomit's**, Menéndez 722. A fast-food institution, cheap snacks and drinks, open when the others are closed, good.

Cafés

Café Cyrano, Bulnes 297 y Maipú, T242749. Popular in evening, less busy at lunchtime, teas, coffee and sandwiches, tortas and cakes.
Café Montt, Pedro Montt 976. Coffees, teas, cakes, pastries and snacks, Wi-Fi.
Coffee Net, Waldo Seguel 670, www.coffeenet.cl. Big internet café opposite the police HQ, good service and music, hot chocolate and coffee.
History Coffee, Lautaro Navarro 1065. Popular for business types in morning.
Jekus, O'Higgins 1021, café restaurant next to La Luna. Open in morning.

Bars and clubs

Punta Arenas *p852, map p853*
La Taberna del Club de la Unión, on the plaza in the basement of the Hotel Nogueira. Smoky but atmospheric bar, good for evening drinks, open Mon-Sat from 1830.
Pub Olijoe, Errázuriz 970. Like a traditional British pub, for beer in a lively atmosphere, plush leather interior. Recommended.

Shopping

Punta Arenas *p852, map p853*
Punta Arenas has certain free-port facilities; Zona Franca, 3½ km north of the centre, opposite Museo Instituto de la Patagonia, is cheaper than elsewhere. Closed 1230-1500 and Sun (bus E or A from Plaza Muñoz Gamero; many colectivos; taxi US$3).
Food and drink **Chocolatta**, Bories 852. Tasty handmade chocolate, good coffee. Also **Chocolates Norweisser**, Carrera 663, open 0930-1230, 1430-1930, Sat 1000-1300.
Secreto de la Patagonia, Sarmiento de Gamboa 1029. Local produce, chocolates, cheese, jams, delicatessen, souvenirs.
Handicrafts **Chile Típico**, Carrera Pinto 1015, T225827.
Supermarkets **Abu-Gosch**, Bories 647, open daily 0900-2200. Others such as **Cofrima 2**, España 01375 and **Líder** 2 km northwest of centre.

Activities and tours

Punta Arenas *p852, map p853*
Skiing **Cerro Mirador**, only 9 km west of Punta Arenas in the Reserva Nacional Magallanes, one of the few places in the world where you can ski with a sea view. **Transtur** buses 090 and 1400 from in front of Hotel Cabo de Hornos, US$5, return, taxi US$12. Daily lift pass, US$28 (high season); equipment rental avialable. Mid-way lodge with food, drink and equipment. Season Jul-Sep, weather and snow permitting. In summer there is a good 2-hr walk on the hill, with labelled flora. Contact **Club Andino**, T241479, www.clubandino.cl. Also skiing at Tres Morros.

Tour operators

Most tour operators organize trips to Torres del Paine, Fuerte Bulnes, the pingüineras on Isla Magdalena and Otway sound and Tierra del Fuego; shop around.
Arka Patagonia, Manuel Señoret 1597, T248167, www.arkapatagonia.com. All types of tours, rafting, fishing, etc.
Cruceros Australis, at Comapa, Magallanes 990, T200200, www.australis.com (in Santiago T02-442 3110, in Buenos Aires T011-4139 8400). Runs cruises on the *Via Australis*, *Mare Australis* and the brand new, larger *Stella Australis* (from Dec 2010) between Punta Arenas and **Ushuaia**, through the Magellan Straits and the 'avenue of glaciers', with stops at Cape Horn and Isla Navarino, glaciers and Isla Magdalena (the itinerary varies according to route). There are opportunities to disembark and see wildlife. 4 nights from Punta Arenas, 3 nights from Ushuaia, service from Sep-Apr, 2010-2011 fares start at US$1,770 pp (US$1,40001 low season), inclusive of all but port tax (US$20 from Punta Arenas, US$10 Ushuaia); check website for promotions. Very safe and comfortable, first-class service, fine dining, daily lectures, an unforgettable experience. Advance booking is essential; check-in is at **Comapa**. Consistently highly recommended.
Kayak Agua Fresca, Lautaro Navarro 975, T613420, www.kayakaguafresca.com. New kayaking company based 27 km south of the city, with own *hostería*, a variety of programmes, good guides and equipment.
Turismo Aonikenk, Magallanes 619, T221982, www.aonikenk.com. Expensive but excellent tailor-made, multi adventure and trekking tours for all levels of fitness, top of the market, French, German, English spoken. Highly recommended. Also has **C Hosp Magallanes** at Magallanes 570, T228616.

Turismo Aventour, Patagonia 779, T241197, www.aventourpatagonia.com. Specialize in fishing trips, organize tours to Tierra del Fuego, helpful, English spoken.
Turismo Comapa, Magallanes 990, T200200, www.comapa.com. Tours to Torres del Paine (responsible, well-informed guides), Tierra del Fuego and to see penguins at Isla Magdalena (3 times a week Dec-Mar, 5 hrs in all, US$40). Sell tickets for sailings Puerto Montt to Puerto Natales. Agents for **Cruceros Australis** (see above).
Turismo Yamana, Errázuriz 932, T710567, www.yamana.cl. Conventional tours, trekking in Torres del Paine, kayaking in the fjords of Parque Nacional De Agostini (Tierra del Fuego), multilingual guides, camping equipment provided. Recommended.
Viento Sur, Fagnano 585, T222590, www.vientosur.com. Horse riding, trekking, kayaking in the Magellan straits and elsewhere, plus Torres del Paine, good tours.
Whale Sound, Lautaro Navarro 1163, T710511, www.whalesound.com. Whale-watching trips in the Magellan Straits.s

Transport

Punta Arenas *p852, map p853*
All transport is heavily booked from Christmas to Mar: advance booking strongly advised.
Air Carlos Ibáñez del Campo Airport, 20 km north of town. Minibus service by **Transfer Austral**, Lautaro Navarro 975, T615100, US$5. **DAP** have their own bus service to town, US$6. Taxi US$14 to city, US$10 to airport. To **Santiago**, **LAN**, via **Puerto Montt** and **Sky** (several stops) daily. To **Porvenir**, **Aerovías DAP** twice daily Mon-Sat, 9 passengers, 12 mins, US$35. To **Puerto Williams**, daily in summer, 1 hr, US$95 one way (book a week in advance for Porvenir, 2 in advance for Puerto Williams). Services to Argentina: To **Ushuaia**, 1 hr, **LAN** three a week in summer (schedules change frequently). **Note** Take passport when booking tickets to Argentina.
Bus Buses leave from company offices: **Pingüino** and **Fernández**, Sanhueza 745, T221429, www.buses fernandez.com. **Pacheco**, Colón 900, T242174, www.busespacheco.cl; **Pullman**, Colón 568, T223359, tickets for all Chile. **Central de Pasajeros**, Colón y Magallanes, T245811, office for booking all tickets, also cambio and tour operator. **Bus Sur**, Menéndez 552, T614224, www.bus-sur.cl. **Ghisoni** and **Tecni Austral**, Lautaro Navarro 975, T613422. Bus services: To **Puerto Natales**, 3-3½ hrs, **Fernández**, **Bus Sur** and **Pacheco**, up to 8 daily, last departure 2015, US$9, US$16 return, look out for special offers and connections to Torres del Paine. Buses may pick up at the airport with advance booking and payment. **Pacheco** have services through Argentina to **Osorno**, **Puerto Montt** and **Castro**, US$60-75, several weekly, 36 hrs, also **Sur**.

To **Río Grande** and **Ushuaia** via **Punta Delgada** (route is described in Argentina, Tierra del Fuego, Ins and outs, Getting there; no buses via Porvenir) **Pacheco**, **Sur**, **Tecni-Austral** and others, 8-10 hrs, US$33, heavily booked; US$46-50 to Ushuaia, 12 hrs. Some services have to change in Río Grande for Ushuaia, others direct. Check companies for frequencies. Book well in advance in Jan-Feb. To **Río Gallegos**, Argentina, via Punta Delgada, **Pingüino** daily; **Pacheco**, Sun, Tue, Fri; **Ghisoni**, Mon, Wed, Thu, Sat. Fares US$15, 5-8 hrs, depending on customs, 15 mins on Chilean side, up to 2 hrs on Argentine side.

Ghisoni sell tickets to many Argentine destinations: **El Calafate** US$30, **Comodoro Rivadavia** US$52, **Puerto Madryn** US$76, **Bariloche** US$100, **Buenos Aires** US$140.

To **Otway Sound**: Bus with **Fernández** 1500, return 1900, US$13.50. Tours by several agencies, US$20, entry extra, taxi US$50 return.
Car hire **Payne**, Menéndez 631, T240852, www.payne.cl, also tours, treks, birdwatching, etc. **Lubag**, Colón 975, T242023, www.lubag.cl. Also multinational companies. **Note** You need a hire company's authorization to take a car into Argentina. This takes 24 hrs (not Sat or Sun) and involves mandatory international insurance at US$240.
Ferry For services to **Porvenir** (Tierra del Fuego), see page 874.
Shipping offices: **Navimag**, in the same office as **Comapa**, Magallanes 990, T200263, www.navimag.com, www.comapa.com.
Shipping Services: For Navimag services Puerto Montt-Puerto Natales, see under Puerto Montt (confirmation of reservations is advised). For **Cruceros Australis** to Cape Horn and Ushuaia, see above.

To **Antarctica**: Most cruise ships leave from Ushuaia, but a few operators are based in Punta Arenas. Try **Antarctic Dream Shipping**, Ebro 2740 of 602, Las Condes, Santiago, T02-481 6910, www.antarctic.cl (in UK **Senderos**, T0208-144 8335, info@senderos.co.uk), or **Antarctic XXI**, Lautaro Navarro 987, p 2, T614100, www.antarcticaxxi.com, flight/cruise packages. See under Santiago Tour Operators, page 713. Otherwise, another possibility is with the Chilean Navy. The Navy does not encourage passengers, so you must approach the captain direct. Spanish is essential. Two vessels, Galvarino and Lautaro, sail regularly (no schedule); isotop@mitierra.cl.

To **Monumento Natural Los Pingüinos**: The boat of Agencia Broom (see Ferries to Tierra del Fuego) booked through **Comapa** (see Activities and tours), at 1600, schedules vary monthly, US$40. Take your own refreshments, as they are expensive on board. Highly recommended, but the trip may be cancelled if it's windy. Other agencies sell the trip, US$40-60, eg **Solo**, Nogueira 1255, at 0700 daily.

Taxi Ordinary taxis have yellow roofs. Colectivos (all black) run on fixed routes, US$0.70 for anywhere on route. Reliable service from **Radio Taxi Austral**, T247710/244409.

Directory

Punta Arenas *p852, map p853*

Airline officesaeroviasdap.cl. Aerovías **DAP**, O'Higgins 891, T616100, www.dap.cl. Open 0900-1230, 1430-1930. Helpful. **LAN**, Bories 884, T600-526 2000. **Sky**, Roca 933, T710645, or 600-600 2828. **Banks** Most banks and some supermarkets have ATMs; many on the Plaza. Banks open Mon-Fri 0830-1400. **Casas de cambio** open Mon-Fri 0900-1230, 1500-1900, Sat 0900-1230, many on Lautaro Navarro 1000 block. **Consulates** **Argentina**, 21 de Mayo 1878, T261264, cparenas@embargentina.cl, open Mon-Fri 0900-1800, visas take 24 hrs. **Belgium**, Roca 817, of, T241472. **Italy**, 21 de Mayo 1577, T221596. **Netherlands**, Magallanes 435, T248100, c.matheson@ladesur.cl. **Spain**, Av Pdte Ibáñnex del Campo 05730, T213563, extremos@terra.cl. **UK**, The British School, Waldo Seguel 454, T09-7472 6187. **Internet and telephones** All over the centre, about US$1.20 per hr. **Medical services** Hospitals: **Hospital Regional Lautaro Navarro**, Angamos 180, T244040. Public hospital, for emergency room ask for La Posta. Has good dentists. **Clínica Magallanes**, Bulnes 01448, T211527. Private clinic, minimum charge US$45. **Hospital Naval**, Av Bulnes 200 esq Capitán Guillermos. Open 24 hrs, good, friendly staff. Recommended. **Post offices** Bories 911 y J Menéndez. Mon-Fri 0830-1930, Sat 0900-1400.

Puerto Natales and around

Beautifully situated on the calm waters of Canal Señoret fjord, an arm of the Ultima Esperanza Sound, edged with spectacular mountains, Puerto Natales, 247 km north of Punta Arenas, is a quiet town of brightly painted corrugated tin houses. It's the base for exploring the magnificent O'Higgins and Torres del Paine national parks, and even when inundated with visitors in the summer, retains an unhurried feel, and is a place to relax for a few days. Puerto Natales has suffered from a decline in tourism since 2008, because of a combination of global economic crises and Chilean Patagonia's reputation as being one of the most expensive places in South America. No immediate upturn is predicted.

Ins and outs

Tourist office At the Sernatur office ⓘ *on the waterfront, Av Pedro Montt 19, T412125, info natales@sernatur.cl, Mon-Sat 0900-1900.*, there's no English spoken, but good leaflets available on Puerto Natales and Torres del Paine in English, and bus and boat information in the park. Also at Municipalidad, Bulnes 285, T411263. CONAF, Baquedano 847, T411843, michael.arcos@conaf.cl.

Sights

Museo Municipal ⓘ *Bulnes 285, T411263, Mon-Fri 0900-1300, 1500-2000, weekends afternoon only, free,* has displays and photos of early colonizers, as well as a small collection of archaeological and natural history exhibits. There are lovely walks along the waterfront or up to Cerro Dorotea, which dominates the town, with superb views. Take any bus going east and alight at the road for summit (Km 9.5).

Monumento Natural Cueva Milodón ⓘ *25 km north, 0830-2030, US$6 to enter park (US$3 low season), camping allowed, getting there: regular bus from Prat 517, T412540, leaves 0945 and 1500, returns 1200 and 1700. US$8; taxi US$30 return or check if you can get a ride with a tour; Adventur and Fernández tour buses to Torres del Paine stop at the cave.* In this cave (70 m wide, 30 m high and 220 m deep), formed by ice-age glacial lakes, remains were found of a prehistoric ground-sloth, together with evidence of occupation by early Patagonian humans some 11,000 years ago. There is a small, well-presented visitor centre, with restaurant and toilets.

Puerto Natales

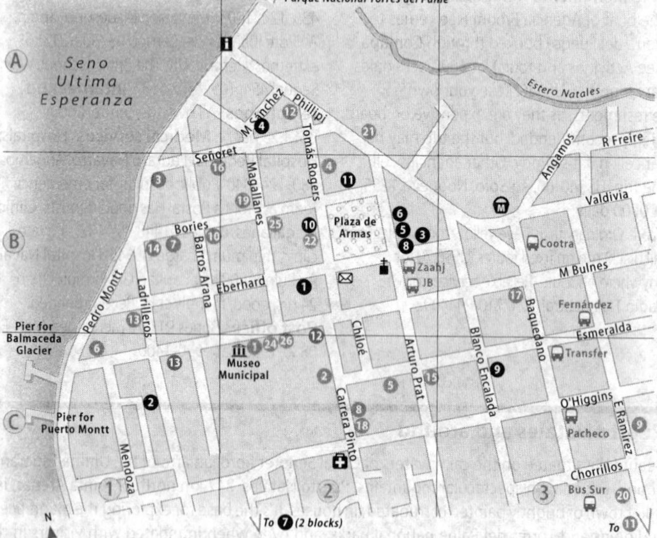

N

200 metres
200 yards

Sleeping
1 Aquaterra *C2*
2 Blanquita *C2*
3 Capitán Eberhard *B1*
4 Casa Cecilia *B2*
5 Casa Teresa *C2*
6 Costaustralis *C1*
7 Hosp Casa Lili *B1*
8 Hosp Chila *C2*
9 Hosp Nancy *C3*
10 Hostal Dos Lagunas *B1*
11 Hostal Las Carretas *C3*
12 Hostal Sir Francis Drake *A2*
13 Hostel Natales *B1*
14 Indigo Patagonia *B1*
15 Josmar 2 Camping *C2*
16 Keoken *B1*
17 Lady Florence Dixie *B3*
18 Los Inmigrantes *C2*
19 Martín Gusinde *B2*
20 Niko's *C3*
21 Niko's II *A2*
22 Patagonia Adventure & Sendero Aventura *B2*
23 Remota *A2*
24 Res Dickson *C2*
25 Res El Mundial *B2*
26 Res Gabriela *C2*
27 Weskar Patagonian Lodge *A2*

Eating
1 Afrigonia *B2*
2 Andrés *C1*
3 Angelica's *B2*
4 Cormorán de las Rocas *A2*
5 El Asador Patagónico *B2*
6 El Living *B2*
7 El Rincón de Don Chicho *C2*
8 La Mesita Grande *B2*
9 La Picada de Carlitos *C3*
10 Oveja Negra *B2*
11 Parrilla Don Jorge *B2*

Bars & clubs
12 El Bar de Ruperto *B2*
13 Kaweshkar *C1*

Parque Nacional Bernardo O'Higgins

Usually referred to as the **Parque Nacional Monte Balmaceda** ⓘ *US$5*, the park is at the north end of Ultima Esperanza Sound and can only be reached on boat trips from Puerto Natales (recommended). After a three-hour journey up the Sound, the boat passes the Balmaceda Glacier which drops steeply from the eastern slopes of Monte Balmaceda (2,035 m). The glacier is retreating; in 1986 its foot was at sea level. The boat docks further north at Puerto Toro, from where it's a 1-km walk to the base of Serrano Glacier on the north slope of Monte Balmaceda. On the trip dolphins, sea-lions (in season), black-necked swans, flightless steamer ducks and cormorants can be seen. There is a route from Puerto Toro on the eastern side of the Río Serrano for 35 km to the Torres del Paine administration centre; guided tours are available on foot or on horseback. It is also possible to travel to the Paine administration centre along the river by boat or zodiac (four hours, US$85). Better going to the park than from the park (the view suddenly opens up and then just gets better and better).

Border with Argentina

There are three crossing points: **Villa Dorotea**, 16 km east of Puerto Natales. On the Argentine side the road continues to a junction, with alternatives south to Río Turbio and north to La Esperanza and Río Gallegos. Chilean immigration is open all year 0800-2400. **Paso Casas Viejas**, 16 km northeast of Puerto Natales. On the Argentine side this joins the Río Turbio–La Esperanza road. Chilean immigration is open 0800-2400 in summer, 0800-2200 in winter. **Cerro Castillo**, 65 km north of Puerto Natales on the road to Torres del Paine, open 0800-2400 in summer, 0800-2200 in winter. On the Argentine side, Paso Cancha Carrera (14 km), the road leads to La Esperanza and Río Gallegos. All buses from El Calafate go via Cerro Castillo, making it possible to transfer to a bus passing from Puerto Natales to Torres del Paine. Chilean immigration is open all year 0800-2200, and the small settlement has several hospedajes and cafeterías. Sheep shearing in December, and rodeo and rural festival third weekend in January. See also Argentina, page 248.

Puerto Natales listings

For Sleeping and Eating price codes and other relevant information, see Essentials, pages 38-40.

Sleeping

Puerto Natales and around *p859, map p860*

In season cheaper accommodation fills up quickly after the arrival of the Navimag ship from Puerto Montt. Hotels in the countryside open only in summer months: dates vary. Good deals in upper range hotels may be available while tourism remains in decline (2010); out of season especially prices may be 50% lower.

LL Costaustralis, Pedro Montt 262, T412000, www.hoteles-australis.com. Very comfortable, tranquil, lovely views (but not from inland-facing rooms), lift, English spoken, waterfront restaurant serves international and local seafood.

LL Indigo Patagonia, Ladrilleros 105, T413609, www.indigopatagonia.com. Relaxed atmosphere, on the water front, great views, a boutique hotel with roof-top spa, rooms and suites, breakfast included, café/restaurant serves good seafood and vegetarian dishes, internet access.

LL Remota, Ruta 9 Norte, Km 1.5, Huerto 279, T414040, www.remota.cl. Boutique hotel just outside town, unique design with big windows, lots of trips, activities and treks offered, spa, all-inclusive packages, good food, first-class.

L Hostería y Refugio Monte Balmaceda, T220174, turismo@aventourpatagonia.com. Beautifully situated on Ultima Esperanza Sound, close to the Río Serrano. Comfortable rooms and refugio (**D**) with well-lit, giant tents, beds and bathrooms, restaurant. Also organize tours and rent equipment. Handy for boat trip up Río Serrano. Recommended.

L Weskar Patagonian Lodge, Ruta 9, Km 1, T414168, www.weskar.cl. Quiet lodge overlooking the fjord, simple rooms with good views, onces and dinner served, internet, bicycle rental, many activities offered, helpful.

L-AL Cisne de Cuello Negro, T244506, T411498 (Av Colón 782, Punta Arenas), www.pehoe.com. In a splendid lakeside setting, about 5 km north of town at Km 275 near Puerto Bories. Comfortable, excellent cooking.

L-AL Martín Gusinde, Bories 278, T412770, www.hotelmartingusinde.com. American buffet breakfast included, modern 3-star standard, smart, parking, expensive restaurant.

AL-A Aquaterra, Bulnes 299, T412239, www.aquaterrapatagonia.com. Good restaurant with vegetarian options, 'resto-bar' downstairs, alternative therapy centre, understated design, safe, warm and comfortable but not cheap, very helpful staff.

AL-A Lady Florence Dixie, Bulnes 655, T411158, www. hotelflorencedixie.cl. Modern 3-star hotel, hospitable, variable room standards, superior are good value.

A Hostel Natales, Ladrilleros 209, T414731, www.hostelnatales.cl. **D** pp in dorms in this luxury hostel, very comfortable, with breakfast, internet.

A Hostal Sir Francis Drake, Phillipi 383, T411553, www.hostalfrancisdrake.com. Calm and welcoming, tastefully decorated, smallish rooms with cable TV, filling breakfast, good views. Recommended.

A Keoken, Señoret 267, T413670, www.keokenpatagonia.com. New cosy, upmarket B&B, spacious living room, some rooms with views. All rooms have bathroom but not all are en suite, English spoken.

A-B Capitán Eberhard, Pedro Montt 58, T411208, www.busesfernandez.com. Refurbished, cosy, modern, most rooms have sea view, Wi-Fi, cable TV, laundry, café, superb service. Recommended.

B-C Casa Cecilia, Tomás Rogers 60, T613560, redcecilia@entelchile.net. Welcoming, popular, with small simple rooms, some with bath, great breakfast. English, French and German spoken, Wi-Fi, rents camping gear and bicycles, booking for tours and information for Torres del Paine, also shared rooms with bunk beds. Warmly recommended.

B-C Hostal Las Carretas, Galvarino 745, T414584. Tastefully decorated and spotless B&B 15 mins' walk to the centre, comfortable rooms, some with bath, good beds, kitchen facilities, Wi-Fi, English spoken. Recommended.

C Blanquita, Carrera Pinto 409, T411674. Looks like a giant portacabin from the outside but is quiet, simple rooms, heating, stores luggage. Recommended.

C Hosp Nancy, Ramírez 540, T410022, www.nataleslodge.cl. Good breakfast, some rooms with bath, warm and hospitable, use of kitchen, information, internet, laundry service, runs tours. Recommended.

C Hostal Dos Lagunas, Barros Araña 104, T415733, doslagunas@hotmail.com. Lovely hospitable place with good breakfast, dinner available, shared bath, use of kitchen, TV and reading room, excursions and buses booked, lots of information.

C Patagonia Adventure, Tomás Rogers 179, T411028, www.apatagonia.com. Lovely old house, bohemian feel, shared bath, **E-F** pp in dorms, good value, homemade bread for breakfast, luggage store, internet, Wi-Fi, equipment hire, bike and kayak tours and tour arrangements for Torres del Paine (see Sendero Aventura, below); no kitchen. Recommended.

C-D Niko's, Ramírez 669, T412810, nikoresidencial@hotmail.com. With breakfast, basic rooms, some rooms with bath, good meals, also dorm accommodation. Recommended.

C-D Niko's II, Phillipi 528, ½ block from Plaza de Armas, T413543, residencial.nikos2@gmail.com. Breakfast included, some rooms with bath, heating, English spoken, book exchange, kitchen, internet for guests if staff/family not using it, information, tours, tent hire. Recommended.

C-D Res Dickson, Bulnes 307, T411871, patagoniadickson@ hotmail.com. Good value, with good breakfasts, helpful, internet, cooking and laundry facilities.

D Los Inmigrantes, Carrera Pinto 480, T413482, losinmigrantes@hotmail.com. Good breakfast, kitchen facilities, equipment rental, luggage store. Recommended.

D Res El Mundial, Bories 315, T412476, omar@fortalezapatagonia.cl. Large breakfast, good value meals, use of kitchen when owners do not need it, luggage stored.

D Res Gabriela, Bulnes 317, T411061. Good breakfast, owner Gabriela is very helpful, heating in rooms, luggage store. Recommended.

E Casa Teresa, Esmeralda 463, T410472, freepatagonia@hotmail.com. Good value, warm and quiet, breakfast included, also cheap meals, tours to Torres del Paine arranged.

E Hosp Chila, Carrera Pinto 442, T412328. Use of kitchen, welcoming, laundry facilities, luggage store, bakes bread. Recommended.

F pp **Hosp Casa Lili**, Bories153, T414063, lilinatales@latinmail.com. Dorms, also has private rooms, small, family-run, use of kitchen, internet, breakfast from 0600, rents equipment and can arrange tickets to Paine.

Camping **Josmar 2**, Esmeralda 517, in centre, T414417. Family run, convenient, hot showers, parking, barbecues, electricity, café, US$2.50 per site or **E** pp in double room.

Border with Argentina *p861*

L-AL Hostería El Pionero, Cerro Castillo, 56 km north of Puerto Natales, T613531, www.baqueanozamora.com. Comfortable country house ambience, good service, horse riding.

D pp **Hosp Loreto Belén**, Cerro Castillo, T413063, or 691932 (public phone, ask to speak to Loreto Belén). Rooms for 4, all with bath, breakfast included, also offers meals, good home cooking.

Eating

Puerto Natales *p859, map p860*

TTT Afrigonia, Eberhard 343, T412232. An unexpected mixture of Patagonia meets East Africa in this Kenyan-Chilean-owned fusion restaurant, considered by many to be the best, and certainly the most innovative, in town.

TTT-TT Angelicas, Eberhard 532, T410365. Elegant Mediterranean style, well-prepared food with quality ingredients. Pricy but recommended.

TTT-TT Cormorán de las Rocas, Miguel Sánchez 72, T413723, www.cormoran delasrocas.com. Patagonian specialties with an innovative twist, wide variety of well- prepared dishes, *pisco sours*, good service and attention to detail, incomparable views. Recommended.

TTT-TT El Asador Patagónico, Prat 158 on the Plaza. Spit-roast lamb, salads, home-made puddings, attractive. Recommended, book in advance.

TTT-TT Parrilla Don Jorge, Bories 430, on Plaza, T410999. Also specializes in spit-roast lamb, but serves fish, too, good service.

TT El Rincón de Don Chicho, Luis Martínez 206, T414339. All-you-can-eat *parrillada*. Vegetarian options on request. 15 mins' walk from centre. Recommended.

TT La Mesita Grande, Prat 169 on the Plaza, T411571. Fresh pizzas from the wood-burning oven, also pasta and good desserts.

TT Oveja Negra, Tomás Rogers 169, Plaza de Armas. Excellent local food, also book exchange.

TT-T La Picada de Carlitos, Blanco Encalada y Esmeralda. Good, cheap traditional Chilean food, popular with locals at lunchtime, when service can be slow.

T Andrés, Ladrilleros 381. Recommended for fish, nice owner, good service.

T El Living, Prat 156, Plaza de Armas, www.el-living.com. Just what you need: comfy sofas, good tea, magazines in all languages, book exchange, good music, delicious vegetarian food, British run, popular.

Cafés

Café + Books, Blanco Encalada 226, T414725. Cosy café with a 2 for 1 book exchange, Wi-Fi and computer terminals, travel services, good place for travellers.

Patagonia Dulce, Barros Arana 233. For the best hot chocolate in town.

Bars and clubs

Puerto Natales *p859, map p860*

El Bar de Ruperto, Bulnes 371, T414302. Lively place with DJs, live music, lots of drinks and some food. 2100-0500.

Kaweshkar, Bulnes 43, T415821. Groovy laid-back bar, serving empanadas, hamburgers, vegetarian food. Club at night with lounge music.

Murciélagos, Bulnes 731. Popular bar with late-night music and dancing.

Shopping

Puerto Natales *p859, map p860*

Camping equipment Check all camping equipment and prices carefully. Average charges per day: whole set US$15, tent US$6-8, sleeping bag US$3-6, mat US$1-2, raincoat US$1, also cooking gear, US$2. (**Note** Deposits required: tent US$200, sleeping bag US$100.) Camping gas is widely available in hardware stores. See under Sleeping and Activities and tours for

places that hire equipment, eg **Casa Cecilia**, **Patagonia Adventure**, **Erratic Rock**.
Supermarkets **Abu Gosch**, Bulnes y Ramírez. **Don Bosco**, Baquedano 358. The town markets are also good.

Activities and tours

Puerto Natales *p859, map p860*
Many agencies along Eberhard. It is better to book tours direct with operators in Puerto Natales than through agents in Punta Arenas or Santiago. Several agencies offer tours to the Perito Moreno glacier in Argentina, 1 day, US$65, 14-hr trip, 2 hrs at the glacier, without food or park entry fee. You can then leave the tour in Calafate to continue into Argentina.
Baguales Group, Galvarino 661, T412654, www.bagualesgroup.com. Specialists in the route from the park back to Puerto Natales. Tailor made multi-activity tours that can incorporate zodiacs, horse riding, kayaking and trekking, mostly off the beaten track. Recommended.
Bella Patagonia, Barros Arana 160, T412 489, www.bellapatagonia.com. Belgian-run operator specializing in kayak trips and trekking.
Criollo Expediciones, Huerto 157-B, T09-8528 4225, www.criolloexpediciones.com. Guided horse rides around Natales and Last Hope Sound as well as the edge of Parque Nacional Torres del Paine, multi-day trips to the Sierra Baguales, US/Chilean-run, attentive guides, well-kept horses. Recommended.
Erratic Rock, Baquedano 719, T410355, www.erraticrock.com. Trekking experts offering interesting expeditions from half a day to 2 weeks. Also hire out good-quality equipment.
Estancia Travel, Casa 13-b, Puerto Bories, Puerto Natales, T412221, www.estanciatravel.com. Based at the Estancia Puerto Consuelo, 5 km north of Puerto Natales, offer horse riding trips from 1 to 10 days around southern Patagonia and Torres del Paine, with accommodation at traditional estancias. Also kayaking trips, British/Chilean run, bilingual, professional guides, at the top end of the price range. Recommended.
Sendero Aventura, at Hostal Patagonia Adventure, Tomás Rogers 179, T415636, www.senderoaventura.com. Adventure tours, including trekking to Torres del Paine, boats in Balmaceda PN, camping equipment, bike hire.
Skorpios, www.skorpios.cl. 2-3 day cruises up the southern fjords to Puerto Edén and the Pío XI Glacier. No office in Puerto Natales; book online or through an agency.

Transport

Puerto Natales *p859, map p860*
Bus In summer book ahead. Buses leave from company offices: **Bus Fernández**, E Ramírez 399, T411111. **Pacheco**, Baquedano y O'Higgins, T414513. **Bus Sur**, Baquedano 668, T614220. **Transfer**, Baquedano 414, T421616. **Zaahj**, Prat 236, T412260.

To **Punta Arenas**, several daily, 3-3½ hrs, US$9, Fernández, Pacheco, Bus Sur and others. To Argentina: to **Río Gallegos** direct, **Bus Sur**, **El Pingüino** and **Ghisoni**, 2-3 weekly each, US$18, 4-5 hrs. Hourly to **Río Turbio**, **Cootra**, and other companies, US$5, 2 hrs (depending on Customs – change bus at border). To **El Calafate**, US$20, **Cootra** via Río Turbio, daily, 4 hrs; or **Zaahj** (3 a week, 4½ hrs) via Cerro Castillo. Otherwise travel agencies run several times a week depending on demand, US$60 one way, not including Perito Moreno glacier entry fee (12 hr trip), shop around, reserve 1 day ahead. **Bus Sur** also runs 3 buses a week to **Ushuaia** Oct-Apr, 15 hrs, US$63. **Note** See Torres del Paine section for buses from Puerto Natales into the park, page 870.
Car hire **Motor Cars**, Blanco Encalada 330, T415593, www.motorcars.cl. **EMSA Avis**, Bulnes 632, T410775. **Punta Alta**, Blanco Encalada 244, T410115, www.puntaalta.cl, good reports. Hire agents can arrange permission to drive into Argentina, takes 24 hrs to arrange, extra insurance required.
Ferry See services from Puerto Montt. **Comapa**, Eberhard 555, T414300, www.comapa.com. **Navimag**, Pedro Montt 308, T411642, www.navimag.com.

To **Parque Nacional Bernardo O'Higgins**: Sailings to **Balmaceda Glacier** daily at 0815 in summer, returning 1630, Sun only in winter (minimum 10 passengers). Bookings direct from **Turismo 21 de Mayo**, Eberhard 560, T614420, www.turismo21demayo.cl (also offers estancia accommodation). Heavily booked in high season. Take warm clothes, hat and gloves. Also **Punta Alta**, see Car Hire, above, same route as 21 de Mayo but in a faster boat and then a zodiac to the Pueblito Serrano at the Park's southern edge. There is an option to return to Natales on the same day by minibus along the southern access road, thus avoiding park entry fees. All agencies can arrange boat trips: Balmaceda and Serrano US$110-130. Combined trip on boat and with horses to Glaciar Geikie, US$300. Glaciar Tyndall, Pueblito Serrano, Salto Río Serrano and back US$90 and one way Puerto Natales to Puerto Toro, US$60-75.

Directory

Puerto Natales *p859, map p860*

Banks Rates for TCs, which can't be changed into US$ cash, are poor. **Banco Santiago**, ATM; several others. Casas de cambio on Blanco Encalada, eg 266 (**Enio América**). Others on Bulnes and Prat. **Bicycle repairs** **El Rey de la Bicicleta**, Ramírez 540. Good, helpful. **Internet and telephones** Several in town. **Post offices** Eberhard 417, open Mon-Fri 0830-1230, 1430-1745, Sat 0900-1230.

Parque Nacional Torres del Paine → *Colour map 9, B1.*

Nothing prepares you for the spectacular beauty of Parque Nacional Torres del Paine. World renowned for its challenging trekking, the park's 242,242 ha contain 15 peaks above 2,000 m. At its centre is the glacier-topped granite massif Macizo Paine, from which rise the vertical pink granite Torres (Towers) del Paine and, below them, the Cuernos (Horns) del Paine, swooping buttresses of lighter granite under caps of darker sedimentary rock. From the vast Campo de Hielo Sur icecap on its western edge, four main glaciers (ventisqueros), Grey, Dickson, Zapata and Tyndall, drop into vividly coloured lakes formed by their meltwater: turquoise, ultramarine and pistachio expanses, some filled with wind-sculpted royal blue icebergs. Wherever you explore, there are constantly changing views of dramatic peaks and ice fields. The park enjoys a micro-climate especially favourable to wildlife and plants: there are 105 species of birds including condors, ibis, flamingos and austral parakeets, and 25 species of mammals including guanaco, hares, foxes, pumas and skunks. Allow 7-10 days to see it all properly.

Ins and outs

Information The park is administered by CONAF: the Administration Centre (T691931, ptpaine@conaf.cl) is in the south of the park at the northwest end of Lago del Toro (open 0830-2030 in summer, 0830-1230, 1400-1830 off season). There are entrances at Laguna Amarga, Lago Sarmiento, Laguna Azul and the Puente Serrano, and you are required to **register** and show your passport when entering the park, since rangers (*guardeparques*) keep a check on the whereabouts of all visitors. You must also register before setting off on any hike. Phone the administration centre for information (in Spanish) on weather conditions. It also has videos and exhibitions with summaries in English of flora and fauna, but no maps to take away. There are six ranger stations (*guarderías*) staffed by rangers, who give help and advice. They will also store luggage (except at Laguna Amarga where they have no room). Entry for foreigners: US$30 (low season US$15.50, Chilean pesos only; proceeds are shared between all Chilean national parks); climbing fees US$1,000. If you are based outside the park and plan on entering and leaving several times explain this when you are paying your entrance to be given a multiple entry stamp. The impact of huge numbers of visitors to the park, over 100,000 a year, is often visible in litter around the refugios and camping areas. Take all your rubbish out of the park including toilet paper.

Getting around and accommodation The park is well set up for tourism, with frequent bus services running from Puerto Natales through the park, to pick up and drop off walkers at various hotels, to start treks, and to connect with boat trips. For details, see Transport below. Accommodation is available on three levels: there are hotels (expensive, over US$100 pp per night), nine *refugios*, six of which are privately run, well-equipped, staffed, offering meals and free hot water for tea, soup, etc, and 10 campsites with amenities and 10 basic *campamentos*. All options fill up quickly in peak summer months, Jan-Feb, so plan your trip and book hotels and refugios in advance. Pay in dollars to avoid IVA (tax). See Sleeping for more details. ▸▸ *See listings, page 868.*

Safety warning It is vital to be aware of the unpredictability of the weather (which can change in a few minutes, see Climate below) and the arduousness of some of the stretches on the long hikes. Rain and snowfall are heavier the further west you go and bad weather sweeps off the Campo de Hielo Sur without warning. The only means of rescue are on horseback or by boat; the nearest helicopter is in Punta Arenas and high winds usually prevent its operation in the park.

Forest fires are a serious hazard. Follow all instructions about lighting fires to the letter. An unauthorized campfire in 2005 led to the destruction of 10% of the northeast sector of the national park.

Equipment and maps A strong, streamlined, waterproof tent gives you more freedom than crowded refugios and is essential if doing the complete circuit. Also essential at all times of year are protective clothing against cold, wind and rain, strong waterproof footwear, a compass, a good sleeping bag, sleeping mat, camping stove and cooking equipment. Most refugios will hire camping equipment for a single night. Sun-screen and sunglasses are also necessary, and you'll want shorts in summer. At the entrance you are asked what equipment you have. Take your own food: the small shops at the refugios and at the Posada Río Serrano are expensive and have a limited selection. Maps (US$7) are obtainable at CONAF offices in Punta Arenas or Puerto Natales. Other Torres del Paine maps are published by Mattassi and (more accurate) Cartografía Digital and Patagonia Interactiva; all three have a few mistakes, however.

Climate Do not underestimate the severity of the weather here. The Park is open all year round, although snow may prevent access in the winter. The warmest time is December to March, but also the most unstable; strong winds often blow off the glaciers, and rainfall can be heavy. It is most crowded in the summer holiday season, January to mid-February, less so in December or March. October and November are recommended for wild flowers. In winter there can be good, stable conditions and well-equipped hikers can do some good walking, but some treks may be closed and boats may not be running.

Hikes

There are about 250 km of well-marked trails, and walkers must keep to the paths: cross-country trekking is not permitted. The times indicated should be treated with caution: allow for personal fitness and weather conditions.

El Circuito (Allow at least seven days) The most popular hike is a circuit round the Torres and Cuernos del Paine: it is usually done anticlockwise starting from the Laguna Amarga *guardería*. From Laguna Amarga the route is north along the west side of the Río Paine to Lago Paine, before turning west to follow the Río Paine to the south end of Lago Dickson. From here the path runs along the wooded valley of the Río de los Perros before climbing steeply to Paso John Gardner (1,241 m, the highest point on the route), then dropping to follow the Grey Glacier southeast to Lago Grey, continuing to Lago Pehoé and the administration centre. There are superb views, particularly from the top of Paso John Gardner.

Camping gear must be carried. The circuit is often closed in winter because of snow. The longest lap is 30 km, between Refugio Laguna Amarga and Refugio Dickson (10 hours in good weather; two campsites, Serón and Cairon), but the most difficult section is the very steep slippery slope between Paso John Gardner and Campamento Paso, a poorly-signed section exposed to strong westerly winds. The major rivers are crossed by footbridges, but these are occasionally washed away.

The 'W' (Allow five days) A popular alternative to El Circuito, it can be completed without camping equipment by staying in refugios, and can be done in either direction. It combines several of the hikes described separately below. From Laguna Amarga the first stage runs west via Hotel Las Torres and up the valley of the Río Ascensio via Refugio Chileno to the base of the Torres del Paine

Parque Nacional Torres del Paine

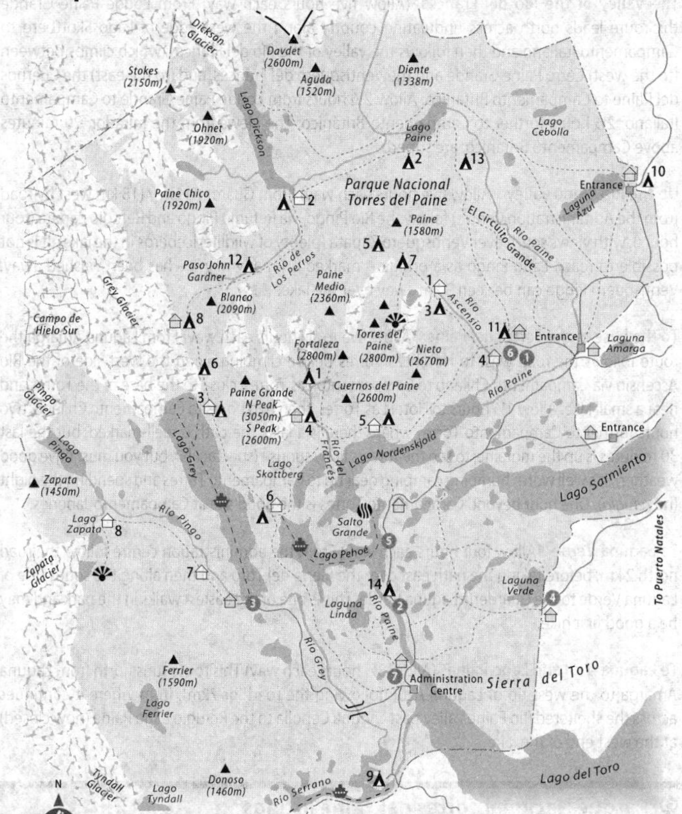

3 km

3 miles

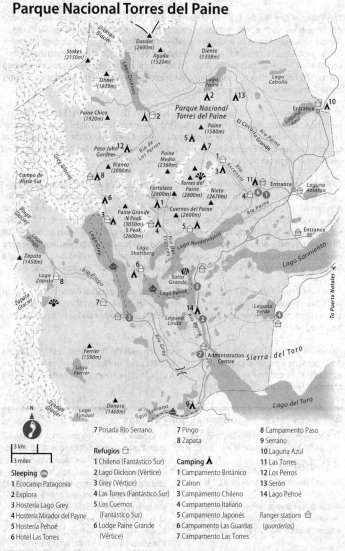

Sleeping
1 Ecocamp Patagonia
2 Explora
3 Hostería Lago Grey
4 Hostería Mirador del Payne
5 Hostería Pehoé
6 Hotel Las Torres
7 Posada Río Serrano

Refugios
1 Chileno (Fantástico Sur)
2 Lago Dickson (Vértice)
3 Grey (Vértice)
4 Las Torres (Fantástico Sur)
5 Los Cuernos (Fantástico Sur)
6 Lodge Paine Grande (Vértice)
7 Pingo
8 Zapata

Camping
1 Campamento Británico
2 Cairon
3 Campamento Chileno
4 Campamento Italiano
5 Campamento Japonés
6 Campamento Las Guardas
7 Campamento Las Torres
8 Campamento Paso
9 Serrano
10 Laguna Azul
11 Las Torres
12 Los Perros
13 Serón
14 Lago Pehoé

Ranger stations (*guarderías*)

(see below). From here return to the Hotel Las Torres and then walk along the northern shore of Lago Nordenskjold via Refugio Los Cuernos to Campamento Italiano. From here climb the Valley of the Río del Francés (see below) before continuing to Lodge Paine Grande. From here you can complete the third part of the 'W' by walking west along the northern shore of Lago Grey to Refugio Grey and Glaciar Grey before returning to Lodge Paine Grande.

The Valley of the Río del Francés (Allow five hours each way) From Lodge Paine Grande this route leads north across undulating country along the west edge of Lago Skottberg to Campamento Italiano and then follows the valley of the Río del Francés, which climbs between (to the west) Cerro Paine Grande and the Ventisquero del Francés, and (to the east) the Cuernos del Paine to Campamento Británico. Allow 2½ hours from Lodge Paine Grande to Campamento Italiano, 2½ hours further to Campamento Británico. The views from the mirador, 20 minutes above Campamento Británico, are superb.

Up the Río Pingo valley (Allow five hours each way) From Guardería Grey (18 km west by road from the Administration Centre) follow the Río Pingo, via Refugio Pingo and Refugio Zapata (four hours), with views south over Ventisquero Zapata (plenty of wildlife, icebergs in the lake). It is not possible to reach Lago Pingo as a bridge – marked on many maps – has been washed away. Ventisquero Pingo can be seen 3 km away over the lake.

To the base of the Torres del Paine (Allow five to six hours each way) From Laguna Amarga the route follows the road west to Hotel Las Torres before climbing along the west side of the Río Ascensio via Campamento Chileno to Campamento Las Torres, close to the base of the Torres and near a small lake. Allow 1½ hours to Hotel Las Torres, then two hours to Campamento Chileno, two hours further to Campamento Torres where there is a lake: the path is well-marked, but the last 30 minutes is up the moraine; to see the towers lit by sunrise (spectacular, but you must have good weather), it's well worth humping camping gear up to Campamento Torres and spending the night (no *refugio*). One hour beyond Campamento Torres is the good site at Campamento Japonés.

To Laguna Verde (Allow four hours each way) From the administration centre follow the road north 2 km, before taking the path east over the Sierra del Toro and then along the south side of Laguna Verde to the Guardería Laguna Verde. This is one of the easiest walks in the park and may be a good first hike.

To Laguna Azul and Lago Paine (Allow 8½ hours each way) This route runs north from Laguna Amarga to the west tip of Laguna Azul (following the road for 7km), from where it continues across the sheltered Río Paine valley past Laguna Cebolla to the Refugio Lago Paine (now closed) at the west end of the lake.

Parque Nacional Torres del Paine listings

For Sleeping and Eating price codes and other relevant information, see Essentials, pages 38-40.

Sleeping

Parque Nacional Torres del Paine *p865, map p867*

All the park's hotels are expensive, many feel overpriced. Agencies in Puerto Natales offer accommodation and transfers or car hire.

LL Explora, T411247. The park's most expensive and exclusive is nestled into a nook at Salto Chico on edge of Lago Pehoé, spectacular views. Everything is included: pool, gym, horse riding, boat trips, tours, can arrange packages from Punta Arenas (reservations: Av Américo Vespucci 80, p 7, Santiago, T02-206 6060, www.explora.com).

LL Hostería Lago Grey, head office Lautaro Navarro 1077, Punta Arenas, T712100, www.turismolagogrey.com. Great views over

Lago Grey, but small rooms, glacier walks, decent restaurant.

LL Hotel Las Torres, T617450, www.lastorres.cl. Superb, comfortable rooms, beautiful lounge with wood fire and great views of the Cuernos, excellent restaurant with evening buffet, good service, horse-riding, transport from Laguna Amarga ranger station, spa, disabled access. Recommended. Visitor centre and confitería open to non-residents, prices double after 1900.

L Hostería Mirador del Payne, Estancia Lazo, lovely location on Laguna Verde on east edge of the park, 52 km from Sarmiento entrance, reservations from Fagnano 585, Punta Arenas, T226930, www.miradordelpayne.com. Comfortable, meals extra, but inconvenient for park itself, riding, hiking, birdwatching. Private transport essential, or hike there from the park.

L-AL Hostería Pehoé, T411390, www.pehoe.com, 5 km south of Pehoé ranger station, 11 km north of park administration. Beautifully situated on an island with spectacular view across Lago Pehoé, but rather run down, restaurant.

AL Posada Río Serrano, reservations through Baqueano Zamora, Baquedano 534, Puerto Natales, T061-613530, www.baqueanozamora.com. An old estancia, some rooms with bath, some without, cable TV, near park administration, with expensive but good restaurant and a shop, horse riding tours in the national park. Recommended.

Refugios

Two companies between them run the refugios in the park, providing dormitory space only (bring your own sleeping bag, or hire one for US$8). Prices are about US$40 pp b&b, full board about US$75. Refugios have kitchen facilities, hot showers, and space for camping, US$7.50. All refugios hire tents for US$12 per night. Most close in winter, although one or 2 may stay open, depending on the weather. Advance booking essential in high season; service can be poor.

Fantástico Sur refugios Book in agencies in Puerto Natales or direct on T061-710050, www.wcircuit.com:

Refugio Chileno, in the Valley of Río Ascencio, at the foot of the Torres.

Refugio Las Torres, 2 refugios next to the Hotel Las Torres (see above), good facilities, especially in the newer **Torre Central**.

Refugio Los Cuernos, on the northern shore of Lago Nordenskjold.

Vértice refugios (book through agencies in Puerto Natales or via www.verticepatagonia.cl) runs:

Lodge Paine Grande, on the northwest tip of Lago Pehoé (expensive food, has internet).

Refugio Grey, on the eastern shore of Lago Grey (has facilities for ice climbing).

Refugio Lago Dickson, on the northern part of the circuit.

Camping

Fires may only be lit at organized camping sites, not at campamentos. The guardaparques expect people to have a stove if camping.

In addition to sites at the above refugios there are the following sites: **Camping Lago Pehoé**, www.campingpehoe.com, US$15 pp, tent rental US$12 pp, hot showers, shop, restaurant. **Camping Laguna Azul**, hot showers. **Los Perros** (run by Vértice Patagonia, tent US$12, sleeping bag US$10, full board US$37), shop and cold showers. **Camping Serón** and **Camping Las Torres** (at Hotel Las Torres) both run by **Fantástico Sur** (see above), US$7, hot showers. Free camping is permitted in 10 other locations in the park: these sites are known as campamentos. The wind tends to rise in the evening so pitch tent early. Mice can be a problem around camping sites and the free refugios; do not leave food in packs on the ground. Equipment hire in Puerto Natales (see above). Other campsites in or near the park: fixed sites, such as the indigenous Kaweskar-influenced domes of **Ecocamp Patagonia** (Don Carlos 3219, Las Condes, Santiago, T02-232 9878, www.ecocamp.travel), the only IS014001, environmental sustainability-certified hotel in Chile, and the luxury yurts of **Patagonia Camp** at Lago Toro, www.patagoniacamp.com.

Camping Río Serrano, at Estancia Vista al Paine, www.campingchile.com, also has a cosy cabaña, horse rides and hikes, recommended.

Activities and tours

Parque Nacional Torres del Paine *p865, map p867*

See under Puerto Natales, Activities and tours, page 864, for recommendations. There are increasingly mixed reports of tours. Before booking a tour, check carefully on details and get them in writing.

Experience Chile, T570 9436, www.torresdelpaine.org, www.experiencechile.org. Specialize in tailor-made itineraries for individuals, couples and small groups.

Boat trips From Refugio Lago Pehoé to Refugio Pudeto, US$19 one way with 1 backpack (US$8 for extra backpacks), from Pudeto 0930, 1200, 1800, from Paine Grande 1000, 1230, 1830, 30 mins in high season, reserve in advance at the refugios at either end or at Catamarán Hielos Patagónicos, Los Arrieros 1517, Puerto Natales, T411380, maclean@entelchile.net. Reduced service off season, no service May-Oct. At all times check in advance that boats are running. See Parque Nacional Bernardo O'Higgins above for entry by 3-hr zodiac trip up the Río Serrano from Balmaceda glacier. Boat to face of glacier from **Hostería Grey**, twice daily, 3½ hrs, US$70 return. A one-way trip can be made via the glacier face to/from the Hostería to the **Refugio Grey** for US$50.

Transport

Parque Nacional Torres del Paine *p865, map p867*

Bus The park administration is 147 km northwest of Puerto Natales by the old road, with a shorter new road, 85 km, opened to the south side of the park in 2007. After mid-Mar there is little public transport and trucks are irregular. From early Nov-mid Apr, there are several companies running daily services into the park, leaving Puerto Natales between 0630 and 0800, and again at around 1430, using the old road, 2½ hrs to Laguna Amarga, 3½ hrs to Refugio Pudeto and 4½ hrs the administration centre. Transport on the new road takes 1½ hr to park. To go to the Administration centre, all charge US$16 one way, US$30 open return (return tickets are not interchangeable between different companies). Buses will stop anywhere en route, but all stop at Laguna Amarga entrance, Salto Grande del Paine and administration centre near Posada Serrano. Services are provided by **Bus Gómez** ⓘ *Prat 234, T411971*; **JB** ⓘ *Prat 258, T410242*; and **Trans Via Paine** ⓘ *Bulnes 518, T413672*. In high season the buses fill quickly so it is best to board at Administration for the return to Puerto Natales. All buses wait at Refugio Pudeto until the 1200 boat from Refugio Paine Grande arrives. Travel between two points within the park (eg Pudeto-Laguna Amarga) US$6. At other times services by travel agencies are dependent on demand: arrange return date with driver to coincide with other groups to keep costs down. **Luis Díaz** is reliable, about US$17 pp, minimum 3 people. Hotel Las Torres sometimes runs an employee bus back to Puerto Natales at 1700, US$5, ask at reception.

In season there are frequent minibus connections within the park: from Laguna Amarga to Hotel Las Torres, US$6.50, and from the administration centre to Hostería Lago Grey, US$17.65. Other than these routes getting around the park without your own transport is difficult and expensive. From Torres del Paine to **Calafate** (Argentina): take the direct bus run by **Chaltén Travel**, US$80, or take services from Puerto Natales (see above); alternatively take a bus from the park to Cerro Castillo (106 km south of administration centre) then catch a direct service to Calafate (see Puerto Natales Buses).

Car hire Hiring a pick-up in Punta Arenas is an economical proposition for a group (up to 9 people): US$400-420 for 4 days. If driving there yourself, the shorter new road from Puerto Natales is narrow with lots of blind corners and sudden gusts of wind and can be rough in patches. In the park, the roads are also narrow and winding with blind corners: use your horn a lot. Petrol available at Río Serrano, but fill up in case.

Tierra del Fuego

The western side of this, the largest island off the extreme south of South America, belongs to Chile and the eastern to Argentina. Here the Andes cordillera runs from west to east, so that the north of the island is flat, covered with vast sheep farms, while the south has mountains, glaciers, lakes and forests. The major population centres, Ushuaia and Río Grande, are on the Argentine side, but Chile has the most southerly town in the world, Puerto Williams, on the island Isla Navarino below Tierra del Fuego. See Argentine Tierra del Fuego for Background.

Porvenir and around → *Phone code: 061. Colour map 9, C2. Population: 5,100.*

Porvenir is a quiet, pleasant place with many inhabitants of Croatian descent. Founded in 1894 in the gold boom, when many people came seeking fortunes from Croatia and Chiloé, it's a quiet, pleasant place with neat, painted tin houses and neatly trimmed yew trees lining the main avenue. There is a small museum, the **Museo Fernando Cordero Rusque** ⓘ *Jorge Schythe y Zavattaro 402, Mon-Thu 0800-1700, Fri 0800-1600, Sat-Sun 1030-1330, 1500-1700, US$1*, with archaeological and photographic displays on the Selk'nam (Onas); good displays on natural history and the early colonisers. **Mirador de la Ciudad** is a walkable excursion round the bay from Porvenir and uphill to the radio aerials. There is a bank ⓘ *just below the Plaza on Phillippi , open Mon-Fri 0900-1400*, changes cash and has a Maestro ATM. Post office on Plaza, on Phillipi. **Tourist information**: the best information is at the Museum. There are tourist notice boards outside the Municipalidad, on seafront and elsewhere; they wrongly suggest that ferries dock in town. A handicrafts stall in a kiosk on the seafront gives tourist information (opposite Comercial Tuto, No 588).

Porvenir is the base for exploring the wonderfully wild virgin territory of Tierra del Fuego. Excursions in the south, the more interesting half, must be totally self-sufficient. There are no hotels, shops, petrol stations or public transport. The only town in the south is Cameron, on the southern shore of Bahía Inútil. In the north, there is fuel and lodging at **Cerro Sombrero**, 46 km south of Primera Angostura, a village built to administrate oil drilling in the area, and a hostal and a place to eat in San Sebastián. There is no car hire on the island and no public transport to Argentina.

North of Porvenir, 6 km, is the **Monumento Natural Laguna de los Cisnes**. Access is across private land; the owner will give permission. Another place to see wildfowl, including black-necked swans from December is **Laguna Santa María**, not far from Porvenir on road to **Bahía Inútil**, a wonderful windswept bay. Cabo Boquerón, the headland at the start of Bahía Inútil, has great views on a clear day, as far as Cabo Froward, Isla Dawson and the distant Cordillera Darwin's snow peaks. Driving east along the bay you pass Los Canelos, with trees, a rare sight, and then the junction for the Cordón Baquedano, on the **Circuito de Oro**. This is a recommended tour, on which you can see gold panning using the same techniques since mining began in 1881, a four-hour, 115-km round trip. Miner Sr Jorge Gesell Díaz is happy to show tourists his workings (very enthusiastic), in summer only. Write in his visitors' book and leave a tip.

The main road east goes to **Onaisin**, 99 km east of Porvenir, and the Argentine border at San Sebastián. A road south at Onaisin passes Caleta Josefina, a handsome ex-estancia built in 1833, where some old buildings remain. To the most southerly point by road, Estancia Lago Fagnano, and the most southerly habitation at Río Azopardo is 4 hours. The government is hoping to complete the road to **Yendegaia** with a view to having a summer route, including ferry, to Puerto Navarino, for Puerto Williams, by 2012. Other options are sailing from Porvenir to **Río Cóndor** across Bahía Inútil, south of Cameron, with trekking or riding from Cameron to **Seno Almirantazgo**, a beautiful, wild and treeless place, where mountains sink into blue fjords with icebergs. A large part of the peninsula between Bahía Inútil and Seno Almirantazgo is the **Karukinka** nature reserve, www.karukinkanatural.cl, run by the Wildlife Conservation Society. Also sailing to **Marinelli glacier**, where you can sail, kayak and dive. Fly fishing, until recently the secret of Hollywood stars, is becoming world-renowned. The area is rich in brown trout, sea-run brook trout and steelheads, weighing 2-14 kg.

Border with Argentina → *Argentine time is 1 hr ahead of Chilean time, Mar-Oct.*
The only legal border crossing between the Chilean and Argentine parts of Tierra del Fuego is 142 km east of Porvenir at **San Sebastián**; open 0800-2200. On the Argentine side the road continues to Río Grande. **Note** There are two settlements called San Sebastián, on each side of the border but they are 14 km apart; taxis are not allowed to cross. No fruit, vegetables, dairy produce or meat permitted on entry to Chile. For entry to Argentina, see page 254.

Puerto Williams → *Phone code: 061. Colour map 9, C2. Population: 2,300, less than ½ civilian.*
Puerto Williams is a Chilean naval base on **Isla Navarino**, south of the Beagle Channel. About 50 km south east of Ushuaia (Argentina) at 54° 55′ 41″ south, 67° 37′ 58″ west, it is small, friendly and remote. The island is totally unspoilt and beautiful, offering great geographical diversity, thanks to **Dientes de Navarino** range, with peaks over 1,000 m, covered with southern beech forest up to 500 m, and, south of that, great plains covered in peat bogs, with many lagoons and abundant in flora. The island was the centre of the indigenous Yaganes culture and there are 500 archaeological sites, the oldest from 3,000 years ago. The town is a mixture of neat naval housing and the more haphazard civilian building with some impressive, modern municipal and school buildings. On an inlet at western edge is the Micalvi, an old naval vessel which is now HQ of the yacht club. **Museo Martín Gusinde** ⓘ *Mon-Thu 1000-1300, 1500-1800, Sat-Sun 1500-1800, Fri closed (subject to change), US$1*, is also known as the Museo del Fin del Mundo ('End of the World Museum'). It is full of information about vanished tribes, local wildlife, and voyages including Charles Darwin and Fitzroy of the Beagle, a must. Businesses in town accept US dollars; there are minimarkets and a hospital. **Tourist information** ⓘ *Municipalidad de Cabos de Hornos, O'Higgins y Prat, T621011, isotop@mitierra.cl, closed in winter*. They may have maps and details on hiking, but it is probably as good, if not beter, to get information from agencies, such as Shila (see Activities and tours, below). **CONAF** ⓘ *Carabinero M Leal 106, T621303, area.cabodehornos@gmail.com.*

Around Puerto Williams
For superb views, climb **Cerro Bandera** (3-4 hours' round trip, steep, take warm clothes). **Villa Ukika**, 2 km east of town, is where the last descendants of the Yaganes people live, relocated from their original homes at Caleta Mejillones (an old, overgrown cemetery marks the spot on the road to Puerto Navarino). There is excellent trekking around the **Dientes de Navarino**, the southernmost trail in the world, through impressive mountain landscapes, with superb views of Beagle Channel (challenging, 53 km in five days, November-March, snowfall permitting, good level of fitness needed). Also to Laguna Windhond, four days, and others all over island.

Cape Horn
It is possible to catch a boat south from Isla Navarino to Cape Horn (the most southerly piece of land on earth apart from Antarctica). There is one pebbly beach on the north side of the island; boats anchor in the bay and passengers are taken ashore by motorized dinghy. A stairway climbs the cliff above the beach, up to the building where a naval officer and his family run the lighthouse and naval post. A path leads from here to the impressive monument of an albatross overlooking the wild, churning waters of the Drake Passage below. Cruceros Australis ships call here (see page 857).

Tierra del Fuego listings

For Sleeping and Eating price codes and other relevant information, see Essentials, pages 38-40.

Sleeping

Porvenir *p871*

B **España**, Croacia 698, T580160. Expanded and upgraded, with bath, hot water, cable TV, central heating, internet, helpful and friendly. Good restaurant with fixed price lunch and dinner, also serves tea.

C **Rosas**, Phillippi 296, T580088, hotelrosas@chile.com. Heating, hot water, with breakfast, restaurant and bar, internet. Recommended.

D **Central**, Phillipi 298, T580077, opp **Rosas**. All rooms with bath, TV, heating and breakfast.

E pp **Hostal Kawi**, Pedro Silva 144, T581638, hostalkawi@yahoo.com. Comfortable, rooms for 3, with bath, TV, meals available, breakfast included, heating, offers fly-fishing trips.

Elsewhere in Chilean Tierra del Fuego

C-F **Hostería Tunkelen**, Arturo Prat Chacón 101, Cerro Sombrero, T061-212757, hosteria_tunkelen@hotmail.com. Also dorm E pp. Recommended.

Border with Argentina: San Sebastián *p872*

C-F **Hostería de la Frontera**, T061-696004, frontera@entelchile.net. Where some buses stop for meals and cakes, cosy, with bath (the annex is much more basic), good food.

Puerto Williams *p872*

LL **Lakutaia**, 2 km west of town, T621721, www.lakutaia.cl. A "base camp" for a range of activities and packages (riding, trekking, birdwatching, sailing, flights), 24 double rooms in simple but attractive style, good bath, no TV, lovely views from spacious public areas, library, maps, internet, uses local personnel and produce, bikes for hire, modern stables, 3 golf 'holes' – most southerly in world! Sailing on SV *Victory* (1986 wooden schooner), 3 crew, 10 pax on overnight trips, 23 on day trips. Everyone becomes a crew member.

B pp **Hostería Camblor**, Vía 2 s/n, a bit out of town, T621033, hostalcamblor@hotmail.com. Full board, full choice at meals, all wine included, also a short tour, free airport pick-up, for 4-passengers will include tour of Cementerio Indígeno. 2 backpacker rooms available, D with breakfast.

B-C **Hostal Akainij**, Austral 22, T621173, www.turismoakainij.cl. Smallish but comfortable rooms, very helpful, excellent, filling meals, kitchen facilities, basic English spoken, adventure tours and transfers. Recommended.

D pp **Forjadores de Cabo de Hornos**, Uspashun 64, Plaza B O'Higgins, near Centro Comercial, T621140, www.hostalforjadoresdelcabodehornos.cl. With breakfast, bath, TV, heating, agency for tours and transport, welcoming.

D pp **Hostal Coirón**, Ricardo Maragaño 168, T621227, or through **Ushaia Boating** or **Sim Ltda** (see Activities and tours). With breakfast, shared bath, helpful, good food, relaxed, quite basic, but OK.

D pp **Hostal Pusaki**, Piloto Pardo 222, T621116, www.hostalpusaki.com. Breakfast, cheaper without bath, use of kitchen, heated by stove, good meals available, laundry, luggage store, internet, owner Patty is helpful and fun.

D pp **Hostal Yagan**, Piloto Pardo 260, T621118, 8749 0166, hostalyagan@hotmail.com. Comfortable, some rooms with bath, central haeting, includes breakfast, lunch and dinner available US$12, run by Daniel Yevenes, who offers tours and transport to Ushuaia.

Camping

At **Hostal Bella Vista**, Tte Muñoz 118, T621010, US$10 per night (also has rooms). See Victory Adventures, below.

Eating

Porvenir *p871*

¶¶ **Club Croata**, Señoret entre Phillippi y Muñoz Gamero, next to the bus stop on the waterfront. A lively place where you can get a good lunch.

¶¶-¶ **El Chispa**, Señoret 202, T580054. Good restaurant for seafood and other Chilean dishes.

¶¶-¶ **La Picá de Pechuga**, Bahía Chilote s/n, by ferry dock. Good fresh seafood and fish. Owner Juan Bahamonde runs **Cordillero de Darwin** tours (see below):

¶ **Panadería El Paine**, Sampaio 368. Shop and tea room, very friendly.

Puerto Williams *p872*

₸₸-₸ Café Angelus, Centro Comercial Norte 151, T621080. Also travel agent and transport. Run by Loreto Camino, friendly cheerful atmosphere, small, good simple cooking, coffee (including Irish), beer. Best place for tourists.

₸ Los Dientes de Navarino, Centro Comercial Sur. Popular with locals, limited fare.

Panaderías and minimarkets: **Simón & Simón** and **Temuco** are opposite each other on Piloto Pardo, junction Condell. The former seems to be centre of reference in town.

Activities and tours

Porvenir *p871*

For adventure tourism and trekking activities contact tour operators in Punta Arenas (see Activities and tours above, page 857).

Turismo Cordillera de Darwin, run by Juan "Pechuga" Bahamonde, T09-9888 6380, or 061-580167, gerencia@cordilleradarwin.com or jebr_darwin@hotmail.com. Runs land, fishing and boating tours. Oro circuit costs US$120 for 4 without lunch, 4 hrs; US$60 pp with lunch, 0800-1700 including Laguna Santa María. Costs of tours to far south vary according to circumstances. Boat and fishing trips, 6 days allowing a day for unforeseen delays.

Puerto Williams *p872*

Boat trips **Victory Adventures**, Tte Muñoz 118, Casilla 70, T061-621010, www.victory-cruises .com, Captain Ben Garrett and his family run this recommended online travel agency for many tours and expeditions around Tierra del Fuego, Patagonia and the southern oceans to Antarctica. They also have the **A Hostal Bella Vista** (**B** without bath, **D** pp in bunks) B&B, internet services and a minimarket. **Cruceros Australis**, Av El Bosque Norte 0440, p 11, Las Condes, Santiago, T02-442 3110, www.australis. com (see page 857), call at Wulaia Bay on the west side of Isla Navarino after visiting Cape Horn; you can disembark to visit the museum and take a short trek.

Trekking You must register first with Carabineros on C Piloto Pardo, near Brito. Tell them when you get back, too. Sometimes they will not allow lone trekking.

Tour operators

Akainij, see Sleeping.

Sea, Ice and Mountains, Ricardo Maragaño 168, T621150, www.simltd.com. Sailing trips, trekking tours and many other adventure activities, including kayaking and wildlife spotting.

Shila, O'Higgins 322 (a hut at entrance to Centro Comercial), T621366, www.turismoshila.cl. Luis Tiznado Gonzales is an adventure guide, trekking and fishing, equipment hire (bikes, tents, sleeping bags, stoves, and more). Lots of trekking information, sells photocopied maps.

Transport

Ferries to Tierra del Fuego

There are 2 crossings. The ferry company accepts no responsibility for damage to vehicles.

Punta Arenas to Porvenir The **Cruz Australis**, sails from Tres Puentes (5 km north of Punta Arenas, bus A or E from Av Magallanes, or colectivo 15, US$1; taxi US$5) at 0900 or 1500-1600, no service Mon in season; less frequent sailings off season. **Tabsa/ Transboradora Austral Broom**, Bulnes 5075 (Tres Puentes), T218100, www.tabsa.cl or through **Comapa**, see Punta Arenas Tour operators. 2½-hr crossing (can be rough and cold, watch for dolphins), US$9.50 pp, US$61 per vehicle. Boat disembarks at Bahía Chilota, 5 km from Porvenir, bus US$1.40; bus drops you where you want to go in town. Return from Porvenir varying times in afternoon between 1400 and 1900, daily except Mon. Timetable dependent on tides and subject to change; check in advance. **Tabsa** website gives monthly schedules. Reservations for cars essential, especially in summer. Tabsa have an office on Señoret, seafront in Porvenir, T580089, open Mon-Fri 0900-1200, 1400-1830.

Punta Delgada to Punta Espora (Bahía Azul) This crossing is via the Primera Angostura (First Narrows), 170 km northeast of Punta Arenas (Punta Espora is 80 km north of Porvenir). There are two boats working continuously, *Pionero* and *Patagonia*. On board is a café, lounge, toilets and decks for getting splashed. Buses can wait up to 90 minutes to board. Boats run 0830-2345, 20 mins' crossing, US$27 per vehicle, foot passengers US$3, www.tabsa.cl. The ferries takes about 4 trucks and 20 cars; before 1000 most space is taken by trucks. There is no bus service to or from this crossing. If hitching, this route is preferable as there is more traffic.

Porvenir *p871*

Air From Punta Arenas – weather and bookings permitting, **Aerovías DAP**, Señoret s/n, T580089, Porvenir, www.dap.cl, details under Punta Arenas, Transport. Heavily booked so make sure you have your return reservation confirmed.

Bus The only public transport on Chilean Tierra del Fuego is Jorge Bastian's minibus Porvenir-Cerro Sombrero, T345406/8503-3662, jorgebastian@hotmail.com, or the driver axelvig20@hotmail.com. Mon, Wed, Fri, leaves Sombrero 0830, 0700 on Mon, returns from Porvenir Municipalidad, 2 hrs, US$4.50.

Road All roads are good *ripio* except paved from Bahía Chilota to Porvenir and in Porvenir itself.

Puerto Williams *p872*

Air From Punta Arenas with DAP (details under Punta Arenas). Book well in advance; long waiting lists (be persistent). The flight is beautiful (sit on right from Punta Arenas) with superb views of Tierra del Fuego, the Cordillera Darwin, the Beagle Channel, and the islands stretching south to Cape Horn. Also army flights available (they are cheaper), but the ticket has to be bought through DAP. Also from the Aeroclub in Ushuaia (see Ushuaia, Transport). Airport is in town.

Boat **Broom** ferry, www.tabsa.cl, from **Punta Arenas** once a week, 24 passengers, US$175 for chair, US$210 for bunk, 34-hr trip through beautiful channels. Will not take passengers if carrying petrol, so ask in advance. From **Ushuaia** with **Ushuaia Boating**, US$100 each way, which includes a 20-40 minute crossing in a semi-rigid boat to Puerto Navarino, a jetty, the Alcaldía del Mar and 4 more houses, plus a few horses and cows. Despite Ushuaia Boating dealing with documents when you buy the ticket, there is a lot of hanging around at Puerto Navarino, but the setting is nice and they sometimes offer coffee and pastries for impatient passengers. Then it's a1-hr ride in a combi on a lovely, *ripio* road past inlets and forests, river outflows, Bahía Mejillones and birdlife to Williams. For return make sure you are clear about transport arrangements.

Directory

Puerto Williams *p872*

Centro Comercial has **Aerovías DAP**, T621 051, **Cape Horn Net Cyber Café** on Centro Comercial Sur, also at Tte Muñoz 118, caphorn@victory-cruises.com, US$4 per hr, **post office** selling post-cards, stamps and maps, and a **telephone office**, Mon-Sat 0930-2230, 1000-1300, 1600-2200.

Chilean Pacific Islands

Chile has two national parks in the Pacific: Juan Fernández Islands, a little easier to reach (and leave) now than in Robinson Crusoe's time, and the remarkable Easter Island.

After the February 2010 earthquake, the Juan Fernández archpelago was hit by a tsunami which destroyed much of the town of San Juan Bautista, causing three deaths and several persons missing. At the time of writing the national park which comprises the islands was closed.

Juan Fernández Islands → *Phone code: 032. Population: 500.*

This group of small volcanic islands is administered by CONAF and is situated 667 km west of Valparaíso. The **CONAF** office ⓘ *Vicente González 130, T275 1004, parquenjfernandez@yahoo.cl,* can give information on flora, fauna and services. Check with CONAF if the park has reopened before trying to visit. Declared a UN World Biosphere Reserve in 1977, the islands enjoy a mild climate and the vegetation is rich and varied. Fauna includes wild goats, hummingbirds and seals. The best time to visit is October-March; take insect repellent. The islands are named after Juan Fernández, the first European to visit in 1574. There are three islands, Robinson Crusoe, the largest, which was the home (1704-1709) of Alexander Selkirk (the original of Defoe's Robinson Crusoe), Alejandro Selkirk and Santa Clara, the smallest. Selkirk's cave on the beach of Robinson Crusoe, about 4 km northwest of the village, can be visited on a boat trip. The only settlement is San Juan Bautista on Robinson Crusoe Island, a fishing village of wooden frame houses, located on Bahía Cumberland on the north coast of the island: many facilities close to the shore were affected by the February 2010 tsunami. The islands are famous for langosta de Juan Fernández (a pincerless lobster) which is sent to the mainland.

Robinson Crusoe Island The remains of the **Fuerte Santa Bárbara**, the largest of the Spanish fortresses, overlook San Juan Bautista. The island has long been the target for treasure-seekers who claim that looted gold from Inca times is buried there. Near Santa Bárbara are the **Cuevas de los Patriotas**, home to the Chilean independence leaders, deported by the Spanish after the Battle of Rancagua. South of the village is the **Mirador de Selkirk**, the hill where Selkirk lit his signal fires. A plaque was set in the rock at the look-out point by British naval officers from HMS Topaze in 1868; nearby is a more recent plaque placed by his descendants. (Selkirk, a Scot, was put ashore from *HMS Cinque Ports* and was taken off four years and four months later by a privateer, the *Duke*.) The Mirador is the only easy pass between the north and south sides of the island. Further south is the anvil-shaped **El Yunque**, 915 m, the highest peak on the island, where Hugo Weber, a survivor from the *Dresden*, lived as a hermit for 12 years. (The *Dresden* was a German cruiser, cornered by two British destroyers in Bahía Cumberland in 1915; the scuttled *Dresden* still lies on the seabed and a monument on the shore commemorates the event.) The only sandy beach on Robinson Crusoe is **Playa Arenal**, in the extreme southwest corner, two hours by boat from San Juan Bautista.

Each February, a **yachting regatta** visits the islands; setting out from Algarrobo, south of Valparaíso, the yachts sail to Isla Robinson Crusoe, then to Talcahuano and Valparaíso. At this time Bahía Cumberland is full of colourful and impressive craft, and prices in restaurants and shops double for the duration. (Thomas G Lammers, Department of Botany, University of Miami.) There are no exchange facilities. Only pesos and US$ cash accepted. No credit cards, no traveller's cheques.

Juan Fernández Islands listings

For Sleeping and Eating price codes and other relevant information, see Essentials, pages 38-40.

Sleeping

Juan Fernández Islands *p876*
Before February 2010 there were several options. At the time of writing it was not known which hotels and cabins were open, or would reopen for the 2010-2011 season. We therefore include only those with websites which may be checked nearer the time.

Crusoe Island Eco Spa, T02-634 5300, www.robinson-crusoe-island.com, which offers many packages, activities and therapies

Refugio Náutico, Av El Palillo s/n, T032-275 1077, www.islarobinson crusoe.cl. Rooms with bath, all meals available, Wi-Fi, hot tub, snorkelling, tours offered, kayak hire included in the price.

Activities and tours

Endémica Expediciones, Sector del Muelle s/n, T032-275 1227, www.endemica.com. Specializes in diving, trekking on the island, also kayaks and fishing. See their website for post-tsunami information and donations.

Transport

Juan Fernández Islands *p876*
Air Air taxis usually Mon, Wed, Fri from 1 Oct to Semana Santa (subject to demand) from **Santiago**, 2¾-3¼ hrs (US$600-700 round trip). For example, **Aerolíneas ATA**, Av Larraín 7941, Hangar 3, La Reina, Santiago, T275 0363, www.aerolineasata.cl; leave from Tobalaba Aerodrome in La Reina (eastern outskirts of city). The plane lands on an airstrip in the west of the island; passengers are taken by boat to San Juan Bautista (1½ hrs, US$2 one way).

Rapa Nui/Easter Island → *Phone code: 032. Always 2 hrs behind the Chilean mainland.*

Known as the navel of the world by the original inhabitants, this is one of the remotest places on earth. Isla de Pascua (Rapa Nui) is just south of the Tropic of Capricorn, 3,790 km west of Chile and 4,050 km from the Great Polynesian Archipelago (at Tahiti). Its nearest neighbour is Pitcairn Island.

The cultural and archeological treasures of Easter Island were the first of any Pacific island nation to be registered by UNESCO on its World Heritage list. From its past the most potent symbols are the giant carved statues, *moai*, that appear trance-like in a stunning landscape, their gaze fixed on a distant horizon on the Pacific. The tangible evidence of these statues, historic dwellings and petroglyphs far exceeds that of any other in Polynesia, Melanesia and Micronesia. Whereas other Pacific Island nations can claim an impressive intangible heritage (story telling, music and dance), but little in terms of structures and artwork, Easter Island has both tangible and intangible heritage of epic proportions. Here are some of the most impressive and mysterious sites on earth. Climb Rano Raraku volcano, dotted with caves and moai, overlooking the magnificent statues of Ahu Tongariki against the backdrop of waves crashing on the rocky coast, or visit Rano Kau volcano with the ancient city of Orongo on its rim, overlooking both the crater lake and the vast Pacific Ocean, and you cannot fail to be overawed.

Ins and outs

Information Isla de Pascua is officially part of V Región of Chile (Valparaíso). **Tourist office Sernatur** ⓘ *Tu'u Maheke s/n esq Apina, T210 0255, ipascua@ sernatur.cl, Mon-Fri 0830-1300, 1400-1730*. **Websites** http://islandheritage.org (Easter Island Foundation, in English, very useful). www.rapanui.co.cl, the Easter Island Newspaper. Average monthly temperatures vary between 15-17°C in August and 24° C in February, the hottest month. Average annual rainfall is 1,100 mm. There is some rain throughout the year, but the rainy season is March to October (wettest in May). The tourist season is from September to April. Anyone wishing to spend time exploring the island would be well-advised to speak to CONAF first ⓘ *Mataveri Otai s/n, T210 0236, enrique.tucki@conaf.cl*; they also give good advice on special interests (biology, archaeology, handicrafts, etc).

Background

The island is triangular in shape, 24 km across, with an extinct volcano at each corner. It is now generally accepted that the islanders are of Polynesian origin (see below for the historical and cultural contexts). European contact with the island began in the 18th century, followed by tragic Peruvian rule from 1862. The island was annexed by Chile in 1888.

The original islanders called the island *Te Pito o te Henua*, the navel of the world. The population was stable at 4,000 until the 1850s, when, for reasons described below, numbers were reduced. The population is now approaching 4,000 again, of whom about 1,000 are from the mainland, mostly living in the village of **Hanga Roa**. Rapa Nui and Spanish are the official languages. Some people speak English and/or French. Rapa Nui has its own script recorded on tablets. Although not widely used, it is being studied and may be implemented again. The islanders have preserved their indigenous songs and dances, and are extremely hospitable. About half the island, of low round hills with groves of eucalyptus, is used for horses and cattle, and over a third constitutes a national park (entry US$11, payable to park rangers at Orongo).

History

The late Thor Heyerdahl's theories, as expressed in *Aku-Aku, The Art of Easter Island* (New York: Doubleday, 1975), are less widely accepted than they used to be, and South American influence is now largely discounted. See box, opposite, for Polynesian origins. Over 1,000 years of isolation and clan rivalry ended in 1722 with the visit of the Dutch admiral, Jacob Roggeven, on Easter Sunday 1722. A Spanish captain, Don Felipe González, arrived in 1770 and claimed the island for the King of Spain, but no Spanish ship came to make it official. British Captain James Cook stopped briefly in 1774, and a French admiral and explorer, le Comte de La Pérouse, spent 11 hours on the island in 1786. Early visitors spent very little time on the island because of the lack of wood and drinking water, but first encounters led to tragic consequences, first with the introduction of diseases, principally venereal, by whalers in the 1800s.

In 1862 eight Peruvian ships kidnapped one third of the population of the island, including the King. Most were sold to hard labour on plantations, others as domestic servants. Many died and international outcry forced Peru to repatriate the islanders. Even this task was handled with utmost neglect, so that, out of 1,407 Rapa Nui originally taken, only 15 made it back to their homeland. Further indignities ensued, first in 1864, when the religious order, Société de Picpus, brought new diseases in its mission to christianize the eastern Pacific, followed by French sea captain Jean-Baptiste Onéxime Dutroux-Bornier, charged with transporting missionaries to the island, deciding to become its sole ruler. Dutroux-Bornier and the missionaries clashed as each shipped islanders out, the former to plantations in Tahiti, the latter to missions elsewhere. With only 175 islanders left, the Frenchman was murdered, but, historians believe, by that time, the culture and traditions of Rapa Nui had been irreversibly destroyed.

In 1888 Captain Policarpo Toro Hurtado took formal possession of the island and the chiefs ceded sovereignty to Chile "for ever". In fact, a single wool company became the new ruler and yet again treatment of the islanders was so appalling that in desperation, the Rapa Nui petitioned the Chilean government to allow them to emigrate en masse to Tahiti. A rebellion erupted in 1914 and the Chilean navy was sent to retore order. In 1953 the Chilean government took over the administration of the island, but it was not until 1967, the year of the first regular commercial flight, that relaxation of colonial rules took place and interests of the islanders were taken into consideration.

Modern Easter Island Although part of Chile, Easter Island is run by an independent Council of Chiefs and elected local officials. Chile provides good education and health care for all and the

The cultural development of Easter Island

Far from being the passive recipient of external influences, Easter Island shows the extent of unique development possible for a people left wholly in isolation. It is believed to have been colonized from Polynesia, possibly the Marquesas Islands or Mangareva, between about AD 400-600: its older altars (ahu) are similar to those of (French) Polynesia, and its older statues (moai) similar to those of the Marquesas Island in the Pacific between 8°-10° S, 140° W. By AD 1000 the island's society was established.

The very precise stone fitting of some of the ahu, and the tall gaunt moai with elongated faces and ears for which Easter Island is best known were later developments whose local evolution can be traced through a comparison of the remains. The moai were sculpted at the Rano Raraku quarry and transported on wooden rollers over more or less flat paths to their final locations; their red topknots were sculpted at and brought from the inland quarry of Puna Pau; and the rounded pebbles laid out checkerboard fashion at the ahu all came from the same beach at Vinapu.

Indigenous Polynesian society, for all its romantic idylls, was competitive, and it seems that the five clans which originally had their own lands demonstrated their strength by erecting these complex monuments. With the growth in sophistication of Easter Island society, almost all the island's trees were felled. The wood was used for building fishing vessels and most probably for transporting and supporting statues. Deforestation led to soil erosion, the extinction of up to half the native plants, drastic alteration of the island's vegetation, loss of nesting sites for birds and, for the people, no means of making fishing boats. Rapa Nui, according to Jared Diamond in his book Collapse, was "the clearest example of a society that destroyed itself by overexploiting its own resources". What followed were brutal wars between the clans that erupted by the end of 17th century.

The birdman cult represented at Orongo is a later development after the islanders had lost their clan territoriality and were concentrated at Hanga Roa, but still needed a non-territorial way to simulate inter-clan rivalry. The central feature of the birdman cult was an annual ceremony in which the heads of the lineages, or their representatives, raced to the islets to obtain the first egg of the sooty tern (known as the Manatara), a migratory seabird which nests on Motu Nui, Motu Iti and Motu Kao. The winning chief was named Bird Man, Tangato Manu, for the following year. It appears that the egg of the tern represented fertility to the cult, although it is less clear what the status of the Tangata Manu actually was. The petroglyphs at Orongo depict the half-man, half-bird Tangata Manu, the creator god Make Make the symbol of fertility, Komari.

local diet is much healthier than on many Pacific islands. The range of services includes a modern mobile phone network, reliable internet, a television station, stadium, gymnasiums, a modern bank and excellent running water and electricity. Foreigners and Chileans from the mainland cannot own land on Easter Island, even if they live and work there, or are married to a local. Nevertheless, islanders own very little land outside Hanga Roa; the national park covers more than a third of the island, but negotiations for land outside this being returned are in progress. In 2009 investment was destined for repair of the runway, construction of a second one, a new wharf for supply ships to dock and a new hospital. Easter Islanders do not pay taxes and they refuse entry to insurance companies, junk food outlets, public buses and other concepts they find hostile to their traditional culture. On 30 July 2007, a constitutional reform gave Easter Island and Juan Fernández the status of special territories. According to Chilean government officials, Rapa Nui is about to gain status as the 16th Region, with extended autonomous rights.

Sights

The unique features of the island are the 600 (or so) *moai*, huge stone figures up to 9 m in height and broad in proportion. One of them, on **Anakena** beach, was restored to its (probably) original state with a plaque commemorating Thor Heyerdahl's visit in 1955. Other moai have since been re-erected.

In theory, a tour of the main part of the island can be done on foot. This would need at least two days, returning to Hanga Roa and setting out again the next day as camping is not permitted in the park (see page 883). To see more, hire a horse or a vehicle. Even with a car you will need at least two nights as to see a minimum of sights requires one long day. Far better is to allow more time to explore. From Hanga Roa, take the road going southeast past the airport; at the oil tanks turn right to Vinapu, where there are two ahu and a wall whose stones are joined with Inca-like precision. Head back northeast along the south coast, past Vaihu (an *ahu* with eight broken moai; small harbour); Akahanga (ahu with toppled moai); Hanga Tetenga (one toppled moai, bones can be seen inside the ahu), Ahu Tongariki (once the largest platform, damaged by a tidal wave in 1960). Turn left to Rano Raraku (20 km), the volcano where the moai were carved. Many statues can be seen. In the crater is a small lake surrounded by reeds (swimming possible beyond reeds). Good views and a good place to watch the sunrise.

The road heads north past 'the trench of the long-ears' and an excursion can be made to **Poike** to see the open-mouthed statue that is particularly popular with local carvers (ask farmer for permission to cross his land). On Poike the earth is red; at the northeast end is the cave where the virgin was kept before marriage to the victor of ceremonies during the birdman cult. The road along the north coast passes Ahu Te Pito Kura, a round stone called the navel of the world and one of the largest moai ever brought to a platform. It continues to Ovahe, where there is a very attractive beach with pink sand, some rather recently carved faces and a cave.

From Ovahe, one can return direct to Hanga Roa or continue to Anakena, site of **King Hotu Matua's village** and Thor Heyerdahl's landing place. From Anakena, a coastal path of variable quality passes interesting remains and beautiful cliff scenery. At Hanga o Teo there appears to be a large village complex, with several round houses, and further on there is a burial place, built like a long ramp with several ditches containing bones. From Hanga o Teo the path goes west then south, inland from the coast, to meet the road north of Hanga Roa.

A six-hour walk from Hanga Roa on the west coast passes **Ahu Tahai** (a moai with eyes and topknot, cave house, just outside town). Two caves are reached, one inland appears to be a ceremonial centre, the other (nearer the sea) has two 'windows' (take a strong flashlight and be careful near the 'windows'). Further north is Ahu Tepeu (broken moai, ruined houses). Beyond here you can join the path mentioned above, or turn right to Te Pahu cave and the seven moai at Akhivi, which look straight into the setting sun. Either return to Hanga Roa, or go to Puna Pau crater (two hours), where the topknots were carved (good views from the three crosses at the top).

Rano Kau, south of Hanga Roa, is another important site to visit; one finds the curious Orongo ruins here. The route south out of Hanga Roa passes the two caves of Ana Kai Tangata, one of which has paintings. If on foot you can take a path from the Orongo road, just past the CONAF sign, which is a much shorter route to Rano Kau crater. 200 m below is a lake with many reed islands. On the seaward side is Orongo, where the birdman cult flourished, with many ruined buildings and petroglyphs. Out to sea are the 'bird islets', Motu Nui, Motu Iti and Motu Kao. It is very windy at the summit; good views at sunset, or under a full moon (it is easy to follow the road back to Hanga Roa in the dark).

In Hanga Roa is **Ahu Tautira**, next to a swimming area marked out with concrete walls and a breakwater (cold water). Music at the 0900 Sunday mass is 'enchanting'. **Museo Arqueológico Padre Sebastián Englert** ⓘ *2 km north of town, very near Ahu Tahai, T255 1020, www.museorapanui.cl, Tue-Fri 0930-1730, Sat, Sun, holidays 0930-1230, closed 25 Dec, 1 Jan,*

Good Friday and 1 May; open morning only 17 Sep, 24, 31 Dec, US$2, small but good collection of original items, history and maps; often arranges exhibitions, films and concerts. It has a good gift shop with books in Spanish and English, handicrafts and paintings and a great little café. In the same complex is the excellent William Molloy Library ⓘ *Tue-Fri 0930-1230, 1400-1730, only locals are allowed to borrow books*. There is a cultural centre next to the football field, with an exhibition hall and souvenir stall.

Rapa Nui/Easter Island listings

For Sleeping and Eating price codes and other relevant information, see Essentials, pages 38-40.

Sleeping

Rapa Nui/Easter Island *p877*

Unless it is a particularly busy season, there is no need to book in advance; mainland agencies make exorbitant booking charges. The airport information desk has an accommodation list. Flights are met by large numbers of hotel and residencial representatives with whom you can negotiate. Alternatively, take a taxi to the centre of Hanga Roa, drop your things in a café and look around. Many places offer accommodation and tours (rates ranging from US$25 to US$150 pp, includes meals). Rates, especially in residenciales, can be cheaper out of season and if you do not take full board.

LL Explora En Rapa Nui, reserve in Santiago T02-206 6060, in US T1-866 750 6699, or through www.explora.com. All inclusive hotel, easily one of the poshest in the South Pacific. Intentionally hard to find (take Cross Island road, turn right about 6 km from town on the wider unpaved road), transport provided for guests, as are all food, drinks and tours. Views of the ocean are tremendous and each room has a jacuzzi.

LL Hanga Roa, Av Pont, T/F210 0299, www.hotelhangaroa.cl. The largest hotel in town and due to reopen after a refit in 2010, within walking distance of centre. Full board, excellent ocean views, no credit cards.

LL Taha Tai, Api Na Nui s/n, T255 1192, www.hoteltahatai.cl. Well kept bright hotel with cabins and sea view, small swimming pool, tours organized.

L O'Tai, Te Pilo Te Henua s/n, T210 0250, otairapanui@entelchile.net. Great location 2 mins from sea, pool, lovely gardens, restaurants, better rooms with terrace, family run. Recommended.

L-AL Taura'a, C Principal s/n, T210 0463, www.tauraahotel.cl. Upmarket B&B, very comfy, good beds, spacious bathrooms, good breakfast,nice garden, good service. **Taura'a Tours** is also recommended.

AL Cabañas Mahevi, Kaituoe s/n, T08-742 3987, maheva_hiturangi@hotmail.com. Cabins for 3-4 people, furnished with kitchen or microwave, breakfast available, near airport, views of Ranu Kau volcano, Packages up to 5 nights available, also car hire, island tours.

AL Gomero, Av Tu'u'Koihu, T210 0313, www.hotelgomero.com. Comfortable place near the beach, spotless, cosy rooms. Restaurant.

AL Mana Nui Inn, Tahai s/n, opp cemetery, T210 0811, www.rapanuiweb.com/mananui. Pleasant cabins on north edge of town, good breakfast with local specialities, tours run.

AL Martín and Anita's hotel, Simón Paoa s/n, opposite hospital in Hanga Roa, T210 0593, www.hostal.co.cl. With breakfast, full board available, hot water, TV, good food. Can arrange car, bike and horse hire, guides and tours.

AL Res Tadeo y Lili, Apina Ichi s/n, T210 0422, tadeolili@entelchile.net. Simple but clean, French-Rapa Nui run, all rooms with sea view and terrace, good breakfast, tours. Recommended.

AL-A Chez Cecilia, Policarpo Toro y Atamu Tekema, near Tahai Moai, T/F255 1965, www.rapanui chezcecilia.com. Cheaper for longer stays, packages with tours offered. With breakfast, excellent food, *cabañas*, quiet, internet, free airport transfer, also good-value camping.

A Cabañas Sunset, near Ahu Tahai site and old cemetery, T255 2171, 08-407 3885. Spotless cabañas overlooking the sea, discounts for Handbook users, ask for the owner, Ms "China" Pakarati. Includes good breakfast, TV, a/c, modern showers. Highly recommended. She also arranges full day tours for groups of 1-4, US$200.

A HI Kona Tau, Avareipua, T210 0321, www.konataurapanui.com. HI hostel, **D** pp in dorms, all rooms with bath, price includes bath and breakfast, kitchen facilities.

A Inaki Uhi, C Principal s/n, opp Taura'a. Simple but clean rooms, shared bath, kitchen facilities, no breakfast, but central, good budget option.

A Orongo, Atamu Tekena s/n, T210 0572, www.hotelorongo.com. ½-board available (excellent restaurant), good service, nice garden.

A Res Tahai, Calle-Rei-Miro, T210 0395. With breakfast, **A** full board, nice garden, good value.

B Ana Rapu, Av Apina, T210 0540, www.anarapu.cl. Camping US$15. Legendary budget lodging with great range of accommodation, from shared bath to comfortable rooms with private bath, all spotless, also cabins, with breakfast.

B-C Mihinoa, Av Pont s/n, T255 1593, www.mihinoa.com. Campsite, which hires out camping equipment, with a few rooms. Clean, breakfast extra, excellent fish barbecues (fishing trips also offered), kitchen facilities, hot showers, laundry, internet, welcoming, exceptional value. Recommended.

Camping Officially, camping is not allowed anywhere in the national park. Many people offer campsites in their gardens, US$8-12 pp, check availability of water first. Some families also provide food.

Eating

Rapa Nui/Easter Island *p877*

Some residenciales offer full board. Vegetarians will have no problems on the island; locally produced fruit and vegetables are plentiful and cheaper than meat and other foodstuffs, which are imported from mainland. Locally caught fish is also good value. Wine and beer are expensive by Chilean standards because of freight charges.

TTT Jardín de Mau, Atanu Tekena s/n. Pasta/fusion using mostly local ingredients. Some of the pasta is freshly made, excellent tuna carpaccio. Friendly staff, better wine list than most, sea views.

TTT Taverne du Pecheur, Hanga Roa. French-run, especially good for fish, lobster and other seafood. Expensive.

TT Kona Nehe Nehe, Policarpo Toro s/n, T255 1516. Good home cooking, fresh fish and *lomo al pobre*. Recommended.

TT Kopa Kavana, Av Te Pito te Henua s/n, T210 0447. Local dishes and a seafood buffet with side dishes.

TT Taha Tai, Apina Nui s/n, T255 1192. Local and Japanese cooking.

Mi Kafé Gelatería, Caleta Hanga Roa near Mike Rapu Diving Center. For real coffee and good ice cream.

For inexpensive local and Chilean food walk down Av Policarpo Toro: several inexpensive restaurants and dives, including **Bar Restaurant Pub Café Takavake**, and home-made *empanadas* shop. On Av Te Pito Ote Henua near Av Policarpo Toro is **Donde el Gordo**, the best place for *completo* (enormous *empanadas*, US$2). **Kotaro Bistro**, on Hotu Matua behind the airport, T255 2074, is small Japanese food shack, run by a Chilean. Passable food, Japanese mangas, free internet for patrons, popular with Asian visitors and expats.

Bars and clubs

Rapa Nui/Easter Island *p877*

There are 2 in Hanga Roa. Action begins after 0100. Drinks are expensive: pisco sour US$5, canned beer US$3. **Piriti**, near airport. Open Thu-Sat. **Toroko**, Caleta Hanga Roa, near harbour. Open daily.

Traditional music and entertainment

Several in town; one of the best is **Kari Kari** at Hotel Hanga Roa, T210 0595. 3 times a week, US$20, very elaborate show.

Festivals and events

Rapa Nui/Easter Island *p877*

Tapati, or **Semana Rapa Nui**, **end-Jan/ beginning-Feb**, lasts about 10 days. Dancing competitions, singing, sports (horse racing, swimming, modified decathlon), body-painting, typical foods (lots of small booths by the football field), necklace-making, etc. Everyone gets involved, many tourists too. Only essential activities continue outside the festival.

Shopping

Rapa Nui/Easter Island *p877*

All shops and rental offices close 1400-1700. On Av Policarpo Toro, the main street, there are lots of small shops and market stalls (which may close during rain) and a couple of supermarkets, cheapest **Kai Nene** or **Tumukai** (good *panadería* inside).

Handicrafts Wood carvings, stone moais, are available throughout Hanga Roa. The expensive Mercado Artesanal, left of church, will give you a good view of what is available – authentic, no compunction to buy. Good pieces cost from US$50 to US$200. Souvenirs at dozens of decent places on Policarpo Toro.

▲ Activities and tours

Rapa Nui/Easter Island *p877*

Diving **Mike Rapu Diving Center**, Caleta Hanga Roa Otai s/n, T255 1055, www.mikerapu.cl. Diving courses and expeditions and fishing trips, US$70 for beginner's course; courses from $US465 (theory, 5 dives). **Orca**, Caleta Hanga Roa, T255 0375, www.seemorca.cl, run by Michael García. Both at the harbour, all equipment provided. After a check dive you will go to more interesting sights; ask for dives that suit your experience.

Hiking To walk around the island in 1 or 2 days you would need to be in great shape. It is more pleasant to take it easy, but once you leave Hanga Roa services (including lodging and food) are scarce. So take plenty of food and water and inform your hotel or park rangers of your exact route. Sample trekking (and cycling) distances and times: Hanga Roa to Anakena Beach, 17 km, 4½ hrs (1¾ hrs by bike); Hanga Roa to Jau-Orongo, 4 km, 1 hr (30 mins); Hanga Roa to Rano Raraku, 25 km, 6½ hrs (3 hrs).

Horse riding The best way to see the island, provided you are fit, is on horseback: horses, US$65 for a day, including guide. **Cabañas Pikera Uri**, T210 0577, www.pantupikerauri.cl, offers several riding tours, as well as cabañas for overnight stays.

Tour operators

Many agencies, residenciales and locals arrange excursions around the island. The English of other tour guides is improving. Good free bilingual tourist maps at Sernatur information office, hotels and tour agencies. More detailed maps (recommended for driving or bicycling) are sold on Av Policarpo Toro for US$15-18, or at the ranger station at Orongo for US$10. A day-long private tour of the island costs US$100-200 for 1-4 people, including guide, without lunch.

Aku-Aku Tours, Tu'u Koihu s/n, T210 0770, akuakuturismo.cl. Wide range of tours.

Hanga Roa Travel, T210 0158, hfritsch@entelchile.net. English, German, Italian and Spanish spoken, good value all-inclusive tours. Recommended.

Haumaka Archeological Guide Services, Av Atamu Tekena y Hotu Matua, T210 0274. English spoken.

Transport

Rapa Nui/Easter Island *p877*

Air The airport runway has been improved to provide emergency landing for US space shuttles! Airport terminal is tiny but it has several reasonably-priced souvenir shops and a good café. No internet, but good mobile phone signal. For those in transit, in the garden at the departure lounge stands one lonely *moai*. Taxi to town centre US$4. **LAN** fly daily a week in high season, less in low season, 5-5½ hrs going east, 3½-4 hrs going west. Most flights continue to **Papeete**, Tahiti. **LAN** office on Av Policarpo Toro y Av Pont, T210 0279. For details of LAN's special sector fare to Easter Island and which must be purchased outside Chile, see Essentials. The cheapest return fare from Santiago, booked well in advance, is about US$550, with occasional special deals available through travel agents. Under 24s and over 65s are often eligible for a 28% discount on some fares. If you fly between Papetee and Santiago or vice versa, you will be considered in transit and will not be allowed to exit the airport. So, if flying to or from Tahiti, check if you can stay over till another flight.

Car hire If you are hiring a car, do the sites from south to north since travel agencies tend to start their tours in the north. Many vehicle hire agencies on the main street. US$50-80 per day for a small 4WD with manual transmission (usually). In theory, a Chilean or international driving licence is necessary, but your national licence will usually do. If a rental company makes a fuss, go next door. **Moira Souvenir Rent a Car**, Te Pito O Te Henua s/n, T210 0718. About US$40 a day for small, beat-up but functional 4WD, no papers asked for, just a reasonable deposit.

There is no insurance available, drive at your own risk (be careful at night, beware deep potholes, horses and speeding). If you have an accident, accounts are usually settled by a few punches and cash. If you are hit, demand that the person who dented your car and the rental car agency settles the bill. If you hit something or someone, you will be expected to pay, cash only. The speed limit in the National Park is under 30 kph. Check oil and water before setting out. There is only one petrol station, near the airport. A basic loop around the island is 50 to 80 km, depending whether you go off road or not. Motorbike hire: about US$40 a day including gasoline (Suzuki or Honda 250 recommended because of rough roads). You can also rent scooters, bicycles (from US$12 or less from your *residencial*) and quadbikes. **Taxi** There are taxis (US$2 within Hanga Roa) and in summer a bus goes from Hanga Roa to Anakena on Sun at 0900, returning in the afternoon (unreliable). **Radiotaxi Vai Reva**, Sergio Cortés, Petero Atamu s/n, T210 0399, 24 hrs, reliable. For touring the island, it is cheaper to hire a car or take a tour if there are more than 3 people sharing.

Directory

Rapa Nui/Easter Island *p877*
Banks US dollars may be accepted, at poor rates. **Banco del Estado**, Av Pont, T210 0221. Mon-Fri 0800-1300, with an ATM. Accepts MasterCard and Cirrus, cash advances on Visa, reasonable rates for dollars or euros. Another reliable ATM at the gas station shop on Av Hotu Matua. Both ATMs can dispense 10,000 pesos per transction. Cash can be exchanged in shops, hotels, etc, at about 5% less than Santiago. Credit cards are widely accepted for purchases, but some places add a surcharge.
Consulates **British Honorary Consul**, James Grant Peterkin, c/o Easter Island Spirit, Tu'u Koihu s/n, T210 0024, james@easterislandspirit.com. Mon-Fri 1700-2000. Can assist most nationalities.
Internet Several cafés with broadband, good connection considering geographical location, sufficient for Skype (headphones and microphones are usually provided free). US$4-6 per hr, most close 2200. **Omotohi Cybercafé**, Av Te Pito o Te Henua; **Isl@net**, Av Atamu Tekena, both recommended. **Medical facilities** Small but well-equipped **Hospital Hanga Roa**, Av Simón Paoa, near the church, T210 0215. **Cruz Verde** pharmacy in town, large, modern. **Post offices** Half a long block up from Caleta Hanga Roa. 0900-1300, 1430-1800, Sat 0900-1230; sells Easter Island stamps.
Telephones Phone calls to the Chilean mainland are subsidized, but still expensive from **Entel**, Centro de Llamadas, near the Bank, look for huge antennae and satellite dish. Calls to Europe, US and Asia cost over US$1 for 1 min. If you have your own mobile phone (not US or Japanese type), you can buy a SIM card from **Entel**. The cheapest way to call home or mainland Chile is by internet from one of the Internet cafés.

Colombia

Contents

888 Planning your trip

898 Bogotá
- 900 Sights
- 917 Around Bogotá

921 Bogotá to the Venezuelan border
- 921 Bogotá to Villa de Leiva
- 927 Tunja to Cocuy
- 930 To Bucaramanga and Cúcuta

938 Cartagena and the north coast
- 938 Cartagena
- 951 To Panama
- 956 Barranquilla
- 958 Santa Marta, Tayrona and Ciudad Perdida
- 966 To Venezuela
- 970 San Andrés and Providencia

976 Medellín and Chocó
- 976 Medellín
- 983 Around Medellín
- 985 Department of Chocó

988 La Zona Cafetera
- 988 Manizales and around
- 991 Pereira to Cartago

998 Cali and the Cauca Valley
- 998 Cali
- 1003 Cauca and the coast

1005 Popayán, Tierradentro and San Agustín
- 1005 Popayán and Tierradentro
- 1010 Popayán to San Agustín

1017 Southern Colombia
- 1017 South to Ecuador
- 1022 Leticia and the Amazon

Footprint features

- 886 Don't miss …
- 889 Driving in Colombia
- 922 The Gilded Man
- 939 The sacking of Cartagena

At a glance

Time required 2-3 weeks.

Best time Dec-Feb generally driest months. Fiestas in many southern towns in Jan and carnival in Barranquilla in Feb/Mar.

When not to go Christmas and Easter are the busiest holiday seasons. Apr/May and Oct/Nov are the wettest months.

★ **Don't miss ...**

1 **Museo de Oro**, page 904.
2 **Zipaquirá**, page 917.
3 **Cartagena**, page 938.
4 **Ciudad Perdida**, page 961.
5 **La Zona Cafetera**, page 988.
6 **San Agustín and Tierradentro**, page 1005.

The adventurous will love this land of sun and emeralds, with its excellent opportunities for climbing, trekking and diving. The gold museum in Bogotá, the Lost City of the Tayrona and San Agustín have superb examples of cultures long gone. Among several fine colonial cities, the jewel is Cartagena, whose history of slavery and pirates can be seen in the massive fortifications. Today, pelicans share the beach with holidaymakers. Colombia's Caribbean, which stretches to the Panamanian isthmus, is the inspiration for Gabriel García Márquez's world of magical realism and is the land of accordion-led vallenato music. Of the country's many snow-capped mountain ranges, the Sierra Nevada de Santa Marta, with its secretive indígenas, is the most remarkable, rising straight out of the Caribbean. Also not to be missed is the cathedral inside a salt mine at Zipaquirá. There are mud volcanoes to bathe in, acres of flowers, coffee farms to visit and a CD library's worth of music festivals. In fact, dancing is practically a national pastime and having a good time is taken very seriously: as García Márquez once said, "five Colombians in a room invariably turns into a party." Despite the drug trade and the guerrilla violence which has scarred the minds and landscape of this beautiful country, Colombia is rebuilding its position on the tourist circuit.

Planning your trip

Where to go

Bogotá, the capital, stands on a plateau in the eastern cordillera of the Andes. It epitomizes the juxtaposition of the historical and the modern, with many important colonial buildings and museums. Among its attractions are La Candelaria, the old centre of the city, and the magnificent Gold Museum, which houses a remarkable collection of prehispanic artefacts, one of the 'musts' of South America. Places to visit around Bogotá include the salt cathedral at Zipaquirá and the Chicaque Parque Natural, a fine preserved area of cloud forest.

Northeast from Bogotá, to Cúcuta on the Venezuelan border, the beautiful colonial town of **Villa de Leiva** is carefully preserved from the 18th century and well worth a visit. Further north, Santander department also has its attractions, including the most dramatic mountain scenery in Colombia in the **Parque Nacional Cocuy. Barichara** is one of the best kept colonial towns and nearby **San Gil** is an important adventure sports centre.

The obvious centre for exploring the north Caribbean coast and the tropical islands of San Andrés and Providencia is **Cartagena**. The city is a fashionable, modern beach resort and also the place where Colombia's colonial past can best be seen. Here are some of the greatest examples of Spanish architecture on the continent are to be found within the city's ramparts. **Santa Marta** to the northeast is a popular beach resort and the centre for the rocky coast to the east, including Taganga and **Parque Nacional Tayrona**. Treks to the **Ciudad Perdida** (Lost City), a major archaeological site, start in Santa Marta. Towards the Venezuelan border, **La Guajira**, a region of arid desert landscape and home to the indigenous group, the Wayúu, is becoming increasingly popular and accessible to visit. Northeast from Cartagena is the northern port of **Barranquilla**, where Carnival rivals some of those in Brazil. Inland from here, up the Río Magdalena, is the fascinating colonial town of **Mompós**.

In northwest Colombia, **Medellín** is a modern, vibrant city with many fine new buildings, old restored architecture and friendly, outgoing people. There are many fascinating places to visit in the surrounding department of Antioquia, including the colonial towns of **Rionegro** and **Santa Fé de Antioquia**. Further west is **Chocó**, one of the world's most biodiverse and wettest regions. Here, the Pacific coast is almost undeveloped for tourism, with pristine forests descending the mountain slopes to the ocean, but resorts such as Bahía Solano and Nuquí on the Atlantic, and Capurganá on the Caribbean coast, are beginning to open up. South of Medellín is the **Zona Cafetera**, with modern and colonial cities such as Manizales and Pereira and where coffee farms, in delightful countryside, welcome visitors.

Further south, in the Cauca Valley, is **Cali**, with its passion for salsa. Like Medellín it is shrugging off its notorious reputation from recent years. Off the Pacific coast, is **Gorgona**, an unspoilt, idyllic island offering excellent diving. From **Popayán**, a city with a strong colonial feel, are the difficult routes to the important archaeological sites of **Tierradentro** and **San Agustín**. South of Popayán is Pasto, a pleasant town in an attractive setting, Ipiales for the border with Ecuador and Tumaco, from where you can visit the coastal national parks.

In Colombia's far southeastern corner, towards the border with Brazil, lies **Leticia** from where jungle treks start.

When to go

The best time to visit is December-February. These are generally the driest months, but many local people are on holiday. It gets busy and very crowded during Christmas and Easter, when many hotels put up their rates and transport can be overloaded. Climate is a matter of altitude: there are no real seasons, though some periods are wetter than others. Height in metres is given for all major towns. Generally, around 2,000 m is 'temperate'; anywhere higher will require warm clothing in the early mornings and evenings. There is heavy rain in

Driving in Colombia

Road Signposting is poor and roads may be in poor condition. There are toll stations every 60-100 km on major roads: toll is about US$3.50. Motorcycles don't have to pay.

Safety Lorry and bus drivers tend to be reckless, and stray animals are often encountered. Always check safety information for your route before setting out. Police and military checks are frequent in troubled areas, keep your documents handy. In town, only leave your car in an attended car park (*parqueadero*). Only park in the street if there is someone on guard, tip US$0.20.

Documents International driving licences are advised, especially if you have your own car. To be accepted, a national driving licence must be accompanied by an official translation if the original is in a language other than Spanish. To bring a car into Colombia, you must also have documents proving ownership of the vehicle, and a tourist card/transit visa. These are normally valid for 90 days and must be applied for at the Colombian consulate in the country which you will be leaving for Colombia. A *carnet de passages* is recommended when entering with a European registered vehicle. Only third-party insurance issued by a Colombian company is valid; there are agencies in all ports. You will frequently be asked for this document while driving. Carry driving documents with you at all times.

Car hire In addition to passport and driver's licence, a credit card may be asked for as additional proof of identity and to secure a returnable deposit to cover any liability not covered by the insurance. If renting a Colombian car, note that major cities have the pico y placa system which means cars are not allowed entry in the city during morning and afternoon rush hour depending on the day and car number plate (does not apply during the weekends and public holidays); www.picoyplaca.info.

Fuel 'Premium 95' octane (only in large cities), about US$4.50 per gallon; 'corriente' 84 octane, US$3.50 per gallon. Diesel US$3.

many places in April-May and October-November though intermittent heavy rain can fall at any time almost anywhere.

Getting around

Air **Avianca**, www.avianca.com, is the main internal airline. Other airlines are **Aires**, www.aires.aero, **AeroRepública** (part of Copa airlines), www.aerore publica.com, **Satena** (government-owned, but linked with Avianca on some flights), www.satena.com, and **Easyfly**, www.easyfly.com.co (a budget airline serving Bogotá, Medellín, Cartagena, Cúcuta, Bucaramanga and other less well-known destinations). Sometimes there are good value reductions on flights advertised in the press and on the internet, eg weekend trips from Bogotá to the north coast and all-inclusive deals to San Andrés. Domestic airports vary in the services they offer and tourist facilities tend to close early on weekdays, and all Sunday. There is a 16% sales tax on one way tickets and an 8% tax on return tickets. Local airport taxes are included in the price. Security checks can be thorough, watch your luggage. ▸▸ *For further information on airport taxes, see page 895.*

Bus Travel in Colombia is exciting. The scenery is generally worth seeing so travel by day: it is also safer and you can keep a better eye on your valuables. Almost all the main routes are paved, but the state of the roads varies considerably between departments. On main routes you usually have choice of company, and type of bus. The cheapest (*corriente*) are basically local buses, stopping frequently, uncomfortable and slow but offering plenty of local colour. Try to keep your luggage with you. *Pullman* (each company will have a different name for the service) are long distance buses usually with a/c, toilets, hostess service, DVDs (almost always violent films, dubbed into Spanish). Sit near the back with your walkman to avoid the movie and the need to keep the blinds down. Luggage is normally carried in a locked compartment against receipt. See the following bus company websites: **Berlinas del Fonce**, www.berlinasdelfonce.com, **Bolivariano**, www.bolivariano.com.co, **Copetran**, www.copetran.com.co, **Expreso Brasilia**, www.expreso brasilia.com, **Expreso Palmira**, www.expresopalmira.com.co. *Colectivos*, also known as *vans* or *busetas*, are usually 12-20 seat vehicles, sometimes seven-seater cars or pick-up trucks, rather cramped but fast, saving several hours on long journeys. When taxis provide this service they are *por puestos* (pay by seat) and do not leave till full. You can keep your eye on luggage in the back of the vehicle. Fares shown in the text are middle of the range where there is a choice but are no more than a guide. Note that meal stops can be few and far between, and short; bring your own food. Be prepared for climatic changes on longer routes and for the vagaries of a/c on buses, sometimes fierce, sometimes none. **If you entrust your luggage to the bus companies' luggage rooms, remember to load it on to the bus yourself; it will not be done automatically.** There are few interdepartmental bus services on holidays. During holidays and high season, arrive at the bus terminal at least an hour before the departure time to guarantee a seat, even if you have bought a ticket in advance. If you are joining a bus at popular or holiday times, not at the starting point, you may be left behind even though you have a ticket and reservation. Always take your passport (or photocopy) with you: identity and luggage checks on buses are frequent and you may be body-searched at army roadblocks.

Cycling Cycling is a popular sport in Colombia. There are good shops for spares in all big cities, though the new standard 622/700 size touring wheel size is not very common. Take your own spare tyres. Around Calle13 with Cra 20 in front of La Sabana train station in Bogotá are several bicycle repair and accessory shops.

Hitchhiking Hitchhiking (*autostop*) is unadvisable and not common. In safe areas, try enlisting the co-operation of the highway police checkpoints outside each town and toll booths. Truck drivers are often very friendly, but be careful of private cars with more than one person inside. Travelling on your own is not recommended.

Taxi Whenever possible, take an official taxi with a meter and ensure that it is switched on. If there is no meter, bargain and fix a price. Official taxis should display the driver's ID with photo and additional legal tariffs that may be charged after 2000, on Sunday and fiestas. Fares are registered in units on the meter, which the driver converts to pesos with a fare table. This should be shown to the passenger. Don't take a taxi which is old; look for 'Servicio Público' on the side. It is safest to call a radio taxi, particularly at night, rather than hailing one down in the street. Bars, hotels and restaurants will order taxis for customers. The dispatcher will give you the cab's number which should be noted in case of irregularities. The last two digits of the number from where the call was made is *el clave*, the security code. Remember it as taxi drivers will ask for the code before setting off. Never get into a taxi if there are already passengers in it. If the taxi 'breaks down', take your luggage and find another taxi immediately.

Sleeping → *See page 38 for our hotel grade price guide.*

Hotels The more expensive hotels charge 16% VAT (IVA). Some hotels add a small insurance charge. From 15 December to 30 April, 15 June to 31 August and bank holidays (*puentes*), hotels in holiday centres may increase prices by at least 20-30%. Prices are normally displayed at reception, but in quiet periods it is always worth negotiating.

Camping Sites are given in the text but also check locally very carefully before deciding to camp. Local tourist offices have lists of official sites, but they are seldom signposted on main roads.

Permission to camp with tent, camper van or car is usually granted by landowners in less populated areas. Many haciendas have armed guards protecting their property: this can add to your safety. Vehicles may camp at truck drivers' restaurants, *balnearios campestres* with armed guards, or ask if you may overnight beside police or army posts.

Youth hostels Federación Colombiana de Albergues Juveniles, Cra 7, No 6-10, Bogotá, T91-280 3041, www.fcaj.org.co. The FCAJ is affiliated to Hostelling International. **Colombian Hostels Association**, www.colombianhostels.com, has 15 members around the country.

Eating and drinking → *See page 40 for our Eating price guide.*

Eating out Colombia's food is regionally varied, most major cities have restaurants with non-local Colombian food. Small towns do not cater for vegetarians. Restaurants in smaller towns often close on Sunday, and early on weekday evenings: if stuck, you will probably find something to eat near the bus station. If economising, ask for the excellent value *menú del día*, also known as *comida corriente* (daily set lunch). This consists of a filling three-course meal (juice, soup, meat or fish dish and dessert) for no more than US$2. More expensive restaurants may add 16% IVA to the bill.

Food Some of the standard items on the menu are: *sancocho*, a meat stock (may be fish on the coast) with potato, corn (on the cob), yucca, sweet potato and plantain. *Arroz con pollo* (chicken and rice), a common Latin American dish, is excellent in Colombia. *Carne asada* (grilled beefsteak), usually an inexpensive cut, is served with *papas fritas* (chips) or rice and you can ask for a vegetable of the day. *Sobrebarriga* (belly of beef) is served with varieties of potato in a tomato and onion sauce. *Huevos pericos,* eggs scrambled with onions and tomatoes, are a popular, cheap and nourishing snack available almost anywhere, especially for breakfast. *Tamales* are meat pies made by folding a maize dough round chopped pork mixed with potato, rice, peas, onions and eggs wrapped in banana leaves (which you don't eat) and steamed. Other ingredients may be added such as olives, garlic, cloves and paprika. Colombians eat *tamales* for breakfast with hot chocolate. *Empanadas* are another popular snack; these are made with chicken or other meats, or vegetarian filling, inside a maize dough and cooked in a light oil. *Patacones* are cakes of mashed and baked *plátano* (large green banana). *Arepas* are standard Colombian fare; these are flat maize griddle cakes served instead of bread or as an alternative. *Pan de bono* is cheese flavoured bread. *Almojábanas*, a kind of sour milk/cheese bread roll, great for breakfast when freshly made. *Buñuelos* are 4-6 cm balls of wheat flour and eggs mixed and deep-fried, also best when still warm. *Arequipe* is a sugar-based brown syrup used with desserts and in confectionery, universally savoured by Colombians.

Regional specialities **Bogotá and Cundinamarca**: *Ajiaco de pollo* is a delicious chicken stew with maize, manioc (yuca), three types of potato, herbs and sometimes other vegetables, served with cream and capers, and pieces of avocado. *Chunchullo* (tripe), and *morcilla* (blood sausage) are popular dishes. *Cuajada con melado* is a dessert of fresh cheese served with cane syrup, or *natas* (based on the skin of boiled milk). **Boyacá**: *Mazamorra* is a meat and vegetable soup with broad and black beans, peas, varieties of potato and cornflour. *Care* is a milk and maize drink, known as *mazamorro* in Antioquia and elsewhere and *peto* in Cundinamarca. *Puchero* is a stew based on chicken with potatoes, yuca, cabbage, turnips, corn (on the cob) and herbs. *Cuchuco*, another soup with pork and sweet potato. *Masato* is a slightly fermented rice beverage. *Longaniza* (long pork sausage) is also very popular. **Santander and Norte de Santander**: *Mute* is a soup of various cereals including corn. *Hormigas culonas* (large-bottomed black ants) is the most famous culinary delight of this area, served toasted, and particularly popular in Bucaramanga at Easter time. *Bocadillo veleño* is similar to quince jelly but made from guava. *Hallacas* are cornmeal turnovers with different meats and whatever else is to hand inside. *Carne oreada* is salted dried meat marinated in a *panela* and pineapple sauce with the consistency of beef jerky.

Cartagena and the north coast: Fish is naturally a speciality the coastal regions. In *Arroz con coco*, rice here is often prepared with coconut. *Cazuela de mariscos*, a soup/stew of shellfish and white fish, maybe including octopus and squid, is especially good. *Sancocho de pescado* is a fish stew with vegetables, usually simpler and cheaper than *cazuela*. *Chipichipi*, a small clam found along the coast in Barranquilla and Santa Marta, is a standard local dish served with rice. *Empanada* (or *arepa*) *de huevo* is deep fried with eggs in the middle. *Canasta de coco* is a pastry containing coconut custard flavoured with wine and surmounted by meringue. **Tolima**: *Lechona*, suckling pig with herbs is a speciality of Ibagué. **Antioquia**: *Bandeja paisa* consists of various types of grilled meats, *chorizo* (sausage), *chicharrón* (pork crackling), sometimes an egg, served with rice, beans, potato, manioc and a green salad; this has now been adopted in other parts of the country. *Natilla*, a sponge cake made from cornflour and *salpicón*, a tropical fruit salad. **Cali and south Colombia**: the emphasis here is on corn, plantain, rice and avocado with the usual pork and chicken dishes. *Manjar blanco*, made from milk and sugar or molasses, served with biscuit is a favourite dessert. *Cuy, curí* or *conejillo de Indias* (guinea pig), is typical of the southern department of Nariño. *Mazorcas* (baked corn-on-the-cob) are typical of roadside stalls in southern Colombia.

Drink *Tinto*, the national small cup of black coffee, is taken at all hours and is usually sweetened. Colombian coffee is always mild. Coffee with milk is called *café perico*; *café con leche* is a mug of milk with coffee added. To make sure you get cold milk with your coffee, ask for it separately at an additional cost. *Agua de panela* is a common beverage (hot water with unrefined sugar), also made with limes, served with cheese. Many decent brands of beer are brewed, including *Costeña*, *Aguila*, *Club Colombia* and *Poker*. The local rum is good and cheap; ask for *ron* eg Ron Viejo de Caldas. *Aguardiente* is a 'rougher' cane-based spirit served with or without aniseed (*aguardiente anisado*). Try *canelazo*, cold or hot *aguardiente* with water, sugar, lime and cinnamon, common in Bogotá. Local table wines include Isabella; none is very good. Wine is very expensive, US$15 in restaurants for an average Chilean or Argentine wine, more for European and other wines.

Fruit and juices As well as fruits familiar in northern and Mediterranean climates, Colombia has a huge variety of local fruits: *chirimoyas* (a green fruit, white inside with pips); *curuba* (banana passion fruit); *feijoa* (a green fruit with white flesh, high in vitamin C); *guayaba* (guava); *guanábana* (soursop); *lulo* (a small orange fruit); *maracuyá* (passion fruit); *mora* (literally 'black berry' but dark red more like a loganberry); *papaya*; the delicious *pitahaya* (taken either as an appetizer or dessert); *sandía* (watermelon); *tomate de árbol* (tree tomato, several varieties normally used as a fruit); and many more. All can be served as juices, either with milk or water. Fruit yoghurts are nourishing and cheap; **Alpina** brand is good; *crema* style is best. Also, **Kumis** is a type of liquid yoghurt. Another drink you must try is *champús*, a corn base, with fruit and lemon.

Essentials A-Z

Accident and emergency

Police: T112; **Ambulance**: T125 or 132; **Fire**: T119; **Red Cross ambulance**: T127; DAS (security police) T153; **CAI Police**: T156. If you have problems with theft or other forms of crime, contact a **Centro de Atención Inmediata** (**CAI**) office for assistance. CAI offices in Bogotá: downtown, C 60 y Cra 9, T2177472, La Candelaria, Cra 7 y C6.

Electricity

110 Volts AC, alternating at 60 cycles per second. A voltage converter may be required if your device does not run on 110 Volts. Most sockets accept both continental European (round) and North American (flat) 2-pin plugs.

Embassies and consulates

Visit www.cancilleria.gov.co for a full list of addresses.

Festivals and events

Public holidays: there are some 18 public holidays. The most important are: 1 Jan: Circumcision of our Lord; 6 Jan: Epiphany*; 19 Mar: St Joseph*; Maundy Thur; Good Fri; 1 May: Labour Day; Ascension Day*; Corpus Christi*; Sacred Heart*; 29 Jun: SS Peter and Paul*; 20 Jul: Independence Day; 7 Aug: Battle of Boyacá; 15 Aug: Assumption*; 12 Oct: Columbus' arrival in America* (Día de la Raza); 1 Nov: All Saints' day*; 11 Nov: Independence of Cartagena*; 8 Dec: Immaculate Conception; 25 Dec: Christmas Day.

When those marked with an asterisk (*) do not fall on a Mon, they will be moved to the following Mon. Public holidays are known as *puentes* (bridges).

Maps

Maps of Colombia are obtainable at the Instituto Geográfico Agustín Codazzi, Carrera 30, Bogotá, No 48-51, T369 4000, www.igac.gov.co, or from their offices in other large cities. They have a wide range of official, country-wide and departmental maps and atlases, but many are a few years old. In Bogotá, they are open Mon-Fri 0800-1630, maps are mainly from US$2.50 to US$6 and you pay at the bank next door. There is a library open until 1630 and refreshments available at lunchtime. A guide with detailed road maps across the country is the annual *Guía de Rutas de Colombia* available at toll booths and some bookshops. Town maps should be available from local tourist offices.

Money → *US$1 = 1878 pesos, € = 2808 pesos (Oct 2009).*

The currency is the peso. There are coins of 50, 100, 200 and 500; there are notes of 1,000, 2,000, 5,000, 10,000, 20,000 and 50,000 pesos (the last can be difficult to change). Change is in short supply, especially in small towns, and in the morning. Watch out for forged notes. The 50,000-peso note should smudge colour if it is real, if not, refuse to accept it. There is a limit of US$10,000 on the import of foreign exchange in cash, with export limited to the equivalent of the amount brought in.

Plastic/TCs/banks

Cash and TCs can in theory be exchanged in any bank, except the **Banco de la República**; go early to banks in smaller places to change these. In most sizeable towns there are *casas de cambio* (exchange shops), which are quicker to use than banks but sometimes charge higher commission. It's best to use euros and, even better, dollars. It can sometimes be difficult to buy and sell large amounts of sterling, even in Bogotá. Hotels may give very poor rates of exchange, especially if you are paying in dollars. It is dangerous to change money on the streets and you may well be given counterfeit pesos. Also in circulation are counterfeit US dollar bills. You must present your passport when changing money (a photocopy is not normally accepted). Take some US$ cash with you for emergencies.

Credit cards

As it is unwise to carry large quantities of cash, credit cards are widely used, especially MasterCard and Visa; Diners Club is also accepted. American Express is only accepted in expensive places in Bogotá. Many banks accept Visa (Visaplus and ATH logos) and Cirrus/MasterCard (Maestro and Multicolor logos) to advance pesos against the card, or through ATMs. There are ATMs for Visa and MasterCard everywhere but you may have to try several machines. All Carulla supermarkets have ATMs. Credit card loss or theft: Visa call collect to (44) 20-7937 8091 or fax (44) 17-3350 3670, MasterCard T0800-912 1303.

ATMs do not retain cards. If your card is not given back immediately, do not proceed with the transaction and do not type in your pin number. There are reports of money being stolen from accounts when cards have been retained. ATMs dispense a frustratingly small amount of cash at a time. The maximum withdrawal is often 300,000 pesos (about US$150), which can accrue heavy bank charges over a period of time. For larger amounts try: **Davivienda** (500,000 per visit) and **Bancolombia** (400,000 per visit).

Note Only use ATMs in supermarkets, malls or where a security guard is present. Don't ask a taxi driver to wait while you use an ATM. Be particularly vigilant around Christmas time when thieves may be on the prowl.

Traveller's cheques

When changing TCs, a photocopy of your passport may be required as well as the original, so take a supply of photocopies with you. The procedure is always slow, maybe involving finger printing and photographs. Take dollar TCs in small denominations; better still, take a credit card (see above). Sterling TCs are practically impossible to change. To change Amex TCs, use major banks. You may have to provide proof of purchase. Obtaining reimbursement for lost Amex TCs can be straightforward if you have the numbers recorded (preferably proof of purchase), a police certificate (*diligencia de queja*) covering the circumstances of loss, and apply to their offices at C 85, No 20-32, T593 4949, Mon-Fri 0800-1800, Sat 0900-1200 (see Bogotá, Banks). Banks may be unwilling to change TCs in remote areas, take local currency. TCs are not normally accepted in hotels, restaurants, shops etc.

Cost of travelling

Prices are generally lower than Europe and North America for services and locally produced items, but more expensive for imported and luxury goods. For the traveller prices are among the lowest in South America. Modest, basic accommodation will cost about US$10-12 pp per night in Bogotá, Cartagena, Santa Marta and colonial cities like Villa de Leiva, Popayán or Santa Fé de Antioquia, but a few dollars less elsewhere. A *comida corriente* (set lunch) costs about US$1.50-2 and breakfast US$1-1.75. *A la carte* meals are usually good value and fierce competition for transport keeps prices low. Typical cost of internet is US$1-4 per hr.

Opening hours

Business hours are generally Mon-Fri 0800-1200, 1400-1700, Sat 0900-1200. A longer siesta may be taken in small towns and tropical areas. Banks in larger cities do not close for lunch. Most businesses such as banks and airline offices close for official holidays while supermarkets and street markets may stay open. This depends a lot on where you are, so enquire locally.

Safety

Travellers confirm that the vast majority of Colombians are polite, honest and will go out of their way to help visitors and make them feel welcome. In general, anti-gringo sentiments are rare. However, in addition to the general advice given in Essentials, see page 47, the following local conditions should be noted. Colombia is part of a major drug-smuggling route. Police and customs activities have greatly intensified and smugglers increasingly try to use innocent carriers. Do not carry packages for other people. Be very polite if approached by policemen in uniform, or if your hotel room is raided by police looking for drugs. Colombians who offer you drugs could be setting you up for the police, who are very active in Cali, on the north coast, San Andrés island and other tourist resorts.

There have been reports of travellers and Colombians being victims of *burundanga*, a drug obtained from a white flower, native to Colombia. At present, the use of this drug appears to be confined to major cities. It is very nasty, almost impossible to see or smell. It leaves the victim helpless and at the will of the culprit. Usually, the victim is taken to ATMs to draw out money. Be wary of accepting cigarettes, food and drink from strangers at sports events and in buses. In bars watch your drinks very carefully.

The internal armed conflict in Colombia is almost impossible to predict and the security situation changes from day to day. For this reason, it is essential to consult regularly with locals for up-to-date information. Taxi and bus drivers, local journalists, soldiers at checkpoints, hotel owners and Colombians who actually travel around their country are usually good sources of reliable information. Travelling overland between towns, especially during the holiday season and bank holiday weekends, has in general become much safer due to increased military and police presence along main roads. However, the government has launched a major offensive against the guerrilla (especially in the south) and in some areas fighting between the armed forces and guerrilla groups has intensified. The following areas are known as *zonas calientes* (hot zones) where there is active presence of guerrilla groups and/or paramilitaries: the rural areas down the eastern part of the country from **Arauca** and **Casanare** to **Meta**; **Caquetá** and **Putumayo**; the **Magdalena Medio** and **Norte de Santander**; from **Urabá** near the border with **Panamá** into northwestern **Antioquia** and parts of **Chocó**; **Sur de Bolívar** and, to a lesser extent, **Carmen de Bolívar** in the department of Bolívar; in and around **La Macarena** national park; the city of **Buenaventura** on the Pacific coast and **Neiva** in the department of Huila. Travellers wishing to go into rural areas in **Cauca** and **Nariño** in the southwest should also seek advice. As a loose rule, the conflict is often most intense in coca growing areas, oil producing regions and along Colombia's borders. Guerrilla activity usually increases in the run up to local and national elections. Incidents in cities, including **Bogotá**, may also occur. Apart from between major cities such as Cartagena, Bogotá, Bucaramanga and Medellín, do not travel between towns by road at night. Parts of the motorway, especially south of Bogotá, may be closed at night between 1800-0600 for security reasons. If venturing into rural areas and hot zones ask first at your embassy. It is essential to follow this up with detailed enquiries at your chosen destination. If arriving overland, go to the nearest hotel favoured by travellers (these are given in the text) and make enquiries. **Note** that rural hot zones are often littered with land mines.

Amazonas and, to a lesser extent, **Los Llanos**, have always been difficult to visit because of their remoteness, the lack of facilities and the huge distances involved (these factors also apply to **La Guajira** in the north). Our text is limited to **Villavicencio**, **Florencia** and the **Letici**a region all of which are comparatively safe. They should only be visited by air, except Leticia where river routes are safe.

Taxes

Airport taxes

The airport departure tax for stays of less than 60 days is about US$33, see www.bogota-dc.com/trans/aviones.htm. It is not included in the ticket price. For stays of over 60 days there is a reduced tax of US$23 (payable in Colombian pesos). Travellers changing planes in Colombia and leaving the same day are exempt from this tax. When you arrive, ensure that all necessary documentation bears a stamp for your date of arrival; without it you will have to pay the full exit tax. There is also an airport tax on internal flights, US$5 (varies according to airport), usually included in the ticket price.

VAT

16%. Ask for an official receipt if you want it documented. Some hotels and restaurants add IVA onto bills, but foreigners do not officially have to pay.

Telephone → *Country code T+57.*

Ringing: equal tones with long pauses.
Engaged: short tones with short pauses.
National and international calls can be made from public phone offices in all major cities and even in rural towns. You are assigned a cabin, place your calls, and pay on the way out. There is usually a screen that tells you how much you are spending. Prices vary considerably. You can also make calls from street vendors who hire out their mobile phones (usually signposted '*minutos*'). It is relatively inexpensive to buy a pay- as-you go SIM card for your mobile phone. Calls are on the whole cheap but there is a complicated system for making calls from mobiles. For calling landlines, 03 must be affixed before the area code and number. For calling mobile numbers, the 0 is dropped.

Time

Official time is 5 hrs behind GMT.

Tipping

Upmarket restaurants 10%, often included in the bill. Porters, cloakroom attendants and hairdressers US$0.05-0.25. It is not customary to tip taxi drivers, but it is appreciated.

Tourist information

National tourism is part of the Ministry of Commerce, Industry and Tourism, Calle 28, No 13A-15, Bogotá, www.mincomercio.gov.co, with its portal, **Proexport**, at the same address, p 35, T427 9000, www.turismocolombia.com. **Posadas Turísticas de Colombia** is a government-sponsored project, with places to stay in selected tourist destinations throughout the country; see www.posadasturisticasde colombia.com. Departmental and city entities have their own offices responsible for tourist information: see the text for local details. These offices should be visited as early as possible for information on accommodation and transport, but also for details on areas that are dangerous to visit. Regional tourist offices are better sources of information on safety than the Bogotá offices; otherwise contact Colombia's representation overseas. See also Websites and Maps, below.

The **National Parks** service is at the Ministerio del Medio Ambiente, Vivienda y Desarrollo Territorial (Ministry of the Environment, www.minambiente.gov.co), Ecotourism office, Carrera 10, No 20-30, p 1, Bogotá, T01-353 2400, ext 138-139, Mon-Fri 0800-1745, www.parquesnacionales.gov.co (which has a list of regional offices). Staff can provide information about facilities and accommodation, and have maps. If you intend to visit the parks, this is a good place to start and ask for up-to-date details and to obtain a permit. The *National Parks Guide* is attractive and informative, US$50, providing lavishly illustrated scientific information. There is a library and research unit (*Centro de Documentación*) for more information. Permits to visit the parks and protected areas must be obtained before going to the park you wish to visit. Do not go directly to the parks themselves. Some prices vary according to high and low seasons. High season includes: weekends, Jun-Jul, Dec-Jan, public holidays and Semana Santa. Permits, transport details and accommodation reservations for some national parks can be obtained from **Aviatur** travel agency, Av 19, No 4-62, Bogotá, T286 5555, or 01-900-331 2222, www.concesionesparquesnaturales.com (addresses given in text, not always efficient). Foreigners over 18 can participate on the voluntary park ranger programme. Details are available from the Ecotourism office in Bogotá. You will have to provide photocopies of ID documents and Colombian entry stamp in your passport. A good level of Spanish is required.

The **Asosiación Red Colombiana de Reservas Naturales de la Sociedad Civil**, C 2 A, No 26-103, San Fernando, Cali, T02-558 5046, www.resnatur.org.co, is a network of privately-owned nature reserves that works with local people to build a sustainable model of environmentally-friendly tourism. See also **www.colparques.net** (Organización para la Promoción de los Parques Naturales de Colombia).

Useful websites

www.colombiajournal.org Interesting photo gallery and good selection of articles about Colombian current affairs, in Spanish and English.
www.humboldt.org.co Site of Institute Von Humboldt, probably the most important environment research organization in Colombia. An excellent site with descriptions of the different ecosystems in the country and projects with ethnic communities (in Spanish).
www.ideam.gov.co Weather forecasts and climate information, in Spanish.
www.natura.org.co **Fundación Natura**, excellent conservation information.
www.poorbuthappy.com/colombia Reliable information on travel, jobs and safety, in English.
www.presidencia.gov.co The government website. You can also access: **www.gobiernoenlinea.gov.co**, in Spanish and English.
www.quehubo.com Colombian Yellow Pages site.
www.terra.com.co for news, sport, entertainment, chat room and more.

Visas and immigration

Tourists are allowed to stay a maximum of 180 days in a calendar year. Make sure that, on entry, you are granted enough days for your visit. If you wish to extend your permission to stay in Colombia, for a further 30 days, apply 2-3 days before your permit expires at the DAS (security police) office in any major city; it costs about US$35. Take 2 passport photos and a copy of your ticket out of Colombia. This does not apply to visas. If you overstay an entry permit or visa, a *salvoconducto* can be applied for at a DAS office. The *salvoconducto* is only issued once for a period of 30 days and is usually processed within 24 hrs; it costs about US$22. Take 2 recent photos and copies of your passport. The DAS head office in Bogotá is, Cra 28, No 17A-00 Paloquemao, T408 8000, www.das.gov.co

(see also under Bogotá, and other cities, Useful addresses). Arrive early in the morning, expect long queues and a painfully slow bureaucratic process. **Note** DAS does not accept cash payments; these are made at the branches of Bancafé with special payments slips. Alternatively, if you have good reason to stay longer (eg for medical treatment), apply at the embassy in your home country before leaving. An onward ticket may be asked for at land borders or Bogotá international airport. You may be asked to prove that you have sufficient funds for your stay.

To visit Colombia as a tourist, nationals of countries of the Middle East (except Israel), Asian countries (except Japan, South Korea, Malaysia, Phillipines, Indonesia and Singapore), Bulgaria, Poland, Russia, Haiti, Nicaragua, and all African countries need a visa. Always check for changes in regulations before leaving your home country. Visas are issued only by Colombian consulates. When a visa is required you must present a valid passport, 3 photographs, the application form (in duplicate), US$23-45 or equivalent (price varies according to nationality), onward tickets, and a photocopy of all the documents (allow 2 weeks maximum).

If you are going to take a Spanish course, you must have a student visa (US$40). You may not study on a tourist visa. A student visa can be obtained while in Colombia on a tourist visa. Proof of sufficient funds is necessary (US$400-600 for a 6-month stay is usually deemed sufficient). You must be first enrolled in a course from a bona fide university to apply for a student visa. Various business and other temporary visas are needed for foreigners who have to reside in Colombia for a length of time. The Ministerio de Relaciones Exteriores (not DAS), C 10, No 5-51, T381 4000, Mon-Fri 0800-1745, processes student and some work visas. In general, Colombian work visas can only be obtained outside Colombia at the appropriate consulate and or embassy. You must register work and student visas at a DAS office within 15 days of obtaining them, otherwise you will be liable to pay a hefty fine. Visas must be used within 3 months. Supporting documentary requirements for visas change frequently. Check with the appropriate consulate in good time before your trip.

When entering the country, you will be given the copy of your DIAN (Customs) luggage declaration. Keep it; you may be asked for it when you leave. If you receive an entry card when flying in and lose it while in Colombia, apply to any DAS office who should issue one and restamp your passport for free. Normally passports are scanned by a computer and no landing card is issued, but passports still must be stamped on entry. Note that to leave Colombia you must get an exit stamp from the DAS. They often do not have offices at the small border towns, so try to get your stamp in a main city.

Note It is highly recommended that you photocopy your passport details, including entry stamps which, for added insurance, you can have witnessed by a notary. Always carry a photocopy of your passport with you, as you may be asked for identification. This is a valid substitute for most purposes though not, for example, for cashing TCs or drawing cash across a bank counter. Generally acceptable for identification (eg to enter government buildings) is a driving licence, provided it is plastic, of credit card size and has a photograph. For more information, check with your consulate.

Weights and measures

Generally metric, but US gallons for petrol.

Bogotá

➔ Phone code: 1. Pop: 8,500,000 million. Colour map 1, B3. Altitude: 2,650 m. Mean temperature: 14°C.
Bogotá, the eighth-largest city in Latin America, is a vast sprawling metropolis where, despite its modernity, it is not uncommon to see the horse and cart still in use on the streets. It is the cultural centre of the country with cosmopolitan restaurants and a vibrant night life. Predictably, there are staggering extremes of wealth and poverty, with the city segregated between the rich north and the poorer south. The capital has advanced in leaps and bounds since the mid-1990s, winning awards for its environmental efforts, libraries and transport systems, as well as improving quality of life. Since 2001, the TransMilenio, a rapid, efficient north-south bus route has helped to unclog Bogotá's gridlocked streets. On Sundays, the city's main streets are closed to traffic for the benefit of cyclists, joggers and rollerbladers. Emerald sellers do deals on street corners, but for a safer view of all that glitters, visit the Gold Museum, one of the most stunning collections of pre-Columbian treasures in the Americas. The old centre of La Candelaria has countless well-preserved colonial buildings and important museums that lie along cobbled streets with fine views over the city. A windy mountain road above the city leads to La Calera, offering panoramic views, a popular place for lunch and horse riding at weekends. As Bogotá is Latin America's third highest city, it gets chilly at night. Warm clothes are needed.

Ins and outs

Getting there El Dorado **airport** has two terminals, El Dorado and Puente Aéreo, 15 km west of the centre. The taxi fare from airport to city is a fixed charge, US$10, more at night and early morning. Make sure you get a registered taxi, normally yellow, found to your right as you leave the main terminal. You can also go left to the far end of the main terminal to domestic arrivals where you can get a ticket, from the booth just inside the building, which will fix the price of your journey – recommended. There are *colectivos* (US$1 plus luggage pp) from airport to centre. Be vigilant with your belongings when coming out of the arrivals hall into the street. The long-distance **bus terminal**, Terminal de Transportes, is in the same direction as the airport, but not as far out. To get into town from the terminal take buses marked 'La Candelaria', 'Centro' or 'Germania'; ask the driver where to get off (the 'Germania' bus goes up to the centre and La Candelaria). Note there are two areas called La Candelaria, one in the north of the city and one in the south. Be sure to ask for La Candelaria in 'el centro histórico'.To get to North Bogotá from the terminal, take a bus heading in that direction on Cra 68. If taking a taxi, obtain a slip (as at the airport), to fix the fare: to the centre, about US$5. At airport and bus terminal, unofficial taxis are dangerous and must be avoided. ▸▸ *See also Transport, page 913.*

Getting around **Bus**: Several types of bus cover urban routes. All stop when flagged down. There are also the red **TransMilenio** buses on dedicated lanes. **Taxi**: Have meters which calculate units starting at 25. Taxis are relatively cheap and easy to come by. If you are carrying valuables and especially at night, call for a radio taxi rather than taking one on the street. For more details, see Transport, page 913. **Street numbering**: The Calles (abbreviated 'C', or 'Cll') run at right angles across the Carreras ('Cra' or 'K'). It is easy to find a place once the address system, used throughout Colombia, is understood. The address Calle 13, No 12-45 would be the building on Calle 13 between Carreras 12 and 13 at 45 paces from Carrera 12; however transversals (Tra) and diagonals (Diag) can complicate the system. The Avenidas (Av), broad and important streets, may be either Calles (like 26) or Carreras (like 14) or both (like 19 which is Calle in the Centre and Carrera in the North). Avenida Jiménez de Quesada, one of Bogotá's most well known streets, owes its lack of straightness to having been built over a river bed (opened up again in 2000). The Calles in the south of the city are marked 'Sur' or 'S'; this is an integral part of the address and must be quoted.

Orientation The mountains of the eastern cordillera lie east, a useful landmark for getting your bearings. Most of the interesting parts of the city follow the foot of the cordillera in a north-south line. **La Candelaria**, full of character, occupies the area bounded by Av Jiménez de Quesada, C 6, Cra 3 and Cra 10. There is some modern infill but many of the houses are well preserved in colonial style, of one or two storeys with tiled roofs, projecting eaves, wrought ironwork and carved balconies. The main colonial churches, palaces and museums are concentrated around and above the Plaza Bolívar. Some hotels are found in this part, more along the margins, eg Avenida Jiménez de Quesada. **Downtown Bogotá** runs in a band northeast along Cra 7 from Av Jiménez de Quesada to C26. It is a thorough mix of styles including modern towers and run-down colonial and later buildings, together with a few notable exceptions. The streets are full of life and can be paralysed by traffic at busy times. The pavements can be congested too, particularly Cra 7 and Av 19. From C 50 to C 68 is **El Chapinero**, once the outskirts of the city and now a commercial district with a sprinkling of old, large, middle-class mansions. It doubles up as the epicentre of Bogotá's gay scene, with many bars and clubs. Next to the National Park, along La Séptima is **La Merced**, a cluster of English country-style houses. A few blocks further south, along Cra 4 between C 25 and C 27, is the Bohemian area of **La Macarena**, which was formerly inhabited by struggling artists, now becoming fashionable with many good restaurants and bars. Beyond C 60, the main city continues to **North Bogotá**, which is split into various points of interest. Most of the best hotels, restaurants and embassies are in this area, which is regarded as the safest in Bogotá. See below.

Due to the **altitude**, go easy and be careful with food and alcoholic drinks for the first day or so. Walking in the downtown area and in La Candelaria by day is recommended as distances are short and traffic is heavy. North Bogotá is more spacious and buses and taxis are more convenient. Between the two and elsewhere, transport is necessary. Taxis, preferably radio taxis, are especially recommended at night; keep the doors locked. La Candelaria is relatively safe by day, but there have been several reports of muggings and robberies by night. You may also be hassled by beggars. As in any city of this size, take care not to tempt thieves by careless display of money or valuables. Anyone approaching you with questions, offering to sell something or making demands, may well be a thief or a con-artist. They may be well-dressed and plausible, may pose as plain-clothes officials, and often work in pairs. They are frequently active in and near the Plaza de Bolívar. Best to ignore anyone who approaches – a wave of the hand is sufficient. Watch where you are going, particularly in wet weather. Potholes in both roads and pavements can be very deep.

Tourist offices **Instituto Distrital de Turismo**, Cra 5, No 36-21, p 2, www.bogotaturismo.gov.co. There are 13 tourist-information kiosks dotted around the city. **La Candelaria** ⓘ *Cra 8 y C 10, T283 7115, Mon-Sat 0800-1800, Sun and holidays 1000-1600.* . Good local guide books and maps. **El Dorado airport** ⓘ *International terminal T414 7014, daily 0700-2200. Puente Aéreo T414 7935, same hours.* **Bus station** ⓘ *Módulo 5, local 127, T295 4460, Mon-Sat 0700-1900, Sun and holidays 1000-1600.* **Parque de la Independencia** ⓘ *Cra 7, C 26, T284 2664, Mon-Sat 1000-1800, Sun and holidays 1000-1600.* **Unicentro shopping centre** ⓘ *Entrada 8, 1st floor, T612 1967, Mon-Sat 1200-2000, Sun 1000-1600.* Also at TransMilenio stops Las Aguas, Alcalá and El Tintal. **Cundinamarca tourist office** ⓘ *C 26, No 47-73, T426 1079. Guía del Ocio* (known as GO) has listings on restaurants and clubs, as do *Plan B* online (www.planb.com.co - Spanish only) and *Vive.in* (www.vive.in - Spanish only). **Note** Most museums and tourist attractions are open Tuesday to Sunday, 0900-1700, but may be closed for a period in the middle of the day. Times are frequently changed. Entry is often free but may be a modest US$1 or so. Very little is open on Mondays. The best time to visit the churches is before or after Mass (not during). Mass times are 0700, 1200 and 1800.

Sights

La Candelaria

When the conquistadores first arrived in the 16th century, the area was inhabited by the Chibcha people. The district, named after Nuestra Señora de la Candelaria, is where the conquistador Gonzalo Jiménez de Quesada founded Santafé (later renamed Bogotá) in 1538.

1 Bogotá

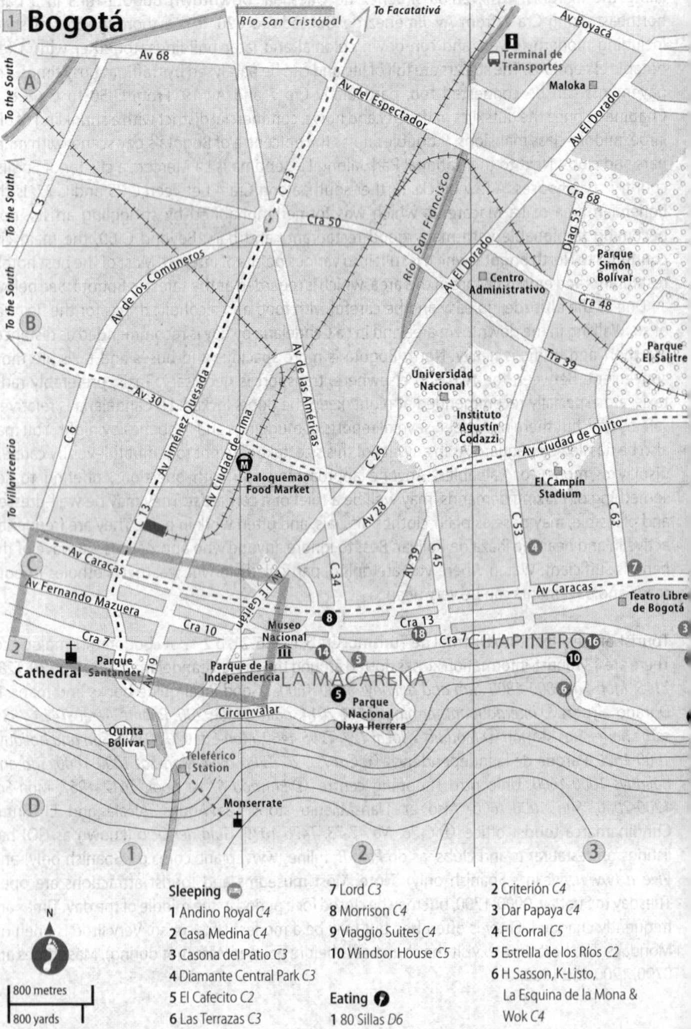

Sleeping
1 Andino Royal *C4*
2 Casa Medina *C4*
3 Casona del Patio *C3*
4 Diamante Central Park *C3*
5 El Cafecito *C2*
6 Las Terrazas *C3*
7 Lord *C3*
8 Morrison *C4*
9 Viaggio Suites *C4*
10 Windsor House *C5*

Eating
1 80 Sillas *D6*
2 Criterión *C4*
3 Dar Papaya *C4*
4 El Corral *C5*
5 Estrella de los Ríos *C2*
6 H Sasson, K-Listo, La Esquina de la Mona & Wok *C4*

Events in 1810 made La Candelaria synonymous with the Independence movement (see below), while the Franciscans and Jesuits founded schools and monasteries giving La Candelaria a reputation as a centre of learning. Among the oldest educational establishments is the **Colegio Nacional de San Bartolomé** ① *Calle 10, No 6-57*, across from the Chapel of **El Sagrario**, founded 1573, now a prestigious school. The **Colegio Mayor de Nuestra Señora del Rosario** ① *Calle 14, No 6-25* (1653), is a beautiful colonial building well worth a look (you can buy a good cheap

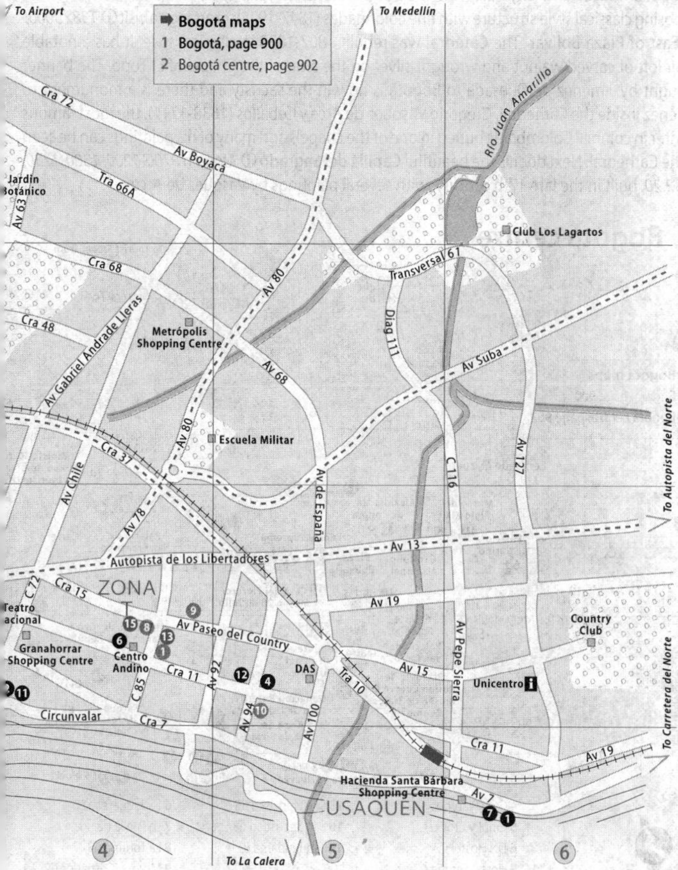

7 Kathmandu *D6*
8 La Casa de las Sopas *C2*
9 La Cigale *C3*
10 mini-mal *C3*
11 Oia *C4*
12 Salto de Angel *C5*

Bars & clubs
13 Alma *C4*
14 Cha Cha *C2*
15 Gótica *C4*
16 In Vitro *C3*
17 Monkey Pub *C3*
18 Son Salomé *C2*

Trans Milenio bus route - - -

lunch at the cafetería). The heart of the city and government is **Plaza Bolívar**, a good starting point for exploring the colonial district. It is claimed that the first ever statue of South America's liberator, Simón Bolívar, stands here. Around the Plaza are the narrow cobbled streets and mansions of the Barrio La Candelaria. On the northern side of the Plaza is the **Corte Suprema de Justicia** (the supreme court of justice) destroyed by fire in 1985 after the now defunct M-19 guerrilla group stormed in. The court was wrecked and the present building was completed in 1999. On the west side of the plaza is the **Alcaldía Mayor de Bogotá** (the office of Bogotá's influential mayor and City Hall). On the south side is the **Capitolio Nacional** (congress), an imposing classical style structure with fine colonnades (1847-1925); to arrange a visit ⓘ *T382 3000.*

East of Plaza Bolívar The **Catedral** was rebuilt 1807-1823 in classical style. It has a notable choir loft of carved walnut and wrought silver on the altar of the Chapel of El Topo. The banner brought by Jiménez de Quesada to Bogotá is now in the sacristy and there is a monument to Jiménez inside the Cathedral. Gregorio Vásquez de Arce y Ceballos (1638-1711), the most famous painter in colonial Colombia, is buried in one of the chapels and many of his paintings can be seen in the Cathedral. Next door is the beautiful **Capilla del Sagrario** ⓘ *Mon-Fri 0700-1200, 1300-1730, US$2.20*, built in the late 17th century, with several paintings by Vásquez de Arce.

2 Bogotá centre

Sleeping
1 Abadia Colonial *C2*
2 Ambala *C3*
3 Bacata *B4*
4 Casa Platypus *C4*
5 Cranky Croc *C3*
6 DN Hostel *C2*
7 Hostal Fátima *C3*
8 Hostal Sue *C4*
9 Hostal Sue Candelaria *C3*
10 Hotel de la Opera *C2*
11 Hotel del Parque *C5*
12 Oceanía *C3*
13 Platypus *C4*
14 Quinta Bolívar *C4*
15 San Francisco *B5*
16 San Sebastían *C3*
17 Tequendama *B5*

Eating
1 Al Wadi *C6*
2 Asociación Construimos Futuro *C3*
3 Enobra *B6*
4 Food Rice *B6*
5 La Hamburgueseria *C6*
6 La Juguetería *B6*
7 La Paella *C2*
8 La Totuma *C3*
9 Moros y Cristianos *C2*
10 Rock & Pizza *C3*
11 Rosita *C2*
12 Sopas de Mamá y Postres de la Abuela *B2*
13 Tábula *C6*
14 Urbano *C6*
15 Yumi Yumi *C4*

At the southeastern corner of the plaza is the **Palacio Arzobispal**, with splendid bronze doors. See the **Casa del Florero** or **Museo 20 de Julio** ⓘ *on the corner of Plaza Bolívar at C 11, No 7-94, Tue-Fri, 0900-1700, Sat-Sun 1000-1600, US$1.70 (reduction with ISIC)*. It was here that the first rumblings of independence began and it houses the famous flower vase that featured in the 1810 revolution. Its ten rooms display the history of Colombia's independence campaigns and boasts portraits and personal belongings of heroes such as Simón Bolívar and Antonio Nariño. It still has original early 17th-century Spanish-Moorish balconies.

In the block behind it is the colonial **Plazuela de Rufino Cuervo**. Here is the house of Manuela Sáenz, the mistress of Bolívar. Inside is the **Museo de Trajes Regionales** ⓘ *Calle 10, No 6-36, Mon-Fri 0930-1630, Sat 1000-1600*, a small collection of traditional costumes from indigenous groups of Colombia. Beside it is the house in which Antonio Nariño printed in 1794 his translation of Thomas Paine's 'The Rights of Man' which had a profound influence on the movement for independence. You can read an extract of the text in Spanish on the wall of the building. Across from Plazuela de Rufino Cuervo is **San Ignacio**, a Jesuit church built in 1605 (being renovated in 2007). Emeralds from the Muzo mines in Boyacá were used in the monstrance and it has more paintings by Gregorio Vásquez de Arce. The **Museo de Arte Colonial** ⓘ *Cra 6, No 9-77, Tue-Fri 0900-1700, Sat-Sun 1000-1600, US$1.10, less with ISIC*, is a fine colonial brick building. It belonged originally to the Society of Jesus, and was once the seat of the oldest University in Colombia and of the National Library. It has a splendid collection of colonial art and paintings by Gregorio Vásquez de Arce, all kinds of utensils, and two charming patios. Across Cra 6 is the **Palacio de San Carlos** ⓘ *Calle 10, No 5-51, Mon-Fri 0900-1200, 1400-1700* , where Bolívar lived, which now houses the Foreign Ministry. Bolívar is said to have planted the huge walnut tree in the courtyard. On 25 September 1828, there was an attempt on his life. His mistress, Manuela, thrust him out of the window and he hid for two hours under the stone arches of the bridge across the Río San Agustín (now Calle 7). Santander, suspected of complicity, was arrested and banished.

South of the Palacio de San Carlos is the **Iglesia de María del Carmen** ⓘ *Cra 5, No 8-36*, the most striking church building in Bogotá, in neo-Gothic style, with excellent stained glass and walls in bands of red and white. Almost opposite the Palacio de San Carlos is the **Teatro Colón** ⓘ *Calle 10, No 5-32, T341 6141 tickets (average cost US$20), guided tours Mon- Fri 0900-1700, ask if you can have a look around when it is not in use*. It is considered Colombia's most prestigious theatre. Its opulent style is typical of late 19th-century Italian architecture. Opera, dance and ballet events are held here. One block northeast of here is the **Casa de la Moneda** (Mint) ⓘ *Calle 11, No 4-93, Mon-Sat*

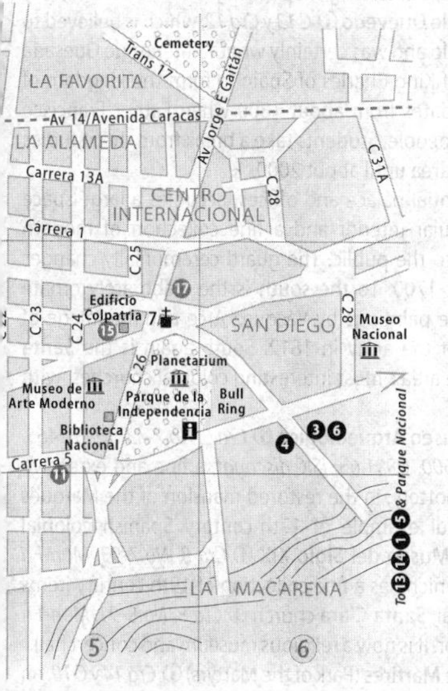

Bars & clubs
16 Escobar y Rosas *C3*
17 Quiebra Canto *C4*

Churches
1 Catedral *B2*
2 Capilla del Sagrario & Palacio Arzobispal *B2*
3 La Tercera Orden *B4*
4 La Veracruz *B3*
5 Mária del Carmen *C2*
6 San Augustín *B2*
7 San Diego *B5*
8 San Francisco *B3*
9 San Ignacio *B2*
10 Santa Bárbara *B1*
11 Santa Clara *B2*

Trans Milenio - - - - - - bus route

1000-2000, Sun and holidays, 1000-1600, closed Tue, free. The building dates back to 1620 when Felipe III of Spain ordered its construction, making this the first mint in South America to produce gold coins. It houses Colombian and European art and sculptures and the machines used to produce gold and silver coins. The courtyard is worth seeing. Next door is the **Donación Botero Museum** ⓘ *Calle 11, No 4-93, Wed-Mon 1000-1700, free.* A well-displayed, excellent collection of Botero's own sculptures and paintings, this includes his fine modern and impressionist art including Picasso, Miró, Dalí and Monet. Well worth a visit. In the same street is the Banco de la República's modern **Biblioteca Luis Angel Arango** ⓘ *No 4-14, library 0800-2000, closed Sun, free,* one of the best endowed and arranged in South America, with three heavily used reading rooms, research rooms, art galleries and a splendid concert hall. There are exhibitions and regular concerts. Free internet usage, but book a computer in advance. There is a good cafetería on the sixth floor.

A few blocks north of here is **Casa de Poesía Silva** ⓘ *C 14, No 3-41, T286 5710, www.casadepoesiasilva.com, Mon-Fri 0900-1300, 1500-1800, free,* house of the poet José Asunción Silva until his death in 1895. The restored colonial house, with a peaceful patio, has a museum, bookshop and a fine audio and book library with taped readings of almost every Spanish-speaking author. CDs are sold in the bookshop. There are also lectures and poetry readings.

Up from the Casa de Poesía to Calle 14/Carrera 2, turn right up a delightful narrow alleyway (Callejón del Embudo) to the **Plaza del Chorro de Quevedo** ⓘ *C 13 y Cra 12,* which is believed to be the centre of the Muisca village of Teusaquillo and was certainly where Jiménez de Quesada took possession of the territory in the name of King Charles of Spain to form the kingdom of New Granada on 6 August 1538. The name dates from about 1800 when Father Francisco Quevedo provided a *chorro* (well) for the local people. Students take a break from their studies here, adding to the activity (and safety) of the area until about 2000.

The **Palacio de Nariño** (1906), the presidential palace and offices, occupies a large space due south of Plaza Bolívar. It has a spectacular interior and a fine collection of modern Colombian paintings. It is occasionally open to the public. The guard ceremonially changes Monday, Wednesday and Friday, normally at 1700. To the south is the elaborately ornate Church of **San Agustín** (1637). It, too, has fine paintings by Vásquez Arce and the Image of Jesus, which was proclaimed Generalísimo of the army in 1812. South again is the **Santa Bárbara** church (mid-16th century), one of the area's most interesting colonial churches, with paintings by Gregorio Vásquez Arce.

Up Calle 7 from the Palacio Nariño is the **Museo Arqueológico** ⓘ *Cra 6, No 7-43, T243 0465, Tue-Fri 0830-1700, Sat 0930-1700, Sun 1000-1600, US$1.65, ISIC discount,* a fine and extensive collection of Latin American, pre-Columbian pottery, in the restored mansion of the Marqués de San Jorge. The house itself is a beautiful example of 17th-century Spanish colonial architecture. Below the Palacio Nariño is the **Museo del Siglo XIX** ⓘ *Cra 8, No 7-93, Mon-Fri 0830-1730, Sat 0900-1300, guided tours only,* which has a fine collection of 19th century items within a restored mansion. Nearby, the colonial **Santa Clara** church ⓘ *Cra 8, No 8-91, Mon-Fri 0900-1700, Sat-Sun 1000-1600,* has a fine interior. It is now a religious museum and concert hall.

Several blocks west of Plaza Bolívar is **Parque Mártires** (Park of the Martyrs) ⓘ *Cra 14 y C 10,* on the site of the plaza in which the Spanish shot and killed many during the independence struggle.

Downtown Bogotá

Midway between Plaza Bolívar and Avenida Jiménez de Quesada, which marks the La Candelaria and Downtown boundary, is the **Palacio de Comunicaciones** ⓘ *Cra 7 y C 12A,* built on the site of the colonial church of Santo Domingo. Across the Avenida Jiménez de Quesada, in the commercial district, is **Parque Santander**, with a bronze statue of Santander, who helped Bolívar to free Colombia and was later its President. There is a handicraft market most days.

Next to Parque Santander is the **Banco de la República**, beside which is the wonderful **Museo del Oro** (the Gold Museum) ⓘ *C 16, No 5-41, T343 2222, www.banrep.gov.co/museo/,*

Tue-Sat 0900-1800 (leave by 1900), Sun and holidays 1000-1600 (leave by 1700), closed 1 Jan, Good Friday, 1 May, 24, 25, 31 Dec, US$1.20, free on Sun, audioguides in Spanish, English and French, also guided tours in Spanish and English,renovated and expanded in 2008. This unique collection is a must and a poignant reminder of why the *conquistadores* found Colombia and the rest of the continent so appealing. There are more than 35,000 pieces of pre-Columbian gold work in the total collection, most of which is held here. The rest are in other Museos de Oro sponsored by the Banco de la República throughout Colombia. The ancient gold objects discovered in Colombia were not made by primitive hammering alone, but show the use of virtually every technique known to modern goldsmiths. A tasteful light show in the Salón Dorado (The Gold Room) highlights some 8,000 pieces and should not be missed. Opposite the Gold Museum is **Galería Artesanal de Colombia** ⓘ *Mon-Sun 0900-1900*, a permanent arts/crafts market.

Also around Parque Santander: **San Francisco** church (mid-16th century), with paintings of famous Franciscans, choir stalls, a famous ornate gold high altar (1622), and a fine Lady Chapel with blue and gold ornamentation. The remarkable ceiling is in Spanish-Moorish (mudéjar) style. Try to see this church when it is fully illuminated. **Palacio de San Francisco** ⓘ *Av Jiménez No 7-50*, built 1918-1933 in the Corinthian style on the site of the Franciscan friary, is now part of the Rosario University. Church of **La Veracruz**, first built five years after the founding of Bogotá, rebuilt in 1731, and again in 1904. In 1910 it became the Panteón Nacional e Iglesia de la República. José de Caldas, the famous scientist, was buried along with many other victims of the 'Reign of Terror' under the church. It has a bright white and red interior and a fine decorated ceiling. Fashionable weddings are held here. **La Tercera Orden** is a colonial church famous for its carved woodwork along the nave and a high balcony, massive wooden altar reredos, and confessionals, built by the Third Franciscan Order in the 17th century.

Continuing north along Carrera 7, at Calle 26 you reach **Parque de la Independencia**, adorned with wax palms. In the park is the **Planetarium** ⓘ *Tue-Sun 1100, 1430, 1630*. There is a good internet café (US$1 per hour) in the building, and good cappuccino served on a nice terrace overlooking the park. Behind is the impressive Moorish- style brick bullring, **La Santamaria**, Cra 6, No 26-50, see under Sports. Also at this junction (Carrera 7 and Calle 26) are the church and monastery of **San Diego**, a picturesque, restored old building. The Franciscan monastery with fine mudéjar ceiling was built in 1560 and the church in 1607 as its chapel. Local craft items are sold in one part of the old monastery. Across the street is the **Tequendama Hotel**. Near the park is the **Biblioteca Nacional**, with its entrance on Calle 24. On the corner is the **Museo de Arte Moderno** (Mambo) ⓘ *Calle 24, No 6-00, T286 0466, www.mambogota.com, Tue-Sat 1000-1800, Sun-holidays 1200-1700, US$1.80, students US$0.90*, with a well-displayed collection of Colombia's modern artists and foreign artists including Picasso, Dalí and Ernst. There is also a good bookshop. **Edificio Colpatria** ⓘ *Cra 7, No 24-89, US$1.70*, the tallest building in this area and illuminated at night, is open Saturday, Sunday and holidays 1100-1700 for good views of the city from the top, 46 floors and 176 m up.

Museo Nacional ⓘ *Cra 7, No 28-66, T334 8366, www.museonacional.gov.co, Tue-Sat 1000-1800, Sun 1000-1700, US$1.25, students US$0.80 (free on Sun), various tours available*, is an old prison converted into a museum, founded by Santander in 1823. There is an excellent archaeological collection. Its top floor houses a fine art section, comprising national paintings and sculptures. Allow at least two hours to look round. The restaurant, Sala 18, is open Mon-Fri 1200-1600; the café, open Tue-Sun 1000-1800, serves good salads and desserts.

In the link between Central and North Bogotá is Colombia's main state university, **Universidad Nacional** (about 13,000 students), housed in the Ciudad Universitaria shown on the map, page 900. Be aware that the university's main entrance on Cra 30 is periodically the focal point of protests (sometimes violent) between students and riot police. Avoid the area during these times. There is an interesting, peaceful and well-organized **Jardín Botánico José Celestino Mutis** ⓘ *Av 63, No 68-95, T437 7060, www.jbb.gov.co, Mon-Fri 0800-1700, Sat-Sun and* *holidays 0900-1700, US$1.10, pensioners free, guided tours at weekends*. It has a large collection of orchids, plus roses, gladioli and trees from all over the country.

Maloka ⓘ *Cra 68D, No 40A-51, near the bus terminal, www.maloka.org, Mon-Fri 0900-1800, Sat 1000-1900, Sun and holidays 1100-1900, US$13.50 including everything*, is a complex of science and technology exhibits, screen cinema, internet café, all under a dome. Entry is cheaper without cinema ticket.

Monserrate

ⓘ *T284 5700 (answer service in English too). The fare up to Monserrate is US$9 adult return, children half price, cheaper on Sun. The funicular works Mon-Sat 0730-0900, every 30 mins; the cable car operates Mon-Sat 0900-2400 every 20 mins; both Sun and holidays 0530-1800. Times change frequently.*

There is a very good view of the city from the top of **Monserrate** (3,210 m), the lower of the two peaks rising sharply to the east. It is reached by a funicular railway and a cable car. The new convent at the top is a popular shrine and pilgrimage site. At the summit, near the church, a platform gives a bird's-eye view of the city's tiled roofs and of the plains beyond stretching to the rim of the Sabana. Sunrise and sunset can be spectacular. The Calle del Candelero, a reconstruction of a Bogotá street of 1887, has plenty of street stalls and snack bars. Behind the church are popular picnic grounds. There are two upmarket touristy restaurants at the top, both overpriced and closed Sunday. If you wish to walk up, possibly the safest time is at the weekend about 0500, before the crowds arrive but when there are people about. At this time you will catch the sunrise. The path is dressed stone and comfortably graded all the way up with refreshment stalls at weekends every few metres and police presence at weekends. It takes about 1¼ hours up (if you don't stop). It is best not to go alone; do not display cameras openly. On no account walk down in the dark. On weekdays, it is not recommended to walk up and especially not down. You should also take a bus or taxi to the foot of the hill Monday-Friday and, at all times, from the bottom station into town. There are usually taxis waiting by the footbridge across the road. There have been reports of tourists being mugged at the summit and the bottom, even during the day. The walk up to Guadalupe, the higher peak opposite Monserrate, is not recommended.

At the foot of Monserrate is the **Quinta de Bolívar** ⓘ *Calle 20, No 2-91 Este, T336 6419, Tue-Fri, 0900-1700, Sat-Sun 1000-1500, US$1.30, reductions for students and children, guided tours*. This is a fine colonial mansion, with splendid gardens and lawns. There are several cannons captured at the battle of Boyacá. The elegant house, once Bolívar's home, is now a museum showing some of his personal possessions and paintings of events in his career. Opposite the Quinta is the attractive campus of the prestigious private university, Los Andes.

North Bogotá

North of Cra 68 are expanding wealthy suburbs, shopping malls and classy restaurants, an area regarded as relatively safe with the best hotels. Between Cra 4 and Cra 5 and C 68 and C 71 is the **Zona G** (for 'gourmet'), home to some of Bogotá's best (and most expensive) restaurants. The T-shaped pedestrianized area made up by C 83 and Cra 13 is Bogotá's **Zona Rosa** (also known as the Zona T) with many fashionable bars, clubs and restaurants. Further north the streets around Parque 93 have more expensive bars and restaurants, while at the very limits of the city, off Cra 7 between C 117 and C119, is **Usaquén**, formerly a satellite town with a pleasant plaza, a popular evening and weekend excursion for *bogotanos* wishing to escape the metropolis.

North Bogotá is noted for its huge, lavish shopping malls, which are worth a visit even if the prices don't grab you. The **Hacienda Santa Bárbara** has been constructed within a large country mansion, and parts of the colonial architecture, even some of the old gardens have been retained. **Museo Mercedes de Pérez** ⓘ *Cra 7, No 94-17, Mon-Fri 1000-1700, Sat 0800-1200, guided tours US$1.40*, formerly the Hacienda de El Chicó, is a fine example of colonial architecture. It contains a world-wide collection of mostly 18th-century porcelain, furniture and paintings.

Bogotá listings

Hotel and guesthouse prices
LL over US$200 **L** US$151-200 **AL** US$101-150
A US$66-100 **B** US$46-65 **C** US$31-45
D US$21-30 **E** US$12-20 **F** US$7-11
G US$6 and under
Restaurant prices
🍴🍴🍴 over US$12 🍴🍴 US$7-12 🍴 under US$6

Sleeping

Book hotels in advance whenever possible. IVA tax of 16% is charged by middle and more expensive hotels. It is additional to the bill but included in our price classification. See also the Colombian Hostel Association, page 891, www.colombianhostels.com.

Note Taxi drivers at the airport or bus station occasionally say that the hotel you have chosen is "closed", "not known" etc, especially the cheaper ones. Ask them to take you to the address we quote. There are many small, unregistered hotels and *hostales* in other parts of the city, not listed here, many of which are cheap, some of which are clean. Such areas may be unsafe for tourists and are remote from places of interest.

La Candelaria *p900, map p902*

LL-L Hotel de la Opera, C 10, No 5-72, T336 2066, www.hotelopera.com.co. Once the residence of Simón Bolívar's personal guard. Opulent, period pieces in exquisite rooms, 2 rooftop restaurants with superb views, sauna, gym and pool. Junior suites have original bathtubs.

AL-A Abadia Colonial, C 11, No 2-32, T341 1884, www.abadiacolonial.com. Fine colonial building in the heart of this area. Comfortable rooms if a bit small, ask for a street-facing room, Wi-Fi, cable TV, safe, Italian restaurant. Recommended.

A Casa Platypus, Cra 3, No 16-28, T281 1801, www.casaplatypus.com. From the owner of the Platypus Hostel, this hotel is aimed at 'the parents of backpackers' or anyone with a larger budget. Beautiful colonial building overlooking the Parque de los Periodistas, excellent rooms with extra large beds and duvets, kitchen, roof terrace with views of Monserrate. Breakfast included, free Wi-Fi. Highly recommended.

B-C DN (Destino Nomada) Hostel, C 11, No 00-38, T352 0932, T312- 300 6895, www.dnhostels.com. Dorms (**E-F** pp), doubles with en suite, breakfast included.

C San Sebastián, Av Jiménez, No 3-97, T337 5031. Fashionable once upon a time, rooms are a little dated, but functional, hot water, internet, Wi-Fi, good writing desks, views of Monserrate.

D Ambala, Cra 5, No 13-46, T341 2376, www.hotelambala.net. In a pretty colonial building, rooms clean but a bit small, dated décor.

D The Cranky Croc, C 15, No 3-46, T342 2438, www.crankycroc.com. New in 2008, Aussie-run hostel in a beautiful 300-year-old building, carefully restored to retain many of the original features. Excellent facilities, Wi-Fi and internet, free luggage storage, lounge with a fireplace. Has several private rooms with bath and dorms with bunks (**F**).

D Hostal Fátima, C 14, No 2-24, T281 6389, www.hostalfatima.com. A maze of brightly

coloured rooms and sunny patios with lots of stained-glass windows and potted plants. Sauna, jacuzzi, TV room, dance studio teaching contemporary and jazz dance, yoga and pilates. Has several private rooms with bath as well as dorms with bunks (**F**).

D Hostal Sue, C 16, No 2-55 and **Hostal Sue Candelaria**, Cra 3, No 14-18, T334 8894 and T341 2647, www.suecandelaria.com. A new Sue (pronounced 'Su-ay') seems to spring up every year, so popular have these hostals become. A 3rd has just opened up (enquire at first 2 for details). All have excellent facilities, including Wi-Fi, internet, kitchen, free lockers, laundry service and places to relax in hammocks. The first attracts a younger crowd, keener on partying, the other 2 for those seeking a quieter atmosphere. Dorms with bunks (**F**) available.

D Oceanía, C 14, No 4-48, T342 0560. Large building, with faded grandeur, rooms are relatively clean, with bath; restaurant serves a *menú ejecutivo* for US$4.

D Platypus, C 16, No 2-43, T341 3104, www.platypusbogota.com. As the first backpackers' hostel to open in Colombia, the Platypus has all the facilities you would expect, internet access, Wi-Fi, book exchange, kitchen and remains popular. Owner Germán Escobar's knowledge of Colombia is encyclopaedic. Has 12 private rooms with and without bath and several dorms with bunks (**F**), simple showers.

Downtown Bogotá *p904, maps p900 and p902*

The downtown area of Bogotá suffers from petty crime and muggings by night.

LL Tequendama, Cra 10, No 26-21, T360 0988, www.cptequendama.com.co. One of Bogotá's traditional grand hotels, witness to some of Colombia's most important political events since its inauguration in 1953. With 2 restaurants, a spa, Wi-Fi throughout and large rooms it is well equipped for the conferences it invariably hosts.

AL Bacata, C 19, No 5-20, T283 8300, www.hotelbacata.com.co. Another traditional Bogotá hotel, large rooms with minibar, cable TV and Wi-Fi, spa, gym and pizzería.

AL-A Hotel del Parque, C 24, No 4A-79 (esq Cra 5), T284 2200, www.hoteldelparqueclasico.com. In the heart of the Centro Internacional, large rooms, cable TV, safe, business facilities, Wi-Fi and breakfast included, taxi service.

A San Francisco, Cra 10, No 23-63, T286 1677, www.sfcol.com. Good-sized rooms, restaurant, Wi-Fi, free breakfasts and free airport transfer.

B Quinta de Bolívar, Cra 4, No 17-59, T337 6500, www.hotelquintadebolivar.com. On the edge of the Candelaria, this Republican- era building has cosy rooms and breakfast is included.

B Las Terrazas, C 54, No 3-12, T255 5777. Well-placed in a quiet area of Chapinero Alto, popular with foreigners. Each room has a large balcony with excellent views of the city, Wi-Fi, cable TV. First 2 floors are student residences.

C Diamante Central Park, C 53, No 10-78, T210 2463, www.hoteldiamantecentralpark.com. In the heart of El Chapinero, a bit ugly, but good value, Wi-Fi, cable TV and safes in each room.

C Lord, C 63, No 14-62, T211 1880, hotel_lord@yahoo.com.ar. Popular with Colombian businessmen, some of the rooms are a little small with windows onto corridors, ask for a street-facing room with cable TV and good light. Has an internet room and restaurant.

D-F El Cafecito, Cra 6, No 34-70, T285 8308, www.cafecito.net. Same owners as the popular hostales in Ecuador, an excellent alternative to staying in La Candelaria. Well located in La Merced, near the restaurants of La Macarena and the clubs of Carrera 7. The building has an interesting history. It has an excellent Wi-Fi-enabled café serving crêpes and cocktails and rooms with and without bath, as well as bunks in dorms. Recommended.

North Bogotá *p906, map p900*

LL Andino Royal, C 85, No 12-28, T651 3092, www.hotelesroyal.com. Well placed between Parque 93 and the Zona Rosa, all the conveniences including gym, Wi-Fi and cable TV. The rooms are light and airy with large windows.

LL Casa Medina, Cra 7, No 69A-22, T312 0299, www.hotelescharleston.com. Built in 1945 by Santiago Medina, with its stone columns and carved wooden doors this hotel is Bogotá at its most refined. It has a gym, Wi-Fi, iPod docks and a fine restaurant in a wood-panelled room.

LL Morrison Hotel, C 84 Bis, No 13-54, T622 3111, www.morrisonhotel.com. Conveniently located near the Zona T, contemporary British design, large rooms with Wi-Fi, LCD TVs and thermo-acoustic windows. It looks out onto the beautiful Parque León de Greiff.

L Windsor House, C 95, No 9-97, T634 3630, www.ghlhoteles.com. English-style luxury, large rooms, some with jacuzzis, all have safe, minibar and use of gym and Turkish bath.

A Casona del Patio, Cra 8, No 69-24, T212 8805, www.lacasonadelpatio.net. With 14 immaculate rooms set around a sunny patio and well situated near the Zona G, this is one of the best mid-range options, cable TV, Wi-Fi. Recommended.

A Viaggio Suites, Cra 18, No 86A-36, Edif Virrey, T622 2525, www.viaggio.com. Excellent value short- and medium-term apartments. Spacious, modern with fitted kitchens, daily housekeeper and breakfast included. All apartments have Wi-Fi and laundry service. Prices drop for longer stays. Recommended.

Eating

The more exotic and fashionable places to eat are in North Bogotá, but Candelaria has its bistros and good value, typical Colombian food. Take local advice if you want to eat really cheaply in markets or from street stalls. Few restaurants in La Candelaria are open in the evening.

La Candelaria *p900, map p902*

La Paella, C 11, No 5-13. Opposite the Centro Cultural García Márquez, serves Spanish food and specializes in paellas.

Rosita, C 13A, No 1A-26. On Plazoleta Chorro de Quevedo, this is an excellent little lunchtime spot. Sells cookbooks.

Asociación Construimos Futuro, C 15A, No 2-21. Good breakfasts served by a neighbourhood cooperative. Has Wi-Fi.

La Totuma, Cra 2, No 13A-58. On the hip Callejón del Embudo, economic sushi and an excellent lunchtime deal of a bowl of teppanyaki for just US$3. Colourful surroundings.

Moros y Cristianos, C 9, N0 3-11. Cuban food served in a sunny, glass-covered patio. Open till midnight on Fri, otherwise lunchtime only.

Rock and Pizza, Cra 2, No 13A-56. Great pizzas at reasonable prices. Upstairs is a chicha bar.

Sopas de Mamá y Postres de la Abuela, Cra 9, No 10-59. A real institution, traditional Colombian dishes such as *ajiaco* and *sancocho* in a beautiful 2nd-floor gallery with stained-glass windows and large panelled wooden doors. Its other speciality is puddings, which include a secret formula for fried ice cream!

Yumi Yumi, Cra 3, No 16-40. Tiny hole-in-the-wall restaurant serving sandwiches, crêpes, fruit juices and cocktails. Open late most nights and offers free tickets to clubs in the Zona Rosa.

Downtown Bogotá *p904, maps p900 and p902*

Many good restaurants and cafes along Carrera 4 in Barrio La Macarena (behind the Bull Ring).

Criterión, C 69A, No 5-75, T310 2810. Minimalist decor, French-influenced menu, with shellfish and steak, large wine list.

Estrella de los Ríos, C 26B, No 4-50, T337 4037, www.estrelladelosrios.com. Costeña Estrella calls her small place an 'anti-restaurant'. Her idea is that your dining experience should feel much like she is cooking for you at home. You must book 24-hours in advance and she reserves the right to turn you away if she doesn't like you! Estrella, the author of several cookbooks, conjures up *costeño* and Cuban food for US$35 for 5 courses, excluding alcohol. Highly recommended.

Dar Papaya, C 69A, No 4-78, T541 5013. Smart restaurant offering a fusion of Asian and Latin American cuisine. *Dar papaya* roughly translates as 'to expose yourself'.

Enobra, Cra 4, No 26-37. Fashionable, chic restaurant with sparse decor serving tapas and various cuts of steak.

La Cigale, C 69A, No 4-93, T249 6839. French restaurant a variety of Gallic specialities.

La Juguetería, C 27, No 4-03, www.restaurantelajugueteria.com. Excellent steaks in an atmosphere dominated by dolls: they hang everywhere. Some of the tables are even made out of dolls' heads.

mini-mal, Cra 4A, No 57-52, T347 5464, www.mini-mal.org. The focus of this restaurant/bar/design shop is on minimalism. The menu is contemporary Colombian cuisine with alternative takes on Pacific, Caribbean, Andean and Amazonian recipes.

Oia, C 70A, No 5-67, T8117846. Popular restaurant serving food and tapas from the Mediterranean – French, Greek, Italian and Spanish, lovely surroundings with a pleasant outdoor patio. It also has a bistro which serves quiches, paninis and juices.

Tábula, C 29 bis, No 5-90. Gourmet international menu in stylish surroundings a couple of blocks from La Macarena.

🍴🍴🍴 **Urbano**, Cra 4, No 27-09. Excellent chicken, steaks and fish in interesting sauces. It has some quirky touches, including bizarre revolving menus.

🍴 **Al Wadi**, C 27, No 4-14. Healthy Lebanese food, including kebabs, falafel and rice dishes.

🍴 **El Cafecito**, Cra 6, No 34-70. Café belonging to the hostel of the same name, varied menu that includes rosti, pancakes, salads, sandwiches, coffees and herbal teas, cocktails.

🍴 **Food Rice**, Cra 4, No 26-13. A simple but effective formula of rice dishes from around the world, from Chinese to Malaysian to Indian. Good vegetarian options. Does home delivery.

🍴 **La Casa de las Sopas**, C 34, No 13-20. Excellent lunchtime venue serving traditional Colombian soups and broths, including ajiaco, mondongo and sancocho.

🍴 **La Hamburguesería**, Cra 4A, No 27-27, www.lahamburgueseria.com. Popular fast-food chain with high quality hamburgers and hotdogs. Several more outlets around town, eg C118, No 7-40, Usaquén, T214 1943. Does home delivery.

North Bogotá *p906, map p900*

North of C 76 there are 3 popular areas for eating and drinking: Zona T, also known as the Zona Rosa, C 83 and Cra 13; further north is Parque 93, for many years the most exclusive address in Bogotá, C 117 with Cra 7 in Usaquén.

🍴🍴🍴 **H Sasson**, C 83, No 12-49. Harry Sasson is one of Colombia's best known chefs and owns a number of Bogotá's most popular restaurants. H Sasson does contemporary Asian food such as crispy duck and curries in stylish surroundings.

🍴🍴 **Kathmandu**, Cra 6, No 117-26, Usaquén, T213 3276. Asian, Chinese and Arabic food in a series of rooms brimming with gilt Buddha statues and other Asian decorations.

🍴🍴 **Salto del Angel**, Cra 13, No 93A-45, T622 6427. This enormous restaurant on Parque 93 has a large, varied menu including steaks, ceviches and some international options which include fish and chips. At weekends, after dinner, the tables are cleared and it becomes a popular upmarket disco.

🍴🍴 **Wok**, Cra 13, No 82-74. Fashionable Asian cuisine restaurant.

🍴 **80 Sillas**, C 118, No 6-05, Usaquén, T619 2471. All kinds of ceviches and other seafood served in wooden elevated patios with encroaching ferns.

🍴 **El Corral**, C 93A, No 14-30. Popular chain serves mainly large hamburgers.

🍴 **La Esquina de la Mona**, C 82, No 14-32. Cheap but good fast food, including parrillas, pinchos, ribs and burgers.

🍴 **K-Listo**, C 83, No 12A-36. Fast-food chain serving stuffed *arepas* and *empanadas*.

Bars and clubs

La Candelaria *p900, map p902*

Escobar y Rosas, Cra 4, No 15-07. One of the few good bars in La Candelaria. Converted old chemist, popular student hangout, packed Fri-Sat nights, trendy, DJs, acid jazz and funk. Wed-Sat 1730-0300.

QuiebraCanto, Cra 5, No 17-76. In colonial house, world music, funk and salsa, best nights Wed, Thu, friendly crowd.

Downtown to North Bogotá *p906, map p900*

Most bars and clubs are concentrated in the Cra 11-13, C 80-86 region, known as the Zona Rosa. Some of these have live entertainment. Further south along Cra 7, from C 32 up to C 59 draws an edgier crowd of filmmakers, artists and students.

Alma Bar, C 85, No 12-51, T622 8289, Wed-Sat 1900-0300, entry US$11-27. Relatively new bar/club playing crossover Colombian/Western music.

Bogotá Beer Company, Cra 12, No 83-33, T802 6737, www.bogotabeercompany.com. Also at Parque 93, Usaquén, C 83, No 13-06 and 4 more. Microbrewery with 8 types of beer, good pubs.

Cha Cha, Cra 7, No 32-16, p 41, www.elchacha.com. In what used to be the old Hilton hotel, on 41st floor with spectacular views of the city, very fashionable, attracting the city's richest and most beautiful. European DJs play electronic music.

Gótica, Cra 14, No 82-50, T218 0727, open Wed-Sat 1000-0400, entry US$8. Plays a mixture of hip hop, electronica and crossover.

In Vitro, C 59, No 6-38. What started as a weekly meeting of friends to show their short films and documentaries has developed into one of Bogotá's hippest clubs. Shows short films during the week while the weekends are reserved for an eclectic mix of salsa, rock'n'roll and indie music. Tue and Wed night are especially popular as entrance is free. Frequented by filmmakers, artists and students.

The Monkey Pub, Cra 5, No 71-45, Edif La Strada, p 2. English pub serving draught beers and the occasional Guinness.

Son Salomé, Cra 7a, No 40 -31, 2nd floor. Good local salsa bar, intimate, cosy atmosphere, Thu-Sat. Recommended.
Theatrón, C 58, No 10-42. In old large theatre, gay and mixed crowd, attracts international DJs, good atmosphere. Be careful coming out of the club at night, use a taxi. Cover US$8.

Entertainment

Bogotá *p900, maps p900 and p902*
Cinema Consult *El Espectador* or *El Tiempo*, and *www.planb.com.co*; there are frequent changes to programmes. **Cine Bar Lumiere**, Cra 14, No 85-59, T636 0485, US$5 weekends and holidays, cheaper mid-week, comfortable airplane-style seats, food and drink. **Cine Bar Paraíso**, Cra 6, No 119B-56, Usaquén, T215 5361, foreign art films. **Cinemania**, Cra14, No 93A-85, mainstream and foreign art films. **Museo de Arte Moderno** shows Colombian and foreign films daily, all day.

There are cinema complexes in the principal shopping centres (see below). The best are **Centro Comercial Andino**, **Unicentro**, and **Atlantis**. Most discount rates on Tue. For times call *CineColombia* T404 2463. Foreign films, old and new, are shown on weekend mornings in some commercial cinemas and there are many small screening rooms running features. Admission, US$2-4. There's an international film festival in Oct (*Festival de Cine de Bogotá*) and a European film festival (*Eurocine*) in Apr/May.
Dance classes **Galería Café Libro**, Cra 11A, No 93-42, T218 3435. Weekly salsa classes, about US$7 pp. **Punta y Taco**, Salón de Baile, Cra 14, No 75-15, T481 9534, www.puntaytaco.com. Tango and salsa classes Mon-Fri 0800-2130, Sat 0800-1930, flexible class times, professional. Individual class US$20, for a group US$8.
Theatre Many of the theatres are in the Candelaria area. Tickets usually from about US$5 up. For **Teatro Colón**, see details on page 903.

Festivals and events

Bogotá *p900, maps p900 and p902*
There are many local religious festivals and parades at Easter and Christmas. One of the best is the **Jan Fiesta de Reyes Magos** (Three Kings) in the suburb of Egipto (up the hill to the east of Candelaria) with traditional processions.

Bogotá hosts the biennial **Iberoamerican Theatre Festival** (**Mar-Apr 2010**, next 2012), www.festivaldeteatro.com.co. **Temporada de Opera y Zarzuela** held in the Teatro Colón in **May, Jun and Sep** with international artists. In **Jun** there is **Rock al Parque**, the biggest annual rock festival in Latin America (www.rockalparque.gov.co). In **Aug Feria Internacional del Libro** (book fair) is held in *Corferias*, Cra 37, No 24-67, www.corferias.com. **Aug-Sep** is opera season. **Candelaria Festival** in **Sep** street theatre, music and dance events. In **Sep**, **Festival Internacional de Jazz**. In **Dec** at Corferias is the **Expoartesanía** fair, an excellent selection of arts and crafts and regional food from across Colombia. Highly recommended.

Shopping

Bogotá *p900, maps p900 and p902*
16% value-added tax on all purchases. Heavy duty plastic for covering rucksacks etc, is available at several shops around C 16 and Av Caracas; some have heat sealing machines to make bags to size. In Barrio Gaitán, Cr 30 y C 65, are rows of leather shops. This is an excellent area to buy made-to-measure leather jackets, good value; not safe at night, go during the day. Designer labels are cheaper in Colombia than in Europe.
Bookshops Ateneo, C 82, No 13-19, north of the city. Good selection of Colombian titles, knowledgeable staff. **Authors**, C 70, No 5-23, T217 7788, www.authors.com.co. American owner, sells English books. **Exopotamia**, C 70, No 4-47. Good selection of books and Latin music, also branch in *Biblioteca Luis Angel Arango* in Candelaria. **Forum**, C 93, No 13A-49, just off Parque 93. Foreign magazines, CDs, pleasant atmosphere. **Librería Central**, C 94, No 13-90. English and German books. **Librería Nacional** bookstores across town eg Unicentro and Santa Bárbara shopping centres. Good Colombian history and current affairs section and some foreign press. **Panamericana**, Cra 7, No 14-09. Disorganized, but has some guidebooks and maps. Other branches in the city. **Taschen**, C 26, No 10-18, next to *Hotel Tequendama*. Art books, small selection of English books and foreign magazines. Also at Museum of Modern Art. **Villegas Editores**, Av 82, No 11-50, int 3. Great coffee-table books on Colombia. **Tower Records** in Andino shopping centre, C 82, Cra 3, sells foreign press.
Camping equipment **Monodedo**, Cra 16, No 82-22, T616 3467. Good selection of camping and climbing equipment. Enquire here for

information about climbing in Colombia. **Tatoo**, Cra 15, No 96-67, loc 2, T218 1125, C 122, No 18-56, T612 5355, and CC Andino, Cra 11, No 82-71, loc 340, T616 8898, www.tatoo.ws. Complete outdoor gear suppliers.

Handicrafts **Artesanías de Colombia**, Claustro de Las Aguas, next to the Iglesia de las Aguas, Cra 3, No 18A-58; Cra 11 No 84-12 by CC Andino; and in **Plaza de los Artesanos**, Tr 48, No 63A-52. Beautiful but expensive designer crafts. **Tienda Fibrarte**, Cra 3, No 11-24. *Artesanías* from around Colombia and Latin America. Good fique products, coca tea. Credit cards accepted. **Galerías Cano**, Ed Bavaria, Cra 13, No 27-98 (Torre B, Int 119), also at Unicentro, and Loc 218, Airport. Sell textiles, pottery, and gold and gold-plated replicas of some of the jewellery on display in the Gold Museum. **Mercado de Pulgas** (fleamarket) on Cra 7/C 24, in car park beside *Museo de Arte Moderno*, on Sun afternoons and holidays. A better fleamarket can be found at the Usaquén market around the plaza on Sun, also a good arts and crafts market at the top of the hill in Usaquén. **Pasaje Rivas**, C10 y Cra10. Persian-style bazaar. Hammocks, ceramics, cheap. A small arts and crafts market is open on most days opposite *Hotel Tequendama* in the centre.

Jewellery The pavements and cafés along Av Jiménez, below Cra 7, and on Plazoleta del Rosario are used on weekdays (especially Fri) by emerald dealers. Rows of jewellers and emerald shops also along C 12 with Cra 6. Great expertise is needed in buying: bargains, but synthetics and forgeries abound. **La Casa de la Esmeralda**, C 30, No 16-18. Wide range of stones. **Emerald Trade Centre**, Av Jiménez, No 5-43, p 1. German/ English spoken. **GMC Galería Minas de Colombia**, C20, No 0-86, T281 6523, at foot of Monserrate diagonal from Quinta de Bolívar. Good selection of gold and emerald jewellery at reasonable prices.

Markets **Paloquemao food market**, Cra 27, entre C19 y 22. Bogotá's huge central market, good to visit just to see the sheer abundance of Colombia's tropical fruits and flowers. Cheap stalls serving *comida corriente*. Safe. **San Andresito**, Cra 38 y C12. Popular contraband market, cheap alcohol, designer sports labels, electrical goods, football shirts. Relatively safe.

Shopping centres **Unicentro**, large shopping centre on Cra 15, No 127, www.unicentro bogota.com (take 'Unicentro' bus from centre, going north on Cra 10 takes about 1 hr). **Centro Granahorrar**, Av Chile (Calle 72), No 10-34, www.centrogranahorrar.com, is another good shopping centre; **Hacienda Santa Bárbara**, Cra 7 Nº 115-60, www.haciendasantabarbara.com.co; **Bulevar Niza**, Av 58, No 125A-59; **Centro Comercial Andino**, Cra 11, No 82-71, www.centroandino.com.co; **Centro Comercial Unilago**, Cra 15, No 78-33, www.unilago.com, **Centro Comercial Santa Fe**, Autopista Norte y C 185. For computers, gadgets and repairs. **Exito**, **Pomona** and **Carulla** chains are probably the best supermarket groups in Bogotá.

Activities and tours

Bogotá *p900, maps p900 and p902*

Bullfighting On Sun during the season (Jan), and occasionally for the rest of the year, at the municipally owned **Plaza de Toros de Santamaría**, Cra 6, No 26-50, T334 1482, near Parque Independencia. In season, the bulls weigh over 335 kg; out of season they are "comparatively small and unprofessional". (Local bullfight museum at bullring, door No 6.) The **Corporación Taurina de Bogotá**, C 70A, No 6-24, T334 1628, www.ctaurina.com, holds a summer festival in early Aug. Boxing matches are also held here.

Cycling The *Ciclovía* is a set of streets leading from Cra 7 to the west, closed to motor traffic every Sun morning and bank holidays, 0700-1400 for cyclists, joggers, rollerskaters etc. There are also the extensive *Cicloruta* paths.

Football Tickets for matches at El Campín stadium can be bought in advance at **Federación Colombiana de Futbol**, Av 32, No 15-42, www.colfutbol.org. It is not normally necessary to book in advance, except for the local Santa Fe-Millionarios derby, and internationals. Take a cushion, matches Sun at 1545, Wed at 2000. Big matches can be rowdy and sometimes violent.

Horse riding **Cabalgatas Carpasos**, Km 7 Vía La Calera, T368 7242, www.carpasos.com, about US$15 pp for 90 mins for groups of 4-5. Horse riding at night too. **Cabalgatas San Francisco**, C 51A, No 76A-15, T295 7715. Daily rides around coffee farms, in the mountains, by rivers and lakes, US$10 per hr.

Rafting and kayaking **Fundación Al Verde Vivo**, Calle 95 Nº 32-40 of 203, T218 3048, www.alverdevivo.org, organizes adventure water sports while trying to minimize environmental impact. Natura Vive, T311-809 4207, www.naturavive.com. Specialists in these sports, plus climbing, in various locations.

Rock climbing **La Gran Pared**, Cra 7, No 50-02, T285 0903, www.granpared.com. Artificial rock-climbing wall in the centre of Bogotá. US$5 per hr including equipment.

Trekking **Sal Si Puedes**, hiking group arranges walks every weekend and sometimes midweek on trails in Cundinamarca, and further afield at national holiday periods eg Semana Santa; very friendly, welcomes visitors. Hikes are graded for every ability, from 6 km to 4-day excursions of 70 km or more, camping overnight. Groups are often big (30-60), but it's possible to stray from the main group. Reservations should be made and paid for a week or so in advance at Cra 7, No 17-01, offices 640, T283 3765, open Mon-Thu 0900-1700, Fri 0900-1400, www.salsipuedes.org. **Corporación Clorofila Urbana**, Cra 33, No 96-13, T616 8711, www.clorofilaurbana.org, offers similar walking opportunities with an emphasis on environmental awareness. **Confraternidad de Senderismo Ecológico El Respiro**, Transversal 48, No 96-48, T253 0884, is another group offering walks. There are several other groups, good information on Fri in *El Tiempo* newspaper, *Eskape* section and in the monthly *Guía del Ocio* guide (has a small section in English and French). A recommended operator is **Caminar por Colombia**, Cra 7, No 22-31, of 226 B, T286 7487, caminarcolombia@hotmail.com, walks around the capital every Sun, US$10 for small groups, includes transport and guide.

Tour operators

Aji Colombia, C 16, No.1-05, La Candelaria, T243 7855/301-362 7065, www.ajicolombia.com. Bespoke tours of Colombia, specialising in the Caribbean region, run by British ex-pats.

Aviatur, Av 19, No 4-62, T234 7333, http://site.aviatur.com. Good, efficient, lots of branches across the country.

Bienvenidos, Cra 78A, No 127C-82, T253 1754, www.bienvenidosturismocolombia.com. Cultural, trekking, beach and adventure tours and can advise on diving. Caters to tourists and business travellers, English spoken, helpful.

Colombia Oculta, Cra 29, No 74-19, T630 3172, www.colombiaoculta.org. Aventure tours throughout Colombia, ecotourism, programmed or personalized tours.

Colombia Quest, C 125, No 19-89, T704 3936, www.colombiaquest.com. Specializes in trips around Bogotá, especially around La Candelaria and Zipaquirá. Also shopping and clubbing tours. Very knowledgeable guides. English, French, German and Japanese spoken. Recommended.

De Una Colombia Tours, Cra 26a, No 40-18, Apto 202, T368 1915, www.deunacolombia.com. Dutch-run tour agency with tailor-made trips throughout Colombia and an emphasis on introducing tourists to the country's people as well as its landscapes. Particularly experienced in Los Nevados and Sierra Nevada del Cocuy.

Doble Vía, Carrera 11, No 77-20, T211 2754. National and international flights. Best for fights to Leticia with **AeroRepública**.

Eco-Guías, T347 5736 or 212 1423, www.ecoguias.com. Colombian/English team specializes in tailor- made trips, ecotourism, adventure sports, trekking, riding and tourism on coffee fincas, efficient, knowledgeable and well organized. Highly recommended.

Edutravel Victoria Reps, C 140, No 16-04, T648 3327, vjaramill4@epm.net.co. Efficient, knowledgeable and helpful, excellent English spoken by the owner, Victoria Jaramillo. Books hotels in Chocó and stays on coffee farms and in Los Llanos, open Sat morning. Recommended.

Somos Aventureros, Cra 28, No 42-50, T605 7400, www.somosaventureros.com. Open Mon-Fri 0900-1200, 1400-1800, Sat 0900-1300. Arranges tours from Bogotá to Parque de los Nevados during bank holiday weekends, rafting, trekking, rock climbing, extreme sports.

Vivir Volando, Cra 16, No 96-64, T601 4676, www.vivirvolando.com. Flights and packages to Pacific, Amazon and Caribbean coast. Strong links with **Satena**.

Transport

Bogotá *p900, maps p900 and p902*

Air

There are 2 terminals on Av El Dorado, the Puente Aéreo terminal being 1 km before the main terminal (T425 1000 for flight information for both terminals). All **Avianca** domestic flights and some **Avianca** international flights use Puente Aéreo. **Note** You must check which terminal your flight will use. (See Ins and outs, page 898, for transport to the city.) The departure area at **El Dorado** has the usual duty-free shops and is comfortable. Many snack bars and restaurants on 1st floor with Wi-Fi points throughout. International calls can be made from **Telecom** on 1st floor open till 2100, credit cards accepted; post office in main arrivals lounge. Exchange rates are marginally lower in the city. Airport bank changes TCs, but is not open at holiday times. There is a *casa de cambio* alongside, which changes cash only. When closed, ask airport police where to change money. Allow at least 2 hrs for checking in and security. Use only uniformed porters. There is no baggage deposit. There are 2 tourist offices, in international arrivals and in domestic arrivals, open late. Both are near respective exits for taxis. **Puente Aéreo** has ATMs which accept international credit cards. There is a **Presto** fast-food restaurant, **Telecom** with international call facilities but no exchange service, and an internet cafe. Otherwise, services are similar to those at El Dorado.

For internal flights, which serve all parts of the country, see page 889. Sometimes, flights are overbooked, so check in well in advance. Reconfirm all flights 48 hrs before departure.

Bus

Local Fares start at US$0.55, depending on length of route and time of day. Most buses have day/night tariff advertised in the window. **Busetas** (green) charge a litle more and can be dirty. There are some *ejecutivo* routes (red and white) with plush seats, US$0.70, and *colectivos* (small vans), cramped but fast, charge US$0.80. Fares are also higher on holidays. The **TransMilenio** (www.trans milenio.gov.co), an articulated bus system running on dedicated lanes connects North, Central and South Bogotá from C 170 (on the Autopista del Norte) to Portal de Usme (where the road to Villavicencio leaves the city). There is a spur to the west along C 80 and a link to Candelaria (Parque de Los Periodistas on Av Jiménez de Quesada with a stop at the Gold Museum). **Corriente** services stop at all principal road intersections, *expresos* limited stops only. The journey from the centre to the north takes under 30 mins. Journey cost US$0.65. Using the TransMilenio is a good, quick way of getting around but tends to be crowded.

Long distance If going to towns in Boyacá or Cundinamarca for a long weekend, leave Bogotá before Fri 1200 as it can take 1½ hrs to get from Terminal to outskirts. Try to arrive back before 1300, or ask to be set down in North Bogota and take TransMilenio bus to centre.

The **Terminal de Transportes** is at C 33B, No 69-59, near Av Boyacá (Cra 72) between El Dorado (Av 26) and Av Centenario (C 13), T295 1100, www.terminaldetransporte.gov.co. There is also access from Cra 68. It is divided into modules serving the 4 points of the compass; each module has several bus companies serving similar destinations. If possible, buy tickets at the ticket office before travelling to avoid over-charging and to guarantee a seat, especially during bank holidays. Fares and journey times are given under destinations below. If you are travelling north, you can significantly cut down on the journey time by taking the *Transmilenio* to Portal del Norte, thus avoiding an arduous journey through Bogotá's traffic. *Velotax busetas* are slightly quicker and more expensive than ordinary buses, as are colectivos, which go to several long-distance destinations. The terminal is well-organized and comfortable, but, as usual, watch out for thieves. Free self- service luggage trolleys are provided. There are shops and restaurants, as well as showers at the terminal (between Nos 3 and 4). At the terminal's medical centre (modelo 4), it is possible to get yellow fever injections, 0700-1900, US$24 for non-Colombians. To get to the terminal take a bus marked '**Terminal terrestre**' from the centre or a *buseta* on Cra 10. A taxi costs around US$4.40 from the centre, with a surcharge at night. As with the airports there is an effective system to stop drivers overcharging. Give your desired address at a kiosk, which will print out a slip with the address and price.

International bus It is better not to buy a through ticket to Caracas with **Berlinas de Fonce** as this does not guarantee a seat and is only valid for 2 Venezuelan companies; no refunds are given in Cúcuta. Ideally, if you have time, make the journey to Cúcuta in 2 stages to enjoy the scenery to the full. Bus connections from San Antonio de Táchira in Venezuela to Caracas are good. **Ormeño**, bus terminal modelo 2, T410 7522, has a weekly Lima-Caracas service via Cúcuta; there is also a Lima-Bogotá service weekly (US$170). Bogotá-Caracas by this service US$60. International tickets with Ormeño can only be bought only at bus terminal. Much better (and cheaper) is to do the trip in stages and enjoy the countries you are travelling through.

Taxi

See Taxis, page 890. Taxis are relatively cheap, minimum fare US$2. Average fare from North Bogotá to the centre US$8. Check for additional charges above what the meter states eg: night charge and rides to the airport. At busy times, empty taxis flagged down on the street may refuse to take you to less popular destinations. If you are going to an address out of the city centre, it is helpful to know the neighbourhood (barrio) you are going to as well as the street address, eg Chicó, Chapinero (ask at your hotel). Radio taxis are recommended for safety and reliability; when you call the dispatcher gives you a cab number, confirm this when it arrives. Try these numbers: T2111111, T3111111, T4111111 and T2233333.

Directory

Bogotá *p900, maps p900 and p902*

Airline offices Domestic: **AeroRepública**, Cra 10, No 27-51, Local 165, reservations T320 9090. **Aires**, Cra 7, No 16-36, T336 6038, and Aeropuerto El Dorado Entrada 1, T01-800-052 4737. **Avianca**, C 19, No 4-37, Local 2, T401 3434, airport T413 9862, or 01-800-012 3434. **Easyfly**, T414 8111. **Satena**, Cra 10, No 26-21, of 210, T337 5000, or 01-800-091 2034, military airline, not the best for comfort and delays.

International: Most airlines, local and international, have offices in both central and North Bogotá. Many international airline offices are closed on Sat and Sun. **Air Canada**, C 100, No 8A-49, Tr B, p 8, T296 6353; **Air Comet**, Cra 9, No 113-52, of 1701, T01-800-700 7587, or 742 5744. **Air France**, Cra 9A, No 99-07, Torre 1 p 5, T650 6002. **American**, C 71A, No 5-90, loc 101, T439 7777. **Continental**, Cra 7, No 71–21, Torre A, of 2, or C 14, No 9-45, Torre B, loc 112, T01-800-944 0219. **Iberia**, Cra 19, No 85-11, T610 5066, airport, T413 8715. **LAN**, C 100, No 8A-49, Torre B, p 7, T01-800-956 4509. **Lufthansa**, C 100, No 8A-49, Torre B, p 8 T296 6333. **Mexicana**, Av 15, No 112-36, of 108, T215 2626. **TACA/LACSA**, C 113, No 7-21, loc 124, T01-800-951 8222.

Banks Some head offices are grouped around the Avianca building and the San Francisco church, others are in North Bogotá on or near C 72. The best way to obtain pesos in Bogotá is to use ATMs. Any other method will require your passport and, often, queues. Since it will probably require at least 2 or 3 attempts, either go downtown or in the north, where there are many banks. Unfortunately, there are no rules; there are countless ATMs accepting MasterCard, Visa and other cards; but machines may be down or out of cash, or just don't accept the cards stated.

Titan, Cra 7, No 18-42, Local 116, T3413875. Another good one at Cra 7, No 32-33, loc 5-114, T352 2026, close Sun. **Cambios Country**, Cra 11, No 71-40, Of 201, and at El Dorado airport, T413 8979. Several other city offices, good rates, speedy service. **Orotur**, Cra 10, No 26-05 (below Hotel Tequendama in pedestrian subway) is quick and efficient, cash only, including sterling. **Cambios New York Money**, in CC Unicentro, Av 15, No 123-30, loc 1-118, accepts sterling, efficient. Other *cambios* on Av Jiménez de Quesada, between Cras 6 and 11, and in the north of the city. On Sun exchange is virtually impossible except at the airport. CC Hacienda Santa Bárbara has several *cambios*. To replace lost Amex TCs, *American Express*, Expreso Viajes y Turismo, C 85, No 20-32, T593 4949 or 313 1146 (has other branches), open 0800-1900, Sat 0900-1400, with full details, a police report of the loss and preferably proof of purchase. They first authorize cash advance on Amex cards and then direct you to the appropriate bank (Banco Unión Colombia).

Car hire See Planning your trip, Car hire, for agencies with continent-wide distribution. Car hire is expensive in Colombia, although one of the cheapest options is **Dollar**, at airport, T266 3835, and Av El Dorado, No 98-50, T413 5599. **Colombia Rent a Car**, Av Boyacá, No 63-12, T300-811 6016.

Cultural centres **British Council**, Cra 9, No 76-49, p 5, T325 9090, www.britishcouncil.org/es/colombia. New modern centre, open Mon-Fri 0900-1700, good TEFL library, British newspapers. **Centro Colombo Americano**, C 19, No 2-49, T334 7640, or in the north, C110, No 15-36, T275 5052, www.colombobogota.edu.co. English and Spanish courses. Recommended. **Alianza Colombo-Francesa**, Cra 3, No 18-15, T341 3148 and Cra 7A, No 84-72, T236 8605, www.alianzafrancesa.org.co. Films in French, newspapers, library monthly bulletin etc. Other branches in major cities across Colombia. **Goethe Institut**, Cra 7, No 81-57, T254 7600, www.goethe.de/ins/co/bog/deindex.htm.

Embassies and consulates Opening times and rules for visas are changing continuously, phone before you go. Few embassies are open in the afternoon, best to go early morning. **Austria**, T326 3680 (emergencies) **Australia**, Cra 18, No 90-38, T636 5247. **Belgium**, Apt 3564, C 26, No 4A-45, p 7, T282 8881, bogota@diplobel.org. **Brazil**, C 93, No 14-20, p 8, T218 0800. **Canada**, Cra 7, No 114-33, p 14, T657 9800, open Mon-Thu 0800-1230, 1330-1700, Fri 0800-1330, www.dfait-maeci.gc.ca. **Ecuador**, C 89, No 13-07, T635 0322. **France**, Cra 11, No 93-12, T638 1400. **Germany**, Cra 69, No 25B-44, p 7, T423 2600, www.bogota.diplo.de. **Israel**, Edif Caxdac, C 35, No 7-25, p 14, T327 7500. **Italy**, C 93B, No 9-92, T218 7206, www.ambbogota.esteri.it. **Japan**, Cra 7, No 71-21, Torre B p 11, T317 5001. **Netherlands**, Cra 13, No 93-40, p 5, T617 4915. **Panama**, C 92, No 7-70, T257 5067. Mon-Fri, 0900-1300. **Spain**, C 92, No 12-68, T622 0090. **Switzerland**, Cra 9, No 74-08, oficina 101, T349 7230, open Mon-Thu 0900-1200, Fri 0900-1100. **UK**, Cra 9, No 76-49, p 9, T326 8300, www.ukincolombia.fco.gov.uk. **USA**, C 22D bis, No 47-51, T315 0811, consulate/visas, T315 1566, http://bogota.usembassy.gov. **Venezuela**, Cra 11, No 87-51, piso 5, T640 1213 (610 6622 visa information), embajada@embaven.org.co, 0830-1200. Visas can be collected the following day 1200-1630. Enquire by telephone first.

Immigration DAS: Bogotá office (for extending entry permits), C 100, No 11B-27, T601 7269, www.das.gov.co. Open Mon-Thu 0730-1600, Fri 0730-1530. Cundinamarca office: C 58, No 10-51. DAS will not authorize photocopies of passports; look in Yellow Pages for notaries.

Internet Most hotels and hostels and some restaurants are now Wi-Fi-enabled and provide several computers for surfing the net. There are many internet cafés, charging US$1-2 per hr. **Listelnet Communications**, Cra 3, No 15-47. Skype and heaphones. International calls. **Café Xanaledra**, Cra 4, No 12-78. Skype and headphones as well as coffee, tea and cake. **Café del Cubo**, Cr 4, No 13-57, Mon-Sat 0900-2200. **Coffeemail**, CC Santa Bárbara. Mon-Sat 1030-2000, Sun 1400- 1800. Helpful staff. **Foto and Internet Café**, Tequendama Hotel/Centro Internacional complex (2nd floor), loc 164, helpful, good service, Mon-Fri 0700-2000, Sat 0900-1600, US$0.90 per hr. **Web Café**, Diag 27, No 6-81, Mon-Fri 0900-2000, Sat 1000-1800.

Language courses You need a student visa, not a tourist visa, to study. Some of the best Spanish courses are in the **Universidad Nacional** (see map, page 900), T316 5000, www.unal. edu.co, about US$180 for 2 months, 8 hrs per week, or **Universidad de los Andes**, T339 4949, www.uniandes.edu.co, US$300, 6 weeks, and **Pontificia Universidad Javeriana**, T320 8320 ext 4620, www.javeriana.edu.co. Good value Spanish courses at the **Universidad Pedagógica**, C 72, No 11-86, T594 1894. Good reports, around US$90 for 40 hrs, 2 hrs per day, one of the cheapest. Enquire at Platypus hostel for more information. **Carmen Trujillo**, T315-874 1325, carmen.trujillo@colombiaquest.com, is recommended. English, French and Italian spoken.

Medical services 24-hr emergency health service, T123 or 125. **Cruz Roja Nacional**, Av 68, No 66-31, T428 0111. 0830-1800, consultations/inoculations US$12.50. **Santa Fe de Bogotá**, C 119, No 9-33, T629 3066, and **El Bosque**, C 134, No 12-55, T274 0577, are both modern, private hospitals, with good service. **Farmacity**, is a chain of well-stocked chemists open 24 hrs across the city. For 24-hr home deliveries in Bogotá, T530-0000, C 93A, No-13-41, off Parque de la 93, Cra 13, No 63A-67, among others.

Post offices Main Avianca ticket office and Deprisa airmail office in basement of Ed Avianca, Cra 7, No 16-36, open 0730-1900 Mon to Fri, 0800-1500 Sat, closed Sun and holidays (*poste restante* 0730-1800, Mon-Sat, letters kept for only a month, US$1 per letter). Parcels by air are sent from here too. Also Cra 7 y C 26-27, near Planetarium; C 140 between Cra 19 y Autopista. Parcels by air, contact *Avianca*. **Adpostal**, Cra 7, No 27-54, handles international parcels.

Telephones International calls from several *Telecom* offices in central Bogotá (eg in the *Tequendama Hotel*/Centro Internacional complex); all close within 30 mins of 2000. Phone cards are recommended for call boxes. See also page 895.

Around Bogotá

The basin on which Bogotá stands, with high ranges of the Cordillera to the east, is known as La Sabana de Bogotá and is the centre of Colombia's important cut-flower industry. Around La Sabana are many places of interest in nearby towns for weekend excursions out of the city.

Zipaquirá → *Phone code: 1. Colour map 1, B3. Population: 62,000. Altitude: 2,600 m.*
Twenty kilometres beyond Chía, on La Sabana with its flower greenhouses and dairy farms, is the famous rock salt mine, still producing salt after centuries. Within the mines, the **Salt Cathedral** ⓘ *0900-1800, Sun mass at 1300, admission by ticket, US$8, including 1¼ hr guided tour, car park US$2,* is one of the major attractions of Colombia. The entrance is in hills about 20 minutes' walk west of the town from Parque Villaveces. At the site, there is an information centre and the **Museo de la Salmuera** ⓘ *US$0.50,* which explains how salt is produced. The original underground cathedral was dedicated in 1954 to Nuestra Señora del Rosario (patron saint of miners). Continuing deterioration made the whole cave unsafe and it was closed. A remarkable, new salt cathedral, minimalist in style, was opened on 16 December 1995. Inside, near the entrance, are the 14 Stations of the Cross, each sculpted by a different artist. Other sections of the cathedral follow to the Nave, 180 m below the surface, with huge pillars "growing" out of the salt. All is discreetly illuminated and gives an austere impression.

Zipaquirá has a pleasant colonial plaza, which is dominated by a brick cathedral (see www.zipaquira.gov.co). Tuesday is market day. In the town is the **Museo Quevedo Zornoza** ⓘ *Calle 3, No 7-69, Tue-Fri 0930-1200, 1400-1600, Sat-Sun 0900-1700, US$1,* which displays musical instruments and paraphernalia including the piano of General Santander. The **Museo Arqueológico** ⓘ *Calle 1, No 6-21, T852 3499, next to the Parque Villaveces entrance, Mon-Sun 0930-1800, US$1.30,* houses more than 1,500 pieces of pre-Columbian pottery. For eating and partying at weekends, a recommended place in **Chía** is **Andrés Carne de Res** (see Eating, below).

Around Zipaquirá
Nemocón, 15 km northeast of Zipaquirá, has salt mines (now closed) and a church with original 17th century frescos (currently under restoration). There is a small but interesting **Museo de Sal** ⓘ *on the plaza, Tue-Sun 0800-1700, closed Tue after bank holiday, US$0.90,* which includes history of the salt industry in the time of the Chibcha. ATM on main plaza. A side road connects with the Bogotá-Cúcuta highway. Some 8 km beyond Nemocón, with its own access to the main Tunja road, is **Suesca**, a centre of rock climbing on sandstone cliffs overlooking the Río Bogotá. ▸▸ *See Transport, page 920.*

Southwest of Bogotá
The Simón Bolívar Highway runs from Bogotá to Girardot; this 132 km stretch is extremely picturesque, running down the mountains. **Girardot**, is the former main river port for Bogotá, but only small boats can go upriver from here. Girardot is a popular second-home resort for Bogotanos looking for heat and sun. It's a relaxed place with a market on the main plaza. About 20 km along this road from the centre of Bogotá is Soacha, now the end of the built-up area of the city. A right fork here leads past the Indumil plant to the **Chicaque Parque Natural** ⓘ *daily 0800-1600, US$9 for foreigners; take a bus to Soacha and ask for continuing transport to the park, T368 3114/3118, if driving, there is a better route via Mosquera on the Honda road, left towards La Mesa and in 11 km left again on the road to Soacha, the park sign is 6 km along this road,* a privately owned 300 ha park, principally cloud forest between 2,100 m and 2,700 m on the edge of the Sabana de Bogotá. It is a popular spot for walkers and riders at weekends with good facilities for day visitors and a Swiss-style *refugio*, about one hour down the trail from the entrance, which provides meals and accommodation for 70 or so costing US$20-25 per day including meals.

Northwest of Bogotá

The Sabana de Bogotá is dotted with white farms and groves of eucalyptus. The road passes through the small towns of Fontibón and Madrid, before reaching **Facatativá** (*Population: 67,000; Altitude: 1,800 m*) 40 km from Bogotá. Some 3 km from Facatativá, on the road to the west, is the park of Piedras de Tunja, a natural rock amphitheatre with enormous stones, numerous indigenous pictographs and an artificial lake. **Villeta**, 71 km from Facatativá (*Population: 13,000*) is a popular weekend resort. The road continues to Honda, half way to which is the interesting historical town of **Guaduas** (*Population: 23,000; Altitude: 1,000 m; Phone code: 1*). In the main plaza is a statue of the liberator Policarpa Salavarrieta, the cathedral and one of several museums in the town. Sunday market. Best local dish is *quesillos*. Nearby La Piedra Capira offers great views of Río Magdalena. Bus to Honda, US$2.50, one hour. The surrounding countryside is beautiful, including waterfalls at Versalles (10 km). Transport for Facatativá, Villeta and Guaduas: take Bogotá-Honda buses.

Honda On the west bank of the river, Honda is 32 km upstream from La Dorada. Founded in 1539, it's a pleasant old town with many colonial houses, including Colombia's oldest pharmacy, a lively indoor market and three museums. The streets are narrow and picturesque, and the town is surrounded by hills. Many of the colonial buildings are slowly and lovingly being restored to their former glory and a small group of expats has settled here, opening up new hotels and restaurants. Popular with visitors from much colder Bogotá, Honda is gradually being discovered by international travellers. El Salto de Honda (the rapids which separate the Lower from the Upper Magdalena) is just below the town. Honda is well-known for its many bridges, some very old and rickety, spanning the Ríos Magdalena and Guali, at whose junction the town lies. In February the Magdalena rises and fishing is unusually good. People come from all over the region for the fishing and the festival of the Subienda, the fishing season. There is a row of good cheap restaurants across the Río Magdalena bridge in Puerto Bogotá.

Gateway to the Llanos

Through Colombia's impressive longest tunnel, Buenavista, and along a 110-km road running southeast from Bogotá lies **Villavicencio** (*Phone code: 8; Population: 384,000; Altitude: 498 m*), capital of Meta Department. **Instituto de Turismo del Meta** ⓘ *Cra 32, No 38-70, Edif Romarco, T671 6666, turismo@etell.net.co*. Villavicencio, a modern town, is a good base for visiting Los Llanos (the plains), at the foot of the eastern slopes of the Eastern Cordillera stretching more than 800 km east as far as Puerto Carreño, on the Orinoco in Venezuela. Los Llanos is cowboy country and the never ending expanse of fertile plains makes it ideal for cattle raising, the area's main industry. The area is also rich in oil and the flames from oil refineries based in Puerto Rico can be seen flickering on the distant horizon.

From Villavicencio, three roads run into the Llanos. To the north is a popular route known as the Ruta del Piedemonte Llanero. Around 3 km northeast is the **Bioparque Los Ocarros** ⓘ *Km 3 via Restrepo, T664 8490, www.bioparquelosocarros.com, US$4.70, children US$3.70*, a 5.5-ha thematic park set around lakes and forests with nearly 200 species endemic to the Llanos.

Two km beyond is the **Centro Cultural Etno Turístico El Maguare** ⓘ *Km 5 via Restrepo, Vereda La Poyata, T664 8464, www.etniasvivas.org, US$2.20*, a community project set up and managed by the Uitoto (ancestral dances in a traditional *maloca*, talks about the state of Colombia's indigenous people and workshops). Further along the road are the pleasant town of **Restrepo**, famous for its salt mines and pretty church, and **Cumaral** which has palm tree plantations and is known as the best place to eat meat in the Llanos.

The road east from Villavicencio, known as the Amanecer Llanero, passes through the Apiay oil field before reaching **Puerto López** on the Río Meta, while the road south, the Ruta del Embrujo Llanero, leads to the Parque Nacional Natural Sumapaz ⓘ *entry US$9*, páramo at 3000-3600 m, and where adventure sports such as whitewater rafting, paragliding and abseiling can be practised, and the Parque Nacional Natural Serranía de la Macarena. See Safety, page 894.

Around Bogotá listings

For Sleeping and Eating price codes and other relevant information, see Essentials, pages 38-40.

Sleeping

Zipaquirá *p917*

C Cacique Real, Cra 6, No 2-12, T851 0209, www.hotelcaciquereal.com. Recently declared a Patrimonio Cultural, fine little hotel, lovely courtyard with hanging baskets, good rooms with cable TV, hot water, Wi-Fi in the lobby, car park.

D Casa Virrey, C 3, No 6-21, T852 3720, casavirreyorani@hotmail.com. Housed in a new building with comfortable rooms, laundry service.

E Torre Real, C 8, No 5-92, T851 1901. Light and airy rooms with large beds. Also laundry service.

Around Zipaquirá: Suesca *p917*

B La Esperanza, Km 1 along railway from Suesca, T856 3339, www.hotellaesperanza.com.co. With breakfast, restaurant, conference centre, sauna, horse riding US$17 per hr, camping at Campamento Zhay, US$4pp, or rent a house or room sleeping 3-5, good for groups.

Northwest of Bogotá *p918*

Guadas

D Hostería Colonial, on plaza, T846 6041. Great value, delightful restored mansion, TV, bath.

Honda

C Casa Belle Epoque, C 12, No 12A-21, Cuesta de San Francisco, T8251 1176/310-481 4090, www.casabelleepoque.com. A lovely old house with spacious, high-ceilinged rooms, all with bath and fan, beautiful roof terrace with jacuzzi, pool, free Wi-Fi, lots of antique, period touches. British-Colombian run, excellent breakfasts, advance booking preferred. Also arranges horse-riding, boat and fishing trips. Recommended.

C-D Calle Real , Cra 11, No 14-40, T251 7737. Central, safe, with a/c or fan, parking, restaurant, small pool on rooftop.

D Asturias Plaza, Cra 11, No 16-38, T251 3326. Large, rambling hotel near bus terminal, pool, cable TV. Rooms are a bit dusty but OK.

D Riviera Plaza, C 14, No 12-09, T312-893 7520. Clean rooms around a large pool. If you get the rooms at the end there are good views over the river Gualí and the colonial part of town.

Gateway to the Llanos: Villavicencio *p918*

AL Hotel del Llano, Cra 30, No 49-77, T671 7000, hotellan@etell.net.co. Tucked under the forested hills of the Cordillera Oriental, a smart option with good rooms, spa, sauna, pool, restaurant, tour agency and Wi-Fi throughout.

AL María Gloria, Cra 38, No 20-26, T672 0197. In an ugly building, with a good pool area with sauna and Turkish bath. A/c, TV and Wi-Fi.

B Savoy, C 41, No 31-02, T662 5007. Simple rooms, a/c, cable TV. Vegetarian restaurant downstairs.

C Hotel de Oriente, C 38A, No 29A-43, T662 6391. Good, large rooms, cheaper with fan. Good security.

C San Jorge Llanos, C 38, No 31-21, T662 1682, hotelsanjorgellanollano@telecom.com.co. Good, a/c and cable TV.

D Delfín Rosado, C 35, No 23-15, T662 6896. The rooms may open up off dark corridors but they are comfortable with fan, cable TV and a restaurant serving decent breakfasts.

E El Caporal, C 39, No 33-35, T662 4011. Clean, simple rooms in a small hotel 1 block from the Parque Principal.

E Granja Los Girasoles, Barrio Chapinerito, T664 2712. Youth hostel, 160 beds, 3 km from bus station.

E Turista del Llano, C 38, No 30A-42, T662 6207. Rooms are a bit musty but it's in the centre of town, with cable TV, bath, towels and soap.

One of the best ways to get to know the Llanos is to stay on a cattle ranch: **Fincas y Eventos**, C 47 Bis, No 28-09, T310-285 6641, www.fincasy eventos.com, has over 90 homesteads.

Eating

Several eating places sell typical local food, also Chinese restaurants in the centre: others, some with pools, on the road to Puerto López.

Zipaquirá *p917*

Many restaurants on and around the main plaza.

TT Parque Restaurante Funzipa, C 1A, No 9-99. Colombian food served in a converted salt mill.

T La Antigua, Cra 8, No 3-35. Cheap and cheerful *almuerzo ejecutivo* for US$3. There are several more similar options near the plaza.

Chía

🍴🍴🍴 **Andrés de Res**, C 2, No 11-94. Open Thu-Sun. This arty, rustic restaurant and bar has become an institution with great typical food, highly original decor, 'performers' to liven things up and free arts and crafts workshops for children.

Northwest of Bogotá: Guaduas *p918*

🍴 **Zaguán del Virrey**, C 4, No 5-68. Good *comida corriente* in pleasant patio with art work.

Honda *p918*

There are many economical fish restaurants by Río Magdalena a short walk from town behind the bus station, serving fresh catch of the day, including **El Corralito de Tuky-Tuky**, Av Pacho María, Bahía 3.

Gateway to the Llanos: Villavicencio *p918*

🍴🍴 **Chop Suey**, C 38, No 30A-44, T662 6852. Popular Chinese restaurant.

🍴 **Asadero La Llanerita**, C 35, No 27-16, T662 3001. Slow-roasted meats cooked on a open barbecue, including *falda de Costilla*.

🍴 **Fonda Quindiana**, Cra 32, No 40-40, T662 6857. Great atmosphere, one of the oldest restaurants, typical dishes as well as *parrillas*.

🍴 **La Posada del Arriero**, C 41, No 30-08, T664 1319. Also serves typical dishes as well as fish, chicken and steak, on a pleasant terrace.

🍴 **Toy-Wan**, C 40A, No 28-69, T6641758. Smart oriental restaurant.

Festivals and events

Gateway to the Llanos: Villavicencio *p918*

Jun-Jul Torneo Internacional del Joropo, involving parades, singers and over 3000 couples dancing the *joropo* in the street.

Encuentro Mundial de Coleo festival in mid **Oct**. Colourful event, similar to rodeo in which cowboys tumble young calves by grabbing their tails and twisting them until they lose their balance.

Activities and tours

Around Zipaquirá: Suesca *p917*

Rock climbing For information call **Hernán Wilke**, T310-216 8119, or visit his climbing centre **Monodedo**, www.monodedo.com. In Suesca turn right at the entrance to Las Rocas, past *Rica Pizza* restaurant. He speaks English and German, experienced and knowledgeable. US$30 for half day climbing with guide, US$45 full day, open weekends and holidays 0830-2100. Also 5-day trips to Cocuy from US$70 pp per day. **Ricardo Cortés**, the owner of *Rica Pizza*, also arranges climbing trips and local accommodation.

Transport

Zipaquirá *p917*

Bus The Zipaquirá bus station is 15 mins walk from the mines and cathedral. Many buses from **Bogotá**: Cra 30 (Av Ciudad de Quito), marked 'Zipa', **Flota Alianza**, or others from the C 170 terminus of the TransMilenio in North Bogotá opposite *Exito* supermarket, US$2 each way, 1¼ hrs. Zipaquirá can also be reached from Tunja (see page 921), by taking a Bogotá-bound bus and getting off at La Caro for connection to Zipaquirá, US$2.40. Note when arriving to C170 terminus from Zipaquirá you need to buy a TransMilenio bus ticket to leave the station. To avoid this, ask the driver to drop you off before the bus station.

Train La Sabana station at C 13, No 18-24, Bogotá. A slow tourist steam train runs on Sat, Sun and holidays at 0830 calling at Usaquén in the north of Bogotá (see map), going north to Zipaquirá (1130) andCajicá, back in Bogotá, La Sabana at 1740. (All times variable.) Cost: adult US$15, child up to 10, US$9.40. Tickets should be bought in advance at La Sabana station, T375 0557, or Usaquén station, C100 y Cr 10, or from travel agents. See www.turistren.com.co.

Honda *p918*

From **Bogotá** by **Velotax** and **Rápido Tolima**, US$11, 4 hrs. **Manizales**, US$10.50. **Rápido Tolima** run ½-hourly buses to **La Dorada** (1 hr), and beyond, to **Puerto Boyacá** (3 hrs). The new Bogotá–Medellín highway bypasses the town.

Gateway to the Llanos: Villavicencio *p918*

Air Aires and Satena to **Bogotá** daily. Satena flies to Medellín, Puerto Carreño and to destinations in the Llanos.

Bus Station outside town, taxi US$1.50. To/from **Bogotá** *colectivos* and mini vans leave 20 times a day from 0400-2000, US$12, 1½ hrs.

Bogotá to the Venezuelan border

The main road route from Bogotá to Venezuela has some beautiful stretches and passes through, or near, several colonial towns. In Cundinamarca and Boyacá it gives access to the Laguna de Guatavita, perhaps the nearest place the Spaniards came to finding their El Dorado, historical battle sites and the Sierra Nevada del Cocuy, excellent climbing and hiking country. The principal towns, both with a strong colonial heritage, are Tunja and charming Villa de Leiva.

The highway crosses Santander and Norte de Santander Departments on its way to Cúcuta. That this was an important route for the Spaniards can be seen in the colonial villages, like Barichara, and the more important centres like Bucaramanga and Pamplona. There is also some grand scenery in the Chicamocha canyon and the eastern cordillera, with possibilities for adventure sports.

Bogotá to Villa de Leiva

Guatavita → *Phone code: 1. Colour map 1, B4. Population: 6,000. Altitude: 2,650 m.*

The modern town of Guatavita Nueva, 75 km from Bogotá, is a popular haunt for Bogotanos. It was rebuilt in replica colonial style when the old town of Guatavita was submerged by the reservoir. There is a small bullring, cathedral and two small museums, one devoted to the Muisca people and the other to relics of the old Guatavita church. The many artisan shops are good places to buy ruanas. Market day is Sunday. The tourist information booth can find accommodation for visitors.

Laguna de Guatavita, a sacred lake of the Muisca, is where the legend of El Dorado (see box opposite) originated. Access is only allowed with a permit from the **Corporación Autónoma Regional de Cundinamarca** (CAR) ⓘ *Cra 7, No 36-45/11, T320 9000, www.car.gov.co, US$6.50*. The lake is a quiet, beautiful place; you can walk right round it, 1½ hours, or climb to the rim of the crater. Opinions differ on whether the crater is volcanic or a meteorite impact, but from the rim at 3,100 m there are extensive views over the countryside. Just before the road reaches Boyacá Department, it passes the Sisca reservoir where there is fishing and windsurfing. At the *Refugio de Sisca* restaurant, try *empanadas de trucha* (cornmeal and trout snack), US$0.60, excellent.

Tunja → *Phone code: 8. Colour map 1, B4. Population: 152,000. Altitude: 2,780 m.*

Tunja, capital of Boyacá Department and 137 km from Bogotá, has some of the finest, well-preserved colonial churches of Colombia. When the Spaniards arrived in what is now Boyacá, Tunja was already an indigenous city, the seat of the Zipa, one of the two Chibcha kings. It was refounded as a Spanish city by Gonzalo Suárez Rendón in 1539. The **Cathedral** and five other churches are all worth visiting, particularly for their colonial woodwork and lavish decoration. These include **Santo Domingo**, begun in 1594, **Santa Bárbara** (1592) and the **Santa Clara La Real** chapel (1580).

The **Casa del Fundador Suárez Rendón** ⓘ *Plaza de Bolívar, daily 0800-1200, 1400-1600, US$0.70*, is one of Colombia's few mansions of a Spanish *conquistador* (1539-1543) and has a peaceful courtyard with fine views of the valley; see the unique series of plateresque paintings on the ceilings. The helpful **tourist office** ⓘ *T742 7548, cultura.turismo@boyaca.gov.co*, is also here.

The market, near Plaza de Toros on the outskirts of town, is open every day (good for *ruanas* and blankets). Friday is main market day. During the week before Christmas, there is a lively festival with local music, traditional dancing and fireworks.

The battle of Boyacá was fought about 16 km south of Tunja, on the road to Bogotá. Overlooking the bridge at Boyacá is a large **monument to Bolívar** ⓘ *daily 0800-1800, US$1.50 per car. There are several other monuments, an exhibition hall and restaurant at the site. Bus*

The Gilded Man

The basis of the El Dorado (Gilded Man) story is established fact. It was the custom of the Chibcha king to be coated annually with resin, on which gold dust was stuck, and then to be taken out on the lake on a ceremonial raft. He then plunged into the lake and emerged with the resin and gold dust washed off. The lake was also the repository of precious objects thrown in as offerings; there have been several attempts to drain it (the first, by the Spaniards in colonial times, was the origin of the sharp cut in the crater rim) and many items have been recovered over the years. The factual basis of the El Dorado story was confirmed by the discovery of a miniature raft with ceremonial figures on it, made from gold wire, which is now one of the most prized treasures of the Museo del Oro in Bogotá. Part of the raft is missing; the story is that the gold from it ended up in one of the finder's teeth! (Read John Hemming's *The Search for El Dorado* on the subject.)

from Tunja, US$0.60, ask for "El Puente". Bolívar took Tunja on 6 August 1819, and next day his troops, fortified by a British Legion, the only professional soldiers among them, fought the Spaniards on the banks of the swollen Río Boyacá. With the loss of only 13 killed and 53 wounded they captured 1,600 men and 39 officers. Only 50 men escaped, and when these told their tale in Bogotá the Viceroy Samao fled in such haste that he left behind him half a million pesos of the royal funds.

Villa de Leiva ➔ *Phone code: 8. Colour map 1, B4. Population: 6,800. Altitude: 2,144 m.*

About 40 km west is the beautiful and unmissable colonial town of **Villa de Leiva** (also spelt Leyva) which has one of the largest plazas in the Americas. It is surrounded by cobbled streets, a charming, peaceful place. The town dates back to the early days of Spanish rule (1572), but unlike Tunja, it has been declared a national monument so will not be modernized. The first president of Nueva Granada, Andrés Días Venero de Leiva, lived in the town. Many of the **colonial houses** are now hotels, others are museums, such as the restored birthplace of the independence hero, **Casa de Antonio Ricaurte** ⓘ *Cra 8 y C 15, Wed-Fri 0900-1200, 1400-1700, Sat, Sun and holidays 0900-1200, 1400-1800, US$1*. Ricaurte was born in Villa de Leiva and died in 1814 at San Mateo, Venezuela, fighting with Bolivár's army. The house has a nice courtyard and garden. **Casa de Nariño** ⓘ *Cra 9 entre 10 y 11, Fri-Tue 0900-1200, 1400-1600, US$1.70*, recently restored, displays documents from the Independence period. The **Casa del Primer Congreso** ⓘ *C 13 y Cra 9, on the corner of the plaza, free, Tue-Thu 0800-1300, 1400-1700, Sat 0800-1300, 1400-1700*, in which the first Convention of the United Provinces of New Granada was held, is worth a visit. On the Plaza Mayor the **Casa-Museo Luis Alberto Acuña** ⓘ *US$1.10, Mon-Sun 0900- 1800*, houses fascinating examples of Acuña's work.

A **palaeontological museum** ⓘ *15 mins' walk north of the town on Cra 9, US$1.10, Tue-Sat 0900-1200, 1400-1700, Sun and holidays 0900-1500*, has well-displayed exhibits. The **Monasterio de las Carmelitas Descalzas** ⓘ *Calle 14 y Cra 10, Sat, Sun and holidays 1000-1300, 1400-1700, US$0.80*, has one of the best museums of religious art in Colombia. Part of the monastery is the **Iglesia del Carmen** and the **Convento**, all worth a visit. The shops in the plaza and adjoining streets have a great selection of Colombian handicrafts.

Some colonial houses close Monday to Friday out of season, but the trip is worthwhile for the views and for long, peaceful walks in the hills. Many places are closed Monday and Tuesday. Market day is Saturday, held in the Plaza de Mercado 0400-1300. During weekends and public holidays, the town is very crowded with Bogotanos. The **tourist office** ⓘ *Cra 9, No 13-04 just off the plaza, T732 0232, 0800-1800 daily*, has local maps, gives advice on cheaper accommodation and bus schedules and is most helpful.

The wide valley to the west of Villa de Leiva abounds in fossils. Some 5 km along the road to Santa Sofía is the fossil of a dinosaur (possibly a Kronosaurus) found in 1977, now with a museum built around it. A second fossil found in 2000 nearby has been put alongside. Look for road signs to **El Fósil** ⓘ *daily 0900-1700, US$1.40.* About 2 km from El Fósil along this road is the turning for (1 km) the archaeological site of **Parque Arqueológico de Monquirá** or **El Infiernito** ⓘ *Tue-Sun 0900-1200, 1400-1700, US$1.80 with guide*, where there are several carved stones believed to be giant phalli and a solar calendar. About 1 km beyond El Infiernito is the **Cactus Nursery of Fibas** ⓘ *T311-222 2399, www.fibas.org, free, meditation US$5.50 (with free plant), Wed-Sun 0800-1730, Mon and Tue with forewarning*, which sells many varieties of cactus and desert plants. It features two mazes, based on indigenous designs, in which meditation exercises are held.

Some 6 km after the Infiernito turning is the **Monastery of Ecce-Homo** (founded 1620) ⓘ *open normal hours, just knock on the door*; note the fossils on the floor at the entrance. It was built by the Dominicans between 1650 and 1695. It was reclaimed from the military in 1920, since when it has been repeatedly robbed; some of the religious art is now in the Chiquinquirá museum. What can be seen of the monastery is impressive, but the fabric and roof are in a poor state. There are buses from Villa de Leiva (0800-1615) to Santa Sofía, US$1.20; it is 30 minutes to the crossing, then a 2-km walk to the monastery. Beyond Santa Sofía is La Cueva de Hayal, a cave set in beautiful scenery. A tour of most of these attractions leaves the plaza at 0930, Saturday/Sunday, US$5.

Villa de Leiva

Sleeping
1 Candelaria
2 Colombian Highlands & Hostal Renacer
3 Duruelo
4 El Marqués de San Jorge
5 El Molino la Mesopotamia
6 Hostal Sinduly
7 Plaza Mayor
8 Posada de los Angeles
9 Posada Don Blas
10 Posada San Antonio

Eating
1 Casa Blanca
2 Casa Quintero (La Cocina de la Gata, Savia, Zarina)
3 Don Quijote
4 Olivas & Especias

About 20 km north of Villa de Leiva is a right turn for the **Santuario de Fauna y Flora de Iguaque** ⓘ *US$16.50 for foreigners, contact Organización Comunitaria Naturar Iguaque, T312-585 9892, naturariguaque@yahoo.es*. The 6,750-ha park is mainly high cloudforest of oak, fig and other temperate trees, many covered with epiphytes, lichens and bromeliads. There is a series of lakes at over 3,400 m, and the mountains rise to 3,800 m. At the visitors centre, Furachiogua, there is accommodation for 48, US$15.50 per person; camping with showers, toilets and cooking facilities, US$2.70. **Colombian Highlands** in Villa de Leiva are recommended for organized tours to the park.

Ráquira → *Market day Sun.*

In the Chibcha language, **Ráquira** means 'city of pots' and with over 100 *artesanía* shops selling earthenware pottery in a village of just a dozen blocks, it is rightly considered the capital of Colombian handicrafts. In recent years there has been an influx of cheap products from Ecuador, somewhat diluting its appeal. The village itself, 25 km from Villa de Leiva, has been painted in an array of primary colours and has a picturesque plaza embellished with terracotta statues. Accommodation (**D-E**) and places to eat on or near the plaza.

About 7 km along a very rough road, which winds up above Ráquira affording spectacular views, is the beautiful 16th-century **Monasterio Desierto de La Candelaria** ⓘ *daily 0900-1200, 1300-1700, US$1.10 plus US$0.55 to Hermit's Cave*. On the altar of the fine church is the painting of the Virgen de La Candelaria, dating from 1597, by Francisco del Pozo of Tunja. The painting's anniversary is celebrated each 1 February, in addition to 28 August, the saint's day of San Agustín. The convent has two beautiful cloisters, one featuring a 170-year-old dwarf orange tree, the other virtually untouched since the 17th century. They are lined with anonymous 17th-century paintings of the life of San Agustín.

Chiquinquirá → *Phone code: 8. Colour map 1, B3. Population: 38,000. Altitude: 2,550 m.*

On the west side of the valley of the Río Suárez, 134 km from Bogotá and 80 km from Tunja, this is a busy market town for this large coffee and cattle region. In December thousands of pilgrims honour a painting of the Virgin whose fading colours were restored by the prayers of a woman, María Ramos. The picture is housed in the imposing **Basílica**, but the miracle took place in what is now the **Iglesia de la Renovación** ⓘ *Parque Julio Flores*. In 1816, when the town had enjoyed six years of independence and was besieged by the Royalists, this painting was carried through the streets by Dominican priests from the famous monastery, to rally the people. The town fell, all the same. There are special celebrations at Easter and on 26 December, the anniversary of the miracle. The town is known for making guitars.

Bogotá to Villa de Leiva listings

For Sleeping and Eating price codes and other relevant information, see Essentials, pages 38-40.

Sleeping

Tunja *p921*

Several smart, central hotels in our **A-B** ranges.

AL Hunza, C 21, No 10-66, T742 4111, www.hotelhunza.com. Tunja's grandest hotel, fine views of Iglesia San Francisco. Spacious rooms, Wi-Fi, swimming pool, Turkish bath, restaurant.

C Alicante, Cra 8, No 19-15, T744 9967, hotelalicante@hotmail.com. Minimalist design, sunny patio fringed by varieties of cactus, bright rooms with cable TV, Wi-Fi in reception, great value.

C Posada San Agustín, C 23, No 8-63, T743 0245. Beautiful colonial building on the Parque Pinzón, balustraded courtyard, antiques and photographs of Tunja down the ages, comfortable rooms, modern conveniences such as Wi-Fi, "a bit of a gem".

D Casa Real, C 19, No 7-65, T743 1764, hotelcasareal@yahoo.es. A real bargain, comfortable rooms in a lovely colonial building with varnished wooden floorboards. Highly recommended.

D Conquistador de América, C 20, No 8-92, T742 3534. Lovely foyer with a bright skylight, rooms are small but comfortable, cable TV.
E Imperial, C 19, No 7-43, T742 3056. Nothing outstanding about this small hotel but it's clean, with cable TV and bath.

Villa de Leiva *p922, map p923*
The town tends to be full of visitors at weekends and bank holidays when booking is advisable. It's essential to book in advance for the Festival of Light. There many beautifully restored colonial houses, now hotels, to stay in.
AL Duruelo, Cra 3, No 12-88, T732 0222, www.duruelo.com.co. Villa de Leiva's most exclusive hotel, on a hill above the town. Comfortable rooms, 4 swimming pools and spa and massage services. Non-guests can buy a 'Plan Día' for US$15.50.
AL La Posada de San Antonio, Cra 8, No 11-61, T732 0583, adelgo@hotmail.com. On Parque Nariño, thick adobe walls, colourful décor, enormous antique beds, popular. Wi-Fi in the lobby.
AL Plaza Mayor, Cra 10, No 12-31, T732 0425, www.hotelplazamayor.com.co. On the plaza, delightful octagonal courtyard with lemon trees, comfortable rooms, plus Wi-Fi, parking and a good (expensive) restaurant.
A Candelaria, C del Silencio, No 8-12, T732 0534, www.hotelcandelaria villadeleyva.com. Delightful location, newly refurbished colonial building with 9 rooms of "monastic simplicity". Its restaurant serves international cuisine.
A El Molino la Mesopotamia, C del Silencio, T732 1832, www.hosterialamesopotamia.addr.com. A beautifully restored colonial mill filled with antiques, excellent home cooking, beautiful gardens, fresh water swimming pool (US$2.80 for non-guests), memorable. Recommended.
B El Marqués de San Jorge, C 14, No 9-20, T732 0240, hospederia_elmarquesdesanjorge@yahoo.com. Simple little place with rooms around a courtyard, cable TV, parking, breakfast included.
C Posada de los Angeles, Cra 10, No 13-94, T732 0562. Basic, clean rooms in a fine building 2 blocks from the plaza, restaurant, ask for a room overlooking the Iglesia del Carmen.
D Posada Don Blas, C 12, No 10-61, T732 0986. This sweet and simple little place is 1 block from the plaza, small, clean rooms with cable TV.
D-E Casa Viena, Cra 10, No 19-114, T732 0711, www.casaviena.com. 10 mins from plaza, comfortable hostel with rooms and dorms, kitchen and social area
D-E Colombian Highlands and Hostal Renacer, Cra 9, No 11-02, T732 1379/ T311-308 3739, www.colombianhighlands.com. 15-min walk from town, this hostel, belonging to English-speaking biologist Oscar Gilède, has some of the most comfortable rooms you are likely to find in a Colombian hostel. Extensive gardens, kitchen, wood-fired pizza oven, hammocks, bike hire, internet and dorms with bunks. Tour agency offering a variety of trips including horse rental and adventure sports, excellent local information. Camping US$3.30 with own tent or US$13.80 for a 4-person tent.
D-F Hostal Sinduly, Cra 11, No 11-77, T314-345 0384, noconadelsol@hotmail.com. Run by Austrian Manfred, 1 private room with bath and

a couple of dorms in a colonial house 1 block from the plaza, use of kitchen, hot water. Manfred arranges trips to a *finca* he owns near the Iguaque National Park. English and German spoken.

Chiquinquirá *p924*

C El Gran, C 16 No 6-97, T726 3700. Central, secure, comfortable, includes breakfast, good restaurant, laundry service, parking.

D Sarabita, C 16, 8-12, T726 2068. Business hotel, pool, sauna (when working), restaurant, building is a national monument.

E Moyba, Cra 9, No 17-53, T726 2649, facing plaza. Cheaper without bath, dingy.

Eating

Tunja *p921*

Café Colonial, Cra 9, No 19-92. On the main plaza, good coffee.

El Maizal, Cra 9, No 20-30, T742 5876. Good varied menu of local specialities.

La Cascada, Pasaje Vargas, No 10-82. Popular at lunchtime, *almuerzo* US$2.20.

La Mojarrita, C 18, No 7-43, T743 8330. Seafood restaurant, famous in Tunja.

Pizza Nostra, C 19, No 10-36, T740 2040. Pizzas and lasagnes on a pedestrianized street in the centre of town.

Son y Sabor, Pasaje Vargas, No 10-71, T740 2970. Typical restaurant with good, varied menu.

Villa de Leiva *p922, map p923*

Villa de Leiva has dozens of good restaurants with varied international and local menus. Most, but not all, are concentrated in the town's upmarket foodcourts, Casa Quintero (on the plaza) and La Guaca (on C Caliente).

Savia, Cra 9, No 11-75 (Casa Quintero). Excellent range of organic salads as well as interesting main dishes.

Zarina, Cra 9, No 11-75 (Casa Quintero). Good Lebanese dishes as well as the usual chicken and steak.

Casa Blanca, C 13, No 7-06. Popular for regional specialities.

Don Quijote, La Guaca, C Caliente (Cra 9), Local 12. Award-winning Spanish restaurant with a 400-year-old kitchen.

La Cocina de la Gata, Casa Quintero. Pleasantly decorated fondue restaurant, which also serves chicken and steak.

Olivas & Especias, Cra 10, No 11-99. On the corner of the plaza, pizzas and pastas in homely surroundings.

Chiquinquirá *p924*

Plenty of reasonable places to eat around and near Parque Julio Flores.

Festivals and events

Villa de Leiva *p922, map p923*

Beginning-Feb Astronomical festival, telescopes are set up in the Plaza for public use. **Virgen del Carmen, 13-17 Jul** annually. In **Aug** (check dates) an **international kite festival** is held in the Plaza Major. **Nov Festival de Gastronomía** for the best individual dish cooked by the town's restaurants. **Festival of Light** is held every year from **7 Dec**.

Shopping

Chiquinquirá *p924*

Many delightful toys are made locally. Along the south side of the Basilica are shops specializing in musical instruments.

Transport

Guatavita: Laguna de Guatavita *p921*

Bus Bogotá-Guatavita Nueva, **Flota Aguila**, at bus terminal, US$3, 2-3 hrs, several departures morning; last return bus at 1730. You can walk (2-3 hrs) or ride (US$7 per horse) from Guatavita Nueva to the lake. An easier approach is from a point on the Sesquilé-Guatavita Nueva road (the bus driver will let you off) where there is a sign 'via Lago Guatavita'. There is a good campsite and places to eat nearby. From the main road to the lakeside the road is paved as far as a school, about half way. Follow the signs. This road and track can be driven in a good car to within 300 m of the lake where there is a car park and good restaurant. Taxi tour from Bogotá US$60 full day.

Tunja *p921*

Bus Bus station is 400 m steeply down from city centre. From **Bogotá** several companies, 2½-3 hrs, 4½-5 hrs weekends and holidays, US$5.50. To **Bucaramanga**, frequent services, 7 hrs, US$19.

Villa de Leiva *p922, map p923*
Bus The bus station is on Cra 9 between C 11 and C 12. Advisable to book the return journey on arrival at weekends. Buses to/from **Tunja**, 45 mins, US$2.75, 5 companies, or microbus every 15 mins from 0530 to 1830. To **Bogotá** via Tunja, takes 3-4 hrs, US$10, several companies, and via Zipaquirá and Chiquinquirá, US$10. To **Chiquinquirá**, 1 hr, US$3.30, 6 a day. To **Ráquira** see below. To **Moniquirá, 1000** connects with bus to **Bucaramanga**, thus avoiding Tunja. To **Iguaque National Park entrance**, 50 mins, US$1.70 at 0915, 1300, 1630.

Ráquira *p924*
Buses leave Villa de Leiva at 0730, 0830, 1230, 1630, 30 mins, US$2.20. The return journey is more complicated, with only one direct service at 0430; you may have to change at Ramera. Taxi US$15 one way from Villa de Leiva. There are also buses to Tunja and Bogotá.

Chiquinquirá *p924*
Bus To **Villa de Leiva** 1¾ hrs, US$3.30. To **Tunja**, 3 hrs, US$6. To **Zipaquirá**, US$6. To **Bogotá**, 2½ hrs, US$5.50.

Directory

Villa de Leiva *p922, map p923*
Banks 2 banks and a Visa ATM in Plaza Mayor. **Internet** Redside, Cra 9, No 9-99. Skype, headphones and international calls. **Post office** In **Telecom** building, C 13, No 8-26.

Tunja to Cocuy

Paipa and around

Along the road 41 km northeast of Tunja is **Paipa**, noted for the **Aguas Termales** complex ⓘ *3 km to the southeast, facilities daily 0600-2200, US$5, children US$3*. The baths and the neighbouring **Lago Sochagota** (boat trips possible) are popular with Colombians and foreign tourists. From Paipa there is a minibus service, US$0.50, a taxi costs US$1.50, or you can walk in 45 minutes. There are innumerable hotels (**D-F**) and restaurants on the main street and on the approach road to the Aguas Termales. Paipa is a good place to buy carpets, hammocks and handicrafts.

Sogamoso → *Phone code: 8. Colour map 1, B4. Population: 70,000. Altitude: 2,569 m.*

At Duitama, a town 15 km beyond Paipa known for basket weaving, turn right and follow the valley of the Río Chicamocha for **Sogamoso**, a large, mainly industrial town. This was an important Chibcha settlement, and a **Parque Arqueológico** ⓘ *Tue-Sun 0900-1300, 1400-1800, US$1.50, US$0.80 children*, has been set up on the original site. It has a good museum and a cafetería.

Lago de Tota and around

South of Sogamoso the road winds through a grassy valley to the colonial village of **Iza** (Population 2080). A quiet place, it has one of the most beautiful parques principales in Colombia. On Sundays, it is lined with stalls selling all types of sugary puddings. There is good hiking here and hot springs 1 km away. The most popular is Piscina Erika, entrance US$3.30, with restaurant, changing rooms and showers. There are also two simple rooms for overnight stays (**C**). Beyond Piscina Erika there is free access to natural pools, popular with locals at weekends.

Beyond Iza the road rises sharply, passing through Cuitiva and the indigenous village of Tota before dropping down to **Lago de Tota** (3,015 m), ringed by mountains. Virtually all round the lake, onions are grown near water level, and the whole area has an intriguing 'atmosphere' of pine, eucalyptus and onion. **Aquitania** is the principal town on the lake. There are plenty of food shops and restaurants, and a bright, restored church with modern stained glass windows. Above the town is a hill (El Cumbre) with beautiful views.

Monguí and around

Tópaga, 9 km northeast of Sogamoso, has a colonial church, unusual topiary in the plaza and the bust of Bolívar to commemorate the battle of Peñón of 11 July 1819. Turn south before Topagá to **Monguí**, once voted the 'most beautiful village of Boyacá'. The upper side of the plaza is dominated by the beautiful basilica and convent. There are interesting arts and crafts shops in all directions. Walk down Cra 3 to the Calycanto Bridge, or up C 4, to the Plaza de Toros. A recommended excursion is east to the **Páramo de Ocetá** with particularly fine *frailejones* and giant wild lupins, a 3-hr walk from Monguí. Local craftwork includes leather and wool items.

Sierra Nevada del Cocuy → *Entrance fee, US$15.50 for foreigners, payable at the park office (on the corner of the main plaza in Cocuy), where you can also obtain a map with the main walking paths.*

By the bridge over the Río Chicamocha at **Capitanejo** is the turning to the attractive **Sierra Nevada del Cocuy** in the Eastern Cordillera, the best range in Colombia for mountaineering and rock climbing. The Sierra consists of two parallel north-south ranges about 30 km long, offering peaks of rare beauty (more than 22 are snow-covered), lakes and waterfalls. The flora is particularly interesting, notably the thousands of *frailejones*.

The park is accessible in the south from the small town of **El Cocuy** or further north from **Güicán**. Either town is a perfect start or end point for hiking or climbing in the park. On the central plaza of El Cocuy is a model of the mountain area. One of the most spectacular hikes is from south to north (or vice versa), during which you will see a great part of what the park has to offer. It might appear an easy marked trail, but it is highly recommended to go with a guide as sudden changes in weather can cause visibility to drop to less than 10 m. You will need to know where to camp and where to get drinking water.

There is no accommodation in the park, so you must take all equipment. Basic food supplies can be bought in El Cocuy or Güicán, otherwise you should buy your food in Bogotá. There is no need to take ice axe or crampons. Temperatures can drop below 0°C at night as most campsites are around 4,000 m. The peak holiday periods (the last week in December, the first two weeks of January and Easter week) can get very busy. Dry seasons are December to April and July to August but even in those months it can rain or be very foggy.

La Laguna de La Plaza is probably the most beautiful lake in the Sierra Nevada del Cocuy, surrounded by the snow tops of **Pan de Azúcar** and **Toti** in the west and Picos **Negro** and **Blanco** to the east. Just below Pan de Azúcar is **Cerro El Diamante**. At sunrise, this rock can change from grey to yellow, gold, red and orange if you are lucky with the weather. **Laguna Grande de la Sierra** is surrounded by Pan de Azúcar, Toti, Portales, Concavo and Concavito and is a perfect base camp for climbing one of these. **El Púlpito de Diablo** is an enormous, altar-shaped rock at 5,000 m. From El Púlpito you can continue to climb up to the top of **Pan de Azúcar** (5,100 m) overlooking Laguna de la Plaza on one side and Laguna Grande de la Sierra on the other. **Valle de los Cojines** is an enormous valley surrounded by snow peaks, filled with *cojines* (pillow plants). **Ritacuba Blanco** is the highest mountain of all (5,322 m) and is not too difficult to climb. The views at the top over the Valle de Cojines and many other parts of the park are stunning.

Tunja to Cocuy listings

For Sleeping and Eating price codes and other relevant information, see Essentials, pages 38-40.

Sleeping

Paipa *p927*

AL Casona del Salitre, Vía Toca, Km 3, T785 1508. 5 mins' drive from town. A national monument and a memorable place to stay near the baths and lake in a well preserved hacienda where Simón Bolívar stayed before the Battle of Boyacá. Hot pools, spa, good restaurant, quiet, fireplace. Recommended.

Sogamoso *p927*

E Bochica, C 11, No 14-33, T770 7381. Good value, comfortable, hot water, TV, tourist information, restaurant.

E Valparaíso, C 11A, No 17-56, T771 6935, near bus station. With bath and TV, restaurant, sauna, tourist information.

Lago de Tota and around *p927*

B Pozo Azul, 3 km beyond Camino Real, in a secluded bay on the lake, T619 9524 (Bogotá), also cabins up to 6. With breakfast. Suitable for children, comfortable, watersport facilities, good food.

C Camino Real, Km 20 Vía Sogamoso a Aquitania, T770 0684, on the lake. Pleasant public rooms, colourful gardens, boat slipway, boats for hire, restaurant, sauna, tourist info.

D Posada del Virrey Solis, C 4A, No 4A-75, Iza, T779 0245. Just off the main plaza, a National Monument, baroque rooms full of religious paintings, old books and Egyptian statuettes. Breakfast, US$2.20. Room price includes access to the thermal springs at Piscina Erika.

E Residencia Venecia, C 8, No 144, Aquitania. Clean, basic, reasonable.

Camping **Playa Blanca**, US$2.20 for tent up to 5 people. US$4.40 for over 5.

Monguí *p928*

C La Casona, Cra 4, No 3-41, T782498, chopo11110@yahoo.es. Small, comfortable rooms, behind restaurant of the same name, lovely views. Recommended.

Other places to stay **C-E**.

Sierra Nevada del Cocuy *p928*

F pp **Cabañas Guaicany**, El Cocuy, at the entrance to Valle de Lagunillas, shared bath, great views of Ritacuba Blanco and other peaks. Also possible to camp and to hire horses and/or guide.

F pp **Cabañas Kanwarra**, El Cocuy, at the foot of Ritacuba Blanca, the perfect starting point to climb the mountain or to walk to Laguna Grande de los Verdes. Shared bath.

F pp **Casa Muñoz**, El Cocuy, on the main plaza. With private bathroom.

F pp **Hotel Villa Real**, El Cocuy. Shared bath.

G pp **Finca La Esperanza**, El Cocuy, at the entrance to Valle de Frailejones. Convenient for the walk to Laguna Grande de la Sierra. Simple rooms with shared bath.

Eating

Sogamoso *p927*

Susacá, Cra 16, No 11-35, T770 2587. One of the best restaurants near the centre, specialities include trout, good *comida*, large portions.

Transport

Sogamoso *p927*

Bus To **Bogotá**, 4-4½ hrs, US$11; to **Tunja**, 1-2 hrs, US$5.50.

Lago de Tota and around *p927*

Bus From **Sogamoso** to **Iza** with **Flota Alianzana**, US$2.20. If no buses from terminal in Sogamoso, take a taxi to Puente de Pesca, 5 or 6 blocks away, and catch from there. Same company to **Tota** and **Aquitania**, US$2.80, 1½ hr.

Monguí *p928*

Bus Buses leave from the plaza. To **Sogamoso**, every 20 mins by buseta, US$1, 45 mins.

Sierra Nevada del Cocuy *p928*

Bus El Cocuy and Güicán can be reached by direct bus (early morning or late in the evening) from **Bogotá** (10-12 hrs) with **Paz del Río**, **Libertadores** and **Concorde**, US$15. Coming from Bucaramanga, change buses in Capitanejo. Around 0600 milk trucks leave the main plaza of El Cocuy. They can take you to the **Cabañas Guaicany** (the southern entrance of the park), **Finca la Esperanza** (for Laguna Grande de la Sierra) or to **Hacienda Ritacuba**, from where it is about an hr's walk to the **Cabañas Kanwarra**. An *expreso* (private transport), about US$34, can be arranged at the main plaza in El Cocuy.

To Bucaramanga and Cúcuta

Socorro ➔ *Phone code: 7. Colour map 1, B4. Population: 23,020. Altitude: 1,230 m.*
The main road goes northeast for 84 km to Socorro, with steep streets and single storey houses set among graceful palms. It has a singularly large stone cathedral. The **Casa de Cultura** museum (opening hours vary) covers the local history and the interesting part played by Socorro in the fight for Independence. It is well worth a visit. There is a daily market.

San Gil ➔ *Phone code: 7. Colour map 1, B4. Population: 28,000. Altitude: 1,140 m.*
About 21 km beyond Socorro, northeast on the main road to Bucaramanga, is San Gil, an attractive colonial town with a good climate. It's a friendly, relaxed place and its main square is lively at night. San Gil is a centre for adventure sports (rafting, kayaking, parapenting, paragliding and caving) and is also a good place for biking, horse riding and walking. See Activities and tours, page 936. Tourist office: **Instituto Municipal de Turismo y Cultura** ⓘ *C 15, No 14-66, T727 3529.* **El Gallineral** ⓘ *daily, US$2.25, guides , some English-speaking, tip them as they are not paid*, a delightful riverside park, covers 4 ha where the Quebrada Curití runs through a delta to the Río Fonce. It has a superb freshwater swimming pool and beautiful trees covered with moss-like tillandsia. Good view from La Gruta, the shrine overlooking the town (look for the cross). Visit Juan Curri waterfalls for abseiling or hiking (take a bus, US$2, towards Charalá and ask to be dropped off. There are two approaches, passing through private *fincas*. You may have to pay a small fee for access, about US$2. A return taxi fare is US$20).

Barichara ➔ *Phone code: 7. Colour map 1, B4. Population: 10,000. Altitude: 1,300 m.*
From San Gil a paved road leads 22 km to Barichara, a beautiful, quiet colonial town founded in 1741 and designated as a national monument. Among Barichara's places of historical interest are the Cathedral and three churches, the cemetery and the house of the former president Aquileo Parra Gómez (the woman next door has the key). There is a superb wide-ranging view from the *mirador* at the top of Carrera 10 across the Río Suárez to the Cordillera de los Cobardes, the last section of the Cordillera Oriental before the valley of the Magdalena.

An interesting excursion is to **Guane**, 9 km away by road, or two hours' delightful walk by *camino real* (historic trail), where there are many colonial houses and an archaeological museum in the *Parroquia San Isidro* ⓘ *daily 0800-1200, 1430-1700, US$1.20*. It has an enormous collection of fossils found in the local area (which is constantly being added to), as well as Guane textiles and a mummified woman. Three good restaurants on the plaza serve regional food. From San Gil there is a three-day walk to the villages of Barichara, Guane, Villanueva, Los Santos, and the ghost town of Jérico, involving a spectacular descent of the Chicamocha canyon. Speak to Shaun at the *Macondo Hostal* in San Gil for more details of hostales and eating places on the way.

Between San Gil and Bucamaranga is the spectacular Río Chicamocha canyon, with the best views to the right of the road. There is a Parque Nacional new visitors' centre with panoramic views, activities, parking, snack bars and toilets and a 6.3-km cable car across the canyon ⓘ *Tue-Thu 0900-1800, Fri-Sun 0900-1900, US$4, cable car US$12.20, children half-price (C 44, No. 35- 27, San Pío, Bucaramanga, T657 4400, www.parquenacionaldelchicamocha.com)*.

Bucaramanga ➔ *Phone code: 7. Colour map 1, B4. Population: 539,000. Altitude: 959 m.*
The capital of Santander, 420 km from Bogotá, was founded in 1622 but was little more than a village until the latter half of the 19th century. The city's great problem is space for expansion. Erosion in the lower, western side topples buildings over the edge after heavy rain. The fingers of erosion, deeply ravined between, are spectacular. The metropolitan area of this modern, commercial city, has grown rapidly because of the success of coffee, tobacco and staple crops. It is known as the 'city of parks' for its fine green spaces, eg Mejoras Públicas, de los Niños, San Pío and Las Palmas.

The **Parque Santander** is the heart of the modern city, while the **Parque García Rovira** is the centre of the colonial area. On it stands the city's oldest church, Capilla de Los Dolores ⓘ *C 35/Cra 10*, a national monument. Just off Parque García Rovira is the **Casa de Cultura** ⓘ *C 37, No 12-46, Mon-Sat 0900-1800, US$1*, in a fine colonial building with exhibitions, films and an *artesanía* display. The **Casa de Bolívar** ⓘ *Calle 37, No 12-15, Tue-Sat 0900-1200, 1400-1800, US$1*, where Bolívar stayed in 1828. It is interesting for its connections with Bolívar's campaign in 1813. On the way out of the city northeast (towards Pamplona) is the **Parque Morrorico**, well-maintained with a fine view. There is a sculptured Saviour overlooking the park, a point of pilgrimage on Good Friday. The **tourist office** is in the Instituto Municipal de Cultura ⓘ *C 30, No 26-117, T634 1132, Mon-Fri 0800-1200, 1400-1830*, is friendly and knowledgeable. The departmental **Coordinadora de Cultura y Turismo** is at ⓘ *C 37, No 10-30, Of 235, T684 4848*. The **National parks office** is at ⓘ *Av Quebrada Seca No 30-44, T634 9418*.

Around Bucaramanga

In **Floridablanca**, 8 km southwest, is the **Jardín Botánico Eloy Valenzuela** ⓘ *Tue-Sun 0800-1100, 1400-1700, US$0.50, take a* Florida Villabel *bus from Cra 33, US$0.80, or* Florida Autopista *to the plaza and walk 1 km; taxi from centre, US$3*, belonging to the national tobacco agency. **Girón** a tobacco centre 9 km southwest of Bucaramanga on the Río de Oro, is a quiet and attractive colonial town. Its white buildings, beautiful church, bridges and cobbled streets are well preserved and the historic part of town unspoilt by modernization. Girón can be easily reached from Bucaramanga and makes a good day trip. By the river are *tejo* courts and open-air restaurants with *cumbia* and *salsa* bands. Bus from Cra 15 or 22 in Bucaramanga, US$0.80, taxi US$4.50. **Piedecuesta** is 18 km southeast of Bucaramanga. Here you can see cigars being handmade, furniture carving and jute weaving. Cheap, hand-decorated *fique* rugs can be bought. There are frequent buses to all the surrounding towns; taxi costs US$6. Corpus Christi processions in these towns in June are interesting. Bus from Cra 22, 45 minutes.

Bucaramanga to Pamplona

The road (paved but narrow) runs east to Berlín, and then northeast (a very scenic run over the Eastern Cordillera) to Pamplona, about 130 km from Bucaramanga. **Berlín** is an ideal place to appreciate the grandeur of the Eastern Cordillera and the hardiness of the people who live on the *páramo*. The village lies in a valley at 3,100 m, the peaks surrounding it rise to 4,350 m and the temperature is constantly around 10°C, although on the infrequent sunny days it may seem much warmer. There is a tourist complex with cabins and there are several basic eating places. Camping (challenging but rewarding) is possible with permission. At the highest point on the road between Bucaramanga and Berlín, 3,400 m, is a café where you can camp on the porch.

Pamplona → *Phone code: 5. Colour map 1, B4. Population: 68,000. Altitude: 2,200 m.*

Founded in the mountains in 1548, it became important as a mining town but is now better known for its university. It is renowned for its Easter celebrations. The climate is chilly. Pamplona is a good place to buy *ruanas* and has a good indoor market. The **Cathedral** in the spacious central plaza is the most attractive feature of this otherwise unprepossessing city. The earthquake of 1875 played havoc with the monasteries and some of the churches: there is now a hotel on the site of the former San Agustín monastery, but it is possible to visit the ex-monasteries of San Francisco and Santo Domingo. The **Iglesia del Humilladero**, adjoining the cemetery, is very picturesque and allows a fine view of the city. The **Casa Colonial** ⓘ *Calle 6, No 2-56, Mon-Fri 0800-1200, 1400-1800; Sat 0800-1200, US$0.50*, archaeological museum, is a little gem. **Casa Anzoátegui** ⓘ *Cra 6, No 7-48, Mon-Fri 0800-1200, 1400-1800*, houses a museum of the Independence period. One of Bolívar's generals, José Antonio Anzoátegui, died here in 1819, at the age of 30, after the battle of Boyacá. The state in northeast Venezuela is named after him. Tourist office ⓘ *C 5, No 6-45, T568 0960, cortourpamplona@yahoo.es*, next to *alcaldía*, off Plaza Central. Very helpful, organizes tours and guides.

Cúcuta → *Phone code: 5. Colour map 1, B4. Population: 585,000. Altitude: 215 m.*

Some 72 km from Pamplona is the city of **Cúcuta**, capital of the Department of Norte de Santander, 16 km from the Venezuelan border. Founded in 1733, destroyed by earthquake 1875, and then rebuilt, its tree-lined streets offer welcome respite from the searing heat, as does the **cathedral**, on Avenida 5 between Calles 10 and 11. The **Casa de Cultura** (also known as Torre de Reloj) ⓘ *Calle13 No 3-67*, has art exhibitions and the **Museo de la Ciudad** which covers the city's history and its part in the Independence Movement. For a border town, it is a surprisingly pleasant place to visit, with plenty of green spaces and a busy but non-threatening centre, but see Warning, page 937. Corporación Mixta de Promoción de Santander, ⓘ *Calle 10, No 0-30, T571 8981, www.cucutaturistica.com*, helpful. Tourist police at the bus station and airport. The international bridge between Colombia and Venezuela is south-east of the city.

Just short of the border is the small town of **Villa Rosario**, where the Congress met which agreed the constitution of Gran Colombia in the autumn of 1821, one of the high points of the career of Simón Bolívar. The actual spot where the documents were signed is now a park beside which is the **Templo del Congreso**, in which the preliminary meetings took place. Also nearby is the **Casa de Santander**, where General Santander, to whom Bolívar entrusted the administration of the new Gran Colombia, was born and spent his childhood.

Border with Venezuela → *Phone code: 7*

Venezuela is 30 minutes ahead of Colombia. If you do not obtain an exit stamp, you will be turned back by Venezuelan officials and the next time you enter Colombia, you will be fined.

Colombian immigration ⓘ *DAS, Av 1, No 28-57, T583 5912, Mon-Fri 0730-1600.* Take a bus from the city centre to Barrio San Rafael, south towards the road to Pamplona. Shared taxi from border is US$6, then US$1 to bus station. Exit and entry formalities are also handled at the DAS office, the white building on the lefthand side of road just before the international border bridge. Another DAS office is at the airport and deals with land travellers. See page 1621 for Venezuelan immigration. There is no authorized charge at the border. For exchange, see Banks, page 937.

Venezuelan consulate ⓘ *Av Camilo Daza y C 7, Zona Industrial, near airport, Mon-Fri 0800-1300.* Nationals not requiring a visa are issued an automatic free tourist card by the Venezuelan immigration officers at the border. Overland visitors requiring a visa to Venezuela can get one here, or at the Venezuelan Embassy in Bogotá, although

Cúcuta

Sleeping
1 Acora
2 Arizona Suites
3 Casa Blanca
4 Hotel de la Paz
5 Lady Di
6 Lord
7 República Bolivariana
8 Tonchalá
9 Zaraya

Eating
1 La Embajada Antioqueña
2 La Mazorca
3 Pinchos & Asados
4 Rodizio
5 Venezia

they may send you to Cúcuta. As requirements change frequently, it is recommended that all overland visitors (whether requiring a visa or not) check with a Venezuelan consulate in advance. Apply for visa at 0800 to get it by 1300. If you know when you will arrive at the border, get your visa in your home country.

Leaving and entering Colombia by private vehicle Passports must be stamped with an exit stamp at the white DAS building before the crossing. If not you will have to return later. Expect very long queues. Car papers must be stamped at the SENIAT office in Venezuela, see page 1621. With all the right papers, the border crossing is easy and traffic flows smoothly.

To Bucaramanga and Cúcuta listings

For Sleeping and Eating price codes and other relevant information, see Essentials, pages 38-40.

Sleeping

San Gil *p930*

Some **A-C** options on the outskirts.

B Mansión del Parque, C 12, No 8-71, T724 5622, mansiondelparque@hotmail.com. Colonial building on the corner of the Parque, most picturesque, large rooms (ask for one with balcony), internet.

C La Posada Familiar, Cra 10, No 8-55, T724 8136. Small, 6 rooms set around a sunny courtyard, with TV. Recommended.

D Abril, C 8, No 10 Esquina, T724 8795, hotelabrilsangilss@yahoo.es. Strangely laid out, but rooms have comfortable antique beds, hot water, TV.

D Posada del Conde, Cra 10, No 13-17, T724 2170, posadadelconde@yahoo.es. Fine old building off the Parque, restaurant, Wi-Fi. Double rooms have no windows. Prices tend to double during high season.

E Hostal Monkora, C 9, No 8-65, T315-400 6018, hostalcasamonkora@ hotmail.com. Backpackers' hostel in a 150-year-old house 3 blocks from the Parque; 2 private rooms and 2 dorms, all with shared bath, use of kitchen, mountain bikes for hire and good information on the local area. Camping available.

E San Carlos, Cra 11, No 11-25, T7242542. Sweet little place, rooms with TV and bath, some have no windows.

E Santander Alemán, C 12, No 7-63, T724 2535, igarnica@hotmail.com. Tiny new place with simple but comfortable rooms, good-value restaurant serves breakfast and home-cooked food for US$2.55.

E-F Macondo Guesthouse, C12, No 7-26, T724 4463, T311-828 2905, www.macondohostel.com. With a communal area decked out with hammocks, and an honesty system for drinks and internet, Australian Shaun Clohesy has created more of a home-from-home than a hostel. Board games, free coffee, BBQs on Thu, internet, comfortable dormitory rooms (**F**), but the biggest asset is the wealth of information on local activities. Recommended.

F Sam's VIP Hostel, Cr 10, No 12-33, p 2, main plaza, T724 2746, samshostel@gmail.com. New, good reports on value and services, with breakfast, rooftop pool, use of kitchen, adventure activities, bar, sauna, Wi-Fi, English spoken.

Barichara *p930*

A Hostal Misión Santa Bárbara, C 5, No 9-12, T726 7163 (or Bogotá T288 4949), www.hostalmisionsantabarbara.info. The place to stay if looking for some luxury. Each room is individually decorated with great taste and all open onto a delightful plant-filled courtyard. Has a good restaurant and a swimming pool.

B Coratá, Cra 7, No 4-08, T726 7110. Delightful colonial building with a fine courtyard, TV, hot water, no fan or a/c but high ceilings keep you cool.

B La Mansión de Virginia, C 8, No 7-26, T726 7170. Impeccable colonial house with rooms around a lovely courtyard, comfortable beds, hot water. Recommended.

D Chia-Ty, Cra 6, No 4-51, T726 7727. A good, cheap option, run by a nice old couple. Rooms are simple but clean with bath, pretty garden.

D La Posada de Pablo 2, C 3, No 7-30, T726 7070. One of several places belonging to Pablo. This one is next to the Iglesia de Jesús Resucitado and a gorgeous park. TV, good beds, rooms 10 and 11 have fine views.

E Los Tiestesitos, Cra 5, No 7-62, T726 7224. The only real budget option in town and a good one, run by a couple of old ladies. Lots of plants, good rooms, comfortable beds. Also doubles as an *artesanía* shop selling ceramics.

Camping Just outside Barichara on the road to San Gil is **La Chorrera**, a natural swimming pool, T726 7422, US$0.30 to bathe, US$1.60 to camp, meals by arrangement, clean, attractive.

Guane

D Posada Mi Tierra Guane, Parque Principal, opposite museum, T315-630 6878, hildaui@hotmail.com. Comfortable and charming small hostel with a pleasant courtyard. Some rooms have bunk beds. Recommended.

D Shia Shue, C Real, T724 7753. Just off the plaza. Fine, comfortable rooms in a colonial house. Also recommended.

Bucaramanga *p930*

Due to being a centre for national conventions, it's sometimes hard to find a room. The **Dann** hotel chain, www.hotelesdann.com, is well represented here, C 47, No 28-83, T643 1919, top of the range, business class.

A Guane, C 34, No 22-72, T634 7014, www.hotel-guane.com. Smart hotel with large rooms, pool and solarium. Breakfast is included.

B El Pilar, C 34, No 24-09, T634 7207, www.hotelpilar.com. Good rooms and lots of extras, parking, internet, restaurant and accident insurance. Cheaper with fan.

B Ruitoque, Cra 19, No 37-26, T633 4567, www.hotelruitoque.com. May not look much from the outside, but rooms are good, restaurant, Wi-Fi, close to Parque Santander.

D Balmoral, Cra 21/C 35, T630 3723. Good budget option, cable TV, hot water, convenient, but street- facing rooms are noisy while back rooms have no windows.

D Colonial Plaza, C 33, No 20-46, T645 4125. It's certainly not colonial but rooms are clean, hot water. Slightly cheaper with fan.

D Kasa Guane, C 49, No 28-21, T657 6960, www.kasaguane.com. The best budget option in town. Owned by paragliding instructor Richi Mantilla of Colombia Paragliding, it's decorated with Guane culture artefacts, has private rooms and dorms, internet, use of kitchen, table games, a pool table and good information on the local area.

Around Bucaramanga: Girón *p931*

D Girón Chill Out, C 25, No 32-06, T646 1119, www.gironchillout.com. Italian-owned hostel, 6 private rooms in a colonial house, plus a studio flat, Wi-Fi, cable TV, use of washing machine and kitchen, Italian meals in hostal's restaurant, VW kombi for local tours.

D-E Hotel Las Nieves, C 30, No 25-71, T681 0144, www.hotellasnievesgiron.com. Characterful colonial buidling on the main plaza, large rooms, TV and hot water. Street-facing rooms have balconies, Wi-Fi, good value restaurant. Much cheaper with fan.

Pamplona *p931*

Accommodation may be hard to find at weekends, when Venezuelans visit the town.

A-B El Solar, C 5, No 8-10, T568 2010, miosolar@hotmail.com. Beautifully restored colonial building. Rooms upstairs are enormous and have kitchen and balconies. Rooms downstairs, without kitchen, are cheaper. Also has by far the best restaurant in town.

B 1549 Hostal, C 8B, No 5-84, T568 0451, 1549hostal@gmail.com. Another lovingly restored colonial building. Rooms are light and airy and decorated with great taste by owners Ricardo and Kokis. Wi-Fi, coffee bar and *panadería* in a large courtyard. Highly recommended.

D-E Orsúa, C 5, No 5-67, T568 2470. Probably the best budget option in town. Crumbling but characterful building east side of Plaza, good restaurant. Cheaper rooms without plaza view.

E Imperial, Cra 5, No 5-36, T568 2571. Large modern building on the Plaza, youth hostel vibe. Rooms are a little grubby but staff are friendly. Cable TV and hot water.

Cúcuta *p932, map p932*

AL Arizona Suites, Av 0, No 7-62, T573 1884, www.hotelarizonasuites.net. Newly refurbished, central, all mod cons including Wi-Fi, safety boxes, Italian restaurant.

AL Tonchalá, C 10/Av 0, T575 6444, www.hoteltonchala.com. Professional staff, large pool, spa, internet and Wi-Fi. Breakfast included.

A Casa Blanca, Av 6, No 14-55, T572 2888, www.hotelcasablanca.com.co. Partly refurbished, with large pool, restaurant serving regional and international food. More expensive suites have hot water, also has cheaper rooms with fan.

B Lord, Av 7a, No 10-58, T571 3609. On a busy street, light and airy rooms, cheaper with fan, parking, laundry service.
B Zaraya, C 11, No 2-46, T571 9436. Central, with cable TV, a/c, restaurant and bar.
C Acora, C 10, No 2-75, T573 1846. Cosy, with TV, fan, fridge (cheaper without), good restaurant (closed Sat), good view for 7th floor, laundry service.
D Hotel de la Paz, C 6, No 3-48, T571 8002. Basic rooms, but has a pool. 10% discount for stays longer than 5 days. Next to **La Embajada Antioqueña** restaurant.
D Lady Di, Av 7, No 13-80, T583 1922. An enormous photo of Princess Diana above the doorway and more photos throughout. Rooms are clean but basic.
D República Bolivariana, Av 6, No 11-77, T571 8099. Well placed near Parque Santander, this hotel is dedicated to Simón Bolívar. Rooms are cheaper with fan.

Eating

San Gil *p930*
Few places open in the evening. The market, Cra 11 entre C13/14, is good for breakfast, fruit salads and juices.
🍴 **Donde Betty**, Cra 9 y C 12, Parque Principal. Good for breakfast, *arepas*, scrambled eggs and fruit juices.
🍴 **El Maná**, C 10, No 9-12. Many set menus for under US$4. Open at lunchtime and evenings except Mon.
🍴 **Pizzeria Pierrot**, Cra 9, No 9-130. Best pizzas in town. Open in the evenings, home delivery.
🍴 **Rogelia**, Cra 10, No 8-09. Good for lunch, local specialities. *Menú ejecutivo* US$2.50.
🍴 **Saludable Delicia**, C 11, No 8-40. Excellent vegetarian restaurant with lots of choice. Also has honey, nut and cereal products for sale.

Barichara *p930*
🍴 **Color de Hormiga**, C 8, No 8-44. Specializes in the *hormiga culona* (see below), here used in inventive ways. On a terrace with a pretty garden and views to the town below.
🍴 **El Compa**, C 5, No 4-48. Family-run restaurant serving regional food.

Bucaramanga *p930*
Try the *hormigas culonas* (a large, winged ant often eaten as a snack), a local delicacy mainly eaten during Holy Week (sold in shops, not restaurants).
🍴🍴🍴 **La Carreta**, Cra 27, No 42-27. Established by football legend Roberto Pablo Janiot, tastefully restored colonial building, *parrillas* and seafood.
🍴🍴🍴 **Mercagán**, C 45, No 33-47. Steaks and hamburgers in a fine setting opposite the beautiful Parque San Pío.
🍴🍴 **D'Marco**, C 28, No 54-21. Excellent meat.
🍴🍴 **El Viejo Chiflas**, Cra 33, No 34-10. Well-established, good, typical food from the region, generous portions. Recommended.
🍴🍴 **La 22**, Cra 22, No 45-18. So popular is this local canteen that at weekends you will struggle to be seated.
🍴🍴 **Los Kioskos**, C 45, No 22-45. Thatched huts serving regional food. There is often live *vallenato* music.
🍴🍴 **Los Tejaditos**, Cra 28, No 34. Popular for its varied menu of meat, seafood, pastas and salads.
🍴🍴 **Tony**, Cra 33A, No 33-67. Typical food, popular. Good *tamales* and *arepas*.
🍴 **La Pamplonesa**, C 35, No 18-29. Just off Parque Santander, this *panadería* does good breakfasts as well as sandwiches, cakes and fruit juices.

Pamplona *p931*
Pamplona is famous for its bread. Particularly well known *panaderías* are **Chávez**, Cra 6, No 7-36 and **Araque**. Try *pastel de horno*, *queso de hoja*, *pan de agua* or *cuca*, a kind of black ginger biscuit often topped with cheese. Pamplona even has a *cuca* festival in Sep/Oct of each year.
🍴🍴 **El Portón Pamplonés**, C 5, No 7-83. Specializes in locally caught trout and other fish.
🍴🍴 **La Casona**, C 6, No 7-58, T5683555. Local favourite serving meats and seafood.
🍴🍴 **Piero's Pizza**, C 9 / Cra 5. Pizzas cooked by an Italian family.
🍴🍴-🍴 **Delicias del Mar**, C 6, No 7-60, T568 4558. Popular lunchtime venue specializing in fish.
🍴 **Calle Real**, Cra 6, No 7-60. Family home that serves a decent lunchtime *menú ejecutivo*.

Cúcuta *p932, map p932*
🍴🍴 **Rodizio**, Av Libertadores, No 10-121, Malecón II Etapa. Elegant, good service, big choice of meat dishes, seafood, salad bar.
🍴 **La Embajada Antioqueña**, C 6, No 3-48, T5731874. Local and antioquian food in a fine open-air setting.

La Mazorca, Av 4, No 9-67. Comida criolla in a pleasant courtyard decorated with hanging baskets. *Menú ejecutivo* US$3.50.

Pinchos & Asados, Av Libertadores, No 10-121. Next to **Rodizio**. Good value fast food and snacks served on terrace. Nice and popular place for evening drinks, good atmosphere. Open late and on Sun.

Venezia, Condominio La Riviera, Av Libertadores, T575 0006. Oven-fired pizzas.

Lots of fast food outlets on the 3rd level of **Centro Comercial Ventura Plaza**, C 10 y 11 Diagonal Santander, also cinema and shops.

Festivals and events

Bucaramanga *p930*

Mar, or Apr **Feria de artesanías** (Handicraft Fair) at the Centro de Exposiciones y Ferias (CENFER). The annual **international piano festival** is held here in **Aug-Sep** in the Auditorio Luis A Calvo at the Universidad Industrial de Santander, one of Colombia's finest concert halls. The university is worth a visit for beautiful grounds and a lake full of exotic plants.

Activities and tours

San Gil *p930*

There are many adventure companies in San Gil, some better equipped than others. Main activities, with 2008 prices: **Abseiling** (rappel) At Juna Curri waterfall, US$20. **Horse riding** US$14 pp for day trip. **Kayaking** 3-day beginner's course US$195 on Río Fonce. **Parapenting** Chicamocha canyon US$94 for 30-60 mins; Curiti, 20-30 mins US$33. **Rafting** Río Fonce, best for beginners, US$14; Ríos Chicamocha and Suárez, more advanced US$67-84. Also caving, cycling (bike hire US$1 per hr), hiking and swimming.

Colombia Rafting Expeditions, Cra 10, No 7-83, T724 5800, www.colombiarafting.com. The best for rafting, with International Rafting Federation-qualified guides. Also does hydrospeed.

Exploracion Colombia Guides, C 8, No 10-38, T723 8080, exploracol@hotmail.com. Caving, canyoning, paragliding and whitewater rafting.

Páramo Santander Extremo, Parque Principal, Páramo, T311-251 3785. Based in nearby Páramo, this company is best for abseiling and canyoning. But it also has caving, rafting and horse riding.

Bucaramanga *p930*

Parapenting At Mesa del Ruitoque and Cañón de Chicamocha. Good schools are **Las Aguilas**, Km 2 vía Mesa de Ruitoque, Floridablanca, T635 2470, www.voladero lasaguilas.com, and **Colombia Paragliding**, T432 6266, www.colombia paragliding.com, which also has a hostel for those taking lessons.

Transport

San Gil *p930*

Bus Station 5 mins out of town by taxi on road to Tunja. To **Bogotá**, US$17-19, 7-8 hrs; **Bucaramanga**, US$10, 2½ hrs; **Barichara** from Cra 12, US$1.40, 45 mins, hourly.

Bucaramanga *p930*

Air Palonegro, on 3 flattened hilltops south of city. Taxi US$4, colectivo US$1. Spectacular views on take-off and landing. Daily **Avianca** flights to **Bogotá** (also **AeroRepública**), and to **Cúcuta** and **Medellín** with **Aires** and **Satena**.

Bus Local buses cost US$0.80. The long distance terminal is on the Girón road, T637 1000, with cafés, shops and showers. Taxi to centre, US$1.50; bus US$0.80. To **Bogotá**, 8-11 hrs, US$43 (Pullman) with **Berlinas del Fonce** (C 53, No 20-40, T630 4468, www.berlinas del fonce.com, or at bus terminal), and **Copetran**, www.copetran.com.co. Same company to **Cartagena**, US$62, 14 hrs, 7 a day (one with Berlinas). **Barranquilla**, 13 hrs, US$55, **Berlinas**. **Santa Marta**, 11 hrs, US$50. To **Valledupar**, 10 hrs, US$39 with **Copetran**, 5 a day. To **Pamplona**, US$14.50, 4-5 hrs. To **Cúcuta**, 6 hrs, US$22 (Pullman), *colectivo* US$22. The trip to Cúcuta is spectacular and passes through cloud forests and *páramos*. Best to start the journey early morning as thick fog usually covers the mountains by afternoon. **Barrancabermeja**, 2 hrs, US$8, paved road, scenic journey. To **El Banco** on the Río Magdalena, US$25, 7 hrs, several companies, direct or change at Aguachica. Hourly buses to **San Gil**, 2½ hrs, US$10. Other companies with local services to nearby villages on back roads, eg the folk-art buses of **Flota Cáchira** (C 32, Cra 33-34).

Taxi Most have meters, minimum fare US$1.80; beware of overcharging from bus terminals.

Pamplona *p931*
Bus To **Bogotá**, US$40, 136 hrs. To **Cúcuta**, US$7.25, 2½ hrs. To **Bucaramanga**, US$14.50, 4-5 hrs. Colectivos or shared taxis to **Bucaramanga** and **Cúcuta** cost a few dollars more and usually cut the journey by 1 hr, with door-to-door pick up and delivery. Try **Cooptmotilon** on the north west corner of Plaza Central, C 5. To **Berlín**, US$5. Buses leave from Cra 5 y C 4, minibuses to Cúcuta from Cra 5 y C 5.

Cúcuta *p932, map p932*
Air The airport is 5 km north of the town centre, T587 9797, 15 mins by taxi in normal traffic from the town and border, US$4, US$10 at night, US$10 to border. There are only domestic flights from Cúcuta airport. To **Bogotá** 3 daily and direct to other Colombian cities with **Avianca** (T587 4884), **AeroRepública** (T587 5497) and **Aires** (T587 6724). It is cheaper to buy tickets in Colombia for these flights than in advance in Venezuela.
Bus Bus station: Av 7 and C 0 (a really rough area). Taxi from bus station to town centre, US$1.50. **Copetran**'s private terminal is on Avenida Camilo Daza, via Aeropuerto; taxi to town centre, US$2.40. The **Berlinas de Fonce** terminal is on the continuation of Diagonal Santander. To **Bogotá**, 15-17 hrs, US$56, frequent with **Berlinas del Fonce** and **Copetran**, 2 stops, including **Bucaramanga**. To **Bucaramanga**, US$20, 6 hrs. To **Cartagena**, **Berlinas** and **Copetran**, 16-19 hrs, US$59-72. Reliable taxis service at the bus terminal, **Cotranol**, T572 6139, 314-413 2316 (Sr Orlando).
Warning Cúcuta and the surrounding area is a large centre for smuggling and guerrilla activity. Be careful. Travellers have been reporting for years that the bus station is overrun with thieves and conmen. This is still true. You must take great care, there is little or no police protection. The safest bets are the **Berlinas del Fonce** and **Copetran** terminals. Go straight to them. Otherwise, on the 1st floor of the main terminal there is a tourist office for help and information and a café/snack bar where you can wait in comparative safety. Go straight to a bus going in your direction, get on it, pay the driver and don't let your belongings out of your sight. For San Cristóbal, only pay the driver of the vehicle, not at the offices upstairs in the bus station. If you are told, even by officials, that it is dangerous to go to your destination, double check. Report any theft to the DAS office, who may be able to help.

Border with Venezuela *p932*
Bus **San Cristóbal**, US$1.40 (**Bolivariano**), colectivo US$3; **San Antonio**, taxi US$8, bus and colectivo from C 7, Av 4/5, US$0.50 to DAS office, then US$0.40 to ONIDEX in San Antonio. From Cúcuta to **Mérida** or beyond, go to San Antonio or (better) San Cristóbal and change. On any form of transport which is crossing the border, make sure that the driver knows that you need to stop to obtain exit/entry stamps etc. You will have to alight and flag down a later colectivo.

❶ Directory

Bucaramanga *p930*
Banks HSBC, Cra 19, No 36-41. **BBVA**, C 35, No 18-02. Many banks in the city, many with ATMs. Cash (€ and US$) changed at **Cambiamos SA**, Centro Comercial Cabecera, Level IV, local 104, Cra 35A y C 49. **Internet** **Setelco**, Cra 27, No 19-15. **Iter-Mega**, Cra 29, No 32-58. **Colombia On Line**, C 13, No 29-16. There is free Wi-Fi in all parks and in many shopping centres.

Pamplona *p931*
Banks **Banco de Bogotá**, main plaza, gives Visa cash advances. ATMs nearby. **Post offices** Cra 6 y C 6, in pedestrian passage. **Telephones** C 7, No 5-79.

Cúcuta *p932, map p932*
Banks For the best exchange rates, it is recommended to change pesos to bolívares in Cúcuta and not in Venezuela. Exchange rates fluctuate throughout the day. There is an ATM tucked away on the left side of the international bridge in Venezuela. Good rates of exchange at the airport, or on the border. It is difficult to change pesos beyond San Antonio in Venezuela. **Banco Ganadero/BBV** and **Banco de Los Andes** near the plaza will give cash against Visa cards. **Banco de Bogotá**, Parque Santander, advances on Visa. Money changers on the street all round the main plaza and many shops advertise bolívares exchange. **Casa de Cambio** **Casas de Cambio Invercambios**, Av 5, No 13-32, Casa de Cambio Unidas, Av 5, No 11-39, L-3 C.C. **Cúcuta Plaza**, El Bolívar de Oro, C 10, No 4-48. Several others, including **Italcambio**, on Parque Santander.

Cartagena and the north coast

Caribbean Colombia is very different in spirit from the highlands: the coast stretches from the Darién Gap, through banana and palm plantations and swamps to the arid Guajira.

Cartagena → *Phone code: 5. Colour map 1, A2. Population: 1,090,000.*

Cartagena should not be missed. Besides being Colombia's top tourist destination and a World Heritage Site, it is one of the most vibrant and beautiful cities in South America. It's an eclectic mix of Caribbean, African and Spanish tastes and sounds. The colonial heart of Cartagena lies within 12 km of ramparts. Within the walled city, El Centro, is a labyrinth of colourful squares, churches, mansions of former nobles and pastel houses along narrow cobbled streets. Most of the upmarket hotels and restaurants are found here. The San Diego quarter, once home to the middle classes, and Plaza Santo Domingo perhaps best capture the lure of Cartagena. Less touristy and developed is the poorer Getsemaní neighbourhood, where colonial buildings of former artisans are being rapidly restored. Here are most of the budget hotels. Immediately adjoining Getsemaní is the downtown sector known as La Matuna, where vendors and fruit juice sellers crowd the pavements and alleys between the modern commercial buildings and banks. Cartagena is also a popular beach resort and along Bocagrande and El Laguito are modern high-rise hotels on the seafront. During the high season the walled city becomes a playground for the rich and famous, while cruise liners dock at its port. Don't miss a drink at night in the cafés next to the city's oldest church, Santo Domingo, and in Plaza San Diego. Beyond Crespo on the road to Barranquilla is a fast-growing beach resort lined with luxury apartments. Trade winds during December-February provide relief from the heat.

Ins and outs

Getting there and around Rafael Núñez **airport** is 1½ km from the city in Crespo district, reached by local buses from Blas de Lezo, southwest corner of inner wall. Bus from one block from airport to Plaza San Francisco US$0.40. Taxi to Bocagrande US$4, to town US$3 (official prices). *Casa de cambio* (T656 4943, open, Monday-Friday 0830-2030, Saturday 0830-1700, Sunday 0830-2100), cashes Amex TCs but not *Bank of America*. Better rates in town. For information, ask at travel agents offices on upper level. Daily flights to all main cities and international destinations. **Bus terminal** is 30 minutes from town on the road to Barranquilla, taxi US$7, or take city buses 'Terminal de Transportes', US$0.60-0.80. ▸▸ *For further information, see Transport, page 948.*

Information **Turismo Cartagena de Indias**: the main office is in the Plaza de las Aduanas, T660 1583, Mon- Fri 0900-1300, 1500-1900, Sat 0900-190, Sun 0900-1700, and there are kiosks in Plaza de los Coches and Plaza de San Pedro Claver. **Corporación de Turismo Cartagena de Indias** ⓘ *Av Blas de Lezo, Muelle Turístico, La Bodeguita, p 2, T655 0277, turismoctg@epm.net.co.* The **Instituto de Patrimonio y Cultura de Cartagena** ⓘ *C del Curato de Santo Toribio No 38-161, Edif Aquilar, p 1, T664 5361*, may provide information. See also www.cartagenacaribe.com (in Spanish). For maps, **Instituto Agustín Codazzi** ⓘ *Calle 34, No 3-37, Edificio Inurbe.*

History

Cartagena de Indias was founded by Pedro de Heredia on 1 June 1533 and grew to be the most important port in the 'New World'. The core of the city was built on an island separated from the mainland by marshes and lagoons close to a prominent hill – the perfect place for a defensive port. There were then two approaches to it, Bocagrande, at the northern end of Tierrabomba island – the direct entry from the Caribbean – and Bocachica, a narrow channel at the south leading to the great bay of Cartagena, 15 km long and 5 km wide. (Bocagrande was

The sacking of Cartagena

Despite its daunting outer forts and encircling walls, Cartagena was challenged repeatedly by enemies. Sir Francis Drake, with 1,300 men, broke in successfully in 1586, leading to the major reconstruction of the ramparts we see today. Nevertheless the Frenchmen Baron de Pointis and Ducasse, with 10,000 men, beat down the defences and sacked the city in 1697. But the strongest attack of all, by Sir Edward Vernon with 27,000 men and 3,000 pieces of artillery, failed in 1741 after besieging the city for 56 days; it was defended by the one-eyed, one-armed and one-legged hero Blas de Lezo, whose statue is at the entrance to the San Felipe fortress.

blocked after Admiral Vernon's attack in 1741 – see box, page 939.) The old walled city lies at the north end of the Bahía de Cartagena, with the Caribbean Sea to the west.

Cartagena was one of the storage points for merchandise sent out from Spain and for treasure collected from the Americas to be sent back to Spain. A series of forts protected the approaches from the sea, and the formidable walls around the city made it almost impregnable.

Entering Bocachica by sea, the island of Tierrabomba is to the left. At the tip of a spit of land is the fortress of **San Fernando**. Opposite, right on the tip of Barú island, is the **Fuerte San José**. The two forts were once linked by heavy chains to prevent surprise attacks by pirates. Close to the head of the bay is Manga island, now a leafy residential suburb. At its northern end a bridge, **Puente Román**, connects it with the old city. This approach was defended by three forts: **San Sebastián del Pastelillo** built between 1558 and 1567 (the Club de Pesca has it now) at the north western tip of Manga Island; the fortress of **San Lorenzo** near the city itself; and the very powerful **Castillo San Felipe de Barajas** ⓘ *daily 0800-1800, US$7, guides are available*, the largest Spanish fort built in the Americas. Built on San Lázaro hill, 41 m above sea level, to the east of the city, initial construction began in 1656 and was finished by 1741. Under the huge structure are tunnels lined with living rooms and offices. Some are open and lit; visitors pass through these and on to the top of the fortress. Good footwear is advisable for the damp sloping tunnels. Baron de Pointis, the French pirate, stormed and took it, but Admiral Vernon failed to reach it.

Yet another fort, **La Tenaza**, protected the walled city from a direct attack from the open sea. The huge encircling walls were started early in the 17th century and finished by 1798. They were on average 12 m high and 17 m thick, with six gates. They contained a water reservoir.

In order to link Cartagena with the Río Magdalena, the most important route to the interior of the continent, the Spaniards built a 114 km canal from the Bahía de Cartagena to Calamar on the river. Called the Canal del Dique, it is still in use.

Independence Cartagena was the first Colombian city to declare independence from Spain, in 1811. A year later Bolívar used the city as a jumping-off point for his Magdalena campaign. After a heroic resistance, Cartagena was retaken by the royalists under Pablo Morillo in 1815. The patriots finally freed it in 1821.

Historic centre

The **Puente Román** leads from the island of Manga into Getsemaní. North of the bridge, in an interesting plaza, is the church of **Santísima Trinidad**, built 1643 but not consecrated until 1839. North of the church, at Calle Guerrero 10 lived Pedro Romero, who set the revolution of 1811 going with his cry of "Long Live Liberty". The chapel of **San Roque** (early 17th century), near the hospital of Espíritu Santo, is by the junction of Calles Media Luna and Espíritu Santo.

If you take Calle Larga from Puente Román, you come to the two churches and monastery of **San Francisco**. The oldest church (now a cinema) was built in 1590 after the pirate Martin Côte had destroyed an earlier church built in 1559. The first Inquisitors lodged at the monastery. From its courtyard a crowd surged into the streets claiming independence from Spain on

Cartagena historic centre

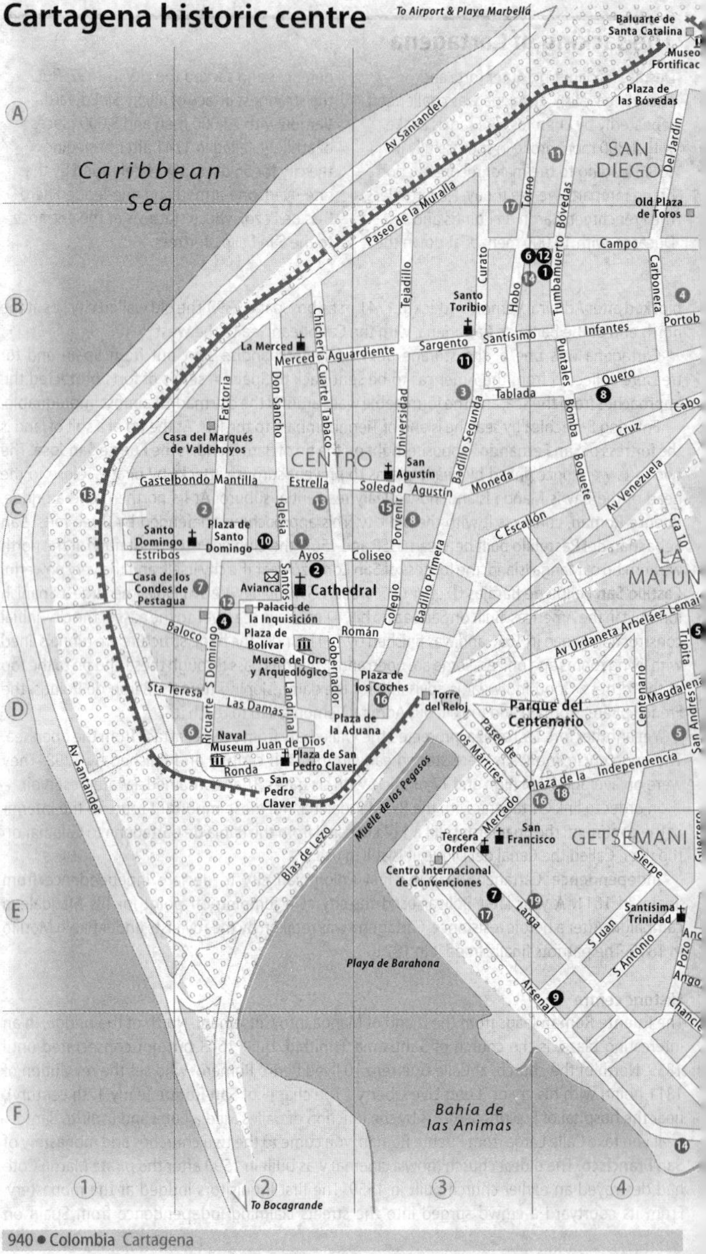

Sleeping

1 Agua *C2*
2 Casa de Pestagua *C2*
3 Casa La Fe *B3*
4 Casa Marco Polo *B4*
5 Casa Viena *D4*
6 Charleston/Santa Teresa *D2*
7 El Marqués *C2*
8 El Viajero *C3*
9 Familiar *D4*
10 Holiday & Hostal Baluarte *D5*
11 Hostal San Diego *A4*
12 Hostal Santo Domingo *C2*
13 La Passion *C2*
14 Las Tres Banderas *B3*
15 Marlin *D5*
16 Monterrey *D4*
17 Santa Clara *B3*
18 Villa Colonial *D5*

Eating

1 Barandales *B4*
2 Bistro *C2*
3 Café Havana *D4*
4 Donde Olano *D2*
5 El Coroncoro *D4*
6 Juan del Mar *B4*
7 La Casa de Socorro *E3*
8 La Mulata *B4*
9 Oh Lá lá *E4*
10 Pelikano *C2*
11 Pizza en el Parque *B3*
12 Teriyaki & Zebra *B4*

Bars & clubs

13 Café del Mar *C1*
14 Casa de la Cerveza *F4*
15 Discoteca Lincon *C3*
16 Diva, Donde Fidel & Tu Candela *D3*
17 Mister Babilla *E3*
18 Quiebra Canto *D4*
19 Studio 54 *E4*

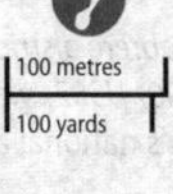

11 November 1811. The monastery is now used by the Corporación Universitaria Rafael Núñez. Originally part of the Franciscan complex, the **Iglesia de la Tercera Orden** on the corner of Calle Larga is worth a visit.

Past the San Francisco complex is **Plaza de la Independencia**, with the landscaped **Parque del Centenario** beyond. At right angles to the Plaza runs the **Paseo de los Mártires**, flanked by the busts of nine patriots executed in the square on 24 February 1816 by the royalist Morillo when he retook the city. At its western end, the **Torre del Reloj** (clock tower) is one of Cartagena's most prominent landmarks. Through its arches (the main entrance to the inner walled city), slaves from Africa were brought to the **Plaza de los Coches**, which served as a slave market. Around almost all the plazas of Cartagena arcades offer refuge from the tropical sun. On the west side of this plaza is the **Portal de los Dulces**, a favourite meeting place, where sweets are still sold. At night, the area becomes a popular place for an evening drink.

The **Plaza de la Aduana**, which has a statue of Columbus, is flanked by the **Palacio Municipal** and the old Customs House. The **Museo de Arte Moderno** ⓘ *Mon-Fri 0900-1200, 1500-1800, Sat 1000-1300, US$1.30*, exhibits modern Colombian artists and has a shop. The **Art Gallery and Museum** ⓘ *Banco Ganadero, Plaza de la Aduana*, has contemporary Latin American paintings. Continue southwest to the **Church of San Pedro Claver and Monastery** ⓘ *Mon-Sat 0800-1730, Sun 0830-1700, US$2.20 (reduction with ISIC), guides US$6 for 20-30 mins.* Built by Jesuits in 1603, it was later dedicated to San Pedro Claver, a monk in the monastery, who was canonized 235 years after his death in 1654. Known as the Slave of the Slaves (El Apóstol de los Negros), he used to beg from door to door for money to give to the black slaves brought to the city. His body is in a glass coffin on the high altar and his cell and the balcony from which he sighted slave ships are shown to visitors. The monastery has a pleasant courtyard filled with flowers and trees in which Pedro Claver baptised slaves.

The church and convent of **Santa Teresa** on the corner of C Ricaurte, was founded in 1609. It is now a hotel, renamed the **Charleston Santa Teresa**; see page 944. Opposite is the **Museo Naval del Caribe** ⓘ *Tue-Sun 1000-1730, open Mon during high season, US$3.50 (sometimes free), children half price*, displaying the naval history of Cartagena and the Caribbean.

The **Plaza de Bolívar** (the old Plaza Inquisición) has a statue of Bolívar. On its west side is the **Palacio de la Inquisición** ⓘ *Mon-Fri 0900-1700, US$2.75*. First established in 1610, the present building dates from 1706. The stone entrance with its coats of arms and ornate wooden door is well preserved. The whole building, with its balconies, cloisters and patios, is a fine example of colonial baroque. It has been restored with air-conditioned rooms. The small museum contains photos of Cartagena from the 20th century, paintings of historical figures, models of colonial houses and a torture chamber (with reproductions of actual instruments). On the opposite side of the Plaza de Bolívar is the **Museo del Oro Zenú** ⓘ *Tue-Fri 0800-1200, 1400-1800, Sat 0900-1700, Sun 1100-1600, free*. It has well displayed pre-Columbian gold and pottery.

The **Cathedral**, in the northeast corner of Plaza de Bolívar, was begun in 1575 and partially destroyed by Francis Drake. Reconstruction was finished by 1610. Great alterations were made between 1912 and 1923. It has a severe exterior, with a fine doorway and a simply decorated interior. See the gilded 18th century altar, the Carrara marble pulpit, and the elegant arcades which sustain the central nave.

The church and monastery of **Santo Domingo**, Santo Domingo y Estribos, was built 1570 to 1579 and is now a seminary. Inside, a miracle-making image of Christ, carved towards the end of the 16th century, is set on a baroque 19th century altar. There is also a statue of the Virgin with a crown of gold and emeralds. Opposite the church is a fine bronze sculpture by Fernando Botero, the *Gertrudis*, presenting an interesting juxtaposition between the colonial and the modern.

Plaza Santo Domingo and Calle Santo Domingo have lots of pavement cafés, restaurants and wandering musicians, an excellent place to go in the evening. In Calle Santo Domingo, No 33-29, is one of the great patrician houses of Cartagena, the **Casa de los Condes de Pestagua** (now a hotel). North of Santo Domingo is the magnificent **Casa del Marqués de Valdehoyos** ⓘ *C de la Factoria 36-57*, home of some of the best woodcarving in Cartagena (under refurbishment, not open to visitors).

The monastery of **San Agustín** (1580) is now the Universidad de Cartagena (at Universidad y La Soledad). From its chapel, today occupied by a printing press, the pirate Baron de Pointis stole a 500-pound silver sepulchre. It was returned by the King of France, but the citizens melted it down to pay their troops during the siege by Morillo in 1815. The church and convent of **La Merced**, Merced y Chichería, was founded 1618. The convent was a prison during Morillos reign of terror and its church is now the Teatro Heredia, beautifully restored. Building of the church of **Santo Toribio** ⓘ *Badilla y Sargento*, began in 1729. In 1741, during Admiral Vernon's siege, a cannon ball fell into the church during Mass and lodged in one of the central columns; the ball is now in a recess in the west wall. The font of Carrara marble in the Sacristy is a masterpiece. There is a beautiful carved ceiling (mudéjar style) above the main altar. Opens for Mass at 0600 and 1800, closed at other times. The church and monastery of **Santa Clara de Assisi**, built 1617-1621, have been converted into a fine hotel (*Santa Clara*, see below). Near the hotel is the orange **Casa de Gabriel García Márquez**, the most famous living Colombian author, on the corner of Calle del Curato.

North of Santa Clara is the **Plaza de las Bóvedas**. The walls of Las Bóvedas, built 1799, are some 12 m high and 15 to 18 m thick. From the rampart there is a grand view. At the base of the wall are 23 dungeons, now containing tourist shops. Both a lighted underground passage and a drawbridge lead from Las Bóvedas to the fortress of La Tenaza at the water's edge (see above). In the neighbouring Baluarte de Santa Catalina is the **Museo Fortificación de Santa Catalina** ⓘ *daily 0800-1800, US$1.50*, inside the city walls.

Casa de Núñez ⓘ *just outside the walls of La Tenaza in El Cabrero district opposite the Ermita de El Cabrero, Calle del Coliseo, Mon-Sat 1000-1200, 1400-1800, US$2*, was the home of Rafael Núñez, president (four times) and poet (he wrote Colombia's national anthem). His grandiose marble tomb is in the adjoining church.

Four of the sights of Cartagena are off our map. Two of them, the Fortress of San Fernando and the Castillo San Felipe de Barajas, across the Puente Heredia, have been described above. At **La Popa** hill (named after an imagined likeness to a ship's poop) ⓘ *daily 0800-1730, US$1.50, children US$0.75*, nearly 150 m high, is the church and monastery of **Santa Cruz** and restored ruins of the convent dating from 1608. The only reason to visit is for good views of the harbour and the city. In the church is the beautiful little image of the Virgin of La Candelaria, reputed a deliverer from plague and a protector against pirates. Every year, in her honour, nine days before 2 February thousands of pilgrims go up the hill and on the day itself carry lighted candles. It is dangerous to walk up on your own; either take a guided tour, or take a public bus to Teatro Miramar at the foot of the hill (US$0.50), then bargain for a taxi up, about US$7 return. If driving, take Cra 21 off Av Pedro de Heredia and follow the winding road to the top.

Beaches

Take a bus south from the Torre del Reloj (10 minutes), taxi US$2.20, or walk to **Bocagrande**, a spit of land crowded with hotels and apartment blocks. Sand and sea can be dirty and you will be hassled by vendors. But do not ignore the *palenqueras*, the black women who majestically carry bowls of fruits on their heads, serving excellent fruit salads on the beach. The **Hilton** hotel beach, at the end of the peninsula, is cleaner and has fewer vendors. A better option is **Marbella** , a locals' beach, just north of Las Bóvedas. During the week, it is quieter and less crowded than Bocagrande. It is decent for swimming though sometimes has dangerous currents.

The **Bocachica** beach, on Tierrabomba island, is also none too clean. Boats leave from Muelle Turístico. The round trip can take up to two hours each way and costs about US$10. To ensure you are not stranded on the island do not pay the whole fare up front; pay the remainder on your return. *Ferry Dancing*, about half the price of the faster, luxury boats, carries dancing passengers. Boats taking in Bocachica and the San Fernando fortress include *Alcatraz*, which runs a daily trip from the Muelle Turístico. Recommended. The *Alcatraz* company goes to Islas del Rosario (see below), stops at the San Martín aquarium, then to Barú-Playa Blanca and leaves around 1530, returning to Cartagena around 1730.

Boats to the Islas del Rosario (see below) may stop at the San Fernando fortress and **Playa Blanca** on the Isla Barú for one hour. Many consider this to be the best beach in the region, with stretches of white sand and shady palm groves. Take food and water since these are expensive on the island. Playa Blanca is crowded in the morning, with armies of hawkers, but the tour boats leave at 1400. If snorkelling, beware drunken jetski drivers. There are several fish restaurants on the beach. If staying the night at Playa Blanca in *cabañas* or tents, take repellent against ferocious sandflies. Most restaurants allow you to camp on their premises for a nominal fee (but you must use their restaurant). If arriving by road (see Transport, below), turn right for cabañas. When taking boat trips be certain that you and the operator understand what you are paying for. You can arrange to be left and collected later, or you can try to catch an earlier boat on to Islas del Rosario or back to Cartagena with a boat that has dropped off people at the beach.

Islas del Rosario

The **Parque Nacional Corales del Rosario** embraces the Rosario archipelago (a group of 30 low-lying, densely vegetated coral islets 45 km southwest of the Bay of Cartagena, with narrow strips of fine sand beaches and mangroves) and the Islas de San Bernardo, a further 50 km south (see page 951). **Isla Grande** and some of the smaller islets are easily accessible by day trippers. Permits from National Parks office in Bogotá are needed for the rest, US$3 entrance fee; in Cartagena, C 4, No 3-20, Bocagrande, T665 6698, see also www.ecohotellacocotera.com. **Rosario** (the best conserved) and **Tesoro** both have small lakes, some of which connect to the sea. There is an incredible profusion of aquatic and birdlife. The **San Martín de Pajarales Aquarium** ⓘ *US$5.50, not included in boat fares (check that it's open before setting out)* is an open sea aquarium; there are guides, but also shark and dolphin shows (Footprint does not endorse dolphins in captivity, see www.wdcs.org/captivity). Many of the smaller islets are privately owned. Apart from fish and coconuts, everything is imported from the mainland, fresh water included. *Hotel Caribe* in Bocagrande has scuba lessons in its pool and diving at its resort on Isla Grande, US$230 and up. Enquire in Bocagrande for other places to stay on the islands. Diving permits are organized by diving companies and are included in the tour price.

North of Cartagena

The little fishing village of **La Boquilla**, northeast of Cartagena, is near the end of a sandy promontory between the Ciénaga de Tesca and the Caribbean, about 20 minutes past the airport. Poor wooden shacks line the beach. It is a popular weekend haunt, known for its many good beachfront fish restaurants (average US$8 for a meal), but visitors may be pestered for money by children. Sometimes people dance local dances, such as *la champeta*, on weekend evenings. Mangrove swamps tours are good for birdwatching, around US$12 for three-hour trip.

A good road continues beyond La Boquilla. On the coast, 50 km northeast, is **Galerazamba**, no accommodation but good local food. Nearby are the clay baths of **Volcán del Totumo** ⓘ *US$1, a bathe will cost you US$2, masseurs available for a small extra fee,* in beautiful surroundings. The crater is about 20 m high and the mud lake, at a comfortable temperature, 10 m across, is reputed to be over 500 m deep.

Cartagena listings

For Sleeping and Eating price codes and other relevant information, see Essentials, pages 38-40.

Sleeping

Cartagena: Historic centre *p939, map p940*

Hotel prices rise substantially, up to 50%, during high season: Jun-Jul and 1 Nov-31 Mar, especially 15 Dec-31 Jan (dates are not fixed and vary at each hotel). Bargain in low season. There are a growing number of attractive boutique hotels in Cartagena. Most budget hostels are on and around Calle Media Luna in Getsemaní. This area can be unsafe, but although it can be dirty and run down, it is still very popular with travellers. Muggings are reported here, even during the day, so take care walking in and around Calle Media Luna and do not walk alone, especially at night.

LL Agua, C de Ayos, No 4-29, T664 9479, www.hotelagua.com.co. Exclusive, expensive, small boutique hotel, colonial, quiet, very pleasant patio.

LL Casa de Pestagua, C Santo Domingo, No 33-63, T664 9510, www.casapestagua.net. Former house of Conde de Pestagua, restored by architect Alvaro Barrera Herrera with great care. Beyond the colonnaded courtyard is a swimming pool and spa, and on the top floor a sun terrace with jacuzzi and sea views.

LL El Marqués, C Nuestra Señora del Carmen, No 33-41, T664 7800, www.elmarqueshotelboutique.com. Another house belonging to the Pestagua family, famous in the 1970s for its celebrity guests. The central courtyard has giant birdcages, hanging bells and large palm trees. The rooms are crisp, white and have Wi-Fi and iPod docks. Exquisite.

LL La Passion, C Estanco del Tabaco, No 35-81, T664 8605, www.lapassionhotel.com. Moroccan-style chic, elegant and discreet comfort, helpful staff, breakfast included, served by the roof top pool, very pleasant.

LL Santa Clara, C del Torno, No 39-29, T650 4700, www.hotelsantaclara.com. French Sofitel group, magnificently restored 16th-century convent, superb lunch buffet, lovely pool, garden with birds in cloisters, Aviatur office. A special place.

LL-L Charleston/Santa Teresa, Cra 13, No 31-23, T664 9494, www.hotelcharlestonsantateresa.com. Formerly a convent, elegantly converted, stylish pool on roof with great views of the colonial district and sea.

AL Casa La Fe, Parque Fernández de Madrid, C 2a de Badillo, No 36-125, T664 0306, www.casalafe. com. Discreet sign (pink building), run by British/ Colombian team. Very pleasant converted colonial house, quiet, jacuzzi on roof, includes breakfast served in patio, Wi-Fi, free bicycle use. Recommended.

AL Monterrey, Paseo de los Mártires Cra 8 B, No 25-103, T664 8560. Colonial style, nice terrace with jacuzzi, business centre, comfortable rooms, a/c, internet.

AL-A Las Tres Banderas, C Cochera de Hobo 38-66, T660 0160, www.hotel3 banderas.com. Off Plaza San Diego, popular, helpful owner, very pleasant, safe, quiet, good beds, spacious rooms, small patio. Price depends on standard of room and season. Free ferry transport to sister hotel on Isla de la Bomba.

A Casa Marco Polo, C de los Siete Infantes, No 9-89, T316-874 9478, cantolindo1@ hotmail.com. Private rooms in a 450-year-old colonial mansion belonging to a local *cumbia* musician. 2 rooms, 1 cheaper (**B**), have a/c, cable TV and share a roof terrace with stunning views. A 3rd room and swimming pool are still being converted, hence the excellent price. Highly recommended.

A Hostal San Diego, C de las Bóvedas 39-120, T660 1433, www.hostalsandiego.com. Near the delightful Plaza San Diego, this colonial building has modern rooms opening onto a tiled courtyard.

B Hostal Santo Domingo, C Santo Domingo 33-46, T664 2268, hsantodomingopiret@ yahoo.es. Prime location, rooms are simple but clean and open onto a sunny patio. Breakfast included, laundry service, gate is always locked, so security is good.

C El Viajero, C del Porvenir, No 35-68, p 2, T664 3289, hotelviajero664@ hotmail.com. Ideally located, more practical than attractive. Organizes tours, has a/c, TV, internet and use of kitchen.

C Villa Colonial, C de las Maravillas 30-60, Getsamaní, T664 4996, hotelvillacolonial@ hotmail.com. Safe, well kept hostel run by friendly family, English spoken, a/c, cheaper with fan, TV, tours to Islas del Rosario. Has a sister hotel on C de la Media Luna.

D Hostal Baluarte, Calle Media Luna No 10-81, Getsemaní, T664 2208. Small rooms in colonial house, family-run, fan, TV, laundry service. Can arrange tours to the Islas del Rosario.

D Marlin, C de la Media Luna, No 10-35, T664 3507, www.hotelmarlincartagena.com. Aquatic-themed hostel with a fine balcony, internet, free coffee. Rooms are a little dark, otherwise recommended.

D-E Casa Viena, C San Andrés 30-53 Getsemani, T664 6242, www.casaviena.com. Popular traveller hostel, Austrian/Colombian run with very helpful staff. Owner, Hans, is an excellent source of information. Cooking facilities, washing machine, TV room, book exchange and internet, range of rooms, some with cable TV and private bath, cheaper in dormitory. Enquire here for information about boats to Panama.

E Familiar, C El Guerrero No 29-66, Getsemaní, T664 2464. Fresh and bright, family-run hotel with rooms set around a colonnaded patio. Has a good noticeboard full of information, a laundry service and use of a kitchen.

E Holiday, Media Luna, No 10-47, T664 0948. Rooms open on to a patio with potted plants and tables. There's a small kitchen and a good information board. Some rooms with shared bath.

Beaches *p943*

Bocagrande

LL El Caribe, Cra 1, No 2-87, T665 0155, www.hotelcaribe.com. The first hotel to be

built in Cartagena, retaining some splendour of bygone years. Beautiful grounds, large pool, beach bar. Has 2 newer annexes, various tour agencies and a dive shop.
LL-L Cartagena Hilton, Av Almte Brion, El Laguito, T665 0660, www.cartagena.hilton.com. Excellent, good bookshop with foreign press, ATM, family-oriented pool area, tennis courts, gym, spa, convention centre and restaurants. Overlooks the sea, own beach area.
L-AL Cartagena Millenium, Av San Martín No 7-135, T665 8499, www.hotelcartagena millennium.com. Range of different suites and spacious rooms at various prices. New, chic and trendy, minimalist decor, small pool, restaurant, good service.
L-AL Charlotte, Av San Martín 7-126, T665 9201, www.hotelescharlotte.com. Colonial, Mediterranean-style decor, comfortable rooms, small pool, a/c, Wi-Fi, Italian restaurant, good.
AL-A Playa, Av San Martín, No 4-87, T665 0112, www.cartagenahotelplaya.com. Good, colourful rooms, inviting pool and direct access to the beach. TV, a/c and breakfast included.
AL-A San Martín, Av San Martín No 8-164, T665 4631, www.hotelsanmartincartagena.com. Bright and airy, small rooms some with balcony, pool.
B Casa Grande, Av del Malecón, No 9-128, T665 6806. Yellow and blue house set back from the beach with spacious rooms off a tranquil garden at the back. Recommended.
C Leonela, Cra 3, No 7-142, T665 4761, www.hostaleonela.com. One of the best *residencias* on Cra 3, long-established. Helpful staff, nice atmosphere, restaurant.
E pp **Mi Casa**, Av 1 No 2-70, El Laguito, T665 8963, micasacartagena@hotmail.com. Entrance through restaurant, welcoming, homely, dorms only, good sea views, dipping pool, right on beach. A good budget option in Bocagrande.

Playa Blanca
LL Baruchica, on private beach on Isla Barú, T312-670 3893, www.paulhiac.us/Realty/BaruChica/default.htm. Rental home owned and run by Olga Paulhiac, organic food, yoga available, evening cocktails, attentive service, delightful. Sleeps 6.
E-F Hugo's Place, T310-716 1021. Hammocks with mosquito nets, fish meals served, camping.
E-F Wintenberg, ask for Gilberto, 'el francés', T311-436 6215. Hammocks with mosquito nets, from US$3, dorms, good cabañas, food served, including vegetarian (at the time of writing the owner was in dispute with local authorities who want to build high rise hotels on his property). Gilberto owns a boat and is often found at Casa Viena on Mon when transport to Playa Blanca can be arranged.
Other places are **Mama Root** (recommended) and **El Paraíso**.

Islas del Rosario *p943*
L Isla del Pirata, book through **Excursiones Roberto Lemaitre**, T665 5622, www.hotel islapirata.com. Simple, comfortable *cabañas*, activities include diving, snorkelling, canoeing and petanque, good Caribbean resturant. Prices include transport to the island, food and non-guided activities. Highly recommended.
L Kokomo Islas del Rosario, Caño Ratón–Isla Grande, reservations with Yolanda Paz T310-741 8616 or through tour operators, www.hotelkokomo.com. All-inclusive private beach resort, pool and restaurant, transport to and from island. Ask about sleeping in hammocks.

Eating

There is a wide range of excellent, upmarket restaurants. All are busy during high season, reservations recommended.

Cartagena: Historic centre *p939, map p940*
TT Donde Olano, C Santo Domingo e Inquisición, T664 7099. Tucked away, Art Deco style, intimate atmosphere, great seafood with French influence.
TT Juan del Mar, Plaza San Diego, No 8-12. Two restaurants in one: inside for expensive seafood, outside for fine, thin-crust pizzas, though you are likely to be harassed by street hawkers.
TT Teriyaki, Plaza San Diego, No 8-28. Next to **Zebra**, serves sushi and Thai food in smart surroundings.
TT Zebra, Plaza San Diego, No 8-34. Café with wide selection of coffees, hot sandwiches and African dishes.
TT-T Bistro, C de los Ayos, No 4-46. German-run restaurant with a relaxed atmosphere, closed

Sun. Sofas, music, European menu at reasonable prices. Recommended.

¶¶-¶ **La Casa de Socorro**, C Larga, No 8B -112, Getsemaní, T664 4658. Busy at lunchtime, excellent seafood restaurant and Caribbean dishes. There are 2 restaurants of the same name on the street. This is the original and better.

¶¶-¶ **Oh! lá lá…**, Callejón Vargas, No 9a-6. Good French food at reasonable prices.

¶¶-¶ **Pelikano**, C Santo Domingo, No 2-98. Atmospheric seafood and meat restaurant offering set menu of starter, main course and 2 glasses of wine for under US$15.

¶ **Barandales**, C de Tumbamuertos, No 38-65, Piso 2. Small restaurant serving typical dishes from Santander. Has a nice balcony overlooking the Plaza de San Diego.

¶ **Café Havana**, C de la Media Luna y C del Guerrero. A fantastic Cuban bar and restaurant, live bands play most nights. Highly recommended.

¶ **El Coroncoro**, C Tripita y Media, No 31-28. Typical restaurant, popular at lunchtime with locals, *comidas corrientes* from US$2.

¶ **La Mulata**, C Quero, No 9-58. Popular lunch venue for a selection of set menu dishes. Wi-Fi. Offers 50% discount if it's your birthday.

¶ **Pizza en el Parque**, C 2a de Badillo, No 36-153. Small kiosk with good pizzas.

Outside the centre

¶¶¶ **Club de Pesca**, San Sebastián de Pastelillo fort, Manga island, T660 5863. Wonderful setting, excellent fish and seafood. Recommended.

Beaches: Bocagrande *p943*

¶¶¶-¶¶ **Arabe**, Cra 3A, No 8-83, T665 4365. Upmarket Arab restaurant serving tagines, etc. A/c, indoor seating or pleasant outdoor garden.

¶¶ **Carbón de Palo**, Av San Martín, No 6-40. Steak heaven, cooked on an outdoor *parrilla*.

¶¶ **La Fonda Antioqueña**, Cra 2, No 6-164. Traditional Colombian.

¶¶ **Ranchería's**, Av 1A, No 8-86. Seafood and meats in thatched huts just off the beach. *Comida corriente*, US$8.

¶ **Jeno's**, Av San Martín, No 7-162. Eat in or take away pizza.

¶ **Juan Valdez Café**, Av San Martín, No 7-17, Starbucks-style chain serving various types of coffee and sandwiches. Has Wi-Fi.

Bars and clubs

Cartagena *p938, map p940*

Most night life is found in the historic district. Many of the hotels have evening entertainment and can arrange *chiva* tours, usually with free drinks and live music on the bus.

Most places don't get going until after 2400, though the Cuban bars **Donde Fidel**, Paseo de los Dulces, and **Café Havana** (see above) start a little earlier and are recommended for Cuban salsa. The majority of clubs are on C del Arsenal. Most bars play crossover music.

Café del Mar, on Baluarte de Santo Domingo, El Centro. The place to go for a drink at sundown.

Casa de la Cerveza, at the end of C del Arsenal. Low sofas around the battlements.

Diva, C del Arsenal. Next door to **Tu Candela**. A 3-level bar playing salsa and electronic music, 2000-0400.

Mister Babilla, C del Arsenal. The most popular and exclusive bar. Take something warm with you, the a/c is fierce!

Quiebra Canto, C Media Luna at Parque Centenario, next to **Hotel Monterrey**, Getsemaní. The best place for salsa. Nice atmosphere, free admission.

Tu Candela, C del Arsenal. Where you can dance in the vaults to 'crossover'.

Gay bars

Discoteca Lincon, C del Porvenir.

Studio 54, C Larga, No 24, Getsemaní.

Festivals and events

Cartagena *p938, map p940*

Mid-Jan Festival Internacional de Música, www.cartagenamusicfestival.com, classical music festival with associated education programme for young musicians. **End-Jan Hay Festival Cartagena**, www.hay festival.com. Franchise of the famous UK literary festival, with internationally renowned writers. **Jan-Feb La Candelaria**, religious processions and horse parades (see La Popa). There is an **international film festival 2nd week of Mar**, www.festicine cartagena.com. **Independence** celebrations, **2nd week of Nov**: masked people in fancy dress dance to the sound of *maracas* and drums. There are beauty contests, battles of flowers and general mayhem.

Shopping

Cartagena *p938, map p940*

Bookshops Abaco, C de la Iglesia y C Mantilla, No 3-86. Popular hangout for writers and poets, delightful atmosphere with café. **Forum Discos y Libros**, Playa de la Artillería, No 33-12, T664 2457.

Handicrafts and jewellery Shopping is better in Bogotá. Handicraft and emerald shops around Plaza de Bolivar and in Plaza de las Bóvedas are good and have the best selection in Cartagena. In the Pierino Gallo building in Bocagrande are reputable jewellery shops.

El Centavo Menos, C Román, No 5-08, Plaza de la Proclamación. Good selection of Colombian handicrafts. **Santo Domingo**, C Santo Domingo, No 3-34. Recommended for jewellery. **Upalema**, C San Juan de Dios, No 3-99. Good for handicrafts.

Supermarket Supermarket **Olympica**, Cra 3, No 5-18, Bocagrande, open 24 hrs. **Vivero**, Av Venezuela y C del Boquete. A/c, with *cafetería*. Shopping malls with cinemas outside the city centre, eg **Los Caracoles** and **Santa Lucía**.

Activities and tours

Cartagena *p938, map p940*

Bullfighting Bullfights take place in Jan in the new Plaza de Toros at the Villa Olímpica on Av Pedro de Heredia, away from the centre. The old, wooden Plaza de Toros is a fine structure, but is no longer used.

Diving Discounts are sometimes available if you book via the hotels, enquire. Recompression chamber at the naval hospital, Bocagrande.

Cultura del Mar, C del Pozo, No 25-95, Getsemaní, T664 9312, www.culturadelmar.com. Run by team of young, well-informed Colombians, diving, snorkelling and tours to Islas del Rosario, English spoken, environmentally responsible.

Diving Planet, Estanco del Aguardiente, No 5-94, T664 2171, also dive shop in Isla Grande (*Hotel Cocoliso*), www.divingplanet.org. PADI open certificate course, snorkelling trips, English spoken. Associated hotel in Cartagena, **Puertas de Cartagena**, www.hotelpuertasdecartagena.com.

La Tortuga Dive Shop, Edif Marina del Rey, Av del Retorno 2-23, El Laguito, Bocagrande, T/F665 6995, www.tortugadive.com. 2 dives US$105. Fast boat, which allows trips to Isla Barú as well as Los Rosarios, same price at *Hotel Caribe Dive shop*, T665 3517, www.caribediveshop.com.

Tour operators

Aventure Colombia, C del Santísimo, No 8-55, T314-588 2378, www.aventurecolombia.com. The only tour organizer of its kind in Cartagena, French/Colombian run, alternative tours of the Sierra Nevada de Santa Marta, local and national activities and expeditions, working (wherever possible) with local and indigenous groups. They also organize boat trips. Highly recommended.

Transport

Cartagena *p938, map p940*

Air

Flights to major Colombian cities and daily to Miami with **Avianca** (C del Arzobispado, No 34-52, T664 7376; in Bocagrande, C 7, No 7-17, L 7, T655 0287, or T01-8000-953434). To **San Andrés**, **AeroRépublica** (Cra 6, No 8-116, Bocagrade, T665 0428) and Avianca. Flights can be overbooked Dec-Mar; even reconfirming and turning up 2 hrs early doesn't guarantee a seat; best not to book a seat on the last plane of the day.

Bus

Local Within the city large buses (with no glass in windows) cost US$0.30 (a/c buses US$0.50, green and white **Metrocar** to all points recommended). From bus terminal to centre, 35 mins or more depending on traffic with Metrocar, US$0.50.

Long distance Colectivos for **Barranquilla** leave from C 70, Barrio Crespo, every 2 hrs, US$14, centre-to- centre service. Several bus companies to **Barranquilla**, every 15 mins, 2-3 hrs, US$8. To **Santa Marta**, hourly, US$14, 4 hrs. Few buses go direct to Santa Marta from Cartagena, most stop in Barranquilla. To **Medellín** 665 km, US$55-60, more or less hourly from 0530, 13-16 hrs. **Rápido Ochoa** is slightly cheaper than others, book early (2 days in advance at holiday times). The road is paved throughout, but in poor condition. To/from **Bogotá** via Barranquilla and Bucaramanga, 16 a day, 21-28 hrs (depending on number of check-points), US$75-83, several companies. To **Magangué** on the Magdalena US$12, 4 hrs with **Brasilia**; to **Mompós**, **Unitransco**, 0700 daily, 12 hrs including ferry crossing from Magangué,

US$17. To **Riohacha**, US$22. Bus to **Maicao** on Venezuelan border, every hour 0500-1200, 2 in the evening, 12 hrs, US$26, with **Brasilia**.

Sea

Intermittent boats go from Cartagena to **Porvenir** in the San Blas Islands (**Panama**); the journey takes about 2 days and costs US$350 pp, including food and 3 nights touring the San Blas archipelago. The journey will normally end in **San Blas** from where you can continue by air or overland to Panama City. The skippers will help with immigration paperwork.

Three boats provide a regular service between Cartagena and San Blas. Highly recommended is **Stella Luna**, T312-681 7833 (Colombia) or T507-6768 6121 (Panama), captained by Hernando Higuera, a key figure in Cartagena's sailing club, with strong links with many indigenous Cuna of San Blas. Also try: **Tango**, French skipper David T314-558 8945, or German captain Guido T316-243 6324, who also owns a backpackers' hostel in Panama.

Take your time before choosing a boat. Some captains are irresponsible and unreliable. The journey is cramped so it's best to get on with the captain. **Aventure Colombia**, see above, can provide reliable information on trustworthy boats and skippers. They also organize 8-day tours to San Blas via the Islas del Rosario, Islas de San Bernardo, Isla Fuerte and Sapzurro in the Darién, US$500 pp, including food. Also try noticeboards at backpacker hotels such as **Casa Viena** or ask around at the Yacht Club (**Club Náutico**, Av Miramar on Isla Manga across the Puente Román, T660 5582). Also on Isla Manga is **Sailing Koala**, Av Miramar 19-50, T805 1816, www.sailingkoala.com.

Taxi

There are no meters; journeys are calculated by zones, each zone costing about US$1.25, though the minimum fare is $2.50. Thus Bocagrande to Centro, two zones, is US$2.50. It is quite common to ask other people waiting if they would like to share, but, in any case, always agree the fare with the driver before getting in. Fares go up at night. A horse-drawn carriage can be hired for US$17, opposite *Hotel El Dorado*, Av San Martín, in Bocagrande, to ride into town at night (short ride). Also, a trip around the walled city, up to 4 people, US$18, from Torre del Reloj.

Beaches: Playa Blanca *p943*

There are three ways of getting to Playa Blanca. The most common is to take a bus from the centre to **Pasacaballo**, US$0.60. From there take a 5-min ferry over the Río Magdalena, US$0.30. Then take a motortaxi or colectivo to **Santa Ana** (45 mins), US$3, and then another colectivo along a rough dirt road to Playa Blanca (45 mins). Do not give money or gifts to children dancing on the roadway. Alternatively, boats to Playa Blanca leave **Bazurto** market, near La Popa, from 0700-0930 daily, US$9 one way. Neither the area nor the boats are particularly safe and boatmen can be persistent. Be sure to pay the captain and not his 'helpers' and arrange a return pick-up time. There are also touristy, expensive boats from the tourist dock (**Muelle Turístico**) at 0830 which stop at Playa Blanca as part of a tour (but you'll have to pay for the whole tour).

Islas del Rosario *p943*
Travel agencies and hotels offer launch excursions from the Muelle Turístico, leaving 0700-0900 and returning 1600-1700, costing US$45, lunch included; smaller boats take 50 mins less. The boat trip is free if staying in one of the hotels. See Sleeping, above. Also, the *Santa Clara Hotel* has San Pedro de Majagua on Isla Grande, and *Cultura de Mar* (see Diving, above) has an ecohotel. Note that there is an additional 'port tax' of US$5 payable at the entrance to the *Muelle* or on the boat. Book in advance. For 5 or more, try hiring your own boat for the day and negotiate a price.

North of Cartagena: Volcán del Totumo *p944*
Bus from **Cartagena** bus terminal to Galerazamba in the morning, US$1.50, 2 hrs, ask to be dropped off at Lomito Arena and walk 2 km along the main road to a right turn signposted 'Volcán del Totumo', 1½ km along a poor road. Hitching possible. Taking a tour from Cartagena will cost more but will save a lot of time. **Aventure Colombia** (see above), organizes tours for US$22, including transport and lunch at La Boquilla or Playa de Manzanillo. A tour of both the volcano and the mangroves is US$38.

Directory

Cartagena *p938, map p940*
Banks There are many ATMs, the most convenient are in the Plaza de la Aduana, where there are **BBVA**, **Bancolombia**, **Davivienda** and **Santander** offices. In Bocagrande a number of banks can be found around Av San Martín y C 8. If you are changing TCs make sure you have your passport with you or you will probably be charged the 3% tax applicable to residents. Never change money on the street in any circumstances. There are *cambios* in the arcade at Torre Reloj and adjoining streets which change Amex TCs; **Cambiamos**, Cra 2, No 1-100, Edif Seguros Bolívar, Bocagrande, T665 1600; **Comisiones Las Bóvedas**, C del Colegio, No 34-53, T664 1692; **Comisiones Royal**, Cra 2, No 5-52, Centro Comercial Michel Center, Bocagrande, T655 1556. **Western Union**, Av Venezuela, No 8A-87, Edif City Bank. **Embassies and consulates** Panama, Cra 1, No 10-10, Bocagrande, T655 1055. **Venezuela**, Cra 3, No 8-129, p 14, T665 0382, consuladodevenezuela@ costa.net.co. Possible to get a visa the same day. **Language classes** Amaury Martelo, amartesi@yahoo.com. Good, professional teacher, polite, all levels catered for. **Internet** Many placess around town. **Post offices** a courier service in Avianca office near cathedral, open Mon-Fri 0800-1830, Sat 0800-1500. Main Post office at Plazaleta Telecom 13, off Av Venezuela. **Security** Carry your passport, or a photocopy, at all times. Failure to present it on police request can result in imprisonment and fines. Generally, central areas are safe and friendly (although Getsemaní is less secure, especially at night), but should you require the police, there is a station in Matuna (Central Comercial La Plazoleta), another in Barrio Manga. In Bocagrande there is a police station on Parque Flanaga.

On the street, do not be tempted by offers of jobs or passages aboard ship: jobs should have full documentation from the Seamen's Union office. Passages should only be bought at a recognized shipping agency.
Telephones Telecom, Av Urdaneta Arbeláez near corner of C 34; long distance phones behind this building; long distance also in Bocagrande. **Useful addresses** DAS: C 20B, No 29-18, T666 0438, open 0730-1100, 1400-1600. **Volunteering**: If you are interested in working with local foundations/NGOs, contact cartagenitos@ yahoo groups.com, who will find places for volunteers.

To Panama

Apart from the towns inland on the road to Medellín and the beaches around Tolú and Coveñas, this section is concerned with the troubled area of the Colombia/Panama border at Darién. Before going by road south of Cartagena, check the latest information on security.

South from Cartagena

The highway south towards Medellín goes through **Turbaco**, 24 km (**Botanical Garden** ⓘ *1½ km before village on the left, Tue-Sun 0900-1600*), **Malagana**, 60 km, and San Jacinto, 90 km, known for its cumbia music using gaitas and local craft work (hand woven hammocks).

Mompós and Magangué

A road runs east from the highway to **Magangué** (*Phone code: 5; Population: 65,000; Altitude: 30 m*), on the western loop of the Río Magdalena. It is the port for the savannas of Bolívar. From here boats go to the small town of **Mompós**, also spelt Mompox (*Phone code: 5; Colour map 1, A3; Population: 41,585*), a UNESCO World Heritage Site on the eastern arm of the river. Alfonso de Heredia (brother of the founder of Cartagena) founded the town in 1540, but due to the silting up of the Río Magdalena here, little has changed in this sweltering, humid town since the early 20th century. Simón Bolívar stayed here frequently and wrote, "If I owe my life to Caracas, I owe my glory to Mompós." Today, Mompós is one of Colombia's most beautiful colonial towns. Opposite the river are the mansions of Spanish merchants for whom this was an important stopping-off point on the Cartagena trade route. Rows of well-preserved, white one-storey buildings have served as a backdrop in many Colombian films. Its six churches, cemetery and plazas are well signed. Mompós is packed during Easter week when visitors flock to see its ornate traditional processions. It is also known for its handworked silver jewellery and its wicker rocking chairs. The town is safe and peaceful and, with improved security in the surrounding area and roads, tourism has increased significantly. But it is still recommended to check safety before setting off. Guided tours of the city on foot or motortaxi cost US$6 per hour. Boat trips can be taken along the Río Magdalena and into the surrounding wetlands, which provide excellent opportunities for birdwatching. Tourist office: **Secretaría de Turismo Municipio de Mompox** ⓘ *Calle Real del Medio, Palacio de San Carlos, T685 5919*. Ferocious mosquitoes and the odd bat are a nuisance after dusk; take insect repellent and wear long sleeves.

Tolú to Turbo

On the coast, 35 km northwest of Sincelejo (the capital of Sucre Department) is **Tolú**, a fast developing holiday town popular for its mud volcanoes, offshore islands and diving. Along the *malecón* (promenade), there are plenty of bars and restaurants. Bicycle rickshaws armed with loud soundsystems blasting out vallenato, salsa and reggaeton spend much of their time trying to outdo each other with the volume of their music. From Cartagena, the best approach is south from Malagana through San Onofre. This is also an easier and safer way for cyclists. For safety reasons, it is recommended not to travel this route at night. There are two mud volcanoes to visit. The nearer is in San Antero, 30 minutes' drive from Tolú, and farther is in San Bernando del Viento, 1¼ hours (turn off the main road at Lorica). Both make good day trips. From Tolú, another good trip is by boat three hours to Múcura island or Titipán in the **Islas de San Bernardo**, about US$20. With all tour boats converging on the island at the same time, it gets very crowded, attracting plenty of beach vendors. There is a charge for everything, including sitting at a table. To enjoy the islands at your leisure, it is better to stay overnight. If camping, take your own supplies. Trips to the mangrove lagoons also recommended.

There are good beaches at **Coveñas**, 20 km further southwest (several *cabañas* on the beach and hotels). This is the terminal of the oil pipeline from the oilfields in the Venezuelan border area. Buses and *colectivos* from Tolú.

The main road south from Tolú passes **Montería** the capital of Córdoba Department, on the east bank of the Río Sinú. It can be reached from Cartagena by air, by boat, or from the main highway to Medellín (US$38, 9 hours), but as it is in a drug-trafficking area, it is best not to linger here.

Arboletes

Southwest of Tolú is the unremarkable town of Arboletes, near which is the largest mud volcano in the area. Dipping into this swimming pool-sized mud bath is a surreal experience – like swimming in treacle. It´s also very good for your skin. You can wash the mud off with a dip in the sea by walking down to the beach 100 m below. Arboletes is also a convenient stopover on the way to Turbo and the Darién coast. The **Volcán de Lodo** is a 15-minute walk from town on the road to Montería or a two-minute taxi ride (US$5.50 return – the driver will wait for you while you bathe). A mototaxi costs US$1. There is a small restaurant and changing rooms (US$ 0.30), plus a locker room (US$1 per bag) and showers (US$0.50).

To Capurganá

On the Gulf of Urabá is the port of **Turbo** (*Phone code: 4; Colour map 1, A2; Population: 127,000*), an important centre of banana cultivation. It is a rough community so it's best to move on quickly. There are various routes involving sea and land crossings around or through the **Darién Gap**, which still lacks a road connection linking the Panamanian Isthmus and South America.

The trek across the Darién is held in high regard by adventurers but we strongly advise against it, not simply because it is easy and fatal to get lost, but also because bona fide travellers are not welcome (indigenous communities still living in Darién have never truly accepted trekkers passing through) and this area still has a heavy guerrilla and drug-trafficking presence. It is virtually deserted by police and the military and it is a hostile environment for any tourist. As recently as 2008 there were reports of kidnappings in the Darién. For the moment only the foolhardy will attempt the land crossing. However, the Caribbean coastline, heavily patrolled by Colombian and Panamanian forces, is safe, though you should exercise caution if venturing into the forest beyond.

Acandí

Acandí is a small fishing village on the Caribbean side of the Darién (populaton about 7,000). It has a spectacular, forest-fringed bay with turquoise waters. To the south are other bays nad villages, such as **San Francisco**. In March-June, thousands of leatherback turtles come here to lay their eggs. There are several cheap *residencias* in Acandí.

Capurganá → *Colour map 1, A2. Phone code: 4.*

For many years, Capurganá and neighbouring Sapzurro have been one of the best kept secrets in Colombia: a glistening, untouched shore of crystal waters, coral reefs and quiet villages. Capurganá has developed into a resort popular with Colombians but little visited by foreigners. There are no banks or cars, just two motorbikes. Taxi rides are provided by horse and cart. The village has two beaches, La Caleta at the northern end, with golden sand, and Playa de los Pescadores, south of the village, fringed by palm and almond trees but with grey sand and pebbles. Ask the fishermen about fishing trips from here (US$ 15-20 in rowing boats).

Several half- and full-day trips can be made by launch to neighbouring beaches, for example Aguacate, near which is a natural jacuzzi known as '*La Piscina*', and Playa Soledad, perhaps the most attractive beach in the area. A return trip by launch boat costs US$11 per person, minimum five people. You can also walk to Aguacate, 1½ hours along the coast, though not to Playa Soledad. Note that it can be difficult to obtain a return by launch if you walk.

A delightful half-day excursion is to **El Cielo**, a small waterfall in the jungle (entry US$2; 40-minute walk, take flip flops or waterproof boots for crossing a stream several times). Take the path to the left of the airport and keep asking for directions. Just before the waterfall a small restaurant serves *patacones* and drinks. Alternatively, you can hire horses to take you there (US$7). Another horse-ride is to El Valle de Los Ríos. The primary forest in this area is rich in wildlife, but you should take a guide. The trip includes lunch at a *ranchería*. For details of excursions, enquire at **Capurganá Tours** (see below).

Another trip is to **Sapzurro**, a few kilometres north and the last outpost before Panama and Central America. The houses of this tiny village are linked by intersecting paths bursting with tropical flowers. It is set in a shallow horseshoe bay dotted with coral reefs, excellent for snorkelling, with a couple of underwater caves to explore. A day's walking trip (there are no cars here) is to the village of **La Miel**, on a gorgeous white-sand beach in Panama. This could qualify as the most relaxed border crossing in the world. The Colombian and Panamanian immigration officers share a hut and copy each other's notes. Be sure to take your passport; if only going to La Miel they won't stamp it but they will take your details. There are breathtaking views of Panama and back into Sapzurro at the frontier on the brow of the hill. You can arrange for a launch to pick you up and take you back to Sapzurro or Capurganá.

Colombian immigration DAS Office is in Capurganá, on the waterfront next to the police station, between the jetty and Playa de los Pescadores, Monday-Friday 0800-1500, Saturday, Sunday and holidays 0900-1600, T311-746 6234. If leaving for Panama you must get your passport stamped here. There are other offices in **Acandí**, Calle Principal, T824 3838, and **Turbo**, Embarcadero Wafe, Barrio Puerto, T827 3815, both open 24 hours.

Entering Panama Panamanian immigration at Puerto Obaldía will check all baggage for drugs. Requirements for entry are proof of US$600 in the bank and a yellow fever certificate. There is a **Panamanian consul** in Capurganá: T824 3173. **Note** Colombian pesos are impossible to change at fair rates in Panama.

To Panama listings

For Sleeping and Eating price codes and other relevant information, see Essentials, pages 38-40.

Sleeping

Mompós *p951*

It is essential to book in advance for Semana Santa and other festival periods, when prices go up.

A Hostal Doña Manuela, C Real del Medio (Cra 2), 17-41, T685 5612/5142, mabe642@yahoo.com. A converted colonial merchant's house, a/c, quiet and peaceful, restaurant is the best in town, pool also open to the public for the day US$2. Good service, knowledgeable managers. Art gallery and jewellery shop. Recommended. Under same management is **C Hacienda San Ignacio**, a few kilometres out of town on the road to Talaigua, modern, with pool and horse riding.

B-E La Casa Amarilla, C 13, No 1-05, T685 6326, www.lacasaamarillamompos.com. 1 block up from the Iglesia Santa Bárbara on the riverfront, 6 luxury rooms with a/c, bath and cable TV, 3 economic rooms with bath and fan (**E**), and an a/c dorm (**F** pp), beautifully decorated. All rooms open onto a cloister-style colonial garden. English owner Richard McColl is an excellent source of information on Colombia. TV, DVD player, book exchange, use of kitchen, tours arranged to silver filigree workshops and to wetlands for birdwatching and swimming (US$10 pp).

C Casa Hotel Villa de Mompós, 500 m east of Parque Bolívar, T685 5208. Charming, family-run, decorated with antique bric-a-brac, internet US$1 per hr. Also arranges rooms for families during festivals.

C La Casona, Cra 2, No 18-58, T685 5307, eusedeal@yahoo.es. Fine colonial building with delightful courtyards and plants. Billiard table, TV, a/c, laundry service and internet access.

C San Andrés, Cra 2, No 18-23, T685 5886. Another fine, restored colonial building. The patio has parrots and aquariums. Has own water and electricity supply and can arrange guides.

Tolú to Turbo: Tolú *p951*
B Alcira, Av La Playa, No 21-151, T288 5016, alcirahotel@yahoo.com. On the promenade, a/c, laundry service, parking, Wi-Fi. Breakfast included.
B Playamar, Av La Playa, No 22-22, T286 0587, playamar@yahoo.es. On the *malecón* with lemon trees outside. Wi-Fi, a/c, minibar, parking, TV. Small restaurant serving breakfast for US$3-5.
D Altamar, Cra 3, No 17-36, T288 5421. Bright rooms, has own water and electricity supply. Prices more than double in high season.
D Darimar, C 17, No 1-60, T2885153. Just off the beach, small but clean rooms, TV, parking, helpful.
D Mar Adentro, Av La Playa 11-36, T2860079. Belonging to tour agency of same name. Nice rooms, **E** with fan.
D-E pp **Estado Natural Ecolodge**, 7 km from San Bernardo del Viento, T311-691 0325, www.estado-natural.com. Rustic cabins on a beach, composting toilets and other sustainable practices, meals not inlcuded, cabins have kitchen, activities include birdwatching, windsurfing, trips to Isla Fuerte, riding and guided tours.
E Villa Babilla, C 20, No 3-40, Barrio el Cangrejo, T288 6124, www.villababillahostel. com. Run by Colombian/German team. 3 blocks from beach, well-organized, dorms, new rooms with bath, good restaurant, Wi-Fi, laundry service, good information on diving and island tours. Recommended travellers' hostel.
F El Turista, Av La Playa, No 11-20, T288 5145. The cheapest option in town and good value for money. Next to all the tour agencies.

Arboletes *p 952*
E Ganadero, C Principal, T820 0086. Basic but clean rooms. Restaurant serves basic fare for US$3.50.
E La Floresta, C Principal, T820 0034. Opposite **Ganadero**. Simple rooms with bath, street-facing rooms have windows.

To Capurganá: Turbo *p952*
C Castilla de Oro, T827 2185. C 100, No 14-07, T827 2185. Best in town, a/c, safety box, good restaurant, pool, reliable water and electricity. Helpful staff.
C Simona del Mar, Km 13 Vía Necoclí, T824 5682, www.simonadelmar.com. A few km outside town, so a good, safe option. *Cabañas* in a tranquil setting near the beach, good restaurant. A taxi to Turbo US$11. You can also ask *colectivos* to drop you there.
C-E Hotel 2000, C 101, No 11-115, T827 2333. Near bus terminal, TV, bath, less with fan.

Acandí: San Francisco *p952*
C pp **Al Vaivén de Hamacas**, San Francisco, T321-643 1171, http://alvaivenreserva. blogspot.com. Price is half board, cheaper without bath, Thai and Colombian food, a resort accessible by boat from Turbo (0900, 1200) or Capurganá (0730, 1 hr), with trekking and horse riding on the beach or in the jungle, boat tours, kayak tours to nearby islands, fishing and river bathing, English spoken.

Capurganá *p952*
Accomodation and food are generally more expensive than in other parts of Colombia, but there are cheaper options. Luxury and cheaper *cabañas* are available. There are several private houses for rent.
A Playa de Capurganá, T04-331 8680 (Medellín) T316-482 5781, www.jardin botanicodarien.com/condominio.htm. In tropical gardens, comfortable rooms, fine veranda with hammocks, swimming pool on the beach. Price includes breakfast and dinner. Recommended.
B Marlin Hostal, Playa de los Pescadores, T824 3611, capurgana marlin@yahoo.es. The best mid-range option in town, good rooms, also bunks (**F**), good restaurant serving excellent fish.
C Cabaña Darius, T314-622 5638, www.cabanadarius.com. In the grounds of Playa de Capurganá, excellent value, simple, comfortable rooms in tropical gardens, fan, breakfast included.
D Hostal Capurganá, C del Comercio, T316-743 3863, www.hostalcapurgana.net. Comfortable, pleasant patio, well situated. Recommended.

Sapzurro
D Zingara Canañas, Camino La Miel, T313-673 3291. Almost the last building in Colombia, 2 lovely *cabañas* overlooking the bay. The owners have a herb and vegetable garden and sell home-made chutneys. This also doubles up as the village pharmacy.
E Paraíso Sapzurro, T824 4115, 313-685 9862, paraisosapzurro@yahoo.com. *Cabañas*on the

beach at the southern end of the village, Chilean-run (ask for El Chileno). Also has space for camping (US$3 or US$4 with tent hire).

Eating

Mompós *p 951*

Fuafua's, on Parque Bolívar. Grand old dining hall overlooking the plaza, serves *comida corriente*.

La Pizzería, opposite San Agustín church. Good pizzas in a lovely setting.

D'La Villa, C 18, No 2-49. Bakery/ ice cream parlour also serving crêpes.

Tolú to Turbo: Tolú *p951*

La 15, Av La Playa, No 15 esquina. Good quality steaks with swift service. Recommended.

La Red, Av La Playa, No 20. Cheap but good seafood, steaks, burgers and hotdogs.

Punto B, C 15, No 2-02. Cheap and cheerful restaurant and *panadería, comida corriente*, US$3.

Capurganá *p952*

Donde Josefina, Playa La Caleta, T316-779 7760. Exquisite seafood, served under a shady tree on the beach.

El Patacón, C del Comercio. Serves good, simple seafood.

Pizzería Mi Ciclo, T314-789 1826. Delicious pizzas from an oven in the dueña's bedsit. Ask around for her on C del Comercio, near Capurganá Tours.

Activities and tours

Tolú to Turbo: Tolú *p951*

Club Náutico Mundo Marino, Av La Playa, No 14-40, T288 4431, www.clubnauticomundo marino.com. Daily tours to San Bernardo Islands at 0800, returning at 1600, US$20, including the aquarium on Isla Palma, includes a 3-hr stay on Múcura where there are shacks serving seafood. Mar Adentro, Av La Playa 11-36, T286 0079, www.club nauticomaradentro.com. A good agency.

Capurganá *p952*

Capurganá Tours, C del Comercio, T682 8858, www.capurganatours.com. Organizes walking tours with knowledgeable guides, as well as horse riding, diving and birdwatching. Trips to San Blas islands in Panama arranged if enough people. Can assist in booking flights from Puerto Obaldía to Panama City. English spoken, internet with Skype, will exchange cash on credit cards for a 6.5% commission. Highly recommended.

Dive and Green, near the jetty, T682 8825, www.diveandgreen.com. The only dive centre in town that does PADI. Excursions to San Blas. English spoken. Ask about house for rent: **Cabaña de los Alemanes**.

Transport

Mompós *p951*

Bus and ferry From **Cartagena**: with **Unitransco**, direct at 0700, US$17, bus returns at 0600 from outside Iglesia Santa Bárbara; or colectivo to La Bodega, US$3 pp, *chalupa* (motorized canoe) to Magangué, US$3.50, and finally bus to Cartagena. **Asotranstax** runs a door-to-door colectivo service between Mompós and **Santa Marta**, US$20; and Mompós and Taganga, US$25. To **Medellín**, taxi to La Bodega, then *chalupa* to Magangué and finally bus with **Brasilia**, 10-12 hrs, US$43, or from Magangué take a bus to **Sincelejo**, then a **Brasilia** or **Rápido Ochoa** bus to Medellín, 8-10 hrs, US$35. **Unitransco** has direct service to **Barranquilla**, leaving at 0600. From **Bogotá**, **Copetran** and **Omega** have services to **El Banco** at 1700, 13 hrs, US$35, then take a 4WD to Mompós, US$12 (US$12.50 a/c), 1 hr. From **Bucaramanga**, **Cotransmagdalena** direct early morning bus, or this company, **Copetran** or **Cotaxi** bus to El Banco, several daily, US$25, then 4WD to Mompós, 8 hrs in all.

Tolú to Turbo: Tolú *p951*

Tolú

Brasilia hourly to **Cartagena** between 0715 and 1730, US$15. 12 a day to **Medellín** with **Brasilia** and **Rápido Ochoa**, US$53, via Montería except at night. **Bogotá**, 3 a day, US$83. To **Barranquilla**, **Santa Marta** and **Riohacha**, 5 a day, US$33.

To Capurganá: Turbo *p952*

Buses From **Medellín**, buses every 1½ hrs to Turbo, 10-12 hrs, US$25-30. To **Montería**, US$12.50, 4-5 hrs. Fewer from **Cartagena**. Check safety carefully before travelling by road to/from Turbo.

Ferries Launches for **Acandí**, **Capurganá** and **Sapzurro** leave daily at 0800, US$26, 3 hrs.

Turbo's port is know as El Waffe. It's a spectacular journey that hugs the Caribbean shoreline of Darién. Rush for a seat at the back as the journey is bumpy and can be painful in seats at the front. **Note** There is a 10 kg limit on baggage, excess is US$0.30 per kg. From mid-Dec to end-Feb the sea is very choppy and dangerous. We advise you not to make the journey at this time.

Capurganá *p952*
Air 1 flight daily to **Medellín** with **Aerolíneas de Antioquia** (ADA), US$400 return. Same company Medellín-Acandí US$150 one way. Twin Otter biplanes with16 passenger capacity. Be sure to book ahead. Baggage limit of 10 kg. Excess is US$2 per kg. You may be asked to allow your baggage to follow on a later plane if seriously overweight.
Ferries Daily launch to **Turbo**, 0800, US$27. Launch Capurganá-**Sapzurro** US$11 (5 people minimum), 30 mins. There are daily launches to **Puerto Obaldía** in Panama, US$20. From here it is possible to fly to **Panama City** with **Aeroperlas**. It is also possible to catch a further launch from Puerto Obaldía to **Mulatuto**, US$20, and from there on to **Colón**, US$66.

Directory

Tolú to Turbo: Tolú *p951*
Banks There are several banks with ATMs on the Parque Principal. **Internet** Cyber Blue, C 15, No 2, headphones and camera.

Barranquilla → *Phone code: 5. Colour map 1, A3. Population: 1,109,000.*

Barranquilla lies on the western bank of the Río Magdalena, about 18 km from its mouth, which, through deepening and the clearing of silted sandbars, makes it a seaport as well as a river port. During recent years, the city's commercial and industrial importance and its port have declined. Few colonial buildings remain. In the northwest of the city are pleasant leafy residential areas and parks. **Tourist information**: available at hotels and the **tourist police** ⓘ *Cra 43, No 47-53, T351 0415/340 9903*. The tourist office is at ⓘ *C 40, No 45-46, Edif de la Gobernación p 5, T351 0311*.

The main reason people visit Barranquilla is for its famous annual **Carnival**, held 40 days before Easter week, end-February/beginning of March. It's one of the oldest in Latin America and less commercial and touristy than the Rio Carnival. In 2003 UNESCO declared it a "masterpiece of the oral and intangible heritage of humanity". Pre-carnival parades and dances last through January until an edict that everyone **must** party is read out. Carnival itself lasts from Saturday, with the Batalla de las Flores, through the Gran Parada on Sunday, to the funeral of Joselito Carnaval on Tuesday. The same families going back generations participate, keeping the traditions of the costumes and dances intact. Prepare for three days of intense revelry and dancing with friendly and enthusiastic crowds, spectacular float processions, parades and beauty queens. The main action is along Calle 17, Carrera 44 and Vía 40. Tickets for the spectator stands are sold in major restaurants and bars, eg **Froggs Leggs** (see Bars and clubs). **La Casa de Carnaval** ⓘ *Cra 54, No 49B-39, T379 3787, www.carnavaldebarranquilla.org*, is the official office and the best place for information.

The church of **San Nicolás**, formerly the Cathedral, stands on Plaza San Nicolás, the central square, and before it is a small statue of Columbus. The new **Catedral Metropolitana** ⓘ *Cra 45, No 53-120, opposite Plaza de la Paz*, has an impressive statue of Christ inside by the Colombian sculptor, Arenas Betancur. The commercial and shopping districts are round Paseo Bolívar, the main boulevard, a few blocks north of the old Cathedral, and in Avenida Murillo. The **Museo Romántico** ⓘ *Cra 54, No 59-199*, covers the city's history with an interesting section on Carnival.

Barranquilla also attracts visitors because the most important national and international football matches are held here in Colombia's largest stadium, **Estadio Metropolitano** ⓘ *Av Murillo, outside the city*. The atmosphere is considered the best in the country. Regular buses run from Paseo Bolívar and the church at Calle 33 y Carrera 41 to the attractive bathing resort of **Puerto Colombia**, 20 minutes. The **Pradomar Hotel** ⓘ *Calle 2, No 22-61, T309 6011* (**B** good beach bar and restaurant), offers surfing lessons. South along the Magdalena, 5 km from the city, is **Soledad** (*Population: 16,000*); around the cathedral are narrow, colonial streets.

Barranquilla listings

For Sleeping and Eating price codes and other relevant information, see Essentials, pages 38-40.

Sleeping

Barranquilla *p956*

Hotel prices rise significantly during Carnival, essential to book well in advance.

LL El Prado, Cra 54, No 70-10, T369 7777, reservas@hotel pradosa.com. A landmark in Barranquilla, 1930s building, traditional service. Fantastic pool shaded by palm trees, various restaurants, tennis courts and a gym.

AL Barranquilla Plaza, Cra 51B, No 79-246, T361 0333, www.hbp.com.co. Popular business hotel, 360° views from the 26th floor restaurant. All amenities including gym, spa, sauna and Wi-Fi.

A Majestic, Cra 53, No 54-41, T349 1010, hotelmajestic@metrotel.net.co. An oasis of calm, fine pool, large, fresh rooms, restaurant.

C San Francisco, C 43, No 43-128, T379 2927. Bright rooms, courtyard full of songbirds, a good, safe bet, laundry service, restaurant, internet.

D Girasol, C 44, No 44-103, T379 3191, www.elhotelgirasol.com. Safe, restaurant, Wi-Fi in all rooms.

E Hotel del Mar, C 42, No 35-57, T341 3703. Popular with locals, probably the best budget option. Good rooms and service, good value including in restaurant.

F El Diamante, C 41, No 38-65, T379 0157. With fan, more with a/c, TV room, laundry, parking.

Eating

Barranquilla *p956*

Many places, for all tastes and budgets, on C 70 from **Hotel El Prado** towards Cra 42. At C 70 y 44B are several *estaderos*, bars with snacks and verandas. Many upmarket restaurants along Carrera 53. There are numerous good Arab restaurants, especially Lebanese, in Barranquilla due to waves of Arab immigration in the 20th century.

TTT-TT **Arabe Gourmet**, Cra 49C, No 76-181. More formal and expensive than others.

TTT-TT **La Cueva** C 59 y Cra 43. Formerly a high-class brothel and a favourite haunt of Gabriel García Márquez and his literati friends during the 1950s. Now its bohemian charm has gone, but it's still worth a visit for the interesting photos. Good typical food, live Cuban music at the weekends.

TT **Arabe Internacional**, C 93, No 47-73, T378 2803. Good Arab cuisine in informal setting.

T **Don Pepe**, Cra 53, No 53-90, T379 9234. Opposite the **Hotel Majestic**, serves *comida santandereana.*

T **La Fonda Antioqueña**, Cra 52, No 70-73, T360 0573. And T **Los Helechos**, Cra 52, No 70-70, T356 7493. Opposite each other, both offer *comida antioqueña* in a good atmosphere.

T **Pescadero del Centro**, Cra 44, No 42-43. A favourite, seving local seafood.

Bars and clubs

Barranquilla *p956*

Froggs Leggs, C 93, No 43-122. Popular bar, good atmosphere.

Henry's Bar, C 80, No 53-18, CC Washington. Popular US-style bar, pizzería downstairs. Open daily from 1600.

Shopping

Barranquilla *p956*

Bookshop Librería Nacional, in CC Buenavista (see below). Small selection of English books.

Market San Andrecito, or Tourist Market, Vía 40, is where smuggled goods are sold at very competitive prices; a good place to buy film. Picturesque and reasonably safe. Any taxi driver will take you there.

Shopping centres Centro Comercial **Buenavista**, Cra 53, C 98, has a good selection of shops, cinemas and fast food outlets.

Transport

Barranquilla *p956*

Air Ernesto Cortissoz airport is 10 km from the city. Daily flights to **Bogotá**, **Cartagena** and **Medellín**, also to **Bucaramanga**, **Montería** and **Valledupar**. International flights to **Aruba**, **Curaçao**, **Miami** and **Panama City**. City bus from airport to town, US$0.35 (US$0.40 on Sun). Taxi to town, US$7 (taxis do not have meters, fix fare in advance). To town, take only buses marked 'centro' from 200 m to right when leaving airport; the bus to the airport (marked Malambo) leaves from Cra 44 up C 32 to Cra 38, then up C 30 to Airport. Taxi to Cartagena,

US$15 pp, leave when full. **Avianca**, C 72, No 57-79, T353 4691.

Bus The main bus terminal is south of the city near the Circunvalación. Some bus companies have offices around C 34 and Cra 45. Take a bus marked 'Terminal' along C 45. To **Santa Marta**, US$5.50, **Brasilia**, 2 hrs, also direct to Santa Marta's Rodadero beach. To **Valledupar**, 5-6 hrs, US$14. To **Bucaramanga**, US$55 with **Copetran**, a/c, first class, departures at 1130 most days, 9 hrs. To **Bogotá**, 24 hrs, frequent, US$78 direct with **Berlinas del Fonce**. To **Maicao**, US$22, 6 hrs (with **Brasilia**, every 30 mins from 0100-1200). To **Cartagena**, 2½-3 hrs, US$6.50-8, several companies; by *Brasilia Van Tours* mini-bus, from their downtown offices as well as the bus terminals, 2 hrs by colectivo, US$14.

Taxi Taxis within the town cost US$1.60 (eg downtown to northern suburbs).

Directory

Barranquilla *p956*

Banks Bancolombia, Banco de Bogotá, etc, and many ATMs. *Casa de cambio* **El Cairo**, C 76, No 48-30, T360 6433, and at C 34, No 43-177, Paseo Bolívar, T379 9441. TCs, euros, dollars but not sterling, Mon-Fri and Sat 0900-1200. **Consulates** **Germany**, C 77B, No 57-141, Of 309, T368 5384. **Netherlands**, Cra 77B, No 57-141, of 806, T368 8387. **USA**, C 77B, No 57-141, of 511, T353 2001 (visas obtainable only in Bogotá). **Venezuela**, Edif Bancafé, Cra 52, No 69-96, p 3, T358 0048, cvenezbq@metrotel.net.co, 0800-1500, visa issued same day, but you must be there by 0915 with photo and US$30 cash; onward ticket may be requested. **Post offices** Plaza Bolívar. **Useful addresses** DAS: C 54, No 41-133, T371 7510.

Santa Marta, Tayrona and Ciudad Perdida

Santa Marta is a port with strong historical associations and popular beaches. Nearby are the Tayrona national park with pre-Columbian remains and the unspoilt Sierra Nevada de Santa Marta coastal range.

Santa Marta → *Phone code: 5. Colour map 1, A3. Population: 309,000.*

Santa Marta is Colombia's third largest Caribbean port and capital of Magdalena Department. It lies on a deep bay with high shelving cliffs to the north and south, at the mouth of the Río Manzanares. The snow-clad peaks of the Sierra Nevada, less than 50 km east, are occasionally visible. The main promenade (Carrera 1) along the sea front is lined with hotels, restaurants and bars and a beach reaching the port. Much more attractive beaches are to be found around Taganga and Parque Nacional Tayrona. Santa Marta is the base for treks to La Ciudad Perdida. For tourist information, go to **Alcaldía Distrital de Santa Marta** ⓘ *C 17, No 3-120, T300-816 1695, turismo@santamarta.gov.co*, which is helpful with lots of maps and brochures. For Magdalena department: ⓘ *Cra 1, No 15-16, Palacio Tayrona, T421 1356.*

Santa Marta was the first town founded by the *conquistadores* in Colombia, in 1525 by Rodrigo de Bastidas. Most of the famous sea-dogs – the brothers Côte, Drake and Hawkins – sacked the city despite the forts on the mainland. It was here that Simón Bolívar, his dream of Gran Colombia shattered, came to die. Almost penniless, he stayed at San Pedro Alejandrino *hacienda*, see below. He died, aged 47, on 17 December 1830, apparently from tuberculosis, and was buried in the Cathedral, but his body was taken to the Pantheon at Caracas 12 years later.

In the city centre, well-preserved colonial buildings and early churches still remain and more are currently being restored. On **Plaza de la Catedral** is the impressive white cathedral ⓘ *Cra 4, C 16/17, open for Mass daily at 0600 and 1800 (more frequently on Sun), possibly also at 1000*, on the site of what is claimed to be Colombia's oldest church and one of the oldest in Latin America. **Casa de la Aduana/Museo del Oro Tairona** ⓘ *Calle 14, No 2-07 on main plaza, Tue-Sat 0800-1200, 1400-1800, Sun and holidays 0800-1200 (tourist season), Mon-Fri 0800-1200, 1400-1800 (the rest of the year), free*, has an excellent archaeological collection, Tayrona culture exhibits and precolombian gold artefacts; visit recommended before going to Ciudad Perdida.

Museo Etnográfico de la Universidad del Magdalena ⓘ *Cra 1, C 22, 0800-1900, US$3*, traces the history of Santa Marta, its port and the Tayrona culture, well-displayed.

Quinta de San Pedro Alejandrino ⓘ *daily 0930-1630, US$3; take a bus or colectivo from the waterfront, Cra 1 C, in Santa Marta to Mamatoca and ask for the Quinta, US$0.25*, a 17th-century villa surrounded by gardens 5 km southeast of the city. Here is the simple room in which Simón Bolívar died, with a few of his belongings. Other paintings and memorabilia of the period are on display. This is an elegant memorial to Colombia's most revered man.

Sandy beaches and headlands stretch all along this coast, surrounded by hills, green meadows and shady trees. The largest sandy bay is that of Santa Marta, with Punta Betín, a rocky promontory protecting the harbour to the north and a headland to the south. The rugged Isla El Morro lies 3 km off Santa Marta, topped by a lighthouse. **Playa El Rodadero** is a crowded, tacky beach resort, 4 km south of the city (local bus service, taxi, US$3). Many of the buses coming from Barranquilla and Cartagena stop at Rodadero on the way to Santa Marta.

Launches leave Rodadero beach every hour for the Aquarium, US$3 entry, last boat back 1600. From the Aquarium, it's a 10-minute walk to Playa Blanca where swimming is less crowded than elsewhere. Food is available at beach.

Around Santa Marta

The paved coast road to Santa Marta from Barranquilla passes salt pans and skirts the **Ciénaga de Santa Marta** *entry US$9*, where all types of water birds, plants and animals may be seen. Cutting off the egress to the sea to build the coast road caused an ecological disaster, but a National Environment Programme is working to reopen the canals and restore the area. There are several villages built on stilts in the lake. On the east shore of the lagoon is **Ciénaga** (*Population: 75,000*), famous for *cumbia* music.

Aracataca, 60 km south of Ciénaga and 7 km before Fundación, is the birthplace of **Gabriel García Márquez**, fictionalized as Macondo in some of his stories (notably *100 Years of Solitude*). His home, now a modest museum, may be seen in the backyard of La Familia Iriarte Ahumada; it

Santa Marta

Sleeping
1 Bahía
2 Bahía Blanca
3 Casa Vieja
4 Hospedaría Casa Familiar
5 Miramar
6 Nueva Granada
7 Residencias El Titanic
8 Tayromar
9 Turismar

Eating
1 Donde Chucho
2 El Balcón Colonial
3 Manuel
4 Mañe Cayon
5 Merkabar
6 Ricky's

Bars & clubs
7 La Puerta

N
200 metres
200 yards

is 1½ blocks from the plaza, ask for directions. There are *residencias* (under US$3) and a restaurant, but it is better to stay in **Fundación**.

Along the Santa Marta-Riohacha road is **Quebra de Valencia** ⓘ *US$1.20*, several natural swimming pools amid waterfalls, with good views. From the marked roadside entrance, it is a pleasant 20 minutes' walk along a clear path, or horse ride, to the waterfalls. It can get overcrowded during high season. Drinks and snacks available along the way.

Taganga

Close to Santa Marta is the popular fishing village and beach of Taganga, set in a little bay with good views. It is peaceful, laid back and Taganga's small community is very welcoming, which lures most visitors to stay far longer than planned. Swimming is good, especially on Playa Grande, 25 minutes' walk round coast or US$2-3 by boat, but watch out for thieving. Taganga is quiet during the week, but it is crowded on Sunday. Good fresh fish is served at places along the beach. Taganga is a popular place for diving and several well-established dive shops offer good value PADI courses. There is a good book exchange shop but no ATMs.

Parque Nacional Tayrona

ⓘ *0800-1700, US$16.50 foreigners, US$3.20 motorcycle, US$4.75 car. During high season, the park is very crowded. Sometimes it closes temporarily for a variety of reasons, but never for long. Best to arrive early. Park accommodation in Arrecifes and Cañaveral is managed by Aviatur, C 15, No 3-20, T421 3848, reservasparques@aviatur.com.co, T01-900-331 2222/01-382 1616, or Bogotá, T381 7111. National parks office: C 17, No 4-06, Santa Marta, T422 0655.*

Stretching north of Taganga for some 85 km is the beautiful and mostly unspoilt coastline of Tayrona National Park, where, in its lush vegetation, you can see monkeys, iguanas and maybe snakes. The park entrance is at the east end of the park, at El Zaino, 35 km from Santa Marta. Tickets are sold here. It is a one hour walk into the park from the gate, or take a colectivo from the park entrance, US$0.50. The road goes to **Cañaveral**. 45 minutes west of Cañaveral on foot, or by horse, is **Arrecifes**, from where it is 45 minutes' walk to Cabo, then 1½ hours on a clear path up to the archaeological site of **Pueblito**. A guided tour around the site is free, every Saturday or as arranged with a park guard. Other Tayrona relics abound. At Pueblito there are indigenous people; do not photograph them. From Pueblito you can either return to Cañaveral, or continue for a pleasant two-hour walk up to Calabazo on the Santa Marta- Riohacha road. A circuit Santa Marta, Cañaveral, Arrecifes, Pueblito, Calabazo, Santa Marta in one day needs a 0700 start at least. It is easier (more downhill) to do the circuit in reverse, ask to be dropped at Calabazo. Tours can be arranged at several hotels and agencies in Santa Marta. Bathing near Cañaveral must take account of frequent heavy pounding surf and treacherous tides. Every year, people drown because they do not heed the warnings. Some 40 minutes' walk left along the beach is Arrecifes, but because of rocks and the dangerous surf, authorities do not recommend this route. Beyond Arrecifes, walk 30 minutes to La Piscina, a beautiful, safe natural swimming pool, excellent snorkelling. Neguangue beach can be reached by colectivo from Santa Marta Market at 0700, return 1600, US$7. For good snorkelling, take a 10-minute boat ride from Neguangue beach to Playa Cristal/Playa Muerto. There are other beaches accessible by coastal path, or by boat.

It is advisable to inform park guards when walking in the park. Wear hiking boots and beware of bloodsucking insects. Take food and water, but no valuables as robbery is common. You can hire horses to carry you and your luggage from Cañaveral to Arrecifes (US$8) and El Cabo de San Juan (US$18). Generally, the main trails and campsites are badly littered. The best information on the Park is in Santa Marta. See Transport, below, for how to get there.

Beyond Cañaveral, at Km 33.5 on the Santa Marta–Riohacha road, is **Los Angeles**, a camp site with access to fine empty beaches, excellent for surfing (hammocks or tents US$10 - less if you bring your own, simple meals available). Owner is Nohemi Ramos, see **Ecoturt**, page 965.

Ten minutes west of Los Angeles is the mouth of the Río Piedras, the border of Tayrona Park, where you can bathe and enjoy sights to rival those in the park. The paved coastal road continues from Tayrona and crosses into Guajira Department at **Palomino**, 80 km from Santa Marta, which has a fine beach and cheap *cabañas*.

Ciudad Perdida → *Colour map 1, A3.*

Ciudad Perdida was called Teyuna by the Tayrona, meaning mother nature. The city covers 400 ha and was built around AD 700. It was the political and trading centre of the Tayrona. The circular and oval stone terraces were once the living quarters for some 1,400-3,000 people. The city was also an important religious and burial site. The Tayrona built sophisticated irrigation systems and walls to prevent erosion. By around 1600, the Tayrona were almost wiped out by the conquistadores and the few who survived were forced to flee. For the next four centuries, the city disappeared under the forest growth. In 1973, tomb looters searching for gold known to exist in burial urns and graves, rediscovered the city by chance. By 1975, the city was officially re-found, attracting local and international anthropologists and archeologists who started to excavate, leading to the first tourist groups in 1984. Today the area is a protected indigenous reserve, where three main indigenous groups, the Koguis, Arhuacos and Arsarios, continue to live.

The 20-km trek to the Lost City is, at times, gruelling and challenging. It is not a leisurely walk, but is well worth the effort for a rewarding and memorable experience. The trek is perhaps more spectacular than the archeological site itself. Along with lush tropical humid and dry forests, abundant flora and fauna, there are crystal clear rivers, waterfalls and natural swimming pools. There are some 1,200 steep slippery steps to climb to the summit of the city. Watch out for snakes. Along the way, you will pass friendly Kogui villages. Archaeologists and army guards will ask you for your permit (obtainable in Santa Marta, at the national parks office, Turcol - see page 965, or ask at tourist office). Don't forget that Ciudad Perdida is in a National Park: it is strictly forbidden to damage trees and collect flowers or insects.

Sierra Nevada de Santa Marta

ⓘ *Entry US$9. For the latest information check with National Parks offices in Santa Marta and Bogotá, ICANH, C 12, No 2-41, Bogotá, T286 0021, www.icanh.gov.co, and the Fundación Pro-Sierra Nevada C 17, No 3-03, Santa Marta, T431 0551, www.prosierra.org, for guidance on what may be possible.*

The Sierra Nevada, covering a triangular area of 16,000 sq km, rises abruptly from the Caribbean to 5,800 m snow peaks in about 45 km, a gradient comparable with the south face of the Himalaya, and unequalled along the world's coasts. Pico Colón is the highest point in the country. The area is a drugs-growing, processing and transporting region. For this reason, the reluctance of some local *indígenas* to welcome visitors, plus the presence of guerrilla and paramilitary groups makes much of the Sierra Nevada de Santa Marta a no-go area. This is a tragedy since here can be found the most spectacular scenery and most interesting indigenous communities in the country.

In the foothills, there are places to visit: **Minca**, 20 km from Santa Marta, is a village surrounded by coffee *fincas* and begonia plantations, with several charming places to stay. Horse riding, birdwatching and tours further into the Sierra Nevada can be arranged from here. About 45 minutes' walk beyond the village is **El Pozo Azul**, a local swimming spot under a waterfall, which is popular at weekends but almost always empty during the week. Beyond Minca, the partly paved road rises steeply to San Lorenzo which is surrounded by a forest of palm trees. On the way to San Lorenzo is **La Victoria**, a large coffee *finca* which offers tours to demonstrate the coffee-making process. It is possible to stay in *cabañas* run by the park authorities near San Lorenzo.

Santa Marta, Tayrona and Ciudad Perdida listings

For Sleeping and Eating price codes and other relevant information, see Essentials, pages 38-40.

Sleeping

Santa Marta *p958, map p959*

In town

Av Rodrigo de Bastidas (Cra 1) has several high-rise hotels on the seafront while Cra 2 and connecting streets have a good choice of budget *residencias*. For groups of 4 or more, ask about apartments for short rent. It's essential to book ahead during high season, when some hotels increase their prices by 50%.

B Bahía Blanca, Cra 1A, No 11-13, T421 4439, www.hotelbahiablanca.com. Rooms around pleasant courtyard, helpful staff, a/c, less with fan. 30% cheaper in low season. Good.

C Casa Vieja, C 12, No 1-58, T431 1606, www.hotelcasavieja.com. A/c, less with fan, welcoming, good popular restaurant.

C Nueva Granada, C 12, No 3-17, T421 0685, www.hotelnuevagranada.com. Colonial building with rooms round a pleasant courtyard, quiet, cheaper with fan, safety-deposit in rooms, small pool, internet, bike hire, includes breakfast. Accepts credit cards, 45% cheaper in low season.

C Tayromar, C 20, No 1C-71, T421 7324, one block from beach, www.hoteltayromar.com. Helpful owners, well-organized, safety-deposit in rooms, modern, a/c (cheaper with fan), secure parking, good service. Recommended.

D Bahía, C 12, No 2-70, T4214057. Clean and modern but lacking character, a/c or fan, safe, restaurant, parking service.

D Turismar, Cra 1, No 11-41, T421 2408. A good option if you opt for a dorm but individual rooms are dark and spartan. Beachside, with pleasant courtyard.

F Hospedaría Casa Familiar, C 10 C, No 2-14, T421 1697, www.hospederiacasafamiliar.freeservers.com. Run by an extremely helpful family, rooms with fan, roof terrace where you can cook your own food. Has its own dive shop and organizes trips to Tayrona and Ciudad Perdida. Recommended.

F Miramar, C 10C, No 1C-59, T423 3276, 2 blocks from beach. Under new joint ownership, Jairo is very knowledgeable and helpful. Guides to the Ciudad Perdida hang around here, sells tours at the official price, also good for tours to Tayrona and Taganga (where they have *Hotel Ramarim*). Can be crowded, basic dorms and some nicer more expensive private rooms, luggage store, motorbike parking, Wi-Fi internet, cheap restaurant. Often full. Reservations via the internet (www.hosteltrail.com) and are held until 1500 on the day of arrival. Airline tickets also sold here.

F Residencias El Titanic, C 10C, No 1C-68, T421 1947. Fan, basic, safe, good value, motorbike parking, tours to Ciudad Perdida can also be bought here.

G The Dreamer Hostel, Cra 51, No 26D, 161 Los Trujillos, Mamatoco, T300-251 6534, www.thedreamerhostel.com. New hostel, opened in Dec 2009.

Playa El Rodadero

There are various short-let apartments available. Prices start from US$40 for 2 people with a/c, TV and balcony, near the beach. There are also many hotels ranging from luxury (our L grade) to more simple places (C). 3 recommendations are:

A La Sierra, Cra 1, No 9-47, T422 7960, lasierra@germanmoraleshijos.com. Fine hotel with pleasant terrace set back from beach, rooms with balcony and Wi-Fi.

B El Rodadero, C 11, No 1-29, T422 8323, www.hotelrodadero.com. Stylish, modern building with a touch of art deco. Excellent pool, rooms with fine views of the beach and breakfast is included.

B La Guajira, Cra 4, No 23F-05, entrance to El Rodadero, T422 0918. Pleasant, modern, Wayúu manageress can advise about travel to La Guajira. Good breakfast, pool, safe parking, includes 2 meals.

Around Santa Marta *p959*

Fundación

E Caroli, Cra 8, No 5-30, T414 0273, is the best.

E Centro del Viajero, with a/c, good value. Also **Hotel Milán**, T414 0227.

Taganga *p960*

A La Ballena Azul, Cra 1, No 18-01, T421 9009. Attractive hotel with French riveria touch, comfortable, spacious rooms with sea views, fan or a/c, breakfast included, Wi-Fi available, also run boat tours to secluded beaches, horses for hire. Nice restaurant on the beach, terrace bar. Works cosely with **Magic Tour Taganga**, T421 9432, www.magic tourstaganga.com.

B Bahía Taganga, C 4, No 1B-35, T421 9049, www.bahiataganga.com/index.php/lang-en. Unmissable sign on the cliff face. Overlooking bay, breakfast served on lovely terrace, hospitable, a/c, cheaper with fan, tastefully decorated.

B Casa Blanca, Cra 1, No 18-161, at the southern end of the beach, barbus85@ latinmail.com. Crumbling but characterful, each room has its own balcony with hammock, but security is poor. Good roof terrace.

C Techos Azules, Sector Dunkarinca, Cabaña 1-100, T421 9141, www.techosazules.com. Off the road leading into town, *cabañas* with good views over the bay, internet, free coffee, laundry service.

D La Casa de Felipe, Cra 5A, No 19-13, 500 m from beach behind football field, T421 9101, www.lacasadefelipe.com. Cosy traveller place run by knowledgeable French team of Jean Phillipe and Sandra Gibelin. Good kitchen facilities, excellent restaurant, Wi-Fi/internet, laundry, hospitable, relaxing hammock and spacious garden area with sea views, studio apartments, dorms and rooms. Good information on trips to Tayrona (maps provided), English spoken. Highly recommended.

E Bayview Hostel, Cra 4, No 178-57, T421 9128, bayviewhostel@gmail.com. With a technicolour façade, pleasant rooms, cheaper dorms, kitchen, 2 lounges with DVD player, Wi-Fi.

E Pelikan Hostal, Cra 2, No 17-04, T421 9057. Characterful, rooms with fan and bath, laundry service.

E-F pp **Divanga**, C 12, No 4-07, T421 9092, divangacolombia@yahoo.fr. French-owned hostel, doubles with private bath or 3-person dorm, includes great breakfast, comfortable, 5-mins' walk from beach, nice views, attentive service, lovely atmosphere, good pool, HI affiliated, Wi-Fi, internet. Recommended.

F Hostal Moramar, Cra 4, No-178-83, T421 9202, www.hostalmoramar.com. New, 2 blocks uphill from beach opposite football pitch. Simple, quiet, rooms with bath and fan, bright, airy, patio area, laundry, attentive owners, welcoming.

F-G Hotel Ramarim, C 12 entre Cra 3 y 4, T423 3276. Probably the cheapest option in Taganga. You get what you pay for. Basic rooms, camping is allowed in the patio but space is limited.

Parque Nacional Tayrona *p960*
Comfortable up-market cabins with thatched roofs (*ecohabs*) for 1-4 people cost from US$100-113 pp (4 people sharing) at **Cañaveral**, cabins for 1-5 people at **Arrecifes** cost from US$69-82 pp (both half board, full board and other packages available), prices fixed by **Aviatur** (address above). They offer privacy, great views over sea and jungle; both have decent restaurants. Both have campsites US$4.50-6.10 pp in 5-person tent; hammocks US$6.75; there are facilities, but only a tiny store at Cañaveral, take all supplies. Take insect repellant and beware falling coconuts and omnivorous donkeys.

On the path to Pueblito there is a campsite at **Cabo de San Juan** where there is excellent bathing. There is also a small restaurant and hammocks for hire (US$13 in high season, US$10 in low season); there are 2 *cabañas* on the rock that divides the 2 bays (US$50 high season, US$43 low); pitching your own tent costs US$7, tent hire for 2 people US$19. There are other camping and hammock places en route. There is nowhere to stay at Pueblito.

Sierra Nevada de Santa Marta *p961*
C Sierra's Sound, C Principal, Minca, T421 9993, www.sierra sound.es.tl. Italian-owned, overlooking a rocky river, hot water, home-made pasta, organized tours into the Sierra Nevada.
D La Casona, on the hill to the right as you enter Minca, T421 9958, lacasona@colombiaexotic.com. Converted convent with views of the valley below, owned by a sculptor from Bogotá, who runs the hostel with his family: "magical".
D Sans Souci, Minca, T421 9968, sanssouciminca@yahoo.com. Rambling house in beautiful garden, German owned, rooms in the house or separate apartments, swimming pool, kitchen, discount in exchange for gardening. Stunning views.

Eating

Santa Marta *p958, map p959*
In town
TTT Mañe Cayon, Cra 1a, No 26-37. Next to **Manuel** on the south side of town. Quality seafood in a good atmosphere.
TTT Manuel, Cra 1, No 26-167, T423 1449. Pricey but excellent seafood, popular at lunchtime.
TT Donde Chucho, Cra 2, No 16-39. A little expensive but well situated in the corner of Parque Santander. Serves seafood and pasta.
TT Ricky's, Cra 1a, No 17-05. Beachside restaurant serving international food, including Chinese. Reasonably priced.
T Merkabar, C 10C, No 2-11. Pastas, great pancakes, good juices and seafood. Family-run, good value and provides tourist information.
T Restaurante El Balcón Colonial, C 15, No 3-35. Serves typical and cheap food.

Taganga *p960*
T Donde Juanita, Cra 1, No17-1. Fine home-cooked food, fish, meat and good vegetarian options.
T Yiu Nu Sagu, C 12, No 1-08. Beachside pizzería, large helpings.

Bars and clubs

Santa Marta *p958, map p959*
Santa Marta is a party town with many new clubs, discos and bars opening every week. The website www.samarios.com is an excellent resource for finding out what's going on at night.
Barrio Sumario, C 17, between Cra 3 and 4. Popular bar playing local music in colonial setting and patio.
La Escollera, C 5, No 4-107, Lagunita (Rodadero), T422 9590, www.la-escollera.com. Huge club under open straw roof, one of the best, open till late, concerts.
La Puerta, C 17, between Cra 3 and 4. Excellent bar and atmosphere in colonial house. Recommended.

Taganga *p960*
El Garaje, C 8, No, 2-127, T421 9003. Plays hip hop and other forms of electronic music. Starts late, finishes late.
Mojito Net, C 14, No 1B-61. Open 0800-0200, happy hour 1400-2100. Live music, open mic sessions, wine, cocktails, food and internet.

Activities and tours

Santa Marta *p958, map p959*
Sendero Tairona, Cra 3, No 18-46, T4229505, clubsenderotayrona@gmail.com. A hiking club, trips to Tayrona Park and the Sierra Nevada from US$130, with transport, food, guides and accommodation included.

Sierra Tours, C 22, No 16-61, Santa Marta, www.sierratours-trekking.com. Also in Taganga, C 17, No 1-18, highly recommended for tours. Ciudad Perdida prices start at US$250 for a minimum of 5 people.
Turcol, Cra 1C, No 20-15, T421 2256, www.buritaca2000.com. Arranges trips to Ciudad Perdida, Tayrona, Pueblito, Guajira and provides a guide service.

Taganga *p960*

Diving

Aquantis, B&B and Diving, C 18, No 1-39, T316-818 4285, www.aquantisdivecenter.com. Belgian-run, PADI-certified, passionate team, PADI course US$285. Recommended.
Oceano Scuba, Cra 1A, No 17-07, T421 9004, www.oceano scuba.com.co. PADI courses, 2, 3 and 4 days from US$70.
Octopus Diving Center, C 15, No 1b-14, T317-327 7570, octopusdivingcenter@ gmail.com. PADI, NAUI and BIS courses. Night and wreck dives are offered. English spoken.
Poseidon Dive Center, C 18, No 1-69, T421 9224, www.poseidondivecenter.com. PADI courses at all levels and the only place on the Colombian Caribbean coast to offer an instructor course. Offers a tourist package with no sales tax. German owner, with English and Croatian spoken. Own pool for beginners, also has rooms to rent.
Tayrona Dive Center, Cra 2, No 18a-22, T421 9195, www.tayronadivecenter.com. Mini course with 2 dives is US$77.

Tayrona National Park *p960*

Ecoturt, Nohemi Ramos or Jarven Rodríguez, T3163738846, ecoturt@ latinmail.com. Highly recommended for guided tours of Pueblito and other parts of the park. Some English spoken.

Ciudad Perdida *p961*

Tours

Six-day trips can be organized by the tourist office and **Turcol** in Santa Marta. Ask also at hotels in Santa Marta (eg **Hotel Miramar**) or Taganga. The cost is about US$250 pp. Under no circumstances should you deal with unauthorized guides, check with the tourist office if in doubt, and try to get views of the quality of guides from travellers who have already done the trip.

It is 3 days there, 1 day (2 nights) at the site, and 2 days back. You will need to take a tent or a hammock and mosquito net (on organized tours these may be supplied by the guide), a good repellent, sleeping bag, warm clothing for the night, torch, plastic bags to keep everything dry, and strong, quick-drying footwear. Small gifts for the indigenous children are appreciated. Be prepared for heavy rain. Check conditions, especially information on river crossings, and ensure you have adequate food, a water bottle and water purifying tablets before you start. Leave no rubbish behind and encourage the guides to ensure no one else does. Going on your own is discouraged and dangerous. Route finding is very difficult and unwelcoming *indígenas*, paramilitaries and drug traders increase the hazards. Scores of tours leave Santa Marta every 3-4 days during the year, experiencing no problems.

Transport

Santa Marta *p958, map p959*

Air Simón Bolívar, 20 km south of city; bus, US$0.35, taxi from Santa Marta, US$7, from Rodadero, US$4. Daily flights to **Bogotá** and **Medellín**; connections to other cities. During the tourist season, get to the airport early and book well ahead (the same goes for bus reservations).
Bus Terminal southeast of the city, towards Rodadero, minibus US$0.30; taxi US$2.50 to centre, US$3.50 to Rodadero. To **Bogotá**, 7 daily, 16 hrs, US$72, **Brasilia** or **Berlinas del Fonce**. To **Medellín**, 6 daily, 15 hrs, US$70, **Brasilia** or **Copetran**. **Copetran** and **Brasilia** to **Bucaramanga** about 9 hrs, US$50, frequent departures 0700-2200. Journey time is dependent on the number of police checks. Buses to **Barranquilla**, 7 daily, 2 hrs, US$5.50. To **Cartagena**, 5 hrs US$14, **Brasilia**. To **Riohacha** US$12, 4 hrs. Frequent buses to **Maicao**, US$17.25 a/c, also cheaper non a/c, 4-5 hrs.
Car (port) Without a *carnet de passages*, it can take up to 4 working days to get a car out of the port, but it is usually well guarded and it is unlikely that anything will be stolen.

Around Santa Marta: Aracataca and Fundación *p959*

Bus **Ciénaga**-Fundación, US$1; Fundación-Aracataca, US$0.25; **Santa Marta**-Fundación, US$6; **Barranquilla**, goes via Ciénaga, US$2.50.

Taganga *p960*

Minibus from **Santa Marta** US$0.60 (frequent, 0600-2130), **taxi** US$3, 15-20 mins.

Parque Nacional Tayrona *p960*

Bus To get to the park entrance in El Zaino, take a minibus from the market in Santa Marta, Cra 11 y C 11, about US$2, 45 mins, frequent service from 0700, last back about 1630 (check on the day with the bus driver). Tourist bus from **Hotel Miramar** in Santa Marta daily at 1100, US$4.50. This returns early afternoon; visitors normally stay overnight. Other hotels help in arranging tours, but there is no need to take guides (who charge US$20 or more pp for a day trip). Hire a boat in Taganga to Arrecifes, about 2 hrs along the scenic coast, US$110 for 8.

Directory

Santa Marta *p958, map p959*

Airline offices **Avianca**, Edif de los Bancos, Cra 2B y C 14, T214 4018, T432 0106 at airport. **Banks** Most banks and ATMs in Plaza Bolívar. eg **Banco Occidente** (good rates for MasterCard). Plenty of cash machines. *Casas de cambio* in 3rd block of C 14. **Immigration** **DAS Office**, C 26, No 8-15, T423 1961. Mon-Fri, 0730-1200, 1400-1800. **Internet** **Mundo Digital**, C 15, No 2B-19, Edif Los Bancos, just off Plaza Bolívar, Mon-Sat 0700-2000, Sun 0900-1700. International calls too. **Tama Café**, C16 with Cra 13, open 0800-1230 and 1400-1830, sells delicious food too.

Taganga *p960*

Banks ATM, all major credit cards, next to the police station half a block up from **Poseidon Dive Center**. **Internet** **Playanet**, Cra 1, No 15-9, T421 9296, also sells credit for mobile phones. Another at Cra 3 y C 14.

To Venezuela

Roads head for the insalubrious border town of Maicao, but on the way is plenty of interest: lagoons where flamingos feed, the pleasant city of Valledupar, which is home to Colombia's famous vallenato music, and the arid, empty Guajira Peninsula with its wildlife and special Wayúu culture.

Riohacha and around → *Phone code: 5. Colour map 1, A4. Population: 142,000.*

The port of Riohacha, 160 km east of Santa Marta and capital of Guajira Department, comes alive at the weekend, when it fills with party-goers and music (almost always vallenato) springs up all over the place. It was founded in 1545 by Nicolás Federmann, and in early years its pearling industry was large enough to tempt Drake to sack it (1596). Pearling almost ceased during the 18th century and the town was all but abandoned. Today, there is a pleasant stretch of beach with shady palms and a long wooden pier. A promenade along the beachfront (Calle 1) is lined with banks, hotels, restaurants and tour agencies. It is common to see Wayúus selling their wares and beautiful handmade *mochilas* (bags) along the seafront. Riohacha is a useful base for exploring the semi-desert landscape of La Guajira. Tourist office: **Dirección de Turismo de la Guajira** ⓘ *C 1 y Cra 4, Antigua Terraza Marina, T727 1015*, little information, better to ask tour operators. Ask for the University of the Guajira, which has an excellent resource centre related to the region and the Wayuú culture (ID is necessary to get in).

Santuario Los Flamencos

ⓘ *US$16.50. 95 km east of Santa Marta and 25 km short of Riohacha.*

There are several small and two large saline lagoons (Laguna Grande and Laguna de Navío Quebrado), separated from the Caribbean by sand bars. The latter is near Camarones (colectivo from Riohacha, new market) which is just off the main road. About 3 km beyond Camarones is 'La Playa', a popular beach to which some colectivos continue at weekends. Flamingos normally visit the large lagoons between October and December, during the wet season, though some birds are there all year. They are believed to migrate to and from the Dutch Antilles, Venezuela and Florida. Across Laguna de Navío Quebrado is a warden's hut on the sand bar, ask to be ferried across by local fishermen or the park guards. The national parks office has comfortable cabins (**E**) for up to eight, open all year. Showers available; meals at the tiendas by the entrance. There are several bars and two stores on the beach.

Valledupar ➔ *Phone code: 55. Colour map 1, A4. Population: 348,000. Altitude: 110 m.*
South of Riohacha on an alternative road to Maicao and the Venezuelan border is **Cuestecita** (*Hotel Turismo*), where you can turn southwest to **Barrancas**, with one of the largest coal mines in the world, **El Cerrejón** ⓘ *T350 5705, for information about pre-arranged visits to the mine.* Continuing on this road, which takes you either round the Sierra Nevada to Barranquilla and Santa Marta via Fundación (see above) or south to Bucaramanga, you come to **Valledupar**, capital of César Department. Valledupar claims to be the home of the *vallenato* music. Each April (26-30), *La Festival de la Leyenda Vallenata* draws thousands of visitors. There are *casas de cambio* on Calle 16. Tourist office in Gobernación, C 16, No 12-120, T574 6011.

Guajira Peninsula
Beyond Riohacha to the east is the arid and sparsely inhabited Guajira Peninsula, the leading producer of natural gas in Colombia. The *indígenas* here collect dividivi (the curved pods of trees used in tanning and dyeing), tend goats, and fish. They are Wayúu (or Guajiros), and of special interest are the coloured robes worn by the women. There language is Wayuunaiki; beyond Cabo de Vela little Spanish is spoken. Sunsets in the Guajira are magnificent.

Note The Guajira peninsula is not a place to travel alone, parties of three or more are recommended. If going in your own transport, check on safety before setting out. Also remember it is hot, easy to get lost, and there is little cover and very little water. Locals, including police, are very helpful in giving lifts. Stock up with provisions and water in Riohacha or Maicao. Elsewhere, what little there is expensive.

To visit a part of the Peninsula take a tour from Riohacha, or a shared taxi (see Transport, below) through fields of cactus but offering fine views of flamingos and other brightly coloured birds. **Manaure** is known for its salt flats southwest of the town. If you walk along the beach past the salt works, there are several lagoons where flamingos congregate the year round (take binoculars). Local children hire out bicycles for US$3 per day to travel to the lagoons and salt flats. Take plenty of sunblock and water and a torch/flashlight for returning in the evening. 14 km from Manaure in this direction is **Musichi**, an important haunt of the flamingos, sometimes out of the wet season. From Manaure there are *busetas* to **Uribia** (US$1), which has a Wayúu festival in May (no other reason to stop here), and thence to Maicao. You can get *busetas* from Uribia to Puerto Bolívar (from where coal from El Cerrejón is exported) and from there transport to **Cabo de Vela**, where the lagoons seasonally shelter vast flocks of flamingos, herons and sandpipers. It costs about US$3 from Uribia to Cabo de Vela. There are fine beaches, but very strong currents offshore. Good walks through desert scrubland, eg to Pan de Azúcar hill (one hour from beach) and El Faro, with superb views of the coastline and desert. Tourism in Cabo de la Vela has boomed recently. To enjoy deserted beaches, avoid Christmas and Easter when the *cabañas* and beaches are crowded and full of cars. Jeep tours to Cabo de la Vela from Riohacha can be easily arranged.

Parque Nacional Macuira
ⓘ *For information, T5-728 2636 in Riohacha. Entry US$14.50.*
Towards the northeast tip of the Guajira peninsula is the Serranía de Macuira, a range of hills over 500 m which create an oasis of tropical forest in the semi-desert. Moisture comes mainly from clouds that form in the evening and disperse in the early morning. Its remoteness gives it

interesting flora and fauna and indigenous settlements little affected by outsiders. To reach the area, you must travel northeast from Uribia either round the coast past Bahía Portete, or direct across the semi-desert, to the Wayúu village of **Nazareth** on the east side of the park. Macuira can be seen on two-day trips from Nazareth. The best way to visit is to contract your own jeep and guide, recommended is **Kaí Eco Travel** see Activities and tours, below. Beyond Cabo de la Vela we strongly advise you take a tour, as there is no public transport, little Spanish is spoken and the locals can be hostile. **Eco-Guías** in Bogotá and **Aventure Colombia** in Cartagena also arrange trips here from time to time.

Maicao → *Phone code: 5. Colour map 1, A4. Population: 59,000. Altitude: 50 m.*

The paved Caribbean coastal highway runs direct from Santa Marta to Riohacha, then paved to Maicao. Maicao, 12 km from the Venezuelan border, is hot and dusty. It is full of Venezuelan contraband and petrol and is an important drug-running route. There is a strong Arab presence, with several mosques and restaurants selling Arabic food. The streets surrounding the main plaza are teeming with clothes stalls. Many of its streets are unsurfaced; most commercial premises close before 1600 and after 1700 the streets are unsafe. The market area is run-down and also unsafe at times. Plenty of *Telecom* offices and internet cafés.

Border with Venezuela

Colombian immigration is at the border. DAS address: C 16, No 3-25, Los Olivos, Maicao, T726 8200, open 0730-1200, 1400-1800. Entering Colombia by *por puesto* make sure the driver stops at the Colombian entry post. It is essential to have an exit stamp from Venezuela and make sure you get an entry stamp at DAS. If not you will have to return later to complete formalities. With all the right papers, the border crossing is easy and there are few traffic delays. There are plenty of money changers hanging around at the border crossing.

There is no Venezuelan consul in Maicao. If you need a visa, get it in Barranquilla, Cartagena or Riohacha. Entering Venezuela, a transit visa will only do if you have a confirmed ticket to a third country within three days. See 'Entering Venezuela', page 1602.

To Venezuela listings

For Sleeping and Eating price codes and other relevant information, see Essentials, pages 38-40.

Sleeping

Riohacha *p966*

A Arimaca, C 1, No 8-75, T727 3481, arimaca@col3.telecom.com.co. Impressive high tower with light, spacious rooms, some with reception room, all with balconies and magnificent sea views, pool on 2nd floor.

B Gimaura, Av La Marina, T727 0019. Light, airy rooms with balconies looking out to sea. Breakfast included, helpful staff, swimming pool, tour agency. 5-min walk to town.

C Almirante Padilla, Cra 6, No 3-29, T727 2328. Much cheaper with fan, patio, laundry, restaurant with cheap *almuerzos*.

D Tunebo, Cra 10, No 12A-02, T727 3326, marytunebo@hotmail.com. Helpful staff, some a/c, rooms are a little dark, some way from the centre.

E Internacional, Cra 7, No 13-37, T727 3483. Down an alleyway off the market, not easy to find. Small, basic rooms with fan and bath. Pleasant restaurant on the patio, a good option.

E Yalconia del Mar, Cra 7, No 11-26, T727 3487. Private bath, cheaper with fan, small rooms, safe, helpful, half way between beach and bus station.

Valledupar *p967*

B Vajamar, Cra 7, No 16A-30, T574 3939. With breakfast, pool, expensive food.

E Hotel/Restaurant Nutibara, C 19, No 9-19, T574 3225. A/c, with breakfast. Several others on C 19.

Guajira Peninsula *p967*

Manaure

D Palaaima, Cr 6, No 7-25, T717 8195, is the best in town. Comfortable, cool rooms with a/c or fan, helpful. There are always Wayúu locals hanging around the hotel who are eager to talk about their culture and traditions.

Uribia

Basic hotels and 1 *residencia* (no running water); most transport stops in Uribia.

Cabo de Vela

This area becomes very crowded during high season. Many huts along the beach to stay in, some have TV, a/c. There is a telecom centre. Most places have hammock space on the beach, US$4-6. Fish meals cost US$4-6, including a large breakfast.

Maicao *p968*

B Hotel Maicao Internacional, C 12, No 10-90, T726 7184. Good rooms with a/c, rooftop swimming pool and bar. A good option in Maicao, attentive staff.

B Maicao Plaza, C 10, No 10-28, T726 0310. Spacious rooms, a/c, cable TV, with bath and cold water.

C Los Mádanos, Cra 10, No 11-25, T726 0467. Large rooms, a bit dark, cold water, a/c, cable TV, minibar, restaurant and disco.

D El Dorado, Cra 10, No 12-45, T726 7242. A little dilapidated, but it has a/c, TV and a good water supply.

Eating

Riohacha *p966*

Many ice cream and juice bars, and small *asados*, serving large, cheap selections of barbecued meat at the western end of the seafront.

TT Malecón, C 1A, No 3-43. Good selection of seafood and meat served in a palm-thatched barn looking out to sea, music and dancing in the evening.

TT Papillón, Cra 7, No 3-27. Crêpes, salads and sandwiches, served on a peaceful patio. The owner is a knowledgeable, Belgian ex-photojournalist.

T Monik, Cra 7, No 5-16. Cheap and cheerful, serving typical Guajira dishes.

Maicao *p968*

T El Oriente, Cra 9, No 11-16. Near main plaza, good, cheap Arabic food, great falafel. Closes 2000.

Shopping

Riohacha *p966*

Market 2 km from town on Valledupar road; hammocks and bags woven by the Wayúu of the Guajira are sold. See also **Operadora Turística Wayúu**, in Activities and tours, below.

Activities and tours

Guajira Peninsula *p967*

Trips to the Guajira Peninsula are best arranged in Riohacha. Tours to Cabo de la Vela, 1-2 days usually include Manaure (salt mines), Uribia, Pilón de Azucar and El Faro. Leave about 0600 and sometimes 0830-0900, return 1900-2000. All organise tours to Wayúu *rancherías* in the afternoon (includes typical goat lunch).

Guajira Total, stand in front of *Hotel Almirante Padilla* on sea front, T727 2328, T315-714 8057. Trips to Wayúu *rancherías*, Manaure and Cabo de Vela.

Guajira Viva, C 3, No 5-08, loc 1, T727 0607. 5-day tours to Alta Guajira, Cabo de la Vela, Santuario de Fauna y Flora los Flamencos. Recommended.

Lucho Freyle, T728 2885, T312-647 1434. Recommended Wayúu guide in Riohacha, jeep tours around La Guajira and Cabo de la Vela.

Operadora Turística Wayúu, C 1A, No 4-35, T311-400 7985. Wayúu-run, on seafront. Sells beautiful, colourful Wayúu *mochilas*. Organizes tours to *rancherías* and Cabo de la Vela.

Uribia

Kaí Eco Travel, T717 7713, T311-436 2830, www.kaiecotravel.com. Run by a network of Wayúu families, organizes tours to Cabo de la Vela, Parque Natural Nacional Macuira, Punta Gallinas, the northernmost point of South America, costs US$540 per person, including transport, accommodation and food. Highly recommended.

Kaishi, T311-429 6315/316-429 6315. Speak to Andrés Orozco, organizes jeep tours around La Guajira.

Transport

Riohacha *p966*

Bus Main terminal is on C 15 (El Progreso). (It is best to travel from Riohacha in a luxury bus, early morning as these buses are less likely to be stopped and searched for contraband.) **Coopcaribe Taxis** travel throughout the region and can be picked up almost anywhere in town, especially close to the old market area near the *Hotel Internacional*: daily to **Uribia**, US$7, 1½ hrs, **Manaure** US$8, 1¾ hrs. Leave when full (4 people), be prepared to pay slightly more if there are no travellers. Early morning best for travel, transport is scarce in the afternoon. No buses leave from Riohacha direct to Cabo de la Vela: travel to Uribia and wait for a jeep (leaves when full, irregular service) to Cabo de La Vela, long and uncomfortable. Take plenty of water with you. It is much easier and recommended to take a tour from Riohacha to Cabo de La Vela.

Valledupar *p967*
Air Aires Mon-Fri to Barranquilla.
Bus The bus and air terminals are 3 km southeast of the town, close to each other, taxi, US$2.50. From **Santa Marta**, 4 hrs, US$15.50, from **Cartagena**, US$22 (with **Expreso Brasilia**). To **Barranquilla**, 5-6 hrs, US$14. To **Bucaramanga**, 8 hrs US$39.

Maicao *p968*
Bus Buses to **Riohacha**, US$5.50, every 30 mins with **Brasilia** from 0630-1700, 1-1½ hr. **Santa Marta** 3 hrs, US$17.25. **Barranquilla**, US$22. **Cartagena**, US$27. Trucks leave regularly for **Cabo de Vela**, 2½-3 hrs, US$6 (can be uncomfortably crowded). Take water. **Fleta** is the local name for the faster taxis. Colectivos, known as *por puestos* in Venezuela, Maicao-**Maracaibo**, US$18, or microbus, US$13, very few buses to Venezuela after midday. Buses leave from the bus terminal where you can change money; buy bus tickets and food before journey. Taxis from Maicao to Maracaibo will stop at both immigration posts and take you to your hotel; safe, easy transfer. Ask the taxi/bus driver to stop at DAS for a Colombian exit stamp.

Directory

Riohacha *p966*
Banks Most banks are on Parque Almirante. Banco de Bogotá, Cra 7, between C 2/3, for Visa. Mon-Fri, 0800-1600, Sat, 0900-1200. **Consulates** Venezuela, Cra 7, No 3-08, p7-B, T727 4076, consuven@telecom.com.co (0900-1300, and closed from 1500 Fri to 0900 Mon). If you need a visa, you should check all requirements for your nationality before arriving at this consulate. It is easier to get a Venezuelan visa in Barranquilla. **Immigration** DAS, C 5, T727 2407, No 4-48, 0730-1200, 1400-1800. **Internet and telephone** On Parque Almirante. **Post offices** C 2, Cra 6/7.

San Andrés and Providencia

Colombia's Caribbean islands of the San Andrés and Providencia archipelago are 480 km north of the South American coast, 400 km southwest of Jamaica, and 180 km east of Nicaragua. This proximity has led Nicaragua to claim them from Colombia in the past. In 2000, the Archipelago of San Andrés, Old Providence and Santa Catalina were declared a World Natural Heritage Site called the Seaflower Biosphere Reserve. San Andrés is larger and more developed than Providencia and has lost much of its colonial Caribbean feel. Both are very expensive by South American standards. Nevertheless, their surrounding islets and cays, good diving, white sand beaches and spectacular turquoise waters make them popular holiday resorts with Colombians and North Americans looking for sun during winter months. San Andrés is very crowded with Colombian shoppers looking for foreign-made, duty-free bargains. Alcoholic drinks are cheap, but international shoppers will find few bargains, and essentials and eating out are expensive. The original inhabitants, mostly descendants of Jamaican slaves, speak English, but the population has swollen with unrestricted immigration from Colombia. There are also Chinese and Middle Eastern communities. The islands are one of the few Colombian departments not affected by the internal armed conflict but drugs running abounds.

Ins and outs

Getting there Air A cheap way to visit San Andrés is by taking a charter flight from Bogotá or other major city, accommodation and food included. See supplements in the local

Colombian press. The airport at San Andrés is 15 mins' walk to town centre; buses to centre and San Luis from across the road from the airport. Airline offices in town.

Boat Cruise ships and tours go to San Andrés; there are no other official passenger services by sea.
▸▸ *See also Transport, page 975.*

San Andrés Tourist office ⓘ *at airport and Circunvalar Av Newball, diagonal Club Náutica, T512 5058, Mon-Fri 0800-1200, 1400-1800*, helpful, English spoken, maps and hotel lists. On arrival in San Andrés, you must buy a tourist card, US$9. It is also valid for Providencia. Do not lose it. You must also have an onward or return ticket. On Providencia, in the Palacio de la Alcaldía, T514 8054, alcalde@providencia.gov.co.

San Andrés → *Phone code: 8. Population: 77,000.*

The 11 km long San Andrés island is made of coral and rises at its highest to 104 m. The town, commercial centre, resort hotel sector and airport are at the northern end. A picturesque road circles the island. Places to see, besides the beautiful cays and beaches on the less developed southern side, include the Hoyo Soplador (South End), a geyser-like hole through which the sea spouts into the air when the wind is in the right direction. The west side is less spoilt, but there are no beaches. Instead there is The Cove, the islands deepest anchorage, and Morgan's Cave (Cueva de Morgan, reputed hiding place for the pirate's treasure) which is penetrated by the sea through an underwater passage. Next to Cueva de Morgan is a **museum** ⓘ *US$2.70*, with exhibitions telling the history of the coconut, lots of paraphernalia salvaged from wrecks around the island and a replica pirate ship. The museum is run by Jimmy Gordon, author of *Legado de Piratas*, who has extensive knowledge of the island's history.

San Andrés town

Sleeping
1 Hernando Henry
2 La Posada de Lulu
3 Los Delfines
4 Portobelo
5 Posada Doña Rosa

Eating
1 Fonda Antioqueña
2 Guillos Café
3 Margherita e Carbonara
4 Niko's

About 1 km south from Cueva de Morgan is **West View** ⓘ *daily 0900-1700, entry US$1.10 (including bread to feed the fish - ecologically unsound), small restaurant opposite entrance*, an excellent place to see marine life as the sea is very clear (you can hire old-fashioned diving equipment with oxygen piped through a tube to a helmet, US$50 for 30 minutes). At The Cove, a road crosses up to the centre of the island and back to town over La Loma, on which is a Baptist Church, built in 1847.

San Andrés is famous in Colombia for its music, whose styles include the local form of calypso, soca, reggae and church music. Concerts are held at the **Old Coliseum** (every Saturday at 2100 in the high season).

Boats leave from San Andrés in the morning for El Acuario and Haynes Cay, and continue to Johnny Cay in the afternoon, which has a white beach and parties all day Sunday (US$17 return). El Acuario has crystalline water and is a good place to snorkel. You can wade across to Haynes Cay where there is good food and a reggae bar at **Bibi's Place**. If you want to avoid the crowds, hire a private boat (US$110 for the day) and do the tour in reverse. Boats for the cays leave from Tonino's Marina between 0930 and 1030, returning at 1530, or from Muelle Casa de la Cultura on Avenida Newell. On San Andrés the beaches are in town and on the east coast. Best are at San Luis and Bahía Sonora/Sound Bay.

Providencia → *Phone code: 8. Population: 5,500. 80 km north-northeast of San Andrés.*

Commonly called Old Providence, **Providencia** is mountainous, of volcanic origin. The barrier reef that surrounds it, the third largest in the world, is called Old Providence McBean Lagoon; it is easily visited (entry US$6.45). Providencia and its sister island **Santa Catalina** (an old pirate lair separated from Providencia by a channel cut to improve their defence) have an approximate surface of 22 sq km. The official languages of its 5,000 inhabitants are Spanish and Caribbean English. Musical influences are the mento from the Antilles, calypso from Trinidad and reggae from Jamaica. The average temperature is 27°C; the rainiest months are October and November, while the driest are January to April. There are no high-rises, apartment blocks or shopping malls and its quieter atmosphere than San Andrés attracts more European visitors.

Superb views can be had by climbing from Casabaja/Bottom House or Aguamansa/Smooth Water to the peak (about one hour, US$13.80 with a guide). There are relics of the fortifications built on the island during its disputed ownership. Horse riding is available, and boat trips can be made to Santa Catalina and, to the northeast, Cayo Cangrejo/Crab Cay (entrance US$1.50, good snorkelling – see Tours, below). Santa Catalina is joined to the main island by the wooden Lover's Bridge (Malecón de los Enamorados). Go left after crossing this bridge (right is a dead end) and walk for about 500 m. Climb stairs to the Virgin statue for excellent views of Providencia. If you continue past the Virgin and go down the flight of stairs you will arrive at a very small beach (nice snorkelling). On the west side is a rock formation called Morgan's Head; from the side it looks like a profile.

Of the three main beaches, Manzanillo is the best preserved and wildest. Not much space for lying out, but pleasant for walking. **Roland's Roots Bar** has excellent live, traditional island music on weekends. South West Bay/Suroeste has stunning beaches and is the best for hanging out. There is access at each end. Two Rasta bars, **Richard's** (the oldest) and **Olibert's Fuente**, are recommended. Agua Dulce is where most hotels and restaurants are. Between April-May, the island is awash with migrating black crabs.

San Andrés and Providencia listings

For Sleeping and Eating price codes and other relevant information, see Essentials, pages 38-40.

Sleeping

San Andrés *p971, map p971*

Hotels quote rates pp, but we list prices for double rooms. Prices include half board, but most can be booked without meals. Most raise prices by 20-30% on 15 Dec. All this also applies to Providencia.

LL Casa Harb, C 11, No 10-83, T512 6348, www.casaharb.com. Just outside town, this boutique hotel takes its inspiration from the Far East and is the most stylish on the island. Each room is individually decorated with antique furniture, enormous granite baths, infinity pool and home-cooked meals.

AL Los Delfines, Av Colombia, No 1B-86, T512 1800, www.decameron.com. One of 6 Decameron hotels on the island, this one achieves some individuality. Comfortable rooms set around a fine pool, restaurant on a jetty.

A Sunset Hotel, Carretera Circunvalar Km 13, T513 0433, sunsetsai@hotmail.com. On the western side of the island, ideal for diving or for getting away from the crowds. Bright, fresh rooms set around a salt-water swimming pool. Restaurant serves international and regional food in a typical clapboard house, dive shop next door.

B La Posada de Lulu, Av Antioquia, No 2-18, T512 2919, www.laposadadelulu.descansorural.com. Brightly coloured hostel, comfortable rooms and 2 apartments to rent for longer stays, excellent restaurant. Recommended.

B Portobelo, Av Colombia, No 5A-69, T512 7008, www.portobelohotel.com. In a couple of buildings at the western end of the *malecón*, large beds, a/c, cable TV. Breakfast included.

B-C Hernando Henry, Av Las Américas, No 4-84, T512 3416. At the back of town, shoddy but passable rooms, cheaper with fan, TV and laundry service.

C Posada Doña Rosa, Av Las Américas con Aeropuerto, T512 3649. A 2-min walk from the airport, this is a reasonable an economical option, use of kitchen, TV room, a short walk from the beach. Also has 2 apartments to rent.

Private houses

D pp **Red Crab**, Av Circunvalar, San Luis, T513 0314, www.arriendos. biz/RedCrab.html. A villa on the beach with 4 independent apartments, each with a capacity for 6. Price includes use of pool and the services of a housekeeper.

Providencia *p972*

Rooms can be rented at affordable prices in local houses or *posadas nativas*. Try Captain 'Hippie', T514 8548, 311-485 4805, who offers home-cooking and lodging in his house (**E** pp).

Hotels in Agua Dulce are 10 mins by motor taxi (US$1) from centre or 1 hr walk. Suroeste is a 20-min walk from Agua Dulce. The **Decameron** group represents 5 properties on the island.

AL Cabañas Miss Elma, Aguadulce, T514 8229, philhuffington@yahoo.es (www.decameron.com). Wood-panelled *cabañas* with terraces, right on the beach. Large rooms, some with reception rooms and baby cots. Cable TV and a/c.

AL Sol Caribe Providencia, Agua Dulce, T514 8230, www.solarhoteles.com. Chain hotel offering 2-5 night packages, pool, sea views, a/c, TV, fridge, bright.

AL-A Sirius, Suroeste, T514 8213, www.siriushotel.net. Large, colourful house set back from the beach, run by a Swiss family. Large, light rooms, some with balconies, on the beach. A/c, TV, internet, use of kitchen, dive centre, kayaks, wakeboarding, horse riding, massage. The owner speaks German, Italian and English. Half-board and diving packages available.

A Cabañas Miss Mary, South West Bay, T514 8454 (www.decameron.com). On the beach at South West Bay, comfortable rooms with cable TV and hot water, breakfast included.

A Posada del Mar, Aguadulce, T514 8168, posadadelmar@latinmail.com (www.decameron.com). Pink and purple clapboard house with comfortable rooms, each with a terrace and hammock, cable TV, a/c, minibar and hot water.

C Old Providence, diagonal Alcaldía Municipal, Santa Isabel (centre), T514 8691. Above supermarket **Erika**, rooms are basic but clean, a/c, cable TV, fridge.

Eating

San Andrés *p971, map p971*

Good fish and seafood meals at San Luis beach.

TTT-TT Margherita e Carbonara, Av Colombia, No 1-93. Good Italian, pizzas and coffee.

Bibi's Place, Haynes Caye, T513 3767, caritoortega@hotmail.com. Reggae bar and restaurant on cay next to El Acuario serving seafood, including crab and lobster. Organizes full moon parties and civil and rasta weddings.

Fonda Antioqueña, Av La Playa, No 1-16. On the main beach in San Andrés town, serves good, cheap *paisa* food.

Niko's, Av Colombia, No 1-93. Bills itself as a seafood restaurant though its steaks are actually better. Lovely setting by the water.

Guillos Café, Av Peatonal next to **Portobelo Hotel**. Fast-food restaurant serving sandwiches and burgers, as well as local specialities.

Providencia *p972*

Typical dish is *rondón*, a mix of fish, conch, yucca and dumplings, cooked in coconut milk. Fish and crab are most common. Corn ice cream is also popular – it tastes a little like vanilla but a little sweeter.

As well as hotels, good places include: **Arturo**, on Suroeste beach, next to Miss Mary. Ask for mix for 2 people, US$13.50 for 2 fish, snail, crab and crayfish with *patacón* fries **Café Studio**, between Agua Dulce and Suroeste. Great pies and spaghetti. **Donde Martín**, Agua Dulce. Good food.

Caribbean Place (Donde Martín), Aguadulce. *Bogoteño* chef Martín Quintero uses local ingredients. Specialities include lobster in crab sauce, fillet of fish in ginger and corn ice cream.

Roland's Reggae bar, Playa Manzanillo, T514 8417, rolandsbeach@hotmail.com. Parties at Roalnd's bar-restaurant are legendary. The menu is mainly seafood. He also hires tents for camping (**F**).

Festivals and events

San Andrés *p971, map p971*

Jun Jardín del Caribe. A folkloric festival. **20 Jul**: **independence** celebrations on San Andrés with various events. **Dec Rainbow Festival**. Reggae and calypso music.

Providencia *p972*

The island holds its **carnival** in **Jun**.

Shopping

Providencia *p972*

There are 3 supermarkets in Santa Isabel town.

Arts and Crafts Café, Agua Dulce, T514 8297. French owners Maria Blancard and Frenchy DelPlace sell local crafts and delicious homemade cookies and ice cream.

Activities and tours

San Andrés *p971, map p971*

Canopying

Canopy La Loma, Vía La Loma-Barrack, T314-447 9868. Site at the top of the hill in San Andrés. 3 'flights' over the trees at 450 m, 300 m and 200 m asl with spectacular views out to sea, US$17. Safety precautions and equipment are good.

Diving Diving off San Andrés is good; depth varies from 3 to 30 m, visibility from10 to 30 m. There are 3 types of site: walls of seaweed and minor coral reefs, different types of coral, and underwater plateaux with much marine life. It is possible to dive in 70% of the insular platform. Diving trips to the reef:

Banda Dive Shop, **Hotel Lord Pierre**, Local 102, T512 2507, www.bandadiveshop.com. PADI qualified, mini courses from US$83. Fast boat and good equipment.

Sharky Dive Shop, Carretera Circunvalar Km 13, T513 0420, www.sharkydiveshop.com. Good equipment and excellent, English- speaking guides. PADI qualifications and a beginner's course held in the Sunset Hotel's saltwater swimming pool.

Watersports and boat trips

Bar Boat, on the road to San Luis (opposite the naval base), daily 1000-1800. Wind-surfing, and sunfish sailing rental and lessons. Also has floating bar, English and German spoken.

Centro Comercial New Point Plaza, No 234, T512 8787. Morning boats to El Acuario Cay, off Haynes Cay. Using a mask and wearing sandals as protection against sea-urchins, you watch the colourful fish. They also run the *Nautilus*, a glass hull semi-submarine, US$17.

Cooperativa Lancheros, on the beach in San Andrés town. Can arrange fishing trips, windsurfing, jet skiing and kite surfing. Snorkelling equipment can be hired for US$10.

Windsurf Spot, Hotel El Isleño, Av Colombia, No 5-117; and **Water Spot**, Decameron Aquarium, Av Colombia, No 1-19, www.decameron.com.

Providencia *p972*

Diving Recommended diving spots on the Old McBean Lagoon reef are Manta's Place, a good place to see manta rays; Felipe's Place where there is a submerged figure of Christ; and Stairway to Heaven, which has a large wall of coral and big fish.

Felipe Diving, South West Bay, T851 8775, www.felipediving.com. Mini courses from US$80, also rents snorkel equipment. Owner Felipe Cabeza even has a diving spot on the reef named after him. Warmly recommended. See also **Hotel Sirius**, above. PADI qualifications, mini course US$80.

Snorkelling and boat trips Recommended snorkelling sites include the waters around Santa Catalina, where there are many caves to explore as well as Morgan's Head and lots of starfish; Hippie's Place, which has a little bit of everything; and El Faro (The Lighthouse), the end of the reef before it drops into deep sea.

Valentina Tours, T514 8548. Lemus Walter, aka Captain 'Hippie', organizes snorkelling, and boat trips (US$17 pp) to the outlying cays and reefs, US$140 for a day's boat hire.

Tour operators **Body Contact**, Aguadulce, T514 8283. Owner Jennifer Archbold organizes excursions, fishing and hiking trips, currency exchange, accommodation, and more. Recommended.

Walking A good 1.5-km walk over Manchineel Hill, between Bottom House (Casa Baja) and South West Bay, through tropical forest, fine views, many types of bird, iguanas and blue lizards. Guided tours depart twice a day at 0900 and 1500 from Bottom House. Enquire at **Body Contact**, see above, or Coralina, T514 9003.

Transport

San Andrés *p971, map p971*

Air Flights to **Bogotá**, **Cali**, **Medellín** and **Cartagena** with **AeroRepública**, **Avianca**, **Satena** and **Searca** (booked through Decameron). **Copa** once daily to **Panama City**. Sunday flights are always heavily booked, similarly Jul-Aug, Dec-Jan.

Bus Buses run every 15 minutes on the eastern side of the island, US$0.30, and more often at night and during the holidays. **Taxis** around the island cost US$11, but in town fares double after 2200. To airport US$5.50 (colectivo US$0.70).

Vehicle and bicycle hire Motorbikes are easy to hire, as are golf buggies. Cars can be hired for US$22 for 2 hrs, US$65 for a day. Passport may be required as deposit. Bikes are easy to hire, but they may be in poor condition. Eg opposite **Los Delfines Hotel** on Av Colombia, US$2 per hr or US$7 per day.

Providencia *p972*

Air **Satena** and **Searca** fly from San Andrés twice a day. Bookable only in San Andrés. Essential to confirm flights to guarantee a seat. Schedules change frequently. Taxi from airport to centre, US$6.50 (fixed).

Boat Cargo boat trips leave from San Andrés, taking 7-8 uncomfortable hrs, 3 times a week, US$22. They usually leave at 2200, arriving in the early morning. *Miss Isabel*, *Doña Olga* and *Raziman* make the trip regularly. Speak directly to the captain at the port in San Andrés, or enquire at the Port Authority (*Capitanía del Puerto*) in San Luis.

Motoped hire US$27 per day from many hotels. No licence or deposit needed. Golf buggies are also available for US$83 per day.

Directory

San Andrés *p971, map p971*

Banks Banks close 1200-1400. **Banco de Bogotá** will advance pesos on a Visa card. **Banco Occidente** for MasterCard. ATMs available in town and at the airport (**Davivenda**, in the lobby at the foot of the stairs). Some shops and most hotels will change US$ cash; it is impossible to change TCs at weekends. **Titan** casa de cambio, inside CC Leda, Av de las Américas, open Mon-Fri, and Sat, 0830-1200, changes TCs, US$ and euros.

Immigration DAS, Cra 7, No 2-70, T512 3667.

Internet Cafés downtown. **Bistronet**, Av Colón, Edif Bread Fruit, Local 105, headphones and Skype, also, international calls. **Varieteam Shop**, Av Providencia, CC Leda, Loc 111, headphones and Skype, photocopying, fax and scanner, CDs and DVDs sold. **Post offices** Deprisa at airport and Av Colón, Edif Salazar.

Providencia *p972*

Banks **Banco de Bogotá**, Santa Isabel, Mon-Thu 0800-1130, 1400-1600, Fri 0800-1130, 1400-1630. An ATM is tucked away just before the Lover's Bridge, on the road to Santa Catalina.

Internet In Santa Isabel. **Telephone** Telecom in Santa Isabel (centre), open Mon-Sat 0800-2200; Sun 0900-1230, 1400-1900. International long distance: 191. International phone enquiries: 198.

Useful numbers Police: T2. Medical: T11. Ambulance: T514 8016 at hospital.

Medellín and Chocó

Antioquia is the largest of the western departments, full of diversity and an important agricultural and commercial region. With its roots in the Cordilleras, it still has 100 km of Caribbean coastline. The people of Antioquia, called 'paisas', are known for their efficiency, hospitality and astute business practices.

Stretching between the Cordillera Occidental and the Pacific Coast, from Panamá to Valle del Cauca, Chocó is one of Colombia's least developed and most beautiful departments.

Medellín → *Phone code: 4. Colour map 1, B2. Population: 2,223,000. Altitude: 1,487 m.*

Medellín, capital of Antioquia, is considered by many to be the engine of Colombia and *paisas* are known for their canny business sense. Previously the home and headquarters of notorious narco-trafficker Pablo Escobar, Medellín has, since his death, shaken off its association with drugs and violence in what is one of the most remarkable turnarounds in Latin America. It is now a fresh, vibrant, prosperous city known for its progressive social politics and culture. In the centre, few colonial buildings remain, but large new buildings must, by law, incorporate modern works of art. Music, arts and gastronomy festivals attract many visitors and the flower festival, the *Desfile de Silleteros*, in August, is the most spectacular parade in Colombia. Known as 'The City of Eternal Spring', Medellín has a pleasant, temperate climate year-round; warm during the day and cool in the evening.

Ins and outs

Getting there **International airport** José María Córdova airport (also called Rionegro), 28 km from Medellín by a new highway, and 9 km from the town of Rionegro; good shops and services, no left luggage, but tourist office may oblige. Taxi to town US$26; *buseta* to centre, US$3, frequent service from 0400-2100, taking about one hour to the small road (Carrera 50A/Calle 53) next to **Hotel Botero Plaza.** To Rionegro from the airport US$0.20 bus, US$8 taxi. The **city airport**, Enrique Olaya Herrera, has regional flights to some destinations in Colombia. Taxi to centre or El Poblado, US$3.30.

The terminal for long-distance buses going north and east is **Terminal del Norte** at Cra 64 (Autopista del Norte) y Transversal 78 (Cra 64C, No 78-58), T230 8514, about 3 km north of the centre, with shops, cafés, left luggage, ATMs and other facilities. It is well policed and quite safe, though best not to tempt fate. Metro stop: Caribe. Taxi to/from the centre US$2.70-US$4.40. For buses going south, **Terminal del Sur**, Cra 65, No 8B-91, T361 1499, alongside the Olaya Herrera airport. Similar services to Terminal del Norte. Take No 143 bus marked 'Terminal del Sur' from C 51 (in front of the Banco Popular) along Cra 46, or metro to Poblado on Línea A, then a taxi for the remaining 1.5 km to the bus station. » *See also Transport, page 982.*

Getting around The city is centred around the old and the new cathedrals, the former on Parque Berrío and the latter overlooking Parque de Bolívar. The main commercial area is three blocks away on Carrera 46. In the centre, Pasaje Junín (Cra 49) is closed to traffic from Parque de Bolívar to Parque San Antonio (C 46). In the south, El Poblado has become an upmarket commercial and residential area and many companies have moved their headquarters there. This is where the best hotels and restaurants can be found. The area around Parque Lleras, known as the Zona Rosa, is where most of the bars and nightclubs are situated. West of the centre between Cerro El Volador and the Universidad Pontificia Bolivariana, Cra 70 and C 44 are busy commercial and entertainment sectors with many new hotels, shopping centres and the huge **Atanasio Girardot** sports stadium nearby. Unlike most other Colombian cities, many central streets are named as well as being numbered. Particularly important are: Cra 46, part of the inner ring road, which has several names but is known popularly as 'Av Oriental'; Cra 80/Cra 81/Diagonal 79, the outer ring road to the west, which is called 'La Ochenta' throughout; C 51/52, east of the centre is 'La Playa'; and C 33, which crosses the Río Medellín to become Calle 37, is called 'La Treinta y Tres'.

For your first view of the city, take the Metro, which runs overground. There are two lines: A from Niquía in the east to Itagüí in the south, B from San Javier to San Antonio, where they intersect, and two connecting cable cars, known as Metro Cable: J from San Javier to La Aurora, and K, serving the areas on the mountain slopes up to Santo Domingo Savio, currently being extended to El Tambo. Change at Acevedo on line A for this cable car. The cable cars give great views over the city, especially at dusk. **Taxi**: make sure meters are used; minimum charge US$2.

Tourist offices Oficina de Turismo de Medellín ⓘ *C 41, No 55-80, of 302, T261 6060*. For information on the city, helpful staff. **Departamento de Antioquia** tourist office ⓘ *C 42B, No 52-106, of 603, T385 8637, turismoantioquia@antioquia.gov.co*. There are tourist booths at both airports and the bus stations. **National parks office** ⓘ *C 49, No 79A-29, T234 6566*; **Aviatur** ⓘ *Cra 49, No 55-25, T576 5000, http://site.aviatur.com, and other branches.*

El Poblado

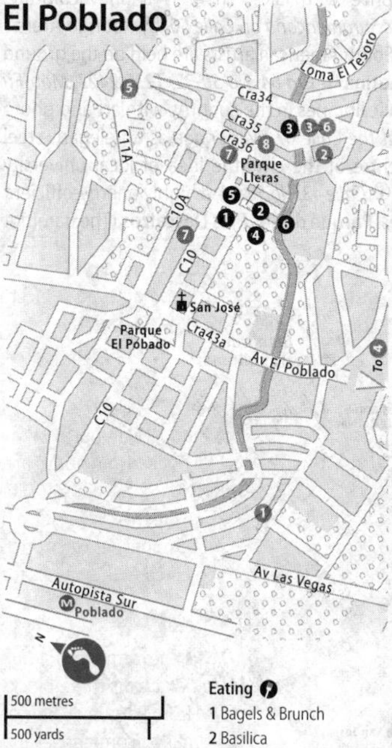

500 metres
500 yards

Sleeping
1 Black Sheep Hostal
2 Casa Kiwi
3 Global Hostel
4 La Habana Vieja
5 Park 10
6 Provenza
7 Tiger Paw

Eating
1 Bagels & Brunch
2 Basilica
3 Donde Paco
4 Le Bon
5 Thaico
6 Triada

Bars & clubs
7 Bar Blue
8 B-lounge

Centre

Plaza Botero (or de las Esculturas) ⓘ *C 52 y Cra 52*, is dotted with 23 bronze sculptures by **Fernando Botero**, Colombia's leading contemporary artist, born in Medellín in 1932. One side of the plaza has **El Palacio de la Cultura Rafael Uribe**, formerly the governor's office, which is now a cultural centre and art gallery (free entry). Across, is the **Museo de Antioquia** ⓘ *Cra 52, No 52-43, T251 3636, Mon-Sat, 0930-1730, Sun and holidays, 1000-1600, US$4, metro stop: Parque Berrío*, well-displayed works of contemporary Colombian artists, including a large collection by Botero. The gift shop sells clothes by up-and-coming Colombian fashion designers. More works by Botero can be seen in **Parque San Antonio** ⓘ *between C 44/46 and Cra 46*. It includes the 'Torso Masculino' (which complements the female version in **Parque Berrío**), and the 'Bird of Peace' which was severely damaged by a guerrilla bomb in 1996. At Botero's request, it has been left unrepaired as a symbol of the futility of violence and a new one has been placed alongside to make the point yet more dramatically. **Parque de Bolívar** is dominated by the **Catedral Metropolitana**, built between 1875 and 1931, claimed to be the third largest brick building in the world. There are three early churches near the centre, **San Benito**, **La Veracruz** and **San José**, and three 18th century churches survive: **San Ignacio**, in Plaza San Ignacio, **San Juan de Dios**, and **San Antonio**.

Outside the centre

To the north are **Joaquín Antonio Uribe botanical gardens** ⓘ *Cra 52, No 73-298, Mon-Say 0800-1700, Sun 0900-1800, US$2.70, metro Universidad* are near the University of Antioquia campus, with 5,500 species of plants, orchids and trees. There are two restaurants, one more economical than the other. Opposite the botanical gardens is the brand new **Parque Explora** ⓘ *Cra 52, No 73-75, T516 8300, www.parque explora.org, Tue-Fri 0830-1730, Sat, Sun and holidays 1000-1830, US$4-9 depending on how many rooms you see, full tour approximately 6-8 hrs*, a science and technology museum. With more than 300 interactive scientific puzzles and games, this is fun for adults and heaven for kids. It has four state-of-the-art rooms, **Territorios Digitales, Colombia Geodiversa, Conexión de la Vida** and **Física Viva**, each of which take one to two hours to explore. **Fundación Casa Museo Pedro Nel Gómez** ⓘ *Cra 51B, No 85-24, T233 2633, free, Mon-Sat 0900-1700, Sun and holidays 0900-1600, may be closed in school holidays, metro station: Universidad,* is the house of the painter and sculptor (1899-1984).

West of the centre **Museo de Arte Moderno** ⓘ *Cra 64B, No 51-64, Mon-Fri 1000-1300, 1400-1800, Sat 1000-1700, US$1.80, half price with ISIC,* has a small collection and shows foreign films daily (not Wednesdays, US$2.65, half price with ISIC). There is a fine sculpture, **Monumento a la Vida** ⓘ *next to the Edif Seguros Suramericana on Calle 50*, by Rodrigo Arenas Betancur, where exhibitions of work by leading South American artists are held on the ground floor. **Biblioteca Pública Piloto para América Latina** ⓘ *Cra 64, No 50-32, T230 2422, Mon-Fri 0830-1900, Sat 0900-1800* is one of the best public libraries in the country, with art and photo exhibitions, readings and films. **Puntocero** ⓘ *at the Calle 67 river bridge*, is an elegant steel double arch with a pendulum marking the centre of the city (the idea of local university students). Southwest are **El Edificio Inteligente** ⓘ *Calle 43, No 58-01*, a highly energy-efficient building used jointly by Medellín's public services. **Parque de Los Pies Descalzos** (The Barefoot

2 Medellín centre

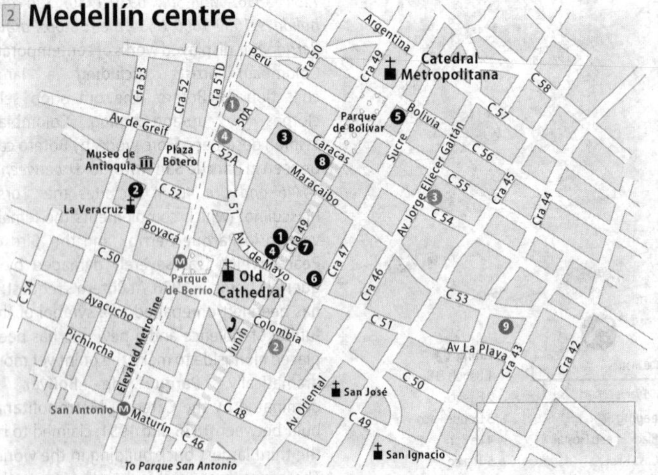

N

200 metres

200 yards

Sleeping
1 Botero Plaza
2 Casa Dorada
3 Gran
4 Nutibara

Eating
1 123...Cazuelas
2 Café Botero
3 Chung Wah
4 Deli Lunch
5 Fonda Parque Bolívar
6 Hato Viejo
7 Salón de Té Astor
8 Versalles

Bars & clubs
9 La Boa

Park) ⓘ *Cra 57, No 42-139*, is a relaxing space with cafés, sand pits, Zen garden and fountains. It serves as a good example of how Medellín is reclaiming and renovating public areas. It also has the **Museo Interactivo EPM** ⓘ *US$3.50, Tues-Sun 0800-2000*, an interactive science and technology museum with 22 rooms on 4 levels.

Museo Etnográfico Miguel Angel Builes ⓘ *Cra 81, No 52B-120, T421 6259, www.yarumal.org, Mon-Fri 0800-1200, 1400-1700, Sat 0830-1200, free but voluntary contributions appreciated*, has an extensive collection of artefacts from indigenous cultures, two floors dedicated to Colombia, one to other Andean countries and another to Africa. It also has a library and bookshop.

As you ride the Metro you will notice three prominent hills in the Aburrá valley: **Cerro Nutibara** ⓘ *Calle 30A y Cra 55, T235 8370*, in the southwest with good views over the city, where there is a stage for open air concerts, sculpture park, miniature Antioquian village (known as Pueblito Paisa), souvenir shops and restaurants; **Cerro El Volador** (seen as the Metro turns between Universidad and Caribe stations), tree-covered and the site of an important indigenous burial ground; and **Morro El Salvador** (to the east of Alpujarra station) with a cross and statue on top, now mostly built over and not recommended for visits.

Medellín listings

For Sleeping and Eating price codes and other relevant information, see Essentials, pages 38-40.

Sleeping

Medellín: centre *p977, map p978*

Most of the city's better accommodation options are situated away from the centre. Many of the cheaper hostels in the centre are *acostaderos*, pay-by-the-hour brothels with questionable security that we advise you to avoid.

A Botero Plaza, Cra 50A, No 53-45, T511 2155, www.hotelboteroplaza.com. Just 1 min's walk from Parque Botero, convenient, on the street where *busetas* leave for the airport. Continental breakfast included. Internet café, sauna, gym, Turkish bath, but the area can be dangerous at night.

A Gran, C 54, No 45-92, T513 4455, www.granhotel.com.co. A few blocks from Parque de Las Esculturas, swimming pool, room service, restaurant, Wi-Fi in lobby.

A Nutibara, C 52A, No 50-46, T511 5111, www.hotelnutibara.com. The city's first major hotel. It retains a certain art-deco charm and has all modern amenities, including pool, sauna, Turkish bath, internet room and Wi-Fi

C Casa Dorada, C 50, No 47-25, T512 5300, www.granhotel.com.co. Part of the Gran Hotel, one of the few safe budget options in the centre, hot water, cable TV, rooms a bit dark and musty.

Medellín: outside the centre *p977, map p977*

Cra 70 is full of hotels in roughly the same price range. Although standards can vary they are good value and within easy reach of the Metro. There are plenty of eateries, bars and discos as well.

AL Mediterráneo, Cra 70, Circular 5a-23, T410 2510, www.mediterraneomedellin.com. Smart, airy rooms, spa with different treatments, business centre, Wi-Fi, good value restaurant. Recommended.

A Florida, Cra 70, No 44B-38, T260 4900, www.hotelfloridamedellin.com. Standard hotel, internet, Wi-Fi, laundry service, car park and restaurant. Some rooms lack windows.

A Lincoln, Circular 3a, No 70-28, T409 1200, www.hotellincoln.com.co. Excellent rooms, TV, stereo, safe and Wi-Fi in every room, free parking, American breakfast, gym, jacuzzi and Turkish bath. Popular with business clients, discounts at weekends.

B Lukas, Cra 70, No 44A-28, T260 1761, www.lukashotel.com. Crisp rooms with safe, a/c, cable TV, internet and Wi-Fi. Breakfast included.

B Parque 70, C 46B, No 69A-11, T260 3339. Good little mid-range hotel in a quiet cul-de-sac off Cra 70, cheper without a/c. Minibar, stereo, TV, DVD and Wi-Fi. 1 block from Estadio metro.

D-F pp **Hostal Casa del Sol**, C 49, No 81A-24, Calasanz, T422 0531, www.hostalcasadelsol.com. 3 mins walk metro Floresta, then 5 mins to centre. Owned by Luis Felipe Botero Osorio. Private rooms or dorms, large communal areas and gardens, kitchen, internet, Wi-Fi, TV, hammocks, breakfast included, Spanish classes.

D-F Hostal Medellín, Cra 65, No 48-144, T230 0511, www.hostalmedellin.com. Spacious hostel, private rooms and dorms, good cooking facilities, German/Colombian run, popular with bikers. Garden with a hammock, organizes tours, close to Metro.

E-F Palm Tree Hostal, Cra 67, No 48D-63, T260 6142, www.palmtreemedellin.com. Good backpackers' hostel, use of kitchen, Wi-Fi, TV and DVD room, bike hire, book exchange and hammocks. Private rooms and dorms, with breakfast, free BBQ on Fri.

El Poblado and around

See also Getting around, page 976.

L Park 10, Cra 36B No 11-12, T310 6060, www.hotelpark10.com.co. Quiet location, smart, all rooms have a reception area. Buffet breakfast, sauna, gym, Wi-Fi, business centre and spa, among other facilities.

A La Habana Vieja, C 10 Sur, No 43A-7, T321 2557, www.hotellahabanavieja.com. Small, cosy, colonial style with antiques, good location, with breakfast.

A Provenza, Cra 35, No 7-2, T326 5600, provenzahostal@gmail.com. A few blocks from Zona Rosa, airy, Wi-Fi, TV, laundry service and breakfast.

B Global Hostel, Cra 35, No 7-58, T311 5418, www.globalhostelcolombia.com. Excellent mid-range option, nice artwork and photography on walls, close to the Zona Rosa, breakfast included, Wi-Fi. Highly recommended.

C-D Tiger Paw, Cra 36, No 10-49, T311 6079, www.tigerpawhostel.com. A variety of rooms, **E-F** in dorms, US-owned, free internet and Wi-Fi, laundry service, tourist packages, sports bar and lots of activities.

C-F Black Sheep Hostel, Transversal 5A, No 45-133 (tell taxi drivers it's in Patio Bonito), T311 1589, T311-341 3048, www.blacksheepmedellin.com (informative website about travelling in Colombia). Recently expanded to 2 floors, run by welcoming Kiwi, Kelvin, homely feel, well-organized, TV areas, good kitchen facilities, popular weekly BBQ, free Wi-Fi, washing machine, excellent service, salsa and Spanish lessons arranged. Information on paragliding. Recommended.

D-F Casa Kiwi, Cra 36, No 7-10, T268 2668, www.casakiwihostel.com. 11 private rooms, also semi-dorms and dorms. Good travellers' hostel, internet, kitchen facilities, laundry, hammock terrace, roof-top pool, bar area and TV room with theatre seating. Near Parque Lleras, Wi-Fi, welcoming, paragliding arranged. Highly recommended.

Eating

Medellín: centre *p977, map p978*

TT Café Botero, Cra 52, No 52-43. Excellent lunchtime venue next to the Museo de Antioquia. Fish, fine steaks and delicious puddings.

TT Chung Wah, C 54, No 49-75. The oldest and best Chinese restaurant in town.

TT Hato Viejo, Cra 47, No 52-17. Typical dishes such as *ajiaco*, *sudao* and *mondongo* as well as the usual steaks and fish. Open lunchtime until late.

TT Versalles, Pasaje Junín, No 53-59. Famous Argentine-run restaurant, *parrillas* and empanadas in a room filled with photographs of renowned Latin American philosophers. Lovely coffees and breakfasts too. Highly recommended.

TT T 1,2,3… Cazuelas, CC Unión, Cra 49, No 52-107, loc 219. Local fast food in what was once Medellín's most exclusive social club, now a shopping mall with numerous restaurants.

TT T Salón de Té Astor, Cra 49, No 52-84. Delightful traditional tea and pastry house, famous for its chocolate delicacies.

T Unión CC food court, Cra 49, No 52-81. Many eateries and outlets in this basement food court of a shopping mall.

T Fonda Parque Bolívar, C 55, No 47-27. Just off Parque Bolívar, popular, quaint-looking lunchtime venue.

Medellín: outside the centre *p977, map p977*

TT La Margarita No 2, Cra 70, No 45E-11. Antioquian dishes in a nice, friendly atmosphere.

TT T Pomodoro, C 42, No 71-24. Wide variety of pastas and sauces at reasonable prices.

T Fenicia, Cra 73, No 2-41. Family-run Lebanese restaurant, takeaway service available.

T Opera Pizza, C 42, No 70-22. *Paisas* swear these are the best pizzas in town, full of Italian expats.

T ¡Orale!, C 41, No 70-138. Excellent little Mexican cantina with tables on the street. Another branch at Cra 43B, 10-49, El Poblado, does Mexican and pizza.

El Poblado and around

TTT Basílica, Cra 38, No 8A-42. Steaks, sushi and Peruvian specialities on an open terrace on Parque Lleras.

ŦŦŦ **Triada**, Cra 38, No 8-8. Enormous restaurant/bar/club in the heart of the Zona Rosa, steaks, sushi, salads and Tex Mex, good atmosphere. Packed on weekends.
ŦŦŦ ŦŦ **Thaico**, C 9, No 37-40. Good Thai food, popular spot for watching televised sports.
Ŧ **Bagels & Brunch**, C9A, No 38-26. Breakfast venue with stuffed bagels, pancakes and fruit smoothies.
Ŧ **Donde Paco**, Cra 35, No 8A-80. Economic Colombian or oriental food in a nice atmosphere.
Ŧ **Le Bon**, C 9, No 39-09. French café with lovely atmosphere. Often has jazz in the evening.

Bars and clubs

Medellín *p977, maps p977 and p978*
In the centre, the area around Parque de Los Periodistas attracts Goths, punks, and students. In El Poblado, the best bars and clubs are in the Zona Rosa, around Parque Lleras. If the prices of the Zona Rosa get too much, an alternative after-hours location is Sabaneta, 11 km from the centre, with an attractive plaza. It's popular with young and old alike. There are several excellent bars and restaurants with lots of local history. Take a taxi from El Poblado, US$5.50.
B Lounge, Cra 35, No 10-38, El Poblado. The place to see and be seen on Wed nights, with karaoke.
Blue Bar, C 10, No 40-20, El Poblado. Open Thu-Sat, plays rock and Colombian music. Small and crowded, entry often includes a free drink. Also **Red** bar opposite, worth checking out.
Canalón, Cra 40, No 75S-25, Sabaneta. A popular club in this area, open Fri and Sat.
El Viejo John, Cra 45, No 70 Sur-42, Sabaneta. A popular local spot with strings of chorizo hanging from the ceiling. Also serves typical dishes.
Fonda Sitio Viejo, C 70 Sur, No 44-33, Sabaneta. Another bar full of character. This one has photographs of every church in Medellín.
La Herrería, Cra 45, No 70 Sur-24, Sabaneta. Packed to the ceiling with pictures of local characters, Mexican sombreros, saddles and bananas.
Trilogía, Cra 43G, No 24-08, T262 6375, Barrio San Diego. Attracts an older crowd and has live cover bands playing a mix of rock and Colombian music. Arrive before 2230 on Fri and Sat.

Entertainment

Medellín *p977, maps p977 and p978*
Cinema Free foreign films daily at Universidad de Medellín or Universidad de Antioquia. **Centro Colombo Americano**, Cra 45, No 53-24, T513 4444. Shows foreign art films. The main shopping malls have multiplexes.
Live music Monthly concerts by the **Antioquia Symphony Orchestra**. Band concerts and other entertainments in the Parque Bolívar every Sun.
Tango Universidad de Medellín theatre has monthly shows. There are popular tango bars in El Envigado, a **Museo Casa Gardeliana**, Cra 45, No 76-50, T212 0968, commemorating Carlos Gardel who died in a plane crash in Medellín in 1935, and an annual **Festival Internacional de Tango** in Jun. **Salón Málaga**, Cra 51, No 45-80, T231 2658, is one of Medellín's oldest tango bars (its 50th anniversary was in 2008). Owner Gustavo Arteaga is considered one of the principle collectors of tango in Colombia.
Theatre **Teatro Metropolitano**, C 41, No 57-30, T232 4597, www.teatrometropolitano.com, major artistic presentations. Many other theatres of all types, check the press for details.

Festivals and events

Medellín *p977, maps p977 and p978*
Easter Semana Santa (Holy Week) has special Easter religious parades. **Jul International Poetry Festival**, see www.festivaldepoesiade medellin.org.**Flower fair (Feria de las Flores/Desfile de Silleteros)** is held annually in the **1st week of Aug** with spectacular parades and music, one of the finest shows in Colombia. **International Jazz and World Music Festival** in **Sep**. There are many other music and cultural festivals throughout the year.

Shopping

Medellín *p977, maps p977 and p978*
Bookshops La Anticuaria, C 49, No 47-46, T511 4969. Sells antique and secondhand books, including some in English, helpful. **Centro Colombo Americano**, Cra 45, No 53-24, T513 4444, www.colomboworld.com. Good selection of books in English (including *Footprint Handbooks*).
Handicrafts There are *artesanía* shops on the top of Cerro Nutibara and a small handicrafts

market at C 52 near Cra 46 with many stalls. **Aluzia Correas y Cinturones**, Oviedo Shopping Center, Poblado, Unicentro Medellín, also in Bogotá, for a wide selection of belts, US$10-30. **Mercado San Alejo**, Parque Bolívar, open on the first Sat of every month except Jan, and before Christmas on Sat and Sun (handicrafts on sale at good prices). Good shopping generally around Parque de Bolívar. Many textile mills have discount clothing with good bargains; ask your hotel.

Maps Instituto Geográfico Agustín Codazzi, Fundación Ferrocarril building, Cra 52, No 43-42, T381 0561, office in the basement. Local and national maps.

▲ Activities and tours

Medellín *p977, maps p977 and p978*

Bullfights At the bullring of La Macarena, C 44 and Cra 63, in Jan and Feb; cheapest US$12, usually fully booked.

Dance classes Academia Dance, Cra 46, No 7-9, T266 1522. Salsa classes. **Black Sheep** residents get 10% discount. Individual lessons US$6, good reports.

Sports complex Estadio Atanasio Girardot, Cra 74, C 50, football, baseball, velodrome, swimming, next to the *Estadio* Metro station.

Tour operators **Destino Colombia**, C 50, No 65-42, CC Contemporáneo, loc 225, T260 6868, www.destinocolombia.com. Tours to nearby attractions in Antioquia and nationwide. Very well-informed English-speaking guides. Can also arrange flights. Recommended. **Turixmo**, C 9, No 43A-31, turixmo@geo. net.co. City and regional tours. Airport pick-ups. Helpful and professional.

Trekking Instituto de Deportes y Recreación (Inder), T576 0780. Organize walking tours around Medellín on Sun.

Transport

Medellín *p977, maps p977 and p978*

Air Airport information, T562 2828. Frequent services to **Bogotá**, **Cartagena**, and all major Colombian cities. Municipal airport: **Olaya Herrera**, 10 mins by taxi from the centre, national flights only including to **Quibdó** (change here for **Nuquí**), **Acandí**, **Capurganá** and major cities, with **easyfly**, **Satena** and **Aerolíneas de Antioquia (ADA)**.

Bus From **Terminal del Norte**, T230 8514: To/ from **Bogotá**, 9-12 hrs, US$33.50, every 40 mins or so, with 5 companies. To **Cartagena**, 15 hrs, by **Pullman** bus, US$55-60 (take food with you, the stops tend to be at expensive restaurants). To **Santa Marta**, 18 hrs, US$70. To **Arboletes**, **Rápido Ochoa**, US$35, 12 hrs. To **Turbo**, US$27 with **Gómez** (the best), 14 hrs. To **Magangué** (for Mompós), US$46, with **Rápido Ochoa** or **Brasilia**.

From **Terminal del Sur**, T361 1499. To **Quibdó**, 12-13 hrs, US$25. Frequent buses to **Manizales**, 6 hrs US$17, by **Empresa Arauca**. To **Pereira**, 6-8 hrs, US$12-17. Frequent buses for **Cali**, **Flota Magdalena**, **Palmira** US$18-22, 10-12 hrs. To **Popayán**, US$31, 12 hrs, **Flota Magadalena**. To **San Agustín**, **Rápidos Tolima**, 0600, US$34. To **Ipiales**, US$43, 22 hrs, **Expreso Bolivariano** (takes Visa).

Metro 0430-2300 weekdays, 0500-2200 Sun and holidays. 1 journey (anywhere on the system) US$0.72.

Taxi Minimum charge US$2. Radio taxis: **Taxi Bernal**, T444 8882, **Taxi Andaluz**, T444 5555. For airport pickups, try **Turixmo**, T266 2846.

Directory

Medellín *p977, maps p977 and p978*

Airline offices AeroRepública, C 5A, No 39-141, T268 4500. **Aires**, Cra 65A, No 13-157, T361 1331. **Avianca**, Cra 43A, No 1A Sur-35, T311 5833, and at both airports. **Easyfly**, T363 1651. **Satena**, Olaya Herrera airport, or C 9, No 41-56, T266 2185. **Aerolíneas de Antioquia**, C 10, No 35-32 or at Olaya Herrera airport. **Banks** Most banks in the business zones have ATMs. Many accept international cards. **Bancolombia**, in El Poblada, cash against MasterCard, Amex, good rates for TCs and cash. Many banks open late and on Sat. Main hotels will cash TCs for residents when banks are closed, but at less favourable rates. Most **casas de cambio** are found in the shopping malls, eg **CC El Tesoro**. **Consulates** France, Cra 49, No 44-94, Local 258, T513 6688, alliamed@epm.net.co, open Tue and Thu only. **Germany**, Cra 48, No 26 Sur-181, Local 106, T334 6474. **Panama**, C 10, No 42-45, Of 266, T312 4590. **UK**, Cra 42, No 53-26, Autopista Sur – Itagüi, T377 9966, consulado britanico@une.net.co, open 0900-1230. **Cultural centres** Centro Colombo Americano, Cra 45,

No 53-24, T513 4444. See Bookshops, above. **Alianza Francesa**, Cra 49, No 44-94, T576 0780. **Immigration** DAS, C 19, No 80A-40 in Belén La Gloria section, T340 5800, and at main airport. **Internet** Plenty of internet cafés in El Poblado, travellers' hostels and most shopping centres. **Language classes** **Eafit University**, Cra 49, No 7 Sur 50, Av Las Vegas, T261 9500. US$265 for 2½ months, 2 hrs a day, popular, well-organized Spanish courses, good reports. **Medical services** Hospital San Vicente de Paul, C 64/Cra 51D, T444 1333, one of the best. **Clínica Soma**, C 51, No 45-93, T576 8400, good doctor and general services. There is an emergency health clinic the Rionegro airport building. **Post offices** Main **Deprisa** office, C 10, No 56-06, Mon-Fri 0730-2100, Sat, 0730-1800. Also Cra 46, No 52-36 and in all **Exito** supermarkets. **Telephones** Telecom, C 49, No 49-73. **Useful addresses** Tourist **Police** T230 8110; local police T112.

Around Medellín

Medellín southeast to Bogotá

Five kilometres from Medellín airport is **Rionegro** (*Phone code: 4*) in a delightful valley of gardens and orchards. The **Casa de Convención** and the **cathedral** are worth a visit. There are colourful processions in Easter Week. There are various hotels (**C-F**) and many places to eat in and near the plaza. Around Rionegro is some very attractive country, popular at weekends with delightful places to spend the day eg El Retiro and nearby **Fizebad**, an old estate house, restored with original furniture and artefacts, and a display of flowering orchids.

On the Medellín-Bogotá highway is **Marinilla**, 46 km from Medellín. A road north goes 25 km to **El Peñol** ⓘ *US$1.30, parking US$1*, a precipitous, bullet-shaped rock which towers above the surrounding hills and the Embalse del Peñol reservoir. It has been eroded smooth, but a spiral staircase has been built into a crack from the base to the summit (649 steps). The views from the top re spectacular. At the entrance and summit are snack bars. From Terminal del Norte in Medellín, many bus companies leave for the rock and to the pretty town of **Guatapé** (*Phone code: 4; Population: 5,000; Altitude: 1,900 m*), US$2.70. Ask to be dropped off at the small road leading to El Peñol, from where it's a 10-minute walk uphill to the entrance. Guatapé is 3 km further along the main road; several places to stay (**B-E**) and plenty of restaurants. During the week it's a quiet town and at weekends there are lots of visitors from Medellín, the malecón lined with pleasure boats.

Another popular trip from Medellín is to **Reserva Natural Cañón del Río Claro**, three hours along the Medellín- Bogotá highway. The crystal-clean Claro river is lined with limestone cliffs and is a beautiful, tranquil place to relax and take leisurely walks along its banks. The reserve is noted for its incredible biodiversity with over 50 new species of plants discovered and more than 370 different species of bird identified since its foundation.

Santa Fé de Antioquia → *Phone code: 4. Colour map 1, B2. Population: 12,000. Altitude: 530m.*

Santa Fé de Antioquia (usually called Santa Fé), is 78 km from Medellín, just west of the Río Cauca, surrounded by mountainous green countryside. It is a safe, peaceful, well-preserved colonial town from where it is best to explore on horseback or bicycle. It is a popular weekend haunt with Antioquians. Santa Fé was founded as a gold mining town by the Spaniards in 1541 and became famous for its gold jewellery. Today, most of the gold mines have been abandoned but there is still some gold mining in the Río Cauca. In 1813, Santa Fé was declared the capital of the short-lived independent state of Antioquia, but in 1826, its status had collapsed and political control was lost to Medellín. The lively main plaza is dominated by a fine old Cathedral. There are several other churches worth seeing, notably Santa Bárbara. Next door is a **Museo de Arte Religioso/Museo Juan del Corral** ⓘ *C 11, open weekends and holidays, 1000-1700*, which has a collection of historical items, paintings, gold objects etc from colonial and more recent times. Opposite the Plaza Santa Bárbara is the site of a former slave market. About 6 km from the town is the 300-m long Puente de Occidente, an impressive suspension bridge with great views; best to take a taxi or motortaxi from the main plaza, round trip US$3.50. Major local festivals at Easter, Christmas and New Year.

South from Medellín

Santa Bárbara (*Altitude: 1,857 m*), 57 km south of Medellín on the main road via the town of Caldas, with stunning views in every direction of coffee, banana and sugar plantations, orange-tiled roofs and folds of hills. Hotels and restaurants on main plaza; bus from Medellín, US$1.20. A further 26 km is **La Pintada** (camping; hotels **E-F**). Here the road crosses the Río Cauca, then splits. To the left is the particularly attractive road through Aguadas, Pácora and Salamina, all perched on mountain ridges, to Manizales.

Alternatively, from La Pintada, the main road goes up the Cauca valley through **Supía**, a pleasant town 140 km south of Medellín and **Riosucio**, a delightful town with fine views, a large church and many restaurants and shops. At Anserma the road turns east to Manizales via Arauca. There is beautiful country on the west side of the Río Cauca.

Shortly after Caldas, a road to the right (west) descends through Amagá to cross the Cauca at Bolombolo. From here, several attractive towns can be visited. **Jericó**, is an interesting Antioquian town with a large cathedral, several other churches, two museums and a good view from **Morro El Salvador. Andes** is a busy coffee-buying centre, several places to stay and to eat, all on Carrera 50/51; attractive waterfalls in the neighbourhood. **Jardín** is 16 km southeast of Andes. This pretty Antioquian village is surrounded by cultivated hills and trout farms. The plaza is full of flowering shrubs and trees. There is a delightful festival (*Fiesta de las Rosas)* in January. The **Templo Parroquial de la Inmaculada Concepción** is a National Monument and the small museum in the Casa Cultura has paintings and local artifacts. The bank accepts Visa cards.

Around Medellín listings

For Sleeping and Eating price codes and other relevant information, see Essentials, pages 38-40.

Sleeping

Medellín southeast to Bogotá *p983*

A-D Refugio Río Claro, reservations in Medellín, T268 8855, T311-354 0119, www.rioclaro elrefugio.com. Tranquil spot, good value, delightful wooden lodges with great views of river. Includes 3 meals, restaurant service, cheaper rooms in hostel and camping (**F**). Book ahead. Rafting trips along river, also zip-lines over canyon. Recommended.

Santa Fé de Antioquia *p983*

It's best to book in advance at weekends and public holidays. Rates can be 40% more in high season and bank holiday weekends. Most hotels organize horse rides and town tours and offer a *día de sol* (lunch and entry to pool) US$15-20.

A Guaracú, C 10, No 8-36, T853 1097. Colonial mansion with antique furniture and a large pet tortoise. Rooms are very comfortable, lovely pool, the speciality of the restaurant is fish.

A Hostal Tenerife, Cra 8, No 9-50, T853 2261. Beautifully decorated colonial house, a/c, cable TV, minibar. Free use of house bikes, internet, pool. Breakfast incuded. Recommended.

A Mariscal Robledo, Cra 10, No 9-70, T853 1111. Stylish colonial hotel. Nice pool area with palms. Good weekend lunch buffet. Recommended.

B Caserón Plaza, C 9, No 9-41, T853 2040, www.hotelcaseronplaza.com.co. Large colonial building, comfortable rooms, some with balconies looking onto pool. Sun deck has fantastic views, internet, Wi-Fi, bike hire, a/c.

B Hostería de la Plaza Menor, C 9A, No 13-21, T853 1133. Round the corner from the Plaza Menor, comfortable, with swimming pool, Turkish bath, gym and a children's playground.

C Las Carnes del Tío, C 10, No 7-22, T853 3385. A restaurant that also offers good rooms with huge bathrooms. Also dorms with shared bath.

D Hostal Plaza Mayor, Parque Principal, T853 3448. Popular with backpackers. There are hammocks, a small pool and a small *cabaña* with bunk beds (**E**). The owner also has a ranch outside town where he will take guests for a BBQ.

E Alejo, C 9, No 10-56, T853 1091. One block from the Parque Principal, small, basic but clean rooms, TV, restaurant serves cheap food.

South from Medellín: Jardín *p984*

Several *residencias* and restaurants by the plaza.

A Hacienda Balandú, Vía Jardín Río Sucio, 800 m from town, T845 6850, www.comfenalcoantioquia.com. Comfortable rooms, pool, gardens, lake, spa, sports, used by birdwatching groups, good restaurant.

Eating

Santa Fé de Antioquia *p983*

Don Roberto, C 10, No 7-37. Colonial building with swimming pool (US$4.50), simple menu.

La Comedia, C 11, No 8-03. This novel restaurant lets you buy any of the furniture or utensils you use, all of which are made by *artesanos* from Barichara. Jazz and art exhibitions. Colombian and international arthouse films every Thu evening, projected in the bar or in the parque.

Macías, Parque Principal. Established over 35 years, serves regional and national dishes.

Transport

Medellín southeast to Bogotá *p983*

Bus To **El Peñol** from Rionegro, take a colectivo to Marinilla from near market, US$0.60. To **El Retiro**, US$2.50. To **Fizebad**, catch a **La Ceja** or **El Retiro** bus from Terminal del Norte. To **Río Claro**, take a Bogotá-bound bus and tell the driver you want to get off at Río Claro, 3 hrs.

Santa Fé de Antioquia *p983*

Bus The station is on the road to Turbo at the north end of Cras 9 and 10 (5 mins' walk to main plaza). To **Medellín** US$5 (numerous companies), colectivo US$7, 1 hr. To **Turbo**, US$20, 8-9 hrs, every 2 hrs or so.

South from Medellín: Jardín *p984*

Bus From Medellín (Terminal Sur), 4-5 hrs; to **Riosucio**, 3 hrs, US$4.40.

Department of Chocó

Chocó is one of the most biodiverse regions in the world and is all in the heavy rainbelt along Colombia's northwest coast, densely forested and sparsely inhabited. It is also one of the rainiest regions on earth ('dry' season: December to March). In the northern part of the department, the mountain ranges rise directly from the ocean to reach a height of about 500 m. Transport is limited to water routes along the Pacific coast from Buenaventura in the south and up the rivers. Road access is via two unpaved routes across the Cordillera Occidental, one from Medellín via Bolívar, the other from Pereira to the southeast via La Virginia and Pueblo Rico (see page 992).

Chocó is home to a number of indigenous groups, including the Embera, whose communities are based on hunting, fishing, and subsistence farming. The coastline is also dotted with poor black fishing communities. The main small tourist resorts are concentrated in Nuquí, Bahía Solano on the Pacific coast and the more developed and expensive resort of Capurganá on the Caribbean (see page 952). The best time to go to Chocó is when humpback whales visit the area (beginning of July-late October). Hotels usually offer all-inclusive packages for a three-night stay and arrange boat transport to and from the airport. Along the Río San Juan, in the south, there is gold prospecting around the towns of Tadó and Istmina. Precautions against malaria, yellow fever, and dengue are recommended. **Warning** The Department of Chocó, especially the lower Atrato, remains a very dangerous area (guerrillas, paramilitaries, kidnappings, drug running). Much caution and detailed advance enquiry are recommended. The best advice is to fly to Nuquí or Bahía Solano.

Quibdó → *Phone code: 4. Colour map 1, B2. Population: 131,000. Altitude: 50 m.*

Quibdó is on the eastern bank of the Río Atrato. It is the jumping-off point for most military operations in this part of the country and, apart from the unstoppable partying during the city's fiestas, there is little to detain the visitor here. The San Pacho festival (20 September-4 October), for instance, has parades and a San Francisco de Asís procession. There is an interesting mural in the cathedral. Hordes of birds fly in to roost at dusk and there are magnificent sunsets, which locals watch from the waterfront promenade, El Malecón.

It is not safe to travel beyond Quibdó by road.

Pacific coast

On the Gulf of Tribugá, surrounded by estuaries, mangroves and virgin beaches, **Nuquí** is gaining popularity among Colombian sports fishermen and vacationers, not so much the town itself, but the beaches and ecolodges up and down the coast. Visitors have to pay a US$2 tourism tax. To the south lies the wide curve of Playa Olímpica. To the north is the even smaller hamlet of Tribugá and a splendid beach. About 50 km north of Nuquí along the coast, **El Valle** has the best bathing and surfing beaches in the area. Between Nuquí and El Valle is **Parque Nacional Ensenada de Utría** *entry US$16.50, contact Corporación Mano Cambiada, T311-872 7887, corporacionmano cambiada@yahoo.es*, home to two varieties of whales, corals, needlefish, and many other aquatic species. The surrounding hillsides are covered with pristine rainforest and there are several magnificent white sand beaches. Most hotels organize day trips to the Park, or you can hire a boat with a group from El Valle, takes 1½ hours, or from Nuquí. Isla Playa Blanca is recommended as part of the trip. Boat prices start at US$150 and vary considerably, depending on time and number of passengers. Ask at hotels for information. Insist on a life jacket.

Bahía Solano → *Phone code: 816.*

The town lies on a large bay set against jungle covered hills. As a resort, it gets busy during holiday periods (the whale season and Easter), otherwise it's a functional fishing town (with a lucrative sideline in collecting discarded shipments of cocaine on their way north). Good bathing beaches may be reached by launch or by walking about 1½ hours at low tide (for example Playa Mecana. Be sure to return before the tide rises or you will be stranded). Diving and sport fishing are also popular. Tourist information from the Alcaldía, *T682 7049, alcaldiabahiasolano@hotmail.com*. There are no ATMs in the town.

Department of Chocó listings

For Sleeping and Eating price codes and other relevant information, see Essentials, pages 38-40.

Sleeping

Quibdó *p986*

There are few decent places to stay, but centrally located and safe is the **Malecón**, T4-671 4662.

Pacific Coast: Nuquí *p986*

Along the beach at the north end of town, there are several tourist hotels usually fully booked during the holiday period, best to make arrangements through travel agents in Medellín or Bogotá. It is possible to stay in Nuquí and Bahía Solano cheaply if you rent a basic room in a family house, around US$10 pp. Ask locals or look for rent signs on windows. Negotiate prices during low season.

The following are environmentally aware, award-winning and design-oriented locations:

Cabañas Pijiba, T4-474 5221 or Medellín 234 3502, www.pijibalodge.com. Award-winning ecotourism development with full board. Comfortable wooden lodges with thatched roofs. Arranges guided trips, diving, forest walks, airport pick-up (45-min boat ride to hotel), from US$285 pp double for 3 nights, longer packages available.

El Cantil, T4-252 0707, www.elcantil.com. 35 mins south of Nuquí, prices start at US$220 pp double for a 2-nights, full board, transfers and a trail walk included. Wooden cabins with sea view, bath, mosquito nets. Also surfing courses, hot springs trips, diving, whale watching in season.

A pp **MorroMico**, T8-521 4172, www.morromico.com. Small hotel with spacious, rustic cabins, restaurant serving fresh food. Activities include whale-watching, birdwatching, boat and beach trips, visits to Ensenada de Utría,and more.

B Lodge Piedra Piedra, 45 mins south of Nuquí, T2-893 1258, www.piedrapiedra.com. Price is for 2 days, 1 night, transport (US$28.50). Meals extra (US$20 full board). Also all-inclusive, whale-watching and fishing packages from 3 to 7 days (from US$278 pp). Organizes local tours, wood and thatched lodges, dorms and private rooms, camping, use of kitchen and kayak rental.

Pacific Coast: El Valle *p986*

AL Cabañas El Almejal, reservations T230 6060 (Medellín), www.almejal.com.co. Cabins with private bath, the best, full board, Price depends on the package. In private reserve, turtle conservation programme, educational programmes, lots of wildlife-watching opportunities.

Other cabins and rooms also available in El Valle.

Bahía Solano *p986*

Mapara Crab, www.mapara crab.com, T2-331 9464, 315-488 7679. Run by Nancy and Enrique Ramírez, small, comfortable place on a private beach, 20 mins by boat from Bahía Solano, private rooms with fan and breakfast. Enrique is a master sports fisherman and diving enthusiast. There are hotels in Bahía Solano itself.

Transport

Quibdó *p986*

Air Flights daily to **Medellín**, **Bogotá** and nearby towns with **Satena** (fare from Medellín from US$62 one way) and **Aires**.

Bus **Flota Occidental** to **Medellín** via Pereira, daily at 0600, 13 hrs, US$25. It is unsafe to take buses in this region. Check with locals first before setting off.

Ferry It is not advisable to take boats in any direction at this time.

Pacific Coast: Nuquí *p986*

Air Satena, **Searca** and **ADA** fly to Nuquí from **Medellín**, **Cali** and **Bogotá** Mon, Wed, Fri and Sun (**Satena** Medellín-Nuquí one way US$87).

As yet there is no **road** access for regular vehicles to Nuquí. A rough road runs 18 km from El Valle to Bahía Solano (passes by airport before town). Jeeps leave every morning, 1 hr, US$4.50, tickets can be purchased 1 day in advance.

Bahía Solano *p986*

Air There are flights from Medellín to Bahía Solano with **Satena** Mon, Wed, Fri, Sun, from US$88 one way.

Daily **jeep** service to **El Valle** and frequent trucks during the day, US$4.50, 1 hr (see above).

Directory

Quibdó *p986*

Banks Several ATMs. **Banco de Bogotá**, cash against Visa, other banks do not change money. A few shopkeepers sometimes change US$ cash, but rates are poor. It is best to buy pesos before arriving.

Useful addresses DAS Office: C 25, No 6-08, T671 1402. No entry or exit stamps.

La Zona Cafetera

Modern and colonial cities line the fertile western slopes of the Cordillera Central which is the centre of Colombia's coffee production. The three departments of Caldas, Quindío and Risaralda are generally known as the 'Zona Cafetera'. Much of the land here is between the critical altitudes for coffee of 800- 1,800 m, and has the right balance of rain and sunshine. The area has beautiful rolling countryside of coffee plantations, interspersed with bamboo, plantain and banana trees. The best way to enjoy the Zona Cafetera is to stay on a coffee farm, where you can tour the plantations and see how coffee is produced at harvest time (October to December). And of course, there is excellent, fresh, coffee all year round. In recent years, the Zona Cafetera has been building a reputation as an adventure sports destination, including rafting, kayaking and canopying (whizzing across ravines on steel cables).

Manizales and around

Rich in coffee and flowers, Manizales is one of the principal starting points for excursions to the Parque Nacional Los Nevados, which, as its name suggests, is dominated by snow-capped mountains. Earthquakes and volcanoes have been a feature of this volatile region.

Manizales ➔ *Phone code: 6. Colour map 1, B2. Population: 335,000. Altitude: 2,153 m.*

Manizales, 309 km from Bogotá, is dominated by its enormous concrete Cathedral and the Nevado del Ruiz volcano, which erupted catastrophically in November 1985. It sits on a mountain saddle, which falls away sharply from the centre into the adjacent valleys. The climate is humid (average temperature is 17°C, annual rainfall is 3,560 mm), encouraging prodigious growth in the flowers that line the highways to the suburbs north and south. Frequently the city is covered in cloud. The best months of the year are from mid-December to early March. The area known as **El Cable**, east of the centre, is the Zona Rosa, with good restaurants and bars. The city looks down on the small town of Villa María, "the village of flowers", now almost a suburb.

Several earthquakes and fires have destroyed parts of the city over the years, so the architecture is predominantly modern with high-rise office and apartment blocks. Traditional styles are still seen in the suburbs and the older sections of the city. The departmental **Gobernación** building, opposite the Cathedral in the Parque de Bolívar, is an imposing example of neocolonial architecture and a national monument. Inside are a tourist office (*C 22 y Cra 21, T884 2400 ext 444-315*) and a local arts and crafts shop. The **bullring**, on Avenida Centenario, is an impressive copy of the traditional Moorish style. Along Avenida 12 de Octubre to the suburb of Chipre is a park, providing a great view to the west and paragliding opportunities (well visited on Sunday); El Tanque, on the Avenida, is a popular landmark and viewpoint.

Banco de la República ⓘ *Cra 23, No 23-06 (behind the cathedral), 0900-1000, 1100-1130, 1430-1830, Mon-Fri, free,* has a gold and anthropology museum with classical music concerts in the afternoon. **Universidad de Caldas** ⓘ *C 65 No 26-10, Mon-Fri 0800-1200, 1400-1800 (take a 'Fátima' bus to the University),* has a natural history museum with a selection of butterflies, moths and birds. The **Centro de Museos** ⓘ *Cra 23, No 58-65, T885 1374, Mon-Fri, 0800-1200, 1400-1600,* also part of Caldas University, has an art gallery and exhibitions on geology and archaeology. **La Galería del Arte** ⓘ *Av Santander at C 55,* has exhibitions of work, which can be bought, by local artists. **Tourist office** Fomento y Turismo ⓘ *C 31, No 22-47, T884 6211, guidebook and maps available, open Mon-Fri 0800-1200, 1400-1800.* See also Gobernación, above.

About 8 km from Manizales is the **Parque Ecológico Río Blanco**, a 4343-ha protected cloudforest, considered by the World Wildlife Fund the best place for birdwatching in Colombia. To date, 335 species of bird have been identified, including 33 species of hummingbird. There are also 350 species of butterfly and 40 types of orchid. Mammals include spectacled bear, ocelot and the white-tailed deer. The park is owned by **Aguas de Manizales** ⓘ *entry is free but you must take a guide (recommended tip US$10) and you must get permission from the Oficina de Recursos Naturales, T886 7777*. There are several hikes of between 20 minutes and eight hours as well as a rangers' hut where 22 species of hummingbird come to feed, managed by the **Fundación Ecológica Gabriel Arango Restrepo** ⓘ *T886 7777, ext 1164, contact Technical Director Sergio Ocampo, www.fundegar.com: basic dorms US$17 pp, food US$12.50*.

Parque Nacional Los Nevados

The park has all the wild beauty of the high Cordillera, towering mountains (snowcapped above 4,850 m), dormant volcanoes, hot springs and recent memories of tragic eruptions. The park comprises 58,000 ha and straddles the departments of Caldas, Quindío, Risaralda, and Tolima. Visitors should come prepared for cold, damp weather, and remember to give themselves time to acclimatize to the altitude. See under Ibagué, page 994, for Nevado del Tolima.

Information **Oficina del Parque de Los Nevados** ⓘ *C 76B, No 18-14, Manizales, T/F886 4104*, for information and entrance fees, US$16.50 for non-Colombians. If you intend to do some serious mountain climbing and or mountain biking, apply in writing to the above office, 5 days in advance. Book accommodation in the Park at the **Aviatur** office in the park ⓘ *T01-900-331 2222, or 01-382 1616; in Manizales C 56, No 23-16, T886 3300, and C 21, No 22-39, T884 2277*. The tourist office in Manizales can put you in touch with agencies who organize day trips to Nevado del Ruiz, only at weekends (US$35 for 1 day, for transport, guide, entrance fees, return via hot pools). Guides can be arranged and trips extended to the Parque Nacional de los Nevados and Nevado del Tolima. **Mountain House**, a traveller hostel in Manizales, has information on trips and provides maps, which are also available at the **Instituto Geográfico** in Manizales ⓘ *C 24, No 25-15, T884 5864*.

The recommended route to visit **Nevado del Ruiz** (5,400 m) with a vehicle is to take the Bogotá road from Manizales, to La Esperanza (22 km). Leave the main road here to the right for excursions towards the volcano. For an alternative, shorter route (4WD only), make for the Barrio La Anea (next to the airport) continuing on an unpaved, rough road for 22 km. This leads first to the hot pools of **Termales de Otoño** ⓘ *US$15*, then towards La Gruta, followed by the hot pools at **Termales del Ruiz** at 3,400 m. Both hot pools have hotels attached (T874 0280). 7 km further on, this road meets the road coming from La Esperanza. Turning right, and continuing 2 km brings you to Las Brisas (small restaurant 2 km beyond). You can walk from Las Brisas down to Manizales in 8 hours, start early and stop on the way at *Hotel Termales del Ruiz* (see Sleeping).

Past Las Brisas the road forks. To the left it continues over huge landslides caused by the 1985 Nevado del Ruiz eruption, to the village of Ventanas (a very scenic drive) and on to Murillo in Tolima department. To the right it climbs steeply for 1 km to reach the **park entrance and visitors' centre** ⓘ *US$17, vehicle US$2, open 0700-1430*, at 4,050 m. In 2.5 km at 4,150 m is *Arenales* (see Sleeping). The turnoff (left) to Nevado del Ruiz is 10 km beyond the park entrance and you can drive to 2 km of the snow line. On foot from 4,050 m to the summit takes six to seven hours if you are acclimatized. At 4,800 m, there is a basic hut, no water, no beds nor any facilities, but there may be refreshments during the day. Ask at the entrance if it is open. From here, it is about three hours to the summit. An authorized guide is obligatory if you wish to climb from the snowline to the crater (beware of fumaroles of toxic gas). Another climb nearby is La Olleta (4,850 m), the ash cone of an extinct volcano. You can go into the crater, but note your route well as fog can obliterate landmarks quickly. The road continues (south) below the Nevados del Cisne and de Santa Isabel (4,950m) between which you can visit the Laguna Verde. A guide to Santa Isabel costs US$53 for a day. Four-wheel drive vehicles are necessary beyond Nevado del Ruiz. 20 km further along the road and 39 km beyond the turnoff to Nevado del Ruiz is Laguna del Otún at the southern end of the park, trout fishing and camping with permission of *Parques Nacionales*. **Note** There are no kitchen facilities or meals at Laguna del Otún.

The main road from Manizales to Bogotá goes east to Honda (see page 918). It passes through **Mariquita** (21 km before Honda). From Mariquita a road turns south to (32 km) **Armero**, which was devastated by the eruption of the Nevado del Ruiz volcano in November 1985. Over 25,000 people were killed as 10% of the ice core melted, causing landslides and mudflows. (Armero can be reached by colectivo from Honda; nearest lodging at **Lérida**, 12 km south.)

Manizales and around listings

For Sleeping and Eating price codes and other relevant information, see Essentials, pages 38-40.

Sleeping

Manizales *p988*

When planning a trip here, take into account price rises during the popular Feria de Manizales in Jan.

AL Las Colinas, Cra 22, No 20-20, T884 2009, www.hotelesestelar.com. Just off Plaza Bolívar, large rooms, cable TV, Wi-Fi, business centre, sauna, bars and restaurant.

AL Varuna, C 62, No 23C-18, T881 1122, www.varunahotel.com. New, slick, minimal look, good restaurant. Rooms are large and comfortable, hydro massage showers, Wi-Fi.

A Carretero, C 23, No 35A-31, T884 0255, www.hotelcarretero.com. Well placed, smart, large, comfortable rooms, breakfast included, Wi-Fi, sauna. Can organize car hire.

A Escorial, C 21, No 21-11, T884 7696, escorial@une.net.co. Nicely decorated, central, Wi-Fi, parking, cable TV, restaurant, breakfast included.

A-B Regine's, C 65A, No 23B-113, T887 5360, regineshotel@hotmail.com. In a quiet suburban street behind El Cable, good rooms, internet access, Wi-Fi, cable TV, laundry service. Breakfast can be served in a small garden where there are smaller, cheaper rooms. Recommended.

D Bolívar, Cra 20, No 23-09, T884 4066, www.hotelesmanizales.com. Small and basic but clean rooms with bath, TV. Also in this group, **Bolívar Plaza**, C 22, No 22-40, T884 7777, and **Roma Plaza**, C 21, No 22-30, T882 8440, both **B**, more upmarket. As with all central hotels, be careful at night and avoid La Galería area.

D California, C 19, No 16-39, T897 3487, lgt71@hotmail.com. Opposite bus station, simple rooms, good mattresses, TV, hot water, Wi-Fi. Some windows don't lock properly.

D-F Mountain House, C 66, No 23B-137, Barrio Guayacanes, T887 4736, www.mountainhousemanizales.com. Near Zona Rosa. Popular, homely travellers' hostel, includes breakfast, kitchen and laundry facilities, Wi-Fi, hammocks, TV room, book exchange, bike rental, hot showers, free coffee, restaurant. Dorms and rooms with bath. Excellent information about trips to Los Nevados and coffee farms. Recommended.

Parque Nacional Los Nevados *p989*

Apart from the hotels at the Termas del Ruiz and Termas del Otoño (see above):

C pp **El Cisne** visitors centre, run by Parques Nacionales, 22 km from Las Brisas, ask at Aviatur (see above). From US$44-52 pp in shared cabin, half board, price depends on season. Private single and double rooms also available.

Camping At **El Cisne** and **Arenales**, US$4.50-5.55 pp at either; both have toilets, showers. Arenales has a cafetería and a medical station. Advance reservations recommended.

Eating

Manizales *p988*

Apart from the hotels, the best restaurants are on or near Cra 23 in El Cable and Barrio Milán, a taxi ride from Cable Plaza, in the east of the city.

TT Chung Mi No. 2, Cra 23, No 30-10. Chinese, good atmosphere, opposite Parque Caldas.

T Don Juaco Snaks, C 65A, No 23A-44, Barrio Milán. Sandwiches, burgers and typical dishes.

T Il Forno, Cra 23, No 73-86, Barrio Milán. Italian, pleasant, pastas, pizzas and salads. Good vegetarian options.

T Juan Valdez, Cra 23, No 64-55, Barrio Milán. Part of the ubiquitous coffee chain, next to the old cable car line, free Wi-Fi.

T Las Cuatro Estaciones, C 65, No 23A-32, Barrio Milán. Good selection of pastas and pizzas.

T Las Vegas, C 23, No 22-15. Traditional Colombian fare served as a buffet. Open 0600 until 2200 depending on custom.

T Pollo y Asado, C 23, Cra 22. Traditional Colombian *asadero* with the best rotisserie chicken in downtown. Also burgers and steaks.

Entertainment

Manizales *p988*

Cinema and theatre Centro Cultural y Convenciones los Fundadores has interesting wood-carved mural by Guillermo Botero, who also has murals in the *Club Manizales* and *Hotel Las Colinas*. Events held here and at other locations during **Jazz and Theatre Festival** in **Sep/Oct**. Free films at the *Universidad Nacional*, on Tue and Thu.

Festivals and events

Manizales *p988*

The **Feria de Manizales** held in early **Jan** includes a coffee festival, bullfights, beauty parades and folk dancing as well as general partying.

Activities and tours

Manizales *p988*

Colombia57, T313-401 5691/T0800-0789157 (UK freephone), www.colombia57.com. British ex-pats Simon Locke and Russell Coleman organize tailor-made trips around the coffee zone and the rest of Colombia. Well-organized, thoroughly researched with a commitment to sustainability. Highly recommended.

Parque Nacional Los Nevados *p989*

Ecosistemas, Cra 21, No 23-21, Manizales, T880 8300, www.hosteltrail.com/ecosistemas. Charges US$47 for group of 4 to Los Nevados for a day. Trips normally arranged only at weekends. Longer trips to Los Nevados can be arranged, also paragliding, rafting and abseiling.

De Una, based in Bogotá, www.deunacolombia.com, organize several treks, see page 913.

Transport

Manizales *p988*

Air Airport 7 km east; flights are often delayed by fog. Buses to the centre US$1, taxi US$4. **Avianca** and **Aires** fly to **Bogotá**, **Aires** and ADA to Medellín.

Bus Terminal with good restaurant, C 19 between Cras 15 and 17, T884 9183. To **Medellín**, 14 a day 0430-2000, 6 hrs, US$17 with **Arauca**; by **Flota Ospina** *kia* mini van, 4½ hrs, US$18. Many buses to **Bogotá**, **Bolivariana**, US$22-27, 9 hrs. To **Honda**, US$14. **Cali**, hourly, 6 hrs, US$17, by **Flota Ospina** US$18, 4½ hrs. **Pereira**, ½-hourly, 2 hrs, excellent road, beautiful scenery, US$5, or **Flota Ospina**, 1½ hrs. **Armenia**, 3 hrs, US$8 with **Expreso Palmira**, hourly 0600-1800.

Parque Nacional Los Nevados *p989*

As the park entrance closes at 1430, it is advisable to start your journey to the park early in the morning. For those without transport, it is possible to catch a daily *chiva* which leaves opposite El Casino de Suboficiales del Batallón Ayacucho between 0430-0500, US$2.20. For further information contact **Mountain House Hostel** or Victor who runs the *chiva*, T880 9891, T311-380 0796. The **Rápido Tolima** bus daily, usually 1400, from the Terminal in Manizales to Murillo passes near the entrance to the Park, US$3, 2½ hrs. See under Pereira for access from there.

Directory

Manizales *p988*

Banks Banks are along Cra 23.

Immigration DAS Office: C 53, No 25A-35, T881 0600, Mon-Fri, 0730-1200, 1400-1730.

Pereira to Cartago

Still in the shadow of the Nevados, this is a region of modern cities (in several cases rebuilt after earthquakes), delightful scenery and botanical parks and gardens. Coffee is still by far the most important agricultural product of the area, but with the fall in international coffee prices, many fincas have had to diversify into other crops, from flowers and asparagus to bamboo and plantains. Recently, coffee farms have also been opening up to tourism, from day visits to overnight stays. No two fincas are the same; they range from beautiful historic country mansions to more modest accommodation options.

Pereira → *Phone code: 6. Colour map 1, B3. Population: 576,000. Altitude: 1,411 m.*

Capital of Risaralda Department and 56 km southwest of Manizales, Pereira stands within sight of the *Nevados* of the Cordillera Central. A severe earthquake on 5 February 1995 badly damaged several buildings and the city was also affected by the earthquake which devastated Armenia in 1999 (see below). Pereira is a pleasant modern city, founded in 1863. The central **Plaza de Bolívar**, is noted for the striking sculpture of a nude Bolívar on horseback, by Rodrigo Arenas Betancur. There are other fine works of his in the city. The **Cathedral** is unimpressive from the outside but has an elegant and interesting interior. The **Museo Quimbaya de Oro y La Cerámica** ⓘ *in the Banco de la República building, Av 30 de Agosto, No 35-08, free*, features Quimbaya pottery and gold items. Alongside is a library and a music auditorium with a daily programme of classical music. The botanical garden, on the campus of Universidad Tecnológica de Pereria ⓘ *T321 2523, US$4.50, Mon-Sat, 0700-1600, must book a visit in advance and use a guide*, is good for bird watching and has bamboo forests and two hour nature walks.

Tourist information: **Oficina de Desarrollo Turístico** for Risaralda ⓘ *C 19, No 13-17, Edif de la Gobernación, p 6, T335 8860*. **Corporación Autónomo Regional de Risaralda** (Carder) ⓘ *Avenida de las Américas, C 46, No 46-40, T314 1455, www.carder.gov.co (in Spanish)*, has information but does not deal with park permits. Contact **Aviatur** ⓘ *Av.30 de Agosto, No.34-38 L1/15, T326 3630, http://site.aviatur.com*, for park permits. **Turiscafé** ⓘ *C 19, No 5-48, office 901 (inside Novacentro shopping centre), T325 4157, www.turiscafe.net*, for good information on coffee farms in Risaralda in Spanish.

Fifteen kilometres from Pereira is **Santa Rosa de Cabal**, from where several thermal pools can be reached, including Termales de Santa Rosa/Los Arbeláez ⓘ *0800-2400, US$8*. An 9 km unpaved road from Santa Rosa leads to the hot baths (early morning *chiva* or taxi, US$9 to entrance). The Termales de Santa Rosa are surrounded by forests, with waterfalls and nature walks. It's packed at the weekend, quiet during the week. Hotel **Termales de Santa Rosa de Cabal** (attached to the hot baths, **A**), *T364 1322*, comfortable, chalet style, with restaurant. Further along this road, midway between Pereira and Manizales is **Chinchiná**, in the heart of the coffee zone. A coffee hacienda which takes day and overnight visitors (**A**) is **Finca Guayabal** ⓘ *T06-850 7831, www.haciendaguaybal.com*, with a nature trail, full explanations of the coffee-growing process and lunch, US$12.

Northwest of Pereira, 30 km towards the Río Cauca, is **Marsella**, and the **Alexander von Humboldt Gardens**, a carefully maintained botanical display with cobbled paths and bamboo bridges. Just outside the town is the **AL Ecohotel Los Lagos** *T368 6529, www.eco hotelloslagos.com*, previously a gold mine, then a coffee *hacienda*, and now restored as a hotel and nature park with lakes.

Parque Ucumari

From Pereira it is possible to visit the beautiful **Parque Ucumari** ⓘ *park office, T06-325 4781, open daily for information. If visiting for the day and not staying overnight, entrance is free*, one of the few places where the Andean spectacled bear survives. From Pereria, a *chiva* leaves daily (0900, 1500, more frequently during high season) with Transporte Florida from C12, No 9-40 to the village of El Cedral. From El Cedral it is a 2-2½ hour walk to *La Pastora*, the park visitors' centre and refuge. There is excellent camping, US$2.20 per person or US$6 at a refuge, meals extra. From La Pastora it is a steep, rocky 1-2 day hike to Laguna de Otún through beautiful scenery of changing vegetation (see page 989). The **Otún Quimbaya** flora and fauna sanctuary ⓘ *entry US$16.50, run by Aviatur, T01-900-331 2222, or 01-382 1616, reservasparques@aviatur.com.co, transport with La Florida, C 12, N 9-40, T334 2721, 3 a day, 4 on Sat-Sun*, forms a biological corridor between Ucumari and Los Nevados; it protects the last remaining area of Andean tropical forest in Risaralda. There are marked paths as well as *cabañas*, camping and meals available.

Pereira to Armenia

A 44 km road runs through the heart of the *Zona Cafetera*. A turn off at the *Posada Alemana* goes east for 9 km to **Salento** (*Phone code: 6; Population: 9,400; Altitude: 1,985 m*), well into the foothills of the Cordillera. This small town is brightly painted with an attractive plaza surrounded by traditional houses. Up Carrera 6 (continuation of the north side of the plaza), now lined with attractive craft shops and restaurants, is a 250-step climb. The 14 stations of the cross measure your progress to an outstanding viewpoint, overlooking the upper reaches of the Quindío and Cárdenas rivers known as the Cocora valley, possibly one of the finest views in Colombia. It is a popular weekend resort for Colombians for walking, riding and trekking but is usually quiet during the week. More places to eat and to stay are opening up constantly, but try to make arrangements early in the day, particularly at the weekend. Fiesta is in the first week of January and every Sunday night after mass the plaza is taken over by food, drink and craft stalls - lively atmosphere. Tourist information: **Alcaldía de Salento** ⓘ *Parque Principal, T759 3183.* **Plantation House** is also an excellent source of information.

Valle de Cocora

The centre of the Cocora valley is 12 km up from Salento along a rough track, a picturesque 2-hour walk, or by jeep, 35 minutes, US$1.60, leave daily from the main plaza, 0610, 0730, 0930, 1130, 1600, returning 0830, 1230,1500, 1700, more frequent services at weekends and holidays. Some 5 km beyond Cocora at 2,770 m is the **Acaime Natural Reserve** with visitor centre, ponies for hire, beds for 20 and a small restaurant. There are humming birds, cloud forest and the most important area of wax palm (the national tree and one of the tallest trees of the world). In January is the Wax Palm Festival. Above Acaime there are many trails into the high mountains.

Armenia → *Phone code: 6. Colour map 1, B2. Population: 324,500. Altitude: 1,838 m.*

The capital of Quindío Department was founded in 1889. In January 1999, an earthquake flattened much of the city. Impressive reconstruction continues and Armenia is as busy as ever. The fine example of Rodrigo Arenas Betancur's work, the **Monumento al Esfuerzo**, in the Plaza de Bolívar poignantly portrays the spirit of the local people. The two main churches, the cathedral and San Francisco church were both badly damaged but have reopened. The **Museo Quimbaya** ⓘ *Avenida Bolivar, C 40 norte, US$ 0.50*, houses a well-displayed collection of ceramics and textiles of the Quimbaya indigenous group. There is also the **Museo del Oro Quimbaya** ⓘ *Banco de República, Cra 23, No 23-14, Tue-Sat, 0900-1630, Sun and holidays, 1000-1630.* **Parque de la Vida**, north of the city, has bamboo structures, waterfalls and a lakeside theatre.

Near Calarca, 6 km from Armenia, is **Jardín Botánico y Mariposario** ⓘ *T742 7254, Tue-Sun 0900-1600, US$3.50, children half price*, a huge covered butterfly house, with some 50 species of butterflies. There is also an insect zoo and forest walks. 20 minutes south of Calarcá or Armenia is **Recuca** ⓘ *0900-1500, US$7 for day visit, US$12 with lunch, reserve in advance, T310-830 3779, www.recuca.com, take bus Armenia-Barcelona,* a coffee farm with tours experiencing all aspects of coffee-growing, also tastings. Tourist information: **Fondo Mixto de Promoción del Quindío** ⓘ *C 20, No 13-22, T744 0264, www.turismo cafeyquindio.com*, and **Corporación de Cultura y Turismo** ⓘ *Centro Administrativo Municipal CAM, p 4, T741 2991, www.armeniainolvidable.com.*

Parque Nacional del Café

Some 12 km northwest of Armenia is **Montenegro**, near which is Pueblo Tapao (4 km) and the **Parque Nacional del Café** ⓘ *T741 7417, in high season, daily 0900-1600, low season, Wed-Sun and public holidays, 0900-1600, general entrance, US$5.50, or US$12-21 for additional activities and rides, parking US$1; take a bus or colectivo (US$0.45) from Armenia to Montenegro and then a jeep marked 'Parque' (US$0.25) or taxi (US$2) to the entrance.* There are restaurants, a Juan Valdez coffee shop, a botanical garden, ecological walks, a Quimbaya cemetery, a tower with a fine view and an interesting museum which covers all aspects of coffee. A cableway links to a children's theme park (roller coasters, water rides etc). Beyond Montenegro is **Quimbaya**, known for its **Fiesta de Velas y Faroles** in December each year. 7 km away is the **Parque Nacional de la Cultura Agropecuaria** (Panaca), an educational theme park ⓘ *T758 2830, Tue-Sun 0900-1800, US$18,* with many varieties of horses (and a very good show/display), cattle and other animals. A good family outing.

Ibagué and around → *Phone code: 8. Colour map 1, B2. Population: 347,000.*

Quindío Pass, 3,350 m (known as *La Línea* after the power lines that cross the mountains) is on the Armenia to Ibagué road (105 km), across the Cordillera Central. On the east side of the Pass is **Cajamarca**, a friendly town in a beautiful setting at 1,900 m (**F** *Residencia Central; Nevado*, both on same street). *Bar El Globo*, on the main plaza, serves excellent coffee. Interesting market on Sunday.

Ibagué (*Altitude: 1,248 m*), capital of Tolima Department, lies at the foot of the Quindío mountains. See the Colegio de San Simón and the market (good tamales). The Parque Centenario is pleasant and there is a famous music conservatory. Try the local alcoholic drink called *mistela*. **Tourist office** ⓘ *Cra 3 entre C 10 y 11, p 2, T261 1934, turismotolima@tolima.gov.co.*

Just outside, on the Armenia road, a dirt road leads up the Río Combeima to El Silencio and the slopes of **Nevado del Tolima**, the southernmost *nevado* in the **Parque Nacional Los Nevados**. The climb to the summit (5,221 m) takes two to three days, camping at least one night over 4,000 m, ice equipment necessary. For safety reasons, visit Nevado del Tolima from Ibagué and not Manizales. A milk truck (*lechero*) leaves Ibagué marketplace for El Silencio between 0630 and 0730, US$2.50, two hours. A guide in Ibagué is: **Maklin Muñoz**, Cra 1, No 5-24, T261 5865, T300-675 6216.

Cartago → *Phone code: 2. Colour map 1, d B2. Population: 130,000. Altitude: 920 m.*

From Pereira and Armenia roads run west to Cartago, at the northern end of the rich Cauca Valley, stretching south for 240 km but no more than 30 km wide. The road, the Panamericana, goes south along this valley to Cali and Popayán, at the southern limit of the valley. There it mounts the high plateau between the Western and Central Cordilleras and goes through to Ecuador.

Founded in 1540 and noted for its fine embroidered textiles, Cartago, 25 km southwest of Pereira, has some colonial buildings, like the fine **Casa del Virrey**, Calle 13, No 4-29, and the **cathedral**.

Pereira to Cartago listings

For Sleeping and Eating price codes and other relevant information, see Essentials, pages 38-40.

Sleeping

Pereira *p991*

L Hacienda San José, Entrada 16 cadena El Tigre, Km 4 Vía Pereira–Cerritos, T313 2615, www.haciendahotelsanjose.com. One of the oldest houses in the region, almost all of the features have been preserved. Breakfast included. Activities include horse riding and visits to one of the largest bamboo reserves in the region.

L Hotel de Pereira, Cra 13, No 15-73, T335 0770, www.hoteldepereira.com. Best in town, comfortable, Wi-Fi, pool, sauna, conference centre, travel agency, excellent service. Discounts available at weekends.

AL Soratama, Cra 7, No 19-20, T335 8650, www.hotelsoratama.com. Recently refurbished, helpful staff, lots of services including Wi-Fi, massage therapist and internet. Breakfast included. Discounts available at the weekend.

C Cataluña, C 19, No 8-61, T335 4527. 2 floors up, airy rooms with hot water, TV, popular restaurant, good value.

D Bolívar Suite, Cra 8, No 18-54, T333 0505. Clean rooms with good light near the Parque Bolívar, cable TV, hot water.

D Colonial, C 17, No 5-50, T333 7206. Clean but windowless rooms, good security.

Coffee farms

There are far too many coffee farms in the Pereira/Armenia region to list here. They range from huge traditional haciendas to smaller, more modern farms. See **www.clubhaciendasdelcafe.com** for a good selection.

C Finca Villa María, 12 km from Pereira, via Marsella, follow the signs, turning before La Bodega, unpaved 3-km road, T333 8977/3410. 25 mins taxi from Pereria, US$9. Charming typical coffee-*hacienda* set in beautiful countryside. Large rooms, peaceful, full board. Coffee plantations tours. Recommended.

C Villa Martha, from Pereria, via Marsella Km 9, Corregimiento Combia, via La Convención,

T322 9994, 310-421 5920, www.fincavillamartha.com. Modern *finca* with bamboo decor, pool and lovely gardens. Comfortable rooms, excellent service, includes breakfast and dinner (vegetarians catered for), free internet, Wi-Fi. Free pick-ups from airport/bus terminal in Pereria. Serves probably the best coffee in La Zona Cafetera.

D-F Cabaña del Recuerdo, Km 5 Vía Filandia-Montenegro, T311-628 5149, reservaselrecuerdo@hotmail.com. A few kilometres outside Filandia (7 km off Pereira-Armenia road), on a *finca* surrounded by banana and coffee plantations, swimming pool, great walks. Free pick up from Filandia with enough notice.

Pereira to Armenia: Salento *p992*

C La Posada del Café, Cra 6, No 3-08, T759 3012, malenacafe@yahoo.com. Breakfast, traditional house with rooms set around a garden, helpful.

C Las Nubes, Cra 9, No 7-31, T321 3522. Another traditional building, simple rooms with character and one of the best views in Salento.

D Hostal Ciudad de Segorbe, C 5, No 4-06, T759 3794, hostalciudaddesegorbe@hotmail.com. Splendid old house around a courtyard, with tapas bar attached, very pleasant, helpful Spanish owners.

D-E La Casona de Lili, C Real 3-45, T612 3988, www.hosteltrail.com/hostallacasonadelili. Good beds, tasteful decorations, excellent breakfast, hot water, use of kitchen, laundry service, Lili is an enthusiastic hostess.

D-F Camping Monteroca, Km 4 Vía Pereira–Salento, T315-413 6862, www.geocities.com/campingmonteroca. Beside the Río Quindío. Owner Jorge knows the area, its history and wildlife well. Well-maintained campsite with clean showers, communal cooking area, TV lounge. Also has themed cabins with stove and hot showers. Museum of fossils and meteorites, a room dedicated to Simón Bolívar and a serpentarium.

D-F Plantation House, Alto de Coronel, C 7, No 1-04, T316-285 2603, www.theplantationhousesalento.com. Popular backpackers' hostel, now expanded to 2 buildings, with private rooms and dorms, brand new kitchen and outdoor seating area. Gorgeous views, book exchange, internet access. English/Colombian owned, the best local information, have recently bought a coffee plantation to which they offer tours. It's also possible to stay the night on the top floor of the finca. Highly recommended.

E Las Palmas, C 6, No 3-02, T759 3065. Small, traditional hostel, comfortable rooms, hot water, use of kitchen, good value.

Valle de Cocora *p993*

B Las Palmas de Cocora, Km 10 Valle de Cocora, T759 3190. Comforable rooms with beds and bunks. Restaurant serving trout (🍴). Horses for hire (US$5.50 per hr, guide US$5.50 per hr).

E Finca San José, Km 11 Vía Cocora, T310-227 5091 (Mariela Pérez in Armenia). 100-year-old farm, basic but characterful rooms, spectacular views, an excellent base for hiking.

E Bosques de Cocora, Km 11 Vía Cocora, T749 6831, juanb@valledecocora.com. Restaurant, hires tents, mattresses and bedding. Shower facilities and free coffee and hot chocolate.

Armenia *p993*

AL Hacienda Bambusa, T311-506 9915, bambusa@haciendabambusa.com. Traditional hacienda in banana plantations, great for relaxing but activities include canopying, horse riding, birdwatching. Has a restaurant and free pick up from airport or bus station. "Enchanting".

A Centenario, C 21, No 18-20, T7443143, www.hotelcentenario.com. Bright rooms, attentive staff, Wi-Fi, internet, cable TV, parking, breakfast included.

B Zuldemayda, C 20, No 15-38, T741 0580, hzuldemayda@telecom.com.co. Popular, Wi-Fi, internet, parking. Refurbished in 2008. Breakfast included.

C Café Plaza, Cra 18, No 18-09, T741 1500, hotelcafeplaza@hotmail.com. Near the Plaza Bolívar, a little noisy but simple, clean rooms with bath and TV, breakfast included.

E Imperial, C 21, No 17-43, T744 9151. Also basic and clean, TV, safe, cold water.

F Alferez, Cra 17, No 17-47, T743 4096. Very basic but safe, TV, laundry service.

Parque Nacional del Café: Montenegro *p993*

See also **Coffee farms**, above.

A El Delirio, Km 1 vía Montenegro-Parque del Café, T745 0405, casadelirio@hotmail.com. Beautiful, traditional *finca* restored with immaculate taste, a "perfect place to unwind", pool, large gardens, delicious food.

C El Carriel, Km 1 vía Quimbaya-Filandia, T746 3612, elcarriel@hotmail.com. An excellent option if you are looking for an economic stay on a working coffee *finca*. Simple but comfortable rooms, hot water, restaurant. The coffee tour takes you through the whole coffee-making process from plant to cup.

Ibagué *p994*
B Ambala, C 11, No 2-60, T261 3888, F263 3490. Breakfast, TV, pool, sauna, parking, restaurant.
E Sandremo, C 16, No 2-88, T261 3339. Fan, TV.

Cartago *p994*
Many hotels in area around bus terminals (Cra 9) and railway station (Cra 9 y C 6).
C Don Gregorio, Cra 5, No 9-59, T211 5111. A/c, pool, sauna, cheaper with fan, includes breakfast.
E Río Pul, Diag 3, No 2-142, T211 0623. With fan and bath, TV. Recommended.

Eating

Pereira *p991*
₸₸ Mediterráneo, Av Circunvalar, No 4-47. Steaks, seafood, fondus and crêpes in a relaxed atmosphere.
₸ Delicias de mi Tierra Pereirana, Cra 5, No 16-52. Cheap canteen serving typical dishes for just over US$2.
₸ Delight, Cra 16, No 4B-35. Popular, more upmarket place also with typical dishes.
₸ La Terracita Paisa, C 17, No 7-62. Typical regional food served on a 2nd-floor terrace decorated with antiques.
₸ La Tienda del Recuerdo, Cra 7, No 18-32. *Paisa* restaurant with live mariachi bands.

Pereira to Armenia: Salento *p992*
₸₸-₸ Balcones del Ayer, C 6, No.5-40. Serving trout, the local speciality, as well as good quality meat dishes. Friendly and efficient.
₸ La Fonda de los Arrieros, Cra 6, No 6-02. Restaurant on the plaza serving good trout and steaks, open until 2100.
₸ El Rincón de Lucy, Cra 6, corner after the plaza. Excellent breakfasts, lunches and dinners, limited menu, but great value and tasty local food. Recommended.

Armenia *p993*
₸₸ Café Quindío, Cra 19, No 33N-41. Gourmet coffee shop and restaurant next to Parque de la Vida, serving recipes such as chicken or steak in coffee sauce as well as international dishes. Also sells coffee products from its own farm.
₸₸ Keizaki, Cra 13, No 8N-39. Sushi and other Asian dishes. There are several other good restaurants on the same block.
₸₸ La Fogata, Cra 13, No 14N-47. One of Armenia's most popular restaurants, serving steaks, pork chops and typical dishes.
₸₸-₸ Anis, C 10N, No 13-94. Excellent restaurant with a varied menu: steaks, pasta, salads, sandwiches, crêpes and other brunch options.
₸ Donde Nelson, Cra 13 with C 15. Family-run hole-in-the-wall, popular with locals.
₸ La Puerta Quindiana, C 17, No 15-40. Cheap *comida corriente* and good fruit juices.
₸ Natural Food Plaza, Cra 14, No 18N-40. Vegetarian, varied menu and fruit juices. Also has a wholefood shop.

Festivals and events

Ibagué *p994*
National Folklore Festival, in **Jun**. Tolima and Huila commemorate **San Juan** (**24 Jun**) and SS Pedro y Pablo (**29 Jun**) with fireworks, and music.

Activities and tours

Pereira *p991*
D'p@seo, Cra 13, No 14-60, local 109, T334 9883, www.dpaseo.com. Opposite **Hotel Pereira**. Arranges weekend trips to Los Nevados, trips on Río la Vieja. Mon-Sat 0800-1200, 1400-1900.

Pereira to Armenia: Salento *p992*
Jesús Bedoya, Cra 6, No 6-14 (coffee shop), T316-620 7760, www.cafejesusmartinbedoya.com. 1-hour tours of local coffee roasting factory, Mon-Wed any time between 0800-1000, but tours can also be arranged at other times, US$3, fun and informative. Also 4-5 hr tours taking in Jesús' father's working finca, Santana, and large parts of the Quindío coffee-growing area including Filandia, Quimbaya, Montenegro and Armenia, US$40. Recommended.

pottery. Another church worth seeing is the Gothic-style **La Ermita**, on the river between Calles 12 and 13. **Museo del Oro** (also called Museo Calima) ⓘ *Calle 7, No 4-69, Banco de la República building, Tue-Sat 1000-1700, free*, has pre-Columbian gold work and pottery.

The **Museo de Arte Moderno La Tertulia** ⓘ *Av Colombia, No 5-105 Oeste, Tue-Sun 1000-1800, US$2.50*, exhibits South American, including local, modern art. To view the city, take a taxi to the **Monumento Las Tres Cruces**, northwest of the city (best on Sunday when people sell fruit on the way up), or to the **Monumento Cristo Rey**, 1,470 m, to the west of the city. The huge statue of Christ can be seen 50 km away across the Río Cauca. The neighbourhood of **San Antonio** (located behind the **Intercontinental Hotel**) is the city's oldest area, where Cali's colonial past can still be felt. The area has a relaxed, bohemian atmosphere, especially at weekends when it's livelier. There are good views of the city from the 18th-century church of San Antonio.

Cali

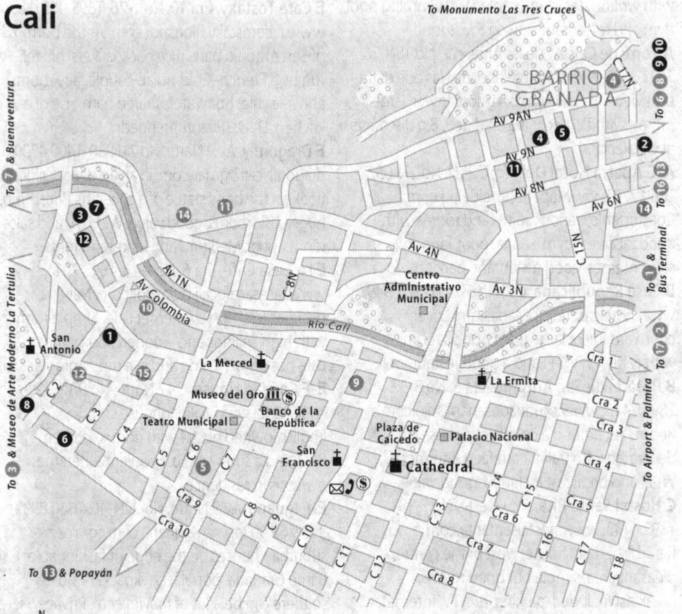

Sleeping
1 Apartahotel Colombia
2 Aparta Hotel Del Río
3 Café Tostaky
4 Calidad House
5 Casa Republicana
6 Dragonfly
7 Hostal Santa Rita
8 Iguana
9 Imperial
10 Intercontinental & La Terraza Restaurant
11 Kaffee Erde
12 La Casa Café
13 Pelican Larry
14 Pensión Stein
15 Posada de San Antonio
16 Sartor
17 Torre de Cali

Eating
1 Bahareque
2 D'Toluca
3 El Balcón de Salo
4 El Solar
5 Granada Faro
6 La Colina
7 La Tartine
8 Ojo de Perro Azul
9 Pampero
10 Pizza al Paso
11 Platillos Voladores
12 Tortelli

Bars & clubs
13 Tin Tin Deo
14 Zaperoco

Cali listings

For Sleeping and Eating price codes and other relevant information, see Essentials, pages 38-40.

Sleeping

Cali *p998, map p999*

AL Intercontinental, Av Colombia, No 2-72, T882 3225, www.intercontinental.com. On the edge of San Antonio, the most expensive hotel in town. Elegant restaurant, **La Terraza**, along with 4 others. Prices drop at weekends.

A Pensión Stein, Av 4 Norte, No 3-33, T661 4927, www.hotelstein.com.co. Owned by the Swiss consulate (next door). Comfortable rooms with writing desks and cable TV, swimming pool, gym and restaurant serving Swiss food.

A Torre de Cali, Av de las Américas, No 18N-26, T683 3535, www.glhhoteles.com. Has one of the best views in Cali from its 41-floor tower, large rooms, with TV, decor is a bit dated. Big discounts at weekends.

A-C Aparta Hotel Del Río, C 21N, No 2N-05, T660 2707, www.apartahoteldelrio.com. Comfortable, various suites and rooms with good facilities (gym, sauna, pool, laundry), safe, internet, good restaurant, parking.

B Casa Republicana, C 7, No 6-74, T896 0949, www.hotelcasarepublicana.com. Lovely courtyard full of large plants, good rooms with cable TV, Wi-Fi and a good restaurant.

B Posada de San Antonio, Cra 5, No 3-37, T893 7413, www.posadadesanantonio.com. Rooms set around a couple of patios, decorated with Calima artefacts, internet, Wi-Fi and breakfast included, good value.

C Hostal Santa Rita, Av 3 Oeste, No 7-131, T892 6143, www.hostalsantarita.com. Refurbished old house, west of the centre, pleasant area, simple but good rooms, breakfast included, parking, a/c, TV, internet.

C Imperial, C 9, No 3-93, T889 9571, www.hotelimperialdecali.com. A bit dated but has good facilities, a/c, internet, cable TV, parking, sauna, pool and restaurant on a terrace.

C Sartor, Av 8 Norte, No 20-50, T668 6482, hotelsartor@yahoo.com. Entrance has 2 large pine trees in a tiny courtyard. Rooms are basic, hot water, small beds, Wi-Fi, cable TV and laundry service.

C-D Apartahotel Colombia, C 31 Norte, No2 Bis-48, T660 8081, http://nelhenao1.googlepages.com/home. One block from bus terminal and clos to Barrio Granada, hot water, cable TV, internet and Wi-Fi, steam room, restuarant, secure, English spoken.

D-E Pelican Larry, C 23 Norte, No 8N-12, Santa Mónica, T396 8659, www.pelicanlarrycali.com. Rooms with and without bath, **F** in dorms. Close to Zona Rosa restaurants and bars, 15 mins walk from bus terminal, hot water, laundry and internet extra, kitchen, Sun night BBQ, Spanish lessons arranged, TV room, helpful staff.

E Café Tostaky, Cra 10, No 1-76, T893 0651, www.cafetostaky.blogspot.com. At the bottom of San Antonio park, nice backpackers' hostel, run by a French- Colombian couple, airy rooms above a café, hot water, shared bath, use of a kitchen, DVDs. Recommended.

E Dragonfly, Av 9 Norte, No 21N-30, T400 4200, dragonflycali@gmail.com. In an art deco building (look for the brass statue of a cheetah), British-run, huge basic rooms, good value. Wi-Fi, TV and salsa rooms, pool. Medium- and long-term rents.

E La Casa Café, Cra 6, No 2-13, T893 7011, www.lacasacafecali.blogspot.com. New backpackers' hostel/internet café. Simple rooms with high ceilings and wooden floorboards; café hosts storytelling and live music nights.

E-F Calidad House, C 17 Norte, No 9AN-39, T661 2338, www.calidadhouse.com. English-owned hostel with dorms, kitchen, BBQ, and a sunny patio. Excellent when the owner is in residence.

E-F Iguana, Av 9 Norte, No 22N-46, T660 8937, 313-768 6024, www.iguana.com.co. In 2 suburban houses on the edge of fashionable Barrio Granada, popular backpackers' hostel so there can be a lot of *movimiento*. Private rooms, some with bath, kitchen, garden, TV room with DVDs, Spanish and salsa classes and good local information. Yoga weekends.

F pp **Kaffee Erde**, Av 4 Norte, No 4N-79, T661 5475, www.hosteltrail.com/kaffeeerde/. Small hostel with dorms and a private room, use of kitchen, meals available, salsa lessons and tours.

Eating

Cali *p998, map p999*

In the centre, Parque de Peñón, just north of San Antonio, has an excellent selection of restaurants serving all types of international food, while San Antonio itself has several good cafés. In the north, Barrio Granada has an enormous number of eating places to choose from.

TTT **El Solar**, C 15 Norte, No 9N-62, Barrio Granada, T653 4628. Great atmosphere and a varied international menu, popular.

TTT **Granada Faro**, Av 9 Norte, No 15AN-02, Barrio Granada, T6674625, www.granfaro.com. Also popular, serves Mediterranean-Peruvian fusion.

TTT **Platillos Voladores**, C 14 Norte, No 9N-32, Barrio Granada, T6687588, www.platillos voladores.com. One of Cali's smartest restaurants, serves excellent Asian-Colombian fusion food.

TT **Pampero**, C 21N, No 9-17, Barrio Granada, T6613117. Argentine steaks on pleasant terrace with good service. Recommended.

TT **La Tartine**, C 3 Oeste, No 1-74, T893 6617. Classic French-owned restaurant in an eccentric setting.

TT **Tortelli**, C 3 Oeste, No 3-15, T893 3227. Little Italian restaurant serving home-made pasta.

T **Bahareque**, C 2, No 4-23. Laid-back, open till 0400 at weekends, often has live music, owners Marly and José are a wealth of information on the local music and dance scene. Serves typical Colombian food and salads.

T **El Balcón de Salo**, Cra 3 Oeste, No 2-65, T893 3235. Arabic restaurant with a outdoor patio serving *kofte*, kebabs and salads as well as steaks.

T **La Colina**, C 3, No 10-35. Great pizzas, crêpes and particularly good puddings.

T **D'Toluca**, C 17N, No 8N-46, Barrio Granada, T6618390. Good little Mexican restaurant serving fajitas, tacos and burritos at reasonable prices.

T **Ojo de Perro Azul**, Cra 9, No 1-27. Bright bohemian hangout with games, mixed drinks, *picadas*, *tostadas* and traditional Colombian dishes.

T **Pizza al Paso**, C 18N, No 9N-29, Barrio Granada, T683 6974. Pizzas, pastas and salads in very agreeable surroundings, this chain of restaurants also puts on art and music events.

Bars and clubs

Cali *p998, map p999*

Cali's nightlife is legendary, especially the *salsatecas* – salsa-playing discos. Clubs in the city have to shut at 0200, apart from in Menga and Juanchito districts and in Dec. The most popular with *caleños* can be found on Av 6 Norte where there are dozens to choose from, although salsa purists would direct you to **Zaperoco**, Av 5N, No 16-46, www.zape roco.com. An alternative is **Tin Tin Deo**, C 5, No 38-71, T514 1537, which attracts students and teachers and is more forgiving of salsa beginners. But it's not just salsa, there are bars playing rock, jazz, blues and electronic music as well.

Babel, C 16N, No 9N-18, Barrio Granada. Crossover music over 3 floors, open bar on Fri, US$12.75 for men, less for women.

Blues Brothers, Av 6AN, No 21-40. Jazz and live rock bands.

Escondité, Cra 37, C5-14, Barrio Estadio/ Tequendama. Crossover music, sometimes stays open (illegally) on Sat until 0400 if enough people are there, not too expensive.

Kukara Makura, C 28N, No 2bis-97. Was the in place in Cali at the time of writing, playing electronic music.

Forum, C 25N, No 5-68. Electronic music.

Talberts Pub and **Bourbon St**, C 17N, 8N, Barrio Granada. English and American themed bars, with same owner, English music generally, good live bands on Fri and good atmosphere in general.

Barrio Juanchito has a range of salsa bars and discos, from thatched roofs to huge, hi-tech salsatecas (eg the popular **Don José**). It is worth visiting just to watch couples dancing salsa and to join in, if you dare! Go with locals and couples; groups of foreign male tourists might have a hard time getting in. Most advisable to take a registered radio taxi there and back; 15-min ride out of Cali, across the bridge over the Río Cauca.

Entertainment

Cali *p998, map p999*

Cinema **Alianza Colombo-Francesa**, Av 6 N, No 21-34, T661 3431, and **Centro Colombo-Americano**, C 13N, No 8-45, T667 3539, both show films. **Museo La Tertulia**, Av Colombia, No 5-105 Oeste. Shows unusual films.

Theatre Teatro Experimental, C 7, No 8-63, T884 3820. **Teatro Municipal**, Cra 5, No 6-64, T883 9107. Major cultural activities, including opera and concerts. **Teatro La Máscara**, Cra 10, No 3-40, San Antonio. Women's theatre group.

Festivals and events

Cali *p998, map p999*

Feria de Cali (Cali Fair) from **25 Dec-3 Jan**, biggest Salsa festival in Latin America, bullfights at the Canaveralejo bull-ring, carnival in streets, horse parades, masquerade balls, sporting contests and general heavy partying.

Sep AjazzGo festival, www.ajazzgo festival.com, with international artists.

Shopping

Cali *p998, map p999*

Best shopping districts are: Av 6N, from Río Cali to C 30 Norte and on Cra 5 in the south with several new shopping malls including:

Chipichape, at the end of Av 6N. Vast, cinemas, **Librería Nacional** bookstore, good choice of restaurants and shops, supermarket.

Bookshops Bookstalls on the sidewalk on Cra 10 near C 10. **Librería Nacional**, Cra 5, No 11-50, Plaza de Caicedo. Has a café, as do branches elsewhere in the city.

Handicrafts Artesanías Pacandé, Av 6N, No 17A-53. Typical regional handicrafts.

La Caleñita, Cr 24, No 8-53. Good selection of typical handicrafts. **Parque Artesenal Loma de la Cruz**, C 5, Cras 15/16. Permanent handicraft market, nice setting and pleasant neighbourhood, safe, cafés around the park. Open 1130-2030. **Platería Ramírez**, C 1A, No 4B-44 Oeste, San Antonio. Good selection of jewellery, lessons offered in jewellery making.

Maps Instituto Geográfico Agustín Codazzi, Cra 6, No 13-56, T885 5611.

Activities and tours

Cali *p998, map p999*

Ciclovida On Sun, 0700-1400, C 9 is closed from north to south to allow people to cycle, run and exercise on the roadway.

Diving Casco Antiguo Diving Centre, Cra 34, No 3-89 (Parque del Perro), cascoantiguo@ telesat.com.co. PADI certified. Organize all-inclusive expensive weekend diving tours to Gorgona Island, US$600 pp and 8 day advanced diving tours to Isla Malpelo (36 hrs boat ride from Buenaventura US$2,500). Contact **Rafael Lozano**, T313-767 6099, for diving trips to Isla Gorgona and Malpelo. Speaks English, lots of experience and very responsible. Recommended.

Paragliding Speak to **Rob Ottomani**, T314-678 7972. German and English spoken.

Tours

Aviatur, Cra 5, No 8-12, T889 3121, http://site.aviatur.com; and other branches. For tours to Isla Gorgona, and other services.

Panturismo, C 18N, No 8-27, T668 2255, and at airport, T666 3021, www.panturismo.com.co. Organizes all inclusive trips to Gorgona.

Transport

Cali *p998, map p999*

Air Frequent services to **Bogotá**, **Medellín**, **Cartagena**, **Ipiales** and other Colombian cities with **Satena** and **Avianca**. International flights to Miami, New York, and Panama. Minibus from airport, from far end of pick-up road outside arrivals, to bus terminal (2nd floor), every 10 mins from 0500 up to 2100, approximately 30 mins, US$2.50. Taxi to city US$25, 30 mins.

Bus Urban: **MIO** metro buses US$0.75 a ride, single tickets sold at the stations; to use pre-trunk routes you need a smart card that you pre-charge, www.metrocali.gov.co.

Long-distance: Busetas (**Velotax** and others) charge 50% more than buses but save time; taxi-colectivos are about 2½ times bus prices and even quickier. To **Popayán**, US$9, 2½-3 hrs, also colectivos, US$14. To **Pasto**, US$19, 8-9 hrs. To **Ipiales** (direct), US$22, 12 hrs; to **San Agustín**, 9 hrs, US$14-16. To **Cartago**, 3½ hrs, US$10. To **Armenia**, US$12.25. To **Manizales**, US$17, 7 hrs. To **Medellín**, US$15-22, 8-10 hrs. To **Bogotá**, 10-15 hrs, by **Magdalena**, T668 7504 (recommended), and others, US$25-33 (sit on left of the bus).

Directory

Cali *p998, map p999*

Banks BanColombia, Cra 5, No 10-79, for Visa cash advances (take passport and a photocopy). Many other banks and *casas de cambio* in the main commercial areas. **Casas de Cambio Cambiamos**, Av 5N, No 23DN-40.

Consulates French, Av 3N, No 18N-24, Of 405, T883 5904. **German**, C 1B, No 66B-29, Barrio El Refugio, T323 8402. **Swiss**, Av 4N, No 3-33, T661 4927 (same building as *Pensión Stein*). **UK**, C 22N, No 6-42, Of 401, Edif Centro Granada, T667 7725, britishcali@uniweb.net.co.
Immigration DAS office: Av 3A, No 50N-20, T650 7500, Mon-Fri 0730-1200, 1400-1700.
Internet Many in the north, along Av 6A, and centre of the city. **Unimegas**, Av 6, No 17A-57, T6603853. Skype and head- phones. **Cosmonet**, Av 6N, No 17N-65, T6535228. Skype, headphones, scanning, photocopying and international calls. **Post offices** **Adpostal** for national service, C 10, No 6-25; **Deprisa** for international service, C 9, No 4-45.

Cauca and the coast

To reach the Pacific you have to cross the western arm of the Andes, with a number of parks and recreational areas. There are plenty of beaches to the northwest of the port of Buenaventura while away to the south is the isolated national park islands of Gorgona and Mapelo.

Lago Calima

If you take the road from the colonial city of Buga (northeast of Cali, south of Cartago on the Panamericana), to Buenaventura you pass the **Laguna de Sonso** reserve, good for birdwatching, before crossing the Río Cauca. Beyond the river, near the crest of the Cordillera, is another park, **Reserva Natural Bosque de Yotoco**, noted for orchids. The road continues to the man-made **Lago Calima**. Many treasures of the Calima culture are said to have been flooded by the lake, when the dam was built. This is an important centre for watersports, riding and other activities. The northern route round the lake goes through **Darién** at 1,500 m with an **archaeological museum** ⓘ *Tue-Fri 0800-1700, Sat-Sun 1000-1800*, with good displays of Calima and other cultures. There are hotels in the village, as well as cabins available at a Centro Náutico on the lakeside. Camping is possible near the village. Direct buses from Buga to Darién (one hour), and Cali (two hours).

From Cali to the coast

Both the toll and (unpaved) ordinary roads from Cali to Buenaventura give beautiful views of mountains and jungle, and from the old road you can reach the **Parque Nacional Farallones** ⓘ *entry US$9, but closed to tourists, details from MA in Cali, page 998*. The area around Pance, however, and the **Ecoparque del Río Pance**, 20 minutes from the centre of Cali, is a popular weekend haunt, with nature walks, swimming and camping all possible. To reach Pance, take a Blanco y Negro bus, Ruta 1, from Calle 5 or Avenida 6, US$0.60.

A popular excursion from Cali is to **San Cipriano**, 30 km on the road to Buenaventura. Get off the bus at Córdoba, from where rail cars, man-powered or motorbike-powered (US$5 return), go to the village in beautiful scenery. There are crystal-clear rivers and waterfalls and inner tubes can be rented for US$2.70 per day for floating downstream. The village and its surroundings are a national reserve of 8,564 ha, entry US$1.

Buenaventura → *Phone code: 2. Colour map 1, B2. Population: 202,000. 145 km from Cali.*

Through a pass in the Western Cordillera is Buenaventura, Colombia's most important port handling some 80% of total exports, including coffee, sugar and frozen shrimp. It was founded in 1540, but not on its present site. It now stands on the island of Cascajal, on the Bay of Buenaventura, 20 km from the open Pacific. For excursions and beaches, see below. The commercial centre is now paved and has some impressive buildings, but the rest of the town has steep unpaved streets lined with shacks on stilts. There is a festive atmosphere every night and the *Festival Folklórico del Litoral* is held in July. South of the town a swampy coast stretches as far as Tumaco (see page 1018); to the north lies the deeply jungled Chocó Department.

Tourist information: Asturias travel agency, T240 4048, barcoasturias@hotmail.com, for information on trips around Buenaventura. **Warning** This town is one of Colombia's main drug- and people-trafficking centres and has severe poverty; this has led to high levels of violent crime and homicide. Do not walk about at night and stick within a couple of blocks of the seafront. There are still problems with malaria.

Beaches around Buenaventura

Beaches are plentiful northwest of Buenaventura along the coast of the **Bahía de Málaga**. There is stunning scenery with virgin jungle, waterfalls and empty, black sand beaches. About 40 km from Buenaventura, near the mouth of the Río San Juan, is **Juanchaco**, a small fishing village, the location of spectacular **dolphin** and **humpback whale** sightings between July and early October. By frequent launch from Buenaventura (*muelle turístico*), one hour, slower boats available. Beyond Juanchaco is **Ladrilleros**, a 30-minute walk, or take a jeep (5 minutes). One of the best and longest beaches, which turns into a football pitch at low tide to provide entertainment as you drink your beer or *cocoloco* (coconut milk and rum). Simple accommodation in Juanchaco (**E-F**) but better in Ladrilleros: **B** Reserva Aguamarina, www.reservaaguamarina.com, which also owns Eco-Guías, T313-750 6430, who organize whale watching and boat trips, as well as diving, snorkelling and kayaking excursions; **B** Palma Real, www.hotelpalmarealcolombia.com, good. Smaller places include **D** Doña Francia, T246 0373. Several small restaurants (good fish) and snack bars at the town end of the beach. Other beaches include Playa Dorada, Juan de Dios and Chucheros. Trips to sea canals and mangrove forests cost US$14.

Gorgona Island → *Colour map 1, B1. 150 km down the coast from Buenaventura.*

ⓘ *Visits to the island are managed and run by* Aviatur, *T01-900-331 2222, or 01-382 1616, www.concesionesparques naturales.com. Accommodation is available in various houses and Aviatur offers 3-night packages from Bogotá, Medellín and Cali. All visitors must have a permit before arriving at the island, obtainable from Aviatur. It is recommended to book accommodation and boat tickets well in advance during high season. Entrance fee US $16.50 for foreigners.*

Until 1984 the island of **Gorgona** was Colombia's high security prison (a sort of Alcatraz). The prison is derelict but some parts can still be clearly seen. Convicts were dissuaded from escaping by the poisonous snakes on the island and the sharks patrolling the 30 km to the mainland (both snakes and sharks are still there). The national park boasts many unspoilt, deserted sandy beaches. From the paths you can see monkeys, iguanas, and a wealth of flora and fauna. (Rubber boots are provided and recommended.) There is an abundance of birds (pelicans, cormorants, geese, herons) that use the island as a migration stop-over. Snorkelling and diving is rewarding, equipment can be hired (but take your own if possible), exotic fish and turtles to be seen. Killer whales visit the area from July-September.

Isla Malpelo

Declared a UNESCO site in 2006, Isla Malpelo is located 506 km from Buenaventura in the Pacific and is an acclaimed birdwatching haven with great diving opportunities. The island is considered to be one of the world's best places to observe hammerhead sharks in great numbers. Boats leave from Buenaventura, a 36-hour bumpy voyage. There are no places to stay on the island and camping is not allowed. Contact national parks office in Bogotá for more information, T243 2009. Embarcaciones Asturias in Buenaventura (see above) offer an eight-day tour, with transport and accommodation. National park embarkation tax US$52; diving fee US$97/day.

Cauca and the coast listings

For Sleeping and Eating price codes and other relevant information, see Essentials, pages 38-40.

Sleeping

Buenaventura *p1003*

AL Estelar Estación, C 2, No 1A-08, T243 4070, www.hotelesestelar.com. Best in town, charming, grand old white building on seafront, good restaurant, pool, helpful. Weekend discounts. Organizes trips to beaches and runs tours mid/late Jul to end Sep for whale sighting: 3 nights/4 days, including all meals and boat trip, US$264 pp.

D Los Delfines, C 1, No 5A-03, T241 5450, hotellosdelfines@mibuenaventura.com. 4 blocks up the hill from the *muelle*, good value, a/c, cable TV, has a breezy terrace.

D Titanic, C 1, No 2A-55, T241 2046. About a block from the *muelle turístico*, good rooms and beds with crisp, white sheets, cable TV, safe. 6th-floor restaurant for *almuerzos* and á la carte, internet, a good option.

Eating

Buenaventura *p1003*

Most hotels have their own restaurant, or there are several cheap places along the promenade.

Transport

Buenaventura *p1003*

Air Flights to **Cali** and **Bogotá**, **Satena**.

Road There are plenty of buses to **Cali**, US$8, 4 hrs. Colectivos and taxis run at ½-hourly intervals to Cali. The **toll road** to Cali is fully paved; the toll is about US$1.30 for cars and US$0.30 for motorcycles.

Gorgona Island *p1004*

It is recommended to book tours through **Aviatur**, they arrange permits, transport and accommodation; their packages include a fast launch service to the island from the seaside town of **Guapi**, 1½ hrs one way, and transfer from airport to dock; embarkation tax US$4. **Satena** flies from Cali or Popayán to Guapi. **Embarcaciones Asturias** at the Muelle Turístico in Buenaventura, T240 4048, barcoasturias@hotmail.com, offer a weekend package leaving Buenaventura on Fri 1900, returning Mon, US$290 pp, including accommodation on boat, food, permit and snorkelling equipment. Alternatively, launches can be contracted in Buenaventura, 4 hrs to Gorgona, US$130.

Directory

Buenaventura *p1003*

Banks Several banks will change cash and TCs.

Immigration DAS, C 8A, No 3-104, Barrio Las Mercedes, T241 2144.

Popayán, Tierradentro and San Agustín

The Pan-American Highway climbs out of the valley to Popayán, a historic city which gives access to the páramo of Puracé in the Cordillera Central and serves as a good base from which to visit some of Colombia's most exciting sights, including the burial caves of Tierradentro and, to the south, the remarkable archaeological site of San Agustín. The Cauca valley has strong indigenous cultures, notably the Páez people.

Popayán and Tierradentro

Popayán has retained its colonial character, even though it had to be fully restored after the March 1983 earthquake. The streets of two-storey buildings are in rococo Andalucian style, with beautiful old monasteries and cloisters of pure Spanish classic architecture. In contrast, the tombs of Tierradentro reveal much of the northern Andean world before the Spaniards arrived.

Popayán ➔ *Phone code: 2. Colour map 1, C2. Population: 258,000. Altitude: 1,760 m.*

Founded by Sebastián de Belalcázar, Francisco Pizarro's lieutenant, in 1536, Popayán became the regional seat of government, until 1717, to the Audiencia of Quito, and later to the Audiencia of Bogotá. It is now the capital of the Department of Cauca. The city lies in the Pubenza valley, a peaceful landscape of palm, bamboo, and the sharp-leaved agave. The early settlers, after setting up their sugar estates in the hot, damp Cauca valley, retreated to Popayán to live, for the city is high enough to give it a delightful climate. To the north, south, and east the broken green plain is bounded by mountains. The cone of the volcano Puracé (4,646 m) rises to the southeast.

Sights **The Cathedral** ⓘ *Calle 5, Cra 6*, beautifully restored, has a fine marble Madonna sculpture behind the altar by Buenaventura Malagón and the unusual statue of Christ kneeling on the globe. Other churches are **San Agustín** ⓘ *C 7, Cra 6*, note the gilt altar piece; **Santo Domingo** ⓘ *C 4, Cra 5*, used by the Universidad del Cauca; **La Ermita** ⓘ *C 5, Cra 2*; **La Encarnación** ⓘ *C 5, Cra 5*, also used for religious music festivals; **San Francisco** ⓘ *C 4, Cra 9* (partly restored); and **El Carmen** ⓘ *C 4, Cra 3*. Walk to **Belén** chapel ⓘ *C 4 y Cra 0*, seeing the statues en route, and then continue to **El Cerro de las Tres Cruces** if you have the energy, and on to the equestrian statue of

Sleeping
1 Campobello Bed & Breakfast *A2*
2 Casa Familiar El Descanso *B2*
3 Casa Familiar Turística *B2*
4 Hosteltrail Guesthouse *B1*
5 La Casona del Virrey *B2*
6 La Plazuela *B2*
7 Los Balcones *B2*
8 Los Portales *B1*
9 Monasterio *B1*
10 Pass Home *B1*

Eating
1 El Muro *B2*
2 Italiano *B2*
3 Jengibre *B2*
4 Juan Valdez *B2*
5 Kaldivia *B2*
6 La Cave *B3*
7 La Viña *B2*
8 Madeira Café *B3*
9 Pan Tolima *B2*
10 Verde y Mostaza *B2*

Bars & clubs
11 El Sotareño *B2*
12 Iguana Afro-Club *B1*
13 Tijuana *B2*

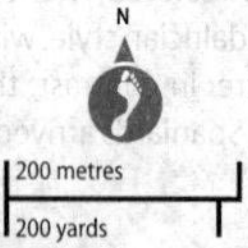

Belalcázar on the **Morro de Tulcán** which overlooks the city; this hill is the site of a pre-Columbian pyramid. It is said that Bolívar marched over the **Puente Chiquito** ⓘ *C 2 y Cra 6*, built in 1713. **Museo Negret** ⓘ *C 5, No 10-23, Mon-Fri 0900-1200, 1400-1800, US$0.60*, has works, photographs and furniture of Negret. **Museo Guillermo Valencia** ⓘ *Cra 6 No 2-69*, is the birthplace of the poet. **Museo de Historia Natural** ⓘ *Cra 2, No 1A-25, US$1*, has good displays of archaeological and geological items with sections on insects (particularly good on butterflies), reptiles, mammals and birds. During the week, the open markets are interesting – **Mercado Bolívar** ⓘ *C 1N, Cra 5*, is best in the early morning – local foods such as *pipián, tamales* and *empanadas*.

The **tourist office** on the Parque Caldas has a good selection of maps and brochures. **Cámara de Comercio de Cauca, Cultura y Turismo** ⓘ *Cra 7, No 4-36, T824 3625, www.cccauca.org.co.* National parks office ⓘ *C 25, No 9-00, Barrio Palacé, T823 1279.*

Note Museums are closed on Monday.

Silvia → *Phone code: 2. Colour map 1, C2. Population: 5,000. Altitude: 2,520 m.*

Silvia, in a high valley 59 km northeast of Popayán, is best known for its Tuesday market when the friendly local Guambianos come to town in their distinctive blue and fuchsia clothes. The market (also full of Otavalo from Ecuador) is at its best between 0600 and 0830 and is very colourful. A typical *indígena* settlement, La Campana, is 45 minutes on the bus; 2½ hours' walk downhill back to Silvia. Tourist information 1½ blocks up from plazuela on the right hand side (keeps irregular hours). *Banco Agrario* gives cash against Visa. For horse hire enquire at tourist office or hotels.

Tierradentro → *Colour map 1, C2*

East of Popayán is **Inzá** which is 67 km beyond **Totoró**. There are several stone statues in the new plaza. 9 km beyond Inzá is the Cruce de Pisimbalá (or Cruce de San Andrés or just El Cruce), where a road turns off to **San Andrés de Pisimbalá** (4 km). The village, at the far end of the Tierradentro Park, has a unique and beautiful colonial church with a thatched roof; for the key ask behind the church. 2 km or so before Pisimbalá is the **Tierradentro Museum** ⓘ *0800-1600, may close for lunch*, of indigenous culture. It has very good local information. The second floor is dedicated to the work of the Páez, not to be missed. The Páez people in the Tierradentro region can be seen on market days at Inzá (Saturday), and Belalcázar (Saturday); both start at 0600. The setting is spectacular, with small indigenous mountain villages (get exact directions before leaving).

Parque Arqueológico Tierradentro ⓘ *Park and Museum open 0800-1600, US$3.80, valid for 3 days. Walking between the sites, take a hat and plenty of water. It gets crowded at Easter.* At the archway opposite the museum or at Pisimbalá village you can hire horses (US$2 per hour) or you can walk to the **Tierradentro** man-made burial caves painted with geometric patterns. There are four cave sites: Segovia, El Duende, Alto de San Andrés and El Aguacate. The main caves are lit, but a torch is advisable. At Segovia (15 minutes' walk up behind the museum across the river), the guards are very informative (Spanish only) and turn lights on in the main tombs. Segovia has about 30 tombs, five of which can be lit. 15 minutes up the hill beyond Segovia is El Duende (two of four tombs are very good, faint paintings can be seen but take torch/flashlight). From El Duende continue directly up to a rough road descending to Pisimbalá (40 minutes). El Tablón, with eight stone statues, is just off the road 20-30 minutes walk down. El Alto de San Andrés is 20 minutes from Pisimbalá. From the back of El Alto it is 1½ hours up and down hill, with a long climb to El Aguacate (superb views). Only one tomb is maintained although there may be 30 more. Guides are available. The area is good for birdwatching.

Popayán and Tierradentro listings

For Sleeping and Eating price codes and other relevant information, see Essentials, pages 38-40.

Sleeping

Popayán *p1006, map p1006*

Prices can rise by 100% for Holy Week and festivals, eg 5-6 Jan, when it's essential to book in advance. It is not safe walking alone at night outside the central area and even in the historic centre it's quiet enough to warrant caution.

L Monasterio, C 4, No 10-14, T824 2191, hdannmo@tvoconectado.com. Run by the Dann group, in what was the monastery of San Francisco, includes breakfast, lovely grounds, swimming pool, very good.

A La Plazuela, C 5, No 8-13, T824 1084, hotellaplazuela@hotmail.com. Opposite Iglesia San José, beautiful colonial building, good-sized rooms with antique furniture set around a courtyard, Wi-Fi, cable TV, breakfast included.

A Los Balcones, Cra 7, No 2-75, T824 2030, hotel losbalcones@emtel.net.co. Huge and small rooms, antique furniture but also has Wi-Fi, free internet.

B La Casona del Virrey, C 4, No 5-78, T824 0836, hotellacasonadelvirrey@hotmail.com. Superlative colonial building with a spiral staircase up to rooms that look down on a cobbled courtyard. Many of the rooms have original wood panelling. Modern services include Wi-Fi. Recommended.

C Los Portales, C 5, No 10-125, T821 0139, losportaleshotel@yahoo.com. Pleasant, rooms set around 3 leafy courtyards with water features, cable TV, internet.

D Pass Home, C 5, No 10-114, T316-448 9513. A rabbit warren with basic rooms opening onto narrow corridors, but they have bath, hot water and cable TV.

E Casa Familiar El Descanso, Cra 5, No 2-41, T824 0029. Popular backpackers' choice, lots of plants and antiques, peaceful, family-run, 5 rooms and 3 shared bathrooms. The owners speak German and English, plenty of local information.

E Casa Familiar Turística, Cra 5, No 2-07, T824 4853. Also popular, simple rooms with high ceilings, good notice boards for information and messages from other travellers.

E-F HostelTrail Guesthouse, Cra 11, No 4-16, T314-696 0805, www.hosteltrail.com. This excellent, efficient backpackers' hostel is run by Scottish couple Tony and Kim. The rooms are comfortable and clean (most with shared bath), cheaper dorms, Wi-Fi, good communal areas, kitchen, DVD room, and lock-up. Extensive knowledge of the local area.

Just outside town

C Campobello Bed & Breakfast (Myriam and Andre), C 33AN, No 14A-14, T823 5545, www.hostalcampobello.com. Off the Pan-American Highway, 300 m down road opposite *Torremolino* restaurant. Swiss/Colombian owners speak French, English, Spanish and Italian, safe, family atmosphere, nicely decorated, terrace, breakfast included, internet, Wi-Fi, laundry service. Near bus station. Recommended.

Tierradentro *p1007*

Near the museum

E Residencias Pisimbalá, near the museum, T311-612 4645. Rooms with bath and hot water, cheaper with shared bath with cold-water, good restaurant. Camping costs US$1.20 pp.

E-F Hospedaje Ricabet, near the museum, T312-795 4636. Flower-filled courtyard, clean rooms with bath and hot water. Rooms with a shared bath are a little cheaper.

F Hospedaje Luzerna, next to the museum. Run by a lovely couple, this little place has clean, basic rooms and good showers (with 30 mins' notice).

In the village

F El Cauchito. Family run, with 3 basic rooms, attentive service, shared bath, no hot water.

F El Viajero. Another family home, basic but clean rooms, unheated shower. Food available.

F Los Llanos, 100 m past the church. Pleasant colonial building with clean, basic rooms and a colourful courtyard.

Eating

Popayán *p1006, map p1006*

Popayán has a tradition of good food. In 2005 the city was named a UNESCO City of Gastronomy.

TT-T Italiano, C 4, No 8-83, T824 0607. Swiss-run, excellent selection of pastas, pizzas, crêpes and fondues. Recommended.

El Muro, Cra 8, No 4-11, T824 0539. Serves vegetarian *almuerzos* with daily menus. At night it converts into a dimly-lit bar.
Jengibre, Cra 7, No 2-71, T820 5456. Good lunchtime venue serving *almuerzos* as well as á la carte options.
La Cave, C 4, No 2-07. French-owned bistro is famous for its salad dressing, also for pastries and tartes. French music too.
La Viña, C 4, No 7-07, T824 0602. Open 24 hrs, *parrillada*, huge selection of steaks and salads.
Pan Tolima, C 4, No 5-84. On the corner of the Parque, good selection of breads and other breakfast snacks.
Verde y Mostaza, Cra 4 y C 4. Popular with students for cheap fast food such as crêpes, pizzas and burgers.

Cafés

Popayán has a thriving café culture, with many in colonial buildings.
Juan Valdez, Cra 7, No 4-40. Part of the ubiquitous chain, in a beautiful courtyard. Large selection of coffees and merchandise on sale. Has Wi-Fi.
Kaldivia, C 5, No 5-63. Popular with the locals, excellent frappes, brownies and ice creams.
Madeira Café, C 3 y Cra 4. Good selection of coffee, milkshakes, brownies, juices and cheesecakes.

Autopista Norte

There is a good selection of typical food from the Cauca region in Popayán. For good food at reasonable prices, take a short taxi ride to the road to Cali to: **Rancho Grande**, Autopista Norte 32N-50, T823 5788. 2 thatched restaurants, delicious *chuzos* (barbecued beef), credit cards accepted, open Sun.

Tierradentro *p1007*

Pisimbalá. Good, cheap. Recommended.
La Portada, bamboo building at jeep/bus stop in village. Excellent *comida corriente*, fresh soups.

Bars and clubs

Popayán *p1006, map p1006*

El Sotareño, C 6, No 8-05. This eccentric bar plays old tango LPs from the 1940s and 50s as well as *bolero* and *ranchero* music.
Iguana Afro-Club, C 4, No 9-67. Good music, jazz, salsa, friendly owner.
Tijuana, Cra 9, No 4-68. Mix of music, very popular.

Festivals and events

Popayán *p1006*

Easter processions, every night of **Holy Week** until Good Friday, are spectacular; at the same time there is an **International Religious Music Festival** and local handicraft fairs. The city is very crowded in Semana Santa. The children's processions in the following week are easier to see. As at Pasto (but less violent), there are the **Día de los Negros** on **5 Jan** and **Día de los Blancos** on **6 Jan**; drenching with water is not very common. These are part of the *Fiestas de Pubenza*, with plenty of local music.

Activities and tours

Popayán *p1006, map p1006*

Tour operators

Aviatur, C 4, No 8-69, T820 9332. For information on national parks and general travel services.
Luna Paz Tours, C 8, No 7-61, T315-513 9593. Organizes tours to Tierradentro as well as further afield destinations in Colombia.

Tierradentro *p1007*

Cayo Oidos Galindo, T310-229 2971, based in La Plata, spent 15 years working with archaeologists from Banco de la República. Organizes tours of Tierradentro and surrounding villages with accommodation and food provided. Can arrange English-speaking guides. Recommended.

Transport

Popayán *p1006, map p1006*

Air The airport is 20 mins' walk from the centre. Service daily to **Bogotá** and **Guapi** three a week with **Satena** (ticket office, Cra 9, No 4-14, T822 0215). All passengers need a DAS stamp on their boarding pass from the DAS office in the airport, a quick formality.

Bus The bus terminal is opposite the airport, 15 mins walk from the centre (Ruta 2-Centro bus, terminal to centre, US$0.35, or taxi, US$1.65). Luggage can be stored safely (receipt given). From the bus station, walk up Carrera 11 and take a left at Calle 4 to reach the centre. Take care if you cross any of the bridges over the river going north, especially at night. To **Bogotá**, **Expreso Bolivariano**, US$36, 12-16 hrs. To **Cali**,

US$7-9, 2½-3 hrs, or **Velotax** microbus, US$14, colectivos leave from the main plaza. To **Pasto**, US$15, 4-6 hrs, spectacular scenery (sit on right - night buses are not safe). To **Ipiales, Expreso Bolivariano**, US$16, 6-7 hrs, runs every hour but many buses arrive full from Cali, book in advance. To **San Agustín** via La Plata, **Coomotor**, 13 hrs, US$13, once a day. Via Isnos **Cootranshuila** or **Estelar**, several a day mainly mid morning to afternoon, US$15.50, 6-8 hrs. Sit on the left for the best views. To **Tierradentro** (Cruce de Pisimbalá, also known as Cruce de San Andrés or San Andrés de Pisimbalá), 5 daily 0500-1500, US$8, 4-6 hrs on to La Plata. To **La Plata**, US$9, 5 hrs, with **Cootranshuila** also **Sotracauca**. To **Puracé**, **Cootranshuila** US$1.20, 2 hrs.

Taxi No meters; normal price within city is US$1.65.

Silvia *p1007*

Bus From **Popayán**, daily **Coomotorista** and **Belalcázar**, several *busetas* in the morning, US$2.50.

Tierradentro *p1007*

Bus The road from Popayán to **Tierradentro** is difficult and narrow, but with beautiful scenery. There are 4 daily buses from Pisimbalá to **Popayán**, but services are erratic. Otherwise, you must go to El Cruce. From Popayán daily 1030, US$8, 4-6 hrs to **Cruce Pisimbalá**. Best to take early buses, as afternoon buses will leave you at the Cruce in the dark. Walk uphill (about 2 km, 30 mins) to the museum and on, 20 mins, to the village. If you want to go to **Silvia**, take this bus route and change to a colectivo (US$1.50) at Totoró. Buses and *camionetas* from the Cruce to **La Plata** (en route to San Agustín, see below) US$4.50, 4-5 hrs or more frequent colectivo jeeps, US$6. If you cannot get a direct Cruce–La Plata bus, take one going to Páez (Belalcázar) (US$1.50), alight at Guadualejo, 17 km east of Inzá, from where there is a more frequent service to La Plata.

Directory

Popayán *p1006, map p1006*

Banks Banco Cooperativo, Cra 6, **Banco del Estado**, and others will change TCs. Some, eg **Banco Popular**, will give cash advances against Visa cards or **Banco del Occidente** against MasterCard. Several ATMs on main plaza. Good rates offered at **Titan**, Cra 7, No 6-40, T824 4659, inside CC Luis Martínez, Mon-Fri 0800-1200, 1400-1700, Sat 0830-1200. They also offer an international money transfer service. There are other *cambios*, but their rates are poor. **Immigration** DAS, C 4N, No 10B-66, T823 1889, Mon-Fri 0700-1800, opposite bus terminal next to fire station, go early to extend visas. **Internet** Many places in the centre, about US$0.70 per hr. **Post offices Adpostal**, C 4, No 2-56. **Safety** Ask the Tourist Police about which areas of the city are unsafe. **Telephones** Telecom, Cra 4 y C 3; closes 2000.

Popayán to San Agustín

The two routes from Popayán to San Agustín go through the highlands of the Puracé national park, with its vocanoes, hot springs and the sources of four great rivers. The goal of the journey is one of South America's great, but mysterious archaeological sites, which is also one of Colombia's main tourist destinations.

Puracé and Parque Nacional Puracé

ⓘ *The park is open all week, 0800-1700, US$9, cars US$3.80, motorcycles US$2.25. For information contact Parque Nacional Puracé office in Popayán, C 25, No 9-00, Barrio Palacé, T823 1212/823 1279, Mon-Fri 0800-1745. It is recommended to book for the park here in advance, especially at Easter.*

Some 30 km from Popayán is the small town of Puracé, at Km 12, which has several old buildings. Behind the school a 500 m-long path leads to Chorrera de las Monjas waterfalls on the Río Vinagre, which is notable for the milky white water due to concentrations of sulphur and other minerals.

At Km 22, look for the spectacular San Francisco waterfall on the opposite side of the valley. At Km 23 is the turning right to Puracé sulphur mines (6 km) which can be visited by applying to **Industrias Puracé SA** ⓘ *Calle 4, No 7-32, Popayán*, best through the Popayán tourist office. About 1 km along this road is a turning left leading in 1½ km to **Pilimbalá** in the **Parque Nacional Puracé** at 3,350 m. Here there is a park office, and seven sulphur baths (cold, no bathing). At Pilimbalá, near the park entrance, there is a restaurant and lodging (see below). The national park contains Volcán Puracé (4,640 m) (for climbing see below), Pan de Azúcar (4,670 m) with its permanent snow summit, and the line of nine craters known as the Volcanes los Coconucos (a strenuous two-day hike can be made around the summits requiring high-altitude camping and mountaineering equipment). The park also encompasses the sources of four of Colombia's greatest rivers: the Magdalena, Cauca, Caquetá and Patía. Virtually all the park is over 3,000 m. The Andean Condor is being reintroduced to the wild here from Californian zoos. There are many other birds to be seen and fauna includes the spectacled bear and mountain tapir. Pilimbalá is a good base from which to explore the northern end of the park.

Climbing Volcán Puracé On the hike to the summit, loose ash makes footholds difficult. Avoid getting down wind of the fumaroles, and do not climb down into the crater. Although the best weather is reported to be December-March and July-August, this massif makes its own climate, and high winds, rain and sub-zero temperatures can come in quickly at any time. A marked trail goes from behind the park office and eventually joins the road leading to a set of telecommunications antennae. **The area around these installations is mined, don't take shortcuts**. The summit is about one hour beyond the military buildings, total time from Pilimbalá at least four hours up and 2½ hours down. A guide is recommended.

Around Puracé

Continuing on the main road from Volcá Puracé to **La Plata** (whose central plaza has an enormous ceiba, planted in 1901) at Km 31 there is a viewpoint for Laguna Rafael, at Km 35 the **Cascada de Bedón** (also chemically charged water) and at Km 37 the entrance to the most northerly part of the Parque Nacional Puracé. Here there is a visitor centre, a **geology/ ethnology museum** ⓘ *US$1*, and the very interesting **Termales de San Juan** ⓘ *700 m from the road, US$0.50*, where 112 hot sulphur springs combine with icy mountain creeks to produce spectacular arrays of multi-coloured mosses, algae and lichens, a must if you are in the area (no bathing; accommodation available). The visitor centre has a *cafetería* (arrange meals beforehand through Popayán Tourist Office).

Southeast of La Plata is Pital where the road forks, southeast to **Garzón** (*Phone code: 88; population: 44,000; altitude: 830 m*), and south to near Altamira. Garzón is a pleasant cathedral town set in mountains, 54 km southeast of La Plata, 92 km south of Neiva (see below).

At Altamira, some 29 km further southwest, the main road heads to **Timaná** (basic accommodation, **F**) and continues paved on to San Agustín. Another road goes southeast to Florencia, capital of the Department of Caquetá. **Florencia**, was originally established in 1908. The plaza contains sculptures, fountains, a large forest tree (*saba*) and flower beds. The local saint's day is 16 July: candlelit procession in the evening.

Note Florencia has been the focus of intense guerrilla activity. From Florencia the road runs northeast as far as San Vicente del Caguán, the centre of the demilitarized zone arranged between President Pastrana's government and the FARC guerrillas in November 1998. After the breakdown of peace negotiations in February 2002, government armed forces evicted the FARC guerrillas from the '**zona de despeje**', which was centred on San Vicente and Cartagena del Chairá. The area should not be entered by tourists.

Pitalito (*Phone code: 8; Population: 63,000; Altitude: 1,231 m*) has little to offer the tourist, save convenient access to the **Parque Nacional Cueva de los Guácharos** ⓘ *US$15.50, cafetería, accommodation US$12.25-16 per night, pp, camping US$3.35-4.45, equipment for hire*, which lies to the south. Between December and June swarms of oilbirds (*guácharos*) may be seen; they are nocturnal, with a unique radar- location system. The reserve also contains many of the unusual and spectacular cocks-of-the-rock and the limestone caves are among the most interesting in Colombia. The rangers are particularly friendly, providing tours and basic accommodation; permission to visit the park must be obtained from the national parks offices in Popayán, or Bogotá. Check with them if the park is open.

Popayán to San Agustín direct

South of Puracé towards San Agustín is **Coconuco** (*Altitude*: 2,460 m). Coconuco's baths, **Agua Hirviendo** ⓘ *1½ km beyond the Hotel de Turismo (see Sleeping), on a paved road (mostly), US$1*, have one major and many individual pools with an initial temperature of at least 80°C. There is one pool where you can boil an egg in five minutes. A track from town is quicker than the road. It gets crowded at weekends, but during the week it is a fine area for walking and relaxing in the waters. About 6 km beyond Coconuco, near the road, are Aguas Tibias, warm rather than hot, with similar facilities for visitors. South of Coconuco by 24 km is **Paletará** with high grassland on a grand scale with the Puracé/Pan de Azúcar volcanoes in the background. Below the village (roadside restaurant and MA post) flows the infant Río Cauca. 10 km south of Paletará, the road enters the Parque Nacional Puracé and there is a track northeast to Laguna del Buey. The road then enters a long stretch of virgin cloud forest. This section links Paletará with Isnos and San Agustín. Heavy rain has weakened this stretch, 25 km of which are impassable to light vehicles and very tedious for buses and trucks. No efforts are being made currently to improve this road. Some 62 km from Paletará at the end of the cloud forest is Isnos (see page 1013) followed by a steep drop to a dramatic bridge over the Río Magdalena and shortly to the main road between Pitalito and San Agustín. **Warning** Avoid travelling by night between Popayán and San Agustín, the roads are dangerous. Cyclists should avoid taking the direct route. Reports of theft on the buses between these towns; do not trust 'helpfuls' and do not put bags on the luggage rack.

San Agustín → *Phone code: 8. Colour map 1, C2. Population: 7,000. Altitude: 1,700 m.*

The little town of San Agustín, near the source of the Río Magdalena, is a peaceful place with a few colonial houses and cobbled streets still intact. It is on every travellers' itinerary because of its proximity to the 'Valley of the Statues', where hundreds of large rough-hewn stone figures of men, animals and gods, dating from roughly 3300 BC to just before the Spanish conquest. Little is known of the culture which produced them or what exactly the stone sculptures represent. One theory suggests that this culture came from the Amazon region. The sculptures also display indigenous and Asian influences. No evidence of writing has been discovered, but traces of small circular bamboo straw-thatched houses have been found. The sites were burial and ceremonial sites where it is thought sacrifices, including of children, were made to the gods. Some sites were also residential areas. Various sculptures found here are exhibited in the National Museum at Bogotá. Only about 30% of the burial mounds in the area have been excavated and many of those that have been opened were previously ransacked by grave diggers, who had looted their precious statues. There are about 20 well-kept sites, described below. The area offers excellent opportunities for hiking, although some trails to remote sites are not well marked, and other adventure sports. The rainy season is April-June/ July, but it rains almost all year, hence the beautiful green landscape; the driest months are November-March.

For impartial advice visit the **Oficina Municipal de Turismo** on the Plaza Cívica or the tourist police at **Oficina de Policía de Turismo** ⓘ *C 3, No 11-86*. For cultural information there is a **Casa de Cultura** ⓘ *Cra 3, No 3-61*. There are also four tour agencies calling themslеves 'tourist offices'. While they may give out useful advice, they also hold contracts with hotels and other operators.

Warning Enquire about safety before walking to the more distant monuments. Beware of 'guides' and touts who approach you in the street. Have nothing to do with anyone offering drugs, pre-Columbian objects, gold, emeralds or other precious minerals for sale.

Sights near San Agustín The whole area leaves an unforgettable impression, from the strength and strangeness of the statues, and the great beauty of the rolling green landscape. The nearest archaeological sites are in the **Parque Arqueológico** ⓘ *0800-1600, US$4 including museum, Parque Arqueológico and Fuente de Lavapatas; if, at the end of the day, you wish to visit the following day for free, enquire first at the ticket office, it is recommended to hire a guide to gain a better understanding of the statues and what they represent. Guidebook in Spanish/English US$3.75.* The park is 3 km from San Agustín. The 130 statues and graves in the Parque are *in situ*, though those in the Bosque (a little wood) have been moved and rearranged, and linked by gravel footpaths. Originally, the statues were found lying down and covered in the graves. Those excavated have been placed upright next to the graves and fenced in. Beyond the central area are the carved rocks in and around the stream at the **Fuente de Lavapatas** in the park, where the water runs through carved channels. The **Alto de Lavapatas** ⓘ *closes at 1600, expensive refreshment stands at 'Fuente' and on the way up to Lavapatas*, above the Fuente, has an extensive view. You can get a good idea of the Parque, the Bosque and the museum in the course of three hours' walking, or add in El Tablón and La Chaquira (see below) for a full day. The **Museo Arqueológico** ⓘ *park entrance, 0800-1800*, displays pottery and information about San Agustín culture (Spanish only).

Around San Agustín

El Tablón is reached up Carrera 14, over the brow of the hill and 250 m to a marked track to the right. El Tablón (five sculptures brought together under a bamboo roof) is shortly down to the left. Continue down the path, muddy in wet weather, ford a stream and follow signs to the Río Magdalena canyon. **La Chaquira** (figures carved on rocks) is dramatically set half way down to the river. To walk to and from San Agustín, two hours. Many houses offer refreshments.

At **La Pelota**, two painted statues were found in 1984 (three-hour return trip, six hours if you include El Tablón and La Chaquira, 15 km in all). Discoveries from 1984/86 include some unique polychromed sculptures at **El Purutal** near La Pelota and a series of at least 30 stones carved with animals and other designs in high relief. These are known as **Los Petroglifos** and can be found on the right bank of the Río Magdalena, near the **Estrecho** (narrows) to which jeeps run.

Alto de los Idolos ⓘ *0800-1600, US$2.70*, is about 10 km by horse or on foot, a lovely (if strenuous) walk, steep in places, via **Puente de la Chaquira**. Here on a levelled hill overlooking San Agustín are 13 uncovered tombs and statues dating from 100 BC-AD 600. These statues, known as *vigilantes*, each guard a burial mound. One is an unusual rat totem; stone crocodiles are believed by some to have strong links with the Amazon region. The few excavated have disclosed large stone sarcophagi. It is not certain whether the vigilantes bear a sculpted resemblance of the inmate.

Alto de los Idolos can also be reached from **San José de Isnos** (5 km northeast) 27 km by road from San Agustín. The road passes the **Salto del Mortiño**, a 170 m fall 7 km before Isnos, 500 m off the road. The main plaza in Isnos has restaurants and cafés, eg **El Turista** (lunch, US$1.80) and a **Cootranshuila** bus office. Isnos' market day is Saturday (bus 0500, US$1.20, return 1100, 1300, otherwise bus from Cruce on Pitalito road, or hitch).

6 km north of Isnos is **Alto de las Piedras** ⓘ *0800-1700*, which has seven interesting tombs and monoliths, including the famous 'Doble Yo' and the tombs of two children. There are still over 90 tombs waiting to be excavated. Only less remarkable than the statues are the orchids growing nearby. 8 km further is Bordones; turn left at end of the village and there is (500 m) parking for the **Salto de Bordones** falls ⓘ *US$0.50*. Good for birdwatching.

Bogotá to San Agustin

ⓘ *Before travelling by road south to Neiva, check on safety.*

A lot of people travelling from Bogotá to San Agustín will pass through **Neiva**. The capital of Huila Department. Neiva is a pleasant, modern city on the east bank of the Río Magdalena, surrounded by rich coffee plantations. There is a large and colourful market every day. *Bancolombia*, near Parque Santander, will change US$ cash and traveller's cheques. South of Girardot, about 50 km before Neiva, is a small area (300 sq km) of scrub and arid eroded red soil known as the **Tatacoa** desert, with large cacti, isolated mesas and unusual wildlife. Four- or five-hour guided walks through the desert cost US$10-12 per person per day. From Villavieja hire a taxi to Tatacoa desert, US$22 return. There is also a museum next to Santa Bárbara church showing prehistoric finds in the area, entry US$2.70. On top of a small incline some 15 minutes' drive from Villavieja is the **Observatorio Astronómico de la Tatacoa** ⓘ *www.tatacoa-astronomia.com*, run by Javier Fernando Rua who gives an excellent talk every evening at 1830, US$2.70 per person (camping permitted, US$5.50 to hire tent). Accommodation available in Villavieja (**E-F**, or several *posadas nativas*, run by local families, enquire at the Asociación de Operadores Turísticos on the Parque Principal, T314-315-2067). Daily bus from Neiva to Villavieja (Coomotor from Neiva bus terminal) 1 hour, US$4. You can cross the Magdalena by motorized canoe near Villavieja for US$1.10, then 1½ km to Aipe for buses on the Neiva-Bogotá road.

Popayán to San Agustín listings

For Sleeping and Eating price codes and other relevant information, see Essentials, pages 38-40.

Sleeping

Puracé *p1010*

G Residencias Cubina, safe, cold showers, secure parking.

Parque Nacional Puracé: Pilimbalá *p1011*

Saloon cars will struggle up the last stretch to the centre, but it's an easy 2½ km walk from Km 23. Picnic shelters, restaurant and lodging in room with bath, US$12.25-16 pp. Camping US$2.75-3.85 pp (tents and sleeping bags can be hired). Firewood is provided. Sleeping bags or warm clothing recommended to supplement bedding provided.

Around Puracé *p1011*

La Plata

E Cambis, C 4, No 4-28, T837 1890. TV, helpful, near bus station. Recommended.

E El Portal de Valencia, C 6, No 3-58, T837 6394. With bath, TV, no hot water.

There are other basic places to stay.

Garzón

D Casablanca, Cra 9 y C 5, T833 0997. Restaurant, bar, parking, safe.

D Damasco, C 16, No 10-75, T833 2091. Colonial building, good meals, fan, fridge, a/c, near bus terminal. Recommended.

Florencia

The better hotels are round the plaza.

C pp **Kamani**, C 16, No 12-27, T435 4101, www.hotelkamani.com. Breakfast and diner included, other packages available, a/c, cable TV, internet, restaurant.

Pitalito

C Calamó, Cra 5, No 5-41, T836 0832. Hot water, pool, cafetería, parking.

D Yoritania, C 7, No 3-51, T836 6044. Helpful, with bath, TV, laundry service, no hot water.

F Sevillana, Cra 5, No 3-52, T836 0305. Next to **Taxis Verdes**, no hot water, free coffee, bath, TV.

Popayán to San Agustin: Coconuco *p1012*

C Hotel de Turismo, 500 m out of town, 10 mins' drive to the baths, the best, comfortable, hot water, price is full board, colonial style hotel, restful atmosphere. There are several other modest hotels and restaurants in town.

At **Agua Hirviendo**, T827 7013/14/15, are 3 cabins at US$20 per day that will hold up to 6.

San Agustín *p1012*

Some hotels increase prices during Easter and Christmas by around 10-20%.

B Yalconia, Vía al Parque Arqueológico, T837 3013, hyalconia@gmail.com. By municipal pool, the only mid-range hotel in town, modern building, cleanish rooms, a bit faded.

D El Jardín, Cra 11, No 4-10, T837 3455, www.hosteltrail.com/eljardin. In town, colonial house with a colourful patio, simple rooms, dorms (**F** pp), restaurant with fixed-menu lunches. There are also dorms, which cost US$10pp.

E Casa de Nelly, Km 2 Vía Parque Archeológico, T311-535 0412, hotelrestaurantebar casadenelly@yahoo.com. On top of the hill on the road to the archeological park, colourful rooms and *cabañas* set in a gorgeous garden, home- cooked pastas and pizzas, hammocks.

E Casa del Sol Naciente, T311-587 6464, www.refugioecologicocasadelsolnaciente.com. 1 km from town, rustic *cabañas*, some with spectacular views, rooms in main house (a bit dark), vegetable and herb garden.

E La Casa de François, T314-358 2930, 200 m via El Tablón, www.lacasade francois.com. Just outside town, French-run, private rooms and dorms set in 2 ha of gardens, recently extended, use of kitchen, good breakfast, meals, crêpes and home-baked bread available, bike and horse hire, Wi-Fi.

F Posada Campesina, Cra 14, Camino al Estrecho (on the route to El Tablón), 1 km from town, T837 3956. A recommended farmhouse, owned by Doña Silviana Patiño, who makes good pizza and cheese bread, meals with family, simple working farm, shared bath, use of kitchen, camping possible, good walks nearby.

Camping Camping San Agustín, 1 km from town towards Parque Arqueológico, opposite clean public swimming pool, Las Moyas, T837 3804. US$1.60 pp with own tent, US$5.50 pp to hire tent, clean, pleasant, safe (guards), showers, toilets, lights, laundry service, horse hire.

Just outside San Agustín

D Hacienda Anacaona, Vía al Estrecho del Magdalena, 2 km from town, T837 9390, www.anacaona-colombia.com. Elegant traditional finca, attractive, beautiful views and garden, hammocks, hot water, restaurant, quiet. Camping allowed on grounds. Good.

E El Maco, 1 km from town, 400 m past Piscina Las Moyas, T837 3437, www.elmaco.ch. Swiss owned, working organic farm with colourful gardens, rustic, peaceful, cosy cabins, also teepee, welcoming, basic kitchen facilities, internet, laundry service, very good restaurant (reserve in advance), excellent local information; see **Chaska Tours** below.

E pp **Finca El Cielo**, 3 km from San Agustín, Vía El Estrecho/Obando, T837 9398, www.fincaelcielo.com. Guesthouse and organic farm, overlookig Río Magdalena, restaurant, camping **F** pp, swimming pool, tours organized in the area and beyond, also live music, dance and riding classes.

Around San Agustín: Alto de los Idolos and around *p1013*

Several basic, budget hotels (**E-F**) around main plaza in Isnos.

Bogotá to San Agustín: Neiva *p1013*

A Neiva Plaza, C 7, No 4-62, T871 0806. Neiva's traditional smart hotel for more than 50 years, good, comfortable rooms, restaurant and pool.

D Andino, C 9, No 5-82, T871 0184. Central, rooms are a little small and dark but clean and with cable TV.

E Tayronas, C 8, No 3-46, T871 3038. Pre-Columbian artefacts in the lobby, dark, small rooms with bath.

Eating

San Agustín *p1012*

Tap water in San Agustín is not safe to drink.

TT Donde Richard, C 5, No 23-45, T312-432 6399. On the outskirts of town. Good steaks, chicken and fish, soups and salads, agreeable surroundings. Recommended.

TT-T Surabhi, C 5, No 14-09, T313-345 7519. Tasty regional specialities and set lunches.

T Brahama, C 5, No 15-11, T301-417 1077. This small restaurant serves Colombian fare and some good vegetarian options.

T El Fogón, C 5 No 14-30, T837 3431. Family run, good *comida* and juices, fresh salads. Recommended.

T La Rana Verde, Cra 11, No 2-26, T314-267 8123. Good little lunchtime venue serving fixed-menu meals.

Bogotá to San Agustín: Neiva *p1013*

T Carbonara, C 9, No 6-41. Cheap *almuerzos* served on a pleasant terrace. Next door is an internet café.

T Frutería y Heladería Alaska, Cra 6, No 8-40. Delicious fruit salads and ice creams (tell them if you don't want ice cream with your breakfast fruit salad).

T La Casona, Cra 4, No 12-37. Cheap *almuerzos* in the smart courtyard of an old house. Also à la carte dishes.

T Yoga Inbound, C 9, No 5-74. Indian-influenced vegetarian restaurant serving lunchtime buffets.

Festivals and events

San Agustín *p1012*

Santa María del Carmen in **mid-Jul** (date varies) in San Agustín. 2 festivals in **Jun** are San Juan (24th) with horse races and dances, and **San Pedro** (29th) with horse races, dances, fancy dress, and more. In the **1st week of Oct**, the

Casa de Cultura celebrates **La Semana Cultural Integrada**, with folklore events from all parts of the country.

Bogotá to San Agustín: Neiva *p1013*
Late Jun/early Jul Festival Nacional del Reinado del Bambuco, incorporating San Juan and San Pedro: dancing competitions, parades of beauty on yhe river and of women ride horses through the streets.

Activities and tours

San Agustín *p1012*
Guides There are countless guides in town offering tours of the various sites. Some give a better service than others. Enquire at your hotel or at the tourist office for advice. Some recommended names are **Marino Bravo**, T313-221 4006, takes walking, riding and minibus tours, authorized, professional, speaks English, French and Italian; **Gloria**, T312-440 2010, and **Carlos Bolaños**, T311-459 5753; **Fabio Burbano**, T311-867 5665, professional, reliable and knowledgeable; **Jorge Hurtado**, T311-292 4241, speaks English; **Luis Alfredo Salazar**, speaks English, French, Italian. They charge US$15 for a half day, US$30 for a full day. **Chaska Tours**, T837 3437, www.chaskatours.net. Run by Swiss René Suter (who also owns **El Maco**), organizes tours around San Agustín and to Tierradentro, Puracé and the Tatacoa desert. English and German spoken. Recommended.
Horse hire You are strongly advised to hire horses for trips around San Agustín through hotels, The centre for horses, **Asociación de Acompañantes y Alquiladores de Caballos**, along C 5 on the road to the park, costs about US$12 per hr, per rider. If you require a guide, you must add the hire cost of his horse. **Pacho**, T311-827-7972 (also does tours to Lago Magdalena, the source of the Río Magdalena, US$27 for guidance plus US$20 pp), and **Abuy**, T311-453 3959, are recommended and are contactable through **El Maco** or **La Casa de Nelly**. There are fixed tariffs for 20 standard trips.
Rafting Magdelana Rafting, Km 2 Vía Parque Arqueológico, T311-271 5333, www.magdalenarafting.com. Run by the experienced Frenchman Amid Bouselahane, offers various rafting, kayaking and caving tours.
Vehicle tours Jeeps may be hired for between 4-5 people. Prices vary according to the number of sites to be visited, but the daily rate is about US$16.50 pp with a minimum of 4 people.

Transport

Parque Nacional Puracé *p1011*
Bus Several daily to Puracé from **Popayán**, last returning 1700. Bus stops 3½ km from Pilimbalá. All the places beyond Puracé village can be reached by bus from **Popayán** to La Plata or Garzón. The bus service can be erratic so check time of last daylight bus to Popayán and be prepared to spend a cold night at 3,000 m. The rangers will allow you to stay in the centre.

Around Puracé *p1011*
La Plata
Bus To **Bogotá**, via Neiva, **Coomotor**, 9 hrs, in the evening, **Cootranshuila**, 5 a day, US$27. To **Garzón**, bus or jeep 1½ hrs, US$4.50. To **Popayán** 0500 and others, US$9, 5½ hrs. To **San Agustín**, direct US$12 or take a colectivo to Garzón or Pitalito and change. For **Tierradentro** take a bus towards Popayán (leaves 0600-0630) and alight at the Cruce US$6. Private jeep hire La Plata- Tierradentro US$40, cheaper if you pick up other passengers. To **Pitalito**, 3½ hrs, US$10.

Florencia
Air Aires and **Satena** fly frequently to **Bogotá**, the former via Neiva.
Bus There are regular services from **Neiva** (US$15, 4-6 hrs), **Garzón** and **Altamira** (bus Altamira to Florencia, US$7). To **Bogotá** US$35.

Pitalito
Bus At the bus stations, both off and on buses, in Pitalito, Garzón and Neiva, theft is common.

Plenty of buses and colectivos to **San Agustín**, US$2.70. Bus to **La Plata**, 3½ hrs, US$10. Buses in Pitalito go from the new bus station. **Taxis Verdes** from the main plaza (US$20 to Bogotá). Bus to Bogotá US$24. Bus to **Mocoa** (in the Putumayo), US$15, 7-8 hrs, also jeeps from market square, 0200. To **Parque Nacional Cueva de los Guácharos** take a bus/*chiva* to Palestina, US$2, 1 hr, then a 40-min *chiva* to Mensura. From there, 8-km walk or horse ride to visitor's centre.

San Agustín *p1012*

Bus To **Bogotá** by colectivo (**Taxis Verdes**, C 3, No 11-02, T837 3068) 3 daily, direct or change at Neiva, go early US$23, 9-11 hrs, or by bus (**Coomotor**, C 3, No 10-71), 4 a day, US$21.50-29, 10-12 hrs. From **Bogotá**, **Taxis Verdes** will pick up at hotels (extra charge), T01-355 5555. Alternatively there are frequent services from Bogotá to **Neiva** as well as some to Pitalito. Most services going to Bogotá will stop at Garzón and Neiva. To **Tierradentro**, check first if any of the tourist offices is running a jeep, otherwise, **Taxis Verdes** or colectivos leave frequently to **Garzón** or **Pitalito** (30 mins), then a colectivo jeep from Pitalito to La Plata, US$10, 3½ hrs. Usually you can get a **chiva**, bus or colectivo, 2-3 hrs to Tierradentro (San Andrés de Pisimbalá) the same day. Daily buses to **Garzón**, US$4.50, 2½-3 hrs, from where more buses go to La Plata for Tierradentro. Do not take a night bus to Tierradentro. There are several daily buses from San Agustín to **Popayán** via Isnos with **Cootranshuila** (office on C 3, No 10-81) and Estelar, slow, bad unpaved road, 6-8 hrs, US$15.50; and **Coomotor** via La Plata, 13 hrs, US$13. Do not travel between San Agustín and Popayán at night. The road is isolated and dangerous. It's best to book seats the day before.

Bogotá to San Agustin: Neiva *p1013*

Air **La Marguita**, 1½ km from city. Daily flights to/from **Bogotá** and principal cities, **Aires** and **Satena**. Taxi to bus terminal US$1.50.

Bus Station out of town; bus from the centre leaves from the old terminal (Cra 2, Cs 5 y 6). To **Bogotá**, 6 hrs, US$15. **Coomotor** to **San Agustín**, US$9, 6 hrs. To **Garzón**, US$4.50, 2 hrs with **Cootranshuila**. To **Pitalito**, US$9, 3 hrs. To **La Plata**, for Tierradentro, US$7, 2 hrs, frequent services (especially early morning, 0400, 0500). To **Popayán**, US$18, 8-11 hrs, poor road in parts. To **Florencia**, US$15.

Directory

San Agustín *p1012*

Banks Change TCs before arriving in San Agustín. **Banco Agrario** and **Ultrahuilca Redeban**, Cra 3, No 12-7, cash advances against Visa. **Almacén de Todo**, opposite the town hall, will cash TCs but at a bad rate. **Internet** Connections are slow. **Weblive.com**, Cra 12, No 4-14.

Southern Colombia

This region includes the routes from Popayán to the border with Ecuador, Colombia's furthest stretch of Pacific coast and its toehold on the Amazon river. Pasto is the commercial outlet for the agricultural produce of the southern highlands and its history is tied up with the struggle for independence from Spain and the subsequent wrangling over Simón Bolívar's dream of Gran Colombia. The country's Amazonian port is Leticia, gateway to the jungle, Brazil and Peru.

South to Ecuador

From Popayán to Ecuador is scenic highland country, much of it open páramo intersected here and there by spectacular deep ravines. To the west is the long slope down to the Pacific including the mangrove swamps of much of the coast and the small port of Tumaco. To the east is the continental divide of the Cordillera Oriental and the beginning of the great Amazonian basin. The route rises still further to the border with Ecuador.

Pasto → *Phone code: 2. Population: 399,000. Altitude: 2,534 m.*

The Pan-American Highway continues south from Popayán to Pasto (285 km, five hours driving). The road drops to 700 m in the valley of the Río Patía before climbing to Pasto with big temperature changes. 38 km before Pasto is **Chachagüi**.

Pasto, 88 km from Ecuador, is overlooked from the west by Volcán Galeras (when not in cloud) and to the east by green hills not yet suburbanized by the city, and is in a very attractive setting. The city, capital of the Department of Nariño, stands upon a high plateau in the southwest and retains some of its colonial character. It was founded in the early days of the conquest. During the wars of independence, it was a stronghold of the Royalists and the last town to fall into the hands of the patriots after a bitter struggle. Then the people of Nariño Department wanted to join Ecuador when that country split off from Gran Colombia in 1830, but were prevented by Colombian troops. Today Pasto is a centre for agricultural and cattle industries. Pasto varnish (*barniz*) is mixed locally, to embellish the colourful local wooden bowls.

There are several churches worth visiting, the ornate churches of **San Juan Bautista** and **La Merced** ⓘ *Calle 18A, No 25-11*, **Cristo Rey** ⓘ *Calle 20, No 24-64* and **Santiago** ⓘ *Cra 23 y Calle 13*, which has good views over the city to the mountains.

The **Museo de Oro del Banco de la República** ⓘ *Calle 19, No 21-27, T721 5777, Mon-Fri 0800-1200, 1400-1800, Sat 0800-1300*, has a small well-displayed collection of pre-Columbian pieces from the cultures of southern Colombia, a library and auditorium **Museo Zambrano** ⓘ *C 20, No 29-78*, houses indigenous and colonial period arts, especially *quiteño* (from Quito). The **tourist office** ⓘ *just off the main plaza, C 18, No 25-31, p 2, T723 4962, turnarino@gmail.com, Mon-Fri 0800-1200, 1400-1800*, is friendly and helpful.

Volcán Galeras and around

The volcano, Galeras (4,276 m), quiescent since 1934, began erupting again in 1989 and has been doing soon frequently since (last in 2009). Check at the tourist office whether it is safe to climb on the mountain and whether you need a permit (entry US$1). A road climbs up the mountain to a ranger station and police post at 3,700 m. At the last report, you were not permitted beyond this point.

On the north side of the volcano lies the village of **Sandoná** ⓘ *frequent buses and colectivos daily, US$3, 1½ hrs from Pasto*, where panama hats are made; they can be seen lying in the streets in the process of being finished. Sandoná market day is Saturday. There are good walks on the lower slopes through Catambuco and Jongovito (where bricks are made).

The 284 km road west from Pasto to Tumaco on the coast is paved, but is subject to landslides – check in Pasto. It leaves the Panamericana 40 km south of Pasto at El Pedregal, passing the brick factories of the high plains of the Cordillera Occidental. In **Túquerres** (*Altitude: 3,050 m*) the market is on Thursday, good for ponchos. Ask in Túquerres about walking and climbing in the Laguna Verde/Volcán Azufral area.

About 90 km from Túquerres, at the village of **Chucunez**, a dirt road branches south to **Reserva Natural La Planada**, set up by the WWF and Fundación para la Educación Superior (FES) in 1982 ⓘ *www.fundacionfes.org/Ambiental.html*, a private 3,200 ha nature reserve. This patch of dense cloud forest on a unique flat-topped mountain is home to a wide variety of flora and fauna, and believed to have one of the largest concentrations of native bird species in South America. Day visitors are welcome but camping is prohibited. Accommodation, meals and guides are available.

Tumaco → *Phone code: 2. Colour map 1, C2. Population: 169,000.*

Tumaco has two-storey wooden houses and a predominantly black population, and the roads, water and electricity supplies are not good. It is in one of the world's rainiest areas; the yearly average temperature is about 30°C. The northern part of the town is built on stilts out over the sea (safe to visit only in daylight). The town's beaches are polluted, but swimming is safe at El Morro beach, north of the town (watch out for poisonous rays). There are many discos specializing in Afro/South American rhythms. A few shops may buy dollars at a poor rate; change money in Cali or Pasto. The area around is noted for the archaeological finds associated with the Tumaco culture.

The coastal area around Tumaco is mangrove swamp, with many settlements on the rivers and inlets; negotiate with boatmen for a visit to the swamps or the beautiful island tourist resort of **Boca Grande**. The trip takes 30 minutes, US$8 return. There are several places to stay in the **F** category.

Border with Ecuador

It is possible to travel to Ecuador (San Lorenzo) by boat. Part of the trip is by river, which is very beautiful, and part on the open sea, which can be very rough; a plastic sheet to cover your belongings is essential. Take suncream. It is possible to go overland crossing the Río Mira to reach Ecuador, but there are no immigration offices so you cannot cross officially. Even if you could, it is not advisable to use this route (or the sea crossing) as narcotics/guerrilla activity makes this a dangerous area.

Colombian immigration is at DAS, C 7, No. 23 - Casa 18, Manzana 10, Barrio Pradomar, T727 2010, Tumaco; Mon-Fri 0730-1800, obtain stamp for leaving Colombia here. Visas for Ecuador (if required) should be obtained in Cali or Pasto. Entry stamps for Ecuador must be obtained in the coastal towns.

Entering Colombia through Tumaco: you will have to go to Ipiales to obtain the entry stamp. Apparently the 24/48 hours 'unofficial' entry is not a problem, but do not obtain any Colombian stamps in your passport before presentation to DAS in Ipiales.

The Putumayo

About 25 km east of Pasto, on the road to Mocoa is **Laguna La Cocha**, the largest lake in south Colombia (sometimes called Lago Guamuez). By the lake, 3 km from the main road, is the **Chalet Guamuez**, T721 9306, with chalets, boat and jeep trips. Recommended. In the lake is the **Isla de La Corota** nature reserve with interesting trees (entry US$0.55, 10 minutes by boat from the **Hotel Sindanamoy**, camping possible, information from the national parks office in Popayán, or Bogotá). There are also cheap and friendly places to stay in and near El Encano (often marked El Encanto on maps) where there are also many restaurants serving trout.

Beyond El Encano there is a steep climb over the Sierra where a large statue of the Virgin marks the entry into the Putumayo. The road then descends steeply to Sibundoy, Mocoa and Puerto Asís. For many years this has been guerrilla territory and a drug growing and processing area. It is also the centre of the government-led coca eradication programme. There are hotels on the plaza in Mocoa. The road Pasto-Mocoa is poor.

Ipiales → *Phone code: 2. Colour map 1, C2. Population: 72,000. Altitude: 2,898 m.*

Passing through deep valleys and a spectacular gorge, buses on the paved Pan-American Highway cover the 84 km from Pasto to Ipiales in 1½-2 hours. The road crosses the spectacular gorge of the Río Guáitara at 1,750 m, near El Pedregal, where *choclo* (corn) is cooked in many forms by the roadside. **Ipiales**, "the city of the three volcanoes", is famous for its colourful Friday morning indigenous market. The **Catedral Bodas de Plata** is worth visiting but the real attraction is the Sanctuary of the Virgin of **Las Lajas** (US$0.55), about 7 km east of Ipiales. Seen from the approach road, looking down into the canyon, the Sanctuary is a magnificent architectural conception, set on a bridge over the Río Guáitara: close up, it is very heavily ornamented in the gothic style. The altar is set into the rock face of the canyon, which forms one end of the sanctuary with the façade facing a wide plaza that completes the bridge over the canyon. There are walks to nearby shrines in dramatic scenery. It is a 10-15 minutes' walk down to the sanctuary from the village. There are great pilgrimages to it from Colombia and Ecuador (very crowded at Easter) and the Sanctuary must be second only to Lourdes in the number of miracles claimed for it. Colectivo taxis from Ipiales bus terminal go direct to Las Lajas (10 minutes), US$6 one way. Several basic hotels and a small number of restaurants at Las Lajas. You may also stay cheaply at the Casa Pastoral: amazing views of the Sanctuary.

Border with Ecuador

Ipiales is 2 km from the Rumichaca bridge across the Río Carchi into Ecuador. The border post stands on a concrete bridge, beside a natural bridge, where customs and passport examinations take place 0600-2200. All Colombian offices are in one complex: DAS (immigration, exit stamp given here), customs, INTRA (Dept of Transportation, car papers stamped here; if leaving Colombia you must show your vehicle entry permit) and ICA (Department of Agriculture for plant and animal quarantine). There is also a restaurant, Telecom, clean bathrooms (ask for key, US$0.10) and ample parking. See page 1086 for the Ecuadorean side and see also Documents in Ecuador, Essentials A-Z, page 1035. The **Ecuadorean consulate** ⓘ *Cra 7, No 14-10, p2, T773 2292, weekdays 0900-1230, 1430-1700*, is in the DAS complex. There are many money changers near the bridge on both sides. There are better rates on the Colombian side but check all calculations.

South to Ecuador

For Sleeping and Eating price codes and other relevant information, see Essentials, pages 38-40.

Sleeping

Pasto *p1017*

AL Morasurco, Av de los Estudiantes, T731 3250, www.hotelmorasurco.com. On the northern outskirts, Pasto's most expensive hotel, large beds, cable TV, Wi-Fi, parking and Turkish bath.

A Don Saul, C 17, No 23-52, T722 4480, hoteldonsaul@computronix.com.co. Jordanian owner. Recently refurbished, large beds, sauna, Turkish bath, cable TV, Wi-Fi, breakfast included, restaurant serves Middle Eastern food.

A Galerías, Cra 26, No 18-71, p 3, T723 7390, www.hotel-galerias.com. In the town's main shopping centre, good-sized rooms, Wi-Fi, parking, good restaurant.

A Loft Hotel, C 18, No 22-33, T722 6733, www.lofthotelpasto.com. Comfortable, with minimalist decor, Wi-Fi, internet, spa. 20% discount if you show a copy of *Footprint Colombia*.

B Casa Madrigal, Cra 26, No 15-37, T723 4592, hotelcasamadrigal@hotmail.com. Spacious rooms with good beds, cable TV, Wi-Fi, parking, restaurant, breakfast included.

B Fernando Plaza, C 20, No 21B-16, T729 1432, www.hotelfernandoplaza.com. Smart, lots of good details such as orthopaedic mattresses, Wi-Fi in every room, restaurant.

D Chambu, Cra 20 y No 17, T721 3129. Clean, basic rooms, Wi-Fi, internet, parking, restaurant, helpful staff.

E Koala Inn, C 18, No 22-27, T72 21101. The best backpackers' option in town. Large, antiquated rooms, some with bath, good information on the local area. There is a small café serving decent breakfasts.

E Metropol, C 15, No 21-41, T721 2498. Decent hotel with small but clean rooms with bath, cable TV.

Tumaco *p1018*

Children meet arriving buses to offer accommodation; most cheap places are in C del Comercio, many houses and restaurants without signs take guests – most have mosquito nets. Be careful of food and water, there are many parasites.

E El Dorado, C del Comercio, T727 2565, near water-front and *canoa* dock. Basic, TV, private and shared bath (half the price).

E Imperial, C Mosquera, No 11-23, T727 4746. A basic option.

Ipiales *p1019*

C Los Andes, Cra 5, No 14-44, T773 4338, www.hotellosandes.com. 1 block from the Parque Principal, with breakfast, large rooms, parking, Wi-Fi, gym and sauna.

D Santa Isabel 2, Cra 7, No 14-27, T773 4172. Smart, central, good services, Wi-Fi and internet, parking, restaurant.

E Emperador, Cra 5, No 14-43, T7252413. Central, best budget option, good rooms, cable TV, hot water, parking.

E Metropol, Cra 2, No 6-10, T773 7976. Opposite the bus station, passable rooms, cable TV, hot water, small café. Take care walking around at night.

E Señorial, C 14, No 4-36, T773 4610. Basic, clean, with bath, hot water, TV.

F Belmonte, Cra 4, No 12-11, T773 2771. Basic but clean, cable TV, shared bath.

Eating

Pasto *p1017*

🍴 El Gastronom', Av los Estudiantes, No 32A-68, T731 3477. In the northern part of town, French-run, à la carte Gallic dishes and *almuerzo* for US$5.

🍴 Guadalquivir Café, C 19, No 24-84, T723 9504. Well-established atmospheric café, good snacks.

🍴 Inca Cuy, C 29, No 13-65, T723 8050. Down a narrow corridor behind the Plaza de Bombona, specializes in fried guinea pig (*cuy*); book ahead as it takes an hour to prepare.

Loto Verde, Cra 24, No 13-79. Hare Krishna-run café with vegetarian lunches.

Parrilla Chipichape, C 18, No 27-88, T729 1684. Very popular, barbecued steaks, steamed pork and Sun specials.

Picantería Ipiales, C 19, No 23-37, T723 0393. Typical food from Nariño, specifically pork-based dishes, and *almuerzos*.

Ipiales *p1019*

Mi Casita, C 9, No 6-12. A local favourite for typical Colombian dishes.

Rancho Grande, Cra 7, No 14-51. For steaks, chicken, seafood and fast food.

Festivals and events

Pasto *p1017*

During the new year's *fiesta* there is a **Día de los Negros** on **5 Jan** and a **Día de los Blancos** next day. On 'black day' people smear each others' faces in black grease. On 'white day' they throw talc or flour at each other. Local people wear their oldest clothes. On **28 Dec** and **5 Feb**, there is also a **Fiesta de las Aguas** when anything that moves gets drenched with water from balconies and even from fire engines' hoses. All towns in the region are involved in this legalized water war! In Pasto and Ipiales (see page 1019), on **31 Dec**, is the **Concurso de Años Viejos**, when huge dolls are burnt; they represent the old year and sometimes lampoon local people.

Shopping

Pasto *p1017*

Handicrafts Leather goods shops are on C 17 and C 18. Try the municipal market for handicrafts. **Artesanía-Mercado Bomboná**, C 14 y Cra 27. **Artesanías Mopa-Mopa**, Cra 25, No 13-14, for *barniz*. **Artesanías Nariño**, C 26, No 18-91. **Casa del Barniz de Pasto**, C 13, No 24-9.

Markets and supermarkets Ley on C 18. **Supermercado Confamiliar de Nariño**, C 16B, No 30-53. Recommended.

On the main plaza (C 19 y Cra 25) is a shopping centre with many shops and restaurants.

Maps Maps of Colombia and cities from **Instituto Geográfico Agustín Codazzi**, C 18A, No 21A-18, limited selection.

Activities and tours

Pasto *p1017*

Every Sun paddle ball is played on the edge of the town (bus marked 'San Lorenzo') similar to the game played in Ibarra, Ecuador.

Emproturn, C 19, No 31B-44, T731 0975, emproturn@gmail.com. Organizes tours in and around Pasto.

Transport

Pasto *p1017*

Air Daily with **Satena** (Cosmocentro 2000, C 19, No 27-05, loc 208, T729 0442) to **Bogotá**, 3 a week to **Cali** and **Puerto Asís**. The airport is at Cano, 40 km from Pasto; by colectivo (beautiful drive), 45 mins, US$2.50 or US$15 by taxi. There are no currency exchange facilities, but the shop will change US$ bills at a poor rate.

Bus All interurban buses leave from the terminal at Cra 6, C 16, 4 km from centre, taxi, US$1. **Bogotá**, 18-23 hrs, US$47 (**Bolivariano Pullman** most direct, recommended). **Ipiales**, 2 hrs, US$3.50, sit on the left for the views. **Popayán**, ordinary buses take 10-12 hrs, US$8; expresses take 5-8 hrs, cost US$15. **Cali**, US$16-19, expresses, 8½ to 10 hrs. **Tumaco**, 9 hrs by bus, 7 hrs by minibus, US$10.

Volcán Galeras and around: Túquerres *p1018*

Bus To **Pasto** US$4.50, 2 hrs, **Trans Ipiales**; jeep to **Ipiales** from Carrera 14, C 20, US$3, 1½ hrs.

Tumaco *p1018*

Air There are daily flights to and from **Cali**, with **Satena**, T727 2329.

Bus To **Pasto**, 6-9 hrs, US$15, **Supertaxis del Sur** or **Trans Ipiales**, 4 a day, interesting ride; minibus 7 hrs. From Ipiales go to El Espino (US$1, colectivo, US$1.50) and change buses for Tumaco (US$6).

Border with Ecuador: Tumaco *p1019*

Boat Seek advice on safety before taking a boat to **San Lorenzo**, 7 hrs (can take 14). Ask on C del Comercio, the waterfront or the fishing centre, El Coral del Pacífico.

The Putumayo: Laguna La Cocha *p1019*

To La Cocha take a taxi from **Pasto**, a colectivo from C 20 y Cra 20, or a **bus** to **El Encano** and walk the remaining 5 km to the chalets of **Chalet**

Guamuez, or 20 mins from bus stop direct to lake shore and take a *lancha* to the chalets.

Ipiales *p1019*

Air San Luis airport is 6½ km out of town. Satena to **Cali** and **Puerto Asís**. Taxi to Ipiales centre, US$4.

Bus Bus companies have individual departure points: *busetas/colectivos* mostly leave from main plaza. To **Popayán**, **Expreso Bolivariano**, US$12, 7½-8 hrs, hourly departures, 0800-2000; also colectivo taxis, US$16. **Expreso Bolivariano** to **Cali**, US$22, 10-12 hrs. To **Pasto** US$3.50, 2-3 hrs. Frequent buses to **Bogotá** every 2 hrs, 20-24 hrs, US$53 (check if you have to change buses in Cali). To **Medellín**, 2 daily, 20-22 hrs, US$43.

Border with Ecuador: Ipiales *p1019*

Bus From Ipiales to **Tulcán**: *colectivo* from C 14 y Cra 11, US$0.80 to the border (buses to Ipiales arrive at the main plaza – they may take you closer to the colectivo point if you ask). Colectivo from border to **Tulcán** US$0.75, to Tulcán bus station, US$1. Ask the fare at border tourist office. Easiest to take a taxi from Ipiales to the border, US$3.50.

Car If entering Colombia by car, the vehicle should be fumigated against diseases that affect coffee trees, at the ICA office. The certificate must be presented in El Pedregal, 40 km beyond Ipiales on the road to Pasto. (This fumigation process is not always carried out.) You can buy insurance for your car in Colombia at Banco Agrario, in the plaza.

Directory

Pasto *p1017*

Banks For changing TCs, **Bancolombia**, C 19, No 24-52. Visa advances. **Banco de Bogotá** will change TCs 0930-1130. If going to Tumaco, this is the last place where TCs can be cashed. *Casas de cambio*, **Titan**, Cra 26, No 18-71, at Cra 25, No 18-97, and C 19, No 24-86, by the main plaza. **Immigration** DAS: C 17, No 29-70, T731 1500, will give exit stamps if you are going on to Ecuador. **Internet** Pc-Rent, Pasaje Corazón de Jesús, C 18, No 25-36. **Post offices** Cra 23, 18-42. **Telephones** Long-distance calls, C 17 y Cra 23.

Ipiales *p1019*

Banks It is not possible to cash TCs, but cash against Visa is no problem at **Bancolombia**, C 14, No 5-32. *Casa de Cambio* on the plaza. Money changers on street, in plaza and at border, but they may take advantage if the banks are closed. Coming from Ecuador, peso rates compare well in Ipiales with elsewhere in Colombia. **Immigration** DAS:, Cra 4, No 10A-33, Libertad, T773 2578. **Telephones** International calls from Cra 6 y C 6/7.

Leticia and the Amazon

The extensive cattle lands from the Cordillera Central to the Orinoco are a good place to get away from it all in the dry season. Leticia, Colombia's port on the Amazon, is on the southern tip of a spur of territory which gives Colombia access to the great river, 3,200 km upstream from the Atlantic. There is a land border with Brazil a short distance to the east beyond which are Marco and Tabatinga. Directly south across the river is another important Brazilian port, Benjamin Constant, which is close to the border with Peru. On the north side of the Amazon, Colombia has a frontage on the river of 80 km to the land border with Peru.

Leticia → *Phone code: 8. Colour map 3, A5. Population: 35,000. Altitude: 82 m.*

Capital of Amazonas Department, the city is clean, modern, though run down near the river. Parque Santander y Orellana is pleasant and is a popular meeting place. It is rapidly merging into one town with neighbouring Marco in Brazil. There is a modern, well-equipped hospital. The best time to visit the area is in July or August, the early months of the dry season. At weekends, accommodation may be difficult to find. Leticia is a good place to buy typical products of Amazon *indígenas* (for example *Almacen Uirapuru*, C 8, No 10-35, T592 7056; it also has a small museum at the back), and tourist services are better than in Tabatinga or Benjamin Constant. The **Museo**

Etnográfico del Hombre Amazónico ⓘ *Cra 11 y Calle 9*, has displays on local ethnography and archaeology, in a beautiful building with a library and a terrace overlooking the Amazon. For the border with Brazil, Colombia and Peru see the Brazil chapter, page 640, where Colombian, Brazilian and Peruvian procedures are detailed in one section. The **tourist office** is at ⓘ *C 10, No 10-47, T592 5944*. **Note** There is an obligatory US$7 environment tax payable upon arrival in Leticia. You may also be asked for a yellow fever inoculation certificate on arrival; if you do not have this, an innoculation will be administered on the spot (not recommended).

Jungle trips from Leticia

Monkey Island (La Isla de los Micos) Visits can be made to the Yagua and Ticuna people. There are few monkeys on the island now, those left are semi-tame. Agencies run overnight tours.

Parque Nacional Amacayacu *0700-1700, US16.50 for foreigners*, 60 km upstream, at the mouth of the Matamata Creek, 2 hours from Leticia. There is a jungle walk to a lookout (guides will point out plants, including those to avoid) and a rope bridge over the forest canopy, with wonderful views over the surrounding jungle (US$8). There are various other guided day treks through the jungle. Boats go to a nearby island to see Victoria Regia water lilies. Accommodation on 2-5 night packages is managed by **Aviatur** ⓘ *C 7, No 10-78, T592 6812 in Leticia (helpful), or T01-900-331 2222/01-382 1616, reservasparques@aviatur.com.co; for the park direct T592 5600.* The Leticia office will also give information and arrange transport to the park.

Puerto Nariño A small, attractive settlement on the Río Loretoyacu, a tributary of the Amazon, beyond the Parque Nacional Amacayacu, 75 km from Leticia. Where the two rivers meet is a popular place to watch dolphins. Tours include Lago de Tarapoto de see pink river dolphin and caiman (US$27-44 per person by motorized canoe) and walks to indigenous communities. **Fundación Natütama** ⓘ *www.natutama.org, Mon-Fri (except Tues) 0800-1200, 1400-1700, free but contributions appreciated* works to preserve the marine life of this part of the Amazon by organizing educational programmes with local communities. They have an informative visitor centre.

Leticia and the Amazon listings

For Sleeping and Eating price codes and other relevant information, see Essentials, pages 38-40.

Sleeping

Leticia *p1022*

LL Decalodge Ticuna, Cra 11, No 6-11, T5926600, www.decameron.com. Spacious apartments, hot water, a/c, pool, bar and restaurant. Can arrange stays in Amacayacu National Park and trips to Monkey Island, to which they hold concessions.

A Amira, C 9, No 9-69, T592 7767. Comfortable rooms with a/c (cheaper with fan), cable TV, hot water.

B Fernando Real, Cra 9, No 8-80, T592 7362. Intimate atmosphere, rooms open onto a flower-filled patio.

B La Frontera, Cra 11, No 6-106, T592 5111, paraisoecologico@hotmail.com. On the border, so convenient if you are heading to Brazil, clean.

B Yurupary, C 8, No 7-26, T592 4743, www.hotelyurupary.com. Good, large rooms, hot water, pool fringed with tropical plants. Also arranges tours into the Amazon through **Yurupary Amazonas Tours**.

D Los Delfines, Cra 11, No 12-85, T592 7488, losdelfinesleticia@hotmail.com. Lovely patio, rooms with bath, fan and Wi-Fi.

E Mahatu Guesthouse, Cra 7, No 9-69, T311-539 1265, www.mahatu.com. One private room in a *maloca* in an overgrown garden and a couple of dorms (**F**), kitchen, bike hire. Owner speaks English, Flemish, French and Portuguese and organizes alternative tours of the Amazon. Check the website before arriving as may be moving.

E Mochileros, Cra 5, No 9-117, T592 5991. Basic hostel with bunks-only rooms and shared bath. Organizes economical tours.

Puerto Nariño *p1023*
Increasingly travellers are choosing to stay in Puerto Nariño. Several options available.
B Casa Selva, Cra 6, No 6-78, T311-521 9297, www.casaselvahotel.com. Comfortable, airy, spotless rooms. Trips to nearby Lago de Tarapoto.
D Malocas Napu, C 4, No 5-72, 2 blocks from river, T310-488 0998, olgabeco@yahoo.com. Simple private wooden rooms, hammocks US$6 pp, quiet and relaxing. Breakfast provided.
E Hospedaje Manguaré, C 4, No 5-52, T311-276 4873. Comfortable cabin-style rooms with fans and shared bath. Bunks in dorms are **F** pp. It also doubles up as the town chemist.

Eating

Leticia *p1022*
Several small sidewalk restaurants downtown, serving good value *platos del día*. Cheap food (fried banana and meat, also fish and pineapples) is sold at the market near the harbour. Cheap fruit for sale. Many café/bars overlook the market on the river bank. Take your own drinking water.
TT Amazon Sazón, Cra 9, No 7-56. Regional food.
TT-T El Sabor, C 8, No 9-25. Recommended for meat grills and *comidas corrientes*.
T Tierras Amazónicas, C 8, No 7-50. Also popular, restaurant/bar, good local dishes.
T Tierras Antioqueñas, C 8, No 9-19. Good *almuerzos* of steak, chicken and river fish.

Activities and tours

Leticia *p1022*
SelvAventura, T311-287 1307, selva ventura@gmail.com. Tailor-made trips to the Río Tacana to indigenous communities, sleeping in *posadas*, with kayaking, caiman spotting and forest observation from canopy platforms. Prices from US$80 pp. English, Portuguese and Spanish spoken.
Steve McAlear, T313-313 1106, stevemcalear@hotmail.com. Personalized tours to some of the area's more remote locations.

Puerto Nariño *p1023*
Tour guides
Ever Sinarahua, Clarindo López and **Milciades Peña** are recommended for their local knowledge of flora and fauna and indigenous customs; enquire through **Casa Selva.** Also, **Pedro Nel Cuello**, enquire through **Fundación Natutama**, also recommended.

Transport

Leticia *p1022*
Air Airport is 1½ km from town, taxi US$2.40; small terminal, few facilities. Taxi direct to Brazilian immigration (Police Station) US$8. Expect to be searched before leaving Leticia airport, and on arrival in Bogotá from Leticia. **Aero República** and **Satena** fly to Leticia (Tabatinga airport if Leticia's is closed) from **Bogotá**, daily. **Satena** has flights to local Amazonas destinations. Taxi to Tabatinga, US$5.50, colectivo US$0.80.

Jungle trips from Leticia *p1023*
Parque Nacional Amacayacu
Boat From Leticia US$1 one way, 2 hrs; 2 operators (check that your operator also runs the day you wish to return). *Rápido* launches leave the wharf (Puerto Civil) daily 1000 and 1400.

Puerto Nariño *p1023*
Boat From **Leticia**, daily at 0800, 1000 and 1400 (check times as they often change), 2 hrs, US$14, with **Tres Fronteras**.

Directory

Leticia *p1022*
Banks Street money changers, *cambios*, and banks for exchange, shop around. TCs cannot be changed at weekends, and are hard to change at other times, try **Banco de Bogotá**. **Immigration** DAS, C 9, No 9-62, T592 4878, Mon-Fri 0700-1800. **Internet** Very few places, slow connections. **Centel.net**, C 9, No 9-09. Skype and local and international calls. **Aloha.net**, C 11, No 7-22. Skype and headphones. **Post offices** Adpostal, C 8, No 9-65, T592 7977. **Telephones** Cra 11, near Parque Santander. **Tourist police**, T592 5060.

Puerto Nariño *p1023*
Internet/telephone Internet and international calls (expensive) next to the school.

Ecuador

Contents

1028 Planning your trip

1036 Quito
1067 Around Quito

1074 Northern Ecuador
1074 Quito to Otavalo
1077 Otavalo and around
1083 Otavalo to the Colombian border

1091 Cotopaxi, Latacunga and Quilotoa
1091 Cotopaxi and Latacunga
1099 Quiltoa Circuit
1102 Ambato

1104 Baños and Riobamba
1104 Baños and around
1111 Riobamba and around

1119 Cuenca and around

1130 Cuenca to the Peruvian border
1136 Vilcabamba to Peru

1139 Guayaquil and south to Peru
1141 Guayaquil
1149 South to Peru

1152 Pacific lowlands
1152 Guayaquil to Puerto López
1160 Manta and Bahía de Caráquez
1167 Northern lowlands

1174 The Oriente
1175 Northern Oriente
1181 Central and southern Oriente

1190 Galápagos Islands
1190 Background
1190 Ins and outs

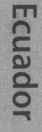

Footprint features

1026 Don't miss …
1031 Driving in Ecuador
1066 Language schools in Quito
1198 Galápagos tourist vessels
1197 Overseas agencies

At a glance

Time required 2-5 weeks.

Best time Jun-Aug, Christmas and New Year are good for fiestas.

When not to go Jun-Sep and Dec-Jan are the busiest times. All year is good from a climatic point of view. In the highlands, the wettest months are Oct-Nov and Feb-May; Jan-May are hottest and rainiest on Pacific coast. In the jungle, wet months are Mar-Sep.

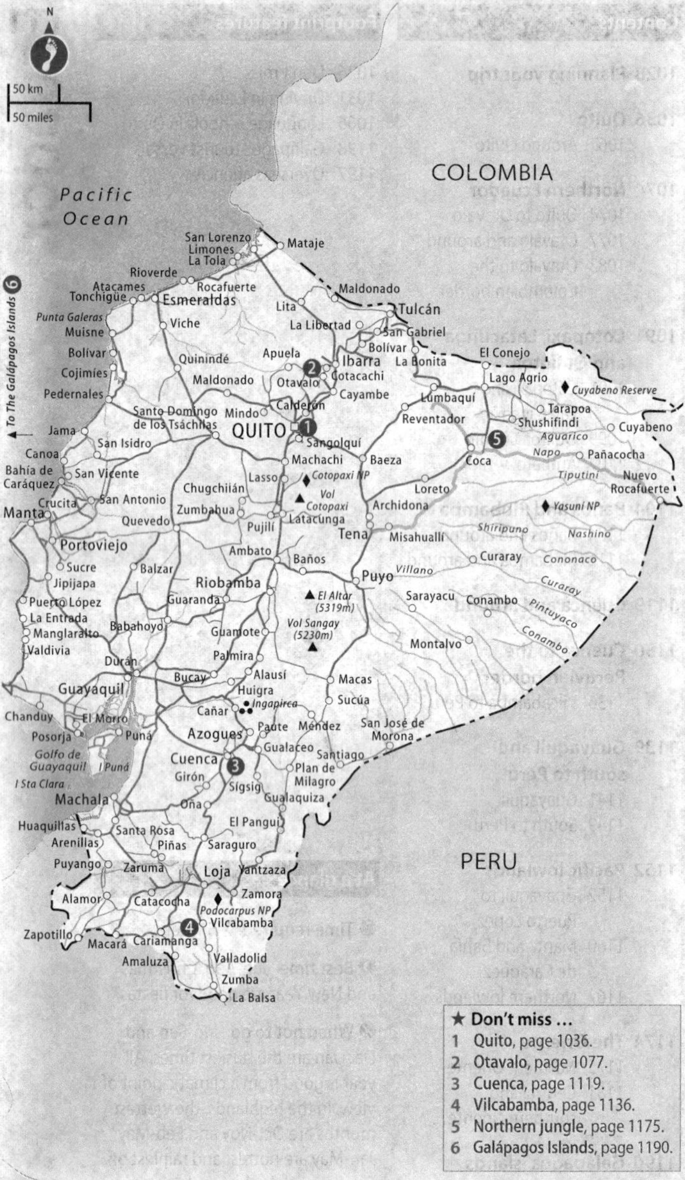

★ Don't miss ...

1 Quito, page 1036.
2 Otavalo, page 1077.
3 Cuenca, page 1119.
4 Vilcabamba, page 1136.
5 Northern jungle, page 1175.
6 Galápagos Islands, page 1190.

Tucked in between Peru and Colombia, this country is small enough for you to have breakfast with scarlet macaws in the jungle, lunch in the lee of a snow-capped peak and, at tea time, be eyeballed by an iguana whose patch of Pacific beach you have just borrowed.

A multitude of national parks and conservation areas emphasise the incredible variety of Ecuador. They include mangroves; an avenue of volcanoes – many of them active – striding across the Equator; forests growing on the dry Pacific coast, in the clouds and under the Amazonian rains; not forgetting all the animals and birds which flourish in these habitats. In fact, as Ecuador is one of the richest places in the world for birds, with some of the planet's most beautiful species, the country is a prime birdwatching destination.

The capital, Quito, has become one of the gringo centres of South America, bursting at the seams with language schools, travel agencies and restaurants. The smaller towns and villages of Ecuador offer the most authentic experience. Indulge your senses at one of their many markets: dizzying arrays of textiles, ceramics, carvings and other crafts, not to mention the cornucopia of fresh produce.

The exotic wildlife of the Galápagos Islands will also keep you enthralled, whether it's sympathizing with Lonesome George, the last giant tortoise of his race, watching an albatross take off on its flight path, or admiring the sexual paraphernalia of the magnificent frigatebird. If the Galápagos are beyond your budget, then Isla de la Plata is a more accessible alternative for seeing marine life.

Planning your trip

Where to go

The capital, **Quito**, boasts some of the best-preserved colonial architecture in South America in its 'colonial city', while the 'modern Quito' is where you'll find most accommodation, restaurants, tour operators and language schools. From the capital many of the country's attractions are accessible by road in only a few hours. Day trips include nature reserves, hot springs, and, of course, the Equator. There is also good mountaineering and white-water rafting nearby. North of Quito is **Otavalo** with its outstanding handicrafts market, a regular one-day tour, but equally popular as a base for exploring nearby villages, more nature reserves and hiking or cycling routes. Carrying on towards the Colombian border is **Ibarra**, another good centre for visiting the north and the starting point for the journey to San Lorenzo on the Pacific.

In the Central Sierra, south of Quito is the national park surrounding **Cotopaxi**, one of Ecuador's most frequently climbed volcanoes. Further south is the **Quilotoa circuit**, a 200-km loop through small villages and beautiful landscapes, with lots of possibilities for trekking, cycling and riding. The starting point is Latacunga on the Pan-American Highway. On one of the main routes from the Sierra to the eastern jungle is **Baños**, a very popular spa town with climbing, hiking, riding and volcano watching opportunities close at hand. The heart of the central highlands is **Riobamba**, beneath Chimborazo volcano. This is another good base for climbing, biking and trekking, as well as the starting point for a very popular railway ride over La Nariz del Diablo (The Devil's Nose) – when the often-damaged line is open. The Inca ruin of **Ingapirca** is between Riobamba and **Cuenca**, a lovely colonial city in the Southern Sierra. Nearby is the Cajas National Park. En route from Cuenca towards Peru are the provincial capital of **Loja**, close to the Parque Nacional Podocarpus, and **Vilcabamba**, with a delightful climate and a favourite with backpackers. Several border crossings to Peru are accessible from Loja.

Ecuador's Pacific capital is **Guayaquil**, 45 minutes by air from Quito (eight hours by bus) and only four hours by bus south to the Peruvian border via Machala. Key areas of the city have been renewed, such as its historic riverfront. To the north stretch the **Pacific Lowlands** with beaches, pre-Columbian archaeological sites and small resorts like Puerto López, Montañita, Canoa and Mompiche, as well as a few highly developed ones like Salinas, Bahía de Caráquez and Atacames. Near Puerto López the **Parque Nacional Machalilla** contains dry tropical forest, offshore islands and marine ecosystems. It is a good place for riding, diving, whale watching, birdwatching and relaxing on the beautiful Los Frailes beach.

The **Oriente** (eastern lowlands) offers good opportunities for nature tourism, with a number of specially designed jungle lodges, mainly in the north. A stay in one of these places is best booked in Quito or from home, but you can head for jungle towns like Coca, Tena, Puyo or

Ecuador and Galapagos Reservation Center
Direct operators of the M/C Galapagos Journey, M/V Galapagos Odyssey, M/V Galapagos Voyager and Cotococha Amazon Lodge.
Galapagos Odyssey
Galapagos Journey
Galapagos Voyager
Mention this Ad when booking with us and get 10% discount in your purchase.
· Andes
· Amazon Rain Forest
· Pacific Coast
· Cultural and Adventure Tours,
· Special Interest and custom made itineraries according to your needs and budget.
Contact Us
Av. Amazonas N24-03 y Wilson, Tercer Piso.
T: ECU + 593 2 222 8385 /
+ 593 2 2286 0355 / USA + 1 646 415 7758
E: reservations@galapagosodyssey.com
W: www.galapagosodyssey.com
Cotococha amazon lodge

Misahuallí to arrange a tour with a local agency or guide. The southern Oriente is less developed for tourism, but interest is growing, with Macas or Zamora as the places to aim for.

Ecuador is famous for its **hot springs** and, on either side of the Andes, there is great **birdwatching** in a wide variety of protected areas. Other special interest activities include **diving**, **whitewater rafting** and various **volunteer programmes**. The nature destination par excellence, though, is the **Galápagos Islands**, 970 km west of the mainland. Tours, which are best arranged in Quito, Guayaquil or from home, involve cruising from island to island to see new species with each landfall.

When to go

Ecuador's climate is highly unpredictable. As a general rule, however, in the **Sierra**, there is little variation by day or by season in the temperature: this depends on altitude. The range of shade temperature is from 6°C to 10°C in the morning to 19°C to 23°C in the afternoon, though it can get considerably hotter in the lower basins. Rainfall patterns depend on whether a particular area is closer to the eastern or western slopes of the Andes. To the west, June to September are dry and October to May are wet (but there is sometimes a short dry spell in December or January). To the east, October to February are dry and March to September are wet. There is also variation in annual rainfall from north to south, with the southern highlands being drier. **Quito** is within 25 km of the Equator, but it stands high enough to make its climate much like that of spring in England, the days pleasantly warm and the nights cool. Rainy season is October to May with the heaviest rainfall in April. Rain usually falls in the afternoon. The day length (sunrise to sunset) is almost constant throughout the year.

Along the **Pacific coast**, rainfall also decreases from north to south, so that it can rain throughout the year in northern Esmeraldas and seldom at all near the Peruvian border. The coast, however, can be enjoyed year-round, although it may be a bit cool from June to November, when mornings are often grey with the *garúa* mists. January to May is the hottest and rainiest time of the year. Like the coast the **Galápagos** suffer from the *garúa* from May to December; from January to April the islands are hottest and brief but heavy showers can fall. In the **Oriente**, heavy rain can fall at any time, but it is usually wettest from March to September.

Ecuador's **high season** is from June to early September, which is also the best time for climbing and trekking. There is also a short tourist season in December and January. In resort areas at major fiestas, such as Carnival, Semana Santa and over New Year, accommodation can be hard to find. Hotels will be full in individual towns during their particular festivals, but Ecuador as a whole is not overcrowded at any time of the year.

Getting around

Air TAME ⓘ *reservations: T1-800-500800 or 02-397 7100, www.tame.com.ec*, is the main internal airline, flying to all major airports and the Galápagos. Enquire locally for up-to-date routes and timetables as they change constantly. TAME offices are listed under each relevant town or city. Smaller airlines include **Aerogal** ⓘ *T1-800-237642 or 02-294 2800, www.aerogal.com.ec*, flies from Quito to Guayaquil, Cuenca, Manta and the Galápagos; **Icaro** ⓘ *T1-800-883567, www.icaro.aero*, flies from Quito to Guayaquil, Manta and Coca. **LAN** ⓘ *T1-800-101075, www.lan.com*, serves Quito, Guayaquil and Cuenca; **Saereo** ⓘ *T1-800-723736 or 02-330 2280, www.saereo.com*, flies from Quito to Macas and Machala, and from Guayaquil to Loja; **VIP** ⓘ *contact through Aerogal*, flies from Quito to Lago Agrio and Coca.

Bus Bus travel is generally more convenient and regular than in other Andean countries. Several companies use comfortable air-conditioned buses on their longer routes; some companies have their own stations, away from the main bus terminals, exclusively for these better buses. **Note** Throughout Ecuador, travel by bus is safest during the daytime.

Driving in Ecuador

Roads A good network of paved roads runs throughout most of the country. Maintenance of major highways is franchised to private firms, who charge tolls of US$0.50-1. Roads are subject to damage during heavy rainy seasons. Always check road conditions before setting out.

Safety Unexpected potholes and other obstructions, the lack of road signs, and local drivers' tendency to use the middle of the road make driving 'an experience'. Beware the bus drivers, who often drive very fast and rather recklessly. Driving at night is not recommended.

Documents To bring a foreign vehicle or motorcycle into the country, its original registration document (title) in the name of the driver is required. If the driver is not the owner, a notarized letter of authorization is required. All documents must be accompanied by a Spanish translation. A 90-day permit is granted on arrival, extensions are only granted if the vehicle is in the garage for repairs. No security deposit is required and you can enter and leave at different land borders. Procedures are generally straightforward but it can be a matter of luck. Shipping a vehicle requires more paperwork and hiring a customs broker. The port of Guayaquil is prone to theft and particularly officious. Manta and Esmeraldas are smaller and more relaxed, but receive fewer ships. A valid driver's licence from your home country is generally sufficient to drive in Ecuador and rent a car, but an international licence is helpful.

Car hire To rent a car you must be 21 and have an international credit card. Surcharges may apply to clients aged 21-25. You may pay cash, which is cheaper and may allow you to bargain, but they want a credit card for security. You may be asked to sign two blank credit card vouchers, one for the rental fee itself and the other as a security deposit, and authorization for a charge of as much as US$5,000 may be requested against your credit card account. The uncashed vouchers will be returned to you when you return the vehicle. Make sure the car is parked securely at night. A small car suitable for city driving costs around US$450 per week including unlimited milage, tax and insurance. A 4WD (recommended for the Oriente and unpaved roads) costs about US$750 a week.

Fuel There are two grades of petrol, 'Extra' (82 octane, US$1.48 per US gallon) and 'Super' (92 Octane, US$1.98-2.30). Both are unleaded. Extra is available everywhere, while Super may not be available in more remote areas. Diesel fuel (US$1.03) is notoriously dirty and available everywhere.

Hitchhiking Public transport in Ecuador is so abundant that there is seldom any need to hitchhike along the major highways. On small out-of-the-way country roads however, the situation can be quite the opposite, and giving passers-by a ride is common practice and safe, especially in the back of a pick-up or truck. A small fee is usually charged, check in advance.

Train Empresa de Ferrocarriles Ecuatorianos ⓘ *www.efe.gov.ec*. A few segments of the spectacular Ecuadorean railway system have been restored. In 2010, tourist rides were being offered: from **Riobamba to Sibambe**, from **Quito to Latacunga** via Parque Nacional Cotopaxi, from **Ibarra to Primer Paso** and from **El Tambo to Baños del Inca**.

Maps and guide books Instituto Geográfico Militar (IGM) ⓘ *Senierges y Telmo Paz y Miño, on top of the hill to the east of Parque El Ejido. From Av 12 de Octubre, opposite the Casa de la Cultura, take Jiménez (a small street) up the hill. Cross Av Colombia and continue uphill on Paz y Miño behind the Military Hospital, then turn right to the guarded main entrance. You have to deposit your passport or identification card. T02-397 5100, ext 2502, www.igm.gov.ec. Map sales room open Mon-Fri 0800-1600.* They sell country maps and topographic maps, covering most areas of Ecuador, in various scales, original, US$2, colour copy (pick-up next day), US$3.36, colour plotted copy US$3.08 (1-hour wait). Maps of border areas and the seacoast are 'reservado' (classified) and not available for sale without a military permit (requires extra time). Buy your maps here, they are rarely available outside Quito. Map and geographic reference libraries are located next to the sales room. There is a beautiful view from the grounds. Two recommended road atlases, *Guía Vial* and *Guía de Quito*, published by **Ediguías** in Quito, are available in book shops. Online maps of major Ecuadorean cities are found on www.guiame.com.ec.

Sleeping → *See page 38 for our hotel grade price guide.*

Hotels Outside the provincial capitals and a few resorts, there are few higher-class hotels, although a number of *haciendas* have opened their doors to paying guests. A few are in the **Exclusive Hotels & Haciendas of Ecuador** group ⓘ *Av 12 de Octubre E11-14 y Orellana, Edif Lincoln, p 2, T02-254 4719, www.ehhec.com*, but there are many other independent haciendas of good quality. Some are mentioned in the text. Larger towns and tourist centres often have more hotels than we can list. This is especially true of Quito. The hotels that are included are among the best in each category, selected to provide a variety of locations and styles. Service of 10% and tax of 12% are added to better hotel and restaurant bills. Some cheaper hotels apply the 12% tax, but check if it is included. Many hotel rooms have very low wattage bulbs, keen readers are advised to take a head torch.

Camping Camping in protected natural areas can be one of the most satisfying experiences during a visit to Ecuador. Organized campsites, car or trailer camping on the other hand are virtually unheard-of. Because of the abundance of cheap hotels you should never *have to* camp in Ecuador, except for cyclists who may be stuck between towns. In this case the best strategy is to ask permission to camp on someone's private land, preferably within sight of their home for safety. It is not safe to pitch your tent at random near villages and even less so on beaches. *Bluet Camping Gas* is easily obtainable, but white gas, like US Coleman fuel, is hard to find. Unleaded petrol (gasoline) is available everywhere and may be an alternative for some stoves.

Eating and drinking → *See page 40 for our restaurant price guide.*

Eating out Upmarket restaurants add 22% to the bill, 12% tax plus 10% service. All other places add the 12% tax, which is also charged on non-essential items in food shops. The cuisine varies with region. The following are some typical dishes.

In the highlands *Locro de papas* (potato and cheese soup), *mote* (corn burst with alkali, a staple in the region around Cuenca, but used in a variety of dishes in the Sierra), *caldo de patas* (cowheel soup with *mote*), *llapingachos* (fried potato and cheese patties), *empanadas de morocho* (fried snacks: a ground corn shell filled with meat), *sancocho de yuca* (vegetable soup with manioc root), roast *cuy* (guinea pig), *fritada* (fried pork), *hornado* (roast pork), *humitas* (tender ground corn steamed in corn leaves), and *quimbolitos* (similar to *humitas* but prepared with wheat flour and steamed in *achira* lily leaves). *Humitas* and *quimbolitos* come in both sweet and savoury varieties.

On the coast *Empanadas de verde* (fried snacks: a ground plantain shell filled with cheese, meat or shrimp), *sopa de bola de verde* (plantain dumpling soup), *ceviche* (marinaded fish or seafood, popular everywhere, see below), *encocados* (dishes prepared with coconut milk, may be shrimp, fish, etc, very popular in the province of Esmeraldas), *cocadas* (sweets made with coconut), *viche* (fish or seafood soup made with ground peanuts), and *patacones* (thick fried plantain chips served as a side dish).

In Oriente Dishes prepared with yuca (manioc or cassava root) and river fish. *Maitos* (in northern Oriente) and *ayampacos* (in the south) are spiced meat, chicken or palm hearts wrapped in special leaves and roasted over the coals.

Throughout the country If economizing ask for the set meal in restaurants, *almuerzo* at lunch time, *merienda* in the evening – very cheap and wholesome; it costs US$2-3. *Fanesca*, a fish soup with beans, many grains, ground peanuts and more, sold in Easter Week, is very filling (it is so popular that in Quito and main tourist spots it is sold throughout Lent). *Ceviche*, marinated fish or seafood which is usually served with popcorn and roasted maize (*tostado*), is very popular throughout Ecuador. Only *ceviche de pescado* (fish) and *ceviche de concha* (clams) which are marinated raw, potentially pose a health hazard. The other varieties of *ceviche* such as *camarón* (shrimp/prawn) and *langostino* (jumbo shrimp/king prawn) all of which are cooked before being marinated, are generally safe (check the cleanliness of the establishment). *Langosta* (lobster) is an increasingly endangered species but continues to be illegally fished; please be conscientious. Ecuadorean food is not particularly spicy. However, in most homes and restaurants, the meal is accompanied by a small bowl of *ají* (hot pepper sauce) which may vary in potency. *Colada* is a generic name which can refer to cream soups or sweet beverages. In addition to the prepared foods mentioned above, Ecuador offers a large variety of delicious fruits, some of which are unique to South America.

Drink The best fruit drinks are *naranjilla*, *maracuyá* (passion fruit), *tomate de árbol*, *piña* (pineapple), *taxo* (another variety of passion fruit) and *mora* (blackberry), but note that fruit juices are sometimes made with unboiled water. Main beers available are *Pilsener*, *Club*, and *Brahma*. Argentine and Chilean wines are available in the larger cities. Good *aguardiente* (unmatured rum, *Cristal* is recommended), also known as *puntas*, *trago de caña*, or just *trago*. The usual soft drinks, known as *colas*, are available. Instant coffee or liquid concentrate is common, so ask for *café pasado* if you want real coffee. In tourist centres and many upscale hotels and restaurants, good cappuccino and espresso can be found.

Essentials A-Z

Accident and emergency

Emergency telephone numbers: T911 in Quito and Cuenca, T112 in Guayaquil, T101 for police everywhere.

Electricity

AC throughout, 110 volts, 60 cycles. Sockets are for twin flat blades, sometimes with a round earth pin.

Embassies and consulates

For a complete list of Ecuadorean embassies and consulates, visit www.mmrree.gov.ec.

Festivals and events

1 Jan: **New Year's Day; 6 Jan**: **Reyes Magos y Día de los Inocentes**, a time for pranks, which closes the Christmas-New Year holiday season. **27 Feb**: **Día del Civismo**, celebrating the victory over Peru at Tarqui in 1829. **Carnival**: Mon and Tue before Lent, celebrated everywhere in the Andes, except Ambato, by throwing water at passers-by: be prepared to participate. **Easter**: **Holy Thu, Good Fri, Holy Sat. 1 May**: **Labour Day; 24 May**: **Battle of Pichincha, Independence. Early Jun**: **Corpus Christi**. **10 Aug**: first attempt to gain the Independence of Quito. **9 Oct**: **Independence of Guayaquil. 2 Nov**: **All Souls' Day. 3 Nov**: **Independence of Cuenca. 1-6 Dec**: **Foundation of Quito. 25 Dec**: **Christmas Day.**

Money → *US$1=€0.74 (Apr 2010).*

The **US dollar** (US$) is the official currency of Ecuador. Only US$ bills circulate. US coins are used alongside the equivalent size and value Ecuadorean coins. Ecuadorean coins have no value outside the country. Many establishments are reluctant to accept bills larger than US$20 because of counterfeit notes or lack of change. There is no substitute for cash-in-hand when travelling in Ecuador. Euros are slowly gaining acceptance, but US$ cash in small denominations is by far the simplest and the only universally accepted option. Other currencies are difficult to exchange outside large cities and fetch a very poor rate.

Plastic/traveller's cheques/banks/ATMs
The most commonly accepted **credit cards** are Visa, MasterCard, Diners and, to a lesser extent, American Express. Cash advances on credit cards can be obtained through many ATMs (only Banco de Guayaquil for Amex), but daily limits apply. Larger advances on Visa and MasterCard are available from the main branches of the following banks: **Banco Bolivariano, Banco de Guayaquil** (Visa only), **Banco del Austro** and **Banco del Pacífico**. Paying by credit card may incur a surcharge (at least 10%). TCs are not accepted by most merchants, hotels or tour agencies in Ecuador. They can be exchanged for cash at **Banco del Pacífico** (main branches) and some **casas de cambio** including **Vaz Corp** (in Quito, Otavalo, Guayaquil, Cuenca, Loja and Machala). A passport is always required to exchange TCs. **American Express** is the most widely accepted brand, but they are no longer replaced in Ecuador; if they are lost or stolen, you must file a claim from home. A police report is required if TCs are stolen. Internationally linked **ATMs** are common, although they cannot always be relied on. Debit cards are less easy to use. ATMs are a focus for scams and robberies, use them judiciously. Funds may be rapidly wired to Ecuador by **Western Union**, high fees and taxes apply.

Cost of living/travelling Despite dollarization, prices remain modest by international standards and Ecuador is still affordable for even the budget traveller. A very basic daily travel budget in 2010 was US$15-20 per person based on two travelling together, but allow for higher costs in Quito and Guayaquil. For US$50 a day you can enjoy a good deal of comfort. Internet use is about US$0.60-1 per hour. An **International Student Identity Card** (**ISIC**) may help you obtain discounts when travelling. ISIC cards are sold in Quito by **Idiomas Travel** ⓘ *Roca 130 y 12 de Octubre, p 2, T250 0264, www.idiomas.com.ec*. They need proof of full-time enrolment in Ecuador or abroad (minimum 20 hrs/week), 2 photos and US$15.

Opening hours
Banks open Mon-Fri 0900-1600. **Government offices** variable hours Mon-Fri, but most close for lunch. **Other offices** 0900-1230, 1430-1800. **Shops** 0900-1900; close at midday in smaller towns, open till 2100 on the coast.

Safety
Urban street crime, bag snatching and slashing, and robbery along the country's highways are the most significant hazards. In an effort to fight crime, army and police patrols operate in some cities and along some highways. Don't be taken aback to see these troops on duty. Secure your belongings, be wary of con tricks, avoid crowds and travel only during the daytime. The countryside and small towns are generally safest, but theft and robbery have been reported from several places where tourists gather. It is the big cities, Guayaquil, Quito, Santo Domingo, and to a lesser extent Cuenca, which call for the greatest care. The northern border with Colombia, including the provinces of Esmeraldas, Carchi, and especially Sucumbíos, call for additional precautions. Armed conflict in Colombia has caused an influx of refugees, and parts of these provinces have come under the influence of insurgents. Enquire locally before travelling to and in any northern border areas.

Occasional social unrest is part of life in Ecuador and you should not overreact. Strikes and protests are usually announced days or weeks in advance, and their most significant impact on tourists is the restriction of overland travel.

Drug use or purchase in Ecuador is punishable by up to 16 years' imprisonment.

Ecuador's active volcanoes are spectacular, but have occasionally threatened nearby communities. The **National Geophysics Institute** provides updates at **www.igepn.edu.ec**.

Tourist information
Ministerio de Turismo ⓘ *Eloy Alfaro N32-300 y Carlos Tobar, Quito, T02-250 7559, www.ecuador.travel*. Local offices are given in the text. The ministry has a Public Prosecutors Office (Fiscalía, T ext 1018) where serious complaints should be reported. Outside Ecuador, tourist information can be obtained from Ecuadorean Embassies. National parks, of which Ecuador has an outstanding array, are controlled by the **Ministerio del Ambiente** ⓘ *Edificio MAG, p 8, Amazonas y Eloy Alfaro, Quito, T02-250 6337*. The ministry has less information than the park offices in the cities nearest the parks themselves.

Useful websites

www.ecuador.org A good introduction.
www.explored.com.ec General information in Spanish, including a guide to national parks.
www.ecuadorexplorer.com; **www.ecuador-travel-guide.org**; and **www.ecuaworld.com** are all travel guides.
www.saexplorers.org South American Explorers has information about volunteering.
www.thebestofecuador.com/volunt.htm Volunteering ideas page on a comprehensive guide to the country.

Tax

Airport tax International flights at Quito airport US$40.80; at Guayaquil it is US$28.27. 12% tax on air tickets for flights originating in Ecuador. Domestic airport tax of US$7.60 (for Quito) is included in the ticket price.
VAT/IVA 12%. Taxes on imported luxury items are high.

Telephone

International phone code: +593. **Note** Many non-Ecuadorean mobile phone networks cannot connect in Quito. Outside the capital, connectivity is a little better, but for local use, buy an Ecuadorean chip (US$3-5).

Time

Official time is GMT -5 (Galápagos, -6).

Tipping

In restaurants 10% may be included in the bill. In cheaper restaurants, tipping is uncommon but welcome. It is not expected in taxis. Airport porters, US$0.50-1, according to number of cases.

Visas and immigration

All visitors to Ecuador must have a passport valid for at least 6 months and an onward or return ticket. The latter is seldom asked for. Visas are not required for tourists, regardless of nationality, unless they wish to stay more than 90 days. Upon entry all visitors must complete an international embarkation/disembarkation card. Keep your copy, you will be asked for it when you leave.

Note You are required by Ecuadorean law to carry your passport at all times. Whether or not a photocopy is an acceptable substitute is at the discretion of the individual police officer. In addition, travellers must carry an **international vaccination certificate**, although the latter is almost never asked for. Tourists are not permitted to work under any circumstances.

Length of stay Tourists are granted 90 days upon arrival and there are no extensions except for citizens of the Andean Community of Nations. Visitors staying over 90 days will be fined US$200. The fine must be payed 48 hrs prior to departure at a *jefatura provincial* (provincial head-quarters) of the **Policía Nacional de Migración** (www.migracion.gov.ec), most are located in provincial capitals; in Quito, **Jefatura Provincial de Migración de Pichincha** ① *Amazonas 171 y República, T227 6394, open Mon-Fri 0800-1200 and 1500-1800*. The maximum stay is 90 days per 12 month period. Visitors will not be allowed back in the country if they have already stayed for 90 days. If you want to spend more time studying, volunteering etc, you can get a purpose specific visa ('12/9' category) at the end of your 90 days as a tourist.

Visas for longer stays are issued by the **Ministerio de Relaciones Exteriores** (Foreign Office, www.mmrree.gov.ec), through their diplomatic representatives abroad and administered in Quito by the **Dirección General de Asuntos Migratorios** (non-immigrant visas) and the **Dirección Nacional de Extranjería** (immigrant visas).

Weights and measures

Metric, US gallons for petrol, some English measures for hardware and weights and some Spanish measures for weights.

Quito

➔ *Phone code: 02. Colour map 11, A4. Population: 1,700,000. Altitude: 2,850 m.*

Few cities have a setting to match that of Quito, the second highest capital in Latin America after La Paz. The city is set in a hollow at the foot of the volcano Pichincha (4,794 m). The city's charm lies in its colonial centre – the Centro Histórico as it's known – a UNESCO World Heritage Site, where cobbled streets are steep and narrow, dipping to deep ravines. From the top of Cerro Panecillo, 183 m above the city level, there is a fine view of the city below and the encircling cones of volcanoes and other mountains.

North of the colonial centre is modern Quito with broad avenues lined with contemporary office buildings, fine private residences, parks, embassies and villas. Here you'll find Quito's main tourist and business area in the district known as La Mariscal, bordered by Avenidas Amazonas, Patria, 12 de Octubre and Orellana.

Ins and outs

Getting there Mariscal Sucre airport is about 5 km north of the main hotel district. It is served by taxis (US$6 to La Mariscal, US$8 to colonial Quito, recommended as the safest option), the *Trole* and *Metrobus* transit systems and city buses. Long-distance bus services leave from terminals at the extreme edges of the city, Quitumbe in the south and Carcelén in the north. It is safest to arrive and leave terminals by taxi, although both new terminals are served by public transit systems. Some bus services run to their own offices in modern Quito. ➧ *See also Transport, page 1061.*

Getting around Both colonial Quito and La Mariscal in modern Quito can be explored on foot, but getting between the two requires some form of public transport, which is plentiful and usually slow. Using taxis is the best option, as it's convenient and cheap (starting at US$1); authorized taxis display a unit number, driver's photograph and have a meter. There are city buses and three parallel transit lines running north to south on exclusive lanes: the *Trole*, *Ecovía* and *Metrobus*. Public transit is not designed for carrying heavy luggage and is often crowded. Quito's main arteries run north-south and traffic congestion along them is a serious problem. Avenida Occidental is a somewhat more expedite road to the west of the city. The Corredor Periférico Oriental is a bypass to the east of the city running 44 km between Santa Rosa in the south and Calderón in the north. Roads through the eastern suburbs in the Valle de los Chillos and Tumbaco can be taken to avoid the city proper. **Note** Colonial Quito is closed to vehicles Sunday 0900-1600.

Orientation Most places of historical interest are in colonial Quito, while the majority of the hotels, restaurants, travel agencies and facilities for visitors are in the modern city to the north. The street numbering system is based on N (Norte), E (Este), S (Sur), Oe (Oeste), plus a number for

1 Quito orientation

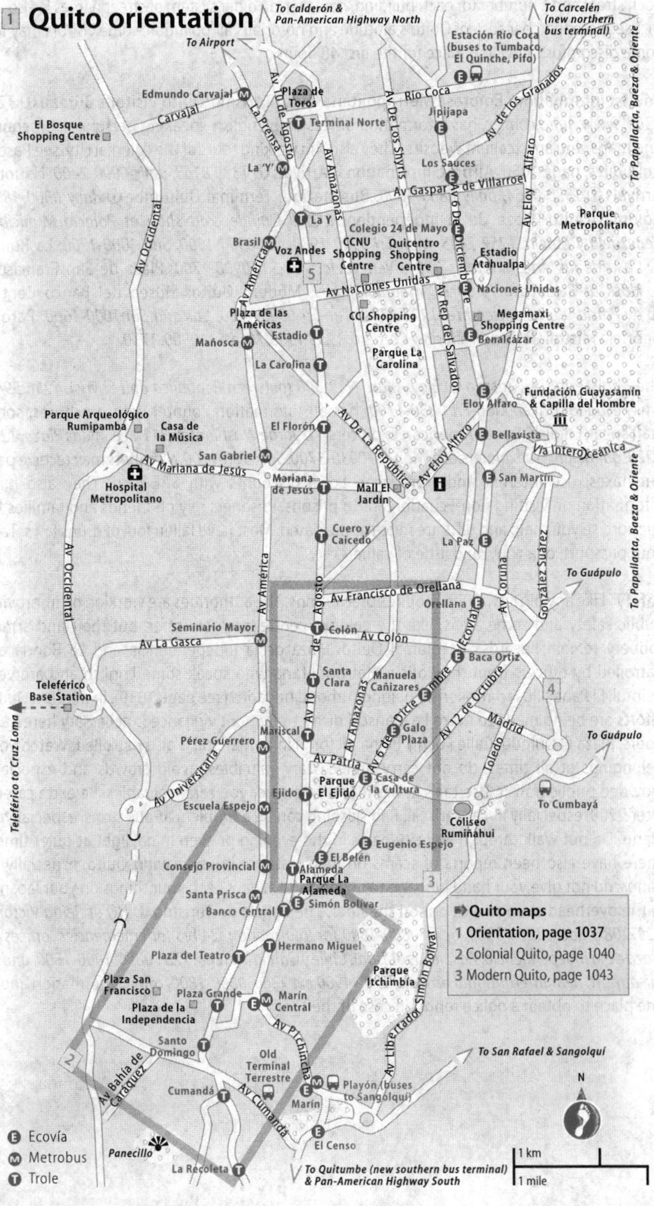
To Calderón & Pan-American Highway North
To Carcelén (new northern bus terminal)
To Airport
Estación Río Coca (buses to Tumbaco, El Quinche, Pifo)
To Papallacta, Baeza & Oriente
Edmundo Carvajal
Plaza de Toros
Río Coca
Av de los Granados
Jipijapa
Carvajal
El Bosque Shopping Centre
Terminal Norte
La Prensa
Av 10 de Agosto
Av Amazonas
Av De Los Shyris
La 'Y'
Los Sauces
Av Gaspar de Villarroel
Av Eloy Alfaro
Av 6 De Diciembre
La Y
Parque Metropolitano
Colegio 24 de Mayo
Brasil
Voz Andes
CCNU Shopping Centre
Quicentro Shopping Centre
Estadio Atahualpa
Av Occidental
Av América
Av Naciones Unidas
Naciones Unidas
Plaza de las Américas
CCI Shopping Centre
Megamaxi Shopping Centre
Estadio
Mañosca
Benalcázar
Av Rep del Salvador
Parque La Carolina
La Carolina
Fundación Guayasamín & Capilla del Hombre
Eloy Alfaro
Parque Arqueológico Rumipamba
Casa de la Música
El Florón
Av De La República
Bellavista
Vía Interoceánica
San Gabriel
Av Mariana de Jesús
Av Eloy Alfaro
Hospital Metropolitano
Mariana de Jesús
Mall El Jardín
San Martín
Cuero y Caicedo
La Paz
Av Occidental
González Suárez
Av Coruña
To Guápulo
Av Francisco de Orellana
Orellana
Seminario Mayor
Colón
Av Colón
Av La Gasca
Baca Ortiz
Teleférico Base Station
Santa Clara
Manuela Cañizares
Teleférico to Cruz Loma
Av 12 de Octubre
Madrid
Toledo
Galo Plaza
To Guápulo
Mariscal
Pérez Guerrero
Av Universitaria
Av Patria
Parque El Ejido
Casa de la Cultura
Ejido
To Cumbayá
Escuela Espejo
Coliseo Rumiñahui
Eugenio Espejo
El Belén
Consejo Provincial
Alameda
Parque La Alameda
Santa Prisca
Simón Bolívar
Banco Central
Quito maps
1 Orientation, page 1037
2 Colonial Quito, page 1040
3 Modern Quito, page 1043
Hermano Miguel
Plaza del Teatro
Parque Itchimbía
Av Simón Bolívar
Plaza San Francisco
Plaza Grande
Marín Central
Plaza de la Independencia
Av Pichincha
Santo Domingo
Av Libertador
To San Rafael & Sangolquí
Av Bahía de Caráquez
Old Terminal Terrestre
Cumandá
Av Cumandá
Playón (buses to Sangolquí)
Marín
El Censo
Ecovía
Metrobus
Trole
Panecillo
La Recoleta
To Quitumbe (new southern bus terminal) & Pan-American Highway South
1 km
1 mile
N

each street and a number for each building, however, an older system of street names is also still in use. Note that, because of Quito's altitude and notorious air pollution, some visitors may feel some discomfort: slow your pace for the first 48 hours.

Tourist information **Empresa Metropolitana Quito Turismo/Quito Visitor's Bureau** ⓘ *T299 3300, www.quito.com.ec*, has information offices with English-speaking personnel, brochures and maps, and an excellent website. They also run walking tours of the colonial city, see Paseos Culturales, page 1056. **Airport**: International Arrivals ⓘ *T330 0163, daily 0900-2400*; National Arrivals ⓘ *T330 0164, daily 0800-1600*. **Bus station**: Terminal Quitumbe ⓘ *daily 0800-1800*. **Colonial Quito**: Plaza de la Independencia ⓘ *El Quinde craft shop at Palacio Municipal, Venezuela y Espejo, T257 2445, Mon-Fri 0900-1930, Sat 0900-1900, Sun 1000-1700*; La Ronda ⓘ *Casa de las Artes, Morales 999 y Venezuela, Tue-Sat 0900-1700*; Plaza de San Francisco ⓘ *kiosk at Benalcázar y Sucre, irregular hours*. **Modern Quito**: Museo del Banco Central ⓘ *Av Patria y 6 de Diciembre, T222 1116, Tue-Fri 0900-1700, Sat and Sun1000-1600*; Parque Gabriela Mistral ⓘ *Reina Victoria y Cordero, T255 1566, Mon-Sat 0900-1730*.

The **Ministerio de Turismo** ⓘ *Eloy Alfaro N32-300 (between República and Shyris), T256 5947, www.ecuador.travel, Mon-Fri 0830-1700*, has an information counter with brochures, some staff speak English. **South American Explorers** ⓘ *Jorge Washington 311 y Leonidas Plaza, T222 5228, quitoclub@saexplorers.org, Mon-Fri 0930-1700, Sat 0900-1200*. Members may receive post and faxes, use internet and store gear. Local discounts with SAE card. They also have information on visiting non-Ecuadoreans in prisons. Prisoners rely on friends and families for support, so your help and gifts are much appreciated. Most have fallen foul of drugs laws. Take your passport, or a copy, and little of value.

Safety Like any big city, Quito requires precautions. The authorities are working on improving public safety and some areas, like the colonial centre, are now safer, but theft and armed robbery remain hazards. In colonial Quito, Plaza de la Independencia and La Ronda are patrolled by officers from the **Policía Metropolitana** who speak some English and are very helpful. El Panecillo is patrolled by neighbourhood brigades (see page 1039). In modern Quito, efforts are being made to make La Mariscal district safer, but vigilance is necessary here at all hours. Plaza El Quinde (Calle Foch y Reina Victoria) in La Mariscal is also patrolled. Watch your belongings at all times, do not carry unnecessary valuables, avoid crowds and especially crowded public transit. Use taxis at night and whenever you carry valuables. Be extra careful after 2200, especially in La Mariscal. Bag slashing can be a problem at bus stops, especially La Marín. Do not walk through any city parks in the evening or even in daylight at quiet times. There have also been reports of scams on long distance buses leaving Quito, especially to Baños; do not give your hand luggage to anyone and always keep your things on your lap, not in the overhead storage rack nor on the floor. The **Policía de Turismo** ⓘ *HQ at Reina Victoria N21-208 y Roca, T254 3983, open 0800-1800 for information, 24 hrs for emergencies, offices at Plaza de la Independencia, Pasaje Arzobispal, Chile y García Moreno, T251 0896, 1000-1800, and at the airport, near international arrivals, T294 4900 ext 2360, 0800-1800*, offers information and is one place to obtain a police report in case of theft.

Sights

Colonial Quito

Quito's revitalized colonial district is a pleasant place to stroll and admire the architecture, monuments and art. At night, the illuminated plazas and churches are very beautiful. The heart of the old city is **Plaza de la Independencia** or **Plaza Grande**, whose pink-flowered arupo trees bloom in September. It is dominated by a somewhat grim **Cathedral** ⓘ *entry through museum, Venezuela N3-117, T257 0371, Mon-Sat 0930-1600, no entry during mass, US$1.50 for the museum, night visits to church and cupolas on request*, built 1550-1562, with grey stone porticos and green tile cupolas. On its outer walls are plaques listing the names of the founding fathers of Quito, and inside are the tomb of Sucre and a famous Descent from the Cross by the indigenous painter Caspicara. There are many other 17th and 18th century paintings; the interior decoration shows Moorish influence. Facing the Cathedral is the **Palacio Arzobispal**, part of which now houses shops. Next to it, in the northwest corner, is the **Hotel Plaza Grande** (1930), with a baroque façade, the first building in the old city with more than two storeys. On the northeast side is the concrete **Municipio**, which fits in quite well. The low colonial **Palacio de Gobierno** or **Palacio de Carondelet**, silhouetted against the flank of Pichincha, is on the northwest side of the Plaza. On the first floor is a gigantic mosaic mural of Orellana navigating the Amazon. The ironwork on the balconies looking over the main plaza is from the Tuilleries in Paris. With the government motto "Ahora Carondelet es de todos", visitors can take tours ⓘ *T258 4000, ex 218, Tue-Sun 0900-1130, 1300-1615, take passport or copy.*

From Plaza de la Independencia two main streets, Venezuela and García Moreno, lead straight towards the Panecillo. Parallel with Venezuela is Calle Guayaquil, the main shopping street. These streets all run south from the main plaza to meet Calle Morales, better known as **La Ronda** ⓘ *www.callelaronda.com*, one of the oldest streets in the city. This narrow cobbled pedestrian way and its colonial homes with wrought iron balconies have been refurbished and house restaurants, bars, cultural centres and shops. It is a quaint corner of the city growing in popularity for a night out or an afternoon stroll. On García Moreno N3-94 is the beautiful **El Sagrario** ⓘ *daily, 0700-1800, no entry during mass, free*, church with a gilded door. The **Centro Cultural Metropolitano** is at the corner of Espejo, housing the municipal library, a museum for the visually impaired, temporary exhibits and the **Museo Alberto Mena Caamaño** ⓘ *T258 4362 ext 135, www.centrocultural-quito.com, Tue-Sun 0900-1630, US$1.50*. This wax museum depicts scenes of Ecuadorean colonial history. The scene of the execution of the revolutionaries of 1809 in the original cell is particularly vivid. The fine Jesuit church of **La Compañía** ⓘ *García Moreno N3-117 y Sucre, T258 4175, www.ficj.org.ec, Mon-Fri 0930-1730, Sat and holidays 09300-1630, Sun 1330-1630, US$2*, has the most ornate and richly sculptured façade and interior. Many of its most valuable treasures are in vaults at the Banco Central. Opposite is the **Casa Museo María Augusta Urrutia** ⓘ *García Moreno N2-60 y Sucre, T258 0103, Tue-Fri 1000-1800, Sat-Sun 0930-1730, US$2.00*, the home of a Quiteña who devoted her life to charity, showing the lifestyle of 20th century aristocracy.

Housed in the fine restored, 16th Century Hospital San Juan de Dios, is the **Museo de la Ciudad** ⓘ *García Moreno 572 y Rocafuerte, T228 3882, www.museociudadquito.gov.ec, Tue-Sun 0930-1730, US$3, foreign language guide service US$6 per group (request ahead)*. It takes you through Quito's history from prehispanic times to the 19th century, with imaginative displays.

On **Cerro Panecillo** ⓘ *Mon-Thu 0900-1700, Fri-Sun 0900-2100, US$1 per vehicle or US$0.25 per person if walking, for the neighbourhood safety brigade; entry to the interior of the monument US$2*, there is a statue to the Virgen de Quito and a good view from the observation platform. Although the neighbourhood patrols the area, it is safer to take a taxi (US$6 return from the colonial city, US$10 from La Mariscal, with a short wait). In the museum of the monastery of **San Diego** (by the cemetery of the same name, just west of Panecillo) ⓘ *Calicuchima 117 y Farfán, entrance to the right of the church, T295 2516, 0930-1300, 1430-1730*

Colonial Quito

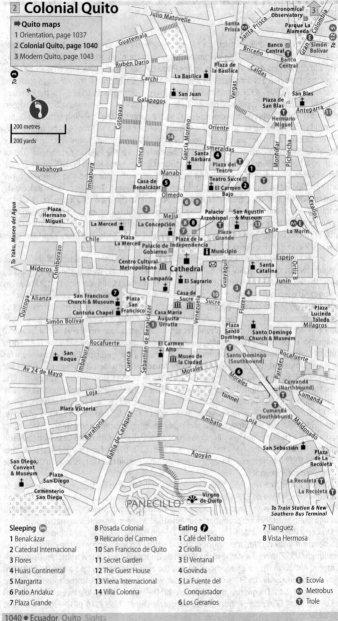

Quito maps
1 Orientation, page 1037
2 Colonial Quito, page 1040
3 Modern Quito, page 1043

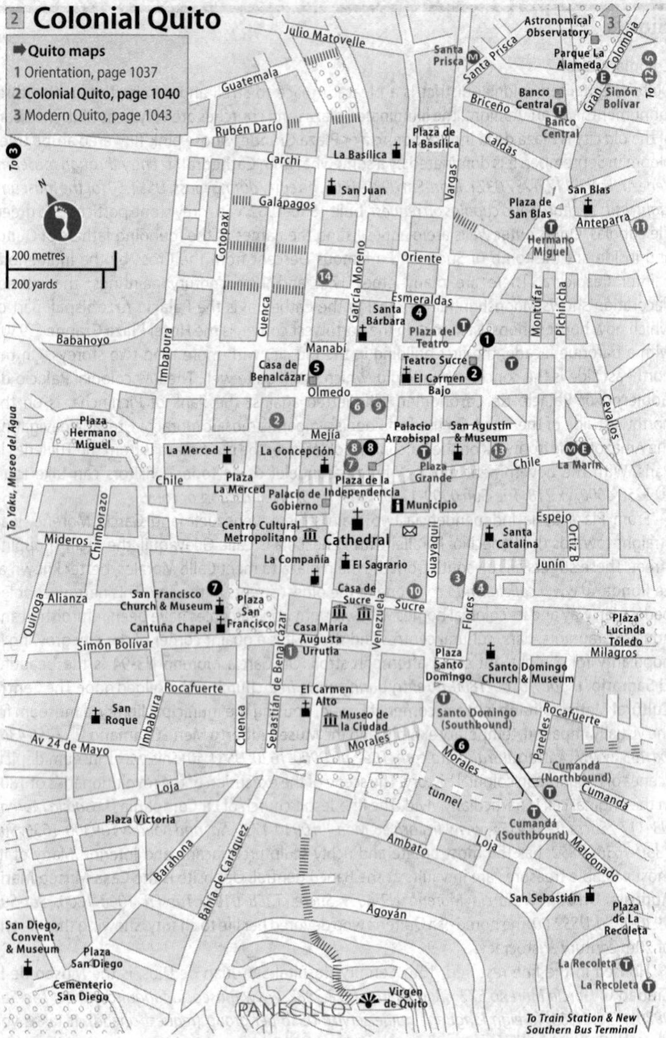

Sleeping
1 Benalcázar
2 Catedral Internacional
3 Flores
4 Huasi Continental
5 Margarita
6 Patio Andaluz
7 Plaza Grande
8 Posada Colonial
9 Relicario del Carmen
10 San Francisco de Quito
11 Secret Garden
12 The Guest House
13 Viena Internacional
14 Villa Colonna

Eating
1 Café del Teatro
2 Criollo
3 El Ventanal
4 Govinda
5 La Fuente del Conquistador
6 Los Geranios
7 Tianguez
8 Vista Hermosa

E Ecovía
M Metrobus
T Trole

daily, US$2, guided tours (Spanish only) take you around four colonial patios where sculpture and painting are shown. Of special interest are the gilded pulpit by Juan Bautista Menacho and the Last Supper painting in the refectory, in which a *cuy* and *humitas* have taken the place of the paschal lamb.

Plaza de San Francisco (or Bolívar) is west of Plaza de la Independencia; here are the great church and monastery of the patron saint of Quito, **San Francisco** ⓘ *Mon-Sat 0900-1200, 1500-1700, Sun 0900-1200*. The church was constructed by the Spanish in 1553 and is rich in art treasures. A modest statue of the founder, Fray Jodoco Ricke, the Flemish Franciscan who sowed the first wheat in Ecuador, stands at the foot of the stairs to the church portal. See the fine wood-carvings in the choir, a high altar of gold and an exquisite carved ceiling. There are some paintings in the aisles by Miguel de Santiago, the colonial *mestizo* painter. The **Museo Franciscano Fray Pedro Gocial** ⓘ *Cuenca 477 y Sucre, T228 1124 , Mon-Fri 0900-1300, 1400-1800, Sat 0900-1800, Sun 0900-1300, US$2*, has a collection of religious art. Adjoining San Francisco is the **Cantuña Chapel** ⓘ *0800-1700*, with sculptures. Not far away to the north along Calle Cuenca is the church of **La Merced** ⓘ *entrance on C Chile, 0630-1200, 1400-1800, free*. In the monastery of La Merced is Quito's oldest clock, built in 1817 in London. Fine cloisters are entered through a door to the left of the altar. La Merced contains many splendidly elaborate styles; note the statue of Neptune on the main patio fountain.

At **Plaza de Santo Domingo** (or Sucre), southeast of Plaza de la Independencia, is the church and monastery of **Santo Domingo**, with its rich wood-carvings and a remarkable Chapel of the Rosary to the right of the main altar. In the monastery is the **Museo Dominicano Fray Pedro Bedón** ⓘ *T228 0518, Tue-Sun 1000-1700, US$2*, another fine collection of religious art. In the centre of the plaza is a statue of Sucre, pointing to the slopes of Pichincha where he won his battle against the Royalists. Nearby is the **Museo Casa de Sucre** ⓘ *Venezuela N3-117 y Sucre, T295 2860, Mon-Fri 0930-1630, Sat-Sun 1000-1600, US$1*, a military museum in the beautiful house of Sucre.

Museo de Santa Catalina ⓘ *Espejo 779 y Flores, T228 4000, Mon-Fri 0830-1700, Sat 0830-1200, free*, said to have been built on the ruins of the Inca House of the Virgins, depicts the history of cloistered life. Many of the heroes of Ecuador's struggle for independence are buried in the monastery of **San Agustín** (Flores y Chile), which has beautiful cloisters on three sides where the first act of independence from Spain was signed on 10 August 1809. Here is the **Museo Miguel de Santiago** ⓘ *Chile 924 y Guayaquil, T295 5225, www.migueldesantiago.com, Mon-Fri 0900-1230, 1430-1700, Sat 0900-1300, US$1*, with religious art.

The **Basílica** ⓘ *on Plaza de la Basílica, Carchi 122 y Venezuela, northeast of Plaza de la Independencia, T228 9428, Mon-Sat 0930-1730, Sun 0900-1300, US$2*, is very large, has many gargoyles (some in the shape of Ecuadorean fauna), stained glass windows and fine, bas relief bronze doors (begun in 1926; some final details remain unfinished due to lack of funding). A coffee shop in the clock tower gives good views over the city. The **Centro de Arte Contemporáneo** ⓘ *Luis Dávila y Venezuela, San Juan, T398 8800, Tue-Sun 0900-1600, US$2*, in the beautifully restored Antiguo Hospital Militar, built in the early 1900s, has an exhibition on the Quito Revolution (www.revolucionquito.com) in place till end-2010. To the west of the city, the **Yaku Museo del Agua** ⓘ *El Placer Oe11-271, T257 0359, www.yakumuseoagua.gov.ec, Tue-Sat 0900-1700, Sun 0900-1700, US$2*, has great views of the city. Its main themes are water and nature, society and heritage. The best way there is take a taxi or walk up Calle Chile, go under the tunnels road then left to El Placer. East of the colonial city is **Parque Itchimbía** ⓘ *T228 2017, www.parqueitchimbia.org.ec*; a natural look- out over the city with walking and cycle trails and a cultural centre housed in a 19th century "crystal palace" which came from Europe, once the Santa Clara market.

3 Modern Quito

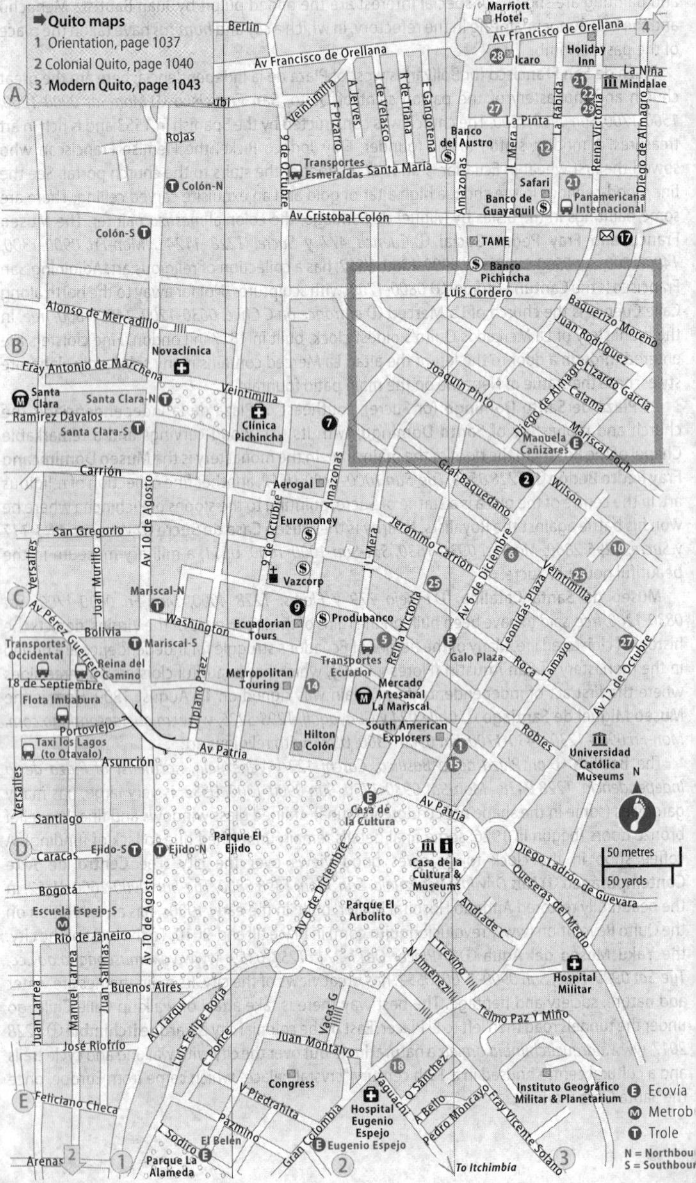

La Mariscal detail

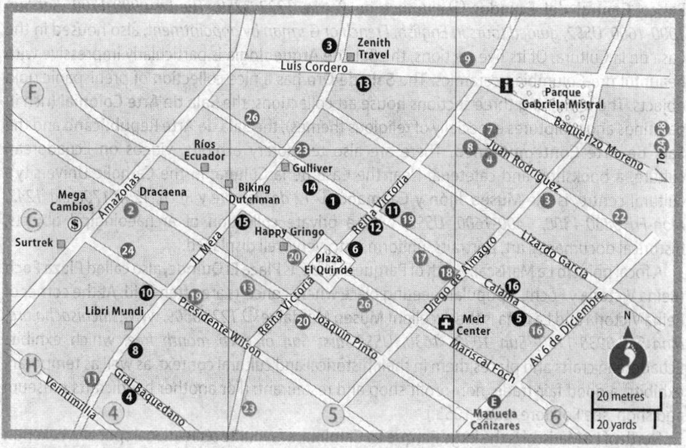

Sleeping

1 Amaranta *D3*
2 Amazonas Inn *detail G4*
3 Antinea *detail G6*
4 Backpackers Inn *detail G6*
5 Café Cultura *C2*
6 Casa Helbling *C3*
7 Cayman *detail F6*
8 El Arupo *detail F6*
9 El Cafecito *detail F6*
10 Fuente de Piedra I *C3*
11 Fuente de Piedra II *detail H4*
12 Hostal de la Rábida *A3*
13 Hostelling International *detail G5*
14 Hothello *C2*
15 La Cartuja *D3*
16 La Casa Sol *detail H6*
17 La Galería *detail G5*
18 L'Auberge Inn *E2*
19 Mansión del Angel *detail G4*
20 Nü House *detail G5*
21 Posada de la Abuela *A3*
22 Posada del Maple *detail G6*
23 Queen's Hostel *detail H5*
24 Rincón Escandinavo *detail F6*
25 Sierra Madre *C3*
26 Titisee *detail H5*
27 Travellers Inn *A3*
28 Villa Nancy *detail F6*

Eating

1 Adam's Rib *detail G5*
2 Baalbek *C3*
3 Chandani Tandoori *detail F5*
4 Chez Alain *detail H4*
5 Coffee & Toffee *detail H6*
6 Coffee Tree *detail G5*
7 El Hornero *B2*
8 Este Café *detail H4*
9 Ethnic Coffee *C2*
10 Kallari *detail G4*
11 La Boca de Lobo *detail G5*
12 Mama Clorinda *detail G5*
13 Paléo *detail F5*
14 Sushi *detail G5*
15 The Magic Bean *detail G5*
16 Uncle Ho's *detail G6*
17 Yu Su *B3*

Bars & clubs

18 Bungalow Six *detail G5*
19 El Aguijón *detail G5*
20 Finn McCool's *detail H5*
21 Ghoz *A3*
22 Kings Cross *A3*
23 No Bar *detail F5*
24 Patatu's *detail G4*
25 Reina Victoria Pub *C2*
26 Santurrón *detail F5*
27 Seseribó *C3*
28 Turtle's Head *A3*
29 Varadero *A3*

Modern Quito

Parque Alameda has the oldest **astronomical observatory** in South America dating to 1873. Refurbished in 2009, it is still operational and houses a museum ⓘ *T257 0765, museum Tue-Sun 1000-1700, US$2, observations on clear nights Tue-Fri 1830-1930*. Just north of the observatory, there is an excellent free light and music show with water fountains Friday and Saturday from 1900-2100, dress warmly. There is also a splendid monument to Simón Bolívar, lakes, and in the northwest corner a spiral lookout tower with a good view. A short distance north of Parque Alameda, opposite Parque El Ejido, at the junction 6 de Diciembre and Patria, there is a large cultural and museum complex housing the **Casa de la Cultura** ⓘ *T222 3392, ext 320, Tue-Fri 1000-1800, Sat 1000-1400, US$2, good toilets*, and the Museo Nacional del Banco Central del Ecuador (see below). Museums belonging to the Casa de la Cultura are: **Museo de Arte Moderno**, paintings and sculpture since 1830; **Museo de Traje Indígena**, traditional dress and adornments of indigenous groups; **Museo de Instrumentos Musicales**, an impressive collection of musical instruments, said to be the second in importance in the world.

If you have time to visit only one museum in Quito, it should be the **Museo Nacional del Banco Central del Ecuador** ⓘ *entrance on Patria, T222 3259, Tue-Fri 0900-1700, Sat-Sun 1000-1600, US$2, guided tours in English, French or German by appointment*, also housed in the Casa de la Cultura. Of its five sections, the **Sala de Arqueología** is particularly impressive with beautiful pre-Columbian ceramics. The **Sala de Oro** has a nice collection of prehispanic gold objects. The remaining three sections house art collections: the **Sala de Arte Colonial** (rich in paintings and sculptures especially of religious themes), the **Sala de Arte Republicano** and the **Sala de Arte Contemporáneo**. There are also temporary exhibits, videos on Ecuadorean culture, a bookshop and cafeteria. Near the Casa de la Cultura, in the Catholic University's cultural centre, is the **Museo Jijón y Caamaño** ⓘ *12 de Octubre y Roca, T299 1700 ext 1242, Mon-Fri 0830-1300, 1400-1600, US$2*, with a private collection of archaeological objects, historical documents, art, portraits, uniforms, etc, very well displayed.

A focal point in La Mariscal, north of Parque El Ejido, is **Plaza El Quinde**, also called **Plaza Foch** (Reina Victoria y Foch), a popular meeting place where concerts are often held. At the corner of Reina Victoria and La Niña is the excellent **Museo Mindalae** ⓘ *T223 0609, www.sinchisacha.org, Mon-Sat 0930-1730, Sun 1030- 1630, US$3, first Sun of each month free*, which exhibits Ecuadorean crafts and places them in their historical and cultural context, as well as temporary exhibits, a good fair-trade, non-profit shop and restaurant. (For another handicrafts museum and shop, see **Folklore**, page 1055.)

North of La Mariscal is the large **Parque La Carolina**, a favourite recreational spot at weekends. Around it is the banking district, several shopping malls and hotels and restaurants. In the park is the **Jardín Botánico** ⓘ *T333 2516, daily 0900-1700 US$3.50, www.jardinbotanicoquito.com*, which has a good cross section of Andean flora. Also the **Vivarium** ⓘ *T227 1799, Tue-Sun 0930-1730, US$3*, dedicated to protect endangered snakes, reptiles and amphibians, and the **Museo de Ciencias Naturales** ⓘ *T244 9824, Mon-Fri 0830-1630, US$2*.

Quito suburbs

East The **Santuario de Guápulo** ⓘ *mass Mon-Fri 1900, Sat 0700, Sun 0700-1200,1600-1700* (1693, built by Indian slaves), perched on the edge of a ravine east of the city, is well worth seeing for its many paintings, gilded altars, stone carvings and the marvellously carved pulpit. The **Museo Fray Antonio Rodríguez** ⓘ *Plaza de Guápulo N27-138, T256 5652, Mon-Thu 0900-1200, 1500-1730, Fri-Sat 0900-1200, US$1.50*, has religious art and furniture, from the 16th to the 20th centuries. Guided tours (Spanish only) include a visit to the beautiful Santuario.

Museo Guayasamín ⓘ *Bosmediano 543, Bellavista, northeast of La Mariscal, T244 6445, Mon-Fri 1000-1700, US$3*, is highly recommended. Take a a taxi. As well as the eponymous artist's works there is a pre-Columbian and colonial collection. Works of art may be purchased (ask to see the whole collection) and also modern jewellery. Also presenting Guayasamín's work and 5 blocks from the museum is **La Capilla del Hombre** ⓘ Mariano Calvache y Lorenzo Chávez, *Bellavista, T244 8492, www.capilladelhombre.com, Tue-Sun 1000-1730, US$3 (US$1 discount if visiting both sites)*, a collection of murals depicting the fate of Latin America from pre-Columbian to modern times.

In the eastern suburb of San Rafael is **La Casa de Kingman Museo** ⓘ *Portoviejo 111 y Dávila, 1 block from San Rafael park, Valle de los Chillos, T286 1065, www.fundacionkingman.com, Thu-Sun1000-1600, US$3*. This is a collection of the renowned artist's work and other colonial, republican and 20th-century art. Take a taxi or a *Vingala* bus from Isabel La Católica y Mena Caamaño, behind Universidad Católica.

West For spectacular views ride the **Teleférico** ⓘ *Av Occidental above La Gasca, T222 1320, www.telefericoquito.com, daily 0800-2000, US$8 express (tourists may not use the US$4.50 regular service), children $6, seniors US$4, service vans pick up at Trole terminals Norte and Recreo, and shopping malls Quicentro, El Jardín, CCI, no fixed schedule, more frequent at weekends, also from big* *hotels, Swiss, Hilton, Marriott and others for groups, US$1 each way*. The cable car is part of a complex with an amusement park, shops and food courts. It climbs to 4,050 m on the flanks of Pichincha, where there are walking trails, including one to the summit of Rucu Pichincha, and horse riding just past the fence, see page 1056.

Parque Arqueológico y Ecológico Rumipamba ⓘ *east side of Av Occidental just north of Mariana de Jesús, T295 7576, www.fonsal.gov.ec, Wed-Sun 0800-1630, free, some English speaking guides*, is a 32-ha park on the slopes of Pichincha, where vestiges of human occupation of several pre-Inca periods, dating from 1500 BC to AD 1500, have been found. Excavated strata show the different ages, with debris from Pichincha's 1660 eruption being the most recent. On one site,several superimposed dwellings separated by mud flows can be seen. There are stone walls, circular mud dwellings, burials of different periods, grindstones and ceramics. The Quitus (AD 500-1500) farmed the area and traded with coast and Amazon until the invasion of the Incas. In 2010, the site continues to be studied. Pastures cover most of the grounds, in a few forested pockets, 36 native species of plants including three endemics have been identified. There are some walking trails including a **colunco**, a path in a gully surrounded by vegetation, characteristic of the trade routes which linked Quito with the lowlands to the west.

Northwest of Rumipamba, in the neighbourhood of San Vicente de la Florida is **Museo de Sitio La Florida** ⓘ*, C Antonio Costas y Román,T258 4962, www.fonsal.gov.ec, Wed-Sun 0800-1630, free, some English speaking guides*. At this necropolis of the Quitus people, ten 17-metre deep burial chambers, dating to AD 220-640, have been excavated. The elaborate dress found in the tombs suggests most were prominent citizens; for example one body was dressed in fine cotton, highly decorated, topped with poncho adorned with 50 pieces of gold, 50 of copper and semi-precious stones. A less important person was just buried inside a sack. The women measured 1.55 m, the men 1.60-1.65 m. Their faces had aquiline features, not the wide nostrils or prominent cheek bones associated normally with Andean peoples.Burials also included ceramics, garnments decorated with spondylus and mother of pearl shells, and gold.

Mitad del Mundo and around

The location of the equatorial line here (23 km N of central Quito, the suburbs stretch almost to the monument) was determined by Charles-Marie de la Condamine and his French expedition in 1736, and agrees to within 150 m with modern GPS measurements. The monument forms the focal point of a park and leisure area built as a typical colonial town, with restaurants, gift shops, Post Office with philatelic sales, travel agency, and has a very interesting **ethnographic museum** inside ⓘ *Mon-Thu 0900-1800, Fri-Sun 0900-1900 (very crowded on Sun), US$2, children US$1, includes entrance to the pavilions; entry to the ethnographic museum US$3 (includes guided tour of museum in Spanish or English)*. In the museum; a lift takes you to the top, then you walk down with the museum laid out all around with different indigenous cultures every few steps. There is a **Planetarium** ⓘ *US$1.50, group of 15 minimum*, with hourly 30-minute shows and an attractive and interesting **model of old Quito**, about 10 m square, with artificial day and night, which took seven years to build. **Museo Inti-Ñan** ⓘ *200 m north of the monument, T239 5122, www.museointinan.com.ec, 0930-1730 daily, US$3*, eclectic, very interesting and lots of fun activities, gives Equator certificates for visitors. Research about the equator and its importance to prehistoric cultures is carried out near Cayambe, by an organization called **Quitsa-to** ⓘ *www.quitsato.org*.

Quito listings

Hotel and guesthouse prices
LL over US$200 **L** US$151-200 **AL** US$101-150
A US$66-100 **B** US$46-65 **C** US$31-45
D US$21-30 **E** US$12-20 **F** US$7-11
G US$6 and under

Restaurant prices
TTT over US$12 **TT** US$7-12 **T** under US$6

Sleeping

wsww.hotelesquito.com lists many establishments. There are no good places to stay near the airport. A few simple places have opened near the Quitumbe bus terminal and there is one lodging opposite the Carcelén bus terminal, along busy Avenida Eloy Alfaro. Plan ahead about what type of lodgings and what part of town best suit you, and take a cab to your first choice. Large international chain hotels are represented in the city and meet their international standards. For more information see: www.sheraton.com, www.radisson.com, www.swissotel.com, www.hilton.com, www.hojo.com (Howard Johnson), www.hiexpress.com (Holiday Inn) www.danncarltonquito.com, www.marriott.com, www.mercure.com, www.bestwestern.com, www.hotelquito.com (Compass).

Colonial Quito *p1039, map p1040*

LL Patio Andaluz, García Moreno N6-52 y Olmedo, T228 0830, www.hotelpatioandaluz.com. 5-star boutique hotel in the heart of the colonial city, beautifully reconstructed 16th century mansion with large arches, balconies and patios, exclusive restaurant with Ecuadorean and Spanish cuisine, 22 rooms, library, Folklore Olga Fisch gift shop.

LL Plaza Grande, García Moreno N5-16, Plaza de la Indpendencia, T251 0777, www.plazagrandequito.com. Exclusive top-of-the-line hotel with an exceptional location, 15 suites including a presidential suite for US$2000, 3 restaurants including La Belle Epoque, gourmet French cuisine and a wine cellar, Jacuzzi in all rooms, climate control, mini-spa, 110/220V outlets.

LL Villa Colonna, Benalcázar 11-28 y Esmeraldas, T295 5805, www.villacolonna.ec. Exclusive boutique bed and breakfast with 6 elegant suites, includes breakfast in elegant kitchen/dinning room, personalized attention from the owners who live here, no smoking.

AL Relicario del Carmen, Venezuela 1041 y Olmedo, T228 9120, www.hotelrelicariodelcarmen.com. Beautifully refurbished colonial house, includes breakfast, good restaurant, cafeteria, Wi-Fi, good rooms and service, no smoking.

B Posada Colonial, García Moreno 1160 y Mejía, T228 0282, posadacolonial@yahoo.com. Nicely refurbished colonial house in a good location, includes breakfast, restaurant serves economical set meals, electric shower, Wi-Fi, a bit pricey.

B-C San Francisco de Quito, Sucre Oe3-17 y Guayaquil, T295 1241. Converted colonial building, includes breakfast in attractive patio or underground cloisters, restaurant, sauna, Jacuzzi, Wi-Fi, suites are particularly good value, well run by owners, rooms to the street can be noisy.

C Catedral Internacional, Mejía Oe6-36 y Cuenca, T295 5438, catedralinternacional@yahoo.es. Nicely restored colonial house with 15 carpeted rooms, small patio with fountain, includes breakfast, popular restaurant, heaters, spa, Wi-Fi, under new management and completely refurbished in 2009.

C Viena Internacional, Flores 600 y Chile, T295 9611. Nice rooms and courtyard, good restaurant (0700-1900).

D-E Huasi Continental, Flores N3-08 y Sucre, T295 7327. Colonial house, restaurant, cheaper with shared bath, hot water, Wi-Fi, parking, good value.

E Flores, Flores N3-51 y Sucre, T228 0435, www.hotelflores.com.ec. Nicely refurbished and decorated, private bath, hot water, laundry facilities, good value.

E-F Benalcázar, Benalcázar N1-88 y Bolívar, Plaza de San Francisco, T295 8302, hotelbenalcazar@hotmail.com. Refurbished colonial house, cheaper with shared bath, hot water, clean basic rooms, good value and location.

In between the colonial and modern cities

L-AL Mansión del Angel, Los Rios N13-134 y Pasaje Gándara, T254 0293, www.mansiondelangel.com.ec. Luxurious hotel decorated with antiques in a beautifully renovated old house, 15 ample rooms and a palacial suite, includes breakfast, internet, nice gardens, lovely atmosphere. Relocated late 2009.

E Chicago, Los Ríos N17-30 y Briceño, T228 1695. Popular family-run hostel, small rooms, includes breakfast, cheaper with shared bath, hot water, internet in sitting room, laundry and cooking facilities, a good economy option.

E L'Auberge Inn, Colombia N15-200 y Yaguachi, T255 2912, www.auberge-inn-hostal.com. Nice spacious rooms, duvets on beds, cheaper with shared bath, excellent hot water, restaurant, spa, Wi-Fi, cooking facilities, parking, lovely garden, terrace and communal area, pool table, helpful, good atmosphere. Recommended.

E Margarita, Los Ríos N12-118 y Espinoza, T295 0441, www.hostalmargarita2.com. Private bath, hot water, Wi-Fi, parking, good beds, sheets changed daily, great value. Recommended.

E Revolution Quito, Los Rios N13-11 y Julio Castro, T254 6458, www.hostelrevolution quito.com. Small hostel with a couple of private rooms and dorms (F per person), Wi-Fi, cooking facilities, games room, difficult to find, Australian-Ecuadorean run.

E Secret Garden, Antepara E4-60 y Los Ríos, T295 6704, www.secretgardenquito.com. Restored old house, some rooms small and dark, lovely roof-top terrace restaurant for breakfast and dinner (vegetarian available), 4 rooms with private bath, cheaper in dorm, hot water, popular meeting and party place, can be noisy. Ecuadorean-Australian owned, also run a rustic lodge between Pasochoa and Cotopaxi, www.secretgardencotopaxi.com.

E The Guest House, Julio Castro E6-16 y Valparaíso, near Parque Itchimbía, T252 5834, info@tours-unlimited.com. Rooms with bath for long stays in a nicely restored house, private bath, hot water, Wi-Fi, laundry and cooking facilities, nice views, helpful, US$240/month/couple.

New City *p1043, map p1043*

LL Le Parc, República de El Salvador N34-349 e Irlanda, T227 6800, www.leparc.com.ec. Modern hotel with 30 executive suites, full luxury facilities and service, includes buffet breakfast, restaurant, spa, gym, includes airport transfers.

LL Nü House, Foch E6-12 y Reina Victoria, T255 7845, www.nuhousehotels.com. Modern luxury hotel with minimalist decor, includes breakfast, restaurant, some suites with Jacuzzi, plug-in internet, all furnishings and works of art are available for sale.

L-AL Café Cultura, Robles E6-62, relocating to Washington y Páez in late 2010, T250 4078, www.cafecultura.com. A well-established hotel relocating to a renovated early 1900s mansion (www.cafecultura.com/new_project) with ample suites, social areas including wood-paneled library with fireplace, restaurant, attentive service.

A Hostal de la Rábida, La Rábida 227 y Santa María, T222 2169, www.hostalrabida.com. Lovely converted home, bright comfortable rooms, good restaurant, Wi-Fi, parking, British-Italian run. Recommended.

A G House, Plaza 170 y 18 de Septiembre, T252 3662, www.hotelacartuja.com. (Formerly La Cartuja). In the former British Embassy, includes breakfast, cafeteria, Wi-Fi, parking, beautifully decorated, spacious comfortable rooms, lovely garden, very helpful and hospitable. Highly recommended.

A La Casa Sol, Calama 127 y 6 de Diciembre, T223 0798, www.lacasasol.com. Small hotel with courtyard , includes breakfast, 24-hour cafeteria, Wi-Fi downstaFMagicirs, very helpful, English and French spoken, also run Casa Sol in Otavalo. Recommended.

A Sol de Quito, Alemania N30-170 y Vancouver, T254 1773, www.soldequito.com. Lovely converted home with large sitting room and library decorated with antiques, includes breakfast, restaurant, Wi-Fi, parking, comfortable rooms, suites have beautiful carved doors. Recommended.

B Cayman, Rodríguez E7-29 y Reina Victoria, T256 7616, www.hotelcaymanquito.com. Pleasant hotel, includes breakfast in lovely bright diningroom, cafeteria, Wi-Fi, parking, rooms a bit small, sitting room with fireplace, garden, very good.

B Finlandia, Finlandia N32-129 y Suecia, T224 4288, www.hotelfinlandia.com.ec. Pleasant small hostel in residential area, buffet breakfast, restaurant, Wi-Fi, parking, spacious rooms, sitting room with fireplace, small garden, airport pick-up extra, helpful staff.

B Fuente de Piedra I & II, Wilson E9-80 y Tamayo and JL Mera N23-21 y Baquedano, T290 0323, www.ecuahotel.com. Nicely decorated modern hotels, comfortable, includes breakfast, Wi-Fi, some rooms are small, nice sitting areas, pleasant.

B Posada de la Abuela, Santa María 235 y La Rábida, T222 5334. Cosy little inn, includes breakfast, Wi-Fi, parking, some rooms with fireplace, safety deposit box. Lovely refurbished 1920s home with pleasant sitting room in a covered patio. Recommended.

B Sierra Madre, Veintimilla E9-33 y Tamayo, T250 5687, www.hotelsierramadre.com. Fully renovated old-style villa, restaurant, Wi-Fi, parking, nice sun roof, comfortable.

B Villa Nancy, Muros N27-94 y 12 de Octubre, T256 2483, www.hotelvillanancy.com. Quaint hotel in quiet residential area, includes buffet breakfast, Wi-Fi, parking, airport transfers extra, homey and comfortable, helpful multilingual staff. Recommended.

C El Arupo, Juan Rodríguez E7-22 y Reina Victoria, T255 7543, www.hostalelarupo.com. Good hostel, includes breakfast, Wi-Fi, laundry and cooking facilities, English and French spoken. Recommended.

C Hothello, Amazonas N20-20 y 18 de Septiembre, T256 5835, www.hothello.com. Small modern hotel, bright and tastefully decorated rooms, , includes nice breakfast, Wi-Fi in café, heating, helpful multilingual staff.

C Rincón Escandinavo, Plaza N24-306 y Baquerizo Moreno, T222 5965, rinconescandinavo @uio.satnet.net. Small well-furnished modern hotel , includes breakfast, restaurant, Wi-Fi, English spoken.

C-D Casa Helbling, Veintimilla E8-152 y 6 de Diciembre, T222 6013, www.casahelbling.de. Very good, popular hostel, spotless, breakfast available, cheaper with shared bath, Wi-Fi, laundry and cooking facilities, English, French and German spoken, family atmosphere, good information, tours arranged, luggage storage, help for motorcyclists, parking. Highly recommended.

C-D Hostelling International, Pinto E6-12 y Reina Victoria, T254 3995, hostellingquito@gmail.com. Pricey modern hostel with capacity for 75, includes breakfast, cafeteria, Wi-Fi, coin-operated laundry, a variety of simple rooms from double with private bath to dorms (**F** per person), discounts for IYHF members.
C-D Posada del Maple, Rodríguez E8-49 y 6 de Diciembre, T254 4507, www.posadadelmaple.com. Popular hostel, includes breakfast, cheaper with shared bath and in dorm, cooking facilities, warm atmosphere, free tea and coffee.
C-D Travellers Inn, La Pinta E4-435 y Amazonas, T255 6985, www.travellersecuador.com. In a nicely converted home, includes good breakfast, other meals on request, cheaper with shared bath, parking, pleasant common area, bike rentals.
D Amazonas Inn, Pinto E4-324 y Amazonas, T222 5723, www.amazonasinn.com. Very nice, hot water, café, Wi-Fi, carpeted rooms, some are noisy, 1st floor best, spotless. Recommended.
D Queen's Hostel/Hostal De La Reina, Reina Victoria N23-70 y Wilson, T255 1844, hostaldelareina@hotmail.com. Nice small hotel, popular among travellers and Ecuadoreans, cafeteria, private bath, hot water, Wi-Fi, cooking facilities, sitting room with fireplace. Recommended.
D Titisee, Foch E7-60 y Reina Victoria, T252 9063, www.hostaltitisee.com. Nice place, large rooms, cheaper with shared bath, hot water, internet, cooking facilities, lounge, book exchange, helpful owner. Recommended.
D Villa Nancy, 6 de Diciembre N24-398 y Cordero, T256 3084, www.villa-nancy.com. Nice place, includes buffet breakfast, most rooms with private bath, hot water, Wi-Fi, cooking facilities, sitting room, terrace, airport pickup, travel information, Swiss-Ecuadorean run, helpful.
E Backpackers Inn, Rodríguez E7-48 y Reina Victoria, T250 9669, www.backpackersinn.net. Popular hostel, breakfast available, cheaper with shared bath or in dorm (F), hot water, Wi-Fi, laundry and cooking facilities, adequate dorms.
E Casona de Mario, Andalucía 213 y Galicia (La Floresta), T254 4036, www.casonademario.com. Popular hostel, shared bath, hot water, laundry facilities, well equipped kitchen, parking, sitting room, nice garden, book exchange, long stay discounts, Argentine owner. Repeatedly recommended.
E El Cafecito, Cordero E6-43 y Reina Victoria, T223 4862, www.cafecito.net. Popular with backpackers, good café including vegetarian, cheaper in dorm (**F**), 1 room with bath, hot water, relaxed atmosphere but can get noisy at night, Canadian owned.
E La Galería, Calama 233 y Almagro, T250 0307, hostallagaleria@hotmail.com. Nice family run hostel, private bath, hot water, internet in sitting-room, cooking facilities, carpeted rooms, patio with tables, English spoken.

Quito suburbs *p1044*

LL Hacienda Rumiloma, Obispo Díaz de La Madrid, final de la calle, T254 8206, www.haciendarumiloma.com. Luxurious hotel in a 40ha hacienda on the slopes of Pichincha. Sumptuous suites, each one individually designed with lots of attention to detail, lounges decorated with antiques, includes breakfast, Pricey restaurant offers good quality Ecuadorean and international cuisine, bar with fireplace, nice views, personalized attention from dynamic owners Amber and Oswaldo Freire, ideal for someone looking for a luxurious escape not far from the city.
AL-A Hostería San Jorge, Km 4 via antigua Quito-Nono, to the west of Av Occidental, T339 0403, www.eco-lodgesanjorge.com. Converted 18th century hacienda on a 80 ha private reserve on the slopes of Pichincha, includes breakfast, full board available, good pricey restaurant, heating, pool, sauna and Jacuzzi, Wi-Fi in lounge, airport transfers, horse riding and birdwatching. Nature reserve (part of a group of reserves) has páramo and one of the few remnants of native forest near Quito. Recommended.

Apartments

B Amaranta, Leonidas Plaza N20-32 y Washington, T254 3619, www.aparthotelamaranta.com. Includes breakfast, good restaurant, Wi-Fi in restaurant and some rooms, parking, comfortable, well-equipped suites, from US$950/month.
A Antinea, Rodríguez 175 y Almagro, T250 6839, www.hotelantinea.com. Rooms, suites and apartments in nicely refurbished house with a French touch, includes breakfast, heating, Wi-Fi, parking, tastefully decorated, from $1160/month, good service.

C Apartamentos Modernos, Amazonas N31-181 y Mariana de Jesús, T223 3766 ext 800, www.apartamentosmodernos.com.ec. Convenient location near El Jardín Mall and Parque La Carolina, 1 and 2 bedroom flats from US$600/month, wi-Fi extra, parking, English and German spoken, good value.

Eating

Eating out in Quito is excellent, varied, upmarket and increasingly cosmopolitan. In colonial Quito there are a number of elegant restaurants offering Ecuadorean and international food. Small simple places serving set meals for US$2-4 are everywhere; most close by early evening and on Sun.

Colonial Quito *p1039, map p1040*

TTT El Ventanal, Carchi y Nicaragua, west of the Basílica, in Parque San Juan, take a taxi to the parking area and a staff member will accompany you along a footpath to the restaurant, T257 2232, www.elventanal.ec, Tue-Sat 1200-1500, 1800-2200, Sun 1200-1700. International nouvelle cuisine with a varied menu including a number of seafood dishes, fantastic views over the city.

TTT Mea Culpa, Palacio Arzobispal, Plaza de la Independencia, T295 1190, www.meaculpa.com.ec, Mon-Fri 1215-1530, 1900-2300, Sat 1900-2300. Formal and elegant, international and Mediterranean gourmet food, reservations required.

TTT Theatrum, Plaza del Teatro, second floor of Teatro Sucre, T228 9669, www.theatrum.com.ec, Mon-Fri 1230-1600, 1930-2330, Sat-Sun 1900-2300. Excellent creative gourmet cuisine in the city's most important theatre, wide selection of fruit desserts which come with an explanatory card.

TTT-TT Los Geranios, Morales Oe1-134, T228 3889, daily 0900-0100. Upscale comida típica, in a nicely restored La Ronda house.

TT Hasta la Vuelta Señor, Pasaje Arzobispal, 3rd floor, Mon-Sat 1100-2300, Sun 1100-2100. A Fonda Quiteña perched on an indoor balcony with Ecuadorean comida típica and snacks, try their empanadas (pasties) or a seco de chivo (goat stew).

TT Tianguez, Plaza de San Francisco under the portico of the church, Mon-Tue- 0930-1830, Wed-Sun 0930-2400. International and local dishes, good coffee, snacks, sandwiches, popular, also craft shop (closes 1830), run by Fundación Sinchi Sacha.

TT-T La Fuente del Conquistador, Benalcázar N7-44 y Olmedo, Mon-Sat 1200-1530. Economical set lunches, grill, local and international food à la carte.

T Criollo, Flores N7-31 y Olmedo, Mon-Sat 0800-2130, Sun 0800-1700. Economical set meals (a bit pricier at weekends), tasty chicken dishes and Ecuadorean food à la carte.

T Govinda, Esmeraldas Oe3-115 y Venezuela, Mon-Sat 0800-1600. Vegetarian dishes, good value economical set meals and à la carte, also breakfast.

Cafés

Café del Teatro, Plaza del Teatro opposite Teatro Sucre, daily 1000-2100, open later when there are events at the theatres. Snacks, cakes, drinks and some meals, nice location and atmosphere.

Vista Hermosa, Mejía 453 y García Moreno, Mon-Sat 1400-0000, Sun 1200-2100. Drinks, pizza, light meals, live music on weekends, lovely terrace-top views of the colonial centre.

New City *p1043, map p1043*

TTT Alkimia, Valladolid N24-519 y Salazar, La Floresta, T252 7855, www.alkimiarestaurante.com, daily 1200-1530, 1900-2200. Very innovative Andean and international cuisine, excellent food and service, same ownership as Theatrum.

TTT Chez Jérôme, Whymper N30-96 y Coruña, T223 4067, Mon-Fri 1230-1530, 1930-2330, Sat 1930-2330. Excelent French cuisine, traditional and modern dishes with a touch of local ingredients, good ambiance and service.

TTT La Choza, 12 de Octubre N24-551 y Cordero, T223 0839, Mon-Fri 1200-1600, 1800-2200, Sat-Sun 1200-1700. Traditional Ecuadorean cuisine, good music and décor.

TTT La Jaiba, Coruña y San Ignacio, T254 3887, daily 1100-1600, Tue-Sat also 1900-2130. An old favourite for seafood, good service.

TTT **La Viña**, Isabel la Católica y Cordero, T256 6033, Mon-Fri 1230-1500, 1930-2300, Sat 1930-2300. Classy restaurant with an extensive and unusual menu, many French and Italian dishes, very good food, presentation, comfort and service, top of the line.

TTT **Los Troncos**, Los Shyris N35-80 y Portugal, T243 7377, Mon-Sat 1230-2200, Sun 1230-1600. Good Argentine grill, serves meats, fish, pasta, salads, small and friendly, busy on Sundays.

TTT **Rincón de La Ronda**, Bello Horizonte 406 y Almagro, T254 0459, www.rinconlaronda.com, daily 1200-2300. Very good local and international food, huge Sun buffet, sun night folklore show, gets many tour groups. Touristy.

TTT **Sake**, Paul Rivet N30-166 y Whymper, T252 4818, www.sakerestaurants.com, Mon-Sat 1230-1530, 1830-2300, Sun 12305-1600, 1830-2200. Sushi bar and other Japanese dishes, very trendy, great food, nicely decorated.

TTT **Zazu**, Mariano Aguilera 331 y La Pradera, T254 3559, www.zazuquito.com, Mon-Fri 1230-1500, 1900-2230, Sat 1900-2230. Very elegant and exclusive dinning. International and Peruvian specialties, extensive wine list, attentive service, reservations required.

TTT-TT **La Briciola**, Toledo 1255 y Salazar, T254 7138, daily 1200-2400. Extensive Itaslian menu, excellent food, homey atmosphere, very good personal service.

TT **Adam's Rib**, Calama E6-16 y Reina Victoria, Sun-Fri 1030-2230, happy hour 1730-1900. Ribs, steaks, good BBQ, great pecan pie, daily brunch 1030-1330, popular.

TT **Coffee & Toffee**, Calama E8-28 y Almagro, open 24 hours. Very good international food, breakfasts, coffee and snacks, generous portions, pleasant atmosphere, Wi-Fi.

TT **Il Risotto**, Eloy Alfaro N34-447 y Portugal, Sun-Fri 1200-1500, 1800-2300. Very popular and very good italian cooking, live music Thu and Fri. A Quito tradition.

TT **La Boca del Lobo**, Calama 284 y Reina Victoria, Sun-Wed 1700-2330, Thu-Sat 1700-0030, bar closes 1 hour later. Stylish bar-restaurant with eclectic food, drink, decor, and atmosphere , good food and cocktails, popular, good meeting place.

TT **Mama Clorinda**, Reina Victoria N24-150 y Calama, daily 1100-2300. Ecuadorean cuisine à la carte and set meals, filling, good value.

TT **Paléo**, Cordero E5-36 y JL Mera, Mon-Sat 1230-1530 1830-2100. Authentic Swiss specialties such as rösti and raclette. Also good economical set lunch, pleasant ambiance. Recommended.

TT **Pekín**, Whymper N26-42 y Orellana, Mon-Sat 1200-1500, 1900-2230, Sun 1200-2030. Excellent Chinese food, very nice atmosphere.

TT **Sushi**, Calama E5-104 y JL Mera, Mon-Sat 1200-2300, Sun 1200-1600. Sushi bar, pleasant atmosphere with nice balcony, good value happy hour 1700-1900.

TT **The Magic Bean**, Foch E5-08 y JL Meral, daily 0700-2200. Specializes in fine coffees and natural foods, more than 20 varieties of pancakes, good salads, large portions, outdoor seating (also offers popular lodging, **D**).

TT-T **Baalbek**, 6 de Diciembre N23-123 y Wilson, daily 1200-1800. Authentic Lebanese cuisine, great food and atmosphere, friendly service.

TT-T **El Hornero**, Veintimilla y Amazonas, República de El Salvador y Los Shyris and on Gonzalez Suárez, daily 1200-2300. Very good wood oven pizzas, try one with choclo (fresh corn). Recommended.

TT-T **Las Palmeras**, Japón N36-87 y Naciones Unidas, opposite Parque la Carolina, daily 0800-1700. Very good comida Esmeraldeña, try their hearty viche soup, outdoor tables, popular, good value. Recommended.

TT-T **Uncle Ho's**, Calama E8-29 y Almagro, Mon-Sat 1200-2230. Good Asian cooking, especially a number of Vietnamese dishes, set meals for lunch and à la carte, cocktails, Wi-Fi, popular.

T **Chandani Tandoori**, JL Mera 1312 y Cordero, Mon-Sat 1100-2200. Good authentic Indian cuisine, economical set meals, popular, good value. Recommended.

T **Chez Alain**, Baquedano E5-26 y JL Mera, Mon-Fri 1200-1530. Choice of good 4-course set meals for lunch, pleasant relaxed atmosphere, good value. Recommended.

T **Sakti**, Carrión E4-144 y Amazonas, Mon-Fri 0830-1830. Vegetarian food, breakfast, set lunches and à la carte, fruit juices, great desserts, a few hostel rooms at the back.

T **Yu Su**, Almagro y Colón, edif Torres de Almagro, Mon-Fri 1230-01600, 1800-2000, Sat 1230-1600. Very good suhi bar, pleasant, Korean run, takeaway service.

Cafés

Coffee Tree, Reina Victoria y Foch, Plaza El Quinde, also at Plaza de los Presidentes and Museo Mindalae (La Niña y Reina Victoria), open 24 hours. Popular cafés serving a variety of snacks, pasta, burguers, coffee, Wi-Fi .

Este Café, JL Mera N23-94 y Baquedano, Cordero E10-18 y Tamayo, and Amazonas N32-135 y La Granja, www.estecafe.com, Mon-Fri 0800-0100, Sat-Sun 0900-2000. Popular chain serving good organic coffee, healthy snacks, salad bar on weekdays, cocktails, also have live music and other cultural events.

Ethnic Coffee, Amazonas N21-81 y Robles, Mon-Sat 0800-2000. Nice café in one of the Ethnic Collection craft shops, offers gourmet coffee as well as a wide range of desserts, meals and drinks.

Kallari, Wilson y JL Mera, www.kallari.com, Mon-Fri 0800-1830, Sat 0900-1830. Fair trade café, breakfast, snacks, salad and sandwich set lunches, organic coffee and chocolate, crafts, run by an association of farmers and artisans from the Province of Napo working on rainforest and cultural conservation. Repetedly recommended.

Mirador de Guápulo, Rafael León Larrea, behind Hotel Quito, Tue-Sat 1600-0000 or later. Snacks such as empanadas, crèpes, sandwiches, drinks, live music Thu-Sat from 2130, great views, portable heaters for outdoor seating at night.

Bars and clubs

New City *p1043, map p1043*

Bungalow Six, Calama N24-139 y Almagro, T09-520 8955, Tue-Sat 1900-0200, Sun 1200-1900. US-style sports bar and club. Popular place to hang out and watch a game or a film, dancing later on, varied music, cover US$5 (Thu free), ladies' night on Wed, happy hour 2000-2200.

El Aguijón, Calama E7-35 y Reina Victoria, T256 9014, www.elaguijon.com.ec, Tue-Sat 2100-0300. Bohemian bar/club, varied music, nice atmosphere, after 2200 entry US$6 with 1 free drink. Also concerts, theatre, art.

El Pobre Diablo, Isabel La Católica E12-06 y Galicia, La Floresta, T222 5194, Mon-Sat 1230-0200. Relaxed atmosphere, friendly, jazz, sandwiches, snacks and nice meals, live music Wed, Thu and Sat, a popular place to hang out and chill.

Finn McCool's, Pinto E7-38 y Reina Victoria, T256 4953, daily 1100-0200. Irish-run pub, Irish and international food, darts, pool, table football, English football and other sports on TV, Wi-Fi, popular meeting place.

Flash Back, González Suárez N27-205 y Muros, T322 6922, opposite Hotel Quito. Club, mostly English music, rock and 1980s music, older crowd, cover US$12.

Ghoz, La Niña E6-62 y Reina Victoria, T255 6255, Tue-Sat 1800-0200. Swiss food, pool, darts, videos, games, music.

Kings Cross, Reina Victoria N26-155 y La Niña, T09-972 3379, Mon-Fri 1730-0200, Sat 1830-0100. Classic rock, BBQ, best hamburgers, wings. Popular with all ages. Recommended.

La Juliana, 12 de Octubre N24-722 y Coruña, T604 1569, www.lajuliana.com.ec, Thu-Sat 2130-0300. Popular club, live 1990s Latin music, cover US$12.

Mario's, Roca E4-115 y Amazonas, at Hotel Windsor, T222 4033, Mon-Sat 1600-0100. Elegant place to relax, listen to classical music and enjoy tropical drinks, older crowd.

No Bar, Calama y JL Mera, Mon-Sat 1900-0300, good mix of Latin and Euro dance music, busy at weekends. Free drinks for women until 2200, Thu-Sat after 2200 entry US$5 with 1 free drink.

Patatu's, Wilson 758 y JL Mera, T250 5233. Mon-Sat 1900-0200. Good drinks, pool table, happy hour all night Mon, loud music, dancing, owner speaks English and German.

Ramón Antiguo, Mena Caamaño e Isabel la Católica, 2100-0200. Live music Fri-Sat, cover US$5-10 depending on band. Great for salsa and other hip tropical music, popular with locals.

Reina Victoria Pub, Reina Victoria 530 y Roca, T222 6369, Mon-Sat 1700-2400. Relaxed English-style pub, good selection of microbrews and of Scottish and Irish whiskys, moderately priced bar meals, darts, popular meeting point for British and US expats.

Santurrón, Calama E4-363 y Amazonas, T254 9684, Tue-Sat 1800-0300. Classy, a good place to hang out, listen to music (live some nights) and dance, no entry fee, happy hour 1800-2100. Good service from English speaking owner

Seseribó, Veintimilla 325 y 12 de Octubre, T256 3598, Thu-Sat 2100-0100. Caribbean music and salsa, a must for salseros, very popular, especially Thu and Fri, cover US$8. Recommended.

Turtle's Head, La Niña 626 y JL Mera, T256 5544, Mon-Tue 1700-0300, Wed-Sat 1230-0300. Microbrews, fish and chips, curry, pool table, darts, fun atmosphere.
Varadero, Reina Victoria N26-99 y La Pinta, T254 2575, Mon-Thu1200-2400, Fri-Sat 1800-0300. Bar-restaurant, live Cuban music Wed-Sat, meals, snacks, good cocktails, older crowd and couples.

Entertainment

Quito *p1036, maps p1037, p1040 and p1043*
There are always many cultural events taking place in Quito, usually free of charge. For events at **Casa de la Cultura**, see http://cce.org.ec. Films are listed daily in *El Comercio*, www.elcomercio.com.

Cinema

Casa de la Cultura, Patria y 6 de Diciembre, T290 2272. Shows foreign films, often has documentaries, film festivals.
Ocho y Medio, Valladolid N24-353 y Guipuzcoa, La Floresta, T290 4720. Cinema and café, good for art films, programme available at *Libri Mundi* and elsewhere. There are several multiplexes, eg **Cinemark**, www.cinemark.com.ec, **Multicines**, www.multicines.com.ec, and **Supercines**. www.supercines.com.

Dance schools

One-to-one or group lessons are offered for US$4-6 per hr.
Son Latino, Reina Victoria N24-211 y García, T223 4340, several varieties of salsa.
Salsa y Merengue School, Foch E4-256 y Amazonas, T222 0427, also cumbia.
Universal Salsa, García E5-45 y JL Mera, T09-631 7757, salsa, capoeira and other dances.

Music

Folk Free folk shows at Palacio Arzobispal (entrance on C Venezuela), Fri at 1900, Sat at 1830 and Sun at 1130. Local folk music is popular in *peñas*; most places do not come alive until 2230:
Noches de Quito, Washington E5-29 y JL Mera, T223 4855. Thu-Sat 2000-0300, show starts 2130, varied music, entry US$6.
Ñucanchi, Av Universitaria Oe5-188 y Armero. T254 0967. Thu-Sat 2000-0300, show starts at 2130, Ecuadorean and other music, including Latin dance later in the night, entry US$8-10.

Ecuadorean folk ballet: **Ballet Andino Humanizarte**, at **Teatro Humanizarte**, Plaza N24-226 y Baquerizo Moreno, T222 6116, www.humanizarte.com, Wed at 1930, US$10; plays and comedies are also often in their repertoire, restaurant on the premises.
Jacchigua, at **Teatro Demetrio Aguilera Malta**, Casa de la Cultura, 6 de Diciembre y Patria, T295 2025, www.jacchiguaesecuador.com, Wed at 1930; entertaining, colourful and touristy, reserve ahead, US$25. **Surimanda**, at Palacio Arzobispal, Plaza de la Independencia, Fri 1900-2030, free.
Classical the **Orquesta Sinfónica Nacional**, T250 2815, performs at **Teatro Sucre, Casa de la Música**, in the colonial churches and regionally.
Casa de la Música, Valderrama s/n y Mariana de Jesús, T226 7093, www.casadelamusica.ec, concerts by the Orquesta Sinfónica Nacional, Orquesta Filarmónica del Ecuador, Orquesta de Instrumentos Andinos and invited performers, Excellent acoustics.

Theatre

Many old theatres have been restored by the municipality, see www.teatrosucre.com.
Agora, open-air theatre of Casa de la Cultura, 12 de Octubre y Patria. Stages plays, concerts.
Teatro Bolívar, Espejo 847 y Guayaquil, T258 2486, www.teatrobolivar.org. Despite restoration work there are tours, presentations and festivals.
Teatro Sucre, Plaza del Teatro, Manabí N8-131 y Guayaquil, T295 1661, www.teatrosucre.com. Beautifully restored 19th century building, the city's main theatre.

Festivals and events

Quito *p1036, maps p1037, p1040 and p1043*
New Year, Años Viejos: life-size puppets satirize politicians and others. At midnight on 31 Dec a will is read, the legacy of the outgoing year, and the puppets are burnt; good along Amazonas between Patria and Colón, very entertaining and good humoured. On New Year's day everything is shut. The solemn **Good Friday** processions are most impressive. **24 May** is **Independence**, commemorating the Battle of Pichincha in 1822 with early morning cannon-fire and parades, everything closes. **Aug**: **Agosto Arte y Cultura**, organized by the municipality, cultural events, dance and music in different places throughout the city. The city's main festival, **Día de Quito**,

celebrated **1-6 Dec**, commemorates the foundation of the city with elaborate parades, bullfights, performances and music in the streets, very lively. Hotels charge extra, everything except a few restaurants shuts on 6 Dec. Foremost among **Christmas** celebrations is the **Misa del Gallo**, midnight mass. Nativity scenes can be admired in many public places. Over Christmas, Quito is crowded, hotels are full and the streets are packed with vendors and shoppers.

O Shopping

Quito *p1036, maps p1037, p1040 and p1043*

Shops open generally 0900-1900 on weekdays, some close at midday and most shut Sat afternoon and Sun. Shopping centres are open at weekends. The main shopping districts are along Av Amazonas in the north and C Guayaquil in the colonial city. In modern Quito much of the shopping is done in malls (see list under Foodstuffs). For maps see Planning your trip, page 1031.

Bookshops

Abya-Yala, 12 de Octubre 14-30 y Wilson. Good for books about indigenous cultures and anthropology, also has excellent library and museum.

Confederate Books, Calama 410 y JL Mera. Open 1000-1900, excellent selection of secondhand books, including travel guides, mainly English but also German and French.

Damas Norteamericanas y Británicas Library, see page 1065. Cheap secondhand English books.

Libri Mundi, JL Mera N23-83 y Veintimilla, Plaza El Quinde, Centro Cultural Metropolitano and Quicentro Shopping, www.librimundi.com. Excellent selection of Spanish, English, French, German, and some Italian books, sells Footprint *Ecuador, South American Handbook* and other titles, knowledgeable and helpful staff, noticeboard of what's on in Quito. Highly recommended.

Libro Express, Amazonas 816 y Veintimilla, also at Quicentro Shopping and airport. Has a good stock of maps, guides and international magazines.

Mr Books, Mall El Jardín, 3rd floor. Good stock, many in English including Footprint travel guides, open daily. Recommended.

The English Bookshop, Calama 217 y Almagro. Daily 1000-1800, good selection of secondhand books.

Camping

Camping gas is available many of the shops listed below, white gas (*combustible para lámpara Coleman, gasolina blanca*) at times from **Kywi**, Centro Comercial Olímpico, 6 de Diciembre, north of the stadium and 10 de Agosto N24-59. They also have rubber boots.

Los Alpes, Reina Victoria N23-45 y Baquedano. Local and imported equipment, also rentals.

Antisana, Centro Comercial El Bosque, ground floor. Local and imported, sales only.

Aventura Sport, Quicentro Shopping, top floor. Tents, good selection of glacier sunglasses, upmarket.

Camping Sports, Colón E6-39 y Reina Victoria. Sales only, well stocked.

Eko,Wilson y JL Mera. Kayaking supplies, ski jackets, fleeces.

Equipos Cotopaxi, 6 de Diciembre N20-36 y Patria. Ecuadorean and imported gear for sale.

Mono Dedo, JL Mera N23-84 y Wilson and Rafael León N24-36 y Coruña, www.monodedo.com. Climbing equipment, part of a rock climbing club.

Tatoo, JL Mera N23-54 y Wilson and CC La Esquina in Cumbayá, www.tatoo.ws. Quality backpacks and outdoor clothing.

The Altar, J L Mera N22-93 y Veintimilla. Imported and local gear for sale, good prices for rentals.

The Explorer, Reina Victoria y N24-43 Pinto. Sales and rentals, very helpful, will buy US or European equipment.

Foodstuffs

Cacaoyere, Calle D, Los Eucaliptos, by Av Eloy Alfaro in the far north. T248 1851, ext 107, www.ecuatorianadechocolates.com. Makes chocolate from 4 different regions of Ecuador, nicely presented, good chocolate. Offers free factory tours, just phone in advance.

Mi Comisariato, a well-stocked supermarket and department store, at Quicentro Shopping (Naciones Unidas y Shyris) and García Moreno y Mejía in the colonial city.

Santa María, Av Iñaquito y Pereira, Bolívar 334 y Venezuela and Versalles y Carrión. Good value supermarkets.

Supermaxi at Mall El Jardín (Amazonas y República), CCI (Amazonas y Naciones Unidas), El Bosque (Occidental y Carvajal), Multicentro (6 de Diciembre y La Niña), Megamaxi (6 de Diciembre y Julio Moreno), and El Recreo. (Av Maldonado). Very well stocked supermarket and department store, local and imported goods.

Handicrafts

Note that there are controls on export of arts and crafts. Unless they are obviously new handicrafts, you may have to get a permit from the **Instituto Nacional de Patrimonio Cultural** (Colón Oe1-93 y 10 de Agosto, T254 3527, offices also in other cities), before you can mail or take things home. Permits cost US$6 and take time.

A wide selection can be found at the following craft markets: **Mercado Artesanal La Mariscal**, Jorge Washington, between Reina Victoria and JL Mera, daily 1000-1800, interesting an worthwhile; **El Indio**, Roca E4-35 y Amazonas, daily 0900-1900; **Centro de Artesanías CEFA**, 12 de Octubre1738 y Madrid, Mon-Fri 0900-1900, Sat 0900-1700.

On weekends, crafts are sold in stalls at **Parque El Ejido** and along the Av Patria side of this park, artists sell their paintings (www.arte ejido.com). There are souvenir shops on García Moreno in front of the Palacio Presidencial in the colonial city. At the north end of the **Plaza de Santo Domingo** and along the nearest stretch of C Flores, local garments (for natives rather than tourists) can be seen and bought.

Recommended shops with an ample selection are:

Camari, Marchena 260 y Versalles. Fair Trade shop run by an artisan organization.

Folklore, Colón E10-53 y Caamaño, the store of the late Olga Fisch (died 1989), who came to Ecuador from Hungary in 1939 and who encouraged craftspeople to excel. Attractive selection of handicrafts and rugs, expensive but very good quality, open Mon-Fri 0900-1900, Sat 1000-1800; small museum upstairs, voluntary donations welcomed. Also at *Hotel Hilton Colón* and *Hotel Patio Andaluz*.

Galería Latina, JL Mera 823 y Veintimilla. Fine selection of alpaca and other handicrafts from Ecuador, Peru and Bolivia, visiting artists sometimes demonstrate their work.

Hilana, 6 de Diciembre N23-10 y Veintimilla Beautiful unique 100% wool blankets with Ecuadorean motifs, excellent quality, purchase by metre possible,. reasonable prices.

Homero Ortega, Isabel La Católica N24-100 and Plaza San Francisco, facing the church. Outlet for Cuenca Panama hat manufacturer.

K Dorfzaun, at Quicentro mall, ground floor. Outlet for Cuenca Panama hat manufacturer.

Kallari, Crafts from Oriente at café, page 1052.

La Bodega, JL Mera 614 y Carrión. Recommended for antiques and handicrafts.

Marcel Creations, Roca 766, entre Amazonas y 9 de Octubre. Panama hats.

Mindalae. Nice crafts at museum, page 1044.

Productos Andinos, Urbina 111 y Cordero. Artisan's co-op, good selection, including unusual items.

Saucisa, Amazonas 2487 y Pinto, and a couple other locations in La Mariscal. Very good place to buy Andean music CDs and instruments.

The Ethnic Collection, Amazonas N21-81and N21-187 y Robles, www.ethniccollection.com. Wide variety of clothing, leather, bags, jewellery and ceramic items. Also café at N21-81.

Jewellery

Argentum, JL Mera 614. Excellent selection, reasonably priced.

Ari Gallery, Bolívar Oe6-23, Plaza de San Francisco, www.ushinajewellery.com. Fine silver with ancestral motifs.

Jeritsa, Mall El Jardín, local 234. Good selection, prices and service.

Taller Guayasamín, at the museum, see page 1044. Jewellery with native designs.

Markets

Main produce markets, all accessible by Trole: **Mercado Central**, Av Pichincha y Olmedo (also on the Ecovía), **Mercado Santa Clara**, Versalles y Ramírez Dávalos and **Mercado Iñaquito**, Iñaquito y Villalengua.

Activities and tours

Quito *p1036, maps p1037, p1040 and p1043*

Birdwatching and nature

The following operators specialize in birdwatching tours: **Andean Birding**, www.andeanbirding.com; **BirdEcuador**, www.birdecuador.com; **Neblina Forest**, www.neblinaforest.com; **Pluma Verde Tours**, www.plumaverdetours.com.

City tours

Paseos Culturales, at Plaza de la Independencia tourist information office, Venezuela y Espejo, T257 2445. Walking tours of the colonial city led by English-speaking officers of the Policía Metropolitana. Daily at 1000, 1100 and 1400, 2½-3 hrs, US$15, children and seniors US$7.50, includes museum entrance fees; Mon is not a good day because many museums are closed. Night tours require a minimum of 8 people, walking tours at 1800 and 1900, US$8; bus tours include El Panecillo and La Cima de la Libertad lookouts, US$20 pp, advance booking required.
Coches Victoria, horse-drawn carriages with an English-speaking guide will take you on a 20-min tour of the colonial heart. Tickets sold at booth on corner García Moreno y Sucre, T09-980 0723, Mon-Fri 1700-2300, Sat-Sun 1000-2300, US$4 pp, children and seniors US$2, reservations recommended at weekends.
Chiva Don Otto, tours of colonial Quito in a *chiva*, an old-fashioned open-sided bus. Sat and Mon-Thu. Contact **Klein Tours**, page 1059.

Climbing and trekking

Climbs and trekking tours can be arranged in Quito and several other cities; the following Quito operators specialize in this area, see Tour operators below for their contact information: **Andes Explorer, Campo Base, Campus Trekking, Climbing Tour, Compañía de Guías, Cotopaxi Cara Sur, Ecuador Treasure, Gulliver, Latitud 0°, Safari, and Sierra Nevada.**

Note that independent guides do not normally provide a full service (ie transport, food, equipment, insurance) and, without a permit from the Ministerio del Ambiente, they will be refused entry to national parks, especially Cotopaxi. You must ensure that your operator, guide and transport have the requisite permits (*patentes*). A cheap tour may leave you stranded at the national park gates.

Cycling and mountain biking

Quito has a couple of bike paths including one around the perimeter of Parque La Carolina and another in the south, along Quebrada Ortega in the Quitumbe neighbourhood. The city organizes a **ciclopaseo**, a cycle day, every Sun 0900-1500. Key avenues are closed to vehicular traffic and thousands of cyclists cross the city in 29 km from north to south. This and other cycle events are run by **Fundación Ciclópolis**, Equinoccio N17-171 y Queseras del Medio, T322 6502, www.ciclopolis.ec (in Spanish); they also hire bikes, US$5.60 per *ciclopaseo* (must book Mon-Fri), US$11.20/day on other days. Rentals also from *La Casa del Ciclista* (see below), near the *ciclopaseo* route. **Biciacción**, www.biciaccion.org, has information about cycling routes in the city and organizes trips outside Quito.

Mountain bike tours Many operators offer bike tours, the following are specialists:
Aries, T09-981 6603, www.ariesbikecompany.com. 1- to 3-day tours, all equipment provided.
Biking Dutchman, Foch E 4-313 y JL Mera, T256 8323, after hours T09-420 5349, www.biking-dutchman.com. One- and several-day tours, great fun, good food, very well organized, English, German and Dutch spoken, pioneers in mountain biking in Ecuador.

Bicycle shops **Bike Stop**, 6 de Diciembre N34-113 e Irlanda,T224 1192, www.bikestop.com.ec.
La Casa del Ciclista, Eloy Alfaro 1138 y República, T254 0339, open daily. Sales, repairs and rentals (US$2 per hr, US$12 per day).
The Bike Shop, Río Coca y Los Shyris, CC Paseo del Río 13, T227 0330.

Horse riding

APROSAR, T269 9508 (evenings) or T09-903 0887. An association of 7 local horse-people, offers guided rides from just above the gate of the teleférico (see p 1044), to a waterfall nearby or longer rides to Rucu Pichincha or beyond, US$10/hr. Book ahead for large groups and long rides.
Green Horse Ranch, see page 1068.

Juan Carlos Andrade, T246 4694, www.horse backriding.com.ec. Rides from the teleférico to Rucu Pichincha returning via an hacienda, US$45 for 4 hrs, minimum 4 riders, reserve in advance.

Paragliding

Escuela Pichincha de Vuelo Libre, Carlos Endara Oe3-60 y Amazonas, T225 6592 (office hours) T09-993 1206, parapent@uio.satnet.net. Offers complete courses for US$400 and tandem flights for US$60.

Swimming

There are a number of good, clean, heated public pools in the city. Swimming cap, towel and soap are compulsory for admission.
Miraflores, at the upper end of Av Universitaria, Tue-Sun 0900-1600. **Batán Alto**, Cochapata y Abascal, off Gaspar de Villaroel. **Colegio Benalcázar**, 6 de Diciembre y Portugal, also sauna. **La Cascada**, Flores N41-47 y Chile, T295 8200, also spa.

Tour operators

National park fees are rarely included in prices.
Advantage Travel, El Telégafo E10-63 y Juan de Alcántara, T246 2871, www.advantagecuador.com. Tours to Machalilla and Isla de la Plata. Also 4-5 day tours on a floating hotel on Río Napo.
Andando Tours – Angermeyer Cruises, Mariana de Jesús E7-113 y Pradera, T323 7186, www.andandotours.com. Operate several Galápagos vessels.
Andean Travel Company, Amazonas N24-03 y Wilson, p 3, T222 8385, www.andeantc.com. Dutch-owned operator, offers a wide range of tours including trekking, operate **Cotococha Amazon Lodge** and the *Galapagos Voyager* and *Galapagos Odyssey* vessels.
Andes Explorer, Reina Victoria 927 y Pinto, T290 1493, www.andes-explorer.com. Good value budget mountain and jungle trips and sells Galápagos tours.
Campo Base, T259 9737, www.campobase-ecuador.com. Climbing, trekking and cycling tours, run by Manuel and Diego Jácome, very experienced climbing guides, they also have a mountain lodge 15 km south of Sangolquí, good for acclimatization at 3050 m.
Campus Trekking, Joaquina Vargas 99 y Calderón, Conocoto, Valle de los Chillos, T234 0601, www.campustrekking.com. Good value trekking, climbing and cultural tours, 8-15 day biking trips, taylor made itineraries, Galápagos. Also run **Hostería Pantaví** near Ibarra, 8 languages spoken.
Climbing Tours, Amazonas N21-221 y Roca, T254 4358, www.climbingtour.com. Climbing, trekking and other adventure sports, tours to regional attractions, also sell Galápagos and jungle tours.
Creter Tours, Pinto 356 y JL Mera, www.cretertours.com.ec. Galápagos tours.
Compañía de Guías, Washington E7-42 y 6 de Diciembre, p2, T290 1551, www.compania deguias.com. Climbing and trekking specialists, but sell other tours, English, German, French and Italian spoken.
Cotopaxi Cara Sur, Veintimilla E9-26 y L Plaza Edif Uziel, of 308, T09-800 2681, www.cotopaxi carasur.com. Climbing and trekking tours, run by experienced climbing guide Eduardo Agama, also own Albergue Cara Sur on Cotopaxi.

Dracaena, Pinto 446 y Amazonas, T254 6590, www.dracaenaecuador.com. Runs good budget jungle tours to Cuyabeno and climbing and trekking trips, popular.

EcoAndes, Baquedano E5-27 y JL Mera, T255 7650, www.ecoandestravel.com. Run by experienced guide Hugo Torres, for classic tours, adventure travel, Galápagos and Amazon. Also operate hotels in Quito.

Ecoventura, Almagro N31-80 y Whymper, T290 7396, www.ecoventura.com. Operate first-class Galápagos cruises and sell tours throughout Ecuador.

Ecuador Journeys, Cordero 1204 y JL Mera, p9, T254 9684, www.ecuadorianjourney.com, www.cheapgalapagoscruises.com. Adventure tours to off-the-beaten-path destinations, choice of day tours, treks to volcanos including Reventador, jungle trips.

Ecuador Treasure, Amazonas N24-157 y Calama, T223 6607, www.ecuadortreasure.com. Climbing, horse riding, cycling and cultural tours, also sell Galápagos and jungle.

Ecuadorian Tours, Amazonas N21-33 y Washington, several other locations, T256 0488, www.ecuadoriantours.com. Airline tickets and tours in all regions.

Enchanted Expeditions, de las Alondras N45-102 y de los Lirios, T334 0525, www.enchanted expeditions.com. Operate Galápagos cruises, sell jungle trips to Cuyabeno and highland tours. Very experienced.

Equateur Voyages Passion, in L'Auberge Inn, Gran Colombia N15-200 y Yaguachi, T254 3803, www.equateurvoyages.com. Full range of adventure tours, run a 4- to 5-day jungle tour on the Shiripuno River, sell Galápagos cruises.

Exclusive Hotels & Haciendas of Ecuador, 12 de Octubre E11-14 y Orellana, p2, 254 4719, www.ehhec.com. A reservation centre for a range of high-end hotels, haciendas, lodges and spas, also offer private transport in 4WD vehicles with English speaking chauffeur/guide from US$170 per day.

Galacruises Expeditions, 9 de Octubre N22-118 y Veintimilla, T252 3324, www.galacruises.com. Operate Galápagos cruises in their fleet of catamarans and yachts.

Galasam, Cordero N24-214 y Amazonas, T290 3909, www.galasam.com. Has a fleet of boats in different categories for Galápagos cruises. City tours, full range of highland tours and jungle trips to *Siona Lodge* in Cuaybeno.

Galextur, Portugal E10-271 y 6 de Diciembre, T226 9626, www.galextur.com. Run 4- to 8-day land-based Galápagos tours with daily sailings to different islands and **Hotel Silberstein** in Puerto Ayora. Good service.

Geo Reisen, El Telégrafo E9-39 y Juan de Alcántara, T244 6224, www.georeisentours.com. Specializing in cultural, adventure and nature tours adapted for individuals, groups or families.

Gulliver, JL Mera N24-156 y José Calama, T252 9297, www.gulliver.com.ec. Wide range of options from guided vehicle tours to extreme outdoor pursuits. Operate **Hostería Papagayo** south of Quito and **Cocoa Inn** near Puerto Quito. .Also sell Galápagos and jungle tours and airline tickets.

Happy Gringo, Foch E6-12 y Reina Victoria, T222 0031, www.happygringo.com, open daily. Operate tours to Otavalo and in Quito and surroundings. Sell Galápagos, jungle and other tours, good service.

Kempery Tours, Ramírez Dávilos 117 y Amazonas, Ed Turismundial, p 2, T250 5599, www.kempery.com. Good-value tours, 4- to 14-day jungle trips to **Bataburo Lodge** in Huaorani territory, operate the *Angelique* and *Archipel II* vessels in Galápagos, multilingual service.

Klein Tours, Eloy Alfaro N34-151 y Catalina Aldaz, also Shyris N34-280 y Holanda, T226 7000, www.kleintours.com. Operate the *Galapagos Legend* and *Coral I* and *II* cruise ships also *Chiva Don Otto* Quito city tour (page1056) and *Chaski Antawa* train (page 1090). Tailor-made itineraries, English, French and German spoken.

Latin Trails, Rumiñahui 221 y 1ra Transversal, San Rafael, T286 7832, www.latintrails.com, www.galapagoscatamarans.com. Run the *Galapagos Journey I* and *II* catamarans and offer a variety of land trips in several countries.

Latitud 0°, Mallorca N24-500 y Coruña, La Floresta, T254 7921, www.latitud0.com. Climbing specialists.
Mallku Expeditions, Av 10 de Agosto N26-117 y Gnal Aguirre, of 301/2, T255 50090, www.mallkexopeditions.com
Metropolitan Touring, Av Las Palmeras N45-74 y Las Orquídeas, Amazonas N20-39 y 18 de Septiembre and at shopping centres, T298 8200, www.metropolitan-touring.com. A large organization that operates tours throughout Ecuador and Peru, Chile and Argentina. Operate several luxury Galápagos vessels, **Finch Bay Hotel** in Puerto Ayora and the *Chiva Express* private rail journey along the Devil's Nose route. Also adventure, cultural and gastronomy tours.
Palmar Voyages, Alemania N31-77 y Av Mariana de Jesús, T256 9809, www.palmarvoyages.com. Small specialist company, custom-made itineraries to all areas of Ecuador or Peru, good rates.
Positiv Turismo, Jorge Juan N33-38 y Atahualpa, T600 9401, www.positivturismo.com. Swiss-Austrian-run company. Galápagos, cultural trips, trekking and special interest tours.
Quasar Náutica, José Jussieu N41-28 y Alonso de Torres, T244 6996,. T1-800 247 2925 (USA), www.quasarnautica.com. Highly recommeded 7-10 day naturalist and diving Galápagos cruises on 8-16 berth luxury and power yachts.
Rolf Wittmer Turismo/Tip Top Travel, Foch E7-81 y Diego de Almagro, Quito, T252 6938, www.rwittmer.com. Run first class yachts: *Tip Top II*, *III* and *IV*. Also tailor-made tours throughout Ecuador.
Safari, Reina Victoria N25-33y Colón, p 11, of 1101, T255 2505, www.safari.com.ec. Excellent adventure travel, personalized itineraries, climbing, cycling, rafting, trekking and cultural tours. Also book Galápagos tours, sell jungle trips and run a glacier school. A good source of travel information. Recommended.

Sangay Touring, Cordero E4-358, T255 0176, www.sangay.com. Operate a variety of custom designed tours, particularly in Oriente, and sell Galápagos trips, efficient service.
Sierra Nevada, Pinto E4-150 y Cordero, T252 8264, www.sierranevada.ec. Specialized multiple-day adventure expeditions: climbing, trekking, rafting and jungle, experienced multi-lingual guides, good service.
Surtrek, Amazonas 897 y Wilson, T250 0530, www.surtrek.com. Custom designed trips with personalized itineraries for individuals and small groups, cultural and adventure trips throughout Ecuador, Galápagos tours, also sell domestic flights.
Terrasenses, T98-215621, www.terrasenses.com. Specialize in reponsible tourism, eco-honeymoons and destination weddings.
Tierra de Fuego, Amazonas N2323 y Veintimilla, T250 4018, www.ecuadortierradefuego.com. Provide land service and tours throughout the country, as well as Galápagos Islands (www.galapagosprograms.com).
Tours Unlimited, Julio Castro E6-16 y Valparaíso, T252 5834, www.tours-unlimited.com. Custom-made itineraries in all regions, city and regional tours including the Tulipe-Pachijal private cloudforest reserve, www.tulipecloudforest.org.
Tropic Journeys in Nature, La Niña E7-46 entre Diego de Almagro y Reina Victoria, T222 5907, www.tropiceco.com. Environmental and cultural tours to the **Huaorani Ecolodge** (page 1179), the highlands, coast and Galápagos, including walking tours on Isabela. Founder Andy Drumm works closely with conservation and indigenous groups. General Manager is Jascivan Carvalho. A percentage of all profits supports **Conservation in Action**. Winner of several awards for responsible tourism.
Zenith Travel, JL Mera N24-234 y Cordero, T252 9993, www.zenithecuador.com. Economical Galápagos cruises as well as various land tours in Ecuador and Peru. All gay Galápagos cruises available. Multilingual service, knowledgeable helpful staff, good value.

Whitewater rafting

Ríos Ecuador/Yacu Amu, Foch 746 y JL Mera, T290 4054, www.riosecuador.com. Australian-owned (Steve Nomchong), very professional, rafting and kayaking trips of 1-6 days, also kayak courses, good equipment. For level 4 and 5 runs, contact freelance guide **Dan Dixon** here. Highly recommended.
Sierra Nevada (see Tour operators above), excellent trips from 1 to 3 days, chief guide Edison Ramírez (fluent English/French) is certified by *French Association*.

All charge about US$50-80 per day.

Mitad del Mundo *p1045*

Calimatours, Manzana de los Correos, Oficina 11, Mitad del Mundo, T239 4796, www.calimaecuador.com. Tours to all the sites in the vicinity. Offers beautiful certificates to record your visit. Recommended.

Transport

Quito *p1036, maps p1037, p1040 and p1043*

Air

Mariscal Sucre Airport, T294 4900, www.quiport.com. The safest and easiest way to travel between airport and town is by **taxi**. You can catch one from the rank outside arrivals. Buy a ticket first at the booth: fixed fare from the airport to La Mariscal US$6; to the colonial city US$8; to Quitumbe terminal US$15; to Carcelén terminal US$6. Alternatively, the **Trans-Rabbit** or **Achupallas** van services are good value for groups of 4 or more. Individuals who buy a ticket for a van must either pay more or wait until they get enough passengers. **Public buses** are not recommended unless you have virtually no luggage or are desperately low on funds. Buses and trolley alike are too crowded to enter with even a small backpack so the risk of theft is very high. The bus stop is 1 block west of terminal, in front of Centro Comercial Aeropuerto. For modern Quito take a southbound bus marked 'Carcelén-Congreso' along Av Amazonas, fare US$0.25. For colonial Quito take a green *alimentador* (feeder bus line) from the same stop to the northern terminus of the trolley line, combined fare US$0.25. There is no bus or trolley service late at night when most flights from North America arrive. There is a hotel booking service at international arrivals. **Moneyzone** cambio in international departures, open 0430-2100, poor rates for 12 currencies. There are duty-free shops in the international departures lounge. Details of internal services are given in the respective destinations. A new airport is scheduled to open in 2011.

Bus

Local Quito has 3 parallel mass transit lines running from north to south on exclusive lanes, covering almost the length of the city. Feeder bus lines (*alimentadores*) go from the terminals to outer suburbs. The combined fare is US$0.25. **Trole** (T266 5016, Mon-Fri 0500-2345, weekends and holidays 0600-2145) is system of trolley buses which runs along Av 10 de Agosto in the north of the city, C Guayaquil (southbound) and C Flores (northbound) in colonial Quito, and mainly along Av Maldonado and Av Teniente Ortiz in the south. The northern terminus is north of 'La Y', the junction of 10 de Agosto, Av América and Av de la Prensa; south of the colonial city are important transfer stations at El Recreo, known as Terminal Sur, and Morán Valverde; the southern terminus is at the Quitumbe bus station. Trolleys do not necessarily run the full length of the line, the destination is marked in front of the vehicle. Trolleys have a special entrance for wheelchairs. **Ecovía** (T243 0726, Mon-Sat 0500-2200, Sun and holidays 0600-2200), articulated buses, runs along Av 6 de Diciembre from Estación Río Coca, at C Río Coca east of 6 de Diciembre, in the north, to La Marín transfer station, east of colonial Quito. The route will be extended to the south along Av Napo. **Metrobus** (T346 5149, Mon-Fri 0530-2230, weekends and holidays 0600-2100) also runs articulated buses along Av de la Prensa and Av América from Terminal La Ofelia in the north to La Marín in the south. There are plans to extend the Ecovía and Metrobus lines. There are also 2 types of **city buses**: *Selectivos* are red, take mostly sitting passengers and a limited number standing and *Bus Tipo* are royal blue, take sitting and standing passengers, both cost US$0.25. Many bus lines go through La Marín transfer station. Extra caution is advised here: it is a rough area, pickpockets abound and it is best avoided at night.

Short distance Outer suburbs are served by green *Interparroquial* buses. Those running east to the valleys of Cumbayá, Tumbaco and beyond leave from the Estación Río Coca (see Ecovía above). Buses southeast to Valle de los Chillos leave from La Marín and from Isabel la Católica y Mena Caamaño, behind Universidad Católica. Buses going north (ie Calderón, Mitad del Mundo) leave from La Ofelia Metrobus station. Regional destinations to the north (ie Cayambe) and northwest (ie Mindo) leave from a regional station adjacent to La Ofelia Metrobus station. Buses south to Machachi from La Villaflora and Quitumbe.

Long distance Two modern terminals opened in 2009. **Terminal Quitumbe** in the southwest of the city, T398 8200, for destinations south, the coast via Santo Domingo, Oriente and Tulcán (in the north). It is served by the Trole (line 4: El Ejido- Quitumbe, best taken at El Ejido) and the Metrobus is being extended towards it, however it is advisable to take a taxi, about US$6, 30-45 mins to the colonial city, US$8-10, 45 mins-1 hr to La Mariscal. Arrivals, tourist information, phone/internet office, bank, ATMs and Trole entrance are on the ground floor. Ticket counters (destinations grouped and colour coded by region), departures and ATMs are at the upper level. Left luggage (US$0.90 per day) and food stalls are at the adjoining shopping area. The terminal is large, allow extra time to reach your bus. Terminal use fee US$0.20. Watch your belongings at all times. On holiday weekends it is advisable to reserve the day before. **Terminal Carcelén**, Av Eloy Alfaro, where it meets the Panamericana Norte, T3961600, serves destinations to the north (including Otavalo) and the coast via the Calacalí–La Independencia road. It is served by feeder bus lines from the northern terminals of the Ecovía and Metrobus, a taxi costs about US$5, 30-45 mins to La Mariscal, US$7, 45 mins-1hr to colonial Quito. Ticket counters are organized by destination. See under destinations for fares and schedules.
A convenient way to travel from Quitumbe to Carcelén is to take a bus bound for Tulcán, **Trans Vencedores** or **Unión del Carchi** (Booth 12), every 30 mins during the day, hourly at night, US$1, 1 hr; taxi between terminals, US$15. There are plans for direct city buses between terminals, these were not running at the time of writing.

Several companies run better quality coaches on the longer routes, those with terminals in modern Quito are: **Flota Imbabura**, Larrea 1211 y Portoviejo, T223 6940, for **Cuenca** and **Guayaquil**; **Transportes Ecuador**, JL Mera N21-44 y Washington, T250 3842, to **Guayaquil**; **Transportes Esmeraldas**, Santa María 870 y Amazonas, T250 9517, for **Esmeraldas**, **Atacames**, **Coca**, **Lago Agrio**, **Manta** and **Huaquillas**. **Reina del Camino**, Larrea y 18 de Septiembre, T321 6633, for **Bahía**, **Puerto López** and **Manta**; **Carlos Aray** Larrea y Portoviejo, T256 4406, for **Manta** and **Puerto López**; **Transportes Occidentales**, 18 de Septiembre y Versalles, T250 2733, for **Esmeraldas**, **Atacames**, **Salinas** and **Lago Agrio**; **Transportes Baños**, for Baños and Oriente destinations, has a ticket counter at Santa María y JL Mera, but buses leave from Quitumbe. **Panamericana Internacional**, Colón E7-31 y Reina Victoria, T255 7133, ext 126 for national routes, ext 125 for international, for **Huaquillas**, **Machala**, **Cuenca**, **Loja**, **Guayaquil**, **Manta** and **Esmeraldas**. They also run an international service: 4 weekly to **Bogotá**, changing buses in Tulcán and Ipiales, US$85, 28 hrs; **Caracas,** 1 weekly, US$130, 3 days; to **Lima**, daily, changing buses in Aguas Verdes and Túmbes, US$85, 38 hrs. **Ormeño Internacional**, from Perú, Shyris N34-432 y Portugal, T246 0027, Tue and Thu 0200 to **Lima** US$80, **La Paz**, US$170, 2½ days, **Santiago** US$210, 4 days, **Buenos Aires** US$280, 6 days, To **Cali**, 2 weekly, US$50 and **Bogotá** US$70. To **Caracas**, 1 weekly, US$100. **Rutas de América**, Selva Alegre Oe1-72 y 10 de Agosto, T250 3611, www.rutasenbus. com, to **Lima**, 1 weekly, US$65; to **Caracas** , 2 weekly, US$135, 2½ days, does not go into Colombian cities, but will let passengers off by the roadside (eg Popayán, Palmira for Cali or Ibagué for Bogotá, all US$55). The route to **Peru** via Loja and Macará takes much longer than the Huaquillas route, but is more relaxed. Don't buy Peruvian (or any other country's) bus tickets here, they're much cheaper outside Ecuador.

Shared taxis and vans offer door-to-door service and avoid the hassle of reaching Quito bus terminals. **Lucy Express**, T09-786 4264, www.lucyexpress.com, daily vans to **Guayaquil**, US$21.50, excellent comfortable service with a/c. **Servicio Express**, T255 1225, T03-242 6828 (Ambato) or T09-924 2795, 6 daily departures to **Ambato** (US$12), they will also drop passengers off in **Latacunga** (US$10), or continue to **Baños** (US$20 extra per vehicle), reserve at least 2 days ahead. **Taxis Lagos** shared taxis to **Otavalo** and **Ibarra**, see page 1082. **Sudamericana Taxis**, to **Santo Domingo**, see page 1166.

Taxi

Taxis are a safe, cheap (from US$1) and efficient way to get around the city. For airport and bus terminal taxis, see above. All taxis must have working meters by law, but make sure the meter is running (if it isn't, fix the fare before). Expect to pay US$1-2 more at night when meter may not be used. All legally registered taxis have the number of their co-operative and the individual operator's number prominently painted on the side of the vehicle and on a sticker on the windshield. They are safer and cheaper than unauthorized taxis. Note the registration and the licence plate numbers if you feel you have been seriously overcharged or mistreated. You may then complain to the transit police or tourist office. Be reasonable and remember that the majority of taxi drivers are honest and helpful. At night it is safer to use a radio taxi, there are several companies including: **Taxi Amigo**, T222 2222; **City Taxi**, T263 3333; and **Central de Radio Taxis**, T250 0600. Make sure they give you the taxi number so that you get the correct vehicle, some radio taxis are unmarked. To hire a taxi by the hour costs from US$8. For trips outside Quito, agree the fare beforehand: US$70-85 a day. Outside luxury hotels cooperative taxi drivers have a list of agreed excursion prices and most drivers are knowledgeable. For taxi tours with a guide, try **Hugo Herrera**, T226 7891. He speaks English and is recommended.

Train

Regular passenger service has been discontinued throughout the country. A tourist train runs from **Quito** to **Latacunga**, Wed, Fri-Sun and holidays at 0730, returns 1400. US$10 return, children under 12 and seniors US$5, Purchase tickets in advance from **Empresa de Ferrocarriles Ecuatorianos** , Bolívar Oe5-43 y

García Moreno, colonial Quito, T258 2930 or T1-800-873637, www.efe.gov.ec, Mon-Fri 0830-1630, you need each passenger's passport number and age to purchase tickets. You can alight at any of the stops and will be picked up on the return trip. The tour starts at the lovely refurbished **Estación Chimbacalle** (Maldonado y Sincholagua, 2 km south of the colonial city, T265 6142), with a visit to a railway museum. There is a breakfast stop at either **Tambillo** or **Machachi**, next stop is **El Boliche**, with views of Cotopaxi and Los Ilinizas. If you wish to spend a few hours until the train returns at about 1500, here is **Area Nacional de Recreación El Boliche** entrance fee US$10, a protected area abutting on Parque Nacional Cotopaxi. The train continues to **Latacunga**, where you have a couple of hours until the return trip at 1400. You cannot purchase tickets to board at Latacunga. **Metropolitan Touring** and **Klein Tours**, see above, offer tours involving train travel.

Mitad del Mundo and around *p1045*

Bus From Quito take a 'Mitad del Mundo' feeder bus from La Ofelia station on the Metrobus (transfer ticket US$0.15), this bus continues to the turnoff for Pululahua. An excursion by **taxi** to Mitad del Mundo (with 1 hr wait) is US$25, or US$30 to include Pululahua. Just a ride from La Mariscal costs about US$15.

Directory

Quito *p1036, maps p1037, p1040 and p1043*

Airline offices National: **Aerogal**, Amazonas 607 y Carrión, República de El Salvador y Suiza and booths at Quicentro Shopping and CCI, T294 2800 and 1-800-237642, www.aerogal.com.ec. **Icaro**, JL Mera N26-221 y Orellana, Shyris N34-108 y Holanda, T299 7400, T1-800-883567. **TAME**, Amazonas N24-260 y Colón and 12 de Octubre N24-383 y Baquerizo Moreno, T1-800-500800. **VIP**, sales through Aerogal. **International: Air France/ KLM**, 12 de Octubre N26-27 y Lincoln, T298 6820. **American**, Amazonas 4545 y Pereira and booth at Mall El Jardín, T299 5000. **Avianca**, Bello Horizonte E11-44 y Coruña, T1-800- 003434. **Continental**, 12 de Octubre 1942 y Cordero, World Trade Center, Mezzanine and Naciones Unidas E10-44 y 6 de Diciembre, T225 0905, 1-800-222333. **Copa**, República de El Salvador N31-201 y Moscú, T227 3082. **Delta**, Los Shyris y Suecia, edif Renazzo Plaza PB, T333 1691 T1-800-101080. **Iberia**, Eloy Alfaro 939 y Amazonas, edif Finandes, p 5, T256 6009. **LAN**, Orellana E11-28 y Coruña and Quicentro Shopping, T299 2300, 1-800-101075. **Santa Bárbara**, República de El Salvador 354 y Moscú, T02-227 9650. **TACA**, República de El Salvador N36-139 y Suecia, T292 3170, T1-800-008222. **Banks** The highest concentration of banks and ATMs is in modern Quito. Many are along Av Amazonas, both in La Mariscal and La Carolina, and along Naciones Unidas between Amazonas and Los Shyris. In colonial Quito there are banks near the main plazas. To change TCs, casas de cambio and **Banco del Pacífico**, Naciones Unidas E7-95 y Los Shyris. **Casas de cambio**: All open Mon-Fri 0900-1730, Sat 0900-1245. **Euromoney**, Amazonas N21-229 y Roca, T252 6907. Change 7 currencies, 2% commission for Amex US$ TCs **Mega Cambios**, Amazonas N24-01 y Wilson, T255 5849. 3% commission for US$ TCs, change cash euros, sterling, Canadian dollars. **Vazcorp**, Amazonas N21-147 y Roca, T252 9212. Change 11 currencies, 1.8% comission for US$ TCs, good rates, recommended. **Car hire** All the main car rental companies are at the airport. For multinational rental agencies, see Essentials, page 35. City offices of local companies: **Expo**, Av América N21-66 y Bolívia, T222 8688, T1-800-736822. **Rent 4WD**,12 de Octubre E11-14 y Orellana, p 2, T254 4719, www.rent-4wd.com. 4WD vehicles with driver, from US$170 per day all inclusive. **Simon Car Rental**, Los Shyris 2930 e Isla Floreana, T243 1019, good rates and service. **Achupallas Tours**, T330 1493, www.achupallasturismo.com and **Trans-Rabbit**, T330 1496, both at the international arrivals section of the Airport, rent vans for 8-14 passengers, with driver, for trips in Quito and out of town.

Cultural centres **Alliance Française**, Eloy Alfaro N32-468, T245 2017, www.afquito.org.ec. French courses, films and cultural events. **Casa Humboldt**, Vancouver E5-54 y Polonia, T02-254 8480, www.asociacion-humboldt.org. Goethe Institute, films, theatre, exhibitions. **Centro Cultural Con Manos de Ébano**, 6 de Diciembre N23-43 y Baquedano, T222 8969, www.azucar afroe.com. Cultural events run by Afro- Ecuadorean community, also restaurant.

Damas Norteamericanas y Británicas, 12 de Octubre N26-138 y Orellana, T222 8190, http://damasnyb.com. The Library, Wed-Sat 1000-1200 plus Fri 1500-1700, is an excellent resource, non-members can join, a charitable foundation, deposite required. **Embassies and consulates** **Austria**, Gaspar de Villaroel E9-53 y Los Shyris, p 3, T244 3272, przibra@interactive.net.ec, 1000-1200. **Belgium** (Cooperation office), República de El Salvador 1082 y Naciones Unidas, p 10, T227 6145, www.diplomatie.be/quitoes. Consular affairs handled in Lima. **Canada**, Amazonas N37-29 y Unión Nacional de Periodistas, p 3, T245 5499, www.quito.gc.ca, 0900-1200. **Colombia** (consulate), Atahualpa 955 y República, edif Digicom p 3, T245 8012, consulado enquito@ andinanet.net. 0900-1300 1400-1600. **Finland**, Whimper N30-91 y Coruña, T290 1501. **France**, Plaza 107 y Patria, T294 3800, www.amba france-ec.org. Mon-Thu 0900-1300. 1430-1730, Fri 0830-1330. **Germany**, Naciones Unidas E10-44 y República de El Salvador, edif City Plaza, T297 0820, www.quito.diplo.de. 0830-1130. **Ireland**, Yanacocha y Juan Prócel, El Condado, T600 1166, dominiquekennedy@gmail.com, 0900-1200. **Israel**, Coruña E25-58 y San Ignacio,T397 1500, http://quito.mfa.gov.il, 0900-1300. **Italy**, La Isla 111 y H Albornoz, T256 1077, www.ambitalquito.org. 0830-1230. **Japan**, Amazonas N39-123 y Arízaga, p11, T227 8700, embapon@uio.satnet.net. 0930-1200, 1400-1700. **Netherlands**, 12 de Octubre 1942 y Cordero, World Trade Center, p 1, T222 9229, www.embajadadeholanda.com, 0830-1300, 1400-1730. **Norway**, República de El Salvador 1082 y Naciones Unidas, Ed Mansión Blanca, Torre París, p4, T2461523, knietoconsula donoruega@uio.satnet.net, 0900-1200. **Peru**, República de El Salvador N34-361 e Irlanda, T246 8410, www.embajadadelperu.org.ec, 0900-1300, 1500-1800. **Spain**, La Pinta 455 y Amazonas, T256 4373. 0900-1200. **Sweden**, Almagro N32-27 y Whymper, edif TorrésWhymper p11, T223 3793, vconsuec@uio.satnet.net, Mon-Thu 0930-1230., **Switzerland**, Juan Pablo Sanz 3617 y Amazonas, edif Xerox p 2, T243 4949, www.eda.admin.ch/quito. 0900-1200. **United Kingdom**, Naciones Unidas y República de El Salvador, edif Citiplaza, p 14, T297 0800, britembq@uio.satnet.net. Mon-Thu 0800-1230, 1330- 1600, Fri 0830-1230. **USA**, Av Avigiras E12-170 y Eloy Alfaro, T398 5000, http://ecuador.usembassy.gov/. 0800-1230, 1330-1700.

Internet Quito has very many cyber cafés, particularly in La Mariscal . Rates start at about US$0.60 pe r hr, but US$1 is more typical.

Language schools The following schools have received favourable reports. **In modern Quito**: **Academia de Español Quito**, Marchena Oe1-30 y Av 10 de Agosto, T255 3647, www.academiaquito.edu.ec. **Amazonas**, Washington 718 y Amazonas, edif Rocafuerte, p3, T250 4654, www.eduamazonas.com. **Andean Global Studies**, El Mercurio E10-23 y la Razón, T02-225 4928 www.andeanglobal studies.org. Customized travel-study programs. **Beraca**, Amazonas N24-66 y Pinto, p 2, T290 6642, www.beraca.net. **Bipo & Toni's**, Carrión E8-183 y Plaza, T254 7090, www.bipo.net. **Colón**, Colón Oe2-56 y Versalles, T250 6508, www.colonspanish school.com. Also offer courses in Baños and Otavalo and have a hostel. **Equinox**, Pinzón N25-106 y Colón, T222 6544,

Language schools in Quito

Quito is one of the most important centres for Spanish language study in Latin America with over 80 schools operating. There is a great variety to choose from. Identify your budget and goals for the course: rigorous grammatical and technical training, fluent conversation skills, getting to know Ecuadoreans or just enough basic Spanish to get you through your trip.

Visit a few places to get a feel for what they charge and offer. Prices vary greatly, from US$4 to US$12 per hour, but you do not always get what you pay for. There is also tremendous variation in teacher qualifications, infrastructure and resource materials. Schools usually offer courses of four or seven hours tuition per day. Many correspondents suggest that four is enough. Some schools offer packages which combine teaching in the morning and touring in the afternoon, others combine teaching with travel to various attractions throughout the country. A great deal of emphasis has traditionally been placed on one-to-one teaching, but remember that a well-structured small classroom setting can also be very good.

The quality of homestays likewise varies, the cost including meals runs from US$12 to US$25 per day. Try to book just one week at first to see how a place suits you. For language courses as well as homestays, deal directly with the people who will provide services to you, avoid intermediaries and always get a detailed receipt.

If you are short on time then it can be a good idea to make your arrangements from home, either directly with one of the schools or through an agency, who can offer you a wide variety of options. If you have more time and less money, then it may be more economical to organize your own studies after you arrive. South American Explorers provides a list (free to members) of recommended schools and these may give club members discounts.

We list schools for which we have received positive recommendations each year. This does not imply that schools not mentioned are not recommended.

www.ecuador spanish.com. Small school. **Instituto Superior**, Darquea Terán 1650 y 10 de Agosto, T222 3242, www.instituto-superior.net. Also have schools in Otavalo (Sucre 1110 y Morales, p 2, T06-292 2414) and Galápagos (advanced booking required). **La Lengua**, Colón 1001 y JL Mera, p 8, T250 1271, www.la-lengua.com. Also have a school at Puerto López (book in advance) and offer a 4 week study and travel programme. Recommended. **Mitad del Mundo**, Barrio Ponceano Calle C N71-193 y Calle B, in northern Quito, T254 6827, www.mitadmundo.com.ec. Offer special courses for business, health and other professionals. Repeatedly recommended. **Quito S.I. Spanish Institute**, 9 de Octubre N27-09 y Orellana, T255 0377, www.quito spanish.com. Spanish courses and examination centre for DELE Spanish proficiency diplomas. **Sintaxis**, 10 de Agosto N20-53 y Bolivia, edif Andrade, p 5, T252 0006, www.sintaxis.net. Consistently recommended. **South American**, Amazonas N26-59 y Santa María, T254 2715, www.southamerican.edu.ec. Also have a school in Guayaquil. **Universidad Católica**, 12 de Octubre y Roca, Sección de Español, T299 1700 ext 1388, mejaramillo@puce.edu.ec. **Vida Verde**, Plaza N23-100 y Wilson, T02-222 6635, www.vida verde.com. Part of profits go to support social and environmental projects. **Medical services** Most embassies have the telephone numbers of doctors and dentists who speak non-Spanish languages. **Hospitals: Hospital Voz Andes** Villalengua Oe 2-37 y Av 10 de Agosto, T226 2142 (Trole, la Y stop). Emergency room, quick and efficient, fee based on ability to pay, run by Christian HCJB organization, has out- patient dept, T243 9343. **Hospital Metropolitano**, Mariana de Jesús y Occidental, T226 1520, ambulance T226 5020. Very professional and recommended, but expensive. **Clínica Pichincha**, Veintimilla E3-30 y Páez, T256 2296, ambulance T250 1565. Another very good, expensive hospital. **Clínica Pasteur**, Eloy Alfaro

552 y 9 de Octubre, T223 4004. Also good and cheaper than the above. **Novaclínica Santa Cecilia**, Veintimilla 1394 y 10 de Agosto, T254 5390, emergency T254 5000. Reasonable prices, good. **Med Center Travel Clinic** (Dr John Rosenberg), Foch 476 y Almagro, T252 1104, 09-973 9734. General and travel medicine with a full range of vaccines, speaks English and German, very helpful GP. **Fybeca** is a reliable chain of 33 pharmacies throughout the city. Their 24-hr branches are at Amazonas y Tomás de Berlanga near the Plaza de Toros, and at C C El Recreo in the south. **Post offices** All branches open Mon-Fri 0800-1800, Sat 0800-1200. In principle all branches provide all services, but your best chances are at Colón y Almagro in the Mariscal district, and at the main sorting centre on Japón near Naciones Unidas, behind the CCI shopping centre. The branch on Eloy Alfaro 354 y 9 de Octubre frequently loses mail; best avoided. There is also a branch in the colonial city, on Espejo entre Guayaquil y Venezuela. The branch at Ulloa and Ramírez Dávalos, behind Mercado Santa Clara is the centre for parcel post, and you may be directed there to send large packages. *Poste Restante* at the post offices at Espejo and at Eloy Alfaro (less efficient). All *poste restante* letters are sent to Espejo unless marked 'Correo Central, Eloy Alfaro', but you are advised to check both *postes restantes*, whichever address you use. *South American Explorers* hold mail for members. **Telephones** There are cabins (*cabinas*) all over the city for national and international calls. The latter will be cheaper from internet cafés. There are also debit cardcell phones throughout the city. **Useful addresses** **Emergencies**: T911 for all types of emergency in Quito. **Immigration Offices**: see Planning your trip. **Police**: T101. **Servicio de Seguridad Turística, Policía de Turismo**, Reina Victoria y Roca, T254 3983. Report robberies here. Also at **Fiscalía de Turismo, Ministerio de Turismo**, Eloy Alfaro N32-300 y Tobar, T250 7559 (ext 1018), Public Prosecutors Office, Mon-Fri 0800-1200, 1400-1800.

Around Quito

Papallacta

At the **Termas de Papallacta** ⓘ *64 km east from Quito, 2 km from the town of Papallacta, 0600-2100, T02-256 8989, www.papallacta.com.ec*, the best developed hot springs in the country, are ten thermal pools, three large enough for swimming, and four cold plunge pools. There are two public complexes of springs: the regular pools ⓘ *US$7*, and the spa centre ⓘ *US$17 (massages and other special treatments extra)*. For accommodation, the hotel (**AL**) has heated rooms with private bath (one with private jacuzzi) surrounding small private pools (access only to guests). A set of cabins for families or groups of up to six people (**LL**-**L**), surround more private pools. Guests are provided with identification and can enter any part of the pools; massages and other treatments at the spa centre have 50% discount. Meals are extra. For weekends and holidays book a room at least a month in advance. The complex is tastefully done and recommended. The view, on a clear day, of Antisana while enjoying the thermal waters is superb. There are several self-guided routes in the **Rancho del Cañón** private reserve behind the pools ⓘ *US$2 for use of a short trail, to go on longer walks you are required to take a guide for US$6-15 per person*. To the north of this private reserve is **Reserva Cayambe Coca** ⓘ *T/F02-211 0370, entry US$10*. A scenic road starts by the Termas information centre, crosses both reserves and leads in 45 km to Oyacachi. A permit from Cayambe Coca headquartes (request by fax) is required to travel this road even on foot. It is a lovely 2-day walk, there is a ranger's station and camping area 1½ hours from Papallacta. Reserva Cayambe Coca is also accesed from La Virgen, the pass on the road to Quito. **Fundación Ecológica Rumicocha** ⓘ *T02-321 4833, www.rumicocha.org.ec* offers guiding service. In addition to the Termas there are municipal pools in the village of Papallacta and several more economical places to stay (some with pools) on the road to the Termas and in the village.

Refugio de Vida Silvestre Pasochoa
ⓘ *US$10, very busy at weekends, 45 mins southeast of Quito by car.*
This natural park set in humid Andean forest is run by the **Fundación Natura** ⓘ *Elia Liut N45-10 y El Telégrafo, T227 2863 ext 328, www.fnatura.org*. Situated between 2,700 m and 4,200 m, the reserve has more than 120 species of birds (unfortunately some of the fauna has been frightened away by the noise of the visitors) and 50 species of trees. There are walks of 30 minutes to eight hours. There is a refuge (US$6-10 per person per night, with hot shower and cooking facilities) but take a sleeping bag; camping is US$4 per person. Meals must be requested in advance, or take food and water as there are no shops.

To the western slopes of Pichincha → *Altitude: 1,200-2,800 m.*
Despite their proximity to the capital (two hours from Quito), the western slopes of **Pichincha** and its surroundings are surprisingly wild, with fine opportunities for walking and bird-watching. This scenic area has lovely cloud forests and many nature reserves. The main tourist town in this area is Mindo. To the west of Mindo is a warm subtropical area of clear rivers and waterfalls, where a growing number of tourist developments are springing up.

Paseo del Quinde Two roads go from Quito northwest over the western Cordillera before dropping into the western lowlands. The old, rough route via Rundupamba, Nono (the only town of any size along this route), Alambi and Tandayapa, is dubbed the Paseo del Quinde or **Ecoruta** (Route of the Hummingbird, see www.ecorutadelquinde.org. It begins towards the northern end of Avenida Occidental, Quito's western ring road, at the intersection with Calle Machala. With increased awareness of the need to conserve the cloud forests of the northwest slopes of Pichincha and of their potential for tourism, the number of reserves here is steadily growing. Keen birdwatchers are no longer the only visitors, and the region has much to offer all nature lovers. Infrastructure at reserves varies considerably. Some have comfortable upmarket lodges offering accommodation, meals, guides and transport. Others may require taking your own camping gear, food, and obtaining a permit. There are too many reserves and lodges to mention here; see *Footprint Ecuador* for more details.

At Km 62 on the old road is **Bellavista Cloud Forest Reserve**, a 700-ha private reserve with excellent birdwatching and botany in the cloudforest, There are 20 km of trails ranging from wheelchair access to the slippery/suicidal. See *Hostería Bellavista* below.

The paved route From the Mitad del Mundo monument the road goes past **Calacalí**, whose plaza has an early monument to the Mitad del Mundo. Beyond Calacalí is a toll (US$0.80 for cars) where a road turns south to Nono. Another road at Km 52 goes to Tandayapa and Bellavista. The main paved road, with heavy traffic at weekends, twists as it descends to Nanegalito (Km 56), Miraflores (Km 62), the turn-offs to the old road and to Mindo (Km79), San Miguel de los Bancos, Pedro Vicente Maldonado and Puerto Quito, before joining the Santo Domingo– Esmeraldas road at La Independencia.

Pululahua ⓘ *US$5.* is a geobotanical reserve in an inhabited, farmed volcanic caldera. A few kilometres beyond the Mitad del Mundo, off the paved road to Calacalí, a lookout on the rim gives a great view, but go in the morning, as the cloud usually descends around 1300. If walking, you can get to the reserve and experience the rich vegetation and warm micro-climate inside. From the mirador: walk down 30 minutes to the agricultural zone then turn left. A longer road allows you to drive into the crater via Moraspungo. To walk out this way, starting at the mirador, continue past the village in the crater, turn left and follow the unimproved road up to the rim and back to the main road, a 15-20 km round trip.

Yunguilla ⓘ *T09-114 4610, www.yunguilla.org*, 5 km north of the Calacalí-La Independencia road (turnoff at Km3, opposite the turn for Nono), is a community-run eco-tourism project selling cheese, jam, handicrafts and footballs. It is located at the upper elevation border of Maquipucuna Reserve (see below). It has a cabin (**B**) with shared bath, full board. Also organizes lodging with families (same price) and camping. Access by pick-up from Calacalí US$4, guiding US$25 per day.

In **Nanegalito**, the transport hub for this area is a tourist information office ⓘ *T02-211 6222, Mon-Sun 0900-1700*. Just past the town is the turn-off to Nanegal and the cloud forest in the 18,500-ha **Maquipucuna Biological Reserve**, which contains a tremendous diversity of flora and fauna, including over 325 species of birds. The reserve has 40 km of trails on eight trails of varying length, from 15 minutes to full day (US$10 per person). See Sleeping, below for the lodge. For information: **Fundación Maquipuicuna** ⓘ *www.maqui.org*, which supports reforestation, recuperation of habitats, eg for migratory birds, and aims for a protective corridor linking all areas of the country. Local guides are good and knowledgeable, US$25 (Spanish), US$100 (English) per day for a group of nine.

Next to Maquipucuna is **Santa Lucía** ⓘ *T02-215 7242, www.santaluciaecuador.com*. Access to this reserve is 30 minutes by car from Nanegal. Day tours combining Pululahua, Yunguilla and Santa Lucía are available. Bosque Nublado Santa Lucía is a community-based conservation and eco-tourism project protecting a beautiful 650-ha tract of cloud forest. The area is very rich in birds (there is a Cock-of-the-rock lek) and other wildlife. There are waterfalls and walking trails and a lodge (see below).

At Armenia (Km 60), a few km beyond Nanegalito, a road heads northwest through Santa Elena, with a popular handicrafts market on Sunday, to the village and archaeological site of **Tulipe** (14 km; 1,450m). The site consists of severalr man-made "pools" linked by water channels. Another path leads beside the Río Tulipe in about 15 minutes to a circular pool amid trees. The site museum ⓘ *T02-285 0635, www.fonsal.gov.ec, US$2, Wed-Sun 0900-1600, guided tours in Spanish, tip guide* has exhibits in Spanish on the Yumbos culture and the Colonos (contemporary settlers). There is an orchidarium and a restaurant serving trout lunches, US$5. There are other restaurants in Tulipe.

The Yumbos were traders who linked the Quitus and the coastal civilizations between AD 800-1600. Their trails are called *coluncos*, 1 m wide and 3 m deep, covered in vegetation for coolness. Several treks in the area follow them. Also to be seen are *tolas*, raised earth platforms for housing; there are some 1,500 in four parishes around Tulipe. **Turismo Comunitario Las Tolas** ⓘ *6 km from Tulipe, T02-286 9488, www.lastolas.org*, offers lodging, food, artesanal workshops and guides to *tolas* and *coluncos*. There are some reserves in the area, see www.tulipecloudforest.com and www.cloudforestecuador.com.

Mindo → *Phone code: 02. Colour map 10, A3. Regional population: 2,900. Altitude: 1250 m.*

Mindo, a small town surrounded by dairy farms and lush cloud forest climbing the western slopes of Pichincha, is the main access for the 19,500-ha Bosque Protector Mindo-Nambillo. The town gets very crowded with Quiteños at weekends and holidays. The reserve, which ranges in altitude from 1,400 to 4,780 m, features beautiful flora (many orchids and bromeliads), fauna (butterflies, birds including the cock of the rock, golden-headed quetzal and toucan-barbet) and spectacular cloud forest and waterfalls. The region's rich diversity was threatened in 2010 by proposed mining in the area. **Amigos de la Naturaleza de Mindo** ⓘ *1½ blocks from the Parque Central, T217 0115, US$1, guide US$20 for group of 10*, runs the **Centro de Educación Ambiental** (CEA), 4 km from town, within the 17 ha buffer zone, capacity for 25-30 people. Lodging **E** per person, full board including excursion **B** per person. Take food if you wish to prepare your own (nice kitchen facilities US$1.50). Arrangements have to be made in advance. During the rainy season, access to the reserve can be rough. Mindo also has orchid gardens and butterfly farms. Activities include visits to waterfalls, with rappelling in the La Isla waterfalls, 'canopy', and 'tubing' regattas in the rivers. **Note** There are no ATMs in Mindo, the nearest one is in San Miguel de Los Bancos.

West of Mindo

The road continues west beyond the turn-off to Mindo, descending to the subtropical zone north of Santo Domingo de los Tsáchilas. It goes via San Miguel de los Bancos, Pedro Vicente (PV) Maldonado and Puerto Quito (on the lovely Río Caoni) to La Independencia on the Santo Domingo-Esmeraldas road. The entire area is good for birdwatching, swimming in rivers and natural pools, walking, kayaking, or simply relaxing in pleasant natural surroundings. There are many reserves, resorts, lodgings and places to visit along the route, of particular interest to birdwatchers. There are tours from Quito. See Sleeping, below, for resorts.

Around Quito listings

For Sleeping and Eating price codes and other relevant information, see Essentials, pages 38-40.

Sleeping

Papallacta *p1067*

C-D Antizana, on road to the Termas, a short walk from the complex, T232 0626. Simple rooms, restaurant, cheaper with shared bath, 2 thermal pools , a good option.

D La Choza de Don Wilson, at intersection of old unpaved road and road to Termas, T232 0627. Simple rooms with nice views of the valley, includes breakfast, good popular restaurant, hot water, pool, massage, spa run by physiotherapist, very attentive proprietors.

D-E Coturpa, next to the Municipal baths in Papallacta town, T232 0640. Restaurant open weekends, hot water, thermal pool and sauna, rooms are functional but very small.

East of Papallacta

A Guango Lodge, near Cuyuja, 9 km east of Papallacta, T02-290 9027 (Quito), www.cabanasanisidro.com. In a 350 ha temperate forest reserve along the Río Papallacta. Includes 3 good meals, nice facilities, excellent birdwatching (Grey-breasted Mountain Toucans are regularly seen here). Day visits cost US$5 per person. Reservations required.

To the western slopes of Pichincha *p1068*

Paseo del Quinde

L Tandayapa Bird Lodge, T244 7520 (Quito), www.tandayapa.com. Designed and owned by birders. Full board, 12 very comfortable rooms with hot water, some rooms have a canopy platform for observation, large common area for socializing, packages available including guide and transport from Quito.

AL-A Hostería Bellavista, T211 6232 (Bellavista), in Quito at Jorge Washington E7-25 y 6 de Diciembre, T290 1536, www.bellavista cloudforest.com. A dramatic dome-shaped lodge perched in beautiful cloud forest, includes full board (good food, vegetarian on request), 5 rooms with private bath; **B** pp in dorm, simple accommodation in research area, also a hill cottage away from main building, camping US$7 pp. Package tours can be arranged including transport from Quito and guide, best booked in advance. Recommended.

AL-A San Jorge, T339 0403, www.eco-lodge sanjorge.com. A series of reserves with lodges in bird-rich areas. One is 4 km from Quito (see **Hostería San Jorge**, page 1049), one in Tandayapa at 1500 m and another in Milpe, off the paved road, at 900 m.

The paved route

L-AL Maquipucuna Lodge, T02-250 7200, 09-237 1945, www.maqui.org. Comfortable rustic lodge, includes full board with good meals using ingredients from own organic garden (vegetarian and vegan available). Rooms range from shared to rooms with bath, hot water, electricity. Campsite is 20 mins' walk from main lodge, **G** pp (food extra), cooking lessons, chocolate massages, bar.

AL Santa Lucía, T02-215 7242, www.santaluciaecuador.com. The lodge with panoramic views is a 1½-hr walk from the access to the reserve. Price includes full board with good food and guiding. There are cabins with private bath, rooms with shared composting toilets and hot showers and dorms (**D** per person including food but not guiding).

E Posada del Yumbo, Tulipe, T286 0121, laposadadelyumbo@hotmail.com. Up a side street off the main road. Large property with cabins with bath and river view, also simple rooms (thin walls), some with bath, electric shower, full board available, pool, horse riding. In same family is restaurant **La Aldea**, beside the archaeologic site.

Mindo *p1069*

L Casa Divina, 1.2 km on the road to Cascada de Nambillo, T09-172 5874, www.mindocasa divina.com. Comfortable 2-storey wooden cabins in a lovely location surrounded by 2.7 forested ha, includes breakfast and dinner, rooms with bathtub, bird-guiding extra, US-Ecuadorean run.

L El Monte, 2 km form town on road to Mindo Garden, then opposite Mariposas de Mindo, cross river on tarabita (rustic cable car), T217 0102, Quito T02-255 8881 (Quito), www.ecuador cloudforest.com. Beautifully-constructed lodge in 44-ha property, newer cabins are spacious and very comfortable, lovely bathroom opening onto outside, includes 3 meals, some (but not all) excursions with a native guide and tubing, other adventure sports and horse riding are extra, no electricity, reserve in advance. Recommended.

L-AL El Carmelo de Mindo, 1 km W of town, T217 0109, Quito T02-222 2837, www.mindo. com.ec. Lodge set in a 32-ha reserve. Rooms, cabins on stilts and tree houses surrounded by nice grounds, price includes full board, walk with a native guide and tubing;, river bathing, pool and spa, camping U$10 pp, fishing, horse riding, butterfly farm, cable car under construction in 2009, mid-week discounts.

AL Séptimo Paraíso, 2 km from Calacalí-La Independencia road along Mindo access road, then 500 m right on a small side road, well signed, T09-368 4420, Quito T02-289 3160, www.septimoparaiso.com. All wood lodge in a 420 ha reserve, comfortable, includes breakfast, expensive restaurant, pool and Jaccuzi, parking, lovely grounds, great birdwatching, walking trails, open to non-guests for US$10. Recommended.

B Hacienda San Vicente (Yellow House), 500 m south of the plaza, T217 0124, Quito 02-223 6275, www.yellowhousetrails.com. Family-run lodge set in 200 ha of very rich forest, includes excellent breakfast and dinner, nice rooms, good walking trails open to non-guests for US$5, reservations required, good value. Highly recommended for nature lovers.

B Mindo Garden, 3 km form Mindo on road to CEA, T09-733 1092, Quito T02-225 2077, www.mindogardens.com. Comfortable, tastefully decorated cabins in a beautiful setting by the Río Mindo, includes breakfast, restaurant, parking, good birdwatching in 300-ha property.

C Caskaffesu, Sixto Durán Ballén (the street leading to the stadium) y Av Quito, T217 0100, caskaffesu@yahoo.com. Pleasant hostal with

nice courtyard, includes breakfast, restaurant serves international food, uS-Ecuadorean run.
C El Descanso, 300 m from main street, take 1st right after bridge, T217 0213, www.eldescanso.net. Nice house with comfortable rooms, includes breakfast, cheaper in loft with shared bath, ample parking. Recommended.
D Jardín de los Pájaros, 2 blocks from the main street, 1st right after bridge, T217 0159. Family-run hostel, includes good breakfast, hot water, small pool, parking, large covered terrace, good value. Recommended.
D-E Rubby, by the stadium, T09-340 6321, rubbyhostal@yahoo.com. Well maintained hostal with homey feel, includes breakfast, meals on request, cheaper with shared bath, electric shower, nice balcony with hammocks, good value. English spoken, owner Marcelo Arias is a birding guide.
E Sandy, 1 block from the main street, 1st right after bridge, T217 0212, vinicioperez@andinanet.net. Family run hostel in a wooden house, includes breakfast, hot water, nice, good value.

West of Mindo *p1070*
LL Arashá, 4 km west of PV Maldonado, Km 121, T02-390 0007, 2449881 (Quito) for reservations, www.arasharesort.com. Well run resort and spa with pools, waterfalls (artificial and natural) and hiking trails. Comfortable thatched cabins with good bathrooms, price includes all meals (world class chef), use of the facilities (spa extra) and tours, can arrange transport from Quito, attentive staff, popular with families, elegant and very upmarket.
A Cocoa, 2 km from Puerto Quito on the road to El Achiote which starts at the town bypass, T02-215 6233, Quito T02-252 9297, www.cocoa.com.ec. Wooden lodge with river views in a tropical fruit growing area, includes full board and guided tours, shared bath, porch with hammocks, trails in the forest leading to waterfalls.
A Selva Virgen, at Km 132, east of Puerto Quito, T02-390 1317, www.selvavirgen.com.ec. Nice *hostería* set in a 100 ha property owned by the Universidad Técnica Equinoccial (UTE). The hotel is staffed by students. Includes breakfast, restaurant, spacious comfortable cabins with a/c, fridge, Jacuzzi, and nice porch, cheaper in rooms with ceiling fan, pool, lovely grounds, part of the property is forested and has trails, facilities also open to restaurant patrons.
B Itapoá, 2 km north of the main road, turn-off at Km 142., west of Puerto Quito, T09-478 4992, itapoa_25@hotmail.com. A small lodge within a 12 ha reserve, botanical gardens, tropical fruit farm and native forest, full board and guided tours included, shared bath, owneris a biologist and runs a 100 ha reserve at Río Gualpí in Esmeraldas. Volunteer programmes and 5-day tours available.
D Grand Hotel Puerto Quito, along the highway bypass, T02-215 6363, www.granhotelpuertoquito.com. Pleasant hotel, restaurant, fan, pool and sauna, parking.
E Mirador Río Blanco, San Miguel de los Bancos, main road, at the east end of town, T02-277 0307. Popular hotel/restaurant serving tropical dishes, rooms a bit small, hot water, parking, terrace with bird feeders (many hummingbirds and tanagers) and magnificent views overlooking the river.

Eating

To the western slopes of Pichincha *p1068*
Pululahua
El Cráter, on the rim of the crater, access right along road to the Mirador, T239 6399, open 1200- 1600. Popular upscale restaurant with excellent views. Also has a fancy hotel, www.elcrater.com.

Activities and tours

To the western slopes of Pichincha *p1068*
Pululahua
Horse riding The Green Horse Ranch, Astrid Muller, T08-612 5433, www.horseranch.de. 1- to 9-day rides, among the options is a 3-day ride to **Bellavista**.

Mindo
Mindo Bird, Sector Saguambi, just out of town on the road to CEA, T217 0188, www.mindobird.com, birdwatching, regattas, cycling, hiking, visits to waterfalls, English spoken, very helpful.
Vinicio Pérez, T09-947 6867, www.birdwatchershouse.com, is a recommended birding guide, he speaks some English.

Transport

Papallacta *p1067*

Bus From **Quito**, Terminal Quitumbe, 2 hrs, US$2: some buses take the unpaved road through Papallacta village, if going to the Termas, ask to be let off at the turn-off to the springs before town; it is a 30-min walk up the hill to the complex or a taxi service runs from the road entrance to the termas, US$0.50 shared, US$2 private hire.At the turn-off is Restaurante La Esquina, if the bus stays on the paved road, get off at the intersection with the old road past town, from there a taxi to the Termas is US$2. The Termas also offer a van service fromtheir office in Quito and some 5-star hotels, US$110-180 depending on the number of passengers. Travelling back to Quito at night is not recommended.

Refugio de Vida Silvestre Pasochoa *p1068*

Bus From Quito buses run from Playón de La Marín to Amaguaña US$0.50 (ask the driver to let you off at the 'Ejido de Amaguaña'); from there follow the signs. It's about 8-km walk, with not much traffic except at weekends, or book a pick-up from Amaguaña, about US$6 for up to 3 people. There is a **Movistar** public phone at the information centre (take a debit card) to call **Cooperativa Pacheco Jr** in Amaguaña, T287 7047.

To the western slopes of Pichincha *p1068*

Pululahua

Bus 'Mitad del Mundo' buses from La Ofelia Metrobus terminal end their route just at the turnoff for the Mirador (crater rim); it is a 30 min walk from the turnoff to the rim.

Tulipe

Bus From **Quito**, Estación La Ofelia, from 0615, US$1.50, 1¾ hrs: **Transportes Otavalo**, 6 daily, continue to Pacto (US$2, 2 hrs) and **Transportes Minas** 4 daily, continue to Chontal (US$2.50, 3 hrs). To **Las Tolas**, **Tranporstres Minas**, daily at 1730, US$2, 2½ hrs or take pick-up from Tulipe, US$5.

Mindo *p1069*

Bus From **Quito**, Estación La Ofelia, **Cooperativa Flor del Valle**, T236 4393. Mon-Fri 0800, 0900, 1600, Sat 0740, 0820, 0920, 1600, Sun 0740, 0820, 0920, 1400, 1700. Mindo-Quito: Mon-Fri 0630, 1345, 1500 Sat 0630, 1400, 1530, 1700, Sun 0630, 1400, 1500, 1600, 1700, US$2.50, 2 hrs. Weekend buses fill quickly, buy ahead. You can also take any bus bound for Esmeraldas or San Miguel de los Bancos (see below) and get off at the turn-off for Mindo from where there are taxis until1930, US$0.50 pp or US$3 without sharing. **Cooperativa Kennedy** to/from **Santo Domingo** 6 daily, US$4, 3½ hrs, 0400 service from Mindo continues to **Guayaquil**, US$9, 9 hrs.

West of Mindo *p1070*

From **Quito**, Terminal Carcelén, departures every 30 min (**Coop Kennedy** and associates) to Santo Domingo via: **Nanegalito** (US$1.50, 1½ hrs), **San Miguel de los Bancos** (US$2.50, 2½ hrs), **Pedro Vicente Maldonado** (US$3, 3 hrs) and **Puerto Quito** (US$3.75, 3½ hrs). **Trans Esmeraldas** frequent departures from Terminal Carcelén and from their own station in La Mariscal, Santa María 870, also serve these destinations along the Quito-Esmeraldas route.

Northern Ecuador

The area north of Quito to the Colombian border is outstandingly beautiful. The landscape is mountainous, with views of the Cotacachi, Imbabura, and Chiles volcanoes, as well as the glacier-covered Cayambe, interspersed with lakes. The region is also renowned for its artesanía.

Quito to Otavalo

On the way from the capital to the main tourist centre in northern Ecuador, the landscape is dominated by the Cayambe volcano.

Quito to Cayambe

Calderón, 32 km north of the centre of Quito, is where the famous bread figurines are made. You can see them being made, though not on Sunday, and prices are lower than in Quito, ranging from about US$0.50 to US$10. On 1-2 November, the graves in the cemetery are decorated with flowers, drinks and food for the dead. The Corpus Christi processions are very colourful. Take a feeder bus at La Ofelia Metrobus terminal.

The Pan-American Highway goes to Guayllabamba where it branches, one road goes through Cayambe and the second through Tabacundo before rejoining at Cajas. At 8 km before Cayambe a globe carved out of rock by the Pan-American Highway is at the spot where the French expedition marked the Equator(small shop sells drinks and snacks). A few metres north is **Quitsato** ⓘ *T02-236 3042, www.quitsato.org,* where studies about the equator and its importance to ancient cultures are carried out. There is a sun dial, 54 m in diameter, and the **Museo de la Cultura Solar** with information about native cultures and archaeological sites along the equator, they have special events for the solstices and equinoxes. At 10 km past Guayllabamba and 8 km before Tabacundo, just north of the toll booth, a cobbled road to the left (signed Pirámides de Cochasquí) leads to Tocachi and further on to the **Tolas de Cochasquí** ⓘ *T254 1818, www.pichincha.gov.ec, 0900-1600, US$3, entry only with a 1½ hr guided tour,* archaeological site. The protected area contains 15 truncated clay pyramids, nine with long ramps, built between AD 950 and 1550 by the Cara or Cayambi- Caranqui Indians. Festivals with dancing at the equinoxes and solstices. There is a site museum and views from the pyramids, south to Quito, are marvellous. From Terminal Carcelén, be sure to take a bus that goes on the Tabacundo road and ask to be let off at the turnoff. From there it's a pleasant 8-km walk; if you arrive at the sign around 0800, you could get a lift from the site workers. A taxi from Tabacundo costs US$12 or US$20 round trip with 1½-hour wait, from Cayambe US$15, US$25 round trip.

Cayambe → *Phone code: 02. Colour map 11, A4. Regional population: 60,500.*

Cayambe, on the eastern (righthand) branch of the highway, 25 km northeast of Guayllabamba, is overshadowed by the snow-capped volcano of the same name. The surrounding countryside consists of a few dairy farms and many flower plantations. The area is noted for its *bizcochos* (biscuits) served with *queso de hoja* (string cheese). At the Centro Cultural Espinoza-Jarrín, is the **Museo de la Ciudad** ⓘ *Rocafuerte y Bolívar, Wed-Sun 0800-1700, free* with displays about the Cayambi culture and ceramics found at **Puntiachil**, an important but poorly preserved archaeologic site at the edge of town. There is a *fiesta* in March for the equinox with plenty of local music; also Inti Raymi during the summer solstice blends into the San Pedro celebrations on 29 June. Market day is Sunday, in the traditional plaza up the hill on Calle Rocafuerte.

Volcán Cayambe → *Altitude: 5,790 m.*

Cayambe, Ecuador's third highest peak, lies within the **Reserva Ecológica Cayambe-Coca** (US$10). It's the highest point in the world to lie so close to the Equator (3¼ km north), but the

Northern Ecuador

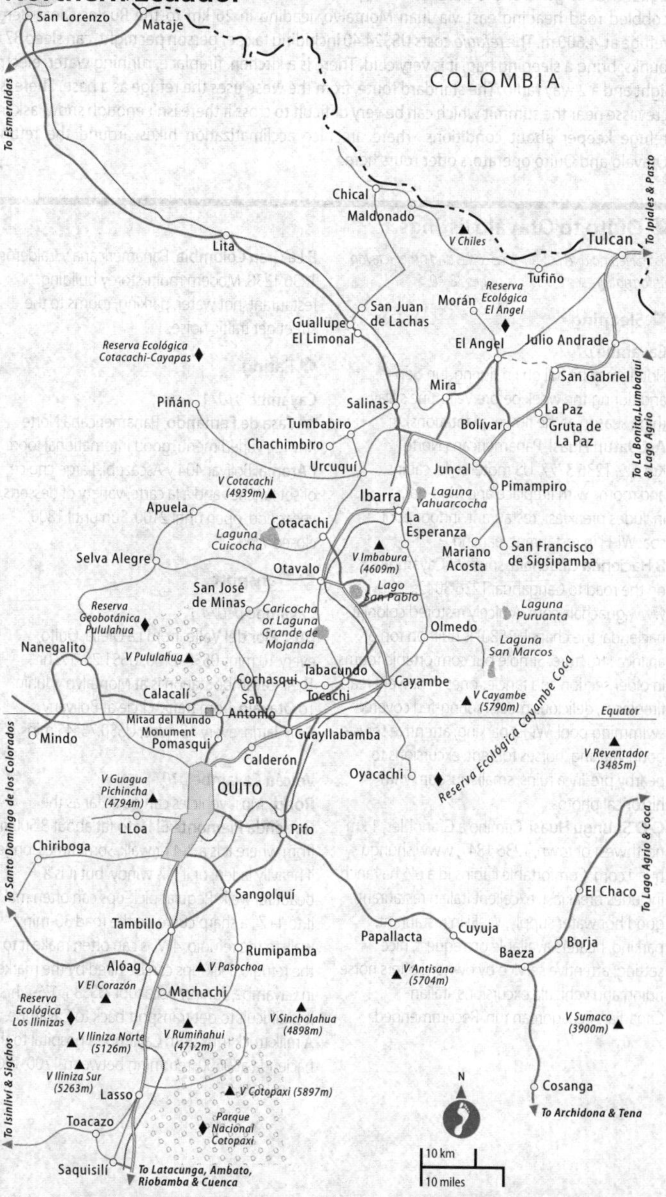

equator does go over the mountain's slope. About 1 km south of Cayambe is an unmarked cobbled road heading east via Juan Montalvo, leading in 26 km to the Ruales-Oleas-Berge refuge at 4,600 m. The *refugio* costs US$24.40 including tax per person per night, can sleep 37 in bunks; bring a sleeping bag, it is very cold. There is a kitchen, fireplace, running water, electric light and a 2 way radio. The standard route, from the west, uses the refuge as a base. There is a crevasse near the summit which can be very difficult to cross if there isn't enough snow, ask the refuge keeper about conditions. There are nice acclimatization hikes around the refuge. Otavalo and Quito operators offer tours here.

Quito to Otavalo listings

For Sleeping and Eating price codes and other relevant information, see Essentials, pages 38-40.

Sleeping

Cayambe *p1074*

Hotels may be full on Fri during Jun-Sep and during the week before Valentine's Day (high season at the flower plantations).

A-C Jatun Huasi, Panamericana Norte Km 1½, T236 3777. US motel style, cabins and rooms with fireplace and frigo-bar, includes breakfast, restaurant, indoor pool, spa, Wi-Fi in restaurant, parking.

B Hacienda Guachalá, south of Cayambe on the road to Cangahua, T236 3042, www.guachala.com. A nicely restored colonial hacienda, the chapel (1580) is built on top of an Inca structure. Simple but comfortable rooms in older section and fancier ones in newer area, fireplaces, delicious meals, spring-fed covered swimming pool, Wi-Fi, parking, attentive service, good walking, horses for rent, excursions to nearby pre-Inca ruins, small museum with historical photos.

C-D Shungu Huasi, Camino a Granobles, 1 km northwest of town, T236 1847, www.shungu huasi.com. Comfortable cabins in a 6½ ha ranch, includes breakfast, excellent Italian restaurant, good hot water supply, Wi-Fi in restaurant, parking, heaters available on request, nice setting, attentive service by owners, offers horse riding and vehicule excursions, Italian-Canadian-Ecuadorean run. Recommended.

E La Gran Colombia, Panamericana y Calderón, T236 1238. Modern multi-storey building, restaurant, hot water, parking, rooms to the street get traffic noise.

Eating

Cayambe *p1074*

TTT Casa de Fernando, Panamericana Norte Km 1.5. Varied menu, good international food.

T Aroma, Bolívar 404 y Ascázubi. Large choice of set lunches and à la carte, variety of desserts, very good, open until 2100, Sun until 1800, closed Wed.

Transport

Cayambe *p1074*

Bus Flor del Valle, from La Ofelia, Quito, every 10 mins 0530-2100, US$1.25, 1½ hrs. Their Cayambe station is at Montalvo y Junín. To **Otavalo**, from traffic circle at Bolívar y Av N Jarrín, every 15 mins, US$0.75, 45 mins.

Volcán Cayambe *p1074*

Road Most vehicles can go as far as the **Hacienda Piemonte El Hato** (at about 3,500 m) from where it is a 3-4 hr walk, sometimes longer if heavily laden, or if it is windy, but it is a beautiful walk. Regular pick-ups can often make it to 'la Z', a sharp curve on the road 30-mins' walk to the refugio. 4WDs can often make it to the refugio. Pick-ups can be hired by the market in Cayambe, Junín y Ascázubi, US$35, 1½-2 hrs. It is difficult to get transport back to Cayambe. A milk truck runs from Cayambe's hospital to the hacienda at 0600, returning between 1700-1900.

Otavalo and around

→ *Phone code: 06. Colour map 11, A4. Population: 60,500. Altitude: 2,530 m.*

Otavalo, only a short distance from the capital, is a must on any tourist itinerary in Ecuador. The main paved road from Cayambe crosses the *páramo* and suddenly descends into the land of the *Otavaleños*, a thriving, prosperous group, famous for their prodigious production of woollens. The town itself, consisting of rather functional modern buildings, is one of South America's most important centres of ethno-tourism and its enormous Saturday market, featuring a dazzling array of textiles and crafts, is second to none and not to be missed. Men here wear their hair long and plaited under a broad-brimmed hat; they wear white, calf-length trousers and blue ponchos. The women's colourful costumes consist of embroidered blouses, shoulder wraps and many coloured beads. Native families speak Quichua at home, although it is losing some ground to Spanish with the younger generation. Otavalo is set in beautiful countryside, with mountains, lakes and small villages nearby. The area is worth exploring for three or four days.

Ins and outs

Tourist offices Contact **iTur** ⓘ *corner of Plaza de Ponchos, Jaramillo y Quiroga, T292 7230, www.visitaotavalo.com, Mon-Fri 0830-1300, 1400-1800, Sat 0900-1400, Sun 0900-1200*, for local and regional information. **Cámara de Turismo** ⓘ *Sucre y Quiroga, p2, T292 1994, www.otavaloturismo. com, Mon-Fri 0900-1300*, has information and pamphlets.

Otavalo

The **Saturday market** comprises four different markets in various parts of the town with the central streets filled with vendors. The *artesanías* market is held 0700-1800, based around the Plaza de Ponchos (Plaza Centenario). The livestock section begins at 0500 until 1000, outside town in the Viejo Colegio Agrícola; go west on Colón from the town centre. The produce market lasts from 0700 till 1400, in Plaza 24 de Mayo. The *artesanías* industry is so big that the Plaza de Ponchos is filled with vendors every day of the week. The selection is better on Saturday but prices are a little higher than other days when the atmosphere is more relaxed. Wednesday is also an important market day with more movement than other weekdays. Polite bargaining is appropriate in the market and shops. Otavaleños not only sell goods they weave and sew themselves, but they bring crafts from throughout Ecuador and from Peru and Bolivia. Indigenous people in the market respond better to photography if you buy something first, then ask politely. The **Instituto Otavaleño de Antropología** ⓘ *At Universidad de Otavalo, Av de los Sarances y Pendoneros, 1 block west of the Panamericana Norte, T292 0321, Mon-Thu 0830-1200, 1430-1800, Fri 0830- 1200, 1430-1700, free,* has a library, an archaeological museum with artefacts from the northern highlands, a collection of musical instruments, and an ethnographic display of regional costumes and traditional activities. **Museo de Tejidos El Obraje** ⓘ *Sucre 6-08 y Olmedo, T292 0261, US$2, Mon-Sat 0900-1200, 1500-1800,* shows the process of traditional Otavalo weaving from shearing to final products.

Around Otavalo

Otavalo weavers come from dozens of communities. In all these villages many families weave and visitors should shop around as the less known families often have better prices. The easiest villages to visit are Ilumán (there are also many felt hatmakers in town and *yachacs*, or shamen, mostly north of the plaza – look for signs); Agato; Carabuela (many homes sell crafts including wool sweaters); Peguche. These villages are only 15-30 minutes away and all have a good bus service; buses leave from the Terminal and stop at Plaza Copacabana (Atahualpa y Montalvo). You can also take a taxi. Allow 1-1½ hours each way.

To reach the lovely **Cascada de Peguche**, from Peguche's plaza, facing the church, head right and continue straight until the road forks. Take the lower fork to the right, but not the road that heads downhill. From the top of the falls (left side, excellent views) you can continue the walk to Lago San Pablo. The *Pawkar Raimi* festival is held in Peguche during carnival. At the falls there is a small information centre (contributions are appreciated).

Lago San Pablo

There is a network of old roads and trails between Otavalo and Lago San Pablo, none of which takes more than two hours to explore. It is worth walking either to or back from the lake for the views. Going in a group is recommended for safety. A nice half-day excursion is via Cascada de Peguche, **Parque Cóndor** ⓘ *on a hill called Curiloma, near the community of Pucará Alto, T292*

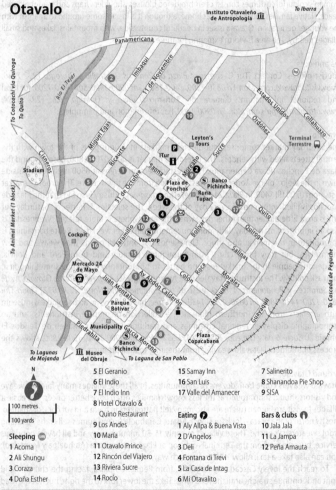

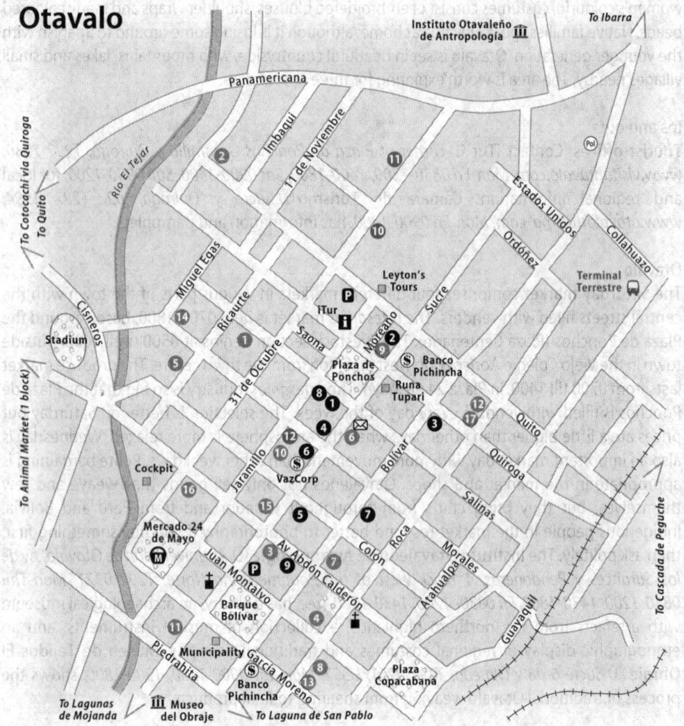

N

100 metres
100 yards

Sleeping
1 Acoma
2 Ali Shungu
3 Coraza
4 Doña Esther
5 El Geranio
6 El Indio
7 El Indio Inn
8 Hotel Otavalo & Quino Restaurant
9 Los Andes
10 María
11 Otavalo Prince
12 Rincón del Viajero
13 Riviera Sucre
14 Rocío
15 Samay Inn
16 San Luis
17 Valle del Amanecer

Eating
1 Aly Allpa & Buena Vista
2 D'Angelos
3 Deli
4 Fontana di Trevi
5 La Casa de Intag
6 Mi Otavalito
7 Salinerito
8 Shanandoa Pie Shop
9 SISA

Bars & clubs
10 Jala Jala
11 La Jampa
12 Peña Amauta

4429, www.parquecondor.org, Tue-Sun 0930-1700, raptor flight demonstrations at 1100, 1500 and 1600, US$3, crowded on weekends*, a reserve and birds of prey rehabilitation centre, and back via **El Lechero**, a lookout by a tree considered sacred among indigenous people. From **San Pablo del Lago** it is possible to climb **Imbabura** volcano (4,630 m, frequently under cloud), allow at least six hours to reach the summit and four hours for the descent. An alternative access is from La Esperanza (see below). Easier, and no less impressive, is the nearby Cerro Huarmi Imbabura, 3,845 m, it is not signed but several paths lead there. Take a good map, food and warm clothing.

Otavalo and around listings

For Sleeping and Eating price codes and other relevant information, see Essentials, pages 38-40.

Sleeping

Otavalo *p1077, map p1078*

In town

Hotels may be full on Fri night before market.

B Ali Shungu, Quito y Miguel Egas, T292 0750, www.alishungu.com. Nicely decorated hotel with lovely garden, comfortable rooms, good restaurant with live music on weekends, parking, no smoking, safe deposit boxes, can arrange transport from Quito, credit cards only accepted over the internet using Paypal, surcharge for credit cards and TCs, US run. Recommended.

B El Indio Inn, Bolívar 9-04 y Calderón, T292 2922, www.hotelelindioinn.com. Attractive hotel, includes breakfast, restaurant, parking, carpeted rooms and suites, spotless.

C Acoma, Salinas 07-57 y 31 de Octubre, T292 6570, www.hotelacoma.com. Lovely modern hotel built in colonial style, includes breakfast, cafeteria, cheaper with shared bath, parking, nice comfortable rooms, some with balcony, one room with bathtub, 2 suites with kitchenette B.

C Coraza, Calderón y Sucre, T292 1225, www.hotelcoraza.com. Modern hotel, includes breakfast, good restaurant, Wi-Fi, nice rooms, quiet and comfortable. Recommended.

C Doña Esther, Montalvo 4-44 y Bolívar, T292 0739, www.otavalohotel.com. Nicely restored colonial house, restaurant downstairs, sparsely furnished rooms with nice wooden floors, colourful décor.

C Hotel Otavalo, Roca 5-04 y J Montalvo, T292 3712. Refurbished colonial house, includes good breakfast, restaurant offers set meals, large rooms, patio, good service, helpful, a bit pricey.

D El Indio, Sucre 12-14 y Salinas, near Plaza de Ponchos, T292 0060. In multi-storey building, breakfast, restaurant, hot water, helpful service.

D Riviera Sucre, García Moreno 380 y Roca, T292 0241, www.rivierasucre.com. Older hotel renovated in 2009, ample rooms, good breakfast, cafeteria, 1 room with shared bath **E**, hot water, laundry facilities, book exchange, nice garden, good meeting place.

D-E Rincón del Viajero, Roca 11-07 y Quiroga, T292 1741, www.hostalrincondelviajero.com. Very pleasant hostel and meeting place. Simple but nicely decorated rooms, includes a choice of good breakfasts, cheaper with shared bath, hot water, Wi-Fi, laundry facilities, parking, rooftop hammocks and pool table, sitting room with fireplace, camping, US-Ecuadorean run, good value. Recommended.

E Los Andes, Sucre y Quiroga by Plaza de Ponchos, T292 1057. Modern building, cheaper with shared bath, hot water, simple small rooms, good value.

E Otavalo Prince, Sucre 7-05 y García Moreno, near Parque Bolívar, T292 2540. Modern hotel, hot water, comfortable rooms, can be a bit noisy at the front.

E Rocío, Morales y Egas, T292 0584. Cheaper with shared bath, hot showers, helpful, popular, good value. Also offers cabañas at the edge of town.

E Samay Inn, Sucre 10-09 y Colón, T292 1826, www.samayinnhotel.com. Nice modern hotel, hot water, small comfortable rooms.

E San Luis, Abdón Calderón 6-02 y 31 de Octubre, T292 0614. Cheaper with shared bath, hot water, basic, family run.

E Valle del Amanecer, Roca y Quiroga, T292 0990, www.hostalvalledelamanecer.com. Small rooms around a nice courtyard, includes breakfast, hot water, popular, bike hire.

F El Geranio, Ricaurte y Morales, T292 0185, hgeranio@hotmail.com. Breakfast available, cheaper with shared bath, electric shower, laundry and cooking facilities, quiet, family run, helpful, popular, runs trips. Good value, recommended.

F María, Jaramillo y Colón, T292 0672. Modern multi-storey building, hot water, parking for small car, bright rooms. Very good value, recommended.
G Camping, in Punyaro, Km 2 vía a Mojanda. US$3 per person, Camping area in a rural property, hot shower and Wi-Fi, arrange through Rincón del Viajero, above.

Out of town

L Ali Shungu Mountaintop Lodge, 5 km west of Otavalo by the village of Yambiro, T292 0750, www.alishungumountaintoplodge.com. Country inn on a 16 ha private reserve. Four comfortable nicely decorated guest houses with capacity for 6, each with living room and kitchenette. Includes full board, vegetarian available, arrangements through Hotel Ali Shungu in Otavalo.
L Casa Mojanda, Vía a Mojanda Km 3.5, T09-972 0890, www.casamojanda.com. Comfortable cabins set in a beautiful gorge. Includes breakfast and tasty dinner prepared with ingredients from own organic garden and short guided hike to waterfall, each room is decorated with its own elegant touch, outdoor hot tub with great views, quiet, good library, horse riding. Recommended.
AL Hacienda Pinsaquí, Panamericana Norte Km 5, 300 m north of the turn-off for Cotacachi, T294 6116, www.haciendapinsaqui.com. Converted hacienda with 20 suites, some with Jacuzzi, includes breakfast, restaurant with lovely dining room, Wi-Fi, lounge with fireplace, beautiful antiques, colonial ambience, gardens, horse riding, biking.
A Las Palmeras de Quichinche, outside Quichinche, 15 minutes by bus from Otavalo, T292 2607, www.laspalmerasinn.com. Cabins and rooms with terrace and fireplace in a rural setting, includes breakfast, restaurant, Wi-Fi, parking, nice grounds and views, pool table and ping-pong, English owned.
B La Casa de Hacienda, Entrance at Panamericana Norte Km 3, then 300 m east, T269 0245, www.casadehacienda.com. Tasteful cabins with fireplace, includes breakfast, restaurant serves Ecuadorean and international food, parking, advance reservations required for horse riding.
D-E La Luna de Mojanda, On a side-road going south off the Mojanda road at Km 4, T09-315 6082, www.hostallaluna.com. Pleasant country hostel in nice surroundings, some rooms with fireplace and private bath, others shared, cheaper in dorm, terrace with hammocks, pleasant dining room-lounge, restaurant, hot water, parking, camping possible, taxi from Otavalo US$4, bus information on hostel's web site, excursions arranged, popular. Recommended.

Around Otavalo: Peguche *p1077*

A La Casa Sol, near the Cascada de Peguche, T269 0500, www.lacasaandina.com. Hacienda-style modern hotel built on a hillside. Rooms and suites with balcony, some with fireplace, lovely attention to detail, price includes breakfast and dinner, restaurant.
D Aya Huma, on the railway line in Peguche, T269 0164, www.ayahuma.com. In a country setting between the unused rail tracks and the river. Restaurant, hot water, quiet, pleasant atmosphere, live music Sat night, Dutch run, popular. Recommended.

Lago San Pablo *p1078*

AL Cusín, by the village of San Pablo del Lago to the southeast of the lake, T291 8013, www.haciendacusin.com. A converted 17th century hacienda with lovely courtyard and garden, includes breakfast, fine expensive restaurant, Wi-Fi, 25 rooms with fireplace, sports facilities (pool, horses, bikes, squash court, games room), library, book in advance, British run. Recommended.
A Puerto Lago, 6 km from Otavalo, just off the Panamericanaon the west side of the lake, T292 0920, www.puertolago.com. Modern hostería in a lovely setting on the lakeshore, good expensive restaurant overlooking the lake, Wi-Fi, rooms and suites with fireplace, very hospitable, a good place to watch the sunset, includes the use of row-boats, pedalos and kayaks, other water sports extra.

Eating

Otavalo *p1077, map p1078*

TT Fontana di Trevi, Sucre 12-05 y Salinas, 2nd floor, 1130-2200. Overlooking Calle Sucre, good pizza and pasta, nice juices, friendly service.
TT Quino, Roca 7-40 y Juan Montalvo, Tue-Sun 1030-2300, Mon1730-2300. Traditional coastal cooking and some meat dishes, pleasant seating around patio.

ΨΨ-Ψ **Buena Vista**, Salinas entre Sucre y Jaramillo, www.buenavistaotavalo.com, 1200-2200, Sat from 0800, closed Tue. Bistro with balcony overlooking Plaza de Ponchos. International food, sandwiches, salads, vegetarian options, trout, good coffee, Wi-Fi.

ΨΨ-Ψ **Deli**, Quiroga 12-18 y Bolívar, Sun-Thu 1100-2000, Fri 1100-2200, Sat 0800-2200. Small place serving good Mexican and international food, also pizza, nice desserts, good value.

ΨΨ-Ψ **SISA**, Abdón Calderón 4-09 y Sucre. Good cultural centre, restaurant, bookstore and cinema, closed for renovations in early 2010.

Ψ **Aly Allpa**, Salinas 509 at Plaza de Ponchos. Good value set meals, breakfast and à la carte including trout, vegetarian, meat. Recommended.

Ψ **D'Angelos**, Sucre y Quito, daily 1000-2200. Very good pizza and lasagna, good service.

Ψ **Mi Otavalito**, Sucre y Morales. Good for set lunch and international food à la carte.

Cafés

La Casa de Intag, Colón 465 y Sucre, Mon-Sat 0800-2000, Sun 0900-2000. Fair trade cafeteria/shop run by Intag coffee growers and artisans associations. Good organic coffee, breakfast, pancakes, salads, sandwiches, sissal crafts, fruit pulp and more.

Salinerito, Bolívar 10-08 y Morales, daily 0800-2200. Café/deli run by the Salinas de Guaranda coop. Good sanwiches, breakfast, coffee and juices. A good place to buy supplies such as cheese, coldcuts and chocolate.

Shanandoa Pie Shop, Salinas y Jaramillo, 1100-2100, Sat from 0900. Good pies, milk shakes and ice-cream, popular meeting place, book exchange.

Bars and clubs

Otavalo *p1077, map p1078*

Otavalo is generally safe but avoid deserted areas at night. Nightlife is concentrated at C 31 de Octubre. Peñas are open Fri-Sat from 1930, entrance US$3.

Peña Amauta, Morales 5-11 y Jaramillo. Good local bands, welcoming, mainly foreigners.

Jala Jala, 31 de Octubre y Quito. Live dancing music on Fri and Sat night.

La Jampa, 31 de Octubre y Panamericana, www.lajampa.com. Andean and dancing music, popular with Ecuadoreans and foreigners.

Festivals and events

Otavalo *p1077, map p1078*

The **end of Jun** combines the **Inti Raymi** celebrations of the summer solstice (**21 Jun**), with the **Fiesta de San Juan** (**24 Jun**) and the **Fiesta de San Pedro y San Pablo** (**29 Jun**). These combined festivities are known as **Los San Juanes** and participants are mostly indigenous. Most of the action takes place in the smaller communities surrounding Otavalo, each one celebrates separately on different dates (www.otavaloturismo.com posts schedule), some of them for a full week. The celebration begins with a ritual bath, the Peguche waterfall is used by Otavalo residents (a personal spiritual activity, best carried out without visitors and certainly without cameras). In Otavalo, indigenous families have costume parties, which at times spill over onto the streets. In the San Juan neighbourhood, near the Yanayacu baths, there is a week-long celebration with food, drink and music. **Fiesta del Yamor** and **Colla Raimi 1st 2 weeks of Sep**, local dishes are cooked, amusement parks are set up, bands in the plaza and there are sporting events. **Oct Mes de la cultura**, cultural events throughout the month. **30 or 31 Oct Mojanda Arriba** is an annual hike from Malchinguí over Mojanda to reach Otavalo for the foundation celebrations. Participants are bused from Quito and Otavalo to the start at 0400.

Activities and tours

Otavalo *p1077, map p1078*

Mountain bikes Several tour operators rent bikes and offer cycling tours for US$35-60 a day trip. **Hostal Valle del Amanecer** (see Sleeping), US$8 per day. **La Tierra** craft shop, Salinas 503 y Sucre, Plaza de Ponchos, good equipment.

Taller Ciclo Primaxi, Atahualpa 2-49 y García Moreno and at the entrance to Peguche, good bikes, US$1 per hr.

Horse riding Several operators offer riding tours. Half-day trips to nearby attractions cost US$20-25. Full day trips such as Cuicocha or Mojanda run US$35-40.

Tour operators

Most common tours are to native communities, Cuicocha and Mojanda, US$20-30 pp. Independent travel to the Lagunas de Mojanda is not recommended because of armed robbery and public safety problems. Only go with a tour.

All about EQ, Los Corazas 433 y Albarracín, at the north end of town, T292 3633, www.all-about-ecuador.com. Interesting itineraries, trekking and horse riding tours, climbing, cycling, trips to Intag, Piñán, Cayambe, Oyacachi, rafting and kayaking on the Río Intag. English and French spoken, guides carry radios. Recommended.

Chachimbiro Tours, Los Corazas 433 y Albarracín, T292 3633, www.chachimbiro.com. Trips to the Termas Hostería Chachimbiro 1 hr northwest of Otavalo.

Ecomontes, Sucre y Morales, T292 6244, www.ecomontestour.com. A branch of a Quito operator, trekking, climbing, rafting, also sell tours to Cuyabeno and Galápagos.

Leyton's Tours, Quito y Jaramillo, T292 2388. Horseback and bike tours.

Runa Tupari, Sucre y Quiroga, Plaza de Ponchos T292 5985, www.runatupari.com. Arranges indigenous homestays in the Cotacachi area, also the usual tours, trekking, horse riding and cycling trips.

Zulaytur, Sucre y Colón, p 2, T292 2791, www.geocities.com/zulaytur. Day trips to artisans' communities, Mojanda, Imbabura, horse riding.

Transport

Otavalo *p1077, map p1078*

Note: Never leave anything in your car or taxi, There are public car parks at Juan Montalvo y Sucre, by Parque Bolívar, and on Quito between 31 de Octubre and Jaramillo.

Bus Terminal at Atahualpa y Ordóñez (see map). To **Quito** 2½ hrs, US$2, every 10 mins; all depart from the Terminal Carcelén in Quito, **Coop Otavalo** and **Coop Los Lagos** go into Otavalo, buses bound for Ibarra or Tulcán drop you off at the highway, this is not safe at night. From **Quito** by taxi takes 1½ hrs, US$50 one way, US$80 return with 3 hours wait; shared taxis with **Taxis Lagos** (in Quito, Asunción y Versalles T256 5992; in Otavalo, Roca 8-04, T292 3203) who run a hotel to hotel service (to/from modern Quito only) and will divert to resorts just off the highway; hourly Mon-Fri 0700-1900, Sat 0700-1600, Sun 0800-1800, 2 hrs, US$7.50 pp, buy ticket the day before, they continue to Ibarra. Bus to **Ibarra**, every 5 mins, US$0.50, 45 mins. To **Peguche**, city bus on Av Atahualpa, every 10 mins, bus stops in front of the terminal and at Plaza Copacabana, US$0.20. To the **Intag region**, 5 daily.

Lago San Pablo *p1078*

Bus From **Otavalo**-San Pablo del Lago every 25 mins, more often on Sat, US$0.25, 30 mins; taxi US$4.

Directory

Otavalo *p1077, map p1078*

Banks **Banco del Austro**, Sucre y Quiroga. **Banco del Pacífico**, Bolívar 614 y García Moreno. **Fax Cambios**, Salinas y Sucre, T292 0501, Mon-Sat 0745-1900, poor rates for cash

(7 currencies), 3% commission on TCs. **Vaz Corp**, Sucre 11-13 y Morales, T292 3500, Tue-Sat 0830-1700, exchange 8 currencies, 1.8% comission on TCs (minimum US$2).

Internet Prices about US$1 per hr. Many in town, specially on C Sucre. **Language schools** Instituto Superior de Español, Sucre 11-10 y Morales, p 3, T299 2414, www.instituto-superior.net. **Mundo Andino Internacional**, Salinas 404 y Bolívar, T292 1864, www.mandinospanishschool.com. Salsa and cooking classes included. **Otavalo Spanish Institute**, 31 de Octubre 47-64 y Salinas, p 3, T292 1404, www.otavalospanish.com, also offers Quichua lessons. **Post offices** Corner of Plaza de Ponchos, entrance on Sucre, 1st floor, Mon-Fri 0700-1500, Sat 0800-1200.

Otavalo to the Colombian border

Northwest of Otavalo is Cotacachi from where a road goes west to the Cotacachi-Cayapas reserve and the subtropical Intag region. The main highway goes north to the city of Ibarra and beyond into the hotl Chota Valley from where a branch road goes west to the subtropical valley of the Río Mira and the coastal town of San Lorenzo. The Panamericana reaches the border at the busy town Tulcán, with its fantastic topiary.

Cotacachi

West of the road between Otavalo and Ibarra is Cotacachi, where leather goods are made and sold. There is also access along a paved road from Otavalo through Quiroga. The **Casa de las Culturas** ⓘ *Bolívar 1334 y 9 de Octubre, T291 5140*, a beautifully refurbished 19th century building is a monument to peace. It houses a library, internet café, temporary exhibits and shows. Municipal information office, **iTur** ⓘ *being relocated in 2010, T291 5086, ext 109, www.cotacachi.gov.ec*. The **Museo de las Culturas** ⓘ *García Moreno 13-41 y Bolívar, T291 5945, Mon-Fri 0900-1200, 1400-1700, Sat 1400-1700, Sun 1000-1300, US$1*, has good displays about early Ecuadorean history, regional crafts and traditions (some English explanations). Local festivals include *Inti Raymi/San Juan* in June and *Jora* during the September equinox.

Laguna Cuicocha → *Altitude: 3,070 m.*

ⓘ *15 km from Cotacachi. US$1 to visit the lake and visitor centre, which has good natural history and cultural displays. US$5 park fee must be paid if going on longer hikes into the national park.*

The area is part of the **Reserva Ecológica Cotacachi-Cayapas**, which extends from Cotacachi volcano to the tropical lowlands on the Río Cayapas in Esmeraldas. This is a crater lake with two islands, although these are closed to the public for biological studies. There is a well-marked, 8-km path around the lake, which takes 4-5 hours and provides spectacular views of the Cotacachi, Imbabura and, occasionally, Cayambe peaks. The best views are in the morning, when condors can sometimes be seen. There is lookout at 3 km, two hours from the start. It's best to go anticlockwise; take water and a waterproof jacket. Motor boat rides around the islands, US$2.25 per person for minimum eight persons.

Warnings Enquire locally about safety before heading out and don't take valuables. Do not eat the berries which grow near the lake, as some are poisonous. The path around the lake is not for vertigo sufferers.

To the northwest of Otavalo lies the lush subtropical region of **Intag**, reached along a road that follows the southern edge of Cuicocha and continues to the town of **Apuela**. (See **Defensa y Conservación Ecológica de Intag** (Decoin), www.decoin.org, for conservation through community projects.) The **Asociación Agroartesanal de Café Río Intag** (AACRI) ⓘ *on the main street opposite the health centre, T06-264 8489, www.consorciotoisan.org*, a fair trade organic coffee grower's association, offers tours of coffee, sisal and sugar cane plantations and processing plants, also lodging and volunteer opportunities. Beyond, are pleasant thermal baths at **Nangulví**. The area is rich in cloudforest and has several nature reserves. On the southwest boundary of the Cotacachi-Cayapas reserve is **Los Cedros Research Station** ⓘ *T08-460 0274, www.reservaloscedros.org*, 6,400 ha of pristine cloudforest, with abundant orchids and bird life. Full board in **a** range.

Ibarra and around → *Phone code: 06. Colour map 11, A4. Pop: 137,000. Altitude: 2,225 m.*
Once a pleasant colonial town (founded in 1606), Ibarra has grown to become the main commercial centre of the northern highlands. The city has an interesting ethnic mix, with blacks from the Chota valley and Esmeraldas alongside Otavaleños and other highland *indígenas*, mestizos and Colombian immigrants. **Dirección de Turismo de Imbabura** ⓘ *Bolívar y Oviedo, T295 5832, www.imbaburaturismo.gov.ec, Mon-Fri 0800-1300, 1500-1800*, is helpful. In the same building **Ecored Sierra Norte** ⓘ *T295 5225, ecored_sierranorte@yahoo.es*, represents 10 different community tourism projects in northern Ecuador. Municipal tourist office, **i-Tur** ⓘ *Sucre y Oviedo, T260 8489, www.ibarraturismo.com, free Wi-Fi*.

On **Parque Pedro Moncayo** stand the Cathedral, the Municipio and Gobernación. One block away is the smaller Parque 9 de Octubre, at Flores y Olmedo, more commonly called **Parque de la Merced** after its church. A walk down Pérez Guerrero leads to the large covered **Mercado Amazonas** ⓘ *on Cifuentes, by the railway station, daily, busiest Sat and Sun*. The **Museo Regional Sierra Norte** ⓘ *Sucre 7-21 y Oviedo, T260 2093, Mon-Fri, 0830-1700, Sat 1000-1300, 1400-1600, US$1*, run by the Banco Central, has interesting displays about cultures from northern Ecuador. Virgen del Carmen festival is on 16 July and Fiesta de los Lagos is in the last weekend of September, Thursday-Sunday.

Off the main road between Otavalo and Ibarra is **San Antonio de Ibarra**, well known for its wood carvings. It is worth seeing the range of styles and techniques and shopping around in the galleries and workshops. Buses leave from Mercado Amazonas, 13 km, 10 minutes, US$0.20. About 8 km from Ibarra on the road to Olmedo is **La Esperanza**, a pretty village in beautiful surroundings. Some 15 km further along, by Angochagua is the community of **Zuleta**. The region is known for its fine embroidery. West of La Esperanza, along a road that starts at Avenida Atahualpa, and also 8 km from Ibarra, is the community of **San Clemente**, which has a very good grassroots tourism project, **Pukyu Pamba**, see Sleeping below. From either La Esperanza or San Clemente you can climb **Cubilche** volcano and **Imbabura**, more easily than from San Pablo del Lago. From the top you can walk down to Lago San Pablo (see page 1078). Native guides are available for these climbs.

Ibarra to the coast The spectacular train ride from Ibarra to San Lorenzo on the Pacific coast no longer operates. A tourist train runs on a small section of this route, see page 1090.

Some 24 km north of Ibarra is the turn-off west for **Salinas**, a mainly Afro-Ecuadorean village with a **Museo de la Sal**, and the very scenic paved road along the Río Mira down to San Lorenzo. At 41 km from the turn-off are the villages of **Guallupe**, **El Limonal** (see Sleeping, below), and **San Juan de Lachas**, in a lush subtropical area. Ceramic masks and figurines are produced at the latter. In **Lita**, 33 km from Guallupe, there is nice swimming in the river. Beyond is the Río Chuchubi with waterfalls and swimming holes; here is **Las Siete Cascadas** ⓘ *entry US$10* resort (see Sleeping below). It is 66 km from Lita to **Calderón**, where this road meets the coastal highway coming from Esmeraldas. Two kilometres before the junction, on the Río Tululbí, is **Hostería Tunda Loma** (see San Lorenzo Sleeping). About 7 km beyond is San Lorenzo (see page 1169).

Northwest of Ibarra Along a secondary road to the northwest of Ibarra is the pretty town of **Urcuquí** with a basic hotel. Urcuquí is one of the access points to the **Piñán lakes**, a beautiful, remote, high *páramo* region, part of the Reserva Ecológica Cotacachi-Cayapas. The local community of Piñán has a tourism programme (www.pinantrek.com), with a well equipped refuge (US$10 pp), native guides (US$15 per day) and muleteers1(US$12 per day, per horse). The lakes are one-hour walk from Piñán. They can also be reached from the community of Sachapamba which offers meals and muleteers and from Cuellaje in the Intag area. Otavalo agencies and Chachimbiro hotels also offer trekking tours to Piñán. Beyond Urcuquí is **Tumbabiro** which is just opening up to tourism (several lodgings, see Sleeping below). The area has great potential for linking the local communities to the wildlife reserves that surround it. Some 8 km from Tumbabiro, along a side road is **Termas Hostería Chachimbiro** ⓘ *entry to recreational pools US$3.50, to medicinal pools and spa US$6, www.chachimbiro.com*, with clean hot mineral pools, lodging and restaurants (see Sleeping); weekends can be crowded. Tours and reservations through Chachimbiro Tours in Otavalo (see above).

North to Colombia

From Ibarra the Pan-American highway goes past Laguna Yahuarcocha (with a few hotels and restaurants) and then descends to the hot dry Chota valley, a centre of Afro-Ecuadorean culture. Beyond the turn-off for Salinas and San Lorenzo, 30 km from Ibarra, is a police checkpoint at **Mascarilla**: have your documents at hand. After Mascarilla the highway divides. One branch follows an older route through Mira and El Angel to Tulcán on the Colombian border. At Mascarilla village, 1 km along this road, ceramic masks are made (hostal run by the women's craft group, **El Patio de mi Casa**, 09-449 4029, **C** full-board). This road is paved and in good condition as far as **El Angel** (3,000 m), but deteriorates thereafter. It is passable with 4WD and is a great mountain bike route.

El Angel's main plaza retains a few trees sculpted by José Franco (see Tulcán Cemetery, below); market day Monday. The **Reserva Ecológica El Angel** ⓘ *T/F297 7597, US$10, office in El Angel near the Municipio, information available; best time to visit the reserve May to Aug*, nearby protects 15,715 ha of *páramo* ranging in altitude from 3,400 to 4,768 m. The reserve contains large stands of the velvet-leaved *frailejón* plant, also found in the Andes of Colombia and Venezuela. Also of interest are the spiny *achupallas* with giant compound flowers. The fauna includes *curiquingues* (caracara), deer, foxes, and a few condors. From El Angel follow the poor road north towards Tulcán for 16 km to **El Voladero** ranger station, where a self-guided trail climbs over a low ridge (30 minutes' walk) to two crystal-clear lakes. Pickups or taxis from the main plaza of El Angel charge US$25 return with one-hour wait for a day trip to El Voladero. A longer route to another area follows an equally poor road to Cerro Socabones, beginning at **La Libertad**, 3½ km north of El Angel (transport El Angel-Cerro Socabones, US$30 return). It climbs gradually to reach the high *páramo* at the centre of the reserve and, in 40 minutes, the **El Salado** ranger station. From Socabones the road descends to the village of **Morán** (lodging and guides, transport with Sr Calderón, T09-128 4022).

Eastern route to the border

The second branch (the modern Pan-American Highway), in good repair but with many heavy lorries, runs east through the warm Chota valley to El Juncal, before turning north to reach Tulcán via Bolívar and San Gabriel. A good paved road runs between Bolívar and El Angel, connecting the two branches.

Bolívar is a neat little town where the houses and the interior of its church are painted in lively pastel colours. There is a Friday market.

Some 16 km north of Bolívar is **San Gabriel**, an important commercial centre. The nice 60-m high **Paluz** waterfall is 4 km north San Gabriel, beyond a smaller waterfall. Follow C Bolívar out of the main plaza and turn right after the bridge, or take a taxi (US$6.50). To the southeast, 11 km from town on the road to Piartal is **Bosque de Arrayanes**, a 16-ha primary forest with a predominace of myrtle trees, some reaching 20 m, taxi US$5.

East of San Gabriel by 20 km is the tiny community of **Mariscal Sucre**, also known as Colonia Huaqueña, the gateway to the **Guandera Reserve and Biological Station** ⓘ *the reserve is part of the Fundación Jatun Sacha. Reservations should be made at Pasaje Eugenio de Santillán N34- 248 y Maurián, Quito, T02-331 7163, www.jatunsacha.org*. You can see bromeliads, orchids, toucans and other wildlife in temperate forest and *frailejón páramo*. From San Gabriel, take a taxi to Mariscal Sucre, one hour, then walk 30 minutes to the reserve, or make arrangements with Jatun Sacha.

Between San Gabriel and Tulcán is the little town of Julio Andrade, with Saturday market (good for horses and other large animals) and, afterwards, paddleball games. This is the beginning of the road to La Bonita, Lumbaqui and Lago Agrio. The road follows the frontier for much of the route. Make enquiries about safety before taking this beautiful route.

Tulcán → *Phone code: 06. Colour map 11, A4. Population: 65,800. Altitude: 2,960 m.*
The chilly town of Tulcán is the busy capital of the province of Carchi. There is a great deal of informal trade here with Colombia, a textile and dry goods fair takes place on Thursday and Sunday. The two branches of the Panamericana join at Las Juntas, 2 km south of the city. In the cemetery, two blocks from Parque Ayora, the art of topiary is taken to beautiful extremes. Cypress bushes are trimmed into archways, fantastic figures and geometric shapes in *haut* and *bas* relief. To see the stages of this art form, go to the back of the cemetery where young bushes are being pruned. The artistry, started in 1936, is that of the late Sr José Franco, born in El Angel (see above), now buried among the splendour he created. The tradition is carried on by his sons.

Safety Don't wander about at night. The area around the bus terminal is unsafe. Tulcán and the traditionally tranquil border province of Carchi have seen an increase in tension due to druf trafficking and the guerrilla conflict in Colombia. Do not travel outside town (except along the Panamericana) without advance local inquiry. The **tourist office**, **Unidad de Turismo** ⓘ *entrance to the cemetery, T298 5760, daily 0800-1300, 1500-1800*, is helpful, some English spoken.

Border with Colombia
The border at Rumichaca is open 0600-2200. It is well organized. There is an iTur tourist office ⓘ *T06-298 5107, Mon-Fri 0830-1700*, and a snack bar. Opposite the complex is a telephone office. Watch your belongings while going through immigration and customs. See page 1019 for Colombian immigration.

Otavalo to the Colombian border listings

For Sleeping and Eating price codes and other relevant information, see Essentials, pages 38-40.

Sleeping

Cotacachi *p1083*
LL La Mirage, 500 m west of town, T291 5237, www.mirage.com.ec. Luxurious converted hacienda with elegant suites and common areas, includes breakfast and dinner, excellent restaurant, pool, gym and spa (treatments extra), beautiful gardens, tours arranged.
A Mesón de las Flores, García Moreno 1376 y Sucre, T291 6009, mesondelasflores@hotmail.com. Refurbished colonial house in the heart of town, includes breakfast, restaurant in lovely patio, live music at lunch Sat-Sun, sauna, Wi-Fi, parking. Recommended.
B Runa Tupari, the municipality has set up a system of homestays in nearby villages. Visitors experience life with a native family by taking part in daily activities. The comfortable rooms have space for 3, fireplace, bathroom and hot shower, and cost US$30 pp including breakfast, dinner and transport from Otavalo. Arrange with *Runa Tupari*, www.runatupari.com, or other Otavalo tour operators.
C Sumac Huasi, Montalvo 11-09 y Moncayo, T291 5873. Pleasant hotel with adequate rooms, includes breakfast, nice rooftop terrace.
D Munaylla, 10 de Agosto y Sucre, T291 6169. Multi-storey building, hot water, rooms a bit small, good value.
E-F Bachita, Sucre 16-82 y Peñaherrera, T291 5063. Simple place, cheaper with shared bath and cold water, quiet.

Laguna Cuicocha *p1083*
A Hostería Cuicocha, Laguna Cuicocha, by the pier, T264 8040, www.cuicocha.org. Modern comfortable rooms overlooking the lake, includes breakfast and dinner, restaurant with lake views.
D Cabañas Mirador, on a lookout above the pier, follow the trail or by car follow the road to the left of the park entrance, T08-682 1699, miradorde

cuicocha@yahoo.com. Rustic cabins with fireplace and modern rooms overlooking the lake, good economical restaurant, trout is the specialty, hot water, parking, transport provided Quiroga (US$4), Otavalo (US$10) Otavalo, owner Ernesto Cevillano is knowledgeable about the area and arranges trips.

Ibarra *p1084*

A Ajaví, Av Mariano Acosta 16-38 y Circunvalación, along main road into town from south, T295 5221, www.hotelajavi.com. Slightly upscale hotel, comfortable rooms, includes breakfast, good restaurant, pool, Wi-Fi, parking, gets tour groups for Sat lunch.

B Hacienda Chorlaví, Panamericana Sur Km 4, T06-293 2222, www.haciendachorlavi.com. In an old hacienda, comfortable rooms, includes breakfast, very good expensive restaurant, excellent parrillada, pool and spa, Wi-Fi, parking, popular, busy on weekends, folk music and crafts on Sat.

C Montecarlo, Av Jaime Rivadeneira 5-61 y Oviedo, T295 8266, montecarlohotel@gmail.com. Nice comfortable hotel by the obelisk, restaurant, heated pool open on weekends, Wi-Fi, parking.

C Nueva Estancia, García Moreno 7-58 y Sánchez y Cifuentes, Parque La Merced, T295 1444, nuevaestancia@andinanet.net. Modern hotel in a central location, small rooms, includes breakfast, restaurant, parking, decoration a bit kitch.

C Royal Ruiz, Olmedo 9-40 y P Moncayo, T264 1999. Modern, comfortable carpeted rooms , includes breakfast, restaurant, solar heated water, parking, long-stay discounts.

D El Callejón, Moncayo 7-38 y Sánchez y Cifuentes, T261 1577. Hot water, parking, comforatble rooms.

D Masters, Larrea 3-53 y Bolívar, T295 8686, www.mastershostalsuite.com. Modern hotel, restaurant on ground floor, parking.

E El Retorno, Pasaje Pedro Moncayo 4-32 entre Sucre y Rocafuerte, T295 7722. Ample rooms, restaurant, cheaper with shared bath, hot water, nice views from terrace. Good value, recommended.

E Las Garzas, Flores 3-13 y Salinas, T295 0985, paulpita@yahoo.com. Simple comfortable rooms, hot water, sitting room doubles as café-bar with a pleasant atmosphere.

F Colón, Chica Narváez 8-62 y Velasco, T295 8695. A friendly basic place, cheaper with shared bath, electric shower, laundry facilities, patio.

Around Ibarra

LL Hacienda Zuleta, By Angochahua, along the Ibarra-Cayambe road, T266 2182, Quito T02-603 6874, www.zuleta.com. A 2000-ha working historic hacienda, among the nicest in the country. Superb accommodation and food, 15 rooms with fireplace, price includes all meals (prepared with organic vegetables, trout and dairy produced on the farm) and excursions, advance reservations required.

A-B Pukyu Pamba, In San Clemente, T266 0045, www.sclemente.com (in French). Part of a community-run program. Nicely built cottages with hot water on family properties, cheaper in more humble family homes, price includes 3 tasty meals and a guided tour, you are expected to participate in the family's activities. Horses and native guides available for more extended treks and visits to other communities.

E Casa Aída, In La Esperanza village, T266 0221. Simple rooms with good beds, breakfast extra, restaurant, shared bath, hot water, some English spoken, meeting place for climbing Imbabura.

Ibarra to the coast *p1084*

C Las Siete Cascadas, 15 km past Lita, T09-430 7434. A-frame' cabins with balconies, excursions to waterfalls, price includes full board.

C-D Bosque de Paz, in El Limonal, about 600 m uphill from the main square, T264 8692, www.bospas.org. Small family-run reserve focusing on fruit and bamboo, rich in bird life. Three private rooms with terrace, cheaper in dorm, splendid views of the valley, includes good breakfast with delicious home-made bread, tasty meals available, small pool, camping G pp, treks and horse-riding trips, can arrange excursions to mangroves, volunteer opportunities, Belgian-Ecuadorean run. Knowledgeable and recommended.

F Residencial Villalobos, in Lita, uphill from the unused train station, T09-237 4616. Wooden house with basic but clean rooms, shared bath, cold water.

Northwest of Ibarra *p1084*

AL Aguasavia Termas, 500 m from the Tumbabiro-Chachimbiro road, turnoff at Km 7.5 , T292 3633, aguasavia@gmail.com.

Spa resort in a beautiful setting in the crater of La Viuda Volcano. Thermal water pools, includes buffet breakfast, restaurant, some rooms have Jacuzzi with thermal water, Wi-Fi, horseriding, hiking, tours to Piñán. Owned by a cooperative of 9 communities, opened in 2010.

A-B Termas Hostería Chachimbiro, at the thermal baths complex, reserve through office in Otavalo (see Tour operators), T264 8133, www.chachimbiro.com. Cabins with private bath, some with Jacuzzi, includes 3 meals and access to spa and pools, 2 restaurants, part of a recreational and spa complex, noisy and chaotic on weekends.

B Hostería Pantaví, 7 km from Salinas, at the entrance to Tumbabiro, T293 4185, Quito reservations T02-234 7476, www.hosteria pantavi.com. Stylish inn in a tastefully restored old hacienda. Very comfortable rooms, includes breakfast, good restaurant, pool, gardens, games room, excursions to Piñan lakes, good value.

North to Colombia *p1085*

El Angel

AL Polylepis Lodge, abutting the reserve, 14 km from El Angel along the road to Socabones, T295 4009, www.polylepislodge.com. Rustic cabins with fireplace by a lovely 12-ha forest, price includes 3 meals (vegetarian on request) and 3 guided walks, Jacuzzi.

C Las Orquídeas, in the village of Morán, T08-641 6936, castro503@yahoo.com. Mountain cabin with bunk beds, shared bath, includes 3 meals, horseback riding and guide, run by Carlos Castro, a local guide and conservation pioneer.

E-F Paisajes Andinos, Riofrío y 2a Transversal, T297 7557. Adequate hostel, some rooms with private bath, hot water.

Eastern Route to the border *p1085*

San Gabriel

D Gabrielita, Mejía y Los Andes, above the agricultural supply shop, T229 1832. Modern hostel, includes breakfast, best in town.

Tulcán *p1086*

Many hotels on C Sucre.

A Sara Espíndola, Sucre y Ayacucho, on plaza, T298 6209. Comfortable rooms, best hotel with nicest restaurant in town, spa, helpful.

C Machado, Bolívar y Ayacucho, T298 4221. Includes breakfast, comfy, parking.

D Lumar, Sucre y Rocafuerte, T298 0402. Modern, hot water, comfortable.

D Torres de Oro, Sucre y Rocafuerte, T298 0296. Hot water, restaurant, parking, modern, nice.

E Sáenz Internacional, Sucre y Rocafuerte, T298 1916. Very nice, modern, hot water, good value.

E Los Alpes, JR Arellano next to bus station, T298 2235. Restaurant, hot water, OK, good value.

F Florida, Sucre y 10 de Agosto, T298 3849. Cheaper without bath, hot water, modern section at back, good value.

Eating

Cotacachi *p1083*

A local specialty is *carne colorada* (spiced pork).

Asadero La Tola, Rocafuerte 0-18 y 9 de Octubre. Grill, in an old courtyard.

𝌆-𝌆 La Marqueza, 10 de Agosto y Bolívar, daily 0730-2130. 4-course set lunches and à la carte.
El Viejo Molino, 10 de Agosto 10-65 y Moncayo. Set meals and à la carte, good value.

Ibarra *p1084*
El Argentino, Sucre y P Moncayo, at Plazoleta Francisco Calderón, Tue-Sun. Good mixed grill and salads, small, pleasant, outdoor seating.
Pizza El Horno, Rocafuerte 6-38 y Flores. Italian dishes, live music Sat night, closed Mon.
Aroma Gourmet, Sánchez y Cifuentes 8-80 y Oviedo. Popular for a good set lunch.
Casa Blanca, Bolívar 7-83. Family run, in colonial house with seating around a central patio with fountain, great food, closed Sun. Recommended.
El Chagra, Olmedo 7-48 y Flores. *Platos típicos*, good trout. Recommended.
Inti Raymi, Av Pérez Guerrero 6-39 y Bolívar. Good simple vegetarian lunches.

Cafés and heladerías

Antojitos de Mi Tierra, Sucre y P Moncayo, at Plazoleta Francisco Calderón, afternoons. Outdoor seating, local drinks and snacks.
Café Arte, Salinas 5-43 y Oviedo, daily from1700. Café-bar with character, drinks, Mexican snacks, sandwiches, live music Fri-Sat night.
Heladería Rosalía Suárez, Oviedo y Olmedo. Excellent homemade *helados de paila* (fruit sherbets made in large copper basins), an Ibarra tradition since 1896. Highly recommended.
Olor a Café, Flores y Bolívar. Café/bar/cultural centre in an historic home, music, library

Tulcán *p1086*
Café Tulcán, Sucre 52-029 y Ayacucho. Café, snacks, desserts, juices, set lunches.
El Patio, Bolívar 50-050 y 10 de Agosto. For Colombian specialities.
Mama Rosita, Sucre entre Boyacá y Atahualpa. Typical Ecuadorean dishes, set lunch.
Tequila, Sucre entre Junín y Boyacá. Varied à la carte menu.

Bars and clubs

Ibarra *p1084*
At the corner of Bolívar and Oviedo are cafés, bars and clubs, a popular Fri and Sat hangout.
El Coyote, Sucre y Pedro Moncayo, at Plazoleta Francisco Calderón. Outdoor seating, drinks and Mexican food.
Rincón de Myer, Olmedo 9-59. A bar with lots of character, attractively restored.
Sambucos and **Dream Cocktails**, Flores y Sucre. Bars/clubs, the in-places among Ibarreño youth.

Activities and tours

Ibarra *p1084*
A unique form of paddle ball, **pelota nacional**, is played in the afternoon at Yacucalle, south of the bus station. Players have huge studded paddles for striking the 1 kg ball.

Cycling

Cycling Zone, Flores y Borja. Well-stocked shop, repairs, rentals, route information.

Paragliding

Fly Ecuador, Oviedo 9-13 y Sánchez Cifuentes, T295 3297, www.flyecuador.com.ec. Tandem flight US$60, course US$400, arrange ahead.

Tour operators

EcuaHorizons, Bolívar 4-67 y García Moreno, T295 9904, ecuahorizons@andinanet.net. Bilingual guides for regional tours.
Intipungo, Rocafuerte 6-08 y Flores, T295 7766. Regional tours.
Metropolitan Touring, Flores 5-76 y Sucre.

Transport

Cotacachi *p1083*
Bus Terminal at 10 de Agosto y Salinas by the market. Every 10 min from the Otavalo terminal; US$0.25, 25 mins; service alternates between the Panamericana and the Quiroga roads. To **Ibarra**, every 15 mins, US$0.45, 45 mins.

Laguna Cuicocha *p1083*
Pick-ups From **Otavalo** US$10. From **Cotacachi**, US$5 one way, US$10 return with short wait. From **Quiroga** US$4. Return service from the lake available from **Cabañas El Mirador**, same rates.

Los Cedros Research Station

Bus From Estación La Ofelia in Quito, **Trans Minas**, daily at 0615, 1000, 1530, 1800 to **Chontal**, US$2.50, 3 hrs; then a 5-hr **walk**; ask in Chontal for mules to carry luggage up. If the road is passable, 1 daily bus from Otavalo to Chontal.

Ibarra *p1084*

Bus Terminal is at Av Teodoro Gómez y Av Eugenio Espejo, to the south of the centre, T264 4676. At the terminal there are small shops, 2 food courts and a telephone office. All inter-city transport runs from here. City buses go from the terminal to the centre or you can walk in 15 mins. To/from **Quito**, Terminal Carcelén, frequent service, US$3, 3 hrs. Shared taxis with **Taxis Lagos** (Quito address and schedules under Otavalo above, in Ibarra at Flores 924 y Sánchez Cifuentes, Parque La Merced, T295 5150), buy ticket at their office the day before travelling, US$7.50 pp, 2½ hrs. To **Tulcán**, hourly, US$2, 3 hrs. To **Otavalo**, frequent service, US$0.50, 30 mins. To **Cotacachi**, US$0.45, 45 mins, some continue to **Quiroga**. To **the coast** several companies leave from the Terminal Terrestre, some go all the way to **San Lorenzo** US$4, 3 hrs, others only as far as **Lita**, US$3.50, 2 hrs. To **Ambato**, **CITA** goes via El Quinche and bypasses Quito, 8 daily, US$5, 5 hrs. To **Baños**, **Expreso Baños**, also bypasses Quito, 2 daily, US$6, 5½ hrs. To **Lago Agrio**, **Valle de Chota**, daily mid-morning, US$9, via La Bonita. Buses to La Esperanza, Zuleta and San Clemete leave from Parque Germán Grijalva (east of the Terminal Terrestre, follow C Sánchez y Cifuentes, south from the centre). To **La Esperanza**, every 20 mins, US$0.25, 30 mins. To **Zuleta**, hourly, US$0.52, 1 hr. To **San Clemente**, frequent, weekdays 0650-1840, Sat-Sun 0720-1500, US$0.25, 30 mins. To **Urcuquí**, **Coop Urcuquí**, from the Terminal Terrestre, every 20 mins, US$0.50, 30 mins. To **Tumbabiro** and **Chachimbiro**, **Coop Urcuquí**, at 0730 and 1200, returning at 1230 and 1500, US$1.25, 1½ hrs, taxi US$40 return, also transport from **Chachimiro Tours** in Otavalo.

Train Station at Espejo y Colón, T295 5050, Mon-Fri 0800-1200, 1400-1800, Sat 0800-1200. **Autoferro** to **Primer Paso**, 45 km out of Ibarra, leaves Wed-Sun 0830, with a minimum of10 passengers if small railcar is available, minimum of 18 passengers if only the larger railcar for 38 is available. It takes 2-2½ hrs with stops to Primer Paso where it turns back. Here is **Cañón del Primer Paso**, T09-968 2689, a resort by the river with pool. On the way back it stops at Salinas where it arrives around 1200 for people to visit the town, the **Museo de la Sal**, eat, experience the Afro-Ecuadorean atmosphere and departs for Ibarra at 1400, US$7.60. Reservations advised on weekends, but you will have to make a deposit for them to hold the seats. **Note** in early 2010 the autoferro was running only as far as Salinas due to repairs on the line. Following the same route, Klein Tours in Quito runs the **Chaski Antawa** (messenger train), from Ibarra to Salinas. Two traditional coaches take a maximum of 34 passengers, www.ecuadortrain.com. You can continue by bus to San Lorenzo from Salinas.

North to Colombia *p1085*

El Angel

Bus from **Ibarra** Terminal Terrestre to **Mira**, every 30 mins, US$0.90, 1 hr; to **El Angel**, hourly, US$1.30, 1½ hrs. El Angel to **Mira**, every 30 mins, US$.50, 20 mins. El Angel to **Tulcán**, US$1.30, 1½ hrs. El Angel to **Quito**, US$4, 4 hrs.

Eastern route to the border *p1085*

San Gabriel

Bus From **San Gabriel** to **Tulcán**, vans and jeeps US$0.70, shared taxis US$0.95, 30 mins, all from the main plaza. From San Gabriel to **Ibarra**, buses, US$1.65, 2 hrs. From San Gabriel to **Quito**, buses, US$3.50, 3½ hrs.

Tulcán *p1086*

Air TAME (Sucre y Ayacucho, T298 0675) no scheduled service in 2010.

Bus The bus terminal is 1½ km uphill from centre; best to take a taxi, US$1. To **Quito**, US$4, 5 hrs, every 15 mins, service to Terminal Carcelén and on to Quitumbe. To **Ibarra**, 3 hrs, US$2. **Otavalo**, US$3, 3 hrs (they don't go in to the Otavalo Terminal, alight at the highway turnoff where taxis are available or transfer in Ibarra). To **Guayaquil**, 20 a day, 13 hrs, US$13. To **Lago Agrio**, 2 a day with **Putumayo**, US$7, 7 hrs, spectacular, but it does go close to the Colombian border.

Border with Colombia *p1086*

Tulcán-Ipiales

Bus Minivans (US$0.75 pp) and shared taxis (US$0.85 pp) Tulcán-border leave when full from Parque Ayora (near the cemetery), private taxi US$3.50. **Note** These vehicles cross the international bridge and drop you off on the Colombian side, where onward transport waits.

Remember to cross back over the bridge for Ecuadorean immigration. Shared taxi border-Tulcán bus terminal, US$1 pp.

Directory

Ibarra *p1084*
Banks Banco del Pacífico, Olmedo 715 y Moncayo. **Banco Pichincha**, Sucre 581 y Flores; **Cambio**, Sánchez y Cifuentes yVelasco, several currencies and TCs. **Internet** Several places in town centre; US$0.75 per hr. **Language courses** Centro Ecuatoriano Canadiense de Idomas (CECI), Pérez Guerrero 6-12 y Bolívar, T295 1911, US$3.50 per hr. **Medical services** Instituto Médico de Especialidades, Egas 1-83 y Av Teodoro Gómez de La Torre, T295 5612. **Post offices** Flores opposite Parque Pedro Moncayo, 2nd floor.

Tulcán *p1086*
Banks Banco del Austro, Ayacucho y Bolívar. **Banco Pichincha**, 10 de Agosto y Sucre. Few places accept credit cards. Nowhere in Tulcán to change TCs. Pesos Colombianos can easily be changed on Parque La Independencia, the bus terminal and the border. **Consulates** Colombia: Av R Arellano y García Moreno, p3, near Parque Ayora, T298 7302, consulcoltulcan@andinanet.net, Mon-Fri 0800-1300, 1430-1530, visas require up to 20 days. **Internet** Prices US$1 per hr, many places in town. **Post offices** Bolívar 53-27.

Cotopaxi, Latacunga and Quilotoa

An impressive roll call of towering peaks lines the route south of Quito, appropriately called the Avenue of the Volcanoes. This area obviously attracts its fair share of trekkers and climbers, while the less active tourist can browse through the many colourful indigenous markets and colonial towns that nestle among the high volcanic cones. The Panamericana heads south from Quito towards the central highlands' hub of Ambato. The perfect cone of Cotopaxi volcano is ever-present and is one of the country's main tourist attractions. Machachi and Lasso are good places to acclimatize, while Latacunga is a good base for the region, and for the impossibly beautiful Quilotoa circuit of small villages and vast expanses of open countryside.

Cotopaxi and Latacunga

Machachi ➔ *Phone code: 02. Colour map 11, A3. Population: 26,000. Altitude: 2,900 m.*

In a valley between the summits of Pasochoa, Rumiñahui and Corazón, lies the town of **Machachi**, famous for its horsemen (*chagras*), hore riding trips, mineral water springs and crystal clear swimming pools (open 0800-1530 daily). The water, 'Agua Güitig' or 'Tesalia', is bottled in a plant 4 km from the town and sold throughout the country, plant tours 0800-1200. Annual highland 'rodeo', El Chagra, third week in July; tourist information office on the plaza.

Reserva Ecológica Los Ilinizas

Machachi is a good starting point for a visit to the northern section of the **Reserva Ecológica Los Ilinizas** *US$5*. There is a *refugio*, a shelter below the saddle between the two peaks, at 4,740 m, with capacity for 20 and cooking facilities, take a mat and sleeping bag, US$15 per night, camping US$5 per tent (renovated in 2009-2010). Iliniza Norte (5,105 m) although not a technical climb, should not be underestimated, a few exposed, rocky sections require utmost caution. Some climbers suggest using a rope and a helmet is recommended if other parties are there because of falling rock; allow 2-4 hours for the ascent from the refuge, take a compass, it's easy to mistake the descent.Iliniza Sur (5,245 m) involves ice climbing despite the deglaciation: full climbing gear and experience are absolutely necessary. Access to the reserve is through a turnoff west of the Panamericana 6 km south of Machachi, then it's 7 km to the village of El Chaupi. A dirt road continues from here 9 km to 'La Virgen' (statue). Nearby are woods where you can camp. El Chaupi hotels arrange for horses with muleteer (US$15 per animal).

Parque Nacional Cotopaxi ➔ *Colour map 11, B4.*

ⓘ *Visitors to the park must register at the entrance. Entrance fee: US$10. Park gates are open 0700-1500, although you can stay until 1800. Visitors arriving with guides not authorized by the park are turned back at the gate. The park administration, a small museum (0800- 1200, 1300-1700) and the Paja Blanca restaurant and shelter, are 10 km from the park gates, just before Limpio Pungo. (See also Transport section below.) The museum has a 3D model of the park, information about the volcano and stuffed animals.*

Cotopaxi volcano (5,897 m) is at the heart of a much-visited national park. This scenic snow-covered perfect cone is the second highest peak in Ecuador and a very popular climbing destination. Cotopaxi is an active volcano, one of the highest in the world, and its most recent eruption took place in 1904. Volcanic material from former eruptions can be seen strewn about the *páramo* surrounding Cotopaxi; there is a high plateau with a small lake (Laguna Limpio Pungo), a lovely area for walking and admiring the delicate flora, and fauna including wild horses and native bird species such as the Andean Lapwing and the Chimborazo Hillstar hummingbird. The lower slopes are clad in planted pine forests, where llamas may be seen.

The **main entrance** to the Parque Nacional Cotopaxi is approached from Chasqui, 25 km south of Machachi, 6 km north of Lasso, and is marked by a Parque Nacional Cotopaxi sign. Once through the national park gates, go past Laguna Limpio Pungo to a fork, where the right branch climbs steeply to a parking lot (4,600 m). From here it's a 30-minutes to one-hour walk to the José Ribas refuge, at 4,800 m; beware of altitude sickness. Walking from the highway to the refuge takes an entire day or more. The **El Pedregal entrance**, from the northwest, is accessed from Machachi via Santa Ana del Pedregal (21 km from the Panamericana), or from Sangolquí via Rumipamba and the Río Pita Valley. From Pedregal to the refuge car park is 14 km. There are infrequent buses to Pedregal (2 a day) then the hike in is shorter but still a couple of hours. The **Ticatilín access** approaches Cotopaxi from the south. From the Panamericana, 1 km north of Lasso, at 'Aglomerados Cotopaxi' (the northern access to Saquisilí) a road goes east to the village of San Ramón and on to Ticatilín (a contribution of US$1-2 per vehicle may be requested at the barrier here) and Rancho María. Remember to close all gates. From the south, San Ramón is accessed from Mulaló. Beyond Rancho María is a less impacted páramo and the private Albergue Cotopaxi Cara Sur (see below). Walking four hours from here you reach Campo Alto, a tent camp used by climbers. There are other access points from the north, east and south, which go through private land.

Climbing Cotopaxi The ascent from the refuge takes 5-8 hours, start climbing at 0100 as the snow deteriorates in the sun. A full moon is both practical and a magical experience. Check out snow conditions with the guardian of the refuge before climbing. The route changes from year to year due to deglaciation. Because of the altitude and weather conditions, Cotopaxi is a serious climb, equipment and experience are required. To maximize your chances of reaching the summit, make sure to be well acclimatized beforehand. Take a guide if you are inexperienced on ice and snow. Agencies in Quito and throughout the Central Highlands offer Cotopaxi climbing trips. Note that some guides encourage tourists to turn back at the first sign of tiredness, don't be pressured, insist on going at your own pace. There is no specific best season to climb Cotopaxi, weather conditions are largely a matter of luck year-round. Just north of Cotopaxi are the peaks of Sincholagua (4,873 m), Rumiñahui (4,722 m) and Pasochoa (4,225 m). To the southeast is Quilindaña (4,890 m). The southwest flank has not received as much impact as the west side. There is good walking, and you can climb Morurco (4,881 m) as an acclimatization hike. Condors may sometimes be seen. To climb to the summit in one day you have to stay at Campo Alto (see above, and Sleeping below). The route is reported easier and safer than the north face, but a little longer. The last hour goes around the rim of the crater with impressive views.

Lasso ➔ *Phone code: 03. Colour map 11, B3. Altitude: 3,000 m.*

The railway and the Pan-American Highway cross one another at Lasso, a small town, 33 km south of Alóag. In the surrounding countryside are several *hosterías*, converted country estates, offering accommodation and meals. There are roadside restaurants along the Panamericana.

Latacunga ➔ *Phone code: 03. Colour map 11, B3. Population: 95,000. Altitude: 2,800 m.*

The capital of Cotopaxi Province is a place where the abundance of light grey pumice has been artfully employed. Volcán Cotopaxi is much in evidence, though it is 29 km away. Provided they are not hidden by clouds, which unfortunately is all too often, as many as nine volcanic cones can be seen from Latacunga; try early in the morning. The colonial character of the town has been well preserved. The central plaza, **Parque Vicente León**, is a beautifully maintained garden (locked at night). There are several other gardens in the town including **Parque San Francisco** and **Lago Flores**. **Casa de los Marqueses de Miraflores** ⓘ *Sánchez de Orellana y Abel Echeverría, T280 1382, Mon-Fri 0800-1200, 1400-1800, Sat 0900-1300, free*, in a restored colonial mansion has a modest museum, with exhibits on Mama Negra (see Festivals and events, below), colonial art, archaeology, numismatics and a library (free).

Casa de la Cultura ⓘ *Antonia Vela 3-49 y Padre Salcedo T281 3247, Tue-Fri 0800-1200, 1400-1800, Sat 0800-1500, US$1*, built around the remains of a Jesuit Monastery and the old Monserrat watermill, houses a nice museum with pre-Columbian ceramics, weavings, costumes and models of festival masks; also art gallery, library and theatre. It has week-long festivals with exhibits and concerts for all the local festivities. There is a Saturday **market** on the Plaza de San Sebastián (at Juan Abel Echeverría). Goods for sale include *shigras* (fine stitched, colourful straw bags) and homespun wool and cotton yarn. The produce market, Plaza El Salto has daily trading and larger fairs on Tuesday and Saturday. A tourist **train** runs from Quito to Latacunga, see page 1063.

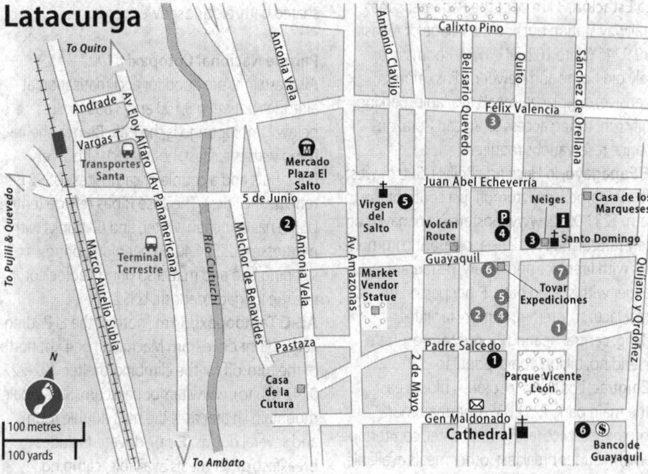

Sleeping
1 Central
2 Estambul
3 Makroz
4 Rodelú
5 Rosim
6 Tiana
7 Villa de Tacunga

Eating
1 Café Colonial
2 Chifa China
3 Coffee Andes Alpes
4 La Fornace
5 Parilladas La Española
6 Pizzería Buon Giorno

Tourist offices: **Cámara de Turismo de Cotopaxi** ⓘ *Sánchez de Orellana y Guayaquil, at Plaza de Santo Domingo, T281 4968, Mon-Fri 0800-1200, 1400-1700*, local and regional information, Spanish only. **Oficina de Turismo**, at the Terminal Terrestre, second floor ⓘ *Mon-Fri 0900-1200, 1330-1800, Sat 0900-1600, Sun 0900-1400*, staffed by high school students, local and some regional information.

Cotopaxi and Latacunga listings

For Sleeping and Eating price codes and other relevant information, see Essentials, pages 38-40.

Sleeping

Machachi *p1091*

LL Hacienda Umbria, 4 km from Aloasí, T231 4237, www.haciendaumbria.com. A gourmet experience with meals cooked by the owner, fine wines, helpful staff, open fires, fine views of several mountains. Overnight stays include everything except alcoholic drinks, activities are horse riding, mountain biking, hiking, tours of the working hacienda. Day visits are also arranged.

B Sierra Loma, near Aloasí, 700 m south of Machachi train station, T09-593 8256, www.sierraloma.com. Cabins for 4 with fireplace in the forest, includes breakfast, other meals on requests, camping **G** pp, package with meals, activities and transport from Quito available.

C La Estación, 3 km W of the Panamericana, by railway station outside the village of Aloasí, T230 9246 Quito T02-241 3784. Rooms in a lovely old home and newer cabins (more expensive), fireplaces, meals available, parking, family run, hiking access to Volcán Corazón, advance reservations required.

C-E Papagayo, in Hacienda Bolívia, 500 m west of the Panamericana, turnoff just south of the toll booth, T231 0002, www.hosteria-papagayo.com. Nicely refurbished hacienda, pleasant communal areas with fireplace and library, restaurant, cheaper with shared bath, **F** per person in dorm, Jacuzzi, internet, laundry facilities, parking, central heating, homey atmosphere, horseriding, biking, tours, popular.

D Chiguac, Los Caras y Colón, 4 blocks east of the main park, T231 0396, germanimor@punto.net.ec. Nice family-run hostel, comfortable rooms, includes breakfast, other meals available, shared bath, hot water.

Reserva Ecológica Los Ilinizas *p1091*

D Hacienda San José del Chaupi, 3 km southwest of El Chaupi, T09-467 1692, haciendasanjosedelchaupi@yahoo.com. Converted hacienda house and wood cabins in a working farm. Shared rooms for 4 and cabins for 6, includes breakfast, meals available on request, hot water, parking, fireplaces in common areas and cabins, horse riding and rentals, visitors are welcome to participate in farm activities, reforestation with native species, call in advance.

E La Llovizna, 100 m behind the church, on the way to the mountain, T09-969 9068. Pleasant hostel, sitting room with fireplace, includes breakfast, restaurant, some rooms with bath, hot water, pool table, ping pong, horse rental.

E Posada El Chaupi, in front of bus stop, T286 0830. Simple family run hostel, includes breakfast, other meals with family on request, cheaper with shared bath, electric shower, very nice.

Parque Nacional Cotopaxi *p1092*

All these inns are good for acclimatization at altitudes between 3,100 and 3,800 m. Just below Limpiopungo is the **Paja Blanca** shelter (**E** pp with breakfast, hot water) with 2 very basic huts and a couple of campsites (US$2 per tent, no facilities). The **José Ribas refuge** (entry US$1) has a kitchen, water, and 60 bunks with mattresses; US$24.40 pp per night, bring sleeping bag and mat, also bring padlock or use the luggage deposit, US$2.50.

AL-C Tambopaxi, 3 km south of the El Pedregal access (1 hr drive from Machachi) or 4 km north of the turn-off for the climbing shelter, T02-222 0242 (Quito), www.tambopaxi.com. Straw-bale mountain shelter at 3,750 m. 3 double rooms and several dorms (**E** pp), duvets, includes breakfast, other meals available, camping $7.50 pp, horse riding with advance notice.

E Albergue Cotopaxi Cara Sur, at the southwestern end of the park, at the end of the Ticatilín road, T08-461 9264 (see Quito, Tour operators), www.cotopaxicarasur.com. Mountain shelter at 4000m, day use US$1. Total capacity 40, meals available with advance notice, use of kitchen, outhouses, hot shower, sauna, bunk beds (**F** pp) and blankets, transport from Quito and climbing tours available. Campo Alto tent camp (4780m, US$5 pp) is 4 hrs walk from the shelter, horse to take gear to Campo Alto US$12, muleteer US$12, equipment rental.

Outside the park

LL San Agustín de Callo, two access roads from the Panamericana, one just north of the main park access (6.2 km); the second, just north of Lasso (4.3 km), T03-271 9160, Quito T02-290 6157, www.incahacienda.com. Exclusive hacienda, the only place in Ecuador where you can sleep and dine in an Inca building, the northernmost imperial-style Inca structure still standing. Rooms and suites with fireplace and bathtub, includes breakfast and dinner, horse rides, treks, bicycles and fishing. Restaurant () and buildings open to non-guests (US$5-10).

To the southeast of the park lies an area of rugged *páramos* and mountains dropping down to the jungle. The area has several large *haciendas* which form the **Fundación Páramo**, a private reserve with restricted access.

LL Hacienda Yanahurco, by Quilindaña, Quito T02-224 1593, www.haciendayanahurco.com. Ranch style rooms with fireplace or heater, includes meals, 2-4 day programs, all-inclusive.

L Hacienda Santa Ana, in Santa Ana del Pedregal, T222-4950, www.santaanacotopaxi.com. Luxurious 17th century former-Jesuit hacienda in beautiful surroundings, activities on offer include horse riding, biking, trekking, climbing.

A-C Tierra del Volcán, T09-972 7934, Quito T02-223 1806, www.tierradelvolcan.com. Three lodges: **Hacienda El Porvenir,** a working ranch by Rumiñahui, between El Pedregal and the northern access to the park, sitting-room with fireplace, 3 types of rooms, includes breakfast, set meals available, horses and mountain bikes for hire, camping $3 per person; **Hacienda Santa Rita**, by the Río Pita, on the Sangolquí-El Pedregal road; and the more remote, rustic and economical **Hacienda El Tambo** by Quilindaña, southeast of the park. Also packages including full board and transport from Quito.

B-C Cuello de Luna, 2 km northwest of the park's main access on a dirt road, T09-970 0330, www.cuellodeluna.com. Comfortable rooms with fireplace, includes breakfast, meals available cheaper in dorm (a very low loft). Can arrange tours to Cotopaxi, horse riding and biking.

B-C Huagra Corral, 200 m east of Panamericana along the park's main access road, T03-271 9729, www.huagracorral.com. Nicely decorated, includes breakfast, restaurant, some rooms with private bath, portable heaters, convenient location, helpful.

Lasso *p1093*

L Hacienda Hato Verde, Panamericana Sur Km 55, by entry to Mulaló, southeast of Lasso, T271 9348, www.haciendahatoverde.com. Lovely old hacienda and working dairy farm near the south flank of Cotopaxi, tastefully restored. 9 rooms with wood-burning stoves, includes breakfast, other meals US$20; activities such as horse riding (for experienced riders), trekking, trip up Cotopaxi Cara Sur, US$80, charming hosts. Recommended.

A Hostería La Ciénega, 2 km south of Lasso, west of the Panamericana, T271 9052, www.hosterialacienega.com. An historic *hacienda* with nice gardens, an avenue of massive eucalyptus trees, rooms with heater or fireplace, good expensive restaurant.

A San Mateo, 4 km south of Lasso west of the Panamericana, T271 9015, www.hosteriasanmateo.com. Bright rooms and cabañas, pricey restaurant, horse riding included, small but nice, adjoining working *hacienda* can be visited.

E Cabañas Los Volcanes, at the south end of Lasso, T271 9524, maexpediciones@yahoo.com. Small roadside hostel, nice rooms, cheaper with shared bath, hot water, laundry facilities, discounts for HI members. Tours to Cotopaxi.

Latacunga *p1093, map p1093*

A-B Villa de Tacunga, Sanchez de Orellana y Guayaquil, T281 2352, www.villadetacunga.com. Nicely restored colonial house, includes breakfast, restaurant serves set meals and à la carte, Wi-Fi, parking, opened in 2009.

C Rodelú, Quito 16-31, T280 0956, www.rodelu.com.ec. Comfortable popular hotel, restaurant, nice suites and rooms except for a few which are too small.

C-D Makroz, Valencia 8-56 y Quito, T280 0907, hotelmakroz@latinmail.com. Modern hotel with nicely decorated comfortable rooms, restaurant, parking.

D Rosim, Quito 16-49 y Padre Salcedo, T280 2172, www.hotelrosim.com. Centrally located, breakfast available, hot water, Wi-Fi, carpeted rooms, quiet and comfortable. Discounts in low season.

D-E Estambul, Belisario Quevedo 6-46 y Padre Salcedo, T280 0354. Simple quiet hostel long-popular with travellers, cheaper with shared bath, ageing but well maintained although beds are a bit saggy, offer tours to Cotopaxi and Quilotoa.

E Central, Sánchez de Orellana y Padre Salcedo, T280 2912. A multi-storey hotel in the centre of town, breakfast available, hot water, a bit faded but very helpfuls.

E Tiana, Guayaquil 5-32 y Quito, T281 0147, www.hostaltiana.com. Old house with simple rooms around a stone patio, includes breakfast, nice heated restaurant/café, spotless shared bathrooms, hot water, Wi-Fi, reservations advised for double rooms, **F** pp in dorm. Owners (English and Dutch spoken) have trekking maps, travel information and offer tours. Popular meeting place. Recommended.

Eating

Machachi *p1091*

TTT-TT Café de la Vaca, 4 km south of town on the Panamericana, open daily 0800-1730. Very good meals using produce from own farm, very popular.

TT El Chagra, 3 blocks west of veggie market. Good Ecuadorean food.

Lasso *p1093*

Several *paradores* (diners) along the Panamericana.

Latacunga *p1093, map p1093*

Few places are open on Sun.

TT Parilladas La Española, 2 de Mayo 7-175 y JA Echeverría, Mon-Sat 1230-2100. Good grill, popular with locals.

TT-T Chifa China, Antonia Vela 6-85 y 5 de Junio, daily 1030-2200. Good Chinese food, large portions.

TT-T Pizzería Buon Giorno, Sánchez de Orellana y Maldonado, Mon-Sat 1300-2200. Great pizzas and lasagne, large selection. Popular and recommended.

T Café Colonial, Padre Salcedo 4-62. Set lunches.

Cafés

Coffee Andes Alpes, Guayaquil 6-07 y Quito, by Santo Domingo church, Mon-Sat 1400-2100, Sun 1600-2100. Pleasant café/bar, strong drinks, sweets and sandwiches.

La Fornace, Quito 17-49 y Guayaquil, daily 1000-2100. Good pizza, coffee, snacks and the best ice-cream.

Bars and clubs

Latacunga *p1093, map p1093*

Galaxy, Barrio El Calvario, on a hill east of the centre. Disco, varied music, nice atmosphere.

Nefertari's,2 de Mayo 71-45 y Padre Salcedo. Bar, varied music, alternative, rock, salsa, etc.

Festivals and events

Latacunga *p1093, map p1093*

The **La Mama Negra** is held **23-24 Sep**, in homage to *the Virgen de las Mercedes*. There are 5 main characters in the parade and hundreds of dancers, some representing the black slaves, others the whites. Mama Negra herself (portrayed by a man) is a slave who dared to ask for freedom in colonial times. The colourful costumes are called the *Santísima Trajería*. The civic festival of **Mama Negra**, with similar parade, is on **the first or second Sat in Nov** (but not 2 Nov, Día de los Muertos). It is part of the Fiestas de Latacunga, 11 Nov.

Shopping

Latacunga *p1093, map p1093*

Artesanía Otavalo, Guayaquil 5-50 y Quito. A variety of souvenirs from Otavalo.

Karoma Artesanía: Quito 76-45. A variety of crafts.

Activities and tours

Latacunga *p1093, map p1093*

All operators offer day trips to **Cotopaxi** and **Quilotoa** (US$40 pp, includes lunch and a visit to a market town if on Thu or Sat, minimum 2 people). Climbing trips to Cotopaxi are around US$170 pp for 2 days (plus park entrance fee and *refugio*), minimum 2 people. Trekking trips US$70-80 pp per day. **Note** Many agencies require passport as deposit when renting gear.

Metropolitan Touring, Guayaquil 5-26 y Quito, T280 2985. See Quito operators. Airline tickets.

Neiges, Guayaquil 6-25, Plaza Santo Domingo, T281 1199, neigestours@hotmail.com. Day trips and climbing.

TribuTrek, at Hostal Tiana, www.tributrek.com. Quality trekking around Quilotoa and Cotopaxi, also sell Galápagos cruises and jungle tours.

Tovar Expediciones, Guayaquil 5-38 y Quito, T281 1333, www.expedicionestovar.com. Climbing and trekking.

Volcán Route, Belisario Quevedo y Guayaquil, T281 2452, www.volcanroute.com. Tour to Cotopaxi follows a secondary road through interesting country, instead of the Panamericana. Also cloud forest treks.

Transport

Machachi *p1091*

Bus To **Quito**, from C Barriga, 8 blocks south and 2 blocks east of the park – *Especiales* go to Redondel de la Villaflora, Rodrigo de Chávez y Maldonado, south of the colonial city, US$0.75, 1 hr, *Populares* to Terminal Quitumbe, US$0.55. To **Latacunga**, from the monument to El Chagra at the Panamericana, US$0.55, 1 hr.

Reserva Ecológica Los Ilinizas *p1091*

Bus From Av Amazonas opposite the market in Machachi, every 30 mins, 0600-1930, to **El Chaupi** (40 min, US$0.36), from where you can walk to the *refugio* in 7-8 hrs. A pick-up from El Chaupi to 'La Virgen' costs US$10, from Machachi US$25. It takes 3 hrs to walk with a full pack from 'La Virgen' to the *refugio*. Horses can be hired at any of the lodgings in El Chaupi.

Parque Nacional Cotopaxi *p1092*
Note that only authorized vehicles with a special permit and licensed guide are allowed to take tourists into the park. Others are turned back

Main park entrance and Refugio Ribas, take a Latacunga bus from Quito and get off at the main access point. Do not take an express bus as you can't get off before Latacunga. At the turnoff to the park there are usually vehicles from a local operator which go to the park. US$25 to the parking lot before the refuge for up to 3 passengers. From **Machachi**, pick-ups go via the cobbled road to El Pedregal on to Limpio Pungo and the refugio parking lot, US$35. From **Lasso**, full day trip to the park, US$70 return, contact **Cabañas los Volcanes**. From **Latacunga**, arrange with tour operators or **Hotel Estambul**.

To **Cara Sur** from Quito, **Agama Expediciones** offer transport to the **Albergue Cara Sur**, US$60 per vehicle up to 5 passengers. Alternatively take a Latacunga bound bus and get off at **Aglomerados Cotopaxi** and take a pick-up from there, US$15 per vehicle for up to 5 passengers.

Latacunga *p1093, map p1093*
Bus Buses leave from the terminal on the Panamericana just south of 5 de Junio, except **Transportes Santa**, which has its own terminal at Eloy Alfaro 28-57 y Vargas Torres, 3 blocks north of the Terminal Terrestre along the Panamericana, T281 1659, serving **Cuenca**, **Loja**, and **Guayaquil** via Riobamba and Pallatanga. To **Quito**, every 15 mins, 2 hrs, US$2; also shared door to door taxi service with **Servicio Express**, see page 1063. To/from **Ambato**, 1 hr, US$1. To **Guayaquil**, US$7, 7 hrs. To **Saquisilí**, every 20 mins (see below). Through buses, which are more frequent, do not stop at Latacunga Terminal. During the day (0600-1700), they go along a bypass road 4 blocks west of the Terminal, and stop at Puente de San Felipe. At night they stop at the corner of Panamericana and Av 5 de Junio. To **Otavalo,** and **Ibarra**, bypassing Quito, **Cita Express**, hourly from Puente de San Felipe. To **Baños**, every 20 mins from Puente de San Felipe. Buses on the Zumbahua, Quilotoa, Chugchilán, Sigchos circuit are given below. **Note** On Thu most buses to nearby communities leave from Saquisilí market instead of Latacunga.

Ⓒ Directory

Latacunga *p1093, map p1093*
Banks Banco de Guayaquil, Maldonado y Sánchez de Orellana. **Banco Pichincha**, C Quito, Parque Vicente León. **Internet** Prices around US$1 per hr. **Medical services** **Clínica Latacunga**, Sánchez de Orellana 11-79 y Marqués de Maenza, T281 0260. Private, 24 hrs. **Post office** Belisario Quevedo y Maldonado.

Quilotoa Circuit

The popular and recommended round trip from Latacunga to Pujilí, Zumbahua, Quilotoa crater, Chugchilán, Sigchos, Isinliví, Toacazo, Saquisilí, and back to Latacunga can be done in two to three days by bus (times given below are approximate; buses are often late owing to the rough roads or requests for photo stops). It is 200 km in total. It is also a great route for biking and only a few sections of the loop are cobbled or rough. Access is from either Lasso or Latacunga. Hiking from one town to another can be challenging, especially when the fog rolls in. For these longer walks hiring a guide might not be unreasonable if you don't have a proper map or enough experience.

Latacunga to Zumbahua

A fine paved road leads west to **Pujilí** ⓘ *15 km, bus US$0.25*, which has a beautiful church. Good market on Sunday, and a smaller one on Wednesday. Colourful Corpus Christi celebrations. Beyond Pujilí, many interesting crafts are practised by the *indígenas* in the **Tigua** valley: paintings on leather, hand-carved wooden masks and baskets. **Chimbacucho**, also known as Tigua, is home to the Toaquiza family, most famous of the Tigua artists. The road goes on over the Western Cordillera to Zumbahua, La Maná and Quevedo. This is a great downhill bike route. It carries very little traffic and is extremely twisty in parts but is one of the most beautiful routes connecting the highlands with the coast. Beyond Zumbahua are the pretty towns of **Pilaló** (two restaurants and petrol pumps), **Esperanza de El Tingo** (two restaurants and lodging at *Carmita's*, T03-281 4657) and **La Maná**.

Zumbahua

Zumbahua lies ½ km from the main road, 65 km from Pujilí. It has an interesting Saturday market (starts at 0600) for local produce, and some tourist items. Just below the plaza is a shop selling dairy products and cold drinks. Friday nights involve dancing and drinking. Take a fleece, as it can be windy, cold and dusty. There is a good hospital in town, Italian-funded and run. The Saturday trip to Zumbahua market and the Quilotoa crater is one of the best excursions in Ecuador.

Quilotoa

Zumbahua is the point to turn off for a visit to Quilotoa, a volcanic crater filled by a beautiful emerald lake. From the rim of the crater, 3,850 m, several snowcapped volcanoes can be seen in the distance. The crater is reached by a paved road which runs north from Zumbahua (about 12 km, 3-5 hours' walk). Entry fee to Quilotoa US$2. There's a 300-m drop down from the crater rim to the water . The hike down takes about 30 minutes (an hour or more to climb back up). The trail starts to the left of the parking area down a steep, canyon-like cut. You can hire a mule to ride up from the bottom of the crater (US$5), but arrange it before heading down. Take a stick to fend off dogs. There is a basic hostel by the lake and kayaks for rent. Everyone at the crater tries to sell the famous naïve Tigua pictures and carved wooden masks, so expect to be besieged (also by begging children). To hike around the crater rim takes 4½-6 hours in clear weather. Be prepared for sudden changes in the weather, it gets very cold at night and can be foggy.

Chugchilán, Sigchos and Isinliví → *Phone code: 03.*

Chugchilán, a village in one of the most scenic areas of Ecuador, is 22 km by road from the Quilotoa crater. An alternative to the road is a 5-6-hour walk around part of the crater rim, then down to Guayama, and across the canyon (Río Sigüi) to Chugchilán, 11 km. Chugchilán has a woodcarving shop and a cheese factory outside town, and good walking opportunities.

Continuing from Chugchilán the road runs through Sigchos, the starting point for the Toachi Valley walk, via Asache to San Francisco de las Pampas (0900 bus daily to Latacunga). There is also a highland road to Las Pampas, with two buses from Sigchos. Southeast of Sigchos is Isinliví, on the old route to Toacazo and Latacunga. It has a fine woodcarving shop and a pre-Inca pucará. Trek to the village of Guantualó, which has a fascinating market on Monday. You can hike to or from Chugchilán (5 hours), or from Quilotoa to Isinliví in 7-9 hours.

From Sigchos, a paved road leads to Toacazo (**C La Quinta Colorada**, T271 6122, price includes breakfast and dinner, very nice) and on to Saquisilí (there are petrol stations at Toacazo and Yalo, below Sigchos).

Saquisilí → *Phone code: 03.*

Some 16 km southwest of Lasso, and 6 km west of the Panamericana is the small but very important market town of Saquisilí. Its Thursday market (0500-1400) is famous throughout Ecuador for the way in which its seven plazas and some of its streets become jam-packed with people, the great majority of them local *indígenas* with red ponchos and narrow-brimmed felt hats. The best time to visit the market is 0900-1200 (before 0800 for the animal market). Be sure to bargain, as there is a lot of competition. Saquisilí has colourful Corpus Christi processions.

Quilotoa Circuit listings

For Sleeping and Eating price codes and other relevant information, see Essentials, pages 38-40.

Sleeping

Latacunga to Zumbahua *p1098*

Pujilí

C El Capulí, Garcia Moreno y Juan Salinas, near the park, T272 4986. Beautifully renovated colonial house, but with an empty feel to it, nice comfortable rooms, includes breakfast, meals on request, Wi-Fi.

Tigua-Chimbacucho

B Posada de Tigua, 3 km east of Tigua-Chimbacucho, 400 m north of the road, T281 3682, laposadadetigua@latinmail.com. Refurbished hacienda, part of a working dairy ranch, 5 rooms, wood-burning stove, includes tasty home-cooked breakfast and dinner, pleasant family atmosphere, horses for riding, trails, nice views.

Zumbahua *p1099*

There are only a few phone lines in town, which are shared among several people. Expect delays when calling to book a room.

E Cóndor Matzi, overlooking the market area, T08-906 1572 or 03-281 2953 to leave message. Basic but best in town, shared bath, hot water, dinning room with wood stove, kitchen facilities, try to reserve ahead, if closed when you arrive ask at Restaurante Zumbahua on the corner of the plaza.

E Quilotoa, at the north end (bottom) of the plaza, next to the abbatoir, T09-955 2154. Fancy fixtures but a bit run down, hot water, not too clean.

F Richard, opposite the market on the road in to town, T09-015 5996. Basic shared rooms and one shower with hot water, cooking facilities, parking.

Quilotoa *p1099*

C Quilotoa Crater Lake Lodge, on the main road facing the access to Quilotoa, T09-794 2123, 12fausto@hotmail.es. Chilly hacienda-style lodge, includes breakfast, restaurant with fireplace and views, new management in 2009.

D Hostal Pachamama, at the top of the hill by the rim of the crater, T09-212 5962. Includes breakfast and dinner, some rooms with bath, hot water.

D-E Cabañas Quilotoa, on the left side of the access road, T09-212 5962. Includes breakfast and dinner, cheaper with shared bath, hot water, wood-burners. Owned by Humberto Latacunga, a good painter who will also organize treks.

Chugchilán *p1099*

Note that conventional phones (landlines) were not working in Chugchilán in early 2010.

L-A Black Sheep Inn, a few mins below the village on the way to Sigchos , T09-963 5405, www.blacksheepinn.com. A lovely eco-friendly resort which has received several awards. Nice private rooms with fireplace, includes 3 excellent vegetarian meals, drinking water and hot drinks all day, cheaper with shared bath, **C** pp in dorm, composting toilets, Wi-Fi extra, book exchange, organic garden, sauna, hot tub, gym, waterslide, arrange excursions, discounts for long stays, ISIC, seniors, SAE and EcoClub members, and cyclists, no credit cards, reservations advised. Highly recommended.

C-D Hostal Mama Hilda, 100 m from centre on the road in to town, T09-044 7451 (Quito), www.hostalmamahilda.org. Pleasant family-run hostel, warm atmosphere, large rooms some with wood stoves, includes good dinner and breakfast, cheaper with shared bath, **E** pp in dorm, parking, arrange horse-riding and walking trips, good value. Highly recommended.

E Hostal Cloud Forest, at the entrance to town, 150 m from the centre, T08-954 5634, josecloudforest@gmail.com. Simple but nice family-run hostel, sitting room with stove, includes dinner (good local fare or vegetarian) and breakfast, cheaper with shared bath, hot water, parking, very helpful owners.

Sigchos *p1099*

F Jardín de los Andes, Ilinizas y Tungurahua, T03-271 2114. Private bath, hot water, parking, basic but quite clean and friendly.

Isinliví *p1099*

C Llullu Llama, T281 4790, www.llullullama.com. Nicely refurbished house, cosy sitting room with wood-burning stove, tastefully decorated rooms, private, semi-private and dorm (**E** pp), includes good hearty dinner and breakfast, also coffee and tea, shared composting toilet with great views, abundant hot water, organic vegetable garden, warm and relaxing atmosphere, a lovely spot. Recommended.

Saquisilí *p1099*

D-E Gilocarmelo, by the cemetery, 800 m from town on the road north to Guaytacama, T09-966 9734, T02-340 0924, carlosrlopezc@yahoo.com. Restored hacienda house in a 4 ha property. Plain rooms with fireplace, cheaper in dorm, restaurant, heated pool, sauna, Jacuzzi, nice garden.

F San Carlos, Bolívar opposite the Parque Central. A multi-storey building, electric shower, parking, good value, but watch your valuables. Will hold luggage for US$1 while you visit the market.

Transport

Zumbahua *p1099*

Bus Many daily on the Latacunga-Quevedo road (0500-1900, US$1.25, 1½ hrs). Buses on Sat are packed full; ride on roof for best views, get your ticket the day before. A pick-up truck can be hired from Zumbahua to **Quilotoa** for US$5-10 depending on number of passengers; also to **Chugchilán** for around US$30. On Sat mornings there are many trucks leaving the Zumbahua market for Chugchilán which pass Quilotoa. Pick-up Quilotoa-Chugchilán US$25.

Taxi Day-trip by taxi to Zumbahua, Quilotoa, return to **Latacunga** is US$40.

Quilotoa *p1099*

Bus From the terminal terrestre in Latacunga **Trans Vivero** daily at 1000, 1130, 1230 and 1330, US$2, 2 hrs. Note that this leaves from Latacunga, not Saquisilí market, even on Thu. Return bus direct to Latacunga at 1300. Buses returning at 1400 and 1500 go only as far as Zumbahua, from where you can catch a Latacunga bound bus at the highway. Also, buses going through Zumbahua bound for Chugchilán will drop you at the turnoff, 5 mins from the crater, where you can also pick them up on their way to Zumbahua and Latacunga.

Chugchilán *p1099*

Bus From **Latacunga**, daily at 1130 (except Thu) via Sigchos, at 1200 via Zumbahua; on Thu from **Saquisilí market** via Sigchos around 1130, US$2.25, 3 hrs. Buses return to Latacunga daily at 0300 via Sigchos, at 0400 via Zumbahua. On Sun there are 2 extra buses to Latacunga leaving 0900-1000. There are extra buses going as far as Zumbahua Wed 0500, Fri 0600 and Sun between 0900-1000; these continue towards the coast. Milk truck to Sigchos around 0800. On Sat also pick-ups going to/from market in Zumbahua and Latacunga. Taxi from Latacunga US$60. From **Sigchos**, through buses as indicated above, US$0.60, 1 hr. Pick-up hire to Sigchos US$25, up to 5 people, US$5 additional person. Pick-up to **Quilotoa** US$25, up to 5 people, US$5 additional person. Taxi from Latacunga about US$60, from Quito US$100.

Sigchos *p1099*

Bus From **Latacunga** frequent daily service US$1.50, 2 hrs. From/to **Quito** direct service on Fri and Sun, US$3, 3 hrs. To **La Maná** on the road to Quevedo, via Chugchilán, Quilotoa and Zumbahua, Fri at 0500 and Sun at 0830, US$3.50, 6 hrs (returns Sat at 0730 and Sun at 1530). To **Las Pampas**, at 0330 and 1400, US$2.50, 3 hrs. From Las Pampas to **Santo Domingo**, at 0300 and 0600, US$2.50, 3 hrs.

Isinliví *p1099*

From **Latacunga** daily (except Thu), via Sigchos at 1215 (**14 de Octubre**) and direct at 1300 (**Trans Vivero**), on Thu both leave from Saquisilí market around 1100, on Sat the direct bus leaves at 1100 instead of 1300, US$1.80, 2½ hrs. Both buses return to Latacunga 0100-0330, except Wed at 0700 direct and Sun at 1245 direct. Connections to Chugchilán, Quilotoa and Zumbahua can be made in Sigchos. Bus schedules are posted on www.llullullama.com.

Saquisilí *p1099*

Bus Frequent service between **Latacunga** and Saquisilí, US$0.30, 20 mins; many buses daily to/from **Quito**, depart from the Quitumbe terminal, 0530-1300, US$2, 2hrs. Buses and trucks to many outlying villages leave from 1000 onwards. Bus tours from Quito cost US$45 pp, taxis charge US$60, with 2 hrs wait at market.

Ambato → *Phone code: 03. Colour map 11, B3. Population: 191,000. Altitude: 2,700 m.*

Almost completely destroyed in the great 1949 earthquake, Ambato lacks the colonial charm of other Andean cities, though its location in the heart of fertile orchard-country has earned it the nickname of 'the city of fruits and flowers' (see annual festival below). It is also the principal supply town of the central highlands. **Tourist office**: Ministerio de Turismo ⓘ *Guayaquil y Rocafuerte, T282 1800. Mon-Fri 0830-1300, 1430-1700*, helpful.

The modern cathedral faces **Parque Montalvo**, where there is a statue of the writer Juan Montalvo (1832-1889). His **house** is at ⓘ *Bolívar y Montalvo, T282 4248, US$1*. The **Museo de la Provincia** in the Casa del Portal (built 1900), facing Parque Montalvo ⓘ *Sucre entre Castillo y Montalvo*, has a photo collection, the elegant Samaria restaurant and a café. The main **market**, one of the largest in Ecuador, is held on Monday, with smaller markets on Wednesday and Friday. They have few items for the tourist.

Northeast of Ambato is the colonial town of **Píllaro**, gateway to **Parque Nacional Los Llanganates**, a beautiful rugged area (for tours see Sachayacu Explorer, page 1111). The town is known for its colourful festivals: a *diablada* (devils parade) 1-6 January and Corpus Christi.

Ambato to Baños

To the east of Ambato, an important road leads to **Salasaca**, where the *indígenas* sell their weavings; they wear distinctive black ponchos with white trousers and broad white hats. Further east, 5 km, is **Pelileo**, the blue jean manufacturing capital of Ecuador with good views of Tungurahua. From Pelileo, the road descends to Las Juntas, where the Patate and Chambo rivers meet to form the Río Pastaza. About 1 km east of Las Juntas bridge, the junction with the closed road to Riobamba is marked by a large sculpture of a macaw and a toucan (locally known as Los Pájaros – the lower bird is buried by volcanic debris). It is a favourite volcano watching site. The road to Baños then continues along the lower slopes of the volcano.

Eight kilometres northeast of Pelileo on a paved side-road is **Patate**, centre of the warm, fruit growing Patate valley. There are excellent views of Volcán Tungurahua from town. *Arepas*, sweets made of squash (unrelated to the Colombian or Venezuelan variety), are the local delicacy; sold around the park. The fiesta of Nuestro Señor del Terremoto is held on the weekend leading up to **4 February**, featuring a parade with floats made with fruit and flowers.

Ambato to Riobamba and Guaranda

After Ambato, the Pan-American Highway runs south to Riobamba (see page 1111). About half way is **Mocha**, where guinea pigs (*cuy*) are bred for the table. You can sample roast *cuy* and other typical dishes at stalls and restaurants by the roadside, *Mariadiocelina* is recommended. The highway climbs steeply south of Mocha and at the pass at **Urbina** (one hostal) there are fine views in the dry season of Chimborazo and Carihuairazo.

To the west of Ambato, a paved road climbs through tilled fields, past the páramos of Carihuairazo and Chimborazo to the great Arenal (a high desert at the base of the mountain), and down through the Chimbo valley to Guaranda (see page 1113). This spectacular journey on the highest paved road in Ecuador takes about three hours. It reaches a height of 4,380 m and vicuñas can be seen.

Ambato listings

For Sleeping and Eating price codes and other relevant information, see Essentials, pages 38-40.

Sleeping

Ambato *p1102*

L-A Casino Emperador, Cevallos y Lalama esquina, T242 4460, www.hotelcasino emperador.com. Luxury hotel with casino. Rooms and suites, includes buffet breakfast, restaurant, pool and spa.

L-A Hotel Ambato, Guayaquil 01-08 y Rocafuerte, T242 1791, www.hotelambato.com. A modern hotel near the heart of the city, includes breakfast, good restaurant, casino, squash court.

A-B Florida, Av Miraflores 1131, T242 2007. Pleasant hotel in a nice setting, includes breakfast, restaurant with good set meals, Wi-Fi, parking, spa, weekend discounts.

D Colony, 12 de Noviembre 124 y Av El Rey, near the bus terminal, T282 5789. A modern hotel with large rooms, includes breakfast, hot water, internet, parking, spotless.

D Pirámide Inn, Cevallos y Mariano Egüez, T242 1920. Comfortable hotel, includes breakfast, cafeteria, hot water, English and Italian spoken.

E Royal, Cevallos 05-60 y Vargas Torres, T282 3528. A small modern hotel, hot water, rooms are small, comfortable, good value.

F Madrid, Juan Cajas y Cumandá, near bus station, T282 8679. Adequate hostel, restaurant, cheaper with shared bath, hot water, disco.

Ambato to Baños *p1102*

Salasaca and Pelileo

D Runa Huasi, in Salasaca, 1 km north off main highway, look for signs and ask around, T09-984 0125, alonsopilla@hotmail.com. Simple hostel, includes breakfast, other meals on request, cooking facilities, nice views, guided walks.

E Hostal Pelileo, Eloy Alfaro 641, T287 1390. Shared bath, hot water, simple.

Patate

L Hacienda Leito, on the road to El Triunfo, T285 9329, www.haciendaleito.com. Classy hacienda, spacious rooms, includes breakfast and dinner, facing Tungurahua, good.

L Hacienda Manteles, in the Leito valley on the road to El Triunfo, T09-871 5632, 02-223 3484 (Quito), www.haciendamanteles.com. Nice converted hacienda with wonderful views of Tungurahua and Chimborazo, includes breakfast, dinner, snacks, walk to waterfalls, hiking and horse riding. Reserve ahead.

B Hostería Viña del Río, 3 km from town on the old road to Baños, T287 0314, www.hosteriavina delrio.com. Cabins on a 22 ha ranch, includes breakfast, restaurant, pool, spa and mini golf, US$4 for day use of facilities.

Ambato to Riobamba *p1102*

Urbina

D Posada de la Estación, in the solitary old railway station at 3,619 m, Urbina (signed), 2 km west of the highway, T03-294 2215, aventurag@yahoo.com. Meals available, shared bath, hot water, magnificent views, comfortable but very cold at night. A good place for acclimatization, helpful, horses, trips and equipment arranged. Recommended.

Eating

Ambato *p1102*

El Alamo Chalet, Cevallos 1719 y Montalvo, open 0800-2300 (2200 Sun). Ecuadorean and international food. Set meals and à la carte, Swiss-owned, good quality.

Govinda's, JB Vela 8-24 y Montalvo, Mon-Sat 0800-2030, Sun 0800-1600. Vegetarian set meals and à la carte.

La Buena Mesa, Quito 924 y Bolívar. Mon-Sat 0900-2200. French, also set lunches, elegant. Recommended.

La Fornace, Cevallos 1728 y Montalvo. Wood oven pizza. Opposite is **Heladería La Fornace**, Cevallos y Castillo. Good coffee, snacks, sandwiches, ice-cream, very popular.

Cafés

Crème Brulée, Juan B Vela 08-38 y Montalvo, daily 0900-2100. Very good coffee and pastries.

Pasterlería Quito, JL Mera y Cevallos, daily 0700-2100. Coffee, pastries, good for breakfast.

Festivals and events

Ambato *p1102*

Ambato has a famous festival in **Feb** or **Mar**, the **Fiesta de frutas y flores**, during carnival when there are 4 days of bullfights, festivities and parades (best Sun morning and Mon night). Must book ahead to get a hotel room.

Shopping

Ambato *p1102*

Leather Ambato is a centre for leather: stores for shoes on Bolívar; jackets, bags, belts on Vela between Lalama and Montalvo. Take a local bus up to the leather town of Quisapincha for the best deals, everyday, but big market on Sat.

Transport

Ambato *p1102*

Bus The main bus station is on Av Colombia y Paraguay, 2 km north of the centre. City buses go there from Plaza Cevallos in the centre, US$0.20. To **Quito**, 3 hrs, US$2.50. To **Cuenca**, US$8, 7 hrs. To **Guayaquil**, 6 hrs, US$6. To **Baños**, 1 hr, US$1. To **Riobamba**, US$1.25, 1 hr. To **Guaranda**, US$2, 3 hrs. To **Ibarra**, bypassing Quito, **CITA**, 8 daily, 5hrs, US$5. To **Santo Domingo de los Tsáchilas**, 4 hrs, US$4. To **Tena**, US$5, 5 hrs. To **Puyo**, US$3, 3 hrs. To **Macas**, US$7, 7 hrs. To **Esmeraldas**, US$8, 8 hrs. Through buses do not go into the terminal, they take the Paso Lateral, a bypass road.

Shared taxi Servicio Express, T242 6828 or T09-924 2795, 6 daily departures to **Quito**, US$12, door to door service.

Directory

Ambato *p1102*

Banks Banco del Pacífico, Cevallos y Lalama, and Cevallos y Unidad Nacional. Visa. **Produbanco**, Montalvo y Sucre. MasterCard. **Pacificard**, Bolívar 17-66 y Montalvo.

Internet Rates US$1 per hr.

Baños and Riobamba

Baños and Riobamba are both good bases for exploring the Sierra and their close proximity to high peaks gives great opportunities for climbing, cycling and trekking (but check for volcanic activity before you set out). The thermal springs at Baños are an added lure and the road east is one of the best ways to get to the jungle lowlands. On the other hand, anyone with the faintest interest in railways stops in Riobamba to ride the train on the last remaining section of the famous line from the Andes to Guayaquil, around the Devil's Nose.

Baños and around

→ *Phone code: 03. Colour map 11, B4. Population: 12,000. Altitude: 1,800 m.*

Baños is nestled between the Río Pastaza and the Tungurahua volcano, only 8 km from its crater. Baños bursts at the seams with hotels, *residenciales*, restaurants and tour agencies. Ecuadoreans flock here on weekends and holidays for the hot springs, to visit the Basílica and enjoy the local *melcochas* (toffees), while escaping the Andean chill in a sub-tropical climate (wettest in July and August). Foreign visitors are also frequent; using Baños as a base for trekking, organizing a visit to the jungle, making local day trips on horseback or by mountain bike, or just plain hanging out.

Ins and outs

Tourist offices iTur ⓘ *Oficina Municipal de Turismo, at the Municipio, Halflants y Rocafuerte, opposite Parque Central, Mon-Fri 0800-1230, 1400-1730, Sat-Sun 0800-1600*. Helpful, have colourful maps of the area, some English spoken. There are several private 'tourist information offices' run by travel agencies near the bus station; high-pressure tour sales, maps and pamphlets available. Local artist, J Urquizo, produces an accurate pictorial map of Baños, 12 de Noviembre y Ambato, also sold in many shops. Enquire with iTur (see above) or at your hotel about the current safety situation. Robberies have taken place along the trail to the Bellavista cross and on the cycling route to Puyo. Also thefts targeting tourists on Quito-Baños buses, take extra care of your hand-luggage.

In 1999, after over 80 years of dormancy, Tungurahua became active again and has remained so until the close of this edition (mid-2010). The level of activity is variable, the volcano can be quiet for days or weeks. Baños continues to be a safe and popular destination and will likely remain so unless the level of volcanic activity greatly increases. **Tungurahua is closed to climbers** and the road to Riobamba is closed, but all else is normal. Since the level of volcanic activity can change, you should enquire locally before visiting Baños. The National Geophysical Institute posts reports on the web at www.igepn.edu.ec.

Baños

The **Manto de la Virgen** waterfall at the southeast end of town is a symbol of Baños. The **Basílica** attracts many pilgrims. The paintings of miracles performed by Nuestra Señora del Agua Santa are worth seeing; also a **museum** ⓘ *0800-1200, 1300-1700, US$0.50*, with stuffed birds and

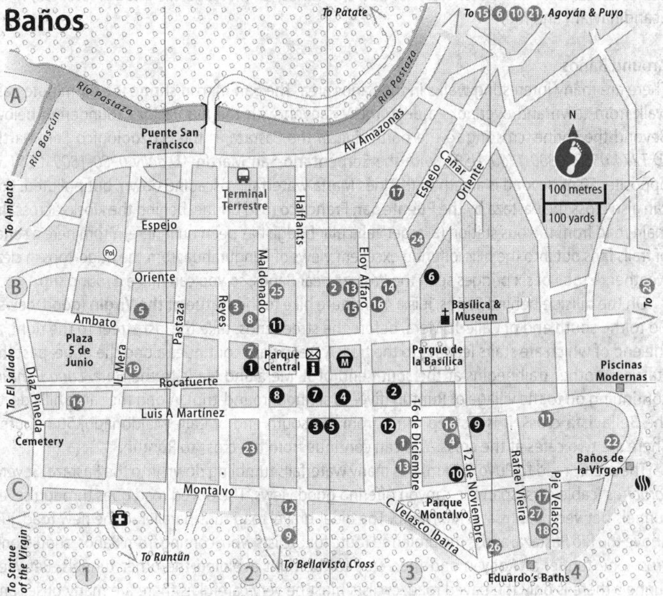

Sleeping
- 1 Carolina *C3*
- 2 Dinastía *B3*
- 3 El Belén *B2*
- 4 El Edén *C3*
- 5 El Oro *B1*
- 6 Finca Chamanapamba *A4*
- 7 Flor de Oriente *B2*
- 8 Hostal Rainforestur *B2*
- 9 Isla de Baños *C2*
- 10 La Casa Verde *A4*
- 11 La Chimenea *C4*
- 12 La Floresta *C2*
- 13 La Petite Auberge & Le Petit Restaurant *C3*
- 14 Llanovientos *C1*
- 15 Luna Runtún *A3*
- 16 Plantas y Blanco *C3*
- 17 Posada del Arte *C4*
- 18 Posada El Marqués *C4*
- 19 Princesa María *B1*
- 20 Puerta del Sol *B4*
- 21 Samari *A4*
- 22 Sangay *C4*
- 23 Timara *C2*
- 24 Transilvania *B3*
- 25 Verde Vida *B2*
- 26 Villa Santa Clara *C4*
- 27 Volcano *C4*

Eating
- 1 Ali Cumba & Café Hood *B2*
- 2 Buon Giorno *B3*
- 3 Café Blah Blah *B2*
- 4 Casa Hood *C3*
- 5 Coffee House *C2*
- 6 La Chimenea *B3*
- 7 Mariane *C2*
- 8 Pancho's *C2*
- 9 Pizzería El Napolitano *C3*
- 10 Quilombo *C3*
- 11 Rico Pan *B2*
- 12 Swiss Bistro *C3*

Bars & clubs
- 13 Buena Vista *B3*
- 14 Ferchos *B3*
- 15 Jack Rock *B3*
- 16 Leprechaun *B3*
- 17 Peña Ananitay *B3*

Nuestra Señora's clothing. There are various thermal baths in town, all charge US$2 unless otherwise noted. The **Baños de la Virgen** ⓘ *0430-1700*, are by the waterfall opposite the *Hotel Sangay*. They get busy so best visit very early morning. Two small hot pools open evenings only (1800-2200, US$3). The **Piscinas Modernas** ⓘ *weekends and holidays only, 0800-1700*, with a water slide, are next door. **El Salado baths** ⓘ *0600-1700*, several hot pools, plus icy cold river water, repeatedly destroyed by volcanic debris and in poor shape in 2010, 1½ km out of town off the Ambato road. **Eduardo's baths** ⓘ *0800-1800, spa US$5*, at the south end of C Rafael Viera, with a 25-m covered cold pool (the best for serious swimming) and a small warm pool. The **Santa Ana baths** ⓘ *Fri-Sun and holidays 0800-1700*, have hot and cold pools, just east of town on the road to Puyo. All the baths can be very crowded at weekends and holidays; the brown colour of the water is due to its high mineral content.

As well as the medicinal baths, there is a growing number of spas, in hotels, as independent centres and massage therapists. These offer a combination of sauna, steam bath (Turkish or box), Jacuzzi, clay and other types of baths, a variety of massage techniques (Shiatsu, Reiki, Scandinavian) and more.

Around Baños

There are many interesting **walks** in the Baños area. The **San Martín shrine** is a 45-minute easy walk from town and overlooks a deep rocky canyon with the Río Pastaza thundering below. Beyond the shrine, crossing to the north side of the Pastaza, is the **Ecozoológico San Martín** ⓘ *T274 0552, 0800-1700, US$2*, with the **Serpentario San Martín** ⓘ *daily 0900-1800, US$1.50* opposite. 50 m beyond is a path to the **Inés María waterfall**, cascading down, but polluted. You can also cross the Pastaza by the **Puente San Francisco** road bridge, behind the kiosks across the main road from the bus station (a larger vehicular bridge has been built here). From here a series of trails fans out into the hills, offering excellent views of Tungurahua from the ridge-tops in clear weather. A total of six bridges span the Pastaza near Baños, so you can make a round trip.

On the hillside behind Baños, it is a 45-minute hike to the **statue of the Virgin** (good views). Go to the south end of Calle JL Mera, before the street ends, take the last street to the right, at the end of which are stairs leading to the trail. A steep path continues along the ridge, past the statue. Another trail begins at the south end of JL Mera and leads to the *Hotel Luna Runtún*, continuing on to the village of Runtún (five- to six-hour round-trip). Along the same hillside, to the **Bellavista cross**, it is a steep climb from the south end of Calle Maldonado, 50 minutes. There are two cafés at the cross. You can continue from the cross to Runtún.

The scenic road to Puyo (58 km) has many waterfalls tumbling down into the Pastaza. Several *tarabitas* (cable cars) span the canyon offering good views. The paved road goes through seven tunnels between Baños and Río Negro. The older gravel road runs parallel to the new road, just above the Río Pastaza, and is the preferred route for cyclists who, coming from Baños, should only cross one tunnel at Agoyán and then stay to the right avoiding the other tunnels. Between tunnels there is only the paved road, cyclists must be very careful as there are many buses and lorries. The area has excellent opportunities for walking and nature observation.

At the junction of the Verde and Pastaza rivers, 17 km from Baños is the town of **Río Verde** with snack bars, restaurants and a few places to stay. The Río Verde has crystalline green water and is nice for bathing. The paved highway runs to the north of town, between it and the old road, the river has been dammed forming a small lake where rubber rafts are rented for paddling. Before joining the Pastaza the Río Verde tumbles down several falls, the most spectacular of which is **El Pailón del Diablo** (the Devil's Cauldron). Cross the Río Verde on the old road and take the path to the right after the church, then follow the trail down towards the suspension bridge over the Pastaza, for about 20 minutes. Just before the bridge take a side trail to the right (signposted) which leads you to **Paradero del Pailón**, a nice restaurant, and viewing platforms above the falls (US$1). The **San Miguel Falls**, smaller but also nice, are some five minutes' walk from the town along a different trail. Cross the old bridge and take the first path to the right, here is **Falls Garden** (US$1), with lookout platforms over both sets of falls. Cyclists can leave the bikes at one of the snack bars while visiting the falls and return to Baños by bus. Do not take valuables when cycling this route and enquire about safety before setting out.

Baños and around listings

For Sleeping and Eating price codes and other relevant information, see Essentials, pages 38-40.

Sleeping

Baños *p1105, map p1105*

Baños has plenty of accommodation but can fill during holiday weekends.

LL Samari, Vía a Puyo Km 1, T274 1855, www.samarispa.com. Upmarket resort-spa opposite the Santa Ana baths, includes breakfast, restaurant, pool and spa (included), tastefully decorated hacienda-style rooms and suites on nice grounds.

LL-AL Luna Runtún, Caserío Runtún Km 6, T274 0882, www.lunaruntun.com. A classy hotel in a beautiful setting overlooking Baños. Includes dinner and breakfast and use of spa, very comfortable rooms with balconies and superb views, lovely gardens. Excellent service, English, French and German spoken, hiking, horse riding and biking tours, nanny service available.

A Finca Chamanapamba, on the east shore of the Río Ulba, a short ride from the road to Puyo, T274 2671, www.chamanapamba.com. Two nicely finished wooden cabins in a spectacular location overlooking the Río Ulba and just next to the Chamanapamba waterfalls, includes breakfast and dinner, very good café-restaurant serves German food.

A-B Sangay, Plazoleta Isidro Ayora 100, next to waterfall and thermal baths, T274 0490, www.sangayspahotel.com. A comfortable hotel and spa with 3 types of rooms, includes buffet breakfast, good restaurant specializes in Ecuadorean food, pool and spa open to non-residents 1600-2000 (US$6), Wi-Fi, parking, tennis and squash courts, games room, car hire, disco, attentive service, British-Ecuadorean run. Recommended.

B Posada del Arte, Pasaje Velasco Ibarra y Montalvo, T274 0083, www.posadadelarte.com. Nice cosy inn, includes breakfast, vegetarian restaurant, Wi-Fi, pleasant sitting room, more expensive rooms have fireplace, terrace.

B Volcano, Rafael Vieira y Montalvo, T274 2140, www.volcano.com.ec. Nice spacious modern hotel, large rooms with fridge, some with views of the waterfall, includes buffet breakfast, restaurant, heated pool, massage, Wi-Fi, nice garden.

C La Floresta, Halflants y Montalvo, T274 1824, www.lafloresta.banios.com. Nice hotel with large comfortable rooms set around a lovely garden, includes excellent breakfast, other meals on request, Wi-Fi, parking, pleasant service. Recommended.

C La Petite Auberge, 16 de Diciembre y Montalvo, T274 0936, www.lepetit.banios.com. Rooms around a patio, some with fireplace, includes breakfast, good French restaurant, parking, quiet.

C-D Isla de Baños, Halflants 1-31 y Montalvo, T274 0609, islabanos@andinanet.net. Nicely decorated comfortable hotel, includes European breakfast and steam bath, Wi-Fi, internet US$1.50, glass-enclosed spa operates when there are enough people, pleasant garden.

D Flor de Oriente, Ambato y Maldonado on Parque Central, T274 0418, www.flordeoriente.banios.com. Very good hotel in a multi-storey building, includes breakfast, cafeteria, private bath, hot water, parking, can get noisy at weekends.

D Hostal Rainforestur, Maldonado y Ambato, T274 0046, www.rainforestur.com.ec. Includes breakfast, hot water, same owners as Rainforestur agency.

D La Casa Verde, in Santa Ana, 1.5 Km from town on Camino Real, a road parallell and north of the road to Puyo, T08-659 4189, www.lacasaverde.com.ec. Very nice spacious hotel decorated in pine, the largest rooms in Baños , includes breakfast, hot water, Wi-Fi, laundry and cooking facilities, very quiet, organic vegetable garden, New Zealand-run, opened in 2009.

D Posada El Marqués, Pasaje Velasco Ibarra y Montalvo, T274 0053, www.marques.banios.com. Hot water, Wi-Fi, spacious, good beds, video room, garden, quiet area.

D Puerta del Sol, Ambato y Arrayanes (east end of C Ambato), T274 2265. Modern hotel, nicer than it looks on the outside, large well appointed rooms, includes breakfast served in a pleasant dinning area, hot water, parking, opened in 2009.

D Villa Santa Clara, 12 de Noviembre y Velasco Ibarra, T274 0349, www.hotelvillasantaclara.com. Nice cabins in a quiet location, cheaper with shared bath, hot water, laundry facilities, parking, garden and spa.

E Carolina, 16 de Diciembre y Martínez, T274 0592. Restaurant, good hot water supply, good kitchen facilities, terrace, discounts for longer stays, popular. Recommended.

E Dinastía, Oriente y Alfaro, T274 0933. Hot water, nice, quiet, good value.

E El Belén, Reyes y Ambato, T274 1024, www.hotel-elbelen.com. Nice hostel, hot water, cooking facilities, parking, helpful staff.

E El Edén, 12 de Noviembre y Montalvo, T274 0616. Pleasant wheelchair-accessible hotel with a patio. Restaurant, hot water, internet, parking, rooms with balconies, pool table, ping pong.

E La Chimenea, Martínez y Rafael Vieira, T274 2725, www.hostalchimenea.com. Nice hostel with terrace café, breakfast available, cheaper with shared bath, **G** pp in dorm, abundant hot water, small pool, Jacuzzi extra, internet, parking for small cars, quiet, helpful and good value. Recommended.

E Llanovientos, Martínez 1126 y Sebastián Baño, T274 0682, www.llanovientos.banios.com. A modern breezy hostel with wonderful views. Comfortable rooms, cafeteria, plenty of hot water, internet, cooking facilities, parking, nice garden. Recommended.

E Princesa María, Rocafuerte y Mera, T274 1035. Spacious rooms, hot water, Wi-Fi, laundry and cooking facilities, parking, popular budget travellers' meeting place, helpful and good value.

E Transilvania, 16 de Diciembre y Oriente, T274 2281, www.hostal-transilvania.com. Multi-storey building with simple rooms, includes breakfast, Middle Eastern restaurant, hot water, internet, nice views from balconies, large TV and many movies in sitting room, pool table, luggage storage, popular meeting place.

E Verde Vida, Maldonado y Oriente, T274 2947. Nice modern hostel, hot water, small terrace with views, attentive service, good value.

E-F El Oro, Ambato y JL Mera., T274 0736. With bath, **G** pp in dorm, hot water, internet, laundry and cooking facilities, cheaper in dorm, good value, popular. Recommended.

E-F Plantas y Blanco, 12 de Noviembre y Martínez, T274 0044, option3@hotmail.com. Pleasant popular hostel decorated with plants, a variety of rooms and prices, cheaper with shared bath, **G** pp in dorm, hot water, Wi-Fi, excellent breakfast, fruit salads and self service drinks in rooftop cafeteria, steam bath, classic films, bakery, French owned, good value. Repeatedly recommended.

E-F Timara, Maldonado 381 y Martínez, T274 0599, www.timara.banios.com. Small, British-Ecuadorean-run hostel, nice new rooms with bath, cheaper with shared bath, hot water, laundry and cooking facilities, nice garden.

Around Baños *p1106*

B Miramelindo, Río Verde, just north of the paved road, T249 3004, www.miramelindo.banios.com. Lovely hotel and spa, nicely decorated rooms, includes breakfast, good restaurant, pleasant gardens include an orchid collection with over 1000 plants.

D Hostería Río Verde, between the paved road and town, T288 4207 (Ambato). Simple cabins in a rural setting, restaurant specializes in trout and tilapia, hot water, large pool, spa.

Eating

Baños *p1105, map p1105*

TTT Le Petit Restaurant, 16 de Diciembre y Montalvo, T274 0936, closed Wed. Very good French cuisine, their onion soup is particularly recommended, also vegetarian dishes, fondue, great atmosphere.

TT Buon Giorno, Ambato y Pasaje Ermita de la Vírgen west of the market, and Rocafuerte y 16 de Diciembre, Tue-Sun 1130-2230. Italian dishes, pizza, mixed reports on service.

TT Mariane, Halflants y Rocafuerte, daily 1600-2300. Excellent authentic Provençal cuisine, large portions, pleasant atmosphere, good value and attentive service. Highly recommended.

TT Quilombo, Montalvo y 12 de Noviembre, Wed-Sun 1200-2200. Good quality Argentine grill.

TT Swiss Bistro, Martínez y Alfaro, Tue-Sat 1200-2300, Sun 1200-1700, Mon 1800-2300. International dishes and Swiss specialties, Swiss run.

¥¥-¥ **Pizzería El Napolitano**, 12 de Noviembre y Martínez, daily 1200-2300. Good pizza, pasta and antipasto. Also some Ecuadorean dishes. Pleasant atmosphere, pool table, economical pizza and soft drink for lunch.

¥ **Café Hood**, Maldonado y Ambato, at Parque Central, 1000-2200, closed Wed. Mainly vegetarian but also some meat dishes, excellent food, English spoken, always busy. Also rents rooms.

¥ **Casa Hood**, Martínez between Halflants and Alfaro, Thu-Mon 1600-2300. Largely vegetarian, but also serve some meat dishes, juices, milkshakes, good desserts, varied menu including Indonesian and Thai dishes. Travel books and maps sold, book exchange, repertory cinema, occasional cultural events, nice atmosphere. Popular and recommended.

¥ **La Chimenea**, Oriente y 16 de Diciembre, 1830-2300, closed Tue. Simple place serving good filling and economical grilled chicken.

Cafés

Ali Cumba, Maldonado opposite Parque Central, daily 0700-1900. Excellent breakfasts, salads, best coffee in town (filtered, espresso), muffins, cakes, homemade bread, large sandwiches (also take-out), book exchange. Pricey but good, Danish-Ecuadorean run. Recommended.

Café Blah Blah, Halflants y Matrínez, daily 0900-2000. Cosy café serving very good breakfasts, coffee, cakes, snacks and juices, a popular meeting place.

Coffee House, Martínez y Halflants, Tue-Sun 0900-0000. Snacks, drinks, coffee, capuccino, good cakes and pastries. Pleasant atmosphere, books, games, pool table, ping-pong. German-Ecuadorean run and recommended.

Pancho's, Rocafuerte y Maldonado at Parque Central, daily 1500-2200. Hamburgers, snacks, coffee, friendly owner.

Rico Pan, Ambato y Maldonado at Parque Central, Mon-Sat 0700-2000, Sun 0700-1200. Good breakfasts, hot bread (including whole wheat), fruit salads and pizzas, also meals, friendly owners.

Bars and clubs

Baños *p1105, map p1105*

Eloy Alfaro, between Ambato and Oriente has many bars including:

Buena Vista, Alfaro y Oriente. A good place for salsa and other Latin music.

Ferchos, Oriente entre Alfaro y 16 de Diciembre, Tue-Sun 1600-2400. Café-bar, modern decor, snacks, cakes, good varied music, German-run.

Jack Rock, Alfaro y Ambato. A favourite traveller hangout.

Leprechaun, Alfaro y Oriente. Popular for dancing, bon-fire on weekends, ocassional live music.

Entertainment

Baños *p1105, map p1105*

Chivas, open-sided buses, cruise town playing music, they take you to different night spots and to a volcano lookout when Tungurahua is active.

Peña Ananitay, 16 de Diciembre y Espejo. Good live music and dancing.

Festivals

Baños *p1105, map p1105*

During Carnival and Holy Week hotels are full and prices rise.

Oct: **Nuestra Señora de Agua Santa** with daily processions, bands, fireworks, sporting events and partying through the month. Week-long celebrations ending **16 Dec**: the town's anniversary, parades, fairs, sports, cultural events. The night of **15 Dec** is the **Verbenas**, when each *barrio* hires a band and there are many parties.

Shopping

Baños *p1105, map p1105*

Look out for jaw-aching toffee (*melcocha*) made in ropes in shop doorways, or the less sticky *alfeñique*.

Handicrafts Crafts stalls at Pasaje Ermita de la Vírgen, off C Ambato, by the market. Tagua (vegetable ivory made from palm nuts) crafts on Maldonado entre Oriente y Espejo. Leather shops on Rocafuerte entre Halflants y 16 de Diciembre.

Latino Shop, Ambato y Alfaro and 4 other locations. For T-shirts.

Las Orquídeas, Ambato Y Maldonado by Parque Central and at *Hostal La Floresta*. Excellent selection of crafts, some guides and coffee-table books.

Recuerdos, on road to Ambato. For balsa-wood birds and to see crafts-people at work.

Activities and tours

Baños *p1105, map p1105*

Potentially hazardous activities are popular in Baños, including mountaineering, white water rafting, canyoning, canopying and bridge jumps. Safety standards vary greatly. There is seldom any recourse in the event of a mishap so these activities are entirely at your own risk.

Canopying or zip line Involves hanging from a harness and sliding on a steel cable. Prices vary according to length, about US$10-15.

Canyoning Many agencies offer this sport, rates US$30-35.

Climbing and trekking There are countless possibilities for walking and nature observation near Baños and east towards Oriente. Baños operators offer climbing and trekking tours to several destinations. Remember that Tungurahua has been officially closed to climbers since 1999. There is nobody to stop you from entering the area, but the dangers of being hit by flying volcanic bombs are very real. Unless volcanic activity has completely ceased, do not be talked into climbing to the crater or summit.

Cycling Many places rent bikes, quality varies, rates from US$5 per day; check brakes and tyres, find out who has to pay for repairs, and insist on a helmet, puncture repair kit and pump. The following have good equipment:

Carrillo Hermanos, 16 de Diciembre y Martínez. Rents mountain bikes and motorcycles (reliable machines with helmets, US10 per hr).

Hotel isla de Baños, cycling tours US$15-20.

Horse riding There are several places, but check their horses as not all are well cared for. Rates around US$5-6 per hr. The following have been recommended:

Angel Aldaz, Montalvo y JL Mera (on the road to the statue of the Virgin).

Hotel Isla de Baños, see above. Horses for rent; 3½ hrs with a guide and jeep transport costs US$30 per person, English and German spoken.

José & Two Dogs, Maldonado y Martínez, T274 0746. Flexible hours.

Ringo Horses, 12 de Noviembre y Martínez (*Pizzeria El Napolitano*). Nice horses, offers rides outside Baños.

Puenting Many operators offer this bungee-jumping-like activity from the bridges around Baños, US$10-15 per jump, heights and styles vary.

River rafting Fatal accidents have occurred, but not with the agencies listed here. Rates US$25-30 for half-day, US$50-70 for full-day. The Chambo, Patate and Pastaza rivers are all polluted.

Adventure Equatorland, see below.

Geotours, see below.

Tour operators

There are many tour agencies in town, some with several offices, as well as 'independent' guides who seek out tourists on the street (the latter are generally not recommended). Quality varies considerably; to obtain a qualified guide and avoid unscrupulous operators, it is best to seek advice from other travellers who have recently returned from a tour. We have received some critical reports of tours out of Baños, but there are also highly respected and qualified operators here. In all cases, insist on a written contract. Most agencies and guides offer trips to the jungle (US$30-50 per day pp) and 2 day climbing trips to Cotopaxi (approximately US$120-180 pp plus entrance fee and refugio) or Chimborazo (approximately US$120-200 pp plus entrance fee and refugio). There are also volcano-watching, trekking and horse tours, in addition to the day-trips and sports mentioned above. Several companies run tours abord a chiva (open-sided bus). The following agencies and guides have received positive recommendations but the list is not exhaustive and there are certainly others.

Adventure Equatorland, Martínez y 16 de Diciembre, T274 0360, www.adventure equatorland.com.

Deep Forest Adventure, no storefront, T09-837 4530, deepforestadventure@hotmail.com. German, English and French spoken, off-the-beaten-track destinations.

Expediciones Amazónicas, Oriente 11-68 y Halflants, T274 0506, www.expediciones amazonicas.com.

Explorsierra, Halflants y Oriente, T274 2771, explorsierra1@hotmail.com. Also rent equipment.

Geotours, Ambato y Halflants, next to Banco Pichincha, T274 1344, www.geotoursbanios.com. Also offer paragliding for US$60.

Marberktour, Eloy Alfaro entre Ambato y Rocafuerte, info_marberktour@yahoo.es, T274 1695,. English and Dutch spoken.

Rainforestur, Ambato 800 y Maldonado, also in Quito, T274 0046, www.rainforestur.com.ec. Environmentally conscious operator.
Sachayacu Explorer, Bolívar 229 y Urbina, in Píllaro, T287 3292, www.rio-amazonas.banios.com. Trekking in the Llanganates, jungle tours as far as Peru, English spoken.

Transport

Baños *p1105, map p1105*
Bus City buses run throughout the day from Alfaro y Martínez east to Agoyán and from Rocafuerte by the market, west to El Salado and the zoo. To **Rio Verde** take any Puyo bus from Maldonado y Amazonas, opposite Baños bus station, 20 mins, US$0.50.

The long distance bus station is on the Ambato-Puyo road (Av Amazonas) a short way from the centre, and is the scene of vigorous volleyball games most afternoons. To/from **Quito**, via Ambato, US$3, 4 hrs, frequent service; going to Quito sit on the right for views of Cotopaxi, buy tickets early for weekends and holidays. For shared taxis to Quito, see **Servicio Express**, p 1104. To **Ambato**, 1 hr, US$1. To **Riobamba**, the direct Baños-Riobamba road is closed due to Tungurahua's volcanic activity, buses go via Ambato, 2 hrs, US$2. To **Latacunga**, 2 hrs, US$2. To **Otavalo** and **Ibarra** direct, bypassing Quito, **Expreso Baños**, 2 daily, US$6, 5½ hrs. To **Guayaquil**, one bus per day and one overnight, 6-7 hrs. To **Puyo**, 1½ hrs, US$2. Sit on the right. You can cycle to Puyo and take the bus back (passport check on the way). To **Tena**, 3 hrs, US$4. To **Misahuallí**, change at Tena, or at the Río Napo crossing, and **Macas**, 6 hrs, US$6 (sit on right).

Directory

Baños *p1105, map p1105*
Banks Banco del Austro, Halflants y Rocafuerte, ATM. **Banco del Pacífico**, Halflants y Rocafuerte, Parque Central, ATM and TCs. **Don Pedro**, Halflants y Martínez, hardware store, open weekends, 3% commission on TCs. Also exchanges Euros and other currencies. **Internet** Plenty of cyber cafés in town, prices US$1 per hr. **Language schools** Spanish lessons cost US$5-6 per hr. **Baños Spanish Center**, Oriente 820 y Julio Cañar, T274 0632, baniosspanishcenter@hotmail.com. Proprietor Elizabeth Barrionuevo, English and German-speaking, flexible, salsa lessons, recommended. **Ciudad de Baños**, Ambato y Eloy Alfaro, T274 0317, www.escueladeidiomas.banios.com. **Mayra's**, Montalvo y 16 de Diciembre T274 2850, www.mayraspanish school.com. **Raíces**, 16 de Diciembre y Pablo A Suárez, T274 0090, www.spanishlessons.org. **Post offices** Halflants y Ambato, across from Parque Central.

Riobamba and around

Guaranda and Riobamba are good bases for exploring the Sierra. Riobamba is the bigger of the two and is the starting point for what remains of the famous railway which used to go to Guayaquil. Because of their central location Riobamba and the surrounding province are known as 'Corazón de la Patria' – the heartland of Ecuador – and the city boasts the nickname 'La Sultana de Los Andes' in honour of lofty Mount Chimborazo.

Riobamba → *Phone code: 03. Colour map 11, B3. Population: 169,000. Altitude: 2,754 m.*
The capital of Chimborazo Province is built in the wide **Tapi Valley** and has broad streets and many ageing but impressive buildings. **Tourist office**: iTur ⓘ *Av Daniel León Borja y Brasil, T294 7389, Mon-Fri 0800-1230, 1430-1800, English spoken*, municipal information office. The **Ministerio de Turismo** ⓘ *3 doors from iTur, in the Centro de Arte y Cultura, T294 1213, Mon-Fri 0800-1300, 1400-1700; also at the train station, Mon-Fri 1400-1800*, is very helpful and knowledgeable, English spoken.

The main square is **Parque Maldonado** around which are the **Cathedral**, the **Municipality** and several colonial buildings with arcades. The Cathedral has a beautiful colonial stone façade and an incongruously modern interior. Four blocks northeast of the railway station is the

Parque 21 de Abril, named after the Batalla de Tapi, 21 April 1822, the city's independence from Spain. The park, better known as **La Loma de Quito**, affords an unobstructed view of Riobamba and Chimborazo, Carihuairazo, Tugurahua, El Altar and occasionally Sangay. It also has a colourful tile tableau of the history of Ecuador. The **Convento de la Concepción** ⓘ *Orozco y España, entrance at Argentinos y J Larrea, T296 5212, Mon 0900-1230, Tue-Sat, 1500-1730, US$3*, is a religious art museum. Its priceless one-metre high gold monstrance, Custodia de Riobamba Antigua, the museum's greatest treasure, was stolen and melted down in 2007. A replica can be seen in the museum. **Museo del Banco Central** ⓘ *Veloz y Montalvo, T296 5501, Mon-Fri 0900-1700, Sat 1000-1600, US$1*, has well displayed exhibits of archaeology and colonial art. **Museo de la Ciudad** ⓘ *Primera Constituyente y Espejo, at Parque Maldonado, T295 1906, Mon-Fri 0800-1230, 1430-1800, Sat 0900-1600, free*, in a beautifully restored colonial building, has displays on regional national parks, paintings, photographs and temporary exhibits.

Riobamba is an important **market** centre where people from many communities congregate. Saturday is the main day when the city fills with colourfully dressed *indígenas* from all over Chimborazo, each wearing their distinctive custome; trading overflows the markets and buying and selling go on all over town. Wednesday is a smaller market day. The 'tourist' market is in the small **Plaza de la Concepción or Plaza Roja** ⓘ *Orozco y Colón, Sat and Wed only, 0800-1500*, south of the Convento de la Concepción (see above). It is a good place to buy local handicrafts and authentic Indian clothing. The main produce market is **San Alfonso**, Argentinos y 5 de Junio, which on Saturday spills over into the nearby streets and also sells clothing, ceramics, baskets and hats. Other markets in the colonial centre are **La Condamine** ⓘ *Carabobo y Colombia, daily*, largest market on Fridays, **San Francisco** and **La Merced**, near the churches of the same name.

Guano is a carpet-weaving, sisal and leather working town 8 km north of Riobamba. Many shops sell rugs and you can arrange to have these woven to your own design. Buses leave from the Mercado Dávalos, García Moreno y New York, every 20 minutes, US$0.25, last bus returns to Riobamba at 1900. Taxi US$3 by day, US$4 at night.

Riobamba

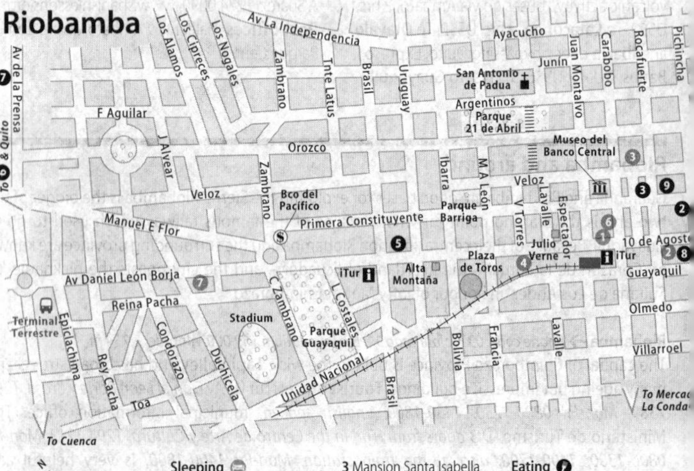

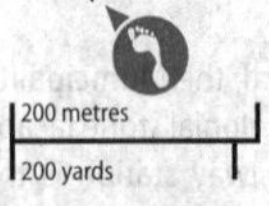

Sleeping
1 El Libertador, San Pedro de Riobamba & La Fogata Restaurant
2 Los Shyris
3 Mansion Santa Isabella
4 Metropolitano
5 Oasis
6 Tren Dorado
7 Zeus

Eating
1 Ave María
2 Café VIP
3 El Delirio
4 Helados de Paila

Guaranda → *Phone code: 03. Colour map 11, B3. Population: 60,000. Altitude: 2,650 m.*
This quaint town, capital of Bolívar province, proudly calls itself 'the Rome of Ecuador' because it is built on seven hills. There are fine views of the mountains all around. Locals traditionally take an evening stroll in the palm-fringed main plaza, **Parque Libertador Simón Bolívar**, around which are the Municipal buildings and a large stone **Cathedral**. Towering over the city, on one of the hills, is an impressive statue of **El Indio Guaranga**, a local Indian leader; museum (free) and art gallery. Although not on the tourist trail, there are many sights worth visiting in the province, for which Guaranda is the ideal base. Of particular interest is the highland town of **Salinas**, with its community development projects (accommodations and tours available, see Sleeping), as well as the *subtrópico* region, the lowlands stretching west towards the coast.

Market days are Friday (till 1200) and Saturday (larger), when many indigenous people in typical dress trade at the market complex at the east end of Calle Azuay, by Plaza 15 de Mayo (9 de Abril y Maldonado), and at Plaza Roja (Avenida Gen Enríquez). Carnival in Guaranda is among the best known in the country. **Tourist office**: Oficina Municipal de Turismo ⓘ *García Moreno entre 7 de Mayo y Convención de 1884, T298 0181 ext 3019, Mon-Fri 0800-1200, 1400-1800.* Provides Information in Spanish and maps.

Reserva Faunística Chimborazo → *See also Riobamba Tour operators.*
ⓘ *US$10 entrance fee, US$5 with student card.* The most outstanding features of this reserve, created to protect the camelids (vicuñas, alpacas and llamas) which were re-introduced here, are the beautiful snow-capped volcano of **Chimborazo** and its neighbour **Carihuairazo**. Chimborazo, inactive, is the highest peak in Ecuador (6,310 m), while Carihuairazo, 5,020 m, is dwarfed by its neighbour. Day visitors can enjoy lovely views, a glimpse of the handsome vicuñas and the rarefied air above 4,800 m. There are great opportunities for trekking on the eastern slopes and of course climbing Ecuador's highest peak. Horse riding tours are offered along the Mocha Valley between the two peaks and downhill cycling from Chimborazo is popular. Many agencies run tours here.

To the west of the reserve runs the Vía del Arenal which joins San Juan, along the Riobamba-Guaranda road, with Cruce del Arenal on the Ambato-Guaranda road. A turn-off from this road leads to the main park entrance and beyond to the **Refugio Hermanos Carrel**, a shelter at 4,800 m, from where It is a 45-minute walk to **Refugio Whymper** at 5,000 m. Both shelters have bunk beds, cooking facilities and toilets and where undergoing renovations in 2010. The access from Riobamba (51 km, paved to the park entrance) is very beautiful. Along the Vía del Arenal past San Juan are a couple of small native communities which grow a few crops and raise llamas and alpacas. They offer lodging and native guides. The *arenal* is a large sandy plateau at about 4,400 m, to the west of Chimborazo, just below the main park entrance. It can be a harsh, windy place, but it is also very beautiful; take the time to admire the tiny flowers which grow here. This is the best place to see vicuñas, which hang around either in family groups, one male and its harem, or lone males which have been expelled from the group.

5 Jamones La Andaluza & Naranjo's
6 L'Incontro
7 Mónaco Pizzería
8 Puro Café
9 Sierra Nevada

Climbing Chimborazo At 6,310 m, this is a difficult climb owing to the altitude. No-one without mountaineering experience should attempt the climb, and rope, ice-axe, helmet and crampons must be used. It is essential to have at least one week's acclimatization above 3,500 m. The best seasons are December and June-September. Ice pinnacles, *penitentes*, sometimes prevent climbers reaching the main, Whymper summit.

The Devil's Nose Train

In 2010, the line along the most spectacular part of the trip – the **Devil's Nose** and **Alausí Loop** – was undergoing extensive repairs. Service was restricted to an *autoferro* (a bus on rails) running between **Riobamba** and **Palmira**, some 75 km to the south (see Transport). The repairs are part of the **Empresa de Ferrocarriles Ecuatorianos'** ⓘ *www.efe.gov.ec* efforts to rehabilitate the railway network.

Alausí ➔ *Phone code: 03. Colour map 11, B3. Population: 9,500. Altitude: 2,350 m.*
This picturesque town perched on a hillside is where many passengers join the train for the amazing descent over *La Nariz de Diablo* to Sibambe. There is good walking, a Sunday market, in the plaza by the church, up the hill from the station; and a *Fiesta de San Pedro* on 29 June.

Sangay National Park

Riobamba provides access to the central highland region of **Parque Nacional Sangay** ⓘ *US$10, information from Ministerio del Ambiente, Avenida 9 de Octubre y Quinta Macají, at the western edge of Riobamba, T261 0029, Mon-Fri 0800-1300, 1400-1700*, a beautiful wilderness area with excellent opportunities for trekking and climbing. A controversial road runs from Riobamba to Macas in the Oriente, cutting through the park. At Cebadas (with a good cheese factory) a branch road joins from **Guamote**, a quiet, mainly indigenous town on the Pan-American highway, which comes to life during its colourful Thursday market. The road through Sangay makes a spectacular ride, with five-hour bus services Riobamba-Macas. At **Atillo**, south of Cebadas, an area of lovely **páramo** dotted with lakes, there is lodging at **F** pp **Cabaña Saskines**, T03-262 6620. **Sangay** (5,230 m) is an active volcano, access to the mountain takes at least three days and is only for those who can endure long, hard days of walking and severe weather. Climbing Sangay can be dangerous even on a quiet day and a helmet to protect against falling stones is vital, November to January is a good time to climb it. Agencies in Quito and Riobamba offer tours or you can organize an expedition independently. A guide is essential, porters can be hired in the access towns of **Alao** and **Guargualla**. The latter has a community tourism project with accommodation (**D** pp demi-pension, T03-260 6774) and native guides. Also in Sangay National Park is the beautiful **El Altar** volcano (5,315 m), whose crater is surrounded by nine summits. The most popular climbing and trekking routes begin beyond Candelaria at Hacienda Releche (see Sleeping).

Riobamba and around listings

For Sleeping and Eating price codes and other relevant information, see Essentials, pages 38-40.

Sleeping

Riobamba *p1111, map p1112*
Many of the upmarket hotels are out of town.
A Mansion Santa Isabella, Veloz 28-48 y Carabobo, T296 2947, mansionasantaisabella@hotmail.com. Nicely refurbished house with pleasant patio, comfortable rooms, most with bathtub, includes breakfast, Wi-Fi, British-Ecuadorean run, opened in 2010.
A San Pedro de Riobamba, Daniel L Borja 29-50 y Montalvo, opposite the train station, T294 0586, www.hotelsanpedroderiobamba.com. Elegant hotel in a beautifully restored house in the centre of town, ample comfortable rooms, includes breakfast, cafeteria, bathtubs, Wi-Fi, parking, covered patio, reservations required. Recommended.

AL-A Abraspungo, Km 3 on the road to Guano, T236 4275, www.haciendaabraspungo.com. Beautiful house in a country setting, comfortable rooms, excellent restaurant, Wi-Fi in lobby, parking, attentive service. Recommended.
A-B La Andaluza, 16 km north of Riobamba along the Panamericana, T294 9370. An old hacienda with modern facilities, nice rooms with heaters and roaring fireplaces , includes breakfast, good restaurant, parking, lovely views, good walking in the area. Recommended.
B Rincón Alemán, Remigio Romero y Alfredo Pareja, Ciudadela Arupos del Norte, T260 3540, www.hostalrinconaleman.com. Family-run hotel in a quiet residential area, nice ample rooms, includes breakfast, Wi-Fi, laundry and cooking facilities, parking, fireplace, sauna, gym, garden, terrace, nice views, German spoken. Recommended.
B-C Zeus, Daniel L Borja 41-29, T296 8036, www.hotelzeus.com.ec. Includes buffet breakfast, restaurant, bar and casino, gym, Wi-Fi, parking, more expensive rooms are nice, some have bathtubs with views of Chimborazo.
D El Libertador, Daniel L Borja 29-22 y Carabobo, across from the train station, T294 7393, www.hotelellibertador.com. Modern hotel with comfortable rooms, hot water, Wi-Fi.
D Metropolitano, Daniel L Borja y Lavalle, near the train station, T296 1714. One of the oldest hotels in Riobamba, built in 1912 and nicely restored in 2009. Ample rooms, breakfast available, hot water, patio.
D Tren Dorado, Carabobo 22-35 y 10 de Agosto, near the train station, T296 4890, www.hoteltrendorado.com. Modern hotel with nice large rooms, buffet breakfast available (starting 0530 on train days, open to non-guests), restaurant, reliable hot water, good value. Recommended.
E Los Shyris, Rocafuerte 21-60 y 10 de Agosto, T296 0323, hshyris@yahoo.com. An old-time budget travellers favourite, cheaper with shared bath, hot water, internet extra, simple adequate rooms, those at the back are quieter.
E Oasis, Veloz 15-32 y Almagro, T296 1210, oasishostel@hotmail.com. Small, pleasant, family-run hostel in a quiet location, hot water, Wi-Fi, laundry facilities, some rooms with kitchen and fridge, shared kitchen for the others, parking, nice garden, popular with backpackers. Recommended.

Guaranda *p1113*
B La Colina, Av Guayaquil 117, on the road to Ambato, T298 0666, www.complejolacolina.com. Nicely situated on a hillside overlooking the city. Bright attractive rooms, includes breakfast, small covered swimming pool, sauna, parking, restful, tours available, best in town.
D Bolívar, Sucre 704 y Rocafuerte, T298 0547. Pleasant hotel with courtyard, small rooms, restaurant next door serves economical breakfasts and lunches, hot water, best quality in the centre of town.
D Cochabamba, García Moreno y 7 de Mayo, T298 1958, hotelcochabamba@yahoo.es. An older hotel refurbished in 2009, good restaurant, hot water, parking.
D Hostal de las Flores, Pichincha 402 y Rocafuerte esquina, T298 4396. Nice hostel in renovated colonial house with covered courtyard and flowers, simple rooms, hot water, popular with backpackers.
D-E Hotel Refugio Salinas, in the town of Salinas, 45 min from Guaranda, T221 0044, www.salinerito.com. Pleasant community-run hotel, meals on request, cheaper with shared bath or in dorm, hot water, dining-sitting area with fireplace, visits to community projects, walking and horse riding tours, advance booking advised.
D-E El Marquez, 10 de Agosto y Eloy Alfaro, T298 1306. Pleasant hotel with family atmosphere, hot water, parking, newer rooms are clean and modern, older ones are cheaper.

Alausí *p1114*
A Posada de las Nubes, on the north side of the Río Chanchán, 7 or 11 km from Alausí depending on the route, best with 4WD, pick-up from Alausí US$7, T293 0535 or 09-315 0847 . Rustic hacienda house at 2,600 m near cloud forest. Simple rooms, some with bath, full board, good for hiking and horse riding, advance booking required.
A-B La Quinta, Eloy Alfaro 121 y M Muñoz, T293 0247, www.hosteria-la-quinta.com. Nicely restored old house near the train station, ample rooms, includes breakfast, restaurant, gardens, nice views, book in advance.
D Gampala, 5 de Junio 122 y Loza, T293 0138. Decent rooms, includes breakfast, restaurant and bar with pool table, hot water.

D San Pedro, 5 de Junio y 9 de Octubre, T293 0089, hostalsanpedro@hotmail.com. Modern hotel with very comfortable rooms, restaurant downstairs for breakfast and simple set meals, hot water, parking, nice owner, good value.
E-F Europa, 5 de Junio 175 y Orozco, T293 0200. Rooms vary from functional to comfortable, cheaper with shared bath, hot water, ample parking.

Sangay National Park *p1114*
D Hostal Capac Urcu, at Hacienda Releche, near the village of Candelaria, T294 9761, 296 0848 (Riobamba). Pleasant and relaxing small working hacienda. Use of kitchen (US$6) or good meals prepared on request, rents horses for the trek to Collanes, US$8 per horse each way, plus US$10 per muleteer. Also runs the **E** pp *refugio* at Collanes, by the crater of El Altar: thatched- roof rustic shelters with solar hot water, kitchen facilities ($6). The *refugio* is cold and dirty, take a warm sleeping bag.

Guamote
D-E Inti Sisa, Vargas Torres y García Moreno, T291 6529, www.intisisa.org. A nice hostel, part of a community development project, run by Belgian and Dutch volunteers, meals available, most rooms with bath, **F** pp in dorm, dining room and communal area with fireplace, horse riding and cycling tours to highland villages, reservations necessary.

Eating

Riobamba *p1111, map p1112*
Most places closed after 2100 and on Sun.
TTT-TT El Delirio, Primera Constituyente 2816 y Rocafuerte, T296 6441, Tue-Sun 1200-2130. Ecuadorean and international food served in a historic house with patio. Set meals and à la carte, nice setting but overpriced and touristy.
TT Ave María, 5 de Junio 21-46 y 10 de Agosto, Mon-Sat 0700-2230. Varied menu for meals, also cafeteria, home-made ice-cream.
TTT-TT L'Incontro, Av Lizarzaburu by the airport, T260 7901, 1200-1500, 1800-2200, closed Tue. Exclusive restaurant with Sicilian chef serving varied European cuisine, set meal of the day and à la carte, chef also plays the piano for guests.
TT Mónaco Pizzería, Av de la Prensa y Francisco Aguilar, Mon-Fri 1500-2200, Sat-Sun 1200-2200. Delicious pizza and pasta, nice salads, very good food, service and value, recommended.
TT-T Café VIP, Pichincha y Primera Constituyente, Mon-Sat 1200-2400. Economical set lunch with vegetarian options, café/bar and cultural centre in the evening. A good place to meet locals.
TT-T Sierra Nevada, Primera Constituyente y Rocafuerte, Mon-Sat 1130-2200, Sun 1130-1600. Good value set lunch, vegetarian on request. Nice atmosphere. Recommended.
T La Fogata, Av Daniel L Borja y Carabobo, opposite the train station, daily 0700-2200. Good economical Ecuadorean food, set meals and breakfast.
T Naranjo's, Daniel L Borja 36-20 y Uruguay, Tue-Sun 1100-1500. Good quality and value set lunch, friendly service, popular with locals.

Cafés and bakeries
Helados de Paila, Espejo y 10 de Agosto, 0900-1900. Good ice cream, café, sweets, popular.
Jamones La Andaluza, Daniel L Borja y Uruguay, 0900–2300. Indoor and outdoor seating, good coffee, sandwiches, salads, variety of cold-cuts and cheeses, tapas.
La Abuela Rosa, Brasil y Esmeraldas, Mon-Sat 1600-2100. Cafetería in grandmother's house serving typical Ecuadorean snacks. Nice atmosphere and good service.
La Vienesa, Larrea 2116 y Guayaquil and Daniel L Borja y Brasil. A Riobamba tradition, try their fresh *palanquetas* (buns).
Puro Café, Pichincha 21-37 y 10 de Agosto, Mon-Sat 1000-1300, 1600-2200. Very nice small European-style coffee shop, good coffee and sandwiches, a good place to hang out.

Guaranda *p1113*
See also Sleeping. Most places closed on Sun.
TT Pizza Buon Giorno, Sucre at Parque Bolívar, Tue-Sun 1200-2200. Pizza and salads.
TT-T La Bohemia, Convención de 1884 y 10 de Agosto, Mon-Sat 0800-2100. Very good economical set meals and pricier international dishes à la carte, nice decor and ambiance, very popular. Recommended.
TT-T La Estancia, García Moreno y Sucre, Mon-Sat 1200-2100. Good buffet lunch for quality, variety and value, à la carte in the evening, nicely decorated, pleasant atmosphere. Recommended.
T La Puerta de Alcalá, García Moreno y Eloy Alfaro, daily 1200-1400. Economical set lunch.

Cafés

Cafetería 7 Santos, Convención de 1884 y Olmedo, Mon-Sat 1000-2200. Pleasant café and bar with open courtyard. Good coffee and snacks, fireplace, live music at weekends, pouplar.
Juad's, Convención de 1884 y Azuay, Mon-Sat 0900-1300, 1500-1900. Very good, popular, cappuccino, hot chocolate, sandwiches, fruit salad, pastries, go early. Recommended.
Salinerito, Plaza Roja, daily 0800-1300, 1430-1900. Salinas cheese shop also serves coffee, sandwiches and pizza.

Bars and clubs

Riobamba *p1111, map p1112*
El Tentadero, Daniel Borja y Miguel Angel León, daily 2000-2400,US$2 cover. Salsa and reggaeton, popular.
La Rayuela, Daniel L Borja 36-30 y Uruguay, daily 1200-2200. Trendy bar/restaurant, live music on Fri, sandwiches, coffee, salads, pasta.
Romeo Bar, Vargas Torres y Daniel L Borja, US$2 cover. Popular, nice bar and club, from Latin to Rythm and Blues, pleasant sitting area on the 2nd floor.
San Valentín, Daniel L Borja y Vargas Torres. Very popular bar with small dance floor. Good Mexican dishes, pizza, hamburgers and snacks.

Entertainment

Riobamba *p1111, map p1112*
Casa de la Cultura, 10 de Agosto y Rocafuerte, T296 0219. Cultural events, cinema on Tue.

Festivals and events

Riobamba *p1111, map p1112*
Fiesta del Niño Rey de Reyes, street parades, music and dancing, starts in Dec and culminates on **6 Jan**. Around **21 Apr** there are **independence** celebrations lasting several days, hotel prices rise. **29 Jun Fiestas Patronales** in honour of San Pedro. **11 Nov** is the festival to celebrate the **first attempt at independence from Spain**.

Shopping

Riobamba *p1111, map p1112*
Camping gear Some of the tour operators hire camping and climbing gear. **Hobby Sport**, 10 de Agosto y Rocafuerte. Sleeping bags, tents, fishing supplies. **Protección Industrial**, Rocafuerte 24-51 y Orozco, T296 3017. For waterproof ponchos and suits, fishing supplies, ropes.
Handicrafts Crafts sold at Plaza Roja on Wed and Sat. Tagua carvings and other crafts sold at *Alta Montaña* (see Tour operators). **Almacén Cacha**, Colón y Orozco, next to the Plaza Roja. A cooperative of native people from the Cacha area, sells woven bags, wool sweaters, other crafts and honey, good value (closed Sun-Mon).
Supermarkets Akí, Colón y Olmedo and Costales y Daniel L Borja. **Camari**, Daniel L Borja y Lavalle, p 2. **La Ibérica**, Daniel L Borja 37-62.

Activities and tours

Riobamba and around *p1111*
Mountain biking Guided tours with support vehile average US$40 pp per day. **Pro Bici**, Primera Constituyente 23-51 y Larrea, T295 1759,

www.probici.com. Tours and rentals. **Julio Verne** (see Tour operators), tours, good equipment and routes.

Tour operators

Most companies offer climbing trips (US$180 pp for 2 days to Chimborazo or Carihuayrazo) and trekking (US$75-85 pp per day).

Alta Montaña, Daniel L Borja 35-17 y Diego Ibarra, T294 2215, www.altamontana.co.cc. Trekking, climbing, birdwatching and horse riding tours, transport, equipment rental, English spoken. Run **Posada de la Estación** on the east flank of Chimborazo (see p). Recommended.

Andes Trek, Colón 22-25 y 10 de Agosto, T294 0964, www.andes-trek.com. Climbing and trekking , transport, equipment rental.

Expediciones Andinas, Vía a Guano, Km 3, across from *Hotel Abraspungo*, T296 4915, www.expediciones-andinas.com. Climbing expeditions run by Marco Cruz, a certified guide of the *German Alpine Club*, operate **AL Estrella del Chimborazo** lodge on south flank of mountain. Recommended.

Julio Verne, El Espectador 22-25 y Daniel L Borja, 2 blocks from the train station, T296 3436, www.julioverne-travel.com. Climbing, trekking, cycling, jungle and Galápagos trips, transport, equipment rental, English spoken, Ecuadorean-Dutch-run, very conscientious and reliable. Highly recommended.

Veloz Coronado, Chile 33-21 y Francia, T296 0916 (after 1900). Climbing and trekking.

Transport

Riobamba *p1111, map p1112*

Bus **Terminal Terrestre** on Epiclachima y Av Daniel L Borja for most long distance buses including to Quito, Guayaquil and Cuenca. **Terminal Oriental**, Espejo y Cordovez, for Baños and the Oriente. Taxi from one terminal to another, US$1. To **Quito**, US$4, 4 hrs, about every 30 mins. To **Guaranda**, US$2, 2 hrs (sit on the right). To **Ambato**, US$1.25, 1 hr. To **Alausí**, see below. To **Cuenca**, 8 a day via Alausí, 6 hrs, US$6. To **Guayaquil** via Pallatanga, frequent service, US$5, 5 hrs, the trip is spectacular for the first 2 hrs. To **Baños**, the direct Riobamba-Baños road is closed due to Tungurahua's volcanic activity, buses go via Ambato, 2 hrs, US$2. To **Puyo** US$4, 4 hrs. To **Macas** from Terminal Oriental at 0230, 0545, 1000, 1300, 1600, 1700, 5 hrs, US$5 (sit on the left).

Guaranda *p1113*

Bus Terminal at Eliza Mariño Carvajal, on road to Riobamba and Babahoyo; if you are staying in town get off closer to the centre. Many daily buses to: **Ambato**, US$2, 2 hrs. **Riobamba**, see above. **Babahoyo**, US$3, 3 hrs, beautiful ride. **Guayaquil**, US$4, 5 hrs. **Quito**, US$5, 5 hrs.

Reserva Faunística Chimborazo *p1113*

There are no buses that will take you to the shelters. You can take a tour or arrange transport with a tour operator or taxi from Riobamba (same price, US$30 one way). You can also take a Riobamba-Guaranda bus, alight at the turn-off for the refuges and walk the remaining steep 5 km to the first shelter. For the eastern slopes, take a trekking tour, arrange transport from an agency or take a bus between Riobamba and Ambato, get off at the turnoff for **Posada La Estación** and Urbina and walk from there.

The Devil's Nose Train *p1114*

In early 2010, a motorized rail-car (*autoferro*) ran Wed, Fri and Sun at 0630 from **Riobamba** (station at 10 de Agosto y Carabobo, T296 1038, riobambatren@efe.gov.ec) to **Palmira**, return at 1000, US$11 return (US$10 one way). Reservations several days in advance at the station or by e-mail, followed by a bank deposit are required. Once track repairs are completed (after Sep 2010), service to Alausí and the Nariz del Diablo is expected to resume. **Metropolitan Touring**, T09-973 2392, runs a private *autoferro* on the Alausí-Sibambe- Alausí route (when track is open),US$30 pp . A minimum number of passengers is required.

Alausí *p1114*

Bus From **Riobamba**, 1½ hrs, US$1.50, 84 km. To **Quito**, from 0600 onwards, 8 a day, 5 hrs, US$5; often have to change in Riobamba. To **Cuenca**, 4 hrs, US$5. To **Ambato** hourly, 3 hrs, US$3. To **Guayaquil**, 4 a day, 4 hrs, US$5. **Coop Patria**, Colombia y Orozco, 3 blocks up from the main street; **Trans Alausí**, 5 de Junio y Loza. Many through buses don't go into town, but have to be caught on the highway.

Sangay National Park *p1114*
To **Atillo** from Juan de Velasco y Olmedo, daily at 0545, 1200, 1520, 1820, US$2, 2½ hrs. Also Riobamba-**Macas** service goes through Atilio, see above. To **Alao**, from Parque La Dolorosa, Puruhá y Primera Constituyente in Riobamba, Mon-Sat 0530, 0630 and hourly 1145-1845, Sun 0630, US$1, 1½ hrs. A milk truck goes to **Guargualiá Chico** from Parque La Dolorosa, daily at 0400, returns 0830, US$1.50, 2 hrs. A bus and pickups go from 10 de Agosto y Benalcázar to Guargualiá Grande (from where it is a 25-min walk to Guargualiá Chico with accommodation), Mon, Wed, Fri, Sat around 1330-1400, US$1.75, 2 hrs.To **Candelaria**, fromTerminal Oriental, Mon-Sat 0630, 1215 and 1700, Sun 0630; get there early, sometimes they leave ahead of schedule, US$1, 1½ hrs. Alternatively, take a bus from the same terminal to Penipe, every ½ hr, US$0.40, 40 mins, and hire a pickup truck from there to Candelaria, US$15, 40 mins.

Directory

Riobamba *p1111, map p1112*
Banks Several banks with ATMs at Primera Costituyente y García Moreno. **Banco del Pacífico**, Daniel L Borja y Zambrano. **Internet** Many places, US$1 per hr. **Post office** 10 de Agosto y Espejo. **Useful addresses** **Immigration**, Av Leopoldo Freire, by the Police station, Barrio Pucará, T296 4697.

Guaranda *p1113*
Banks **Banco Pichincha**, Azuay y 7 de Mayo, ATM only. **Internet** **Compumás**, 10 de Agosto y 7 de Mayo. **Tortilla Net**, 10 de Agostoy Sucre, US$1. **Post office** Azuay y Pichincha. **Useful addresses** **Immigration**, Guayaquil y Manabí 231, T298 0108.

Cuenca and around

➔ Phone code: 07. Colour map 11, C3. Population: 360,000. Altitude: 2,530 m.
Founded in 1557 on the site of the Inca settlement of Tomebamba, much of Cuenca's colonial air has been preserved, with many of its old buildings recently renovated. Its cobblestone streets, flowering plazas and whitewashed buildings with old wooden doors and ironwork balconies make it a pleasure to explore. The climate is spring-like, but the nights are chilly. In 1999 Cuenca was designated a UNESCO World Heritage Site.

Ins and outs

Getting there The **Terminal Terrestre** is on Avenida España, 20 minutes' walk northeast of the centre, T282 4811. The **airport** is five minutes' walk from the Terminal Terrestre, T2886 2203. Both can be reached by city bus. The **terminal for local buses** in the province is at the Feria Libre on Avenida Las Américas. Many city buses pass here. ▸▸ *See Transport, page 1128, for details.*

Getting around The city is bounded by the Río Machángara to the north and the Ríos Yanuncay and Tarqui to the south. The Río Tomebamba separates the colonial heart from the newer districts to the south. Avenida Las Américas is a ring road around the north and west of the city and the *autopista*, a multi-lane highway bypasses the city to the south.

Tourist offices **Ministerio de Turismo** ⓘ *Sucre y Benigno Malo, on Parque Calderón next to the Municipio, T282 2058, helpful. Mon-Fri, 0830-1700.* **Cámara de Turismo** ⓘ *Terminal Terrestre, T286 8482. Mon-Sat 0830-1200, 1230-1800.* General information from www.cuenca.com.ec.

Safety Though safer than Quito or Guayaquil, routine precautions are advised. Outside the busy nightlife area around Calle Larga, the city centre is deserted and unsafe after 2300. Around Cruz del Vado (south end of Juan Montalvo), the Terminal Terrestre and all market areas, are not safe after dark.

Sights

On the main plaza, **Parque Abdón Calderón**, are the Old Cathedral, **El Sagrario**, begun in 1557, and the immense 'New' **Catedral de la Inmaculada**, started in 1885. It contains a famous crowned image of the Virgin, a beautiful altar and an exceptional play of light and shade

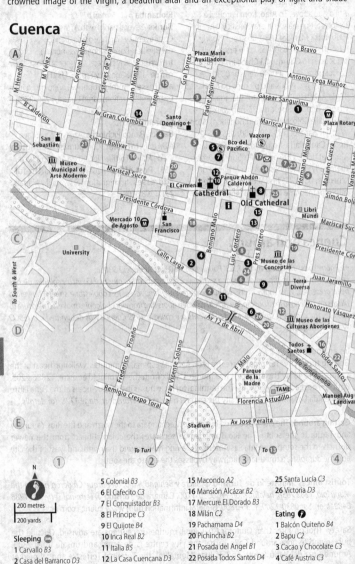

Cuenca

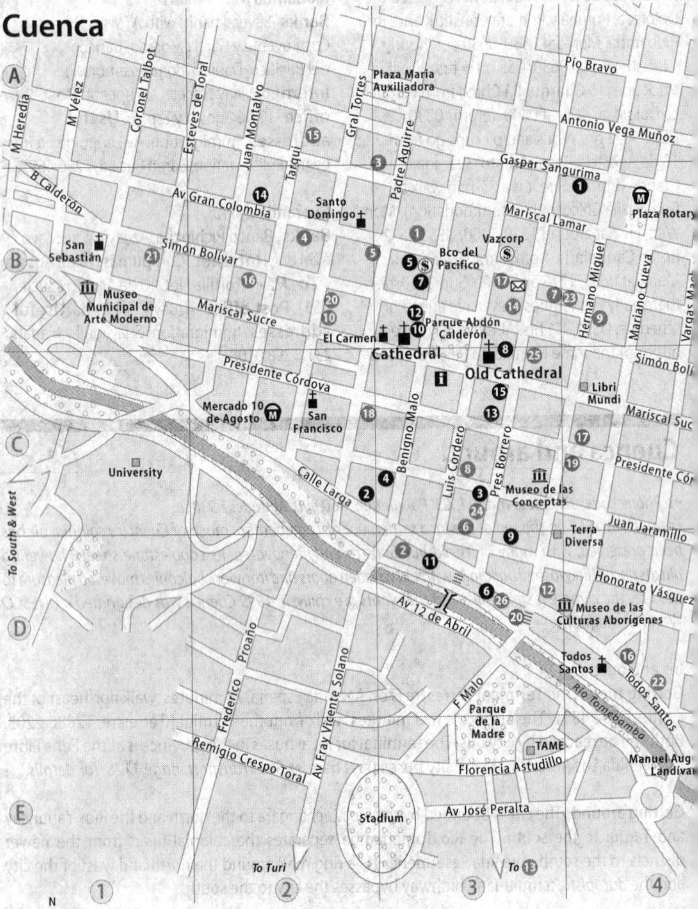

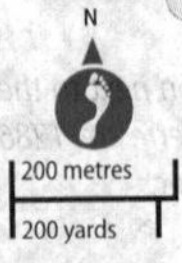

Sleeping
1 Carvallo *B3*
2 Casa del Barranco *D3*
5 Colonial *B3*
6 El Cafecito *C3*
7 El Conquistador *B3*
8 El Príncipe *C3*
9 El Quijote *B4*
10 Inca Real *B2*
11 Italia *B5*
12 La Casa Cuencana *D3*
15 Macondo *A2*
16 Mansión Alcázar *B2*
17 Mercure El Dorado *B3*
18 Milán *C2*
19 Pachamama *D4*
20 Pichincha *B2*
21 Posada del Angel *B1*
22 Posada Todos Santos *D4*
25 Santa Lucía *C3*
26 Victoria *D3*

Eating
1 Balcón Quiteño *B4*
2 Bapu *C2*
3 Cacao y Chocolate *C3*
4 Café Austria *C3*

through modern stained glass. Other churches which deserve a visit are **San Blas, San Francisco** and **Santo Domingo**. Many churches are open at irregular hours only and for services. The church of **El Carmen de la Asunción**, close to the southwest corner of La Inmaculada, has a flower market in the tiny **Plazoleta El Carmen** in front. There is a colourful daily market in **Plaza Rotary** where pottery, clothes, guinea pigs and local produce, especially baskets, are sold. Thursday is the busiest.

6 El Jordán *D3*
7 Heladería Holanda *B3*
8 La Fornace *C3*
9 Molienda *D3*
10 Raymipampa *B3*
11 Sankt Florian *D3*
12 Tutto Freddo *B3*
13 Viejo Rincón *C3*

Bars & clubs
16 Café del Tranquilo *D4*
17 Gabia *C4*
18 La Mesa Salsoteca *B4*
19 San Angel *C4*
20 Wunderbar *D3*

Museo del Monasterio de las Conceptas ⓘ *Hermano Miguel 6-33 entre Pdte Córdova y Juan Jaramillo, T283 0625, www.museodelasconceptas.org.ec. Mon-Fri 0900-1830, Sat and holidays 1000-1300, US$2.50*, in a cloistered convent founded in 1599, houses a well displayed collection of religious and folk art, in addition to an extensive collection of lithographs by Guayasamín.

The **Banco Central 'Pumapungo'** ⓘ *C Larga y Huayna Capac, entrance is on the far left of the building, T283 1255, Mon-Fri 0900-1800, Sat 0900-1300, US$3*, is a museum complex on the edge of the colonial city at the actual site of Tomebamba excavations. It has a **Parque Arqueológico Pumapungo**. The **Museo Arqueológico** section contains all the Cañari and Inca remains and artifacts found at this site. Other halls in the premises house the **Museo Etnográfico**, with information on different Ecuadorean cultures, including a special collection of *tsantsas* (shrunken heads from Oriente), the **Museo de Arte Religioso**, the **Museo Numismático** and temporary exhibits. There are also book and music libraries, free cultural videos and music events. Three blocks west of Pumapungo, **Museo Manuel Agustín Landívar** ⓘ *Larga 2-23 Y Manuel Vega. T282 1177, Mon-Fri 0800-1700, Sat 0900-1300, US$1*, is at the site of the Todos los Santos ruins, with Cañari, Inca and colonial remains.

Museo de las Culturas Aborígenes ⓘ *Larga 5-24 y Hermano Miguel, T283 9181, Mon-Fri 0830-1800, Sat 0900-1400, US$2; guided tours in English, Spanish and French, has a craft shop and restaurant*, the private collection of Dr J Cordero López, has a impressive selection of pre-Columbian archaeology. **Museo del Sombrero** ⓘ *C Larga 1041 y Torres, T283 6972, Mon-Fri 0900-1800, free*, has all the old factory machines for hat finishing.

On Plaza San Sebastián is **Museo Municipal de Arte Moderno** ⓘ *Sucre 1527 y Talbot, T282 0638, Mon-Fri 0830-1300, 1500-1830, Sat-Sun*

0900-1300, free, has a permanent contemporary art collection and art library. It holds a biennial international painting competition and other cultural activities. Across the river from the Museo del Banco Central, the **Museo de Artes de Fuego** ⓘ *Las Herrerías y 10 de Agosto, Mon-Fri, except for lunchtime, and Sat morning.* has a display of wrought iron work and pottery. It is housed in a beautifully restored old building. Also south of city, accessed via Avenida Fray Vicente Solano, beyond the football stadium, is **Turi church, orphanage and mirador**. It's a two-hour walk or take a taxi; a tiled panorama explains the magnificent views.

There are sulphur baths at **Baños**, with a domed, blue church in a delightful landscape, 5 km southwest of Cuenca. These are the hottest commercial baths in Ecuador. Above Hostería Durán (see Sleeping) are three separate complexes of warm baths, **Merchán, Rodas and Durán** ⓘ *dawn till 2100 or 2200, US$3.50*. The latter is by far the largest and best maintained, there are numerous hot pools and tubs and steam baths.

Ingapirca → *Phone code: 07. Colour map 1a, B3. Altitude: 3,160 m.*

ⓘ *Daily 0800-1800, US$6, including museum and tour in Spanish; bags can be stored. Small café.*
Ecuador's most important Inca ruin, at 3,160 m, lies 8½ km east of the colonial town of **Cañar** (hostales in **D-F** range, www.imcanar.gov.ec). Access is from Cañar or **El Tambo**. The Inca Huayna Capac took over the site from the conquered Cañaris when his empire expanded north into Ecuador in the third quarter of the 15th century. Ingapirca was strategically placed on the Royal Highway that ran from Cuzco to Quito and soldiers may have been stationed there. The site shows typical imperial Cuzco-style architecture, such as tightly fitting stonework and trapezoidal doorways. The central structure may have been a solar observatory. Nearby is a throne cut into the rock, the **Sillón del Inga** (Inca's Chair) and the **Ingachugana**, a large rock with carved channels. The site is, unfortunately, run-down. A 10-minute walk away from the site is the **Cara del Inca**, or 'face of the Inca', an immense natural formation in the rock looking over the landscape. On Friday there is an interesting indigenous market at Ingapirca village.

A tourist train runs on weekends from El Tambo 7 km to the small Cañari-Inca archaeological site of **Baños del Inca** or **Coyoctor** ⓘ *site open daily 0800-1700, US$1; return train ride US$7, includes entry to El Tambo museum and Coyoctor site*, a massive rock outcrop carved to form baths, showers, water channels and seats overlooking a small amphitheatre. There is an interpretation centre with information about the site, a hall with displays about regional fiestas and an audiovisual room with tourist information about all of Ecuador.

Inca Trail to Ingapirca

The three-day hike to Ingapirca starts at **Achupallas**, 25 km from Alausí. The walk is covered by three 1:50,000 *IGM* sheets, Alausí, Juncal and Cañar. The Juncal sheet is most important, the name Ingapirca does not appear on the latter, you may have to ask directions near the end. Also take a compass. Good camping equipment is essential. Take all food and drink with you as there is nothing along the way. A shop in Achupallas sells basic foodstuffs. There are persistent beggars the length of the hike, especially children. Tour operators in Riobamba and Cuenca offer this trek for about US$200-250 per person, three days, everything included.

East of Cuenca

Northeast of Cuenca, on the road to Méndez in the Oriente, is **Paute**, with a pleasant park and modern church. South of Paute, **Gualaceo** is a rapidly expanding, modern town set in beautiful landscape, with a charming plaza and Sunday market. The **iTur** ⓘ *at the Municipio, Gran Colombia y 3 de Noviembre, Parque Central, T225 5131, Mon-Fri 0800-1300, 1400-1700* is very helpful, Spanish only. **CIDAP** ⓘ *Loja y Sucre, Wed-Sun 0900-1300, free*, is a small crafts museum. A scenic road goes from Gualaceo to Limón in Oriente.

South of Gualaceo is **Chordeleg**, a touristy village famous for its crafts in wood, silver and gold filigree, pottery and panama hats. At the Municipio is the **Centro de Interpretación** ⓘ *C 23* *de Enero, Mon-Fri 0800-1300, 1400-1700*, an exhibition hall with fascinating local textiles, ceramics and straw work, some of which are on sale at reasonable prices. It's a good uphill walk from Gualaceo to Chordeleg, and a pleasant hour downhill in the other direction. South of Gualaceo, 83 km from Cuenca, **Sígsig**, an authentic highland town where women can be seen weaving hats 'on the move'. It has a Sunday market, two *residenciales* and an archaeology museum. A poor but scenic road goes from Sígsig to Gualaquiza in Oriente.

Parque Nacional Cajas

ⓘ *The park office is at Presidente Córdova 7-56 y Luis Cordero, Edif Morejón, p 2, T282 9853, www.etapa.com.ec, Mon-Fri 0800-1300 and 1500-1800. Park entry is US$10, payable at the entrance gates at Laguna Toreadora, Laguna Llaviuco or Soldados.*

Northwest of Cuenca, Cajas is a 29,000 ha national park with over 230 lakes. Near the entrance is an altar and pilgrim area where a teenager saw 'Our Lady of the Faith' in 1988. The *páramo* vegetation, such as chuquiragua and lupin, is beautiful and contains interesting wildlife. Cajas is very rich in birdlife; 125 species have been identified, including the condor and many varieties of hummingbird (the Violet-tailed Metaltail is endemic to this area). On the lakes are Andean gulls, Speckled Teal and Yellow-billed Pintails. On a clear morning the views are superb, even to Chimborazo, some 300 km away.

There are two access roads. The paved road from Cuenca to Guayaquil via Molleturo goes through the northern section and is the main route for Laguna Toreadora, the visitors' centre and Laguna Llaviuco. Skirting the southern edge of the park is a poor secondary road, which goes from Cuenca via San Joaquín to the Soldados entrance and the community of Angas beyond. (See Transport, page 1128.) There is nowhere to stay after the *refugio* at Laguna Toreadora (see Sleeping, below) until you reach the lowlands between Naranjal and La Troncal.

The park offers ideal but strenuous walking, at 3,150 m-4,450 m altitude, and the climate is rough. There have been deaths from exposure. The best time to visit is August-January, when you may expect clear days, strong winds, night-time temperatures to -8°C and occasional mist. From February-July temperatures are higher but there is much more fog, rain and snow. It is best to arrive in the early morning since it can get very cloudy, wet and cool after about 1300. Cuenca tourist office has a good, one-page map of Cajas, but other local maps are not always exact. It is best to get the *IGM* maps in Quito (Chaucha, Cuenca, San Felipe de Molleturo, or Chiquintad 1:50,000) and take a compass. It is easy to get lost as signs are of little help.

Cuenca and around listings

For Sleeping and Eating price codes and other relevant information, see Essentials, pages 38-40.

Sleeping

Cuenca and around *p1119, map p1120*

L Mansión Alcázar, Bolívar 12-55 y Tarqui, T282 3918, www.mansionalcazar.com. Beautifully restored house, a mansion indeed, central, very nice rooms, includes breakfast, restaurant serves gourmet international food, lovely gardens, quiet relaxed atmosphere.

AL Mercure El Dorado, Gran Colombia 787 y Luis Cordero, T283 1390, www.eldorado hotel.com.ec. Elegant modern hotel, includes buffet breakfast, cafeteria open 0530-2300, spa, gym, Wi-Fi, business centre, parking, a meeting place among Cuencanos.

AL Oro Verde, Av Ordóñez Lazo, northwest of the centre towards Cajas, T409 0000, www.oroverdehotels.com. Elegant hotel, includes buffet breakfast, excellent international restaurant offers buffet lunch and à la carte dinner, small pool, parking.

AL Santa Lucía, Borrero 8-44 y Sucre, T282 8000, www.santaluciahotel.com. An elegantly renovated colonial house with 20 very nice comfortable rooms, includes buffet breakfast, excellent Italian restaurant in the patio, Wi-Fi, fridge, safe deposit box.

A Carvallo, Gran Colombia 9-52, entre Padre Aguirre y Benigno Malo, T283 2063, www.hotelcarvallo.com.ec. Combination of an elegant colonial-style hotel and art/antique gallery. Very nice comfortable rooms all have bath tubs , includes breakfast, restaurant, Wi-Fi, boutique with exclusive crafts and clothing.

A El Conquistador, Gran Colombia 665 y Hermano Miguel (second location at Sucre 6-78 y Borrero), T284 2888, www.hotelconquistador.com.ec. Modern hotel in the heart of the colonial city, includes buffet breakfast, good restaurant with Ecuadorean and international food, cafeteria, Wi-Fi, fridge, safety deposit box, airport tranfers.

A Victoria, C Larga 6-93 y Borrero, T283 1120, www.grupo-santaana.net. Elegant refurbished hotel overlooking the river, comfortable modern rooms , includes breakfast, excellent expensive restaurant, Wi-Fi, nice views, attentive service.

B Inca Real, Gral Torres 8-40 entre Sucre y Bolívar, T282 3636, www.hotelincareal.com.ec. Refurbished colonial house with comfortable rooms around patios, includes breakfast, Wi-Fi, Spanish restaurant, parking.

B Italia, Av España y Huayna-Cápac, by Terminal Terrestre, T284 0060, www.hotelitaliaec.com. Modern hotel with comfortable rooms, includes buffet breakfast, restaurant, Wi-Fi, parking, english spoken.

B Posada del Angel, Bolívar 14-11 y Estévez de Toral, T284 0695, www.hostalposadadelangel.com. A nicely restored colonial house, comfortable rooms, includes breakfast, good Italian restaurant (0630-2230), Wi-Fi, parking, sitting area in patio with plants, some noise from restaurant, English spoken, helpful staff. Recommended.

B Presidente, Gran Colombia 659 y Hermano Miguel, T283 1341. Comfortable hotel in a convenient location, includes breakfast, good restaurant, Wi-Fi, group tours in a chiva. Good value.

C Apartamentos Otorongo, Av 12 de Abril y Guayas, T281 8205, www.otorongo.com.ec. Furnished 1 or 2 bedroom suites with kitchenette, 10-15 min walk from centre, breakfast extra, TV, phone, Wi-Fi, parking, daily cleaning service, friendly owners, US$410-510 per month.

C Casa Naranja, Lamar 10-38 y Padre Aguirre, T285 3234, www.hotelnaranja.com. Artistically decorated colonial house with 2 inner patios, breakfast available, cheaper with shared bath, hot water, Wi-Fi, cooking facilities, terrace, safety deposit boxes, storage room, long stay discounts, refurbished in 2009.

C El Príncipe, J Jaramillo 7-82 y Luis Cordero, T284 7287, www.hotelprincipecuenca.com. A refurbished 3-storey colonial house, comfortable rooms around a nice patio with plants, includes breakfast, restaurant, Wi-Fi, parking.

C El Quijote, Hermano Miguel 9-58 y Gran Colombia, T284 3197, www.hotelquijote.com. Nicely restored old building with patio, carpeted rooms, includes breakfast, restaurant.

C La Casona, Miguel Cordero 2-134, near the stadium, T281 0823, www.lacasonahotel.com.ec. Very nice refurbished family home in a residential area, comfortable carpeted rooms, includes breakfast in a nice dining room, restaurant, Wi-Fi.

C La Orquídea, Borrero 9-31 y Bolívar, T282 4511, www.hostalorquidea.com. Nicely refurbished colonial house, bright rooms, restaurant serves economical set meals, fridge, discounts in low season, good value.

C-D Casa Naranja, Lamar 10-38 y Padre Aguirre, T285 3234, www.hotelnaranja.com. Artistically decorated colonial house with 2 inner patios, breakfast available, cheaper with shared bath, Wi-Fi, cooking facilities, terrace, safety deposit boxes, storage room, long stay discounts, refurbished in 2009. Owner has upmarket alpaca clothing store.

C-D Colonial, Gran Colombia 10-13 y Padre Aguirre, T284 1644. Refurbished colonial house with beautiful patio, carpeted rooms, some to the street others interior, includes breakfast, restaurant serves lunch, English spoken.

D Casa del Barranco, Calle Larga 8-41 entre Benigno Malo y Luis Cordero, T283 9763, www.casadelbarranco.com. Nicely restored colonial house, some rooms with lovely views over the river, includes breakfast, cafeteria overlooking the river, hot water, Wi-Fi in common areas, refurbished in 2009.

D Macondo, Tarqui 11-64 y Lamar, T284 0697, www.hostalmacondo.com. Nice restored colonial house, large rooms, includes buffet breakfast, cheaper with shared bath, hot water, Wi-Fi, laundry and cooking facilities, pleasant patio with plants, garden, very popular, US run. Highly recommended.

D Milán, Pres Córdova 989 y Padre Aguirre, T283 1104, www.hotelmilan.com.ec. Multi-storey hotel with views over market, includes breakfast, restaurant, hot water, laundry facilities, popular and good value, refurbished in 2009.
D Posada Todos Santos, C Larga 3-42 y Tomás Ordóñez, near the Todos Santos Church, T282 4247. Nice tranquil hostel decorated with murals, includes breakfast, hot water, Wi-Fi, very good, attentive service, English spoken, refurbished in 2009.
D-E El Cafecito, Honorato Vásquez 7-36 y Luis Cordero, T283 2337, www.cafecito.net. Colonial house, restaurant and bar in nice patio, cheaper with shared bath, **G** pp in dorm, hot water, Wi-Fi, happy hour daily, popular with travellers and noisy.
D-E Santa Fé, Borrero 5-57 y Juan Jaramillo, T282 2025, hostalsantafe2010@yahoo.com. In a refurbished old house, includes breakfast, cheaper in dorm, hot water, family run, good value.
E La Casa Cuencana, Hermano Miguel 436 y C Larga, T283 4941, lacasacuencana@hotmail.com. Nicely furnished family run hostal in the heart of the action, cheaper with shared bath, hot water, cooking facilities. **Bananas Café** next door for good breakfast.
E Pachamama, Calle Larga 2-38 y Manuel Vega, T282 9465. Convenient for nightlife, shared rooms, breakfast available, cheaper with shared bath, cooking facilities, family atmosphere, helpful.
E-F Pichincha, Gral Torres 8-82 y Bolívar, T282 3868, hpichincha@etapanet.net. Spacious rooms, shared bath, hot water, cooking facilities, noisy, helpful. Second location on Montalvo 9-78 y Bolívar, **D** with bath and breakfast.

Baños
A Hostería Durán, Km 8 Vía Baños, T289 2485, www.hosteriaduran.com. Includes breakfast, restaurant, has well-maintained, very clean pools, US$4 for non-residents, steam bath, camping is allowed. There are also a couple of cheap *residenciales*.

Ingapirca *p1122*
A Posada Ingapirca, 500 m uphill from ruins, T221 7116, or T283 0064 (Cuenca), www.grupo-santaana.net. Converted hacienda, comfortable rooms, heating, including typical breakfast, excellent restaurant, good service, great views.
E El Castillo, opposite the ruins, T09-998 3650. Two simple cabins, private bath, hot water, restaurant, a good choice.
There are a couple of simple places in the village.

El Tambo
This is the nearest town to Ingapirca.
D-E Chasky Wasy, Montenegro next to Banco del Austro, 1 block from the park, T09-854 7845, tenezaca@hotmail.com . Nice hostel with ample rooms, hot water, parking nearby.
E-F Sunshine, Panamericana y Ramón Borrero, at north end of town, T223 3394. Simple, family run, not always staffed, cheaper with shared bath, hot water, traffic noise.

Inca Trail to Ingapirca *p1122*
F Ingañán, Achupallas, T293 0652. Basic, with bath, hot water, meals on request, camping.

East of Cuenca *p1122*
Paute
A Hostería Uzhupud, 10 km from Paute, T225 0329, www.uzhupud.com. Set in the beautiful Paute valley, deluxe, relaxing, rooms at the back have best views, swimming pool and sauna (US$6 for non-residents), sports fields, gardens, lots of orchids. Recommended.
F Cutilcay, Abdón Calderón, by the river, T225 0133. An older hostel, basic, cheaper with shared bath and cold water.

Gualaceo
D Peñon de Cuzay, Sector Bullcay El Carmen on the main road to Cuenca, T220 3815. In one of the weaving communities, with spa and pool.
E-F Residencial Gualaceo, Gran Colombia 302 y FA Piedra, T225 5006. Older hotel with clean basic rooms, cheaper with shared bath, hot water, parking, good value.

Parque Nacional Cajas *p1123*
There is a *refugio* at **Laguna Toreadora**, cold, cooking facilities, and camping at **Laguna Llaviuco**. Other shelters in the park are primitive.
B Hostería Dos Chorreras, Km 14½ vía al Cajas, sector Sayausí, T285 3154, doschorreras@etapaonline.net.ec. Hacienda style inn outside the park. Heating, includes breakfast, restaurant serves excellent fresh trout, reservations recommended, horse rentals with advanced notice.

Eating

Cuenca *p1119, map p1120*

Most places are closed on Sun evening. There are cheap *comedores* at the Mercados 9 de Octubre (cleanest) and 10 de Agosto.

TTT **Villa Rosa**, Gran Colombia 12-22 y Tarqui, T283 7944, Mon-Fri 1200-1430, 1900-2230. Very elegant restaurant in the centre of town, excellent international food and service. A meeting place for business people.

TTT-TT **Balcón Quiteño**, Sangurima 6-49 y Borrero, and Av Ordoñez Lazo 311 y los Pinos, T283 1926, open until 0200. Good Ecuadorean food and service, 1960's décor. Popular with the locals after a night's hard partying.

TTT-TT **El Jordán**, C Larga 6-111, T285 0517, www.eljordanrestaurante.com. International, Middle Eastern and Ecuadorean dishes. Also serves a more economical set lunch. Elegant decor.

TTT-TT **Molinos del Batán**, 12 de Abril y Puente El Vado, T281 1531, Wed-Sat 1200-1500, 1830-2300, Sun 1200-1600. Excellent comida típica Cuencana in a nice setting by the river.

TT **Café Austria**, Benigno Malo 5-99 y J Jaramillo, daily 0900-0000. A traditional Cuenca café serving international food and great Austrian pastries, pleasant atmosphere, recommended.

TT **Café Eucalyptus**, Gran Colombia 9-41 y Benigno Malo, Mon-Fri 1700-2300 or later, Sat 1900-0200. A pleasant restaurant, café and bar in an elegantly decorated two storey house. Large menu with dishes from all over the world. British-American run, popular and recommended.

TT **Raymipampa**, Benigno Malo 8-59, at Parque Calderón, Mon-Fri 0830-2300, Sat-Sun 0930-2230. Good typical and international food in a nice central location, economical set lunch on weekdays, fast service, very popular, at times it is hard to get a table.

TT **Zöe**, Borrero 761 y Sucre, Mon-Sat 1700-2300 (bar open until 0200 Thu-Sat). International food, live music most Fri nights, popular with expats.

TT-T **Bapu**, C Larga 9-34 y Benigno Malo, daily 230-2300. Excellent Indian food, good value and service.

TT-T **La Fornace**, Remigio Crespo 5-13 e Imbabura, Borrero 8-29 y Sucre, and other locations, at Remigio daily 1200-1500 and 1800-2300, 1030-2130 at other locations. Good pizza and ice cream, the one on Remigio Crespo is a full restaurant with good Italian food , attentive service.

TT-T **Sankt Florian**, Calle Larga 7-119 y Luis Cordero, www.sanktflorian.com, Mon-Sat 1100-2200 (later on weekends). Nicely decorated restaurant overlooking the river, good set lunch and international food à la carte.

TT-T **Viejo Rincón**, Pres Córdova 7-46 y Borrero, Mon-Fri 1200-2200. Tasty Ecuadorean food, very good set lunch and à la carte, nice atmosphere, popular.

T **Good Afinity**, Av Ordoñez Lasso y Av Américas, Mon-Sat 1100-1500. Very good vegetarian food, economical set lunch, nice garden seating.

T **Grecia**, Gran Colombia y Padre Aguirre, Mon-Sat 1200-1500. Good quality and value set lunch.

T **Molienda**, Honorato Vásquez y Hermano Miguel, daily 1100-2200. Tasty Colombian food, friendly service.

Cafés

Cacao y Chocolate, Juan Jaramillo y Borrero. Chocolate in every imaginable form. Pleasant atmosphere at night. Recommended.

Heladería Holanda, Benigno Malo 9-51, daily 0930-2000. Yoghurt for breakfast, ice-cream, fruit salads, cream cakes. Popular.

Monte Bianco, Bolívar 2-80 y Ordóñez and a couple of other locations. Good ice-cream and cream cakes, good value.

Panesa, Benigno Malo entre Gran Colombia y Sucre. Bakery with good bread and sweets.

Tutto Freddo, Bolívar 8-09 y Benigno Malo and several other locations, daily 0900-2200. Good ice-cream, crêpes, pizza sandwiches and sweets, reasonable prices, popular.

Bars and clubs

Cuenca *p1119, map p1120*

Calle Larga is a major destination for night life, with lots of bars with snacks and some restaurants. Av Remigio Crespo, behind the university also has night spots, but the atmosphere is unpleasant, with people drinking on the street. Most bars open Wed-Thu until 2300, Fri-Sat until 0200.

Café del Tranquilo, C Larga y Vargas Machuca. Pleasant popular bar, live music, US$5 cover.

Gabia, Pres Córdova y Hermano Miguel. Dress code, Latin and other music, young crowd, US$5 cover.

La Mesa Salsoteca, Gran Colombia 3-36 entre Vargas Machuca y Tomás Ordoñez (no sign). Latin music, salsa, popular among travellers and locals, young crowd.

San Angel, Hermano Miguel 6-88 y Presidente Córdova. Popular bar and dance spot, live music, mixed-age crowd.

Wunderbar, entrance from stairs on Hermano Miguel y C Larga, Mon-Fri 1100-0200, Sat 1500-0200. A café-bar- restaurant, drinks, good coffee and food including some vegetarian. Nice atmosphere, German magazines, book exchange, German-run.

Entertainment

Cuenca *p1119, map p1120*

Cinemas **Multicines**, Av José Peralta, complex of 5 theatres and food court, also at Mall del Río.

Dance Classes **Cachumbambe**, Remigio Crespo 7-79 y Guayas, above *Restaurante Charito*, T288 2023. Salsa, merengue and a variety of other rhythms.

Festivals and events

Cuenca *p1119, map p1120*

On **24 Dec** there is an outstanding parade: **Pase del Niño Viajero**, probably the largest and finest Christmas parade in all Ecuador. Children and adults from all the *barrios* and surrounding villages decorate donkeys, horses, cars and trucks with symbols of abundance. Little children in colourful indigenous costumes or dressed up as Biblical figures ride through the streets accompanied by musicians. The parade starts at about 1000 at San Sebastián, proceeds along C Simón Bolívar and ends at San Blas about 5 hrs later. In the days up to, and just after Christmas, there are many smaller parades. **12 Apr** is the **Foundation of Cuenca**. On **Good Friday** there is a fine procession through the town to the Mirador Turi. **May-Jun** **Septenario**, the religious festival of Corpus Christi, lasts a week. On **3 Nov** is **Independence of Cuenca**, with street theatre, art exhibitions and night-time dances all over the city. Cuenca hosts an internationally famous art competition every 2 years, which begins in **Apr** or **May**. The next *bienal* is due in 2011. Information from Bolivar 13-89, T283 1778.

Shopping

Cuenca *p1119, map p1120*

Books **BC Carolina**, Hermano Miguel 4-46 y C Larga. Good selection of English books for sale and exchange. Friendly service. **Librimundi**, Hermano Miguel 8-14 y Sucre, www.librimundi.com. Nice bookshop with good selection and a café/reading area. Stocks Footprint guides.

Camping equipment **Bermeo Hnos**, Borrero 8-35 y Sucre, T283 1522. **Explorador Andino**, Borrero 7-39 y Sucre. **Tatoo/Cikla**, Av Remigio Tamariz 2-52 y Federico Proaño, T288 4809, www.tatoo.ws. Good camping, hiking, climbing and biking gear. Also rent bikes, US$12 per day. Several other shops near the university, on or near Av Remigio Crespo. Equipment rental from **Apullacta**, see Tour operators.

Handicrafts Good souvenirs are carvings, leather, basketwork, painted wood, onyx, ceramics, woven stuffs, embroidered shirts, jewellery. There are many craftware shops along Gran Colombia, Benigno Malo and Juan Jaramillo alongside Las Conceptas. There are several good leather shops in the arcade off Bolívar between Benigno Malo and Luis Cordero. *Polleras*, traditional skirts worn by native women are found along Gral Torres, between Sucre and Pres Córdova, and on Tarqui, between Pres Córdova and C Larga. For basketwork, take a 15-min bus ride from the Feria Libre (see below) to the village of **San Joaquín**.

Arte Artesanías y Antigüedades, Borrero y Córdova. Textiles, jewellery and antiques.

Artesa, L Cordero 10-31 y Gran Colombia, several branches. Modern Ecuadorean ceramics at good prices. **Centro Artesanal Municipal 'Casa de la Mujer'**, Gral Torres 7-33, T284 5854. Crafts market with a great variety of handicrafts.

Colecciones Jorge Moscoso, Juan Jaramillo 6-80 y Borrero, T282 2114. Weaving exhibitions, ethnographic museum, antiques and crafts.

El Barranco, Hermano Miguel 3-23 y Av 3 de Noviembre. Artisans' cooperative selling a wide variety of crafts. **El Tucán**, Borrero 7-35. Good selection. Recommended. **Galápagos**, Borrero 6-75. Excellent selection.

Jewellery **Galería Claudio Maldonado**, Bolívar 7-75, has unique pre-Columbian designs in silver and precious stones.

Unicornio, Gran Colombia y Luis Cordero. Good jewellery, ceramics and candelabras.

Panama hats Manufacturers have displays showing the complete hat making process.
K Dorfzaun, Gil Ramírez Dávalos 4-34, near bus station, T280 7563, www.kdorfzaun.com. Good selection of hats and straw crafts, nice styles, good prices. English-speaking guides. **Homero Ortega P e Hijos**, Av Gil Ramírez Dávalos 3-86, T280 1288, www.homero ortega.com. Highest quality.
Markets **Feria Libre**, Av Las Américas y Av Remigio Crespo, west of the centre. The largest market, also has dry goods and clothing, busiest Wed and Sat.
Mercado 9 de Octubre, Sangurima y Mariano Cueva, busiest on Thu. Nearby at **Plaza Rotary**, Sangurima y Vargas Machuca, crafts are sold, best selection on Thu. Note this area is not safe.
Mercado 10 de Agosto, C Larga y Gral Torres. Daily market with a prepared foods and drinks section on the 2nd floor.

Activities and tours

Cuenca *p1119, map p1120*
Day tours to Ingapirca US$40 pp. Trekking in Cajas about US$40-45 pp per day.
Almíbar, Córdova 5-33 y Mariano Cueva, T07-282 6117. Local and regional tours, English and Italian spoken.
Apullacta, Gran Colombia 11-02 y Gral Torres, T283 7815, www.apullacta.com. Offers the usual tours and also hires tents, sleeping bags and other camping equipment.
Metropolitan Touring, Sucre 6-62 y Borrero, T283 7000, www.metropolitan-touring.com. A branch of the Quito operator, also sells airline tickets.
Terra Diversa, Hermano Miguel 5-42 entre Honorato Vázquez y Juan Jaramillo, T282 3782, www.terradiversa.com. Lots of useful information, helpful staff, a pleasant sitting area, small library and bulletin boards. Ingapirca, Cajas, community tourism in Saraguro, jungle trips, horse riding, mountain biking and other options. The more common destinations have fixed departures. Also sell Galápagos tours and flights. Recommended.

Transport

Cuenca *p1119, map p1120*
Air Airport is 5 mins walk beyond the terminal. No ticket reservations at the airport. To **Quito**, US$70 and **Guayaquil**, US$55, with **Aerogal**, **LAN** and **TAME**. Schedules change often so ask. Arrive at least 1 hr before departure.
Bus Terminal for local services is at the Feria Libre on Av Las Américas. Many city buses pass here. City buses US$0.25. For **Baños**, city buses every 5-10 mins, 0600-2330, buses pass the front of the Terminal Terrestre, cross the city on Vega Muñoz and Cueva, then down Todos los Santos to the river, along 12 de Abril and onto Av Loja.

The long distance Terminal Terrestre is on Av España, northeast of centre, take a taxi. Take daytime buses to enjoy scenic routes. To **Riobamba**, 6 hrs, US$6. To **Ambato**, 7 hrs, US$8. To **Quito**, 10 hrs, US$12. To **Loja**, 5 hrs, US$7. To **Machala**, 4 hrs, US$5, sit on the left, wonderful scenery. To **Guayaquil**, via Cajas and Molleturo, 4 hrs, or via Zhud, 5 hrs, both US$5. To **Cajas National Park**, see below. To **Macas** via Guarumales or Limón, 8 hrs, US$8.50; spectacular scenery but prone to landslides, check in advance if roads are open. To **Huaquillas**, 5 hrs, US$6. To **Saraguro**, US$5, 3 hrs. To **Gualaquiza**, in the southern Oriente, there are 2 routes, via Gualaceo and Plan de Milagro, 7 hrs, US$5 and via Sígsig, 6 hrs, US$6.25. To **Alausí**, 4 hrs, US$5; all Quito-bound buses pass through.
Taxi US$1 for short journey; US$2 to airport, US$1.50 to the bus station. To **Baños** costs US$5.

Ingapirca *p1122*
Bus **Transportes Cañar** has 2 direct buses daily from **Cuenca** to Ingapirca, at 0900 and 1300, returning 1300 and 1600, US$2.50, 2 hrs. From **Cañar**, corner of 24 de Mayo and Borrero, local buses leave every 15 mins for Ingapirca, 0600-1800, US$0.50, 30 mins; last bus returns at 1700. The same buses from Cañar go through **El Tambo**, US$0.50, 20 mins. If coming from the north, transfer in El Tambo. Pick-up from Cañar US$8, from El Tambo US$5. From **Alausí to Achupallas**, for the Inca Trail to Ingapirca, small buses and pickups leave as they fill between 1100 and 1600, US$1, 1hr. Alternatively, take any bus along the Panamericana to **La Moya**, south of Alausí, at the turn-off for Achupallas, and a shared pick-up from there (best on Thu and Sun), US$0.50. To hire a pick-up from Alausí costs US$15, from La Moya US$10.

East of Cuenca *p1122*

Bus From Terminal Terrestre in Cuenca: to **Paute**, every 15 mins, US$0.75, 1 hr; to **Gualaceo**, every 15 mins, US$0.60, 50 mins; to **Chordeleg**: every 15 mins from Gualaceo, US$0.25; 15 mins or direct bus from Cuenca, US$0.70, 1 hr; to **Sigsig**, every 30 mins via Gualaceo, US$1.25, 1½ hrs.

Parque Nacional Cajas *p1123*

Bus From Cuenca's Terminal Terrestre take any **Guayaquil** bus that goes via Molleturo (not Zhud), US$2, 30 mins to turn-off for Llaviuco, 45 mins to Toreadora. **Coop Occidental** to Molleturo, 8 a day from the Feria Libre (an unsafe area). For the Soldados entrance, catch a bus from Puente del Vado in Cuenca, daily at 0600, US$1.25, 1½ hrs; the return bus passes the Soldados gate at about 1600.

Directory

Cuenca *p1119, map p1120*

Airline offices **Aerogal**, Aurelio Aguilar 159 y Solano and Av España near the airport, T286 1041. **Icaro**, Av España 1114, T280 2700. **LAN**, Bolívar 9-18, T283 8078. **TAME**, Florencia Astudillo 2-22 and at the airport, T288 9581. **Banks** Banco del Pacífico, Gran Colombia 23-120 y Av Las Américas, ATM and TCs. Many banks with ATMs around the old cathedral. **Vazcorp**, Gran Colombia 7-98 y Cordero, T283 3434, Mon-Fri 0830-1730, Sat 0900-1245, change 11 currencies, good rates, 1.8% comission for US$ TCs. **Car rental** Avis, Av España 10-87 and at the airport, T286 0174, www.avis.com.ec. **Bombuscaro**, España y Elia Liut, opposite the airport, T286 6541. **Hertz**, at the airport, T280 6147, www.hertz.com.ec. **Internet** Rates US$0.60-1 per hr. Many to choose from. **Language courses** Rates US$6-10 per hr. **CEDEI, Centers for Interamerican Studies**, Luis Cordero 5-66 y Juan Jaramillo, T283 9003, www.cedei.org. Spanish and Quichua lessons, immersion/volunteering programmes, also run Hostal Macondo. Recommended. **Centro Abraham Lincoln**, Borrero 5-18 y Honorato Vásquez, T282 3898. Small Spanish language section. **Estudio Internacional Sampere**, Hermano Miguel 3-43 y C Larga, T284 1986, www.sampere.es. At the high end of the price range. **Sí Centro de Español e Inglés**, Borrero 7-67 y Sucre, T282 0429, www.sicentrospanishschool.com. Good teachers, competitive prices, homestays, volunteer opportunities, helpful and enthusiastic, tourist information available. Recommended. **Medical services** **Hospital Monte Sinaí**, Miguel Cordero 6-111 y Av Solano, near the stadium, T07-288 5595, several English-speaking physicians. **Hospital Santa Inés**, Av Toral 2-113, T281 7888; Dr Jaime Moreno Aguilar speaks English. **Post office** Gran Colombia y Borrero, helpful. **Useful addresses** Emergencies: T911. **Immigration**: E Muñoz 1-42 y Ordoñez Lasso, T282 1112.

Cuenca to the Peruvian border

From Cuenca various routes go to the Peruvian border, fanning out from the pleasant city of Loja, due south of which is Vilcabamba, famous for its invigorating climate, lovely countryside and, nowadays, its excellent services for tourists.

South to Loja

From Cuenca, the Pan-American Highway runs south to La Y, about 20 km away. Here the road divides: one continues as the Pan-American to Loja, the other runs southwest through Girón, the Yunguilla valley (with a small bird reserve, see www.fjocotoco.org) and Santa Isabel, several hotels with pools and spas, some cloud forest and waterfalls. The last stretch through sugar cane fields leads to Pasaje and Machala. The scenic road between Cuenca and Loja undulates between high, cold páramo passes and deep desert-like canyons.

Saraguro ➔ *Phone code: 07. Colour map 11, C3. Population: 7,500. Altitude: 2,500m.*
On the road to Loja is this old town, where the local people, the most southerly native Andean group in Ecuador, dress all in black. The men are notable for their black shorts and a particular kind of saddle bag, the *alforja*, and the women for their pleated black skirts, necklaces of coloured beads and silver *topos*, ornate pins fastening their shawls. The town has a picturesque Sunday market and interesting mass and easter celebrations. Traditional festivities are held during solstices and equinoxes in surrounding communities. Necklaces and other crafts are sold around the plaza. Saraguro has a community tourism programme with tours and home-stay opportunities with native families. Contact **Fundación Kawsay** ⓘ *18 de Noviembre y Av Loja, T220 0331, www.kawsay.org*, or the **Oficina Municipal de Turismo** ⓘ *C José María Vivar on the main plaza, T220 0100 ext 18, www.turismosaraguro.com, Mon-Fri 0800-1200, 1400-1800. See also www.saraguro.org*. **Bosque Washapampa**, 6 km south has good birdwatching.

Loja ➔ *Phone code: 07. Colour map 11, C3. Population: 172,000. Altitude: 2,060 m.*
This friendly, pleasant highland city, encircled by hills, is a traditional gateway between the highlands and southern Amazonia. It was founded on its present site in 1548, having been moved from La Toma, and was rebuilt twice after earthquakes, the last of which occurred in the 1880s. The city has two universities, with a well-known law school. The Universidad Nacional has good murals on some of its buildings. Loja has won international awards for its beautiful parks and its recycling programme. **Tourist offices**: iTur ⓘ *José Antonio Eguiguren y Bolívar, Parque Central, T258 1251, www.municipiodeloja.gov.ec, Mon-Fri 0800-1300, 1500-1800, Sat 0900-1300*. Local and regional information and map, helpful, some English spoken. **Consejo Provincial** ⓘ *Bernardo Valdivieso y Eguiguren, T257 0234 ext 170, www.gobierno deloja.gov.ec, Mon-Fri 0800-1300, 1500-1800*, information on Loja, city and province. **Ministerio de Turismo** ⓘ *Bolívar 12-39 y Lourdes, p 3, Parque San Sebastián, T257 2964, www.surecuadorturismo.gov.ec, Mon-Fri 0830-1330, 1430-1700*. Regional information, helpful, Spanish only.

The **Cathedral** and **Santo Domingo church**, Bolívar y Rocafuerte, have painted interiors. The 16th century **El Valle** church, on the north edge of the city, has a lovely interior and a small religious art museum in the bell-tower. Housed in a beautifully restored house on the main park is the **Centro Cultural Loja** home of the **Museo del Banco Central** ⓘ *10 de Agosto 13-30 y Bolívar, T257 3004, Mon-Fri 0900-700, free*, with well displayed archaeology, ethnography, art, and history halls. There are also temporary exhibits, a library and an auditorium. The **Museo de las Concepcionistas** ⓘ *10 de Agosto 12-78 y Bernardo Valdivieso, T256 1109, Mon-Fri 0900-1200, 1400-1700, Sat 0900-1200, US$1*, has a religious art collection. Loja is famed for its musicians and has one of the few musical academies in the country and two symphonic orchestras. Musical evenings and concerts are often held around the town and it's a good place to find guitar lessons. The **Museo de Música** ⓘ *Valdivieso 09-42 y Rocafuerte, T256 1342. Mon-Fri 0830-1230,*

1500-1900, free, housed in the restored Colegio Bernardo Valdivieso, honours ten Lojano composers. It also has rotating exhibits, not necessarily about music, and a café. At Puente Bolívar, by the northern entrance to the centre of town, is a fortress-like monument and a lookout over the city, known as **La Puerta de la Ciudad** ⓘ *Mon-Fri 0830-2130, Sat-Sun 0900-2130*. It has art exhibits at ground level and a small café upstairs, a good place to take pictures. Also in the north of the city, a couple of blocks east of the Terminal is the **Parque Recreacional Jipiro**, a well maintained, clean park, good to walk and relax in. It is popular at weekends. Take the city bus marked 'Jipiro', a five-minute ride from the centre.

Parque Universitario Francisco Vivar Castro (Parque La Argelia) ⓘ *on road south to Vilcabamba, Tue-Sun 0800-1700, US$1, city bus marked 'Capulí-Dos Puentes' to the park or 'Argelia' to the Universidad Nacional and walk from there*, is superb, with trails through the forest to the *páramo*. Across the road is the **Jardín Botánico Reynaldo Espinosa** ⓘ *Mon-Fri 0800-1600, Sat-Sun 0900-1730, US$1*, which is nicely laid out.

Parque Nacional Podocarpus

ⓘ *Park entry is US$10, officially valid only at the entrance where bought. Headquarters at Cajanuma entrance, T302 4852. Information from Ministerio del Ambiente in Loja, Sucre 04-55 y Quito, T257 9595, parquepodocarpus@gmail.com, Mon-Fri 0800-1700. In Zamora at Sevilla de Oro y Orellana, T260 6606. Their general map of the park is not adequate for navigation.*

Podocarpus (950 to 3,700 m) is one of the most diverse protected areas in the world. It is particularly rich in birdlife, including many rarities and some newly discovered species, and includes one of the last major habitats for the Spectacled Bear. The park protects stands of *romerillo* or podocarpus, a native, slow-growing conifer. UNESCO has declared Podocarpus-El Cóndor (Cordillera del Cóndor) as a biosphere reserve. It includes a large area (1.14 million has) in the provinces of Loja and Zamora Chinchipe. The park itself is divided into two areas, an upper premontane section with spectacular walking country, lush cloud forest and excellent birdwatching; and a lower subtropical section, with remote areas of virgin rainforest and unmatched quantities of flora and fauna. Both zones are quite wet (rubber boots recommended) but there are sometimes periods of dry weather October to January. The upper section is also very cold, so warm clothing and waterproofs are indispensable year-round. **Cajanuma** is the trailhead for the eight-hour hike to **Lagunas del Compadre**, 12 lakes set amid rock cliffs, camping is possible there. At **San Francisco**, the *guardianía* (ranger's station) operated by Fundación Arcoiris, offers nice accommodation (see below). This section of the park is a transition cloud forest at around 2,200 m, very rich in birdlife. This is the best place to see podocarpus trees: a trail (four hours return) goes from the shelter to the trees.

Entrances to the upper section: at Cajanuma, 8 km south of Loja on the Vilcabamba road, from the turn-off it is a further 8 km uphill to the guard station; at San Francisco, 24 km from Loja along the road to Zamora; the southwestern section of the park can be reached by trails from Vilcabamba, Yangana and Valladolid. Entrances to the lower section: Bombuscaro is 6 km from Zamora; Romerillos is two hours south of Zamora. Conservation groups working in and around the park include: **Arcoiris**, Ciprés 12-202 y Acacias, La Pradera, T257 2926, www.arcoiris.org.ec; **Naturaleza y Cultura** Internacional, Avenida Pío Jaramillo y Venezuela, T257 3691, www.natureandculture.org.

Zamora → *Phone code 07. Colour map 11, C3. Population: 13,000. Altitude: 950 m.*

The road to the Oriente crosses a low pass and descends rapidly to Zamora, an old mission settlement about 65 km away at the confluence of the Ríos Zamora and Bombuscaro. The road is beautiful as it wanders from *páramo* down to high jungle, crossing mountain ranges of spectacular cloud forest, weaving high above narrow gorges as it runs alongside the Río Zamora. The town itself is hilly, with a pleasant climate. As well as being the gateway to the lowland portion of Parque Nacional Podocarpus, it also gives access to Alto Nangaritza (see page 1184). There are two *orquidearios*, **Tzanka** ⓘ *José Luis Tamayo y Jorge Mosquera, T260 5692, US$2* and **Pafinia** ⓘ *Av del Ejército Km 2, T260 5911*. For information about the town: **iTur** ⓘ *booth outside the Terminal Terrestre, T260 7526, Mon-Fri 0800-1230, 1400-1730*; A couple ATMs in town, but not always reliable, bring cash.

Loja to the Peruvian border

Of all the crossings from Ecuador to Peru, by far the most efficient and relaxed is the scenic route from Loja to Piura via Macará. Other routes are from Vilcabamba to La Balsa (see page 1137), Huaquillas (see page 1150) and along the Río Napo in the Oriente (see page 1177). There are smaller border crossings without immigration facilities (passports cannot be stamped) at Jimbura, southeast of Macará; and Lalamor, west of Macará.

Leaving Loja on the main paved highway going west, the airport at **La Toma** (1,200 m) is reached after 35 km. La Toma is also called **Catamayo**, where there is lodging. At Catamayo, where you can catch the Loja-Macará-Piura bus, the Pan-American Highway divides: one branch runs west, the other south.

On the western road, at San Pedro de La Bendita, a road climbs to the much-venerated pilgrimage site of **El Cisne**, dominated by its large incongruous French-style Gothic church. There is a small museum, two basic *pensiones* (other houses open to lodgers at pilgrimage time) and places to eat. Vendors and beggars fill the town and await visitors (see Festivals and events, below). Continuing on the western route, **Catacocha** is spectacularly placed on a hilltop. Visit the Shiriculapo rock for the views. There are pre-Inca ruins around the town; small archaeological **Museo Hermano Joaquín Liebana** ⓘ *T268 3201, 0800-1200, 1400-1800*. From Catacocha, the road runs south to the border at Macará.

The south route from Catamayo to Macará is via Cariamanga. The road goes to **Cariamanga**, via **Gonzanamá**, a pleasant, sleepy little town (basic *hostales*), famed for the weaving of beautiful *alforjas* (multi-purpose saddlebags). It is 27 km to Cariamanga (six hotels, banks), then the road twists along a ridge westwards to **Colaisaca**, before descending steeply through forests to **Utuana** with a nature reserve (www.fjocotoco.org) and **Sozoranga** (one hotel), then down to the rice paddies of **Macará**, on the border. There is a choice of accommodation here and good road connections to Sullana and Piura in Peru.

Border with Peru **Ecuadorean immigration** is open 24 hours. Formalities last about 30 minutes. It is a much easier crossing than at Huaquillas. During the day there are money changers dealing in soles at the international bridge and in Macará at the park where taxis leave for the border. The international bridge over the Río Macará is 2½ km from town; shared taxi US$0.30, private US$1. On the Peruvian side, minivans and cars run to Sullana; avoid arriving in Sullana after dark.

Cuenca to the Peruvian border listings

For Sleeping and Eating price codes and other relevant information, see Essentials, pages 38-40.

Sleeping

Saraguro *p1130*

D Achik Huasi, on a hillside above town, T220 0058 or through Fundación Kawsay, www.kawsay.org. Community-run hostería in a nice setting, breakfast available, private bath, hot water, parking, views, tours, taxi to centre US$1.

E-F Saraguro, Loja No 03-2 y A Castro, T220 0286. Cheaper with shared bath, nice courtyard, electric shower, family-run, basic, good value.

Loja *p1130*

L-AL Howard Johnson, Av Zoilo Rodríguez y Antisana, T258 9000, www.ghlhoteles.com. Part of the US hotel chain, lovely views of the city from rooms and dining room, includes buffet breakfast, restaurant offers set lunch with salad bar, Ecuadorean and international food , small indoor pool and spa, safety box in room, weekend discounts, opened in 2009.

AL Grand Victoria, B Valdivieso 06-50 y Eguiguren, half a block from the Parque Central, T258 3500, www.grandvictoriabh.com. Rebuilt early-20th century home with 2 patios, comfortable modern rooms and suites, includes buffet breakfast, Mediterranean restaurant, small pool, spa, gym, Wi-Fi, business centre, frigobar, safety box, parking.

A La Casa Lojana, París 00-08 y Zoilo Rodríguez, T258 5984, www.casalojana.com.ec. A refurbished residence elaborately decorated in colonial style. Rooms are plain compared to the opulent common areas. Includes breakfast, restaurant in elegant dining room, Wi-Fi, parking, lovely grounds and views of the city. Run by the Universidad Técnica Particular de Loja and staffed by their Hotel School students.

B Libertador, Colón 14-30 y Bolívar, T256 0779, www.hotellibertador.com.ec. A very good hotel in the centre of town, comfortable rooms, suites available, includes buffet breakfast, good restaurant, indoor pool (US$4 for non-guests), spa, Wi-Fi, parking.

C Bombuscaro, 10 de Agosto y Av Universitaria, T257 7021, www.bombuscaro.com.ec. Comfortable rooms and suites, includes buffet breakfast and airport transfers, restaurant, Wi-Fi, car rental, good service. Recommended.

D Acapulco, Sucre 07-61 y 10 de Agosto, T257 0651. Pleasant hotel in the centre of town. Nicely furnished but small rooms, includes basic breakfast, cafeteria, private bath, hot water, Wi-Fi and computer for guests' use, quieter away from breakfast room.

D América, 18 de Noviembre entre Imbabura y Quito, T256 2887, hostalamerica@gmail.com. Modern multi-storey hotel with spacious, comfortable rooms, includes breakfast, good restaurant downstairs for breakfast and set meals, hot water, Wi-Fi.

E Chandelier, Imbabura 14-82 y Sucre, T256 3061, chandelierhotel@hotmail.com. Simple but adequate, cheaper with shared bath, electric shower, parking, hospitable.

F Londres, Sucre 07-51 y 10 de Agosto, T256 1936. Hostel in a well maintained old house, shared bath, electric shower, basic but very clean, good value.

Parque Nacional Podocarpus *p1131*

At **Cajanuma**, there are cabins for US$3 pp per night, bring warm sleeping bag, stove and food. At **San Francisco**, the *guardianía* (ranger's station), operated by **Fundación Arcoiris** offers nice rooms with shared bath, hot water and kitchen facilities, US$8 pp if you bring a sleeping bag, US$10 if they provide sheets. Ask to be let off at Arcoiris or you will be taken to Estación San Francisco, 8 km further east. At **Bombuscaro** there are cabins with beds for US$2pp.

Zamora *p1131*

A-C Copalinga, Km 3 on the road to the Bombuscaro entrance of Parque Nacional Podocarpus, T304 0027, T09-347 7013, www.copalinga.com. Nice comfortable cabins with balcony in a lovely setting, includes very good breakfast, other delicious meals available if arranged in advance, more rustic cabins with shared bath are cheaper, excellent birdwatching. Belgian run, English, French and Dutch spoken, attentive, reserve ahead. Highly recommended.

C Samuria, 24 de Mayo y Diego de Vaca, T260 7801, hotelsamuria@hotmail.com. Modern bright hotel, comfortable well furnished rooms, includes breakfast, restaurant, parking.

D Wampushkar, Diego de Vaca y Pasaje Vicente Aldeán, T260 7800. Nice modern hotel, ample rooms, includes breakfast, hot water, Wi-Fi, parking, good value, opened in 2009.

E Betania, Francisco de Orellana entre Diego de Vaca y Amazonas, T260 7030, hotel-betania@hotmail.com. Modern, functional, breakfast available, hot water.

E Chonta Dorada, Pío Jaramillo y Diego de Vaca, T260 6384. Small rooms, electric shower, parking for small vehicles, adequate and good value.

Loja to the Peruvian border *p1132*

Catamayo

B-D MarcJohn's, Isidro Ayora y 24 de Mayo, at the main park, T267 7631, granhotelmarcjohns@hotmail.com. Modern multi-storey hotel, functional rooms, suites with Jacuzzi and fridge, restaurant, Wi-Fi, includes airport transfers. Best in town.

C Rosal del Sol, a short walk from the city on the main road west of town, T267 6517, www.rosaldelsol.com.ec. Ranch-style building, rooms are comfortable but hot and you might need insect repellent, restaurant (not always

open), small pool, parking, includes airport transfer, business centre, welcoming owner.
E-F Reina del Cisne, Isidro Ayora on the park, T267 7414. Simple adequate rooms, cheaper with shared bath, cold water, fan, small pool, parking.

Macará

E Colina, Olmedo y Loja, T269 4871. Pleasant modern hostal in a quiet location, some rooms have electric showers, fan, small rooftop terrace, good value.
E El Conquistador, Bolívar y Abdón Calderón, T269 4057. Comfortable hotel, some rooms are dark, request one with balcony, includes simple breakfast, electric shower, fan, parking.
F Bekalus, Valdivieso entre 10 de Agosto y Rengel, T269 4043. Cold water, parking, simple but adequate.

Eating

Saraguro *p1130*

Several restaurants around the main plaza serve economical meals.
¥¥-¥ Turu Manka, 100 m uphill from Hostal Achik Huasi. Wide selection. The food is average, but it is still one of the better choices in town.

Loja *p1130*

¥¥ Parrilladas Uruguayas, Juan de Salinas y Av Universitaria, Sun 1100-1800, Mon 1800-0030, Tue-Sat 1100-0030. Good grilled meat, helpful Uruguayan owner.
¥¥-¥ Casa Sol, 24 de Mayo 07-04 y José Antonio Eguiguren, daily 0830-2330. Small place serving breakfast, economical set lunches and regional dishes in the evening. Pleasant seating on balcony.
¥¥-¥ Pizzería Forno di Fango, Bolívar 10-98 y Azuay, also at 24 de Mayo y Azuay, Tue-Sun 1200-2230. Excellent wood-oven pizza, salads and lasagne. Large portions, good service and value. Recommended.
¥ Angelo's, José Félix de Valdivieso y Av Universitaria, Mon-Sat 0900-2100. Good quality set lunches, international dishes à la carte in the evening , nice decor and above average service.
¥ Rizzoto, Bolívar 10-11 y Riofrío (no sign, upstairs inside La Casona shopping gallery), Mon-Sat 0900-1500. Breakfast and vegetarian set lunches, also some meat options.
Alivinatu, 10 de Agosto 12-53 y Bernardo Valdivieso, in the health food shop. Very good fresh fruit or vegetable juices, you choose the ingredients and it is prepared on the spot. Also a few snacks and set lunches.

Cafés

Café Ruskina, Sucre 07-48 y 10 de Agosto, Mon-Sat 0845-1300, 1500-2030. Coffee, cream cakes, other sweets and regional snacks such as humitas.
El Jugo Natural, José Antonio Eguiguren 14-18 y Bolívar, Mon-Fri 0700-2000, Sat-Sun 0800-1800. Very good fresh juices and breakfast.
El Sendero, Bolívar 13-13 y Mercadillo, upstairs, Tue-Sat 1530-2200. Fruit juices, coffee and snacks, nice balcony overlooking Plaza San Sebastián, ping pong and other games, library.
El Tamal Lojano, 18 de Noviembre 05-12 e Imbabura, Mon-Sat 0800-2030. Good tamales and other local snacks, drinks.

Zamora *p1131*

¥ Flor de Canela, Sevilla de Oro y Av Héroes de Paquisha, Mon-Fri 0700-2000. Good set meals.
¥ King Ice, Diego de Vaca y José Luis Tamayo, by the plaza, daily 0900-0000. Snacks and a few à la carte dishes.
Spiga Pan, 24 de Mayo, ½ block downhill from the plaza. Great bakery with a variety of hot bread, cream cakes and fresh fruit yoghurt. A very good option in this otherwise un-gastronomic town.

Loja to the Peruvian border *p1132*

Catamayo

¥ Don Leo, Isidro Ayora y 9 de Octubre, daily 0700-2200. Set meals and huge portions à la carte.

Festivals and events

Loja *p1130*

Aug-Sep Fiesta de la Virgen del Cisne, hundreds of faithful accompany the statue of the Virgin in a 3-day 74 km walk from El Cisne to Loja cathedral, beginning **16 Aug**. A religious festival with serenades at the cathedral is held **8 Sep**, a week long commercial and agricultural exhibition begins on the same day. The image remains in Loja until **1 Nov** when the return pilgrimage starts. Town is crowded Aug-Sep.

Activities and tours

Loja *p1130*

Aratinga Aventuras, Lourdes 14-84 y Sucre, T/F258 2434, aratinga@loja.telconet.net.

Specializes in birdwatching tours, over-night trips to different types of forest. Pablo Andrade is a knowledgeable guide.
Blaue Berge, Bernardo Valdivieso 11-71 y Mercadillo, T258 6805, sisacunatours@gmail.com. Tours in Loja, Zamora and El Oro.

Zamora *p1131*
BioAventura, at **Refugio Tzanka** (see above), T09-381 4472. Fernado Ortega offers downhill bike rides along the old road Loja-Zamora.
Cabañas Yankuam, see p, offer tours to the Alto Nangaritza.
Wellington Valdiviezo, T09-380 2211, manacus_manacus@yahoo.es. Tours to the Alto Nangaritza, Shuar communities, adventure sports, visits to shamans. Contact in advance.

Transport

Saraguro *p1130*
Bus To **Cuenca** US$5, 3 hrs. To **Loja**, US$1.75, 2 hrs. Check if your bus leaves from the plaza or the Panamericana.

Loja *p1130*
Air The airport is at La Toma (Catamayo), 35 km west (see Loja to the Peruvian border above): taxi from airport to Catamayo bus station US$1.50, to Loja shared taxi US$4-5 pp, to hire US$15-20 (cheaper from Loja) eg with Jaime Gonzales, T256 3714, to Vilcabamba, US$30-40 . There are daily **TAME** (24 de Mayo y E Ortega, T257 0248) flights to Quito (US$79-85) and daily **Saereo** (Av Cuxibamba y Ancón, T256 2401) flights to **Guayaquil** (US$75). Flights are often cancelled due to strong winds or fog.
Bus All buses leave from the Terminal Terrestre at Av Gran Colombia e Isidro Ayora, at the north of town, 10 mins by city bus from the centre; left luggage, information desk, shops, US$0.10 terminal tax. Taxi from centre, US$1. To **Cuenca**, 5 hrs, US$7. **Machala**, 10 a day, 5-6 hrs, US$6 (3 routes, all scenic: via Piñas, for **Zaruma**, unpaved and rough; via Balsas, paved; and via Alamor, for **Puyango petrified forest**). **Quito**, US$14, 13 hrs. **Guayaquil**, US$10, 8 hrs.
To **Huaquillas**, US$6, 6 hrs direct. To **Zumba** (for Peru border at La Balsa), several daily including **Sur Oriente** at 0500 to make connections to Peru same day, US$7.50, 7 hrs but delays possible. To **Catamayo** (for airport) every 20 min 0600-2000, US$1, 1hr. To **Macará**, see below. To **Piura (Peru)**, **Loja Internacional**, via Macará, at 0700, 1300 and 2300 daily, US$8, 8 hrs including border formalities; buy ticket 24 hrs in advance. Also **Unión Cariamanga** at 2400 and 0600.

Parque Nacional Podocarpus *p1131*
For **Cajanuma**, take a Vilcabamba bound bus, get off at the turnoff, US$1, it is a 8-km walk from there. Direct transport by taxi to the park gate, about US$10 (may not be feasible in the rainy season) or with a tour from Loja. You can arrange a pick up later from the guard station.
To the **San Francisco section**, take any bus between Loja and Zamora, make sure you alight by the Arcoiris *guardianía* and not at Estación Científica San Francisco which is 8 km east.
To the **lower section**: **Bombuscaro** is 6 km from Zamora, take a taxi US$6 to the entrance, then walk 1 km to the visitor's centre.

Zamora *p1131*
Bus Leave from Terminal Terrestre. To **Loja**, frequent, 1½-2 hrs, US$2.40; to **Gualaquiza**, US$3.50, 3 hrs, where you can change buses for Macas.

Loja to the Peruvian border *p1132*
Macará
Bus **Transportes Loja** and **Cariamanga** have frequent buses, daily from Macará to **Loja**; 6 hrs, US$6. Direct Loja-**Piura** buses can also be boarded in Macará, US$4 to Piura, 3 hrs. *Transportes Loja* also has service to **Quito**, US$15, 15 hrs, and **Guayaquil**, US$11, 8 hrs.

Directory

Loja *p1130*
Banks Several banks with ATMs around the Parque Central. **Vazcorp**, B Valdivieso entre 10 de Agosto y Rocafuerte, change euros, Peruvian soles and other South American currencies, also TCs, 1.8% comission. A couple of shops along José Antonio Eguiguren change cash euros and soles.
Embassies and consulates Peru, Zoilo Rodríguez 03-05, T258 7330, Mon-Fri 0900-1300, 1500-1700. **Internet** US$1 per hr. **Medical services** Clínica San Agustín, 18 de Noviembre 10-72 y Azuay, T257 3002. **Post offices** Colón y Sucre; no good for sending parcels.

Vilcabamba ➔ *Phone code: 07. Colour map 11, C3. Population: 4,400. Altitude: 1,520 m.*

Once an isolated village, Vilcabamba has become increasingly popular with foreign travellers, an established stop along the gringo trail between Ecuador and Peru. The whole area is beautiful and tranquil, with an agreeable climate (17°C minimum, 26°C maximum, the rainy season is November to April; July and August can be very dry and windy). There are many places to stay and several good restaurants. There are many great day-walks and longer treks throughout the area, as well as ample opportunities for horse riding. A number of lovely private nature reserves are situated east of Vilcabamba, towards Parque Nacional Podocarpus. Trekkers can continue on foot through orchid-clad cloud forests to the high cold *páramos* of Podocarpus. Artisans sell their crafts in front of the church on weekends. **Tourist office**: iTur ⓘ *Diego Vaca de*

Vilcabamba

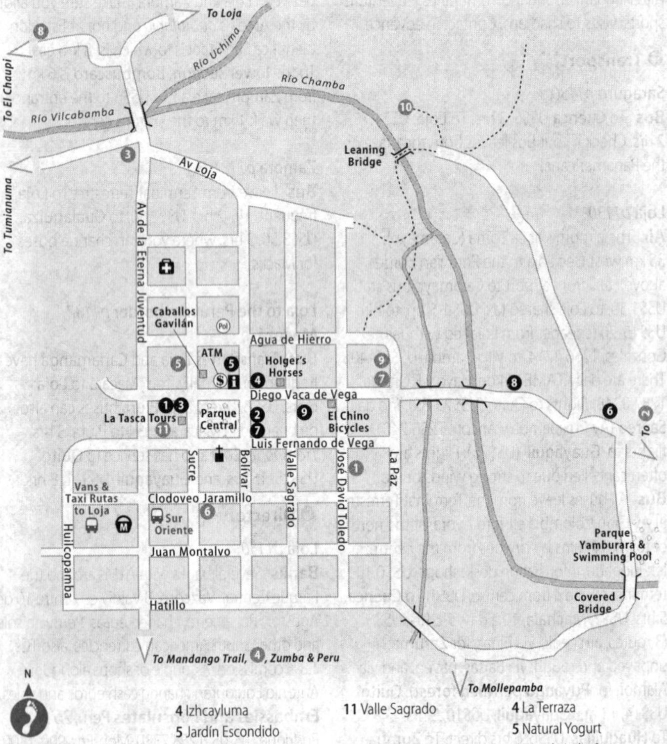

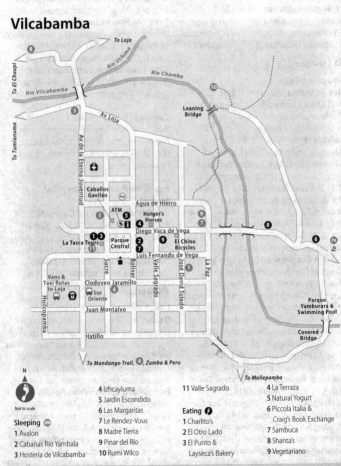

Sleeping
1 Avalon
2 Cabañas Río Yambala
3 Hostería de Vilcabamba
4 Izhcayluma
5 Jardín Escondido
6 Las Margaritas
7 Le Rendez-Vous
8 Madre Tierra
9 Pinar del Río
10 Rumi Wilco
11 Valle Sagrado

Eating
1 Charlito's
2 El Otro Lado
3 El Punto & Layseca's Bakery
4 La Terraza
5 Natural Yogurt
6 Piccola Italia & Craig's Book Exchange
7 Sambuca
8 Shanta's
9 Vegetariano

Vega y Bolívar, on the corner of the main plaza, T264 0090, daily 0800-1300, 1500-1800, has various pamphlets, helpful. See www.vilcabamba.org.

Rumi Wilco ⓘ *10-min walk northeast of town, take C Agua de Hierro towards C La Paz and turn left, follow signs, US$2 valid for the duration of your stay in Vilcabamba.* This 40-ha private nature reserve has several signed trails. Many of the trees and shrubs are labelled with their scientific and common names. There are great views of town from the higher trails, and it is a very good place to go for a walk. Over 100 species of birds have been identified here. Volunteers are welcome.

Climbing **Mandango**, 'the sleeping woman' mountain (US$2, includes a small bottle of mineral water and a small bag of panela, local raw sugar), is a popular and scenic half-day walk. The signed access is along the highway, 250 m south of the bus terminal. Be careful on the higher sections when it is windy and be sure to enquire about safety before going.

Vilcabamba to Peru

Many daily buses run from Loja via Vilcabamba to **Zumba** (see Loja, Transport), 112 km south of Vilcabamba (paving underway in 2010). It is a 1½ -hour rough ride by *ranchera* (open-sided bus) from Zumba to **La Balsa**, where there is an immigration post (supposedly open 24 hours). Passports may also be checked at Pucapamba, north of La Balsa. A modern vehicle bridge over the Río Canchis leads to the Peruvian border post (open 0800-1300, 1500-2000); entering Peru, visit immigration and the PNP office. On the Peruvian side a minibus service runs to **Namballe**, 15 minutes away, and cars run to Namballe and **San Ignacio** (Peru) when full, two hours, from where there is transport to **Jaén**. This opens a faster, more direct route between **Vilcabamba and Chachapoyas**, which can be done in two days, parts of the route are rough.

Vilcabamba to Peru listings

For Sleeping and Eating price codes and other relevant information, see Essentials, pages 38-40.

Sleeping

Vilcabamba *p1136, map p1136*

Note Over the years we have received many serious complaints about the hotel **Ruinas de Quinara**, renamed in 2009 **El Agua de Hierro**.

A-C Madre Tierra, 2 km north on road to Loja, then follow signs west, T264 0269, www.vilcabambamadretierra.com. A variety of rooms from ample to small and simple, eclectic colourful decor, includes breakfast, restaurant, nice grounds, pool, spa (massage and other treatments extra), Wi-Fi, videos, ping-pong, English spoken.

B Hostería de Vilcabamba, by the bridge at the northern entrance to town, T264 0271, www.vivavilcabamba.com. Modern, spacious and comfortable rooms, family bungalows, includes breakfast, restaurant, parking, nice ample grounds, pool and spa, all well maintained. Popular with Ecuadorean families.

C-D Izhcayluma, 2 km south on road to Zumba, T264 0095, www.izhcayluma.com. Popular inn with comfortable rooms and cabins with terrace and hammocks. Includes very good buffet breakfast, excellent restaurant with wonderful views, cheaper with shared bath, **F** pp in dorm, Wi-Fi in dining room, nice grounds, pool, massage centre, lively bar, billiards, ping-pong and other games, parking, walking map and route descriptions, English and German spoken, helpful. Highly recommended.

C-E Jardín Escondido, Sucre y Diego Vaca de Vega, T264 0281, www.jardin-escondido.com. Nicely refurbished old house around a lovely patio, bright comfortable rooms, includes very good and generous breakfast, excellent Mexican restaurant, cheaper in shared rooms, small pool, Jacuzzi extra, parking for small vehicle, English spoken.

D Avalon, José David Toledo 12-26 y Luis Fernando de la Vega, T264 0184, www.avalon-vilcabamba.de. Bed and breakfast in a nicely refurbished adobe house. Three comfortable rooms, includes good breakfast, shared bath, hot water, tastefully decorated, nice common areas, garden, English, German and French spoken, opened in 2009.

D-E Le Rendez-Vous, Diego Vaca de Vega 06-43 y La Paz, T09-219 1180, www.rendezvousecuador.com. Very comfortable rooms with terrace and hammocks around a lovely garden. Includes good breakfast, cheaper with shared bath, hot water, pleasant atmosphere, attentive service, French and English spoken. Highly recommended.

D-E Rumi Wilco, 10-min walk northeast of town, take C Agua de Hierro towards C La Paz and turn left, followi the signs from there, www.rumiwilco.com. Nice adobe or wood cabins in the Rumi Wilco reserve. Lovely setting on the shores of the river, very tranquil, cheaper with shared bath, hot water, laundry facilities, fully furnished kitchens, discounts for long stays and volunteers, camping US$3.50 pp, friendly Argentine owners, English spoken. Recommended.

E Cabañas Río Yambala, Yamburara Alto, 4 km east of town, T09-106 2762, www.vilcabamba-hotel.com. Cabins in a beautiful tranquil setting on the shores of the Río Yambala , meals available on request, cheaper with shared bath, hot water, sauna, cooking facilities, tours to Las Palmas private nature reserve with waterfalls and good birdwatching. English spoken.

E Las Margaritas, Sucre y Clodoveo Jaramillo, T264 0051, www.vilcabamba.org/lasmargaritas. Small family-run hotel with very comfortable and nicely-furnished rooms, includes good breakfast, intermittent solar-heated water, small pool, parking, nice garden, good value.

E Valle Sagrado, Luis Fernando de Vega y Av de la Eterna Juventud, T264 0386, www.vilcabamba.org/vallesagrado. Nice ample grounds, simple rooms, breakfast available, cheaper with shared bath and in dorm, electric shower, laundry and cooking facilities, parking.

F Pinar del Río, La Paz y Agua de Hierro, T264 0459. Family-run hostel, simple rooms, some small, meals on request, hot water, cooking facilities, patio with hammocks, pool table, good value.

Vilcabamba to Peru: Zumba *p1137*

E El Emperador, Colón y Orellana, T230 8063. Simple adequate rooms, cheaper with shared bath, cold water.

E San Luis, 12 de Febrero y Brasil, T230 8017. Simple, shared bath, electric shower.

Eating

Vilcabamba *p1136, map p1136*

There are excellent restaurants at hotels **Izhcayluma** and **Jardín Escondido**. Around the Parque Central are many café/bar/restaurants with pleasant sidewalk seating, see map.

TT Shanta's, 800 m from the centre on the road to Yamburara, Mon 1700-2200, Tue-Sun 1300-2200. Good international food, specialties are trout, frogs legs, filet mignon. Also vegetarian options, tasty pizza, good fruit juices and drinks. Nicely decorated rustic setting just outside town, good atmosphere and attentive service. Recommended.

TT-T Natural Yogurt, Bolívar y Diego Vaca de Vega, daily 0800-2200. Breakfast, home-made yoghurt, a variety of savoury and sweet crêpes, some pasta dishes.

TT-T Piccola Italia, Yamburara, 1 km east of town, follow Diego Vaca de Vega, 1100-2100, closed Tue. Italian dishes and Ecuadorean set lunches. Here is **Craig's Book Exchange** with 2,500 books in 12 languages.

T Charlito's, Diego Vaca de Vega y Sucre, Tue-Sun 1000-2200. Salads, pasta, pizza, sandwiches with tasty homemade wholemeal bread, popular with expats.

T Vegetariano, Valle Sagrado y Diego Vaca de Vega, 0900-1930, closed Wed evening. Small family-run vegetarian restaurant in a nice garden setting. Very good 3-course set meals and a few à la carte dishes, also breakfasts.

Activities and tours

Vilcabamba *p1136, map p1136*

See under Sleeping, above, for more options.

Cycling **El Chino**, Diego Vaca de Vega y José David Toledo. Mountain bike tours (US$15-22), rentals (US$1.50/hr, US$8/day) and repairs.

Horse riding Short trips US$5-8 per hour, half day US$15-25, full day with lunch US$30-35, overnight trips US$30-40 per day full board.

Caballos Gavilán, Sucre y Diego Vaca de Vega, T08-632 3285, gavilanhorse@yahoo.com. Run by New Zealander Gavin Moore, lots of experience, good horseman.

Centro Ecuestre, Diego Vaca de Vega y Bolívar. A group of local guides, helpful.

Holger's Horses, Diego Vaca de Vega y Valle Sagrado, T08-296 1238. Holger Granda, good horses and saddles, German spoken.

La Tasca Tours, Sucre at the plaza, T09-184 1287. Tours with experienced guides, René and Alvaro León.
Refugio Solomaco, T08-914 4812, 1- to 3-day guided or independent riding or walking tours to a private reserve by Podocarpus.
Massage **Beauty Care**, Bolívar y Diego Vaca de Vega, T09-326 1944, daily 1000-1800, Karina Zumba, facials, waxing, Reiki, 1 hr US$10. **Shanta's** (see Eating, above), T08-562 7802, Lola Encalada is a physiotherapist, 1¼ hr therapeutic massage US$14, waxing, very good. Recommended.

Transport

Vilcabamba *p1136, map p1136*
Loja to Vilcabamba, a nice 1-hour bus ride; from Loja's Terminal Terrestre, **Vilcabambaturis** mini-buses, every 15-30 mins, 0545-2115, US$1, 1 hr; or *taxirutas* (shared taxis) from José María Peña y Venezuela, 0600-2000, US$1.20, 45 min. To **Loja**, vans and shared taxis leave from the small terminal behind the market.

To **Zumba** buses originating in Loja pass Vilcabamba about 1 hr after departure and stop along the highway in front of the market (1st around 0600), US$6.50, 5-6 hrs. From Zumba to **La Balsa**, *rancheras* at 0800, 1400 and 1700, US$1.75, 1½ hrs. From La Balsa to Zumba at 1200, 1730 and 1900. Taxi Zumba-La Balsa, US$20.

Directory

Vilcabamba *p1136, map p1136*
Airline offices TAME agent, Bolívar y Montalvo, T264 0437. **Banks** No banks, only one standalone ATM (sometimes out of order) at Diego Vaca de Vega y Bolívar, next to iTur; bring some cash. **San Pablo grocery store** on Clodoveo Jaramillo across from the bus station may change cash euros and soles, poor rates. **Internet** US$1 per hr. **Language courses** Spanish classes with **Catalina Carrasco**, T08-267 8960, catycarrasco@yahoo.com; **Marta Villacrés**, T09-751 3311.

Guayaquil and south to Peru

→ *Phone code: 04. Colour map 11, B2. Population: 2,500,000. Altitude: 4 m.*

Guayaquil is hotter, faster and brasher than the capital. It is Ecuador's largest city and the country's chief seaport; an industrial and commercial centre, some 56 km from the Río Guayas' outflow into the Gulf of Guayaquil. The Puerto Marítimo handles three-quarters of the country's imports and almost half of its exports. Industrial expansion continually fuels the city's growth. Founded in 1535 by Sebastián de Benalcázar, then again in 1537 by Francisco Orellana, the city has always been an intense political rival to Quito. Guayaquileños are certainly more lively, colourful and open than their Quito counterparts. Since 2000, Guayaquil has cleaned-up and 'renewed' some of its most frequented downtown areas, there is a modern airport terminal, the Metrovía transit system, and a rebuilt bus station. The city as a whole is becoming more attractive and the authorities are trying hard to encourage tourism.

Thriving and ever increasing banana plantations, with shrimp farms among the mangroves, are the economic mainstay of the coastal area bordering the east flank of the Gulf of Guayaquil. Rice, sugar, coffee and cacao are also produced. The Guayas lowlands are subject to flooding, humidity is high and biting insects are fierce. Mangroves characterize the coast leading south to Huaquillas, the main border crossing to Peru.

Ins and outs

Getting there José Joaquín de Olmedo International **airport** is 15 minutes north of the city centre by taxi (recommended for safety, US$4). Neither the Metrovía nor buses to the centre (eg Línea 130 'Full 2') are safe or practical with luggage. For groups, **Trans Rabbit** (T216 9228) has van service (US$12 downtown). If going straight on to another city, get a cab directly to the **Terminal Terrestre** (bus station), which is close by; US$3. The northern terminus of the Metrovía is opposite the Terminal Terrestre, it and many city buses go from the bus station to the city centre, (eg Línea 84 to Plaza Centenario) but these are not safe with luggage; take a taxi (US$3-4). ▸▸ *See also Transport, page 1147.*

Getting around Not surprisingly for a city of this size, you will need to get around by public transport. A number of hotels are centrally located in the downtown core. The Metrovía crosses the city from north to south with articulated buses. A second line goes east-west along C Sucre in the centre and on to the suburbs. There are also city buses and *furgonetas* (minibuses), all cost US$0.25 and get overcrowded at rush hour, watch out for pickpockets. Taxis are the safest and most comfortable option, insist that the driver use the meter. The rates are slightly lower for taxis taken in the street, outside the airport or bus terminal. In the street take only yellow taxis with an antenna; there are also radio taxis (eg Vipcar, T239 3000). Short trips costs US$2.50, the fares from the centre to Urdesa, Policentro or Alborada are around US$3-4.

Orientation The centre is on the west bank of the Río Guayas, the city's suburbs sprawl to the north and south of the centre, with middle-class neighbourhoods and some very upscale areas in the north and poorer working-class neighbourhoods and slums to the south. A road tunnel under Cerro Santa Ana links the northern suburbs to downtown. Outside downtown, adresses are complicated and hard to find; ask for a nearby landmark to help orient your taxi driver.

Tourist offices Centro de Información Turística del Municipio ⓘ *Clemente Ballén y Pichincha, at Museo Nahim Isaías, T232 4182, Tue-Sat 0900-1700, English spoken*, has pamphlets and city maps. There are also information booths at Malecón 2000, by the 9 de Octubre entrance, and at the Terminal Terrestre, by the first entrance next to Banco Bolivariano. **Ministerio de Turismo,**

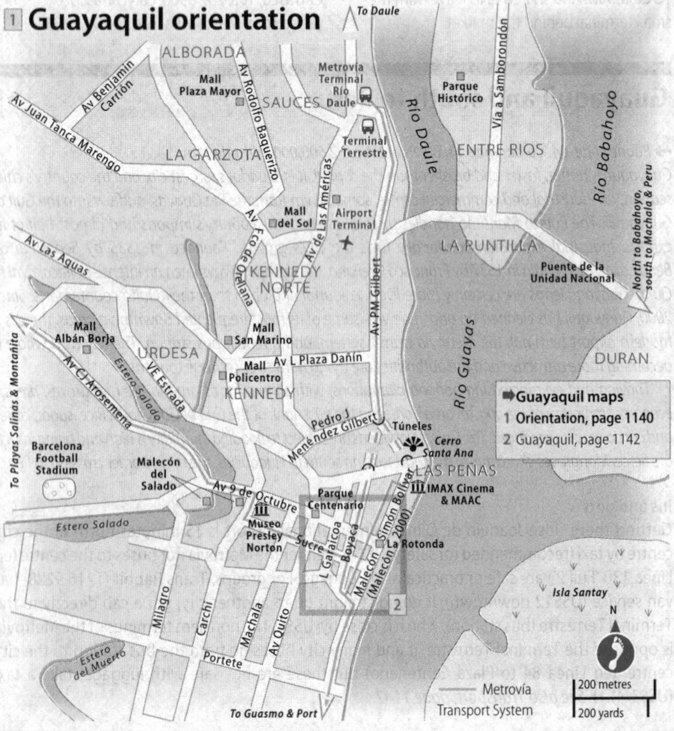

➡Guayaquil maps
1 Orientation, page 1140
2 Guayaquil, page 1142

Subsecretaría del Litoral ⓘ *Av Francisco de Orellana, Edif Gobierno del Litoral, p 8 and counter on the ground floor, Ciudadela Kennedy, T268 4274, www.ecuador.travel, Mon-Fri 0900-1700.* Information about the coastal provinces of Ecuador and whale watching regulations, Spanish only. The municipality publishes a bilingual guide to Guayaquil's attractions and services, available in bookstores, US$15; see www.guayaquilguides.com. Websites with information about Guayaquil and the coast include www.visitaguayaquil.com, www.guayaquil.gov.ec, and www.turismoguayas.com. Website for eating and night life: www.farras.com.

Climate From May-December it is dry with often overcast days but pleasantly cool nights, whereas the hot rainy season from January-April can be oppressively humid.

Safety Despite an ongoing public safety campaign by the municipal authorities, residential neighbourhoods hide behind bars and protect themselves with armed guards. The Malecón 2000, parts of Avenida 9 de Octubre, Las Peñas and Malecón del Estero Salado are heavily patrolled and reported safe. The area around Parque Centenario is not safe, day or night. Gangs are a problem in some peripheral neighbourhoods such as Sauces. The rest of the city carries all the usual risks of a large seaport and metropolis, so it is best not to walk anywhere with valuables, in the street take only yellow taxis with an antannae and at night call a radio-taxi. Pirate taxis, sometimes fancy unmarked cars, have been involved in scams whereby they take a passenger from ATM to ATM and force them to take out money.

Guayaquil

Sights

A wide, tree-lined waterfront avenue, the Malecón Simón Bolívar runs alongside the Río Guayas from the Palacio de Cristal, past **Plaza Olmedo**, the Moorish clock tower, by the imposing **Palacio Municipal** and **Gobernación** and the old Yacht Club to Las Peñas. The riverfront along this avenue is an attractive promenade, known as **Malecón 2000**, where visitors and locals can enjoy the fresh river breeze and take in the views. There are gardens, fountains, monuments and walkways. You can dine at upmarket restaurants, cafés and food courts. Towards the south end are souvenir shops, a shopping mall and the **Palacio de Cristal** (prefabricated by Eiffel 1905-1907), used as a gallery housing temporary exhibits.

At the north end of the Malecón are gardens, a food court and an IMAX cinema, with a historical and maritime museum underneath ⓘ *US$3.50, open till 1830*. Beyond is the **Museo Antropológico y de Arte Contemporaneo** (MAAC) ⓘ *T230 9400, www.museomaac.com, Tue-Sat 1000-1730, US$1,50; Sun and holidays 1100-1500, free*, with excellent collections of ceramics and gold objects from coastal cultures and an extensive modern art collection.

North of the Malecón 2000 is the old district of **Las Peñas**, the last picturesque vestige of colonial Guayaquil with its brightly painted wooden houses and narrow, cobbled main street (Numa Pompilio Llona). It is an attractive place for a walk to **Cerro Santa Ana**, which offers great views of the city and the mighty Guayas. The area is heavily guarded and safe. It has a bohemian feel, with bars and restaurants. A large open-air exhibition of paintings and sculpture is held here during the *fiestas julianas* (24-25 July). North of La Peñas is the new **Puerto Santa Ana,** with upmarket apartments, a promenade and three museums: to the romantic singer Julio Jaramillo, to beer in the old brewery, and to football. **Santo Domingo**, the city's first church founded in 1548, stands just by Las Peñas. Other churches of note are **San Francisco**, with its restored colonial interior, off 9 de Octubre and P Carbo, and the beautiful **Basílica de La Merced**.

In the pleasant, shady **Parque Bolívar** stands the **Cathedral**, in Gothic style, inaugurated in the 1950s. In the park are many iguanas and the park is popularly referred to as Parque de las Iguanas. The nearby **Museo Municipal** ⓘ *in the Biblioteca Municipal, Sucre y Chile, Tue-Sat*

0900-1700, free, city tours on Sat, also free has paintings, gold and archaeological collections, shrunken heads, a section on the history of Guayaquil and a good newspaper library.

Between the Parque Bolívar and the Malecón is the **Museo Nahim Isaías** ⓘ *Pichincha y Clemente Ballén, Plaza de la Administración, T232 4283, Tue-Sat 0830-1700, US$1.50*, a colonial art museum with a permanent religious art collection and temporary exhibits.

2 Guayaquil centre

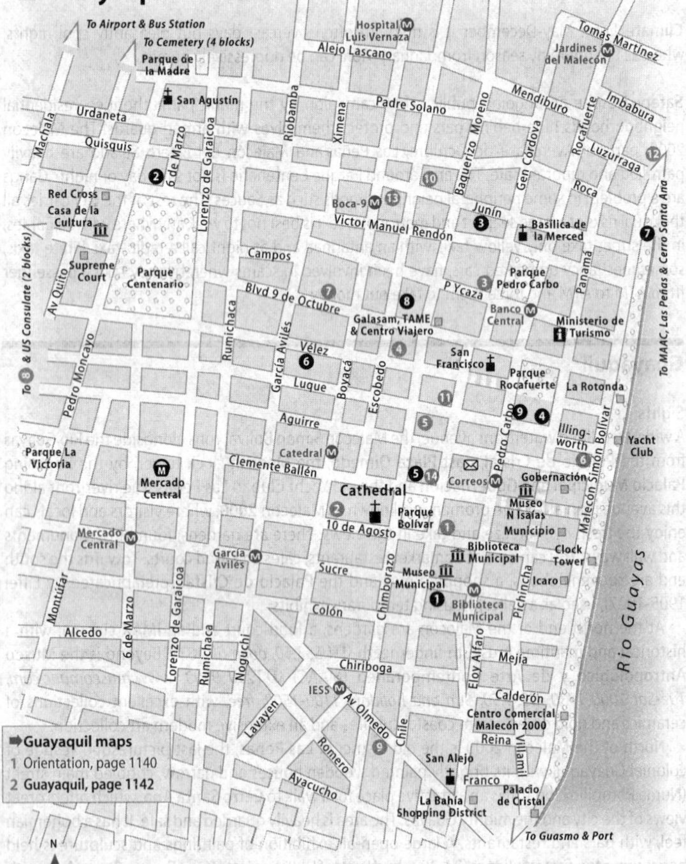

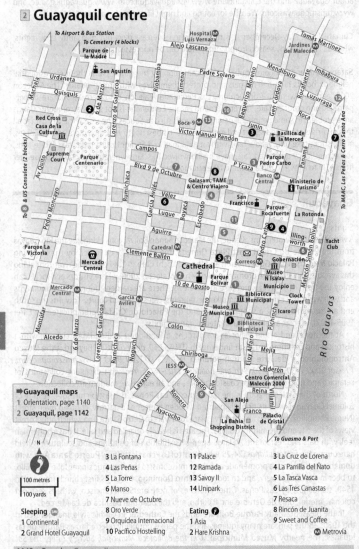

➡Guayaquil maps
1 Orientation, page 1140
2 Guayaquil, page 1142

N

100 metres

100 yards

Sleeping
1 Continental
2 Grand Hotel Guayaquil
3 La Fontana
4 Las Peñas
5 La Torre
6 Manso
7 Nueve de Octubre
8 Oro Verde
9 Orquídea Internacional
10 Pacífico Hostelling
11 Palace
12 Ramada
13 Savoy II
14 Unipark

Eating
1 Asia
2 Hare Krishna
3 La Cruz de Lorena
4 La Parrilla del Ñato
5 La Tasca Vasca
6 Las Tres Canastas
7 Resaca
8 Rincón de Juanita
9 Sweet and Coffee

Ⓜ Metrovía

Halfway up 9 Octubre is **Parque Centenario** with a towering monument to the liberation of the city erected in 1920. Overlooking the park is the museum of the **Casa de la Cultura** ⓘ *9 de Octubre 1200 y P Moncayo,T230 0500 Tue-Fri 1000-1800, Sat 0900-1500. US$1. English-speaking guides available* which houses an impressive collection of prehistoric gold items in its archaeological museum. Also here is the **Pinacoteca Manuel Rendón Seminario**, a photo collection of old Guayaquil.

West of Parque Centenario, the **Museo Presley Norton** ⓘ *Av 9 de Octubre y Carchi, T229 3423, www.museopresleynorton.com, Tue-Sat 0900-1700, free*, has an archaeological collection from the coast near Salango (see page 1154). At the west end of 9 de Octubre is the **Malecón del Estero Salado**, another pleasant waterfront promenade along a brackish estuary. It has various monuments, eateries specializing in seafood, and rowboats and pedal-boats for hire.

North of Parque Centenario, below Cerro El Carmen, the huge, spreading **Cemetery** with its dazzling, high-rise tombs and the ostentatious mausoleums of the rich is worth a visit. A flower market over the road sells the best selection of blooms in the city. Go on a Sunday when there are plenty of people about.

Sights outside the city

Parque Histórico Guayaquil ⓘ *Vía Samborondón, near Entreríos, T283 3807, www.parquehistorico.com, Wed-Sun 0900-1630, US$3, (Sun US$4.50), children US$1.50, seniors US$1, CISA buses to Samborondón leave from the Terminal Terrestre every 20 mins, US$0.25.* The park recreates Guayaquil and its rural surroundings at the end of the 19th century. There is a natural area with native flora and fauna, a traditions section where you can learn about rural life and how crafts are made, an urban section with wooden architecture and an educational farm. A pleasant place for a stroll. The **Botanical Gardens** are northwest ⓘ *Av Francisco de Orellana, in Ciudadela Las Orquídeas, T289 9689, daily 0800-1600, US$3, guiding service US$5. bus line 63 or furgoneta Orquídeas.* Good views and a long but pleasant walk. There are over 3,000 plants, including 150 species of Ecuadorean and foreign orchids (most flower August to December).

Bosque Protector Cerro Blanco ⓘ *Vía a la Costa, Km 16, T287 4947, www.bosquecerroblanco.com, US$4, additional guiding fee US$7-12 depending on trails visited, camping US$7 pp, lodge available.* The reserve, run by **Fundación Pro-Bosque**, is set in tropical dry forest with an impressive variety of birds (over 200 species), many reptiles and with sightings of monkeysand other mammals. Unfortunately it is getting harder to see the animals due to human encroachment in the area. Reservations required during weekdays and for groups larger than 8 at weekends, and for birders wishing to arrive before or stay after normal opening hours (0800-1530). Take a **CLP** bus from the Terminal Terrestre or a taxi (from US$5 up). On the other side of the road, at Km 18 is **Puerto Hondo** ⓘ T 287 1900. Canoe trips through the mangroves can be arranged on the spot at weekends from the *Fundación Pro-Bosque* kiosk for US$12 for a group of 8, or during the week with the Cerro Blanco office (see above).

Heading east then south from Guayaquil, 22 km beyond the main crossroads at Km 50 on the road to Machala, lies the **Ecological Reserve of Manglares Churute** ⓘ *US$10, basic cabins US$5, camping US$3. Boat tour US$15 per hr for up to15 passengers (2-4 hrs recommended to appreciate the area), arrange several days ahead through the Dirección Regional, Ministerio del Ambiente in Guayaquil, 9 de Octubre y Pichincha, Edif Banco Central, p 6, T230 6645, ext 106. Buses (CIFA, Ecuatoriano Pullman, 16 de Junio) leave the Terminal Terrestre every 30 mins, going to Naranjal or Machala; ask to be let off at the Churute information centre. The reserve can also be reached by river.* It is a rich natural area with five different ecosystems created to preserve mangroves in the Gulf of Guayaquil and forests of the Cordillera Churute. Many waterbirds, monkeys, dolphins and other wildlife can be seen. There is a trail through the dry tropical forest (1½ hours' walk) and you can also walk (one hour) to Laguna Canclón or Churute, a large lake where ducks nest. Abutting the park is **Monoloco Lodge** (**D-E**), www.monoloco.ec, tours available.

Guayaquil listings

For Sleeping and Eating price codes and other relevant information, see Essentials, pages 38-40.

Sleeping

Guayaquil *p1141, maps p1140 and p1142*
Guayaquil has some of the best top-class accommodation in Ecuador. For major chain hotels see: www.hilton.com (Hilton Colón and Hampton Inn Boulevard, both excellent), www.oroverdehotels.com (Oro Verde and Unipark), www.hotelcontinental.com.ec, www.hojo.com (Howard Johnson), www.hdoral.com (Best Western) and www.sheraton.com. Decent economy hotels are few and far between. They are mostly downtown and concentrated around Parque Centenario, an unsafe area at all hours.

L-AL Grand Hotel Guayaquil, Boyacá 1600 y 10 de Agosto, T232 9690, www.grandhotel guayaquil.com. A traditional Guayaquil hotel, central, includes buffet breakfast, good restaurants, pool (US$6 for non-guests), gym and sauna, internet.

L-AL Palace, Chile 214 y Luque, T232 1080, www.hotelpalaceguayaquil.com.ec. Modern, completely refurbished in 2009, includes breakfast, restaurant, 24-hour cafeteria, traffic noise on Av Chile side, good value for business travellers. Recommended.

AL-A Ramada, Malecón 606 e Imbabura, T256 5555, www.hotelramada.com. Excellent location right on the Malecón, rooms facing the river are more expensive, includes buffet breakfast, restaurant, a/c, pool, spa, Wi-Fi.

A Castell, Av Miguel H Alcivar y Ulloa, by the Parque Japonés, Kennedy Norte, T268 0190, www.hotelcastell.com. Modern comfortable hotel in a quiet location in the north of the city, includes buffet breakfast, restaurant, a/c, convenient for the a irport.

A-B Iguanazú, Ciudadela La Cogra, Manzana 1, Villa 2, off Av Carlos Julio Arosemena Km 3½ (taxi from bus terminal US$5, Metrovía '28 de Mayo' stop, best without luggage), T220 1143, www.iguanazuhostel.com. Lovely suburban guesthouse, a variety of rooms including suite with Jacuzzi, includes breakfast, E per person in dorm, a/c, pool and Jacuzzi, Wi-Fi, cooking facilities, parking, terrace with hammocks and views of the city, French spoken.

A-B La Fontana, P Ycaza y Córdova, T230 3967. Nice hotel in an excellent location, bright ample rooms, suites with balconies, includes breakfast, restaurant, bar with live music, a/c, Wi-Fi in some rooms, no lift, discounts on weekends, reserve ahead.

A-C Manso, Malecón 1406 y Aguirre, p1, T252 6644, www.manso.ec. Beautifully refurbished 6-room hostel in a great location opposite the Malecón. Nicely decorated rooms vary from fancy with a/c, private bath and river view, to simpler with shared bath and fan and even a 4-bed dorm (E per person), includes breakfast, good mainly vegetarian restaurant (1230-2100) also offers set lunches, internet, good service, owner speaks English and German, can arrange tours to Isla Santay, opened in 2009.

B Las Peñas, Escobedo 1215 y Vélez, T232 3355. Nice hotel in a refurbished part of downtown, ample modern rooms, includes breakfast, cafeteria, a/c, Wi-Fi, quiet despite being in the centre of town, good value. Recommended.

B Tangara Guest House, Manuela Sáenz y O'Leary, Manzana F, Villa 1, Ciudadela Bolivariana, T228 4445, www.tangara-ecuador.com. Comfortable hotel in a nice area by the university and near the Estero Salado, includes breakfast, a/c, fridge, airport transfers, convenient for airport and bus terminal but also along the flight path, so it is noisy.

B-D Casa Alianza, Av Segunda 318 y Calle 12, Los Ceibos (taxi from bus terminal US$6-7, 15 min walk from 'Fe de Guayas' Metrovía stop (only without luggage), T235 1261, www.casaalianza.com. Good hostel, far from the centre, a variety of rooms and prices, cafeteria, a/c, cheaper with shared bath and fan, also have a dorm with a/c for groups, Wi-Fi, run by a Norwegian NGO, also have a Spanish school, completely refurbished in 2009.

C La Torre, Chile 303 y Luque, p 13-15, T253 1316. Popular hotel in a downtown office tower, long flight of stairs to get into the building, comfortable rooms, includes breakfast, cafeteria, a/c, Wi-Fi, nice views, reasonably quiet for where it is, busy, advance booking advised, good value.

C Orquídea Internacional, Olmedo 309 y Chile, T240 2686, elenavalverderamirez@hotmail.com. Nicely refurbished hotel, ample rooms, includes breakfast, cafeteria, a/c, internet.

C-D Dream Kapture, Alborada Etapa 12, Manzana 2, Villa 21, near Centro Comercial La Rotonda (taxi from bus terminal US$3, from inside airport US$5, tell driver it's in the same street as Restaurante El Colorado), T224 2909, www.dreamkapture.com. Family-run hostel. Simple rooms, includes breakfast, electric shower, a/c, cheaper with shared bath or with fan, F per person in dorm, small pool, Wi-Fi, cooking facilities, lounge with TV, airport or bus terminal transfers extra, English and French spoken, travel agency.
D-E Pacífico Hostelling, Escobedo 811 y Junín, T230 2077. Central hostel with adequate rooms, hot water, a/c, Wi-Fi.
D-E Savoy II, Junín 627 y Boyacá, T231 0206. Modern hotel in a central location, cafeteria, hot water, a/c, good value.
E Nueve de Octubre, 9 de Octubre 736 y García Avilés, T256 4222. Eight-storey hotel in a good central location. Small comfortable rooms, cafeteria, cold water, a/c, cheaper with fan, parking extra.

Eating

Guayaquil *p1141, maps p1140 and p1142*
Main areas for restaurants are the centre with many in the larger hotels, around Urdesa and the residential and commercial neighbourhoods to the north.
TTT Kioto, at Hotel Hilton Colón, Av Francisco de Orellana, Kennedy Norte, T232 9690, Tue-Sun 1200-1500, 1900-2330. Excellent sushi.
TTT Lo Nuestro, VE Estrada 903 e Higueras, Urdesa, T238 6398, daily 1100-1530, 1900-2330. Luxury restaurant with typical coastal cooking, good seafood platters and stuffed crabs, colonial décor.
TTT Manny's, Av Miraflores 112 y Segunda, Miraflores, T220 2754, daily 1000-2200. Well known crab house with specialties such as cangrejo al ajillo (crab in garlic butter), good quality and value.
TTT-TT Cangrejo Criollo, Av Rolando Pareja, Villa 9, La Garzota, T223 2018, daily 0900-0100. Excellent, varied seafood menu.
TTT-TT La Parrilla del Ñato, VE Estrada 1219 y Laureles in Urdesa; Av Francisco de Orellana opposite the Hilton Colón; Luque y Pichincha downtown; and several other locations, T238 7096, daily 1200-0000. Large variety of dishes, salad bar, also pizza by the meter, good quality, generous portions. Try the parrillada de mariscos, available only at the Urdesa and Kennedy locations. Recommended.
TTT-TT La Trattoria da Enrico, Bálsamos 504 y las Monjas, Urdesa, T238 7079, Mon-Sat 1230-1530, 1930-1130, Sun 1230-2230. Very exclusive Italian restaurant since 1980, the best in food and surroundings, good antipasto.
TTT-TT María Bonita, VE Estrada 1202 y Laureles, Urdesa, T288 0173, 1200-1500, 1900-2300. Good Mexican food, pleasant atmosphere.
TTT-TT Riviera, VE Estrada 702 y Ficus, Urdesa, and Mall del Sol, T288 3790, daily 1230-0030. Extensive Italian menu, good pasta, antipasto, salads, bright surroundings, good service.
TTT-TT Sion Lung, VE Estrada 619 y Ficus, Urdesa, also Av Principal, Entre Ríos, T288 8213, daily 1200-2300. Chinese food, a variety of rice (chaulafán) and noodle (tallarín) dishes.
TT La Canoa, at Hotel Continental, open 24 hrs. Regional dishes rarely found these days, with different specials during the week, a Guayaquil tradition.
TT La Tasca Vasca, Clemente Ballén 422 y Chimborazo, downtown, Mon-Fri 1000-0000, Sat 1000-2200, Sun 1000-1500. Spanish cuisine, specialties include paella and pulpo a la gallega (octopus).
TT-T Asia, Sucre 321 y Chile, downtown, also VE Estrada 508 y Las Monjas, Urdesa and in shopping centres in the north, daily 1100-2130. Good Chinese food, vegetarian dishes on request, large portions, popular, good value.
T Hare Krishna, VM Rendón 1130 y 6 de Marzo, Parque Centenario, Mon-Sat 1100-1900. Vegetarian set meals.
T La Cruz de Lorena, Junín 417 y Córdova, downtown, Mon-Sat 1200-1700. Good economical set lunches and international dishes à la carte.
T Ollantay, Tungurahua 508 y 9 de Octubre, west of downtown. The best choice for vegetarian food.
T Rincón de Juanita, Escobedo 1115 y 9 de Octubre, downtown, Mon-Sat 0730-2200. Cheap set meals, ceviches, busy and noisy.

Cafés and snacks

Aroma Café, Malecón 2000 by Tomás Martínez, daily 1200-0000. Café, also serves regional food, nice garden setting.

California Gourmet, Escobedo 1215 y Vélez, below Hotel Las Peñas, Mon-Sat 0700-2000, Sun 0700-1400. Breakfast, snacks, drinks, sweets.
Fruta Bar, Malecón e Imbabura, VE Estrada 608 y Monjas, Urdesa. Excellent fruit juices and snacks, unusual African decor, good music.
Las Tres Canastas, Vélez y García Avilés and several other locations. Breakfast, snacks, safe fruit juices and smoothies.
Sweet and Coffee, Luque y Pedro Carbo, and in all shopping centres. Popular chain of cafés with good coffee and reasonable prices.

Bars and clubs

Guayaquil *p1141, maps p1140 and p1142*
Guayaquil nightlife is not cheap. Most discos charge a cover of around US$5-10 on weekdays, US$10-15 at weekends, and drinks are expensive. There are clubs, bars and casinos in most of the major hotels, as well as in the northern suburbs, especially at the **Kennedy Mall**. Also in vogue are the **Las Peñas** area, and the **Zona Rosa**, bounded by the Malecón Simón Bolívar and Rocafuerte, C Loja and C Roca. Both these areas are considered reasonably safe.
La Paleta, Escalón 176, Las Peñas. Tue-Sat from 2000. Good music, great drinks and snacks. US$10-12 cover Fri and Sat, popular, reserve.
Praga, Rocafuerte 636 y Mendiburo. Tue-Sat from 1830. US$10-16 cover, live music Fri-Sat. Pleasant atmosphere, several halls, varied music.
Resaca, Malecón 2000, at the level of Junín. Daily 1130-2400. Lovely setting, live tropical music Fri-Sat night. Also serves set lunches on weekdays and regional dishes and pricey drinks.
Vulcano, Rocafuerte 419 y Padre Aguirre. Fri-Sat from 2230. Cover US$7-8. Popular gay bar which attracts a mixed crowd, varied modern music.

Entertainment

Guayaquil *p1141, maps p1140 and p1142*
Boat parties See Activities and tours below.
Cinemas are at the main shopping centres and cost US$3-4. The **IMAX Cinema**, Malecón 2000, projects impressive films on its oversize screen.
Theatre **Centro Cívico**, Quito y Venezuela, excellent theatre/concert facility, home to the Guayaquil Symphony which gives free concerts. **Teatro Centro de Arte**, on the road to the coast, is another first-class theatre complex.

Festivals and events

Guayaquil *p1141, maps p1140 and p1142*
The **foundation of Guayaquil** is celebrated on **24-25 Jul**, and the **city's independence** on **9-12 Oct**. Both holidays are lively and there are many public events; cultural happenings are prolonged throughout Oct.

Shopping

Guayaquil *p1141, maps p1140 and p1142*
There are lots of shopping malls – ideal for cooling off on hot days.
Bookshops **El Librero**, in the Ríocentro. Has English books. **Librimundi**, at San Marino, Ríocentro, Los Ceibos and Etreríos shopping centres. Good selection including English books. **Mr Books**, at Mall del Sol. Good selection including some English books and travel guides. **Nuevos Horizontes**, 6 de Marzo 924. For book exchange. **Sagitario**, Mall del Sol. Excellent bookstore, has English books.
Camping equipment **Casa Maspons**, Ballén 517 y Boyacá. For camping gas.
Handicrafts **Mercado Artesanal del Malecón 2000**, at the south end of the Malecón, has many kiosks selling varied crafts. **Mercado Artesanal**, Baquerizo Moreno between Loja and J Montalvo. Greatest variety, almost a whole block of permanent stalls with good prices. In Albán Borja Mall are: **El Telar** with a good variety of *artesanías* and **Ramayana**, with nice ceramics.
Malls **Centro Comercial Malecón 2000** is at the south end of the Malecón. **Centro Comercial San Marino**, Av Francisco de Orellana y L Plaza Dañín. Huge, one of the largest in South America. **Mall del Sol** is near the airport on Av Constitución y Juan Tanca Marengo. It has craft shops. **Las Bahías**, is a huge bazaar area on either side of Olmedo from Villamil to Chile, by the south end of the Malecón. It was traditionally where contraband was sold from boats which put into the bay. It's still very popular for electrical appliances, clothing and shoes. Watch your valuables and be prepared to bargain.

Activities and tours

Guayaquil *p1141, maps p1140 and p1142*
Boat tours The gulph islands and mangroves can be visited on tours from Guayaquil, Puerto Hondo and Puerto El Morro. **Isla Santay**, a Ramsar site wetland with walking trails has a community tourism programme, as does **Puná**,

the largest of the islands. **Xavier Ávalos**, T239 6583 or T09-709 8400, xavier_avalos@yahoo.com.mx, an English-speaking biologist offers tours to the islands and all natural sites in the region. **Capitan Morgan**, Muelle Malecón y Sucre, T251 7228, 1-hr tours on the river with nice city views, Mon-Fri at 1730 and 1900, Sat and Sun at 1200, 1400, 1600 and 1930, US$3. Also party cruises, Thu-Sat from 2200, with live music, pricey drinks, food and dancing.
Cruceros Discovery, Muelle Malecón y Tomás Martínez, T2304824, www.crucerosdiscovery.com, tours to Isla Santay Tue-Fri 1300-1600, Sat and Sun 1100-1600, 2½ hrs, US$8, minimum 8 passengers. Also 1-hr river cruises, Tue-Fri from1500, Sat-Sun from 1300 and party trips.

Tour operators Details about agencies operating Galápagos cruises page 1194. A 3-hr city tour costs about US$14 pp in a group. Tours to coastal haciendas, large plantations, offer a glimpse of rural life.
Canodros, Urb Santa Leonor, Mz 5, Solar 10, T228 5711, www.canodros.com. Runs luxury Galápagos cruises and arange tours to the Kapawi Ecological Reserve in the southern Oriente.
Centro Viajero, Baquerizo Moreno 1119 y 9 de Octubre, No 805, T230 1283, T09-235 7745 24-hr service, cetrovi@telconet. net. Custom-designed tours to all regions, travel information and bookings, car and driver service, well informed about options for Galápagos, helpful, English spoken. Recommended.
Ecoventura, Km 1.5 Vía Samborondón, Edif Samborondón Business Center, Torre A p 3, T283 9390, www.ecoventura.com. Excellent high-end Galápagos tours. Recommended.
Galasam, Edif Gran Pasaje, 9 Octubre 424, ground floor, T230 4488, www.galapagos-islands.com. Galápagos cruises, city tours, tours to reserves near Guayaquil, diving trips, also run highland and jungle tours.
Guayaquil Visión, ticket booth next to IMAX theatre at the north end of Malecón 2000, T288 5800. City tours on a double-decker bus, US$6-17 depending on route, departs from Plaza Olmedo, the Rotonda or IMAX cinema at Malecón 2000. Also tours to attractions outside the city and night-time party tours.
Kleintours, Av Alcívar, Mz 410 y Angel Barrera, Kennedy Norte, T268 1700, www.kleintours.com. Land and Galápagos tours.
La Moneda, Av de las Américas 809 y C 2, and P Ycaza 115 y Pichincha T269 0900, www.lamoneda.com.ec. City and coastal tours, whale watching.
Metropolitan Touring, Edif Megamaxi, Mall del Sol, T208 2507, www.metropolitan-touring.com. High-end land tours and Galápagos cruises.

⊖ Transport

Guayaquil *p1141, maps p1140 and p1142*
Air The information booth outside international arrivals (T216 9000, open 24 hrs) has hotel and transport information. On the ground floor are a Banco de Guayaquil (Mon-Fri 0830-1800, ATM, changes euros at poor rates, no TCs), post office, luggage storage (0800-2200, US$5 for 24 hours) and car hire agencies. There is also a food court, several ATMs, phone office and internet. For transport, see Ins and outs, above. Many flights daily to **Quito**, US$62-71. Sit on the right side for the best views. Also to **Cuenca**, **Esmeraldas** and **Loja**. Daily to **Galápagos** (see page 1191).
Bus **Metrovía** (T213 0402, www.metrovia-gye.com, US$0.25) is an integrated transport system of articulated buses running on exclusive lanes and *alimentadores* (feeder buses) serving suburbs from the terminuses. One line runs from the Terminal Río Daule, opposite the Terminal Terrestre, in the north, to the Terminal El Guasmo in the south. In the city centre it runs along Boyacá southbound and Pedro Carbo northbound. The second line goes from the centre (transfer points at Biblioteca Municipal and IESS) to the northwest as far as Bastión Popular and provides access to neighbourhoods such as Urdesa, Miraflores, and Los Ceibos. The Metrovía is a good way of getting around if you do not have luggage or valuables.

City buses and *furgonetas* (vans) are only permitted on a few streets in the centre; northbound buses go along Rumichaca or the *Malecón*, southbound along Lorenzo de Garaicoa or García Avilés, US$0.25.
Long distance The Terminal Terrestre, just north of the airport, is off the road to the Guayas bridge. It doubles as a shopping centre with supermarket, shops, bank, internet, food courts. Incoming buses arrive on the ground floor, where the ticket offices are also located. Regional buses depart from the second level and long distance (interprovincial) buses depart from the third level. The terminal is very large, so you

need to allow extra time to get to your bus. Check the board at the entrance for the location of the ticket counters for your destination, they are organized and colour-coded by region (eg Sierra Norte, Sierra Sur, Oriente, etc). Several companies to/from **Quito** (Terminal Quitumbe), 8 hrs, US$9; also non-stop, a/c services, eg **Transportes Ecuador**, Av de las Américas y Hermano Miguel, opposite the airport terminal, T229 4788; door to door van service, **Lucy Express**, T280 1524, www.lucyexpress.com. To **Cuenca**, 4 hrs via Molleturo/Cajas, 5 hrs via Zhud, both US$5, both scenic. **Riobamba**, 5 hrs, US$5. To **Santo Domingo de los Tsáchilas**, 5 hrs, US$5. **Manta**, 4 hrs, US$4. **Esmeraldas**, 8 hrs, US$8. To **Bahía de Caráquez**, 6 hrs, US$5. To **Ambato**, 6 hrs, US$6. Regular and frequent buses to **Playas**, 2 hrs, US$2.60; and to **Salinas**, 2½ hrs, US$3.70. To **Santa Elena**, 2hrs, US$2.50, change here for **Puerto López**. To **Montañita** and **Olón**, **CLP**, at 0520, 0620, 0900, 1300, 1500 and 1640, 3¼hrs, US$5.70. For the **Peruvian border**, to/from **Huaquillas** direct, 4½ hrs, US$6; to/from **Machala**, 3 hrs, US$5, also hourly vans with **Oro Guayas**, Clemente Ballén y Chile, T232 0934, US$10, 2¾ hrs. . Direct bus to **Tumbes** 10 daily, 5½ hrs, US$6 and to **Piura** with **CIFA**, T214 0379, regular service at 0720, 1750 and 2100, 10 hrs, US$11 and double- decker *bus-cama* at 1950 and 2330, US$13-15. To **Lima**, with **Ormeño**, Centro de Negocios El Terminal, near Terminal Terrestre, T214 0847, daily at 1130, 27 hrs, US$60, also to **Bogotá**, Tue and Fri, 38 hrs, US$90.

Directory

Guayaquil *p1141, maps p1140 and p1142*
Airline offices Aerogal, Junín 440 y Cordova, T231 0346, T1-800-237642. **Air France/KLM**, at the airport, p3, T216 9070. **American Airlines**, Policentro Mall, T259 8800. **Avianca**, at the airport, p2 and Galerías Hilton Colón, T239 9048, T1-800- 003434 **Continental**, Av 9 de Octubre 100 y Malecón, T1-800-222333. **Iberia**, Av 9 de Octubre 101 y Malecón, T232 9558. **Icaro**, at the airport, p3, T390 560, T1-800-883567. **LAN**, Galerías Hilton Colón, T1-800-101075. **TACA**, Luque 406 y Pichincha, T1-800-008222. **TAME**, 9 de Octubre 424, edif Gran Pasaje, and Galerías Hilton Colón,T1-800-500800. **Banks** Most banks have their main branches (with ATMs) downtown and other branches in the shopping malls. The airport and Terminal Terrestre have several ATMs. **Banco del Pacífico**, PYcaza 200, p 4 for TCs and cash advances. **Cambios Internacionales**, CC Albán Borja for currency exchange. **Car hire** All the main car rental agents are at the airport. **Embassies and consulates** Australia, Rocafuerte 520. **Austria**, Circunvalación Sur 718 y Guayacanes, Urdesa, T246 9700. **Belgium**, JA Campos 101 y García Avilés, T231 0505. **Canada**, Av J Tanca Marengo y J Orrantia, Edif Nobis Executive Center, p7, T229 6837. **Colombia**, Av Francisco de Orellana , Edif World Trade Center, torre B, p11, T263 0674. **France**, José Mascote 909 y Hurtado, T232 8442. **Germany**, Av Las Monjas 10 y C J Arosemena Km 2.5, Edif Berlín, T220 6868. **Italy**, P Ycaza 423 y Córdova, T256 8358. **Netherlands**, Quisquis 1502 y Tulcán, p 1, T228 0156. **Peru**, Av Francisco de Orellana y Alberto Borges, Edif Centrum, p 14, Kennedy Norte, T228 0135. **Spain**, Tungurahua y Vélez, T601 7460. **Sweden**, Km 6.5 vía a Daule, T225 4111. **Switzerland**, Av J Tanca Marengo Km 1.8 y S Castillo, Edif Conauto, p5, T268 1900. **UK**, Gen Córdova 623 y Padre Solano, T256 0400. **USA**, 9 de Octubre 1571 y García Moreno, T232 3570. **Internet** There are many cyber cafés in the centre and suburbs alike, the greatest number are concentrated in shopping malls. Prices around US$1 per hr. **Medical services** For doctors and dentists, contact your consulate for recommendations. **Emergencies** T112. **Hospitals**: the main hospital used by the foreign community is the **Clínica Kennedy**, Av San Jorge y la 9na, T228 9666. Also has a branch in Ciudadela La Alborada XIII, Mz-1227. It contains the consulting rooms of almost every kind of specialist doctor and diagnostic laboratory (Dr Roberto Morla speaks German); very competent emergency department. Also reliable are: **Clínica Alcívar**, Coronel 2301 y Azuay, T258 0030; **Clínica Guayaquil**, Padre Aguirre 401 y General Córdova, T256 3555 (Dr Roberto Gilbert speaks English and German). **Post offices** Central Post office at Pedro Carbo y Aguirre. **DHL**, Malecón 2000, Galería B or 9 de Octubre y P Carbo, edif San Francisco 300, T1-800-989898. Recommended for international service. **Servientrega**, offices throughout the city, for deliveries within Ecuador. **Useful addresses** **Immigration**: Av Río Daule, near the bus terminal, T214 0002.

South to Peru

Machala → *Phone code: 07. Colour map 11, C2. Population: 290,000.*

The capital of the province of El Oro is a booming agricultural town in a major banana producing and exporting region with an annual banana fair in September. It is not particularly attractive, somewhat dirty, oppressively hot and unsafe. For the tourist, the only reasons for stopping here are to go to the beautiful tranquil uplands of El Oro, and to catch a through CIFA bus to Peru (if not caught in Guayaquil) for the beaches around Máncora. **Tourist office** ⓘ *25 de Junio y 9 de Mayo, Municipio, iturmachala@hotmail.com, Spanish only, open Mon-Fri 0800-1230, 1500-1800.* Some 30 km south along the road to Peru is **Santa Rosa** with the regional airport.

Puerto Bolívar, on the Estero Jambelí among mangroves, is a major export outlet for over two million tonnes of bananas annually. From the old pier canoes cross to the beaches of **Jambelí** (hourly 0730-1800, US$2.40 return) on the far side of the mangrove islands which shelter Puerto Bolívar from the Pacific. The beaches are crowded at weekends, deserted during the week and not very clean. Boats can be rented for excursions to the **Archipiélago de Jambelí**, a maze of islands and channels just offshore, stretching south between Puerto Bolívar and the Peruvian border. These mangrove islands are rich in birdlife (and insects for them to feed on, take repellent), the water is very clear and you may also see fish and reefs.

Zaruma → *Phone code: 07. Colour map 11, C3. Population: 8,600. Altitude: 1,300 m.*

Southeast from Machala is the lovely old gold-mining town of Zaruma (118 km). It is reached from Machala by paved road via Piñas, by a scenic dirt road off the main Loja-Machala road, or via Pasaje and Paccha on another scenic dirt road off the Machala-Cuenca road.

Founded in 1549 on orders of Felipe II to try to control the gold extraction, Zaruma is a delightful town perched on a hilltop, with steep, twisting streets and painted wooden buildings. The **Oficina de Turismo** ⓘ *in the Municipio, at the plaza, T297 3533, www.vivezaruma.org, Mon-Fri 0800-1200, 1300-1700, Sat 0900-1600, Sun 0900-1300* is very friendly and helpful. They can arrange for guides and accommodation with local families. Next door is the small **Museo Municipal** ⓘ *free, ask for the key at the tourist office if closed.* It has a collection of local historical artefacts. The Zaruma area has a number of pre-Hispanic archaeological sites and petroglyphs are also found in the region. Tours with **Oroadventure** ⓘ *at the Parque Central, T297 2761* or with English speaking guide **Ramiro Rodríguez** ⓘ *T297 2523.* Zaruma is also known for its excellent Arabica coffee freshly roasted in the agricultural store basement, the proud owner will show you around if the store isn´t busy. On top of the small hill beyond the market is a public swimming pool (US$1), from where there are amazing views over the hot, dry valleys. For even grander views, walk up **Cerro del Calvario** (follow Calle San Francisco); go early in the morning as it gets very hot. At **Portovelo** (www.portovelo.com) south of Zaruma is the largest mine in the area. Its history told inside a mine shaft at the **Museo Magner Turner** ⓘ *T294 9345, daily 0900-11, 1400-1700, US$1.* The area has virtually no tourists and is well worth a visit.

Piñas, 19 km west of Zaruma, along the road to Machala is a pleasant town which conserves just a few of its older wooden buildings. There are buses along scenic secondary roads to **Paccha**, up in the hills to the north, and to **Ayapamba** and many other old gold mining villages. Northwest of Piñas, 20 minutes along the road to Saracay and Machala, is **Buenaventura**, to the north of which lies an important area for bird conservation, with over 310 bird species recorded, including many rare ones. The area is also rich in orchids. **The Jocotoco Foundation** (www.fjocotoco.org) protects a 1,500-ha forest in this region, entry US$15, **L** category lodge, advance booking required.

Bosque Petrificado Puyango

ⓘ *110 km south of Machala, west of the Arenillas-Alamor road, T293 2106 (Machala), bosquepuyango@hotmail.com, 0800-1530, US$2 includes tour (tips appreciated), camping US$3.*

At Puyango, a dry-forest reserve, a great number of petrified trees, ferns, fruits and molluscs, 65 to 120 million years old, have been found. Over 120 species of birds can be seen. No accommodation in the village, but ask around for floor space or try at the on-site information centre. If not, accommodation is available in **Las Lajas**, 20 minutes north (one residencial) and **Alamor**, 20 km south (several hotels, eg **E** Rey Plaza *T07-268 0256*). Campsites are also provided.

Huaquillas → *Phone code: 07. Colour map 11, C2. Population: 50,000.*

The stiflingly hot Ecuadorean border town of Huaquillas is something of a shopping arcade for Peruvians. The border runs along the Río Zarumilla and is crossed by two international bridges, one at the western end of Avenida La República in Huaquillas and a second one, opened in 2010, further south outside Chacras.

Border with Peru

The border is open 24 hours. In early 2010, an Ecuadorean border complex was under construction near the new international bridge; but only customs was operating there, not immigration. The turn off for the new bridge is about 4 km from Huaquillas on the road to Machala. Passports were still being stamped at the old complex, 3 km from Huaquillas along the road to Machala, where customs was also operating; taxi Huaquillas-immigration US$1.50. In Peru, both a new complex with customs, immigration and Policía Nacional del Perú (PNP), a few metres from the new bridge; and the old complex at Zarumilla, 3 km from Aguas Verdes, were operational. At the time of writing, it was possible to cross at either international bridge. These details will likely change. Allow at least one hour for border formalities. The **Huaquillas-Tumbes** crossing has traditionally been harrowing, made worse by the crowds and heat. You must always watch your belongings carefully. In addition to cheating by money changers and cab drivers, this border is known for its thefts and con tricks on traveller. Those on the direct CIFA bus Guayaquil- or Machala-Tumbes or Piura should have fewer hassles, otherwise it is best to cross in a group. Women are advised not to cross alone. Perhaps things will improve once the new border complex away from the busy towns of Huaquillas and Aguas Verdes is fully operational. Those seeking a more relaxed crossing to or from Peru should consider Macará (see page 1132) or La Balsa (see page 1136).

South to Peru listings

For Sleeping and Eating price codes and other relevant information, see Essentials, pages 38-40.

Sleeping

Machala *p1149*

LL Oro Verde, Circunvalación Norte in Urbanización Unioro, T293 3140, www.oroverdehotels.com. Includes buffet breakfast, 2 restaurants, nice pool (US$6 for non-guests), beautiful gardens, tennis courts, casino, full luxury. Best in town.

B Royal, Junín entre Sucre y Olmedo, T293 8444, www.royalhotel.com.ec. Modern multi-storey hotel, includes breakfast, Wi-Fi.

C Oro Hotel, Sucre y Juan Montalvo, T293 0032, orohotel@yahoo.com. Includes breakfast, pricey restaurant and cheaper café downstairs, a/c, fridge, parking, nice comfortable rooms but those to the street are noisy, helpful staff. Recommended.

E Julio César, 9 de Mayo 1319 entre Pasaje y Boyacá, T293 7978. Private bath, cold water, fan, basic.

E San Miguel, 9 de Mayo y Sucre, T292 2625. Good quality and value, some rooms without windows, hot water, a/c, cheaper with fan, fridge, helpful staff.

Zaruma *p1149*

C Hostería El Jardín, Barrio Limoncito, 10 min walk from centre (taxi US$1.50), T297 2706. Lovely palm garden and terrace with views, includes breakfast, internet, parking, comfortable rooms, small zoo, family-run. Recommended.

C-D Roland, at entrance to town on road from Portovelo, T297 2800. Comfortable rooms (some are dark) and nicer more expensive cabins, restaurant with lovely views, pool, parking.

E Aguila Dorada, Sucre 156, T297 2755. Hot water, simple but adequate, rooms 6 and 11 are best.

E Blacio, C Sucre, T297 2045. Hot water, modern, ask for rooms with balcony.

Huaquillas *p1150*

D-E Hernancor, 1 de Mayo y 10 de Agostso, T299 5467. Cafeteria, a/c, internet, best in town.

D-E Vanessa, 1 de Mayo y Hualtaco, T299 6263. A/c, internet, fridge, parking, pleasant.

Eating

Machala *p1149*

The best food is found in the better hotels.

¶¶ Mesón Hispano, Av Las Palmeras y Sucre. Very good grill, attentive service, outstanding for Machala.

¶ Chifa Central, Tarqui y 25 de Junio. Good Chinese.

¶ Chifa Gran Oriental, 25 de Junio entre Guayas y Ayacucho. Good food and service, clean place. Recommended.

Zaruma *p1149*

¶¶ Giuseppe, Pichincha s/n, T297 3118. Good pizzas, open Mon-Sat 1100-2100.

¶¶-¶ 200 Millas, Av Honorato Márquez, uphill from bus station. Good seafood.

¶ Cafetería Uno, C Sucre. Good for breakfast and Zaruma specialties, best *tigrillo* in town.

Transport

Machala *p1149*

Air The regional airport is at Santa Rosa, 32 km from Machala along the road to the border; taxi US$12. **Saereo** (office at the airport, T390 3210, has 1-2 daily flights to **Quito**, US$94 one way.

Bus There is no Terminal Terrestre. Do not take night buses into or out of Machala as they are prone to hold-ups. To **Quito**, with **Occidental** (Buenavista entre Sucre y Olmedo), 10 hrs, US$10, 8 daily, with **Panamericana** (Colón y Bolívar), 7 daily. To **Guayaquil**, 3 hrs, US$5, hourly with **Ecuatoriano Pullman** (Colón y Rocafuerte), **CIFA** (Bolívar y Guayas) and **Rutas Orenses** (Tarqui y Rocafuerte); also hourly vans with **Oro Guayas**, Guayas y Pichincha, T293 4382, US$10, 2¾ hrs. There are 3 different routes to **Loja**, each with bus service. They are, from north to south: via **Piñas** and **Zaruma**, partly paved and rough but very scenic; via **Balsas**, fully paved and also scenic; and via **Arenillas** and **Alamor**, for **Puyango** petrified forest. Fare to **Loja**, 6 hrs, US$6. To **Cuenca**, half-hourly with **Trans Azuay** (Sucre y Junín), 4 hrs, US$5. To **Huaquillas**, with **CIFA** and **Ecuatoriano Pullman**, direct, 1½ hr, US$2, every 30 mins. To **Piura**, in Peru, with **CIFA**, 4 a day, US$8-10, 6 hrs; also to **Máncora**, 5 daily, US$6, 5hrs and **Tumbes**, 7 daily, US$3, 3 hrs.

Zaruma *p1149*

Bus To/from Machala with **Trans Piñas** or **TAC**, half-hourly, US$3.50, 3 hrs. To **Piñas**, take a Machala bound bus, US$1, 1 hr. Also 8 daily to **Guayaquil**, US$7, 6½ hrs, **Quito**, 5 daily, US$11, 12 hrs, note that TAC has a terminal in Quito at Almagro y La Niña; to **Cuenca**, 3 daily (**Trans Azuay** at US$7, 6 hrs and **Loja**, 4 daily, US$5, 5 hrs (may have to change at Portovelo).

Puyango *p1149*

Puyango is west of the highway: alight from bus at turn-off at the bridge over the Río Puyango. Bus from **Machala**, **Trans Loja** 0930, 1300 and 2200, **CIFA** at 0600 and 1500, US$3.50, 2½ hrs. From **Loja**, **Trans Loja** 0900, 1430 and 1930, US$5, 5 hrs. From **Huaquillas**, **Trans Loja** at 0730 and **Unión Cariamanga** at 1130, US$2, 1½ hrs. You might be able to hire a pick-up from the main road to the park, US$3. Pick-up from Alamor to Puyango US$25 return, including wait. There may be military checkpoints between Puyango and Machala, have your passport at hand.

Huaquillas *p1150*

Bus There is no Terminal Terrestre, each bus company has its own office, many on Teniente Cordovez. If you are in a hurry, it can be quicker to change buses in Machala or Guayaquil. There are checkpoints along the road north from Huaquillas, keep your passport to hand. To **Machala**, with **CIFA** (Santa Rosa y Machala) and **Ecuatoriano Pullman**, direct, 1½ hrs, US$2, every hour between 0800 and 2000; via Arenillas and Santa Rosa, 2 hrs, every 20 mins. To **Quito**, with **Occidental**, every 2 hrs, 12 hrs, US$10; with **Panamericana**, 11½ hrs, 3 daily via Santo Domingo; 2 daily via **Riobamba** and **Ambato**,

12 hrs. To **Guayaquil**, frequent service with **CIFA** and **Ecuatoriano Pullman**, fares above. To **Cuenca**, 8 daily, 5 hrs, US$6. To **Loja**, 6 daily, 6 hrs, US$5.

Directory

Machala *p1149*
Banks **Banco del Pacifico**, Rocafuerte y Junín, ATM and TCs. For ATM: **Banco de Guayaquil** and **Banco Pichincha**, both a t Rocafuerte y Guayas. **Embassies and consulates** **Peruvian Consulate**, Urb Unioro, Mz 14, V 11, near Hotel Oro Verde, T293 0680, Mon-Fri 0900-1800. **Internet** Prices around US$1 per hr. **Post offices** Bolívar y Montalvo.

Huaquillas *p1150*
Banks Banks do not change money here. Many street changers, recognized by their black briefcases, deal in soles and US$ cash. Check the rate beforehand on the internet or with travellers leaving Peru, as there are many tricks and travellers are often cheated. Do not change more US$ than you need to get to Tumbes, where there are reliable cambios, but get rid of all your soles here as they are difficult to exchange further inside Ecuador. Do your own arithmetic – there have been reports of 'doctored' calculators, count your change carefully and watch out for counterfeit bills. Especially avoid those changers who chase after you. Only clean, crisp US$ bills are accepted in Peru. **Internet** Several on Av La República, US$1.50 per hr.

Pacific lowlands

This vast tract of Ecuador covers everything west of the Andes and north of the Guayas delta. Though popular with Quiteños and Guayaquileños, who come here for weekends and holidays, the Pacific Lowlands receive relatively few foreign visitors, which is surprising given the natural beauty, diversity and rich cultural heritage of the coast. Here you can surf, watch whales, visit archaeological sites, or just relax and enjoy some of the best food this country has to offer. The Parque Nacional Machalilla protects an important area of primary tropical dry forest, pre-Columbian ruins, coral reef and a wide variety of wildlife. Further north, in the province of Esmeraldas, there are not only well-known party beaches, but also opportunities to visit the remaining mangroves and experience two unique lifestyles: Afro-Ecuadorean on the coast and native Cayapa further inland. Coastal resorts are busy and more expensive from December to April, the temporada de playa.

Guayaquil to Puerto López

Southwest of Guayaquil is the beach resort of Playas and, west of it, the Santa Elena Peninsula, with Salinas at its tip. From the town of Santa Elena, capital of the province of the same name (created in 2008), the coastal road stretches north for 737 km to Mataje on the Colombian border; along the way are countless beaches and fishing villages, and a few cities. The coastal strip is known as 'Ruta del Sol'. Puerto López is the perfect base for whale watching and from which to explore the beautiful Parque Nacional Machalilla.

Playas and Salinas → *Phone code: 04. Colour map 11, B1. Population: 38,000 and 38,900 respectively.*
The beach resorts of Playas and Salinas remain as popular as ever with vacationing Guayaquileños. The paved toll highway from Guayaquil divides after 63 km at El Progreso (Gómez Rendón). One branch leads to **Playas** (General Villamil), the nearest seaside resort to Guayaquil. Bottle-shaped ceibo (kapok) trees characterise the landscape as it turns into dry, tropical thorn scrub. In Playas a few single-sailed balsa rafts, very simple but highly ingenious, can still be seen among the motor launches returning laden with fish. The same rafts without sails are used to spread nets close offshore, then two gangs of men take 2-3 hours to haul them in. In high season (*temporada* - December to April), and at weekends, Playas is prone to severe

crowding, although the authorities are trying to keep the packed beaches clean and safe (thieving is rampant during busy times). Out of season or midweek, the beaches are almost empty especially north towards Punta Pelado (5 km). Playas has six good surf breaks. There are showers, toilets and changing rooms along the beach, with fresh water, for a fee. Many hotels in our **B-F** ranges. Excellent seafood and typical dishes from over 50 beach cafés (all numbered and named). Many close out of season. **Tourist office** ⓘ *on the Malecón, Tue-Fri 0800-1200, 1400-1800, Sat-Sun 0900-1600.*

Salinas, surrounded by miles of salt flats, is Ecuador's answer to Miami Beach. **Turismo Municipal** ⓘ *Eloy Alfaro y Mercedes de Jesús Molina, Chipipe, T277 3931, Tue-Fri 0800-1700, Sat 0800-1400.* There is safe swimming in the bay and high-rise blocks of holiday flats and hotels line the seafront. More appealing is the (still urban) beach of Chipipe, south of the exclusive Salinas Yacht Club. In December-April it is overcrowded, its services stretched to the limit. Even in the off season it is not that quiet. On the south shore of the Santa Elena peninsula, 8 km south of La Libertad, built on high cliffs is **Punta Carnero**, with hotels in the **A-C** range. To the south is a magnificent 15-km beach with wild surf and heavy undertow, there is whale watching in season.

North to Puerto López

The '**Ruta del Sol**' north to Puerto López in the province of Manabí parallels the coastline and crosses the Chongón-Colonche coastal range. Most of the numerous small fishing villages along the way have good beaches and are slowly being developed for tourism. Beware of rip currents and undertow.

Valdivia → *Phone code: 04. Colour map 11, B2.*

San Pedro and Valdivia are two unattractive villages which merge together. There are many fish stalls. This is the site of the 5,000 year-old Valdivia culture. Many houses offer 'genuine' artefacts (it is illegal to export pre-Columbian artefacts from Ecuador) and one resident at the north end of the village will show you the skeletons and burial urns dug up in his back garden. Ask for Juan Orrala, who makes excellent copies, and lives up the hill from the **Ecomuseo Valdivia** ⓘ *T08-011 9856, daily, US$1.50*, which has displays of original artefacts from Valdivia and other coastal cultures. There is also a handicraft section, where artisans may be seen at work, and lots of local information. At the museum is a restaurant and 5 rooms with bath to let. Most of the genuine artefacts discovered at the site are in museums in Quito and Guayaquil.

Manglaralto → *Phone code: 04. Colour map 11, B2.*

Located 180 km northwest of Guayaquil, this is the main centre of the region north of Santa Elena. There is a tagua nursery; ask to see examples of worked 'vegetable ivory' nuts. It is a nice place, with a quiet beach, good surf but little shade. **Pro-pueblo** is an organization working with local communities to foster family run orchards and cottage craft industry, using tagua nuts, paja toquilla (the stuff Panama hats are made from), and other local products. They have a craft shop in town (opposite the park), an office in San Antonio south of Manglaralto, T278 0230, and headquarters in Guayaquil, T268 3569, www.propueblo.com. **Proyecto de Desarrollo Ecoturístico Comunitario** ⓘ *T252 9968, coorcpr@interactive.net.ec, or contact Paquita Jara T09-174 0143*, has a network of simple lodgings with local families (US$9 per person), many interesting routes into the Cordillera Chongón Colonche and whale watching and island tours.

Montañita and Olón → *Phone code: 04. Colour map 11, B2.*

About 3 km north of Manglaralto, **Montañita** (www.montanita.com) has mushroomed over the past few years into a major surf resort, packed with hotels, restaurants, surf-board rentals, tattoo parlours and craft/jewellery vendors. There are periodic police drug raids in Montañita and several foreigners are serving long sentences in jail. At the north end of the bay, 1 km away, is another hotel area with more elbow-room, Baja Montañita (or Montañita Punta, Surf Point).

Between the two is a lovely beach where you'll find some of the best surfing in Ecuador. Various competitions are held during the year and at weekends, in season, the town is full of Guayaquileños. Beyond an impressive headland and a few minutes north of Montañita is **Olón**, with a spectacular long beach. Nearby is **El Cangrejal**, a 7-ha dry tropical forest with mangroves.

Ayampe to Salango ➔ *Phone code: 04. Colour map 11, B2.*
North of Montañita, by **La Entrada**, the road winds up and inland through lush forest before continuing to the small, poor village of **Ayampe** (many popular places to stay at south end of the beach). North of Ayampe are the villages of **Las Tunas**, **Puerto Rico** and **Río Chico**. There are places to stay all along this stretch of coast. Just north of Río Chico is **Salango**, worth visiting for the excellent **Salango archaeological museum** ⓘ *at the north end of town, daily 0900-1200, 1300-1700, US$1*, housing artefacts from excavations right in town. It also has a craft shop and, in back, nice rooms with bath in the **E** range.

Puerto López ➔ *Phone code: 05.*
Colour map 11, B2. Population: 10,000.
This pleasant fishing town is beautifully set in a horseshoe bay. The beach is best for swimming at the far north and south ends, away from the fleet of small fishing boats moored offshore. The town is popular with tourists for whale watching, approximately mid-June to September, Parque Nacional Machalilla and Isla de la Plata. Scooters can be hired in town for getting about.

Parque Nacional Machalilla
ⓘ *US$12 for mainland portions, US$15 for Isla de la Plata, US$20 if visiting both areas (ask for 5-6 days), payable at the park office in Puerto López (C Eloy Alfaro y García Moreno), daily 0800-1200, 1400-1600, or directly to the park rangers (insist on a receipt).*
The Park extends over 55,000 ha, including Isla de la Plata, Isla Salango, and the magnificent beach of **Los Frailes** and preserves marine ecosystems as well as the dry tropical forest and archaeological sites on shore. At the north end of the beach is a trail through the forest leading to a lookout with great views and on to the town of Machalilla (don't take valuables). The land-based part of the park is divided into three sections which are separated by private land, including the town of Machalilla. Recommended for birdwatching, especially in the cloud forest of Cerro San Sebastián; also several species of mammals and reptiles.

About 5 km north of Puerto López, at Buena Vista, a dirt road to the east leads to **Agua Blanca** (park kiosk at entry). Here, 5 km from the main road, in the national park, amid

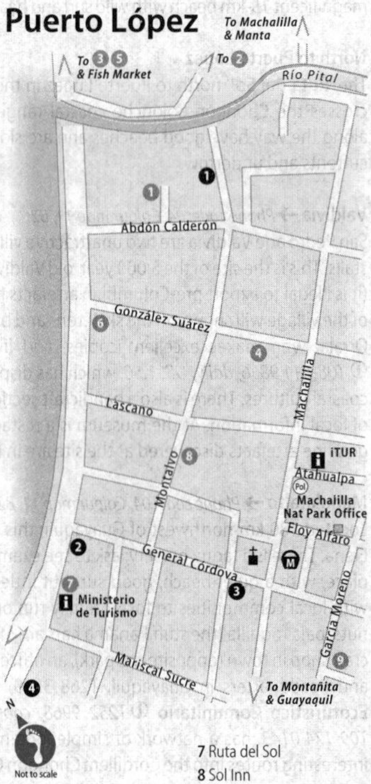

Sleeping
1 Itapoa
2 La Terraza
3 Mandála
4 Máxima
5 Oceanic
6 Pacífico
7 Ruta del Sol
8 Sol Inn
9 Villa Colombia

Eating
1 Bellitalia
2 Carmita
3 Flipper
4 Whale Café

hot, arid scrub, is a small village and a fine, small **archaeological museum** ⓘ *0800-1800, US$3 for a 2-3 hr guided tour of the museum, ruins (a 45-min walk), funerary urns and sulphur lake, horses can be hired for the visit, camping is possible and there's a cabin and 1 very basic room for rent above the museum for US$5 per person; pick-up from Puerto López US$7*, containing some fascinating ceramics from the Manteño civilization. **San Sebastián**, 9 km from Agua Blanca, is in tropical moist forest at 800 m; orchids and birds can be seen and possibly howler monkeys. Although part of the national park, this area is administered by the Comuna of Agua Blanca, which charges its own fees in addition to the park entrance, you cannot go independently. It's five hours on foot or by horse. A tour to the forest costs US$40 per day including guide, horses and camping (minimum two people), otherwise lodging is with a family at extra cost.

About 24 km offshore is **Isla de la Plata**. Trips are popular because of the similarities with the Galápagos. Wildlife includes nesting colonies of waved albatross (April-November), frigates and three different booby species. Whales can be seen from June to September, as well as sea lions. It is also a pre-Columbian site with substantial pottery finds, and there is good diving and snorkelling, as well as walks. Take a change of clothes, water, precautions against sun and seasickness (most agencies provide snorkelling equipment). Staying overnight is not permitted.

Puerto López to Manta

North of Machalilla, the road forks at **Puerto Cayo**, where whale-watching tours may be organized July-August. One road follows the coast, partly through forested hills, passing Cabo San Lorenzo with its lighthouse. The other route heads inland through the trading centre of **Jipijapa** to **Montecristi**, below an imposing hill, 16 km before Manta. The town is renowned as the centre of the panama hat industry. Also produced are varied straw- and basketware, and wooden barrels which are strapped to donkeys for carrying water. Ask for José Chávez Franco, Rocafuerte 203, where you can see panama hats being made; wholesale and retail. Some 23 km east of Montecristi is **Portoviejo**, capital of Manabí province, a sweltering commercial city.

Guayaquil to Puerto López listings

For Sleeping and Eating price codes and other relevant information, see Essentials, pages 38-40.

Sleeping

Salinas *p1152*

LL-L Barceló Colón Miramar, Malecón entre C 38 y C 40, T277 1610, www.barcelocolon miramar.com. Package includes 3 buffet meals, **AL** for accommodation and breakfast only, restaurant, pool and spa, high-rise by the sea, most luxurious in town.

B El Carruaje, Malecón 517, T277 4282. Comfortable rooms, some with ocean view, all facilities, good restaurant, electric shower, a/c, fridge, parking.

B Francisco I and II, Enríquez Gallo y Rumiñahui, T277 4106; Malecón y Las Palmeras, T277 3751. Both are very nice, comfortable rooms, restaurant, a/c, fridge pool.

C Travel Suites, Av 5 Y C 13, T277 2856, maguerra@telconet.net. Modern, a/c, kitchenette with fridge, very good value in low season.

D Las Olas, C 17 y Av Quinta, T277 2526, pachecobolivar@hotmail.com. Hot water, a/c, spotless, good value.

D-E Porto Rapallo, Av Edmundo Azpiazu y 24 de Mayo, T277 1822. Modern place in a quiet area, hot water, a/c, cheaper with fan, good value.

Valdivia *p1153*

C Valdivia Ecolodge, at Km 40, just south of San Pedro, T291 6128. Screened cabins without walls in a nice location above the ocean, fresh and interesting. Includes breakfast, restaurant, pool and access to nice bathing beach.

Manglaralto *p1153*

See also *Proyecto de Desarollo Ecoturístico Comunitario*, page 1153.

E Manglaralto, half a block north of the plaza, T290 1369. Pleasant hotel, restaurant, with fan.

E Manglaralto Sunset, one block from the Plaza, T290 1405, manglaralto_beach@ yahoo.com. Nice modern place, comfortable rooms, hammocks, cafeteria bar, electric shower, parking.

Montañita *p1153*

There are many places to stay in town; the quieter ones are on the outskirts of the village.

A Baja Montañita, in Montañita Punta, T09-189 8542. A small resort off on its own, comfortable rooms, buffet breakfast, restaurant, a/c, pool, Wi-Fi, parking.

B La Casa del Sol, in Montañita Punta, T09-129 3222, www.casasol.com. Buffet breakfast, restaurant, a/c, Wi-Fi, minibar, large rooms available, surfing lessons, packages and tours.

C Charo's, Malecón, in town by the beach, T206 0044, www.charoshostal.com. Very nice, ample rooms, restaurant, a/c, pool and Jacuzzi, nice garden, hammocks, English spoken.

C La Barranca, on the road to the sanctuary, T283 2095. A nice hotel in a privileged setting with lovely views. Spacious impeccable rooms, terrace with hammocks, includes breakfast, restaurant, a/c, Jacuzzi.

C Swiss Point, on the road to the sanctuary, T206 0083, www.swisspointmontanita.com. Good breakfast, fine restaurant upstairs serving Swiss and international food, fan, spotless.

D Sole Mare, on the beach at the north end of Montañita Punta, T236 4962, solemare_ecuador@hotmail.com. Very nice, quiet, Italian-run.

D Tabuba, away from centre at south end of town, T206 0145. Modern place with large rooms, restaurant, hot water, parking, quiet and good, very good value in low season.

E La Casa Blanca, C Guido Chiriboga, T09-918 2501. Includes breakfast, good restaurant, private bath, sporadic hot water, mosquito nets, hammocks.

E Ricky, in town by the bus stop, T09-931 7386, loboricky@hotmail.com. A simple hostel, cheaper with shared bath and in tents with beds, electric shower, cooking facilities, mosquito net, balcony with hammocks. Relaxed, good meeting place, free surfing lessons, also organizes tours.

Olón *p1153*

A-B Finca El Retiro, Km 1.5 Vía a San Vicente de Loja, turnoff by the police just north of Olón , T09-450 1520, Guayaquil T04-239 9213, www.elretiro.com.ec. Comfortable rural inn with rooms and a cabin for 8, includes breakfast, a/c, pool, fridge, nature trail, horse riding (extra), climbing wall, zip line.

D-E Susi's Boon, C Othmar Staheli 217, across from the church, 3 blocks from the beach, T278 0202, www.hosteriasusiboon.com. Two storey hotel with a variety of rooms, balconies with hammocks.

Ayampe to Salango *p1154*

L Atamari, on the headland south of Ayampe, a 15-min walk from the highway, T04-278 0430, www.resortatamari.com. Beautiful cabins with rooms and suites in spectacular surroundings on cliffs above the sea, restaurant with wonderful food, pool, packages including half board available May-Oct.

A-C Alandaluz, T04-278 0690, T02-224 8604 (Quito), www.alandaluz.com. Just south of Puerto Rico. Cabins range from bamboo with thatched roofs and compost toilets to more luxurious with flush toilets, all with bath. Good homegrown organic food, vegetarian or seafood, bar, all at extra cost. Very peaceful, clean beach, pool, stunning organic vegetable and flower gardens in the middle of the desert, camping with own tent **F** pp, tours, zip line. Often busy, book ahead. Highly recommended.

B Islamar, on a hilltop south of Salango, T09-385 7580, Guayaquil T04-228 7001, www.hosteria-islamar.com.ec. Ample comfortable cabins, restaurant, lovely views of Isla Salango, camping in your own tent **F** pp. Offers paragliding, diving, and has a climbing wall. Swiss-Ecuadorean run.

B-D Azuluna, in Las Tunas, on a hill near La Barquita (the restaurant boat on the beach), T278 0693, Quito T02-241 0756, www.azuluna-ecuador.com. Comfortable cabins with incredible views and beautifully decorated common areas, restaurant, bar, a variety of different rooms and prices, cheaper with shared bath.

C La Barquita, by Las Tunas, 4 km north of Ayampe and 1 km south of Alandaluz, T04-278 0051, www.labarquita-ec.com. Restaurant and bar are in a boat on the beach with good ocean views, rooms with fan and mosquito nets, tours, games, Swiss run; French, English and German spoken.

C-D Finca Punta Ayampe, south of other Ayampe hotels, T04-278 0616, info@fincapuntaayampe. com. Bamboo structure high on a hill with great ocean views, restaurant, hot water, mosquito nets, helpful staff.

E Cabañas de la Iguana, Ayampe, T04-278 0605, ayampeiguana@hotmail.com. Cabins for 4, mosquito nets, meals with advance notice, cooking facilities US$2, quiet, Swiss-Ecuadorean run, family atmosphere, knowledgeable and helpful, organizes excursions. Recommended.

Puerto López *p1154*

A Mantaraya Lodge, 3 km south of town, T02-244 8985, www.mantarayalodge.com. Restaurant and bar, pool, comfortable rooms, nice view, colourful decor, horse riding, fishing and diving trips organized.

B-C Mandála, Malecón at north end of the beach, T230 0181, www.hosteriamandala.info. Nice cabins decorated with art, lovely garden, excellent restaurant, fan, mosquito nets, Wi-Fi, games, music room, Swiss-Italian run, English spoken, knowledgeable owners. Recommended.

B-D Pacífico, Malecón y González Suárez, T230 0147, hpacific@manta.ecua.net.ec. Includes breakfast, restaurant, a/c, comfortable, cheaper in old wing with fan and shared bath, nice grounds, pool, boat tours. Recommended.

C La Terraza, on hill north behind the clinic, T230 0235, www.laterraza.de. Spacious cabins, great views over the bay, hot water, good breakfast available , gardens, small pool and Jacuzzi, German spoken. Recommended.

C Oceanic, at the north end, past Mandala, T09-621 1065. Nice thatch roofed cabins with balcony and hammocks right at the beach, restaurant, pool, Wi-Fi, parking, ample grounds, flowers and trees.

D Ruta del Sol, Malecón y Mariscal Sucre, T230 0236. Nice hotel opposite the beach, restaurant, hot water, some rooms with a/c.

E Itapoa, on a lane off Abdón Calderón, between the Malecón and Montalvo, T09-314 5894. Cabins around large garden, sauna and Jacuzzi, includes breakfast, hot water, Wi-Fi, English and Portuguese spoken.

E Máxima, González Suárez y Machalilla, T09-953 4282, www.hotelmaxima.org. Restaurant and bar, cheaper with shared bath, mosquito nets, laundry and cooking facilities, parking, modern, comfortable, English spoken, good value.

E Sol Inn, Montalvo entre Eloy Alfaro y Lascano, T230 0248, hostal_solinn@ hotmail.com. Cheaper with shared bath, hot water, fan, laundry and cooking facilities, parking, garden, pool table. Popular, nice atmosphere, English and French spoken, good value.

E-F Villa Colombia, García Moreno behind market, T230 0105. Pleasant hostel, with hot water, fan, cheaper in dorm, cooking facilities, mosquito nets, garden with hammocks.

Puerto López to Manta *p1155*

There are other places to stay; many close out of season.

D Luz de Luna, 5 km north of Puerto Cayo on the coastal road, T261 6031, T02-240 0562 (Quito), www.hosterialuzdeluna.com. On a clean beach, comfortable spacious rooms with balcony, full board **C**, restaurant, cold water in cabins, shared hot showers available, fan and mosquito net, pool, disco, quieter in low season when discounts are available.

D Puerto Cayo, south end of beach, Puerto Cayo, T261 6019, T09-752 1538. Good restaurant, fan, comfortable rooms with hammocks and terrace overlooking the sea.

Eating

Salinas *p1152*

A couple of blocks inland from the Malecón are food stalls serving good *ceviches* (US$4-5) and freshly cooked seafood: **Cevichelandia**, María González y Las Palmeras; **La Lojanita**, Enríquez Gallo y Leonardo Avilés, recommended; others are around the Libertad Peninsular bus station at María González y León Avilés.

TTT La Bella Italia, Malecón y C 17, near Hotel El Carruaje. Good pizza and international food. Recommended.

TTT-TT Amazon, Malecón near Banco de Guayaquil, T277 3671. Elegant upmarket eatery, grill and seafood specialties, good wine list.

TT Oyster Catcher, Enríquez Gallo entre C 47 y C 50, open Oct-May. Restaurant and bar, friendly place, safe oysters, enquire here here about birdwatching tours with local expert Ben Haase.

TT-T Mariner, Malecón y José Estrella. Recommended for seafood.

T El Mayquito, Av 2 y C 12. Simple place with very good food and friendly service.

Manglaralto *p1153*

T El Alegre Calamar, at the north end of town. À la carte seafood.

Montañita *p1153*

ΨΨΨ-ΨΨ Tikilimbo, opposite Hotel Casa Blanca. Good quality, vegetarian dishes available.

ΨΨ Happy Donkey, near the beachfront. Good grill, Chinese food, seafood, frequently recommended.

ΨΨ Machu Picchu, in the centre of town. Rustic setting, seafood and international dishes, popular.

ΨΨ Marea Pizzeria Bar, opposite Hotel Montañita. Real wood-oven pizza, very tasty, recommended.

Ψ Tiburón, on the main street, south of the centre. Seafood and international dishes.

Olón *p1153*

Several cheap, simple places to eat seafood, many close in low season.

Salango *p1154*

ΨΨ El Delfín Mágico. Order meal before visiting museum because all food is cooked from scratch (very fresh and safe), try the *spondilus* (spiny oyster) in fresh coriander and peanut sauce with garlic coated *patacones*.

ΨΨ-Ψ El Pelícano, behind the church. Excellent seafood, also caters for vegetarians.

Puerto López *p1154*

ΨΨ Bellitalia, Montalvo y Abdón Calderón, one block back from the Malecón and near the river, open from 1800. Excellent Italian food, try their spinach soup. Pleasant garden setting, Italian run. Highly recommended.

ΨΨ Carmita, Malecón y General Córdova. Tasty fish and seafood, a Puerto López tradition.

ΨΨ Whale Café, towards the south end of the Malecón. Good pizza, stir-fried Asian dishes, Thai specialties, sandwiches, vegetarian salads, cakes and pies. Nice breakfast, famous for pancakes. US-run, owners Diana and Kevin are very helpful and provide travel information. Recommended.

Ψ Flipper, Gen Córdova next to Banco Pichincha, open until 1700. Good set meals.

The *panadería* behind the church serves good banana bread and other sweets.

▲ Activities and tours

Salinas *p1152*

Avista Travel, Malecón by Banco de Guayaquil, T277 0331, avistatravel@hotmail.com. Whale watching, local attractions and Ruta del Sol.

Ben Haase, at Museo de Ballenas, Av Enríquez Gallo entre C47 y C50, T277 7335, T09-961 9257, bhaase@ecua.net.ec. Expert English speaking naturalist guide runs birdwatching tours to the Ecuasal salt ponds, US$40 for a small group. Also whale watching and trips to a sea-lion colony.

Fernando Félix, T38 4560, T09-09-827 4475, fernandofelix@femm.org. English-speaking marine biologist, can guide for whale watching and other nature trips, arrange in advance.

Montañita *p1153*

Surfboard rentals from US$4/hr, US$15/day.

Montañita Adventures, around the corner from **Hotel Casa Blanca**, kayaks, bicycles, surfing lessons, snorkelling tours.

Puerto López *p1154*

Whale watching Puerto López is a major centre for trips from Jun to Sep/Oct, with many more agencies than we can list. **Note** Whales can also be seen further north. There is a good fleet of small boats (16-20 passengers) running excursions, all have life jackets and a toilet. All agencies offer the same tours for the same price. In high season: US$40 pp for whale watching, Isla de la Plata and snorkelling, with a snack and drinks, US$25 for whale watching only (available Jun and Sep). Outside whale season, tours to Isla de la Plata and snorkelling cost US$25. These rates don't include the National Park fee. Trips depart around 0800 and return around 1700. Agencies also offer tours to the mainland sites of the national park. A day tour combining Agua Blanca and Los Frailes costs US$25 pp. There are also hiking, birdwatching, kayaking and other trips.

Bosque Marino-Expediciones Oceánicas, Malecón y Sucre, T260 4106 or T09-707 1067, www.bosquemarino.com. Experienced guides, some speak English.

Cercapez, at the Centro Comercial on the highway, T230 0173. All-inclusive trips to San Sebastián, with camping, local guide and food run US$40 pp per day. Also offer trips further north with **Guacamayo Bahía Tours** in Bahía de Caráquez and transport to the airport and other cities.

Excursiones Pacífico, Malecón at **Hotel Pacífico**, T230 0133. Good boat and service.

Exploramar Diving, Malecón y Gral Córdova, T230 0123, www.exploradiving.com. French-run, Quito based (T02-256 3905). Have 2 boats for 8-16 people and their own compressor to fill dive tanks. PADI divemaster accompanies qualified divers to various sites, but advance notice is required, US$95 pp for all-inclusive diving day tour (2 tanks). Also offer diving lessons. Recommended.

Machalilla Tours, Malecón y Eloy Alfaro and Gral Córdova y Machalilla, T230 0234, machalillatours @yahoo.com. Also surf lessons.

Manta Raya, on Malecón Norte, T09-727 6759. Comfortable spacious boat. Also diving for US$90-130 pp, all inclusive.

Mares Dive Center, Malecón y Gral Córdova, T09-951 5215. 1 day (2 tanks) US$95, also offer a 4-day course.

Orcados Aventura, Gral Córdova y Montalvo, T230 0106, avenorca@yahoo.com. Good boat. They also have diving equipment and charge US$130 pp, all inclusive.

Transport

Buses to this area depart from the second level of the Terminal Terrestre in Guayaquil.

Playas *p1152*

Bus Trans Posorja and **Trans Villamil** leave from stations along Av Menéndez Gílbert, a couple of blocks back from the beach. To **Guayaquil**, frequent, 2 hrs, US$2.60; taxi US$25.

Salinas *p1152*

Bus To **Guayaquil**, **Coop Libertad Peninsular (CLP)**, María González y León Avilés, every 5 mins, US$3.70, 2½ hrs. For **Montañita**, **Puerto López** and points north, transfer at La Libertad (not safe, take a taxi between terminals) or Santa Elena. From La Libertad, every 30 mins to Puerto López, US$4, 2½ hrs; or catch a Guayaquil-Olón bus in Santa Elena.

Manglaralto *p1153*

Bus To **Santa Elena** and **La Libertad**, US$1.25, 1½ hrs. Transfer in Santa Elena for Guayaquil. To **Guayaquil** direct, see Olón schedule below. To **Puerto López**, 1 hr, US$1.50.

Montañita and Olón *p1153*

Bus Montañita is just a few mins south of Olón, from where **CLP** has direct buses to **Guayaquil** at 0520, 0620, 0900, 1300, 1500 and 1640 (same schedule from Guayaquil), US$5.70, 3¼ hrs; or transfer in Santa Elena, US$1.50, 1½ hrs. To **Puerto López**, every 30 mins, US$1.50, 45 mins.

Puerto López *p1154*

Bus To **Santa Elena** or **La Libertad**, every 30 mins, US$2.50, 2½ hrs. To **Montañita** and **Manglaralto**, US$1.50, 1 hr. To **Guayaquil**, transfer in Olón or Santa Elena. Pick-ups for hire to nearby sites are by the market, east of the highway. To/from **Manta**, direct, every 2 hrs, US$3, 3 hrs. To **Quito** with **Reina del Camino** office in front of market, 2 a day and **CA Aray**, 5 daily, 9-10 hrs, US$10-13; some buses go to Quitumbe others to their private stations.

Parque Nacional Machalilla *p1154*

Bus **To Los Frailes**: take a bus towards Jipijapa (US$0.25), or a pick-up (US$7), and alight at the turn-off just south of the town of Machalilla, then walk for 30 mins. Show your national park ticket on arrival. No transport back to Puerto López after 2000 (but check in advance). **To Agua Blanca**: take tour, a pick-up (US$7) or a bus bound for Jipijapa (US$0.25); it is a hot walk of more than 1 hr from the turning to the village. **To Isla de la Plata**: the island can only be visited on a day trip. Many agencies offer tours, see Puerto López above.

Puerto López to Manta *p1155*

Bus From Jipijapa (terminal on the outskirts) to **Manglaralto** (2 hrs, US$2), to **Puerto López** (1 hr, US, 1, these go by Puerto Cayo), to **Manta** (1 hr, US$1), to **Quito** (10 hrs, US$9).

Directory

Salinas *p1152*

Banks **Banco de Guayaquil**, Malecón y 24 de Mayo. **Banco Pichincha**, Malecón y Armando Barreto. **Internet** Several places, US$1 per hr.

Montañita *p1153*

Banks **Banco Bolivariano**, ATM (not always working, bring cash). **Internet** US$1-1.50/hr. **Language courses** **Montañita Spanish School**, opposite Disco Caña Grill, T09-758 5207, www.montanitaspanishschool.com.

Puerto López *p1154*

Banks **Banco Pichincha**, on the main road, for ATM; only one in town, best bring some cash. **Internet** Several places, US$1.20 per hr. **Language courses** **La Lengua**, Abdón Calderón y García Moreno, east of the highway, T09-233 9316 or Quito T02-250 1271, www.la-lengua.com.

Manta and Bahía de Caráquez

Two quite different seaside towns: Manta is the quintessential maritime city, growing fast and prospering on fishing and trade. Bahía de Caráquez is a relaxed town and a pleasant place to spend a few days. It is proud of its 'eco' credentials. Just beyond Bahía, on the other side of the Río Chone estuary, is the village of Canoa, boasting some of the finest beaches in Ecuador.

Manta and around → *Phone code: 05. Colour map 11, B2. Population: 250,000.*
Ecuador's second port after Guayaquil is a busy town that sweeps round a bay filled with all sorts of boats. A constant sea breeze tempers the intense sun and makes the city's *malecones* pleasant places to stroll. The Malecón Escénico, at the gentrified west end of town has a cluster of bars and seafood restaurants. It is a lively place especially at weekends, when there is good music, free beach aerobics and lots of action. Playa Murciélago is a popular beach with wild surf (flags indicate whether it is safe to bathe), with good surfing from December to April. The **Museo del Banco Central** ⓘ *Malecón y C 19, T262 6998 Tue-Sat 0930-1630, US$2, Sun 1100-1430, free,* has a small but excellent collection of archaeological pieces from seven different civilizations which flourished on the coast of Manabí between 3500 BC and AD 1530. Three bridges join the main town with its seedy neighbour, **Tarqui**. **Tourist offices**: Ministerio de Turismo ⓘ *Paseo José María Egas 1034 (Av 3) y C 11, T262 2944, Mon-Fri 0900-1230, 1400-1700*; **Dirección Municipal de Turismo** ⓘ *C9 y Av 4, T261 0171, www.informanta.com, Mon-Fri 0800-1700*; and. **Oficina de Información ULEAM** ⓘ *Malecón Escénico, T262 4099, daily 0900-1700*; all helpful and speak some English.

Crucita → *Phone code: 05. Colour map 11, B2. Population: 14,000.*
A rapidly growing resort, 45 minutes by road from either Manta or Portoviejo, Crucita is busy at weekends and holidays when people flock here to enjoy ideal conditions for paragliding, hang-gliding and kite-surfing. The best season for flights is July to December. There is also an abundance of sea birds in the area. There are many restaurants serving fish and seafood along the seafront. Motumbo is very good, try their *viche*, they also offer interesting tours and rent bikes.

North to Bahía
About 60 km northeast of Manta (30 km south of Bahía de Caráquez) are **San Clemente** and, 3 km south, **San Jacinto**. The ocean is magnificent but be wary of the strong undertow. Both get crowded during the holiday season and have a selection of *cabañas* and hotels. Some 3 km north of San Clemente is **Punta Charapotó**, a high promontory clad in dry tropical forest, above a lovely beach. Here are some nice out-of-the way accommodations and an out-of-place upmarket property development.

Bahía de Caráquez and around → *Phone code: 05. Colour map 11, B2. Population: 27,000.*
Set on the southern shore at the seaward end of the Chone estuary, Bahía has an attractive riverfront laid out with parks along the Malecón which goes right around the point to the ocean side. The beaches in town are nothing special, but there are excellent beaches nearby between San Vicente and Canoa and at Punta Bellaca (the town is busiest July-August). Bahía has declared itself an 'eco-city', where recycling projects, organic gardens and ecoclubs are common. Tricycle rickshaws called 'eco-taxis' are a popular form of local transport. The city is also a centre of the less than ecologically friendly shrimp farming industry, which has boosted the local economy but also destroyed much of the estuary's precious mangroves. With awareness of the damage done, Bahía now boasts the first certified organic shrimp farm in the world. Information about the eco-city concept can be obtained from the **Planet Drum Foundation**, www.planetdrum.org. **Tourist offices**: Ministerio de Turismo, T269 1124 and Dirección Municipal, T264 1044, www.bahiade caraquez.com, both at Bolívar y Padre Laennen,

Mon-Fri 0800-1300, 1400-1700, Sat 0800-1300, Spanish only. The **Museo Bahía de Caráquez** ⓘ *Malecón Alberto Santos y Aguilera, T269 0817, www.museobahiadecaraquez.com, Tue-Sat 0900-1600, Sun 1100-1430, US$1*, of the Banco Central, has an interesting collection of archaeological artefacts from prehispanic coastal cultures, a life-size balsa raft and modern sculpture. Bahía is an important port for international yatchs with good service at Puerto **Amistad** ⓘ *T269 3112, www.puertoamistadecuador.com*.

The Rio Chone estuary has several islands with mangrove forest. The area is rich in birdlife, dolphins may also be seen, and conditions are ideal for photographers because you can get really close, even under the mangrove trees where birds nest. The male frigate birds can be seen displaying their inflated red sacks as part of the mating ritual; best from August to January. **Isla Corazón** has a boardwalk through an area of protected mangrove forest. There are bird colonies at the end of the island which can only be accessed by boat. The village of **Puerto Portovelo** is involved in mangrove reforestation and runs an eco-tourism project (tour with native guide US$6 per person). You can visit independently, taking a Chone-bound bus from San Vicente or with an agency. Agency tours might do part of the trip by boat, which has the advantage of travelling through the estuary and seeing several islands. Visits here are tide-sensitive, so even if you go independently, it is best to check with the agencies about the best time to visit; agency tours are US$20-30 per person. Inland near Chone is **La Segua** wetland, very rich in birds; Bahía agencies offer tours here. **Saiananda** ⓘ *5 km from Bahía along the bay, T239 8331, www.sainanda.com, owner Alfredo Harmsen, biologist, reached by taxi or any bus heading out of town, US$2*, is a private park with extensive areas of reforestation and a large collection of animals, a cactus garden and spiritual centre. Also offer first-class accommodation (**B** including breakfast) and vegetarian meals served in an exquisite dining area over the water.

San Vicente and Canoa → *Phone code: 05. Colour map 11, B2.*

On the north side of the Río Chone, San Vicente is reached by ferry from Bahía (bridge under construction in 2010) or by road west from Chone. The **Santa Rosa church**, 100 m to the left of the wharf, contains excellent mosaic and glass work by **José María Peli** (better known as Peli).

Canoa, once a quiet fishing village with a splendid 200-m wide beach, has grown rapidly and is increasingly popular with Ecuadorean and foreign tourists. It has lost some of its charm along the way, but it is still pleasant on weekdays, crowded, noisy and dirty on weekends and especially holidays. The choice of accommodation and restaurants is very good.The beautiful 17-km beach between San Vicente and Canoa is a good walk, horse or bike ride. Horses and bicycles can be hired through several hotels. Surfing is good, particularly during the wet season, December to April. In the dry season there is good wind for windsurfing. Canoa is also a good place for hang-gliding and paragliding. Tents for shade and chairs are rented at the beach for US$3 a day. About 10 km north of Canoa, the **Río Muchacho organic farm** (see Activities and tours) accepts visitors and volunteers, it's an eye-opener to rural coastal (*montubio*) culture and to organic farming.

North to Pedernales → *Phone code: 05. Colour map 10, A2. Population: 32,000.*

The coastal road cuts across Cabo Pasado to **Jama** (1½ hours; cabins and several *hostales*), then runs parallel to the beach past coconut groves and shrimp hatcheries, inland across some low hills and across the Equator to **Pedernales**, a market town and crossroads with nice undeveloped beaches to the north. In town, where beaches are less attractive, they cater to the *quiteño* holiday market. A mosaic mural and stained glass windows on the church overlooking the plaza are among of the best pieces of work by Peli (see above). A poor unpaved road goes north along the shore to Cojimíes. The main coastal road, fully paved, goes north to Chamanga, El Salto and Esmeraldas. Another important road goes inland to El Carmen and on to Santo Domingo de los Tsáchilas: this is the most direct route to Quito.

Santo Domingo de los Tsáchilas → *Phone code: 02. Colour map 11, A3. Population: 382,000.* In the hills above the western lowlands, Santo Domingo, 129 km from Quito, is an important commercial centre and transport hub. It is capital of the eponymous province, created in 2008. The city is noisy and dangerous, caution is recommended at all times in the market areas, including the pedestrian walkway along 3 de Julio and in peripheral neighbourhoods. Sunday is market day, shops and banks are closed Monday instead. It was known as 'Santo Domingo de los Colorados', a reference to the traditional red hair dye, made with *achiote* (annatto), worn by the native Tsáchila men. Today the Tsáchila only wear their native dress on special occasions. There are less than 2,000 Tsáchilas left, living in eight communities off the roads leading from Santo Domingo towards the coast. Their lands make up a reserve of some 8,000 ha. Visitors interested in their culture are welcome at the *Complejo Turístico Huapilú*, in the Comunidad Chigüilpe, where there is a small but interesting museum (contributions expected). Access is via the turn-off east at Km 7 on the road to Quevedo, from where it is 4 km. Tours are run by travel agencies in town. The Santo Domingo area also offers opportunities for nature trips and sports activities, such as rafting. **Cámara de Turismo** ⓘ *Río Mulaute y Av Quito, T275 2146, Mon-Fri 0830-1300, 1430-1800, English spoken.*

Manta and Bahía de Caráquez listings

For Sleeping and Eating price codes and other relevant information, see Essentials, pages 38-40.

Sleeping

Manta and around *p1160*

All streets have numbers; those above 100 are in Tarqui (those above C110 are not safe).

L Howard Johnson Plaza, Barrio Umiña, 1½ km on the way to Barbasquillo, T262 9999, www.ghlhoteles.com. Part of the US chain, buffet breakfast, restaurant, pool and gym, modern, full facilities.

L Oro Verde, Malecón y C 23, T262 9200, www.oroverdehotels.com. Includes buffet breakfast, restaurant, pool, all luxuries.

A Vistalmar, C M1 y Av 24B, at Playa Murciélago, T262 1671. Exclusive hotel overlooking the ocean. Ample cabins and suites tastefully decorated with art, includes breakfast, a/c, pool, Wi-Fi, cabins have kitchenettes, gardens by the sea. A place for a honeymoon.

B Manakin, C 20 y Av 12, T262 0413. Includes breakfast, a/c, Wi-Fi, comfortable rooms, small patio, nice common areas.

C YorMar, Av 14 entre C 19 y C 20, T262 4375. Nice rooms with small kitchenette and patio, includes breakfast, electric shower, a/c, parking.

E Centenario, C 11 #602 y Av 5, enquire at nearby Lavamatic Laundry, T262 9245, josesanmartin@hotmail.com. Pleasant hostel in a nicely refurbished old home in the centre of town. Shared bath, hot water, fan, cooking facilities, nice views, quiet location, good value. Recommended.

Tarqui

C-D Chávez Inn, Av 106 y C 106, T262 1019. Modern hotel, a/c, fridge, small bright rooms.

E Astoria, C 106 y Av 105, T262 1904. Cold water, a/c, cheaper with ceiling fan, simple decent rooms.

Crucita *p1160*

D Italia, C 9 y 25 de Mayo, at the south end of town, T234 0291. Pleasant place, restaurant serves pizza, electric shower, small pool, parking, nice patio.

E Cruzita, towards the south end of beach, T234 0068, www.ecuadorcrucita.com. Very nice hostel with great views right on the beach, meals on request, cold water, fan, small pool, use of kitchen in the evening, parking, good value. Owner Raul Tobar offers paragliding flights and lessons. Recommended.

E Hostal Voladores, at south end of beach, T234 0200, www.parapentecrucita.com. Simple but nice, restaurant, cheaper with shared bath, hot water, small pool, sea kayaks available. Owner Luis Tobar offers paragliding flights and lessons.

North to Bahía *p1160*

AL Palmazul, between San Clemente and Punta Charapotó, T09-824 7454, www.palmazul ecuador.com. An upmarket resort hotel in an odd location, includes breakfast, restaurant, fan, mosquito nets, frigobar, large pool, tennis court, nice beach. Pricey and a bit pretentious.

D Hotel San Jacinto, on the beach between San Jacinto and San Clemente, T261 5516, www.hotelsanjacinto.com. Pleasant location right by the ocean, restaurant, hot water, fan, older place under new management, gradually being refurbished and looking good.

D Peñón del Sol, on the hillside near Punta Charapotó, T09-941 4149, penondelsol@hotmail.com. Located on a 250 ha dry tropical forest reserve, meals on request, shared bath, cold water, great views, camping possible.

F Sabor de Bamboo, on the ocean side of the road to Punta Charapotó, T08-562 8146. Nice simple wooden cabins with sea breeze, restaurant and bar, cold water, wonderfully relaxed place, friendly owner Meier, German spoken.

Bahía de Caráquez *p1160*

LL-L Casa Ceibo, Km 5 on the road to Chone, T239 9399, www.casaceibo.com. An opulent luxury hotel, includes breakfast, restaurant, pool, ample manicured grounds, large comfortable rooms, opened in 2009.

A-B La Piedra, Circunvalación near Bolívar, T269 0154, www.hotellapiedra.com. Modern hotel with access to the beach and lovely views, good expensive restaurant, a/c, pool (US$2 for non-guests, only in low season), good service, bicycle rentals for guests.

C-E La Herradura, Bolívar e Hidalgo, T269 0446. Older well-maintained hotel, restaurant, a/c, cheaper with fan and cold water, nice common areas, cheaper rooms are good value.

E Bahía Hotel, Malecón y Vinueza, T269 0509. A variety of different rooms, those at the back are nicer, fan, parking.

E Centro Vacacional Life, Octavio Viteri 504 y Muñoz Dávila, T269 0496. Private facilities for company employees but rents to public if there is space (not available Jul-Aug), hot water, parking, fully furnished 2-bedroom cottages, good value.

E Coco Bongo, Cecilio Intriago y Arenas, T08-544 0978, www.cocobongohostal.com. Nice hostel with a pleasant atmosphere, breakfast available, electric shower, ceiling fan, mosquito nets, cooking facilities, Australian-owned.

E-F Bahía Bed & Breakfast Inn, Ascázubi 322 y Morales, T269 0146, jacob.santos@live.com. Older place with renovated common area, simple rooms, includes breakfast, cheaper with shared bath and cold water, fan, discount for Canadians.

San Vicente *p1161*

There are several hotels along the road to Canoa.

E Vacaciones, on the Malecón, T267 4116, hotelvacaciones@hotmail.com. Hot water, a/c, cheaper with fan, pool could be cleaner, fridge, parking, showing its age but OK for the price.

Canoa *p1161*

A Hostería Canoa, 1 km south of town, T261 6380. Comfortable cabins and rooms, includes breakfast, good restaurant and bar, a/c, pool, sauna, whirlpool.

D Sol y Luna, 2 km south of town, T261 6434. Good hostel, restaurant, hot water, fan, small pool, comfortable rooms, no palms for shade by the beach since paragliders land here.

D-E Coco Loco, on the beach toward the south end of town, T09-544 7260. Pleasant breezy hotel with nice views, café serves breakfast and snacks, bar, cheaper with shared bath and in dorm, hot showers, cooking facilities, surfboard rentals, excellent horse riding, English spoken, popular.

D-E País Libre, by the river, 3 blocks from the beach, T261 6387, www.hotelpaislibre.com. Four-storey wood and bamboo construction. Spacious rooms, upper floors have pleasant breeze and good views, restaurant, cheaper with shared bath, pool, parking.

D-F Bambú, on the beach just north of C Principal, T08-926 5225, www.hotelbambuecuador.com. Pleasant location and atmosphere. A variety of rooms and prices, good restaurant including vegetarian options, cheaper with shared bath and in dorm, camping possible (US$3 pp with your own tent), hot water, fan, surfing classes and board rentals. Dutch-Ecuadorean run, very popular and recommended.

D-F Olmito, at the south end of the beach, T05-261 6374, www.olmito.org. Cane and thatch construction in a quiet location, a variety of rooms and prices, some have mosquito nets, cheaper with shared bath, cold water, cooking

facilities, balconies with ocean views, nice palm garden with hammocks, good value.
E Baloo, on the beach at south end of the village, T261 6355, baloo_canoa@yahoo.com. Wood and bamboo cabins, restaurant, cheaper with shared bath, hot water, British run.
E Posada de Daniel, C principal, 6 blocks from the beach, T09-750 8825. An attractive homestead on nice ample grounds. Pleasant bamboo cabins, bar, fan, pool, surf boards and bicycles for rent. Discounts for long stays.
F-G Camping Iguana, towards the south end of town, one block from the beach, behind Hotel La Vista, www.camping-iguana.com. Camping or rent a tent. Cooking facilities over an open fire, also 3 simple but clean cabins with balcony and bath. German run.

North to Pedernales *p1161*
Jama
A Samvara, 300 m from the highway, turnoff 13 km north of Jama, T09-128 2278, www.samvara-ecolodge.com. Thatched cabins on 6 ha of land, includes breakfast and dinner, beach and pool, lovely secluded setting, camping possible (US$15 pp in on-site tents, US$8 pp in your own tent), Swiss-Ecuadorean run.
A-B Punta Prieta Guest House, by Punta Prieta, T09-225 9146, Quito T02-286 2986, www.puntaprieta.com. Gorgeous setting on a headland high above the ocean with access to pristine beaches. Meals available, comfortable cabins with fridge, suites and rooms with shared bath, balcony with hammocks, nice grounds.
E-F Palo Santo, C Melchor Cevallos, by the river in Jama town, T241 0441, luchincevallos@hotmail.com. Thatched cabins on pleasant grounds, cold water, ceiling fan.

Pedernales
There are many other hotels in all price ranges.
C Agua Marina, Jaime Roldós 413 y Velasco Ibarra, T268 0491. Modern hotel, includes breakfast, cafeteria, a/c, pool, parking.
C Cocosolo, on a secluded beach 20 km north of Pedernales (pickups from main park US$1, 30 min), T09-921 5078. A lovely hideaway set among palms. Includes breakfast, restaurant, clean cabins and rooms, camping possible, horses for hire, French and English spoken.
E Mr John, Plaza Acosta y Malecón, 1 block from the beach, T268 0235. Modern hotel, cold water, fan, parking, rooms facing the beach can be noisy at weekends. Good value.

Santo Domingo de los Tsáchilas *p1162*
A Grand Hotel Santo Domingo, Río Toachi y Galápagos, T276 7947, www.grandhotelsd.com. Includes breakfast, restaurant, a/c, pool and spa, Wi-Fi, parking, modern three-storey hotel, comfortable rooms.
A Tinalandia, 16 km from Santo Domingo, on the road to Quito, poorly signposted, look for a large rock painted white; T09-946 7741, in Quito T244 9028, www.tinalandia.com. Includes full board, nice chalets in cloud forest reserve, great food, spring-fed pool, good birdwatching, entry US$10 for non-guests.
A Zaracay, Av Quito 1639, 1½ km from the centre, T275 0316, www.hotelzaracay.com. Includes breakfast, restaurant, gardens and swimming pool, parking, good rooms and service. Advance booking advised, especially on weekends.
C-E Royal Class, Cadmo Zambrano y César López, near the bus station, T274 3348. Multi-storey modern hotel, a/c, cheaper with fan, Wi-Fi, parking, the best choice near the bus station, reasonably quiet location, good value.
D Puerta del Sol, 29 de Mayo y Cuenca, T275 0370. Cafeteria, hot water, fan, nice rooms, good value.
E Safiro Internacional, 29 de Mayo 800 y Loja, T276 0706. Comfortable modern hotel, cafeteria, hot water, a/c, good value.

Eating

Manta *p1160*
Restaurants on Malecón Escénico serve local seafood.
Club Ejecutivo, Av 2 y C 12, top of Banco Pichincha building. First class food and service, great view.
El Marino, Malecón y C 110, Tarqui. Classic fish and seafood restaurant, for *ceviches*, *sopa marinera* and other delicacies, open for lunch only. Recommended.
Martinica, Via Barbasquillo, near Howard Johnson. Elegant place, varied menu, good food.

¶¶-¶ **Beachcomber**, C 20 y Av Flavio Reyes. Cheap set lunch and mid-range grill in the evening.
¶ **Café Trovador**, Av 3 y C 11, Paseo José María Egas, closes 2100. Very good coffee, snacks, sandwiches and economical set lunches.
¶ **Peberes**, Av 1 entre C 13 y C 14. Good quality and value set lunch, popular with local office workers.

Bahía de Caráquez *p1160*
¶¶ **Puerto Amistad**, on the pier at Malecón y Vinueza, Mon-Sat 1200-2400. Nice setting over the water, international food and atmosphere, popular with yachties.
¶¶-¶ **Arena-Bar Pizzería**, Riofrío entre Bolívar y Montúfar, T05-269 2024, daily 1700-2400. Restaurant/bar serving good pizza, salads and other dishes, nice atmosphere, also take-away and delivery service. Recommended.
¶¶-¶ **El Rey del Burrito**, Hurtado e Hidalgo, daily 1800-2200. Small family-run place serving good Mexican food.
¶¶-¶ **Muelle Uno**, by the pier where canoes leave for San Vicente, daily 1000-2400. Good grill and seafood, lovely setting over the water.
¶ **Doña Luca**, Cecilio Intriago y Sergio Plaza, towards the tip of the peninsula, daily 0800-1800. Simple little place serving excellent local fare, *ceviches, desayuno manabita* (a wholesome breakfast), and set lunches. Friendly service, recommended.

Canoa *p1161*
¶¶ **Amalur**, behind the soccer field, daily 1200-2100. Fresh seafood and authentic Basque specialties, try the *lomo de chancho adobado*, attentive service, modest portions.
¶¶ **Café Flor**, behind La Vista hotel, Mon-Sat 0900-1500, 1800-2130. Nicely decorated café-restaurant, good breakfast, pizza, Mexican and vegetarian dishes. Friendly owners.
¶¶-¶ **Surf Shak**, at the beach, daily 0800-2400. Good for pizza, burgers and breakfast, best coffee in town, Wi-Fi US$1/hr, popular hangout for surfers, English spoken.
¶ **Ché**, at the beach across from Coco Loco hotel. Very good pizza and cocktails served right on the beach, Argentine chef.
¶ **Oasis**, C Principal, 2 blocks from the beach. Good set meals, tasty and abundant.

Pedernales *p1161*
There are a great many other seafood places along the beach.
¶¶-¶ **La Choza**, Malecón y Eloy Alfaro. A variety of seafood and barbeque.

Santo Domingo de los Tsáchilas *p1162*
¶¶¶ **Parrilladas Che Luis**, on the road to Quito, Tue-Sun1200-2300. One of the best grills in town.
¶¶-¶ **La Cocina de Consuelo**, Av Quito y Chimbo, 0700-2230, Sun and Mon to 1700. Very good à la carte dishes and 4-course set meals.

▲ Activities and tours

Manta *p1160*
Delgado Travel, Av 6 y C 13, T262 2813, vtdelgad@hotmail.com. City and regional tours, whale watching trips, Parque Nacional Machalilla, run *Hostería San Antonio* at El Aromo, 15 km south of Manta.
Metropolitan Touring, Av 4 y C 13, T262 3090. Local, regional and nationwide tours.

Bahía de Caráquez *p1160*
Ceibos Tours, Av Bolívar 200 y Checa, T269 0801, www.ceibostours.com. Runs tours to Isla Corazón and Cerro Seco. Also rent bikes.
Guacamayo Bahía Tours, Av Bolívar y Arenas, T269 1412, www.riomuchacho.com. Tours to islands, wetlands, Río Muchacho farm, helps with environmental work and sells crafts. Part of tour fees go to community environmental programmes. Discounts for Kiwis and SAE members.

Canoa *p1161*
Canoa Thrills, at the beach next to **Surf Shak**, www.canoathrills.com. Surfing tours and lessons, sea kayaking. Also rent boards and bikes. English spoken.
Río Muchacho/Guacamayo Bahía Tours, C Principal, 2 blocks from the beach, T261 6384. Bookings for **Río Muchacho organic farm** and other tours offered by Guacamayo in Bahía. Helpful with local information.
Wings and Waves, T08-519 8507 or ask around for Greg. Paragliding flights and lessons.

Santo Domingo de los Tsáchilas *p*
Turismo Zaracay, 29 de Mayo y Cocaniguas, T275 0546, zaratur@andinanet.net. Tours to Tsáchila commune, minimum 5 persons; rafting, fishing trips, bird/butterfly watching tours, English spoken.

⊖ Transport

Manta *p1160*
Air Eloy Alfaro airport. **Aerogal** (T262 8899), **TAME** (T262 2006) and **Icaro** (T262 7327) to **Quito** daily, US$73-77.
Bus All buses leave from the terminal on C 7 y Av 8 in the centre. A couple of companies have their own private terminals nearby. To **Quito**, 9 hrs, US$7-8, some go to Quitumbe, others continue to private terminals further north. **Guayaquil**, 4 hrs, US$4, hourly. **Esmeraldas**, 3 daily, 10 hrs, US$8. **Santo Domingo**, 7 hrs, US$6. **Portoviejo**, 45 mins, US$0.75, every 10 mins. **Jipijapa**, 1 hr, US$1, every 20 mins. **Bahía de Caráquez**, 3 hrs, US$3, hourly.

Crucita *p1160*
Bus Run along the Malecón. There is frequent service to **Portoviejo**, US$1, 1 hr and **Manta**, US$1.20, 1½ hrs.

North to Bahía *p1160*
Bus From San Clemente to **Portoviejo**, every 15 mins, US$1.25, 1¼ hrs. To **Bahía de Caráquez**, US$0.50, 30 mins, a few start in San Clemente in the morning or wait for a through bus at the highway. Mototaxis from San Clemente to Punta Charapotó, US$0.50.

Bahía de Caráquez *p1160*
Boat Motorized canoes (*lanchas* or *pangas*) cross the estuary to **San Vicente**, from the dock opposite C Ante. Frequent service 0615-1800, US$0.29; larger and slower boats make the crossing every 40 mins from 1800-2200, US$0.35, later rent a boat. A **ferry** runs from a ramp near the obelisk, opposite C Ascázubi every 20 mins tides permitting (there may be long waits), 0630-2000, small vehicles US$3, motorcycles US$0.50, free for footpassengers. Due to silting of the estuary, ferry service is becoming increasingly tide-dependent and erratic. In 2010 a bridge was under construction, it will eventually replace the ferry boats.
Bus The Terminal Terrestre is at the entrance to town. To **Quito**, **Reina del Camino**, regular service to Quitumbe at 0620 and 2145 (from Quitumbe 1030, 2300), 8 hrs, US$7.50, Ejecutivo to their own station (18 de Septiembre y Larrea) at 0800 and 2215 (from Quito 1200, 2300), US$10. To **Santo Domingo**, 5 hrs, US$5-7.50. To **Guayaquil**, every 30 mins, 6 hrs, US$6-7. To **Portoviejo**, 2 hrs, US$2. To **Manta**, 3 hrs. US$3. To **Puerto López**, change in Manta, Portoviejo or Jipijapa.

San Vicente and Canoa *p1161*
San Vicente
Bus The terminal is by the market on the San Isidro road, take an eco-taxi tricycle to get there. To **Portoviejo**, US$2.50, 2½ hrs. To **Guayaquil**, US$6, 6½ hrs. To **Quito** (Quitumbe), with **Reina del Camino** at 1000 and 2100 (from Quitimbe 0830 and 2100), US$7.50, 7½ hrs, more services from Bahía, or take a bus to **Pedernales** US$3, 2½ hrs and change. For **Esmeraldas** and northern beaches, take a bus to **Chamanga**, at 0810, 1430 or 1700, US$4.50, 3¼ hrs, and transfer there.

Canoa
Bus To/from **San Vicente**, every 30 mins, 0600-1900, 30 mins, US$0.50; taxi US$5. To **Pedernales**, hourly 0600-1800, 2 hrs, US$2.50. To **Quito** direct, **Trans Vencedores** from C Principal Ramón Centeno at 2400 (from Quitumbe at 1430), 7½ hrs, US$8.50 or transfer in Pedernales or San Vicente.

Pedernales *p1161*
Bus To **Santo Domingo**, every 15 mins, 3½ hrs, US$4, transfer to Quito. To **Quito** (Quitumbe) direct **Trans Vencedores**, 6 daily, 6 hrs, US$6.25. To **Chamanga**, hourly 0600-1700, 1½ hrs, US$2, change there for **Esmeraldas**, 3½ hrs, US$3.50.

Santo Domingo de los Tsáchilas *p*
Bus The bus terminal is on Av Abraham Calazacón, at the north end of town, along the city's bypass. Long distance buses do not enter the city. Taxi downtown, US$1, bus US$0.25. As it is a very important transportation centre, you can get buses going everywhere in the country. To **Quito** via Alóag US$3, 3 hrs; via San Miguel de los Bancos, 5 hrs; also **Sudamericana Taxis**,

Cocaniguas y 29 de Mayo, p 2, T275 2567, door to door shared taxi service, 6 daily 0500-1700, US$13, 3 hrs. To **Ambato** US$4, 4 hrs. To **Loja** US$13, 11 hrs. To **Guayaquil** US$5, 5 hrs. To **Huaquillas** US$10, 10 hrs, via Guayaquil. To **Esmeraldas** US$3, 3 hrs. To **Atacames**, US$4, 4hrs. To **Manta** US$6, 7 hrs. To **Bahía de Caráquez** US$5, 6 hrs. To **Pedernales** US$4, 3½ hrs.

Directory

Manta *p1160*

Banks Many banks with ATMs in the centre, Banco del Pacífico, Av 2 y C 13. **Banco de** Guayaquil, Malecón y C14. **Internet** US$1 per hr. **Language courses** Academia Sur Pacífico, Av 24 y C 15, Edif Barre, 3rd floor, T05-261 0838, www.surpacifico.k12.ec.

Bahía de Caráquez *p1160*

Banks Banco de Guayaquil, Av Bolívar y Riofrío. ATM. **Internet** US$1per hr.

San Vicente and Canoa *p1161*

Banks Banco Pichincha in San Vicente for ATM. No ATMs in Canoa. **Internet** US$1 per hr in both locations. **Language courses** Sundown, at Sundown Inn, in Canoa, on the beach, 3 km toward San Vicente, contact Juan Carlos, T09-143 6343, www.ecuadorbeach.com, US$7 per hr.

Santo Domingo de los Tsáchilas *p*

Banks Banco del Pacífico, 29 de Mayo y Av de los Tsáchilas, ATM. Many other ATMs in town. **Internet** Many in the centre, US$0.50-0.80 per hr. **Post offices** Av de los Tsáchilas y Río Baba.

Northern lowlands

A mixture of beaches, mangroves (where not destroyed for shrimp production), tropical forests and Cayapa Indian communities characterize this part of Ecuador's Pacific lowlands as they stretch to the Colombian border.

North to Atacames

North of Pedernales the coastal highway veers northeast, going slightly inland, then crosses into the province of Esmeraldas near **Chamanga** (*San José de Chamanga, Population: 4,500*), an authentic little hub with houses built on stilts on the freshwater estuary. This is a good spot from which to explore the nearby mangroves, there is one basic *residencial* and frequent buses north and south. Town is 1 km from the highway. Inland, and spanning the provincial border is the **Reserva Ecológica Mache-Chindul**, administered by the **Jatun Sacha Foundation** (www.jatunsacha.org). North of Chamanga by 31 km and 7 km from the main road along a poor side road is **Mompiche** with a lovely beach and one of Ecuador's best surfing spots. The town and surroundings are changing rapidly with the construction of an international resort complex and holiday real-estate development two kilometres south at Punta Portete. The main road continues through El Salto, the crossroads for **Muisne**, a town on an island with a selection of beachside hostels and a mangrove protection group which offers tours.

The fishing village of **Tonchigüe** is 25 km north of El Salto. South of it, a secondary road goes west and follows the shore to **Punta Galera**, along the way is the secluded beach of **Playa Escondida** (see Sleeping below). Northeast of Tonchigüe by 3 km is Playa de **Same**, with a beautiful, long, clean, grey sandy beach, safe for swimming. The accommodation here is mostly upmarket, intended for wealthy Quiteños, but it is wonderfully quiet in the low season. There is good birdwatching in the lagoon behind the beach and some of the hotels offer whale watching tours in season. Ten kilometres east of Same and 4 km west of Atacames, is **Súa**, a friendly little beach resort, set in a beautiful bay. It gets noisy on weekends and the July to September high season, but is otherwise tranquil.

Atacames ➔ *Phone code: 06. Colour map 11, A2. Population: 13,000.*

One of the main resorts on the Ecuadorean coast, Atacames, 30 km southwest of Esmeraldas, is a real 24-hour party town during the high season (July-September), at weekends and national holidays. Head instead for Súa or Playa Escondida (see above) if you want peace and quiet. Most hotels are on a peninsula between the Río Atacames and the ocean. The main park, most services and the bus stops are south of the river. Information from **Oficina Municipal de Turismo** ⓘ *on the road into town from Esmeraldas, T273 1912, Mon-Fri 0800-1230, 1330-1600, municipioatacamesturismo@andinanet.net.*

Camping on the beach is unsafe and along the beach from Atacames to Súa there is a high risk of mugging. Also the sea can be very dangerous, there is a powerful undertow and many people have been drowned. The sale of black coral jewellery has led to the destruction of much of the offshore reef. Consider the environmental implications before buying.

Esmeraldas ➔ *Phone code: 06. Colour map 11, A2. Population: 94,000.*

This eponymous provincial capital has little to offer and suffers from water shortages. Some visitors nonetheless enjoy the very relaxed swinging atmosphere. Marimba groups can be seen practising in town, enquire about schedules at the tourist office. Ceramics from La Tolita culture (see below) are found at the **Museo del Banco Central** ⓘ *Bolívar y Piedrahita, US$1, English explanations.* At the **Centro Cultural Afro** ⓘ *Malecón y J Montalvo, T06-271 0424, Mon-Fri 0800-1200, 1430-1800, free*, you can see 'La Ruta del Esclavo', an exhibit showing the harsh history of Afro-Ecuadoreans brought as slaves to Ecuador (some English explanations). Despite its wealth in natural resources (gold mining, tobacco, cacao, cattle ranching), Esmeraldas is among the poorest provinces in the country. Shrimp farm development has destroyed much mangrove and timber exports are decimating Ecuador's last Pacific rainforest. **Tourist office**: **Ministerio de Turismo** ⓘ *Bolívar y Ricaurte, Edif Cámara de Turismo, p3, T271 1370, Mon-Fri 0900-1200, 1500-1700.* Mosquitoes and malaria are a serious problem throughout Esmeraldas province, especially in the rainy season (January-May). Most *residenciales* provide mosquito nets (*toldos* or *mosquiteros*), or buy one in the market near the bus station. Take care in town, especially on arrival at the bus terminal.

North of Esmeraldas

From Esmeraldas, the coastal road goes northeast to Camarones and Río Verde, with a nice beach, from where it goes east to **Las Peñas**, once a sleepy seaside village with a nice wide beach, now a holiday resort. The completion of a paved highway from Ibarra has made Las Peñas the closest beach to any highland capital, only four hours by bus. Ibarreños pack the place on weekends and holidays. From Las Peñas, a secondary road follows the shore north to **La Tola**, 122 km from Esmeraldas (San Mateo bridge), where you can catch a launch to Limones. Here the shoreline changes from sandy beaches to mangrove swamp; the wildlife is varied and spectacular, especially the birds. The tallest mangrove trees in the world (63.7 m) are found by **Majagual** to the south. In the village of **Olmedo**, just northwest of La Tola, the Unión de Mujeres runs an ecotourism project; they have accommodation, cheap meals and tours in the area. La Tola is not a pleasant place to stay, women especially may be harassed; Olmedo is a better option, see Sleeping below. To the northeast of La Tola and on an island on the northern shore of the Río Cayapas is **La Tolita**, a small, poor village, where the culture of the same name thrived between 300 BC and AD 700. Many remains have been found here, several burial mounds remain to be explored and looters continue to take out artefacts to sell.

Limones (also known as Valdez) is the focus of traffic downriver from much of northern Esmeraldas Province, where bananas from the Río Santiago are sent to Esmeraldas for export. The Cayapa Indians live up the Río Cayapas and can sometimes be seen in Limones, especially during the crowded weekend market, but they are more frequently seen at Borbón (see below). Two shops in Limones sell the very attractive Cayapa basketry. There has been a great deal of migration from neighbouring Colombia to the Limones, Borbón and San Lorenzo areas. Smuggling, including drugs, is big business and there are occasional searches by the authorities. Accommodations are basic.

Borbón ➔ *Phone code: 06. Colour map 11, A2. Population: 8,300.*
From Las Peñas, the coastal highway runs inland to **Borbón**, upriver from La Tola, at the confluence of the Cayapas and Santiago rivers, a lively, dirty, busy and somewhat dangerous place, with a high rate of malaria. It is a centre of the timber industry that is destroying the last rainforests of the Ecuadorean coast. Ask for Papá Roncón, the King of Marimba, who, for a beer or two, will put on a one-man show. Cayapa handicrafts are sold in town and at the road junction outside town, Afro musical instruments are found at **Artesanía** on 5 de Agosto y Valdez. The local fiestas with marimba music and other Afro-Ecuadorean traditions are held the first week of September. The bakery across from the churh is good for breakfast. Sra Marcia, one block from the Malecón serves good regional food.

Upriver from Borbón are Cayapa or Chachi Indian villages and Afro-Ecuadorean communities, you will see the Chachis passing in their canoes and in their open long-houses on the shore. To visit these villages, arrangements can be made through **Hostal Brisas del Río**. Alternatively, around 0700, canoes arrive at the malecón in Borbón and return to their homes around 1000. You can arrange to go with them. For any independent travel in this area take a mosquito net, some food and means of water purification. Upriver along the Río Cayapas are the villages of **Pichiyacu** and **Santa María**, above the confluence with the Río Onzole (2 hours), **Zapallo Grande**, a friendly village with many gardens (3½ hours) and **San Miguel**, beautifully situated on a hill at the confluence of the San Miguel and Cayapas rivers (4 hours). Along this river are a couple of lodges, the ride is none to comfortable but it is an interesting trip. San Miguel is the access point to **Reserva Ecológica Cotacachi-Cayapas**, about 30 minutes upriver. The community also runs its own 1,200 ha forest reserve, abutting on the national reserve, and has an ecotourism project with accommodation and guiding service.

From Borbón, the costal road goes northeast towards **Calderón** where it meets the Ibarra-San Lorenzo road. Along the way, by the Río Santiago, are the nature reserves of **Humedales de Yalare**, accessed from **Maldonado**, and **Playa de Oro** (see below). From Calderón, the two roads run together for a few kilometres before the coastal road turns north and ends at **Mataje** on the border with Colombia. The Ibarra road continues to San Lorenzo.

San Lorenzo ➔ *Phone code: 06. Colour map 1a, A3. Population: 19,000.*
The hot, humid town of San Lorenzo stands on the Bahía del Pailón, which is characterized by a maze of canals. It is a good place to experience the Afro-Ecuadorean culture including marimba music and dances. There is a local festival August 6-10 and groups practise throughout the year; ask around. At the seaward end of the bay are several beaches without facilities, including San Pedro (1hr away) and Palma Real (1¾ hrs). On weekends canoes go to the beaches around 0700-0800 and 1400-1500, the cost is about US$3. Note that this area is close to the Colombian border and it may not be safe, enquire with the Navy (Marina). Like elsewhere in the region, the area's rich forests are threatened by logging. From San Lorenzo you can visit several natural areas; launches can be hired for excursions (see Transport below) and trips are organized by **Bosque de Paz** (page 1087). There are mangroves at **Reserva Ecológica Cayapas-Mataje** (REMACAM), which protects most of the islands in the estuary northwest of town. The **Reserva Playa de Oro** ⓘ *www.touchthejungle.org, see Sleeping below*, 10,406 ha of Chocó rainforest, rich in wildlife, along the Río Santiago. Access is from **Selva Alegre** (a couple of basic *residenciales*), off the road to Borbón.

Border with Colombia

The Río Mataje is the border with Colombia. From San Lorenzo, the port of Tumaco in Colombia can be reached by a combination of boat and land transport. Boats leave San Lorenzo on most days from 0700 for Puerto Palma (Colombia), US$10, one hour. From here *rancheras* and other vehicles run 45 minutes to the Río Mira, which you cross in a canoe, before continuing in another vehicle five minutes to Tumaco; total land transport costs about US$6. Ecuadorean immigration is located in the main police station in San Lorenzo, T278 1548, open daily 0730-1200, 1500-1830. Colombian immigration is on the road from Tumaco to the airport. Travel in this area can be dangerous; if you want to risk it, then check about current conditions in advance in San Lorenzo.

Northern lowlands listings

For Sleeping and Eating price codes and other relevant information, see Essentials, pages 38-40.

Sleeping

North to Atacames *p1167*

Mompiche

There are several economical places in the town. Camping on the beach is not safe.

B Mompiche's Land, 1 km east of town along the beach, T08-849 8399, Quito T02-242 8200, www.mompichesland.com. Includes breakfast, cold water, nice rooms and cabins with sea breeze, great views, wonderful setting.

D-E Gabeal, 300 m east of town, T09-969 6543. Lovely quiet place with ample grounds and beachfront. Bamboo construction with ocean views, balconies, small rooms and cabins, restaurant serves breakfast and lunch in season, discounts in low season. The owner can arrange visits to his 80 ha forest reserve, good for birdwatching. Recommended.

Tonchigüe to Punta Galera

C Playa Escondida, 10 km west of Tonchigüe and 6 km east of Punta Galera, T273 3106, www.playaescondida.com.ec. A charming beach hideaway set in 100 ha with 500 m beachfront stretching back to dry tropical forest. Run by Canadian Judith Barett on an ecologically sound basis. Nice rustic cabins overlooking a lovely little bay , excellent restaurant (not cheap), private showers, shared composting toilets, camping US$8 pp, good swimming and walking along the beach at low tide. Also offers volunteer opportunities. Recommended.

Same

A-B Cabañas Isla del Sol, at south end of beach, T273 3470, www.cabanasisladelsol.com. Comfortable cabins, meals available in high season, electric shower, a/c, cheaper with fan, pool, boat tours and whale watching in season.

B Casa de Amigos, by the entrance to the beach, T247 0102, www.casadeamigosecuador.com. Includes breakfast, restaurant, electric shower, a/c, nice rooms with balconies, use of kayaks and surfboards included, English and German spoken.

D La Terraza, on the beach, T247 0320, pepo@hotmail.es. Nice rooms and cabins for 3-4 with balconies, hammocks and large terrace, spacious, hot water, a/c, fan, mosquito net, some rooms have fridge, good restaurant open in season, Spanish run.

E Luna del Mar, near entrance from highway, ask around, T09-468 3945. Some rooms with bath, cold water, a/c, bunk beds, good value for Same.

Súa

D Chagra Ramos, on the beach, T273 1006. Ageing hotel with balconies overlooking the beach, restaurant, cold water, fan, parking, good service.

E Buganvillas, on the beach, T273 1008. Nice, room 10 has the best views, pool, helpful owners.

E Los Jardines, 200 m from the beach on road from highway, T273 1181. Cold water, fan, nice pool, parking, popular with families.

E Sol de Súa, across from beach toward west end of town, T273 1021, www.folklorehotelsua.com. Cold water, ceiling fan, mosquito net, simple cabins on ample grounds with palm trees, camping possible.

Atacames *p1168*

Prices rise on holiday weekends, discounts may be available in low season.

AL-A Juan Sebastián, towards the east end of the beach, T273 1049, www.hoteljuansebastian.com. Large upmarket hotel with cabins and suites , includes breakfast, restaurant, a/c, 3 pools and small spa (US$10 for non-guests), fridge, parking, popular with Quiteños.

A El Marqués, Malecón y Los Crotos, T276 0182, www.hotelelmarques.com.ec. Includes breakfast, restaurant, a/c, gym, pool (US$5 for non-guests), parking, large modern multi-storey urban hotel by the sea.

B Carluz, behind the stadium, T273 1456. Nice hotel in a good, quiet location. Comfortable suites for 4 and apartments for 6, includes breakfast, good restaurant, a/c, fan, pool, fridge, parking.

B Cielo Azul, on the beach near the stadium, T273 1813, www.hotelcieloazul.com. Restaurant, fan, pool, fridge, rooms with balconies and hammocks, comfortable and very good.

C Le' Castell, on the beach, T273 1476, www.lecastell.com.ec. Restaurant, cold water, a/c, pool, fridge, parking, rooms and family cabins on ample grounds.

C-D Tahiti, toward east end of beach, T276 0085, lucybritogarcia@yahoo.com.ar. Good restaurant, cheaper with cold water, pool, parking, large grounds.

D Der Alte Fritz, at the beach, T273 1610, www.deraltefritz-ecuador.com. Nice large bright rooms, some with balconies, can be noisy, restaurant serving German and international food, cold water, fan, German and English spoken.

E Jarfi, 1 block from the beach by the footbridge, T273 1089, www.hoteljarfi.com.ec. Hot water, pool, simple bungalows, good value.

E Las Vegas, Julio Estupiñán y Malecón del Río, T273 1039. Older place, electric shower, pool, parking, simple rooms, patio with hammocks.

Esmeraldas *p1169*

Hotels in the centre are poor; better to stay in the outskirts.

B Apart Hotel Esmeraldas, Libertad 407 y Ramón Tello, T272 8700, www.aparthotelesmeraldas.net. Includes breakfast, good restaurant, casino, a/c, Wi-Fi, fridge, parking, excellent quality.

D Galeón, Piedrahita 330 y Olmedo, T272 3820. Cold water, a/c, cheaper with fan, good.

E Andrés, Sucre 812 y Piedrahita, T272 5883. Simple hostel in a multi-storey building, cold water, fan.

E Zulema 2, Malecón y Rocafuerte. Modern concrete hostel with large rooms, cold water, fan, parking.

North of Esmeraldas *p1168*

Las Peñas

D Mikey, by the beach, T278 6031. Cabins with kitchenettes, private bath, hot water, pool.

Olmedo

D Casa del Manglar, a 20-min walk or short boat ride from La Tola, T278 6126 (Catalina Montes or her son Edwin). A wood cabin with porch by the shore. Dormitory for 15 people, meals available, shared bath, mosquito nets, quiet and pleasant. Take drinking water or means of purification. Organizes tours to mangroves, La Tolita and other sights.

Limones

E Colón, next to the church at the main park, T278 9311. A good hostel for where it is, with bath, cold water, fan.

Borbón *p1169*

E Brisas del Río Santiago, Malecón y 23 de Noviembre, T278 6211. Basic concrete hostel with good air circulation, private bath, cold water, fan, mosquito net, meeting point for travellers going upriver. Owner Sr Betancourt can arrange canoes for excursions.

E Castillo, 5 de Agosto, near Trans Esmeraldas, T278 6613. With bath, cold water, fan, parking.

San Miguel

In villages like **Pichiyacu** (ethnic Chachi) and **Santa María** (Afro-Ecuadorean), local families can provide accommodation.

A Eco-Lodge San Miguel, above the village of San Miguel, contact Fundación Verde Milenio, Quito, T02-290 6192, www.verdemilenio.org. Community-run lodge with lovely views, 7 bedrooms, shared bath. Price includes transport from Borbón, 3 meals and excursion to the forest. The community also manages the basic ranger's house next door which might be a more economical option. Advance booking advised.

San Lorenzo *p1169*
Expect to be mobbed by children wanting a tip to show you to a hotel or restaurant. Also take insect repellent.
A Playa de Oro, on the Río Santiago, upriver from Borbón, contact Ramiro Buitrón at Hotel Valle del Amanecer in Otavalo, T06-292 0990, www.touchthejungle.org.
Basic cabins with shared bath, includes 3 meals and guided excursion.
B Tunda Loma, Km 17 on the road to Ibarra (taxi from San Lorenzo US$5), T278 0367. Beautifully located on a hill overlooking the Río Tululbí. Wood cabins, includes breakfast, restaurant, warm water, fan, organizes tubing trips on the river and hikes in the forest.
E Pampa de Oro, C 26 de Agosto y Tácito Ortiz, T278 0214. Adequate family run hotel, with bath, cold water, fan, mosquito net.
E San Carlos, C Imbabura near the train station, T278 0284. Simple concrete hotel, cheaper with shared bath, cold water, fan, mosquito nets.

Eating

North to Atacames *p1167*
Mompiche
ΨΨ-Ψ Pizza Luz, on the beach between town and Hotel Gabeal, opens around 1830. Excellent pizza prepared fresh on the spot, bar-stool seating, popular, worth looking and waiting for.
Ψ Comedor Margarita, on main street, 2 blocks from the beach, daily from 0730. Basic *comedor* serving tasty local fare, mostly fish and seafood.

Same
ΨΨΨ Seaflower, by the beach at the entrance road. Excellent international food.

Súa
ΨΨ-Ψ Kikes, on the Malecón. à la carte seafood, sometimes also serves set meals, could be friendlier.
Ψ Churuco's, diagonally across from the park, 100 m from the beach, Wed-Sun 0900-2100. Simple *comedor* serving good set meals and local snacks, generous portions, good value.

Atacames *p1168*
The beach is packed with bars and restaurants offering seafood, too many to list.
ΨΨ Da Giulio, on the Malecón, weekdays 1700-2300, weekends from 1100.
Spanish & Italian cuisine, good pasta.
ΨΨ-Ψ El Tiburón, on the Malecón. Good seafood.
ΨΨ-Ψ Le Cocotier, on the Malecón. Very good pizza.
Ψ Sabor Manabita, Montalvo y Malecón del Río, near the Trans Esmeraldas bus station, daily 0600-2100. Variety of set meals and à la carte.

Esmeraldas *p1169*
There are restaurants and bars by Las Palmas beach offering regional specialties.
ΨΨ Chifa Asiático, Cañizares y Bolívar.
Chinese and seafood, a/c, excellent.
ΨΨ-Ψ El Manglar, Quito y Olmedo.
Good *comida esmeraldeña*.
Ψ Tapao.con, 6 de Diciembre 1717 y Piedrahita. A popular place for typical dishes such as *tapado*, *encocado* and *ceviche*.

San Lorenzo *p1169*
Ψ El Chocó, C Imbabura. Good fish and local specialties. Also economical set lunches and the best *batido de borojó* (milkshake) in town.

Bars and clubs

Esmeraldas *p1169*
Expresiones, Sucre y Manabí, opposite the cathedral. Bar and gallery displaying paintings by local artists. By the beach in Las Palmas there are a great variety of bars blasting salsa, merengue and regaetón.

Transport

North to Atacames *p1167*
Bus Hourly from **Chamanga** to **Esmeraldas**, US$3.50, 3½ hrs, and to **Pedernales**, US$2, 1½ hrs. **Mompiche** to/from **Esmeraldas**, 5 a day, US$3, 3½ hrs, the last one from Esmeraldas about 1630. To **Playa Escondida**: take a ranchera or bus from Esmeraldas or Atacames for Punta Galera or Cabo San Francisco, 5 a day, US$2, 2 hrs. A taxi from Atacames costs US$12 and a pick-up from Tonchigüe US$5. To **Súa** and **Same**: Buses every 30 mins to and from **Atacames**, 15 mins, US$0.35. Make sure it drops you at Same and not at Club Casablanca.

Atacames *p1168*

Bus To **Esmeraldas**, every 15 mins, US$0.80, 1 hr. To **Guayaquil**, US$9, 8 hrs, **Trans Esmeraldas** at 0830 and 2245. To **Quito**, various companies, about 10 daily, US$8, 7 hrs, **Trans Esmeraldas** has service from its own terminal in La Mariscal, Quitumbe and Carcelén. To **Pedernales**, **Coop G Zambrano**, 4 daily, $4, 4 hrs or change in Chamanga.

Esmeraldas *p1169*

Air Gen Rivadeneira Airport is near the town of Tachina, on the east shore of the Río Esmeraldas, along the coastal road heading north. A taxi to the city centre (30 km) costs US$6, buses to the Terminal Terrestre from the road outside the airport pass about every 30 mins. If headed north towards San Lorenzo, you can catch a bus outside the airport. **TAME** (Bolívar y 9 de Octubre, T272 6863) , 1-2 daily flights to **Quito**, US$79, continuing to to Cali (Colombia) Mon, Wed, Fri, US$123; also 3 a week to **Guayaquil**, US$106.

Bus **Trans-Esmeraldas** (10 de Agosto at Parque Central, recommended) and **Panamericana** (Colón y Salinas) have *servicio directo* or *ejecutivo* to Quito and Guayaquil, a better choice as they are faster buses and don't stop for passengers; they also run to their own terminals in La Mariscal in Quito. Frequent service to **Quito** via Santo Domingo or via Calacalí, US$7, 6 hrs; ask which terminal they go to before purchasing ticket. To **Ibarra**, 9 hrs, US$10, via Borbón. To **Santo Domingo**, US$3, 3 hrs. To **Ambato**, 6 a day, US$8, 8 hrs. To **Guayaquil**, hourly, US$8, *directo*, 8 hrs. To **Bahía de Caráquez**, via Santo Domingo de los Tsáchilas, US$8, 9 hrs. To **Manta**, US$8, 10 hrs. **La Costeñita** and **El Pacífico**, both on Malecón, to/ from **La Tola** 8 daily, US$3.75, 3 hrs. To **Borbón**, frequent service, US$3.50, 3 hrs. To **San Lorenzo**, 8 daily, US$4.50, 4 hrs. To **Súa**, **Same** and **Atacames**, every 15 mins from 0630-2030, to Atacames US$0.80, 1 hr. To **Chamanga**, hourly 0500-1900, US$3.50, 3½ hrs, change here for points south.

North of Esmeraldas *p1168*

Ferry There are launches between **La Tola** and **Limones** which connect with the buses arriving from Esmeraldas, US$3, 1 hr, and 3 daily Limones- **San Lorenzo**, 2 hrs US$3. You can also hire a launch to **Borbón**, a fascinating trip through mangrove islands, passing hunting pelicans, approximately US$10 per hr.

Borbón *p1169*

Bus To/from **Esmeraldas**: frequent service, US$3.50, 3 hrs. To San Lorenzo, US$1.60, 1 hr.

Ferry 4 launches a day run to communities upriver, 1030-1100. Check how far each one is going as only one goes as far as **San Miguel**, US$8, 4 hrs.

San Lorenzo *p1169*

Bus Buses leave from the train station or environs. To **Ibarra**, 10 daily, 4 hrs, US$4. To **Esmeraldas**, via Borbón, 8 daily, US$4.50, 4 hrs.

Ferry Two companies that offer launch service are **Coopseturi**, T/F278 0161; and **Costeñita**, both near the pier. All services are subject to change and cancellation. To **Limones**, 3 daily, 2 hrs, US$3. To **La Tola**, US$6, 4 hrs. To **Palma Real**, for beaches, 2 daily, US$3, 2 hrs. To hire a boat for 5 passengers costs US$20 per hr.

Directory

Atacames *p1168*

Banks **Banco Pichincha**, Espejo y Calderón by the plaza, for ATM. There are a few other stand-alone ATMs in town and along the beach. **Internet** US$1 per hr.

Esmeraldas *p1169*

Banks For ATMs, several banks on C Bolívar in the centre. **Internet** Many in town.

San Lorenzo *p1169*

Banks **Banco Pichincha**, C Ponce y Garcés, has the only ATM in town; bring some cash.

The Oriente

East of the Andes the hills fall away to tropical lowlands. Some of this beautiful wilderness remains unspoiled and sparsely populated, with indigenous settlements along the tributaries of the Amazon. Large tracts of jungle are under threat, however: colonists are clearing many areas for agriculture, while others are laid waste by petroleum development. The Ecuadorean jungle, especially the Northern Oriente, has the advantage of being relatively accessible and tourist infrastructure here is well developed. The eastern foothills of the Andes, where the jungle begins, offer the easiest access and a good introduction to the rainforest for those with limited time or money. Further east lie the remaining large tracts of primary rainforest, teeming with life, which can be visited from several excellent (and generally expensive) jungle lodges. Southern Oriente is as yet less developed for tourism, it offers good opportunities off the beaten path but is threatened by large mining projects.

Ins and outs

Getting there There are scheduled commercial flights from Quito to Lago Agrio, Coca and Macas. From Quito, Macas and Shell, light aircraft can be chartered to any jungle village with a landing strip. Much of western Oriente is also accessible by roads which wind their way down from the highlands. Quito, via Baeza, to Lago Agrio and Coca, Baños to Puyo, and Loja to Zamora are fully paved, as is most of the lowland road from Lago Agrio all the way south to Zamora. Other access roads to Oriente are: Tulcán to Lago Agrio via Lumbaqui (parts run along the Colombian border and public safety is a concern); Riobamba to Macas; Cuenca to Méndez, Plan de Milagro or Gualaquiza, via Guarumales, Paute or Sígsig, respectively. Some roads are narrow and tortuous and subject to landslides in the rainy season, but all have regular bus service and all can be attempted in a jeep or in an ordinary car with good ground clearance. Deeper into the rainforest, motorized canoes provide the only alternative to air travel.

Jungle tours These fall into four basic types: **lodges; guided tours, indigenous ecotourism** and **river cruises**. When staying at a jungle lodge (normally a *cabaña* complex located in a natural setting), you will need to take a torch (flashlight), insect repellent, protection against the sun and a rain poncho that will keep you dry when walking and when sitting in a canoe. See also Lodges on the lower Napo, page 1178. **Guided tours** of varying length are offered by tour operators and independent guides. These should, in principle, be licensed by the Ecuadorean **Ministerio de Turismo**. Tour operators and guides are mainly concentrated in Quito, Baños, Puyo, Tena, Misahuallí, Coca, and, to a lesser extent, Macas and Zamora.

A number of indigenous communities and families offer **ecotourism** programmes in their territories. These are either community- controlled and operated, or organized as joint ventures between the indigenous community or family and a non-indigenous partner. These programmes usually involve guides who are licensed as *guías nativos* with the right to guide within their communities. You should be prepared to be more self-sufficient on such a trip than on a visit to a jungle lodge or a tour with a high-end operator. Take a light sleeping bag, rain jacket, trousers (not only shorts), long-sleeve shirt for mosquitoes, binoculars, torch, insect repellent, sunscreen and hat, water-purifying tablets, and a first aid kit. Wrap everything in several plastic bags to keep it dry. Most lodges provide rubber boots, indepedent guides may not.

River cruises offer a better appreciation of the grandeur of Amazonia, but less intimate contact with life in the rainforest. Passengers sleep and take their meals onboard comfortable river boats, stopping on route to visit local communities and make excursions into the jungle.

Though it may seem attractive from a financial point of view, jungle travel without a guide is not recommended. Some native groups prohibit the entry of outsiders to their territory, navigation in the jungle is difficult, and there are a variety of dangerous animals. Additionally, public safety is a concern north of the Río Napo, especially along the Colombian border. For your own safety as well as to be a responsible tourist, the jungle is not a place to wander off on your own.

Health and safety A yellow fever vaccination is required. Anti-malarial tablets are recommended, as is an effective insect repellent. There are police and military checkpoints in the Oriente, so always have your passport handy. Northern Oriente is affected by ongoing armed conflict in neighbouring Colombia. Caution is particularly required in the province of Sucumbíos. Always enquire about public safety before visiting any remote sites north of the Río Napo, and avoid all areas adjacent to the Colombian border.

Northern Oriente

Much of the Northern Oriente is taken up by the Parque Nacional Yasuní, the Cuyabeno Wildlife Reserve and most of the Cayambe-Coca Ecological Reserve. The main towns for access are Baeza, Lago Agrio and Coca.

Quito to the Oriente

From Quito to Baeza, a paved road goes via the Gaumaní pass (4,064 m). It crosses the Eastern Cordillera just north of **Volcán Antisana** (5,705 m), and then descends via the small village of **Papallacta** (hotsprings, see page 1067) to the old mission settlement of Baeza. The trip between the pass and Baeza has beautiful views of Antisana (clouds permitting), high waterfalls, *páramo*, cloud forest and a lake contained by an old lava flow. **Antisana** is a very difficult climb; experience is essential.

Baeza→ *Phone code: 06 Colour map 11, A4 Population: 2,400, Altitude 1,900 m.*

The mountainous landscape and high rainfall have created spectacular waterfalls and dense vegetation. Orchids and bromeliads abound. Baeza, in the beautiful Quijos valley, is about 1 km from the main junction of roads from Lago Agrio and Tena. The town itself is divided in two parts: a faded but pleasant **Baeza Colonial** (Old Baeza) and **Baeza Nueva** (New Baeza), where most shops and services are located. There are hiking trails in the area which generally can be done without a guide.

Beyond Baeza

From Baeza a road heads south to Tena , with a branch going east via Loreto to Coca, all paved. Another paved road goes northeast from Baeza to Lago Agrio, following the Río Quijos past the villages of **Borja** (8 km from Baeza, very good *comedor* Doña Cleo along the highway) and **El Chaco** (12 km further, simple accommodation and kayaking at **E La Guarida del Coyote**) to the slopes of the active volcano **Reventador**, 3,560 m. Check www.igepn.edu.ec and inquire locally about volcanic activity before trekking here; simple **D Hostería El Reventador** at the bridge over the Río Reventador; **Ecuador Journeys** offers tours, see page 1058. Half a kilometer south of the bridge is signed access to the impressive 145-m **San Rafael Falls** ⓘ *part of Reserva Ecológica Cayambe-Coca, entry US$10*, believed to be the highest in Ecuador. It is a pleasant 1-hour round trip hike through cloud forest to *miradores* with stunning views of the thundering cascade. A trail to the bottom of the falls is steep and slippery. Many birds can be spotted along the trail, including cock-of-the-rock, also monkeys and coatimundis. In 2010 the falls could still be visited but the former ranger station had been converted to headquarters of a hydro-electric project (www.cocasinclair.com) which would use up to 70% of the water in the Río Quijos, leaving only 30% to go over the falls – the death knell for Ecuador's most beautiful cascade.

Lago Agrio → *Phone code: 06 Colour map 11, A5 Population: 56,000, Altitude 300 m.*
The capital of Sucumbíos is an old oil town with close ties to neighbouring Colombia, and among the places in Ecuador which has been most affected by conflict there. The name comes from Sour Lake, the US headquarters of Texaco, the first oil company to exploit the Ecuadorean Amazon in the 1970s. It is also called Nueva Loja or just 'Lago'. If taking a Cuyabeno tour from Lago Agrio, it is worth leaving Quito a day or two early, stopping en route at Papallacta, Baeza or San Rafael falls. Lago Agrio is not a safe place, return to your hotel by 2000. Alternatively you can overnight at more tranquil **Cascales** (small, clean, friendly **E Paraíso Dorado**), 35 minutes before Lago Agrio, and still meet your tour party in Lago the following morning. There is a border crossing to Colombia north of Lago Agrio but it is also unsafe. As well as violence, the area is threatened by the spraying of herbicides to destroy coca plantations across the border. Seek local advice from the **Ministerio de Turismo** ⓘ *Narváez y Añazco, upstairs, T06-283 2488, Mon-Fri 0830-1300, 1400-1800.*

Cuyabeno Wildlife Reserve → *entrance fee US$20.*
This large tract of rainforest, covering 602,000 ha, is located about 100 km east of Lago Agrio along the Río Cuyabeno, which eventually drains into the Aguarico. In the reserve are many lagoons and a great variety of wildlife, including river dolphins, tapirs, capybaras, five species of caiman, ocelots, 15 species of monkey and over 500 species of birds. This is among the best places in Ecuador to see jungle animals. The reserve is very popular with visitors and has not had safety problems in recent years, but best inquire before booking a tour. Access is either by road from Lago Agrio, or by river along the Río Aguarico. Within the reserve, transport is mainly by canoe. In order to see as many animals as possible and minimally impact their habitat, seek out a small tour group which scrupulously adheres to responsible tourism practices. Most Cuyabeno tours are booked through agencies in Quito or other popular tourist destinations.

Coca → *Phone code: 06. Colour map 11, A5. Population: 31,000. Altitude 250 m.*
Officially named **Puerto Francisco de Orellana**, Coca is a hot, noisy, bustling oil town at the junction of the Ríos Payamino and Napo. It is the capital of the province of Orellana and is a launch pad from where to visit more exciting jungle parts. The view over the water is nice, and the riverfront **Malecón** can be a pleasant place to spend time around sunset; various native groups have craft shops here. Hotel and restaurant provision is adequate, but electricity, water and, ironically for an oil-producing centre, petrol supplies are erratic. Information from **iTur** ⓘ *Chimborazo y Amazonas, by the Malecón, T288 0532, Mon-Sat 0800-1200, 1400-1800, www.orellanaturistica.gov.ec* and the **Ministerio de Turismo** ⓘ *Cuenca y Quito, upstairs, T06-288 1583, Mon-Fri 0830-1700.*

Jungle tours from Coca Coca provides access to **Parque Nacional Yasuní** and the **Reserva Huaorani**. Tours into the park and reserve really need a minimum of five days but shorter visits of 3-4 days are worthwhile along the Río Napo, where the lodges are concentrated. Wildlife in this area is under threat: insist that guides and fellow tourists take all litter back and ban all hunting and shooting; it really makes a difference. The majority of tours out of Coca are booked through agencies in Quito and other tourist centres but there are a few local operators. Quality varies so try to get a personal recommendation, prices are around US$60-70 per person per day. **Note** If a guide offers a tour to visit the Huaorani, ask to see his/her permission to do so, which should be issued by the Huaorani organization *NAWE*.

The paved road to Coca via Loreto passes through **Wawa Sumaco**, where a rough road heads north to **Sumaco National Park**; 7 km along it is **AL Wildsumaco** ⓘ *www.wildsumaco.com, full board*, a comfortable birdwatching lodge with excellent trails and many rare species. Just beyond is the village of Pacto Sumaco from where a trail runs through the park to the *páramo*-clad summit of **Volcan Sumaco** (3732 m), 6-7 days round-trip. Local guides may be hired, there are 3 nice shelters along the route and a basic community-run hostel in the village (try T06-287 0187 but not always staffed).

Coca to Nuevo Rocafuerte and Iquitos

Pañacocha is halfway between Coca and Nuevo Rocafuerte, near a magnificent lagoon. Here is the **Amazon Dolphin Lodge** (see Lodges on the Río Napo) and Coca agencies and guides also run tours to the area (see Tour operators). There are basic places to stay and eat in Pañacocha village.

Following the Río Napo to Peru is rough, adventurous and requires plenty of patience. There are two options: by far the least expensive is to take a motorized canoe from Coca to **Nuevo Rocafuerte** on the border. This tranquil riverside town has simple hotels, eateries, a phone office and shops. It can be a base for exploring the southeastern section of Parque Nacional Yasuní; ask around for a local guide. Ecuadorean immigration for exit stamps is next to the navy dock; if the officer is not in, enquire in town. Peruvian entry stamps are given in Pantoja, where there is a decent municipal *hospedaje*, **F Napuruna**. Shopkeepers in Nuevo Rocafuerte and Pantoja change money at poor rates. In addition to immigration, you may have to register with the navy on either side of the border so have your passport at hand. See Transport, page 1181, for boat services Coca-Nuevo Rocafuerte and onward to Pantoja and Iquitos. See also the Peru chapter, under Iquitos, Transport.

The second option for river travel to Iquitos is to take a tour with a Coca agency, taking-in various attractions on route, and continuing to Iquitos or closer Peruvian ports from which you can catch onward public river transport. Ask carefully about these tours as they may involve many hours sitting in small, cramped craft; confirm all details in advance.

Northern Oriente listings

For Sleeping and Eating price codes and other relevant information, see Essentials, pages 38-40.

Sleeping

Baeza *p1175*

E Bambús, Av de los Quijos, at the east end of the new town, T232 0003. Well suited to families, hot water, indoor pool, parking, busy and noisy at weekends and holidays.

E Gina, Jumandy y Batallón Chimborazo, just off the highway in the old town, T232 0471. Hot water, parking, pleasant, good value.

E La Casa de Rodrigo, in the old town, T232 0467, rodrigobaeza@andinanet.net. Modern and comfortable, hot water, friendly owner offers rafting trips, kayak rentals and birdwatching.

E-F Samay, Av de los Quijos, in the new town, T232 0170. Cheaper with shared bath, electric shower, older place but friendly and adequate, simple rooms, good value.

Around Baeza

L Cabañas San Isidro, near Cosanga, 19 km south of Baeza, T02-290 9027 (Quito), www.cabanasanisidro.com. A 1,200-ha private nature reserve with rich bird life, comfortable accommodation and warm hospitality. Includes three excellent meals, reservations required. Recommended.

D Hostería El Reventador, on main highway next to bridge over the Río Reventador, turismovolcanreventador@yahoo.com. Meals on request, hot water, pool, simple rooms, busy at weekends, mediocre service but well located for San Rafael Falls and Volcán Reventador.

Lago Agrio *p1176*

Virtually everything can be found on the main street, Av Quito.

A Gran Hotel de Lago, Km 1½ Vía Quito, T283 2415. Includes breakfast, restaurant, a/c, pool, Wi-Fi, parking, cabins with nice gardens, quiet. Recommended.

B Arazá, Quito 536 y Narváez, T283 1287, www.hotel-araza.com. Quiet location away from centre. Buffet breakfast, restaurant, a/c, pool (US$5 for non-residents), Wi-Fi, fridge, parking, comfortable, nice. Recommended.

C El Cofán, 12 de Febrero 3915 y Quito, T283 0526. Includes breakfast, restaurant, a/c, internet, fridge, parking, older place but well maintained.

C-D Lago Imperial, Colombia y Quito, T283 0453, hotellagoimperial@hotmail.com. A/c, cheaper with fan and cold water, Wi-Fi, central location, good value.
D-E Gran Colombia, Quito y Pasaje Gonzanamá, T283 1032. Good restaurant, hot water, a/c, cheaper with fan and cold water, more expensive rooms also have fridge, parking, centrally located, modern and good value.
E Americano, Quito 224 y Colombia, T283 0555. Cold water, a/c, cheaper with fan.
E-F Casa Blanca, Quito 228 y Colombia, T283 0181. Electric shower, fan, nice bright rooms.

Cascales

E Paraíso Dorado, on the highway at the east end of town, T09-471 6998. A small place, meals on request, cold water, mosquito nets, very helpful.

Coca *p1176*

A Gran Hotel del Coca, Camilo del Torrano y Esmeraldas, away from centre, T288 2666, granhoteldelcoca@hotmail.com. Modern upmarket hotel with little character, buffet breakfast, restaurant, a/c, Wi-Fi, ample rooms, suites have Jacuzzi and fridge.
B Heliconias, Cuenca y Amazonas, T288 2010, heliconiaslady@yahoo.com. Includes breakfast, upmarket restaurant, pool (US$5 for non-guests), Wi-Fi, spotless. Recommended.
B-C El Auca, Napo y García Moreno, T288 0600, helauca@ecuanex.net.ec. Restaurant, disco on weekends, a/c, cheaper with fan, Wi-Fi, parking, a variety of different rooms and mini-suites. Comfortable, nice garden with hammocks, English spoken. Popular and centrally located but can get noisy.
C La Misión, by riverfront 100 m downriver from the bridge, T288 0260, www.hotelamision.com. A larger hotel, restaurant and disco, a/c and fridge, pool (US$2 for non-guests), Wi-Fi, parking, a bit faded but still adequate.
C Puerto Orellana, Av Alejandro Labaka, at the entrance to town from Lago Agrio, T288 0129, jesseniabrito@andinanet.net. Includes breakfast, a/c and fridge, parking, out of the way but modern and very nice. Popular, book in advance.
C-D Amazonas, 12 de Febrero y Espejo, T288 0444, hosteriacoca@hotmail.com. Nice quiet setting by the river, away from centre, restaurant, electric shower, a/c, Wi-Fi, parking.
C-D Río Napo, Bolívar entre Napo y Quito, T288 0872. A/c, cheaper with fan, small modern rooms.
D Omaguas, Cuenca y Quito, T288 2436, h_omaguas@hotmail.com. Restaurant, hot water, a/c, parking, small modern rooms.
D-E San Fermín, Bolívar Y Quito, T288 0802, www.wildlifeamazon.com. Hot water, a/c (cheaper with fan, shared bath and cold water), Wi-Fi, ample parking, variety of different rooms, nicely furnished, popular and busy, good value, owner organizes tours. Recommended.
E Coca, Inés Arango entre Cuenca y Rocafuerte, T288 2088. Cold water, fan, parking for small vehicle, basic but OK for the price.

Jungle tours from Coca *p1176*

Lodges on the lower Napo

All Napo lodges count travel days as part of their package, which means that a '3-day tour' spends only 1 day actually in the forest. Most lodges have fixed departure days from Coca (eg Mon and Fri) and it is very expensive to get a special departure on another day.
Amazon Dolphin Lodge, Quito office: Amazonas N24-236 y Colón, T02-250 4037, www.amazondolphinlodge.com. Opened in 2009 on Laguna de Pañacocha, 4½ hours downriver from Coca. Special wildlife here includes Amazon river dolphins and giant river otters as well as over 500 species of birds. Cabins with private bath, US$450-600 for 4 days.
Napo Wildlife Center, Quito office: Pje Yaupi N31-90 y Mariana de Jesús, T02-252 8261, USA T1-866-750-0830, UK T0-800-032-5771, www.ecoecuador.org. Operated by and for the local Añangu community, 2½ hrs downstream from Coca. This area of hilly forest is rather different from the low flat forest of some other lodges, and the diversity is slightly higher. There are big caimans and good mammals, including giant otters, and the birdwatching is excellent with 2 parrot clay-licks and a 35-m canopy tower. US$720 for 4 days. Recommended.
La Selva, Quito office: Mariana de Jesús E7-211 y La Pradera, T02-255 0995, www.laselvajunglelodge.com. An upmarket lodge, 2½ hrs downstream from Coca on a picturesque lake. Surrounded by excellent forest, especially on the far side of Mandicocha. Bird and animal life is exceptionally diverse. Many species of monkey are seen regularly. A total of 580 bird species

have been found, one of the highest totals in the world for a single elevation. Comfortable cabins and excellent meals. High standards, most guides are biologists. 45-m canopy tower. US$717 for 4 days.

Sacha, Quito office: Julio Zaldumbide 397 y Valladolid, T02-256 6090, www.sachalodge.com. An upmarket lodge 2½ hrs downstream from Coca. Very comfortable cabins, excellent meals. The bird list is outstanding; the local bird expert, Oscar Tapuy (Coca T06-2881486), can be requested in advance. Canopy tower and 275-m canopy walkway. Several species of monkey are commonly seen. Nearby river islands provide access to a distinct habitat. US$690 for 4 days.

Sani, Quito office: Roca E4-49 y Amazonas, T02-255 8881, www.sanilodge.com. All proceeds go to the Sani Isla community, who run the lodge with the help of outside experts. It is located on a remote lagoon which has 4- to 5-m-long black caiman. This area is rich in wildlife and birds, including many species such as the scarlet macaw which have disappeared from most other Napo area lodges. There is good accommodation and a 35-m canopy tower. An effort has been made to make the lodge accessible to people who have difficulty walking; the lodge can be reached by canoe (total 3½ hrs from Coca) without a walk. US$510 for 4 days. Good value, recommended.

Yachana, Quito office: Málaga N24-739 y Valladolid, T02-252 3777, www.yachana.com. Located in the village of Mondaña, 2½ upstream from Coca. Proceeds go toward supporting community development projects. US$400-630 for 4 days depending on type of accommodation. Recommended.

Lodges in the Reserva Huaorani *p1176*

Bataburo, Quito office: **Kempery Tours**, see page 1059. A lodge in Huaorani territory near Parque Nacional Yasuní, on the Río Tiguino, a 3-6 hr canoe ride from the end of the Vía Auca out of Coca. Some cabins have private baths and there are shared showers. Guides are mostly local. The birds here have been little studied but macaws and other large species are present. The mammal population also appears to be quite good. US$330 for 4 days.

Huaorani Ecolodge, operated by **Tropic Journeys in Nature** in Quito (see page 1061), a joint venture with several Huaorani communities who staff the lodge; winner of sustainable tourism awards. Small (10 guests), no frills accommodation, solar lighting, a spontaneous, rewarding and at times challenging experience. Includes much community involvement, rainforest hikes, conservation area, kayaks, dug out canoe trips. Tours arrive by small plane from Shell and leave after non-motorized river journeys on the Vía Auca to Coca. US$850 for 4 days includes land and air transport from Quito.

Otobo's Amazon Safari, www.rainforest camping.com. 8 day/7 night camping expeditions in Huaorani territory, access by flight from Shell to Bameno (US$1,540 pp), or by road from Coca then 2-day motorized canoe journey on the Ríos Shiripuno and Cononaco (US$1,050 pp) All meals and guiding included.

Shiripuno, Quito T02-227 1094, www.shiripuno lodge.com. A lodge with capacity for 20 people, very good location on the Río Shiripuno, a 4-hr canoe ride downriver from the Vía Auca. Cabins have private bath. The surrounding area has seen relatively little human impact to date. US$360 for 4 days.

Coca to Nuevo Rocafuerte and Iquitos *p1177*

E Casa Blanca, Malecón y Nicolas Torres, T238 2184. Cold water, fan, nice simple place, welcoming, refurbished in 2009.

A couple of other basic places to stay in town.

Eating

Baeza *p1175*

El Viejo, east end of Av de los Quijos, the road to Tena in the new town, daily 0700-2100. Good set meals and à la carte.

Gina, Batallón Chimborazo, just off the highway in the old town, daily 0730-2200. Trout is the speciality, popular.

Lago Agrio *p1176*

There are good restaurants at the larger hotels (see above); also many cheap *comedores*.

Ecuatorianísimo, 18 de Noviembre y Guayaquil, Mon-Sat 0930-1800. Ecuadorian specialties, à la carte only, clean.

Coca *p1176*

Denny's, Alejandro Labaka by the airport, Mon-Sat 0800-2000, Sun 1200-1400. Steaks, ribs and other US-style meals and drinks, friendly.

🍴🍴 **Las Tablitas**, 9 de Octubre y Espejo, Mon-Sat 1700-2300. Grill.

🍴🍴-🍴 **Pizza Choza**, Rocafuerte entre Napo y Quito, daily 1800-2200. Good pizza, friendly owner, English spoken.

🍴 **La Casa del Maito**, Espejo entre Quito y Napo, daily 0700-1700. *Maitos* in AM, and other local specialties.

🍴 **Media Noche**, Napo y Rocafuerte (no sign), daily 1700-2400. Chicken dishes, large portions, popular and busy.

🍴 **Ocaso**, Eloy Alfaro entre Napo y Amazonas, Mon-Sat 0600-2100, Sun 0600-1400. Set meals and à la carte, popular with locals.

Activities and tours

Cuyabeno Wildlife Reserve *p1176*

To visit Cuyabeno it is best to shop around Quito Tour operators (see page 1057), including the following. Prices do not include US$20 park fee nor transport to Lago Agrio.

Dracaena, page 1058. US$200 for 4 days. Recommended.

Ecuador Verde País, Calama E6-19 y Reina Victoria, T02-222 0614, www.cabanasjamu.com. Run *Jamu Lodge*, good service, US$190-225 for 4 days.

Galasam, page 1059. US$340 for 4 days.

Neotropic Turis, Pinto E4-360, Quito, T02-252 1212, www.neotropicturis.com. Operate the *Cuyabeno Lodge* by the Laguna Grande, English speaking guides, US$220-350 for 4 nights. Recommended.

Coca *p1176*

Jungle tours from Coca

See also page 1057.

Luis Duarte, at **Casa del Maito** (see Eating above), T06-288 2285, cocaselva@hotmail.com.

Ecu-Astonishing, near **Hotel La Missión**, 06-288 0251, jjarrin1@msn.com. Julio Jarrín offers tours to his own cabins near Pañacocha.

Wildlife Amazon, Robert Vaca at **Hotel San Fermín** (see Sleeping above), T06-288 0802, www.wildlifeamazon.com. Jungle tours and trips to Iquitos.

Sachayacu Explorer, in Píllaro near Baños (see page 1111), T03-287 3292, www.rio-amazonas.banios.com. Although not based in Coca, experienced jungle guide Juan Medina offers recommended jungle tours and trips to Iquitos. Advance arrangements required.

River cruises on the lower Río Napo

Manatee, Quito office: **Advantage Travel**, El Telégrafo E10-63 y Juan de Alacántara, T02-246 2871, www.manateeamazonexplorer.com. This 30-passenger vessel sails between Coca and Pañacocha. US$601 for 4 days. First-class guides, excellent food, en suite cabins.

Coca to Nuevo Rocafuerte and Iquitos *p1177*

Juan Carlos Cuenca, Nuevo Rocafuerte, T06-238 2257, is a native guide who offers tours to Parque Nacional Yasuní, US$50-60 per day plus park fees.

Transport

Baeza *p1175*

Bus Buses to and from**Tena** pass right through town. If arriving on a **Lago Agrio** bus, get off at the crossroads (La "Y") and walk or take a pick-up for US$0.25. From **Quito**, 5 daily (3 on Sun), with**Trans Quijos**, T02-295 0842, from Don Bosco y Av Pichincha (under the overpass at La Marín, an unsafe area), US$3, 2½ hrs.

Lago Agrio *p1176*

Air Airport is 5 km southeast of the centre. **TAME** (Orellana y 9 de Octubre, T283 0133) and **VIP** (at the airport, T283 0333) to **Quito**, US$70. Book 1-2 days in advance. If there is no space available to **Lago Agrio** then you can fly to **Coca** instead, from where it is only 2 hrs by bus on a good road.

Bus *Terminal terrestre* is north of town, but buses for Coca leave from the market area on Orellana, 3 blocks south of Av Quito. To **Quito** (2 routes: through Cascales, and, slightly longer via Coca and Loreto), US$8, 7-8 hrs. **Baeza** 5 hrs. **Coca**, US$3, 2 hrs. **Tena**, US$7, 8 hrs.

Coca *p1176*

Air Flights to **Quito** with **Icaro** (office in *Hotel La Misión*, T288 2767), **TAME** (Napo y Rocafuerte, T288 1078) and **VIP** (at the airport T288 1742), US$68, several daily (fewer on weekends), reserve as far in advance as possible.

Bus Long distance buses depart from company offices in town; local destinations, including **Lago Agrio**, are served from the terminal on 9 de Octubre north of the centre. To **Quito**, 10 hrs, US$10, several daily 1030-2200. To **Tena**, 6 hrs, US$7. To **Baeza**, US$7.50, 8 hrs. To **Baños**, US$11, 9 hrs.

River Down the Río Napo to **Nuevo Rocafuerte** on the Peruvian border, 50-passenger motorized canoes leave Sun, Tue, Thu, Fri at 0700, 10-12 hrs; returning same days at 0500, 12-14 hrs; US$15-20. **Coop de Transporte Fluvial Orellana**, inside the **iTur** office, T288 0532; **Kamu Kamu**, kiosk near the dock, T288 0799. Details change often, inquire locally, buy tickets a day in advance and be at the dock early.

From Nuevo Rocafuerte boats can be hired for the 30 km trip down river to the Peruvian border town of **Pantoja**, US$50-60 per boat, try to share the ride. Departure dates of riverboats from **Pantoja** to **Iquitos** are irregular, be prepared for a long wait. Try to call Iquitos or Pantoja from Coca to inquire about the next sailing; full details are given in the Peru chapter under Iquitos, Transport. For the journey, take a hammock, cup, bowl, cutlery, extra food and snacks, drinking water or purification, insect repellent, toilet paper, soap, towel, cash dollars and soles in small notes; soles cannot be purchased in Coca.

Directory

Lago Agrio *p1176*

Banks For ATMs: **Banco de Guayquil**, Quito y 12 de Febrero; **Banco Pichincha**, 12 de Febrero y Añasco. Several **Casas de Cambio** on Quito between Colombia and Pasaje Gonzanamá, change euros and Colombian *pesos*.

Coca *p1176*

Banks For ATMs: **Banco Pichincha**, Quito y Bolívar; **Banco Internacional**, 9 de Octubre y Cuenca. **Internet** Several places, about US$1 per hr. **Post office** Napo y Guayaquil, north of centre.

Central and southern Oriente

Quito, Baños, Puyo, Tena and Puerto Misahuallí are all starting points for cental Oriente. Further south, Macas, Gualaquiza and Zamora are the main gateways. All have good road connections.

Archidona → *Phone code: 06. Colour map 11, B4. Population: 11,000. Altitude: 550 m.*

Archidona, 65 km south of Baeza and 10 km north of Tena, has a striking, small painted church and not much else but there are some interesting reserves in the surrounding area. The road leaving Archidona's plaza to the east goes to the village of **San Pablo**, and beyond to the Río Hollín. Along this road, 15 km from Archidona, is **Reserva El Para** ⓘ *owned by Orchid Paradise (see Archidona hotels below); groups pay US$30 for a guide plus US$40 for transport.* This 500-ha forest reserve has many rare birds and a nice waterfall.Tours can also be arranged to the **Izu Mangallpa Urcu (IMU) Foundation** ⓘ *contact Elias Mamallacta in Archidona, T08-045 6942 or T06-288 9383, www.izu-mangallpa-urcu.freehomepage.com, US$35 per day for accommodation (private rooms, mosquito nets) and guiding, minimum 2 people.* This reserve was set up by the Mamallacta family to protect territory on Galeras mountain. It is tough going but the forest is wonderful.

Tena and around → *Phone code: 06. Colour map 11, B4. Population: 34,000. Altitude: 500 m.*

Relaxed and friendly, Tena is the capital of Napo Province. Like Archidona, it was founded in 1560 and both were important colonial missionary and trading posts. It occupies a hill above the confluence of the Ríos Tena and Pano, there are nice views of the Andean foothills often shrouded in mist. Tena is popular with visitors for whitewater rafting and ethno-tourism and it makes a good stop en route from Quito to points deeper in Oriente. The road from the north passes the airstrip and market and heads through the town centre as Avenida 15 de Noviembre on its way to the bus station, nearly 1 km south of the river. Tena is quite spread out. A pedestrian bridge and a vehicle bridge link the two halves of town. **iTur** ⓘ *García Moreno between Calderón and JL Mera, near the river, T06-288 6536, Mon-Fri 0800-1230, 1330-1700,* municipal and regional tourist information offices all under one roof.

Misahuallí → *Phone code: 06. Colour map 11, B4. Population: 5,000. Altitude: 400 m.*

This small port, at the junction of the Napo and Misahuallí rivers, is perhaps the best place in Ecuador from which to visit the 'near Oriente', but your expectations should be realistic. The area has been colonized for many years and there is no extensive virgin forest nearby (except at Jatun Sacha, see Lodges on the upper Río Napo). Access is very easy however, prices are reasonable, and while you will not encounter large animals in the wild, you can still see birds, butterflies and exuberant vegetation – enough to get a taste for the jungle. There is a fine, sandy beach on the Río Misahuallí, but don't camp on it as the river can rise unexpectedly. A narrow suspension bridge crosses the Río Napo at Misahuallí and joins the road along the south shore. There is an interesting *mariposario* (butterfly farm) ⓘ *US$2.50*, 4 km west of Misahuallí. Several colourful species can be observed and photographed close up. Make arrangements through *Ecoselva*. (See Activities and tours, below).

Tena

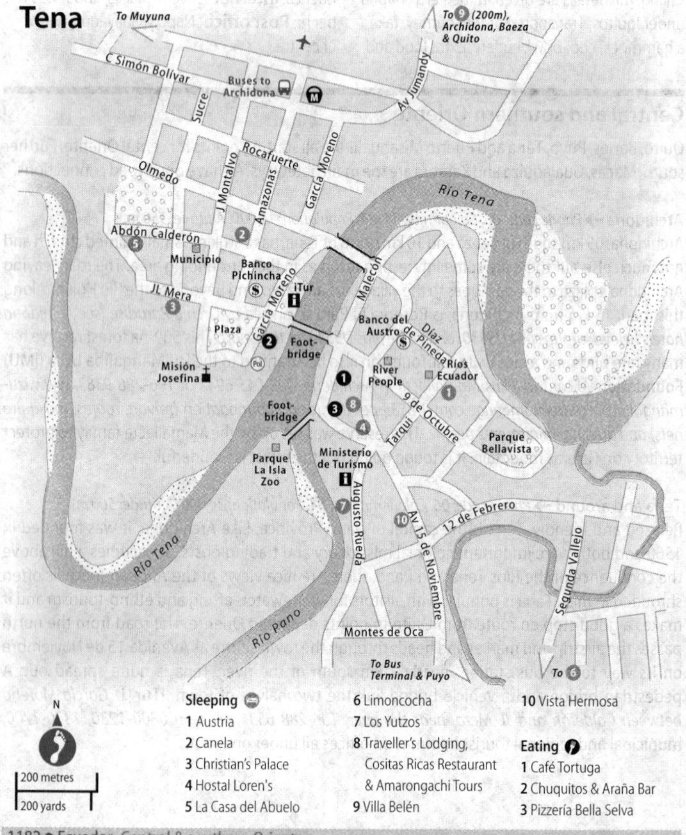

Sleeping
1 Austria
2 Canela
3 Christian's Palace
4 Hostal Loren's
5 La Casa del Abuelo
6 Limoncocha
7 Los Yutzos
8 Traveller's Lodging, Cositas Ricas Restaurant & Amarongachi Tours
9 Villa Belén
10 Vista Hermosa

Eating
1 Café Tortuga
2 Chuquitos & Araña Bar
3 Pizzería Bella Selva

Puyo ➔ *Phone code: 03. Colour map 11, B4. Population: 39,000. Altitude: 950 m.*
The capital of the province of Pastaza feels more like a lowland city anywhere in Ecuador rather than a typical jungle town. Visits can nonetheless be made to nearby forest reserves and tours deeper into the jungle can also be arranged from Puyo. It is the junction for road travel into the northern and southern Oriente (80 km south of Tena, 130 km north of Macas), and for traffic heading to or from Ambato via Baños; all on paved roads. The Sangay and Altar volcanoes can occasionally be seen from town. The **Museo Etno-Arqueológico** ⓘ *Atahualpa y General Villamil, p 3*, has displays of the traditional dwellings of various cultures of the province of Pastaza. **Tourist offices: iTur** ⓘ *Francisco de Orellana y 9 de Octubre, T288 5122, daily 0800-2000.* **Ministerio de Turismo** ⓘ *Ceslao Marin y Juan de Velasco, upstairs, T288 5819, Mon-Fri 0830-1230, 1330-1700, helpful.*

Omaere ⓘ *T288 7656, daily 0800-1700, US$3*, is a 15.6-ha ethnobotanical reserve located 2 km north of Puyo on the road to Tena. It has three trails with a variety of plants, an orchidarium and traditional native homes.There are other small private reserves of varying quality in the Puyo area and visits are arranged by local tour operators (see below). You cannot however expect to see large tracts of undisturbed primary jungle here. Sites include: **Criadero de Vida Silvestre Fátima** ⓘ *9 km north on the road to Tena, US$2*, which attempts to 'rehabilitate' captive jungle animals; **Jardín Botánico Las Orquídeas** ⓘ *3 km south on the road to Macas, US$6*, orchids and other tropical plants; **Fundación Ecológica Hola Vida**, 27 km from Puyo near **Porvenir**, rustic accommodation in the forest and a 30-minute canoe trip.

Shell is 13 km west of Puyo, 50 km (1 hour) east of Baños. It has a busy airfield.

Macas ➔ *Phone code: 07. Colour map 11, B4. Population: 19,000, Altitude: 1,050 m.*
Capital of Morona-Santiago province, Macas is situated high above the broad Río Upano valley. It is a pleasant tranquil place, established by missionaries in 1563. **Sangay volcano** (5,230 m) can be seen on clear mornings from the plaza, creating an amazing backdrop to the tropical jungle surrounding the town. The modern cathedral, with beautiful stained-glass windows, houses the much-venerated image of La Purísima de Macas. Five blocks north of the cathedral, in the Parque Recreacional, which also affords great views of the Upano Valley, are a butterfly garden and a small orchid collection. **Fundación Chankuap** ⓘ *Soasti y Bolívar, T270 1176, www.chankuap.org*, sells a nice variety of locally produced crafts and food products. **Tourist office**: **Cámara de Turismo** ⓘ kiosk at *Domingo Comín y Pje Proaño, T270 1606, Mon-Fri 0800-1200.* Macas provides access to **Parque Nacional Sangay** ⓘ *US$10, information from Ministry of the Environment in Macas, Juan de la Cruz y Guamote, T270 2368, Mon-Fri 0800-1300, 1400-1700.* The lowland area of the park has interesting walking with many rivers and waterfalls. See also Sangay (page 1114) for notes on the road from Macas to Riobamba.

Macas to Gualaquiza

South of Macas lies one of Ecuador's least touristed areas, promising much to explore. In 2010 the road was paved as far as Limón (see below), with work in progress to Gualaquiza. **Sucúa**, 23 km from Macas, is the administrative centre of the Shuar native people who inhabit much of southern Oriente. The town has most services and little else of interest but there are walks and rivers for bathing in the area. **Logroño**, 24 km further south, has a large limestone cave nearby; to visit contact Mario Crespo, T07-391 1013. It is another 31 km to (Santiago de) **Méndez**, a crossroads with a modern church. A partly paved road descends from Cuenca via Paute and Guarumales to Méndez, and another road heads east from Méndez via Patuca to Santiago and San José de Morona, near the Peruvian border. Some 26 km south of Méndez is **Limón** (official name General Leónidas Plaza Gutiérrez), a busy, friendly place, surrounded by impressive hills. From Limón the road climbs steeply 10 km to **Plan de Milagro**, another crossroads, where a rough and beautiful road, great for birdwatching, descends from Cuenca via Gualaceo. Next are **Indanza**, 5 km south, then **San Juan Bosco**,16 km further, with striking views of Cerro Pan de Azucar (2,958 m) rising abruptly out of the jungle, before the road reaches Gualaquiza, 55 km ahead.

Gualaquiza → *Phone code 07. Colour map 11, C3. Population 10,000. Altitude 850 m.*

A pleasant town with an imposing church on a hilltop, Gualaquiza's pioneer-settlement charm is threatened by large international mining projects in the area. Fortunately, tourism offers an alternative as there are also lovely waterfalls, good rivers for tubing, caves, and undeveloped archaeological sites nearby. Information and tours from the **Oficina Municipal de** Turismo ⓘ *García Moreno y Gonzalo Pesántez, T278 0783, Mon-Fri 0730-1230, 1330-1630*, and from Leonardo Matoche at **Canela y Café** (see Eating, below).

At Gualaquiza a very rough and narrow road forks northwest to climb steeply to Cuenca via **Sígsig**. The paved road south from Gualaquiza passes El Pangui and Yantzaza (55 km), 8 km south of which is **Zumbi**, with basic hotels on the plaza. At Zumbi, a bridge crosses the Río Zamora and a side road goes southeast to Guayzimi and the beautiful **Alto Nangartiza** region, with **Reserva El Zarza**. The upper Río Nangaritza flows through Shuar territory and a magnificent jungle-covered gorge with 200-m-high walls. There are also oilbird caves and other natural attractions. There is bus service to the area from Zamora, and tours are available form **Cabañas Yankuam** (see Sleeping, below). South of Zumbi along the 35 km paved road to **Zamora** (page 1131), the broad valley of the Río Zamora becomes progressively narrower, with forested mountains and lovely views.

Central and southern oriente listings

For Sleeping and Eating price codes and other relevant information, see Essentials, pages 38-40.

Sleeping

Archidona *p1181*

A Hakuna Matata, Vía Chaupi Shungu Km 3.9, off the road between Tena and Archidona, T09-802 0518, www.hakunamat.com. Comfortable cabins in a lovely setting by the Río Inchillaqui. Includes breakfast, other meals available, walks, river bathing and horse riding. Very good food, Belgian hosts, pleasant atmosphere. Warmly recommended.

A Orchid Paradise, 2 km north of town, T288 9232. Cabins in nice secondary forest with lots of birds. Includes breakfast, other meals available, owner organizes tours in the area.

E Regina, Rocafuerte 446, 1 block north of the plaza, T288 9144. Cheaper with shared bath, cold water, ample parking, pleasant, family-run.

Tena *p1181, map p1182*

B Christian's Palace, JL Mera y Sucre, T288 6047. Includes breakfast, restaurant, a/c, cheaper with fan, pool and small spa, modern and comfortable.

B-C Los Yutzos, Augusto Rueda 190 y 15 de Noviembre, T288 6717, www.uchutican.com. Comfortable rooms and beautiful grounds overlooking the Río Pano, quiet and family-run. A/c, cheaper with fan, Wi-Fi, parking, simple annex next door is cheaper. Recommended.

C-E Traveler's Lodging, 15 de Noviembre 438 y 9 de Octubre, T288 8204. Many different rooms and prices, front ones noisy, best to Look around and choose for yourself, **Cositas Ricas** restaurant and **Amarongachi Tours** on the premises. Some rooms with a/c, cheaper with fan, Wi-Fi.

D Canela, Amazonas y Abdón Calderón, T288 6081, canelahostal@yahoo.com. Hot water, fan, modern, spacious, mixed reports on service.

D Hostal Loren's, 15 de Noviembre y Augusto Rueda, T287 0232. Very pleaasant, modern, hot water, fan, opened in 2009.

D La Casa del Abuelo, JL Mera 628, T288 6318, runanambi@yahoo.com. Nice quiet place, hot water, ceiling fan, Wi-Fi, parking, comfortable rooms.

E Austria, Tarqui y Diaz de Pineda, T288 7205. Includes breakfast, electric shower, fan, ample parking, spacious rooms, quiet, good value, popular and often full. Recommended.

E Villa Belén, on Baeza road (Av Jumandy) just north of town near the airport, T288 6228. Hot water, fan, laundry and cooking facilities, parking, excellent rooms, quiet. Recommended.

E Vista Hermosa, 15 de Noviembre 622 y Marañón, T288 6521. Restaurant, hot water, fan, parking, nice rooftop terrace with views over river.

E-F Limoncocha, Sangay 533, Sector Corazón de Jesús, on a hillside 4 blocks from the bus station, ask for directions, T288 7583, http://limoncocha.tripod.com. Concrete house with terrace and hammocks. Cafeteria, cheaper with shared bath, hot water, fan, Wi-Fi, laundry and cooking facilities, parking, German- Ecuadorean run, enthusiastic owners organize tours. Out of the way in a humble neighbourhood, nice views, pleasant atmosphere, good value.

Misahuallí *p1182*

L Jardín Alemán, on the shores of the Río Misahuallí, 3 km from town, T289 0122, www.eljardinaleman.com. Includes 3 meals and river tour, restaurant and bar, ceiling fans and balconies, internet, comfortable rooms and cabins on a 120 ha reserve, ample grounds with captive animals.

C France Amazonia, on road to Tena across from the high school, T289 0009, www.france-amazonia.com. Includes breakfast, electric shower, pool, parking, nice grounds with river views, small rooms (not suitable for very tall people), French run, very helpful.

C Hostería Misahuallí, across the river from town, T289 0063, www.misahuallijungle.com. Meals available on request, electric shower, fan, pool and tennis court, cabins for up to 6, nice setting, lovely sunsets.

E Centro de Recreación Ecológico, on Santander at entrance to town, T289 0061. Electric shower, fan, parking, ample rooms and grounds.

E El Paisano, Rivadeneyra y Tandalia, T289 0027. Restaurant, hot water, mosquito nets, newer ample rooms upstairs are nice, cheaper ones downstairs, helpful owner.

E Shaw, Santander on the Plaza, T289 0019, ecoselva@yahoo.es. Includes breakfast, good restaurant, hot water, fan, simple rooms, operate their own tours, English spoken, very knowledgeable. Good value. Recommended.

Lodges on the upper Río Napo

Casa del Suizo, Quito office: Julio Zaldumbide 397 y Valladolid, T02-256 6090, www.casadelsuizo.com. On north shore at Ahuano, resort with capacity for 200, comfortable rooms, well-tended grounds, pool, gift shop, great river views. Swiss-Ecuadorean owned. US$89 per night.

Cotococha, Quito office: Amazonas N24-03 and Wilson, p 2, Quito, T02-223 4336, www.cotococha.com. Comfortable well-screened cabins with road access. Jungle walks, tubing, waterfalls and community visits. US$216 for 4 days.

Gareno, contact Michael Saur, T02-234 4350, or Roeland Van Lede, T02-224 9225 (both in Quito), www.guaponi.com. Located in Huarorani territory, accessible by road. Sightings of nesting Harpy Eagles have been reported, and the area is of special interest to birdwatchers. US$55 per night plus a one-time US$20 contribution to the Huaorani community. Recommended.

Jatun Sacha Biological Station, Quito T02-331 7163, www.jatunsacha.org. A 1300-ha reserve for education, research and tourism. Accessible by road. 507 birds, 2500 plants and 765 butterfly species have been identified. Good trails and views. US$30 per night, guiding extra.

Liana Lodge, on Río Arajuno near its confluence with the Napo, accessible by road, T09-980 0463, www.amazoonico.org. 6 cabins with terraces and river views. German spoken. *Centro de rescate* has captive animals on site. US$175 for 4 days.

Puyo *p1183*

LL Las Cascadas Lodge, book via Surtrek, Av Amazonas 897 y Wilson, Quito, T02-250 0530, www.surtrek.com. First-class accommodation (8 rooms), near waterfalls. US$700 for 4 days/ 3 nights including meals, guide and transport to/from Quito.

L Altos del Pastaza Lodge, access from Km 16 of Puyo-Macas road, Quito office: Leonardo Murialdo E11-04 y los Nardos, T09-767 4686, www.altosdelpastazalodge.com. Attractive lodge in 76-ha reserve overlooking the Río Pastaza. Don't expect much wildlife, but a nice place to relax, 3- to 5-day packages.

B El Jardín, Paseo Turístico, Barrio Obrero, T288 6101. Nice rooms and garden, includes breakfast, Wi-Fi, good upmarket restaurant, disco, noisy at weekends.

C Delfín Rosado, Ceslao Marín y Atahualpa, T288 8757, www.delfinrosadohotelspa.com. Includes breakfast, pool, Wi-Fi, modern rooms.

C Turingia, Ceslao Marín 294, T288 5180, www.hosteriaturingia.com. Restaurant, fan, small pool, Wi-Fi, parking, comfortable rooms, nice garden.

D-E Las Palmas, 20 de Julio y 4 de Enero, 5 blocks from centre, T288 4832, hostal_las palmas_puyo@yahoo.com. Includes breakfast, hot water, comfortable multi-storey hotel.

E Colibrí, C Manabí entre Bolívar y Galápagos, T288 4768, www.hostalcolibri.com. Hot water, Wi-Fi, parking, away from centre, simple but nice, good value. Offers tours and volunteer opportunities. Recommended.

E Libertad, Francisco de Orellana y Villamil, T288 3282. Restaurant, electric shower, parking, basic but good value.

Jungle lodges

Kapawi, Quito office: Foch E7-38 y Reina Victoria, T02-600 9333, www.kapawi.com. A top-of-the-line lodge located on the Río Capahuari near its confluence with the Pastaza, in the heart of Achuar territory not far from the Peruvian border. Accessible only by small aircraft and motor canoe. The lodge was built in partnership with the local Achuar community and fully turned over to them in 2008. The biodiversity is good, but more emphasis is placed on ethno-tourism here than at other upmarket jungle lodges. US$955 for 4 days includes land and air transport from Quito.

Macas *p1183*

A Arrayan & Piedra, Vía a Puyo Km 7, T304 5930, arraynp@hotmail.com. Upmarket hotel well suited to groups and meetings, includes breakfast, large restaurant, pool, comfortable rooms with terrace and hammock, manicured grounds, opened in 2009.

B Casa Upano, Av La Ciudad, Barrio La Barranca, 1 km from centre, T270 2674, www.realnature travel.com. A family run B&B in a private home, includes breakfast, full board available, excellent food, Wi-Fi, parking, ample comfortable rooms, huge garden with many birds. Very helpful, English spoken, organize birdwatching tours. Warmly recommended.

D Casa Blanca, Soasti 14-29 y Sucre, T270 0195. Includes breakfast, hot water, small pool, modern and comfortable, very helpful, good value. Often full, best book in advance. Recommended.

D Heliconia, Soasti y Tarqui, T270 1956. Hot water, nice spacious rooms.

E Esmeralda, Cuenca 6-12 y Soasti, T270 0130. Hot water, family run, pleasant, adequate, but some rooms are small.

E Nivel 5, Juan de la Cruz y Amazonas, T270 1240. Nice modern multi-storey hotel, hot water, fan, pool, parking, opened in 2009.

E Plaza, 10 de Agosto y Amazonas, T270 1683, lilipo29_64@hotmail.com. Nice rooms but those in front are noisy, helpful staff, good value.

Macas to Gualaquiza *p1184*

Sucúa

D Arutam, Vía a Macas Km 1, north of town, T274 0851. Restaurant, pool and sauna, parking, modern comfortable rooms, nice grounds, sports fields, well suited to families.

D Athenas, Domingo Comín y Serafín Solís, T274 0216. Breakfast available, Wi-Fi, parking, modern, large rooms.

Méndez

E Interoceánico, C Quito on the plaza, T276 0245. Hot water, parking, smart and modern, good value.

Limón

E Dream House, Quito y Bolívar, T277 0166. With restaurant, shared bath, hot water, adequate.

San Juan Bosco

E Antares, on the plaza, T304 2128. Restaurant, hot water, indoor pool, Wi-Fi, simple functional rooms, helpful owner.

Gualaquiza*p1184*

E Gran Hotel, Orellana y Gran Pasaje, T278 0722. Modern concrete building, hot water, fan, parking, small rooms, some without windows.

E Internacional, C Cuenca y García Moreno, T278 0637. Includes breakfast, restaurant, hot water, small simple rooms, most have fan.

E-F Wakis, Orellana 08-52 y Domingo Comín, T278 0138. Older simple place with small rooms, cheaper with shared bath, cold water, enthusiastic owner speaks English.

Alto Nangaritza

C Cabañas Yankuam, at the end of the road, 3 km south of Las Orquideas, T260 5739 (Zamora), www.lindoecuadortours.com. Rustic cabins in a lovely setting , includes breakfast, other tasty meals on request, some rooms with private bath, good walking in surrounding jungle-clad hills, organizes trips up the Río Nangaritza. Family-run. Reservations required, one week advance notice preferred. Recommended.

Eating

Tena *p1181*

Chuquitos, García Moreno by the plaza, Mon-Sat 0730-2130, Sun 1100-2130. Good food, à la carte only, seating on a balcony overlooking the river. Pleasant atmosphere, attentive service and nice views. Popular and recommended.

Pizzería Bella Selva, Malecón near the foot-bridge to the zoo, daily 1100-2300. Good pizza.

Cafés

Café Tortuga, Malecón between the two footbridges, open 0730-2100, closed Sun midday and Mon PM. Juices, snacks and sweets, nice location, spotlessly, friendly Swiss owner. Recommended.

Misahuallí *p1182*

Doña Gloria, Arteaga y Rivadeneyra by corner of plaza, daily 0730-2030. Good set meals.

Ecocafé, at **Hotel Shaw**, on the plaza. Good breakfast, meat and vegetarian dishes, set meals and à la carte, capuccino, nice atmosphere, attentive service.

Puyo *p1183*

La Carihuela, Mons Alberto Zambrano, near the bus station, Tue-Sun 0900-1600, 1800-2100. Good set lunch and à la carte.

Pizzería Buon Giorno, Orellana entre Villamil y 27 de Febrero, Mon-Sat 1200-2300, Sun 1400-2300. Good pizza, lasagne and salads, pleasant atmosphere, very popular and recommended.

El Alcázar, 10 de Agosto 936 y Sucre, Mon-Sat 0900-2300, Sun 0900-1500. Very good restaurant with an unexpectedly Spanish-European flavour in the Ecuadorean Amazon. Good value set meals and varied à la carte. Recommended.

Cafés

El Fariseo, Atahualpa entre 27 de Febrero y General Villamil, 0700-2200. Good cakes and the best coffee in town.

Macas *p1183*

Pagoda China, Amazonas y Domingo Comín, daily 1030-2230. Very good Chinese food, generous portions, authentic décor, popular and recommended.

La Napolitana, Amazonas y Tarqui, daily 0800-2300. Open-air seating, pizza, grill and set lunch.

Charloth, Soasti 15-24 y Bolívar, Mon-Fri 0630-1500, 1730-2100, Sat AM only. Small simple place in an old wooden house, good local breakfast and set meals, popular.

Cafés

Sports Café, Soasti y Bolívar, daily 0900-2200. Very good ice-cream from **Tutto Freddo** in Cuenca, capuccino, sandwiches and set meals, popular.

Gualaquiza *p1184*

Cabaña Los Helechos, 12 de Febrero y Gonzalo Pesántez, near bus station, daily 0730-2200. Set meals and à la carte.

Canela y Café, Gonzalo Pesántez y García Moreno, daily 0930-1200, 1700-2400. Burgers, desserts and good fruit juices, nice atmosphere. Owner Leonardo Matoche has information about the area and runs tours.

Activities and tours

Tena *p1181*

Rafting tours cost US$50-70 per day, safety standards vary between operators.

Amarongachi Tours at **Hostal Traveler's Lodging**, see Sleeping, above.

Limoncocha, at **Hostal Limoncocha**, see Sleeping, above. German spoken.

Ríos Ecuador, Tarqui 230 y Díaz de Pineda, T06-288 6346, www.riosecuador.com. Highly recommended whitewater rafting and kayak trips, and a 4-day kayaking school.

River People, 15 de Noviembre y 9 de Octubre, T06-288 8384, www.riverpeoplerafting.com. Whitewater rafting and kayaking.

Ricancie, Av del Chofer y Hugo Vasco, 2 blocks from bus terminal, T06-288 8479, http://ricancie.nativeweb.org. This local NGO fosters community development through eco/ethnotourism. Various Kichwa communities may be visited, US$40-45 per day, also volunteer opportunities.

Runa Ñambi at **La Casa del Abuelo** hotel, see Sleeping, above.

Misahuallí *p1182*

Jungle tours (US$25-50 per person per day) can be arranged by most hotels as well as the following:

Ecoselva, Santander on the plaza, T06-289 0019, ecoselva@yahoo.es. Recommended guide Pepe Tapia speaks English and has a biology background. Well organized and reliable.

Selva Verde, Santander on the plaza, T06-289 0165. Guide Luis Zapata speaks English and offers a variety of tours.

Puyo *p1183*

All of the following offer jungle tours of varying lengths, US$25-50 per person per day.

Amazonía Touring, Atahualpa y 9 de Octubre, T03-288 3219.

Coka Tours, 27 de Febrero y Ceslao Marín, T03-288 6108.

Naveda Santos, at the Terminal Terrestre, T03-288 3974. Owner, Marco Naveda.

Papangu Tours, 27 de Febrero y Sucre, T03-2887684, papangu@andinanet.net.

Operated by the **Organización de Pueblos Indigenas de Pastaza** (OPIP). Native guides.

Macas *p1183*
Tours to native communities and lowland portions of **Parque Nacional Sangay**, cost about US$50 per day.
Insondu, Bolívar y Soasti, T270 2533, www.mundoshuar.com.
Planeta Tours, Domingo Comín 7-35 y Soasti, T270 1328, planeta_ms@hotmail.com.
Real Nature Travel Company, at **Casa Upano**, see Sleeping, above. Run by RhoAnn Wallace and professional birdwatching guide Galo Real, English spoken.

Transport

Tena *p1181*
Bus Run-down Terminal Terrestre on 15 de Noviembre, 1 km from the centre (taxi US$1). To **Quito**, US$6, 5 hrs. To **Ambato**, via Baños, US$5, 5 hrs. To **Baños**, 4 hrs, US$4. To **Riobamba**, via Ambato, 6 hrs, US$6. To **Puyo**, US$3, 2 hrs. To **Coca** and **Lago Agrio**, fares given above. To **Misahuallí**, hourly, US$1, 45 mins. To **Archidona**, from Amazonas y Bolívar by market, every 20 mins, US$0.25, 15 mins.

Misahuallí *p1182*
Bus Local buses run from the plaza. To **Tena**, hourly 0700-1800, US$1, 45 mins. Make long-distance connections in Tena, or get off at Puerto Napo to catch southbound buses although you may not get a seat. To **Quito**, 1 direct bus a day at 0830, US$7, 5 hrs.
River No scheduled passenger service, but motorized canoes for 8-10 passengers can be chartered for the journey to **Coca** (5-7 hrs, US$200) or other destinations.

Puyo *p1183*
Air The nearest airport to Puyo is at Shell, 13 km. Military flights to jungle villages are not open to foreigners, but light aircraft can be chartered starting around US$300 per hr.
Bus Terminal Terrestre on the outskirts of town, a 10- to 15-min walk from the centre; taxi US$1. To **Baños**, US$2, 1½ hrs. To **Ambato**, US$3, 3 hrs. To **Quito**, US$5, 5 hrs via Ambato. To **Riobamba**, US$4, 4 hrs. To **Tena**, see above. To **Macas**, US$5, 3 hrs.

Macas *p1183*
Air Airport within walking distance, at Cuenca y Amazonas. To **Quito**, daily except Sat with **Saereo** (T270 2764), US$74. Sit on left for best views of Volcán Sangay. Air taxis available to jungle villages, US$600 per hr for 9 passengers.
Bus Terminal Terrestre by the market. To **Puyo**, see above. To **Quito**, via Puyo, Baños and Ambato, US$8, 8 hrs. To **Riobamba** through Parque Nacional Sangay, a beautiful ride, US$5, 5 hrs. To **Cuenca**, US$8, 8 hrs, via Méndez and Guarumales (partly paved) or via Plan de Milagro and Gualaceo (rough road). To **Gualaquiza**, US$8, 8 hrs, where you can get a bus to Zamora and Loja (see below). To **Sucúa**, every hour, US$0.90, 30 min. To **9 de Octubre**, for access to **Parque Nacional Sangay**, US$1.50, 1½ hrs

Gualaquiza *p1184*
Bus To **Macas**, see above. To **Cuenca**; via Sígsig, 4 daily, US$6.25, 6 hrs; via Plan de Milagro and Gualaceo at 2130, US$5, 7hrs. To **Zamora**, US$3.50, 4 hrs. To **Loja**, US$6, 6hrs.

Directory

Tena *p1181*
Banks For ATMs: **Banco del Austro**, 15 de Noviembre y Díaz de Pineda; **Banco Pichincha**, Amazonas y JL Mera.

Puyo *p1183*
Banks For ATM: **Banco del Austro**, Atahualpa entre 10 de Agosto y Dávila.

Macas *p1183*
Banks For ATMs: **Banco del Austro**, Soasti y Domingo Comín; **Banco Pichincha**, Soasti y 10 de Agosto. **Internet** US$1 per hr. **Post offices** 9 de Octubre y Domingo Comín, next to the park.

Gualaquiza *p1184*
Banks For ATMs: **CACPE**, 12 de Febrero y Cuenca; **Banco de Loja**, C Cuenca; but don't count on them, bring some cash.
Internet Several places, US$1/hr.

Galápagos Islands → *Phone code: 05. Colour map 10.*

A trip to the Galápagos Islands is an unforgettable experience. The islands are world-renowned for their fearless wildlife but no amount of hype can prepare the visitor for such a close encounter with nature. Here you can snorkel with penguins and sea-lions, and encounter the odd hammerhead shark, watch giant 200 kg tortoises lumbering through cactus forest and enjoy the courtship display of the blue-footed booby and magnificent frigate bird, all in startling close-up.

Lying on the Equator, 970 km west of the Ecuadorean coast, the Galápagos consist of six main islands (San Cristóbal, Santa Cruz, Isabela, Floreana, Santiago and Fernandina – the last two uninhabited), 12 smaller islands (Baltra and the uninhabited islands of Santa Fe, Pinzón, Española, Rábida, Daphne, Seymour, Genovesa, Marchena, Pinta, Darwin and Wolf) and over 40 islets. The islands have an estimated population of almost 31,000, but this does not include temporary inhabitants. The largest island, Isabela (formerly Albemarle), is 120 km long and forms half the total land area of the archipelago. Its notorious convict colony was closed in 1958; some 2,600 people live there now, mostly in and around Puerto Villamil, on the south coast. San Cristóbal (Chatham) has a population of 7,100 with the capital of the archipelago, Puerto Baquerizo Moreno. Santa Cruz (Indefatigable) has 21,000, with Puerto Ayora the main tourist centre; and Floreana (Charles) about 100.

Background

The Galápagos have never been connected with the continent. Gradually, over many hundreds of thousands of years, animals and plants from over the sea somehow migrated there and as time went by they adapted themselves to Galápagos conditions and came to differ more and more from their continental ancestors. Unique marine and terrestrial environments, due to the continuing volcanic formation of the islands in the west of the archipelago and its location at the nexus of several major marine currents, has created laboratory-type conditions where only certain species have been allowed access. The formidable barriers which prevent many species from travelling within the islands, has led to a very high level of endemism. A quarter of the species of shore fish, half of the plants and almost all the reptiles are found nowhere else. In many cases different forms have evolved on the different islands. Charles Darwin recognized this speciation within the archipelago when he visited the Galápagos on the *Beagle* in 1835 and his observations played a substantial part in his formulation of the theory of evolution.

This natural experiment has been under threat ever since the arrival of the first whaling ships and even more so since the first permanent human settlement. New species were introduced and spread very rapidly, placing the endemic species at risk. Quarantine programmes have since been implemented in an attempt to prevent the introduction and spread of even more species, but the rules are not easy to enforce. There have also been campaigns to eradicate some of the introduced species on some islands, but this is inevitably a very slow, expensive and difficult process.

One extraordinary feature of the islands is the tameness of the animals. The islands were uninhabited when they were discovered in 1535 and the animals still have little instinctive fear of man.

Plant and animal species are grouped into three categories. **Endemic species** are those which occur only in the Galápagos and nowhere else on the planet. Examples are the **marine** and **land iguana, Galápagos fur seal, flightless cormorant** and the **'daisy tree'** (*Scalesia pedunculata*). **Native species** make their homes in the Galápagos as well as other parts of the world. Examples include all three species of **boobies, frigate birds** and the various types of **mangroves**. Although not unique to the islands, these native species have been an integral part of the Galápagos ecosystems for a very long time. **Introduced species** on the other hand are very recent arrivals, brought by man, and inevitably the cause of much damage. They include **cattle, goats, donkeys, pigs, dogs, cats, rats** and over 500 species of plants such as **elephant grass** (for grazing cattle), and fruit trees. The unchecked expansion of these introduced species has upset the natural balance of the archipelago. The number of tourists also continues to grow every year: from 11,800 in 1979, to 68,900 in 2000, to 163,000 in 2009. In July 2007, as a result of the myriad pressures that accompany human activity, the Galápagos were placed on the UNESCO list of endangered World Heritage Sites.

Ins and outs

Getting there

Air There are two airports which receive flights from mainland Ecuador, but no international flights to Galápagos. The most frequently used airport is at **Baltra**, across a narrow strait from Santa Cruz, the other at **Puerto Baquerizo Moreno**, on San Cristóbal. The two islands are 96 km apart and on most days there are local flights in light aircraft between them, as well as to **Puerto Villamil** on Isabela. There is also boat service between Puerto Ayora, Puerto Baquerizo Moreno, Puerto Villamil and occasionally Floreana.

TAME has two daily flights from Quito to Baltra, one stops on route in Guayaquil. TAME also operates Mon, Wed, Fri and Sat to San Cristóbal. **AeroGal** likewise flies twice daily to Baltra, and on Tue, Thu, Fri, Sat and Sun to San Cristóbal. The return fare in high season is US$422 from Quito, US$371 from Guayaquil. The low season fare (1 May-15 June, 16 September-31 October) is US$365 from Quito, US$327 from Guayaquil. The same prices apply regardless of whether you fly to San Cristóbal or Baltra; you can arrive at one and return from the other. You can also depart from Quito and return to Guayaquil or vice versa, but you may not buy a one-way ticket. The above prices are subject to change without notice. Discount fares for Ecuadorean nationals and residents of Galápagos are not available to foreigners and these rules are strictly enforced. A 15% discount off the high season fare is available to students with an ISIC card.

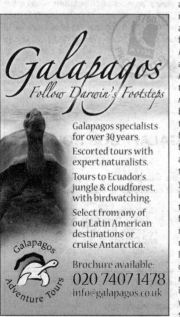

Airport transfer Two buses meet flights from the mainland at Baltra: one runs to the port or *muelle* (10 mins, no charge) where the cruise boats wait; the other goes to Canal de Itabaca, the narrow channel which separates Baltra from Santa Cruz. It is 15 minutes to the Canal, free, then you cross on a small ferry for US$1, another bus waits on the Santa Cruz side to take you to Puerto Ayora in 45 minutes, U$2. If you arrive at Baltra on one of the local inter-island flights (see below) then you have to wait until the next flight from the mainland for bus service, or hire two pick-up trucks and a motorboat at the canal (total US$25). For the return trip to the airport, two buses per flight leave Puerto Ayora from the *Terminal Terrestre* on Avenida Baltra, 2 km from the pier. A kiosk near the pier sells bus tickets to the airport but it is seldom open, best to confirm details locally with your airline. Pickup truck from town to bus station, US$1. ▸▸ *See also Transport, page 1208.*

Getting around

Emetebe Avionetas ⓘ *Guayaquil T04-229 2492, www.emetebe.com, see Directory for local offices*, offers inter-island flights in two light twin-engine aircraft. Two daily flights operate between **Puerto Baquerizo Moreno** (San Cristóbal), **Baltra** and **Puerto Villamil** (Isabela), most days except Sun, but this varies with passenger demand. Baggage allowance 25 lbs, strictly enforced. All fares US$158 one way, US$263 return, including taxes.

Fibras (fibreglass motor launches for about 15 passengers) operate daily between Puerto Ayora and Puerto Baquerizo Moreno, 2½ hours, and between Puerto Ayora and Puerto Villamil, three hours. They charge US$30, one way. The *fibras* leave Puerto Baquerizo Moreno and Puerto Villamil early each morning and return from Puerto Ayora around 1400. Tickets are sold by several agencies in Puerto Baquerizo Moreno, at the pier in Puerto Ayora, and across the street from the police station in Puerto Villamil. This can be a wild wet ride, life vests are supposed to be carried but check. Take sun protection, your own drinking water, and avoid single-engine boats.

Information and advice

A recommended web site is **www.galapagospark.org**. It describes each visitor site and gives details of tourist vessels operating in the islands.

Tourist offices **Santa Cruz** (Puerto Ayora): **Ministerio de Turismo** ⓘ *Av Charles Darwin y Tomás de Berlanga, T252 6174, mturgal@gpsinter.net, Mon-Fri 0800-1230, 1400-1730*. **iTur** (Dirección Municipal de Turismo) ⓘ *at the bus terminal, 2 km from town, daily 1000-1700, and another at Baltra airport, www.santacruz.gov.ec*, has information about Puerto Ayora and Santa Cruz Island. **CAPTURGAL** ⓘ *Galápagos Chamber of Tourism, Av Charles Darwin y Charles Binford, T252 6206, www.galapagos tour.org, Mon-Fri 0730-1200, 1400-1730*, English spoken. This is the place to present any serious complaints about cruise vessels, agencies or other tourist services. **San Cristóbal** (Puerto Baquerizo Moreno): **CATURCRIST** ⓘ *Hernández y 12 de Febrero, T252 0592, ctcsancrist@easynet.net.ec, Mon-Fri 0730-1230, 1400-1700*, is the San Cristóbal Chamber of Tourism. **Municipal tourist office** ⓘ *Malecón Charles Darwin y 12 de Febrero, T252 1166, Mon-Fri 0730-1230, 1400-1700*, is at the Municipio.

Entry fees On arrival, every foreign visitor to Galápagos must pay a **US$100 National Park fee** plus an additional **US$10 INGALA fee**, both cash only. Be sure to have your passport to hand at the airport and keep all fee receipts throughout your stay in the islands.

Basic rules Do not touch any of the animals, birds or plants. Do not transfer sand, seeds or soil from one island to another. Do not leave litter anywhere; nor take food on to the islands. Uninhabited islands are no-smoking zones.

What to take A remedy for seasickness is recommended; the waters south of Santa Cruz are particularly choppy. A good supply of sun block and skin cream to prevent windburn and chapped lips is essential, as are a hat and sunglasses. You should be prepared for dry and wet landings, the latter involving wading ashore. Take plenty of memory cards or film with you; the animals are so tame that you will use far more than you expected; a telephoto lens is not essential, but if you have one, bring it. Also take filters suitable for strong sunlight. Snorkelling equipment is particularly useful as much of the sea-life is only visible under water. Most of the cheaper boats do not provide equipment and those that do may not have good snorkelling gear. If in doubt, bring your own, rent in Puerto Ayora, or buy it in Quito. Always bring some US$ cash to Galápagos. There is only one bank and ATM system, which may not work with all cards.

Tipping A ship's crew and guides are usually tipped separately. The amount is a very personal matter; you may be guided by suggestions made onboard or in the agency's brochures, but the key factors should always be the quality of service received and your own resources.

If you have problems Raise any issues first with your guide or ship's captain. Additional complaints may be made to **CAPTURGAL** in Puerto Ayora, see above.

Best time to visit The Galápagos climate can be divided into a hot season (December-May), when there is a possibility of heavy showers, and the cool or *garúa* (mist) season (June-November), when the days generally are more cloudy and there is often rain or drizzle. July and August can be windy, force 4 or 5. Daytime clothing should be lightweight. (Clothing generally, even on 'luxury cruises', should be casual and comfortable.) At night, however, particularly at sea and at higher altitudes, temperatures fall below 15°C and warm clothing is required. Boots and shoes soon wear out on the lava terrain. The sea is cold July-October; underwater visibility is best January-March. Ocean temperatures are usually higher to the east and lower at the western end of the archipelago. The islands climate and hence its wildlife are also influenced by the El Niño phenomenon. Despite all these variations, conditions are generally favourable for visiting Galápagos throughout the year.

The authorities At least six different authorities have a say in running the Galápagos islands and surrounding marine reserve: 1) **Instituto Nacional Galápagos** (INGALA), under control of the president of Ecuador, which issues residency permits; 2) the **National Park Service**, under the authority of the Ministerio del Ambiente, which regulates tourism and manages the 97% of the archipelago which is parkland; 3) the **Charles Darwin Research Station** (www.darwinfoundation.org), part of an international non-profit organization which supporting scientific research, advises other authorities regarding conservation, and channels funds for this purpose; 4) the **Ecuadorean Navy**, which patrols the waters of the archipelago and attempts to enforce regulations regarding both tourism and fishing; 5) **SICGAL**, in charge of controlling movement of live animals, plants and many foods including fresh fruit, vegetables and dairy products (all forbidden). They check bags at Quito and Guayaquil airport, and also when travelling independently between islands. 6) local **elected authorities** including municipalities, the provincial council, and a member of the national Congress. There are also various other **international NGOs** working in Galápagos, each with its own agenda.

Choosing a tour

There are two ways to travel around the islands: a cruise (*tour navegable*), where you sleep on the boat, or shore-based tours on which you take day trips to the islands. On the former you travel at night, arriving at a new landing site each day, with more time ashore. On a land-based tour you spend less time ashore at wildlife sites, cover less ground and cannot visit the more distant islands. Itineraries are controlled by the National Park to distribute tourism evenly throughout the islands. A third option is independent travel on the populated islands. Although neither cheap nor a substitute for either of the above, it allows those with plenty of time to explore a small part of the archipelago at their leisure. If taking a day trip by boat (*tour diario*), you should check with one of the information offices if a boat is authorized for such trips; many are not. All tours begin with a morning flight from the mainland on the first day and end on the last day with a midday flight back to the mainland.

The less expensive boats are normally smaller and less powerful so you see less and spend more time travelling; also the guiding may be mostly in Spanish. The more expensive boats will probably have air conditioning, hot water and private baths. All boats have to conform to certain minimum safety standards; more expensive boats are better equipped. A water maker can be a great asset. Note that boats with over 18 passengers take quite a time to disembark and re-embark people, while the smaller boats have a more lively motion, which is important if you are prone to seasickness. Note also that there may be limitations for vegetarians on the cheaper boats, enquire in advance. The least expensive boats (economy class) cost about US$175 per person per day and a few of these vessels are dodgy. For around US$200-300 per day (tourist and tourist superior class) you will be on a better, faster boat which can travel more quickly between visitor sites, leaving more time to spend ashore. Over US$350 per day are the first-class and luxury brackets, with far more comfortable and spacious cabins, as well as a superior level of service and cuisine. No boat may sail without a park-trained guide.

The table on page 1198 lists live-aboard tour vessels, it does not include dive boats nor day-trippers. The sailing vessels listed also have motors, and many frequently operate under engine power. All details are subject to change, for updates see www.galapagospark.org. Captains, crews and guides regularly change on all boats. These factors, as well as the sea, weather and your fellow passengers will all influence the quality of your experience.

Note Over the years, we have received repeated serious complaints about the vessel *Free Enterprise*, sometimes also called *Intrepid* or *Discovery*. The *Gaby* (also known as *Friendship*) has likewise received negative reports.

Booking a tour in advance You can book a Galápagos cruise in several different ways: 1) over the internet; 2) from either a travel agency or directly though a Galápagos wholesaler in your home country; 3) from one of the very many agencies found throughout Ecuador, especially in Quito but also in other tourist centres and Guayaquil; or 4) from agencies in Puerto Ayora but not Puerto Baquerizo Moreno. The trade-off is always between time and money: booking from home is most efficient and expensive, Puerto Ayora cheapest and most time-consuming, while Quito and Guayaquil are intermediate. Prices for a given category of boat do not vary all that much however, and it is not possible to obtain discounts or make last-minute arrangements in high season. When looking for a last-minute cruise in Puerto Ayora it is best to pay your hotel one night at a time since hoteliers may not refund advance payments. Especially on cheaper boats, check carefully about what is and is not included (eg drinking water, snorkelling equipment, etc).

Cruising It is possible but expensive to cruise the islands in your own yacht. The same rules apply regarding national park fees and being accompanied by a park-trained guide. See under Puerto Ayora, Directory (page 1208), for agents who can help organize logistics, paperwork and cruises on local vessels.

The islands

Santa Cruz: Puerto Ayora → *Phone code: 05. Population: 18,000.*

Santa Cruz is the most central of the Galápagos islands and the main town is Puerto Ayora. About 1½ km from Puerto Ayora is the **Charles Darwin Research Station** ⓘ *at Academy Bay, office Mon-Fri 0700-1600, visitor areas 0600-1800 daily.* A visit to the station is a good introduction to the islands as it provides a lot of information. Collections of several of the rare sub-species of giant tortoise are maintained on the station as breeding nuclei, together with tortoise-rearing pens for the young. See their website for more information, page 1194.

One of the most beautiful beaches in the Galápagos Islands is at **Tortuga Bay**, 45 minutes easy walk (2.5 km each way) west from Puerto Ayora on an excellent cobbled path through cactus forest. Start at the west end of Calle Charles Binford; further on there is a gate where you must register, open 0600-1800 daily, free. Make sure you take sun screen, drinking water, and beware of the very strong undertow. Also, do not walk on the dunes above the beach, which are a marine tortoise nesting area. Ten minutes' walk to the west end of Tortuga Bay is a trail to a lovely mangrove-fringed lagoon, with calmer and warmer water and shade under the mangroves.

Las Grietas is a beautiful gorge with a pool at the bottom which is splendid for bathing. Take a water taxi from the port to the dock at Punta Estrada (5 minutes, US$0.50). It is a 5-minute walk from here to the *Finch Bay* hotel and 15 minutes further over rough lava boulders to Las Grietas – well worth the trip. The highest point on Santa Cruz Island is **Cerro Crocker** at 864 m. You can hike here and to two other nearby 'peaks' called **Media Luna** and **Puntudo**. The trail starts at Bellavista (7 km from Puerto Ayora) where a rough trail map is painted as a mural on the wall of the school. The round trip from Bellavista takes six to eight hours. A permit and guide are not required, but a guide may be helpful. Always take food, water and a compass or GPS.

There are a number of sites worth visiting in the interior, including **Los Gemelos**, a pair of twin sinkholes, formed by a collapse of the ground above a fault. They straddle the road to Baltra, beyond Santa Rosa. You can take a *camioneta* all the way, otherwise take a bus to Santa Rosa (see below), then walk. It's a good place to see the Galápagos hawk and barn owl. There are several **lava tubes** (natural tunnels) on the island. Some are at **El Mirador**, 3 km from Puerto Ayora on the road to Bellavista. Barn owls can be seen here. Two more lava tubes are 1 km from Bellavista. They are on private land, it costs US$1.50 to enter the tunnels (bring a torch) and it takes about 30 minutes to walk through the tunnels. Tours to the lava tubes can be arranged in Puerto Ayora.

Another worthwhile trip is to the **El Chato Tortoise Reserve**, where giant tortoises can be seen in the wild during the dry season. The trail starts at Santa Rosa, 22 km from Puerto Ayora. Past the school in Santa Rosa, a Parque Nacional Galápagos sign warns that tourists have been lost along the trail. Turn left here and follow a badly overgrown path south between 2 barbed wire fences. After 3 km you reach a wooden memorial to an Israeli tourist and a better trail running east-west. Turn right and follow the trail west for 20 minutes to a sign, "Entrada Al Chato". There are many confusing trails in the reserve itself; take food, water and a compass or GPS. The round trip on foot takes a full day, or horses can sometimes be hired at Santa Rosa. It is best to take a guide if you have no hiking experience; tours can also be arranged in Puerto Ayora.

Near the reserve is the **Butterfly Ranch** (Hacienda Mariposa) ⓘ *US$2, camping possible for $10-15 pp*, where you can see giant tortoises in the pastures, but only in the dry season. In the wet season the tortoises are breeding down in the arid zone. The ranch is beyond Bellavista on the road to Santa Rosa (the bus passes the turn-off, walk 1 km from there).

San Cristóbal: Puerto Baquerizo Moreno → *Phone code: 05. Population: 7,100.*
Puerto Baquerizo Moreno, on San Cristóbal island to the east, is the capital of the archipelago. It is a pleasant place to spend a few days, with interesting excursions in the area. The town's attractive *malecón* has a tidepool with a water shute, a fountain with a 3-D map of the islands and many shaded seats.

In town, the **cathedral** ⓘ *on Av Northía, 2 blocks up from the post office, 0900-1200, 1600-1800*, has interesting artwork combining religious and Galápagos motifs. To the north of town, opposite Playa Mann, is the Galápagos National Park visitor centre or **Centro de Interpretación** ⓘ *T252 0138, ext 102, daily 0700-1700, free.* It has an excellent display of the natural and human history of the islands.

A good trail goes from the Centro de Interpretación to the northeast through scrub forest to **Cerro Tijeretas**, a hill overlooking town and the ocean, 30 minutes away (take water). Side trails branch off to lookouts on cliffs over the sea. Frigate birds nest in this area and can be observed gliding about, there are sea lions on the beaches below. To go back, if you take the trail which follows the coast, you will end up at **Playa Punta Carola,** a popular surfing beach, too rough for swimming. Closer to town is the small **Playa Mann** (follow Avenida Northía to the north), more suited for swimming, and in town is **Playa de Oro**, where some hotels are located. Right in the centre of town, along the sand by the tidal pool, sea lions can be seen, be careful with the male who 'owns' the beach. To the south of town, 20 minutes' walk past the airport, is **La Lobería,** a rocky bay with shore birds, sea lions and marine iguanas.

Around San Cristóbal There are five buses a day inland from Puerto Baquerizo Moreno to **El Progreso** ⓘ *6 km, 15 mins, US$0.20*, then it's a 2½ hour walk to El Junco lake, the largest body of fresh water in Galápagos. There are also frequent pick-up trucks to El Progreso ⓘ *US$2*, or you can hire a pick-up in Puerto Baquerizo Moreno for touring: US$18 to El Junco, US$30 continuing to the beaches at Puerto Chino on the other side of the island, past a man-made tortoise reserve. Prices are return and include waiting. At El Junco there is a path to walk around the lake in 20 minutes. The views are lovely in clear weather but it is cool and wet in the *garúa* season, so take adequate clothing. Various small roads fan out from El Progreso and make for pleasant walking. **Jatun Sacha** (www.jatunsacha.org) has a volunteer centre on an old hacienda in the highlands beyond El Progreso working on eradication of invasive species and a native plants nursery (US$15 taxi ride from town), take repellent.

It's a three-hour hike from the landing site at **Caleta Tortuga**, on the northwest shore of the island, to **La Galapaguera Natural** where you can see tortoises in the wild. **Isla Lobos** is an islet with a large sea lion colony and nesting site for sea birds northeast of Puerto Baquerizo Moreno. It is also a dive site.

Boats go to **Puerto Ochoa**, 15 minutes, for the beach; to **Punta Pitt** in the far north where you can see all three species of booby (US$65 for tour). Off the northwest coast is **Kicker Rock** (León Dormido), the basalt remains of a crater; many seabirds, including Nazca and blue- footed boobies, can be seen around its cliffs (five hour trip, including snorkelling, recommended, US$35).

Note: Always take food, plenty of water and a compass or GPS when hiking on your own on San Cristóbal. There are many crisscrossing animal trails and it is easy to get lost. Also watch out for the large-spined opuntia cactus and the poisonwood tree (*manzanillo*), which is a relative of poison ivy and can cause severe skin reactions.

Overseas agencies

Galapagos Classic Cruises, 6 Keyes Rd, London NW2 3XA, T020-8933 0613, www.galapagoscruises.co.uk. Specialists in tailor-made cruises and diving holidays to the islands with additional land tours to Ecuador and Peru on request.
Galápagos Holidays, 14 Prince Arthur Av, Suite 311, Toronto, Ontario M5R 1A9, T416-413 9090, T1-800-661 2512 (toll free), www.galapagosholidays.com.
Galápagos Network, 5805 Blue Lagoon Dr, Suite 160, Miami, FL 33126, T305-2626264, www.ecoventura.com.
INCA, 1311 63rd St, Emeryville, CA 94608, T510-420 1550, www.inca1.com.
Select Latin America, 3.51 Canterbury Court, 1-3 Brixton Road, London SW9 6DE, T020-7407 1478, www.selectlatinamerica.com. David Horwell arranges quality tailor-made tours to Ecuador and the Galápagos islands.
International Expeditions, 1 Environs Park, Helena, Alabama, 35080, T205-428 1700, T1-800-633 4734, www.internationalexpeditions.com.
Sol International, PO Box 1738, Kodak, TN 37764, T931-536 4893, T1-800-765 5657, www.solintl.com.
Wilderness Travel, 1102 Ninth St, Berkeley, CA 94710, T510-558 2488, T1-800-368 2794, www.wildernesstravel.com.

Isabela Island➔ *Phone code: 05.*
This is the largest island in the archipelago, formed by the extensive lava flows from six volcanoes. Five of the volcanoes are active and each has (or had) its own separate sub-species of giant tortoise. Isabela is developing for land-based tourism. If you have a few days to spare and are looking for tranquillity in a South-Pacific-island setting, this may be just the place. Most residents live in **Puerto Villamil** (population 2,500). In the highlands, there is a cluster of farms at Santo Tomás. There are several lovely beaches right by town, but mind the strong undertow and ask locally about the best spots for swimming. It is 2½ hours walk west to **Muro de las Lágrimas**, a gruesome place built by convict labour under hideous conditions. Along the same road 30 minutes from town is the **Centro de Crianza**, a breeding centre for giant tortoises surrounded by lagoons with flamingos and other birds. In the opposite direction, 30 minutes east toward the *embarcadero* (fishing pier) is **Concha Perla Lagoon**, with a nice access trail through mangroves and a little dock from which you can go swimming with sea lions and other creatures. Fishermen can take you to **Las Tintoreras** a set of small islets in the harbour where white-tipped reef sharks may be seen in the still crystalline water (US$20 per person for a three-hour tour). **Sierra Negra Volcano** has the largest basaltic caldera in the world, 9 x 10 km. It is 19 km (30 minutes) by pickup truck to the park entrance (take passport and National Park entry receipt), where you switch to horses for the one-hour beautiful ride to the crater rim at 1,000m. It is a further 1½ hours walk along bare brittle lava rock to **Volcán Chico**, with several fumaroles and more stunning views. You can camp on the crater rim but must take all supplies, including water, and obtain a permit the day before from the National Park office in Puerto Villamil. A half-day tour including transport, horses and lunch costs US$40 per person (US$45 with English-speaking guide).

A visit to **Punta Moreno**, on the southwest part of the island, starts with a dinghy ride along the beautiful rocky shores where penguins and shore birds are usually seen. After a dry landing there is a hike through sharp lava rocks. **Elizabeth Bay**, on the west coast, is home to a small colony of penguins living on a series of small rocky islets and visited by dinghy. **Tagus Cove**, on the west coast across the narrow channel from Fernandina island, is an anchorage that has been used by visiting ships going back to the 1800s, and the ships' names can still be seen painted on the cliffs. A trail leads inland from Tagus Cove past Laguna Darwin, a large saltwater lake, and then further uphill to a ridge with lovely views.

Galápagos tourist vessels

Name	Description	Capacity	Website
Galápagos Explorer II	cruise ship	100	www.canodros.com
Galápagos Legend	cruise ship	100	www.kleintours.com
Xpedition	cruise ship	100	www.galapagosxpedition.co.uk
Santa Cruz	cruise ship	90	www.galapagosvoyage.com
Nat Geo Polaris	cruise ship	80	www.expeditions.com
Eclipse	cruise ship	48	www.galapagos-eclipse.com
Nat Geo Islander	cruise ship	48	www.expeditions.com
Isabela II	cruise ship	40	www.galapagosvoyage.com
Millenium	cruise ship	40	www.galasam.com
Coral I	motor yacht	36	www.kleintours.com
Evolution	cruise ship	32	www.quasarnautica.com
La Pinta	cruise ship	32	www.lapintagalapagoscruise.com
Coral II	motor yacht	20	www.kleintours.com
Eric	motor yacht	20	www.ecoventura.com
Flamingo I	motor yacht	20	www.ecoventura.com
Galápagos Adventure	motor yacht	20	various
Letty	motor yacht	20	www.ecoventura.com
Lammer Law	2-mast trimaran	18	www.lammerlaw.com
Aida Maria	motor yacht	16	www.galapagostours.net
Alta	3-mast ketch	16	www.quasarnautica.com
Amigo I	motor vessel	16	various
Anahí	motor catamaran	16	various
Angelique	2-mast sailer	16	www.kempery.com
Angelito I	motor yacht	16	www.angelitogalapagos.com
Archipel II	motor yacht	16	various
Athala II	motor catamaran	16	www.athalacruise.com
Beluga	motor yacht	16	www.enchantedexpeditions.com
Cachalote	2-mast schooner	16	www.enchantedexpeditions.com
Carina	motor yacht	16	various
Cormorant II	motor catamaran	16	various
Cruz del Sur	motor yacht	16	www.galasam.com
Daphne	motor yacht	16	various
Darwin	motor vessel	16	various
Edén	motor yacht	16	www.galapagostours.net
Estrella de Mar	motor yacht	16	www.galasam.com
Floreana	motor yacht	16	www.yatefloreana.com

Floreana Island → *Phone code: 05. Population: about 100.*
Floreana is the island with the richest human history and the fewest inhabitants, most in Puerto Velasco Ibarra, the rest in the highlands. Unless you visit with one of the few boats which land at Black Beach for a few hours, it is difficult to get onto and off the inhabited part of the island. Services are limited; you should be very flexible about travel times and self-sufficient, unless staying with the Wittmers or at Lava Lodge (see Sleeping, below). Margret Wittmer died in 2000, however you can meet her daughter and granddaughter. The climate in the highlands is fresh and comfortable, good for birdwatching. Places to visit include the **Devil's Crown** snorkelling site, **Punta Cormorant**, a green beach near which is a lake normally inhabited by flamingos and **Post Office Bay**, on the north side. There is a custom for visitors to Post Office Bay

Name	Description	Capacity	Website
Fragata	motor yacht	16	various
Galap Adventure II	motor yacht	16	various
Galaxy	motor yacht	16	various
Genovesa	motor vessel	16	www.galapagostours.net
Golondrina I	motor vessel	16	various
Gran Monserrat	motor yacht	16	various
Guantanamera	motor yacht	16	various
Integrity	motor yacht	16	various
Liberty	motor yacht	16	various
Mary Anne	3-mast barquentine	16	www.angermeyercruises.com
Monserrat	motor vessel	16	various
Monserrat II	motor vessel	16	various
Nina	motor catamaran	16	various
Parranda	motor yacht	16	various
Pelíkano	motor vessel	16	www.galapagos-tours.com
Queen Beatriz	motor catamaran	16	various
Queen of Galap	motor catamaran	16	www.galasam.com
Reina Silvia	motor yacht	16	www.reinasilvia.com
Rumba	motor vessel	16	www.galapagostours.net
Sagitta	3-mast sailing ship	16	www.angermeyercruises.com
Samba	motor yacht	16	www.angermeyercruises.com
San José	motor yacht	16	various
San Juan II	motor vessel	16	various
Sea Man II	motor yacht	16	various
The Beagle	2-mast schooner	16	www.angermeyercruises.com
Tip Top II	motor vessel	16	www.rwittmer.com
Tip Top III	motor yacht	16	www.rwittmer.com
Tip Top IV	motor yacht	16	www.rwittmer.com
Xavier III	motor vessel	16	various
Yolita II	motor yacht	16	various
Albatros	motor yacht	14	various
Amazonía	1-mast catamaran	12	various
Flamingo	motor vessel	12	various
Galapágos Vision I	1-mast catamaran	10	various
Merak	1-mast sailer	8	various

since 1793 to place unstamped letters and cards in a barrel, and deliver, free of charge, any addressed to their own destinations.

Unpopulated islands

Bartolomé is a small island in Sullivan Bay off the eastern shore of Santiago. It is probably the most visited and most photographed of all the islands with its distinctive **Pinnacle Rock** (a trail leads to the summit). A second visitor site has a lovely beach from which you can snorkel or swim and see the penguins. **Daphne**, west of Baltra, has very rich bird-life, in particular the nesting boobies, but visits are limited to one a month. **Española** is the southernmost island of the Galápagos and, following a successful programme to remove all the feral species, is now the most pristine of the islands. Gardner Bay, on the northeastern coast, is a beautiful white sand beach with excellent swimming and snorkelling. Punta Suárez, on the western tip of the island, has a trail through a rookery. As well as a wide range of seabirds (including blue-footed and Nazca boobies) there are sea lions, the largest and most colourful marine iguanas of the Galápagos and the original home of the waved albatrosses. **Fernadina** is the youngest of the islands, about 700,000 years old, and the most volcanically active. At Punta Espinosa, on the northeast coast, a trail goes up through a sandy nesting site for huge colonies of marine iguanas. You can also see flightless cormorants and go snorkelling in the bay.

Genovesa, at the northeast part of the archipelago, is an outpost for many sea birds. It is an eight to ten hour all-night sail from Puerto Ayora. Like Fernandina, Genovesa is best visited on smaller vessels with longer range; large ships are not allowed. One of the most famous sites is Prince Phillip's Steps, an amazing walk through a seabird rookery that is full of life. You will see tropic birds, all three boobies, frigates, petrels, swallow-tailed and lava gulls, and many others. There is also good snorkelling at the foot of the steps, with lots of marine iguanas. The entrance to Darwin Bay, on the eastern side of the island, is very narrow and shallow and the anchorage in the lagoon is surrounded by mangroves, home to a large breeding colony of frigates and other seabirds.

One of the closest islands to Puerto Ayora is **Plaza Sur**. It has a combination of both dry and coastal vegetation. Walking along the sea cliffs is a pleasant experience as the swallowtail gull, shearwaters and red-billed tropic-birds nest here. There are also lots of blue-footed boobies and a large population of land iguanas on the island. **Rábida**, just south of Santiago, has a salt water lagoon, occasionally home to flamingos. There is an area of mangroves near the lagoon where brown pelicans nest. You can snorkel and swim from the beach. On **Santa Fe**, between Santa Cruz and San Cristóbal, the lagoon is home to a large colony of sea lions who are happy to join you for a swim. This little island has its own sub-species of land iguana.

Santiago, a large island, also known as James, is east of Isla Isabela. It has a volcanic landscape full of cliffs and pinnacles, and is home to several species of marine birds. James Bay, on the western side of the island, has a wet landing on the dark sands of Puerto Egas. Fur seals are seen nearby. Espumilla Beach is another visitor site with a walk through a mangrove forest to a lake usually inhabited by flamingos, pintail ducks and stilts. Sea turtles dig their nests at the edge of the mangroves. Buccaneer Cove, in the northwest, was a haven for pirates during the 1600s and 1700s. Sullivan Bay, on the eastern coast opposite Bartolomé (see above) has a trail across an impressive lunar landscape of lava fields. Just off the southeastern tip is Sombrero Chino island, noted for its volcanic landscape. On **Seymour Norte**, just north of Baltra, the tourist trail leads through mangroves in one of the main nesting sites for blue-footed boobies and frigates in this part of the archipelago.

Galápagos Islands listings

For Sleeping and Eating price codes and other relevant information, see Essentials, pages 38-40.

Sleeping

Puerto Ayora *p1195*

Reservations are essential in high season.

LL Finch Bay Hotel, On a small bay south of Puerto Ayora, accessible only by boat, T252 6297, www.finchbayhotel.com. A luxury hotel on a beautiful beach. Buffet breakfast, restaurant, pool, fine restaurant and bar, good service, comfortable rooms. Book through **Metropolitan Touring** in Quito.

LL Red Mangrove, Darwin y las Fragatas, toward the Charles Darwin station, T252 6564, Quito T02-225 0166, www.redmangrove.com. A beautiful hotel with plenty of character. Includes breakfast, restaurant, jacuzzi, deck bar and lovely Japanese dining room. Very tasteful rooms all overlooking the water, ample bathrooms. Owner Hernan Rodas offers day tours and diving. Recommended.

LL Royal Palm, in the highlands of Santa Cruz, T252 7409, www.royalpalmgalapagos.com. Includes breakfast, villas and suites with all luxuries, Jacuzzi in rooms, private lounge at airport, part of Millennium international chain.

LL Silberstein, Darwin y Piqueros, T252 6047, www.hotelsilberstein.com. Modern and very comfortable, with lovely grounds and a small pool, buffet breakfast, restaurant and bar, spacious rooms and common areas, very nice.

LL-L Angemeyer Waterfront Inn, by the dock at Punta Estrada, T09-472 4955, tangermeyer@yahoo.com. Gorgeous location overlooking the bay. Includes breakfast, very comfortable modern rooms and apartments, some with kitchenettes.

L Sol y Mar, Darwin y Binford, T252 6281, www.hotelsolymar.com.ec. Right in town but with a nice location overlooking the bay. Buffet breakfast, restaurant and bar, pool and spa.

AL Lobo de Mar, 12 de Febrero y Darwin, T252 6188, www.lobodemar.com.ec. Modern building with balconies and rooftop terrace, great views over the harbour. Includes breakfast, a/c, two pools, Wi-Fi, fridge, modern and comfortable, attentive service. Recommended.

A Estrella de Mar, by the water on a lane off 12 de Febrero, T252 6427. Nice quiet location with views over the bay. Includes breakfast, a/c, fan, fridge, spacious rooms, sitting area.

A Santa Fe Suites, Charles Binford entre Juan Montalvo y Las Ninfas, T252 6419, www.santafeii.com.ec. Rooms with small kitchenettes in a quiet area, includes breakfast, fan, pool.

A-B Gardner, Berlanga y Islas Plaza, T252 6979, pensiongardner@yahoo.com. Pleasant and quiet, spacious rooms, includes breakfast, a/c, older rooms with fan are cheaper, small sitting area with hammocks and outdoor cooking facilities. Recommended.

B Castro, Los Colonos y Malecón, T252 6113. Pleasant, older but well maintained place on a quiet street. Includes breakfast, restaurant, a/c, Wi-Fi, rooftop terrace.

C Peregrino, Darwin e Indefatigable, T252 6323. Away from the centre of town, includes breakfast, electric shower, a/c, nice rooms, small garden, family run, homey atmosphere.

C Salinas, Islas Plaza y Berlanga, T252 6107. Cheaper with cold water, fan, simple and adequate.

D-E Santa Cruz, Av Baltra e Indefatigable, T252 4326. Electric shower, a/c, cheaper with fan, good value.

E Los Amigos, Darwin y 12 de Febrero, T252 6265. Small place with a couple of 3-bed rooms, two rooms with private bath, cold water, laundry facilities, basic but friendly.

Puerto Baquerizo Moreno *p1196*

AL Miconia, Darwin y Melville, T252 0608, www.miconia.com. Includes breakfast, restaurant, a/c, small pool, large well-equipped gym, modern if somewhat small rooms, some with fridge.

A-B Chatham, Northía y Av de la Armada Nacional, on the road to the airport, T252 0137, chathamhotel@hotmail.com. Patio with hammocks, meals on request, electric shower, rooms in newer section have a/c and fridge, older rooms with fan are cheaper, well maintained and nice.

A-C Gran Hotel Mar Azul, Northía y Esmeraldas, T252 0091, www.granhotelmarazul.com.ec. Modern multi-storey hotel, comfortable rooms with a/c and fridge, good service.

B Casablanca, Mellville y Darwin, T252 0392, jacquivaz@yahoo.com. Large white house with lovely terrace and views of harbour. Breakfast available, each room is individually decorated by the owner who has an art studio on the premises.

B Suites Bellavista, Darwin y Melville, above the supermarkert, T252 0352. Good location right on the *malecón*, a/c, cooking facilities, ample modern rooms.

C Casa de Nelly, Northía y Roldos, T252 0112. Three storey building in a quiet location, fan, cooking facilities, bright comfortable rooms with a fresh sea breeze.

C Mar Azul, Northía y Esmeraldas, T252 0139, hotelmarazul-ex@hotmail.com. Nice comfortable lodgings, electric shower, a/c, cheaper with fan, pleasant. Recommended.

D León Dormido, Villamil y Darwin, T252 0169. Nice simple place, hot water, good value.

E Doña Pilo, Northía y Quito, T252 0098. Electric shower, fan, family run, simple but adequate and good value, often full.

E San Francisco, Darwin y Villamil, T252 0304. Cold water, fan, rooms in front are nicer, simple but good value.

Isabela Island *p1197*

LL Red Mangrove, Conocarpus y Opuntia, T252 9030, www.redmangrove.com. Reception and common areas are in older wooden building, bungalows across the road are more modern, with a/c, but only the front ones have a sea view. Pricey for what it offers.

L-AL La Casa de Marita, at east end of beach, T252 9238, www.galapagosisabela.com. Definitely upscale, even chic. Includes breakfast, other meals on request, a/c and fridge, Jacuzzi, very comfortable, each room is a bit different and some have balconies. A little gem. Recommended.

AL Albemarle, on the beachfront, T252 9489, www.hotelalbemarle.com. Attractive Mediterranean-style construction, includes breakfast, a/c, bright comfortable rooms with wonderful ocean views, English-Ecuadorean run.

B San Vicente, Cormoranes y Pinzón Artesano, T252 9140. Very popular hotel which also offers tours and kayak rentals, includes breakfast, cold water, a/c, use of cooking facilities and fridge, meals on request, rooms a bit small but nice, camping possible, family run. Recommended.

C-E La Casa Rosada, Antonio Gil at at west end of the beach, T252 9330, claudiahodari@gmail.com. Nicer inside than outside, fan, terrace overlooking the ocean, comfortable rooms with antique-style furniture, fridge.

D Posada del Caminante, C Cormorán behind the lagoon, T252 9407. A bit out of the way, hot water, fan, ample rooms with kitchen, friendly owner.

Floreana Island *p1198*

L Lava Lodge, on the beach, T252 6564, www.redmangrove.com. Part of Red Mangrove chain, includes breakfast, other meals on request, restaurant, fan when there is electricity, simple cabins. Advance booking required.

AL Pensión Wittmer, right on Black Beach, T252 9506. Includes 3 delicious meals, fan when there is electricity, simple and comfortable, a very special place, reservations required.

Eating

Puerto Ayora *p1195*

TTT Angermeyer Point, across the bay, take a water-taxi from the port, T252 7007, Tue-Sat 1900-2200, Sun brunch 1100-1600. Former home of Galápagos pioneer and artist Carl Angermeyer, with his works on display. Gorgeous setting over the water (take insect repellent). Excellent, innovative and varied menu, attentive service. Reservations advised. Highly recommended.

TTT La Dolce Italia, Charles Darwin entre Islas Plaza y 12 de Febrero, daily 1100-1500, 1800-2200. Italian and seafood, wine list, a/c, pleasant atmosphere, attentive owner.

TTT The Rock, Charles Darwin e Islas Plaza, 0900-2300, closed Tue. Very popular restaurant and bar, international food, sushi on Fri night.

TTT-TT Hernán, Av Baltra y Opuntia, daily 0730-2230. Restaurant and bar, international menu, pizza, burgers, cappuccino.

TTT-TT La Garrapata, Charles Darwin between 12 de Febrero and Tomás de Berlanga, Mon-Sat 0900-2200, Sun 1700-2200. Good food, attractive setting and good music, juice bar, sandwiches and set lunch during the day, à la carte at night.

TT Chocolate Galápagos, Charles Darwin entre Tomas de Berlanga y Charles Binford, daily 0700-2200. Breakfast, snacks, meals, and desserts, outdoor seating, popular.

T El Descanso del Guía, Charles Darwin y Los Colonos. Good value set meals, very popular with locals.

T Kiosks, Along Charles Binford between Padre Herrera and Rodríguez Lara. Many kiosks selling traditional food, including reasonably priced seafood. **Kiosko de Renato** is especially good; **Pelícano Goloso**, **Servi-Sabrosón** and **William** also cook well. All with simple outdoor seating and a lively atmosphere, popular with locals and busy at night.

Cafés

La Casa del Lago, Moisés Brito y Juan Montavo, Barrio Las Ninfas, a quiet area away from the main drag, www.galapagoscultural.com, Mon-Sat 0700-2200. Drinks, snacks and ice cream, live music, art and cultural activities, owners Enrique and Helena also rent apartments nearby.

Puerto Baquerizo Moreno *p1196*

TTT La Playa, Av de la Armada Nacional, by the navy base, T252 1511, daily 0930-2330. Varied menu, fish and seafood specialties, nice location.

TTT Miramar, on beachfront around the corner from Capitanía, daily 1800-2400. Seafood and international dishes, variety of cocktails, lovely ocean views, great sunsets.

TTT-TT Rosita, Ignacio de Hernández y General Villamil, daily from 1100, closed Sun PM. Set meals and varied à la carte, old-time yachtie hangout.

🍴 **Deep Blue**, Darwin y Española. Ceviches in morning, good set lunch, closed evenings.
A few other simple places serve set meals.

Cafés

Mockingbird Café, Española y Hernandez. Fruit juices, brownies, snacks, internet.
Panadería Fragata, Northía y Rocafuerte. Excellent bread and pastries, good selection.

Isabela Island *p1197*
🍴 **El Encanto de la Pepa**, Antonio Gil on the Plaza. Set meals and à la carte, lots of character, good food, pleasant outdoor seating.
🍴 **La Choza**, Antonio Gil y Las Fragatas. Varied menu, a bit pricey, pizza must be ordered the morning before.
🍴-🍴 **Tropical**, Las Fragatas 1/2 block from Plaza, open daily. Good quality and value set meals, popular with locals.

Bars and clubs

Puerto Ayora *p1195*
La Panga, Av Charles Darwin y Berlanga and **Bar Bongo**, upstairs, are both popular.
Limón y Café, Charles Darwin y 12 de Febrero. Snacks and drinks, lots of music, pool table.

Puerto Baquerizo Moreno *p1196*
Calypso, Darwin y Manuel J. Cobos, daily 1800-2400. Snacks and drinks, pleasant outdoor seating.
Iguana Rock, Quito y Juan José Flores, some live music, pool table, popular.

Isabela Island *p1197*
Beto's Beach Bar, Antonio Gil y Los Flamencos along the beach. Pleasant location, irregular hours, very relaxed. Has one room to rent.

Shopping

Most items can be purchased on the islands, but cost more than on the mainland. Do not buy items made of black coral as it is an endangered species.

Puerto Ayora *p1195*
There is an attractive little **Mercado Artesanal** (craft market) at Charles Darwin y Tomás de Berlanga. **Proinsular**, opposite the pier, is the largest and best stocked supermarket.

There are various T-shirt, souvenir, and highbrow jewellery shops along the length of Av Charles Darwin, all touristy and expensive.
Camping gear Tatoo, opposite Capitanía del Puerto, T252 4101, www.tatoo.ws.

Puerto Baquerizo Moreno *p1196*
Galamarket, Isabela y Juan José Flores, is a modern well-stocked supermarket. **Fabo Galería de Arte**, Malecón Charles Darwin y Melville, 2nd floor of **Hotel Casa Blanca**. Paintings by the owner Fabricio, and silk-screened T-shirts. A few souvenir shops along the Malecón sell T-shirts and crafts.

Activities and tours

Galápagos operators on the mainland

Details of the following are given under their respective cities. **Quito** (see page 1057):

Andando Tours-Angermeyer Crusies, Andes Explorer, Creter Tours, Ecoventura, Enchanted Expeditions, Galacruises Expeditions, Surtrek, Galasam, Go Galapagos, Latin Trails, Mallku Expeditions, Nature Galapagos and Ecuador, Zenith Travel. **Guayaquil**: Canodros. See also page 1194.

Puerto Ayora *p1195*

Cycling Mountain bikes can be hired from travel agencies in town. Prices and quality vary.

Diving Only specialized diving boats are allowed to do diving tours. It is not possible to dive as part of a standard live-on-board cruise.

National Park rules prohibit collecting samples or souvenirs, spear-fishing, touching animals, or other environmental disruptions. Experienced dive guides can help visitors have the most spectacular opportunities to enjoy the wildlife. There are several diving agencies in Puerto Ayora offering courses, equipment rental, dives within Academy Bay (2 dives for US$90), and other central islands (2 dives, US$140), daily tours for 1 week in the central islands and several day live-aboard tours. There is a hyperbaric chamber in Puerto Ayora to treat divers in case of decompression sickness (US$1,500 per hr, 50% discount if your dive operator is affiliated): Rodríguez Lara y 12 de Febrero, T252 6911, www.sssnetwork.com. Confirm in advance whether your diving insurance is accepted and make sure you have adequate cover. To avoid the risk of decompression sickness, divers are advised to stay an extra day on the islands after their last dive before flying to the mainland, especially to Quito at 2,840 m above sea level.

DiveCenter Silberstein, opposite Hotel Silberstein, T2526028, www.divinggalapagos.com. Trips for beginners up to PADI divemaster.

Galápagos Sub-Aqua, Av Charles Darwin e Isla Floreana, T252 6633, www.galapagos-sub-aqua.com (Guayaquil: Orellana 211 y Panamá, No 702, T04-230 5514). Open Mon-Sat 0800-1230, 1430-1830. Instructor Fernando Zambrano offers full certificate courses up to PADI divemaster level. Repeatedly recommended.

Nautidiving, Av Charles Darwin, T252 7004, www.nautidiving.com. Offers 8-day, 7-night trips.

Scuba Iguana, Charles Darwin near the research station, T252 6497, www.scubaiguana.com. Matías Espinoza runs this long-time reliable and recommended dive operator. Courses up to PADI divemaster.

Horse riding For riding at ranches in the highlands, enquire at **Moonrise Travel**.

Snorkelling Masks, snorkels and fins can be rented from travel agencies and dive shops, US$5 a day, deposit required. Closest place to snorkel is by beaches near Darwin Station.

Surfing There is surfing at Tortuga Bay and at other more distant beaches accessed by boat. There is better surfing near Puerto Baquerizo

Moreno on San Cristóbal. The **Lonesome George** agency (see below) rents surfboards for US$10-$15 per half-day.

Tour operators

Avoid touts who approach you at the airport or in the street offering cheap tours. Also be wary of agencies who specialize in cut-rate cruises.

Lonesome George, Av Baltra y Enrique Fuentes, T252 6245, lonesomegrg@yahoo.com. Run by Victor Vaca. Sells tours and rents: bicycles, surfboards, snorkelling equipment and motorcycles.

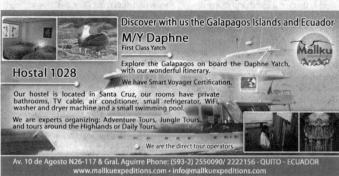

Moonrise Travel, Av Charles Darwin y Charles Binford, opposite Banco del Pacífico, T252 6348, www.galapagosmoonrise.com. Last-minute cruise bookings, day-tours to different islands, bay tours, airline reservations. Owner Jenny Devine speaks English, she is helpful, reliable and

very knowledgeable. Highly recommended.
Naugala Yacht Services, Barrio El Eden, T252 7403, www.naugala.com.

Puerto Baquerizo Moreno *p1196*

Cycling Hire bikes from travel agencies, US$20 per day.

Diving There are several dive sites around San Cristóbal, most popular being Kicker Rock, Roca Ballena and Punta Pitt (at the northeastern side). See Tour operators (below) who offer dives. The nearest hyperbaric chamber is in Puerto Ayora.

Surfing There is good surfing in San Cristóbal, the best season is Dec-Mar. **Punta Carola** near town is the closest surfing beach; popular among locals. There is a championship during the local *fiesta*, the 2nd week of Feb.

Tour operators

Chalo Tours, Española y Hernandez, T252 0953, www.chalotours.com. Bay tours to Kicker Rock and Isla de los Lobos, boat tours to the north end of the island, highland tours, diving tours, bike rentals, snorkelling gear, book exchange.

Galakiwi, Española y Darwin, T252 1562, galakiwi@yahoo.com.au. Owned by New-Zealander Tim Cooney. Highland and diving tours, kayaks and other gear rentals.
Sharksky, Española y Charles Darwin, T252 1188, http://sharksky.com. Adventure tours, diving, volunteering, has a popular café, helpful.

Isabela Island *p1197*
Hotels can arrange visits to local attractions, mostly operated by Antonio Gil at **Hotel San Vicente**, reliable and recommended.
Carapachudo Tours, Escalecias y Tero Real, Puerto Villamil, T05 252 9451, info@carapachudotours.com. Mountain biking tours, downhill from Sierra Negra and to other attractions, US$42 for a full day including lunch. Also rentals: bikes for US$3/hr, US$20/day; surf boards US$4/hr.
Isabela Dive Center, Escalecia y Alberto Gil, T05-252 9418, www.isabeladivecenter.com.ec. Diving, land and boat tours.

Transport

Puerto Ayora *p1195*
Pick-ups may be hired for transport throughout town, US$1-2, agree fare in advance. Up to the highlands, they leave throughout the day from in front of the Tropidurus store, Padre Herrera corner Jaime Roldos, 2 blocks past the market: to **Bellavista** US$0.25, 10 min; to **Santa Rosa** US$1, 20 min; to **Playa Garrapatero** US$30 for the vehicle round trip including wait. **Water taxis** (*taxis marítimos*) from the pier to anchored boats and Punta Estrada, US$0.60 pp from 0600 until 1900 and then US$1. Several taxis work until midnight. There is always one on duty 24-hr but you might have to wait awhile when lots of boats are in port, especially Fri and Sat. If you have access, call them on channel 14.

Directory

Puerto Ayora *p1195*
Airline offices Aerogal, Rodrigues Lara y San Cristóbal, T252 6798. **TAME**, Av Charles Darwin y 12 de Febrero, T252 6527. **Emetebe**, Av Charles Darwin near port, 2nd floor of Ferroinsular hardware store next to Proinsular supermarket, T252 6177. **Banks** **Banco del Pacífico**, Av Charles Darwin y Charles Binford, T252 6282, Mon-Fri 0800-1530, Sat 0930-1230. US$5 commission per transaction for TCs, maximum US$500 per transaction. ATM works with Cirrus, Plus and MC but not Visa; cash advances from tellers on Visa and MC. **Embassies and consulates** British Consul, David Balfour, T252 6159. **Medical services** Hospitals: there is a hospital on Av Baltra for first aid and basic care. For anything serious, locals usually fly to the mainland. Also see hyperbaric chamber under Diving, above. **Internet** There are several cybercafés throughout town, US$2/hr. **Post offices** by the port, unreliable; it often runs out of stamps, never leave money and letters. **DHL courier and Western Union**, across the street from Hotel Silberstein. **Useful addresses** **Yacht agents** Galapagos Ocean Services (Peter Schiess), Charles Darwin next to Garrapata restaurant, T09-477 0804, www.gos.ec. **Naugala Yacht Services** (Jhonny Romero), T252 7403, www.naugala.com.

Puerto Baquerizo Moreno *p1196*
Airline offices Aerogal, at the airport, T252 1118. **TAME**, Charles Darwin y Manuel J Cobos, T252 1351, airport counter T252 1089. **Emetebe**, at the airport T252 0615. **Banks** **Banco del Pacífico**, Charles Darwin entre Española y Melville. Same hours and services as in Puerto Ayora. **Internet** US$2 per hr. **Laundry** **Lavandería Limpio y Seco**, Av Northía y 12 de Febrero. Wash and dry US$2. Open daily 0900-2100. **Medical services** There is a hospital providing only basic medical services. **Dr David Basantes**, opposite Hotel Mar Azul, T252 0126, is a helpful GP. **Farmacia San Cristóbal**, Villamil y Hernández. **Post offices** Malecón Charles Darwin y 12 de Febrero.

Isabela Island *p1197*
Airline offices Emetebe, Antonio Gil y Las Fragatas, T252 9155. **Banks** There are no banks on Isabela, no ATMs, and nowhere to use credit cards or change TCs. You must bring US$ cash. **Money Gram**, Terro Real y Escalecias, in Hotel Insular, for international funds transfer.If stuck without funds, ask **Emetebe** if they can give cash against Visa or Mastercard; it may take a day or two for the cash to arrive. **Internet** There are a couple of slow cyber-cafés in town, US$2/hr.

Paraguay

Contents

1212 **Planning your trip**

1217 **Asunción**
1217 Sights

1230 **Región Oriental: East of Asunción**

1237 **Región Oriental: South of Asunción**

1243 **North of Asunción**

1247 **The Chaco**

Footprint features

1210 Don't miss …
1214 Driving in Paraguay

At a glance

Time required 1-3 weeks.

Best time Sep/Oct and Mar-May are not too hot or wet.

When not to go Heaviest rains Nov-Mar; Dec-Feb can be excessively hot.

★ Don't miss …
1 Plaza de los Héroes, Asunción, page 1219.
2 Itaipú, page 1234.
3 Jesuit missions, page 1238.
4 The Chaco, page 1247.
BOLIVIA
BRAZIL
ARGENTINA
BRAZIL
Mayor Pablo Lagerenza
PN Defensores del Chaco
Bahía Negra
Gral Eugenio A Garay
FN Madrejón
PN Tte Agripino Enciso
Fuerte Olimpo
Fortín Infante Rivarola
Mariscal Estigarribia
Filadelfia
Loma Plata
Neuland
Chaco
Río Verde
Vallemí
PN Serranías San Luís
Bella Vista
PN del Cerro Corá
Pedro Juan Caballero
Yby Yaú
Concepción
Horqueta
Pozo Colorado
Pirahú
Puerto Antequera
Paraguay
San Pedro
Rosario
Mbaracayú Forest Reserve
Salto del Guaíra
Tacuara
Curuguaty
San Estanislao
Benjamin Aceval
Villa Hayes
Represa de Itaipu
ASUNCION
San Lorenzo
Coronel Oviedo
Paraguarí
Colonia Independencia
Ciudad del Este
Villarrica
Ybicuí NP
Ybicuí
Caapucú
Caazapá
Villa Florida
Pilar
San Juan Bautista
Santa Rosa
Obligado
Jesús
Hohenau
San Ignacio Guazú
Trinidad
Paso de Patria
Encarnación
Ayolas
San Cosme y Damián
Luque
Altos
Tobatí
ASUNCIÓN
Aregua
Lago Ypacaraí
San Bernardino
San Lorenzo
Capiatá
Nemby
Itauguá
Ypacaraí
Caacupé
San Antonio
Ypané
Piribebuy
Río Paraguay
Guarambaré
Pirayú
Itá
Villeta
Chololó
Yaguarón
Puerto Paraíso
Nueva Italia
Paraguarí
N
100 km
100 miles

An air of mystery hangs over this under-explored pocket of South America, a country of farmland, nature and folklore. From the hot, wild impenetrable Chaco in the northwest to the lush forests of the southeast, there is abundant birdlife, a number of rivers to navigate and fantastic opportunities to experience rural tourism. Although dwarfed by its giant neighbours Brazil and Argentina, Paraguay covers some 440,000 sq km, roughly the same size as California. It is at the confluence of six ecorregion types, Atlantic forest, cerrado, humid chaco, dry chaco, pantanal and pampa grasslands, resulting in a variety of landscapes and panoramas as well as rich flora and fauna.

Land-locked Paraguay has had a strange history of charismatic leaders, steadfastness and isolation. Paraguayans are proud of their Guaraní culture and heritage, evident in the widespread use of the officially-recognized indigenous language, which is still taught in schools. Although apparently impossible to enunciate by an outsider, the Guaraní language cannot mask the warmth of Paraguayan hospitality. Music, too, marks Paraguay apart from its neighbours: emotive songs and European dances accompanied by virtuoso harp players and guitarists.

In other ways, Paraguay is not so separate. It shares with Argentina and Brazil remains of the Mission settlements built by Jesuits near the banks of the Río Paraná, testimony to one of the major social experiments on the continent. Paraguayans are renowned for their passion for football and a dedication to a daily consumption of yerba mate (*Ilex paraguariensis*); either with ice cold water (*tereré*) on hot days, or hot water (*mate*) on cold days. Today the country is part of the Mercosur economic union, with trade routes to Argentina and Brazil well established and the road to Bolivia recently completed: the Trans-Chaco is one of the great road adventures in South America.

Planning your trip

Where to go

Paraguay is divided into two main regions separated by the Río Paraguay. The capital, **Asunción**, sits between the two; to the east of the river lies the Región Oriental (approximately 40%) and to the west the Región Occidental (approximately 60%), or Chaco. It is best to plan your travels to either of these regions from Asunción.

The capital, Paraguay's largest city with some 1.4 million inhabitants, stands on a bay of the Río Paraguay. The expansion of the metropolitan area means it now rubs shoulders with the neighbouring cities of San Lorenzo, Fernando de la Mora, Lambaré, Luque, Mariano Roque Alonso, Ñemby, San Antonio, Limpio, Capiatá and Villa Elisa. Together, these form Gran Asuncion (population approximately 2.8 million). Asunción is the political and commercial heart and much of its architecture dates from the early 1800s. Paraguayan history is marked by bloody wars and charismatic dictators, which is somehwat unexpected given the warmth and serenity of its people.

Región Oriental makes up most of the fertile agricultural part of the country. The towns and villages are quiet and traditional in their way of life. Many have unique crafts associated with them. There are also many signs of the Jesuit heritage, which is best exemplified at the ruins of the reductions at Santísima Trinidad de Paraná and Jesús de Tavarangüé, declared World Heritage Sites by UNESCO in 1993 (along with a third, Santos Cosme y Damián), close to the city of Encarnación. From here you can cross the Río Paraná to the Argentine city of Posadas in the province of Misiones. Paraguay's eastern border with Brazil has several frontier posts, but the main one is Ciudad del Este, a duty-free shopper's paradise (or hell, depending on your point of view), where you can visit Itaipú, until recently the largest hydroelectric dam in the world. Across the Friendship Bridge from Ciudad del Este is Foz do Iguaçu in Brazil and the magnificent Iguaçu Falls.

North of Asunción there is one main town, Concepción, and the most interesting route there, if you have the time, is by river boat from the capital. The boat ride takes at least a day, so quicker ways are via the Chaco, along part of the Trans-Chaco Highway or across the Cordillera and San Pedro Departments along Ruta 3. Beyond Concepción, the Río Paraguay leads to the Brazilian Pantanal, which can also be reached by road.

Región Occidental, or Chaco makes up the western half of the country. Divided into three departments, Presidente Hayes (also known as Bajo Chaco), Boquerón and Alto Paraguay (or Alto Chaco), the Chaco begins as a marshy palm savanna, but becomes an increasingly impenetrable and dry scrub forest as it approaches the border with Bolivia. The Trans-Chaco Highway crosses the Chaco and, apart from scattered military outposts, there are few urbanized areas for 400 kilometres until you reach the Mennonite colonies of Filadelfia, Loma Plata and Neuland which make up the Chaco Central region. A relatively short distance further northwest is the former military base of Mariscal Estigarribia. The Chaco is possibly the best place in Paraguay to see wildlife, especially birds, but you should not venture off the beaten track alone and unprepared in this part of the country.

National parks and nature tourism Paraguay is a confluence of globally important ecoregions and is rich in biodiversity. This abundance of wildlife is especially visible in the still largely pristine Chaco, especially in its remote national parks, along the Río Pilcomayo, and the frontier with Bolivia. Current estimates include around 7,000 plant species, 100,000 invertebrates (including 765 of butterfly), 300 species of fish, 120 reptiles, 100 amphibians, 687 birds and 171 mammals. For more details, visit **Fauna Paraguay** (www.faunaparaguay.com). Paraguay has an extensive network of state-protected areas, including 11 national parks, plus seven reserves under the management of the Itaipú (6) and Yacyretá (1) dam companies. More recently, the number of private reserves has increased to 33, of which 17 are legally recognized. Unfortunately, many of these protected areas exist solely on paper, and the whole system is under- funded. Visiting the protected areas is not always easy; contact the relevant institutions and authorities. For a list of all protected areas (public and private), visit the **Secretaría Nacional de Turismo** (www.senatur.gov.py). For state-protected area visit **Secretaría del Ambiente** (SEAM, www.seam.gov.py). For Itaipú and Yacyretá reserves go to the relevant environmental departments. For private reserves contact the following conservation NGOs: **Guyra Paraguay** (Gtna Martino 215 esq Tte Ross, Asunción, T21-229097, www.guyra.org.py), which has a wealth of information for birdwatchers, naturalists and biologists as well as the capacity, infrastructure and expertise to organize tailor-made ecotours to all parts of the country, including some of the more remote locations not provided by other tour operators (highly recommended); **Fundación Moisés Bertoni para la Conservación de la Naturaleza** (www.mbertoni.org.py), which manages the Mbaracayú Reserve, one of the few remaining pristine Atlantic Forest reserves in the region. **Desarrollo Turístico Paraguayo** (DTP, www.dtp.com.py) can organize adventure tours to different parts of the country.

When to go

The climate is sub-tropical, with a marked difference between summer and winter and often from one day to the next. December to February (summer) can be very hot and humid, with temperatures from 25° to 43°C. From March to May (autumn) and September to November (spring) the heat is less oppressive, a good time for travelling. During winter (June-August) the temperature can range from 0°C at night to 28°C in the day. Temperatures below freezing are very rare, and it never snows. Some rain falls each month, but the heaviest rains tend to occurs from October to April.

Getting around

Air There are scheduled services to most of the main parts of the country from Silvio Pettirossi airport. Domestic fares are subject to US$2 tax.

Bus Along most main roads, buses will stop at almost any junction to collect or drop off passengers, so all timetables are approximate.

Train Most of the 441-km rail network has been closed since early 2001, although freight trains continue to make sporadic trips to Encarnación, and a recently extended tourist steam train service (**Tren del Lago**) now runs from Asunción, Botánico station, to Sapucaí via Aregua each Sunday (see page 1228). Visit www.ferrocarriles.com.py.

Driving in Paraguay

Road Around 10% of roads are paved. Roads serving the main centres are in good condition and are continually being upgraded. A highway links Asunción with Iguazú Falls (six hours). Potholes are a hazard, especially in Asunción. Unsurfaced roads may not be passable in bad weather, especially November-April. There are regular police checks; it's advisable to lock doors.
Safety Beware of stray cattle on the road at night. Driving at night is not advisable.
Documents Neither a carnet de passages *nor libreta de pasos por aduana* is required for a car or motorcycle, but the carnet may make entry easier. Temporary admission for a private vehicle is usually 30 days.
Organizations Touring y Automóvil Club Paraguayo (TACP), 25 de Mayo y Brasil, p 2, Asunción, T021-210550, www.tacpy.com.py, produces a road map and provides information about weather and roads. TACP is also in charge of **Rural Tourism**. Information also from the office of the traffic police in Asunción, T021-493390.
Car hire Weekly and free-km rates available. Rates are from US$45 per day to US$150 for 4WD.
Fuel Unleaded only (some has sugar-cane alcohol added). Most vehicles are diesel-powered. 95 octane US$0.74 per litre; 97 octane US$0.86 per litre; diesel US$0.70 per litre. Motor fuel and oil are sold by the litre. There are few service stations in the Chaco.

Maps A general map of the country can be purchased at most bookstores in Asunción, at bus terminals and the **Touring y Automóvil Club Paraguayo** (TACP), but more detailed maps are available from **Instituto Geográfico Militar** ⓘ *Av Artigas casi Av Perú*; make sure to have your passport.

Sleeping ➔ *See page 38 for our hotel grade price guide.*
There are a few hotels in our **G** range and many good ones in our **D-F** ranges, with private shower and toilet. Most hotels have two rates – one for a room with a/c, the other without. Almost all include breakfast.

Eating and drinking ➔ *See page 40 for our restaurant price guide.*
Eating out Lunch is usually served between 1130-1300 in most restaurants and bars. Evening meals are hard to find in small towns, but options exist in larger cities.

Food Typical local foods include *chipa*, a cheese bread that comes in a number of varieties: *almidón*, made with yuca flour; *barrero*, made with corn flour; *manduví*, made with peanuts (better warm than cold). *Chipa so'o* is maize bread with minced meat filling; *chipa guazú* is made with fresh corn; *sopa paraguaya* is a kind of sponge of ground maize and cheese. These make a great side dish, or can be enjoyed on their own. *Soyo* is a soup of different meats and vegetables; *albóndiga* a soup of meat balls; *bori bori* another type of soup with diced meat, vegetables, and small balls of maize mixed with cheese. The beef is excellent in the better restaurants (best cuts are *lomo* and *lomito*) and can be enjoyed with *chorizo* (sausage), *morcilla, chipa guazú, sopa paraguaya* and a variety of salads. *Parrillada completa* is recommended and there are many *churrascarías* serving huge quantities of meat, with salad, vegetables and pasta. River fish include *surubí* and *dorado*, which are prepared in many different ways. Although vegetarian restaurants are scarce, there are lots of fruits, salads and vegetables, as well as the non-meat varieties of *empanada*, such as *choclo, palmito* or *cuatro quesos*.

Drink The most popular national drink is *tereré* (cold mate with digestive herbs) for warm days and hot mate to warm you up on cold days. *Cocido* is a type of tea made by burning (traditionally with a red ember) the yerba with some sugar; this can be served with or without milk. Paraguayan beers are very good, the better brands being *Baviera*, *Pilsen* and *Munich*. These are lager-types, but you can sometimes find darker beers in the winter. The better brands of the national sugarcane-based spirit, *caña*, include *Aristocrata* (known as 'Ari'), *Fortín* and *Tres Leones*. You can find most global brand soft drinks, including *guaraná* (originally from Brazil). *Mosto* is a very sweet but refreshing juice from sugarcane. And there is a wonderful variety of fresh fruit juices.

Essentials A-Z

Accident and emergency

Ambulance and police emergency T911.

Electricity

220 volts AC, 50 cycles, but power surges and voltage drops are frequent. European 2 round pin plugs are used. Visitors from North America should bring an inexpensive adaptor, as few hotels outside Asunción offer 110-volt service.

Embassies and consulates

See www.mre.gov.py, the Ministry of Foreign Affairs' website.

Festivals and events

Public holidays

1 Jan; 3 Feb (San Blas, patron of Paraguay); 1 Mar (anniversary of the death of former president Francisco Solano López); Maundy Thu, Good Fri; 1 (Labour Day), 15 May (Independence); 12 Jun (Paz del Chaco), 24 Jun (San Juan); 15 Aug (founding of Asunción), 16 Aug (Children's Day, in honour of the boys who died at the Battle of Acosta Ñu, see page 1219); 29 Sep (victory of Boquerón, decisive battle in the Chaco War); 12 Oct (Día de la Raza); 8 Dec (Virgen de Caacupé), 25 Dec.

Internet

The average cost of internet in urban areas is US$0.75-1.25 per hour.

Money → *US$1=G4,609, €1=G6,258 (Feb 2010).*

The guaraní (plural guaraníes) is the unit of currency, symbolized by the letter G (crossed). There are bank notes for 1,000, 5,000, 10,000, 50,000 and 100,000 guaraníes and coins for 1, 5, 10, 50, 100, 500 and 1,000 guaraníes. Get rid of all your guaraníes before leaving Paraguay; there is no market for them elsewhere (except in some cambios in Buenos Aires).

Plastic/TCs/banks Asunción is a good place for obtaining US$ cash on MasterCard or Visa especially if heading for Brazil. ATMs for Visa and MasterCard are common in Asunción and offer good rates of exchange. Many banks in Asunción (see page 1229) give US$ cash, but charge up to 5.5% commission. Rates for most other foreign currencies are reasonable. Casas de cambio may want to see customers' records of purchase before accepting TCs. Visitors are advised to check on the situation on changing TCs in advance. Visa and MasterCard cash advances are possible in Asunción, Ciudad del Este and Encarnación, but only for credit (not debit) cards. Street dealers operate from early morning until late at night, even on public holidays, but double check that they are giving you the right exchange.

Cost of travelling Allow US$40-45 per person per day to cover all expenses, unless staying in the cheapest hotels and not moving around much.

Opening hours

Shops, offices and businesses open around 0700; some may close 1200-1500 for lunch and siesta. **Commercial office hours** are 0730-1100 or 1300, and 1430 or 1500-1800 or 1900. **Banks:** 0845-1500, closed Sat-Sun. **Government offices:** 0700-1130 in summer, 0730-1200 in winter, open Sat.

Safety

Paraguay is generally safe and visitors are treated courteously. At election times there may be demonstrations in the capital, but the country as a whole is very calm. Beware police seeking bribes, especially at Asunción bus station and at border crossings. See **www.policia.gov.py** for all matters related to the police and **www.mspbs.gov.py** for current health risks in Paraguay.

Tax

Airport tax US$18, payable on departure in US$ or guaraníes (cheaper).
VAT/IVA 10%.

Telephone → *Country code +595.*
Ringing: equal long tones with long pauses.
Engaged: equal short tones with equal pauses.
Directory enquiries and information: T112.

Time

Standard time GMT -4 hrs begins first Sun in Mar. Summer time GMT -3 hrs begins second Sun in Oct.

Tipping

Restaurants, 10%. Porters US$0.15 per suitcase. Taxis, 10%. Porters at docks US$0.40 per suitcase. In supermarkets, tip the check-out boys who pack bags; they are not paid.

Tourist information

Secretaría Nacional de Turismo Palma 468 y 14 de Mayo, Asunción, T021-494110 or 021-441530, www.senatur.gov.py.

Useful websites

www.paraguay.gov.py Official site for general country information.
www.guidetoparaguay.com A blog about living and travelling in Paraguay.
www.paraguay-hotel.com/py Links to hotels, tourism, embassies and consulates.
www.paraguayglobal.com Business and cultural news.
www.presidencia.gov.py The official government website (in Spanish).
www.maxicambios.com.py For currency exchange rates.
www.yagua.com Paraguayan portal with news and links.
www.abc.com.py ABC Color (local newspaper).
www.ultimahora.com Última Hora (local newspaper).
www.lanacion.com.py La Nación (local newspaper).

Visas and immigration

A passport valid for 6 months after the intended length of stay is required to enter Paraguay and tourist visas are issued at the point of entry for a stay of up to 90 days. Visitors are registered on arrival by the immigration authorities and proof of onward travel is required (although not always asked for). Citizens of the following countries do not require visas in advance: EU member states, Israel, Japan, Norway, South Africa, Switzerland, countries of South and Central America. All others (including Australia, Canada, New Zealand and USA) must apply for a visa prior to travel, which costs £36, multiple entry £52, presenting a valid passport and 2 photos (for a business visa, a supporting letter from one's employer should suffice). Double check at a consulate or www.mre.gov.py before arrival which nationalities need a visa and which Paraguayan consulates issue them. Make sure you're stamped in and out of Paraguay to avoid future problems. If you do not get an entrance stamp in your passport you can be turned back at the border, or have to pay a fine when leaving Paraguay.

Weights and measures

Metric.

Asunción → *Phone code: 021. Colour map 6, C6. Population: over 1.4 million.*

Asunción was founded in 1537 on the eastern bank of a calm bay in the Río Paraguay. It is the longest continually inhabited area in the River Plate Basin and is sometimes referred to as the "Mother of Cities" because it was from here that colonial expeditions set off to establish other cities. The centre is a testament to 19th-century ideals, with names reflecting its heroes and battles. Tree-lined avenues, parks and squares break up the rigid grid system. In July and August the city is drenched in colour with the prolific pink bloom of the lapacho trees, which grow everywhere.

Ins and outs

Getting there The international **airport** is in Luque, 16 km northeast of the city centre, from which taxis, buses and an airport-to-hotel minibus service run. It takes from 30-45 minutes from the airport to town. The **bus terminal** is south of the centre, also 30-45 minutes away. You can go by taxi or by city bus (see page 1227 for the correct one). Both the airport and bus terminal have tourist information desks. ▸▸ *See also Transport, page 1227.*

Getting around Most of the historical sights of interest are in a relatively small area by the river, so walking between them is not a problem. Similarly, there are many central hotels within walking distance of these sights. Places outside this zone are easily reached by taxi or bus. If going by taxi, give driver the specific street address but also the name of the nearest intersection. Almost all locations in Asunción are referred to in this manner. Note also that the often-used "casi" (near) generally means "at the corner of". The bus system is extensive and runs 0600-2400; buses stop at signs before every street corner. Asunción is very spread out and transport so slow that you need to allow 60-90 minutes to get beyond its limits.

Tourist offices Secretaría Nacional de Turismo ⓘ *Palma 468, T494110/441530, Mon-Fri 0800-1300 (phone Mon-Sat 0800-1900 for information).* Good free map (ask for it), information on all parts of Paraguay, but you may need to be persistent. Other maps are sold in bookshops. Information on Asunción at www.asu-cvb.org.py (Spanish and English). The city of Asunción's municipal web site ⓘ *www.mca.gov.py* also has excellent, up-to-date information in Spanish.

Sights

Historic centre

At the bottom of Avenida Colón, just before it joins El Paraguayo Independiente, are the colonial façades of **La Recova**, shops selling local arts and crafts. The main river port and **La Aduana** (Customs) are at this same junction. Continue along El Paraguayo Independiente to a small plaza on your left with a statue of the former dictator, Alfredo Stroessner. After his deposition, the statue was crushed and placed inside a block of concrete, only his hands and face protruding. Next to this is the **Palacio de Gobierno**, built in the style of Versailles by Alan Taylor as a palace for Francisco Solano López (1860-1869). During the later years Taylor was forced to use child labour as all adult men were enlisted to fight in the Triple Alliance War. It now houses government departments. Down the side of the palace towards the river is a platform for viewing the back of the building. Directly opposite the Palace is the **Manzana de la Rivera** ⓘ *Ayolas 129 y El Paraguayo Independiente, T445085, Mon-Sat 0700-2000, library Mon-Fri 0700-1900, Sat 0800-1200,* nine restored buildings and a patio area dating from 1700s including **Casa Viola** with Museo Memoria de la Ciudad with historical photos and city information, **Casa Clari**, with exhibition halls and a bar, and **Casa Vertua**, the municipal library. These collectively represent the most complete set of colonial era buildings in the city.

Next to the Palace is the new **Congreso Nacional**, built in steel and glass representing a huge ship moored on the river bank and incorporating part of the old congress building. On **Plaza de la Independencia** (often referred to as Plaza Constitución or Plaza Juan de Salazar) there is a small memorial to those who died in the struggle for democracy (also look out for statues of the frog and the dog). On the Plaza are the **Antiguo Colegio Militar** (1588) originally a Jesuit College, now home to government ministries, the **Cabildo** ⓘ *Mon-Fri 0900-1900, Sat 0800-1200, free*, now the **Centro Cultural de la República**, with temporary exhibitions, indigenous and religious art, museum of music, film and video on the top floor, and the **Catedral Metropolitana** (mid-17th century, rebuilt in the mid-19th century) ⓘ *not always open, possible to view the interior before, after or during mass, usually around 1100 daily*. The altar, decorated with Jesuit and Franciscan silver, is very beautiful. Between the river and the historical buildings is **La Chacarita**, a shanty town which is home to many poor families who have moved from the countryside in search of work. It is not recommended to wander through this place unaccompanied. From the Plaza turn right onto Alberdi and to your right is the **Oficina de Correo** (post office), a colonial building with a lovely planted courtyard and a small museum; it also has public toilets. At Alberdi and Presidente Franco is the **Teatro Municipal**

Asunción

Sleeping
1 Adelia *C6*
2 Amalfi *C4*
3 Aspen Apart Hotel *C1*
4 Asunción Palace *B1*
5 Bavaria *B6*
6 Cardel *C6*
7 Cecilia *B6*
8 Chaco *B4*
9 City *C3*
10 El Lapacho *A6*
11 Excelsior *C3*
12 Granados Park *B2*
13 Gran Armele *B1*
14 La Española *C4*
15 Paramanta *A6*
16 Portal del Sol *A6*
17 Res Itapúa *C6*
18 Sabe Center *B4*
19 Sheraton *A6*
20 Westfalenhaus *A6*
21 Yasy *C6*

Eating
1 Bistro *B2*
2 Bolsi *B3*
3 Café Literario *B4*

Ignacio Pane ⓘ *T448820 for information on events,* fully restored to its former Belle Époque glory and re-opened in 2007. The **Estación San Roque** ⓘ *Ayala y México, just below Plaza Uruguaya, T447848,* was built in 1856 with British and European help. Paraguay had the first passenger carrying railway in South America. No trains now run from the station, but it has a small **museum** ⓘ *0700-1200, free,* featuring the old ticket office, machinery from Wolverhampton and Battersea and the first steam engine in Paraguay, the **Sapucaí** (1861). **Plaza Uruguaya**, at the nexus of Calles México, Eligio Ayala, 25 de Mayo and Antequera, with its shady trees and fountain is another spot to stop and rest. From here take Mariscal Estigarribia towards Plaza de Los Héroes. The **Museo Nacional de Bellas Artes** ⓘ *Mcal Estigarribia e Iturbe, T447716, Tue-Fri 0700-1900, Sat-0700-1200, closed Sun-Mon,* has some interesting 20th-century Paraguayan art and a good small collection of European paintings including works by Tintoretto and Murrillo.

Mariscal Estigarribia becomes Palma at the intersection with Independencia Nacional (the names of all streets running east to west change at this point). On **Plaza de los Héroes** is the **Panteón Nacional de los Héroes** ⓘ *Palma y Chile, open daily,* which is based on Les Invalides in Paris, begun during the Triple Alliance War and finished in 1937. It contains the tombs of Carlos Antonio López, Mariscal Francisco Solano López, Mariscal Estigarribia, the victor of the Chaco War, an unknown child-soldier, and other national heroes. The child-soldiers honoured in the Panteón were boys aged 12-16 who fought at the battle of Acosta Ñu in the War of the Triple Alliance, 15 August 1869. Most of the boys died and nine out of 10 adult Paraguayan men were killed during the war. Sight-seeing here is strictly on your own. Plaza de los Héroes is made up of four separate squares with different names but these are very rarely used; it is sometimes referred to as Plaza de la Democracia.

- 4 Dali *B2*
- 5 El Mirasol *B4*
- 6 Estrella *B2*
- 7 La Flor de la Canela *A5*
- 8 La Vida Verde *B2*
- 9 Le Saint Tropez *B4*
- 10 Lido *B3*
- 11 Metropol *B6*
- 12 Oliver's (Hotel Presidente) *C3*
- 13 San Roque *B5*
- 14 Taberna Española *C1*

Bars & clubs

- 15 Britannia Pub *B5*

On the Plaza at Chile y Oliva (Plaza Libertad) there are **covered market stalls** selling traditional Paraguayan arts and crafts in wood, cotton and leather. Along Palma indigenous women sell colourful woven bags, beads and baskets. You may be approached by indigenous men selling whistles, bows and arrows or feather headdresses. A few blocks further along Palma is the **tourist information office**; it has craft stalls for those not wishing to buy on the street. On Saturday morning, till 1200, Palma becomes a pedestrian area, with stalls selling arts, crafts, clothes and during the summer there is entertainment outside the tourist office. On Sunday there are stalls selling second-hand or antique items around Plaza de los Héroes. From Palma turn right at 14 de Mayo to the **Casa de la Independencia** ⓘ *14 de Mayo y Presidente Franco, www.casadelaindependencia.org.py, Mon-Fri 0700-1830, Sat 0800-1200, free* (1772), with a historical collection; the 1811 anti-colonial revolution was plotted here. The **Iglesia de Encarnación** ⓘ *14 de Mayo y Víctor Haedo*, partially restored after a fire in 1889 by an Italian immigrant who offered his services free of charge under the condition that he would be free to select the best materials, is a tranquil place to end your tour.

Heading out of the centre along Avenida Mariscal López

The **Museo Histórico Militar** ⓘ *in the Ministry of National Defence, Mariscal López y 22 de Septiembre (surrender passport on entry)*, has articles from both the Triple Alliance and the Chaco Wars. These include blood-stained flags from the Triple Alliance as well as clothes and personal possessions of Francisco Solano López and his Irish mistress, Eliza Lynch. The national cemetery, **Cementerio Recoleta** ⓘ *Av Mariscal López y Chóferes del Chaco*, resembles a miniature city with tombs in various architectural styles. It contains the tomb of Madame Lynch (ask guide to show you the location), and, separately, the tomb of her baby daughter Corrine (Entrada 3 opposite Gran Unión supermarket). Eliza Lynch's home at the corner of Yegros and Mariscal Estigarribia was, until 1999, the Facultad de Derecho.

On the outskirts of Asunción is **San Lorenzo** (Km 12). Reached via Ruta 2 (Mariscal Estigarribia Highway) or take buses 12, 56, 26 and get off at central plaza with blue, 18th-century neo-Gothic cathedral. The **Museo Guido Boggiani** ⓘ *Bogado 888 y Saturio Ríos, T584717, 1½ blocks from plaza, daily until 1900, ring the bell if door is shut*, is staffed by a very helpful lady who explains the exhibits, which include rare Chamacoco feather art, and a well-displayed collection of tribal items from the northern Chaco from the turn of the 20th century. The shop across the road sells crafts at good prices. There's also a small Museo Arqueológico near the church and a daily market. The **Facultad de Ciencias Agrarias** ⓘ *on the campus of the Universidad Nacional de Asunción, Mon-Fri 0800-1530, closed Jan, free*, has an interesting small museum with natural history collections. Ask guard at gate for directions.

Heading out of the centre along Avenida España

Museo Etnográfico Dr Andrés Barbero ⓘ *España 217 y Mompox, T441696, www.museobarbero.org.py, Mon-Fri 0700-1100, Mon, Wed, Fri 1500-1700, free*, houses a good collection of tools and weapons of the various Guaraní cultures. The Centro de Artes Visuales includes the **Museo del Barro** and the **Museo de Arte Indígena** ⓘ *Grabadores del Cabichuí entre Cañada y Emeterio Miranda, T607996, www.museodelbarro.com, exhibitions open Thu-Sat, 1530-2000, US$2.50, free on Fri, shop and café Wed-Sat 1530-2000, take bus 30 or 44A from the centre past Shopping del Sol, ask driver for Cañada.* Contains both contemporary and indigenous art, bookshop, café. Highly recommended.

Luque (take bus 30), founded 1636, has an attractive central plaza with some well-preserved colonial buildings and a pedestrianized area with outdoor cafes. It is famous for the making of Paraguayan harps and guitars (**Guitarras Sanabria** ⓘ *Km 13, T021-2291*, is one of the best-known firms), and for fine filigree jewellery in silver and gold at very good prices, many shops on the main street. Tourist information at Plaza General Aquino. There are some fine musical instrument shops on the road to Luque along Av Aviadores del Chaco.

Other sights

The best of several parks is **Parque Carlos Antonio López**, set high to the west along Colón and, if you can find a gap in the trees, with quite a grand view. Another place for good views is **Cerro de Lambaré**, 7 km south (buses 9 and 29 from Gral Díaz).

The **Jardín Botánico** (250 ha) 6 km east, on Av Artigas y Primer Presidente, lies along the Río Paraguay, on the former estate of the López family. The gardens are well-maintained, with signed walks and a rose garden, and arbordered by the 18-hole Asunción Golf Club. In the gardens are the former residences of Carlos Antonio López, a one-storey typical Paraguayan country house with verandas, now housing a **Museo de Historia Natural** and a library, and of Solano López, a two-storey European-inspired mansion which is now the **Museo Indigenista** (neither in good condition). ⓘ *Both museums are free, Mon-Sat 0730-1130, 1300-1730, Sun 0900-1300. Getting there: by bus (Nos 2, 6, 23, and 40, US$0.15, 35 mins from Luis A Herrera, or Nos 24, 35 or 44B from Oliva or Cerro Corá).* The church of **Santísima Trinidad** (on Santísimo Sacramento, parallel to Avenida Artigas), where Carlos Antonio López was originally buried, dating from 1854 with frescoes on the inside walls, is well worth a visit. Nearby is the wreck of the **Ycuá Bolaños supermarket** ⓘ *Santísima Trinidad y Artigas*, which was destroyed by fire in August 2004, killing 396 people when the doors were ordered locked by the owners (now in jail) to prevent looting. It is now a memorial with a donation box for the families of the dead. The **Maca indigenous community** ⓘ *US$0.30, guide US$0.50, take bus 42 or 44*, is just north of the Botanical Gardens. The *indígenas* live in poor conditions and expect you to photograph them (US$0.15).

Around Asunción

Many villages close to Asunción can be visited on a day trip: eg Aregua and San Bernadino on Lago Ypacari (see page 1231), Altos, great views over the lake, Itauguá. Alternatively take a tour from any travel agent (see Activities and tours, page 1226) of the **Circuito de Oro**: destinations vary but tend to include, Itá, Yaguarón, Paraguarí, Piribebuy, Caacupé, San Bernardino, Aregua, Itauguá, 200 km on paved roads, seven hours. The route goes through the rolling hills of the Cordilera, no more than 650 m high, which are beautiful, with hidden waterfalls and a number of spas: Chololó, Pirareta (near Piribebuy) and Pinamar (between Piribebuy and Paraguarí) are the most developed. The **Camino Franciscano** is similar, including the historical towns of Ypané, Altos, Itá, Atyra, Yaguarón, Piribebuy, Tobatí, Caacupé, Valenzuela, Villarrica, Caazapá and San Juan Neopomuceno.

Asunción listings

Hotel and guesthouse prices

LL over US$200	**L** US$151-200	**AL** US$101-150
A US$66-100	**B** US$46-65	**C** US$31-45
D US$21-30	**E** US$12-20	**F** US$7-11
G US$6 and under		

Restaurant prices

ΨΨΨ over US$12	ΨΨ US$7-12	Ψ under US$6

Sleeping

The hotel bill does not usually include a service charge. Look out for special offers. For Asunción's **Sheraton** (**LL-L**), see www.sheraton-asuncion.com.py.

Asunción *p1217, map p1218*

LL-L Granados Park, Estrella y 15 de Agosto, T497921, www.granadospark.com.py. Luxury, top quality hotel, range of suites with breakfast, all facilities, WiFi, good restaurant *Il Mondo*.

LL-L Hotel Casino Yacht y Golf Club Paraguayo, 14 km from town, at Lambaré, on own beach on the Río Paraguay, T906121, www.hotelyacht.com.py. 7 restaurants and cafés, super luxury, with pool, gym, spa, golf, tennis, airport transfers; many extras free, special deals.

LL-AL Sabe Center, 25 de Mayo y México, T450093, www.sabecenterhotel.com.py. Luxury hotel in modern tower, with all facilities, discounts available.

AL Excelsior, Chile 980, T495632, www.excelsior.com.py. Luxurious, stylish, gym, pool, tennis, internet, cell phone rental, bar and restaurant.

AL-A Aspen Apart Hotel, Ayolas 581 y Gral Díaz, T496066, www.aspen.com.py. Modern, lots of marble, 50 suites and apartments, with breakfast, pool, sauna, gym, internet, cheaper longer stays.

AL-A Cecilia, Estados Unidos 341 y Estigarribia, T210365, www.hotelcecilia.com.py. Comfortable suites, breakfast included, weekend specials, internet, good restaurant, *La Preferida* (ΨΨΨ), pool with a view, sauna, gym, airport transfers, parking, medical service.

AL-A Paramanta, Av Aviadores del Chaco 3198, T607053, www.paramanta-hotel.com. 4-star, mid-way between airport and centre, buses stop outside, with breakfast, TV, WiFi internet, bar, restaurant, pool, gym, gardens, and many other services. English and German spoken.

AL-A Hotel Westfalenhaus, Sgto 1° M Benítez 1577 C Stma Trinidad, T292374, www.paraguay-hotels.com. Comfortable, German-run, breakfast included, half board, weekly rates and self-catering apartments available, with pool, Wi-Fi, safe deposit box, a/c, international restaurant, *Piroschka*, gym, massage and spa, English, German and Spanish spoken.

A Chaco, Caballero 285 y Estigarribia, T492066, www.hotelchaco.com.py. Central 1970s hotel, with breakfast, parking nearby, rooftop swimming pool, Wi-Fi, internet, bar, good restaurant (TTT).

B Asunción Palace, Colón 415 y Estrella, T492153, www.geocities.com/aphotel. Historic building dating from 1858. 24 rooms, with breakfast, a/c, TV, fridge, very helpful, elegant, laundry, internet.

B Bavaria, Chóferes del Chaco 1010, T600966, www.hotel-bavaria-py.com. Comfortable, colonial style, beautiful garden, pool, a/c, good value rooms and suites with kitchens, TV, fridge, German spoken, very helpful staff.

B El Lapacho, República Dominicana 543, casi Av España, T210662. Family-run, welcoming, comfortable, a bit run down, rooms available at lower prices. Favourite with backpackers and students. Convenient for local services, 10 mins from centre by bus, pool, 24-hr internet, parking.

B Portal del Sol, Av Denis Roa 1455 y Santa Teresa, T609395, www.hotelportaldelsol.com. Comfortable hotel with breakfast, some rooms sleep 4, free airport pick-up and internet, pool.

C Amalfi, Caballero 877 y Fulgencio R Moreno y Manuel Domínguez, T494154, www.hotelamalfi.com.py. Modern, comfortable, spacious rooms, breakfast included, internet and restaurant. Recommended.

C City Hotel, Humaitá 209 y NS de la Asunción, T491497, www.cityhotel.com.py. A/c, good, with breakfast in City Cafetería in lobby.

C Gran Armele, Palma 999 y Colón, T444455, www.hotelarmele.com.py. With breakfast, a/c, gym, sauna, restaurant, Wi-Fi, pool, large hotel used by tour groups.

D La Española, Herrera 142 y F Yegros, T449280. Central, comfortable, breakfast included, a/c, internet access, credit cards accepted, airport pick-up, laundry, luggage storage, restaurant, parking. Recommended.

F Cardel, Ygurey 1145 and Av Dr. Eusebio Alaya, T/F214586, cardel@highway.com.py. Halfway between bus station and centre of town, breakfast included.

F Residencial Itapúa, Fulgencio R Moreno 943, T445121. Breakfast available at small cost, a/c, cheaper with fan, kitchen for drinks and snacks, no cooking, quiet, comfortable.

Near the bus terminal

F Adelia, Av F de la Mora y Rep Argentina y Lapacho, T553083. With breakfast, modern, TV a/c.

F Yasy, Av F de la Mora 2390, T551623. A/c and TV, cheaper with fan; both are overpriced. Many more behind these in Calle Dolores.

Out of the city: San Lorenzo

Estancia Oñondivemi, Tourism farm, Km 27.5 on Ruta 1 just past the turn off to Ruta 2 at San Lorenzo, 30 mins from Asunción, T0295-20344, www.onondivemi.com.py. A pleasant escape from the city. Serves all meals, food organically grown on site. Horse riding, fishing, swimming, nature walks (they have a nearby property with a waterfall, lovely for swimming), attractive accommo dation with a/c. Contact for prices (includes meals).

Camping If camping, take plenty of insect repellent. The pleasant site at the **Jardín Botánico** is US$2.50 pp plus tent, cars also permitted, cold showers and 220v electricity, busy at weekends.

You can camp at rear of **Restaurant Westfalia**, Av Perón y Av F Bogado, T331772, hotelrestaurant westfalia@hotmail.com. Owner speaks English, French, German, knowledgeable, US$1 per night for car, showers, laundry, noisy, animals. Take Av General Santos, towards Lambaré. Restaurant Westfalia is 5 km from Asunción (bus 19, 23 or 40).

Eating

Asunción *p1217, map p1218*

Many restaurants are outside the scope of the map. A few restaurants close at weekends, but may open at night. A good meal in the food halls at the shopping malls, which you pay for by weight, as you do in some of the city centre restaurants, is about US$3.25. Average price of a good meal in quality restaurants: US$18. The following are open most days of the week, day and night.

TTT **Acuarela**, Mariscal López casi San Martín, T601750. Very good churrascaría and other Brazilian dishes.

TTT **Bistro**, 15 de Agosto y Estrella. Excellent, US$25.

TTT **Bolsi**, Estrella 399 y Alberdi, T491841. One of Asunción's longest-operating eateries. Enormously popular. Wide choice of wines, good for breakfast, excellent food (Sun 1200-1430) in large servings. Has great diner next door, lower prices, also popular.

TTT **Churrasquería Sajón**, Av Carlos A López, bus 26 from centre. Good Paraguayan harp/ guitar group; restaurant serving meat.

TTT **Fabio Rolandi's**, Mariscal López y Infante Rivarola, T610447. Delicious pasta, steak and fish. Recommended.

TTT **Fina Estampa**, Senador Long 789 y Tte Vera, T601686, www.finaestampa.com.py. Peruvian food. Good Sun lunch buffet.

TTT **La Pergola Jardín**, Perú 240 y José Bergés, T214014. Under the same ownership as Bolsi, excellent.

TTT **Le Saint Tropez**, México entre Cerro Corrá y 25 de Mayo, T441141. Beautiful setting. Bar and restaurant, pizzería, open for lunch and dinner. Premises for sale (2008), so call ahead.

TTT **Mburicao**, González Rioboó 737 y Chaco Real, T660048. Mediterranean food. Highly recommended.

TTT **Oliver's**, Hotel Presidente, Azara e Independencia Nacional, T494941. Very good, pricey, live music.

TTT **Shangrilá**, Aviadores del Chaco y San Martín, T661618. Very good food at upmarket Chinese.

TTT **Sukiyaki**, in Hotel Uchiyamada, Constitución 763 y Luis A de Herrera, T222038. Good Japanese, about US$12 pp.

TTT **Taberna Española**, Ayolas 631 y General Díaz, T441743. Spanish food, very good.

TT **Dali**, Estrella 695 y Juan E. O' Leary, T490890. Snack-bar-style eatery. Good Italian (and other) food, nice terrace. Recommended.

TT **Hacienda Las Palomas**, Guido Spano y Senador Long 644, T605111. Mexican food, popular.

TT **Hiroshima**, Chóferes del Chaco 1803 y Av Moreno, T662945. Authentic Japanese.

TT **Lido**, Plaza de los Héroes, Palma y Chile, T446171. An institution in Asunción, great location across from Panteón, loads of character. Good for breakfast, empanadas and watching the world go by. Good quality and variety, famous for fish soup, delicious. Open daily 0700-2300, very popular. Recommended.

TT **San Roque**, Eligio Ayala y Tacuary, T446015. Traditional, relatively inexpensive.

TT-T **Paulista Grill**, San Martín casi Mariscal López, T662185, www.paulistagrill.com.py. Another good churrascaría, good value, cheaper in the week, popular with groups.

T **El Cheff Peruano**, General Garay 431 y Del Maestro, T605756, www.elchefperuano.com.

Good quality Peruvian food, also popular with large groups.

🍴 **El Mirasol**, 25 de Mayo 241, entre Yegros e Iturbe. Vegetarian and Chinese, open till 1600 for buffet lunch, closed Sun.

🍴 **La Vida Verde**, Palma 634 y 15 de Agosto, T446611. Vegetarian, Chinese influenced, with buffet lunch, open till 1700, closed Sun.

🍴 **Tapei**, Tte Fariña 1049 y Brasil y Estados Unidos, T201756. Serves stylish vegetarian by weight. Recommended.

🍴 **Tembi'u he**, Dr Francisco Fernández y Av Stma Trinidad, T293324. Paraguayan food.

Cafés and snacks

Most cheap lunch places close around 1600.

Café Literario, Palma casi México, T491640. Mon-Fri from 1600, cosy café/bar, books and good atmosphere. Occasional cultural events with Alianza Francesa.

El Molino, España 382 y Brasil, T225351, www.confiteriaelmolino.com. Good value, downstairs for sandwiches and homemade pastries, upstairs for full meals in a nice setting, good service and food (particularly steaks) but pricey. Recommended.

Estrella, Estrella y 15 de Agosto. Pizza, *empanadas*.

Heladería París, 3 locations: Brasilia y Siria, San Martín y Pacheco and NS de Asunción y Quinta Avenida. Café/bar/ice cream parlour. Popular.

La Flor de la Canela, Tacuary 167 y Eligio Ayala, T498928. Cheap Peruvian lunches.

Metropol, Estados Unidos 341 y 25 de Mayo, T202222, www.hotelcecilia.com.py/mp/menu.php. Café and shop with European food, sandwiches, cheese and meats. Part of **Hotel Cecilia**.

Michael Bock, Pres Franco 828, T495847. Excellent bread and sweet shop.

Quattro D (4d), San Martín y Dr Andrade, T497604. Ice cream parlour offering great range of flavours, also weekday lunches from US$1.85.

Sugar's, several branches including most Shopping Centres and Brasilia 662.

Bars and clubs

Asunción *p1217, map p1218*

Bars

The best up to date online source for bars and clubs in Asunción, Ciudad del Este and anywhere else in Paraguay is www.asunfarra.com.py.

Paseo Carmelitas, Av Espana y Malutin, tiny but upscale mall has several popular bars, such as **El Bar**, **Kamastro**, **Kilkenney Irish Pub**, **Liquid** and the very chic **Sky Resto & Lounge** (T600940, www.skylounge.com.py) as well as restaurants and shops.

Britannia Pub, Cerro Corá 851, T443990, www.britannia-pub.com. Evenings only, closed Mon, good variety of drinks, German spoken, popular expat hangout, book exchange.

Café Bohemia Senador Long 848 casi España, T662191. Original decor and atmosphere, Mon and Tue live blues/jazz.

Déjà Vu, Galería Colonial, Av España casi San Rafael, T615098. Popular.

Refuel, Galería Colonial, Av España casi San Rafael. Yet another popular bar, more upscale than most and with live music nightly.

Clubs

Av Brasilia has a collection of clubs such as **Arena & Café, Ristretto Café & Bar** (No 671 y Siria, T224614) and **Mouse Cantina** (No 803 y Patria, T 228794).

Asunción Rock, Mariscal Estigarribia 991 y Estados Unidos, T442034. Wed-Sat, 2200 till late. 2 dance floors, rock and alternative music.

Coyote Night & Fun, Sucre casi Av San Martín, T622816, www.coyote.com.py. Fri, Sat. Several dance floors and bars, retractable roof, affluent crowd, see website for other events in different locations including Ciudad del Este and San Bernardino. Recommended.

El Sitio Disco, Av Rep Argentina 1035 y McMahon, T612822. Latin and retro, Fri-Sat, 2100 till 0300.

Face's, Av Mariscal López 2585 (technically in Fernando de la Mora), T671421/672768, www.faces.com.py. Also in Ciudad del Este. Largest club in Paraguay, shows nightly.

Glam, Av San Martin 1155 y Agustín Barrios, T331905, www.glam.com.py. Along with Coyote and Face's (see above), one of Asunción's most popular clubs. Thu, Fri and Sat. Same owners as **Caracol Club**, Av Perón y Concepción Yegros, T332848, www.caracol.com.py. Electronic music, several dance floors, 20 mins' drive from centre.

Pirata Bar, Benjamín Constant y Ayolas, T452953, www.piratabar.com.py. Fri-Sat, 2100 till 0300.

Trauma, 25 de Mayo y Antequera y Tacuary. Gay/transvestite/mixed, Fri, Sat, 2300.

Entertainment

Asunción *p1217, map p1218*

Cinema Cinema programmes are given in the press; latest releases, admission US$4 (Wed and matinées half price). Modern cinemas at: **Shopping del Sol**, 6 screens, **Shopping Villa Mora** 6 screens, and **Mall Excelsior**, **Hiperseis** (see Supermarkets and shopping centres, below). **Centro Cultural de la Ciudad**, Haedo 347, T442448, for quality foreign films, US$1.50.

Theatre See newspapers for performances of concerts, plays, ballets. Various Cultural centres also put on theatrical productions. For online listings, check **ABC Digital** (www.abc.com.py), **Última Hora** (www.ultimahora.com) and **La Nación** (www.lanacion.com.py). **Teatro Municipal**, Alberdi y Presidente Franco, T445169. Restored 2007. Ticket sales Mon-Sat 0800-2200. **Banco Central**, T6192243, the Paraguay Philharmonic gives monthly recitals May-Dec. **Teatro de las Américas**, J Bergés 297, concerts are given here.

Festivals and events

Asunción *p1217, map p1218*

Two weeks in **Jul**, **Expo**, an annual trade show at Mariano Roque Alonso, Km 14.5 on the Trans-Chaco Highway, www.expo.com.py. The biggest fair in the country with local and international exhibitors. Bus from centre takes 30 mins.

Shopping

Asunción *p1217, map p1218*

Bookshops 'Books', at Shopping del Sol and Mariscal López 3971, also opposite Villa Morra shopping centre, very good for English books, new titles and classics. **El Lector** at Plaza Uruguaya y 25 de Mayo, T491966, also at San Martín y Austria, T614256 (has café and internet connection), www.ellector.com.py. Has a selection of foreign material and a range of its own titles on Paraguay. **Librería Alemana**, Av Luis A de Herrera 292, warmly recommended for German books. **Librería Internacional**, Oliva 386, Estrella 723 and Palma 595. Good for maps, indigenous cultures; sometimes sponsors concerts and recitals in stores.

Camping **Camping 44**, Av Artigas 2061, T297240, www.camping44.com.py; **Gauchito Deportes**, Av Fernando de la Mora 2477 y Cedro, T555953, or **Unicentro**, Palma y 15 de Agosto; Nueva Americana, Mcal Estigarribia 111 esq Independencia Nacional, T492021, www.nuevaamericana.com.py.

Crafts Check the quality of all handicrafts carefully, lower prices usually mean lower quality. Many leading tourist shops offer up to 15% discount for cash; many others will not accept credit cards, so ask even if there are signs in window saying they do. For leather goods there are several places on Colón and on Montevideo including: **Boutique Irene**, No 463; **Boutique del Cuero**, No 329; and **Galería Colón 185** (recommended). Also **La Casa del Portafolio**, Av Palma 302, T558228. **Artes de Madera** at Ayolas 222. Wooden articles and carvings. **Casa Overall 1**, Mariscal Estigarribia y Caballero, T448657, good selection. Also **No 2** at 25 de Mayo y Caballero, T447891. **Casa Vera**, Estigarribia 470, T445868, for Paraguayan leatherwork, cheap and very good. **Doña Miky**, O'Leary 215 y Pres Franco, recommended. **Folklore**, Mcal Estigarribia e Iturbe, T/F494360, good for music, woodcarvings and other items. **Victoria, Arte Artesanía**, Iturbe y Ayala, T450148, interesting selection of wood carvings, ceramics etc. Recommended.

Electronic goods Cheap electronic goods in the Korean-run shops along Palma.

Markets **Mercado Cuatro** on Pettirossi, a huge daily market selling food, clothing, electrical items, DVDs, CDs, jewellery, toys, is a great place to visit. Good, cheap Chinese restaurants nearby. There is a daily market on Av Dr Francia, best visited during the week. See also under Historic centre, Sights. **Shopping Mariscal López** (see below) has a fruit and vegetable market, Tue, in the car park, and a small plant/flower market, including orchids, Wed, at the entrance.

Shopping centres Asunción has a number of modern Shopping Malls with shops, ATMs, cafés, supermarkets, cinemas and food halls all under one a/c roof. **Shopping Villa Morra** (Av Mariscal López y San Roque González). **Shopping Mariscal López** (Quesada 5050 y Charles de Gaulle, behind Shopping Villa Morra, T611272, www.mariscallopez.com.py). **Shopping del Sol** (Av Aviadores de Chaco y D F de González, T611780, www.delsol.com.py). **Mall Excelsior** (Chile y Manduvirá). **Supermarkets** Hiperseis at Boggiani y Mariscal López; **Stock** at Shopping del Sol and Mall Excelsior. **Superseis** at Shopping Villa Morra; **Casa Rica**, Av San Martín y Aviadores del Chaco, good for speciality foods and some European imports. **Real Villa Mora**, Boggiani y Av Argentina, has an imported food aisle, mainly from USA.

Activities and tours

Asunción *p1217, map p1218*

Football Asunción (technically next-door Luque) is the permanent home of the **South American Football Confederation**, CONMEBOL (www.conmebol.com), on the autopista heading towards the airport, opposite Ñu Guazú Park. This imposing building with its striking 'football' fountain houses offices, a hall of fame, extensive football library and a new museum with interactive exhibits, T494628 in advance for visits. See also **Asociación Paraguaya de Futbol**, www.apf.org.py. **Estadio Defensores del Chaco**, Mayor Martínez 1393 y Alejo García, T480120, is the national stadium, hosting international, cup and major club matches.

Horse riding **Club Hípico Paraguayo**, Av Gral Andrés Rodríguez y Cleto Romero, Barrio Mariano Roque Alonso, T290921. Actually 9 different athletic clubs in one; scene of many Asunción society events. Members club (US$55 per month but daily rates available) open to the public. Friendly and helpful.

Nature tourism See page 1212.

Rural tourism *Turismo rural* has become one of the most enjoyable ways to visit the country and get a feel for a Paraguayan way of life that revolves around agriculture and ranching. The **Touring y Automóvil Club Paraguayo** (25 de Mayo y Brasíl, p 2, T210550, www.tacpy.com.py) is officially in charge of rural tourism, through the **Paraguayan Rural Tourism Association** (APATUR) T210550, int 126-230, and its own travel agency, **Touring Viajes**. They organize visits to ranches and farms all over Paraguay. One-day tour prices start at about US$55 pp including accommodation, food and drink (not alcohol); tours of three or more days for groups of 2-12, US$60-125. All the ranches listed under APATUR have good facilities. Transport to and from these ranches from Asunción is sometimes included in the package. Visitors experience living and working on a ranch, can participate in a variety of activities, and enjoy typical food, horse riding, photo safaris and nature watching. Another agency for visiting *estancias* in Misiones Province only is **Emitur**, T0782-20286, T021-222081 or T0975-626780, and see www.paraguay.gov.py for a list of these and other ranches.

Tennis **Academia de Tenis** at Parque Seminario, 25 de Mayo y Kubicheck, T206379 to reserve a court. Price US$4 per hr daytime and US$5 per hr evening. Coaching available.

Tours

Many agencies offer day tours of the Circuito de Oro or Camino Franciscano (from US$50). Trips to local estancias, Encarnación and the Jesuit Missions, Itaipú and Iguazú or the Chaco region are all offered as 1, 2 or 4-day tours. Prices from US$100. Most agencies will also provide personalized itineraries on request. City tours also available. For more information contact **Dirección General de Turismo** or the **Paraguayan Association of Travel Agencies and Tourism** (ASATUR), Juan O'Leary 650, p 1, T491755/491728.

Alda Saguier, Yegros 941, p 2, T446492. For the Chaco and indigenous regions. English and German spoken.

Aries Travel, Paraguari 743 y Herrera, T450473, ariestravel@emociones.org.py.

Canadá Viajes, Rep de Colombia 1061, T2211192, www.canadaviajes.com.py. Good Asunción and Chaco tours.

Crucero Paraguay, Pdte Franco 982, Edif Mocipar, p 3, T452328, www.crucero paraguay.info. Specialists in Chaco and Pantanal. 4-10 day cruises on the Río Paraguay, visits historical and ecological sites along the river, on-board entertainment, international menu, pool and cinema.

Inter Tours, Perú 436 y España, T211747, www.intertours.com.py. One of Paraguay's biggest full-service tour agencies. Tours to Chaco, Iguazú and Jesuit missions. Highly recommended.

Itra Travel, Venezuela 663 y España, T200020, www.itra.com.py. Also offer ecotourism, national park tours.

Menno Travel, Rep de Colombia 1042 y Brasil, T493504, mennotravel@gmx.net. German spoken.

Natura Express, Cruz del Defensor 137 y Mariscal López, Villa Morra, T610353, www.natura-express.com. Adventure tourism, offering hiking, rappelling, kayaking, microlight flights, caving, riding and other activities, various packages.

Paraguay Natural, Barka Viajes, Gral Santos y 18 de Julio, T302027, www.paraguaynatural.com.py. Specialists in nature tourism throughout the country and to Brazilian Pantanal.

Time Tours, 15 Agosto y Gral Díaz, T449737, also at O'Higgins 891 y Austria in Villa Mora, T611649, www.timetours.com.py. Fluent English, runs Camino Franciscano tours. Recommended.

Vips Tour, México 782 entre Fulgencio R Moreno y Herrera, T/F441199, www.vipstour.com.py. Asunción, estancia and Chaco tours.

Transport

Asunción *p1217, map p1218*

Air Silvio Pettirossi Airport, T645600. Several agencies have desks where you can book a taxi to your hotel, US$15-22. Bus 30 goes every 15 mins between the red bus stop outside the airport and Plaza de los Héroes, US$0.40, difficult with luggage. Minibus service from your hotel to airport run by **Tropical**, T424486, book in advance, US$8 (minimum 2 passengers, or pay for 2). The terminal has a tourist office (free city map and hotel information), bank (turn right as you leave customs – better rates in town), post office (0800-1800), handicraft shop, restaurant and several travel agencies who arrange hotel bookings and change money (very poor rates). Left luggage US$4.25 per day per item.

Bus City buses: Journeys within greater Asunción US$0.40. Buses can be busy at rush hours. Turnstiles are awkward for large backpacks. Keep your ticket for inspection until you leave bus.

Long-distance: The Terminal de Omnibus is south of the centre at República Argentina y Fernando de la Mora (T551740/1, www.mca.gov.py/webtermi.html). Local bus No 8 is the only direct one from Oliva, which goes via Cerro Corá and Av Brasil from the centre, and stops outside the terminal, US$0.40. From the terminal to the centre it goes via Av Estados Unidos, Luis A Herrera, Antequera and E Ayala; get off at Chile y Díaz. Other buses Nos 10, 25, 31, 38 and 80, follow very circuitous routes. Taxi to/from centre, recommended if you have luggage, US$3.35, journey time depends on the amount of traffic, about 30 mins. The terminal has a bus information desk, free city/country map, restaurant (quite good), café, casa de cambio (poor rates), post office, phone booths and shops. There are many touts for bus companies at the terminal. Allow yourself time to choose the company you want and don't be bullied, or tricked, into buying the wrong ticket. Better companies include: **Nuestra Señora de la Asunción**, T551725 or 289 1000, www.nsa.com.py, has booking office at main terminal and at Mariscal Estigarribia y Antequera, off Plaza Uruguaya. **RYSA**, T444244, rysa1@supernet.com.py. Bus company offices on the top floor are in 3 sections: short-distance, medium and long. Local departures, including for Yaguarón and Paraguarí, are boarded from the basement. Hotels nearby: turn left from front of terminal, 2 mins' walk. Bus times and fares within Paraguay are given under destinations.

To Argentina There is a road north from Asunción (passing the Jardín Botánico on Primer Presidente) to a concrete arch span bridge (Puente Remanso – US$1.25 toll, pedestrian walkway on upstream side, 20 mins to cross) which leads to the border at Puerto Falcón (about 40 km) and then to **Clorinda** in Argentina. The border is open 24 hrs; local services are run by **Empresa Falcón** to Puerto Falcón (US$0.60, every hr, last bus from Falcón to the centre of Asunción 1830; from Falcón to Clorinda costs US$0.40), but it is cheaper overall to book direct from Asunción to Argentina. Buses don't wait for you to go through formalities: wait for the same company's next bus, or buy a new ticket.

Buses to **Buenos Aires** (18 hrs) daily, many companies, via Rosario and Santa Fe (average fare US$53 luxury, US$39-43 diferencial, US$25-31 común). To **Formosa**, 4 a day, **El Pulqui** and **Godoy** (US$5.30-6, plus US$0.50 luggage) many drug searches on this road. To **Salta**, take **Brújula** (T551664) at 0600, 0830, and other companies, to **Resistencia**, 8 hrs, US$9, then change (after long wait) to **La Veloz del Norte**.

To Brazil Many Paraguayan buses advertise that they go to destinations in Brazil, when, in fact you have to change buses and book again at the frontier. Services to **Campo Grande** and **Corumbá** via Pedro Juan Caballero and Ponta

Porã do not stop for immigration formalities. Check all details carefully. **Nuestra Señora de la Asunción** and the Brazilian company **Pluma** (T551758) have direct services via Ciudad del Este to **Foz do Iguaçu** (Brazil), US$16.50-20, 5-7 hrs. Seat reservations recommended.
To **Curitiba**, with **Pluma** and others, buses daily, 15½ hrs, US$47. To **Florianópolis Catarinense** (T551738, Tue, Wed, Thu, Sat, Sun), 17 hrs, US$112 and **Pluma** (Mon, Wed, Fri), US$60.
To **Porto Alegre**, **Uneleste** (T442679), Tue, Thu, US$56. To **São Paulo**, **Pluma** and **Brújula**, 20 hrs, US$60. **Pluma** to **Rio de Janeiro**, US$80; **Transcontinental** (T557369) to **Brasília** 3 a week, US$89.

To Bolivia Via the Chaco, to Santa Cruz, **Yacyretá**, T551725, most reliable, Mon, Wed, Fri, and Sat at 2000. **Stel Turismo**, T558196, daily at 2000, **Pycazú,** Thu and Sat at 2100, but you cannot get on in Mariscal Estigarribia. All fares US$55. All buses normally travel via Mariscal Estigarribia, for Paraguayan immigration where foreigners must get an exit stamp; La Patria; Infante Rivarola at the border; Ibibobo, for Bolivian immigration; and Villamontes, to Santa Cruz de la Sierra. Advertised as 21 hrs, the trip can take 5 days if the bus breaks down. Some food provided but take your own, plus extra water just in case; also take toilet paper. The buses can be very crowded. In summer the route can be very hot and dusty, but in winter, it can be cold at night. Alternative route to Bolivia via Salta, Argentina (see above).

Unless specifically advertised, buses to Bolivia do not go through Filadelfia or the other Mennonite colonies, so take a local services from Asunción (see page 1252). After visiting the Chaco, you can usually get on a Bolivia-bound bus in Mariscal Estigarribia, where the bus companies have agents (see page 1250), but enquire in advance with their offices in Asunción.

To Uruguay EGA (Eligio Ayala 693, T492473, www.egakeguay.com) runs to **Montevideo** 3 times a week 20 hrs, US$115, as does **Brújula/Cynsa** (Pres Franco 995, T441720). The route is Encarnación, Posadas, Paso de los Libres, Uruguaiana, Bella Unión, Salto, Paysandú; the only customs formalities are at Bella Unión; passport checks here and at Encarnación.

River boat To escape the city take a short trip across the river to the **Mbiguá Club** to sunbathe and relax. Ask at Aduanas for information. A small launch leaves every 20 mins from the pier at the bottom of Montevideo to **Chaco-i**, a strip of land between the Ríos Paraguay and Pilcomayo, US$0.65 each way. The Argentine town of Clorinda is just the other side of the Pilcomayo. Ferry to **Puerto Pilcomayo** (Argentina) about every 30 mins, US$0.65 (Argentine immigration closed at weekends for tourists).

Boats for **Concepción** leave from the bottom of Montevideo. Offices for information/ prices El Paraguayo Independiente 813 y Ayolas (not always staffed), T492829. Sailings weekly (Wed), 27-30 hrs, US$22.50 1st class, US$14.25 2nd, US$6 deck space (not recommended). Sleeping space is sometimes available. Take food, water, toilet paper, warm clothes, sleeping bag and mosquito repellent. If you want more luxury take a 5-star cruise on the **Crucero Paraguayo**, see **Tours**, above. Reservations also available through larger tour operators.

Taxi Minimum fare in Asunción : US$0.40, and US$0.08 per 100 m. The average journey costs about US$1.70. Minimum fare is about 30-50% more at night. There are many taxi ranks throughout the city. Taxis can eitehr be hailed or call **Radiotaxi** (recommended), T550116/311080.

Train A **tourist steam train** runs from Estación Botánico, outside the Jardín Botánico, to Aregua and Sapucaí, Sun 1030, return 1930, US$22 for foreigners, US$6 for Paraguayans, price includes soft drink, *empanadas* and on-board entertainment (actors presenting 19th-century scenes); 4-hr stop in Aregua for lunch and sightseeing. Highly recommended. You can buy tickets on the day or in advance from Estación San Roque, Ayala y Plaza Uruguaya. See page 1238 for the locomotive workshops at Sapucaí.

Directory

Asunción *p1217, map p1218*

Airline offices Aerolíneas Argentinas, España 2220, T450577, arasugsa@sap.com.py. **AeroSur**, Senador Long 856 y España, T614743, www.aerosur.com. **Gol**, contact via webpage: www.voegol.com.br. **Iberia**, Mariscal López 995, T214246, asuuu@iberia.es. **LAB**, 14 de Mayo 563, ground floor, T441586, susklb@rieder.net.py.

Lan, Juan de Salazar y Washington, T233487-9, www.lan.com. **Lufthansa**, N S de la Asunción 208, T447962, lhasu@cmm.com.py, admin and cargo only, ticket information from travel agents. **TAM**, Oliva 761 y Ayolas, T645500, www.tam.com.py. **United Airlines**, Mariscal López 310, T213019, viase@supernet.com.py.

Banks Be careful to count money received from street money changers (Palma and surrounding area – their rates are poor when banks and cambios are closed). See Money section in Planning your trip. Lots of ATMs, accepting credit and debit cards, give dollars and guaraníes. **HSBC**, Palma y O'Leary, T419 7000, (as well as several other branches in Greater Asunción). Accepts Visa. **Citibank**, CitiCenter, Av Mariscal López 3794 y Cruz del Chaco, T6202000. Will change Citibank TCs into US$ cash, and gives US$ cash on MasterCard credit card. **ABN AMRO**, Estrella 443 y Alberdi (main office), T419000, clientes@py.abnamro.com; also at Av San Martín 763 y Lillo, T611513; Eusebio Ayala y Mayor Bullo, T225854; and Shopping Mariscal López, T608977, accepts several cards. **Interbanco**, Oliva 349 y Chile, T494992, ATM at Shopping Del Sol, accepts Visa. **Amex**, at Inter-Express, Yegros 690, T490111, iexpress@interexpress.com.py. To change TCs other than American Express you must go to Banco Santander, Banespa, Independencia Nacional y Moreno, good rates, proof of purchase required. Many **casas de cambio** on Palma, Estrella and nearby streets (open Mon-Fri 0730-1200, 1500-1830, Sat 0730-1200). All rates are better than at frontiers. They change dollars, euros, Brazilian reais, Argentine pesos and a few will accept sterling notes. Some **casas de cambio** change only dollar-denominated TCs. **Cambios Chaco**, on Palma and at Shopping Mscal López. **Maxi Cambio**, in Shopping del Sol. Good rates for dollars cash. **Parapiti Cambios/ Financiera Guaraní**, Palma 449, T490032, change TCs (small fee). Mon-Fri 0830-1730, Sat 0830-1200. **Sudamérica Express**, 14 de Mayo 340, T445305, www.tupi.com.py, 3 other locations in capital. Decent rates for TCs. **Cambios Yguazú**, 15 de Agosto 451, T448018, no commission.

Car hire **Fast Rent a Car**, Prof Chávez 1276 y Santa Rosa, T605462, www.fastrentacar.com.py. Good, helpful. Also other companies at the airport. See Planning your trip for international rental agencies.

Cultural centres **Alianza Francesa**, Mariscal Estigarribia 1039 y Estados Unidos, T210503, www.alianzafrancesa.edu.py. Snack bar. **Centro Cultural Paraguayo Americano**, España 352 entre Brasil y Estados Unidos, T224831, www.ccpa.edu.py. Has a good library (Mon-Fri 0900-2000, Sat 0900-1200, also has snack bar). **Centro Paraguayo-Japonés**, Av Julio Corea y Domingo, T607276, www.centroparaguayojapones.blogspot.com. Has a good theatre. **Instituto Cultural Paraguayo Alemán**, Juan de Salazar 310 y Artigas, T226242, www.icpa-gz.org.py. Recommended. All institutes have special events, films, etc.

Embassies and consulates **Argentina**, España y Perú, T212320, www.embajada-argentina.org.py. Visas issued at Edif Banco Nacional de Argentina, Palma 319, p1, T442151, open 0800-1300, 1500-1800, 2-hr service, photo needed (if you require a multiple entry visa, get it in your country of residence). **Australia**, nearest embassy Buenos Aires. **Austrian Consulate**, Aviadores del Chaco 1690, T613316. Mon-Fri 0730-1100. **Belgian Consul**, Daniel Ceuppens, Ruta 2, Km 17, Capiatá, T0228-633326. Mon-Fri 1000-1400. **Bolivia**, Campos Cervera 6427 y Rl Ytororó, T660620. Mon-Fri 0900-1300. **Brazil**, Coronel Irrazabal y Eligio Ayala, T248 4000, www.embajadabrasil.org.py, open 0800-1400, Mon-Fri, US$25 for visa. **Canada**, Prof Ramírez 3 y Juan de Salazar, T227207. Mon-Fri 0800-1300. **Danish Consulate**, N S de la Asunción 76, T493160, Mon-Fri 0730-1130 and 1500-1830. **Dutch Consulate**, Artigas 4145, T 283665, Mon-Fri 0900-1600. **Finland**, Honourary Consulate, Capitán Elias Ayala 295 y Yasy, T291175 (the nearest embassy is in Brasilia). **France**, España 893 y Padre Pucheu, T212449, www.ambafrance-py.org, Mon-Fri 0800-1200. **Germany**, Av Venezuela 241,T214009, www.asuncion.diplo.de. 0800-1100 Mon-Fri. **Israel**, De la Residentas 685 y Boquerón, T221486, consulis@gmail.com. **Italy**, Quesada 5871 y Bélgica, T615620, consolare@cmm.com.py. **Japan**, Av Mariscal López 2364, T604616. Mon-Fri 0800-1200, 1500-1730. **New Zealand**, O'Leary 795 esquina Humaitá, T496498. **Spain**, Yegros 435, p 6, T490686/7. Mon-Fri 0830-1300. **Swedish Consulate**, Artigas

1945, T214114. Mon-Fri 0730-1200, 1330-1730. **Switzerland**, O'Leary 409, p 4, of 423, T490848. 0800-1230 Mon-Fri. **UK**, Honorary Consulate, Eulogio Estigarribia 4846 y Monseñor Bogarin, T210405, guillermo.peroni@ pstbn.com.py, Mon-Fri 0800-1300 and 1500-1900, nearest Embassy in Buenos Aires. **Uruguay**, Guido Boggiani 5832 y Alas Paraguayas, T664244, conurupar@telesurf.com.py. Visas processed immediately if exit ticket from Uruguay, overland travel to Uruguay and onward country visas can be shown. Mon-Fri 0700-1730. **US Embassy and Consulate**, Av Mariscal López 1776, T213715. Mon-Fri 0730-1730. **Immigration** Caballero y Eligio Ayala, T446066, www.migraciones.gov.py.

Internet Lots of internet cafés in and around Asunción. The average price is US$1 per hr. **Cyber Shop**, Estrella 480 and Alberdi y 14 de Mayo, T446290, helpful. **Interspace Internet**, 25 de Mayo y Antequera, T119190. **Patio de Luz Internet Café**, Azara 248, T449741. Also bar, restaurant, occasional live music. Internet near food hall in Shopping Villa Morra. **Unicom**, Papa Juan XXIII y Gómez (behind Shopping del Sol), T/F610902. Very helpful, fax and DVD rental.

Language schools **Idipar** (Idiomas en Paraguay), Manduvirá 963, T447896, www.idipar.edu.py. Offers courses in Spanish or Guaraní. Private or group lessons available, also offers accommodation with local families and volunteer opportunities. 60 hrs per week from US$340 in groups, US$21 per hr for private lessons. Good standard.

Medical services Private hospitals: **Bautista**, Av Argentina y Cervera, T600171/4. **Sanatorio San Roque**, Eligio Ayala y Pai Pérez, T212499/ 228700, 24 hrs. Public hospital: **Emergencias Médicas**, Brasil y FR Moreno, T204800/204715. Pharmacies: There are numerous pharmacies throughout Asunción, many offering 24-hr service. **Farmacia Vicente Scavone**, Palma y 15 de Agosto, T490396. **Farmacia Catedral Centro**, Palma e Independencia Nacional, Plaza de los Héroes. Both reliable. **Post offices** Alberdi, between Benjamín Constant y El Paraguayo Independiente, T498112. Mon-Fri 0700-2000, Sat 0700-1200. **Poste Restante** (ask at the Casillas section) charges about US$0.40 per item, but you may have to insist they double-check if you are expecting letters (poste restante closes 1100). Postcards for sale, but better ones in nearby bookshops. Packages under 2 kg should be handed in at the small packages window, over 2 kg at the 'Encomiendas' office in the same building, but on other end at corner of Alberdi and Benjamín Constant. A faster and more reliable way to send parcels is by EMS, the post office courier service from the same office. Customs inspection of open parcel required. Register all important mail. There are sub-offices at Shopping del Sol, Shopping Villa Morra and in certain suburbs, but mail takes longer to arrive from these offices. **Telephones** Phone booths can be found on almost every block of central or international calls and fax, 24 hrs.

Región Oriental: East of Asunción

To the east of the Río Paraguay lie the most fertile lands and the most populated region of the country. Of the vast rainforests that once covered it, only a few isolated patches have not been converted to farmland. Ruta 2 and Ruta 7 head east towards the border with Brazil, taking the traveller through tranquil villages known for their arts and crafts, German colonies and small towns associated with the country's bloody past. In contrast to the quiet of the countryside, Ciudad del Este is a crossroads for all manner of merchandise, much of it illegal, and the world's largest stolen car market, while the giant Itaipú dam has irreversibly changed the landscape. Just over the border are the Iguazú Falls.

Itauguá → *Phone code: 0294. Population: 94,896.*

At Km 30, founded in 1728, Itauguá, now Paraguay's fastest-growing city, is where the famous *ñandutí*, or spiderweb lace, is made. There are over 100 different designs. Prices are lower than in Asunción and the quality is better; there are many makers, but try Taller Artesanal (Km 29), Mutual Tejedoras (Km 28), or Casa Miryam (Km 30, T20372). To watch the lace being made, ask around. The old town lies two blocks from the main highway. Worth seeing are the **market** ⓘ *0800-1130, 1500-1800, closed Sun*, the church and the **Museo de Historia Indígena** ⓘ *Km 25, daily 0800-1130, 1500-1800, US$0.60*, a beautiful collection of carvings of Guaraní mythological creatures, and the **Museo Parroquial San Rafael** ⓘ *daily 0800- 1130, 1500-1800*, with a display of indigenous art and Franciscan artefacts. There is a four-day **Festival de Ñandutí** in early July, including processions and the crowning of Señorita Ñandutí. Many of Paraguay's best traditional musicians perform during the festival. Itauguá is also the birthplace of Juan Crisóstomo Centurión, the only Paraguayan military leader to win a battle in the War of the Triple Alliance and an architect of the country's rebirth.

Aregua ➔ *Phone code: 0291. Population: 13,323.*

At **Capiatá** (Ruta 2, Km 20, fine colonial church), a left turn goes to **Aregua**. Founded in 1541 this is a pretty colonial village on the slopes above **Lago Ypacaraí**. From its attractive church at the highest point in town there is one of the best views of the lake and surroundings. It has an interesting ceramics cooperative, a museum, arts and crafts exhibition and a convent. There is a good German-run restaurant in the centre of the village. From here boat trips run across the lake at weekends to San Bernadino and the tourist steam train comes here each Sunday from Asunción on its way to Supacaí.

San Bernardino and Lago Ypacaraí ➔ *Phone code: 0512. Population, 5,729.*

At Km 40 on Ruta 2 a branch road, 8 km long, leads off to **San Bernardino**, originally a German colony, known locally as 'San Ber', on the east bank of Lago Ypacaraí. The lake, 24 km by 5 km, has facilities for swimming and watersports and sandy beaches (ask locally about pollution levels in the water). There are frequent cruises from the pier during the tourist season. This is the main vacation spot for Asunción from December-February, which means that it is lively and crowded at weekends in the summer, with concerts, pubs and nightclubs, but as a result it is commercialized. During the week and off season it is a tranquil resort town, with lakeside tourism clearly the main draw. Boats can be hired and there is good walking in the neighbourhood, for example from San Bernardino to **Altos**, which has one of the most spectacular views of the lake, wooded hills and valleys (round trip three hours). Shortly after the turn off from the main road towards San Bernardino is a sign to **La Gruta**; turn right here to a secluded park (Ypacaraí). There are grottos with still water and overhanging cliffs. No buses run after 2000 and taxis are expensive. Tourist information is in the centre of town between General Morinigo and Emilio Hassler.

Caacupé ➔ *Phone code: 0511. Colour map 6, C6. Population: 25,797. www.caacupe.com.py*

At Km 54 on Ruta 2, this is a popular resort and religious centre on the Azcurra escarpment. The centre is dominated by the modern Basilica of Our Lady of the Miracles, with a copper roof, stained glass and polychrome stone esplanade, consecrated by Pope John Paul II in 1988 (US$0.25 to climb the tower). There is an ATM on the plaza between the supermarket and Hotel El Mirador.

Thousands of people from Paraguay, Brazil and Argentina flock to the shrine, especially for the **Fiesta de la Inmaculada Concepción** on 8 December. Besides fireworks and candlelit processions, pilgrims watch the agile gyrations of Paraguayan bottle-dancers; they weave in intricate measures whilst balancing bottles pyramided on their heads. The top bottle carries a spray of flowers and the more expert dancers never let drop a single petal.

Tobati, a town north of Caacupé, specializes in woodwork. The *villa artesenal* is a short walk from the bus stop outside the house of Zenon Páez, a world famous sculptor. There are some amazing rock formations on the way to Tobati. To get there, take a bus from the corner below the park on the main Asunción road in Caacupé; ask the driver to let you off at Páez' house.

Piribebuy ➔ *Phone code: 0515. Population: 11,726.*
Beyond Caacupé, at Km 64, a paved road runs 13 km southeast to the small town of Piribebuy, founded in 1640 and noted for its strong local drink, *caña*. In the central plaza is the church (1640), with fine sculptures, high altar and pulpit. The town was the site of a major battle in the War of the Triple Alliance (1869), commemorated by the **Museo Histórico Pedro Juan Caballero** ⓘ *free*. Buses from Asunción by Transportes Piribebuy. Near the town are the attractive falls of Piraretá. The road continues via Chololó, 13 km south, and reaches Ruta 1 at Paraguarí, 28 km from Piribebuy (see page 1238). Between Pirbebuy and Paraguarí is an outdoor and adventure centre, **Eco-reserva Mbatoví**, with a visitor centre ⓘ *US$3, T0971-299250, for reservations and information visit www.mbatovi.com.py*. It includes an outdoor pursuits course ⓘ *US$35*, and a 2-hr guided walk ⓘ *US$15*, taking in early settlements, local folklore and beautiful scenery.

Vapor Cué National Park
A turn-off from Eusebio Ayala (Km 72) goes 23 km to **Caraguatay**, 5 km from which is the Vapor Cué National Park, where boats from the War of the Triple Alliance are preserved. Although officially a national park, it is more of an open-air museum. Next to the (indoor) museum is a pleasant hotel, **Hotel Nacional de Vapor Cué** (**D**, T0517-222395). Frequent buses run from Asunción to Caraguatay.

North from Coronel Oviedo
Coronel Oviedo (Phone code 0521; colour map 6, C6; population: 58,120), at the junction of west-east highway and the major north-south Ruta 8, is an important route centre, although hardly worth a stop. Buses drop passengers for connections at the junction (El Cruce). Ruta 8 runs north to **Mbutuy**, continuing as Ruta 3 to Yby Yaú, where it meets Ruta 5 (Concepción-Pedro Juan Caballero). At Mbutuy (Km 56, parador, restaurant, petrol station) Ruta 10 branches off northeast to the Brazilian frontier at **Salto del Guaíra** (*Phone code: 046*), named after the waterfalls now under the Itaipú lake. There is a 900-ha wildlife reserve, Refugio Biológico Mbaracayú. Salto del Guaíra, a free port, can also be reached by a paved road which runs north from Hernandarias, via Itaquyry to meet Ruta 10 at Cruce Carambey.

Mbaracayú Forest Reserve ⓘ *To visit you must book and pay in advance, and sign a disclaimer at the Moisés Bertoni Foundation in Asunción (see National Parks, page 1212); entry US$6.50, lodging US$16.25 pp, camping US$12 per tent, take your own food, cook available US$9 per day plus US$3 per day for gas, transport US$0.35 per km. You must hire a guide for US$22.50 per day. There is public transport to Villa Ygatimi from where they pick you up, 20 km to the park. Pay ahead for transport you will require within the park. Buses from Asunción to Curuguaty: La Coruguateña and Santa Ana, 0900 and 1430, 6 hrs, US$5.80. From Curuguaty to Ygatimi local buses take 1 hr.* Not to be confused with the nearby Refugio Biológico Mbaracayú mentioned above, this federally protected reserve covers more than 66,000 ha of Paraguay's rapidly disappearing Interior Atlantic forest. It is the largest area representative of this ecosystem in good conservation status in Paraguay. It contains 48% of all mammal species and 63% of all bird species (over 400) found in eastern Paraguay. There are trails, waterfalls and spectacular view points. There are also two indigenous communities, the Aché and Guaraní. There is a visitor centre and small museum at Villa Ygatimi.

At Santa Rosa, 143 km north of Mbutuy, there is petrol, pensión and restaurants. A dirt road runs southwest for 27 km to **Nueva Germania** founded in 1866 by Bernhard Förster and Elisabeth Nietzsche (the philosopher's sister) to establish a pure Aryan colony. This road goes on to San Pedro and Puerto Antequera on the Río Paraguay (88 km). A further 23 km north of Santa Rosa, a dirt road runs northeast through jungle to the interesting **Capitán Badó** (120 km), which forms the frontier with Brazil. From here a road follows the frontier north to Pedro Juan Caballero (100 km). About 50 km north of the turn off to Capitán Badó is Yby Yaú, see page 1244.

Villarrica ➔ *Phone code: 0541. Colour map 6, C6. Population: 47.173.*

Villarrica, 42 km south of Coronel Oviedo, is delightfully set on a hill rich with orange trees. A very pleasant, friendly place, it has a fine cathedral, built in traditional style with veranda, and various pleasant parks. The museum (closed weekends) behind the church has a foreign coin collection; please contribute. Products of the region are tobacco, cotton, sugar, yerba mate, hides, meat and wine produced by German settlers. There is a large student population.

There are several German colonies near Villarrica. Some 7 km north is an unsigned turn off to the east, then 20 km to tiny **Colonia Independencia**, which has some beautiful beaches on the river (popular in summer). German-speaking travellers can also visit the German cooperative farms (these are not Mennonite communities, but rather German settlements established in the early 20th century). A great mate and wine producing area and, at harvest time, there is a wine festival. They also have beer festival in October.

East from Coronel Oviedo

The paved Ruta 7 runs 195 km through farmed areas and woods and across the Caaguazú hills. From here it continues to the spectacular 500-m single span 'Friendship Bridge' across the Paraná (to Brazil) at Ciudad del Este.

Ciudad del Este

Ciudad del Este ➔ *Phone code: 061. Colour map 7, C1. Population: 320,782.*

Originally founded as Ciudad Presidente Stroessner in 1957, this was the fastest growing city in the country until the completion of the Itaipú hydroelectric project, for which it is the centre of operations. Ciudad del Este has been described as the biggest shopping centre in Latin America, attracting Brazilian and Argentine visitors who find bargain prices for electrical goods, watches and perfumes. However, it is a counterfeiter's paradise and can be quite dangerous. Check everything properly before making a purchase and ensure that shops pack what you actually bought. The main shopping street is Avenida San Blas, lined with shopping malls and market stalls, selling a huge variety of goods, both original and imitations – usually the latter. Almost any vehicle advertised for sale, should you be tempted, was stolen in Brazil. Watch the exchange rates if you're a short-term visitor. Parts are of the city are dirty and frantic during business hours, but away from the shopping arcades people are friendly and more relaxed. The leather market is well worth a visit, be sure to bargain. **Tourist office** ⓘ *Coronel Rafael Franco entre Pampliega y Curupayty, Edificio Líbano p 1 of 104, T866264 (mob), senaturcde @senatur.gov.py.*

Around Ciudad del Este The **Monday falls** ⓘ *0700-1700, US$0.45, taxi US$20 return*, where the Río Monday drops into the Paraná gorge, are worth seeing. Nearby is the popular beach resort and biological refuge called **Tatí Yupí** ⓘ *www.itaipu.gov.py*. Two other biological reserves border the Itaipú dam, **Itabó** and, further north, **Limoy**. Take the unpaved road north from Ciudad del Este towards Salto del Guaíra. Itabó is at the first turn off to Dorila, and Limoy the turnoff at Colonia San Lorenzo.

Border with Brazil

The border crossing over the Friendship Bridge to Foz do Iguaçu is very informal, but is jammed with vehicles and pedestrians all day long. No passport stamps are required to visit Ciudad del Este for the day. Motorcycle taxis (helmet provided, hang on tight) are a good option if you have no luggage. Otherwise, to enter Paraguay here, hire a taxi and go very early in the morning, or take your gear to the Paraguayan bus terminal (left luggage facilities) by city bus, then shuttle back and forth on foot to get passport stamped; it is a long and tiring process. (Make sure you get a Paraguayan entry stamp; without it you will be fined. If you do get fined, get a receipt.) Immigration formalities for Paraguay and Brazil are dealt with on opposite sides of the bridge. There is a friendly tourist office in the customs building on the Paraguayan side. Remember to adjust your watch to local time (Brazil is one hour ahead). The **Brazilian consulate** ⓘ *Ciudad del Este, Pampliega 205, T500984, consulbr@cde.rieder.net.py, Mon-Fri 0700*, issues visas. The Argentine Consulate is at ⓘ *Av Boquerón y Adrián Jara, Edificio China p 7, T500638, ccest@mrecic.gov.ar.*

Itaipú and around

ⓘ *www.itaipu.gov.py. Mon-Fri 0730-1200, 1330-1700, Sat, Sun and holidays 0800-1100. Bus tours Mon-Fri 0800, 0930, 1400, 1500, Sat 0800, 0930, 1030, 1400, 1500 (morning only Sun and holidays). Free tours of the project with film show (several languages). Take passport. Buses going to Hernandarias will drop you at the visitor centre.*

The Itaipú project (a huge hydroelectric project covering an area of 1,350 sq km and still subject to controversy among environmental groups) is close to Ciudad del Este, and well worth a visit.

On the way to Itaipú is **Flora y Fauna Itaipú Binacional** ⓘ *0730-1130, 1400-1700*, a zoo and museum containing native animals and plants; it is about 2 km from the visitor's centre on the road back to Ciudad del Este. At the Centro Ambiental de Itaipú is the **Museo de la Tierra Guaraní** ⓘ *T061-599 8040, Tue-Sat 0800-1130, 1430-1700 (Mon afternoon only, Sun morning only)*, which offers a view of the science and culture of the Guaraníes via natural history displays and interactive screens.

Hernandarias, just north of Ciudad del Este grew rapidly with the building of Itaipú. A paved road runs north to Cruce Carambey, where it meets Ruta 10 (see above, page 1232). From Hernandarias, boat trips on Lago Itaipú go to Puerto Guaraní where there is a museum.

East of Asunción listings

For Sleeping and Eating price codes and other relevant information, see Essentials, pages 38-40.

Sleeping

San Bernardino *p1231*

There are plenty of hotels other than those listed, many with good restaurants (eg **de Sol** and **Los Alpes**, US$3.50 for buffet lunch and use of pool).

L Sol de San Ber, Rosa Mendola y Tte Weiler, T233138, pueblo@telesurf.com.py. New, super luxury.

A-B Del Lago, Tte Weiler 401 y Mcal López, near lake in town, T232201, www.hoteldellago.org. With breakfast, attractive 1888 building recently renovated as a museum, upgraded, a/c, fan, safe, Wi-Fi, regional decor, restaurant, bar and grill, pool, lovely gardens.

B San Bernardino Pueblo, C 8 entre C 5 y Mbocayá, T232195, pueblohotel@hotmail.com. Swimming pool, a/c, by the lake. Weekend packages, 2 nights for US$68 pp.

B Los Alpes, Ruta General Morínigo Km 46.5, 3 km from town, T232083, www.hotellos alpes.com.py. A/c, cable TV, Wi-Fi, internet, lovely gardens, 2 pools, excellent self-service restaurant, children's playground, beach 1 km away, frequent buses to centre.

Camping Brisas del Mediterraneo, Ruta Kennedy a 2000 m from Copaco, T232459, www.campingparaguay.org. With beach, games.

Caacupé *p1231*

Cheaper than Lago Ypacaraí. Prices increase during the Fiesta de la Inmaculada Concepción.

D Virgen Serrana, plaza, T242366, www.hotelvirgenserrana.turismoparaguay.net/VirgenpcccCCCC.htm. A/c, **E** with fan.

E El Mirador, T242652, on plaza. With bath.

E Katy María, Eligio Ayala y Dr Pino, T242860, beside Basílica. Well-kept, welcoming.

Camping West of Tobati is **Atyrá** (15km from Caacupé), 2 camp grounds: **Chorro Carumbey** and **Balneario Atyrá**.

Tourism farm

AL Estancia Aventura, Km 61.5, Ruta 2, T0981-441804, www.estancia-aventura.com. 225 acres of countryside, 7-day packages. Good, horse riding, tennis swimming, can arrange airport pickup from Asunción.

Piribebuy *p1232*

C pp **La Quinta**, 10 km from Piribebuy, 19 km from Paraguarí, 82.5 km from Asunción (take bus to Piribebuy then bus to Chololó, bus passes in front of hotel), T971-117444, www.laquinta.com.py. Price based on 4 sharing in cabins, also suites, also open for day visits, own stream and is close to falls at Piraretá and Chololó.

F Viejo Rincón, Maestro Fermín López esq Tte Horacio Gini, T0515-212251. Reasonable.

Coronel Oviedo and around: Salto del Guaíra *p1232*

D-E Peralta, Av Paraguay y Capitán Capii Pery, T242235. Pleasant, with breakfast and bath, **F** without.

Villarrica *p1233*

A-B Villarrica Palace Hotel, Ruta 8 Blas Garay, turn right on road entering Villarrica, T42832, www.sosahoteles.com. Large modern hotel, restaurant, parking, pool, sauna.

C Ybytyruzú, C A López y Dr Bottrell, T42390. Best in town, breakfast, more with a/c, restaurant.

E Guairá, Mariscal López y Talavera, T42369. With bath and a/c, cheaper with fan, friendly.

F Central Comuneros y Pa'i Anasagasti, by Plaza Ybaroty at entrance to town. With bath, a/c, electric shower, family run.

German colonies near Villarica:

Colonia Independencia *p1233*

D Hotel Tilinski, out of town, T0548-265240. Peaceful, German spoken, swimming pool (filled with river water), meals for residents.

Camping There is camping nearby at Melgarejo.

East from Coronel Oviedo *p1233*

B pp **Estancia Golondrina**, José Domingo Ocampo, Km 235, T0527-20122 or 0971-417440 (mob), www.ges-py.com, or Asunción office T/F021-201521 (weekdays only), or through APATUR (see Rural tourism, page 1226). Take the unpaved road to the right, 17 km to the ranch. A good place for combining rural and ecotourism. The ranch has extensive agricultural land as well as 12,000 ha of protected virgin forest (Reserva Ypetí) and abundant wildlife. There are trails for walking or horse riding, boat trips on the river, picturesque accommodation (a/c, private bathroom, very comfortable) overlooking the river. Price includes all meals and transportation from the main road.

Ciudad del Este *p1233, map p1233*

B-C Convair, Adrián Jara y Pioneros del Este, T508555. In shopping district. A/c, comfortable, breakfast included, cheaper rooms without bath. Restaurant good, pasta festival on Thu, pool. Bus to Foz do Iguaçu stop across the road.

C California, C A López 180, T500378, www.hotelcalifornia.com.py. Including breakfast, TV, a/c, several blocks from commercial area, large, modern with swimming pool, lit clay tennis court, attractive gardens, restaurant, good local surubi fish.

C Panorama Inn Pampliega y Eusebio Alaya, T500110, www.hotelpanoramainn.com.py. Modern, corporate atmosphere, breakfast.

D New Cosmos Apart-Hotel, Edif Cosmopolitan 1, Paí Pérez y Pampliega, T511030. Apartment style with kitchenette and living room.
D-E Austria (also known as Viena), E R Fernández 165, T504213, www.hotelaustriarestaurante.com. Above restaurant, good breakfast, a/c, Austrian family, good views from upper floors. Warmly recommended.
E Munich, Fernández y Miranda, T500347. With breakfast, a/c, garage. Recommended.
F Caribe, Miranda y Fernández, opposite Hotel Austria, T512450. A/c, hot water, nice, garden, helpful owner. Recommended.
F Tía Nancy, Arturo Garcete y Cruz del Chaco, by terminal, T502974. With electric shower, clean and convenient for bus station.

Eating

Villarrica *p1233*
Many eating places on CA López and General Díaz. Good restaurants are **La Tranquera** (good value, more expensive at weekends), **Asunción**, **Casa Vieja** and **La Cocina de Mamá**. At night on the plaza with the Municipalidad stands sell tasty, cheap steaks. Good nightclubs are **Monasterio** (the most popular) and **La Tirana**, great atmosphere.

German colonies near Villarica: Colonia Independencia *p1233*
Che Valle Mi, Sr Jacob Esslinger, Correo Melgarejo. Recommended.
Ulli y Klaus, restaurant next door. Recommended.

Ciudad del Este *p1233, map p1233*
Cheaper restaurants along García and the market. Fast food chains in centre.
Hotel Austria (see above). Good-value Austrian fare.
Mi Ranchero, Adrián Jara. Good food and prices.
New Tokyo, Arco Iris supermarket, Bernandino Caballero. Good, authentic Japanese.
Osaka, Adrián Jara. Good, authentic Japanese.
Patussi Grill, Monseñor Francisco Cedzich casi Av Alejo García. Good churrasquería.

Transport

Itauguá *p1230*
Bus Frequent from **Asunción**, 1 hr, US$0.40.

Aregua *p1231*
Bus From **Asunción**, **Transportes Ypacaraínse**, every 30 mins, but do not leave from the terminal; alternatively take local bus to Capiatá and change.

San Bernardino *p1231*
Bus From **Asunción**, 3 companies: **Altos**, **Loma Grande** and **Ciudad de San Bernadino**, every 10 mins, 45 km, 1-2 hrs, US$0.60.

Caacupé *p1231*
Bus From **Asunción**, US$0.60, get off at Basilica (closer to centre) rather than Caacupé station.

Coronel Oviedo and around: Salto del Guaíra *p1232*
Bus To **Asunción**, US$11.75, 5 daily; to **Ciudad del Este**, US$8. **To Brazil** Regular launches cross the lake to Guaíra, 20 mins, US$1.30. Also hourly bus service, 30 mins, US$1.30. Buses run north of the lake to Mondo Novo, where they connect with Brazilian services. Brazilian Consulate is at Destacamento de Caballería y Defensores del Chaco, T24-2305.

Villarrica *p1233*
Bus To **Coronel Oviedo**, US$1.65. To **Asunción**, frequent, US$3.30, 3½ hrs (Empresa Guaireña). Also direct service to **Ciudad del Este**, 4 daily, US$3.65, 4 hrs.

German colonies near Villarrica: Colonia Independencia *p1233*
Bus Direct to **Asunción**, 3 daily (US$1.65, 4 hrs), as well as to **Villarrica**.

Ciudad del Este *p1233, map p1233*
Air Full jet airport, Aeropuerto Guaraní. To **Asunción**, TAM daily en route from São Paulo. **TAM**, Curupayty 195 y Eusebio Alaya, T506030-35.
Bus Terminal is on the southern outskirts, T510421 (No 4 bus from centre, US$0.50, taxi US$2.70, recommended). Many buses to and from **Asunción**, US$16 rápido, 4½ hrs, at night only; US$8-10 común, 5 hrs. **Nuestra Señora** recommended (they also have an office in Shopping Mirage, Pampliega y Adrián Jara), **Rysa** (T501201) and others. To **Villarrica**, 10 a day, last 1620, 4 hrs, US$3 (**Guaireña**). To **Pedro Juan Caballero**, 7 hrs, overnight

US$8.50. To **Concepción**, **García**, 11 hrs, 2 per day. To **Encarnación** (for Posadas and Argentina), paved road, frequent, 4 hrs, US$5.50 (this is probably cheaper than via Foz do Iguaçu).

Border with Brazil *p1234*

Bus The international bus goes from outside the Ciudad del Este terminal to the Rodoviária in Foz. There are also local buses from the terminal and along Av Adrián Jara, every 15 mins, 0600-2000, US$0.60, which go to the city terminal (terminal urbana) in Foz. Most buses will not wait at immigration, so disembark to get your exit stamp, walk across the bridge (10 mins) and obtain your entry stamp; keep your ticket and continue to Foz on the next bus free. Paraguayan taxis cross freely to Brazil (US$20-22), although they are not keen to, and it is cheaper and easier to walk across the bridge and then take a taxi, bargain hard. You can pay in either currency (and often in Argentine pesos). Obtain all necessary exit and entry stamps.
To Argentina Direct buses to **Puerto Iguazú**, leave frequently from outside the terminal, US$1. If continuing into Argentina, you need to get Argentine and Paraguayan stamps (not Brazilian), but bus may not stop, so ask driver if he will. Also check what stamps you need, if any, if making a day visit to Puerto Iguazú.

Itaipu and around: Hernandarias *p1234*
Bus Frequent from **Ciudad del Este**, US$0.50.

Directory

Ciudad del Este *p1233, map p1233*
Banks Local banks (open Mon-Fri 0730-1100). **Citibank**, Adrián Jara y Curupayty. ATM, changes TCs, 0830-1200. **Amex**, Curupayty casi Adrián Jara, T502259. Dollars and guaraníes can be changed into reais in town. Several casas de cambio: **Cambio Guaraní**, Av Monseñor Rodríguez, changes TCs for US$0.75, branch on Friendship Bridge has good rates for many currencies including dollars and reais, but there is a long wait. **Cambios Alberdi**, Adrián Jara by Hotel Puerta del Sol, good rates. Casa de cambio rates are better than street rates. Money changers (not recommended) operate at the bus terminal but not at the Brazilian end of the Friendship Bridge. **Internet** Setik Technology, Av Tte Morales y 29 de Setiembre, T509009. **Cyber Café**, Shopping Mirage, Pampliega y Adrián Jara. **Telephones** Copaco, Alejo García y Pai Pérez, near centre on road to bus terminal, for international calls.

Región Oriental: South of Asunción

Ruta 1 runs south from Asunción to Encarnación and the Argentine border. This is an attractive area of fertile landscapes, sleepy towns and the historically important Jesuits settlements, the ruins of some of which have been extensively restored and have interpretive exhibits.

Itá (Km 37) is famous for rustic pottery, but also sells wood, leather and textile items including hammocks. You can visit the workshop of **Rosa Brítez**, a local ceramics artist and Paraguay's most famous artisan, recognized by UNESCO. Its church, San Blas, was built in 1585 and the town has a lagoon which is reputed never to dry up.

Yaguarón

Founded in 1539, Yaguarón, Km 48, was the centre of the Franciscan missions in colonial times. At the centre of the town, marooned on an island of green, mown grass, stands the church of **San Buenaventura**, with its external bell-tower ⓘ *daily 0700-1100, 1330-1630, on Sun morning only*. The simplicity and symmetry of the exterior is matched by the ornate carvings and paintings of the interior. The tints, made by the *indígenas* from local plants, are still bright on the woodcarvings and the angels have Guaraní faces. Built in Hispano-Guaraní Baroque style by the Franciscans between 1755 and 1772, it was reconstructed in 1885 and renovated in the late 20th century. Stations of the Cross behind the village lead to a good view of the surroundings.

Museo Dr José Gaspar Rodríguez de Francia ⓘ *leaving the church, 500 m down the road to your left, Tue-Sun 0730-1130, free guided tour in Spanish*, with artefacts from the life of Paraguay's first dictator, 'El Supremo', plus paintings and artefacts from the 18th century. The 18th-century single-storey adobe building with bamboo ceilings and tiled roof belonged to Francia's father. The fiesta patronal is in mid-July. There are a few basic hotels.

Paraguarí and around
➔ Colour map 6, C6. Phone code: 531. Population: 11,379.

Founded 1775 (Km 63), the north entrance to the mission area, at the foot of a range of hills. Its restored church has two bell towers, separate from the main structure. Buses between Asunción and Encarnación stop here. There is an interesting Artillery Museum inside the nearby military base with cannons and artefacts from the Chaco War. You can stroll to the top of Cerro Perõ for views from the cross on top. More challenging is a one-hour climb through dense forest to the summit of Cerro Jhu, ask for directions in Barrio San Miguel behind the abandoned train station. Paraguarí retains many customs from its Spanish founders, and is seen as Paraguay's capital of bullfighting.

Supucaí, 25 km east of Paraguarí, the terminus of the tourist train from Asunción, is the location of the **workshops** ⓘ *Mon-Fri, take a bus from Asunción at 0700, 1200, 88 km, 3 hrs, US$1.25*, where you can see old and abandoned wood-burning steam locomotives. There are also some cheap *hospedajes*.

Northeast from Paraguarí 15 km is **Chololó** ⓘ *bus US$0.55*, with a small but attractive series of waterfalls and rapids with bathing facilities and walkways, mainly visited in the summer.

Parque Nacional Ybycuí

At **Carapeguá**, Km 84 (*hospedaje* on main street, basic, friendly; blankets and hammocks to rent along the main road, or buy your own, made locally and cheaper than elsewhere), a road turns off to Acahay, Ybycuí and the **Parque Nacional Ybycuí** ⓘ *0800-1700, www.salvemoslos.com.py/pny.htm. For camping get a permit from the Environmental Department, Madame Lynch 3500, in Asunción (see National parks, page 1212)*, 67 km southeast. This is one of the most accessible national parks, if you have a car, and one of the few remaining areas of rainforest in eastern Paraguay. It contains 5,000 ha of virgin forest and was founded in 1973. Good walks, a beautiful campsite and lots of waterfalls. At the entrance is a well set out park and museum, plus the reconstructed remains of the country's first iron foundry (La Rosada). Crowded on Sunday but deserted the rest of the week. Guides available. The only shops (apart from a small one at the entrance selling drinks, eggs, etc, and a good T-shirt stall which helps support the park) are at **Ybycuí**, 30 km northwest.

Ruta 1 continues through **Villa Florida**, 162 km from Asunción, on the banks of the Río Tebicuary. It's a popular spot in January-February for its sandy beaches and the fishing is first-rate. The **Hotel Nacional de Villa Florida** (**D**, T083-240207), one of three such places run by Senatur (see also Vapor Cué, page 1232 and Ayolas, below, www.paraguay.gov.py) would make a convenient place to stop when travelling on this route.

The Jesuit missions

In 1578 Jesuit missionaries came to what is now the border region of Brazil, Argentina and Paraguay to convert the Guaraníes to Christianity. The first mission was established in 1610 at San Ignacio Guazú. Together these two groups developed a pioneering economic and social system that emphasized collaboration and, to some extent, integration between the two societies. In 1767, by decree of Charles III of Spain, the missions were abandoned and local wealthy landowners took the Guaraníes as slave workers. Thirty missions, or *reducciones*, were built. Eight of these remain in Paraguay in varying states of repair and three have been inscribed as UNESCO World Heritage Sites. See *The Mission*, Films, in Background.

San Ignacio Guazú and around

At Km 226, this is a delightful town on the site of a former Jesuit *reducción* (*guazú* means big in Guaraní). Several typical Hispano-Guaraní buildings survive. Each Sunday night at 2000 a folklore festival is held in the central plaza, free, very local, "fabulous". The **Museo Jesuítico** ⓘ *daily 0800-1130, 1400-1730, US$0.75*, housed in the former Jesuit art workshop, reputedly the oldest surviving civil building in Paraguay, contains a major collection of Guaraní art and sculpture from the missionary period. The attendant is very knowledgeable, but photos are not allowed. Nearby is the **Museo Histórico Sembranza de Héroes** ⓘ *Mon-Sat 0745-1145, 1400-1700, Sun 0800-1100*, with displays on the Chaco War. For tours of the area or to visit local ranches contact Emi Tours, T078-220286.

Santa María de Fé is 12 km northeast along a cobbled road. Here there is another fine **museum** ⓘ *0900-1300, 1500-1800, US$0.40 (photos allowed)*, in restored mission buildings containing 60 Guaraní sculptures among the exhibits. The modern church has a lovely altarpiece of the Virgin and Child (the key is kept at a house on the opposite side of the plaza). There is also the **Santa María Cooperative and Educational Fund**, begun by English journalist Margaret Hebblethwaite, which sponsors education and craftwork (notably appliqué) and organizes local activities for visitors. It also has a hotel on the plaza, see www.santamariahotel.org and www.santamariadefe.org.

At **Santa Rosa** (Km 248), founded 1698, only a chapel of the original church survived a fire. The chapel houses a museum; on the walls are frescoes in poor condition; exhibits include a sculpture of the Annunciation considered to be one of the great works of the Hispanic American Baroque (ask at the parroquia next door for entry). Buses from San Ignacio Guazú.

Southwest to Pilar Ruta 4 (paved) from San Ignacio (see above) goes southwest to **Pilar** (*phone code: 086*; hotels in **E-G** range), on the banks of the Río Paraguay. Capital of Neembucú district, the town is known for its fishing, manufacturing and its historical Cabildo. This area saw many bloody battles during the War of the Triple Alliance and you can visit **Humaitá**, with the old church of San Carlos, **Paso de Patria**, **Curupayty** and other historic battle sites.

Ayolas, Santiago and San Cosme

At Km 262 on Ruta 1 a road leads to the reduction at Santiago and the town of **Ayolas** standing on the banks of the Aña Cuá river. **Santiago** is another important Jesuit centre (1669) with a modern church containing a fine wooden carving of Santiago slaying the saracens. More wooden statuary in the small museum next door (ask around the village for the key-holder). There is an annual **Fiesta de la Tradición Misionera**, 2-3 February. Beyond is **Ayolas**, good for fishing and influenced by the construction of the Yacyretá dam. There is an archaeological museum and, 12 km from Ayolas, the **Refugio Faunístico de Atinguy** ⓘ *Mon-Sat 0830-1130 and 1330-1630, Sun and holidays 0830-1130*, run as a research and educational facility by the **Entidad Binacional Yacyretá** (EBY) to study the fauna affected by the dam. EBY also has a biological reserve on the **island of Yacyretá** itself ⓘ *visits to the project at 0830, 1000, 1400, T072-222141, or 021-445055, www.eby.gov.py*. Cross the river to Ituzaingó, Argentina (linked via road to Corrientes and Posadas). Follow the unpaved road from Ayolas to the **San Cosme y Damián** *reducciones* or leave Ruta 1 at Km 306. When the Jesuits were expelled from Spanish colonies in 1767, the **church and ancillary buildings** ⓘ *0700-1130, 1300-1700 US$1*, were unfinished. A huge project has followed the original plans. Some of the *casas de indios* are still in use.

Encarnación → *Phone code: 071. Colour map 6, C6. Population: 85,149.*

A bridge connects this busy port, the largest town in the region (founded 1614), with the Argentine town of Posadas across the Alto Paraná. The old town was badly neglected at one time as it was due to be flooded when the Yacyretá-Apipé dam was completed. Since the flooding, however, what is not under water has been restored and a modern town has been built higher up. This is less interesting than the lower part, once the main commercial area selling a wide range of cheap goods to visitors from Argentina and Brazil. The town exports the products of a rich area: timber, soya, mate, tobacco, cotton, and hides; it is fast losing its traditional, rural appearance. The town is a good base for visiting nearby Jesuit mission sites. Given its proximity to the border, the cost of living is higher than in most other parts of Paraguay. The **tourist office** ⓘ *by Universidad Católica, T204515, 0800-1200*, is very helpful and has a street map. In the afternoon maps are available from the Municipalidad, Estigarribia y Kreusser, Oficina de Planificación.

Border with Argentina

The new San Roque road bridge connects Encarnación with **Posadas**. Formalities are conducted at respective ends of the bridge. Argentine side has different offices for locals and foreigners; Paraguay has one for both. **Note** Paraguay is one hour behind Argentina, except during Paraguayan summer time.

Santísima Trinidad del Paraná and Jesús de Tavarangüé

Northeast from Encarnación along Ruta 6 towards Ciudad del Este are the two best-preserved Jesuit *reducciones*, see box, page 1753. These are both recognized as UNESCO World Cultural Heritage sites (whc.unesco. org/en/list/648). The hilltop site of **Trinidad** ⓘ *US$2.50, Oct-May 0700-1900, Apr-Sep 0700-1730*, built 1706-1760, has undergone significant restoration. Note the partially restored church, the carved stone pulpit, the font and other masonry and relief sculpture. Also partially rebuilt is the bell-tower near the original church (great views from the top). You can also see another church, a college, workshops and indigenous living quarters. It was founded in 1706 by Padre Juan de Anaya; the architect was Juan Bautista Prímoli. For information or tours (in Spanish and German), ask at the visitor centre. The Jesuito Snack Bar at the turn off from the main road has decent food. 1 km from Trinidad is **Ita Cajón**, an enormous clearing where the stone was quarried for the Jesuit *reducción*.

About 10 km northwest of Trinidad, along a rough road (which turns off 300 m north from Trinidad entrance) is **Jesús**, now a small town where another group of Jesuits settled in 1763. In the less than five years before they were expelled they embarked on a huge

Encarnación

construction programme that included the church, sacristy, residencia and baptistry, on one side of which is a square tower. ⓘ *Oct-May 0700-1900, Apr-Sep 0700-1730, US$2.50*. (Camping is permitted at entrance to ruins.) There is a fine front façade with three great arched portals in a Moorish style. The ruins have been restored. There are beautiful views from the main tower.

German colonies on the road to Ciuidad del Este

From Trinidad the road goes through or near a number of German colonies including **Hohenau** (Km 36) and **Parque Manantial** ⓘ *Km 35, 500 m from main road, www.manantial.itapua.net*. The park is in a beautiful location and has two pools (open 0830-2200), a good restaurant, bar, very nice camping ground and complete facilities (US$5.75 per day including use of a swimming pool and all facilities), horse riding, tour of the countryside by jeep and cross country tours to the nearby Jesuit ruins. It's a good place to stop off on the way to Ciudad del Este. Owner Rubén Pretzle is always willing to help visitors, whatever the problem. Major credit cards accepted and local and national phone calls can be made at no extra charge.

The next colony is **Obligado**; it has an ATM in the centre of town. About 5 km further north is **Bella Vista** (Km 42, also has ATM), where it's possible to visit various yerba mate plantations. The most geared up for visitors is **Pajarito** ⓘ *T0767-240240, www.pajarito.com.py*.

South of Asunción listings

For Sleeping and Eating price codes and other relevant information, see Essentials, pages 38-40.

Sleeping

Paraguarí and around *p1238*

E pp **Estancia Mónica**, Camino a Cerro Corá, near Acahay, Paraguarí, T03771-216394 or 0983-756996, info@paraguay-magazin.com. German/Paraguayan run ranch with B&B and full board for maximum 7 people, offers tours as far as Iguazú, German, English, Spanish spoken. Owner Jan Paessler runs www.wochenblatt-online.com, German language newspaper.

Ybycuí *p1238*

E Hotel Pytu'u Renda, Av General Caballero 509 y Quyquyho, T0534-226364. Good food, cooking facilities.

Tourism farm B Estancia Santa Clara, Km 141, Ruta 1, Caapucú, T021-605729, www.estanciasantaclara.com.py. Rural activites in a beautiful setting between Paraguarí and San Ignacio Guazú, full board or visit for the day (mini-zoo). Reserve in advance.

San Ignacio Guazú and around *p1239*

C Parador Altamirano-Piringó, Ruta 1, Km 224, T082- 232334. Modern, on outskirts, with a/c, (**E** pp without), recommended, 24-hr restaurant.

E La Casa de Loly, Mariscal López y Última, San Ignacio, T082-232362, lacasadeloly@ yahoo.com, on outskirts. Nice atmosphere, pool, a/c, with breakfast, other meals on request.

Camping is possible outside the town.

Ayolas, Santiago and San Cosme *p1239*

D Hotel Nacional de Ayolas, Av Costanera, T072-222273. Overlooking the river, popular with fishing groups. More info from Asunción tourist office, www.paraguay.gov.py.

Encarnación *p1239, map p1240*

A-B Encarnación Resort Hotel, Villa Quiteria, on outskirts, Ruta 1, Km 361, T207250, www.encarnacionresorthotel.com.py. First class, comfortable, very well run. Highly recommended.

B De La Costa, Av Rodríguez de Francia 1240 con Cerro Corá, T205694, www.delacostahotel.com.py. Smart new hotel, pool, garden, Wi-Fi, parking, restaurant, breakfast included.

C Acuario, J L Mallorquín 1550 y Villarrica, T/F202676, www.acuario.com.py. Pool, a/c, with breakfast.

D Cristal, Mariscal Estigarribia 1157 y Cerro Corá, T202371, cristalh@telesurf.com.py. Pool, restaurant, TV and a/c, helpful staff.

D Paraná, Estigarribia 1414 y Tomas R Pereira y Villarrica, T204440. Good breakfast, helpful. Recommended.

D Viena, PJ Caballero 568, T205981, beside Copaco. With breakfast, German-run, good food, garage.

E Central, Mariscal López 542 y C A López, Zona Baja, T203454. With breakfast, nice patio, German spoken.
E Germano, General Cabañas y C A López, opposite bus terminal, T203346. **G** without bath or a/c, German and Japanese spoken, small, very accommodating. Highly recommended.
E Itapúa, C A López y General Cabañas, T205045, opposite bus station. Dark rooms, modern.
E Liz, Av Independencia 1746, T202609. Comfortable, restaurant, recommended.

Santísima Trinidad del Paraná and Jesús de Tavarangüé *p1240*
E-F pp **Hotel a las Ruinas**, a good hotel and restaurant next to the entrance to the hilltop site of the Jesuit reducción at Trinidad, T0985-828563, a.weisbach@gmx.net. German-owned, helpful, pool, nice garden.
Centro Social, Trinidad. Food and shower available, take sleeping gear.
Camping is permitted behind the souvenir stall at Trinidad. No facilities and beware theft.

German colonies on the road to Ciuidad del Este *p1241*
A Biorevital Hotel and Spa, Av Mariscal López 275 y Itapúa (Km 38½), Obligado, T0717-20073, www.spa-kur.com.py. German run, includes organic meals, mineral water pools, sauna, mud baths, yoga, internet, homeopathic treatments and various packages offered.
B Papillón, Ruta 6, Km 45, Bella Vista, T0767-240235, www.papillon.com.py. A/c, internet, pool, gardens, very pleasant, German, French, English, Flemish spoken, excellent and popular restaurant, full and half-board available. Highly recommended. Organizes excursions in the area including in a light aircraft.
E Plaza, Samaniego 1415, Bella Vista, T0757-240236.

Eating

Paraguarí and around *p1238*
La Frutería, about 2½ km before the town. Wide selection of fruit, outdoor seating and a restaurant serving *empanadas*, hamburgers, beer, fruit salad. Highly recommended.

Encarnación *p1239, map p1240*
TT American Grill, Av Irrazábal just before International Bridge. Good *churrasquería*.
TT Parrillada las Delicias, Mariscal Estigarribia 1694. Good steaks, comfortable, Chilean wines.
TT Provenza, Dr Mallorquín, just past the rail tracks. International cuisine.
TT Tokio, Mariscal Estigarribia 472. Good Japanese, real coffee.
TT-T Cuarajhy, Mariscal Estigarribia y Pereira. Terrace seating, good food, open 24 hrs.
TT-T Hiroshima, 25 de Mayo y L Valentinas (no sign), T206288. Excellent Japanese, wide variety, fresh sushi, Tue-Sun 1130-1400, 1900-2330.
T Rubi, Mariscal Estigarribia 519. Chinese, good.

Transport

Yaguarón *p1237*
Bus Every 15 mins from **Asunción**, US$0.60.

Paraguarí and around *p1238*
Bus City buses leave from lower level of the Asunción terminal every 15 mins throughout the day, but much faster to take an Encarnación-bound bus from the upper level, same fare US$0.90.

Parque Nacional Ybycuí *p1238*
Bus There are 2 per day, 1000 and 1600 from **Ybycuí**, US$0.60, take bus going to the Mbocaya Pucú colony that stops in front of the park entrance. From Asunción take a bus to Acahay, **Transportes Emilio Cabrera**, 8 daily and change, or bus to Ybycuí, 0630, US$1.30.

San Ignacio Guazú *p1239*
Bus Regular services to/from **Asunción**, US$4.30 común, US$6.80 rápido; to **Encarnación**, frequent, US$5.25 común, US$7.80 rápido.

Santa María
Bus From **San Ignacio** from the Esso station, 6 a day from 0500, 45 mins.

San Cosme y Damián
Bus From **Encarnación**, **La Cosmeña** and **Perla del Sur**, US$2.70, 2½ hrs.

Encarnación *p1239, map p1240*

Bus The bus terminal is at Estigarribia y Memmel. Good cheap snacks. To/from **Asunción**, **Alborada, La Encarnaceña** (recommended, T203448), **Flecha de Oro, Rysa**, at least 4 a day each, 6 hrs, US$12. Stopping (común) buses are US$9.50, but much slower (6-7 hrs). To **Ciudad del Este**, US$5.75, several daily, 4 hrs.

Border with Argentina *p1240*

Bus Take any 'Posadas/Argentina' bus from opposite bus terminal over the bridge, US$0.65, 30 mins. Bus passengers should keep all luggage with them and should retain bus ticket; buses do not wait. After formalities (queues common), use ticket on next bus. **Taxi** costs US$5.50 (at least). **Cycles** are not allowed to use the bridge, but officials may give cyclists a lift. **Ferry** costs US$1.25. Immigration formalities must be undertaken at the main offices.

Santísima Trinidad del Paraná and Jesús de Tavarangüé *p1240*

Bus Many go from **Encarnación** to and through Trinidad, take any bus from the terminal marked Hohenau or Ciudad del Este, US$1.25 (beware overcharging). A **taxi** tour from Encarnación costs about US$22. Bus direct **Encarnación-Jesús** 0800; buses run **Jesús-Trinidad** every hr (30 mins, US$0.55), from where it is easy to get back to Encarnación, so do Jesús first. Last bus Jesús-Trinidad 1700; also collective taxis, return Trinidad-Jesús US$3.65. No buses on Sun. Enquire locally as taxis may overcharge.

Directory

Encarnación *p1239, map p1240*

Banks Most banks now in the upper town, eg **Banco Continental**, Mariscal Estigarribia 1418, Visa accepted. **Citibank**, Mariscal Estigarribia y Villarrica, ATM. Casas de cambio for cash on Mariscal Estagarribia (eg **Cambios Financiero** at No 307, **Cambio Iguazú** at No 211). **Cambio Chaco Irrazábal y Memmel**, inside Superseis supermarket. Moneychangers at the Paraguayan side of the bridge but best to change money in town. **Consulates Argentina**, Artigas 960, T201066, consuldorep@click.com.py, Mon-Fri 0800-1300. **Brazil**, Memmel 452, T206335, brvcconcep@tigo.com.pyS. **Germany**, Memmel 631, T204041, con_alemana@itacom.com.py. **Telephones Copaco**, Capitán PJ Caballero y Mariscal López, 0700-2200, only Spanish spoken.

North of Asunción

The winding Río Paraguay is 400 m wide and is still the main trade route for the products of northern Paraguay, in spite of a paved highway built to Concepción. Boats carry cattle, hides, yerba mate, tobacco and timber. On the river, a boat trip to Concepción is probably one of the most interesting ways to see the countryside and wildlife. s

Asunción to Concepción

Travelling north from Asunción by river, you first come across Puente Remanso, the bridge that marks the beginning of the Trans-Chaco Highway. Just further upstream is Villa Hayes, founded in 1786 but renamed in 1879 after the US president who arbitrated the territorial dispute with Argentina in Paraguay's favour. Further upstream is Puerto Antequera and 100 km beyond is Concepción. By road there are two alternative routes. One is via the Trans-Chaco Highway and Pozo Colorado. The Pozo Colorado-Concepción road, 146 km, is completely paved and offers spectacular views of birdlife. The other route is Ruta 2 to Coronel Oviedo, Ruta 3 to Yby Yaú (paved) and then west along Ruta 5 (paved). North of Coronel Oviedo, at Tacuara (Km 225), a road heads west to Rosario, from where you can visit the Mennonite community of **Colonia Volendam**, nine hours by bus from Asunción (two a day, San Jorge, US$3.30). German and Spanish are spoken here.

Concepción → *Phone code: 0331. Colour map 6, B6. Population: 54,441.*
Concepción, 312 km north of Asunción, stands on the east bank of the Río Paraguay. It is known as La Perla del Norte for its climate and setting. To appreciate the colonial aspect of the city, walk away from the main commercial streets. At Plaza La Libertad are the Catedral and recently restored Municipalidad. Sunsets from the port are beautiful. The town is the trade centre of the north, doing a considerable business with Brazil. The **Brazilian Consulate** ⓘ *Pdte Franco 972, T242655, Mon-Fri 0800-1400, brvcconcep@tigo.com.py*, issues visas, but go early to ensure same-day processing. The market, a good place to try local food, is east of the main street, Agustín Pinedo (which is a kind of open-air museum). From here Avenida Presidente Franco runs west to the port. Along Avenida Agustín Pineda is a large statue of María Auxiliadora with Christ child. There are stairs to balconies at the base of the monument which offer good views of the city. The **Museo Municipal** ⓘ *Mariscal López y Cerro Corá, Mon-Fri 0700-1200*, contains a collection of guns, religious art and other objects. Plaza Agustín Fernando de Pinedo has a permanent craft market. About 9 km south is a bridge across the Río Paraguay, which makes for an interesting walk across the shallows and islands to the west bank and the Chaco, about an hour return trip, taxi US$6. The island in the Río Paraguay facing Concepción is Isla Chaco'i, where you can stroll through the fields. Row boats take passengers to the island from the shore next to the port, US$0.25 per person. For more information visit the town's own blog, http://concepcionparaguay.blogspot.com.

East of Concepción
There is a 215-km road (Ruta 5 – fully paved) from Concepción, eastwards to the Brazilian border. This road goes through Horqueta, Km 50, a cattle and lumber town of 10,000 people. Further on the road is very scenic. From **Yby Yaú** (junction with Ruta 8 south to Coronel Oviedo) the road continues to Pedro Juan Caballero.

Six kilometres east of Yby Yaú a road branches off to the pleasant **Parque Nacional Cerro Corá** (22,000 ha), the site of Mariscal Francisco Solano López' death and the final defeat of Paraguay in the War of the Triple Alliance. There is a monument to him and other national heroes; the site is constantly guarded. It has hills and cliffs (some with pre-Columbian caves and petroglyphs), camping facilities, swimming and hiking trails. The rocky outcrops are spectacular and the warden is helpful and provides free guides. When you have walked up the road and seen the line of leaders' heads, turn right and go up the track passing a dirty-looking shack (straight on leads to a military base). Administration office is 5 km east of the main entrance at Km 180 on Ruta 5.

Pedro Juan Caballero → *Phone code: 0336. Colour map 7, B1. Population: 75,109.*
This border town is separated from the Brazilian town of Ponta Porã, by a road (Dr Francia on the Paraguayan side, on the Brazilian side either Rua Marechal Floreano or Avenida Internacional): which anyone can cross at their leisure (see below for immigration formalities). Ponta Porã is the more modern and prosperous of the two. In addition to liquor and electronics, everything costs less on the Paraguayan side. **Shopping China** is a vast emporium on the eastern outskirts of town and **Maxi** is a large well stocked supermarket in the centre. You can pay in guaraníes, reais or US$, at good exchange rates. **Arte Paraguaya**, Mariscal López y Alberdi, has a good selection of crafts from all over the country.

Border with Brazil
This is a more relaxed crossing than Ciudad del Este. For day crossings you do not need a stamp, but passports must be stamped if travelling beyond the border towns (ask if unsure whether your destination is considered beyond). Paraguayan immigration ⓘ *T0336-272195, Mon-Fri 0700-2100, Sat 0800-2100, Sun 1900-2100, take bus line 2 on the Parguayan side, or any Brazilian city bus that goes to the Rodoviária, taxi US$4*, is in the customs building on the

eastern outskirts of town near *Shopping China*. Then report to Brazilian federal police in Ponta Porã (closed Sat-Sun). The Brazilian consulate ⓘ *Mariscal Estigarribia 250, T0336-273562, Mon-Fri 0800-1300*, issues visas, fees payable only in guaraníes, take passport and a photo, go early to get visa the same day. There is another crossing to Brazil at Bella Vista on the Río Apá, northwest of PJ Caballero; buses run from the Brazilian border town of Bela Vista to Jardim and on to Campo Grande. There is a Paraguayan immigration office at Bella Vista, but no Brazilian Policia Federal in Bela Vista. To cross here, get Paraguayan exit stamp then report to the local Brazilian police who may give a temporary stamp, but you must later go to the Policia Federal in either Ponta Porã or Corumbá. Do not fail to get the proper stamp later or you will be detained upon re-entering Paraguay.

North of Asunción listings

For Sleeping and Eating price codes and other relevant information, see Essentials, pages 38-40.

Sleeping

Asunción to Concepción *p1243*

B pp **Estancia Jejui**, set on the Río Jejui, 65 km north of Tacuara on Ruta 3, address in Asunción, Telmo Aquino 4068, T021-600227, www.coinco.com.py/jejui. All rooms with a/c, bathroom and hot water, fishing, horse riding, tennis, boat rides extra, US$60 pp including all meals.

E pp **Hotel Waldbrunner**, Colonia Volendam, T0451-20175. Bath, **F** without a/c, also has a good restaurant.

Concepción *p1244*

C Francés, Franco y C A López, T242750, www.hotelfrancesconcepcion.com. With a/c, **D** with fan, breakfast, rooms are ageing, nice grounds with pool (US$1.50 non-guests), restaurant, parking.

C Victoria, Franco y Caballero, T242256. Pleasant rooms, a/c, fridge, **D** with fan, restaurant, parking.

D Concepción, Don Bosco y Cabral near market, T242360. With simple breakfast, a/c, **E** with fan, family run, good value.

Pedro Juan Caballero *p1244*

A Hotel Casino Amambay, Av Dr Francia 1 y José Bergés at the west end of town, T271140, hcassino@uol.com.br. A posh establishment centred around its casino, simple rooms compared to its surroundings, include buffet breakfast, a/c, fridge, balcony, lovely grounds with large pool.

B Eiruzú, Mariscal López y Mariscal Estigarribia, T272435. With breakfast, a/c, fridge and pool, starting to show its age but still good.

B Porã Palace, Alberdi 30 y Dr Francia, T273021. With breakfast, a/c, fridge, balcony, restaurant, pool, aging but still OK, rooms in upper floor have been refurbished and are nicer.

E La Victoria, Teniente Herrero y Alberdi, near bus station, T272733. With breakfast, electric shower and a/c, cheaper with fan, family run, simple.

Eating

Concepción *p1244*

ǂ **Hotel Francés**, good value buffet lunch, à la carte in the evening.

ǂ **Hotel Victoria**, set lunches and à la carte, grill in *quincho* across the street.

ǂ **Pollería El Bigote**, Pdnte Franco y E A Garay. Simple, good chicken, sidewalk seating.

ǂ **Ysapy**, Yegros y Mariscal Estigarribia at Plaza Pineda. Pizza and ice-cream, terrace or sidewalk seating, very popular, daily 1630-0200.

Pedro Juan Caballero *p1244*

ǂ **Mr Grill** at *Maxi* supermarket, Mariscal López y J Estigarribia. Good quality buffet by the kilo.

ǂ **Pepes**, Dr Francia y Alberdi. Buffet, à la carte.

ǂ **Pizza House**, Mariscal López y José de J Martínez.

Transport

Concepción *p1244*

Bus The terminal is on the outskirts, 8 blocks north along General Garay, but buses also stop in the centre, Av Pinedo, look for signs Parada Omnibus. A shuttle bus (Línea 1) runs between the terminal and the port. Taxi from terminal or port to centre, US$2; terminal to port U$2.65. To **Asunción**, 7 a day with **Nasa/Golondrina**, 2 with **Santaniana**, plus other companies,

US$13, 5½ hrs via Pozo Colorado, 9 hrs via Coronel Oviedo. To **Pedro Juan Caballero**, frequent service, several companies, **Amambay** is best, US$4.75, 4-5 hrs. To **Horqueta**, 1 hr, US$1.10. To **Filadelfia**, **Nasa/Golondrina** direct at 0730 daily, US$12, 5 hrs, otherwise change at Pozo Colorado. To **Ciudad del Este**, **García** direct at 1230 daily, US$13, 9 hrs, or change at Coronel Oviedo.

Boat To **Asunción**, the Cacique II sails Mon between 0600 and 0700 (if enough passengers), 22-24 hrs, tickets sold on board in advance of departure (fares and other services on page 1228). To **Fuerte Olimpo**, **Bahía Negra**, and intermediate points along the upper Río Paraguay, the **Río Aquidabán** sails Tue 1100, arriving Bahía Negra on Fri morning and returning immediately to arrive back in Concepción on Sun, US$18 to Bahía Negra plus US$8.50 for a berth if you want one. Take food and water. Tickets sold in office just outside the port, T242435, Mon-Sat 0700-1200. There are sporadic ferries from Concepción to Isla Margarita, across from Porto Murtinho, Brazil. Ask for prices and times at dock and note that service does not include anything other than standing room. Motorboats (*deslizadores*) may be hired but beware overcharging and seek advice from the Prefectura Naval. **Note** There is an immigration office in Concepción (see below), but not further towards Brazil. Check well in advance, even in Asunción, about obtaining an exit stamp in good time. In all, a time consuming, adventurous and expensive journey.

Pedro Juan Caballero *p1244*

Air TAM, Curupayty y Mariscal López, T274501, to **Asunción**, Mon-Fri. Airport is 30 km from town on road to Yby Yaú, TAM has free shuttle bus before flights, taxi US$19 (ask for fare before getting in).

Bus To **Concepción**, frequent, 4-5 hrs, US$4.75. To **Asunción**, 5-6 hrs via 25 de Diciembre, 7½ hours via Coronel Oviedo. **Santaniana** has nicest buses, *bus cama* US$13.35; *semicama* US$11.10. **Amambay** 0700 via Oviedo US$11.10, twice via 25 de Diciembre, US$11.75. **Nasa** 2 a day US$11.10. To **Bella Vista**, **Perpetuo Socorro** 3 a day, US$4.50, 4 hrs. To **Campo Grande** **Amambay** 3 a day, US$13.75, 5 hrs, they stop at Policia Federal in Ponta Porã for entry stamp.

Directory

Concepción *p1244*

Banks TCs cannot be changed. **Norte Cambios**, Pdte Franco y 14 de Mayo, Mon-Fri 0830-1700, Sat 0830-1100, fair rates for US$ and euros, cash only. **Financiera Familiar**, Pdte Franco y General Garay, US$ cash only. **Immigration** Registro Civil, Pdte Franco y Caballero, T0972-193143. **Internet** **Cybercom Internet Café**, Pdte Franco y 14 de Mayo, open until 2230. **Post office** Pdte Franco. **Telephone** **Copaco** and other cabinas on Pdte Franco.

Pedro Juan Caballero *p1244*

Banks Many *cambios* on the Paraguayan side, especially on Curupayty between Dr Francia and Mariscal López. Good rates for buying guaraníes or reais with US$ or euros cash, better than inside Brazil, but TCs are usually impossible to change and there is only one ATM. Banks on Brazilian side do not change cash or TCs but have a variety of ATMs. **BBVA**, Dr Francia y Mariscal Estigarribia. Mon-Fri 0845-1300, changes US$ cash to guaraníes only, and has Cirrus ATM. **Norte Cambios**, Curupayty entre Dr Francia y Mariscal López, Mon-Fri 0830-1630, Sat 0830-1100, fair rates for cash, 5% commission for TCs. **Internet** Several places including **Maxi supermarket**, spacious, quiet, a/c, US$0.80 per hr. **Telephones** **Copaco**, behind the bus station, plus many *cabinas*.

The Chaco

West of the Río Paraguay is the Chaco, a wild expanse of palm savanna and marshes (known as Humid, or Bajo Chaco, closest to the Río Paraguay) and dry scrub forest and farmland (known as Dry, or Alto Chaco, further northwest from the river). The Chaco has a substantial population of indigenous peoples. Birdlife is spectacular and abundant. Large cattle estancias dot the whole region, but otherwise agriculture has been developed mainly by German-speaking Mennonites from Russia in the Chaco Central. Through this vast area the Trans-Chaco Highway runs to Bolivia. Most of the region is pristine, perfect for those who want to escape into the wilderness with minimal human contact and experience nature at its finest. It is also considerably lacking in infrastructure, so travellers should prepare accordingly.

Ins and outs

Getting there The Paraguayan Chaco covers 24 million ha, but once away from the vicinity of Asunción, the average density is far less than one person to the sq km. A single major highway, the Ruta Trans-Chaco, runs in an almost straight line northwest towards the Bolivian border, forming part of the *corredor bi-oceánico*, connecting ports on the Pacific and Atlantic oceans. The elevation rises very gradually from 50 m opposite Asunción to 450 m on the Bolivian border. Paving of the Trans-Chaco to the Bolivian border (Infante Rivarola) was completed in 2007. However, sections paved earlier, such as La Patria to Mariscal Estigarribia (the first Paraguayan immigration post coming from Bolivia) are already showing signs of wear and tear, with repairs to potholes few and far between. From the border to Villamontes, the road is gravel and in good condition even after rain, and a 4WD is no longer indispensable. The first 40 km out of Villamontes are paved, and the remainder is in progress. Although road conditions are much improved, motorists and even travellers going by bus should carry extra food and especially water; climatic conditions are harsh and there is little traffic in case of a breakdown. ▸▸ *See also Transport, page 1252.*

Getting around Most bus companies have some a/c buses on their Chaco routes (a great asset December-March), enquire in advance. There is very little local public transport between the main Mennonite towns, you must use the buses heading to/from Asunción to travel between them as well as Mariscal Estigarribia. No private expedition should leave the Trans-Chaco without plentiful supplies of water, food and fuel. No one should venture onto the dirt roads alone and since this is a major smuggling route from Bolivia, it is unwise to stop for anyone at night. There are service stations at regular intervals along the highway in the Bajo and Chaco Central, but beyond Mariscal Estigarribia there is one stop for diesel only and no regular petrol at all until Villamontes, a long drive. Winter temperatures are warm by day, cooler by night, but summer heat and mosquitoes can make it very unpleasant (pyrethrum coils, *espirales*, are sold everywhere).

Information Consejo Regional de Turismo Chaco Central (CONRETUR) coordinates tourism development of the three cooperatives and the private sector. Contact **Hans Fast** ⓘ *T492-52422, Loma Plata, fast@telesurf.com.py*. The **Fundación para el Desarrollo Sustentable del Chaco** ⓘ *Deportivo 935 y Algarrobo, Loma Plata, T492-52235, www.desdelchaco.org.py*, operates conservation projects in the area and has useful information but does not offer tours. ▸▸ *For Tour operators, see page 1252. See also under individual towns for local tourist offices.*

Background

The Bajo Chaco begins on the riverbank just west of Asunción across the Río Paraguay. It is a picturesque landscape of palm savanna, much of which is seasonally inundated because of the impenetrable clay beneath the surface, although there are 'islands' of higher ground with forest vegetation. Cattle ranching on huge estancias is the prevailing economic activity; some units lie several hundred kilometres down tracks off the highway. Remote estancias have their own airfields, and all are equipped with two-way radios. Never wander into one unless you have prior permission from the owner, except in an emergency. There have been cases of guards shooting travellers mistaken for smugglers.

In the **Chaco Central**, the natural vegetation is dry scrub forest, with a mixture of hardwoods and cactus. The palo borracho (bottle tree) with its pear-shaped, water-conserving, trunk, the palo santo, with its green wood and beautiful scent, and the tannin-rich *quebracho* (literally meaning axe-breaker) are the most noteworthy native species. This is the best area in Paraguay to see large mammals, especially once away from the central Chaco Mennonite colonies.

The **Alto Chaco** is characterized by low dense thorn and scrub forest which has created an impenetrable barricade of spikes and spiny branches resistant to heat and drought and very tough on tyres. Towards Bolivia cacti become more prevalent as rainfall decreases. There are a few estancias in the southern part, but beyond Mariscal Estigarribia there are no towns, only occasional military checkpoints. Summer temperatures often exceed 45°C.

Reserva de la Biósfera del Chaco

This is the crown jewel of Paraguay's national park system, albeit one without infrastructure and nearly impossible to visit. Guyra Paraguay, who currently co-manages the national parks in this region, is possibly the best option for arranging a tour (see page 1213).The 7.4-million-ha biosphere reserve in the Chaco and Pantanal eco- systems includes six national parks, monuments and indigenous reserves: Defensores del Chaco, Médanos del Chaco, Teniente Enciso, Cerro Cabrera-Timane, Cerro Chovoreca, and Río Negro. All are north of the Trans-Chaco and most are along the Bolivian border. Teniente Enciso is the smallest park and the only one accessible by public transport, although not easily, see below. The others can only be visited with a private 4WD vehicle, or on expensive tours from Loma Plata and Asunción. Most of Paraguay's few remaining jaguars are found here. Puma, tapir and peccary also inhabit the area, as well as taguá (an endemic peccary) and a short-haired guanaco. The best time to see them is around waterholes at nightfall in the dry season, but with great patience. **Cerro León** (highest peak 600 m), one of the only hilly areas of the Chaco, is located within this reserve. Roads from Filadelfia through this area are very rough, for 4WDs only.

Parque Nacional Defensores del Chaco, some 220 km from Filadelfia, has three visitor centres with accommodation, a/c, kitchen and shared bathroom. Distances between sites are long, visitors may be able to travel with rangers. **Parque Nacional Teniente Enciso**, 20 km from La Patria, has a good visitor centre with accommodation, one room with bathroom, others shared, a/c, take sleeping bag and all food. Nasa minibuses run from Filadelfia to Teniente Enciso via Mariscal Estigarribia and La Patria, see Transport, page 1252.

The Trans-Chaco Highway

To reach the Ruta Trans-Chaco, you leave Asunción behind and cross the Río Paraguay to Villa Hayes. Birdlife is immediately more abundant and easily visible in the palm savanna (binoculars and camera highly recommended), but other wildlife is usually only seen at night, and otherwise occurs mostly as road kills. The first service station after Asunción is at Km 130. **Pirahú**, Km 252, has a service station and is a good place to stop for a meal; it has a/c, delicious empanadas and fruit salad. The owner of the parador owns an old-fashioned carbon manufacturing site 2 km before Pirahú. Ask for him if you are interested in visiting the site. At Km 271 is **Pozo Colorado** abd the turning for Concepción (see page 1244). There are two restaurants, a basic hotel (**F** pp with fan, cheaper without), supermarket, hospital, a service station and a military post. The Touring y Automóvil Club Paraguayo provides a breakdown and recovery service from Pozo Colorado (T0981-939611, www.tacpy.com.py). At this point, the tidy Mennonite homesteads, with flower gardens and citrus orchards, begin to appear. At Km 282, 14 km northwest of Pozo Colorado, is **Rancho Buffalo Bill**, T021-298381, one of the most pleasant places to stop off or eat, beside a small lake. The estancia has limited but good accommodation (**D**), ask at restaurant. Horse riding, nature walks and camping are good options here. At Km 320 is **Río Verde**, with fuel, police station and restaurant. The next good place to stay or eat along the Trans-Chaco is **Cruce de los Pioneros**, at Km 415, where accommodation (**D** Los Pioneros, T491-432170, hot shower, a/c), limited supermarket, vehicle repair shop, and fuel are available. A new paved road has been built from Cruce Boquerón, just northwest of Cruce de los Pioneros, to Loma Plata. In mid-September the country's biggest motorsport event, the Trans-Chaco Rally (www.transchacorally.com.py), is held.

Mennonite communities

The Chaco Central has been settled by Mennonites, Anabaptists of German extraction who began arriving in the late 1920s. There are three administratively distinct but adjacent colonies: Menno (from Russia via Canada); Fernheim (directly from Russia) and Neuland (the last group to arrive, also from Russia, after the Second World War). Among themselves, the Mennonites speak 'plattdeutsch' ('Low German'), but they readily speak and understand 'hochdeutsch' ('High German'), which is the language of instruction in their schools. Increasingly, younger Mennonites speak Spanish and some English. The people are friendly and willing to talk about their history and culture. Altogether there are about 80 villages with a population of about 18,000 Mennonites and 20,000 *indígenas*. Increasing numbers of Paraguayans are migrating to the area in search of economic opportunities while indigenous people (eight distinct groups) occupy the lowest rung on the socioeconomic ladder.

The Mennonites have created a remarkable oasis of regimented prosperity in this harsh hinterland. Their hotels and restaurants are impeccably clean, services are very efficient, large modern supermarkets are well stocked with excellent dairy products and all other goods, local and imported. Each colony has its own interesting museum. All services, except for hotels, a few restaurants and one gas station in Filadelfia, close on Saturday afternoon and Sunday. The main towns are all very spread out and have no public transport except for a few expensive taxis in Filadelfia, most residents use their private vehicles. Walking around in the dust and extreme heat can be tiring. Transport between the three main towns is also limited, see Transport, page 1252.

Filadelfia → *Phone code: 0491. Colour map 6, B5. Population: 9,713.*

Also known as Fernheim Colony, Filadelfia, 466 km from Asunción, is the largest town of the region. The **Jacob Unger Museum** ⓘ *US$1 including video*, provides a glimpse of pioneer life in the Chaco, as well as exhibiting artefacts of the indigenous peoples of the region. The manager of the Hotel Florida will open the museum upon request, when things are not too busy. Next to the museum is **Plaza de los Recuerdos**, a good place to see the *samu'u* or *palo borracho* (bottle tree). A bookstore-cum-craft shop, **Librería El Mensajero**, next to Hotel Florida, is run by Sra Penner, very helpful and informative.

The Fernheim community does not encourage tourism, but there is a good website, www.filadelfiaparaguay.com. Apart from that, there is no tourist infrastructure in Filadelfia. General information may be obtained from the co-op office.

Loma Plata → *Phone code: 0492. Population: 4,118.*

The centre of Menno Colony, Loma Plata is 25 km east of Filadelfia. Although smaller than Filadelfia, it has more to offer the visitor. It has a good museum **Museo de la Colonia Menno** ⓘ *Mon-Fri 0700-1130, 1400-1800; Sat 0700-1300, US$1.65*. **Balneario Oasis swimming complex** ⓘ *Nord Grenze, 700 m past airport north of Loma Plata, T52704, US$1.65, Sep-Apr 1500-2100, except Sun and holidays, 1100-2100* has three pools with slides and snack bar, a welcome break from the summer heat. **Tourist office** (contact Walter Ratzlaff) ⓘ *next to the Chortitzer Komitee Co-op, T492-52301, turismo@chortitzer.com.py, Mon-Fri 0700-1130, 1400-1800, Sat 0700-1300*, very helpful. For general information about the colony, not tourism, www.chortitzer.com.py.

Wetlands around Loma Plata To the southeast of Loma Plata is the Riacho Yacaré Sur watershed, with many salt water lagoons, generally referred to as Laguna Salada. This is a wonderful place to see waterbirds such as Chilean flamingos, swans, spoonbills and migratory shorebirds from the Arctic. There are extensive walks though the eerily beautiful landscape. **Laguna Capitán**, a 22-ha recreation reserve, 30 km from town, has several small lagoons, a swimming lake, basic bunk bed accommodation (**F** per person, shared bath), kitchen facilities, meals on request, camping (US$1 per person). Reserve directly at T0991-650101 or through the Cooperative information office in Loma Plata. There is no public transport. Taxi US$22 one way; full-day tour combining Laguna Capitán with visit to the Cooperative's installations and museum, US$64 per group plus transport. **Laguna Chaco Lodge**, a 2,500-ha-private reserve, 70 km from town, is a Ramsar wetland site (no accommodation despite the name). The lovely Laguna Flamenco is the main body of water surrounded by dry forest. Large numbers of Chilean flamingos and other water birds may be seen here. **Campo María**, a 4,500-ha reserve within the co-operative's land 90 km from town, also has a large lake and can be visited on a tour.

Indigenous Foundation for Agricultural and Livestock Development (FIDA) ⓘ *30 km from Neuland, Filadelfia and Loma Plata, T0491-32116*. Located within Yalve Sanga, this is the first indigenous version of the Mennonite cooperative colonies and provides an interesting insight into the lives of the communities. Limited handicrafts are sold in the Yalva Sanga supermarket (better selection in Neuland).

Neuland → *Phone code: 0493. Population: 3,429.*

Neuland, also known as Neu-Halbstadt, is 33 km south of Filadelfia. There is a small museum of historical objects brought by the first Mennonites from Russia, set in the building of the first primary school of the area. **Neuland Beach Park** ⓘ *US$1.55, pool, snack bar with a/c*. **Parque la Amistad**, 500 m past pool, is 35 ha of natural vegetation where paths have been cleared for nature walks. Most spectacular are the wild orchids (September-October), cacti and birdlife. Enrique (Heinz) Weibe is the official guide of the Neuland colony; also ask for Harry Epp ⓘ *contact through Neuland Co-op office, T493- 240201, www.neuland.com.py, Mon-Fri 0700-1130, 1400-1800, Sat 0700-1130*, who is very knowledgeable about the flora and fauna and is an informative and entertaining guide. He also gives tours of Neuland in a horse drawn carriage. Phone booths and post office are in centre of town next to the supermarket.

Fortín Boquerón, 27 km from Neuland, is the site of the decisive battle of Chaco War (September 1932) and includes a memorial, a small, well-presented museum and walks around the remainder of the trenches. **Campamento Aurora Chaqueña** is a park 15 km from town on the way to Fortín Boquerón, there is simple accommodation with fan (**G** per person, take your own food and water). **Parque Valle Natural**, 10 km from Neuland on the way to Filadelfia, is an *espartillar*, a dry riverbed with natural brush around it and a few larger trees. Camping is possible although there is only a small covered area.

Mariscal Estigarribia and on to Bolivia → *Colour map 6, B5.*

Around 525 Km from Asunción, Mariscal Estigarribia is a former garrison town with aspirations of becoming a transport hub. The few services are spread out over four km along the highway: three gas stations (no fuel stations between Mariscal Estigarribia and Villamontes on the Bolivian side), a couple of small supermarkets (**La Llave del Chaco** is recommended), two mediocre hotels, and one remarkably excellent restaurant (see listings below). Better services are found in Filadelfia, Loma Plata and Neuland. The immigration office (supposedly 24 hours, but often closed in the small hours) is at the southeast end of town near the Shell station. All buses stop at the terminal (**Parador Arami**), at the northwest end of town, where travellers entering from Bolivia are subject to thorough searches for drugs. The people are friendly and helpful. There is good birdwatching nearby along the dirt road called Picada 500, as well as some indigenous communities nearby where crafts are made.

There are no reliable services of any kind beyond Mariscal Estigarribia. At **La Patria**, 125 km northwest, the road divides: 128 km west to Infante Rivarola continuing to Villamontes, Bolivia, with Bolivian immigration and customs at Ibibobo; 128 km northwest to General Eugenio A Garay continuing to Boyuibe, Bolivia (hardly used as shifting sand makes it treacherous). Immigration posts are at Mariscal Estigarribia and Ibibobo (the latter often closed). There are customs posts at either side of the actual border in addition to the main customs offices in Mariscal Estigarribia and Villamontes.

In Bolivia, from Villamontes or Boyuibe, a paved road runs north to Santa Cruz and south to Yacuiba on the Argentine border, see page 375. Take small denomination dollar notes as it is impossible to buy bolivianos before reaching Bolivia (if entering from Bolivia street changers in Santa Cruz sometimes sell guaraníes at good rates, but often only casas de cambio have them).

The Chaco listings

For Sleeping and Eating price codes and other relevant information, see Essentials, pages 38-40.

Sleeping

Filadelfia *p1249*

C-E Golondrina, Av Hindenburg 635-S at entrance to town, T432643, www.hotelgolondrina.com. Modern, 4 types of room with breakfast, a/c, TV and fridge in the best (cheapest with fan, shared bath, no breakfast), restaurant.

D Florida, Av Hindenburg 165-S opposite park, T432152/4, hotelflorida@telesurf.com.py. Breakfast, a/c, fridge, **F** in basic annex with shared bath, fan and without breakfast. Pool (US$1.40/hr for non-guests), restaurant (🍴) for buffet and à la carte.

D Safari, Industrial 194-E, T432218, www.hotel-safari.com. Modern, clean, spacious common areas with game room. Spanish and German spoken.

Loma Plata *p1249*

D-E Palace, Av Fred Engen, T252180, hpalace@telesurf.com.py. With breakfast, TV, a/c, mini bar, decent restaurant set around indoor pool (free for diners), friendly staff, best facilities in town.

E Mora, Sandstrasse 803, T252255. With breakfast, a/c, new wing has spacious rooms with fridge, nice grounds, family run, good value, good breakfast, basic meals available on request. Recommended.

E Pensión Loma Plata, J B Reimer 1805, T452829. A/c, breakfast, comfortable rooms, homely atmosphere, very helpful, good value. Includes breakfast, other meals on request. Recommended.

Neuland *p1250*

D-E Hotel Boquerón, Av 1 de Febrero opposite the Cooperative, T0493-240311, cfiss@telesurf.com.py. With breakfast, a/c, cheaper in older wing without TV, restaurant.

F Parador, Av 1 de Febrero y C Talleres, T0493-240567. With breakfast, a/c, **G** with fan and shared bath, restaurant.

Mariscal Estigarribia *p1250*

D-E Parador Arami, northwest end of town and far from everything, also known as *la terminal*, T0494-247230. Functional rooms, a/c, meals on request, agents for Stel Turismo and Nasa buses.

Eating

Filadelfia *p1249*

🍴🍴 **El Girasol**, Unruh 126-E y Hindenburg. Good buffet and *rodizio*, cheaper without the meat. Mon-Sat 1100-1400, 1800-2300, Sun 1100-1400.

Loma Plata *p1249*

🍴🍴 **Chaco's Grill**, Av Dr Manuel Gondra, T52166. Buffet, *rodizio*, very good, patio, live music.

🍴 **Norteño**, opposite supermarket. Good, simple, lunch till 1400 then open for dinner.

🍴 **Pizzería San Marino**, Av Central y Dr Gondra. Pizza and German dishes, daily 1800-2300.

Mariscal Estigarribia *p1250*

🍴🍴 **Italiano**, at the southwest end of town behind the Shell station, T0494-247231. Excellent, top quality meat, large portions, an unexpected treat in the outback. Italian owner Mauricio is friendly and helpful, open daily for lunch and dinner.

Activities and tours

Many agencies in Asunción offer Chaco tours. Note that some are just a visit to Rancho Buffalo Bill and do not provide a good overview of attractions. Hans Fast and Harry Epp also run tours to national parks. In Loma Plata ask around for bicycle hire to explore nearby villages. For more complete tailor-made tours, contact **Guyra Paraguay** (www.guyra.org.py).

Transport

Filadelfia *p1249*

Bus From **Asunción**, **Nasa/Golondrina**, at least 2 daily; **Stel Turismo**, 1 overnight; 6-7 hrs, US$14. To **Loma Plata**, **Nasa/Golondrina** 0800 going to Asunción, 0600 and 1900 coming from Asunción, 1 hr, US$2.25. To **Neuland**, local service Mon-Fri 1130 and 1800, 1 hr, US$2.25. Also **Stel Turismo** at 1900 and **Nasa/Golondrina** at 2130, both coming from Asunción. To **Mariscal Estigarribia**, **Ovetense** at 1800 coming from Asunción, 1½ hrs, US$2.40. Also **Nasa** at 0500 Mon and Fri, continuing to La Patria and Parque Nacional Teniente Enciso (see page 1248), 5-6 hrs, US$9, returns around 1300 same day (confirm all details in advance).

Loma Plata *p1249*

Bus **Asunción**, **Nasa/Golondrina**, 0600 daily, 7-8 hrs, US$14. To **Filadelfia**, Mon-Fri 1300, Sat 1100, Sun 1200, daily 2130, all continuing to Asunción, 1 hr, US$2.25.

Neuland *p1250*

Bus To **Asunción**, **Nasa/Golondrina** at 1945, and **Stel Turismo** at 1800, via Filadelfia, 7-8 hrs, US$14. Local service to Filadelfia, Mon-Fri 0500, 1230, 1 hr, US$2.25.

Mariscal Estigarribia *p1250*

Bus From **Filadelfia Nasa/Golondrina** 1100 daily, **Ovetense** 1200 and 2000 daily; **Asunción Nasa/Golondrina**, daily 1430; **Stel**, 2 a day, and **Pycasu** 3 daily, 7-8 hrs, US$14, 0700. Buses from Asunción pass through town around 0300-0400 en route to Bolivia: **Yaciretá** on Tue, Thu, Sat, Sun (agent at Barcos y Rodados petrol station, T0494-247320); **Stel Turismo** daily (agent at Parador Arami, T0494-247230). You can book and purchase seats in advance but beware overcharging, the fare from Mariscal Estigarribia should be about US$10 less than from Asunción.

Directory

Filadelfia *p1249*

Banks There are no ATMs in the Chaco, neither in the Mennonite colonies nor in Mariscal Estigarribia. **Fernheim Cooperative Bank**, Hindenburg opposite the Cooperative building, changes US$ and euro cash, no commission for US$ TCs (although must be from major issuer). **Internet** At **Shopping Portal del Chaco** and opposite **Radio ZP30**. **Telephone** **Copaco** on Hindenburg, opposite supermarket, Mon-Sat 0700-2100, Sun 0700-1200, 1500-2000.

Loma Plata *p1249*

Banks **Chortitzer Komitee Co-op**, Av Central, Mon-Fri 0700-1730, Sat 0700-1100, good rates for US$ and euros, US$1.25 commission per TC. **Internet** **Microtec**, Fred Engen 1229, Mon-Sat 0800-1130, 1400-2200, US$0.80 per hr. **Telephone** **Copaco**, Av Central near supermarket, Mon-Sat 0700-2000, Sun 0700-1200, 1500-2000.

Neuland *p1250*

Banks Neuland Cooperative changes US$ cash and TCs, Mon-Fri 0700-1130, 1400-1800, Sat 0700-1130.

Mariscal Estigarribia *p1250*

Banks No banks. Shell station best for US$, cash only. **Telephones** **Copaco**, one street back from highway, ask for directions.

Peru

Contents

1256 Planning your trip

1266 Lima

1297 Huaraz and the Cordilleras
- 1297 Huaraz
- 1307 Cordillera Blanca
- 1315 Cordillera Huayhuash

1317 North coast
- 1317 North of Lima
- 1320 Trujillo and around
- 1331 Chiclayo and around
- 1339 Piura and around
- 1342 North to Ecuador

1350 Northern Highlands
- 1350 Trujillo to Cajamarca
- 1357 Chachapoyas region
- 1364 Chachapoyas to the Amazon
- 1368 Chachapoyas to Ecuador and the coast

1370 South coast
- 1370 South from Lima
- 1376 Nazca and around

1382 Arequipa and the far south
- 1382 Arequipa
- 1394 Colca Canyon
- 1399 Cotahuasi Canyon
- 1400 South to Chile

1405 Lake Titicaca
- 1413 The islands
- 1415 To Cuzco
- 1417 Border with Bolivia

1419 Cuzco
- 1445 Southeast from Cuzco

1446 Sacred Valley of the Incas
- 1454 Machu Picchu
- 1459 Inca trails
- 1462 Vitcos and Vilcabamba
- 1463 West from Cuzco

1464 Central Highlands
- 1464 Lima to Huancayo
- 1466 Huancayo and around
- 1472 Huancavelica
- 1474 Ayacucho
- 1479 Ayacucho to Cuzco
- 1481 East and north of La Oroya

1486 Amazon Basin
- 1486 North from Huánuco to Pucallpa
- 1490 Yurimaguas and Pacaya-Samiria
- 1492 Iquitos and around
- 1499 Southeastern jungle

Footprint features

1254 Don't miss …
1259 Driving in Peru
1420 Inca society

At a glance

Time required 2-6 weeks.

Best time Dec-Apr on the coast; Oct-Apr in the sierra; Apr-Oct driest in the jungles. Jun for fiestas, especially in Cuzco; carnival is celebrated everywhere.

When not to go 28-29 Jul is a major holiday; transport and hotels are booked up. Roads in sierras and jungle can be impassable Nov-Apr. Coast is dull and damp May-Nov.

★ **Don't miss ...**

1 **Cordillera Blanca and Huaraz**, page 1307.
2 **Kuélap**, page 1358.
3 **Nazca Lines**, page 1376.
4 **Colca Canyon**, page 1394.
5 **Machu Picchu**, page 1454.
6 **Manu Biosphere Reserve**, page 1500.

Cuzco, capital of the Inca world, is now South America's main gringo hangout, with its access to Machu Picchu, the Sacred Urubamba Valley and a buzzing nightlife. On the border with Bolivia is Lake Titicaca, blessed with a magical light and fascinating islands. But in Peru, the Egypt of the Americas, this is just the tip of the pyramid.

The coastal desert may sound uninhabitable, yet pre-Inca cultures thrived there. They left their monuments in sculptures etched into the surface of the desert, most famously at Nazca. Civilization builders welcomed gods from the sea and irrigated the soil to feed great cities of adobe bricks. After the Incas came the Spanish conquistadores, who left some of their own finest monuments. You can trek for ever amid high peaks and blue lakes, cycle down remote mountainsides, look into canyons deeper than any others on earth, or surf the Pacific rollers. There are enough festivals to brighten almost every day of the year, while the spiritual explorer can be led down mystical paths by a shaman.

East of the Andes the jungles stretch towards the heart of the continent with some of the richest biodiversity on earth. And, should you tire of nature, there is always Lima: loud, brash, covered in fog for half the year, but with some of the best museums, most innovative restaurants and liveliest nightlife in the country.

Planning your trip

Where to go

Lima, the sprawling capital, is daunting at first sight, but worth investigating for its museums, colonial architecture and nightlife. Routes radiate in every direction and great steps have been taken to improve major roads linking the Pacific with the highlands. Travelling overland does, however, take time, so if on a short visit, try to stick to one area.

North of Lima it is only seven hours to Huaraz, in the Cordillera Blanca, the country's climbing and trekking centre. Mountaineering and hiking can be easily linked with the archaeological site at Chavín, east of Huaraz, or with the pre-Inca cities Sechín, Chan Chán and the Huaca de la Luna, the last two close to the colonial city of Trujillo. Heading up the coast, there is plenty of evidence of pre-Columbian culture, particularly around Chiclayo, beaches for surfing (eg Chicama) or watching traditional fishing techniques, and wildlife parks in the far north near Tumbes. (Tumbes, and the nearby Piura-Sullana route are the gateways to Ecuador.) In the northern highlands, Cajamarca is a pleasant base for exploring more archaeological sites, thermal baths and beautiful countryside. From here, or by a route from Chiclayo, there is access to the remote Chachapoyas region where a bewildering number of prehispanic cities and cultures are beginning to be opened up to visitors. Going east from here is one of the less-travelled, but nonetheless beautiful roads into the jungle lowlands.

South of Lima are Peru's most deservedly famous tourist destinations. The chief focus is Cuzco, where Spanish colonial and Inca architecture are united, and the Sacred Valley of the Incas, with the mountain-top city of Machu Picchu as the highlight of a historical and cultural treasure trove. Regular trips from Cuzco extend to Puno on the shores of Lake Titicaca (on the overland route to Bolivia), in which islands are frequently visited to see a unique way of life. Arequipa, a fine city at the foot of El Misti volcano, gives access to the canyons of Colca and, for those with more time, the even deeper Cotahuasi. A much-travelled railway links Cuzco, Puno and Arequipa, but the Cuzco-Puno road has now been paved, offering new opportunities for exploring these high-altitude regions. On the southern coastal route is the Paracas Peninsula (near Pisco), reputed to be home to the largest sea-lion colony on earth, and offshore Ballestas islands, one of the best places to see marine birdlife in the world. The mysterious Nazca Lines, whose meanings still stir debate, etched in the stony desert, should not be missed if you are on the Lima-Arequipa road, or taking the Pan-American Highway south to Tacna and Chile.

The **Central Highlands** can be reached by roads from Lima, Pisco and Nazca, the main centres being Huancayo, Huancavelica and Ayacucho. There is much of historical interest here and the Mantaro Valley and Ayacucho are good areas for buying handicrafts. From Ayacucho you can continue to Cuzco by bus, a rough journey until you reach Abancay, but well worth the discomfort. Roads in this part of the Sierra are being improved considerably, but check conditions if going far off the beaten track.

Another route into the **Peruvian jungle** runs from the Central Highlands to Pucallpa, but the most popular journeys are by air to the Amazon city of Iquitos, from where boats can be taken to Brazil, or from Cuzco to the spectacular Manu Biosphere Reserve and the Tambopata area (accessed from Puerto Maldonado). This has some of the highest levels of biodiversity in the world, providing wonderful opportunities for animal and plant lovers.

When to go

Each of Peru's geographical zones has its own climate. The **coast**: December-April, summertime, temperatures from 25°C to 35°C; hot and dry. These are the best months for swimming. Wintertime, May-November; the temperature drops a bit and it is cloudy. On the coast, climate is determined by cold sea-water adjoining deserts: prevailing inshore winds pick up so little moisture over the cold Peruvian current that only from May to November does it condense. The resultant blanket of cloud and sea-mist extends from the south to about 200 km north of Lima. This *garúa* dampens isolated coastal zones of vegetation (called *lomas*) and they are grazed by livestock driven down from the mountains. During the *garúa* season, only the northern beaches near Tumbes are warm enough for pleasant swimming.

The **sierra**: April-October is the dry season, hot and dry during the day, around 20-25°C, cold and dry at night, often below freezing. November-April is the wet season, dry and clear most mornings, some rainfall in the afternoon, with average temperatures of 18°C (15°C at night).

Peru's high season is June-September, which is the best time for hiking the Inca trails or trekking and climbing elsewhere in the country. At this time the days are generally clear and sunny, though nights can be very cold at high altitude. The highlands can be visited at other times of the year, though during the wettest months November-April some roads become impassable and hiking trails can be very muddy.

The **jungle**: April-October, dry season, temperatures up to 35°C. This is the best time to visit the jungle. In the south, a cold front can pass through at night. November-April, wet season, heavy rainfall at any time, humid and hot. During the wet season, it only rains for a few hours at a time, which is not enough to spoil your trip, but enough to make some roads virtually impassable.

Getting around

Air Carriers serving the major cities are **Star Perú**, www.starperu.com and **LAN** *www.lan.com*. For destinations such as Andahuaylas, Ayacucho, Cajamarca, Huancayo, Huánuco and Huaraz flights are offered by **LC Busre** *www.lcbusre.com.pe*. **Grupo Taca** *www.grupotaca.com*, offers a service on the Lima-Cuzco route. **Peruvian Airlines**, *www.peruvianairlines.pe*, started flying from Lima in 2009 to Arequipa, Cuzco, Iquitos and Tacna. See page 1294 for airline phone numbers. Flights start at about US$100 one-way anywhere in the country from Lima. Prices often increase during holiday times (Semana Santa, May Day, Inti Raymi, 28-29 July, Christmas and New Year), and for elections. During these times you should book early, especially on the Lima-Cuzco-Lima route. Flight schedules and departure times often change and delays are common. In the rainy season cancellations occur. Flights into the mountains may well be put forward one hour if there are reports of bad weather. Flights to jungle regions are also unreliable. Always allow an extra day between national and international flights, especially in the rainy season. Internal flight prices are fixed in US dollars (but can be paid in soles) and have 19% tax added. Time-keeping tends to be better early morning than later. **Note** If possible travel with hand luggage only to avoid the risk of losing baggage. Flights must be reconfirmed in the town you will be leaving from at least 24 hours in advance; be at the airport well ahead of your flight. About 30 minutes before departure, the clerk is allowed by law to let standby passengers take the seats of those who haven't turned up.

Bus Services along the coast to the north and south as well as inland to Huancayo, Ayacucho and Huaraz are generally good, but since 2008 the number of accidents and hold-ups on buses has increased. On long-distance journeys it is advisable to pay a bit extra and take a reliable company. All major bus companies operate modern buses with two decks on interdepartmental routes. The first deck is called *bus cama*, the second *semi cama*. Both have seats that recline, *bus cama* further than *semi cama*. These buses usually run late at night and are more expensive than ordinary buses which tend to run earlier in the day. Many buses have toilets and show movies. Each company has a different name for its regular and *cama* or *ejecutivo* services. **Cruz del Sur** and **Ormeño** are bus lines covering most of the country. **Cruz del Sur**, generally regarded as a class above the others, accepts Visa cards and gives 10% discount to ISIC and Under26 cardholders (you may have to insist). There are many smaller but still excellent bus lines that run only to specific areas. For bus lines, see page 1292. Take a blanket or warm jacket when travelling in the mountains. Where buses stop it is possible to buy food on the roadside. With the better companies you will get a receipt for your luggage, which will be locked under the bus. On local buses watch your luggage and never valuables on the luggage rack or floor, even when on the move. If your bus breaks down and you are transferred to another line and have to pay extra, keep your original ticket for refund from the first company. If possible, on country buses avoid the back seats because of the bumpiness, and the left side because of exhaust fumes.

Combis operate between most small towns on one- to three-hour journeys. This makes it possible, in many cases, just to turn up and travel within an hour or two. On rougher roads, combis are minibuses, while on better roads there are also slightly more expensive and much faster car colectivos, often called *autos*, or *cars*. These usually charge twice the bus fare. They leave only when full. They go almost anywhere in Peru; most firms have offices. Book one day in advance and they pick you up at your hotel or in the main plaza. Trucks are not always much cheaper than buses. Always try to arrive at your destination in daylight: much safer.

Note Prices of bus tickets are raised by 60-100%, 2-3 days before Semana Santa, 28 July (Independence Day – Fiestas Patrias), Christmas and special local events. Tickets are sold out 2-3 days in advance at this time and transport is hard to come by.

Hitchhiking Hitchhiking is difficult. Freight traffic has to stop at the police *garitas* outside each town and these are the best places to try (also toll points, but these are further from towns). Drivers usually ask for money but don't always expect to get it. In mountain and jungle areas you usually have to pay drivers of lorries, vans and even private cars; ask the driver first how much he is going to charge, and then recheck with the locals. Private cars are very few and far between. Readers report that mining trucks are especially dirty to travel in, avoid if possible.

Taxi Taxi prices are fixed in the mountain towns, about US$0.75-1.20 in the urban area. Fares are not fixed in Lima although some drivers work for companies that do have standard fares. Ask locals what the price should be and always set the price beforehand; expect to pay US$2-4 in the capital. The main cities have taxis which can be hired by phone, which charge a little more, but are reliable and safe. Many taxi drivers work for commission from hotels. Choose your own hotel and get a driver who is willing to take you. Taxis at airports are more expensive; seek advice about the price in advance. In some places it is cheaper to walk out of the airport to the main road and flag down a cab. Keep all hand luggage out of sight in taxis; smash-and-grab thieves are very quick. Another common form of public transport is the mototaxi, a three-wheel motorcycle with an awning covering the double-seat behind the driver. Fares are about US$1.

Train The main railways are Puno–Juliaca–Cuzco, Cuzco–Machu Picchu and Lima–Huancayo, with a continuation to Huancavelica in the Central Highlands. Details of services are given in the text below.

Maps The **Instituto Geográfico Nacional** in Lima sells a selection of maps, see page 1288. Other official sites are: **Ministerio de Transporte**, Jr Zorritos 1203, Lima centre, T01-615 7800, www.mtc.gob.pe, and **Instituto Geológico Minero Y Metalúrgico** (Ingemmet), Av Canadá 1470, San Borja, T01-225 3128, www.ingemmet.gob.pe. Lima 2000's *Mapa Vial del Perú* (1:2,200,000) is probably the most correct road map available. Maps can be obtained from the **South American Explorers**, who will give good advice on road conditions. The **Touring y Automóvil Club del Perú** ⓘ *Av Trinidad Morán 689, Lince, Lima, T614 9999, www.touring peru.com.pe*, with offices in most provincial cities, gives news about the roads and hotels (for the most up-to-date information also try bus and colectivo offices). It sells a very good road map at US$5 (Mapa Vial del Perú, 1:3,000,000, Ed 1980) and route maps covering most of Peru (available as pdf on website). The *Guía Toyota* (Spanish), which is published annually, is one of the best guides for venturing off the beaten track. Other maps can be bought from street vendors in Colmena and Plaza San Martín, Lima. 'Westermanns Monatshefte; folio Ecuador, Peru, Bolivien' has excellent maps of Peru, especially the archaeological sites.

A good tourist map of the Callejón de Huaylas and Cordillera Huayhuash, by Felipe Díaz, is available in many shops in Huaraz, including Casa de Guías. **Alpenvereinskarte Cordillera Blanca Nord 0/3a** and **Alpenvereinskarte Cordillera Blanca Süd 0/3b** at 1:100,000 are the best maps of

Driving in Peru

Road About 10% of Peru's roads are paved, including the Pan-American Highway which runs north-south through the coastal desert. Tolls, US$1.35-2.60, are charged on most major paved roads. Total tolls from Ecuador to Chile on main roads, about US$30. Mountain roads dirt, some good, some very bad. Each year they are affected by heavy rain and mud slides, especially on the east slopes of the mountains. Repairs can be delayed due to lack of funds. Some of these roads can be dangerous or impassable in the rainy season. Check with locals (not with bus companies, who only want to sell tickets) as accidents are common at these times.

Documents You must have an international driving licence and be over 21 to drive in Peru. If bringing in your own vehicle you must provide proof of ownership; a libreta de pasos por aduana or carnet de passages is accepted and recommended, although not officially required. You cannot officially enter Peru with a vehicle registered in someone else's name, but it is possible with a notarized letter of authorization and insurance documents stating that Peru is incorporated. On leaving Peru there is no check on the import of a vehicle.

Organizations The Touring y Automóvil Club del Perú, Av Trinidad Morán 689, Lince, Lima, T614 9999, www.touringperu.com.pe, offers help to tourists and particularly to members of the leading motoring associations. Good maps available of the whole country; regional routes and the South American sections of the Pan-American Highway available (US$5).

Car hire The minimum age for renting a car is 25. If renting a car, your home driving licence will be accepted for up to six months. Car hire companies are given in the text. Prices reflect high costs and accident rates. Hotels and tourist agencies will tell you where to find cheaper rates, but you will need to check that you have such basics as spare wheel, toolkit and functioning lights etc.

Fuel 84 octane petrol/gasoline costs US$3.15/gallon; 90 octane, US$3.60; 95 octane, US$4.55; 97 octane, US$4.80. Diesel costs US$3.35. Unleaded fuel (90, 95 and 97 octane) is available in large cities and along the Panamericana, but rarely in the highlands.

that region, US$24, available in Huaraz and Lima, but best bought outside Peru. **Cordillera Huayhuash map**, 1:50,000 (The Alpine Mapping Guild, 2nd ed, 2004) is recommended, available in Huaraz at Café Andino, US$15.

Sleeping → *See page 38 for our hotel grade price guide.*

Hotels All deluxe and first class hotels charge 19% in state sales tax (IGV) and 10% service charges. Foreigners should not have to pay the sales tax on hotel rooms. Neither is given in the accommodation listings, unless specified. By law all places that offer accommodation now have a plaque outside bearing the letters H (Hotel), Hs (Hostal), HR (Hotel Residencial) or P (Pensión) according to type. A hotel has 51 rooms or more, a hostal 50 or fewer; the categories do not describe quality or facilities. Many hotels have safe parking for motor cycles. All hotels seem to be crowded during Christmas and Easter holidays, Carnival and at the end of July; Cuzco in June is also very busy. iPeru advises that all accommodations registered with them are now listed on their web site: www.peru.info.

Camping Camping is easy in Peru, especially along the coast. There can be problems with robbery when camping near a small village. Avoid such a location, or ask permission to camp in a backyard or *chacra* (farmland). Most Peruvians are used to campers, but in some remote places, people have never seen a tent. Be casual about it, do not unpack all your gear, leave it inside your tent (especially at night) and never leave a tent unattended. Camping gas in little blue bottles is available in the main cities. Those with stoves designed for lead-free gasoline should use *ron de* *quemar*, available from hardware shops (*ferreterías*). White gas is called *bencina*, also available from hardware stores.

Youth hostels Contact **Asociación Peruana de Albergues Turísticos Juveniles** ⓘ *Av Casimiro Ulloa 328, Miraflores, Lima, T446 5488, www.limahostell.com.pe or www.hostellingperu.com.pe.*

Eating and drinking → *See page 40 for our Eating price guide.*

Eating out A normal lunch or dinner costs US$5-8, but can go up to about US$80 in a first-class restaurant, with drinks and wine. Middle and high-class restaurants may add 10% service, but not include the 19% sales tax in the bill (which foreigners do have to pay); this is not shown on the price list or menu, check in advance. Lower class restaurants charge only tax, while cheap, local restaurants charge no taxes. Lunch is the main meal and most restaurants serve one or two set lunch menus, called *menú ejecutivo* or *menú económico* (US$1.50-2.50). The set menu has the advantage of being served almost immediately and it is usually cheap. The *menú ejecutivo* costs US$2 or more for a three-course meal with a soft drink and it offers greater choice and more interesting dishes. Chinese restaurants (*chifas*) serve good food at reasonable prices. For really economically minded people the *comedores populares* in most cities of Peru offer a standard three-course meal for US$1.

Peruvian cuisine The best **coastal** dishes are seafood based, the most popular being *ceviche*. This is a dish of raw white fish marinated in lemon juice, onion and hot peppers. Traditionally, *ceviche* is served with corn-on-the-cob, *cancha* (toasted corn), yucca and sweet potatoes. *Tiradito* is *ceviche* without onions made with plaice. Another mouth-watering fish dish is *escabeche* – fish with onions, hot green pepper, red peppers, prawns (*langostinos*), cumin, hard-boiled eggs, olives, and sprinkled with cheese (it can also be made with chicken). For fish on its own, don't miss the excellent *corvina*, or white sea bass. You should also try *chupe de camarones*, which is a shrimp stew made with varying ingredients. Other fish dishes include *parihuela*, a popular bouillabaisse which includes *yuyo de mar*, a tangy seaweed, and *aguadito*, a thick rice and fish soup said to have rejuvenating powers. A favourite northern coastal dish is *seco de cabrito*, roasted kid (baby goat) served with the ubiquitous beans and rice, or *seco de cordero* which uses lamb instead. Also good is *aji de gallina*, a rich and spicy creamed chicken, and duck is excellent. *Humitas* are small, stuffed dumplings made with maize. The *criollo* cooking of the coast has a strong tradition and can be found throughout the country. Two popular examples are *cau cau*, made with tripe, potatoes, peppers, and parsley and served with rice, and *anticuchos*, which are shish kebabs of beef heart with garlic, peppers, cumin seeds and vinegar.

The staples of **highland** cooking, corn and potatoes, come in a variety of shapes, sizes and colours. *Causa* is a dish of yellow potatoes, lemons, pepper, hard-boiled eggs, olives, lettuce, sweet cooked corn, sweet cooked potato and fresh cheese, served with onion sauce (it can be made with tuna, avocado or prawns). Another potato dish is *papa a la huancaína*, which is topped with a spicy sauce made with milk and cheese. *Ocopa* is a similar dish in which slices of potato are served with a sauce made from milk, herbs and pecan nuts. *Papa rellena* is a deep-fried mashed potato ball stuffed with vegetables, egg and meat. The most commonly eaten corn dishes are *choclo con queso*, corn on the cob with cheese, and *tamales*, boiled corn dumplings filled with meat and wrapped in a banana leaf.

The main ingredient in jungle cuisine is fish, especially the succulent, dolphin-sized *paiche*, which comes with the delicious *palmito*, or palm-hearts, and yucca and fried bananas. *Juanes* are a jungle version of tamales, stuffed with chicken and rice.

A dish almost guaranteed to appear on every restaurant menu is *lomo saltado*, a kind of stir-fried beef with onions, vinegar, ginger, chilli, tomatoes and fried potatoes, served with rice. *Rocoto relleno* is spicy bell pepper stuffed with beef and vegetables, *palta rellena* is avocado filled with chicken salad, Russian salad or prawns. *Estofado de carne* is a stew which often contains wine and *carne en adobo* is a cut and seasoned steak. Others include *fritos*, fried pork, usually eaten in the morning, *chicharrones*, deep fried chunks of pork ribs and chicken or fish, and *lechón*, suckling pig. A delicacy in the highlands is *cuy*, guinea pig. Filling and good value are the many kinds of soup, such as *yacu-chupe*, a green soup made from potato, with cheese, garlic, coriander, parsley, peppers, eggs, onions, and mint, *and sopa a la criolla* containing thin noodles, beef heart, egg, vegetables and pleasantly spiced.

Peruvian fruits are of good quality: they include bananas, the citrus fruits, pineapples, dates, avocados (*paltas*), eggfruit (*lúcuma*), custard apple (*chirimoya*) which can be as big as your head, quince, papaya, mango, guava, the passion-fruit (*maracuyá*) and the soursop (*guanábana*).

Drink The most famous local drink is *pisco*, a clear brandy which, with egg whites and lime juice, makes the famous pisco sour. The most renowned brands come from the Ica valley. The best wines are from Ica, Tacama and Ocucaje. Tacama blancs de blancs and brut champagne have been recommended, also Gran Tinto Reserva Especial. Viña Santo Tomás, from Chincha, is reasonable and cheap. Casapalca is not recommended. Beer is best in lager types, especially the *Cusqueña* and *Arequipeña* brands (lager) and *Trujillo Malta* (porter). In Lima only *Cristal* and *Pilsener* (not related to true Pilsen) are readily available, others have to be sought out. Look out for the sweetish 'maltina' brown ale, which makes a change from the ubiquitous pilsner-type beers. *Chicha de jora* is a maize beer, usually homemade and not easy to come by, refreshing but strong, and *chicha morada* is a soft drink made with purple maize. The local rival to Coca Cola, the fluorescent yellow *Inca Cola*, is made from lemongrass. Peruvian coffee is good, but the best is exported and many cafés only serve coffee in liquid form or Nescafé. There are many different kinds of herb tea: the commonest are *manzanilla* (camomile) and *hierbaluisa* (lemon grass). *Mate de coca* is frequently served in the highlands to stave off the discomforts of altitude sickness.

Essentials A-Z

Accident and emergency

Tourist Police administrative office at Jr Moore 268, Magdalena at the 38th block of Av Brasil, Lima, T460 1060, daily 24 hrs; for public enquiries etc, Jr Pachitea at the corner of Belén, Lima, T424 2053 and Colón 246, Miraflores, T243 2190. You should come here if you have had property stolen. They are friendly, helpful and speak English and some German.

Electricity

220 volts AC, 60 cycles throughout the country, except Arequipa (50 cycles). Most 4- and 5-star hotels have 110 volts AC. Plugs are American flat-pin or twin flat and round pin combined.

Embassies and consulates

Visit www.rree.gob.pe, the Ministry of Foreign Affairs website, for details of Peruvian embassies and consulates.

Festivals and events

Two of the major festival dates are **Carnaval**, which is held over the weekend before Ash Wed, and **Semana Santa** (Holy Week), which ends on Easter Sun. Carnival is celebrated in most of the Andes and Semana Santa throughout Peru. Another important festival is **Fiesta de la Cruz**, held on the first of May in much of the central and southern highlands and on the coast. In Cuzco, the entire month of Jun is one huge *fiesta*, culminating in **Inti Raymi**, on 24 Jun, one of Peru's prime tourist attractions. Another national festival is **Todos los Santos** (All Saints) on 1 Nov, and on 8 Dec is **Festividad de la Inmaculada Concepción**. A full list of local festivals is listed under each town. Apart from those listed above, the main holidays are: 1 Jan, New Year; 6 Jan, **Bajada de Reyes**; 1 May, Labour Day; 28-29 July, Independence (Fiestas Patrias); 7 Oct, Battle of Angamos; 24-25 Dec, Christmas. **Note** Most businesses close for the official holidays but supermarkets and street markets may be open. Sometimes holidays that fall mid-week will be moved to the following Mon. The high season for foreign tourism in Peru is Jun-Sep while national tourism peaks at Christmas, Semana Santa and Fiestas Patrias. Prices rise and rooms and bus tickets are harder to come by.

Money → *US$1 = S/2.87; 1€ = S/3.64 (May 2010).*
Currency The new sol (s/) is divided into 100 céntimos. Notes in circulation are: S/200, S/100,

S/50, S/20 and S/10. Coins: S/5, S/2, S/1, S/0.50, S/0.20, S/0.10 and S/0.05 (being phased out). Some prices are quoted in dollars (US$) in more expensive establishments, to avoid changes in the value of the sol. You can pay in soles, however. Try to break down large notes whenever you can.

Warning Forged US$ notes and forged soles notes and coins are in circulation. Always check your money when you change it, even in a bank (including ATMs). Hold sol notes up to the light to inspect the watermark and that the colours change according to the light. The line down the side of the bill spelling out the bill's amount should appear green, blue and pink. Fake bills are only pink and have no hologram properties. There should also be tiny pieces of thread in the paper (not glued on). In parts of the country, forged 1-, 2- and 5-sol coins are in circulation. The fakes are slightly off-colour, the surface copper can be scratched off and they tend to bear a recent date. Posters in public places explain what to look for in forged soles. There is a shortage of change in museums, post offices, railway stations and even shops, while taxi drivers are notorious in this regard – one is simply told 'no change'. Do not accept this excuse.

Credit cards, traveller's cheques (TCs), banks and ATMs Visa (by far the most widely accepted card in Peru), MasterCard, American Express and Diners Club are all valid. There is often an 8-12% commission for all credit card charges. Bank exchange policies vary from town to town, but as a general rule the following applies (but don't be surprised if a branch has different rules): **BCP** ⓘ *Mon-Fri 0900-1830, Sat 0900-1300*, changes US$ cash and TCs (Amex only) to soles in some branches, changes TCs to US$ cash for US$11.50 commission per transaction; cash advances (until 1800) on Visa in soles only; ATM for Visa/Plus/Electron, MasterCard/Maestro/Cirrus and Amex. **Interbank** ⓘ *Mon-Fri 0900-1815, Sat 0900-1230*, changes US$ cash and TCs to soles (in main cities also changes euros cash), TCs to US$ cash for US$5 per transaction up to US$500; branches have **Global Net** ATMs (www.globalnet.com.pe), which appear to accept many different types of credit cards. **Scotiabank** ⓘ *Mon-Fri 0915-1800, Sat 0915-1230*, changes US$ cash and TCs (Amex only) to soles, cash advances on Visa and MasterCard; ATM for Visa, MasterCard and Cirrus. **BBVA Continental** changes US$ cash to soles, some branches change TCs; ATM for Visa/Plus and MasterCard. **Banco de la Nación** operates **Multi-Red** ATMs, often in small towns. They accept Visa only, but maybe only cards issued in Peru.There are also **Red Unicard** ATMs which accept Visa, Plus, MasterCard, Maestro and Cirrus. ATMs usually give US$ if you don't request soles and their use is widespread. The compatibility of ATMs across Peru is increasing all the time. Your card has to be pretty obscure not to be able to obtain cash from an ATM, but availability decreases outside large towns. In smaller towns, take some cash. Businesses displaying credit card symbols, on the other hand, are less likely to take foreign cards. For credit card loss: **American Express** ⓘ *Travex SA, Av Santa Cruz 621, Miraflores, Lima, T01-710 3900, info@travex.com.pe*; **Diners Club** ⓘ *Canaval y Moreyra 535, San Isidro, T01-221 2050*; **MasterCard** ⓘ *T0800-307 7309*; **Visa** ⓘ *T0800-890-0623*.

All banks' exchange rates are considerably less favourable than *casas de cambio* (exchange houses). Long queues and paperwork may be involved. US$ and euros are the only currencies which should be brought into Peru from abroad (take some small bills). There are no restrictions on foreign exchange. Few banks change euros. Some banks demand to see two documents with your signature for changing cash. Always count your money in the presence of the cashier. Street changers give the best rates for changing small amounts of US$ or euros cash, avoiding paperwork and queuing, but take care: check your soles before handing over your US$, check their calculators, etc, and don't change money in crowded areas. If using their services think about taking a taxi after changing, to avoid being followed. Street changers congregate near an office where the exchange 'wholesaler' operates; they will probably offer better rates than on the street. Soles can be exchanged into US$ at the exchange desks at Lima airport, and you can change soles for US$ at any border. US$ can also be bought at the various borders.

Note No one, not even banks, will accept US$ bills that look 'old', damaged or torn.

Cost of travelling The average budget is US$30-40 pp a day for living comfortably, including transport, or US$15-20 a day for low budget travel. Your budget will be higher the longer you stay in Lima and Cuzco and depending on how many flights you take between destinations. Rooms range from US$5 pp for the most basic *alojamiento* to US$15-30 for mid-range places, to over US$90 for top-of-the range hotels (more in Lima). Living costs in the provinces are 20-50% below those in Lima and Cuzco. The cost of using the internet is generally US$0.60-1 per hr, but where competition is not fierce, rates vary from US$1.50 to US$4.

Students can obtain very few reductions in Peru with an international students' card, except in and around Cuzco. To be any use in Peru, it must bear the owner's photograph. An ISIC card can be obtained in Lima from **Intej** ⓘ *Av San Martín 240, Barranco, T247 3230; Portal de Panes 123, of 107 (CC Los Ruiseñores), Cuzco, T084-256367; Santo Domingo 123, of 401, Arequipa, T054-284756; José Sabogal 913, Cajamarca, T076-362522; Edificio de Administracion y Gobierno, p 7, Universidad Nacional del Centro del Perú, Km 5 – Carretera Central, Huancayo, T064-481081 ext 6056; www.intej.org.*

Opening hours

Shops: 0900 or 1000-1230 and 1500 or 1600-2000. In the main cities, supermarkets do not close for lunch and Lima has some that are open 24 hrs. Some are closed on Sat and most are closed on Sun. **Banks**: most banks around the country are open 0930-1200 and 1500-1800. Banks in Lima and Cuzco are open 0900/0945-1700/1830. Many banks in Lima and Cuzco have Sat morning hours from 0900-1200 or 1300. **Offices**: Continuous hours 0900-1700 and most close on Sat. **Government offices**: Mon-Fri 0830-1130, Jan-Mar. The rest of year Mon-Fri 0900-1230, 1500-1700, but this changes frequently.

Safety

The following notes on personal safety should not hide the fact that most Peruvians are hospitable and helpful. For general hints on avoiding crime, see Security, Essentials, page 47. All the suggestions given there are valid for Peru. Always use licensed taxis: anyone can stick a taxi label on the windscreen and pick up a fare, but "pseudo taxis" are not safe. The police presence in Lima and Cuzco, and to a lesser extent Arequipa and Puno, has been greatly stepped up. Nevertheless, there has been an alarming increase in aggressive assaults in Lima and centres along the Gringo Trail. Places like Arequipa, Puno and in particular Cuzco have, at times, been plagued by waves of strangle muggings. Also watch for scammers who ask you, "as a favour", to change dollars into (fake) soles and for strangers who shake your hand, leaving a chemical which will knock you out when you next put your hand to your nose. Outside the Jul-Aug peak holiday period, there is less tension, less risk of crime, and more friendliness.

Although certain illegal drugs are readily available, anyone carrying any is almost automatically assumed to be a drug trafficker. If arrested on any charge the wait for trial in prison can take a year and is particularly unpleasant. If you are asked by the narcotics police to go to the toilets to have your bags searched, insist on taking a witness. **Drug use or purchase is punishable by up to 15 years' imprisonment. The number of foreigners in Peruvian prisons on drug charges is still increasing.**

Many places in the Amazon and in Cuzco offer experiences with Ayahuasca or San Pedro, often in ceremonies with a shaman. These are legal, but always choose a reputable tour operator or shaman. Do not go with the first person who offers you a trip. Single women should not take part. There are plenty of websites for starting your research.

Tricks employed to get foreigners into trouble over drugs include slipping a packet of cocaine into the money you are exchanging, being invited to a party or somewhere involving a taxi ride, or simply being asked on the street if you want to buy cocaine. In all cases, a plain clothes 'policeman' will discover the planted cocaine, in your money, at your feet in the taxi, and will ask to see your passport and money. He will then return them, minus a large part of your cash. Do not get into a taxi, do not show your money, and try not to be intimidated. Being in pairs is no guarantee of security, and single women may be particularly vulnerable. Beware also thieves dressed as policemen asking for your passport and wanting to search for drugs; **searching is only permitted if prior paperwork is done**.

In Cuzco many clubs and bars offer coupons for free entry and a free drink. The drinks are made with the cheapest, least healthy alcohol; always watch your drink being made and never leave it unattended. Sadly, the free entry-and-drink system doesn't appear to apply to Peruvians who are invariably asked to pay for entry to a disco, even if their tourist companions get in for nothing. We have also received reports of nightclubs and bars in Lima and Cuzco denying entrance to people solely on the basis of skin colour and assumed economic status. This discrimination should be discouraged.

Insurgency Until 2008 the activities of Sendero Luminoso and MRTA had seemed to be a thing of the past, but neither organization was completely non-functional. Reports indicate that Sendero Luminoso was mobilising again in the areas where its remants had gone to ground, the drug-growing zones of the Huallaga Valley and the jungle east of Ayacucho. In 2010 it was still safe to travel to all parts of Peru except those just mentioned, but it is important to inform yourself of the latest situation before going.

For up-to-date information contact the **Tourist Police** (see Accident & emergency), your embassy or consulate, fellow travellers, or **South American Explorers**, who issue the pamphlet *How Not to Get Robbed in Peru* (Lima T445 3306, Cuzco T245484, or in Quito). You can also contact the **Tourist Protection Bureau** (Indecopi). As well as handling complaints, they will help if you have lost, or had stolen, documents.

Tax

Airport taxes US$31 on international flight departures, payable in US$ or soles; US$6.82 on internal flights (when making a domestic connection in Lima, you don't have to pay airport tax; contact airline personnel at baggage claim to be escorted you to your departure gate). 19% state tax is charged on air tickets; it is included in the price of the ticket.

VAT/IVA 19%.

Telephone → *Country code+51.*

The numbering system for digital phones is as follows: for Lima mobiles, add 9 before the number, for the departments of La Libertad 94, Arequipa 95, Piura 96, Lambayeque 97; for other departments, add 9 – if not already in the number – and the city code (for example, Cuzco numbers start 984). Note also that some towns are dominated by Claró, others by Movistar (the two main mobile companies). As it is expensive to call between the two you should check, if spending some time in one city and using a mobile, which is the best account to have.

Red Privada Movistar (RPM) and **Red Privada Claró** (RPC) are operated by the respective mobile phone companies. Mobile phone users who subscribe to these services obtain a 6-digit number in addition their 9-digit mobile phone number. Both the 6- and 9-digit numbers ring on the same physical phone. The RPM and RPC numbers can be called from anywhere in Peru without using an area code, you just dial the 6 digits, and the cost is about 20% of calling the 9-digit number. This 80% discount usually also applies when calling from *locutorios*. Many establishments including hotels, tour operators and transport companies have both RPM and RPC numbers.

Time

GMT -5.

Tipping

Restaurants: service is included in the bill, but tips can be given directly to the waiter for exceptional service. Taxi drivers: none (bargain the price down, then pay extra for good service). Cloakroom attendants and hairdressers (very high class only): US$0.50-1. Porters: US$0.50. Car wash boys: US$0.30. Car 'watch' boys: US$0.20. If going on a trek or tour, it is customary to tip the guide as well as the cook and porters.

Tourist information

Tourism promotion and information is handled by **PromPerú** ⓘ *Edif Mincetur, C Uno Oeste 50, p 13, urb Córpac, San Isidro, T01-224 3131, www.peru.info.* PromPerú runs an information and assistance service, **i perú** ⓘ *T01-574 8000 (24 hrs). Main office: Jorge Basadre 610, San Isidro, Lima, T421 1627, iperulima@promperu.gob.pe, Mon-Fri 0830-1830. Also a 24-hr office at Jorge Chávez airport; and throughout the country.*

There are tourist offices in most towns, either run by the municipality, or independently. Outside Peru, information can be obtained from Peruvian embassies/consulates. **Indecopi** ⓘ *in Lima T224 7800, www.indecopi.gob.pe,* is the government-run consumer protection and tourist complaint bureau. They are friendly, professional and helpful. An excellent source of information is **South American Explorers**, in Lima (see page 1266) and Cuzco. See also Essentials, page 52. They have information on travellers held in prison, some for up to 1 year without sentencing, and details on visiting regulations. A visit will be really appreciated!

Useful websites

www.minam.gob.pe Ministerio del Ambiente (Spanish).
www.adonde.com portal.
www.terra.com.pe Click 'Turismo' to get to travel page (in Spanish).
www.livinginperu.com Informative guide in English for people living in Peru.
www.aboutcusco.com, **www.cuscoonline.com** and **www.cusco.net** are websites about Cuzco.
www.machu-picchu.info On Machu Picchu.
www.yachay.com.pe/especiales/nasca Nazca lines (in Spanish).
www.andeanexplorer.com For Huaraz and the Callejón de Huaylas, in English.
www.leaplocal.org Recommends good quality guides, helping communities benefit from socially responsible tourism.
www.xanga.com/TrujilloPeru Mainly for the north of the country, packed full of links.
www.caretas.com.pe The most widely read weekly magazine, *Caretas*.

Visas and immigration

Tourist cards No visa is necessary for citizens of countries in the EU, most Asian countries, North and South America, and the Caribbean, or for citizens of Andorra, Iceland, Israel, Liechtenstein, Norway, Switzerland, Australia, New Zealand and South Africa. A Tourist Card (TAM – Tarjeta Andina de Migración) is free on flights arriving in Peru, or at border crossings for visits up to 183 days. The form is in duplicate, the original given up on arrival and the copy on departure. A new tourist card must be obtained for each re-entry. If your tourist card is stolen or lost, get a new one at **Migraciones** ⓘ *Digemin, Av España 730, Breña, Lima, T417 6900/433 0731, www.digemin.gob.pe, Mon-Fri 0800-1300.*

Tourist visas For citizens of countries not listed above (including Turkey), visas cost US$31 or equivalent, for which you require a valid passport, a departure ticket from Peru (or a letter of guarantee from a travel agency), 2 colour passport photos, 1 application form and proof of economic solvency. Tourist visas are valid for 183 days.

Keep ID, preferably a passport, on you at all times. You must present your passport when reserving travel tickets. To avoid having to show your passport, photocopy the important pages of your passport – including the immigration stamp, and have it legalized by a 'Notario público' (US$1.50). We have received no reports of travellers being asked for onward tickets at the borders at Tacna, Aguas Verdes, La Tina, Yunguyo or Desaguadero. Travellers are not asked to show an onward flight ticket at Lima airport, but you will not be able to board a plane in your home country without one.

Under Decree 1043 of Jun 2008, once in Peru tourists may not extend their tourist card or visa. It's therefore important to insist on getting the full number of days to cover your visit on arrival (it's at the discretion of the border official). If you exceed your 90 days, you'll pay a US$1-per-day fine.

Business visas If receiving money from Peruvian sources, visitors must have a business visa: requirements are a valid passport, 2 colour passport photos, return ticket and a letter from an employer or Chamber of Commerce stating the nature of business, length of stay and guarantee that any Peruvian taxes will be paid. The visa costs US$31 (or equivalent). On arrival business visitors must register with the *Dirección General de Contribuciones* for tax purposes.

Student visas These must be requested from Migraciones (address above) once you are in Peru. In addition to completing the general visa form you must have proof of adequate funds, affiliation to a Peruvian body, a letter of consent from parents or tutors if you are a minor. The cost is US$20. Full details are on the Digemin website (in Spanish).

If you wish to change a tourist visa into another type of visa (business, student, resident, etc), you may do so without leaving Peru. Visit Inmigraciones and obtain the relevant forms.

Weights and measures

Metric.

Lima

→ Phone code: 01. Colour map 3, C2. Population: 8.2 million (metropolitan area).

Lima's colonial centre and suburbs, shrouded in fog which lasts eight months of the year, are fringed by the pueblos jóvenes which sprawl over the dusty hills overlooking the city. It has a great many historic buildings, some of the finest museums in the country and its food, drink and nightlife are second to none. Although not the most relaxing of South America's capitals, it is a good place to start before exploring the rest of the country.

Ins and outs

Getting there All international flights land at Jorge Chávez **airport**, 16 km northwest of the Plaza de Armas. Transport into town by taxi or bus is easy. If arriving in the city by **bus**, most of the recommended companies have their terminals just south of the centre, many on Av Carlos Zavala. This is not a safe area and you should take a taxi to and from there. ▸▸ *For more detailed information including getting away from the airport, see Transport, page 1291.*

Getting around Downtown Lima can be explored on foot by day; at night a taxi is safest. Miraflores is 15 km south of the centre. Many of the better hotels and restaurants are here and in neighbouring San Isidro. Transport between the centre and the suburbs is not a problem. Three types of bus provide an extensive public transport system; all vehicles stop when flagged down. The route of the bus is posted on a coloured sticker on the windscreen; ignore destinations written on the side. **Taxis** do not use meters. Agree the price of the journey beforehand and insist on being taken to the destination of your choice. On both buses and taxis be ready to pay the exact fare. At night, on Sunday and holidays expect a surcharge of 35-50% is made in taxis.

Addresses Several blocks, with their own names, make up a long street, a jirón (often abbreviated to Jr). Street corner signs bear both names, of the jirón and of the block.

Climate Only 12° south of the equator, one would expect a tropical climate, but Lima has two distinct seasons. The winter is May-November, when a *garúa* (Scotch mist) hangs over the city, making everything look grey. It is damp and cold, 8-15°C. The sun breaks through around November and temperatures rise to as high as 30°C. Note that the temperature in the coastal suburbs is lower than the centre because of the sea's influence. Protect against the sun's rays when visiting the beaches around Lima, or elsewhere in Peru.

Tourist information **i perú** has offices at Jorge Chávez international airport ⓘ *T574 8000, open 24 hrs*; Casa Basadre ⓘ *Av Jorge Basadre 610, San Isidro, T421 1627, Mon-Fri 0830-1830*; and Larcomar shopping centre ⓘ *Módulo 10, Plaza Principal, Miraflores, T445 9400, Mon-Fri 1100-1300, 1400-2000*. Ask for the free, *Peru Guide* published in English by Lima Editora, T444 0815, available at travel agencies. **South American Explorers** ⓘ *Piura 135 (Casilla 3714), Miraflores, T445 3306 (dial 011-51-1 from USA) www.saexplorers.org*. See also Essentials, page 52.

Background

Lima, capital of Peru, is built on both sides of the Río Rímac, at the foot of Cerro San Cristóbal. It was originally named *La Ciudad de Los Reyes*, in honour of the Magi, at its founding by conquistador Francisco Pizarro in 1535. From then until the independence of the South American republics in the early 19th century, it was the chief city of Spanish South America. The name Lima, a corruption of the Quechua name *Rimac* (speaker), was not adopted until the end of the 16th century.

The Universidad de San Marcos was founded in 1551, and a printing press in 1595, both among the earliest of their kind in South America. Lima's first theatre opened in 1563, and the Inquisition was introduced in 1569 (it was not abolished until 1820). For some time the Viceroyalty of Peru embraced Colombia, Ecuador, Bolivia, Chile and Argentina. There were few cities in the Old World that could rival Lima's power, wealth and luxury, which was at its height during the 17th and early 18th centuries. The city's wealth attracted many freebooters and in 1670 a protecting wall 11 km long was built round it, then destroyed in 1869. The earthquake of 1746 destroyed all but 20 houses, killed 4,000 inhabitants and ended its pre-eminence. It was only comparatively recently, with the coming of industry, that Lima began to change into what it is today.

Modern Lima is seriously affected by smog for much of the year, and is surrounded by 'Pueblos Jóvenes', or settlements of squatters who have migrated from the Sierra. Villa El Salvador, a few kilometres southeast of Lima, may be the world's biggest 'squatters' camp' with 350,000 people building up an award-winning self-governing community since 1971.

Over the years the city has changed out of recognition. Many of the hotels and larger business houses have relocated to the fashionable suburbs of Miraflores and San Isidro, thus moving the commercial heart of the city away from the Plaza de Armas.

Half of the town-dwellers of Peru now live in Lima. The metropolitan area contains eight million people, nearly one-third of the country's total population, and two-thirds of its industries. Callao, Peru's major port, runs into Lima; it is a city in its own right, with over one million inhabitants. Within its boundaries is the Jorge Chávez airport. The docks handle 75% of the nation's imports and some 25% of its exports. Callao has a serious theft problem, avoid being there in the evening.

Sights

The traditional heart of the city, at least in plan, is still what it was in colonial days. Although parts of it are run down, much of the old centre is undergoing restoration and many colonial buildings have been cleaned. It is worth visiting the colonial centre to see the architecture and works of art. Most of the tourist attractions are in this area. Churches open between 1830 and 2100 unless otherwise stated. Many are closed to visitors on Sunday. Some museums are only open 0900-1300 from January-March, and some are closed in January.

Plaza de Armas

One block south of the Río Rímac lies the Plaza de Armas (also called Plaza Mayor since 1998), which has been declared a World Heritage Site by UNESCO. Running along two sides are arcades with shops: Portal de Escribanos and Portal de Botoneros. In the centre of the plaza is a bronze fountain dating from 1650. The **Palacio de Gobierno**, on the north side of the Plaza, stands on the site of the original palace built by Pizarro. The changing of the guard is at 1200. To take a tour register two days in advance at the Oficina de Turismo, (ask guard for directions); the free, 45-minute tours are in Spanish and English Monday-Friday, 1400-1730. The **Cathedral** ⓘ *T427 9647, Mon-Sat 0900-1630, US$3.30,* was reduced to rubble in the earthquake of 1746. The reconstruction, on the lines of the original, was completed 1755. Note the splendidly carved stalls (mid-17th century), the silver-covered altars surrounded by fine woodwork, mosaic-covered walls bearing the coats of arms of Lima and Pizarro and an allegory of Pizarro's commanders, the 'Thirteen Men of Isla del Gallo'. The supposed remains of Franscisco Pizarro lie in a small chapel, the first on the right of the entrance, in a glass coffin, though later research indicates that they reside in the crypt. Museo de Arte Religioso in the cathedral, free guided tours (English available, give tip), ask to see the picture restoration room. Next to the cathedral is the **Archbishop's Palace**, rebuilt in 1924, with a superb wooden balcony.

Around the Plaza de Armas

Just off the plaza is the **Philatelic Museum** ⓘ *at the Central Post Office, Mon-Sun 0815-1300, 1400-1800, free.* Incomplete collection of Peruvian stamps and information on the Inca postal system. There is a stamp exchange in front of the museum every Saturday and Sunday,

0900-1300. Commemorative issues can be bought here. Nearby is the **Casa Aliaga** ⓘ *Unión 224. Lima Tours has exclusive rights to include the house in its tours (T424 5110).* It is still occupied by the Aliaga family but has been opened to the public. The house contains what is said to be the oldest ceiling in Lima and is furnished entirely in the colonial style.

The baroque church of **San Francisco** ⓘ *on the 1st block of Jr Lampa, corner of Ancash, a few blocks from the Plaza de Armas, T427 1381, daily 0930-1645, church and monastery US$1.65, US$0.50 children, only with guide, Spanish and English (recommended),* was finished in 1674 and withstood the 1746 earthquake. The nave and aisles are lavishly decorated in Mudéjar style. The monastery is famous for the Sevillian tilework and panelled ceiling in the cloisters (1620). The Catacombs under the church and part of the monastery are well worth seeing. The late 16th-century **Casa de Jarava** or **Pilatos** ⓘ *Jr Ancash 390,* is opposite San Francisco church. Close by, **Casa de las Trece Monedas** ⓘ *Jr Ancash 536,* still has the original doors and window grills. **Parque de la Muralla** ⓘ *open 0900-2000, US$0.50,* on the south bank of the Rímac, incorporates a section of the old city wall, fountains, stalls and street performers.

The **Palacio Torre Tagle** (1735) ⓘ *Jr Ucayali 363, Mon-Fri during working hours,* is the city's best surviving example of secular colonial architecture. Today, it is used by the Foreign Ministry, but visitors are allowed to enter courtyards to inspect the fine, Moorish-influenced

1 Lima

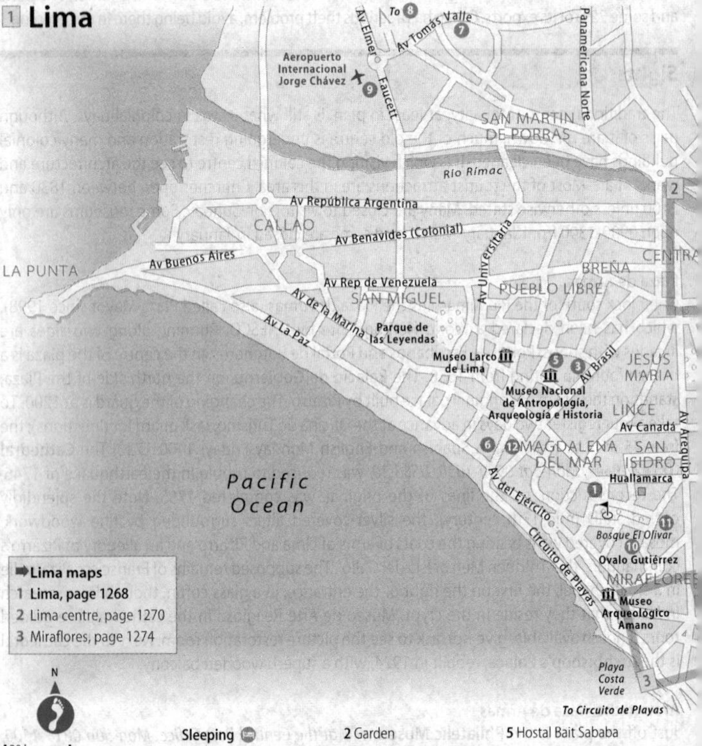

wood-carving in balconies and wrought iron work. **Casa de la Rada**, or **Goyoneche** ⓘ *Jr Ucayali 358*, opposite, is a fine mid-18th-century French-style town house which now belongs to a bank. The patio and first reception room are open occasionally to the public. **Museo Banco Central de Reserva** ⓘ *Jr Ucayali at Jr Lampa, T01-613 2000 ext 2655, http://museobcr.perucultural.org.pe/, Tue-Fri 1000-1630, Wed 1000-1900, Sat-Sun 1000-1300, free, photography prohibited*. This is a large collection of pottery from the Vicus or Piura culture (AD 500-600) and gold objects from Lambayeque, as well as 19th and 20th-century paintings: both sections highly recommended. **San Pedro** ⓘ *3rd block of Jirón Ucayali, Mon-Sat 0930-1145, 1700-1800*, finished by Jesuits in 1638, has marvellous altars with Moorish-style balconies, rich gilded wood carvings in choir and vestry, and tiled throughout. Several Viceroys are buried here; the bell called La Abuelita, first rung in 1590, sounded the Declaration of Independence in 1821.

Between Avenida Abancay and Jr Ayacucho is **Plaza Bolívar**, where General José de San Martín proclaimed Peru's independence. The plaza is dominated by the equestrian statue of the Liberator. Behind lies the Congress building which occupies the former site of the Universidad de San Marcos; visit recommended. Behind the Congress is Barrio Chino, with many *chifas* and small shops selling oriental items. **Museo del Tribunal de la Santa Inquisición** ⓘ *Plaza Bolívar, C Junín 548, near the corner of Av Abancay, T311 7777, www.congreso.gob.pe/museo.htm, Mon-Sun 0900-1700, free, students offer to show you round for a tip; good explanations in English.* The main hall, with a splendidly carved mahogany ceiling, remains untouched. The Court of Inquisition was held here from 1584; 1829-1938 it was used by the Senate. In the basement there is a recreation *in situ* of the gruesome tortures. A description in English is available at the desk.

8 Pay Purix
9 Ramada Costa del Sol
10 Sofitel Royal Park
11 Sonesta El Olivar
12 Tambopacaya

The 16th-century **Santo Domingo church and monastery** ⓘ *T427 6793, monastery and tombs open Mon-Sat 0900-1230, 1500-1800; Sun and holidays morning only, US$1.65*, is on the first block of Jr Camaná. The Cloister, one of the most attractive, dates from 1603. The second Cloister is less elaborate. Beneath the sacristy are the tombs of San Martín de Porres, one of Peru's most revered saints, and Santa Rosa de Lima (see below). In 1669, Pope Clement presented the alabaster statue of Santa Rosa in front of the altar. Behind Santo Domingo is **Alameda Chabuca Granda**, named after one of Peru's greatest singers. In the evening there are free art and music shows and you can sample foods from all over Peru. A few blocks away, **Casa de Oquendo** or **Osambela** ⓘ *Conde de Superunda 298, 0900-1300*, stages art exhibitions. A few blocks west is **Santuario de Santa Rosa** ⓘ *Av Tacna, 1st block, T425 1279, daily 0930-1300, 1500-1800, free to the grounds*, a small but graceful church. A pilgrimage centre; here are preserved the hermitage built by Santa Rosa herself, the house in which she was born, a

2 Lima centre

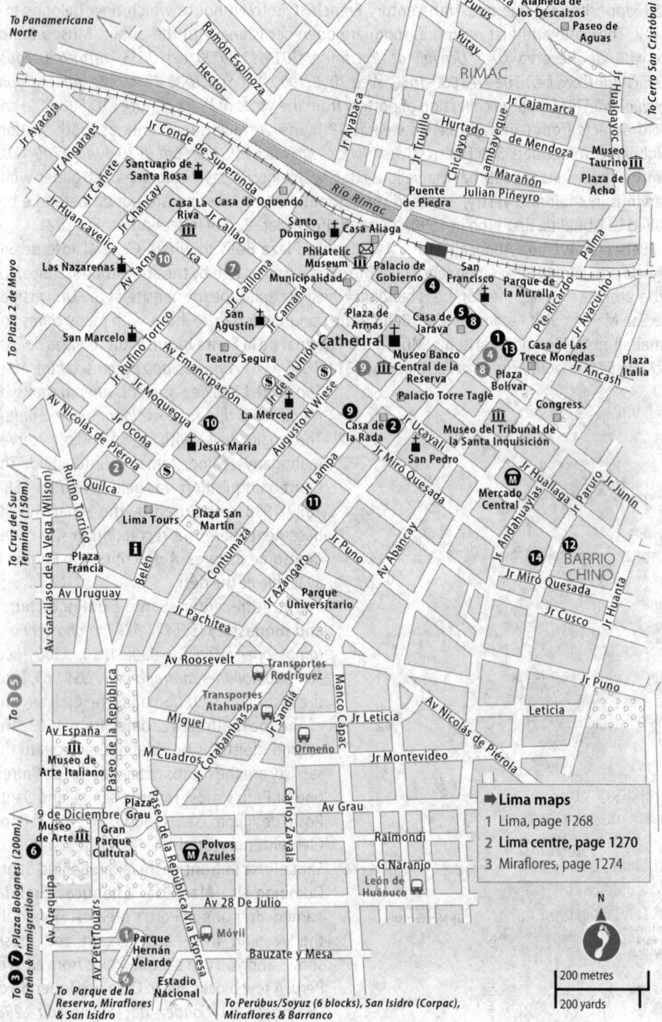

Sleeping
1 Clifford
2 Familia Rodríguez
3 Hostal de las Artes
4 Hostal España
5 Hostal Iquique
6 Hostal La Posada del Parque
7 Hostal Roma & Café Carrara
8 Hostal San Francisco
9 Maury
10 Pensión Ibarra

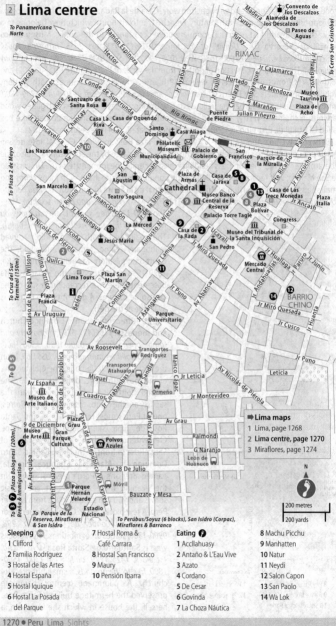

Eating
1 Acllahuasy
2 Antaño & L'Eau Vive
3 Azato
4 Cordano
5 De Cesar
6 Govinda
7 La Choza Náutica
8 Machu Picchu
9 Manhatten
10 Natur
11 Neydi
12 Salon Capon
13 San Paolo
14 Wa Lok

section of the house in which she attended to the sick, her well, and other relics. Nearby, **Casa La Riva** ① *Jr Ica 426,* has an 18th-century porch and balconies, a small gallery with 20th-century paintings.

San Agustín ① *Jr Ica 251, T427 7548, daily 0830-1130, 1630-1900, ring for entry,* is west of the Plaza de Armas: its façade (1720) is a splendid example of churrigueresque architecture. There are carved choir stalls and effigies, and a sculpture of Death, said to have frightened its maker into an early grave. The church has been restored after the last earthquake, but the sculpture of Death is in storage. **Las Nazarenas Church** ① *Av Tacna, 4th block, T423 5718, daily 0700-1200, 1600-2000,* is built around an image of Christ Crucified painted by a liberated slave in 1655. This, the most venerated image in Lima, and an oil copy of El Señor de los Milagros (Lord of Miracles), encased in a gold frame, are carried on a silver litter the whole weighing nearly a ton through the streets on 18, 19, and 28 October and again on 1 November (All Saints' Day). *El Comercio* newspaper and local pamphlets give details of times and routes.

Northeast of Plaza de Armas

From the Plaza, passing the Palacio de Gobierno on the left, straight ahead is the **Desamparados** ① *free,* railway station, which now houses fascinating exhibitions on Peruvian themes. **The Puente de Piedra**, behind the Palacio de Gobierno, is a Roman-style stone bridge built in 1610, crossing the Río Rímac to the district of that name. On Jr Hualgayoc is the bullring in the **Plaza de Acho**, inaugurated on 20 January 1766, with the **Museo Taurino** ① *Hualgayoc 332, T482 3360, Mon-Sat 0800-1600, US$1, students US$0.50, photography US$2.* Apart from matador's relics, the museum contains good collections of paintings and engravings, some of the latter by Goya. There are two bullfight seasons: October to first week in December and during July. They are held in the afternoons on Sunday and holidays. The **Convento de Los Descalzos** ① *on the Alameda de Los Descalzos in Rímac, T481 0441, daily 1000-1300, 1500-1800, except Tue, US$1, guided tour only, 45 mins in Spanish (worth it),* was founded in 1592. It contains over 300 paintings of the Cuzco, Quito and Lima schools which line the four main cloisters and two ornate chapels. The chapel of El Carmen was constructed in 1730 and is notable for its baroque gold leaf altar. The museum shows the life of the Franciscan friars during colonial and early republican periods. The cellar, infirmary, pharmacy and a typical cell have been restored.

Cerro San Cristóbal dominates downtown Lima and can be visited in a one-hour tour, run by *Ofistur*, departing from in front of Santo Domingo, Jr Camaná ① *Sat and Sun 1000-2100; departures every 15 mins, US$1.50.* It includes a look at the run-down Rímac district, passes the Convento de los Descalzos (see above), ascends the hill through one of the city's oldest shanties with its brightly painted houses and spends about 20 minutes at the summit, where there is a small museum and café. Excellent views on a clear day.

South of Plaza de Armas

The Jr de La Unión, the main shopping street, runs to the Plaza de Armas. It has been converted into a pedestrian precinct which teems with life in the evening. In the two blocks south of Jr Unión, known as C Belén, several shops sell souvenirs and curios. **La Merced** ① *Unión y Miró Quesada, T427 8199, 0800-1245, 1600-2000 (Sun 0700-1300, 1600-2000); monastery daily 0800-1200 and 1500-1730,* is in Plazuela de la Merced. The first mass in Lima was said here on the site of the first church to be built. The restored façade is a fine example of colonial Baroque. Inside are some magnificent altars and the tilework on some of the walls is noteworthy. A door from the right of the nave leads into the Monastery. The cloister dates from 1546. Jr de la Unión leads to **Plaza San Martín**, which has a statue of San Martín in the centre. The plaza has been restored and is now a nice place to sit and relax.

Museo de Arte ① *9 de Diciembre 125,T423 4732, http://museoarte.perucultural.org.pe/, Thu-Tue 1000-1700, US$3.65, free guide, signs in English,* is in the Palacio de la Exposición, built in 1868 in Parque de la Exposición (designed by Gustave Eiffel). There are more than 7,000 exhibits, giving a chronological history of Peruvian cultures and art from the Paracas civilization up to today. It includes excellent examples of 17th- and 18th-century Cuzco paintings, a beautiful display of carved furniture, heavy silver and jewelled stirrups and also pre-Columbian pottery. The Filmoteca (movie club) is on the premises and shows films just about every night. See the local paper for details, or look in the museum itself. The **Gran Parque Cultural de Lima** ⓘ *0800-2030,* is in the grounds. Inaugurated in January 2000, this large park has an amphitheatre, Japanese garden, food court and children's activities. Relaxing strolls through this green, peaceful and safe oasis in the centre of Lima are recommended.

Museo de Arte Italiano ⓘ *Paseo de la República 250, T423 9932, Tue-Fri 0900-1900, Sat-Sun 1100-1700, US$1,* is in a wonderful neo-classical building, given by the Italian colony to Peru on the centenary of its independence. Note the remarkable mosaic murals on the outside. It consists of a large collection of Italian and other European works of art and houses the Instituto de Arte Contemporáneo, which has many exhibitions.

In **Parque de la Reserva** is the **Circuito Mágico del Agua** ⓘ *block 8 of Av Arequipa and going up towards the centre, Santa Beatriz, www.circuitomagicodelagua.com.pe, Wed-Sun and holidays 1600-2200, US$1.40,* a display of 13 fountains, the highest reaching 80 m, enhanced by impressive light and music shows four times a night, great fun and very popular.

San Borja

Museo de la Nación ⓘ *Javier Prado Este 2465, T476 9876, Tue-Sun 0900-1700, closed major public holidays, US$2.50. 50% discount with ISIC card, see http://inc.perucultural.org.pe/agenda.asp for details of temporary exhibitions* in the huge *Banco de la Nación* building, is the museum for the exhibition and study of the art and history of the aboriginal races of Peru. ⓘ *From Av Garcilaso de la Vega in downtown Lima take a combi with a "Javier Prado/Aviación" window sticker. Get off at the 21st block of Javier Prado at Av Aviación. From Miraflores take a bus down Av Arequipa to Av Javier Prado (27th block), then take a bus with a "Todo Javier Prado" or "Aviación" window sticker. Taxi from downtown Lima or Miraflores US$2.* There are good explanations in Spanish and English on Peruvian history, with ceramics, textiles and displays of almost every ruin in Peru. Guided tours in English/Spanish. It is arranged so that you can follow the development of Peruvian precolonial history through to the time of the Incas. A visit is recommended before you go to see the archaeological sites themselves. There are displays of the tomb of the Señor de Sipán, artefacts from Batán Grande near Chiclayo (Sicán culture), reconstructions of the friezes found at Huaca La Luna and Huaca El Brujo, near Trujillo, and of Sechín and other sites. Temporary exhibitions are held in the basement, where there is also an Instituto Nacional de Cultura bookshop. The museum has a cafetería.

Pueblo Libre

The original museum of anthropology and archaeology is **Museo Nacional de Antropología, Arqueología e Historia** ⓘ *Plaza Bolívar in Pueblo Libre, not to be confused with Plaza Bolívar in the centre, T463 5070, http://museonacional.perucultural.org.pe/, Tue-Sat 0900-1700, Sun and holidays 0900-1600, US$3.65, students US$1, guides available for groups.* On display are ceramics of the Chimú, Nazca, Mochica and Pachacámac cultures, various Inca curiosities and works of art, and interesting textiles. **Museo Nacional de Historia** ⓘ *T463 2009, Tue-Sat 0900-1700, Sun and holidays 0900-1600, US$3.65,* in a mansion occupied by San Martín (1821-1822) and Bolívar (1823-1826) is next door. It exhibits colonial and early republican paintings, manuscripts and uniforms. Take any public transport on Avenida Brasil with a window sticker saying "Todo Brasil." Get off at the 21st block called Avenida Vivanco. Walk about five blocks down Vivanco. The museum will be on your left. From Miraflores take bus SM 18 Carabayllo-Chorrillos, marked "Bolívar, Arequipa, Larcomar", get out at block 8 of Bolívar by the Hospital Santa Rosa, and walk down Av San Martín five blocks until you see the 'blue line'; turn left. The 'blue line' marked on the pavement, very faded, links the Museo

Nacional de Antropología, Arqueología e Historia to the Museo Larco (see below), 10 minutes' walk. Taxi from downtown US$2.50-3; from Miraflores US$4.

Museo Larco de Lima ⓘ *Av Bolívar 1515, T461 1312, www.museolarco.org, 0900-1800; texts in Spanish, English and French, US$10 (half price for students), disabled access, photography not permitted.* Located in an 18th-century mansion, itself built on a seventh-century pre-Columbian pyramid, this museum has a collection which gives an excellent overview on the development of Peruvian cultures through their pottery. It has the world's largest collection of Moche, Sicán and Chimú pieces. There is a Gold and Silver of Ancient Peru exhibition, a magnificent textile collection and a fascinating erotica section. Don't miss the storeroom with its vast array of pottery, unlike anything you'll see elsewhere. It is surrounded by beautiful gardens.Take any bus to the 15th block of Avenida Brasil. Then take a bus down Avendia Bolívar. From Miraflores, take the SM 18 Carabayllo-Chorrillos, see above, to block 15 of Bolívar. Taxi from downtown, Miraflores or San Isidro, 15 minutes, US$3.50. Follow the 'blue line' marked on the pavement to the Museo Nacional de Antropología, Arqueología e Historia (see above), 10 minutes' walk.

San Isidro

To the east of Avenida La República, down Calle Pancho Fierro, is **El Olivar**, an olive grove planted by the first Spaniards which has been turned into a park. 32 species of birds have been recorded there. Between San Isidro and Miraflores, is **Huallamarca** ⓘ *C Nicolás de Rivera 201 and Av Rosario, 0900-1700, closed Mon, US$1.75. Take bus 1 from Av Tacna, or minibus 13 or 73 to Choquechaca, then walk.* An adobe pyramid of the Maranga culture, it dates from about AD 100-500. There is a small site museum. There are many good hotels and restaurants in San Isidro; see Sleeping, page 1278 and Eating, page 1283.

South of San Isidro is the rundown seaside resort of **Magdalena del Mar**, inland from which is Pueblo Libre (see above). **Parque las Leyendas** ⓘ *T464 4282, daily 0900-1730, US$2,* is arranged to represent the three regions of Peru: the coast, the Sierra, and the tropical jungles of the Selva, with appropriate houses, animals and plants, children's playground. It gets very crowded at weekends. Take bus 23 or colectivo on Avenida Abancay, or bus 135. A or colectivo from Avenida La Vega, is reached from the 24th block of Avenida de La Marina in San Miguel: take Avenida Parque Las Leyendas to the entrance on Avenida La Mar.

Miraflores

Avenida Arequipa continues to the coast, to the most important suburb of Lima (see Sleeping, page 1278, Youth hostel, page 1281 and eating, page 1283). Together with San Isidro and Barranco this is the social centre of Lima.

Parque Kennedy, the Parque Central de Miraflores is located between Avenida Larco and Avenida Mcal Oscar Benavides (locally known as Avenida Diagonal). This extremely well kept park has a small open-air theatre with performances Thursday-Sunday and an arts and crafts market most evenings of the week. The house of the author **Ricardo Palma** ⓘ *Gral Suárez 189, T445 5836, Mon-Fri 0915-1245, 1430-1700, small entrance fee,* is now a museum. At the end of Avenida Larco and running along the Malecón de la Reserva is the renovated **Parque Salazar** and the very modern shopping centre called **Centro Comercial Larcomar**. Here you will find expensive shops, hip cafés and discos and a wide range of restaurants, all with a beautiful ocean view. The 12-screen cinema is one of the best in Lima and even has a 'cine-bar' in the twelfth theatre. Don't forget to check out the Cosmic Bowling Alley with its black lights and fluorescent balls. A few hundred metres to the north is the famous **Parque del Amor** where on just about any night you'll see at least one wedding party taking photos of the newly weds.

Museo Arqueológico Amano ⓘ *Retiro 160, 11th block of Av Angamos Oeste, Miraflores), T441 2909, visits by appointment Mon-Fri in afternoons only, free (photography prohibited).* The collection is of artefacts from the Chancay, Chimú and Nazca periods, owned by the late

Mr Yoshitaro Amano. It has one of the most complete exhibits of Chancay weaving, and is particularly interesting for pottery and pre-Columbian textiles, all superbly displayed and lit. Take a bus or colectivo to the corner of Avenida Arequipa y Avenida Angamos and another one to the 11th block of Avenida Angamos Oeste. Taxi from downtown US$3; from Parque Kennedy US$2.

Poli Museum ⓘ *Almte Cochrane 466, T422 2437, tours cost US$10 per person irrespective of the size of the group, allow 2 hrs, call in advance to arrange tours.* This is one of the best private collections of colonial and pre-Columbian artefacts in Peru, including material from Sipán. At General Borgoño, eighth block s/n, turn off Avenida Arequipa at 45th block, is **Huaca Pucllana** ⓘ *T01-445 8695, http://pucllana.perucultural.org.pe/, US$2.50, includes 45-min tour in Spanish or English, 0900-1600, closed Tue,* a 5th to 8th- century AD, pre-Inca site which is under excavation. It has a small site museum with some objects from the site itself, and a handicrafts shop (see Eating, below).

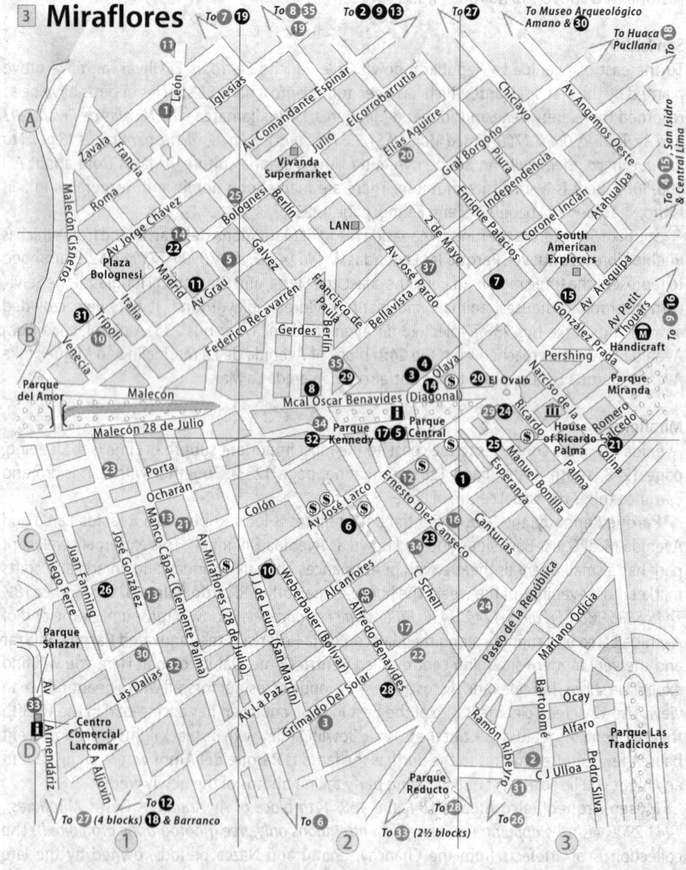

Barranco

This suburb further south was already a seaside resort by the end of the 17th century. Nowadays, a number of artists have their workshops here and there are several chic galleries. The attractive public library, formerly the town hall, stands on the plaza. Nearby is the interesting *bajada*, a steep path leading down to the beach. The **Puente de los Suspiros** (Bridge of Sighs), leads towards the Malecón, with fine views of the bay. Barranco is quiet by day but comes alive at night (see Eating and Bars sections) in the bars focussed around the main plaza. Take a colectivo to Miraflores then another. Some run all the way to Barranco from Lima centre; check on the window or ask. The 45-minute walk from Miraflores to Barranco along the Malecón is nice in summer. **Museo de Arte Colonial Pedro de Osma** ⓘ *Av Pedro de Osma 423, T467 0141, www.museopedrodeosma.org, Tue-Sat 1000-1800, by appointment Sun and holidays, US$3.35, students half price.* A private collection of colonial art of the Cuzco, Ayacucho and Arequipa schools. Take bus 2, 54 or colectivo from Avenida Tacna.

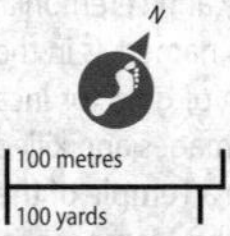

Sleeping

1 Adventures House *A2*
2 Albergue Turístico Juvenil Internacional *D3*
3 Albergue Verde *D2*
4 Alemán *A3*
5 Antigua Miraflores *B1*
6 Casa Andina *D2*
7 Casa de Baraybar *A2*
8 Casa del Mochilero *A2*
9 Casa Rodas *B3*
10 El Carmelo *B1*
11 Explorer's House *A1*
12 Flying Dog *C2*
13 Friend's House *C1*
14 Hitchhikers B&B Backpackers *A1*
15 Home Perú *A3*
16 Hostal El Patio *C2*
17 Hostal La Castellana *C2*
18 HQ Villa *A3*
19 Inka Frog *A2*
20 Inka Lodge *A2*
21 José Antonio *C1*
22 La Casa Nostra *D2*
23 Lex Luthor's House *C1*
24 Lion Backpackers *C3*
25 Loki Backpackers *B3*
26 Mansión San Antonio *D3*
27 Miraflores Park *D1*
28 Pakacuna Backpackers *D3*
29 Pariwana *B3*
30 Perú Backpackers Miraflores Guesthouse *D1*
31 San Antonio Abad *D3*
32 Señorial *D1*
33 Sipán *D2*
34 Sonesta Posadas del Inca *C2*
35 The Lighthouse *A2*

Eating

1 Astrid y Gaston *C3*
2 Bohemia *A2*
3 Café Beirut *B2*
4 Café Café *B2*
5 Café de la Paz *B2*
6 Café Tarata & Mama Olla *C2*
7 Café Voltaire *B3*
8 Café Zeta *B2*
9 C'est si Bon *A2*
10 Chef's Café *C2*
11 Coco de Mer *B1*
12 Dalmacia *D1*
13 Dino's Pizza *A2*
14 Dove Vai, Sandwich.com & Shehadi *B2*
15 El Huarike *B3*
16 El Kapallaq *B3*
17 El Parquetito *B2*
18 El Rincón Gaucho *D1*
19 El Señorío de Sulco *A2*
20 Haiti *B3*
21 Il Postino *C3*
22 Las Brujas de Cachiche *B1*
23 Las Tejas *C2*
24 La Tiendecita Blanca *B3*
25 La Trattoria *C3*
26 Lobo del Mar – Octavio Otani *C1*
27 Madre Natura *A3*
28 Pardo's Chicken *D2*
29 Pizza Street *B2*
30 San Antonio *A3*
31 Sí Señor *B1*
32 Super Rueda *B2*

Bars & clubs

33 Bartinis *D1*
34 Media Naranja *B2*
35 The Old Pub *B2*
36 Treff Pub Alemán *C2*
37 Voluntarios Pub *B2*

➡**Lima maps**
1 Lima, page 1268
2 Lima centre, page 1270
3 Miraflores, page 1274

Lima beaches

In summer (December-April) the city's beaches get very crowded at weekends and lots of activities are organized. Even though the water of the whole bay has been declared unsuitable for swimming, Limeños see the beach more as part of their culture than as a health risk. Do not camp on the beaches as robbery is a serious threat and, for the same reason, take care on the walkways down. Don't take any belongings with you to the beach, only what is really necessary.

The *Circuito de Playas*, which begins with Playa Arica (30 km from Lima) and ends with San Bartolo (45 km from Lima), has many great beaches for all tastes. The beaches of Miraflores, Barranco and Chorrillos are very popular and sand and sea get dirty. It's much better to take a safe taxi 40 km south to Punta Rocas, Señoritas or Silencio. Punta Hermosa has frequent surfing and volleyball tournaments. If you really want the height of fashion head to **Asia**, Km 92-104, some 20 beaches with boutiques, hotels, restaurants and condos.

Pachacámac

ⓘ *T430 0168, http://pachacamac.perucultural.org.pe, www.ulb.ac.be/philo/ychsma, 0900-1700, closed 1 May, US$2.50, includes the museum, guide US$6.*

When the Spaniards arrived, Pachacámac in the Lurín valley was the largest city and ceremonial centre on the coast. A wooden statue of the creator-god, after whom the site is named, is in the site museum. Hernando Pizarro was sent here by his brother in 1533 in search of gold for Inca emperor Atahualpa's ransom. In their fruitless quest, the Spaniards destroyed images and killed the priests. The ruins encircle the top of a low hill, whose crest was crowned with a **Temple of the Sun**, now partially restored. Hidden from view is the reconstructed **House of the Mamaconas**, where the 'chosen women' spun fine cloth for the Inca and his court. An impression of the scale of the site can be gained from the top of the Temple of the Sun, or from walking or driving the 3-km circuit, which is covered by an unmade road for cars and tour buses. The site is large and it is expected that tourists will be visiting by vehicle. There is also a parking area.

Puruchuco

ⓘ *At the end of Av Javier Prado Este, T494 2641, http://museopuruchuco.perucultural.org.pe, Tue-Fri 0830-1600, Sat-Sun 0900-1600, US$1.85. Take a bus to Carretera Central and get off at Km 4.5 asking for Museo Puruchuco (take a Covida bus or combis going up to Carretera Central)*

In the eastern outskirts of Lima, near La U football stadium, is Puruchuco, the reconstructed palace of a pre-Inca Huacho noble. There is a very good museum, Jiménez Borja, with ceramics and textiles from the lower Rímac or Lima valley. This is also the site of a major archaeological find (2002): under a shanty town called Túpac Amaru, over 2,000 intact mummy bundles have been uncovered in an Inca cemetery known as **Puruchuco-Huaquerones**. The quantity and completeness of the mummies, plus the tens of thousands of accompanying objects, should reveal a wealth of information about the last century of Inca society before the Spanish conquest. To see the tombs, ask the guards on Saturday morning if you can visit the archaeologists at work.

Lima listings

Hotel and guesthouse prices
LL over US$200 **L** US$151-200 **AL** US$101-150
A US$66-100 **B** US$46-65 **C** US$31-45
D US$21-30 **E** US$12-20 **F** US$7-11
G US$6 and under
Restaurant prices
¥¥¥ over US$12 ¥¥ US$7-12 ¥ under US$6

Sleeping

Central Lima is not as safe at night as the more upmarket areas of Miraflores, San Isidro and Barranco. If you are only staying a short time and want to see the main sites, it is convenient, but do take care. San Isidro is the poshest district while Miraflores has a good mix of places to stay, great ocean views, bookstores, restaurants and cinemas. From here you can then commute to the centre by bus (30-45 mins) or by taxi (20-30 mins). Barranco is a little further out. All hotels in the upper price brackets charge 19% state tax and service on top of prices. In hotels foreigners pay no tax and the amount of service charge is up to the hotel. Neither is included in the prices below, unless otherwise stated. All those listed below have received good recommendations.

Lima *p1267, maps p1268 and p1270*

Near the airport

L Ramada Costa del Sol, Av Elmer Faucett s/n, T711 2000, www.ramada.com. Within the airport perimeter. Offers day rates as well as overnights if you can't get into the city.

B-D Hostal Residencial Victor, Manuel Mattos 325, Urb San Amadeo de Garagay, Lima 31, T01-569 4662, hostalvictor@terra.com.pe. 5 mins from the airport by taxi, or phone or email in advance for free pick-up, large comfortable rooms, with bath, hot water, cable TV, free luggage store, free internet and 10% discount for Footprint book owners, American breakfast, evening meals can be ordered locally, 2 malls with restaurants, shops, cinemas, etc nearby, very helpful.

D Pay Purix, Av Bertello Bolatti, Mz F, Lote 5, Urb Los Jazmines, 1ra Etapa, Callao, T484 9118, www.paypurix.com. 3 mins from airport, can arrange pick-up (taxi US$6, US$2 from outside airport). Hostel with doubles and dorms (**E-F** pp), convenient, with breakfast, Wi-Fi, washing machine, English spoken, CDs, DVDs, games and use of kitchen.

Central Lima

B The Clifford Hotel, Parque Hernán Velarde 27, near 2nd block of Av Petit Thouars, Sta Beatriz, T433 4249, www.thecliffordhotel.com.pe. Nicely converted, republican town house in a quiet and leafy park. Also has suites (**A**), includes breakfast, a welcome drink and one airport transfer, has a bar and conference room.

B Maury, Jr Ucayali 201, T428 8188, http://ekeko2.rcp.net.pe/hotelmaury/. Fancy, secure, breakfast included, most luxurious hotel in the historical centre.

C Hostal La Posada del Parque, Parque Hernán Velarde 60, near 2nd block of Av Petit Thouars, Santa Beatriz, between centre and San Isidro, T433 2412, www.incacountry.com. A charmingly refurbished old house in a safe area, excellent bathrooms, cable TV, breakfast US$2 extra, airport transfer 24 hrs for US$14 for up to 3 passengers, no credit cards, free internet 0830-2200. The owners speak good English. Recommended as excellent value.

D Hostal Roma, Jr Ica 326, T/F427 7576, www.hostalroma.8m.com. **E** without bath, cheaper in low season, hot water, basic, often full, internet extra, motorcycle parking (**Roma Tours**, arranges city tous - but shop around if you want to, flight reservations, Errol Branca speaks English).

D Hostal Iquique, Jr Iquique 758, Breña (discount for SAE members), T433 4724, www.hostal-iquique-lima.com. Rooms on top floor at the back are best, well-kept if a bit noisy and draughty, use of kitchen, warm water, storage facilities, safe, internet. Repeated recommendations.

E Hostal de las Artes, Jr Chota 1460, T433 0031, www.hostaldelasartes.net. **F** without bath (no singles with bath), **G** pp in dormitory, Dutch owned, English spoken, safes in rooms and safe luggage store, nice colonial building, solar hot water system, book exchange, gay friendly, airport transfer US$12.

F Hostal España, Jr Azángaro 105, T427 9196, www.hotelespanaperu.com. **E** with private bath (3 rooms), **G** pp in dormitory, fine old building, shared bathroom, internet, motorcycle parking, luggage store (free), laundry service, don't leave valuables in rooms, roof garden, good café, can be very busy.

F Hostal San Francisco, Jr Azángaro 127, T426 2735, hostalsf@lanpro.com.pe. Dormitories with and without bathrooms, safe, Italian/Peruvian owners, good service, internet and *cafetería*.

G pp **Familia Rodríguez**, Av Nicolás de Piérola 730, p 2 no 3, T423 6465, jotajot@ terra.com.pe. With breakfast, popular, some rooms noisy, will store luggage, also has dormitory accommodation with only one bathroom (same price), transport to airport US$10 pp for 2 people, US$4 pp for 3 or more, good information, secure.

G Pensión Ibarra, Av Tacna 359, p 14-16, T/F427 8603 (no sign), pensionibarra@ekno.com. Breakfast US$2, discount for longer stay, use of kitchen, balcony with views of the city, very helpful owner, hot water, full board available (good small café next door).

Pueblo Libre *p1272, map 1268*

F pp **Guest House Marfil**, Parque Ayacucho 126, at the 3rd block of Bolívar, T463 3161, cosycoyllor@yahoo.com. English spoken, breakfast, kitchen facilities and laundry free of charge, internet, Spanish classes arranged, family atmosphere.

G Hostal Bait Sababa, Av San Martín 743, near the hospital, T01-261 4990, www.baitsababa.com. The home of a Jewish family who also speak Spanish and English, very helpful, Fri evening meal provided, restaurants, laundry, internet and phone nearby.

San Isidro *p1273, map 1268*

LL Country Club, Los Eucaliptos 590, T611 9000, www.hotelcountry.com. Excellent, fine service, luxurious rooms, safes in rooms, cable TV, free internet for guests, good bar and restaurant, classically stylish.

LL Libertador Hotels Peru, Los Eucaliptos 550, T518 6300, www.libertador.com.pe (reservations: Las Begonias 441, office 240, T518 6500). Overlooking the golf course, full facilities for the business traveller, large comfortable rooms in this relatively small hotel, fine service, good restaurant.

LL Sonesta El Olivar, Pancho Fierro 194, T712 6000, www.sonesta.com/Lima/. Excellent, one of the top 5-star hotels in Lima overlooking El Olivar park, modern, many superb eating options, bar, garden, swimming pool, quiet, very attentive, popular.

L Sofitel Royal Park, Av Camino Real 1050, T215 1616, www.sofitel.com. Excellent rooms, charming, part of the French group, prices can be negotiated.

AL Garden, Rivera Navarrete 450, T442 1771, www.gardenhotel.com.pe. Includes breakfast, good beds, small restaurant, ideal for business visitors, convenient, free internet, good value.

D-E Hospedaje Elizabeth Ballon, Av del Parque Norte 265, San Isidro, T9980 07557, http://chezelizabeth.typepad.fr. Family house in residential area 7 mins' walk from Cruz del Sur bus station. Shared or private bathrooms, TV room, laundry, luggage storage, breakfast included, airport transfers US$13 for 4.

San Miguel and Magdalena del Mar *p1268*

C Hostal Mami Panchita, Av Federico Gallessi 198 (ex-Av San Miguel), San Miguel, T263 7203, www.mamipanchita.com. Dutch-Peruvian owned, English, French, Dutch, Spanish and German spoken, includes breakfast and welcome drink, comfortable rooms with bath, hot water, living room and bar, patio, email service, book exchange, Raymi Travel agency (good service), 15 mins from airport, 15 mins from Miraflores, 20 mins from historical centre. Frequently recommended.

F Tambopacaya, Jr Manco Capac 212 (block 31 of Av Brasil), Magdalena del Mar, T261 6122, www.tambopacaya.com. **G** in dorm, hot water, private rooms have bath, use of kitchen, internet, luggage store, laundry, convenient for airport and centre.

Miraflores *p1273, map p1274*

LL Miraflores Park, Av Malecón de la Reserva 1035, T610 8300/4000, www.mirafloresspark.com. An Orient Express hotel, excellent service and facilities, beautiful views over the ocean, top class. Rooftop, open-air, heated pool and spa which looks out over the ocean, open to the public when you buy a spa treatment.

L-A Sonesta Posadas del Inca, Alcanfores 329, T241 7688, www.sonesta.com/Miraflores/. Part of renowned chain of hotels, convenient location, cable TV, a/c, restaurant.

AL-A Antigua Miraflores, Av Grau 350 at C Francia, T01-241 6116, www.peru-hotels-inns.com. A small, elegant hotel in a quiet but central location, very friendly service, tastefully furnished and decorated, gym, cable TV, good restaurant. Recommended.

AL-A Casa Andina, Av 28 de Julio 1088, T241 4050, www.casa-andina.com. Also at Av Petit Thouars 5444 and Av La Paz 463 (**Private Collection, LL**) in Miraflores. A recommended chain, all with similar facilities and decor (others in the Cuzco area, Puno, Arequipa and Nazca). Very neat, with many useful touches, comfortable beds, free internet and Wi-Fi, a/c, fridge, safe, laundry service, buffet breakfast, other meals available. Check website for discounts.

A José Antonio, 28 de Julio 398 y C Colón, T445 7743, www.hotelesjoseantonio.com. Good in all respects, including the restaurant, huge rooms, jacuzzis, internet, swimming pool, business facilities, helpful staff speak some English.

A Mansión San Antonio, Av Tejada 531, T01-445 9665, www.mansionsanantonio.com. Bed and breakfast, 7 suites of varying standards on 3 floors in a quiet residential area, safe, bar, coffee shop, Wi-Fi in public areas, swimming pool, stylish and gay friendly.

B Hostal La Castellana, Grimaldo del Solar 222, T444 4662, lacastellan@terra.com.pe. Pleasant, good value, nice garden, safe, expensive restaurant, laundry, English spoken, special price for South American Explorers (SAE) members.

B San Antonio Abad, Ramón Ribeyro 301, T447 6766, www.hotelsanantonioabad.com. Secure, quiet, helpful, tasty breakfasts, Wi-Fi, internet cabina next door, 1 free airport transfer with reservation, justifiably popular.

B-C Hostal El Patio, Diez Canseco 341, T444 2107, www.hostalelpatio.net. Includes breakfast, reductions for long stays, very nice suites and rooms, comfortable, English and French spoken, convenient, *comedor*, gay friendly. Very popular, reservations are essential.

C Alemán, Arequipa 4704, T241 1500, www.hotelaleman.com.pe. No sign, comfortable, quiet, garden, excellent breakfast included, enquire about laundry service, smiling staff, free internet.

C El Carmelo, Bolognesi 749, T446 0575, carmelo@amauta.rcp.net.pe. With TV, great location a couple of blocks from the Parque del Amor, small restaurant downstairs serving *criolla* food and *ceviche*, price includes breakfast, good value, comfortable.

C La Casa Nostra, Av Grimaldo del Solar 265, T241 1718, www.lacasanostraperu.com. Variety of rooms (**E** pp in 4-bed room), good service, convenient, with breakfast, internet, safe, money exchange, laundry, tourist information. Popular.

C Señorial, José González 567, T445 0139, www.senorial.com. With breakfast, comfortable, nice garden, Wi-Fi, restaurant, good services. Recommended.

C Sipán, Paseo de la República 6171, T447 0884, www.hotelsipan.com.pe. Breakfast and tax included, very pleasant, on the edge of a residential area next to the Vía Expresa (which can be heard from front rooms), TV, fridge, security box, internet access. Free airport transfers available.

C-D Flying Dog, Diez Canseco 117, T445 6745, www.flyingdogperu.com. Also at Lima 457 and Olaya 280, all with dorms **F** pp. At Pershing 155 is a house for monthly rentals and they have hostels in Cuzco and Arequipa. All on or near Parque Kennedy, with kitchen, internet, lockers, but all with different features.

D Casa de Baraybar, Toribio Pacheco 216, T441 2160, www.casadebaraybar.com. 1 block from the ocean, extra long beds, breakfast included, TV, 24-hr room service, laundry, airport transfers free for stays of 3 nights. Bilingual staff, internet. Recommended.

D Inka Frog, Gral Iglesias 271, T445 8979, www.inkafrog.com. **E** with SAE discount. Renovated hostel, self-styled "Exclusive B&B", comfortable, nice décor, lounge with huge TV, all rooms with bath and cable TV, rooftop terrace. Breakfast included, great value.

D The Lighthouse, Cesareo Chacaltana 162, T446-8397, www.thelighthouseperu.com. **F** in shared dorm. Near Plaza Morales Barros, British/Peruvian run, relaxed, small dorm or private rooms with shared bath. Free internet and Wi-Fi, use of kitchen, small indoor patio. Breakfast included. Recommended.

D-E Casa Rodas, Av Petit Thouars 4712, T447 5761, and Tarapacá 250, T242 4872, www.casarodas.com. Both houses have rooms for 2, 3, or 4, good beds, hot water, with breakfast, use of kitchen, Wi-Fi, helpful staff.

D-E Home Perú, Av Arequipa 4501 (no sign), T241 9898, www.homeperu.com. In a 1920s mansion with huge rooms (private or dorms), **E-F** pp with shared bath, group discounts, use of kitchen, luggage store, English spoken, laundry service, internet, Wi-Fi in lounge, garden, large friendly dog. Can help with bus and plane tickets, connected to other *hostales* in Peru.

D-E Lion Backpackers, Grimaldo del Solar 139, T447 1827, www.lionbackpackers.com. 3 blocks from Parque Kennedy, double and dorms, good atmosphere, safe, breakfast, very helpful.

E pp **Inka Lodge**, Elías Aguirre 278, T242 6989, www.inkalodge.com. Also with dorms (**F** pp), convenient, excellent breakfast included, internet, laundry, very helpful.

E-F pp **Perú Backpackers Miraflores Guesthouse**, José González 526, T447 7044, www.backpackersperu.com. **D** in double, has a girls-only dorm, good breakfast included, good service, cooking facilities, internet, DVD, safe, book exchange.

F pp **Adventures House**, Alfredo Leon 234, T241 5693, www.adventureshouse.com. Rooms for up to 4, with bath and hot water, free internet, national calls, pleasant, quiet, a short walk from all main facilities, airport transfer, use of kitchen, bike rental US$15/day. Associated with **Fly Adventures**, see Paragliding, below.

F pp **Albergue Verde**, Grimaldo del Solar 459, T445 3816, www.albergueverde.com. Nice small hostal, comfortable beds, **D** pp in double, friendly owner, Arturo Palmer, breakfast included, airport transfers US$15 (second location in preparation).

F pp **Explorer's House**, Av Alfredo León 158, by 10th block of Av José Pardo, T241 5002, explorers_ house@yahoo.es. No sign, but plenty of indications of the house number, with breakfast, dorm with shared bath, or double rooms with bath, hot water, use of kitchen, laundry service, Spanish classes, English spoken, very welcoming, internet, small roof patio.

F Friend's House, Jr Manco Cápac 368, T446 6248, friendshouse_peru@yahoo.com.mx. Dormitory accommodation with hot water, cable TV, use of kitchen, includes breakfast, very popular with backpackers, near Larcomar shopping centre, plenty of good information and help. Highly recommended. They have another branch at José Gonzales 427, T446 3521, **E** pp with bath, same facilities, except private rooms only and more like a family home. Neither branch is signed.

F pp **Hitchhikers B&B Backpackers**, Bolognesi 400, T242 3008, www.hhikersperu.com. Located close to the ocean, mixture of dorms (one girl-only) and private rooms with bath (**D**), use of kitchen, nice patio, internet, plenty of parking.

F pp **HQ Villa**, Independencia 1288, T221 3221, info@hqvilla.com. Peruvian/British owned hostel with mixed and girls-only dorms and doubles (**C**) in a modern house, garden, lounge, double kitchen, receptionists speak 3 languages, airport pick-up, with breakfast, internet, Wi-Fi, spacious, nice atmosphere.

F pp **Loki Backpackers**, José Galvez 576, T651 2966, www.lokihostel.com. In a quiet area, the capital's sister to the party hostel of the same name in Cuzco, **D** in double room, good showers, with breakfast (cooked breakfast extra), Fri barbecues, use of kitchen, free internet, lockers, airport transfer extra.

F pp **Pakacuna Backpackers**, Juan de la Fuente 647, T445 3205, www.pakacuna.com. Rooms with or without bath, price includes breakfast, internet, kitchen, cable TV and movies, garden.

F Pariwana, Av Larco 189, T242 4350, www.pariwana-hostel.com. New in 2009, party hostel with dorms and shared bath, individual lockers with power outlets so you can leave your gadgets charging in a safe place.

F pp **Stop & Drop Backpacker Hotel & Guesthouse**, Berlín 168, p2, T243 3101, www.stopanddrop.com. **D** Double rooms with private bath. Backpacker hotel and guesthouse, also surf and Spanish school. Bar, kitchen facilities, luggage store, laundry, TV, movies, internet, games, comfy beds, safe, hot showers 24 hrs, adventure sports (including diving, horse riding) and vounteer jobs. Airport pick up.

G pp **Casa del Mochilero**, Cesareo Chacaltana 130A, T444 9089, pilaryv@hotmail.com. Ask for Pilar or Juan, dorms or **E** in double room on terrace, all with shared bath, breakast and internet extra, hot water, Wi-Fi, use of kitchen. lots of information. Not to be confused with **Mochilero's Inn** at No 136, which also has dorms in G range.

G pp **Lex Luthor's House**, Porta 550 (look for the green lights), T242 7059, luthorshouse@hotmail.com. Breakfast included, pleasant house, small and basic but clean, use of kitchen, good value.

Barranco *p1275*

C Domeyer, C Domeyer 296, T247 1413, www.domeyerhostel.net. Hot water 24 hrs, laundry service, secure, gay friendly.

E pp **Barranco's Backpackers Inn**, Malecón Castilla 260, T247 1326, www.barrancobackpackers.com. Ocean view, colourful rooms, all ensuite, shared and private rooms (with cable TV), free internet with Wi-Fi, kitchen facilities. Breakfast included. Discount for SAE members.

E Casa Barranco, Av Grau 982, T477 0984, www.lacasabarranco.8m.com. No sign on the street, just ring. All rooms with shared bath, dormitory **F**, also monthly rentals available (US$150). Has kitchen, DVD room, cable TV and PS1. Helpful owner, Felipe. Discount for SAE members.

E Safe in Lima, Alfredo Silva 150, T252 7330, www.safeinlima.com. Quiet, Belgian-run hostal with family atmosphere in new premises, with breakfast, very helpful, airport pick-up US$14, good value, reserve in advance, lots of information for travellers.

F pp **The Point**, Malecón Junín 300, T628 7952, www.thepointhostels.com. Rooms range from doubles to large dormitories, all with shared bath, very popular with backpackers (book in advance at weekends), breakfast included, internet, cable TV, laundry, kitchen facilities, gay friendly, party atmosphere most of the time, *The Pointless Pub* open 2000 till whenever, weekly barbecues, therapeutic massage next door, can arrange bungee jumping, flight tickets and volunteering.

Youth hostels *map p1274*

F Albergue Juvenil Malka, Los Lirios 165 (near 4th block of Av Javier Prado Este), San Isidro, T442 0162, www.youthhostelperu.com. Youth hostel, 20% discount with ISIC card, dormitory style, 4-8 beds per room, also doubles (**D**, **E** without bath), breakfast US$2, English spoken, cable TV, Wi-Fi, laundry, kitchen, climbing wall, nice café. Airport transfer US$14.

F pp **Albergue Turístico Juvenil Internacional**, Av Casimiro Ulloa 328, San Antonio, T446 5488, www.limahostell.com.pe. Dormitory accommodation, **C** in a double private room, basic cafeteria, travel information, cooking (minimal) and laundry facilities, swimming pool often empty, extra charge for kitchen facilities, safe, situated in a nice villa; 20 mins walk from the beach. Bus No 2 or colectivos pass Av Benavides to the centre; taxi to centre, US$2.50.

Eating

19% state tax and 10% service will be added to your bill in middle and upper class restaurants. Chinese is often the cheapest at around US$5 including a drink.

Lima *p1267, map p1270*

Central Lima

ΨΨ Antaño, Ucayali 332, opposite the Torre Tagle Palace, T426 2372. Good, typical Peruvian food, nice patio. Recommended.

ΨΨ L'Eau Vive, Ucayali 370, also opposite the Torre Tagle Palace, T427 5612. Run by nuns, open Mon-Sat, 1230-1500 and 1930-2130, fixed-price lunch menu, Peruvian-style in interior dining room, or à la carte in either of dining rooms that open onto patio, excellent, profits go to the poor, Ave Maria is sung nightly at 2100.

ΨΨ Manhatten, Jr Miró Quesada 259. Open Mon-Fri 0700-1900, low end executive-type restaurant, local and international food from US$5-10, good.

ΨΨ Wa Lok, Jr Paruro 864, Barrio Chino, T427 2656. Good dim sum, cakes and fortune cookies (when you pay the bill). Owner Liliana Com speaks fluent English, very friendly.

ΨΨ-Ψ De Cesar, Ancash 300, T428 8740. Open 0700-2300 for seafood, including *ceviche* and meat dishes. Good food.

ΨΨ-Ψ San Paolo, Ancash 454, T427 4600. Open 0600 till midnight for Peruvian food, also has a good *menú diario* for US$3-4.

Ψ Cordano, Jr Ancash 202. Typical old Lima restaurant/watering hole, slow service and a bit grimy but full of character. Definitely worth the time it takes to drink a few beers.

Ψ Govinda, Av Garcilaso de la Vega 1670, opposite Gran Parque de Lima. Vegetarian food and natural products, good.

Ψ Kin Ten, Ucayali y Paruro, Barrio Chino. Excellent vegetarian options at this *chifa*.

Ψ Machu Picchu, Jr Ancash 312. Huge portions, grimy bathrooms (to say the least), yet very popular, closed for breakfast.

Ψ Natur, Moquegua 132, 1 block from Jr de la Unión, T01-427 8281. The owner, Humberto Valdivia, is also president of the South American Explorers' board of directors; the casual conversation, as well as his vegetarian restaurant, is certainly recommended.

Ψ Neydi, Puno 367. Good, cheap seafood, open daily 1100-2000, popular.

Ψ Salon Capon, Jr Paruro 819. Good dim sum, at this recommended *chifa*. Also has a branch at Larcomar shopping centre, which is ΨΨΨ, elegant and equally recommended.

Cafés

Acllahuasy, Jr Ancash 400. Around the corner from **Hostal España**, open daily 0700-2300, good Peruvian dishes.

Café Carrara, Jr Ica 330, attached to **Hostal Roma**. Open daily from breakfast until 2300, pancakes, sandwiches.

La Catedral del Pisco, Av Uruguay 114, T330 0079, lacatedraldelpisco@hotmail.com. Café/bar open 0800-2200, serving comida criolla, complementary coffee or pisco sour for Footprint owners, associated with **Victor Travel Service** (see below), internet.

Breña

ΨΨ La Choza Náutica, Jr Breña 204 and 211 behind Plaza Bolognesi, T423 8087. Good *ceviche* and friendly service.

Ψ Azato, Av Arica 298, 3 blocks from Plaza Bolognesi, T423 4369. Excellent and cheap Peruvian dishes.

A variety of Lima's better-known restaurants and cafés have branches on Avenida Primavera: eg **Antica Pizzería** (No 275, T372 2698) and **Delicass** (No 654, T372 5203), both also in San Isidro, a branch of the **San Antonio Café** chain (see Miraflores, Cafés, below), and the main branch of **T'Anta** (No 692, T372 3528), a coffee shop-cum-restaurant which specializes in the Novo Andino cuisine of Gastón Acurio (of *Café* *del Museo* and *Astrid & Gastón*, see below); also 28 de Julio 888, Miraflores, Pancho Fiero 115, San Isidro, and Pasaje N de Rivera 142, behind the Plaza de Armas.

Pueblo Libre *p1272*

TT-T Antigua Taberna Quierolo, Av San Martín 1090, 1 block from Plaza Bolívar. Atmospheric old bar with glass-fronted shelves of bottles, marble bar and old photos, owns bodega next door. Serves simple lunches, sandwiches and snacks, good for wine, does not serve dinner.

TT-T Café del Museo at the Museo Larco, Av Bolívar 1515, Pueblo Libre, T462 4757. Daily 0900-1800, seating inside and on the terrace. Specially designed interior, offers a selection of salads, fine Peruvian dishes, pastas and seafood, a tapas bar of traditional Peruvian foods, as well as snacks, desserts and cocktails. Highly regarded.

San Isidro *p1273*

TTT Alfresco, Santa Lucía 295 (no sign), T422 8915. Best known for its tempting seafood and ceviche, also pastas and rice dishes, expensive wines.

TTT Antica Pizzería, Av Dos de Mayo 728, T222 8437. Very popular, great ambience, excellent food, Italian owner. Also **Antica Trattoria** in Barranco at Alfonso Ugarte 242, and an excellent bar, **Antica Taberna**, with a limited range of food at Conquistadores 605, San Isidro, very good value, fashionable, get there early for a seat.

TTT Asia de Cuba, Conquistadores 780, T222 4940. Popular, serving a mix of Asian, Cuban and Peruvian dishes. It also has a reputation for its bar and nightclub; try the martinis.

TTT Matsuei, C Manuel Bañon 260, T422 4323. Sushi bar and Japanese dishes, very popular, among the best Japanese in Lima.

TTT Valentino, Manuel Bañon 215, T441 6174. One of Lima's best international restaurants, formal, look for the tiny brass sign.

TT Chez Philippe, Av 2 de Mayo 748, T222 4953. Pizza, pasta and crêpes, wood oven, rustic decor (same owners as Pizza B&B in Huaraz).

TT Como Agua Para Chocolate, Pancho Fierro 108, T222 0297. Dutch-Mexican owned restaurant, specializing in Mexican food as the name suggests, also has a very amusing Dutch night once a month. SAE members get a discount.

TT Delicass, Miguel Dasso 131. Great deli with imported meats and cheeses, good coffee, open late.

TT Segundo Muelle, Av Conquistadores 490, T421 1206, and Av Canaval y Moreyra (aka Corpac) 605. Excellent *ceviche* and other very good seafood dishes, popular with the younger crowd.

Cafés

Café Olé, Pancho Fierro 115 (1 block from *Hotel El Olívar*). Huge selection of entrées and desserts, very smart with prices to match.

Café Positano/Café Luna, Miguel Dasso 147. Popular with politicians, café and bistro.

News Café, Av Santa Luisa 110. Great salads and desserts, popular and expensive.

Miraflores *p1273, map p1274*

Calle San Ramón, known as 'Pizza Street' (across from Parque Kennedy), is a pedestrian walkway lined with outdoor restaurants/bars/discos open until the wee small hours. It's very popular, with good-natured touts trying to entice diners and drinkers with free offers.

TTT Astrid y Gaston, Cantuarias 175, T242 5387. Exceptional local/Novo Andino and international cuisine, one of the best in Lima, owners are Gastón Acurio and his wife Astrid. Also has a bar.

TTT Las Brujas de Cachiche, Av Bolognesi 460, T447 1883. An old mansion converted into bars and dining rooms, traditional food (menu in Spanish and English), best Lomo Saltado in town, live *criollo* music.

TTT Café Voltaire, Av Dos de Mayo 220, T447 4807. International cuisine with emphasis on French dishes, beautifully cooked food, pleasant ambience, good service, closed Sun.

TTT Coco de Mer, Av Grau 400, T243 0278. Run by Englishwoman Lucy Ralph, popular, Mediterranean and Peruvian dishes, cocktails, events, open daily 1200 till whenever.

TTT El Señorío de Sulco, Malecón Cisneros 1470, T441 0183. Overlooking a clifftop park, with ocean views from upstairs. Forget the Footprint grading, this is a 'five-fork' restaurant which some believe is the best in Lima, all Peruvian food, à la carte and buffet, piscos, wines, piano music at night.

TTT Huaca Pucllana, Gral Borgoño cuadra 8 s/n, alt cuadra 45 Av Arequipa, T445 4042. Facing the archaeological site of the same name,

contemporary Peruvian fusion cooking, very good food in an unusual setting, popular with groups.
ΨΨΨ El Kapallaq, Av Petit Thouars 4844, T444 4149. Prize-winning Peruvian restaurant specializing in seafood and fish, excellent *ceviches*. Open Mon-Fri 1200-1700 only.
ΨΨΨ El Rincón Gaucho, Av Armendáriz 580, T447 4778. Good grill, renowned for its steaks.
ΨΨΨ Sí Señor, Jr Bolognesi 706, T445 3789. Mexican food, cheerful, interesting décor, huge portions.
ΨΨΨ Rosa Náutica, T445 0149, www.larosanautica.com. Built on old British-style pier (Espigón No 4), in Lima Bay. Delightful opulence, finest fish cuisine, experience the atmosphere by buying an expensive beer in the bar at sunset, open 1230-0200 daily.
ΨΨΨ Las Tejas, Diez Canseco 340, T444 4360. Open 1100- 2300 daily, good, typical Peruvian food, recommended for ceviche.
ΨΨΨ La Trattoria, Manuel Bonilla 106, T446 7002, 1 block from Parque Kennedy. Italian cuisine, popular, good desserts. Has another branch, **La Bodeguita**, opposite entrance to Huaca Pucllana.
ΨΨ Bohemia, Av Santa Cruz 805, Ovalo Gutiérrez, T446 5240. Large menu of international food, great salads and sandwiches.
ΨΨ Café Tarata, Pasaje Tarata 260, T446 6330. Good atmosphere, family-run, good varied menu.
ΨΨ Dalmacia, San Fernando 401, T445 7917. Spanish-owned, casual gourmet restaurant, excellent.
ΨΨ El Huarike, Enrique Palacios 140, T241 6086. Fashionable, delicious combinations of ceviche and sushi.
ΨΨ Il Postino, Colina 401, T446 8381. Great Italian food.
ΨΨ Lobo del Mar - Octavio Otani, Colón 587, T242-1871. Basic exterior hides one of the oldest *cevicherías* in Miraflores, excellent, a good selection of other seafood dishes.
ΨΨ Mama Olla, Pasaje Tarata 248. Charming café on a pedestrian walkway, huge menu, big portions.
ΨΨ-Ψ Café Beirut, Mártir Olaya 204. Excellent Middle-Eastern restaurant, close to the centre of Miraflores, enthusiastic waiters, superb falafel and Arabic favourites, both sweet and savoury. Also has a good choice of international dishes.
ΨΨ-Ψ Shehadi, Av Diagonal 220. Facing Parque Kennedy, US-owned, brightly lit restaurant specializing in pizza but also serving typical Peruvian fare. Good value daytime menus. Popular with locals and foreigners.
Ψ Dino's Pizza, Av Cdte Espinar 374 and many other branches, T242 0606. Great pizza at a good price, delivery service.
Ψ El Parquetito, Diez Canseco 150. Good cheap menu, serves breakfast, eat inside or out.
Ψ Madre Natura, Chiclayo 815. Natural foods shop and eating place, very good, closes 2100.
Ψ Pardo's Chicken, Av Benavides 730. Chicken and chips, very good and popular (branches throughout Lima).
Ψ Sandwich.com, Av Diagonal 234. Good, cheap sandwiches with interesting combinations of fillings.
Ψ Super Rueda, Porta 133, also Av Pardo 1224. Mexican food a-la Peru, fast-food style.

Cafés

Café Café, Martin Olaya 250, at the corner of Av Diagonal. Very popular, good atmosphere, over 100 different blends of coffee, good salads and sandwiches, very popular with 'well-to-do' Limeños. Also in Larcomar.
Café de la Paz, Lima 351, middle of Parque Kennedy. Good outdoor café right on the park, expensive, great cocktails.
Café Zeta, Mcal Oscar R Benavides 598 y José Gálvez. American owned, excellent Peruvian coffee, teas, hot chocolate, and the best homemade cakes away from home, cheap too.
C'est si bon, Av Cdte Espinar 663. Excellent cakes by the slice or whole, best in Lima.
Chef's Café, Av Larco 763. Nice place for a sandwich or coffee. Also has a little cart in Parque Kennedy until 2200 with good hot coffee to go.
Dove Vai, Diagonal 228. A bright *heladería* in this block of eating places; try the *encanto* with lumps of chocolate brownie.
Haiti, Av Diagonal 160, Parque Kennedy. Open almost round the clock daily, great for people watching, good ice cream.
La Tiendecita Blanca, Av Larco 111 on Parque Kennedy. One of Miraflores' oldest, expensive, good people-watching, very good cakes, European-style food and delicatessen.
San Antonio, Av Angamos Oeste 1494, also Vasco Núñez de Balboa 770, Rocca de Vergallo 201, Magdalena del Mar and Av Primavera 373, San Borja. Fashionable *pastelería* chain, good, not too expensive.

Barranco *p1275*

TTT Canta Rana, Génova 101, T01-477 8934. Open Sun-Mon 1200-1800, Tue-Sat 1200-2300, good *ceviche* but expensive, small portions. Very popular on Sun.

TTT La Costa Verde, on Barranquito beach, T441 3086. Excellent fish and wine, expensive but recommended as the best by Limeños, open 1200-2400 daily, Sun buffet.

TT El Hornito, Grau 209 (corner of the main plaza), T252 8183. Beautiful pizza and pasta restaurant with covered outdoor seating, romantic under the fairy-lights in the evening. Good quality food and selection of drinks. Recommended.

TT Las Mesitas, Av Grau 341, open 1200-0200. Traditional tea rooms-cum-restaurant, serving creole food and traditional desserts which you won't find anywhere else.

TT-T Iskay, Pedro de Osma N 106, T01-247 2102, iskay@iskayperu.com. Mon-Sat 0900-2300. Cultural café, art gallery and handicrafts, excellent service, well-decorated, daily *menú* US$2.50. Recommended.

Bars and clubs

Lima *p1267, map p1270*

Central Lima

The centre of town, specifically Jr de la Unión, has many discos. It's best to avoid the nightspots around the intersection of Av Tacna, Av Piérola and Av de la Vega. These places are rough and foreigners will receive much unwanted attention.

For latest recommendations for gay and lesbian places, check out www.deambiente.com, www.gayperu.com and http://lima.queercity.info/index.html.

El Rincón Cervecero, Jr de la Unión (Belén) 1045, www.rinconcervecero.com.pe. German pub without the beer, fun.

Estadio Futbol Sports Bar, Av Nicolás de Piérola 926 on the Plaza San Martín, T428 8866. Beautiful bar with a disco, international football theme, good international and creole food.

Piano Bar Munich, Jr de la Unión 1044 (basement). Small and fun.

Yacama Arte & Rock Bar, Jr de la Unión 892, T01-427 7897. Unpretentious rock bar on 2nd floor; serving cheap beer.

Miraflores *p1273, map p1274*

Bartinis, in Larcomar, T241 1299, www.bartini-larcomar.com. Good cocktails, trendy crowd; expensive.

La Tasca, Av Diez Canseco 117, very near Parque Kennedy, part of the **Flying Dog** group and under one of the hostels (see Sleeping, above). Spanish-style bar with cheap beer (for Miraflores). An eclectic crowd including ex-pats, travellers and locals. Gay-friendly. Small and crowded.

Media Naranja, Schell 130, at bottom of Parque Kennedy. Brazilian bar with drinks and food.

The Old Pub, San Ramón 295 (Pizza Street), www.oldpub.com.pe. Cosy, with live music most days.

Treff Pub Aleman, Av Benavides 571-104, T444 0148, www.treff-pub-aleman.com (hidden from the main road behind a cluster of tiny houses signed "Los Duendes"). A wide range of German beers, plus cocktails, good atmosphere, darts and other games.

Voluntarios Pub, Independencia 131, T445 3939, www.voluntariospub.com.pe. All staff are volunteers from non-profit organizations which benefit by receiving 90% of the profits made by the pub. Good atmosphere, music and drinks, nice to know that while you are partying other people are benefiting.

Barranco *p1275*

Barranco is the capital of Lima nightlife. The following is a short list of some of the better bars and clubs. Pasaje Sánchez Carrión, right off the main plaza, and Av Grau, just across the street from the plaza, are lined with bars, eg El Ekeko, Av Grau 266, and Las Terrazas, Av Grau 290. Many of the bars in this area turn into discos later on.

Ayahuasca, San Martín 130. In the stunning Berninzon House from the Republican era, chilled out lounge bar with several areas for eating, drinking and dancing. Food is expensive and portions are small, but go for the atmosphere.

Bosa Nova, Bolognesi 660. Chilled student-style bar with good music.

El Dragón, N de Piérola 168, T797 1033, www.eldragon.com.pe. Popular bar and venue for music, theatre and painting.

El Grill de Costa Verde, part of the *Costa Verde* restaurant on Barranco beach. Young crowd, packed at weekends.
Juanitos, Av Grau, opposite the park. Barranco's oldest bar, and perfect to start the evening.
La Noche, Bolognesi 307, at Pasaje Sánchez Carrión. A Lima institution and high standard, live music, Mon is jazz night, kicks off around 2200.
La Posada del Angel, three branches, two on Pedro de Osma 164-222, T247 0341, and the third at Av Prol San Martín 157, T247 5544. These are popular bars serving snacks and meals, worth a visit for their crazy décor.
La Posada del Mirador, Ermita 104, near the Puente de los Suspiros (Bridge of Sighs). Beautiful view of the ocean, but you pay for the privilege.
Mochileros, Av Pedro de Osma 135. Good pub in a beautiful house, holds events at weekends.
Sargento Pimienta, Bolognesi 755. Live music, always a favourite with Limeños. Opposite is the relaxed **Trinidad**.

Entertainment

Lima *p1267, maps p1268, p1270 and p1274*

Cinemas

The newspaper *El Comercio* lists cinema information in the section called *Luces*. Tue is reduced price at most cinemas. Most films are in English with subtitles and cost US$2 in the centre and around US$4-5 in Miraflores. The best cinema chains in the city are **Cinemark, Cineplanet** and **UVK Multicines**. Some *Cine Clubs* are **Cine Club Miraflores**, Av Larco 770, in the Miraflores Cultural Centre building, T446 2649. **Filmoteca de Lima**, Av 9 de Diciembre 125 (better known as Colón), T331 0126.
Cinematógrafo de Barranco, Pérez Roca 196, Barranco , T264 4374/247 4782. Small independent cinema showing a good choice of classic and new international films.

Peñas

De Cajón, C Merino 2nd block, near 6th block of Av Del Ejército, Miraflores. Good *música negra*.
De Rompe y Raja, Manuel Segura 127, T01-247 3271, www.derompeyraja.pe. Popular, open Thu, Fri, Sat for music, dancing and criolla food.
Del Carajo, Catalino Miranda 158, Barranco, T247 7977, www.delcarajo.com.pe. All types of traditional music.
La Candelaria, Av Bolognesi 292, Barranco, T247 1314, www.lacandelariaperu.com. A good Barranco *peña*, open Fri-Sat 2130 onwards.
La Estación de Barranco, at Pedro de Osma 112, T477 5030, www.laestaciondebarranco.com. Good, family atmosphere, varied shows.
Las Brisas de Titicaca, Pasaje Walkuski 168, at 1st block of Av Brasil near Plaza Bolognesi, T332 1901, www.brisasdeltiticaca.com. A Lima institution.
Sachun, Av del Ejército 657, Miraflores, T441 0123, www.sachunperu.com. Great shows on weekdays as well.

Theatre

Most professional plays are staged at **Teatro Segura**, Jr Huancavelica 265, T427 9491. There are many other theatres in the city, some of which are related to Cultural centres (see below). The press gives details of performances. Theatre and concert tickets booked through Teleticket, T01-610 8888, Mon-Fri 0900-1900, www.e-teleticket.com.

Festivals and events

Lima *p1267, maps p1268, p1270 and p1274*
18 Jan: **Founding of Lima**. **Semana Santa**, or Holy Week, is a colourful spectacle with processions. **28-29 Jul**: is **Independence**, with music and fireworks in the Plaza de Armas on the evening before. **30 Aug**: **Santa Rosa de Lima**. **Oct**: is the month of **Our Lord of the Miracles**; see Las Nazarenas church, above page 1271.

Shopping

Lima *p1267, maps p1268, p1270 and p1274*

Bookshops

Crisol, Ovalo Gutiérrez, Av Santa Cruz 816, San Isidro, T221 1010, Below *Cine Planet*. Large bookshop with café, titles in English, French and Spanish. Also in Jockey Plaza Shopping Center, Av Javier Prado Este 4200, Surco, T436 004.
Epoca, Av Cdte Espinar 864, Miraflores, T241 2951. Great selection of books, mostly in Spanish.
Ibero Librerías, Av Diagonal 500, T01-242 2798, Larco 199, T01-445 5520, and in Larcomar, Miraflores. Stocks Footprint Handbooks as well as a wide range of other titles.

Special Book Services, Av Angamos Oeste 301, Miraflores, T01-241 8490, www.sbs.com.pe. Holds stock of international books in several languages. Has a branch in Larcomar and others around the country.
Virrey chain has a great selection, but few in English: Larcomar Shopping Center (local 210), Miraflores, Pasaje Nicolás de Rivera, Lima centre behind the Municipalidad, T427 5080, and Miguel Dasso 141, San Isidro (next door is **Librería Sur**, No 143).

Camping equipment

It's better to bring all camping and hiking gear from home. Camping gas (the most popular brand is **Doite**, which comes in small blue bottles) is available from any large hardware store or bigger supermarket, about US$3.
Alpamayo, Av Larco 345, Miraflores at Parque Kennedy, T445 1671. Sleeping mats, boots, rock shoes, climbing gear, water filters, tents, backpacks etc, very expensive but top quality equipment. Owner speaks fluent English and offers good information. Open Mon-Fri 1000-1330, 1430-2000, Sat 1000-1400.
Altamira, Arica 880, Parque Damert, behind Wong on Ovalo Gutiérrez, Miraflores, T445 1286. Sleeping bags, climbing gear, hiking gear and tents.
Camping Center, Av Benavides 1620, Miraflores, T242 1779, www.campingperu.com. Selection of tents, backpacks, stoves, camping and climbing gear. Open Mon-Fri 1000-2000, Sat 1000-1400.
El Mundo de las Maletas, Preciados 308, Higuereta-Surco, T449 7850. 0900-2200 daily for suitcase repairs.
Minex, Gral Borgoño 394 y Piura, Miraflores, T445 3923 (ring bell). Quality camping gear for all types of weather, made to order products as well.
Tatoo, CC Larcomar, locs 123-126, T242 1938 and CC Jockey Plaza loc 127, Av Javier Prado 4200, T436 6055, www.tatoo.ws. For top quality imported ranges and own brands of equipment.
Todo Camping, Av Angamos Oeste 350, Miraflores, near Av Arequipa, T447 6279. Sells 100% deet, blue gas canisters, lots of accessories, tents, crampons and backpacks.

Handicrafts

Miraflores is a good place for high quality, expensive handicrafts; there are many shops on and around Av La Paz.
Agua y Tierra, Diez Canseco 298 y Alcanfores, Miraflores, T444 6980. Fine crafts and indigenous art.
Artesanía Santo Domingo, Plaza Santo Domingo, by the church of that name, in Lima centre, T428 9860. Good Peruvian crafts.
Centro Comercial El Alamo, corner of La Paz y Diez Canseco, Miraflores. *Artesanía* shops with good choice.
Cuy Arts & Crafts, Av Larco 1175 and 874, Miraflores, T628 1076, http://cuy-arts.com. Slightly more unusual souvenirs, T-shirts, even Paddington bears.
Kuntur Wasi, Ocharan 182, Miraflores, T444 0557. English-speaking owner very knowledgeable about Peruvian textiles, often has exhibitions of fine folk art and crafts.
La Casa de la Mujer Artesana, Juan Pablo Ferandini 1550 (Av Brasil cuadra 15), Pueblo Libre, T423 8840, www.casadelamujerartesana.com. A cooperative run by the Movimiento Manuela Ramos, excellent quality work mostly from *pueblos jóvenes*, open Mon-Fri 0900-1300, 1400-1700.
Las Pallas, Cajamarca 212, 5th block of Av Grau, Barranco, T477 4629, Mon-Sat 0900-1900. Very high quality handicrafts, English, French and German spoken.
Luz Hecho a Mano, Berlín 399, Miraflores, T446 7098, www.luzhechoamano.com. Lovely hand made handbags, wallets and other leather goods including clothing which last for years and can be custom made.
There are bargains in high quality Pima cotton. Shops selling **alpaca** items include:
Alpaca 859, Av Larco 859, Miraflores. Good quality alpaca and baby alpaca products.
Da Capo, Aramburú 920, dpto 402, San Isidro, T441 0714. Beautiful alpaca scarves and shawls in new designs.
Dédalo, Paseo Sáenz Peña 295, Barranco, T477 0562. A labyrinthine shop selling furniture, jewellery and other items, as good as a gallery. It also has a nice coffee shop and has cinema shows.

Kuna by Alpaca 111, Av Larco 671, Miraflores, T447 1623, www.kuna.com.pe. High quality alpaca, baby alpaca and vicuña items. Also in Larcomar, loc 1-07, Pasaje Nicolás de Rivera El Viejo 125, and Swissôtel, San Isidro.

Jewellery **Ilaria**, Av 2 de Mayo 308, San Isidro, T221 8575. Jewellery and silverware with interesting designs. There are other branches in Lima, Cuzco and Arequipa. Recommended. On Cs La Esperanza and La Paz, Miraflores, dozens of shops offer gold and silverware at reasonable prices.

Silvania Prints, Diéz Canseco 337A, Miraflores. Modern silk-screen prints on Pima cotton with pre-Columbian designs.

Maps

Instituto Geográfico Nacional, Av Aramburú 1190, Surquillo, T618 9800, ext 119, www.ign.gob.pe. Open Mon-Fri 0800-1730. It has topographical maps of the whole country, mostly at 1:100,000, political and physical maps of all departments and satellite and aerial photographs. They also have a new series of tourist maps for trekking, eg of the Cordillera Blanca, the Cuzco area, at 1:250,000. You may be asked to show your passport when buying these maps. **South American Explorers** (see page 1266) also stocks a selection of the most popular maps.

Lima 2000, Av Arequipa 2625, Lince (near the intersection with Av Javier Prado), T440 3486, www.lima2000.com.pe. Open Mon-Fri 0900-1300 and 1400-1800. Has an excellent street map of Lima (the only one worth buying), US$10, or US$14 as booklet. Provincial maps and a country road map as well. Good for road conditions and distances, perfect for driving or cycling. **South American Explorers** (see page 1266) also stocks these maps.

Markets

All are open 7 days a week until late.

Av Petit Thouars, in Miraflores. At blocks 51-54 (near Parque Kennedy, parallel to Av Arequipa). An unnamed crafts market area, usually called **Mercado Inca**, with a large courtyard and lots of small flags. This is the largest crafts arcade in Miraflores. From here to Calle Ricardo Palma the street is lined with crafts markets.

Parque Kennedy, the main park of Miraflores, hosts a daily crafts market from 1700-2300.

Polvos Azules, on García Naranjo, La Victoria, just off Av Grau in the centre of town. The 'official' black market, sells just about anything; it is generally cheap and very interesting; beware pickpockets.

Supermarkets

Supermarket chains include **E Wong**, **Metro**, **Plaza Vea**, **Santa Isabel** and the upmarket **Vivanda**. They are all well stocked and carry a decent supply of imported goods.

▲ Activities and tours

Lima *p1267, maps p1268, p1270 and p1274*

Cycling

Best Internacional, Av Cdte Espinar 320, Miraflores, T446 4044. Open Mon-Sat 1000-1400, 1600-2000. Sells leisure and racing bikes, also repairs, parts and accessories.

BiciCentro, Av Paseo de la República 4986, Miraflores, T475-2645. Bicycle repairs and rentals.

Biclas, Av Conquistadores 641, San Isidro, T440 0890. Open Mon-Fri 1000-1300, 1600-2000, Sat 1000-1300. Knowledgeable staff, tours possible, good selection of bikes, repairs and accessories, cheap airline boxes for sale.

BikeMavil, Av Aviación 4023, Surco, T449 8435. Open Mon-Sat 0930-2100. Rental service, repairs, tours, selection of mountain and racing bikes.

Bike Tours of Lima, Bolívar 150, Miraflores, T445 3172, www.biketoursoflima.com. Offer a variety of day tours through the city of Lima by bike, also bicycle rentals.

Casa Okuyama, Manco Cápac 590, La Victoria, T330 9131. Open Mon-Fri 0900-1300, 1415-1800, Sat 0900-1300. Repairs, parts, try here for 28-in tyres, excellent service.

Cycloturismo Peru, Jr Emilio Fernández 640, Santa Beatriz; T433 7981, www.cicloturismo peru.com. Offers good value cycling trips around Lima and beyond, as well as bike rental. The owner, Aníbal Paredes, speaks good English, is very knowledgeable and is the owner of **Mont Blanc Gran Hotel**.

Perú Bike, Gonzales Prada 331, Miraflores, T260 8225, www.perubike.com. Experienced agency leading tours, professional guiding, mountain bike school and workshop.

Willy Pro (Williams Arce), Av Javier Prado Este 3339, San Borja, T346 4082. Open Mon-Sat 0800-2000. Selection of specialized bikes, helpful staff.

Diving

Peru Divers, Santa Teresa 486, Chorrillos, T251 6231, www.perudivers.com. Open Mon-Fri 0900-1900, Sat 0900-1700. Owner Lucho Rodríguez is a certified PADI instructor who offers certification courses, tours and a wealth of good information.

Horse racing

Hipódromo Monterrico, Tue and Thu evenings (1900) and Sat and Sun (1400) in summer, and in winter on Tue evening and Sat and Sun afternoons. For *Caballos de Paso*, which move in 4- step amble, extravagantly paddling their forelegs, **National Paso Association**, Miraflores, T447 6331, www.anpcpp.org.pe.

Mountaineering

Asociación de Andinismo de la Universidad de Lima, Universidad de Lima, Javier Prado Este s/n, T437 6767. Meetings on Wed 1800-2000, offers climbing courses.

Base Camp Perú, E Diez Canseco 234, Miraflores, www.basecampperu.com. Open climbing gym and climbing excursions.

Club de Montañeros Américo Tordoya, Francisco Graña 378, Magdalena, T460 6101, www.clubamericotordoya.org. Meetings Thu 2000, contact Gonzalo Menacho. Climbing excursions ranging from easy to difficult.

Club de Montañismo Camycam, see www.camycam.org for contact numbers. Expeditions, climbing, trekking, courses, guiding and help with community projects.

Trekking and Backpacking Club, Jr Huáscar 1152, Jesús María, Lima 11, T423 2515, 99-773 1959 (mob), www.angelfire.com/mi2/ tebac. Sr Miguel Chiri Valle, treks arranged, including in the Cordillera Blanca.

Paragliding

Fly Adventure, Alfredo León 234, of 202, Miraflores, T241 5693, 99-754 2011, www.flyadventure.net. US$40 for 15-min tandem flight over the cliffs, 1-day course US$80, 7-day course US$450. Recommended.

Surfing

Focus, Leonardo Da Vinci 208, San Borja, T475 8459. Shaping factory and surf boards, knows about local spots and conditions, rents boards.

Klimax, José González 488, Miraflores, T447 1685. New and second-hand boards, knowledgeable.

To buy Aussie-made boards, all sizes, contact **Segundo**, T99-902 7112, segundodurangarcia@hotmail.com.

Tour operators

Do not conduct business anywhere other than in the agency's office and insist on a written contract.

4 Star Turismo del Peru, Jr Elias Aguires 141, of 313, Miraflores, T719 7792 (USA/Canada T1-888 206 9546, www.4starperu.com). Tours throughout Peru.

Amazing Peru, Calle Ramán Ribeyro 264, Urb San Antonio, Miraflores (9 Alma Rd, Manchester M19 2FG, T0808 2346805), www.amazingperu.com.

Andean Tours, Schell 319 oficina 304-305, Miraflores, T241 1222, www.andean-tours.com. Recommended for bespoke arrangements.

AQP (Travex), Av Santa Cruz 621, Miraflores, T710 3900, www.saaqp.com.pe. Comprehensive service, tours offered throughout the country.

Aracari Travel Consulting, Schell 237, of 602, Miraflores, T651 2424, www.aracari.com. Regional tours throughout Peru, also 'themed' and activity tours, has a very good reputation.

Class Adventure Travel (CAT), San Martin 800, Miraflores, T444 1652, www.classadventure.travel. Dutch-owned and run, one of the best, with 11 years experience of tailor-made travel solutions throughout the continent. Highly recommended.

Coltur, Av Reducto 1255, Miraflores, T615 5555, www.coltur.com.pe. Very helpful, experienced and well-organized tours throughout Peru.

Condor Travel, Armando Blondet 249, San Isidro, T615-3000, www.condortravel.com. Peruvian HQ of highly-regarded, South America-wide travel company, offices in Cuzco, Arequipa, commitment to social responsibility with Misminay Project near Cuzco, and others.

Dasatariq, Jr Francisco Bolognesi 510, Miraflores, T513 4400, www.dasatariq.com. Also in Cuzco. Well-organized, helpful, with a good reputation.

Domiruth Travel Service S.A.C, Jr Rio de Janeiro 216-218, Miraflores, T610 6022, www.domiruth.com.pe. Tours throughout Peru, from the mystical to adventure travel. See also **Peru 4x4 Adventures**, part of Domiruth, T610 6000, www.peru4x4adventures.com, for exclusive 4WD tours with German, English, Spanish, Italian and Portuguese-speaking drivers.

Explorandes, C San Fernando 320, Miraflores, T715 2323, www.explorandes.com. Award-winning company. Offers a wide range of adventure and cultural tours throughout the country. Also offices in Cuzco and Huaraz (see page 1304).

Fertur Peru, C Schell 485, Miraflores, T445 1760, and Jr Junín 211, Plaza de Armas, T427 1958 (USA/Canada T(1) 877-247 0055 toll free, UK T020-3002 3811), www.fertur-travel.com. Open 0900-1900. Siduith Ferrer de Vecchio, CEO of this agency, is highly recommended; she offers up to date, correct tourist information on a national level, but also great prices on national and international flights, discounts for those with ISIC and Youth cards and **South American Explorers** members. Other services include flight reconfirmations, hotel reservations and transfers to and from the airport or bus stations. Also tours.

Il Tucano Peru, Elías Aguirre 633, Miraflores, T444 9361, 24-hr number 01-975 05375. Personalized tours for groups or individuals throughout Peru, also 4WD overland trips, first-class drivers and guides, good service. Recommended.

Info Perú, Jr de la Unión (Belén) 1066, of 102, T431 0117, www.infoperu.com.pe. Mon-Fri 0900-1800, Sat 0930-1400. Run by a group of women, ask for Laura Gómez, offering personalized programmes, hotel bookings, transport, free tourist information, sale of maps, books and souvenirs, English and French spoken.

InkaNatura Travel, Manuel Bañon 461, San Isidro, T440 2022, www.inkanatura.com. Also in Cuzco and Chiclayo, experienced company offering good tours with knowledgeable guides, special emphasis on both sustainable tourism and conservation, especially in Manu and Tambopata,

also birdwatching, and on the archaeology of all of Peru. Very helpful. Recommended.

Lima Tours, Jr Belén 1040, Lima centre, T619 6900, www.limatours. com.pe. Recommended for tours in the capital and around the country.

Masi Travel Sudamérica, Porta 350, Miraflores, T446 9094, www.masitravel.com. Tours throughout Peru, plenty of information on the website. Contact Verónika Reategui for an efficient service.

Peru For Less, ASTA Travel Agent, Luis Garcia Rojas 240, Urb Humboldt, US office: T1-877-269 0309; UK office: T+44-203-002 0571; Peru (Lima) office: T273 2486, Cuzco T084-254800, www.peruforless. com. Will meet or beat any published rates on the internet from outside Peru. Good reports.

Peru Rooms, Av Dos de Mayo 1545 of205, San Isidro, T422 3434, www.perurooms.com. Internet-based travel service offering 3- to 5-star packages throughout Peru, cultural, adventure and nature tourism. Often recommended.

Peru World Travel Tour Agency, C Bolognesi 400, T242 3008, www.peruworldtravel.com.

Rutas del Peru SAC, Av Enrique Palacios 1110, Miraflores, T445 7249, www.rutasdelperu.com. Bespoke trips and overland expeditions in trucks.

Viajes Pacífico (Gray Line), Av La Mar 163, T610 1900, www.graylineperu.com. Expanded service with tours throughout Peru and within South America.

Victor Travel Service, Jr de la Unión (Belén) 1068, T01-433 5547, 9958 3303, www.victortravelservice.com. Tours throughout Peru, hotel, bus and air reservations, free maps of Lima and Peru, Mon-Fri 0830-1930, Sat-Sun 0830-1400, very helpful.

Viracocha, Av Vasco Núñez de Balboa 191, Miraflores, T445 3986, peruviantours@ viracocha.com.pe. Very helpful, especially with flights, adventure, cultural, mystical and birdwatching tours.

Private guides The **MITINCI** (Ministry of Industry Tourism, Integration and International Business) certifies guides and can provide a list. Most are members of **AGOTUR** (Asociación de Guías Oficiales de Turismo), La Venturosa 177, Surco, T448 5167, agoturlima@yahoo.com. Book in advance. Most guides speak a foreign language.

⊖ Transport

Lima *p1267, maps p1268, p1270 and p1274*

Air

Arrivals or departures flight information T511 6055, www.lap.com.pe. **Jorge Chávez Airport**, 16 km from the centre of Lima. At the customs area, explain that you are a tourist and that your personal effects will not be sold in Peru; items such as laptops, cameras, bicycles, climbing equipment are exempt from taxes if they are not to be sold in Peru.

Information desks can be found in the national and international foyers. There is also a helpful desk in the international arrivals hall. It can make hotel and transport reservations. The **Perú Perú** shops sell gifts and books, including some English-language guidebooks. **Global Net ATM** (accepting American Express, Visa, MasterCard and the Plus, Maestro and Cirrus systems), a **Casa de Cambio** (money changing desk) and a bank can be found at the same end as the stairs up to national departures. There are also exchange facilities for cash in the international arrivals hall, but rates are poorer than outside. There are **public telephones** around the airport and a **Telefónica del Peru** *locutorio*, open 0700-2300 daily. Internet facilities are more expensive than in the city. Most of the terminal has free Wi-Fi. There are postal services.

Transport from the airport *Remise* taxis from desks outside International Arrivals and National Arrivals: **Taxi Green**, T484 4001, www.taxigreen.com.pe, US$8 to San Miguel, US$13 to the city centre, US$11.50 to San Isidro, US$15 to Miraflores and Barranco; **Mitsui**, T349 7722, remisse@mitsuiautomotriz.com, US$27 to centre, US$31 to San Isidro and Miraflores, US$36 to Barranco, and **CMV**T422 4838, cmv@ exalmar.com.pe, a little cheaper. There are many taxi drivers offering their services outside Arrivals with similar or higher prices (more at night). The **Bus Super Shuttle**, T517 2556, www.supershuttleairport.com, runs from the airport to San Miguel and the centre, US$15, San Isidro, Miraflores and Barranco for US$19 (prices for 6 people sharing), US$25 for private hire. To get to Miraflores by combi, take the "Callao-Ate" with a big red "S" ("La S"), the only direct link from the airport to Miraflores. Catch it outside of the airport, on Av Faucett, US$0.45. From downtown Lima go to the junction of Alfonso

Ugarte and Av Venezuela where many combis take the route "Todo aeropuerto – Avenida Faucett", US$0.35-0.45. At busy times (anytime other than very late at night or early in the morning) luggage may not be allowed on buses. **Note** Do not take the cheapest, stopping buses to the centre along Av Faucett. They are frequently robbed. Pay more for a non-stop bus. Nor go to the car park exit and find a taxi outside the perimeter. Although much cheaper than those inside, they are not safe.

Bus

Local The bus routes are shared by buses, combis (mid-size) and colectivos (mini-vans or cars); the latter run from 0600-0100, and less frequently through the night, they are quicker and stop wherever requested. Buses and combis charge US$0.35, colectivos a little more. On public holidays, Sun and from 2400 to 0500 every night, a small charge is added to the fare. **Lima centre–Miraflores**: Av Arequipa runs 52 blocks between downtown Lima and Parque Kennedy in Miraflores. There is no shortage of public transport on this avenue; they have 'Todo Arequipa' on the windscreen. When heading towards downtown from Miraflores the window sticker should say 'Wilson/Tacna'. To get to Parque Kennedy from downtown look on the windshield for 'Larco/Schell/ Miraflores', 'Chorrillos/Huaylas' or 'Barranco/Ayacucho'.

Lima centre–Barranco: Lima's only urban freeway, Vía Express, runs from Plaza Grau in the centre of town, to the northern tip of Barranco. This 6-lane thoroughfare, locally known as *El Zanjón* (the Ditch), with a separate bus lane in the middle, is the fastest way to cross the city. In order from Plaza Grau the 8 stops are: 1) **Av México**; 2) **Av Canadá**; 3) **Av Javier Prado**; 4) **Corpac**; 5) **Av Aramburu**; 6) **Av Angamos**; 7) **Av Ricardo Palma**, for Parque Kennedy; 8) **Av Benavides**. Buses downtown for the Vía Expresa can be caught on Av Tacna, Av Wilson (also called Garcilaso de la Vega), Av Bolivia and Av Alfonso Ugarte. These buses, when full, are of great interest to highly skilled pickpockets who sometimes work in groups. If you're standing in the aisle be extra careful.

Long distance There are many different bus companies, but the larger ones are better organized, leave on time and do not wait until the bus is full. For approximate prices, frequency and duration of trip, see destinations. **Note** In the weeks either side of 28/29 Jul (Independence), and of the Christmas/ New Year holiday, it is practically impossible to get bus tickets out of Lima, unless you book in advance. Bus prices double at these times.

Cruz del Sur, Jr Quilca 531, Lima centre, T431 5125, www.cruzdelsur.com.pe. This terminal has routes to many destinations in Peru with *Imperial* service, quite comfortable buses and periodic stops for food and bathroom breaks, a cheap option with a quality company. The other terminal is at Av Javier Prado Este 1109, San Isidro, T225 5748. This terminal offers the *Cruzero* service (luxury buses) and *VIP* service (super luxury buses). The website accepts Visa bookings without surcharge and tickets can be delivered to any address in Lima.

Ormeño and its affiliated bus companies depart from and arrive at Av Carlos Zavala 177, Lima centre, T427 5679; also Av Javier Prado Este 1059, Santa Catalina, T472 1710, www.grupo-ormeno. com.pe. **Ormeño** offers *Royal Class* and *Business Class* service to certain destinations. These buses are very comfortable with bathrooms, hostess, etc. They arrive and depart from the Javier Prado terminal, but *Business* buses stop at both terminals. Javier Prado is the best place to buy any Ormeño ticket.

Other companies include: **Oltursa,** Aramburú 1160, San Isidro, T708 5000, www.oltursa.com.pe. A reputable company offering top end services to **Nazca, Arequipa** and destinations in **northern Peru**, mainly at night. **Tepsa**, Javier Prado Este 1091, La Victoria, T202 3535, www.tepsa.com.pe, also at Av Paseo de la República 151-A, T427 5642 and Av Carlos Izaguirre 1400, Los Olivos, T386 5689 (not far from the airport, good for those short of time for a bus connection after landing in Lima). Services to the north as far as **Tumbes** and the south to **Tacna**.

Transportes Chanchamayo, Av Manco Cápac 1052, La Victoria, T265 6850. To **Tarma, San Ramón** and **La Merced**. **Ittsa**, Paseo de la República 809, T332 1665. Good service to the north, **Chiclayo, Piura, Tumbes**. **Transportes León de Huánuco**, Av 28 de Julio 1520, La Victoria, T424 3893. Daily to **Huánuco, Tingo**

María and **Pucallpa**. **Línea**, José Gálvez 999, Lima Centre, T424 0836, www.transportes linea.com.pe, also has a terminal at Av Carlos Izaguirre 1058, Los Olivos (see above under Tepsa), T522 3295. Among the best services to destinations in the **north**. **Móvil**, Av Paseo de La República 749, Lima Centre near the national stadium, T332 9000 (has a 2nd terminal at Los Olivos), www.moviltours.com.pe, to **Huaraz** and **Chiclayo** by *bus cama*, and Chachapoyas (should you want to go straight through). **Soyuz**, Av México 333, T205 2370, www.soyuz.com.pe. To **Ica** every 7 mins, well-organized. As **PerúBus**, the same company runs north to **Huacho** and **Barranca**, www.perubus.com.pe. **Rodríguez**, Av Roosevelt 393, Lima Centre, T428 0506. **Huaraz, Caraz, Yungay, Carhuaz**. Recommended to arrive in Huaraz and then use local transportation to points beyond. Good. Various levels of bus service. **Vía**, Av N Arriola 539, La Victoria, T719 9185, www.via.com.pe, to **Trujillo** and **Chimbote**.

Bus or colectivo to Pachacámac from Lima: From the Pan American Highway (southbound) take a combi with a sticker in the window reading "Pachacámac/ Lurín" (US$0.85). Let the driver know you want to get off at the ruins. A taxi will cost approximately US$5.50, but if you don't ask the driver to wait for you (an extra cost), finding another to take you back to Lima may be a bit tricky. **Mirabus**, T242 6699, www.mirabusperu.com, goes from Parque Kennedy at 1000 to Pachacámac and back with a stop at Pántanos de Villa wildlife sanctuary, US$19, 3½ hrs tour.

International buses: **Ormeño**, Av Javier Prado 1059, Santa Catalina, T472 1710. To: **Guayaquil** (29 hrs with a change of bus at the border), **Quito** (38 hrs), **Cali** (56 hrs), **Bogotá** (70 hrs), **Caracas** (100 hrs), **Santiago** (54 hrs), **Mendoza** (78 hrs), **Buenos Aires** (90 hrs). A maximum of 20 kg is allowed pp. **Cruz del Sur** also has a service to **Buenos Aires**. **El Rápido**, Av Rivera Navarrete 2650, Lince, T422 9508. Service to Argentina and Uruguay only. **Rutas de América**, Av Paseo de la República 569 y Av 28 Julio, CIVA Terminal, T431 6165, and Av Alfredo Mendiola 1501, T534 3195, www.rutasenbus.com. To Guayaquil, Quito, Cali, Bogotá, Cucutá and Caracas, Tue and Sat. Also has connecting routes to Bolivia, Chile, Argentina and Brazil. Bear in mind that international buses are more expensive than travelling from one border to another on national buses.

Warning The area around the bus terminals is very unsafe; thefts and assaults are more common in this neighbourhood than elsewhere in the city. You are strongly advised either to take a bus from a company which has a terminal away from the Carlos Zavala area (eg Cruz del Sur, Oltursa, Ormeño), or to take a taxi to and from your bus. Make sure your luggage is well guarded and put on the right bus. It is also important not to assume that buses leave from the place where you bought the tickets.

Taxi

The following are taxi fares for some of the more common routes, give or take a sol. From downtown Lima to: Parque Kennedy (Miraflores), US$3-3.50. Museo de la Nación, US$3. South American Explorers, US$3. Archaeology Museum, US$3. Immigration, US$2.15. From Miraflores (Parque Kennedy) to: Museo de la Nación, US$2. Archaeology Museum, US$3. Immigration, US$3, Barranco, US$4. Whatever the size or make, yellow taxis are usually the safest since they have a number, the driver's name and radio contact. A large number of taxis are white, but as driving a taxi in Lima (or for that matter, anywhere in Peru) simply requires a windshield sticker saying "Taxi", they come in all colours and sizes. Licensed and phone taxis are safest and, by law, all taxis must have the vehicle's registration number painted on the side. There are several reliable phone taxi companies, which can be called for immediate service, or booked in advance; prices are 2-3 times more than ordinary taxis; eg to the airport US$11-15, to suburbs US$8-9. Some are **Moli Taxi**, T479 0030; **Taxi Real**, T470 6263, www.taxireal.com; **Taxi Seguro**, T241 9292, www.taxiseguro.com.pe; **Taxi Tata**, T274 5151; **TCAM**, run by Carlos Astacio, T99-983 9305, safe, reliable. If hiring a taxi for over 1 hr agree on price per hr beforehand. Recommended, knowledgeable drivers: **César A Canales N**, T436 6184, T99-687 3310, or through *Home Perú*, only speaks Spanish, reliable. **Hugo Casanova Morella**, T485 7708 (he lives in La Victoria), for city tours, travel to airport, etc. **Mario Salas Pantoja**, T99-908 1888. Very reliable and helpful, airport transfers for US$12 or hourly rate for city tours/museum visits etc. Speaks basic English. **Mónica Velásquez Carlich**, T425 5087, T99-943 0796, vc_monica@ hotmail.com. For airport pick-ups, tours (US$10 per hr, minimum 5 hrs), speaks English, most helpful, frequently recommended. **Note** Drivers don't expect tips; give them small change from the fare.

Train

Details of the service on the Central Railway to Huancayo are given under Huancayo, page 1471.

Directory

Lima *p1267, maps p1268, p1270 and p1274*

Airline offices **Domestic**: LAN, Av José Pardo 513, Miraflores, T213 8200. **LC Busre**, Los Tulipanes 218, San Eugenio-Lince, T619 1300. **Peruvian Airlines**, Av José Pardo 495, Miraflores, T716-6000. **Star Perú**, Av Cdte Espinar 331, Miraflores, T213 8813, Av José Pardo 485, T705 9000. **Taca Perú**, Av Cdte Espinar 331, Miraflores, T511 8222. **International**: **Aerolíneas Argentinas**, Carnaval y Moreyra 370, p 1, San Isidro, T01-513 6565, www.aerolineas.com.ar. **Air France-KLM**, Av Alvarez Calderón 185, p 6, San Isidro, T01-213 0200, Reservations.Peru@ klm.com. **American Airlines**, Las Begonias 471, San Isidro, and Av Pardo 392 y Jr Independencia, T211 7000. **Avianca**, Av José Pardo 140, Miraflores, T01-445 6895, or 0800-51936. **Continental**, Av V A Belaúnde Via Principal 110, Edif Real 5 of 101, San Isidro, and in the Hotel Marriott, Av Larco 1325, Miraflores, T01-712 9230, or 0800-70030. **Copa**, Canaval y Moreyra y Los Halcones, Centro Empresarial Torre Chocavento of 105 , T01-610 0808. **Delta**, Av V A Belaúnde 147 Via Principal 180, Edif Real 3 of 701, San Isidro, T211 9211. **Iberia**, Av Camino Real 390, p 9 of 902, San Isidro, T411 7800. **Lacsa**, Av 2 de Mayo 755, Miraflores, T01-444 7818. **LAN**, see above. **Lufthansa**, Av Jorge Basadre 1330, San Isidro, T442 4455, lhlim@terra.com.pe. **Tame**, Av La Paz 1631, Miraflores, T01-422 6600.

Banks **BCP**, Jr Lampa 499, Lima Centre (main branch), Av Larco at Pasaje Tarata, Miraflores, and others. **Banco de Comercio**, Jr Lampa 560, Lima Centre (main branch), Av José Pardo 272, Miraflores. **BBVA Continental**, corner of Av Larco and Av Benavides and corner of Av Larco and Pasaje Tarata, Miraflores, Jr Cusco 286, Lima Centre near Plaza San Martín. **Banco Financiero**, Av Ricardo Palma 278, near Parque Kennedy (main branch). TCs (Amex), ATM for Visa/Plus. **Banco Santander Central Hispano (BSCH)**, Av Augusto Tamayo 120, San Isidro (main branch), Av Pardo 482 and Av Larco 479, Miraflores. TCs (Visa and Citicorp). ATM for Visa/Plus and Mastercard. **Citibank**, main branch at Av Canaval y Moreyra 480, also Miguel Dasso 121, San Isidro, and in all *Blockbuster* stores, other branches in Miraflores. *Blockbuster* branches open Sat and Sun 1000-1900. **HSBC**, Av Pardo 269, Miraflores, Jr Carabaya 451, Lima. **Interbank**, Jr de la Unión 600, Lima Centre (closed Sat morning), also Av Pardo 413, Av Larco 690 and in Larcomar, Miraflores, Av Grau 300, Barranco, and others including some supermarkets. **Scotiabank**, Av Diagonal 176 on Parque Kennedy, Av José Pardo 697, Miraflores, and others. **Exchange houses** There are many *casas de cambio* on and around Jr Ocoña off the Plaza San Martín. On the corner of Ocoña and Jr Camaná is a large concentration of *cambistas* (street changers) with huge wads of US$, euros and soles in one hand and a calculator in the other. They should be avoided. Changing money on the street should only be done with official street changers wearing an identity card with a photo. This card doesn't *automatically* mean that they are legitimate but you're less likely to have a problem. Around Parque Kennedy and down Av Larco in Miraflores are dozens of official *cambistas* with ID cards and, usually, blue, sometimes green vest. A repeatedly recommended *casa de cambio* is **LAC Dolar**, Jr Camaná 779, 1 block from Plaza San Martín, p 2, T428 8127, also at Av La Paz 211, Miraflores, T242 4069. Open Mon-Sat 0930-1800, good rates, very helpful, safe, fast, reliable, 2% commission on cash and TCs, will come to your hotel if you're in a group. Another recommended *casa de cambio* is **Virgen P Socorro**, Jr Ocoña 184, T428 7748. Open daily 0830-2000, safe, reliable and friendly. **Moneygram**, Ocharan 260, Miraflores, T447 4044. Safe and reliable agency for sending and receiving money. Locations throughout Lima and the provinces. Exchanges most world currencies and TCs. **Car hire** Most companies have an office at the airport, where you can arrange everything and pick up and leave the car. It is recommended to test drive before signing the contract as quality varies. It can be much cheaper to rent a car in a town in the Sierra for a few days than to drive from Lima; also companies don't have a collection service. See page 35 for international rental agencies. Cars can be hired from: **Paz Rent A Car**, Av Diez Canseco 319, of 15, Miraflores, T446 4395, 9993 9853 (mob), pazrent@latin mail.com. Prices range from US$40 to US$60 depending on type of car. **Budget**, T475 1055, www.budgetperu.com. Make sure that your car is in a locked garage at night. **Cultural centres** **Alianza Francesa**, Av Arequipa 4595, Miraflores, T446 5524, www.alianz afrancesalima. edu.pe. Various cultural activities, library. **CCPUCP** (cultural centre of the Universidad Católica), Camino Real 1075, San Isidro, T616 1616, http://cultural.pucp. edu.pe. Excellent theatre (tickets US$7.15), European art films (US$1.45 Mon-Wed), galleries, good café and a bookshop selling art and literature titles. Recommended. **Centro Cultural Peruano Japonés**, Av Gregorio Escobedo 803, Jesús María, T463 0606, postmast@apjp.org.pe. Has a concert hall, cinema, galleries, museum of Japanese immigration, cheap and excellent restaurant, lots of activities. Recommended. **Goethe Institute**, Jr Nazca 722, Jesús María, T433 3180, www.goethe.de. Mon-Fri 0800-2000, library, German papers. **Instituto Cultural Peruano- Norteamericano**, Jr Cusco 446, Lima Centre, T428 3530, with library. Central office at Av Angamos Oeste 120, Miraflores, T242 6300, www.icpna. edu.pe. Theatre productions, modern dance performances etc. Also Spanish lessons; see Language schools, below.

Embassies and consulates **Note** During the summer, most embassies open only in the morning. **Australia**, Av Víctor Andrés Belaúnde 147, Vía Principal 155, Ed Real 3, of 1301, San Isidro, Lima 27, T222 8281, info.peru@ austrade.gov.au. **Austria**, Av República de Colombia 643, p 5, San Isidro, T442 0503, lima-ob@bmeia.gv.at. **Belgian Consulate**, Angamos Oeste 380, Miraflores, T241 7566, www.diplomatie.be/lima. **Bolivian Consulate**, Los Castaños 235, San Isidro, T442 3836, embajada@boliviaenperu.com (0900-1330), 24 hrs for visas (except those requiring clearance from La Paz). **Brazil**, José Pardo 850, Miraflores, T512 0830, www.embajadabrasil.org.pe, Mon-Fri 0930-1300. **Canada**, Libertad 130, Casilla 18-1126, Lima, T444 4015, lima@dfait-maeci.gc.ca. **Chilean Consulate**, Javier Prado Oeste 790, San Isidro, T710 2211, embchile@ mail.cosapidata.com.pe. Open 0900-1300, need appointment. **Ecuadorean Consulate**, Las Palmeras 356, San Isidro (6th block of Av Javier Prado Oeste), T212 4161, embajada@mecuador peru.org.pe. **French Embassy**, Arequipa 3415, San Isidro, T215 8400, www.ambafrance-pe.org. **Germany**, Av Arequipa 4202, Miraflores, T212 5016, emergency number 99-927 8338, www.lima.diplo.de. **Israel**, Natalio Sánchez 125, p 6, Santa Beatriz, T418 0500, http://lima.mfa. gov.il. **Italy**, Av Giusepe Garibaldi 298, Jesús María, T463 2727. **Japan**, Av San Felipe 356, Jesús María, T463 0000. **Netherlands Consulate**, Torre Parque Mar, Av José Larco 1301, p 13, Miraflores, T01-213 9800, info@nlgovlim.com, open Mon-Fri 0900-1200. **New Zealand Consulate**, Los Nogales 510, p 3, San Isidro, T422 7491, alfonsorey1@gmail.com. Open Mon-Fri 0830-1300, 1400-1700. **Spain**, Jorge Basadre 498, San Isidro, T212 5155, open 0900-1300. **Sweden**, C La Santa María 130, San Isidro, T442 8905, konslima@speedy.com.pe. **Switzerland**, Av Salaverry 3240, Magdalena, Lima 17, T264 0305, www.eda.admin.ch/lima. **UK**, Torre Parque Mar, p 22, T617 3000, www.britishembassy.gov.uk/ peru. Open 1300-2130 (Dec-Apr to 1830 Mon and Fri, and Apr-Nov to 1830 Fri), good for security information and newspapers. **USA**, Av Encalada block 17, Surco, T618 2000, for emergencies after hours T434 3032, http://lima.usembassy.gov. The Consulate is in the same building.

Internet Lima is completely inundated with internet cafés, so you will have absolutely no problem finding one regardless of where you are. An hour will cost you S/2-3 (US$0.60-0.90).

Language schools **Conexus**, Av Paseo de la República 3195, of 1002, San Isidro, T421 5642, www.conexusinstitute.com. Reasonably priced and effective. **Hispana**, San Martín 377, Miraflores, T446 3045, www.hispanaidiomas. com. 5-day travellers' programme and other courses, afternoon cultural activities. **Instituto Cultural Peruano- Norteamericano**, see Cultural centres, above. Classes are on Mon-Fri from 0900 to 1100, US$80 per month, no private classes offered. **Instituto de Idiomas (Pontífica Universidad Católica del Perú)**, Av Camino Real 1037, San Isidro, T442 8761. Classes Mon-Fri 1100-1300, private lessons possible. Recommended. **El Sol School of Languages**, Grimaldo del Solar 469, Miraflores, T242 7763, http://elsol.idiomasperu. com. US$20 per hr for private tuition, also small groups. Family homestays and volunteer programmes available. **Independent teachers** (enquire about rates): **Srta Susy Arteaga**, T534 9289, T99-989 7271 (mob), susyarteaga@ hotmail.com, or susyarteaga@yahoo.com. Recommended. **Srta Patty Félix**, T521 2559, patty_fel24@ yahoo.com. **Luis Villanueva**, T247 7054, www.acspanishclasses.com. Flexible, reliable, helpful. **Medical services** (Also worth contacting consulate for recommendations.) **Hospitals: Clínica Anglo Americano**, Av Salazar 3rd block, San Isidro, a few blocks from Ovalo Gutiérrez, T616 8900, www.clinanglo americana.com.pe. Stocks Yellow Fever for US$18 and Tetanus. Dr Luis Manuel Valdez recommended. **Clínica Internacional**, Av Garcilaso de la vega 1421 (main), Jr Washington 1471 y Paseo Colón (9 de Diciembre - emergencies), downtown Lima, T619 6161. Good, clean and professional, consultations up to US$35, no inoculations. **Instituto Médico Lince**, León Velarde 221, near 17th and 18th blocks of Av Arenales, Lince, T471 2238. **Instituto de Medicina Tropical**, Av Honorio Delgado 430 near the Pan American Highway in the Cayetano Heredia Hospital, San Martín de Porres, T482 3903, www.upch.edu.pe/tropicales/. Good for check-ups after jungle travel. Recommended. **Clínica del Niño**, Av Brasil 600 at 1st block of Av 28 de Julio, Breña, T330 0066, www.isn.gob.pe. **Centro Anti-Rabia de Lima**, Jr Austria 1300, Breña, T425 6313. Open Mon-Sat 0830-1830. Consultation is about US$2.50. **Clínica Padre Luis Tezza**, Av El disorders etc, expensive; for stomach or intestinal problems. **Clínica Ricardo Palma**, Av Javier Prado Este 1066, San Isidro, T01-224 2224, www.crp.com.pe. For general medical consultations, English spoken. **Dr José Luis Calderón**, general practitioner recommended. **Backpackers Medical Care**, T99-735 2668, backpackersmc@yahoo.com. The 'backpackers' medic', Dr Jorge Bazán, has been recommended as professional and good value, about US$13 per consultation. **International Health Department**, at Jorge Chávez airport, T517 1845. Open 24 hrs a day for vaccinations. **Pharmacy**: Pharmacy chains are modern, well-stocked, safe and very professional. They can be found throughout the city, often in or next to supermarkets. Some offer 24-hr delivery service. **Post offices** The central post office is on Jr Camaná 195 in the centre of Lima near the Plaza de Armas. Mon-Fri 0730- 1900 and Sat 0730-1600. Poste Restante is in the same building but is considered unreliable. In Miraflores the main post office is on Av Petit Thouars 5201 (same hours). There are many small branches around Lima, but they are less reliable. For express service: EMS, next to central post office in downtown Lima, T533 2020. **Telephones** Easiest to use are the many independent phone offices, *locutorios*, all over the city. They take phone cards, which can be bought in *locutorios*, or in the street nearby. There are payphones all over the city. Some accept coins, some only phone cards and some both. **Useful addresses Tourist Police**, Jr Moore 268, Magdalena at the 38th block of Av Brasil, T460 1060, open daily 24 hrs. For public enquiries, Jr Pachitea at the corner of Belén (Jr de la Unión), Lima, T424 2053. They are friendly and very helpful, English spoken. It is recommended to visit when you have had property stolen. **Immigration:** Av España 734, Breña, open 0800-1300. . Provides new entry stamps if passport is lost or stolen. **Intej**, Av San Martín 240, Barranco, T477 2846. They can extend student cards, change flight itineraries bought with student cards. **National library**, Av Abancay 4th block, with Jr Miró Quesada, T428 7690. Open Mon-Sat 0800-2000, Sun 0830-1330.

Huaraz and the Cordilleras

The spectacular Cordillera Blanca is an area of jewelled lakes and snowy mountain peaks attracting mountaineers and hikers in their thousands. Huaraz is the natural place to head for. It has the best infrastructure and the mountains, lakes and trails are within easy reach. This region, though, also has some sites of great archaeological significance, the most notable of which must be Chavín de Huantar, one of Peru's most important pre-Inca sites. Mining is bringing new prosperity to the area.

Ins and outs

North from Lima the Pan-American Highway parallels the coast. A series of roads climb up to Huaraz, in the Callejón de Huaylas, gateway to Parque Nacional Huascarán. Probably the easiest route to Huaraz is the paved road which branches east off the Pan-American Highway north of Pativilca, 203 km from Lima. The road climbs increasingly steeply to the chilly pass at 4,080 m (Km 120). Shortly after, Laguna **Conococha** comes into view, where the Río Santa rises. A dirt road branches off from Conococha to **Chiquián** (see page 1315) and the **Cordilleras Huayhuash** and **Raura** to the southeast. After crossing a high plateau the main road descends gradually for 47 km until **Catac**, where another road branches east to Chavín and on to the **Callejón de Conchucos** (the eastern side of the Cordillera Blanca). Huaraz is 36 km further on and the road then continues north between the towering Cordillera Negra, snowless and rising to 4,600 m, and the snow-covered Cordillera Blanca. The alternative routes to the Callejón de Huaylas are via the Callán pass from Casma to Huaraz (see page 1319), and from Chimbote to Caraz via the Cañon del Pato (page 1318).

Huaraz → *Phone code: 043. Colour map 3, B2. Population: 80,000. Altitude: 3,091 m.*

The main town in the Cordillera Blanca, 420 km from Lima, Huaraz is expanding rapidly as a major tourist centre, but it is also a busy commercial hub, especially on market days. It is a prime destination for hikers and a Mecca for international climbers.

Ins and outs

Tourist offices iPerú ⓘ *Pasaje Atusparia, of 1, Plaza de Armas, T428812, iperuhuaraz@ promperu. gob.pe, Mon-Sat 0800-1830, Sun 0830-1400.* Also at Jr San Martín cuadra 6 s/n, open daily 0800-1100, and at Anta airport when flights arrive. **Policía de Turismo** ⓘ *on 2nd floor of main iPerú building, T421341 ext 315, Mon-Fri 0900-1300, 1600-1900, Sat 0900-1300*, is the place to report crimes and mistreatment by tour operators, hotels, etc. **Indecopi** ⓘ *Jr José de Sucre 767 y Bolívar, p 2, T423899, jcvela@indecopi.gob.pe*. Huaraz has its share of crime, especially since the arrival of mining and during the high tourist season. Women should not go to surrounding districts and sites alone.

Sights

Huaraz, capital of Ancash department, was almost completely destroyed in the earthquake of May 1970. The Plaza de Armas has been rebuilt, with a towering, white statue of Christ. A new **Cathedral** is still being built. The setting, at the foot of the Cordillera Blanca, is spectacular. The main thoroughfare, Avenida Luzuriaga, is bursting at the seams with travel agencies, climbing equipment hire shops, restaurants, cafés and bars. A good district for those seeking peace and quiet is La Soledad, 6 blocks uphill from the Plaza de Armas on Avenida Sucre. Here, along Sucre as well as Jr Amadeo Figueroa, every second house seems to rent rooms, most without signs. **Museo Arqueológico de Ancash** ⓘ *Instituto Nacional de Cultura, Plaza de Armas, Mon-Sat 0900-1700, Sun 0900-1400, US$1.80,* contains stone monoliths and *huacos* from the Recuay culture, well labelled. The **Sala de Cultura SUNARP** ⓘ *Av Centenario 530, Independencia, T421301, Mon-Fri 1700-2000, Sat 0900-1300, free,* often has interesting art and photography exhibitions by local artists.

About 8 km to the northeast is **Willkawain** ⓘ *US$1.50, take a combi from 13 de Diciembre and Comercio, US$0.55 direct to Willkawain*. The ruins (AD 700-1000, Huari Empire) consist of one large three-storey structure with intact stone roof slabs and several small structures. About 500 m past Willkawain is Ichiwillkawain with several similar but smaller structures. Take a torch if it's late. If walking, go past the Hotel Huascarán. After crossing a small bridge take a second right marked by a blue sign, it is about two hours' uphill walk; ask directions as there are many criss-crossing paths used regularly by local people. North of Huaraz, 6 km along the road to Caraz, are the thermal baths at **Monterrey** (at 2,780 m). ⓘ *The lower pool is US$0.85; the upper pool, which is nicer (closed Mon for cleaning), US$1.35; also individual and family tubs US$1.35 per person for 20 mins; crowded at weekends and holidays*. There are restaurants and hotels (**B-C**). City buses along Av Luzuriaga go as far as Monterrey (US$0.22), until 1900; taxi US$2-3. There is also an alternative road from Willkawain to Monterrey.

Huaraz listings

For Sleeping and Eating price codes and other relevant information, see Essentials, pages 38-40.

Sleeping

Huaraz *p1297, maps p1299 and p1300*
Hotels fill up rapidly during high season (May-Sep), especially during public holidays and special events when prices rise (beware overcharging). Touts meet arriving buses and aggressively "suggest" places to stay; do not be put off your choice of lodging and ring in advance to confirm bookings. Unless otherwise stated, all hotels listed are recommended.

AL Andino Club, Pedro Cochachín 357, some way southeast from the centre (take a taxi after dark), T421662, www.hotelandino.com. Good international standard hotel with restaurant, free internet, safe parking, Swiss run, upper floors have views of Huascarán. New section has suites with sauna, among other details (more expensive).

A Hostal Colomba, Francisco de Zela 278, just off Centenario across the river, T421501, www.huarazhotelcolomba.com. Lovely old hacienda, family-run, garden, safe parking, gym and well-equipped rooms with cable TV, comfortable beds, internet connection.

A-C The Lazy Dog Inn, 30 mins' drive from Huaraz (US$8-10 by taxi), close to the boundary of Huascarán National Park, 3.1 km past the town of Marian, close to the Quebrada Cojup, T943 789330, www.thelazydoginn.com. Eco-tourism lodge actively involved in community projects, water recycling systems and composting toilets. Beautifully designed in warm colours, great location gives access to several mountain valleys. Owners Wayne and Diana can organize horse-riding and hiking trips, excellent home cooking on request.

B El Patio, Av Monterrey, 250 m downhill from the Monterrey baths, T424965, www.elpatio. com.pe. Very colonial-style with lovely gardens, comfortable rooms, some with balconies. Meals on request, bar.

B San Sebastián, Jr Italia 1124, T426960, www.hotelhuaraz.com. Elegant, modern hotel, comfortable beds with duvets, parking available, internet, helpful, buffet breakfast included, good views.

B-D The Way Inn Lodge, at 3,712 m, close to the border of Huascarán National Park, address in town Jr Buenaventura Mendoza 821, T943 466219, www.thewayinn.com. Rooms in bungalows, dorm rooms and camping **F** and **G** respectively; accommodation includes breakfast, other meals available, 60% of vegetables are grown on site. Many activities available, from paragliding to yoga classes and mountain biking.

C Steel Guest House, Alejandro Maguiña 1467 (a fair walk from the centre – take taxi late at night), T429709, www.steelguest.com. Comfortable, excellent view from the roof terrace, small but comfortable rooms with TV, sauna, kitchen for guests, internet access, good value.

D Albergue Churup, Jr Figueroa 1257, T422584, www.churup.com. Price includes breakfast, **F** in dormitory without breakfast, hot water, fire in sitting room on 4th floor, internet (WiFi) access, cafeteria, use of kitchen, sauna and massage room, roof terrace, lots of information, luggage store, laundry, book exchange, English spoken, Spanish classes, extremely helpful.

D Apu Wasi, Jr Federico Sal y Rosas 820, T426 035, h_apuwasi@yahoo.com. Modern but simple, with TV, very comfortable beds, includes a basic breakfast. Discounts for longer stays.

D Hostal Montañero, Plaza Ginebra 30-B, T426 386, www.trekkingperu.com. Includes breakfast, hot water, comfortable, good contact point for quality mountain and trekking guides, climbing equipment rental and sales.

D Olaza Guesthouse, J Argüedas 1242, T422529, www.andeanexplorer.com. Recently upgraded, comfortable rooms, run by Tito Olaza. Safe, stylish, luggage stored, nice terrace with views, breakfast included. Pick up from bus station with room reservation. Downstairs there's an office for **Mountain Bike Adventures** (see below), run by Julio Olaza. They have a second office closer to the centre at Jr Lúcar y Torre 530.

D-E Alojamiento Soledad, Jr Amadeo Figueroa 1267, T421196, www.lodgingsoledad.com. Breakfast, some hard beds, hot water, kitchen, use of internet, family-run, secure, trekking information given. More expensive in high season.

D-E Monte Blanco, José de la Mar 620, T426 384, http://monteblancohotel.com. Very comfortable, good showers, cable TV, helpful staff (no English), good value, breakfast, nice views from roof terrace.

D-E Residencial NG, Pasaje Valenzuela 837, T421831, www.residencialng.com. Breakfast, hot water, TV, good value, helpful, has restaurant.

E Angeles Inn, Av Gamarra 815, T422205, solandperu@yahoo.com. No sign, look for *Sol Andino* travel agency in same building (www.solandino.com), kitchen and laundry facilities, garden, hot water, owners Max and Saul Angeles are official guides, helpful with trekking and climbing, rent equipment.

E Benkawasi, Parque Santa Rosa 928, 10 mins from centre, T423150, www.huarazbenkawasi.com. Doubles, cheaper without breakfast, also rooms for 3, 4 and dorm, hot water, use of kitchen and laundry, games room, pick-up from bus station. Owner Benjamín Morales also has **Xtreme Bar**, **Infinite Adventures** tour operator (Plazuela Belén 1035, T427304, www.infiniteadventures peru.com) and a lodge at Playa Tortugas, near Casma (aranges downhill biking from Huaraz).

E Edward's Inn, Bolognesi 121, T/F422692, www.edwardsinn.com. Cheaper without bath, nice garden, laundry, breakfast extra, insist on proper rates in low season, popular. Edward speaks English and has 30 years' experience trekking, climbing and guiding in the area. He also rents gear.

E La Casa de Zarela, J Arguedas 1263, T421694, www.lacasadezarela.com. Hot water, use of

2 Huaraz centre

Sleeping
1 Cayesh Guesthouse
2 Familia Meza
3 Hostal Gyula
4 Hostal Montañero
5 Hostal Tany
6 Monte Blanco
7 Oscar's Hostal

Eating
1 Café Andino
2 Chifa Jim Hua
3 Chilli Heaven
4 Créperie Patrick
5 El Horno Pizzería Grill
6 El Querubin & Rinconcito Minero
7 Encuentro
8 Las Tulpas y Chimichurri
9 Monte Rosa
10 Piccolo
11 Pizza B & B
12 Pizzería Landauro
13 Sabor Salud

Bars & clubs
14 '13 Buhos' & Makondo's
15 Amadeus
16 Monttrek Disco
17 Taberna Tambo
18 Vagamundo

kitchen, laundry facilities, popular with climbers and trekkers, owner Zarela who speaks English organizes groups and is very knowledgeable.

E-F Hatun Wasi, Jr.Daniel Villayzán 268, T425 055, www.hatunwasi.net. New family-run hotel next to *Jo's place*. Spacious rooms, with hot water, pleasant roof terrace, ideal for breakfasts, with great views of the Cordillera.

F Alojamiento Marilla, Sucre 1123, T428160, alojamaril@latinmail.com. Good views, modern, rooms with and without bath (**G**), also dormitory, hot water, breakfast available, kitchen facilities, luggage store, knowledgeable owners.

F Alojamiento Nemy's, Jr Figueroa 1135, T422949. Secure, hot shower, breakfast US$2.40, good for climbers, luggage store. Recommended. **F Alojamiento Norma**, Pasaje Valenzuela 837, near Plaza Belén, T421831, www.residencialng.com. Includes breakfast, cheaper without bathroom, hot water.

1 Huaraz

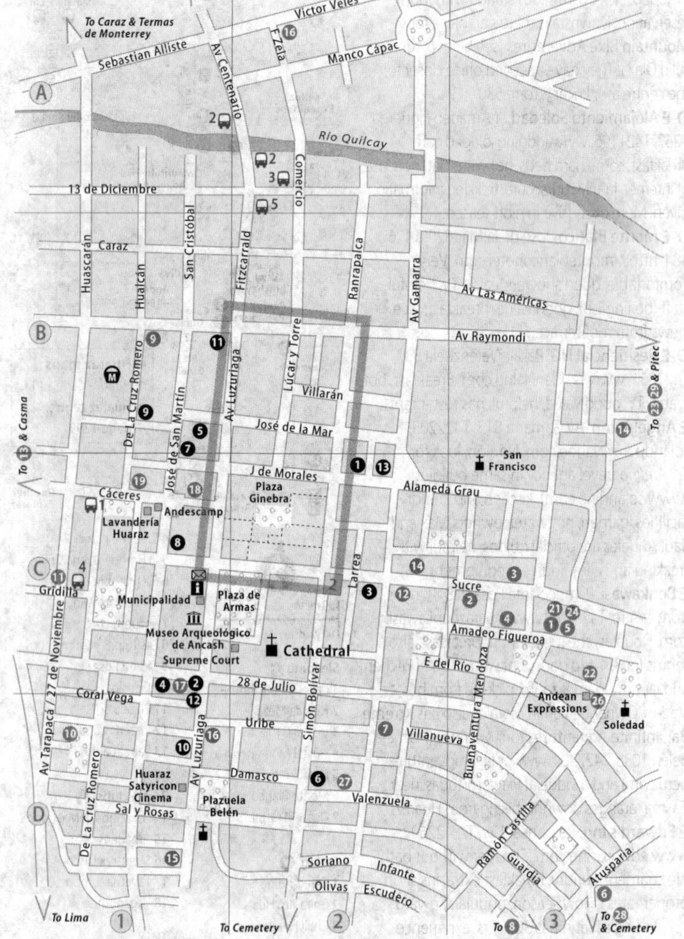

F Familia Meza, Lúcar y Torre 538, T426367, familiameza_lodging@hotmail.com. Shared bath, hot water, use of kitchen, laundry facilities, popular with trekkers, mountaineers and bikers.

F Hostal Estoico, San Martín 635, T422371. Cheaper without bath, safe, hot water, laundry facilities, good value.

F Hostal Gyula, Parque Ginebra 632, opposite the Casa de Guías, T421567, www.madeinhuaraz.com. Hot water, helpful but noisy at weekends, has good information on local tours, stores luggage.

F Hostal Quintana, Mcal Cáceres 411, T426060, www.hostal-quintana.com. Cheaper without bath, hot shower, laundry facilities, basic, stores luggage, popular with trekkers.

F Hostal Tany, Lúcar y Torre 468A, T422534. Cheaper without bath, hot water at night, spotless, money exchange, tours, café/restaurant.

F Jo's Place, Jr Daniel Villayzan 276, T425505, www.josplacehuaraz.com. Safe, hot water at night, nice mountain views, garden, terrace, kitchen facilities, English owner, warm atmosphere, popular.

F La Cabaña, Jr Sucre 1224, T423086, www.huaraz.org/lacabana. Shared and double rooms, hot showers, laundry, kitchen, computer, popular, safe for parking, bikes and luggage, english and French spoken, good value.

F Lodging Caroline, Urb Avitentel Mz D-Lt 1, T422588, carolinelodging@gmail.com, 10 min walk from centre. Price includes breakfast, free pick-up from bus station (phone in advance), hot water, kitchen facilities, tourist information, laundry, very popular, keep valuables secure. If buying a tour here, make it clear in advance what you require and compare prices with those of established operators.

F Lodging Casa Sucre, Sucre 1240, T422264, filibertor@terra.com.pe. Private house, kitchen, laundry facilities, hot water, English, German and French spoken, mountaineering guide, Filiberto Rurush, can be contacted here.

F Oscar's Hostal, La Mar 624, T/F422720, cvmonical@hotmail.com. Hot water, cheap breakfast next door, good beds, cheaper in low season, helpful.

F-G Alojamiento El Jacal, Jr Sucre 1044, T424612, reservaseljacal@yahoo.es. With or without shower, hot water, helpful family, garden, use of kitchen, laundry facilities, luggage store, internet café.

F-G Casa Jansy's, Jr Sucre 948. Hot water, meals, laundry, owner Jesús Rivera Lúcar is a mountain guide.

F-G pp **Cayesh Guesthouse**, Jr Julián de Morales 867, T428821, www.cayesh.net. Comfortable hostel with good location, solar hot water system, kitchen, TV lounge with over 250 DVDs. Owner is an enthusiastic climber and happy to provide advice.

G pp **Backpackers**, Av Raimondi 510, T429101, http://huaraz.com/backpackers. Without breakfast, spacious, hot showers, good views, a real bargain.

N

200 metres

200 yards

Sleeping

1 Albergue Churup *C3*
2 Alojamiento El Jacal *C3*
3 Alojamiento Marilla *C3*
4 Alojamiento Nemy's *C3*
5 Alojamiento Soledad *C3*
6 Andino Club *D3*
7 Angeles Inn *D2*
8 Apu Wasi *D3*
9 Backpackers *B1*
10 Benkawasi *D1*
11 Casa de Jaimes *C1*
12 Casa Jansy's *C2*
13 Edward's Inn *B1*
14 El Patio *B3*
15 Hatun Wasi *A1*
16 Hostal Colomba *A2*
17 Hostal Continental *C1*
18 Hostal Estoico *C1*
19 Hostal Quintana *C1*
20 Jo's Place *A2*
21 La Cabaña *C3*
22 La Casa de Zarela *C3*
23 Lazy Dog Inn *B3*
24 Lodging Casa Sucre *C3*
25 Lodging House Ezama *A3*
26 Olaza Guesthouse *D3*
27 Residencial NG *D2*
28 Steel Guest House *D3*
29 Way Inn Lodge *B3*

Eating

1 Bistro de los Andes *C2*
2 Café El Centro *C1*
3 Cafetería y Jugería *C2*
4 California Café *C1*
5 Fuente de Salud *B1*
6 Huaraz Querido *D2*
7 Las Puyas *B1*
8 Pachamama *C1*
9 Panadería La Alameda *B1*
10 Panadería Montserrat *D1*
11 Pepe's Place *B1*
12 Pizza Bruno *D1*
13 Siam de Los Andes *C2*

Bars & clubs

14 Chacraraju/Chill-Out *C2*
15 La Cascada *D1*
16 Xtreme *D1*

Transport

1 Sandoval Chavín Express *C1*
2 Combis to Caraz *A1, A2*
3 Combis to Wilcawain *A2*
4 Terminal de Transportistas Zona Sur & Trans Rodríguez *C1*
5 Trans Huandoy *A2*

Huaraz maps
1 Huaraz, page 1300
2 Huaraz centre, page 1299

G Casa de Jaimes, Alberto Gridilla 267, T422281, 2 blocks from the main plaza, www.casajaimes. com. Dormitory with hot showers, laundry facilities, has maps and books of the region, use of kitchen, 1 hr free internet use per day. Noisy but otherwise good.

G Hostal Continental, 28 de Julio 586 near Plaza de Armas, T424171. Hot water, cafeteria serving good breakfasts. Good, but avoid rooms on street as there are 2 noisy *peñas* nearby.

G pp **Lodging House Ezama**, Mariano Melgar 623, Independencia, T423490, 15 mins' walk from Plaza de Armas (US$0.50 by taxi). Light, spacious rooms, hot water, safe, helpful.

Eating

Huaraz *p1297, maps p1299 and p1300*

ΨΨΨ Créperie Patrick, Luzuriaga 422. Excellent crepes, fish, quiche, spaghetti and good wine.

ΨΨΨ Monte Rosa, J de la Mar 691, www.huaraz. com/monterosa. Open 1000-2300, pizzería, fondue and other Swiss specialities. Swiss owner is Victorinox representative, offering knives for sale and repair service, also has climbing and trekking books to read, excellent postcards for sale, climbing equipment and vehicles for rent.

ΨΨΨ Pizza Bruno, Luzuriaga 834. Best pizza, excellent crêpes and pastries, good service, open from 1600-2300, French owner Bruno Reviron also has a 4WD with driver for hire.

ΨΨΨ Siam de Los Andes, Gamarra corner J de Morales. Authentic Thai cuisine, good food and atmosphere.

ΨΨ Bistro de los Andes, J de Morales 823 and Plaza de Armas 2nd floor, T/F426249. Great food, owner speaks English, French and German. Plaza branch has a nice view of the plaza. Wide range of dishes including breakfasts.

ΨΨ Chilli Heaven, Parque Ginebra, T396085. Run by a British biker, specializing in spicy food (Mexican, Indian, Thai), book exchange. Recommended.

ΨΨ El Horno, Pizzería Grill, Parque del Periodista, T043-424617. Good atmosphere, fine grilled meats and nice location.

ΨΨ Fuente de Salud, J de la Mar 562. Vegetarian, also meat and pasta dishes, serves good soups and breakfast.

ΨΨ Huaraz Querido, Bolívar 981. Open for lunch only, very popular place for great ceviche and other fish dishes .

ΨΨ Pachamama, San Martín 687. Bar, café and restaurant, concerts, art gallery, garden, nice place to relax, pool table and table-tennis, trekking info, Swiss-owned. Recommended.

ΨΨ Pepe's Place, Raymondi 624. Good pizza, chicken, meat, warm atmosphere.

ΨΨ Piccolo, J de Morales 632. Pizzería, very popular with gringos.

ΨΨ Pizza B&B, La Mar beside laundry of same name. Recommended for its traditional sauces for pizza and pasta, and desserts.

ΨΨ Pizzería Landauro, Sucre, on corner of Plaza de Armas. Very good for pizzas, Italian dishes, sandwiches, breakfasts, nice atmosphere, closed 1200-1800 and Sun.

ΨΨ Rinconcito Minero, J de Morales 757. Swiss-run, breakfast, lunch, vegetarian options, coffee and snacks, also has a video bar.

ΨΨ Sabor Salud, Luzuriaga 672, upstairs. Restaurant and pizzería specializing in vegetarian and Italian food.

ΨΨ-Ψ Chifa Jim Hua, Luzuriaga 645, upstairs. Large, tasty portions, *menú* US$1.15, open Mon-Sat 0900-1500, 1800-2400, Sun 1800-2200.

ΨΨ-Ψ Encuentro, Parque Ginebra, off Luzuriaga cuadra 6. Opens 0700, breakfast, lunch and dinners, very busy, good.

Ψ El Querubín, J de Morales 767. Good breakfast and set meals, also vegetarian, snacks and à la carte.

Ψ Las Puyas, Morales 535. Popular with gringos, good *sopa criolla* and trout, also serves breakfast.

Cafés

Café Andino, Lúcar y Torre 538, cafeandino@ hotmail.com. American-run café and bar, book exchange, extensive lending library in many languages, a nice place to relax, great atmosphere, good meeting place, owner guides treks in Cordilleras Blanca and Huayhuash.

Café El Centro, 28 de Julio 592. Good breakfast for US$1.30-2, great chocolate cake and apple pie.

Cafetería y Juguería, Sucre 806. Cheap café just above the Plaza. Serves excellent yogurt and honey drinks, among other treats.

California Café, 28 de Julio 562, T428354, http://huaylas.com/californiacafe/california.htm. Excellent breakfast, great coffee and chocolate cake, book exchange. Californian owner is a good source of information on trekking in the Cordillera Huayhuash and security issues.

Las Tulpas y Chimichurri, J de Morales 756. Open 0730-2300, nice garden. Good breakfasts and good value lunchtime menu, keen to promote Peruvian cuisine with Western standards of presentation.

Panadería La Alameda, Juan de La Cruz Romero 523 near market. Excellent bread and sweets.

Panadería Montserrat, Av Luzuriaga 928. Good bakery and café, cheap, pleasant atmosphere, good for a snack.

Bars and clubs

Huaraz *p1297, maps p1299 and p1300*

13 Buhos Bar, José de la Mar 2nd floor, above Makondo's. With good music, games, nice atmosphere.

Amadeus, Parque Ginebra. Bar-disco.

Chacraraju/Chill-out Bar, Jr Sucre 959, next of the agency of the same name. Good pizzas, good atmosphere, and, on occasion, a good DJ or two.

La Cascada, Luzuriaga 1276. Disco tavern.

Makondo's, José de la Mar, opposite Cruz del Sur bus station. Bar, nightclub and restaurant, safe, popular.

Monttrek Disco, Sucre just off Plaza de Armas. In converted cinema, reasonable prices.

Taberna Tambo, José de la Mar 776. Folk music daily, disco, open 1000-1600, 2000-early hours, full on, non-stop dance mecca. Very popular with both locals and gringos.

Vagamundo, J de Morales 753. Popular bar with snacks and football tables.

Xtreme, Jr Gabino Uribe, near Luzuriaga, upstairs. Popular with *gringos*, soft music, open 1900-0200.

Entertainment

Huaraz *p1297, maps p1299 and p1300*

Cinema

Huaraz Satyricon, Luzuriaga 1036, T043-955 7343. American-run café and movie theatre, big screen, comfortable sofas. Movies range from 60's classics to cutting edge Latin American, plus occasional showings of *Touching the Void*, the mountaineering classic set and partially shot in the Huayhuash.

Festivals and events

Huaraz *p1297, maps p1299 and p1300*

Patron saints' day, **El Señor de la Soledad**, week starting **3 May**. **Semana del Andinismo**, in **Jun**, international climbing week. **San Juan** and **San Pedro** throughout the region during the last week of **Jun**. **Aug**, **Inkafest mountain film festival**, dates change each year.

Shopping

Huaraz *p1297, maps p1299 and p1300*

Clothing For local sweaters, hats, gloves and wall hangings at good value, Pasaje Mcal Cáceres, off Luzuriaga, in the stalls off Luzuriaga between Morales and Sucre, Bolívar cuadra 6, and else- where. **Andean Expressions**, Jr J Arguedas 1246, near La Soledad church, T422951, www.andeanexpressions.com. Open 0800-2200, run by Lucho, Mauro and Beto Olaza, recommended for hand-printed clothing and gifts. The family also runs the **Andean Explorer** agency and produces a free map-guide of the Huaraz area.

Markets The central market offers a wide variety of canned and dry goods, as well as fresh fruit and vegetables. Beware pickpockets in this area.

Supermarkets **Ortiz**, Luzuriaga 401 corner Raymondi (good selection).

Activities and tours

Huaraz *p1297, maps p1299 and p1300*

Try to get a recommendation from someone who has recently returned from a tour, climb or trek, or see South American Explorers' recommendations in the Lima office. All agencies run conventional tours to Llanganuco (US$12 per person, very long day) and Chavín (8-10 hrs, US$14 per person), entry tickets not included. Many hire equipment.

Horseriding

Sr Robinson Ayala Gride, T423813. Contact him well in advance for half-day trips (enquire at **El Cortijo** restaurant, on Huaraz-Caraz road, Km 6.5). He is a master paso rider.

Posada de Yungar, at Yungar (about 20 km on the Carhuaz road), T421267, 967 9836 (mob). Swiss run. Ask for José Flores or Gustavo Soto. US$4.50 per hr on nice horses; good 4-hr trip in the Cordillera Negra.

Mountain biking

Mountain Bike Adventures, Lúcar y Torre 530, T424259, julio.olaza@terra.com.pe, or www.chakinaniperu.com. Contact Julio Olaza. US$20 for 5 hrs, various routes, excellent standard of equipment. Julio speaks excellent English and also runs a book exchange, sells topo maps and climbing books. Recommended.

Trekking and climbing

Trekking tours cost US$40-70 pp per day, climbing US$90-140 pp per day. Many companies close in low season.

Active Peru, Av Gamarra 699, T423339, 943-553447, www.activeperu.com. Offers the classic treks, climbing, plus the standard tours to Chavín and Llanganuco, among others, good in all respects, Belgian owner speaks Dutch, German and English.

Andean Kingdom, Parque Ginebra next to Casa de Guías , T425555, www.andeankingdom.com. Free information, maps, climbing wall, rock and ice climbing, including multi-day courses, treks, equipment rental, English and some Hebrew spoken, can be very busy. The company is building a lodge near the rock climbing site of Hatun Machay.

Andean Sport Tours, Luzuriaga 571, T421612. Have a basic practice wall behind the office. Also organize mountain bike tours, ski instruction and river rafting.

Andeno Viaggio, Av Luzuriaga 627, T428047, www.andenoviaggio.com. Offers the usual range of day tours (Llanganuco, Chavin) plus trekking and climbing, reputable.

Andescamp, Jr Mcal Cáceres 418, T423325, www.andescamp.com. Popular, especially with budget travellers, qualified climbing guides, a great variety of treks on offer, plus rafting, paragliding and more.

Chacraraju Expeditions, Jr.José de Sucre 959, T426172, www.chacrarajuexpedition.com. Tours and equipment for hire, plus a small climbing wall and the **Chill-out Bar** next door.

Cordillera Blanca Adventures, run by the Mejía Romero family, Los Nogales 108, T421934, www.cordillerablanca.org. Experienced, quality climbing and trekking trips, good guides and equipment.

Explorandes, Av Centenario 489, T421960, postmast@exploran.com.pe.

Galaxia Expeditions, Jr Mariscal Cáceres 428, T425691, galaxia_expeditions@hotmail.com. Reputable agency with the usual range of tours, equipment rental, etc.

Huascarán, Jr Pedro Campos 711, Soledad, T424504, www.huascaran-peru.com. Contact Pablo Tinoco Depaz, one of the brothers who run the company. 4-day Santa Cruz trip recommended. Good food and equipment, professional service, free loan of waterproofs and pisco sour on last evening. Recommended.

Kallpa, José de la Mar y Luzuriaga, p 2, T427868, www.peruviantrek.com. Organizes treks, rents gear, arranges arrieros and mules, very helpful.

Montañero, Parque Ginebra 30-B, T426386, www.trekkingperu.com. Run by veteran mountain guide Selio Villón, German, French and English spoken.

Monttrek, Luzuriaga 646, upstairs, T421124, monttrek@terra.com.pe. Good trekking/ climbing information, advice and maps, run ice and rock climbing courses (at Monterrey), tours to Laguna Churup and the 'spectacular' Luna Llena tour; they also hire mountain bikes, run ski instruction and trips, and river rafting. Helpful, conscientious guides. Next door in the Pizzería is a climbing wall, good maps, videos and slide shows. For new routes and maps contact Porfirio Cacha Macedo, 'Pocho', at Monttrek or at Jr Corongo 307, T423930.

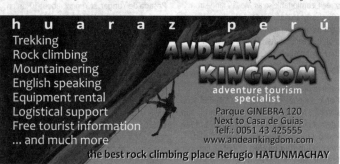

Peruvian Andes Adventures, José Olaya 532, T421864, www.peruvianandes.com, www.perutrekkingclimbing.com. Run by Hisao and Eli Morales, professional, registered

mountain and trekking guides. All equipment and services for treks of 3-15 days, climbing technical and non-technical peaks, or just day walks. Vegetarians catered for.
Quechua Explorer, Jr José de Sucre 705 of 4, T422886, www.quechuaexplorer.com. Hiking, mountaineering, rock and ice climbing, rafting, biking, cultural and ecological tourism, experienced and friendly guides.

Guides

Aritza Monasterio, through *Casa de Guías*. Speaks English, Spanish and Euskerra.
Augusto Ortega, Jr San Martín 1004, T424888, is the only Peruvian to have climbed Everest.
Casa de Guías, Plaza Ginebra 28-g in Huaraz, T421811, casa_de_guias@hotmail.com. Mon-Sat 0900-1300, 1600-1800. This is the climbers' and hikers' meeting place. Has a full list of all members of the Asociación de Guías de Montaña del Perú (AGMP) throughout the country. It is useful with information, books, maps, arrangements for guides, *arrieros*, mules, etc, but as it is no longer not-for-profit, it operates as an agency and sells tours. Notice board, postcards and posters for sale and has a very good restaurant (open 0700-1100, 1700-2300).
Christopher Benway, La Cima Logistics, T421 203, cafeandino@hotmail.com. American, leads treks in the Huayhuash.
Filiberto Rurush Paucar, Sucre 1240, T422264 (*Lodging Casa Sucre*), speaks English, Spanish and Quechua.
Genaro Yanac Olivera, T422825, speaks good English and some German, also a climbing guide.
Hugo Sifuentes Maguiña and his brother **César** (speaks English and a little French), at **Siex** (Sifuentes Expeditions), Av Centenario 687, T426529, www.siex.org.
Koky Castañeda, T421694, or through *La Casa de Zarela* or *Café Andino*. Speaks English and French, AGMP certified.
Max and Saul Angeles, T422205 (*Sol Andino* agency), speak some English, know Huayhuash well.
Ted Alexander, Skyline Adventures, Jr José de San Martín 637, T427097, www.skyline-adventures.com. US outward bound instructor, very knowledgeable.
Tjen Verheye, Jr Carlos Valenzuela 911, T422 569, is Belgian and speaks Dutch, French, German, and reasonable English, runs trekking and conventional tours and is knowledgeable about the Chavín culture.
Vladimiro and Máximo Hinostrosa, Mountain Shop Chacraraju, T943 692395. Trekking guides with knowledge of the entire region.
Prices: The Dirección de Turismo issues qualified guides and *arrieros* (muleteers) with a photo ID. Note down the name and card number in case you should have any complaints. Prices are set at: *arriero*, US$10 per day; donkey or mule, US$6 per day; trekking guides US$40-70 per day (more for foreign guides); climbing guides US$90-140 per day (more for foreign guides), depending on the difficulty of the peak; cooks US$30 per day. You are required to provide or pay for food and shelter for all *arrieros*, porters, cooks and guides. Associations of arrieros: **Humacchuco-Llanganuco** (for porters and cooks), T943-786497, victorcautivo@hotmail.com. **Pashpa Arrieros**, T830540/83319. **Musho Arrieros**, T230003/814416. **Collon Arrieros** (for Llama trekking), T833417/824146.
Camping gear The following agencies are recommended for hiring gear: **Anden Sport Tours**, **Galaxia Expeditions**, **Monttrek**, **Kallpa** and **Montañero**. Also **Skyline**, **Alpandes**, Luzuriaga 557, T424646, and **MountClimb**, Jr Mcal Cáceres 421, T426060, mountclimb@ yahoo.com. **Tatoo**, on Parque Ginebra, T422966, www.tatoo.ws, is good for climbing and outdoor clothes and gear, locally produced and international brands. Casa de Guías rents equipment and sells dried food. Check all camping and climbing equipment very carefully before taking it. Gear is of variable quality and mostly second hand, left behind by others. Also note that some items may not be available, so it's best to bring your own. All prices are standard, but not cheap, throughout town.
All require payment in advance, passport or air ticket as deposit and rarely give any money back if you return gear early. Many trekking agencies sell camping gas cartridges. White gas is available from *ferreterías* on Raymondi below Luzuriaga and by Parque Ginebra. Campers have complained that campsites are dirty, toilet pits foul and that rubbish is not taken away by groups.

Tour operators

Amazing Peru, Jr Sucre 1214 (9 Alma Rd, Manchester M19 2FG, T0808 2346805), www.amazingperu.com.

Chavín Tours, Luzuriaga 502, T421578, F724 801. All local tours, long-standing agency. **Pablo Tours**, Luzuriaga 501, T421142/ 421145. For all local tours, also with many years of operation.

Transport

Huaraz *p1297, maps p1299 and p1300*

Air LC Busre flies daily to/from **Lima**, 1 hr. Office at Av Toribio de Luzuriaga 904, Belén, T424734.

Bus To/from **Lima**: 7-8 hrs, US$7-15. There is a large selection of ordinary service and luxury coaches throughout the day. Many of the companies have their offices along Av Raymondi and on Jr Lúcar y Torre. Some recommended companies are: **Cruz del Sur**, Bolívar Mz C Lote 12, T728726; **Transportes Rodríguez**, Tarapacá y Rodríguez, T421353; **Civa**, Morales opposite Lúcar y Torre; **Móvil**, Av Confraternidad Oeste 4451, T422555 (2 standard and 2 cama services a day); **Empresa 14**, Fitzcarrald 216, T421282, terminal at Bolívar 407.

Other long distance buses: To **Casma** via the Callán pass and Pariacoto (150 km) 7 hrs, US$6, the lower section of the road is very poor, landslides and closures are common (sit on the left for best views): **Transportes Huandoy**, Fitzcarrald 261, T427507 (terminal at Caraz 820), daily at 0800, 1000 and 1300. **Yungay Express**, Raymondi 930, T424377, 3 a day. They continue to Chimbote, 185 km. To Chimbote via Caraz and the Cañon del Pato (sit on the right for the most exciting views) *Yungay Express*, daily, US$7, 10 hrs. Other companies go to **Chimbote** via Pativilca; US$8.30, 7 hrs (to **Pativilca**, 160 km, 4 hrs, US$3.50). Most continue to **Trujillo**, all buses go at night, 8-9 hrs, US$12-20.50: **Chinchaysuyo** (J de Morales 650, T426417), **Línea** (Simón Bolívar 450, T726 666), **Móvil** and **Empresa 14**, addresses above.

Within the Cordillera Blanca: Several buses and frequent minivans run daily, 0500-2000, between Huaraz and **Caraz**, 1¼ hrs, US$1.50, from the parking area under the bridge on Fitzcarrald and from the open space beside the bridge on the other side of the river (beware of thieves here). To **Chavín**, 110 km, 2 hrs (sit on left side for best views), US$3: **Sandoval/Chavín Express**, Mcal Cáceres 338, T424652, 3 a day. Also **Trans Río Mosna**, Mcal Cáceres 265, T426632, 3 a day, US$3.30; both have buses that go on to Huari, 4 hrs, US$4.10. **Renzo**, Raymondi 821, T425371, runs to Carhuaz, Chacas and San Luis (5½ hrs) at 0600, 1400, 2000, continuing to Yanama, Piscobamba and Pomabamba. **Los Andes**, same office as Yungay Express, T427362, goes daily at 0630 to Yungay, US$0.75, Lagunas de Llanganuco, US$3.45, Yanama, US$3.45, Piscobamba, US$5.20 and Pomabamba, US$6 (8 hrs). Also to **Pomabamba** via Yungay, Lakes Llanganuco and Yanama, **La Perla de Alta Mayo**, 0630, 8 hrs, US$6. To **Sihuas**, **Sandoval/Chavín Express**, Tue and Fri 0800, and **Perú Andino**, 8 hrs, US$8. Colectivos to **Recuay**, US$0.45, and **Catac**, US$0.55, leave daily at 0500-2100, from Gridilla, just off Tarapacá (Terminal de Transportistas Zona Sur). To **Chiquián** for the Cordillera Huayhuash (see below). To **Huallanca** (Huánuco), the route now taken is the paved road through Conococha, Chiquián, Aquia to Huansala, then by dirt road to Huallanca and La Unión (paving began in 2008). Departs Huaraz twice a day, first at 1300, with **Trans El Rápido**, Bolognesi 216, T043-422887, US$4.80. There are regular colectivos from Huallanca to La Unión from the corner of Comercio y 28 de Julio, 1 hr, US$0.75.

Taxi Standard fare in town is about US$0.60, US$0.70 at night; radio taxis T421482 or 422512.

Directory

Huaraz *p1297, maps p1299 and p*

Banks BCP, on Plaza de Armas, closed 1300-1630. **Interbank**, on Plaza de Armas. **Scotiabank**, Sucre 766. **Casa de Cambio**: **Oh Na Nay**, opposite *Interbank*, cash only, good rates. Street changers and *casas de cambio* on Luzuriaga (be careful). **Internet** There are internet places everywhere, US$0.30 per hr on average. **Sayuri**, Bolívar 683. As well as internet, has digital photo services and international phone calls. Cafés usually offer videophones, scanning, CD burning and printing services. **Post offices** Serpost, Luzuriaga 702, open Mon-Sat 0800-2000. **Telephones** **Telefónica**, Sucre y Bolívar, Plaza de Armas, national and international phone and fax, open 0700-2300 daily. Many calling centres on Luzuriaga.

Cordillera Blanca

Apart from the range of Andes running along the Chile-Argentina border, the highest mountains in South America lie along the Cordillera Blanca and are perfectly visible from many spots. From Huaraz alone, you can see more than 23 peaks of over 5,000 m, of which the most notable is Huascarán (6,768 m), the highest mountain in Peru. Although the snowline is receding, the Cordillera Blanca still contains the largest concentration of glaciers found in the world's tropical zone and the turquoise-coloured lakes, which form in the terminal moraines, are the jewels of the Andes. Here also is one of Peru's most important pre-Inca sites, at Chavín de Huantar.

Parque Nacional Huascarán

Established in July 1975, the park includes the entire Cordillera Blanca above 4,000 m, with an area of 3,400 sq km. It is a UNESCO World Biosphere Reserve and part of the World Heritage Trust. The park's objectives are to protect the flora, fauna, geology, archaeological sites and scenic beauty of the Cordillera. Take all your rubbish away with you when camping. The park office charges visitors US$1.65 for a day visit. For visits of up to seven days (ie for trekking and climbing trips) a permit costing US$22 (65 soles) must be bought. If you stay longer than seven days, you will need another permit. Fees for visiting the national park are collected at rangers posts at Llanganuco and Huascarán (for the Llanganuco to Santa Cruz trek), and at Collón on the way up the Quebrada Ishinca. The park office ⓘ *Jr Federico Sal y Rosas 555, by Plazuela Belén, T722086, pnh@terra.com.pe; Mon-Fri 0830-1300, 1430-1700*, is principally administrative.

INRENA has implemented new regulations governing the Huascarán national park. Local guides are mandatory for everywhere except designated 'Recreation Zones' (areas accessible by car). Tourists must hire a licensed tour operator for all activities and those operators may only employ licensed guides, cooks, *arrieros* and porters. Anyone wishing to trek, climb or ski in Huascarán should seek advice from INRENA or a local tour operator.

Trekking and climbing in the Cordillera Blanca

The Cordillera Blanca offers popular backpacking and trekking, with a network of trails used by the local people and some less well-defined mountaineers' routes. Most circuits can be hiked in five days. Although the trails are easily followed, they are rugged with high passes, between 4,000 and 5,000 m, so backpackers should be fit and acclimatized to the altitude, and carry all equipment. Essential items are a tent, warm sleeping bag, stove, and protection against wind and rain (the weather is unreliable and you cannot rule out rain and hail storms even in the dry season). Less stamina is required if you hire mules to carry equipment. The season is from May to September, although conditions vary from year to year. The rainy season in Huaraz is December-March.

Advice to climbers The height of the Cordillera Blanca and the Callejón de Huaylas ranges and their location in the tropics create conditions different from the Alps or even the Himalayas. Fierce sun makes the mountain snow porous and glaciers move more rapidly. Deglaciation is rapidly changing the face of the Cordillera. Older maps do not provide a reliable indication of the extent of glaciers and snow fields (according to some studies 15% of the range's glaciers have disappeared since the 1970s), so local experience is important. If the new INRENA rules preventing independent treks or climbs have not been instigated (see above), move in groups of four or more, reporting to the Casa de Guías (see also above) or the office of the guide before departing, giving the date at which a search should begin, and leaving your embassy's telephone number, with money for the call. International recommendations are for a 300 m per day maximum altitude gain. Be wary of agencies wanting to sell you trips with very fast ascents (but ask around if this is what you want). The **Unidad de Salvamento de Alta Montaña** (USAM) ⓘ *Calles Inés de Salas y Jaime Gonzales, Yungay, T043-793333/793327, usam@pnp.gob.pe*, has a rescue team with 24-hour phone service and vhf/uhf radio dispatch. They have a helicopter and trained search-and-rescue dogs. At present, they will rescue anyone – climbers, trekkers, tourists – without asking for cash up front. Insured climbers will be billed, but rescues for the uninsured are currently free. This policy is likely to change. USAM will only take the injured person as far as Caraz or Huaraz hospitals, from where additional costly medical evacuation may be required. It therefore remains imperative that all climbers carry adequate insurance (it cannot be purchased locally). Be well prepared before setting out on a climb. Wait or cancel your trip when the weather is bad. Every year climbers are killed through failing to take weather conditions seriously. Climb only when and where you have sufficient experience.

Note Before heading out on any route, always enquire locally about public safety. The Cordillera Blanca is generally safe, but muggings have taken place on the way to Laguna Churup, to the Mirador Rataquena above Huaraz, the Mirador above Monterrey, and at Wilkawain. On all treks in this area, respect the locals' property, leave no rubbish behind, do not give sweets or money to children who beg and remember your cooking utensils and tent would be very expensive for a *campesino*, so be sensitive and responsible.

Huaraz to Chavín ➔ *For Guides and prices, see Huaraz listings, page 1304.*

South of Huaraz is **Olleros** (*Altitude: 3,450 m*). The spectacular and relatively easy three to four-day hike to Chavín, along a pre-Columbian trail, starts from Olleros. Some basic meals and food supplies available. At 38 km via the main road from Huaraz is **Catac** (two basic hotels and a restaurant), where a paved road branches east for Chavín. About 7 km south of Catac on the main road is **Pachacoto** from where a road goes to **Huallanca** (Huánuco) on the other side of the Cordillera Blanca (133 km, 4½ hours). Buses to Huallanca do not take this route, but the paved road via Chiquián.

A good place to see the impressive Puya Raimondi plants is the Pumapampa valley. A 14 km gravel road from Pachacoto goes to the park entrance (4,200 m), where there is a park office. You can spend the night here. Walking up the road from this point, you will see the gigantic plants, whose flower spike, which can reach 12 m in height, takes 100 years to develop. The final flowering (usually in May) is a spectacular sight. (This is the route to Pastoruri, a popular tour from Huaraz, until its closure in 2008.) Another good spot, and less visited, is the **Queshque Gorge**. Follow the Río Queshque from Catac (see above); it's easy to find.

From Catac to Chavín is a magnificent journey. The road passes Lago Querococha, has good views of the Yanamarey peaks and, at the top of the route, is cut through a huge rock face, entering the Cahuish tunnel at 4,550 m. (The tunnel has no light and is single lane; a small stream runs inside. Cyclists must have a strong light so that trucks and buses can see them.) On the other side it descends the Tambillo valley, then the Río Mosna gorge before Chavín.

Chavín de Huantar

ⓘ *Tue-Sun 0800-1700, US$3, US$5 for a group with Spanish-speaking guide (many at the entrance).* Chavín de Huantar, a fortress temple, was built about 800 BC. It is the only large structure remaining of the Chavín culture which, in its heyday, is thought to have held influence in a region between Cajamarca and Chiclayo in the north to Ayacucho and Ica in the south. In December 1985, UNESCO designated Chavín a World Heritage Trust Site. The site is in good condition despite the effects of time and nature. The main attractions are the marvellous carved stone heads and designs in relief of symbolic figures and the many tunnels and culverts which form an extensive labyrinth throughout the interior of the pyramidal structure. The carvings are in excellent condition, though many of the best sculptures are in Huaraz and Lima. The famous Lanzón dagger-shaped stone monolith of 800 BC is found inside one of the temple tunnels. In order to protect the site some areas are closed to visitors. All the galleries open to the public have electric lights. The guard is also a guide and gives excellent explanations of the ruins. The main **museum** ⓘ *1 km north of the town on the road to San Marcos, closed Mon, US$3.75* has a comprehensive collection of items not exhibited before, gathered from several deposits and museums.

In high season, the site is busy with tourists all day through. You will receive an information leaflet in Spanish at the entrance.

The town of Chavín ➔ *Altitude: 3,140 m.*
Just north of the ruins, Chavín, painted colonial yellow and white, has a pleasant plaza with palm and pine trees. Several good, simple hotels and restaurants have benefitted recently from the influence of the nearby mines. The streets are now paved and mobile phone signals reach here, but not as yet anywhere to change money. Local *fiesta* July 13-20.

Chavín to Pomabamba ➔ *225 km in total, gravel road, parts rough.*
From Chavín one circuit by road back to Huaraz is via Huari, San Luis, Yanama and Yungay (see page 1311) but the bus service is infrequent. The road north from Chavín descends into the Mosna river canyon. The scenery is quite different from the other side of the Cordillera Blanca, very dry and hot. After 8 km it reaches **San Marcos**, a small, friendly town with a nice plaza and a few basic restaurants and *hostales*. Further on 32 km is **Huari**, perched on a hillside at 3,150 m, with various basic hotels (**F**) and restaurants. *Fiesta* of *Nuestra Señora del Rosario* first two weeks of October, main day 7th.

There is a spectacular **two-three days' walk** from Huari to Chacas via Laguna Purhuay. Alberto Cafferata of Caraz writes: "The Purhuay area is beautiful. It has splendid campsites, trout, exotic birds and, at its north end, a 'quenoal' forest with orchids. This is a microclimate at 3,500 m, where the animals, insects and flowers are more like a tropical jungle, fantastic for ecologists and photographers." A day walk to Laguna Purhuay is possible for those who don't want the longer walk to Chacas, but this does not allow time to walk above the lake. A new road has been built to the lake where there are kayaks and boat rides.

In **Chacas**, 10 km south of San Luis by a new road, is a fine church. The local *fiesta* (Virgen de la Asunción) is on 15 August, with bullfights, a famous *carrera de cintas* and fireworks. Seek out the Taller Don Bosco, a woodcarving workshop run by an Italian priest. There are hostels (**E**), shops, good restaurants and a small market.

It is a three-day hike from Chacas to Marcará via the Quebradas Juytush and Honda (lots of condors to be seen). The Quebrada Honda is known as the Paraíso de las Cascadas because it contains at least seven waterfalls. From Huari the road climbs to the Huachacocha pass at 4,350 m and descends to **San Luis** at 3,130 m, 60 km from Huari (**E Hostal Puñuri**, Ramón Castilla 151, T043-830408, swith bath and hot water, a few basic restaurants, shops and a market).

Some 20 km north of San Luis, a road branches left to **Yanama**, 45 km from San Luis, at 3,400 m. It has a recommended hotel, **Andes Lodge Peru**, T043-943 847423, www.andeslodgeperu.com (**B-Ds**, full board available, excellent food and services, fabulous views). The village retains many traditional features and is beautifully surrounded by snow-capped peaks. A day's hike to the ruins above the town affords superb views.

A longer circuit to Huaraz can be made by continuing from San Luis 62 km to **Piscobamba**. There is a basic, but clean and friendly hotel, and one other, both **G**; also a few shops and small restaurants. Beyond Piscobamba by 22 km, is **Pomabamba**, worth a visit for some very hot natural springs (the furthest are the hottest). There are various hotels (**F-G**) near the plaza and restaurants.

Several good walks into the Cordillera Blanca start from near Pomabamba, some day walks, others of several days, eg: via Palo Seco or Laurel to the Lagunas Safuna. From there you can go on to Nevado Alpamayo, dubbed 'the most beautiful mountain in the world'. The glacier of Alpamayo is an incredible sight. From there, continue down to Santa Cruz and Caraz.

From Pomabamba a dusty road runs up the wooded valley crossing the puna at Palo Seco, 23 km. The road then descends steeply into the desert-like Sihuas valley, passing through the village of Sicsibamba. The valley is crossed half an hour below the small town of **Sihuas**, a major connection point between the Callejón de Conchucos, Callejón de Huaylas, the upper Marañón and the coast. It has a few **F-G** hotels and places to eat. From Sihuas it is possible to travel, via Huancaspata, Tayabamba, Retamas and Chahual to Huamachuco along a road which is very poor in places and involves crossing the Río Marañón twice. A bridge over the river means that it is now possible to travel from Cuzco to Quito through the Andes entirely by public transport. This journey is best undertaken in this direction though the road may be almost impassable in the wet season.

Caraz → *Altitude: 2,290 m. Colour map 3, B2.*

This pleasant town is a good centre for walking, parasailing and the access point for many excellent treks and climbs. Tourist facilities are expanding as a more tranquil alternative to Huaraz, and there are great views of Huandoy and Huascarán as well as the northern Cordilleras in July and August. In other months, the mountains are often shrouded in cloud. Caraz has a milder climate than Huaraz and is more suited to day trips. The ruins of **Tunshukaiko** are 1 km from the Plaza de Armas in the suburb of Cruz Viva, to the north before the turn-off for Parón. There are seven platforms from the Huaraz culture, dating from around 2000-1800 BC. The tourist office, at Plaza de Armas, in the municipality, T391029, has limited information. On 20 January is the fiesta *Virgen de Chiquinquirá*. In the last week of July is *Semana Turística*.

Treks from Caraz

A good day hike with good views of the Cordillera Blanca is to **Pueblo Libre** (about four hours round trip, or you can take a colectivo back to Caraz). A longer day walk of six to seven hours in total with excellent views of Huandoy and Huascarán follows the foothills of the Cordillera Blanca, from Caraz south. It ends at Puente Ancash on the Caraz-Yungay road, from where transport goes back to Caraz.

A large stand of **Puya Raimondi** can be seen in the Cordillera Negra west of Caraz. Beyond Pueblo Libre the road which continues via Pamparomas and Moro joins the coastal highway between Casma and Chimbote. After 45 km (two hours) are the Puya Raymondi plants at a place called **Winchos**, with views of 145 km of the Cordillera Blanca and to the Pacific. The plants are usually in flower May or October. Take warm clothing, food and water. You can also camp near the puyas and return the following day. The most popular way to get there is to rent a bike (US$15/day), go up by public transport (see below), and ride back down in 4-5 hours. Or form a group (eg via the bulletin board at Pony's Expeditions, Caraz) and hire a car which will wait for you (US$50 for 8, including guide). From Caraz, a combi for Pamparomas leaves from Grau y Ugarte between 0800 and 0900, US$2, two hours. From the pass (El Paso) or El Cruce it is a short walk to the plants. Return transport leaves between 1230 and 1300. If you miss the bus, you can walk back to Pueblo Libre in four hours, to Caraz in 6-8 hours, but it is easy to get lost and there are not many people to ask directions along the way.

Laguna Parón From Caraz a narrow, rough road goes east 32 km to beautiful Laguna Parón ⓘ *US$3.50*, in a cirque surrounded by several, massive snow-capped peaks, including Huandoy, Pirámide Garcilazo and Caraz. The gorge leading to it is spectacular. It is a long day's trek for acclimatized hikers (25 km) up to the lake at 4,150 m, or a 4-5 hour walk from the village of Parón, which can be reached by combi. Camping is possible.

Santa Cruz Valley One of the finest treks in the area is the 4-5 days route over the path from the Santa Cruz valley, by Mount Huascarán to the Lagunas de Llanganuco (described below). The most popular way to do this famous hike starts at Cashapampa in the Santa Cruz valley (see Transport below). It takes four to five days over the pass of Punta Unión, 4,750 m, to Vaquería or the Llanganuco lakes. Many recommend this 'anticlockwise' route as the climb is gentler, giving more time to acclimatize, and the pass is easier to find. You can hire an *arriero* and mule in Cashapampa, prices given in Listings, Activities and tours, see page 1313. Campsites are at Llamacorral and Taullipampa before Punta Unión, and Quenoapampa (or Cachina Pampa) after the pass. You can end the hike at Vaquería on the Yanama-Yungay road, or, a day later with a night at the Paccha Pampa campsite, at the Llanganuco lakes, from where cars go back to Yungay.

Yungay → *Colour map 3, B2.*
The main road goes on 12 km south of Caraz to Yungay which was completely buried during the 1970 earthquake by a massive mudslide; a hideous tragedy in which 20,000 people lost their lives. The earthquake and its aftermath are remembered by many residents of the Callejón de Huaylas. The original site of Yungay, known as Yungay Viejo, desolate and haunting, has been consecrated as a *camposanto* (cemetery). The new settlement is on a hillside just north of the old town, and is growing gradually. It has a pleasant plaza and a concrete market, good on Wednesday and Sunday. October 17 is the *Virgen del Rosario* fiesta and October 28 is the anniversary of the founding of the town. The tourist office is on the corner of the Plaza de Armas.

Lagunas de Llanganuco
The Lagunas de Llanganuco are two lakes nestling 1,000 m below the snowline beneath Huascarán and Huandoy. The first you come to is Laguna Chinancocha (3,850 m), the second Laguna Orconcocha (3,863 m). The park office is situated below the lakes at 3,200 m, 19 km from Yungay. Accommodation is provided for trekkers who want to start the Llanganuco-Santa Cruz trek from here, US$2 per person. From the park office to the lakes takes about five hours (a steep climb). For the last 1½ hours, a nature trail, Sendero María Josefa (sign on the road), takes 1½ hours to walk to the western end of Chinancocha where there is a control post, descriptive trail and boat trips on the lake. Walk along the road beside the lake to its far end for peace and quiet among the quenoal trees, which provide shelter for 75% of the birdlife found in the park

Carhuaz → *Colour map 3, B2.*
After Yungay, the main road goes to **Mancos** (8 km south, 30 minutes) at the foot of Huascarán. There is a dormitory at *La Casita de mi Abuela*, some basic shops and restaurants. From Mancos it is 14 km to Carhuaz, a friendly, quiet mountain town with a pleasant plaza. There is very good walking in the neighbourhood (eg to thermal baths; up the Ulta valley). Market days are Wednesday and Sunday (the latter is much larger). The local fiesta of *Virgen de las Mercedes*, 14-24 September, is rated as among the best in the region.

Cordillera Blanca listings

For Sleeping and Eating price codes and other relevant information, see Essentials, pages 38-40.

Sleeping

Huaraz to Chavin: Olleros *p1308*
D Altas Montañas, Av Puyhuan s/n, T422569, www.altasmontanas.com/index9.htm. Small 3-star lodge, Belgian- run, with hot showers, good breakfast included, dinner available, bar, birdwatching, guided treks, information, laundry, recommended for start or end of trek, phone 24 hrs in advance, preferably at 2000, to arrange free pick-up from Huaraz.

Chavín *p1309*
D Ri'kay, on 17 de Enero 172N, T454027, www.hotelrickay.com. Set around 2 patios, modern, best in town, TV, hot water, restaurant does Italian food in the evening. Recommended.
E Inca, Wiracocha 170, T454021, www.huaraz.com/hotelinca. In a renovated house, cheaper without bath, good beds, hot water on request, nice garden.
E La Casona, Wiracocha 130, Plaza de Armas, T454116, lacasonachavin@peru.com. In a renovated house with attractive courtyard, cheaper without bath, insufficient hot water, 1 double room, motorcycle parking.
F Hostal Chavín, Jr San Martín 141-151, half a block from the plaza, T/F454055. Pleasant courtyard, hot water, will provide breakfast for groups, best of the more basic hotels but beds are poor.
Camping Inside park gates at archaeological site for vehicles, ask for permission.

Caraz *p1310*

AL-C O'Pal Inn, Pativilca/Caraz Km 265.5, T043-391015, www.opalsierraresort.com. Scenic, bungalows and rooms, swimming pool. Recommended.

D Chamanna, Av Nueva Victoria 185, 25 mins walk from centre, T943 595343 (mob), www.chamanna.com. Cabañas in beautiful garden, hot water, secure, excellent French and international cuisine if reserved in advance, German run. Recommended.

D-F Los Pinos, Parque San Martín 103, 5 blocks west of plaza, T391130, lospinos@apuaventura.com. Rooms with and without bath, hot water, comfortable and airy, garden open to all travellers, camping US$2.50, use of internet US$0.50 per hr, use of kitchen US$3, laundry service, safe, book exchange, information and travel agency Apu-Aventura. Breakfast and dinner are available, bar with movies every night. Recommended.

E Caraz Dulzura, Sáenz Peña 212, about 10 blocks from the city centre, T391523, hostalcarazdulzura@hotmail.com. Modern building in an old street, hot water, cheaper without bath and TV, comfortable, great service, airy rooms, breakfast extra. Recommended.

E La Alameda, Av Noé Bazán Peralta 262, T391177, jtorres@viabcp. com.pe. Comfortable rooms, hot water, breakfast, parking, gardens. Recommended.

E La Perla de los Andes, Plaza de Armas 179, T/F392007. Comfortable rooms, hot water, TV, helpful, average restaurant, has a large new annex 1 block up San Martín.

F Chavín, San Martín 1135 just off the plaza, T391171, hostalchavin@hotmail.com. Warm water, good service but a bit grubby, breakfast extra, guiding service, tourist info.

F Regina, Los Olivos s/n y Gálvez, at the south end of town, 1 block west of road to Yungay, T391520. Modern, hot water, good value.

G Alojamiento Caballero, D Villar 485, T391637, or ask at *Pony's Expeditions* on the plaza. Shared bath, hot water, laundry facilities, stores luggage, basic, family run.

G Hostal La Casona, Raymondi 319, 1 block east from the plaza, T391334. Cheaper without bath, hot water, lovely little patio.

Yungay *p1311*

D Complejo Turístico Yungay (COMTURY), Prolongación 2 de Mayo 1019, 2.5 km south of the new town, 700 m east of main road in Aura, the only neighbourhood of old Yungay that survived, T788656, http://comtury.com. Nice bungalows, pleasant country setting, hot water, fireplace, restaurant with regional specialities, camping possible.

F Hostal Gledel, Av Arias Graziani, north past plaza, T393048, rugamboa@viabcp.com. Owned by Sra Gamboa, who is hospitable and a good cook, shared bath, hottish water, no towels or soap, cheap meals prepared on request, nice courtyard.

F Hostal Sol de Oro, Santo Domingo 07, T393 116. With bath, hot water, comfortable, good value, best in town.

G Hostal Mery, 28 de julio s/n. Hot water, simple but OK, rooms at front noisy.

Lagunas de Llanganuco *p1311*

AL-D Llanganuco Lodge, Lago Keushu, Llanganuco Valley, close to Huascarán park entrance (booking office in Huaraz: Gamarra 699), T943 672849, www.llanganucolodge.com. Room price depends on type of room and season, dorms (**E** pp), modern, camping area, meals extra, excellent food in restaurant, helpful staff, fine views and limitless possibilities for trekking (equipment rental and logistics), British-owned.

Carhuaz *p1311*

B-C El Abuelo, Jr 9 de Diciembre y Tumbes, T394149, www.elabuelohostal.com. Modern, comfortable but overpriced, café, parking, ask at *Heladería El Abuelo* on main plaza.

C pp **Casa de Pocha**, 1 km out of town towards Hualcán, at foot of Nevado Hualcán, ask directions in town, T943 613058 (mob, 1800-2000), www.socialwellbeing.org/lacasadepocha.htm. Including breakfast and dinner, country setting, entirely solar and wind energy powered, hot water, sauna and pool, home-produced food (vegetarian available), horses for hire, camping possible, many languages spoken. Recommended. Book in advance.

F Hostal Señor de Luren, Buin 549, 30 m from Plaza de Armas. Hot water, TV, safe motorcycle parking, very hospitable. **F** four family run *hospedajes* have been built as part of a community development project. All have private bath and hot water. The better 2 are: **Hospedaje Robri**, Jr Comercio 935, T394505. Modern. **Alojamiento Las Torresitas**, Jr Amazonas 603, T394213.

G Hostal La Merced, Ucayali 724, T394241 (Lima 442 3201). Hot water (usually), "like going back to the 1950s", luggage store.

Eating

Chavín *p1309*

TT-T Chavín Turístico, middle of 17 de Enero. The best in town, good *menú* and à la carte, delicious apple pie, nice courtyard, internet.

TT-T La Portada, towards south end of 17 de Enero. In an old house with tables set around a pleasant garden. Recommended.

T La Ramada, towards north end of main street, 17 de Enero. Regional dishes, also trout and set lunch.

Caraz *p1310*

TT-T La Punta Grande, D Villar 595, 10 mins' walk from centre. Best place for local dishes, closes 1700.

T Esmeralda, Av Alfonso Ugarte 404. Good set meal, breakfast. Recommended.

T Heladería Caraz Dulzura, D Villar on the plaza. Excellent home made ice cream, good value meals, pastries.

T Jeny, Daniel Villar on the plaza. Good food at reasonable prices.

Cafés

Café de Rat, Sucre 1266, above *Pony's Expeditions*. Serves breakfast, vegetarian dishes, pizzas, drinks and snacks, darts, travel books, nice atmosphere. Recommended.

El Turista, San Martín 1117. Open in morning and evening only. Small, popular for breakfast, ham omelettes and ham sandwiches are specialities.

Panificadora La Alameda, D Villar y San Martín. Very good bread and pastries, ice cream, popular with locals. Also **Establo La Alameda**, D Villar 420. Excellent *manjar blanco* (they let you try it first), cakes and sweets.

Yungay *p1311*

TT Alpamayo, Av Arias Graziani s/n. At north entrance to town, good for local dishes, lunchtime only.

T Café Pilar, on the main plaza. Good for juices, cakes and snacks.

Carhuaz *p1311*

TT El Abuelo, Plaza de Armas. International and local food , produce from own garden including all natural ice cream.

TT La Bicharra, just north of Carhuaz on main road, T943 780893 (mob). Innovative North African/ Peruvian cooking, lunch only, busy at weekends, call ahead to check if they are open on weekdays.

Bars and clubs

Caraz *p1310*

Taberna Disco Huandy, Mcal Cáceres 119. Good atmosphere.

Shopping

Caraz *p1310*

Camping supplies Fresh food in the market. Some dried camping food is available from **Pony's Expeditions**, who also sell camping gaz canisters and white gas.

Activities and tours

Caraz *p1310*

Agencies in Caraz arrange treks in the Cordillera Huayhuash, as well as more local destinations.

Apu-Aventura, at **Hotel Los Pinos** (see above), www.apuaventura.com. Offer all sorts of adventure sports and equipment rental.

Pony's Expeditions, Sucre 1266, near the Plaza de Armas, T/F391642, www.ponyexpeditions.com. Mon-Sat 0800-2200, English, French and Quechua spoken. Owners Alberto and Aidé Cafferata are knowledgeable about treks and climbs. They arrange local tours, trekking and transport (US$30 for up to 4 people) for day excursions, maps and books for sale, also equipment for hire, mountain bike rental (US$15 for a full day); agents for Cruz del Sur buses and LC Busre flights. Visa cards accepted. Highly recommended.

Mariano Araya, ask at the municipality. He is a trekking guide who is also keen on photography and archaeology.

Transport

Chavín *p1309*

Bus It is much easier to get to Chavín (even walking!) than to leave the place by bus. All buses to **Huaraz** originate in Huari or beyond. They pass through Chavín at irregular hours and may not have seats available. Buying a ticket at an agency in Chavín does not guarantee you will get a seat or even a bus. For buses from **Huaraz**, see under Huaraz. **Sandoval/Chavín Express** goes through around 1200, 1600 and 1700 daily, **Río Mosna** at 0430 and then 4 between 1600-2200. Bus to Huaraz takes 2 hrs, US$3-3.30. To **Lima**: 438 km, 12 hrs, US$9, with **Trans El Solitario** and **Perú Andino** daily. Locals prefer to travel to Huaraz and then take one of the better companies from there.

To other destinations in the Callejón de Conchucos, either use buses coming from Huaraz or Lima, or hop on and off combis which run between each town. To **San Marcos**, 8 km, and **Huari**, 38 km, take one of the combis which leave regularly from the main plaza in Chavín, 20 mins and 30 mins respectively. There are buses during the day from Lima and Huaraz which go on to **Huari**, with some going on to **San Luis**, a further 61 km, 3 hrs; **Piscobamba**, a further 62 km, 3 hrs; and **Pomabamba**, a further 22 km, 1 hr; such as **El Solitario** which passes through Chavín at 1800. Gasoline is available at north end of Chavín.

Chavín to Pomabamba *p1309*

Huari

Bus Terminal Terrestre at Av Circunvalación Baja. To **Huaraz**, 4 hrs, US$4.10, **Sandoval/Chavín Express** 3 a day. Services also to **San Luis** and **Lima**.

Yanama

Bus Daily between **Yungay** and Yanama over the 4,767 m Portachuelo de Llanganuco (3 hrs, US$4.50), continuing to Pomabamba.

Pomabamba

To **Piscobamba**, combis depart hourly, 1 hr, US$1.20. There are no combis from Piscobamba to San Luis. To **Lima**, 18 hrs, US$11, via San Luis (4 hrs, US$3), Huari (6 hrs, US$4.50) and Chavín (9 hrs, US$6) with **El Solitario** Sun, Mon and Thu at 0800; via **Yungay** and **Huaraz** with **La Perla del Alto Mayo**, Wed, Thu, Sat, Sun, 16 hrs, US$11.

Sihuas

Bus To **Pomabamba**, combi from Av 28 de Julio near the market at 1100, 4 hrs, US$3.80 (returns 0200). To **Huaraz**, via Huallanca, with **Cielo Azul**, daily at 0830, 10 hrs, US$8. To **Tayabamba**, for the Marañón route north to Huamachuco and Cajamarca: **Andía** passes through from Lima on Sat and Sun at 0100, **La Perla del Alta Mayo** passes through Tue, Thu 0000-0200; also **Garrincha** Wed, Sun around 0800; all 8 hrs, US$8, the beginning of a long wild ride. To **Huacrachuco**, **Andía**, passes through Wed, Sat 0100. To **Chimbote**, **Corvival** on Wed, Thu and Sun morning, 9 hrs, US$6.50; **La Perla del Alta Mayo** Tue, Thu, Sun, US$9. To **Lima** (19 hrs, US$14.50) via Chimbote, **Andía** Tue, Sun 0200, Wed, Sat 1600; and 3 other companies once or twice a week each.

Caraz *p1310*

Bus From Caraz to **Lima**, 470 km, 5 companies on D Villar and Jr Córdova, daily, US$7 (**El Huaralino**, **Expreso Ancash**, T391509, **Móvil**, **Rodríguez**, T391184), 10-11 hrs. All go via Huaraz and Pativilca. To **Chimbote**, **Yungay Express** (D Villar 318), via Huallanca and Cañon del Pato 0830 every day, US$6.60, 8 hrs. Sit on right for best views. To **Trujillo**, via Huaraz and Pativilca, **Chinchaysuyo** (Córdova 830, T791930), 1845 daily, US$9.10, 11-12 hrs, stops in Casma (US$7.60) and Chimbote (US$7.60). To **Huaraz**, combis leave 0400-2000, 1¼ hrs, US$1.35. They leave from a terminal on the way out of town, where the south end of C Sucre meets the highway. To **Yungay**, 12 km, 15 mins, US$0.30. To **Huallanca** (for the Cañon del Pato), combis and cars leave from Córdova y La Mar, 0700-1730, US$1.50.

Treks from Caraz *p1310*

Laguna Parón

To the village of **Parón** pickups from Santa Cruz y Grau by the market, Mon to Sat 0400 and 1300, Sun 0300 and 1300, 1 hr, US$1.30. They return from Parón at 0600 and 1400. From **Caraz**, colectivos go to the lake if there are enough passengers and only in the dry season, US$3-4 pp. **Pony's Expeditions** have a pool of well-trained drivers who make daily departures to Laguna Parón at 0800, US$30 for 4, including 1-hr visit to the lake and 1-hr walk downhill to the bridge, where diver will pick up the group (extra hours at US$3). Also, you can hire a bike (US$15 per day), take a car up (US$6 with 4 passengers) and ride back down.

Santa Cruz Valley
To **Cashapampa** (Quebrada Santa Cruz) buses from Santa Cruz y Grau, Caraz, hourly from 0830 to 1530, 2 hrs, US$1.50. Yanama to Yungay combis can be caught at Vaquería between 0800-1400, US$3, 3 hrs.

Yungay *p1311*
Buses and colectivos run the whole day to **Caraz**, 12 km, US$0.30, and **Huaraz**, 54 km, 1½ hrs, US$1. To lakes **Llanganuco**, combis leave when full, especially 0700-0900, from Av 28 de Julio 1 block from the plaza, 1 hr, US$1.50. To **Yanama**, via the Portachuelo de Llanganuco Pass, 4,767m, 58 km, 3½ hrs, US$3; stopping at María Huayta (for the Llanganuco-Santa Cruz trek), after 2 hrs, US$2. To **Pomabamba**, via Piscobamba, **Trans Los Andes**, daily at 0800, the only company with a ticket office in Yungay; **Transvir** and **La Perla de Alta Mayo** buses coming from Huaraz, 0730, stop if they have room, 6-7 hrs, US$6. After passing the Llanganuco lakes and crossing the Portachuelo the buses descend to Puente Llacma, where it is possible to pick up buses and combis heading south to San Luis, Chacas and Huari.

Carhuaz *p1311*
All transport leaves from the main Plaza. To **Huaraz**, colectivos and buses leave 0500-2000, US$0.75, 40 mins. To **Caraz**, 0500-2000, US$0.75, 1 hr. There are **trucks** (only 1 or 2 a day) and 1 minivan (0800) going up the Ulta valley to **Chacas** (see page 1309), 87 km, 4-5 hrs, US$4.50. The road works its way up the Ulta valley to the pass at Punta Olímpica from where there are excellent views. The dirt road is not in a very good condition owing to landslides every year (in the wet season it can be closed). **Renzo** daily buses pass through en route to **San Luis** (see page 1309), a further 10 km, 1½ hrs.

Directory

Chavín *p1309*
Internet Librería Aquariu's, 17 de Enero y Túpac Yupanqui, US$1 per hr. **Post offices** 17 de Enero 365N; open 0630-2200. **Telephones** Payphones all over town.

Chavín to Pomabamba *p1309*
Internet and telephones Best in Huari.

Caraz *p1310*
Banks BCP, D Villar 217, ATM for Visa, Mastercard and AmEx. **Importaciones América**, Sucre 721, T391479, good rates and service, open weekends and evenings. **Internet** Many places around the Plaza and throughout town, US$0.30. **Post offices** San Martín 909. **Telephones** National and international phone and fax at Raymondi y Sucre. Also several others, eg at Sucre y Santa Cruz, and on Plaza de Armas next to *Jeny*. No collect calls can be made except from private lines. Very few of the coin boxes take phone cards.

Cordillera Huayhuash

The Cordillera Huayhuash, lying south of the Cordillera Blanca, has azure trout-filled lakes interwoven with deep quebradas and high pastures around the hem of the range and is perhaps the most spectacular cordillera for its massive ice faces that seem to rise sheer out of the Puna's contrasting green. You may see tropical parakeets in the bottom of the gorges and condors circling the peaks. The complete circuit is very tough; allow 10-12 days. Trekkers have to pay US$70 per person at the Huascarán national park office in Huaraz, of which some goes to the local communities in a bid to improve safety for tourists. The trail head is at **Cuartel Huain**, between Matacancha and the **Punta Cacanan** pass (the continental divide at 4,700 m). There are up to eight passes over 4,600 m, depending on the route. A half-circuit is also possible, but there are many other options. Both ranges are approached from Chiquián in the north, **Oyón**, with links to Cerro de Pasco to the southeast, **Churín** in the south or Cajatambo to the southwest. The area offers fantastic scenery and insights into rural life.

Chiquián is a town of narrow streets and overhanging eaves. *Semana Turística*: first week of July. Buy all your food and supplies in Huaraz as there are only basic supplies in Chiquián and almost nothing in the hamlets along the route. **Mule hire** It may take a day to bring the mules to your starting point from Llamac or Pocpa where they are kept. (Very basic supplies only can be bought in either village.) Ask for mules (US$4-5 per day) or horses (US$7 per day) at the hotels or restaurants in Chiquián. A guide for the Huayhuash is **Sr Delao Callupe**, ask for him in Chiquián.

Cajatambo is the southern approach to the Cordillera Huayhuash, a small market town with a beautiful 18th-century church and a lovely plaza. There are various hotels (**G**) and some good restaurants around the plaza. Note that the road out of Cajatambo is not for the fainthearted. For the first 3-4 hours it is no more than a bus-width, clinging to the cliff edge.

Cordillera Huayhuash listings

For Sleeping and Eating price codes and other relevant information, see Essentials, pages 38-40.

Sleeping

Cordillera Huayhuash *p1315*

E Gran Hotel Huayhuash, 28 de Julio 400, Chiquián, T447049, www.hotelhuayhuash.com. Private bathroom, hot water, TV, restaurant, laundry, parking, modern, great views, information and tours.

F Hostal San Miguel, Jr Comercio 233, Chiquián, T447020. Nice courtyard and garden, clean, many rooms, popular.

G pp **Los Nogales de Chiquián**, Jr Comercio 1301, T447121 (in Lima T460 8037), hotel_nogales_chiquian@yahoo.com. Cheaper without bath, hot water, cable TV, cafeteria, parking. Recommended.

Eating

Cordillera Huayhuash *p1315*

¶ El Refugio de Bolognesi and **Yerupajá**, on Tarapacá, both offer basic set meals.

¶ Panificadora Santa Rosa, Comercio 900, on the plaza, Chiquián, for good bread and sweets, has coin-operated phones and fax.

Transport

Cordillera Huayhuash *p1315*

Coming from Huaraz, the road is now paved beyond Chiquián to Huansala, on the road to Huallanca (Huánuco). Two bus companies run from **Huaraz to Chiquián**, 120 km, 3½ hrs: **El Rápido**, at Bolognesi 216, T422887, at 1345, and **Chiquián Tours**, on Tarapacá behind the market. From Chiquián to Huaraz: buses leave the plaza at 0500 daily, US$1.75, except **El Rápido**, Jr Figueredo 216, T447049, at 0500 and 1330, US$3.65. Also colectivo Chiquián-Huaraz 1500, 3 hrs, US$2.45 pp. There is also a connection from Chiquián to Huallanca (Huánuco) with buses coming up from Lima in the early morning and combis during the day, which leave when full, 3 hrs, US$2.50. From Huallanca there are regular combis on to La Unión, 1 hr, US$0.75, and from there transport to Huánuco. From Cajatambo buses depart for **Lima** at 0600, US$8.80, daily with **Empresa Andina** (office on plaza next to Hostal Cajatambo), **Tour Bello**, 1 block off the Plaza, and **Turismo Cajatambo**, Jr Grau 120 (in Lima, Av Carlos Zavala 124 corner of Miguel Aljovin 449, T426 7238).

North coast

The north of Peru has been described as the Egypt of South America, as it is home to many ruined pre-Inca treasures. Many tourists pass through without stopping on their way to or from Ecuador, missing out on one of the most fascinating parts of the country. Along a seemingly endless stretch of desert coast lie many of the country's most important pre-Inca sites: Chan-Chán, the Moche pyramids, Túcume, Sipán, Batán Grande and El Brujo. The main city is Trujillo, while Chiclayo is more down-to-earth, with one of the country's largest witchdoctors' market. The coast is also famous for its deep-sea fishing, surfing, and the unique reed fishing boats at Huanchaco and Pimentel. Inland lies colonial Cajamarca, scene of Atahualpa's last stand. Further east, where the Andes meet the jungle, countless unexplored ancient ruins await the more adventurous traveller.

North of Lima

The Pan-American Highway is four-lane (several tolls, about US$2) to Km 101, by **Huacho**, which is by-passed, 19 km east of **Puerto Huacho** (several hotels in Huacho, and good restaurants, eg Cevichería El Clásico, C Inca s/n, open 1000-1800; **La Estrella**, Av 28 de Julio 561). The beaches south of the town are clean and deserted. The journey inland from Huacho, up the Huaura valley, is splendid. Beyond Sayán the road follows the Huaura valley which narrows almost to a gorge before climbing steeply to **Churín**, with hot, sulphurous springs which are used to cure a number of ailments, and various hotels and restaurants. The climate is dry: temperatures range from 10° to 32°C. The area is famous for cheese, yoghurt and other natural products. Other hot springs nearby are **Huancahuasi**, **Picoy** (both good) and **Chiuchín** (neglected).

Caral and Paramonga → *Phone code: 01.*

A few kilometres before Barranca (by-passed by the Highway) a turning to the right (east) at Km 184 leads to **Caral** ⓘ *0900-1700; all visitors must be accompanied by an official guide, US$7 per group, in the car park is the ticket office, toilets, handicrafts stalls; for details, Proyecto Especial Caral, Av Las Lomas de la Molina 327, Urb Las Lomas, Lima 12, T205 2500 ext 517, www.caralperu.Gob.pe, UNESCO World Heritage Site*. This ancient city, 26 km from the coast, dates from about 2600 BC. Many of the accepted theories of Peruvian archaeology have been overturned by Caral's age and monumental construction. It appears to be easily the oldest city in South America. The dry, desert site lies on the southern fringes of the Supe valley, along whose flanks there are more ruins, 19 out of 32 of which have been explored. Caral covers 66 ha and contains eight significant pyramidal structures. To date seven have been excavated by archaeologists from the University of San Marcos, Lima. They are undertaking careful restoration on the existing foundations to re-establish the pyramidal tiers. It is possible to walk around the pyramids. A viewpoint provides a panorama across the whole site. The site is well organized, criss-crossed by marked paths which must be adhered to. Allow at least two hours to visit the site. You can stay or scamp at the **Casa del Arqueólogo**. See Listings for tours and transport.

Some 4 km beyond the turn-off to Huaraz, beside the Panamericana, are the well preserved ruins of the Chimú temple of **Paramonga** ⓘ *US$1.70; caretaker may act as guide.* Set on high ground with a view of the ocean, the fortress-like mound is reinforced by eight quadrangular walls rising in tiers to the top of the hill.

Casma and Sechín → *Phone code: 043. Colour map 3, B2. Population: 22,600.*

Casma has a pleasant Plaza de Armas, several parks and two markets including a good food market. It is a base from where to explore **Sechín** ⓘ *www.xanga.com/sechin, the site is open daily 0800-1800, photography best around midday, US$1.70 (children and students half price); ticket also valid for the Max Uhle Museum by the ruins and Pañamarca, an archaeological site in the*

Nepeña Valley, north of Casma. Frequent colectivos leave from in front of the market in Casma, US$0.50 pp, or motorcycle taxi US$1, one of the most important ruins 5 km away on the Peruvian coast. It consists of a large square temple completely faced with about 500 carved stone monoliths narrating, it is thought, a gruesome battle in graphic detail. The style is unique in Peru for its naturalistic vigour. The complex as a whole is associated with the pre-Chavín Sechín culture, dating from about 1600 BC. Three sides of the large stone temple have been excavated and restored, but you cannot see the earlier adobe buildings inside the stone walls because they were covered up and used as a base for a second storey, which has been completely destroyed.

Chimbote → *Phone code: 043. Colour map 3, B2. Population: 296,600.*

The port of Chimbote serves the national fishing industry and the smell of the fishmeal plants is overpowering. As well as being unpleasant it is also unsafe. Take extensive precautions, always use taxis from the bus station to your hotel and don't venture far from the hotel. **Note** The main street, Avenida Víctor Raul Haya de la Torre, is also known by its old name, José Pardo. At weekends boat trips go around the bay to visit the cliffs and islands to see the birdlife and rock formations.

Chimbote to Callejón de Huaylas

Just north of Chimbote, a road branches northeast off the Pan-American Highway and goes up the Santa valley following the route of the old Santa Corporation Railway which used to run as far as **Huallanca** (Ancash – not to be confused with the town southeast of Huaraz), 140 km up the valley. At Chuquicara, three hours from Chimbote (paved – very rough thereafter), is Restaurante Rosales, a good place to stop for a meal (you can sleep here, too, but it's very basic). At Huallanca there are also places to stay and eat. Fuel is available. At the top of the valley by the hydroelectric centre, the road goes through the very narrow and spectacular **Cañon del Pato**. You pass under tremendous walls of bare rock and through almost 40 tunnels, but the flow of the river has been greatly reduced by the hydroelectric scheme. After this point the road is paved to the Callejón de Huaylas and the road south to Caraz and Huaraz.

An alternative road for cyclists (and vehicles with a permit) is the 50-km private road known as the 'Brasileños', used by the Brazilian company Odebrecht which has built a water channel for the Chavimochic irrigation scheme from the Río Santa to the coast. The turn-off is 35 km north of the Santa turning, 15 km south of the bridge in Chao, on the Pan-American Highway at Km 482. It is a good all-weather road via Tanguche. Permits are obtainable from the Chavimochic HQ at San José de Virú, US$6.50, or from the guard at the gate on Sunday.

North of Lima listings

For Sleeping and Eating price codes and other relevant information, see Essentials, pages 38-40.

Sleeping

Casma and Sechín *p1317*

D Hostal El Farol, Túpac Amaru 450, T711064, hostalfaro@yahoo.com. Very nice, cheaper in low season, hot water, swimming pool, pleasant garden, good restaurant, parking, information.

E Las Dunas, Luis Ormeño 505, T/F711057. An upgraded and enlarged family home, friendly.

E-F Hostal Celene Ormeño 595, T711065. Large pleasant rooms.

F Gregori, Luis Ormeño 530, T711073. Cheaper without bath, café downstairs.

F Monte Carlo, Nepeña 370, T711421. TV, internet, laundry, good value.

F Rebeca, Huarmey 377, T711258. Modern, hot water only at night, good.

Chimbote *p1318*

Plenty of hotels, so try to negotiate a lower rate.

B Cantón, Bolognesi 498, T344388. Modern, higher quality than others, has a good but pricey chifa restaurant.

C Ivansino Inn, Haya de la Torre 738, T321811, ivansino@hotmail.com. Including breakfast, comfortable, modern.

D D'Carlo, Villavicencio 376, on the plaza, T/F321047. Friendly, TV, mini-bar, restaurant.

D San Felipe, Haya de la Torre 514, T323401. Hot water, comfortable, restaurant.

E Felic, Haya de la Torre 552, T325901. **F** without bath, quiet. Recommended.

E Hostal Karol Inn, Manuel Ruiz 277, T/F321216. Hot water, good, family run, laundry, cafetería.

E Residencial El Parque, E Palacios 309, on plaza, T323963. Converted old home, hot water, nice, secure.

F Hostal El Ensueño, Sáenz Peña 268, 2 blocks from Plaza Central, T328662. **G** without bath, very good, safe, welcoming.

F Tany, Palacios 553, T/F323411. Includes breakfast, TV, good value.

Eating

Casma and Sechín *p1317*

Cheap restaurants on Huarmey. The local ice-cream, *Caribe*, is available at Ormeño 545.

Tío Sam, Huarmey 138. Specializes in fresh fish.

Venecia, Huarmey 204. Local dishes, popular.

Activities and tours

Casma and Sechín *p1317*

Sechín Tours, in Hostal Monte Carlo, Casma, T711421. Organizes tours in the local area. The guide, Renato, only speaks Spanish but has knowledge of local ruins and can be contacted on T712528, renatotours@yahoo.com. US$3 per hr, including use of mototaxi.

Transport

North of Lima *p1317*

Bus Litsa to **Huacho** from **Lima** 2½ hrs, US$2.75, or **Comité 18**, daily colectivos, US$3. To **Churín Estrella Polar, Espadín** and **Beteta** have several times a day from **Lima**, 4-5 hrs, US$6.75.

Caral and Paramonga *p1317*

Bus To **Barranca** stops opposite the service station (*el grifo*) at the end of town. From **Lima** to Barranca, 3½ hrs, US$3. As bus companies have their offices in Barranca, buses will stop there rather than at Pativilca or Paramonga. Bus from Barranca to **Casma** 155 km, several daily, 2½ hrs, US$3. From Barranca to **Huaraz**, take a minibus from C Lima to the gas station in Pativilca where you can catch a bus, colectivo or truck on the good, paved road to Huaraz.

To **Caral**, **Empresa Valle Sagrado Caral** leave from terminal at Berenice Dávila, cuadra 2, Barranca, US$1.75 shared, or US$28 private service with 1½ hrs at the site. The ruins are 25 km along a road which runs up the Supe valley from Km 184 of the Panamericana (signed). Between Kms 18 and 19 of this road a track leads across the valley to the ruins, though the river may be impassable Dec-Mar, 30 mins. Tours from Lima usually allow 1½ hrs at Caral, with a 3-hr journey each way, stopping for morning coffee and for lunch in Huacho on the return.

Buses run only to Paramonga port (3 km off the Highway, 4 km from the Paramonga ruins, about 15 mins from Barranca). **Taxi** From Paramonga to the ruins and return after waiting, US$6, otherwise take a Barranca-Paramonga port bus, then a 3 km walk.

Casma and Sechín *p1317*

Bus Half hourly from **Lima** to **Chimbote** which can drop you off in Casma, 370 km, 5½ hrs, US$6.75. If going to **Lima** many of the buses from Trujillo and Chimbote stop briefly opposite the petrol station, block 1 of Ormeño or, if they have small offices, along blocks 1-5 of Av Ormeño.

To **Chimbote**, 55 km, it is easiest to take a **Los Casmeños** colectivo, huge old Dodge cars, which depart when full from in front of the petrol station, block 1 of Ormeño, or from Plaza Poncianos, 45 mins, US$1.65. To **Trujillo** it is best to go first to Chimbote bus station and then take an **América Express** bus. To **Huaraz** (150km), via Pariacoto, buses come from Chimbote, 6-7 hrs, US$6. **Transportes Huandoy**, Ormeño 166, T712336, departs at 0700, 1100 and 1400, while **Yungay Express**, Ormeño 158, departs at 0600, 0800 and 1400. This difficult but beautiful trip is worth taking in daylight. From Casma the first 30 km are paved, a good dirt road follows for 30 km to **Pariacoto** (basic lodging). From here to the **Callán** pass (4,224 m) the road is rough (landslides in rainy season), but once the Cordillera Negra has been crossed, the gravel road is better with lovely views of the Cordillera Blanca (150 km to Huaraz). Most Huaraz buses go via Pativilca, which is further but the road is much better, 6 hrs, US$6, **Móvil Tours** and **Trans Chinchaysuyo**, all run at night.

Chimbote *p1318*
Warning Under no circumstances should you walk to the centre: minibus costs US$0.50, taxi US$1.30. There are no hotels near the terminal; some companies have ticket offices in the centre.
Bus The station is 4 km south on Av Meiggs. From **Lima**, to Chimbote, 420 km, 5½ hrs, US$9.50-12.25, US$25-34 *cama*, several buses daily, **Trans Isla Blanca** has the most frequent service. To **Trujillo**, 130 km, 2 hrs, US$2.85, **América Express** buses every 20 mins. To **Huaraz** most companies, with the best buses, go the 'long way round', ie down the Pan- americana to Pativilca, then up the paved highway, 7 hrs, US$6. The main companies start in Trujillo and continue to **Caraz**. To Huaraz via Pariacoto, 7 hrs, US$6, **Trans Huandoy** (Etseturh), T354024, at 0600, 1000 and 1300, 7 hrs, and **Yungay Express** at 0500, 0700 and 1300. To **Caraz** via Cañón del Pato, 7-8 hrs, US$7.60, **Yungay Express** at 0830 (for a description of this route see above). Sit on the left-hand-side for the best views. If arriving from Caraz via the Cañón del Pato there is usually time to make a connection to Casma or Trujillo/Huanchaco and avoid overnighting in Chimbote. If travelling to Caraz, take **Línea** 0600 or earlier from Trujillo to make the 0830 bus up the Cañón del Pato. If overnighting is unavoidable, Casma is near enough to stay in but you will need to buy your Caraz ticket the day before; the bus station is on the Casma side of Chimbote.

Directory

Casma and Sechín *p1317*
Banks Good rates for cash and TCs, no commission, at **BCP**, Bolívar 181. **Internet** Café on west side of Plaza, 0900-2100.

Chimbote *p1318*
Banks **BCP** and **Interbank**, on Bolognesi and M Ruiz. *Casas de cambio* and street changers along M Ruiz between Bolognesi and VR Haya de la Torre.

Trujillo and around → *Phone code: 044. Colour map 3, B2. Population: 1,539,774.*

The capital of La Libertad Department, 548 km from Lima, disputes the title of second city of Peru with Arequipa. The compact colonial centre, though, has a small-town feel. The greenness surrounding the city is a delight against the backcloth of brown Andean foothills and peaks. Founded by Diego de Almagro in 1534 as an express assignment ordered by Francisco Pizarro, it was named after the latter's native town in Spain. Nearby are some of Peru's most important Moche and Chimú archaeological sites and a stretch of the country's best surfing beaches.

Ins and outs

Getting there The **airport** is west of the city; the entry to town is along Avenida Mansiche. There is no central bus terminal. **Bus stations** are spread out on four sides the city beyond the inner ring road, Avenida España. There are few hotels around them, but plenty of taxis. Insist on being taken to your hotel of choice. ▸▸ *See also Transport, page 1329.*

Getting around Trujillo is best explored on foot. Taxis in town charge US$0.85-1.20; always use official taxis, which are mainly yellow, or cooperative txis, which have the company logo on the side. The major sites outside the city, Chan Chán, the Moche pyramids and Huanchaco beach are easily reached by public transport, but take care when walking around. A number of recommended guides run tours to these and other places. **Note** The city is generally safe but be careful at bus stations when arriving or leaving. Also take care beyond the inner ring road, Avenida España, as well as obvious places around bus stops and terminals, and at ATMs and internet cafés.

Tourist offices **i perú** ⓘ *Diego de Almagro 420, Plaza de Armas, T294561, iperutrujillo@promperu.gob.pe, Mon-Sat 0900-1800, Sun 1000-1400.* Useful websites include www.xanga.com/TrujilloPeru and www.laindustria.com/industria. The **Tourist Police** ⓘ *Independencia 572, in the INC building, policia_turismo_tru@hotmail.com, open Mon-Sat 0800-2000,* provide useful information and can help with reports of theft, some speak English. **Indecopi** ⓘ *Santo Toribio de Mogrovejo 518, Urb San Andrés II etapa, T295733, sobregon@indecopi.gob.pe,* for tourist complaints. **Gobierno Regional de la Libertad** ⓘ *Dirección de Turismo, Av España 1800, T296221*, for information on regional tourism.

Sights

The focal point is the pleasant and spacious **Plaza de Armas**. The prominent sculpture represents agriculture, commerce, education, art, slavery, action and liberation, crowned by a young man holding a torch depicting liberty. Fronting it is the **Cathedral** ⓘ *0700-1230, 1700-2000*, dating from 1666, with its museum of religious paintings and sculptures next door ⓘ *Mon-Fri 0900-1300, 1600-1900, Sat 0900-1300, US$1.40*. Also on the Plaza are the *Hotel Libertador*, the colonial style Sociedad de Beneficencia Pública de Trujillo and the Municipalidad. The **Universidad de La Libertad**, second only to that of San Marcos at Lima, was founded in 1824. Two beautiful colonial mansions on the plaza have been taken over. The Banco Central de Reserva is in the Colonial-style **Casa Urquiaga (or Calonge)** ⓘ *Pizarro 446, Mon-Fri 0900-1515, Sat-Sun 1000-1330, free 30-min guided tour, take passport*, which contains valuable pre-Columbian ceramics. The other is **Casa Bracamonte (or Lizarzaburu)** ⓘ *Independencia 441*, with occasional exhibits. Opposite the Cathedral on Independencia, is the **Casa Garci Olguín** (*Caja Nuestra Gente*), recently restored but boasting the oldest façade in the city and Moorish-style murals. The buildings that surround the Plaza, and many others in the vicinity, are painted in bright pastel colours. Near the Plaza de Armas is the spacious 18th-century **Palacio Iturregui**, now occupied by the **Club Central** ⓘ *Jr Pizarro 688, Mon-Sat 0800-1800, free entry to patio, US$1.75 to see the ceramics, 0830-1000*. An exclusive and social centre of Trujillo, it houses a private collection of ceramics.

Other mansions, still in private hands, include **Casa del Mayorazgo de Facalá** ⓘ *Pizarro 314, Mon-Fri 0915-1230* now Scotiabank. **Casa de la Emancipación** ⓘ *Jr Pizarro 610 (Banco Continental), Mon-Sat, 0900-1300, 1600-2000*, is where independence from Spain was planned and was the first seat of government and congress in Peru. The **Casa del Mariscal de Orbegoso** ⓘ *Orbegoso 553, closed for refurbishment, 2010*, is the Museo de la República owned by the *BCP* bank.

One of the best of the many churches is the 17th-century **La Merced** ⓘ *at Pizarro 550, 0800-1200, 1600-2000, free*, with picturesque moulded figures below the dome. **El Carmen** ⓘ *at Colón y Bolívar, open for mass Sun 0700-0730*, church and monastery, has been described as the 'most valuable jewel of colonial art in Trujillo' but it is rarely open. Likewise **La Compañía** ⓘ *near Plaza de Armas*,now an auditorium for cultural events.

Museo de Arqueología ⓘ *Junín 682 y Ayacucho, Casa Risco, T249322, www.unitru.edu.pe/cultural/arq, Mon-Fri 0830-1430, US$1.85*, houses a large and interesting collection of thematic exhibits. The **Museo del Juguete** ⓘ *Independencia 705 y Junín, Mon-Sat 1000-1800, Sun 1000-1300, US$1.85, children US$0.70, café open 0900-2300*, is a toy museum containing examples from prehistoric times to 1950, collected by painter Gerardo Chávez. Downstairs is the Espacio Cultural Angelmira with a café bar; in a restored *casona*, worth a visit. Gerardo Chávez has opened the **Museo de Arte Moderno** ⓘ *Av Industrial, 3½ km from centre, T215668, 0930-1730, Sun 0930-1400, US$3.50, students half price*, which has some fine exhibits, a peaceful garden and friendly staff. The basement of the **Cassinelli garage** ⓘ *Av N de Piérola 607, T231801, behind a petrol station, 1000-1300, 1430-1800, US$2.45*, contains a private collection of Mochica and Chimú pottery which is recommended. **Museo de Zoología de Juan Ormea** ⓘ *Jr San Martín 368, Mon-Fri 0700-1850, US$0.70*, has interesting displays of Peruvian animals.

Huacas del Sol and de la Luna

ⓘ *0900-1600 (last entry, but site open till sunset), US$3.80 with guide, some of whom speak European languages (students US$2, children US$0.35), booklet in English or Spanish US$2.85. You have to go with a guide on a 1-hr tour in English, French or Spanish. Groups can be up to 25 people and quite rushed. See Proyecto Huaca de la Luna, Jr Junín 682, Trujillo, T297430,* *www.huacadelaluna.org.pe; www.huacas.com. The visitors' centre (T834901) has a café showing videos and a souvenir shop and good toilets.*

A few kilometres south of Trujillo are the huge and fascinating Moche pyramids, the Huaca del Sol and the Huaca de la Luna. Until the Spaniards destroyed a third of it in a vain search for treasure, Huaca del Sol was the largest man-made structure in the western hemisphere, at

Trujillo

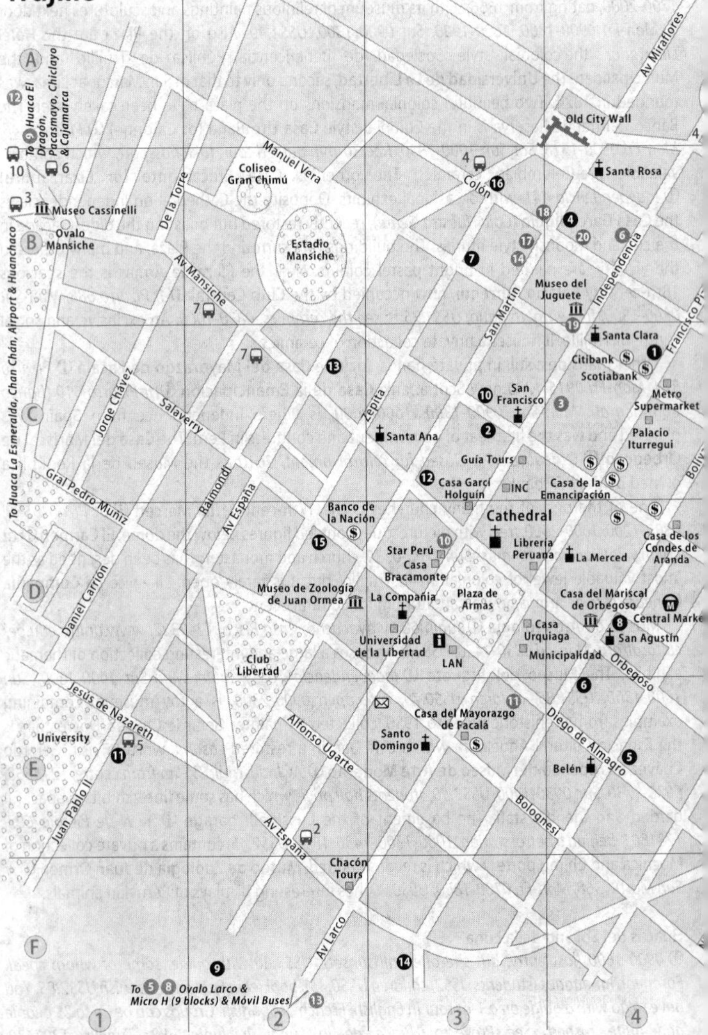

45 m high. It consisted of seven levels , with 11 or 12 phases of construction over the first six centuries AD. Today, about two-thirds of the pyramid have been lost and it is closed to the public. Huaca de la Luna, 500 m away, received scant attention until extensive polychrome moulded decorations were uncovered since 1990. The colours on these remarkable geometric patterns and deities have faded little and it is now possible to view impressive friezes of the

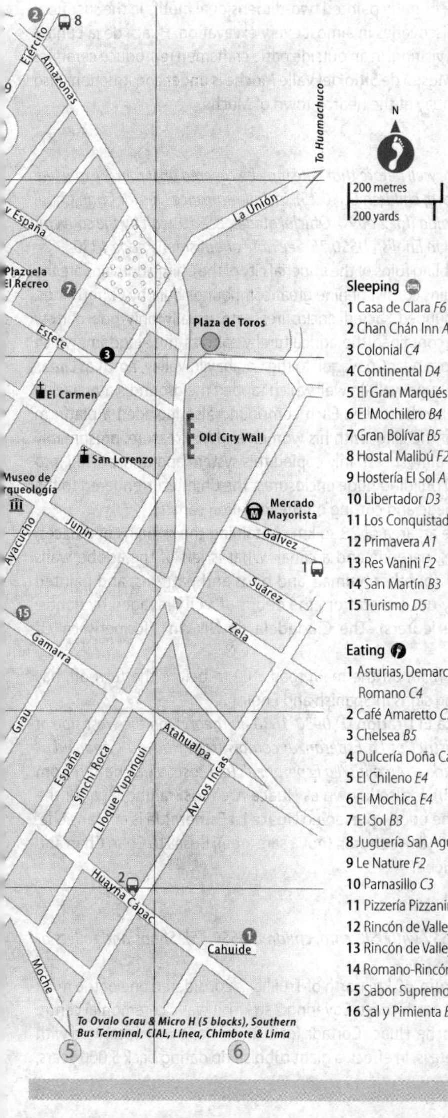

Bars & clubs

17 Canana *B3*
18 El Estribo *B4*
19 Juguete *C4*
20 Stradivarius *B4*

Transport

1 Buses to Huaca del Sol y de la Luna *D6*
2 Combi A to Chan Chán & Huanchaco *E2, E5*
3 Combis A & B; & Micros B, H & H-Corazón: to Chan Chán & Huanchaco *B1*
4 Combi B & Micro B: to Chan Chán & Huanchaco *A4, B3*
5 Micro H to Chan Chán & Huanchaco *E1*
6 El Dorado *B1*
7 Ittsa *B2, C2*
8 Oltursa & Flores *A5*
9 Ormeño *A5*
10 Turismo Díaz, Horna & Tarapoto Tours *B1*

Sleeping

1 Casa de Clara *F6*
2 Chan Chán Inn *A5*
3 Colonial *C4*
4 Continental *D4*
5 El Gran Marqués *F2*
6 El Mochilero *B4*
7 Gran Bolívar *B5*
8 Hostal Malibú *F2*
9 Hostería El Sol *A1*
10 Libertador *D3*
11 Los Conquistadores *E3*
12 Primavera *A1*
13 Res Vanini *F2*
14 San Martín *B3*
15 Turismo *D5*

Eating

1 Asturias, Demarco & Romano *C4*
2 Café Amaretto *C3*
3 Chelsea *B5*
4 Dulcería Doña Carmen *B4*
5 El Chileno *E4*
6 El Mochica *E4*
7 El Sol *B3*
8 Juguería San Agustín *D4*
9 Le Nature *F2*
10 Parnasillo *C3*
11 Pizzería Pizzanino *E1*
12 Rincón de Vallejo *C3*
13 Rincón de Vallejo 2 *C2*
14 Romano-Rincón Criollo *F3*
15 Sabor Supremo *D2*
16 Sal y Pimienta *B3*

upper four levels on the northern exterior wall of the huaca. The highest mural is a 'serpent' which runs the length of the wall, beneath it there are repeated motifs of 'felines' holding decapitated heads of warriors, then repeated motifs of 'fishermen' holding fish against a bright blue background and, next, huge 'spider/crab' motifs. The bottom two levels show dancers or officials grimly holding hands and, below them, victorious warriors following naked prisoners past scenes of combat and two complex scenes, similar to those at Huaca Cao Viejo at El Brujo (see below). Combined with intricate, brightly painted two-dimensional motifs in the sacrificial area atop the huaca, and with new discoveries in almost every excavation, Huaca de la Luna is now a truly significant site well worth visiting. In an outside patio craftsmen reproduce ceramics in designs from northern Peru and a **Museo de Sitio del Valle Moche** is under construction. Also good toilets. Food is available on Sunday at the nearby town of Moche.

Chan Chán

ⓘ *5 km from Trujillo. 0900-1600, arrive well before that. Site may be covered up if rain is expected. Tickets cost US$3.80 (US$2 with ISIC card, children US$0.35), include entrance fees for Chan Chán, Huaca El Dragón and Huaca La Esmeralda (for 2 days). Official guides, US$10, wait by the souvenir shops, toilets here too. Map and leaflet in English US$0.75. See note about safety, page 1330.*

These vast, unusually decorated crumbling ruins of the imperial city of the Chimú domains are the largest adobe city in the world. The ruins consist of nine great compounds built by Chimú kings. The 9-m high perimeter walls surrounded sacred enclosures with usually only one narrow entrance. Inside, rows of storerooms contained the agricultural wealth of the kingdom, which stretched 1,000 km along the coast from near Guayaquil to the Carabayllo Valley, north of Lima.

Most of the compounds contain a huge walk-in well which tapped the ground water, raised to a high level by irrigation further up the valley. Each compound also included a platform mound which was the burial place of the king, with his women and his treasure, presumably maintained as a memorial. The Incas almost certainly copied this system and transported it to Cuzco where the last Incas continued building huge enclosures. The Chimú surrendered to the Incas around 1471 after 11 years of siege and cutting off the irrigation canals.

The dilapidated city walls enclose an area of 28 sq km containing the remains of palaces, temples, workshops, streets, houses, gardens and a canal. What is left of the adobe walls bears well-restored decorations of fish, other animals and birds and patterns, and painted designs have been found on pottery unearthed from the debris of a city ravaged by floods, earthquakes, and *huaqueros* (grave looters). The **Ciudadela de Nik-An** (formerly called Tschudi) is the part that visitors see.

The **site museum** ⓘ *US$1, 0830-1630,* on the main road, 100 m before the turn-off, has objects found in the area, displays and signs in Spanish and English.

The partly restored temple, **Huaca El Dragón** ⓘ *0930-1630 (in theory), on the west side of the Pan-American Highway in the district of La Esperanza; combis from Huayna Cápac y Los Incas, or Av España y Manuel Vera marked 'Arco Iris/La Esperanza', taxi costs US$2,* dating from Huari to Chimú times (AD 1000-1470), is also known as **Huaca Arco Iris** (rainbow), after the shape of friezes which decorate it. The poorly preserved **Huaca La Esmeralda** is at Mansiche, between Trujillo and Chan Chán, behind the church (not a safe area). Buses to Chan Chán and Huanchaco pass the church at Mansiche.

El Brujo

ⓘ *open daily 0900-1600, US$3.80 (US$2 with ISIC card, children US$0.35). Shops and toilets at the entrance.*

A complex collectively known as **El Brujo**, 60 km north of Trujillo, is considered one of the most important archaeological sites on the north coast. Covering 2 sq km, it was a ceremonial centre for up to 10 cultures, including the Moche. Huaca Cortada (or El Brujo) has a wall decorated with high relief stylized figures. Huaca Prieta is, in effect, a giant rubbish tip dating back 5,000 years, which once housed the very first settlers. Huaca Cao Viejo has extensive friezes, polychrome reliefs up to 90 m long, 4 m high and on five different levels. The mummy of a tattooed woman, La Señora de Cao, dating from AD 450, has also been found. Her mausoleum, with grave goods, can be visited in a purpose-built museum, opened in 2009. In front of Cao Viejo are the remains of one of the oldest Spanish churches in the region. It was common practice for the Spaniards to build their churches near these ancient sites in order to counteract their religious importance. Excavations will continue for many years. Trujillo travel agencies run tours.

Huanchaco and around

An alternative to Trujillo is this fishing and surfing village, full of hotels, guest houses and restaurants (but little nightlife). It is famous for its narrow pointed fishing rafts, known as *caballitos* (little horses) *de totora*, made of totora reeds and depicted on Mochica, Chimú and other cultures' pottery. Unlike those used on Lake Titicaca, they are flat, not hollow, and ride the breakers rather like surfboards (fishermen offer trips on their *caballitos* for US$1.75, be prepared to get wet; groups should contact Luis Gordillo, El Mambo, T461092). You can see fishermen returning in their reed rafts at about 0800 and 1400 when they stack the boats upright to dry in the fierce sun. Overlooking Huanchaco is a huge church (1535-40) from the belfry of which are extensive views. Post Office at Grau y Manco Capac, open Mon-Sat 1300-1800.

Puerto Chicama (**Malabrigo**), is claimed by surfers as the best surf beach in Peru, with the longest left-hand point-break in the world. The best waves are March-October. It is 70 km north of Trujillo, turn off Panamericana at Paiján. There are simple places to eat in town and a few hospedajes, but a string of small places line the clifftop south of town, Distrito El Hombre, from the exclusive **Chicama Surf Resort**, www.chicamasurfresort.com, to the 3-star **Chicama Beach**, www.chicamabeach.com, and other humbler places (several close out of season).

Trujillo and around listings

For Sleeping and Eating price codes and other relevant information, see Essentials, pages 38-40.

Sleeping

Trujillo *p1320, map p1322*

LL-L Libertador, Independencia 485, Plaza de Armas, T232741, www.libertador.com.pe. Comfortable rooms, excellent service, swimming pool in a flower-filled patio, sauna, cafetería and restaurant, breakfast extra, excellent buffet lunch on Sun. Recommended.

L El Gran Marqués, Díaz de Cienfuegos 145-147, Urb La Merced, T/F249366, www.elgran marques.com. Price includes breakfast, modern, free internet connection in rooms, pool, sauna, jacuzzi, restaurant. Recommended.

AL Los Conquistadores, Diego de Almagro 586, T203350, losconquistadores@viabcp.com. Includes American breakfast, internet, bar, restaurant, very comfortable.

B Gran Bolívar, Bolívar 957, T222090, www.granbolivarhotel.net. Includes breakfast, in converted 18th-century house, internet, café, bar, parking.

B Hostal Malibú, Av Larco 1471, Urb La Merced, T284811, www.hostalmalibu.com. Variety of rooms, restaurant, room service, Wi-Fi, mini-bar, laundry, massage, currency exchange. Also sister hotel of same name at Av Larco 1000, Huanchaco.

C Continental, Gamarra 663, T241607, F249881. Opposite market, good breakfast, helpful, safe.

C San Martín, San Martín 749, T/F252311, www.deperu.com/sanmartin. Good value, attractive, TV, good for breakfast, Wi-Fi, noisy, otherwise recommended.

C-D Colonial, Independencia 618, T258261, hostalcolonialtruji@hotmail.com. Attractive but small rooms, hot showers, basic breakfast, good restaurant, especially for set lunch. Recommended.

D Almagro, Jr Almagro 748, T223845. New hotel with cable TV, hot water, cafetería (breakfast extra), good.

D Chan Chán Inn, Av Ejército 307, T298583, chanchaninn@hotmail.com. Close to several bus terminals so noisy, includes breakfast (cheaper without), popular with backpackers, luggage store, café, laundry, internet, money exchange, information.

D Turismo, Gamarra 747, T244181. Includes continental breakfast, central, good services TV, restaurant, parking, travel agency.
E Hostería El Sol, Brillantes 224, Urb Santa Inés, T231933, near bus terminals on Av Nicolás de Piérola. With hot shower, restaurant, all meals available for US$2.60.
E Primavera, Av N de Piérola 872, Urb Primavera, T231915. Hot water, restaurant, bar, pool.
F pp **Casa de Clara**, Cahuide 495, T243347, www.xanga.com/CasadeClara. Cheaper without bath, hot water, good food (breakfast US$0.90, lunch US$1.50, dinner US$2.10), very helpful, loads of information available, laundry US$1.50/kg, meeting place and lots going on, internet and Wi-Fi, many languages spoken (see Clara Luz Bravo and Michael White, Activities and tours below). Recommended. Restaurants nearby.
E-F Mochica's B&B, La Arboleda E-19, T422006, www.mochicas.com. 5 mins by taxi from centre near Av América Sur and bus terminals. Shared rooms for 1, 2 or 4 with bath, safe residential area, quiet, very helpful, good breakfast, internet, TV and DVDs, use of kitchen, hot water.
F Residencia Vanini, Av Larco 237, outside Av España, T200878, enriqueva@hotmail.com. Youth hostel in a converted private house, a good option but not in the centre, some rooms with bath, others with shared shower.
F-G pp **El Mochilero**, Independencia 887, T297842, 992-305471, http://elmochilero.blogia.com/ New in 2009, variety of dorms and rooms, only one with bath (E), electric showers, internet, Wi-Fi, breakfast US$1.75, fridge for guests' use. Tours arranged, information.

Huanchaco *p1325*
B Bracamonte, Los Olivos 503, T461166, www.hotelbracamonte.com.pe. Comfortable rooms, pool, own water supply, rents bicycles, secure, good restaurant, with lunch menu and some vegetarian dishes, laundry service, English spoken, Wi-Fi. Highly recommended.
B Hostal Huankarute, La Rivera 233, T044-461705, www.hostalhuankarute.com. On the sea-front, with small pool, bar, sun terrace, Wi-Fi, bicycle rental; some rooms larger, more luxurious and more pricey. Recommended.
C Alojamiento Sol y Mar, La Rivera 400, T461120, ctsolymar1@hotmail.com. Breakfast extra, TV, with pool, restaurant and garden.
C Las Palmeras, Av Larco 1150, sector Los Tumbos, T461199, www.lasplamerasdehuanchaco.com. One of the best, rooms with terrace, bath, TV, hot water, dining room, pool and gardens.
D El Malecón, Av La Rivera 225, T461275, hostalelm@yahoo.com. Overlooking the sea, some rooms with terrace, Wi-Fi, hot water, TV, café, helpful staff.
D Hostal Huanchaco, Larco 287 on Plaza, T461272, www.huanchacohostal.com. With breakfast, TV, hot water, pool, good but pricey cafetería, video, pool table. Recommended.
D Huanchaco Inn, Los Pinos 528, T461158, www.huanchacoinn.net. Rooms with and without bath, new and still expanding, hot water, cable TV, internet cabins, use of kitchen, laundry service, small pool.
D La Casa Suiza, Los Pinos 308, T461285, www.lacasasuiza.com. This Huanchaco institution has been fully revamped, variety of rooms with and without bath, small restaurant, barbecue on the roof, Wi-Fi, book exchange.
D-E Huanchaco Gardens, Av Circunvalación 440, El Boquerón, T461194, www.huanchacogardens.com. Family-run, bungalows (**D** with kitchenette), cable TV, also camping, hot water, use of kitchen, free luggage store, helpful, garden with two pools (one for children), Wi-Fi, parking, laundry. Frequently recommended.
D-E Ñaylamp, Prolongación Víctor Larco 1420, northern end of seafront in El Boquerón, T461 022, www.hostalnaylamp.com. Rooms set around a courtyard, dorms **G** pp, hammocks, garden, good beds, hot water, camping US$3.50, US$4,65 with hired tent, laundry, safe, internet, Italian food, good breakfasts. Recommended.
E Hostal Los Esteros, Av Larco 618, T461300, huanchacoesteros@yahoo.com. Hot water, restaurant, safe motorcycle parking, can arrange surfing and *caballitos de totora* trips.
F pp **Hostal Solange**, Los Ficus 258, 1 block from the beach, T461410, hsolange@yahoo.es. Hot showers, dorm **G** pp, good food, laundry facilities, limited use of kitchen, popular meeting point. Recommended.
E Las Brisas, Raymondi 146, T461186, lasbrisas@hotmail.com. Hot water, café, cable TV, comfortable.
E McCallum Lodging, Los Ficus 460, T501813. Private rooms and shared triples (**F**), hot water,

use of kitchen, family atmosphere, highly considered by locals and tourists, especially for longer stays.

F pp **Cherry's**, Los Pinos 448, T462520, juancarlos160@yahoo.es. Owner Juan Carlos speaks English, cheaper without bath, hot water, use of kitchen, shop, bar, even a small swimming pool.

G Casa Hospedaje Los Ficus, Los Ficus 516, T461719. Breakfast and laundry extra. Family run, hot water, use of kitchen. Recommended.

G pp **Hospedaje El Boquerón**, R Palma 330, T461968, maznaran@hotmail.com. 1 block from beach, modern, shared bathrooms, hot water, kitchen, laundry, internet, fair.

G Hospedaje My Friend, Los Pinos 533, T461 080, myfriendhuanchaco@hotmail.com. Popular place with surfers and foreigners, good for meeting others and for a meal in the restaurant (closed 0700-2200), with hot water, TV room, information. Tours arranged, but service is erratic.

G Hostal Ilalo, La Orquídeas 312, T94 9579753. Hot water, TV, use of kitchen, roof terrace, welcomes US and local visitors.

G pp **Sra Mabel Díaz de Aguilar**, Túpac Amaru 248, T461232, mabel_minerva@hotmail.com. Near football ground, shared bath, hot water, English spoken.

Eating

Trujillo *p1320, map p1322*

A speciality is *shambar*, a thick minestrone made with pork, served on Mon. All along Pizarro are restaurants to suit all tastes and budgets. On the west side of the central market at Grau y Ayacucho are several small, cheap restaurants.

TT **Chelsea**, Estete 675, T257032, www.chelsea.com. Restaurant/bar, open 1145-1645, 1700-0100, on Sun Buffet Criollo US$8.70, special shows on Fri (live music, fee US$3.50) and Sat (Marinera dance show, US$5.25). Recommended.

TT **Demarco**, Pizarro 725. Popular at midday for lunchtime menus and for its cakes and desserts.

TT **El Mochica**, Bolívar 462. Good typical food and occasional live music. Warmly recommended.

TT **Le Nature**, Marcelo Corne 338,T209674. In a residential district off Av Larco, probably the best vegetarian food in town. Open Mon-Thu 1000-2200, Fri, Sun 1000-1600, Sat 1900-2200.

TT **Pizzería Pizzanino**, Av Juan Pablo II 183, Urb San Andrés, opposite University. Recommended for pizzas, pastas, meats, desserts, evening only.

TT **Romano**, Pizarro 747. International food, good *menú*, breakfasts, coffee, excellent milkshakes, cakes, has internet.

TT **Romano-Rincón Criollo**, Estados Unidos 162, Urb El Recreo, 10-min walk from centre, T244207. Northern Peruvian cuisine, *menú* for US$5.60, smart.

T **Asturias**, Pizarro 741. Nice café with a reasonable *menú*, good pastas, cakes and sandwiches.

T **Café Oviedo**, Pizarro 737. With vegetarian options, good salads and cakes, helpful.

T **El Sol**, Zepita 203, T345105. Vegetarian, lunch menú and à la carte, open Mon-Sat 0800-2200, Sun 0800-1600.

T **Juguería San Agustín**, Bolívar 526. Good juices, good *menú*, popular, excellent value.

T **Parnasillo**, Gamarra 368, T234715, Mon-Sat 1300-1530. Restaurant and hotel school, good *menú* US$2.60-3, food nicely presented, good value.

T **Rincón de Vallejo**, Orbegoso 303. Good *menú*, typical dishes, very crowded at peak times. Second branch at Av España 736.

T **Sabor Supremo**, Diego de Almagro 210, T220437. Menú US$1.75, also à la carte, vegetarian food, vegan on special request.

T **Sal y Pimienta**, Colón 201. Very popular for lunch, US$1 and US$1.85, close to buses for Huanchaco and Chan Chán.

Cafés

Café Amaretto, Gamarra 368. Smart, good selection of real coffees, "brilliant" cakes, sweets, snacks and drinks.

Dulcería Doña Carmen, San Martín 814. Serves local specialities such as *alfajores*, *budin*, *king kong*, etc.

El Chileno, Ayacucho 408. Café and ice cream parlour, popular.

Fitopán, Bolívar 406. Good selection of breads, also serves lunches.

Huanchaco *p1325*

There are about 30 restaurants on the beachfront. Many close in the low season and at night.

TTT **Big Ben**, Víctor Larco 1182, near A Sánchez, T461869. Seafood and international, very good. Open 1130-1730.

TTT **Club Colonial**, La Rivera 514, on the beachfront, T461015. A smart restaurant and bar, open 1100-2300, French-speaking Belgian owner.

¥¥¥ **El Kero**, Av La Ribera 612, T461184. Open 0800-midnight, very popular meeting place and good restaurant.

¥¥¥ **El Mochica**, Av Larco 700, T293441. Same owners and quality as this restaurant in Trujillo, very nice dining area and panorama, open 1200-1800.

¥¥¥ **Huanchaco Beach**, Av Larco 602, T461484. One of the best for quality in town, popular with tours.

¥¥ **Casa Tere**, Plaza de Armas, T461197. For best pizzas in town, also pastas, burgers and breakfasts.

¥¥ **Estrella Marina**, Av Víctor Larco 740, T461850. Open 1100-2400. Great value for fish, chicken after 1800.

¥¥ **La Barca**, Raimondi 117, T461855. Very good seafood, well-run, popular.

¥¥ **Los Herrajes**, Av Larco 1020, T461397. Excellent seafood, low-priced *menú*, good sea view, closes at sunset. Recommended.

¥¥ **Lucho del Mar**, Av Víctor Larco 750. On seafront road, serves excellent sea food.

¥¥ **Sabes?**, V Larco 920, T461555. Pub with food, internet café, popular, British-owned, oens at 2000.

¥¥-¥ **Otra Cosa**, Av Larco 1312, T461346, www.otracosa. info. Overlooking the sea, vegetarian and other dishes, Dutch owners, can arrange tours in Peru, 2 rooms for rent, open 0830-2030.

¥ **La Charapita**, Huáscar 162. Modest but popular restaurant serving large portions.

Cafés

Arcimboldo, Las Gardenias 611, T462621. 100% vegetarion food (vegan optional), Peruvian/Italian owner.

Chocolate, Av Rivera 772. Dutch management, open 0730-1900, serves breakfast, also some vegetarian food, coffee and cakes.

Bars and clubs

Trujillo *p1320, map p1322*

Bar/Café Juguete, Junín y Independencia. An old style café serving good coffee. Open to midnight. Has a good pasta restaurant attached.

Bar/Café Stradivarius, Colón 327. An attractive café with sofas, open in the evenings only.

Canana, San Martín 788. Bars and restaurant, disco, live music at weekends (US$1.50-3), video screens (also has travel agency). Recommended, but take care on leaving.

El Estribo, San Martin 809, T204053. A club playing a wide genre of sounds and attracting a mixed crowd.

Festivals and events

Trujillo *p1320, map p1322*

The 2 most important festivals are the **National Marinera Contest** (end of **Jan**) and the **Festival Internacional de La Primavera** (last week of **Sep**), with cultural events, parades, beauty pageants and Trujillo's famous **Caballos de Paso**.

Huanchaco *p1325*

In the 1st week of **May** is the **Festival del Mar**, a celebration of the disembarkation of Taycanamo, the leader of the Chimú period. A procession is made in Totora boats. **30 Jun**, **San Pedro**, patron saint of fishermen: his statue is taken out to sea on a huge totora-reed boat. Also the annual **Olímpiadas Playeral** and **El Festival Internacional de la Primavera** (see Trujillo above). There are also surf competitions. Carnival and New Year are also popular celebrations.

Shopping

Trujillo *p1320, map p1322*

Bookshops **Librería Peruana**, Pizarro 505, just off the Plaza. Best selection in town, also postcards, ask for Sra Inés Guerra de Guijón. **SBS**, Jr Bolívar 714 and in Mall Aventura, Av Mansiche block 20, also in Plaza Real Mall, Prol Av César Vallejo (behind UPAO University), California (take taxi or green California micro A).

Handicrafts **120 Artesanía por Descubriur**, Las Magnolias 403, California, www.tienda120.blogspot.com. Art gallery designs and handmade crafts, near Real Plaza. **APIAT**, craft market, Av España y Zela. The largest craft market in the city, good for ceramics, totora boats, woodwork and leather, competitive prices. **Artesanía del Norte**, at Dulcería La Libertad, Jr Pizarro 758, and at the Huacas del Sol y de la Luna, www.artesaniadelnorte.com. Sells items mostly to the owner, Mary Cortijo's, design using traditional techniques. **Trama Perú**, Pizarro 754, T287897, www.tramaperu.com. Mon-Fri 1000-2130. High quality, handmade art objects, authorized Moche art replicas.

Markets **Mercado Central**, on Gamarra, Ayacucho and Pasaje San Agustín. **Mercado Unión**, between Av Santa and Av Perú. A little safer than others, also has repairs on shoes, clothes and bags.

Huanchaco *p1325*

El Quibishi, entrance to Huanchaco at south end of beach. Main artesanía market; also has a food section.

Activities and tours

Trujillo *p1320, map p1322*

Tour operators

Prices vary and competition is fierce so shop around for the best deal. Few agencies run tours on Sun and often only at fixed times on other days. To Chan Chán, **El Dragón** and **Huanchaco**, 4-4½ hrs for US$7-8.50 pp. To **Huacas del Sol** and **de la Luna**, 2½-3 hrs for US$7-8.50 pp. To **El Brujo**, US$27-34 pp, 5-8 hrs. **City tours** cost US$3.50 pp, 2-2½ hrs. Prices do not include entrance fees.

Chacón Tours, Av España 106-112, T255212. Sat afternoon and Sun morning. Recommended for flights etc, not local tours.

Guía Tours, Independencia 580, T234856, guitour@amauta.rcp.net.pe. Also Western Union agent. Recommended.

Guides

Many hotels work on a commission basis with taxi drivers and travel agencies. If you decide on a guide, make your own direct approach and always agree what is included in the price. The Tourist Police (see Directory) has a list of guides; average cost US$7 per hr. Beware of cowboy outfits herding up tourists around the plazas and bus terminals for rapid, poorly translated tours. Also beware scammers offering surfing or salsa lessons and party invitations. **Clara Bravo**, Cahuide 495, T243347, www.xanga.com/trujilloperu. An experienced tourist guide who speaks Spanish, English, German and understands Italian. She takes tourists on extended circuits of the region (archaeological tour US$20 for 6 hrs, city tour US$7 pp, US$53 per car to El Brujo, with extension to Sipán, Brüning Museum and Túcume possible – tours in Lambayeque involve public transport, not inlcuded in cost). Clara works with English chartered accountant **Michael White** (same address, microbewhite@ yahoo.com, also speaks German, French and Italian), who provides transport. He is very knowledgeable about tourist sites. They run tours any day of the week; 24-hr attention, accommodate small groups. **Luis Ocas Saldaña**, Jr José Martí 2019, T949-339593, guianorteperu@hotmail.com. Very knowledgeable, helpful, covers all of northern Peru. Recommended. **Gustavo Prada Marga**, at Chan Chán, an experienced guide. **Alfredo Ríos Mercedes**, riosmercedes@hotmail.com, T949-657978. Speaks English. **Jannet Rojas Sánchez**, Alto Mochica Mz Q 19, Trujillo, T94 9344844, jannarojas@hotmail.com. Speaks English, enthusiastic, works also for *Guía Tours*. **José Soto Ríos**, Atahualpa 514, dpto 3, T251489. He speaks English and French.

Huanchaco *p1325*

Surfing

There are plenty of surf schools. Cost of equipment rental US$8.75/day, one lesson US$14-15.50.

Indigan, Deán Saavedra 582 (next to soccer field), T462591, indigansurf@hotmail.com. Jhon and Giancarlos Urcía for lessons, surf trips and rentals. Also offer lodging at their home.

Muchik, Av Larco 650, T462535, www.escuelatablamuchik.com. Instructors Chico and Omar Huamanchumo are former surf champions, also repairs. Arrange trips to other surf sites.

Onechako, Av Larco 640, T633242, escuelasurfonechako@hotmail.com. Owner Tito Lescano. Also offer *caballito de totora* riding lessons. Surf trips to other surf beaches in the North, with restaurant/bar.

Yenth Ccora, Av Larco 500, T94 9403871, ycc_mar@hotmail.com. Surfing equipment manufacture, repair, rental and surfing school.

Transport

Trujillo *p1320, map p1322*

Air To **Lima**, 1 hr, daily flights with **LAN** and **Star Perú**. Taxi to airport, US$4.

Bus Micros (small buses with 25 or more seats) and combis (up to 15 passengers), on all routes, cost US$0.30-0.45; colectivos (cars carrying 6 passengers), US$0.40, tend to run on main avenues starting from Av España. None is allowed inside an area bounded by Av Los Incas in the east to Ovalo Mansiche in the west and the north and south perimeters of Av España.

A large new bus terminal for southbound buses is being built between Ovalos Grau and

La Marina. Meanwhile, better bus companies maintain their own terminals. To and from **Lima**, 561 km, 7½ hrs in the better class buses, average fare US$24-34, 10 hrs in the cheaper buses, US$10-17. There are many bus companies doing this route, among those recommended are: **Cruz del Sur**, Amazonas 437 near Av Ejército, T261801; **Turismo Díaz**, Nicolás de Piérola 1079 on Panamericana Norte, T201237; **Línea**, Av América Sur 2857, T297000, 3 levels of service, also to **Chimbote** hourly, **Huaraz**, 9 hrs, **Cajamarca** 5 a day, **Chiclayo**, hourly, US$4.75 (from Carrión by Av Mansiche, T235847, on the hour), and **Piura**, 2300. Also **Flores** (Av Ejército 346, T208250), **Ittsa** (Av Mansiche 145, T251415; No 431 for northern destinations – good service, T222541), **Móvil**, Av América Sur 3959, T286538. **Oltursa**, Av Ejército 342, T263055, 3 *bus cama* services to Lima.

Small **Pakatnamú** buses leave when full, 0400-2100, from Av N de Piérola 1092, T206594, to **Pacasmayo**, 102 km, 1¼ hrs, US$3.40. To **Chiclayo**, 3 hrs from Trujillo, US$4.75, several companies. Among the best are **Emtrafesa**, Av Túpac Amaru 185, T471521, on the half-hour every hour; also to **Jaén**, 1930, 9 hrs, US$10; **Piura**, 6 hrs, US$9.25 (**Ittsa**'s 1330, or **Línea**'s 1415 buses are good choices).

Direct buses to **Huaraz**, 319 km, via Chimbote and Casma (169 km), with **Línea** and **Móvil**, 8 hrs, US$12-20.50. There are several buses and colectivos to **Chimbote**, with **América Express** from Av La Marina 315, 135 km, 2 hrs, US$2.85, departures every 30 mins from 0530 (ticket sales from 0500); then change at Chimbote (see above – leave Trujillo before 0600 to make a connection from 0800). Ask Clara Bravo and Michael White (see Guides, above) about transport to Caraz avoiding Chimbote (a very worthwhile trip via the Brasileños road and Cañon del Pato).

To **Cajamarca**, 300 km, 7-8 hrs, US$7-29: with **Línea**, **Emtrafesa**, see above, at 2145, and **Horna**, Av N de Piérola 1249, T225303. To **Huamachuco**, 170 km, 6 hrs, US$7-8.55, **Trans Horna**, 5 a day, also Tunesa, Prol Av Vallejo 1390, T210725. To **Chachapoyas**, *Móvil*'s Lima-Chiclayo-Chachapoyas service passes through Trujillo at 1600 and Chiclayo at 2000, US$22.

To **Tarapoto**, via Moyobamba, **Tarapoto Tours**, US$21-29, Av N de Piérola 1239, T470318, at 2230, and **Ejetur** Av N de Piérola 1238, T222228, at 1300, 1500, also to Yurimaguas at 0700, and to Jaén at 1700, US$10.

Taxi Town trip, US$0.85 within Av España and US$1.05 within Av América. To airport US$4. Beware of overcharging, check fares with locals. Taxi from in front of Hotel Libertador, US$10 per hr, about the same rate as a tour with an independent guide or travel agent for 1-2 people.

Huacas del Sol and de la Luna *p1321*

Combis every 15 mins from Ovalo Grau and, less safe, Galvez y Los Incas. They leave you a long walk from the site. On the return go to Ovalo Grau for onward connections. US$0.40. Taxis about US$5; few at site for return, unless you ask driver to wiat.

Chan Chán *p1324*

Take any transport between Trujillo and Huanchaco (see below) and ask to get out at the turn-off to Chan Chán, US$0.40. A taxi is US$3 from Trujillo to the ruins, US$0.85 from museum to ruins, US$2 to Huanchaco.

Note There are police at the entrance to the site, but it is a 25 min walk to the ticket office. Take care if not taking a car on this track. On no account walk the 4 km from Chan Chán to, or on, Buenos Aires beach as there is serious danger of robbery and of being attacked by dogs.

El Brujo *p1324*

The complex can be reached by taking one of the regular buses from Trujillo to Chocope, US$1, and then a colectivo (every 30 minutes) to Magdalena de Cao, US$0.50, then a mototaxi to the site, including wait, US$5, or a 5 km walk to the site.

Huanchaco *p1325*

Two combi routes run between Trujillo and Huanchaco, A and B. Four micros run between Trujillo and Huanchaco: A, B (also known as Mercado Mayorista), H (UPAO) and H-Corazón (with red heart, Mercado Hermelinda). They run 0500-2030, every 5-10 mins. Fare is US$0.50 for the journey (25-45 mins). The easiest place to pick up any of these combis or micros is Ovalo Mansiche, 3 blocks northwest of Av España in front of the Cassinelli museum. In Trujillo, combi

A takes a route on the south side of Av España, before heading up Av Los Incas. Combi B takes the northerly side of Av España. From Huanchaco to the **Línea**, **Móvil Tours** and southern bus terminals, take micro H. It also goes to Ovalo Grau where you can catch buses to the Huacas del Sol and de la Luna. For **Cruz del Sur, Ormeño, Flores, Oltursa**, etc, take combi or micro B from Huanchaco. Taxis US$4.10-5.10.

Puerto Chicama

Micros from Santa Cruz terminal, Av Santa Cruz, 1 block from Av America Sur, US$1.55. Also **Dorado** buses, Av N de Piérola 1062, T291778 (via Paiján) buses stop just off Plaza Central, opposite Comisaria, US$1.55 (US$0.35 from Paiján 16 km).

Directory

Trujillo *p1320, map p1322*

Airline offices LAN, Diego de Almagro 490, Plaza de Armas, T221469. **Star Perú**, Independencia 463, T226948. **Banks** **Banco de la Nación**, Diego de Almagro 297. **BBVA Continental**, Pizarro 620. **BCP**, Gamarra 562. **Citibank**, Junín 468. **Interbank**, Pizarro y Gamarra. **Scotiabank**, Pizarro 314, *Casa de Mayorazgo de Facalá*; also opposite Metro supermarket, Pizarro y Junín. There are many *casas de cambio* and street changers on Gamarra block 5 and Bolívar blocks 5 and 6. **Cultural centres** **Alianza Francesa**, San Martín 858-62, T231232, www.ucv.edu.pe/alianzafrancesa-trujillo. **Instituto de Cultura Peruano Norteamericano**, Av Venezuela 125, Urb El Recreo, T232512, www.elcultural.com.pe. **Consulates** **UK**, Honorary Consul, Mr Winston Barber, Jr Alfonso Ugarte 310, T245935, winstonbarber@terra.com.pe. Mon-Fri 0900-1700. **Internet** There are internet offices all over the centre, mostly on Pizarro blocks 1 and 6, and Av España blocks 1 and 8. **Medical services** Hospital: **Hospital Belén**, Bolívar 350, T245281. **Clínica Peruano Americana**, Av Mansiche 810, T242400, English spoken, good. **Pharmacies** Several pharmacy chains in the centre (on Pizarro and Gamarra) and others on either side of Belén hospital on Bolognesi. **Post offices** Independencia 286 y Bolognesi. 0800-2000, Sun 0900-1300. **DHL**, Almagro 579. **Telephones** **Telefónica**, headquarters at Bolívar 658. Private call centres all over town. **Useful addresses** **Immigration:** Av Larco 1220, Urb Los Pinos, T282217. Open Mon-Fri 0815-1230, 1500-1630.

Chiclayo and around

Lambayeque department, sandwiched between the Pacific and the Andes, is a major agricultural zone, especially for rice and sugar cane. The boasts a distinctive cuisine and musical tradition, and an unparalleled ethnographic and archaeological heritage. Chiclayo's witchcraft market is famous and excavations at nearby adobe pyramid cities are uncovering fabulous treasures.

Chiclayo → *Phone code: 074. Colour map 3, B1. Population: 411,536.*

Since its inception in the 16th century, Chiclayo has grown to become a major commercial hub. The city has an atmosphere all of its own and a distinctive musical tradition featuring Afro-indian rhythms, but is best known for the spectacular cache of archaeological treasures that lie at its doorstep. **Tourist offices**: **i perú** ⓘ *Sáenz Peña 838, T205703, iperuchiclayo@promperu.gob.pe, 0900-1900, Sun 0900-1300*; also at the airport (open daily). For complaints and tourist protection, **Indecopi** ⓘ *Los Tumbos 245, Santa Victoria, T206223, aleyva@indecopi.gob.pe, Mon-Fri 0800-1300, 1630-1930*. The **tourist police** ⓘ *Av Sáenz Peña 830, T236700, ext 311, 24 hrs a day*, are very helpful and may store luggage and take you to the sites themselves. There are tourist kiosks on the Plaza and on Balta.

In the city itself, on the Plaza de Armas, is the 19th-century neoclassical **Cathedral**, designed by the English architect Andrew Townsend. The private **Club de la Unión** is on the Plaza at the corner of Calle San José. Continue five blocks north on Balta to the **Mercado Modelo**, one of northern Peru's liveliest and largest daily markets. Don't miss the handicrafts stalls (see *Monsefú*) and the well-organized section (off C Arica on the south side) of ritual paraphernalia used by traditional curers and diviners (*curanderos*): herbal medicines, folk charms, curing potions, and exotic objects including dried llama foetuses to cure all manner of real and imagined illnesses. At *Paseo de Artesanías*, 18 de Abril near Balta, stalls sell handicrafts in a quiet, custom-built open-air arcade.

Monsefú and the coast

The traditional town of **Monsefú**, southwest, is known for its music and handicrafts; good market, four blocks from the plaza. Handicraft stalls open when potential customers arrive (see

Chiclayo

100 metres
100 yards

Sleeping
1 América *B2*
2 Casa de la Luna *B1*
3 Costa del Sol *C3*
4 El Sol *B1*
5 Garza *C3*
6 Gran Hotel Chiclayo *B1*
7 Hosp Concordia *C3*
8 Hosp San Eduardo *C3*
9 Inti *B2*
10 Las Musas *C3*
11 Pirámide Real *C3*
12 Santa Rosa *B2*
13 Sicán *C2*
14 Sol Radiante *C2*

Eating
1 Boulevar *B2*
2 Café Astoría *C2*
3 D'Onofrio *C3*
4 El Huaralino *C1*
5 Fiesta *B1*
6 Hebrón *C3*
7 Kaprichos *A3*
8 La Panadería *B2*
9 La Parra *C3*
10 La Plazuela *B1*
11 Las Américas *B3*
12 Roma *C3*
13 Romana *C3*
14 Tradiciones *C3*

Transport
1 Brüning Express to Lambayeque *B1*
2 Cial *C1*
3 Civa C3
4 Colectivos to Lambayeque *A2*
5 Colectivos to Puerto Etén *A3*
6 Cruz del Sur *C3*
7 Emtrafesa *C3*
8 Línea *C2*
9 Móvil *C2*
10 Oltursa *B1*
11 Tepsa *C2*
12 Transportes Chiclayo *B1*

also Festivals above). Beyond Monsefú are three ports serving the Chiclayo area. **Pimentel**, 8 km from Chiclayo, is a beach resort which gets very crowded on Sunday. You can walk along the decaying pier for US$0.25. There are several seafood restaurants. The surfing between Pimentel and the Bayovar Peninsula is excellent, reached from Chiclayo (14½ km) by road branching off from the Pan-American Highway. Sea-going reed boats (*caballitos de totora*) are used by fishermen and may be seen returning in the late afternoon. Nearby **Santa Rosa** has little to recommend it and it is not safe to walk there from Pimentel. The most southerly is **Puerto Eten**, a quaint port with some nice wooden buildings on the plaza, 24 km by road from Chiclayo. Its old railway station has been declared a national heritage. In the adjacent roadstead, Villa de Eten, panama hats are the local industry, but it is not as picturesque.

The ruined Spanish town of **Zaña**, 51 km south of Chiclayo, was destroyed by floods in 1726, and sacked by English pirates on more than one occasion. There are ruins of five colonial churches and the convents of San Agustín, La Merced and San Francisco.

Lambayeque

About 12 km northwest from Chiclayo is Lambayeque, its narrow streets lined by colonial and republican houses, many retaining their distinctive wooden balconies and wrought iron grill-work over the windows, but many in very bad shape. On Calle 2 de Mayo see especially **Casa de la Logia o Montjoy**, whose 64 m long balcony is said to be the longest in the colonial Americas. It is being restored. At 8 de Octubre 345 is **Casona Descalzi**, which is well-preserved as a good restaurant ⓘ *T284341, 1100-1700 daily*. It has 120 carved iguana heads on the ceiling. Opposite, at No 328, **Casona Cúneo**, and **Casona Iturregui Aguilarte**, No 410, are, by contrast, seriously neglected. Also of interest is the 16th-century **Complejo Religioso Monumental de San Francisco de Asís** and the baroque church of the same name which stands on the **Plaza de Armas 27 de Diciembre**.

The reason most people visit is to see the town's two museums. The older of the two is the **Brüning Archaeological Museum** ⓘ *0900-1700, US$3.50, a guided tour costs an extra US$2.75*, in a modern building, specializing in Mochica, Lambayeque/Sicán and Chimú cultures. Three blocks east is the more recent **Museo de las Tumbas Reales de Sipán** ⓘ *0900-1700, closed Mon, US$3.45, http://sipan.peru cultural.org.pe, mototaxi from plaza US$0.35*, shaped like a pyramid. The magnificent treasure from the tomb of 'The Old Lord of Sipán' (see below), and a replica of the Lord of Sipán's tomb are displayed here. A ramp from the main entrance takes visitors to the third floor, from where you descend, mirroring the sequence of the archaeologists' discoveries. There are handicrafts outside and a tourist office ⓘ *Tue-Sun 1030-1400, 1500-1730*.

On the plaza in **Mórrope**, on the Pan-American Highway 20 km north of Lambayeque, is one of the earliest churches in northern Peru, **San Pedro de Mórrope** (1545), an adobe and algarrobo structure (under reconstruction, ask for Carlos Tejada in the restuarant on the plaza, who has the key). It contains the tomb of the cacique Santiago Cazusol. Next to it is the more modern parish church.

Sipán

ⓘ *Daily 0900-1700, entrance for tombs and museum is US$2.75; guide at site US$3.75 (may not speak English). To visit the site takes about 3-4 hrs.*

At this imposing complex a short distance east of Chiclayo (turn-off well-signed in the centre of Pomalca), excavations since 1987 in one of three crumbling pyramids have brought to light a cache of funerary objects considered to rank among the finest examples of pre-Columbian art. Peruvian archaeologist Walter Alva, leader of the dig, continues to probe the immense mound that has revealed no less than 12 royal tombs filled with 1,800-year-old offerings worked in precious metals, stone, pottery and textiles of the Moche culture (circa AD 1-750). In the most extravagant Moche tomb discovered, El Señor de Sipán, a priest was found clad in gold (ear ornaments, breast plate, etc), with turquoise and other valuables. A site museum features photos and maps of excavations, technical displays and replicas of some finds. A new site museum is under construction.

In another tomb were found the remnants of what is thought to have been a priest, sacrificed llama and a dog, together with copper decorations. In 1989 another richly appointed, unlooted tomb contained even older metal and ceramic artefacts associated with what was probably a high-ranking shaman or spiritual leader, called 'The Old Lord of Sipán'. Three tombs are on display, containing replicas of the original finds. You can wander around the previously excavated areas to get an idea of the construction of the burial mound and adjacent pyramids. For a good view, climb the large pyramid across from the Sipán excavation. A 4,000-year old temple, Ventarrón, with murals, was uncovered nearby in 2007.

East from Pomalca is Chongoyape, just before which is the turning to the **Chaparrí** private ecological reserve, 34,000 ha, set up and run by the Comunidad Muchik Santa Catalina de Chongoyape, 75 km from Chiclayo. Visitors can go for the day or stay at the **Chaparrí EcoLodge** ⓘ *US$3 for a day visit. US$10 entry if intending to stay overnight, www.chaparri.org*. All staff and guides are locals; for every 10 people you have to have a local guide (this provides work and helps to prevent rubbish). There are no dogs or goats in the area so the forest is recuperating; it contains many bird and mammal species of the dry forest, including White-winged Guan and Spectacled Bear. The Tinajones reservoir is good for birdwatching.

Túcume

ⓘ *Open 0900-1700, entry US$3, students US$1, children US$0.30, guide US$7, T835026, www.museodesitiotucume.com.*

About 35 km north of Chiclayo, not far from the Panamericana and Túcume Nuevo, lie the ruins of this vast city built over 1,000 years ago. A short climb to the two *miradores* on **Cerro La Raya** (or **El Purgatorio**) offers the visitor an unparalleled panoramic vista of 26 major pyramids, platform mounds, walled citadels and residential compounds flanking a ceremonial centre and ancient cemeteries. One of the pyramids, Huaca Larga, where excavations are still being undertaken, is the longest adobe structure in the world, measuring 700 m long, 280 m wide and over 30 m high. There is no evidence of occupation of Túcume previous to the Sicán, or Lambayeque people who developed the site AD 1000-1375 until the Chimú conquered the region, establishing a short reign until the arrival of the Incas around 1470. The Incas built on top of the existing structure of **Huaca Larga** using stone from Cerro La Raya. Among the other pyramids which make up this huge complex are: **Huaca El Mirador** (90 m by 65 m, 30 m high), **Huaca Las Estacas, Huaca Pintada** and **Huaca de las Balsas** which is thought to have housed people of elevated status such as priests.

Not much of the site is open to view, only the miradores mentioned above and the walk through the site there, as lots of study is going on. There is a pleasant dry forest walk to Huaca I, with shade, bird- and lizard-watching. **A site museum** contains architectural reconstructions, photographs and drawings. There is a good hostel, **Los Horcones**, www.loshorconesdetucume.com, rustic luxury in the shadow of the pyramids, with adobe and algarrobo rooms set in lovely garden with lots of birdlife. Note that if rice is being grown nearby in January-May there can be a serious mosquito problem.

The town of Túcume Viejo is a 20 minute walk beyond the site. Look for the side road heading towards a new park, opposite which is the ruin of a huge colonial church made of adobe and some brick. The surrounding countryside is pleasant for walks through mango trees and fields of maize. *Fiesta de la Purísima Concepción*, the festival of the town's patron saint, is eight days prior to Carnival in February, and also in September.

Ferreñafe and Sicán

The colonial town of **Ferreñafe**, 20 km northeast of Chiclayo, is worth a visit, especially for the **Museo Nacional Sicán** ⓘ *T286469, Tue-Sun 0900-1700, US$2.75, students US$1.10,* *http://sican.perucultural.org.pe*. This excellent new museum on the outskirts of town houses objects of the Sicán (Lambayeque) culture from near Batán Grande. **Tourist office**: helpful **Mincetur** office on the Plaza de Armas ⓘ *T282843, citesipan@mincetur.gob.pe*.

The entrance to **El Santuario Histórico Bosque de Pómac** ⓘ *free, visitors' centre, dalemandelama@gmail.com, 0900-1700, a guide (Spanish only) can be hired with transport, US$3.45, horses for hire US$6*, which includes the ruins of **Sicán**, lies 20 km beyond Ferreñafe along the road to Batán Grande (from the Panamericana another entrance is near Túcume). Visiting is not easy because of the arid conditions and distances involved: it is 10 km to the nearest huaca (pyramid). At the visitors' centre food and drinks are available and camping is permitted. The guide covers a two-hour tour of the area which includes at least two huacas, some of the most ancient carob trees and a mirador (viewpoint), which affords a beautiful view across the emerald green tops of the forest with the enormous pyramids dramatically breaking through. Sicán has revealed several sumptuous tombs dating to AD 900-1100. The ruins comprise some 12 large adobe pyramids, arranged around a huge plaza, measuring 500 by 250 m, with 40 archaeological sites in total. The city, of the Sicán (or Lambayeque culture), was probably moved to Túcume (see above), 6 km west, following 30 years of severe drought and then a devastating El Niño related flood in AD 1050-1100. These events appear to have provoked a rebellion in which many of the remaining temples on top of the pyramids were burnt and destroyed. The forest itself has good birdwatching possibilities.

Two hours beyond Pómac is **Laquipampa Wildlife Refuge** ⓘ *contact zr_laquipampa@inrena.gob.pe*, 8,329 ha, in a green and fertile high Andean valley. The dry forest here, from 500-2,500 m, is the habitat of many birds endemic to the Tumbesian zone, also the spectacled bear and rare flora. Take a passing bus for Incahuasi.

North of Chiclayo

On the old Pan-American Highway 885 km from Lima, **Olmos** is a tranquil place (several hotels and *Festival de Limón* last week in June). A paved road runs east from Olmos over the Porculla Pass, branching north to Jaén and east to Bagua Grande (see page 1368). The old Pan-American Highway continues from Olmos to Cruz de Caña and Piura. At Lambayeque the new Pan-American Highway, which is in good condition, branches off the old road and drives 190 km straight across the Sechura Desert to Piura. There is also a coast road, narrow and scenic, between Lambayeque and Sechura via Bayovar.

Olmos is the best base for observing the critically endangered White-winged Guan, a bird thought extinct for 100 years until its rediscovery in 1977. On the outskirts is the White-winged Guan captive breeding centre, **Zoocriadero Bárbara d'Achille** ⓘ *Km 103, Olmos*, which also has an aviary of rescued birds, and the **Asociación Cracidae Perú** (director Fernando Angulo Pratolongo) ⓘ *Torres Paz 708, Chiclayo, T074-238748, cracidae@llampayec.rcp.net.pe*. Captive breeding started in 1979 and the first reintroduction into the wild was made in 2001 at Chaparrí (see page 1334). One place where the guans can be seen in the wild is Quebrada Limón (or Frejolillo), where guides from the local community check on the guans' whereabouts in order to take visitors to see them in the early morning. Ask at the breeding centre for how to get there.

Sechura Desert is a large area of shifting sands separating the oases of Chiclayo and Piura. Water for irrigation comes from the Chira and Piura rivers, and from the Olmos and Tinajones irrigation projects which bring water from the Amazon watershed by means of tunnels (one over 16 km long) through the Andes to the Pacific coast. **Note** Solo cyclists should not cross the desert as muggings have occurred. Take the safer, inland route. In the desert, there is no water, no fuel and no accommodation. Do not attempt this alone.

Chiclayo and around listings

For Sleeping and Eating price codes and other relevant information, see Essentials, pages 38-40.

Sleeping

Chiclayo *p1331, map p1332*

AL Costa del Sol, Balta 399, T227272, www.costadelsolperu.com. Non-smoking rooms, smart, TV, mall pool, sauna, jacuzzi, Wi-Fi, ATM. *Páprika* restaurant, good value Sun buffets US$7.50, vegetarian options.

AL Gran Hotel Chiclayo, Villareal 115, T234911, www.granhotelchiclayo.com.pe. With breakfast, a/c, pool, safe car park, changes dollars, jacuzzi, entertainments, restaurant. Warmly recommended.

AL-A Garza, Bolognesi 756, T228172, www.garzahotel.com. A/c, excellent bar/restaurant, pool, car park, airport transfers, Wi-Fi, close to bus stations so activity at all hours. Recommended.

A Casa de la Luna, José Bernardo Alcedo 250, T270156, www.hotelcasadelaluna.com.pe. Good modern, business class hotel, a/c, excellent showers, internet, Wi-Fi, pool, restaurant, parking.

A Inti, Luis Gonzales 622, T235931, www.intihotel.com.pe. More expensive rooms with jacuzzi, family rooms available, welcome cocktail, airport transfer included, with buffet breakfast, parking, Wi-Fi, a/c, safe and fridge in room, restaurant, helpful staff.

A Las Musas, Los Faiques 101, Urb Santa Victoria, T273445, lasmusas@terra.com.pe. Large rooms, afable service, TV, mimibar, internet and Wi-Fi, karaoke and fiestas at weekends.

C El Sol, Elías Aguirre 119, T232120, hotelvicus@hotmail.com. Hot water, big rooms, restaurant, pool by car park, TV lounge, comfortable, good value.

C-D Santa Rosa, L González 927, T224411, www santarosahotelchiclayo.com. Hot water, fan, laundry, with breakfast, Wi-Fi, good value.

D América, Av L González 943, T229305, hotelamericasac@hotmail.com. Comfortable, restaurant, good value, breakfast included, Wi-Fi, frigobar. Recommended.

D-E Hospedaje Concordia, 7 de Enero Sur 235, Urb San Eduardo, T209423. Rooms on 2nd floor bigger than 3rd, modern, pleasant, discounts for long stays, TV, no meals, Wi-Fi, laundry service, view of Parque San Eduardo.

D-E Hospedaje San Eduardo, 7 de Enero Sur 267, Urb San Eduardo, T208668. No meals, colourful decor, modern bathrooms, fan, Wi-Fi, public phone, quiet, cable TV, hot water.

D-E Sol Radiante, Izaga 392, T237858. Hot water, comfortable, TV, pleasant, family-run, Wi-Fi, laundry, tourist information. Pay in advance.

E Pirámide Real, MM Izaga 726, T224036. Compact and spotless, good value, no meals, safe in room, TV, fan, Wi-Fi, very central.

E Sicán, MM Izaga 356, T208741, hsican@hotmail.com. With breakfast, hot water, TV, internet cabin, fan, comfortable, welcoming and trustworthy.

Lambayeque *p1333*

B Hostería San Roque, 2 de Mayo 437, T282860, www.hosteriasanroque.com. In a fine, extensive 19th-century house, beautifully refurbished, helpful staff, bar, swimming pool, with breakfast, lunch on request. Recommended. The owners are also rebuilding **Hostería Santa Lucía**, 8 de Octubre y San Martín, with hotel, upmarket café, promises to be equally impressive.

D Hostal Libertad, Bolívar 570, T283561, www.hostallibertad.com. 1½ blocks from plaza, big rooms, fridge, TV, meals extra, good, arranges tours.

E Posada La Norteña, Panamericana Norte Km 780, 3 blocks from town, T282602. Quiet, safe, hot water, fan, more expensive with TV, meals extra.

Sipán: Chaparrí *p1334*

A-B EcoLodge Chaparrí, T074-97 9685626 or 074-452299, www.chaparrilodge.com. A delightful oasis in the dry forest, 6 beautifully decorated cabins, built of stone and mud, nice and cool, solar power. Price is for all-inclusive package (except horse hire). Complimentary cup of wine on arrival, first-class food. Sechuran foxes in the gardens; hummingbirds bathe at the pool about 0600 every day. Recommended.

North of Chiclayo: Olmos *p1335*

D El Remanso, San Francisco 100, T427158, elremansolmos@yahoo.com. Like an hacienda with courtyards, small pool, whitewashed rooms, colourful bedding, flowers and bottled water in room, hot water (supposedly). Price is full board, good restaurant. Charming owner.

Eating

Chiclayo *p1331, map p1332*

For delicious, cheap ceviche, go to the Nativo stall in the Mercado Central, a local favourite.

El Huaralino, La Libertad 155, Santa Victoria. Wide variety, international and creole.

Fiesta, Av Salaverry 1820 in 3 de Octubre suburb, T201970, www.restaurantfiesta gourmet.com. Gourmet local dishes, excellent food and service, beautifully presented, daily and seasonal specials, fabulous juices, popular business lunch place.

Hebrón, Balta 605. For more upmarket than average chicken, but also local food and *parrilla*, good salads. Also does an excellent breakfast and a good buffet at weekends.

Kaprichos, Pedro Ruíz 1059, T232721. Chinese, delicious, huge portions.

Las Américas, Aguirre 824. Open 0700-0200, good service. Recommended.

Roma, Izaga 706. Wide choice, open all day for breakfasts, snacks and meals.

Romana, Balta 512,T223598. First-class food, usually good breakfast, popular with locals.

Tradiciones, 7 de Enero Sur 105, T221192. Open 0900-1700 daily. Good variety of local dishes, including ceviche, and drinks, nice atmosphere and garden, good service.

Boulevar, Colón entre Izaga y Aguirre. Good, friendly, *menú* and à la carte.

Café Astoria, Bolognesi 627. Open 0800-1200, 1530-2100. Breakfast, good value *menú*.

La Parra, Izaga 746. Chinese and creole, *parrillada*, very good, large portions, cheerful place.

La Plazuela, San José 299, Plaza Elías Aguirre. Good food, seats outside.

Greycy, Elias Aguirre y Lapoint. Good local ice cream.

D'Onofrio, Balta y Torres Paz. Good ice cream.

La Panadería, Lapoint 847. Good choice of breads, including *integral*, snacks and soft drinks.

Festivals and events

Chiclayo *p1331, map p1332*

6 Jan: **Reyes Magos** in **Mórrope**, **Illimo** and other towns, a recreation of a medieval pageant in which pre-Columbian deities become the Wise Men. On **4 Feb**: **Túcume** devil dances (see below). **Holy Week**, traditional Easter celebrations and processions in many villages. **2-7 Jun**: **Divine Child of the Miracle**, Villa de Eten. **27-31 Jul**: **Fexticum** in **Monsefú**, traditional foods, drink, handicrafts, music and dance. **5 Aug:** pilgrimage from the mountain shrine of **Chalpón** to **Motupe**, 90 km north of Chiclayo; the cross is brought down from a cave and carried in procession through the village. At **Christmas** and **New Year**, processions and children dancers (*pastorcitos* and *seranitas*) can be seen in many villages, eg **Ferreñafe**, **Mochumi**, **Mórrope**.

Activities and tours

Chiclayo *p1331, map p1332*

The Lambayeque's museums, Sipán and Túcume (see Around Chiclayo) can easily be visited by public transport. Local operators run 3-hr tours to Sipán; Túcume and Lambayeque (5 hrs); Sicán is a full-day tour including Ferreñafe and Pómac; also to Zaña and coastal towns.

InkaNatura, in Gran Hotel Chiclayo (address above), T209948, www.inkanatura.net. Run historical and nature tours throughout northern Peru. Good service, open Mon-Fri 0915-1315, 1515-1915, Sat 0915-1315.

Horse riding

Rancho Santana, in Pacora, T074-97-971 2145 (mob), www.cabalgatasperu.com. Relaxing tours on horseback, half-day (US$15.50), one-day (US$22.50) or three-day tours, including to Santuario Bosque de Pómac, Sicán ruins and Túcume, Swiss run (Andrea Martin), good horses. lodging in Pacora, **F** pp at **Hospedaje Naylamp**, 28 de Julio 117, T691674, with swimming pool, free camping with cooking and laundry facilities, meals available. Frequently recommended.

Transport

Chiclayo *p1331, map p1332*

Air José Abelardo Quiñones González airport 1 km from town, T233192; taxi from centre US$1. Daily flights to/from **Lima** and **Piura** with LAN (MM Izaga 770).

Bus No terminal terrestre; most buses stop outside their offices on Bolognesi. To **Lima**, 770 km, US$18-21.50 and US$28.55-32 for *bus cama*: **Civa**, Av Bolognesi 714, T223434; **Cruz del Sur**, Bolognesi 888, T225508; **Ormeño**, Haya de la Torre 242, 2 blocks south of Bolognesi, T234206; **Ittsa**, Av Bolognesi 155, T233612; **Línea**, Bolognesi 638, T222221, *especial* and *bus cama* service; **Móvil**, Av Bolognesi 195, T271940 (goes as far as Tarapoto); **Oltursa**, ticket office at Balta e Izaga, T237789, terminal at Vicente de la Vega 101, T225611; **Tepsa**, Bolognesi 504-36 y Colón, T236981; **Transportes Chiclayo**, Av L Ortiz 010, T223632. Most companies leave from 1900 onwards. To **Trujillo**, 209 km, with **Emtrafesa**, Av Balta 110, T234291, almost hourly from 0530-2015, US$4.75, and *Línea*, as above. To **Piura**, US$4.50, **Línea** and **Transportes Chiclayo** leave hourly throughout the day; also **Emtrafesa** and buses from the **Cial/Flores** terminal, Bolognesi 751, T239579. To **Sullana**, US$5.50. To **Tumbes**, US$6, 9-10 hrs; with **Cial**, **Cruz del Sur** or **El Dorado**. Some companies on the route northwards arrive full from Lima. Many buses go on to the **Ecuadorean border** at **Aguas Verdes**. Go to the *Salida* on Elías Aguirre, mototaxi drivers know where it is, be there by 1900. All buses stop here after leaving their terminals to try and fill empty seats, so discounts may be possible. To **Cajamarca**, 260 km, US$6.25-15.50, eg **Línea**, 4 a day; others from Tepsa terminal, Bolognesi y Colón, eg **Días**, T224448. To **Chachapoyas**, US$11-16: **Civa** 1730 daily, 10-11 hrs; **Turismo Kuélap**, in Tepsa station, 1830 daily, **Móvil**, address above, at 2000. To **Jaén**, US$5.50-10: eg **Móvil**, and **Transcade** (Av Saenz Peña 106, T232552). To **Tarapoto**, 18 hrs, US$12.50-23, with **Móvil**, also **Tarapoto Tours**, Bolognesi 751, T636231. **Taxi** Mototaxis are a cheap way to get around; US$0.70 anywhere in city.

Monsefú and the coast *p1332*
Combis to **Monsefú** cost US$0.50 from Balta y Pedro Ruiz, or Terminal Epsewl, Av Quiñónez. The **ports** may be visited on a half-day trip. Combis leave from Av L Ortiz y San José, Chiclayo, to Pimentel, US$0.50. Colectivos to Eten leave from 7 de Enero y Arica.

Lambayeque *p1333*
Colectivos from **Chiclayo** US$0.50, 25 mins, from Pedro Ruíz at the junction with Av Ugarte. Also **Brüning Express** combis from Vicente de la Vega entre Angamos y Av L Ortiz, every 15 mins, US$0.25.

Sipán *p1333*
Combis to Sipán leave from Plaza Elías Aguirre, US$0.50, 1 hr.

Chaparrí
Take a public bus from Leoncio Prado y Sáenz Peña, Chiclayo, to **Chongoyape** (1¼ hrs, US$1.10), then a mototaxi to **Chaparrí**, US$7.50.

Túcume *p1334*
Combis from **Chiclayo**, Av Leguía, 15 m from Angamos, US$0.75, 45 mins; mototaxi from highway/new town to ruins US$0.35. Combi Túcume-**Lambayeque**, US$0.45, 25 mins.

Ferreñafe and Sicán *p1334*
Colectivos from Chiclayo to the centre of Ferreñafe leave every few mins from 8 de Octubre y Sáenz Peña, 15 mins, U$0.75, take a mototaxi to the museum, 5 mins, US$0.50. Alternatively, combis for Batán Grande depart from the Terminal Nor-Este, Av N de Piérola in Chiclayo, and pass the museum every 15-20 mins, 20 mins, US$0.85.

Directory

Chiclayo *p1331, map p1332*
Banks Beware of counterfeit bills, especially among street changers on 6th block of Balta, on Plaza de Armas and 7th block of MM Izaga. **BCP**, Balta 630. **Scotiabank**, Bolognesi, opposite Cuglievan. **Interbank**, on Plaza de Armas. All open Sat morning. **Consulates** Honorary German Consul, Armin Dietrich Bülow, José Francisco Cabrera Cdra 1 (Casa Comunal de la Juventud), T237442, abm@ddm.com.pe. **Cultural centres** Alianza Francesa, Cuglievan 644, T237571, www.universidadperu.com/alianza-francesa-de-chiclayo.php. **Instituto de Cultura Peruano-Norteamericana**, Av Izaga 807, T231241, icpnachi@mail.udep.edu.pe. **Instituto Nacional de la Cultura**, Av L González 375, T237261, occasional poetry readings, information on local archaeological sites, lectures, etc. **Internet** Lots of places, particularly on San José and Elías Aguirre, average price US$0.60 per hr. **Medical services** Ambulance: Max Salud, 7 de Enero 185, T234032, maxsalud@telematic.edu.com. **Post offices** On 1 block of Aguirre, 6 blocks from Plaza. **Telephones** Telefónica, headquarters at Aguirre 919; bank of phone booths on 7th block of 7 de Enero behind Cathedral for international and collect calls. Phone card sellers hang around here.

Piura and around → *Phone code: 073. Colour map 3, A1. Population: 377,500.*

A proud and historic city, Piura was founded in 1532, three years before Lima, by the conquistadores left behind by Pizarro. The city has two well-kept parks, Cortés and Pizarro (with a statue of the *conquistador*, also called Plaza de las Tres Culturas), and public gardens. Old

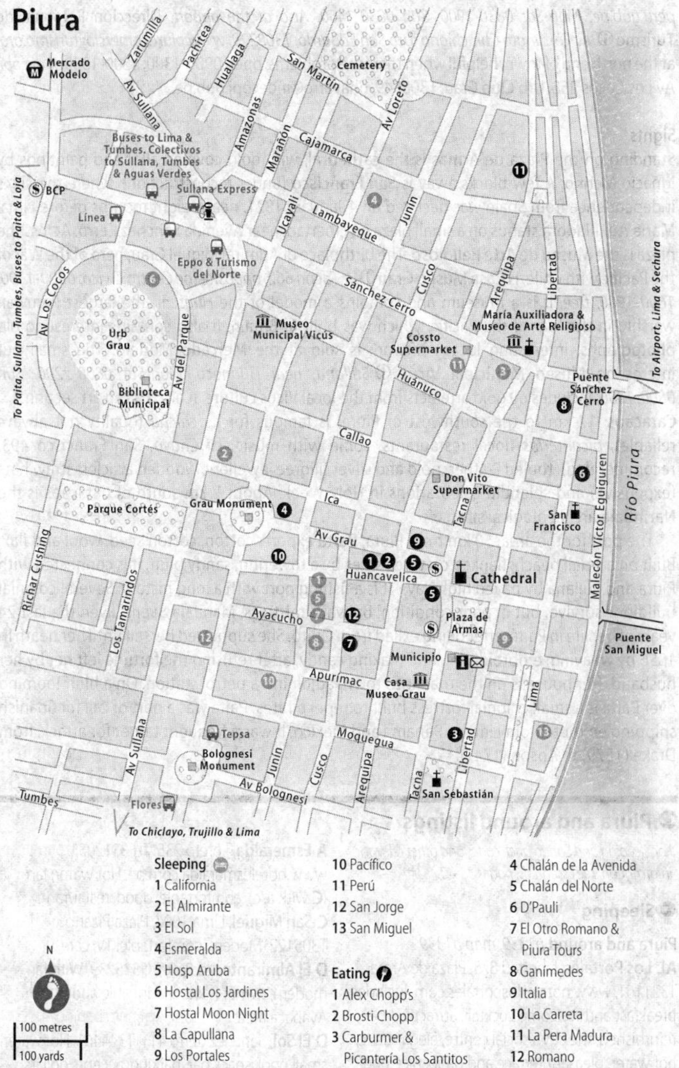

Sleeping
1 California
2 El Almirante
3 El Sol
4 Esmeralda
5 Hosp Aruba
6 Hostal Los Jardines
7 Hostal Moon Night
8 La Capullana
9 Los Portales
10 Pacífico
11 Perú
12 San Jorge
13 San Miguel

Eating
1 Alex Chopp's
2 Brosti Chopp
3 Carburmer & Picantería Los Santitos
4 Chalán de la Avenida
5 Chalán del Norte
6 D'Pauli
7 El Otro Romano & Piura Tours
8 Ganímedes
9 Italia
10 La Carreta
11 La Pera Madura
12 Romano

buildings are kept in repair and new buildings blend with the Spanish style of the old city. Three bridges cross the Río Piura to Castilla, the oldest from Calle Huancavelica, for pedestrians (Puente San Miguel), another from Calle Sánchez Cerro, and the newest from Avenida Panamericana Norte, at west end of town. The winter climate, May-September, is very pleasant although nights can be cold and the wind piercing; December to March is very hot.

Tourist offices Information at the tourist office ⓘ *Ayacucho 377, T320249, iperupiura@promperu.gob.pe, Mon-Sat 0830-1900, Sun 0830-1400. Also at the airport.* **Dirección Regional de Turismo** ⓘ *Av Fortunato Chirichigno, Urb San Eduardo, T308229, www.piuracomercioyturismo.org,* at the north end of town, helpful when there are problems, open 0900-1300, 1600-1800. *Indecopi*, Av Los Cocos 268, Urb Club Grau, T308549, dnavarro@indecopi.gob.pe.

Sights

Standing on the **Plaza de Armas** is the **cathedral**, with gold covered altar and paintings by Ignacio Merino. A few blocks away is **San Francisco** (under reconstruction), where the city's independence from Spain was declared on 4 January 1821, nearly eight months before Lima. **María Auxiliadora** stands on a small plaza on Libertad, near Avenida Sánchez Cerro. Across the plaza is the **Museo de Arte Religioso**. The birthplace of Admiral Miguel Grau, hero of the War of the Pacific with Chile, is **Casa Museo Grau** ⓘ *Jr Tacna 662, opposite the Centro Cívico, 0800-1300, 1600-1900, free*. It is a museum and contains a model of the *Huáscar*, the largest Peruvian warship in the War of the Pacific, which was built in Britain. It also contains interesting old photographs. Interesting local craftwork is sold at the **Mercado Modelo**. The small but interesting **Museo Municipal Vicús** ⓘ *Sullana, near Huánuco, Mon-Sat 0800-2200, Sun 0800-1200*, includes 60 gold artefacts from the local Vicús culture. It also has an art section.
Catacaos 12 km to the southwest of Piura, is famous for its *chicha* (quality not always reliable), *picanterías* (local restaurants, some with music, *La Chayo*, San Francisco 493, recommended), tooled leather, gold and silver filigree jewellery, wooden articles, straw hats (expensive) and splendid celebrations in Holy Week. About 2 km south of Catacaos is the **Narihualá** archaeological site.

The port for the area, 50 km from Piura, **Paita** exports cotton, cotton seed, wool and flax. Built on a small beach, flanked on three sides by a towering, sandy bluff, it is connected with Piura and Sullana by paved highways. It is a fishing port with a long history. Several colonial buildings survive, but in poor condition. Bolívar's mistress, Manuela Sáenz, lived the last 24 years of her life in Paita, after being exiled from Quito. She supported herself until her death in 1856 by weaving, embroidering and making candy, after refusing the fortune left her by her husband. Her house is on the road into town, adjoining a petrol station. On a bluff looming over Paita is a small colonial fortress built to repel pirates. Paita was a port of call for Spanish shipping en route from Lima to Panama and Mexico. It was a frequent target for attack, from Drake (1579) to Anson (1741).

Piura and around listings

For Sleeping and Eating price codes and other relevant information, see Essentials, pages 38-40.

Sleeping

Piura and around *p1339, map p1339*

AL Los Portales, Libertad 875, Plaza de Armas, T321161, www.hoteleslosportales.com. Includes breakfast and welcome cocktail, attractively refurbished, the city's social centre, elegant, a/c, hot water, pleasant terrace and patio, nice pool.

A Esmeralda, Loreto 235, T/F331205, www.hotelesmeralda.com.pe. Hot water, fan (**C** with a/c), comfortable, good, restaurant.

C San Miguel, Lima 1007, Plaza Pizarro, T305122. Modern, comfortable, TV, café.

D El Almirante, Ica 860, T/F335239. With fan, modern, owner is knowledgeable about the Ayabaca area.

D El Sol, Sánchez Cerro 411, T324461. Hot water, small pool, snack bar, parking, accepts dollars cash or TCs but won't change them. Recommended.

D San Jorge, Jr Loreto 960, T327514. With fan, cheaper without cable TV, hot water.

E Hostal Los Jardines, Av Los Cocos 436, T326 590. Hot water, TV, laundry, parking, good value.

E Perú, Arequipa 476, T333919. With fan, safe, laundry service, cold water, modern small rooms, all meals in restaurant are extra.

F La Capullana, Junín 925, T321239. Some cheap single rooms, welcoming.

F Pacífico, Apurímac 717, T303061. With bath, hot water and fan, simple, good value.

F Hostal Moon Night, Junín 899, T336174. Comfortable, modern, spacious, **G** without bath or TV, cold water, good value.

G pp **California**, Jr Junín 835, upstairs, T328789. Shared bath, own water-tank, mosquito netting on windows, roof terrace, brightly decorated. Recommended (some short stay, though).

G Hospedaje Aruba, Junín 851, T303067. Small rooms but comfortable, shared bath, fan on request. Recommended.

Eating

Piura and around *p1339, map p1339*

TTT Carburmer, Libertad 1014, T332380. Very good lunches and dinners, also serves pizza.

TTT Picantería Los Santitos, in the same precinct is Carburmer. Lunch only, wide range of traditional dishes in a renovated colonial house.

TT Alex Chopp's, Huancavelica 538, T322568. A la carte dishes, seafood, fish, chicken and meats, beer, popular at lunchtime.

TT Brosti Chopp, Arequipa 780, T303753. Similar, but with lunch *menú* for US$1.45.

TT La Carreta, Huancavelica 726, T304231. Popular for roast chicken.

TT Romano, Ayacucho 580. Popular with locals, extensive menu, excellent set meal for US$1.55, Mon-Sat 0700-2300. Recommended. Also has **TT El Otro Romano**, Ayacucho 579, offering the same fare, Tue-Sun 0900-1700.

T Ganímedes, Lima 440, T329176. A good vegetarian restaurant, very popular set lunch, à la carte is slow but well worth it, try the excellent yoghurt and fruit.

T Italia, Grau 172. For breakfasts, snacks, desserts and juices.

Cafés

Chalán del Norte several branches for sweets, cakes and ice cream, Tacna 520 on Plaza de Armas, Grau 173 and 450 (*Chalán de la Avenida*).

D'Pauli, Lima 541. Sweets, cakes and ice-cream.

La Pera Madura, Arequipa 168, next to Cine Municipal, daily 1700-2300. For local specialities, eg turket sandwiches, plus tamales and other snacks.

Activities and tours

Piura and around *p1339, map p1339*

Piura Tours, C Ayacucho 585, T326778, piuratours@cpi.udep.edu.pe. The manager Mario speaks very good English.

Transport

Piura and around *p1339, map p1339*

Air Capitán Guillermo Concha airport is in Castilla, 10 mins from the centre by taxi (US$1). It has gift shops and two car rental agencies (see below). Daily flights with **Lan** (Av Grau 140) to **Lima** via **Chiclayo**.

Bus Most companies are on Av Sánchez Cerro, blocks 11, 12 and 13 (see www.munipiura.gob.pe/turismo/transporte.shtml). To **Lima**, 1,038 km, 14-15½ hrs, US$18-32, on the Panamericana Norte. Most buses stop at the major cities on route; **Ittsa**, Sánchez Cerro 1142, T308645; **Línea**, Sánchez Cerro 1215, T327 821; **Tepsa**, Loreto 1195, T323721. To **Chiclayo**, 190 km, 3 hrs, US$4.50, several buses daily. Also several daily buses to **Trujillo**, 7 hrs, 487 km, US$9.25, to travel by day change in Chiclayo. To **Tumbes**, 282 km, 4½ hrs, US$5, several buses daily, eg **Cruz del Sur** (Av Circunvalación 160, T337094, also to Lima), **Cial** (Bolognesi 817, T304250) and **Emtrafesa** (Los Naranjos 255, T337093, also to Chiclayo and Trujillo); also colectivos, US$7. To **Talara**, US$2, 2 hrs, with **Eppo**, T304543. To **Paita**, **Trans Dora**, Sánchez Cerro 1391, every 20 mins, 1 hr, US$1; also from Paita terminal on Av Gullman, just off Sánchez Cerro. To **Máncora**, US$3.15, 3 hrs, with **Eppo**.

To Ecuador: To **Machala** and **Guayaquil**, the fastest route if you are heading directly to Quito, **CIFA**, Los Naranjos y Sánchez Cerro (cuadra 11-12) opposite Emtrafesa, T305925, 5 a day, Machala US$6, 6 hrs, Guayaquil US$10,

9 hrs. **Ecuatoriana Pullman**, on Av Loreto, 0830, 2030 to **Guayaquil** via Sullana, Tumbes and Machala, US$9, 10 hrs. Otherwise, go to Tumbes and travel on from there for the Aguas Verdes crossing. To **Loja**, the best option if you want to visit the southern or central highlands of Ecuador, **Transportes Loja**, Sánchez Cerro 1480, T309407, 4 daily, US$8, 8 hrs, to **Macará** US$4. Or **Unión Cariamanga**, Sánchez Cerro (cuadra 18) y Av Vice, Urbanización Santa Ana, T96 9900135 (mob), at 1330 and 2000. Alternatively take a bus to **Sullana**, 38 km, 30 mins (US$0.50), **Eppo, Sullana Express** and **Turismo del Norte**, all on 1100 block of Sánchez Cerro; also colectivos (US$1). To **La Tina** on the Ecuadorean frontier, is a further 128 km, 1¾ hrs, US$3.40. It's best to take an early bus to Sullana (start at 0430, leave when full), then a colectivo (see under Sullana).

Catacaos *p1340*

Combis From **Piura** to Catacaos leave when full from bus terminal at block 12 of Av Sánchez Cerro, US$0.30, 20 mins.

Directory

Piura and around *p1339, map p1339*

Banks BCP, Grau y Tacna. **BBV Continental**, Plaza de Armas. **Interbank**, Grau 170. *Casas de cambio* are at Arequipa 600 block and 722, and Ica 366, 456 and 460. Street changers can be found on Grau outside *BCP*. **Car hire** Vicús, T342051, http://vicusr entacar.com.pe; **Ramos**, T348668, www.ramosrentacars.com. Both at airport. **Consulates** Honorary British Consul, c/o American Airlines, Hancavelica 223, T305990. **Honorary German Consul**, Dr Percy Cavero, La Ribera MZ B Lote 6, Urb La Ribera, T300243, percy.garcia@udep.pe. **Internet** Several in the centre. 10 machines in the Biblioteca Municipal, Urb Grau, US$0.60 per hr. **Post offices** Libertad y Ayacucho on Plaza de Armas. **Telephones** Loreto 259, national and international phone and fax. Also at Ovalo Grau 483. **Useful addresses** Immigration: Av Integración Urbana y Av Sullana, T335536.

North to Ecuador

Sullana, built on a bluff over the fertile Chira valley, is a busy, modern place 38 km north of Piura. Here the Pan-American Highway forks. To the east it crosses the Peru-Ecuador border at La Tina and continues via Macará to Loja and Cuenca. The excellent paved road is very scenic. The more frequently used route to the border is the coastal road which goes from Sullana northwest towards the Talara oilfields, and then follows the coastline to Máncora and Tumbes.

Border at La Tina-Macará The border crossing is problem-free; **Peruvian immigration** is open 24 hours and officials are helpful. Go to Peruvian immigration at the end of the bridge, get a stamp, walk across and then go to Ecuadorean immigration. When entering Peru, after getting the exit stamp from Ecuador, go to Peruvian immigration to get the TAM immigration form, fill it out, go across the street to the police (PNP) to get their stamp, then back to immigration for the entry stamp. If you forget the last step, you will have a serious problem when leaving Peru. There are no customs searches (vehicles, including colectivos, are subject to full searches, though). There are no money changers right at the bridge, only in Macará. At the border, only Banco Financiero on the Peruvian side, Monday-Friday 0900-1600, US$ cash only. There is one *hospedaje* and several eating places on the road down to the bridge.

To the border at Tumbes **Talara**, 112 km north of Piura, is the main centre of the coastal oil area. It has a State-owned, 60,000 barrel-a-day oil refinery and a fertilizer plant. Set in a desert oasis 5 km west of the Panamericana, the city is a triumph over formidable natural difficulties, with water piped 40 km from the Río Chira. La Peña beach, 2 km away, is unspoilt. There is a range of hotels and many cheap restaurants on the main plaza.

Máncora and Punta Sal

Máncora, a small, attractive resort stretching along 3 km of the Panamerican Highway is popular with young Limeños and Argentines and as a stop-off for travellers, especially surfers, on the Peru-Ecuador route. Bathing is safe on a long, sandy beach and excellent beaches such as Las Pocitas and Vichayito are being developed to the south. Surfing on this coast is best November-March and boards and suits can be hired from several places on Avenida Piura, US$1.50 each per hour. It is 32 km north of the port of Cabo Blanco. Tourist office ⓘ *iPerú, Av Piura 250, Thu-Sun 1000-1700.*

At 22 km north of Máncora, Km 1187, is the turn-off for **Punta Sal Grande**, marked by a large white arch (El Arco) over the track leading into Punta Sal (2 km). Punta Sal boasts a 3-km long white sandy beach and a more upmarket clientèle than Máncora, with accommodation (and prices) to match. There is no town centre nor services such as restaurants independent of hotels; it is very quiet in the low season. Taxi from Máncora, 20 minutes, US$14, mototaxi 40 minutes, US$10, otherwise take any combi going between Mancorá and Tumbes and tell the driver you want to get out at Punta Sal, then look out for the arch marking the entrance. It takes about half an hour to walk down to the beach. **Zorritos**, 27 km south of Tumbes, is an important fishing centre with a good beach. At **Caleta La Cruz** is the only part of the Peruvian coast where the sea is warm all year, 16 km southwest of Tumbes. It was here that Pizarro landed in 1532. Regular colectivos, US$0.30 each way.

Tumbes and around → *Phone code: 072. Colour map 3, A1. Population: 94,750.*

The most northerly of Peruvian towns (265 km north of Piura), Tumbes is a garrison town: do not photograph the military or their installations – they will destroy your film and probably detain you. Most tourists stop only briefly to get transport connections to the beaches to the south, or to Ecuador to the north. The most striking thing is the bright and cheery modern public buildings. The **Malecón Benavides**, a long promenade beside the Tumbes river, has rainbow-coloured archways and a monstrous statue called El Beso (the Kiss). The Plaza de Armas sports a large structure of many colours and even the **cathedral** (1903, restored in 1985) has green and pink stripes ⓘ *entry during morning and evening mass*. Calles Bolívar and San Martín (Paseo de la Concordia) make for a pleasant wander and there is a small artesans' market at the top end of San Martín (approaching Plaza Bolognesi). On Calle Grau, there are the tumble-down colonial houses, many of which are no longer in use. **Tourist office** is in the Centro Cívico ⓘ *Bolognesi 194, 2nd level, on the plaza*. Pronaturaleza ⓘ *Jr Tarapacá 4-16, Urb Fonavi, T524764, www.pronaturaleza.org*, for specialized information about National Parks and resources in the area.

The Río Tumbes is navigable by small boat to the mouth of the river, an interesting two hour trip with fantastic birdlife and mangrove swamps. The **Santuario Nacional los Manglares de Tumbes** protects 3,000 ha of Peru's remaining 4,750 ha of mangrove forest. It contains examples of all five species of mangroves as well as being home to over 200 bird species, especially pelicans. It is best visited via the CECODEM centre near Zarumilla, but arrange day before with *Pronaturaleza* in Tumbes.

The **Parque Nacional Cerros de Amotape** protects 90,700 ha of varied habitat, but principally the best preserved area of dry forest on the west coast of South America. Species that may be sighted include the black parrot, white-backed squirrels, foxes, deer, tigrillos, pumas and white-winged guan. *Inrena* permission is needed to enter the area (which Pronaturaleza in Tumbes can arrange). All water must be carried which is why most visitors choose to visit by tour. Access is via the road which goes southeast from the Pan-American Highway at Bocapán (Km 1,233) to Casitas and Huásimo, it takes about two hours by car from Tumbes, and is best done in the dry season (July-November). Also access via Quebrada Fernández from Máncora and via Querecotilo and Los Encuentros from Sullana.

The **Zona Reservada de Tumbes** (75,000 ha) lies northeast of Tumbes between the Ecuadorean border and Cerros de Amotape National Park. It protects dry equatorial forest and tropical rainforest. Wildlife includes monkeys, otters, wild boars, small cats and crocodiles. The Río Tumbes crocodile, which is a UN Red-data species, is found at the river's mouth, where there is a small breeding programme (near Puerto Pizarro), and in its upper reaches. Access from Tumbes is via Cabuyal, Pampas de Hospital and El Caucho to the Quebrada Faical research station or via Zarumilla and Matapalo. The best accessible forest is around El Narango, beyond the research station.

Border with Ecuador The border is open 24 hours. In early 2010, a new border complex with customs, immigration and Policía Nacional del Perú (PNP) was opened, a few metres from a new international bridge. The old complex at **Zarumilla**, 3 km from **Aguas Verdes**, was also operational. At the time of writing, it was possible to cross at either bridge. An Ecuadorean border complex was under construction near the new bridge. These details will likely change. Allow at least one hour for border formalities. The Huaquillas-Tumbes crossing has traditionally been harrowing, made worse by the crowds and heat. You must always watch your belongings carefully. In addition to cheating by money changers and cab drivers, this border is known for its thefts and con tricks on traveller. Those on the direct CIFA bus from Piura or Tumbes to Guayaquil or Machala should have fewer hassles, otherwise it is best to cross in a group. Women are advised not to cross alone. Perhaps things will improve once the new border complex away from the busy towns of Huaquillas and Aguas Verdes is open. Those seeking a more relaxed crossing to or from Peru should consider La Tina-Macará.

Tumbes

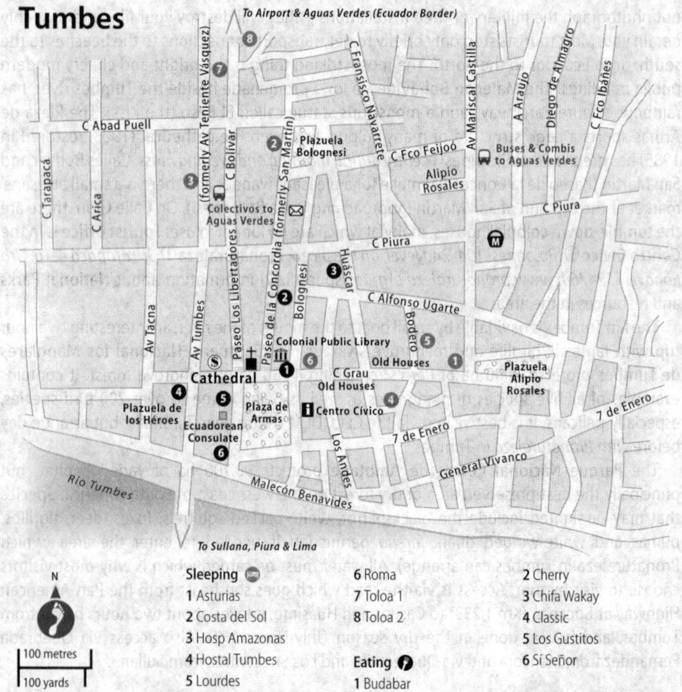

Sleeping
1 Asturias
2 Costa del Sol
3 Hosp Amazonas
4 Hostal Tumbes
5 Lourdes
6 Roma
7 Toloa 1
8 Toloa 2

Eating
1 Budabar
2 Cherry
3 Chifa Wakay
4 Classic
5 Los Gustitos
6 Sí Señor

North to Ecuador listings

For Sleeping and Eating price codes and other relevant information, see Essentials, pages 38-40.

Sleeping

North to Ecuador: Sullana *p1342*
Take care by the market. Do not arrive at night.
B Hostal La Siesta, Av Panamericana 400, T/F502264. At entrance to town, hot water, fan, **C** with cold water, pool, restaurant, laundry.
E El Churre, Tarapacá 501, T/F507006. TV, laundry, café. Recommended.
F Hospedaje San Miguel, C J Farfán 204, T502 789. **G** without bath, basic, helpful, good showers, will spray rooms against mosquitoes, cafetería.
F Hostal Lion's Palace, Grau 1030, T502587. With fan, patio, pleasant, quiet, no breakfast.

Máncora and Punta Sal *p1343*
Máncora town
The main strip of the Panamericana is known as Av Piura from the bridge for the first couple of blocks, then Av Grau to the end of town. The better hotels are at the southern end of town, with a small concentration of mid-range hotels just over the bridge. Hotels to the left look onto the beach directly in front of the best surf and often have beach entrances as well as road entrances. As the most popular with tourists, they are all quite noisy at night from nearby discos, which go until around 0200 week nights and 0600 at weekends. Prices can increase by up to 100% in high season (Dec-Mar). Many hotels have special rates for Christmas, New Year, Easter and Independence Day holidays when the resort is full to bursting with partying Limeños. When checking into any hotel, expect to pay up front and make sure you get a receipt as you will most likely be asked to pay again the next time the receptionist sees you.
C Del Wawa, beachfront, T258427, www.delwawa.com. This relaxed and spacious hotel is popular with serious surfers.
C-D Las Olas, beachfront, T258099, www.lasolasmancora.com. Smart, cabin-style rooms, hammocks and gardens, half and full-board rates available.
D Punta Ballenas, south of Cabo Blanco bridge at the south entrance to town, T258136, www.puntaballenas.com. **C** in high season, lovely setting on beach, garden with small pool, includes breakfast, expensive restaurant.
D Loki del Mar, Av Piura 262, T258484, www.lokihostel.com. Latest addition to the Loki group, seafront, modern hostel, **F** pp in dorm, with breakfast, bar, pool, internet, surf board hire.
E Casa del Turista, Av Piura 224, T258126. Family-run, TV, roof terraces giving sea views. Recommended but all but the top floor suites are noisy at night due to nearby Sol y Mar disco.
F Sol y Mar, beachfront, T258106, hsolymar@hotmail.com. One of the oldest hotels in Máncora, very popular with young travellers out for a good time. Has the loudest disco in town, and offers basic but clean room with bath and fan. Mixed reports.
F-G Hospedaje Crillon, Paita 168, 1 block back from Panamericana in centre, T258001. Basic rooms with 4 or more beds, shared bath, plenty of water. Recommended.

Quebrada Cabo Blanco
Crossing the bridge into Máncora, a dirt track leads downhill to the right, to the Quebrada Cabo Blanco, signed to La Posada Youth Hostel. The 4 hotels at the end of the track require better lighting for guests returning at night, but they are quiet and relaxing. Robberies have occurred so take a mototaxi at night (US$0.35).
C Kimbas Bungalows, T258373, www.vivamancora.com/kimbas. Chilled out spot with charming thatched bungalows, central complex with restaurant and bar, and a small pool.
C La Quebrada, T01-99 8300623, www.vivamancora.com/laquebrada/index.html. Smart, modern, large rooms with glass patio doors and hammocks, shared kitchen and TV.
C-E El Pirata, T258459, www.vivamancora.com/elpirata. Impressive (if wobbly) bamboo rooms, large, airy, mosquito nets; downstairs rooms are sturdier but lack light and some are very small. Use of basic kitchen and BBQ. Staff are helpful.

Las Pocitas
South of Máncora, a stretch of beautiful beach with rocks on the shore, behind which little pools (or pocitas) form at low tide. Being developed with luxury resorts and hotels, popular with more up-market tourists and families.

L La Casita de Sueños, T258389, www.mancora-peru.com. 3 luxury bungalows on the beach, fully equipped, secluded, self-catering, but a cook can be provided.

AL Casa Del Muelle, Km 1215 Antigua Panamericana Norte, www.casadelmuellemancora.com. Just before the pier, elegant, aimed at families. Use of well-equipped, clean kitchen, spacious, airy rooms sleep up to 5, views of the pool, beach and sea.

AL Grandmare, T258716, www.grandmaremancora.com. Individual beach bungalows around a central pool, rooms all have safes, a/c and cable TV, internet.

AL Las Arenas de Máncora, Antigua Panamericana Norte 1213, T258240, www.lasarenasdemancora.com. Smart bungalow-style accommodation, hot water, cable TV, with central bar and restaurant serving imaginative dishes, beautiful pool, palm-lined beach frontage, includes breakfast, very romantic.

C Puerto Palos, along the old Pan-American Highway south of town (10 mins by mototaxi, US$1.45), T258199, www.puertopalos.com. Excellent, nice pool overlooking ocean, good but expensive restaurant.

D Mancoral, 1 km south of Máncora pier, T516107, www.vivamancora.com/mancoral. A good budget option, basic but clean, good sea views, small, hospitable.

North of Máncora

L Samana Chakra, T01-99 411 6877, www.samanachakra.com. A well-being retreat with peaceful beachside bungalows, home-cooked food and yoga and meditation classes in a studio looking out over the pool and ocean.

D Laguna Surf Camp, T01-99 401 5628, www.vivamancora.com/lagunacamp. 100 m from the sea near new breakwater, thatched roofs, hammocks, cabins sleeping up to 6 people, helpful. Relaxed atmosphere, cabins surround small communal area with hammocks.

Punta Sal

A Caballito De Mar, T01-241 4455, www.hotelcaballitodemar.com. Immaculate beach-front rooms and small bungalows built into the cliff behind the road, pool and bar area facing the ocean. Very professional and helpful staff.

D Los Delfines, T617804, near the beach at the entrance to Playa Punta Sal. Shared bath, nice rooms, restaurant open in high season, meals on request in low season, vegetarian available, full board **AL**, more during high season for full board, **A** for a room only in high season.

D pp **Hospedaje El Bucanero**, at the entrance to Playa Punta Sal, set back from the beach, T381 125, www.elbucaneropuntasal.com. The most happening place in Punta Sal, popular with travellers, a variety of rooms, pool, restaurant, bar, gardens and billiards, great view.

E Huá, on the beach at the entrance to Playa Punta Sal, T540023, www.huapuntasal.com. **B** in the high season. A rustic old wooden building, pleasant terrace overlooking ocean, discount for IYHF card holders, camping permitted on the beach beside the hotel, meals available.

E pp **Las Terrazas**, opposite Sunset Punta Sal, T540001, lasterrazaspuntasal@yahoo.com. One of the more basic and cheaper hotels in Punta Sal, restaurant has sea view, some rooms better than others, those with own bath and sea view twice the price. Helpful owners.

Zorritos

F pp **Casa Grillo Centro Ecoturistico Naturista**, Los Pinos 563, between Bocapán and Los Pinos, 30 km from Tumbes, T01-99 764 2836, www.casagrillo.net. Take colectivo from Tumbes market to Los Pinos, or get off bus on Panamericana at Km 1236.5. Youth Hostel, excellent restaurant including vegetarian, great place to relax, 6 rooms for up to 4, made of local materials, shared bath, hot water, laundry, surfing, scuba diving, fishing, cycling, trekking, horse riding, camping available.

Tumbes and around *p1343, map p1344*

Av Tumbes is still sometimes referred to by its old name of Teniente Vásquez. At holiday times it can be very difficult to find a room.

B Costa del Sol, San Martín 275, Plazuela Bolognesi, T523991, www.costadelsolperu.com. The only high class hotel in town, hot water, minibars, a/c, good restaurant, garden, pool, excellent service. Parking for an extra fee. Rooms which look onto the Plaza Bolognesi are noisy.

C Asturias, Av Mcal Castilla 305, T522569, turismoasturiasrl@hotmail.com. Comfortable, hot water, a/c, cable TV, restaurant, bar and laundry. Accepts credit cards.

E Lourdes, Mayor Bodero 118, 3 blocks from main plaza, T522966. Welcoming place. Narrow corridor leading to cell-like rooms which are plushly decorated with a mixture of antique and modern furniture. Good bathrooms, fans in each room.
E Roma, Bolognesi 425, Plaza de Armas, T524137. Best of the budget hotels in a great location, light and spacious rooms, hot water, cable TV, fan. 2nd floor terrace looks out over the Plaza. Recommended.
F Hospedaje Amazonas, Av Tumbes 317, T525266. Large, noisy, with basic facilities, feels run down, smallish dark rooms but is relatively clean and secure. Unreliable water supply in the mornings.
F Hostal Tumbes, Filipinas s/n, off Grau, T522203, or 972 852954. Small, dark, basic but cleanish rooms with fans and bath. Good cheap option.
F Toloa 1, Av Tumbes 436, T523771. No frills hostal, standard rooms have bath, fan and cable TV, noisy as on the Panamericana, popular with travelling businessmen, which may be an uncomfortable environment for women travelling alone.
F Toloa 2, Bolívar 458, T524135. Same as Toloa 1 but slightly more run-down, and 5 soles less per room.

Border with Ecuador *p1344*

Zarumilla/Aguas Verdes

If stuck overnight in the border area there is a hotel in Aguas Verdes **F Hostal Francis**, Av República de Perú 220, T561177, OK. Aguas Verdes also has phone booths and airline ticket offices. There are 4 hotels in Zarumilla, at Km 1290 on the Pan-American Highway, 5 km south of Aguas Verdes.

Eating

Máncora and Punta Sal *p1343*

Máncora

A small open-air commercial centre called **The Birdhouse** has some of the best eateries in town, including: **Green Eggs and Ham**, open 0730-1300 for great breakfasts at US$3.35, 8 options including waffles, pancakes or eggs and bacon, plus optional extra portions, juice or coffee included. **Papa Mo´s** milk bar, directly underneath Green Eggs and Ham, with comfy seats which are practically on the beach and a selection of drinks.

Along the main strip of the Panamericana:

TT Pizzería Chan-Chan, Av Piura, udoliliana@terraplus.com.pe. Good pizza and pasta, fairly expensive but delicious.
TT-T El Faro, Av Piura 233, elfarodemancora@hotmail.com. One of the most popular restaurants, a large variety of seafood, chicken and meat dishes for lunch or dinner, as well as a cheap set menu at lunch times. In the evening it becomes a crowded spot for drinks.
TT-T El Tuno, Av Piura 233. Probably the best restaurant in Máncora, gourmet food at everyday prices. Specialties are grilled tuna steaks and homemade pastas.
T Angela's Place/Cafetería de Angela, Av Piura 396, www.vivamancora.com/deangela. A great option for a healthy breakfast or lunch and heaven for vegetarians and whole-food lovers, homemade rye bread and whole grain bread featuring 10 grains, as well as natural yogurts, fresh fruit etc. Free tourist information on the back of the menus.
T Café La Bajadita, has an impressive selection of delicious homemade deserts and cakes including cheesecake with a choice of 3 fruit toppings. Other food is disappointing – go here for desserts.
There are many cheaper restaurants further north along Av Piura and at the entrance to the beach, all offering ceviche and other popular local fish and seafood dishes. **La Espada** and **Don Pedro** are good choices for quality and quantity. Remember that beachfront restaurants don't have as high hygiene standards as the more established restaurants along the highway.

Tumbes and around *p1343, map p1344*

Cheap restaurants on the Plaza de Armas, Paseo de la Concordia and near the markets.
TT-T Budabar, Grau 309, on Plaza de Armas, T525493. One of a kind chill out lounge offering traditional food and comfy seating with outdoor tables and cheap beer, very popular in the evenings.
TT-T Chifa Wakay, Huáscar 413. A large, well-ventilated smart restaurant offering the usual Chifa favourites. Open evenings only.
TT-T Classic, Tumbes 185. Look for it almost under the bridge over the river, heading south. Popular for local food. Recommended.
TT-T Los Gustitos, Bolívar 148. Excellent menús and à la carte. Popular, good atmosphere at lunchtime.
T Sí Señor, Bolívar 119 on the plaza. Good for snacks, cheap lunch menus.

Fuente de Soda Cherry, San Martín 116, open 0800-1400, 1700-2300. Tiny café offering an amazing selection of cakes and desserts, also fresh juices, shakes, sandwiches, hot and cold drinks and the traditional *cremoladas* (fruit juice with crushed ice).

Activities and tours

Máncora and Punta Sal *p1343*

Iguanas Trips, Av Piura 245, T01-99 8262476, www.vivamancora.com/iguanastrips. Run by Ursula Behr, offers a variety of adventure tourism trips including white-water rafting, horseriding and camping trips in the nearby national parks and reserve zones.

Michel Expediciones Perú, Martín Weise 521, T258715, www.vivamancora.com/michelexp/index.html. New company run by Michel Lemoine, a Peruvian guide and ecologist with 25 years experience in tourism. Wildlife watching, surf and kite-surfing and cultural tours, plus hotel reservations, transport and car rental and off the beaten track tours to circuits being developed.

Tumbes and around *p1343, map p1344*

One-day trips to the Manglares at Puerto Pizarro, US$25 pp (including entrance to the crocodile breeding center), or to the Zona Reservada de Tumbes for US$30-50 pp (including INRENA entrance fee). Day trip to Cerros de Amotape costs US$35-55 pp, including visits to ruins at Rica Playa. Also available is a 1-day Historical Tour, including the Huaca Gran Chilimasa and site museum, the place where petrol was first extracted, and hot springs (*hervideros*) and the beach at Puntal Sal, US$35 pp.

Cocodrilos Tours, San Martín 131, T972 619 204, www.cocodrilotours.com. Tours with an emphasis on sustainable tourism, sale of transport tickets, tourist information and equipment hire.

Mapa Mundi Tours, Jr Simón Bolívar 338, Paseo Los Libertadores, T526813, mapamundi tours@terra.com. Tours with more of an ecological focus.

Rosillo Tours, Tumbes 293, T523892, rosillotours@speedy.com.pe. Operate all of the above tours and are equipped to handle large groups.

Transport

North to Ecuador: Sullana *p1342*

Bus Several bus companies including **Ormeño** use a new Terminal Terrestre. To **Tumbes**, 244 km, 4-5 hrs US$5, several buses daily. To **Chiclayo** and **Trujillo** see under Piura. To **Lima**, 1,076 km, 14-16 hrs, US$20, several buses daily, most coming from Tumbes or Talara, luxury overnight via Trujillo with **Ittsa** (T503705), also with **Ormeño**. To **Talara**, **Eppo**, US$1.25. To **Máncora**, *Eppo*, 5 a day, 2½ hrs, US$4.

Border with Ecuador: La Tina-Macará *p1342*

Buses leave frequently from Ecuadorean side for Loja, so if you are not taking the through bus (see under Piura), you can go from Sullana to Loja in a day. From the border to Sullana, cars may leave before they are full, but won't charge extra.

Combis Leave from Sullana to the international bridge from Terminal Terrestre La Capullana, off Av Buenos Aires, several blocks beyond the canal. They leave when full, US$3.40 per person, 1¾ hrs (US$24 for whole car, US$30 border-Piura). It's best to take a taxi or mototaxi to and from the terminal. From the border to Macará is 4 km: walk over the bridge and take one of the pick-ups which run from the border (10 mins, US$0.30, or US$1.25 for whole car).

To the border at Tumbes: Talara *p1342*

Air To/from **Lima**, **Star Perú** (T98-900 6864), via Cajamarca, Tue, Thu, Sun.

Bus To **Tumbes**, 171 km, 3 hrs, US$4, most coming from Piura and stopping at major towns going north; several daily. To **Piura**, 2 hrs, US$2.

Máncora and Punta Sal *p1343*

Bus **Talara** to **El Alto** (Cabo Blanco), 32 km, 30 mins, US$1, continuing to Máncora, 28 km, 30 mins, US$1. To **Talara/Sullana/ Piura** with **Eppo**, 5 a day, US$4; to **Tumbes** (and points in between), combis leave when full, US$4, 2 hrs.

Tumbes and around *p1343, map p1344*

Air Daily flights to and from **Lima** (**Lan**, Bolognesi 250).

Bus Daily to and from **Lima**, 1,320 km, 18-20 hrs, depending on stopovers, US$22 (Ormeño *business*), US$45 (Cruz del Sur regular and Ormeño *Royal* services), US$54 (Cruz del Sur *cruzero*). Several buses daily, all on Av Tumbes: **Civa**, No 518, T525120; **Ormeño**, Av Tumbes s/n, T522228; **Cruz del Sur**, No 319, T896163; **Trans Chiclayo**, No 466, T525260. Cheaper buses usually leave 1600-2100, more expensive ones 1200-1400. Except for luxury service, most buses to Lima stop at major cities en route. Tickets to anywhere between Tumbes and Lima sell quickly, so if arriving from Ecuador you may have to stay overnight. Piura is a good place for connections in the daytime. To **Sullana**, 244 km, 3-4 hrs, US$5, several buses daily. To **Piura**, 4-5 hrs, 282 km, US$5 with **Trans Chiclayo, Cruz del Sur, El Dorado** (Piura 459, T523480) 6 a day; **Comité Tumbes/Piura** (Tumbes N 308, T525 977), US$7 pp, fast cars, leave when full, 3½ hrs. To **Chiclayo**, 552 km, 6 hrs, US$6, several each day with *Cruz del Sur*, *El Dorado*, and others. To **Trujillo**, 769 km, 10-11 hrs, US$10-19, *Ormeño*, *Cruz del Sur*, *El Dorado*, *Emtrafesa*, Tumbes Norte 397, T525850. Transport to the Border with Ecuador, see below.

To **Ecuador**: CIFA to **Machala** and **Guayaquil**, 6 a day, luxury bus at 1000, US$8, 5 hrs to Guayaquil, recommended for crossing the border.

Santuario Nacional los Manglares de Tumbes

Combis From Tumbes market to **Zarumilla**, 20 mins, US$0.50. In Zarumilla hire a mototaxi for the 7 km run (20 mins, US$1.50) to the Centre. A 2½-hr guided visit costs US$12, for up to 6 people.

Border with Ecuador *p1344*

Zarumilla/Aguas Verdes

Between Tumbes and the border Colectivos leave from block 3 of Av Tumbes, US$1.25 pp or US$8 to hire car. Combis leave from the market area along Mcal Castilla across from Calle Alipio Rosales, US$0.75, luggage on roof. Old, slow city buses ply the same route as combis, US$0.60. All vehicles only leave when full. From the border to Zarumilla by mototaxi costs US$0.75 pp. Taxi to Tumbes, including wait at immigration, US$8. With the construction of the new border faciliteis and bridge, all transport details may change. Make sure the driver takes you all the way to the border post that is operating.

Entering Peru It is easier to take a colectivo to Tumbes and then a bus south, rather than trying to get on a bus from the border to a southern destination. When driving into Peru, vehicle fumigation is not required, but there is one outfit who will attempt to fumigate your vehicle with water and charge US$10. Beware of officials claiming that you need a *carnet* to obtain your 90-day transit permit; this is not so, cite Decreto Supremo 015-87-ICTI/TUR. Frequent road tolls between Tumbes and Lima, US$1.35-2.60 each.

❶ Directory

North to Ecuador: Sullana *p1342*

Banks BCP, San Martín 685. *Casas de cambio* and street changers on San Martín by Tarapacá. **Internet** Several in the centre, on San Martín and Av Lama. **Post offices** San Martín 778, Mon-Sat 0800-1930, Sun 0800-1300. **Telephones** Telephone and fax at Miró Quesada 213.

Máncora and Punta Sal *p1343*

Banks Two ATMs which accept all major cards. Several places to change money, but rates tend to be lower than in major cities. **Internet** Several places on Av Piura, relatively fast connection. **Medical services** 24-hr emergency clinic, Av Piura 306, T258712. Mon-Sat 0800-1400, 1600-2100. Has good lab for clinical tests. **Boticas BTL**, Av Piura 621 (next to police station). Chemist/pharmacy with good stock, 0700-2300. Delivery within Máncora T258587. **Botica Mariluz** (next to Casa de Betty), 24-hr delivery T258214. **Telephones** Several places on Av Piura for local, national and international calls, good rates.

Tumbes and around *p1343, map p1344*

Banks Several large banks on the Plaza de Armas and 3 ATMS which accept all major cards. **Scotiabank**, Av Bolognesi 111, with ATM in the plaza. Changes TCs and cash. **BBV Continental**, Bolívar 121, cash and Amex TCs only, US$5 commission. **Cambios Internacionales**, Av Bolívar 259-A, cash only, good rates, open 0800-1300, 1530-1900. Minimum exchange US$20. Money changers on the street (on Bolívar, left of the Cathedral) give a much better rate than banks or cambios, but don't accept the first offer you are given. None changes TCs. Be extremely careful, only use them if you are confident of being able to recognize the fake bank notes. **Consulates** **Ecuadorean Consulate**, Bolívar 129, Plaza de Armas, T521739, consultum@speedy.com.pe. **Internet** Widely available in many cheap cafés and major hotels. **Medical services** 24 Hour Emergency Clinic, Av Mariscal Castilla 305, T525341. Consultancy hours Mon to Fri 0800-1400. **Post offices** San Martín 208. **Telephones** San Martín 210.

Northern Highlands

Leaving the Pacific coast behind, you climb in a relatively short time up to the Sierra. It was here, at Cajamarca, that the defeat of the Incas by the Spaniards began, bringing about cataclysmic change to this part of the world. But, unlike this well-documented event, the history of the Incas' contemporaries and predecessors has to be teased out of the stones of their temples and fortresses, which are shrouded in cloud in the 'Eyebrow of the Jungle'.

Trujillo to Cajamarca

To the northeast of Trujillo is Cajamarca, an attractive colonial town surrounded by lovely countryside and the commercial centre of the northern mountain area. It can be reached by the old road via Huamachuco and Cajabamba, or by paved road via Ciudad de Dios. The former road is being improved, but, for cyclists especially, is lonely, taking a couple of days by bus (as opposed to 9 hours via Ciudad de Dios, see below), but it is more interesting, passing over the bare puna before dropping to the Huamachuco valley.

Huamachuco → *Colour map 3, B2. Altitude: 3,180 m. www.munihuamachuco.gob.pe.*
This colonial town formerly on the royal Inca Road, 181 km from Trujillo, has the largest main plaza in Peru, with fine topiary, and a controversial modern **cathedral**. There is a colourful **Sunday market**, with dancing in the plaza, and the Founding of Huamachuco festival, second week in August, with spectacular fireworks and the amazing, aggressive male dancers, called *turcos*. **Museo Municipal Wamachuko** ⓘ *Sucre 195, Mon-Sat 0900-1300, 1500-1900, Sun 0900-1200, free*, displays artefacts found at nearby Cerro Amaru (a hill-top system of wells and water worship) and **Marca Huamachuco**: access is via a poor vehicle road or a mule track (preferable for walking), off the road to Sanagorán, there is an archway at the turnoff, 5 km from Huamachuco, mototaxi to turnoff US$2; combis to Sanagorán in the morning. These hilltop pre-Inca fortifications rank in the top 10 archaeological sites in Peru. They are 3 km long, dating back to at least 300 BC though many structures were added later. Its most impressive features are: El Castillo, a remarkable circular structure with walls up to 8 m high located at the highest point of the site, and El Convento complex, five circular structures of varying sizes towards the northern end of the hill. The largest one has been partially reconstructed. The extensive Huari ruins of **Wiracochapampa** are 3 km north of town, 45 minutes' walk. Although much of the site is overgrown the Waman Raymi festival is held here on the second Sunday in August (a northern version of Cuzco's Inti Raymi).

Cajabamba is a small market town and a useful stop-over point between Cajamarca and Huamachuco.

Pacasmayo → *Colour map 3, A2. Population: 12,300.*
Pacasmayo, 102 km north of Trujillo, is the port for the next oasis north. It has a nice beach front with an old Customs House and a very long pier. Resort El Faro is 1 km away, with surfing at the point and kite- and windsurfing closer to town. There are maritime festivals at New Year and Semana Santa. Away from the front it is a busy commercial centre.

20 km further north on the Panamericana is the main road connection from the coast to Cajamarca at a junction called **Ciudad de Dios**. The paved 175 km road branches off the Pan-American Highway soon after it crosses the Río Jequetepeque. The river valley has terraced rice fields and mimosas may often be seen in bloom, brightening the otherwise dusty landscape.

Cajamarca → *Phone code: 076. Colour map 3, B2. Population: 201,000. Altitude: 2,750 m.*

At Cajamarca Pizarro ambushed and captured Atahualpa, the Inca emperor. This was the first showdown between the Spanish and the Incas and, despite their huge numerical inferiority, the Spanish emerged victorious, executing Atahualpa in the process. The nearby **Yanacocha gold mine** ⓘ *www.yanacocha.com.pe*, has brought new wealth to the town (and major ecological concerns and social problems) and Cajamarca is the hub of tourism development for the whole of the northwest via the *Circuito Turístico Nororiental* (Chiclayo-Cajamarca-Chachapoyas). **Tourist offices**: Dirección Regional de Turismo and Instituto Nacional de Cultura ⓘ *in the Conjunto Monumental de Belén, Belén 631, T362601, www.regioncajamarca.gob.pe, www.inccajamarca.org, Mon-Fri 0900-1300, 1500-1730*. Sub-Gerencia de Turismo of the Cajamarca Municipality ⓘ *Cruz de Piedra 635, T602233, ext 253, www.municajamarca.gob.pe*, will move in 2010 to the new municipal Capac Ñan building, opposite UNC university on the road to Baños del Inca. The University tourist school has an office at Del Batán 289, T361546, offering free advice and leaflets, open Mon-Fri 0830-1300, 1500-2200. The **Indecopi** office is at Apurímac 601, T363315, mcastillo@indecopi.gob.pe.

Complejo Belén ⓘ *Tue-Sat 0900-1300, 1500-1800, Sun 0900-1300, US$1.55, valid for more than 1 day, a ticket is also valid for the Cuarto de Rescate, a guide for all the sites costs US$2.85 (US$5.75-8.50 for guides in other languages)*. The complex comprises the tourist office and

Cajamarca

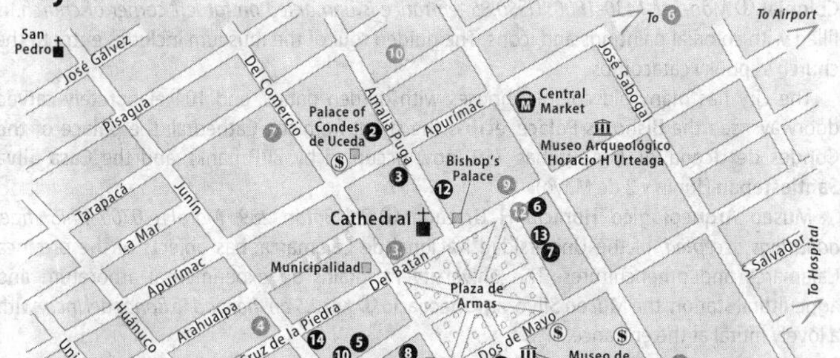

Sleeping
1 Cajamarca
2 Casa Blanca & La Casona del Inca
3 Costa del Sol
4 El Cabildo
5 El Cumbe Inn
6 El Ingenio
7 El Portal del Marqués
8 Hosp Los Jazmines
9 Hostal Becerra
10 Hostal Los Pinos
11 Hostal Olympo
12 Hostal Perú
13 Los Balcones de La Recoleta

Eating
1 Bella's Café Lounge
2 Casa Club
3 Cascanuez
4 Don Paco
5 El Pez Loco
6 El Zarco
7 Heladería Holanda
8 Om-Gri
9 Pascana
10 Pizzería El Marengo
11 Pizzería Vaca Loca
12 Querubino
13 Salas
14 Sanguchón.com

Institute of Culture, a beautifully ornate church, considered the city's finest. See the inside of the dome, where eight giant cherubs support an intricate flowering centrepiece. In the same courtyard is the **Museo Médico Belén**, which has a collection of medical instruments. Across the street is a maternity hospital from the colonial era, now the **Archaeological and Ethnological Museum**, Junín y Belén. It has a range of ceramics from all regions and civilizations of Peru. The **Cuarto de Rescate** ⓘ *entrance at Amalia Puga 750*, is not the actual ransom chamber but in fact the room where Atahualpa was held prisoner. A red line on the wall is said to indicate where Atahualpa reached up and drew a mark, agreeing to have his subjects fill the room to the line with treasure. The chamber is roped off but can be viewed from the outside. Pollution and weather have had a detrimental effect on the stone.

You can also visit the plaza where Atahualpa was ambushed and the stone altar set high on **Santa Apolonia hill** ⓘ *US$0.60, take bus marked Santa Apolonia/Fonavi, or micro A*, where he is said to have reviewed his subjects. There is a road to the top, or you can walk up from Calle 2 de Mayo, using the steep stairway. The view is worth the effort, especially at sunrise (but go in a group).

The **Plaza de Armas**, where Atahualpa was executed, has a 350-year-old fountain, topiary and gardens. The **Cathedral** ⓘ *0800-1000, 1600-1800*, opened in 1776, is still missing its belfry, but the façade has beautiful baroque carving in stone. On the opposite side of the plaza is the 17th century **San Francisco Church** ⓘ *Mon-Fri 0900-1200, 1600-1800*, older than the Cathedral and with more interior stone carving and elaborate altars. The attached **Museo de Arte Colonial** ⓘ *Mon-Sat 1430-1800, US$0.85, entrance is unmarked on far left corner of church*, is filled with colonial paintings and icons. The guided tour of the museum includes entry to the church's spooky catacombs.

The city has many old colonial houses with garden patios, and 104 elaborately carved doorways: see the **Bishop's Palace**, across the street from the Cathedral; the **palace of the Condes de Uceda**, at Jr Apurímac 719 (now occupied by BCP bank); and the **Casa Silva Santiesteban** (Junín y 2 de Mayo).

Museo Arqueológico Horacio H Urteaga ⓘ *Del Batán 289, Mon-Fri 0700-1445, free, donations accepted*, of the Universidad Nacional de Cajamarca, has objects of the pre-Inca Cajamarca and other cultures. The university maintains an experimental arboretum and agricultural station, the **Museo Silvo-agropecuario** ⓘ *Km 2.5 on the road to Baños del Inca*, with a lovely mural at the entrance.

Excursions About 6 km away are the sulphurous thermal springs of **Los Baños del Inca** ⓘ *0500-2000, T348249, US$0.70, combis marked Baños del Inca cost US$0.20, 15 mins, taxis US$2.30*. The water temperature is at least 72° C. Atahualpa tried the effect of these waters on a festering war wound and his bath is still there. The complex is renewed regularly, with gardens and various levels of accommodation (see Sleeping, below). The main baths are divided into five categories, with prices ranging from US$1.75-2.10, all with private tubs and no pool. Sauna US$3.50, massage US$7 (take your own towel; soaps are sold outside). Only spend 20 minutes maximum in the water; obey instructions; many of the facilities allow bathers in shifts, divided by time and/or sex.

Other excursions include **Llacanora**, a typical Andean village in beautiful scenery (13 km south- east; nice walk downhill from Baños del Inca, two hours). **Ventanillas de Otusco** ⓘ *8 km, 0800-1800, US$1.10, combi US$0.20*, part of an old pre-Inca cemetery, has a gallery of secondary burial niches. There are good day walks in this area; local sketch maps available.

A road goes to **Ventanillas de Combayo** ⓘ *occasional combis on weekdays; more transport on Sun when a market is held nearby, 1 hr*, some 20 km past the burial niches of Otusco. These are more numerous and spectacular, being located in an isolated, mountainous area, and distributed over the face of a steep 200 m high hillside.

Cumbe Mayo, a *pampa* on a mountain range, is 20 km southwest of Cajamarca. It is famous for its extraordinary, well-engineered pre-Inca channels, running for 9 km across the mountain tops. It is said to be the oldest man-made construction in South America. The sheer scale of the scene is impressive and the huge rock formations of Los Frailones ('big monks') and others with fanciful names are strange indeed. On the way to Cumbe Mayo is the Layzón ceremonial centre. There is no bus service; guided tours run from 0900-1300 (recommended in order to see all the pre-Inca sites); taxi US$15. To walk up takes 3-4 hours (take a guide, or a tour, best weather May-September). The trail starts from the hill of Santa Apolonia (Silla del Inca), and goes to Cumbe Mayo straight through the village and up the hill; at the top of the mountain, leave the trail and take the road to the right to the canal. The walk is not difficult and you do not need hiking boots. Take a good torch. The locals use the trail to bring their goods to market.

The **Porcón** rural cooperative, with its evangelical faith expressed on billboards, is a popular excursion, 30 km northwest of Cajamarca. It is tightly organized, with carpentry, bakery, cheese and yoghurt-making, zoo and vicuñas. A good guide helps to explain everything. If not taking a tour, contact **Cooperativa Agraria Atahualpa Jerusalén** ⓘ *Chanchamayo 1355, Fonavi 1, T/F825631.*

Some 93 km west of Cajamarca is the mining town of Chilete, 21 km north of which on the road to San Pablo is **Kuntur Wasi**. The site was devoted to a feline cult and consists of a pyramid and stone monoliths. Extensive excavations are under way and significant new discoveries are being made (excellent site museum). There are two basic *hostales* in Chilete; very limited facilities.

Trujillo to Catamarca listings

For Sleeping and Eating price codes and other relevant information, see Essentials, pages 38-40.

Sleeping

Huamachuco *p1350*

C-E Real, Bolívar 250, T441402, www.hotelreal peru.com. New, TV, sauna, internet, majority of fittings are wood. Recommended.

D-F Hostal Santa Fe, San Martín 297, T441019, hs_turistico_santafe@hotmail.com. New, TV, hot water. Recommended.

E Hospedaje Colonial Plaza, Castilla 208, on the plaza, T441760. An old colonial house, some rooms retain original furniture, hot water, laundry facilities. Can arrange horse-riding.

E Hostal Gran Colonial, Castilla 537, T511101, grancolonialhostal@hotmail.com. An attractive old colonial house, with hot water, TV, restaurant is good value. Recommended.

F Hostal Noche Buena, San Román 401 on the main plaza, T441435. Clean with hot showers, TV, laundry, overlooking the plaza.

F Huamachuco, Castilla 354, on the plaza, T441393. With hot showers (**G** without), good value, has parking.

Cajabamba

F Hostal La Casona, Jr Alfonso Ugarte 586, Plaza de Armas, T848385. Small rooms, electric shower, with restaurant.

F Jhoel, Jr Grau 633, T551653. With electric shower, patio, pleasant, good value.

Pacasmayo *p1350*

C La Estación, Malecón Grau 69, T521515, www.hotellaestacion.com.pe. Restaurant on ground floor, all meals extra, 4 rooms with terrace overlooking sea, internet, fan, good beds.

C Libertad, Leoncio Pardo 1-D, T521937, www.hotellibertad.com.pe. 2 km from beach by petrol station, with breakfast, Wi-Fi and internet, safe, restaurant/bar, parking, efficient and nice.

C Pakatnamú, Malecón Grau 103, T522368, hotelpakatnamu@hotmail.com. Older building on seafront, one suite, new rooms have seaview, with breakfast.

D-E Duke Kahanamoku, Ayacucho 44, T521889, eldukepacasmayo.com. Surfing place, with classes and board rental, breakfast extra, hot water, Wi-Fi, free internet.

Cajamarca *p1351, map p1351*

L-AL Costa del Sol, Cruz de la Piedra 707, T344040, www.costadelsolperu.com. On the Plaza de Armas, part of a Peruvian chain, with breakfast, airport transfer, welcome drink, internet, Wi-Fi; restaurant, café and bars, pool, spa.

L-AL Posada del Puruay, 5 km north of the city, T367928, www.posadapuruay.com.pe. A 17th-century *hacienda* converted into a 'hotel museum', high standards and beautiful colonial furnishings. Good food and a range of activities, including horseriding. Recommended.

B El Ingenio, Av Vía de Evitamiento 1611-1709, T367121, www.elingenio.com. 1½ blocks from new El Quinde shopping mall. With solar-powered hot water, spacious, very relaxed, helpful. Highly recommended.

B El Portal del Marqués, Del Comercio 644, T368464, www.portaldelmarques.com. Attractive converted colonial house, TV, internet, laundry, safe, parking, leased restaurant *El Mesón del Marqués* has good lunch *menú*. Recommended.

B-C Casa Blanca, Dos de Mayo 446 on Plaza de Armas, T362141. Safe, nice old building with garden, café/bar.

B-C Hostal Los Pinos, Jr La Mar 521, T365992, www.lospinosinn.com. Includes breakfast, lovely colonial house with a new extension, decorated in extravagant style, comfortable, also has 2 apartments, other meals on request.

C Cajamarca, Dos de Mayo 311, T362532, hotelcajamarca@gmail.com. 3-star in beautiful colonial mansion, sizeable rooms, hot water, food excellent in *Los Faroles* restaurant, Wi-Fi. Recommended.

C La Casona del Inca, 2 de Mayo 458-460, Plaza de Armas, T367524, www.casonadelincaperu.com. Upstairs, old building, traditional style, some rooms overlooking plaza, some with interior windows, good beds, TV, Wi-Fi, breakfast in café on top floor, tours, luggage store, laundry.

C El Cabildo, Junín 1062, T827025, cabildoh@latinmail.com. Includes breakfast, in historic monument with patio and modern fountain, full of character, elegant local decorations, comfortable, breakfast served, internet, Wi-Fi. Recommended.

C El Cumbe Inn, Pasaje Atahualpa 345, T826858, www.elcumbeinn.com. Includes breakfast and tax, comfortable, variety of rooms, hot water, internet, Wi-Fi, evening measl on request, small gym, will arrange taxis, very helpful. Recommended.

C Los Balcones de la Recoleta, Amalia Puga 1050, T363302, luchi9200@hotmail.com. Beautifully restored 19th-century house, central courtyard full of flowers, some rooms with period furniture, internet, breakfast extra. Recommended.

D Hospedaje Los Jazmines, Amazonas 775, T361812, hospedajelosjasmines@yahoo.com. In a converted colonial house with courtyard and café, 11 rooms with bath, 2 without, all profits go to disabled children (some staff are disabled), guests can visit the project's school and help. Recommended.

D Hostal Becerra, Del Batán 195, T367867. With hot water and TV, modern, pleasant, will store luggage until late buses depart.

D Hostal Perú, Amalia Puga 605, on Plaza, T365568, hostal_peru@elzarco.org. With bath, hot water, Wi-Fi, functional rooms in old building around central patio used by El Zarco restaurant, wooden floors, credit cards taken.

E Hostal Olympo, Av Atahualpa 439, T324105. Near buses, rooms with TV, internet.

Baños del Inca

L-AL Laguna Seca, Av Manco Cápac 1098, T584300, www.lagunaseca.com.pe. In pleasant surroundings with thermal streams but has seen better days, private hot thermal baths in rooms, swimming pool with thermal water, restaurant, bar, health spa with a variety of treatments, disco, horses for hire.

A Hostal Fundo Campero San Antonio, 2 km off the Baños road (turn off at Km 5), T/F348237, jc_luna@viabcp.com. An old *hacienda*, wonderfully restored, with open fireplaces and gardens, 15 mins walk along the river to Baños del Inca, includes breakfast, riding on *caballos de paso*, own dairy produce, fruit and vegetables, catch your own trout for supper; try the *licor de sauco*. Recommended.

Eating

Huamachuco *p1350*

Café Somos, R Castilla 670. Good coffee, large turkey/ham sandwiches and excellent cakes.

La Casona, Sánchez Carrión 294. Open daily 0700-0900, 1200-1430, 1900-2030. Serves good value and quality set meals and local dishes, popular. Also places on the Plaza de Armas.

Cajabamba

Don Lucho, Jr Leoncio Prado 227. Good local trout and other à la carte dishes.

Quengococha at Bolognesi 790. Tasty local dishes.

Cajamarca *p1351, map p1351*

Pascana, Av Atahualpa 947. Well-known and recommended as the best in town, near the new Capac Ñan Municipality. Their **Taberna del Diablo** is the top disco in town.

Querubino, Amalia Puga 589. Mediterranean-style decoration, a bit of everything on the menu, including pastas, daily specials, breakfasts, cocktails, coffees, expensive wines otherwise reasonable, popular.

Casa Club, Amalia Puga 458-A, T340198. Open 0800-2300. Menú, including vegetarian, and extensive selection à la carte, family atmosphere, slow but attentive service.

Don Paco, Amalia Puga 390, T362655. Opposite San Francisco. Typical, including novo andino, and international dishes, tasty food, desserts, drinks.

El Pez Loco, San Martín 333. Good for fish.

Om-Gri, San Martín 360, near the Plaza de Armas. Good Italian dishes, small, informal, French spoken, opens 1300 (1830 Sun).

Pizzería El Marengo, Junín 1201. Good pizzas and warm atmosphere, T368045 for delivery.

Salas, Amalia Puga 637, on the main plaza, T362867. A Cajamarca tradition, open 0700-2200. Fast service, excellent local food (try their *cuy frito*), best *tamales* in town.

El Zarco, Jr Del Batán 170, T363421. Open Sun-Fri 0700-2300. Very popular, also has short *chifa* menu, good vegetarian dishes, excellent fish, popular for breakfast.

Pizzería Vaca Loca, San Martín 330. Popular, best pizzas in town.

Cafés

Bella's Café Lounge, Junín 1184, T345794. For breakfasts, sandwiches, great desserts and coffee from Chanchamayo, Wi-Fi, a place to linger, check emails and relax, owner Raul speaks English. Popular with visitors to the city.

Cascanuez, Amalia Puga 554. Great cakes, extensive menu including *humitas*, breakfasts, ice creams and coffees, highly regarded.

Heladería Holanda, Amalia Puga 657 on the Plaza de Armas, T340113. Dutch-owned, easily the best ice-creams in Cajamarca, 50 flavours (but not all on at the same time), try *poro poro, lúcuma* or *sauco*, also serves coffee. Four branches, including at Baños del Inca. Ask if it is possible to visit their factory. They assist deaf people and single mothers.

Sanguchón.com, Junín 1137. Best burgers in town, sandwiches, also popular bar.

Festivals and events

Cajamarca *p1351, map p1351*

The **pre-Lent Carnival** is very spectacular and regarded as one of the best in the country; it is also one of the most raucous. In Porcón, 16 km to the northwest, **Palm Sunday** processions are worth seeing. On **24 Jun**: is **San Juan** in Cajamarca, Chota, Llacanora, San Juan and Cutervo. An agricultural fair is held in **Jul** at Baños del Inca; on the first Sun in **Oct** is the **Festival Folklórico** in Cajamarca.

Shopping

Cajamarca *p1351, map p1351*

Handicrafts Cheap, but bargain hard. Specialities including gilded mirrors and cotton and wool saddlebags (*alforjas*). Items can be made to order. The market on Amazonas is good for *artesanía*; also daily handicraft market on block 5 of Belén. There are several shops on 300 block of Dos de Mayo.

Shopping malls

El Quinde, Av Hoyos Rubio, blocks 6 and 7, Fonavi. Shopping centre on road to airport, with well-stocked supermarket, cinema, food mall, popular.

Activities and tours

Cajamarca *p1351, map p1351*

Agencies around the Plaza de Armas offer trips to local sites and further (eg Kuntur Wasi, Kuélap), trekking on Inca trails, riding *caballos de paso* and handicraft tours. 2010 prices: Cumbe Mayo, US$6.50-8.50, 4-5 hrs at 0930. Porcón, US$6.50-8.50, 4-5 hrs at 0930. Otusco, US$4.50-7,

3-3½ hrs at 1530. City tour, US$7, 3 hrs at 0930 or 1530. Kuntur Wasi is a full day. There are also 2 day/3 night tours to Kuélap and Cutervo National Park.

Atahualpa Inca Tours, La Mar 435, T367014. Conventional tours and trekking (in Hostal El Mirador).

Mega Tours, Amalia Puga 691 on the plaza, T341876, www.megatours.org. Conventional tours, full day and further afield, ecotourism and adventures.

Saelma Tours, Junín 1100, T341305. Conventional, full days and strong emphasis on trekking.

Socio Adventures, Ben Eastwood, Pje Chota 123, Dpto 1A, Urb Ramón Castilla, Cajamarca, T341118, or contact via www.socio adventures.com. They offer a Stove Trek Tour, where you donate materials and help a local family build a cooking stove while taking a 5-day, 5-night guided tour of the area. You stay at their lodge called the *Blur Poncho* near Chota, excellent food and accommodation.

Tacabamba Tours, Dos de Mayo 458, Plaza de Armas, T976 680638 (mob), morales2251@ hotmail.com. Comprehensive local tours and further afield, eg to areas in Chachapoyas.

Transport

Huamachuco *p1350*

Bus From **Trujillo**, 170 km, 6 hrs, US$7-8.50: **Horna** (San Martín 875, T440114) 5 a day, also **Tunesa** (Balta y Suárez, T441157). To **Cajabamba**, **Trans Los Andes**, Pje Hospital 109, 3 combis a day, 3 hrs, US$3.50.

Cajabamba

Bus To/from **Cajamarca**, 127 km, US$4, 4 hrs, several companies; combis 3 hrs, US$5.

Cajamarca *p1351, map p1351*

Air To/from **Lima**: **LC Busre** (Comercio 1024, T076-361098), daily except Sat, **LAN** (Cruz de Piedra 657) and **Star Perú** (Junín 1300, T367243). Airport 5 km from town; taxi US$4.20.

Bus Buses in town charge US$0.25. To **Lima**, 870 km, 12-14 hrs, *económico* US$18-79, from economy to Super VIP, including **Civa** and **Cruz del Sur**'s luxury service, several buses daily. To **Trujillo**, 295 km, 7 hrs, US$7-29, regular buses daily 0900-2230 most continue to Lima. To **Chiclayo**, 265 km, 6 hrs, US$6.25-15.50, several buses daily; you have to change buses to go on to Piura and Tumbes. To **Celendín**, 107 km, 3½ hrs, US$3.45, usually 2 a day with **Atahualpa**, CABA (in same office, T366665), **Royal Palace's** and **Rojas**. **Móvil** has a service to **Chachapoyas**, 336 km, 11-12 hrs, US$18, to **Leymebamba**, US$12.50, 9-10 hrs. The route follows a road (paved as far as Encañada) through beautiful countryside. Among the bus companies are: **Atahualpa**, Atahualpa 299, T363060 (Lima, Celendín, Cajabamba); **Civa**, Ayacucho 753, T361460 (Lima); **Cruz del Sur**, Atahualpa 664, T361737 (Lima). **Emtrafesa**, Atahualpa 315, T369663 (to Trujillo). **Horna**, Atahualpa 313, T363218 (Trujillo, Cajabamba, Huamachuco). **Línea**, Atahualpa 318, T363956 (Lima, Trujillo, Chiclayo). **Móvil**, Atahualpa 405, T340873 (Lima, Chachapoyas). **Rojas**, Atahualpa 309, T340548 (to Cajabamba, buses not coming from Lima; Celendín); **Royal Palace's**, Reina Forje 130, T343063 (Lima, Trujillo, Celendín); **Tepsa**, Sucre y Reina Forje, T363306 (Lima); **Turismo Días**, Av Evitamiento s/n, T344322 (to Lima, Chimbote, Trujillo, Chiclayo).

Taxi US$1 within city limits. Mototaxis US$0.50.

Directory

Cajamarca *p1351, map p1351*

Banks BCP, Apurímac 719. **Scotiabank**, Amazonas 750. **Interbank**, 2 de Mayo 546, on Plaza. **Telebanco 24 Horas** ATM (Visa) at the gas station next to Línea buses on Av Atahualpa. Dollars can be changed in most banks and travel agencies on east side of Plaza, but euros hard to change. Casa de cambio in **Casa del Artefacto** musical and electrical store at Amazonas 537. Good rates, cash only. Casas de cambio also at Jr del Comercio y Apurímac and at Amalia Puga 673. **Street changers** on Jr Del Batán by the Plaza de Armas and at Del Batán y Amazonas. **Internet** Cabins everywhere, US$0.35 per hr. **Post offices** Serpost, Apurímac 626. Mon-Sat 0800-2000. **Telephones** Public phone offices can be found all over the centre.

Chachapoyas region

Cajamarca is a convenient starting point for the trip east to the department of Amazonas, which contains the archaeological riches of the Chachapoyans, also known as Sachupoyans. Here lie the great pre-Inca cities of Vilaya (not yet developed for tourism), Cerro Olán and the immense fortress of Kuélap, among many others. The road is unpaved and prone to landslides in the rainy season. It follows a winding course through the mountains, crossing the wide and deep canyon of the Río Marañón at Balsas. The road climbs steeply with superb views of the mountains and the valleys below. The fauna and flora are spectacular as the journey alternates between high mountains and low forest.

Celendín ➔ *Phone code: 076. Colour map 3, B2.*

East from Cajamarca, this is the first town of note, with a pleasant plaza and cathedral, predominantly blue. Festival 16 July to 3 August (Virgen del Carmen). There is also a fascinating local market on Sunday which is held in three distinct areas. At 0630 the hat market is held by the Alameda, between Ayacucho and 2 de Mayo at Jorge Chávez. You can see hats at every stage of production, but it is over within an hour or so. Then at 0930 the potato market takes place at 2 de Mayo y Sucre and, at the other end of town, the livestock market on Túpac Amaru. The most popular local excursion is to the hot springs and mud baths at **Llanguat**, 20 km, US$2.75 by limited public transport. Multired ATM beside Banco de la Nación on 2 de Mayo may not accept all foreign cards; take cash.

Leymebamba and around ➔ *Phone code: 041. Colour map 3, B2. Altitude: 2,250 m.*

There are plenty of ruins – many of them covered in vegetation– and good walking possibilities around this pleasant town at the source of the Utcubamba River. See www.leymebamba.org. The main attraction in the area is its spectacular museum, see below.

La Congona, a Chachapoyan site, is well worth the effort, with stupendous views. It consists of three hills: on the vegetation-covered conical hill in the middle, the ruins are clustered in a small area, impossible to see until you are right there. The other hills have been levelled. La Congona is the best preserved of three sites in this area, with 30 round stone houses (some with evidence of three storeys) and a watch tower. The two other sites, El Molinete and Pumahuanyuna, are nearby. All three sites can be visited in a day but a guide is advisable. It is a brisk three hours' walk from Leymebamba, first along the road to Fila San Cristóbal (under construction in 2010), then a large trail. The road starts at the bottom of Jr 16 de Julio.

At **Laguna de los Cóndores**, in 1996, a spectacular site consisting of six burial *chullpas*, containing 219 mummies and vast quantities of ceramics, textiles, woodwork, *quipus* and everyday utensils from the late Inca period, was discovered near a beautiful lake in a lush cloudforest setting. The trip to Laguna de los Cóndores takes 10-12 hours on foot and horseback from Leymebamba. Guides and muleteers for the three-day muddy trek can be arranged at Leymebamba hotels or with Chachapoyas operators. The artefacts were moved to the excellent **Museo Leymebamba** ⓘ *outside San Miguel, on the road to Celendín, T041-816803, www.museoleymebamba.org, Tue-Sun 1000-1630, entry US$3.60. Taxi from Leymebamba US$2.50.* From Leymebamba, walk 3 km south to San Miguel, then take the footpath uphill, the road is much longer. It is beautifully laid-out and very informative. Across the road is **Kentikafe**, offering snacks and observation of hummingbirds attracted to their feeders; accommodations where under construction in 2010.

The road to Chachapoyas follows the Utcubamba River north. In the mountains rising from the river, are a number of archaeological sites. Before **Yerbabuena** (important Sunday market, basic *hospedaje*), a road heads east to **Montevideo** (basic *hospedaje*) and beyond to the small village of San Pedro de Utac . The Chachapoyan site of **Cerro Olán** is a 30 minute walk from San Pedro. Here are the remains of towers, some archaeologists claim they had roofs like medieval European castles.

The burial *chullpas* of **Revash**, of the Revash culture (AD 1250), are reached from either **San Bartolo** (30-45 minutes walk) or a trail starting past **Puente Santo Tomás** (1½-2 hours walk). Both access points are along roads going west from Yerbabuena.The town of **Jalca Grande** (or La Jalca), at 2,800 m, is reached along a road going east at **Ubilón**, north of Yerbabuena. Along the way are the ruins of **Ollape,** with intricate fretwork. Jalca Grande has the remains of a Chachapoyan roundhouse, a stone church tower, a small **museum** ⓘ *entry US$1.80*, with ceramics and textiles, and one very basic *hospedaje*.

Tingo → *Phone code: 041. Colour map 3, B2. Altitude: 1,800 m.*
Situated at the junction of the Tingo and Utcubamba rivers, 25 km north of Leymebamba and 37 km south of Chachapoyas, Tingo is the access for Kuelap. A road climbs steeply from Tingo to Choctámal, where it divides. The left branch climbs east to Lónguita, María, Quizango and Kuélap.

Kuélap → *Altitude: 3,000 m.*
ⓘ *0800-1700, US$4.30, guides available for US$7 per group (Rigoberto Vargas Silva has been recommended). A small Centro de Interpretaciones has a good model of the site.*
Kuélap is a spectacular pre-Inca walled city which was re-discovered in 1843. It was built over a period of 600 years, from AD 500 to 1100 and contained three times more stone than the Great Pyramid at Giza in Egypt. The site lies along the summit of a mountain crest, more than 1 km in length. The massive stone walls, 585 m long by 110 m wide at their widest, are as formidable as those of any pre-Columbian city. Some reconstruction has taken place, mostly of small houses and walls, but the majority of the main walls on all levels are original, as is the inverted, cone-shaped 'dungeon'. The structures have been left in their cloud forest setting, the trees covered in bromeliads and moss, the flowers visited by hummingbirds.

Chachapoyas → *Phone code: 041. Colour map 3, B2. Population: 25,000. Altitude: 2,350 m.*
The capital of the Department of Amazonas, founded in 1538 retains its colonial character. The city's importance as a crossroads between the coast and jungle began to decline in the late 1940s, however archaeological and ecological tourism have grown gradually since the 1990s and have brought increasing economic benefits to the region. The modern cathedral (being rebuilt in 2010) stands on the spacious Plaza de Armas. **INC Museum** ⓘ *Ayacucho 904, Tue-Sat 0830-1230, 1345-1730, US$2*, contains a small collection of artefacts and mummies, with explanations in Spanish. The **Museo Santa Ana** ⓘ *Jr Santa Ana 1054, T790988, Mon-Fri 0800-1800, Sat-Sun 0900-1300, 1500-1800, US$2.50*, has colonial religious art and pre-Hispanic ceramics and textiles. **Tourist offices**: **iPerú** ⓘ *Jr Ortiz Arrieta 588, Plaza de Armas, T477292, iperuchachapoyas@promperu.gob.pe, Mon-Sat 0900-1300, 1400-1800, Sun 0900-1300.* **Dirección Regional de Turismo** ⓘ *Jr Santa Ana 1162, T478355, Mon-Fri 0800-1300, 1400-1700.* A useful site is *http://camayoc peru.com/lerche.htm* of the German ethnologist, Doctor Peter Lerche, mayor of Chachapoyas (2006-2010).

Huancas ⓘ *autos leave from Jr Ortiz Arrieta 370, 0600-1800, 20 min, US$1 or 2-hour walk*, is a small village to the north of Chacha where rustic pottery is produced. Walk uphill from town to the **Mirador** ⓘ *1 km from the plaza, US$0.35, viewing tower, crafts on sale*, for magnificent views into the deep canyon of the Río Sonche, with tumbling waterfalls. At **Huancaurco**, 5 km from Huancas, past the large prison complex, are ruins, remains of an Inca road and another *mirador* with fine views including Gocta Waterfall in the distance.

Levanto, due south of Chachapoyas, was built by the Spaniards in 1538, directly on top of the previous Chachapoyan structures, as their first capital of the area. Nowadays Levanto is an unspoilt colonial village overlooking the massive canyon of the Utcubamba River. Kuélap can, on a clear day, be seen on the other side of the rift. A 30-minute walk from Levanto towards Chachapoyas are the overgrown ruins of **Yalape**, which seems to have been a massive residential complex, extending over many hectares. Local people can guide you to the ruins.

East of Chachapoyas

Off the road to Mendoza are the pre-Inca ruins of **Purunllacta** or **Monte Peruvia**, hundreds of white stone houses with staircases, temples and palaces. The ruins have been cleared by local farmers and some houses have been destroyed. The ruins are two-hours walk from **Cheto**, which is south of the main road . A guide is useful. There are no hotels in Cheto but a house high on the hill above the town with a balcony has cheap bed and board. The same family also has a house on the Plaza.

The road east from Chachapoyas continues on to **Mendoza**, centre of the coffee producing region of Rodríguez de Mendoza. It is the starting point of an ethnologically interesting area in the Guayabamba Valley, where there is an unusually high incidence of fair-skinned people.

Northwest of Chachapoyas

On a turn-off on the Chachapoyas-Pedro Ruiz road, at Km 37, is the village of **Luya**. Here the road divides, one branch goes north to **Lamud**, a convenient base for several interesting sites, such as San Antonio and Pueblo de los Muertos, and the Quiocta cave. The second road goes

Chachapoyas

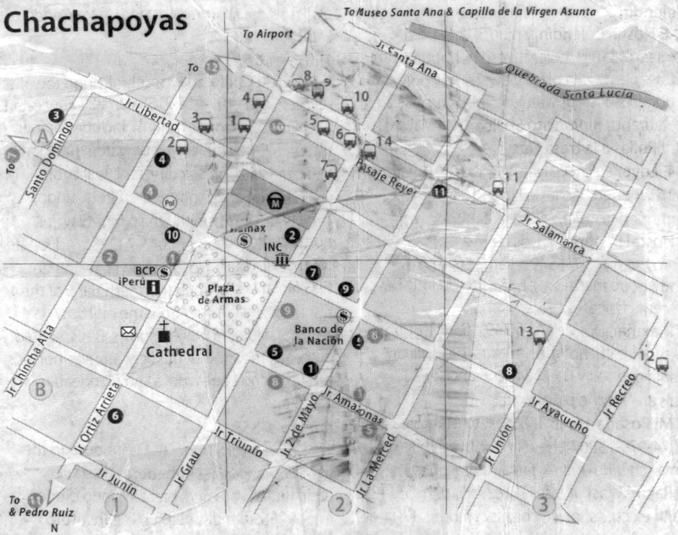

Sleeping
1 Belén *A1*
2 Casa Vieja *A1*
3 Casona Monsante *B2*
4 El Dorado *A1*
5 Gocta *B2*
6 Gran Vilaya *B2*
7 Las Orquídeas *A1*
8 Puma Urco *B2*
9 Revash *B2*
10 Rumi Huasi *A1*
11 Villa París *B1*
12 Vista Hermosa *A1*

Eating
1 Dulcería Santa Elena *B2*
2 El Edén *A2*
3 El Tejado *A1*
4 Fusiones *A1*
5 Heladería San Antonio *B2*
6 La Tushpa *B1*
7 Mari Pizza *B2*
8 Matalaché *B3*
9 Panadería Café San José *B2*
10 Romana *A1*
11 Sabores del Perú *A2*

Transport
1 Cars to Huancas & Mendoza *A2*
2 Cars to Lamud & Luya *A1*
3 Combis to Pedro Ruiz *A1*
4 Trans Zelada *A2*
5 Cars to Celendín *A2*
6 Trans Rollers to María *A2*
7 Cars to Pedro Ruiz & Bagua Grande *A2*
8 Civa *A2*
9 Virgen del Carmen to Mendoza and Celendín *A2*
10 Karlita to Leymebamba *A2*
11 Trans Kuélap *A3*
12 Movil Tours *B3*
13 GH Bus *B3*
14 Combis to Pizuquia *A2*

south and west to Cruzpata, the access for **Karajía** ⓘ *entry US$1, take binoculars*, where remarkable, 2½-m high sarcophagi set into an impressive cliff face overlook the valley. The viewpoint is 2½ hours' walk from Luya or 30 minutes from Cruzpata (*autos* from Luya to Cruzpata, 0600-1700, US$2.90, 1hr). **Chipuric** is another site 1½ hours' walk fro Luya. In a lush canyon, 1½ hours' walk from the road to Luya is **Wanglic**, a funeral site with large circular structures built under a ledge. Nearby is a beautiful waterfall, a worthwhile excursion. Ask for directions in Luya. Best to take a local guide (US$3.50-5 a day). The road to Luya and Lamud is unpaved, see Chachapoyas Transport for how to get there.

Chachapoyas region listings

For Sleeping and Eating price codes and other relevant information, see Essentials, pages 38-40.

Sleeping

Celendín *p1357*

C-E Hostal Celendín, Unión 305, Plaza de Armas, T555041, hcgustavosd1@hotmail.com. Some rooms with plaza view, central patio and wooden stairs, hot water, TV, pleasant, has 2 restaurants: **Rinconcito Shilico**, 2 de Mayo 816, and **Pollas a la brasa Gusys**.

E-F Loyer's, José Gálvez 410, T555210. Patio with wooden balcony all round, cheaper without bath, nice, all meals extra.

F Hostal Imperial, Jr Dos de Mayo 568, 2 blocks from the plaza, T555492. Large rooms with bath, good mattresses, hot water, colour TV, decent choice.

F Maxmar, Dos de Mayo 349, T555330. Cheaper without bath, hot shower extra, basic, clean, parking, good value, owners Francisco and Luis are very helpful.

F Mi Posada, Pardo 388, next to Atahualpa bus, T074-979-758674. New in 2009, with breakfast, small cheerful rooms, family atmosphere.

F Raymi Wasi, Jr José Gálvez 420, T976-551133. With electric shower, cheaper without, TV, large rooms, has patio, quiet, parking, good value, restaurant and karaoke.

Leymebamba *p1357*

B-C La Casona, Jr Amazonas 223, T830106. Nicely refurbished house, attractive common area, includes breakfast, simple rooms with bath and hot water, arrange tours and horses, very friendly. Recommended.

E La Petaca, Jr Amazonas 426, on the plaza, T830105. Good rooms with bath and hot water.

E Laguna de los Cóndores, Jr Amazonas 320, half a block from the plaza, T830104, www.loscondoreshostal.com. With bath, cheaper without, electric shower, nice courtyard, friendly, also runs the shelter at Laguna de los Cóndores.

Tingo *p1358*

A Estancia Chillo, 5 km south of Tingo towards Leymebamba, T01-265 9158 (Lima), www.estanciachillo.com. On a 9-ha farm, includes dinner and breakfast, with bath, hot water, transport, tours, trekking, horse riding. The walk from Chillo to Kuélap, is shorter than from Tingo.

E-F Hosp Tingo, on the main highway, just north of the Río Tingo, T941-732251. Adequate rooms with bath, electric shower, restaurant.

F-G Hosp León, along the south bank of the Río Tingo, just upriver from the highway, T941 715685, hildegardlen@yahoo.es. Basic, shared bath, electric shower, guiding, arrange horses, run by Lucho León who is knowledgeable.

Kuélap *p1358*

Walking up from Tingo, the last house to the right of the track (**El Bebedero**) offers very basic rooms with bed, breakfast and dinner from US$6, friendly, helpful. The **Instituto Nacional de Cultura** (INC) hostel is 100 m below the ruins, with a dorm for 12, US$1.75 pp, no running water, lovely setting, simple meals. Free camping. These options may be fully booked by archaeologists, but **Gabriel Portocarrero**, the caretaker, runs a hostel just below the ruins, basic, sleeping on a mat on the floor, friendly. **María**, 2-½ hrs from Kuelap on the vehicle road to Choctámal has 10 *hospedajes* in the **F** range, some with bath and hot water; meals available.

Choctámal

C Choctámal MS Lodge, 3 km from village towards Kuelap, T041-478838, www.marvelous spatuletail.com. Book ahead with Chachapoyas Tours, address below. Heated rooms, hot showers, hot tub, telescope for star- gazing. Meals US$6-8. Arrange treks to ruins, chance to see the endangered Marvellous Spatuletail Hummingbird.

F Gran Shubet, at the entrance to town from Tingo. Very basic, shared bath, restaurant.

Chachapoyas *p1358, map p1359*

B-C Casa Vieja, Chincha Alta 569, T477353, www.casaviejaperu.com. Converted old house with lovely courtyard, very nicely decorated, all rooms different, family atmosphere, living room and *comedor* with open fire, includes breakfast, Wi-Fi and library. Repeatedly recommended.

B-C Casona Monsante, Amazonas 746, T477702, www.lacasonamonsante.com. Converted colonial house with patio, comfortable rooms decorated with antiques, Wi-Fi in lobby, breakfast available.

B-C Villa París, 2 km from centre off road to Pedro Ruiz, T792332, www.hostalvillaparis.com. Comfortable rooms and cabins in a rural setting, Includes breakfast, good restaurant, small pool, nice grounds, parking.

C Puma Urco, Amazonas 833, T477871. Comfortable rooms, includes breakfast, Wi-Fi, **Café Café** next door, hotel and café receive good reports, run tours.

C-D Revash, Grau 517, Plaza de Armas, T477391, www.chachapoyaskuelap.com.pe. Traditional house with patio, steaming hot showers, Wi-Fi, breakfast available, friendly helpful owners, good local information, popular. Operate tours and sell local crafts.

D Gocta, Amazonas 721, T477698, carlaam6@hotmail.com. Brightly painted rooms with private bath, hot water, Wi-Fi, new in 2009.

D Gran Vilaya, Ayacucho 755, T477664, www.hotelvilaya.com. Comfortable rooms, firm beds, includes breakfast, Wi-Fi, parking, English spoken. Knowledgeable owner: Gumer Zegarra.

D Las Orquídeas, Ayacucho 1231, T478271. Converted home, includes breakfast, private bath, hot water, large garden, Wi-Fi, friendly.

D-E Belén, Jr Ortiz Arrieta 540, Plaza de Armas, T477830, www.hostalbelen.com. With private bath, hot water, nicely furnished, pleasant sitting room overlooking the Plaza, good value.

E El Dorado, Ayacucho 1062, T477047, ivvanovt@hotmail.com. With bathroom, electric shower, clean and helpful.

E Vista Hermosa, Puno 285, T477526. Nice ample rooms, some have balconies, private bath, electric shower, Wi-Fi, good value.

F Rumi Huasi, Ortiz Arrieta 365, T791100. With private bath, cheaper without, electric shower, small rooms, opened in 2009.

Levanto

D Levanto M S Lodge, behind the church, T041-478838, www.marvelousspatuletail.net. Two circular buildings with tall thatched roofs, can accommodate 12 people (**G** pp with own sleeping bag), external bathrooms, hot shower, lounge with fireplace and kitchen, meals US$6-8, book ahead with Chachapoyas Tours.

Northwest of Chachapoyas *p1358*

D Hostal Kuélap, Garcilaso de la Vega 452, on the plaza, Lamud. Cheaper without bath or hot water, basic. A few doors down is **Restaurant María**, cheap, excellent value, popular, the owner's son is a good local guide.

Eating

Celendín *p1357*

TT-T La Reserve, José Gálvez 313. Good quality and value, extensive menu, from Italian to chifa.

T Carbón y Leña, 2 de Mayo 410. For chicken, *parrillas* and pizzas.

T Juguería Carolin, Bolognesi 384. One of the few places open for early, from 0700-2200 daily, for juices, breakfasts and caldos.

Orange King, Ayacucho 491. Café, bar and disco, with good cocktails, snacks, music and lounge. Very friendly owner, Vilzeth, has information on trekking in the area.

Leymebamba *p1357*

T Cely Pizza's, Jr La Verdad 530, 2 blocks from Plaza de Armas, daily 0700-1900. Good food, value and service, pizza and vegetarian dishes with advance notice, great for breakfast, clean and very friendly. Recommended.

Chachapoyas *p1358, map p1359*

¥¥ El Tejado, Santo Domingo 424, Mon-Fri 1200-1600, 1900-2100, Sat-Sun midday only, but hours vary. Excellent upscale *comida criolla*. Large portions, attentive service, nice atmosphere and setting. Also serves good value *menu ejecutivo* on weekdays. Recommended.

¥¥ La Tushpa, Jr Ortiz Arrieta 753, Mon-Sat 1300-2300. Good grilled meat and *platos criollos*, wine list, very clean kitchen, attentive service.

¥¥-¥ Romana, Ayacucho 1013, daily 0700-2300. Choice of set meals and à la carte, good service.

¥ El Edén, Grau y Ayacucho by the market, Sun-Thu 0700-2100, Fri 0700-1800. Good vegetarian, large helpings.

¥ Mari Pizza, Ayacucho 832, daily 1630-0100. Good pizza, homemade pasta and fruit juices.

¥ Matalaché, Ayacucho y Unión, Mon-Sat 0700-2100, Sun 0800-1600. Famous for their huge *milanesa* (breaded beef); also serves *menú*.

¥ Sabores del Perú, Jr 2 de Mayo 321, daily 0700-2200. Breakfast, good value and quality *menú* at lunch, à la carte at night.

Dulcería Santa Elena, Amazonas 800, 0900-2230. Old-fashioned homemade desserts.

Fusiones, Chincha Alta 445, Mon-Sat 0730-1130, 1600-2100. Breakfast, fair-trade coffee, juices, snacks, Wi-Fi, book exchange, volunteer opportunities.

Heladería San Antonio, 2 de Mayo 521 and Amazonas 856. Good homemade ice-cream, try the *lúcuma* and *guanábana* flavours.

Panadería Café San José, Ayacucho 816, Mon-Sat 0700-1300, 1500-2200. Bakery and café, good breakfasts, sweets and snacks.

Activities and tours

Chachapoyas *p1358, map p1359*

Full-day trips cost US$12.50-25 pp, depending on season (higher Jul-Sep), distance to a site, number of passengers and whether meals are included. Several operators have daily departures to Kuélap and Gocta. Other popular destinations are Karajía, Quiocta, Leymebamba, and Revash. All inclusive trekking tours cost about US$45 pp per day, Gran Vilaya and Laguna de los Cóndores are most popular.

Andes Tours, at **Hostal Revash**. Daily trips to Kuélap and Gocta, other tours to ruins, caves and trekking. Also less-visited destinations, combining travel by car, on horseback and walking.

Chachapoyas Tours, Santo Domingo 432, T478078 www.kuelapperu.com, USA T1-866-396 9582 or T1-407-325 0499. Reliable, with 20 years' experience, benefiting local communities, multilingual staff and guides, volunteer opportunities, good service. Recommended.

Nuevos Caminos, at **Café Fusiones**, T479170, www.nuevoscaminostravel.com. Alternative community tourism throughout northern Peru, volunteer opportunities.

Turismo Explorer, Jr Grau 509 and at **Hotel Puma Urcu**, T478162, www.turismoexplorer peru.com. Daily tours to Kuélap, Gocta and other destinations, trekking tours including Laguna de los Cóndores and other archaeological sites, transport service.

Vilaya Tours, c/o **Gran Hotel Vilaya**, T477506, www.vilayatours.com. All-inclusive treks to off-the-beaten-path destinations throughout northern Peru. Run by Robert Dover, a very experienced and knowledgeable British guide, book ahead. Recommended.

Guides Martín Chumbi, contact through **Restaurante Las Rocas**, Jr Ayacucho, at the Plaza.

Transport

Celendín *p1357*

Bus To **Cajamarca**, 107 km, 3½ hrs: with **Atahualpa**, 2 de Mayo 707, Plaza de Armas, T555256, at 1230 daily, US$3.40; **Royal Palace's**, Jr Unión y José Gálvez, by Plaza de Armas, at 1400 daily; also **CABA** 2 a day, and **Rojas** 3 a day. Cars to Cajamarca leave when full from Ovalo Agusto Gil, Cáceres y Amazonas, 2½ hrs, US$6.75 pp. From the same place they go to **Chachapoyas**, 6 hrs, US$18 pp; also **Chachapoyas Express** combis to **Leymebamba**, Thu and Sun, 0800, US$7.15. Also here is **Móvil**, to Cajamarca daily 1500, to Chachapoyas, 0900, US$12.50, 9 hrs. **Virgen del Carmen**, Cáceres 117 by Ovalo A Gil, T792918, to Chachapoyas, daily except Tue and Sat at 1000, US$11, 6 hrs to Leymebamba, US$7.

Leymebamba and around *p1357*

To **Chachapoyas** (fills quickly, book ahead), 2½ hrs, **Transportes Karlita**, Jr Amazonas corner16 de Julio on the plaza, *combis* at 0400 and 0500, US$3.60, and cars as they fill early in the morning, US$7.15; with **Raymi Express**, Jr 16 de Julio at the plaza, cars as they fill, US$5.40;

also *combis* from Jr Bolívar 347, at 0500 and 1400; **Móvil Tours**, Jr Amazonas 420, Cajamarca-Chachapoyas bus passes around 1500, US$3.60. To **Celendín** (6-7 hrs) and **Cajamarca** (9-10 hrs), **Móvil Tours**, Jr Amazonas 420, passes Leymebamba about 0800, Celendín US$8.90 , Cajamarca US$12.50; **Chachapoyas Express**, 16 de Julio below the plaza, *combis* to Celendín, Tue and Fri at 0600, US$7.15.

Kuélap *p1358*
There are 4 options: 1) Take a tour from Chachapoyas (3 hrs each way in vehicle, including lunch stop on return, 3 hrs at the site). 2) Hire a vehicle with driver in Chachapoyas, US$43 per vehicle. 3) Take a combi from Chachapoyas , see below, to Kuelap, María, or Choctámal (all have accommodations), then walk along the road to the site (4-5 hrs from Choctámal, 2-2½ hrs from María). Some combis to María will continue to the end of the road, near the ruins. Alternatively, go early from Chachapoyas to Tingo, hike up to Kuélap then walk down to María and spend the night there. 4) Take a combi from Chachapoyas to Tingo, spend the night, then take the 5 hrs' strenuous walk uphill from Tingo; take waterproofs, food and drink, and start early as it gets very hot. Only the fit should try to ascend and descend in one day on foot. In the rainy season it is advisable to wear boots; at other times it is hot and dry (take all your water with you as there is nothing on the way up).

Chachapoyas *p1358, map p1359*
Air Service was scheduled to resume in May 2010: **LC Busre**, to **Chiclayo** daily at 0735, US$89 one way, 50 min; from Chiclayo at 0615. The airport is to the north of the city, taxi US$2.
Bus To **Chiclayo** (9 hrs, US$11-16), **Trujillo** (12 hrs, US$22) and **Lima** (20-22 hrs, US$29-41), best is **Móvil**, Libertad 464, T478545; to Lima daily at 1000; to Trujillo and Chiclayo at 1930. Most buses to Lima leave 1500-1600: **Trans Zelada**, Ortiz Arrieta 310, T478066. **Civa**, Salamanca y Ortiz Arrieta, T478048 (to Chiclayo also at 1815). **Turismo Kuélap**, Salamanca 726, T478128, to Chiclayo Tue and Sat at 1900, other days at 2000. **GH Bus**, Jr Unión 330, T479200, to Lima at 1000, to Chiclayo at 1900. To **Celendín** (8-9 hrs) and **Cajamarca** (11-12) hrs: **Móvil**, at 0600 daily, Celendín US$12.50, Cajamarca US$18; to Celendín with **Virgen del Carmen**, Salamanca 956, Mon at 1700, Thu and Sat at 0500, US$11. Cars to Celendín, **Raymi Express**, Salamanca 909, US$18, 8 hrs, arrange ahead. To **Pedro Ruiz** (1 hr), for connections to Chiclayo, Jaén, or Tarapoto, cars leave from Grau 310 y Salamanca, 0600-2100 (2100-2300 they depart from Grau in front of the market), US$3.60; combis every 2 hrs 0600-1800, from Ortiz Arrieta 370, US$2, also from Libertad y Ortiz Arrieta. To **Bagua Grande** for connections to Jaén, cars from Grau between Libertad and Salamanca 0600-2100 and Grau by the market 2100- 0600, US$8, 2 hrs (road works between Pedro Ruiz and Bagua Grande in 2010).
Regional For **Kuélap** US$7.15, 3½ hrs (will only go to Kuélap if they have enough passengers); **María** US$5.40, 3 hrs; **Lónguita** US$4.30, 2½ hrs; **Choctámal** US$3.60, 2 hrs; **Tingo** US$2.90, 1½ hrs: with **Roller's**, Grau y Salamanca, combi or car, at 0300 (return from Kuélap around 1200); with **Sr José Cruz**, Grau 331, combi or car at 0530 (returns from María at 0800); with **Trans Shubet**, Pasaje Reyes off Grau, cars to Lónguita around 1400-1500. To **Tingo**, also with **Brisas del Utcubamba**, Grau 332, cars bound for Magdalena, 0500-1800 or transport going to Yerbabuena or Leymebamba. Vehicles going to Chachapoyas pass Tingo from 0500. To **Leymebamba**, 83 km, 2½ hrs, reserve ahead: **Transportes Karlita**, Salamanca cuadra 9, *combis* 1200, 1600, US$3.60, and cars as they fill early in the morning US$7.15; with **Raymi Express**, Salamanca 909, cars US$5.40; also *combis* from Grau below Libertad, 1400, 1600, US$3.60. For **Cerro Olán**, **Comité Santo Tomás**, Grau y Pasaje Reyes, 1200, 1400 (return 0300, 0400) to **Montevideo** US$3.60, and **San Pedro de Utac**, US$5.35. For **Revash**, **Comité Santo Tomás**, to **Santo Tomás**, at 1000, 1300, 1500 (return at 0300, 0400, 0500), US$4.30, 3 hrs; get off at **Cruce de Revash** (near Puente Santo Tomás), US$4.30, 2½ hrs; or with the same company to **San Bartolo** at 1400 (return 0600), US$4.30, 3 hrs. To **Jalca Grande**, from Jr Hermosura y Salamanca, 2 combis depart Mon-Fri from 1330 onwards, US$4.30, 3 hrs (return 0300-0400). To **Levanto**, cars from Av Cuarto Centenario y Sociego southeast end of town, daily 1200-1300, US$2.90. For **Purunllacta**: to **Cheto** from Salamanca y Jr Hermosura, Mon-Fri 0700-1400,

cars US$2.90 and *combis* US$2.15. To **Mendoza** (86 km) **Trans Zelada**, Ortiz Arrieta 310, bus at 1800 (return at 0900), US$5.40, 4 hrs; cars 0500-1900, with **Guayabamba**, Ortiz Arrieta 372, US$9, 3½ hrs. To **Luya** and **Lamud**, from Libertad y Chincha Alta, cars 0400-1800, US$2.85, 1 hr to Lamud, same price to Luya.

Directory

Chachapoyas *p1358, map p1359*
Banks BCP, Ortiz Arrieta 576, Plaza de Armas. Visa and MC ATM. **Banco de la Nación**, Ayacucho corner 2 de Mayo, Visa ATM. **Isamax** clothing store, Ayacucho 940, Plaza de Armas, US$ cash only, fair rates. **Hostal Revash** changes US$ cash and sometimes Euros. There is nowhere to change TCs. Exchange rates in Chacha are lower than in other cities. **Internet** Many places around town, US$0.35 per hr. **Post office** Jr Ortiz Arrieta 632.

Chachapoyas to the Amazon

From Chachapoyas the road heads north through the beautiful river canyon for one hour to a crossroads, **Pedro Ruíz** (two hotels; basic restaurants), where you can return to the coast, head to Jaén for Ecuador, or continue east to Tarapoto and Yurimaguas, making the spectacular descent on a paved road from high Andes to jungle. In the rainy season, the road may be subject to landslides. On route to Tarapoto are **Rioja** (198 km, with several hotels) and Moyobamba.

Gocta

South of Pedro Ruíz is the spectacular **Gocta Waterfall** (771 m, the upper waterfall is 231 m, the lower waterfall is 540 m), third highest in the world (or 5th, or 14th, according to various ratings). From Pedro Ruiz, take the Chachapoyas road for 18 km to Cocahuayco where there are two roads up to Gocta, along either bank of the Cocahuayco River. The first turn-off leads up to the village of **San Pablo de Valera** (20 min by car) from which it is a 1-hour walk to a mirador, and another hour to the base of the upper waterfall. The second turn-off, 100 m further on the main road, leads up to the village of **Cocachimba** (5.3 km, 20 min), from which it is a 2 hour walk to the base of the lower waterfall. Both routes go through about 2 kms of lovely forest and offer fine views of the falls; the San Pablo trail is somewhat flatter. There is the possibility of connecting from one trail to the other. Both communities offer similar services: entry fee is US$1.80, local guides cost US$1.80 pp, horses can be hired for US$7 (they can only go part of the way), meals run US$1.80-3.60, rubber boots and rain ponchos are available for hire (it is always wet by the falls) and they offer basic accommodations. Chachapoyas operators offer tours to the falls (US$12.50-21).

Moyobamba → *Phone code: 042. Colour map 3, B2. Population: 14,000. Altitude: 915 m.*

Moyobamba, capital of San Martín department, is a pleasant town, in the attractive Río Mayo valley. The area is renowned for its orchids and there is a Festival de la Orquídea over three days around 1 November. Among several places to see orchids is **Orquideario Waqanki** ⓘ *www.waqanki.com, 0700-1800, US$0.55*, where the plants have been placed in trees. Just beyond are **Baños Termales San Mateo**, ⓘ *5 km southeast, 0600-2200, US$0.55*, which are worth a visit. **Puerto Tahuishco** is the town's harbour, a pleasant walk north of the centre, where boat trips can be taken. **Morro de Calzada** ⓘ *Rioja combi to the Calzada turnoff, US$0.55, mototaxi to the start of the trail US$2.50*, is an isolated outcrop in white sand forest, good for birdwatching. A path through forest leads to the top and a lookout (1½ hrs). In the foothills to the west are nature reserves, see www.tingana.org and www.lloros.org.

Tourist offices: Oficina Municipal de Información ⓘ *Jr Pedro Canga 262, at Plaza, T562191, Mon 0800-1300, 1430-1700, Tue-Fri 0800-1300, 1430-2000, Sat 0900-1300, 1600-2000, Sun 0900-1300*, helpful, English spoken. **Dircetur** ⓘ *Jr San Martín 301, T562043, www.turismosanmartin.com*, has leaflets and map. Also see www.moyobamba.net.

Tarapoto → *Phone code: 042. Colour map 3, B2. Altitude: 500 m.*
Tarapoto, the largest commercial centre in the region, is a very friendly place. Information from: **Oficina Municipal de Información** ⓘ *Jr Gregorio Delgado 260, at plaza, Mon-Sat 0830-1230, 1500-1900, Sun 0900-1300* and **Dircetur** ⓘ *Jr Angel Delgado Morey, cuadra 1, T522567, tarapoto@mincetur.gob.pe*. **Lamas** 22 km from Tarapoto, off the road to Moyobamba, has a native community, descendants of the Chancas people, who live in the Wayku neighbourhood below the centre. There is a small **museum** ⓘ *Jr San Martín 1157, daily 0830-1300, 1430-1800, US$0.90*, with ethnological and historical exhibits. In upper part of town is a *mirador*, opposite is **E Hosp Girasoles**, T042-543439, stegmaiert@yahoo.de, with breakfast, nice views, pizzeria and friendly knowledgeable owners. Cars from Tarapoto: Av Alfonso Ugarte, cuadra 11, US$1.45, 30 minutes.

Laguna Azul or Laguna de Sauce is a big lake 52 km south of Tarapoto, off the road to Juanjui. There are motor boats for hire, a couple of waterfalls nearby and a choice of accommodations including: **A El Sauce Resort**, T522588, www.elsauceresort.com, full service cottages by the lake, includes breakfast, restaurant, pool, kayaks.

About 15 km from Tarapoto on the spectacular road to Yurimaguas are the 50-m falls of **Ahuashiyacu** ⓘ *US$0.70, tours available or transport from La Banda de Shilcayo*. This is a popular place with locals. There are many other waterfalls in the area. Past Ahuashiyacu, the road climbs to a tunnel (stop at the police control for birdwatching, mototaxi US$6), after which you descend through beautiful forest perched on rocky cliffs to Pongo de Caynarachi (several basic *comedores*), where the flats start.

Chachapoyas to the Amazon listings

For Sleeping and Eating price codes and other relevant information, see Essentials, pages 38-40.

Sleeping

Moyobamba *p1364*

A-B Puerto Mirador, Jr Sucre, 1 km from the centre, T562050. Includes buffet breakfast, lovely grounds and views overlooking the river valley, pool, Wi-Fi, good restaurant.

B-C Río Mayo, Jr Pedro Canga 415, T564193, www.riomayo.com. Includes breakfast, central location, modern comfortable rooms, frigobar, Wi-Fi, small indoor pool, parking.

D La Casona, Alonso de Alvarado 682, T563858. Nicely refurbished old home, lovely courtyard with orchids, comfortable rooms, includes breakfast. Recommended.

D Orquídea del Mayo, Jr San Martín 432, T561049, orquideadelmayohostal@hotmail.com. Includes breakfast, modern comfortable rooms with bath, hot water, internet, opened in 2010.

E Atlanta, Alonso de Alvarado 865, T562063, atlantainn@hotmail.com. With bath, hot water (cheaper without), parking, TV, fan, clean and good but front rooms noisy.

E-F La Cueva de Juan, Jr Alonso de Alvarado 870, T562488, lacueva870@hotmail.com. Small courtyard, private bath, hot water, restaurant, central but reasonably quiet, good value.

F Cobos, Jr Pedro Canga 404, T562153. Private bath, cold water, simple but good.

Tarapoto *p1365*

Several **E** alojamientos on Alegría Arias de Morey, cuadra 2, and cheap basic hotels by the bus terminals.

AL Puerto Palmeras, in La Banda de Shilcayo, T524100, www.puertopalmeras.com. Includes breakfast, good restaurant, nice rooms, helpful staff, pleasant grounds with horses and small zoo. Private reserve outside town.

A Río Shilcayo, Pasaje Las Flores 224, 1 km east of town in La Banda de Shilcayo, T522225, www.rioshilcayo.com. Includes buffet breakfast, excellent meals, pool (US$3.50 for non-guests), airport transfers.

B Nilas, Jr Moyobamba 173, T527331, www.hotelnilas.com. Includes breakfast, a/c, fridge, Wi-Fi, pool, Jacuzzi, gym, airport transfers, conference facilities.

C Río Sol, Jiménez Pimentel 407, T523154, www.riosoltarapotohotel.com. Includes breakfast and airport transfers, small pool, restaurant and bar. Modern comfortable rooms with a/c, fridge, Wi-Fi.

C-D La Posada Inn, San Martín 146, T522234, laposada_inn@ yahoo.es. Good central hotel, ageing but well maintained, comfortable rooms with a/c (cheaper with fan), private bath, hot water, fridge, Wi-Fi, nice atmosphere.

C-D Luna Azul, Jr Manco Capac 276, T525787, www.lunaazulhotel.com. Includes breakfast and airport transfers, with bath, hot water, a/c (cheaper with fan), Wi-Fi, frigobar.

D El Mirador, Jr San Pablo de la Cruz 517, 5 blocks uphill from the plaza T522177, www.elmiradortarapoto.blogspot.com. With bath, electric shower (cheaper with cold water), fan, Wi-Fi, laundry facilities, very clean, breakfast available (US$3.50), hammocks on rooftop terrace with nice views, tours arranged. Family-run and very welcoming. Recommended.

D La Patarashca, Jr San Pablo de la Cruz 362, T528810, www.lapatarashca.com. Very nice hotel with ample rooms, includes breakfast, restaurant, private bath, electric shower, Wi-Fi, large garden with hammocks, tours arranged.

E-F San Antonio, Jr Jiménez Pimentel 126, T525563. Small simple rooms with private bath, hot water and fan.

Eating

Moyobamba *p1364*

ΨΨ-Ψ La Olla de Barro, Pedro Canga 398, Mon-Sat 0900-2200, Sun to 1600. Typical regional food, upmarket compared with other places in town.

ΨΨ-Ψ Kikeku, Jr Pedro Canga 450, next to casino, open 24 hrs. Good *chifa*, also *comida criolla*, large portions, noisy.

Ψ El Avispa Juane, Jr Alonso de Alvarado 1003, closed Sun. Regional specialties and snacks.

Ψ La Buena Salud, 25 de Mayo 227, by market, Sun-Fri 0800-1500. Vegetarian set meals, breakfast and fruit juices.

Helados La Muyuna, Jr Pedro Canga 549. Good natural jungle fruit ice cream.

Tarapoto *p1365*

ΨΨ Real Grill, Jr Moyobamba on the plaza, daily 0830-2400. Regional and international food. One of the best in town, expensive.

ΨΨ La Patarashca Restaurant, Jr Lamas 261, daily 1200-2300. Tourist restaurant serving regional specialties à la carte.

ΨΨ-Ψ Chifa Cantón, Jr Ramón Castilla 140, Mon-Fri 1200-1600, Sat-Sun 1200-2400. Chinese, very popular and clean.

ΨΨ-Ψ El Merendero, Jr San Martín cuadra 1, daily until 2300. *Comida criolla* à la carte.

ΨΨ-Ψ Tambo's Pizza, Jr San Pablo de la Cruz 299, Mon-Sat 1830-0000, Sun 1830-2200. Pizza and pasta.

Ψ El Maguaré, Jr Moyobamba corner Manco Cápac, Mon-Sat 1100-1530. Choice of set meals and à la carte, good food and service.

Café Plaza, Jr Maynas corner Martínez, at the plaza, closed midday. Breakfast, coffee, snacks, juices, Wi-Fi, popular.

Helados La Muyuna, Jr Ramón Castilla 271, open 0800-2400 except closed Fri from 1700 until Sat at 1830. Good natural ice cream and drinks made with jungle fruits, fruit salads,

Transport

Chachapoyas to the Amazon *p1364*

Pedro Ruíz Many buses on the **Chiclayo-Tarapoto** and Chiclayo-**Chachapoyas** routes pass through town. There is no way to reserve a seat and buses are usually full. Better to take cars or combis. To **Chachapoyas**, cars US$3.60, combis US$2, 1 hr. To **Bagua Grande**, cars US$4.30, 1hr; in 2010 traffic was restricted because of road construction. To **Jaén**, **Trans Fernández** bus from Tarapoto passes Pedro Ruiz about 1400-1500 or take a car to Bagua Grande and transfer there. To **Moyobamba**, cars US$10.70, 4 hrs. To **Nueva Cajamarca**, cars US$9, combis US$5.35, 3-3½ hrs, then a further 20 min to **Rioja**, car US$1.40, combi US$0.55. From Rioja to **Moyobamba**, 21 km, 20 min, car US$1.45, combi, US$0.55.

Gocta *p1364*
There are 3 options: 1) Take a tour from Chachapoyas. 2) Take a taxi from Pedro Ruiz to either Cocachimba or San Pablo, US$25 with 5-6 hrs wait. 3) To go independently, start early. From Pedro Ruiz, cars depart as they fill to **San Pablo de Valera**, US$2.15, 50 min, to **Cocachimba,** US$1.80, 50 min. Transport may be difficult on the way back. If there are no cars, from either town it takes 1-1½ hrs to walk down to Cocahuayco on the main road. Wait for transport to Pedro Ruiz or Chachapoyas, but space is not always available.

Moyobamba *p1364*
Long distance The bus terminal is 12 blocks from the centre on Av Grau (mototaxi US$0.55). No service originating in Moyobamba, all buses are on-route to/from Tarapoto. Several companies to **Tarapoto**, US$3.60-5.35, 2 hrs. Also many heading west to **Pedro Ruiz** (US$9, 4 hrs), **Jaén** (US$9, 7 hrs), **Chiclayo** (US$14.30-US$23, 12 hrs), **Piura** (US$18, 14 hrs) and **Lima** (US$32-46, cama US$57, 23-25 hrs). To book on long-haul buses, you may have to pay the fare to the final destination even if you get off sooner.
Regional **Empresa San Martín**, Benavides 276, and **ETRISA**, Benavides 244: cars to **Tarapoto**, US$7.15, 2 hrs; to **Rioja** US$1.45, 20 mins; to **Nueva Cajamarca**, US$1.80, 40 mins. Combis cost about 50% less on all routes. Taxi (for 4 passengers) to **Pedro Ruiz**, US$43, to **Chachapoyas** US$54.

Tarapoto *p1365*
Air US$3 per taxi airport to town, mototaxi US$1.50. To **Lima**, with **Lan** (Ramírez Hurtado 183, on the plaza, T529318), 2 daily, US$180-225, and **Star Perú** (San Pablo de la Cruz 100, T528765), daily, US$97-117. Star Perú to **Iquitos**, Tue, Thu and Sat, US$107-127.
Buses From Av Salaverry, blocks 8-9, in Morales; mototaxi from centre, US$0.70, 15 mins. To **Moyobamba**, 116 km, US$3.60-5.35, 2 hrs; to **Pedro Ruiz**, US$7.10 (companies going to Jaén or Chiclayo), 6 hrs; **Chiclayo**, 690 km, 15-16 hrs, US$12.50-23; and **Lima**, US$32-46, cama US$57, 29-30 hrs. To **Jaén**, US$11, 10 hrs, **Fernández** at 0700, 1400 and 1600, and **Jaén Express**, at 1200. For **Chachapoyas**, take a Jaén or Chiclayo bus to Pedro Ruiz (paying full fare to final destination) and a car from there. To **Piura** US$21.50, 18 hrs, with **Sol Peruano**, at 1200. To **Tingo María** and **Pucallpa**, daily except Sun at 0800, **Transamazónica** and **Transmar** alternate days, Pucallpa, US$32, 22-24 hrs; there have been armed holdups on this route.
Regional To **Moyobamba**, cars with **Empresa San Martín**, Av Alfonso Ugarte 1456, T526327 and **ETRISA**, Jr Limatambo 504, T521944, both will pick you up from your hotel, US$7.15, 2 hrs; combis with **Turismo Selva**, Av Alfonso Ugarte, cuadra 11, US$3.60, 2½ hrs. To **Yurimaguas**, **Gilmer Tours**, Av Alfonso Ugarte 1480, hourly minibuses, 0500-1200, 1400-1800, US$5.35, 2½ hrs; cars with **Empresa San Martín**, see above, US$7.15, 2 hrs .

❶ Directory

Moyobamba *p1364*
Banks For ATMs (Visa/MC), US$ cash and TCs: **BCP**, Alonso de Alvarado 903 y San Martín; **BBVA**, San Martín 494; **Interbank**, San Martín y Callao; **Scotiabank**, Alonso de Alvarado y San Martín. **Lizana Cambio**, Alonso de Alvarado, cuadra 10, US$ and Euros, cash only, good rates. **Internet** Several places in town.

Tarapoto *p1365*
Banks For ATMs (Visa/MC) and US$: **Scotiabank**, Ramírez Hurtado y Grau, corner of plaza; **BBVA**, Ramírez Hurtado, on plaza; **Interbank**, Grau 119, near the plaza; also ATM at **La Inmaculada Supermarket**, Martínez de Compagñón, just off plaza. **Cambio Popi**, Jr Maynas 174, US$ and Euros, cash only, good rates. **Internet** Several places in the centre, US$0.55 per hour.

Chachapoyas to Ecuador and the coast

The road from Pedro Ruiz (see page 1364) goes west to Bagua Grande and then follows the Río Chamaya. It climbs to the Abra de Porculla (2,150 m) before descending to join the old Pan-American Highway at Olmos (see page 1335). From Olmos you can go southwest to Chiclayo, or northwest to Piura. **Bagua Grande** is the first town of note heading west. It has several hotels (eg **E Hotel Bagua Grande**, Av Chachapoyas) but is hot, dusty and unsafe. Pedro Ruiz or Jaén are more pleasant places to spend the night.

To Ecuador

Some 50 km west of Bagua Grande, a road branches northwest at Chamaya to **Jaén** (*Phone code: 076; Colour map 3, B2; Population: 25,000*), a convenient stopover en route to the jungle or Ecuador. It is a modern city surrounded by rice fields. Festival, *Nuestro Señor de Huamantanga*, 14 September.

A road runs north to **San Ignacio** (109 km, first 55 km are paved), near the border with Ecuador. San Ignacio (*fiesta* 30 July) is a pleasant town with steep streets in the centre of a coffee growing area. The nearby hills offer excursions to waterfalls, lakes, petroglyphs and ancient ruins. From San Ignacio the narrow, unpaved road runs 45 km through green hills to **Namballe**. Just north of Namballe a dirt road goes west to the **Santuario Tabaconas-Namballe** ⓘ *ProSNTN, Av Santa Rosa 800, San Ignacio, T076-356490, prosntn@gmail.com*, a 29,500-ha reserve, at 1,200-3,800 m protecting the Spectacled Bear and several ecosystems. The border is 15 minutes from town at **La Balsa**, with a simple *comedor*, a few small shops and money changers, but no lodgings. To leave Perú head directly to immigration, when entering see immigration first, then the PNP and return to immigration. From the frontier transport goes to Zumba and then to Vilcabamba and Loja. See Transport, page 1369.

Chachapoyas to Ecuador and the coast listings

For Sleeping and Eating price codes and other relevant information, see Essentials, pages 38-40.

Sleeping

To Ecuador *p1368*

Jaén

C El Bosque, Mesones Muro 632, T431184, hotelerael bosque@speedy.com.pe. On main road by bus terminals. Includes breakfast, quiet rooms in back, gardens, a/c, frigobar, solar hot water, Wi-Fi, nice pool, good restaurant.

D Hostal Valle Verde, Mcal Castilla 203, Plaza de Armas, T432201. Very clean and modern, large comfortable rooms and beds, a/c (cheaper with fan), hot water, frigobar, Wi-Fi, parking, includes breakfast. Recommended.

D Prim's, Diego Palomino 1341, T431039. Includes breakfast, good service, comfortable, hot water, a/c (cheaper with fan), frigobar, Wi-Fi, friendly, small pool. Recommended.

D-E César, Mesones Muro 168, T431491, hotelcesar-jaen@hotmail.com. Spacious comfortable rooms, fan, phone, TV, Wi-Fi in lobby, parking.

E Cancún, Diego Palomino 1413, T433511. Good rooms with bath, hot water, fan and Wi-Fi.

F-G Santa Elena, Sánchez Carrión 142, T803020. Cold water, cheaper with shared bath, basic rooms, some with fan.

North of Jaén

E Sol de la Frontera, 1 km north of Namballe, 4 km from La Balsa, soldelafrontera@yahoo.es. British-run by Isabel Wood. Comfortable rooms, bathtubs, gas water heaters, continental breakfast (other meals not available), set in 2.5 ha of countryside. A good option if you have your own vehicle or bring some food.

D-E Gran Hotel San Ignacio, Jr José Olaya 680 at the bottom of the hill,T076-356544, www.granhotelsanignacio.com.pe. Includes breakfast, restaurant **Mi Tierra**, Wi-Fi, modern comfortable rooms, upmarket for San Ignacio.

E-F La Posada, Jr Porvenir 218, T076-356180. Simple rooms with private bath and hot water (cheaper with shared bath and cold water), restaurant, internet, small terrace upstairs.

F-G Hostal Maldonado, near the plaza, Namballe, T076-830011. Private bath (cheaper without), cold water, basic.

Eating

To Ecuador *p1368*

Jaén

TT-T La Cabaña, Bolívar 1332 at Plaza de Armas, daily 0700-0000. Daily specials at noon, à la carte in the evening, popular.

TT-T Lactobac, Bolívar 1378 at Plaza de Armas, daily 0730-0000. Variety of à la carte dishes, snacks, desserts, good *pollo a la brasa*. Very popular and recommended.

T Claudy Chicken, Diego Palomino 1284, Sun-Fri 0700-2300. Selection of set meals at noon, Chinese and chicken in the evening.

Transport

Chachapoyas to Ecuador & the coast *p1368*

Many buses pass through **Bagua Grande** en route from Chiclayo to Tarapoto or Chachapoyas and vice versa. You can book for Lima (US$16-28) or Chiclayo (US$5.50), but for Tarapoto (US$8) or Chachapoyas (US$5) you must wait and see if there is space; better to take a car or combi. Cars to **Jaén** from Mcal Castilla y Angamos at the west end of town, US$3.20, 1 hr. From Jr B Alcedo at the east end of town, cars leave to **Pedro Ruiz**, US$4.30, 1 hr (in 2010 traffic was restricted because of road construction); to **Chachapoyas**, US$7.85, 2½ hrs.

To Ecuador *p1368*

Jaén

Bus Terminals are strung along Mesones Muro, blocks 4-7, south of centre; many ticket offices, always enquire where the bus actually leaves from. Some companies also have offices in the centre: eg **Civa**, Mcal Ureta 1300 y V Pinillos (terminal at Bolívar 935). To **Chiclayo**: US$5.50-7, 6 hrs, many companies, eg **Móvil**, *bus cama* at 1330 and 2300, US$10; **Turismo Jaén**, 0900, 1220, 1430, 2230, 2300, 2320. Cars to Chiclayo from terminal at Mesones Muro cuadra 4, US$18, 5 hrs. To **Lima**: **Móvil** at 1600, 16 hrs, *bus cama* US$39, *semi-cama* US$32. **Civa**, 1700, US$32. Service to Lima also goes through **Trujillo**. To **Piura** via Olmos: **Sol Peruano**, at 2230, US$14, 8 hrs. To **Tarapoto**: 490 km, US$11, 9 -10 hrs; **Jaén Express** at 1000 and 1700, **Fernández**, 1000, 1700 and 2100; **Sol Perú** and **Sol Peruano**, both at 2030. To **Moyobamba**: US$9, 7 hrs, same service as Tarapoto, likewise to **Pedro Ruiz**: US$7, 3½hrs. To **Bagua Grande**: cars from Mesones Muro cuadra 6, 0400-2000, US$3.20, 1hr; combis from cuadra 9, US$1.80. To **Chamaya**: cars from Mesones Muro cuadra 4, 0500-2000, US$1, 15 min. To **San Ignacio** (for Ecuador), cars from Av Pacamuros, cuadra 19, 0400-1800, US$5.40, 2 hrs; combis from cuadra 17, US$3.60 , 3 hrs.

North of Jaén

Bus From San Ignacio to **Chiclayo**, with **Civa**, Av San Ignacio 386, daily at 1830, US$9, 10-11 hrs; with **Trans Chiclayo**, Av San Ignacio 406, 1845 daily.To **Jaén**, from *óvalo* at south end of Av Mariano Melgar (many touts): cars US$5.40, 2 hrs; combis US$3.60, 3 hrs.

To **Namballe** and **La Balsa** (border with Ecuador), cars leave from Jr Porvenir y Jr Santa Rosa: to Namballe US$3.60, 1¾ hrs; to La Balsa US$4.30, 2 hrs. In Ecuador, only *rancheras* (open -sided buses) run from La Balsa to Zumba at 1230, 1730 and 1930, US$1.75, 1¾ hrs; Zumba to La Balsa 0800, 1430 and 1730. There are Ecuadorean military controls before and after Zumba; keep your passport to hand.

Directory

To Ecuador *p1368*

Jaén

Banks **BCP**, Bolívar y V Pinillos, at the Plaza. ATM (Visa/MC), US$ cash and TCs; **BBVA**, Ramón Castilla y San Martín, at the plaza, ATM (Visa/MC) and US$ cash. Many **cambios** on V Pinillos 1 block north of Plaza, US$ cash only.

Internet many places, US$0.40/hr.

North of Jaén

Banks In San Ignacio: **Banco de la Nación**, Av San Ignacio 150; and **Comercial Unión**, Av San Ignacio 454, change US$ cash only. **Multi-Red ATM** on the Plaza may accept some Visa cards, but always bring cash. **Internet** places in both San Ignacio and Namballe.

South coast

The Pan-American Highway runs all the way south from Lima to the Chilean border. This part of Peru's desert coast has its own distinctive attractions. The most famous, and perhaps the strangest, are the mysterious Nazca Lines, whose origin and function continue to puzzle scientists the world over. But Nazca is not the sole archaeological resource here: remains of other pre-Columbian civilizations include outposts of the Inca empire itself. Pisco and Ica are the main centres before Nazca. The former, which is near the famous Paracas marine reserve, is named after the latter's main product, the pisco grape brandy and a number of places are well-known for their bodegas.

South from Lima

Beyond the beaches which are popular with Limeños the road passes near several towns worth a stop: eg Chincha with its Afro-Peruvian culture. The Paracas peninsula, near Pisco, is one of the world's great marine bird reserves and was home to one of Peru's most important ancient civilizations. Further south, the Ica valley, with its wonderful climate, is home to that equally wonderful grape brandy, pisco. Most beaches have very strong currents and can be dangerous for swimming; if unsure, ask locals.

Cañete Valley

A paved road runs inland from Cañete, mostly beside the Río Cañete, to **Lunahuaná** (40 km). It is 8 km beyond the Inca ruins of **Incawasi**, which dominated the valley. On Sunday the town is full of life with pisco tastings from the valley's bodegas, food and handicrafts for sale in the Plaza and lots of rafting, abseiling and other activities round about. Several places offer rafting and kayaking: from November-April rafting is at levels 4-5. May-October is low water, levels 1-2 only. A festival of adventure sports is held every February. *Fiesta de la Vendimia*, grape harvest, first weekend in March. At the end of September/beginning October is the *Fiesta del Níspero* (medlar festival). There are several hotels, ranging from **B** to **F**, and *restaurantes campestres* in the area. Tourist office in the Municipalidad (T284 1006, mlunah@mixmail.com), opposite the church, open daily.

Beyond Lunahuaná the road ascending the Cañete Valley leaves the narrow flood-plain and runs 41 km, paved, through a series of gorges to the San Jerónomo bridge. A side road heads to Huangáscar and the village of Viñac, where Mountain Lodges of Peru has its **Viñak-Reichraming Lodge** (**AL-A** pp full board, T01-421 7777, www.refugiosdelperu.com, see page 1461), a wonderful place to relax or go horseriding or walking (superb views, excellent food). The main road carries on to market town of **Yauyos** (basic accommodation, 5 km off the road). After the attractive village of **Huancaya**, the valley is transformed into one of the most beautiful upper valleys in all Peru, on a par with Colca. Above Huancaya the high Andean terrain lies within the **Nor-Yauyos National Reserve** and the river descends through a series of absolutely clear, turquoise pools and lakes, interrupted by cascades and white-water rapids. Culturally, the valley is fascinating for its dying indigenous languages and perhaps the best pre-Columbian terracing anywhere in Peru. Further upstream **Llapay** is a good base because it is in the middle of the valley (**G** *Hostal Llapay*, basic but very friendly, will open at any hour, restaurant). 17 July Fiesta Nor-Yauyina in Llapay, large and popular. Beyond Llapay, the Cañete valley narrows to an exceptionally tight canyon, with a road squeezed between nothing but rock and rushing water for the steep climb to the 4,600-m pass. Beyond, the road drops to Huancayo (see page 1466).

Pisco and around → *Phone code: 056. Colour map 3, C3. Population: 82,250.*

The largest port between Callao and Matarani is a short distance to the west of the Pan-American Highway and 237 km south of Lima. In August 2007, an earthquake of 7.9 on the

Richter scale struck the coast of Peru south of Lima killing 519 people, with 1,366 injured and 58,500 homes destroyed. Hardest hit was the province of Ica; in the city of Pisco almost half of all buildings were destroyed. Three years later many people are still without homes and NGOs are hard at work rebuilding communities. Also affected was **Chincha Alta**, 35 km north of Pisco, where the negro/criollo culture thrives. The famous festival, *Verano Negro*, is at the end of February while, in November, the *Festival de las Danzas Negras* is held in El Carmen, 10 km south.

A 317-km paved road goes to Ayacucho in the sierra, with a branch to Huancavelica. At Castrovirreyna it reaches 4,600 m. The scenery on this journey is superb. **Tambo Colorado** ⓘ *US$1.50,* one of the best-preserved Inca ruins in coastal Peru, is 38 km from the San Clemente junction, up the Pisco valley. It includes buildings where the Inca and his retinue would have stayed. Many of the walls retain their original colours. On the other side of the road is the public plaza and the garrison and messengers' quarters. The caretaker will act as a guide, he has a small collection of items found on the site. Tours US$45 with guide, minimum 2 people.

Paracas National Reserve

ⓘ *US$1.75 pp; agency tours cost US$5.25 in a bus..*

Down the coast 15 km from Pisco Puerto is the bay of **Paracas**, sheltered by the Paracas peninsula. The name means 'sandstorm' (these can last for three days, especially in August; the wind gets up every afternoon, peaking at around 1500). Paracas can be reached by the coast road from San Andrés, passing the fishing port and a large proportion of Peru's fishmeal industry. Alternatively, go down the Pan-American Highway to 14½ km past the Pisco turning and take the road to Paracas across the desert. Many of the tour agencies which used to be in Pisco have moved to Paracas town, where new hotels and restaurants have opened.

The peninsula, a large area of coast to the south and the Ballestas Islands is a National Reserve, and one of the best marine reserves, with the highest concentration of marine birds in the world. It's advisable to see the peninsula as part of a tour: it is not safe to walk alone and it is easy to get lost. The **Julio Tello site museum** was being refurbished in early 2010. Tours follow a route through the Reserve, including to a *mirador* of **La Catedral** rock formation, which collapsed in 2007. Longer tours venture into the deserts to the south. About 14 km from the museum is the pre-Columbian Candelabra (**Candelabro** in Spanish) traced in the hillside, at least 50 m long, best seen from the sea. The tiny fishing village of **Lagunilla** is 5 km from the museum across the neck of the peninsula. Eating places there are poor value (watch out for prices in dollars) and unhygienic.

Ballestas Islands

Trips to the **Islas Ballestas** leave from the jetties in Paracas town. The islands are spectacular, eroded into numerous arches and caves (*ballesta* means bow, as in archery), which provide shelter for thousands of seabirds, some of which are very rare, and hundreds of sea lions. The book *Las Aves del Departamento de Lima* by Maria Koepcke is useful (see also www.avesdelima.com/playas.htm). You will see, close up, thousands of inquisitive sea lions, guano birds, pelicans, penguins and, if you're lucky, dolphins swimming in the bay. Most boats are speedboats with life jackets, some are very crowded; wear warm clothing and protect against the sun. The boats pass Puerto San Martín and the Candelabra en route to the islands.

Ica and Huacachina ➔ *Phone code: 056. Colour map 3, C3. Population: 161,410.*

Ica, 70 km southeast of Pisco, is Peru's chief wine centre and is famous for its *tejas*, a local sweet of *manjarblanco*. It suffered less damage than Pisco, but one side of the Plaza de Armas collapsed in the earthquake. The **Museo Regional** ⓘ *Av Ayabaca, block 8, T234383, Mon-Wed 0800-1900, Thu-Sun 0900-1800, US$4, students US$2, tip guides US$4-5, take bus 17 from the Plaza de Armas (US$0.50),* has mummies, ceramics, textiles and trepanned skulls from the Paracas, Nazca and Inca cultures; a good, well-displayed collection of Inca counting strings (*quipus*) and clothes made of feathers. Behind the building is a scale model of the Nazca lines with an observation tower; a useful orientation before visiting the lines. The kiosk outside sells copies of motifs from the ceramics and textiles. **Dircetur** is at ① *Av Grau 148, T238710, ica@mincetur.gob.pe*. Some tourist information is available at travel agencies. Also try **Touring y Automóvil Club del Perú** ① *Camino a Huacachina s/n, T235061, ica@touringperu.com.pe*.

Wine bodegas that you can visit are: **La Caravedo**, Panamericana Sur 298, T01-446 0478, with organic production and sophisticated presentation; **El Carmen**, on the right-hand side when arriving from Lima (has an ancient grape press made from a huge tree trunk); **El Catador** ① *José Carrasco González, T962629, elcatadorcristel@yahoo.es, 1000-1800, US$1.50, 10 km outside Ica, in the district of Subtanjalla, combi from the 2nd block of Moquegua, every 20 mins, US$0.40, taxi takes 10 mins, good tours in Spanish*. The shop sells homemade wines and pisco, and traditional crafts associated with winemaking. In the evening it is a restaurant-bar with dancing and music, best visited during harvest, late February to early April, wine and pisco tasting usually possible. Near El Catador is **Bodega Alvarez**, whose owner, Umberto Alvarez, is very hospitable and won the gold medal for the best pisco in Peru in 1995. Ask about *pisco de mosto verde* and the rarer, more expensive *pisco de limón*. The **Ocucaje** winery (www.ocucaje.com), 30 km south of Ica, makes wines and *pisco*. Half the winery's hotel, which also has a collection of fossilized whale and other sea creatures' bones in the garden, fell down in the earthquake. The winery's restaurant has a limited menu but serves good food.

About 5 km from Ica, round a palm-fringed lake and amid amazing sand dunes, is the oasis and summer resort of **Huacachina** ① *take a taxi from Ica for under US$1*, an increasingly popular gringo spot to warm up after the Andes. Its green sulphur waters are said to be curative and thousands of visitors come to swim here. There are lots of eating places and bars with music around the lake. Sometimes the water and shore get dirty and polluted. Sandboarding on the dunes is a major pastime here; board hire US$1.50 per hour. **Note** For the inexperienced, sandboarding can be dangerous on the big dunes. Dune buggies also do white-knuckle, rollercoaster tours for US$13 (not including municipal fee of US$1.05), most start between 1600 and 1700, beautiful sunsets, some at 1000, 2½ hours, recommended but not for the faint-hearted.

South from Lima listings

For Sleeping and Eating price codes and other relevant information, see Essentials, pages 38-40.

Sleeping

Pisco and around *p1370*

C-D La Hostería del Monasterio, Av Bolognesi 326, T531383, sister hotel of **Posada Hispana** (see below). has 3 triple rooms and 8 doubles, hot water, cable TV; breakfast terrace.

C-D Posada Hispana Hostal, Bolognesi 222, T536363, www.posadahispana.com. Rooms with loft and bath, also rooms with shared bath (not all rooms survived the 'quake), hot water, can accommodate groups, comfortable, breakfast extra, has **Café de la Posada** (lunch US$2), information service, English, French, Italian and Catalan spoken. Recommended.

D Hostal El Candelabro, Callao y Pedemonte, T532620, hostalelcandelabro@hotmail.com. Modern, pleasant, all rooms with bath, fridge, cable TV.

D Hostal Los Inkas Inn, Prol Barrio Nuevo Mz M, Lte 14, Urb San Isidro, T536634, www.losinkasinn.com. Affordable, rooms have safes, rooftop games area, internet, **G** pp in dorm, small pool. Soon to open **Inkas Inn II** on the other side of the road with bar/disco on top floor.

D Hostal Tambo Colorado, Av Bolognesi 159, T531379, www.hostaltambocolorado.com. Welcoming, helpful owners are knowledgable about the area, hot water, cable TV, small café/bar.

D-E Residencial San Jorge, C Barrio Nuevo 133, T532885, www.hotelsanjorgeresidencial.com. Cable TV, hot water, internet, secure parking, restaurant serves breakfast (not included), lunch and dinner.

E pp **Hostal San Isidro**, San Clemente 103, T/F536471. **F** in dorm, hot water, safe, laundry facilities, use of kitchen, breakfast extra, English spoken, parking, arranges dune buggies. Recommended.

Paracas *p1371*

LL Doubletree Guest Suites Paracas, Lote 30-34, Urb Santo Domingo on the outskirts, T01-617 1000, www.doubletree.com. Low rise, clean lines and a comfortable size, built around a lovely pool, on beach, water sports, spa, all mod cons and popular with families.

LL Hotel Paracas Luxury Collection Resort, Av Paracas 173, T581333, www.libertador.com.pe. The reincarnation of the famous **Hotel Paracas**, as a resort with spa, pools, excellent rooms in cottages around the grounds, access to beach, choice of restaurants, bar. Recommended.

L La Hacienda Bahía Paracas, Lote 25, Urb Santo Domingo, T01-213 1000, www.hoteleslahacienda.com. Next to Doubletree but not connected, rooms and suites, some with access straight to pool, spa, choice of restaurants, bar.

B-C El Mirador, at the turn-off to El Chaco, T545086, www.elmiradorhotel.com. Hot water, good service, boat trips arranged, meals available, large pool, tranquil gardens, relaxing.

C Santa María, Av Paracas s/n, T545045, www.santamariahostal.com. Smart rooms, hot water, internet and **El Chorito** restaurant, mainly fish and seafood.

D Hostal El Amigo, El Chaco, T545042, hostalelamigo@hotmail.com. Simple, hot water, breakfast not yet available, good reports.

D Los Frayles, Av Paracas Mz D lote 5, T545141, www.hostallosfrayles.com. Variety of simple, well-kept rooms, breakfast extra, free internet 30 mins, roof terrace, tourist information.

D Mar Azul, Alan García Mz B lote 20, T534542, hmarazulparacas@hotmail.com. Family run, all female staff, comfortable, also dorm **F** pp, hot water, breezy roof terrace for breakfast (included), helpful owner Yudy Patiño.

Also **Ballestas Expeditions** for local tours.

Ica and Huacachina *p1371*

Hotels are fully booked during the harvest festival and prices rise. Many hotels are in out of town residential neighbourhoods, insist taxis go to the hotel of your choice.

LL-AL Las Dunas, Av La Angostura 400, T256224, www.lasdunashotel.com. Lima office: Av Vasco Núñez de Balboa 259, Lima, T213 5000. Prices do not include service, about 20% cheaper on weekdays. Highly recommended, in a complete resort with restaurant, swimming pool, horse riding and other activities, it has its own airstrip for flights over Nazca, 50 mins.

C Villa Jazmín, Los Girasoles Mz C-1, Lote 7, Res La Angostura, T258179, www.villajazmin.net. Modern hotel in a residential area near the sand dunes, 8 mins from the city centre, solar heated water, restaurant, pool, Wi-Fi, internet, tours arranged, airport and bus transfers, helpful staff, tranquil and very good.

D La Florida Inn, Residencias La Florida B-01, Urb San Luis, T237313. Not too easy to find, with 16 rooms, cheaper without bath, restaurant.

E Princess, Urb Santa María D-103, T215421, hotel_princess@yahoo.com. Taxi ride from the main plaza, small rooms, hot water, TV, pool, tourist information, helpful, peaceful, very good.

F Hostal El Paraíso, Bolívar 418, T227582. Hot water, cable TV, affordable basic accommodation.

Huacachina

AL-A Mossone east end of the lake, T213660, mossone@dematourhoteles.com. Elegant, hacienda- style, full board available, lovely patio, pool, bicycles and sandboards. Recommended. On quiet days, at the staff's discretion you can pay US$3.45 to use large, clean swimming pool

A-C Hostería Suiza, Malecón 264, T238762, hostesuiza@terra.com.pe. Overlooking lake, lovely grounds, quiet, includes breakfast, safe parking, internet. Recommended.

C-D Hostal Huacachinero, opposite Hostal Salvatierra, T217435, http://elhuacachinero.com. Breakfast US$3, comfortable, nice atmosphere, pool, outside bar and restaurant only for guests, parking, offers tours and buggy rides.

E Casa de Arena, Av Perotti s/n, T215274, casadearena@ hotmail.com. Basic rooms, cheaper without bath, bar, small pool, laundry facilities, board hire, popular with backpackers but grubby, check your bill and change carefully, don't leave valuables unattended.

F Carola del Sur (also known as **Casa de Arena II**), Av Perotti s/n, T215439. Basic rooms, also popular, small pool, restaurant/bar, hammocks, access to Casa de Arena's bigger pool.
F Hostal del Barco, Balneario de Huacachina 180. A very relaxed place with hammocks on the front terrace, basic rooms, bar, use of kitchen, can arrange tours.
F Hostal Rocha, T222256, kikerocha@hotmail.com. Hot water, **G** without bath, family run, kitchen and laundry facilities, board hire, small pool, popular with backpackers, but a bit run-down.
F Hostal Salvatierra, T232352, hospedaje salvatierra@hotmail.com. An old building, cheaper without bath, not on waterfront, charming, pool, relaxing courtyard, rents sandboards, good value.
G Hostal Titanic, T229003. Small rooms, pool and café, clothes washing, board hire, good value for lodging and set meals.

Eating

Pisco and around *p1370*

As de Oro, San Martín 472, T532010. Good food, not cheap but always full at lunchtime, swimming pool, closed Mon.
Café Pirata , Callao 104, T534343. Open 0630-1500, 1800-2200, desserts, pizzas, sandwiches, coffee and lunch menu, closed Sun.
Chifa Lisen, Av San Martín 325, T535527. 1230-1530, 1800-2200. Chinese food and delivery.

Paracas *p1371*

Several eating places on the Malecón by Playa El Chaco, all with similar menus and prices (in our range) and open for breakfast, eg **Bahía**; **Brisa Marina**, varied menu, mainly seafood, good; **Johnny y Jennifer**, also serves vegetarian.

Ica and Huacachina *p1371*

Anita, Libertad 133, Plaza de Armas. Local dishes, no set breakfast, a bit expensive for what's offered, but fully operational.
Las Carnes , Av San Martín, distance from centre. Typical Peruvian fare with an emphasis on chicken, US$5 all-day *menú*, popular with locals.
Caine y pescao, Av Juan José Elías 417, T228157. Seafood and, at night, grilled chicken and *parrilladas*.
Plaza 125, C Lima 125, T211816. On the plaza, regional and international food as well as breakfast.
Tejas Helena, Cajamarca 137. The best *tejas* in town are sold here.

Huacachina

La Casa de Bamboo, Av Perotti s/n, next to Hostería Suiza, T776649. Café-bar, English breakfast, marmite, Thai curry, falafel, vegetarian and vegan options, TV, book exchange, games.
Moroni, T238471. Only restaurant right on the lake shore, serving a variety of Peruvian and international foods. Open 0800 till late.

Festivals and events

Ica and Huacachina *p1371*

Wine harvest festival in early **Mar**. The image of El Señor de Luren, in a fine church in Parque Luren, draws pilgrims from all Peru to the twice-yearly festivals in **Mar** and **Oct (15-21)**, when there are all-night processions.

Activities and tours

Paracas *p1371*

There are agencies all over town offering trips to the Islas Ballestas, the Paracas reserve, Ica, Nazca and Tambo Colorado. A 2-hr boat tour to the islands US$12-14 pp. Usually, agencies will pool clients together in 1 boat. A private boat trip costs US$25-30, minimum 2 people. Do not book tours on the street. An agency that does not pool clients is **Huacachina,** based in Ica, with an office in Paracas, T056-215582, www.huacachinatours.com.

Ica and Huacachina *p1371*

In Ica, agencies offer city tours, Nazca Lines, Paracas, Islas Ballestas, buggies and sand boarding: **A Dolphin Travel**, C Municipalidad 132, of 4, T256234; **Desert Travel**, Lima 171, inside Tejas Don Juan on Plaza, T227215, desert_travel@hotmail.com.
Desert Adventures, Huacachina, T228458, www.desertadventure.net. Frequently recommended for sandboarding and camping trips into the desert by 4WD and buggies, French, English and Spanish spoken. Also to beaches, Islas Ballestas and Nazca Lines flights.

Ica Desert Trip, Bolívar 178, T237373, www.icadeserttrip.com. Roberto Penny Cabrera (speaks Spanish and English) offers 1, 2 and 3-day trips off-road into the desert, archaeology, geology, etc. US$50 pp per day, 4 people maximum, contact by email in advance. Take toilet paper, something warm for the evening, a long-sleeved loose cotton shirt for daytime and long trousers. Recommended, but "not for the faint-hearted".

Over Sand Adventures, Huacachina, T956-757601/956-357402, ruben1985_6@hotmail.com. Buggies, sandboarding and beaches tours.

Transport

Cañete Valley *p1370*

Soyuz bus Lima-**Cañete** every 7 mins, US$3; combi Cañete-**Lunahuaná**, US$1.75. **ETAS** run from **Cañete** (in front of AEDO petrol station, T01-287 8831 or 01-9771 1254) to **Huancayo** (Loreto 744, T215424). Information about ETAS buses on posters in the villages. Daily bus from **Lunahuaná** between 1900-2200 to **Yauyos** stops at a shop on the road on request. Bus from Yauyos to **Llapay** between 0100-0230, arrives 0200-0400, final destination **Huancayo** arriving 0900.

Pisco and around *p1370*

Bus Buses drop passengers at San Clemente on Panamericana Sur, known as **El Cruce**; many bus companies and tour agencies have their offices here. It's a 10-km taxi ride from the centre, US$5, US$8 to Paracas. Colectivos leave from outside the Banco Continental in the plaza for El Cruce when full, US$2. To **Lima**, 242 km, 4 hrs, US$4. The best companies are: **Ormeño**, **Cruz del Sur**, 2 a day each, and **Soyuz**, every 7 mins. **Ormeño** has an office in Pisco plaza and will take you to El Cruce to meet their 1600 bus. **Flores** is the only company that goes into Pisco town, from Lima and Ica, but buses are poor and services erratic. To **Ica**, US$0.90 by bus, 45 mins, 70 km, with **Ormeño**, also colectivos. To **Nazca**, 210 km, take a bus to Ica and then change to a colectivo. To **Ayacucho**, 317 km, 8-10 hrs, US$7.55-15.15, several buses daily, leave from El Cruce, book in advance to ensure seat and take warm clothing as it gets cold at night. To **Huancavelica**, 269 km, 12-14 hrs, US$7, with **Oropesa**, coming from Ica. To **Arequipa**, US$12, 10-12 hrs, 2 daily. To **Tambo Colorado** from near the plaza in Pisco, 0800, US$1.60, 3 hrs; also colectivos, US$1.20 pp. Alight 20 mins after the stop at Humay; the road passes right through the site. Return by bus to Pisco in the afternoon. For transport back to Pisco wait at the caretaker's house. Taxi from Pisco US$25. Tours from Pisco agencies US$10-15 with guide, minimum 2 people.

Paracas *p1371*

Cruz del Sur, **Oltursa** and **Ormeño** buses between Lima and Nazca stop at the Double Tree Hotel near Paracas, Cruz del Sur 4 a day, US$20-26 from **Lima**, US$12-15 to **Nazca**. Others have 1-2 a day, US$19-22.

Taxi From **Pisco** to Paracas about US$2.50-3; combis when full, US$0.50, 25 mins.

Ica and Huacachina *p1371*

Bus All bus offices are on Lambayeque blocks 1 and 2 and Salaverry block 3. To **Pisco**, 70 km, as above. To **Lima**, 302 km, 4 hrs, US$5-10, several daily including **Soyuz** (Av Manzanilla 130 – every 7 mins 0600-2200), **Flores** and **Ormeño** (at Lambayeque 180). To **Nazca**, 140 km, 2 hrs, several buses (US$1.50) and colectivos (US$3.75) daily, including **Ormeño**, **Flores**, 4 daily, and **Cueva** (José Elias y Huánuco), hourly on the hour 0600-2200. To **Arequipa** the route goes via Nazca, see under Nazca.

Directory

Pisco and around *p1370*

Banks ATMs at banks on Plaza, Visa and Globalnet. Also **BCP** on Fermín Tangüis in a **Repsol** service station. **Telephones** On Plaza de Armas between Av San Martín y Callao.

Ica and Huacachina *p1371*

Banks Avoid changing TCs if possible as commission is high. If necessary, use **BCP**. **Post offices** At Callao y Moquegua.
Telephones At Av San Martín y Huánuco.

Nazca and around

Set in a green valley amid a perimeter of mountains, Nazca's altitude puts it just above any fog which may drift in from the sea. The sun blazes the year round by day and the nights are crisp. Nearby are the mysterious, world-famous Nazca Lines. Overlooking the town is Cerro Blanco (2,078 m), the highest sand dune in the world, popular for sandboarding and parapenting.

Nazca Town ➔ *Phone code: 056. Colour map 3, C3. Population: 50,000. Altitude: 598 m.*
In the town of Nazca (140 km south of Ica via Pan-American Highway, 444 km from Lima) there are two important museums. **Museo Antonini** ⓘ *Av de la Cultura 600, eastern end of Jr Lima, T523444, cahuachi@terra.com.pe, 0900-1900, ring the bell, US$3, including guide. 10-min walk from the plaza, or short taxi ride.* This museum houses the discoveries of Professor Orefici and his team from the huge pre-Inca city at Cahuachi (see below), which, Orefici believes, holds the key to the Nazca Lines. Many tombs survived the *huaqueros* and there are displays of mummies, ceramics, textiles, amazing *antaras* (panpipes) and photos of the excavations. In the garden is a prehispanic aqueduct. Recommended. The **Maria Reiche Planetarium** ⓘ *Hotel Nazca Lines, T522293, shows usually at 1900 and 2115 in English, 2000 in Spanish; US$6 (students half price), very good,* was opened in May 2000 in honour of Maria Reiche (see below). Stimulating lectures are given every night about the Nazca Lines, based on Reiche's theories, which cover archaeology and astronomy. The show lasts about 45 minutes, after which visitors are able to look at the moon, planets and stars through sophisticated telescopes. There is a small market at Lima y Grau and the Mercado Central at Arica y Tacna. The *Virgen de la Guadalupe* festival takes place 29 August-10 September. **Tourist police** ⓘ *Av Los Incas cuadra 1, T522105.*

Nazca

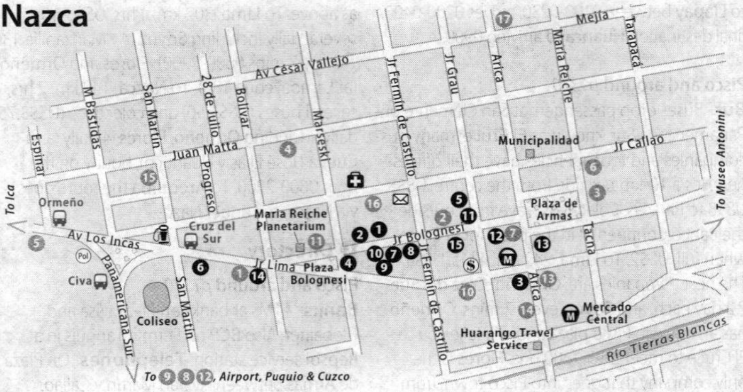

N

200 metres
200 yards

Sleeping
1 Alegría
2 Casa Andina
3 El Mirador de Nasca
4 Friends House
5 Hostal Alegría
6 Internacional
7 Las Líneas
8 Maison Suisse
9 Majoro
10 Nasca
11 Nasca Lines
12 Nido de Cóndor
13 Paredones Inn
14 Perugia Hostal
15 Posada Guadalupe
16 Sol de Nasca
17 The Walk On Inn

Eating
1 Chifa Guang Zhou
2 Coffee Break
3 Concordia
4 El Portón
5 Fuente de Soda Jumbory
6 Kañada
7 La Carreta
8 La Choza
9 La Taberna
10 Los Angeles
11 Panadería
12 Picante's
13 Plaza Mayor
14 Rico Pollo
15 Vía La Encantada

Nazca Lines

Cut into the stony desert about 22 km north of Nazca, above the Ingenio valley on the Pampa de San José, along the Pan-American Highway, are the famous Nazca Lines. Large numbers of lines, not only parallels and geometrical figures, but also designs such as a dog, an enormous monkey, birds (one with a wing span of over 100 m), a spider and a tree. The lines, best seen from the air, are thought to have been etched on the Pampa Colorada sands by three different groups – the Paracas people 900-200 BC, the Nazcas 200 BC-AD 600 and the Huari settlers from Ayacucho at about AD 630.

The Nazcas had a highly developed civilization which reached its peak about AD 600. Their polychrome ceramics, wood carvings and adornments of gold are on display in many of Lima's museums. The Paracas was an early phase of the Nazca culture, renowned for the superb technical quality and stylistic variety in its weaving and pottery. The Huari empire, in conjunction with the Tiahuanaco culture, dominated much of Peru from AD 600-1000.

Origins of the lines The German expert, Dr Maria Reiche, who studied the lines for over 40 years, mostly from a step ladder, died in 1998, aged 95. She maintained that they represent some sort of vast astronomical pre-Inca calendar. In 1976 Maria Reiche paid for a platform, the mirador, from which three of the huge designs can be seen – the hands, the Lizard and the Tree. Her book, *Mystery on the Desert*, is on sale for US$10 (proceeds to conservation work) in Nazca. In January 1994 Maria Reiche opened a small **museum** ⓘ *US$1. 5 km from town at the Km 416 marker, take micro from in front of Ormeño terminal, US$0.70, frequent*. Viktoria Nikitzhi, a colleague of Maria Reiche, gives one-hour lectures about the Nazca Lines at **Dr Maria Reiche Center** ⓘ *US$5, Av de los Espinales 300, 1 block from Ormeño bus stop, T969 9419, viktorianikitzki@hotmail.com*. She also organizes tours in Jun and Dec (phone in advance to confirm times; also ask about volunteer work). See the Planetarium, above. Another good book is *Pathways to the Gods: the mystery of the Nazca Lines*, by Tony Morrison (Michael Russell, 1978), available in Lima.

Other theories abound: Georg A von Breunig (1980) claims that the lines are the tracks of running contests, and a similar theory was proposed by the English astronomer Alan Sawyer; yet another is that they represent weaving patterns and yarns (Henri Stirlin) and that the plain is a map demonstrating the Tiahuanaco Empire (Zsoltan Zelko). *The Nazca Lines – a new perspective on their origin and meaning* (Editorial Los Pinos, Lima 18), by Dr Johan Reinhard, brings together ethnographic, historical and archaeological data, including current use of straight lines in Chile and Bolivia, to suggest that the Lines conform to fertility practices throughout the Andes.

Another theory is that the ancient Nazcas flew in hot-air balloons, based on the idea that the lines are best seen from the air, and that there are pieces of ancient pottery and tapestry showing balloonists, and local legends of flying men (see *Nazca, The flight of Condor 1*, by Jim Woodman, Murray, 1980, Pocket Books, NY 1977). This in part accords with research carried out by the BBC series 'Ancient Voices'. Clues to the function of the lines were found in the pottery and textiles of the ancient Nazcans, some of which show a flying creature emitting discharge from its nose and mouth. This is believed to portray the flight of the shaman who consumes certain psycho-active drugs that convince him he can fly and so enter the real world of spirits in order to rid sick people of evil spirits. In this way, the lines were not designed to be seen physically from above, but from the mind's eye of the flying shaman. This also explains the presence of creatures such as a monkey or killer whale which possess qualities needed by the shaman in his spirit journeys.

After six years' work at La Muña and Los Molinos, Palpa (43 km north of Nazca), and using photogrammetry (mapping from aerial photographs), Peruvian archaeologist Johny Isla and Markus Reindel of the Swiss-Liechtenstein Foundation deduced that the lines on both the Palpa and Nazca plains are offerings dedicated to the worship of water and fertility. These two elements were paramount to the coastal people in this arid environment and they expressed their adoration not only in the desert, but also on their ceramics and on the engraved stones of the Paracas culture. Isla and Reindel believe that the Palpa lines predate those at Nazca and that the lines and drawings themselves are scaled up versions of the Paracas drawings. In addition, objects in the shape of drops of water, whales and chilis, found in the grave of El Señor de Palpa, are repeated in the desert. This new research proposes that the Nazca culture succumbed not to drought, but to heavy rainfall, probably during an El Niño event.

Other excursions

The Nazca area is dotted with over 100 cemeteries and the dry, humidity-free climate has perfectly preserved invaluable tapestries, cloth and mummies. At **Chauchilla** ⓘ *30 km south of Nazca, last 12 km a sandy track, US$1.65*, grave robbing *huaqueros* ransacked the tombs and left bones, skulls, mummies and pottery shards littering the desert. A tour takes about two hours and should cost about US$7 per person with a minimum of three people. Gold mining is one of the main local industries and a tour usually includes a visit to a small family processing shop where the techniques used are still very old-fashioned. Some tours include a visit to Sr Andrés Calle Benavide, a local potter, who makes Nazca reproductions and is particularly recommended.

To the Paredones ruins and aqueduct: the ruins, also called Cacsamarca, are Inca on a pre-Inca base. They are not well preserved. The underground aqueducts, built 300 BC-AD 700, are still in working order and worth seeing. By taxi it is about US$10 round trip, or go with a tour.

Cantalloc is a 30 minutes to one hour walk through Buena Fe, to see markings in the valley floor. These consist of a triangle pointing to a hill and a *tela* (cloth) with a spiral depicting the threads. Climb the mountain to see better examples.

Cahuachi, to the west of the Nazca Lines, comprises several pyramids and a site called **El Estaquería** ⓘ *to visit the ruins of Cahuachi costs US$17 pp on a tour, US$12-15 in private taxi, minimum 2 people. See also the Museo Antonini, above.* The latter is thought to have been a series of astronomical sighting posts, but more recent research suggests the wooden pillars were used to dry dead bodies and therefore it may have been a place of mummification.

Road from Nazca towards Cuzco

Two hours out of Nazca on the newly paved road to Abancay and Cuzco is the **Reserva Nacional Pampas Galeras** at 4,100 m, which has a vicuña reserve. There is an interesting Museo del Sitio, also a military base and park guard here. It's best to go early as entry is free. At Km 155 is **Puquio**, then it's another 185 km to **Chalhuanca**. Fuel is available in both towns. There are wonderful views on this stretch, with lots of small villages, valleys and alpacas.

South of Nazca

Chala (*Phone code: 054*), 173 km from Nazca, is a fishing village with beaches. There are dozens of restaurants. There are several hotels (**D-G**), all in Chala Sur, 10 minutes' walk south from where the buses stop in Chala Norte. No banks or ATMs, but several internet places. Colectivos from Nazca cost US$3.50. Lima-Arequipa buses pass Chala about 0600.

About 10 km north of Chala are the large pre-Columbian ruins of **Puerto Inca** on the coast. This was the port for Cuzco. The site is in excellent condition: the drying and store houses can be seen as holes in the ground (be careful where you walk). On the right side of the bay is a cemetery, on the hill a temple of reincarnation, and the Inca road from the coast to Cuzco is clearly visible. The road was 240 km long, with a staging post every 7 km so that, with a change of runner at every post, messages could be sent in 24 hours. The site is best appreciated when there is no *garúa* (ie when the sun is shining).

Nazca and around listings

For Sleeping and Eating price codes and other relevant information, see Essentials, pages 38-40.

Sleeping

Nazca *p1376, map p1376*

If arriving by bus beware of touts who tell you that the hotel of your choice (notably *Alegría*) is closed, or full, and no longer runs tours. If you phone or email the hotel they will pick you up at the bus station free of charge day or night.

AL-A Maison Suisse, opposite airport, T/F522 434, www.aeroica.net. Comfortable, safe car park, expensive restaurant, pool, suites with jacuzzi, accepts Amex, good giftshop, shows video of Nazca Lines. Also has camping facilities. Ask for packages including flights over Nazca Lines.

AL-A Majoro, Panamericana Sur Km 452, T522490, www.hotelmajoro.com. A charming old hacienda about 5 km from town past the airstrip, beautiful gardens, pool, restaurant, quiet and homely, attentive service, serene surroundings, good arrangements for flights and tours.

AL-A Nazca Lines, Jr Bolognesi 147, T522293, reservanasca@derramajae.org.pe. With a/c, comfortable, rooms with private patio, hot water, peaceful, American breakfast included, restaurant, good but expensive meals, safe car park, pool (US$4.50 for non-guests, or free if having lunch), they can arrange package tours which include 2-3 nights at the hotel plus a flight over the lines and a desert trip. Recommended.

A Casa Andina, Jr Bolognesi 367, T523563, www.casa-andina.com. One of this chain of hotels, which all offer standardized services in distinctive style. Bright, modern decor, a/c, pool, TV, internet, restaurant open all day.

B Nido del Cóndor, opposite the airport, Panamericana Sur Km 447, T522424, www.nidodelcondornasca.com. Large rooms, hot water, good restaurant, bar, shop, swimming pool, camping US$3, parking, English, Italian German spoken, free pick-up from town, reservation advised.

C pp **Hotel Alegría**, Jr Lima 168, T522497, www.nazcaperu.com. Rooms with bath, a/c, continental breakfast, bungalows with hot shower, or spartan rooms with shared bath and no breakfast **E**, hot water, café, garden, pool, English, Italian, German and Hebrew spoken, laundry facilities, safe luggage deposit, book exchange, Wi-Fi, email facilities for US$2 per hr, netphone also US$2, free video on the Lines at 2100, very popular. Recommended. Efraín Alegría also runs a tour agency (see Activities and tours), flights and bus tickets arranged.

D Paredones Inn, Jr Lima 600, T522181, www.paredonesinn.com. 1 block from the Plaza de Armas, ample rooms with cable TV, minibar, microwave, great views from roof terrace, laundry service, bar, suites with jacuzzi, helpful staff.

E Internacional, Av Maria Reiche, T522744. Hot water, garage, café and nice bungalows.

E Las Líneas, Jr Arica 299, T522488. Spacious, cheaper without bath, restaurant. Recommended.

E El Mirador de Nasca, Tacna 436, T523121, www.actiweb.es/hotelmiradordenasca. On main plaza, comfortable, cheaper with shared bath, TV, new, modern.

E Nasca, C Lima 438, T522085, marionasca13@hotmail.com. Hot water, cheaper without bath, laundry facilities, luggage store, new annexe at the back, nice garden, safe motorcycle parking.

E Perugia Hostal, Arica 520, T521484, perugiahostal@hotmail.com. Hot water, cable TV, internet and tours around Nazca.

F pp **Hostal Alegría**, Av Los Incas 117, opposite *Ormeño* bus terminal, T522497. Basic, hot water, hammocks, nice garden, camping, restaurant.

F Posada Guadalupe, San Martín 225, T522249. Family run, lovely courtyard and garden, hot water, **G** without bath, good breakfast, relaxing (touts selling tours are nothing to do with hotel).

F Sol de Nasca, Callao 586, T522730, reservasnazca@hotmail.com. Rooms with and without hot showers, TV, restaurant, pleasant, don't leave valuables in luggage store.

F Friends House, Juan Matta 712, T524191, www.friendshousenazca.com. Popular backpackers' hang out, with cheap dorm room, rooftop rest area with hammocks, open kitchen, breakfast, single and shared rooms, internet and buggy rides.

F pp **The Walk On Inn**, José María Mejía 108, 3 blocks from Plaza de Armas, T/F056-522566, www.walkon inn.com. Rooms with bathroom, hot water, family feel, small swimming pool, TV room, excellent and cheap restaurant on top floor for breakfast and salads, very helpful staff, internet, Wi-Fi, luggage store, works with **Nasca Trails** for flights and tours. Recommended.

South of Nazca *p1378*

A Puerto Inka, 2 km along a side road from Km 610 Panamericana Sur (reservations T054-778458), www.puertoinka.com.pe. Bungalows on the beautiful beach, hammocks outside, great place to relax, use of pool US$7 for non-guests, boat hire, diving equipment rental, pleasant camping US$3, low season discounts, used by tour groups, busy in summer.

Eating

Nazca *p1376, map p1376*

ΨΨ-Ψ **Concordia**, Lima 594. Good, also rents bikes at US$1 an hour.

ΨΨ-Ψ **El Portón**, Moresky 120, in front of Hotel Nazca Lines. Popular with tours, specializes in Peruvian food of all types, indoor/outdoor setting. Recommended.

ΨΨ-Ψ **La Carreta**, Bolognesi, next door to Los Angeles. Nuevo Andino dishes using traditional ingredients, rustic, lively atmosphere, live music.

ΨΨ-Ψ **La Choza**, Bolognesi 290. Nice décor with woven chairs and thatched roof, all types of food, live music at night. Single women may be put off by the crowds of young men hanging around the doors handing out flyers.

ΨΨ-Ψ **La Taberna**, Jr Lima 321, T521411. Excellent food, live music, popular with gringos, it's worth a look just for the graffiti on the walls.

ΨΨ-Ψ **Plaza Mayor**, on the Plaza. Rustic style, specializes in barbecue of all types, roasted chicken, steaks, anticuchos and great salads. Recommended.

Ψ **Chifa Guang Zhou**, Bolognesi 297, T522036. Very good.

Ψ **Kañada**, Lima 160, nazcanada@yahoo.com. Cheap, good *menú*, excellent pisco sours, nice wines, popular, display of local artists' work, email service, English spoken, helpful. Recommended.

Ψ **Los Angeles**, Bolognesi 266. Good, cheap, try *sopa criolla*, and chocolate cake.

Ψ **Rico Pollo**, Lima 190. Good local restaurant.

Ψ **Vía La Encantada**, Jr Bolognesi 282, www.vialaencantada.com. Restaurant/bar with a good variety of dishes, pleasant, with balcony, good coffee, Wi-Fi.

Coffee Break, Bolognesi 219, open 0700-2300 except Sat. For real coffee.

Fuente de Soda Jumbory, near the cinema. Good *almuerzo*.

Panadería, Bolognesi 387.

Picante's, Av Bolognesi 464. Delicious real coffee, good cakes. The owner, Percy Pizzaro is very knowledgeable about the Lines.

Activities and tours

Nazca *p1376, map p1376*

All guides must be approved by the Ministry of Tourism and should have an official identity card. As more and more touts (*jaladores*) operate at popular hotels and the bus terminals, they are using false ID cards and fake hotel and tour brochures. They are all rip-off merchants who overcharge and mislead those who arrive by bus. Only conduct business with agencies at their office, or phone or email the company you want to deal with in advance. Some hotels are not above pressurising guests to purchase tours at inflated prices. Taxi drivers usually act as guides, but most speak only Spanish. Do not take just any taxi on the plaza for a tour, always ask your hotel for a reputable driver.

Air Nasca Travel, Jr Lima 185, T521027, guide Susi recommended. Very helpful and competitive prices. Can do all types of tours around Nazca, Ica, Paracas and Pisco. Recommended.

Algería Tours, Lima 186, T522444, www.nazcaperu.com. Offers inclusive tours which have been repeatedly recommended. Guides with radio contact and maps can be provided for hikes to nearby sites. Guides speak English, German, French and Italian. They also offer adventure tours, such as mountain biking from 4.000 m in the Andes down to the plain, sandboarding, and more.

Mystery Peru, Ignacio Morsesky 126, Parque Bolognesi, T522379, 956-691155, www.mysteryperu.com. Owned by Enrique Levano Alarcón, based in Nazca with many local tours, also packages throughout Peru.

Jesús Erazo Buitrón, Juan Matta 1110, T523005. Very knowledgeable, he speaks a little English but his Spanish is easy to follow.

Fernández family, who run the *Hotel Nasca*, also run local tours. Ask for the hotel owners and speak to them direct.

Huarango Travel Service, Arica 602, T522141, huarangotravel@yahoo.es. Tours around Ica, Paracas, Huacachina, Nazca and Palpa. Also has a restaurant with family atmosphere and breezy terrace.

Nanasca Tours, Jr Lima 160, T/F522917, T962 2054 (mob), nanascatours@yahoo.com. Very helpful.

Nasca Trails, Juan Tohalino Vera, Bolognesi 550, T522858, nascatrails@terra.com.pe. English, French, German and Italian spoken. Recommended.

Félix Quispe Sarmiento, 'El Nativo de Nazca', Fedeyogin5@hotmail.com. He has his own museum, Hantun Nazca, at Panamericana Sur 447 and works with the Instituto Nacional de Cultura, tours off the beaten track, can arrange flights, knowledgeable, ask for him at Kañada restaurant. Recommended.

Tours of the Nazca Lines

On land Taxi-guides to the mirador, 0800-1200, cost US$4-6 pp, or you can hitch, but there is not always much traffic. Travellers suggest the view from the hill 500 m back to Nazca is better. Go early as the site gets very hot. Or take a taxi and arrive at 0745 before the buses.

By air Small planes take 3-5 passengers to see the Nazca Lines. Flights last 30-35 mins and are controlled by air traffic personnel at the airport to avoid congestion. The price for a flight is US$40-80 pp from low to high season. You also have to pay US$3 airport tax. It is best to organize a flight with the airlines themselves at the airport. Flights are bumpy with many tight turns – many people get airsick so it's wise not to eat or drink just before a flight. Best times to fly are 0800-1000 and 1500-1630 when there is less turbulence and better light (assuming there is no fog). Make sure you clarify everything before getting on the plane and ask for a receipt. Also let them know in advance if you have any special requests. Taxi to airport, US$3.35, bus, US$0.10 (most tours include transport). These companies are recommended; there are others.

Aero Ica in Jr Lima and at the airport. In Lima, T01-446 3026, www.aeroica.net. Offers full-day packages from Ica and Lima with lunch at Maison Suisse, plus flight over the lines.
Can be booked at the **Maison Suisse**.

Alas Peruanas, T522444, www.alasperuanas.com. Flights can also be booked at Hotel Alegría. Experienced pilots. They also offer 1-hr flights over the Palpa and Llipata areas, where you can see more designs and other rare patterns (US$75 pp, minimum 3). They can also organize flights from Pisco (US$140) and Ica (US$130). All *Alas Peruanas* flights include the BBC film of Nazca.

Transport

Nazca *p1376, map p1376*

Bus It is worth paying the extra for a good bus – reports of robbery on the cheaper services. Over-booking is common.

To **Lima**, 446 km, 6 hrs, several buses and colectivos daily. **Ormeño**, T522058, *Royal Class* at 0530 and 1330 US$21.50 from Hotel Nazca Lines, normal service from Av Los Incas, 6 a day, US$12.50; **Civa**, Av Guardia Civil, T523019, normal service at 2300, US$6; **Cruz del Sur**, Lima y San Martín, T523713, 4 daily via Ica and Paracas, luxury service. Ormeño's *Royal Class* arrives in Santa Catalina, a much safer area of Lima. **Ormeño** to Ica, 2 hrs, US$1.50, 4 a day. For **Pisco** (210 km), 3 hrs, buses stop 5 km outside town (see under Pisco, Transport), so change in Ica for direct transport into Pisco. To **Arequipa**, 565 km, 9 hrs, US$10, or US$32-46 *bus cama* services: **Ormeño**, from Av Los Incas, *Royal Class* at 2130, 8 hrs. **Cruz del Sur** has 4 buses daily. Also **Oltursa**, Av los Incas 103, T522265, reliable, comfortable and secure on this route. **Civa**, 8 hrs. Delays are possible out of Nazca because of drifting sand across the road or because of mudslides in the rainy season. Travel in daylight if possible. Book your ticket on previous day.

Buses to **Cuzco**, 659 km, via **Chalhuanca** and **Abancay** (13 hrs). The highway from Nazca to Cuzco is paved and is safe for bus travellers, drivers of private vehicles and motorcyclists. To Cuzco with **Ormeño**, US$46, and **Cruz del Sur**, 2015, 2100, US$46; also **Cial** (opposite Hotel Alegría), 2000, US$35, but theft reported with this company on this route.

South of Nazca: Puerto Inca *p1378*

Taxi from **Chala** US$5, or take a colectivo to Nazca as far as the turnoff for Puerto Inca, Km 610, if it has space, about US$1 pp, beware overcharging.

Directory

Nazca *p1376, map p1376*

Banks BCP, Lima y Grau. **Globalnet** ATM on Bolognesi. Some street changers will change TCs for 8% commission. **Internet** Many places on Jr Bolognesi and hotels. **Post offices** At Fermín de Castillo 379, T522016. **Telephones** Telefónica for international calls with coins on Plaza Bolognesi; also on Plaza de Armas and at Lima 359. **Useful addresses** Police: at Av Los Incas, T522105, or T105 for emergencies.

Arequipa and the far south

The colonial city of Arequipa, with its guardian volcano, El Misti, is the ideal place to start exploring southern Peru. It is the gateway to two of the world's deepest canyons, Colca and Cotahuasi, whose villages and terraces hold onto a traditional way of life and whose skies are home to the magnificent condor. From Arequipa there are routes to Lake Titicaca and to the border with Chile.

Arequipa → *Phone code: 054. Colour map 6, A1. Population: 1 million. Altitude: 2,380 m.*

The city of Arequipa, 1,011 km from Lima, stands in a beautiful valley at the foot of El Misti volcano, a snow-capped, perfect cone, 5,822 m high, guarded on either side by the mountains Chachani (6,057 m), and Pichu-Pichu (5,669 m). The city has fine Spanish buildings and many old and interesting churches built of sillar, a pearly white volcanic material almost exclusively used in the construction of Arequipa. The city was re-founded on 15 August 1540 by an emissary of Pizarro, but it had previously been occupied by Aymara Indians and the Incas. It is the main commercial centre for the south, and its people resent the general tendency to believe that everything is run from Lima. It has been declared a World Cultural Heritage site by UNESCO.

Ins and outs

Getting there Transport to and from the **airport** (7 km west) is described below under Transport. It takes about half an hour to town. The main **bus terminal** is south of the centre, 15 minutes from the centre by colectivo, 10 minutes by taxi. ▸▸ *See also Transport, page 1392.*

Getting around The main places of interest and the hotels are within walking distance of the Plaza de Armas. If you are going to the suburbs, take a bus or taxi. A cheap tour of the city can be made in a *Vallecito* bus, 1½ hours for US$0.35. It is a circular tour which goes down Calles Jerusalén and San Juan de Dios. Alternatively an open-top bus tours the city and nearby attractions from Portal San Agustín, Plaza de Armas at 0900 and 1400 daily ⓘ *US$8 for 2½ hrs, US$12 for 4½ hrs, Bus Tour, T203434, www.bustour.com.pe, and Tours Class Arequipa, T220551, tourclassarequipa@hotmail.com.*

Climate The climate is delightful, with a mean temperature before sundown of 23°C, and after sundown of 14½°C. The sun shines on 360 days of the year. Annual rainfall is less than 150 mm.

Security There have been recent reports of taxi drivers in collusion with criminals to rob both tourists and locals. Ask hotels, restaurants, etc, to book a safe taxi for you. Theft can be a problem in the market area and the park at Selva Alegre. Be very cautious walking anywhere at night. The police are conspicuous, friendly, courteous and efficient, but their resources are limited.

Tourist office i perú: central office is in the Plaza de Armas ⓘ *Portal de la Municipalidad 110, T223265, iperuarequipa@promperu.gob.pe, Mon-Sat 0830-1930, Sun 0830-1600*, also at Casona Santa Catalina ⓘ *C Santa Catalina 210, T221227, Mon-Sun 0900-1900*, and in the airport arrivals hall, T444564, only open when flights are arriving. **Municipal tourist office** is in the Municipalidad ⓘ *on the south side of the Plaza de Armas, No 112 next to iperu, T211021*. See www.arequipa-tourism.com. **Indecopi** ⓘ *Hipólito Unanue 100-A, Urb Victoria, T212054, mlcornejo@indecopi.gob.pe*. The **Tourist Police** ⓘ *Jerusalén 315, T201258, open 24 hrs*, are very helpful with complaints or giving directions.

Sights

The elegant **Plaza de Armas** is faced on three sides by arcaded buildings with many restaurants, and on the fourth by the massive **Cathedral**, founded in 1612 and largely rebuilt in the 19th century. It is remarkable for having its façade along the whole length of the church (entrance on

Santa Catalina and San Francisco). Inside is the fine Belgian organ and elaborately carved wooden pulpit. In the June 2001 earthquake which devastated much of southern Peru, one of the cathedral's twin towers famously collapsed. It has been rebuilt. Behind the Cathedral there is an alley with handicraft shops and places to eat.

1 Arequipa

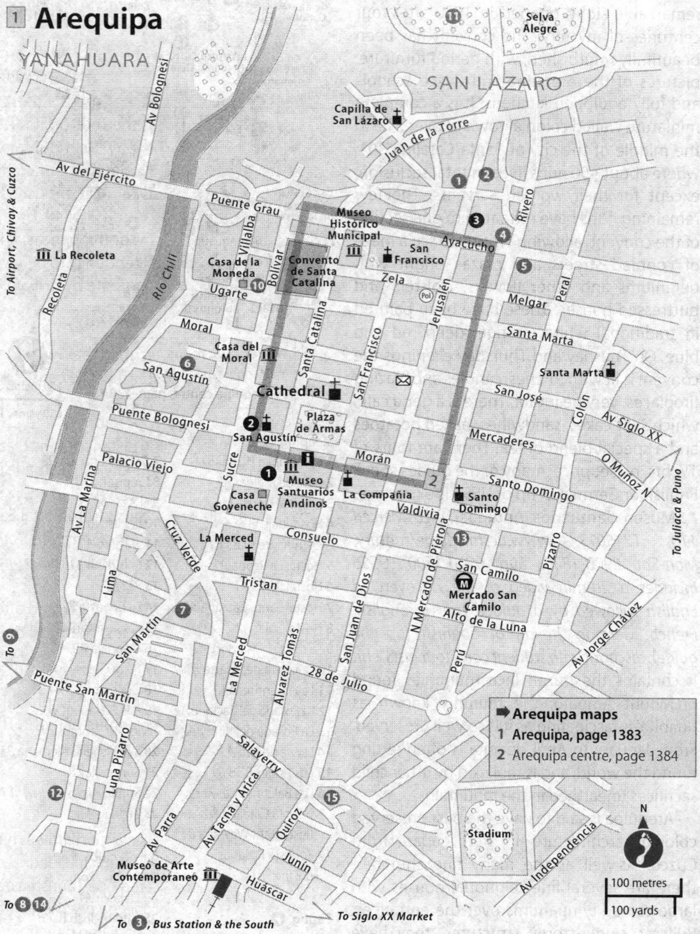

Sleeping
1 Casa Andina
2 Casa de Mi Abuela
3 El Indio Dormido
4 Home Sweet Home
5 Hostal Rivero
6 Hostal Tumi de Oro
7 La Casa de Avila
8 La Casa de Tintin
9 La Estación
10 Las Torres de Ugarte
11 Libertador Arequipa
12 Point Arequipa
13 Posada del Parque
14 Posada el Castillo
15 Tambo Viejo

Eating
1 Cusco Coffee Co
2 El Herraje Argentino
3 La Quinta

Santa Catalina Convent ⓘ *Santa Catalina 301, T608282, www.santacatalina. org.pe, 0900-1700 (high season from 0800, last admission 1600), evening visits till 2000 on Tue and Thu, US$12.* This is by far the most remarkable sight, opened in 1970 after four centuries of mystery. The convent has been beautifully refurbished, with period furniture, pictures of the Arequipa and Cuzco schools and fully equipped kitchens. It is a complete miniature walled colonial town of over 2 ha in the middle of the city at Santa Catalina 301, where about 450 nuns lived in total seclusion, except for their women servants. The few remaining nuns have retreated to one section of the convent, allowing visitors to see a maze of cobbled streets and plazas bright with geraniums and other flowers, cloisters and buttressed houses. These have been painted in traditional white, orange, deep red and blue. On Tuesday and Thursday evenings the convent is lit with torches, candles and blazing fireplaces, very beautiful. There is a good café, which sells cakes, sandwihes, baked potatoes and a special blend of tea. There are tours of 1½ hrs, no set price, many of the guides speak English or German (a tip of US$6 is expected).

Museo Santuarios Andinos ⓘ *La Merced 110, T215013, www.ucsm.edu.pe/santury, Mon-Sat 0900-1800, Sun 0900-1500, US$6 includes a 20-min video of the discovery in English followed by a guided tour in English, French, German, Italian or Spanish (tip the guide), discount with student card, tour lasts 1 hr.* It contains the frozen Inca mummies found on Mount Ampato; the mummy known as 'Juanita' is fascinating as it is so well preserved. From January to April, Juanita is often jetting round the world, and is replaced by other child sacrifices unearthed in the mountains.

Arequipa is said to have the best preserved colonial architecture in Peru, apart from Cuzco. As well as the many fine churches, there are several fine seignorial houses with large carved tympanums over the entrances. Built as single-storey structures, they have mostly withstood earthquakes. They have small patios with no galleries, flat roofs and small windows, disguised by superimposed lintels or heavy grilles. Since many of these buildings are now banks and have heavy

2 Arequipa centre

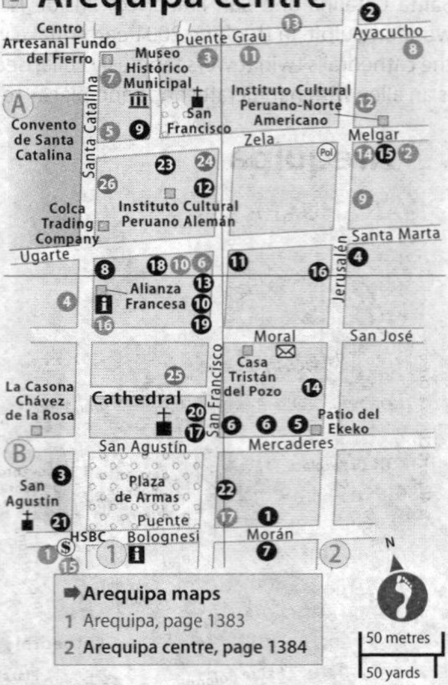

Sleeping
1 Casablanca Hostal *B1*
2 Casa de Melgar *A2*
3 Colonial House Inn *A1*
4 Hospedaje El Caminante Class *B1*
5 Hostal La Reyna *A1*
6 Hostal Regis *A1*
7 Hostal Santa Catalina *A1*
8 Hostal Solar *A2*
9 La Casa de Margott *A2*
10 La Casita de Ugarte *A1*
11 La Fiorentina *A2*
12 La Posada del Cacique *A2*
13 La Posada del Virrey *A2*
14 Lluvia de Oro *A2*
15 Los Andes B&B *B1*
16 Los Balcones de Moral y Santa Catalina & Restaurant Wayrana *B1*
17 Sonesta Posadas del Inca *B1*

Eating
1 Antojitos de Arequipa *B2*
2 Ary Quepay *A2*
3 Bóveda San Agustín *B1*
4 Bruno Pizzería *A1*
5 Café Capriccio *B2*
6 Café Manolo *B2*
7 Café Valenzuela *B2*
8 Crepisimo *A1*
9 El Asador *A1*
10 El Místico *B1*
11 El Turko *A2*
12 El Turko II *A1*
13 Fez *B1*
14 La Canasta *B2*
15 Lakshmivan *A2*
16 Mandala *A2*
17 Pizza Golosa *B1*
18 Qochamama *A1*
19 Ras El Hanout y los 40 Sabores *B1*
20 Salchichería Alemana *B1*
21 Sonccollay *B1*
22 Suri *B2*
23 Zig Zag *A1*

Bars & clubs
24 Casona Forum & Dejá Vu *A1*
25 Farren's Irish Bar *B1*
26 Las Quenas *A1*

security it can sometimes be difficult to get inside for a good look around. Good examples are the 18th-century **Casa Tristán del Pozo**, or **Gibbs-Ricketts house** ⓘ *San Francisco 108, 0915-1245, 1600-1800*, with its fine portal and puma-head waterspouts (now *Banco Continental*). **Casa del Moral** ⓘ *Moral 318 y Bolívar, Mon-Sat 0900-1700, Sun 0900-1300, US$1.80, US$1 for students*, also known as Williams house. It is now the *Banco Industrial* and has a museum. **Casa Goyeneche** ⓘ *La Merced 201 y Palacio Viejo*, now an office of the *Banco Central de la Reserva*, ask the guards to let you view the courtyard and fine period rooms. The oldest district is **San Lázaro**, a collection of tiny climbing streets and houses quite close to the **Hotel Libertador**, where you can find the ancient **Capilla de San Lázaro**.

Among the many fine churches is **La Compañía** ⓘ *General Morán y Alvarez Thomas*, the main façade (1698) and side portal (1654) are striking examples of the florid Andean *mestizo* style. To the left of the sanctuary is the **Capilla Real** (Royal Chapel) ⓘ *Mon-Fri 0900-1230, 1500-1930, Sat 1130-1230, 1500-1800, Sun 0900-1230, 1700-1800, with mass every day at 1200, free but donations box by the main altar*. Its San Ignacio chapel has a beautiful polychrome cupola. Also well worth seeing is the church of **San Francisco** ⓘ *Zela 103, US$1.65*, opposite which is the interesting **Museo Histórico Municipal** ⓘ *Plaza San Francisco 407, Mon-Fri 0900-1700, US$0.70*, with much war memorabilia and some impressive photos of the city in the aftermath of several notable earthquakes. **La Recoleta** ⓘ *Jr Recoleta 117, T270966, Mon-Sat 0900-1200, 1500-1700, US$1.50*, a Franciscan monastery built in 1647, stands on the other side of the river, on Recoleta. A seldom-visited gem it contains a variety of exhibits. As well as several cloisters and a religious art museum, the pre-Columbian art museum contains ceramics and textiles produced by cultures of the Arequipa area. Most impressive however is the museum of Amazon exploration featuring many artifacts as well as photos of early Franciscan missionaries in the Amazon. The library, containing many antique books, is available for supervised visits at 45 minutes past the hour for 15 minutes when the museum is open.

The central **San Camilo market**, between Perú, San Camilo, Piérola and Alto de la Luna, is worth visiting, as is the Siglo XX market, to the east of the rail station. **Museo de Arte Contemporaneo** ⓘ *Tacna y Arica 201, T221068, Tue-Fri 1000-1700, Sat-Sun 1000-1400, US$1*, in the old railway station, is a new museum dedicated to painting and photography from 1900 onwards. The building is surrounded by gardens and has a Sunday market. The **archaeological museum** of the Universidad de San Agustín ⓘ *Alvarez Thomas y Palacio Viejo, T288881, Mon-Fri 0815-1700*, has an interesting collection of ceramics and mummies, tracing the region's history from pre-Columbian times to the Republican era.

Excursions near Arequipa

At **Yanahuara**, 2 km northwest, is a 1750 *mestizo*-style church, with a magnificent churrigueresque façade, all in *sillar* (opens 1500). On the same plaza is a *mirador*, through whose arches there is a fine view of El Misti with the city at its feet, a popular spot in the late afternoon. The **Museo Pre Inca de Chiribaya** ⓘ *Miguel Grau 402, www.museochiribaya.org, Mon-Sat 0830-1900, Sun 0900-1500*, has a good collection of vessels and well-preserved textiles from a culture that had a high importance in the area before the arrival of the Incas. To get to Yanahuara, cross the Puente Grau, turn right up Av Bolognesi. In the hillside suburb of **Cayma** is the delightful 18th-century church ⓘ *open until 1700*. There are many old buildings associated with Bolívar and Garcilaso de la Vega. Many local buses go to Cayma.

Tingo ⓘ *bus 7, US$0.20*, which has a very small lake and three swimming pools, should be visited on Sunday for local food. Some 3 km past Tingo, beside the Río Sabandía on the Huasacanche road, is **La Mansión del Fundador** ⓘ *0900-1700, US$2.50*. Originally owned by the founder of Arequipa, Don Garcí Manuel de Carbajal, it has been restored as a museum with original furnishings and paintings; also has cafetería and bar.

About 8 km southeast of Arequipa is the **Molino de Sabandía** ⓘ *US$1.50, ring bell for admission; round trip by taxi US$6*. This is the first stone mill in the area, built in 1621. It has been fully restored and the guardian diverts water to run the grinding stones when visitors arrive. Adjoining Sabandía is **Yumina** ⓘ *tourist fee of US$6 payable, which may be asked for on the bus to Chivay*, with many Inca terraces which are still in use and between Sabandía and Arequipa is Paucarpata, with an old church and views of terraces, El Misti and Chachani.

Climbing El Misti and Chachani At 5,822 m, El Misti volcano offers a relatively straightforward opportunity to scale a high peak. Start from the hydroelectric plant, after first registering with the police there, then you need one day to the Monte Blanco shelter, at 4,800 m. Start early for the four to six hours to the top, to get there by 1100 before the mists obscure the view. If you start back at 1200 you will reach the hydroelectric plant by 1800. Alternatively, take a jeep at 3,300 m to the end of the rough road, then four to five hours hike to the campground at 4,600 m. Only space for three tents. Buses leave Arequipa for Baños Jesús, then on to Chiguata, from where you can walk to the base of El Misti. Guides may be available at Cachamarca. Be sure to take plenty of food, water and protection against the weather; it takes two days to reach the crater.

Climbing Chachani (6,057 m), northwest of El Misti, is also popular. This peak retains it's icy covering longer than El Misti, though this is fast disappearing. Remember that both summits are at a very high altitude and that this, combined with climbing on scree, makes it hard going for the untrained. Recent reports of hold-ups of climbers make it inadvisable for you to go alone. Join a group or take a guide. Further information is available from travel agencies and professional guides (see Activities and tours, page 1390).

Arequipa listings

For Sleeping and Eating price codes and other relevant information, see Essentials, pages 38-40.

Sleeping

Arequipa *p1382, maps p1383 and p1384*
When arriving by bus, do not believe taxi drivers who say the hotel of your choice is closed or full. This applies to many of the popular hotels, drivers will try to take you to another hotel which pays them a high commission. Phone in advance, or ring the door bell and check for yourself.

LL-L Libertador Arequipa, Plaza Simón Bolívar, Selva Alegre, T215110, www.libertador.com.pe. Safe, large comfortable rooms, good service, swimming pool (cold), gardens, good meals, pub-style bar, cocktail lounge, squash court.

L-A Sonesta Posadas del Inca, Portal de Flores 116, T215530, www.sonestaperu.com. On the Plaza de Armas, all the services associated with this chain, Inkafé café and bar with good views, restaurant, tiny outdoor pool, business centre with internet.

AL-B Casa Andina, C Jerusalén 603, T202070, www.casa-andina.com. Part of the attractive Casa Andina chain, with breakfast, comfortable and colourful, central, modern, good restaurant, safe, cable TV, phones, car parking.

B Casa de Mi Abuela, Jerusalén 606, T241206, www.lacasadmiabuela.com. Safe, hot water, laundry, cable TV, swimming pool, rooms at the back are quieter and overlook the garden, **E** without bath, self-catering if desired, English spoken, parking, internet access US$3 per hr, tours and transport organized in own agency (*Giardino*, T221345, www.giardinotours.com), which has good information, breakfast or evening snacks on patio or in beautiful garden, restaurant behind pool for evening meals.

C Casablanca Hostal, Puente Bolognesi 104, a few metres from the Plaza de Armas, T221327, www.casablancahostal.com. Super stylish hostal, lovely minimalist rooms in a colonial building. Ambient lighting, most rooms with bath (hot water) and balcony.

C La Casa de Tintin, Urbanización San Isidro F1, Vallecito, T284700, www.hoteltintin.com. 15 mins' walk, 5 mins by taxi from the Plaza de Armas, Belgian/Peruvian owned, hot water, cable TV, garden, terrace, sauna, laundry service, restaurant, café and bar and internet, mountain bike rental, very pleasant and comfortable, breakfast included. Recommended.

C De La Fuente, Urb La Campiña Paisajista D-14A, San Lázaro, T203996, delafuente_hostal@hotmail.com. With breakfast, family-style, welcoming, cable TV, free internet, safe.

C Hostal Solar, Ayacucho 108, T241793, www.hostalsolar.com. Nice colonial building, TV, bath, hot water, includes good breakfast served in nice patio, sun lunge on roof, very secure. Warmly recommended.

C Posada el Castillo, Pasaje Campos 105, Vallecito, T201828, www.posadaelcastillo.com. Dutch-owned hotel in colonial style 15 mins walk south of Plaza de Armas. Variety of rooms and suites, some with balcony and view of El Misti, free internet, TV, pool, wonderful breakfast, expensive laundry. Recommended.

D La Casa de Avila, San Martín 116, T213177, www.casadeavila.com. All rooms with bathroom and hot water, price includes good breakfast, spacious, sunny garden, guests' kitchen, internet, can arrange airport/bus station pick-up, recommended Spanish courses held in the garden and other activities.

D La Casa de Margott, Jerusalén 304, T229517, www.lacasademargott.com. Family run, bright with a massive palm tree in patio, spacious, convenient, small bar/café, cable TV, phone, security box, Wi-Fi, being renovated in 2010. Recommended.

D Casa de Melgar, Melgar 108, T/F222459, www.lacasademelgar.com. 18th-century building, excellent rooms with bath, hot water (solar), safe, courtyard, good breakfast in café (open am and 1730-2100). Good taxi driver (Angel). Recommended.

D Las Torres de Ugarte, Ugarte 401, T/F283532, hostaltorresdeugarte@star.com.pe. Round the corner from Santa Catalina convent, hot water, cable TV, laundry service, reflexology, roof terrace, parking, safe, luggage store, price includes breakfast. Some rooms are bungalow style in colonial part at the back. Recommended

D Los Balcones de Moral y Santa Catalina, Moral 217, T201291, www.balconeshotel.com. Convenient, 1 block from Plaza de Armas and close to Santa Catalina, large rooms, comfy beds, hot water, laundry, café, tourist information.

D-G Tambo Viejo, Av Malecón Socabaya 107, IV Centenario, T288195, www.tamboviejo.com. 5 blocks south of the plaza near the rail station. 15 rooms ranging from double with bath to dormitory, quiet, English and Dutch spoken, walled garden, hot water, choice of 8 fresh breakfasts (extra), vegetarian restaurant, laundry service, cable TV, safe deposit, coffee shop, bar, book exchange (2 for 1), money changed, tourist information for guests, internet, phone for international calls, bike rental, luggage store extra, tours and volcano climbs arranged. For a small fee, you can use the facilities if passing through. Free pick-up from bus terminal (call when arriving), US$5 for airport pick-up.

E La Estación, Loreto 410, Umacollo, T273852, www.backpackerperu.com. Unusual dormitory accommodation in 2 train carriages, includes breakfast, hot water, restaurant next door. 10 mins' walk from Plaza, ask directions for 'el Ovalo del Vallecito', English spoken.

E Home Sweet Home, Rivero 509A, T405982, www.homesweethome-peru.com. Run by María and daughter Cathy, who runs a travel agency and speaks Spanish, English, Italian, French, very helpful, warm and inviting atmosphere, substantial fresh breakfast included. Private or shared bath, hot water all day, simple rooms.

E Hospedaje El Caminante Class, Santa Catalina 207-A, 2nd floor, T203444, www.elcaminanteclass.com. Cheaper without bath, hot water, comfortable, laundry service and facilities, sun terrace, very helpful owners. Recommended. Second location at Santa Catalina 223.

E Hostal Regis, Ugarte 202, T226111, regis@qnet.com.pe. Colonial house, French-style interior, hot water all day, use of fridge and laundry facilities, sun terrace with good views, street-facing rooms with sound-proofed windows, safe deposit, luggage store, video rental and guide books and English language magazines for reference, tours arranged, but poor breakfast.

E Hostal Tumi de Oro, San Agustín 311A, 2½ blocks from the Plaza de Armas, T/F281319. French and English spoken, hot water, roof terrace, book exchange, tea/coffee facilities, safe.

E Lluvia de Oro, Jerusalén 308, T214252, lluvia_de_oro@hotmail.com. Cheaper without bath, English-spoken, breakfast US$2, laundry service, good views, beautiful colonial house with cheerful décor.

E La Posada del Cacique, Puente Grau 219 and at Jerusalén 404, T202170, www.laposadadelcacique.com. At Puente Grau is an old house with tall ceilings, teeny patio, sun terrace, hot water, English spoken, family atmosphere, **F** without bath, also dorm accommodation, safe storage facilities, breakfast available, laundry service, will pick up from terminal. Recommended.

E La Posada del Virrey, Puente Grau 103, T224050, www.usuarios.multimania.es/posadavirrey/. Spacious rooms with and without bath (**F**), dorms **G** pp, hot water, kitchen and laundry facilities, helpful, café bar, small patio, free internet for guests.

E Lula's B&B, in Cayma, T272517, 959 992995, www/bbaqpe.com. Same owner as Ari Quipay language school, Lula speaks English, German and French, discount for long stay, with breakfast and airport/bus terminal pick-up, modern, charming, free internet, quiet, meals available.

F Casa Itzhak, Av Parra 97, T204596. With and without bath, includes breakfast, cable TV, laundry service, restaurant, free transport to bus station, very helpful.

F Colonial House Inn, Puente Grau 114, T223533, colonial houseinn@hotmail.com. Hot water, quieter rooms at the back, laundry facilities and service, kitchen facilities, roof terrace, good choice of breakfasts, owners speak English.

F pp **El Indio Dormido**, Av Andrés Avelino Cáceres B-9, T427401, the_sleeping_indian@yahoo.com. Close to bus terminal, free transport to centre, some rooms with bath, TV, very helpful.

F Hostal La Reyna, Zela 209, T286578, hostalreyna@yahoo.com. With or without bath, two more expensive rooms at the top of the house, hot water, the daughter speaks English, laundry, breakfast for US$1.15, rooftop seating, will store luggage, ask about rips to the Colca Canyon and volcanoes. Opposite Arequipa nightlife and popular with young backpackers so can be noisy at night.

F Hostal Santa Catalina, Santa Catalina 500, T243705, www.hostalsantacatalinaperu.com. Comfortable rooms arranged around a courtyard, roof terrace with great views, charming and helpful staff. Can arrange trips and accommodation in other cities.

F Hostal Rivero, Rivero 420, T229266, hostal_rivero@yahoo.com. Cheaper with shared bath, hot water, cable TV extra, medical assistance, laundry facilities, very helpful, good value.

F Los Andes Bed & Breakfast, La Merced 123, T330015, losandesaqp@hotmail.com. A good value option just off the Plaza de Armas with free internet, kitchen use, breakfast included, hot water, 2 shared TV rooms, cheaper rates for long stays. Recommended.

F Piccola Daniela, Bolivar 400, T054-405727, piccoladanielaaqp@hotmail.com. Includes breakfast, **F** without bath, good value, cable TV, hot water, tiny patio, no English.

F pp **The Point Arequipa**, Lima 515, Vallecito, T286920, www.thepointhostels.com. In a relaxed suburb, free airport/bus station pick-up. Nice building with big garden, great place to meet other travellers, lots of services (free internet, laundry, DVDs etc) and a big party pad.

G La Casita de Ugarte, Ugarte 212, T204363. English/Peruvian run, large basic rooms in a colonial building, new, good value.

G La Fiorentina, Puente Grau 110, T202571, lafiorentinahostal@hotmail.com. Cheaper without bath, hot water, comfortable, family atmosphere, tours arranged, laundry facilities, café bar and TV room.

G Posada del Parque, Deán Valdivia 238-A, T212275. Opposite Parque de la Madre, comfortable private or shared rooms, hot water, internet, Wi-Fi, cable TV, breakfast is served on rooftop terrace.

Eating

Arequipa *p1382, maps p1383 and p1384*

TTT La Quinta, Jerusalén 522. Excellent food, large portions of local food but limited menu, some vegetarian dishes, attentive service, quiet garden, aimed primarily at the tourist market. Also has a *peña*, weekends mainly, US$1.50 cover.

TTT Wayrana, Santa Catalina 200, T285641. Traditional Arequipeñan dishes with a modern twist, in a beautiful colonial building with stylish interior design.

TTT Zig Zag, Zela 210, T206020. In a colonial house, European (including Swiss) and local dishes, meats include ostrich and alpaca, delicious. They also have **Crepisimo** at Santa Catalina 208, T206620, which has great coffee and a huge variety of sweet and savoury crepes, magazines and board games.

TT Ary Quepay, Jerusalén 502. Excellent local meat and vegetarian dishes, open 1000-2400, very touristy but fun.

TT Café-Restaurante Bóveda San Agustín, Portal San Agustín 127-129, T243596. Attractive, downstairs bar type atmosphere, upstairs balcony overlooking the Plaza de Armas, good value breakfasts and lunches, evening specials, opens at 0700.

🍴🍴 **El Místico**, San Francisco 123. Good lounge/restaurant with interesting menu of Peruvian dishes, nice atmsophere, good value.
🍴🍴 **Sonccollay**, Portal de San Agustin 149, www.sonccollay.com. Serving 'Inca and Pre-Inca' dishes, stone-cooked alpaca steaks and meats are a speciality (you can view the kitchen), entertaining owner, copious *chicha* and generous pisco sours, open 0800-2200. It has a seafood branch, **Qochamama**, Ugarte 300 p 2, T231407, which is more of a bar in the evening.
🍴🍴-🍴 **El Asador**, Zela 201, T223414. Good value for alapca steaks, parrillada, pleasant atmosphere, good music.
🍴 **Bruno Pizzería**, Jerusalén y Santa Marta. Pizzas and pastas with good lunch and dinner menus.
🍴 **El Herraje Argentino**, Puente Bolognesi 127. Argentine *parrilladas* and grilled chicken, good value *menúes* with salad bar.
🍴 **El Turko**, San Francisco 216-A. Kebabs, coffee, breakfasts recommended, good sandwiches, open 0700-2200. Also 🍴🍴 **El Turko II** at San Francisco 315, also very good, more of a restaurant atmosphere than El Turko. **El Turko III** is at the airport.
🍴 **Fez**, San Francisco 229 and **Istanbul**, San Francisco 231-A. More up-market restaurants run by same company as **El Turko**. Delicious falafel and Middle-Eastern fast food, including vegetarian. Good coffee, pleasant courtyard at **Fez**.
🍴 **Lakshmivan**, Jerusalén 408, T228768. Vegetarian whole food restaurant, set breakfast, lunch and dinner options for under US$2, pleasant courtyard, good value and healthy, but slow service.
🍴 **Mandala**, Jerusalén 207, T229974. Good-value vegetarian, breakfast, 3 set menus for lunch, buffet, dinner, friendly staff. Recommended.
🍴 **Pizza Golosa**, Portal San Agustín 13, T772177. Make up your own pizza, also does delivery.
🍴 **Ras El Hanout y los 40 Sabores**, San Francisco 227, T227779. Morrocan "resto-lounge", breakfast, tagines, keftas, salads, juices and World Music .

Cafés

Antojitos de Arequipa, Morán 125-A. An Arequipeñan institution, sells traditional sweets.
Café Capriccio, Mercaderes 121. Not that cheap, but excellent coffee, cakes, etc. Very popular with local business people, free internet upstairs in lounge for customers, as well as Wi-Fi. Recommended.
Café Manolo, Mercaderes 107 and 113. Great cakes and coffee, also cheap lunches.
Café Valenzuela, Morán 114. Fantastic coffee (also sells beans and ground coffee), locals' favourite.
La Canasta, Jerusalén 115. Excellent baguettes twice daily, also serves breakfast and delicious apple and brazil nut pastries, courtyard seating.
Cusco Coffee Co, La Merced 135, T281152. Good variety of coffees, cakes, average sandwiches, comfy sofas, Wi-Fi.
Salchichería Alemana, San Francisco 137. Wide choice of sausages, plus very good empanadas and sandwiches. Good value and popular.
Suri, Portal de Flores 128, T237202. The best chicken pie in Arequipa and more, great for a cheap, quick snack while you look out on the Plaza.
Typical Arequipeño food is available at the San Camilo market. The local chocolate is excellent: **La Ibérica**, in Patio del Ekeko, Mercaderes 141 (see Shopping), is top quality, but expensive.

Bars and clubs

Arequipa *p1382, maps p1383 and p1384*
Casona Forum, San Francisco 317, www.forumrockcafe.com. Huge complex which hosts the **Retro Bar**, **Zero** pool bar, **Forum Rock Café**, **Terrasse** lounge and **Chill Out Sofa Bar**. With live music, underground club with huge imitation waterfall and top floor classy restaurant with great views of the city. Opens 1800 every day.
Déjà Vu, San Francisco 319-B. Café/restaurant and bar, good food, DJ evenings, shows movies, has rooftop bar and often live music, weekend drinks specials, popular, 2000-2400.
Farren's Irish Bar, Pasaje Catedral. Good meeting place, pool table, great music.
Las Quenas, Santa Catalina 302, T281115, call to reserve. For *peña* music, traditional food and live show Mon-Fri 2100.

Festivals and events

Arequipa *p1382, maps p1383 and p1384*
A full list of the department's many festivals is available locally from iperú.

10 Jan: **Sor Ana de Los Angeles y Monteagudo**, festival for the patron saint of Santa Catalina monastery. **Mar-Apr**: **Semana Santa** celebrations involve huge processions every night, culminating in the burning of an effigy of Judas on Easter Sunday in the main plazas of Cayma and Yanahuara, and the reading of his will, containing criticisms of the city authorities. **27 Apr**: the celebration of the apostle Santiago. **May** is known as the **Mes de Las Cruces**, with ceremonies on hilltops throughout the city. **3 Aug**: a procession through the city bearing the images of Santo Domingo and San Francisco. **6-31 Aug**: **Fiesta Artesanal del Fundo El Fierro** is a sale and exhibition of *artesanía* from all parts of Peru, taking place near Plaza San Francisco. **6-17 Aug**: celebration of the city's anniversary (the 15th, many events including a mass ascent of El Misti). **2 Nov**: Day of the Dead celebrations in cemeteries.

Shopping

Arequipa *p1382, maps p1383 and p1384*

Bookshops

For international magazines, look along C San Francisco, between Mercaderes and San José. **Librería El Lector**, San Francisco 221. Wide selection, including of Peruvian authors, book exchange in various languages (2 for 1), stocks *Footprint*.

Librerías San Francisco has branches at Portal de Flores 138, San Francisco 102-106 and 133-135. Books on Arequipa and Peru, some in English.

SBS Book Service, San Francisco 125, T205317. Has a good selection of travel books etc.

Handicrafts

Alpaca 21, Jerusalén 115, of 125, T213425. Recommended.

Colca Trading Company, Santa Catalina 300B, T242088, info@perunaturtex.com. Sells a wide variety of naturally coloured ecological and organic cotton and alpaca clothing for adults and children.

Michell y Cia, Juan de la Torre 101, T202525, www.michell.com.pe. Factory outlet, excellent place for alpaca yarn in huge variety of colours, also a clearance room for baby and adult alpaca yarn is sold. They also sell other types of wool. Alpaca garments also for sale. 1920s machinery on display. Michell has opened a new outlet, Sol Alpaca, Santa Catalina 210 (inside La Casona Santa Catalina), T221454, with branches in Lima and Cuzco, for their latest lines in alpaca and pima cotton clothing.

Millma's Baby Alpaca, Pasaje Catedral 117, T205134, millmas@hotmail.com. 100% baby alpaca goods, run by Peruvian family, high quality, beautiful designs, good prices.

Mundo Alpaca, Alameda San Lorenzo 101, T202525, www.mundoalpaca.com.pe. Helpful staff, informative on all aspects of alpaca fibre production, good quality.

Markets

The covered market opposite the Teatro Municipal in C Mercaderes is recommended for knitted goods, bags, etc.

Fundo del Fierro, the large handicraft market behind the old prison on Plaza San Francisco, is also worth a visit. Shop 14 sells alpaca-wool handicrafts from Callalli in the Colca canyon.

Shopping centres

Patio del Ekeko, Mercaderes 141, www.patiodelekeko.com. A commercial centre with upmarket handicrafts, *Kuna by Alpaca 111* (www.kuna.com.pe, recommended for high-quality alpaca and vicuña products, other branches in the city), **Ilaria** for fine jewellery, *La Ibérica* chocolate shop, café, internet, cinema and **Museo de Arte Textil** upstairs (Mon-Sat 1000-2030, Sun 1000-1530).

Activities and tours

Arequipa *p1382, maps p1383 and p1384*

Climbing, cycling, rafting and trekking

International recommendations are for a 300 m per day maximum altitude gain. Be wary of agencies wanting to sell you trips with very fast ascents.

Julver Castro, who has an agency called *Mountrekk*, T601833, julver_mountrekk@hotmail.com. A climbing guide recommended as experienced and "full of energy".

Colca Trek, Jerusalén 401 B, T206217, www.colcatrek.com.pe. Knowledgeable and English-speaking Vlado Soto is one of the best guides for the Cotahuasi Canyon and is recommended for climbing, trekking and mountain biking in the Colca Canyon. He also rents equipment and has topographical maps.

Cusipata, Jerusalén 408, T203966, www.cusipata.com. Recommended as the best local rafting operator, run 6-day trips on the Río Colca. May-Dec, Río Chili 1-day kayak courses, also trekking and mountain bike tours.
Naturaleza Activa, Santa Catalina 211, T204182, naturactiva@yahoo.com. Experienced guides, knowledgeable, climbing and trekking.
Peru Adventures Tours, Jerusalén 410, T221658, www.peruadventurestours.com. Downhill mountain biking with 4WD support, 3-hr trip into Misti and Chachani mountains, stopping along the way for sightseeing. Cycle ride starts at Azufrero, 5,000 m, finishing in Arequipa at 1600, all equipment, oxygen and snack provided, English-speaking guide. Also climbing, trekking, in southern Peru.
Sacred Tours, Jerusalén 400, T330408, sacred_road@hotmail.com. Arranges hiking and rock climbing in Colca Canyon and elsewhere, experienced guides, equipment available.
Selern Services, Urb Puerta Verde F13, José LB y Rivero, Arequipa, T348685, www.selernexpediciones.com. Trekking, adventure tourism, mountain climbing.
Volcanyon Travel, C Villalba 414, T205078, mario-ortiz@terra.com.pe. Trekking and some mountain bike tours in the Colca Canyon, also volcano climbing.
Carlos Zárate Aventuras, Santa Catalina 204, of 3, T202461, www.zarateadvenures.com. Run by Carlos Zárate of the Mountaineering Club of Peru. Good family run business that always works with qualified mountain guides. A specialist in mountaineering and exploring, with a great deal of information and advice and some equipment rental. Carlos also runs trips to the source of the Amazon, Nevado Mismi, as well as trekking in the Cotahuasi canyon and climbing tougher peaks such as Coropuna.

Tour operators

Many agencies on Jerusalén, Santa Catalina and around Plaza de Armas sell air, train and bus tickets and offer tours of Colca, Cotahuasi, Toro Muerto and city. Prices vary greatly so shop around. As a general rule, you get what you pay for, so check carefully what is included in the cheapest of tours. Always settle the details before starting the tour and check that there are enough people for the tour to run. Travel agents frequently work together to fill buses (even the more expensive agencies may not have their own transport) and there are lots of touts. Many tourists prefer to contract tours through their hotel. If a travel agency puts you in touch with a guide, make sure he/she is official. The following have been recommended as helpful and reliable.
AI Travel Tours, Santa Catalina 203, Office 1, T222052, www.aitraveltours.com. Peruvian-Dutch tour operator offering cultural and adventure tours for groups or individuals, volunteer work and Spanish courses, large book exchange.
Andina Travel Service, Jerusalén 309-402A, T220462, www.andinatravelaqp.com. Good tours of Colca Canyon, guide Gelmond Ynca Aparicio is very enthusiastic.
Holley's Unusual Excursions, T/F258459 (home) any day 1700-0700, or all day Sat and Sun, or Mon-Fri 0800-1600 T222525 and leave a message, angocho@terra.com.pe. Expat Englishman Anthony Holley runs trips in his Land Rover to El Misti, Toro Muerto, the desert and coast.
Land Adventure, Santa Catalina 118-B, T204872, www.landadventures.net. "Sustainable" tour operator with good guides for communities in Colca, trekking, climbing, downhill biking.
Pablo Tour, Jerusalén 400-AB-1, T203737, www.pablotour.com. Family-run agency, owns several hostals in Cabanaconde and know area well, 3-day mixed tours in the Colca Canyon with mountain biking, trekking and rafting, free tourist information, maps for sale, bus and hotel reservation service. Son Edwin Junco Cabrera can sometimes be found in the office, he speaks fluent French and English.
Santa Catalina Tours, Santa Catalina 219-223, T284292, www.santacatalinatours.com. Offer unique tours of Collagua communities in the Colca Canyon, open daily 0800-1900.
Transcontinental Arequipa, Puente Bolognesi 132, of 5, T213843, transcontinental-aqp@terra.com.pe. Cultural and wildlife tours in the Colca Canyon.
Vita Tours, Jerusalén 302, T284211, www.vitatours.com.pe. Tours in the Arequipa area, including to the coast, and in the Colca Canyon where they have a hotel, **La Casa de Lucila**.

Transport

Arequipa *p1382, maps p1383 and p1384*

Air

Rodríguez Ballón airport is 7 km from town, T443464. To and from **Lima**, 1 hr 10 mins, several daily with **LAN**, **Peruvian Airlines** (also toTacna) and **Star Perú**. **LAN** also serves **Juliaca**, 30 mins, continuing to **Cuzco**, 1 hr 10 mins from Arequipa. Transport to the airport may be arranged when buying a ticket at a travel agency, US$1.50 pp, but not always reliable. Or use a radio taxi company listed below. Local buses go to about ½ km from the airport.

Bus

There are 2 terminals at Av Andrés A Cáceres s/n, Parque Industrial, south of the centre, 15 mins by colectivo US$0.35, or taxi US$1.50. The older Terminal Terrestre contains a tourist office, shops and places to eat. The newer Terrapuerto, across the carpark, has a tourist office (which makes hotel reservations) and its own hostal (**E** without breakfast), T421375. Terminal tax US$0.30. Buses may not depart from the terminal where you bought your ticket. All the bus companies have offices in Terminal Terrestre and several also have offices in Terrapuerto.

Note Theft is a serious problem in the bus station area. Take a taxi to and from the bus station and do not wander around with your belongings. No one is allowed to enter the terminal 2100-0500, so new arrivals cannot be met by hoteliers between those hours; best not to arrive at night.

To **Lima**, 1,011 km, 16-18 hrs, economy service US$12, US$30 with video, toilets, meals, etc, US$40-48 *bus cama*, several daily; **Enlaces** (T430333, Terrapuerto stands 39-40), **Tepsa** (T054-608079), **Ormeño** (T424187) and **Cruz del Sur** (T427728) are recommended (prices quoted are of Cruz del Sur). The road is paved but drifting sand and breakdowns may prolong the trip.

To **Nazca**, 566 km, 9 hrs, US$10 (US$32-46 on luxury services), several buses daily, mostly at night and most buses continue to Lima. Also US$7.25 to **Chala**, 8 hrs. Some bus companies charge the same fare to Nazca as to Lima. To **Moquegua**, 213 km, 3 hrs, US$4-8, several buses and colectivos daily. To **Tacna**, 320 km, 6-7 hrs, US$9-15, 17 buses daily with *Flores*, also **Cruz del Sur** 3 recommended *Cruzero* buses a day.

To **Cuzco**, all buses go via Juliaca or Puno, US$21-23, US$32-39 with **Cruz del Sur**, 10 hrs. Most companies go overnight, eg **Enlaces, Cial, Ziva** and **Ormeño**, running one morning and, some companies, one afternoon bus. There is a new, quick paved road to **Juliaca**, US$6.50- 13.50, 4-5 hrs, and **Puno**, 5 hrs, US$5-7, US$20-30 **Cruz del Sur**. Most buses and colectivos continue to Puno. **Flores**, **Sur Oriente** and **Julsa** recommended.

Taxi

US$5-6 airport to city (can be shared). US$0.85-1 around town. **Alo 45**, T454545; **Taxitel**, T452020; **Taxi 21**, T212121; **Turismo Arequipa**, T458888.

Directory

Arequipa *p1382, maps p1383 and p1384*

Airline offices LAN, Santa Catalina 118-C, T201100. **Peruvian Airlines**, La Merced 202-B, T202697. **Star Perú**, Santa Catalina 105A, T221896. **Taca**, Av Cayma 636 y Av Ejército, p 1, T0800 18222. Most tour agencies sell air tickets. **Banks** ATM **Globalnet** cash machines everywhere, eg on the Plaza, at **i perú** offices. Many give cash in soles or US$ and they accept a wide range of cards. **BCP**, San Juan de Dios 125. **BBV Continental**, San Francisco 108. **BSCH**, C Jerusalén, close to Post Office, will change TCs, low rates, Visa and Mastercard ATM. **HSBC**, La Merced y Puente Bolognesi, Plaza de Armas. **Interbank**, Mercaderes 217. **Interbank Direct** money exchange office in the Portal de Flores, Plaza de Armas, 0800-2200. Also *cambios* on Jerusalén and San Juan de Dios, and several travel agencies. **Sergio A del Carpio D**, Jerusalén 126, T242987, good rates for dollars. **Via Tours**, Santo Domingo 114, good rates. **Casa de Cambio**, San Juan de Dios 109, T282528, good rates. **Consulates** **Belgium**, Francisco de la Rosa C 13, Mza 1, lote 2, Parque I, T285508. **Bolivia**, Rivero 408, Edif Cáceres Of 5-6, T213391. **Chile**, Mercaderes 212, p 6, Galerías Gameza, T223947, entrance to lift 30 m down passageway down Mercaderes on left. Mon-Fri 0900-1300, present passport 0900-1100 if you need a visa. **France**, Edif Magnus 1301 esq Av Cayma, T232438. **Germany**, Instituto Cultural Peruano-Alemán, Ugarte 207, T218567.

Italy, Los Cerezos 110, Cayma, T254686. **Netherlands**, González Prada 122 y Juana Ezpinoza, Umacollo-Arequipa, T252649. **Spain**, Ugarte 218, p 2, T214977. Mon-Fri 1100-1300, Sat 0900-1300. **Sweden**, Quezada 107, Yanahuara T251499. **Switzerland**, Av Miguel Forga 348, Parque Industrial, T229998. **UK**, Mr Roberts, Tacna y Arica 156, T606600, gerencia@gruporoberts. com. Mon-Fri 0830-1230, 1500-1830, reported as very friendly and helpful. **Cultural centres** Alianza Francesa, Santa Catalina 208, T215579, www.afarequipa. org.pe. **Instituto Cultural Peruano-Norte Americano**, Casa de los Mendiburo, Melgar 109, T891020, www.ccpna. edu.pe, has an English Library. **Instituto Cultural Peruano Alemán**, Ugarte 207, T228130, www.icpa.org.pe. **Instituto Nacional de Cultura**, Alameda San Lázaro 120, T213171.

Internet Many places throughout the centre, about US$0.30 per hr. **Language courses Centro de Intercambio Cultural Arequipa (CEICA)**, Urb Universitaria G-9, T/F231759, www.ceica-peru.com. Individual classes at US$6 per hr, US$4.50 for groups, accommodation with families arranged, with board (US$70 per week) or without (US$30), also excursions. Recommended. **Escuela de Español Ari Quipay (EDEAQ)**, T272517, 959 992995 (mob), www.edeaq.com. Peruvian-Swiss run, experienced, multilingual staff, recognized by Peruvian Ministry of Education, in a colonial house near the Plaza de Armas, one-to-one and group classes, home stay available (see **Lula's B&B** under Sleeping). Recommended. **Llama Education**, Casabella, lote A6, Cerro Colorado, T274069, www.arequipaspanish.com/index. html. Professional, with personal attention, owner María Huaman is very helpful. Individual and small group tuition, home stays and cultural exchanges. **Silvana Cornejo**, 7 de Junio 118, Cerrito Los Alvarez, Cerro Colorado, T254985, silvanacor@yahoo.com. US$6 per hr, negotiable for group, she speaks German fluently and is recommended. Her sister Roxanna also is a teacher. **Liz and Edwin Pérez**, T264068, edwinett@mixmail.com. US$5 per hr one-to-one tuition, will go to the hotel you are staying at. Classes are also available at the Instituto Peruano-Norte Americano and Instituto Cultural Peruano Alemán (see Cultural Centres), the latter is US$4 per hr, compared with US$10 at the former, good. **Cecilia Pinto Oppe**, Puente Grau 108 (in Hostal La Reyna), T959 961638, www.cepesmaidiomasceci.com. Good value lessons, held in a café which helps orphaned children. **Carlos Rojas Núñez**, Filtro 405, T285061, carlrojas@mixmail.com. Private or group lessons to students of all levels, encourages conversation, knowledgeable on culture and politics. Recommended.

Medical services Only use reputable hospitals or clinics, not practitioners who advertise independent services. Hospitals: **Regional Honorio Delgado**, Av A Carrión s/n, T238465/231818 (inoculations). **Central del Sur**, Filtro y Peral s/n, T214430 in emergency. Clinics: **Clínica Arequipa SA**, Puente Grau y Av Bolognesi, T599000, www.clinicaarequipa. com.pe, fast and efficient with English-speaking doctors and all hospital facilities, consultation costs US$18, plus US$4 for sample analysis and around US$7 for a course of antibiotics. **Paz Holandesa**, Villa Continental, C 4, No 101, Paucarpata, T432281, www.pazholandesa.com. Dutch foundation dedicated to helping the impoverished, which also has a travel clinic for tourists. Dutch and English spoken, 24-hr service. Highly recommended (see their website if you are interested in volunteering). **Emergencies**: Ambulance T289800; also **San Miguel**, T283330 (24 hrs). Pharmacy: **Farmacia Libertad**, Piérola 108, owner speaks English.

Post offices The central office is at Moral 118, Mon-Sat, 0800-2000, Sun 0800-1400. **DHL**, Santa Catalina 115, T234288 for sending documents and money, also Western Union rep.

Telephones Alvarez Thomas y Palacio Viejo. Many **locutorios** and internet cafés offer cheap international calls, from around US$0.25 per min.

Colca Canyon

→ *You must buy a tourist ticket for US$24, at a checkpoint on the road to Chivay when entering the canyon.*

The Colca Canyon is deep: twice as deep as the Grand Canyon. The Río Colca descends from 3,500 m above sea level at Chivay to 2,200 m at Cabanaconde. In the background looms the grey, smoking mass of Sabancaya, one of the most active volcanoes in the Americas, and its more docile neighbour, Ampato (6,288 m). Unspoiled Andean villages lie on both sides of the canyon, inhabited by the Cabana and Collagua peoples, and some of the extensive pre-Columbian terraced fields are still in use. High on anyone's list for visiting the canyon is an early-morning trip to the Cruz del Cóndor, to see these majestic birds at close quarters. From January to April is the rainy season, but this makes the area green, with lots of flowers. This is not the best time to see condors. May to December is the dry, cold season when there is more chance of seeing the birds. Conditions vary annually, though.

From Arequipa there are two routes to **Chivay**, the first village on the edge of the Canyon: the old route, via Cayma, and the new route, through Yura, following the railway, longer but quicker. It can be cold in the morning, reaching 4,825 m in the Pata Pampa pass, but the views are worth it. Cyclists should use the Yura road; better condition and less of a climb at the start. The main road from Arequipa to Chivay has been paved. The old dirt route runs north from Arequipa, over the altiplano. About an hour out of Arequipa is the **Aguada Blanca National Vicuña Reserve**. If you're lucky, you can see herds of these rare animals near the road. This route affords fine views of the volcanoes Misti, Chachani, Ampato and Sabancaya. The road from Chivay to Puno via Pata Pampa, Patahuasi, Imata and Juliaca has been improved with a daily tourist transport service (see Transport, below).

Chivay is the chief linking point between the two sides of the canyon; there is a road bridge over the river here (others at Yanque and Lari). The road continues northeast to **Tuti** (small handicrafts shop), and **Sibayo** (*pensión* and grocery store). A long circuit back to Arequipa heads south from Sibayo, passing through **Puente Callalli**, **Chullo** and **Sumbay**. This is a little-travelled road, but the views, with vicuña, llamas, alpacas and Andean duck are superb. Crossing the river at Chivay going west to follow the canyon on the far side, you pass the villages of **Coporaque**, **Ichupampa** (a footbridge crosses the river between the two villages and foot and road bridges connect the road between Coporaque and Ichupampa with Yanque), **Lari**, **Madrigal** (footbridge to Maca) and **Tapay** (connected to Cabanaconde by a footbridge).

Chivay to Cabanaconde

Chivay (3,600 m) is the gateway to the canyon. The **Maria Reiche Planetarium and Observatory** ⓘ *in the grounds of the Casa Andina hotel, 6 blocks west of the Plaza between Huayna Capac and Garcilazo (www.casa-andina.com), US$6, discounts for students*, makes the most of the Colca's clear Southern Hemisphere skies with a powerful telescope and two 55-minute presentations per day at 1830 (Spanish) and 1930 (English). There is a very helpful **tourist office** in the Municipalidad on the west side of the plaza (closed at weekends). The tourist police, also on the plaza, can give advice about locally trained guides. **Traveller's Medical Center** (TMC) ⓘ *T531037, Ramón Castilla 232, tmc.colcaperu@hotmail.com*. There is a Globalnet ATM close to the plaza.

The hot springs of **La Calera** ⓘ *US$3.50, regular colectivos (US$0.25) or a 1 hr walk from town*, are 4 km away and are highly recommended after a hard day's trekking.

From Chivay, the main road goes west along the Colca Canyon. The first village encountered is **Yanque** (8 km, excellent views), with an interesting church, a museum on the opposite side of the plaza, and a bridge to the villages on the other side of the canyon. A large thermal swimming pool is 20 minutes walk from the plaza, beside the renovated Inca bridge on the Yanque-Ichupampa road, US$0.75. The road continues to **Achoma** (Hospedaje Cruz del Cóndor on the plaza and a campsite) and **Maca**, which barely survived an earthquake in November

1991. Then comes the tiny village of **Pinchollo**, with **Hospedaje Refugio del Geyser**, C Melgar s/n, behind municipality, T054-959-007441/958-032090, basic with good local information. From here it is a 30-minute walk on a dirt track to the geyser **Hatun Infiernillo**. The Mirador, or **Cruz del Cóndor** ⓘ *where you may be asked to show your tourist ticket*, is at the deepest point of the canyon. The view is wonderful and condors can be seen rising on the morning thermals (0900, arrive by 0800 to get a good spot) and sometimes in the late afternoon (1600-1800). Camping here is officially forbidden, but if you ask the tourist police in Chivay they may help. Milagros' 0630 bus from Chivay stop here very briefly at around 0800 (ask the driver to stop), or try hitching with a tour bus at around 0600. Buses from Cabanaconde stop at about 0700 (Andalucía) or 0830 (Reyna), which leave Cabanaconde's plaza 30 minutes earlier.

From the Mirador it is a 20-minute ride in tourist transport, 40 minutes by local bus to **Cabanaconde** (3,287 m), a friendly, typical village, but very basic (it does have 24-hour electricity). It is the last village in the Colca Canyon. The views are superb and condors can be seen from the hill just west of the village, a 15-minute walk from the plaza, which also gives views of the agrcultural terraces, arguably the most attractive in the valley, to the south of the village. Cabanaconde is an excellent base for visiting the region, with interesting trekking, climbing, biking and horse riding. Many are keen to encourage respectful tourism in the area and several locally-owned tourism businesses have opened in the village.

There's a friendly tourist information office, T280212, willing to give plenty of advice, if not maps. It's a good place to find trekking guides and muleteers (US$30 a day mule and guide).

Two hours below Cabanaconde is **Sangalle**, an 'oasis' of palm trees and swimming areas and three campsites with basic bungalows and toilets (three-4½ hours back up, ask for the best route in both directions, horses can be hired to carry your bag up, US$5.85), a beautiful spot, recommended. A popular hike involves walking east on the Chivay road to the Mirador de Tapay (before Cruz del Cóndor), then descending to the river on a steep track (four hours, take care). Cross the bridge to the north bank. At the village of San Juan de Chuccho you can stay and eat at a basic family hostel, of which there are several. Hostal Roy and Casa de Rebelino (**G**) are both good. US$2 will buy you a good meal. From here pass **Tapay** (also possible to camp here) and the small villages of Malata and Cosnirhua, all the time heading west along the north side of the Río Colca (take a guide or ask local directions – there are many trails). After about three hours walking, cross another bridge to the south bank of the Río Colca, follow signs to Sangalle, spend the night and return to Cabanconde on the third day. This route is offered by many Arequipa and local agencies.

Colca Canyon listings

For Sleeping and Eating price codes and other relevant information, see Essentials, pages 38-40.

Sleeping

Colca Canyon *p1394*
Families in the Colca Canyon offer meals for about US$2 and lodging at US$3.

Chivay to Cabanconde *p1394*

Chivay

AL Estancio Pozo del Cielo, C Huáscar B-3, Sacsayhuaman-Chivay over the Puente Inca from Chivay amid pre-Inca terraces, T531041 (Alvarez Thomas 309, Arequipa, T205838), www.pozodelcielo.com.pe. Very comfortable, warm rooms, good views, good service and restaurant. Recommended.

A Casa Andina, Huayna Cápac s/n, T531020, www.casa-andina.com. Attractive cabins with hot showers and a cosy bar/dining area, another member of this recommended hotel chain, heating, internet, parking.

C Colca Inn, Salaverry 307, T531111, www.hotelcolcainn.com. Good mid-range option, modern, spick and span, hot water, decent restaurant.

C Cóndor Wasi, on the road to La Calera hot springs, 1 km from Chivay, T959 444956, condorwasi@hotmail.com. Rustic rooms with bath, hot water, very tranquil.

D Posada del Colca, Salaverry 325, T531032, posadachivay@hotmail.com. Central, good rooms, hot water, breakfast included.
D Wasi Kolping, Siglo XX, 10 blocks south of town opposite Plaza de Toros, T531076, www.hoteleskolping.net/colcawasi/index.html. Comfortable cabins with hot shower, quiet, good views.
D Yaravi Hostal-Restaurant, Plaza de Armas 604, T489109, www.yaravigourmet.com.pe. Small rooms, modern installations and stylish décor, ask for a 2nd floor room with plaza view, cable TV, hot water, breakfast included. The restaurant has Arequipeña food, vegetarian options and the most impressive coffee machine in town. Recommended.
E La Casa de Lucila, M Grau 131, T607086. Comfortable, coffee, guides available.
E La Pascana, Puente Inca y C Siglo XX 106, T531001, hrlapascana@hotmail.com. Northwest corner of the Plaza. Excellent value with spacious en-suite rooms, hot water, most rooms overlook a pleasant garden. Includes breakfast, parking, a good restaurant.
E-F Hospedaje Restaurant Los Portales, Arequipa 603, T531164, www.losportales chivay.com. Good value, though beds have rather 'floppy' mattresses, breakfast included. Restaurant downstairs.
F Hostal La Casa de Anita, north side of plaza No 607, T531114. Rooms with bath look onto a small garden. Recommended.
G pp **Rumi Wasi**, Sucre 714, 6 blocks from plaza (3 mins' walk), T531114. Good rooms, breakfast included, hot water, helpful, mountain bike rental (in poor condition).

Yanque

LL Las Casitas del Colca, Parque Curiña s/n, Yanque, T054-1 610 8300, www.lascasitas delcolca.com. An Orient Express hotel, with luxury bungalows made of local materials. Has a restaurant, vegetable garden and farm, offers cookery courses, the Samay Spa offers a variety of treatments, swimming pool.
LL-L Colca Lodge, across the river between Coporaque and Ichupampa at Fundo Puye-Yanque-Caylloma, T531191, office at Mariscal Benavides 201, Selva Alegre, Arequipa, T054-202587, www.colca-lodge.com. Very relaxing, with beautiful hot springs beside the river, spend at least a day to make the most of the activities on offer. Day pass US$22 pp. Recommended.
A Collahua, Av Collahua cuadra 7, in Arequipa at Mercaderes 212, Galerías Gamesa, T226098, www.hotelcollahua. com. Modern bungalows just outside Yanque, with heating, solar-powered 24 hr hot water and plush rooms.
C Tradición Colca, on main road. In Arequipa C Argentina 108, Urb Fecia JL Bustamante y Rivero, T054-424926, 935 7117 (mob) for reservations, www.tradicion colca.com. Price is per unit, **D** in low season, includes breakfast, with gardens, restaurant, bar, games room, guided hiking tour to Ullu Ullu, also has a travel agency in Arequipa. Recommended.
E Casa Bella Flor Sumaq Wayta Wasi, Cuzco 303, T253586, www.casabellaflor.com. Charming small lodge run by Sra Hilde Checca, flower-filled garden, tasteful rooms, good meals (also open to non-residents), Hilde's uncle, Gregorio, guides visitors to pre-Columbian sites.

Cabanaconde

B Kuntur Wassi, C Cruz Blanca s/n, on the hill above the plaza, T812166, www.arequipa colca.com. Excellent, 3-star, **D** in low season, breakfast included, fine traditional meals on request. Creative design with rooms spaced between rock gardens and waterfalls. Viewing 'tower' and conference centre above. Owners Walter and María very welcoming and knowledgeable about treks. Recommended.
C Posada del Conde, C San Pedro, T440197, www.posadadelconde.com. Smart hotel and a lodge. Cheaper in low season, with hot shower, excellent value, very good food.
E Majestic Colca, Miguel Grau s/n near C San Pedro, T958-962129, www.majesticcolca.com. Modern, new, hot water, roof-top terrace and restaurant, includes breakfast.
E-F Hostal Valle del Fuego, 1 and 2 blocks from the plaza on C Grau y Bolívar, T830032, www.pablotour.com. 2 places, both with restaurants serving meals for around US$3. Rooms with comfortable beds, all with bath and hot water, laundry facilities. The Junco family have plenty of information, with a small family 'empire', including the Arequipa agency **Pablo Tour**, the **Oasis Paradise** in Sangalle (discounts for clients of Valle del Fuego) and a new bar, the

asa de Pablo Club at the end of the street. hey usually meet the incoming buses. Popular.

-G Pachamama Home, San Pedro 209, 253879, 959-316322, www.pachamama ome.com. Backpacker hostel, with and ithout bath, family atmosphere, with breakfast, ot water, lots of information, good bar/pizzería ext door, you can help with teaching and ctivities for village children. Recommended.

; Virgen del Carmen, Av Arequipa s/n, 832159, 5 blocks up from the plaza. Hot howers, may even offer you a welcoming lass of chicha. Recommended.

Eating

:hivay *p1394*

everal restaurants serve buffet lunches for our groups, US$5 pp, also open to the general ublic. Of the few that open in the evening, nost have folklore shows and are packed vith tour groups. For local cheeses and dairy roducts, visit **Productos del Colca**, Av 22 de gosto in the central market.

¥ El Balcón de Don Zacarías, Av 22 de Agosto 02 on plaza, T531108. Breakfast, the best lunch uffet in town, à la carte menu, novo andean nd international cuisine. Recommended.

¥-¥ Lobos Pizzería, José Gálvez 101, T531081. Has good pizzas and pastas, fast service and good bar, popular. Has mountain biking nformation and **Isuiza Turismo y Aventura** gency, T959-860870.

¥-¥ McElroys's Irish Pub, on the plaza. Bar run y a Peruvian and an Irishman, warm, good election of drinks (sometimes including xpensive Guinness), sandwiches, pizza, pasta nd music. Mountain bikes for hire. Accepts Visa.

¥-¥ Witite, Siglo XX 328. Good international ood and some local dishes.

¥ Innkas Café-Bar, main plaza No 706, T531209. Coffee, sandwiches, *menú*, pizzas, pool table, nice atmosphere.

¥ La Pascana, near the Plaza de Armas. Another place serving local food; also has lodging (**D**).

¥ Ruadhri Irish Pub, Av Salaverry 202. Nothing rish about it, but still a popular hang-out offering pizzas, pastas and sandwiches, has happy hour and a pool table.

Cabanaconde *p1395*

¥¥-¥ Casa de Pablo Club, C Grau. Excellent fresh juices and pisco sour, cable TV (football!), small book exchange and some equipment hire.

¥ Las Brisas del Colca, main plaza, T631593. Pleasant, serves breakfast, tourist menu, à la carte dishes, juices and sandwiches. Recommended.

¥ Don Piero, signposted just off main plaza. Excellent choice and good information.

¥ Limeño, just to the north of the Plaza. Excellent value breakfasts, friendly service.

¥ Pizzería Bar Bon Appetit, Jorge Chávez s/n, main plaza, T630171. Pizzas, pastas, breakfast, and vegetarian.

¥ Rancho del Colca, on the plaza. Serves mainly vegetarian food.

Festivals and events

Colca Canyon *p1394*

Many in the Colca region: **2-3 Feb**: **Virgen de la Candelaria**, Chivay, Cabanaconde, Maca, Tapay. **Feb**: **Carnaval**, Chivay. **3 May**: **Cruz de la Piedra**, Tuti. **13 Jun**: **San Antonio**, Yanque, Maca. **14 Jun**: **San Juan**, Sibayo, Ichupampa. **21 Jun**: anniversary of Chivay. **29 Jun**: **San Pedro y San Pablo**, Sibayo. **14-17 Jul**: **La Virgen del Carmen**, Cabanaconde. **25 Jul**: **Santiago Apóstol**, Coporaque. **26 Jul-2 Aug**: **Virgen Santa Ana**, Maca. **15 Aug**: **Virgen de la Asunta**, Chivay. **8 Dec**: **Immaculada Concepción**, Yanque, Chivay. **25 Dec**: **Sagrada Familia**, Yanque. Many of these festivals last several days and involve traditional dances and customs.

Activities and tours

Colca Canyon *p1394*

Trekking

There are many hiking possibilities in the area, with *hostales* or camping for longer treks. Make sure to take enough water, or purification, as it gets very hot and there is not a lot of water available. Moreover, sun protection is a must. Some treks are impossible if it rains heavily in the wet season, but this is very rare. Ask locals for directions as there are hundreds of confusing paths going into the canyon. In Cabanaconde trekking and adventure sports can be organized quite easily at short notice. Buy food for longer hikes in Arequipa. Topographical maps are available at the *Instituto Geográfico Nacional* in Lima (IGN 1:100,000 Huambo and Chivay sheets give the best coverage), and at Colca Trek or Pablo Tour in Arequipa, and good information from *South American Explorers*. From Chivay you can hike to Coporaque and Ichupampa, cross the river by the footbridge and climb up to Yanque, a 1-day hike. It is a 2-hr walk from the Mirador to Cabanaconde (or the other way round – horses can be hired) by a short cut, following the canyon instead of the road, which takes 3 hrs. It takes 2-3 days to walk from Chivay to Cabanaconde (70 km), you can camp along the route, then take a bus back. See above for the main trek from Cabanaconde.

Tours

It is not always possible to join a tour in Chivay; it is best to organize it in Arequipa and travel with a group. From Arequipa a 'one-day' tour to the Mirador at Cruz del Cóndor costs US$20-25: depart Arequipa at 0400, arrive at the Cruz del Cóndor at 0800-0900, expensive lunch stop at Chivay and back to Arequipa by 2100. For many, especially for those with altitude problems, this is too much to fit into one day (the only advantage is that you don't have to sleep at high altitude). Two-day tours are about US$25-30 pp with an overnight stop in Chivay or Yanque; more expensive tours range from US$45 to US$90. Most agencies will have a base price for the tour and then different prices depending which hotel you pick. Allow at least 2-3 days to appreciate the Colca Canyon fully, more if planning to do some trekking.

Chivay *p1394*

Ampato Adventure Sports, Plaza de Armas (close to **Lobos Pizzería**), Chivay, T531073, www.ampatocolca.com. Offer information and rent good mountain bikes, but rarely open.

Colca-Turismo, Av Salaverry 321, Chivay, T503368, and guide **Zacarías Ocsa Osca**, zacariasocsa@hotmail.com, seem to offer a professional service.

Cabanaconde *p1395*

Chiqui Travel & Expeditions, San Pedro s/n, T958-063602, chiquitravel_expeditions@hotmail.com. Small, but professional and reliable, organizes trekking, biking and horse riding.

Guías Locales Aproset, T958-099332, cabanatours@hotmail.com. Association of local guides, can organize *arrieros* and mules for independent treks.

Transport

Colca Canyon *p1394*

Bus Trans Milagros, T531115, **La Reyna** (T430612, recommended) and **Andalucía**, T694060, have almost hourly departures daily from Arequipa to **Chivay**, some continuing to **Cabanaconde**, a further 75 km, 2 hrs, US$1. **La Reyna** has the quickest service, about 6 hrs, US$5, others US$4. Buses return to Arequipa from bus station in Chivay, 3 blocks from the main plaza, next to the stadium. Combis and colectivos leave from the terminal to any village in the area. Ask the drivers. **Chivay-Cabanaconde** Bus at 0500. Buses run infrequently in each direction, fewer on Sun. Buses leave Cabanaconde for Arequipa from 0730 to 1500 from the Plaza de Armas, US$6. To **Puno**, with **4M Express**, www.4m-express.com, 5¾ hrs, US$40, at 1330. It is difficult to go to Cuzco from Chivay: you can take a colectivo to Puente Callalli, but the police there are unwilling to let passengers wait for a passing Cuzco-bound bus, which may not stop anyway. Best to go back to Arequipa.

ːotahuasi Canyon

ɔro Muerto

ⅰ *US$2; entrance 10 mins' drive from the petroglyphs.*

'est of Arequipa, a dirt road branches off the Pan-American to Corire, Aplao (small museum ɔntaining Wari cultural objects from the surrounding area) and the Río Majes valley. The **orld's largest field of petroglyphs** at Toro Muerto is near Corire, where there are several ɔtels and restaurants near the plaza. For Toro Muerto, turn off on the right heading back out of ɔrire; one hour walk; ask directions. The higher you go, the more interesting the petroglyphs, ıough many have been ruined by graffiti. The designs range from simple llamas to elaborate ɹman figures and animals and are thought to be Wari in origin. The sheer scale of the site, ɔme 6,000 sculpted rocks, is awe-inspiring and the view is wonderful (UNESCO World Heritage te). Take plenty of water, sunglasses and sun cream.

otahuasi Canyon

eyond Aplao the road heads north through **Chuquibamba**, where the paving ends (festivals 0 January; 2-3 February; 15 May), traversing the western slopes of Nevado Coropuna (6,425 m), efore winding down into **Cotahuasi** (*Phone code: 054; Population: 3,200; Altitude: 2,600 m*). The eaceful colonial town nestles in a sheltered hanging valley beneath Cerro Huinao. Its streets 're narrow, the houses whitewashed. Local festival is 4 May.

Several kilometres away a canyon has been cut by the Río Cotahuasi, which flows into the acific as the Río Ocuña. At its deepest, at Ninochaca (just below the village of Quechualla), the anyon is 3,354 m deep, 163 m deeper than the Colca Canyon and the deepest in the world. rom this point the only way down the canyon is by kayak and it is through kayakers' reports nce 1994 that the area has come to the notice of tourists (it was declared a Zona de Reserva urística in 1988). There is little agriculture apart from some citrus groves, but in Inca times the ɔad linking Puerto Inca and Cuzco ran along much of the canyon's course. Note that the area is ot on the tourist route and information is hard to come by.

Following the Río Cotahuasi to the northeast up the valley, you come to **Tomepampa** (10 km), neat hamlet at 2,700 m, with painted houses and a chapel. The hotsprings of **Luicho** (33° to 8°C) ⓘ *18 km from Cotahuasi, 24 hrs, US1.50*, are a short walk from the road, across a bridge. Beyond **Alca** (20 km, one hostal), above which are the small ruins of Kallak, Tiknay and a "stone library" of ɔck formations. All these places are connected by buses and combis from Cotahuasi. Buses leave ılca for Arequipa around 1400, combis when full. **Puica** ⓘ *connected to Alca by combi (2 hrs, 'S$1.50*, is the last village of any significance in the valley, hanging on a hillside at nearly 3,700 m. learby attractions include: Churca and a vast prairie of Puya Raimondi cacti; the Ocoruro geysers; nd the ruins of Maucallacta. Horses can be hired for US$3 a day, and locals can act as guides.

One of the main treks in the region follows the Inca trade road from Cotahuasi to Quechualla. rom the football pitch the path goes through Piro, the gateway to the canyon, and Sipia (three ours, two suspension bridges to cross), near which are the powerful, 150 m high Cataratas de Sipia ːake care near the falls if it is windy). Combis from Cotahuasi go to within an hour's walk of the 'ataratas; they leave 0600 and 1930, return 0900 and 1400. It's best to visit at midday. A road is eing built from this point to the falls, and may be complete by the time you read this. The next hree-hour stretch to Chaupo is not for vertigo sufferers as the path is barely etched into the canyon vall, 400 m above the river in places. At Chaupo ask permission to camp; water is available. Next is 'elinga, then the dilapidated but extensive ruin of Huña, then the charming village of **Quechualla**. ısk Sr Carmelo Velásquez Gálvez for permission to sleep in the schoolhouse.

Several tour operators in Arequipa run four-day trips to Cotahuasi, taking in the Sipia falls nd the Puya Raimondi cacti. They can also organize adventure activities. **Cotahuasi Trek** www.cotahuasitrek.com) is a specialist adventure company based in Cotahuasi, owned by ʌarcio Ruiz, locally renowned guide.

Cotahuasi Canyon listings

For Sleeping and Eating price codes and other relevant information, see Essentials, pages 38-40.

Sleeping

Cotahuasi *p1399*

F Hostal Alcalá II, Arequipa 116, T581090. Very good, hot showers, excellent beds, doubles and triples. Recommended. Run by same family as **F-G Hostal Alcalá**, main plaza, Alca, T280450. One of the best hostales in the valley, 2 rooms with shower, others shared, hot water, restaurant, good food. Prices vary according to season and demand.

G Alojamiento Chávez, Jr Cabildo 125, T581028. Basic rooms around a flower-filled court- yard, Sr José Chávez is helpful on places to visit.

G Hostal Fany Luz, Independencia 117, T581002. Basic but amenable, shared hot showers, double room with cold water only.

G Valle Hermoso, Tacna 108-110, T581057, www.hotelvallehermoso.com. Nice and cosy, beautiful views of the canyon, comfortable rooms.

Eating

Cotahuasi *p1399*

Three small restaurants/bars on Jr Arequipa offer basic fare, best is **BuenSabor**, opposite Hostal Alcalá II. There are many well-stocked tiendas, particularly with fruit, vegetables and local wine.

El Pionero, Jr Centenario. Clean, good menú.

Las Quenas and **Las Delicias**, both on main square, have decent menus.

Transport

Toro Muerto *p1399*

Empresa Del Carpio buses to **Corire** leave from **Arequipa** main terminal hourly from 0500, 3-4 hrs, US$3. Ask to be let out at the beginning of the track to Toro Muerto, or from the plaza in Corire take a taxi, US$6-10 including 2-hr wait.

Cotahuasi *p1399*

Buses daily from **Arequipa** bus terminal, 11-12 hrs US$9: **Alex** at 1530; **Reyna** at 1600; all return from the plaza in Cotahuasi at the same times. They stop for refreshments in Chuquibamba, about halfway. Both companies continue to Alca.

Directory

Cotahuasi *p1399*

Useful services No money exchange. **PNP**, on plaza; advisable to register with them on arrival and before leaving. **Maps:** some survey maps in Municipalidad and PNP; they may let you make photocopies (shop on the corner of the plaza and Arequipa). Sr Chávez has photocopies of the sheets covering Cotahuasi and surroundings. The *Lima 2000* 1:225,000 map of the Colca and Cotahuasi canyons has information about the small villages throughout the canyon as well as about interesting places to visit.

South to Chile

Moquegua → *Phone code: 053. Colour map 6, A1. Population: 110,000. Altitude: 1,412 m.*

This town 213 km from Arequipa in the narrow valley of the Moquegua River enjoys a sub tropical climate. The old centre, a few blocks above the Pan-American Highway, has winding cobbled streets and 19th-century buildings. The Plaza de Armas, with its mix of ruined and well maintained churches, colonial and republican façades and fine trees, is one of the most interesting small-town plazas in the country. **Museo Contisuyo** ⓘ *on the Plaza de Armas, within the ruins of the Iglesia Matriz, T461844, http://bruceowen.com/contisuyo/Museo E.html, Mon-Sun 0800-1300, 1430-1730, Tue 0800-1200, 1600-2000, US$0.45,* covers the cultures which thrived in the Moquegua and Ilo valleys, including the Huari, Tiahuanaco, Chiribaya and Estuquiña, who were conquered by the Incas. Artefacts are well-displayed explained in Spanish and English. Día de Santa Catalina, 25 November, is the anniversary of the founding of the colonial city. There are several email offices on or near the Plaza de Armas. Municipal **tourist office** on the plaza ⓘ *Ayacucho y Ancash, Mon-Fri 0800-1600.*

A highly recommended excursion is to **Cerro Baúl** ⓘ *30 mins by colectivo, US$1.70*, 2,590 m, a abletop mountain with marvellous views and many legends, which can be combined with the pleasant town of Torata, 24 km northeast.

The Carretera Binacional, from the port of Ilo to La Paz, has a breathtaking stretch from Aoquegua to Desaguadero at the southeastern end of Lake Titicaca. It skirts Cerro Baúl and limbs through zones of ancient terraces to its highest point at 4,755 m. On the altiplano there re herds of llamas and alpacas, lakes with waterfowl, strange mountain formations and now-covered peaks. At Mazo Cruz there is a PNP checkpoint where all documents and bags are hecked. Approaching Desaguadero the Cordillera Real of Bolivia comes into view. The road is ully paved and should be taken in daylight.

acna → *Phone code: 052. Colour map 6, A1. Population: 174,366. Altitude: 550 m.*

)nly 36 km from the Chilean border and 56 km from the international port of Arica, Tacna has ee-trade status. It is an important commercial centre and Chileans come for cheap medical nd dental treatment. Around the city the desert is gradually being irrigated. The local economy ncludes olive groves, vineyards and fishing. Tacna was in Chilean hands from 1880 to 1929, vhen its people voted by plebiscite to return to Peru. Above the city (8 km away, just off the anamericana Norte), on the heights, is the **Campo de la Alianza**, scene of a battle between

Sleeping
1 Camino Real
2 Copacabana
3 Dorado
4 El Mesón
5 Gran Hotel Tacna
6 Hostal Anturio
7 Hostal Bon Ami
8 La Posada del Cacique
9 Maximo's
10 Roble 18 Residencial

Eating
1 Café Zeit
2 Cusqueñita
3 Da Vinci
4 El Conquistador
5 Fu-Lin
6 Il Pomodoro
7 Koyuki
8 Un Limón
9 Verdi

Peru and Chile in 1880. The cathedral, designed by Eiffel, faces the Plaza de Armas, which contains huge bronze statues of Admiral Grau and Colonel Bolognesi. They stand at either end of the Arca de los Héroes, the triumphal arch which is the symbol of the city. The bronze fountain in the Plaza is said to be a duplicate of the one in the Place de la Concorde (Paris) and was also designed by Eiffel. The **Parque de la Locomotora** ⓘ *daily 0700-1700, US$0.30; knock at the gate under the clock tower on Jr 2 de Mayo for entry*, near the city centre, has a British-built locomotive, which was used in the War of the Pacific. There is a very good railway museum at the station. The house of **Francisco Zela** ⓘ *Zela 542, Mon-Sat 0830-1230, 1530-1900*, who gave the Cry of Independence on 20 July 1811, is a museum.

Tourist office, i perú ⓘ *Av San Martín 491, Plaza Principal, T425514, iperutacna@promperu.gob.pe, 0830-1930, Sun 0830-1400*. Also at the Terminal Internacional ⓘ *Mon-Sat 0830-1500*, city map, helpful, list of official taxi rates, at the airport for when flights arrive and at the border crossing at Santa Rosa. **Tranvía Tour** ⓘ *daily 0845 and 1245, 4 hrs, US$12 pp, www.tranviatour.com* on an open top double decker bus, covers the highlights of the city centre and the valley around Tacna. **Tourist police** ⓘ *Pasaje Calderón de la Barca 353, inside the main police station, T414141 ext 245*. **Indecopi** ⓘ *Bolognesi 91-93, T427938, jvela@indecopi. gob.pe*. **Touring y Automóvil Club del Perú** ⓘ *Av 2 de Mayo 67, T744237, tacna@touringperu.com.pe*.

Border with Chile

There is a checkpoint before the border, which is open 0800-2300 (24 hours Friday and Saturday). You need to obtain a Peruvian exit stamp and a Chilean entrance stamp; formalities are straightforward (see below). If you need a Chilean visa, you have to get it in Tacna (address below). Peruvian time is 1 hour earlier than Chilean time March-October; two hours earlier September/October to February/March (varies annually). No fruit or vegetables are allowed into Chile or Tacna.

Crossing by private vehicle For those leaving Peru by car buy *relaciones de pasajeros* (official forms, US$0.45) from the kiosk at the border or from a bookshop; you will need four copies. Next, return your tourist card, visit the PNP office, return the vehicle permit and finally depart through the checkpoints.

Exchange See under Banks, below. Changers can also be found at counters in the international bus terminal; rates are much the same as in town.

South to Chile listings

For Sleeping and Eating price codes and other relevant information, see Essentials, pages 38-40.

Sleeping

Moquegua *p1400*

Most hotels do not serve breakfast.

D Alameda, Junín 322, T463971. Includes breakfast, large comfortable rooms, welcoming.

E Hostal Adrianella, Miguel Grau 239, T/F463469. Hot water, TV, safe, helpful, tourist information, close to market and buses, bit faded.

E Hostal Plaza, Ayacucho 675, T461612. Modern and comfortable, good value.

F Hostal Carrera, Jr Lima 320-A (no sign), T462113. Hot water (**F** shared bath, solar-powered hot water, best in afternoon), laundry facilities on roof, good value. Recommended.

G pp **Hospedaje Cornejo**, Tarapacá 281-A, T507681. Shared bath, electric showers, basic, clean.

Tacna *p1401, map p1401*

B Gran Hotel Tacna, Av Bolognesi 300, T424193, www.derrama.org.pe. Includes breakfast, internet access in rooms US$1/hr, pool open to non-guests with US$8 purchases in restaurant or bar, best in town, gardens, safe car park, English spoken.

C Dorado, Arias Araguez 143-5, T415741, www.doradohotel.com. Includes breakfast, restaurant, modern and comfortable.

D Camino Real, Av San Martín 855-7, T242010, www.caminorealtacna.com. Restaurant, bar, coffee shop, Wi-Fi, cable TV and fridge.

El Mesón, H Unánue 175, T425841, 'ww.mesonhotel.com, . With breakfast, TV, entral, modern, comfortable, safe, wireless iternet in rooms. Recommended.

Maximo's, Arias Araguez 281, T242604, ww.maximoshotel.com. With breakfast, odern rooms with frigo-bar, Wi-Fi, sauna.

Roble 18 Residencial, H Unánue 245, 241414, roble18@gmail.com. Hot water, ible TV, internet, Wi-Fi, English, Italian, erman spoken.

Copacabana, Arias Araguez 370, T421721, ww.copahotel.com. With breakfast, good rooms.

Hostal Anturio, 28 de Julio 194 y Zela, 244258, www.hostalanturio.es.tl. Cafeteria ownstairs, breakfast extra, clean, modern id good value.

La Posada del Cacique, Arias Aragues 300-4, 47424, laposada_hostal@hotmail.com. itique style in an amazing building built ound a huge spiral staircase.

Hostal Bon Ami, 2 de Mayo 445, T411873. eaper without bath, hot water best in ernoon, simple, secure.

Eating

oquegua *p1400*

Pizzería Casa Vieja, Moquegua 326. on-Sat 1830-2300, pizza and pasta.

Ioraly, Lima y Libertad. The best place for eals. Breakfast, good lunches, *menú* US$1.75, en Mon-Sat 1000-2200, Sun 1000-1600.

cna *p1401, map p1401*

DaVinci, San Martín 596 y Arias Araguez, 44648. Mon-Sat 1100-2300, pizza and other hes, nice atmosphere, bar upstairs Tue-Sat 00-0200.

l Pomodoro, Bolívar 524 y Apurimac. Closed n evening and Mon midday, upscale Italian ving set lunch on weekdays, pricey à la carte he evening, attentive service.

usqueñita, Zela 747, 1100-1600, excellent ourse lunch, large portions, good value, iety of choices. Recommended.

Conquistador, Av San Martín 884, T412496. grills and *anticuchos*.

u-Lin, Arias Araguez 396 y 2 de Mayo. n-Sat 0930-1600, vegetarian Chinese.

oyuki, Bolívar 718. Generous set lunch daily, food and other à la carte in the evening, closed Sun evening. Several other popular lunch places on the same block.

Un Limón, Av San Martín 843, T425182. Ceviches and variety of seafood dishes.

Café Zeit, Pasaje Vigil 51, www.cafezeitperu.com. German-owned coffee shop offering cultural events and live music as well as good quality coffee and cakes. Also at Deústua 150.

Verdi, Pasaje Vigil 57. Café serving excellent *empanadas* and sweets, also set lunch.

Transport

Moquegua *p1400*

Bus All bus companies are on Av Ejército, 2 blocks north of the market at Jr Grau, except **Ormeño**, Av La Paz casi Balta. From **Lima**, US$15-30, 15 hrs, many companies with executive and regular services. To **Tacna**, 159 km, 2 hrs, US$3, hourly buses with **Flores**, Av del Ejército y Andrés Aurelio Cáceres. To **Arequipa**, 3½ hrs, US$4-8, several buses daily. Colectivos for these two destinations leave when full from Av del Ejercito y Andrés Aurelio Cáceres, almost double the bus fare – negotiate. To **Desaguadero** and **Puno**, **San Martín- Nobleza**, 4 a day, 6 hrs, US$7.50; the 2130 bus continues to Cuzco; to **Cuzco** direct at 1100, 13 hrs, US$13.50. **Mily Tours**, Av del Ejército 32-B, T464000, colectivos to Desaguadero, 4 hrs, US$15.

Tacna *p1401, map p1401*

Air The airport (T314503) is at Km 5 on the Panamericana Sur, on the way to the border. To go from the airport directly to Arica, call the bus terminal (T427007) and ask a colectivo to pick you up on its way to the border, US$4. Taxi from airport to Tacna centre US$2-3. To **Lima**, 1½ hrs; daily flights with **LAN** (Av San Martín 259, T428346) and **Peruvian Airlines** (Av San Martín 670 p2, T412699, also to **Arequipa**).

Bus Two bus stations on Hipólito Unánue, T427007, 1 km from the plaza (colectivo US$0.25, taxi US$0.60 minimum). One terminal is for international services (ie Arica), the other for domestic, both are well-organized, local tax US$0.30, baggage store, easy to make connections to the border, Arequipa or Lima. To **Moquegua** (prices above) hourly buses with **Flores** (Av Saucini behind the Terminal Nacional, T426691). **Trans Moquegua Turismo** have direct services to Moquegua and Arequipa in comfortable bus camas from 1030 to 2130 daily. To **Arequipa**, 6 hrs, US$9-150, several buses daily, most with **Flores**. **Cruz del Sur** has an executive service. To **Nazca**, 793 km, 12 hrs, several buses daily, en route for Lima (fares about US$3 less than to Lima). Several companies daily to **Lima**, 1,239 km, 21-26 hrs, US$15-20 regular, US$30-40 *bus-cama*, eg **Flores**, **Cruz del Sur** and **Ormeño** (on Arias Araguez by the petrol station), recommended. Buses to **Desaguadero, Puno** and **Cuzco** leave from Terminal Collasuyo (T312538), Av Internacional in Barrio Altos de la Alianza neighbourhood; taxi to centre US$0.75. **San Martín-Nobleza** in early morning and at night to **Desaguadero**, US$13.50, and **Puno**, US$10, 8-10 hrs; to Cuzco direct at 0830, US$15, 15 hrs, or change in Moquegua.

At **Tomasiri**, 35 km north of Tacna, passengers' luggage is checked, whether you have been out of the country or not. Do not carry anything on the bus for anyone else, just your own belongings. Passports may be checked at Camiara, a police checkpoint some 60 km from Tacna. **Inrena** also has a post where any fruit will be confiscated in an attempt to keep fruit fly out of Peru.

To **La Paz**, Bolivia, the quickest and cheapest route is via Moquegua and Desaguadero; it also involves one less border crossing than via Arica and Tambo Colorado.

Border with Chile: Tacna *p1401*

Road 56 km, 1-2 hrs, depending on waiting time at the border. Buses to Arica charge US$1.80 and colectivo taxis US$4-5 pp. All leave from the international terminal in Tacna throughout the day. Colectivos which carry 5 passengers only leave when full. As you approach the terminal you will be grabbed by a driver or his agent and told that the car is "just about to leave". This is hard to verify as you may not see the colectivo until you have filled in the paperwork. Once you have chosen a driver/agent, you will be rushed to his company's office where your passport will be taken from you and the details filled out on a Chilean entry form. You can change your remaining soles at the bus terminal. It is 30 mins to the Peruvian border post at Santa Rosa, where all exit formalities are carried out. The driver will hustle you through all the procedures. A short distance beyond is the Chilean post at Chacalluta, where again the driver will show you what to do. All formalities take about 30 mins. It's a further 15 mins to Arica's bus terminal. A Chilean driver is more likely to take you to any address in Arica.

Train Station is at Av Albaracín y 2 de Mayo. *Autoferro* to Arica, Mon-Sat 0600 and 1600 (from Arica at 0900 and 2000 Peruvian time), US$1.50, 1½ hrs, customs and immigration at railway stations. Ticket office 0800-0900 and 1430-1600; for the morning train best buy the morning before as it sells out.

Directory

Moquegua *p1400*

Banks **BCP**, Moquegua y Tarapacá. Street changers at Mercado Central. **Internet** Many places all over town, US$0.35 per hr.

Tacna *p1401, map p1401*

Banks BCP, San Martín 574. **Scotiabank**, San Martín 476. **Interbank**, San Martín 646. Several *casas de cambio* at San Martín y Arias Araguez, all offering good rates for dollars cash, also change euros, pesos chilenos and bolivianos. Street changers stand outside the Municipalid[ad]. **Consulates** **Bolivia**, Av Bolognesi 1721 y Pi[...], T715125, Mon-Fri 0900-1500. **Chile**, Presbítero Andía block 1, T723063. Open Mon-Fri 0800-1300. **Internet** Many on San Martín, several open 24 hrs. Others around the centre. Average price US$0.35 per hr. **Post offices** Av Bolognesi 361. Open Mon-Sat 0800-2000. **Telephones** Public *locutorios* everywhere; shop around for best prices. **Useful addresses** Immigration, Av Circunvalación s/n, Urb El Triángulo, T243231.

Lake Titicaca

Straddling Peru's southern border with Bolivia are the sapphire-blue waters of mystical Lake Titicaca, a huge inland sea which is the highest navigable lake in the world. Its shores and islands are home to the Aymara and Quechua, who are among Peru's oldest peoples. Here you can wander through traditional villages where Spanish is a second language and where ancient myths and beliefs still hold true. Newly paved roads climb from the coastal deserts and oases to the high plateau in which sits Lake Titicaca (Arequipa-Yura-Santa Lucía-Juliaca-Puno; Moquegua-Desaguadero-Puno). The steep ascents lead to wide open views of pampas with agricultural communities, desolate mountains, small lakes and salt flats. It is a rapid change of altitude, so be prepared for some discomfort and breathlessness.

Puno and around

➔ *Phone code: 051. Colour map 6, A2. Population: 100,170. Altitude: 3,855 m.*

On the northwest shore of Lake Titicaca, Puno is capital of its department and Peru's folklore centre with a vast array of handicrafts, festivals and costumes and a rich tradition of music and dance. Puno gets bitterly cold at night: from June to August the temperature at night can fall to -25°C, but generally not below -5°C.

Ins and outs

Tourist offices: **i perú** ⓘ *Jr Lima y Deústua, near Plaza de Armas, T365088, iperupuno@promperu.gob.pe, daily 0830-1930*. Helpful English-speaking staff, good information and maps. **Dircetur** ⓘ *Ayacucho 684, T364976, puno@mincetur.gob.pe*, with a desk at the Terminal Terrestre. **Indecopi**, the consumer protection bureau, has an office at ⓘ *Jr Deústua 644, T363667, jpilco@indecopi.gob.pe*. **Tourist police** ⓘ *Jr Deústua 558, T354764, daily 0600-2200. Report any scams, such as unscrupulous price changes, and beware touts (see page 1411).*

Sights

The **Cathedral** ⓘ *Mon-Fri 0800-1200, 1500-1800, Sat-Sun until 1900*, completed in 1657, has an impressive baroque exterior, but an austere interior. Across the street from the Cathedral is the **Balcony of the Conde de Lemos** ⓘ *Deústua y Conde de Lemos, art gallery open Mon-Fri 0800-1600* where Peru's Viceroy stayed when he first arrived in the city. The **Museo Municipal Dreyer** ⓘ *Conde de Lemos 289, Mon-Sat 1030-2200, Sun 1600-2200, US$5 includes 45 min guided tour*, has been combined with the private collection of Sr Carlos Dreyer. A short walk up Independencia leads to the **Arco Deústua**, a monument honouring those killed in the battles of Junín and Ayacucho. Nearby, is a mirador giving fine views over the town, the port and the lake beyond. The walk from Jr Cornejo following the Stations of the Cross up a nearby hill, with fine views of Lake Titicaca, has been recommended, but be careful and don't go alone (the same applies to any of the hills around Puno, eg Huajsapata).

Avenida Titicaca leads to the port from where boats go to the islands. From its intersection with Avenida Costanera towards the pier, one side of the road is lined with the kiosks of the **Artesanos Unificados de Puno**, selling crafts. Closer to the port are food kiosks. On the opposite side of the road is a shallow lake where you can hire pedal boats ⓘ *US$0.70 pp for 20 mins*. At the pier are the ticket counters for transport to the islands. The **Malecón Bahía de los Incas**, a lovely promenade along the waterfront, extends to the north and south; it is a pleasant place for a stroll and for birdwatching. The *Yavari*, the oldest ship on Lake Titicaca ⓘ *0800-1700, free but donations of US$6 welcome to help with maintenance costs*, is berthed near the entrance to the Sonesta Posada del Inca hotel and is you have to go through the hotel to get to it. Alternatively, a boat from the port costs US$2 return, with wait. The ship was built in England in 1862 and was shipped in kit form to Arica, then by rail to Tacna and by mule to Lake Titicaca. The journey took six years. The *Yavari* was launched on Christmas Day 1870. Project addresses: England: 61 Mexfield Rd, London SW15 2RG, T/F44- 20-8874 0583, Yavarilarken@talktalk .net. Peru/Lima: Giselle Guldentops, T01-999 985071, yavariguldentops@ hotmail.com; in Puno: T051-369329. Visit www.yavari.org. Another old ship is the MN *Coya* ⓘ *moored in Barrio Guaje, beyond the Hotel Sonesta Posada del Inka, T368156, daily 0800-1700*, built in Scotland and launched on the lake in 1892. Its museum is similar to the Yavari. Its restaurant serves Peruvian specialties, set menu US$7, buffet US$8, if they have dinner reservations they stay open in the evening. Berthed next to Coya is Hull (UK)-built MS *Ollanta*, which sailed the lake from 1926 to the 1970s.

Around Puno

Anybody interested in religious architecture should visit the villages along the western shore of Lake Titicaca. An Inca sundial can be seen near the village of **Chucuíto** (19 km), which has an interesting church, La Asunción, and houses with carved stone doorways. Visits to Chucuíto usually include the Templo de la Fertilidad, **Inca Uyo**, which boasts many phalli and other fertility symbols. The authenticity and original location of these objects is the subject of debate.

Puno

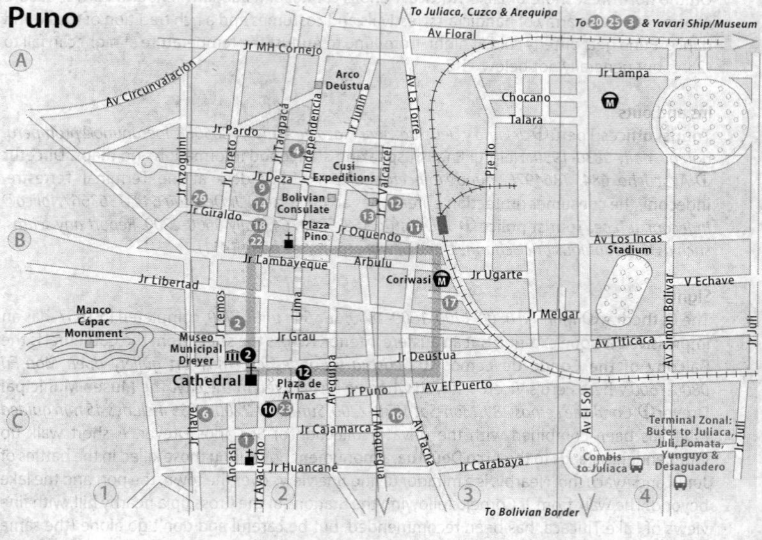

Sleeping

1 Balsa Inn *C2*
2 Casa Andina Plaza *B2*
3 Casa Andina Private Collection Puno *A4*
4 Casa Andina Tikarani *B2*
5 Colón Inn *Puno centre*
6 Conde de Lemos *C2*
7 El Buho *Puno centre*
8 Hacienda Puno *Puno centre*
9 Hosp Res Margarita *B2*
10 Hostal Europa *Puno centre*
11 Hostal Illampu *B3*
12 Hostal Imperial & Los Uros *B3*
13 Hostal Italia *B2*
14 Hostal Los Pinos *B2*
15 Hostal Pukara *Puno centre*
16 Hostal Rubi 'Los Portales' *C3*
17 Inka's Rest *B3*
18 Intiqa *B2*
19 Julio César *Puno centre*
20 Libertador Lago Titicaca *A4*
21 Plaza Mayor *Puno centre*
22 Posada Don Giorgio *B2*
23 Puno Plaza *C2*
24 Sillustani *Puno centre*
25 Sonesta Posadas del Inca *A4*
26 Tambo Real *B2*

Eating

1 Cafetería Mercedes *Puno centre*
2 Casa del Corregidor *C2*
3 Casa Grilll La Estancia *Puno centre*
4 Chifa Nan Hua *B2*
5 Don Piero *Puno centre*
6 Govinda *Puno centre*
7 IncAbar *Puno centre*
8 Internacional *Puno Centre*
9 La Hostería *Puno Centre*
10 La Plaza *C2*

Juli, 80 km, has some fine examples of religious architecture. **San Pedro** on the plaza, is the only functioning church ⓘ *open 0630-1130, 1400-1600, except Tue when only for mass at 0700 and Sun for mass at 0730, 1100 and 1800, free, but donations appreciated*. It contains a series of paintings of saints, with the Via Crucis scenes in the same frame, and gilt side altars above which some of the arches have baroque designs. **San Juan Letrán** ⓘ *daily 0800-1600, US$1.20*, has two sets of 17th-century paintings of the lives of St John the Baptist and of St Teresa, contained in sumptuous gilded frames. San Juan is a museum. It also has intricate *mestizo* carving in pink stone. **Santa Cruz** is closed to visitors, but there is a view of the lake from the plaza in front. The fourth church, **La Asunción** ⓘ *daily 0800-1630, US$1.20*, is also a museum. The nave is empty, but its walls are lined with colonial paintings with no labels. The original painting on the walls of the transept can be seen. Its fine bell tower was damaged by earthquake or lightning. Outside is an archway and atrium which date from the early 17th century. Needlework, other weavings, handicrafts and antiques are offered for sale in town. Near Juli is a small colony of flamingos. Many other birds can be seen from the road. Colectivo Puno-Juli US$1.20; return from Juli outside market at Ilave 349.

Puno centre

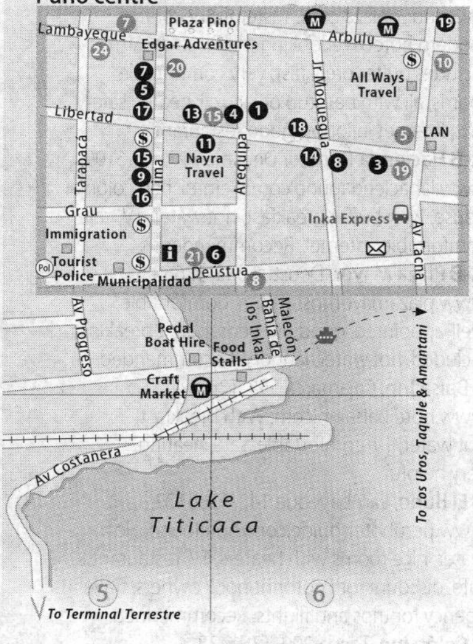

11 Los Balcones de Puno *Puno Centre*
12 Mojsa *C2*
13 Pizzería/Trattoria El Buho *Puno centre*
14 Remembranzas *Puno Centre*
15 Ricos Pan *Puno centre*
16 Tradiciones del Lago *Puno centre*
17 Tulipans *Puno centre*
18 Ukukus *Puno centre*
19 Vida Natural *C3*

Bars & clubs
20 Pub Ekeko's *Puno Centre*

A further 20 km along the lake is **Pomata** (bus from Juli US$0.50, US$1.70 from Puno), whose red sandstone church of Santiago Apóstol ⓘ *daily 0700-1200, 1330-1600, US$0.70, but if guardian is not there, leave money on the table* has a striking exterior and beautiful interior, with superb carving and paintings. At **Zepita**, near Desaguadero, the 18th-century Dominican church is also worth a visit.

Near Puno are the *chullpas* (pre-Columbian funeral towers) of **Sillustani** ⓘ *32 km from Puno on an excellent road, US$1.90, take an organized tour; about 3-4 hrs, leave 1430, US$8.50-10, tours usually stop at a Colla house on the way, to see local products*, in a beautiful setting on a peninsula in Lake Umayo. John Hemming writes: "Most of the towers date from the period of Inca occupation in the 15th century, but they are burial towers of the Aymara-speaking Colla tribe. The engineering involved in their construction is more complex than anything the Incas built – it is defeating archaeologists' attempts to rebuild the tallest 'lizard' *chullpa*." There is a museum and handicraft sellers wait at the exit. Photography is best in the afternoon light, though this is when the wind is strongest. The scenery is barren, but impressive. There is a small community at the foot of the promontory.

Llachón → *Population: 1,300.*

At the eastern end of the Península de Capachica, which encloses the northern side of the Bahía de Puno, is Llachón, a farming village which has introduced community-based tourism. It has electricity and one phone (T051-832323). On Capachica there are currently six community tourism organizations, each with a dozen or more families and links to different tour operators in Puno, Cuzco or abroad. The scenery is very pretty, with sandy beaches, pre-Inca terracing, trees and flowers. The view of the sunset from the Auki Carus hill is reckoned to be better even than from Taquile. Visitors share in local activities and 70% of all produce served is from the residents' farms. Throughout the peninsula the dress of the local women is very colourful, with four-cornered hats called *monteros*, matching vests and colourful *polleras*. The peninsula is good for hiking, mountain biking and sailing; boats can be hired.

Puno and around listings

For Sleeping and Eating price codes and other relevant information, see Essentials, pages 38-40.

Sleeping

Puno *p1405, map p1406*

A number of luxury hotels are opening in and around the city. You can expect lower prices in the low season. Many touts try to persuade tourists to go to a hotel not of their own choosing. Be firm.

LL Titilaka Lodge, on a private peninsula near Chucuíto, www.inkaterra.com/en/puno. This boutique luxury hotel offers all- inclusive 2- to 4-day packages in an exclusive environment on the lake. Plenty of activities.

L-A Sonesta Posadas del Inca, Av Sesquicentenario 610, Huaje, 5 km from Puno on the lakeshore, T364111, www.sonesta.com/laketiticaca/. 62 rooms with heating, facilities for the disabled, friendly, local textile decorations, good views, *Inkafé* restaurant has an Andean menu, folklore shows.

AL Casa Andina Private Collection Puno, Av Sesquicentenario 1970, T363992. This recommended chain's lakeshore property. The group also has **A Casa Andina Plaza**, Jr Grau 270, 1 block from plaza, T367520, includes breakfast, TV, heating, non-smoking rooms, safe, central. Business centre with internet, parking; and **A Casa Andina Tikarani**, Independencia 185, T367803, similar to the **Plaza**, but further from the centre. Visit www.casa-andina.com.

AL Libertador Lago Titicaca, on Isla Esteves linked by a causeway 5 km northeast of Puno (taxi US$3), T367780, www.libertador.com.pe. Built on a Tiahuanaco-period site, spacious, good views, phone, bar, good restaurant, disco, good service, electricity and hot water all day, parking.

A Intiqa, Jr Tarapacá 272, T366900, www.intiqahotel.com. New in 2009, built around a sunny courtyard with good restaurant. Stylish, rooms have heaters, phone, Wi-Fi, professional staff. Associated with **La Casa de Wiracocha**, at No 260, for select Peruvian handicrafts.

A Puno Plaza, Jr Puno 425, T351424, www.punoplaza.com. Tastefully decorated modern hotel overlooking the Plaza de Armas, includes buffet breakfast, very comfortable rooms, all with bathtub or jacuzzi, heater, safety box, internet in lobby, good restaurant.

A-B Hacienda Puno, Jr Deústua 297, T356109, www.lahaciendapuno.com. Refurbished colonial house, with buffet breakfast, hot water, TV, café, comfortable, internet. Recommended.

A-B Plaza Mayor, Deústua 342, T366089, www.plazamayorhostal.com. Comfortable, well-appointed, good big beds, buffet breakfast included, hot water, laundry. Recommended.

B Balsa Inn, Cajamarca 555, T363144, www.hotelbalsainn.com. With breakfast, hot water, TV, comfortable, safe, heating, very helpful.

B El Buho, Lambayeque 142, T366122, www.peruhotelsguide.com/hotelbuho. Hot water, nice rooms with heaters, TV, restaurant, safe, discount for Footprint book owners, travel agency for trips and flights. Recommended.

B Colón Inn, Tacna 290, T351432, www.coloninn.com. Colonial style, good rooms with hot shower, price includes tax and buffet breakfast, Wi-Fi, internet, good service, safe, restaurant *Sol Naciente* and pizzería *Europa*, the Belgian manager Christian Nonis is well known, especially for his work on behalf of the people on Taquile island. Recommended.

B Conde de Lemos, Jr Puno 675, T369898, www.condelemosinn.com. Convenient, comfortable, colonial style, with breakfast, heating, washing machine, internet, Wi-Fi, elevator, wheel chair friendly, restaurant.

Sillustani, Tarapacá 305 y Lambayeque, 51881, www.sillustani.com. Price includes eakfast and taxes, hot water, cable TV, safety posit, heaters, internet, well-established, pular, reservations advised.

Tambo Real, Jr Santiago Giraldo 362, T366060, ww.tamborealtitikaka.com. Good value, bright oms, price includes breakfast, upgraded throoms in 2009, family-owned, helpful, Wi-Fi, mputers for guests' use (20 mins free), tea and ffee in the lobby all day. Recommended.

Hostal Imperial, Teodoro Valcarcel 145, 52386, www.hostalimperial.com. **D** in low ason, basic but big rooms, good hot showers, fe, helpful, stores luggage, comfortable.

Hostal Italia, Teodoro Valcarcel 122, T352521, ww.hotelitaliaperu.com. 2 blocks from the ation. With breakfast, cheaper in low season, od, safe, hot water, good food, small rooms, aff helpful.

Hostal Pukara, Jr Libertad 328, T368448, kara@terra.com.pe. Excellent, English spoken, ntral, quiet, free coca in evening, breakfast.

Posada Don Giorgio, Tarapacá 238, T363648, ww.posadadongiorgio.com. Breakfast, TV, hot ater, large rooms, nicely decorated, comfortable.

D Hostal Rubi 'Los Portales', Jr Cajamarca 2-154, T353384, www.mancocapacinn.com/ ubilodge_espanol.htm. Safe, breakfast US$2, hot ater, TV, good, tours arranged. Recommended.

Julio César, Av Tacna 336, T366026, ww.juliocesarhoteles.com. Hot water, with eakfast, welcoming, some English spoken.

Hospedaje Residencial Margarita, Tarapacá 130, T352820, www.hostalmargarita no.com. Large building, family atmosphere, t water most of the day, stores luggage, urs can be arranged. Recommended.

F Hostal Illampu, Av La Torre 137-interior, 53284, www.illampu.3a2.com. Warm water, eakfast and TV extra, café, laundry, safe box o not leave valuables in room), exchange oney, arranges excursions (ask for Santiago).

F Hostal Los Pinos, Tarapacá 182, T367398, stalpinos@hotmail.com. Family run, breakfast $2, hot showers, safe, luggage store, laundry ilities, helpful, cheap tours organized. commended.

F Los Uros, Teodoro Valcarcel 135, T352141, ww.losuros.com. Cheaper without bath, **F** in v season, hot water, breakfast available, quiet at back, good value, small charge to leave luggage, laundry, often full, changes TCs at a reasonable rate. Recommended.

F Hostal Europa, Alfonso Ugarte 112, near train station, T353026, heuropa@terramail.com. Very popular, cheaper without bath, luggage may be stored (don't leave valuables in your room), hot water sometimes, garage space for motorcycles.

F pp **Inka's Rest**, Pasaje San Carlos 158, T368720. Includes breakfast, several apartments each with shared sitting area and shared bath, hot water, free internet, rooms a bit small, cooking and laundry facilities, a place to meet other travellers, reserve ahead.

Around Puno: Chucuíto *p1406*

E pp **Albergue Juvenil Las Cabañas**, Jr Tarapacá 538, T369494, 951-751196, www.chucuito.com. Great wee cottages, meals, will collect you from Puno if you phone in advance. Highly recommended.

F pp **Sra Nely Durán Saraza**, Chucuíto Occopampa, T951 586240 (mob). 2 nice rooms, one with lake view, shared bath, hot water, breakfast and dinner available, very welcoming and interesting.

Llachón *p1407*

Families offer accommodation on a rotational basis and, as the community presidents change each year, the standard of facilites changes from year-to-year and family-to family. All hosts can arrange boat transport to Amantaní. Among those who offer lodging (**F** per bed, meals extra) are: Tomás Cahui Coila, **Centro Turístico Santa María Llachón**, T951 923595, www.explore titicaca.com; **Primo Flores**, Santa María, T051-951 680040, primopuno@hotmail.com; **Valentín Quispe**, T051-951 821392 (mob), llachon@yahoo.com. But do recognise that there are other families who accept guests.

Eating

Puno *p1405, map p1406*

IncAbar, Lima 348, T368031. Open for breakfast, lunch and dinner, interesting dishes in creative sauces, fish, pastas, curries, café and couch bar, nice decor.

Internacional, Moquegua 201, T352502. Very popular, excellent trout, good pizzas, service variable.

🍴🍴 **La Hostería**, Lima 501, T365406. Good set meal and à la carte dishes including local fare like alpaca and cuy, pizza, also breakfast, music in the evening.
🍴🍴 **La Plaza**, Puno 425, Plaza de Armas. Good food, international dishes and *comida nueva andina*, good service.
🍴🍴 **Los Balcones de Puno**, Jr Libertad 345, T365300. Peruvian and international food, daily folklore show 1900-2100.
🍴🍴 **Mojsa**, Lima 635 p 2, Plaza de Armas. Good international and *novo andino* dishes, also has an arts and crafts shop. Recommended.
🍴🍴 **Tradiciones del Lago**, Lima 418, T368140, www.tradicionesdelago.com. Buffet, à la carte and a big selection of Peruvian food.
🍴🍴 **Tulipans**, Lima 394, T351796. Sandwiches, juices and a lunchtime menu are its staples. One of the few places in Puno with outdoor seating in a pleasant colonial courtyard, a good option for lunch.
🍴🍴-🍴 **Don Piero**, Lima 360. Huge meals, live music, try their 'pollo coca-cola' (chicken in a sweet and sour sauce), slow service, popular, tax extra.
🍴🍴-🍴 **Pizzería/Trattoria El Buho**, Lima 349 and at Jr Libertad 386, T356223. Excellent pizza, lively atmosphere, open 1800 onwards, pizzas US$2.35-3.
🍴 **Casa Grilll La Estancia**, Libertad 137, T51-365469 . Salad bar, huge steaks, grilled meat and peruvian food. Very popular with locals for huge lunches and a few beers.
🍴 **Chifa Nan Hua**, Arequipa 378. Tasty Chinese, big portions.
🍴 **Govinda**, Deústua 312. Cheap vegetarian lunch menus, closes at 2000.
🍴 **Remembranzas**, Jr Moquegua 200. Pizzas as well as local food. Open 0630-2200.
🍴 **Ukukus**, Libertad 216 and Pje Grau 172, T367373, 369504. Good combination of Andean and novo andino cuisine as well as pizzas and some Chinese chifa style.
🍴 **Vida Natural**, Tacna 141. Breakfast, salads, fruits, also vegetarian meals midday and evening.

Cafés

Cafetería Mercedes, Jr Arequipa 144. Good menú US$1.50, bread, cakes, snacks, juices.
Casa del Corregidor, Deústua 576, aptdo 2, T365603. In restored 17th-century building, sandwiches, good snacks, coffee, good music, great atmosphere, nice surroundings with pati
Also has a Fair Trade store offering products directly from the producers.
Ricos Pan, Jr Lima 424. Café and bakery, great cakes, excellent coffees, juices and pastries, breakfasts and other dishes, Mon-Sat 0600-2300 Branches at Arequipa cuadra 3 and Moquegua 33

Bars and clubs

Puno *p1405, map p1406*
Dómino, Libertad 443. "Megadisco", happy hour 2000-2130 Mon-Thu, good.
Positive, Jr Lima 382. Drinks, large screen TV, modern music, occasional heavy metal rock groups.
Pub Ekeko's, Lima 355. Live music every night, happy hour 2000-2200.

Festivals and events

Puno *p1405, map p1406*
Feb: at the **Fiesta de la Virgen de la Candelari** 1st 2 weeks in **Feb**, bands and dancers from all the local towns compete in a *Diablada*, or Devil Dance. The festivities are better at night on the streets than the official functions in the stadium Check the dates in advance as Candelaria may be moved if pre-Lentern carnival coincides with it. A candlelight procession through darkened streets takes place on **Good Friday**. **3 May**: **Festividad de las Cruces**, celebrated with masses, a procession and the Alasita festival of miniatures. **29 Jun**: colourful festival of **San Pedro**, with a procession at Zepita (see page 1407). **4-5 Nov**: pageant dedicated to the founding of Puno and the emergence of Manco Cápac and Mama Ocllo from the waters of Lake Titicaca.

Shopping

Puno *p1405, map p1406*
Markets Puno is the best place in Peru to bu alpaca wool articles, bargaining is appropriate. Along the avenue leading to the port is the larg **Mercado Artesanal Asosiación de Artesanos Unificados**, daily 0900-1800. Closer to the cent are **Mercado Coriwasi**, Ugarte 150, daily 0800-2100 and **Mubel Artesanías**, Jr Deústua 576, http://asociacion.ciap.org, fair trade alpaca goods. The **Mercado Central**, in the blocks bound by Arbulú, Arequipa, Oquendo and Tac has all kinds of food, including good cheeses as

'ell as a few crafts. Beware pickpockets in the ıarket. You will be hassled on the street and utside restaurants to buy woollen goods, so ıke care.

Activities and tours

uno *p1405, map p1406*

/atch out for unofficial tour sellers, *jalagringos*, 'ho offer hotels and tours at varying rates, epending on how wealthy you look. They are /erywhere: train station, bus offices, airport and otels. Ask to see their guide's ID card. Only use gencies with named premises, compare prices ıd only hand over money at the office, never ı the street or in a hotel.

Agencies organize trips to the Uros floating 'ands (see page 1413) and the islands of ıquile and Amantaní, as well as to Sillustani, ıd other places. Make sure that you settle all etails before embarking on the tour. We have ceived good reports on the following:

ll Ways Travel, Tacna 285 of 102-104, also in ısa del Corregidor, Deústua 576, T/F355552, ww.titicacaperu.com. Very helpful, kind and liable, speak German, French, English and ılian. They offer a unique cultural tour to e islands of Anapia and Yuspique in Lake 'iñaymarka, beyond the straits of Tiquina, he Treasure of Wiñaymarka", departures ıu and Sun.

ısi Expeditions, Jr T Varcarcel 164, T369072, servascusi@terra.com.pe. They own most of the ɔats which operate the standard tours of the ands. You will very likely end up on a Cusi tour it's best to buy from them directly to get the ɛst price and the most accurate information.

lgar Adventures, Jr Lima 328, T/F353444, ww.edgaradventures.com. English, German and ench spoken, very helpful and knowledgeable. ɔnstantly exploring new areas, lots of off-the-aten-track tours, eg kayaking tour of Llachón. ɔmmunity-minded, promote responsible urism. Consistently recommended.

ıfer Viajes, Arequipa 179, T352701, ww.kafer-titicaca.com. Efficient and helpful.

ntiki Tours, Jr Melgar 188. T353473, ww.kontikiperu.com. Receptive tour agency ecializing in special interest excursions.

ıyra Travel, Jr Lima 419, of 105, T337934, ww.nayratravel.com. Small agency run by ian Cotrado and her helpful staff, traditional local tours and a variety of options in Llachón. Can organize off-the-beaten track excursions for a minimum of 2 people. Recommended.

Pirámide Tours, Jr Rosendo Huirse 130, T366107, www.titikakalake.com. Out of the ordinary and classic tours, flexible, personalized service, modern fast launches, very helpful, works only via internet, overseas clients.

Titikaka Explorers, Jr Puno 633 of 207, T368903, www.titikaka-explorer.com. Good service, helpful.

Transport

Puno *p1405, map p1406*

Bus All long-distance buses, except some Cuzco services and buses to La Paz (see below), leave from the Terminal Terrestre, which is at 1 de Mayo 703 y Victoria, by the lake, T364733. It has a tourist office, snack bars and toilets. Platform tax US$0.35. Small buses and colectivos for Juliaca, Ilave and towns on the lake shore between Puno and Desaguadero, including Yunguyo, leave from Av Bolívar between Jrs Carabaya and Palma. To **Juliaca**, 44 km, 45 mins, bus US$0.70, combi US$0.85. Daily buses to **Arequipa**, 5 hrs via Juliaca, 297 km, most buses take this route, US$5-7 (**Cruz del Sur**, T368524, **Destinos**, **Julsa**, **Señor de Milagros**, or **Sur Oriente**, most have a morning and evening bus – better quality buses go at night).

4M Express, Jr Arequipa 736, T364887, www.4m-express.com, to Arequipa US$30, also to **Chivay** at 0630, US$40. To **Moquegua**, US$4.50-6, and **Tacna**, US$10. To **Lima**, 1,011 km, 21 hrs, US$27-51, all buses go through **Arequipa**, sometimes with a change of bus. See Arequipa, page 1392. For services to La Paz or Copacabana (Bolivia), see page 1418.

To **Cuzco**, 388 km, 5-7 hrs. There are 3 levels of service: regular via Juliaca, US$5-7, 7 hrs; direct, without stopping in Juliaca, with **Tour Perú**, Jr Tacna, T352991, www.tourperu.com.pe, at 0800, US$8.50 and 2130 (*bus cama* US$10), 6 hrs; tourist service with 5 stops (Pukará, Sicuani for lunch, La Raya, Raqchi and Andahuaylillas), leave at 0730, US$30 plus museum entry fees (US$7), includes lunch, 10 hrs, with **Inka Express**, Jr Tacna 346 and at the Terminal Terrestre, T365654, www.inkaexpress.com (leaves from the Terminal and may pick up from hotel on request), **First Class**, Tacna 280-300, T364640, firstclass@terra.com.pe, or **Turismo Mer**, Jr Tacna 336, T367223, www.turismomer.com. In high season, reserve 2 days ahead. **Note** It is advisable to travel by day, for safety as well as for the views. If you wish to travel by bus and cannot go direct, it is no problem to take separate buses to Juliaca, then to Sicuani, then to Cuzco.

Boats on Lake Titicaca Boats to the islands leave from the terminal in the harbour (see map); *trici-taxi* from centre, US$1.

Taxi 3-wheel 'Trici-Taxis', cost about US$0.20 per km and are the best way to get around.

Trains The railway runs from Puno to Juliaca (44 km), where it divides, to Cuzco (381 km) and Arequipa (279 km; no passenger service). To **Cuzco** *Andean Explorer*, US$220 (no other class) Mon, Wed, Fri and Sat at 0800, arriving in Cuzco at about 1800 (no Fri train Nov-Mar); try to sit on the right hand side for the views. The train stops at La Raya. The ticket office is open from 0630-1030, Mon-Sun. Ticket office Mon-Fri 0700-1300, 1400-1700, Sat 0700-1200, in high season buy several days in advance, passport required. The station is well guarded by police and sealed off to those without tickets.

Llachón *p1407*

Boats Only 1 weekly public boat from Llachón to Puno, Fri 0900, returning to Llachón Sat 1000, US$1.20, 3½ hrs. The daily 0800 boat to Amantantí may drop you off at Colata (at the tip of the peninsula), a 1 hr walk from Llachón, confirm details in advance. Returning to Puno, you can try to flag down the boat from Amantaní which passes Colata between 0830 and 0930. In Santa María (Llachón), boats can be hired for trips to Amantaní (40 mins) and Taquile (50 mins), US$20 return, minimum 10 passengers. **Combis** run daily from Bellavista market (known as El Contrabando) in Puno to **Capachica**, from 0700 to1600, 1½ hrs, US$1.35, where you get another *combi* or bus to **Llachón**, leave when full, 30 mins, US$0.70.

Directory

Puno *p1405, map p1406*

Airline offices LAN, Tacna y Libertad, T367227. **Star Perú**, Melgar 106, T364615.
Banks BCP, Lima 510. **Banco Continental**, Lima 411. **Interbank**, Lima 444. **Scotiabank**, Lima y Deústua. For cash go to the *cambios*, the travel agencies or the better hotels. Best rates with money changers on Jr Lima, many on 400 block, and on Tacna near the market, eg Arbulu y Tacna. Check your Peruvian soles carefully. Rates for bolivianos are sometimes better in Puno than in Yunguyo; check with other travellers. **Consulates** Bolivia, Jr Arequipa 136, T351251, consular visas take about 48 hrs, Mon-Fri 0830-1400. **Internet** There are offices everywhere in the centre, upstairs and down. Average price US$0.45 per hr. Particularly good is **Choz@net**, Lima 339, p 2, fast computers and a small snack bar. **Post offices** Jr Moquegua 268, Mon-Sat 0800-2000. **Telephones** Locutorios all over the centre. **Useful addresses** Immigration: Ayacucho 280, T357103, Mon-Fri 0800-1300, 1500-1700.

The islands

The Uros

ⓘ *US$1.70 entry.*

The people of Uros or the 'floating islands' in Puno Bay fish, hunt birds and live off the lake plants, most important of which are the reeds they use for their boats, houses and the very foundations of their islands. Visitors to the floating islands encounter more women than men. These women wait every day for the tour boats to sell their handicrafts. The few men one does see might be building or repairing boats or fixing their nets. The rest are out on the lake, hunting and fishing. The Uros cannot live from tourism alone and it is better to buy handicrafts or pay for services than just to tip. They glean extra income from tourists offering overnight accommodation in reed houses, selling meals and providing Uro guides for two-hour tours, US$3.40. Organized tour parties are usually given a boat building demonstration and the chance to take a short trip in a reed boat (US$0.70 pp). Some islanders will also greet boat loads of tourists with a song and will pose for photos. The islanders, who are very friendly, appreciate gifts of pens, paper, etc for their two schools. This form of tourism on the Uros Islands is now well-established and, whether it has done irreparable harm or will ultimately prove beneficial, it takes place in superb surroundings. Take drinking water as there is none on the islands.

Taquile

ⓘ *US$1 to land.*

Isla Taquile, 45 km from Puno, on which there are numerous pre-Inca and Inca ruins, and Inca terracing, is only about 1 km wide, but 6-7 km long. Ask for the (unmarked) **museum of traditional costumes**, which is on the plaza. There is a co-operative shop on the plaza that sells exceptional woollen goods, which are not cheap, but of very fine quality. Shops on the plaza sell postcards, water and dry goods. You are advised to take some food, particularly fruit, bread and vegetables, water, plenty of small-value notes, candles and a torch. Take precautions against sunburn. The principal festivals are from 2-7 June, and the *Fiesta de Santiago* from 25 July to 2 August, with many dances in between. Native guides in Taquile, some speaking English and/or German, charge US$3.40 for two-hour tours. It is worth spending a night on Taquile to observe the daily flurry of activity around the boatloads of tourists: demonstations of traditional dress and weaving techniques, the preapartion of trout to feed the hordes. When the boats leave, the island breathes a gentle sigh and people slowly return to their more traditional activities.

Amantaní

ⓘ *US$1 to land.*

Another island worth visiting, is Amantaní, very beautiful and peaceful. There are six villages and ruins on both of the island's peaks, **Pacha Tata** and **Pacha Mama**, from which there are excellent views. There are also temples and on the shore there is a throne carved out of stone, the **Inkatiana**. On both hills, a fiesta is celebrated on 15-20 January, Pago a la Tierra or San Sebastián, the main day being Thursday. The festivities are very colourful, musical and hard-drinking. There is also a festival the first Sunday in March with brass bands and colourful dancers and a Feria de Artesanías, 8-16 August. The residents make beautiful textiles and sell them quite cheaply at the Artesanía Cooperativa. They also make basketwork and stoneware. The people are Quechua speakers, but understand Spanish. Islanders arrange dances for tour groups (independent travellers can join in), visitors dress up in local clothes and join the dances. Small shops sell water and snacks.

Anapia and Yuspique

In the Peruvian part of the Lago Menor are the islands of **Anapia**, a friendly, Aymara-speaking community, and **Yuspique**, on which are ruins and vicuñas. The community has organized committees for tourism, motor boats, sailing boats and accommodation with families (All Ways Travel, see page 1411, arranges tours). To visit Anapia independently, take a colectivo from Yunguyo to Tinicachi and alight at Punta Hermosa, just after Unacachi. Boats to Anapia leave Punta Hermosa on Sunday and Thursday at 1300 (they leave Anapia for Yunguyo market on the same days at 0630); bus from Puno Sunday, Tuesday, Thursday, US$3. It's two hours each way by boat. On the island ask for José Flores, who is very knowledgeable about Anapia's history, flora and fauna. He sometimes acts as a guide.

The islands listings

For Sleeping and Eating price codes and other relevant information, see Essentials, pages 38-40.

Sleeping

The Uros *p1413*

Oscar Coyla, T051-951 824378 (mob) is the representative for the Uros community. Accommodation costs US$5 pp, simple meals are extra or US$10 pp full board including tour. **René Coyla Coila**, T051-951 743533 (mob) is an official tour guide who can advise on lodging and **Armando Suaña**, T051-951 341374 is another native guide offering accommodation in Kantati.

Taquile *p1413*

The **Presidente del Comité Turístico de Taquile** is Leucario Huata Cruz, T051-951 830433 (mob). Lodging rates US$20-25 pp full board. Where possible try to support the communal system and ask the Jefe which families are in need of a visit from tourists. Since some families have become the favourites of tour groups they have been able to build better facilities (eg with showers and loos) and those which are in need of the income are often shunned as their facilities may be more basic. Instead of staying in the busy part around the main square, the Huayllano community is hosting visitors. This is on the south side of the island. Contact **Alipio Huatta Cruz**, T951 668551 or 951 615239 (mob) or you can arrange a visit with **All Ways Travel**.

Amantaní *p1413*

The **Presidente del Comité Turístico de Amantaní** is Senón Tipo Huatta, T051-951 832 308 (mob). Rate is up to US$25 pp full board. If you are willing to walk to a more distant communities, you might get a better price and you are helping to share the income. Some families that one can contact are: **Kantuta Lodge**, T051-789290, 951 636172, www.kantutalodge.com; **Hospedaje Jorge Cari**, basic, but nice family, great view of lake from room, or j.manani.cari@eudoramail. com; or **Familia Victoriano Calsin Quispe**, Casilla 312, Isla Amantaní, T051-360220 or 363320.

Eating

Taquile *p1413*

There are many small restaurants around the plaza and on the track to the Puerto Principal (eg Gerardo Huatta's **La Flor de Cantuta**, on the steps; **El Inca** on the main plaza). Meals are generally fish, rice and chips, omelette and *fiambre*, a local stew. Meat is rarely available and drinks often run out. Breakfast consists of pancakes and bread.

Amantaní *p1413*

There is 1 restaurant, **Samariy**. Food at the family lodgings is frequently reported to be dreadful (a reflection of the artificially low price), so take your own supplies, especially bread and fruit.

Transport

The Uros *p1413*

Boat Asociación de Transporte los Uros, at the port, T368024, aeuttal@hotmail.com, 0800-1600. Motorboat US$3.40, from 0600-1600 or whenever there are 10 people. Agencies charge US$7-10.

Taquile *p1413*

Boats Centro de Operadores de Transporte **Taquile**, at the port, T205477, 0600-1100, 1400-1800. In high season, boats go at 0730 and 0800, returning at 1400 and 1430, in low season only one boat travels, US$3.40 one way. Organized tours cost US$10-13.50.

Amantaní *p1413*

Boats Transportes Unificados Amantaní, at the port, T369714, 0800-1100. Two daily boats at 0815, one direct, the 2nd one stops at Uros, they return at 0800 the next day, one direct to Puno, the 2nd one stops at Taquile. US$3.40 one way direct, US$10 return with stops at Uros and Taquile. Amantaní-Taquile costs US$1.70. If you stop in Taquile on the way back, you can continue to Puno at 1200 with the Amantaní boat or take a Taquile boat at 1400 (also 1430 in high season). Purchasing one way tickets gives you more flexibility if you wish to stay longer on the islands.

To Cuzco

Juliaca → *Phone code: 051. Colour map 6, A2. Population: 134,700. Altitude: 3,825 m.*
Freezing cold at night, Juliaca, 289 km northeast of Arequipa, is not particularly attractive. As the commercial focus of an area bounded by Puno, Arequipa and the jungle, it has grown very fast into a chaotic place with a large impermanent population, lots of contraband and more *tricitaxis* than cars. Monday, market day, is the most disorganized of all. A Sunday woollens market, La Dominical, is held near the exit to Cuzco. The handicrafts gallery, *Las Calceteras*, is on Plaza Bolognesi. Túpac Amaru market, on Moquegua seven blocks east of railway line, is a cheap market. There are several internet places in the centre. **Tourist office**, Dircetur ⓘ *Jr Noriega 191, p 3, T321839, ceturjuliaca@yahoo.es, open Mon-Fri 0730-1530*. See also www.juliacavirtual.com/indexj.htm.

The unspoiled little colonial town of **Lampa**, 31 km northwest of Juliaca is known as the 'Pink City'. It has a splendid church, La Inmaculada, containing a copy of Michelangelo's 'Pietà' (guided tours US$1.70), many Cuzqueña school paintings and a carved wooden pulpit. **Kampac Museo** ⓘ *Jr Ayacucho y Alfonso Ugarte, T951 820085 (mob), owner Profesor Jesús Vargas can be found at the shop opposite, no charge for admission and tour but contributions appreciated*, small private museum featuring an eclectic collection of sculptures and ceramics from a number of Peruvian cultures. Lampa has a small Sunday market. Cars (US$0.65) and combis (US$0.50) leave when full from Jr Huáscar y R Palma, 1 block from Mercado Santa Bárbara, 30 minutes to Lampa.

Puno to Cuzco

The road Puno-Juliaca-Cuzco is now fully paved and in good condition. Bus services are consequently an acceptable alternative to the train, at an average altitude of 3,500 m. There is much to see on the way, but neither the daytime buses nor the trains make frequent stops. You would have to be using your own transport, or taking buses from town to town to sample what the places en route have to offer, eg pottery bulls at Pucará (rooms available at the station); knitted alpaca ponchos and pullovers and miniature llamas at Santa Rosa (rooms available). There are also hotels in **Ayaviri**, whose speciality is a mild, creamy cheese (US$4 per kg).

The road and railway crosses the altiplano, climbing to **La Raya**, the highest pass on the line; 210 km from Puno, at 4,321 m (local market; toilets US$0.20). Up on the heights breathing may be a little difficult, but the descent along the Río Vilcanota is rapid. To the right of **Aguas Calientes**, the next station, 10 km from La Raya, are steaming pools of hot water in the middle of the green grass; a startling sight *US$0.15*. The temperature of the springs is 40°C, and they show beautiful deposits of red ferro-oxide. Communal bathing pools and a block of changing rooms have been opened. At **Maranganí**, the river is wider and the fields greener, with groves of eucalyptus trees.

At 38 km beyond La Raya pass is **Sicuani** (*Phone code: 084; Altitude: 3,690 m*), an important agricultural centre. Excellent items of llama and alpaca wool and skins are sold on the railway station and at the Sunday morning market. Around Plaza Libertad there are several hat shops. (For more information about places between Sicuani and Cuzco, see page 1445.)

To Cuzco listings

For Sleeping and Eating price codes and other relevant information, see Essentials, pages 38-40.

Sleeping

Juliaca *p1415*

There are water problems in town, especially in the dry season.

AL-A Suites Don Carlos, Jr M Prado 335, T321571, www.hotelesdon carlos.com. Good facilities, quiet, continental breakfast US$6.50, lunch or dinner US$13.

A-B Hostal Don Carlos, Jr 9 de Diciembre 114, Plaza Bolognesi, T323600, www.hotelesdon carlos.com. Comfortable, modern facilities, hot water, TV, heater, good service, breakfast, restaurant and room service. Recommended.

C Hostal La Casona, Plaza Bolognesi, **Lampa**, T01-99 903 8321, lacosnalampa@yahoo.com. Nicely refurbished 17th-century house decorated with antiques, includes breakfast, other meals available for US$7, hot water, heater in room and hot water bottles in beds, advanced booking required, caters to groups, tours arranged.

C La Maison, Jr 7 de Junio 535, T321444, www.lamaisonhotel.com. Hot water, one room with jacuzzi, no breakfast, restaurant next door, parking, a bit pricy but OK.

B-C Royal Inn, San Román 158, T321561, www.royalinnhoteles.com. Decent place with hot water, heaters, TV, safe, laundry, good restaurant (♈♈-♈). Recommended.

E Hostal Luquini, Jr Brasesco 409, Plaza Bolognesi, T321510. Comfortable, patio, helpful, reliable hot water in morning only, motorcycle parking.

E Sakura, San Román 133, T322072, hotelsakura@ hotmail.com. Includes breakfast, cable TV, hot water, cheaper basic rooms in older section **F** with shared bath, cafeteria, internet extra.

F Hospedaje Samay Huasi, Jr San Martín 1220, T323314. Very basic, family-run, helpful, clean and well situated just around the corner from the Cruz del Sur office. Private rooms with shared bath on second floor with access to hot water and cable TV. On the ground floor are dorm rooms used by locals.

Puno to Cuzco: Sicuani *p1415*

The bus terminal is in the newer part of town, which is separated from the older part and the Plaza by a pedestrian walkway and bridge.

F Samariy, Av Centenario 138, T352518. West side of old pedestrian bridge. Good value.

G José's, Av Arequipa 143, T351254. With bath, good.

Eating

Juliaca *p1415*

♈ **Dory's**, Jr San Martín 347. Sun-Thu 0800-2000, Fri 0800-1400, simple vegetarian.

♈ **El Asador**, Unión 119. Chicken, grill and pizza, good food and service, pleasant atmosphere, open 1800-2400.

Ricos Pan, San Ramón. Bakery with café, popular. Recommended.

Puno to Cuzco: Sicuani *p1415*

♈ **El Fogón**, C Zevallos. Good chicken and chips.

♈ **Pizzería Bon Vino**, 2 de Mayo 129, p 2. Good Italian.

♈ **Mijuna Wasi**, Jr Tacna 146. Closed Sun. Serves local dishes in a dilapidated, atmospheric courtyard.

Transport

Juliaca *p1415*

Air Airport is small but well organized. To/from **Lima**, 2¼ hrs, 3 a day with **Lan** (T322228 or airport T324448) via **Arequipa** (30 mins), **Cuzco** and direct. Minibus 1-B on Núñez, US$0.15; from airport to town they take you to your hotel. Beware overcharging for transport from Juliaca airport. If you have little luggage, combis stop just outside the airport parking area. Taxi from Plaza Bolognesi, US$1.75; taxi from airport US$3.40. Airport transfers from **Puno** US$3.40 pp with **Camtur**, Jr Tacna 336, of 104, T951 967652 and **Rossy Tours**, Jr Tacna 308, T366709, www.rossytours.tk. Many Puno hotels offer an airport transfer. Taxi to the airport US$17-24. If taking regular public transport to Juliaca and a taxi to the airport from there, allow extra time as the combis might drive around looking for passengers before leaving Puno.

Bus To **Puno**, buses leave when full throughout the day from Piérola y 8 de Noviembre, US$0.65, 1 hr. Combis from inside courtyard on Loreto by Plaza Bolognesi, US$0.85, 45 min. **Virgen de Fátima** "sprinters" or minibuses leave from the same place, faster, more confortable and same price. To **Capachica** for Llachón, from Cerro

Colorado market, leave when full 0500-1700, US$0.65, 1½ hrs.

Long distance: The terminal terrestre at the east end of San Martín (cuadra 9, past the Circunvalación) was not in use in early 2010. Most bus companies have their offices nearby on San Martín. To **Lima**, US$27 normal, US$44 'Imperial', 20 hrs; with **Ormeño** 1630, 2000. To **Cuzco**, US$5-12, 5-6 hrs; **Power** (T321952) hourly, several others. To **Arequipa**, US$6.50-13.50, 4-5 hrs, **Julsa** (T331952) hourly, several others. To **Puerto Maldonado**, along a rough but dramatic road via the San Gabán gorge and Mazuco, US$17, 16-18 hrs; buses leave M Nuñez cuadra 11 by the exit to Cuzco; **Aguilas/Tahuamanu** (M Núñez 1130, T323840) daily at 1200 and 1600, **Tambopata** (M Núñez 1130) daily at 1600. See below for how to get to the Bolivian border and page 1418 for transport.

Train See information under Puno or Cuzco. The station at Juliaca is the junction for services between **Arequipa** (no passenger services), **Puno** and **Cuzco.** Prices to Cuzco are the same as from Puno. There is no ticket office. You can get on the train in Juliaca, but you must buy the ticket in Puno or Cuzco.

Puno to Cuzco: Sicuani *p1415*

Bus To **Cuzco**, 137 km, US$1.25.

Border with Bolivia → *Peruvian time is 1 hr behind Bolivian time.*

There are three different routes across the border:

Puno-La Paz via Yunguyo and Copacabana **Peruvian immigration** is five minutes' drive from **Yunguyo** and 500 m from the Bolivian post; open 0700-2000 (but Bolivian immigration is only open 0830-1930). Ninety days is normally given when entering Peru. Leaving Peru, you must first go to the Policía Judicial, then to Peruvian immigration for your exit stamp. Be aware of corruption at customs and look out for official or unofficial people trying to charge you a fee, on either side of the border (say that you know it is illegal and ask why only gringos are approached to pay the 'embarkation tax').

Bolivian consulate is at Jr Grau 339, T856032, near the main plaza in Yunguyo, open Monday-Friday 0830-1500, for those who need a visa; some nationalities have to pay. Note that US citizens now need a visa for Bolivia; US citizens must pay US$100 cash and must have a passport valid for at least 6 months plus a photocopy, proof of sufficient funds (showing a credit card is acceptable) and an international vaccination certificate. For **Bolivian immigration**, see page 303. There are a couple of *casas de cambio* on the Peruvian side of the border offering slightly lower rates than in Yunguyo, but better rates than the shops on the Bolivian side. US$ cash and soles can also be exchanged at *cambios* in Copacabana, there are no ATMs in Copacabana. In Yunguyo best rates for US$ cash and Bolivianos at **Farmacia Loza**, Jr Bolognesi 567, Plaza 2 de Mayo. Also *cambios* on Plaza de Armas, and street changers who deal in dollars, bolivianos and euro.

Puno-Desaguadero **Desaguadero** is an unscrupulous place, with poor restaurants and dubious accommodation. Friday is the main *feria* day, with a smaller one onTuesday. There is no need to stop in Desaguadero as all roads to it are paved and if you leave La Paz, Moquegua or Puno early enough you should be at your destination before nightfall. Combis and minibuses Puno-Desaguadero hourly 0600-1900, 2½ hrs, US$2. Taxi US$33. **Peruvian border office** is open 0700-2000, Bolivian 0830-2030 (both local time). It is easy to change money on the Peruvian side. This particular border crossing allows you to stop at Tiahuanaco en route.

Along the east side of Lake Titicaca This is the most remote route, via **Huancané** and **Moho** (several *hostales*, **F-G**). Some walking may be involved as there is little traffic between Moho and **Puerto Acosta**, Bolivia. Make sure you get an exit stamp in Puno, post-dated by a couple of days. From Juliaca there are buses to Huancané, Moho and Tilali, the last village in Peru with basic lodgings (see Transport, above). The road is paved to Huancané. From Tilali it is 2-km walk to the **Peruvian**

customs post and a further 2-km steep climb to the international frontier at Cerro Janko Janko (see page 303). Puerto Acosta in Bolivia is a further 10 km. You must get a preliminary entry stamp at the police station on the plaza, then the definitive entry stamp at Migración in La Paz.

Border with Bolivia listings

For Sleeping and Eating price codes and other relevant information, see Essentials, pages 38-40.

Sleeping

Border with Bolivia: Yunguyo *p1417*
A few places to stay in **G** range.
F Hostal Isabel, San Francisco 110, near Plaza de Armas, T951 794228 (mob). Cheaper without bath, nice rooms and courtyard, electric shower, parking, friendly.

North shore of Lake Titicaca
LL Hotel Isla Suasi, T051-962 2709, a Casa Andina Private Collection hotel, www.casa-andina.com. The hotel is the only house on this tiny, tranquil island. There are beautiful terraced gardens, best Jan-Mar. The non-native eucalyptus trees are being replaced by native varieties. You can take a canoe around the island to see birds and the island has six vicuñas, a small herd of alpacas and one vizcacha. The sunsets from the highest point are beautiful. Facilities are spacious, comfortable and solar-powered, rooms with bath, hot water, hot water bottles. Price includes full board, national drinks, entrance to island, all transport, services and taxes. Massage room and sauna, internet US$20 per hr.

Transport

Border with Bolivia: Yunguyo *p1417*
Bus The road is paved from Puno to Yunguyo and the scenery is interesting. From Puno to **Copacabana**, US$5, 3 hrs, and **La Paz**, US$8.50-10, the best direct services are with **Tour Peru**, Jr Tacna, www.tourperu.com.pe, direct service to Copacabana leave Puno daily at 0730, and to La Paz at 0700. **Panamericano**, Jr Tacna 245, T369010, and **Litoral** (at Terminal Terestre, cheaper, but thefts reported in late 2009 on night buses).
To **Yunguyo**, from the Terminal Zonal in Puno, combis and mini buses hourly 0600-1900, 2½ hrs, US$1.70 (return from Jr Cusco esq Arica, 1 block from Plaza 2 de Mayo). From Yunguyo to the border (Kasani), from Jr Titicaca y San Francisco, 1 block from Plaza de Armas, cars and combis US$0.15 pp, mototaxi, US$0.35, taxi US$1, 5 mins. From Kasani to Copacabana, minibuses US$0.35, shared taxi US$0.40, taxi US$2, 20 mins. **Note** Don't take a taxi Yunguyo- Puno without checking its reliability first, driver may pick up an accomplice to rob passengers.

To La Paz by hydrofoil or catamaran
There are luxury services from Puno/Juli to La Paz by **Crillon Tours** hydrofoil, with connections to tours, from La Paz, to Cuzco and Machu Picchu. In Puno their office is at **Arcobaleno Tours** (see Activities and tours), or contact head office in La Paz. The itinerary is: Puno-Copacabana by bus; Copacabana-Isla del Sol-Huatajata (Bolivia) by hydrofoil; Huatajata-La Paz by bus; 13 hrs. Similar services, by catamaran, are run by **Transturin**, whose dock is at Chúa, Bolivia; bookings through **Transturin** in La Paz.

Along the east side of Lake Titicaca *p1417*
Combis to from Juliaca to **Huancané**, 51 km, from Grifo San Juan del Oro, Sucre y Ballón, US$0.45, 1 hr. From Hunacané, combis leave for Julica when full throughout the day. Buses to **Moho** (40 km from Huancané), from Moquegua 1179, T326820, 4 daily, 2-2½ hrs, US$1.50. From Moho to Juliaca, buses leave at 0130, 0800 and 1300 daily. Buses to **Tilali**, **Transportes Lucero**, 1 or 2 daily in early morning, **Aguila del Sur**, 1 daily in morning, both from Circunvalación y Lambayeque, 4 hrs, US$2.50 (schedules change daily; ask in advance). Daily buses from Tilali to Juliaca, around 0100, plus a morning bus, 0800-1000 on Sun, Tue and Fri. On market days trucks go to Puerto Acosta and La Paz. Try hitching to catch bus from Puerto Acosta to La Paz (daily) about 1400 (note Bolivian time is 1 hr ahead of Peru), more frequent service on Sun, 5 hrs, US$3.75. If you are in a hurry and miss the bus, ask the truck to drop you off 25 km further in Escoma, from where there are frequent minivans to La Paz. Buses leave La Paz for Puerto Acosta at 0600 daily. Transport from Puerto Acosta to border only operates on market days, mostly cargo trucks.

Cuzco → *Phone code: 084. Colour map 3, C4. Altitude: 3,310 m.*

The ancient Inca capital is said to have been founded around AD 1100, and since then has developed into a major commercial and tourism centre of 326,000 inhabitants, most of whom are Quechua. The city council has designated Qosqo (Cuzco in Quechua) as the official spelling. Today, colonial churches, monasteries and convents and extensive pre-Columbian ruins are interspersed with countless hotels, bars and restaurants that cater for the hundreds of thousands of visitors. Almost every central street has remains of Inca walls, arches and doorways; the perfect Inca stonework now serves as the foundations for more modern dwellings. This stonework is tapered upwards (battered); every wall has a perfect line of inclination towards the centre, from bottom to top. The curved stonework of the Temple of the Sun, for example, is probably unequalled in the world.

Ins and outs

Getting there The **airport** is to the southeast of the city and the road into the centre goes close to Wanchac station, at which **trains** from Juliaca and Puno arrive. The **bus terminal** is near the Pachacútec statue in Ttio district. Transport to your hotel is not a problem from any of these places by taxi or in transport arranged by hotel representatives. ▸▸ *See also Transport, page 1441.*

Getting around The centre of Cuzco is quite small and possible to explore on foot. Taxis in Cuzco are cheap and recommended when arriving by air, train or bus and especially when returning to your hotel at night. Cuzco is only slightly lower than Puno, so respect the altitude: two or three hours rest after arriving makes a great difference; avoid meat and smoking, eat lots of carbohydrates and drink plenty of clear, non-alcoholic liquid; remember to walk slowly. To see Cuzco and the surrounding area properly (including Pisac, Ollantaytambo, Chinchero and Machu Picchu) you need five days to a week, allowing for slowing down because of the altitude.

Tourist information **Official tourist information** ⓘ *Portal Mantas 117-A, next to La Merced church, T263176, open 0800-2000.* There is also an **i perú** tourist information desk at the airport ⓘ *T237364, open daily for flights*, and another at ⓘ *Av Sol 103, of 102, Galerías Turísticas, T252974, iperucusco@promperu.gob.pe, daily 0830-1930.* **Dircetur** ⓘ *Plaza Túpac Amaru Mz 1 Lte 2, Wanchac, T223761, open Mon-Fri 0800-1300*, gives out good map. Other information sources include **South American Explorers** ⓘ *Atocsaycuchi 670, T245484, www.saexplorers.org, Mon-Fri 0930-1700, Sat 0930-1300.* It's worth making the climb up the steps to the large new clubhouse which has a garden. Sells good city map, members get many local discounts, has comprehensive recycling centre. As with SAE's other clubhouses, this is the place to go for specialized information, member-written trip reports and maps. Also has rooms for rent. For full details on South American Explorers, see page 52. Many churches close to visitors on Sunday; 'official' opening times are unreliable. No photographs are allowed in any museums. **Automóvil Club del Perú** ⓘ *Av Sol 349, nivel 2, T/F224561, cusco@touringperu.com.pe*, has some maps. Motorists beware; many streets end in flights of steps. Apart from South American Explorers' comprehensive map, there are few good maps of Cuzco.

Visitors' tickets A combined entry ticket, called *Boleto Turístico de Cusco* (BTC), is available to most of the sites of main historical and cultural interest in and around the city, and costs as follows: 130 soles (US$45/€33.50) for all the sites and valid for 10 days; or 70 soles (US$24/€18) for either the museums in the city, or Sacsayhuaman, Qenqo, Puka Pukara and Tambo Machay, or Pisac, Ollantaytambo, Chinchero and Moray; the 70 soles ticket is valid for one day. Tickets can be bought at the **OFEC offices** ⓘ *Casa Garcilaso, Plaza Regocijo, esquina Calle Garcilaso, T226919, Mon-Sat 0800-1600, Sun 0800-1200; Cosituc, Av Sol 103 of 102, T261465, www.cosituc.gob.pe, Mon-Fri 0800-1800, Sat 0830-1230*, or at any of the sites included in the ticket. For students with a

Inca society

Cuszo was the capital of the Inca empire – one of the greatest planned societies the world has known – from its rise during the 11th century to its death in the early 16th century. (See John Hemming's *Conquest of the Incas* and B C Brundage's *Lords of Cuzco* and *Empire of the Inca*.) It was solidly based on other Peruvian civilizations which had attained great skill in textiles, building, ceramics and working in metal. Immemorially, the political structure of the Andean *indígena* had been the ayllu, the village community; it had its divine ancestor, worshipped household gods, was closely knit by ties of blood to the family and by economic necessity to the land, which was held in common. Submission to the ayllu was absolute, because it was only by such discipline that food could be obtained in an unsympathetic environment. All the domestic animals, the llama and alpaca and the dog, had long been tamed, and the great staple crops, maize and potatoes, established. What the Incas did – and it was a magnificent feat – was to conquer enormous territories and impose upon the variety of ayllus, through an unchallengeable central government, a willing spiritual and economic submission to the State. The common religion, already developed by the classical Tiwanaku culture, was worship of the Sun, whose vice-regent on earth was the absolute Sapa Inca. Around him, in the capital, was a religious and secular elite which never froze into a caste because it was open to talent. The elite was often recruited from chieftains defeated by the Incas; an effective way of reconciling local opposition. The mass of the people were subjected to rigorous planning. They were allotted land to work, for their group and for the State; set various tasks (the making of textiles, pottery, weapons, ropes, etc) from primary materials supplied by the functionaries, or used in enlarging the area of cultivation by building terraces on the hill-sides. Their political organization was simple but effective. The family, and not the individual, was the unit. Families were grouped in units of 10, 100, 500, 1,000, 10,000 and 40,000, each group with a leader responsible to the next largest group. The Sapa Inca crowned the political edifice; his four immediate counsellors were those to whom he allotted responsibility for the northern, southern, eastern and western regions (suyos) of the empire.

Equilibrium between production and consumption, in the absence of a free price mechanism and good transport facilities, must depend heavily upon statistical information. This the Incas raised to a high degree of efficiency by means of their quipus: a decimal system of recording numbers by knots in cords. Seasonal variations were guarded against by creating a system of state barns in which provender could be stored during years of plenty, to be used in years of scarcity. Statistical efficiency alone required that no one should be permitted to leave his home or his work. The loss of personal liberty was the price paid by the masses for economic security. In order to obtain information and to transmit orders quickly, the Incas built fine paved pathways along which couriers sped on foot. The whole system of rigorous control was completed by the greatest of all their monarchs, Pachacuti, who also imposed a common language, Quechua, as a further cementing force.

green ISIC card the BTC costs 70 soles (US$24), which is only available at the OFEC office (Casa Garcilaso) upon presentation of the ISIC card. Take your ISIC card when visiting the sites, as some may ask to see it. Photography is not allowed in the churches, and museums.

Entrance tickets for the Santo Domingo/Qoricancha, the Inka Museum (El Palacio del Almirante) and La Merced are sold separately, while the Cathedral and churches of El Triunfo, La Sagrada Familia, La Compañia and San Blas and the Museo de Arte Religioso del Arzobispado are included on a religious buildings ticket which costs 36 soles (US$13) and is alid for 10 days. Machu Picchu ruins and Inca trail entrance tickets are sold at the **Instituto acional de Cultura** (INC) ⓘ *San Bernardo s/n entre Mantas y Almagro, T236061, Mon-Fri 900-1300, 1600-1800, Sat 0900-1100.*

ecurity Police patrol the streets, trains and stations, but one should still be vigilant. On no ccount walk back to your hotel after dark from a bar or club, strangle muggings and rape are 'equent. For safety's sake, pay the US$1 taxi fare, but not just any taxi. Ask the club's doorman ɔ get a taxi for you and make sure the taxi is licensed. Other areas in which to take care include an Pedro market (otherwise recommended), the San Cristóbal area, and at out-of-the-way uins. Also take special care during Inti Raymi. The **Tourist Police**, C Saphi 510, 249665/221961. If you need a *denuncia* (a report for insurance purposes), which is available 'om the Banco de la Nación, they will type it out. Always go to the police when robbed, even hough it will cost you a bit of time. The Consumer Protection Bureau (**Indecopi**) is at Av Manco ıca 209, Wanchac, T252987, mmarroquin@indecopi.gob.pe. Toll free 0800-44040 (24-hour otline, not available from payphones).

ights

he heart of the city in Inca days was *Huacaypata* (the place of tears) and *Cusipata* (the place of appiness), divided by a channel of the Saphi River. Today, Cusipata is Plaza Regocijo and uacaypata is the Plaza de Armas, around which are colonial arcades and four churches. To the ortheast is the early 17th-century baroque **Cathedral** ⓘ *until 1000 for genuine worshippers – uechua mass is held 0500-0600. Tourists may visit Mon, Tue, Wed, Fri, Sat 1000-1130, 1400-1730, hu and Sun 1400-1730.* It is built on the site of the Palace of Inca Wiracocha (*Kiswarcancha*). he high altar is solid silver and the original altar *retablo* behind it is a masterpiece of Andean ood carving. The earliest surviving painting of the city can be seen, depicting Cuzco during he 1650 earthquake. In the far right hand end of the church is an interesting local painting of he Last Supper replete with *cuy*, *chicha*, etc. In the sacristy are paintings of all the bishops of uzco. The choir stalls, by a 17th-century Spanish priest, are a magnificent example of colonial aroque art. The elaborate pulpit and the sacristy are also notable. Much venerated is the rucifix of El Señor de los Temblores, the object of many pilgrimages and viewed all over Peru as guardian against earthquakes. The tourist entrance to the Cathedral is through the church of **esús María** (1733), which stands to its left as you face it. Its gilt main altar has been renovated. **l Triunfo** (1536), on its right of the Cathedral, is the first Christian church in Cuzco, built on the ite of the Inca Roundhouse (the *Suntur Huasi*). It has a statue of the Virgin of the Descent, eputed to have helped the Spaniards repel Manco Inca when he besieged the city in 1536.

On the southeast side of the plaza is the beautiful **La Compañía de Jesús**, built on the site f the Palace of the Serpents (*Amarucancha*, residence of Inca Huayna Capac) in the late 7th century. Its twin-towered exterior is extremely graceful, and the interior rich in fine murals, aintings and carved altars. Nearby is the **Santa Catalina** church ⓘ *Arequipa at Santa Catalina ngosta, daily 0900-1200, 1300-1700, except Fri 0900-1200, 1300-1600, joint ticket with Santo omingo US$6*, convent and museum, built upon the foundations of the *Acllahuasi* (House of he Chosen Women). There are guided tours by English-speaking students; tip expected.

La Merced ⓘ *on Calle Márquez, church 0830-1200, 1530-1730; monastery and museum 430-1700, except Sun, US$1.* The church was first built 1534 and rebuilt in the late 17th entury. Attached is a very fine monastery with an exquisite cloister. Inside the church are uried Gonzalo Pizarro, half-brother of Francisco, and the two Almagros, father and son. The hurch is most famous for its jewelled monstrance, which is on view in the monastery's nuseum during visiting hours.

Much **Inca stonework** can be seen in the streets and most particularly in the Callejón Loreto, unning southeast past La Compañía de Jesús from the main plaza. The walls of the *Acllahuasi* House of the Chosen Women) are on one side, and of the *Amarucancha* on the other. There are also Inca remains in Calle San Agustín, to the east of the plaza. The stone of 12 angles is in Call Hatun Rumiyoc halfway along its second block, on the right-hand side going away fror the Plaza. The **Palacio Arzobispal** stands on Hatun Rumiyoc y Herrajes, two blocks northeas of Plaza de Armas. It was built on the site of the palace occupied in 1400. It contains th **Museo de Arte Religioso** ⓘ *Mon-Sat, 0830-1130, 1500-1730,* a collection of colonial painting and furniture. The collection includes the paintings by the indigenous master, Diego Quisp Tito, of a 17th-century Corpus Christi procession that used to hang in the church of Santa Ana.

The **Palacio del Almirante**, just north of the Plaza de Armas on Ataud, is impressive. It house the **Museo Inka** ⓘ *Mon-Sat 0800-1900, Sat 0900-1600, US$3, students guide visitors for a tip*

1 Cuzco

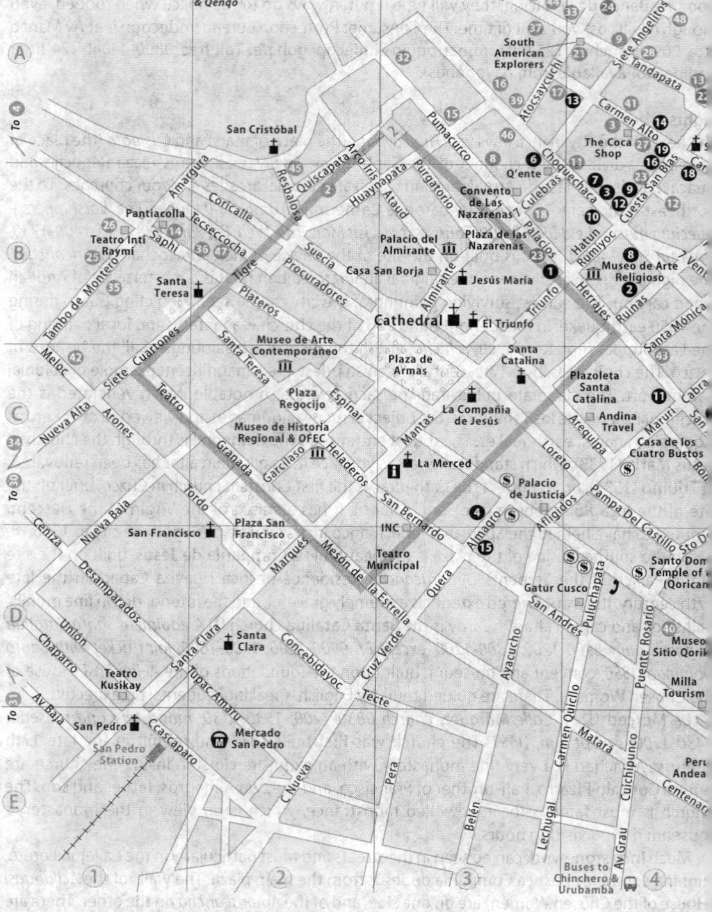

hich is run by the Universidad San Antonio de Abad, the museum exhibits the development of ılture in the region from pre-Inca, through Inca times to the present day: textiles, ceramics, ıetalwork, jewellery, architecture, technology. See the collection of miniature turquoise gures and other offerings to the gods. Weaving demonstrations are given in the courtyard. On ıe northwest side of the Plaza de las Nazarenas is **Museo de Arte Precolombino** ⓘ *daily 900-2200, US$6, US$3 with student card, shops, MAP Café (see Eating, below)*, housed in the **Casa abrera**. This beautiful museum is set around a spacious courtyard and contains many superb ‹amples of pottery, metalwork (largely in gold and silver), wood carvings and shells from the ıoche, Chimú, Paracas, Nazca and Inca cultures. There are some vividly rendered animistic

➡ Cuzco maps

1 **Cuzco, page 1422**
2 Around Plaza de Armas, page 1427

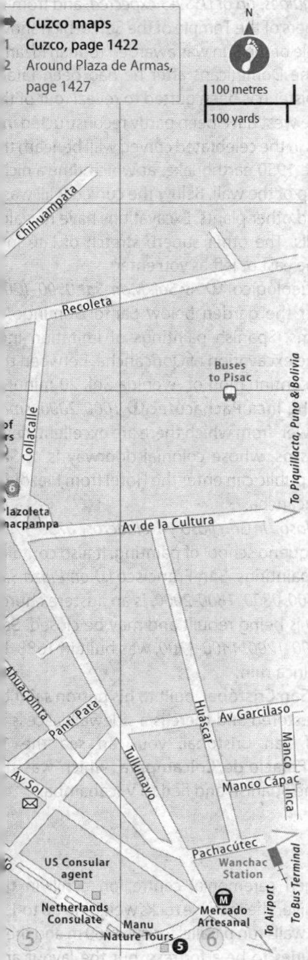

Sleeping

1 Albergue Casa Campesina *C5*
2 Albergue Municipal *B2*
3 Andes de San Blas *A4*
4 Cahuide *A1*
5 Casa Andina Koricancha *C4*
6 Casa Andina Private Collection Cusco *C5*
7 Casa Andina San Blas *B5*
8 Casa Cartagena *A3*
9 Casa de la Gringa 1 *A4*
10 Casa de la Gringa 2 *B4*
11 Casa Elena *A4*
12 Casa San Blas *B4*
13 Casona Les Pleiades *A4*
14 Cuzco Plaza 2 *B1*
15 El Arqueólogo *A3*
16 El Balcón Colonial *A3*
17 El Grial *A3*
18 El Monasterio *B3*
19 Estrellita *C5*
20 Hosp El Artesano de San Blas *A4*
21 Hosp Familiar Inti Quilla *A4*
22 Hosp Inka *A5*
23 Hostal Amaru *B4*
24 Hostal Casa de Campo *A3*
25 Hostal El Balcón *B1*
26 Hostal Familiar *B1*
27 Hostal Familiar Carmen Alto *A4*
28 Hostal Familiar Mirador del Inka *A4*
29 Hostal Kuntur Wasi *A3*
30 Hostal Loki *C1*
31 Hostal Luzerna *D1*
32 Hostal María Esther *A3*
33 Hostal Pakcha Real *A4*
34 Hostal Qorichaska *C1*
35 Hostal Rickch'airy *B1*
36 Hostal San Isidro Labrador *B2*
37 Hostal Tikawasi *A3*
38 Libertador Palacio del Inka *C4*
39 Los Apus Hotel & Mirador *A3*
40 Maison de la Jeunesse *D4*
41 Marani *A4*
42 Niños Hotel *C1*
43 Novotel *C4*
44 Pensión Alemana *A3*
45 Piccola Locanda & L'Osteria Restaurant *B2*
46 Rumi Punku *A3*
47 Suecia II *B2*
48 The Blue House *A4*

Eating

1 A Mi Manera *B3*
2 Baco *B4*
3 Café Cultural Ritual *B4*
4 Café El Ayllu *C3*
5 Café Manu *E6*
6 Café Punchay *A3*
7 Chocolate *B4*
8 El Encuentro *B4*
9 Granja Heidi *B4*
10 Inka...fe *B4*
11 Inkanato *C4*
12 Jack's Café *B4*
13 Juanito's Sandwich Bar *A4*
14 La Bodega *A4*
15 Los Toldos *D3*
16 Macondo *A4*
17 Moni *C4*
18 Pachapapa *B4*
19 Panadería El Buen Pastor *A4*
20 Witches Garden *B4*

Bars & clubs

21 Bar 7 *A3*
22 Km 0 (Arte y Tapas) *A4*
23 Marcelo Batata *B3*
24 Siete Angelitos *A4*

designs, giving an insight into the way Peru's ancient people's viewed their world and t
creatures that inhabited it. Every exhibit carries explanations in English and Spanish. Hig
recommended. The **Convento de las Nazarenas**, also on Plaza de las Nazarenas, is now
annex of Orient Express' *Monasterio* hotel. You can see the Inca-colonial doorway with
mermaid motif, but ask permission to view the lovely 18th-century frescos inside. In the S
Blas district, now firmly on the tourist map, the small church of **San Blas** ⓘ *Carmen Ba, 0800-1130 (except Thu), 1400-1730* has a beautiful carved *mestizo* cedar pulpit, which is w
worth seeing. See Shopping Local crafts, below.

Santo Domingo, southeast of the main Plaza, was built in the 17th century on the walls of t **Qoricancha, Temple of the Sun** ⓘ *Mon-Sat 0830-1730, Sun 1400-1700 (closed holidays), US$2, joint ticket with Santa Catalina US$6, English-speaking guides, tip of US$2-3 expected*, and from stones. Excavation has revealed more of the five chambers of the Temple of the Sun, which sho the best Inca stonework to be seen in Cuzco. The Temple of the Sun was awarded to Juan Pizar the younger brother of Francisco, who willed it to the Dominicans after he had been fata wounded in the Sacsayhuaman siege. The baroque cloister has been gutted to reveal four of t original chambers of the great Inca temple – two on the west have been partly reconstructed in good imitation of Inca masonry. The finest stonework is in the celebrated curved wall beneath t west end of Santo Domingo. This was rebuilt after the 1950 earthquake, at which time a nic that once contained a shrine was found at the inner top of the wall. Below the curved wall wa garden of gold and silver replicas of animals, maize and other plants. Excavations have reveal Inca baths below here, and more Inca retaining walls. The other superb stretch of late In stonework is in C Ahuacpinta outside the temple, to the east or left as you enter.

Museo de Sitio Qorikancha (formerly Museo Arqueológico) ⓘ *Av Sol, Mon-Sat 0900-120 1300-1700, Sun 0800-1400, entrance by BTC* is under the garden below Santo Domingo. contains a limited collection of pre-Columbian items, Spanish paintings of imitation In royalty dating from the 18th century, and photos of the excavation of Qoricancha. Between t centre and the airport on Alameda Pachacútec, the continuation of Avenida Sol, 20 minut walk from the Plaza de Armas, there is a **statue of the Inca Pachacútec** ⓘ *1000-2000, sm galleries and coffee shop*, placed on top of a lookout tower, from which there are excellent vie of Cuzco. The palace called **Casa de los Cuatro Bustos**, whose colonial doorway is at S Agustín 400, is now the **Hotel Libertador**. The general public can enter the Hotel from Plazole Santo Domingo, opposite the Temple of the Sun/Qoricancha.

Museo de Historia Regional ⓘ *in the Casa Garcilaso, Jr Garcilaso y Heladeros, 0730-170 entrance by BTC* tries to show the evolution of the Cuzqueño school of painting. It also contai Inca agricultural implements, colonial furniture and paintings. **San Francisco** ⓘ *on Plaza S Francisco, 3 blocks southwest of the Plaza de Armas, 0600-0800, 1800-2000*, is an austere chur reflecting many indigenous influences. Its monastery is being rebuilt and may be closed. **Sa Pedro** ⓘ *in front of the San Pedro market, Mon-Sat 1000-1200, 1400-1700*, was built in 1688. two towers were made from stones brought from an Inca ruin.

Above Cuzco, on the road up to Sacsayhuamán, is **San Cristóbal**, built to his patron saint b Cristóbal Paullu Inca. The church's atrium has been restored and there is a sidewalk access the Sacsayhuamán Archaeological Park. North of San Cristóbal, you can see the 1 doorway-sized niches of the great Inca wall of the **Palacio de Colcampata**, which was th residence of Manco Inca before he rebelled against the Spanish and fled to Vilcabamba.

Sacsayhuaman

ⓘ *Daily 0700-1730; free student guides, give them a tip.*

There are some magnificent Inca walls in this ruined ceremonial centre, on a hill in th northern outskirts. The Incaic stones are hugely impressive. The massive rocks weighing up to 1 tons are fitted together with absolute perfection. Three walls run parallel for over 360 m and the are 21 bastions. Sacsayhuaman was thought for centuries to be a fortress, but the layout ar architecture suggest a great sanctuary and temple to the Sun, which rises exactly opposite the place previously believed to be the Inca's throne – which was probably an altar, carved out of the solid rock. Broad steps lead to the altar from either side. The hieratic, rather than the military, hypothesis was supported by the discovery in 1982 of the graves of priests, who would have been unlikely to be buried in a fortress. The precise functions of the site, however, will probably continue to be a matter of dispute as very few clues remain, owing to its steady destruction. The site is about a 30-minute walk up Pumacurco from Plaza de las Nazarenas.

Along the road from Sacsayhuaman to Pisac, past a radio station, is the temple and amphitheatre of **Qenqo** with some of the finest examples of Inca stone carving *in situ*, especially inside the large hollowed-out stone that houses an altar. On the same road are **Puka Pukara** (Red Fort, but more likely to have been a *tambo*, or post-house), wonderful views; and the spring shrine of **Tambo Machay**, which is in excellent condition. Water still flows by a hidden channel out of the masonry wall, straight into a little rock pool traditionally known as the Inca's bath. Take a guide to the sites and visit in the morning for the best photographs. Carry your multi-site ticket, there are roving ticket inspectors. You can visit the sites on foot, a pleasant walk of at least half a day through the countryside; take water, sun protection, and watch out for dogs. Alternatively, take the Pisac bus up to Tambo Machay (US$0.35) and walk back, or arrange a horseback tour with an agency.

Cuzco listings

For Sleeping and Eating price codes and other relevant information, see Essentials, pages 38-40.

Sleeping

Cuzco *p1419, maps p1422 and p1427*

In Jun and other busy times, double-booking occurs so double-check reservations. Book more expensive hotels well in advance, particularly for the week or so around Inti Raymi, when prices are greatly increased. Prices given are for the high season in Jun-Aug. When there are fewer tourists hotels may drop their prices by as much as half. Always check for discounts. Train passengers are approached by unlicensed hotel agents for medium-priced hotels who are often misleading about details; their local nickname is *jalagringos* (gringo pullers), or *piratas*. Taxis and tourist minibuses meet the train and (should) take you to the hotel of your choice for US$0.75-1, but be insistent. Since it is cold here and many hotels have no heating, ask for an *estufa*, a heater which some places will provide for an extra charge.

LL Andean Wings, Siete Cuartones 225, T243166, www.andeanwingshotel.com. In a restored 17-th century house, in the same group as Casa de la Gringa, Mandela's Bar and Another Planet, 5-star, intimate, suites, some with jacuzzi, are individually designed one is accessible for the disabled), restaurant and bar.

LL Casa Cartagena, Pumacurco 336, T261171, www.casacartagena.com. In a converted monastery and national heritage building, super-deluxe facilities with Italian design and colonial features, 4 levels of suite from US$700 to US$1,800 a night, La Chola restaurant, extensive Qoya spa, enriched oxygen system, Wi-Fi, and all services to be expected in a "boutique" hotel (in the Luxury Properties group).

LL El Monasterio, C Palacios 136, Plazoleta Nazarenas, T604000, www.monasteriohotel.com. 5-star, beautifully restored Seminary of San Antonio Abad (a Peruvian National Historical Landmark), including the Baroque chapel, spacious comfortable rooms with all facilities (some rooms offer an oxygen- enriched atmosphere to help clients acclimatize, US$25 extra), very helpful staff, price includes buffet breakfast (US$19 to non-residents, will fill you up for the rest of the day), good restaurants, lunch and dinner à la carte, business centre with email for guests (US$3 per hr).

LL La Casona Inkaterra, Plazoleta Las Nazarenas 113, T245314, www.inkaterra.com. A private, colonial-style boutique hotel in a converted 16th-century mansion, built on the site of Manco Cápac's palace. 11 exclusive suites, all facilities, concierge service with activities and excursions, highly-regarded (prices from US$600).

LL Libertador Palacio del Inka, Plazoleta Santo Domingo 259, T231961, www.libertador.com.pe. 5-star, price includes buffet breakfast, good, especially the service, warm and bright, *Inti Raymi* restaurant, excellent, folk music in the evening.
LL Novotel, San Agustín 239, T881030, www.novotel.com. 4-star, cheaper in modern section; price includes buffet breakfast, converted from colonial house with beautiful glass-roofed courtyard, spacious rooms, cable TV, central heating, 2 restaurants and a French chef.
L-A Casa San Blas, Tocuyeros 566, just off Cuesta San Blas, T237900, www.casasanblas.com. A boutique hotel, bright and airy rooms with traditional textiles, breakfast and Wi-Fi internet included, attentive service; excellent **Tika Bistro** downstairs.
AL Casa Andina Private Collection Cusco, Plazoleta de Limacpampa Chico 473, T232610, www.casa-andina.com. Upmarket chain hotel in 16th-century mansion, very high standards, gourmet restaurant, good *piscos*.
AL Sonesta Posadas del Inca, Portal Espinar 108, T227061, www.sonesta.com. Includes buffet breakfast, warmly decorated rooms with heating and cable TV, safe, some rooms on 3rd floor with view of Plaza, very helpful, English spoken, restaurant with Andean food, excellent service. They are also to open a new hotel on Av Sol 954, T224322.
A Casa Andina Plaza, Portal Espinar 142, T231 733, www.casa-andina.com. 40 rooms, new hotel near plaza, cable TV, private bathroom, internet access, ATM and safe deposit box. Equally recommendable are **Casa Andina Koricancha**, San Agustín 371, T252633, **Casa Andina Catedral**, Santa Catalina Angosta 149, T233661, and the **A Casa Andina San Blas**, Chihuampata 278, San Blas, T263964, all of which are in the same vein.
A Cuzco Plaza 2, Saphi 486, T263000, www.cuscoplazahotels.com. Same management as **A-B Cuzco Plaza 1** (Plaza Nazarenas 181, T246161). Nicely decorated rooms set around 3 charming covered patios, includes American breakfast, cable TV and heating.
A El Arqueólogo, Pumacurco 408, T232569, www.hotelarqueologo.com. Includes breakfast, hot water, heating extra, helpful, French and English spoken, will store luggage, garden, cafeteria and kitchen. Also has a B&B hostal at Carmen Alto 294, T232760, **C-D. Vida Tours**, Ladrillo 425, T227750, www.vidatours.com. Traditional and adventure tourism.
A Los Apus Hotel & Mirador, Atocsaycuchi 515 y Choquechaca, San Blas, T264243, www.losapushotel.com. Includes breakfast and airport transfer, full of character, very smart, central heating, disabled facilities.
A Royal Inka I, Plaza Regocijo 299, T263276, www.royalinkahotel.com (also *Royal Inka II* Santa Teresa 335, T222284, a little pricier). Price includes taxes and breakfast, bar, dining room, good service. These hotels run a bus to Pisac at 1000 daily, returns 1800, free for guests.

2 Around Plaza de Armas

➡ **Cuzco maps**

1 Cuzco, page 1422

2 **Around Plaza de Armas, page 1427**

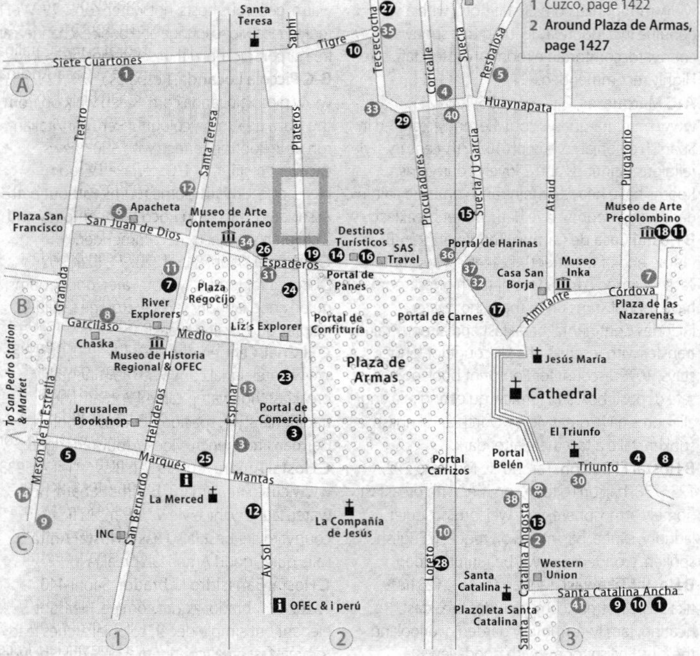

Plateros detail

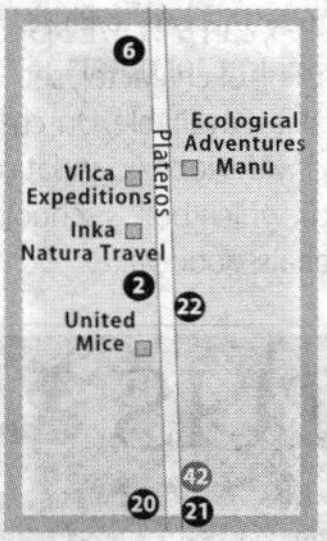

Sleeping

1 Andean Wings *A1*
2 Casa Andina Catedral *C3*
3 Casa Andina Plaza *C2*
4 El Procurador del Cusco *A2*
5 Hostal Resbalosa *A3*
6 Hostal Royal Frankenstein *B1*
7 La Casona Inkaterra *B3*
8 Marqueses *B1*
9 Pariwana *C1*
10 Pensión Loreto *C2*
11 Royal Inka I *B1*
12 Royal Inka II *A1*
13 Sonesta Posadas del Inca *B2*
14 The Point *C1*

Eating

1 Al Grano *C3*
2 Amaru *Plateros detail*
3 Bembos *C2*
4 Bistrot 370 *C3*
5 Café El Ayllu *B3*
6 Café Halliy *Plateros detail*
7 Chicha, El Truco & Taberna del Truco *B1*
8 Cicciolina *C3*
9 Dolce Vita *C3*
10 El Encuentro *A2, C3*
11 Fallen Angel *B3*
12 Fusiones & Maikhana *C2*
13 Incanto & Greens Organic *C3*
14 Inka Grill *B2*
15 Kusikuy *B3*
16 La Retama *B2*
17 Limo *B3*
18 MAP Café *B3*
19 Pachacútec Grill & Bar *B2*
20 Pucará *Plateros detail*
21 The Muse *Plateros detail*
22 The Real McCoy *Plateros detail*
23 Trotamundos *B2*
24 Tunupa *B2*
25 Tupananchis *C1*
26 Varayoc *B2*
27 Víctor Victoria *A2*
28 Witches Garden *C2*
29 Yaku Mama *A2*

Bars & clubs

30 Cross Keys Pub *A2*
31 El Garabato Video Music Club *B2*
32 Extreme *B3*
33 Indigo *A2*
34 Kamikaze *B2*
35 Los Perros *A2*
36 Mama Africa *B2*
37 Mythology *B3*
38 Norton Rat's Tavern *C3*
39 Paddy Flaherty's *C3*
40 Roots *A2*
41 Rosie O'Grady's *C3*
42 Ukuku's *Plateros detail*

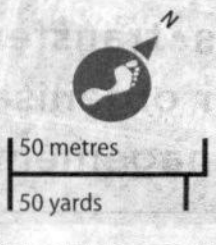

A Rumi Punku, Choquechaca 339, T221102, www.rumipunku.com. 3-star hotel with a genuine Inca doorway leading to a sunny courtyard, comfortable rooms, helpful staff, safe. Highly recommended.

A-C Marqueses, Garcilaso 256, T264249, www.hotelmarqueses.com. Recently restored in Spanish colonial style, with 16/17th-century style religious paintings and 2 lovely courtyards. Rooms have heavy curtains and some are a little dark; luxury rooms have bath. Buffet breakfast.

B Hostal Casa de Campo, Tandapata 296-B (at the end of the street), T244404, www.hotelcasadecampo.com. Some of the highest rooms have a *lot* of steps up to them, hot water, includes Continental breakfast and airport/ rail transfer with reservations, discount for longer stays, 10% discount for Footprint book owners, safe deposit box, sun terrace, quiet and relaxing, all rooms have great views, Dutch and English spoken, take a taxi there after dark.

B Hostal El Balcón, Tambo de Montero 222, T236738, balcon1@terra.com.pe. With breakfast, homely atmosphere, very welcoming, quiet, laundry, sauna, bar, meals on request, English spoken, wonderful views, beautiful garden.

B Hostal Tikawasi, Tandapata 491, T231609, tikawasi@hotmail.com. Includes breakfast, heating, family-run, lovely garden overlooking the city. Stylish rooms with good views, comfortable beds.

B Pensión Alemana, Tandapata 260, San Blas, T226861, www.cuzco.com.pe. Swiss owned, welcoming, price includes American breakfast, comfortable, discount in low season.

B-C Casona Les Pleiades, Tandapata 116, T506430, www.casona-pleiades.com. Small guesthouse in renovated colonial house, cosy and warm, generous hosts, hot water, cable TV, Wi-Fi, roof terrace, video lounge and book exchange, café, free airport pickup with reservation, lots of info.

B-C Piccola Locanda, Resbalosa 520, T252551, www.piccolalocanda.com. Steep walk up from the Plaza de Armas, colourful Peruvian/Italian run B&B. Rooftop terrace with 360° views, excellent restaurant **L'Osteria**, a TV room, pleasant courtyard. Some rooms without bath. Associated with **Perú Etico** tour company and 2 children's projects. Recommended.

C Cahuide, Saphi 845, T222771, F248262. Discount for long stay, hot water, good rooms, quiet, good laundry service, storage facilities, helpful, good value breakfasts.

C El Grial, Carmen Alto 112, T223012, San Blas, www.hotelelgrial.com. With continental breakfast, hot water, cable TV, charming, traditional style, spacious, books in English, German and French, videos, tours arranged.

C Hostal Amaru, Cuesta San Blas 541, T225933, www.cusco.net/amaru. **E** without bath, hot water, laundry, nice views, rooms in first courtyard are best (also has **E Hostal Anita**, safe, quiet, good American breakfast).

C Hostal San Isidro Labrador, Saphi 440, T226241, labrador@qnet.com.pe. Pleasant, elegant but simple decor, colonial arches lead to breakfast area (continental breakfast included) and 2 lovely patios, hot water, heating.

C Marani, Carmen Alto 194, San Blas, T/F249462, www.hostalmarani.com. Full of character, set around a courtyard, breakfast available, Dutch-owned hostel associated with Hope Foundation (www.stichtinghope.org), which builds schools, helps teachers and hospitals, good value.

C Niños Hotel, Meloc 442, T/F231424, www.ninos hotel.com. Hot water, excellent breakfast extra, restaurant, laundry service, luggage store, Dutch, English, German and French spoken, run as part of the Dutch foundation *Niños Unidos Peruanos* and all profits are invested in projects to help street children. Also has *Niños 2*, on C Fierro, with all the same features, and the **Niños Hacienda** in Huasao, 25 mins from Cuzco, with rooms and bungalows, breakfast and dinner included, also weekend packages.

C Pensión Loreto, Pasaje Loreto 115, Plaza de Armas, T/F226352, loreto@hloreto.com. Rooms with Inca walls and electric heaters, a bit dark, cheap laundry service, comfortable and secure, taxis and other travel can be arranged, Lucio here is a good guide, safe luggage deposit.

C-D Hostal Familiar Mirador del Inka, Tandapata 160, off Plaza San Blas, T261384, www.miradordelinka.info. **E** without bath, hot water, laundry, the son Edwin rents trekking equipment.

D Casa Elena, Choquechaca 162, T241202, www.casaelenacusco.com. French/Peruvian hostel, very comfortable, good choice, breakfast.

D Hostal Kuntur Wasi, Tandapata 352-A, San Blas, T227570, www.kunturws.com. Great views, **F** without bath, use of kitchen US$0.60, laundry service, owner speaks a bit of English and is very helpful and welcoming, a pleasant place to stay.

D Hostal Royal Frankenstein, San Juan de Dios 260, 2 blocks from the Plaza de Armas, T236999, www.hostal-frankenstein.net. Eccentric place but a frequent favourite, **E** with shared bath, hot water, safe, kitchen, free Wi-Fi, small charge for internet and laundry, German-owned, German and English spoken.

D (from **G** pp) **Hostal Loki**, Cuesta Santa Ana 601, T243705, www.lokihostel.com/en/cusco. Huge hostel in a restored viceroy's residence on the steep Cuesta Santa Ana, dorms and rooms set around a beautiful courtyard, comfortable beds, hot water, free internet. A great meeting place.

D Hostal María Esther, Pumacurco 516, T224382, http://hostalmariaesther.free.fr/. Very comfortable, helpful, includes breakfast, garden.

D-E Hostal Pakcha Real, Tandapata 300, San Blas, T237484, www.hostalpakchareal.com. Family run, hot water, relaxed, cheaper without bath. Breakfast, cooking and laundry facilities extra. Airport/train/bus pick-up, but call ahead if arriving late.

E pp **Casa de La Gringa 1**, Tandapata y Pasñapacana 148, San Blas, T241168, www.casa delagringa.com. Individually decorated rooms, hot water, cable TV, kitchen, Wi-Fi, relaxed atmsophere. Also **E** pp **Casa de la Gringa 2**, Carmen Bajo 226, San Blas, T254387. Rooms with and without bath, with breakfast, internet. See also **Another Planet** (Tour operators), below.

E El Balcón Colonial, Choquechaca 350, T238129, balconcolonial@hotmail.com. Accommodation for 11 people in 6 rooms, hot showers, breakfast, kitchen and laundry facilities all extra, comfortable, safe, generous hosts.

E Hostal Familiar, Saphi 661, T239353. **E** without bath, hot water, good beds, popular.

E Hostal Rickch'airy, Tambo de Montero 219, T236606. **G** with shared bath, hot water in the morning, laundry service, free luggage store, breakfast available, nice garden with good views, will collect guests from train station, tourist information, mixed reports.

E Hostal Qorichaska, Nueva Alta 458, some distance from centre, T228974, www.qoricha skaperu.com. Hot water, includes breakfast, use of kitchen, will store luggage, safe, great value.

E Hostal Resbalosa, Resbalosa 494, T224839, www.hostalresbalosa.com. Cheaper without bath, hot water in the mornings and evenings, ask for a room with a view, luggage stored, laundry facilities, full breakfast for US$1.45.

E Suecia II, Tecseccocha 465, T239757. **G** without bath, good security, breakfast US$1.40 from 0500, beautiful building, good meeting place, water not always hot or bathrooms clean, best to book in advance (if full, they'll find alternative accommodation, which may not be as good).

E-F Andes de San Blas, Carmen Alto 227, T242346, www.andesdesanblas.com. Family run, excellent location with good views from rooftop terrace and some rooms. Basic breakfast included, internet access, can arrange budget tours. Generally good.

F Albergue Casa Campesina, Av Tullumayo 274, T233466, www.cbc.org.pe/casacampesina. Includes breakfast, shared bath, lovely place, funds support the Casa Campesina organization (www.cbc.org.pe/casacamp/), which is linked to local campesina communities (see also

Store of the Weavers under Shopping, below). 23% discount for SAE members.

F Estrellita, Av Tullumayo 445, parte Alta, T234134. Includes breakfast, basic kitchen for guests, most rooms with shared bath, 2 with private bath, basic but excellent value, safe parking available for bikes.

F Hostal Familiar Carmen Alto, Carmen Alto 197, T224367, 1st on the right down steps (there is no sign), 3 blocks from central plaza, carmencitadelperu@hotmail.com. If there's no answer at the bell, go to the shop next door. Tranquil and full of character, family run, use of kitchen and washing machine, breakfast US$2, shared bath.

F Hostal Luzerna, Av Baja 205, near San Pedro train station (take a taxi at night), T232762. Hot water, safe to leave luggage, good beds, nice family, with breakfast, use of kitchen.

F pp **Pariwana**, Mesón de la Estrella 136, T233751, www.pariwana-hostel.com. Also doubles (**C-D**, cheaper without bath), in a converted colonial mansion, restaurant, bar/lounge, with breakfast, kitchen, internet and Wi-Fi, lockers, English spoken, lots of activities.

F pp **The Blue House**, Kiskapata 291 (parallel and above Tandapata), T242407, www.aschisite02.activesbs.co.uk. Cosy hostal, good value. Reductions for longer stays, includes breakfast, DVDs, shared kitchen, great views.

F pp **The Point**, Mesón de la Estrella 172, T252266, www.thepointhostels.com. Dormitory accommodation, also has doubles **E**, includes breakfast, free internet, hot showers, good party atmosphere.

G Hospedaje El Artesano de San Blas, Suytucato 790, San Blas, T263968, manosandinas@yahoo.com. Many bright and airy rooms, taxis leave you at Plaza San Blas, then it's a steep walk uphill for 5-10 mins.

G pp **Hospedaje Inka**, Suytuccato 848, T231995. Also steep walk up from Plaza San Blas, or phone the hostal. Includes breakfast, wonderful views, spacious rooms, kitchen, internet, Wi-Fi, owner Américo is very helpful.

G Hospedaje Familiar Inti Quilla, Atocsaycuchi 281, T252659. Shared rooms around a pleasant little courtyard, hot water 24 hrs, no breakfast or kitchen.

Youth hostels

D-E Maison de la Jeunesse (affiliated to HI), Av Sol, Cuadra 5, Pasaje Grace, Edif San Jorge (down a small side street opposite Qoricancha) T235617, hostellingcusco@hotmail.com/maisondelajeunesse@hotmail.com. French/Peruvian run, dormitories and private rooms, TV and video room, cooking facilities and very hot water, includes breakfast.

E-F El Procurador del Cusco, Coricalle 440, Prolongación Procuradores, T243559, http://hostelprocuradordelcusco.blogspot.com. Price includes use of the basic kitchen (no fridge) and laundry area, basic rooms, but upstairs is better, helpful, good value. Recommended.

F Albergue Municipal, Quiscapata 240, San Cristóbal, T252506, albergue@municusco.gob.pe. Dormitories and double rooms, helpful staff, luggage store, great views, bar, cafeteria, laundry, safe deposit, discount for members.

Eating

Cuzco *p1419, maps p1422 and p1427*

There are many good cheap restaurants on Procuradores, Plateros and Tecseccocha.

TTT Bistrot 370, Triunfo 370, p 2. 'Fusion' cuisine, menu with Peruvian and Oriental touches, smart and highly regarded, good bar and wine list, cosy seating areas.

TTT Chicha, Plaza Regocijo 261, p 2 (above El Truco), T240520, daily 1200-2400. Opened by restaurateur Gastón Acurio (see under Lima, Eating), Peruvian cuisine of the highest standards in a renovated colonial house, at one time the royal mint, tastefully decorated, open-to-view kitchen, bar, good service.

TTT Cicciolina, Triunfo 393, 2nd floor, T239510, www.cicciolinacuzco.com. Sophisticated cooking focusing largely on Italian/Mediterranean cuisine, impressive wine list. Good atmosphere, great for a special occasion.

TTT Fallen Angel, Plazoleta Nazarenas 320, T258 184, www.fallenangelincusco.com. International and Novo Andino gourmet cuisine, great steaks, genuinely innovative interior design, worth checking out their events. Sun from 1500. Also has **'The' Small Luxury Guest House** (**A**) at No 221.

TTT Incanto, Santa Catalina Angosta 135, T254753. Under same ownership as Inka Grill and with the same standards, restaurant has Inca stone work and serves Italian dishes (pastas, grilled meats, pizzas), and desserts, accompanied by an extensive wine list. Open daily 1100-2400. Also Peruvian delicatessen. Upstairs is **Greens Organic** with exclusively organic, but not wholly vegetarian, ingredients in fusion cuisine and a fresh daily buffet, very good.

TTT Inka Grill, Portal de Panes 115, Plaza de Armas, T262992. According to many the best food in town, specializing in Novo Andino cuisine (the use of native ingredients and 'rescued' recipes), also homemade pastas, wide vegetarian selection, live music, excellent coffee and homemade pastries 'to go'.

TTT Limo, Portal de Carnes 236. On 2nd floor of a colonial mansion overlooking the Plaza de Armas, Peruvian cuisine with strong emphasis on fish and seafood, pisco bar, good service and atmosphere.

TTT MAP Café, in Museo de Arte Precolombino, Plaza de las Nazarenas 231. Café by day (1000-1830), from 1830 to 2200 serves superb international and Peruvian-Andean cuisine, innovative children's menu, minimalist design and top-class service.

TTT Maikhana, Av El Sol 106 (2 p), T252044, www.maikhana.net. Authentic Indian restaurant, serving curry, unlimited rice and lassies. Free internet and phone.

TTT Pachacútec Grill and Bar, Portal de Panes 105, Plaza de Armas, www.pachacutec restaurant.com. International cuisine, seafood and Italian specialities, folk music nightly.

TTT La Retama, Portal de Panes 123, 2nd floor. Good food (also Novo Andino) and service, live music and dance, art exhibitions.

TTT El Truco, Plaza Regocijo 261. Excellent local and international dishes, buffet lunch 1200-1500, nightly folk music at 2045, next door is **Taberna del Truco**, open 0900-0100.

TTT Fusiones Restaurant–Bar, Av El Sol 106, T233341. In the new commercial centre La Merced, 2nd floor, very close to Plaza de Armas. Novo Andino and international cuisine, fine wines. Accepts credit cards. Open 1100-2300.

TTT Tunupa, Portal Confiturias 233, p 2, Plaza de Armas. Large restaurant, small balcony overlooking Plaza, international, Peruvian and Novo Andino cuisine, good buffet US$15, nicely decorated, cocktail lounge, live music and dance at 2030.

TTT Tupananchis, Portal Mantas 180, T245159. Tasty Novo Andino and Fusion cuisine in a sophisticated atmosphere. Recommended.

TTT-TT La Cosa Nostra, Plateros 358A, p 2, T232992, open 1200-2300. Sicilian/Peruvian owned Italian place with good food and service, à la carte, wine list, unpretentious and intimate.

TT A Mi Manera (Culturas Peru), Triunfo 393, T222 219, www.culturasperu.com. Imaginative Novoandina cuisine with open kitchen. Great hospitality and atmosphere.

TT Al Grano, Santa Catalina Ancha 398, T228032. Authentic Asian dishes, menu changes daily, excellent food, best coffee in town, vegetarian choices, open 1000-2100, closed on Sun.

TT Baco, Ruinas 465, T242808. Wine bar and bistro-style restaurant, same owner as *Cicciolina*. Specializes in BBQ and grilled meats, also veggie dishes, pizzas and good wines. Unpretentious and comfy, groups welcome.

TT Inkanato, San Agustín 280, T222926. Good food, staff dressed in Inca outfits and dishes made only with ingredients known in Inca times, calls itself a "living museum".

TT Jack's Café, Choquechaca y San Blas. Excellent varied menu, generous portions, relaxed atmosphere, can get very busy at lunchtime, expect a queue in high season.

TT Kusikuy, Suecia 339, T292870. Open 0800-2300 Mon-Sat, local, national and international dishes, good service, set lunch unbeatable value at only US$2.

TT La Bodega, Carmen Alto 146, San Blas. Snug Dutch and Peruvian-owned café/restaurant, good food, salads, drinks.

TT Los Toldos, Almagro 171 and San Andrés 219. Grilled chicken, fries and salad bar, also *trattoria* with homemade pasta and pizza, delivery T229829.

TT Macondo, Cuesta San Blas 571, T229415. Interesting restaurant with an imaginative menu, good food, well-furnished, gay friendly.

TT Pachapapa, Plazoleta San Blas 120, opposite church of San Blas, T241318. A beautiful patio restaurant in a colonial house, good Cusqueña and other dishes, at night diners can sit in their own, private colonial dining room, attentive staff. Recommended.

ǂǂ **Pucará**, Plateros 309. Mon-Sat 1230-2200. Peruvian and international food (no language skills required as a sample plate of their daily menu is placed in the window at lunchtime), nice atmosphere.

ǂǂ **The Real McCoy**, Plateros 326, 2nd floor, T261111, www.bookingbox.org.uk/realmccoy/. A retreat for homesick Brits and Aussies, the full English and good value breakfast buffet, English classics for dinner, puddings too. Wi-Fi, comfy sofas and well stocked book exchange.

ǂǂ **Varayoc**, Espaderos 142, T232404. Swiss restaurant, including Peruvian ingredients (cheese fondue US$10-13); also has a variety of pastas, good desserts, literary atmosphere.

ǂǂ **Witches Garden**, Loreto 125, T244077, www.witchesgarden.net. Good Novo Andino and international food and desserts, warmly decorated, videos for patrons to choose.

ǂǂ-ǂ **Yanapay**, Ruinas 415, p 2. Good café serving breakfast, lunch and dinner. Run by a charity which supports children's homes (www.aldeayanapay.org).

ǂ **Bembos**, Portal Comercio 153, Plaza de Armas. Cuzco branch of the successful chain of Peruvian-style burger restaurants. Coffee shop and internet on the second floor.

ǂ **Café Cultural Ritual**, Choquechaca 140. Good value and tasty vegetarian food, including some good Indian dishes, US$ 2.20.

ǂ **El Encuentro**, Santa Catalina Ancha 384, Choquechaca 136 and Tigre 130. One of the best value eateries in Cuzco, 3 courses of good healthy vegan food and a drink for US$1.35, very busy at lunchtime.

ǂ **Inka...fe**, Choquechaca 131-A. Great food and value in a nice setting, English spoken.

ǂ **Víctor Victoria**, Tecseccocha 466, T252854. Israeli and local dishes, first-class breakfasts, good value.

Cafés

Amaru, Plateros 325, 2nd floor. Limitless coffee and tea, great bread and juices, even on ´non-buffet´ breakfasts (US$1.15 for simple), colonial balcony. Also has bar.

Café El Ayllu, Almagro 133,T232357, and Marqués 263, T255078. Classical/folk music, good atmosphere, superb range of milk products, wonderful apple pastries, good selection for breakfast, great juices, quick service. (Rumours abound that El Ayllu is to become a Starbucks franchise, but this hasn't happened yet.)

Café Halliy, Plateros 363. Popular meeting place, especially for breakfast, good for comments on guides, has good snacks and 'copa Halliy' (fruit, muesli, yoghurt, honey and chocolate cake), also good vegetarian *menú* and set lunch.

Café Manu, Av Pardo 1046. Good coffee and good food too.

Café Punchay, Choquechaca 229. German-owned café with speciality coffees, cocktails, pastas, sandwiches, cakes, garden and big screen for live sports broadcasts.

Chocolate, Choquechaca 162. Good for coffee and cakes, but don't miss the gourmet chocolates.

Granja Heidi, Cuesta San Blas 525. Delicious yoghurt, granola, ricotta cheese and honey and other great breakfast options, vegetarian dishes.

Dolce Vita, Santa Catalina Ancha 366. Delicious Italian ice cream, open 1000-2100.

Juanito's Sandwich Café, Qanchipata 596 esq Carmen Alto. Great grilled veggie and meaty burgers and sandwiches, coffee, tea and hot chocolate. Juanito himself is a great character and the café stays open late.

Moni, San Agustín 311, T231029. Peruvian/English-owned, good fresh food and breakfast, British music, magazines, bright and comfortable.

The Muse, Plateros 316. Fresh coffee, locally grown in Quillabamba, good food, including vegetarian, often live music in the afternoons/evenings. English owner Clair is helpful when she is in town.

Trotamundos, Portal Comercio 177, 2nd floor. Balcony overlooking the plaza, nice atmosphere, especially at night with open fire, good coffees and cakes, safe salads, internet service, open Mon-Sat 0800-2400.

Yaku Mama, Procuradores 397. Good for breakfast, unlimited fruit and coffee.

Panaderías

Panadería El Buen Pastor, Cuesta San Blas 579. Very good bread, *empanadas* and pastries, proceeds go to a charity for orphans and street children.

Bars and clubs

Cuzco *p1419, maps p1422 and p1427*

Bars

Bar 7, Tandapata 690, San Blas, T506472. Good food and drinks in a trendy bar which specializes in local ingredients.

Cross Keys Pub, Triunfo 350 (upstairs), www.cross-keys-pub-cusco-peru.com. Open 1100-0130, run by Barry Walker of **Manu Expeditions**, a Mancunian and ornithologist, new cosy location, darts, cable sports, pool, bar meals, plus daily half price specials Sun-Wed, great pisco sours, very popular, great atmosphere.

Indigo, Tecseccocha 2, p 2, T260271. Shows 3 films a day. Also has a lounge and cocktail bar and serves Asian and local food. A log fire keeps out the night-time cold.

Km 0 (Arte y Tapas), Tandapata 100, San Blas. Mediterranean themed bar tucked in behind San Blas, good snacks and tapas, with live music every night (around 2200 – lots of acoustic guitar etc).

Los Perros Bar, Tecseccocha 436. Open 1100-0100. Great place to chill out on comfy couches, excellent music, welcoming, good coffee, tasty meals available (including vegetarian), book exchange, English and other magazines, board games. Opened a take-away only branch in 2009 at Suecia 368, open 2400 midnight to 0600 for good quality, post-club food.

Marcelo Batata, Palacio 121, p 3, T222424, www.cuzcodining.com. Bar/restaurant offering sandwiches and international food, slow service but worth going to sit on the rooftop for the great 360° panorama and enjoy the Cuzco sunshine.

Norton Rat's Tavern, Santa Catalina Angosta 116, www.nortonrats.com. New location on the corner of the Plaza de Armas, fine balcony, open 0700-0230, also serves meals, cable TV, popular, English spoken, pool, darts, motorcycle theme with information for motorcyclists from owner, Jeffrey Powers.

Rosie O'Grady's, Santa Catalina Ancha 360, T247935. Good music, tasty food, English and Russian spoken, good value, open 1100 till late (food served till 2400).

Paddy Flaherty's, Triunfo 124 on the corner of the plaza. Irish theme pub, deservedly popular, open 1300-0100, good grub.

Clubs

El Garabato Video Music Club, Espaderos 132, p 3. Open daily 1600-0300, dance area, lounge for chilling, bar, live shows 2300-0030 (all sorts of styles) and large screen showing music videos.

Extreme, Suecia, next to Magtas's. Movies in the late afternoon and early evening, but after midnight this place really gets going with an eclectic range of music, from 60's and 70's rock and pop to techno and trance.

Kamikaze, Plaza Regocijo 274, T233865. *Peña* at 2200, good old traditional rock music, candle-lit cavern atmosphere, entry US$2.50.

Mama Africa, Portal de Panes 190. Cool music and clubber's spot, good food with varied menu, happy hour till 2300, good value.

Mythology, Portal de Carnes 298, p 2. Mostly an early 80's and 90's combination of cheese, punk and classic, popular. Food in served in the jungle-themed **Lek Café**. They also show movies in the afternoons.

Roots, Huaynapata 194 (just off Suecia). Plays mostly reggae, but there are other styles too, good atmosphere and popular.

Siete Angelitos, Siete Angelitos 638. Tiny club, just a couple of rooms, but spectacular cocktails, a friendly owner by the name of Walter and an awesome atmosphere when things get going. **Ukuku's**, Plateros 316. US$1.35 entry, very popular, good atmosphere, good mix of music including live shows nightly.

Entertainment

Cuzco *p1419, maps p1422 and p1427*

Folklore Regular nightly folklore show at **Centro Qosqo de Arte Nativo**, Av Sol 604, T227901. Show from 1900 to 2030, entrance on BTC ticket. **Teatro Inti Raymi**, Saphi 605, nightly at 1845, US$4.50, well worth it. **Teatro Kusikay**, Unión 117, T255414, www.kusikay.com (tickets from the theatre Mon-Sat 0900-2100 or, out of hours, **Inka Grill** or **Incanto** restaurants, or at the **Mayu Café** at Ollantaytambo train station). Mon-Sat 1930, US$35, thriliing show with spectacular dances based on the Mamacha Carmen festival of Paucartambo, with lavish costumes, special effects and a troupe of 30. **Teatro Municipal**, C Mesón de la Estrella 149 (T227321 for information 0900-1300 and 1500-1900). Plays, dancing and shows, mostly Thu-Sun. They also run classes in music and dancing from Jan to Mar which are great value.

Festivals and events

Cuzco *p1419, maps p1422 and p1427*

Carnival in Cuzco is a messy affair with flour, water, cacti, bad fruit and animal manure being thrown about in the streets. **Easter Monday**: procession of **El Señor de los Temblores** (Lord of the Earthquakes), starting at 1600 outside the Cathedral. A large crucifix is paraded through the streets, returning to the Plaza de Armas around 2000 to bless the tens of thousands of people who have assembled there. **2-3 May**: **Vigil of the Cross** takes place at all mountaintops with crosses on them, a boisterous affair. **Jun**: **Q'Olloriti**, the Snow Star Festival, is held at a 4,700 m glacier north of Ocongate (Ausangate) 150 km southeast of Cuzco. Several agencies offer tours. (The date is moveable.) On **Corpus Christi** day, the Thu after Trinity Sunday, all the statues of the Virgin and of saints from Cuzco's churches are paraded through the streets to the Cathedral. The Plaza de Armas is surrounded by tables with women selling *cuy* (guinea pig) and a mixed grill called *chiriuchu* (*cuy*, chicken, *tortillas*, fish eggs, water-weeds, maize, cheese and sausage) and lots of Cusqueña beer. **24 Jun**: the pageant of **Inti Raymi**, the Inca festival of the winter solstice, is enacted in Quechua at 1000 at the Qoricancha, moving on to Sacsayhuaman at 1300. Tickets for the stands can be bought a week in advance from the Emufec office, Santa Catalina Ancha 325, US$80, less if bought Mar-May. Travel agents can arrange the whole day for you, with meeting points, transport, reserved seats and packed lunch. Those who try to persuade you to buy a ticket for the right to film or take photos are being dishonest. On the night before Inti Raymi, the Plaza de Armas is crowded with processions and food stalls. Try to arrive in Cuzco 15 days before Inti Raymi. **28 Jul**: Peruvian Independence Day. Prices shoot up during these celebrations. **Aug**: on the last Sun is the **Huarachicoy** festival at Sacsayhuaman, a spectacular re-enactment of the Inca manhood rite, performed in dazzling costumes by boys of a local school. **8 Sep**: **Day of the Virgin** is a colourful procession of masked dancers from the church of Almudena, at the southwest edge of Cuzco, near Belén, to the Plaza de San Francisco. There is also a splendid fair at Almudena, and a free bull fight on the following day. **1 Nov**: **All Saints Day**, celebrated everywhere with bread dolls and traditional cooking. **8 Dec**: Cuzco day, when churches and museums close at 1200. **24 Dec**: **Santuranticuy**, 'the buying of saints', with a big crafts market in the plaza, very noisy until early hours of the 25th.

Shopping

Cuzco *p1419, maps p1422 and p1427*

Arts and crafts

In the Plaza San Blas and the surrounding area, authentic Cuzco crafts still survive. A market is held on Sat. Many leading artisans welcome visitors. Among fine objects made are Biblical figures from plaster, wheatflour and potatoes, reproductions of pre-Columbian ceramics and colonial sculptures, pious paintings, earthenware figurines, festive dolls and wood carvings.

Cuzco is the weaving centre of Peru and excellent textiles can be found at good value. Be very careful of buying gold and silver objects and jewellery in and around Cuzco.

Agua y Tierra, Plazoleta Nazarenas 167, and also at Cuesta San Blas 595, T226951. Excellent quality crafts from rainforest communities.
Apacheta, San Juan de Dios 250, T238210, www.apachetaperu.com. Replicas of Pre-Inca and Inca textiles, ceramics, alpaca goods, contemporary art gallery, books on Andean culture.
Inkantations, Choquechaca 200. Radical baskets made from natural materials in all sorts of weird and wonderful shapes. Also ceramics and Andean weavings. Interesting and original.
La Mamita, Portal de Carnes 244, Plaza de Armas, sells the ceramics of Pablo Seminario (see under Urubamba, page 1447), plus cotton, basketry, jewellery, etc.
Mercado Artesanal, Av Sol, block 4, is good for cheap crafts.
Pedazo de Arte, Plateros 334B. A tasteful collection of Andean handicrafts, many designed by Japanese owner Miki Suzuki.
La Pérez, Urb Mateo Pumacahua 598, Huanchac, T232186. A big co-operative with a good selection; they will arrange a free pick-up from your hotel.

Bookshops

Centro de Estudios Regionales Andinos Bartolomé de las Casas, Av Tullumayo 465, T233472, www.cbc.org.pe. Good books on Peruvian history, archaeology, etc, Mon-Sat 1100-1400, 1600-1900.
Jerusalem, Heladeros 143, T235408. English books, guidebooks, music, postcards, book exchange (3 for 1).
Special Book Services, Av El Sol 781-A, T248106.
Book exchange, 1 for 1, at **The Sun**, Plazoleta Limacpampa Chico 471, café/restaurant, run by an Aussie.

Camping equipment

For renting equipment, there are several places around the Plaza area. Check the equipment carefully as it is common for parts to be missing. A deposit of US$100 is asked, plus credit card, passport or plane ticket. White gas (*bencina*), US$1.50 per litre, can be bought at hardware stores, but check the purity. Stove spirit (*alcoól para quemar*) is available at pharmacies; blue gas canisters, costing US$5, can be found at hardware stores and camping shops. You can also rent equipment through travel agencies.
Edson Zuñiga Huillca, Mercado Rosaspata, Jr Abel Landeo P-1, T802831, 993 7243 (mob). 3 mins from Plaza de Armas, for repair of camping equipment and footwear, also equipment rental, open 24 hrs a day, 7 days a week, English and Italian spoken.
Tatoo, C del Medio 130, T254211, www.tatoo.ws. High-quality hiking, climbing and camping gear, not cheap, but western brand names and their own lines.

Fabrics and alpaca clothing

Alpaca 3, Ruinas 472 (English spoken). For quality items.
Arte Vivo del Cusco al Mundo, beside Capilla San Ignacio, Plaza de Armas. Open 1030-1300, 1530-2100. Outlet for 2 weaving co-ops.
The Center for Traditional Textiles of Cuzco, Av Sol 603, T228117, www.textilescusco.org. A non-profit organization that seeks to promote, refine and rediscover the weaving traditions of the Cuzco area. Tours of workshops, weaving classes, you can watch weavers at work. Over 50% of the price goes direct to the weaver. Recommended.
Hilo, Carmen Alto 260, T254536. Fashionable items designed individually and hand made on-site. Run by Eibhlin Cassidy, she can adjust and tailor designs.
Josefina Olivera, Portal Comercio 173, Plaza de Armas. Sells old textiles and weavings, expensive but worth it to save pieces being cut up to make other items, open daily 1100-2100.
Kuna by Alpaca 111, Plaza Regocijo 202, T243233, www.kuna.com.pe. High quality alpaca clothing with outlets also in hotels *El Monasterio, Libertador* and *Machu Picchu Sanctuary Lodge*.
Store of Weavers (Asociación Central de Artesanos y Artesanas del Sur Andino Inkakunaq Ruwaynin), Av Tullumayo 274, T233466, www.cbc.org.pe/tejidosandinos. Store run by 6 local weaving communities, some of whose residents you can see working on site. All profits go to the weavers themselves.

Food and natural products

Casa Ecológica Cusco, Triunfo 393 and Portal de Carnes 236, interior 2, Plaza de Armas. Organic foods, wild honey, coffee, granola. Casa Ecológica also offers natural medicines, indigenous art and weavings.

La Cholita, Portal Espinar 142-B and at airport. Special chocolates made with local ingredients.
The Coca Shop, Carmen Alto 115, San Blas, T260774, www.thecocashop.com. Tiny shop selling an interesting selection of sweets and chocolates made using coca leaf flour. There is also plenty of information about the nutritional values of coca leaves.
Tik'a, www.tikasoapperu.com. Eco-friendly soaps, oils and beauty products made from local ingredients by Fiona Cameron and Carmen Pedraza.

Jewellery

Calas, Siete Angelitos 619-B, San Blas. Hand-made silver jewellery in interesting designs and alpaca goods from the community of Pitumarca.
Carlos Chaquiras, Triunfo 375 y Portal Comercio, T227470, www.carloschaquiras.com. Very upmarket, with lots of Inca figures, among other designs.
Ilaria, Portal Carrizos 258, T246253. Branches in hotels *Monasterio, Libertador* and at the airport. For recommended jewellery and silver.
Mullu, Triunfo 120, T229831. Contemporary silver jewellery with semi-precious stones and cotton clothing with interesting designs, open Mon-Sat 1000-2100.
Spondylus, Cuesta San Blas 505 and Plazoleta San Blas 617, T226929. A good selection of interesting gold and silver jewellery and fashion tops with Inca and pre-Inca designs.
Typical Peru Gifts, Av El Sol 106, Módulo 101 B, Galerías La Merced, T330491. Handmade silver jewellery with natural stones.

Music

Taki Museo de Música de los Andes, Hatunrumiyoq 487-5. Shop and workshop selling and displaying musical instruments, owner is an ethno- musicologist. Recommended for anyone interested in Andean music.

Markets

Wanchac, Av Garcilaso (southeast of centre) and **San Pedro Market**, opposite Estación San Pedro, sell a variety of goods.

Activities and tours

Cuzco *p1419, maps p1422 and p1427*

For a list of recommended Tour operators for Manu, see page 1506.

There are many travel agencies in Cuzco. The sheer number and variety of tours on offer is bewildering and prices for the same tour can vary dramatically. Always remember that you get what you pay for and that, in a crowded market, organization can sometimes be a weak point. In general you should only deal directly with the agencies themselves. You can do this when in town, or you can raise whatever questions you may have in advance (or even in Cuzco), and get replies in writing, by email. Other sources of advice are visitors returning from trips, who can give the latest information, and the trip reports for members of the South America Explorers. Students will normally receive a discount on production of an ISIC card. Do not deal with guides who claim to be employed by agencies listed below without verifying their credentials. City tours cost about US$7 for 4 hrs; check what sites are included and that the guide is experienced.

Only a restricted number of agencies are licensed to operate **Inca Trail** trips. INRENA, Av José Gabriel Cosio 308, Urb Magisterial, 1 etapa, T229297, verifies operating permits (see Visitors' tickets, above, for INC office). Unlicensed agen cies will sell Inca Trail trips, but pass clients on to the operating agency. This can cause confusion and booking problems at busy times. There is a quota for agencies and groups to use the Trail, but modifications to the procedures encouraged some agencies to make block bookings way in advance of departure dates. This made it much harder for agencies to guarantee their clients places on the Trail. Current advice is to book your preferred dates as early as possible, between 2 months and a year in advance, depending on the season when you want to go, then confirm nearer the time. There have been many instances of disappointed trekkers whose bookings did not materialize. Don't wait to the last minute and check your operator's cancellation fees. **Note** See page 1459, under Inca Trails, for regulations governing the Trail.

Inca Trail and general tours

Amazing Peru, Calle Yepez Miranda C-6, Magisterio (9 Alma Rd, Manchester M19 2FG, T0808 2346805), www.amazingperu.com. Highly recommended, professional and well-organized, "perfect tour", knowledgeable guides.

Andean Treks, Av Pardo 705, T225701, www.andeantreks.com. Manager Tom Hendrickson uses high-quality equipment and satellite phones. This company organizes itineraries, from 2 to 15 days with a wide variety of activities in this area and further afield.

Andina Travel, Plazoleta Santa Catalina 219, T251892, www.andinatravel.com. Specializes in trekking and biking, notably the Lares Valley, working with traditional weaving communities. Recommended.

Big Foot, Triunfo 392 (oficina 213), T238568, 984-913851, www.bigfootcusco.com. Tailor-made hiking trips, especially in the remote corners of the Vilcabamba and Vilcanota mountains; also the Inca Trail.

Chaska, Garcilaso 265 p 2, no 6, T240424, www.chaskatours.com. Dutch-Peruvian company offering cultural, adventure, nature and esoteric tours. They specialize in the Inca Trail, but also llama treks to Lares, treks to Choquequirao.

Culturas Peru, Tandapata 354A, T243629, www.culturasperu.com. Swiss-Peruvian company offering adventure, cultural, ecological and spiritual tours. Also specialize in alternative Inca trails.

Destinos Turísticos, Portal de Panes 123, oficina 101-102, Plaza de Armas, T228168, www.destinosturisticosperu.com. The owner speaks Spanish, English, Dutch and Portuguese and specializes in package tours from economic to 5-star budgets. Advice on booking jungle trips and renting mountain bikes. Very helpful.

EcotrailPeru, Av El Sol 106, # 205, 2 p, T233357, www.ecotrailperu.com. Operates treks, tours and adventure trips throughout Peru for all fitness levels. Committed to sustainable travel.

Enigma, Jirón Clorinda Matto de Turner 100, Magisterio 1a Etapa, T222155, www.enigmaperu.com. Run by Spaniard Silvia Rico Coll. Well-organized, innovative trekking expeditions including a luxury service, Inca Trail and a variety of challenging alternatives. Also

cultural tours to weaving communities, Ayahuasca Therapy, climbing and biking itineraries on demand.
Explorandes, Av Garcilaso 316-A (not to be confused with C Garcilaso in the centre), T238380, www.explorandes.com. Experienced high-end adventure company. Arrange a wide variety of mountain treks; trips available in Peru and Ecuador, book through website also arranges tours across Peru for lovers of orchids, ceramics or textiles. Award-winning environmental practices.
Fertur, Procuradores 341, p 1 int F, T221304, www.fertur-travel.com. Mon-Fri 0900-1900, Sat 0900-1200. Cuzco branch of the Lima tour operator, see page1290.
Gatur Cusco, Puluchapata 140 (a small street off Av Sol 3rd block), T223496, www.gaturcusco.com. Esoteric, ecotourism, and general tours. Owner Dr José (Pepe) Altamirano is knowledgeable in Andean folk traditions. Excellent conventional tours, bilingual guides and transportation. Guides speak English, French, Spanish and German. They can also book internal flights.
Gravity Peru, C Santa Catalina Ancha 398, T228032, www.gravityperu.com. From the same team that pioneered MTB in Bolivia.
Hiking Peru, Portal de Panes 109, office 6, T247942, 984 651414, www.hikingperu .com. 8-day treks to Espíritu Pampa; 7 days/6 nights around Ausangate; 4-day/3-night Lares Valley Trek.
Inca Explorers, Ruinas 427, T241070, www.inca explorers.com. Specialist trekking agency for small group expeditions in socially and environmentally responsible manner. Also 2-week hike in the Cordillera Vilcanota (passing Nevado Ausangate), and Choquequirao to Espíritu Pampa.
InkaNatura Travel, Ricardo Palma J1, T255255, www.inkanatura.com. Offers tours with special emphasis on sustainable tourism and conservation. Knowledgeable guides.
Liz's Explorer, Medio 114B, T246619, www.lizexplorer.com. 4-day/ 3-night Inca Trail trek (minimum group size 10, maximum 16), other lengths of trips available. Reports of good trips but haphazard organization.
Llama Path, San Juan de Dios 250, T240822, www.llamapath.com. A wide variety of local tours, specializing in Inca Trail and alternative treks, involved in environmental campaigns and porter welfare. Many good reports.
Machete Tours, Nueva Alta 432, Int B, T224829, T984 631662, www.machetetours.com. Many innovative trekking trips: eg 9-day traverse of the Cordillera Vilcabamba, expeditions to Espíritu Pampa, Ausangate and the Inca Trail. Also have rainforest lodge on Río Blanco, south of the Manu Biosphere Reserve. Not all guides speak English.
Manu Expeditions, C Clorinda Matto de Turner 330, Urb Magisterial Primero Etapa, T225990, www.manuexpeditions.com. Natural history and birding tours, Machu Picchu and horse riding.
Peru Planet, Suecia 318, T251145, www.peru-planet.net. Peruvian/Belgian owned agency offering tours of Inca Trail, other treks around Cuzco and packages within Peru, also Bolivia and Patagonia.
Peru Treks and Adventure, Avenida Pardo 540, T222722, www.perutreks.com. Trekking agency set up by Englishman Mike Weston and his wife Koqui González. They pride themselves on good treatment of porters and support staff and have been consistently recommended for professionalism and customer care, a portion

of profits go to community projects. Treks offered include Salkantay, the Lares Valley and Vilcabamba Vieja. Mike also runs the **Andean Travel Web**, www.andeantravelweb.com.
Q'ente, Choquechaca 229, p 2, T222535, www.qente.com. Their Inca Trail service is recommended. Also private treks to Salkantay, Ausangate, Choquequirao, Vilcabamba and Q'eros. Horse riding to local ruins costs US$35 for 4-5 hrs. Very good, especially with children.
Sky Travel, Santa Catalina Ancha 366, interior 3-C (down alleyway next to Rosie O'Grady's pub), T261818, www.skyperu.com. English spoken. General tours around city and Sacred Valley. Inca Trail with good-sized double tents and a dinner tent (the group is asked what it would like on the menu 2 days before departure). Other trips include Vilcabamba and Ausangate (trekking).
SAS Travel, Portal de Panes 143, T237292, www.sas travel.com. Discount for students. Inca Trail includes the bus down from Machu Picchu to Aguas Calientes and lunch on the last day. SAS have their own hostel in Aguas Calientes. Offer alternatives to the classic Inca Trail, including Salkantay and Santa Teresa. Also mountain bike, horse riding and jungle tours. All guides speak some English. They can book internal flights at cheaper rates than from overseas. Recent reports increasingly mixed.
Tambo Tours, 4405 Spring Cypress Rd, Suite 210, Spring, TX 77388, USA, T1-888-2-GO-PERU (246-7378), T001-281 528 9448, www.2GO PERU.com. Long established adventure and tour specialist with offices in Peru and the US. Customized trips to the Amazon and archaeological sites of Peru, Bolivia and Ecuador.
Trekperu, Av República de Chile B-15, Parque Industrial, Wanchac, T261501, www.trekperu.com. Experienced trek operator as well as other adventure sports and mountain biking. Offers 'culturally sensitive' tours. Cusco Biking Adventure includes support vehicle and good camping gear (but providing your own sleeping bag).
Tucan Travel, T241123, cuzco@tucantravel.com. Offer adventure tours and overland expeditions.
United Mice, Plateros 351y Triunfo 392, T221139, www.unitedmice.com. Inca Trail and alternative trail via Salkantay and Santa Teresa, including entrance to Machu Picchu. Good English-speaking guides; Salustio speaks Italian and Portuguese. Discount with student card, good food and equipment. City and Sacred Valley tours and treks to Choquequirao. Cheaper than most.
Wayki Trek, Av Pardo 510, T224092, www.waykitrek.net. Budget travel agency with a hostel attached, recommended for their Inca Trail service. Owner Leo knows the area very well. Treks to several almost unknown Inca sites and interesting variations on the 'classic' Inca Trail with visits to porters' communities. Also treks to Ausangate, Salkantay and Choquequirao.

Rafting, mountain biking and trekking

When looking for an operator please consider more than just the price of your tour. Competition between companies in Cuzco is intense and price wars can lead to compromises in safety. Consider the quality of safety equipment (lifejackets, etc) and the number and experience of rescue kayakers and support staff. On a large and potentially dangerous rivers like the Apurímac and Urubamba (where fatalities have occurred - most recently March 2010), this can make all the difference.
Amazonas Explorers, Av Collasuyo 910, Miravalle, PO Box 722, Cuzco, T252846, www.amazonas- explorer.com. Experts in rafting, hiking and biking; used by BBC. English owner Paul Cripps has great experience, but takes most bookings from overseas (in UK, T01874-658125). However, he may be able to arrange a trip for travellers in Cuzco. Rafting includes Río Apurímac and Río Tambopata including Lake Titicaca and Cuzco, with all transfers from Lima. Also 5-day/4-night Inca Trail, alternatives to the Inca Trail, Choquequirao to Machu Picchu, and an excellent variation of the Ausangate Circuit. Multiactivity and family trips are a speciality. All options are at the higher end of the market and are highly recommended.
Apumayo, Av Garcilaso 316, Wanchaq, T246018, www.apumayo.com. Mon-Sat 0900-1300, 1600-2000. Urubamba rafting (from 0800-1530 every day); 3- to 4-day Apurímac trips. Also mountain biking to Maras and Moray in Sacred Valley, or from Cuzco to the jungle town of Quillabamba. This company also offers tours for disabled people, including rafting.
Apus Perú, Cuichipunco 366, www.apus-peru.com. Conducts most business by internet, specializes in alternatives to the Inca Trail, strong commitment to sustainability, well-organized.

Camp Expeditions, Av Manco Capac 414, of 403, T431468, www.campexpedition.net. All sorts of adventure tours, but specialists in climbing, for which they are recommended as most reliable, and trekking.

Cusco Adventure Team, Santa Catalina Ancha 398 (under Al Grano), T228032, www.cuscoadventureteam.com. With the combined experience of **Amazonas Explorers** (see above) and **Gravity Peru**, CAT offer ½-3 day bike rides and rafting and canoe trips for small groups or individuals, state of the art equipment, adventurous, safe and environmentally-aware. Part of **Grupo Inca**, www.grupo-inca.com, and member of www.onepercentfortheplanet.org (1% of the price of each trip is donated to a local tree planting project).

Eric Adventures, Velasco Astete B-8-B, T234 764, www.ericadventures.com. Specialize in adventure activities, but not rafting. They clearly explain what equipment is included in their prices and what you will need to bring. Mountain biking to Maras and Moray; Inca Trail to Machu Picchu, rent motorcross bikes for US$45 (guide is extra). Prices are more expensive if you book by email. A popular company.

Medina Brothers, contact Christian or Alain Medina on T225163 or 965 3485/969 1670 (mob). Family-run rafting company with good equipment and plenty of experience. They usually focus on day rafting trips in the Sacred Valley, but services are tailored to the needs of the client.

Pachatusan Trek, Psje Esmeralda 160, Santiago, T231817, www.pachatusantrek.com. Offers a wide variety to treks, as alternatives to the Inca Trail, professional and caring staff.

River Explorers & Peru Treks Explorers, Garcilaso "Casa del Abuelo" 210, Of 128, T779619, 984-909249, www.riverexplorers.com. Offers mountain biking, trekking and rafting trips (on the Apurímac and Urubamba). Experienced and qualified guides and appear to present a good emphasis on safety and environmental awareness.

Terra Explorer Peru, T237352, www.terraexplorerperu.com. Offers a wide range of trips from high-end rafting in the Sacred Valley and expeditions to the Colca and Cotahuasi canyons, trekking the Inca Trail and others, mountain biking, kayaking (including on Lake Titicaca) and jungle trips. All guides are bilingual.

Cultural tours

Milla Tourism, Av Pardo 689 and Portal Comercio 195 on the plaza, T231710, www.millaturismo.com. Mon-Fri 0800-1300, 1500-1900, Sat 0800-1300. Mystical tours to Cuzco's Inca ceremonial sites such as Pumamarca and The Temple of the Moon. Guide speaks only basic English. They also arrange cultural and environmental lectures and courses. **Mystic Inca Trail**, Unidad Vecinal de Santiago, bloque 9, dpto 301, T221358, ivanndp@ terra.com.pe. Specialize in tours of sacred Inca sites and study of Andean spirituality. This takes 10 days but it is possible to have shorter 'experiences'.

Shamans and drug experiences

San Pedro and Ayahuasca have been used since before Inca times, mostly as a sacred healing experience. If you choose to experience these incredible healing/teaching plants, only do so under the guidance of a reputable

agency or shaman and always have a friend with you who is not partaking. If the medicine is not prepared correctly, it can be highly toxic and, in rare cases, severely dangerous. Never buy from someone who is not recommended, never buy off the streets and never try to prepare the plants yourself.
Another Planet, Triunfo 120, T984 602609 (mob), www.incaplanetcusco.com. Run by Lesley Myburgh, who operates all kinds of adventure tours and conventional tours in and around Cuzco, but specializes in jungle trips anywhere in Peru. Lesley is an expert in San Pedro cactus preparation and she arranges San Pedro journeys for healing at physical, emotional and spiritual levels in beautiful remote areas. The journeys are thoroughly organized and a safe, beautiful, unforgettable experience.
Eleana Molina, T975 1791 (mob), misticanativa@yahoo.com. For Ayahuasca ceremonies.

Paragliding and ballooning

Richard Pethigal, T984 937333. For a condor's-eye view of the Sacred Valley, from May-Sep Richard runs half-day tandem paraglider flights, very experienced, high-quality equipment. Magnificent scenery, soaring close to snow-capped mountains makes this an awesome experience. He is licensed and charges US$70, but if weather conditions are good, for US$120 he can fly you all the way back to Cuzco, touching down in the ruins of Sacsayhuaman above the city.
Globos de los Andes, Av de la Cultura 220, suite 36, T232352, www.globosperu.com. Hot-air ballooning in the Sacred Valley and expeditions with balloons and 4WD lasting several days.

Private guides

As most of the sights do not have any information or signs in English, a good guide can really improve your visit. Either arrange this before you set out or contract one at the sight you are visiting. A tip is expected at the end of the tour. Set prices: City tour US$15-20 per day; Urubamba/Sacred Valley US$25-30, Machu Picchu and other ruins US$40-50 per day. **South American Explorers** has a list and contact details for recommended local guides. See also www.leaplocal.org.

Transport

Cuzco *p1419, maps p1422 and p1427*

Air

The airport is at Quispiquilla, near the bus terminal, 1.6 km from centre, airport information T222611/ 601. **Note** Check in 2 hrs before flight. Reconfirm 48 hrs before your flight. Flights may be delayed or cancelled during the wet season, or may leave early if the weather is bad. To **Lima**, 55 mins, daily flights with **Taca**, **Star Perú**, **LAN** and **Peruvian Airlines**. To **Arequipa**, 30 mins daily with **LAN**. To **Puerto Maldonado**, 30 mins, with **LAN** and **Star Perú**. To/from **La Paz**, **Aero Sur** Thu and Sun. Taxi to and from the airport costs US$2 (US$4.50 by radio taxi). Colectivos cost US$0.30 from Plaza San Francisco or outside the airport car park. Many representatives of hotels and travel agencies operate at the airport, with transport to the hotel with which they are associated. Take your time to choose your hotel, at the price you can afford. There is a post office, ATMs, phone booths, restaurant and cafeteria.

Bus

Long distance Terminal on Av Vallejo Santoni, block 2 (Prolongación Pachacútec), colectivo from centre US$0.30, taxi US$1. Platform tax US$0.35. Buses to **Lima** (20-24 hrs) go via **Abancay**, 195 km, 5 hrs (longer in the rainy season), and **Nazca**, on the Panamerican Highway. This route is paved but floods in the wet season often damage large sections of the highway. If prone to travel sickness, be prepared on the road to Abancay, there are many, many curves, but the scenery is magnificent. At Abancay, the road forks, the other branch going to **Andahuaylas**, a further 138 km, 10-11 hrs from Cuzco, and **Ayacucho**, another 261 km, 20 hrs from Cuzco. On both routes at night, take a blanket or sleeping bag to ward off the cold. All buses leave daily from the Terminal Terrestre. **Molina**, who also have an office on Av Pachacútec, just past the railway station, have buses on both routes. They run 3 services a day to Lima via Abancay and Nazca, and one, at 1900, to Abancay and Andahuaylas. **Cruz del Sur**'s service to Lima via Abancay leaves at 0730 and 1400, while their more comfortable services depart at 1500 and 1600. **San Jerónimo** and **Los Chankas** have buses to Abancay, Andahuaylas and Ayacucho at 1830. **Turismo Ampay** and **Turismo Abancay** go 3 times a day to Abancay, and

Expreso Huamanga once. **Bredde** has 5 buses a day to Abancay. Fares: Abancay US$10, Andahuaylas US$14, Nazca up to US$46, Lima also US$46; also US$51-64 (*Cruz del Sur Cruzero* and *VIP* classes). In Cuzco you may be told that there are no buses in the day from Abancay to Andahuaylas; this is not so as **Señor de Huanca** does so. If you leave Cuzco before 0800, with luck you'll make the connection at 1300 – worth it for the scenery. **Ormeño** has a service from Cuzco to Lima via Arequipa which takes longer (22 hrs), but is a more comfortable journey.

To Lake Titicaca and Bolivia: To **Juliaca**, 344 km, 5-6 hrs, US$5-12. The road is fully paved, but after heavy rain buses may not run. To **Puno**, via Juliaca, US$5-12; direct, US$8.50 (*bus cama* US$10), 6 hrs. Tourist service with 5 stops, **First Class**, Av Sol 930, and **Inka Express**, Av La Paz C-32, Urb El Ovalo, Wanchac, T247887, www.inkaexpress.com, calling at Andahuaylillas church, Raqchi, La Raya, Sicuani and Pucará, US$30, lunch but not entrance tickets included. **Note** It is safest to travel by day on the Juliaca-Puno-Cuzco route.

To **Arequipa**, 521 km, US$21; **Cruz del Sur** use the direct paved route via Juliaca and have a *Cruzero* service at 2030, 10 hrs, US$32-39. Other buses join the new Juliaca-Arequipa road at Imata, 10-12 hrs (eg **Carhuamayo**, 3 a day).

To the **Sacred Valley**: To **Pisac**, 32 km, 1 hr, US$0.85, from C Puputi on the outskirts of the city, near the Clorindo Matto de Turner school and Av de la Cultura. Colectivos, minibuses and buses leave whenever they are full, between 0600 and 1600. Buses returning from Pisac are often full. The last one back leaves around 2000. An organized tour can be fixed up with a travel agent for US$5pp. Taxis charge about US$20 for the round trip. To Pisac, **Calca** (18 km beyond Pisac) and **Urubamba** a further 22 km, buses leave from Av Tullumayo 800 block, Wanchac, US$1. Combis and colectivos leave from 300 block of Av Grau, 1 block before crossing the bridge, for **Chinchero**, 23 km, 45 mins, US$0.60; and for **Urubamba** a further 25 km, 45 mins, US$0.45 (or US$1 Cuzco-Urubamba direct, US$1.15 for a seat in a colectivo taxi). To **Ollantaytambo** from Av Grau, 0745, 1945, US$2.85, or catch a bus to Urubamba. Direct taxi-colectivo service to Ollantaytambo from C Pavitos, leaves when full, US$3.50. Tours can be arranged to Chinchero, Urubamba and Ollantaytambo with a Cuzco travel agency. To Chinchero, US$6 pp; a taxi costs US$25 round-trip. Usually only day tours are organized for visits to the valley, US$20-25. Using public transport and staying overnight in Urubamba, Ollantaytambo or Pisac allows more time to see the ruins and markets.

Taxi

In Cuzco they are cheap and recommended when arriving by air, train or bus. They have fixed prices: in the centre US$0.60 (after 2200 US$0.90); to the suburbs US$0.85-1.55. In town it is safest to take taxis which are registered; these have a sticker with a number in the window and a chequerboard pattern on the sides. Taxis on call are reliable but more expensive, in the centre US$1.25: **Ocarina** T247080, **Aló Cuzco** T222222. Trips to **Sacsayhuaman** US$10; ruins of **Tambo Machay** US$15-20 (3-4 people); day trip US$40-70.

Recommended taxi drivers: **Manuel Calanche**, T227368, T984 695402 (mob), enthusiastic, attentive (Spanish only). **Carlos Hinojosa**, T251160. **Angel Marcavillaca Palomino**, Av Regional 877, T251822, amarcavillaca@yahoo.com. Helpful, patient, reasonable prices. **Movilidad Inmediata**, Juan Carlos Herrera Johnson, T984-623821 (mob), local tours with English-speaking guide. **Ferdinand Pinares Cuadros**, Yuracpunco 155, Tahuantinsuyo, T225914, T984 681519 (mob), English and French spoken, reasonable prices. **Angel Salazar**, Marcavalle 1-4 Huanchac, T224679, English speaking, helpful, arranges good tours. **Milton Velásquez**, T222638, T984 680730 (mob), an anthropologist and tour guide who speaks English.

Train

To Juliaca and Puno, **Perú Rail** trains leave from the Av Sol station, Estación Wanchac, T238722. When arriving in Cuzco, a tourist bus meets the train to take visitors to hotels whose touts offer rooms. Machu Picchu trains leave from Estación San Pedro, opposite the San Pedro market.

The train to **Juliaca/Puno** leaves at 0800, Mon, Wed, Fri and Sat, arriving at Puno at 1800, sit on the left for views (no Fri train Nov-Mar). The train makes a stop to view the scenery at La Raya. Always check whether the train is running, especially in the rainy season, when services may be cancelled. Only one class, *Andean Explorer*, US$220. Ticket office is open Mon-Fri 0700-1700, Sat 0700-1200 (take you passport or a copy when buying tickets, and be patient). Buy tickets on www.perurail.com, or through a travel agent. Meals are served on the train. To **Ollantaytambo** and **Machu Picchu**, see page 1457.

❶ Directory

Cuzco *p1419, maps p1422 and p1427*

Airline offices Lan, Av Sol 627-B, T225552. Peruvian Airlines, C del Medio 117, T254890. Star Perú, Av Sol 679 of 1, T262768. Taca, Av Sol 602, T249921. **Banks** Most of the banks are on Av Sol, and all have ATMs from which you can withdraw dollars or soles. BCP, Av Sol 189. Interbank, Av Sol y Puluchapata. Next door is Banco Continental. BSCH, Av Sol 459. Scotiabank, Maruri entre Pampa del Castillo y Pomeritos. There are ATMs around the Plaza de Armas, in San Blas and on Av La Cultura. Many travel agencies and *casas de cambio* (eg on Portal de Comercio, Plaza de Armas, and Av Sol) change dollars; some of them change TCs as well, but charge 4-5% commission. LAC Dollar, Av Sol 150, T257762, Mon-Sat 0900-2000, with delivery service to central hotels, cash and TCs. The street changers hang around Av Sol, blocks 2-3, every day; they will also change TCs. In banks and on the street check the notes. Dollars are accepted at many restaurants and at the airport. Western Union, Santa Catalina Ancha 165, T233727, money transfers in 10 mins; also at *DHL*, see below. **Consulates** Belgium, Av Sol 954, T224322. France, Jorge Escobar, C Michaela Bastidas 101, p4, T233610. Germany, Sra Maria-Sophia Júrgens de Hermoza, San Agustín 307, T235459, acupari@terra.com.pe, open Mon-Fri, 1000-1200, appointments may be made by phone, also book exchange. Ireland, Charlie Donovan, Santa Catalina Ancha 360 (Rosie O'Grady's), T243514. Italy, Sr Fedos Rubatto, Av Garcilaso 700, T224398. Mon-Fri 0900-1200, 1500-1700. Netherlands, Sra Marcela Alarco, Av Pardo 827, T241897, marcela_alarco@yahoo.com, Mon-Fri 0900-1500. Spain, Sra Juana María Lambarri, Av Pardo 1041, T984-650106. Switzerland, Av Regional 222, T243533. UK, Barry Walker, Av Pardo 895, T239974, bwalker@amauta.rcp.net.pe. US Agent, Dra Olga Villagarcía, Av Pardo 845, T231474, CoresES@state.gov.

Internet You can't walk for 5 mins in Cuzco without running into an internet café, and new places are opening all the time. Most have similar rates, around US$0.50 per hr, although if you look hard enough there are cheaper places. The main difference between cafés is the speed of internet connection and the facilities on offer. The better places have scanners, webcams and CD burners, staff in these establishments can be very knowledgeable. **Language schools** Academia Latinoamericana de Español, Plaza Limacpampa 565, T243364, www.latinoschools.com. The same company also has schools in Ecuador (Quito) and in Bolivia (Sucre). They can arrange courses that include any combination of these locations using identical teaching methods and materials. Professionally run with experienced staff. Many activities per week, including dance lessons and excursions to sites of historical and cultural interest. Good homestays. Private classes US$170 for 20 hrs, groups, with a maximum of 4 students US$125, again for 20 hrs. Acupari, the German-Peruvian Cultural Association, San Agustín 307, T242970, www.acupari.com. Spanish classes are run here. Amauta Spanish School, Suecia 480, T241 1422, www.amautaspanish.com. Spanish classes, one-to-one or in small groups, also Quechua classes and workshops in Peruvian cuisine, dance and music, US$11.50 per hr one-to-one, group tuition (2-6 people), US$114 for 20 hrs. They have pleasant accommodation on the same street, as well as a free internet café for students, and can arrange excursions and help find voluntary work. They also have a school in Pisac and can arrange courses in Tambopata, Lima and also in Argentina. Amigos Spanish School, Zaguán del Cielo B-23, T/F242292, www.spanish cusco.com. Certified, experienced teachers, friendly atmosphere. All profits support a foundation for disadvantaged children. Private lessons for US$8 per hr, US$108 for 20 hrs of classes in a small group. Comfortable homestays and free activities available, including a 'real city tour' through Cuzco's poor areas. Cusco Spanish School, Garcilaso 265, of 6, p 2, T226928, www.cuscos panishschool.com. US$175 for 20 hrs private classes, cheaper in groups. School offers homestays, optional activities including dance and music classes, cookery courses, ceramics, Quechua, hiking and volunteer programmes. They also offer courses on an *hacienda* at Cusipata in the Vilcanota valley, east of Cuzco. **Excel**, Cruz Verde 336, T235298, www.excel-spanishlanguageprograms-peru.org. Very professional, US$7 per hr for private one-to-one lessons. US$229 for 20 hrs with 2 people, or US$277 with homestay, one-on-one for 20 hrs. **Fairplay Spanish School**, Pasaje Zavaleta C-5, Wanchac, T984 789252, www.fair play-peru.org. This relatively new NGO teaches Peruvians who wouldn't normally have the opportunity (Peruvian single mothers, for example) to become Spanish teachers themselves over several months of training. The agency then acts as an agent, allowing these same teachers to find work with visiting students. Classes with these teachers cost US$4.50 or US$6 per hr, of which 33% is reinvested in the NGO, the rest going direct to the teachers. Can also arrange volunteer work and homestay programmes. **La Casona de la Esquina**, Purgatorio 395, corner with Huaynapata, T235830. US$5 per hr for one-to-one classes. Recommended. **Mundo Verde**, COVIDUC h-14 San Sebastián, T274574, www.mundoverde spanish.com. Spanish lessons with the option to study in the rainforest and the possibility of working on environmental and social projects while studying. Some of your money goes towards developing sustainable farming practices in the area. US$250 for 20 hrs tuition with homestay. **San Blas Spanish School**, Carmen Bajo 224, T247898, www.spanish schoolperu.com. Groups, with 4 clients maximum, US$90 for 20 hrs tuition (US$130 one-to-one). **Massage and therapies** Casa **de la Serenidad**, Santa María P-8, San Sebastián, T792224, www.shamanspirit.net. A shamanic therapy centre run by a Swiss- American healer and Reiki Master who uses medicinal 'power' plants. It also has bed and breakfast and has received very good reports. **Healing Hands**, based at *Loki Hostel*, faery amanita@hotmail.com. Angela is a Reiki, Shiatsu and CranioSacral Therapist. Very relaxing and recommended. **Medical services** Clinics: **Hospital Regional**, Av de la Cultura, T227661, emergencies 223691. **Clínica Pardo**, Av de la Cultura 710, T240387, www.clinica pardo.com. 24 hrs daily, trained bilingual personnel, complete medical assistance coverage with international insurance companies, highly regarded. **Clínica Panamericana**, Urb Larapa Grande C-17, T270000, T984 785303 (mob), www.cusco health.com. 24-hr emergency and medical attention. Good. **Motorcycle hire** **Perú Mototours**, Saphi 578, alc@perumoto tours. com. Helpful, good prices and machines. **Post offices** Av Sol, block 5, Mon-Sat 0730-2000; Sun and holidays 0800-1400. Stamps and postcards available. *Poste restante* is free and helpful. **DHL**, Av Sol 627, T244167. **Telephones** Phone offices around town. **Telefónica**, Av Sol 386, for telephone and fax, open Mon-Sat 0700-2300, Sun and holidays 0700-1800. International calls by pay phone or go through the operator (long wait possible), deposit required. **Useful addresses** **Migraciones**, Av Sol s/n, block 6 close to post office, T222741, Mon-Fri 0800-1300. **ISIC-Intej office**, Portal de Panes 123, of 107 (CC Los Ruiseñores), T256367. Issues international student cards.

Southeast from Cuzco

There are many interesting villages and ruins on this road. **Tipón** ruins ⓘ *US$3.50,* between the villages of Saylla and Oropesa, are extensive and include baths, terraces, irrigation systems, possibly an agricultural laboratory and a temple complex, accessible from a path leading from just above the last terrace (5 km climb from village; take a combi from Cuzco to Oropesa, then a taxi, or taxi from Cuzco US$7). **Oropesa**, whose church contains a fine ornately carved pulpit, is the national 'Capital of Bread'. Try the delicious sweet circular loaves known as *chutas*.

At **Huambutío**, north of the village of Huacarpay, the road divides; northwest to Pisac and north to **Paucartambo**, on the eastern slope of Andes. This remote town, 80 km east of Cuzco, has become a popular tourist destination. The *Fiesta de la Virgen del Carmen* (Mamacha Carmen) is a major attraction, with masked dancers enacting rituals and folk tales: 15-17 July. (There is basic accommodation in town.) From Paucartambo, in the dry season, you can go 44 km to **Tres Cruces**, along the Pilcopata road, turning left after 25 km. Tres Cruces gives a wonderful view of the sunrise in June and July: peculiar climactic conditions make it appear that three suns are rising. Tour agencies in Cuzco can arrange transport and lodging.

Further on from Huacarpay are the Huari (pre-Inca) ruins of **Piquillacta** ⓘ *daily 0700-1730, US$3.50.* Buses to Urcos from Avenida Huáscar in Cuzco will drop you at the entrance on the north side of the complex, though this is not the official entry. The Piquillacta Archaeological Park also contains the Laguna de Huacarpay (known as Muyna in ancient times) and the ruins that surround it: Kañarakay, Urpicancha and the huge gateway of Rumicolca. A guide will help to find the more interesting structures. It's good to hike or cycle and birdwatch around the lake.

Andahuaylillas is a village 32 km southeast from Cuzco, with a fine early 17th-century church (the 'Andean Sistine Chapel'), with beautiful frescoes, a splendid doorway and a gilded main altar. Taxi colectivos go there from block 17 of Av La Cultura (opposite university), as does the *Oropesa* bus (from Avenida Huáscar in Cuzco) via Tipón, Piquillacta and Rumicolca. The next village, **Huaro**, also has a church whose interior is entirely covered with colourful frescoes.

Beyond Andahuaylillas is **Urcos**, whose lake is a popular picnic spot (follow the clear path). There are three very basic hostales. A spectacular road from Urcos crosses the Eastern Cordillera to Puerto Maldonado in the jungle (see page 1500). Some 47 km after passing the snow line Hualla-Hualla pass, at 4,820 m, the super-hot thermal baths of **Marcapata** ⓘ *173 km from Urcos, US$0.10,* provide a relaxing break.

Some 82 km from Urcos, at the base of **Nevado Ausangate** (6,384 m), is the town of **Ocongate**, which has two hotels on the Plaza de Armas. Beyond Ocongate is **Tinqui**, the starting point for hikes around Ausangate and in the Cordillera Vilcanota. On the flanks of the Nevado Ausangate is Q'Olloriti, where a church has been built close to the snout of a glacier. This place has become a place of pilgrimage (see Cuzco, Festivals, page 1434).

Hiking around Ausangate The hike around the mountain of Ausangate takes six days: spectacular, but quite hard, with three passes over 5,000 m, so you need to be acclimatized. Temperatures in high season (April-October) can drop well below zero at night. It is recommended to take a guide or *arriero*. *Arrieros* and mules can be hired in Tinqui for US$7 per day for an *arriero*, US$6 for a mule, but more for a saddle horse. *Arrieros* also expect food. Make sure you sign a contract with full details. Buy all food supplies in Cuzco. Maps are available at the IGN in Lima or **South American Explorers**, who also have latest information.

From Urcos to Sicuani (see page 1415), the road passes **Cusipata** (with an Inca gate and wall), **Checacupe** (with a lovely church) and **Tinta**, 23 km from Sicuani (church with brilliant gilded interior and an interesting choir vault). There are frequent buses and trucks to Cuzco, or take the train from Cuzco. Continuing to Sicuani, **Raqchi** is the scene of the region's great folklore festival starting on 24 June, *Wiracocha*, when dancers come from all over Peru. Raqchi is also the site of the **Viracocha Temple** ⓘ *US$3.50, take a bus or truck from Cuzco towards Sicuani, US$1.50.* John Hemming wrote: "What remains is the central wall, which is adobe above and Inca masonry below. This was probably the largest roofed building ever built by the Incas. On either side of the high wall, great sloping roofs were supported by rows of unusual round pillars, also of masonry topped by adobe. Nearby is a complex of barracks-like buildings and round storehouses. This was the most holy shrine to the creator god Viracocha, being the site of a miracle in which he set fire to the land – hence the lava flow nearby. There are also small Inca baths in the corner of a field beyond the temple and a straight row of ruined houses by a square. The landscape is extraordinary, blighted by huge piles of black volcanic rocks."

Southeast from Cuzco listings

For Sleeping and Eating price codes and other relevant information, see Essentials, pages 38-40.

Sleeping

Ausangate *p1445*

G Ausangate, Tinqui. Very basic, but warm, friendly atmosphere. Sr Crispin (or Cayetano), the owner, is knowledgeable and can arrange guides, mules, etc. He and his brothers can be contacted in Cuzco on F227768. All have been recommended as reliable sources of trekking and climbing information, for arranging trips.

G Hostal Tinqui Guide, on the right-hand side as you enter Tinqui. Meals available, the owner can arrange guides and horses.

Transport

Southeast from Cuzco: Paucartambo *p1445*

Bus A minibus leaves for Paucartambo from Av Huáscar in **Cuzco**, every other day, US$4.50, 3-4 hrs; alternate days Paucartambo-Cuzco. Trucks and a private bus leave from the Coliseo, behind Hospital del Segur0 in Cuzco, 5 hrs, US$2.50. Agencies in Cuzco can arrange round trip on 15-17 Jul, US$30.

Ausangate *p1445*

Bus from Cuzco, to **Tinqui** from Av Tomasatito Condemayta, corner of the Coliseo Cerrado in Cuzco, Mon-Sat 1000, 6-7 hrs, US$3.50. **Huayna Ausangate** is a recommended company, ticket office near the Coliseo Cerrado.

Sacred Valley of the Incas

The name conjures up images of ancient rulers and their god-like status, with the landscape itself as their temple. And so it was, but the Incas also built their own tribute to this dramatic land in monuments such as Machu Picchu, Ollantaytambo, Pisac and countless others. For the tourist, the famous sights are now within easy reach of Cuzco, but the demand for adventure, to see lost cities in a less 21st-century context, means that there is ample scope for exploring. But if archaeology is not your thing, there are markets to enjoy, birds to watch, trails for mountain-biking and a whole range of hotels to relax in. The best time to visit is April to May or October to November. The high season is June-September, but the rainy season, from December to March, is cheaper and pleasant enough.

Pisac → *Phone code: 084. Colour map 3, C4.*

Pisac, 30 km north of Cuzco, has a traditional Sunday morning **market**, at which local people sell their produce in exchange for essential goods. It is also a major draw for tourists who arrive after 0800 until 1700. Pisac has other, somewhat less crowded but more commercial markets on Tuesday and Thursday morning. Each Sunday at 1100 there is a Quechua mass. On the plaza are the church and a small interesting **Museo Folklórico**. The **Museo Comunitario Pisac** ⓘ *Av Amazonas y Retamayoc K'asa, museopisac@gmail.com, daily 1000-1700, free but donations welcome* was opened in 2009, with a display of village life, created by the people of Pisac. There are many souvenir shops on Bolognesi. Local fiesta: 15 July.

High above the town on the mountainside is a superb **Inca fortress** ⓘ *0700-1730, guides charge about US$5, if you do not show your BTC multi-site ticket on the way up, you will be asked to* *do so by the warden, or pay US$13.50.* The walk up to the ruins begins from the plaza (but see below), past the Centro de Salud and a new control post. The path goes through working terraces, giving the ruins a context. The first group of buildings is Pisaqa, with a fine curving wall. Climb then to the central part of the ruins, the Intihuatana group of temples and rock outcrops in the most magnificent Inca masonry. Here are the Reloj Solar ('Hitching Post of the Sun') – now closed because thieves stole a piece from it, palaces of the moon and stars, solstice markers, baths and water channels. From Intihuatana, a path leads around the hillside through a tunnel to Q'Allaqasa, the military area. Across the valley at this point, a large area of Inca tombs in holes in the hillside can be seen. The end of the site is Kanchiracay, where the agricultural workers were housed. Road transport approaches from this end. The descent takes 30 minutes. At dusk you will hear, if not see, the *pisaca* (partridges), after which the place is named. Even if going by car, do not rush as there is a lot to see and a lot of walking to do. Road transport approaches from the Kanchiracay end. The drive up from town takes about 20 minutes. Walking up, although tiring, is recommended for the views and location. It's at least one hour uphill all the way. The descent takes 30 minutes on foot. Horses are available for US$3 per person. Combis charge US$0.60 per person and taxis US$3 one way up to the ruins from near the bridge. Then you can walk back down (if you want the taxi to take you back down negotiate a fare). Overnight parking allowed in the parking lot.

Pisac to Urubamba

Calca, 2,900 m, is 18 km beyond Pisac. The plaza is divided in two: Urubamba buses stop on one side; and Cuzco and Pisac buses on the other side of the dividing strip. *Fiesta de la Vírgen Asunta* 15-16 August. There are basic hotels and eating places in town.

The **Valle de Lares** is beautiful for walking and cycling, with its magnificent mountains, lakes and small villages. You start near an old hacienda in Huarán (2,830 m), cross two passes over 4,000 m and end at the hot springs near Lares. From this village, transport runs back to Calca. Alternatively, you can add an extra day and continue to Ollantaytambo. Several agencies in Cuzco offer trekking and biking tours to the region and some offer this trek as an alternative Inca Trail.

About 3 km east of Urubamba, **Yucay** has two grassy plazas divided by the restored colonial church of Santiago Apóstol, with its oil paintings and fine altars. On the opposite side from Plaza Manco II is the adobe palace built for Sayri Túpac (Manco's son) when he emerged from Vilcabamba in 1558. In Yucay monks sell milk, ham and eggs from their farm on the hillside.

Urubamba → *Phone code: 084. Altitude: 2,863 m.*

Like many places along the valley, Urubamba is in a fine setting with snow-capped peaks in view. Calle Berriózabal, on the west edge of town, is lined with pisonay trees. The large market square is one block west of the main plaza. The main road skirts the town and the bridge for the road to Chinchero is just to the east of town. Visit **Seminario-Bejar Ceramic Studio** ⓘ *Berriózabal 111, T201002, www.ceramicaseminario.com*, in the beautiful grounds of the former Urpihuasi hostal. They investigate and use pre-Columbian techniques and designs, highly recommended. ATM on the main road not far from the bridge. For local festivals, May and June are the harvest months, with many processions following ancient schedules. Urubamba's main festival, *El Señor de Torrechayoc*, occupies the first week of June.

About 6 km west of Urubamba is **Tarabamba**, where a bridge crosses the Río Urubamba. Turn right after the bridge to **Pichingoto**, a tumbled-down village built under an overhanging cliff. Also, just over the bridge and before the town to the left of a small, walled cemetery is a salt stream. Follow the footpath beside the stream to Salineras, a small village below which are a mass of terraced Inca salt pans which are still in operation (entry US$1.80); there are over 5,000. The walk to the salt pans takes about 30 minutes. Take water as this side of the valley can be very hot and dry.

Chinchero and Moray

Chinchero (3,762 m) ⓘ *site 0700-1730, US$2.45, or on the BTC combined entrance ticket (see page 1419)*, is just off a direct road to Urubamba. It has an attractive church built on an Inca temple. The church has been restored to reveal in all their glory the interior paintings. The ceiling, beams and walls are covered in beautiful floral and religious designs. The church is open on Sunday for mass and at festivals; ask in the tourist office in Cuzco for other times. Recent excavations there have revealed many Inca walls and terraces. The food market and the handicraft market are separate. The former is held every day, on your left as you come into town. The latter, on Sunday only, is up by the church, small, but attractive. On any day but Sunday there are few tourists. Fiesta, day of the Virgin, on 8 September.

At Moray, there are three 'colosseums', used by the Incas, according to some theories, as a sort of open-air crop nursery, known locally as the laboratory of the Incas. The great depressions contain no ruined buildings, but are lined with fine terracing. Each level is said to have its own microclimate. It is a very atmospheric place which, many claim, has mystical power, and the scenery is absolutely stunning (entry US$3.50, or by BTC). The most interesting way to get to Moray is from Urubamba via the Pichingoto bridge over the Río Urubamba. The climb up from the bridge is fairly steep but easy. The path passes by the spectacular **salt pans**, still in production after thousands of years, taking 1½-2 hours to the top. The village of Maras is about 45 minutes further on, then it's 9 km by road or 5 km through the fields to Moray. Tour companies in Cuzco offer cycle trips to Moray. There are no hotels at all in the area, so take care not to be stranded. (See Transport, for further details on how to get there.)

The Sacred Valley

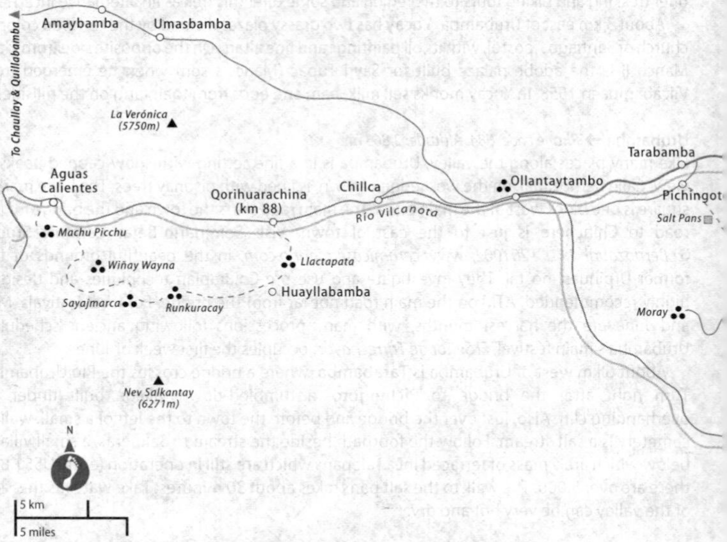

Ollantaytambo → *Colour map 3, C4. Phone code: 084. Altitude: 2,800 m.*
ⓘ *Inca ruins open 0700-1730. If possible arrive very early, 0700, before the tourists. Admission is by BTC visitor's ticket, which can be bought at the site (otherwise US$6.50).*
The Inca town, or *Llacta*, on which the present-day town is based is clearly seen in the fine example of Inca *canchas* (blocks), which are almost entirely intact and still occupied behind the main plaza. Entering Ollantaytambo from Pisac, the road is built along the long wall of 100 niches. Note the inclination of the wall: it leans towards the road. Since it was the Inca's practice to build with the walls leaning towards the interiors of the buildings, it has been deduced that the road, much narrower then, was built inside a succession of buildings. The road out of the plaza leads across a bridge, down to the colonial church with its enclosed *recinto*. Beyond is a plaza (and car park) with entrances to the archaeological site.

The so-called **Baño de la Ñusta** (bath of the princess) is of grey granite, and is in a small area between the town and the temple fortress. Some 200 m behind the Baño de la Ñusta along the face of the mountain are some small ruins known as Inca Misanca, believed to have been a small temple or observatory. A series of steps, seats and niches have been carved out of the cliff. There is a complete irrigation system, including a canal at shoulder level, some 6 ins deep, cut out of the sheer rock face (under renovation). The flights of terraces leading up above the town are superb, and so are the curving terraces following the contours of the rocks overlooking the Urubamba. These terraces were successfully defended by Manco Incas warriors against Hernando Pizarro in 1536. Manco Inca built the wall above the site and another wall closing the Yucay valley against attack from Cuzco. These are visible on either side of the valley.

The temple itself was started by Pachacútec, using Colla Indians from Lake Titicaca – hence the similarities of the monoliths facing the central platform with the Tiahuanaco remains. The massive, highly finished granite blocks at the top are worth the climb to see. The Colla are said to have deserted halfway through the work, which explains the many unfinished blocks lying about the site.

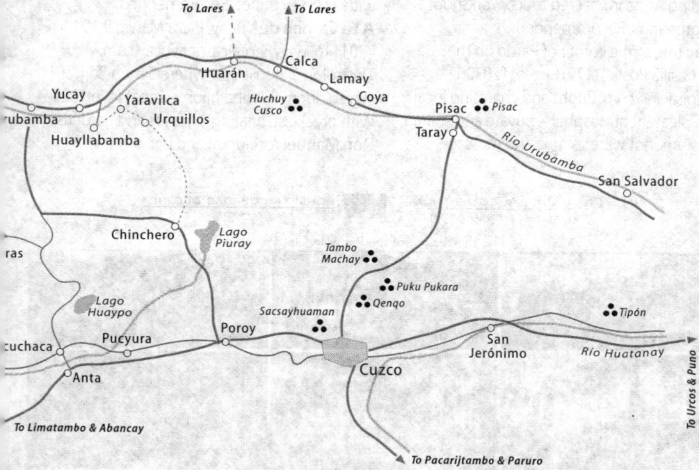

El Museo Catcco ① *1 block from plaza in the Casa Horno, T084-204024, 0900-1900, US$1.50 requested as donation.* The museum has good displays of textiles, findings from local ruins, ethnographic and archaeological information. Tourist information and details of heritage trails are available in the museum.

On the west side of the main ruins, a two-dimensional 'pyramid' has been identified in the layout of the fields and walls of the valley. A fine 750 m wall aligns with the rays of the winter solstice on 21 June. It can be appreciated from a high point about 3½ km from Ollantaytambo.

Sacred Valley of the Incas

For Sleeping and Eating price codes and other relevant information, see Essentials, pages 38-40.

Sleeping

Pisac *p1446*

A Royal Inka Pisac, Carretera Ruinas Km 1.5, T267236, www.royalinkahotel.com/ hpisac.html. Including breakfast, converted hacienda with olympic-size swimming pool (US$3.50 per day), sauna and jacuzzi for guests only, very pleasant, provides guides.

C Hostal Varayoc, Mcal Castilla 380, T223638, luzpaz3@hotmail.com. Renovated hotel around a colonial courtyard with working bread oven. Décor is smart and bathrooms are modern.

C Paz y Luz, T203204, www.pazyluzperu.com. 10-15 mins walk from Pisac Plaza, close to the river. American-owned, pleasant garden, nicely designed rooms, breakfast included. Diane Dunn offers healing from many traditions (including Andean), sacred tours, workshops and gatherings. Recommended.

C Pisac Inn, at the corner of Pardo on the Plaza, Casilla Postal 1179, Cuzco, T203062, www.pisacinn.com. Bright and charming local decor, pleasant atmosphere, private and shared bathrooms, hot water, sauna and massage. Good breakfast, the **Cuchara de Palo** restaurant serves meals using local ingredients, plus pizza and pasta, café.

F Res Beho, Intihuatana 642, T/F203001. Ask for room in main building, good breakfast for US$1, owner's son will act as guide to ruins at weekend.

G pp **Parador**, on the Plaza, T203061. Shared bathrooms, breakfast extra, hot water, restaurant.

Pisac to Urubamba *p1447*

Yucay

AL Sonesta Posadas del Inca Sacred Valley, Plaza Manco II de Yucay 123, T084-201107, www.sonestaperu.com. Converted 300-year-old monastery, it is like a little village with plazas, chapel, 69 comfortable, heated rooms, price includes buffet breakfast. Lots of activities can be arranged, canoeing, horse riding, mountain biking, etc. **Inkafe** restaurant is open to all, serving Peruvian, fusion and traditional cuisine with a US$15 buffet. Recommended.

A La Casona de Yucay, Plaza Manco II 104, T201116, www.hotelcasonayucay.com. This colonial house was where Simón Bolívar stayed during his liberation campaign in 1824. With breakfast, heating, 2 patios and gardens, **Don Manuel** restaurant and bar.

B The Green House, Km 60.2 Huaran, T984-770130, www.thegreenhouseperu.com. A charming retreat, only 4 rooms, comfortable lounge, restaurant, beautiful garden. Information on walks and day trips in the area.
C-D Hostal Y'Llary, on Plaza Manco II 107, T201112, www.hostalyllary.com. Including breakfast, hot water, parking.

Urubamba *p1447*
LL Tambo del Inka, Av Ferrocarril s/n, T581777, www.libertador.com.pe. Completely remodelled luxury resort on the edge of town, by the river, spa and health centre, swimming pools, **Hawa** restaurant, lots of activities arranged.
L Valle Sagrado Lodge, Río Sagrado, T201631, www.riosagrado.com. 4 km from Urubamba, set in beautiful gardens overlooking the river with views of surrounding mountains.
AL Casa Andina Private Collection Sacred Valley, Yanahuara, between Urubamba and Ollantaytambo, T976 5501, www.casa-andina.com. In its own 3-ha estate, with all the facilities associated with this chain, plus 'Sacred Spa, gym, internet and planetarium, good restaurant, adventure options.
AL Sol y Luna, west of town, T201620, www.hotelsolyluna.com. Nice bungalows set off the main road, pool, excellent buffet in restaurant, wine tastings, spa. Has **Viento Sur** adventure travel agency, for horse riding, mountain biking, trekking and paragliding.
D Posada Las Tres Marías, Zavala 307, T201006, www.posadatresmarias.com. Hot water, welcoming, beautiful gardens. Recommended.
D-E Hospedaje Los Jardines, Jr Convención 459, T201331. An attractive guesthouse with comfortable rooms, non-smoking, delicious breakfast extra (vegans catered for), safe, lovely garden, laundry. Sacred Valley Mountain Bike Tours also based here.
E pp **Las Chullpas**, 3 km from town, T201568, www.uhupi.com/chullpas. Very peaceful, includes excellent breakfast, vegetarian meals, English and German spoken, Spanish classes, natural medicine, treks, riding, mountain biking, camping US$3 with hot shower. Mototaxi from town US$0.85, taxi (ask for Querocancha) US$2.
F Hostal Urubamba, Bolognesi 605, T201062. Basic, pleasant, cold water, cheaper without bath.

Chinchero *p1448*
C La Casa de Barro, T306031 www.lacasadebarro.com. Modern hotel, price includes American breakfast, with hot water, bar, restaurant, tours arranged.

Ollantaytambo *p1449*
AL Pakaritampu, C Ferrocarril s/n, T204020, www.pakaritampu.com. Includes breakfast, modern, TV room, restaurant and bar, internet service for guests, laundry, safe and room service. Adventure sports can be arranged. Meals are extra: buffet US$20, dinner US$17. Excellent quality and service.
A-B El Albergue Ollantaytambo, within the railway station gates, T204014, www.rumbosperu.com/elalbergue/. Owned by North American Wendy Weeks, only 8 rooms, full of character, charming and relaxing. Price includes breakfast; packed lunch available, full dinner on request. Courtyard and lovely gardens, eucalyptus steam sauna, interesting handicrafts are on sale, plus Wendy's digestif, Compuesto Matacuy. It's convenient for the Machu Picchu train, good information, private transport can be arranged to the salt pans, Moray, Abra Málaga for birdwatching and taxi transfers to the airport. Highly recommended.
A-B Ñustayoc Mountain Lodge and Resort, about 5 km west of Ollantaytambo, just before Chillca and the start of the Inca Trail, T01-275 0706, www.nustayoclodge.com. Large lodge in a wonderful location with great views of the Verónica massif and other peaks. Lovely flower-filled garden and grounds, nicely decorated, spacious rooms, includes continental breakfast.
C Apu Lodge, Calle Lari, T797162, www.apulodge.com. On the edge of town, great views of the ruins and surrounding mountains. Run by Scot Louise Norton and husband Arturo, good service, can help organize tours and treks. They work with Leap Local (www.leaplocal.org) guides project.
C Hostal Munay Tika, on the road to the station, T204111, www.munaytika.com. Price includes breakfast, dinner served by arrangement. To use the sauna costs US$5 with prior notice, also has a nice garden, good.
C Hostal Sauce, C Ventiderio 248, T204044, www. hostalsauce.com.pe. Smart, simple décor and views of the ruins from some rooms.

C Hotel Sol Ollantay, C Ventiderio s/n by the small brigde between the two plazas, T204130, www.sol-ollantay.com. Tastefullly renovated in 2009 with new bathrooms. Good views from most rooms.

C-E KB, between the main plaza and the ruins, T204091, www.kbperu.com. Spacious, comfortable rooms, cheaper without bath, also has budget lodging (**G**), hot water, flower-filled garden, very good restaurant (🍴🍴). Also offers adventure tours.

D Albergue Kapuly, at the end of the station road, T204017. Prices are lower in the off season, quiet, spacious rooms, with or without bath, includes a good continental breakfast. Nice garden. Recommended.

E Hostal La Ñusta, C Ocobamba, T204035. Ask about accommodation in the shop/restaurant of the same name on the plaza or in the **Gran Tunupa** restaurant. A decent although uninspiring option. Proprietor Rubén Ponce loves to share his knowledge of the ruins with guests. Good view of the ruins from the balcony.

E Hostal Tambo, T084-204003, walk up Calle Lari that heads north from the plaza. After 20 m or so you'll see an unmarked blue door on the left-hand side; bang on the door. If this doesn't work keep walking, turn left down the first small alley and bang on that blue door instead! Past this unassuming exterior is a garden of fruit trees, flowers, dogs, cats and domesticated parrots. Three basic rooms with shared bath (some hot water), very friendly family and the *señora* is a real character.

E Las Orquídeas, near the start of the road to the station, T204032. Good accommodation, price includes breakfast and meals are available.

F Hostal Chaskawasi, Calle del Medio (also C Taypi) north of the plaza, T204045, katycusco@yahoo.es. A *hostal* snuggled away in the small alleys behind the plaza. Owner Anna is very friendly.

F Hostal Ollanta, south side of the plaza, T204116. Basic but in a great location. All rooms with shared bath.

G Hostal Choza, just below the main plaza in town, T204113. Very pleasant, safe motorcycle parking, TV in front room for guests, ask for the room with the view of the ruins and Nevado Verónica. Recommended.

Eating

Pisac *p1446*

🍴🍴-🍴 Miski Mijuna Wasi, on the Plaza de Armas, T203266. Serves tasty local food, typical and Novo Andino, also international dishes. Has a *pastelería* also.

🍴🍴-🍴 Mullu, Mcal Castilla 375, T208182. Open Tue-Sun 0900-1900. Café/restaurant related to the Mullu store in Cuzco, also has a gallery promoting local artists.

🍴 Doña Clorinda, Bolognesi at the plaza, tasty food, including vegetarian.

🍴 Valle Sagrado, Av Amazonas 116 (the main street where buses go towards Urubamba). Good quality, generous portions and a lunchtime buffet that includes vegetarian options. Go early before the tour groups arrive. **Valle Sagrado II** due open in 2010.

Bakery, Mcal Castilla 372. Sells excellent cheese and onion *empanadas* for US$0.25, suitable for vegetarians, and good wholemeal bread.

Blue Llama Café, corner of the plaza opposite Pisac Inn, T203135, www.bluellamacafe.com. Cute, colourful café with a huge range of teas, good coffee, breakfasts and daily menus.

Ulrike's Café, Plaza de Armas 828, ulrikescafe@terra.com.pe. Has possibly the best apple crumble with ice cream, excellent coffee, smoothies and a wide range of international dishes. Good value 3-course daily *menú*. A good place to chill out.

Urubamba *p1447*

🍴🍴🍴 Tunupa, on road from Urubamba to Ollantaytambo, on riverbank, zappa@terra.com.pe. Same owners as Tunupa in Cuzco, colonial-style hacienda, excellent food and surroundings, pre-Columbian and colonial art exhibitions, buffet lunch 1200-1500, US$15, dinner 1800-2030.

🍴🍴 El Fogón, Parque Pintacha, T201534. Peruvian food. Recommended.

🍴🍴 El Maizal, on the main road, before the bridge, T201454. Country-style restaurant, buffet service with a variety of Novo Andino and international choices, beautiful gardens, open daytime only. Recommended.

🍴 La Chepita, Av 1 de Mayo, M6, in a small plaza. The place to go on Sun for regional food in the biggest portions you have ever seen. Get 1 plate between 2.

Pintacha, Bolognesi 523. Pub/café serving sandwiches, burgers, coffees, teas and drinks, games, book exchange, cosy, open till late.

Pizza Wasi, Av Mcal Castilla 2nd block. Pizzas and pastas, good value.

The Muse Too, Comercio 347 y Grau, on the corner of the plaza, T984 807970, themusecusco@yahoo.com. New version of the Cuzco Muse, similar idea with colourful walls, comfortable sofas, good coffee and breakfasts.

Ollantaytambo *p1449*

Fortaleza, 2 branches, one on Plaza Ruinas, the other on the north side of the main Plaza. Basic but good food, breakfasts, pizza and pasta – gringo favourites and some local dishes.

Heart´s Café, on Plaza de Armas, T204078, www.heartscafe.org. Wholefood restaurant serving western and Asian dishes, including chicken and fish, owned by SAE member Sonia, whose expertise is in vegetarian food. Bright, open from 0700, run by villagers with all proceeds going to local communities. Popular and warmly recommended.

Il Cappuccino, just before the bridge on the right hand side. The best cappuccino in town, good continental and American breakfasts, slightly more sophisticated than others in town.

Kusicoyllor, on the Plaza Ruinas. Same owners as Il Cappuccino, pizza, pasta and good coffee.

Mayupata, Jr Convención s/n, across bridge on the way to the ruins, on the left, T204083 (Cuzco). International choices and a selection of Peruvian dishes, desserts, sandwiches and coffee, opens 0600 for breakfast, and serves lunch and dinner. Bar has fireplace; river view, relaxing atmosphere.

Alcázar Café, C del Medio, 50m from Plaza, T204034. Vegetarian, but also offers meat and fish, and pasta. Arranges excursions to Andean communities.

La Ñusta, on the Plaza, with the same owner as the hostel – see above. Popular, good food; snacks available.

Festivals and events

Ollantaytambo *p1449*

On the Sun following Inti Raymi, there is a colourful festival, the **Ollanta-Raymi**. **6 Jan**: the **Bajada de Reyes Magos** (the Magi), with dancing, a bull fight, local food and a fair. **End-May/early-Jun**: 50 days after Easter, **Fiesta del Señor de Choquekillca**, patron saint of Ollantaytambo, with several days of dancing, weddings, processions, masses, feasting and drinking. **29 Oct**: the town's anniversary, with lots of dancing in traditional costume and many local delicacies for sale.

Activities and tours

Urubamba *p1447*

Agrotourism **Chichubamba**, Casa de ProPerú, Jr Rejachayoc, T201562, www.agrotourismsacredvalley.com. A community tourism project which lets visitors take part in a number of traditional activities (culinary, horticulture, textiles, ceramics, beekeeping, etc, US$3 pp, cheaper for groups), hiking US$10, lodging **E** pp and local meals, US$5. 20 mins' walk from Urubamba; follow the signs.

Horse riding **Perol Chico**, 5 km from Urubamba at Km 77, T01-99 8223297 (mob), office 054-284732, www.perolchico.com. Dutch/Peruvian owned, 1- to 14-day trips out of Urubamba, good horses, Peruvian Paso style. Recommended.

Trekking **Haku Trek**, contact Javier Saldívar, T984 613001 (mob). Cooperative tourism project in the Chicón valley (the mountain valley above Urubamba), run by residents of the community, 1- and 2-day hiking trips based at a simple eco-lodge; profits are used to fund reforestation of the area.

Transport

Urubamba *p1447*

Bus Terminal, west of town on the main road, about 3 km from centre. From Urubamba to **Calca**, **Pisac** (US$0.80, 1 hr) and **Cuzco**, about 2 hrs, US$1, with Caminos del Inca, from 0530; also buses to Cuzco via Chinchero. Combis run to **Ollantaytambo**, 45 mins, US$0.30.

Chinchero and Moray *p1448*

Road There is a paved road from the main road between Chinchero and Urubamba to the village of Maras and from there an unmade road in good condition leads to Moray, 9 km. Ask in Maras for the best route to walk, other than on the main road. Any bus between Urubamba and Cuzco via

Chinchero passes the clearly marked turning to Maras. From the junction taxi colectivos charge US$1.50 pp to Maras, or you can walk (30 mins). There is public transport from Chinchero to Maras; it stops running between 1700 and 1800. Taxi to Moray, 1-hr wait then take you to the salt pans, from where you can walk back to the Urubamba-Ollantaytambo road, US$20.

Ollantaytambo *p1449*

Bus Direct bus Ollantaytambo to **Cuzco** at 0715 and 1945, US$2.85. The station is 10-15 mins walk from the plaza. Colectivos leave all day, when full, for Urubamba, from 1 block east of the main plaza. There are colectivos at the plaza for the station when trains are due. Check in advance the time trains pass through here (see also under trains to and from Machu Picchu, page 1457). You won't be allowed on the station unless you have previously bought a ticket (and it is best to buy tickets in Cuzco).

❶ Directory

Pisac *p1446*

Banks ATM on the plaza next to **Ulrike's Café**, sometimes hard to find behind the market stalls. Also money excange at the **Blue Llama Café**.

Ollantaytambo *p1449*

Banks ATM at C Ventiderio 248, between the Plaza and Av Ferrocarril, and at Hostal Sauce. **Internet** Several places in town. **Medical services** Hampi Traveller's Clinic, Plaza de Armas, www.hampiland.com. Has ambulance and evacuation service and professional medical care.

Machu Picchu → *Colour map 3, C4.*

There is a tremendous feeling of awe on first witnessing Machu Picchu. The ancient citadel (42 km from Ollantaytambo by rail) straddles the saddle of a high mountain (2,380 m) with steep terraced slopes falling away to the fast-flowing Urubamba river snaking its hairpin course far below in the valley floor. Towering overhead is Huayna Picchu, and green jungle peaks provide the backdrop for the whole majestic scene. Machu Picchu is a complete Inca city. For centuries it was buried in jungle, until Hiram Bingham stumbled upon it in 1911. It was then explored by an archaeological expedition sent by Yale University. The ruins – staircases, terraces, temples, palaces, towers, fountains and the famous Intihuatana (the so-called 'Hitching Post of the Sun') – require at least a day. Take time to appreciate not only the masonry, but also the selection of large rocks for foundations, the use of water in the channels below the Temple of the Sun and the surrounding mountains.

In early 2010 torrential rain caused loss of life, many landslides and other damage in many parts of south-central Peru, Machu Picchu included. The site was closed for a while and the railway connection broken. At the time of writing the site had reopened and the railway had been repaired on schedule. Not all services were fully back to normal, though, so visitors are advised to seek advice in advance from local sources.

Ins and outs

Entrance to Machu Picchu The site is open from 0600 to 1730. Entrance fee is 126 soles, 64 for Peruvians, 63 with ISIC card (US$45 and 22 approximately), payable only in soles. Normally, tickets must be bought in advance from **Instituto Nacional de Cultura** (INC) in Aguas Calientes ⓘ *Av Pachacútec cuadra 1, 0500-2200 (also i perú here, of 4, T211104, iperumachupicchu@promperu.gob.pe, daily 0900-1300, 1400-2000)*, or Cuzco (see page 1421), www.inc-cusco.gob.pe, but in April 2010 were supposedly only available in Cuzco and upon presentation of a return train ticket. Ask in Cuzco before going. Site museum and botanical garden, just over the bridge by the road up to the ruins, US$7. You can deposit your luggage at the entrance for US$1. Guides are available at the site, they are often very knowledgeable and worthwhile, US$20 for 2½ hours (but may take groups of up to 15). Site wardens are also informative, in Spanish only. After 1530 the ruins are quieter, but note that the last bus down from the ruins leaves at 1730. Monday and Friday are bad days in high season because there is usually a crowd of people on guided tours who are going or have been to Pisac market on Sunday. The hotel is located next to the entrance, with a self-service restaurant. Take your own food and drink if you don't want to pay hotel prices, and take plenty of drinking water. Note that food is not officially allowed into the site and drink can only be carried in canteens/water bottles. In the dry season sandflies can be a problem, so take insect repellent and wear long clothes.

Around the site

Huayna Picchu, the mountain overlooking the site (on which there are also ruins), has steps to the top for a superlative view of the whole site, but it is not for those who are afraid of heights and you shouldn't leave the path. The climb takes up to 90 minutes but the steps are dangerous after bad weather. Visitors are given access to the main path at 0700 and 1000 daily, latest return time 1500 (maximum 200 people per departure). Check with the INC in Aguas Calientes or Cuzco for current departure times and to sign up for a place. The other trail to Huayna Picchu, down near the Urubamba, is via the Temple of the Moon, in two caves, one above the other, with superb Inca niches inside. For the trail to the Temple of the Moon: from the path to Huayna Picchu, take the marked trail to the left. It is in good shape, although it descends further than you think it should. After the Temple you may proceed to Huayna Picchu, but this path is overgrown, slippery in the wet and has a crooked ladder on an exposed part about 10 minutes before reaching the top (not for the faint-hearted). It is safer to return to the main trail to Huayna Picchu, although this adds about 30 minutes to the climb. The round trip takes about four hours. Before doing any trekking around Machu Picchu, check with an official which paths may be used, or which are one-way.

The famous Inca bridge is about 45 minutes along a well-marked trail south of the Royal Sector. The bridge (on which you cannot walk) is spectacularly sited, carved into a vertiginous cliff-face. East of the Royal Sector is the path leading up to **Intipunku** on the Inca Trail (45 minutes, fine views).

Aguas Calientes

Those with more time should spend the night at Aguas Calientes and visit the ruins early in the morning, when no one's around. Most hotels and restaurants are near the railway station, on the plaza, or on Avenida Pachacútec, which leads from the plaza to the **thermal baths** ⓘ *0500-2030, US$3.15, 10 mins walk from the town* (a communal pool, smelling of sulphur) good bar for cocktails in the pool. You can rent towels and bathing costumes (US$3) at several places on the road to the baths; basic toilets and changing facilities and showers for washing *before* entering the baths; take soap and shampoo, and keep an eye on valuables. The **Museo Manuel Chávez Ballon** ⓘ *Carretera Hiram Bingham, Wed-Sun 0900-1600, US$7*, displays objects found at Machu Picchu.

Machu Picchu listings

For Sleeping and Eating price codes and other relevant information, see Essentials, pages 38-40.

Sleeping

Machu Picchu *p1454*

LL Machu Picchu Sanctuary Lodge, reservations as for the *Hotel Monasterio* in Cuzco, which is under the same management (Peru Orient Express Hotels), T084-984 816956, www.sanctuarylodge.net. Comfortable, good service, helpful staff, food well-cooked and presented. Electricity and water 24 hrs a day, prices are all-inclusive, restaurant for residents only in the evening, but the buffet lunch is open to all. Usually fully booked well in advance, try Sun night as other tourists find Pisac market a greater attraction.

Aguas Calientes *p1456*

LL Inkaterra Machu Picchu, T211122, Km 110, 5 mins walk along the railway from the town. For reservations: Jr Andalucía 174, Miraflores, Lima, T01-610 0404; in Cuzco at Plaza las Nazarenas 167 p2, T245314, www.inkaterra.com. Beautiful colonial-style bungalows in village compound surrounded by cloud forest, lovely gardens with a lot of steps between the public areas and rooms, pool, restaurant, also campsite with hot showers at good rates, offer tours to Machu Picchu, several guided walks on and off the property, great buffet breakfasts included in price. Also has the Café Inkaterra by the railway line. Recommended.

LL Sumaq Machu Picchu, Av Hermanos Ayar Mz 1, Lote 3, T211059, www.sumaqhotelperu.com. New 5-star on the edge of town, between railway and road to Machu Picchu. Suites and luxury rooms with Wi-Fi, heating, cable TV, etc, restaurant and bar, spa.

AL-A Gringo Bill's (**Hostal Q'oñi Unu**), Colla Raymi 104, T211046, www.gringobills.com (in Cuzco Av El Sol 520, T223663). With breakfast, hot water, laundry, money exchange, luggage stored, good beds, lot of coming and going, good restaurant, breakfast from 0530, packed lunch available. Sadly the monstrous new municipal building has been plonked right in front of the hotel, obscuring the views from rooms which once looked out over the plaza.

A La Cabaña, Av Pachacútec M20-3, T211048, www.lacabanamachupicchu.com. With breakfast, hot water, café, laundry service, helpful, popular with groups.

A Presidente, at the old station, T211034 (Cuzco T244598), www.hostalpresidente.com. Adjoining Hostal Machu Picchu, see below, more upmarket but little difference, rooms without river view cheaper, price includes breakfast.

A-B Rupa Wasi, Huanacaure 180, T211101, www.rupawasi.net. Charming 'eco-lodge' up a small alley off Collasuyo, laid back, comfortable, great views from the balconies, purified water available, organic garden, good breakfasts, half-board available, excellent restaurant, **The Tree House**, and cookery classes.

C Hostal Machu Picchu, at the old station, T211065, sierrandina@gmail.com. Functional, quiet, Wilber, the owner's son, has travel information, hot water, nice balcony over the Urubamba, grocery store, price includes breakfast. Recommended.

C Hostal Pachakúteq, up the hill beyond *Hostal La Cabaña*, T/F211061. Hot water, good breakfast, quiet, family-run. Recommended.

C Hostal Wiracocha Inn, C Wiracocha, T211088, www.wiracochainn.com. Hot water, breakfast included, small garden, helpful, popular with groups, also has higher-priced suites.

D Hospedaje Quilla, Av Pachacútec between Wiracocha and Tupac Inka Yupanki, T/F211 009. Price includes breakfast, hot water, rents bathing gear for the hot springs.

D-E Las Bromelias, Colla Raymi, T211145, just off Plaza before Gringo Bill's. Cheaper without bath, small, hot water.

E pp **Hostal Los Caminantes**, Av Imperio de los Incas 140, by the railway just beyond the old station, T211083. With bath and hot water, breakfast extra, basic but clean.

E Terrazas del Inca, C Wiracocha s/n, T211113, www.terrazasdelinca.com. Safety deposit box, continental breakfast included, kitchen use, helpful staff. Recommended.

Camping The only official campsite is in a field by the river, just below Puente Ruinas station, toilets, showers, US$3.50 pp. Do not leave your tent and belongings unattended.

Eating

Aguas Calientes *p1456*

Pizza seems to be the most common dish in town, but many of the *pizzerías* serve other types of food as well. The old station and Av Pachútec are lined with eating places. Tax is often added as an extra to the bill.

Café Inkaterra, on the railway, just below the Machu Picchu Pueblo Hotel. US$15 for a great lunch buffet with scenic views of the river.

Inka Wasi, Av Pachacútec. Very good choice, has an open fire, full Peruvian and international menu available.

Indio Feliz, C Lloque Yupanqui, T/F211090. Great French cuisine, excellent value and service, set 3-course meal for US$10, good pisco sours in the new bar, great atmosphere. Highly recommended.

Inka's Pizza Pub, on the plaza. Good pizzas, changes money and accepts TCs. Next door is **Illary**, which is popular.

Pueblo Viejo, Av Pachacútec (near plaza). Good food in a spacious but warm environment. Price includes use of the salad bar.

Toto's House, Av Imperio de los Incas, on the railway line. Same owners as Pueblo Viejo. Good value and quality *menú*, buffet from 1130-1500.

Discovery, Plaza de Armas, T211355. The best coffee and internet connection in Aguas Calientes. Several computers and Wi-Fi.

Govinda, Av Pachacútec y Túpac Inka Yupanki. Vegetarian restaurant with a cheap set lunch. Recommended.

Paraguachayoc, Av Pachacútec, at the top near the baths. Charming little restaurant with trout farm where you can catch your own dinner. US$5 for a whole trout with chips and drink.

Bars and clubs

Aguas Calientes *p1456*

Waisicha Pub, C Lloque Yupanqui. For good music and atmosphere.

Activities and tours

Aguas Calientes *p1456*

Peru Sightseeing, www.perusightseeing.com. The only agency in Aguas Calientes, guided trips to Machu Picchu with audio tours as well as local guides, 2 or 3 day packages, or just the Machu Picchu tour. Also half-day tours in the area to Mandor and the Machu Picchu musuem. Can make onward travel arrangements.

Transport

Machu Picchu *p1454*

Bus Buses leave **Aguas Calientes** for Machu Picchu every 30 mins from 0630 until 1300, 25 mins. US$12 return, US$6 single, valid 48 hrs. The bus stop in Aguas Calientes is 50 m from the railway station, with the ticket office opposite. Tickets can also be bought in advance at **Consetur**, Sta Catalina Ancha, Cuzco, which saves queuing when you arrive in Aguas Calientes. Buses return from the ruins to Aguas 0700-0900 and 1200-1730. The walk up from Aguas Calientes follows an Inca path, but it is in poor condition and crosses the motor road (take care).

Train Two companies operate: **PerúRail** (Av Pachacútec, Wanchac Station, T581414, www.perurail.com) to Machu Picchu from Poroy, near Cuzco, and from Ollantaytambo. **Inca Rail** (Av El Sol 611, Cuzco, T233030, or Lima T613 5288, www.incarail.com) from Ollantaytambo to Machu Picchu. A third company, **Andean Railways**, was due to start running in 2010 (no published details). They go to Aguas Calientes (the official name of this station is 'Machu Picchu'). The station for the tourist trains at Aguas Calientes is on the outskirts of town, 200 m from the Pueblo Hotel and 50 m from where buses leave for Machu Picchu ruins. The ticket office is open Mon-Fri 0700-1700, Sat, Sun and holidays 0700-1200, T238722; there is a guard on the gate. There is a paved road in poor condition between Aguas Calientes and the start of the road up to the ruins. **Note** In Feb 2010, the annual threat to schedules from mudslides in the rainy season became a grim reality. Many communities were engulfed in this and other areas, Machu Picchu was closed and the railway line was broken. Services were restored in Apr, but trains ran from a temporary station at Km 82, Piscacucho. Confusion reigned over who should provide buses to Km 82, but consult the rail companies in the first instance to see if they are permitted to run buses from Cuzco or Ollantaytambo. Owing to the temporary schedules we do not list full details below. Make all enquiries in Cuzco when you are there, and consult www.perurail.com and www.incarail.com before you travel.

There are 3 classes of **PerúRail** tourist train: **Vistadome** (US$71 one-way from Poroy); **Backpacker** (US$48 Poroy-Machu Picchu one-way); and the luxurious **Hiram Bingham** service (US$641 return), each scheduled once a day from July 2010. PerúRail is also scheduling Vistadome and Backpacker services from Ollantaytambo, 11 a day from 0510-2100, with fares from US$31-60 depending on service and time of day. Seats can be reserved even if you're not returning the same day. The Vistadome tickets include food in the price. These trains have toilets, video, snacks and drinks for sale. Tickets for all trains can be bought at Wanchac station in Cuzco, on Av Pachacútec. You must have your original passport to travel on the trains to Machu Picchu. Tickets can also be bought through PerúRail's website, www.perurail.com and from travel agents.

The **Hiram Bingham** service departs Poroy at 0905 Mon-Sat, brunch is served on board, and arrives at Machu Picchu 1224 (the timing is good because you can enter the site at a time when most visitors are leaving for their journey back to Cuzco). Return journey is at 1750 (pre-dinner cocktails in bar accompanied by live entertain- ment, and then a 4-course dinner) reaching Poroy at 2116 with bus service to Cuzco hotels.

Inca Rail has 3 trains a day Ollantayambo-Machu Picchu (Sunrise, Morning and Sunset), with fares at US$50 one way executive class, US$75 one way 1st class. Coaches have a/c and heating, snacks are available

Tourists may not travel on the local train to Machu Picchu, but there is a way to avoid the train altogether. Take a bus from Cuzco towards Quillabamba at 1900, US$6 (other buses in the day may not connect with onward transport). Get out at **Santa María** (about 7 hrs) where minibuses wait to go to **Santa Teresa**, 2 hrs, US$2.10. Your reach Santa Teresa by sunrise in time to buy breakfast. From Santa Teresa you have to cross the Río Urubamba. Cross the new bridge and walk 6 km to the Central Hidroeléctrica, a nice, flat road, or take a combi, US$10-15. From the Hidroeléctrica train station it's 40 mins on the local train to Aguas Calientes at 1520, US$8 for tourists, or you can walk along the railway in 2-3 hrs (at Km 114.5 is **F** pp **Hospedaje Mandor**, about 2 km from bridge to Machu Picchu). To return, at 0600 walk from Aguas Calientes to Santa Teresa to catch a bus at 1000 to Santa María, arrive at 1200. At 1300 take a bus back to Cuzco, arriving between 1900-2000. Or take the local train from Aguas Calientes to Santa Teresa at 1210, stay in a hostal, then take the 1000 bus to Santa María. If using this route, don't forget to buy your ticket for Machu Picchu in Cuzco, unless you want to buy it in Aguas Calientes. **Note** At the time of writing, this route was open, but badly affected by landslides. Timings may be much altered.

Directory

Aguas Calientes *p1456*
Banks Several ATMs in town, but they may run out of cash at weekends. **BCP** changes TCs. **Internet** Many interent shops, average price US$1 per hr; slow connection. **Post offices Serpost** agencies: just off the plaza, between the Centro Cultural Machu Picchu and Galería de Arte Tunupa. **Telephones** Office is on C Collasuyo and there are plenty of phone booths around town.

Inca trails

The most impressive way to reach Machu Picchu is via the centuries-old Inca Trail that winds its way from the Sacred Valley near Ollantaytambo, taking three to five days. The spectacular hike runs from Km 88, Qorihuayrachina (2,299 m), a point immediately after the first tunnel 22 km beyond Ollantaytambo station. A sturdy suspension bridge has now been built over the Río Urubamba. Guided tours often start at Km 82, Piscacucho, reached by road. New rules for hiking the trail are detailed below. What makes this hike so special is the stunning combination of Inca ruins, unforgettable views, magnificent mountains, exotic vegetation and extraordinary ecological variety.

Ins and outs

Equipment The Inca Trail is rugged and steep (beware of landslides), but the magnificent views compensate for any weariness which may be felt. It is cold at night, however, and weather conditions change rapidly, so it is important to take not only strong footwear, rain gear and warm clothing but also food, water, water purification for when you fill bottles from streams, insect repellent, a supply of plastic bags, coverings, a good sleeping bag, a torch/flashlight and a stove for preparing hot food and drink to ward off the cold at night. A stove using paraffin (kerosene) is preferable, as fuel can be bought in small quantities in markets. A tent is essential, but if you're hiring one in Cuzco, check carefully for leaks. Walkers who have not taken adequate equipment have died of exposure. Caves marked on some maps are little better than overhangs, and are not sufficient shelter to sleep in.

All the necessary equipment can be rented; see page 1435 under Camping equipment and Activities and tours. Good maps of the Trail and area can be bought from **South American Explorers** in Lima or Cuzco. If you have any doubts about carrying your own pack, reasonably priced porters/guides are available. Carry a day-pack for your water, snacks, etc in case you walk faster than the porters and you have to wait for them to catch you up.

Tours Travel Agencies in Cuzco arrange transport to the start, equipment, food, etc, for an all-in price for all treks that lead to the Machu Picchu Historical Sanctuary. Prices vary from US$420 to US$520 per person for a four day/three night trek on the Classic Inca Trail. If the price is significantly lower, you should be concerned as the company will be cutting corners and may not be paying the environment the respect the new rules were designed to instil. All are subject to strict rules introduced in 2001 and must be licensed. Tour operators taking clients on any of the Inca Trails leading to the Machu Picchu Historical Sanctuary have to pay an annual fee. Groups of up to seven independent travellers who do not wish to use a tour operator will be allowed to hike the trails if they contact an independent, licensed guide to accompany them, as long as they do not contact any other persons such as porters or cooks. There is a maximum of 500 visitors per day allowed on the Classic Inca Trail. Operators pay US$12 for each porter and other trail staff; porters are not be permitted to carry more than 20 kg. Littering is banned, as is carrying plastic water bottles (canteens only may be carried). Pets and pack animals are prohibited, but llamas are allowed as far as the first pass. Groups have to use approved campsites only.

Trail tickets On all hiking trails (Km 82 or Km 88 to Machu Picchu, Salkantay to Machu Picchu, and Km 82 or Km 88 to Machu Picchu via Km 104) adults must pay US$86, students and children under 15 US$43. On the Camino Real de los Inkas from Km 104 to Wiñay-Wayna and Machu Picchu the fee is US$51 per adult, US$28 for students and children and Salkantay to Huayllabamba and Km 88, US$51. The Salkantay trek is subject to a trekking charge of US$45. All tickets must be bought at the INC office on Calle San Bernardo in Cuzco; tickets are only sold on presentation of a letter from a licensed tour operator on behalf of the visitor, including full passport details. Tickets are non-refundable and cannot be changed so make sure you provide accurate passport details to your tour operator. None is sold at the entrance to any of the routes. See page 1436 on the need to reserve your place on the Trail in advance. You can save a bit of money by arranging your own transport back to Ollantaytambo in advance, either for the last day of your tour, or by staying an extra night in Aguas Calientes and taking the early morning train, then take a bus back to Cuzco. If you take your own tent and sleeping gear, some agencies give a discount. Make sure your return train ticket to Cuzco has your name on it (spelt absolutely correctly) for the tourist train, otherwise you have to pay for any changes.

The Trail is closed each February for cleaning and repair. The Annual Inca Trail Clean-up takes place usually in September. Many agencies and organizations are involved and volunteers should contact South American Explorers in Cuzco for full details of ways to help.

Advice Four days would make a comfortable trip (though much depends on the weather). Allow a further day to see Machu Picchu when you have recovered from the hike. You cannot take backpacks into Machu Picchu; leave them at ticket office, US$1. The first two days of the Trail involve the stiffest climbing, so do not attempt it if you're feeling unwell. Leave all your valuables in Cuzco and keep everything inside your tent, even your shoes. Security has, however, improved in recent years. Always take sufficient cash to tip porters and guides at the end (S/.50-100 each, but at your discretion). Avoid the July-August high season and check the conditions in the rainy season from November to April (note that this can vary). In the wet it is cloudy and the paths are very muddy and difficult. Also watch out for coral snakes in this area (black, red, yellow bands).

The Trail

The trek to the sacred site begins either at Km 82, **Piscacucho**, or at Km 88, **Qorihuayrachina**, at 2,600 m. In order to reach Km 82 hikers are transported by their tour operator in a minibus on the road that goes to Quillabamba. From Piri onward the road follows the riverbank and ends at Km 82, where there is a bridge. You can depart as early as you like and arrive at Km 82 faster than going by train. The Inca Trail equipment, food, fuel and field personnel reach Km 82 (depending on the tour operator's logistics) for the Inrena staff to weigh each bundle before the group arrives. When several groups are leaving on the same day, it is more convenient to arrive early. Km 88 can only be reached by train, subject to schedule and baggage limitations. The train goes slower than a bus, but you start your walk nearer to Llaqtapata and Huayllabamba. Note that the route from Km 82 goes via **Cusichaca**, rather than Llaqtapata. (See below for details of variations in starting points for the Inca Trail.)

The walk to **Huayllabamba**, following the Cusichaca River, needs about three hours and isn't too arduous. Beyond Huayllabamba, a popular camping spot for tour groups, there is a camping place about an hour ahead, at **Llulluchayoc** (3,200 m). A punishing 1½ hour climb further is **Llulluchapampa**, an ideal meadow for camping. If you have the energy to reach this point, it will make the second day easier because the next stage, the ascent to the first pass, **Warmiwañuska** (Dead Woman's Pass) at 4,200 m, is tough; 2½ hours.

Afterwards take the steep path downhill to the Pacamayo valley. Beware of slipping on the Inca steps after rain. You could camp by a stream at the bottom (1½ hours from the first pass). It is no longer permitted to camp at **Runkuracay**, on the way up to the second pass (a much easier climb, 3,850 m). Magnificent views near the summit in clear weather. A good overnight place is about 30 minutes past the Inca ruins at **Sayacmarca** (3,500 m), about an hour on after the top of the second pass.

A gentle two-hour climb on a fine stone highway leads through an Inca tunnel to the third pass. Near the top there's a spectacular view of the entire Vilcabamba range. You descend to Inca ruins at **Phuyopatamarca** (3,650 m), well worth a long visit, even camping overnight. There is a 'tourist bathroom' here where water can be collected (but purify it before drinking).

From there steps go downhill to the impressive ruins of **Wiñay-Wayna** (2,700 m, entry US$5.75), with views of the recently cleared terraces of Intipata. Access is possible, but the trail is not easily visible. There is a basic hostel with bunk beds, **G** per person, showers and a small restaurant. There is a small campsite in front of the hostel. After Wiñay-Wayna there is no water and no camping till Machu Picchu. The path from this point goes more or less level through jungle until the steep staircase up to the **Intipunku** (two hours), where there's a magnificent view of Machu Picchu, especially at dawn, with the sun alternately in and out, clouds sometimes obscuring the ruins, sometimes leaving them clear.

Get to Machu Picchu as early as possible, preferably before 0830 for best views but in any case before the tourist trains in high season. **Note** Camping is not allowed at Intipunku; guards may confiscate your tent. You may only camp in the field by the river below Puente Ruinas station.

Alternative Inca trails

The **Camino Real de los Inkas** starts at Km 104, where a footbridge gives access to the ruins of Chachabamba and the trail which ascends, passing above the ruins of Choquesuysuy to connect with the main trail at Wiñay-Wayna. This first part is a steady, continuous ascent of three hours (take water) and the trail is narrow and exposed in parts. Many people recommend this short Inca Trail. Good hiking trails from Aguas Calientes (see page 1456) have been opened along the left bank of the Urubamba, for day hikes crossing the bridge of the hydroelectric plant to Choquesuysuy. A three-night trek goes from Km 82 to Km 88, then along the Río Urubamba to Pacaymayo Bajo and Km 104, from where you take the Camino Real de los Inkas.

Two treks involve routes from **Salkantay**: one, known as the **High Inca Trail** joins the classic Trail at Huayllabamba, then proceeds as before on the main Trail through Wiñay Wayna to Machu Picchu. To get to Salkantay, you have to start the trek in Mollepata, northwest of Cuzco in the Apurímac valley. *Ampay* buses run from Arcopata on the Chinchero road, or you can take private transport to Mollepata (three hours from Cuzco). Salkantay to Machu Picchu this way takes three nights. The second Salkantay route, known as the **Santa Teresa Trek**, takes four days and crosses the 4,500-m Huamantay Pass to reach the Santa Teresa valley, which you follow to its confluence with the Urubamba. The goal is the town of Santa Teresa from where you can go to La Hidroeléctrica station for the local train to Aguas Calientes (see page 1458). On this trek, **Machu Picchu Lodge to Lodge** ⓘ *Mountain Lodges of Peru, T084-243636 (in Lima T01-421 6952, in North America T1-949-679 1872, in Europe 43-664-434 3340), www.mountainlodgesofperu.com*, a series of lodges have been set up. Fully guided tours take 7 days, going from lodge to lodge, which are at Soraypampa (**Salkantay Lodge and Adventure Resort**), Huayraccmachay (**Wayra Lodge**), Collpapampa (**Colpa Lodge**) and Lucmabamba (**Lucma Lodge**). Contact **Mountain Lodges of Peru** for rates, departure dates and all other details.

There are other routes which approach the Inca trails to Machu Picchu, such as Km 77, Chillca, up the Sillque ravine in the Qente valley, which is commonly called the Lago Ancascocha route. A common starting point for this trek is the community of Huarocondo. You can end this trek either at Huayllabamba, where you join the Classic Inca Trail (for further walking), or at the railway line at Km 82 (for transport to the Sacred Valley) or Km 88 (for the train to Aguas Calientes). Then there is another access through the Millpo Valley in the Salkantay area. From the Vilcabamba mountain range, one can reach Machu Picchu by hiking down from Huancacalle to Chaulla by road, getting to Santa Teresa and walking to La Hidroeléctrica station. Tour operators which specialize in trekking can advise on these routes.

Inca Jungle Trail This is offered by several tour operators in Cuzco: on the first day you cycle downhill from Abra Málaga to Santa María (see Train, above, page 1457, also check if landslides have affected this route), 4-5 hours of beautiful, easy riding. The second day is a hard seven-hour trek from Santa María to Santa Teresa. It involves crossing three adventurous bridges and bathing in the hot springs at Santa Teresa (US$1.65 entry). The third day is a six-hour trek from Santa Teresa to Aguas Calientes and the final day is a guided tour of Machu Picchu. Average price is US$200 per person.

Vitcos and Vilcabamba

The Incas' last stronghold is reached from **Chaullay**, a village on the road between Ollantaytambo and Quillabamba. The road passes through Peña, a beautiful place with snowy peaks on either side of the valley, then the climb to the pass begins in earnest – on the right is a huge glacier. Soon on the left, Verónica begins to appear in all its huge and snowy majesty. After endless zig-zags and breathtaking views, you reach the Abra Málaga pass (road is paved to here). The descent to the valley shows hillsides covered in lichen and Spanish moss. At Chaullay, the road crosses the river on the historic Choquechaca bridge.

From Chaullay you can drive, or take a daily bus or truck (4-7 hours) to the village of **Huancacalle**, the best base for exploring the nearby Inca ruins of **Vitcos**, with the palace of the last four Inca rulers from 1536 to 1572, and **Yurac Rumi** (or **Chuquipalta**), the impressive sacred white rock of the Incas. There are a few restaurants, shops and basic places to stay at Huancacalle. There is a hostal, **F Sixpac Manco** (managed by the Cobos family). Alternatively villagers will let you stay on their floor, or you can camp near the river below the cemetery. Allow time for hiking to, and visiting Vitcos. It takes one hour to walk from Huancacalle to Vitcos, 45 minutes Vitcos-Chuquipalta, 45 minutes Chuquipalta-Huancacalle. Horses can be hired.

The road from Chaullay continues to **Vilcabamba La Nueva**. You can also hike from Huancacalle; a three-hour walk through beautiful countryside with Inca ruins dotted around. There is a missionary building run by Italians, with electricity and running water, where you may be able to spend the night.

Vilcabamba Vieja

Travellers with ample time can hike from Huancacalle to **Espíritu Pampa**, the site of the **Vilcabamba Vieja** ruins (entry US$11), a vast pre-Inca ruin with a neo-Inca overlay set in deep jungle at 1,000 m. The site is reached on foot or horseback from Pampaconas. From Chaullay, take a truck to Yupanca, Lucma or Pucyura: there rent horses or mules and travel through breathtaking countryside to Espíritu Pampa. From Huancacalle a trip will take 3-4 days on foot, with a further day to get to Chaquiri and transport back to Quillabamba. The INC charge for this trek is US$38, students US$19. It is advisable to take local guides and mules. Maps are available from the South American Explorers in Cuzco and Lima. Ask around in Huancacalle for guides. The Sixpac Manco hostal has various guides and other people in the village will offer their services. Distances are considerable and the going is difficult. *Sixpac Manco*, by Vincent R Lee (available in Cuzco), has accurate maps of all archaeological sites in this area, and describes two expeditions into the region by the author and his party, following in the footsteps of Gene Savoy, who first identified the site in the 1960s. His book, *Antisuyo*, is also recommended reading. The best time of year is May to November, possibly December. Outside this period it is very dangerous as the trails are very narrow and can be thick with mud and very slippery. Insect repellent is essential, also pain-killers and other basic medicines.

Vitcos and Vilcabamba listings

For Sleeping and Eating price codes and other relevant information, see Essentials, pages 38-40.

Transport

Huancacalle *p1462*

Bus Four companies leave Cuzco's bus terminal for **Quillabamba**, taking 8-14 hrs for the 233 km, depending on season, US$6 (**Ampay** is best company). Then take a **combi** from Quillabamba, 0900 and 1200, US$3.30 to Huancacalle, 4-7 hrs. On Fri they go all the way to Vilcabamba.

West from Cuzco

Beyond Anta on the Abancay road, 2 km before Limatambo at the ruins of **Tarahuasi** (US$3.50), a few hundred metres from the road, is a very well-preserved **Inca temple platform**, with 28 tall niches, and a long stretch of fine polygonal masonry. The ruins are impressive, enhanced by the orange lichen which give the walls a honey colour.

Along the Abancay road 100 km from Cuzco, is the exciting descent into the Apurímac canyon, near the former Inca suspension bridge that inspired Thornton Wilder's *The Bridge of San Luis Rey*.

Choquequirao

ⓘ *Entry US$13, students US$6.25.*

Choquequirao is another 'lost city of the Incas', built on a ridge spur almost 1,600 m above the Apurímac. Although only 30% has been uncovered, it is reckoned to be a larger site than Machu Picchu, but with fewer buildings. The main features of Choquequirao are the **Lower Plaza**, considered by most experts to be the focal point of the city. The **Upper Plaza**, reached by a huge set of steps or terraces, has what are possibly ritual baths. A beautiful set of slightly curved agricultural terraces run for over 300 m east-northeast of the Lower Plaza.

Usnu is a levelled hilltop platform, ringed with stones and giving awesome 360-degree views. The **Ridge Group**, still shrouded in vegetation, is a large collection of unrestored buildings some 50-100 m below the Usnu. The **Outlier Building**, isolated and surrounded on three sides by sheer drops of over 1½ km into the Apurímac Canyon, possesses some of the finest stonework within Choquequirao. **Capuliyoc**, nearly 500 m below the Lower Plaza, is a great set of agricultural terraces, visible on the approach from the far side of the valley. One section of terraces is decorated with llamas in white stone.

There are three ways in to Choquequirao. None is a gentle stroll. The shortest way is from **Cachora**, a village on the south side of the Apurímac, reached by a side road from the Cuzco-Abancay highway, shortly after Saywite. It is four hours by bus from Cuzco to the turn-off, then a two-hour descent from the road to Cachora (from 3,695 m to 2,875 m). Guides (Celestino Peña is the official guide) and mules are available in Cachora. From the village you need a day to descend to the Río Apurímac then seven hours to climb up to Choquequirao. Allow 1-2 days at the site then return the way you came. This route is well-signed and in good condition, with excellent campsites and showers en route. Horses can be hired to carry your bags. The second and third routes take a minimum of eight days and require thorough preparation. You can start either at Huancacalle, or at Santa Teresa, between Machu Picchu and Chaullay. Both routes involve an incredible number of strenuous ascents and descents. You should be acclimatised for altitudes ranging from 2,400 m to between 4,600 and 5,000 m and be prepared for extremes of temperature. In each case you end the trail at Cachora. It is possible to start either of these long hikes at Cachora, continuing even from Choquequirao to Espíritu Pampa.

Saywite → *3 km from the main road at Km 49 from Abancay, 153 km from Cuzco, US$3. Altitude: 3,500 m.*
Beyond the town of Curahuasi, 126 km from Cuzco, is the large carved rock of Saywite. It is a UNESCO World Heritage Site. The principal monolith is said to represent the three regions of jungle, sierra and coast, with the associated animals and Inca sites of each. It is fenced in, but ask the guardian for a closer look. It was defaced, allegedly, when a cast was taken of it, breaking off many of the animals' heads. Six further archaeological areas fall away from the stone and its neighbouring group of buildings. The site is more easily reached from Abancay than Cuzco.

West from Cuzco listings

For Sleeping and Eating price codes and other relevant information, see Essentials, pages 38-40.

Sleeping

Choquequirao *p1463*

B pp **Los Tres Balcones**, Jr Abancay s/n, Cachora, www.choquequirau.com. Hostel designed as start and end-point for the trek to Choquequirao. Breakfast included, comfortable, hot showers (**E** pp without bath), restaurant and pizza oven, camping. Shares information with the town's only internet café. They run a 5-day trek to Choquequirao, US$550, with camping gear (but not sleeping bag), all meals and lunch at the Hostel afterwards, entrance to the ruins, horses to carry luggage (US$650 including transport from Cuzco and bilingual tour guide).

D pp **Casa de Salcantay**, Prolongación Salcantay s/n, T984-397336, www.salcantay.com. Price includes breakfast, dinner available if booked in advance. Dutch-run hostel with links to community projects, comfortable, small, Dutch, English, German spoken, can help with arranging independent treks, or organize treks with tour operator.

F pp **La Casona de Ocampo**, San Martín 122, T237514, lacasonadeocampo@yahoo.es. Rooms with hot shower all day, free camping, owner Carlos Robles is knowledgeable.

Transport

Choquequirao *p1463*

From Cuzco take the first Abancay bus of the morning with **Bredde** at 0600, buy your ticket the night before to get a seat. Buses run from Abancay (Jr Prado Alto entre Huancavelica y Núñez) to **Cachora** at 0500 and 1400, return 0630 and 1100, 2 hrs, US$1.50. Cars run from the Curahuasi terminal on Av Arenas, Abancay, US$10 for whole vehicle. Trek from Cachora to Choquequirao.

Central Highlands

The Central Andes are remote mountain areas with small, typical villages. The vegetation is low, but most valleys are cultivated. Roads, all dirt, are in poor condition, sometimes impassable in the rainy season; the countryside is beautiful with spectacular views and the people are friendly. The road into the central Andes has been improved and is paved throughout, offering fine views. Huancayo lies in a valley which produces many crafts; the festivals are very popular and not to be missed.

Lima to Huancayo

The Central Highway more or less parallels the course of the railway between Lima and Huanacayo (335 km). With the paving of roads from Pisco to Ayacucho and Nazca to Abancay, there are now more options for getting to the Sierra and the views on whichever ascent you choose are beyond compare. You can also reach the Central Highlands from Cuzco (via Abancay and Andahuaylas) and from Huaraz (via La Unión and Huánuco), so Lima is not the sole point of access overland.

Chosica and Marcahuasi

Chosica (860 m) is the real starting place for the mountains, 40 km from Lima. It's warm and friendly and a great place to escape Lima's grey cloud. Beyond the town looms a precipitous range of hills almost overhanging the streets. There are some basic *hostales* and, outside town, weekend resorts (see www.chosica.com). Up the Santa Eulalia valley 40 km beyond Chosica, is **Marcahuasi**, a table mountain (US$3) about 3 km by 3 km at 4,200 m, near the village of **San Pedro de Casta**. There are three lakes, a 40-m high 'monumento a la humanidad', and other mysterious lines, gigantic figures, sculptures, astrological signs and megaliths, which late Daniel Ruzo describes in his book, *La Culture Masma*, Extrait de l'Ethnographie, Paris, 1956. Others say that the formations are the result of wind erosion. The trail starts behind the village of San Pedro, and bends to the left. It's three hours to the *meseta*; guides cost about US$3 a day and are advisable in misty weather. Mules for carrying bags cost US$4 to hire, horses US$4.45. Tourist information at the municipality on the plaza sells a map of the plateau for US$1.50. At a shop on the plaza in San Pedro you can buy everything for the trip, including bottled water. Tours can be arranged with travel agencies in Lima.

Chosica to Huancayo

For a while, beyond Chosica, each successive valley looks greener and lusher, with a greater variety of trees and flowers. Between Río Blanco and **Chicla** (Km 127, 3,733 m), Inca contour-terraces can be seen quite clearly. After climbing up from **Casapalca** (Km 139, 4,154 m), there are glorious views of the highest peaks, and more mines, at the foot of a deep gorge. The road ascends to the Ticlio Pass, before the descent to **Morococha** and **La Oroya**. A large metal flag of Peru can be seen at the top of Mount Meiggs, not by any means the highest in the area, but through it runs Galera Tunnel, 1,175 m long, in which the Central Railway reaches its greatest altitude, 4,782 m. The railway itself is a magnificent feat of engineering, with 58 bridges, 69 tunnels and six zigzags, passing beautiful landscapes. It is definitely worth the ride on the new tourist service (see Transport, below). **La Oroya** (3,755 m) is the main smelting centre for the region's mining industry. It stands at the fork of the Yauli and Mantaro rivers. Any traveller, but asthmatics in particular, beware, the pollution from the heavy industry causes severe irritation. (For places to the east and north of La Oroya, see page 1481.)

Jauja The old town of Jauja (*Phone code: 064; Population: 105,000; Altitude: 3,330 m*), 80 km southeast of La Oroya, was Pizarro's provisional capital until the founding of Lima. It has a colourful Wednesday and Sunday market. The **Museo Arqueológico Julio Espejo Núñez** ⓘ *Jr Cusco 537, T361163, Mon and Wed 1500-1900, Sun 0900-1200, 1400-1700, donations welcome, knock on door of La Casa del Caminante opposite where the creator and curator lives*, is a quaint but endearing mix of relics from various Peruvian cultures, including two mummies, one still wrapped in the original shroud. The **Cristo Pobre** church is supposedly modelled after Notre Dame and is something of a curiosity. **Tourist Office** for department of Junín ⓘ *Jr Grau 528, T362897, junin@mincetur.gob.pe (unlikely they will reply!)*. On a hill above Jauja there is a fine line of Inca storehouses, and on hills nearby the ruins of hundreds of circular stone buildings from the Huanca culture (John Hemming). There are also ruins near the **Paca lake**, 3½ km away. The western shore is lined with restaurants; many offer weekend boat trips, US$0.75 (combi from Avenida Pizarro US$0.30).

On the road to Huancayo 18 km to the south, is **Concepción** (*Altitude: 3,251 m*), with a market on Sunday. From Concepción a branch road (6 km) leads to the **Convent of Santa Rosa de Ocopa** ⓘ *0900-1200 and 1500-1800, closed Tue, 45-min tours start on the hour, US$1.10, colectivos from the market in Concepción, 15 mins, US$0.25*, a Franciscan monastery set in beautiful surroundings. It was established in 1725 for training missionaries for the jungle. It contains a fine library with over 20,000 volumes, a biological museum and a large collection of paintings.

Lima to Huancayo listings

For Sleeping and Eating price codes and other relevant information, see Essentials, pages 38-40.

Sleeping

Chosica and Marcahuasi: San Pedro de Casta *p1464*

Locals in town will put you up for US$0.60 pp; ask at tourist information at the municipality on the plaza, T01-571 2087. Take all necessary camping equipment for Marcahuasi trek.

F Marcahuasi, just off the plaza. **G** pp without bath, the best hotel in San Pedro; it also has a restaurant. There are 2 other restaurants.

Chosica to Huancayo: La Oroya *p1465*

F Hostal Chavín, Tarma 281; and **G Hostal Inti**, Arequipa 117, T391098. Both basic.

Jauja *p1465*
D-E Hostal Manco Cápac, Jr Manco Cápac 575, T361620, bbonierbale@terra.com.pe. Central, good rooms, **F** pp in sghared rooms, garden, good breakfast and coffee. Recommended.
F Hostal María Nieves, Jr Gálvez 491, 1 block from the Plaza de Armas, T362543. Safe, helpful, large breakfast, hot water all day, parking. Good.

Eating

Chosica to Huancayo: La Oroya *p1465*
El Tambo, 2 km outside town on the road to Lima. Good trout and frogs, sells local cheese and *manjar*, recommended as the best in and around town, buses on the Lima route stop here.

Jauja *p1465*
Centro Naturista, Huarancayo 138 (no sign). Fruit salad, yoghurt, granola, etc, basic place.
D'Chechis, Jr Bolívar 1166, T368530. Lunch only, excellent.
Ganso de Oro, R Palma 249, T362166. Good restaurant in hotel of same name (which is not recommendable), varied prices, unpretentious.
La Rotonda, Tarapacá 415, T368412. Good lunch menú and pizzas in the evening.

Transport

Chosica *p1464*
Colectivos for Chosica leave from Av Grau, **Lima**, when full, between 0600 and 2100, US$0.75. Most **buses** on the Lima-La Oroya route are full; colectivo taxi to La Oroya US$4, 3 hrs, very scenic, passing the 2nd highest railway in the world.

San Pedro de Casta/Marcahuasi
Bus To San Pedro de Casta leave **Chosica** from Parque Echenique, opposite market, 0900 and 1500, 4 hrs, US$2.50; return 0700 and 1400.

Chosica to Huancayo: La Oroya *p1465*
Bus To **Lima**, 4½ hrs, US$5.50. To **Jauja**, 80 km, 1½ hrs, US$1. To **Tarma**, 1½ hrs, US$1.50. To **Cerro de Pasco**, 131 km, 3 hrs, US$2.20. To **Huánuco**, 236 km, 6 hr, US$4.35. Buses leave from Zeballos, adjacent to the train station. Colectivos also run on all routes.

Jauja *p1465*
Air LC Busre has a daily flight from **Lima** to Francisco Carle airport, just outside Jauja, 45 mins, price includes transfer to Huancayo (marketed 'Lima-Huancayo').
Bus To **Lima**: with **Cruz del Sur**, Pizarro 220, direct, 6 hrs, US$8. Most companies have their offices on the Plaza de Armas, but their buses leave from Av Pizarro. To **Huancayo**, 44 km, takes 1 hr and costs US$1.25. Combis to Huancayo from 25 de Abril y Ricardo Palma, 1¼ hrs, US$1. To **Cerro de Pasco**, **Turismo Central** from 25 de Abril 144, 5 hrs, US$3.55. **Turismo Central** also goes to **Huánuco**, 8 hrs, US$10. To **Tarma**, US$2, hourly with **Trans Los Canarios** and **Angelitos/ San Juan** from Jr Tarma; the latter continues to **Chanchamayo**, US$5.25. Colectivos to Tarma leave from Junín y Tarma when full.

Directory

Jauja *p1465*
Banks Dollar Exchange Huarancayo, on Jr Huarancayo, gives a much better rate than BCP (no TCs). If closed, US$ exchanged at clothes shop at Junín y Bolívar, just off the Plaza. **Internet** All along Junín blocks 9 to 12. **Post offices** Jr Bolívar. **Telephones** Ricardo Palma, opposite *Hotel Ganso de Oro*.

Huancayo and around

→ *Phone code: 064. Colour map 3, C3. Population: over 500,000. Altitude: 3,271 m.*

The city is in the beautiful Mantaro Valley. It is the capital of Junín Department and the main commercial centre for inland Peru. All the villages in the valley produce their own original crafts and celebrate festivals all year round. At the important festivals in Huancayo, people flock in from far and wide with an incredible range of food, crafts, dancing and music. The Sunday market gives a little taste of this every week (it gets going after 0900), but it is better to go to the villages for local handicrafts. Jr Huancavelica, 3 km long and four stalls wide, still sells clothes, fruit, vegetables, hardware, handicrafts and traditional medicines and goods for witchcraft. There is also an impressive daily market behind the railway station and a large handicrafts market between Ancash and Real, block 7, offering a wide selection.

Tourist offices **Huancayo**: Regional office is in Jauja; see above. **Small tourist information booth** ⓘ *Plaza Huamanmarca, Real 481, T238480/233251.* **Indecopi** ⓘ *Moquegua 730, El Tambo, T245180, abarrientos@indecopi.gob.pe.* **Touring y Automóvil Club del Perú** ⓘ *Jr Lima 355, T231204, huancayo@touringperu.com.pe.*

The **museum** at the Salesian school, north of the river on Pasaje Santa Rosa ⓘ *Mon-Fri 0900-1800, Sun 1000-1200, US$1.75, www.hyoperu.com/huancayo/museos/1*, is a fascinating cabinet of curiosities with everything ranging from two-headed beasts to a collection of all the

Huancayo

200 metres
200 yards

Sleeping
1 Casa Alojamiento de Aldo y Soledad Bonilla *C2*
2 El Marquez *A2*
3 Hosp Familiar Tachi *B2*
4 Hostal Santo Domingo *B1*
5 Kiya *B2*
6 La Casa de La Abuela *B3*
7 Los Balcones *A2*
8 Peru Andino *A3*
9 Presidente *C2*
10 Retama Inn *C2*
11 Santa Felicita *B2*
12 Turismo *B2*

Eating
1 A La Leña *B2*
2 Café El Parque *B2*
3 Chifa El Centro *B2*
4 Chifa Xu *B2*
5 Detrás de la Catedral *B2*
6 Donatelo's *B2*
7 El Inka *A2*
8 El Olímpico *B2*
9 El Paraíso *C2*
10 ImaginArte *A2*
11 La Cabaña *B3*
12 La Pérgola *A2*
13 Panadería Koky *B2*
14 Pizzería Antojitos *B2*

coins of the United States of America. The **Parque de Identidad Wanka** ⓘ *on Jr San Jorge in the Barrio San Carlos northeast of the city, entry free, but contributions are appreciated,* is a fascinating mixture of surrealistic construction interwoven with indigenous plants and trees and the cultural history of the Mantaro Valley.

Mantaro Valley

The whole Mantaro valley is rich in culture. On the outskirts of town is **Torre-Torre**, impressive, eroded sandstone towers on the hillside. Take a bus to Cerrito de la Libertad and walk up. The ruins of **Warivilca** (15 km) ⓘ *1000-1200, 1500-1700 (museum mornings only), US$0.15, take a micro for Chilca from C Real* are near **Huari**, with the remains of a pre-Inca temple of the Huanca tribe. Museum in the plaza, with deformed skulls, and modelled and painted pottery of successive Huanca and Inca occupations of the shrine. Between Pilcomayo and Huayo (15 km) is the **Geophysical Institute of Huayo**, on the 'Magnetic Equator' 12½° south of the geographical equator (best to visit in the morning, or when the sun is shining). Take bus from Jr Giráldez to Chupaca, but get out by bridge before Chupaca, where the road splits, then take a colectivo.

East of the Mantaro River The villages of **Cochas Chico** and **Cochas Grande**, 11 km away, are where the famous *mate burilado*, or gourd carving, is done. You can buy them cheaply direct from the manufacturers, but ask around. Beautiful views of the Valle de Mantaro and Huancayo. *Micros* leave from the corner of Amazonas and Giráldez, US$0.25.

Hualahoyo (11 km) has a little chapel with 21 colonial canvases. **San Agustín de Cajas** (8 km) makes fine hats, and **San Pedro** (10 km) makes wooden chairs; **Hualhuas** (12 km) fine alpaca weavings which you can watch being made. The weavers take special orders; small items can be finished in a day. Negotiate a price.

The town of **San Jerónimo** is renowned for the making of silver filigree jewellery; Wednesday market. Fiesta on the third Saturday in August. There are ruins 2-3 hours' walk above San Jerónimo, but seek advice before hiking to them.

Between Huancayo and Huancavelica, **Izcuchaca** is the site of a bridge over the Río Mantaro. On the edge of town is a fascinating pottery workshop whose machinery is driven by a water turbine (plus a small shop). A nice hike is to the chapel on a hill overlooking the valley; about one to 1½ hours each way.

Huancayo and around listings

For Sleeping and Eating price codes and other relevant information, see Essentials, pages 38-40.

Sleeping

Huancayo *p1466, map p1467*

Prices may be raised in Holy Week. **Note**: The Plaza de Armas is called Plaza Constitución.

A-B Turismo, Ancash 729, T231072, www.hoteles-del-centro.com. Restored colonial building, same owner as Presidente, with more atmosphere, elegant, rooms quite small, TV, Wi-Fi extra, quiet. Restaurant (TT-T) serves good meals, fine service.

B El Marquez, Puno 294, T219202, www.elmarquezhuancayo.com. With breakfast, TV, free internet access, Wi-Fi, good value, efficient, popular with local business travellers, safe parking.

B Presidente, C Real 1130, T231735, www.hoteles-del-centro.com. Helpful, classy, safe, serves breakfast, restaurant. Recommended.

D Kiya, Giráldez 107, T214955, www.hotelkiya.com. Comfortable although ageing, hot water, helpful staff. Spectacular view of Plaza.

D-E Santa Felicita, Giráldez 145, Plaza Constitución, T235285, irmaleguia@hotmail.com. Hot water, cheaper without TV, good, breakfast extra.

E pp **Casa Alojamiento de Aldo y Soledad Bonilla**, Huánuco 332, ½ block from Mcal Cáceres bus station, T232103. Cheaper without full board, colonial house, owners speak English, laundry, secure, relaxing, nice courtyard, tours arranged, best to book ahead, renovated in 2009.

E La Casa de la Abuela, Av Giráldez 691, T223303, www.incasdelperu.org/casa-de-la-abuela. Hot shower, breakfast included, some rooms with antique beds, dormitory **G**, laundry facilities, meals available, internet and Wi-Fi, sociable staff, owner speaks English, good meeting place, free pickup from bus station if requested in advance.

E Los Balcones, Jr Puno 282, T211041/214881. Very comfortable rooms, Wi-fi, cable TV, hot water, helpful staff, elevator (practically disabled-accessible). View of the back of the Cathedral. Highly recommended.

E Retama Inn, Ancash 1079, T219193, retamainn73@hotmail.com. All amenities, comfortable beds, hot water, TV, café/bar, helpful, breakfast US$2.

F pp **Peru Andino**, Pasaje San Antonio 113-115, one block Parque Túpac Amaru, in first block of Francisco Solano (left side of Defensoria del Pueblo), 10-15 mins walk from the centre (if taking a taxi, stress that it's *Pasaje* San Antonio), T223956, www.peruandino.com. Including breakfast, hot showers, several rooms with bath, safe area, cosy atmosphere, run by Sra Juana and Luis, who speak some English, organize trekking and mountain bike tours, cooking and laundry facilities, Spanish classes. Can pick up guests at Lima airport with transfer to pus station. Highly recommended.

G pp **Hospedaje Familiar Tachi**, Huamanmarca 125, T219980, saenz_nildy@hotmail.com. Central but not the safest area, small, comfortable, hot water, shared showers, family run, nice atmosphere and views from terrace.

G Hostal Santo Domingo, Ica 6755, T218890. Set around 2 pleasant patios, basic, good value. Pay up front.

Mantaro Valley *p1468*

Izcuchaca has 1 hotel on the plaza, no bathroom, use the public bath by the river; the other is just off the plaza, a yellow 3-storey house, **G**, no shower, toilet suitable for men only, chamber pot supplied, only blankets on bed, cold. Ask in stores off the plaza. Many locals are enthusiastic about renting a room to a gringo traveller for a night. You may well make a friend for life.

Eating

Huancayo *p1466, map p1467*

Breakfast is served in Mercado Modelo from 0700. Better class, more expensive restaurants, serving typical dishes for about US$4-5, plus 18% tax, drinks can be expensive. Lots of cheap restaurants along Av Giráldez.

TT El Olímpico, Giráldez 199. Long-established, one of the more upscale establishments offering Andean and Creole dishes; the real reason to go is the owner's model car collection displayed in glass cabinets.

TT La Cabaña, Av Giráldez 652. Pizzas, ice cream, *calentitos*, and other dishes, excellent atmosphere, live folk music Thu-Sun.

TT Pizzería Antojitos, Puno 599. Attractive, atmospheric pizzería with live music some nights.

TT-T Chifa Xu, Giráldez 208. Good food at reasonable prices, always-bustling atmosphere.

TT-T Detrás de la Catedral, Jr Ancash 335 (behind Cathedral as name suggests), T212969. Pleasant atmosphere, excellent dishes. Charcoal grill in the corner keeps the place warm on cold nights. Consider by many to be the best in town.

T A La Leña, Paseo la Breña 144 and on Ancash. Good rotisserie chicken and salads, popular.

T Chifa El Centro, Giráldez 238, T217575. Another branch at Av Leandra Torres 240. Chinese food, good service and atmosphere.

T Donatelo's, Puno 287. Excellent pizza and chicken place, with nice atmosphere, popular.

T La Pérgola, Puno 444. Pleasant atmosphere, woody and warm, overlooking the plaza, 4-course *menú*.

Cafés

Café El Parque, Giráldez y Ancash, on the main plaza. Popular place for juices, coffee and cakes.

El Inka, Puno 530. Popular *fuente de soda*, with coffee, Peruvian food, desserts, milkshakes.

El Paraíso, Arequipa 428, and another opposite at No 429. Both vegetarian places, OK.

ImaginArte, Jr.Ancash 260. Principally an art gallery, often displaying work based on ethnic Peruvian culture. Good coffee and cakes. Open from 1800.

Panadería Koky, Ancash y Puno, serves Hotel Marquez. Open 0700-2300, lunch 1230-1530. Good for breakfasts, lunches, sandwiches, capuccino and pastries, fancy atmosphere, free Wi-Fi.

Mantaro Valley *p1468*
Restaurant El Parque on plaza, Izcuchaca. Opens 0700, delicious food.

Bars and clubs

Huancayo *p1466, map p1467*
Clubs Most open around 2000 and close at 0200. Some charge an entrance fee of US$3-4. Eg: **Galileo**, Paseo La Breña 378. High-class bar, live music at night. **La Noche**, Pasaje San Antonio 241. Nice discoteque.
Peñas All the *peñas* have folklore shows with dancing, open normally Fri, Sat and Sun from 1300 to 2200. Entrance fee is about US$2 pp. Eg **Ollantaytambo**, Puno, block 2, and **Taki Wasi**, Huancavelica y 13 de Noviembre.

Festivals and events

Huancayo *p1466, map p1467*
There are so many festivals in the Mantaro Valley that it is impossible to list them all. Nearly every day of the year there is some sort of celebration in one of the villages.

Jan: 1-6, New Year celebrations; 20, **San Sebastián y San Fabián** (recommended in Jauja). **Feb**: there are carnival celebrations for the whole month, with highlights on 2, **Virgen de la Candelaria**, and 17-19 **Concurso de Carnaval**. **Mar-Apr**: **Semana Santa**, with impressive Good Friday processions. **May**: **Fiesta de las Cruces** throughout the whole month. **Jun**: 15 **Virgen de las Mercedes**; 24, **San Juan Bautista**; 29, **Fiesta Patronal**. **Jul**: 16, **Virgen del Carmen**; 24-25, **Santiago**. **Aug**: 4, **San Juan de Dios**; 16, **San Roque**; 30, **Santa Rosa de Lima**. **Sep**: 8, **Virgen de Cocharcas**; 15, **Virgen de la Natividad**; 23-24, **Virgen de las Mercedes**; 29, **San Miguel Arcángel**. **Oct**: 4, **San Francisco de Asís**; 18, **San Lucas**; 28-30 culmination of month-long celebrations for **El Señor de los Milagros**. **Nov**: 1, **Día de Todos los Santos**. **Dec**: 3-13, **Virgen de Guadalupe**; 8, **Inmaculada Concepción**; 25, **Navidad** (Christmas).

Shopping

Huancayo *p1466, map p1467*
Thieves in the market hand out rolled up paper and pick your pocket while you unravel them.
Crafts All crafts are made outside Huancayo in the many villages of the Mantaro Valley, or in Huancavelica. The villages are worth a visit to learn how the items are made.
Casa de Artesano, on the corner of Real and Paseo La Breña, at Plaza Constitución. Has a wide selection of good quality crafts.

Activities and tours

Huancayo *p1466, map p1467*
Tour operators
American Travel & Service, Plaza Constitución 122, of 2 (next to the Cathedral), T211181, 964 830220 (mob), americtr@huncayotravel.com. Wide range of classical and more adventurous tours in the Mantaro Valley and in the Central Jungle. Transport and equipment rental possible. Most group based day tours start at US$8-10 pp.
Dargui Tours, Jr Ancash 367, Plaza Constitución, T233705 (also Lima, Av Conquistadores 1020 of 203, San Isidro. T01-422 7132). Standard local tours.
In the Andes, above **Dargui Tours**, T226933, www.intheandes.com. Peruvian-German owned, trekking and mountaineering tours.
Incas del Perú, Av Giráldez 652, T223303, www.incasdelperu.org. Associated with the **La Cabaña/Otra Lado** restaurants and **La Casa de la Abuela**. Run jungle, biking and riding trips throughout the region, as well as language and volunteer programs. Very popular with travellers in the region.
Peruvian Tours, Plaza Constitución 122, p 2, of 1, T213069, Eaiperu@hotmail.com. Next to the Cathedral and American Travel & Service. Classic tours of the Mantaro valley, plus day trips up to the Huaytapallana Nevados above Huancayo, plus long, 16-hr excursions to Cerro de Pasco and Tarma.

Guides
Marco Jurado Ames, T201260 or 964 227050 (mob), andinismo_peru@yahoo.es. Rock climbing and mountaineering, organizes long-distance treks on the 'hidden paths of Peru'. Many of these include Huancayo, such as a trek from to Machu Picchu from the Amazon lowlands via Choquequirao and Inca Trail to Pariaccacca in the central Andes. Can start in Huancayo or Lima.

Transport

Huancayo *p1466, map p1467*

Bus A new bus terminal for all buses to all destinations is planned 3 km north of the centre. There are regular buses to **Lima**, 6-7 hrs on a good paved road, US$10-13. Travelling by day is recommended for the fantastic views and, of course, for safety. If you must travel by night, take warm clothing. Recommended companies: **Ormeño**, Av Mcal Castilla 1379, El Tambo; **Cruz del Sur**, Ayacucho 281, T235650, **Turismo Central**, Jr Ayacucho 274, T223128 (double-decker *bus cama*), and **Transportes Rogger**, Lima 561, T212687, *cama* and *semi-cama* at 1300 and 2330, comercial at 2230.

To **Ayacucho**, 319 km, 9-10 hrs, US$10-12 with **Molina**, C Angaráes 334, T224501, 3 a day, recommended; 1 a day with **Turismo Central** US$8. The road is paved for the first 70 km, then in poor condition and is very difficult in the wet. Take warm clothing. (**Note** If driving to Ayacucho and beyond, roads are "amazingly rough". Don't go alone. Count kilometres diligently to keep a record of where you are: road signs are poor.) After Izcuchaca, on the railway to Huancavelica, there is a good road to the Quichuas hydroelectric scheme, but after that it is narrow with hair-raising bends and spectacular bridges. The scenery is staggering.

To **Huancavelica**, 147 km, 5 hrs, US$2.85. Many buses daily, including **Transportes Yuri**, Ancash 1220, 3 a day. The road has been paved and is a delightful ride, much more comfortable than the train (if you can find a driver who will not scare you to death). A private car from Huancayo costs US$12-17 pp depending on your negotiating skills.

To **Cerro de Pasco**, 255 km, 5 hrs, US$4. Several departures. Alternatively, take a bus to La Oroya, about every 20 mins, from Av Real about 10 blocks north of the main plaza. From La Oroya there are regular buses and colectivos to Cerro. The road to La Oroya and on to Cerro is in good condition. To **Huánuco**, 7 hrs, **Turismo Central** at 2115, US$6, good service.

To **Chanchamayo**: **Angelitos/San Juan**, Ferrocarril 161 and Plaza Amazonas, every 1½ hrs, and **Tans Los Canarios** hourly service via Jauja to Tarma, 3 hrs, US$3, some of which continue on to La Merced, 5 hrs, US$4.70.

To **Cañete**, 289 km, 10 hrs, US$4, **ETAS/Angoma**, Loreto 744, T215424. It is a poor road with beautiful mountain landscapes before dropping to the valley of Cañete.

To **Jauja**, 44 km, 1 hr. Colectivos and combis leave every few mins from Huamanmarca y Amazonas, and Plaza Amazonas, US$1.50. Ones via San Jerónimo and Concepción have 'Izquierda' on the front. Taxi to Jauja US$10, 45 mins. Most buses to the Mantaro Valley leave from several places around the market area. Buses to **Hualhuas** and **Cajas** leave from block 3 of Pachitea. Buses to **Cochas** leave from Amazonas y Giráldez.

Train There are 2 unconnected railway stations. The Central station serves **Lima**, via La Oroya: Service on this railway with trains at weekends run by **Ferrocarril Centro Andino**, Av José Galvez Barrenechea 566, p 5, San Isidro, Lima, T01-226 6363, www.ferrocarrilcentral.com.pe. The fare is US$75 *turístico*, US$38 *clásico*, one way. The train leaves Lima Thu or Fri 0700 on set weekends (check website), 11 hrs, returns Sun 0700 or 1800. Coaches have reclining seats, heating, restaurant, tourist information, toilets, and nurse with first aid and oxygen. Information on forthcoming departures can be obtained from the websites or travel agents, see Activities and tours, above.

From the small station in Chilca suburb (15 mins by taxi, US$1), trains run to **Huancavelica**, on a narrow gauge (3 ft). There are usually 2 trains a day, but work to improve the line was delayed by heavy rains in early 2010. There are 38 tunnels and the line reaches 3,676 m. This "classic" Andean train journey takes 7 hrs and has fine views, passing through typical mountain villages where vendors sell food and crafts. In some places, the train has to reverse and change tracks.

Directory

Huancayo *p1466, map p1467*

Banks BCP, Real 1039. **Scotiabank**, Real casi Ica. **Interbank** and **Banco Continental** are on block 6 of Real. There are several *casas de cambio* on Ancash. The best place to change money is C Lima, parallel to Plaza Constitución, where a number of kiosks stamp your exchanged bills as a means of guaranteeing them. Establish a relationship with the same person and he will give you a special rate. **Internet** Numerous places round Plaza Constitución on Giráldez, Paseo La Breña; average price under US$0.75 per hr. **Language classes** Incas del Perú (see Activities and tours, above) organizes Spanish courses for beginners for US$100 per week, including accommodation at **Hostal La Casa de La Abuela**, Av Giráldez 691, and all meals, also homestays and weaving, playing traditional music, Peruvian cooking and lots of other things. **Katia Cerna** is a recommended teacher, T225332, katiacerna@hotmail.com. She can arrange home stays; her sister works in adventure tourism.

Huancavelica

→ *Phone code: 064. Colour map 3, C3. Population: 37,500. Altitude: 3,660 m.*

Huancavelica is a friendly and attractive town, surrounded by huge, rocky mountains. It was founded in the 16th century by the Spanish to exploit rich deposits of mercury and silver. It is predominantly an indigenous town, and people still wear traditional costume. There are beautiful mountain walks in the neighbourhood. The Cathedral, located on the Plaza de Armas, has an altar considered to be one of the finest examples of colonial art in Peru. Also very impressive are the five other churches in town. The church of San Francisco, for example, has no less than 11 altars. Sadly, though, most of the churches are closed to visitors. **Tourist office**: **Dircetur** ⓘ *Jr Victoria Garma 444, T452938, dircetur_hcv@hotmail.com*. Very helpful.

Bisecting the town is the Río Huancavelica. South of the river is the main commercial centre. North of the river, on the hillside, are the **thermal baths** ⓘ *0600-1500, US$0.15 for private rooms, water not very hot, US$0.10 for the hot public pool, also hot showers, take a lock for the doors.* The handicraft sellers congregate in front of the Municipalidad on M Muñoz and the Biblioteca on the Plaza de Armas (V Toledo). Most handicrafts are transported directly to Lima, but you can still visit craftsmen in neighbouring villages. The Potaqchiz hill, just outside the town, gives a fine view, about one hour walk up from San Cristóbal. **Instituto Nacional de la Cultura** ⓘ *Plazoleta San Juan de Dios, T453420, inc_huancavelica@yahoo.es*, is a good source of information on festivals, archaeological sites, history, etc. Gives courses on music and dancing, and lectures some evenings. There is also an interesting but small **Museo Regional** ⓘ *Arica y Raimondi, Mon-Sat 1000-1300, 1500-1900.*

Huancavelica to Ayacucho

The direct route from Huancavelica to Ayacucho (247 km) goes via **Santa Inés** (4,650 m), 78 km. Out of Huancavelica the road climbs steeply with switchbacks between herds of llamas and alpacas grazing on rocky perches. Around Pucapampa (Km 43) is one of the highest habitable *altiplanos* (4,500 m), where the rare and highly prized ash-grey alpaca can be seen. Snow- covered mountains are passed as the road climbs to 4,853 m at the Abra Chonta pass, 23 km before Santa Inés. By taking the turnoff to Huachocolpa at Abra Chonta and continuing for 3 km you'll reach the highest drivable pass in the world, at 5,059 m. Nearby are two lakes (Laguna Choclacocha) which can be visited in 2½ hours. 52 km beyond Santa Inés at the Abra de Apacheta (4,750 m), 98 km from Ayacucho, the rocks are all the colours of the rainbow, and running through this fabulous scenery is a violet river. See Transport, below, for road services and lodging options on this route.

There is another route to Ayacucho from Huancayo, little used by buses, but which involves not so much climbing for cyclists. Cross the pass into the Mantaro valley on the road to **Quichuas** . Then to **Anco** and **Mayocc** (lodging). From here the road crosses a bridge after 10 km and in another 20 km reaches **Huanta** in the picturesque valley of the same name. It celebrates the *Fiesta de las Cruces* during the first week of May. Its Sunday market is large and interesting. Then it's a paved road 48 km to Ayacucho. On the road from Huanta, 24 km from Ayacucho, is the site of perhaps the oldest known culture in South America, 20,000 years old, evidence of which was found in the cave of **Pikimachay**. The remains are now in Lima's museums.

Huancavelica listings

For Sleeping and Eating price codes and other relevant information, see Essentials, pages 38-40.

Sleeping

Huancavelica *p1472*

E Ascención, Jr Manco Capac 481 (Plaza de Armas), T451397. A hidden treasure, no sign, use wooden door next to the Comisaría and follow the sign that says "Hote"l. Very comfortable, wooden floors, with bath and cable TV, cheaper without, hot water. Cafetín coming soon. Highly recommended.

E La Portada, Virrey Toledo 252, T453603. Cheaper without bath, hot water, heater extra, very basic, small desks in rooms, secure metal doors. Women may be put off by the public urinal in the shared shower area, but there is a better bathroom by the cafeteria.

E Presidente, Plaza de Armas, T452760, www.hoteles-del-centro.com. Lovely colonial building, higher-priced suites available, cable TV, heating, parking, breakfast included, safe, Wi-Fi, internet, laundry, restaurant and café.

E-F San José, Jr Huancayo 299, T752958. Solar hot water in daytime, cheaper without bath or TV, secure, nice beds, helpful but basic.

F Camacho, Jr Carabaya 481, T453298. Shared showers, hot water morning only, good value, secure, old-fashioned, good value.

F-G Tawantinsuyo, Carabaya 399 y Manchego Muñoz, T452968. Wooden floors, curtains, 24-hr hot water, cheaper without washbasin.

Huancavelica to Ayacucho *p1472*

G Alojamiento Andino, in Santa Inés, a very friendly restaurant, **El Favorito**, where you can sleep, and several others.

G Hostal Recreo Sol y Sombra, in Quichuas. Charming, small courtyard, helpful, basic.

G Hostal Gabi, in Anco. Appalling, but better than anything else.

Eating

Huancavelica *p1472*

ΨΨ-Ψ Mochica Sachún, Av Virrey Toledo 303. Great *menú* US$1.50, full meals available, sandwiches, friendly.

Ψ Chifa El Mesón, Manchego Muñoz 153, T453570. Very popular, standard chifa fare. Delivery available.

Ψ Joy, Virrey Toledo 230. Creole and regional dishes, sandwiches, long-established, award-winning, bright. Also **Joy Campestre**, Av de los Incas 870. Serves typical Peruvian regional dishes in leisurely country environment.

Ψ Roma II, Manco Capac 580, T452608. Open 1800-2300. Pizzas, smells delicious, friendly staff, delivery available.

Festivals and events

Huancavelica *p1472*

The whole area is rich in culture. **Fiesta de los Reyes Magos y los Pastores, 4-8 Jan**. **Fiesta del Niño Perdido** is held on **2nd Sun in Jan**. **Pukllaylay Carnavales**, celebration of the first fruits from the ground (harvest), **20 Jan-mid Mar**. **Semana Santa**, Holy Week. **Toro Pukllay** festival **last week of May, 1st week of Jun**. **Fiesta de Santiago** is held in **May and Aug** in all communities. **Los Laygas** or **Galas** (scissors dance), **22-28 Dec**.

Transport

Huancavelica *p1472*

Bus All bus companies have their offices on, and leave from the east end of town, around Parque M Castilla, on Muñoz, Iquitos, Tumbes and O'Donovan. To **Huancayo**, 147 km, 5 hrs, US$2.85, paved road, **Transportes Yuri** and **Transportes Ticllas** (O'Donovan 500). To **Lima** via Huancayo, 445 km, 13 hrs minimum, US$9. Most buses to Huancayo go on to Lima, there are several a day. The other route is to **Pisco**, 269 km, 12 hrs, US$7 and **Ica**, US$8, 1730 daily, with **Oropesa**, O'Donovon 599. Buy your ticket 1 day in advance. The road is poor until it joins the Ayacucho-Pisco road, where it improves. Most of the journey is done at night. Be prepared for sub-zero temperatures in the early morning as the bus passes snowfields, then for temperatures of 25-30°C as the bus descends to the coast.

Train See under Huancayo; trains leave for Huancayo at 0630 and1300, daily.

Huancavelica to Ayacucho *p1472*

There is no direct transport from Huancavelica to Ayacucho, other than 0430 on Sat with **San Juan Bautista** (Plazoleta Túpac Amaru 107, T803062), US$5.70. Otherwise you have to go to

Rumichaca just beyond Santa Inés on the paved Pisco-Ayacucho road, also with **San Juan Bautista** 0430, 4 hrs, then wait for a passing bus to Ayacucho at 1500, US$2, or try to catch a truck. Rumichaca has only a couple of foodstalls and some filthy toilets. This route is one of the highest continuous roads in the world. The journey is a cold one but spectacular as the road rarely drops below 4,000 m for 150 km. The best alternative is to take a colectivo Huancavelica-**Lircay**, a small village with **F** unnamed hostal at Sucre y La Unión, with bath and hot water, much better than Hostal El Paraíso, opposite, also with bath, **G** without (**Transportes 5 de Mayo**, Av Sebastián Barranca y Cercado, US$4.55, 2½ hrs, leave when full). The same company runs from Lircay Terminal Terrestre hourly from 0430 to Julcamarca (colonial church, **Hostal Villa Julcamarca**, near plaza, no tap water, really basic), 2½ hrs, US$3, then take a minibus from Julcamarca plaza to Ayacucho, US$2, 2 hrs; beautiful scenery all the way. Another option is to take the train to Izcuchaca, stay the night and take the colectivo (see above).

Directory

Huancavelica *p1472*

Banks BCP, Virrey Toledo 300 block. There is a *Multired* ATM on M Muñoz in front of the Municipalidad. **Internet** Despite what they say, internet places open around 0900 till 2100-2200. There are places on V Toledo and M Muñoz. **Librería Municipal**, Plaza de Armas, US$0.60 per hr. **Post offices** Ferrua Jos, at block 8 of M Muñoz. **Telephones** Carabaya y Virrey Toledo.

Ayacucho → *Phone code: 066. Colour map 3, C3. Population: 105,918. Altitude: 2,748 m.*

A week can easily be spent enjoying Ayacucho and its hinterland. The climate is lovely, with warm, sunny days and pleasant balmy evenings, and the people are very hospitable. Semana Santa celebrations are famous throughout South America. Ayacucho was founded on 9 January 1539. On the Pampa de Quinua, on 9 December 1824, the decisive Battle of Ayacucho was fought, bringing Spanish rule in Peru to an end. In the middle of the festivities, the Liberator Simón Bolívar decreed that the city be named Ayacucho, 'City of Blood', instead of its original name, Huamanga.

The city is built round the Plaza Mayor, the main plaza, with the Cathedral, Municipalidad, Universidad Nacional de San Cristóbal de Huamanga (UNSCH) and various colonial mansions facing on to it. It is famous for its Semana Santa celebrations, its splendid market and its 33 churches. **Tourist offices: i perú** ⓘ *Portal Municipal 45, on the Plaza, T318305, iperuayacucho@promperu.gob.pe, daily 0830-1930, Sun 0830-1430*. Very helpful. Also has an office at the airport. **Dirección Regional de Industria y Turismo** (Dircetur) ⓘ *Asamblea 481, T312548. Mon-Fri 0800-1300*, friendly and helpful. **Tourist Police** ⓘ *Arequipa cuadra 1, T312055.*

Sights

The **Cathedral** ⓘ *daily 1700-1900, Sun 0900-1700*, built in 1612, has superb gold leaf altars. It is beautifully lit at night. On the north side of the Plaza Mayor, on the corner of Portal de la Unión and Asamblea, are the **Casonas de los Marqueses de Mozobamba y del Pozo**, also called Velarde-Alvarez. Recently restored as the Centro Cultural de la UNSCH, frequent artistic and cultural exhibitions are held here. The **Museo de Arte Popular Joaquín López Antay** ⓘ *Portal de la Unión 28, in the BCP building, museo@ unsch.edu.pe, Tue-Fri 1030-1700, Sat 1030-1230*, displays local craft work. North of the Plaza is **Santo Domingo** (1548) ⓘ *9 de Diciembre, block 2, Mass daily 0700-0800*. Its fine façade has triple Roman arches and Byzantine towers.

Jr 28 de Julio is pedestrianized for two blocks. A stroll down here leads to the prominent **Arco del Triunfo** (1910), which commemorates victory over the Spaniards. Through the arch is the church of **San Francisco de Asís** (1552) ⓘ *28 de Julio , block 3, daily for morning mass and 1730-1830*. It has an elaborate gilt main altar and several others. Across 28 de Julio from San Fancisco is the **Mercado de Abastos Carlos F Vivanco**, the packed central market. As well as all the household items and local produce, look for the cheese sellers,the breads and the section dedicated to fruit juices.

Ayacucho

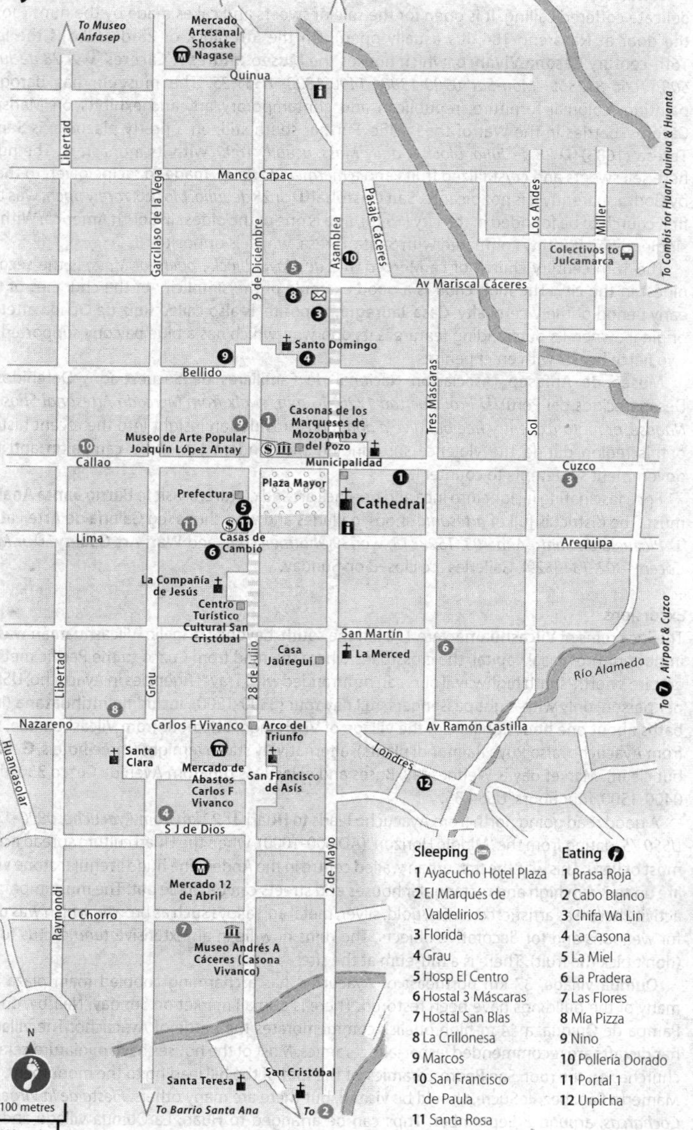
To 2
To Pisco & Lima
To Museo Anfasep
Mercado Artesanal Shosake Nagase
Quinua
Libertad
Manco Capac
Garcilaso de la Vega
9 de Diciembre
Asamblea
Pasaje Cáceres
Los Andes
Miller
Colectivos to Julcamarca
To Combis for Huari, Quinua & Huanta
Av Mariscal Cáceres
Santo Domingo
Bellido
Tres Máscaras
Sol
Casonas de los Marqueses de Mozobamba y del Pozo
Museo de Arte Popular Joaquín López Antay
Municipalidad
Callao
Cuzco
Plaza Mayor
Prefectura
Cathedral
Lima
Casas de Cambio
Arequipa
La Compañía de Jesús
Centro Turístico Cultural San Cristóbal
San Martín
Casa Jaúregui
La Merced
Río Alameda
To 7, Airport & Cuzco
Grau
28 de Julio
Nazareno
Carlos F Vivanco
Arco del Triunfo
Av Ramón Castilla
Huancasolar
Santa Clara
Mercado de Abastos Carlos F Vivanco
San Francisco de Asís
Londres
S J de Dios
2 de Mayo
Mercado 12 de Abril
Raymondi
C Chorro
Museo Andrés A Cáceres (Casona Vivanco)
Santa Teresa
San Cristóbal
To Barrio Santa Ana
To 2
N
100 metres
100 yards
Sleeping
1 Ayacucho Hotel Plaza
2 El Marqués de Valdelirios
3 Florida
4 Grau
5 Hosp El Centro
6 Hostal 3 Máscaras
7 Hostal San Blas
8 La Crillonesa
9 Marcos
10 San Francisco de Paula
11 Santa Rosa
Eating
1 Brasa Roja
2 Cabo Blanco
3 Chifa Wa Lin
4 La Casona
5 La Miel
6 La Pradera
7 Las Flores
8 Mía Pizza
9 Nino
10 Pollería Dorado
11 Portal 1
12 Urpicha

Santa Clara de Asís ⓘ *Jr Grau, block 3, open for Mass*, is renowned for its beautifully delicate coffered ceiling. It is open for the sale of sweets and cakes made by the nuns (go to the door at Nazareno 184, it's usually open). On the 5th block of 28 de Julio is the late 16th-century **Casona Vivanco**, which houses the **Museo Andrés A Cáceres** ⓘ *Jr 28 de Julio 508, T066-812360, Mon-Sat 0900-1300, 1400-1800. US$1.25*. The museum has baroque painting, colonial furniture, republican and contemporary art, and exhibits on Mariscal Cáceres' battles in the War of the Pacific. Further south still, on a pretty plazuela, is **Santa Teresa** (1683) ⓘ *28 de Julio, block 6, daily Mass, usually 1600*, with its monastery. The nuns here sell sweets and crystallized fruits and a *mermelada de ají*, made to recipe given to them by God; apparently it is not picante. **San Cristóbal** ⓘ *Jr 28 de Julio, block 6, rarely open*, was the first church to be founded in the city (1540), and is one of the oldest in South America. With its single tower, it is tiny compared with Santa Teresa, which is opposite.

The 16th-century church of **La Merced** ⓘ *2 de Mayo, block , open for Mass*, is the second oldest in the city. The high choir is a good example of the simplicity of the churches of the early period of the Viceroyalty. **Casa Jáuregui**, opposite, is also called **Ruiz de Ochoa** after its original owner. Its outstanding feature is its doorway, which has a blue balcony supported by two fierce beasts with erect penises.

Museo de Anfasep (Asociación Nacional de Familiares de Secuestrados Detenidos y Desaparecidos del Perú) ⓘ *Prol Libertad 1226, 15 mins' walk from Mercado Artesanal Shosake Nagase, or mototaxi, entry free but give a donation*, provides an insight into the recent history of this region during the violence surrounding the Sendero Luminoso campaign and the government's attempts to counter it.

For a fascinating insight into Inca and pre-Inca art and culture, a visit to **Barrio Santa Ana** is a must. The district is full of *artesanía* shops, galleries and workshops (eg **Galería de Arte Latina** ⓘ *Plazuela de Santa Ana 105, T528315, wari39@hotmail.com*, and **Wari Art Gallery** ⓘ *Jr Mcal Cáceres 302, T312529*). Galleries are closed on Sunday.

Excursions

The Inca ruins of **Vilcashuamán** are 120 km the south, beyond Cangallo. Vilcashuamán was an important provincial capital, the crossroads where the road from Cuzco to the Pacific met the empire's north-south highway. Tours can be arranged with Travel Agencies in Ayacucho, US$13 per person, only with eight passengers, full day tour (0500-1800), including **Intihuatana** (Inca baths about one hour uphill from the village of Vischongo, one hour from Vilcashuamán, five from Ayacucho, also Puya Raimondi plants); alternatively stay overnight (three hotels, **G**, basic but clean). Market day is Wednesday. Buses and colectivos run from Avenida Cuzco 350, daily 0400-1500, four hours, US$4.35.

A good road going north from Ayacucho leads to **Huari** ⓘ *22 km from Ayacucho, 0800-1700, US$0.75*, dating from the 'Middle Horizon' (AD 600-1000), when the Huari culture spread across most of Peru. This was the first urban walled centre in the Andes. The huge irregular stone walls are up to 3-4 m high and rectangular houses and streets can be made out. The most important activity here was artistic: ceramics, gold, silver, metal and alloys such as bronze, which was used for weapons and for decorative objects. The ruins now lie in an extensive *tuna* cactus forest (don't pick the fruit). There is a museum at the site.

Quinua village, 37 km northeast of Ayacucho, has a charming cobbled main plaza and many of the buildings have been restored. There is a small market on Sunday. Nearby, on the Pampa de Quinua, a 44 m-high obelisk commemorates the battle of Ayacucho. The village's handicrafts are recommended, especially ceramics. Most of the houses have miniature ceramic churches on the roof. San Pedro Ceramics, at the foot of the hill leading to the monument, and Mamerto Sánchez, Jr Sucre, should be visited, but there are many others. *Fiesta de la Virgen de Cocharcas*, around 8 September. Trips can be arranged to Huari, La Quinua village and the battlefield; US$7.55 per person, minimum four people. Combis leave from Paradero a Huari

Quinua, corner of Jr Ciro Alegría and Jr Salvador Cavero, when full from 0700; 40 minutes to Huari, US$0.75, then on to Quinua, 25 minutes, US$0.50 (US$1.10 from Ayacucho – ask the driver to go all the way to the Obelisco for an extra US$0.50).

Ayacucho listings

For Sleeping and Eating price codes and other relevant information, see Essentials, pages 38-40.

Sleeping

Ayacucho *p1474, map p1475*

B Ayacucho Hotel Plaza, 9 de Diciembre 184, T312202, hplaza@derrama.org.pe. Beautiful colonial building but the rooms don't match up, comfortable, TV, some rooms overlook the plaza.

D El Marqués de Valdelirios, Alameda Valdelirios 720, T317040. Lovely colonial-style mansion, beautifully furnished, pick-up from the airport for US$3, includes breakfast, hot water, bar, reserve at least 24 hrs in advance. Recommended.

D Marcos, 9 de Diciembre 143, T316867. Comfortable, modern, in a cul-de-sac ½ block from the Plaza, quiet, hot water, TV, price includes breakfast in the cafetería.

D Santa Rosa, Jr Lima 166, T314614, www.hotel-santarosa.com. Lovely colonial courtyard in building with historical associations, roof terrace, warm rooms, hot water, attentive staff, car park, good restaurant with good value menú. Recommended.

D San Francisco de Paula, Jr Callao 290, T312353, www.hotelsanfranciscodepaula.com. A bit like a museum with a nice patio, popular choice. Breakfast included, hot water, TV, comfortable rooms and some suites. Recommended. Will book **El Encanto de Oro** in Andahuaylas.

E Florida, Jr Cuzco 310, T312565, F316029. Small, pleasant, quiet, patio with flowers, TV, hot water from electric showers.

E Hostal 3 Máscaras, Jr 3 Máscaras 194, T314107, hoteltresmascaras@yahoo.com. New rooms with bath better, but with less character, than the old ones without, nice colonial building with patio, hot water, breakfast extra, car park.

E La Crillonesa, El Nazareno 165, T312350, www.hotelcrillonesa.com. Special price for tourists, very good value, hot water, laundry facilities, discount for longer stay, great views from roof terrace, loads of information, very helpful, Carlos will act as a local tour guide and knows everyone. Recommended.

F Grau, Jr San Juan de Dios 192, T312695. Rooms on 3rd floor by the markets, **G** without bath, hot water, laundry facilities, good value, safe but noisy, breakfast extra. Recommended.

F Hospedaje El Centro, Av Cáceres 1048, T313556. Rooms without bath and TV are **G**, large rooms, hot water, good value, on a busy avenue.

F Hostal San Blas, Jr Chorro 167, T312712. Hot water, cheaper with shared bath, laundry facilities, nice rooms, cheap meals available, discount for longer stay, kitchen facilities, laundry service, bicycles to lend. Recommended.

Eating

Ayacucho *p1474, map p1475*

Those wishing to try *cuy* should do so in Ayacucho as it's a lot cheaper than Cuzco. For a cheap, healthy breakfast, try *maca*, a drink of maca tuber, apple and quinoa, sold outside the market opposite Santa Clara, 0600-0800.

TT Las Flores, Jr José Olaya 106, Plaza Conchopata, east of city. Specializes in *cuy*, open 0900-1900 daily. taxi US$1 from centre.

TT Urpicha, Jr Londres 272, T813905. Recommended for typical food.

TT-T La Casona, Jr Bellido 463. Open 1200-2200. Dining under the arches and in dining room, regional specialities, try their *puca picante*, *mondongo* and *cuy*, and a wide menu. Recommended.

TT-T Nino, Jr 9 de Diciembre 205, on small plaza opposite Santo Domingo church, T814537. Open daily, pleasant decor, terrace and garden (look for the owls in the trees); chicken, pastas, pizzas, including take-away.

T Brasa Roja, Jr Cuzco block 1. More upmarket chicken place with food cooked *a la leña*, salads, very good.

T Cabo Blanco, Av Maravillas 198, T818740, close to Shosaku Nagase market (see Shopping). Cebiches, seafood and fish dishes, small place with personal service. Many other **cevicherías** on Av 26 de Enero.

🍴 **Chifa Wa Lin**, Asamblea 257. Very popular Chinese, said to be the best in town.
🍴 **La Pradera**, Lima 145 int 7. Vegetarian, open 0700-2200 daily.
🍴 **Mía Pizza-Pizzería Karaoke**, Av Mcal Cáceres 1045, T313273. Open1800-2400, for pizzas, pastas and karaoke (also has a bar to get you in the mood for singing).
🍴 **Pollería Dorado**, Jr Asamblea 310. Excellent value set menu and chicken dishes in a long, cavernous dining room, has a wood oven.

Cafés

Centro Turístico Cultural San Cristóbal, 28 de Julio 178, some expensive cafés (eg **Lalo's**, No 115, open 0900-2100, **New York**, No 114) as well as other restaurants; all have tables in the pleasant courtyard.
La Miel, Portal Constitución 11-12, 2 locations. Good coffee, hot drinks, juices, shakes, cakes and snacks, also ice creams.
Portal 1, Portal Constitución 1. A good café on the corner of the plaza serving snacks, light meals and ice cream.

Festivals and events

Ayacucho *p1474, map p1475*
The area is well-known for its festivals throughout the year. Almost every day there is a celebration in one of the surrounding villages. Check with the tourist office. **Carnival** in **Feb** is reported as a wild affair. **Semana Santa** begins on the Fri before Holy Week. There follows one of the world's finest Holy Week celebrations, with candle-lit nightly processions, floral 'paintings' on the streets, daily fairs (the biggest on Easter Saturday), horse races and contests among peoples from all central Peru. All accommodation is fully booked for months in advance. Many people offer beds in their homes during the week. Look out for notices on the doors and in windows of transport companies.
25 Apr: anniversary of the founding of Huamanga province. **1-2 Nov, Todos Los Santos** and **Día de los Muertos**.

Shopping

Ayacucho *p1474, map p1475*
Handicrafts Ayacucho is a good place to buy local crafts including filigree silver, which often uses *mudéjar* patterns. Also look out for little painted altars which show the manger scene, carvings in local alabaster, harps, or the pre-Inca tradition of carving dried gourds. The most famous goods are carpets and *retablos*. In both weaving and *retablos*, scenes of recent political strife have been added to more traditional motifs. For carpets, go to Barrio Santa Ana, see under Sights above. **Familia Pizarro**, Jr UNSCH 278, Barrio Belén, T313294. Works in textiles and *piedra huamanga* (local alabaster), good quality.
Mercado 12 de Abril, Chorro y San Juan de Dios. For fruit and vegetables. **Shosaku Nagase**, on Jr Quinua y Av Maravillas, opposite Plazoleta de María Parado de Bellido. A large handicraft market.

Activities and tours

Ayacucho *p1474, map p1475*
Morocuchos, Jr Cuzco 355, T312542, www.morochucos.com. Tours, flight and bus tickets.
Urpillay Tours, Portal Unión 33, T315074, urpillaytours@terra.com. All local tours and flight tickets. **Wari Tours**, Portal Independencia 70, T311415. Recommended for local tours. **Willy Tours**, Jr 9 de Diciembre 107, T314075. Personal guides, also handles flight and bus tickets.

Guides

Adán Castilla Rivera, T315789, 970 1746 (mob), castilla68@hotmail.com. An archaeologist who guides tours to local sites and the city, very knowledgeable.

Transport

Ayacucho *p1474, map p1475*
Air From/to **Lima**, 55 mins, with **LC Busre** (Jr 9 de Diciembre 160, T316 012) daily. To **Cuzco**, **Los Andes** (9 de Diciembre 127, T326316), Fri 0630, US$119, 1 hr, 18 passengers.
Bus Bus terminal at final Av de la Confraternidad, Urb Los Artesanos, northwest of centre, 10 mins. To **Lima**, 8 hrs on a good paved road, via Ica, several companies US$8-13, plus **Cruz del Sur** US$18 *imperial*, US$20 *semi cama* and US$26 *cama*. For **Pisco**, 332 km, take a Ica/Lima bus and get out at San Clemente, 5 hrs, 10 mins from Pisco, and take a bus or combi (same fare to San Clemente as for Ica). Companies include: **Antezana**, Manco Cápac 273, T311348, **Ayacucho Express**, Av Mcal Càceres 1442, T328 277, **Cruz del Sur**, Av Mcal Cáceres 1264, T312813, US$15.15, **Libertadores**,

Tres Máscaras 493, T318 967, **Molina**, 9 de Dicimbre 458 T319 989, and **Reybus**, Pasaje Cáceres 177, T319413. **Ormeño**, Jr Libertad 257, T312485, goes to Ica only.

To **Huancayo**, 319 km, 9-10 hrs, US$10-12, 3 daily with **Molina**, also **Turismo Central**, Manco Cápac 499, T317873, US$8 at 2030. The road is paved but poor as far as Huanta, thereafter it is rough, especially in the wet season, except for the last 70 km (paved). The views are breathtaking.

For **Huancavelica**, take a **Cruz del Sur** 1000, **Libertadores** 0730, or **Molina** 0800 bus as far as **Rumichaca**, US$2, where combis wait at 1030 for Huancavelica, 4 hrs. Otherwise take a Huancayo bus as far as **Izcuchaca**, then take another bus, a longer route.

Directory

Ayacucho *p1474, map p1475*
Banks BCP, Portal Unión 28. **Continental BBVA**, Portal Uniòn 24. **Interbank**, Jr 9 de Diciembre 183. Many street changers and *casas de cambio* at Portal Constitución on Plaza, good rate for cash. **Internet** All over the centre. Connections and machines are good, average price is US$0.60 per hr, some charge US$0.90 at night. All 0800-2300 daily. **Post office** Asamblea 293. **Telephones** Many phone offices in the centre.

Ayacucho to Cuzco

Beyond Ayacucho are two highland towns, Andahuaylas and Abancay, which are possible stopping, or bus-changing places on the road to Cuzco. The road towards Cuzco climbs out of Ayacucho and crosses a wide stretch of high, treeless páramo before descending through Ocros to the Río Pampas (6 hours from Ayacucho). It then climbs up to **Chincheros**, 158 km from Ayacucho, and Uripa (good Sunday market).

Andahuaylas

Andahuaylas is about 80 km further on, in a fertile valley. It offers few exotic crafts, but beautiful scenery, great hospitality and a good market on Sunday. On the north side is the Municipalidad, with a small **Museo Arqueológico**, which has a good collection of pre-Columbian objects, including mummies. A good nearby excursion is to the **Laguna de Pacucha** ⓘ *colectivo from Av Los Chankas y Av Andahuaylas, at the back of the market, US$0.75, 40 mins*. On the shore is the town of Pacucha with a family-run hostal (**G** pp on road from plaza to lake) and various places to eat. A road follows the north shore of the lake and a turn- off climbs to **Sóndor** ⓘ *US$0.65*, an Inca archaeological site at 3,300 m. Various buildings and small plazas lead up to a conical hill with concentic stone terracing and, at the summit, a large rock or *intihuatana*. Each 18-19 June Sóndor Raymi is celebrated. Taxi from Andahuaylas, US$10; walk from Pachuca 8-10 km, or take a colectivo to Argama (also behind Andahuaylas market), which passes the entrance. With any form of public transport you will have to walk back to Pacucha, unless very lucky. **Tourist office:** Dircetur ⓘ *Av Túpac Amaru 374, T421627*.

Abancay ➔ *Phone code: 084; Altitude: 2,378 m*

Nestled between mountains in the upper reaches of a glacial valley, the friendly town of Abancay is first glimpsed when you are many kilometres away. The town is growing in importance now that the paved Lima-Nazca-Cuzco road passes through. **Tourist office** ⓘ *Lima 206, T321664, 0800-1430*, or **Dircetur**, *Av Arenas 121, p 1, T321664*. **Santuario Nacional de Ampay** ⓘ *US$1.50*, north of town, has lagoons called Angasccocha (3,200 m) and Uspaccocha (3,820 m), a glacier on Ampay mountain at 5,235 m and flora and fauna typical of these altitudes. By public transport, take a colectivo to Tamburco and ask the driver where to get off. To get to the glacier you need two days trekking, with overnight camping. See page 1463 for sites of interest between Abancay and Cuzco.

Ayacucho to Cuzco listings

For Sleeping and Eating price codes and other relevant information, see Essentials, pages 38-40.

Sleeping

Andahuaylas *p1479*

D El Encanto de Oro, Av Pedro Casafranca 424, T723066, www.encantodeoro.4t.com. Modern, comfy, good facilities, breakfast included, TV, hot water, laundry service, restaurant, organizes trips on request. Reserve in advance.

E Sol de Oro, Jr Juan A Trelles 164, T721152, soldeorohotel@hotmail.com. Includes breakfast, hot water, TV, laundry service, garage, tourist information, restaurant alongside, near buses.

F El Encanto de Apurímac, Jr Ramos 401 (near Los Chankas and other buses), T723527. With bath, hot water, TV, very helpful.

G Las Américas, Jr Ramos 410, T721646. Near buses, bit gloomy in public areas, ooms are fine if basic, cheaper without bath, hot water, helpful.

G Hostal Waliman, Av Andahuaylas 266. Basic, cold water in shared bathrooms, helpful.

Abancay *p1479*

C-D Turistas, Av Díaz Barcenas 500, T321017, hotursa@terra.com.pe. The original building is in colonial style, rooms (**D**) a bit gloomy, breakfast not included. Newer rooms on top floor (best) and in new block (**C**), including breakfast. Good restaurant (**TT**), wood panelled bar, internet (US$0.60 per hour), parking.

E Imperial, Díaz Barcenas 517, T321538. Great beds, hot water, spotless, very helpful, parking, good value, cheaperwithout bath or breakfast.

F Hostal Arenas, Av Arenas 192, T322107. Brand new hotel almost finished beside the old one, well-appointed rooms, good beds, hot showers, TV, internet, helpful service, restaurant.

G Apurímac Tours, Jr Cuzco 421, T321446. Modern building, rooms with bath have tiny bathrooms, hot water, good value, helpful.

Eating

Andahuaylas *p1479*

T **El Dragón**, Jr Juan A Trellas 279. A recommended chifa serving huge portions, excellent value (same owner as Hotel El Encanto de Apurímac).

T **Il Gatto**, Jr G Cáceres 334. A warm pizzería, with wooden furniture, pizzas cooked in a wood-burning oven.

T **Nuevo Horizonte**, Jr Constitución 426. Vegetarian and health food restaurant, open for breakfast.

Abancay *p1479*

T **Focarela Pizzería**, Díaz Bárcenas 521, T083-322036. Simple but pleasant décor, pizza from a wood-burning oven, fresh, generous toppings, popular (ask for vino de la casa!).

T **Pizzería Napolitana**, Diaz Barcenas 208. Wood-fired clay oven, wide choice of toppings.

Activities and tours

Abancay *p1479*

Apurimak Tours, at Hotel Turistas, see Sleeping. Run local tours and 1 and 2-day trips to Santuario Nacional de Ampay: one-day, 7 hrs, US$40 per person for 1-2 people (cheaper for more people). Also a 3-day trip to Choquequirao including transport, guide, horses, tents and food, just bring your sleeping-bag, US$60 pp.

Carlos Valer, guide in Abancay – ask for him at Hotel Turistas, very knowledgeable and kind.

Transport

Ayacucho to Cuzco *p1479*

Ayacucho to Andahuaylas, 261 km, takes 10-11 hrs (more in the rainy season), the road is unpaved but in good condition when dry, but landslides occur in the wet. The scenery is stunning. Daytime buses stop for lunch at Chumbes (4½ hrs), which has a few restaurants, a shop selling fruit, bread and refrescos, and some grim toilets. **Los Chankas**, Pasaje Cáceres 150, T312391, at 0630 (without toilet) and 1900 (with chemical toilet), US$10. **Celtur**, Pasaje Caceres 174, T313194, 1830, US$10. Los Chankas' 1900 and Celtur are direct to **Cuzco**, but you still have to change buses in Andahuaylas. There are no other direct buses to Abancay or Cuzco.

Andahuaylas to Ayacucho: **Los Chankas**, Av José María Arguedas y Jr Trelles, T722441, 0600 and 1800 or 1840, one coming from Cuzco. To **Abancay**, **Señor de Huanca**, Av Martinelli 170, T721218, 3 a day, 5 hrs, US$3.40; **Los Chankas** at 0630, US$4. To **Cuzco**,

San Jerónimo, Av José María Arguedas 425, T801767, via Abancay, 1800 or 1830, also 1900 Sun, US$14, and **Los Chankas**. To **Lima**, buses go via Ayacucho or Pampachiri and Puquio: US$15.15. On all night buses, take a blanket.

In **Abancay**, 138 km from Andahuaylas, 5 hrs, the new Terminal Terrestre is on Av Pachacútec, on the west side of town. Taxi to centre US$0.60, otherwise it's a steep walk up to the centre. Several companies have offices on or near the El Olivo roundabout at Av Díaz Bárcenas y Gamarra, others on Av Arenas. Buses go to **Cuzco, Andahuaylas**, and **Nazca** (464 km, via Chalhuanca and Puquio), continuing to **Lima**. To **Cuzco**, 195 km, takes 4½ hrs, US$10. The scenery en route is dramatic, especially as it descends into the Apurímac valley and climbs out again.

Bus companies, all leave from Terminal Terrestre; office addresses are given: **Bredde**, Gamarra 423,T321643, 5 a day to Cuzco. **Cruz del Sur**, Díaz Bárcenas 1151, T323028. **Los Chankas**, Díaz Bárcenas 1011, El Olivo, T321485. **Molina**, Gamarra 422, T322646. 3 a day to Cuzco, to Andahuaylas at 2330. **San Jerónimo**, to Cuzco at 2130 and Andahuaylas at 2130. **Señor de Huanca**, Av Arenas 198, T322377, 3 a day to Andahuaylas. Several others to Lima and Cuzco.

Directory

Ayacucho to Cuzco *p1479*

Andahuaylas and **Abancay** have ATMs, **casas de cambio** and plenty of internet cabins.

East and north of La Oroya

A paved road heads north from La Oroya towards Cerro de Pasco and Huánuco. Just 25 km north of La Oroya a branch turns east towards Tarma, then descends to the relatively little-visited jungles of the Selva Central. This is a really beautiful run. North of La Oroya the road crosses the great heights of the Junín pampa and the mining zone of Cerro de Pasco, before losing altitude on its way to the Huallaga Valley. On this route you can connect by road to the Cordillera Blanca via La Unión.

Tarma and around → *Phone code: 064. Colour map 3, C3. Population: 105,200. Altitude: 3,050 m.*
Founded in 1538, Tarma, 60 km from La Oroya, is a growing city but still has a lot of charm. The **Semana Santa celebrations** are spectacular, with a very colourful Easter Sunday morning procession in the main plaza. Accommodation is hard to find at this time, but you can apply to the Municipalidad for rooms with local families. The town is also notable for its locally made fine flower-carpets. Good, friendly market around C Amazonas and Ucayali. The surrounding countryside is beautiful. **Tourist office** ⓘ *2 de Mayo 775 on the Plaza, T321010, ext 107, turismo@munitarma.gob.pe, very helpful. Mon-Fri 0800-1300, 1500-1800. See www.tarma.info*. Around 8 km from Tarma, the small town of **Acobamba** has *tapices* made in San Pedro de Cajas which depict the Crucifixion. There are festivities during May. About 2 km up beyond the town is the **Santuario de Muruhuay**, with a venerated picture painted on the rock behind the altar.

Beyond Tarma the road is steep and crooked but there are few places where cars cannot pass one another. In the 80 km between Tarma and La Merced the road, passing by great overhanging cliffs, drops 2,450 m and the vegetation changes dramatically from temperate to tropical. The towns of San Ramón and La Merced are collectively known as **Chanchamayo** (*Population: 7,000*). **San Ramón** is 11 km before La Merced and has several hotels (**C-G**) and restaurants. There are regular combis and colectivos between the two towns. **La Merced** (*Population: 15,000*), lies in the fertile Chanchamayo valley. Campa Indians can usually be found around the central plaza selling bows, arrows, necklaces and trinkets. There is a festival in the last week of September. There are several hotels (**C-F**) and restaurants.

About 25 km from La Merced along the road to Oxapampa, a road turns northeast to **Villa Rica**, centre of an important coffee growing area (hotels and restaurants). A very poor dirt road continues north to Puerto Bermúdez and beyond to join the Tingo María-Pucallpa road at Von Humboldt, 86 kilometres from Pucallpa. **Puerto Bermúdez** is a great base for exploring further into the San Matías/San Carlos national reserve in the Selva Central Peruana, with trips upriver to the Asháninca communities. Tours arranged by **Albergue Humboldt** cost US$18-28 a day, depending on group size. Boat passages possible from passing traders. To go further downriver to Pucallpa, there is transport via Puerto Palcazu, US$10.

North of La Oroya

A paved road runs 130 km north from La Oroya to Cerro de Pasco. It runs up the Mantaro valley through canyons to the wet and mournful Junín pampa at over 4,250 m, one of the world's largest high-altitude plains. An obelisk marks the battlefield where the Peruvians under Bolívar defeated the Spaniards in 1824. Blue peaks line the pampa in a distant wall. This windswept sheet of yellow grass is bitterly cold and the only signs of life are the youthful herders with their sheep and llamas. The road follows the east shores of the Lago de Junín. The town of **Junín** lies some distance south of the lake and has the somewhat desolate feel of a high puna town, bisected by the railway (two hotels, **E** and **G**).

The **Lago Junín National Reserve** ⓘ *US$5, ticket from Inrena in Junín, Jr San Martín 138, T064-344146, m-junin@inrena.gob.pe,* protects one of the best bird-watching sites in the central Andes where the giant coot and even flamingos may be spotted. It is easiest to visit from the village of Huayre, 5 km south of Carhuamayo, from which it is a 20-minute walk down to the lake. Fishermen are usually around to take visitors out on the lake. Carhuamayo is the best place to stay: *Gianmarco*, Maravillas 454, and *Patricia*, Tarapacá 862, are the best of several basic *hostales*. There are numerous restaurants along the main road.

Cerro de Pasco → *Phone code: 063. Population: 29,810. Altitude: 4,330 m.*

This long-established mining centre, 130 km from La Oroya, is not attractive, but is nevertheless very friendly. Copper, zinc, lead, gold and silver are mined here, and coal comes from the deep canyon of Goyllarisquisga, the 'place where a star fell', the highest coal mine in the world, 42 km north of Cerro de Pasco. The town is sited between Lago Patarcocha and the huge abyss of the mine above which its buildings and streets cling precariously. Nights are bitterly cold. *BCP* is on Jr Bolognesi. Money changers can be found on Jr Bolognesi between the market and the Cathedral.

Southwest of Cerro de Pasco by 40 km is **Huayllay**, near which is the **Santuario Bosque de Piedras** ⓘ *US$1, payable only if the guides, Ernesto and Christian, are there, camping is permitted within the Sanctuary; Inrena in Junín administers the site.* These unique weathered limestone formations are in the shape of a tortoise, elephant, alpaca, etc. At the Sanctuary (4,100-4,600 m), four tourist circuits through the spectacular rock formations have been laid out. The village of Huallay is 30 minutes beyond the sanctuary entrance. The Central Highway from Cerro de Pasco continues northeast another 528 km to Pucallpa, the limit of navigation for large Amazon river boats. The western part of this road (Cerro de Pasco-Huánuco) has been rebuilt into an all-weather highway. The sharp descent along the nascent **Río Huallaga** is a tonic to travellers suffering from *soroche*. The road drops 2,436 m in the 100 km from Cerro de Pasco to Huánuco, and most of it is in the first 32 km. From the bleak high ranges the road plunges below the tree line offering great views. The only town of any size before Huánuco is **Ambo**.

Huánuco → *Phone code: 062. Colour map 3, B3. Population: 118,814. Altitude: 1,894 m.*

This is an attractive Andean town on the Upper Huallaga with an interesting market. **Tourist office** ⓘ *Gen Prado 716, on the Plaza de Armas, T512980*. A website giving local information is www.webhuanuco.com. About 5 km away on the road west to La Unión is **Kótosh** (*Altitude: 1,912 m*) ⓘ *US$0.75, including a guide around a marked circuit which also passes through a small botanical garden of desert plants, taxi US$5 from the centre, with 30 mins' wait*. At this archaeological site, the Temple of Crossed Hands, the earliest evidence of a complex society and of pottery in Peru, dates from 2000 BC. From Huánuco, a spectacular but very poor dirt road leads to **La Unión**, capital of Dos de Mayo district. It's a fast developing town with a couple of hotels

(**F** to **G**) and restaurants, but electricity can be a problem and it gets very cold at night. On the pampa above La Unión are the Inca ruins of **Huánuco Viejo** ⓘ *US$1.50, allow 2 hrs*, a 2½-hour walk from the town, a great temple-fortress with residential quarters (taxi US$6.50-9.50 with wait). It has impressive Inca stonework and a fine section of Inca road running south. The route to the Callejón de Huaylas goes through **Huallanca (Huánuco)**, an attractive town, with mining projects nearby. Check local political conditions before taking this route. See Transport, below.

East and north of La Oroya

For Sleeping and Eating price codes and other relevant information, see Essentials, pages 38-40.

Sleeping

Tarma and around *p1481*

A Los Portales, Av Castilla 512, T321411, www.hoteleslosportales.com. On the edge of town, hot water, heating, quiet, includes breakfast, good restaurant.

B Hacienda La Florida, 6 km from Tarma, T341041, www.haciendalaflorida.com. 18th-century, working hacienda, with hot water, includes breakfast, other meals extra, owned by German-Peruvian couple Inge and Pepe who arrange excursions. Recommended. Also camping for US$4.75.

B Hacienda Santa María, 2 km out of town at Sacsamarca 1249, T321232, www.haciendasantamaria.com. A beautiful (non-working) 17th-century hacienda, beautiful gardens and antique furniture. Includes breakfast and light evening meal. Excellent guides for local day trips. Recommended.

D Hostal Campestre Auberge Normandie, beside the Santuario de Muruhuay, Acobamba, T064-341028, Lima T01-349 5440, www.normandie.com.pe. 16 cabins with hot water, TV in lounge, bar, restaurant, tours offered.

D-E El Caporal, Lima 616, T323636, hostalelcaporal@yahoo.es. Includes breakfast, good location, comfortable, hot water, cable TV. Recommended.

E-F Hostal Aruba, Jr Moquegua 452 near the market, T322057. Hot water, nice rooms with tile floors, good value.

E-F Hostal Central, Huánuco 614, T322625. Cheaper without bath, hot water, laundry facilities, bit rundown but popular, has observatory (opens Fri 2000, US$1 for non-guests).

F La Colmena, Jauja 618, T321157. Well-maintined old building, convenient for Huancayo buses.

G Res El Dorado, Huánuco 488, T321914. Hot water, cheaper without bath, rooms set round a patio, 1st floor better, poor beds, safe, welcoming.

Puerto Bermúdez

G pp **Albergue Cultural Humboldt**, by the river port (La Rampa), T063-830020, www.alberguehumboldt.com. Meals available. The owner, Basque writer Jesús, has created a real haven for backpackers, with maps, library and book exchange. Jesús arranges tours, from day trips to camping and trekking in primary forest. Highly recommended.

Cerro de Pasco *p1482*

D Señorial, in the district of San Juan, 5 mins north of Cerro by taxi, T721026, hotelsenorial@hotmail.com. The most comfortable in town, hot water, TV, fine view back across the mine pit.

E Wong, Carrión 99, T721515. Hot water 24 hrs, TV, run-down and noisy but friendly, motorcycle parking.

F Hostal Arenales, Jr Arenales 162, near the bus station, T723088. Modern, TV, hot water in the morning.

F Welcome, Av La Plata 125, opposite the entrance to the bus station, T721883. Some rooms without window, hot water 24 hrs.

Huánuco *p1482*

B Grand Hotel Huánuco, Jr D Beraun 775, T514222, www.grandhotelhuanuco.com. Includes breakfast, internet, restaurant, pool, sauna, gym, parking. Recommended.

D Hostal Caribe, Huánuco 546, T513645, and adjoining it **D Hostal Mariño**. 2 large modern hotels with big rooms, TV.

D Imperial, Huánuco 581, T518737. Renovated, with breakfast, hot showers, TV, quiet, clean and helpful. Recommended.

E Hostal Miraflores, Valdizan 564, T512848, www.granhostalmiraflores.com. Hot water and cable TV, quiet, safe, laundry service.

F Las Vegas, 28 de Julio 936, on Plaza de Armas, T/F512315. Small rooms, hot water, TV. Restaurant next door. Good.
G El Roble, Constitución 629, T512515. Without bath, clean, good value.

Huallanca
E Hotel Milán, 28 de Julio 107. Modern, TV and hot water, best in town, good restaurant.
G Hostal Yesica, L Prado 507. Hot water, shared bathroom, the best of the basic ones.

Eating

Tarma and around *p1481*
Chavín, Jr Lima 270 at Plaza de Armas, open daily 0730-2230. Very good quality and variety in set meals (weekdays only), also à la carte. Recommended.
Chifa Roberto Siu, Jr Lima 569 upstairs. A good option for Chinese food, popular with locals.
Comedor Vegetariano, Arequipa 695. Open 0700-2100, but closed Fri after lunch and Sat, vegetarian, small and cheap, sells great bread.
Señorial/Pollería El Braserito, Huánuco 138. Good *menú*, extensive choice of à la carte dishes, Señorial is open daily 0800-1530, El Braserito, daily 1800-2300.

Cerro de Pasco *p1482*
Los Angeles, Jr Libertad, near the market. Excellent *menú* for US$1.50. Recommended.
San Fernando, bakery in the plaza. Opens at 0700, great hot chocolate, bread and pastries.

Huánuco *p1482*
Chifa Men Ji, 28 de Julio, block 8. Good prices, nice Chinese food.
Govinda, 2 de Mayo 1044. Reckoned to be the best vegetarian restaurant.
La Olla de Barro, Gral Prado 852, close to main plaza. Serves typical food, good value.
Pizzería Don Sancho, Prado 645. Best pizzas in town.

Festivals and events

Huánuco *p1482*
20-25 Jan: is **Carnaval Huanuqueño**. **3 May**: **La Cruz de Mayo**. **16 Jul**: **Fiesta de la Virgen del Carmen**. **12-18 Aug**: Tourist Week in Huánuco. **28-29 Oct**: **Fiesta del Rey y del Señor de Burgos**, the patron of Huánuco. **25 Dec**: **Fiesta de los Negritos**.

Transport

Tarma and around *p1481*
Bus To **Lima**, 231 km (paved), 6 hrs, US$4.70-6.50 *normal*, US$8 *semi-cama*, US$9.50-11 *cama*. **Transportes Junín**, Amazonas 667, 7 a day, with *bus cama* night bus (in Lima: Av Nicolás Arriola 198, T01-224 9220, www.transpjunin.com). **Trans La Merced**, Vienrich 420, 3 a day. **Trans Los Canarios**, Jr Amazonas 694, (2 daily) start in Tarma. **Transportes Chanchamayo**, Callao 1002, T321882, 2 a day, en route from Chanchamayo. To **Jauja**, US$1.50, and **Huancayo**, US$2.50, **Transportes Angelitos/San Juan**, from the stadium, 0800-1800, every 1½ hrs; **Trans Los Canarios** about 1 per hr, 0500-1800; **Trans Junín** at 1200 and 2400. Colectivos depart when full from Callao y Jauja, 2 hrs, US$4, and 3 hrs, US$6, respectively. To **Cerro de Pasco**, **Empresa Junín**, Amazonas 450, 4 a day, 3 hrs, US$2.50. Also colectivos when full, 2 hrs, US$4. Buses to **La Oroya** leave from opposite the petrol station on Av Castilla block 5, 1 hr, US$1.25, while colectivos leave from the petrol station itself, 45 mins, US$2. To **Chanchamayo**, **Transportes Angleitos/San Juan**, 13 daily, 0600-2100, to La Merced US$1.60; **Trans Junín**, 4 a day, to San Ramón US$1.60, 1½ hrs, La Merced US$2.50, 2 hrs. Combis, US$1.60, and colectivos, US$3.80, from the stadium to La Merced.

Colectivos and **Canary Tours combis** to **Acobamba** and up to **Muruhuay**, 15 mins, US$0.30 and 0.45 respectively.

Note The local names for colectivos are 'carros' and 'stations'.

San Ramón
Air Flights leave from San Ramón. There is a small airstrip where **Aero Montaña**, T064-339191, rfmamsa@hotmail.com, has air taxis that can be chartered (*viaje especial*) to the jungle towns, with a maximum of 3 people, but you have to pay for the pilot's return to base. Flights cost US$250 per hr. **Puerto Bermúdez** takes 33 mins. You can also just go to the air base, across the river, on the east side of town.

La Merced

Bus Many buses go here from **Lima**: **Expreso Satipo, Junín, La Merced** and **Chanchamayo** each have several buses during the day, US$8 *regular*, US$11 *cama* upper level, US$12.50 *cama* lower level, 7-8 hrs. To **Tarma Transportes Angelitos/San Juan**, hourly, 2½ hrs, US$1.60, or colectivos, just over 1 hr, US$3.80. To **Puerto Bermúdez Empresa Transdife** and **Villa Rica** have 4WD pick-ups which leave starting at 0400 and may pick up passengers at their hotels. You must purchase tickets in advance, the vehicles get very full. US$14 in front, US$8 in the back (spending the extra money is suggested because of the extreme crowding), 8-10 hrs or more.

Cerro de Pasco *p1482*

Bus There is a large bus station. To **Lima** several companies including **Carhuamayo** and **Transportes Apóstol San Pedro**, hourly 0800-1200, plus 4 departures 2030-2130, 8 hrs, US$4-5. If there are no convenient daytime buses, you could change buses in La Oroya. To **Carhuamayo, Junín** and **La Oroya**: buses leave when full, about every 20-30 mins, to Carhuamayo 1 hr, US$1; to Junín 1½ hrs, US$1; to La Oroya, 2½ hrs, US$2. Colectivos also depart with a similar frequency, 1½ hrs, US$2.50, to La Oroya. To **Tarma**, **Empresa Junín**, 0600, 1500, 3 hrs, $2.50. Colectivos also depart hourly, 1½ hrs, US$4. To **Huancayo**, various companies leave throughout the day, 5 hrs, US$4. To **Huánuco**, buses and cars leave when full, about half hourly, 2½ hrs and 1½ hrs, US$2 and US$4 respectively.

Huayllay

Minibuses to Huallay from Cerro de Pasco's terminal leave throughout the day, about 1 hr, US$1. They return until 1800-1900.

Huánuco *p1482*

Air Airport T513066. From **Lima**, **LCBusre** (2 de Mayo 1355, T518113), daily, 55 mins.

Bus To **Lima**, US$9, 8 hrs. **León de Huánuco**, Malecón Alomía Robles 821, 3 a day. Also **Bahía Continental**, Valdizan 718, recommended, **Transportes El Rey**, 28 de Julio 1215 (28 de Julio 1192, La Victoria, Lima). The majority of buses of all companies leave 2030-2200, most also offer a bus at 0900-1000. A colectivo to Lima, costing US$20, leaves at 0400, arriving at 1400; book the night before at Gen Prado 607, 1 block from the plaza. Recommended. To **Cerro de Pasco**, 3 hrs, US$2, colectivos under 2 hrs, US$4. All leave when full from the Ovalo Carhuayna on the north side of the city, 3 km from the centre. To **Huancayo**, 7 hrs, US$6: **Turismo Central**, Tarapacá 530, at 2100. Colectivos run to **Tingo María**, from block 1 of Prado close to Puente Calicanto, 2½ hrs, US$5. Also **Etnasa**, 3-4 hrs, US2. For **Pucallpa**, take a colectivo to Tingo María, then a bus from there. This route has many checkpoints and robberies can occur. Travel by day and check on the current situation regarding safety. To **La Unión, Turismo Unión**, daily 0730, 7 hrs, US$5; also **Turismo Marañón** daily 0700. This is a rough road operated also by **El Niño** colectivos, Aguilar 530, leave when full, US$7.15.

La Unión

Bus To **Huánuco**: **Turismo Unión**, Jr Comercio 1224 daily at 0600, US$5, 7 hrs. Also **Turismo Marañón**, Jr Comercio 1309, daily at 0700 (no afternoon/evening departures). *El Niño* colectivos, Jr Comercio 12, T062-515952, 5 hrs, US$7.15.

To **Huallanca (Huánuco)**, combis leave from the market, about half hourly, when full and follow the attractive Vizcarra valley, 1 hr, US$0.75. *El Rápido* runs to **Huaraz** 0400, 4½ hrs, US$4.80, or change in Huallanca. Combis leave when full about half hourly, from the corner of Comercio y 28 de Julio in Huallanca for La Unión.

Directory

Tarma *p1481*

Banks BCP, Lima 401, with ATM (other Visa ATMs in town). Several **cambios** on Jr Moquegua near the Plaza de Armas change cash US$ and €, good rates. **Internet** Internet offices all along Av Lima and Malecón José Gálvez, US$0.30 per hr. *Locutorios* everywhere.

Huánuco *p1482*

Banks BCP, at Dos de Mayo 1005. **Internet** Several in the centre. **Post offices** 2 de Mayo on the Plaza. Open Mon-Sat 0800-2000, Sun 800-1400. **Telephones** 28 de Julio 1170.

Amazon Basin

Cooled by winds sweeping down from the Andes but warmed by its jungle blanket, this region contains important tropical flora and fauna. In the north of the region, Iquitos, on the Amazon itself, is the centre of jungle exploration. It is a very varied landscape, with grasslands and tablelands of scrub-like vegetation, inaccessible swamps, and forests up to 2,000 m above sea level. The principal means of communication in the jungle is by its many rivers, the most important being the Amazon, which rises high up in the Andes as the Marañón, then joins the Ucayali to become the longest river in the world. The northern tourist area is based on the River Amazon itself with, at its centre, a sizeable city, Iquitos. Although it has lost its rubber-boom dynamism, Iquitos is still at the heart of life on the river. There are jungle lodges upstream and down, each with its own speciality and level of comfort, but none more than half a day away by fast boat. To get right into the wilds, head for Peru's largest national reserve, Pacaya-Samiria, accessed by boat from Iquitos or the little town of Lagunas.

North from Huánuco to Pucallpa

Huánuco to Tingo María

The journey to Tingo María from Huánuco, 135 km, is very dusty but gives a good view of the jungle. Some 25 km beyond Huánuco the road begins a sharp climb to the heights of Carpish (3,023 m). A descent of 58 km brings it to the Huallaga River again; it then continues along the river to Tingo María. The road is paved from Huánuco to Tingo María, including a tunnel through the Carpish hills. Landslides along this section are frequent and construction work causes delays. Although this route is reported to be relatively free from terrorism, robberies do occur and it is advisable to travel only by day.

Situated on the middle Huallaga, in the Ceja de Montaña, on the edge (literally 'eyebrow') of the mountains, **Tingo María** (*Phone code: 062; Population: 20,560; Altitude: 655 m; Annual rainfall: 2,642 mm*) is isolated for days in the rainy season. The altitude prevents the climate from being oppressive. The Cordillera Azul, the front range of the Andes, covered with jungle-like vegetation to its top, separates it from the jungle lowlands to the east. The mountain which can be seen from all over the town is called La Bella Durmiente, the Sleeping Beauty. The meeting here of highlands and jungle makes the landscape extremely striking. Bananas, sugar cane, cocoa, rubber, tea and coffee are grown. The main crop of the area, though, is coca, grown on the *chacras* (smallholdings) in the countryside, and sold legitimately and otherwise in Tingo María. A small university outside the town, beyond the *Hotel Madera Verde*, has a little **museum-cum-zoo** ⓘ *free but a small tip would help to keep things in order*; it also maintains botanical gardens in the town. About 6½ km from Tingo, on a rough road, is a fascinating cave, the **Cueva de las Lechuzas** ⓘ *US$0.90 for the cave, take a torch, and do not wear open shoes, getting there: take a motorcycle-taxi from town, US$1.75; cross the Río Monzón by new bridge*. There are many oilbirds in the cave and many small parakeets near the entrance. **Tourist office** ⓘ *Av Ericson 162, T562310, cataperu10@hotmail.com*. Note that Tingo María is a main narco-trafficking centre and although the town is generally safe, it is not safe to leave it at night. Always keep to the main routes.

Tingo María to Pucallpa

From Tingo María to the end of the road at Pucallpa is 255 km, with a climb over the watershed – the Cordillera Azul – between the Huallaga and Ucayali rivers. The road is in poor shape for most of the journey, but some paving is in progress. Travel by day: it is safer the views are tremendous as you go from the high jungle to the Amazon Basin. Sit on the righthand side of the bus. When the road was being surveyed it was thought that the lowest pass over the Cordillera Azul was over 3,650 m high, but an old document stating that a Father Abad had found a pass through these mountains in 1757 was rediscovered, and the road now goes through the pass of Father Abad, a gigantic gap 4 km long and 2,000 m deep. At the top of the pass is a Peruvian Customs house; the jungle land to the east is a free zone. Coming down from the pass the road bed is along the floor of a magnificent canyon, the Boquerón Abad. It is a beautiful trip through luxuriant jungle, ferns and sheer walls of bare rock, punctuated by occasional waterfalls plunging into the roaring torrent below. East of the foot of the pass the all-weather road goes over the flat pampa, with few bends, to the village of **Aguaytía** (narcotics police outpost, gasoline, accommodation in the **F Hostal San Antonio**, clean, and two restaurants). From Aguaytía the road continues for 160 km to Pucallpa – five hours by bus. There is a service station three hours before Pucallpa.

Pucallpa ➔ *Phone code: 061. Colour map 3, B3. Population: 400, 000.*

Pucallpa is a rapidly expanding jungle town on the Río Ucayali, navigable by vessels of 3,000 tons from Iquitos, 533 nautical miles away. Different 'ports' are used depending on the level of the river, they are all just mud banks without any facilities (see Transport, below).The economy of the area includes sawmills, plywood factories, oil refinery, fishing and boat building. Large discoveries of oil and gas are being explored. Local festivals are *Carnival* in February, *San Juan* on 24 June, and the Ucayali regional fair in October. The town is hot and dusty between June and November and muddy from December to May. **Note** There is narcotics activity in the area. The city itself is safe enough to visit, but don't travel at night. **Museo Regional** ⓘ *Carretera Federico Basadre Km 4.2, www.parquenaturalpucallpa.com, park entry US$0.95, Mon-Fri 0800-1630, Sat and Sun 0900-1730,* has some good examples of Shipibo ceramics, as well as some delightful pickled snakes and other reptiles. **Tourist office Dircetur** ⓘ *Jr 2 de Mayo 111, T571303, ucayali@mincetur.gob.pe, Mon-Fri 0730-1300, 1330-1515.* Information also at **Gobierno Regional de Ucayali (GOREU)**, Raimondi block 220, T573240, www.regionucayali.gob.pe.

Around Pucallpa The main attraction is **Lago Yarinacocha**, to the northeast of Pucallpa ⓘ *20 mins by colectivo or bus along Jr Ucayali, US$0.30, or 15 mins by taxi, US$2*, an oxbow lake linked to the Río Ucayali by a canal at the northern tip of its west arm. River dolphins can be seen here. Puerto Callao, also known as Yarinacocha or Yarina, is the main town, at the southern tip, reached by road from Pucallpa. There are a number of restaurants and bars here and it is popular at weekends. From Yarina, a road continues along the western arm to **San José**, **San Francisco** and **Santa Clara** (bus US$0.65). The area is populated by the Shipibo people, who make ceramic and textile crafts. The area between the eastern arm of the lake and the Río Ucayali has been designated as a reserve. Here, towards the northwestern shore of the east arm is the beautifully located **Jardín Botánico Chullachaqui** *free*, which can be reached by boat from Puerto Callao to Pueblo Nueva Luz de Fátima, 45 minutes, then one hour's walk to the garden (ask at Moroti-Shobo on the Plaza de Armas in Puerto Callao).

North from Huánuco to Pucallpa listings

For Sleeping and Eating price codes and other relevant information, see Essentials, pages 38-40.

Sleeping

Tingo María *p1486*

B-C Madera Verde, Av Universitaria s/n, out of town on the road to Huánuco, near the University, T/F561800, www.maderaverde hotel.com. Chalets in beautiful surroundings, with and without bath, restaurant, swimming pool.

E Albergue Ecoógico Villa Jennifer, Km 3.4 Carretera a Castillo Grande, 10 mins from Tingo María, T960 3509, www.villajennifer.net. Danish-Peruvian owned, includes breakfast, weekend packages, US$77, and tours to local sites, pool, minizoo, birdwatching, restaurant, laundry service, phone ahead to arrange bus station pick-up. Rooms are surrounded by local flora, with lots of birdlife.

F Hostal Marco Antonio, Jr Monzón 364, T562201. Quiet, restaurant of the same name next door.

F Nueva York, Av Alameda Perú 553, T562406. Cheaper without bath and TV, laundry, good value, restaurant.

Pucallpa *p1487*

A Sol del Oriente, Av San Martín 552, T575154, www.soldelorientehoteles.com. Price includes breakfast and airport transfer, a/c, pool, minizoo, good restaurant.

B-C Mercedes, Raimondi 610, T575120, ghotelmercedes@hotmail.com. An older hotel with some refurbished rooms, includes breakfast, hot water, a/c, fridge, pool, restaurant.

C-D Antonio's, Jr Progreso 545, T573721, www.antonios-pucallpa.com. A variety of rooms and prices, cheaper in older rooms or with fan, breakfast extra, cable TV, garden, pool, jacuzzi, parking, airport pick-up.

C-D Arequipa, Jr Progreso 573, T571348, www.hostal-arequipa.com. Good, a/c, TV, cheaper with fan, with breakfast, comfortable, safe, restaurant.

E-F Barbtur, Raimondi 670, T572532. Cheaper without bath, central, good beds, cold water, friendly but noisy.

E-F Komby, Ucayali 360, T571562, www.hostalkomby.com.pe. Cold water, fan, ample rooms, pool, very noisy street but back rooms are quiet, good value.

E-F La Suite de Petita's Inn, Jr Fitzcarraldo 171, T572831. Includes simple breakfast, cold water, fan, fridge, free internet, parking.

Around Pucallpa: Yarinacocha *p1487*

B Jana Shobo Amazonian Lodge, Lake Yarinacocha, T596943, www.janashobo.tk. Small lodge is set in 10 ha of forest on the lakeshore. Price includes meals and airport transfer, packages and tours available. Living room, reading room and kitchen.

B Pandisho Amazon Ecolodge, north of the village of 11 de Agosto, towards the northern tip of the eastern shore of the west arm, T061-575041, www.amazon-ecolodge.com. Full-board in resort with cabins by the lakeshore, also offer tours to local (US$15 pp) and rainforest (US$35 pp) destinations. Good.

E-F Los Delfines, opposite Electroucayali in Puerto Callao. With bath, fan, fridge, some with TV.

Eating

Tingo María *p1486*

T El Antojito 2, Jr Chiclayo 458. Local food.

T Girasol, Av Raimondi 253, T562065. Chicken, burgers, cakes and fruit juices.

Pucallpa *p1487*

TT-T C'est si bon, Jr Independencia 560 y Pasaje Zegarra, Plaza de Armas, daily 0800-2400. Chicken, snacks, drinks, sweets, ice cream.

TT-T Chifa Xin Xin, Jr Tarapacá 515 and Av Raimondi 603, daily 1200-1600 and 1830-2300. Authentic Chinese cooking, set meals and à la carte.

TT-T El Viajero, Jr Libertad 374, Sun-Fri 0800-1630. Choice of good set meals, also à la carte, very popular. Recommended.

TT-T La Favorita, Jr Adolfo Morey e Inmaculada, daily 0800-1600. Regional and home cooking, good set meals Mon-Sat and *parrilladas* on Sun, popular.

T Tropitop Heladería, Jr Sucre y Tarapacá 401 (Plaza de Armas). Good, cheap, typical breakfasts.

Shopping

Pucallpa *p1487*

Many Shibipo women carry and sell their products around Pucallpa and Yarinacocha. **Agustín Rivas**, at Jr Tarapacá 861, above a small restaurant whose entrance is at No 863 (ask for it). For local wood carvings visit the workshop of this sculptor, whose work is made from huge tree roots. **Artesanías La Anaconda**, Pasaje Cohen by Plaza de Armas, good selection of indigenous crafts.

Activities and tours

Tingo María *p1486*

Franz Malpartida, T962 659759 (mob), frantur81@hotmail.com. Reliable guide to local sites, eg waterfall climbing, and hikes, good value.

Tingo María Travel Tours, Av Raimondi 460, T562501. For local excursions.

Transport

Tingo María *p1486*

Bus To **Huánuco**, 119 km, 3-4 hrs, US$2 with **Etnasa** (not recommended – theft and drug-trafficking); take a micro, US$2, or colectivo, US$5, 2 hrs, several daily. Direct buses continue to Lima, 10 hrs, with **Trans Rey**, US$15 *bus cama*,

León de Huánuco and **Bahía Continental** (recommended, T01-424 1539), US$11. To **Pucallpa**, 5 hrs, US$15. **Ucayali Express** colectivos leave from Raimondi y Callao and **Selva Express**, Av Tito Jaime 218, T562380. Buses take 7-8 hrs, US$6.50-8, eg **Etposa**.

Pucallpa *p1487*

Air To **Lima** and **Iquitos**, daily 1 hr, flights with **LAN** (Jr Tarapacá 805 y San Martín, T579840) and **Star Perú** (7 de Junio 865, T590585). Airport taxis charge US$6 to town, outside taxis charge US$3.

Bus There are regular bus services to **Lima**, several companies, 18-20 hrs (longer in the rainy season, Nov-Mar), US$11-12.50 *regular*. **Transmar**, Av Raimondi 770, T579778 (in Lima Av Nicolás de Pierrola 197, T01-265 0190), US$16 *regular*, US$25 *bus cama* with a/c, US$22 *bus cama* without a/c. To **Tingo María**, bus US$6.50-8, 7-8 hrs, bound for Lima, also **Etposa**, 7 de Junio 843, at 1700. Or 5 hrs, US$15 by combi, leave from early morning, **Turismo Ucayali**, 7 de Junio 799, T593002, and **Selva Express**, Jr 7 de Junio 841, T579098. Take blankets as the crossing of the Cordillera at night is bitterly cold.

Ferry Boats to all destinations dock around Puerto Inmaculada, 2 blocks downriver from the Malecón Grau, at the bottom of Jr Inmaculada, unless the water level is very high, in which case they dock at Puerto Manantay, 4 km south of town. To **Iquitos** down the Ucayali and Amazon rivers, 3-4 days, longer if the water level is low and larger boats must travel only by day, hammock US$35, berth US$43-65 pp. **Henry** is a large company with departures Mon, Wed, Fri and Sat from Puerto Henry at the bottom of Jr Manco Capac, by Jr Arica; their newer boats, *Henry 6* and *7*, have some cabins with private bath. Another good boat is *Pedro Martín 2* sailing from Puerto Inmaculada.

You must ask around for the large boats to Iquitos. A mototaxi to any of the ports costs US$0.75 from the Plaza de Armas, taxis charge US$3. Departure times are marked on chalk boards on the deck. Schedules seem to change almost hourly. Do not pay for your trip before you board the vessel, and only pay the captain. Some boat captains may allow you to live on board a couple of days before sailing. Bottled drinking water can be bought in Pucallpa, but not cheaply. See General hints for river travel, page 1497.

❶ Directory

Tingo María *p1486*

Internet Several places on Raimondi and near Plaza de Armas, fast and cheap but strange hrs.

Pucallpa *p1487*

Banks BCP, Raimondi y Tarapacá. Also **Interbank**, Av Raimondi y Ucayali, and **Scotiabank**, Av Raimondi 192 y Tacna. **Cambios**, several at Av Raimondi corner Ucayali. **Cultural centres** Art school: **Usko Ayar Amazonian School of Painting**, in the house of artist Pablo Amaringo, a former *vegetalista* (healer), Jr LM Sánchez, Cerro 465-467, www.egallery.com/coll/amazon.php. The school provides art classes for local people, and is dependent upon selling their art. The internationally renowned school welcomes overseas visitors for short or long stays to study painting and learn Spanish and/or teach English with Peruvian students. **Police** **Policia Nacional**, Jr Independencia 3rd block, T575211.

Yurimaguas and Pacaya-Samiria

Yurimaguas

The Río Huallaga winds northwards for 930 km. The Upper Huallaga is a torrent, dropping 15.8 m per kilometre between its source and Tingo María. The Lower Huallaga moves through an enervation of flatness, with its main port, Yurimaguas, below the last rapids and only 150 m above the Atlantic Ocean, yet distant from that ocean by over a month's voyage. Between the Upper and Lower lies the Middle Huallaga: the third of the river which is downstream from Tingo María and upstream from Yurimaguas.

Downriver of Tingo María, beyond Bellavista, the orientation is towards **Yurimaguas** (*Phone code: 065; Population: 25,700*), which is connected by road with the Pacific coast, via Tarapoto and Moyobamba (see page 1365). It's a very relaxed jungle town and, as the roadhead on the lower Río Huallaga, is an ideal starting point for river travel in the Peruvian Amazon. It has a fine church of the Passionist Fathers, based on the Cathedral of Burgos, in Spain. A colourful market is held from 0600-0800, full of fruit and animals. Excursions in the area include the gorge of Shanusi and the lakes of Mushuyacu and Sanango. Tourist information is available from the Consejo Regional building (which also has a small archaeological museum) on the main plaza, T352676.

Pacaya-Samiria

All river traffic to Iquitos stops at **Lagunas**, 12 hours from Yurimaguas. From here there are good jungle trips from Lagunas to the **Pacaya-Samiria Reserve** ⓘ *Reserve office in Iquitos, C Moore 1430, T226944, Mon-Fri 0800-1300, 1500-1800*, has general information and an updated list of tour operators authorized to enter the reserve. You must go here to obtain proof of payment for the park entry fee (US$20 per day), payment itself must be made at Banco de la Nación. Pacaya- Samiria Reserve, at 2,080,000 ha, is the country's largest protected area. It is bounded by the rivers Marañón and Ucuyali, narrowing to their confluence near the town of Nauta. The reserve's waterways and wetlands provide habitat for manatee, tapir, river dolphins, giant otters, black cayman, boas, 193 species of fish and some 330 bird species. Many of the animals found here are in danger of extinction. Trips are mostly on the river, sleeping in hammocks, and include fishing. The main part of the reserve is off-limits to tourists, but some 'eco-tourism zones' have been set up where, with the correct permits, river trips can be undertaken and some controlled camping is possible. As no building is allowed, nor use of motors, trips are limited. Iquitos operators enter through Nauta to Yarina where there is a shelter, also through Requena. Other entry points are the village of **Leoncio Prado** (with a couple of *hospedajes*), on the Marañón, opposite the outflow of the Río Samiria. Also **Bretaña** on the Canal de Puinahua, a shortcut on the Ucayali.

Yurimaguas and Pacaya-Samiria listings

For Sleeping and Eating price codes and other relevant information, see Essentials, pages 38-40.

Sleeping

Yurimaguas *p1490*

B Puerto Pericos, Malecón Paranapura, T352009, www.puertopalmeras.com.pe. Same group as **Puerto Palmeras** in Tarapoto, includes breakfast, with hot water, restaurant and gardens.

D Posada Cumpanama, Progreso 403, T352905, http://posadacumpanama.blogspot.com. Cheaper without a/c, with breakfast, tastefully decorated, pool, very pleasant.

D Hostal Residencial El Naranjo, Arica 318, T352860, hotel_elnaranjo@hotmail.com. Best in town, a/c (**E** with fan), hot water, comfortable, small pool, with good restaurant.

E Luis Antonio, Av Jaúregui 407, T352061, antonio@vibcp.com. With fan C with a/c), cold water, balconies overlooking small pool, very helpful. Recommended.

F Hostal El Caballito, Av Jaúregui 403, T352864. Cold water, fan, pleasant, good value.

F Leo's Palace, Sgto Lores 106, Plaza de Armas, T351404. Good, reasonable value (**D** with a/c), restaurant.

Pacaya-Samiria: Lagunas *p1490*

G Hostal Isabel, Miraflores 1 block from plaza. Shared bath, cold water, basic, meals available. Several other basic places in town.

G Hostal La Sombra, Jr Vásquez 1121. Shared bath, basic, good food.

Pacaya-Samiria *p1490*

Pacaya Samiria Amazon Lodge, Lima office: Av José Pardo 601, of 602, Miraflores, T01-446 5771, www.pacayasamiria.com.pe. In Iquitos at Urbanización Las Palmeras A-9, T065-9657 29179. Beautifully designed, luxurious lodge on a hill overlooking the Marañón, just inside the boundaries of the Reserve but close to road and town. All buildings in indigenous style, with balconies and en-suite bathrooms, restaurant, bar. Community visits and specialist birdwatching trips are included in the price, but boat trips (also included) can be long. Camping trips (with official permits) can be arranged deeper inside the reserve.

Activities and tours

Yurimaguas *p1490*

Manguares Expeditions, Sargento Lores 126, near Plaza de Armas.

Nilo Hidalgo, Maynas 710, T502442. US$50-80 pp per day for guide, transport and food, excluding park entry fees.

Pacaya-Samiria *p1490*

Local guides offer tours to the reserve for about US$40 per day including food and equipment. There are 5 registered operators in Lagunas. In Bretaña the **Gallán** family act as guides. Trips to Pacaya-Samiria can also be arranged in Iquitos. Expeditions must be booked in advance, all equipment and food is provided. **Asiendes** (Asociación Indígena en Defensa de la Ecología Samiria), Tavara 1258, T965-861748, asiendesperu@hotmail.com, Sr Manuel Ahuanari, is a local association which runs trips into Pacaya-Samiria, promoting the jungle and benefiting the community, from 4 to 7 days, US$50 per day, all inclusive except boat passage from Iquitos and price of entry to the park. You stay at rangers' stations or can camp. With all tours make sure you know exactly what is involved on the trip, lodging, food, hunting, etc.

Transport

Yurimaguas *p1490*

Bus The road to Tarapoto is paved. **Paredes Estrella**, office on 5th block of Mariscal Cáceres, 0430 daily to **Lima** (30 hrs, US$32) via **Tarapoto** (US$4), **Moyobamba** (US$9, 5-6 hrs), **Pedro Ruiz** (for Chachapoyas), **Chiclayo** (20 hrs) and **Trujillo**. Also **Ejetur**, 0400 to Lima, 30 hrs, US$36. Faster than the bus to Tarapoto are: **Gilmer Tours**, C Victor Sifuentes 580, hourly mini-buses 0500-1200, 1400-1800, US$5.35, 2½ hrs; cars (eg **San Martín**) US$7.15; and combis (**Turismo Selva**) US$3.60.

Ferry To **Iquitos**, 3 days and 2 nights, **Eduardo** company is best, Elena Pardo 114, T352552 (see under Iquitos, Transport).

Directory

Yurimaguas *p1490*

Banks **Interbank** or travel agents charge poor rates. **Negocios Zerimar**, Jaúregui ½ block from plaza, changes US$ cash, Mon-Sat 0700-2100, Sun 0700-1500. **Internet** Café on Plaza de Armas, US$1.70 per hr.

Iquitos and around → *Phone code: 065. Colour map 3, A4. Population: 600,000.*

Iquitos stands on the west bank of the Amazon and is a chief town of Peru's jungle region. Some 800 km downstream from Pucallpa and 3,646 km from the mouth of the Amazon, the city is completely isolated except by air and river. Its first wealth came from the rubber boom (late 19th century to second decade of 20th century). The main economic activities are logging, commerce and petroleum and it is the main starting point for tourists wishing to explore Peru's northern jungle.

The incongruous **Iron House/Casa de Fierro** stands on the Plaza de Armas, designed by Eiffel for the Paris exhibition of 1889. It is said that the house was transported from Paris by a local rubber baron and is constructed entirely of iron trusses and sheets, bolted together and painted silver. It now houses a pharmacy. Of special interest are the older buildings, faced with *azulejos* (glazed tiles). They date from the rubber boom of 1890 to 1912, when the rubber barons imported the tiles from Portugal and Italy and ironwork from England to embellish their homes. Werner Herzog's film *Fitzcarraldo* is a *cause célèbre* in the town and Fitzcarrald's house, the **Casa de Barro**, still stands on the Plaza de Armas. **Museo Amazónico**, in the Prefectura, Malecón Tarapacá y Morona, has displays of native art and sculptures by Lima artist Letterstein (under renovation, 2010).

Belén, the picturesque, lively waterfront district, is worth visiting, but is not safe at night. Most of its huts are built on rafts to cope with the river's 10 m change of level during floods (January-July); now they're built on stilts. On Pasaje Paquito are bars serving local sugar cane rum. The main plaza has a bandstand made by Eiffel. In the high season canoes can be hired on the waterfront for a tour of Belén, US$3 per hour. The market at the end of the Malecón is well worth visiting, though you should get there before 0900 to see it in full swing.

Tourist offices: i perú ⓘ *C Loreto 201 y Raymondi, by Plaza Castilla, T236144, iperuiquitos@promperu.gob.pe, Mon-Sat 0830-1930, Sun 0830-1400*, also at the airport, at flight times. Both offices are helpful. If arriving by air, go first to this desk. They will give you a list of clean hotels, a map, tell you about the touts outside the airport etc. **Dircetur** ⓘ *Condamine 183, T234609, loreto@mincetur.gob.pe*. www.iquitosnews.com has articles, maps and information. **Indecopi**, the consumer protection service, is at ⓘ *Putumayo 464, T243490, jreategui@ indecopi.gob.pe*.

Excursions

There are pleasant beaches at **Tipishca**, reached in 20 minutes by boat from Puerto de Santa Clara near the airport, it gets quite busy at weekends, and, quieter, **Santa Rita**, reached from Puerto de Pampa Chica, on a turnoff, off the road to the airport. Beaches appear when the river is low, July-September.

Allpahuayo-Mishana Reserve ⓘ *Iquitos office at Instituto de Investigaciones de la Amazonía Peruana (IIAP), Av Quiñones on the way to the airport, T265515, www.siamazonia.org.pe/rnam/*. Some 25 km south of Iquitos by road or 2-3 hours by boat from Bellavista, this reserve protects the largest concentration of white sand jungle (*varillales*) in Peru. Part of the Napo ecoregion, biodiversity here is among the highest in the Amazon basin. It has several endangered species including two primates, several endemic species; the area is rich in birds (500 species have been recorded). It also has a **Jardín de Plantas Medicinales** ⓘ *at Km 24, T267733, 0800-1400, US$3.35*. The beautiful **Lake Quistococha** in lush jungle is 4 km south of the city, with a fish hatchery at the lakeside. There's a two-hour walk through the surrounding jungle on a clearly marked trail, bars and restaurants on the lakeside and a small beach. Boats are for hire on the lake and swimming is safe but take insect repellent against sandflies. The **zoo** ⓘ *US$1, 0900-1700*, is squalid. **Pilpintuhuasi Butterfly Farm** ⓘ *near the village of Padre Cocha, T232665, www.amazon animalorphanage.org, US$5, includes guided tour, Tue-Sun 0900-1600, guided tours at 0930, 1100, 1330 and 1500*, as well as butterflies, has a small well-kept zoo, Austrian-Peruvian run. Colectivo from Bellavista to Padre Cocha takes 20 minutes, walk from there. If the river is high, boats can reach Pilpintuhuasi directly (no need to walk), a speedboat charges US$25 return including waiting time (pay at the end).

Border with Brazil

Details on exit and entry formalities seem to change frequently, so when leaving Peru, check in Iquitos first at Immigration or with the Capitanía at the port. Boats stop in Santa Rosa for Peruvian exit formalities. All details are given in the Brazil chapter.

Iquitos

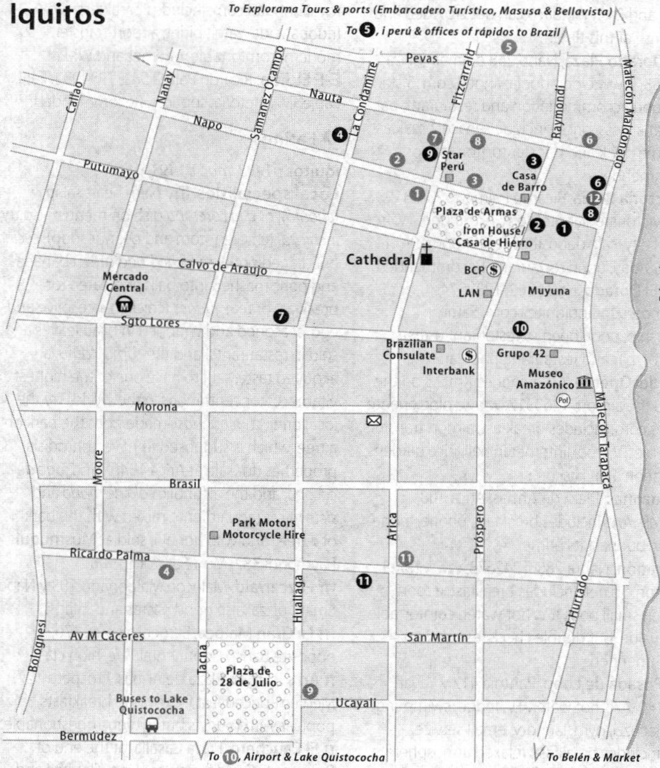

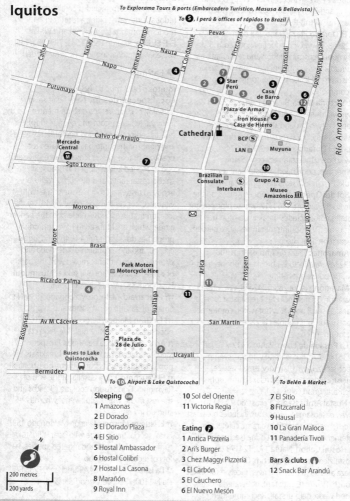

Sleeping
1 Amazonas
2 El Dorado
3 El Dorado Plaza
4 El Sitio
5 Hostal Ambassador
6 Hostal Colibrí
7 Hostal La Casona
8 Marañón
9 Royal Inn
10 Sol del Oriente
11 Victoria Regia

Eating
1 Antica Pizzería
2 Ari's Burger
3 Chez Maggy Pizzería
4 El Carbón
5 El Cauchero
6 El Nuevo Mesón
7 El Sitio
8 Fitzcarrald
9 Hausaí
10 La Gran Maloca
11 Panadería Tivoli

Bars & clubs
12 Snack Bar Arandú

N
200 metres
200 yards

Iquitos and around listings

For Sleeping and Eating price codes and other relevant information, see Essentials, pages 38-40.

Sleeping

Iquitos *p1492, map p1493*

Around Peruvian Independence Day (27 and 28 Jul) and Easter, Iquitos can get crowded and prices rise at this time.

LL El Dorado Plaza, Napo 258 on main plaza, T222555, www.eldoradoplazahotel.com. 5 star, very good accommodation and restaurant, bar, internet access, prices include service, breakfast, welcome drink and transfer to/from airport. Recommended.

AL Victoria Regia, Ricardo Palma 252, T231983, www.victoriaregiahotel.com. A/c, fridge, TV, free map of city, safe deposit boxes in rooms, Wi-Fi US$6.50/day, good restaurant. Recommended.

AL-A El Dorado, Napo 362, T232574, www.hotel doradoiquitos.com. Same ownership, pool (open to restaurant users), cable TV, bar and restaurant, popular.

A Sol del Oriente, Av Quiñónez Km 2.5 on the way to the airport, T260317, www.soldeloriente hoteles.com. Includes breakfast, airport transfers, a/c, cable TV, pool, internet in hall, nice gardens, decoration a bit kitsch.

C Amazonas, Plaza de Armas, Arica 108, T232149. A/c, includes breakfast, phone, fridge bar, TV, but past its prime.

C Marañón, Nauta 285, T242673, www.hotel maranon.cjb.net. Includes breakfast, airport transfer, small pool, a/c, hot water, comfortable, good value, but double check reservations. Recommended.

C La Posada de Lobo, Pantoja 417 y Yavari, T236140. A/c, hot water, TV, fridge, swimming pool, jacuzzi, gym, laundry, email service, price includes breakfast, relaxed atmosphere, pleasant, good value.

D Hostal Ambassador, Pevas 260, T233110, www.paseosamazonicos.com. Includes breakfast, a/c, transport to and from airport, cafeteria, internet, owns Sinchicuy Lodge (see page 1497).

D Hostal Colibrí, Nauta 172, T241737, hostalelcolibri@hotmail.com. One block from Plaza and 50 m from the river, nicely refurbished house, TV, a/c (**E** with fan), hot water, secure, good value, helpful staff. Recommended.

D Hostal La Casona, Fitzcarald 147-A, T234 394, www.lacasonadeiquitos.com. Ample rooms, cold water, fan, kitchen facilities, small patio, internet, Wi-Fi, pool, popular with travellers. Recommended.

D Royal Inn, Aguirre 793, T224244, www.the royalinnhotel.com. Includes breakfast, a/c, frigobar, hot water, bidet, airport transfer, modern, comfortable, internet and Wi-Fi.

E-F El Sitio, Ricardo Palma 541, T234932. Fan, cable TV, cafeteria, spotless. Recommended.

Eating

Iquitos *p1492, map p1493*

Local specialities Try palm heart salad (*chonta*), or *a la Loretana* dish on menus; also try *inchicapi* (chicken, corn and peanut soup), *cecina* (fried dried pork), *tacacho* (fried green banana and pork, mashed into balls and eaten for breakfast or tea), *juanes* (chicken, rice, olive and egg, seasoned and wrapped in bijao leaves and sold in restaurants) and the *camu-camu*, an acquired taste, said to have one of the highest vitamin C concentrations in the world. Try the local drink *chuchuhuasi*, made from the bark of a tree, which is supposed to have aphrodisiac properties (for sale at Arica 1046), and *jugo de cocona*, and the alcoholic *cola de mono* and *siete raices* (aguardiente mixed with the bark of 7 trees and wild honey), sold at **Musmuqui**, Raymondi 382, Mon-Sat from 1900.

TTT **Fitzcarrald**, Malecón Maldonado 103 y Napo. Smart, pizza, also good pastas and salads.

TTT **La Gran Maloca**, Sargento Lores 170, opposite Banco Continental. A/c, high class.

TT **Ari's Burger**, Plaza de Armas, Próspero 127. Medium-priced fast food, good breakfasts, popular with tourists but hygiene questionable.

TT **El Cauchero**, Plaza Castilla, at the end of Raymondi. Good fusion cooking ("Iquitos and the rest of the world"), local chef who has studied in France.

TT **El Nuevo Mesón**, Malecón Maldonado 153. Local specialities include wild boar, alligator, turtle, tapir and other endangered species, has lots of regular dishes, too.

TT **La Isla**, Av Freyre 1647, Punchana, T253177. Daily 1100-1700, very good seafood.

Yellow Rose of Texas, Putumayo 180. Varied food including local dishes, Texan atmosphere. Open 24 hrs so you can wait here if arriving late at night, good breakfasts, lots of information, also has a bar, Sky TV and Texan saddle seats.

Antica Pizzería, Napo 159. Sun-Thu 0700-2400, Fri-Sat 0700-0100, very nice pizza and Italian dishes, pleasant ambiance especially on the upper level, also serves breakfast.

Chez Maggy Pizzería, Raymondi 177. Daily 1800-0100, wood oven pizza and home made pasta.

El Carbón, La Condamine 115. Evenings only, grilled meats, salads, regional side-dishes such as tacacho and patacones.

El Sitio, Sargento Lores 404. Evenings only, a simple place for *anticuchos* for all tastes including vegetarian, popular.

Huasaí, Fitzcarrald 131. Varied and innovative menu, popular, daily 0730-1600. Recommended.

Cafés

Café de María, Pevas 2nd block. Sandwiches, pies and the best cappuccino in Iquitos.
Panadería Tívoli, Ricardo Palma, block 3, a variety of good bread and sweets.

Bars and clubs

Iquitos *p1492, map p1493*

El Pardo, Mariscal Cáceres y Alzamora. Very large, popular dance centre, live Latin music.
Noa Noa, Pevas y Fitzcarrald. Popular disco, varied music, open Tue-Sat.
Snack Bar Arandú, Malecón Maldonado. Good views of the Amazon river.

Festivals and events

Iquitos *p1492, map p1493*

5 Jan: founding of Iquitos. **Feb-Mar**: **Carnival**. **3rd week in Jun**: tourist week. **24 Jun**: San Juan. **28-30 Aug**: Santa Rosa de Lima. **8 Dec**: Immaculate Conception, celebrated in Punchana, near the docks.

Shopping

Iquitos *p1492, map p1493*

Hammocks in Iquitos cost about US$8. **Amazon Arts & Crafts**, Napo block 100. **Mad Mick's Trading Post**, Putumayo 163, top floor, next to the Iron House, hires out rubber boots for those going to the jungle. **Comisesa**, Arica 471, sells rubber boots, torches (flashlights), rain ponchos and other gear. **Mercado Artesanal de Productores**, 4 km from the centre in the San Juan district, on the road to the airport, take a colectivo. Cheapest in town with more choice than elsewhere.

Activities and tours

Iquitos *p1492, map p1493*

Jungle tours from Iquitos Agencies arrange 1-day or longer trips to places of interest with guides speaking some English. Package tours booked in your home country, over the internet or in Lima are much more expensive than those booked locally. Take your time before making a decision and don't be bullied by the hustlers at the airport (they get paid a hefty commission). You must make sure your tour operator or guide has a proper licence (check with i perú). Do not go with a company which does not have legal authorization; there are many unscrupulous people about. Find out all the details of the trip and food arrangements before paying (a minimum of US$45 per day). Speed boats for river trips can be hired by the hour or day at the Embarcadero Turístico, at the intersection of Av de la Marina and Samánez Ocampo in Punchana. Prices vary greatly, usually US$10-20 per hr, US$80 for speedboat, and are negotiable. In fact, all prices are negotiable, except **Muyuna**, **Heliconia Lodge** and **Explorama**, who do not take commissions.

General information and advice Take a long-sleeved shirt, waterproof coat and shoes or light boots on jungle trips and binoculars and a good torch, as well as espirales to ward off the mosquitoes at night – they can be bought from pharmacies in Iquitos. Premier is the most effective local insect repellent. The dry season is from Jul-Sep (Sep is the best month to see flowers and butterflies).

Before taking ayahuasca in a ceremony with a shaman, read the note on page 1263.

Amazon River Expeditions, run trips to Heliconia Lodge, see below for details.

Amazon Yarapa River Lodge, Av La Marina 124, T993 1172, www.yarapa.com. On the Río Yarapa, in a pristine location, award-winning in its use of ecofriendly resources and work with local villages, flexible and responsible, its field laboratory is associated with Cornell University. Rates from US$840 for 2 on a 3 night/4 day package. Arranges trips to Pacaya-Samiria.

Blue Morpho Tours, Av Guardia Civil 515, T263454, www.bluemorphotours.com. A rustic camp on Carretera Nauta, Km 52.5. Centre for shamanic studies and workshops, 9-day shamanic trips US$2,190, all inclusive except for bar and snacks.

Cumaceba Amazonia Tours, Putumayo 184 in the Iron House, T/F232229, www.cumaceba.com. Overnight visits to Cumaceba Lodge, 35 km from Iquitos, and tours of 1-4 nights to the Botanical Lodge on the Amazon, 80 km from Iquitos, bird-watching tours, ayahuasca ceremonies.

Dawn on the Amazon, Malecón Maldonado 185 y Nauta, T223730, www.dawnonthe amazon.com. Offer a variety of day tours around Iquitos on the 14 passenger vessel *Dawn on the Amazon* (US$65 pp) and the luxurious 20 passenger *Dawn on the Amazon III* ($120 pp). Also offer custom-made cruises for several days. Their wooden vessels are decorated with carvings of jungle themes.

Explorama Tours, by the riverside docks on Av La Marina 340, T252530, www.explorama.com, are highly recommended, with over 40 years in existence, certainly the biggest and most established. Their sites are: **Ceiba Tops**, 40 km (1½ hrs) from Iquitos, is a comfortable resort, 75 a/c rooms with electricity, hot showers, pool with hydromassage and beautiful gardens. The food is good and, as in all Explorama's properties, is served communally. There are attractive walks and other excursions, a recommended jungle experience for those who want their creature comforts, US$270 pp for 1 night/2 days, US$115 for each additional night (1-2 people). **Explorama Lodge** at Yanamono, 80 km from Iquitos, 2½ hrs from Iquitos, has palm-thatched accommodation with separate bathroom and shower facilities connected by covered walkways, cold water, no electricity, good food and service. US$365 for 3 days/2 nights and US$100 for each additional day (1-2 people). **Explornapo Lodge** at Llachapa on the Sucusai creek (a tributary of the Napo), is in the same style as Explorama Lodge, but is further away from Iquitos, 160 km (4 hrs), and is set in 105,000 ha of primary rainforest, so is better for seeing wildlife, US$950 for 5 days/ 4 nights. Nearby is the impressive canopy walkway 35 m above the forest floor and 500 m long, 'a magnificent experience and not to be missed'. It is associated with the **Amazon Center for Tropical Studies (ACTS)**, a scientific station, only 10 mins from the canopy walkway. **Explor Tambos**, 2 hrs from Explornapo, offer more primitive accommodation, 8 shelters for 16 campers, bathing in the river, offers the best chance to see fauna. Close to Explornapo is the ReNuPeRu medicinal plant garden, run by a curandero. Members of South American Explorers are offered 15% discount.

Heliconia Lodge, Ricardo Palma 259, T231959 (Lima 01-421 9195), www.amazonrex.com. On the Río Amazonas, 1¼ hrs from Iquitos, the lodge has hot water, electricity for 5 hrs a day, good guiding and staff; rustic yet comfortable, 3 days/2 nights US$282. Under same management as Zungarococha Bungalows 15 km from Iquitos on a lake off the Río Nanay, and in same group as Hotels Victoria Regia and Acosta, see above. They organize trips to Allpahuayo- Mishana, to Pacaya-Samiria and to the ACTS canopy walkway.

Muyuna Amazon Lodge, Putumayo 163, ground floor, T242858, 993 4424, www.muyuna.com. 140 km from Iquitos, also on the Yanayacu, before San Juan village. Packages from 1 to 5 nights available. Everything is included in the price. Good guides, accommodation, food and service, very well organized and professional, flexible, radio contact, will collect passengers from airport if requested in advance. It is easy to see animals here and you can even find rareties such as the piuri (Wattled curaçao, *Crax globulosa*). They offer birdwatching trips. Because of the isolated location they guarantee that visitors will see animals. Highly recommended.

Paseos Amazónicos Ambassador, Pevas 246, T/F231618, operates the **Amazonas Sinchicuy Lodge**. The lodge is 1½ hrs from Iquitos on the Sinchicuy river, 25 mins by boat from the Amazon river. The lodge consists of several wooden buildings with thatched roofs on stilts, cabins with bathroom, no electricity but paraffin lamps are provided, good food, and plenty activities, including visits to local villages. Recommended. They also have Tambo Yanayacu and Tambo Amazónico lodges, organize visits to Pacaya Samiria and local tours.

Tahuayo Lodge, Amazonia Expeditions, 10305 Riverburn Drive, Tampa, FL 33647, toll free T800-262 9669, www.perujungle.com. Near the Reserva Comunal de Tamshiyacu-Tahuayo on the Río Tahuayo, 145 km upriver from Iquitos, comfortable cabins with cold shower, buffet meals, good food, laundry service, wide range of excursions, community visits, excellent staff. An 8-day programme costs US$1,555, all inclusive, extra days US$100. Recommended. The lodge is associated with the Rainforest Conservation Fund, see www.rainforestconservation.org.

Tambo Visits, Alfonso Ugarte 565, T226686, grupotambo@terra.com.pe. Offers day trips in and around Iquitos.

Transport

Iquitos *p1492, map p1493*

Air Francisco Secada Vigneta airport, T260147. Taxi to the airport costs US$4.80; *motocarro* (motorcycle with 2 seats), US$2. A bus from the airport, US$0.55, goes from the main road; most go through the centre of town. To **Lima**, daily; **LAN**, **Peruvian Airlines** and **Star Perú** (direct or via Tarapoto).

Airline offices **Grupo 42**, Sgto Lores 127, T233224. **LAN**, Próspero y Putumayo, ½ block from Plaza de Armas, T224177. **Peruvian Airlines**, Próspero 215, T231074. **Star Perú**, Napo 260, T234173.

Ferry **General hints for river travel**: large passenger and cargo vessels are called *lanchas*, smaller faster craft are called *rápidos* or *deslizadores* (speedboats). *Yates* are small to medium wooden colectivos, usually slow, and *chalupas* are small motor launches used to ferry passengers from the lanchas to shore. For information about boats, go to the corresponding ports of departure for each destination, except for speed boats to the Brazil/Colombian border which have their offices clustered on Raymondi block 3.

Lanchas leave from Puerto Henry and Masusa, 2 km north of the centre, a dangerous area at night. All sailings around 1800-2000, the first night's meal is not included. Always deal directly with boat owners or managers, avoid touts and middle-men. All fares are negotiable. You can buy either a ticket to sling your hammock on deck, or for a berth in a cabin sleeping 2 to 4 people.

A hammock is essential. A double, of material (not string), provides one person with a blanket. Board the boat many hours in advance to guarantee hammock space. If going on the top deck, try to be first down the front; take rope for hanging your hammock, plus string and sarongs for privacy. On all boats, hang your hammock away from lightbulbs (they aren't switched off at night and attract all sorts of strange insects) and away from the engines, which usually emit noxious fumes. Guard your belongings from the moment you board. It's safer to club together and pay for a cabin in which to lock your belongings, even if you sleep outside in a hammock. There is very little privacy; women travellers can expect a lot of attention. There are adequate washing and toilet facilities, but the food is rice, meat and beans (and whatever can be picked up en route) cooked in river water. Stock up on drinking water, fruit and tinned food. Vegetarians must take their own supplies. There is usually a bar on board. Take plenty of prophylactic enteritis tablets; many contract dysentery on the trip. Also take insect repellent and a mosquito net. If arriving in Iquitos on a regular, slow boat, take extreme care when disembarking. Things get very chaotic at this time and theft and pickpocketing is rife.

To **Pucallpa**, 4-5 days up river along the Amazon and Ucayali (can be longer if the water level is low), larger boats must travel only by day, hammock US$35, berth US$43-65 pp. **Henry** (T263948) is a large company with 4 departures per week from Puerto Henry; *Henry 6* and *7* have some cabins with bath. Another good boat is *Pedro Martín II* from Puerto Masusa. To **Yurimaguas**, 3-4 days up river along the Amazon, Marañón and Huallaga, 2nd class hammock space US$17-22 (can be very crowded), 1st class hammock space US$38, berth US$38-48 pp. The **Eduardo** company, T960404, with 8 boats is recommended, they sail from Puerto Henry Mon-Sat; *Eduardo IV* and *Eduardo V* are good vessels. **Islandia** for **Leticia** (Colombia) and **Tabatinga** (Brazil), 2-3 days down river on the Amazon, hammock space US$15-17.50, cabin US$25-30. Passengers disembark in Peru for immigration formalities (no exchange facilities), then take another US$2.50 boat to **Marco**, the port for **Tabatinga**. Most boats for **Manaus** depart from Marco.

Rápidos for **Tabatinga** (Brazil), 8-10 hrs downriver, US$60, depart from the Embarcadero Turístico at 0600 (board 0500-0530) Tue-Sun; be at the port 0445 for customs check. After immigration formalities in **Santa Rosa**, they take passengers to Tabatinga, a few boats may continue to Leticia, Colombia. From Tabatinga departures for Iquitos Tue-Sun 0500-0600, the trip takes slightly longer upriver. All include a small breakfast of a sandwich and coffee, a passable lunch and mineral water (ask for it). All carry life jackets and most have bathrooms. Luggage limit is 15 kg. Purchase tickets in advance from company offices, most are clustered on Raymondi, block 3, and a couple on Arica (open Mon-Sat 0800-1900, some close for lunch, a few open Sun 0800-1200). Not all rápidos are the same; ask around and if possible have a look at the boat before purchasing your ticket. Each company has 3 weekly departures in each direction. **i perú** has a list of companies registered with them, but there are other good ones.

To **Pantoja** (for Ecuador), 5-7 days up river on the Napo, there are 2 boats: the better boat is *Cabo Pantoja*, contact through the Municipio de Torres Causana, Iquitos T226575, or try to inquire at one of the following private phones in Pantoja: T811616, T830055. Hammock space US$35, US$3 per day extra for a berth. The other, shabbier boat is *Jeisawell* Iquitos T965-613049. To shorten the voyage, or visit towns along the way, you can go to **Indiana** from Muelle de Productores (*yates* at 1000 and 1400, returning at 0600 and 1300, US$1.60, 3 hrs; *deslizadores* upon demand, last one returns to Iquitos about 1700, US$3.80, 45 mins), then take a mototaxi to **Mazán** on the Río Napo. From Mazán, there are rápidos to **Santa Clotilde** Mon, Tue, Thu, Fri and Sat around 0900-1100 (Santa Clotilde to Mazán Tue, Wed, Fri, Sat and Sun), US$24 includes a snack, 4-5 hrs, information from **Forestal Export HM**, T251315, or **Familia Ruiz** T251410 (Iquitos). From Mazán to Pantoja the *lancha* costs US$22-25, from Santa Clotilde to Pantoja US$16-19. There is no public transport from Pantoja to **Nuevo Rocafuerte** (Ecuador), you must hire a private boat, US$50-60 per boat. For details of boats to/from Neuvo Rocafuerte, see Ecuador chapter, Coca, Transport, River, see page 1181.

Excursions: Lake Quistococha *p1492*

Combis leave every hour until 1500 from Plaza 28 de Julio, Iquitos; the last one back leaves at 1700. Alternatively take a **motocarro** there and back with a 1 hr wait, which costs US$6. Perhaps the best option is to hire a **motorbike** and spend the day there. The road can be difficult after rain.

Directory

Iquitos *p1492, map p1493*
Banks BCP, Plaza de Armas. Visa ATM around the corner on Próspero. **BBV Continental**, Sgto Lores 171. **Banco de la Nación**, Condamine 478. Good rates. **Interbank**, Próspero y Sgto Lores, cash and TCs at fair rates, ATM. **Casa de cambio** at **Tienda Wing Kong**, Próspero 312, Mon-Sat 0800-1300, 1500-2000, Sun 0900-1200. Western Union, Napo 359, T235182. Don't change money on the streets.
Consulates Brazil, Sargento Lores 363, T235153, www.abe. mre.gov.br. Mon-Fri 0800-1400, visas issued in 2 days. **Colombia**, Calvo de Araujo 431, T231461, Mon-Fri 0900-1230, 1500-1700. **Germany**, Max Axel Georg Druschke, Pevas 133-B, T233466, mdruschke@terra.com.pe. **Note** There is no Ecuadorean consulate. If you need a visa, you must get it in Lima or in your home country. **Internet** There are places everywhere, US$0.5-0.65 per hr. **Medical services** Clínica Ana Stahl, Av la Marina 285, T252535. **Motorcycle hire** **Park Motors**, Tacna 643, US$2.20 per hr, US$19 per day. Addresses of others from tourist office, see above. **Post offices** On the corner of C Arica with Morona, near Plaza de Armas, daily 0700-1700. **Telephones** *Locutorios* everywhere. **Useful addresses** Immigration: Mcal Cáceres 18th block, T235371, Mon-Fri 0800-1615. **Tourist police**: Sargento Lores 834, T231851. In emergency T241000 or 241001.

Southeastern jungle

The southern selva is in Madre de Dios department, which contains the Manu National Park (1.9 million ha), the Tambopata National Reserve (254,358 ha) and the Bahauja-Sonene National Park (1.1 million ha). The forest of this lowland region (*Altitude: 260 m*) is technically called Sub-tropical Moist Forest, which means that it receives less rainfall than tropical forest and is dominated by the floodplains of its meandering rivers. The most striking features are the former river channels that have become isolated as ox-bow lakes. These are home to black caiman and giant otter. Other rare species living in the forest are jaguar, puma, ocelot and tapir. There are also howler monkeys, macaws, guans, currasows and the giant harpy eagle. As well as containing some of the most important flora and fauna on Earth, the region also harbours gold-diggers, loggers, hunters, drug smugglers and oil-men, whose activities have endangered the unique rainforest. Moreover, the construction of the *Interoceánica*, a road linking the Atlantic and Pacific oceans via Puerto Maldonado and Brazil, will certainly bring more uncontrolled colonization in the area, as seen so many times in the Brazilian Amazon.

Ins and outs

Access to Manu The multiple use zone of Manu Biosphere Reserve is accessible to anyone and several lodges exist in the area (see Lodges in Manu below). The reserved zone is accessible by permit only. Entry is strictly controlled and visitors must visit the area under the auspices of an authorized operator with an authorized guide. Permits are limited and reservations should be made well in advance. In the reserved zone the only accommodation is in the comfortable Manu Lodge or in the comfortable but rustic Casa Machiguenga in the Cocha Salvador area. Several companies have tented safari camp infrastructures, some with shower and dining facilities, but all visitors sleep in tents. The entrance fee to the Reserved Zone is 150 soles pp (about US$54) and is included in package tour prices.

Useful addresses **In Lima** **Asociación Peruana para la Conservación de la Naturaleza** (APECO) ⓘ *Parque José Acosta 187, p 2, Magdalena del Mar, T01-264 5804, www.ape co.org.pe*. **Pronaturaleza** ⓘ *Doña Juana 137, Urb Los Rosales, Santiago de Surco,T01-271 2621, and in Puerto Maldonado, Jr Cajamarca cuadra 1 s/n, T082-571585, www.pronaturaleza.org*. **In Cuzco** **Perú Verde** ⓘ *Ricardo Palma J-1, Santa Mónica, T084-226392, www.peruverde.org*. This is a local NGO that can help with information and has free video shows about Manu National Park and Tambopata National Reserve. Friendly and helpful and with information on research in the jungle area of Madre de Dios. The **Amazon Conservation Association** (ACA) ⓘ *Av Oswaldo Baca 402, Urb Magisterio, Cuzco,T084-222329, www.amazonconservation.org, Jr Cusco 499, T082-573237, Puerto Maldonado* is another NGO whose mission is to protect biodiversity by studying ecosystems and developing conservation tools to protect land while suporting local communities. Further information can be obtained from the **Manu National Park Office** ⓘ *Av Micaela Bastidas 310, Cuzco, T084-240898, pqnmanu@terra.com.pe, open 0800-1400*. They issue the permit for the Reserved Zone.

Climate The climate is warm and humid, with a rainy season from Novemer to March and a dry season from April to October. Cold fronts from the South Atlantic, called *friajes*, are characteristic of the dry season, when temperatures drop to 15-16° C during the day, and 13° C at night. Always bring a sweater at this time. The best time to visit is during the dry season when there are fewer mosquitoes and the rivers are low, exposing the beaches. This is also a good time to see nesting and to view animals at close range, as they stay close to the rivers and are easily seen. Note that this is also the hottest time. A pair of binoculars is essential and insect repellent is a must.

Manu Biosphere Reserve

No other reserve can compare with Manu for the diversity of life forms; it holds over 1,000 species of birds and covers an altitudinal range from 200 to 4,100 m above sea-level. Giant otters, jaguars, ocelots and 13 species of primates abound in this pristine tropical wilderness, and uncontacted indigenous tribes are present in the more remote areas, as are indigenous groups with limited access.

The reserve is one of the largest conservation units on Earth, encompassing the complete drainage of the Manu River. It is divided into the **Manu National Park** (1,692,137 ha), where only government sponsored biologists and anthropologists may visit with permits from the Ministry of Agriculture in Lima; the **Reserved Zone** (257,000 ha) within the Manu National Park, set aside for applied scientific research and ecotourism; and the **Cultural Zone** (92,000 ha), which contains acculturated native groups and colonists, where the locals still employ their traditional way of life. Among the ethnic groups in the Cultural Zone are the Harakmbut, Machiguenga and Yine in the Amarakaeri Reserved Zone, on the east bank of the Alto Madre de Dios. They have set up their own ecotourism activities. Associated with Manu are other areas protected by conservation groups, or local people (for example the Blanquillo reserved zone) and some cloud forest parcels along the road. The **Nahua-Kugapakori Reserved Zone**, set aside for these two nomadic native groups, is the area between the headwaters of the Río Manu and headwaters of the Río Urubamba, to the north of the alto Madre de Dios.

Cuzco to Puerto Maldonado via Mazuko

This route is Cuzco-Urcos-Quincemil-Mazuko-Puerto Maldonado. Bus and truck details are given under Transport, below. It's a painfully slow journey on an appalling road; trucks frequently get stuck or break down. **Quincemil**, 240 km from Urcos on the road to Mazuko, is a centre for alluvial gold-mining with many banks. Accommodation is available in **F Hotel Toni**, friendly, clean, cold shower, good meals. Quincemil marks the half-way point and the start of the all-weather road. Gasoline is scarce in Quincemil because most road vehicles continue on 70 km to Mazuko, which is another mining centre, where they fill up with the cheaper gasoline of the jungle region. The changing scenery is magnificent and worth the hardship and discomfort.

Cuzco to Puerto Maldonado via Pilcopata and Itahuania

The arduous 255 km trip over the Andes from Cuzco to Pilcopata takes about 8-12 hours by bus or truck (10 hours to two days in the wet season). On this route, too, the scenery is magnificent. From Cuzco you climb up to the pass before Paucartambo (very cold at night), before dropping down to this mountain village at the border between the departments of Cuzco and Madre de

Dios. The road then ascends to the second pass (also cold at night), after which it goes down to the cloud forest and then the rainforest, reaching **Pilcopata** at 650 m (8 hours).

Pilcopata to Itahuania After Pilcopata, the route is hair-raising and breathtaking, passing through **Atalaya**, the first village on the Alto Madre de Dios River and tourist port for hiring boats to Boca Manu (basic accommodation). The route continues to Salvación, where a Park Office and Park Entrance are situated. There are basic hostals and restaurants. Basic restaurants can be found in Pilcopata and Atalaya.

The road, which bypasses the previous port of **Shintuya**, continues to **Itahuania**, the starting point for river transport. Rain often disrupts wheeled transport, though. The road is scheduled to continue to Nuevo Edén, 11 km away, and Diamante, so the location of the port will be determined by progress on the road. Eventually, the road will go to Boca Colorado. **Note** It is not possible to arrange trips to the Reserved Zone of the National Park from Itahuania, owing to park regulations. All arrangements, including permits, must be made in Cuzco.

Itahuania to Puerto Maldonado Cargo boats leave for the gold mining centre of Boca Colorado on the Río Madre de Dios, via Boca Manu, but only when the boat is fully laden (see Transport below). Very basic accommodation can be found here, but it is not recommended for lone women travellers. From Colorado you can take a colectivo taxi to Puerto Carlos, cross the river, then take another colectivo to Puerto Maldonado; 4½ hours in all.

Boca Manu is the connecting point between the rivers Alto Madre de Dios, Manu and Madre de Dios. It has a few houses, an air strip and some food supplies. It is also the entrance to the Manu Reserve and to go further you must be part of an organized group. The park ranger station is located in Limonal. You need to show your permit here. Camping is allowed if you have a permit. There are no regular flights from Cuzco to Boca Manu. These are arranged the day before, if there are enough passengers. Check at Cuzco airport; or with the tour operators in Cuzco.

To the Reserved Zone Upstream on the Río Manu you pass the *Manu Lodge* (see Sleeping, below), on the Cocha Juárez, 3-4 hours by boat. You can continue to Cocha Otorongo, 2½ hours and Cocha Salvador, 30 minutes, the biggest lake with plenty of wildlife. From here it is 2-3 hours to Pakitza, the entrance to the National Park Zone. This is only for biologists with a special permit.

Between Boca Manu and Colorado is **Blanquillo**, a private reserve (10,000 ha). Bring a good tent with you and all food if you want to camp and do it yourself, or alternatively accommodation is available at the *Tambo Blanquillo* (full board or accommodation only). Wildlife is abundant, especially macaws and parrots at the macaw lick near *Manu Wildlife Centre*. There are occasional boats to Blanquillo from Shintuya; 6-8 hours.

Puerto Maldonado ➔ *Phone code: 082. Colour map 3, C5. Pop: 45,000. Altitude: 250 m.*

Puerto Maldonado is an important starting point for visiting the south eastern jungles of the Tambopata Reserve or departing for Bolivia or Brazil. It overlooks the confluence of the rivers Tambopata and Madre de Dios and, because of the gold mining and timber industries, the immediate surrounding jungle is now cultivated. A bridge, as part of the Interoceánica highway, is being built across the Río Madre de Dios. Even before its completion (late 2010 or 2011, forecasts vary) business activity in the town is growing fast. There are tourist offices at the airport and at **Dircetur** ⓘ *Urb Fonavi, take a moto-taxi to the Posta Médica which is next door.*

The beautiful and tranquil **Lago Sandoval** is a one-hour boat ride along the Río Madre de Dios, and then a 5-km walk into the jungle (parts of the first 3 km are a raised wooden walkway; boots are advisable). Entry to the lake coasts US$9.50. You must go with a guide; this can be arranged by the boat driver. Boats can be hired at the Madre de Dios port for about US$25 a day, minimum two people (plus petrol) to go to Lago Sandoval (don't pay the full cost in advance).

Jungle tours from Puerto Maldonado

Trips can be made to **Lago Valencia**, 60 km away near the Bolivian border, four hours there, eight hours back. It is an ox-bow lake with lots of wildlife. Many excellent beaches and islands are located within an hour's boat ride. Mosquitoes are voracious. If camping, take food and water.

It is quite easy to arrange a boat and guide from Puerto Maldonado (see Tour operators below) to the **Tambopata National Reserve** (TNR) ⓘ *Inrena, Av 28 de Julio 482, Puerto Maldonado, T573278*, between the rivers Madre de Dios, Tambopata and Heath. Some superb ox-bow lakes can be visited and the birdwatching is wonderful.

The **Bahuaja-Sonene National Park**, declared in 1996, stretches from the Heath River across the Tambopata, incorporating the Río Heath National Sanctuary. It is closed to visitors.

Río Las Piedras

Lying to the northeast of, and running roughly parallel to the Río Manu, this drainage runs some 700 km from rainforest headwaters in the Alto Purús region. The lower, more easily accessible section of the river, closer to Puerto Maldonado and outside state protection, runs through rich tropical forests, very similar to those in the Manu and Tambopata areas. Close to 600 species of birds, at least eight primate species and some of the Amazon's larger mammals, giant otter, jaguar, puma, tapir and giant anteater, are all present. Hunting pressure has resulted in wildlife being somewhat shier and more secretive than in Manu or Tambopata, but this remains an excellent wildlife destination.

To Iberia and Iñapari

Daily public transport runs to **Iberia** and **Iñapari** on the border with Brazil. Until paving of this section of the Interoceánica road is complete, there may be delays, especially in the wet season. It takes a lot of traffic and can be dangerous for motorcyclists as a result. Along the road there remains no primary forest, only secondary growth and small *chacras* (farms). There are also picturesque *caseríos* (settlements) that serve as processing centres for the brazil nut. Approximately 70% of the inhabitants in the Madre de Dios are involved in the collection of this prized nut.

Iberia, Km 168, has two hotels, the best is **G Hostal Aquino**, basic, cold shower. Just outside the town the local rubber tappers association has set up an interesting Reserve and Information Centre.

Iñapari, at the end of the road, Km 235, has two basic hotels and a restaurant, but **Assis Brasil** across the border is much more attractive and has three hotels, two restaurants and shops. A suspension bridge now links the two countries.

There is a road from Assis Brasil into Brazil and connections to Cobija in Bolivia from Brasiléia. There are no exchange facilities en route and poor exchange rates for Brazilian currency at Iñapari. Crossing between Peru and Bolivia on this route is not easy.

Crossing to Brazil

Public transport stops near **immigration in Iñapari**. Exit stamps can be obtained at immigration, open 0930-1300, 1500-1930 daily (Brazilian side 0830-1200, 1400-1830). In Assis Brasil, there is no Policía Federal office. You have to travel on to Brasiléia to obtain your Brazil entry stamp at Policía Federal in the Rodoviária (bus station). You must have a yellow fever certificate to enter Brazil.

Southeastern jungle listings

For Sleeping and Eating price codes and other relevant information, see Essentials, pages 38-40.

Sleeping

Manu Biosphere Reserve *p1500*

Lodges in Manu

Amazonia Lodge, on the Río Alto Madre de Dios just across the river from Atalaya, T084-816131, www.amazonialodge.com; in Cuzco at Matará 334, p 3, T084-231370. An old tea hacienda run by the Yabar Calderón family, famous for its bird diversity and fine hospitality, a great place to relax, meals included, birding or natural history tours available, contact Santiago in advance and he'll arrange a pick-up.

Casa Machiguenga, near Cocha Salvador, upriver from Manu Lodge. Contact **Manu Expeditions** or **Apeco** NGO, T084-225595. Machiguenga-style cabins run by local communities with NGO help.

Cock of the Rock Lodge, on the road from Paucartambo to Atalaya at 1,600 m, www.tropicalnaturetravel.com. Next to a Cock of the Rock *lek*, 10 private cabins with en-suite bath, US$495 pp for 3 days/2 nights, including tours, guide and meals.

Erika Lodge, on the Alto Madre de Dios, 25 mins from Atalaya, offers basic accommodation and is cheaper than the other, more luxurious lodges. Contact **Manu Ecological Adventures** (see below).

Manu Cloud Forest Lodge, at Unión, at 1,800 m on the road from Paucartambo to Atalaya, owned by **Manu Nature Tours**, 6 rooms with 16-20 beds.

Manu Lodge, on the Manu river, 3 hrs upriver from Boca Manu towards Cocha Salvador, run by **Manu Nature Tours** and only bookable as part of a full package deal with transport.

Manu Wildlife Centre, 2 hrs down the Río Madre de Dios from Boca Manu, near the Blanquillo macaw lick. Book through **Manu Expeditions** or **InkaNatura**. 22 double cabins, with private bathroom and hot water. Also canopy towers for birdwatching and a Tapir lick.

Pantiacolla Lodge, 30 mins down-river from Shintuya. Owned by the Moscoso family. Book through **Pantiacolla Tours** (see page 1508).

Yanayaco Lodge, Procuradores 46, Cuzco, T084-248122, www.yanayacolodge.com. About 1 hr by boat above Diamante village on the southern bank of the Madre de Dios, close to a small parrot *collpa* (mineral lick). Using local river transport to arrive at the lodge rates are very reasonable, prices depend on length of stay. The lodge also offers several different itineraries in Manu.

Cuzco to Puerto Maldonado via Pilcopata and Itahuania *p1500*

Turismo Indigena Wanamei, Av El Sol 814 p 2, of 212, Cuzco, T234608, 984-754708, or Av 26 de Diciembre 276, Puerto Maldonado, T082-572 539, www.ecoturismowanamei.com. New initiative by the people of the Amarakaeri Communal Reserve, located between Manu and Tambopata. They offer 4-9 day trips starting and ending in Cuzco. Accommodation includes lodges, communities and camping. The trips aim not only to offer excellent wildlife viewing opportunities but also an insight in to the daily life of indigenous peoples. It's advised that you speak Spanish.

D Boca Manu Lodge, book through **Emperadores Tours**, Procuradores 190, Cuzco, T084-239987, empetcusco@hotmail.com. Run by Juan de Dios Carpio, who owns a general store in Boca, reasonably priced.

G Hospedaje Manu, Boca Colorado, on street beside football field. Cell-like rooms, open windows and ceilings but comfy mattresses and mosquito netting.

G Sra Rubella in Pilcopata. Very basic but friendly.

Yine Lodge, next to Boca Manu airport. A cooperative project run between **Pantiacolla Tours** and the Yine community of Diamante, who operate their own tours into their community and surroundings. Also **G** pp **Hostal** in Boca Manu run by the community. Basic accommodation.

Puerto Maldonado *p1501*

New hotels catering for business travellers are springing up.

B Anaconda Lodge, 600m from airport, T982 611039 (mob), www.anacondajunglelodge.com. **D** with shared bath, Swiss/Thai owned bungalows, hot showers, swimming pool, Thai restaurant, tours arranged, has space for camping, very pleasant, family atmsophere.

B Wasai Lodge & Expeditions, Billinghurst opposite the Capitanía, www.wasai.com. In a beautiful location overlooking the Madre de Dios River, with forest surrounding cabin-style rooms, a/c, TV, shower, small pool with waterfall, good restaurant (local fish a speciality). Recommended. They can organize local tours and also have a lodge on the Río Tambopata (see page 1505).

C Cabañaquinta, Cuzco 535, T571045, www.hotelcabanaquinta.com.pe. With breakfast, a/c (cheaper rooms without a/c and hot water), free drinking water, internet, good restaurant, lovely garden, very comfortable, airport transfer. Recommended.

C Paititi Hostal, G Prada 290 y Av León Velarde, T574667, paititihostal@hotmail.com. All mod-cons, executive and standard rooms, TV, a/c, breakfast included, Wi-Fi. Reserve in advance. Recommended.

D Don Carlos, Av León Velarde 1271, T571 029. Nice view over the Río Tambopata, a/c, restaurant, TV, phone, good.

E Amarumayo, Libertad 433, 10 mins from the centre, T573860, residenciamarumayo@hotmail.com. Comfortable, with breakfast, with pool and garden, good restaurant. Recommended.

E Hospedaje Español, González Prada 670, T572381. Comfortable, set back from the road, in a quiet part of town.

E Hospedaje La Bahía, 2 de Mayo 710, T572127. Cheaper without bath or TV, new, large rooms, a good choice.

F Hospedaje El Bambú, Jr Puno 837, T793880. New, basic and small but well-kept rooms with fan, family atmosphere, breakfast and juices not included in price but served in dining room. A good budget option.

F pp **Tambopata Hostel**, Av 26 de Diciembre 234, www.tambopatahostel.com. The only real backpacker hostel in town, dorm beds. Nice atmosphere, they also organize local tours.

Jungle tours from Puerto Maldonado: Tambopata *p1502*

Some of the lodges along the Tambopata river offer guiding and research placements to biology and environmental science graduates. For more details send an SAE to **TReeS**: UK – J Forrest, PO Box 33153, London, NW3 4DR, www.tambopata.org.

Lodges on the Río Madre de Dios

C Casa de Hospedaje Mejía, to book T571428, visit **Ceiba Tours**, L Velarde 420, T573567, turismomejia@hotmail.com. Attractive rustic lodge close to Lago Sandoval, full board can be arranged, canoes are available. 3 days/2 nights cost US$70.

Eco Amazonia Lodge, on the Madre de Dios, 1 hr down-river from Puerto Maldonado. In Lima: Enrique Palacios 292, Miraflores, T01-242 2708, in Cuzco Garcilazo 210, of 206, T084-236159, www.ecoamazonia. com.pe. Basic bungalows and dormitories, good for birdwatching, has its own Monkey Island with animals taken from the forest, US$190 for 3 days/2 nights.

El Corto Maltés, Billinghurst 229, Puerto Maldonado, T571320, cortomaltes@terra.com.pe. On the Madre de Dios, halfway to Sandoval which is the focus of most visits. Hot water, huge diningroom, well run. 3 days/2 nights US$180.

Estancia Bello Horizonte, 20 km northwest of Puerto Maldonado, Jr José María Grain 105, Puerto Maldonado, T572748, www.estanciabellohorizonte.com. In a nice stretch of forest overlooking the Madre de Dios, a small lodge with bungalows for 20 people, with private bath, hammock and pool. 3 days/2 nights US$150. The lodge belongs to APRONIA and profits fund a home for children with difficulties. Suitable for those wanting to avoid a river trip.

Inkaterra Reserva Amazónica, 45 mins by boat down the Madre de Dios. To book: **Inkaterra**, Andalucía 174, Miraflores L18, Lima, T01-610 0400; Plaza Nazarenas 167 p 2, Cuzco T084-245314; www.inkaterra.com. Tastefully redecorated hotel in the jungle with suites and bungalows, solar power, good food in huge dining room supported by a big tree. Jungle tours in its own 10,000 ha plus their new canopy walk; also tours to Lago Sandoval. From US$760 for 3-day/2-night package, but cheaper for longer.

Sandoval Lake Lodge, 1 km beyond *Mejía* on Lago Sandoval, book through **InkaNatura**, address under Manu, Tour operators. Usual access is by canoe after a 3-km walk or rickshaw ride, huge bar and dining area, electricity, hot water. US$215 pp for 3 days/2 nights.

Lodges on the Tambopata

Lodges on the Tambopata are reached by vehicle to Bahuaja port, 15 km up river from Puerto Maldonado by the community of Infierno, then by boat.

Casas de Hospedaje Baltimore, several families in the community of Baltimore on the banks of the Río Tambopata, 60 km upriver, in Puerto Maldonado, Junín cuadra 1, Mz 2-Lte 10F, T572380, www.balti moreperu.org.pe. They offer the opportunity to experience the forest close-up and an insight into daily life in the forest at a more economical price. US$140 double, 4 days/3 nights. First night camping, next two staying in a family home. Guiding in Spanish, English speaking guide can be arranged for US$25. Researchers and volunteers also welcomed by arrangement.

Explorers Inn, book through Peruvian Safaris, Alcanfores 459, Miraflores, Lima, T01-447 8888, www.peruviansafaris.com. Just before the La Torre control post, adjoining the TNR, in the part where most research work has been done, 58 km from Puerto Maldonado. 2½ hrs up the Río Tambopata (1½ hrs return), one of the best places in Peru for seeing jungle birds (580 plus species have been recorded), butterflies (1,230 plus species), also giant river otters, but you probably need more than a 2-day tour to benefit fully from the location. Offers tours through the adjoining community of La Torre. The guides are biologists and naturalists undertaking research in the reserve. They provide interesting wildlife-treks, including to the macaw lick (*collpa*). US$450 for 5 days/4 nights.

Posada Amazonas Lodge, on the Tambopata river, 1½ hrs by vehicle and boat upriver from Puerto Maldonado. Book through **Rainforest Expeditions**, San Francisco de Paula Ugariza 813, Of 201, San Antonio-Miraflores, Lima, T01-241 4880, reservations at 01-997 903650, www.peru nature.com. A collaboration between the tour agency and the local native community of Infierno. Attractive rooms with cold showers, visits to Lake Tres Chimbadas, with good birdwatching including the Tambopata Collpa. Offers trips to a nearby indigenous primary health care project where a native healer gives guided tours of the medicinal plant garden. Service and guiding is very good. Recommended. Prices start at US$225 for a 3 day/2 night package, or US$745 for 5 days/ 4 nights including the **Tambopata Research Centre**, the company's more intimate, but comfortable lodge, about 6 hrs further upriver. Rooms are smaller than Posada Amazonas, shared showers, cold water. The lodge is next to the famous Tambopata macaw clay lick. 2 hrs from Posada Amazonas, Rainforest Expeditions also has the **Refugio Amazonas**, close to Lago Condenados. It is the usual stopover for those visiting the collpa. 3 bungalows accommodate 70 people in en-suite rooms, large, kerosene lit, open bedrooms with mosquito nets, well-designed and run, atmospheric. Prices as for Posada Amazonas.

Tambopata Eco Lodge, on the Río Tambopata, to make reservations Nueva Baja 432, Cuzco, T084-245695, operations office Jr Gonzales Prada 269, Puerto Maldonado, T571726, www.tambopatalodge.com. Rooms with solar-heated water, good guides, excellent food. Trips go to Lake Condenado, some to Lake Sachavacayoc, and to the Collpa de Chuncho, guiding mainly in English and Spanish, package from US$256 pp for 3 days/2 nights, naturalists programme provided.

Wasai Lodge and Expeditions, Río Tambopata, 120 km (4½ hrs) upriver from Puerto Maldonado, T082-572290, owned by Hotel Wasai, www. wasai.com. 20 km of trails around the lodge, guides in English and Spanish. The Collpa de Chuncho is only 1 hr up river; 3 day/2 night trips US$300, 5 day/4 nights US$400.

Río Las Piedras

Amazon Rainforest Conservation Centre, contact Pepe Moscoso, Jr Los Cedros B-17, Los Castaños, Puerto Maldonado, T082-573655. Roughly 8 hrs up Río Las Piedras, overlooking a beautiful oxbow lake, Lago Soledad, which has a family of giant otters. Comfortable bungalows, with bath and hot water. Activities include a viewing platform 35 m up an ironwood tree, a hide overlooking a macaw lick, and walks on the extensive trail network. Most trips break the river journey half way at Tipishca Camp, overlooking an oxbow lake with a family of otters. 6-days/ 5-nights with 5-7 people costs US$985.

Las Piedras Biodiversity Station, T/F082-573922, www.rainforestresearch.netfirms.com. A small lodge in a 4,000-ha concession of 'primary' rainforest 90 km up the Río Las Piedras. Visitors camp en route to the lodge. 20 beds in 10 rooms, central dining-room, shared bath, no electricity, library, guiding in English/ Spanish. Minimum package is for 4 days/3 nights, US$470 pp based on a group of 2-3, falling to US$239 pp for groups of 10-14 people. Birdwatching trips cost more.

Eating

Puerto Maldonado *p1501*

¥¥-¥ **Burgos's**, Billinghurst 480 y Puno. With a lovely terrace overlooking the Madre de Dios, serves traditional dishes and has a good set lunch menu.

¥¥-¥ **Carne Brava**, on the Plaza de Armas. One of the smart new joints for a steak and chips. Similar, also on the Plaza, is **Vaka Loca**.

¥¥-¥ **El Califa**, Piura 266. Some regional specialities. Recommended.

¥¥-¥ **El Hornito/Chez Maggy**, on the plaza. Cosy, good pizzas, busy at weekends.

¥ **D'Caoba**, Madre de Dios 439. Serves the most delicious *pollos a la brasa* in town.

¥ **La Casa Nostra**, Velarde 515. Sells huge fruit juices for US$0.50, as well as *tamales, papas rellenas* and enormous fancy cakes, great coffee.

¥ **Namaste**, Av León Velarde 469. Moroccan and Indian food, sandwiches, breakfasts and set lunches, in chilled out surroundings.

Gustitos del Cura, Loreto 258, Plaza de Armas. Ice-cream and juice parlour run by a project for homeless teenagers, offering an amazing of unusual flavours.

Tu Dulce Espera, Av L.Velarde 475. Good for evening juices and snacks.

Bars and clubs

Puerto Maldonado *p1501*

Coconut, east side of the plaza. Disco.

El Witite, Av León Velarde 153. A popular, good disco, latin music, open Fri and Sat.

Le Boulevard, behind **El Hornito**. Live music, popular. There is a billiard hall at **Puno 520**.

T-Saica, Loreto 335. An atmospheric bar with live music at weekends.

Activities and tours

Manu Biosphere Reserve *p1500*

Warning Beware of pirate operators on the streets of Cuzco who offer trips to the Reserved Zone of Manu and end up halfway through the trip changing the route "due to emergencies", which, in reality means they have no permits to operate in the area. The following companies organize trips into the Multiple Use and Reserved Zones. Contact them for more details.

Amazon Trails Peru, C Tandapata 660, San Blas, Cuzco, T084-236770, or 984 714148 (mob), www.amazontrailsperu.com. Offers tours to Manu National Park and Blanquillo clay lick; runs 2 lodges in Manu. Operated by ornithologist Abraham Huamán who has many years experience guiding in Manu and his German wife Ulla Maennig. Well-organized tours with good guides and guaranteed departure dates. Also trekking in Cuzco area. Run the Amazon Hostel next door to office in Cuzco (T236770).

Bonanza Tours, Suecia 343, T507871, www.bonanzatoursperu.com. 3 to 8-day tours to Manu with local guides, plenty of jungle walks, rafting, kayaking and camp-based excursions. Tours go down the Madre del Dios as far as the Blanquillo clay lick, not to the reserve area.

Expediciones Vilca, Plateros 359, Cuzco, T/F084-244751, www.manuvilcaperu.com. Offers tours at economical prices.

InkaNatura, in Cuzco: Ricardo Palma J1, T084-255255, in Lima: Manuel Bañón 461, San Isidro, T01-440 2022, www.inkanatura.com. Tours to Manu Wildlife Centre and Sandoval Lake Lodge (see above) with emphasis on sustainable tourism and conservation. Knowledgeable guides. They also run treks in Cuzco area.

Manu Ecological Adventures, Plateros 356, Cuzco, T084-261640, www.manuadventures.com. This company operates one of the most physically active Manu programmes, with options for a mountain biking descent through the cloudforest and 3 hrs of white-water rafting on the way to **Erika Lodge** on the upper Río Madre de Dios.

Manu Expeditions, Clorinda Matto de Turner 330, Urb Magisterial, Primera Etapa, Cuzco, T084-225990, www.manuexpeditions.com. Owned by ornithologist, Barry Walker, 3 trips available to the reserve and Manu Wildlife Centre.

Manu Learning Centre, Fundo Mascoitania, a 600-ha private reserve near Salvación, operated by CREES, San Miguel 250, Cuzco, T262433 (in UK 5-6 Kendrick Mews, London, SW7 3HG, T020-7581 2932), www.crees-manu.org.

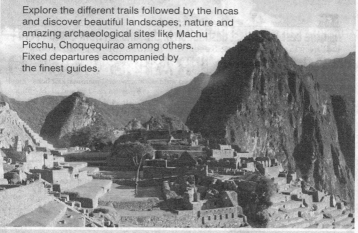

A multi-use centre in the Cultural Zone for ectourism, research, volunteers and school groups for rainforest conservation and commuity development. They run expeditions, tours and field courses.

Manu Nature Tours, Av Pardo 1046, Cuzco, T084-240152, www.manuperu.com. Owned by Boris Gómez Luna, run lodge-based trips, owners of Manu Lodge and part owners of Manu Cloudforest Lodge; Manu is the only lodge in the Reserved Zone, open all year, situated on an ox-bow lake, providing access to the forest, US$130 per night including meals, guides available; activities include river-rafting and canopy-climbing, highly recommended for experiencing the jungle in comfort.

Oropéndola, Av Circunvalación s/n, Urb Guadalupe Mz A Lte 3, Cuzco, T084-241428, www.oropendola peru.org. Guide Walter Mancilla Huamán is an expert on flora and fauna. 5-, 7- and 9-day tours from US$800 pp plus park entrance. Good reports of attention to detail and to the needs of clients.

Pantiacolla Tours SRL, Saphi 554, Cuzco, T084-238323, www.pantiacolla.com. Run by Marianne Von Vlaardingen and Gustavo Moscoso. They have tours to the Pantiacolla Lodge (see Sleeping, above) and also 8-day camping trips. Pantiacolla has started a community-based ecotourism project, called the Yine Project, with the people of Diamante in the Multiple Use Zone.

Puerto Maldonado *p1501*

Guides

All guides should have a carnet issued by the Ministry of Tourism (DIRCETUR), which also verifies them as suitable guides for trips to other places and confirms their identity. Check that the carnet has not expired. Reputable guides are **Hernán Llave Cortez**, **Romel Nacimiento** and the **Mejía** brothers, all of whom can be contacted on arrival at the airport, if available. Also recommended: **Carlos Borja Gama**, a local guide offering specialist bird watching and photography trips as well as traditional jungle tours. Contact him through Wasaí or see www.carlosexpeditions.com. **Víctor Yohamona**, T082-982 686279 (mob), victorguideperu@hotmail.com. Speaks English, French and German. Boat hire can be arranged through the Capitanía del Puerto (Río Madre de Dios), T573003. **Perú Tours**, Loreto 176, T082-573 244, perutoursytravel@hotmail.com. Organize local trips. See also **Ceiba Tours**, under *Casa de hospedaje Mejía*, above.

Transport

Cuzco to Puerto Maldonado: via Urcos and Mazuko *p1500*

Bus There are daily buses from the Terminal Terrestre in **Cuzco** with **Transportes Iguazú** and **Mendivil**. Both on Av Tambopata, blocks 3 and 5 in Puerto Maldonado. 19 hrs (potentially much longer in the wet), US$15, depart 1400 from Puerto Maldonado. Another option is to go from Cuzco to **Urcos**, 1 hr, US$2.25, then look for the **Transportes Juan Carlos** bus in Urcos' main plaza. This is a Volvo truck modified with seats and windows. In the dry season this takes 26 hrs to Puerto Maldonado, US$13; it leaves about 1500 daily. There are also daily buses from **Mazuko** to Puerto Maldonado with **Transportes Bolpebra** and **Transportes Señor de la Cumbre**, 4 hrs, US$3.

Cuzco to Puerto Maldonado: via Pilcopata and Itahuania *p1500*

Road From the Coliseo Cerrado in Cuzco 3 bus companies run to **Pilcopata** Mon, Wed, Fri, returning same night, US$10. They are fully booked even in low season. The best are **Gallito de las Rocas**; also **Unancha** from C Huáscar near the main plaza. Trucks to Pilcopata run on same days, returning Tue, Thu, Sat, 10 hrs in wet season, less in the dry. Only basic supplies are available after leaving Cuzco, so take all your camping and food essentials, including insect repellent. Transport can be disrupted in the wet season because the road is in poor condition; paving is under way as part of the Carretera Interoceánica (tour companies have latest details). *Camioneta* service runs between Pilcopata and **Salvación** to connect with the buses, Mon, Wed, Fri. The same *camionetas* run **Itahuania-Shintuya-Salvacion** regularly, when sufficient passengers, probably once a day, and 2 trucks a day. On Sun, there is no traffic. To **Boca Manu** you can hire a boat in Atalaya, US$212 for a *peke peke*, or US$400 for a motor boat. It's cheaper to wait or hope for a boat going empty up to Boca Manu to pick up passengers, when the fare will be US$12.50 per passenger. Itahuania-Boca Manu in a shared boat with other passengers is US$6.25. A private, chartered boat would be US$105. From Itahuania, cargo boats leave for the gold mining centre of **Boca Colorado** on the Río Madre de Dios, via Boca Manu, but only when the boat is fully laden; about 6-8 a week, 9 hrs, US$15. From Boca Colorado colectivos leave from near football field for Puerto Carlos, 1 hr, US$5, ferry across river 10 mins, US$1.65; colectivo Puerto Carlos-Puerto Maldonado, 3 hrs, US$10, rough road, lots of stops (in Puerto Maldonado **Turismo Boca**

Colorado, Tacna 342, T082-573435, leave when full). Tour companies usually use own vehicles for the overland trip from Cuzco to Manu.

Puerto Maldonado *p1501*

Air To **Lima**, daily with **LAN** and **Star Perú** via Cuzco. Moto-taxi from town to airport US$3, combi US$0.60, 8 km. **Airline offices** LAN, Av León Velarde y 2 de Mayo, T573677. **Star Perú**, Av León Velarde 151, T982 7074. **Road and ferry** A standard journey by **moto-taxi** in town costs US$0.60, a ride on a **motorbike** US$0.30. Routes from Cuzco are given above. For **Boca Manu** and **Itahuania** take a colectivo to **Boca Colorado** (see above) and then take a cargo boat (no fixed schedule). From Itahuania there is transport to Pilcopata and Cuzco. To **Iberia** and **Iñapari** for Brazil, daily buses from Jr Ica y Jr Piura, recommended companies are **Turismo Imperial** and **Real Dorado**. Car colectivos also run from across the river, 4 hrs, US$10. To **Juliaca**, **Aguilas/Tahuamanu**, Fizcarrald 609, and **Tambopata**, Av Tambopata 1000, daily services via San Gabán, at 1900 and 1700 respectively, 18 hrs, US$17. For all routes, ask around the bus offices for colectivo minibuses.

Directory

Puerto Maldonado *p1501*

Banks Open 0900-1300, 1700-1900. **BCP**. **Banco de la Nación**, cash on Mastercard, quite good rates for TCs. The best rates for cash are at the *casas de cambio* on Puno 6th block, eg *Cárdenas Hnos*, Puno 605. **Consulates** **Bolivian Consulate**, on the north side of the plaza. **Internet** All over town. **Motorcycle hire** Scooters and mopeds can de hired from **San Francisco** and others, on the corner of Puno and G Prado for US$1.15 per hr or US$10 per day. Passport and driver's licence must be shown. **Post offices** **Serpost:** at Velarde 6th block, 0800-2000, 0800-1500 Sun. **Telephones** **Telefónica**, on west side of Plaza, next to Municipalidad; also on Plaza next to *El Hornito*, sells phone cards for national and international calls. **Useful addresses** **Peruvian immigration**, Ica 727, p2, T571069, get your exit stamp here.

Uruguay

Contents

1514 **Planning your trip**

1518 **Montevideo**
1519 Sights

1532 **Western Uruguay**

1545 **Eastern Uruguay**
1545 East from Montevideo
1556 Montevideo north to Brazil

Footprint features

1512 Don't miss …
1515 Driving in Uruguay
1535 Wreckers, revolutionaries and gauchos
1536 National pride

At a glance

Time required 1-2 weeks.

Best time Dec-Mar best. Carnival and Holy Week are the biggest festivals, particularly in Montevideo.

When not to go Coastal resorts packed out in Jan and can be all shut up in Jun-Sep.

★ Don't miss ...
1 Mercado del Puerto, page 1524.
2 Estancia tourism, page 1528
3 Colonia del Sacramento, page 1533.
4 Punta del Este, page 1546.
ARGENTINA
BRAZIL
Bella Unión
Río Quaraí
Artigas
Termas del Arapey
Rivera
Salto
Termas de Daymán
Minas de Corrales
Tacuarembó
Termas de Guaviyú
Tambores
Ansina
Aceguá
Curtina
Las Toscas
Paysandú
Guichón
Melo
Río Uruguay
Paso de los Toros
Rincón del Bonete (Lago Artificial)
Tres Bocas
Río Negro
Quebrada de los Cuervos
Fray Bentos
Carlos Reyes
Mercedes
Cerro Chato
Soriano
Palmitas
Durazno
Sarandí del Yi
Treinta y Tres
Trinidad
José R Varela
Dolores
Sarandi Grande
Lascano
Nueva Palmira
Cardona
Pirajá
Calera de las Huérfanas
Cerro Colorado
Velásquez
Carmelo
Nueva Helvecia
Florida
Rosario
San José de Mayo
Aiguá
Castillo
Conchillas
Colonia del Sacramento
Colonia Valdense
Minas
Canelones
Sta Rosa
Solís
Libertad
San Carlos
Atlántida
La Paloma
Río de la Plata
MONTEVIDEO
Piriápolis
Maldonado
Punta del Este
Atlantic Ocean
N
20 km
20 miles

Uruguay is a land of rolling hills, best explored on horseback, or by staying at the many estancias that have opened their doors to visitors. It also has its feet in the Atlantic Ocean and one of the best ways to arrive is by ferry across the shipping lanes of the Río de la Plata. Montevideo, the capital and main port, is refurbishing its historical centre to match the smart seaside neighbourhoods, but its atmosphere is far removed from the cattle ranches of the interior.

West of Montevideo is Colonia del Sacramento, a former smuggling town turned gambling centre, and a colonial gem where race horses take their exercise in the sea. Up the Río Uruguay there are pleasant towns, some with bridges to Argentina, some with thermal springs. Also by the river is Fray Bentos, a town that lent its name to corned beef for generations, which is now an industrial museum.

Each summer, millions of holidaymakers flock to Punta del Este, one of the most famous resorts on the continent, but if crowds are not your cup of *mate* (the universal beverage), go out of season. Alternatively, venture up the Atlantic coast towards Brazil for empty beaches and fishing villages, sea lions, penguins and the occasional old fortress. And anywhere you go, take your binoculars because the birdwatching is excellent.

Planning your trip

Where to go

Montevideo, the capital, is the business heart of the country and has an interesting Ciudad Vieja (old city). The highlights are Mercado del Puerto, the former dockside market, which has become an emporium for traditional food and drink, and the magnificently restored Teatro Solís and the pedestrian Calle Sarandí. Within the city's limits are a number of beaches, which continue along the north shore of the Río de la Plata and on to the Atlantic seaboard. The most famous resort is **Punta del Este** which, in season (December-February), is packed with Argentines, Brazilians and locals taking their summer break. Beyond Punta del Este, there are quieter beaches with less infrastructure, but with sand dunes and other natural features. Along the coast, impressive villas and condominiums blend with their surroundings, a sort of museum of contemporary South American architecture under the open sky.

West of the capital is **Colonia del Sacramento**, a unique remnant of colonial building in this part of the continent. It is well preserved, standing on a small peninsula, and has one of the principal ferry ports for passenger traffic from Buenos Aires. Consequently it is a popular but costly place, but well worth a visit. Continuing west you come to the confluence of the Río Uruguay with the Plata estuary. Up river are the last vestiges of the meat canning industry at **Fray Bentos**, which has a museum commemorating what used to be one of Uruguay's main businesses. Further upstream are towns such as **Paysandú** and the historic **Salto**, from which you can cross to Argentina, and the hot springs which have been developed into resorts.

The centre of the country is mainly agricultural land, used for livestock and crops. Many *estancias* (farms) accept visitors. Daytrips out of Montevideo, Punta del Este, or Colonia, for instance, to an *estancia*, usually involve a meal, handicraft shopping and an educational element. Those ranches which offer lodging let you take part in the daily tasks, as these are working farms; you can do as much or as little as you like. Horse riding is the main activity and is suitable for all.

When to go

The climate is temperate, often windy, with summer heat tempered by Atlantic breezes. Winter (June-September) is damp; temperatures average 10-16°C, but can sometimes fall to freezing. Summer (December-March) temperatures average 21-27°C. There is always some wind and the nights are relatively cool. The rainfall, with prolonged wet periods in July/August, averages about 1,200 mm at Montevideo and some 250 more in the north, but the amount varies yearly.

Most tourists visit during the summer, which is also high season, when prices rise and hotels and transport need advance bookings. Seasonal variations for Montevideo and Punta del Este are given on pages 1523 and 1546. In the low season on the coast many places close.

Getting around

Flight connections If flying from Uruguay to make an international connection in Buenos Aires, make sure your flight goes to Ezeiza International Airport (eg American Airlines or TAM), not Aeroparque (almost all Aerolíneas Argentinas or Pluna flights). Luggage is not transferred automatically to Ezeiza and you will have to travel one hour between the airports by taxi or bus. If you need a visa to enter Argentina, you must get a transit visa (takes up to four weeks to process in Montevideo), just to transfer between airports. See also Tax for airport taxes, page 1517.

Bus and road All main cities and towns are served by good companies originating from the Tres Cruces Terminal in Montevideo (www.trescruces.com.uy, for schedules and fares, but purchase must be made in person and early if travelling to popular destinations at peak holiday time). There are good services to neighbouring countries. Details are given in the text. Driving your own

Driving in Uruguay

Road Driving is very expensive by South American standards: fuel costs are high and many roads have tolls (1-way tolls Montevideo-Colonia US$3.60, payable in UR$, AR$, US$ or Reais). Roads are generally good condition; 23% are paved and a further 60% all-weather. In rural areas, motorists should drive with their head- lights on even in daylight, especially on major roads. Uruguayans are polite drivers: outside Montevideo, trucks will move to let you pass and motorists will alert you of speed traps.
Documents 90-day admission is usually given without any problems. Entry is easier and faster with a *carnet de passages*, but it is not essential. Without it you will be given a temporary import paper which must be surrendered on leaving the country. Insurance is required by law. For more information, see www.aduanas.gub.uy.
Organizations Automóvil Club del Uruguay, Av del Libertador 1532, T1707, www.acu.com.uy. Reciprocity with foreign automobile clubs is available; members do not have to pay for affiliation.
Fuel All gasoline is unleaded: 97 octane, US$1.49 per litre, 95 octane, US$1.44, *especial* 87 octane, US$1.43 per litre; diesel, US$1.38 per litre. Filling stations may close weekends.

or a rented vehicle (see page 1530) is a viable way to explore Uruguay, as it allows flexibility and access to further destinations. **Hitching** is not easy.

Train The passenger services are slow commuter services from Montevideo to Progreso, Canelones, Santa Lucía, 25 de Agosto and San José de Mayo; and from Montevideo to Pando and Sudriers.

Maps Automóvil Club del Uruguay (see box page 1515), publishes road maps of the city and country, as do **Esso** and **Ancap**. A good road map of Uruguay and Montevideo (all in one) is published by **Silveira Mapas**, *Mapa de la República Oriental del Uruguay/Plano de la capital Montevideo*, US$6.50. ITM of Vancouver also publish a country map (1:800,000). Official maps are issued by **Instituto Geográfico Militar**, Abreu y 8 de Octubre, T487 1810.

Sleeping → *See page 38 for our hotel grade price guide.*
Camping There are lots of sites. Most towns have municipal sites (quality varies). Many sites along the Ruta Interbalnearia, but most of these close off season. The Tourist Office in Montevideo issues a good guide to campsites and youth hostels; see references in main text. The annual Guía de Verano is good for sites and prices, particularly at the beach resorts.

Youth hostels Many good quality hostels can be found in Montevideo and other cities and towns (see recommendations in Sleeping sections). **Hostelling International** ⓘ *Paraguay 1212 (y Canelones), Montevideo, T900 5749, www.hosteluruguay.org*, has 20 member hostels.

Eating and drinking → *See page 40 for our restaurant price guide.*
Eating out Dinner hours are generally 2000-0100. Restaurants usually charge *cubierto* (bread and place setting), costing US$1-3, and more in Punta del Este. Lunch is generally served from 1300-1500, when service often stops until dinner. A *confitería* is an informal place which serves meals at any time, as opposed to a *restaurante*, which serves meals at set times. Uruguay does not have a great selection of international restaurants. Vegetarians may have to stick to salads or pasta, as even the dishes which are "meatless" are served with ham or bacon.

Food In general, you have two choices: meat or Italian food. Beef is eaten at almost all meals. Most restaurants are *parrilladas* (grills) where the main cuts are *asado* (ribs); *pulpa* (no bones), *lomo* (fillet steak) and entrecote. Steak prices normally indicate the quality of the cut. Also very popular are *chorizos* and *salchichas*, both types of sausage. More exotic Uruguayan favorites include *morcilla* (blood sausage, salty or sweet), *chinchulines* or *chotos* (small or large intestines), *riñones* (kidneys) and *molleja* (sweetbreads). *Cordero* (lamb) and *brochettes* (skewers/kebabs) are also common. Grilled *provolone*, *morrones* (red peppers), *boniatos* (sweet potatos), and *chimichurri* sauce are also omnipresent. *Chivitos* (large, fully loaded steak burgers) and *milanesa* (fried breaded chicken or beef) are also popular; usually eaten with mixed salad (lettuce, tomato, onion), or chips. All Italian dishes are delicious, from bread to pastas to raviolis to desserts. Pizza is very common and good. Seafood includes squid, mussels, shrimp, salmon, and *lenguado* (sole). For snacks, *medialunas* (croissants) are often filled with ham and/or cheese, either hot or cold; toasted sandwiches and quiche are readily available; *panchos* are hot dogs; *picada* (crackers or breads, cheese, olives, coldcuts) is a common afternoon favourite. Desserts, mostly of Italian origin, are excellent. *Dulce de leche* (similar to caramel) and *dulce de membrillo* (quince cheese) are ubiquitous ingredients. As in Argentina, *alfajores* are a favourite sweet snack. Ice cream is excellent everywhere.

Drink The beers are good (**Patricia** has been recommended). Local wines vary, but tannat is the regional speciality (eg **Don Pascual, Pisano**). See www.vino-uruguay.com and www.uruguaywinetours.com. Whisky is the favourite spirit in Uruguay, normally Johnny Walker. The local spirits include *uvita*, *caña* and *grappamiel* (honey liquor). In the Mercado del Puerto, Montevideo, a *medio medio* is half still white wine, half sparkling white (elsewhere a *medio medio* is half *caña* and half whisky). *Espillinar* is a cross between whisky and rum. Try the *clérico*, a mixture of wine and fruit juices. Very good fresh fruit juices and mineral water are common. *Mate* is the drink of choice between meal hours. Coffee is good, normally served espresso-style after a meal. Milk, sold in plastic containers, is excellent, skimmed to whole (*descremada* to *entera*)

Essentials A-Z

Accident and emergency

Emergency T911. Ambulance T105 or 911. Fire service T104. Road police T108. Tourist Police in Montevideo, at Colonia y Av del Libertador, T0800-8226.

Electricity

220 volts 50 cycles AC. Various plugs used: round 2-pin or flat 2-pin (most common), oblique 2-pin with earth, 3 round pins in a line.

Embassies and consulates

Visit www.mrree.gub.uy for a complete list.

Festivals and events

Public holidays 1 Jan, 6 Jan; Carnival; Easter week; 19 Apr; 1 and 18 May, 19 Jun; 18 Jul; 25 Aug (the night before is **Noche de la Nostalgia**, when people gather in *boliches* to dance to old songs); 12 Oct; 2 Nov; 25 Dec.

Carnival begins in late Jan/early Feb and lasts for some 40 days until Carnival week, officially Mon and Tue before Ash Wed (many firms close for the whole week). The most prominent elements in Carnival are Candombe, representing the rituals of the African slaves brought to the Río de la Plata in colonial times through drumming and dance. The complex polyrhythms produced by the mass of drummers advancing down the street in the 'Llamadas' parades is very impressive. The other main element is Murga, a form of street theatre withparody, satire, singing and dancing by elaboately made-up and costumed performers.

Business also comes to a standstill during **Holy Week**, which coincides with La Semana Criolla (horse-breaking, stunt riding by cowboys, dances and song). Department stores close only from Good Fri. Banks and offices close Thu-Sun. Easter Mon is not a holiday. A weekend of Sep or Oct is chosen annually for celebrating the **Día del Patrimonio** (Heritage Day) throughout the country: hundreds of buildings, both public or private, including embassies, are open to the public for that day only. Also special train services run. Mid-Dec there is a **Fireworks night** at Pocitos beach.

Money ➔ *US$1=19.11, €1=26.31 (Mar 2010).* The currency is the *peso uruguayo*. Bank notes: 5, 10, 20, 50, 100, 200, 500, 1,000 and 2,000 pesos uruguayos. Coins: 50 centésimos, 1, 2, 5 and 10 pesos. Any amount of currency can be taken in or out. Rates change often.

There's no restriction on foreign exchange transactions (so it is a good place to stock up with US$ bills, though AmEx and some banks refuse to do this for credit cards; most places charge 3% commission for such transactions). Those banks that give US$ cash against a credit card are given in the text. Most ATMs in Montevideo can dispense both Uruguayan pesos and US$. Dollars cash can be purchased when leaving the country. Changing Argentine pesos into Uruguayan pesos is usually a marginally worse rate than for dollars. Brazilian *reais* get a much worse rate. US$ notes are accepted for some services, including most hotels and some restaurants.

Cost of travelling Prices vary considerably between summer and winter in tourist destinations, Punta del Este being one of the most expensive summer resort in Latin America. In Montevideo, allow US$60 daily for a cheap hotel, eating the *menú del día* and travelling by bus. Internet price varies around US$0.70 to US$2 per hr.

Credit cards In some places there is a 10% charge to use Visa and MasterCard. Most banks operate with **Banred** ATMs for Visa or MasterCard withdrawals. MasterCard emergency line call collect to USA, T1-636-722 7111, or 02-902 5555. Visa emergency line, call collect T00-044-20-7937 8091. Most cheaper hotels outside major cities do not accept credit cards.

Safety

Personal security offers few problems in most of Uruguay. Petty theft does occur in Montevideo, most likely in tourist areas or markets. Beggars are often seen trying to sell small items or simply asking for money. They are not dangerous. The Policía Turística patrol the streets of the capital.

Tax

Airport tax US$17 on all air travellers leaving Uruguay for Buenos Aires, Aeroparque, but US$31 to Ezeiza and all other countries (payable in US$, local currency or by credit card), and a tax of 3% on all tickets issued and paid for in Uruguay.

VAT/IVA 22%, 10% on certain basic items.

Telephone ➔ *Country code +598.*

Road information: T1954. Ringing: long equal tones, long pauses. Engaged: short tones, short pauses. Mobile phone numbers are prefixed by 098, 099.

Time

GMT -3 (Sep-Mar -2).

Tipping

Restaurant and cafés usually include service, but an additional 10% is expected. Porters at the airport: US$1 per piece of luggage. Taxis: 5-10% of fare.

Tourist information

Ministry of Tourism Edif Depósito Santos, Rambla 25 de Agosto y Yacaré, T02-188 5100, www.turismo.gub.uy and www.uruguaynatural.com. It has information on birdwatching and the best places to see birds. Contact also: **Avesuruguay/Gupeca** Canelones 1164, Montevideo, T02-902 8642, www.avesuruguay.org.uy.

Useful websites

www.welcomeuruguay.com Excellent bilingual regional guide to all tourist related businesses and events.

www.eltimon.com A good Uruguayan portal.

www.turismodeluruguay.com A tourism portal in English, Spanish and Portuguese.

www.brecha.com.uy *Brecha*, a progressive weekly listing films, theatres and concerts in Montevideo and provinces, US$2 (special editions sometimes free). Recommended.

Visas and immigration

A passport is necessary for entry except for nationals of most Latin American countries and citizens of the USA, who can get in with national identity documents for stays of up to 90 days. Nationals of the following countries need a visa for a tourist visit of less than 3 months: Albania, Armenia, China, Egypt, Estonia, Guyana, India, Morrocco and Russia. Visas cost US$42, and you need a passport photo and a ticket out of Uruguay. Visa processing may take 2-4 weeks.

For those living in a country with no Uruguayan embassy, a visa can be applied for online and collected at any Uruguayan consulate before entering the country. Visas are valid for 90 days and usually single entry. Tourist cards (obligatory for all tourists, obtainable on entry) are valid for 3 months, extendable for a similar period at the **Migraciones office** C Misiones 1513, T916 0471, www.dnm.minterior.gub.uy.

Weights and measures

Metric.

Working hours

Shops: Mon-Fri 1000-1900; Sat 1000-1300; **shopping malls**: daily 1000-2200. In small towns or non-tourist areas, there is a break for lunch and siesta, between 1300 and 1600. **Businesses**: 0830-1200, 1430-1830 or 1900. **Banks**: 1200-1700 in Montevideo (some till 1800); Mon-Fri 1300-1700 in Colonia; also in the afternoon in Punta del Este and elsewhere; banks close Sat. **Government offices**: Mon-Fri 1200-1800 in summer; Mon-Fri 1000-1700 (rest of the year).

Montevideo → *Phone code: 02. Colour map 8, B6. Population: 1,325,968.*

Montevideo is a modern city that feels like a town. Barrios retain their personality while the city gels into one. The main areas, from west to east are: the shipping port, downtown, several riverside and central neighbourhoods (Palermo, Punta Carretas, Pocitos), the suburbs and Carrasco International airport, all connected by the Rambla. Everything blends together – architecture, markets, restaurants, stores, malls, stadiums, parks and beaches – and you can find what you need in a short walk.

Montevideo, the capital, was officially founded in 1726 on a promontory between the Río de la Plata and an inner bay, though the fortifications have been destroyed. Spanish and Italian architecture, French and Art Deco styles can be seen, especially in Ciudad Vieja. The city not only dominates the country's commerce and culture: it accounts for 70% of industrial production and handles almost 90% of imports and exports. In January and February many locals leave for the string of seaside resorts to the east. The first football World Cup was held in Centenario Stadium and won by Uruguay in 1930.

Ins and outs

Getting there Carrasco International **airport** is east of the centre, with easy connections by bus or taxi (20-30 minutes to downtown). Many visitors arrive at the port by boat from Buenos Aires, or by boat to Colonia and then bus to the Tres Cruces bus terminal just north of downtown. Both port and terminal have good facilities and tourist information. ▸▸ *See also Transport, page 1528.*

Getting around The Ciudad Vieja can be explored on foot. From Plaza de la Independencia buses are plentiful along Avenida 18 de Julio, connecting all parts of the city. Taxis are also plentiful, affordable and generally trustworthy, although compact. *Remises* (private driver and car) can be rented by the hour. Full details are given in Local Transport, see below. **Note** Street names are located on buildings, not street signs. Some plazas and streets are known by two names: for instance, Plaza de la Constitución is also called Plaza Matriz. It's a good idea to point out to a driver the location you want on a map and follow your routeas you go. Also, seemingly direct routes rarely exist owing to the many one-way streets and, outside the centre, non-grid layout.

Tourist offices Tourist information for the whole country is at the **Tres Cruces bus terminal** ⓘ *T409 7399, Mon-Fri 0800-2200, Sat-Sun 0900-2200*; at the **Ministry of Tourism** ⓘ *Rambla 25 de Agosto y Yacaré (next to the port), T1885 ext 100*, or nearby at Rambla 25 de Agosto 206 1000-1700; and at **Carrasco international airport** ⓘ *T604 0386, 0800-2000*; which has good maps. For information on Montevideo, inside **Palacio Municipal** ⓘ *18 de Julio y Ejido, T1950, 3171 or 1831, Mon-Fri 1000-1600*, all helpful. Check at the municipal website for weekend tours, www.monte video.gub.uy. For the **Tourist Police** ⓘ *Colonia y Av del Libertador, T0800-8226.*

Guía del Ocio is recommended; it's sold at news-stands on Fridays (US$0.90s) and has information on museums, cultural events and entertainment. See also www.pimba.com.uy, www.montevideo.com.uy, www.cartelera.com.uy, www.aromperlanoche.com, www.banda joven.com and www.eltimon.com.

Maps Best street maps of Montevideo are at the beginning of the *Guía Telefónica* (both white and yellow page volumes). Free maps in all tourist offices and some museums. *Eureka Guía De Montevideo* is recommended for streets, with index and bus routes (US$6 from bookshops and newspaper kiosks).

Sights

City centre

In the **Ciudad Vieja** is the oldest square in Montevideo: the **Plaza de la Constitución** or **Matriz**. On one side is the **Catedral** (1790-1804), with the historic **Cabildo** (1804) ⓘ *JC Gómez 1362, T915 9685, Tue-Fri 1230-1730, Sat 1100-1700, free*, opposite. It contains the **Museo y Archivo Histórico Nacional.** The Cabildo has several exhibition halls. On the south side is the **Club Uruguay** (built in 1888), which is worth a look inside. See also the unusual fountain (1881), surrounded by art and antique vendors under the sycamore trees.

West along Calle Rincón is the small **Plaza Zabala**, with a monument to Bruno Mauricio de Zabala, founder of the city. North of this Plaza are: the **Banco de la República** ⓘ *Cerrito y Zabala* and the **Aduana** ⓘ *Rambla 25 de Agosto*. Several historic houses belong to the Museo Histórico Nacional: **Casa de Montero-Roosen, Museo Romántico** ⓘ *25 de Mayo 428, T915 5361, Tue-Fri 1100-1700, free,* first built in 1728, rebuilt by Antonio Montero in 1831, contains late 19th, early 20th century furniture, furnishings and portraits. **Museo Casa de Rivera** ⓘ *Rincón 437, T915 1051, Mon-Fri 1100-1700, Sat 1000-1500, free*, is an 1850 mansion of the first president of the republic. Its rooms are dedicated to various stages of Uruguayan history. Also in the Ciudad Vieja is the **Palacio Taranco, Museo de Artes Decorativos** ⓘ *25 de Mayo y 1 de Mayo, T915 6060, Tue-Sat 1230-1800, Sun 1400-1800, free,* whose garden overlooks Plaza Zabala, a palatial mansion in turn-of-the-20th-century French style, with sumptuously decorated rooms, and a museum of Islamic and Classical pottery and glass. It was first built as a theatre in 1793; in 1908 it was bought by the Ortiz de Taranco family.

The main port is near the Ciudad Vieja, with the docks three blocks north of Plaza Zabala. Three blocks south of the Plaza is the Río de la Plata. Cross the Rambla from the docks to visit the **Mercado del Puerto** (see Eating, page 1524) and the adjacent **Museo Carnaval** ⓘ *Rambla 25 de Agosto 1825, T916 5493, www.museodelcarnaval.org, Tue-Sun 1100-1700, US$3*, a small exhibition with colourful pictures and costumes from the February celebrations. Proceed south one block to Cerrito, east two blocks to the **Banco de la República** and church of **San Francisco** (1864) ⓘ *Solís 1469*, south across Plaza Zabala to Peatonal Sarandí (pedestrian street) and east to Plaza de la Independencia (see next paragraph), stopping at the aforementioned historical sites as desired. Restoration efforts are slow but steady. Although safe by day, with many tourist police, common sense, even avoidance, at night is recommended.

Between the Ciudad Vieja and the new city is the largest of Montevideo's squares, **Plaza de la Independencia**, a short distance east of Plaza de la Constitución. Numerous cafés, shops and boutiques line Peatonal Sarandí. Two small pedestrian zones full of cafés, live music (mostly after 2300) and restaurants, Peatonal Bacacay and Policia Vieja, lead off Sarandí. Below his statue (1923) in the middle of Plaza de la Independencia is the subterranean marble mausoleum of Artigas. Just west of the plaza is **Museo Torres García** ⓘ *Sarandí 683, T916 2663, Mon-Fri 0930-1930, Sat 1000-1800, bookshop, donation requested (US$2 or 5).* It has an exhibition of the paintings of Joaquín Torres García (1874-1949), one of Uruguay's foremost contributors to the modern art movements of the 20th century, and five floors dedicated to temporary exhibitions of contemporary Uruguayan and international artists. At the eastern end is the **Palacio Salvo** ⓘ *Plaza Independencia 846-848*, built 1923-28. The first skyscraper in Uruguay and the tallest South American structure of its time, opinions are divided on its architectural merit. Currently it houses a mixture of businesses and residences. The famous tango, *La Cumparsita*, was written in a former café at its base. On the southern side is the **Casa de Gobierno Histórico** ⓘ *Palacio Estévez, Mon-Fri 1100-1600*, with an exhibition of Uruguay's presidential history. Just off the plaza to the west is the splendid **Teatro Solís** (1842-69) ⓘ *Reconquista y Bartolomé Mitre, T1950 3323, www.teatrosolis.org.uy. Guided visits on Tue-Sun 1100, 1200, 1600 (Sat also at 1300), Wed free, otherwise US$2 for tours in English* (US$1 in Spanish). It has been entirely restored to perfection, with added elevators, access for disabled people, marble flooring and impressive attention to detail. Built as an opera house, Teatro Solís is now used for many cultural events, including ballet, classical music, even tango performances. Check press for listings. Tickets sold daily 1500-2000.

Avenida 18 de Julio runs east from Plaza de la Independencia. The **Museo de Arte Contemporaneo** ⓘ *18 de Julio 965, T900 6662, Wed-Sun 1100-1600,* holds temporary exhibitions. The **Museo del Gaucho y de la Moneda** ⓘ *Av 18 de Julio 998, Edif Banco de la República, T900 8764, Mon-Fri 1000-1700, free,* was renovated in 2003. Museo de la Moneda has a

Montevideo Ciudad Vieja & Centre

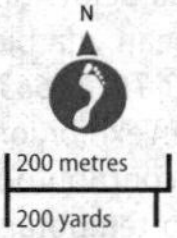

Sleeping
1 Arapey *A4*
2 Balfer *B6*
3 Bremen Apart Hotel *C6*
4 El Viajero Ciudad Vieja Hostel *A3*
5 Embajador *B6*
6 Europa *A6*
7 Hispano *B4*
8 Iberia *B5*
9 Klee Internacional *B6*
10 Lancaster *B5*
11 London Palace *B5*
12 Mediterráneo *A5*
13 Motevideo Hostel *B4*
14 Nh Columbia *B3*
15 Oxford *B5*
16 Palacio *B3*
17 Palermo Art Hostel *C6*
18 Plaza Fuerte *B3*
19 Radisson Victoria Plaza *A4*
20 Red Hostel *C6*
21 Sur Hotel *C5*

survey of Uruguayan currency and a collection of Roman coins; Museo del Gaucho is a fascinating history of the Uruguayan gaucho and is highly recommended. Between Julio Herrera and Río Negro is the **Plaza Fabini**, or **del Entrevero**, with a statue of *gauchos* engaged in battle, the last big piece of work by sculptor José Belloni. Beneath the plaza is the **Centro Municipal de Exposiciones - Subte** ⓘ *Tue-Sun 1530-2100, free,* temporary exhibitions of contemporary art, photography, etc. In the **Plaza Cagancha** (or Plaza Libertad) is a statue of Peace. The restored **Mercado de la Abundancia** ⓘ *San Jose 1312,* is an attractive old market with handicrafts, meat restaurants and tango on Saturday and Sunday evenings. The **Palacio Municipal** (La Intendencia) is on the south side of Avenida 18 de Julio, just before it bends north, at the statue of **El Gaucho**. It often has interesting art and photo exhibitions and there is a huge satellite image of the city displayed on the main hall's floor. The road which forks south from the Gaucho is Constituyente, and leads to the beach at Pocitos. **Museo de Historia del Arte** ⓘ *Ejido 1326, T1950 2191, Tue-Sun 1200-1730* is also in the Palacio Municipal. **Centro Municipal de Fotografía** ⓘ *Palacio Municipal (San José 1360, T1950 1219), Mon-Fri 1000-1900, Sat 0930-1430,* has photography exhibitions.

The immense **Palacio Legislativo** ⓘ *from Plaza Fabini head along Av del Libertador Brig Gen Juan Lavalleja (known as Av Libertador), 5 blocks east of Plaza de la Independencia (buses 150, 173, 175 from C Mercedes), free guided visits hourly Mon-Fri 0900-1800,* was built 1908-1925 from local marble: there are 52 colours of Uruguayan marble in the Salón de los Pasos Perdidos, 12 types of wood in the library. Other rooms are beautiful. Not far, and dramatically changing the city skyline, is the brand new 160-m high **Antel building** ⓘ *Paraguay y Guatemala, Aguada, T928 0000, Mon, Wed, Fri 1530-1700; Tue, Thu 1030-1200, free,* with a public terrace on the 26th floor for panoramic bay views.

Outside the centre

Museo Nacional de Antropología ⓘ *Av de las Instrucciones 948, Prado, T359 3353, Mon-Fri 1300-1800, Sat, Sun and holidays 1000-1800, free, take bus 149 from Ejido,* has a small, well-presented anthropological collection in the hall of a superb, late 19th-century mansion, the ex-Quinta de Mendilaharsu (see particularly the huge Chinese silk tapestry in the Music Room). On the same street, **Centro Cultural y Museo de la Memoria** ⓘ *Av de las Instrucciones 1057, Prado, T355 5891, Tue-Sun 1200-1800, free,* is a fascinating space dedicated to remembering the horrors of Uruguay's 1970s-80s dictatorship. **Museo Municipal de Bellas Artes Juan Manuel Blanes** ⓘ *Millán 4015, Prado, T336 2248, Tue-Sun 1215-1745, free, take buses 148 or 149 from Mercedes,* in the ex-Quinta Raffo (a late 19th-century mansion) is dedicated to the work of the artist Blanes (1830-1901). It also

Eating

1 Albahaca *B4*
2 Café Bacacay & Panini's *B3*
3 El Fogón *B5*
4 Los Leños Uruguayos *B5*
5 Mercado del Puerto *A1*
6 Subte Pizzerías *B6*
7 Tras Bambalinas *B4*
8 Viejo Sancho *B6*

has a room of the works of Pedro Figari (1861-1938), a lawyer who painted strange, naive pictures of peasant life and negro ceremonies, also other Uruguayan artists' work. **Museo Zoológico** ⓘ *Rambla República de Chile 4215, Buceo, T622 0258, Tue-Sun 1300-1715, free, take bus 104 from 18 de Julio*, is well displayed and arranged, recommended, great for children.

In the **Puerto del Buceo**, following the coast eastwards away from the centre, the ship's bell of *HMS Ajax* and rangefinder of the German pocket-battleship, *Graf Spee*, can be seen at the **Naval Museum** ⓘ *Rambla Costanera y Luis A de Herrera, Buceo, T622 1084, 0800-1200, 1400-1800, closed Thu, free*. Both ships were involved in the Battle of the River Plate (13 December 1939) after which *Graf Spee* was scuttled off Montevideo. The museum also has displays of documentation from this battle, naval history from the War of Independence onwards and on the sailing ship *Capitán Miranda*, which circumnavigated the globe in 1937-8. This ship is now in the port (can be visited weekends.

In **Parque Batlle y Ordóñez** (reached eastwards of Avenida 18 de Julio), are statues: the most interesting group is the well-known **La Carreta** monument, by José Belloni, showing three yoke of oxen drawing a wagon. In the grounds is the **Estadio Centenario**, the national 70,000-seater football stadium and a football museum, an athletics field and a bicycle race-track (bus 107). The **Planetarium** ⓘ *next to the Jardín Zoológico, at Av Rivera 3275, www.montevideo.gub.uy/planetario, take bus 60 from Av 18 de Julio, or buses 141, 142 or 144 from San José*, gives good, 40-minute shows on Saturday and Sunday, free.

From the Palacio Legislativo, Avenida Agraciada runs northwest to **Parque Prado**, the oldest of the city's many parks, about 5 km from Avenida 18 de Julio (bus 125 and others). Among fine lawns, trees and lakes is a rose garden planted with 850 varieties, the monument of **La Diligencia** (the stage coach), the Círculo de Tenis and the Sociedad Rural premises. Part of the park is the adjacent **Jardín Botánico**. ⓘ *daily summer 0700-1830, winter 0700-1700, guided tours, T336 4005. It is reached via Av 19 de Abril (bus 522 from Ejido next to Palacio Municipal), or via Av Dr LA de Herrera (bus 147 from Paysandú)*. The largest and most popular park is **Parque Rodó**, on Rambla Presidente Wilson. Here are an open-air theatre, an amusement park, and a boating lake studded with islands. At the eastern end is the **Museo Nacional de Artes Visuales** ⓘ *Tomás Giribaldi 2283, T711 6124, www.mnav.gub.uy, Tue-Sun 1400-1900, free*, a collection of contemporary plastic arts, plus a room devoted to Blanes. Recommended.

Within the city limits, the **Punta Carretas**, **Pocitos** and **Buceo** neighbourhoods are the nicest, with a mix of classical homes, tall condos, wonderful stores, services, restaurants, active beaches, parks, and two major malls. Outside the city along Rambla Sur, the affluent **Carrasco** suburb has large homes, quieter beaches, parks and services. **Parque Nacional Roosevelt**, a green belt stretching north, and the international airport are nearby. The express bus D1 (US$0.75) runs every 30 minutes along Avenida 18 de Julio and the Rambla and is about 30 minutes quicker to Carrasco.

At the western end of the bay is the **Cerro**, or hill ⓘ *getting there: bus from centre to Cerro: 125 'Cerro' from Mercedes*, 139 m high (from which Montevideo gets its name), with the Fortaleza General Artigas, an old fort, on the top. It is now the **Museo Militar** ⓘ *T487 3121, Mon-Fri 1000-1700, free (fort visit US$0.85)*. It houses historical mementos, documentation of the War of Independence and has one of the only panaramoic views of Montevideo. The Cerro is surmounted by the oldest lighthouse in the country (1804).

Bathing **beaches** stretch along Montevideo's water front, from Playa Ramírez in the west to Playa Carrasco in the east. The waterfront boulevard, Rambla Naciones Unidas, is named along its several stretches in honour of various nations. Bus 104 from Aduana, which goes along Avenida 18 de Julio, gives a pleasant ride (further inland in winter) past Pocitos, Punta Gorda and all the beaches to Playa Miramar, beyond Carrasco, total journey time from Pocitos to Carrasco, 35 minutes. The seawater, despite its muddy colour (sediment stirred up by the Río de la Plata), is safe to bathe in and the beaches are clean. Lifeguards are on duty during the summer months.

Montevideo listings

Hotel and guesthouse prices
LL over US$200 **L** US$151-200 **AL** US$101-150
A US$66-100 **B** US$46-65 **C** US$31-45
D US$21-30 **E** US$12-20 **F** US$7-11
G US$6 and under
Restaurant prices
ΨΨΨ over US$12 ΨΨ US$7-12 Ψ under US$6

Sleeping

Hotels may add 23% VAT, but it is usually included in the bill in cheaper and mid-range options; check when booking. High season is 15 Dec-15 Mar, book ahead; many beach hotels only offer full board during this time. After 1 Apr prices are reduced and some hotel dining rooms shut down. During Carnival, prices go up by 20%. The city is visited by Argentines at weekends: many hotels increase prices. Midweek prices may be lower than those posted. When not included, breakfast (*café completo*) costs US$2 or more. Most hotels above an **E** have cable TV and a mini bar or fridge.

The tourist office has information on the more expensive hotels. The **Holiday Inn**, hotel@holidayinn.com.uy, and **Ibis** groups are represented. For more information and reservations contact **Asociación de Hoteles y Restaurantes del Uruguay**, Gutiérrez Ruiz 1213, T908 0141, ahru@montevideo.com.uy.

City centre *p1519, map p1520*

LL Radisson Victoria Plaza, Plaza Independencia 759, T902 0111, www.radisson.com/montevideouy. A/c, excellent restaurant (rooftop, fine views), less formal restaurant in lobby, luxurious casino in basement, with new 5-star wing, art gallery, business centre (for guests only).

AL Embajador, San José 1212, T902 0012, www.hotelembajador.com. Sauna, swimming pool in the summer, TV with BBC World, excellent. Recommended.

AL Nh Columbia, Rambla Gran Bretaña 473, T916 0001, www.nh-hotels.com. 1st class. Rooms have minibar and TV. Breakfast, restaurant, sauna, music show.

A Klee Internacional, San José 1303, T902 0606. Very comfortable, good value in standard rooms, spacious, includes internet use, breakfast, a/c, heater, minibar, good view, satellite TV. Highly recommended.

A London Palace, Río Negro 1278, T902 0024, www.lphotel.com. Reliable, excellent breakfast, internet. Parking.

A Oxford, Paraguay 1286, T902 0046, www.hoteloxford.com.uy. Modern, good breakfast, safes, laundry service, parking. Recommended.

B Balfer, Z Michelini 1328, T902 0135, www.hotelbalfer.com. Good, TV, safe deposit, excellent breakfast.

B Bremen Apart Hotel, Dr Aquiles Lanza 1168, T900 9641, www.bremenmontevideo.com. Recommended for short term rentals.

B Europa, Colonia 1341, T902 0045, www.hoteleuropa.com.uy. Comfortable, spacious rooms, good choice in this price range, restaurant, cybercafé, garage.

B Hispano, Convención 1317, T900 3816, www.hispanohotel.com. A/c, with breakfast, comfortable, laundry, parking.

B Lancaster, Plaza Cagancha 1334, T902 1054, www.lancasterhotel.com.uy. Central; needs a full renovation, but rooms are still quite acceptable with a/c, fridge, and some with nice views over Plaza Cagancha. With breakfast.

B Mediterráneo, Paraguay 1486, T900 5090, www.hotelmediterraneo.com.uy. With breakfast, TV, comfortable, boxy but clean rooms.

B Plaza Fuerte, Bartolomé Mitre 1361, T915 6651, www.plazafuerte.com. Restored 1913 building, historical monument, a/c, safe, internet, restaurant, pub.

B Red Hostel, San José 1406, T908 8514, www.redhostel.com. By the Intendencia, hostel with double rooms and dorms (**E**), all with shared bath, cheerful, cable TV, internet connection in rooms, computers, safe, breakfast, roof terrace and kitchen.

B El Viajero Ciudad Vieja Hostel, Ituzaingó 1436, T915 6192, www.ciudadviejahostel.com. Hostel with lots of services (Spanish lessons, bike hire, city tours, laundry, theatre tickets, football), shared bedrooms (**E**), free internet/Wi-Fi, safes, kitchen, airport transport, helpful staff. Recommended.

B-C Iberia, Maldonado 1097, T901 3633, www.internet.com.uy/hoiberia. Very helpful staff, 1400 check-out, free bike rental, parking, Wi-Fi, stereos, minibar and cable in rooms. US$5.50 for breakfast. Modern, recently refurbished. Highly recommended.

C Arapey, Av Uruguay 925, near Convención, T900 7032, www.arapey.com.uy. Slightly run down old building, but has character and good location, on route to airport. Variety of rooms with bath, TV, fan, heating, no breakfast.

C Palacio, Bartolomé Mitre 1364, T916 3612, www.hotelpalacio.com.uy. Old hotel, a bit run down but safe, balconies, laundry service, stores luggage, no breakfast, frequently booked, good value. Recommended.

C Sur Hotel, Maldonado 1098, T908 2025, www.surhotel.com. Colourful, recently refurbished, welcoming, some rooms with balconies. Good continental breakfast, 24-hr room service, Wi-Fi.

E Montevideo Hostel (members only), Canelones 935, T908 1324, www.montevideohostel.com.uy. Open all year, 24 hrs (seasonal variations, breakfast and internet included), dormitory style, kitchen, lots of hot water, but shortage of bathrooms and noisy, one bedroom (**C**), bicycle hire US$2 per hr.

Outside the centre *p1521*

Tres Cruces, Palermo

A Days Inn, Acevedo Díaz 1821-23, T400 4840, www.daysinn.com.uy. A/c, breakfast, safe, coffee shop and health club, look for promotional offers.

B Tres Cruces, Miguelete 2356 esq Acevedo Díaz, T402 3474, www.hoteltrescruces.com.uy. A/c, TV, safe, café, decent buffet breakfast. Disabled access.

E Palermo Art Hostel, Gaboto 1010, T410 6519, www.palermoarthostel.com. Cosy and colourful, with breakfast, bar and live music, private and shared rooms, some doubles (**C**), near beach and US Embassy. Highly Recommended.

East of the centre
(Punta Carretas, Pocitos)

L Sheraton, Victor Solino 349, T710 2121, www.sheraton.com. Beside Shopping Punta Carretas, all facilities, good views, access to golf club. Recommended. Also a **Four Points Sheraton** at Ejido 1275, T901 7000, in the centre (**AL**).

AL Pocitos Plaza, Juan Benito Blanco 640, Pocitos, T712 3939, www.pocitosplazahotel.com.uy. Modern building in pleasant residential district, next to the river, with large functional rooms, gym and sauna.

A Ermitage, Juan Benito Blanco 783, T710 4021, www.ermitagemontevideo.com. Near Pocitos beach, remodelled 1945 building, rooms, apartments and suites, some with great views, internet, buffet breakfast.

E pp **Pocitos Hostel**, Av Sarmiento 2641 y Aguilar, T711 8780, www.pocitos-hostel.com. Rooms for 2 to 6 (mixed and women only), includes breakfast, use of kitchen, *parrilla*, towels extra, internet, Spanish classes.

Carrasco

LL Belmont House, Av Rivera 6512, T600 0430, www.belmonthouse.com.uy. 5-star, includes breakfast, 28 beautifully furnished rooms, top quality, excellent restaurant Allegro, pub/bar Memories, pool, 3 blocks from beach. Recommended.

L Regency Suites, Gabriel Otero 6428, T600 1383, www.regency.com.uy. Good boutique-style hotel with all services, free internet, safety deposit, fitness centre, pool, restaurant *Tartufo* and pub/wine bar, a couple of blocks from the beach.

AL Cottage, Miraflores 1360, T600 1111, www.hotelcottage.com.uy. In a prime location next to wide beaches and in quiet residential surroundings, very comfortable, simply furnished rooms with fridge and a/c, restaurant, pool in a lovely garden. Excellent value.

Eating

There is a 23% tax on restaurant bills that is usually included, plus a charge for bread and service (*cubierto*) that varies between US$1-3 pp.

City centre *p1519, map p1520*

TTT Los Leños Uruguayos, San José 909, T900 2285. www.parrilla.com.uy. Good and smart *parrilla*, and also fish.

TTT El Mercado del Puerto, opposite the Aduana, Calle Piedras, between Maciel and Pérez Castellanos (take 'Aduana' bus), www.mercadodelpuerto. com.uy. Don't miss eating at this 19th-century market building, open late on Sun, delicious grills cooked on huge charcoal grates (menus are limited to beef, chicken and fish, including swordfish). Best to go at lunchtime, especially Sat; the atmosphere's great. Inside the Mercado del Puerto, those recommended are: **Roldós**, sandwiches, most people start with a *medio medio* (half still, half sparkling white wine).

El Palenque, famed as the finest restaurant. **La Estancia del Puerto, Cabaña Verónica, La Chacra del Puerto. Don Tiburón** has a bar inside and a more expensive and smart restaurant, **La Posada**, with tables outside.

TTT Panini's, Bacacay 1339 (also at 26 de Marzo 3586, Pocitos). Good Italian pasta. Large and lively.

TT Café Bacacay, Bacacay 1310 y Buenos Aires. Good music and atmosphere, food served, try the specials. Recommended.

TT El Fogón, San José 1080. Good value, very friendly, always full.

TT Tras Bambalinas, Ciudadela 1250 y Soriano, T903 2090, www.trasbambalinas.com.uy. Colourful carnival-themed *parrilla*, also featuring pizzas, *picadas* and salads. Live music and stand-up often programmed. Very popular.

TT Viejo Sancho, San José 1229. Excellent, popular, complimentary sherry or vermouth to early arrivals; set menus for US$6 pp.

T Albahaca, W F Aldunate 1311, T900 6189, www.albahaca.com.uy. Great lunchtime specials at this healthy, mostly-vegetarian café, very popular. Open 0800-2000. Recommended.

T Subte Pizzerías, Ejido 1327, T902 3050. An institution, cheap and good. Recommended.

T Restaurant on 6th floor of YMCA building, Colonia 1870. Reasonable for lunch, with good views, ask for Asociación Cristiana de Jóvenes.

Centro Cultural Mercado de la Abundancia, San Jose 1312 (see Sights, above) has good authentic local eateries, with lunch specials. Highly recommended.

Outside the centre *p1521*

In and around Pocitos

TTT Da Pentella, Luis de la Torre 598, esq Francisco Ros, T712 0981. Amazing Italian and seafood, artistic ambience, great wines. Recommended.

TTT Doña Flor, Artigas 1034. Classy French restaurant, limited menu but good, moves to Punta del Este in summer.

TTT La Spaghetteria 23, Scosería 2584, T711 4986. Very good Italian.

TTT Tabare, Zorilla de San Martín 152/54, T712 3242. Wonderful restaurant in a converted old *almacén* (grocery shop). Great wines and entrées.

TTT El Viejo y el Mar, Rambla Gandhi 400 block (on the coast), Punta Carretas, T710 5704. Fishing community atmosphere with a great location by the river.

TT La Otra, Tomás Diago y Juan Pérez, 2 blocks northeast of 21 de Septiembre in Punta Carretas. Specialises in meat, lively. Highly recommended.

TT Pizza Trouville, 21 de Septiembre y Francisco Vidal. A traditional pizza place with tables outside, next to the beach.

TT Tanquilo Bar, 21 de Septiembre 3104. Very popular restaurant/bar, great lunch menu.

Carrasco/Punta Gorda

Several restaurants on Av Arocena close to the beach, packed Sun middle day.

TTT Café Misterio, Costa Rica 1700, esq Riviera, T6018765. Lots of choice on menu, sushi, cocktails. Completely new decor and menu every 6 months. Recommended.

TTT Hacienda Las Palomas, P Murillo 6566. Tue-Sat evenings, Sun lunchtime. A little away from Carrasco beach, good Mexican restaurant and tequila bar.

TTT Hemingway, Rambla Méjico on west side of Punta Gorda, T600 0121. Decent food, worth going for amazing sunset views of river and city, great outdoor seating.

TTT-TT Bistró Latino, Dr Alejandro Schroeder 6415. Sushi, meats, pastas, seafoods, tapas, speciality cocktails. Highly recommended.

TTT-TT García's, Arocena 1587, T600 2703. Spacious, indoor and outdoor seating, large wine selection, rack of lamb is a speciality. Recommended.

Confiterías Brasilero, Ituzaingó 1447, half a block from Plaza Matriz towards the port. Small entrance; easy to miss. A must, one of the oldest cafés in Montevideo and a permanent hangout of one of the greatest Latin American writers, Eduardo Galeano. Others include: **Amaretto**, 21 de Septiembre y Roque Graseras, Punta Carretas. Excellent Italian coffee and pastries. **Café Iberia**, Uruguay esq Florida. Locals' bar. **Conaprole Pocitos**, Rambla Gandhi y Solano Antuña. Ideal at sunset for riverviews, it serves very good strong coffee and quality Conaprole dairy products. A *completo* includes toasts, butter, jam, cheese, a slice of cake, biscuits, juice and coffee or tea, all for US$9. **Manchester Bar**, 18 de Julio 899. Good for breakfasts. **Oro del Rhin**, Convención 1403. Mon-Fri 0830-2000 (Sat till 1400), open since 1927 it retains the feel of an elegant *confitería* serving good cakes and sandwiches or vegetable pies for lunch. **Café de la Pausa**, Sarandí 493, upstairs. Closed Sun.

Options with multiple locations Several good restaurants and establishments have locations in many neighbourhoods and serve typical Uruguayan fare. Among these are family restaurants: **La Pasiva**, **Pony Pisador**, **Don Pepperone** and **Il Mondo della Pizza**. A popular bakery chain is **Medialunas Calentitas**, great for coffee and croissants. Two popular *heladerías* are **La Cigale** and **Las Delicias**.

Bars and clubs

Montevideo *p1518, map p1520*

Boliches

See www.aromperlanoche.com for latest events and recommendations. Head to Sarandí, Bacacay or Bartolomé Mitre in Ciudad Vieja, or to Pocitos and Punta Carretas. Discos charge around US$5. Bars/discos/pubs offering typical local nightlife:

503 Bar, Aguilar 832, just north of Ellauri. Pool tables, only steel tip dart bar in town, small wood frame entrance, no sign, open all day 1930-0400.

Almodobar, Rincón 626, Ciudad Vieja. Electronic and rock music, Fri, Sat 2230.

Bancaria Jazz Club, Sarandí y Zabala p 5. Jazz sessions in the evenings.

Clyde's, Costa Rica y Rivera, Carrasco. Live music from 2000.

Fun-Fun, Ciudadela 1229, Ciudad Vieja, T915 8005. Hangout of local artists, founded in 1895, used to be frequented by Carlos Gardel, where *uvita*, the drink, was born. Great music Fri and Sat. Recommended.

Groove, Rambla República de Mexico 5521, Punta Gorda. Electronic music, Thu-Sat from 2400.

El Pony Pisador, Bartolomé Mitre 1326, Ciudad Vieja. Popular with the young crowd. Live music.

Viejo Mitre, Bartolomé Mitre 1321, Ciudad Vieja. Mixed music, outside tables, open till late all week.

Outside the centre *p1521*

Playa Ramírez (near Parque Rodó)

'W' Lounge, Rambla Wilson y Requena García. Fashionable place for young people, Fri-Sat 2300, live music on Sat, rock, electronica, Latin.

Entertainment

Montevideo *p1518, map p1520*

Cinema Blockbusters often appear soon after release in US, most others arrive weeks or months later. Most films are in English (except non-English and animated features). Modern malls (Montevideo Shopping, Punta Carretas, Portones) house several theatre companies each (Grupo Cines, MovieCenter, Hoyt's, and others). Independent art theatres: **Cine Universitario**, 2 halls: Lumière and Chaplin, Canelones 1280, also for classic and serious films. **Cinemateca** film club has 4 cinemas: 18, 18 de Julio 1286, T900 9056; Salas 1 y 2, Dr L. Carnelli 1311, T418 2460; Linterna Mágica, Soriano 1227, T902 8290; and Sala Pocitos, A Chucarro 1036, T703 7637. The Cinemateca shows great films from all over the world and has an extended archive. It organizes an international film festival, **Festival de invierno**. Entry is US$2.50 for 6 months, which may admit 2.

Tanguerías **El Milongón**, Gaboto 1810, T929 0594, www.elmilongon.com.uy. A show that may include dinner beforehand, Mon-Sat. For tango, milonga, candombe and local folk music. Recommended. **Joven Tango**, at Mercado de la Abundancia, Aquiles Lanza y San José, T901 5561. Cheap and atmospheric venue, Sun 2000. **Tabaris**, Tristán Narvaja 1518, T408 7856. Usually Fri, Sat 2200; check by phone. **Tango a Cielo Abierto**, Tango Under the Open Sky, in front of Café Facal, Paseo Yi and 18 de Julio, T908 7741 for information. Free and very good Uruguayan tango shows every day at noon on a wooden stage. Highly recommended. **La Escuela Universitaria de Música**, Sala Zitarrosa, 18 de Julio 1012. Good, free classical music concerts.

Theatres Montevideo has a vibrant theatre scene. Most performances are only on Fri, Sat and Sun, others also on Thu. Apart from **Teatro Solís** (see Sights, above), recommended are **Teatro del Centro Carlos E Sheck**, Plaza Cagancha 1162/4, T902 8915, and **Teatro Victoria**, Río Negro y Uruguay, T901 9971. See listings in the daily press and *La Brecha*. Prices are around US$4; performances are almost exclusively in Spanish starting at 2100 or at 1900 on Sun. **Teatro Millington-Drake** at the Anglo (see Cultural centres) puts on occasional productions, as do the theatres of the Alianza Uruguay-Estados Unidos and the Alliance Française (addresses below). Many theatres close Jan-Feb.

Shopping

Montevideo *p1518, map p1520*

The main shopping area is Av 18 de Julio. Many international newspapers can be bought on the east side of Plaza Independencia.

Bookshops The Sun market on Tristán Narvaja and nearby streets is good for second-hand books. Every December daily in the evening is a Book and Engraving Fair, at Plazoleta Florencio Sánchez (Parque Rodó), with readings and concerts. The following have a few English and American books, but selection in Montevideo is poor: **Bookshop SRL**, JE Rodó 1671 (at Minas y Constituyente), T401 1010, www.bookshop.com.uy, Cristina Mosca. With English stock, very friendly staff, also at Ellauri 363 and at both Montevideo and Portones Shopping Centers; specializes in travel. **Ibana**, International Book and News Agency, Convención 1485. Specializes in foreign publications. **El Libro Inglés**, Cerrito 483, Ciudad Vieja. **Librería Papacito**, 18 de Julio 1409, T908 7250, www.libreriapapacito.com. Good selection of magazines and books, wide range of subjects from celebrity autobiographies to art. **Puro Verso**, 18 de Julio 1199, T901 6429, puroverso@adinet.com.uy. Very good selection is in Spanish, small secondhand section in English, excellent café, chess tables. It has another branch on Sarandí 675, **Más Puro Verso**. Others include: **Librería El Aleph**, Bartolomé Mitre 1358. Used and rare books in Spanish. **Linardi y Risso**, Juan Carlos Gómez 1435, Ciudad Vieja, lyrbooks@linardiyrisso.com. **Centro de la Cultura Uruguaya**, Plaza Fabini, T901 1714, www.corazon alsur.com.uy. Books on Uruguay in Spanish and Uruguayan music.

Galleries There are many good art galleries. **Galería Latina**, Sarandí 671, T916 3737, is one of the best, with its own art publishing house. Several art galleries and shops lie along C Pérez Castellanos, near Mercado del Puerto.

Handicrafts Suede and leather are good buys. There are several shops and workshops around Plaza Independencia. Amethysts, topazes, agate and quartz are mined and polished in Uruguay and are also good buys. For authentic, fairly- priced crafts there is a marquee on Plaza Cagancha (No 1365), and at Mercado de la Abundancia, San José 1312, T901 0550, auda@minetuy.com. For leather goods, walk around C San José y W Ferreira Aldunate. **Montevideo Leather Factory**, Plaza Independencia 832, www.montevideoleatherfactory.com. Recommended. **Manos del Uruguay**, San José 1111, Sarandí y Bacacay, Ciudad Vieja, and at Shopping Centers, www.manos.com.uy. A non-profit organization that sells very good quality, handwoven woollen clothing and a great range of crafts, made by independent craftsmen and women from all over Uruguay. **Mundo Mineral**, Sarandí 672. Recommended for amethysts, topazes, agate and quartz.

Markets **Calle Tristán Narvaja** (and nearby streets), opposite Facultad de Derecho on 18 de Julio. On Sun, 0800-1400, there is a large, crowded street market here, good for silver and copper, and all sorts of collectibles. **Plaza de la Constitución**, a small Sat morning market and a Sun antique fair are held here. **Villa Biarritz**, on Vásquez Ledesma near Parque Rodó, Punta Carretas. A big market selling fruit, vegetables, clothes and shoes (Tue and Sat 0900-1500, and Sun in Parque Rodó, 0800-1400).

Shopping malls **The Montevideo Shopping Center**, on the east edge of Pocitos (Herrera 1290 y Laguna, 1 block south of Rivera, www.montevideoshopping.com.uy). Open daily 1000- 2000 and has a self-service restaurant, a cinema and *confiterías*. It also has wide range of shops selling leather goods, Foto Martín, bookshop, markets and more (bus 141 or 142 from San José). **Punta Carretas Shopping**, Ellauri 350, close to Playa Pocitos in the former prison, www.puntascarretasweb.com.uy. Open 1000-2200, is large, modern, with all types of shop, also cinema complex and good food patio, popular. Take bus 117 or 121 from Calle San José. Other shopping centres at Portones in Carrasco, www.portones.com.uy, the Tres Cruces bus station, www.trescruces.com.uy, and Plaza Arozena Shopping Mall.

▲ Activities and tours

Montevideo *p1518, map p1520*

Sports

Football (soccer) is the most popular. Seeing a game in **Centenario Stadium** is a must, located in Parque Batlle. If possible, attend a game with Uruguay's most popular teams, **Nacional** or **Peñarol**, or an international match. General admission tickets (US$5-10) can be bought outside before kickoff for sections Amsterdam, América, Colombes, Tribuna Olímpica. Crowds in Uruguay are much safer than other countries, but it's best to avoid the *plateas*, the end zones where the rowdiest fans chant and cheer. Sit in

Tribuna Olímpica under or opposite the tower, at midfield. **Parque Central**, just north of Tres Cruces, **Nacional**'s home field, is the next best venue. Other stadiums are quieter, safer and also fun. For information try www.tenfieldigital.com.uy, but asking a local is also advisable. **Basketball** is increasingly popular; games can be seen at any sports club (**Biguá** or **Trouville**, both in Punta Carretas/Pocitos neighbourhoods) or in **Estadio Cerrado Cilindrón** (the Cylinder), in the north city, in Villa Español. See www.fubb.org.uy for schedules. Rugby, volleyball, tennis, cycling, surfing (www.olasyvientos.com), windsurfing and kite surfing, lawn bowling, running, and walking are also popular. **Golf**: Uruguay has seven 18-hole and two 9-hole courses, between Fray Bentos and Punta del Este. Apart from Jan-Feb, Jul-Aug, you should have no problem getting onto the course, see www.aug.com.uy.

Tours

The **Asociación de Guías de Turismo de Montevideo**, agtmguias202@hotmail.com, runs historical and architecture tours of Ciudad Vieja leaving from the Cabildo every Sat. Check times and availability in English. Tours of the city are organized by the **Municipalidad**, see http://cultura.montevideo .gub.uy (go to Paseos) for details.

Day tours of Punta del Este are run by many travel agents and hotels, US$40-100 with meals.

Estancia tourism Information on *estancias* can be found at **Lares** (see below), which represents many *estancias* and *posadas*; at the tourist offices in Montevideo; or general travel agencies and those that specialize in this field: **Estancias Gauchas**, Cecilia Regules Viajes, agent for an organization of 80 estancias offering lunch and/or lodging, English, French and Portuguese spoken. Full list of estancias at www.turismo.gub.uy. Ask at these organizations about **horse riding**, too.

Cecilia Regules Viajes, Bacacay 1334, T/F916 3011, T09-968 3608 (mob), www.ceciliaregulesviajes.com, very good, knowledgeable, specialist in *estancia*, tango and railway tourism in Uruguay, and skiing in Argentina.

Jetmar, Plaza de la Independencia 725-7, T902 0793, info@jetmar.com.uy. A helpful tour operator.

JP Santos, Colonia 951, T902 0300, www.jpsantos.com.uy. Helpful agency.

Lares, Wilson Ferreira Aldunate 1341, T901 9120, www.lares.com.uy. Specializes in birdwatching and other nature tours, cultural tours, trekking, horse riding and estancia tourism.

Simply, Colonia 971, T900 8880, www.simply.com.uy. Adventure and nature tourism specialists, plus many other national and international packages.

Rumbos, Galería del Libertador, Rio Branco 1377, p 7, T900 2407, www.rumbosturismo.com. Caters specifically for independent travellers, very helpful.

TransHotel, Av 8 de Octubre 2252, T402 9935, www.e-transhotel.com. Accommodation, eco-tourism, sightseeing and tailor-made itineraries.

Turisport Ltda, San José 930, T902 0829, www.turisport.com.uy. American Express for travel and mail services, good; sells Amex dollar TCs on Amex card.

⊖ Transport

Montevideo *p1518, map p1520*

Air

The main airport is at Carrasco, 21 km outside the city, T601 1757, www.aic.com.uy; exchange facilities, but if closed, buses will accept US$ for fares to town. If making a hotel reservation, ask them to send a taxi to meet you; it's cheaper than taking an airport taxi. To Montevideo 30 mins by taxi or *remise* (US$12-21, depending on destination in the city – may be able to pay taxi driver in Argentine pesos or in US$, or charge it to hotel bill if without cash); about 50 mins by bus. Buses, Nos 700, 701, 704, 710 and 711, from Terminal Brum, Río Branco y Galicia, go to the airport US$1 (crowded before and after school hours); dark brown 'Copsa' bus terminates at the airport. **COT** buses connect airport and Punta del Este, US$7.25. **Concorde Travel** (Robert Mountford), Germán Barbato 1358, apto 1302, T902 6346/8, has a service from hotel to plane (almost) US$10-25.

Air services to **Argentina**: for the Puente Aéreo to Buenos Aires, check in at Montevideo airport, pay departure tax and go to immigration to fill in an Argentine entry form before going through Uruguayan immigration. Get your stamp out of Uruguay, surrender the tourist card you received on entry and get your stamp into Argentina. There are no immigration checks on arrival at Aeroparque, Buenos Aires.

Bus

Local City buses are comfortable and convenient. Pay your fare to the driver or to conductor in the centre of the bus, US$0.85; buses D1 (see Sights Carrasco, above), D2, D3, 5, 8, 9, 10, 11 US$0.75. There are many buses to all parts from 18 de Julio; from other parts to the centre or old city, look for those marked 'Aduana'. For Punta Carretas from city centre take bus No 121 from Calle San José.

Remises: US$15 per hr; **Remises Carrasco**, T606 1412, www.remisescarrasco.com.uy; **Remises Elite** , T099-183802; **Remises Urbana**, T400 8665.

Long distance During summer holidays buses are often full; it is advisable to book in advance (also for Fri and weekend travel all year round). **Buses within Uruguay**: excellent terminal, Tres Cruces, Bulevar Artigas y Av Italia, T408 8710 (10-15 mins by bus from the centre, Nos 21, 64, 180, 187, 188 – in Ciudad Vieja from in front of Teatro Solís); it has a shopping mall, tourist office, internet café, restaurants, left luggage (free for 2 hrs at a time, if you have a ticket for that day, then US$2 up to 4 hrs, 12-24 hrs US$4.75), post and phone offices, toilets, good medical centre, **Banco de Montevideo** and **Indumex** cambio (accepts MasterCard). Visit www.trescruces.com.uy for bus schedules. Fares and journey times from the capital are given under destinations.

To Argentina (ferries and buses)

You need a passport when buying international tickets. Direct to **Buenos Aires**: **Buquebus**, at the docks, in old customs hall, Terminal Fluvio-Marítima; Terminal Tres Cruces, Local 28/29, and Punta Carretas Shopping, loc 219; in all cases T130. 1-3 daily, 3 hrs, US$69 tourist class, US$97 1st class, US$111 special; departure tax included in the price of tickets. At Montevideo dock, go to Preembarque 30 mins before departure, present ticket, then go to Migración for Uruguayan exit and Argentine entry formalities. The terminal is like an airport and the seats on the ferries are airplane seats. On board there is duty-free shopping, video and poor value food and drinks. **Services via Colonia**: bus/ ferry and catamaran services by **Buquebus**: from 5 crossings daily from 1 to 3 hrs from Colonia, depending on vessel, fares: US$21 tourist, US$60 1st class or US$47 on slowest *Eladia Isabel*, more expensive on fast vessels. All have 2½-hr bus connection Montevideo- Colonia from Tres Cruces. There are also bus connections to **Punta del Este**, 2 hrs, and La Paloma, 5 hrs, to/from Montevideo. Cars are carried on either route, US$86-112 **Montevideo**, US$51-75 and 68-95 (depending on size of vehicle and boat) **Colonia**; motorcycles US$70 Montevideo, US$34-45 Colonia. Schedules and fares can be checked on www.buquebus.com. Fares increase in high season, Dec-Jan, when there are more sailings. Check the website for promotional discounts that may offer up to almost half the price. If you want to break your journey in Colonia, you will have to buy your own bus ticket in another company to complete the trip to/from Montevideo. **Colonia Express**, W Ferreira Aldunate 1341, T901 9597; also at Tres Cruces bus terminal, T408 8120, www.coloniaexpress.com, makes 2-3 crossings a day between Colonia and Buenos Aires in fast boats (no vehicles) with bus connections to/from Montevideo, Punta del Este and other Uruguayan towns. Fares, including Montevideo-Colonia bus: around US$47 via the website.

Services to **Carmelo** and **Tigre** (interesting trip): bus/ motor launch service by **Trans Uruguay/ Cacciola/Laderban**, 2 a day, at Tres Cruces T402 5721, www.cacciolaviajes.com/ www.transuruguay.com, US$32 (Montevideo to Buenos Aires via Carmelo and Tigre); US$18 boat from Carmelo to Tigre. Advanced booking is advisable on all services at busy periods. On through buses to Brazil and Argentina, you can expect full luggage checks both by day and night.

To Paraguay, Brazil, Chile If intending to travel through Uruguay to Brazil, do not forget to have Uruguayan entry stamped in your passport when crossing from Argentina. Without it you will not be able to cross the Brazilian border. To **Asunción**, Paraguay, US$80, 14 hrs, Mon, Wed, Sat at 1300 with **EGA**, T402 5165 (and Río Branco 1417, T902 5335), recommended, meals served. Alternatively take bus to **Santa Fe**, Argentina (US$58, 10 hrs), via Paysandú bridge, for easy access to Asunción. The through bus route is via Paysandú, Salto, Bella Unión, Uruguaiana, Paso de los Libres, Posadas, Encarnación, to Asunción (there are no passport or customs formalities except passport checks at Bella Unión and at Encarnación). There are very comfortable buses to **Porto Alegre** (US$82, 12 hrs, Mon, Wed, Fri) and **São Paulo** (US$177, 30 hrs, daily except Sat. There is also a Sun service via Camboriú, US$134, 20 hrs, a good place to stop over, and Curitiba, US$153, 23 hrs) with **EGA** and **TTL** (**Tres Cruces** or **Río Branco** 1375, T401 1410/901 9050, www.ttl.com.br), neither daily. Buses to **Florianópolis** run Tue, Fri, Sat and Sun (US$125, 18 hrs). An alternative route (which avoids the risk of being stranded at the border by through-bus drivers) is to Chuy, **COT**, T409 4949, **Cynsa** T402 5363, or **Rutas del Sol**, T403 4657 (US$16, 5-6 hrs), then catch a bus to Porto Alegre (7½ hrs, US$33-40), either direct or via Pelotas. Some private tour companies in Montevideo offer excellent deals on overland bus tours to places like Iguazú, Rio de Janeiro, Salvador, Bariloche and Santiago (eg **MTUR Viajes**, www.mturviajes.com, recommended).

Taxi

The meter starts at about US$1 in *fichas*, which determine fares as shown on a table in taxi. Tipping is not expected but welcomed, usually by rounding up the fare. Do not expect change for large peso notes. Prices go up on Sat, Sun, holidays and late at night.

Train

Uruguayan railways, **AFE**, use outdated trains, but interesting rides for enthusiasts. The old train station has been abandoned, replaced by a nice new terminus next to the Antel skyscraper, known as **Nueva Estación Central** at Paraguay y Nicaragua (Aguada), T924 8080 or 924 9645, www.afe.com.uy. Passenger trains run Mon-Sat only along 2 lines, called 25 de Agosto and Sudriers. Most commuter trains run north between Montevideo and Progreso (about 7 a day), passing some of the country's poorest areas. Fewer services go beyond Progreso. Once a day, a service goes as far as San José de Mayo on the same line and once a day as far as Florida. Another commuter line runs northeast from Montevideo to Sudriers, passing Pando. To Progreso (50 min, US$0.80), to Canelones (1 hr 20 min, US$1), to Santa Lucía (1 hr 35 min, US$1.50), to 25 de Agosto (1 hr 40 min, US$1.50), to San José de Mayo (2½ hrs, US$2), to Pando (1 hr, US$0.80). Occasionally, long distance services and a steam-engine run for special events, such as the 48-hr celebration of the Día del Patrimonio (Heritage Day) in Oct. More information, T924 3924.

Directory

Montevideo *p1518, map p1520*
Airline offices Aerolíneas Argentinas, Plaza Independencia 749 bis, T902 3691. **Air France/KLM**, Río Negro 1354, p 1, T902 5023, www.airfrance.com.uy. **American Airlines**, Sarandí 699 bis y Plaza Independencia, T916 3929. **ASATEJ Uruguay**, Student Flight Centre, Río Negro 1354, p 2, of 1 y 2, T908 0509. **Gol**, T606 0901, www.voegol.com. **Iberia**, Colonia 975, T908 1032. **LAN**, Colonia 993, p 4, T902 3881. **Pluna**, Colonia 1021, T902 1414, www.pluna.aero. **Tam Mercosur**, Plaza Cagancha 1335 of 804, T901 8451. For information on flight arrivals/departures, T604 0262, and www.tam.com.uy. **Banks** Don't trust the few black market money changers offering temptingly good rates. Many are experienced confidence tricksters. **Casas de cambio** on Plaza Cagancha daily until 2200, including Sun; banks only open 1300-1700 (some till 1800). Find most banks along 25 de Mayo, Cerrito or Zabala, and on Plaza Matriz, in Ciudad Vieja, and in the centre along Av 18 de Julio. **Banred**, www.banred.com.uy, is the largest ATM network from where you can withdraw US$ or pesos with a Visa or MasterCard. **HSBC, Lloyds TSB, BBVA, Citibank** all have Banred ATMs. More ATMs in supermarkets. Airport bank daily 0700-2200. **Western Union**, throughout the city in **Abitab** agencies, some exchange houses, and **Disco** or **Devoto** supermarkets. Exchange houses along 18 de Julio, eg **Bacacay**, at 853, **La Favorita** (Amex agents) at 1497, **Suizo** at 1190, **Regul**, at 1126, or in Ciudad Vieja, eg **Continental**, Misiones 1472, **Globus**, 25 de Mayo 466, but shop around for best rates (rates for cash are better than for TCs, but both are often better than in banks, and quicker service). **Brimar**, Misiones 1476, and **Delta**, Río Negro 1341, have been recommended. **Car hire** It is wise to hire a small car (1.3 litre engine) as Uruguay is relatively flat and gas prices are high. A small car can be negotiated for about US$60 per day, free mileage, including insurance and collision damage waiver, if you are hiring a car for at least 3 days (rates are lower out of season). Cheaper weekly rates available. Best to make reservations

before arrival. **Autocar**, Mercedes 863, T900 5925, autocaruruguay@hotmail.com. Economical, helpful. **Punta Car**, Cerro Largo 1383, T900 2772, puntacar@ puntacar.com.uy, also at Aeropuerto Carrasco. **Snappy**, Andes 1363, T900 7728, www.snappy .com.uy. **Sudancar**, Acevedo Díaz 1813, T402 6620, www.sudancar.com.uy. See Essentials, page 35 for international agencies. Most car companies don't allow their cars to be taken abroad. To travel to Argentina or Brazil, you can use **Maxicar** rentals in Salto, see page 1544. **Cultural centres** Alianza Cultural Uruguay- Estados Unidos, Paraguay 1217, T902 5160, www.alianza.edu.uy, library Mon-Fri, 1400-2000, US publications (excellent selection), theatre, art gallery. **Instituto Cultural Anglo-Uruguayo** (known as the 'Anglo'), San José 1426, T902 3773, www.anglo.edu.uy (theatre, recommended, library Mon-Fri 0930-1200, 1430-1930); café at No 1227. **Alliance Française**, Blvr Artigas 1229, T400 0505, www.alianza francesa.edu.uy (theatre, concerts, library, excellent bookshop). **Goethe Institut**, Canelones 1524, T410 5813, www.goethe.de/montevideo (Mon, Tue, Thu, Fri 1000-1300, 1600-1930). **Instituto Italiano de Cultura**, Paraguay 1177, T900 3354, www.iicmontevideo.esteri.it. **Centro Cultural de España**, Rincón 629, Ciudad Vieja, T915 2250, www.cce.org.uy, Mon-Fri 1130-2000, Sat 1130-1800, has art exhibitions and a café. **Embassies and consulates** Argentine Consulate, Wilson Ferreira Aldunate 1281, T902 8623, www.consuladoargentinomonte video.com.uy. Open 1300-1830, visa US$15, 1-day wait, English spoken. **Australian Consulate**, Cerro Largo 1000, T901 0743, payssed@adinet.com.uy. **Belgian Consulate**, Rincón 625, of 26, T916 2719. **Brazilian Consulate**, Convención 1343, p 6, T901 2024, conbras@consbras.org.uy. Open 0930-1230, 1430-1730 (visas takes 24 hrs and the procedure is more complicated than Argentina – need photo, onward ticket, entry ticket, proof of finances). **Canada**, Plaza Independencia 749, of 102, T902 2030, www.canadainternational.gc.ca/ uruguay. **Chile**, 25 de Mayo 575, T916 4090. Open 0900-1400, visa US$5, same day. **France**, Av Uruguay 853, T170-50000, www.ambafrance uruguay.org. **Germany**, La Cumparsita 1417-35, T902 5222, www.monte video.diplo.de. Open Mon-Thu 0745-1230, 1300-1645 (shuts at lunch on Fri). **Israel**, Blvd Gral Artigas 1585, T400 4164, ambassadorsec@montevideo.mfa.gov.il. **Italy**, JB Lamas 2857, T708 4916, ambasciata. montevideo@esteri.it. **Netherlands**, Leyenda Patria 2880, Apt 202, T711 2956, www.holanda.org.uy. **New Zealand Consulate**, Miguel Grau 3789, T622 1543. **Paraguay**, Blvd Artigas 1256, T707 2138, embapur@ netgate.com.uy. Summer 0900-1200, winter 1400-1730. **Portugal**, Av Dr F Soca 1128, T708 4061, portmont@netgate.com.uy. **Spanish Consulate**, Libertad 2738, T708 0048, www.maec.es/consulados/montevideo. **Sweden**, Rambla 25 de Agosto 508, p 5, T917 0289. **Switzerland**, Ing Federico Abadie 2936/40, T711 5545, www.eda.admin.ch/ montevideo. **UK**, Marco Bruto 1073, T622 3630, http://ukinuruguay.fco.gov.uk. **US Embassy** and **Consulate**, Lauro Muller 1776, T418 7777, http://uruguay.usembassy.gov.

Internet Cyber Café Nacho, Av del Libertador 1607 y Cerro Largo, T903 9070. Open till 2200, US$0.75 per hr. **Cyber Café The Night**, Vásquez 1418, T402 1715, US$0.65 per hr. Open till 0300. **Cyber Café Uruguay**, Colonia 1955. **Cyberi@**, San José 933. **Millennium Café**, Paraguay 1325, local 53, in mall. **Phone Box**, Andes 1363, US$0.80 per hr. **Zona Tec**, T908 9042, US$0.75 per hr. **Language schools** Academia Uruguay, Juan Carlos Gómez 1408, T915 2496, www.academia uruguay.com. **Medical services** Hospital Británico, Av Italia 2420, T487 1020. Recommended. **Post offices** Misiones 1328 y Buenos Aires; 0800-1800 Mon-Fri, 0800-1300 Sat and holidays. **Poste restante** at main post office will keep mail for 1 month. Next to Pluna office on Av Libertador, next to Montevideo Shopping Center, 0800-1300, and under Intendencia at corner of Av 18 de Julio and Ejido, Mon-Fri 1000-2000, Sat 1700-2200. **Telephones** Antel, Fernández Crespo 1534 (headquarters) and at San José 1101 (Plaza), 18 de Julio 891 (Plaza Independencia), Arocena 1598 (Carrasco), Ariel 4914 (Sayago), Cádiz Garzón 1929 (Colón), José Belloni s/n (Piedras Blancas).

Western Uruguay

West of Montevideo, Route 1, part of the Pan-American Highway, heads to the UNESCO World Heritage Site of Colonia del Sacramento and the tranquil town of Carmelo. Off the road are the old British mining town of Conchillas and the Jesuit mission at Calera de las Huérfanas. Other roads lead to the Río Uruguay,

Colonia del Sacramento

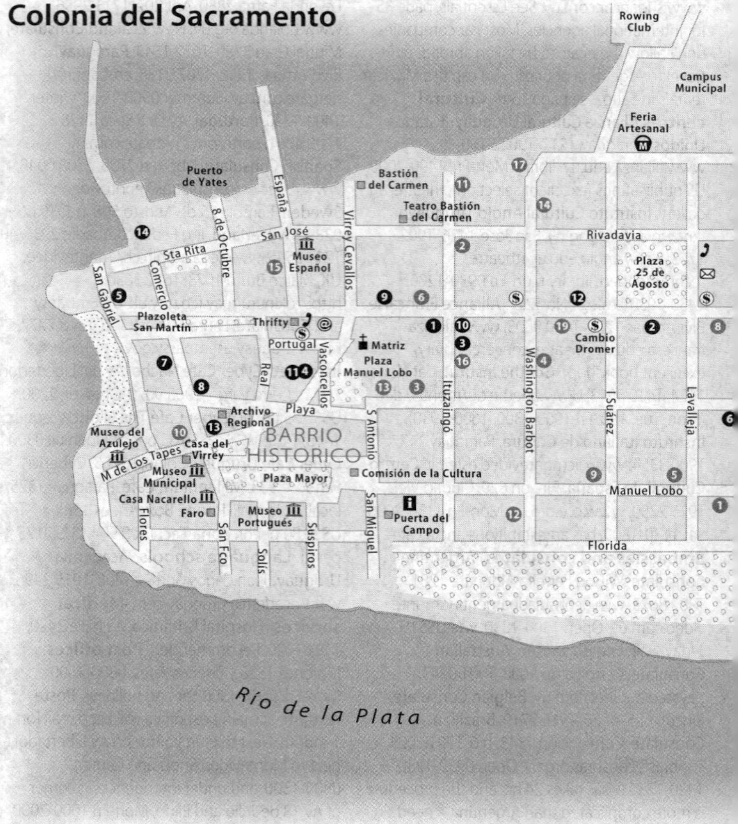

Sleeping
1 Blanca y Juan Carlos
2 Don Antonio Posada
3 El Capullo Posada
4 El Viajero
5 Español
6 Esperanza
7 Hostal de los Poetas
8 Hostel Colonial
9 Italiano
10 Plaza Mayor
11 Posada de la Flor
12 Posada del Angel
13 Posada del Gobernador
14 Posada del Río
15 Posada del Virrey
16 Posada Manuel de Lobo
17 Radisson Colonia de Sacramento & Restaurant Del Carmen
18 Romi
19 Royal

Route 2 from Rosario to Fray Bentos, and Route 3 via San José de Mayo and Trinidad to the historic towns of Paysandú and Salto. The latter passes farms, man-made lakes and the river itself. There are also many hot-spring resorts .

Eating

1 Blanco y Negro
2 Club Colonia
3 El Asador
4 El Drugstore & Viejo Barrio
5 El Torreón
6 La Amistad
7 La Bodeguita
8 Lobo
9 Lo de Renata
10 Mercosur
11 Mesón de la Plaza
12 Parrillada El Portón
13 Pulpería Los Faroles
14 Yacht Club

Colonias Valdense and Suiza

Route 1 to Colonia de Sacramento is a four-lane highway. At Km 121 from Montevideo the road passes Colonia Valdense, a colony of Waldensians who still cling to some of the old customs of the Piedmontese Alps. For tourist information, T055-88412. A road branches off north here to Colonia Suiza, a Swiss settlement also known as **Nueva Helvecia** (*Population: 10,000, Phone code: 0552*), with lovely parks, gardens and countryside. In the town is the Santuario de Nuestra Señora De Schonstatt, all walls are covered by plants, and the first steam mill in Uruguay (1875).The Swiss national day is celebrated with great enthusiasm.

The highway skirts **Rosario** (*Phone code: 052*, 140 km from Montevideo, 60 km before Colonia del Sacramento), called 'the first Uruguayan Museum of Mural Art'. Dozens of impressive murals are dotted around the city, some with bullfights, some abstract designs.

Colonia del Sacramento ➔ *Phone code: 052. Colour map 8, B5. Population: 22,000.*

ⓘ *All museums Fri-Mon 1115-1745, closed either Tue, Wed or Thu, except Archivo Regional (shut Sat-Sun), combined tickets US$2.50.*

Founded by Portuguese settlers from Brazil in 1680, Colonia del Sacramento was a centre for smuggling British goods across the Río de la Plata into the Spanish colonies during the 17th century. The small historic section juts into the Río de la Plata, while the modern town extends around a bay. It is a lively place with streets lined with plane trees, a pleasant Plaza 25 de Agosto and a grand Intendencia Municipal (Méndez y Avenida Gen Flores, the main street). The town is kept very trim. The best beach is Playa Ferrando, 1½ km to the east, easily accessible by foot or hired vehicle. There are regular connections by boat with Buenos Aires and a free port.

The **Barrio Histórico**, with its narrow streets (see Calle de los Suspiros), colonial buildings and reconstructed city walls, is charming because there are few such examples in this part of the continent. It has been declared Patrimonio Cultural de la Humanidad by UNESCO. The old town can be easily seen on foot in a day (wear comfortable shoes on the uneven cobbles), but spend one night there to experience the illuminations by nostalgic replica street lamps. The **Plaza Mayor** is especially picturesque and has parakeets in the palm trees. Grouped around it are the **Museo Municipal**, in a mid- 18th-century Portuguese residence (with indigenous archaeology, historical items, natural history, palaeontology), the **Casa Nacarello** next door (18th century; depicting colonial life), the **Casa del Virrey** (in ruins), the **Museo Portugués** (1720) with, downstairs, an exhibition of beautiful old maps, and the ruins of the Convento de San Francisco, to which is attached the **Faro** (lighthouse, entry US$0.70, daily 1200-1800, on a clear day you can see Buenos Aires). The **Museo Naval** ⓘ *Calle Henrique de la Peña y San Francisco, T25609*, was opened at the end of 2009. At the Plaza's eastern end is the **Puerta del Campo**, the restored city gate and drawbridge. Just north of the Plaza Mayor is the **Archivo Regional** (1750), collection of maps, police records 1876-1898 and 19th-century watercolours. The **Iglesia Matriz**, on Calle Vasconcellos (beside the Plaza de Armas/Manuel Lobo), is the oldest church in Uruguay. Free concerts are held on Friday in the church grounds during the summer months. At the end of Calle Misiones de los Tapes, the Casa Portuguesa is now the tiny **Museo del Azulejo** (partly original floor, collection of French and Catalan tiles, plus the first Uruguayan tile from 1840). The house of Gen Mitre, Calles de San José y España, houses the **Museo Español** (closed for refurbishment, 2010). At the north edge, the fortifications of the **Bastión del Carmen** can be seen; nearby is the Centro Cultural Bastión del Carmen, Rivadavia 223, in a 19th-century glue and soap factory, with frequent theatre productions. In the third week of January, festivities mark the founding of Colonia. The **Feria Artesanal** ⓘ *Campus Municipal, Fosalba y Suárez*, is worth a visit. Kids will love the new **Acuario** in the Barrio Histórico ⓘ *Calle Virrey Cevallos 236, esq Rivadavia, open Wed-Mon 1600-2000, US$1.50*.

Around the bay is **Real de San Carlos** ⓘ *5 km, take 'Cotuc' or 'ABC' buses from Av Gral Flores, leaving Barrio Histórico, US$0.60*, an unusual, once grand but now sad tourist complex, built by Nicolás Mihanovic 1903-1912. The elegant bull-ring, in use for just two years, is falling apart (closed to visitors, bullfighting is banned in Uruguay). The casino, the nearest to Buenos Aires then (where gambling was prohibited), failed when a tax was imposed on Mihanovic's excursions; also disused is the huge Frontón court. Only the racecourse (Hipódromo) is still operational (free, except three annual races) and you can see the horses exercising on the beach.

Tourist offices ⓘ *Flores y Rivera, T26141, daily 0900-1900 (closes at 2000 in peak summer and 1800 in winter), infoturismo@ colonia.gub.uy and www.coloniaturismo.com*, good maps of the Barrio Histórico and the region. Beside the **Old Gate** ⓘ *Manuel Lobo e Ituzaingó, T28506, daily 0800-2000 (0900-1900 in winter)*. Also an information desk at bus terminal. There is a **Ministry of Tourism** office at the passenger terminal at the dock, T24897, and a new tourist board set to open in 2010. Visit www.guiacolonia.com.uy, www.colonianet.com.

Conchillas, 50 km from Colonia and 40 km from Carmelo, is a former British mining town from the late 19th century. It preserves dozens of buildings constructed by C H Walker and Co Ltd. Tourist information is available at the **Casa de la Cultura** (daily 0800-1400) on Calle David Evans. The police station is also a good source of information. Direct buses from Colonia; road well marked on Route 21.

Carmelo → *Phone code: 0542. Population: 22,000.*

From Colonia, Route 21 heads northwest to Carmelo (77 km) on the banks of Arroyo Las Vacas. A fine avenue of trees leads to the river, crossed by the first swing bridge built 1912. Across the bridge is the Rambla de los Constituyentes and the Fuente de las Tentaciones. The church, museum and archive of El Carmen is on Plaza Artigas (named after the city's founder). In the Casa de la Cultura Ignacio Barrios (IMC), 19 de Abril 246, is a tourist office. Historically a mining centre, it is said that many luxurious buildings in Buenos Aires were made from the grey granite

Wreckers, revolutionaries and gauchos

Uruguay's passion for rural life began in 1603 with Hernando Arias and the first shipment of cattle and horses to the Banda Oriental.

Today, a typical day on an *estancia* begins at the hearth, perhaps with a warming *mate*, before a horseride. The fireplace may be decorated with signs of present and past ownership, each brand burnt into the fireplace representing a personal history, but one element unites them all: the myth of the gaucho.

You might be forgiven for imagining yourself a latter-day gaucho as you put your foot in the *copa* (a cupped stirrup) and mount a sturdy Uruguayan horse, perhaps of the same breed as the one that Napoleon had shipped back to carry him around a wintry Europe. However, your thick poncho might well be the only piece of gaucho gear that you are wearing. Gauchos sometimes used ponchos as shields in knife fights, but on the ride you probably won't be needing a *facón* (a large dagger), nor a pair of *bombachas* (baggy trousers gathered at the ankle) or *culero* (an apron of soft leather tied around the waist, open on the left side) to avoid lacerations from a lasso during branding and gelding. Horses on tourism estancias are used to novice riders, and *rebenques* (short whips) are best kept unused by your side. You'll find the Uruguayan horse a compliant platform for launching your *boleadoras* (three stones, covered with hide, on ropes tied at the middle, are used for entangling the legs of cattle). At this point you may learn whether your horse is a *pingo*, a gaucho's favourite horse, or *flete*, an ordinary cargo beast.

Riding along extensive *cuchillas* (ridges) and crossing rivers will bring to mind the nomadic gaucho lifestyle, and the revolutionary (largely gaucho) guerrilla bands. A *montonera* was a band of gauchos organized to drive the Brazilians and Argentinians out of Uruguay. Patriot leader Artigas was a gaucho- caudillo (boss).

Uruguayan life is built from livestock, sometimes quite literally. Houses were occasionally made from cattle hide. And cattle were put to other uses: coastal ranchers in Maldonado Department in the 19th century placed lights on the horns of their cows to lure ships onto the rocks for plunder.

of Cerro Carmelo (mines flooded and used for watersports). It is one of the most important yachting centres on Río de la Plata and its microclimate produces much wine.

Calera de Las Huérfanas (Estancia de las Vacas) is the remains of one of the area's main Jesuit missions. Vines were introduced and lime was exported for the construction of Buenos Aires. After the expulsion of the Jesuits, it became an orphanage. It's in relatively good state and is best reached by car (exit from Route 21 clearly marked, some 10 km before Carmelo).

Between Carmelo and Nueva Palmira, another river port, is the colonial monument, **Capilla de Narbona** (Route 21, Km 263), built in the early 18th century. At **Granja y Bodega Narbona** (T540 4778), wine, cheese and other produce are available, as well as a fine restaurant and two exclusive hotel rooms. Nearby, at Km 262, is the luxurious **Four Seasons Resort**, www.fourseasons.com/carmelo.

Mercedes → *Phone code: 053. Colour map 8, B5. Population: 42,000.*

This livestock centre is best reached by Route 2 from the main Colonia-Montevideo highway. Founded in 1788, it is pleasant town on the Río Negro, a yachting and fishing centre during the season. Its charm (it is known as 'the city of flowers') derives from its Spanish-colonial appearance, though it is not as old as the older parts of Colonia. There is an attractive *costanera* (riverside drive).

National pride

The indigenous Charrúas were remarkably brave, but they were also inhospitable and rallied against European explorers. They killed Spaniard Juan Díaz de Solís, the navigator who first charted Montevideo in 1515. Between early explorer visits, they learned to ride captured horses, still slinging stones on suede straps in defiance of and indifference to the superior Spanish swords. Their aggression, despite the impossible odds, led to their eradication when the last remaining natives were massacred in 1831. Nevertheless, their legacy lives on. *Mate*, the native tea, is now the national beverage, proudly sipped and shared throughout Uruguay. And the national soccer team is nicknamed *Los Charrúas* because, after winning the first and fourth FIFA World Cups in 1930 and 1950, against powerhouses Argentina and Brazil, people recognized that "fight to the finish" attitude in the players. In fact, in Uruguay, it is a great compliment to be described as having *garra Charrúa*, meaning strength, resourcefulness, bravery and determination.

West of town 4 km is the Parque Mauá, dating from 1757. It has a mansion which contains the **Museum of Palaeontology** ⓘ *daily 1100-1800, free,* on the ground floor. The building is worth wandering around to see the exterior, upper apartments and stable block. Camping is possible in season. It takes 45 minutes to walk to the park, a pleasant route passing Calera Real on the riverbank, dating back to 1722, the oldest industrial ruins in the country (lime kilns hewn out of the sandstone). There is a **tourist office** at Colón, on the plaza, where maps and hotel lists are available.

Fray Bentos ➔ *Phone code: 056. Colour map 8, B5. Population: 23,000.*
Route 2 continues westwards (34 km) to Fray Bentos, the main port on the east bank of Río Uruguay 193 km from Buenos Aires. Here in 1865 the Liebig company built its first factory producing meat extract. The original plant, much extended and known as **El Anglo**, has been restored as the **Museo de la Revolución Industrial** ⓘ *Tue-Sun 0800-1930, entry price includes 1½-hr guided tour 1000 and 1600, US$1.50, in Spanish, leaflet in English.* The office block in the factory has been preserved complete with its original fittings. Many machines can be seen. Within the complex is the Barrio Inglés, where workers were housed, and La Casa Grande, where the director lived. There are **beaches** to the northeast and southwest. **Tourist office**: 25 de Mayo 3400, T22233.

Crossing to Argentina
About 9 km upriver from Fray Bentos is the San Martín International Bridge. Owing to a long-running dispute between Argentina and Uruguay over a Uruguayan wood pulp mill, this crossing is effectively closed. Alternatives are at Paysandú, Salto, or one of the crossings on the Río de la Plata.

Paysandú ➔ *Phone code: 072. Colour map 8, A5. Population: 74,575.*
North of Fray Bentos, 110 km, is this undulating, historic city on the east bank of the Río Uruguay. Along Route 3, it's 380 km from Montevideo. Summer temperatures can be up to 42°C. There is a 19th-century **basilica** ⓘ *daily 0700-1145, 1600-2100*. The **Museo Histórico Municipal** ⓘ *Zorrilla de San Martín y Leandro Gómez, Mon-Sat 0800-1300,* has good collection of guns and furniture from the time of the Brazilian siege of 1864-1865. **Museo de la Tradición** ⓘ *north of town at the Balneario Municipal, 0900-1745 daily, reached by bus to Zona Industrial,* gaucho articles, is also worth a visit. **Tourist office** ⓘ *Plaza de Constitución, 18 de Julio 1226, T26220, www.paysandu.com/turismo, Mon-Fri 0800-1900, Sat-Sun 0900-1900 (2000 in summer), and at Puente Gen Artigas, T27574.*

Around Paysandú

The **Termas del Guaviyú** *US$3.50, getting there: 50 mins by bus, US$3, 6 a day*, thermal springs 50 km north, with four pools, restaurant, 3 motels (**A-C**) and private hotel (**B**, **Villagio**) and excellent cheap camping facilities. Along Route 90, 84 km east, are the **Termas de Almirón** ⓘ *T074-02203, www.guichon.com.uy*, five pools, with camping and motels. The **Meseta de Artigas** ⓘ *90 km north of Paysandú, 13 km off the highway to Salto, no public transport, free*, is 45 m above the Río Uruguay, which here narrows and forms whirlpools at the rapids of El Hervidero. It was used as a base by General Artigas during the struggle for independence. The terrace has a fine view, but the rapids are not visible from the Meseta. The statue topped by Artigas' head is very original.

Crossing to Argentina

The José Artigas international bridge connects with Colón, Argentina (US$5 per car, return), 8 km away. Immigration for both countries is on the Uruguayan side in the same office. If travelling by bus, the driver gets off the bus with everyone's documents and a list of passengers to be checked by immigration officials.

Salto ➔ *Phone code: 073. Colour map 8, A5. Population: 99,000.*

A centre for cultivating and processing oranges and other citrus fruit, Salto is a beautifully kept town 120 km by paved road north of Paysandú. The town's commercial area is on Calle Uruguay, between Plazas Artigas and Treinta y Tres. There are lovely historic streets and walks along the river. Next to Club Uruguay, Calle Uruguay, is the *Farmacia Fénix*, "la más antigua de Salto", over

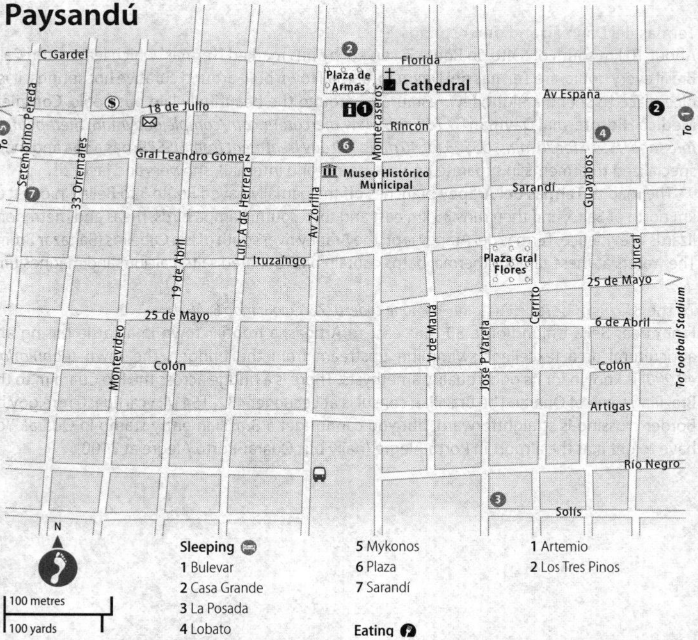

Sleeping
1 Bulevar
2 Casa Grande
3 La Posada
4 Lobato
5 Mykonos
6 Plaza
7 Sarandí

Eating
1 Artemio
2 Los Tres Pinos

100 years old. See the beautiful but run-down **Parque Solari** (Ruta Gral Artigas, northeast of the centre) and the **Parque Harriague** (south of the centre) with an open-air theatre. The **Museo de Bellas Artes y Artes Decorativas** ⓘ *Uruguay 1067, T29898 ext 148, Tue-Sun 1500-2000 (Tue-Sun 1400-1900 in winter)*, in the French-style mansion of a rich *estanciero* (Palacio Gallino), is well worth a visit. **Museo del Hombre y La Tecnología** ⓘ *Brasil 510, T29898, ext 151, Tue-Sun 1400-1900 (Tue-Sun 1300-1800 in winter), free entry and free guided tours in Spanish*, is very interesting, with a small archaeological museum. There is a Shrove Tuesday carnival. **Tourist office** ⓘ *Uruguay 1052, T34096, www.salto .gub.uy, Mon-Sat 0800-1930*, free map; and at the international bridge, T28933.

The most popular tourist site in the area is the large **Presa de Salto Grande** dam and hydroelectric plant 20 km from Salto, built jointly by Argentina and Uruguay ⓘ *taxi to dam US$20.50; tours can be arranged with SOMA, T20329*; small visitors centre at the plant. A road runs along the top of the dam to Argentina. By launch to the **Salto Chico** beach, fishing, camping.

Near the dam (2 km north on the Route 3) is **Parque Acuático Termas de Salto Grande** ⓘ *open all year 1000-2000 (Jan and Feb 1000-2200), US$6, T30902, www.hotelhoracioquiroga.com/parque.htm*, (4 ha) in a natural setting. There are several pools, slides, hydro massages, water jets and a man-made waterfall.

Crossing to Argentina

North of the town, at the Salto Grande dam, there is an international bridge to Concordia, Argentina, open 24 hours a day, all year. Passengers have to get off the bus to go through immigration procedures. Buses don't go on Sundays. Both Argentine and Uruguayan immigration offices are on the Argentine side.

Termas del Daymán and other springs

About 10 km south of Salto on Route 3, served by bus marked 'Termas' which leave from Calle Brasil every hours, are **Termas del Daymán**, a small town built around curative hot springs. It is a nice place to spend a night; few restaurants around the beautifully laid out pools. **Complejo Médico Hidrotermal Daymán** ⓘ *T69090, www.mercotour.com/complejodayman, therapeutical massage US$14 for 20 mins, US$23 for 40 mins, full day treatment from US$29*, has a spa and many specialized treatments in separate pools (external and internal), showers and jacuzzis.

The road to **Termas del Arapey** branches off the partially paved Route 3 to Bella Unión, at 61 km north of Salto, and then runs 35 km east and then south. Pampa birds, rheas and metre-long lizards in evidence. Termas del Arapey is on the Arapey river south of Isla Cabellos (Baltazar Brum). The waters at these famous thermal baths contain bicarbonated salts, calcium and magnesium.

To the Brazilian border: Artigas → *Phone code: 0772. Colour map 8, A6.*

From near Bella Unión Route 30 runs east to Artigas, a frontier town in a cattle raising and agricultural area (excellent swimming upstream from the bridge). The town (*Population: 40,000*) is known for its good quality amethysts. There is a bridge across the Río Cuaraim to the Brazilian town of Quaraí. The Brazilian consul is at Lecueder 432, T5414, vcartigas@mre.gov.br. Border crossing is straightforward, but you cannot get a Brazilian entry stamp in Quaraí. You have to get it at the airport in Porto Alegre (daily bus Quaraí-Porto Alegre at 2100).

Western Uruguay listings

For Sleeping and Eating price codes and other relevant information, see Essentials, pages 38-40.

Sleeping

Nueva Helvecia (Colonia Suiza) *p1533*
L **Nirvana**, Av Batlle y Ordóñez, T44081, www.hotelnirvana.com. Restaurant (Swiss and traditional cuisine), half board available, see website for promotions, sports facilities, gardens. Recommended.
C **Del Prado**, Av G Imhoff, T44169, www.hoteldelprado.info. Open all year, huge buffet breakfast, TV, pool.
Camping Campsite in a park at the turnoff for Col Suiza, on main road, free, toilets, no showers.

Tourism farms
AL pp **Finca Piedra**, Ruta 23, Km 125, Mal Abrigo, northwest of San José de Mayo (convenient for Montevideo or Colonia), T0340-3118, www.fincapiedra.com. Price is full board, various rooms in different parts of this 1930s estancia and vineyard, lots of outdoor activities including riding, tours of the vines, winetasting, pool, caters for children, Wi-Fi.
A **La Vigna**, T558 9234, Km 120 Ruta 51 to Playa Fomento, www.lavignalifestyle.com. Wonderful boutique eco-hotel, solar-powered and recycled furniture. Offers horse-riding and art lessons. Good food, all farm reared and organic. Owner is a cheese farmer, excellent produce. Highly recommended.
B pp **Estancia Don Miguel**, Ruta 1 Km 121 y Ruta 52, T0550-2041, esmiguel@adinet.com.uy. Rustic, working farm, full board, transport extra, good activities, little English spoken.
B **El Terruño**, Ruta 1, Km 140, 35 km before Colonia, T/F0550-6004. Price includes breakfast, horse-rides and activities.

Colonia del Sacramento *p1533, map p1532*
Choice is good including several recently renovated 19th-century posada hotels.

Barrio Histórico
A **El Capullo Posada**, 18 de Julio 219, T30135, www.elcapullo.com. Spacious living area, English owners, stylish boutique-style rooms, outdoor pool and *parrilla*.
A **Plaza Mayor**, Del Comercio 111, T23193, www.colonianet.com/plazamayor. In a 19th-century house, beautiful internal patio with lemon trees and Spanish fountain, lovely rooms with a/c or heating, English spoken.

Centre
AL **Radisson Colonia de Sacramento**, Washington Barbot 283, T30460, www.radissoncolonia.com. Great location overlooking the jetty, casino attached. Internet, 2 pools, 1 indoor, very good.
A **Don Antonio Posada**, Ituzaingó 232, T25344, www.posadadonantonio.com. 1870 building, buffet breakfast, a/c, TV, garden, pool, internet, Wi-Fi, excellent.
A **Esperanza**, Gral Flores 237, T22922, www.hotelesperanzaspa.com. Charming, with sauna, heated pool and treatments.
A **Italiano**, Intendente Suárez 105, T27878, www.hotelitaliano.com.uy. Open since 1928, it has been renovated with comfortable rooms, cheaper rates Mon-Thu. Large outdoor and indoor pools, gym, sauna, good restaurant. Recommended.
A **Posada de la Flor**, Ituzaingó 268, T30794, www.posada-delaflor.com. At the quiet end of C Ituzaingó, next to the river and to the Barrio Histórico, simply decorated rooms on a charming patio and roof terrace with river views.
A **Posada del Angel**, Washington Barbot 59, T24602, www.posadadelangel.net. Early 20th-century house, breakfast, pleasant, warm welcome, gym, sauna, pool.
A **Posada del Gobernador**, 18 de Julio 205, T22918, www.delgobernador.com. Charming, with open air pool, garden and tea room open 1600-2000.
A **Posada del Virrey**, España 217, T22223, www.posadadelvirrey.com. Large rooms, some with view over bay (cheaper with small bathroom and no balcony), with breakfast. Recommended.
A **Posada Manuel de Lobo**, Ituzaingó 160, T22463, www.posadamanueldelobo.com. Built in 1850. Large rooms, huge baths, parking, some smaller rooms, nice breakfast area inside and out.

A Royal, General Flores 340, T22169, www.hotelroyalcolonia.com. Shabby lobby but pleasant rooms, some with Río de la Plata views, pool, noisy a/c but recommended.
B Blanca y Juan Carlos, Lobo 430, T24304. Member of an organization that arranges for visitors to stay with local families, welcoming, garden, safe, with breakfast. Recommended.
B Posada del Río, Washington Barbot 258, T23002, hdelrio@adinet.com.uy. A/c, small breakfast included, terrace overlooking bay.
C Hostal de los Poetas, Mangarelli 677, T31643, hostaldelospoetas@hotelescolonia.com. Some distance from the Barrio Histórico but one of the cheapest, friendly owners, few simple bedrooms and a lovely breakfast room, tiny exuberant garden.
C Romi, Rivera 236, T30456, www.hotelromi.com.uy. 19th-century posada- style downstairs, with lovely tiles at entrance. Airy modernist upstairs and simple rooms. Recommended.
D Español, Manuel Lobo 377, T30759. Good value, **F** pp with shared bath in dorms, breakfast US$4, internet, kitchen. Recommended.
E pp **Hostel Colonial**, Flores 440, T30347. Pretty patio and quirky touches, such as barber's chair in reception. Kitchen, bar with set meals, free internet access and use of bikes (all ancient), run down and noisy, but popular. Some doubles (**D**).
E pp **El Viajero**, Washington Barbot 164, T22683, http://elviajerocolonia.com. Small, friendly hostel with a/c and WiFi, **E** in dorm, HI affiliated, some doubles (**B**).
Camping D Municipal site at Real de San Carlos, T24500, US$5 pp, in mini-cabañas, electric hook-ups, 100 m from beach, hot showers, open all year, safe, excellent. Recommended.

Carmelo *p1534*
B Timabe, 19 de Abril y Solís, T5401, www.ciudad carmelo.com/timabe. Near the swing bridge, with a/c or fan, TV, dining room, parking, good.
Camping At Playa Seré, hot showers.

Mercedes *p1535*
A Rambla Hotel, Av Asencio 728, T30696, www.mercedesramblahotel.com.uy. Riverside 3-star hotel with quite good rooms and Wi-Fi.
C Ito, Eduardo V Haedo 184, T24919, www.sorianototal.com/hotelito/mercedes.htm. Basic though decent rooms with cable TV in an old house.
E Hospedaje Mercedes, F Sánchez 614, T23804, opposite hospital. Shared bath, very helpful.
E Hospedaje El Tigre, Sarandí 505, T28104. Simple, OK, clean showers.
Camping Club de Remeros, De la Ribera y Gomensoro (on the riverside), T22534. Also has dorm (**G** with own sheets), restaurant.
Tourism Farm AL pp **Estancia La Sirena Marinas del Río Negro**, Ruta 14, Km 4, T0530-2726, www.lasirena.com.uy. *Estancia* dating from 1830, picturesque, on the river, birdwatching, fishing, waterskiing, accommodation, meals, price is per person, full board (**C** pp with breakfast) friendly owners Rodney, Lucia and Patricia Bruce. Warmly recommended.

Fray Bentos *p1536*
C Las Cañas, 8 km south, T22224, lascanas@adinet.com.uy. A tourist complex with a beach; pleasant, but crowded in summer. Accommodation in motel rooms with kitchenette and bath, cheaper without kitchen, all with a/c, TV, fridge. Camping US$10 per day minimum.
B Plaza, 18 de Julio y 25 de Mayo, T22363, www.grupocarminatti.com/hot1ha.html. Comfortable, a/c, TV, internet, with breakfast, on the Plaza Constitución.
C Colonial, 25 de Mayo 3293, T22260, www.hotelcolonial.com.uy. Attractive old building with patio. Price includes breakfast.
Camping At the **Club Remeros**, near the river and at Colegio Laureles, 1 km from centre, T22236.

Paysandú *p1536, map p1537*
Book hotels in advance during Holy Week.
A Casa Grande, Florida 1221, Plaza Constitución, T24994, www.paysandu.com/ hotelcasagrande/. A/c, welcoming, parking, very good.
A Mykonos, 18 de Julio 768, T20255. Buffet breakfast, meeting room, cable TV.
B Bulevar, Bulevar Artigas 960, T28835. Bar, garage, internet, cable TV.
B Lobato, Leandro Gómez 1415, T22241, hotellobato@adinet.com.uy. With breakfast, a/c, modern, good.
B Plaza, Leandro Gómez 1211, T22022, www.hotelplaza.com.uy. A/c, balcony, breakfast, parking.

C La Posada, José Pedro Varela 566, T27879. Internet, patio with BBQ, a/c, restaurant and bar.
C Sarandí, Sarandí 931, T23465. Good, comfortable, breakfast not included.
Camping Balneario Municipal, 2 km north of centre, by the river, no facilities. **Camping Club de Pescadores**, Rambla Costanera Norte, T22885, US$7 per day, showers. Also at Parque Municipal.
Tourism farms A pp **La Calera**, near Guichón, 150 km east of Paysandú, T409 7856, www.lacalera.com. 40 luxurious suites with fireplace and kitchenette, pool, riding, rodeo, conference facilities. Self-catering. Highly recommended.
A Estancia La Paz, 15 km south of Paysandú, T720 2272, www.estancialapaz.com.uy. Excellent rustic rooms, pool, customized gaucho experiences, horseriding, birdwatching. Highly recommended.

Salto *p1537*
AL Hotel Horacio Quiroga, near Salto Chico, T34411, www.hotelhoracioquiroga.com. Best in town although some distance from centre, at the Termas complex, sports facilities, staffed by nearby catering school, special packages in season.
B Los Cedros, Uruguay 657, T33984. In centre, comfortable 3-star hotel, internet, buffet breakfast, conference room.
C Argentina, Uruguay 892, T29931. With breakfast, a/c, cafetería, comfortable.
C pp **Concordia**, Uruguay 749, T/F32735. Oldest hotel in Uruguay, founded 1860, Carlos Gardel stayed here, fine courtyard, pleasant breakfast room.
C Hostal del Jardín, Colón 47, T24274, hostalj@adinet.com.uy. Comfortable, TV, fridge, very helpful, spacious garden.

Termas del Daymán *p1538*
A Termas de San Nicanor, 12 km from Termas de Daymán, Km 485, Route 3, T0730-2209, www.termassannicanor.com. Estancia and gaucho experience, excellent nature watching, private pool. Recommended. Also camping (US$10 pp), good facilities.
B Del Pasaje, various addresses near Ruta 3, T69661, www.hoteldelpasaje.com. Hotel rooms, apartments for 2,4, 6 or 7 people and cabañas. Situated in front of the Parque Acuático Acuamanía.
B La Posta del Daymán, Ruta 3, Km 487, T69801, www.lapostadeldayman.com. A/c, half-board or breakfast only (**D** low season, hostel half price), thermal water in more expensive rooms, thermal pool, good restaurant, long-stay discounts, camping. Recommended. Also hydrothermal complex.
D Bungalows El Puente, near the bridge over Río Dayman, T69271, includes discount to thermal baths.
D Estancia La Casona del Daymán, 3 km east of the bridge at Daymán, T073-02137. Well-preserved, but non-operational farm, horse riding.
E pp **La Canela**, Los Sauces entre Los Molles y Calle 1, T69121. Good value.
Camping See **Termas de San Niconor**, above.

Termas del Arapey
A Hotel Termas de Arapey, T0768-2441, www.hoteltermasdelarapey.com. Open all year, a/c, TV, safe, indoor/outdoor pool, restaurant.
Camping US$5 pp, good facilities

Artigas *p1538*
There are a few hotels in town and the **Club Deportivo Artigas**, Pte Berreta and LA de Herrera, 4 km from city, T0772-3860/2532, open all year, rooms (**D**) and camping (US$4.50 pp), restaurant, no cooking facilities.
Camping At Club Zorrilla, T4341.

Eating

Nueva Helvecia (Colonia Suiza) *p1533*
Don Juan, main plaza. Snack bar/restaurant excellent food, pastries and bread.

Colonia del Sacramento *p1533, map p1532*
Blanco y Negro, Gen Flores 248, T22236, www.bynrestojazz.com.uy. Closed Tue-Wed. Set in historic brick building, smart, great range of meat dishes, live jazz every night. Cellar of local wines.
Del Carmen, Washington Barbot 283, T30460. Open from breakfast to dinner, fantastic views, great for evening drink. Recommended.
Lo de Renata, Flores 227, T31061. Open daily. Popular for its lunchtime buffet of meats and salads.
Mesón de la Plaza, Vasconcellos 153, T24807. 140-year old house with a leafy courtyard, elegant dining, good traditional food.

TTT **Viejo Barrio (VB)**, Vasconcellos 169, T25399. Closed Wed. Very good for home-made pastas and fish, renowned live shows.

TTT **Yacht Club** (Puerto de Yates), T31354. Ideal at sunset with wonderful view of the bay. Good fish.

TT **La Amistad**, 18 de Julio 448. Good local grill.

TT **La Bodeguita**, Del Comercio 167, T25329. Tue-Sun evenings and Sat-Sun lunch. Its terrace on the river is the main attraction of this lively pizza place that serves also good *chivitos* and pasta.

TT **Club Colonia**, Gen Flores 382, T22189. Good value, frequented by locals.

TT **El Drugstore**, Portugal 174, T25241. Hip, fusion food: Latin American, European, Japanese, good, creative varied menu, good salads and fresh vegetables. Music and show.

TT **Lobo**, Del Comercio y De la Playa, T29245. Modern interior, good range of salads, pastas and meat. Live music at weekends.

TT **Mercosur**, Flores y Ituzaingó, T24200. Popular, varied dishes. Also café serving homemade cakes.

TT **Parrillada El Portón**, Gral Flores 333, T25318. Best parrillada in town. Small, relatively smart, good atmosphere. House speciality is offal.

TT **Pulpería de los Faroles**, Misiones de los Tapes 101, T30271. Very inviting tables (candlelit at night) on the cobbled streets for a varied menú that includes tasty salads, seafood and local wines.

TT **El Torreón**, end of Av Gen Flores, T31524. One of the best places to enjoy a sunset meal with views of the river. Also a café serving toasties and cakes.

TT-T **El Asador**, Ituzaingó 168. Good *parrillada* and pasta, nice atmosphere, value for money.

Arcoiris, Av Gral Flores at Plaza 25 de Agosto. Very good ice cream.

Mercedes *p1535*

The following serve good food: **La Brasa**, Artigas 426. **Círculo Policial**, C 25 de Mayo. **El Emporio de los Panchos**, Roosevelt 711.

Fray Bentos *p1536*

TT **Los Paraísos**, Inglaterra y Brasil, T27996. Meat and pasta dishes.

Several other cafés and pizzerías on 18 de Julio near Plaza Constitución.

Paysandú *p1536, map p1537*

TT **Artemio**, 18 de Julio 1248. Simple, reputation for serving "best food in town"

TT **Los Tres Pinos**, Av España 1474. *Parrillada*, very good.

Salto *p1537*

TT **La Caldera**, Uruguay 221, T24648. Good *parrillada*, also seafood, closed Mon lunchtime.

TT **Pizzería La Farola**, Brasil 895 esq Soca.

TT-T **La Casa de Llamas**, Chiazzaro 20. Pasta.

T **Club de Uruguay**, Uruguay 754. Breakfast and good-value meals.

Trouville, Uruguay 702. Pizzería.

Shopping

Colonia del Sacramento *p1533, map p1532*

There's a large artist community, Uruguayan and international, with good galleries across town. **El Almacén**, Real 150, creative gifts. Decorative pottery by local artist Eduardo Acosta at **Paseo del Sol**, Del Comercio 158. **Oveja Negra**, De la Playa 114, recommended for woollen and leather clothes. Leather shops on C Santa Rita, next to Yacht Club. **Afro**, 18 de Julio 246, *candombe* culture items from local black community, percussion lessons. **Colonia Shopping**, Av Roosevelt 458, shopping mall on main road out of town (east) selling international fashion brands.

Activities and tours

Colonia del Sacramento *p1533, map p1532*

City tours available with **Destino Viajes**, General Flores 341, T25343, destinoviajes@adinet.com.uy, or or guided tours with **Sacramento Tour**, Av Flores y Rivera, T23148, sacratur@adinet.com.uy. **Asociación Guías de Colonia**, T22309/22796, asociacionguiascolonia@gmail.com, organizes walking tours (1 hr, US$5) in the Barrio Histórico, daily 1100 and 1500 from tourist office next to Old Gate.

Paysandú *p1536, map p1537*

Bodega Leonardo Falcone, Av Wilson Aldunate y Young, T072-27718, www.bodegaleonardofalcone.com.uy. Winery tours at one of Uruguay's finest wine makers.

Transport

Nueva Helvecia (Colonia Suiza) *p1533*

Bus **Montevideo-Colonia Suiza**, frequent, with **COT**, 2-2½ hrs, US$6.50; **Turil**, goes to Colonia Suiza and Valdense; to **Colonia del Sacramento**, frequent, 1 hr, US$3.50. Local services between Colonia Valdense and Nueva Helvecia connect with Montevideo/Colonia del Sacramento buses.

Colonia del Sacramento *p1533, map p1532*

Air Flights to Aeroparque, **Buenos Aires**, most days, generally quicker than hydrofoil. The airport is 17 km out of town along Route 1; for taxi to Colonia, buy ticket in building next to arrivals, US$10.

Road Roadworks on Route 1 west of Montevideo may delay traffic. There are plenty of filling stations. If driving north to Paysandú and Salto, especially on Route 3, fill up with fuel and drinking water at every opportunity, stations are few and far between. From Colonia to Punta del Este by passing Montevideo: take Ruta 11 at Ecilda Paullier, passing through San José de Mayo, Santa Lucía and Canelones, joining the Interbalnearia at Km 46.

Bus All leave from bus terminal between the ferry port and the petrol station (free luggage lockers, ATM, exchange, café and internet). To **Montevideo**, several services daily, 2¼-2¾ hrs, **COT**, T23121, **Chadre** and **Turil**, T25246, US$9. **Turil** to Col Valdense, US$3. **Chadre** to Conchillas, US$2.50. To **Carmelo**, 1½ hrs, **Chadre** and **Berrutti**, US$4. **Chadre** to Mercedes, US$9, Fray Bentos, US$11, Paysandú, US$17 and Salto, 8 hrs, US$23. **Turil** to Tacuarembó, US$29, Rivera, US$34, and Artigas, US$39. **Nossar**, T22934, to Durazno, US$10.

Ferry Book in advance for all sailings in summer. A new terminal opened in 2009. To **Buenos Aires**: from 5 crossings daily, with **Buquebus** (T22975), cars carried, fares and schedules given under Montevideo, Transport. **Colonia Express**, office at the port, T29677, www.colonia express.com, makes 2-3 crossings a day between Colonia and **Buenos Aires** (50 min) in fast boats (no vehicles carried) with bus connections to/from Montevideo, Punta del Este and Uruguayan towns: US$36 Buenos Aires to Colonia (much cheaper if bought in advance online). **Líneas Delta** run a daily bus/boat service, 1245 (Sat-Sun 1400), to Tigre, US$28.

Note Passports must be stamped and Argentine departure tax paid even if only visiting Colonia for 1 day.

Taxi A Méndez y Gral Flores, T22920; Av Flores y Suárez (on plaza), T22556.

Carmelo *p1534*

Bus To **Montevideo**, US$12, **Intertur**, **Chadre** and **Sabelín**. To **Fray Bentos**, **Salto**, with **Chadre** from main plaza 0655, 1540. To **Colonia**, see above. To **Argentina**: via Tigre, across the Paraná delta, an interesting bus/boat ride past innumerable islands: **Cacciola** 2 a day; office in Carmelo, Wilson Ferreira 263, T542 7551, www.cacciolaviajes.com (the Uruguayan company on this route is **Laderban**), see Montevideo page 1529.

Mercedes *p1535*

Bus To **Paysandú**, with **Sabelín**, in bus terminal, T3937, 1½ hrs, US$6; also **Chadre** on the Montevideo-Bella Unión route. To **Montevideo**, US$15, 3½ hrs, **CUT**, Artigas (on plaza, also to **Argentina**), **Agencia Central** and **Sabelín**.

Fray Bentos *p1536*

Bus Terminal at 18 de Julio y Blanes. To/from **Montevideo**, **CUT**, 4 hrs, 5 a day, US$16, also **Agencia Central**. To **Mercedes**, **ETA**, US$1.50, 5 daily.

Crossing to Argentina: Fray Bentos *p1536*

Bus This border has been closed on and off since 2007. To **Buenos Aires**, 6 hrs, US$29.

Paysandú *p1536, map p1537*

Bus Can be hard to get a seat on buses going north. Terminal at Zorilla y Artigas, T23225. To/from **Montevideo**, US$39 (**Núñez, Copay**, T22094, 4 a day), 5-6 hrs, also **Chadre**, **COT** and **Agencia Central**. To **Salto**, **Alonso**, T24318, US$6.50, 3 a day. To **Rivera**, US$11, **Copay**, 0400, 1700 Mon-Sat (Sun 1700 only). To **Fray Bentos**, 2 a day, 2 hrs direct, US$5. To **Colonia** by **Chadre**, 0750, 1750, 4 hrs, US$17.

Crossing to Argentina: Paysandú *p1537*

Bus To **Colón** and **Concepción del Uruguay**, 3 a day (**Copay** 0815, 1645, **Paccot** 1545, 2030), on Sun **Copay** 1645, US$3.75 to Colón, US$4 to Concepción.

Salto *p1537*

Bus Terminal 15 blocks east of centre at Batlle y Blandengues, café, shopping centre, *casa de cambio*. Take taxi to centre. To/from **Montevideo**, 6-7¾ hrs, US$25 (**Norteño, Núñez, Agencia Central** and **Chadre**). **Chadre** to **Termas del Arapey**, 1½ hrs, daily, US$3.50. **Paysandú** US$6.50, 1¾ hrs, 6 a day. To **Rivera**, US$20. To **Bella Unión**, 2 hrs, US$7.50, 2 a day. To **Colonia**, 0555, 1555, 8 hrs, US$23; to **Fray Bentos**, same times, US$11.50.

Crossing to Argentina: Salto *p1537*

Bus To **Concordia**, **Chadre** (0800, 1400, return 1200, 1800) and **Flecha Bus**, 2 a day each, not Sun, US$7.50. To **Buenos Aires**, US$23, **Flecha Bus**.

Ferry To **Concordia, Sanchristobal/Río Lago** joint service, Mon-Fri 5 daily, Sat 3 daily, no service on Sun, US$4, depart port on C Brasil, 15 mins; immigration either side of river, quick and easy.

Artigas *p1538*

Bus To **Salto**, 225 km, Oribe 279, US$10.50. **Turil** and others from **Montevideo** via Durazno, Paso de los Toros and Tacuarembó, US$31.50.

Directory

Colonia del Sacramento *p1533, map p1532*

Banks Banks open afternoon only. Most museums and restaurants accept Argentine pesos or US$, but rarely euros. **HSBC**, De Portugal 183 (Barrio Histórico), Mon-Fri 1300-1700. **Cambio Dromer**, Flores 350, T22070, Mon-Fri 0900-2000, Sat 0900-1800, Sun 1000-1300. **Cambio Colonia** and **Western Union**, Av Flores y Lavalleja, T25032. **Car hire** In bus terminal: **Avis**, T29842, US$100 per day, **Hertz**, T29851, US$90 per day. **Thrifty** by port, also at Flores 172, T22939, where there are bicycles too (US$3per hr), scooters (US$7 per hr) and golf buggies (US$15 per hr) for hire, recommended as traffic is slow and easy to navigate. **Consulates** **Argentine Consulate and Cultural Centre**, Flores 209, T22093, open weekdays 1300-1800. **Internet** Av Flores 172, US$1 per hr, or Av Flores 234, US$1.25 per hr. Bus terminal, US$2.70 per hr. **Post offices** On main plaza. **Telephones** Telecentro Sacramento, Av Flores 172.

Carmelo *p1534*

Banks **Banco de la República**, Zorilla 361, for exchange and ATM.

Mercedes *p1535*

Banks **Cambio Fagalde**, Giménez 709. **Banco Comercial** on Colón (just off plaza) and **Banco de la República**, on plaza.

Fray Bentos *p1536*

Banks For exchange try **Cambio Nelson**, 18 de Julio y Roberto Young, T20409.

Paysandú *p1536, map p1537*

Banks *Casas de cambio* on 18 de Julio: **Cambio Fagalde**, No 1004; **Cambio Bacacay**, No 1008; change TCs, Sat 0830-1230. **Banco de la República**, 18 de Julio y Montevideo. **Consulates** **Argentina**, Gómez 1034, T22253, Mon-Fri 1300-1800. **Internet** **paysandu.com**, 18 de Julio 1250, plaza, US$2 per hr. **Post offices** Montevideo y 18 de Julio. **Telephones** **Antel**, Montevideo 875, T22100.

Salto *p1537*

Banks **Banco Comercial** and **Banco de la República**, both on Uruguay. *casas de cambio* on Uruguay. **Car hire** **Maxicar**, Paraguay 764, T35554, 099-435454, maxirentsalto@hotmail.com. 24 hrs, cars allowed to travel to Argentina and Brazil. **Consulates** **Argentina**, Artigas 1162, T32931, Mon-Fri 0900- 1400. **Post offices** Treinta y Tres y Artigas. **Scooter hire** Agraciada 2019, T29967.

Eastern Uruguay

Resorts line the coast from Montevideo to Punta del Este, the ultimate magnet for summer holidaymakers, especially from Argentina. Out of season, it is quieter and you can have the beaches to yourself, which is pretty much the case the closer you get to Brazil year round. Inland are cattle ranches, some of which welcome visitors, and hills with expansive views.

East from Montevideo

This beautiful coast consists of an endless succession of small bays, beaches and promontories, set among hills and woods. The beach season is from December to the end of February. An excellent four-lane highway leads to Punta del Este and Rocha, and a good two-lane highway to Chuy. This route will give you a chance to see the most important Uruguayan beach resorts, as well as Parque Nacional Santa Teresa and other natural attractions. If driving there are three tolls each way (about US$2), but this route is the easiest and the most comfortable in Uruguay with sufficient service stations along the way.

Piriápolis → *Phone code: 043. Colour map 8, B6. Population: 6,000.*

This resort set among hills, 101 km from Montevideo, is laid out with an abundance of shady trees, and the district is rich in pine, eucalyptus and acacia woods. It has a good beach, a yacht harbour, a country club, a motor-racing track (street circuit) and is particularly popular with Argentines. It was, in fact, founded in the 1890s as a bathing resort for residents of Buenos Aires. Next to the marina is a small cable car (with seats for two) to the top of **Cerro San Antonio** ⓘ *US$4, 10 mins ride, free car park and toilets at lower station*. Magnificent views of Piriápolis and beaches, several restaurants. Recommended, but be careful when disembarking. North of the centre, at **Punta de Playa Colorada**, is a marine rescue centre ⓘ *sos-faunamarina@adinet.com.uy*, that looks after injured sea creatures before releasing them to the wild. **Tourist office**, Asociación de Turismo ⓘ *Paseo de la Pasiva, Rambla de los Argentinos, summer 0900-2400, winter 1000-1800, T25055/22560.*

About 6 km north on the R37 is **Cerro Pan de Azúcar** (Sugar Loaf Hill) ⓘ *getting there: take bus 'Cerro Pan de Azúcar' and get off after 6 km*, crowned by a tall cross with a circular stairway inside, fine coastal views. There is only a steep path, marked by red arrows, up to the cross. Just north of Piriápolis R 37 passes the La Cascada Municipal park (open all year) which contains the house of Francisco Piria, the founder of the resort, **Museo Castillo de Piria** ⓘ *open daily in summer, weekends in winter, 1000-2100*. About 4 km beyond Cerro Pan de Azúcar is the village of Pan de Azúcar, which has a **Museo al Aire Libre de Pintura** where the walls of the buildings have been decorated by Uruguayan and Argentine painters, designers and writers with humorous and tango themes (direct bus every hour from Piriápolis).

Portezuelo and Punta Ballena

R93 runs between the coast and the Laguna del Sauce to Portezuelo, which has good beaches. The **Arboreto Lussich** ⓘ *T78077, 1030-1630*, on the west slope of the Sierra de la Ballena (north of R93) contains a unique set of native and exotic trees. There are footpaths, or you can drive through; two *miradores*; worth a visit. From Portezuelo drive north towards the R9 by way of the R12 which then continues, unpaved, to Minas. Just off R12 is **El Tambo Lapataia** ⓘ *1 km east from Solanas, then 4 km north, T042-220000, www.lapataiapuntadeleste.com*, a dairy farm open to the public, selling ice cream, *dulce de leche*, homemade pizzas and pastas, with an international jazz festival in January.

At Punta Ballena there is a wide crescent beach, calm water and very clean sand. The place is a residential resort but is still quiet. At the top of Punta Ballena there is a panoramic road 2½ km long with remarkable views of the coast. **Casa Pueblo**, the house and gallery of Uruguayan artist Carlos Páez Vilaro, is built in a Spanish-Moroccan style on a cliff over the sea; the gallery can be visited (US$6), there are paintings, collages and ceramics on display, and for sale; open all year. Walk downhill towards the sea for a good view of the house.

Maldonado → *Phone code: 042. Colour map 8, B6. Population: 55,000.*

The capital of Maldonado Department, 140 km E of Montevideo, is a peaceful town, sacked by the British in 1806. It has many colonial remains and the historic centre was restored in 2005. It is also a dormitory suburb of Punta del Este. Worth seeing is the **El Vigia watch tower** ⓘ *Gorriti y Pérez del Puerto*; the Cathedral (started 1801, completed 1895), on Plaza San Fernando; the windmill; the **Cuartel de Dragones exhibition centre** ⓘ *Pérez del Puerto y 18 de Julio, by Plaza San Fernando*, and the **Cachimba del Rey** ⓘ *on the continuation of 3 de Febrero, almost Artigas*, an old well – legend claims that those who drink from it will never leave Maldonado. **Museo Mazzoni** ⓘ *Ituzaingó 687, T221107, Tue1600-2030, Wed-Sat 1030-2130, Sun 1300-2100*, has regional items, indigenous, Spanish, Portuguese and English. **Museo de Arte Americano** ⓘ *José Dodera 648 y Treinta y Tres, T22276, 2000-2200, Dec and Feb Fri-Sun only (closed winter)*, a private museum of national and international art, interesting. **Tourist office** ⓘ *Dirección General de Turismo, Edificio Municipal, T231773, www.maldonado.gub.uy*.

Punta del Este → *Phone code: 042. Colour map 8, B6.*

About 7 km from Maldonado and 139 km from Montevideo (a little less by dual carriageway), facing the bay on one side and the open waters of the Atlantic on the other, lies the largest and best known of the resorts, **Punta del Este**, which is particularly popular among Argentines and Brazilians. The narrow peninsula of Punta del Este has been entirely built over. On the land side, the city is flanked by large planted forests of eucalyptus, pine and mimosa. Two blocks from the sea, at the tip of the peninsula, is the historic monument of El Faro (lighthouse); in this part of the city

Punta del Este

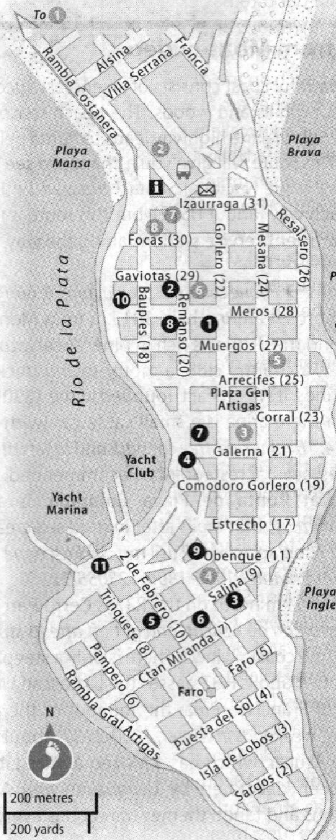

Sleeping

1 Conrad
2 Gaudi
3 Iberia
4 Palace
5 Punta del Este Hostel
6 Remanso
7 Tánger
8 Youth hostel 1949

Eating

1 Cantón Chino
2 El Ciclista
3 Gure-etxe
4 Isidora
5 Juana Enea
6 Lo de Charlie
7 Lo de Tere
8 Los Caracoles
9 Viejo Marino
10 Virazón
11 Yatch Club Uruguayo

no building may exceed its height. On the ocean side of the peninsula, at the end of Calle 25 (Arrecifes), is a shrine to the first mass said by the Conquistadores on this coast, 2 February 1515. Three blocks from the shrine is Plaza General Artigas, which has a *feria artesanal* (handicraft market); along its side runs Avenida Gorlero, the main street. There are two casinos, a golf course, and many beautiful holiday houses. **Museo Ralli of Contemporary Latin American Art** ⓘ *Curupay y Los Arachanes, Barrio Beverly Hills, T483476, Tue-Sun 1700-2100 in Jan-Feb, Sat-Sun 1400-1800 rest of year, free.* Worth a visit but a car is needed.

Punta del Este has excellent bathing **beaches**, the calm *playa mansa* on the bay side, the rough *playa brava* on the ocean side. There are some small beaches hemmed in by rocks on this side of the peninsula, but most people go to where the extensive *playa brava* starts. Papa Charlie beach on the Atlantic (Parada 13) is preferred by families with small children as it is safe. Quieter beaches are at La Barra and beyond.

There is an excellent yacht marina, yacht and fishing clubs. There is good fishing both at sea and in three nearby lakes and the Río Maldonado. **Tourist information** ⓘ *Liga de Fomento, Parada 1, T446519, open summer 0900-2400, winter 1000-1800; in bus station T494042; at Parada 24, Playa Las Delicias (Mansa side), T230050;* and at airports. See the websites www.puntaweb.com, www.puntadeleste.com and www.vivapunta.com.

Isla de Gorriti, visited by explorers including Solís, Magellan and Drake, was heavily fortified by the Spanish in the 1760's to keep the Portuguese out. The island, densely wooded and with superb beaches, is an ideal spot for campers (boats from 0900-1700, return 1015-1815, US$12.70, T446166; *Don Quico*, also does fishing trips, T448945). On **Isla de Lobos**, which is a government reserve within sight of the town, there is a huge sea-lion colony; excursions, US$30-50. Ticket should be booked in advance (T441716). See also Activities and tours, below.

Beaches east of Punta del Este

Between the Peninsula and the mouth of the Río Maldonado, a road runs along the coast, passing luxurious houses, dunes and pines. Some of the most renowned architects of Uruguay and Argentina design houses here. The river is crossed by a unique undulating bridge, like a shallow M, to **La Barra**, a fashionable place, especially for summer nightlife, with beaches, art galleries, bars and restaurants (take a bus from Punta del Este terminal or taxi US$20). The **Museo del Mar Sirenamis** ⓘ *1 km off the coast road, watch for signs, T771817, summer daily 1030-2000 winter 1100-1700, US$5,* has an excellent collection on the subject of the sea, its life and history and on the first beach resorts (it claims to have 5,000 exhibits). The coast road climbs a headland here before descending to the beaches further north, Montoya and **Manantiales** (reached by Condesa bus; taxi US$28). Some 30 km from Punta del Este is the fishing village of **Faro José Ignacio** with a **lighthouse** ⓘ *summer daily 1100-2030, winter 1100-1330, 1430-1830, US$0.75*, a beach club and other new developments, now the road is paved. Coastal R10 runs some way east of José Ignacio, but there is no through connection to La Paloma as a new bridge across the mouth of the Lago Garzón is not operational. A car ferry sometimes runs; rowing boats will take pedestrians and cyclists across.

La Paloma and around → *Phone code: 0479. Colour map 8, B6. Population: 5,000.*

Protected by an island and a sandspit, this is a good port for yachts. The surrounding scenery is attractive, with extensive wetlands nearby. You can walk for miles along the beach. The pace is more relaxed than Punta del Este. **Tourist office** ⓘ *Av Solari y C Paloma at entrance to town, T96088*, very helpful. For the Department of Rocha see www.turismorocha.gub.uy.

Coastal R10 runs to Aguas Dulces (regular bus services along this route). About 10 km from La Paloma is **La Pedrera**, a beautiful village with sandy beaches. Beyond La Pedrera the road runs near pleasant fishing villages which are rapidly being developed with holiday homes, for example **Barra de Valizas**, 50 minutes north. At **Cabo Polonio** (permanent population 80), visits to the islands of Castillos and Wolf can be arranged to see sea lions and penguins. It has two great beaches: the north beach is more rugged, while the south is tamer by comparison. Both have lifeguards on duty (though their zone of protection only covers a tiny portion of the kilometres and kilometres of beach). The village is part of a nature reserve. This limits the number of people who are allowed to stay there since the number of lodgings is limited and camping is strictly forbidden (if you arrive with a tent, it may be confiscated). During January or February (and especially during Carnival), you **have** to reserve a room in one of the few posadas or hotels, or better yet, rent a house (see Sleeping, below). From Km 264 on the main road all-terrain vehicles run 8 km across the dunes to the village (several companies, around US$5). Day visitors must leave just after sundown (see Transport, below). Ask locally in Valizas about walking there, 3-4 hours via the north beach (very interesting, but hot, unless you go early). There are also pine woods with paths leading to the beach or village.

The **Monte de Ombúes** ⓘ *open in summer months, from Jan, free, basic restaurant with honest prices* is a wood containing a few *ombú* trees (Phytolacca dioica – the national tree), *coronilla* (Scutia buxifolia) and *canelón* (Rapanea laetevirens). It has a small circuit to follow and a good hide for birdwatching. To reach the woods from Km 264, go 2 km north along R10 to the bridge. Here take a boat with guide, 30 minutes along the river (*Monte Grande* recommended as they visit both sides of the river, montegrande@adinet.com.uy). You can also walk from Km 264 across the fields, but it's along way and the last 150 m are through thick brush. The bridge is 16 km from Castillos on R9 (see next paragraph): turn onto R16 towards Aguas Dulces, just before which you turn southwest onto R10.

From **Aguas Dulces** the road runs inland to the town of **Castillos** (easy bus connections to Chuy), where it rejoins R9. A tourist office at Aguas Dulces/Castillos crossroads on R9 has details on hotels.

Punta del Diablo

At Km 298 there is a turn to a fishing village in dramatic surroundings, again with fine beaches. Punta del Diablo is very rustic, popular with young people in high season, but from April to November the solitude and the dramatically lower prices make it a wonderful getaway for couples or families. Increased popularity has brought more lodging and services year round, although off-season activity is still extremely low compared to summer. **Note** there is no ATM in Punta del Diablo so bring enough cash with you. The nearest ATM is in Chuy. See www.portaldeldiablo.com.

Parque Nacional Santa Teresa

ⓘ *100 km from Rocha, 308 km from Montevideo, open 0700-1900 to day visitors (open 24 hrs for campers).*

This park has curving, palm-lined avenues and plantations of many exotic trees. It also contains botanical gardens, fresh-water pools for bathing and beaches which stretch for many kilometres (the surf is too rough for swimming). It is the site of the impressive colonial fortress of Santa Teresa, begun by the Portuguese in 1762 and seized by the Spanish in 1793. The fortress houses a **museum** of artefacts from the wars of independence ⓘ *Tue-Sun 0900-1900 (winter 1000-1800), US$0.50*; there is a restaurant opposite, *La Posada del Viajero* (recommended). On the inland side of Route 9, the strange and gloomy Laguna Negra and the marshes of the Bañado de Santa Teresa support large numbers of wild birds. A road encircles the fortress; it's possible to drive or walk around even after closing. From there is a good view of Laguna Negra.

There are countless campsites (open all year), and a few cottages to let in the summer (usually snapped up quickly). At the *capatacia*, or administrative headquarters, campers pay US$4 pp per night. Here there are also a small supermarket, greengrocer, butcher, bakery, medical clinic, petrol station, auto mechanic, post and telephone offices, and the *Club Santa Teresa*, where drinks and meals are available, but expensive. Practically every amenity is closed off-season. The bathing resort of **La Coronilla** is 10 km north of Santa Teresa, 20 south of Chuy; it has several hotels and restaurants, most closed in winter (tourist information T098-169204). Montevideo-Chuy buses stop at La Coronilla.

Chuy → *Phone code: 0474. Colour map 7, inset. Population: 10,400. For details of Chuí in Brazil see page 523.* At Chuy, 340 km from Montevideo, the Brazilian frontier runs along the main street, Avenida Internacional, which is called Avenida Brasil in Uruguay and Avenida Uruguaí in Brasil. The Uruguayan side has more services, including supermarkets, duty-free shops and a casino.

On the Uruguyan side, on a promontory overlooking Laguna Merín and the gaúcho landscape of southern Brazil, stands the restored fortress of **San Miguel** ⓘ *US$0.75, bus from Chuy US$1.50, Rutas del Sol buses from Montevideo go here after passing through Chuy*, dating from 1734 and surrounded by a moat. It is set above a 1500-ha wetland park, which is good for birdwatching and is 10 km north of Chuy along Route 19 which is the border. There is a small museum of *criollo* and *indígena* culture, displaying, among other artefacts, old carriages and presses. Not always open in low season. A fine walk from here is 2 km to the Cerro Picudo. The path starts behind the museum, very apparent. Tours (US$10 from Chuy) end for the season after 31 March.

Border with Brazil

Uruguayan passport control is 2½ km before the border on Ruta 9 into Chuy, US$2 by taxi, 20 minutes' walk, or take a town bus; officials friendly and cooperative. Ministry of Tourism kiosk here is helpful, especially for motorists, T4599. Tourists may freely cross the border in either direction as long as they do not go beyond either country's border post. Taking a car into Brazil is no problem if the car is not registered in Brazil or Uruguay. (Uruguayan rental cars are not allowed out of the country. Although you can freely drive between Chuy and Chuí, if you break down/have an accident on the Brazilian side, car rental insurance will not cover it: park in Chuy, even if only one metre from Brazil, and walk.) From the border post, Ruta 9 bypasses the town, becoming BR-471 on the Brazilian side, leading to Brazilian immigration, also outside town. The Brazilian consulate is at Tito Fernández 147 esq Samuel Priliac, T2049, Chuy. For buses to Brazilian destinations, go to the rodoviária in Chuí (details in the Brazil chapter, page 523). The bus companies that run from Chuy into Brazil ask for passports – make sure you get yours back before boarding the bus.

Entering Uruguay You need a Brazilian exit stamp and a Uruguayan entry stamp (unless visiting only Chuí), otherwise you'll be turned back at customs or other official posts. Those requiring a visa will be charged around US$80 depending on the country.

East from Montevideo listings

For Sleeping and Eating price codes and other relevant information, see Essentials, pages 38-40.

Sleeping

Piriápolis *p1545*

Many hotels along the seafront, most close end-Feb to mid-Dec. Book in advance in high season. Many others than those listed here.

A Argentino, Rambla de los Argentinos y Armenia, T22791, www.argentinohotel.com.uy. A fine hotel and landmark designed by Piria with casino, 2 restaurants, medicinal springs, sauna and good facilities for children.

A Centro, Sanabria 931, T/F22516. With breakfast, cafeteria, helpful about local sites, very near beach.

A Luján, Sanabria 939, T22216. Simple rooms, family run, some rooms have balconies, homeopathist on top floor. Not great value.

A-B Rivadavia, Rambla de los Argentinos y Trápani, T22532, www.hotelrivadavia.com. Cable TV, mini-bar, open all year (much cheaper in winter).

E pp **Hostel Piriápolis**, Simón del Pino 1136 y Tucumán, T20394, www.hostelpiriapolis.com. Rooms for 2-4 (open all year), private rooms **C**, 240 beds, non-HI members pay more, hot showers, cooking facilities, student cards accepted.

Camping Piriápolis, T23275, on the slope of Cerro del Toro, doubles in bungalows, and tents. Site at Misiones y Niza, just behind bus station, poor showers, smelly toilets, US$5.60.

Portezuelo and Punta Ballena *p1545*

LL-L Casa Pueblo, T578611, www.clubhotel.com.ar. Highly recommended hotel and apartments, restaurant, spa and, lower down the hill, a *parrillada*.

LL-L Hotel-Art Las Cumbres, Ruta 12 Km 3.9, 4 km inland, T578689, www.cumbres.com.uy. Some rooms **AL** out of season, themed as an artist's house-studio, on a wooded hill with great views over Laguna del Sauce and the coast, pool, restaurant and tea room (expensive but popular).

Campsite Punta Ballena, Km 120, Parada 45, T042-578902, www.campinginternacional puntaballena.com. US$7 pp per night, many facilities, very clean.

Maldonado *p1546*

Hotel accommodation is scarce in summer; cheaper than Punta del Este, but you will have to commute to the beach. Basic 1-2 star places (**B-E**), open all year, include: **Catedral**, Florida 830 casi 18 de Julio, T242513, hotelcatedral@adinet.com.uy, central, and **A-B Colonial**, 18 de Julio 841 y Florida, T223346, www.elhotelcolonial.com.

B Hospedaje Isla de Gorriti, Michelini 884, T245218. Nice courtyard. Recommended.

E Celta, Ituzaingó 839, T/F230139. Helpful, Irish owner, No 7 bus stop outside.

Camping Parque El Placer, T270034, free.

Punta del Este *p1546*

Note Streets on the peninsula have names and numbers; lowest numbers at the tip. Hotels are plentiful but expensive: we list recommended ones only. Rates in the few hotels still open after the end of Mar are often halved. Visitors without a car have to take a hotel on the peninsula, unless they want to spend a fortune on taxis.

On the peninsula

LL Conrad Hotel y Casino, Parada 4, Playa Mansa, T491111, www.conrad.com.uy. Luxurious hotel with spa, concerts and events, wonderful views. Book in advance in high season.

LL-A Remanso, C 20 y 28, T447412, www.hotelremanso.com.uy. Some rooms **A** low season, comfortable, businesslike, pool, safe, open all year (also suites in **LL** range). Recommended.

L Iberia, C 24, No 685, T440405, iberiapunta@hotmail.com. **A** out of season, breakfast included, open all year, garage opposite.

AL-A Palace, Av Gorlero esq 11, T229596, on www.reservas.net click on Punta del Este (closed in winter). 3-star. Breakfast only (expensive restaurant, *La Stampa*, in the hotel), well kept.

AL-B Tánger, C 31 entre 18 y 20, T441333, www.hoteltanger.com. Open all year, a/c, safe, disabled access, 2 pools.

A-C Gaudi, C Risso, parada 1, by bus terminal, T494116, www.hotelgaudi.com.uy. 2-star. Good, a/c, convenient, safe, fridge, WiFi, bar, open all year.

C pp **Alicia Lorenzo**, Parada 5, T480781. Bed and breakfast room with bath, barbecue.

D pp **Youth hostel 1949**, C 30 y 18, T440719, www.1949hostel.com. 100 m from bus station. Small, **A** in double (in low season only, **C**), kitchen, bar, TV and DVD, close to beaches.

D-E pp **Punta del Este Hostel**, C 25 No 544 y 24, T441632, www.puntadelestehostel.com. US$17-25 in dorm (price depends on season; no doubles), includes breakfast, lockers, central, basic.

Beaches east of Punta del Este *p1547*

San Rafael (Parada 12)

LL-A San Marcos, Av Mar del Plata 191, T482 251, www.hotelsanmarcos.com. Pool (covered in winter), prices fall to **AL-B** in mid and low season, restaurant, bicycle hire, free internet, very pleasant.

L San Rafael, Lorenzo Batlle y Pacheco, Parada 11 Brava, T482161, www.hotelsan rafael.com.uy. Large hotel, open all year, suites cost **LL** in high season, a/c, heating, safe, TV, spa.

AL La Capilla, Viña del Mar y Valparaíso, behind San Marcos, T484059, www.lacapilla.com.uy. Open all year (doubles **LL** at Christmas), includes breakfast, kitchenette in some rooms, safes in rooms, gardens, pool, good, recently upgraded.

La Barra

LL Hostal de la Barra, Ruta 10, Km 161.300, T771521, www.hostaldelabarra.net. A small hotel, not a hostel, with sea view, forest view

and loft rooms, open all year, neat, Christmas, Carnival and Semana Santa require 7 or 4-night minimum stays.
LL La Ballenera Bed and Breakfast, Km 162, just off coast road ½ km east of the hilly promontory, behind Playa Montoya, T771079, www.laballenera.com. Half price in low season, big old wooden mansion, lovely breakfast terrace, kitchen and internet.
LL La Posta del Cangrejo, hotel/restaurant, Ruta 10 Km 160, T770021, www.lapostadel cangrejo.com. Nice location, smart, if a bit old. Recommended.
AL Mantra, Ruta 10, Parada 48, T771000, www.mantraresort.com. Very good, but you will need a car to move around. Open all year, great pool, casino, restaurants, concerts, own cinema and wine bar. Recommended.
D-E pp **Backpacker de La Barra**, C 9, No 2306, ½ km off main road, T772272, www.backpackerdelabarra.com. Closed in low season (except if large group), youth hostel style, price depends on dates and class of room, 6 night package over New Year, café and restaurant, internet, laundry.
Camping Camping San Rafael, www.campingsanrafael.com.uy. Good facilities, US$12, bus 5 from Maldonado.

Faro José Ignacio

LL Posada del Faro, C de la Bahía y Timonel, T0486-2110, www.posadadelfaro.com. Exclusive hotel overlooking the sea, 12 rooms in 4 standards, internet, pool, bar, restaurant, often quoted as the best of the new developments.

Manantiales

Resorts include: **LL Las Dunas**, Ruta 10, Km 163, T771211, hlasdunas@adinet.com.uy, 5-star, opulent (AL in low season), and **LL Las Olas**, Ruta 10, Km 162.5, T770466, www.lasolasresort.com.uy, 4-star.
B El Viajero Manantiales, Ruta 10, Km 164, T774427, www.manantialeshostel.com. **D** in dorm. HI affiliated. Swimming pool, kitchen, bikes and surfboards for rent, lockers, DVDs, laundry, Wi-Fi, bar, open Nov to Apr.

La Paloma *p1547*

AL Palma de Mallorca, on Playa La Aguada, in nearby La Aguada, luxury hotel, T6739, www.hotelpalmademallorca.com. Right on the ocean. Discounts for longer stays, heated pool.
A Bahía, Av del Navío s/n, entre Solari y Del Sol, T6029, www.elbahia.com.uy. Breakfast, rooms for 2-4, clean and simple, quite old-fashioned, TV, Wi-Fi, laundry.
A Embeleco, Virgen y Sol, T6108. Breakfast, half price in winter, welcoming. One block from the beach.
E-F pp **Reserva Ecológica La Laguna**, 2 km north of Aguas Dulces, T0475-2118/099-602410, http://lalagunauruguay.spaces.live.com/. Rustic cabins on the shore a lake, price depends on number of occupants, also day rates (US$55 adults, US$35 children), full and half-board available, close to beach, horse riding, trekking, sailing, hydrobikes, meditation. Always phone in advance for directions and reservation.
Youth hostels **E** pp **Altena 5000** at Parque Andresito, T6396, www.lapalomahostel.com. 50 beds, HI discounts, clean, friendly, good meals, kitchen, open all year. Also **D-E** pp **Ibirapita**, Av Paloma s/n, 250 m from bus station, 200 m from beach, T9303, www.hostelibirapita.com. Cheaper in mixed dorm and for HI members, doubles **B-C**. Buffet breakfast, Wi-Fi, surf boards, bicycles.
Camping In **Parque Andresito**, T6081. Overpriced, thatched *cabañas* for rent, US$50 per day with maid and kitchen facilities, sleep 4-6. *Grill del Camping* for *parrillas*. **La Aguada**, T6239, 1 km east of town, 300 m from beach, US$5-6. Good, each site with BBQ, tap, sink, water and electricity.

Northeast of La Paloma

At **Cabo Polonio** you cannot camp. There are posadas, some listed below, or you can rent a house; see **www.cabopolonio.com** or **www.portaldelcabo.com.uy** for all options. Water is drawn from wells (*cachimba*) and there is no electricity (some houses have generators, some gas lamps, otherwise buy candles). There are 4 shops for supplies, largest is **El Templao**. At **Aguas Dulces** there are various places to stay and lots of cheap cabins for rent.
AL Mariemar, Cabo Polonio, T0470-5164, 099-875260, mariemar@cabopolonio.com. Nice owners, own electricity generator, hot water, with breakfast, restaurant, open all year. Recommended.

AL La Pedrera, La Pedrera, T0479-2001, hpedrera@adinet.com.uy. 2 pools, tennis court, restaurant,good rooms.

AL La Perla, Cabo Polonio, T0470-5125, T099-871017, www.mayoral.com.uy/. Meals US$8-11. Rooms to rent; no credit cards, horse riding, visits to lighthouse, open all year.

AL Posada Eirete, Barra de Valizas, T0475-4011, www.posadaeiretevalizas.com. Small, tasteful, good breakfasts, owned by painter María Beloso. Highly recommended.

D pp **La Cañada**, about 1 km outside Cabo Polonio, T099-550595, posadalacaniada@cabopolonio.com. Shared rooms and a few doubles, friendly, small restaurant. They also rent out a cabin.

D pp **Cabo Polonio Hostel**, T099-445 943, www.cabopoloniohostel.com. Small wooden hostel, hot showers, shared rooms but doubles outside high season (**C**), kitchenettes, solar power, bar, good fresh food, can arrange tours and riding.

Reserva Ecológica La Laguna, about 2 km from Aguas Dulces, T099-602410/0475-2118. Private reserve on a 25 ha lake, with cabins for 4-6 (**E** pp), meals extra, open all year, many languages spoken, pick-up from bus stop in jeep, tours arranged, activities. (Rutas del Sol bus from Montevideo, US$10).

Youth hostels At La Pedrera: **El Viajero**, 500 m from beach, T0479-2252, www.lapedrerahostel.com. Open mid-Nov to 31 Mar, US$26-42 in double with bath, US$16-27 in dorm, kitchen, internet, surf classes, riding. **La Duna**, Carretero 685, Barra de Valizas, T0475-4045, open Dec-Mar, US$14 (HI members) US$18 (non-members), in dorm. Some doubles. Both are HI hostels.

Camping **Camping Esmeralda**, at Km 280.5, 17 km north of Castillos. **La Palomita**, 8 blocks from the sea, La Pedrera. Wooded, electricity, US$5, summer only.

Punta del Diablo *p1548*

In high season you should book in advance; www.portaldeldiablo.com gives a full list of choices.

L Aquarella, Av No 5, ½ block from beach, T0477-2400, www.portaldeldiablo.com. Pool, jacuzzi, great views, restaurant in high season.

A Posada Rocamar, Calle 5 No 3302, T0477-2516, www.posadarocamar.com.uy. Doubles and family suites, tastefully decorated, outdoor patio, peaceful, excursions to Laguna Negra organized.

D Hostería del Pescador, on road into village, Blv Santa Teresa, T0477-2017, www.portaldeldiablo.com. Rooms for 2-5, price vary for season and day of week, with breakfast, restaurant, pool.

D Posada de Maite, Calles 11 y 10, T0477-2335, www.portaldeldiablo.com. Rooms for 2-6 people, English spoken, Wi-Fi, BBQ, pool, very nice.

D-E pp **El Diablo Tranquilo Hostel and Bar**, Av Central, T0477-2647, www.eldiablotranquilo.com, shared and private rooms, double suites with fireplaces (**B-C**), great internet access, breakfast and cooking facilities, year round. Separate bar that is one of the nightlife hotspots. Highly recommended.

E pp **Punta del Diablo Hostel**, Km 298, Ruta 9, T0477-2655, www.puntadeldiablohostel.com. Discounts for HI members. With kitchen, camping (US$8-10 pp), bicycles, free internet, open end-Dec to end-Feb.

Chuy *p1549*

All hotels are open the year round.

A Parador Fortín de San Miguel, Paraje 18 de Julio, near San Miguel fortress, T6607, www.elfortin.com. Excellent, full and half-board, colonial- style hotel. Beautiful rooms, gym, pool, fine food and service. Highly recommended. You don't have to go through Uruguayan formalities to get there from Brazil.

B Alerces, Laguna de Castillos 578, T/F2260, alerces@montevideo.com.uy. 4 blocks from border. Bath, TV, breakfast, heater, pool.

B Nuevo Hotel Plaza, C Artigas y Av Arachanes, T2309, www.hotelplaza.chuynet.com. On plaza, bath, good buffet breakfast, TV, very helpful, good, restaurant *El Mesón del Plaza*.

C Vittoria, Numancia 143, T2280. Price includes breakfast, simple and clean, parking.

Camping From Chuy buses run every 2 hrs to the Barra del Chuy campsite, Ruta 9 Km 331, turn right 13 km, T2425. Good bathing, many birds. *Cabañas* for up to 4 persons cost US$20 daily or less, depending on amenities.

Eating

Portezuelo and Punta Ballena *p1545*

TTT Medio y Medio, Cont Camino Lussich s/n, Punta Ballena, T578791, www.medioymedio.com. Jazz club and restaurant, music nightly and good food.

TTT-TT Las Vertientes, Camino de Los Ceibos, 2 km on the Route 9, T042-669997. Country restaurant, fresh food which all comes from own farm, good salads and sweets.

Maldonado *p1546*

Best ice cream at **Popy's**.

TTT-TT Lo de Rubén, Florida y Santa Teresa, T223059. *Parrillada*, best restaurant in town, open every day.

TTT-TT Taberna Patxi, Dodera 944, T238393. Very good Basque food with authentic recipes.

Punta del Este *p1546, map p1546*

Many enticing ice cream parlours on Gorlero.

TTT La Bourgogne, Pedragosa Sierra y Av del Mar, T482007. Elegant French/South American cuisine, fresh ingredients, chef Jean-Paul Bondoux.

TTT Bungalow Suizo, Av Roosevelt y Parada 8, T482358. Excellent Swiss, must book.

TTT Cantón Chino, Calle 28 y Gorlero, T441316. Creative Chinese food, good.

TTT Los Caracoles, Calle 20 y 28, T440912. Excellent food (international, *parrilla*, seafood) at good prices.

TTT El Ciclista, Calle 20 y 29, T448371. Long-standing, with international cuisine, Italian, *parrilla* and seafood. Recently moved to new building.

TTT Gure-etxe (also in La Coronilla), Calle 9 y 12, T446858. Seafood and Basque cuisine.

TTT Isidora, Rambla del Puerto, esq 21, T449646, www.isidora.com.uy, Smart, by the port, international cuisine beautifully presented.

TTT Juana Enea, Calle 9, No 607, T447236. Restaurant and fishmonger, fresh fish, popular with locals.

TTT Lo de Charlie, Calle 12 y 9, T444183. Fish, including tuna and octopus, plus pasta and *parrilla* standards.

TTT Lo de Tere, Rambla Artigas y 21, T440492, www.lode tere.com. Good local food, open all year but closed Wed in winter, 20% discount if eating lunch before 1300 or dinner before 2100. Highly recommended.

TTT Viejo Marino, Calle 11 entre 14 y 12, Las Palmeras, T443565. Fish restaurant, busy, go early.

TTT Virazón, Rambla Artigas y C 28, T443924. Good food and great view, but expensive. Recommended.

TTT Yatch Club Uruguayo, Rambla Artigas y 8, T441056. Very good, fish, seafood, views over the port (not to be confused with the Yacht Club).

TT Il Barreto, C 9 y 10, T446916. Italian vegetarian, good value, live Italian and Latin music some evenings, in low season open weekends only.

Beaches east of Punta del Este *p1547*

La Barra

TTT Baby Gouda Café, Ruta 10, Km 161, T771874. Alternative food, yoga and Arab dances.

TTT-TT Restaurant T, Ruta 10, Km 49.5, T771356. Old-style, Italian and French as well as local dishes, good wine selection. Claims to be the only "real" bistro in Punta del Este

Faro José Ignacio

TTT La Huella, Los Cisnes on Playa Brava, T0486-2279. Excellent seafood, on the beach.

TTT Marismo, Ruta 10 Km185, T0486-2273. Romantic, outdoor tables around a fire.

Manantiales

TTT Cactus y Pescados, Primera Bajada a Bikini, T774782. Very good seafood, international menu.

La Paloma *p1547*

TT Arrecife, Av Principal, T0479-6837. First class, serving pizzas, *parrilla* and a good range of salads.

TT Da Carlos, Av Solari. Moderate prices, pizzas plus Uruguayan food.

TTT La Marea, Av Solari, near tourist office. Very popular, has outstanding seafood.

Northeast of La Paloma

In **Cabo Polonio**, there are a few restaurants, some with vegetarian options, so you don't have to bring any food with you. Fish is on the menu when the sea is calm enough for the fishermen to go out. The most expensive and fashionable is **La Puesta**, on the south beach. On weekends during the summer there are DJs, dancing and live music. For self-catering, the stores sell fruit, vegetables, meat, etc. There are several restaurants in **Castillos** including ₸₸₸ La Strada, 19 de Abril, and several restaurants in **Punta del Diablo**, mostly colourful huts grouped around the sea front serving excellent fish. A couple of pizza places too.

₸₸ **Chivito Veloz**, Aguas Dulces. Good, large portions for US$5.

Parque Nacional Santa Teresa *p1548*

₸₸ **La Ruta**, La Coronilla. This small round restaurant at the entrance to town may be your only option if you are driving in the evening and off season from Chuy to Punta or Montevideo. Good meat dishes. Off season, other restaurants in Coronilla are closed.

Chuy *p1549*

₸₸-₸ **Fusion**, Av Brasil 387. Good food, not traditional Uruguayan fare. Recommended

₸₸-₸ **Restaurant Jesús**, Av Brasil y L Olivera. Good value and quality.

Bars and clubs

Punta del Este *p1546, map p1546*

Hop, Rambla Artigas, T446061, www.hop.com.uy. Bar and restaurant, popular drinking spot.

Moby Dick, Rambla del Puerto. Mock English-style pub by the port, open until the early hours, very popular.

Ocean Club, Parada 12 de la Brava, T484869, www.oceanclub.com.uy. Very fashionable and smart club playing mostly pop and house. Dress up.

Activities and tours

Punta del Este *p1546, map p1546*

Diving Punta Divers, C 32, No 626, T482481, www.ssila.com. US$290 for 8 dives to caves at Punta Ballena and Gorriti, and to wrecks (eg HMS *Agamemon*, Nelson's favourite ship), courses offered. Trips include refreshments. Also offer dive in a gold mine near Minas. To see right whales at end-Aug to Nov, US$18.

Riding Nueva Escuela de Equitación, at **Cantegril Country Club**, Av Saravia, T223211. Classes, guided rides for all levels and ages.

Transport

Piriápolis *p1545*

Road Piriápolis may be reached either by following the very beautiful R10 from the end of the Interbalnearia, or by taking the original access road (R37) from Pan de Azúcar, which crosses the R93. The shortest route from Piriápolis to Punta del Este is by the Camino de las Bases which runs parallel to the R37 and joins the R93 some 4 km east of the R37 junction.

Bus Terminal on Misiones, 2 blocks from Hotel Argentino, T24141. To/from **Montevideo**, US$5, 1½ hrs. To **Punta del Este**, US$4, 50 mins. To **Maldonado**, US$3, 40 mins. For **Rocha**, **La Paloma** and **Chuy**, take bus to Pan de Azúcar and change.

Maldonado *p1546*

Bus Av Roosevelt y Sarandí. To/from **Montevideo**, US$7; to **Minas**, 2 hrs, 5 a day, US$4.50. To **San Carlos** take a local bus 3 blocks from the main bus station, US$1.50.

Punta del Este *p1546, map p1546*

Air Direct daily Boeing 737 flights from Buenos Aires to brand new Punta del Este airport during the high season. **Laguna del Sauce**, Capitán Curbelo (T559777), which handles flights to Buenos Aires, 40 mins. Airport tax US$30. Exchange facilities, tax-free shopping. Regular bus service to airport from Punta del Este (will deliver to and collect from private addresses and hotels), US$5, 90 mins before departure, also connects with arriving flights. Taxi US$25; *remise* around US$30 depending on destination (T441269). El Jagüel airport is used by private planes.

Bus Local: Traffic is directed by a one-way system; town bus services start from C 5 (El Faro), near the lighthouse. www.puntaweb.com has details of bus routes. **Long distance**: terminal at Av Gorlero, Blvd Artigas and C 32, T486810 (served by local bus No 7); has toilets, newsagent, café and Casa de Cambio. To/from **Montevideo** via Carrasco airport, **COT** (T486810) or **Copsa** (T1975), US$7.50, just over 2 hrs, many in the summer; 19 a day in winter. To **Piriápolis**, US$4. To **San Carlos**

(US$1.50) for connections to Porto Alegre, Rocha, La Paloma, Chuy. Direct to **Chuy**, 4 hrs, US$12. Local bus fare about US$0.50. For transport Montevideo-Buenos Aires, **Buquebus** T488380, at bus terminal, loc 09, buses connect with ferries. Also **Colonia Express**.

La Paloma *p1547*
Bus Frequent to and from **Rocha**, US$1.75, and to and from **the capital** (5 hrs, US$12). 4 buses daily to **Chuy**, US$8, 3½ hrs, 2 a day to San Carlos, Pan de Azúcar and Aguas Dulces, all with **Rutas del Sol**. Northeast of La Paloma, some Montevideo-Chuy buses go into **Punta del Diablo**, 4 km from the main road.

To **Cabo Polonio**, **Rutas del Sol** from Montevideo, US$15, 4-5 hrs, and any of the coastal towns to Km 264, where you catch the truck to the village (see above).

Chuy *p1549*
Bus To **Montevideo** (**COT, Cynsa, Rutas del Sol**) US$17, 4¾-6 hrs, may have to change buses in San Carlos; to **Maldonado** US$7.50. International buses passing through en route from Montevideo to Brazil either stop in Chuy or at the border. Make sure the driver knows you need to stop at Uruguayan immigration. Sometimes everybody must get off for customs check. If looking for onward transport, if there is a free seat, most companies will let you pay on board.

Directory

Piriápolis *p1545*
Banks BROU on Rambla Argentinos changes TCs; **Casa de Cambio Monex**, Argentinos s/n, T25295. **Post office** Av Piria y Tucumán.

Maldonado *p1546*
Banks **Banco Pan de Azúcar**, accepts Master-Card. **Cambio Bacacay**, Florida 803, good rates, TCs.

Punta del Este *p1546, map p1546*
Airline offices **Aerolíneas Argentinas**, Edif Edmos Dumont, Av Gorlero, T444343. **Pluna**, Av Roosevelt y Parada 9, T492050/490101.

Banks Best rates of exchange from **Banco de la República Oriental de Uruguay**, which opens earlier and closes later than the other banks and accepts MasterCard, but no TCs. Many ATMs at banks on the peninsula and at Punta Shopping (Roosevelt). Also *casas de cambio*, eg **Indumex**, Av Gorlero y 28, **Brimar**, C 31 No 610. **Car hire** **Punta Car**, Continuación Gorlero s/n, Hotel Playa, T482112, puntacar@puntacar.com.uy. **Uno**, Gorlero y 21, T445018, ununobat@movinet.com.uy. And others. See Essentials, for international agencies. **Internet** **Locutorio**, Gorlero y 30, T441807, US$2 per hr. Another internet café in **Devoto** shopping centre, Av Roosevelt y Parada 10, T494992. **Post offices** Av Gorlero entre 31 y 32, 0900-1400, 1600-1900, daily (shorter hours out of season). **Scooter hire** US$51 per day, with drivers licence (US$50 fine if caught without it) and ID documents from **Filibusteros**, Av Artigas y Parada 5, T484125. They also rent out bicycles (US$3.50 per hr, US$7.50 per half day, US$10 per day, includes padlocks). **Telephones** Telephone and fax on Calle 24 at Calle 25, by the plaza.

La Paloma *p1547*
Internet **Arrecife**, Av Solari, US$2 per hr, open 1000-0100. **Useful services** Bike rental from **El Tobo**, T0479-7881, US$3.50 a day. One bank which changes TCs; also a supermarket and post office.

Chuy *p1549*
Banks Several *cambios* on Av Brasil, eg **Gales**, Artigas y Brasil, Mon-Fri 0830-1200, 1330-1800, Sat 0830-1200, and in World Trade Center, open 1000-2200; on either side of Gales are Aces and Val. All give similar rates, charging US$1 plus 1% commission on TCs, US$, pesos and reais. On Sun, try the casino, or look for someone on the street outside the *cambios*. **BROU**, Gen Artigas, changes TCs. No problem spending reais in Chuy or pesos in Chuí. **Internet** **MPM**, Gen Artigas 163, T4358. **Post office** On Gen Artigas. **Telephones** **Antel**, S Priliac almost Artigas, open 0700-2300.

Montevideo north to Brazil

Two roads run towards Melo, heart of cattle-ranching country: Route 8 and Route 7, the latter running for most of its length through the Cuchilla Grande, a range of hills with fine views. Route 8 via Minas and Treinta y Tres, is the more important of these two roads to the border and it is completely paved.

Minas and around ➔ *Phone code: 0442. Colour map 8, B6. Population: 38,000.*

This picturesque small town, 120 km north of Montevideo, is set in wooded hills. Juan Lavalleja, the leader of the Thirty-Three who brought independence to the country, was born here, and there is an equestrian statue to Artigas, said to be the largest such in the world, on the Cerro Artigas just out of town. The church's portico and towers, some caves in the neighbourhood and the countryside are worth seeing. Good confectionery is made in Minas; you can visit the largest firm, opposite *Hotel Verdun*. Banks are open 1300-1700 Monday-Friday. There is a tourist office at the bus station.

The Parque Salus, on the slopes of Sierras de las Animas, is 8 km to the south and very attractive; take the town bus marked 'Cervecería Salus' from plaza to the Salus brewery, then walk 2 km to the mineral spring and bottling plant (**A** *Parador Salus*, good). It is a lovely three-hour walk back to Minas from the springs. The Cascada de Agua del Penitente waterfall, 11 km east off Route 8, is interesting and you may see wild rheas nearby. It's hard to get to off season.

To the Brazilian border

Route 8 continues north via **Treinta y Tres** (*Population: 26,000*) to Melo (also reached by Route 7), near Aceguá close to the border. In **Melo** (*Phone code: 0462; Population: 51,000*), there are places to stay and exchange rates are usually better than at the frontier. If crossing to Brazil here, Brazilian immigration is at Bagé, not at the border. At 12 km southeast of Melo is the Posta del Chuy (2 km off Route 26). This house, bridge and toll gate (built 1851) was once the only safe crossing place on the main road between Uruguay and Brazil. It displays gaucho paintings and historical artefacts.

Río Branco was founded in 1914, on the Río Yaguarón. The 1 km-long Mauá bridge across the river leads to Jaguarão in Brazil. The Brazilian vice-consulate in Río Branco is at Calle Ismael Velázquez 1239, T0675-2003, bravcrb@gmail.com. For road traffic, the frontier at Chuy is better than Río Branco or Aceguá. There is a toll 68 km north of Montevideo.

An alternative route to Brazil is via Route 5, the 509-km road from Montevideo to the border town of Rivera, which runs almost due north, bypassing Canelones and Florida before passing through Durazno. After crossing the Río Negro, it goes to Tacuarembó. South of the Río Negro is gently rolling cattle country, vineyards, orchards, orange, lemon and olive groves. North is hilly countryside with steep river valleys and cattle ranching. The road is dual carriageway as far as Canelones.

East of Florida, Route 56 traverses the countryside eastwards to **Cerro Colorado**, also known as Alejandro Gallinal, which has an unusual clock tower.

Durazno ➔ *Phone code: 0362. Colour map 8,B6. Population: 30,700.*

On the Río Yí 182 km from Montevideo, Durazno is a friendly provincial town with tree-lined avenues and an airport. There is a good view of the river from the western bridge.

Dams on the Río Negro have created an extensive network of lakes near **Paso de los Toros** (*Population: 13,000; 66 km north of Durazno, bus from Montevideo US$13*), with camping and sports facilities. Some 43 km north of Paso de los Toros a 55-km road turns east to **San Gregorio de Polanco**, at the eastern end of Lago Rincón del Bonete. The beach by the lake is excellent, with opportunities for boat trips, horse riding and other sports.

Tacuarembó → *Phone code: 063. Colour map 8, B6. Population: 51,000.*
This is an agro-industrial town and major route centre 390 km north of Montevideo. The nearby Valle Edén has good walking possibilities. Some 23 km west of Tacuarembó, along Route 26, is the **Carlos Gardel Museum** ⓘ *US$1, daily 0900-1800*, a shrine to the great tango singer who was killed in an air crash in Medellín (Colombia). Uruguay, Argentina and France all claim him as a national son. The argument for his birth near here is convincing.

Brazilian border
Rivera (*Population: 64,400, Phone code: 062*) is divided by a street from the Brazilian town of Santa Ana do Livramento. Points of interest are the park, the Plaza Internacional, and the dam of Cañapirú. Uruguayan immigration is at the end of Calle Sarandí y Presidente Viera, 14 blocks, 2 km, from the border (take bus along Agraciada or taxi from bus terminal for around US$1.50). There is also a tourist office here, T31900. Luggage is inspected when boarding buses out of Rivera; there are also 3 checkpoints on the road out of town. The Brazilian consulate is at Ceballos 1159, T23278. Remember that you must have a Uruguayan exit stamp to enter Brazil and a Brazilian exit stamp to enter Uruguay.

Montevideo north to Brazil listings

For Sleeping and Eating price codes and other relevant information, see Essentials, pages 38-40.

Sleeping

Minas *p1556*

C Posada Verdun, W Beltrán 715, T24563, posadaverdun@hotmail.com. Good, breakfast extra (**Confitería Nuevo Sabor** nearby serves good food).

F Hostel de Villa Serrana, C Molle s/n off Route 8, Km 145, in Villa Serrana, T09-922 6911, www.villa serranahostel.com. Oldest hostel in Uruguay. US$8 pp, open all year, 28 km beyond Minas on road to Treinta y Tres. Thatched house, kitchen for members, horses for hire, basic, take plenty of food and drink (no shop). Direct bus from Montevideo to Treinta y Tres or Melo, ask to be set down at Km 145 and walk 2 km to Villa Serrana. Or take bus to Minas from Montevideo or Punta del Este then **Cosu** bus Tue, Thu 0900, 1730 to Villa Serrana.

Camping Arequita, Camino Valeriano Magri, T0440-2503, beautiful surroundings, cabañas (for two people with shared bathroom US$12.50), camping US$3 each.

Tourism farm AL Posada El Abra, Puntas de Santa Lucía, 25 km from Minas, T0440-2869, www.elabra.com.uy. Small *estancia* in hills at Río Santa Lucía headwaters, full board, includes transport, guides, horses for riding, good walking, swimming in river, expansive views.

To the Brazilian border *p1556*

Treinta y Tres

D pp **Cañada del Brujo**, Km 307.5, Ruta 8, Sierra del Yerbal, 34 km north of Treinta y Tres, T0452- 2837, T099-297448 (mob), cdelbrujo@latinmail.com. Isolated hostel, no electricity, basic but "fantastic", dorm, local food, owner Pablo Rado drives you there, canoeing, trekking on foot or horseback, trips to Quebrada de los Cuervos. Recommended.

D La Posada, Manuel Freire 1564, T21107, www.hotellaposada33.com. With breakfast, good overnight stop.

Melo

B Virrey Pedro de Melo, J Muñiz 727, T22673, www.hotelvirreypedrodemelo.com. Better rooms in new part, 3-star, TV, minibar, café.

Cerro Colorado

L San Pedro de Timote, Km 142, R7, 14 km west of Cerro Colorado, T0598-310 8086, http://sanpedrodetimote.com.uy. A famous colonial-style *estancia*, working ranch, landscaped park, 3 pools, cinema, gym, horse riding, good restaurant.

A Arteaga, 7 km off R7 north of Cerro Colorado, T02-707 4766, arteaga@paradaarteaga.com. Typical European *estancia*, famous, beautiful interior, pool.

Durazno *p1556*
There are a few hotels (**D-F**).

Camping At 33 Orientales, in park of same name by river, T2806, nice beach, hot showers, toilets, laundry sinks.

Tourism Farm Estancia Albergue El Silencio, Ruta 14 Km 166, 10 km west of Durazno, T2014 (or T0360-2270, HI member), www.estancia elsilencio.net. About 15 mins walk east of bridge over Río Yí where bus stops, clean rooms, friendly, riding, swimming, birdwatching. Recommended.

Paso de los Toros
D Sayonara, Sarandí y Barreto, T0664-2535/2743 2 blocks centre, renovated old residence, rooms with bath, a/c and cable TV. Breakfast extra, US$3.50.

San Gregorio de Polanco
B Posada Buena Vista, De Las Pitangueras 12, T0369-4841, www.san-gregorio-de-polanco.com. Overlooking lake, breakfast extra, good.

Tacuarembó *p1557*
AL Carlos Gardel, Ruta 5 Km 388,500, T30306, www.hotelcarlosgardel.com.uy. Internet, pool, restaurant, meeting room.

AL Tacuarembó, 18 de Julio 133, T22104, www.tacuarembohotel.com.uy. Breakfast, central, TV, Wi-Fi, safe, restaurant, pool, parking.

C Central, Gral Flores 300, T22841. Cable TV, ensuite bathrooms, rooms with or without a/c, laundry service.

C pp **Panagea**, 1 hr from Tacuarembó, T099-836149, http://panagea-uruguay.blogspot.com. Estancia and backpackers' hostel, working cattle and sheep farm, home cooking, lots of riding, electricity till 2200 is only concession to modern amenities, many languages spoken.

Camping Campsites 1 km out of town in the Parque Laguna de las Lavanderas, T4761, and 7 km north on R26 at Balneario Iporá.

Brazilian border: Rivera *p1557*
B Casablanca, Sarandí 484. Shower, breakfast, a/c, TV, comfortable, pleasant.

D Sarandí, Sarandí 777, T33963. Fan, good, cheaper without bath.

Camping Municipal site near AFE station, and in the Parque Gran Bretaña 7 km south along R27.

Eating

Minas *p1556*
Restaurants include **Complejo San Francisco de las Sierras**, Ruta 12 Km 347,500 (4 km from Minas); **Ki-Joia**, Diego Pérez in front of Plaza Libertad. **Irisarri**, C Treinta y Tres 618. Best pastry shop, *yemas* (egg candy) and *damasquitos* (apricot sweets).

Tacuarembó *p1557*
Parrilla La Rueda, W Beltrán 251. Good.

Transport

Minas *p1556*
Bus To **Montevideo**, US$8, 5 companies, 2 hrs. To **Maldonado**, US$4.50, 7 a day, 1½ hrs (**COOM**).

To the Brazilian border: Melo *p1556*
Bus To **Montevideo** US$21, 5 hrs (**Cota, Núñez, Turismar**). Several buses daily to Río Branco.

Durazno *p1556*
Bus To **Montevideo** US$9.50, 2½ hrs.

Tacuarembó *p1557*
Bus From **Montevideo**, US$19.50, 4-5 hrs.

Brazilian border: Rivera *p1557*
Bus Terminal at Uruguay y Viera (1½ km from the terminal in Santa Ana). To/from **Montevideo**, US$25, 5½-6¾ hrs (**Agencia Central, Turil, Núñez**). To **Paysandú, Copay**, T23733, at 0400, 1600, US$18. To **Tacuarembó**, US$5.50 (**Núñez, Turil**), no connections for Paysandú. To **Salto**, Mon and Fri 1630, 6 hrs, US$20. For **Artigas**, take bus from Livramento to Quaraí, then cross bridge.

Venezuela

Contents

1562 Planning your trip

1570 Caracas
- 1573 Sights
- 1585 Around Caracas

1588 West from Caracas
- 1588 Maracay and around
- 1593 Valencia and around
- 1597 Coro and around
- 1601 From Maracaibo to Colombia
- 1605 Barquisimeto and around
- 1607 Valera to Mérida

1609 Mérida and around
- 1609 Mérida
- 1617 Sierra Nevada de Mérida

1626 Los Llanos and Amazonas
- 1626 Los Llanos
- 1629 Amazonas

1631 East coast
- 1631 Caracas to Puerto La Cruz
- 1635 Parque Nacional Mochima
- 1637 Cumaná
- 1640 Araya to Paria
- 1645 Isla de Margarita
- 1653 Los Roques

1655 Canaima and the Orinoco Delta
- 1655 Ciudad Bolívar
- 1660 Canaima and Angel Falls
- 1664 Ciudad Guayana and the Orinoco Delta
- 1667 Ciudad Guayana to Santa Elena de Uairén
- 1675 Mount Roraima

Footprint features

- **1560** Don't miss ...
- **1564** Driving in Venezuela
- **1614** The Lighthouse of Maracaibo

At a glance

Time required 2-3 weeks.

Best time Highlands are driest Oct-May, good for trekking. Llanos best at start of Nov-May rains. Don't miss San Juan Bautista celebrations on 24 Jun.

When not to go Avoid Maracaibo Jul-Sep. High seasons at Carnival, Easter, mid-Jul to mid-Sep and Christmas to New Year.

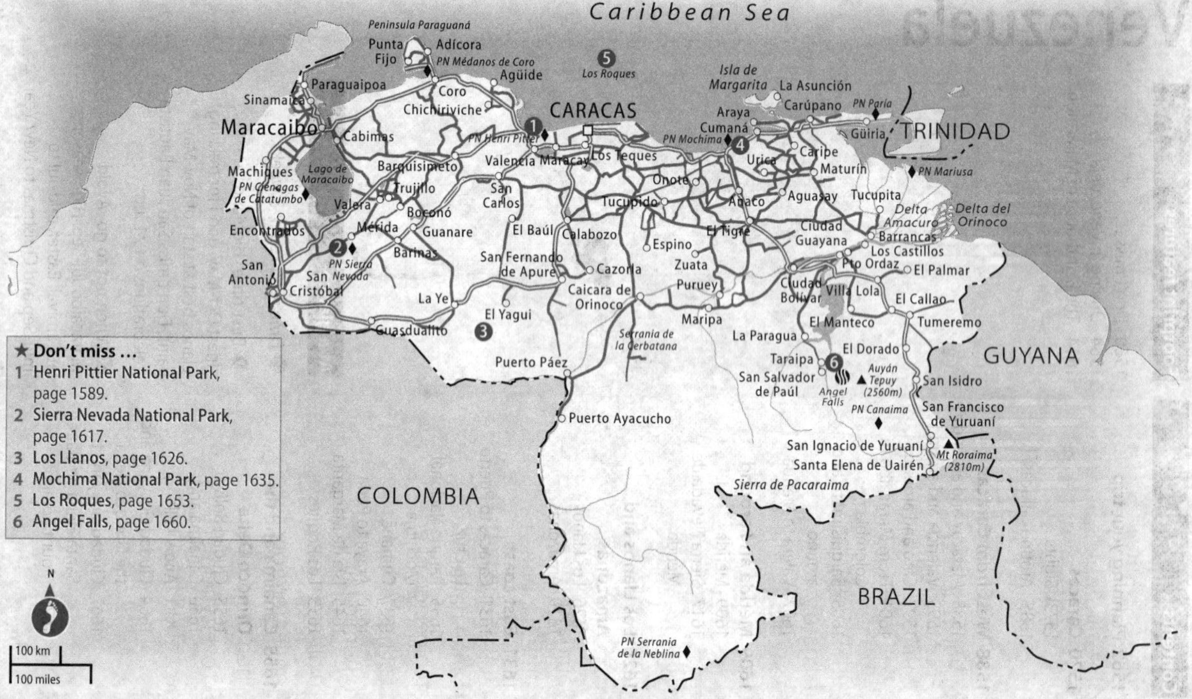

★ **Don't miss ...**

1 Henri Pittier National Park, page 1589.
2 Sierra Nevada National Park, page 1617.
3 Los Llanos, page 1626.
4 Mochima National Park, page 1635.
5 Los Roques, page 1653.
6 Angel Falls, page 1660.

Venezuela is where the Andes meet the Caribbean. The Orinoco river separates great plains from the table-top mountains of the Gran Sabana, where waterfalls tumble in sheer drops into the forest and lost worlds are easy to imagine. More recent innovations – cable cars up to the high peaks, hang gliders for jumping off them – are now part of the scene at Mérida, capital of Venezuela's Andes. Lying at the heart of the country – geographically and spiritually – are the llanos (plains), a vast area of flat savannah the size of Italy and home to an immense variety of birds, exotic mammals and reptiles, such as caiman (alligators), giant anacondas, anteaters, pumas, jaguars and giant otters, to name but a few.

These plains flood seasonally, but when the waters retreat, the birds and animals share their territory with cattle and the llanero cowboys, renowned for their hospitality towards visitors who can stay at one of the many luxurious hatos – cattle ranches – or rough it on a budget tour from Mérida. If the sea is more to your taste, head for the country's seductive coastline – the longest in the Caribbean at over 2,500 km. Venezuela's waters play host to some of the best (and least known) diving in the region with three marine national parks. Pick of the bunch are Islas Los Roques, an archipelago of emerald and turquoise lagoons and dazzling white beaches. At the other end of the country, the Amazon is home to humid rainforests and rare plants and animals as well as over 20 different ethnic groups. This part of Venezuela is very much frontier territory and remains wild and untamed, as it was when the country received its first foreign visitor back in 1498. So overwhelmed was Columbus by what he saw that he described it as 'Paradise on Earth'.

Planning your trip

Where to go

Caribbean coast Venezuela has the longest coastline in the Caribbean with numerous palm-fringed beaches of white sand. **Caracas** is hidden from the Caribbean by Monte Avila, one of Venezuela's national parks, but you don't have to go too far beyond the mountain to find good beaches. Only a few hours west of the capital are some lovely little beaches. Further west is the Parque Nacional Morrocoy, with many islands close to the shore. North of Morrocoy is the historic town of Coro, surrounded by sand dunes, and the Paranaguá Peninsula. Parque Nacional Mochima, east of Caracas, has some excellent beaches and a multitude of islets to explore. Further east are unrivalled beaches on the Paria Peninsula, but they are harder to reach. Besides those islands already mentioned, there is Isla de Margarita, one of the country's principal destinations for local and foreign tourists. The Islas Los Roques, 166 km due north of the central coast, is a beautiful archipelago, still unspoilt despite the growth in tourist interest.

The Andes Venezuela's Andes have some gorgeous scenery, with snow-capped peaks and remote, historic villages. The main centre is Mérida, in the Sierra Nevada of the same name. It has accommodation, other services and tour companies, which can arrange treks, climbing and other excursions. Two of its claims to fame are the highest cable car in the world, ascending the 4,776-m Pico Espejo, and the shop selling the largest number of ice cream flavours in the world.

The Llanos Life in the *llanos* revolves around the cycle of wet and dry seasons; the movement of cattle, the mainstay of the region's economy, depends on it. In the flat grasslands are slow running rivers which flood in the rainy season, creating a huge inland sea. When the rains cease, the whole area dries out completely. South of the cattle lands are forests and the tributaries of the Río Orinoco. Just after the May-November wet season, this is a paradise for nature lovers, with a spectacular variety of birds, monkeys, big cats, anaconda, river dolphins, caiman and capybara. Tours to the *llanos* are run from Mérida and there are ecotourism ranches which offer you the chance to get to know the lifestyle of the plains.

Guayana and the Orinoco Above the grasslands of the Gran Sabana rise *tepuis*, flat-topped mountains from which spring magnificent waterfalls and rivers. The Angel Falls, the highest in the world, are one such wonder, usually seen from a plane, but also reachable by a two- to three-day trip upriver. There are many other falls in the Gran Sabana and a few places to stay, the most popular being Canaima camp on a lagoon on the Río Carrao. Where Venezuela meets Brazil and Guyana is Mount Roraima; to reach its summit is one of the country's most adventurous excursions. The Orinoco delta is remote, but trips can be made from the small town of Tucupita. Amazonas is well off the beaten track, but accessible from Puerto Ayacucho. Much of the rainforest is protected and you need permission from the authorities to visit areas beyond the reach of a tour company.

When to go

The climate is tropical, with changes between the seasons being a matter of wet and dry, rather than hot and cold. Temperature is determined by altitude. The dry season in Caracas is December to April, with January and February the coolest months (there is a great difference between day and night temperatures at this time). The hottest months are July and August. The Caribbean coast is generally dry and rain is particularly infrequent in the states of Sucre, in the east, and Falcón, in the northwest. The lowlands of Maracaibo are very hot all year round; the least hot months are July to September. South of the Orinoco, in the Gran Sabana and Parque Nacional Canaima, the dry season is November to May. The same months are dry in the *llanos*, but the best time to visit is just after the rains, when the rivers and channels are still full of water and the humidity is not too high. In the Andes, the dry season is October to May, the best time for climbing or hiking. The days are clear, but the nights are freezing cold. The rains usually begin in June, but in the mountains the weather can change from day to day. **High season**, when it is advisable to book in advance is: Carnival, Easter, 15 July-15 September and Christmas to New Year.

National parks

Venezuela has 43 national parks, 21 national monuments, three World Heritage sites and various other refuges and reserves, some of which are mentioned in the text. A full list is published by the **Instituto Nacional de Parques** (Inparques), Salida del Distribuidor Santa Cecilia, Edificio Sur del Museo de Transporte, entre Avenida Francisco de Miranda y Autopista Francis Caracas, T273 2811 (Caracas). Each park has a regional director and its own guards (*guardaparques*). Permits (free) are required to stay in the parks (up to five), although this is not usually necessary for those parks visited frequently. For further information on the national parks system, visit the **Ministerio del Poder Popular para el Ambiente**, Centro Simón Bolívar, Torre Sul, Caracas 1010, T481 2209. See also **www.parkswatch.org** for a good run down of the country's most important national parks.

Getting around

Air Most big places are served by **Aeropostal** *www.aeropostal.com*, **Aserca** *www.asercaairlines.com*, **Avior** *www.avior.com.ve*, **Rutaca** *www.rutaca.com.ve* and **Venezolana** *http://ravsa.com.ve*. **Aereotuy/LTA** *www.tuy.com*, connects the coast, the Orinoco Delta and their camp in Canaima National Park, Arekuna. Apart from **Aserca**, which is marginally better than the rest, none is great. Lost luggage is a frequent problem. Delays and cancellations without compensation are common. Beware of overbooking during holidays, especially at Caracas airport; check in at least two hours before departure. If you book a ticket online with a credit card, you may be told at check-in that your tickets is 'reserved but not purchased'. Check with your card company that you have not been charged twice.

Bus and taxi Buses on most long-distance routes come in four standards, *normal*, *semi-ejecutivo*, *ejecutivo* and *bus-cama*. Fares are set by the authorities and you should see them posted on bus office windows. There are numerous services between the major cities and many services bypass Caracas, so you don't have to change buses in the capital. Buses stop frequently, but there may not always be a toilet at the stop. For journeys in a/c buses take a sleeping bag or similar because the temperature is set to freezing. This is most important on night journeys, which otherwise are fine. Also take earplugs and eyemask to protect against the loud stereo and violent Hollywood

Driving in Venezuela

Road Road quality varies. The four-lane *autopistas* are quite good.
Safety As infrastructure is not improving and spare parts for cars are scarce and expensive, serious road accidents are common. The situation is not helped by reckless driving at extremely high speed. If you have an accident and someone is injured, you will be detained as a matter of routine, even if you are not at fault. Carry a spare battery, water, fan belts, the obligatory breakdown triangle, a jack and spanners. Use private car parks whenever possible.
Documents Minimum driving age is 18. A valid driving licence from your own country, or international driving licence (preferred) is required. Neither a *carnet de passages*, nor a *libreta de pasos por aduana* is officially required, but is recommended. Before shipping your vehicle to Venezuela, go to a Venezuelan consul to obtain all necessary documentation. You must also go to a Venezuelan consul in the country in which you land your car if other than Venezuela. An entry permit for a car costs US$10 and requires one photograph (takes 24 hours).
Organizations **Touring y Automóvil Club de Venezuela**, Torre Phelps, p 15, of A y C, Plaza Venezuela, Caracas, T0212-781 9743, www.automovilclubvenezuela.com. Issues *libreta de pasos por aduana*, see www.automovilclubvenezuela.com/documentos.php .
Car hire Although pricey, it is a good idea to hire a car; many best places are off the beaten track. You need a credit card to rent a vehicle. Rates for a car are about US$75 per day, with insurance, unlimited mileage and government tax if you book in advance. Prices are higher paying on the spot. Excess starts at about US$20 per day.
Fuel 91 and 95 octane, unleaded, cost US$0.06-0.10 a gallon; diesel, US$0.06 a gallon. **Warning** There is a US$20 fine for running out of fuel.

screenings. The colectivo taxis and minibuses, known as *por puesto*, seem to monopolize transport to and from smaller towns and villages. For longer journeys they are normally twice as expensive as buses, but faster. They are mostly 1980s US gas-guzzlers, in all states of repair (a shortage of original spare parts and brakeneck driving speeds make *por puestos* a dangerous mode of transport). They are, however, great places to meet the locals, learn about the area and discuss politics. If first on board, wait for other passengers to arrive, do not take a *por puesto* on your own unless you want to pay for the whole vehicle. They may be reluctant to take luggage, but for a bit of comfort you can pay for two front seats and place your luggage between you and the driver. Outside Caracas, town taxis are relatively expensive.

Hitchhiking Hitchhiking (*cola*) is not recommended as it is unsafe. It is illegal on toll roads and, theoretically, for non-family members in the back of pick up trucks. Avoid hitchhiking around Guardia Nacional posts, where foreign travellers, even if travelling on regular buses or *por puestos*, may be subject to harassment.

Maps *Guía Vial de Venezuela*, edited by Miro Popic (Caracas 1999), is a motoring guide with maps and tourist information. The best country map is the late Kevin Healey's, published by International Travel Maps, Vancouver, Canada, www.itmb.com; buy direct or at good travel agents.

Sleeping → *See page 38 for our hotel grade price guide.*
Value for money is very low, with one or two exceptions, but many foreign-run, no-frills places catering for backpackers are opening up. The major cities, Isla Margarita, Los Roques, Guayana and Amazonas have higher room rates (eg US$15-20 in Caracas for a basic room). Add 10-15% for air-conditioning. In the Andean region prices are lower at around US$8-12 per person. If

comfort and cleanliness is what you are after, the price of a basic 3-star (Venezuelan '4 star') hotel room with a/c, private bath and breakfast will be in our A-B range, US$65-100, depending on location and whether it's a hotel or posada. There are no discounts or corporate rates for foreigners, unless arranged long in advance with tedious correspondence. A prior reservation will not guarantee you a room when you arrive. Always insist on seeing the room before paying; if you don't, you will almost certainly be given the worst possible room.

Elizabeth Kline's Guide to Camps, Posadas and Cabins in Venezuela 2009/2010, published every 2 years or so (purchasing information from notkalvin@yahoo.com) is incredibly detailed and doesn't pull its punches. *La Guía Valentina Quintero* also covers the whole country, suggesting routes, where to stay and eat, published biannually, www.valentinaquintero.com.ve. **Casa Tropical** (main office), CC Paseo Las Mercedes, Sector La Cuadra, Local 26, Caracas, T212-613 8343, www.casatropical.com.ve, offers interesting accommodation options in the Andes, Ciudad Bolívar and Tacarigua National Park, among other places.

Camping Camping in Venezuela is popular. Camping, with or without a vehicle, is not possible at the roadside. If camping on the beach, for the sake of security, pitch your tent close to others, even though they play their radios loud.

Eating and drinking → *See page 40 for our restaurant price guide.*

Eating out As with lodging, eating out is, by South American standards, very expensive and locals hardly ever do so. Some cities, like Puerto Ordaz, are notably costly. Midday used to be the cheapest time to eat and the best time to find fresh vegetables, but now many places offer only à la carte, quoting scarcity of supplies. In some places you can still find the three-course *menú ejecutivo* or *cubierto*, but it's increasingly rare. Minimum price for a meal is US$5-7, plus US$1 for drinks. Hotel breakfasts are likely to be poor. It is better and cheaper in a *fuente de soda* and cheaper still in a *pastelería* or *arepería*.

Food There is excellent local fish (such as *pargo* or red snapper, *carite* or king fish), crayfish, small oysters and prawns. Although it is a protected species, turtle may appear on menus in the Península de Paraguaná as *ropa especial*. Of true Venezuelan food there is *sancocho* (vegetable stew with meat, chicken or fish); *arepas*, bland white maize bread; toasted *arepas* served with various fillings or the local salty white cheese, are cheap, filling and nutritious; *cachapas*, a maize pancake wrapped around white cheese; *pabellón*, of shredded meat, beans, rice and fried plantains; and *empanadas*, maize-flour pies of cheese, meat or fish. At Christmas there are *hallacas*, maize pancakes stuffed with chicken, pork, olives, boiled in a plantain leaf. A *muchacho* (boy) on the menu is a cut of beef. *Ganso* is not goose but beef. *Solomo* and *lomito* are other cuts of beef. *Hervido* is chicken or beef with vegetables. *Contorno* with a meat or fish dish is a choice of fried chips, boiled potatoes, rice or yuca. *Caraotas* are beans; *cachitos* are filled *croissants*. *Pasticho* is what Venezuelans call Italian lasagne. The main fruits are bananas, oranges, grapefruit, mangoes, pineapple and pawpaws. *Lechosa* is papaya, *patilla* water melon, *parchita* passion fruit, and *cambur* a small banana. Excellent strawberries are grown at Colonia Tovar, 90 minutes from Caracas, and in the Andes. Delicious sweets are *huevos chimbos*, egg yolk boiled and bottled in sugar syrup, and *quesillo*, made with milk, egg and caramel. **Note** Venezuelans dine late!

Drink Venezuelan rum is very good; recommended brands are *Cacique, Pampero* and *Santa Teresa*. There are five good beers: *Polar* (the most popular, sold as Polar and Ice, and Solera and Solera Light), *Regional* (strong flavour of hops), *Cardenal* and *Nacional* (a *lisa* is a glass of keg beer; for a bottle of beer ask for a *tercio*); Brazilian *Brahma* beer (lighter than *Polar*) is now brewed in Venezuela. There are also mineral waters and gin. There is a good local wine in Venezuela. The *Polar* brewery joined with Martell (France) to build a winery in Carora. **Bodegas Pomar** (www.empresas-polar.com/marca-cerve_vinos.php) also sells a champagne-style sparkling wine. Look out for Pomar wine festivals in March and September. Liqueurs are cheap, try the local *ponche crema*. Coffee is very cheap (*café con leche* is milky, *café marrón* much less so, *café negro* is black); it often has sugar already added, ask for "sin azúcar". Try a *merengada*, a delicious drink made from fruit pulp, ice, milk and sugar; a *batido* is the same but with water and a little milk; *jugo* is the same but with water. A *plus-café* is an after-dinner liqueur. Water is free in restaurants even if no food is bought. Bottled water in *cervecerías* is often from the tap; no deception is intended, bottles are used as convenient jugs. Insist on seeing the bottle opened if you want mineral water. *Chicha de arroz* is a sweet drink made of milk, sugar and vanilla. Fruit juices are very good, ask for "jugo natural, preparado en el momento" for the freshest juice.

Essentials A-Z

Accident and emergency

Dial T171 for the integrated emergency system. **CICPC (Cuerpo de Investigaciones Científicas,** Penales y Criminalísticas), Av Urdaneta entre Pelota y Punceres; Edif Icauca, mezzanina 2, Caracas, T0212-564 7798, www.cicpc.gov.ve. For registering crimes, with agencies throughout the country.

Electricity

110 volts, 60 cycles. Plugs are 2-pin round and flat combined, 2-pin flat and 2-pin flat with optional D-shaped earth.

Embassies and consulates

The Ministry of Foreign Affairs website is www.mre.gov.ve. For a list of Venezuelan embassies and consulates abroad visit www.anuncioscaracas.com.ve/embajadasconsulados.htm and sites such as www.embavenez-uk.org and www.embavenez-us.org.

Festivals and events

Public holidays

1 Jan; **Carnival** on the Mon-Tue before Ash Wed (everything shuts down Sat-Tue; book accommodation in advance), Thu-Sat of Holy Week, **19 Apr**, **1 May**, **24 Jun** (the feast day of San Juan Bautista, celebrated on the central coast where there were once large concentrations of plantation slaves who considered San Juan their special Saint; the best-known events are in villages such as Chuao, Cata and Ocumare de la Costa); **5 Jul**, **24 Jul**, **24 Sep**, **12 Oct**, **2 Nov**, **25 Dec**.

Other holidays

From 24 Dec-1 Jan, museums are closed, most restaurants close 24-25 Dec (except for fast-food outlets) and there is no long-distance public transport on 25 Dec, while other days are often booked solid. On New Year's Eve, everything closes and does not open for at least a day. Business travellers should not visit during Holy Week or Carnival. Extra holidays for banks: **19 Mar** (San José), nearest Mon to **6 Jan**, **Ascension Day**, **29 Jun**, **15 Aug** and **8 Dec**.

See *Atlas de tradiciones venezolanas*, Fundación Bigott/El Nacional (2005), a beautiful book with sections on festivals, gastronomy, music, *artesanías*, architecture and popular art. Also *Calendario de fiestas tradicionales venezolanas*, Cecilia Fuentes and Daría Hernández, Fundación Bigott (2003).

Money → *1 US$=4.29 BsF; €1 = 5.86 BsF (Mar 2010).*

The unit of currency is the bolívar fuerte (BsF). There are coins for 1 bolívar fuerte, 50, 25, 12.5, 10, 5 and 1 céntimos, and notes for 2, 5, 10, 20, 50 and 100 bolívares fuertes. Have small coins and notes to hand, since in many shops and bars and on public transport large notes may be hard to change.

Venezuela has had an exchange control regime since 2003. The government determines the **exchange rate** for the bolívar fuerte, which remains overvalued in relation to the dollar and other currencies despite a devaluation in January 2010. Priority imports are charged at 2.60 BsF to the dollar, non-essential imports at 4.30 BsF (prices in this guide are calculated with this rate, so bear this fact in mind when estimating the cost of your trip). The 'parallel' (ie black) market exchange of currencies is illegal, but it is common practice among importers, exporters and travellers. It fluctuates, depending on many factors, including government foreign currency reserves and the price of oil. In Mar 2010 it stood at about US$1 = 6.70 BsF. Banks, *casas de cambio* and credit card transactions use the official rate; quoted rates in hotels tend to be worse than that.

If you do decide to change cash on the black market, a) find out what the unofficial rate is from as many sources as possible (you can check one of many websites like http://dolarparalelo.blog spot.com), and b) do the transaction with the most trusted person. The best method is with the senior staff in a European or US-run posada. If you don't take this option, the transaction will not be simple. You will probably not be offered the full parallel rate, say 5.50-6 BsF compared with 6.70. If you run short of cash, your best and cheapest bet is to cross the border to Colombia (San Antonio to Cúcuta is easiest), spend the night in Cúcuta and withdraw as much as possible in Colombian pesos from an ATM. Then go to any *casa de cambio* and buy bolívares. Remember to count your money carefully and make sure that you do not receive damaged notes.

Plastic, TCs, banks and ATMs TCs can be changed in *casas de cambio* and some banks at the official rate, but not as easily as dollars cash. To convert unused bolívares back into dollars, you must present the original exchange receipt (up to 30% of original amount changed); only banks and authorized *casas de cambio* can legally sell bolívares. In *casas de cambio* rates for TCs will be poor and they insist on photocopying your passport, ask for proof of purchase of TCs, ask you to sign a form saying where cash dollars came from and may even photograph you. Beware of forged Amex TCs and US$ notes.

You can use Visa/Plus, Mastercard, Cirrus and Maestro for obtaining bolívares at the official rate only. There are cash machines for Visa, Plus, Mastercard, Maestro and Cirrus at Simón Bolívar airport, but they are not reliable. You should be wary of using cash machines; Visa and Mastercard transactions inside banks, although slower, are much safer. Queues at ATM machines attract thieves. Some ATMs require a Venezuelan ID number. **Citibank** will exchange Citicorp cheques and has Visa and Mastercard ATMs. For Visa ATMs, branches of **Banco de Venezuela**. For cash advances on Mastercard and ATM go to branches of **Banco Mercantil**, **Banco de Venezuela**, **Banco Exterior**, **Banco Occidental de Descuento** (BOD) and a few others. **Corp Banca** (part of BOD) is affiliated with American Express, no commission, some branches cash personal cheques from abroad on an Amex card; **American Express** travel services are handled by **Italcambio** agencies around the country. Mastercard assistance T0800-1-002902. Visa assistance T0800-1-002167.

Cost of travelling On the cheapest possible budget at the official exchange rate, you can get by on about US$50-60 pp per day, depending on which part of the country you visit. A less basic budget would be about US$120 per day, rising to US$350 and upwards for first class travel. Remember that these costs will be less if you use the parallel exchange rate. The average cost for using the internet varies from US$0.50-0.80 outside Caracas to US$1-2 per hour in the capital.

Opening hours

See also under Festivals and events, page 1566.

Business hours **Banks**: Mon-Fri 0830-1530 only. **Government offices**: 0800-1200 are usual morning hrs, although they vary. Officials have fixed hrs, usually 0900-1000 or 1500-1600, for receiving visitors. **Businesses**: 0800-1800 with a midday break. **Shops**: Mon-Sat 0900-1300, 1500-1900.

Generally speaking, Venezuelans start work early, and by 0700 everything is in full swing. Most firms and offices close on Sat.

Safety

Venezuela is unfortunately quite a dangerous place to travel around. During the day is mostly trouble-freee, as long as you are aware of where you are going. Ask your hotel where it is safe to go. Carry only as much money as you need, don't wear jewellery or expensive sunglasses. It is not advisable to walk after dark: always take a taxi, preferably a marked car, or get someone to recommend a driver who can give you his number and you can use him for the duration of your stay. This applies even to tourist centres like Mérida and Ciudad Bolívar. In many places services shut after 1800. You **must** speak at least basic Spanish to be able to get yourself around. Very few people in the street will be able to speak English, and even fewer in rural areas. As a tourist you will sand out, so it helps considerably to understand and be understood on a basic level.

Some statistics state that Venezuela's crime rate is the highest in South America and Caracas's murder rate is the world's highest. Muggings are common, particularly in the bigger cities and are often at gunpoint. Rape is sadly very common, but mainly in poor neighbourhoods where police do not dare or want to go after sunset.

Outside of the big cities you will feel less unsafe, but still need to be careful in quieter rural areas as there may not be many tourists around. The more popular destinations (such as beaches and national parks) are used to having travellers and are generally further away from the kind of problems that you might encounter in the large cities. You still need to watch out for scams, cons and petty thieving. Beaches can be packed at weekends and, while empty on weekdays, the detritus left by the weekend crowds may not be cleared up. If you are seeking an isolated beach, make enquiries about which are safe before setting out.

The marked divisions between pro- and anti-Chávez factions can cause tension on the street. Stay away from political rallies (unless you are there to join them). Foreigners may find themselves subject to harassment or abuse, or to thorough police identity and body searches. Carry a copy of your passport and, if searched, watch the police like a hawk, in case they try to plant drugs to your bags. Do not photograph people without permission. Carry a mobile and be prepared to call your embassy or your contact in the country if a police search becomes threatening.

Tax

Airport tax International passengers pay an airport tax of US$39.79 and exit tax of the same amount (at the official 4.30 exchange rate – check latest rates at www.aeropuerto-maiquetia.com.ve). The exit tax may be included in your flight ticket. Only locally-issued credit cards can be used for paying airport tax. Otherwise only dollars or bolívares are accepted, no TCs. (See p 1567 above on ATM machines at the airport.) Children under 2 years do not pay tax. There is an 8% tax on the cost of all domestic flights, plus an airport tax of US$7.55. Exit stamps have to be paid by overland travellers at some borders, US$12.80 (BsF 55). Correct taxes are not advertised and you may be overcharged

VAT/IVA 12%.

Telephone → *Country code +58.*

Ringing: long equal tones with equal long pauses. Engaged: short equal tones, with equal pauses. Mobile phone codes are generally 0412, 0414, or 0416.

Time

4 hrs behind GMT, 1 hr ahead of EST.

Tipping

Taxi drivers are not tipped if you agree the fare in advance. Usherettes are not tipped. Hotel porters, US$1; airport porters US$1 per piece of baggage. Restaurants 5-10% of bill; some even charge on top of the service charge when it is included.

Tourist information

In charge of tourism is the **Ministerio del Poder Popular para el Turismo**, Av Francisco de Miranda con Av Principal de La Floresta, Edif Mintur (Frente al Colegio Universitario de Caracas), Chacao, Caracas, T0212-208 4511, www.mintur.gob.ve and www.inatur.gob.ve. **Venetur**, Final Av Libertador, Edif Nuevo Centro, diagonal al Centro Comercial Sambil, Caracas, T0500-TURISMO (887 4766), www.venetur.gob.ve, is the state-owned and operated travel agency, aimed at facilitating travel for nationals and foreigners, making reservations and arranging tours. In Caracas, go to **Corpoturismo**, Parque Central, Torre Oeste, p 35, 36 y 37, T507 8800.

Outside Venezuela, contact Venezuelan embassies and consulates. Read and heed the travel advice at websites below.

Useful websites

www.gobiernoenlinea.ve Government site.
www.venezuelatuya.com Tourism, history, geography, cuisine, traditions and more.
www.mipunto.com/venezuelavirtual/ Information on the whole country.

www.turismo.net.ve Tourism portal and related blog at **www.turismo.venezuela.net.ve**.
www.auyantepuy.com, **www.terra.com.ve** Useful information and links.
www.bvonline.com.ve or **www.venamcham.org** VenAmCham's Business Venezuela.
Some political websites include:
In Spanish:
www.aporrea.org A good pro-Chávez site.
www.abn.info.ve The government's news agency, sums up daily news in the country.
www.eluniversal.com Anti-government newspaper, good opposition source for analysis.
www.noticias24.com Daily news on Venezuela, opposition leaning.
In English:
www.venezuelanalysis.com Pro-government analysis site. Good links to past articles.
www.caracaschronicles.com Anti-government blog with very good links to information on Venezuela and recent history.

Visas and immigration

See also Embassies and consulates, page 1566.
Entry is by passport and visa, or by passport and tourist card. Tourist cards (*tarjetas de ingreso*) are issued by airlines to visitors from all EU and other Western European countries, Australia, Canada, New Zealand, South Africa, USA and most South and Central American and Caribbean countries. To check if you need a visa, see www.mre.gov.ve. Valid for 90 days, tourist cards cannot be extended. At some overland border crossings (including San Antonio) visitors are given only 30 days. Overstaying your tourist card may lead to arrest and a fine when you try to depart. For a **tourist visa**, you need 1 passport photo, passport valid for 6 months, references from bank and employer, onward or return ticket and a completed and signed application form. The fee is US$75. For a 90-day extension go to the Servicio Administrativo de Identificación, Migración y Extranjería, SAIME, Av Baralt on Plaza Miranda in Caracas, T0800-SAIME00 or 0212-483 2070, www.saime.gob.ve (see also http://pasaporte.saime.gob.ve); take passport, tourist visa, photographs and return ticket; passport with extension returned at end of day. SAIME offices in many cities do not offer extensions. Transit visas, valid for 72 hrs are also available, mostly the same requirements and cost (inward and onward tickets needed). SAIME in Caracas will not exchange a transit for a tourist visa. In Manaus you also need a yellow fever inoculation certificate. Consuls may give a 1-year visa if a valid reason can be given. To change a tourist visa to a business visa, to obtain or to extend the latter, costs US$75.

Work visas also cost US$75 and require authorization from the **SAIME** in Caracas. Student visas need a letter of acceptance from the Venezuelan institution, references from bank and university, signed application form, 1 passport photo, onward or return ticket, passport valid for 6 months and US$75. It takes 2 days to issue a visa.

Note If you are not eligible for a tourist card, you must get a consular visa in advance. Carry your passport with you at all times as police do spot checks and anyone found without ID is immediately detained (carrying a certified copy of your passport and entry stamp is OK, though not always accepted). You will also be asked to provide details like name, address, passport number in restaurants and shops. Military checkpoints are in many areas, especially in border zones (eg on the roads from San Antonio to Maracaibo and Mérida), where all transport is stopped. Have documents ready and make sure you know what entry permits you need; soldiers may not know rules for foreigners. Searches at checkpoints are thorough and foreigners get closer attention than nationals. Business visitors on short visits are advised to enter as tourists, otherwise they'll have to obtain a tax clearance certificate (*solvencia*) before they can leave. Do not lose the carbon copy of your visa as this has to be surrendered when leaving.

Weights and measures

Metric.

Caracas

→ *Phone code: 0212. Colour map 1, A6. Population: about 4 million (city 2 million). Altitude: 960 m.*

Caracas is not the gentlest of introductions to South America. Some enjoy its pleasant, year-round climate, its parks and cosmopolitan nightlife. Others are drawn to see firsthand the Chávez revolution in action. For others, it's more like a slap in the face from a garishly dressed, loud mestizo with a taste for all things American. Founded in 1567, it lies in a rift in thickly forested mountains which rise abruptly from a lush green coast to heights of 2,000 to 3,000 m. The small basin in which the capital lies runs some 24 km east and west. By way of escape, there are several nearby excursions to mountain towns, the colonial district of El Hatillo, the Parque Nacional Monte Avila, beaches and Los Roques, a beautiful Caribbean atoll reached by a short flight.

Ins and outs

Getting there The **airport** is 28 km from Caracas, near the port of La Guaira: Maiquetía and Aeropuerto Auxiliar for national flights and Simón Bolívar for international flights. The terminals are connected by an airconditioned walkway. There are three main **bus terminals** in different parts of the city; where you arrive depends upon where you travelled from. ▸▸ *See also Transport, page 1581.*

Getting around The metro is a/c, clean, safe, comfortable and quick, although poorly signed and often packed, especially at rush hours. MetroBuses are modern, comfortable, recommended

Sleeping
1 Altamira
2 Caracas Palace
3 Continental Altamira
4 Eurobuilding
5 La Floresta & Montserrat
6 Paseo Las Mercedes
7 Tamanaco

but infrequent. Regular buses are overcrowded in rush hour and charge extra after 2100. Bus tickets cost US$0.05-0.15. *Por puesto* minibuses, known as *busetas, carmelitas* or *carritos* run on regular routes; fares depend on the distance travelled within the city. A *metrocable* system opened 2010 serving residents of the San Agustín barrio. A bus system on dedicated lines is still under construction.

Orientation In the centre, each street corner has a name: addresses are generally given as 'Santa Capilla and Mijares' (*Santa Capilla y* - sometimes *a* - *Mijares*), rather than the official 'Calle Norte 2, No 26'. In the east, 'y' or 'con' are used for street intersections. Modern multi-storeyed edifices dominate and few colonial buildings remain intact; many find the city lacking in character. A 10-km strip from west to east, fragmented by traffic-laden arteries, contains several centres: Plaza Bolívar, Plaza Venezuela, Sabana Grande, Chacaíto, Altamira, La California and Petare. The Avila mountain is always north.

Tourist offices **Corpoturismo**, Parque Central, Torre Oeste, p 35, 36 y 37, T507 8800.

Climate Maximum 32°C July-August, minimum 9°C January-February.

Security Safety in Caracas has deteriorated in recent years and crime rates and kidnappings have risen significantly. You should be on the lookout from the moment you arrive; there are many pirate taxis and rip-off merchants operating at the international airport. It is best not to arrive in Caracas at night. Avoid certain areas such as all western suburbs from the El Silencio

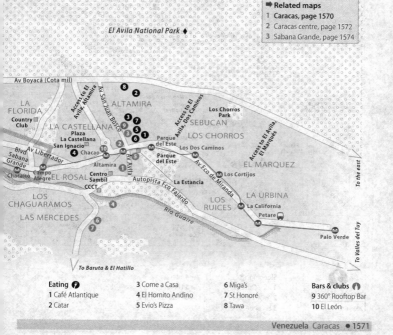

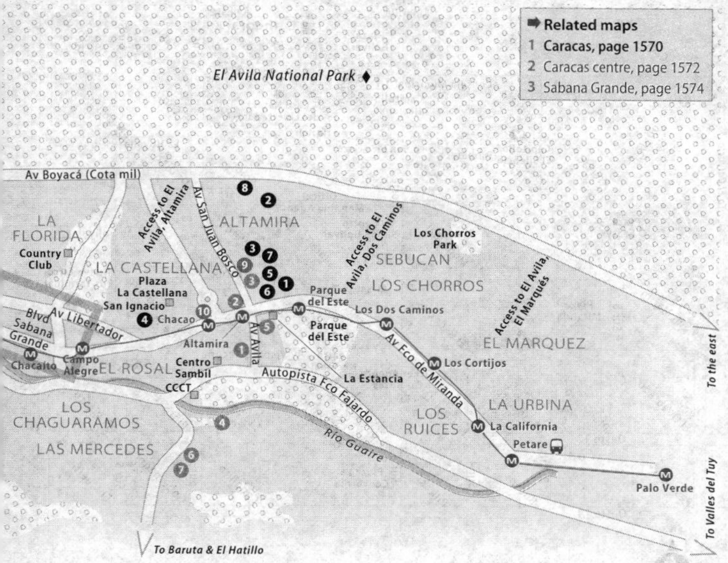

Eating
1 Café Atlantique
2 Catar
3 Come a Casa
4 El Hornito Andino
5 Evio's Pizza
6 Miga's
7 St Honoré
8 Tawa

Bars & clubs
9 360° Rooftop Bar
10 El León

monument to Propatria, the areas around the Nuevo Circo and La Bandera bus stations, the area around the *teleférico*, Chapellín near the Country Club, and Petare. It is not advisable to walk at night in the city, except in the municipality of Chacao (Altamira, Chacao and Los Palos Grandes) and in Las Mercedes. Street crime is common, even armed robbery in daylight. Carry handbags, cameras etc on the side away from the road as motorcycle bag- snatchers are notorious. Do not to wear jewellery, carry valuables or openly display mobile phones or cameras. Car theft is common: always use car parks; never park on the street. Police checks are frequent, thorough and can include on-the-spot searches of valuables. Always carry your passport, or a photocopy (nothing else will be acceptable); bribes are sometimes asked for. If you have entered overland from Colombia, expect thorough investigation. See also Safety, page 1567.

2 Caracas centre

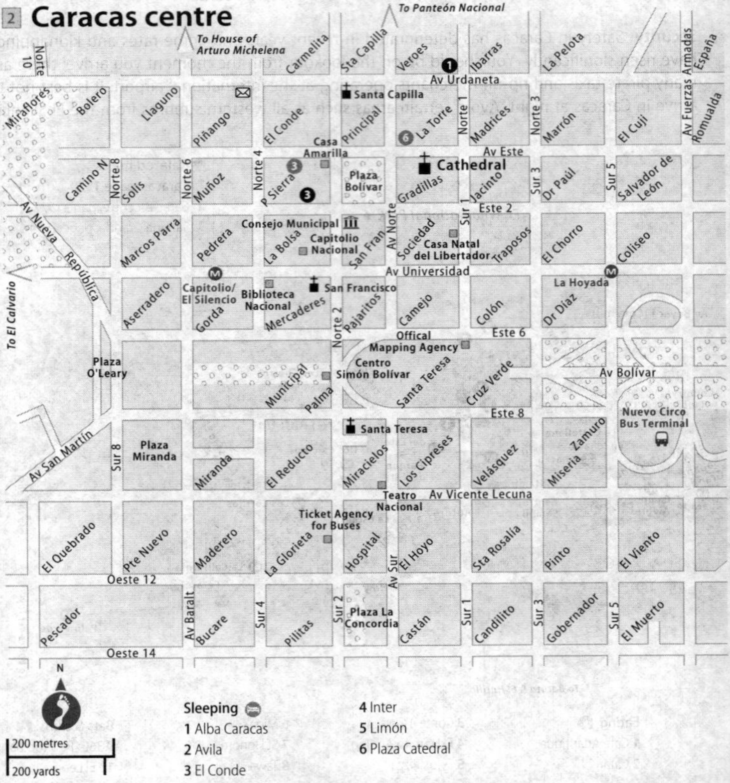

Centre

ⓘ *Many museums close on Mon and at lunchtime.*

The shady **Plaza Bolívar**, with its fine equestrian statue of the Liberator and pleasant colonial cathedral, is still the official centre of the city, though no longer geographically so. Much of its colonial surroundings is being restored. In the **Capitolio Nacional**, the National Assembly, which consists of two neoclassical-style buildings, the Legislative Palace and the Federal Palace ⓘ *Tue-Sun, 0900-1200, 1400-1700,* the Elliptical Salon has some impressive paintings and murals by the Venezuelan artist Martín Tovar y Tovar. The present **Cathedral** dating from 1674 has a beautiful façade, the Bolívar family chapel and paintings by Michelena, Murillo and an alleged Rubens 'Resurrection'. Bolívar was baptized in this Cathedral and the remains of his parents and wife are kept here.

The **Consejo Municipal** (City Hall) on Plaza Bolívar contains three **museums** ⓘ *all 3 open Tue-Fri 0930-1200, 1500-1800; Sat and Sun 0930-1800* and feature a collection of the paintings

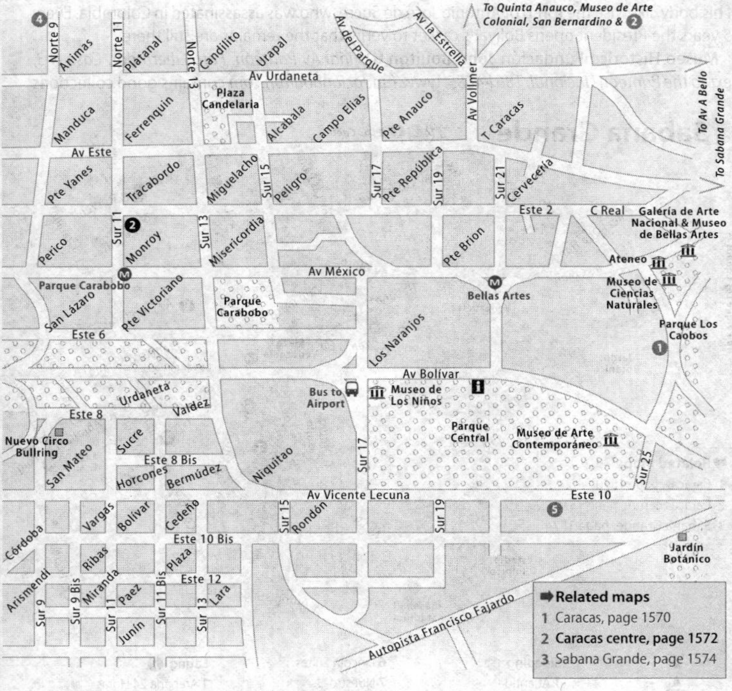

Eating 🅕

1 El Parador

2 La Cocina Criolla de Francy

3 La Indicata

of Emilio Boggio, a Venezuelan painter; the Raúl Santana Museum of the Creole Way of Life, a collection of miniature figures in costumes, all handmade by Raúl Santana; and the Sala de Arqueología Gaspar Marcano, exhibiting ceramics, mostly discovered on the coast.

Casa Natal del Libertador ⓘ *Sur 1 y Este 2, Jacinto a Traposos, opposite Plaza El Venezolano, T541 2563, Tue-Fri 1000-1200, 1400-1700, Sun and holidays 1000-1300, 1400-1700*, is a fascinating reconstruction of the house where Bolívar was born (24 July 1783). Interesting pictures and furniture and murals tell Bolívar's life story. The first house, of adobe, was destroyed by an earthquake. The second became a stable, and was later pulled down. The **Museo Bolivariano** is alongside the Casa Natal and contains the Liberator's war relics.

San Francisco ⓘ *Av Universidad y San Francisco (1 block southwest of Plaza Bolívar)*, the oldest church in Caracas, rebuilt 1641, should be seen for its colonial altars. **Santa Teresa** ⓘ *between La Palma and Santa Teresa, just southeast of the Centro Simón Bolívar*, has good interior chapels and a supposedly miraculous portrait of Nazareno de San Pablo (popular devotions on Good Friday).

Panteón Nacional ⓘ *Av Norte y Av Panteón, Tue-Sun 0900-1200,1400-1630*. The remains of Simón Bolívar, the Liberator, lie here in the Plaza Panteón. The tomb of Francisco Miranda (the Precursor of Independence), who died in a Spanish prison, has been left open to await the return of his body, likewise the tomb of Antonio José de Sucre, who was assassinated in Colombia. Every 25 years the President opens Bolívar's casket to verify that the remains are still there.

Museo Histórico Fundación John Boulton ⓘ *Final Av Panteón, Foro Libertador, Casa N 3, next to the Panteón Nacional, T861 4685, www.fundacionboulton.com* contains good collections

3 Sabana Grande

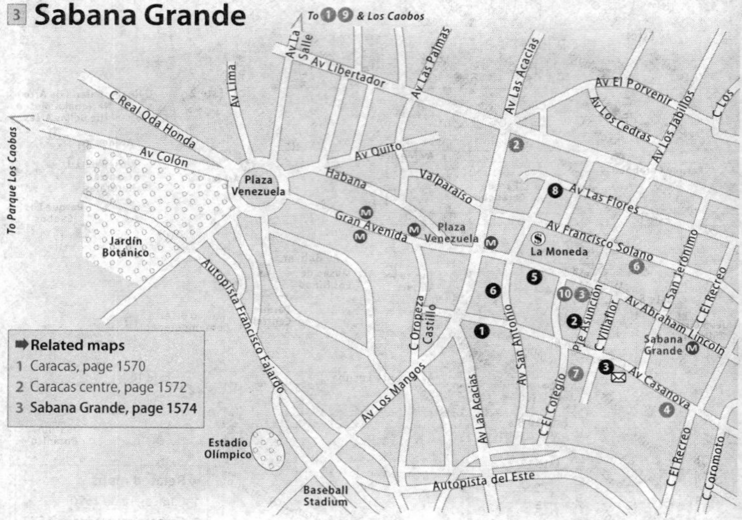

➡ Related maps
1 Caracas, page 1570
2 Caracas centre, page 1572
3 Sabana Grande, page 1574

N

200 metres
200 yards

Sleeping
1 Atlántida
2 Crillón
3 Cristal
4 Gran Meliá
5 Las Américas
6 Lincoln Suites
7 Nuestro
8 Plaza Palace
9 Plaza Venezuela
10 Savoy

Eating
1 Arepería 24 Horas
2 Córdova Pollo's Ceviche
3 El Arabito
4 El Arepazo
5 Gran Café

of 19th century art and objects, furniture, maps, metals and coins and a collection of objects and documents relating to the life of Simon Bolivar.

Museo de Arte Colonial ⓘ *Quinta Anauco, Av Panteón, San Bernardino, T551 4256, www.quintadeanauco.org.ve, Tue-Fri 0900-1130, 1400-1630, Sat-Sun and holidays 1000-1600, US$4.65.* This delightful house in the beautiful suburb of San Bernardino, was built in 1720 and was formerly the residence of the Marqués del Toro. Everything from the roof to the carpet has been preserved and the house contains a wealth of period furniture and sculpture and almost 100 paintings from the colonial era.

Sabana Grande and east of the centre

In the **Parque Central**, a concrete jungle complex between Avenida Lecuna (east end) and the elevated section of Avenida Bolívar, there are two, run-down octagonal towers (56 floors each) and four large, shabby apartment blocks with cafés and shops below. Four museums are located here: **Museo de Arte Contemporáneo** ⓘ *Parque Central, Cuadra Bolívar, T573 8289, www.fmn.gob.ve/fmn_mac.htm entrance beside Alba Hotel, 0900-1700, free.* It has some 3,000 works on display, including modern sculptures and the works by, among others, Miró, Chagall, Matisse and Picasso, one of the finest collections of modern art in South America. The **Museo de los Niños** ⓘ *Parque Central, next to east Tower, Nivel Bolívar, T575 0695, www.maravillosa realidad.com, Mon-Fri 0900-1700, Sat-Sun and holidays 1000-1700, US$5.35, children US$4.65,* is an extremely popular and highly sophisticated interactive science museum. Also in the Parque Central complex, is the **Museo del Teclado** (Museum of Keyboard Instruments) ⓘ *T572 0713, www.museodelteclado.com.ve.*

6 Jaime Vivas
7 La Huerta
8 Sabas Nieves
9 Urrutia

Bars & clubs
10 El Encuentro de los Artistas
11 El Maní Es Así

Parque Los Caobos is a peaceful park with fountains and a cafeteria in the middle. It is a lovely place to wander if you are visiting the Plaza de los Museos (see below). It also contains Bosque de las Esculturas, an open-air sculpture exhibition near the Plaza de los Museos entrance. By the entrance in Avenida México is the cultural centre, **Ateneo de Caracas**, with a cinema, theatre, art gallery, concert room, bookshop and the imposing **Teresa Carreño theatre** complex, www.ateneodecaracas.org. **Museo de Bellas Artes** ⓘ *Plaza de los Museos, T578 0275, www.fmn.gob.ve/fmn_mba.htm, free, Mon-Fri 0900-1600, Sat-Sun and holidays 1000-1700,* the oldest museum in Caracas, designed by Carlos Raúl Villanueva. It contains a good, permanent collection of contemporary and 19th century works by mainly Venezuelan and South American artists and a good café surrounded by outdoor sculptures. Adjacent is the **Galería de Arte Nacional** ⓘ *T576 8707, www.fmn.gob.ve/fmn_gan.htm, Mon-Fri 0900-1700, Sat-Sun and holidays 1000-1700,* displays the history of Venezuelan art, from colonial times to present day, and also houses the **Cinemateca Nacional** ⓘ *www.cinemateca.gob.ve (site under construction - 2010),* an arts and experimental cinemas. **Museo de**

Ciencias Naturales ⓘ *Plaza de los Museos, Los Caobos, T577 5103, www.fmn.gob.ve/fmn_mc.htm, Mon-Fri 0900-1700, Sat-Sun and holidays 1030-1800*, has archaeological, particularly pre- Columbian, zoological and botanical exhibits, interesting temporary shows.

Jardín Botánico ⓘ *near Plaza Venezuela, entrance by Ciudad Universitaria, Mon-Sun 0830-1630, www.fibv.org.ve/jardin*, is worth a visit, with extensive collections of over 2000 species; 10,000 trees belonging to 80 species grow in the arbetorium alone. Here you can see the world's largest palm tree (*Corypha Sp*) and the Elephant Apple with its huge edible fruit.

La Estancia ⓘ *just along from the Altamira metro exit, www.laestancia.pdvsa.com*, is a cultural centre with good exhibitions, regular activities and events including free yoga and music. It is set in a lovely park with beautiful trees and manicured lawns, the perfect place to escape from the hectic city.

Parque Nacional del Este ⓘ *closed Mon, opens 0530 for joggers, 0830 for others, till 1700, reached from Parque del Este metro station*, is the largest park in Caracas and a popular place to relax, especially at weekends. A great place for a leisurely stroll and people watching, it has a boating lake, snake house, cactus garden, a number of different sunken lakes featuring caiman and turtles, monkeys and a caged jaguar as well as the **Humboldt Planetarium** ⓘ *T234 9188, www.planetariohumboldt.com*. **Museo de Transporte** ⓘ *Parque Nacional del Este (to which it is connected by a pedestrian overpass), T234 1621, www.automotriz.net/museo-del-transporte, Sun 0900-1630*, has a large collection of locomotives and old cars.

Other parks and urban excursions

The densely wooded **Parque Caricuao** ⓘ *Tue-Sun 0900-1630: take metro to Caricuao Zoológico, then 5 min walk up Av Principal La Hacienda*, is at the southwest end of the Metro line, and forms part of the Parque Nacional Macuro. A pleasant day out. At the foot of the Avila mountain, the **Parque Los Chorros** ⓘ *Tue-Fri 0830-1630, Sat-Sun 0830-1800, take bus from Los Dos Caminos station to Lomas de Los Chorros* has impressive waterfalls and forest walks. **El Calvario**, west of El Silencio, with the Arch of Confederation at the entrance, has a good view of Centro Simón Bolívar, but muggings have been reported. It has a small Museo Ornitológico, botanical gardens and a picturesque chapel.

El Hatillo ⓘ *take a bus or taxi from central Caracas, about 20-30 mins' drive, depending on traffic*, once a separate village now subsumed by the city sprawl, is one of the few places in Caracas that has retained its colonial architecture. Built around a central plaza, its peaceful streets of multi-coloured houses offer a fine selection of cafés, restaurants, shops and small galleries. It is recommended as a wonderful spot to escape from the city and to shop for handicrafts, but it gets busy at weekends.

See also the cable car ride to the summit of **Monte El Avila** with fantastic views of Caracas, page 1585.

Caracas listings

Hotel and guesthouse prices

LL over US$200	**L** US$151-200	**AL** US$101-150
A US$66-100	**B** US$46-65	**C** US$31-45
D US$21-30	**E** US$12-20	**F** US$7-11
G US$6 and under		

Restaurant prices

¥¥¥ over US$12	¥¥ US$7-12	¥ under US$6

Sleeping

Caracas hotels are not cheap and the range of budget accommodation is poor. The cheapest hotels are in the downtown area, but this is not a safe part of town at night, or even in the day with a backpack. Sabana Grande, which has a wide range of hotels, is not safe at night, either. If you don't want to stay in the suburbs or centre, spend a little more and go to the upmarket Chacao, Altamira, La Castellana districts (all easily reached by metro), where it is relatively safe to stroll around during the day. There are hotels on the coast, close to the airport, if you do not want to go into the city. Some hotels listed below will charge an additional 17% tax; others include it in their price. If you book from abroad, make sure you receive written confirmation before beginning your journey. For apartment rental, consult *El Universal* daily paper, small ads columns. The business and commercial district is southeast of the centre, not on metro.

Central area *p1573, map p1572*

The cheapest hotels are around the Nuevo Circo bus terminal (not a safe area). Plaza Bolívar and its surrounding streets are busy by the day, but by night are deserted and unsafe.

L-AL Alba Caracas, Av Sur 25 with Av Mexico, T503 5000. Ageing luxury hotel, formerly the Hilton, now run jointly by the state and a privately company. Business centre, city views, noisy (traffic and a/c), pool, but for this price there are better options elsewhere in the city.

A El Conde, Av Este esq El Conde, T860 1171. Well located for those wanting to stay in the historic centre, elegant lobby but rooms are a bit run down. Own restaurant and bar.

B Plaza Catedral, Blvd Plaza Bolívar, next to Cathedral, T564 2111. Central location just off Plaza Bolívar, Amex accepted, a/c, English spoken, good views over the Plaza but can be noisy. Good restaurant, includes breakfast. Recommended.

D Inter, Animas a Calero, on corner of Av Urdaneta, near Nuevo Circo, T564 0251. Helpful, English spoken, very popular, poor restaurant, accepts credit cards.

D Limón, Av Lecuna, Frente Parque Central, T571 6457, Bellas Artes metro. Safe, parking, well located for museums and galleries, often recommended.

San Bernardino *map p1572*

Residential area 2 km north of Bellas Artes metro.

AL-A Avila, Av Jorge Washington, T555 3000, www.hotelavila.com.ve. Modern, medium-sized hotel, set in tranquil tropical gardens around 20 mins' drive from the centre, very pleasant, good service, most staff speak English and German, fans, mosquito screens, pool, Metrobus nearby, very good restaurant and poolside bar, travel agency, phones accept Visa/Mastercard.

Sabana Grande/Chacaíto *p1575, map p1574*

This popular area with budget backpackers has restaurants and shops, but most close by early evening. Many hotels are in the Av Las Acacias/ Av Casanova area, the majority are short stay.

LL Gran Meliá, Av Casanova y El Recreo, T762 8111, www.gran-melia.com/en/. Top-ranking hotel with all facilities, business centre, generous gourmet buffets, restaurants (including Japanese and pizzería), fitness centre, spa, great pool area, piano bar.

LL Las Américas, C Los Cerritos, at the end of Av Casanova, T951 7133, www.hotellasamericas.com.ve. Modern tower blocks, tiny roof pool and restaurant, taxi service to airport.

AL Lincoln Suites, Av Francisco Solano, T762 8575, www.lincoln-suites.com.ve. Well-equipped with comfortable rooms, popular bar.

AL-A Crillón, Av Libertador, esq Av Las Acacias, T761 4411, www.hotelcrillon.com.ve. Near Plaza Venezuela metro. High-rise block, good service, comfortable, good bar.

A Plaza Palace, Av Los Mangos, Las Delicias, T762 4821, plaza_palace_hotel@hotmail.com. Old building with good facilities for business travellers, a/c, TV, helpful, English spoken.

A Savoy, Av Francisco Solano López y Av Las Delicias, T762 1971, www.hotelsavoycaracas.com.ve.

Well-established large hotel, good food, terrace, WiFi, secure car park, taxi service to airport.

B Atlántida, Av La Salle, Los Caobos, T793 3211. Modern, comfortable hotel with cable TV, restaurant, pool and fitness club.

B Plaza Venezuela, Av La Salle, Los Caobos, T781 7811. Modern, small but good rooms, helpful staff, good value.

C-D Cristal, C Real de Sabana Grande, Pasaje Asunción, just off Av Abraham Lincoln, near Sabana Grande metro, T761 9131. Comfortable, a/c, safe, good value, restaurant, English spoken, helpful staff.

D Nuestro, also known as **The Backpackers Hostel**, Av Casanova, C El Colegio, T762 1788. Calls itself 'one of the only backpacker hostels in Caracas'. Basic rooms with bath, helpful staff, English spoken, can arrange airport transfers and tours, terrace and luggage lock, snacks and drinks sold. Good value. Works with recommended tour operator **Osprey**, T762 5975, www.ospreyvenezuela.com.

Chuao/Las Mercedes *map p1570*

An upmarket commercial district southeast of the centre and Sabana Grande, no metro station.

LL Tamanaco Inter-Continental, Av Principal Las Mercedes, T909 7111, www.ichotelsgroup.com. One of the better hotels in Caracas, good pool, sauna, luxury business hotel, courteous staff, good facilities, WiFi, excellent food. Midweek discounts available.

LL-L Eurobuilding Hotel & Suites, Calle La Guarita, Chuao, T902 1111, www.eurobuilding.com.ve. 5-star, modern, has all-suite wing, well-furnished, a/c, includes breakfast, efficient service, large pool, gym, restaurants, many services, weekend rates.

AL Hotel Paseo Las Mercedes, CC Paseo Las Mercedes, Las Mercedes, T993 1244, www.hotelpaseolasmercedes.com. Located in the shopping mall with fine restaurants and bars on the doorstep. Comfortable, spacious rooms with good service. Close to the **Tamanaco** but a cheaper option.

Chacao, Altamira, La Castellana *map p1570*

These 3 districts, east of Gran Sabana and the centre, are adjacent to each other, and are a respectable commercial and residential zone.

LL Caracas Palace, Av Luis Roche con Av Francisco Miranda, Altamira, T771 1000, www.caracaspalace.com. Popular high end hotel, good pool and spa.

LL-L Continental Altamira, Av San Juan Bosco, Altamira, T261 0644, www.hotel-continental.org.ve. Smart, with breakfast, gardens and a good pool.

A Residencia Montserrat, Av Avila Sur, T263 3533, F261 1394. Near Plaza Altamira and Altamira metro station, pleasant, well-run, helpful, a/c, hot water, TV, parking. Recommended for long stays.

A-B La Floresta, Av Avila Sur, T263 1955, www.hotellafloresta.com. Near Altamira metro, hot water, cable TV, restaurant, bar, parking, modern, some rooms renovated.

B Altamira, Av José Féliz Sosa, Altamira Sur, T267 4284 (do not confuse with **Altamira Suites Hotel**). Close to Altamira metro. Safe, modern, comfortable, credit cards accepted, helpful and efficient staff, changes dollars, secure parking. Most rooms with balcony. Recommended.

Near airport

See Litoral Central, page 1587.

Eating

Central area *p1573, map p1572*

There are plenty of eating places around Plaza Bolívar and, better still, around Plaza La Candelaria.

TT La Cocina Criolla de Francy, Av Este 2 y Sur 11, La Candelaria, T576 9849. Good Spanish-Venezuelan food, best for weekend breakfasts and lunch. Recommended.

TT The restaurant in the **Museo de Arte Contemporáneo** serves great food, good value.

TT El Parador, Av Urdaneta, esquina Ibarras a Maturín No 18. Great Spanish food and service.

TT-T La Indicata, just off Plaza Bolívar. Good for breakfast, decent arepas, fresh juices and coffee.

Sabana Grande *p1575, map p1574*

This area has some cafés, bars (*tascas*) and restaurants. Good selection in CC El Recreo.

TTT Urrutia, Fco Solano y Los Mangos. Good Basque food in this busy, relaxed restaurant

TTT-TT Jaime Vivas, C San Antonio, T763 4761. Best place to go for traditional Venezuelan food, especially *pabellón*.

TTT-TT La Huerta, Avda Fco Solano con 1ra Av de Las Delicias. A popular *tasca*, very good tapas. Popular with locals for watching Spanish football.

‼ Córdova Pollo's Ceviche, Pasaje Asunción, Edif Rioja, Loc 11. Peruvian-owned ceviche restaurant, hole-in-the-wall, he puts chairs out on alleyway.

‼-ǂ Gran Café, Sabana Grande. Great open air café-restaurant, good place to have a coffee or meal and watch the world go by.

‼-ǂ Sabas Nieves, C Pascual Navarro 12. Homely, good value vegetarian restaurant.

ǂ El Arabito C Villaflor, just off Av Abraham Lincoln between metro stations Sabana Grande and Plaza Venezuela. Arabic food. Others in this area.

ǂ Arepería 24 Horas, Av Casanova y Av Las Acacias. Busy, inexpensive and very popular.

ǂ El Arepazo, 1 block south of Chacaíto metro station. Every kind of arepa filling you could want.

Chuao/Las Mercedes

The area has a good selection of upmarket restaurants and US-style steakhouses and chains.

‼ǂ Astrid y Gaston, Londres entre Av Caroní y Nueva York, T993 1119, Las Mercedes, www.astridygaston.com. Very nice Peruvian restaurant with open kitchen and friendly staff.

‼ǂ Coco Thai and Lounge, CC Tolón, piso 3, Las Mercedes. Excellent Thai food in this sophisticated restaurant with roof terrace

‼ǂ-‼ La Castañuela, C Trinidad con C París. Live music at weekends, bar area, good Spanish food, generous portions, attentive service, popular.

‼ La Carreta, Centro Uruguayo Venezolano, Av Arístides Calvani, Los Chorros, T234 0317. Atmospheric haunt of the Uruguayan community with fantastic meat and tango dancing on Wed and Sun nights.

‼ Nouveau Café, Av Principal De Valle Arribe, cruce con Av Orinoco. Well-priced, tasty Mediterranean food, including pastas, nice décor and terrace. Open Sun.

‼ Persepolis, C California con C Mucuchíes, T993 3987. Good Iranian food.

‼ La Taberna de Félix, Av Principal de las Mercedes, Multicentro las Mercedes. Lively Spanish restaurant and bar with live music and flamenco.

Altamira, La Castellana *map p1570*

‼ǂ Café Atlantique, Av Andrés Bello, Los Palos Grandes. Sophisticated bar and restaurant with good food

‼ǂ-‼ Catar, Cuadra Gastronómica, 6a Transversal. Relaxed, stylish café/restaurant with delicious thin crust pizzas and a melt-in-the-mouth chocolate pudding. Good selection for vegetarians. Closed Mon. Several other good restaurants in this gastronomic block.

‼ Come a Casa, 1ra Avenida con 1ra Transversal, Los Palos Grandes. Popular Italian with terrace, cosy atmosphere and home made pasta dishes.

‼ Evio's Pizza, Av 4 between Transversales 2 y 3, Los Palos Grandes, Altamira. Best pizza in town. Live music from Thu to Sun.

‼ El Hornito Andino, 2da Transversal con 4ta Avenida, Campo Alegre. On the edge of Chacao, excellent, good value Andean breakfasts and lunches, vegetarian options. Good service.

‼ Tawa, 1ra Avenida con 1ra Transversal, Los Palos Grandes. Peruvian fusion restaurant, good food with fine service.

‼-ǂ Miga's, Av Luis Roche con 1ra Transversal, Los Palos Grandes, opposite **Altamira Suites Hotel**, www.migas.com.ve. Busy café/bakery/deli chain with 6 outlets selling fresh breads, cakes, salads, sandwiches and meat dishes, some vegetarian options, open late.

‼-ǂ St Honoré, 1ra Transversal con Av Andrés Bello, Los Palos Grandes. Popular café and bakery with covered terrace, good for lunch. Some of the best bread in town.

Bars and clubs

Caracas *p1570, maps p1570, p1572 and p1574*

Caracas has a vibrant nightlife. Clubs don't usually come to life until after 2300, and then go on to the early hours. Las Mercedes district is full of busy, trendy bars.

Bars

360° Rooftop Bar, 19th floor of **Altamira Suites Hotel**, 1ra Avendia, Los Palos Grandes. Hip, sophisticated wine bar with panaromic views of the city, snack on pizza or sushi and sip delicious cocktails. A must just for the views.

El Encuentro de los Artistas, Callejón Asunción (also known as the Callejón de las Puñaladas - Stab Alley!), Sabana Grande. Crowded, lively jazz bar with regular live music, popular with students.

El León, in Plaza La Castellana, T263 6014. Very popular outdoor bar, heaving at weekends, open daily 1200-2400.

El Naturista, 2da Transversal, La Castellana, next to McDonalds, T263 5350. Arepas by day, beer and bar at night, open daily, popular.

Puto Bar, also known as **NuvoBar**, Av Libertador con C El Muñeco, Chacao. Shoreditch and the Lower East Side meet Caracas, small, hip bar with live music.
Centro Comercial San Ignacio, see Shopping, has many fashionable, though pricey bars and the occasional nightclubs, popular with wealthy young Venzuelans. Try **Whisky Bar** (Nivel Blandín), usually packed, trendy and friendly crowd, long bar with terrace area, open daily. Or **Suka** (Nivel Blandín) with giant hammock and good cocktail menu.
La Suite bar, Centro Comercial Tolón Fashion Mall, PB, Las Mercedes, T300 8858. Another popular lounge bar, lavish décor, attracts wealthy 20-something crowd. Mix of music from house to 80s. Tango on Mon, boleros on Tue, jazz on Wed, varied music with invited DJ nights Thu-Sat.
U-Bar, CC Macaracuay Plaza, Macaracuay. Popular, university bar, giant screen, open 2200-0500.

Clubs

El Maní es Así, Av Francisco Solano y C El Cristo, Sabana Grande, T763 6671, www.elmaniesasi.com. Famous for its live salsa and dancing, casual, open Tue-Sun till 0400/0500.
Moulin Rouge, Av Francisco Solano, Las Mercedes. Club famous for its live rock music

Entertainment

Caracas *p1570, maps p1570, p1572 and p1574*
For details of cinemas and other events, see the newspapers, *El Universal* (the cinema page on www.el-universal.com has full listings), *El Nacional* and *Daily Journal*.

Concerts, ballet, theatre and film festivals at the **Ateneo de Caracas**, Paseo Colón, Plaza Morelos. **Centro de Estudios Latinoamericanos Rómulo Gallegos** (CELARG), Av Luis Roche con 3ra Transversal, Altamira, T285 2721, www.celarg.org.ve. Cultural centre with cinema showing alternative films, theatre, exhibitions, talks.
Trasnocho Cultural, Urb Las Mercedes, Centro Comercial Paseo Las Mercedes, Nivel Trasnocho, T993 1910, www.trasnochocultural.com. Theatre, cinemas, exhibitions, lounge bar with live DJs Thu-Sat, bookshop, café and yoga centre.

Festivals and events

Caracas *p1570, maps p1570, p1572 and p1574*
3 May, Velorio de la Cruz de Mayo still celebrated with dances and parties in some districts. **18-25 Dec**, Yuletide masses at different churches leading up to Christmas. Traditional creole dishes served at breakfasts.

Shopping

Caracas *p1570, maps p1570, p1572 and p1574*
Bookshops **American Bookshop**, Nivel Jardín (bottom level) of CC Centro Plaza, Av Francisco de Miranda, Altamira metro, T286 2230/285 8779. Selection of second-hand English books.
Librorio, C París con Nueva York, Las Mercedes, T993 2841, www.libroria.com, Mon-Sat 0830-1900, Sun 1400-1700. Good selection of English language books and English speaking staff.
Chocolate **La Praline Chocolatier**, Av Andrés Bello con 3ra Transversal, Los Palos Grandes, T284 7986. Ultimate heaven for chocaholics, delicious chocolates crafted from Venezuelan cacao. The packets of hot chocolate make great gifts. **Blue Moon**, C La Paz, Plaza de El Hatillo, T963 3023. Divine chocolatier with small café selling hot chocolate mixes.
Handicrafts Good quality Sun craft market between Museo de Bellas Artes and Museo de Historia Natural (metro Bellas Artes). **Hannsi**, C Bolívar, El Hatillo, T963 5577, www.hannsi.com.ve. A superstore of Venezulean crafts and products made up of numerous small rooms displaying everything from candles to ceramics to hammocks and artesanías from the Amazon. Good adjoining café with wide coffee selection. Well worth a visit.
Jewellery **Edificio La Francia**, 'Esquina Caliente', Plaza Bolívar, Centro. Mon-Fri, 0900-1700, Sat 0900-1400, 10 floors of jewellery stores, central hub of Caracas' gold market.
Malls Most shopping takes place in Caracas' numerous malls.
Centro Sambil, Av Libertador, 1 block south of Chacao Metro. One of the largest in South America, with every type of shop, internet cafés, global brands, bookshops, *cambio*, CANTV centres and cinema. Open Mon-Sun 1000-2100.
San Ignacio, several blocks north of Chacao Metro. Very exclusive. Cinema, banks and smart cafés, bars and restaurants too, open Mon-Sun 1000-2100.

Markets **Mercado Quinta Crespo**, off Av Baralt, El Silencio metro, daily, one of the largest central food markets, shabby but vibrant. **Mercado de Chacao**, Av Avila, 3 blocks north of Chacao metro, 0800-1200, daily except Sun. Good food, fruit and veg market. **Mercado Peruano**, Colegio de Ingenieros metro, Boulevard Amador Bendayán, from 0900 on Sun, popular small Peruvian food market with ceviche stalls.

Activities and tours

Caracas *p1570, maps p1570, p1572 and p1574*

Baseball The popular baseball season is from late Sep-Jan. The capital's local team, Los Leones del Caracas, plays at the Estadio Universitario, Los Chaguaramos. Tickets can be bought at the stadium's box office, www.leones.com.

Gym The gym and pool at **La Gran Meliá** are open to non-guests. A 'día del spa', use of the gym, pool for the day and a massage costs US$35.

Tours

There are numerous companies offering organized tours from standard packages to tailor-made trips. For details on climbing and mountaineering, contact **Asociación Venezolana de Instructores y Guías de Montaña (AVIGM)**, www.avigm.com.

Akanan, C Bolívar, Edf Grano de Oro, pb loc C, Chacao, T715 5433, www.akanan.com. Riding, cycling and other outdoor activities outside Caracas.

Alpiviajes, Av Sucre, Centro Parque Boyacá, Torre Centro, Los Dos Caminos, T283 1433, www.alpi-group.com. Tours throughout Venezuela, including fishing trips and adventure sports, English spoken, good for flights and advice. Flying safari tours in private plane. Recommended.

Backpacker Tours, www.backpacker-tours.com (see page 1673). Numerous tours on offer including roundtrips, trekking, rafting and biking excursions. Good service.

Candes Turismo, Av Francisco de Miranda, Edif Roraima, p 3, of 3C, T953 1632, www.candes turismo.com. Well-established tour operator, range of destinations, helpful, efficient, English, Italian, German spoken.

Cóndor Verde, Av Caura, Torre Humboldt, M 3, Prados del Este, T975 4354, www.condor verdetravel.com. Operate throughout the country, well-established, German run.

Natoura Travel & Adventure Tours, C 31 entre Av Don Tulio y prol Av 6 No 5-27, Mérida 5101, T274-252 4216 (in US T303-800 4639), www.natoura.com. Tailor-made tours. Specialists in adventure tours and ecotourism. See also page 1615.

Natura Raid, Av Principal de la Carlota, Centro Comercial Santa Cecilia, loc 3, T237 2648, www.naturaraid.com. Well-established and experienced agency, bilingual guides, works with local communities.

Orinoco Tours, Edif Galerías Bolívar, p 7, of 75A, Blvd Sabana Grande, T761 8431, www.orinocotours.com. German-owned, flights and tours, including trekking, birdwatching and 'flying safaris.' Very helpful.

Tucaya, Quinta Santa Marta, 1a Av Urbanización Campo Claro, Los Dos Caminos, T234 9401, www.tucaya.com. Small company with good reputation, popular with French speakers.

Transport

Caracas *p1570, maps p1570, p1572 and p1574*

Air

The airport, 28 km from Caracas at La Guaira port, has 2 terminals, Maiquetía (national) and Simón Bolívar (international), which are 5 mins apart, connected by an airconditioned walkway. Airport information: www.aeropuerto-maiquetia.com.ve. Facilities include an **Inatur** tourist office (national terminal), casas de cambio, ATM machines, a bank, cafés, restaurants, car hire offices (national terminal) and duty free shops. In both terminals, many people will offer to change money on the black market. There is no way of knowing if they are trustworthy.

Always allow plenty of time when going to the airport, whatever means of transport you are using: the route can be very congested (minimum 45 mins, can take 2 hrs in daytime) and arrive, if possible, in daylight. Allow at least 2 hrs checking-in time before your flight.

It is vital that you do not arrive at the airport without having arranged a pick up. There has been an increase in foreigners getting taken in what seem to be marked taxis, only to be driven off, robbed and left in the middle of nowhere. If the hotel does not have its own taxis, ask them to contact a taxi company or someone they know for you. It is impossible to verify the trustworthiness of the freelance **taxi** drivers who crowd the terminal. On no account go with an unlicensed driver. There are official taxis. The vehicles are all black, with an oval, yellow logo, which is also displayed at the counter in the arrivals hall where you buy a ticket for the journey into town. You will be accompanied to the taxi by a member of staff. Double check the driver's ID. Prices are listed by the sliding doors, outside which the taxis wait. The fare is US$35-40 (at the official rate) per vehicle to Caracas, depending on time of day and district.

The airport **shuttle bus** (Bus Caracas) leaves from east end of terminal, left out of exit. To airport, catch it under the flyover at Bolívar and Av Sur 17, 250 m from Bellas Artes metro (poorly lit at night, not safe to wait here in the dark), or at metro stations such as Parque Central and Gato Negro. To the city 0700-1930, to the airport 0630-2130, every 30 mins, 1-2 hrs, depending on traffic, US$5. If heading for a hotel in Chacao or Altamira on arrival, get off at Gato Negro metro station (same fare) and take metro from there (with luggage only at off-peak times). The shuttle bus or *por puesto* to airport can also be caught at Gato Negro metro station. Watch your belongings around Gato Negro. A much cheaper alternative is to take a bus to Catia La Mar and get out at the airport.

Airport information Passengers leaving Caracas on international flights must reconfirm their reservations not less than 72 hrs in advance by telephone or in person; not less than 24 hrs for national flights: if you fail to do this, you lose all rights to free accommodation, food, transport, etc if your flight is cancelled and may lose your seat if the plane is fully booked. Beware of forged tickets; buy only from agencies. If told by an agent that a flight is fully booked, try at the airport anyway. International passengers must check in at least two hours before departure or they may lose their seat to someone on a waiting list.

Bus

Local See Getting around, page 1570.

Long distance The *Terminal Oriente* at Guarenas for **eastern destinations** is clean, modern and relatively safe. It can be reached by numerous buses from the city centre and Petare. Take a taxi at night.

The La Bandera terminal for all **western** destinations is a 500 m, unsafe walk from La Bandera metro station on Line 3. City buses that pass are prominently marked 'La Bandera'. Give yourself plenty of time to find the bus you need although there are bus agents who will assist in finding a ticket for your destination. Tickets are sold in advance except for nearby destinations such as **Maracay** and **Valencia**. Those first on get the best seats so it is advisable to arrive an hour before departure. There is a left luggage office, telephone office, cash machines and a restaurant and many food and drink kiosks.

The more upscale **Aeroexpresos Ejecutivos**, Av Principal De Bello Campo, www.aeroexpresos.com.ve (timetables and prices available online), a private bus company, runs regular services to most major destinations. Prices are more expensive than others, but worth it for the more comfortable and modern buses and for the extra security.

Buses to places near Caracas leave from the old Nuevo Circo bus station (eg **Los Teques, Higuerote, Catia La Mar, La Guaira**).

Sat and Sun morning and public holidays are bad for travel into/out of Caracas. Always take identification when booking a long-distance journey. Times and fares of buses are given under destinations.

International buses Ormeño (www.grupo-ormeno.com) has 1 bus a week to **Cúcuta**, **Bogotá**, **Cali**, **Quito**, **Guayaquil**, **Lima**; safe, comfortable, a/c, video, toilet.

Car

Car hire Self-drive cars (**Hertz, Avis, Budget, Dollar, ACO**) are available at the airport (offices open 0700-2100, **Avis** till 2300, good service) and in town. See rates on page 1564.

Metro

Operates 0530-2300, no smoking, luggage allowed only at off-peak times. There are 3 lines: Line 1 (west-east) from Propatria to Palo Verde; Line 2 (north-south), from El Silencio to Las Adjuntas, with connection to Caricuao Zoológico; Line 3, south from Plaza Venezuela via La Bandera to El Valle, plus metrobus El Valle-Los Teques. New stations on Line 3 between El Valle and La Rinconada are under construction. A single ticket costs is BsF0.50,

BsF0.70 return, whereas a 10-journey (*multi abono*) ticket is economical at BsF4.50. Student discounts are available with ISIC card; apply at Parque del Este station. Metrobuses connect with the Metro system: get transfer tickets (*boleto integrado*, BsF0.70-0.90) for services to southern districts, route maps displayed at stations; retain ticket after exit turnstile. Good selection of maps at shops in Altamira and La California stations.

Motorcycle

Motorcycles may not be ridden in Caracas between 2300 and 0500.

Taxi

Even though they are a legal requirement, meters are never used. Negotiate fares in advance; always offer 10% less than the driver's first quote and bargain hard. Most city trips are about US$8-10 during the day. Taxi drivers are authorized to charge an extra 20% on night trips after 1800, on Sun and all holidays, and US$1 for answering telephone calls. After 1800 drivers are selective about destinations. Beware of taxi drivers trying to renegotiate fixed rates because your destination is in 'a difficult area'. See warning above under Air about pirate taxis. See also under Air (or in Yellow Pages) for radio taxis. **Note** Never tell a driver it's your first visit to Caracas.

Directory

Caracas *p1570, maps p1570, p1572 and p1574*

Airline offices Domestic: **Aeropostal**, main office: Av Paseo Colón, Torre Polar Oeste, p 22, Los Caobos, T708 6211. **Aereotuy**, Boulevard de Sabana Grande, Edif Gran Sabana, N-174, T212 3110. **Aserca**, Edif Taeca, C Guaicaipuro, El Rosal, T0800-648 8356 (0700-2000, Sun 0800-1600). **Rutaca**, Centro Seguros La Paz, Av Fco de Miranda, Nivel Mezzanina, loc C-12, La California Sur, T624 5800. See Getting around, page 1563 for websites. **International: Aerolíneas Argentinas**, Calle Guaicaipuro, Torre Hener p 1, of 1A, El Rosal, T951 6395, call centre 0800-100 5655, www.aerolineas.com, closed at weekends. **Air France**, Edif Parque Cristal, Torre Este, p 2, Los Palos Grandes, T208 7200, www.airfrance.com.ve. **American**, Av Principal, La Castellana, Centro Letonia, T209 8111, www.aa.com.ve. **Avianca**, Av Tamanaco, Torre Norte del edif JW Marriott, loc 21 y 22, El Rosal, T200 5725, 0800-100 5022. **Continental**, Centro Lido, Torre E, p 6, Av F de Miranda, T953 3107/0800-100 3198, www.continental.com. **Cubana**, Av Casanova y Av Las Acacias, Torre Banhorient p 5, of 5F, T793 6319, ventascubanacaracas@yahoo.com.ve. **Delta**, Torre E, p 8, Centro Lido, Av Fco de Miranda, El Rosal, T958 1000 . **Iberia**, Av Fco de Miranda, edif Parque Cristal, Torre Este, p 9, Los Palos Grandes, T284 0020. **LAN**, Torre Kleper, of 3-1, Centro San Ignacio, Av Blandín, T263 9663, 0800-100 8600. **Lufthansa**, Centro Torre Conaisa, p 1, of 16, Av San Felipe, La Castellana, closed Sat-Sun.

Banks See also Money, page 1566. Plenty of ATMs around the city and most of the banks have branches in the major shopping centres (Sambil, San Igancio, El Tolón). To change American Express TCs, try **Corp Banca**, Av Principal de La Castellana, Plaza La Castellana, entre Blandín y Los Chaguaramas, Torre Corp Banca, Nivel E-3, La Castellana, T206 4521, mornings and afternoons. They ask for ID and proof of purchase. For money exchange and Amex travel services go to **Italcambio**, the official government exchange office and take ID. They also change Visa TCs, require proof of TC purchase, open Mon-Fri till 1630, Sat till 1200. Offices at Av Urdaneta, esq Animas a Platanal, Edif Camoruco, Nivel Pb, El Centro, T564 4111, Av Francisco de Miranda, CC Lido, Nivel Miranda, T953 9901, at CC Sambil shopping centre, Av Libertador, in Chacao, T265 7423, at Tamanaco Interncontinental Hotel, Las Mercedes, T993 5040, and others. **Italcambio** also at national and international terminals at airport (may limit transaction to US$100, open public holidays). **La Moneda**, Centro Financiero Latino, Av Fco Solano, Edif San Germán, Sabana Grande, open Mon-Fri only. **Viajes Febres Parra**, Av. Libertador, Edif CC Libertador, PB, Loc 4 y 5, La Florida, and at airport.

Cultural centres **British Council**, Torre Credicard, p 3, Av Principal del Bosque, Chacaíto, T952 9965, www.britishcouncil.org/venezuela.htm. Opposite Chacaíto metro, great internet café, magazines, newspapers, film library, courses. **Asociación Cultural Humboldt (Goethe Institut)**, Av Jorge Washington con Juan Germán Roscio, San Bernardino, T552 7634, www.internet.ve/asohum. Library, films, concerts, Spanish and German courses. See also **Centro de Estudios Latinoamericanos Rómulo Gallegos** (CELARG), under Entertainment, and **La Estancia**, page 1576, above.

Embassies and consulates Many are open to the public only in the morning, some are closed on Fri. **Australia** has no embassy in Caracas; apply to Canadian Embassy (below), or Australian Embassy in Brasília. **Austria**, Av La Estancia, Torre Las Mercedes, p 4, of 408, Chuao, T991 3863, caracas-ob@bmaa.gv.at. **Belgium**, 10a Transversal con 9a Transversal, Altamira, T263 3334, www.diplomatie.be/ caracas. **Brazil**, Edif 'Centro Gerencial Mohedano', p 6, between C Los Chaguaramas and Av Mohedano, La Castellana, T918 6000, www.brasil.org.ve, Mon-Fri 0900-1300. **Canada**, Av Francisco de Miranda y Altamira Sur near metro Altamira, T600 3000, www.canadainternational.gc.ca/ venezuela/. Open Mon-Thu 0730-1630, Fri 0730-1300, consular services Mon-Fri 0800-1200. **Colombian consulate**, 2a Av de Campo Alegre con Av Francisco de Miranda, Torre Credival, p 11, T216 9596. **Denmark**, Torre Centuria, p 7, Av Venezuela con C Mohedano, El Rosal, T951 5278, danmark@cantv.net. **Finland**, C Sorocaima entre Av Venezuela y Av Tamanaco, Edif Atrium, p 1, El Rosal, T952 4111, www.finland.org.ve. **France**, C Madrid y Av Trinidad, Las Mercedes, T909 6500, www.francia.org.ve. Mon-Fri 0800-1200. **Germany**, Torre La Castellana, p 10, Av Eugenio Mendoza con C José Angel Lamas, La Castellana, T219 2500, www.caracas.diplo.de/Vertretung/ caracas/es/Startseite.html, nearest metro Altamira. Mon-Wed 0900-1200. **Guyana**, Quinta Roraima, Av El Paseo, Prados del Este, T977 1158, www.guyana.org/spanish/venezuela_embassy. html. **Israel**, Av Principal Los Ruices at Av Fco de Miranda, Centro Empresarial Miranda, p 4, of 4-D, T239 4511. **Italy**, Edif Atrium, C Sorocaima entre Av Tamanaco y Venezuela, El Rosal, T952 7311, www.ambcaracas.esteri.it. **Japan**, Av Principal con 2da Transversal, Edif Bancaracas, p 11, La Castellana, T261 8333. **Netherlands**, Edif San Juan, p 9, San Juan Bosco and Av Transversal 2, Altamira, T263 3622, www.mfa.nl/car, Mon-Thu 0800-1100. **New Zealand** Consulate, Av Francisco de Miranda con Av Libertador, Torre KPMG, p 7, Chacao, T277 7965. **Spain**, Av Mohedano, entre 1 y 2 Transversal, Quinta Marmolejo, La Castellana, T263 2855, www.maec.es/embajadas/caracas/ es/home. **Sweden**, Torre Phelps, p 19, Plaza Venezuela, T781 6976. **Switzerland**, Av Eugenio Mendoza y San Felipe, Centro Letonia, Torre ING-Bank, p 15, La Castellana, T267 9585, www.eda.admin.ch/ caracas. Mon-Fri 0900-1200. **Suriname**, 4a Av de Altamira Norte, Quinta 41, Altamira, T263 8094, embsur1@cantv.net. **Trinidad**, beside the Suriname Embassy, Quinta Serrana, 4a Av de Altamira Norte, between 7a and 8a Transversal, Altamira, T261 5796. **UK**, Torre La Castellana, p 11, Av Principal La Castellana, T263 8411, www.ukinvenezuela.fco.gov.uk. Consular and visa section open Mon-Fri 0800-1200, Wed 1330-1600. **USA**, C F with C Suapure, Colinas de Valle Arriba, take metro to Chacaíto then taxi, T975 6411 (out of office hours 907 8400), http://caracas. usembassy.gov/.

Ferries **Conferry** office for tickets to **Isla de Margarita**, Plaza Venezuela, Av Casanova con Av Las Acacias, Torre Banhorient, PB, Sabana Grande, T0501-2663 3779, www.conferry.com.

Internet Plenty of **CANTV** *centros de comunicaciones* and independent outlets around the city, eg Blvd Sabana Grande (Abraham Lincoln) with broadband, international faxes, and in shopping centres, eg CC Sambil, Chacao. See also **British Council**, above. **Language Schools** **Centro de Idiomas Berlitz**, CC Paseo Las Mercedes, Las Mercedes, www.berlitz.com. **Medical services** **Clínica Avila**, Av San Juan Bosco con 6ta Transversal, Altamira, T276 1111, www.clinicaelavila.com. **Post offices** **Ipostel** main branch at Urdaneta y Norte 4, near Plaza Bolívar, www.ipostel.gov.ve, for poste restante. Overseas package service; packages should be ready to send, also at airport. **MRW**, throughout the city, T0800-304 0000, see www.mrw.com.ve for branches. 24-hr service, more reliable than Ipostel. **Telephones** Public phones in Metro stations and along Blvd Sabana Grande (Abraham Lincoln). **Useful addresses** **SAIME** for visa renewal go to Departamento de Admisión, Av Baralt, Edif 1000, p 2, El Silencio, opposite Plaza Miranda, T483 2070/3581/2706. **Touring y Automóvil Club de Venezuela**, Torre Phelps, p 15, of A y C, Plaza Venezuela, T781 9743, desiree@automovilclubvenezuela.com.

Around Caracas

Between the capital and the Caribbean coast is the national park of El Avila, not only a popular recreational area for caraqueños, but also a refuge for wildlife within earshot of the city and a good place for birdwatching and hiking. The coast itself is also a favourite weekend escape, although it can get busy. Nor, at weekends, can you expect to have Colonia Tovar to yourself, a German immigrant town to which city folk flock for the local produce and mild climate.

Monte Avila → *Colour map 1, A6.*

The 85,192-ha **Parque Nacional El Avila** (renamed **Waraira Repano**) forms the northern boundary of Caracas. The green slopes rise steeply from both the city and from the central Caribbean coast. Despite being so close to the capital, fauna includes red howler monkeys, jaguar and puma. There are also several species of poisonous snake. Access is from Caracas, with several marked entrances along the Cota Mil (Avenida Boyacá), designed for hikers. The park is closed Monday and Tuesday morning. The website **www.el-avila.com** gives hiking routes (see below for suggestions and advice). See also **www.wairairarepano.gob.ve**.

A **cable railway** (*teleférico*) runs up Monte El Avila ⓘ *Tue 1300-1800, Wed-Sat 1000-2100, Sun 0900-1800, US$8, students with card US$4.65 and children 4-12 US$3.50, free for over 60s and under 4s, Final Av Principal de Maripérez (Simón Rodríguez), T901 5555 or 793 5960*. The 20-minute cable car ride offers fantastic views of Caracas on clear days and is highly recommended. Courting couples wander the restaurants, food stalls and skating rink at the summit, El Avila station. From here you can look down the other side of Monte Avila over the village of Galipán all the way to the Caribbean sea. The *Humboldt Hotel* on the summit has been refurbished and is open for guided tours but not for sleeping. From El Avila station you can take a 4WD *carrito* to the village of Galipán, a popular weekend excursion with *caraqueños*. The village has a number of good restaurants and numerous stalls selling food and local produce, strawberries and cream, jams and flowers. There are *posadas* for overnight stays. Also worth visiting is the old coffee hacienda **Los Venados**, where there is a zip wire (known as 'canopy') ⓘ *Senderos Aéreos, T0416-177 4017, www.senderosaereos.com*. El Avila station can also be reached in 45 minutes by shared 4WD *carritos* that leave regularly from the entrance to the park at San Bernardino. A recommended trip is to ride up in a vehicle and hike back down (note that it is cold at the summit, around 13°C).

Listed below are three good places to start a hike. **Advice** Hikers should go in groups of at least three, for mountain and personal safety (Monte Avila is not a dangerous place, but muggings have been reported, especially on more remote paths; leave valuables at home). You should have a park permit from *Inparques* in Caracas to camp. Always take water and something for the cold at altitude. The unfit should not attempt any of the hikes.

Pico Naiguatá (2,765 m) This is a very strenuous hike. Take the metro to La California, then a bus going up Avenida Sanz, ask for the Centro Comercial El Marqués. From there walk up Avenida Sanz towards Cota Mil (Avenida Boyacá), about four blocks. At the end of Avenida Sanz, underneath the bridge, is the entrance to the Naiguatá trail. In about 40 minutes you reach La Julia *guardaparques* station, where you have to pay US$0.50 entrance.

Pico Oriental (2,600 m) From the Altamira metro station take a bus to 'La entrada de Sabas Nieves', where the *Tarzilandia* restaurant is. From here a dirt road leads up to the **Sabas Nieves** *guardaparques* station, a steep 20-40 minute hike with good views of the city, popular with keep-fit *caraqueños*. The path to Pico Oriental starts at the back of Sabas Nieves and is extremely easy to follow. **Note** Paths beyond Sabas Nieves are shut in dry season (roughly February-June depending on the year) to prevent forest fires.

Hotel Humboldt (2,150 m) This is a relatively easy route of three hours. Take the Metro bus from Bellas Artes station to El Avila stop, US$0.50; opposite is a grocery. Turn the corner and walk two blocks up towards the mountain. At the top of the street turn left; almost immediately on your right is the park entrance. **Note** This area is not safe before 0800 or after dark. Plenty of people take this route, starting 0830-0900, giving enough time to get up and down safely and in comfort.

Litoral Central

The Litoral Central is the name given to the stretch of Caribbean Coast directly north of Caracas. A paved road runs east from Catia La Mar, past the airport and then through the towns of Maiquetía, La Guaira and Macuto. This became the state of Vargas in January 1999 and in December that year was the focus of Venezuela's worst natural disaster of the 20th century. Prolonged heavy rains on deforested hillsides caused flash floods and landslides, killing and causing to disappear an estimated 30,000 people and leaving 400,000 homeless. From La Guaira a panoramic road runs to the beaches at Chichiriviche de la Costa, Puerto Cruz (nice beach, no shade, bars) and Puerto Maya (very nice beach with shade and services).

La Guaira, Venezuela's main port dates back to 1567. It achieved its greatest importance in the 18th century when the Basque Guipuzcoana Company held the royal trading monopoly. Much of the city was severely damaged in the 1999 floods.

Colonia Tovar and Guatopo → *Phone code: 0244. Population: 10,000. Altitude: 1,890 m.*

This picturesque mountain town was founded in 1843 by German immigrants from Kaiserstuhl in the Black Forest; a small **museum** ⓘ *1000-1800, Sat-Sun and holidays*, tells the history of the founding pioneers. They retained their customs and isolation until a paved road reached the settlement in 1963. It is now very touristy, attracting hordes of weekend visitors, but the blond hair, blue eyes and Schwartzwald-accented German of the inhabitants remain. This *Tovarense* farming community make great bread, blackberry jam, bratwurst and beer. Colonia Tovar offers delightful landscapes, mild climate, old architecture and dignified hospitality.

From Colonia Tovar, Ruta 4 continues (paved but hair raising) south down the slopes for 34 km to La Victoria on the Caracas-Valencia Highway (see below); bus US$1; glorious scenery.

In **San Francisco de Yare** (*Phone code: 0239; 90 km from Caracas*), a celebration is held at Corpus Christi in early June (the eigth Thursday after Thursday of Semana Santa). Some 80 male 'Diablos' of all ages, dressed all in red and wearing horned masks, dance to the sound of their own drums and rattles. From Santa Teresa make a detour to the beautiful and little frequented **Parque Nacional Guatopo** on the road to Altagracia de Orituco (bus from Nuevo Circo marked 'El Popular', US$1.35). You must return to Santa Teresa to continue your journey to Yare. At the Parque Guatopo are various convenient places to picnic on the route through the forest and a number of good nature trails. Take insect repellent. Free camping at Hacienda La Elvira; take jeep from Altagracia de Orituco (US$1) and ask to be let off at the turn-off to the Hacienda. A permit must be obtained at the Inparques office, which has some accommodation, or baggage can be stored temporarily while walking in the park.

Around Caracas listings

For Sleeping and Eating price codes and other relevant information, see Essentials, pages 38-40.

Sleeping

Litoral Central *p1586*

If you're arriving or leaving the airport at odd times, there are some good choices in Catia La Mar and Macuto as an alternative to Caracas. These places often provide transfers, or a taxi costs about US$5, 5-20 mins depending on traffic.

LL-L Olé Caribe, Final Av Intercomunal, El Playón, 1160, Macuto, T620 2000, www.hotelolecaribe.com. A good, if expensive bet near the airport, a/c, TV, safe in room, breakfast, pool.

L Eurobuilding Express Maiquetía, Av La Armada, T7000 700, maiquetia@eurobuilding.com.ve. Useful business hotel with pool, tennis, tennis, cable TV, internet in rooms, airport transfer.

A-B Posada Il Prezzano, Av Principal de Playa Grande c/c 5, Catia La Mar, T351 2626, www.ilprezzano.com.ve. Italian-run, spotless, pleasant, good value, a/c, restaurant.

B Catimar, Urb Puerto Viejo Av Principal, Catia La Mar, T351 7906, www.hotelcatimar.com. Price includes transfers to and from airport (you may have to phone them from Asistencia al usuario desk), nice bar, restaurant, internet, basic rooms, expensive for what's offered. Near small Puerto Viejo beach, said to be safe, with a few restaurants (**Brisas del Mar, Puerto Mar**), snack bar.

C Santiago, Av La Playa, Urb Alamo, Macuto, T213 3500, www.hotelsantiago.com.ve. Comfortable, restaurant with live music, pool, secure parking, internet,15 mins' drive to airport.

Colonia Tovar *p1586*

There are many hotels, normally full at weekends. Rates, **B** category and above, include good, German-style food. Half-board prices are usually **AL**. Credit cards widely accepted.

Eating

Colonia Tovar *p1586*

Many places serve German delicacies.

El Codazzi, in centre on C Codazzi. Traditional German and Hungarian dishes, strudel and biscuits, Wed-Sun 1100-1600. Recommended.

El Molino, C Molino next to the old mill, 5 min walk from main plaza. Great *jugo de fresas*, wide selection of German dishes, open 0900-1000, 1200-1600, 1800-1900, Mon 0900-1400.

Café Munstall, opposite the church, interesting location in oldest house in Colonia Tovar. Excellent pastries and coffee at weekends.

Fruit, vegetables and flowers sold at **Frutería Bergman**, next to Lagoven station at east entrance to town; across the street is **Panadería Tovar** for delicious bread; many food stalls on weekends along Av Codazzi.

Activities and tours

Monte Avila *p1585*

Centro Excursionista Caracas, Av Santa Sofia Sur, Zona Polideportivo, Urb Santa Sofia. El Cafetal, Caracas, cecaracas@cantv.net. This hiking club meets Sat 1430, day and weekend hikes, very welcoming; some English and German spoken.

Transport

Colonia Tovar *p1586*

The 1½ hrs' windy drive up from Caracas on Ruta 4, through Antímano and El Junquito, is easy during the week, but murder (2½ hrs) on weekends: long traffic jams, few picnic spots or accommodation, definitely not recommended. It is generally easy to get a lift if there are no buses.

Bus From Av Sur 9 y El Rosario, next to Nuevo Circo, or, easier, from La Yaguara metro station, to El Junquito (1 hr, US$0.50), then change for Colonia Tovar (1 hr, US$1). *Por puesto* from Plaza Catia or O'Leary (more frequently), Caracas, 1 hr, US$2. Alternatively, take a *por puesto* from Plaza Capuchino to El Junquito, then one from there to Colonia Tovar, US$1.50. Last bus to Caracas 1800, later at weekends.

West from Caracas

The Central Highlands run through this varied region. North of the highlands is the Caribbean, with secluded coves and popular resorts such as Puerto Colombia. Straddling the mountains is the birders' paradise of Parque Nacional Henri Pittier. Two coastal national parks, Morrocoy, which lies offshore, and Los Médanos, around the old city of Coro, are further highlights of this area. West of Coro is the city and lake of Maracaibo, for most Venezuelans, a region summed up in three letters – oil. For others, it can be summed up in four letters – heat. Both are certainly true. To the south, though, are the eastern extremities of the Andean mountain chain, with quaint villages, lakes and high passes on the way to the Sierra Nevada de Mérida.

Maracay and around

Maracay is a hot, thriving industrial city and is the gateway to Henri Pittier national park. The city has some pleasant leafy residential neighbourhoods and is the centre of an important agricultural area. The great basin in which lies the Lago de Valencia and the industrial town of Valencia is 100 km west of Caracas. The basin, which is only 450 m above sea-level, receives plenty of rain and is one of the most important agricultural areas in the country.

Maracay ➔ *Phone code: 0243. Colour map 1, A6. Population: 607,000. Altitude: 445 m.*

In its heyday Maracay was the favourite city of Gen Juan Vicente Gómez (dictator, 1909-1935) and some of his most fantastic whims are still there. **Jardín Las Delicias** (Avenida Las Delicias, en route to Choroní; take an Ocumare bus from terminal) with its beautiful zoological garden (closed Monday), park and fountain, built for his revels. The **Gómez mausoleum** (Calle Mariño) has a huge triumphal arch. The heart of the city is **Plaza Girardot**, on which stands the attractive, white **Cathedral**, dating back almost to the city's foundation in 1701. There is an interesting collection of prehispanic artefacts in the museum of the **Instituto de Antropología e Historia** ⓘ *south side of the plaza, T247 2521, Tue-Sun 0800-1200, 1400-1800, free.* The opposite end of the same building has rooms dedicated to Gómez and Bolívar. At the rear of the building is the **Biblioteca de Historia** whose walls are lined with portraits of Bolívar. **Plaza Bolívar**, said to be the largest such-named plaza in Latin America, is 500 m east. On one side is the **Palacio del Gobierno**, originally the *Hotel Jardín*, built by Gómez in 1924. Also here are the **Palacio Legislativo** and the **opera house** (1973). The school and experimental stations of the Ministry of Agriculture are worth visiting. The **Museo Aeronáutico de las Fuerzas Aéreas Venezolanas** ⓘ *Av Las Delicias con Av 19 de Abril, 1 block from Plaza Bolívar, T233 3812*, has an interesting collection of aircraft and memorabilia. The San José festival is on 16-25 March.

Parque Nacional Henri Pittier

Tourist office for the state, **Iatur** ⓘ *Hotel Golf Maracay, pb, Urb Catarrana, T242 1967, www.iatur.gob.ve, open Mon-Fri 0800-1200, 1300-1600 (1330 on Fri).*

Parque Nacional Henri Pittier

A land of steep, lush, rugged hills and tumbling mountain streams, the 107,800 ha park, rises from sea-level in the north to 2,430 m at Pico Cenizo, descending to 450 m towards the Lago de Valencia. Named after Swiss conservationist and engineer Henri Pittier, the park was established in 1937 and is the oldest in the country. It has 578 bird species, including seven different eagles and eight kites. It contains 43% of all species in Venezuela.The park is also home to pumas and jaguars. It extends from the north of Maracay to the Caribbean, excluding the coastal towns of Ocumare, Cata and Choroní, and south to the valleys of Aragua and the villages of Vigírima, Mariara and Turmero. The dry season is December-March and the rainy season (although still agreeable) is April-November. The variation in altitude gives a great range of vegetation, including impressive lower and upper cloud forests and bamboo. See *Parque Nacional de Henri Pittier – Lista de Aves*, by Miguel Lentino and Mary Lou Goodwin, 1993.

Two paved roads cut through the Park. The Ocumare (western) road climbs to the 1,128 m high Portachuelo pass, guarded by twin peaks (38 km from Maracay). At the pass is Rancho Grande, the uncompleted palace/hotel Gómez was building when he died (in a state of disrepair). It is close to the bird migratory routes, September and October are the best months. There are many trails in the vicinity. Permits to visit the park and walk the trails near the Rancho Grande biological research station ⓘ *T283 8264, museoebrg@cantv.net* are available here.

Aragua Coast

To Cata and Cuyagua The road to the coast from Rancho Grande goes through **Ocumare de la Costa** (*Population: 6,140, 48 km from Maracay*), to La Boca de Ocumare and **El Playón** (hotels and restaurants at both places). The road is very busy at weekends. 20 minutes west by boat is **La Ciénaga**, a pretty place, but little shade. A few kilometres east is **Bahía de Cata**, now overdeveloped, particularly at the west end, while the smaller beach at **Catita** is reached by fishing boat ferries (10 minutes, US$1), or a 20-minute walk, tricky over rocks at the start. In Cata town (5 km inland, population of town and beach 3,120) is the small colonial church of San Francisco; devil dancers here fulfil an ancient vow by dancing non-stop through the morning of 27 July each year. Cuyagua beach, unspoilt, is 23 km further on at the end of the road. Good surfing, dangerous rips for swimmers. Devil dancers here too, on movable date in July/August.

To Choroní The second twisty and narrow (eastern) road through the Parque Nacional Henri Pittier is spectacular and goes over a more easterly pass (1,830 m), to **Santa Clara de Choroní**, a small colonial town with attractive, pastel single-storey houses (no ATM). The Fiesta de San Juan on 31 May is worth seeing. Choroní is a good base for walking. There are many opportunities for exploring the unmarked trails, some originating in picturesque spots such as the river pools, 'pozos', of El Lajao (beware of the dangerous whirlpool), and Los Colores, 6 km above Choroní. Other recommended 'pozos' are La Virgen, 10 km from Choroní, and La Nevera, 11 km away.

Puerto Colombia and around ➔ *Phone code: 0243. Colour map 1, A6. Population: 7,000.*

Just beyond Choroní is the popular fishing village of Puerto Colombia, a laid back place with several narrow streets lined with colonial buildings. During high season, its small main bay attracts arts and crafts sellers. It is a good place to stay and spend a couple of days beach hopping with boat rides to different bays. Five minutes' walk across the river lies Puerto Colombia's main attraction; the dazzling long stretch of white beach, Playa Grande, lined with palm trees beneath mountains. There is a row of good fish restaurants at the beach entrance. At weekends drummers drum and dancers gyrate and the beach gets crowded with campers and families. At other times it's more peaceful, with brightly painted fishing boats in the river and frigate birds wheeling overhead. If swimming, beware the strong undertow. There are public showers at the entrance. Many fishing boats are for hire in the harbour, US$35 for a day trip. A very bumpy, 30-minute ride east goes to Cepe, another beautiful long beach with good swimming, popular with campers. About US$15, boats usually take 6-10 people, or por puesto fishing boat from the port US$1.50 per person. From the beach, there is a delightful 25-minute walk to **Pueblo de Cepe** through the Henri Pittier park. Several places on the beach serve fish, salad and tostones for US$5. Most locals bring their own supplies in the obligatory beer cooler. From the beautiful unspoiled beach there are fishing and scuba diving trips. The latter, with guide and equipment, explore the only bit of coral on this stretch of the coast. At Cepe's west end, you can climb the hill and descend to **Playa Escondida**, a deserted but more rocky beach. Other beaches include: to the east, before Cepe, Valle Seco (boat US$20, some shade, natural pool protected by reef) and Chuao. To the west are: Diario (small, no shade), Aroa (lovely, with river and palms, rough sea but one safe bathing area, no services, take everything with you, 3 hours' hike from Choroní, go early) and Uricao (also isolated); boat to Uricao US$15.

Maracay and around listings

For Sleeping and Eating price codes and other relevant information, see Essentials, pages 38-40.

Sleeping

Maracay *p1588*

Budget hotels are in streets around Plaza Girardot.

AL Italo, Av Las Delicias, Urb La Soledad, T232 1576, www.hotelitalo.com.ve. A/c, large, modern 4-star, on bus route, pleasant, small rooftop pool, good Italian restaurant, *El Fornaio*. Recommended.

B Posada El Limón, C El Piñal 64, El Limón suburb, near Parque Nacional Henri Pittier, T283 4925, T0414-444 1915, www.posadaellimon.com. Dutch owned, some way from centre, Caracas airport transfers US$125 cash in good car with English-speaking driver, relaxed and pleasant, family atmosphere, spacious rooms with a/c and hot water, **E** in dorm, laundry, pool, internet, good restaurant, parking, trips to Parque with guide.

B Princesa Plaza, Av Miranda Este entre Fuerzas Aéreas y Av Bermúdez, T232 2052. Large commercial hotel, 1 block east of Plaza Bolívar, convenient, a/c, inexpensive restaurant.

D Caroní, Ayacucho Norte 197, Bolívar, T554 4465. A/c, hot showers, comfortable. Recommended.

D Sao Vicente, Av Bolívar 03. Decent budget option, a/c, central location, cable TV.

E Mar del Plata, Av Santos Michelena 23, T246 4313, mardelplatahotel@gmail.com. Central, with a/c, cable TV, hot water, excellent.

Parque Nacional Henri Pittier *p1589, map 1588*

E pp **Campamento El Cocuy**, Choroní (**C** full board), T243-991 1106, 0416-747 3833, www.cocuy.org.ve. Pleasant mountain refuge, beautiful views, sleeping in hammocks. Walking and birdwatching tours, bilingual guides.

F pp **Rancho Grande biological research station**. Plenty of beds in basic dorms, US$7.50 pp per night, use of kitchen facilities, take warm sleeping bag, candles and food; nearest supplies at El Limón, 20 km before Rancho Grande.

Aragua Coast *p1589*

Ocumare de la Costa

A De La Costa Eco-Lodge, California 23, T993 1986, 0414-460 0655, www.ecovenezuela.com. Comfortable, upmarket lodge near beach, with outdoor bar serving food, restaurant, roof terraces with good sea views, pool, landscaped gardens, excursions, equipment hire, specialist bilingual guides. Includes breakfast.

D Posada Mis Tres Tesoros, Anzoátegui 46, T993 1725, 0414-588 0149. 6 blocks from sea, a/c, cable TV, simple rooms, hot water, very good, helpful owners.

La Ciénaga

AL pp all-inclusive **Coral Lagoon Lodge**, La Ciénaga, T0212-762 5975 at Angel-Eco Tours, www.corallagoonlodge.com. A dive resort accessible only by boat. Beautiful location on waterfront with view of mountains. 6 rooms in 2 cabins sleeping 2-4 people, fans, solar power with back-up generator, rainwater and seawater used. Hammocks, deckchairs, kayaks and snorkelling. Diving with PADI and SSI instructors to underwater grottos, canyons, reefs and wrecks.

Choroní

See **www.choroni.info** for listings and locations of many hotels and posadas.

AL Hacienda El Portete, C El Cementerio, T991 1255, www.elportete.com. Restored cocoa plantation, colonial-style large grounds, restaurant, a/c, pool, many children's facilities, excursions.

A Hacienda La Aljorra, 1 km south in La Loma, T0212-252 0002(Caracas), 218 8841 (Choroní), laaljorra@hotmail.com. On roadside, out of town, **C** on weekdays, breakfast included, hot water, 300-year old cacao hacienda in 62 ha of wooded hillside. Large rooms, relaxing and peaceful.

B La Gran Posada, 5 km north of Choroní on a steep hillside above Maracay road, T217 0974. Small hotel right on the roadside with little open space. Neat, a/c pleasant bar and restaurant. Negotiate in low season.

D Posada Colonial El Picure, C Miranda No 34-A, T991 1296, www.hosteltrail.com/posadaelpicure. Colonial house in village centre, backs onto river. Popular with travellers, welcoming, dorms and private rooms, restaurant with vegetarian options.

Puerto Colombia and around *p1589*

There are dozens of posadas for all budgets in town, but most are fully booked during high season when prices rise by around 40%.

A Hostal and Spa Casa Grande (also known as **Coco's**), Morillo 33, T991 1251. One of the best in town, attractive colonial décor, pool, gardens, parking. Excellent.

A Posada Turpial, José Maitin 3, T991 1123, www.posadaturpial.com.Colonial house, a/c, with breakfast, well-organized, cosy, attractive, nice atmosphere, good restaurant, rooms around patio, TV, safety deposit box, German and English spoken. Book in advance. Owners run travel agency www.turpialtravel.com and organize local tours, dive trips. Recommended.

A-B Posada Pittier, on road to Choroní, 10 min walk from Puerto Colombia, T991 1028, www.posadapittier.com. Small, immaculate rooms, more expensive at weekends, a/c, good meals, helpful, WiFi, garden. Recommended.

B Costa Brava, Murillo 9, near Malecón, T991 1057, suarezjf@cantv.net. Cheaper in low season. Basic, cheaper without bath, fans, laundry, good food, parking, English spoken, family run. Recommended.

B La Posada de Choroní, Calle Principal, 2 blocks from Malecón, T991 1191, www.laposadadechoroni.3a2.com. Rooms with a/c and TV, cheaper without TV, cheaper with fan, hot water, colonial with rooms off central garden, parking.

B Posada Alonso, near checkpoint, T0416-546 1412 (mob). Quiet, hammocks, laundry. Recommended.

B Posada Xuchytlan, Av Principal, after Posada Cataquero, T991 1234. Charming, stylish colonial house, beautiful gardens, comfortable rooms, welcoming, a/c, parking, includes breakfast.

C Hostal Vista Mar, C Colón at western end, T991 1250. On seafront, pleasant, terraces with hammocks, some rooms with sea view, some with a/c and TV, helpful, secure parking.

C Posada El Malecón, El Malecón 1, T991 1107. On seafront, a/c, hot water, less with fan, small, basic rooms. Discounts Mon-Thu (same owners as Vista Mar), secure parking.

C Posada La Parchita, Trino Rangel, T991 1233, 0416-832 2790. Including breakfast, rooms set around a lovely patio, very nice. Recommended, book in advance.

C-D La Montañita, Murillo 6, T991 1132, choroni_indio@hotmail.com. Popular, nice courtyard, charming owners, packages available (**B** full board).

D Brisas del Mar, C Principal at the port. Above a bar, noisy but comfortable, a/c, TV, bit overpriced.

D Hostal Colonial, on Morillo, opposite bus stop, T218 5012, colonial@choroni.net. Popular hostel, good value, with fan, laundry, German owner. Also good tours in the Pittier park.

D Posada Doña Enriqueta, Color 3, T991 1158, just off the seafront. Basic rooms, a/c, books tours, helpful, 40% discount Mon-Thu.

E La Abuela, near bridge to Playa Grande. Basic, fan, shared bath.

E Casa Luna, next to Hostal Colonial, Morillo 35, no obvious sign, T951 5318, claudibeckmann@web.de. Colonial house, basic rooms, German and English spoken. Tours to Pittier park, diving trips and airport transfers, jungletrip@choroni.net.

Camping is possible on Playa Grande, no permission needed and showers on beach; beware of theft. Crowded during high season.

Cepe and Chuao

Several *posadas* in Chuao, but some distance from the beach (those listed are closer).

La Luzonera (**C**), on the plaza, T242 1284, is the

best, but there are others (**D-E**), unsigned, basic. Camping is permitted on Chuao and Cepe beaches.

A La Terraza del Morocho, Av Principal Las Tejerías 44, Chuao, T0414-450 3341. A/c, cable TV, helpful, ask about guides for excursions.

B Posada Puerto Escondido, Cepe, T241 4645. Includes 3 meals, drinks and boat from Puerto Colombia, spacious rooms, with bath, hot water and fan, peaceful homely atmosphere, tropical gardens and pool area, diving. Recommended.

C El Gran Cacao, 200 m up the hill from the port at Chuao, T218 3604. Comfortable, with a/c or fan, some rooms with TV. Recommended.

E Rincón del Marino, near El Gran Cacao in Chuao. Basic, with fan.

Eating

Maracay *p1588*

Many excellent restaurants in the Av Las Delicias area (eg **Mansión Imperial**, also has internet, bakery and supermarket). Lots of Chinese eateries and *loncherías*, *tascas* and cheap restaurants in streets around Plazas Girardot and Bolívar.

Puerto Colombia *p1589*

TTT-T Mango, Trino Rangel. Informal setting in patio, delicious catch of the day and pastas, generous portions. Recommended.

TTT-T Willy, Vía Playa Grande 1, just after bridge along the river. Very popular, good seafood and meat dishes. In low season only opens Fri-Sun.

TT Costa Café Terraza, just before bridge to Playa Grande. Upstairs terrace looks onto river, excellent fresh fish and tasty dishes. Good service, accepts credit cards.

TT-T El Abuelo, just before bridge to Playa Grande. Good food and value, accepts credit cards.

Activities and tours

Puerto Colombia *p1589*

Claudia Beckmann and Emilio Espinoza, Unión 4, T951 5318, 0412-435 3056, jungletrip@choroni.net. Good trips in the national park.

Transport

Maracay *p1588*

Bus The bus station is 2 km southeast of the centre, taxi US$4. It has two sections, Terminal Oriente for long distance and Terminal Nacional for regional buses. *Por puesto* marked 'Terminal' for the bus station and 'Centro' for the centre (Plaza Girardot). To **Maracaibo**, **Expresos los Llanos**, US$17.50. To **Valencia**, US$3.50, 1 hr, and **Caracas**, US$4.75 by *autobus*, 5 daily, US$5.70 by *microbus*, 1½- 2 hrs, and US$5.25 by *por puesto*. **Barinas**, US$12, 7 hrs. **Mérida** US$14-22, 12 hrs; **Ciudad Bolívar**, US$17.50, 10 hrs. To **Coro**, US$12, 7¾ hrs.

Parque Nacional Henri Pittier *p1589, map 1588*

Bus Depart from Maracay Terminal; pay full fare to **Ocumare** or hitch from the alcabala at El Limón.

Taxi Hire in Maracay for day in the park, US$50.

Aragua Coast *p1589*

El Playón

Bus From **Maracay**, 2-2½ hours, US$2.75. To **Cata** from El Playón US$0.50 from plaza, from Ocumare de la Costa US$1.

Choroní

Bus There is a single, new bus station between Choroní and Puerto Colombia, serving both. **Maracay-Choroní**, beautiful journey Henri Pittier park, every 2 hrs from 0630-1700, more at the weekend, US$2.75, 2½-3 hrs. Taxi US$7.25. Road congested at holidays and weekends.

Puerto Colombia *p1589*

Bus From **Maracay** terminal leave from platform 5. Buses to Maracay depart every hr from 0500 till 1700, US$4.75, 2-3 hrs. **Taxi** From **Maracay** US$8.50 pp, 1-1½ hrs.

Directory

Maracay *p1588*

Banks See also Money, page 1566. **Italcambio** (Amex), Av Aragua con C Bermúdez, C C Maracay Plaza, p 1, loc 110K, T235 6945, Mon-Fri 0830-1700, Sat 0830-1200. *Cambio* in **Air Mar** travel agency, CADA Centro Comercial, Av 19 de Abril, Local 20, 2 blocks north of Plaza Girardot. 2.5% commission. **Internet** Few places near Plaza Bolívar and CC La Capilla, Av Santos Michelena.

Puerto Colombia *p1589*

Banks The nearest banks are in Maracay. Some *posadas* and restaurants change cash/TCs at poor rates, or give cash against credit cards (passport required). *Licorería San Sebastián*, by the bridge, changes cash and TCs and sells phone cards.

Valencia and around

Founded in 1555, Valencia is the capital of Carabobo State and Venezuela's third largest city. It's the centre of its most developed agricultural region and the most industrialized. Near the city are several groups of petroglyphs while the coast has some very popular beach areas. Best known of these is the Morrocoy national park, but you have to seek out the quiet spots.

Valencia → *Phone code: 0241. Colour map 1, A5. Population: 1,350,000. Altitude: 480 m.*

A road through low hills thickly planted with citrus, coffee and sugar runs 50 km west from Maracay to the valley in which Valencia lies. It is hot and humid with annual rainfall of 914 mm. Like its Spanish namesake, Valencia is famous for its oranges.

The **Cathedral** ⓘ *daily 0630-1130, 1500-1830, Sun 0630-1200, 1500-1900,* built in 1580, is on the east side of **Plaza Bolívar**. The statue of the Virgen del Socorro (1550) in the left transept is the most valued treasure; on the second Sunday in November (during the Valencia Fair) it is paraded with a richly jewelled crown. See also **El Capitolio** ⓘ *Páez, between Díaz Moreno y Montes de Oca,* the **Teatro Municipal** ⓘ *Colombia y Av Carabobo,* the old **Carabobo University** building and the handsome **Plaza de Toros** ⓘ *south end of Av Constitución beyond the ring road,* which is the second largest in Latin America after Mexico City. The magnificent former **residence of General Páez** (hero of the Carabobo battle) ⓘ *Páez y Boyacá, Tue-Sun 0900-1500, free,* is now a museum. Equally attractive is the **Casa de los Celis** (1766) ⓘ *Av Soublette y C Comercio, Tue-Sun 0800-1200, 1500-1700.* This well-restored colonial house and national monument served as a hospital for wounded soldiers during the Battle of Carabobo. It also houses the **Museo de Arte e Historia**, with pre-Columbian exhibits. Most of the interesting sights are closed on Monday.

Around Valencia

Most important of the region's petroglyphs can be found at the **Parque Nacional Piedras Pintadas**, where lines of prehispanic stone slabs, many bearing swirling glyphs, march up the ridges of Cerro Pintado. The **Museo Parque Arqueológico Piedra Pintada** is at the foot of Cerro Las Rosas ⓘ *Sector Tronconero, vía Vigirmia, Guacara, T041-571 596, Tue-Sat 0900-1700, Sun 1000-1600, free,* has 165 examples of rock art and menhirs (tours, parking, café).

Other extensive ancient petroglyphs have been discovered at **La Taimata** near Güigüe, 34 km east of Valencia on the lake's southern shore. There are more sites on rocks by the Río Chirgua, reached by a 10-km paved road from Highway 11, 50 km west of Valencia. About 5 km past Chirgua, at the Hacienda Cariaprima, is a remarkable 35 m-tall geoglyph, a humanoid figure carved into a steep mountain slope at the head of the valley.

At 30 km southwest of Valencia on the highway to San Carlos is the site of the **Carabobo** battlefield, an impressive historical monument surrounded by splendid gardens. The view over the field from the *mirador* where the Liberator directed the battle in 1814 is impressive. Historical explanations are given on Wednesday, weekends and holidays.

Coast north of Valencia

Puerto Cabello (*Colour map 1, A5, Phone code: 0242, Population: 185,000*), 55 km from Valencia, was one of the most important ports in the colonial Americas, from which produce was transported to the Dutch possessions. Puerto Cabello has retained its maritime importance and is Venezuela's key port. Plaza Bolívar and the colonial part of town are by the waterfront promenade at Calle 24 de Julio. The **Museo de Antropología e Historia** ⓘ *C Los Lanceros 43, Tue-Fri 0900-1600, Sat 0900-1230,* is in one of the few remaining colonial houses (1790), in the tangle of small streets between Plaza Bolívar and the sea. It displays the region's history and has a room on Simón Bolívar.

To the east is **Bahía de Patanemo**, a beautiful, tranquil horseshoe-shaped beach shaded by palms. It has three main sectors, Santa Rita, Los Caneyes and Patanemo itself, with the village proper, further from the beach than the other two. All three have lodging, but it may be difficult to find meals midweek (try at posadas). Offshore is the lovely Isla Larga (no shade or facilities), best reached by boat from Quizandal, US$5, 15 minutes. There are several cafés along the beachfront. Nearby are two sunken wrecks that attract divers. From Puerto Cabello, take a *por puesto* from the terminal, 20 minutes, US$0.75, a taxi US$5.75.

Parque Nacional Morrocoy ➔ *Colour map 1, A5.*

Palm-studded islets and larger islands (*cayos*) with secluded beaches make up Parque Nacional Morrocoy. The largest and most popular of the islands within the park is **Cayo Sombrero**, with two over-priced fish restaurants. No alcohol is sold on this or other islands; be aware of hidden extra costs and take your own supplies. It is very busy at weekends and during holidays and is generally dirty and noisy. But there are some deserted beaches, with trees on which to sling a hammock. For peace and quiet, take boats to the farthest cayos. **Playuela** is beautiful and is considered to have one of the nicest beaches of all. It has a small restaurant at weekends and there's a nice walk to Playuelita. **Boca Seca** is also pleasant, with shade and calm water suitable for children, but it can be windy. **Cayo Borracho**, one of the nicest islands, has become a turtle-nesting reserve, closed to visitors. **Playa Azul**, a nice small cayo, has shallow water. The water at **Pescadores** is very shallow. **Los Muertos** has two beaches with shade, mangroves and palms. **Mero**'s beach is beautiful, with palms, but is windy. With appropriate footwear it is possible to walk between some of the islands. Calm waters here are ideal for water-skiing while scuba diving is best suited to beginners. Two things to note, though: a chemical spill in the 1990s destroyed about 50% of the coral in the park, so snorkellers will see very little. Only by diving to deeper waters will you see coral, although in all locations there are still fish to watch. Secondly, take insect repellent against *puri puri* (tiny, vicious mosquitoes) and flies. A number of muggings have been reported around Playa Sur.

Adjoining the park to the north is a vast nesting area for scarlet ibis, flamingos and herons, the **Cuare Wildlife Sanctuary**. Most of the flamingos are in and around the estuary next to Chichiriviche, which is too shallow for boats but you can walk there or take a taxi. Birds are best watched early morning or late afternoon.

Tucacas and Chichiriviche ➔ *Phone code: 0259. Colour map 1, A5*

Tucacas is a hot, busy, dirty town, where bananas and other fruit are loaded for Curaçao and Aruba. Popular and expensive as a beach resort, it has garish high-rise blocks and casinos. Its port area is gaining a reputation for rip-offs and robberies. A few kilometres beyond Tucacas, towards Coro, is Chichiriviche (*Population: 7,000*), smaller, more relaxed, but lined with tacky shops, also dirty and not that attractive. Both provide access to Parque Nacional Morrocoy, each town serving separate *cayos*, but only as far as Cayo Sombrero. Apart from this and the diving options, no one has a good word to say about Tucacas or Chichiriviche.

Valencia and around listings

For Sleeping and Eating price codes and other relevant information, see Essentials, pages 38-40.

Sleeping

Valencia *p1593*

There are hotels for all budgets on Av Bolívar, but it is a long avenue, so don't attempt to walk it.

A Don Pelayo, Av Díaz Moreno y Rondón, T857 8793, www.hoteldonpelayo.com. Central, modern block, restaurant, a/c, includes buffet breakfast.

C Marconi, Av Bolívar 141-65, T823 4843. Small, modern hotel, simple rooms, a/c, helpful, safe, laundry, recommended (next to a petrol station), take bus or colectivo from bus station to stop after 'El Elevado' bridge.

E Carabobo, C Libertad 100-37, esq Plaza Bolívar, T858 8860. Central, cold water, OK, with a/c lobby.

Coast north of Valencia *p1593*

AL-A Posada Santa Margarita, Bolívar 4-36, Puerto Cabello, T361 4112, www.posadasantamargarita.com.ve. Converted colonial house in historic part of town, 2 blocks from the waterfront promenade, local day trips, attractive rooms, roof terrace, restaurant, small pool, breakfast included. Reserve in advance.

At **Patanemo** there are hotels and *posadas* in the village (eg **Patanemo**, **Chachita** and **Iliana**).

A Posada Edén, Final Av Principal Los Caneyes, T0416-442 4955. The best posada in the region, small, comfortable, with a/c, TV, hot water, restaurant and pool.

D Posada Natal Mar, at entrance to Caneyes sector, 100 m from turn-off to Bahía de Patanemo, T0412-536 7961. Small but clean rooms with a/c, TV, but no windows, restaurant upstairs.

Parque Nacional Morrocoy *p1594*

Camping is allowed at **Cayo Paiclás** and **Cayo Sol** but you must first make a reservation with **Inparques** (National Parks), T800 8487, daily 0800-2000; reserve at least 8 working days in advance; US$2.50 pp per night, 7 nights max, pay in full in advance (very complicated procedure). Very few facilities and no fresh water at **Paiclás**. **Playa Azul** and **Paiclás** have ecological toilets. At weekends and holidays it is very crowded and litter-strewn (beware rats).

LL pp **Villa Mangrovia** on the Lizardo Spit between Tucacas and Chichiriviche, the only place to stay in the park. 3 rooms, excellent food and service, charming owner. Book via **Last Frontiers**, T01296-653000, or **Journey Latin America**, T0161-832 1441.

Tucacas *p1594*

For a wider choice of budget accommodation stay at Chichiriviche rather than Tucacas. Most hotels and restaurants in Tucacas are on the long Av Libertador, the town's main street.

B Manaure, T812 0286. Modern, low-rise hotel, a/c, hot water, pool, good.

B Posada Villa Gregoria, C Mariño, 1 block north of bus stop behind the large water tank, T818 6359. Spanish-run, helpful, relaxing, good value, fan or a/c, laundry, small rooms, hammocks, garden, secure parking. Tours, English spoken.

D Posada Amigos del Mar, C Nueva, near bus stop, beyond Hospital Viejo, T812 3962. Helpful staff, organizes trips to cayos and diving, use of kitchen, with fan. A good budget option.

Camping Gas in Tucacas or Puerto Cabello.

Chichiriviche *p1594*

There are plenty of reasonably priced posadas.

C Capri, Av Zamora, T818 6026. Near docks, basic rooms, a bit shabby, shower, fan or a/c, pleasant, Italian owner, good restaurant and supermarket.

C Posada Sol, Mar y Arena, Mariño y Partida, T815 0306, posadasolmaryarena@cantv.net. Small rooms with a/c, TV, welcoming, upstairs terrace with a grill, 1 block from sea, changes US$.

D Morena's Place, Sector Playa Norte, 10 mins walk from bus stop, T815 0936, posadamorenas@hotmail.com. Beautifully decorated house, fan, hammocks, helpful hosts, English spoken.

D Posada Alemania, Cementos Coro, T815 0912. German-run, runs tours, rents snorkel gear, 200 m from Playa Sur, nice garden.

D Posada Res Delia, C Mariño 30, 1 block from Gregoria, T818 6089. Including breakfast, **D** with a/c, shared bath, organizes tours.

D Posada Tío José, on street parallel to main avenue, 1 block off, T898 0215. More pricey in high season, a/c, TV, cosy atmosphere, pleasant decor. Recommended.

Eating

Valencia *p1593*

TT-T La Rinconada, Plaza Bolívar. Recommended, open Sun.

Chichiriviche *p1594*

Many fish restaurants along seafront, eg **TT Txalupa**. Good seafood and Spanish dishes, efficient service. And **Veracruz**. Good fish.

Activities and tours

Tucacas *p1594*

Bicycles can be hired in town.

Diving Equipment can be hired from near the harbour. There are several diving companies.

Submatur, C Ayacucho 6, near Plaza Bolívar, T812 0082, morrocoysubmatur1@cantv.net. Experienced owner, 4-day PADI course US$350, day trip 2 dives from US$65 (US$45 with own equipment); also rents rooms, **F**, fan and cooking facilities.

Transport

Valencia *p1593*

Air The airport is 6 km southeast of centre. Taxi airport-bus terminal US$10.50. **Aeropostal**

flights daily to **Maracaibo** and **Porlamar**. **Aserca** flies to **Caracas, Maracaibo, Puerto Ordaz** and other cities (often via Caracas). **Dutch Antilles Express**, www.flydae.com, and **Insel Air**, www.fly-inselair.com, each fly to **Curaçao** 6 days a week.

Bus Terminal is 4 km east of centre, part of shopping mall *Big-Low* (24-hr restaurants). Entry to platforms by *ficha* (token), US$2. Left luggage. Minibus to centre, frequent and cheap, but slow and confusing route at peak times; taxi from bus station to centre, US$4.50 (official drivers wear ID badges). To **Caracas**, frequent buses with **Aeroexpresos Ejecutivos** from 0600-1900, 2½ hrs, US$5.75. To **Maracay**, US$3.50, 1 hr. **Mérida**, 10-12 hrs, US$13-22; to **San Cristóbal**, 10 hrs, US$19. **Barquisimeto**, US$9, 3½ hrs. To **Maracaibo**, 2 evening buses with **Aeroexpresos Ejecutivos**, US$15.50, 8 hrs. **Puerto Cabello**, US$1, 1 hr. **Tucacas**, US$2.50, or US$5.25 by frequent *por puesto* service. To **Coro** US$8.65, 4½ hrs. To **Ciudad Bolívar**, US$18.25, 10 hrs.

Around Valencia *p1593*

Parque Nacional Piedras Pintadas

Bus To **Vigírima** 20 km northeast of Valencia at regular intervals (US$1), ask to get off at the 'Cerro Pintado' turnoff. Driving from Vigírima, turn left at a small blue 'Cadafe Tronconero' sign, then a further 3 km.

Carabobo

Bus To Carabobo leave from bottom of Av Bolívar Sur y C 75, or from Plaza 5 de Julio, Valencia, US$0.50, ask for Parque Carabobo (1¼ hrs).

Parque Nacional Morrocoy *p1594*

Ferry From Tucacas: prices per boat from US$20 return to **Paiclás** to US$40 return to **Cayo Sombrero** (max 7 per boat). Ticket office is left of the car entrance to the Park. Recommended boatmen are Orlando and Pepe. Boats to Boca Seca and Playuelita only leave from Tucacas. **From Chichiriviche**: tickets can be bought per person or per boat and vary according to distance; US$17.50 per boat to **Los Muertos**, 10 min trip, US$32-60 to **Cayo Sombrero**. Prices are set for each cayo and there are long and short trips. There are 2 ports: one in the centre, one at Playa Sur. Ask for the ticket system to fix price and to ensure you'll be picked up on time for return trip.

Tucacas *p1594*

Bus Frequent *por puesto* from **Valencia**, US$5.25, bus US$2.50; to **Puerto Cabello**, take bus from the intersection of the coastal highway with the main avenue of Tucacas to **Morón** (35 mins, US$1.25), then from Morón to Puerto Cabello (15 mins, US$0.50); Tucacas-Morón bus goes on to Puerto Cabello, if there are enough passengers. To **Coro**, US$5.50, 3 hrs.

Chichiriviche *p1594*

Bus To **Puerto Cabello**, frequent *por puestos* often via Valencia, 2 hrs, US$3.50; to **Barquisimeto** often via Morón, 3 hrs; to **Valera**, 9 hrs. To **Coro**, take a bus from the station on Av Zamora to **Sanare**, US$1, every 20 mins, then another to Coro, US$5.50, 3 hrs. Direct buses from **Valencia**, or take bus from Morón to Coro and get out at turnoff, 1½-2 hrs, US$4.65.

Directory

Valencia *p1593*

Banks See also Money, page 1566. **Corp Banca**, Av Díaz Moreno, CC Colombia. Amex TCs changed. **Italcambio**, Av Bolívar Norte, Edif Talia, loc 2, T821 8173. Amex travel services, Visa TCs, a long way north of centre in Urbanización Los Sauces, get off bus at junction with C 132; also at airport, Mon-Fri 0830-1700, Sat morning only. **Consulates** **British Honorary Consul**, Dalca, Urb Industrial El Recreo, Calle B, Parcela 103, T878 3480, burguesdal@cantv.net.ve. **Telephones** CANTV, Plaza Bolívar, for international calls.

Tucacas *p1594*

Banks Banesco gives cash advance on credit cards. Hotels and travel agents will change money but at very low rates, if they have enough cash. In **Chichiriviche**, many hotels will change dollars and euros but at very low rates.

The relaxed colonial city of Coro, with its sand-dune surroundings, sits at the foot of the arid, windswept Paranaguá Peninsula. Inland from Coro, the Sierra de San Luis is good walking country in fresher surroundings.

Coro → *Phone code: 0268. Colour map 1, A5. Population: 175,025. Mean temperature: 28° C.*

Coro, the capital of the Falcón state and former capital of the country, is a UNESCO World Heritage Site. Founded in 1527, it became an important religious centre for Christians and Jews alike. The city, 177 km from Tucacas, is relatively clean and well kept and its small colonial part has several shaded plazas and beautiful buildings, many of which date from the 18th century. Recently, efforts have been made to preserve and restore its colonial heritage. In the rainy season the centre may flood. The **tourist office** is on Paseo Alameda, T251 8033, English spoken, helpful. See also www.coroweb.com (in English, French and Spanish). State tourist office: **Fondo de Turismo**, Av Bolívar, CC Caribe, p3, loc 7, Punto Fijo, T246 7422, www.visitfalcon.com.

The **Cathedral**, a national monument, was begun in 1583. **San Clemente** church has a wooden cross in the plaza in front, which is said to mark the site of the first mass said in Venezuela; it is believed to be the country's oldest such monument ⓘ *Mass Mon-Sat 1930*. It has been undergoing reconstruction. There are several interesting colonial houses, such as **Los Arcaya** ⓘ *Zamora y Federación, also under reconstruction*, one of the best examples of 18th-century architecture, with the **Museo de Cerámica**, small but interesting, with a beautiful garden. **Los Senior** ⓘ *Talavera y Hernández*, where Bolívar stayed in 1827, has the oldest synagogue in Venezuela (1853), if not South America. It houses a branch of the **Museo de Arte Alberto Henríquez** of the Universidad Francisco de Miranda (UNEFM) ⓘ *open sporadically, usually only in the morning, less often in the rainy season*. Another branch of the museum is on Paseo Talavera entre Bolívar y Comercio. Also on Paseo Talavera is the **Museo de Arte de Coro** ⓘ *T251 5265, www.fmn.gob.ve/fmn_coro.htm, free, Mon-Sat 0900-1900, Sun 0900-1700*, exhibiting some interesting modern artwork. Built 1764-1765, **Las Ventanas de Hierro** ⓘ *Zamora y Colón, Tue-Sat 0900-1200, 1500-1800, Sun 0900-1300, US$0.20*, is now the

Coro

N

200 metres

200 yards

Sleeping

1 El Gallo
2 Intercaribe
3 Miranda Cumberland
4 Posada Casa Tun Tun
5 Posada Don Antonio
6 Posada La Casa de los Pájaros
7 Taima Taima
8 Vila Antigua

Eating

1 Barra del Jacal
2 Dulzura y algo más
3 El Portón de Arturo
4 Mersi
5 Panadería Costa Nova
6 Posada Don Luis

Museo de Tradición Familiar. Just beyond is the **Casa del Tesoro** ⓘ *C Zamora, T252 8701, free,* an art gallery showing local artists' work. There are other handicraft galleries in the centre, such as Centro **Artesanal Generalísimo Francisco de Miranda** near Plaza San Clemente. The **Jewish cemetery** ⓘ *C 23 de Enero esq C Zamora, visit by prior arrangement only, enquire at the Museo de Coro,* is the oldest on the continent. It was founded by Jews who arrived from Curaçao in the early 19th century.

The **Museo de Coro 'Lucas Guillermo Castillo'** ⓘ *C Zamora opposite Plaza San Clemente, T251 1298, Tue-Sat 0900-1200, 1500-1800, Sun 0900-1330, US$0.25,* is in an old monastery, and has a good collection of church relics, recommended.

Coro is surrounded by sand dunes, **Los Médanos de Coro**, which form an impressive **national park** ⓘ *www.losmedanos.com/; outside town on the main road to Punto Fijo: take bus marked 'Carabobo' from C35 Falcón y Av Miranda, or up Av Los Médanos and get off at the end, just after Plaza Concordia, from there walk 500 m to entrance, or take a taxi.* The place is guarded by police and is generally safe, but stay close to the entrance and on no account wander off across the dunes. Kiosk at entrance sells drinks and snacks; open till 2400.

The historic part of the town's port, **La Vela de Coro** (population: 25,275), is included in the UNESCO Heritage Site, with some impressive colonial buildings, lovely sea front, wooden traditional fishing boats and historic church. It has an unmistakable Caribbean feel, but it is in urgent need of facelift (taxi from Coro US$7). On the road to La Vela, near the turning, is the interesting **Jardín Botánico Xerofito Dr León Croizat** ⓘ *Sector Sabana Larga, T277 8451, Mon-Fri 0800-1200, 1300- 1600, Sat and Sun 0900-1700, free, getting there: take Vela bus from corner of C Falcón, opposite Banco Coro, and ask to be let off at Pasarela del Jardín Botánico – the bridge over the road.* It is backed by UNESCO and has plants from Africa, Australia, etc. Tours in Spanish.

Paraguaná Peninsula → *Phone code: 0269. Colour map 1, A5. Population: 210,000.*

Punto Fijo and around This area is a must for windsurfers and is a great place for walking and flamingo spotting. The western side of the peninsula is industrialized, with oil refineries at Cardón and Amuay connected by pipeline to the Lago de Maracaibo oilfields. The main town is **Punto Fijo**, a busy, unappealing place, whose duty-free zone attracts shoppers with cheap electrical goods and alcohol. 5 km away is the residential area of **Judibana**, a much nicer place to stay, with shopping centre, cinema and restaurants.

Adícora A quiet if run-down little resort on the east side of the peninsula. The beaches are very windswept and not great but they are popular with wind- and kitesurfers. There are three windsurfing schools in town. Adícora is also a good base for exploring the beautiful, barren and wild peninsula where goats and wild donkeys roam.

Cerro Santa Ana (830 m) is the only hill on the peninsula and commands spectacular views. The entrance is at El Moruy; take bus to Pueblo Nuevo (0730-0800), then take one to Punto Fijo and ask to be dropped off at the entrance to Santa Ana. From the plaza walk back to the signpost for Pueblo Nuevo and take the dirt road going past a white building; 20 m to the left is Restaurant La Hija. Walk 1 km through scrubby vegetation (watch out for dogs) to the *Inparques* office (closed Monday to Friday but busy at weekends). Register here before attempting the steep three-hour climb. It's safer to go on Saturday or Sunday. Some *posadas* in Coro arrange trips to the Peninsula.

Laguna Boca de Caño (also called Laguna Tiraya) is a nature reserve north of Adícora, inland from Supi, along a dirt track that is usually fit for all vehicles. There is abundant bird life, particularly flamingos. It is the only mangrove zone on the east of the peninsula.

Sierra de San Luis

South of Coro, on the road to Barquisimeto, the Sierra includes the **Parque Nacional Juan C Falcón**, with tropical forest, caves and waterfalls. Visit it from the picturesque village of **Curimagua**; jeeps leave from Coro terminal, US$4.65, 1 hour. The lovely colonial town of **Cabure** is the capital of the Sierra. Jeeps leave from Coro terminal, 58 km, 1¼ hours, US$4.65. As well as hotels, Cabure has restaurants, bars, a bakery, supermarket and pharmacy. A few kilometres up the road is a series of beautiful waterfalls, called the Cataratas de Hueque. **The Spanish Road** is a fantastic three-hour walk through orange groves and tropical forest from Curimagua to Cabure. You will see many butterflies along the way. The path is not well marked, so it is best to hire a guide. Take water. It's very muddy in rains; take insect repellent and good shoes and be prepared to get wet. Ask at any of the hotels listed below. To walk the Spanish Road from Coro in one day, take transport to Cabure, ask to be dropped at the turn-off for the **Posada El Duende** (see below) and walk uphill 1 km to the Posada, where you begin the trek. The path eventually comes out to the Curimagua-Coro paved road, where you can take transport back to Coro.

Coro and around listings

For Sleeping and Eating price codes and other relevant information, see Essentials, pages 38-40.

Sleeping

Coro *p1597, map p1597*

Coro has several excellent *posadas* catering for travellers; book well in advance, especially in Dec.

A Miranda Cumberland, Av Josefa Camejo, opposite old airport, T252 2111, reservas@hotelescumberland.com. Large modern hotel, price includes breakfast, good value, restaurant, good pool area, travel agency.

C Intercaribe, Av Manaure entre Zamora y Urdaneta, T251 1844, intercaribe@cantv.net. Bland, modern, pool, a/c, small rooms.

C Posada Don Antonio, Paseo Talavera 11, T253 9578. Central, small rooms, a/c, internet, parking.

D Posada La Casa de los Pájaros, Monzón 74 entre Ampies y Comercio, T252 8215, www.casadelospajaros.com.ve. Colonial house 6 blocks from centre, being restored by the owners with local art and antiques, rooms with and without bath, hammock space US$3.50, meals available, free internet, use of kitchen for small fee, laundry service, trips to local sights. Recommended.

D Taima Taima, C 35 Falcón (away from centre), T252 1215. Small rooms, a/c, TV, some hot water, parking.

D Villa Antigua, C 58 Comercio 46, T251 6479/0414-683 7433. Colonial style, a/c, TV, fountain in courtyard, restaurant, public phones.

E El Gallo, Federación 26, T252 9481, www.hosteltrail.com/posadaelgallo/. In colonial part, French/ Venezuelan owned, relaxed, spacious, internet, shared baths, courtyard with hammocks, dorms and private rooms, use of kitchen, some English spoken, see Eric for tours to Sierra San Luis, a 1-day tour includes lunch.

E Posada Casa Tun Tun, Zamora 92, entre Toledo y Hernández, T404 4260, www.hosteltrail.com/casatuntun/. Run by knowledgeable and welcoming Belgian couple. Restored colonial house with 3 attractive patios, kitchen facilities, laundry, relaxing hammock areas and dipping pool, dorms and rooms with bath and lovely décor. Good value, nice atmosphere, free morning coffee, changes US$. Highly recommended.

Camping About 30 km east of Coro at **La Cumara**, nice, good beach and dunes.

Punto Fijo *p1598*

B Caraibi, Av Bolivia entre Peninsular y Ayacucho, T247 0227. With breakfast, good restaurant, parking, a/c, modern, accepts credit cards.

C Miami, C Falcón entre Av México y Bolivia, T245 8532. A/c, bit cheaper with fan, parking, restaurant. Recommended.

Judibana

C Jardín, on Av Mariscal y C Falcón, near airport, T246 1727. A/c, pool, restaurant, parking, accepts credit cards, changes US$ cash.

D Luigi, C Oeste, P PB, T246 0970. A/c, pleasant, good restaurant, accepts credit cards.

Adícora *p1598*

A Hacienda La Pancha, Vía Pueblo Nuevo, 5 km from Adícora in the hills, T0414-969 2649. Beautiful, old, colonial-style house set in countryside, nice owners, restaurant, pool, no children.

B-D Archie's Surf Posada, Playa Sur, T988 8285, www.kitesurfing-venezuela.com. At entrance to Adícora, 5 mins' walk to centre. German-run, well established, organizes wind and kite surfing lessons. Also trips, horse riding and airport pick-ups. Furnished bungalows for 4-12, apartments for 2-4, hammocks. Good reports.

D Posada Kitzberger, C Comercio de Adícora, on Malecón, T988 8173. Fan and a/c, German owners, pleasant, cosy, no single rooms, good restaurant. Recommended.

Sierra de San Luís *p1598*

Curimagua

D Finca El Monte, Vía La Soledad, 5 km from the village, T404 0564, fincaelmonte@yahoo.com. Run by a Swiss couple on an eco-friendly basis. Peaceful, beautiful views, colonial style, hot water, meals, hammocks. Tours round the park include birdwatching and cave tours. English, German and French spoken. Highly recommended.

Cabure

In town are several budget options.

B-C Hotel El Duende, 20 mins uphill from village, T808 9066. A beautiful 19th-century posada and garden, price depends on size of room, fan, cold water, good restaurant, horse riding, walking, peaceful. Recommended.

Eating

Coro *p1597, map p1597*

TT Barra del Jacal, Av Manaure y C 29 Unión. Outdoors, pizza and pasta.

TT Mersi, C 56 Toledo y Zamora. Good pizzas and *empanadas*.

TT El Portón de Arturo, C 56 Toledo, towards Plaza Falcón. All kinds of regional meat.

TT Posada Don Luis, opposite airport. Serves local speciality, *chivo*, goat.

Cafés

Dulzura y algo más, on the corner of Paseo Alameda. Good ice cream and local sweets.

Heladería Brudrimar, Paseo Talavera 2, T253 1300. In historic centre, old fashioned, a real institution with good food and good for people watching. Recommended.

Panadería Costa Nova, Av Manaure, opposite *Hotel Intercaribe*. Good bread, sandwiches and pastries, open late.

Punto Fijo *p1598*

T Colonial, C Libertad entre Colombia y Ecuador. Cheap, lunch only. Recommended.

T Good *panadería* opposite bus terminal.

Adícora *p1598*

Hotel Falcon III, C La Marina, Vía Las Cabanas, T697 9267. On beachfront, white hotel, serves excellent, good value seafood and fish soup. Also rents a/c, basic rooms (**B**).

Festivals and events

Coro *p1597, map p1597*

26 Jul, Coro Week. **9-12 Oct**, **state fair**. **24-25 Dec**, **Tambor Coriano** and **Parranda de San Benito** (Coro, La Vela and Puerto Cumarebo).

Activities and tours

Coro *p1597, map p1597*

Contact *posadas* in town for tours, eg **La Casa de los Párajos**.

Transport

Coro *p1597, map p1597*

Air Airport open for domestic flights; see also Las Piedras, below, for flights.

Bus Terminal is on Av Los Médanos, entre Maparari y Libertad, buses go up C 35 Falcón, US$0.35, taxi US$2.75. To/from **Caracas** US$20, 6-8 hrs; **Maracaibo**, US$11.25 (US$15 with a/c), 4 hrs, *por puesto* US$15; **Tucacas**, every 20 mins, US$8, 3-4 hrs; **Punto Fijo**, *por puesto* US$2.

Punto Fijo *p1598*

Air Airport at **Las Piedras**: *por puestos* from C Garcés y Av Bolívar (don't believe taxis who say there are no *por puestos* from airport to town); taxi from Punto Fijo US$5, from bus terminal US$3.50. Daily flights to **Curaçao** with **Insel Air**.

Bus Terminal on C Peninsular entre Colombia y Ecuador; *por puestos* to **Pueblo Nuevo, Adícora, Coro, Valencia** and **Maracaibo**. To **Maracay, Barquisimeto, Maracaibo** and **Caracas**: **Expresos Occidente**, on C Comercio entre Ecuador y Bolivia; to **Mérida, Barinas** and **Caracas**, **Expresos San Cristóbal**, C Carnevali behind Hotel América; **Expresos Alianza**, on Av Colombia between Carnevali and Democracia, to many destinations.

Adícora *p1598*

Bus Several daily to and from **Coro**, from 0630-1700, US$2, 1 hr; to and from **Pueblo Nuevo** and **Punto Fijo**, several daily from 0600-1730.

Directory

Coro *p1597, map p1597*

Banks See also Money, page 1566. **Banco Mercantil**, C 35 Falcón y C 50 Colina, Edif Don Luis, ATM and cash on Mastercard. **Banco Venezuela**, Paseo Talavera. ATM and cash on Visa and Mastercard. Try hotels and travel agents for cash and TCs. **Internet Falcontech**, next door to **Hotel Intercaribe**, Av de Manuare. **CANTV** Centro de Comunicaciones, Av Los Médanos, opposite bus terminal, also international calls.

Punto Fijo *p1598*

Banks Many banks on Av Bolívar y Comercio accept Visa, Mastercard and others, eg **Banco de Venezuela, Banesco. Banco Mercantil**, Av Bolívar y C Girardot. Changes Citicorp TCs. **Casa Fukayama**, Av Bolívar entre C Altagracia y Girardot. Changes US$ cash. **Consulates Dutch Consul** in Punta Cardón, Judibana at Urb La Laguna, C Mucubaji 38, Roque Hernández, T240 7211. **Post offices** Ipostel at C Páez y Av Panamá, collection every 10 days. **Telephones** CANTV at C Falcón y Av México.

From Maracaibo to Colombia

To the heart of Venezuela's oil business on the shores of Lake Maracaibo: not many tourists find their way here. Those that do are usually on their way to Colombia via the border crossing on the Guajira Peninsula to the north. If you've got the time to stop and can handle the heat, Maracaibo is the only town in Venezuela where occasionally you'll see indigenous people in traditional dress going about their business and nearby are reminders of prehispanic and oil-free customs.

Maracaibo → *Phone code: 0261. Colour map 1, A4. Population: 1,800,000.*

Maracaibo, capital of the State of Zulia, is Venezuela's second largest city and oil capital. The region is the economic powerhouse of the country with over 50% of the nation's oil production coming from the Lago de Maracaibo area and Zulia state. The lake is reputedly the largest fresh water reserve in South America. A long cement and steel bridge, Puente General Rafael Urdaneta, crosses Lago de Maracaibo, connecting the city with the rest of the country. Maracaibo is a sprawling modern city with wide streets. Some parts are pleasant to walk around, apart from the intense heat (or when it is flooded in the rainy season), but as in the rest of the country, security is becoming an issue. By the time this edition goes to print, there should be some much-needed improvements in the centre. Plaza Bolívar is undergoing intensive reconstruction and is not considered safe at night. The hottest months are July to September, but there is usually a sea breeze from 1500 until morning. Just north of the regional capital is a lagoon where you can still see the stilt houses that inspired the Spanish invaders to christen it 'Little Venice'. The **tourist office** is **Corzutur** ⓘ *Av 18, esq C 78 (Dr Portillo), Edif Lieja, p 4, T783 4928, www.gobernaciondelzulia.gov.ve.* Zulia state has returned a governor opposed to Chávez in the past two elections and the city is staunchly pro-market. Bear this in mind if expressing political opinions.

Sights The traditional city centre is **Plaza Bolívar**, on which stand the **Cathedral** (at east end), the **Casa de Gobierno**, the **Asamblea Legislativa** and the **Casa de la Capitulación** (or Casa Morales) ⓘ *Mon-Fri, 0800-1600, free,* a colonial building and national monument. The Casa houses the libraries of the Sociedad Bolivariana and of the Academia de Historia de Zulia, a gallery of work by the Venezuelan painter, Carmelo Fernández (1809-1887), several exhibition halls and a stunning interior patio dedicated to modern art. Next door is the 19th-century **Teatro Baralt**, hosting frequent subsidized concerts and performances.

Running west of Plaza Bolívar is the **Paseo de las Ciencias**, a 1970s development which levelled all the old buildings in the area. Only the **Iglesia de Santa Bárbara** stands in the Paseo; a new public park is to be opened here. **Calle Carabobo** (one block north of the Paseo de las Ciencias) is a very good example of a colourful, colonial Maracaibo street. One block south of the

Paseo is **Plaza Baralt** ⓘ *Av 6, stretching to C 100 and the old waterfront market* (**Mercado de Pulgas**). The impressive **Centro de Arte de Maracaibo Lía Bermúdez** ⓘ *in the 19th-century Mercado de Pulgas building, Mon-Fri 0800-1200, 1400-1600, Sat-Sun 0930-1700*, displays the work of national and international artists. It is a/c, a good place to escape the midday heat and a good starting place for a walking tour of the city centre. Its walls are decorated with beautiful photographs of Maracaibo. The Centro has a café, internet, bookshops, cinema and holds frequent cultural events, including the Feria Internacional de Arte y Antigüedades de Maracaibo (FIAAM). The new part of the city round **Bella Vista** and towards the University is in vivid contrast with the small **old town** near the docks. The latter, with narrow streets and brightly painted, colonial style adobe houses, has hardly changed from the 19th century, although many buildings are in an advanced state of decay. The buildings facing **Parque Urdaneta** (three blocks north of Paseo de las Ciencias) have been well-restored and are home to several artists. Also well-preserved are the church of **Santa Lucía** and the streets around. This old residential area is a short ride (or long walk) north from the old centre. **Parque La Marina**, on the shores of the lake, contains sculptures by the Venezuelan artist, Jesús Soto (1923-2005). More of his work can be seen in the **Galería de Arte Brindhaven** (free), near Santa Lucía.

Paseo de Maracaibo, or Vereda del Lago, 25 mins' walk from Plaza Bolívar, is a lakeside park near the *Hotel del Lago*. It offers walks along the shores of the lake, stunning views of the Rafael Urdaneta bridge and of oil tankers sailing to the Caribbean. The park attracts a wide variety of birds. To get there take a 'Milagro' *por puesto* or a 'Norte' bus northbound and ask the driver to let you off at the well-marked entrance. Opposite is the Mercado de los Indios Guajiros (see Shopping).

Maracaibo to Colombia

About one hour north is the Río Limón. Take a bus (US$1, from terminal or Avenida 15 entre C 76 y 77) to **El Moján**, riding with the Guajira Indians as they return to their homes on the peninsula. From El Moján, *por puestos* go to **Sinamaica** (US$2; taxi US$7).

Sinamaica is the entry point to the territory of Añu people (also known as Paraujanos) who live in stilt houses on Sinamaica lagoon. Some 15,000 Añu live in the area, although official numbers say there are only 4,000. Their language is practically extinct (UNICEF is supporting a project to revive it: www.unicef.org/infobycountry/venezuela_37969.html; other reports say that one of the only two women still to speak it died recently aged 100). The Añu use fibers to make handicraft. To get to the lagoon, take a truck (US$1) from Sinamaica's main plaza on the new paved road to Puerto Cuervito (5 minutes), where the road ends at the lagoon. Dozens of indigenous people will be waiting for water transport. You can hitch a ride on a shared boat to one of the settlements for a few bolívares, or you can hire a boat by the hour (US$20 per hour, ask for Víctor Márquez, recommended). Main settlements on the lagoon are El Barro, La Bocita and Nuevo Mundo. Nuevo Mundo has **Posada Nuevo Mundo**, basic bungalows on stilts on lagoon (**E**). There is small shop. There are several small eateries on the lagoon. **Parador Turístico de la Laguna de Sinamaica** has decent food, clean bathrooms and an excellent handicraft shop with local produce.

Beyond Sinamaica, the paved road past the Lagoon leads to the border with Colombia. Along the way you see Guajira Indians, the men with bare legs, on horseback; the women with long, black, tent-shaped dresses and painted faces, wearing the sandals with big wool pom-poms which they make and sell, more cheaply than in tourist shops. The men do nothing: women do all the work, tending animals, selling slippers and raising very little on the dry, hot, scrubby Guajira Peninsula.

Border with Colombia → *Colombia is 1 hr behind Venezuela.*

If you travel on the road between Maracaibo and the border, even if you are planning to visit just Sinamaica and its lagoon, carry your passport with you. This is tough area, with drug gangs and illegal immigrants (mainly from Colombia) attempting to cross the border. Police and army checkpoints are numerous. They are friendly but can get tough if you don't have your documents, or don't cooperate. The border operates 24 hours. You need an exit card and stamp, US$9.30 (BsF 40), to leave Venezuela, payable in bolívares only. Ask for 90 days on entering Colombia and make sure you get an entry stamp from the Colombian authorities (DAS). From the frontier to Macaio, it's a 15-minute drive. Check exchange rates; it may be better to change bolívares into Colombian pesos in Venezuela at the border rather than in Colombia. For entering Colombia, see page 968.

From Maracaibo to Colombia listings

For Sleeping and Eating price codes and other relevant information, see Essentials, pages 38-40.

Sleeping

Maracaibo *p1601*

It is best to reserve well in advance.

Reminder Prices are shown at official exchange rate.

L Best Western Hotel El Paseo, Av 1B y C 74, Sector Cotorrera, T792 4422, www.hotelelpaseo.com.ve. Closest competition to El Lago (see next entry), all rooms with breathtaking view of the lake. Very expensive but good. 𝐓𝐓 **Garisol**, revolving restaurant on top floor with great view, international dishes.

L Hotel del Lago, Av 2 (El Milagro), near Club Náutico, T794 4222, www.venetur.gob.ve. With 368 rooms, some overlooking the lake, this 5-star institution is easily the most luxurious hotel in Maracaibo. It was the Intercontinental, but is now part of Venetur.

L Kristoff, Av 8 Santa Rita entre C 68 y 69, T796 1000, www.hotelkristoff.com. In the north of the city some distance from centre. Being refurbished throughout, a/c, nice pool open to non-residents, disco, laundry service, restaurant.

A Aparthotel Presidente, Av 11 N 68-50, entre C 68 y 69, T798 3133, ahpresi@intercable.com.ve. Self contained units, café and restaurant, pool and travel agency. Good for longer stays.

A Gran Hotel Delicias, Av 15 esq C 70, T797 0983, www.granhoteldelicias.com. North of the city. Old-fashioned modern hotel, bland, a/c, restaurant, pool, disco, accepts credit cards.

B Doral, C 75 y Av 14A, T717 5796, www.hoteldoral.com. North of the city. A/c, safe, decent rooms, with breakfast, helpful. Recommended.

D Paraíso, Av 9B, No 82-70, sector Veritas, T797 6149. With small sitting room, a/c, cable.

E Acuario, C 78 (also known as Dr Portillo) No 9-43, Bella Vista, T797 1123. A/c, shower, safe, small rooms, safe parking, basic.

E San Martín, Av 3Y (San Martín) con C 80, T791 5095. A/c, restaurant next door, accepts credit cards.

E Victoria, Av 6-14, Plaza Baralt, T721 2654. Right in the centre, near Plaza Bolívar, unsafe area at night. Art nouveau structure, basic, private and shared bath, no hot water, a/c, no windows in some rooms, poor value but well located.

Eating

Maracaibo *p1601*

A range of US chain restaurants and Chinese restaurants (mostly on Av 8 Santa Rita, including restaurant **Hue Chie**) and pizzerías in the north of town. Many places to eat and bars on Calle 72 and 5 de Julio. Most restaurants are closed on Sun. Many restaurants on *palafitos* (stilts) in Santa Rosa de Agua district, good for fish (*por puesto* US$0.45 to get there); best to go at lunchtime.

𝐓𝐓𝐓 **El Zaguán**, on C Carabobo (see above). Serves traditional regional cooking, friendly service, good menu and food, pleasant bar.

𝐓𝐓𝐓 **Paparazzi Ristorante**, Av 20 entre C 69 y 70, T783 4979. Part of a nightclub, Italian and international, one of the best in town.

𝐓𝐓 **El Carite**, C 78, No 8-35, T71878. Excellent selection of fish and seafood, delicious and moderately priced.

𝐓𝐓 **Koto Sushi**, Av 11 entre C 75 y 76, Tierra Negra, T798 8954. Japanese food.

𝐓𝐓 **Mi Vaquita**, Av 3H con C 76. Texan steak house, popular with wealthy locals, bar area for dancing, pricey drinks. No sandals allowed.

𝐓𝐓 **Peruano Marisquería**, Av 15 (Delicias) y C 69, T798 1513. Authentic Peruvian seafood dishes and international cuisine.

𝐓𝐓 **Pizzería Napoletana**, C 77 near Av 4. Excellent food but poor service, closed Tue.

𝐓𝐓 **Yal-la**, Av 8 C 68, opposite Hotel Kristoff, T797 8863. Excellent, authentic Lebanese/ Middle Eastern restaurant at very reasonable prices. Great vegetarian food.

Café Baralt, Paseo de las Ciencias, opposite Teatro Baralt. Recommended for good value authentic local lunch, irregular opening hours.
Bambi, Av 4, 78-70. Italian run with good cappuccino, pastries, recommended.
Chips, Av 31 opposite Centro Comercial Salto Angel. Regional fast food, *tequeños* and *patacones*. Recommended. There are many other good restaurants around the Plaza de la República, C77/5 de Julio and Av 31, in Bella Vista.
Kabuki, C 77 entre Av 12 y 13. Nice café with good food.
La Friulana, C 95 con Av 3. Good cheap meal, closes 1900. Repeatedly recommended.

Festivals and events

Maracaibo *p1601*
Virgen del Rosario, 5 Oct; 24 Oct; 18 Nov, NS de Chiquimquira (La Chinita), processions, bullfights – the main regional religious festival.

Shopping

Maracaibo *p1601*
There are several modern malls with all services and amenities, including multiplex cinemas. The most luxurious is **Centro Lago Mall**.
Bookshops **Librería Cultural**, Av 5 de Julio. Best Spanish language bookstore in town. **Librería Italiana**, Av 5 de Julio, Ed Centro América. Postcards and foreign publications. Staff at the public library, Av 2, are helpful to tourists.
Handicrafts and markets **El Mercado de los Indios Guajiros**, open market at C 96 y Av 2 (El Milagro). A few crafts, some pottery, hammocks, etc. **Las Pulgas**, south side of C 100 entre Av 10 y 14. The outdoor market, enormous, mostly clothes, shoes, and household goods. Most of the shops on **C Carabobo** sell regional crafts, eg *La Salita*. **El Turista**, C 72 y Av 3H, in front of Centro Comercial Las Tinajitas, T792 3495.

Transport

Maracaibo *p1601*
Air La Chinita airport is 25 km southwest of city centre (taxis US$20, no *por puestos*). Good bookshop in arrivals sells city map; several good but overpriced eateries; *Italcambio* for exchange, daily 0600-1800, no commission; car hire outside. Frequent flights with **Aserca**, **Aeropostal** and **Avior** to **Caracas, Valencia, Barquisimeto, San Antonio,** and **Porlamar**. International flights to **Miami**.
Bus The bus station is 1 km south of the old town. It is old and chaotic, unsafe at night. Taxi to the city US$6.50-11. Ask for buses into town, local services are confusing. Several fast and comfortable buses daily to **Valencia**, US$15.50, 8 hrs. **San Cristóbal**, US$18.75-20, 6-8 hrs, *por puesto*, US$21. **Barquisimeto**, 4 hrs in buseta, US$10.50. **Coro** US$11.25-15, 4 hrs. **Caracas**, US$19.50, 10-13 hrs **(Aeroexpresos Ejecutivos** from Av 15 con C 90 - Distribuidor las Delicias, T783 0620), *por puesto* US$40. **Mérida**, from US$11, 5-7 hrs, or *por puesto*, US$12.50, 6½ hrs.
Local *Por puestos* go up and down Av 4 from the old centre to Bella Vista. Ruta 6 goes up and down C 67 (Cecilia Acosta). The San Jacinto bus goes along Av 15 (Las Delicias). Buses from Las Delicias also go to the centre and terminal. From C 76 to the centre *por puestos* marked 'Las Veritas' and buses marked 'Ziruma'. Look for the name of the route on the roof, or the windscreen, passenger's side. Downtown to Av 5 de Julio in a 'Bella Vista' *por puesto* costs US$0.45-0.70, depending on distance. Taxis minimum US$4.65; from north to centre US$7 (beware overcharging, meters are not used). Public transport is being completely overhauled, but it will take years to complete. New large and small red public buses (government- owned) connect the north, centre and other parts of the city at US$0.45. Old private buses charge US$0.55.

An elegant light-rail system, **Metro**, is being developed. Six stations of the frst line are in operation, from Altos de la Vanega, southwest of the centre, to Libertador, via Sabaneta and Urdaneta. Basic fare US$0.15. Five more stations are under construction and more lines are planned.

Border with Colombia *p1602*
Maracaibo-Maicao
Bus **Busven** direct at 0400. Other buses operate during the morning, US$15.50. Or take a *colectivo* from Maracaibo bus terminal (5 passengers), US$15.50 pp; shop around, plus US$1 road toll, 2-3 hrs. Lots of police checks en route. There are reports that border police are on the look out for bribes, so make sure your documents are in order. Some drivers are unwilling to stop for formalities; make sure the driver takes you all the way to Maicao and arrive before the last bus to Santa Marta or Cartagena (1630).

ⓘ Directory

Maracaibo *p1601*

Banks See also Money, page 1566. **Banco Mercantil**, on corner of Plaza de la República. Branches of **Banco de Venezuela**, including at airport, for Visa ATMs. Best for dollars and TCs is **Casa de Cambio de Maracaibo**, C 78 con Av 9B. **Italcambio**, C C Montielco, loc PA 1-1, entre Av 20 y C 72, T7832682, Amex rep. **Citibank**, Av 15 (Las Delicias) con C 77 (5 de Julio) for Citicorp TCs. All banks shut at 1530, exchange morning only. *Cambio* at bus terminal will change Colombian pesos into bolívares at a poor rate. **Consulates** **Germany**, Av 3F No 69-26, Sector Bellas Artes, T791 1416, herrmann@cantv.net. **Italy**, Av 17 entre C 71 y 55, Quinta La Querencia, Sector Baralt, T783 0834, consolato.maracaibo@esteri.it. **Norway**, Auto Agro Maracaibo, CA; Av 4 (Bella Vista) No 85-150, T722 9096, autoagromcbo@telcel.net.ve. **UK**, Av 4 Bella Vista, Edif Centro Profesional Norte, of 3A, T797 7003, alexp@inspecciones.com. **Internet** **Cyber Estudio**, Av 10 No 66-110, 1100-2300. **Medical services** *Hospital Coromoto*, Av 3C, No 51, El Lago, T790 0017. **Post offices** Av Libertador y Av 3. **Telephones** CANTV, C 96, No 3-42, just off the main plaza. Centre for internet and international calls.

Barquisimeto and around

→ *Phone code: 0251. Colour map 1, A5. Population: 900,000. Altitude: 565 m. Mean temperature: 25° C*

The arid, fruit-growing area around the city of Barquisimeto leads to the lush Andean foothills of Trujillo state. Venezuela's fourth largest city was largely destroyed by an earthquake in 1812, but is a nice enough place to spend a few days when visiting the area. For information: **División de Turismo y Recreación** ⓘ *Cra 19 esq C 25, Palacio de Gobierno, T233 8239, www.cortulara.gob.ve*. See also www.barquisimeto.com.

Many fascinating corners have been preserved and a law prohibiting demolition of older buildings means more are being restored. The **Museo de Barquisimeto** ⓘ *Av 15 between C 25 and 26, Tue-Fri 0900-1700, Sat-Sun 1000-1700, free,* displays the town's history and contemporary art. More historic buildings line **Plaza Jacinto Lara**. The **San Francisco church** faces the plaza. On the opposite side is the small **Ateneo cultural centre** ⓘ *Cra 17 y C 23, Mon-Fri 0830-1200, 1500-1830, Sat 0900-1200, free,* with exhibitions in an 18th-century house. It also has a restaurant and occasional evening concerts. The **Cathedral** ⓘ *C 30 y Cra 26 (Venezuela)*, is a modern structure of reinforced concrete and glass. At the heart of the old city is **Plaza Bolívar**, with a statue of the Liberator, the white-painted **Iglesia Concepción** and the **Palacio Municipal** ⓘ *Cra 17 y C 25*, an attractive modern building. **Parque Ayacucho** ⓘ *Cra 15 (Av Francisco de Miranda) between C 41-43*, has lush vegetation, fountains and a bronze statue of Mariscal Sucre. On Av Libertador Oeste, just out of the city **El Obelisco**, 75 m high (built 1952 to celebrate 400 years of the city), has a lift to the top, worth a visit.

About 24 km southwest of Barquisimeto is the busy agricultural centre of **Quíbor** (*Phone code: 0253, Population: 40,295*). Festivals on 18 January (NS de Altagracia) and 12 June (San Antonio de Padua). The **Centro Antropológico de Quíbor** exhibits work of the *indígenas* who used to live in the region. South of Quíbor and 40 minutes from Barquisimeto is **Sanaré** (1,360 m), on the edge of the **Parque Nacional Yacambú**, where you can hike through tropical forest up the Fumerola, a sleeping volcano. About 60 km east of Barquisimeto is **Chivacoa** (*Population: 40,400*). South of the town is the sacred mountain of the María-Lionza cult, practised throughout Venezuela. Celebrations are held there at weekends with 12 October (Día de la Raza) being the most important day. There is a Catholic festival, La Inmaculada Concepción, from 8-14 December.

Barquisimeto and around listings

For Sleeping and Eating price codes and other relevant information, see Essentials, pages 38-40.

Sleeping

Barquisimeto *p1605*

Avenidas and Carreras run east to west, Calles run north to south.

B Príncipe, Av 18 entre C 22 y C 23, T231 2344. A/c, TV, pool, restaurant.

C Hevelyn, Av Vargas (Cra 17) entre 20 y 21, T252 3986. Hot water, a/c.

C Yacambú, Av Vargas/Cra 17 entre C 19 y C 20, T251 3022/3229. Accepts credit cards, a/c, bar and restaurant with Mediterranean food.

D Avenue, Av Vargas/Cra 17 entre C 21 y C 22, T231 1367. A/c and fan, TV, parking, secure.

D Lido, Cra 16 entre C 26 y 27, T231 5568. A/c, hot water, some rooms gloomy, cash only, poor value.

E del Centro, Av 20 entre C 26 y C 27, T808 0378. Spacious rooms, a/c or fan, TV, cooled water dispenser on each floor.

E Don Quijote, Cra 18 entre C 21 y C 22. Clean, well-maintained, cash only, parking, next to restaurant.

Sanaré

E Posada Turística El Cerrito, T0414-550 4077. English spoken, small restaurant and bar, tours to local sights and Yacambú. Highly recommended.

Eating

Barquisimeto *p1605*

Barquipán, C 26 entre Cras 17 y 18. Good breakfasts, snacks.

La Maison de la Vargas, Av Vargas entre C 21 y C 22. Panadería y pastelería, excellent choice of cakes, pastries, sandwiches. Lots of places to eat on and around Av Vargas.

Majestic, Av 19 con C 31. Breakfast and vegetarian meals.

Sabor Vegetariano, on C 24 entre Av 20 y 21, next to *El Rincón Griego* restaurant. Snacks.

Festivals and events

Barquisimeto *p1605*

On **28 Dec** (morning) is the fiesta of **La Zaragoza**, when colourfully clad people are accompanied by music and dancing in the street. Huge crowds watch **La Divina Pastora** procession in early **Jan**, when an image of the Virgin Mary is carried from the shrine at Santa Rosa village into the city.

Transport

Barquisimeto *p1605*

Air Jacinto Lara international airport is 8 km southwest of the centre, 10 mins, US$5.75 by taxi. Local buses outside, US$0.25. Flights to **Caracas** and **Maracaibo**.

Bus Terminal is on the edge of the city at Carrera 24 y C 42 (a new terminal, Estación Central Simón Bolívar, is under construction on the western edge of the city). To **Mérida**, 3-4 a day, at 1020 and several between 2000 and 0200, 8 hrs via Agua Viva and El Vigía, US$18.50 *bus cama*; to **Acarigua** (see page 1626), 1 hr, US$4. To **Barinas**, 5 hrs, US$10. To **Valera** *por puesto*, 3½ hrs, US$8.75. To **Tucacas** every 2 hrs; to **Coro** at 1200 and by night, 7 hrs, US$13. To **Caracas**, US$13.25-15, 5½ hrs.

Directory

Barquisimeto *p1605*

Banks See also Money, page 1566. **Banco de Venezuela**, Av 20 y C 31, No 31-08, ATM. **Capital Express**, Av Los Leones, Centro Comercial Paseo, next to C 90. **Italcambio**, Av Los Leones, C C París, loc 1-40, T254 9790, and at airport for Amex. **Post offices** Av 17 con C 25. **Telephones** C 30 entre Avs 24 y 25.

Valera to Mérida

From the lowland heat of Valera, roads climb towards the mountains, passing colonial towns and entering an increasingly rugged landscape.

Valera → *Phone code: 0271. Colour map 1, A5. Population: 130,000.*
This is the most important town in Trujillo state. Here, you can choose between two roads over the Sierra, either via Timotes and Mucuchíes to Mérida, or via Boconó and down to the Llanos at Guanare. There are several upmarket business hotels, few decent budget ones, and lots of good Italian restaurants on the main street.

Trujillo → *Phone code: 0272. Colour map 1, A5. Population: 44,460. Altitude: 805 m.*
From Valera a road runs via the restored colonial village of **La Plazuela** to the state capital, Trujillo. This beautiful historic town consists of two streets running uphill from the Plaza Bolívar. It's a friendly place with a warm, subtropical climate. The **Centro de Historia de Trujillo**, on Avenida Independencia, is a restored colonial house, now a museum. Bolívar lived there and signed the 'proclamation of war to the death' in the house. A 47m-high monument to the **Virgen de la Paz** ⓘ *0900-1700, US$1*, with lift, was built in 1983; it stands at 1,608 m, 2½ hours walk from town and gives good views to Lake Maracaibo but go early. Jeeps leave when full from opposite *Hotel Trujillo*, 20 minutes, US$1 per person. For **tourist information**, Avenida Principal La Plazuela, No 1-03, T236 1455, presidenciactt@hotmail.com, or fondomixto@formitru.org.ve.

Boconó and Niquitao

From Trujillo there is a high, winding, spectacular paved road to Boconó, built on steep mountain sides and famed for its crafts. The **Centro de Acopio Artesanal Tiscachic** is highly recommended for *artesanía* (turn left just before bridge at entrance to town and walk 350 m).

Niquitao, a small town one hour southwest of Boconó, is still relatively unspoilt. Excursions can be made to the Teta de Niquitao (4,007 m), two hours by jeep, the waterfalls and pools known as Las Pailas, and a nearby lake. Southwest of Niquitao, by partly paved road is **Las Mesitas**; continue up towards **Tuñame**, turn left on a good gravel road (no signs), cross pass and descend to **Pueblo Llano** (one basic hotel and restaurant), from where you can climb to the Parque Nacional Sierra Nevada at 3,600 m, passing Santo Domingo. Good hiking in the area.

Road to the high Andes

After **Timotes** the road climbs through increasingly wild, barren and rugged country and through the windy pass of **Pico El Aguila** (4,118 m) in the Sierra de la Culata, best seen early morning, otherwise frequently in the clouds. This is the way Bolívar went when crossing the Andes to liberate Colombia, and on the peak is the statue of a condor. At the pass is the tourist restaurant **Páramo Aguila**, reasonably priced with open fire. People stop for a hot chocolate or a *calentado*, a herb liquor drunk hot. There are also food and souvenir stalls, and horses for hire (high season and weekends). Across from the monument is a small chapel with fine views. A paved road leads from here 2 km to a *CANTV* microwave tower (4,318 m). Here are tall *frailejones* plants; nearby are large storage sheds for vegetables from Piñango cooperatives. Continuing north as a lonely track the road goes to the **Piñango lakes** (45 km) and the traditional village of **Piñango** (2,480 m), 1½ hours. Great views for miles around. Eventually the road reaches the Panamerican and Lago de Maracaibo.

Santo Domingo (*Phone code: 0274; Population: 6,000; Altitude: 2,178 m*), with good handicraft shops and fishing, is on the spectacular road up from Barinas to Mérida, before the Parque Nacional Sierra Nevada. Festival: 30 September, San Gerónimo. The tourist office is on the right leaving town, 10 minutes from the centre.

Valera to Mérida listings

For Sleeping and Eating price codes and other relevant information, see Essentials, pages 38-40.

Sleeping

Trujillo *p1607*
D Los Gallegos, Av Independencia 5-65, T/F236 3193. With hot water, a/c or fan, with or without TV. As well as several other places.

Boconó *p1607*
B-C Estancia de Mosquey, Mosquey, 10 km from Boconó towards Biscucuy, T0272-414 8322, 0414-723 4246, www.estancia-mosquey.com. Family run, great views, rooms and cabañas, good beds, good restaurant, pool, recommended. There are other hotels and posadas **in town**, some on or near Plaza Bolívar, one opposite the bus station.

Niquitao *p1607*
B Posada Turística de Niquitao, T0271-885 2042/0414-727 8217/0416-771 7860, www.ciberexpo.com. Rooms with bath, hot water, TV, some with bunks, restaurant, tours arranged with guide, also has small museum.
D Na Delia, T0271-885 2113, on a hill 500 m out of town. With restaurant.

Road to the high Andes *p1607*
Timotes
B Las Truchas, north entrance to town, T/F0271-828 9158, www.andes.net/lastruchas. 44 cabins, with and without kitchen. Also has a Restaurant.
D Carambay, Av Bolívar 41, T0271-828 9261.

Santo Domingo
AL La Trucha Azul, east end of town, T898 8111, www.latruchaazul.com. Rooms with open fireplace, also suites and cabins, expensive for what it offers.
AL Los Frailes, between Santo Domingo and Laguna Mucubají at 3,700 m. T0274-417 3440 or book through **Hoturvensa**, T/F0212-976 0530/ 976 4984, www.hoturvensa.com.ve, but pay at hotel. Cheaper in low season, includes breakfast. Beautiful former monastery, specializes in honeymoon packages, rooms are simple, international menu and wines. Includes breakfast.
B Moruco, T898 8155/8070, out of town. Good value, beautiful, rooms and cabins, good food, bar.
C Paso Real, on the other side of the river from Los Frailes, no phone. A good place to stay.

Eating

Niquitao *p1607*
₸₸-₸ La Estancia, Plaza Bolívar. Owner Golfredo Pérez, helpful, kind, knows area well, pizzas.

Transport

Valera *p1607*
Bus The bus terminal on the edge of town. To **Boconó**, US$6, 3 hrs; to **Trujillo**, *por puestos*, 30 mins, US$1; to **Caracas**, 9 hrs, US$18.25 (direct at 2230 with **Expresos Mérida**); to **Mérida**, 4 daily with **Trans Barinas**, US$8.50, 4½ hrs; *por puestos* to **Mérida**, 3 hrs, US$11.50, leave when full (travel by day for the views and, especially in the rainy season, safety); to **Maracaibo**, *micros* every 30 mins until 1730, 4 hrs, US$8.

Road to the high Andes *p1607*
Santo Domingo
Bus Buses or *busetas* pass through in either direction at around 2 hr intervals all day. **Mérida** 2 hrs, US$4.25 *por puesto*; **Barinas** 1½ hrs, US$4.75.

Directory

Valera *p1607*
Banks Corp Banca, Av Bolívar con C 5, changes Amex TCs, no commission. **Banco de Venezuela**, C 7 con Av 10, cash on Visa and Mastercard.

Trujillo *p1607*
Banks See also Money, page 1566. **Banco de Venezuela**, 1 block down from cathedral, has ATM.

Mérida and around

Venezuela's high Andes offer hiking and mountaineering, and fishing in lakes and rivers. The main tourist centre is Mérida (674 km from Caracas), but there are many interesting rural villages. The Transandean Highway runs through the Sierra to the border with Colombia, while the Pan-American Highway runs along the foot of the Andes through El Vigía and La Fría to join the Transandean at San Cristóbal.

The Sierra Nevada de Mérida, running from south of Maracaibo to the Colombian frontier, is the only range in Venezuela where snow lies permanently on the higher peaks. Several basins lying between the mountains are actively cultivated; the inhabitants are concentrated mainly in valleys and basins at between 800 m and 1,300 m above sea level. The towns of Mérida and San Cristóbal are in this zone.

Mérida

→ *Phone code: 0274. Colour map 1, A4. Population: 300,000. Altitude: 1,640 m.*

Mérida stands on an alluvial terrace – a kind of giant shelf – 15 km long, 2½ km wide, within sight of Pico Bolívar, the highest in Venezuela. The mountain is part of the Five White Eagles group, visible from the city. The summits are at times covered in snow, but the glaciers and snow are retreating. Founded in 1558, the capital of Mérida State retains some colonial buildings but is mainly known for its 33 parks and many statues. For tourists, its claims to fame are the great opportunities for doing adventure sports and the buzz from a massive student population.

The heart of Venezuelan mountaineering and trekking is the Andes, with Mérida as the base, and there are several important peaks and some superb hikes. Bear in mind that high altitudes will be reached and acclimatization is essential. Suitable equipment is necessary and you may consider bringing your own. In the Sierra Nevada is mountain biking, whitewater rafting, para- penting and horse riding. See also the companies listed in Activities and tours, page 1614.

Ins and outs

Getting around Mérida may seem a safe place, but theft and robbery does occur. Avoid the Pueblo Nuevo area by the river at the stairs leading down from Avenida 2, as well as Avenida 2 itself. The **airport** is on the main highway, 5 km from the centre. *Por puesto* into town US$0.35, taxi US$3.50. The **bus terminal** is 3 km from the centre of town on the west side of the valley, linked by a frequent minibus service to Calle 25 entre Avenidas 2 y 3, US$0.35. City bus fares rise at weekends. A trolley bus system from the southern suburb of Ejido to La Hechicera in the north has been opened for much of its length. » *See also Transport, page 1615.*

Information **Tourist offices** Next to the airport is the **Corporación Merideña de Turismo**, on Avenida Urdaneta y C 45, T262 2371/263 2782, cormetur@merida.gob.ve. It's open Monday-Saturday low season 0800-1200 and 1400-1800, high season 0800-1800. They supply a useful map of the state and town. Also at the airport in the waiting lounge, very informative, for the same low season hours, 0730-1330 in high season; in the bus terminal, same hours, have a map of the city (free). At Parque Las Heroínas, at the zoo in Chorros de Milla park and at the Mercado Principal, low season 0800-1200, 1400-1800, high season 0830-1830. **Inparques** (National Parks) Av Las Américas, C 2, sector Fondur, T262 1356, sierranevada .andigena.org. Map of Parque Nacional Sierra Nevada (mediocre) US$1; also, and easier, at Teleférico for permits.

Sights

In the city centre is the attractive **Plaza Bolívar**, on which stands the **cathedral**, dark and heavy inside, with **Museo Arquidiocesano** beside it, and **Plaza de Milla**, or **Sucre** ⓘ *C 14 entre Avs 2 y 3,* always a hive of activity. The **Parque de las Cinco Repúblicas** ⓘ *C 13, entre Avs 4 y 5, beside the barracks*, is renowned for having the first monument in the world to Bolívar (1842, replaced in

Mérida

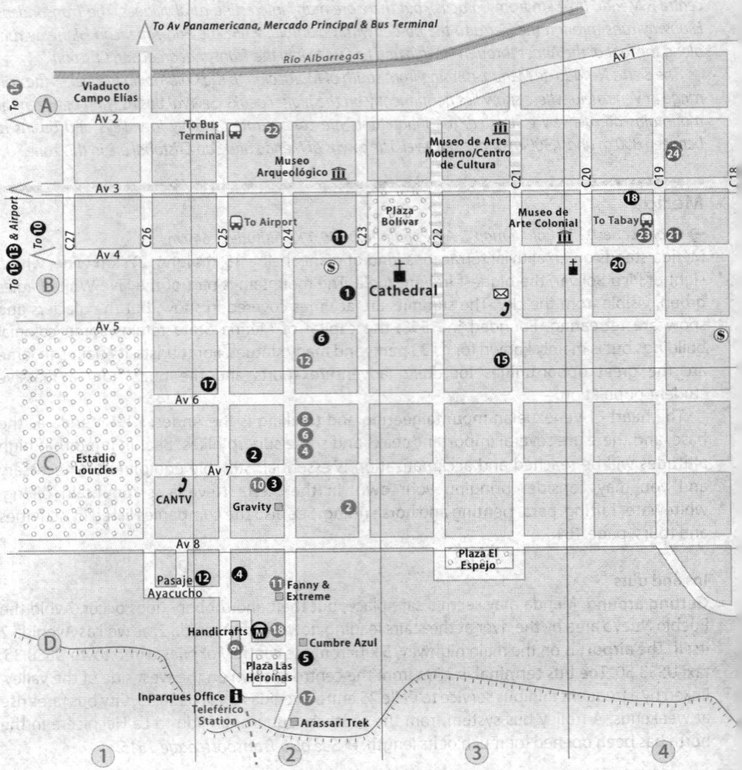

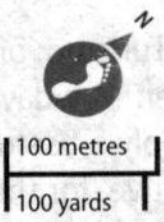

Sleeping 🛏
1 Apart Hotel Central *B5*
2 El Escalador *C2*
3 El Tisure *B5*
4 Encanto Andino *C2*
5 Italia *A4*
6 La Montaña & restaurant *C2*
7 Los Bucares de Mérida *B6*
8 Luxemburgo *C2*
9 Mintoy *D2*
10 Montecarlo *C2*
11 Mundo Mérida *D2*
12 Nevada Palace *B2*
13 Posada Alemania *A5*
14 Posada Casa Alemana-Suiza *A1*
15 Posada Casa Sol *B5*
16 Posada Doña Pumpa *B6*
17 Posada Familiar Mara *D2*
18 Posada Guamanchi & Guamanchi Tours *D2*
19 Posada Luz Caraballo *A6*

Eating 🍴
1 Bimbo *B2*
2 Buona Pizza *C2*
3 Buona Pizza Express *C2*
4 Café Atico *D2*
5 Cheo's Pizzería *D2*
6 Chipen *B2*
7 El Museo *A6*
8 El Sabor de los Quesos *A6*
9 El Sano Glotón *B4*
10 El Tinajero *B1*

1988) and contains soil from each of the five countries he liberated (photography strictly prohibited). Three of the peaks known as the Five White Eagles (Bolívar, 5,007 m, La Silla del Toro, 4,755 m, and León 4,740 m) can be clearly seen from here. **Plaza Las Heroínas**, by the lowest station of the *teleférico* (see below) is busy till 2300, an outdoor party zone, with artists exhibiting their work. Many tour operators have their offices here.

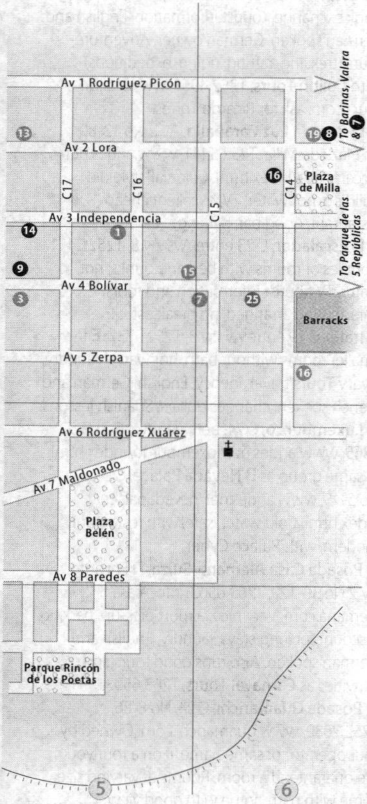

11 Espresso Café *B2*
12 Federico's *D2*
13 Heladería La Coromoto *B1*
14 La Abadía *B5*
15 La Abadía del Angel *B3*
16 La Astilla *A6*
17 La Esquina de Pajarito *C2*
18 La Mamma *B4*
19 T-Café *B1*
20 Zanzibar *B4*

Bars & clubs
21 Alfredo's *B4*
22 Birosco Carioca *A2*
23 El Hoyo del Queque *B4*
24 Kontiki *A4*
25 The Clover *B6*

Less central parks include **Parque La Isla** ⓘ *Prol Av Los Próceres*, which contains orchids, basketball and tennis courts, an amphitheatre and fountains. In the **Plaza Beethoven** ⓘ *Santa María Norte*, a different melody from Beethoven's works chimes every hour; *por puestos/ busetas*, run along Avenida 5, marked 'Santa María' or 'Chorro de Milla', US$0.25. The **Jardín Botánico** ⓘ *on the way to La Hechicera, open daily*, has the largest collection of bromeliads in South America; also a canopy walkway. The **Jardín Acuario**, beside the aquarium ⓘ *high season daily 0800-1800, low season closed Mon, US$0.25; (busetas leave from Av 4 y C 25, US$0.25, passing airport)*, is an exhibition centre, mainly devoted to the way of life and the crafts of the Andean *campesinos*.

Mérida has several museums: **Museo de Arte Colonial** ⓘ *Av 4, Casa 20-8, T252 7860, fundacolonial@latinmail.com, Tue-Fri 0900-1600, Sat-Sun 1400-1700 (1000-1700 high season), US$0.50*. More interesting is the small **Museo Arqueológico** ⓘ *Av 3, Edif del Rectorado de la Universidad de los Andes, just off Plaza Bolívar, T240 2344, museogrg@ula.ve, Tue-Sat 0800-1200, 1400-1800, Sun 1400-1800, US$0.50* with pre-Columbian exhibits from the Andes. **Museo de Arte Moderno** ⓘ *Av 2 y C 21, Mon-Fri 0800-1600, Sat-Sun 0800-1300, free*, is in the Centro Cultural Don Tulio Febres Cordero, a run-down but impressive concrete building with political murals in front of its main entrance, several galleries and theatres. It is open sporadically. Roger Manrique has an impressive butterfly collection (over 10,000), also knowledgeable about Andean wildlife, contact **Arassari Trek**, see Tour operators, page 1614.

Mérida listings

For Sleeping and Eating price codes and other relevant information, see Essentials, pages 38-40.

Sleeping

Mérida *p1609, map p1610*

Book ahead in school holidays and Feria del Sol.

A Posada Casa Sol, Av 4 entre C15 y C16, T252 4164, www.posadacasasol.com. Renovated colonial-era house with lovely rooms in distinctive, tasteful style, modern art on walls, hot water, garden, free internet, large breakfast US$18, very helpful, English, German and Italian spoken, limited parking. Highly recommended.

B El Tisure, Av 4 entre C 17 y 18, T252 6061. Modern, colonial-style, very pleasant, disco.

B-C La Montaña, C 24 No 6-47 entre Av 6 y 7, T252 5977, www.posadalamontana.com. Hot water, TV, safe, fan, fridge, luggage store. Very helpful, English spoken, excellent restaurant.

B-C Posada Doña Pumpa, Av 5 y C 14, T252 7286, www.donapumpa.com. Good showers, spacious rooms, cable TV, quiet, very comfortable, English-speaking owner, no breakfast, parking.

C Apart Hotel Central, Av 3, No 16-11, T252 7629, aparthotelcentral@hotmail.com. Good apartments for up to 12, TV, kitchen and parking.

C Mintoy, C 25 (Ayacucho), No 8-130, T252 0340. 10% discount for cash, comfortably furnished, breakfast, good value, parking, suites with separate sitting area (sleeps 5).

C-D Los Bucares de Mérida, Av 4 No 15-5, T/F252 2841, www.losbucares.com. Cheaper in noisier rooms at front, hot showers, TV, also has family rooms, nice patio with occasional live music, garage, safe, breakfast extra in *cafetín*.

C-D Encanto Andino, C 24 No 6-53, entre Avs 6 y 7, T252 6929. **E** without bath, 5 rooms, easygoing, kitchen with fridge and microwave, no breakfast.

C-D Montecarlo, Av 7 entre C 24 y C 25, T252 5981, F252 5910. Ask for back room with view of mountain, safe, parking, hot water, restaurant.

C-D Posada Alemania, Av 2 entre C 17 y 18, No 17-76, T/F252 4067, www.posadaalemania.com. **E** without bath, quiet, family atmosphere, leafy patio, popular with backpackers, discounts for long stay, breakfast and laundry extra, kitchen, book exchange, tourist information, English and German spoken, German owner. Adventure tours (trekking, rafting, riding, expeditions) with **Colibrí Tours**, T252 4961, www.colibri-tours.com, ask for Ricardo Torres.

C-D Posada Luz Caraballo, Av 2 No 13-80, on Plaza de Milla, T252 5441, www.andes.net/luzcaraballo/index.html. Colonial-style old building, hot water, TV, excellent cheap restaurant, good bar, parking.

D El Escalador, C 23 entre Avs 7 y 8, T252 2411. Doubles or rooms with bed and bunks, hot water, TV, tourist information and tours, parapenting arranged, no breakfast.

D Italia, C 19 entre Av 2 y 3, T252 5737. **E** in smaller rooms without bath, hot water, laundry, **Ayary Tours** travel agency, English, German and French spoken, changes dollars, Spanish lessons.

D Luxemburgo, C 24, between Avs 6-7, T252 6865, www.andes.net/luxemburgo/index.html. In same group as **B Nevada Palace**, C 24, No 5-45, www.andes.net/nevadapalace/index.html. Cold water, safe, with restaurant, modern, with **Palace Cyber**.

D Posada Casa Alemana-Suiza, El Encanto, Av 2 No 38-120, T263 6503, info@casa-alemana.com. Very nice, airport pick-up, parking, discount for long stays, laundry, English and German spoken. Also runs good tours and activities as **Carnaval Tours**, T263 6503.

D Posada Guamanchi, C 24, No 8-86, T252 2080, www.guamanchi.com. Owned by tour operator of same name, if on a tour you are guaranteed a room. Rooms of varying size, some with bath, some with good view, 2 kitchens, cable TV room, terrace with hammocks, good, no parking.

E Mundo Mérida, C 24 y Av 8, on Plaza las Heroínas, T252 6844, jorgemda@hotmail.com. Hot water, shared bath, opposite *Guamanchi Tours*, luggage store, laundry, good.

E Posada Familiar Mara, C 24 No 8-215, T252 5507. Pleasant, hot water, luggage store, no TV, no breakfast.

Eating

Mérida *p1609, map p1610*

Many places offer student lunches for US$1-1.50.

ΨΨ **La Abadía**, Av 3 entre C 17 y 18, T251 0933, www.grupoabadia.com. Excellent, varied menu, including vegetarian, 30 mins free internet time with each meal. Has other outlets including **La Abadía del Angel**, C 21 entre Avs 5 y 6, café and restaurant, with internet.

ΨΨ **Chipen**, Av 5, No 23-67. Good meat.

ΨΨ **El Museo**, Av 2, C12-13. Nice patio, lots of graffiti, good food, pleasant place for a drink.

ΨΨ-Ψ **La Astilla**, C 14, No 2-20, Plaza de Milla. Plants, nostalgic music, bar, varied menu including pizza, frequented by locals and groups.

ΨΨ-Ψ **La Mamma**, Av 3 and C 19. Good pizza, pasta, set lunches and salad bar, popular in the evening, live music at weekends, local wine.

Ψ **Bimbo**, C 23, No 4-48. Clean, popular for lunch.

Ψ **Buona Pizza**, Av 7 entre C 24 y 25, T252 7639, with Express branch opposite and 2 other branches, open 1200-2300 daily, very good pizza.

Ψ **Café Atico**, C 25 near Plaza Las Heroínas. Excellent lunch for US$2.50. Recommended.

Ψ **Cheo's Pizzería**, 3 separate restaurants on Plaza Las Heroínas, one serves pizzas, the 2nd chicken and meat, the 3rd trout. Also hotel on the plaza.

Ψ **El Sabor de los Quesos**, on Plaza de Milla. Very good and cheap pizzería, very busy, painted green and white.

Ψ **El Tinajero**, C 29/Av 4. Clean, simple place.

Ψ **Federico's**, Pasaje Ayacucho No 25-24. Vegetarian and pizza.

Ψ **La Esquina de Pajarito**, C 25 esquina Av 6. Simple but good local food, cheap set lunch.

Ψ **La Montaña**, C 24 between Av 6 and 7 (next to *posada*). Good, cheap food, pleasant setting.

Ψ **El Sano Glotón**, Av 4 y C 18. Vegetarian. Recommended. Next door but one is a great snack bar with excellent *empanadas*.

Ψ **Zanzibar**, Av 4 entre C 19 y 20. Very good value lunches under US$2, German chef.

Cafés

Espresso Café Cyber & Galería, Av 4, No 23-54, upstairs No 2A. With art gallery, good computers and TV, coffee and cakes.

Heladería La Coromoto, Av 3 y C 29, T523525, Tue-Sun 1415-2100, offers 750 flavours of ice cream, at least 60 choices daily, eg trout, avocado.

T-Café, diagonally opposite **Heladería La Coromoto**. Homemade food, good lunches, juices, coffee and cakes.

Bars and clubs

Mérida *p1609, map p1610*

There is no cover charge for nightclubs but always take your passport or a copy.

Alfredo's, C 19 y Av 4, 0900-2300. Bar, popular, also vegetarian café (lunch US$1) and internet.

Birosca Carioca, Av 2 y C 24. Popular, with live music, take care outside.

Café Calypso, C 26, in Centro Comercial El Viaducto. Pop/rock music, a bit more pricey.

The Clover, Av 4 entre C 14 y 15. Irish bar with live music at weekends.

El Hoyo del Queque, Av 4 across the road from *Alfredo's*. Open 1200-2400, usually packed, good meeting place. The best local bands play here, some nights free, sometimes cover can go up to US$8.50 with one drink, good food. Recommended.

Kontiki, Av 3 y C 19. Mérida's oldest club.

Festivals and events

Mérida *p1609, map p1610*

For 2 weeks leading up to Christmas there are daily song contests between local students on Plaza Bolívar, 1700-2200. **Feria del Sol**, held on the week preceding Ash Wednesday. This is also the peak bullfighting season. **1-2 Jan**, **Paradura del Niño**; **15 May**, **San Isidro Labrador**, a popular festival nationwide, but especially in Mérida.

Shopping

Mérida *p1609, map p1610*

Bookshops **Fundación Librerías del Sur**, on Plaza Bolívar. State-run, good for subsidized books, including national, Latin American and world poets. **Librería Ifigenia**, next door, is also very good. **Temas**, Av 3, entre C31 y 32, No 31-24, T252 6068. Very good, amazing stock.

Camping shops **5007**, Av 5 entre C 19 y 20, CC Mediterráneo, T252 6806. Recommended. **Cumbre Azul**, C 24 opposite Plaza Las Heroínas, T416 3231, cumbreazul@hotmail.com. Rents and sells mountaineering equipment (also sells some fishing tackle). **Eco Bike**, Av 7 No 16-34. For mountain bikes and equipment. Many tour operators rent equipment.

The Lighthouse of Maracaibo

In the south and southwest of the Lago de Maracaibo is the **Catatumbo** delta, a huge swamp with fast flowing, navigable rivers, luxurious vegetation and plentiful wildlife, one of the most fascinating trips in the whole country. Its nightly displays of lightning over the lake at the Parque Nacional Ciénagas del Catatumbo, best seen from May to November or December, have yet to be explained. Indigenous people thought that it was produced by millions of fireflies meeting to pay the homage to the creator gods. Early scientific thought was that the constant silent flashing at three to ten second intervals was caused by friction between hot air moving south from Zulia and Falcón and cold currents from Andes. Latest theories suggest it is the result of clashes between the methane particles from the marsh and the lake system between the Catatumbo and Bravo rivers. It has been proved that this phenomenon is a regenerator of the planet's ozone layer.

Whatever its origin, the spectacle is truly unique, best observed from Congo Mirador right after nightfall. Several operators run tours from Mérida, which may be the best way because they have bilingual nature guides, who have information about birds, butterflies and flora and boat transport (see page 1615).

Going independently is a real tropical adventure and not fully safe because of illegal immigration and contraband coming from Colombia. To get to the Mirador takes 3 to 4 hours by motorboat from the port of Encontrados. Travel should be arranged in a group. Boatman will demand about US$70. If staying overnight on the boat, take plenty of water and food, mosquito repellant and antiseptics. Security can be hired at Encontrados, a small town with basic services. It is at the entrance to the Parque Nacional Ciénagas de Juan Manuel de Aguas Blancas y Aguas Negras, known for impressive vegetation and migrating birds. It is open from 0700-1600 and the Catatumbo lightning can be seen from some parts of the park, even from Encontrados. If not going on a tour, you must get a permit from Inparques to enter the park. In town hotels: D Hostería Juancho, Calle Piar 74, T0275-615 0448, basic, and C Hotel La Nona Magdalena, Av Principal, near Plaza Bolívar, T0275-414 2951, central, cable TV, food. Restaurants close around 1600; few basic choices include San Benito and Caballo Viejo, near Plaza Bolívar.

To get to Encontrados takes about 4 hours by car from Maracaibo, 3-4 hours from San Cristóbal. Drive south from Maracaibo on Machiques-Colón road then, at El Manguito, take a road to Encontrados, over 70 km from the intersection. Approximately 90 minutes by por puesto or 2 hours by bus from La Fría and Encontrados. Irregular flights to Santa Bárbara airport near San Carlos del Zulia, 45 km from Encontrados.

Handicrafts Handicraft market on La Plaza de Las Heroínas, opposite *teleférico*. **Mercado Principal** on Av las Américas (buses for bus station pass by), has many small shops, top floor restaurant has regional *comida típica*, bargaining possible.

▲ Activities and tours

Mérida *p1609, map p1610*

Parapenting All agencies offer jumps. Conditions in Mérida are suitable for flying almost all year round. It takes on average 50 mins to get to a launch site and tandem jumps last 25 mins. There are 7 main sites. Price US$60. Can take own equipment and hire a guide. An experienced pilot is Oswaldo, T0414-717 5953. **Xtreme Adventours**, Av 8, C24, Plaza Las Heroínas, T252 7241. Specializes in parapenting (latest equipment, safety) and many other adventure options, plus tours in the region. Also offers tours from Mérida to Canaima, Margarita and Los Roques.

Tour operators

Arassari Trek, C 24 No 8-301 (beside the teleférico), T/F252 5879, www.arassari.com. Run by Tom and Raquel Evenou, and Angel Barreto, English, French and German spoken, good tours with great guides at fair prices, very helpful and hospitable, highly recommended for trekking and climbing in the Sierra Nevada, horse riding, mountain biking, canyoning, caving, rafting, parapenting and canoeing. They also have a book exchange and cybercafé. Their Llanos tour (US$130-140 for 4 days) is excellent with many different activities, have their own, superb purpose-built camp.

Cocolight, T0414-756 2575, www.cocolight.com. Alan Highton and his team specialise in 2-day trips to Catatumbo to see the lightning, visit the communities of the region and experience the variety of habitats between the Andes and the delta. They have a camp at Ologa lagoon. Naturalist tours to other parts of the country offered. Very experienced, several languages spoken.

Fanny Tours, C 24, No 8-30, T252 2952, 0414-747 1349, www.fanny-tours.com. Patrizia Rossi, José Albarrán for parapenting (the first to do it), reliable. Apart from parapenting, specializes in mountain biking, US$30 half-day pp for 2, US$40 whole day without jeep support, US$58 with jeep, all inclusive; bike hire US$16. Also rafting US$140 pp for 4; Llanos, Catatumbo, canyoning, trekking to mountains and some climbing; also tours combining all types of sport; book and money exchange. Recommended.

Gravity Tours, C 24 entre Av 7 y 8, 1 block from cable car, T251 1279, 0424-760 8327, www.gravity-tours.com.ve. Bilingual guides, natural history and adventure tours, some extreme, including rock climbing, rafting, biking, Llanos trips and Gran Sabana.

Guamanchi Tours, C 24, No 8-86, T252 2080, www.guamanchi.com. Owned by John and Joëlle Peña, with Volker on the team. German, French, Italian and English spoken, recommended for hiking, paragliding, horse riding, biking, bird- watching, equipment hire, exchange, information, mountain climbing, also tours to Llanos, Amazonia and Angel Falls, email service for customers, new 4WD jeeps, have a posada in town (see above) and at Los Nevados (see below). Recommended.

Natoura Travel and Adventure Tours, C 31 entre Av Don Tulio y prol Av 6 No 5-27 (Diagonal Bomberos ULA), Mérida 5101, T274-252 4216, in US 303-800 4639, in Germany 05906-303364, in France 0970-449206, www.natoura.com. Open daily 0900-1700, friendly company organizing tours throughout Venezuela, run by Jose Luis Troconis and Renate Reiners, English, French, German and Italian spoken, climbing, trekking, rafting, horse riding, mountain biking, birdwatching and equipment hire. Their self-drive option allows you to rent a car and they will reserve accommodation for your route. Repeatedly recommended.

Drivers Lucio (T252 8416) and Nicolás Savedra (T271 2618) and Juan Medina Yagrumo, C 24, mostalla@hotmail.com.

Transport

Mérida *p1609, map p1610*

Air You can save a lot of time by checking in the day before flight. There are daily flights to **Caracas** (1½ hrs direct). In the rainy season, especially on afternoon flights, planes may be diverted to San Antonio (3-5 hrs by road), or El Vigía (2½ hrs away); both these airports are served by several airlines. *Casa de cambio*, various ATMs, shops, phones and a smart restaurant.

Bus The terminal has 2 levels, the upper one for small buses, minivans and cars to nearby places, the lower for interstate buses. Taxis line up outside the main entrance. A small exit tax of US$0.35 is charged for journeys in the the state, US$0.50 for long-distance, payable at one of 2 kiosks leading to buses. Make sure you pay, officials check buses before departure. On interstate buses, it is essential to book in advance; for buses within the state you pay on board. The terminal has a tourist office, phones, toilets, luggage store and places to eat. Fares: **Caracas**, US$15.50 (*normal*) to US$25 (*bus-cama*); **Maracay**, US$14-22; **Valencia**, US$13-22; **Coro**, US$11.50-22; **Maracaibo**, US$11; **Barquisimeto**, US$18.50; **Puerto La Cruz**, US$26.70.

Bus companies: Expresos Occidente, T263 5844, daily direct to **Caracas**, 12 hrs, or via Valencia and Maracay; to **Coro/ Punto Fijo**, 12-14 hrs. **Expresos San Cristóbal** (T263 1881), daily direct to Caracas, 14 hrs, or via Valencia and Maracay; to **Maracaibo**, 8 hrs. **Expresos Mérida** (T263 3430), to Caracas hourly from 1800, some direct others via Valencia and Maracay; also to **Barquisimeto**, 8 hrs, **Maracaibo**, **Coro** and **Punto Fijo**. **Transportes Barinas** (T263 4651), **Barinas** (US$5.80) via **Apartaderos** (US$2.75), to **Guanare** (US$8.50) and **Valera** (US$8.50). **Expresos Los Llanos** (T265 5927), to Caracas at 1900. **Expresos Coromoto**, T417 1722, to **Maracaibo** 0845, 1345. From upper level of terminal: **Táchira Mérida**, to **San Cristóbal** (US$9.25, 6 hrs) and **San Antonio**. Also to Jaji, Chiguará, Apartaderos, Barinas (US$8.75, 4 hrs), El Vigía, Valera. **Líneas Unidas**, T263 8472, *por puesto* microbus with TV, and car, to **Maracaibo**, 1000, 2130; also **Fraternidad del Transporte**, T263 1187, 1000, 1400, 2145.

Taxi In town US$2.75-4.

Directory

Mérida *p1609, map p1610*

Banks See also Money, page 1566. **Banco Mercantil**, Av 5 y C 18. ATM takes Cirrus (commission lower than Visa). **BBVA Banco Provincial**, Av 4 y C 25, and **Banco de Venezuela**, Av 4 entre C 23 y 24, both ATM and cash advance on Visa and Mastercard. *Italcambio* at airport; this is often the easiest place to change cash and TCs. **Car hire** Several companies at the airport, including **Alquil Auto**, T263 1440, or **Dávila Tours**, Av Los Próceres opposite Urb la Trinidad, T266 0711, or airport T263 4510. **Consulates** **Colombia**, Av Andrés Bello, CC San Antonio, T266 2646, consulbia merida@yahoo.com, open 0800-1400. Visas take 10 min. **UK**, Professor Robert Kirby, honorary vice-Consul, Finca La Trinitaria, Santa Rosa, 10 mins from the town centre towards La Hechicera, T416 8496. **Internet** Places all over town, most with broadband, US$0.40-0.80 per hr. See *La Abadía* and *Arassari Trek* above. **CANTV Centro de Comunicaciones**, Av 7 entre C 25 y 26. Also at Av 6 y C 21, open Sun, has internet next to *Ipostel*. **Language schools** **Iowa Institute**, Av 4 y C 18, T252 6404, cathy@ iowainstitute.com. Run by Cathy Jensen de Sánchez, competitive prices, fully qualified teachers, homestays arranged. Recommended. **Latinoamericano de Idiomas**, CC Mamayeya, p 4, of C-5-38, T/F244 7808. Contact Marinés Asprino, Conjunto Residencial Andrés Bello, Torre C, p 5, Apt 6-1, T271 1209 for private lessons and cheap accommodation. Recommended. **Carolina Tenías**, 17 years' experience in private lessons for travellers, grammar and conversation, T252 4875, or T0416-971 1445. **Medical services** Doctors: **Dr Aldo Olivieri**, Av Principal La Llanita, La Otra Banda, Centro Profesional El Buho, 09, T244 0805, T0414-374 0356, aldrolia250@ cantv.net, very good, gastroenterologist, speaks English and Italian. **Dr Giotto Guillén Echeverria**, Centro Médico La Trinidad, C 42 entre Avs Urdaneta y Gonzalo Picón, T263 9685, T0416-674 0707. Specialist in infections, speaks French. **Post office** **Ipostel**, C 21 entre Avs 4 y 5, 0800-1900 daily. Post office also in bus terminal, 0800-1200, 1400-1700, weekdays only. **Telephone** CANTV, C 21 y Av 5, Mon-Sat 0800-1930. **Useful addresses** **Immigration office:** SAIME, Av 4 y C 6, quinta San Isidro, Parroquia Sagrario, T252 9754, Mon-Sat 0800-1700. **Tourist police:** The **CICPC** will provide a *constancia* reporting the crime and listing the losses. Their office is on Av Las Américas, at Viaducto Miranda, T262 0343. Open daily but they won't issue a *constancia* on Sun. To get there, take any bus marked 'Terminal Sur' or 'Mercado' leaving from C 25. You can also get a *constancia* from the *Prefectura Civil del Municipio Libertador*, but it can take all day and is only valid for a limited period; at Av 4 No 21-69, just off Plaza Bolívar; opening hours variable. Tourist offices may be better than police if you need to register a theft for insurance purposes.

Sierra Nevada de Mérida

The Sierra is a mixture of the wild and isolated and the very touristy. In the latter group fall the cable car up Pico Espejo and villages designed to lure the shopper, but it is not difficult to escape the tour groups. There are routes from the mountains to the Llanos and to Colombia.

Parque Nacional Sierra Nevada (South)

Close to Mérida is the popular hiking area around Los Nevados, with the added attraction of the highest cable car in the world (if it's running). The further you go from Mérida, the greater the off-the-beaten-track possibilities for hiking and exploration that arise.

Since this is a national park, you need a permit from the *Inparques* (National Parks) offices in Mérida (see Ins and outs) to hike and camp overnight. Permits are not given to single hikers (except to Los Nevados), a minimum of two people is needed. Have your passport ready. Return permit after your hike; park guards will radio the start of trek to say you've reached the end. If camping, remember that the area is 3,500-4,200 m so acclimatization is necessary. The night temperatures can fall below freezing so a -12°C sleeping bag is necessary, plus good waterproofs. Conditions are much more severe than you'd think after balmy Mérida. Don't leave litter. Some treks are very difficult so check with the tourist office before leaving. Water purification is also recommended. See Mérida Tour operators and Parque Nacional Sierra Nevada (North) below.

Pico Espejo The world's highest and longest aerial cableway (built by the French in 1957-60) runs to Pico Espejo (4,765 m) in four stages ⓘ *T252 5080/1997. The teleférico was closed in late 2008 and remained so in 2010. A new system is under construction*. When operating, its final station is at Pico Espejo, with a change of car at every station, all of which have cafés, toilets and advice. Beware altitude sickness: there is oxygen and a nursing station at higher points. Barinas is the ground level station, Plaza de las Heroínas; you can hire, or buy, hats, gloves and scarves here, the Venezuelans all do. La Montaña (2,442 m) is the second station with a small Museo del Montañismo. You pass over various levels of forest. Next is La Aguada (3,452 m), then Loma Redonda (4,045 m). From here you can start the trek to Los Nevados (see below); you must inform Inparques if trekking to Los Nevados. Pause for 10 minutes at Loma Redonda before the last stage to Pico Espejo, where there is a statue of Nuestra Señora de las Nieves. As the car nears its final destination, you are welcomed by enormous graffiti of Hugo Chávez waving and smiling from the platform. Next door to Pico Espejo is Pico Bolívar (Mucumbari, where the sun sleeps) with Humboldt behind. It has remnants of a glacier. In the other direction, closest is La Silla del Toro and you can see a statue of Francisco Miranda with the Venezuelan flag on an outcrop. On a clear day you can see the blue haze of the Llanos to the east and, west, as far as Sierra de Cocuy and Guicán in Colombia. Across Río Chama you can see Sierra de la Culata. It is advisable to spend only 30 minutes at Pico Espejo. Apart from Los Nevados trek, the only safe part to walk down is Loma Redonda to La Aguada; a rough but clear trail, two hours; wear boots, not for children or the elderly, take water.

Los Nevados Los Nevados (*Altitude: 2,711 m*) is a colonial town with cobbled streets, an ancient chapel and a famous fiesta on 2 May. From here, it is a very testing two-day trek to **Pico Espejo**, with a strong chance of altitude sickness as the ascent is more than 1,600 m. It is best done November- June early in the morning (before 0830 ideally), before the clouds spoil the view. In summer the summit is clouded and covered with snow and there is no view. **Do not attempt Pico Espejo alone; go with a guide, it is easy to get lost.** Reputable trekking companies provide suitable clothing; temperatures can be 0° C. August is the coldest month.

From Los Nevados to **Loma Redonda** takes five to seven hours, four hours with mules (14 km). The hike is not too difficult; breathtaking views; be prepared for cold rain in the afternoon, start very early. The walk from Los Nevados to the village of **El Morro** (24 km) takes seven to nine hours (very steep in parts). (It's 47 km to Mérida; jeeps do the trip daily.) Sr Oviller Ruiz provides information on the history of the church of San Jacinto (the patron saint, whose fiesta is on 16 August) and the indigenous cemetery. The town, with its red tiled roofs is an interesting blend of the colonial and the indigenous.

It is possible to hike from Pico Espejo to the cloud forest at La Mucuy (see below), two to three days walking at over 4,000 m altitude, passing spectacular snow peaks and Lagos Verde and Coromoto. A tent and a warm sleeping bag are essential, as is a good map (local guides may lend theirs to photocopy). If you start at Pico Espejo you will be at the highest point first, so although you will be descending, you may have altitude sickness from the word go.

Parque Nacional Sierra Nevada (North) and Sierra de La Culata

The Transandean highway snakes its way through the rugged mountain landscape, past neat, little towns of red-tiled roofs, steep fields and terraces of maize and potatoes. Just outside Mérida a side road goes to El Valle, known for *pasteles de trucha*, *vino de mora* and handicraft shops. The snow-tipped peaks of the high sierras watch over this bucolic scene, with Pico Bolívar lording it over them all. Throughout the park you will see a plant with felt-like leaves of pale grey-green, the *frailejón* (or great friar, *espeletia*), which blooms with yellow flowers from September to December. There are more than 130 species; tall ones grow at less than 1 cm a year.

Tabay At 12 km from Mérida, Tabay (30 minutes; altitude 1708 m; population 17,000) is named after an indigenous tribe. Its Plaza Bolívar has an attractive church, trees and plants. Around it are two minimercados, telecommunications, **Pizzería Valentina** (best in town), **Pastelitos** (at bus stop from Mérida, for empanadas in morning), all other transport stops, and other services. Jeeps run a regular service to **La Mucuy** cloud forest, 0600-2200, they are labelled (US$1.50 one way if five passengers, negotiate hard). They drop you at the Guardaparques. There is nothing to pay for a day visit, but you pay per night if making the Travesía to Pico Espejo and the Teleférico (or alternative route) down to Mérida. The distances on the park signs to Lagos Coromoto and Verde would appear to be very ambitious (eg Coromoto is not three hours, but an overnight trip if not continuing). When going back to Tabay, you may have to wait for a jeep; the driver will charge extra for backpacks. Jeeps also go to the **Aguas Termales** (from a different stop, just off Plaza Bolívar, US$1). It is possible to walk and there are signs. The man-made pool has 38°C water. The area is also good for walking and horse riding (see Mano Poderosa, Sleeping), all Mérida agencies go here.

Beyond Tabay the road goes through **Mucurubá** (2,400m) with a pleasant Plaza Bolívar and blue and white church, colonial buildings, handicrafts and Hospedaje Mococón, and passes the **Monumento al Perro Nevado**. It depicts Simón Bolívar, the Indian boy, Tinjaca, the Mucuchíes dog, Snowy, and the father and son who gave Bolívar the dog in 1813. According to legend, both Tinjaca and Nevado were devoted to Bolívar until their death on the same day at the Battle of Carabobo, 1821. At Mucuchíes (*Phone code: 0274; Population: 9,175; Altitude: 2,983 m*) the statue of the Liberator on Plaza Bolívar also features Tinjaca and Snowy. Also on the Plaza is a wooden statue of San Isidro, patron saint of farmers; all rural communities honour him on 15 May. The patron saint of Mucuchíes is San Benito; this festival (and several others) on 27-30 December is celebrated by participants wearing flower-decorated hats and firing blunderbusses. Tourist office on C 9 as you enter from Mérida, internet at C 9 Independencia.

The road leads up from Mucuchíes to **San Rafael de Mucuchíes** (*Altitude: 3,140 m; Fiesta 24 October*). You should visit the remarkable church, pieced together from thousands of stones, by the late Juan Félix Sánchez (born 1900), nationally renowned as a sculptor, philosopher and clown. The chapel is dedicated to the Virgen de Coromoto; it was blessed by Pope John Paul II. The tombs of Sánchez and his companion of 50 years, Epifania Gil, are inside. Next door is his house, now a museum with photos, weavings and sculptures. Opposite is the library given by him to the community. He built a similar chapel at El Tisure. The picturesque road continues to Apartaderos (two hours from Mérida). It follows the Río Chama valley in the heart of the cultivated highlands and the fields extend up to the edge of the *páramo*, clinging to the steep slopes. Main crops are potatoes (four harvests a year) onions, garlic and carrots. East of the Río Chama is the Sierra Nevada; to the west is the Sierra de La Culata. There are handicrafts, *posadas* and eateries.

Apartaderos (*Phone code: 0274; Altitude: 3,342 m*) is at the junction of Route 7 and the road over the Sierra Nevada to Barinas. About 3 km above Apartaderos, a narrow paved road (signposted) turns west off the highway at Escuela Estatal 121 and winds its way to **Llano del Hato** (3,510 m) and on to the **Centro de Investigaciones de Astronomía** (3,600 m) ⓘ *the 4 telescopes and modern facilities are open Wed-Sat 1500-1900, but Mon only Aug-Sep (check website for details), US$1.85 for adults, US$1.15 under-18s, students with card US$0.70, seniorns and under-8s free, www.cida.ve.* At least two view- points on the way in give great views of the Lake Mucubají plateau. A good paved road descends 7 km from Llano del Hato to the Mérida highway at La Toma, just above Mucuchíes. Many prehispanic terraces and irrigation systems, adobe houses and ox-ploughed fields (*poyos*) are visible from the road.

Three kilometres beyond the junction of the roads from Barinas and Valera is the entrance to the **Parque Nacional Sierra Nevada** (*Línea Cultura* bus from Mérida ends at the junction, 2 hours; taxis run from bus stop to Park, US$2.75). At the turn-off to the park is a motel and restaurant. Near the entrance is **Laguna Mucubají**, at 3,600 m, with free campsite; visitors' centre, bookshop, good maps, interesting museum. A 2-2½-hour walk takes you to Laguna Negra and back (1½ hours on horseback, US$2-3 to hire a horse, guide US$2.50). A further 1½-hour walk from Laguna Negra is the beautiful Laguna Los Patos. There are many *frailejón* plants here. Guides (not always necessary) are at Laguna Mucubají or the hotels in Santo Domingo. *Páramo* tours to this area usually include Pico El Aguila (see Road to the high Andes, page 1607).

From Mérida to the Panamericana

There are three routes from Mérida to the Panamericana which runs at the foot of the Andes near the border with Zulia state. The most northerly of them is the most interesting. This beautiful journey, starting in the highlands from Mérida, heads west. It passes La Chorrera waterfall on the way to La Encrucijada (restaurant and Trébol service station), where a side road leads to **Jají** (*Phone code: 0274*), a pretty, restored colonial village with white-washed houses, cobbled streets, arches on the exits to the plaza and a white and blue church. Most houses are given over to handicrafts shops. There are a few hotels and others in the hills, where there is good walking. *Buseta* from Mérida bus terminal, hourly, 50 minutes, US$1. From La Encrujidada the road passes dairy farms before its descent through cloud forest. Towns passed on the way are San Eusebio and Mirabel. This is prime birdwatching territory as the road, paved but rough in parts, twists down through several habitats. **La Azulita**, 73 km, four hours from Mérida, is the base for birdwatching tours, with several lodges nearby. A modern cathedral stands on the Plaza and, overall, it's a modern town. From La Azulita, the road meets the Panamericana at Caño Zancudo, passing en route the Cascada Palmita. Turn south for El Vigía, one of the hottest zones in South America, and routes to Lago de Maracaibo and Catatumbo.

El Vigía is where the second route from Mérida meets the Panamericana. Transandean Route 7 leaves Mérida and passes through El Ejido, originally known as Las Guayabas, or 'the city of honey and flowers'. El Ejido and surrounding villages in the sugar cane zone are known for handicrafts and ceramics. One such historic town is **Mesa de los Indios**, 5 km from El Ejido towards Jaji. It is famous for for the local bands that perform in the main plaza and for its artists. Among them is the sculptor Daniel Camara. The main road follows the Chama valley, to Lagunillas and Tovar.

Lagunillas was founded in the 16th century by Spaniard Juan Rodríguez Suárez on the site of a pre-hispanic ceremonial centre. Its elaborately choreographed dances honouring a beautiful indigenous princess can be seen at festivities taking place on 15 May. More can be learned at **Museo Arqueológico Julio César Salas** ⓘ *on Parque Sucre*. Nearby is Laguna de Urao, whose natural soda crystals have been mined since pre-hispanic times. **San Juan de Lagunillas**, 2 km away, is where Mérida was originally supposed to be built. Locals (and allegedly doctors) say that the climate is one of the healthiest in the world. There are botanical gardens and a colourful fiesta on 24 June.

Near Estanques, a winding road leads towards **Chiguará**, one of the best-preserved coffee towns in Venezuela. Bizarrely, it contains **La Montaña de los Sueños** theme park ⓘ *1700-2400, daily, ticket office open 1700-2000, T0274-245 0053, US$20, children and senior citizens US$15, food available,* devoted to the history of the Venezuelan film industry (1950s to 1970s), complete with sets, old aeroplanes, limousines, cameras and posters. There are also displays of local television, commercial music and theatre. Chiguará is 45 km from Mérida: take bus or por puesto towards El Vigía and ask to be dropped at junction for Chiguará, from where you have to hitch or wait for infrequent bus or por puesto (**C Posada Turística La Peña de Lolito**, Vía La Peña, T0275-836 1109, 0414-532 1334, Mexican-style, 8 rooms with bath and hot water, TV).

Beyond Estanques the main highway for bus and heavy traffic turns off Route 7. Near the intersection on the right is 19th-century **Hacienda La Victoria** with an interesting coffee museum. The highway descends from the grey, scarred mountains before the thickly wooded tropical hillsides above the plains. Buses between Mérida and San Crístobal then belt along the Panamericana to La Fría. The third route leaves the Transandean road at **Tovar** (*Phone code: 0275, 96 km from Mérida*), passing through Zea, a pleasant town in the foothills. A 4-lane motorway between San Cristóbal and La Fría is nearly finished and will cut travel by at least one hour.

From Mérida to Táchira

From Tovar the road continues to **Bailadores** (fiesta from Christmas to Candlemas, 2 February), and **La Grita**, a pleasant town in Táchira state (Sunday market, fiesta 6 August). Near Bailadores is the pleasant Parque La Cascada India Carú, named after a legendary princess whose tears at the death of her warrior lover created the waterfall. Cheap posadas include **C Posada Santa Eduvigis**, C 10 entre Cras 3 y 4, T0275-857 0651, 50 m east of the church, parking, restaurant. This route takes the wild and beautiful old mountain road over Páramo de La Negra to San Cristóbal. Mérida-San Cristóbal buses go via La Fría, not this road; by public transport change in Tovar and La Grita.

San Cristóbal → *Phone code: 0276. Colour map 1, B4. Population: 297,620. Altitude: 830 m.*

The capital of Táchira State was founded in 1561. Today it's a large, busy, but friendly place built over hills and ravines, although a few blocks in historic centre, around the cathedral, retain a colonial air. You need to know which district you are in for orientation, eg La Concordia for the bus station. The **Fiesta de San Sebastián** in second half of January is a major international event, with parades, trade shows, and much more; book ahead, prices rise. **Tourist office: Cotatur,** ⓘ *Av España con Av Carabobo, T357 9655, www.cotatur.gob.ve.* Helpful. **Inparques** ⓘ *Parque Metropolitano, Av 19 de Abril, T346 6544.*

On Sunday, take a taxi to **Peribeca** (US$11 one way), a tiny colonial village with handicraft shops, restaurants and sellers of dairy products, fruit desserts and bewildering variety of liqueurs and infusions. The pretty handicraft alley is next to the modern church. There are two posadas, **La Posada de la Abuela** on the Plaza, and **Posada Turística Doña Meche**, just outside the village. Many restaurants open for Sunday lunch, the best is **El Solar de Juancho**. Alternatively, on Monday, go to the wholesale vegetable market of **Táriba**, just off highway going north. The town's huge white Basílica de la Virgen de la Consolación (1959) can be seen from the highway. Stained glass tells the story of the image. Her fiesta in August attracts great numbers of devotees. The market place is reached by a pedestrian suspension bridge from the plaza in front of the basilica. There are longer trips to colonial villages and handicraft-making communities, but public transport is poor.

San Cristóbal to San Antonio → *Phone code: 0276. Colour map 1, B4. Population: 38,000.*
The border town of San Antonio is 55 km from San Cristóbal by a paved, congested road. At **Capacho** (25 km from San Antonio) is an interesting old Municipal Market building, with lions at the 4 corners. If travelling light and in no hurry, you can go via **Rubio** (45 minutes from San Cristóbal, US$1.40, Líneas Unidas). In the coffee zone, it has a pleasant colonial centre, with an enormous brick church, Santa Bárbara, in neo-Gothic style (1934-1971). It's a busy town with extensive modern outskirts. The roads to it are paved and quieter than the main road, with better scenery, too. Buses congregate around the market. Expreso La Moderna to San Antonio (70 minutes, US$1.15, to/from Av Venezuela in San Antonio) continues to Cúcuta (US$1).

San Antonio is connected by international bridge with Cúcuta on the Colombian side (16 km); continue by road or air to Bogotá. San Antonio has a colonial cathedral and some parks, but is not tourist-oriented. Avenida Venezuela leads to Venezuelan customs. You can catch most transport here, to Cúcuta, San Cristóbal, Rubio, even to Caracas, but the bus terminal is off the road to the airport: at the roundabout at end of Avenida Venezuela, turn left (C 11), take a Circunvalación combi marked Terminal (US$0.50). Also buses to airport. There is a festival on 13-20 May.

Border with Colombia This is the main crossing point between the two countries and the border formalities are geared towards locals. Few foreigners travel overland here. Get a Venezuelan exit stamp at SAIME, Cra 9 entre 6 y 7, Antiguo Hospital San Vicente, T771 2282. You will have to fill out a departure card and pay US$9.50 (BsF 40) departure tax across the street. The Colombian consulate is at Centro Cívico San Antonio, loc 1-8, T771 5890, open 0800-1400; better to get a visa in Mérida. The border is open 24 hours but **note** Venezuelan time is 30 minutes ahead of Colombian. Colombian formalities are taken care of right after the bridge: DAS procedures are straightforward with only a passport check and stamp. Colombian and Venezuelan citizens do not need any immigration formalities. Foreigners can arrange exit and entry stamps 0800-1800, often much later. If you only travel to Cúcuta (even to spend the night), no immigration formalities are needed. Just cross the bridge by bus, taxi or por puesto and return the same way. If you plan to travel further to Colombia, however, you will need both Venezuelan exit stamp and Colombian entry stamp.

Entering Venezuela, get your passport stamp at DAS and take bus, por puesto or taxi across the bridge. Ask the driver to take you to Venezuelan immigration, otherwise you will be taken to the centre of San Antonio and will have to backtrack. You can also cross the bridge on foot, but watch out for robberies. Information centre is at the end of the bridge on Venezuelan side. Go to SAIME for entry formalities then look for a bus or por puesto to San Cristóbal on Av Venezuela, or go to the bus station (taxi from SAIME US$2). If Venezuelan customs is closed at weekends, it is not possible to cross from Cúcuta. There is a customs and Guardia Nacional post at Peracal outside San Antonio; be prepared for luggage and strip searches. There may be more searches en route, as well as searches between San Cristóbal and Mérida, eg at La Jabonosa on the Panamericana.

If crossing by private vehicle, car documents must be stamped at the SENIAT office at the Puente Internacional, just before San Antonio. Two different stamps are needed at separate SENIAT buildings ⓘ *Mon-Fri 0800-1200, 1330-1700, Sat 0800-1200, T771 5411*. It's essential to have proof of car/motorbike ownership. You must check in advance if you need a visa and a *carnet de passages* (see page 37). See Cúcuta, Colombia, page 933, for details on exit formalities. Once in Venezuela, you may find police are ignorant of requirements for foreign cars.

Sierra Nevada de Mérida listings

For Sleeping and Eating price codes and other relevant information, see Essentials, pages 38-40.

Sleeping

Los Nevados *p1617*

E pp **Posada Bella Vista**, behind church. Hot water, hammocks, great views, restaurant. Recommended.

E pp **Posada Guamanchi**, T252 2080, www.guamanchi.com. Solar power, great views, cheaper without bath, 2 meals included. Recommended.

F pp **El Buen Jesús**, T252 5696. Hot water, Meals.

El Morro

E Posada run by Doña Chepa, as you enter from Los Nevados, warm. Recommended.

F pp **Posada El Orégano**, including meals, basic, good food. Recommended.

Tabay *p1618*

C Casa Vieja, Transandina via Páramo, San Rafael de Tabay, inside the Parador Turístico El Paramito, T0274-417 1489, www.casa-vieja-merida.com. Plant-filled colonial house, German and Peruvian owners, good doubles, hot water, breakfast and dinner available, good food, relaxing, very helpful, information on independent trips from Tabay and transport, English, French and German spoken. Travel agency, **Caiman Tours**, for Llanos, wildlife and adventure tours, see also www.birds-venezuela.de. From the bus terminal in Mérida take a bus via Mucuchíes or Apartaderos, 30 mins to Tabay, get off exactly 1.5 km after the gas station in Tabay village (just after you pass Plaza Bolívar); the bus stop is called El Paramito. There is a sign on the road pointing left. Free pick-up from the airport or terminal with reservation. They also have a second posada in the village of Altamira de Cáceres. Warmly recommended.

C La Casona de Tabay, on the Mérida road 1½ km from the plaza, T0274-283 0089, posadala casona@cantv.net. A beautiful colonial-style hotel, surrounded by mountains, comfortable, home cooking, family-run. Take *por puesto*, 2 signposts.

E pp **Posada de la Mano Poderosa**, beyond San Rafael de Tabay on road to Mucuchíes, T0414-742 2862. Dorms, lovely, quiet, hot showers, good food, great value, get off at La Plazuela then walk 15 mins towards Vivero Fruti Flor.

Mucuchíes

C Los Conquistadores, Av Carabobo 14, T872 0350. Nice decor, modern, breakfast, TV, heating, lots of facilities like pool tables and other games, garden, parking, restaurant 0800-2200, tasca, and bike hire. Arranges transport for tours, BBV Provincial and ATM.

E Posada Los Andes, Independencia 25, T872 0151, 0414-717 2313. Old house on street above plaza, run by Las Hermanas Pironi Belli, 5 cosy rooms, hot water, shared bathrooms, TV in living room, excellent restaurant (breakfast extra, criollo and Italian food, 0800-2030). Internet available. Highly recommended.

Mucuposadas is a network of basic lodgings, see www.andestropicales.org/Andes_Vzla.html.

San Rafael de Mucuchíes

C Posada San Rafael del Páramo, just outside San Rafael, 500m from the Capilla de Piedra, on road to Apartaderos, T872 0938. With breakfast or **D** without breakfast in low season. Charming converted house with lots of interesting sculpture and paintings, hot water, heating, TV, also cabin with kitchenette, walking and riding tours (guide extra). Recommended.

D Casa Sur, Independencia 72, T872 0342, 0416-275 1684, njespindola@yahoo.com. Hot water, heating, TV, breakfast extra, other meals on request.

D El Rosal, Bolívar 37, T872 0331, T0416-275 3254. Hot water, TV, good, also cabins with kitchenette (**B**), no breakfast, café nearby, restaurant for groups, tasca at weekends.

Apartaderos *p1619*

A Hotel Parque Turístico, main road, T888 0094. Cheaper in low season. Attractive modern chalet- style building, heating, very hot showers, helpful owner, expensive restaurant. Recommended.

B Hotel y Restaurante Mifafí, on main road, T888 0131, refugioturisticomifafi@hotmail.com. Cheaper without heating, pleasant rooms and cabins, hot water, TV, good food. A welcoming, reliable choice.

D Posada y Restaurant Juan Hilario, Mucuchíes side of town, T888 0145, T0414-747 3779 (mob). 9 big rooms with hot water, double bed and bunks, TV, cold but looks OK, all meals extra, parking.

D Posada Viejo Apartaderos, outside town, coming from Mucuchíes, T888 0003, posadaviejo apartaderos@cantv.net.

Next to *bomba*, with **La Matica de Rosa** restaurant, T271 2209, Sra Marbeles. Open only in high season. Good value, good restaurant with reasonable prices.

From Mérida to the Panamericana *p1619*

Jají

A pp **Estancia La Bravera**, 18 km from Jají towards La Azulita, T0212-978 2627, 414-293 3306, www.estancialabravera.com. Cabins in beautiful flower gardens in the cloud forest, great for bird- watching, hot water, includes breakfast and dinner, lunch extra, uses home produce, holds an annual Estancia Musical (Aug).

B Hacienda Santa Filomena, 5 mins from Jají, T0212-573 1519, 0414-247 9020, santafilomena@hotmail.com. Stay and dine on a 19th-century coffee farm. Used by birders.

B Posada Restaurant Aldea Vieja, C Principal, just off Plaza, T414 6128, or T414-717 3137, http://aldeavieja.com. Colonial style main building, also cabins for 4-8, lovely views, simple rooms, TV, hot water, meals extra (breakfast US$3.40), playground (watch out for the slides).

C Hacienda La Carmen, Aldea La Playa, 2 km from Jají (there is public transport), T414-639 2701, 0414-630 9562, www.haciendaelcarmen.com.ve. On a working dairy and coffee-processing farm, built 1863, fascinating buildings, lovely rooms, one with jacuzzi (**B**), some simpler rooms, breakfast included, coffee tours, owner Andrés Monzón.

E Posada Turística Jají, beside the Prefectura, on the plaza, T416 6333. 4 rooms with hot water, no TV, historic, 2 fountains, restaurant 0800-2100, breakfast included if staying a few days.

La Azulita

3 km before town is a turning left to San Luis and Saysayal Bajo. The sign mentions various *posadas*, but most not working. Recommended are:

B El Tao, on a side road beyond Remanso, 4-5 km, 6 mins in car from La Azulita, T0274-511 3088, 0416-175 0011, www.eltaomerida.com. Taoist owners and oriental- style spa with saunas, and natural therapies, many birds, favoured by birders and other groups, lovely gardens, very safe and peaceful, nice public areas. Cabins for 2-4, with breakfast, TV, hot water. Restaurant, boxed lunches and early breakfast for birding groups.

B-C Remanso del Quebradón, close to junction, T0416-775 7573, www.remanso.com.ve. 4 rooms with bath, on a small coffee farm with fruit trees in the gardens, restaurant, breakfast included, popular with birdwatchers.

E Posada Turística La Azulita, on Plaza Bolívar. Rooms around restaurant in courtyard, OK food. Some other lodgings in town.

Mesa de los Indios

C Posada Papá Miguel, C Piñango 1, T0274-252 2529, 0414-747 9953 (mob). Rustic and characterful.

San Cristóbal *p1620*

Cheapest hotels around the bus station (ugly area), **A-B** business hotels in the centre (**El Faraón, Dinastía**) and more upmarket place in the north- western suburbs (eg **Castillo de la Fantasía, Los Pirineos, Posada Remanso de Pueblo Nuevo**).

AL Lidotel, Sambil San Cristóbal Mall, Autopista Antonio José de Sucre, Las Lomas, T510 3333, www.lidotelhotelboutique.com. Attached to an enormous, posh shopping mall, with all the luxuries of 4-star hotel, pool, very well run. Recommended.

AL Posada Rincón Tachirense, Av Ferrero Tamayo con C 3, N Ft-19, La Popita, T341 8573, www.posadarincontachirense.com. Not central, down hill from **Del Rey**, cheaper with shared bath, comfortable, a/c, TV, Wi-Fi and internet, breakfast and will ring out for pizza. Recommended.

A Del Rey, Av Ferrero Tamayo, Edif El Rey, T343 0561. Good showers, fridge, TV, Wi-Fi, kitchenette, laundry, no breakfast but *panadería* in building, pizzas. Recommended.

D Posada Turística Don Manuel, Cra 10 No 1-104, just off Av 19 de Abril, Urb La Concordia, T347 8082. Rooms are across street; Sra Carmen will direct you. Hot water, family run, TV, fridge, fan, limited kitchen facilities, no breakfast, parking. Sleeps 8, always book in advance, convenient.
E Río de Janeiro, C 1, No 7-27, Urb Juan Maldonado, La Concordia, by bus station, T347 7666. Big rooms, fan, hot shower, no breakfast.
E Tropical, Prol 5ta Av No 7472, opposite bus station, T347 2932. Basic. Other cheapies nearby.

San Cristóbal to San Antonio *p1621*

Capacho

B La Molinera, 20 mins from San Cristóbal at Capacho, municipalidad de Independencia, T788 3117. Rooms and suites in a beautiful, traditional posada with swimming pool and hand-made furniture. Good Tachirense food in its restaurant.

San Antonio

Many hotels near town centre.
C Adriático, C6 y Cra 6, T771 3896. Not far from Av Venezuela, 3-star, functional.
E Neveri, C 3, No 3-13, esq Carrera 3, T771 5702. A/c, TV, safe, parking nearby, 1 block from Customs, opposite Guardia Nacional barracks. No food, dated. Internet next door.

Eating

San Cristóbal *p1620*

El Barrio Obrero has the main concentration of eateries, bars and discos. Try **Rocamar**, Cra 20 y C 14, for seafood. Also pizza places and *pastelerías*.
La Olleta, Cra 21, no 10-171, just off plaza, Barrio Obrero, T356 6944. Smart, simple décor, Venezuelan and international with creative touches, well presented.

Around town there are many *panaderías* and *pastelerías* for snacks as well as bread and cakes, coffee and other drinks, eg **América**, Cra 8, Edif La Concordia, no 4-113, La Concordia (several on Cra 8 y C 4, La Concordia); also **Táchira** branches.

San Antonio *p1621*

Rosmar, Cra 6 y C 6, opposite Hotel Adriático. Very popular for lunch, several choices, OK food.

Transport

Los Nevados *p1617*

Jeep Los Nevados-**Mérida**, late afternoon (depart 0700 from Plaza Las Heroínas in Mérida), 5-6 hrs, US$11 pp, US$48 per jeep, very rough and narrow but spectacular.

Tabay *p1618*

Regular bus service from **Mérida** C 19 entre Avs 3 y 4, every 10 mins, US$0.40; taxi US$4-8 (more at night). Gasoline in Tabay.

Apartaderos *p1619*

Bus To **Mérida** from turn-off to Barinas; bus to **Barinas** on the road over the Sierra Nevada is unreliable, best to catch it in Mérida.

San Cristóbal *p1620*

Air Airport at Santo Domingo, 40 km away. Helpful tourist kiosk with leaflets, map of San Cristóbal US$0.50. Taxi to San Cristóbal US$22, can take as little as 35 mins, but normally much more, lots of traffic, nice scenery (tourist office says no other option). The highway is 30 mins' walk away; it may be possible to catch a bus, 1 hr, US$1.50. Daily flights to/from **Caracas** with **Aserca**, **Aeropostal** and **Rutaca**. Alternatively fly to San Antonio (see below) for better public transport links.
Bus Local: buses cost US$0.35. 'Intercomunal' goes from Av Ferrero Tamayo (northwest) to Bus Terminal. 'Tusca' from Av Ferrero Tamayo to centre. Taxis US$3.50 for a short run. **Línea Pirineos**, T355 1717/355 0405 recommended.

The **bus station** is in La Concordia, in the southeast. It is a bus terminal, shopping mall, market, phone exchange and food court all lumped together. Terminal tax US$0.10, paid on bus before departure. Company offices are grouped together: **Expresos Mérida** (not to Mérida), **Aerobuses**, **Expresos Los Llanos** (to San Fernando), **Expresos Barinas** (direct to San Fernando at 1700, and to Puerto Ayacuccho, T0276-414 6950), many others. **Expresos Occicente** have their own terminal nearby. To **Mérida**, US$9.25, 5 hrs, with **Táchira-Mérida** (buy ticket on bus); **Expreso Unido** to Mérida, 0530, 0830, plus *ejecutivos* 1130, 1430, 1730; also to Tovar 0930, 1430,

4 hrs, US$9.50. Buses to Mérida go via the Panamericana, not over the Páramo. National Guard Control at La Jabonesa, just before San Juan de Colón, be prepared for luggage search. To **Maracaibo**, 6-8 hrs, US$18.50-20. To **Caracas**, US$18-23, 15 hrs; **Valencia**, US$14.25-23. To **Barinas**, US$8.60. To **San Fernando de Apure** via **Guasdualito**, US$19-23. To **San Antonio**, 1¼ hrs (but San Cristóbal rush hour can add lots of time), US$1.50, **Línea San Antonio**, T347 0976 (San Antonio 771 2966) and **Unión de Conductores**, T346 0691 (San Antonio 771 1364). To **Cúcuta**, **Línea Venezuela**, T347 3086 (Cúcuta T0270-583 6413) and **Fronteras Unidas**, T347 7446 (Cúcuta T0270 583 5445) , US$2.75, Mon-Fri 0800-1200, 1400-1800. Opposite terminal on Rugeles, **Coop de Conductores Fronterizos** cars, T611 2256, to **San Antonio**.

San Antonio *p1621*

Air The airport has exchange facilities (mainly for Colombian pesos). Taxis run to SAIME (immigration) in town, and on to Cúcuta airport. Flights to **Caracas** with **Aeropostal** and **Rutaca**.

Bus From terminal several companies to **Caracas**, via the Llanos, Valencia and Maracay. All *bus-cama*: Caracas US$27, Valencia US$22, Maracay US$22. **Expresos San Cristóbal** have office on Av Venezuela, close to Customs, 1800 to Caracas, 13-14 hrs; **Expresos Mérida**, Av Venezuala, No 6-17, at 1900. **Táchira-Mérida** to **Mérida** and **Barquisimeto**, 1600; **Expresos Unidos** to Mérida 1200, 1700. To **San Cristóbal**, catch a bus on Av Venezuela. Taxi from SAIME area to San Cristóbal, 40 mins, they try to charge US$40 but will negotiate down to US$18.

Border with Colombia *p1621*

Air It is cheaper, but slower, to fly **Caracas**-San Antonio, take a taxi to Cúcuta, then take an internal Colombian flight, than to fly direct Caracas- Colombia. The airport transfer at San Antonio is well-organized and taxi drivers make the 25-min trip with all stops. Air tickets out of Cúcuta can be reserved in a Venezuelan travel agency.

Bus On Av Venezuela por puestos/colectivos to **Cúcuta** charge US$1, and buses US$0.70 payable in bolívares or pesos, 30 mins. Some say to terminal, others to centre. Taxi to Cúcuta, US$11. On any transport that crosses the border, make sure the driver knows you need to stop to obtain stamps. *Por puesto* drivers may refuse to wait. Taxi drivers will stop at all the offices. Just to visit Cúcuta, no documents are needed.

Directory

San Cristóbal *p1620*

Banks Plenty of ATMs in town. Major banks on Av 7 between Cs 9 and 10. Mon-Fri 0830-1530. TCs are difficult to change. **Consulates German**, Cra 3 con C 4,CC Dr Toto Gonzáles, p 1, of 7, T343 6218, kmargeit@ hotmail.com. **UK**, CC El Tama, loc 49, Altos de Pirineos, T356 6732, britcon-sc@cantv.net. **Telephones** Many **CANTV** offices and phones; also independent phone tables, with land lines and mobiles, everywhere.

San Antonio *p1621*

Banks Many *casas de cambio* on Av Venezuela near the international bridge will change Colombian pesos, but not all change cheques or even US$ cash. The exchange rate for bolívares to pesos is the same in San Antonio as in Cúcuta.

Los Llanos and Amazonas

A spectacular route descends from the Sierra Nevada to the flat llanos, one of the best places in the world to see birds and animals. This vast, sparsely populated wilderness of 300,000 sq km – one third of the country's area – lies between the Andes to the west and the Orinoco to the south and east. Southwest of the Guayana region, on the banks of the Orinoco, Puerto Ayacucho is the gateway to the jungles of Venezuela. Although it takes up about a fifth of the country, Amazonas and its tropical forests is for the most part unexplored and unspoilt.

Los Llanos

The *llanos* are veined by numerous slow-running rivers, forested along their banks. The flat plain is only varied here and there by *mesas*, or slight upthrusts of the land. About five million of the country's 6.4 million cattle are in the *llanos*, but only around 10% of the human population. When the whole plain is periodically under water, the *llaneros* drive their cattle into the hills or through the flood from one *mesa* to another. When the plain is parched by the sun and the savanna grasses become inedible they herd the cattle down to the damper region of the Apure and Orinoco. Finally they drive them into the valley of Valencia to be fattened.

In October and November, when the vast plains are still partially flooded, wildlife abounds. Animals include capybara, caiman, monkeys, anacondas, river dolphins, pumas and many bird species. Though it's possible to explore this region independently, towns are few and far between and distances are great. It's better to visit the *llanos* as part of a tour from Mérida (see Tour operators, page 1614), or stay at one of the ecotourism *hatos*, or ranches (see below).

Guanare → *Phone code: 0257. Colour map 1, B5. Population: 32,500.*
An excellent road goes to the western *llanos* of Barinas from Valencia. It goes through San Carlos, Acarigua (an agricultural centre and the largest city in Portuguesa state) and Guanare, a national place of pilgrimage with a cathedral containing the much venerated relic of the Virgin of Coromoto. The **Santuario Nacional Nuestra Señora de Coromoto** on the spot where the Virgin appeared to Cacique Coromoto in 1652 ⓘ *25 km frm Guanare on road to Barinas, open 0800-1700, bus from C 20 y Cra 9, Guanare, every 15 mins, US$0.35* is an imposing modern basilica dedicated to the Virgin. It was inaugurated by Pope John Paul II in 1996. Pilgrimages to Coromoto are 2 January and 11 September and Candlemas is 2 February. There is also a large park devoted to María, 4 km from Coromoto. For tourist information: fondomixtoportuguesa@hotmail.com.

Barinas → *Phone code: 0273. Colour map 1, A5. Population: 240,000.*
The road continues to Barinas, the hot, sticky capital of the cattle-raising and oil-rich state of Barinas. A couple of colonial buildings remain: the Palacio del Marqués on the west side of the plaza and the Casa de la Cultura on the north side. On the south side of the plaza is the beautifully restored, 19th-century Escuela de Música; the cathedral is to the east. The shady Parque Universitario, just outside the city on Avenida 23 de Enero, has a botanical garden. **Tourist office** ⓘ *Av Insauste con Av Adonay Parra Jiménez, at entrance to La Ciudad Deportiva, T552 7091, www.corbatur.org.ve*. Helpful, maps, no English spoken; kiosks at airport and bus station.

San Fernando de Apure → *Phone code: 0247. Colour map 1, A6. Population: 135,000.*
At Lagua, 16 km east of Maracay, a good road leads south to San Fernando de Apure. It passes through San Juan de los Morros, with natural hot springs; Ortiz, near the crossroads with the San Carlos-El Tigre road; the Guárico lake and Calabozo. Some 132 km south of Calabozo, San Fernando is the hot and sticky capital of the state of Apure and a fast-growing trade and transport hub for the region. There is *Corp Banca* for American Express, Avenida Miranda, Edif

Chang, PB, and *Bancos Mercantil* (Paseo Libertador) and *Provincial* (Plaza Páez) with Visa and Mastercard ATM and cash advance. From San Fernando you can travel east to Ciudad Bolívar (see page 1655) or south to Puerto Ayacucho (see below).

San Fernando to Barinas

From San Fernando a road heads to head west to Barinas (468 km). It's a beautiful journey, but the road can be in terrible condition, eg between Mantecal, La Ye junction and Bruzual, a town just south of the Puente Nutrias on the Río Apure. In the early morning, many animals and birds can be seen, and in the wet season caiman (alligators) cross the road. **Mantecal** is a friendly cattle-ranching town with hotels and restaurants. *Fiesta*, 23-26 February.

Los Llanos listings

For Sleeping and Eating price codes and other relevant information, see Essentials, pages 38-40.

Sleeping

Guanare *p1626*
Hotels include:
D Italia, Carrera 5, No 19-60, T253 1213. A/c, bar and restaurant, off-street parking.

Barinas *p1626*
B Varyná, Av 23 de Enero, near the airport, T533 2477. A/c, cable TV, hot water, restaurant, parking. Recommended.
C Internacional, C Arzobispo Méndez on Plaza Zamora, T552 2343, hotelinternacional_3@hotmail.com. A/c, safe, cable TV, good restaurant.
D Mónaco, Av Elías Cordero, T533 2096. A/c, cable TV, hot water, parking.
D Motel Don Ripoli, Av 23 de Enero, near the airport, T552 2829. Cold showers, a/c, pool, basic, parking.
E El Palacio, Av Elías Cordero con C 5, T552 6947. A/c, good value, parking, near bus terminal so front rooms are noisy.

Staying at a tourist ranch

An alternative to travelling independently or arranging a tour from Mérida is to stay at one of the tourist ranches. Most of these are in Apure state and can be reached from Barinas or San Fernando de Apure.
AL pp **Hato Piñero**, T0212-991 8935, www.hato pinero.com. A safari-type lodge at a working ranch recently nationalized by the government, near El Baúl (turn off Tinaco-El Sombrero road at El Cantón). Inclusive price, per day, packages can include return overland or air transport from Caracas. Free drinks, good room, bi-lingual nature guide for excellent bird- and animal-watching trips. Highly recommended. No public transport to ranch but ask police in El Baúl for ride with Hato Piñero workers. From Caracas, 6 hrs; from Ciudad Bolívar, 9 hrs.
A Hato Chinea Arriba, the closest *hato* to Caracas, is a 5 mins' drive from Calabozo, T0212-781 4241 or 0414-322 0785, www.haciendachineaarriba.com. Prices all-inclusive. Owner Francisco Leitz speaks French, German and English.
A pp **Hato El Cedral**, about 30 mins by bus from Mantecal (see above). Address: Av La Salle, edif Pancho p 5, of 33, Los Caobos, Caracas, T0212-781 8995, www.elcedral.com. A 53,000-ha ranch, recently nationalized, where hunting is banned. Fully inclusive price, tax extra (high season Dec to Apr), a/c, hot water, land and river safaris, guides, pool. Special offers at certain times of year. Can also rent a room without tour or food.
A Hato La Fe, halfway between Calabozo and San Fernando de Apure in Guárico state, T0414-946 1419, www.hatolafe.com. All-inclusive tours include animal-watching trips and horse riding. Eight bedrooms in a colonial-style house, pool, camping available.
B pp **Rancho Grande**, close to Mantecal, T0240-808 7434. Run by very friendly and knowledgeable Ramón González. All inclusive, good wildlife spotting and horse riding trips.
C pp **Reserva Privada de Flora y Fauna Mataclara**, on road to El Baúl at Km 93 (next to Hato Piñero turn off). Address: Prof Antonio González-Fernández, Universidad de Los Llanos 'Unellez', Mesa de Caracas, Guanare 3323, Estado de Portuguesa, T0241-867 7254. Full board, fishing with own equipment and animal watching trips.

San Fernando de Apure *p1626*
Most hotels are within 1 block of the intersection of Paseo Libertador and Av Miranda.
C Gran Hotel Plaza, C Bolívar, T342 1746, 2 blocks from the bus terminal, www.granhotelplaza.com/index.htm. A/c, cable TV, safe, good, Wi-Fi, parking.
C Trinacria, Av Miranda, near bus terminal, T342 3778. Huge rooms, a/c, cable TV, fridge.
D El Río, Av María Nieves, near the bus terminal, T341 1928. With a/c, cable TV, good value.
D La Fuente, Miranda y Libertador, T342 3233. A/c, TV, phone, safe.
D La Torraca, Av Boulevard y Paseo Libertador by Plaza Bolívar, T342 2777. Excellent rooms, a/c, balcony overlooking centre of town. Recommended.

Eating

Barinas *p1626*
ΨΨ **El Estribo**, C Apure entre Av Garguera y Andrés Varela. Roast and barbecue meat, good, open 1100-2400.
ΨΨ **Sol Llanero**, facing **Hotel Palacio**. Good, cheap.
ΨΨ **Restaurant Pizzería El Budare**, Av 23 de Energo y Mérida. Good pizza, local dishes. 3 restaurants across the street serve similar fare.

Transport

Barinas *p1626*
Air Aeropuerto Nacional, Av 23 de Enero. Flights to **Caracas**.
Bus To **Mérida**, 6 a day with **Transportes Barinas**, US$5.80, spectacular ride through the mountains, 5-7 hrs (sit on right for best views); also to **Valera** at 0730, 1130, US$7.40, 7 hrs. To **Caracas**, US$16.30, 8 hrs, several companies go direct or via **Maracay** and **Valencia**, regularly 0730-2300. To **San Cristóbal**, several daily, US$8.60, 5 hrs; to **San Fernando de Apure**, US$12, 9 hrs with **Expresos Los Llanos** at 0900, 2300; the same company also goes to **Maracaibo** (at 2000 and 2200, US$16.30, 8 hrs) and **Puerto La Cruz** (3 a day, US$23.25, 16 hrs).

From Barinas there is a beautifully scenic road to Apartaderos, in the Sierra Nevada de Mérida (see page 1619). Motorists travelling east to Ciudad Bolívar can either go across the *llanos* or via San Carlos, Tinaco, El Sombrero, Chaguaramas, Valle de la Pascua (see below) and El Tigre. The latter route requires no ferry crossings and has more places with accommodation.

San Fernando de Apure *p1626*
Air Aeropuerto Las Flecheras, Av 1 de Mayo, T341 0139. Flights to **Caracas**.
Bus Terminal is modern and clean, not far from centre; US$3 taxi. To **Caracas**, US$15.80, 7 hrs; to **Barinas**, **Expresos Zamora**, 5 daily, 7 hrs (take food and drink), rough ride, day and night bus, US$12; to **Maracay**, US$11.50; to **Puerto Ayacucho**, US$17.75, 8 hrs; to **Calabozo**, 1½ hrs, US$3.75.

San Fernando to Barinas *p1627*
Bus San Fernando de Apure-Mantecal 3½ hrs, US$6.80; Mantecal-Barinas, 4 hrs, US$8.50.

Directory

Barinas *p1626*
Banks **Banco Mercantil**, Av Marqués del Pumar y Bolívar, and **Banco Provincial**, Av Marqués del Pumar y Carvajal, for Mastercard or Visa cash withdrawals.

Amazonas

Much of Amazonas is stunningly beautiful and untouched, but access is only by river. The more easily accessible places lie on the course of the Orinoco and its tributaries. The best time to visit is October to December after the rains, but at any season, this is a remote part of the country.

San Fernando to Puerto Ayacucho

Due south of San Fernando de Apure is **Puerto Páez** (*Phone code: 0247; Population: 2,600*) at the confluence of the Meta and Orinoco rivers; here there is a crossing to El Burro west of the Caicara-Puerto Ayacucho road. Route 2 runs south from San Fernando to Puerto Páez, crossing several major rivers. Between the Capanaparo and Cinaruco rivers is the **Parque Nacional Cinaruco- Capanaparo** (also called **Santos Luzardo**), reached only from this road. If this road is closed, to get to Puerto Ayacucho from San Fernando involves a minimum 15-hour detour via the Caicara ferry.

From Caicara a new paved road runs 370 km southwest to Puerto Ayacucho. The turn off to **El Burro**, where the boat crosses the Orinoco to Puerto Páez (ferry US$1), is 88 km north of Puerto Ayacucho (*taxi* El Burro-Puerto Ayacucho, two hours US$8.50).

Puerto Ayacucho → *Phone code: 0248. Colour map 1, B6. Population: 41,240.*

The capital of the State of Amazonas is 800 km via the Orinoco from Ciudad Bolívar. At the end of the dry season (April), it is very hot and sticky. It is deep in the wild, but no direct boats do the five day journey up river. **Museo Etnológico Monseñor Enzo Ceccarelli** ⓘ *Av Río Negro, Tue-Sat 0830-1200, 1430-1830, Sun 0900-1300, US$1,* has a library and collection of regional exhibits, recommended. In front of the museum is a market, open every day, where *indígenas* sell handicrafts. One block away is the cathedral. The Salesian Mission House and boys' school on Plaza Bolívar may also be visited. Prices in Puerto Ayacucho are generally higher than north of the Orinoco. **Tourist office** is in the Gobernación building, Av Río Negro, T521 0033, www.amazonas.gob.ve. **Note** Malaria is prevalent in this area; take precautions.

Excursions October to December is the best time, when rivers are high but the worst of the rains has passed. In the low season, May-June, it may be difficult to organize tours for only a few days.

You can walk up **Cerro Perico** for good views of the town, or go to the Mirador, 1 km from centre, for good views of the Ature rapids. A recommended trip is to the village of Pintado (12 km south), where petroglyphs described by Humboldt can be seen on the huge rock **Cerro Pintado**. This is the most accessible petroglyph site of the hundreds scattered throughout Amazonas.

Some 35 km south on the road to Samariapo is the **Parque Tobogán de la Selva**, a pleasant picnic area based around a steeply inclined, smooth rock over which the Río Maripures cascades. This waterslide is great fun in the wet season; crowded on Sunday, take swimsuit and food and drink (stick to the right to avoid crashing into the barrier, few locals slide right from the top; also beware of broken glass). A small trail leads up from the slide to a natural jacuzzi after about 20 minutes. Taxi to Cerro Pintado and Parque Tobogán, US$17 return (organize your return, otherwise you may face a lengthy hike). Agencies in town arrange tours; easier but more expensive.

The well-paved road from Puerto Ayacucho to Samariapo (63 km) was built to bypass the rapids which here interrupt the Orinoco, dividing it into 'Upper' and 'Lower'; the powerful Maripures Rapids are very impressive.

Tours in Amazonas

The best base is Puerto Ayacucho. Do not travel alone. By ascending the Autana or Sipapo rivers, you can see **Autana-tepuy**, a 1,200 m-high mass of rock no-one has climbed from the base. Other *tepuis* in the region include the great mass of the Sierra de la Neblina on the Brazilian border.

San Juan de Manapiare (Population: 3,700) is the regional centre for the middle Ventuari. A beautiful track winds around the Cerro Guanay to get there. The road starts at Caicara and goes through Guaniamo and Sabana de Cardona.

Amazonas listings

For Sleeping and Eating price codes and other relevant information, see Essentials, pages 38-40.

Sleeping

Puerto Ayacucho *p1629*

A Orinoquia Lodge, on the Río Orinoco, 20 mins from airport, book through Cacao Travel, www.cacaotravel.com, or through www.casatropical.com.ves. Nice setting, comfortable lodgings in thatched huts, full board.

B City Center, Av 23 de Enero, on roundabout at entrance to town, T521 0639. Pleasant, safe parking, takes credit cards.

C Apure, Av Orinoco 28, T521 0516, less than 1 km from centre. A/c, good restaurant. Recommended.

D Res Internacional, Av Aguerrevere 18, T521 0242. A/c (cheaper without), comfortable, shower, locked parking, safe but basic, not very clean, good place to find tour information and meet other travellers, if no room available you can sling up your hammock, bus drivers stay here and will drive you to the terminal for early starts.

Private camps in Amazonas There are a number of private river camps on the upper Orinoco but they do not welcome casual guests.

Near Puerto Ayacucho

A Canturama Amazonas Resort, T521 0266, or Caracas 0212-941 8813, 20 mins by vehicle south of town. On the banks of the Orinoco, 40 km from nearest jungle, highly recommended accommodation and food but beware biting insects by the river.

Río Manapiare area

LL Campamento Camani, in a forest clearing on the banks of the Río Alto Ventuari, 2 hrs by launch from San Juan de Manapiare, T521 4865, www.campamentocamani.com. From Puerto Ayacucho daily aerotaxi takes 50 mins. Maximum 26 at any one time, mosquito nets, all amenities, excursions available. Has 2-, 3- and 4-night packages including transport, full board and jungle excursions.

LL Yutajé Camp, on a tributary of Río Manapiare due east of Puerto Ayacucho. Restaurant and bar, full board, fishing, canoes, horses, excursions to indigenous villages, expensive but professional, welcoming. Reached by plane from Puerto Ayacucho or boat up the Ríos Manapiare and Corocoro (take something soft to sit on). Price is for a 3 day/2 night package.

Eating

Puerto Ayacucho *p1629*

ϒϒ **Cherazad**, Aguerrevere y Av Orinoco. Arabic food, relatively expensive.

ϒϒ **El Padrino**, in Urb Andrés Eloy Blanco on Av Belisio Pérez off Av 23 de Enero. Good Italian.

ϒϒ-ϒ **El Espagetazo**, Av Aguerrevere. Mainly pasta, popular with locals.

ϒϒ-ϒ **Las Palmeras**, Av 23 de Enero, 2 blocks from the Redoma. Pizzas and fast food.

ϒ **Capi Fuente de Soda**, on Av Evelio Roa behind *gobernación*. Some vegetarian dishes.

Shopping

Puerto Ayacucho *p1629*

Handicrafts Good *artesanía* in the Plaza del Indio; also in **Artes Amazonas** on Av Evelio Roa, next to **Wayumi**, and in **Topocho** just up from Plaza del Indio. Vicente Barletta, **Típico El Casique**, Av Principal 583, Urb Andrés Eloy Blanco, has a good collection of masks (free); he also works as a guide, recommended, take own food and equipment.

Activities and tours

Tours in Amazonas *p1629*

It is strongly recommended to go on tours organized by tour agents or guides registered in the **Asocación de Guías**, in the Cámara de Turismo de Puerto Ayacucho, Casa de la Piedra, on the Arteria Vial de la Av Orinoco with Av Principal (the house on top of the large rock). Some independent guides may not have permission to visit Amazonas. Those listed below will arrange permits and insurance but shop around.

Coyote Expediciones, Av Aguirrevere 75, T521 4582, 0416-448 7125, coyoteexpedition@cantv.net. Helpful, professional, English spoken, organizes trips staying in indigenous villages.
Expediciones Aguas Bravas Venezuela, Av Río Negro, No 32-2, in front of Plaza Rómulo Betancourt, T521 4458/0541, aguasbravas@cantv.net. Whitewater rafting, 2 daily 0900-1200 and 1500-1800, 3-13 people per boat, reservations required at peak times, take insect repellent, sun protector, light shoes and swimsuit.
Tobogán Tours, Av 23 de Enero 24, near *Instituto del Menor*, T521 4865, tobogant@cantv.net.
Yutajé Tours, in Urb Monte Bello, 1 block from Av Orinoco, past the Mercadito going out of town, T521 0664, turismoamazona@ cantv.net. Good value for money but the organization is erratic.

Transport

Puerto Ayacucho *p1629*
Air Airport 7 km southeast along Av Orinoco.
Bus Expresos del Valle to **Cuidad Bolívar** (US$20, 10 hrs; take something to eat, bus stops once for early lunch), **Caicara, Puerto Ordaz** and **San Félix**; **Cooperativa Cacique** to **San Fernando de Apure**, US$17.75, 8 hrs; both companies in bus terminal. **Expresos La Prosperidad** to **Caracas** and **Maracay** from Urb Alto Parima. Bus from **Caracas**, 2030, 2230 daily, US$25, 12 hrs (but much longer in wet season). *Por puesto* to Ciudad Bolívar, 3 daily, US$25, 10-12 hrs (Caicara Amazonas).
Ferry Ferry service across the Orinoco, US$0.50. Boat to **Caicara**, 1½ days, US$25 including food, but bargain; repellent and hammock required.

Directory

Puerto Ayacucho *p1629*
Banks Changing dollars is difficult.
Internet El Navegante, CC Maniglia, Av Orinoco, or on top floor of Biblioteca Pública Central, Av Río Negro. **Post offices** **Ipostel** on Av Aguerrevere 3 blocks up from Av Orinoco.
Telephones International calls from **CANTV**, on Av Orinoco next to *Hotel Apure*; also from *Las Churuatas* on Av Aguerrevere y C Amazonas, 1 block from Plaza del Indio.

East coast

Beautiful sandy bays, islands, forested slopes and a strong colonial influence all contribute to make this one of the most visited parts of the country. The western part, which is relatively dry, has the two main cities, Puerto La Cruz and Cumaná, which is possibly the oldest Hispanic city on the South American mainland. IAs you go east, you find some splendid beaches. Off shore are two of Venezuela's prime holiday attractions, Isla de Margarita, a mix of the overdeveloped and the quiet, and the island paradise of the Los Roques archipelago.

Caracas to Puerto La Cruz

Very much a holiday coastline, the first part takes its name from the sweeping Barlovento bay in Miranda state. Onshore trade winds give the seaboard a lusher aspect than the more arid landscape elsewhere.

It is some five hours from Caracas to Puerto La Cruz through Caucagua, from which there is a 58 km road northeast to **Higuerote** (*Phone code: 0234. Population: 13,700*); three basic hotels, the best beaches are out of town. A coastal road from Los Caracas to Higuerote has many beaches and beautiful views.

Parque Nacional Laguna de Tacarigua

At 14 km before Higuerote on the road from Caucagua is Tacarigua de Mamporal, where you can turn off to the **Parque Nacional Laguna de Tacarigua**. The 18,400 ha national park enclosing the lagoon is an important ecological reserve, with mangroves, good fishing and many water birds, including flamingos (usually involving a day-long boat trip to see them, best time to see them 1700-1930; permit required from *Inparques* at the *muelle*, US$1). Boats leave from *Muelle Ciudad Tablita*; also from Inparques *muelle* (overcharging is common). Agencies have offices in Sector Belén in the fishing village of **Tacarigua de la Laguna**; fixed price of US$4.60. Boats can be hired to anywhere in the Park and to *Club Miami* beach resort, **B**, on the Caribbean side of the eastern sandspit. Good fish dishes are served at *Bar-Restaurant Poleo Lebranche Asado*. The beaches beyond here are unspoilt and relaxing, but mosquitoes are a problem after sunset.

Puerto La Cruz and around → *Phone code: 0281. Colour map 2, A1.*

Originally a fishing village, Puerto La Cruz (*Population: 185,000*) is now a major oil refining town and busy, modern holiday resort. (Tourist facilities are above average, if expensive, and the sea is polluted.) The seafront avenue, Paseo Colón, extends to the eastern extremity of a broad bay. To the west the bay ends at the prominent El Morro headland. Most hotels, restaurants, bars and clubs are along Paseo Colón, with excellent views of Bahía de Pozuelas and the islands of the Parque Nacional Mochima (see below). Vendors of paintings, jewellery, leather and hammocks are on Paseo Colón in the evening. The *Santa Cruz* festival is on 3 May, while 8 September is the

Puerto La Cruz

Sleeping
1 Caribbean Inn
2 Comercio
3 Cristal Park
4 Gaeta
5 Gran Hotel Puerto La Cruz
6 Marcelino
7 Pippo
8 Rasil
9 Riviera
10 Senador

Eating
1 El Guatacarauzo
2 Heladería Tropic & Galería Colón
3 La Colmena
4 O Sole Mio
5 Salmorejo
6 Trattoria Dalla Nonna
7 Tío Pepe

Virgen del Valle, when boats cruise the harbour clad in palms and balloons; afternoon party at El Faro, Chimana, lots of salsa and beer. The main attractions of Puerto La Cruz lie offshore on the many islands of the beautiful Parque Nacional Mochima and in the surrounding waters. For details of how to get there, see below. The tourist office is **Fondoturismo** ⓘ *C Bolívar, Ed Araya, local 3 PB, T267 1632, Mon-Fri 0800-1300*, very helpful and friendly.

Caracas to Puerto La Cruz listings

For Sleeping and Eating price codes and other relevant information, see Essentials, pages 38-40.

Sleeping

Parque Nacional Laguna de Tacarigua *p1631*

Tacarigua de la Laguna

B Villa del Río, about 3 km before the village on the road. Apart-hotel, price for 1-7 persons, bath, kitchen facilities, fan, connected with *Remigios Tours*, transfer to and from Tacarigua for US$25.

C La Posada de Carlos, C Real, T0234-871 1156. Basic.

Puerto La Cruz *p1632, map p1632*

Newer, up-market hotels are at Lechería and El Morro; cheaper hotels are concentrated in the centre, though it's not easy to find a cheap hotel.

L Gran Hotel Puerto La Cruz, Paseo Colón, east edge of the centre, T500-3611, www.granhotelplc.com.ve. Now part-owned by Venetur, 5-star luxury hotel with all facilities.

A Caribbean Inn, Freites, T267 4292, hotelcaribbean@cantv.net. Big rooms, very well kept with quiet a/c, small pool, very good service.

A Rasil, Paseo Colón y Monagas 6, T262 3000, www.hotelrasil.com.ve. Rooms, suites and bungalows, 3 restaurants, bar, pool, tour office, gym, money exchange, car rental, convenient for ferries and buses.

A Riviera, Paseo Colón 33, T267 2111, hotelriviera@cantv.net. Seafront hotel, noisy a/c, some rooms have balcony, phone, bar, watersports, very good location, restaurant, poor breakfast.

B Cristal Park, Buenos Aires y Libertad, T267 0744. Some with a/c, exchange at a good rate.

B Gaeta, Paseo Colón y Maneiro, T265 0411, gaeta@telcel.net.ve. Very modern, a/c, good location but very small rooms, restaurant, can change money at good rates.

B Senador, Miranda y Bolívar, T267 3522, hotelsenadorplc@cantv.net. A/c, back rooms quieter, phone, restaurant with view, parking.

C Comercio, Maneiro y Libertad, T265 1429. A/c, hot water, safe, cable TV.

D Marcelino, Paseo Colón 109 y Juncal, T268 7545. Large rooms, a bit tatty, a/c, TV, Arabic restaurant next door.

E Pippo, Freites 66 y Municipal, T268 8810. Cold water, some rooms with TV, very noisy and not very clean.

Eating

Puerto La Cruz *p1632, map p1632*

Many on Paseo Colón, eg **Tío Pepe** and **Big Garden**, delicious sea food. **O Sole Mio**, cheap, excellent, wide variety. **Trattoria Dalla Nonna**, Italian food.

🍴🍴 **Celeri**, on Av Municipal, 1 block from Guamaché. Vegetarian, weekdays 1130-1530. Recommended.

🍴🍴 **La Colmena**, next to **Hotel Riviera**. Vegetarian.

🍴🍴 **La Taberna del Guácharo**, C Carabobo, east end of Paseo Colón. Excellent Venezuelan cuisine, good service. Highly recommended.

🍴🍴 **El Guatacarauzo**, Paseo Colón near Pizza Hut. Live music, salsa, good atmosphere and value.

🍴🍴 **Moroco**, Av 5 de Julio 103. Good seafood.

🍴🍴 **Salmorejo**, Miranda y Honduras. For chicken and seafood, with a terrace.

🍴 **El Farao**, east corner of main bus station. Excellent, authentic, spicy Arabic food.

Cafés

Heladería Tropic, Galería Colón on Paseo Colón. Good ice cream.

Sourdough Bakery and Grill, Paseo Colón. Vegetarian options, excellent.

Bars and clubs

Puerto La Cruz *p1632, map p1632*
Most clubs are in El Morro and Lechería.
Casa Latina Av 5 de Julio. Good 1970s salsa.

Activities and tours

Puerto La Cruz *p1632, map p1632*
Diving Several companies, mostly on Paseo Colón, run diving courses. They're a bit more expensive than Santa Fe and Mochima. Hotels and travel agents also organize trips. The nearest recompression chamber is on Isla Margarita. We've received favourable reports on these:
Aquatic Adventures, at end of Paseo Colón in the Marina, T0414-806 3744, or 0414-820 8758 (mob). Very experienced, English spoken, collect you from hotel and provide lunch, US$55 for 2 dives, 2-3 person minimum, 4-day PADI course US$350, rents snorkelling equipment.
Explosub, *Gran Hotel Puerto La Cruz*, T267 3256, explosub@gmail.com. Efficient, helpful, will dive with 1 person, US$75 for 2 dives, good 4-island tour.
Kayaking **Jakera**, www.jakera.com. Sea kayaks for rent from their lodge at Playa Colorada (T0293-808 7057), trips to whole country arranged (lodge in Mérida too, office C 24, No 8-205, Plaza Las Heroínas, Mérida, T0274-252 9577, 0416-887 2239 - mob), Chris and Joanna helpful, English spoken.

General tours

Note Do not buy tours from wandering salespeople not affiliated with a registered tour company.

Transport

Puerto La Cruz *p1632, map p1632*
Bus Bus terminal to the east of town; *por puesto* terminal at Av Juncal y Democracia, many buses also stop here. **Aero- expresos Ejecutivos** to/from **Caracas** 5 a day, 5 hrs, US$13-15 (T267 8855, next to ferry terminal), highly recommended (also to Maracay, Valencia and Barquisimeto). Other cheaper companies to **Caracas** include **Expresos Los Llanos** (T267 0330, recommended, a/c, movies), **Camargüi** and others. To **Mérida**, US$26.70, 16 hrs. To **Ciudad Bolívar** US$12; to **Ciudad Guayana** US$18. To **Cumaná**, bus US$4.60, *por puesto* US$9.50, 1½ hrs. To **Carúpano**, US$8, 5 hrs. *Por puesto* to Playa Colorado US$1 and to Santa Fe US$4.60. There are also services to Maracay, Valencia, Barinas, San Cristóbal, Güiria. Along Av 5 de Julio runs a bus marked 'Intercomunal'. It links Puerto La Cruz with the city of Barcelona (which has the nearest airport) and intervening points. Another Barcelona bus is marked 'Ruta Alternativa' and uses the inland highway via the Puerto La Cruz Golf and Country Club and Universidad de Oriente, US$0.35.
Ferry For details of ferries to **Isla Margarita**, see page 1652.

Directory

Puerto La Cruz *p1632, map p1632*
Banks **Corp Banca** (Amex TCs), Av 5 de Julio y Las Flores, Local No 43. **Banco de Venezuela** and **Banesco** on Av Libertad near Miranda. **Italcambio**, Av Ppal de Lechería, CC Galery Center, Loc 10, T700 0524. Amex representative. **Oficambio**, Maneiro y Honduras, no commission on TCs, open 0800-1645 Mon-Fri. **Internet** In Galería Colón, Paseo Colón, **American Net** and **CANTV Centro de Comunicaciones. North American Connection**, CC Paseo Plaza, C Carabobo, ½ block south of **Hotel Puerto La Cruz**. Fax and scanning facility as well as internet. **Puerto Internet**, C Maneiro. **Post offices and telephones** **CANTV and Ipostel**, Freites y Bolívar, 1 block from Paseo Colón. Telephone office accepts Visa for calls.

Parque Nacional Mochima

Beyond the cities of Barcelona and Puerto La Cruz, the main focus is the Mochima national park, one of the country's most beautiful regions. Hundreds of tiny Caribbean islands, a seemingly endless series of beaches backed by some of Venezuela's most beautiful scenery and tiny coves tucked into bays, all offer excellent snorkelling, fishing and swimming.

Ins and outs Tour companies offer trips to the islands from Puerto La Cruz: for example **Passion**, Paseo Colón, Edif Araya, pb 4, T268 5684/T0414-822 3200; passiontours@cantv.net, manager Gabriel Laclé, day tour around several islands for snorkelling, diving, fishing. Also **Aquatic Adventures**, see Puerto la Cruz, Activities and tours, above. **Transtupaco**, next to *Gran Hotel Puerto La Cruz*, no tours, they act as a taxi to the islands. Alternatively, you can reach the islands with the *Embarcadero de Peñeros*, on Paseo Colón, behind the *Tejas Restaurant*. Departures from 0900- 1000, return at 1600-1630; US$6.50 per person. Tourist office in Puerto La Cruz provides tour operators for day trips to various islands for swimming or snorkelling; six-hour trip to four islands costs US$40 per person, including drinks. The islands to the east (Isla de Plata, Monos, Picuda Grande and Chica and the beaches of Conoma and Conomita) are best reached from the port at **Guanta** (taxi from town, or *por puesto* from C Freites between Avenida 5 de Julio and C Democracia, and ask to be dropped off at the Urb Pamatacualito). **Note** Boat trips to the islands are cheaper from **Santa Fe** or **Mochima** (see below). Bring your own food as the island restaurants are expensive.

When to avoid At Christmas, Carnival and Easter this part of the coast becomes extremely congested so patience is needed as long queues of traffic can develop. Accommodation is very hard to find and prices increase by 20-30%. It can also become littered and polluted, especially on the islands. Robbery may be a problem, but if you take care and use common sense the risk is minimal. Camping on the islands in Parque Nacional Mochima is not advisable.

Around the park Starting east from Puerto La Cruz is the Costa Azul, with the islands of the Parque Nacional Mochima offshore. Highway 9 follows the shore for much of the 85 km to Cumaná. The road is spectacular but if driving take great care between Playa Colorada and Cumaná. It passes the 'paradise-like' beaches of **Conoma** and **Conomita**. Further along is **Playa Arapito** (*posada*, **D-E**, restaurant, parking extra). Here boats can be hired to **La Piscina**, a beautiful coral reef near some small islands, for good snorkelling (with lots of dolphins); US$15 per boat.

Playa Colorada is a popular beach (Km 32) with beautiful red sands and palm trees (take a *por puesto* from corner of terminal in Puerto La Cruz, US$1). Nearby are **Playa Vallecito** (camping free, security guard, car US$1.50, bar with good food and bottled water on sale, plenty of palm trees for slinging a hammock) and **Playa Santa Cruz**. At **Playa Los Hicacos** is a lovely coral reef. **Note** Robberies have been reported on the empty beach at the west end of Playa Colorada.

In Sucre State 40 km from Puerto La Cruz is **Santa Fe** (*Phone code: 0293*), larger and noisier than Mochima, but a good place to relax. The attractive beach is cleaned daily. It has a market on Saturday. Jeep, boat or diving tours available. Fishermen offer trips but their prices are usually high. Boat trips to Playas Colorada or Blanca cost US$23 per person; better to hire your own boat for half the price, or hitch down the road to Colorada.

The little village of **Mochima** beyond Santa Fe, is 4 km off the main road (hitching difficult). It's busy at weekends but almost deserted through the week. The sea is dirty near the town. Boats take tourists to nearby beaches, such as Playa Marita and Playa Blanca (excellent snorkelling, take own equipment). Both have restaurants, but bring food and water to be safe. Boats to the islands cost US$14-18 (up to six people), depending on distance, eg **Semilla Tours** on the main street. Arrange with the boatman what time he will collect you. The tourist office arranges six hour, four-island trips with snorkelling and swimming, US$16. Canoeing trips are available and walks on local trails and to caves (ask for information, eg from Carlos Hernández, or Rodolfo Plaza – see Diving, below).

Parque Nacional Mochima listings

For Sleeping and Eating price codes and other relevant information, see Essentials, pages 38-40.

Sleeping

Parque Nacional Mochima *p1635*

Playa Colorada

A Sunset Inn, Av Principal, T0416- 887 8156. Clean, comfortable, pool, a/c, hot water.

D Carmita, Apdo 46/7, on road from beach to village. Excellent breakfast included, very helpful German-speaking owner. Highly recommended.

E Posada Edgar Lemus, off Av Principal, T0416-795 0574. Very clean, laundry, excellent food. Highly recommended.

E Villa Nirvana, 6-min walk uphill from beach, opposite *Jaly*, run by Sra Rita who is Swiss, T808 7844. Rooms with fan or a/c, also mini-apartments with kitchen for 2-6 people, hot water, kitchen facilities, English, French and German spoken, book exchange, laundry, breakfast extra.

E Quinta Jaly, C Marchán, T808 3246/0416-681 8113. A/c, hot water, very quiet, also one bungalow sleeps 6, family atmosphere, English and French spoken, use of kitchen, laundry facilities, good breakfast extra, multilingual library. Recommended.

Santa Fe

C Café del Mar, first hotel on beach, T231 0009, rogelioalcaraz@hotmail.com. A/c or cheaper with fan, good restaurant. Rogelio Alcaraz speaks English and Italian, arranges tours to islands.

C La Sierra Inn, near *Café del Mar*, T642 3802. A/c, self-contained garden suite with fridge and cooker, run by Sr José Vivas, English spoken, helpful, tours to islands, recommended.

C Siete Delfines, on beach, T808 8064/T0416-317 9290, lossietedelfinessantafe@hotmail.com. Cheaper without breakfast, safe, fan, bar, good meals in restaurant, owner speaks English.

D Bahía del Mar, T231 0073/T0426-481 7242. Pleasant rooms with a/c or fan, upstairs rooms have a cool breeze, owners María and Juan speak French and some English.

D Cochaima, on beach, T642 07828. Run by Margot, noisy, popular, a/c or fan, safe. Recommended.

D Petit Jardin, behind **Cochaima**, T231 0036/T0416-387 5093. A/c, hot water, fan, kitchen, pool, helpful.

D Playa Santa Fe Resort and Dive Center, T808 8249/T0426-620 7133, stafedive@cantv.net. Renovated posada with rooms and suites, laundry service, owner Howard Rankell speaks English, can arrange transport to beaches, kitchen.

E Las Palmeras, T231 0008/T0426-884 0753. Behind **Cochaima**, fan, room for 5 with fridge and cooker. Price negotiable, ask about light work in exchange for longer stays. English, German, Italian and Portuguese spoken

Mochima

Various apartments available for larger groups, look for signs.

A Posada Gaby, at end of road with its own pier next to sea, T431 0842/0414-773 1104. A/c or fan, breakfast available, lovely place.

C Posada Mochimero, on main street in front of *Restaurant Mochimero*, T0414-773 8782. A/c or fan, rooms with bath.

C Villa Vicenta, Av Principal, T414 0868. Basic rooms with cold water and larger rooms with balcony, also cold water, a/c, dining room, owner Otilio is helpful.

C Posada Doña Cruz, T416 6114. A/c, cable TV. Run by José Cruz, family also rents rooms at **Posada Mama Cruz** on the plaza with a/c, cable TV, living room.

Eating

Parque Nacional Mochima *p1635*

Playa Colorada

Daniel's Barraca, at east end of the beach, is good for cheap food.

Santa Fe

Club Naútico, fish and Venezuelan dishes, open for lunch and dinner.

Los Molinos (Julios), open from 0800, beach bar serves sandwiches, hamburgers and cocktails.

Mochima

El Mochimero, on waterfront 5 mins from jetty. Highly recommended for lunch and dinner.

Il Forno de Mochima, main street. Run by Roberto Iorio, for those who would like a change from seafood, homemade pastas and pizza.

Puerto Viejo, on the plaza. Good food, if a bit pricey, good views.

Activities and tours

Parque Nacional Mochima *p1635*

Mochima

Diving **Francisco García**, runs a diving school and shop (*Aquatics Diving Center*, T0426-581 0434/0414-777 4894), C La Marina at Plaza Apolinar. Equipment hire, courses, trips.

Rodolfo Plaza runs a diving school (*La Posada de los Buzos*, T416 0856/T0424-807 7647, mochima rafting@hotmail.com) and hires equipment, also walking, rafting, kayaking and canoeing trips; contact him in Caracas (Los Palos Grandes, Av Andrés Bello entre 3a y 4a transversal, T0212-961 2531).

Transport

Parque Nacional Mochima *p1635*

Santa Fe

Getting there from **Cumaná**, take *por puesto* 1 block down from the Redonda del Indio, along Av Perimetral, US$4.65. It may be difficult to get a bus from **Puerto La Cruz** to stop at Santa Fe, take a *por puesto* (depart from terminal, US$4.60, 1 hr), or taxi, US$25 including wait.

Mochima

Bus From **Cumaná** to Mochima take a bus from outside the terminal and ask to be let off at the street where the transport goes to Mochima, US$2.40; change here to crowded bus or jeep (US$0.50). No buses between Santa Fe and Mochima, take a *por puesto*, bargain hard on the price, US$11-15 is reasonable. Bus to Cumaná, 1400, US$1.20.

Cumaná → *Phone code: 0293. Colour map 2, A1. Population: 343,500.*

Cumaná was founded in 1521 to exploit the nearby pearl fisheries. It straddles both banks of the Río Manzanares. Because of a succession of devastating earthquakes (the last in 1997), only a few historic sites remain. Cumaná is a charming place with its mixture of old and new, but the port area (1½ km from the centre) is not safe at night. Main festivals are 22 January, Santa Inés, a pre-Lenten carnival throughout the state of Sucre and 2 November, the Santos y Fideles Difuntos festival at El Tacal.

A long public beach, **San Luis**, is a short bus ride from the centre of town; take the 'San Luis/Los Chaimas' bus. The least spoilt part is the end by the *Hotel Los Bordones*.

The **Castillo de San Antonio de la Eminencia** (1686) has 16 mounted cannons, a drawbridge and dungeons from which there are said to be underground tunnels leading to the Santa Inés church. Restored in 1975, it is flood-lit at night (but don't go there after dark, it's not safe). The **Castillo de Santa María de la Cabeza** (1669) is a rectangular fortress with a panoramic view of San Antonio and the elegant homes below. **Convento de San Francisco**, the original Capuchin mission of 1514, was the first school on the continent; its remains are on the Plaza Badaracco Bermúdez facing the beach. The **Church of Santa Inés** (1637) was the base of the Franciscan missionaries; earthquakes have caused it to be rebuilt five times. A tiny 400-year-old statue of the Virgen de Candelaria is in the garden. The **home of Andrés Eloy Blanco** (1896-1955) ⓘ *0800-1200, 1430-1730, free,* one of Venezuela's greatest poets and politicians, on Plaza Bolívar, has been nicely restored to its turn-of-the-century elegance. On the opposite side of the plaza is **La Gobernación** around a courtyard lined by cannon from Santa María de la Cabeza; note the gargoyles and other colonial features. There are markets selling handicrafts and food on both sides of the river.

The **Museo Gran Mariscal de Ayacucho** ⓘ *Consejo Municipal in Parque Ayacucho, Tue-Fri 0845-1130, 1545-1830; free tours,* commemorates the battle of Ayacucho: with portraits, relics and letters of Bolívar and José Antonio Sucre (Bolívar's first lieutenant). **Museo del Mar** ⓘ *Av Universidad with Av Industrial, Tue-Sun 0830-1130, 1500-1800, US$0.75, getting there: take San Luis minibus from the cathedral,* has exhibits of tropical marine life, at the old airport.

For information contact **Dirección de Turismo** ⓘ *C Sucre 49, T808 7769/T0414-189 2071, edosucre.gov.ve/turismo/ contenido-turismo.htm, open mornings only*. This office is very helpful, English spoken. See also www.sucreturistico.com.

Cumaná listings

For Sleeping and Eating price codes and other relevant information, see Essentials, pages 38-40.

Sleeping

Cumaná *p1637, map below*

A Nueva Toledo Suites, end of Av Universidad, close to San Luis beach, T494 9311, www.nuevatoledo.com. A/c, hot water, TV, pool, beach bar, good value all-inclusive deals.

A Los Bordones, at end of Av Universidad on the beach, T400 0350, www.losbordones.com. A/c, pool, restaurant, another hotel with all-inclusive options.

C Bubulina's, Callejón Santa Inés, half a block west of Santa Inés church, T431 4025, bubulinas10@hotmail.com. In the historic centre, beautifully restored colonial building, a/c, TV, hot water, good service, German spoken.

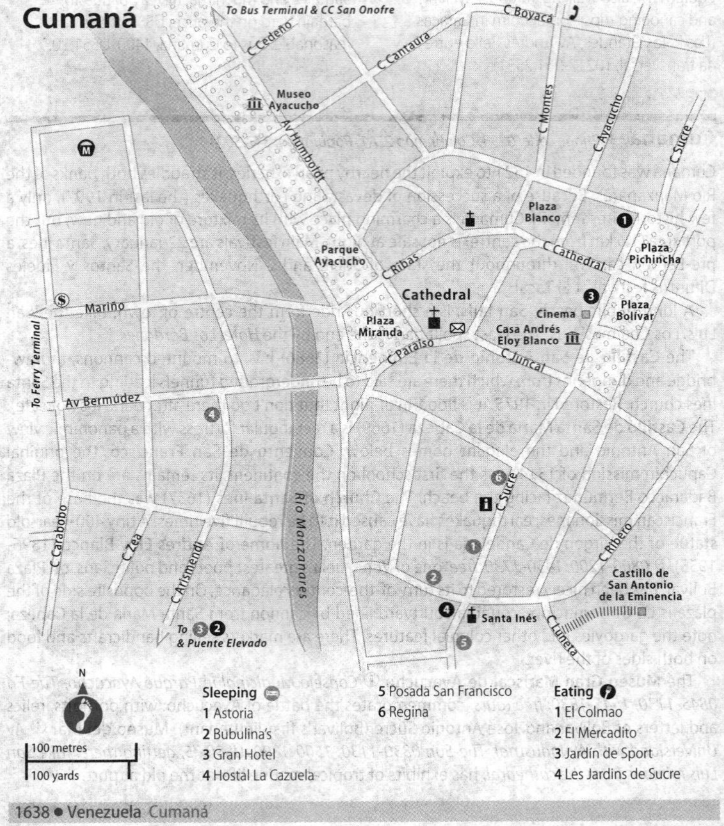

C Gran Hotel, Av Universidad near San Luis beach, T451 0671. A/c, pool, restaurant, includes breakfast.
C Posada San Francisco, C Sucre 16, near Santa Inés, T431 3926. Renovated colonial house, courtyard, spacious rooms, hot water, a/c (cheaper with fan), very helpful, bar, restaurant. Recommended.
C Regina, Arismendi y Av Bermúdez, T432 2581. Hot water, a/c, restaurant, helpful.
C-D Hostal La Cazuela, Sucre 63, T432 1401/T0416-090 1388, narart@hotmail.com. A/c, cable TV, pleasant, personable.
D Astoria, Sucre, T433 2708. A/c, shower, basic, bar, restaurant with good food cooked to order.

Eating

Cumaná *p1637, map p1638*
All central restaurants close Sun lunchtime
Les Jardins de Sucre, Sucre 27, in front of the Santa Inés church. French food, good service, outdoor seating. Recommended.
El Colmao on Plaza Pichincha, C Sucre. Very good fish, charming service, karaoke.
Ali Baba, Av Bermúdez near corner of C Castellón. Excellent middle eastern food. Recommended.
Jardín de Sport, Plaza Bolívar. Outdoor café, good food, noisy atmosphere. Recommended.
El Mercadito at Puente Elevado. For excellent cheap lunches, fish and seafood.
Mi Jardín, on C Humboldt. Cheap, tasty roast chicken.

Activities and tours

Cumaná *p1637, map p1638*
Rosa Theron, T432 5502, rositatheron@sucreturistico.com offers tours. **Posadas San Francisco** and **Bubulina's** can also help arrange local tours, sailing, diving.

Transport

Cumaná *p1637, map p1638*
Bus Terminal 3 km northwest of the centre on Av Las Palomas, just before the junction with the peripheral road. Local bus into centre US$0.45, taxi US$3.50. *Por puesto* to **Puerto La Cruz**, US$9.30, bus US$4.65, 1½ hrs. To **Güiria**, US$11.60, **Expresos Los Llanos** once a day, *por puesto* US$14 (6-7 hrs), beware of overcharging, often stop in Irapa. To **Carúpano**, US$4.65, 2-3 hrs. To **Caripe**, you have to go to **Santa María**, south of Cariaco, and change to *por puesto* there. To **Caracas**, US$14 (7-8 hrs), frequent service; many daily to **Ciudad Guayana** and **Ciudad Bolívar**, US$16.30 and 14 respectively. **Caribe** runs all the way to the border with Brazil, US$16.30. Also to Maturín.
Ferry For Ferries to **Araya Peninsula** and **Isla Margarita**, see below and page 1652.

Directory

Cumaná *p1637, map p1638*
Banks See also Money, page 1566. For cash advance on Mastercard **Banco Mercantil**, Av Bermúdez. ATM and cash advance on Visa and Mastercard. Also **Banco Venezuela**, at Mariño y Rojas and **Banesco** at Mariño y Carabobo. **Corp Banca**, Av Bermúdez y Av Perimetral, edif Don Jesús No 21. Amex TCs changed at good rates, no commission. **Internet** Centro de Comunicaciones CANTV, CC San Onofre at the end of Av Humboldt. **Comiti**, Edif Arismendi p 2, Av Arismendi. Two internet cafes on C Cedral near Plaza Bolívar. **Post offices** Ipostel, next to Cathedral on C Paraíso. **Telephones** CANTV, on C Montés con Boyacá, 2 blocks from Plaza Blanco.

Araya to Paria

This section is bounded by two peninsulas, Araya, which is an area of desert landscapes and pink salt lakes, and Paria, a finger of land stretching out to the most easterly point on Venezuela's Caribbean coast and a place of peaceful, coastal towns, beaches and forest. The eastern mountains, rising to 2,000 m at their highest point, receive abundant rainfall in their tropical forest.

Araya Peninsula

The main settlement is Araya which has an airport and a ferry dock. The major sight is the Fortaleza de Santiago de León, built by Spain to protect the salt mines, but of which very little now remains. Construction began in 1622 and it took 47 years to complete. Entry is free, but the only facilities are a refreshment stand and a picnic area. Today the mines are exploited by a state- owned corporation, ENSAL. Windsurfing is excellent, but only for the experienced.

Carúpano ➔ *Phone code: 0294. Colour map 2, A1. Population: 147,000.*

This is a colonial town dating back to 1647, from which 70% of Venezuela's cocoa is shipped. The area around Plaza Santa Rosa has been declared a national and international heritage site by UNESCO. Buildings include the **Museo Histórico**, containing a comprehensive database on the city, and the **Iglesia Santa Rosa**. The **Casa del Cable** ⓘ *T331 3847/0414-780 0060, merle@telcel.net.ve, www.fundacionthomasmerle.org.ve*, location of the first telecommunications link with Europe, is the headquarters of the Fundación Thomas Merle, run by Wilfried Merle, who has been instrumental in setting up ecotourism and economic development projects in the Paria Peninsula. Carúpano is famous throughout Venezuela as the last place still celebrating a traditional pre-Lenten Carnival: days of dancing, rum drinking, with masked women in black (*negritas*). Book well ahead for places to stay at this time (February). Other local festivals are 3 May, Velorios de la Cruz (street dances); 15 August, Asunción de la Virgen. On the outskirts of Carúpano is **Playa Copey** (ask the *por puesto*/ bus to drop you at Playa Copey if arriving from Cumaná or other westerly points, or take a taxi from town, US$7). See www.carupano.org.

Caripe ➔ *Phone code: 0292. Population: 23,880.*

A paved road runs inland from Carúpano to Caripe via Cariaco and Santa María, two hours. Caripe is an attractive town set in gorgeous mountain scenery. There is a lively daily market. It is 12 km from the famous Cueva del Guácharo and a good place to escape from the beaches. It's especially good for walking and biking. At San Francisco, on the Maturín-Cumaná road (212 km, all paved but twisty; beautiful tropical mountain scenery), is a branch road running 22½ km northeast to Caripe. *Feria de las Flores* is on 2-12 August and *NS del Pilar* is 10-12 October. See http://caripe.net. To get to Caripe from Caracas you must go to **Maturín**, the capital of Monagas state (*Phone code: 0291. Colour map 2, A1, relatively expensive accommodation*), then take a *por puesto*. Alternatively go to Cumaná and then to Santa María for *por puesto* services.

Cueva del Guácharo ➔

ⓘ *0800-1600, US$3.50 with compulsory guide in Spanish, speak some English and German. Leave backpacks at the ticket office, cameras allowed but ask before using flash, to go further into the caves permits from Inparques in Caracas are needed.*

This remarkable cave was discovered by Humboldt and has since been penetrated 10½ km along a small, crystal-clear stream. In the first caves live around 18,000 *guácharos* (oil birds) with an in-built radar system for sightless flight. Their presence supports a variety of wildlife in the cave: blind mice, fish and crabs in the stream, yellow-green plants, crickets and ants. For two hours at dusk (about 1900) the birds pour out of the cave's mouth. Through a very narrow entrance is the *Cueva del Silencio* (Cave of Silence). About 2 km in is the *Pozo del Viento* (Well of the Wind).

Wear old clothes, stout shoes and be prepared to get wet. In the wet season it can be a bit slippery; tours in the cave may be closed in August-September because of rising water level. There is a caving museum with good cafeteria. Opposite the road is a paved path to **Salto Paila**, a 25 m waterfall, about 30 minutes' walk, guides available for US$4.65. A beautiful path, built by Inparqes, starts at the caving museum, with some nice shelters for picnics. Camping is allowed by the cave for US$2.30, or you can sleep without a tent under the roof by the café for free.

Between Cariaco and Casanay, **Las Aguas de Moisés** ⓘ *open 0800-1700, US$11.45, half price for seniors and children, T0414-780 2013, www.lasaguasdemoises.com, ask to be let off from bus or por puesto on Cariaco-Carúpano route* is a tourist park containing eleven large thermal pools. The waters are said to be curative and there are lots of sporting and other activities. Camping (**E**) is available, or **Hotel San Remo Suites** (T555 1036).

Paria Peninsula

Río Caribe This lovely fishing village (*Phone code: 0294; Population: 51,100; 20 km E of Carúpano*) used to be a major cacao-exporting port. It is a good jumping-off point for the beautiful beaches of **Playa Medina** (in an old coconut plantation, 25 km east) and Pui Puy, both famous for their crystal-clear water and golden sands. Playa Medina is safe, has shade for rent and stalls selling food and drink; it is crowded at weekends and holidays. Cabins at the beach are very expensive (**AL-A** per person). To get to Playa Medina, take a taxi, US$35 return trip per car, US$40 to Pui Puy. There are *camionetas* which go quite close to Medina and one which departs from opposite petrol station at exit to village (US$1, one hour), which drops you at entrance to beaches, but it's two hours' walk from there (further to Pui Puy – take great care, armed robberies have been reported). Surfing at Playas Pui Puy and Querepare; visit **Querepare** between May and August to watch sea turtles laying their eggs. Ask at **Posada Shalimar** (see Sleeping, below) about boat trips to Santa Isabel, a small village near a waterfall (stay at **C Posada de Cucha**). There is a Banco Venezuela in Río Caribe for exchange.

Further east is the delightful village of **San Juan de las Galdonas** and some great beaches. Near Chacaracual, 15 minutes' drive from Río Caribe is **Paria Shakti** *T611 8767/T0416-517 9676*, a 4-acre cacao plantation and holistic health centre that offers factory tours and massages. Next door, visit **Aguasana**, a *hacienda* with mineral-rich hot springs and mud pools (see Sleeping, below). Recommended guide: Eli Monroy (T0426-985 7670 or through **Posada Shalimar**). Near Bohordal is **Hacienda Rio de Agua**, a buffalo ranch available for day visits and milk factory tours; many species of birds can be seen (also see Sleeping). Day trips are also available to **Caño de Ajíes** with a visit a waterfall and the estuary which flows into the Golfo de Paria; you can see crocodiles, birds and snakes. It is part of the Parque Nacional Turuépano. A trip by car and boat costs US$130.

Güiria At Bohordal, the paved road from Río Caribe across the mountains meets Route 9, which continues to the pleasant town of Irapa (*Population: 23,710; hotels, bus connections*). The paved highway continues 42 km to Güiria (*Phone code: 0294; Colour map 2, A2; Population: 36,860*), a friendly, peaceful town and a badly littered beach. Feria de la Pesca, 14 July. Gasoline is available.

Macuro A quiet town on the tip of the Peninsula, Macuro (*Population: 1,500*) is accessible by boat (two hours from Güiria) and by a new road from Güiria (20 km paved, the remainder passable by 4WD). It was around here Columbus made the first recorded European landing on the continent on 5 August 1498. Locals like to believe the landing took place at Macuro, and the town's official new name is Puerto Colón. A big party is held here every year on 12 October to mark the official 'discovery' of America. Restaurants only open at weekends (good food at Sra Mercedes, on C Carabobo, round corner from *Posada Beatriz*, blue house). There are also a few basic shops and a pharmacy. The boat to Güiria leaves at 0500, arrive early, US$5 per person.

The beach is unattractive but the coast on the north side of the peninsula is truly wonderful; crystal-clear water and dazzling sands backed by dense jungle. A highly recommended trip for the adventurous is the hike to **Uquire** and **Don Pedro** on the north coast; 4-6 hours' walk, places to hang a hammock or pitch a tent. In Uquire ask for Nestor Mata, the Inparques guard, very helpful. **Note** This part of the peninsula is a national park; you need a permit from Inparques in Caracas.

Araya to Paria listings

For Sleeping and Eating price codes and other relevant information, see Essentials, pages 38-40.

Sleeping

Araya *p1640*

D Araya Mar, El Castillo, T437 1382/T0414-777 3682. A/c, hot water, good restaurant, arranges car and boat tours to the Salinas and around Araya, parking. Good restaurant serves Venezuelan food. Recommended.

D Araya's Wind, beside the Fortaleza in front of beach, T0414-189 0717. A/c, some rooms with bath, cold water, cable TV.

D Lagunasal, C El Progreso ½ block from El Timonel de Fabi, T437 1290/T0414-778 2533. New posada, no sign as yet, a/c, cable TV.

D Posada Helen, behind *Araya's Wind*, T437 1101/T0414- 189 3867. A/c, cold water, cable TV.

Carúpano *p1640*

AL Hotel Euro Caribe Internacional, Av Perimetral Rómulo Gallegos, T331 3911. A/c, cable TV, hot water, breakfast included, parking, good Italian restaurant.

B La Colina, Av Rómulo Gallegos 33, behind *Hotel Victoria*, T332 2915. A/c, cable TV, hot water, includes breakfast, restaurant and bar, beautiful view. Recommended.

C Lilma, Av Independencia, 3 blocks from Plaza Colón, T331 1361, hotellilma@hotmail.com. A/c, hot water, TV, restaurant, *tasca*, cinema.

C Paradise, Av Independencia, T331 1007/T0416-387 7576. A/c, cable TV, hot water.

C San Francisco, Av Juncal 87A y Las Margaritas, T331 1074. A/c, no hot water, TV, parking, restaurant, *tasca*.

C Victoria, Av Perimetral Rómulo Gallegos, T331 1554, hotelvictoria@hotmail.com. Safe but basic, a/c, hot water.

D Bologna, Av Independencia, 1 block from Plaza Santa Rosa, T331 1241. Basic but clean, a/c.

D El Centro, Carabobo 71, close to Iglesia Santa Catalina, T331 3673. A/c, cable TV.

Playa Copey

B Posada Casa Blanca, Av Principal, 5 mins from *Posada Nena*, T331 6896, www.posadacasablanca.com. A/c, hot water, safe, good family atmosphere, private stretch of beach illuminated at night, Spanish restaurant, German spoken, discounts for long stays.

B Posada Nena, 1 block from the beach, T331 7297, www.posadanena.de. A/c, hot water, games room, good restaurant, public phone, good service, German spoken, owner Volker Alsen offers day trips to Cueva del Guácharo, Mochima, Medina and other Venezuelan destinations. Recommended.

Caripe *p1640*

B Finca Agroturística Campo Claro, at Teresén, T555 1013/0414 770 8043 (mob), www.haciendacampoclaro.com. Cabins for 4-15 people with cooking facilities and hot water, also rooms (**C**), restaurant for residents, horse riding.

B Samán, Enrique Chaumer 29, T545 1183, www.hotelsaman.com. Also has more expensive suites, comfortable, pool, parking, not so welcoming to backpackers.

E Caripe Plaza, opposite church on Plaza Bolívar, T744 9185. Hot water, cable TV, parking.

E La Perla, Av Enrique Chaumer 118, 5 mins from centre, T0424-921 1007. Very basic.

Río Caribe *p1641*

As well as those listed, there are other *posadas* and private, unmarked pensions; ask around.

B Posada Caribana, Av Bermúdez 25, T646 1242. Beautifully restored colonial house, tastefully decorated, a/c or fan, with breakfast, restaurant, bar, excursions. Ask about *posada* at Playa Uva.

C La Posada de Arlet, 24 de Julio 22, T/F646 1290. Price includes breakfast, a/c, laundry service, English and German spoken, bar, arranges day trips to local beaches. Recommended.

C Posada de Angel, 2 km away from the beach at **Playa Medina**, T0414-100 7247. Nice place, private bathrooms, fan, mosquito netting on windows.
C Posada Shalimar, Av Bermúdez 54, T646 1135, www.posada-shalimar.com. Francisco González speaks English, very helpful, can arrange tours to and provide information about local beaches and other areas. Beautiful rooms situated around pool have a/c, cable TV. Recommended.
E Pensión Papagayo, 14 de Febrero, 1 block from police station, opposite *liceo*, T646 1868. Charming house and garden, a/c, shared bath with hot water (single sex), use of kitchen, nice atmosphere, owner Cristina Castillo.

San Juan de las Galdonas

C pp **Habitat Paria**, T511 9571. With breakfast and supper, huge, splendid, zodiac theme, fan, bar/restaurant, terraces, garden. The posada is right behind Barlovento beach on the right hand side of San Juan. Can arrange boat tours. Recommended.
C Posada Playa Galdonas, T889 1892. 4-star, overlooking the main beach, a/c, hot water, bar/restaurant, swimming pool, English and French spoken, arranges boat tours to Santa Isabel and beaches.
C Posada Las Tres Carabelas, T0416-894 0914 (mob), carabelas3@hotmail.com. Fans and mosquito nets, restaurant, wonderful view, owner Javier knowledgeable about local area. Ask about new *posada* at Guariquen, as yet untouched by tourism.

Outside Río Caribe

C Hato Río de Agua, T332 0527. Rustic cabins with fans, private bathrooms, restaurant on a buffalo ranch (see above), price includes breakfast and tours of dairy factory.
D Hacienda Posada Aguasana, T416 2944/ T0414-304 5687, www.posadaaguasana.com. Attractive rooms with fans near hot springs, **B** with meals.

Güiria *p1641*

C **Timón de Máximo**, C Bideau, 2 blocks from plaza, T982 1535. A/c, cable TV, fridge, good créole restaurant. Recommended.
C **Vista Mar**, Valdez y Trincheras, T982 1055. A/c, hot water, fridge, cable TV, restaurant.
D Plaza, esq Plaza Bolívar, T982 0022. Basic, restaurant, luggage store, a/c.

Macuro *p1641*

E Posada Beatriz, C Mariño y Carabobo. Basic, clean, with bath, fan.

Eating

Araya *p1640*

Eat early as most places close before 2000. Hamburger stalls around the dock and 2 *panaderías*.
ΨΨ **El Timonel de Fabi**. *Tasca* across from dock, Venezuelan food, karaoke.
Ψ **Las Churuatas de Miguel**, on the beach near dock. Fish and typical food.
Ψ **Eugenía**, in front of *Posada Helen*. For good value meals.

Carúpano *p1640*

ΨΨ-Ψ **El Fogón de La Petaca**, Av Perimetral on the seafront. Traditional Venezuelan dishes, fish.
ΨΨ-Ψ **La Madriguera**, Av Perimetral Rómulo Gallegos, in Hotel Eurocaribe. Good Italian food, some vegetarian dishes, Italian and English spoken.
Ψ **Bam Bam**, kiosk at the end of Plaza Miranda, close to seafront. Tasty hotdogs and hamburgers.
Ψ **La Flor de Oriente**, Av Libertad y Victoria, 4 blocks from Plaza Colón. Open from 0800, arepas, fruit juice and main meals, good, large portions, good, food, reasonable prices, very busy at lunchtime.
Ψ **El Oasis**, Juncal in front of Plaza Bolívar. Open from 1700, best Arabic food in Carúpano.
Other options include the **food stalls** in the market, especially the one next to the car park, and the *empanadas* in the Plaza Santa Rosa.

Caripe *p1640*

ΨΨ **Tasca Mogambo**, next to **Hotel Saman**. Good, local food.
ΨΨ **La Trattoria**, C Cabello. Wide variety of good food, popular with locals and tourists.

Río Caribe *p1641*

ΨΨ **Mi Cocina**, on the road parallel to Av Bermúdez, 3 mins' walk from Plaza Bolívar. Very good food, large portions.
ΨΨ **Mis Manos Benditos**, near the beach.

Güiria *p1641*
Everywhere is closed Sun, except for kiosks on Plaza Bolívar. Restaurants include:
El Limón, C Trinchera near C Concepcion, good value, outdoor seating.
El Milagro, corner of Plaza Bolívar. OK.
Rincón Güireño, corner of Plaza Sucre. Good for breakfast (also rents rooms, **D**).

Activities and tours

Carúpano *p1640*
Corpomedina, T331 5241, F331 3021, at the airport, associated with Fundación Thomas Merle (see Casa del Cable, page 1640), reservations for cabins at Medina or Pui Puy beach: at Medina **LL-AL** depending on numbers, including meals, but not alcoholic drinks or transport; at Pui Puy **A-B**, including breakfast. Transport from the airport to Medina and Pui Puy can be arranged.
Mar y Luna, T/F332 2668, louisa@cantv.net. Offer day trips to Medina, Pui Puy, Caripe, El Pilar, Los Pozos, specialist surfing and diving packages, walking and hiking in the Paria Peninsula, reconfirmation of international flights, reservations for *posadas*, reception of fax and email, information and advice, English, French, Portuguese and a little Italian spoken, very helpful.

Macuro *p1641*
A highly recommended **guide** is Eduardo Rothe, who put together, and lives at, the Museo de Macuro on Calle Bolívar, 1 block from *Posada Beatriz*. He'll take you on walking tours to the north coast, US$4-7 pp per day, or boat trips (US$40 per boat), or fishing trips (US$30 pp per day, including mangroves).

Transport

Araya *p1640*
Ferry Cumaná-Araya ferry with **Naviarca** car ferry, T/F0293-433 5577, www.grancacique.com.ve, shuttles back and forth 24 hrs a day, US$1.40 pp, US$14-18 per car. At weekends it usually makes only 1 trip each way. To get to ferry terminal take taxi in Cumaná, US$3.50 (avoid walking; it can be dangerous). Alternatively, take a *tapadito* (passeger ferry in a converted fishing boat, leave when full, crowded, stuffy, US$1.15) to Manicuare and *camioneta* from there to Araya (15 mins). Return ferries from Araya depart from main wharf at end of Av Bermúdez. Ferries to **Isla de Margarita**, *tapaditos* depart from **Chacopata** (1 hr, US$10.50 one way). To get to Chacopata from Carúpano, take a *por puesto* at the stop diagonal to the market entrance (where the fish is unloaded), US$4.65, 1½ hrs.

Carúpano *p1640*
Air The airport is 15 mins' walk from the centre, US$3.50 by taxi. Check with **Rutaca** (T0212-355 1838), which occasionally offers flights to Caracas through Porlamar.
Bus To **Caracas**, US$16.30-19.75, 9 hrs, to Terminal de Oriente. To **Maracay, Valencia**, US$20, 10 hrs. For other destinations such as **Cumaná**, US$4.65, 2 hrs, **Puerto La Cruz**, US$7, 4 hrs (Mochima/Santa Fé), **Güiria**, US$7, 3 hrs *por puestos* are a better option. They run more frequently and make fewer stops. Buses do not go from Carúpano to Caripe, you have to take a *por puesto* to **Cariaco**, US$2.50, then another to **Santa María**, US$3.50, then another to Caripe, US$3.

Caripe *p1640*
Bus Terminal 1 block south of main plaza. For **Carúpano**, take *por puestos* to Santa María and Cariaco (see above), similarly for **Río Caribe** and **Las Aguas de Moisés**. To get to **Cumaná**, go to Santa María and catch transport from there. Bus to **Maturín** several daily, 2½ hrs, US$6; Maturín-**Caracas** costs US$14-20 (bus cama), 7½ hrs. *Por puestos* run from Maturín to Ciudad Bolívar.

Cueva del Guácharo *p1640*
Bus Frequent from **Caripe** to the caves. If staying in Caripe, take a *por puesto* (a jeep marked Santa María-Muelle), at 0800, see the caves and waterfall and catch the Cumaná bus which goes past the caves between 1200 and 1230. Taxis from Caripe US$3.50, hitching possible. *Por puesto* from Cumaná US$11.60, 2 hrs. Private tours can be organized from Cumaná for about US$21 per person, with guide.

Río Caribe and San Juan de las Galdonas *p1641*
Bus Direct from **Caracas** (Terminal del Oriente) to Río Caribe with **Cruceros Oriente Sur**, 10 hrs, and from **Maturín** with **Expresos Maturín**.

Por puesto **Carúpano**-Río Caribe, US$2.80, or taxi US$9.30. Buses depart Río Caribe from the other Plaza Bolívar, 7 blocks up from pier. Jeep Carúpano-San Juan de las Galdonas 1100, 1½ hrs; *camioneta* from Río Caribe from stop near petrol station, 0600 till 1300, US$3.50.

Güiria *p1641*
Bus Depart Plaza Sucre, at top end of C Bolívar: **Expresos Maturín** to **Maturín** (0400, US$10.50, 6 hrs), **Caripito**, **San Félix**, **Cumaná** (*por puesto*, US$9.30), Puerto La Cruz and **Caracas**; also **Expresos Los Llanos** (recommended).
Ferry To **Macuro**: daily 1100-1200 from the Playita, US$4-7, return 0500, 2 hrs.
To **Trinidad** A ferry leaves every Wed at 1700 for Chaguaramas, Trinidad (leaves Trinidad at 0900, Wed), 3½ hrs, US$92 one way (plus tax), operated by **Pier 1 Cruises**. There is a US$23 exit tax from Venezuela (US$13 from Trinidad). Talk to Siciliano Bottini at the *Agencia Naviera* for other ships to Trinidad. Don't take any old boat that's going; however safe it may appear, you may come under suspicion for drug running.

Directory

Carúpano *p1640*
Banks It is not easy to change foreign currency in Carúpano. American Express TCs can be changed until 1400 at **Corp Banca**, C Güiria y C Carabobo. Cash advance on Visa or Mastercard at **Banco Caribe**, Av Independencia, 4 blocks from Plaza Santa Rosa. ATMs are unreliable for European cards. Good rate at the casino on the waterfront near the bus station. It may be possible to change dollars in *Hotels Lilma, San Francisco* or *Victoria*, but rates are not good.
Internet Centro de Comunicaciones CANTV, C Juncal, opposite *Hotel San Francisco*, 0800-2000. **Cybercafé**, C Las Margaritas entre Juncal y Carabobo, same hours. **Ebenezer**, CC Sahara, C San Félix. **Post offices and telephones** Both **Ipostel** and **CANTV** are at the end of Carabobo, 1 block up from Plaza Santa Rosa.

Güiria *p1641*
Useful services Immigration: visas can't be arranged in Güiria, should you need one; maximum length of stay 14 days (but check). For more than 14 days, get visa in Caracas. Remember to get exit stamp before leaving Venezuela. Officially, to enter Trinidad and Tobago you need a ticket to your home country, but a return to Venezuela is usually enough.

Isla de Margarita → *Colour map 2, A1*

Margarita is the country's main Caribbean holiday destination and is popular with both Venezuelans and foreign tourists. The island's reputation for picture-postcard, white-sand beaches is well-deserved. Some parts are crowded but there are undeveloped beaches and colonial villages. Porlamar is the most built up and commercial part of the island while Juan Griego and La Restinga are much quieter.

If you book a place to stay in advance, it is possible to enjoy the island even on a budget during high season. If you don't reserve ahead, it is almost impossible to find accommodation for under US$25-30 per person a night. Despite the property boom and the frenetic building on much of the coast and in Porlamar, much of the island has been given over to natural parks. Of these the most striking is the Laguna La Restinga.

The western part, the Peninsula de Macanao, is hotter and more barren, with scrub, sand dunes and marshes. Wild deer, goats and hares roam the interior, but 4WDs are needed to penetrate it. The entrance to the Peninsula de Macanao is a pair of hills known as **Las Tetas de María Guevara**, a national monument covering 1,670 ha. There are mangroves in the **Laguna de las Marites** natural monument, west of Porlamar.

Other parks are **Cerro El Copey**, 7,130 ha, and **Cerro Matasiete y Guayamurí**, 1,672 ha (both reached from La Asunción). The climate is exceptionally good and dry. Roads are good and a bridge links the two parts. Nueva Esparta's population is over 377,700, of whom 85,000 live in Porlamar. The capital is La Asunción.

Ins and outs

Getting there and around There are many national, international and charter flights to Isla de Margarita. There also ferries from La Guaira (Caracas), Puerto La Cruz and Cumaná. Car hire is a good way of getting around (see Directory, below). Women should avoid walking alone at night on the island. ▸▸ *See also Transport, page 1651.*

Information **Isla de Margarita**: The private **Cámara de Turismo** is at Av Virgen del Valle in the Jorge Coll sector of Porlamar, T262 0683. They have free maps and are very helpful. The state **tourism department** can be contacted on T262 2322, www.islamargarita.gob.ve. Travel agencies can also provide a tourist guide to Margarita. *MultiGuía de Margarita* (US$4) is published yearly and is a useful directory of tourist information and can be found in kiosks, *panaderías*, cafés and bookshops. The best map is available from *Corpoven*. See also the websites www.islamargarita.com and www.margaritaonline.com. Many offices close for lunch.

Isla de Margarita

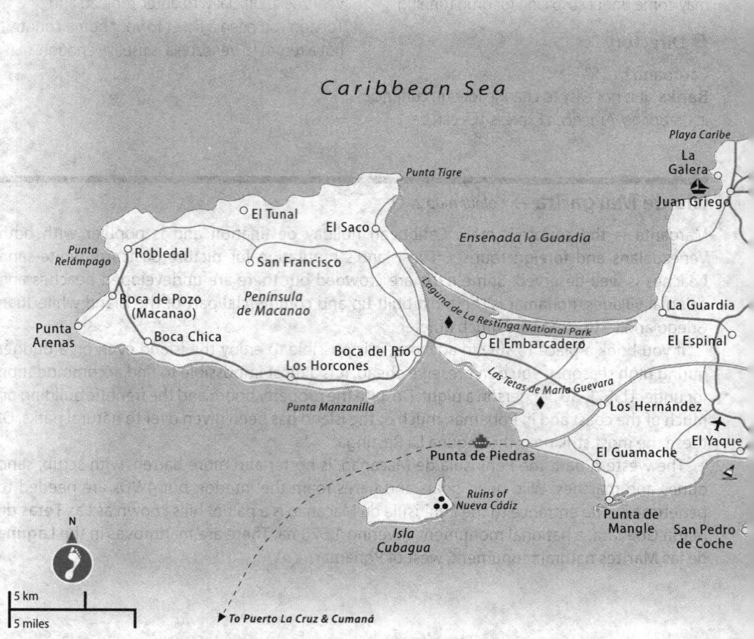

Porlamar ➔ *Phone code: 0295.*

Most of the island's high-rise hotels are at Porlamar which is 20 km from airport and 28 km from Punta de Piedra, where ferries dock. If you're seeking sun and sand, then head for the north coast towns where the beaches tend to be lined with low-rise hotels and thatched restaurants. Porlamar's beaches are nothing special, but it makes up for what it lacks in this department with its shops (see Shopping below). At Igualdad y Díaz is the **Museo de Arte Francisco Narváez**, which has some good displays of the work of this local sculptor. At night everything closes by 2300.

The **Bella Vista** beach is busy but clean and has lots of restaurants lining the seafront. **Playa Concorde** is small, sheltered and tucked by the marina. **Playa Morena** is a long, barren strip of sand for the Costa Azul hotel zone east of the city. **La Caracola** is a popular beach for a young crowd.

Boats go from Punta de Piedra, El Yaque and La Isleta to the **Isla de Coche** (11 km by 6), which has 4,500 inhabitants and one of the richest salt mines in the country (see Transport below). They also go, on hire only, to **Isla de Cubagua**, which is totally deserted, but you can visit the **ruins of Nueva Cádiz** (which have been excavated). Large private yachts and catamarans take tourists on day trips to Coche.

La Asunción ➔ *Population: 27,500.*

The capital of La Asunción located a few kilometres inland from Porlamar. It has several **colonial buildings**, a **cathedral**, and the **fort of Santa Rosa** ⓘ *Mon 0800-1500, the rest of the week 0800-1800*, which features a famous bottle dungeon. There is a **museum** in the Casa Capitular, and a good local **market**, worth browsing for handicrafts. Nearby is the **Cerro Matasiete** historical site, where the defeat of the Spanish on 31 July 1817 led to their evacuation of the island.

Pampatar ➔ *Population: 25,000.*

For a more Venezuelan atmosphere go northeast to Pampatar, which is set around a bay favoured by yachtsmen as a summer anchorage. Pampatar has the island's largest fort, **San Carlos de Borromeo**, which was built in 1662 after the Dutch destroyed the original. It's worth visiting the church of **Cristo del Buen Viaje**, the **Library/Museum** and the **customs house**. Jet skis can be hired on the clean and pretty beach. A fishing boat can be hired for US$20 for 2½ hours, 4-6 passengers; shop around for best price; it's good fun and makes for a worthwhile fishing trip. There is a *casa de cambio* in the Centro Comercial Sambil.

Eastern and northern beaches

Playa Guacuco, reached from La Asunción by a road through the Guayamurí reserve, is a popular local beach with a lot of surf, fairly shallow, palm trees, restaurants and car park; excellent horseriding here or up into the hills,

US$30 for two hours, contact Harry Padrón at the ranch in Agua de Vaca, or phone travel agent on T261 1311. Playa Parguito further up the east coast is best for surfing (strong waves; full public services).

Playa El Agua has 4 km of white sand with many kiosks and shady restaurants. The sea is very rough in winter (dangerous for children), but fairly shallow; beware the strong cross current when you are about waist deep. This beach gets overcrowded at Venezuelan holiday times. The fashionable part is at the south end. The beach is 45 mins by bus from Porlamar (US$0.80). See also www.playaelagua.info.

Manzanillo (*population: 2,000*) is a picturesque bay between the mountains on the northeast point of the island with apartments (**A-B**), beach houses and good places to eat (cheaper than Playa El Agua). Playa Escondida is at the far end. Puerto Fermín/ El Tirano is where Lope de Aguirre, the infamous conquistador, landed in 1561 on his flight from Peru.

The coast road is interesting, with glimpses of the sea and beaches to one side. There are a number of clifftop look-out points. The road improves radically beyond Manzanillo, winding from one beach to the next. **Playa Puerto la Cruz** (wide and windy) adjoins **Pedro González** (*Population: 3,700*), with a broad sweeping beach, running from a promontory (easy to climb) to scrub and brush that reach down almost to the water's edge. **Playa Caribe** is a fantastic curve of white sand with moderate surf. Chairs and umbrellas can be hired from the many beach bars.

Juan Griego (*Population: 25,500*) is further west, a fast-expanding town whose pretty bay is full of fishing boats. The little fort of La Galera is on a promontory at the northern side, beyond which is a bay of the same name with a narrow strip of beach lined with many seafront restaurants.

Playa El Yaque

Playa El Yaque on the south coast, near the airport, is a Mecca for wind- and kitesurfers. The winds are perfect from mid-June to mid-October and the water is shallow enough to stand when you fall off (see Activities and tours, below). Most visitors come on package deals and therefore accommodation is expensive, but cheaper places to stay can be found. There is no public transport; a taxi from Porlamar costs US$14. Cholymar travel agency will change money and there is a *casa de cambio* in the Hotel California. A certified Spanish teacher, Mary Luz Jinete, offers lessons, T0412-094 1651 (mob), spanishwithmaryluz@yahoo.com, which cost US$28 an hour depending on the size of the group.

La Restinga and around

This is the 22-km sandbar of broken seashells that joins the eastern and western parts of Margarita. Behind the *restinga* is the eponymous **national park**, designated a wetland of international importance. More than 100 species of birds live here, including the blue- crowned parakeet, which is endemic to Margarita. There are also marine turtles and other reptiles, dolphins, deer, ocelots, seahorses and oysters. *Lanchas* can be taken into the fascinating lagoon and mangrove swamps to the beach from landing stages at the eastern end (US$4.60 for 30 minutes, US$25 for an hour trip in a boat taking five, plus US$2.50 entrance fee to park). Bus from Porlamar US$1.60. On La Restinga beach you can look for shellfish in the shallows (sun protection is essential) and the delicious oysters can be bought here for around US$1 a dozen.

The **Peninsula de Macanao**, over the road bridge from La Restinga, is mountainous, arid, barely populated and a peaceful place to get away from the holidaymakers on the main part of Isla Margarita. It also has some good beaches that are often deserted and is a good place for horse riding. Punta Arenas is a very pleasant beach with calm water and is the most popular. It has some restaurants, chairs and sunshades. Further on is the wilder Playa Manzanillo. It's best visited in a hire car as public transport is scarce. **Boca del Río**, near the road bridge, has a **Museo Marino** ⓘ *T291-3231, www.museomarino.com, daily 0900-1630, open until 1730 in the high season, US$1, US$0.50 children*, which has interesting collections of marine life, organized by ecosystem, and also features a small aquarium.

Isla de Margarita listings

For Sleeping and Eating price codes and other relevant information, see Essentials, pages 38-40.

Sleeping

Porlamar *p1647*

Many luxury hotels are grouped in the Costa Azul suburb east of Porlamar, but they now pepper most of the northeast coast of the island. Most hotels and tour operators work on a high season/ low season price system. High season prices (Christmas, Easter and Jun-Aug) can be up to 35% higher. Flights and hotels are usually fully booked at this time. In low season, bargaining is possible.

AL Bella Vista, Av Santiago Mariño, T261 7222, www.hbellavista.com. Large, luxury hotel with all services (but not overly helpful), good pool with sea views, beach, car hire, travel agency, French restaurant, and restaurant serving *comida criolla*.

AL Margarita Princess, Av 4 de Mayo, T263 6777, hotelprincess@cantv.net. Large, comfortable rooms, balcony, restaurant, small pool.

B For You, Av Santiago Mariño, T263 8635. Modern, bland, large rooms, good service and roof restaurant, bar.

B Imperial, Av Raul Leoni, via El Morro, T261 6420, www.hotelimperial.com.ve. Modern, best rooms have sea view, parking, balcony, safe, a/c, TV, restaurant, hot water, parking, English spoken.

B María Luisa, Av Raúl Leoni entre Campos y Fermín, T263-7940. A/c, pool, some beach views.

C Posada Casa Lutecia, Final C Campos Cedeño y Marcano, T/F263 8526. Lovely bright rooms with personal touch, a/c, hot water, TV, French-owned, café with outdoor seating near beach.

La Asunción *p1647*

B Ciudad Colonial, C La Margarita, T416 7647. Upmarket apartments minimum 4 people, swimming pool, a/c, accepts credit cards, restaurant.

C Posada Restaurant Ticino Da´Rocco, Crucero de Guacuco, vía Playa El Agua, C San Onofre, sector Camoruco, T242 2727. Pool, a/c, restaurant, accepts credit cards.

Playa Guacuco *p1647*

A Guacuco Resort, Vía Playa Guacuco, T242 3040, www.guacucoresort.com. Stylish, comfortable apartments for up to 4 people with balcony or terrace, 1 km from the beach and 300 m off the road, a/c, self-catering, tranquil, beautiful tropical gardens with birds, spa, pool and bar.

Playa El Agua *p1648*

Most *posadas* are on C Miragua, near the beach.

A Coco Paraíso, Av Principal, T0414-320 5859 (Caracas 0212-578 3922). Pleasant, large rooms, a/c, pool, 3 mins from beach, English and German spoken.

A Costa Linda, C Miragua, T249 1303, www.hotel costalinda.com. Lovely rooms in colonial-style house with a/c, relaxing, TV, safe, pool, restaurant and bar, includes breakfast, accepts credit cards, changes TCs and US$, English and German spoken.

A Costa Linda Beach, C Miragua. T415-9961, hotelcostalinda@cantv.net. Comfortable rooms, pool, bar and restaurant, gym, a/c, TV.

A Doña Romelia, Av 31 de Julio (1 km before Playa Manzanillo), 10 min walk to Playa El Agua, T249 0238, yoya37@cantv.net. Very attractive rustic style hotel, bright rooms with balconies and hammocks, nice pool area and garden. Well-run, helpful staff. Parking, breakfast included. Recommended.

B Chalets de Belén, Miragua 3, T249 1707. 2 chalets for 4 and 6, kitchen, good value, parking TV, no hot water, also 2 double rooms, **D** (discounts in low season).

C Margarita Tropical Villa, C Díaz Ordaz, T249 0558, www.casatrudel.com. Canadian run (formerly Casa Trudel), small place, patio with hammocks, includes breakfast, 5 mins from beach, Wi-Fi, king size beds, hot water shower.

D Hostería El Agua, Av 31 de Julio vía Manzanillo, T249 1297, hosteriaelagua@hotmail.com. Simple, a/c, hot water, safe, restaurant/bar, on roadside 4 mins' walk from beach, English spoken.

Juan Griego *p1648*

C Hostel El Caney, Giulliana Torrico 17, Rue Guevara, T253 5059, elcaney1@hotmail.com. A/c, TV, shared kitchen, small pool, Engish and French spoken.

C Patrick's, El Fuerte, T/F253 6218, www.hotelpatrick.com. Good travellers hostel, a/c rooms with fine sunset views, excellent restaurant and bar, near beach, internet access. English spoken, will arrange salsa and Spanish lessons. Recommended.

D The Sunset Posada Turística, T253 2168, www.sunsetposada.com. Spartan, single rooms with a/c, no TV. Apartments sleep 4-8, good value, some with beachfront balconies.

Playa El Yaque *p1648*

B Hotel El Yaque Paradise, T263 9810, yaque@grupoparadise.com. Upmarket, pleasant, good rooms, a/c, safety deposit box, bar, restaurant, English spoken, includes breakfast.

D El Yaque Motion, T263 9742, www.elyaquemotion.com. 400 m from beach. German run, popular with wind- and kitesurfers (lessons and equipment hire available), well-established, a/c, kitchen, laundry, free internet and Wi-Fi, roof terrace, cheaper with shared bath, rents 3 apartments for 4-8 people, English spoken, good.

D Sail Fast Shop, T263 3449, herbert@sail-fast.com. Basic rooms 300 m from the beach, ask for Herbert Novak at the Sail Fast Shop opposite Hotel Yaque Paradise. Rooms with private bath, some with a/c, kitchen facilities.

La Restinga and around: Peninsula de Macanao *p1648*

AL Makatao, T/F263 6647, www.makatao.com. Run by Dr Alexis Vásquez, price includes transfer, food, some therapies, natural drinks and lodging in the singular rooms. The doctor runs health, 'eco-relax' and therapy programs, and there are mud baths at the *campamento*.

A Posada Río Grande, at *Cabatucan Ranch*, 2 km from Guayacancito on the road to Punta Arenas, T416 8349. Attractive rooms with a/c, hot water, full board available, charming, includes breakfast. Also offer horse riding tours twice a day, T416 3584.

B L'Oasis Posada, Robledal, T291 5339. A/c or fan, hot water, TV, sea view, garden, restaurant. Arrange tours including jeep tours, windsurfing and horse riding.

Eating

Porlamar *p1647*

The upmarket dining, such as Japanese food, is in Urb Costa Azul on Av Bolívar. Plenty of eating places on Campos and 4 de Mayo.

TT-T La Casa del Mero, Av Raúl Leoni. Good place for a cocktail on the water, serves seafood, steaks and chicken.

TT-T La Pimienta, Cedeño entre Campos y Fermín. Good seafood.

TT-T Rancho Grande, C Guevara, near Playa El Agua bus stop. Colombian, good value.

T Dino's Grill, Igualdad y Martínez. Open 0700-1400, buffet lunch, indoor/outdoor seating, grill, home-made sausages, cheap, good service.

T Dragón Chino, 4 de Mayo. Great Chinese.

T El Pollo de Carlitos, Marcano y Martínez. Pleasant location, good food.

T El Punto Criollo, Igualdad near **Hotel Porlamar**. Excellent value *comida margariteña*.

Playa El Agua *p1648*

Several restaurants along C Miragua. Two good restaurants on beach in Playa Agua, **TT El Pacífico**, thatched roof, popular, good fish. Another beach restaurant **TT La Isla** owned by friendly Italian, serves good, fresh Mediterranean-style food, pleasant terrace area and good service.

TT Marlín, with beach view. Serves seafood.

Juan Griego *p1648*

Several restaurants along the beach. **La Calera de mi Caribina** recommended.

Bars and clubs

Porlamar *p1647*

Several bars in the Centro Comercial Costal Azul. **Señor Frog's** is popular.

El Remo, Av 4 de Mayo. Seafood restaurant with disco upstairs, open until 0300, no cover.

Tasca Gaita, C Marcano. Loud music, wood-panelled ceilings.

Many hotels in Urb Costa Azul have relatively inexpensive **casinos**; the best are **Casino del Sol** at the *Hotel Marina Bay*, and **Hilton Margarita**.

Playa El Yaque *p1648*

Several beach bars; best bar is **Los Surf Piratas**, drinks and dancing from 2130.

Juan Griego *p1648*
Los Tucanes for eating and drinking.
Rose's Place for late-night partying.

Festivals and events

Isla de Margarita *p1645, map p1646*
Many religious festivals, including **19 Mar** at Paraguachí (*Feria de San José*, 10 days); **26 Jul** at Punta de Piedras; **31 Jul** (Batalla de Matasiete) and **15 Aug** (Asunción de la Virgen) at La Asunción; **1-8 Sep** at El Valle; **4-11 Nov** at Boca del Río, **4-30 Nov** at Boca del Pozo; **5-6 Dec** at Porlamar; **27 Dec-3 Jan** at Juan Griego See map for locations.

Shopping

Porlamar *p1647*
Margarita's status as a duty-free zone attracts Venezuelan shoppers, who go in droves for clothing, electronic goods and other items. Street sellers lay out their handicrafts on Av Santiago Mariño in the afternoon. When buying jewellery, bargain, don't pay by credit card (surcharges are imposed) and get a detailed guarantee of the item. Av Santiago Mariño and surroundings are the place for designer labels, but decent copies can be found on Blvds Guevara and Gómez and around Plaza Bolívar in the centre. For bargains on denims, T-shirts, shorts, swimming gear and bikinis, take a bus to Conejeros market (from Fraternidad, Igualdad a Velásquez).

Activities and tours

Porlamar *p1647*
Aquanauts Diving, Urb Costa Azul, C Los Almendrones, Centro Comercial Bayside, local No 1-47, PB, T267 1645, www.aquanauts.com.ve. PADI school, snorkelling and fishing trips.
Natura Raid, Av 4 de Mayo con Av Santiago Mariño, Edif Silcat p 4, of 4-1, T261 4419, www.naturaraid.com. Eco-tourism and adventure trips across Venezuela, including diving in Los Roques and sailing (also has an office in Caracas).
Sailing The private yacht **Viola Festival** can be hired for mini cruises to the island of Coche, contact **Festival Tours**, Calle Los Uveros, Caribbean Center Mall, PB, Local 82, Costa Azul, T267 0552, www.violafestival.com. There are other yachts offering island cruises, fishing trips, etc.

Playa El Agua *p1648*
Tour shops in Playa El Agua are the best places to book scuba diving and snorkelling trips: most go to Los Frailes, a small group of islands to the north of Playa Agua, and reputedly the best diving and snorkelling in Margarita, but it's also possible to dive at Parque Nacional La Restinga and Isla Cubagua. Prices from US$75 pp for an all-inclusive full day (2 dives), but bargaining is possible if you have a group of 4 or more. Snorkelling is always about half the price of scuba diving.
Enomis Divers, Av 31 de Julio, CC Turístico, Playa El Agua, loc 2, sector La Mira, T249 0366, www.divemargarita.com. PADI school, diving trips. Open water certification US$250.

Playa El Yaque *p1648*
Sailboards, **kite surf** and **kayaks** can be hired on the beach from at least 5 well-equipped companies, who also offer lessons. Half day including lesson costs US$70 for wind/kite surfing; US14 per hour for kayak. English, German, French and Portuguese spoken. Enquire at **El Yaque Motion** (see Sleeping, above) for more information about wind and kite surfing. See also www.velawind surf.com. A 20-min boat ride to Isla Coche leaves from next door to **El Yaque Motion**, a recommended spot for advanced kiters. Rescue service available at the beach.

La Restinga and around: Peninsula de Macanao *p1648*
Horse riding You can ride on the peninsula at **Ranch Cabatucan**, T416 3584, www.cabatucan.com. Prices start at US$93 pp for 2 hrs.

Transport

Porlamar *p1647*
Air There are too many flight options to list here: check with local offices for details.
Gen Santiago Mariño Airport, between Porlamar and Punta de Piedras, has the international and national terminals at either end. Airport tax US$12.80. Taxi from Porlamar US$28, 20-30 mins. There are scheduled flights to **Frankfurt** and internal flights to almost all Venezuela's airports. All national airlines have routes to **Margarita**. Many daily flights to/from

Caracas, with **Aeropostal**, and **Aserca**, 45 mins flight; tickets are much cheaper if purchased in Venezuela. Reservations made from outside Venezuela are not always honoured. To **Canaima** and to **Los Roques** with **Aereotuy** and **Rutaca**.

Bus Local: *Por Puestos* serve most of the island, minimum fare US$1, few services at night and in low season: Airport, from Centro Comercial AB, Av Bolívar; La Asunción, from Fajardo, Igualdad a Marcano; Pampatar, from Fajardo y La Marina; La Restinga, from Mariño, La Marina a Maneiro; Playa El Agua, from Guevara, Marcano a Cedeño; Juan Griego, from Av Miranda, Igualdad a Marcano; Playa Guacuco, from Fraternidad, La Marina a Mérito (mornings), from Fajardo, Igualdad a Velásquez (afternoons). **Long distance**: Several bus companies in Caracas sell through tickets from Caracas to Porlamar, arriving about midday. Buses return to Caracas from La Paralela bus station in Porlamar.

Ferry From **Puerto La Cruz** to Margarita (**Punta de Piedras**): **Conferry**, Los Cocos terminal, Puerto La Cruz, freefone T0501-2663 3779, www.conferry.com. Terminal has restaurant, CANTV and internet services. Price varies according to speed of ferry and class of seat, 2½-4½ hrs, 4-6 a day, night departures too (check times, extra ferries during high season). Fast ferry, passengers US$17 one way, over-60s and children 2-7 half price (proof of age required), cars US$23. Slow ferries US$10 one way. **Conferry** office in **Porlamar**, Av Terranova con Av Llano Adentro, Mon-Fri 0800-1200, 1400-1730, Sat 0800-1200. **Gran Cacique**, 2-3 fast ferries a day Puerto la Cruz-Punta de Piedras, US$13.25-19 one way, T0281-263 0935 (Puerto La Cruz ferry terminal), T0295-239 8339 (Punta de Piedras, or Av Santiago Mariño, Edif Blue Sky, loc 3, Porlamar, T0295-264 2945). Ferries not always punctual. It is not uncommon for delays up to 6 hours in high season. It is most advisable to book in advance, especially if travelling with a car or motorbike during high season. Insist on a ticket even when you are told it is full. Don't believe taxi drivers at bus terminal who may tell you there's a ferry about to leave. To get to terminal in Puerto La Cruz, take 'Bello Monte' *por puesto* from Libertad y Anzoátegui, 2 blocks from Plaza Bolívar. From **Cumaná** ferry terminal, El Salado, **Gran Cacique**, T0293-432 0011, 2-3 a day, US$14-19 one way (children 3-7 and over-60s cheaper), and **Naviarca**, T0293-433 5577, continuous service, US$9.30 one way for passengers (children 3-7 and over-60s half price), vehicles US$17-19.50. **Note** Ferries are very busy at weekends and Mon.

Taxi Taxi for a day is US$23 per hr. Always fix fare in advance; 30% extra after 2100. Taxi from Playa El Agua to airport, US$28, from Restinga, US$33.

Directory

Porlamar *p1647*

Airline offices **Aeropostal**, Sambil Margarita, local Mn17, T262 2179. **Aereotuy**, T415 5778, sramirez@tuy.com. **Aserca**, Av Bolívar, CC Provemed, PB, local 5, Pampatar, T0800-648 8356. **Rutaca**, Centro Comercial Jumbo, T263 9936, 0501-788 2221. **Banks** Banks on Avs Santiago Mariño and 4 de Mayo, open 0830-1130, 1400-1630. **Casas de cambio**: **Cambio Cussco** at Velásquez y Av Santiago Mariño. **Italcambio**, CC Jumbo, Av 4 de Mayo, Nivel Ciudad, T265 9392. **Car hire** Several offices at the airport and at the entrance to *Hotel Bella Vista*, others on Av Santiago Mariño. **Ramcar II**, at airport and *Hotel Bella Vista*, cheap and reliable. Check the brakes, bodywork and terms and conditions of hire thoroughly. Scooters can also be hired. Motor bikes may not be ridden 2000-0500. **Note** Fill up before leaving Porlamar as service stations are scarce. Roads are generally good and most are paved. Signposts are often nonexistent. Free maps are confusing, but it's worth having one with you. Avoid driving outside Porlamar after dark. Beware of robbery; park in private car parks. **Internet** Several on Av Santiago Mariño. **Post offices** On Maneiro. **Telephones** Several on Av Santiago Mariño.

Pampatar *p1647*

Language school **Centro de Lingüistica Aplicada**, Corocoro Qta, Cela Urb, Playa El Angel between Porlamar and Pampatar, T/F262 8198, http://cela-ve.com (useful website).

Los Roques

➔ *Colour map 1, A6. Phone code: 0237. National park entry US$12, Venezuelans and children 5-12 years half price.*

The turquoise and emerald lagoons and dazzling white sands of the Archipelago de Los Roques make up one of Venezuela's loveliest national parks. For lazing on an untouched beach, or for snorkelling and diving amid schools of fish and coral reefs, these islands cannot be beaten. Diving and snorkelling are best to the south of the archipelago. The islands tend to be very busy in July-August and at Christmas. See www.los-roques.com. Also look out for the excellent *Guía del Parque Nacional Archipiélago Los Roques* (Ecograph, 2004).

The islands of Los Roques, with long stretches of white beaches and over 20 km of coral reef in crystal-clear water, lie 166 km due north of La Guaira; the atoll, of about 340 islets and reefs, constitutes a national park of 225,153 ha. There are many bird nesting sites (eg the huge gull colonies on Francisqui and the pelicans, boobies and frigates on Selenqui); May is nesting time at the gull colonies. For more information visit www.fundacionlosroques.org. This is one of the least visited diving spots in the Caribbean; best visited midweek as Venezuelans swarm here on long weekends and at school holidays, after which there is litter on every island. (Low season is Easter to July.) There are at least seven main dive sites offering caves, cliffs, coral and, at Nordesqui, shipwrecks. There are many fish to be seen, including sharks at the caves of Olapa de Bavusqui. Prices are higher than the mainland and infrastructure is limited but the islands are beautiful and unspoiled. Camping is free, but campers need a permit from **Inparques** ⓘ *T0212-273 2811 in Caracas, or the office on Plaza Bolívar, Gran Roque, Mon-Fri 0830-1200 and 1400-1800, weekends and holidays 0830-1200 and 1430-1730, another small office by the runway.* Average temperature 29°C with coolish nights. You will need strong sunblock as there is no shade and an umbrella is recommended.

Gran Roque (*Population: 900*) is the main and only permanently inhabited island. The airport is here, as is the national guard, a few small grocery stores and souvenir shops, public phones (expensive internet), a bank with an ATM, medical facilities, dive shops, a few restaurants and accommodation. There is nowhere to change traveller's cheques. Park Headquarters are in the scattered fishing village. Tourist information is available free of charge from the very helpful *Oscar Shop*, directly in front as you leave the airstrip. Boat trips to other islands can be arranged here (round trip fares US$7-US$42, depending on distance, more for a tour), which are worthwhile as you can not swim off Gran Roque.

You can negotiate with local fishermen for transport to other islands: you will need to take your own tent, food and (especially) water. **Madrisqui** has a good shallow beach and joins Pirata Cay by a sandspit. **Francisqui** is three islands joined by sandspits, with calm lagoon waters to the south and rolling surf to the north. You can walk with care from one cay to the other, maybe swimming at times. There's some shade in the mangrove near the bar at La Cueva. **Crasqui** has a 3-km beach with beautiful water and white sand. **Cayo de Agua** (1 hour by fast boat from Gran Roque) has an amazing sandspit joining its two parts and a nice walk to the lighthouse where you'll find two natural pools.

Los Roques listings

For Sleeping and Eating price codes and other relevant information, see Essentials, pages 38-40.

Sleeping

In most places on Islas Los Roques, breakfast and dinner are included in the price.

Los Roques: Gran Roque *p1653*

There are over 60 *posadas* on Gran Roque (some bookable through **Aereotuy**), from **D** to **L** pp. In high season, Jul-Aug, Dec, prices are very high. Bargaining is advisable (especially in low season) for stays of more than 2 nights.

L pp **Piano y Papaya**, near Plaza Bolívar towards seafront, T0414-281 0104 (mob), www.pianoypapaya.com. Very tasteful, run by Italian artist, with fan, **AL** pp for bed and breakfast, credit cards and TCs accepted, Italian and English spoken, laundry service.

L pp **Posada Caracol**, on seafront near airstrip, T221 1049, www.caracolgroup.com. Delightful, half-board and bed and breakfast options available, **A** pp, credit cards and TCs accepted, Italian and English spoken, good boats.

L-B pp **El Botuto**, on seafront near *Supermercado W Salazar*, T0416-621 0381 (mob), www.posadaelbotuto.com. Price depends on season and if half board or full board, reservations must be made 50% in advance. Nice airy rooms with fan, good simple food, locally owned. Trips to other islands and watersports arranged.

AL Posada Acquamarina, C 2 No 149, T0412-310 1962, www.posada-acquamarina.com. All-inclusive, rooms have a/c, cable TV, private bathrooms with hot water, terrace. Owner Giorgio very helpful, speaks Italian and some French, can arrange flights from Caracas. Also operates the **Rasqui Island Chalet** (**AL** 3 rooms), the only posada on that island.

A Posada Doña Magalis, Plaza Bolívar 46, T0414-287 7554, www.magalis.com. Simple place, locally owned, with fan, cheaper with shared bath, includes soft drinks, breakfast and dinner, delicious food, mostly fish and rice.

C pp **Roquelusa**, C 3 No 214, behind *Supermercado W Salazar*, T0414-369 6401 (mob). Probably the cheapest option on Gran Roque, basic, with cold water, a/c.

Activities and tours

Los Roques *p1653*

Diving Note For health reasons you must allow 12 hrs to elapse between diving and flying back to the mainland. Companies charge US$70 for 2 dives including equipment and US$95 for an introductory course; lots of courses and packages available.

Cayo de Agua and **Francisqui** recommended for **snorkeling**. Boats and equipment rentals can be arranged.

Ecobuzos, 3 blocks from the airstrip, T0295-262 9811/0414-791 9380, www.ecobuzos.com. Very good, new equipment, modern boats, experienced dive masters. PADI courses (US$350) and beginner dives available.

Recife Divers, past Inparques at the far end of town. PADI courses and beginner dives available.

Sailing Fully equipped yachts can be chartered for US$300-500 per night for 2 people, all inclusive, highly recommended as a worthwhile way of getting some shade on the treeless beaches. Ask at **Angel & Oscar Shop**, or **Posada Pez Ratón**, T0414-257 1067, info@pezraton.com.

Windsurfing and kitesurfing On Francisqui, ask for Elías.

Transport

Los Roques *p1653*

Air Flights from Maiquetía or Porlamar. **Aereotuy**, **Chapi Air**, **Transaven** (T0212-355 1965) and **Los Roques Airlines** (T0212 6352166, www.losroques-airlines.com) all fly from Maiquetía (Aeropuerto Auxiliar) once a day, 40 mins, US$130-150 round trip, more expensive if booked outside of Venezuela. Some carriers charge more at weekends. Remember that small planes usually restrict luggage to 10 kg. They offer full-day packages (return flight, meals and activities), and Aerotuy offers overnight packages as well (see www.tuy.com for details), recommended. It's best to buy a return to the mainland as buying and confirming tickets and finding offices open on the islands is difficult

Directory

Los Roques *p1653*

Banks Banesco, Plaza Bolívar, Mon-Fri 0830-1230, 1430-1700. Cash advances on Visa. **Internet** Many posadas have computers. If not, **Posada Acquamarina** (see Sleeping) has a service for the public. **Public telephones** Plaza Bolívar and Guardia National on seafront.

Canaima and the Orinoco Delta

In Parque Nacional Canaima, one of the largest national parks in the world, you'll find the spectacular Angel Falls, the highest in the world, and the mysterious "Lost World" of Roraima (described under South to Brazil). Canaima is the tourist centre for the park, but indigenous communities are now accepting tourists. The historic Ciudad Bolívar on the Río Orinoco is a good starting place for the superb landscapes further south. Further east, beyond the industrial city of Ciudad Guayana, the Orinoco Delta is developing as a tourist destination.

Guayana, south of the Orinoco River, constitutes half of Venezuela, comprising rounded forested hills and narrow valleys, rising to ancient flat-topped tablelands on the borders of Brazil. These savannahs interspersed with semi-deciduous forest are sparsely populated. So far, communications have been the main difficulty, but a road that leads to Manaus has now been opened to Santa Elena de Uairén on the Brazilian frontier (see page 1670). The area is Venezuela's largest gold and diamond source, but its immense reserves of iron ore, manganese and bauxite are of far greater economic importance.

Ciudad Bolívar → *Phone code: 0285. Colour map 2, A1, Population: 300,000.*

Ciudad Bolívar is on the narrows of the Orinoco, some 300 m wide, which gave the town its old name of Angostura, 'The Narrows'. It is 400 km from the Orinoco delta. It was here that Bolívar came after defeat to reorganize his forces, and the British Legionnaires joined him. At Angostura he was declared President of the Gran Colombia he had yet to build and which was to fragment before his death. With its cobbled streets, pastel buildings and setting on the Orinoco, it is one of Venezuela's most beautiful colonial towns and its status as a UNESCO World Heritage Site is under consideration.

At the Congress of Angostura, 15 February 1819, the representatives of the present day Venezuela, Colombia, Panama and Ecuador met to proclaim Gran Colombia. The building, on **Plaza Bolívar**, built 1766-76 by Manuel Centurión, the provincial governor, houses a museum, the **Casa del Congreso de Angostura**, with an ethnographic museum in the basement. Guides give tours in Spanish only. Also on this plaza is the **Cathedral** (which was completed in 1840), the **Casa de Los Gobernadores de la Colonia** (also built by Centurión in 1766), the **Real Intendencia**, and the **Casa de la Cultura**. Also here, at Bolívar 33, is the house where Gen Manuel Piar, the Liberator of Guayana from the Spanish, was held prisoner before being executed by Bolívar on 16 October 1817, for refusing to put himself under Bolívar's command. The restored **Plaza Miranda**, up C Carabobo, has an art centre. The present legislative assembly and **Consejo Municipal** are between Plaza Bolívar and Plaza Miranda. In 1824, when the town was still known as Angostura a Prussian physician to Bolívar's troops invented the bitters; the factory moved to Port of Spain in 1875.

Museum at **Casa del Correo del Orinoco** ⓘ *Paseo Orinoco y Carabobo, Mon-Fri 0930-1200, 1430-1700*, houses modern art and some exhibits of history of the city. **Museo Casa San Isidro** ⓘ *Av Táchira, Tue-Sun 0900-1700, free, knowledgeable guides*, a colonial mansion where Simón Bolívar stayed for two weeks. It has antique furniture and an old garden. **Museo de Arte Moderno Jesús Soto** ⓘ *Av Germania, 0930-1730, weekends and holidays 1000-1700, free, guide in Spanish only,* is located some distance from the centre in pleasant gardens. It has works by Venezuela's celebrated Jesús Rafael Soto and other modern artists from around the world. Recommended. The best views of the city are from **Fortín El Zamuro** ⓘ *C 28 de Octubre y Av 5 de Julio, open daily except Mon, free, guides available,*, dating from 1902, strategically located at one of the tallest points of the city.

Speedboats take passengers across the river to the small, picturesque town of **Soledad** (US$0.50 one way, 5 minutes) on a journey that offers great views of colonial centre, the bridge and the river itself. Security can be an issue at either end; don't cross at night. There are no other passenger boat services. The Paseo Orinoco leading west out of town goes to the **Angostura Bridge**, which can be seen from town. This is the first bridge across the Orinoco, 1,668 m long, opened in 1967, again with great views (cyclists and walkers are not allowed to cross, you must flag down a car or truck).

West of the centre is **El Zanjón**, an area of vegetation typical of the region. East is **Parque El Porvenir**, with botanical gardens (entrance on C Bolívar, www.jborinoco.org). Outside the airport is the *Río Caroní* aeroplane, which Jimmy Angel landed on top of Auyán Tepuy (see page 1661).

The **tourist office** is **Dirección de Turismo** ⓘ *Av Bolívar, Quinta Yeita 59, T632 2362, Mon-Fri 0800-1200, 1400-1730*. Helpful, English spoken. State website: www.e-bolivar.gov.ve.

To Ciudad Bolívar from the coast and the llanos Ciudad Bolívar can be reached easily by roads south from Caracas and Puerto La Cruz. The Caracas route, via Valle de la Pascua, and the Puerto La Cruz route, via Anaco, meet at El Tigre (*Population*: 122,000), which has good hotels and services. From the *llanos*, from **Chaguaramas** turn south through Las Mercedes (hotel **E**) to **Cabruta** (*Population: 4,300*), 179 km, road in very bad shape, daily bus to Caracas, US$11, basic hotel. Then take a ferry from opposite the airport to **Caicara** (car ferry 1½ hours, *lanchas* for pedestrians 25 minutes). A new bridge across the Orinoco is being built between Cabruta and

Ciudad Bolívar

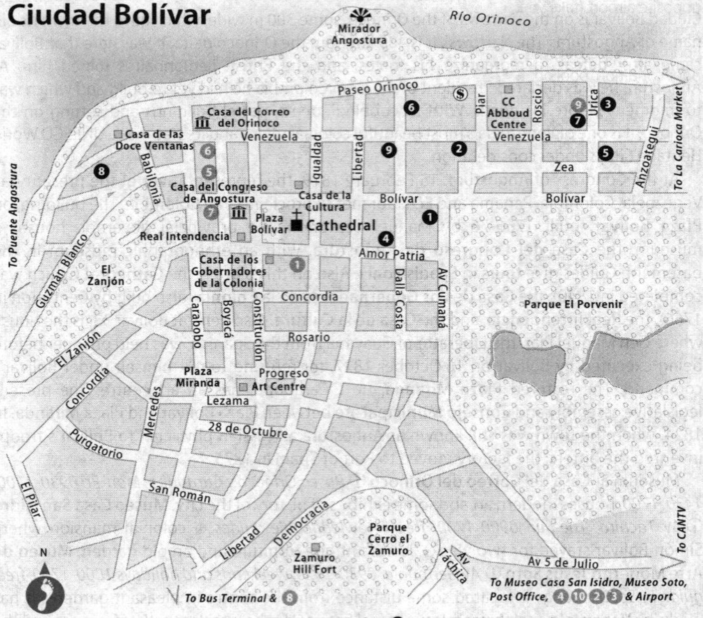

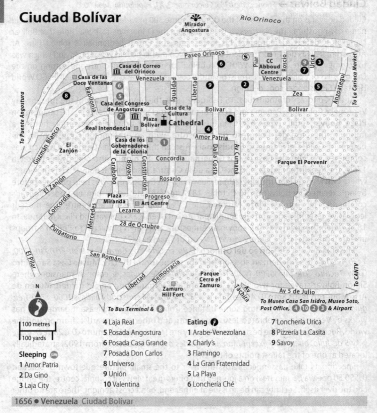

100 metres
100 yards

Sleeping
1 Amor Patria
2 Da Gino
3 Laja City
4 Laja Real
5 Posada Angostura
6 Posada Casa Grande
7 Posada Don Carlos
8 Universo
9 Unión
10 Valentina

Eating
1 Arabe-Venezolana
2 Charly's
3 Flamingo
4 La Gran Fraternidad
5 La Playa
6 Lonchería Ché
7 Lonchería Urica
8 Pizzería La Casita
9 Savoy

Caicara (due to open in 2011). Alternatively, from San Fernando de Apure take a bus to Calabozo (*Population*: 108,000) and *por puesto* from there to El Sombrero (*Population*: 23,000; US$2.25), where you can catch the Ciudad Bolívar bus.

Tours can be made into the area south of the Río Orinoco from **Maripa** (*Colour map 2, A1*), travelling on the Río Caura. These include visits to indigenous villages, river bathing, jungle treks to waterfalls with explanations of wildlife and vegetation, usually starting from Ciudad Bolívar (see Activities and tours, below).

Ciudad Bolívar listings

For Sleeping and Eating price codes and other relevant information, see Essentials, pages 38-40.

Sleeping

Ciudad Bolívar *p1655, map p1656*

Near airport

A Laja Real, Av Andrés Bello y Jesús Soto, opposite airport (take your life in your hands if you walk across), T617 0100, www.lajareal.com. Rooms with a/c, hot water, TV, fridge, in very poor condition, pool open to non-residents for US$5 per day, Wi-Fi being installed in rooms, overpriced restaurant, sauna, gym, parking.

C Valentina, Av Maracay 55, T632 2145. Quiet, a/c, hot water, TV, comfortable, very good restaurant.

D Da Gino, Av Jesús Soto, opposite airport, T632 0313. A/c, hot water, TV, good service and restaurant, changes US$ cash.

In the centre

L Posada Casa Grande. C Boyacá 8, T632 4639, angostura@cacaotravel.com. A beautiful hotel in colonial style, with breakfast, cable TV, a/c, hot water, restaurant, pool on the roof.

B Posada Angostura, same contact details as *Posada Casa Grande* above, also on C Boyacá. Handsome rooms in old colonial house, some rooms have river view, a/c, fan, hot water, travel agency, unwelcoming service. A chef prepares some of the best food in Venezuela for guests.

C Laja City, Av Táchira y Av Bolívar, T/F632 9919, hotellajacity@cantv.net. Quiet, a/c, hot water, TV, restaurant.

B-C Posada Don Carlos, C Boyacá 26 y Amor Patrio, just 30m from Plaza Bolívar, T632 6017, www.hosteltrail.com/posadadoncarlos. Stunning old house, could be museum. Double rooms with a/c and bath, cheaper with fan, hammock and shared facilities **E**, breakfast and dinner available, free internet, lovely patio, bar. Very popular with travellers. Recommended.

E Amor Patria, Amor Patria 30, T632 8819, plazabolivar@hotmail.com. Renovated colonial house, fan, shared bathrooms, kitchen, hammocks for hire (**F**). Run by Gerd Altmann, German and English spoken. Recommended.

E Unión, Calle Urica, T632 3374. Clean, basic with fan, cable TV, helpful, filtered water, good value.

Near the bus terminal

D Universo, Av República, 2 blocks left out of terminal, T654 3732. A/c, hot water, TV, restaurant, accepts credit cards.

Outside town

D Posada La Casita, Av Ligia Pulido, Urb 24 de Julio, PO Box 118, T617 0832, T0414-854 5146, www.posada-la-casita.com. Very nice rooms, with cold water, fan (a/c extra), hammock with mosquito net can be rented, **E**. Beautiful gardens (with small zoo), pool, laundry service, good food and drinks available, German and English spoken, helpful. Free pick up from airport or bus terminal (ring in advance). Free shuttle service into town. The owner runs **Gekko Tours** (see below).

Eating

Ciudad Bolívar *p1655, map p1656*

TTT TT **Mercado La Carioca**, Octava Estrella y Paseo Orinoco, on the banks of the river. The best place for eating tasty local food, open daily from 0600-1500. Great view. Various stalls and excellent local food with a range of prices. The municipality is providing daily security.

TT **Arabe-Venezolano**, on Cumaná near Bolívar. Clean, a/c, good Arabic food, not cheap.

TT **Mirador** Paseo Orinoco. *Comida criolla* with views over the river.

TT-T **La Playa**, C Urica entre Venezuela y Zea. Good for fish, reasonable prices.

Charly's, Venezuela. Good *fuente de soda*, cheap, fast service.

Flamingo, C Urica opposite Hotel Unión. Peruvian dishes, good value if they don't overcharge.

Lonchería Ché, Dalla Cosat y Paseo Orinoco. Good breakfast.

Lonchería Urica, Urica, next to *Hotel Unión*. Good lunch for US$1.25, get there early.

Pizzería La Casita Venezuela, opposite *La Casa de las Doce Ventanas*. Good value pizza and ice cream, views over Puente Angostura.

Restaurant Vegetariano La Gran Fraternidad Amor Patria y Dalla Costa. Lunch only.

Savoy, Venezuela y Dalla Costa. Good value breakfast.

Cafés and fast food

Café Estilo, Av Andrés Bello, opposite **Laja Real Hotel** and very near airport. Open 0900-1200, 1500-1900. Boutique and café with homemade sweets, comfortable, spotless. Run by very nice elderly couple. Recommended.

Several fast food restaurants around **Museo de Arte Moderno Jesús Soto**, including **McDonalds. Café Park**, great ice cream parlour with coffee and simple but decent food, playground for children.

Shopping

Ciudad Bolívar *p1655, map p1656*

Camping equipment White gas (stove fuel) is available at **Lubriven**, Av República 16, near the bus terminal.

Handicrafts Arts and crafts from Bolívar state, basketry from the Orinoco Delta can be found in **La Carioca** market, at the end of Paseo Orinoco and **Tienda Artesanía Guayanesa** at the airport.

Jewellery There are many jewellers on Pasaje Guayana, which runs off Paseo Orinoco.

Supermarket Close to the Museo Soto on Av Germania, large and well-stocked.

Activities and tours

Ciudad Bolívar *p1655, map p1656*

Competition is stiff in Ciudad Bolívar, and among the genuine companies roam phoney salesmen. You are more than likely to have someone attempt to sell you a tour at the bus station. Do not pay any money to anyone in the bus station or on the street. Always ask to be taken to the office. Always ask for a receipt (and make sure that it comes on paper bearing the company logo). Be suspicious of people offering tours that start in another town or city. If you are unfortunate enough to fall prey to a con artist, be sure to make a *denuncio* at the police station and inform genuine travel agents.

Ciudad Bolívar is the best place to book a tour to Canaima, but you may pick up cheaper deals for trips to Roraima and the Gran Sabana from Santa Elena. The main tour operators in Canaima who offer tours at backpacker prices – *Bernal Tours*, *Express Dorado*, *Kawi Travel Adventure* and *Tiuna Tours*. Most other agents in Ciudad Bolívar sell tours run by these operators, but sometimes add commission. Always ask who will be running the actual tour; it may be cheaper to book from the tour operator directly. Service seems to change with the seasons and year-on-year: get independent recommendations on standards of guiding, food, time-keeping, etc. For 3 days/2 nights tours to Canaima expect to pay around US$350 pp (official exchange rate), or US$310 for 1-day tour that includes flights to Canaima, flight near the Angel Falls, boat ride across Canaima lagoon (just a few minutes) and food (see p 1663 for flights to Canaima). A 4 day/3 night tour to Gran Sabana costs about US$250; 5 days/ 4 nights; Río Caura US$245.

Asociación Cooperativa Yajimadu, Servicios y Excursiones Ecoturísticas, T615 2354, dichenedu@hotmail.com, or Miguel Estaba, T0414-099 0568. 5-day trip to Río Caura, 10 and 15-day trips also available, small groups catered for, guides are Ye'kwana from villages on the river, knowledgeable, Spanish spoken (some guides learning English), sleep in hammocks, very good.

Bernal Tours/Sapito Tours, at airport, T632 6890, 0414-854 8234 (mob in Spanish), 414-899 7162 (in English), www.bernaltours.com. Canaima tours slightly more expensive, *indígena* guides and their own eco lodge at Canaima lagoon overlooking the falls. Sapito Tours is the only agent authorized to issue domestic and international tickets at the airport. Also offer day tours to Kavác caves, Gran Sabana, Río Caura, Roraima (6 days/5 nights), Orinoco Delta (3 days/2 nights), Los Roques, Puerto Ordaz and city tours. Agency is run by descendents of

Peruvian adventurer Tomás Bernal from Arequipa (see p 1660).

Di Blasio, Av Cumaná 12, T632 1931. Very helpful for domestic and international air tickets, reconfirmations, hotel bookings in Caracas and other Venezuelan cities.

Expediciones Dearuna, C Libertad 16 (above Inversiones Ruiz), T632 4635. All usual tours at competitive prices.

Gekko Tours, run by Pieter Rothfuss at airport (also *Posada La Casita)*, T632 3223, T0414-854 5146, www.gekkotours-venezuela.de. Gran Sabana, Canaima, Roraima, Orinoco Delta, rafting and river trips.

Kawi Travel Adventure, at the airport, T511 4581, 0414-899 6399 (mob). Offers usual routes in the area, plus US$16.25 for night in hammock in the countryside, 10 mins from the airport, with pool (discount or even free if tour is booked with them).

Miguel Gasca, T0414-923 5210/0166-629 4600 (mob), or find him at *Hotel Italia*. Recommended for tours to Roraima, Gran Sabana and Canaima.

Soana Travel, run by Martin Haars at *Posada Don Carlos*, Boyacá 26, T632 6017, T0414-864 6616 (mob), soanatravel@gmx.de. Tours to Río Caura, Canaima and Gran Sabana, English and German spoken.

Tiuna Tours, at airport, T632 8697. Cheapest option for Canaima (but mixed reports in 2008), have a camp that takes 180 people. Guides speak English, German and Italian.

Turi Express, at airport, T652 9764, T0414-893 9078 (mob), turiexpress@cantv.net. Range of tours plus Guri dam and fishing tours, good English.

Transport

Ciudad Bolívar *p1655, map p1656*

Air Minibuses and buses marked Terminal to town centre. Taxi to Paseo Orinoco US$3. To **Caracas** 5-6 a week, 1 hr, **Aserca** and **Rutaca. Transmandú** (T0285-632 1462, www.transmandu.com) and **Rutaca** (recommended for views) fly daily to **Canaima**. **Transmandú** also flies to **Kamarata, Kavác** and **Santa Elena**. There are international phones at the airport, excellent café with runway view and some food, and car hire. Check where tours start from as some fly from Ciudad Guayana (**Turi Tours**), and charge passengers for taxi transfers. Taxi to Ciudad Guayana or its airport for daily flights to Caracas about US$35.

Bus Terminal at junction of Av República and Av Sucre. Left luggage. To get there take bus marked Terminal going west along Paseo Orinoco (US$0.35). 10 daily to **Caracas** US$16.75, 8-9 hrs with **Aeroexpresos Ejecutivos**; also **Camargüi, Expresos Los Llanos**; *por puesto* US$40. 10 daily to **Puerto La Cruz**, US$8, 5 hrs, with **Caribe** and **Expresos San Cristóbal**, *por puesto*, US$16. 1 daily to **Cumaná**, US$11.50, 7 hrs with **Caribe**. Several daily to **Maracay**, US$14, and **Valencia**, via Maracay, US$14, 8-9 hrs, with **Expresos Los Llanos. Tumeremo** US$8.50; Tumeremo bus through to El Dorado US$9.50, 3 daily. To **Santa Elena de Uairén** direct with **Caribe** US$26.50 (3 daily), **Expresos San Cristóbal**, US$21.50 (2 daily), stopping en route with **Línea Orinoco, Transportes Mundial** (5 daily), spectacular views of Gran Sabana, 12-13 hrs. 1 daily to **Boa Vista** with **Caribe**, US$34, 20 hrs. To **Ciudad Guayana** hourly from 0700, US$1.75, 1½ hrs, *por puesto*, US$5.75, 1½ hrs. To **Ciudad Piar**, US$5.75, 3 hrs, and **La Paragua**, US$8.25, 4 hrs, with **Coop Gran Mcal Sucre**. 2 daily to **Caicara**, US$13.50 (including 2 ferry crossings), 7-8 hrs, with **Coop Gran Mcal Sucre**. To **Maturín** with **Unión Maturín**. 2 daily to **Puerto Ayacucho**, US$16, 10-12 hrs with **Coop Gran Mcal Sucre**, take food.

Taxi US$2 to virtually anywhere in town. US$1.75 from bus station to town centre.

Directory

Ciudad Bolívar *p1655, map p1656*

Banks See also Money, page 1566. TCs difficult to change. ATMs open only in banking hours. **Corp Banca**, Paseo Meneses, Edif Johanna. Amex TCs. **Banco de Venezuela**, Paseo Orinoco near Piar. Cash on Visa, ATM. **Banco Mercantil**, east end of Paseo Orinoco. Changes TCs, has ATM. **BBVA Banco Provincial**, west end of Av Jesús Soto, opposite Mobil petrol station. Cash on Visa, ATM. **Consulates** **Italy**, Av 17 de Diciembre, Edif Terepaima, Local 1, T/F654 4335, agziaconsolarecb@hotmail.com. **Internet** Places in the centre. **Galaxia.com**, C C Abboud Centre, Paseo Orinoco. **Galaxy Computer**, Av República y Jesús Soto, behind Mobil petrol station. **Post offices** Av Táchira, 15 mins walk from centre. **Telephones** *CANTV*, Av 5 de Julio, 100 m from Av Táchira (closed Sun).

Canaima and Angel Falls

➔ *Colour map 2, B1. Park entry US$16 pp paid to Inparques on arrival in Canaima.*

Canaima National Park, a UNESCO World Heritage Site since 1994, is one of the most unspoilt places on earth. At over 3 million ha, it is the second largest national park in Venezuela, the 6th largest on the planet. It is a world apart, with its fantastic table mountains, waterfalls which include the world's highest (Angel Falls), caves, deep forests and indigenous cultures.

At Canaima camp, the Río Carrao tumbles spectacularly over Ucaima, Golondrina and Hacha Falls into the lagoon, which has beautiful tannin-stained water with soft beige beaches. It's a lovely spot, but it also has the air strip and is the centre of operations for river trips to indigenous areas and to Angel Falls. The Falls are named after Jimmie Angel, the US airman who first reported their existence in 1935. Two years later he returned and crash landed his plane, the *Río Caroní*, on top of Auyán Tepuy. The site is marked with a plaque. The sheer rock face was climbed in 1971 by three Americans and an Englishman, David Nott, who recounted the 10-day adventure in his book *Angels Four* (Prentice-Hall). Hugo Chávez has said that the falls should be called by an indigenous name: Kerepakupai Merú.

There is a famous `tunnel' between Sapo and Sapito Falls (where Río Carrao passes behind Isla Anatoliy), where one can walk behind the huge waterfall - a must for any visitor. It is essential to be accompanied by guide. The easiest way to get there is from Tomás Bernal Camp on Isla Anatoliy (5 minutes boat ride from Canaima Camp). It's a 25-minute walk from there. Plastic raincoats are usually provided by the guide, or wear a swim suit. Wrap your camera and other belongings in a plastic bag. No matter what, you will get completely soaked in the middle of the tunnel. The path behind the waterfall is extremely slippery and should be taken only by the reasonably fit. Wrap your hand in an extra plastic bag, otherwise it will be cut by the rough rope. When taking photos from behind the wall of water, experiment with camera speeds for the best effects.

Warning There is one more, invisible, waterfall on Canaima Lagoon, at the opposite end from Canaima Camp. It is called Salto Ara. The lagoon is a terrace and at Salto Ara all the water goes down one step. It is invisible from the surface, the only indicator is foam rising as if from nowhere. This fall is extremely dangerous: do not swim or take a boat near it. This is where Tomás Bernal, the Peruvian discoverer of the above tunnel, lost his life in 1998 after the engine of his boat broke down. He is buried on Isla Anatoliy.

Canaima

There are several tourist lodges at Canaima and some package tours now visit on day trips. Do not forget swimwear, insect repellent and sun cream; waterproof clothing may be advisable. Do not walk barefoot as there are chiggers, or *niguas*, in the lagoon's sand beaches.

Trips to the Angel Falls

The Angel Falls, the highest in the world (979 m – its longest single drop is 807 m), 70 km downriver from Canaima, are best reached by plane to Canaima from Caracas, Ciudad Bolívar or Ciudad Guayana. Trips by boat upriver to the Angel Falls operate May-January, depending on the level of the water in the rivers. Boats literally fly up and down river over the bolders (not for faint-hearted), but even during the rainy season you may have to get out and push in places. Most trips make an overnight stop on one of the islands, continuing to the Falls the next day. There are also bottom-numbing, 12-hour day trips which cost around US$80. More relaxing, with more stops at beauty spots, are 44-hour, 'three day' trips, US$140. **Inparques** is in Ciudad Guayana ⓘ *Av Guayana, Edif Centro Empresarial Alta Vista, p 8, Puerto Ordaz, T0286- 966 2033.* Ask here if you need a *permiso de excursionistas* to go on one tour and come back with another, giving yourself more time at the Falls. You may have to pay extra to do this, up to US$30 (take all food and gear). Trips can be arranged with agencies in Ciudad Bolívar (see above) or at Canaima airport. All *curiaras* (dugouts) must carry first aid, life jackets, etc. Take wet weather gear, swimwear, mosquito net for hammock and insect repellent, lots of film and a plastic bag to protect your camera/day bag. The light is best on the falls in the morning.

The cheapest way to fly over the falls is on scheduled flights from Ciudad Bolívar. From Canaima a 45-minute flight costs US$60 per person (black market rates) and does some circuits over and alongside the falls; departures only if enough passengers.

Kamarata

The largest of the tepuis, **Auyán Tepuy** (700 sq km) is also one of the more accessible. **Kamarata** is a friendly indigenous settlement with a Capuchin mission on the plain at the east foot of the tepuy. It has a well-stocked shop but no real hotels; basic rooms can be found for about US$4 per person, camping also possible at the mission (mosquito nets necessary and anti-malarial pills advised). Take food, although there is one place to eat, and locals may sell you dinner. The whole area is within the Parque Nacional Canaima.

Pemón families in Kamarata have formed co-operatives and can arrange *curiaras*, tents and porters for various excursions: see Activities and tours, below.

Kavác

About a two-hour walk northwest of Kamarata, this is a new indigenous-run resort consisting of a dozen thatched huts (*churuatas*) for guests, a small shop, and an excitingly short airstrip serviced by Cessnas from Ciudad Bolívar, Santa Elena, and Isla Margarita; flights from the north provide excellent views of Angel Falls and Auyán Tepuy. There is a vehicle connection with Kamarata but it is expensive because all fuel has to be flown in.

Parque Nacional Canaima

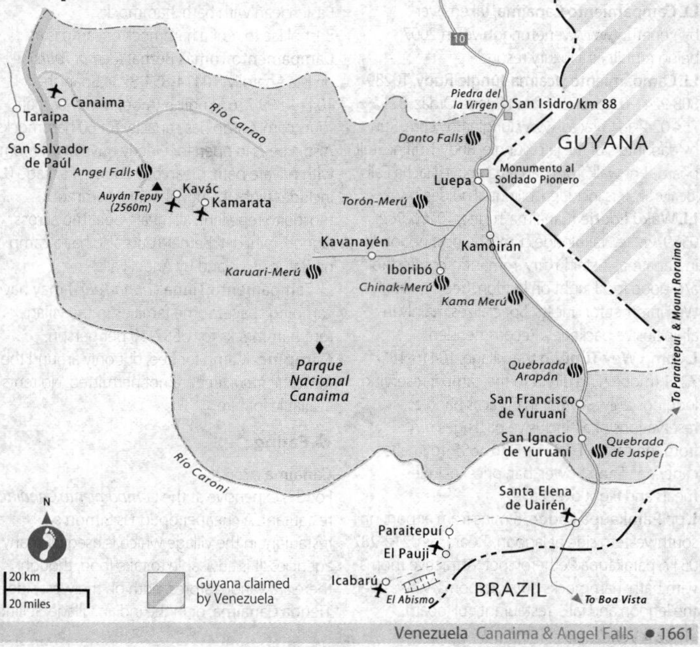

The prime local excursion is to **Kavác Canyon** and its waterfall known as La Cueva, which can be reached by joining a group or by setting out early west up the Río Kavác. A natural jacuzzi is encountered after a 30-minute wade along the sparkling stream, after which the gorge narrows dramatically until the falls are reached. Go in the morning to avoid groups of day-trippers from Porlamar. The sun's rays illuminate the vertical walls of the canyon only for a short time around 1100. Be prepared to get wet; swimwear and shoes with good grip, plus a dry change of clothing are recommended; also insect repellent, as there is a mosquito and midge invasion around dusk. Late afternoon winds off the savannah can make conditions chilly. It costs US$10 per person to stay at the camp (cheaper in hammocks), including a canyon tour. Take food with you.

Uruyén

South of Auyán Tepuy and west of Kamarata, **Uruyén** is similar to Kavác, only smaller and more intimate. It also has a beautiful canyon and is the starting point for treks up Auyán Tepuy. The camp is run by the Carvallo family. For more information, see www.angelconservation.org/lodges.html.

Canaima and Angel Falls listings

For Sleeping and Eating price codes and other relevant information, see Essentials, pages 38-40.

Sleeping

Canaima *p1660*

LL Campamiento Canaima, taken over by Venetur (www.venetur.gob.ve) in 2007, being rebuilt as a luxury resort.

LL Campamiento Ucaima Jungle Rudy, T0289-808 9241, 0286-952 1529 in Puerto Ordaz, 0212-754 0244 in Caracas, www.junglerudy.com. Run by daughters of the late 'Jungle' Rudy Truffino, full board, 1 hr walk from Canaima above Hacha Falls, local transfers included, bilingual guides.

LL Wakü Lodge (Canaima Tours), T0286-962 0559, www.wakulodge.com. The best option in Canaima, 4-star luxury, romantic, comfortable, a/c, good food, right on lagoon, free satellite/WiFi internet for guests. Specializes mainly in all-inclusive packages. Recommended.

L Camp Wey Tüpü, in the village, T0416-185 7231 (mob). Ring direct to the camp if reserving lodgings only, *Roymar* in Caracas handle reservations of all-inclusive packages run from the camp, T/F0212- 576 5655, roymar@cantv.net. Fan, shower, bar, price includes meals and flight over Falls.

L pp **Parakaupa Lodge**, 5 mins from airport, on southwestern side of lagoon, T Caracas 0212-287 0517, parakaupa@etheron.net. Attractive rooms with bath, hammocks outside rooms, views over the lagoon and falls, restaurant, full board.

A Kusary, close to *Parakaupa Lodge*, near airport, T0286-962 0443. Basic but clean, with bath, fan, food available, ask for Claudio at *Tienda Canaima*.

D pp **Kaikusé**, next to *Kusary*, T0414-884 9031. Basic, clean with bath, hammocks.

Best place to rent a hammock or camp is at **Campamento Tomás Bernal** (*Bernal Tours*) on Isla Anatoliy, T0414-854-8234 Spanish, T0414-899 7162 English (mob), www.bernaltours.com. Camp has capacity for 60 hammocks. Also 4 beds in open for elderly travelers, 4 rooms with private bath. Clean bathrooms. Package (**L**) includes flight, bilingual guide, hammock, mosquito repellent, all meals, boat trip across lagoon, raincoat. Bernal Tours also has a camp on Ratoncito Island by Angel Falls.

Campamento Tiuna (*Tiuna Tours*) may have camping space. Some families in the village rent hammocks for US$7-10 per person.

Camping Camp for free, but only around the *fuente de soda*; fires are not permitted. No tents available for hire.

Eating

Canaima *p1660*

Food is expensive at the *Campamiento Canaima* restaurant. A cheaper option is **Simon's** restaurant in the village which is used by many agencies. It is advisable to take food, though there are various stores, both on the west side, **Tienda Canaima**, or in the indian village, selling mainly canned foods. A *fuente de soda* overlooks the lagoon. There is an expensive snack bar at the airport selling basic food, soft drinks and coffee; also souvenir shop.

Activities and tours

Canaima *p1660*

You can do walking expeditions into the jungle to indigenous villages with a guide, but bargain hard on the price. Other excursions are to the Mayupa Falls, including a canoe ride on the Río Carrao (US$30, half day), to Yuri Falls by jeep and boat (US$20, half day); to Isla Orquídea (US$45, full day, good boat ride, beach barbecue); to Saltos de Sapo and Sapito (3 hrs, US$18).

Guides in Canaima Fierce competition at the airport but agencies pretty much offer the same thing at the same price. Some package tours to Canaima are listed under Caracas and Ciudad Bolívar Tour operators. Agents may tell you that guides speak English: some do, but many don't.

Bernal Tours (see above).

Kamaracoto Tours and **Tiuna Tours** for trips to Salto Sapo, Kavác, Salto Angel; they will also help with finding accommodation.

Kamarata *p1661*

Macunaima Tours (Tito Abati), **Excursiones Pemón** (Marino Sandoval), and **Jorge and Antonio Calcaño II** run local tours.

For details on climbing Auyán Tepuy, contact **Kamadac** in Santa Elena, run by Andreas Hauer (T0289-995 1408, T0414-886 6526, www.abenteuer-venezuela.de).

Alechiven and Pemón co-operatives run 6-day river trips from Kamarata to Angel Falls (May-Dec), descending the **Río Akanán** to the Carrao by motorized dugout then turning south up the 'Devil's Canyon' to the Falls; the tours continue downriver to Canaima. Cost is US$240 for the *curiara* (minimum 4), not including flights to Kamarata or food – supply your own food. River trips in this area are easier in the rainy season. Guides for Auyán Tepuy can be hired here for about US$18 per day, if you have your own equipment. Contact Andreas Hauer at *Kamadac*.

Transport

Canaima *p1660*

Air There are no flights from Caracas to Canaima. **Aereotuy** runs 1 day excursions out of **Isla Margarita**, to Canaima, with a possible stopover in Ciudad Bolívar or Puerto Ordaz and overflight of Angel Falls if conditions permit, US$798.14. They also have a camp, Arekuna, near the foot of Nonoy Tepuy, visits to which can be direct from Margarita or with an extension to Canaima; bookable only through **Aereotuy**, recommended (T0212-212 3110, www.tuy.com).

The flight to Canaima from **Ciudad Bolívar** is spectacular and takes approximately 1 hr each way, overflying mining towns of San Isidro and Los Barrancos, as well as the vast artificial lake at Guri and the Yuri Falls. For flights in 5-seater Cessnas to Canaima from Ciudad Bolívar, go to the airport early, 0600-0700. Several companies operate flights: **Rutaca, Sundance, Transmandú, La Montaña**. The first plane leaves at about 0800, and all run on a first- come, first-served basis. The less passengers, the fewer the flights. A one-way ticket costs US$140 pp, flight only. Tickets can also be bought from **Bernal Tours, Kawi Travel, Express Dorado** or **Tiuna Tours**; prices are the same. Bigger groups can negotiate slightly better rates on 19-seater Jetstream if it is available. For tours that include flight over Angel Falls, boat across lagoon, lunch and trip to Salto Sapo, etc, see Ciudad Bolívar and Canaima Tour operators, above.

Kamarata *p1661*

Air Transmandú from **Ciudad Bolívar** (2 hrs).

Kavác *p1661*

Air A day excursion by light plane to Kavác from **Canaima** (45 mins' flight) can be made with any of the tour operators at the airport. There are also flights from **Ciudad Bolívar** with **Transmandú**. Trips from Ciudad Bolívar can be arranged with tour agencies in town or at airport, including flight via Angel Falls, meals, and 1 night's accommodation.

Ciudad Guayana and the Orinoco Delta

Ciudad Guayana ➔ *Phone code: 0286. Colour map 2, A2. Population: 700,000.*

In an area rich in natural resources 105 km downriver from Ciudad Bolívar, Ciudad Guayana was founded in 1961 by merging two towns, San Félix and Puerto Ordaz, on either bank of the Río Caroní where it spills into the Orinoco. Now a single city, it is hot, humid and futuristic. Its wide avenues, lack of sidewalks and public transport reflect the influence of the US-owned Orinoco Mining Company, which had its headquarters here and was nationalized in 1976. East of the Caroní is the commercial port of **San Félix** and the Palúa iron-ore terminal. Across the Caroní by the 470 m concrete bridge is **Puerto Ordaz** (airport), the iron-ore port connected by rail with the Cerro Bolívar open-cast iron mine. The second bridge across the Río Orinoco, Puente Orinoquia, 3,156 m long, was opened in Ciudad Guayana in 2006.

Visitors should be particularly careful while exploring Ciudad Guyana: it is surrounded by some desperately poor neighbourhoods. Violent crime, including rape, is unfortunately very common. And so is police unwillingness to answer 171 calls, let alone to investigate.

Excursions Unlike elsewhere in Venezuela, there is little emphasis on arts and culture. However, you can get beyond the urban functionality into some pleasant parks, all well kept and free to enter. Just up the Caroní at Macagua, some truly beautiful cataracts called Salto Llovizna are in the **Parque Nacional La Llovizna** ⓘ *open from early morning till 1630, taxi, US$8.50*, which covers 26 islands separated by narrow waterways and connected by 36 footbridges. Also in the park are hydroelectric plants, but these do not spoil the views of the larger and smaller falls, diverse fauna, including monkeys, and magnificent plants growing from the falling water. There are several trails. A facility on the hydroelectric dam ⓘ *Tue-Sun 0900-2100*, houses an ecological museum, art exhibitions and displays on the dam's construction, and a café. Near La Llovizna, the iron-tinted waterfall in the pretty **Parque Cachamay** (about 8 km from centre, near the Guayana Hotel; closes 1700) is worth a visit. A third park, adjoining Cachamay, is **Loefling Wildlife Park**, with tapirs, capybaras and capuchin monkeys.

Higher up the Caroní is the massive Guri dam ⓘ *daily 0900-1030, 1415-1515*, take your passport; the area gets busy during holidays, Easter or carnival, powered by the world's second-largest reservoir, which is filled by the Paragua and Caroní rivers. The trip to Guri takes 90 minutes by taxi.

Los Castillos, supposedly where Sir Walter Raleigh's son was killed in the search for El Dorado, are two old forts down the Orinoco from San Félix (one hour by *por puesto*, US$3, or take a tour).

Tucupita ➔ *Phone code: 0287, Colour map 2, A2, Population: 67,000.*

A worthwhile side trip along asphalted roads can be made to Tucupita (*Climate: very humid*), on the Orinoco delta. Though capital of Delta Amacuro state and the main commercial centre of the delta, there's a one-horse feel about it. The **tourist office** is at Calle Dalla Costa beside Sonido Color 2000, fondomixtodeltaamacuro@hotmail.com. Tourists should go there first for tour information. **Note** Banks won't change traveller's cheques.

For a 3-4 day **trip to see the delta**, its fauna and the indigenous *Warao*, either arrange boats through the tourist office (see Ins and outs, above). Boats are not easy to come by and are expensive except for large groups. Bargain hard and never pay up front.

Excursions often only travel on the main river, not in the *caños* where wildlife is most often be seen. To avoid disappointment, be sure to determine where your guide intends to take you before you leave. If the river level rises after a downpour, arrangements may be cancelled. On all trips agree in advance exactly what is included, especially that there is enough food and water for you and your guide. Hammocks and mosquito repellents are essential.

Barrancas → *Colour map 2, A2. Population: 13,000.*

An interesting and friendly village, founded in 1530, Barrancas is one of the oldest villages in the Americas, but its precolonial past dates back to 1000 BC. Situated on the Orinoco, it can be reached by road from Tucupita (63 km), or from Maturín. It has two basic hotels (**E**). The village has a large community of Guyanese people who speak English. It is possible to take a boat to the *Warao* villages of **Curiapo** and **Amacuro** (near Guyana border), check at harbour.

It is possible to take a cargo boat to Mabaruma in Guyana from Curiapo. A trustworthy boatman is Bimbo, who lives at Wirma's guest house, where you can sleep if stuck in Curiapo (very likely). Contact Bimbo in advance through his sister in Tucupita; just ask for the "English woman" on Calle Amacuro – everyone knows her. In Curiapo, find Miss Teresa to get your exit stamp; she is rarely at home at the weekend. Take plenty of dollars cash, be prepared to wait for a boat and to cover yourself with a large plastic sheet once at sea (the mid part of the trip is on the open ocean). If thinking of taking this route, visit the Guyanese Embassy in Caracas first.

Ciudad Guayana and the Orinoco Delta listings

For Sleeping and Eating price codes and other relevant information, see Essentials, pages 38-40.

Sleeping

Ciudad Guayana: Puerto Ordaz *p1664*

LL-L Hotel Guayana, formerly Intercontinental, Av Guayana, technically in Cachamay Park, T713 1000/1240, has been taken over be Venetur (www.venetur.gob.ve); see also www.ichotelsgroup.com. It overlooks La Llovizna, far from centre, highest standard in city but price is high for what is offered.

AL Roraima Inn Express, Carrera La Paragua, T923 28362, 0800-767 2462, www.roraimainn.com. Good rooms but pricey, WiFi, airport transfer, buffet breakfast, cable TV. Casino and entertainment, can get wild.

B Dos Ríos, México esq Ecuador, T924 0679. New rooms have a/c, hot water, TV, pool, restaurant, *loncheria*, hairdresser, helpful.

B Posada Turística Alonga, Urb La Corniza, Av Canadá, manz 10, casa 14, T923 3154, 0414-898 2794 (mob). Quiet residential area, cable TV, internet.

C Residencias Tore, C San Cristóbal y Cra Los Andes, T923 0679, tore@cantv.net. Good rooms with a/c, hot water, TV, meals available.

D in the house of Rolf and Rosa Kampen, C Surinam 03-07, Villa Antillana, 3 km from central Pto Ordaz, T/F923 0516. Room for 6 people, free pick up (best to contact by fax), breakfast US$4, dinner can be arranged. Rolf speaks English, German and Dutch.

E with Wolfgang Löffler of *Lobo Tours*, C Zambia 2, Africana Manzana 39, T961 6286. Room for 8 people, free transfer from airport. 'El Lobo' speaks English and German. Recommended.

Tucupita *p1664*

C Saxxi, on main road into Tucupita, 10 mins from centre, T721 2112, hotelsaxxi@cantv.net. Comfortable, hot water, a/c, bar/restaurant, disco Fri-Sat, pool. Also has camps *Mis Palafitos* and *Orinoco Bujana Lodge*, **AL**, T721 1733. All inclusive.

D Gran Hotel Amacuro, Bolívar 23, T721 0404. A/c, big rooms, dubious, **E** with fan.

D Sans Souci, Centuríon 30, T721 0132. Safe, a/c, OK, **E** with fan. French spoken.

E Pequeño, La Paz, T721 0523. Basic but clean, fan, good value, safe, stores luggage, orchid garden, popular, closes at 2200.

E Residencias San Cristóbal, San Cristóbal 50, T721 4529. Fan, parking.

Eating

Ciudad Guayana *p1664*

There are plenty of restaurants and cafés on Cras Tumeremo and Upata, off Av Las Américas. There is a very good *churrascaría* on Av Las Américas 15 mins' walk from *Hotel Guayana* towards the airport, in an old hacienda building on the left, next to a *cervecería*, recommended. Fast food and upmarket eateries in Ciudad Comercial Altavista and surrounding streets.

Mall Orinokia, on Av Guayana, Altavista. Huge, super-modern shopping centre with restaurants, cafés and travel agencies. Multi-screen cinema.

El Arepazo Guayanés, C La Urbana, Puerto Ordaz, T922 4757, the oldest and best *arepería*

in Ciudad Guyana, open 24 hrs. **Pollos y Parillas El Guayanés**, next door to Arepazo, open until midnight. (Opposite is a good laundry, **Lavandería Villa Brasil.**)
Mi Rinconcito across the street from Mall Orinokia (Altavista), T962 1554, is famous for its *cachapas* and live music at the end of the week.

Tucupita *p1664*
🍴 **Capri**, on Paseo Manamo. Very good.
🍴 **Mi Tasca**, C Dalla Costa. Popular, varied menu, large portions. Recommended.
🍴 **Refresquería La Cascada**, on Paseo Manamo. English spoken.

Activities and tours

Ciudad Guayana *p1664*
Anaconda Tours, PB, loc 2, CC Anto, Av Las Américas, T923 7966, anaconda2@ cantv.net. Trips to Castillos de Guayana, Guri dam, Orinoco Delta, Gran Sabana and Canaima.
Bagheera Tours, p 2, of 86, C C Gran Sabana, Paseo Caroní, near airport, T952 9481, bagheera@telcel.net.ve. Tours to Gran Sabana, Angel Falls, Caura River and Orinoco Delta.
Lobo Tours, C Zambia No 2, Villa Africana Manzana 39, T961 6286. Wolfgang Löffler will tailor his tours to fit your demands. Trips organized to the Gran Sabana and Orinoco Delta, but will put together other excursions. Very helpful, all-inclusive, excellent cooking. English and German spoken. Recommended.
Oridelta, T961 5526, T0416-806 1211, www.deltaorinoko.com.ve. Roger and Ninoska Ruffenach arrange 1, 2 and 3-day tours to their Campamento in the less-visited southern part of the Orinoco Delta (T400 2649, 0414-868 2121, simple facilities), near Piacoa, 25 km from Los Castillos. German and English spoken.
Piraña Tours, at *Hotel Guayana*, Av Guayana, Parque Punta Vista, Puerto Ordaz, T923 6447, www.pirana tours.com. Local trips on the Caroní, Cachamay Falls and Orinoco, Delta and Gran Sabana tours, 25 years' experience.
Recommended guide Richard Brandt, T/F922- 4370 (or in Santa Elena de Uairén at *Cabañas Friedenau*), has own car, speaks English and tailors trips to your requirements.

Tucupita *p1664*
Some boat owners visit hotels in the evenings looking for clients and may negotiate a price. Ask Pieter Rothfuss at *Gekko Tours/Posada La Casita* in Ciudad Bolívar and Roger Ruffenbach of *Oridelta* in Ciudad Guayana about a trip through the southern part of the delta and into the Sierra Imataca highlands. The following (and *Mis Palafitos* – see *Hotel Saxxi*) are registered with the tourist board and have insurance (this does not necessarily guarantee a good tour).
Aventura Turística, C Centurión 62, T/F721 0835, and at bus station, a_t_d_1973@ hotmail.com. Nicolás and Vidalig Montabric have 2 camps in the northern part of the delta, all-inclusive tours, English and French spoken.
Delta Sur, C Mariño and C Pativilca, T/F721 2666, oldest-established company, 3 day tours offered, English spoken.
Tucupita Expeditions, opposite hospital, T0414- 789 8343, www.orinocodelta.com. 2- to 5-night tours to lodges in the delta.

Transport

Ciudad Guayana *p1664*
Air Daily flights from Puerto Ordaz to **Caracas, Maracaibo**, **Porlamar** and short-haul destinations with **Aserca, Aeropostal, Rutaca** and others. Car hire, **Europcar** and **Avis**. Walk 600 m to gas station on main road for buses to San Félix or Puerto Ordaz.
Bus Terminals at San Félix and close to Puerto Ordaz airport; long distance buses at both. Public transport in Ciudad Guayana is very limited. New, free local buses are infrequent. Minibuses are fast and cheap; San Félix-Puerto Ordaz, US$1.40; buses run until 2100. Several buses daily to **Santa Elena de Uairén** (via El Callao), US$18.25, 10 hrs, with **Caribe** (T951 8385, recommended) and **Turgar** (or night bus, which misses the fine scenery, 9 hrs). **El Callao** (US$6), **Tumeremo** (US$7.50), **El Dorado** (US$10) and Km 88 with **Turgar**. **Ciudad Bolívar** US$1.75 (*por puesto* US$5.75), 1 hr. Bus to **Maturín** US$8.75, 2½ hrs. 8 daily to **Caracas**, US$18.50 (**Aeroexpresos Ejecutivos**), 10 hrs. 8 daily to **Puerto La Cruz**, US$18, 6 hrs, with **Caribe**. 2 daily to **Cumaná**, US$16.30, 8 hrs, with **Caribe**.

5 daily to **Valencia**, US$20, 12½ hrs, with **Expresos Occidente**. To **Tucupita**, US$7, 3 hrs, leaving from San Félix bus terminal with **Expresos Guayanesa**, booking office opens 1 hr before departure, be there early, passport check just before Tucupita. San Felix bus terminal is not a safe place, especially at night.

International buses 1 bus daily to **Brazil**, US$33, 14 hrs including 3 stops, departs 2130, arrives Boa Vista 1130, with **Caribe** recommended, a/c (take warm clothes), toilets and reclining seats.

Taxi San Félix-Puerto Ordaz US$4 minimum, Puerto Ordaz-airport US$8, airport-centre US$14, San Félix bus terminal-Puerto Ordaz bus terminal US$11, bus terminal-centre US$6, centre-San Félix bus terminal US$6.50. Some hotels and the airport charge double and only allow their own taxis to enter. Radio taxi **Carlos Manuel Piar**, T931 3948.

Tucupita *p1664*

Bus *Por puesto* from **Maturín** US$11, 2-3 hrs; bus to Maturín, US$5.75, 3-4 hrs, **Expresos Guayanesa**, US$7 with **Expresos Los Llanos** recommended. 2 daily to **San Félix**, US$7, 3 hrs, with **Expresos La Guayanesa**. 2 daily to **Caracas**, US$17, 12-13 hrs, with **Camargüi**. **Puerto La Cruz**, US$12, 7-8 hrs.

Barrancas *p1665*

Bus **Tucupita**-Barrancas, US$2, return at 0945 and 1700.

❶ Directory

Ciudad Guayana *p1664*

Banks See also Money, page 1566. **Corp Banca** (American Express), Av Cuchivero y C Caruachi, Edif Seguros Orinoco, PB, Urb Alta Vista, and C Urbana, Edif Don An, Puerto Ordaz. **Banco de Venezuela**, Av Las Américas y Av Monseñor Zabaleta. Banks will not exchange Brazilian currency. **Car hire** Many agencies at airport, **Margarita Rentals** cars recommended; **Hertz**, Puerto Ordaz, rents 4WD vehicles. A car is very useful here, eg for the Cerro Bolívar mine and Guri dam, or taking a road trip through the Gran Sabana to Brazil. **Consulates** **Brazil**, Cra Tocoma, Edif Eli-Alti, of 4, Alta Vista, T961 2995, www.consbrasguayana.org.ve, 0900-1200-1400-1800. Friendly, helpful, visa issued in 1 hr, no onward ticket requested (some have to pay, eg Australians), good information. **Internet** **Planet Web Café**, Carrera Tumeremo, **Cyberarepa**, CC Altavista. **Internet y Comunicaciones 2015**, C La Urbana, Puerto Ordaz. Open till late. **Medical services** **Clinic Chilemex**, Av Las Américas.

Tucupita *p1664*

Banks **Banesco** C Petíon 35, cash on Visa. **Banco de Venezuela**, Paseo Manamo, Delta a La Paz, ATM and cash advances. **Internet** **Compucenter.com**, in same Centro Comercial on Plaza Bolívar. **Delta Microsystems**, C Pativilca.

Ciudad Guayana to Santa Elena de Uairén

Travelling South from Ciudad Guayana to the Brazilian border is becoming an increasingly popular excursion for Venezuelan tourists, as well as for overland travellers heading into (or out of) Brazil via Boa Vista. The road to the border at Santa Elena de Uairén passes across the beautiful Gran Sabana and is completely paved, with all bridges in place.

Ins and outs

Getting around A 4WD is only necessary off the main road, especially in the rainy season. You may need spare tanks of gasoline if spending a lot of time away from the main road (eg in Kavanayen and El Paují) and have a gas-guzzling vehicle. Carry extra water and plenty of food. Small eating places may close out of season. There are Guardia Nacional checks at the Río Cuyuní (Km 8), at Km 126, and at San Ignacio de Yuruaní (Km 259), and a military checkpoint at Luepa (Km 143); all driving permits, car registration papers, and ID must be shown. ▸▸ *See also Transport, page 1674.*

Advice Camping is possible but a good waterproof tent is essential. A small fee is payable to the *indígenas* living around Kaui, Kama and similar villages (see also under Parque Nacional Canaima). Insect repellent and long-sleeved/trousered clothes are needed against *puri-puri* (small, black, vicious biting insects) and mosquitoes (especially in El Dorado, at Km 88 and at Icabarú); or use baby oil mixed with vitamin B12. Arrange five-day/four-night tours of the Gran Sabana in Caracas or in Ciudad Bolívar (cheaper and easier). See www.lagransabana.com.

To Tumeremo

South from Ciudad Guayana Highway 10 is a four-lane *autopista* as far as **Upata** (*Phone code: 0288; Population: 51,500*). Buy provisions opposite the petrol station. **Note** Water is rationed in Upata and hot water in hotels is rare south of Ciudad Guayana, except in the better hotels of Santa Elena. From Upata to Km 88, the road is partly resurfaced with occasional broad hard shoulders.

At 18 km beyond **Guasipati** is **El Callao** on the south bank of the Río Yuruari, off the highway, a small, clean, bright town (*Population: 12,000*) whose pre-Lenten carnival has a touch of calypso from British Caribbean immigrants who came to mine gold in the late 19th century. The gold mine, 8 km away in El Perú, has a museum of geology and carnival (T762 0336). Sr Rafael, who lives opposite will show you the mine (T762 0662, evenings only). The town has many jewellery shops and restaurants. The *Banco de Venezuela* on main plaza may change US$ cash, but not traveller's cheques. There is a chronic water shortage, check when it's available in your hotel. All prices rise for carnival in February.

On another 41 km is **Tumeremo** (*Colour map 2, A2. Population: 25,000*), which is recommended as the best place to buy provisions. There is *Banco de Orinoco* (Amex, after 1500), and gasoline (all grades) at a normal price (better than El Dorado). About 5 km from Tumeremo towards the Fuerte Tarabay is the beautiful artificial lake of San Pedro with free campsite.

El Dorado ➔ *Phone code: 0288. Colour map 2, B2. Population: 4,000.*

This hot, dirty and very noisy miners' supply centre in dense forest is 76 km from Tumeremo, 278 km from Ciudad Guayana, and 7 km off the road on the Río Cuyuní. On a river island is the prison made famous by Henri Charrière/Papillon's stay there in 1945. The local gold seams have been largely exhausted but mining still continues and the town's nightlife is entirely for the miners, violence is in the air after nightfall. El Dorado's other economic mainstay is its gas station (open 0800-1900, daily).

El Dorado to Santa Elena de Uairén

The turn-off to El Dorado is marked Km 0; distances are measured from here by green signs 2 km apart. About 3 km south of the turnoff to El Dorado, is the Río Cuyuní crossed by a bridge.

Las Claritas, a gold-miners' town at Km 85 has a couple of places to stay, a restaurant, a big market for food and gold, and safe parking at Las Hermanitas de las Pobres (Convent), which can be better reached by the track from Km 88. At **Km 88** (also called **San Isidro**), there is gasoline, a garage, one of the last reliable telephones before Santa Elena and Banco Guayana. Everything is expensive; better food shops at Km 85.

The wall of the Gran Sabana looms above Km 88 and the highway climbs steeply in sharp curves for 40 km before reaching the top. The road is in very good condition and presents no problem for conventional cars. 4WDs may be better in the wet season (May-October). At Km 100 the huge **Piedra de la Virgen** (sandy coloured with black streaks) is passed before the steepest climb (La Escalera) enters the beautiful **Parque Nacional Canaima** (see page 1660).

The landscape is essentially savannah, with clusters of trees, moriche palms and bromeliads. Characteristic of this area are the large abrupt *tepuis* (flat-topped mountains or mesas), hundreds of waterfalls, and the silence of one of the oldest plateaus on earth. At Km 119 (sign can only be seen going north) a short trail leads to the 40 m **Danto ('Tapir') Falls**, a powerful fall wreathed in mosses and mist. If you are paying for your ride, try to persuade the driver to make a short stop; the falls are close to the road (about five minutes slippery walk down on the left-hand side), but not visible from it. (Buses cannot be flagged down here because of dangerous bends.) The **Monumento al Soldado Pionero** (Km 137) commemorates the army engineers who built the road up from the lowlands, finally opened in 1973; barbecues, toilets, shelters are now almost all in ruins. Some 4 km beyond is **Luepa**; all travellers must stop at the *ciudadela* (military checkpoint) a little way south. There is a popular camping place at Luepa, on the right going south which belongs to a tour company. An informative guide on duty will rent you a tent or you can hang a hammock in an open-sided shelter (very cold at night, no water or facilities, possible to buy a meal from a tour group, but expensive). There is a breakfast place, US$4. The Inparques station at Luepa has some guestrooms which are intended for visitors of Inparques, but they may let you stay for a small fee. There is a kitchen at the station and a cafetería for employees of Inparques and Edelca. You can camp at a site right on the Río Aponwao on the left hand side of the road going south.

Some 8 km beyond Luepa, a poor, graded gravel road leads 70 km west to **Kavanayén** (little traffic, best to have your own vehicle with high clearance, especially during the wet season, take snacks; the road can be cycled but is slow, lots of soft, sandy places). Accommodation is at the Capuchin mission, **G**, very friendly, also in private homes. One of the two grocery stores will

Santa Elena de Uairén

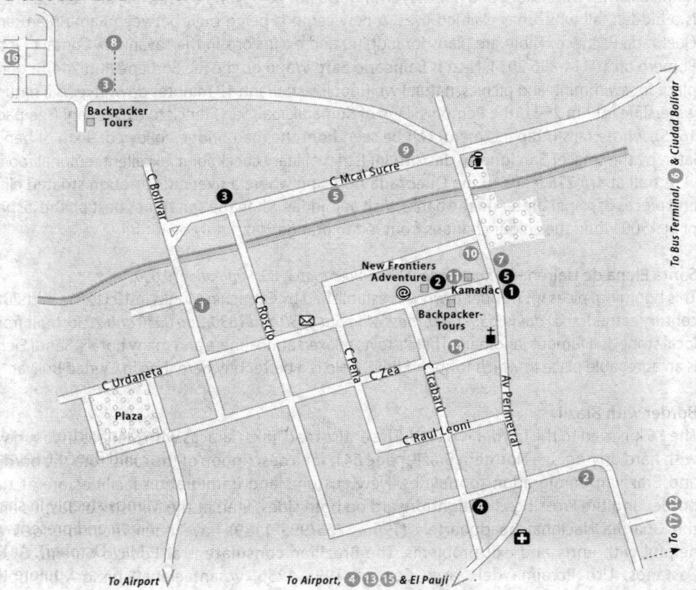

Sleeping
1 Augusta
2 Cabañas Friedenau
3 Cabañas Roraima
4 Gran Sabana
5 Jaspe
6 Kiamantí
7 La Posada Aventura & Adventure Tours
8 Las 5 Jotas
9 Los Castaños
10 Lucrecia
11 Michelle
12 Tavarúa
13 Temiche Camp
14 Tres Naciones
15 Villa Apoipó
16 Villa Fairmont
17 Ya-Koo Ecological Camp

Eating
1 Alfredo's
2 Café Goldrausch & Michelle
3 El Ranchón Criollo
4 Panadería Gran Café
5 Venezuela Primero

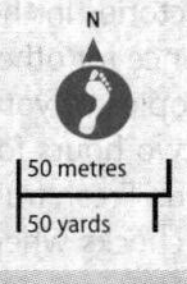

prepare food, or the restaurant opposite serves cheap breakfasts and dinners, order in advance. Medical post in front of the mission, where handicrafts are sold.

The settlement is surrounded by *tepuis*. Off the road to Kavanayén are the falls of **Torón Merú** and **Chinak-Merú** (also called Aponwao), 105 m high and very impressive. Neither is a straightforward detour, so get full instructions before setting out. Chinak-Merú is reached via the very friendly Pemón village of **Iboribó** (there is a small bakery near the junction to Torón). A day's walk west of Kavanayén are the lovely falls on the **Río Karuay**. Ask locals for details.

For the remaining 180 km to Santa Elena de Uairén few people and only a few Pemón Indian villages are to be seen. San Juan and San Rafael de Kamoiran and **Rápidos de Kamoirán** are passed. The 5-m Kawí falls on the **Kaüi** River are at Km 195, while at Km 201.5 are the impressive 55 m high **Kama Merú** falls (US$1 to walk to bottom of falls). Also a small lake, handicrafts, a small shop, canoe trips. Cabins and *churuatas* can be rented, also camping. *Puri-puri* flies descend at dusk. Buses can be flagged down going south or north three times a day; check times in advance.

At Km 237 the Río Arapán cascades over the charming **Quebrada Pacheco** ; pools nearby where you can swim. Tour groups often stop here. A path up the opposite side of the main falls leads to an isolated natural pool 20 minutes walk away, in the middle of the savannah. Nearby are more falls with waterslides and pools. **Warning** Do not go beyond the red line at Pacheco: there is a hidden fall which has claimed lives. A new camp is being built between Kama Merú and Quebrada Pacheco. There are plans for lodging and excursions in the savannah. Contact Oscar Romero on T0414-886 2034. Next is **Balneario Saro Wapo** on the Río Soruapé (Km 244), a good place for swimming and picnics, natural whirlpool, restaurant, 10 minutes downriver is a natural waterslide. At Km 250 is the Pemón village of Kumarakapai, San Francisco de Yuruaní (see page 1675), whose falls (Arapena-merú) can be seen from the road bridge, followed, 9 km of bends later, by the smaller **San Ignacio de Yuruaní** (strict military checkpoint; excellent regional food).

A trail at Km 275 leads to the **Quebrada de Jaspe** where a river cuts through striated cliffs and pieces of jasper glitter on the banks. Visit at midday when the sun shines best on the jasper, or at 1500 when the colour changes from red to orange, dazzlingly beautiful.

Santa Elena de Uairén → *Phone code: 0289. Colour map 2, B2. Population: 9,000.*

This booming, pleasant frontier town was established by Capuchin Monks in 1931. The mid-20th century cathedral ⓘ *daily 0530-1900, mass Mon-Sat 0630 and 1830, Sun 0630 and 2030*, built from local stone, is a famous landmark. Thanks to its relaxed atmosphere and many hotels, Santa Elena is an agreeable place in which to spend time. Gold is a better buy here than in Ciudad Bolívar.

Border with Brazil

The 16 km road to the border is paved. The entire road links Caracas with Manaus in four days with hard driving; see Northern Brazil, page 641, for a description of the road from the border and Brazilian immigration formalities. New customs and immigration facilities are at the border and the crossing is straightforward on both sides. Staff at the Ministry of Justice and the Guardia Nacional headquarters (T960 3765/995 1189) have been recommended as helpful with entry and exit problems. The **Brazilian consulate** is at Edifício Galeno, C Los Castaños, Urb Roraima del Casco Central, T995 1256, vcsantaelena@mre.gov.br; open 0800-1200, 1400-1800. You can get a visa here.

For entry to Venezuela, some nationalities who cross the border from Boa Vista, Brazil, need a visa. It is not required by western Europeans, whose passport must be valid for a year, but check with a consulate before leaving home. Venezuelan consulates are listed in directories in the Brazil chapter. A yellow fever vaccination certificate is required. Ask well in advance for other health requirements (eg malaria test certificate). Entering by car, keep photocopies of your licence, the Brazilian permission to leave and Venezuelan entry stamp. Allow two hours for formalities when crossing by private vehicle and don't cross during the lunch hour. Fresh fruit and vegetables may not be brought into Venezuela. There are frequent road checks when heading north from Santa Elena. Seniat (the customs authority) has its Aduana Principal Ecológica outside the town and there may be up to eight more thorough searches, mainly for drugs. Luggage will be sealed before loading into the bus hold in Santa Elena. These checks may mean you arrive in Ciudad Bolívar after dark. There is no public transport on the Venezuelan side, hitch or take a taxi from Brazil.

El Paují

A road leaves the highway 8 km south of Santa Elena and after passing through a tunnel of jungle vegetation emerges onto rolling savannah dotted with *tepuis*. The road has been considerably improved and has been paved for about 20 km. The rest is graded, but rapidly deteriorating. It can take between 2-4 hours to reach El Pauji. Take advice before setting out, as rain can rapidly degrade the road. At Km 58 is a Guardia Nacional checkpoint at Paraitepuí, waterfall nearby.

El Paují, 17 km further on, is an agricultural settlement with a growing foreign population. It is a lovely area, with good walking. Excellent sights: **Chirica Tepuy**, huge, beautiful, jet black, set in rolling savannah; **Río Surucún**, where Venezuela's largest diamond was found; **Salto Catedral** (61 km off the road), beautiful small hollow, lovely falls, excellent swimming (camping, shop); **Salto La Gruta**, impressive falls, but very slippery; and **Pozo Esmeralda**, 1½ km outside El Paují towards Icabarú (400 m south of road), fine rapids, waterfall you can stand under and pools. At Los Saltos de Paují are many powerful falls; going from El Paují towards Santa Elena, before crossing the first bridge, take track on left for about 500 m. A good walk is to the small hill, 2 km from El Paují beyond the airfield; views from the crest over **El Abismo**, the plunging escarpment marking the end of Gran Sabana highlands and the start of the Amazon rainforest. It takes an hour to reach the top, and the walk is highly recommended. Guides, though not necessary, are in the village. A recommended guide is German-speaking Marco. Small campsite (lovely early morning or sunset).

Apiculture is the main activity of El Paují and there's an International Honey Festival every summer. The honey made in this area is delicious; buy it at the shop in El Paují or Salto Catedral.

Ciudad Guayana to Santa Elena de Uairén listings

For Sleeping and Eating price codes and other relevant information, see Essentials, pages 38-40.

Sleeping

To Tumeremo *p1668*

Upata

C Andrea, Plaza Miranda, T221 3618. Decent rooms, a/c, hot water, TV, fridge in some rooms. Credit cards accepted, Chinese restaurant, safe parking, good.

D Yocoima, C Ayacucho, T221 1305. 25 rooms with a/c, TV, Italian restaurant, accepts credit cards.

E Comercio, C Piar, T221 1156. Excellent.

Guasipati

C Hotel La Reina, Av Orinoco, T767 1357. A/c, hot water, cable TV, good.

D El Mery de Oro, Av Orinoco, T767 1287. Hot water, a/c, helpful if bland.

E Residencias El Agua, southern end of town. Basic, a/c, OK.

El Callao

C Arte Dorado, C Roscio 51, 5 mins from Plaza Bolívar, T762 0535. A/c, TV, parking.

C New Millenium, Plaza Bolívar, T762 0448. Nice rooms, a/c, TV, laundry, parking, cheaper without hot water. Recommended.

D Isidora, on the road to El Perú but in town, T762 0290. A/c.

E Elvira, C Bolívar, 2 blocks from the plaza, T0416-788 7617 (mob). Shared bath, laundry facilities. Recommended.

E Italia Centro, C Ricuarte off Plaza Bolívar, T762 0770. Basic, a/c.

E Ritz, C Ricuarte, T762 0730. Basic, cold beer.

Tumeremo *p1668*

Most hotels here are used for doing business with diamonds and as short-stay accommodation.

C-D Miranda, Zea 33, T771 0202. Cable TV, a/c, parking, comfortable.

D Sinfontes, C El Dorado, T771 0739. Good value, good beds, a/c, TV, bath, has seen better days (1 block down from *Leocar*, Dorado y Paez, next to the bus stop, which is poor value, very basic).
D La Francia, C Bolívar, T711 1477. Clean, a/c, cheaper with fan, TV, basic.
D Pan-hoc, C Piar at Miranda, next to plaza Bolívar, T771 0264. Good value.
D Tumeremo City, on Zea, T771 0281. A/c, TV, parking. Recommended.
E Central, Piar y Miranda, T710 2064. Fan, OK, bakery and snackbar.

El Dorado *p1668*
All hotels have problems with running water and there is lots of short-stay accommodation.
C El Encanto Cuyuní, a camp 3 km down the road at Puente Río Cuyuní, T0288-808 3845. Bruno and Vanessa will pick you up from El Dorado, or buses drop you at the bridge. Hammock space, camping, cabins, guests can prepare food. Boat trips and tours.
D Agua Selva, on right when entering town, T991 1093. Rustic camp, with shared bathrooms, fan, includes breakfast, dinner available at extra cost. Hammocks for rent, **F** including breakfast. Welcoming owner, tours. Recommended.
D Universo, C Cuyuní, running parallel to the river, T991 1151. Clean, safe, a/c, some rooms have TV, safe parking. Recommended.

El Dorado to Santa Elena de Uairén *p1668*
A Campamento Turístico Anaconda, Las Claritas, T0286-923 7996, anaconda@cantv.net. Cabins with bath, fan, well-furnished, bar, including breakfast and dinner, reserved for tour groups (**B** in low season).
A pp **La Barquilla de Fresa**, at Km 84.5. Book via Alba Betancourt in Caracas T0212-256 4162, T0416- 709 7205, barquilladefresa@cantv.net. Run by Henry Cleve, English and German spoken. Bird- watching tours and inventory of bird species for the jungle here has reached more than 300 species. Full board lodging, reservations and deposit required.
D La Pilonera, opposite Vargas store, Km 88. With a/c and hot water, **E** with fan and cold water, safe parking, some rooms with bath, restaurant with good fruit drinks; good food next door.
E Landolfi, Las Claritas, left turn in the centre of town towards the indigenous village of San Lucia de Inaway. A/c, **F** with fan, parking.

Rápidos de Kamoirán
D Campamento Rápidos de Kamoirán, Km 172, T0289-805 1505. Clean, with fan, well-kept, cold water, camping US$4, aiso restaurant, gasoline, and picnic spot by rapids.

Santa Elena de Uairén *p1670, map p1669*
A Gran Sabana, outside town, 10 km from border, T995 1810. Most luxurious in town, good service. Recommended.
A-B Villa Fairmont, Urb Akurimá, T995 1022, at north edge of town. Large, comfortable rooms, a/c, hot water, TV, restaurant, small craft shop.
B pp **Ya-Koo Ecological Camp**, 2 km on unpaved road to Sampai Indian community, up mountain behind Santa Elena, T995 1742, www.ya-koo.com. *Cabañas* in beautiful 10-ha site, full board, spacious rooms, hot water, natural pool. Cheaper in low season. Recommended if you have a car.
C Lucrecia, Av Perimetral, T995 1105, near old terminal. A/c or fan, TV, restaurant, pool, parking, helpful, good.
C Temiche Camp, 5 mins from town on airport road, T962 2693/0414-886 2323. Nice rooms, hot water, meals and use of kitchen extra.
D Kiamantí, outside town near new bus terminal, T995 1952, kiamanti77@hotmail.com. Full board, fan, hot water, comfortable, parking, pool.
D Tavarúa, near *Ya-Koo*, T808 8386, 0416-289 2600, robtavarua1@yahoo.com. Lovely rooms, hot water, meals available, pick-up from town, Roberto Campano is a guide.
E Augusta, C Bolívar, next to Panadería Rico Pan, T995 1654. Hot water, fan, cable TV, clean, central.
E pp **Cabañas Friedenau**, Av Ppal de Cielo Azul, off Av Perimetral, T995 1353, friedenau@cantv.net. Self-contained chalets, price includes breakfast, nice grounds, vegetarian food, parking, transfer to Puerto Ordaz, bikes, horseriding, trips to Roraima (see below), English spoken. Recommended.
E Cabañas Roraima, up road behind old bus terminal, near *Villa Fairmont*, T996 1164. A/c, hot water, fridge, also cabins for up to 8.
E Los Castaños, C Mcal Sucre, near old bus terminal, T995 1450. A/c, TV, cheaper with fan.

E Jaspe, on C Mcal Sucre, T995 1379, 150 m from old bus terminal on opposite side. Hot water, fan, TV, free coffee.

E La Posada Aventura, above *Adventure Tours* on Av Perimetral, T995 1574. Hot water, fan. Good.

E Las 5 Jotas, near *Cabañas Roraima*, T0414-886 1524. Comfortable, good value.

E Michelle, C Urdaneta, next to *Café Goldrausch*, T995 1415, hotelmichelle@cantv.net. Spotless, hot water, fan, helpful, laundry, good value. Credit cards accepted, cash advances on Visa if you're desperate.

E Tres Naciones, on C Zea, T995 1190. Basic, with a/c, hot water, restaurant, parking.

E Villa Apoipó, on the road to the airport, turn left at the *Hotel Gran Sabana*, T492 2626, 0414-886 2049. Very nice rooms, hot water, fan. For groups but will take independent travellers if you ring ahead. Use of kitchen or full board. Bunk beds or hammocks available in large *churuata*.

El Paují *p1671*

A pp **Campamento Amaribá**, 3½ km outside El Paují on road from Santa Elena, transport available from airstrip, T0414-932 2169, Caracas T0212-753 9314, amariba@cantv.net. Comfortable cabins with mosquito nets, separate bathrooms, good facilities, full board, kitchen, tours arranged, very hospitable.

B Campamento El Paují, 3½ km outside El Paují on road from Santa Elena, transport usually available from airstrip, T995 1431, or contact through Maripak. Beautiful cabins with spectacular views over the Gran Sabana, food available, camping US$6 per tent. Recommended.

B Weimure, 2 km out, outside El Paují on road from Santa Elena, pauji0@yahoo.com. Beautiful cabin close to river, dynamic architect owner.

D pp **Chimanta** and **Manoa**, T995 1431. Cosy rooms, restaurant serving vegan food.

D Maripak, near the airstrip and small store, T808 1033, maripaktepuy@hotmail.com, or reserve in Caracas T0212-234 3631. Run by Marielis Gil, cabins for 2/3 with bath, US$10 per meal, good food, tours, camping US$6 per tent, phone.

E Canta Rana tourist camp, 25 km from town. Basic accommodation, breakfast and dinner included in the price, owners, Alfonso and Barbara Borrero, speak German, English and Spanish, waterfall and lovely surroundings.

Eating

Tumeremo *p1668*

Restaurante Las Cuevas, near plaza. Popular, average food and prices, service slow, check your bill. **Restaurante Turístico**, expensive but OK.

El Dorado *p1668*

Archiven, Plaza Bolívar. Good, helpful owner.

El Caney, on right just down from *Agua Selva*, good food. Recommended.

Restaurant by church serves delicious *criolla* food.

Santa Elena de Uairén *p1670, map p1669*

Several restaurants on Mcal Sucre, one of these **El Ranchón Criollo** serves good *criolla* fare.

Alfredo's, Av Perimetral, at the end of C Urdaneta. Tasty pizzas at good prices.

Venezuela Primero, Av Perimetral. Chicken, meat, and seafood.

Pizzería Darwing, C Icabarú, in front of Parque Ferial, T0414-875 5457. Great pizza.

Cafés

On the Plaza is a pay-by-weight buffet restaurant serving very good local food. **Café Goldrausch**, C Urdaneta, next to *Restaurant Michelle*. Makes good breakfasts, also dinners, and internet. Good place to form tour groups with other travellers. **Panadería Gran Café**, C Icabarú. Good breakfasts and coffee. **Gran Sabana Deli**, C Bolívar, CC Augusta, T995 1158. Cosy and good.

Activities and tours

Santa Elena de Uairén *p1670, map p1669*

Santa Elena is the most economical place to book tours of the Gran Sabana, Roraima, and other tepuis. There are many tour operators and freelance guides. Shop around, form larger groups, and haggle. Many tour operators will tailor tours to fit your needs, contact by email to discuss plans before arriving.

Adventure Tours, Av Perimetral at the end of C Urdaneta, T995 1861, adventure3tours@hotmail.com. Tours of Gran Sabana or El Paují, group discounts, all-inclusive 6 days to Roraima (minimum 4 persons). Sleeping bags and camping mats available for hire.

Backpacker Tours, C Urdaneta, T995 1415, T0414-886 7227, www.backpacker-tours.com. 1-5 day, all-inclusive jeep tours through the Gran Sabana, visiting little-known falls in the

Kavanayen area. Trekking to nearby Chirikayen Tepuy, 3-4 days and to Roraima (minimum 4 persons), plus more. German and English spoken. Recommended. Also have own **Posada Los Pinos**, Urb Akurima, 10 mins from airport, T995 1524.

Kamadac, C Urdaneta, T995 1408, T0414-886 6526, www.abenteuer-venezuela.de. Run by Andreas Hauer, tours of Gran Sabana, US$300 pp per day for jeep (4 persons). 6-day, all-inclusive tour to Roraima, US$405 pp (for 4), and also more adventurous tours to Auyán Tepuy from which Angel Falls cascades (5 days, US$785 pp for 4 people), difficult; many other options. Recommended.

New Frontiers Adventure, also on C Urdaneta, next to *Tommy Town*, T0414-886 6040, www.newfrontiers adventures.com. Ecotours and tours for small groups. All the usual tours at standard prices, and 4-day, inclusive walking tours, taking in the different ecosystems of the Gran Sabana, and staying in Pemón villages. English, French, and German spoken. Recommended.

Roberto's Mystic Tours, Icabarú y Urdaneta, mystic-tours@cantv.net. Roberto is very helpful and knowledgeable about local culture (and UFOs), great tours. Recommended.

Recommended guides **Rawllins** and his brother, **Terry** (Guyanese) speak English, excellent cooks, T0414-886 2669, rawllins@ yahoo.com, akawaio@hotmail.com. **Franklin Sierra**, T995 1686, 0414-886 2448, speaks English, Italian and other languages, tailor-made tours, good service and value.

⊖ Transport

Tumeremo *p1668*

Bus To **Santa Elena**, US$14, 8-10 hrs, with **Líneas Orinoco**, 2 blocks from plaza near *Leocar*); **El Dorado**, US$1.75, 1½ hrs. Bus to **Ciudad Bolívar**, US$8.50-9.50, 6 a day, 6½ hrs or *por puesto* (via San Félix and Puerto Ordaz). Bus to **San Félix** (Ciudad Guayana), US$2.75, *por puesto* US$8. To **Caracas**, US$24, direct service at 1600, 14 hrs.

El Dorado *p1668*

Bus All buses stop on main plaza. From **Caracas**, **Expresos del Oriente**, at 1830 daily, US$24.50, 14½ hrs, return at 1400 (925 km). The **Orinoco** bus links with **Ciudad Bolívar** (6 hrs) and **Santa Elena**, as does **Transmundial** (better, leaving 1100, US$11 to **Santa Elena**, US$8.60 to San Félix, 4 hrs).

El Dorado to Santa Elena de Uairén *p1668*

Km 88 (San Isidro)

Bus Km 88-Caracas, US$24.50; to **Ciudad Bolívar** wait at gas station for buses from Las Claritas (depart 0900, 1100, 1500, 1800). Frequent *por puestos* from **El Dorado** to Km 88, 1 hr, US$2.75. Most non-luxury buses stop at the petrol station to refuel. Alternatively get a ride with jeeps and trucks (little passes after 1030).

Santa Elena de Uairén *p1670, map p1669*

Air Airport, 8 km from the centre. **Transmandú** (www.transmandu.com), the only company with flights from **Ciudad Bolívar** in small planes.

Bus The new bus terminal on road to Ciudad Bolívar is 2 km/30 mins walk from town, taxi US$5. Get to terminal 30 mins in advance for SENIAT baggage check for contraband. From **Caracas** it is best to go to Ciudad Bolívar and then take a bus direct to Boa Vista, or Santa Elena. 10 buses daily from Santa Elena to **Ciudad Bolívar**, US$21.50-26.50, with **Expresos Los Llanos** (recommended), **San Cristóbal**, and **Línea Orinoco**, 10-12 hrs. 10 daily to **Ciudad Guayana** and **San Félix**, US$18.25, 10-11 hrs, with **Caribe** (recommended) and **Turgar**. 10 daily to **Puerto La Cruz**, US$24, 14 hrs, with **Caribe** (recommended), **Turgar**, and **Línea Orinoco**. **Expresos Maturín** goes to **Maturín** daily. **Expresos Los Llanos** go to **Maracay** and **Valencia** 3 times a day, US$33, 18- 20 hrs. 3 buses daily to **Boa Vista**, US$8.25, 4 hrs, **Eucatur**; at 0700 to **Manaus** 15 hrs, US$35 (make sure ticket includes the exit tax).

Jeep To **El Paují** (see below), **Canta Rana** (US$17.75), and **Icabarú** (US$20) leave about 0700 from Plaza Bolívar. Also at *Panadería Gran Café*, C Icabarú. PDV gas station on road out of town.

El Paují *p1671*

Road To get further than El Paují – to Canta Rana and Icabarú – a 4WD vehicle is necessary. From Santa Elena, US$8-11 by jeep if full, more if not, daily at around 0600-0700 and 1500-1600 from Plaza Bolívar. Taxi US$11.

ⓘ Directory

El Dorado *p1668*

Banks There is a **Banco de Venezuela**, accepts Visa and Mastercard; exchange with the gold buyer on the main street, cash only, poor rates.

Santa Elena de Uairén *p1670, map p1669*

Banks See also Money, page 1566. ATMs are unlikely to accept non- Venezuelan cards. Try shops in the centre for dollars cash, reais or TCs, eg *Casa de Los Cóchamos*, gold shop south of main plaza that changes TCs at lower rate than bank. **Inversiones Fortaleza**, C Urdaneta on plaza, cash dollars, TCs or Brazilian currency. **La Boutique Zapatería** also changes TCs and cash at good rates. Grocery store **El Gordito**, C Urdaneta, for Brazilian currency (English and French spoken). Try at border with Brazilians entering Venezuela. Generally rates are poor; check with travellers going in opposite direction what rates should be. For better rates you must wait until Ciudad Guayana, or Boa Vista if going to Brazil (change some money into Brazilian currency before bus leaves). **Internet** **Global de Communicaciones**, C Icabarú y Urdaneta. Another place opposite **Panadería Rico Pan**, C Bolívar. **Telephones** **Global de Communicaciones**, **CANTV** at the old bus terminal for international calls and faxes. It is cheaper to buy a card and call from a street phone for international calls.

Mount Roraima → *Altitude: 2,810 m.*

An exciting trek is to the summit of Mt Roraima, at one time believed to be the '**Lost World**' made famous by Arthur Conan Doyle's novel. 'Roroima' is a word in the Pemón Indian language meaning 'The great blue-green'. Due to the tough terrain and extreme weather conditions, this hike is only suitable for the fit. Supplies for a week or more should be bought in Santa Elena. If a tour company is supplying the food, check what it is first; vegetarians may go hungry.

San Francisco de Yuruaní

The starting point is this Pemón village, 9 km north of the San Ignacio military checkpoint (where you must register). There are three small shops selling basic goods but not enough for Roraima hike. Meals are available and tents can be hired, US$5 each per day, quality of tents and stoves is poor; better equipment is available in Santa Elena.

Paraitepui

The road to Paraitepui (which is signposted), the nearest village to the mountain, leaves the highway 1 km south of San Francisco. It is in good condition, with three bridges; the full 25 km can be walked in seven hours. You can sleep for free in the village if hiring a guide; camping is permitted. Few supplies are available; a small shop sells basics. The villagers speak Tauripán, the local dialect of the Pemón linguistic group, but now most of them also speak Spanish.

Climbing Roraima

The foot trail winds back and forth on a more direct line than the little-used jeep track; it is comparatively straightforward and adequately marked descending from the heights just past Paraitepui across rolling hills and numerous clear streams. The goal, Roraima, is the mountain on the right, the other massive outcrop on the left is Mata Hui (known as Kukenán after the river which rises within it). If leaving the village early in the day, you may reach the Río Cuquenán crossing by early afternoon (good camping here). Three hours' walk brings you to a lovely bird-filled meadow below the foothills of the massif, another perfect camping spot known as *campamento base* (10 hours to base camp from Paraitepui). The footpath now climbs steadily upwards through the cloud forest at the mountain's base and becomes an arduous scramble over tree trunks and damp rocks until the cliff is reached. From here it is possible to ascend to the plateau along the 'easy' rock ledge which is the only route to the top. Walkers in good health should take about four hours from the meadow to the top. The summit is an eerie world of stone and water, difficult to move around easily. There are not many good spots to camp; but there are various overhanging ledges which are colourfully known as 'hoteles' by the guides. Red painted arrows lead the way to the right after reaching the summit for the main group of these. A marked track leads to the survey pillar near the east cliff where Guyana, Brazil and Venezuela meet; allow a day as the track is very rough. Other sights include the Valley of the Crystals, La Laguna de Gladys and various sinkholes.

The whole trip can take anywhere between five days and two weeks. The dry season for trekking is November-May (with annual variations); June-August Roraima is usually enveloped in cloud. Do not remove crystals from the mountain; on-the-spot fines up to US$100 may be charged. Thorough searches are made on your return. Take your rubbish back down with you.

Mount Roraima listings

For Sleeping and Eating price codes and other relevant information, see Essentials, pages 38-40.

Sleeping

San Francisco de Yuruaní *p1675*

E **El Caney de Yuruaní**, T995 1307. Clean, basic rooms, fan, restaurant.

F **Arapena Posada**, T01414-890 3314 (mob). Run by Arepena Tours (see below), small, basic.

F **Posada**, run by *Roraima Tours* (see below). Dormitories, usually full.

Sr Casilda Rodriguez has a *churuata* where you can sling a hammock.

Camping Permitted just about anywhere, free. Plenty of mosquitos at night.

Climbing Roraima *p1675*

Camping Full equipment including stove is essential (an igloo-type tent with a plastic sheet for the floor is best for the summit, where it can be wet), wear thick socks and boots to protect legs from snakes, warm clothes for the summit (much mist, rain squalls and lightning at night) and effective insect repellent – biting *plaga (blackflies)* infest the grasslands. The water on the summit and around the foot of Roraima is very pure, but as more do the trek, the waters are becoming dirtied. Bring bottled water or a purifier for the savannah. Fires must not be lit on top of Roraima, only gas or liquid fuel stoves. Litter is appearing along the trail; please take care of the environment.

Activities and tours

Climbing Roraima *p1675*

Guides and tours The National Guard requires all visitors to have a guide beyond Paraitepui; you will be fined. Go with a guide or tour operator from Santa Elena (US$400, 6 days/5 nights) or from San Francisco; those hired on the street or in Paraitepui have no accident insurance cover. Guides can help for the hike's final stages (easy to get lost) and for finding best camping spots. Guides in San Francisco de Yuruaní cost US$40 a day, more if they carry your supplies. Check the camping gear for leaks, etc, and be clear about who is providing the guide's food.

Arapena Tours, T0414-890 3314, arapenatours@latinmail.com. Tours to Roraima and Kavurin, US$40 per day for guide.

Roraima Tours, T808 1037, T0414-886 3405, recommended, Ana Fernández is very helpful, all-inclusive tour (group rates can be arranged), or US$45 per day for guide only.

Guides in Paraitepui cost US$25 a day, Spanish speaking guides. The **Ayuso** brothers are the best-known guides. Ask for El Capitán, he is in charge of guides. Parking at Inparques US$9.

Transport

San Francisco de Yuruaní *p1675*

Bus From **Santa Elena** will let you off here and pick up passengers en route northwards (no buses 1200-1900). Jeep to **Paraitepui** US$100. Cheapest is Oscar Mejías Hernández, ask in village.

Guianas

Contents

1680 Guyana
- 1680 Planning your trip
- 1684 Georgetown
- 1685 Outside Georgetown

1702 Suriname
- 1702 Planning your trip
- 1706 Paramaribo
- 1708 Outside Paramaribo

1717 Guyane
- 1717 Planning your trip
- 1719 Cayenne
- 1721 Outside Cayenne

Footprint features

1678 Don't miss …
1681 Driving in Guyana
1703 Driving in Suriname
1718 Driving in Guyane

At a glance

Time required 1-2 weeks each for Guyana and Suriname; Guyane 1 week, 2 if exploring beyond the coast.

Best time Guyana: coolest months Aug-Oct. Suriname: year-end festival is Surifesta, mid-Dec to 1st week of Jan; Holi Phagwa (Hindu spring festival) in Mar. Guyane: Aug-Nov; Carnival Feb/Mar.

When not to go Guyana: Georgetown is very crowded during Republic Day, 23 Feb; wettest months May-Jul and Dec/Jan. Surinam: Prices highest 15 Mar-15 May, Jul-Sep and during year-end Surifesta. Guyane: Wettest months May-Jul, but rains start Nov.

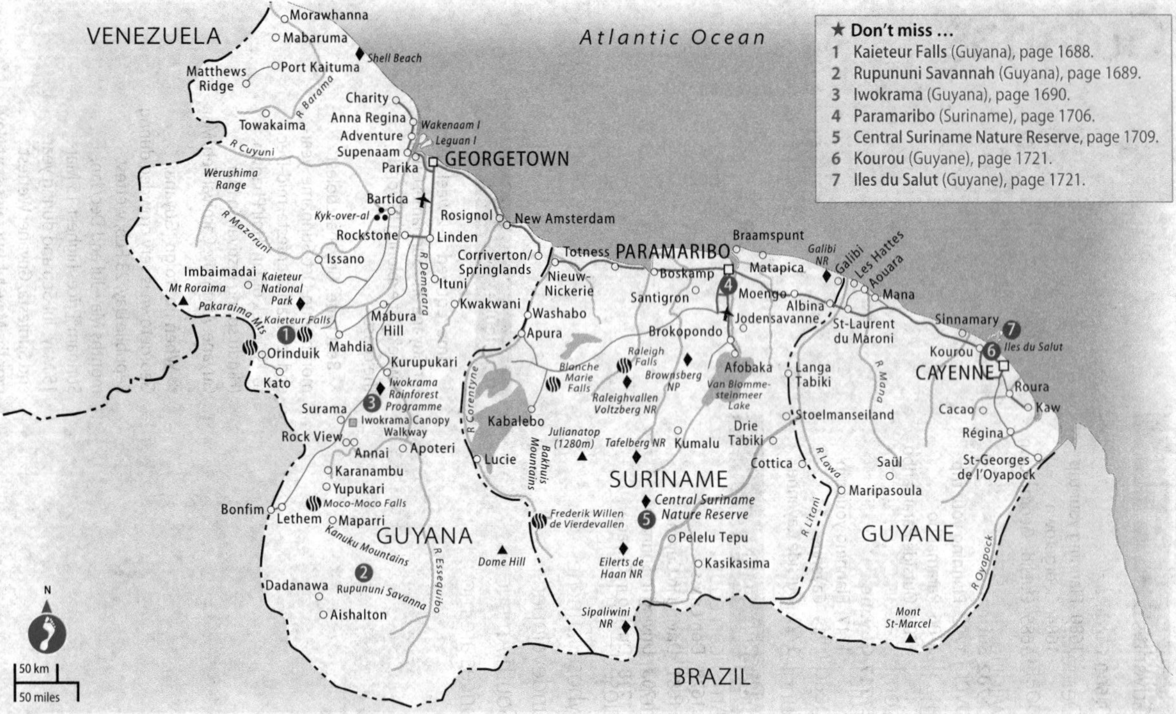
Atlantic Ocean
VENEZUELA
GUYANA
SURINAME
GUYANE
BRAZIL
GEORGETOWN
PARAMARIBO
CAYENNE
Morawhanna
Mabaruma
Shell Beach
Matthews Ridge
Port Kaituma
R Barama
Charity
Towakaima
Anna Regina
Wakenaam I
Adventure
Leguan I
R Cuyuni
Supenaam
Parika
Werushima Range
Bartica
Kyk-over-al
Rosignol
New Amsterdam
R Mazaruni
Rockstone
Linden
Issano
Corriverton/ Springlands
Imbaimadai
Kaieteur National Park
Mt Roraima
Ituni
R Demerara
Kwakwani
Pakaraima Mts
Kaieteur Falls
Mabura Hill
Orinduik
Mahdia
Kato
Kurupukari
Iwokrama Rainforest Programme
Surama
Iwokrama Canopy Walkway
Rock View
Annai
Apoteri
Karanambu
Yupukari
Moco-Moco Falls
Bonfim
Lethem
Maparri
Kanuku Mountains
R Essequibo
Dadanawa
Rupununi Savanna
Aishalton
Dome Hill
Totness
Nieuw-Nickerie
Washabo
Apura
R Corentyne
Kabalebo
Blanche Marie Falls
Lucie
Bakhuis Mountains
Julianatop (1280m)
Frederik Willen de Vierdevallen
Boskamp
Santigron
Brokopondo
Raleigh Falls
Brownsberg NP
Raleighvallen Voltzberg NR
Tafelberg NR
Kumalu
Central Suriname Nature Reserve
Pelelu Tepu
Eilerts de Haan NR
Kasikasima
Sipaliwini NR
Braamspunt
Matapica
Moengo
Jodensavanne
Afobaka
Van Blommesteinmeer Lake
Drie Tabiki
Cottica
Galibi NR
Galibi
Les Hattes
Aouara
Mana
Albina
St-Laurent du Maroni
Langa Tabiki
R Mana
Stoelmanseiland
R Lawa
R Litani
Saül
Maripasoula
Sinnamary
Iles du Salut
Kourou
Roura
Kaw
Cacao
Régina
St-Georges de l'Oyapock
R Oyapock
Mont St-Marcel
N
50 km
50 miles
★ Don't miss ...
1 Kaieteur Falls (Guyana), page 1688.
2 Rupununi Savannah (Guyana), page 1689.
3 Iwokrama (Guyana), page 1690.
4 Paramaribo (Suriname), page 1706.
5 Central Suriname Nature Reserve, page 1709.
6 Kourou (Guyane), page 1721.
7 Iles du Salut (Guyane), page 1721.

Guyana's coastal region is dominated by a mixture of Calypso music, Dutch drainage systems, Hindu temples, rice and Demerara sugar. Leaving the sea behind, travelling by riverboat or by plane, it is a land of rainforests, which gives way to wildlife-rich savannahs and isolated ranches. Waterfalls tumble over jasper rocks, or, at Kaieteur, into a chasm almost five times the height of Niagara. Suriname, too, has the intriguing combination of Dutch, Asian and African, which influences the culture, food and street life. And, like its neighbour, when you head inland, you enter a different world of bronze-tinted rivers, jungles and Amerindian villages.

Despite having geographical features shared by other South American countries, Suriname and Guyana are classed as Caribbean states. Guyane, on the other hand, is an overseas department of France. It has a famous penal colony – now closed – circled by sharks, a European space programme whose launches can be witnessed and jungle adventure in the undeveloped interior. All this within the context of a corner of South America where coffee and croissants are served and the prices are more than Parisian.

Guyana

Planning your trip

Where to go

Despite being on the Atlantic, **Georgetown**, capital of Guyana, is known as the 'Garden City of the Caribbean'. This gives some idea of the country's orientation, in trade and cultural terms. The coast, where most of the population live, is a mix of coconut palms and calypso music, Dutch place names and techniques for draining the land, Hindu temples and Islamic mosques, all of which reflect the chequered history of the country. The thinly populated interior is different again, with life revolving around the rivers in the tropical forest, or, further south, the scattered ranches of the Rupununi Savannah. The improvement of the road from Georgetown to Lethem on the Brazilian border, with a regular bus service, opens up the interior for easier exploration, but this area remains largely untouched, with many places reached by river boat or plane. Highlights include the Kaieteur Falls, among the highest in the world, the Orinduik Falls on the border with Brazil and the Iwokrama Rainforest Reserve, with the Iwokrama Canopy Walkway. Travelling on any of the rivers, many with excellent beaches, is the most interesting way to get around. On the coast there are no beaches for bathing, but in the far northwest is Shell Beach, a protected area for marine turtles and birdlife.

When to go

Although hot, the climate is not unhealthy. Mean shade temperature throughout the year is 27°C; the mean maximum is about 31°C and the mean minimum 24°C. The heat is greatly tempered by cooling breezes from the sea and is most felt from August to October. There are two wet seasons in the north of the country, from May to June, and from December to the end of January, although they may extend into the months either side. The south and the Rupununi receive one wet season, May to July. Rainfall averages 2,300 mm a year in Georgetown. Note that the Republic Day celebrations (23 February, float parade) last for one day, but there are other activities (Children's Costume Competition, etc) which take place during the preceding days. Hotels in Georgetown are very full, as they are also during international cricket.

Getting around

Air Most flights to the interior leave from Ogle, which has been upgraded with an extended runway and new customs and immigration facilities. It's about 15 minutes from Georgetown (taxi about US$6). For scheduled flights between Georgetown and Lethem see page 1700, and services to Kaieteur and Rupununi, see page 1700. Scheduled services to many parts of Guyana are offered by **Trans Guyana Airways, TGA**, Ogle, T222 2525, Monday to Saturday. Charter flights from Ogle are flown by **Roraima Airways, RAL**, Lot 8 Eping Avenue, Bel Air Park, Georgetown, T225 9648, www.roraimaairways.com, and **Air Services Ltd, ASL**, Ogle Aerodrome, T222 4357, asl@solutions2000.net. Domestic airlines are very strict on baggage allowance on internal flights: 20 lb pp (TGA and ASL) and 25 lb (Roraima).

Public road transport Minibuses and collective taxis, an H on their number plate, run between Georgetown and the entire coast from Charity to Corriverton; also to Linden. **Intraserv** bus service has a scheduled route from Georgetown to Lethem. All taxis also have an H on the number plate.

River There are over 960 km of navigable river, an important means of communication. Ferries and river boats are described here; also contact the Transport and Harbours Department, Water St, Georgetown. Six-seater river boats are called *ballahoos*, three- to four-seaters *corials*; they

Driving in Guyana

Roads Most coastal towns are linked by a good 296-km road from Springlands in the east to Charity in the west; the Essequibo river is crossed by ferry, the Berbice by both ferry and bridge and the Demerara by a toll bridge, which, besides closing at high tide for ships to pass through (2-3 hrs) is subject to frequent closures (an alternative ferry operates only one trip daily: from Rosignol to New Amsterdam in the morning, return in the afternoon). Apart from a good road connecting Timehri and Linden, continuing as good dirt to Mabura Hill, and the new Georgetown-Lethem road, most other roads in the interior are very poor.
Safety Traffic drives on the left. There are shortages of car spares.
Documents No *carnet de passages* is required for driving a private vehicle.
Car hire Several companies in Georgetown (most are listed in the Yellow Pages of the phone directory).
Fuel Gasoline costs US$3.45-4 a gallon.

provide the transport in the forest. The ferry across the Corentyne to Suriname carries vehicles; it operates one return trip daily.

Maps Maps of country and Georgetown (US$6) from **Department of Lands and Surveys**, Homestreet Av, Durban Backland (take a taxi). T226 0524 in advance, poor stock. Rivers and islands change frequently, so maps only give a general direction. A local guide can be more reliable. Free country and city maps are available from most tour operators and hotels. Georgetown and Guyana maps in **Explore Guyana**. Guyana ITMB map is recommended.

Sleeping → *See page 38 for our hotel grade price guide.*
The largest hotels in Georgetown have their own emergency electricity generators and water pumps to deal with any interruptions in supply. Other hotels usually provide a bucket of water in your room, fill this up when water is available. When booking an a/c room, ensure it also has natural ventilation.

Eating and drinking → *See page 40 for our eating price guide.*
Local food The blend of different influences – Indian, African, Chinese, Creole, English, Portuguese, Amerindian, North American – gives distinctive flavour to Guyanese cuisine. One well-known dish, traditional at Christmas, is pepper-pot: meat cooked in bitter cassava (casareep) juice with peppers and herbs. Some popular local dishes are cook-up-rice, curry (chicken, beef, mutton) with rice, dhal pouri or roti and metagee. All are available in Creole restaurants. Seafood is plentiful and varied, as are tropical fruits and vegetables. The staple food is rice. In the interior wild meat is often available, eg wild cow, or *labba* (a small rodent).

Drink Rum is the most popular drink. There is a wide variety of brands, all cheap, including the best which are very good and cost US$3.50 a bottle. Demerara Distillers Ltd produces two prize-winning brands, the 12-year-old King of Diamonds premium rum, and the 15-year-old El Dorado (voted the best rum in the world every year since 1999, US$45 in Georgetown, US$25 at duty free in the airport). Demerara Distillers, the makers of these rums, have a distillery tour and visit to their rum heritage, US$15. High wine is a strong local rum. There is also local brandy and whisky (Diamond Club), which are worth trying. D'Aguiar's Cream Liqueur, produced and bottled by Banks DIH Ltd, is excellent (and strong). The local beer, Banks, made partly from rice is good and cheap. There is a wide variety of fruit juices produced by Topco. Mauby, a local drink brewed from the bark of a tree, and natural cane juice are delightful thirst quenchers available from Creole restaurants and local vendors.

Accident and emergency

Police T911; Fire T912; Ambulance T226 9449.

Electricity

110 volts in Georgetown; 220 volts elsewhere, including some Georgetown suburbs. Plugs as in US.

Embassies and consulates

Guianas overseas representatives

Belgium, 12 Avenue du Brésil, 1050 Brussels, T675 6216, embassy9.guyana@skynet.be.
Brazil, SHIS QI 05-Conj 19-Casa 24, CEP71615-190, Brasília DF, T061-3248 0874, embguyana@embguyana.org.br.
Canada, High Commission: Burnside Building, 151 Slater St, suite 309, Ottawa, Ontario, K1P 5H3, 613-235 7249, guyanahcott@rogers.com. Consulate-General: 505 Consumer's Rd, Suite 206, Willowdale, Toronto, Ontario, M2J 4X8, T416-494 6404, info@guyanaconsulate.com.
Suriname, Henck Aaronstraat 82, PO Box 785, Paramaribo, T597-477895, guyembassy@sr.net.
UK, High Commission, 3 Palace Ct, London W2 4LP, T020-7229 7684, guyanahc1@btconnect.com.
USA, Embassy: 2490 Tracy Pl, NW, Washington DC 20008, T265 3834, guyanaembassydc@verizon.net. New York Consulate General: 370 7th Ave 4th Floor, Seven Penn Plaza, NY 10001, T212-947 5115. Miami: 795 NW 72 St, Miami, Florida 33150, T786-235 0431, guyanaconsulate@aol.com.
Venezuela, Quinta Roraima, Av El Paseo, Prados del Este, Aptdo 51054, Caracas 1050, T977 1158, embguy@cantv.net.

Festivals and events

Public holidays 1 Jan, New Years' Day; 23 Feb, Republic Day and Mashramani festival; Good Fri, Easter Mon; Labour Day, 1 May; Arrival Day, 5 May; Independence Day, 26 May (instigated in 1996); Caricom Day, first Mon in Jul; Freedom Day, first Mon in Aug; Christmas Day, 25 Dec, and Boxing Day, 26 Dec. Hindu and Muslim festivals follow a lunar calendar, and dates should be checked as required: Phagwah, usually Mar; Eid el Fitr, end of Ramadan; Eid el Azah; Youm un Nabi; Deepavali, usually Nov.

Money ➔ *US$1 = G$204; €1 = G$271 (Mar 2010).*

The unit is the Guyanese dollar. There are notes for 20, 100, 500 and 1,000 dollars. Coins are for 1, 5 and 10 dollars. Official exchange rate is adjusted weekly in line with the rate offered by licensed exchange houses (*cambios*). There are ATMs in Georgetown. Also take cash dollars or euros. No *cambio* changes TCs. They only buy US or Canadian dollars, euros and pounds sterling. Most *cambios* accept drafts (subject to verification) and telegraphic transfers, but not credit cards. Rates vary slightly between *cambios* and from day to day and some *cambios* offer better rates for changing over US$100. Rates for changing TCs are good on the black market. Banks in Georgetown that accept TCs are **Demerara Bank** (South Road and Camp St), **Guyana Bank of Trade and Industry** (GBTI, 47 Water St) and **Republic Bank** (38-40 Water St). All charge commission. **Republic Bank** and *cambios* accept euros at best rates. Note that to sell Guyanese dollars on leaving, you will need to produce your *cambio* receipt. The black market on America St ('Wall St') in Georgetown still operates, but rates offered are not that better than the *cambio* rate. To avoid being robbed on the black market, or if you need to change money when *cambios* are closed, go by taxi and ask someone (preferably a friend) to negotiate for you. The black market also operates in Molson Creek/Springlands, the entry point from Suriname, and where the bus stops for launches between Bonfim and Lethem at the Brazilian border.

Cost of travelling The devaluation means that, for foreigners, prices for food and drink are low at present. Even imported goods may be cheaper than elsewhere and locally produced goods such as fruit are very cheap. Hotels, tours and services in the interior are subject to energy and fuel surcharges, making them less cheap.

Opening hours

Banks 0800-1400 Mon-Thu, Fri 0800-1430. Shops 0830-1600, Mon-Thu, 0830-1700 Fri, 0830-1200 Sat. Markets 0800-1600, Mon-Sat, except Wed 0900-1200, Sun 0800-1000.

Tax

Airport tax This is G$4,000 (US$20, £12, €14), payable in Guyanese dollars or foreign currency

equivalent at Cheddi Jagan International airport.
VAT 16%.

Telephone → *Country code +592.*
Ringing: a double ring, repeated regularly.
Engaged: equal tones, separated by equal pauses.

Time
4 hrs behind GMT; 1 hr ahead of EST.

Tourist information
Ministry of Tourism, Industry and Commerce, 229 South Rd near Camp St, Georgetown, T226 2505, www.mintic.gov.gy, creates tourism policy. **The Guyana Tourism Authority,** National Exhibition Center, Sophia, Georgetown, T219 0094, www.guyana-tourism.com, promotes the development of the tourism industry. **Tourism and Hospitality Association of Guyana (THAG)**, office and information desk at 157 Waterloo St, T225 0807, www.exploreguyana.com. Private organization covering all areas of tourism, with a 80-page, full-colour magazine called *Explore Guyana*, available from the Association at PO Box 101147, Georgetown, or phone above number. See also www.turq.com/guyana. For information and lots of useful links, visit www.guyana.org. The government agency's site is www.gina.gov. See also www.wwfguianas.org, of **WWF Guianas Programme**, 285 Irving Street, Queenstown, Georgetown, T223 7802, the WWF conservation initiative covering the three Guianas. For birdwatching see www.guyanabirding.com and its associated newsletter, *Guyana Birding News*.

Visas and immigration
The following countries do not need a visa to visit Guyana: Australia, Canada, Japan, New Zealand, Norway, Switzerland, USA, EU countries (except Cyprus, Czech Republic, Estonia, Hungary, Latvia, Lithuania, Malta, Poland, Slovak Republic and Slovenia) and the Commonwealth countries. Visitors are advised to check with the nearest embassy, consulate or travel agent for changes to this list. All visitors require a passport with 6 months' validity and all nationalities, apart from those above, require visas. To obtain a visa, 3 photos, evidence of sufficient funds, a travel itinerary and, if coming from a country with yellow fever, a yellow fever certificate are required. If Guyana has no representation in your country, apply to the Guyana Embassy in Washington DC, or the Guyana Consulate General in New York. Tourist visas cost US$30, 1-entry business visas US$40, multiple entry business visas US$50. Visitors from those countries where they are required arriving without visas are refused entry, unless a tour operator has obtained permission for the visitor to get a visa on arrival. To fly in to Guyana, an exit ticket is required, at land borders an onward ticket is usually not asked for.

Weights and measures
Metric since 1982, but imperial is widely used.

Georgetown → *Colour map 2, B3. Population: 200,000.*

Guyana's capital, and chief town and port, is on the east bank of the mouth of the Demerara river. The climate is tropical, with a mean temperature of 27°C, but the trade winds provide welcome relief. The city is built on a grid plan, with wide tree-lined streets and drainage canals following the layout of the old sugar estates. Parts of the city are very attractive, with white-painted wooden 19th century houses raised on stilts and a profusion of flowering trees. In the evening the sea wall is crowded with strollers and at Easter it is a mass of colourful kites.

Ins and outs

Getting there From the airport, take minibus No 42 to Georgetown US$1.50, one to hours hours (from Georgetown leaves from next to Parliament building); for a small charge they will take you to your hotel (similarly for groups going to the airport). A taxi costs US$20-25 (use approved airport taxis). Internal flights go from Ogle airstrip, 8 km from Georgetown; minibus from Market to Ogle US$0.50. » *See also Transport, page 1699.*

Getting around Minibuses run regularly to most parts of the city, mostly from Stabroek market or Avenue of the Republic, standard fare G$60 (US$0.30) very crowded. It is difficult to get a seat during rush hours. Taxis: charge US$1.50 for short journeys, US$3 for longer runs, with higher rates at night (a safe option) and outside the city limits. Collective taxis ply set routes at a fixed fare; they stop at any point on request. Certain hand signals are used on some routes to indicate the final destination (ask). Special taxis at hotels and airports, marked 'special' on the windscreen, charge US$2 for short journeys around town, US$4 for longer runs, stops and waiting time extra, or you can negotiate a 'by the hour' deal, usually US$7.50.

Security This is a beautiful city, but check with your hotel, tour operator, the police or government authorities about unsafe areas. Don't walk the streets at night: always take a taxi, especially if going to Sheriff Street for the nightlife. At all times, avoid Albouystown (south of the centre) and the Tiger Bay area, just one block west of Main Street. Leave your valuables in your hotel. These problems are restricted to Georgetown and nearby villages; the interior remains as safe as ever.

Sights

Although part of the old centre was destroyed by fire in 1945, there are some fine 19th century buildings, particularly on or near High St and the Avenue of the Republic. **St George's Anglican Cathedral**, which dates from 1889 is 44 m high and is reputed to be the tallest wooden building in the world (it was designed by Sir Arthur Blomfield). Above the altar is a chandelier given by Queen Victoria. The Gothic-style **City Hall** dates from 1888; its interior has been recently restored and may be viewed. Other fine buildings on High St are the City Engineer's Office, the Victoria Law Courts (1887) and the Magistrates' Court. The **Public Buildings**, on Brickdam, which house Parliament, are an impressive neo-classical structure built in 1839. Opposite is **St Andrew's Presbytery** (18th century). **State House** on Main St is the residence of the president. Much of the city centre is dominated by the imposing tower above **Stabroek market** (1881). At the head of Brickdam is an aluminium arch commemorating independence. Nearby is a monument to the 1763 slave rebellion, surmounted by an impressive statue of Cuffy, its best-known leader. Near the *Pegasus* hotel on Seawall Rd is the **Umana Yana**, a conical thatched structure built by a group of Wai Wai Amerindians using traditional techniques for the 1972 conference of the Non-Aligned Movement. The **National Museum** ⓘ *opposite the post office, Mon-Fri 0900-1700, Sat 0900-1200, free*, has exhibits from Guyana and elsewhere, including a model of Georgetown before the fire and a good natural history section. The **Walter Roth Museum of Anthropology** ⓘ *Main St, Mon-Fri 0800-1300, 1400-1640, www.sdnp.org.gy/wrma/waiwai.htm*, has artefacts from Guyana's nine Amerindian tribes and serves as a research centre for indigenous people.

The **Botanical Gardens** (20 minutes' walk from Anglican Cathedral, entry free), covering 50 ha, have Victorian bridges and pavilions, palms and lily ponds (undergoing continual improvements). The gardens are safe in daylight hours, but keep to the marked paths. Do not go to the gardens after dark. Near the southwest corner is the former residence of the president, Castellani House, which now houses the **National Art Collection** (open after extensive renovation), and there is also a large mausoleum containing the remains of the former president, Forbes Burnham, which is decorated with reliefs depicting scenes from his political career. Look out for the rare cannonball tree (*Couroupita Guianensis*), named after the appearance of its poisonous fruit. The Botanical Gardens offer great birdwatching. The city has 200 bird species from 39 families many of which can be seen in the gardens. Flycatchers, tanagers, hummingbirds and many migrating species such as Peregrine Falcons and warblers can be found around the capital, but the true stars are the Blood-coloured Woodpecker, which is endemic to the Guiana Shield, and Festive Parrot. Both are regularly spotted in the gardens. Tour operators offer birdwatching tours.

The **zoo** ⓘ *0800-1800, US$1.50 for adults, half price for children; to use personal video US$11*, is in very poor condition but is supposedly being upgraded. It carries the WWF logo and has educational programmes. It hss a collection of local animals including manatees, which usually surface around 1730. The zoo also boasts a breeding centre for endangered birds which are released into the wild. There are also beautiful tropical plants in the **Promenade Gardens** (open 0830-1630) on Middle St and in the **National Park** on Carifesta Avenue, which has a good public running track. Near the southeast corner of the Botanic Gardens is the well-equipped **Cliff Anderson Sports Hall**. Nearby is the **National Cultural Centre**, an impressive air-conditioned theatre with a large stage. Performances are also given at the **Theatre Guild Playhouse** in Parade St.

The **Georgetown Cricket Club** at Bourda was one of the finest cricket grounds in the tropics. For the **ICC World Cup** in 2007, a new stadium was built at **Providence** on the east bank of Demerara right next to Buddy's International Hotel (8 km from the city on the airport road, take bus 42 or a taxi). It has fine modern stands but not enough protection from sun and rain.

Outside Georgetown

The interior of Guyana is a land of great rivers, dramatic waterfalls, rainforests and savannahs. On the coast are turtle-nesting grounds and sea defences. You can stay at working ranches and secluded resorts. At all times, expect superb nature watching.

Southeast to Suriname

New Amsterdam (*Population: 25,000. 104 km southeast of Georgetown*) On the east bank of the Berbice River, near its mouth, is picturesque New Amsterdam. From Georgetown, take a minibus (44, or express No 50) or collective taxi to Rosignol on the west bank of the Berbice, US$4.50, then cross the river. A new floating bridge from Cotton Tree to Palmyra Village (5 km from New Amsterdam) was opened on 24 December 2008 (a toll is charged). A ferry also runs between Rosignol and New Amsterdam, crossing only takes 15 minutes, but add another 45 minutes for unloading (US$0.30; also takes vehicles).

Corriverton (*Population: 31,000*) The road continues east from New Amsterdam (minibus, No 50, US$1.75-2.50), to **Springlands** and **Skeldon** at the mouth of the Corentyne River. The towns are officially known as **Corriverton** (Corentyne River Town). Springlands is 2 km long, so you need to know where you want to get off the bus. There are the *Republic Bank* and *Guyana National Commercial Bank*. Suriname dollars can officially be changed into Guyanese dollars here. A ferry sails from Moleson, or Crabwood Creek, 13 km south of Springlands, to South Drain in Suriname, 40 km south of Nieuw-Nickerie (see Transport, below).

Georgetown

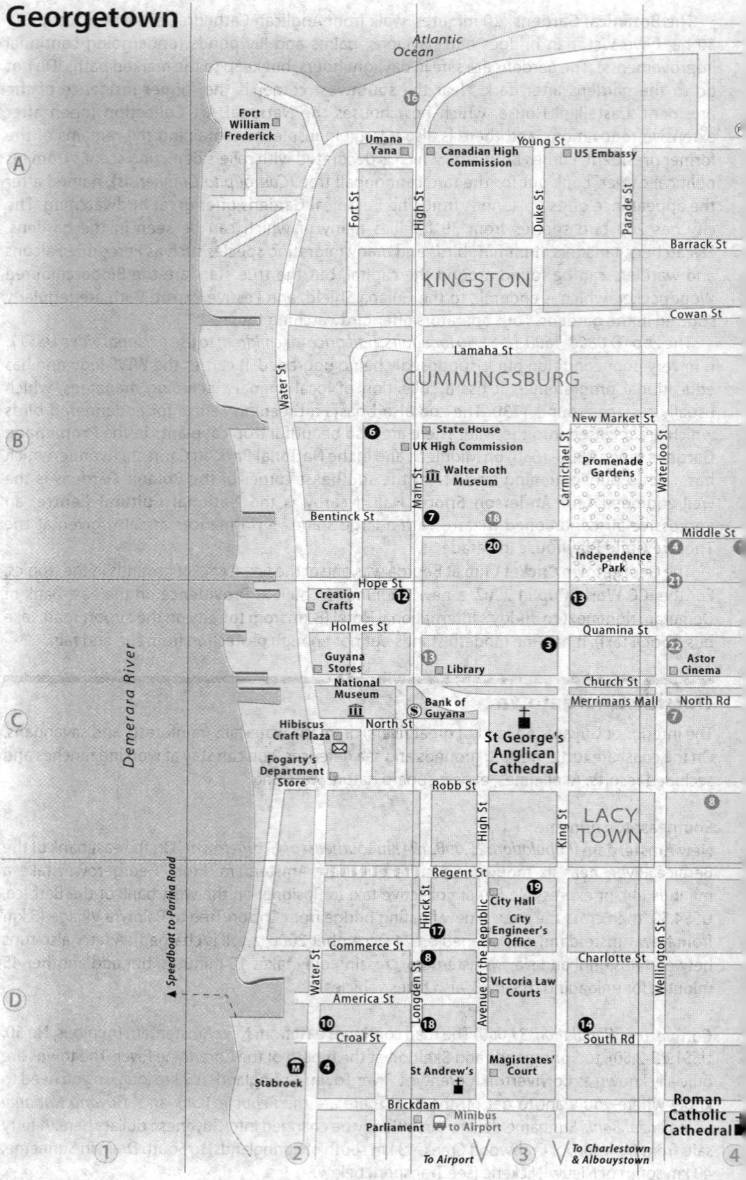

Atlantic Ocean
Fort William Frederick
Umana Yana
Canadian High Commission
Young St
US Embassy
Fort St
High St
Duke St
Parade St
Barrack St
KINGSTON
Cowan St
Lamaha St
CUMMINGSBURG
Water St
New Market St
State House
UK High Commission
Walter Roth Museum
Main St
Carmichael St
Promenade Gardens
Waterloo St
Bentinck St
Middle St
Independence Park
Hope St
Creation Crafts
Holmes St
Quamina St
Guyana Stores
Library
Astor Cinema
National Museum
Church St
Merrimans Mall
North Rd
Bank of Guyana
North St
Hibiscus Craft Plaza
St George's Anglican Cathedral
Fogarty's Department Store
Robb St
Demerara River
LACY TOWN
King St
Regent St
Speedboat to Parika Road
City Hall
City Engineer's Office
Hinck St
Avenue of the Republic
Commerce St
Charlotte St
Wellington St
Longden St
Victoria Law Courts
America St
Croal St
South Rd
Magistrates' Court
St Andrew's
Stabroek
Brickdam
Roman Catholic Cathedral
Parliament
Minibus to Airport
To Airport
To Charlestown & Albouystown
A
B
C
D
1
2
3
4

Sleeping

1 Ariantze & Sidewalk Café *B4*
2 Brandsville's Apartments *B4*
3 Cara Lodge & Bottle Bar & Restaurant *C4*
4 Cara Suites, Bistro 176, Surinam Airways & Wilderness Explorers *B4*
5 El Dorado Inn *C4*
6 Emba-Sea *A4*
7 Florentene's *C4*
8 Friends *C4*
9 Grand Coastal Inn *B4*
10 Grand Coastal Lodge *D4*
11 Herdmanston Lodge *B4*
12 Hotel Glow *B2*
13 Hotel Tower *C3*
14 Melbourne Inn *B4*
15 Ocean Spray International *A4*
16 Pegasus Guyana *A2*
17 Regency Suites *D4*
18 Rima Guest House *B3*
19 Roraima Residence Inn *B4*
20 Sleepin Guesthouse *C4*
21 Tropicana & Jerry's Café *B4*
22 Waterchris *C4*
23 Windjammer International Cuisine & Comfort Inn *A4*

Eating

1 Brazil Churrascaria *D4*
2 Church's Chicken *B4*
3 Coalpot *C4*
4 Demico House *D2*
5 Excellence *C4*
6 German's *B2*
7 Golden Coast *B3*
8 Hacks Halaal *D3*
9 Juice Power *B4*
10 KFC *C4/D2*
11 Mario's Pizza *B4*
12 New Thriving *B4*
13 Oasis Café *C3*
14 Oasis Too *D3*
15 Pizza Hut *B4*
16 Popeye's *B4*
17 Quality Fast Food *D3*
18 Salt and Pepper Food Court *D3*
19 Upscale *D3*
20 Windies Sports Bar *B3*

Bars & clubs

21 Blue Iguana *C4*

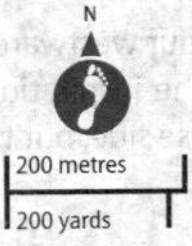

West from Georgetown

The road crosses the 2 km long floating Demerara bridge (opens often for shipping, US$0.25 toll, pedestrians free). Speedboats cross the Demerara from Stabroek market, US$0.30 every 30 minutes. The road continues 42 km, past rice paddies, *kokers* and through villages to **Parika**, a growing town on the east bank of the Essequibo River (minibus US$2.25). It has a Sunday market, 0600-1100, and three banks. Ferries cross the river to **Adventure** on the west bank at 1700 daily and 0830 Wednesday and Friday, returning at 0300 daily and 1330 Wednesday and Friday; or speedboat US$2.40.

The northwest coastal area is mainly accessible by boat only. Speedboats cross from Parika to Supenaam, US$5.55 (can be very wet). From Supenaam minibuses or taxis (US$6.60 per person) go to Charity. From Adventure a road runs north through Anna Regina. Nearby there is a resort at **Lake Mainstay**. You can visit a hot and cold lake, which varies in temperature, and the Wayaka Mainstay Amerindian Community, 13 km from Anna Regina. Mainstay is 2½ hours by road and ferry from Georgetown (depending on tides), 17 minutes by plane from Ogle (US$48). The road goes on to **Charity**, a pleasant town with loud bars, two small hotels (eg **C Xenon**, comfortable) and a lively market on Monday (quiet at other times).

Border with Venezuela Near the border with Venezuela are the small ports of **Morawhanna** (Morajuana to the Venezuelans) and **Mabaruma**. Mabaruma has replaced Morawhanna as capital of the region since it is less at risk from flooding. If arriving from Venezuela, make sure that the official who stamps your passport is not an imposter. You may only be given a five-day temporary visa, to be renewed on arrival in Georgetown.

Shell Beach Part of a protected area of Atlantic coastline, Shell Beach is some 145 km long, from the Pomeroon River to the Venezuelan border. It safeguards the nesting grounds of leatherback, green, hawksbill and olive Ridley turtles. Nesting activity begins in late March and continues, with hatching, until mid-August. Former turtle hunters have been retrained to patrol and identify nest sites, which are logged using global positioning satellite equipment. The project receives support from WWF. The coast consists of areas of mangrove swamps with beaches formed entirely of eroded shell particles. There are large flocks of scarlet ibis. Other birds include Amazon parrots, macaws, toucans, woodpeckers and crab hawks. Iguanas are usually seen in the mangroves, with sightings of rare river dolphin on the narrower stretches of river.

The camp consists of a thatched dining area and huts for the staff and igloo-type tents for guests, with fly-sheets and mosquito netting (vital in the rainy season, when there are 'blizzards' of mosquitos). Showers and toilets are basic. Food is very good. An Arawak family runs the camp and offers daily activities of fishing and birdwatching. They are excellent English-speaking guides. Turtle watching is available in season.

Fort Island and Bartica From Parika (see above) a vehicle ferry runs up the Essequibo River to Bartica on Monday, Thursday and Saturday, returning next day, US$1.60 one way. The 58 km journey takes six hours, stopping at **Fort Island**; boats come out from riverside settlements to load up with fruit. On Fort Island is a Dutch fort (built 1743, restored by Raleigh International in 1991) and the Dutch Court of Policy, built at the same time. There is also a small village; the rest of the island is dairy farms. River taxis run from Parika to Bartica all day, US$20 per person.

Bartica, at the junction of the Essequibo and Mazaruni rivers, is the 'take-off' town for the gold and diamond fields and the interior generally. Opposite Bartica, at the mouth of the Mazaruni, is Kaow Island, with a lumber mill. The *stelling* (wharf) and market in Bartica are very colourful. Bars flank the main street; *Crystal Crest* has a huge sound system and will play requests. Easter regatta, mostly power boats.

Southwest of Bartica The Essequibo is navigable to large boats for some miles upstream Bartica. The Cuyuni flows into the Mazaruni three miles above Bartica, and above this confluence the Mazaruni is impeded for 190 km by thousands of islands, rapids and waterfalls. To avoid this stretch of treacherous river a poor road runs from Bartica to Issano, where boats can be taken up the more tranquil upper Mazaruni. At the confluence of the Mazaruni and Cuyuni rivers are the ruins of the Dutch stronghold **Kyk-over-al**, once the seat of government for the Dutch county of Essequibo. Nearby are the **Marshall Falls** (30-60 minutes by boat from Bartica, US$50 per boat, return), which are beautiful, but too dangerous for swimming. You can swim in the nearby bay, part of the Rainbow River Marshall Falls property (day trippers may have to pay an entrance fee).

Kaieteur National Park ⓘ *Permission to enter park must be obtained from the National Parks Commission, Georgetown, T225 9142 (arranged by tour operators).* The **Kaieteur Falls**, on the Potaro River, nearly five times the height of Niagara, with a drop of 228 m, are almost 100 m wide. Ranking with the Niagara, Victoria, and Iguazú Falls in majesty and beauty, they have the added attraction of being surrounded by unspoilt forest. Lying within a national park, there is also plenty of wildlife: tapirs, ocelots, monkeys, armadillos, anteaters and birds. At the falls themselves, one can see the magnificent silver fox, the Guianan Cock-of-the-rock and the White-collared Swift, also known as Makonaima bird, which lives behind the falls. At dusk the swifts swoop in and out of the gorge before passing through the deluge to roost behind the water. The Golden Poison Arrow frog lives in the Giant Tank bromeliad and are endemic to this area. In the dry months, April and October, the flow of the falls is reduced; in January and June/July the flow is fullest. In the height of the wet season (June), the overland route is impassable.

The **Pakaraima Mountains** stretch from Kaieteur westwards to include the highest peak in Guyana, **Mount Roraima**, once believed to be the inspiration for Conan Doyle's *Lost World*. Roraima is very difficult to climb from the Guyanese side, but *Wilderness Explorers* offer trips via Brazil and Venezuela.

Orinduik Falls Orinduik Falls are on the Ireng River, which forms the border with Brazil; the river pours over steps and terraces of jasper, with a backdrop of the Pakaraima Mountains. There is good swimming at the falls which are a 25-minute flight from Kaieteur. Vincent and Rose Cheong run a tourist shelter and are full of information.

South from Georgetown: to Brazil

Linden (*Population: 60,000. 112 km south of Georgetown*) The second-largest town in Guyana is a bauxite mining town on the banks of the Demerara River. The two towns are linked by a good road (slow for the first part to Timehri); police checks are to stop drug and gun running. Linden's opencast mine is 60-90 m deep and is said to have the world's longest boom walking dragline. The town is dominated by a disused alumina plant and scarred by old bauxite pits. In town is the lovely colonial guesthouse on the Demerara River, run by the mining company.

From Linden rough roads suitable for four-wheel drive vehicles run south to the bauxite mining towns of **Ituni** and **Kwakwani**. The road south to the logging centre at Mabura Hill is in excellent condition; from here a good road runs west to Mahdia, with a pontoon crossing of the Essequibo, and another road continues south from Mabura Hill to Kurupukari on the route to Lethem. A good road goes west from Linden to Rockstone ferry on Essequibo River. From Rockstone roads run north to Bartica and southwest to Issano.

Rupununi Savannah This is an extensive area of dry grassland in the far southwest of Guyana, with scattered trees, termite mounds and wooded hills. The rivers, creeks and ponds, lined with Ite palms and other trees, are good for seeing wildlife. Among a wide variety of birds, look out for macaws, toucan, parrots, parakeets, osprey, hawks and jabiru storks (take binoculars). Many of the animals are nocturnal and seldom seen. The region is scattered with Amerindian villages and a few large cattle ranches which date from the late 19th century: the descendants of some of the Scots settlers still live here. Links with Brazil are much closer than with the Guyanese coast; many people speak Portuguese and most trade is with Brazil.

Avoid the Rupununi in the wet season (mid-May to August); much of the Savannah floods and malaria mosquitoes and *kabura*/sandflies are widespread. The best time is October to April. River bathing is good, but beware of dangerous stingrays and black caiman. Note that a permit from the Home Affairs Ministry is usually required to visit Rupununi, unless you go with a tour operator. Check in advance if your passport is sufficient. A separate permit to visit Amerindian villages is needed from the Minister of Amerindian Affairs, the President's office in Georgetown.

Lethem A small but scattered town on the Brazilian border (see below), this is the service centre for the Rupununi and for trade with Brazil. There are many small stores, a small hospital (T772 2006), a police station (T772 2011) and government offices. A big event at Easter is the rodeo, visited by cowboys from all over the Rupununi. Prices are about twice as high as in Georgetown. About 2½ km south of town at St Ignatius there is a Jesuit mission dating from 1911. In the nearby mountains there is good birdwatching and there are waterfalls to visit.

Border with Brazil The Takutu River separates Lethem from Bonfim in Brazil. The crossing is about 1.6 km north of Lethem and 2½ km from Bonfim. A new bridge across the river has been built. Formalities are tight on both sides of the border and it is important to observe them as people not having the correct papers and stamps will have problems further into either country. Visas for Brazil have to be obtained in Georgetown at the Brazillian Embassy. You must have a yellow fever certificate. All procedures for exit and entry are carried out at the Guyanese immigration office at the border. Immigration is supposedly open 24 hours, but officers usually go home at 1800. If arriving from Brazil, buy some Guyanese dollars in Boa Vista, or use the black market at the river, as there are no exchange facilities in Lethem.

Annai This remote Amerindian village is located in the northern savannahs, south of the Iwokrama Rainforest Programme. It is possible to trek over the plains to the Rupununi River, or through dense jungle to the mountains. About 1-2 hours on foot are the villages of Kwatamang and Wowetta where Raleigh International built a health and community Centre in 1995. Some 25 km north of Annai is the Amerindian village of **Surama** which organizes its own ecotourism activities through the village council and can accommodate guests in the new Ecotourism Lodge 3 km from the river bank near a manakin lek. A Harpy Eagle nest nearby has proven very reliable over the last 18 months, with good sightings. Comfortable chalets (**C**), guided walks and river tours: info@suramaecolodge.com. The forest is beautiful, with many animals especially at dawn on the dirt road between Surama and the Lethem-Georgetown road. Birdwatching (US$6), night trekking (US$9), boating (US$30-60) and Land Rover trips (US$30) arranged; every visitor pays a village fee of US$3. Bookings are made via **Wilderness Explorers** in Georgetown, who have formed a partnership with Surama community to develop tourism, www.wilderness-explorers.com; through **The Rock View Lodge** (see Sleeping, below), or through Iwokrama. Transport to Surama can be arranged from Rock View, who can also organize transport from the Lethem-Guyana road.

Iwokrama Rainforest Programme ⓘ *For information and prices, which change frequently, contact the administrator, Iwokrama International Centre for Rainforest Conservation and Development, 77 High St, Kingston, Georgetown, PO Box 10630, T225 1504, www.iwokrama.org.* This is a 360,000 ha project, set up by Guyana and the Commonwealth to conserve habitats such as primarily tropical forest. As well as conservation, the Programme will involve studies on the sustainable use of the rainforest and ecotourism. It is hoped that the results will provide a database for application worldwide. The Field Station is at Kurukupari, near the Arawak village of Fairview (which has an airstrip), on the northern boundary of the reserve. You can meet research teams, take boat trips and stay at satellite camps deep in the forest (Clearwater on the Burro-burro, Kabocalli and Turtle Mountain on the Essequibo). Fishing is good, especially for peacock bass. Well-trained rangers, who speak their native language and English, escort visitors through the forest on many trails. One goes to Turtle Mountain (45 minutes by boat, then 1½ hours walk), go early for great views of the forest canopy. Another trek is to the top of Mount Iwokrama, a difficult 20 km round trip; for the less fit there is a 10 km trail to the foot of the mountain to a pleasant stream and Amerindian petroglyphs. There are set rates for boat and Land Rover use and for field assistants to accompany you.

There is a 33-m high **Iwokrama Canopy Walkway**, managed by Wilderness Explorers, Surama, Rock View Lodge and Iwokrama International Centre, under the name of Community And Tourism Services (CATS); for information contact Wilderness Explorers (see Georgetown, Tour operators) ⓘ *US$ 20 pp for a day visit including entry to the walkway and qualified guide with good birding knowledge, www.iwokramacanopywalkway.com.* The walkway allows visitors to walk among the treetops and see the birds and monkeys of the upper canopy. Night excursions are available on the walkway. There is a library with birding books and a small arts and crafts shop. See Sleeping below, page 1695, **Atta Rainforest Lodge**.

Guyana listings

Hotel and guesthouse prices

LL over US$200 **L** US$151-200 **AL** US$101-150
A US$66-100 **B** US$46-65 **C** US$31-45
D US$21-30 **E** US$12-20 **F** US$7-11
G US$6 and under

Restaurant prices

TTT over US$12 TT US$7-12 T under US$6

Sleeping

Georgetown *p1684, map p1686*

It's best to book in advance. There isn't much choice in the lower price categories and many small hotels and guesthouses are full of long-stay residents, while some are rented by the hour. If in doubt, go to a larger hotel for first night and look around next day in daylight. Many new hotels opened for the ICC World Cup. There are several business hotels (eg **B Regency Suites** 98 Hadfield St, Werk-en-Rust, T225 4785) and apartments (eg **LL-L** Eddie Grant's **Blue Wave**, 8-9 North Road, Bourda, T227-8897, www.bluewave-gy.com; **AL-B Brandsville's Apartments**, 89 Pike St, Campbellville, T227 0989, bransville@gol.net.gy); **A M's Ville Apartments**, 230 Anaida Avenue, Eccles, East Bank Demerara, T233 2409, mvilleapartment@yahoo.com.

LL Princess International Hotel, Providence, East Bank Demerara, next to Cricket World Cup stadium, 15-20 mins drive out of the city, T265 7001, www.worldofprincess.com. 250 rooms all with a/c, huge pool with 2 poolside bars, restaurants. Casino due open in 2010.

LL Pegasus Guyana, Seawall Rd, PO Box 101147, T225 2856, www.pegasushotelguyana.com. Maintained to highest standard, very safe, a/c, comfortable, fridge, cable TV, lovely swimming pool, gym, tennis, business centre, massage and yoga, 4 restaurants (El Dorado, Poolside, Browne's Café, The Oasis). 24-hr back up electricity.

L-AL Cara Suites, 176 Middle St, T226 1612/5, www.carahotels.com. Luxurious, secure, self-contained rooms with kitchen, grocery, shoeshine, laundry, internet access, airport pick-up.

L-AL Roraima Residence Inn, R8 Eping Avenue, Bel Air Park, T225 9648, www.roraimaairways.com. A small hotel with good standards, a/c and pool.

L-A Ocean Spray International, 46 Stanley Place, Kitty, T227 3763/5, www.oceanspray.co.gy. Small, simple, plain, near the sea wall, with breakfast, fridge, a/c, TV, hot water, free Wi-Fi, but rooms have no windows (some have a door onto a patio).

AL-A Cara Lodge, 294 Quamina St, T225 5301, www.carahotels.com. A Heritage House hotel, 150-year-old converted mansion, 36 rooms, broadband (DSL) internet in rooms, good service, superb, restaurant, bar, taxi service, laundry, business centre with internet, conference room.

AL-A Emba-Sea, 8 Pere St, Kitty, T225 0542. DSL internet ports in rooms, safety deposit bags, pool, craft shop, 24-hr café, mobile phones and car hire, beauty salon and business centre.

AL-A Tropical View International, 33 Delph St, Campbellville, T227 2216/7, http://tropicalviewinternationalhotel.shutterfly.com. Smart, modern hotel in a residential area, rooms with windows, TV, all mod cons, Wi-Fi, breakfast included.

A El Dorado Inn, 295 Quamina and Thomas Sts, T225 3966, www.eldorado-inn.com. Good hotel with nicely appointed rooms in central location. Also has **LL** suites.

A-B Ariantze, 176 Middle St, T227 0152, www.ariantzesidewalk.com. Fans, or a/c in deluxe rooms. Includes small breakfast, see Eating, below. Very good but can be noisy from music and nightclub next door.

A-B Hotel Tower, 74-75 Main St, T227 2015, hoteltower@solutions2000.net. A/c, old-fashioned and overpriced, lively bar, *Main Street Café*, swimming pool (membership for non-residents), gym, Muneshwer's travel agency.

A-C Grand Coastal Inn, 2 Area M Le Ressouvenir, 5 km out of city, T220 1091, www.grandcoastal.com. Three standards of room, with breakfast and drinking water, dining room, laundry, business centre with internet, car rental, tours, good.

A-C Grand Coastal Lodge, 144 W1/2 Regent St, Bourda, T231 7674, www.grandcoastal.com. Convenient location in central Georgetown, internet, rate includes light breakfast, safe deposit boxes, pure water system and back up generator.

A-C Windjammer International Cuisine and Comfort Inn, 27 Queen St, Kitty, T227 7478,

www.windjammergy.com. 30 very comfy, rooms, a/c, hot water, 2 bridal suites.
B Herdmanston Lodge, 65 Peter Rose and Anira Sts, Queenstown, T225 0808, www.herdmanston lodge.com. In a lovely old house, pleasant district, with breakfast, restaurant, Wi-Fi throughout the hotel, very comfortable.
B-C Waterchris, 184 Waterloo St, T227 1980, waterchris@mail.com. A/c (supposedly), TV, hot water, phone (**D** with fan), simple and run-down wooden rooms, some with shared bath next to a noisy TV lounge, poor plumbing.
B-D Friends, 82 Robb St, T227 2383, F227 0762. Renovated with bath, a/c, TV, kitchenette, hot water, safe, cheaper without kitchen or a/c, mosquito net, bar, restaurant with Creole dishes, travel agency (domestic and international). Take care in this area.
B-D Sleepin Guesthouse, 151 Church St, Alberttown, T231-7667, , www.sleepinguest house.com. A/c, cheaper with fan, some rooms with kitchenette, Wi-Fi, meals served, also has car hire. Also **Sleepin International,** 24 Brickdam, Stabroek, T 223-0991, www.sleepininternationalhotel.com. Slightly better.
C Day Star, 314 Sheriff St, Campbellville, T225 4425, F226 2665. Various rooms, bath, fan, mosquito net, no restaurant but several nearby, breakfast available, laundry, 15-20 mins from centre. Recommended.
C-D Melbourne Inn, 29 Sherrif St, Campbell-ville, T226 7050, www.melbourne inn.com. On this famous street, rooms with and without a/c, some with kitchen, all with bath, car hire.
C-E Hotel Glow, 23 Queen St, Kitty, T227 0863. Clean, a/c or fan, some with TV, 24-hr restaurant, breakfast extra, taxi or minibus to centre.
D Rima Guest House, 92 Middle St, T225 7401, rima@networksgy.com. Good central area, well-run, modern, popular with backpackers, no a/c, hot, communal bath and toilets, good value, internet, safe, mosquito nets, restaurant (breakfast US$6, lunch/ dinner US$8). Mrs Nellie Singh is very helpful. Highly recommended, book ahead.
E Florentene's, 3 North Rd, Lacytown, T226 2283. Central, very basic, friendly and safe, not clean, neighbourhood is unsafe at night.
E Tropicana, 177 Waterloo St, T227 5701, www.newtropicanahotel.com. With fan, aimed at backpackers, Wi-Fi, Jerries Café downstairs, central, can accommodate groups, Spanish and Portuguese spoken.

Resorts near Georgetown

AL Emerald Tower Rainforest Lodge, Madewini on Demerara River, T227 2011, F225 6021, day tour US$45, children US$25 (US$8 entrance fee without meals), overnight stays US$120 double (includes lodging, 3 meals, soft drinks), cabins for day rental US$45 (weekends), meals cost US$10, breakfast US$6, activities include swimming, nature trails and birdwatching. Guests must arrange own transport.
AL pp **Timberhead**, operated by **Tropical Adventures Ltd**, 10 Providence, East Bank Demerara, T223-5108, geb@solutions 2000.net. In the Santa Amerindian Reserve (founded 1858), situated on a sandy hill overlooking Savannah and the Pokerero Creek, 3 beautiful native lodges with bath and kitchen facilities, well-run, good food, lovely trip up the Kamuni River to get there, much wildlife to be seen, 212 species of bird have been recorded, activities include swimming, fishing, jungle trails, visit to Santa Mission Arawak village, volleyball, US$79 pp for a day trip (minimum 2 people), US$153 pp per night (including transport, meals, bar, guide, accommodation). Recommended.
Arrowpoint Nature Resort, contact at R8 Eping Av, Bel Air Park, Georgetown, T225 9648. In the heart of the Santa Mission Amerindian reservation, offers a "back to nature experience", excellent birdwatching, with numerous other activities such as mountain biking, canoeing.

New Amsterdam *p1685*

B Little Rock Hotel, 65 Vrymans Erven, T333 3758. **D** without a/c, hot water, a/c, TV, phone, fridge, breakfast US$3-5, lunch/ dinner US$4-5. Also **A-B Little Rock Suites**, 10 Main and Church Sts, T333 2727, irtvs@guyana.net.gy.
B-C Church View Guest House, 3 Main and King Sts, T333 2880. Breakfast US$3-4.50, room rate includes 1 hr in gym, a/c **C** without), phone, TV, clean. Recommended.
C Parkway, 4 Main St, T333 6438, F333 2028. Clean, a/c, safe, with bath, breakfast US$2.55-4, lunch/dinner US$4-5. Recommended.
D Astor, 7 Strand. All rooms self-contained, breakfast US$2.45, charming owner.

Berbice resorts

LL Cortours, Springlands, Berbice, T339 2430, cortoursinc@yahoo.com. Offers package tours to Orealla village, Cow Falls and Wanatoba Falls for overnight visits and Peacock bass fishing.

B pp **Dubalay Ranch**, a working ranch on the Berbice River, 147 km from the river mouth, has forest, savannah and swamp habitats, with some 300 bird species, deer, large cats, water buffalo and Dutch colonial remains. Activities include boat trips (US$25 with guide), riding (US$15 for first hr, then US$10 per hr), birdwatching (US$15), jeep tours (US$30), night time wildlife trips (US$50), custom-made packages, or just relaxing. Price is **C** for scientists or students, includes 3 meals and soft drinks/juices, but not transport to the ranch (US$230 return from/to Georgetown) or activities. Small parties preferred; advance booking essential. Contact **Shell Beach Adventures or Wilderness Explorers**, see Tour operators, Georgetown.

Corriverton *p1685*

B Par Park, in Skeldon. With bath and a/c, hot water, TV, no meals available.

C Mahogony, in Skeldon. With bath, TV, fridge, hot water, clean, lunch/dinner US$2.60-3.25. Recommended.

F pp **Swiss Guest House**, Springlands, T339 2329. Pakistani run, with bath and fan, no meals, helpful, simple accommodation. Others include **C Riverton Suites**, Lot 78 Springlands, T335 3039, F335 3056, and **D-E Paraton Inn**, K & L 78, Corriverton, T335 3025, F335 3093.

West from Georgetown: Lake Mainstay *p1687*

A Lake Mainstay Resort, T226 2975. 40 cabins with a/c, cheaper without lake view, also single rooms, beachfront on the lake, restaurant, bars, swimming, boating, other sports, birdwatching and nature trails, entertainment. Breakfast US$7, lunch US$10.45 and dinner US$12.75. Day trips US$87 pp (8-10 passengers). This fee includes road and boat transport, snacks, activities and entry fees. With own transport entrance fee is US$2.90 without meals and drinks.

Adel's Eco Resort, Akawini Creek, Pomeroon River, T771 5391/617 0398/629 4198, www.adelresort.com. In a pristine location 3 hrs from Georgetown, ideal for relaxation and tours of the Pomeroon river and Akawini Creek, fishing, etc. All-inclusive accommodation.

Border with Venezuela: Mabaruma *p1687*

There is a **Government Guest House**, 2 rooms with bath or shared bath, clean, book in advance. **E Kumaka Tourist Resort**, Maburama, contact **Somwaru Travel Agency**, Georgetown, T225 9276. Meals, bath, run down; offers trips to Hosororo Falls, Babarima Amerindian settlement, rainforest, early examples of Amerindian art.

Bartica *p1688*

A-D Platinum Inn International, Lot 7, 1st Avenue, T455 3041, www.platinumparadise.bravehost.com. Range of rooms from suite with a/c, cable TV and fridge, to fan and TV, weekend packages available, internet, tours arranged, restaurant and bar.

B Marin Hotel, 19 Second Ave, T455 2243. **A** with a/c, with bath, TV, phone, fridge, meals available (breakfast US$5, lunch and dinner US$12).

C-D The New Modern Hotel & Nightclub, 9 First Av, T/F455 2301, near ferry. 2 standards of room, with bath and fan. Recommended. Good food, best to book ahead.

Resorts near Bartica

LL-A Hurakabra River Resort, on the West Bank of the Essequibo, about 2 hrs from Georgetown, booking office 168 Century Palm Gardens, Durban Backlands, Lodge T225 3557/226 0240, www.hurakabragy.com. This nature resort has a choice of three lodgings, the grand Mango Tree Villa, which can sleep up to 8, Bucksands Lodge, 3 mins away by boat, sleeps up to 10, or Bamboo Cottage, for 2-4 people, all are on the waterfront with tropical forest behind, bamboo groves, mango trees and abundant birdlife.

L-A Baganara Island Resort, beautiful house on Baganara Island in Essequibo River a few miles south of Bartica, www.baganara.com. Price depends on season and standard of room, full board, private beach, watersports, airstrip; day trips US$85 pp (minimum 12), includes road and boat transport, snacks, lunch, local soft drinks, VAT, activities and guide. Transport to resort US$30 pp return.

C pp **WilAmo Family House**, 6½ km from Bartica, T226 5558, wilf@networksgy.com.

A family house on the western bank of the Essequibo River. Maid service and cook available but need to bring own food.

Kaieteur Falls *p1688*

F The rest house at the top of the Falls is open for guests, but is basic; enquire and pay first at the National Parks Commission, Georgetown, T225 9142 (if planning to stay overnight, you must be self-sufficient, whether the guesthouse is open or not; take your own food and a hammock, it can be cold and damp at night; the warden is not allowed to collect money). In 2010 the guesthouse was being upgraded.

Linden *p1689*

C Barrow's Dageraad Inn, 82 Manni St, Mackenzie, T444-6799, dunbarr@networksgy.com. Breakfast, US$3.50, all double/twin, hot water, a/c, TV, fridge.

C-D Hotel Star Bonnett, 671 Industrial Area, 1.5 km out of town on Georgetown Rd, T444 6505, F444 6829. Various standards of room, all with a/c and TV, clean, breakfast US$4, good lunches (US$4-5).

D-F Summit Hotel, 6 Industrial Area, McKenzie, T444 6500. Cheaper shared rooms available, breakfast extra.

Resorts in the Rupununi *p1689*

For the first two ranches and Maipaima Eco-Lodge below, contact **Wilderness Explorers**. All transport is arranged.

L pp **Dadanawa Ranch**, Duane and Sandy de Freitas, 96 km south of Lethem, one of the world's largest ranches, each bedroom has a verandah (being upgraded). They can organize trekking and horse riding trips, also camping with *vaqueros*. Tours also to the **Upper Rewa River**, minimum 14 day in conjunction with Wilderness Explorers: one of the most spectacular wildlife destinations in South America. Very remote and expensive but a high chance of seeing big cats, other large mammals and Harpy Eagle.

L pp **Karanambu Ranch**, http://karanambu.com. Dianne McTurk, 96 km northeast of Lethem, on the Rupununi River, unique old home, 5 cottages with bath (1 suitable for a family), mosquito net, toiletries, good meals, Wi-Fi, fishing, excellent birdwatching and boat rides with guides, including to see Victoria Amazonica flowers which open at dusk. 24 km from Yupukari Amerindian village, trips possible. Dianne McTurk rears and rehabilitates orphaned giant river otters.

Caiman House Field Station, at Yupukari village, www.rupununilearners.org. A centre for black caiman research and projects with the community, such as public library, furniture making. There is a guest house, rooms with bath, and rooms in the field station, Wi-Fi. Guests can help with research, walk local trails, and go birdwatching.

Rewa Eco-Lodge, Rewa Village, North Rupununi, shirleyjmelville@yahoo.com. This lodge is on the Rewa River, 2-3 hrs by boat from Kwatamang Landing, which is 5 km from Annai. In 3 benabs, one with dining facilities, 7 bedrooms, separate toilets and bathrooms, hammocks, solar lighting. Packages include sport fishing in Bat Creek, Harpy eagle or wild cats viewing, Arapaima spotting; also excellent birdwatching. 2- and 3-night packages available.

Lethem *p1689*

A Maipaima Eco-Lodge, 56 km from Lethem in Nappi village, Kanuku Mountains, T772 2085, www.fosterparrots.com/etguyana.html. Community-run lodge with plenty of wildlife-viewing opportunities, hikes in rainforest and to waterfalls. Two cabins (with more being built) and a large *benab* (dining hall), each cabin sleeps 4, buildings are elevated and connected by walkways. Hammock accommodation **F**.

D Cacique Guest House, T772 2083. With bath, fan, clean, breakfast extra, lunch/dinner US$8.50-10.50.

D Savannah Inn, T772 2035 (Georgetown T227 4938), savannahinn@futurenetgy.com, or book through **Wilderness Explorers**. Including breakfast, a/c cabins with bath (cheaper with fan), phone, TV, fridge, clean, bar, breakfast US$8, lunch or dinner US$12, changes reais into Guyanese dollars, tours arranged, will take you to airport.

D-E Takutu, T772 2034. Simple a/c and fan-cooled rooms, also hammock space (**F**), fridge, clean, breakfast extra. Lunch/dinner US$8.50-10.50.

Annai *p1690*

AL The Rock View Lodge, Annai, T226 5412, www.rockviewlodge.com, to book, or through **Wilderness Explorers**. Colin Edwards and family, guesthouse with 8 self-contained rooms, hot water, fans, bars, Wi-Fi, natural rock swimming pool; in the Pakaraima foothills, where the savannah meets the Iwokrama Rainforest Programme (see below). Pony treks, nature tours for painting, photography and fishing, regional Amerindian and other local cooking, full board. Recommended.

D The Oasis, Rock View's second facility on the Lethem-Georgetown road. With a bar, churrascaria restaurant, shop, accommodation in comfortable a/c rooms or hammock space (**G**). Onward air tickets and buses can be booked from here and tours from Rock View or for Surama/Iwokrama. Interesting nature trail in front of the Oasis up a forest-covered hill – sweeping views of the savannah – channel billed toucans very common.

Iwokrama *p1690*

A pp **Atta Rainforest Lodge**. For visits to the Iwokrama Canopy Walkway, 8 rooms with shared bath (en-suites planned for 2010), with a bar, dining area and Wi-Fi. Mosquito nets provided. Restaurant serves breakfast, lunch and dinner. The overnight trip rate includes entry to the Iwokrama Canopy Walkway, trained guide, hammock accommodation, 3 meals. Visitors can experience the dawn chorus and be on the walkway at dusk and into the night. Have new and extended trails. Birds include Crimson Fruitcrow, White-winged Potoo and a family of Black Curassow that regularly feed in the lodge's gardens.

At **Iwokrama Field Station**, the rainforest lodge is one of the most comfortable in South America in a beautiful setting on the banks of the Essequibo, next to pristine forest, full of giant Moura trees and Kapoks. It has two types of accommodation, in free standing cabins or in a terrace of rooms. Tourists pay a fee for the bed and a user fee. The cabins are comfortable, with bath and veranda. Meals served in huge dining research area with a library and bar which offers alcoholic beverages at extra cost; breakfast US$8, lunch US$12, dinner US$15. Wi-Fi available. Reservations for all Iwokrama lodges and information from **Wilderness Explorers**, see Georgetown, Tour operators, or from Rock View (see above).

Camps

Maparri Wilderness Camp. Contact **Wilderness Explorers** for rates and bookings. It is on the Maparri River, in the Kanuku Mountains, recognized by Conservation International as one of the few remaining pristine Amazonian areas, rich in flora and fauna. It is easy to watch macaws, herons, toucans, kingfisherm, maybe harpy eagles. With luck, you can see tayra, labba, ocelot, agouti, monkeys, tapir, even jaguar. Various treks are arranged. It can only be reached by air and river. **Maparri Camp** is built of wood, with open sides, and has hammocks with mosquito nets. The site overlooks a waterfall; the river water is crystal clear (unlike most rivers in Guyana) and the fall and surrounding pools are safe for swimming. The camp is merely a framework. Simple, nutritional meals, and fish from the river, are prepared over an open fire.

Eating

Georgetown *p1684, map p1686*

A 10% service may be added to the bill. Many restaurants are closed on public holidays. Restaurants are categorized according to their most expensive dishes. All have much cheaper options on menus.

TTT **Bistro 176**, at *Cara Suites*, see above. Restaurant and bar offering local and international cuisine.

TTT **Bottle Bar and Restaurant** at *Cara Lodge*. Very good, pleasant surroundings, must book, also open for breakfast.

TTT **Golden Coast**, Main and Middle Sts. Chinese, good food, huge portions, classy.

TTT-T **Coalpot**, Carmicheal Street, opposite Bishop's High School in New Town. Good lunches starting at US$1.80, up to US$13.15 (no shorts allowed, cheaper cafetería).

TTT-T **El Dorado**, at *Pegasus* hotel. Good atmosphere, Caribbean, Continental, Guyanese.

TTT-T **Excellence**, 82 Robb St, Bourda, T226 8782. Creole restaurant and night club (free entrance), which also has apartments (**A-B** per day) and a catering service.

$$$-$ New Thriving, Main St, the building before Customs House. A/c, buffet restaurant with large, oily portions.
$$$-$ Poolside, at *Pegasus* hotel. BBQ, pizza, live bands.
$$$-$ Sidewalk Café and Jazz Club in *Ariantze Hotel*, Middle St. Buffet lunches Mon-Sat.
$$ Brazil Churrascaria, 208 Alexander St, Lacytown. All you can eat for US$15. Great.
$$ Church's Chicken, Camp and Middle Sts. For chicken and fries.
$$ JR Burgers, 3 Sandy Babb Str, Kitty. Popular.
$$ Kamboat, 51 Sheriff St, Campbellville. Recommended for Chinese.
$$ Mario's Pizza, Camp and Middle Sts. Oppsite Church's Chicken. Serves a variety of pizza.
$$ Popeye's, 1e Vissengen Rd and Duncan St, T223 6226. Serves chicken.
$$ White Castle Fish Shop, 21 Hadfield and John St, Werk-en-rust, T223 0921. Casual open-air bar, serving really great fried fish and chips. Delivery available.
$$ Windies Sports Bar and Grill, 91 Middle St, T231 3624, dburgess@networksgy.com. Typical sports bar, varied Western menu, outdoor area, popular hang out bar.
$$-$ German's, 8 New Market St, North Cummingsburg, T227 0079. Creole food with and emphasis on traditional soups, for which it is best known.
$$-$ Hacks Halaal, 5 Commerce St. Specilises in creole foods and snacks, local juices etc.
$$-$ Main Street Café, at *Hotel Tower*. Good breakfast and other meals.
$ Jerry's, 177 Waterloo St (at **Tropicana Hotel**), T225 2988. Big portions, slow service, cheap beer, karaoke Wed, Fri, Sat. Also fresh daily baking. Open 24 hrs.
$ Oasis Café, 125 Carmichael St, South Cummingsburg, T226 9916, www.oasiscafegy.com. Fashionable and safe, has Wi-Fi access, proprietor William Walker. A second branch at **Oasis Too**, 216 South Rd, Lacytown, T227 0121. Both serve creole food, mainly lunch. Recommended. Also **Oasis Lounge** at the Cheddi Jagan International Airport. Creole food, snacks, etc.
$ Salt and Pepper Food Court, 14-15 Croal and Longden Sts, T223 6172. Central, serves over 50 different Creole dishes (eg roti and curry, cook-up rice, pepper pot, etc).
$ Upscale, 32 Regent and Hing St, T225 4721. Popular, poetry night Tue, comedy night Fri.

Fast food: KFC, Vlissengen Road, T225 3909, Water and Croal Sts, and Mandela Avenue, T227 3110. **Pizza Hut**, Vissengen and Barima Avenue, T226 6888. **Quality Fast Food**, Commerce St, across from Hack's Halaal, lots of local dishes, snacks and juices.

Cafés

Demico House, opposite Stabroek market. A variety of local snacks, ice cream, pizza and other fast foods.
Juice Power, Middle St, past the hospital. Excellent fruit juices, also sells drinking water.
The Dutch Bottle Café, 10 North Road, Bourda, T231 6560. Serves a mix of Guyanese and international food, has Wi-Fi access.

Corriverton *p1685*
Mansoor, in Skeldon. Good Indian food. Several good Chinese restaurants within a few blocks of Springlands town centre.

Bartica *p1688*
Riverview Beach Bar, at Goshan near Bartica (Camp Silo bible study centre). Popular hotel and bar, disco, nice beach, safe swimming.

Lethem *p1689*
The Airport Shop, good snacks, bar.
Foo Foods, T772 2010. Recommended for snacks.

Bars and clubs

Georgetown *p1684, map p1686*
Surprisingly lively at night, mainly with gold miners, traders and overseas Guyanese throwing US$ around. Most nightclubs sell imported, as well as local Banks beer; many sell drinks by the bottle rather than shot, this works out cheaper. Don't walk home at night; take a taxi.
Blue Iguana, 71 5th St, Alberttown, T223 6266.
El Club Latino, 57 Hadfield and Lime Sts, Werk-En-Rust, T227 4600.
Sidewalk Café and Jazz Club in *Ariantze Hotel*, Middle St. US$3 on Thu, major international artists US$6-12.
The Tunnel, 45 Main St, North Cummingsburg, T225 7775, albert16642004@yahoo.com.

Trump Card, Church St, near St George's. Sometimes has a live band.

Sheriff St is some way from the centre but is 'the street that never sleeps' full of late night Chinese restaurants (eg **Buddy's Mei Tung Restaurant**, No 137); and has some good bars including **Tennessee Lounge** (no cover charge), **Burns Beat** (US$5.50 for night club section), **Royal Castle** (Sheriff and Garnett Sts) for chicken burgers. Also **Cambo**, No 76 (also at 119 Regent St, Lacytown); **VIP Kids Zone**, No 279 with John Smith St.

Entertainment

Georgetown *p1684, map p1686*
Cinema **Astor**, Waterloo and Church Sts. US$1.50-2.50.
Theatre There are 2 theatres.

Shopping

Georgetown *p1684, map p1686*
The main shopping area is Regent St.
Bookshops **Argosy** and **Kharg** both on Regent St. **Austin's Book Services**, 190 Church St, Cummingsburg, T227 7395. **Dimension**, Cummings St. **Georgetown Reading and Research Centre**, Waterloo St, 2 buildings form Jerry's. Offers a wide range of books, used and new, at really great prices. **GNTC**, Water St.
Clothes Good T-shirts are sold at **Guyana Stores** (see below) and in the markets. **Tribal Vibes**, 92 Laluni St, Queenstown, T225 7098. Locally designed T-shirts, shirts, vests and bags.
Crafts Items are a good buy: Amerindian basketwork, hammocks, wood carvings, pottery, and small figures made out of Balata, a rubbery substance tapped from trees in the interior. Look for such items in the markets, or craft shops. **Creations Craft**, Water St; **Amerindian Hostel**, Princess St, **Hibiscus Craft Plaza**, outside General Post Office. Others are advertised in the papers.
Department stores and malls **Guyana Stores**, Church St, and **Fogarty's**, both of which stock a wide range of goods. The **City Mall**, Regent and Camp Sts, T225 6644, is a small mall with everything from food to jewellers. **Giftland OfficeMax**, Water St, wide range of items. **Regent Multiplex**, Regent and Wellington Sts. Also for a wide range of items.
Film Films over ASA400 are normally not available; bring your own stock.
Gold Sold widely, often at good prices but make sure you know what you are buying. Do not buy it on the street.
Markets Most Guyanese do their regular shopping at the 4 big markets: **Stabroek** (don't take valuables), **Bourda**, **La Penitence** and **Kitty**.

Activities and tours

Georgetown *p1684, map p1686*
The tourism sector is promoting ecotourism in the form of environmentally friendly resorts and camps on Guyana's rivers and in the rainforest (see below). There is much tropical wildlife to be seen. See also **Birdwatching and nature tourism** in Planning your trip at the front of the book.
Dagron International, 35 Main St, T227 5525, www.sdnp.org.gy/guytrop/slothisland. Adventure and eco-tours within Guyana and in neighbouring countries and the Caribbean.
Earth Tours Ltd, 106 Lamaha St, North Cummingsburg, T223 7847, navindranarine@hotmail.com. Tours to Iwokrama, Kaieteur Falls and fishing trips to the east coast, Demerara River, Canal no 1 and Canal no 2.
Evergreen Adventures, at **Pegasus Georgetown**, T225 4484, www.evergreen-adventures.com. Tours on the Essequibo River to Baganara Island, bus tickets to Lethem.
Rainforest Tours, 232 Camp and Middle St, T227 2011 or 231 5661, www.rftours.com. Frank Singh, day and overland trips to Kaieteur, Santa Mission, Essequibo/Mazaruni; also Pakaraima Mountain hike, Kukubara to Orinduik, 5 days from one Amerindian village to another.
Roraima Airways, R8 Eping Av, Bel Air Park, T225 9648, F225 9646. Day trips to Kaieteur and Orinduik Falls.
Shell Beach Adventures, office at *Pegasus Guyana*, T225 4483/4, (after hrs T227 4732), www.sbadventures.com. Trips to Shell Beach in northwest Guyana, 2-day trip US$450 pp using light aircraft and camping on beach (minimum 2 people, cheaper rates for larger groups, ask about volunteering), day and overland trips to Kaieteur, trips to inland resorts and other locations.
Splashmin's, 48 High St, Werk-en-rust, Georgetown, T223 7301, www.splashmins.com. A water fun park on the Linden highway, 1 hr from the city, entrance and transportation from Georgetown: adult US$6, child US$5, with own

transport, entry adult US$3.55, children over 7 US$2.50, children 6 and under free. Also has a resort (**A**).

Torong Guyana, 56 Coralita Av, Bel Air Park, T225 0876/226 5298, toronggy@networksgy.com. Air, land and river advice and logistical support to all destinations in Guyana, bespoke tours country-wide and excellent trips to Kaieteur.

Whitewater Adventure Tours, Lot no 3 Sandy Babb St, Kitty, T226 6614, F226 5225. Daytrips to Baracara Island on the Mazaruni River from US$60; trips to Marshall Falls (rapids) available, uses two jetboats for tours.

Wilderness Explorers, Cara Suites, 176 Middle St, T227 7698, www.wilderness-explorers.com. (In London: c/o Claire Antell, 46 Melbourne Rd, London SW19 3BA, T020-8417 1585.) Offer ready-made or custom-designed itineraries. Tours to all of Guyana's interior resorts, day and overland tours to Kaieteur Falls, horse trekking, hiking and general tours in the Rupununi (agents for *Ranches of the Rupununi*) and rainforest (trips to Iwokrama Rain Forest Programme and joint managers of Iwokrama Canopy walkway, see page 1690). Tours also in Suriname, Guyane, Brazil, Venezuela, Barbados, Dominica, St Lucia and Trinidad and Tobago. Specialists in nature, adventure and bird-watching tours. Free tourism information, booklet and advice available. General sales agents for Surinam Airways, Air Services Ltd, Blue Wings airline and Trans Guyana Airways. Recently won Honourable Mention in Pioneers of Prosperity competition. Representatives: North America: Michael McCrystal, 2141 Hayes St, San Francisco, CA 94117, T415-935 4622, michael@wilderness-explorers.com. Europe: Claudia Langer, claudia@wilderness-explorers.com.

Wonderland Tours, 85 Quamina and Carmichael Sts, T225 3122, T/F225 9795. (24 hrs), day trips to Kaieteur and Orinduik Falls, Santa Mission, Essequibo and Mazaruni rivers, city tours; special arrangements for overnight stays available, recommended.

Travel agents

Connections Travel, 6 Ave of the Republic.

Frandec, Main St. Mr Mendoza. Repeatedly recommended (no tours to the interior).

H and R Ramdehol, 215 South Rd, Lacytown.

Jim Bacchus, 34-37 Water St, WM Fogarty Building.

Muneshwers Ltd, 45-47 Water St.

Bartica *p1688*

B Balkarran, 2 Triangle St, T455 2544. A good boatman and guide.

Essequibo Adventure Tours, 52 First Av, Bartica, T455 2441, sbell@guyananet.gy. Jet boat and tours on the Essequibo/Mazaruni and Cuyuni Rivers.

686

…tional Airport is at …of Georgetown. Check in …flights and you contact the … before your flight to hear if it ha… delayed, or brought forward. There are 3 duty-free shops. Some spirits are more expensive than downtown. There is also an exchange house, open usual banking hrs; if closed, plenty of parallel traders outside (signboard in the exchange house says what the rate is). It is difficult to pay for flight tickets at the airport with credit cards or TCs. The exchange desk will change TCs for flight ticket purchases.

Flights are often booked up weeks in advance (especially at Christmas and in August) and are frequently overbooked, so it is essential to reconfirm your outward flight within 72 hrs of arrival, which can take some time, and difficult to change your travel plans at the last minute. A number of travel agents are now computerized, making the process easier. Check for special deals on flights to neighbouring countries. Foreigners must pay for airline tickets in US$ (most airlines do not accept US$100 bills), or other specified currencies. Luggage should be securely locked as theft from checked-in baggage is common.

Bus There are regular services by minibuses and collective taxis to most coastal towns from the Stabroek Market. Minibuses leave early; arrive before 0700. To **Moleson Creek** for the crossing to Suriname, No 65 from opposite the City Hall, Ave of the Republic between Regent and Charlotte Sts, leaves when full, US$12.50. This is not a safe area early in the morning, if there are no other passengers waiting take a taxi to Moleson Creek from Georgetown, US$40-45. **Avenish**, T642 5161, offers this service. Be sure he takes you to the legal ferry, via immigration and not the illegal crossing further north. If, by mistake, you get on a bus going only as far as **Springlands**, US$10, 15 mins before Moleson Creek, 3-4 hrs, the driver will probably take you for a little extra money (check with the driver in Georgetown where his bus is going); you can also break the journey at New Amsterdam. To **Rossignol**, US$3.75; to **Parika**, No 32, US$2.25; to **Linden**, No 43, US$4.50. Ask other passengers what the fare is.

Note *For visiting many parts of the interior,* particularly Amerindian districts, permits are required in advance from the **Ministry of Home Affairs** and the **Minister of Amerindian Affairs**, 236 Thomas St, South Cummingsburg. If venturing out of Georgetown on your own, check beforehand whether you need a permit for where you intend to visit. Permits can be difficult to obtain and may require some time. Apply before arrival in Guyana. **Wilderness Explorers** offer a service for obtaining permits.

Georgetown to Suriname *p1689*

Air **TGA, GUM Air, Blue Wings** and **META** airlines fly Georgetown-Paramaribo.

Boat To Suriname: a ferry from Moleson, or Crabwood Creek, 13 km south of Springlands, to South Drain (40 km south of Nieuw-Nickerie) runs daily at 1100, check-in 0930, US$10 single (US$15 return for 21 days), bicycles free, motorbikes US$5, cars US$15, 30-min crossing. Immigration forms are handed out on board. At the ferry point is a hut/bar where you can buy Suriname dollars.

Bus Direct buses **Georgetown-Moleson Creek**, see above. Entering Guyana, you may be able to join a Paramaribo-Georgetown minibus at Immigration. Direct buses Georgetown-Paramaribo are operated by **Dougla**, T226 2843, US$60 including ferry ticket; they pick up and drop off at hotels. Minibuses to Paramaribo by **Bobby's**, T226 8668, **Lambada**, **Bin Laden**, T264 2993/624 2411 (mob), US$22; they pick up and drop off at hotels. Check visa requirements for Suriname before travelling.

Border with Venezuela: Mabaruma *p1687*

Air **TGA** flies from Georgetown Mon, Wed, Fri, Sat US$80 one way, US$160 return.

Boat A ferry runs every other Tue from Georgetown at 1500 (US$8.35) to Mabaruma. The journey is surprisingly rough and 'you will have to fight for hammock space and watch your possessions like a hawk'. For assistance with transport contact Mr Prince through the Government Guest House. Boats also go from Charity (see page 1687) when there is demand. Ask for Peanut or Gavin. Boats go out to sea so you will get very wet, can be rough, 6 hrs, costs up to US$100 per boat.

Shell Beach *p1687*

Air/Boat Fly Georgetown-Mabaruma, then take a motorized canoe to Shell Beach, 1 hr (good trip in the early morning for birdwatching); the last 20 mins is from the mouth of the Waini River along coast to Shell Beach camp, which can be a jolting ride. Or from Georgetown by canoe along some very interesting waterways. Allow 3-4 days. For information, contact **Shell Beach Adventures** or **Wilderness Explorers**, see above.

Kaieteur and Orinduik Falls *p1688*

Organized tours A trip to the Kaieteur Falls costs US$270 with most operators, minimum 5 people. The trip includes 2 hrs at Kaieteur Falls, 2 hrs at Orinduik Falls, lunch, drinks, park entrance fee and guide; sit on left for best views, take swimming gear. Trips depend on the charter plane being filled; there is normally at least 1 flight per week. Cancellations only occur in bad weather or if there are insufficient passengers. Operators offering this service are **Wilderness Explorers** (guarantees flight to Kaieteur Falls for flights booked as part of a package), **Wonderland Tours**, **Torong Guyana**, **Shell Beach Adventures**, **Rainforest Tours**, and **Nature Tours**. Another option is Kaieteur Falls with **Baganara Island Resort** for US$245 pp. To charter a plane privately costs US$1,200 to Kaieteur and Orinduik. **Air Services** Ltd offer a Kaieteur only flight on Sat and Sun for US$220 (includes national park registration); flight must be full, last minute cancellations not uncommon. **Rainforest Tours** in Georgetown offer overland trips to Kaieteur for US$3,000 for groups of 3 minimum; rate includes all transport, meals, camping gear, guides and flight back to Georgetown. Minibuses run daily from Georgetown as far as Mahdia, via Mabura Hill.

On the Rupununi *p1689*

Transport around the Rupununi is difficult; there are a few 4WD vehicles, but ox-carts and bicycles are more common on the rough roads. From Lethem transport can be hired for day-trips to the Moco-Moco Falls and the Kumu Falls and to the Kanuku Mountains (4WD and driver to Moco-Moco US$72.50, long, rough ride and walk, but worth it). Trucks may also be hired to visit Annai, 130 km northeast (see below) along a poor road, 4 hrs journey, ... leaving town must check with the ...

Lethem *p1689*

The **Airport Shop** can arrange horse hire for US$8 per hr, and Land Rovers and trucks at US$3 per mile. **Savannah Inn** has good 4WD vehicles for hire with driver. For birdwatching trips and transport contact Loris Franklin, T772 2105, or through the Airport Shop. Best time to ask about vehicle hire (with driver), or horse is when plane arrives. Car hire is expensive.

Air TGA flies Georgetown-Lethem-Georgetown daily except Tue and Sun, US$127 one way, US$238 return. Stops are available at Annai, Fair View (Iwokrama) and Karanambu Ranch.

Road The road from Georgetown to Lethem via Mabura Hill and Kurupukari is now all-weather. It provides a through route from Georgetown to Boa Vista (Brazil). After Linden, it runs 100 km to Mabura Hill, then 50 km to Frenchman's Creek and on to the Essequibo. After the river and Iwokrama (see below) the road goes through jungle to **Rock View** (see Sleeping, above), the stop for Annai. Then the road crosses the Rupununi. **IntraServ**, 159 Charlotte St, Lacytown, George- town, T226 0605, Lethem T772 2202, have a scheduled bus service from Georgetown to Linden, Kurupukari, Mabura Hill, Rock View (for Annai) and Lethem Mon, Tue, Thu, Fri at 2100 from near **Tropicana Hotel**, Waterloo and Middle Streets. They leave Lethem Sun, Mon, Wed, Thu at 1000. Baggage allowance: 50 lbs (US$0.80 per lb over). Fares from Georgetown: Mabura Hill, Kurupukari and Iwokrama Canopy Walkway US$40 (US$70 return); Annai US$45 (US$89 return); Lethem US$50 (US$100 return). Also minibuses which leave when full, US$50.

Border with Brazil *p1689*

From Lethem to the crossing (1.6 km), take a taxi, or pickup, US$3-5. There is no toll to cross the bridge.

Buses from **Bonfim** to Boa Vista (Brazil) 4-5 a day, 2½ hrs, US$11; colectivos charge US$25.

Air **Blue Wings** and **META** fly Georgetown-Boa Vista.

Annai *p1690*

Road TGA agent in Annai is Colin Edwards and the Rock View Lodge is beside the airstrip. Rock View-Georgetown by scheduled bus (see under Lethem), or Land Rover US$70 return. From **Karanambu** to **Rock View** by boat and jeep costs US$380 for up to 4 people, fascinating trip.

Iwokrama *p1690*

Road 1¼ hrs by road from Annai or Surama. Coming from Georgetown, you have to cross the Essequibo at Kurupukari; ferry runs 0800-1700, hoot for service, US$35 for a car, pick-up or small minibus, US$55 for 15-seat minibus, US$125 truck.

Directory

Georgetown *p1684, map p1686*

Airline offices International: **Blue Wing Airlines**, www.bluewingairlines.com, flights to Paramaribo, Tue, Thu, Sat 0800. **Caribbean Airlines**, 63 Robb St, Robbstown, T1-800-744 2225, or 221 2202, www.caribbean-air lines.com (Caribbean, Miami, New York, Toronto, London – codeshare with BA). **Delta**, www.delta.com, flies to Guyana from New York 3 times a week. **META**, 303 Church St, Queenstown, T225 5315, metageorgetown@hotmail.com (from Manaus and Boa Vista, Brazil, to Guyana and Suriname). **Surinam Airways**, 176 Middle St, T225 4894. For domestic flights see Getting around, page 1680. **Banks** **Republic Bank**, **Guyana Bank of Trade and Industry** (GBTI), **Bank of Baroda**, **Bank of Nova Scotia** (2 branches) will give cash advance on Visa card. ATMs at Scotia Bank (Robb St and High St - most reliable), **GBTI**, **Pegasus Guyana**, **City Mall** and **Buddy's International Mall**. **Exchange houses:** (*cambios*) in shops may be open longer. A good, safe *cambio* is Kayman Sankar, Lamaha St. There is a *cambio* next to Rima Guest House, Middle St. Roving *cambios* at entrance to Stabroek Market, take care. To buy Suriname dollars, go to **Swiss House**, a *cambio* in the unsafe market area around Water St and America St, known locally as 'Wall St'. There are others that will change Suriname dollars. **Car hire** Available through numerous companies (page 44 in the Guyana Telephone book lists some of them and the rest can be found in the Yellow Pages). **Budget** at *Ocean View Hotel*, US$105, plus US$250 deposit for minimum of 3 days. **Shivraj**, 98 Hadfield St, Werk-en-Rust, T226 0550/225 4785, carl@solution.com. US$54.65 plus US$220 deposit. A permit is needed from local police; rental agencies can advise. **Embassies and consulates** **Brazilian Embassy**, 308 Church St, Queenstown, T225 7970, bragetown@solutions 2000.net. Visa issued next day, 90 days, 1 photo, US$12.75. **Canadian High Commission**, High and Young Sts, T227 2081-5, www.dfait-maeci.gc.ca/latin-america/guyana. **French Consulate**, Lot 7 2nd Ave and Sheriff St, Subbryanville, T227 5435, consulfr@networksgy.com. **Suriname Embassy**, 171 Peter Rose and Crown St, Queenstown, T225 2846/2631, surnmemb@gol.net.gy. Consular section open Mon, Wed, Fri morning only, but visa application can be handed in at any time. **UK High Commission**, 44 Main St, T226 5881, bhcgeo@networks.gy.com. **US Embassy**, 99-100 Young and Duke Sts, Kingston, T226 3938. **Venezuelan Embassy**, 296 Thomas St, South Cummingsburg, T226 6749/1534, embveguy@gol.net.gy. **Internet** **Byte 'N' Surf**, 288 Middle St, South Cummingsburg, T225 6481, US$2.15 per hr. **Internet World**, 16 'B' Duncan St, Newton Kitty, T227 1051, US$1.90 per hr. **Jerry's**, 177 Waterloo St, Georgeotwn, T225 2988, see Eating, above. **Solutions 2000**, 167 Waterloo St, South Cummingsburg, T225 2653/ 1436, US$2.15 per hr. **The Computer Lab**, 32-33 Regent & Hinck Sts, T223 3211. See Eating above for Wi-Fi at **Oasis Café** and **The Dutch Bottle Café**. **Medical services** Well-equipped private hospitals include **St Joseph's**, Parade St, Kingston; **Prashad's**, Thomas St, doctor on call at weekends, 24-hour malaria clinic, T226 7214/9 (US$2 to US$8 per day; medical consultations US$8 to US$15). If admitted to hospital you must bring sheets and food (St Joseph's provides these). The **Georgetown Hospital** is understaffed even though facilities have improved. Recommended doctor, **Dr Clarence Charles**, 254 Thomas St, surgery 1200-1400 hrs. **Post offices** Main one on North Rd, opposite the National Museum. Also on Regent St, opposite Bourda market. Mail can also be sent from postal centres in Lethem and at Rock View Lodge in Annai.

Suriname

Planning your trip

Where to go

Like its neighbours, Suriname has been influenced by a variety of cultures, African, Asian, European and Amerindian. Markets, customs, festivals and food all reflect this. In Paramaribo, the capital, there is some fine wooden architecture, dating from the Dutch colonial period, and important Jewish monuments. Colonial buildings can be seen elsewhere. Probably the main attraction is the tropical, Amazonian flora and fauna in this very sparsely populated country. Much of the interior is untouched and largely uninhabited. Infrastructure is limited, so tourist lodges, Amerindian and Maroon villages can only be reached by small boat or plane. The Maroons, descendants of escaped slaves, have maintained traditional African culture for centuries and, together with the Amerindians, have a special bond with the tropical rainforest and its biodiversity. Nature reserves, such as the Central Suriname Nature Reserve, formed by the Raleigh Falls, Eilerts de Haan mountain and Tafelberg reserves, Brownsberg, Wia-Wia and Galibi are given in the text below. Suriname is famous as nesting ground for marine turtles. There are no beaches to speak of; the sea and rivers around the coast are muddy, and mosquitoes can be a problem. Some recreational facilities have improvised beaches on the riverbanks (eg White Beach Resort, Overbridge, on the Suriname river).

When to go

The climate is tropical and moist, but not very hot, since the northeast trade wind makes itself felt during the whole year. In the coastal area the temperature varies on an average from 23° to 31°C, during the day; the annual mean is 27°C, and the monthly mean ranges from 26° to 28°C. The mean annual rainfall is about 2,340 mm for Paramaribo and 1,930 mm for the western division. The seasons are: minor rainy season, November to February; minor dry season, February to April; main rainy season, April to August; main dry season, August to November. None of these seasons is, however, usually either very dry or very wet. The degree of cloudiness is fairly high and the average humidity is 82. The climate of the interior is similar but with higher rainfall. The high seasons, when everything is more expensive, are 15 March to 15 May, July to September and 15 December to 15 January.

Getting around

Air Internal services are run by **Gum Air** (Doekhieweg 3, Zorg en Hoop Airfield, T498760, www.gumair.com) and **Blue Wing** (Zorg en Hoop Airport, T430370, www.bluewingairlines.com), small air charter firms. **Hi Jet** is a helicopter charter company at Zorg en Hoop airport (T432577).There are no scheduled flights, only charters. The air companies fly to several Amerindian and Maroon villages. Most settlements have an airstrip, but internal air services are limited. These flights are on demand.

Road Details of buses and taxis are given in the text below. **Hitchhiking** is possible but neither common nor advisable.

Sleeping → *See page 38 for our hotel grade price guide.*

Hotels (and restaurants) are rare outside Paramaribo, but accommodation in the interior is excellent if organized through a tour operator. Many have their own resorts. Going alone, you usually have to supply your own hammock and mosquito net, and food and drink. A tent is less useful in this climate. Do not travel independently without taking some local currency.

Time

Official time GMT -3.

Tourist information

Suriname Tourism Foundation Dr J F Nassylaan 2, T424878, www .suriname-tourism.org (in English). Also try **Stinasu** or **METS Travel and Tours**, see Paramaribo Tour operators.

Useful websites

http://lanic.utexas.edu/la/sa/suriname. The University of Texas site, lots of links.
www.kabinet.sr.org Office of the President.
www.ci-suriname.org Conservation International site. Information on Suriname, including the Central Suriname Nature Reserve (site being redeveloped in 2010).
www.scf.sr.org The Suriname Conservation Foundation.
www.nimos.org NIMOS, a local organization, which acts as an advisory body to the Surinamese government on all environmental issues.
http://whc.unesco.org/en/list/940 Information about the Historic Inner City of Paramaribo and the admission to the UNESCO World Heritage list.
www.whsrn.org Western Hemisphere Shorebird Reserve Network, in which are the Bigi Pan, Wia Wia and Coppenamemonding reserves.
www.wwfguianas.org Set up in 1998, the WWF Guianas Programme (Henck Aaronstraat 63, Suite E, Paramaribo, T422357) is a conservation initiative covering the three Guianas.

Electricity

110/127 volts AC, 60 cycles. Plug fittings: usually 2-pin round (European continental type).

Visas and immigration

Visitors must have a valid passport and a visa. Nationalities that do not need a visa include: Israel, Japan, Cuba, some Latin American countries, some Caricom member states and some Southeast Asian states. To obtain a visa in advance, you must apply to a Surinamese Embassy or Consulate at least 3 weeks before your scheduled departure to Suriname. You need to fill an application with a copy of your passport page, date of arrival and flight number. You will then be issued a Visa on Arrival Entry Document and another form to be completed with 2 passport photos abd presented on arrival at Johan Pengel International Airport where the visa fee must be paid. A 2-month tourist visa, single entry: US$45; multiple entry: US$90 for 4 months, US$130 for 6 months, US$210 for 12 months. A visa for US passport holders is US$100 for 3 years, multiple entry. A transit visa costs US$15. A business visa costs from US$60 (2 months) to US$360 (2 years). If arriving by land or sea, you cannot use a Visa on Arrival document; you must obtain a visa sticker from a consulate, for example Amsterdam, Cayenne (normally takes 1 day), or Georgetown (visa applications can be given in at any time, but only collected when the consular section is open on Mon, Wed and Fri 0800-1500; if applying when the consulate is open, visas are usually processed on the same day). Make sure your name on the visa agrees in detail with that on your passport. On entry to Suriname (by land or air) check the number of days in the stamp in your passport given by the military police. Some details may be found on www.consulaatsuriname.nl, www.suriname embassy.org, or www.scgmia.com. It is not possible to enter Suriname on a single-entry visa then extend this in the country. If you wish to stay in Suriname, you must apply at least 3 months in advance for Authorization of Temporary Stay (*Machtiging Kort Verblijf*, MVK) which costs €40 or US$45. An exit stamp is given by the military police at the airport or land border. Useful addresses: the Alien Registration Office (Vreemdelingendienst), Mr J Lachmonstraat 167, at the Department of Civil Works building, Paramaribo, T597-490666, Mon-Fri, 0700-1430. The Ministry of Foreign Affairs, consular section, Henck Arronstraat 23-25 (opposite Surinaamsche Bank), Paramaribo. See also www.capitolvisa.com. **Note** If you arriving from Guyana, Guyane or Brazil you need a certificate of vaccination against yellow fever to be allowed entry.

Weights and measures

Metric.

Paramaribo → *Colour map 2, B5. Population: 487,024 (2004).*

The capital and chief port, lies on the Suriname River, 12 km from the sea. There are many attractive colonial buildings. The **Governor's Mansion** (now the Presidential Palace) is on Onafhankelijkheidsplein (also called Eenheidsplein and, originally, Oranjeplein). Many beautiful 18th- and 19th-century buildings in Dutch (neo-Normanic) style are in the same area. A few have been restored, notably along the waterfront.

Ins and outs

Getting there The airport is 47 km south. There is no central bus station. » *See also Transport, page 1715.*

Getting around There are very few regular **buses**; the few services that are left leave from Heiligenweg. There are privately run 'wild buses', also known as 'numbered buses' which run on fixed routes around the city; they are minivans and are severely overcrowded. **Taxis** generally have no meters, average price US$2.50. The price should be agreed on beforehand to avoid

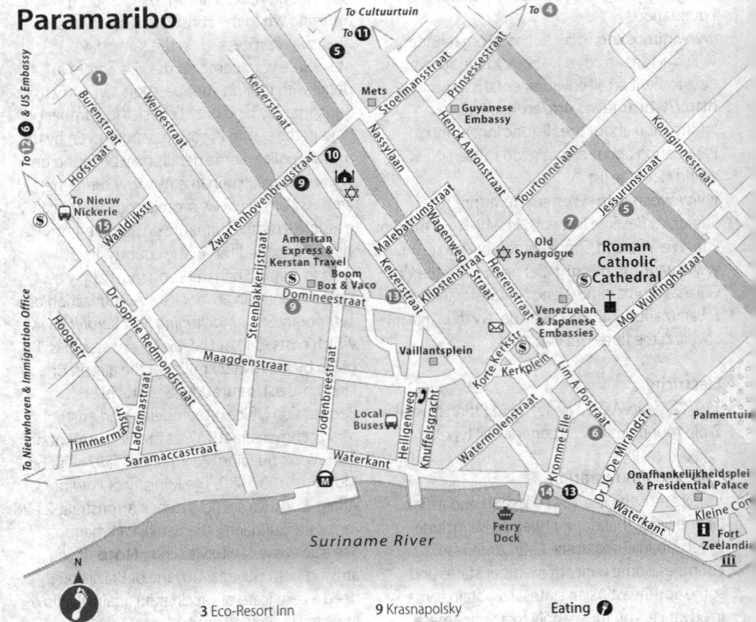

100 metres
100 yards

Sleeping
1 Best Western Elegance
2 Courtyard Paramaribo (Marriott)
3 Eco-Resort Inn
4 Fanna
5 Guest House 24
6 Guest House Albergo Alberga
7 Guesthouse Kolibrie
8 Guesthouses Centre & Sabana
9 Krasnapolsky
10 Queens Hotel & Casino
11 Residence Inn
12 Savoie
13 Spanhoek
14 Torarica
15 Zeelandia Suites

Eating
1 Bali
2 Café de Punt, Mambo, 'T Lekkerbekje & Zanzibar
3 Chi Min
4 DOK 204
5 Dumpling #1
6 Garden of Eden

trouble. Recommended is **Tourtonne's Taxi**, T475734/425380, tourtaxi87@yahoo.com, reliable good value, will collect from airport with advance notice. If hiring a taxi for touring, beware of overcharging. If you're a hotel guest, let the hotel make arrangements.

Tourist information Suriname Tourist Foundation, main office JF Nassylaan 2, T410357, www.suriname-tourism.org. Monday-Friday 0730-1500. Branch office at the Zeelandia Complex, T479200, Monday-Friday 0900-1530. Or ask at operators like **METS**.

Sights

Fort Zeelandia houses the Suriname Museum ⓘ *T425871, Tue-Fri 0900-1400, Sun 1000-1400, US$2,* restored to this purpose after being repossessed by the military. The whole complex has been opened to the public again and its historic buildings can be visited. The fort itself now belongs to the Stichting (foundation) Surinaams Museum ⓘ *www.surinaamsmuseum.net*, and is generally in good condition. The old wooden officers' houses in the same complex have been restored with Dutch finance. Very few exhibits remain in the old museum in the residential suburb of Zorg en Hoop, Commewijnestraat. Look for Mr F H R Lim A Postraat if you wish to see what Paramaribo looked like only a comparatively short time ago. The 19th century **Roman Catholic St Peter and Paul Cathedral** (1885), built entirely of wood, is one of the largest wooden buildings in the Americas. This twin towered, neo-Gothic building with a rose window is both impressive and beautiful, but is currently being restored with funds from the European Union. Much of the old town, dating from the 19th century, and the churches have been restored. Other things to see are the colourful **market** and the waterfront, **Hindu temples** in Koningstraat and Wanicastraat (finally completed after years of construction), one of the Caribbean's largest **mosques** at Keizerstraat (take a magnificent photo at sunset). There are two **synagogues**: one next to the mosque at Keizerstraat 88, the other (1854) on the corner of Klipstenstraat and Heerenstraat (closed, now houses an internet café and IT business unit). The **Numismatich Museum** ⓘ *Mr FHR Lim A Postraat 7, T520016, www.cbvs.sr Mon-Fri 0800-1400,* displaying the history of Suriname's money, is operated by the Central Bank. A new harbour has been constructed about 1½ km upstream. Two pleasant parks are the **Palmentuin**, with a stage for concerts, and the **Cultuurtuin** (with recently renovated zoo, US$1.20, busy on Sunday), the latter is a 20-minute walk from the centre. National dress is normally only worn by the Asians on national holidays and at wedding parties, but some Javanese women still go about in sarong and klambi. A

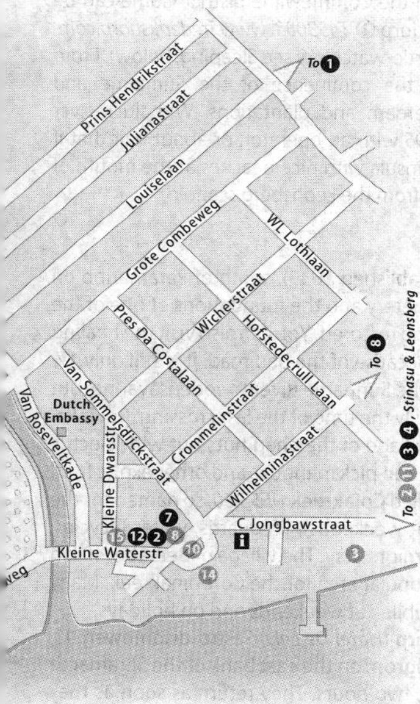

7 Pannekoek en Poffertjes Café
8 Power Smoothie
9 Roopram Rotishop
10 Roti Joose
11 Spice Quest
12 'T VAT'
13 Uncle Ray & Warungs

Bars & clubs
14 Broki
15 Touché

university (Anton de Kom Universiteit van Suriname) was opened in 1968. There is one public pool at Weidestraat, T475700, US$1.80 per person. There is an exotic Asian-flavour market area. There is a Sunday morning flea market on Tourtonnelaan.

An interesting custom throughout Suriname are birdsong competitions, held in parks and plazas on Sunday and holidays. People carrying their songbird (usually a small black tua-tua) in a cage are frequently seen; on their way to and from work or just taking their pet for a stroll.

Outside Paramaribo

Inland from Paramaribo

An interesting excursion for a half or full day is to take minibus four, or taxi, to **Leonsberg** on the Suriname River (**Stardust Hotel**, with mid-priced restaurant, café, pool, games; several nice local restaurants called *warungs* serve *saoto* soup and other Javanese specialities, overlooking the river), then ferry to **Nieuw-Amsterdam**, the capital of the predominantly Javanese district of Commewijne. There's an open-air **museum** ⓘ *open mornings only except Fri 1700-1900, closed Mon*, inside the old fortress that guarded the confluence of the Suriname and Commewijne rivers. There are some interesting plantation mansions left in the Commewijne district (some can be visited on tours and you can stay at the **Hotel Frederiksdorp** ⓘ *T453083, www.frederiksdorp.com*, which dates from around 1760 and is a good base for turtle-watching; see Sleeping, below). From Leonsberg or Paramaribo, there are boat trips to the confluence of the Suriname and Commewijne rivers, calling at villages, Nieuw-Amsterdam and plantations. With luck river dolphins can be seen en route. Tours cost about US$95 with an operator, or about half that if aranged direct with a boat owner. **Braamspunt**, a peninsula with nice beaches at the mouth of Suriname River, is 10 km from Paramaribo. Take a boat from the Leonsberg scaffold.

South of Paramaribo

You can drive to **Jodensavanne** (Jews' Savannah, established 1639), south of Paramaribo on the opposite bank of the Suriname River, where a cemetery and the foundations of one of the oldest synagogues in the Western Hemisphere are being restored. You can also visit the healing well. There is no public transport and taxis won't go because of the bad road. It is still only 1½ hours with a suitable vehicle. There's a bridge across the Suriname River to Jodensavanne, but in early 2010 it was broken so take a ferry; check carefully the time of the last crossing. **Powaka,** about 90 minutes south of the capital, is a primitive village of thatched huts but with electric light and a small church. In the surrounding forest one can pick mangoes and other exotic fruit. 5 km from the International Airport there is a resort called **Colakreek** *US$3.60*, so named for the colour of the water, but good for swimming (busy at weekends), lifeguards, water bicycles, children's village, restaurant, bar, tents or huts for overnight stay. The village of **Bersaba**, 40 km from Paramaribo close to the road to the airport, is popular area for the Coropinakreek. Many people go there and the neighbouring village of Republiek at weekends and on holidays.

About 30 km southwest of Paramaribo, via **Lelydorp** (*Hotel De Lely*, Sastro-disomoweg 41; *The Lely Hills* casino), is the Bush Negro village of **Santigron**, on the east bank of the Saramacca River. Minibuses leave Paramaribo at 0530 and 1500, two hours. They return as soon as they drop off passengers in the village, so make sure you will have a bus to return on. In 2008, new simple accommodation and cultural activities were set up at the **Santigron Eco Park** by Dutchman Gilles Dubbeld ⓘ *1 night's accommodation, meals, activities and transfers cost US$130 pp, www.santigronexperience.com*. Nearby is the Amerindian village of **Pikin Poika**. The two make a good independent day trip. Tour agencies also visit the area about twice a month, including canoe rides on the Saramacca River and a Bush Negro dance performance.

By bus or car to **Afobakka**, where there is a large dam on the Suriname River. There is a government guest house (price includes three meals a day) in nearby **Brokopondo**.

On the way to Brokopondo Lake is the **Bergendal Eco & Cultural River Resort** ⓘ *Domineestraat 37-39, Paramaribo, T597-475050, www.bergendalresort.com. Book online, through STO Suriname, T453083, or via the Hotel Krasnopolsky, T475050* on the Suriname River, 85 km/1½ hours by road and river from the capital. Day visits and overnight stays in three types of comfortable cabins are offered. Activities include canopy tours, hiking, mountain bikes and kayaking.

An hour by car from Brokopondo, are the hills of **Brownsberg National Park** ⓘ *US$5.50*, which overlook the Professor Dr Ir van Blommen- steinmeer reservoir. It features good walking, ample chances to see wildlife and three impressive waterfalls. Stinasu run all-inclusive tours from Paramaribo (one to four-day tours US$70-US$240 , price includes transport, accommodation, food and guide). Independent visits are possible. Minibuses for Brownsweg leave Saramaccastraat in Paramaribo daily when full, be there 0800-0900, two hours. Trucks converted into buses do the trip for less. Go to Stinasu at least 24 hours in advance and pay for accommodation in their guest houses (US$124 sleeping 9 - there are larger houses, or US$15 to camp, US$11 to sling hammock) or to arrange for a vehicle to pick you up in Brownsweg. Take your own food. A one-day tour with an agency costs US$105.

Tukunari Island, in van Blommesteinmeer lake, is about three hours' drive from Paramaribo to Brokopondo then a two-hour canoe ride. The island is near the village of Lebi Doti, where Aucaner Maroons live.

Several tour operators organize boat tours with stays in lodges on the Suriname River. See, for example, **Anaula Nature Resort** and **Danpaati Eco Lodges** in Activities and tours, below.

Saramaka villages and **Awarradam**. There are many Saramaka villages along the Gran and Pikin Rios, both Suriname River tributaries. These are fascinating places, set up in the 17th and 18th centuries by escaped slaves, originally from Ghana, who preserve a ceremonial language, spirituality and traditions. METS have a comfortable lodge on the Gran Rio at Awarradam, in front of a beautiful set of rapids in thick forest, and many other agencies organize culturally sensitive tours to the villages. Independent visitors are not welcome. METS also combines tours to Awarradam with visits to **Kasikasima** and **Palumeu**, in the far south of Suriname, are a series of dramatic granite mountains rising out of pristine forest. The highest is Mount Kasikasima, near the Trio and Wajana Amerindian village of Palumeu. METS have a comfortable river lodge here and organize trips up the mountain, as do other operators. METS tours to Awarradam are 4-5 days, US$655; Awarradam and Palumeu, 8 days, US$1,310; Awarradam and Kasikasima, 8 or 11 days, US$1,564-1,636.

Raleighvallen/Voltzberg Nature Reserve ⓘ *US$15* (78,170 ha) is a rainforest park, southwest of Paramaribo, on the Coppename River. It includes Foengoe Island in the river and Voltzberg peak; climbing the mountain at sunrise is unforgettable. The reserve can be reached by air, or by road (180 km) followed by a 3-4 hour boat ride. This reserve has been joined with Tafelberg and Eilerts de Haan reserves to create the **Central Suriname Nature Reserve** (1.592 million ha – 9.7% of Suriname's total land area). The Reserve is now part of the UNESCO's World Heritage List. New tourist facilities have been opened. Stinasu does 3-4 day tours, all-inclusive with transport, food and guides for US$458-560 (accommodation alone costs US$70 double, camping with own tent US$15).

Stoelmanseiland, on the Lawa River in the interior, and the Maroon villages and rapids in the area can be visited on an organized tour. Price US$520 per person for three days (five people, minimum). They are, however, more easily reached by river from St-Laurent du Maroni and Maripasoula in Guyane.

West of Paramaribo

A narrow but paved road leads through the citrus and vegetable growing areas of **Wanica** and **Saramaca**, linked by a bridge over the Saramaca River. At **Boskamp** (90 km from Paramaribo) is the Coppename River. The Coppename bridge crosses to **Jenny** on the west bank. The Coppename Estuary is the **Coppenamemonding Nature Reserve**, protecting many shorebird colonies, mangrove and other swamps.

A further 50 km is **Totness**, where there was once a Scottish settlement. It is the largest village in the Coronie district, along the coast between Paramaribo and Nieuw-Nickerie on the Guyanese border. There is a good government guesthouse. The road (bad, liable to flooding) leads through an extensive forest of coconut palms. Bus to Paramaribo at 0600. 40 km further west, 5 km south of the main road is **Wageningen**, a modern little town, the centre of the Suriname rice-growing area. The road from Nickerie has been renewed. One of the largest fully mechanized rice farms in the world is found here (*Hotel de Wereld*, T451544, standards are a little inconsistent). A little outside Wageningen is the *Guesthouse Hira*, where you can stay and learn to cook with a Hindustani family ⓘ *T88-10992, or book through STO Suriname, T453083*. The **Bigi-Pan** area of mangroves is a birdwatchers' paradise; boats may be hired from local fishermen. METS includes Bigi Pan in its two-day tours to Nickerie, US$235.

Nieuw-Nickerie (*Population: 13,000, district 45,000, mostly East Indian*) on the south bank of the Nickerie River 5 km from its mouth, opposite Guyana, is the main town and port of the Nickerie district and is distinguished for its rice fields. It's a clean, ordered town with a lot of mosquitoes.

Border with Guyana

Ferry to Moleson Creek (for Springlands) From South Drain/Canawiama (Suriname, 40 km from Nieuw-Nickerie, road due to be paved) to Moleson/Crabwood Creek (Guyana), it's a 30-minute trip on the regular ferry. Immigration forms are handed out on the boat. Suriname is one hour ahead of Guyana.

Apura on the Corantijn can be reached by seagoing vessels (**C**) with three meals, advance booking from Paramaribo advisable, good). **Blanche Marie Falls**, 320 km from Paramaribo on the Apura road, is a popular destination. There is a guesthouse, Dubois, see Sleeping below. **Washabo** near Apura, which has an airstrip, is an Amerindian village. No public transport runs from Paramaribo to the Apura-Bakhuis area, but frequent charter flights go to the Washabo airstrip. Irregular small boats sail from Apura to Nieuw-Nickerie and to Springlands (Guyana).

East of Paramaribo to Guyane

Eastern Suriname was the area most severely damaged during the civil war. A paved road connects Meerzorg (bridge across the river) with Albina, passing through the districts of Commewijne and Marowijne. There is little population or agriculture left here. **Moengo**, 160 km up the Cottica River from Paramaribo, was a bauxite mining and loading centre for Suralco. It can be reached by medium draught ships and by cars. The new bauxite mining centre is at Coermotibo, not far from Moengo.

There are two **nature reserves** on the northeast coast of Suriname. Known primarily as a major nesting site for sea turtles (five species including the huge leatherback turtle come ashore to lay their eggs), **Wia-Wia Nature Reserve** (36,000 ha) also has nesting grounds for some magnificent birds. The nesting season of sea turtles is early February to mid-July, best observed from April. In July you can see adults coming ashore to lay eggs and hatchlings rushing to the sea at high tide. Since the beaches and turtles have shifted westwards out of the reserve, accommodation is now at **Matapica** beach, not in the reserve itself. Stinasu offers 2-day tours which take a bus to Leonsberg, then a boat to Johannes Margareta (one hour), where you change to another boat for the one hour ride through the swamps to Matapica. Lodging is in Stanasu's lodge (round trip cost is US$200 for minimum five people, rooms alone cost US$35 for 2, US$80 for 4), or you can also stay in hammocks. Suitable waterproof clothing should be worn. Book through Stinasu or other agencies; keep your receipts or you will be refused entry. Early booking is essential.

The **Galibi Nature Reserve** ⓘ *US$5 1-day entry; www.stinasu.com*, where there are more turtle-nesting places, is near the mouth of the Marowijne River. There are Carib Indian villages. From Albina it is a three-hour (including 30 minutes on the open sea) boat trip to Galibi. Here you can stay at the **Warana Lodge** (US$50 pp), which has cooking facilities, a refrigerator, rooms with shower and toilet, powered mostly by solar energy. Make arrangements through Stinasu who run all-inclusive, two- to four-day tours, US$215-368 (you can save money by taking your own food and public transport to the river to meet the motorboat).

East of Moengo, the scars of war are most obvious. **Albina** is on the Marowijne River, the frontier with Guyane. Once a thriving, pleasant town and then a bombed-out wreck, it is now showing signs of recovery with shops, a market and restaurants (it's still not very inviting, though). *The Creek Hotel* (with eight rooms) is on the northern outskirts of town; the owner speaks English.

Border with Guyane

Customs and immigration on both sides close at 1900, but in Albina staff usually leave by 1700. Be wary of local information on exchange rates and transport to Paramaribo. Changing money on the Suriname side of the border is illegal; see Money, page 1704. Suriname dollars are not recognized in Guyane; when crossing to Suriname, pay for the boat in euros, or get the minivan driver to pay and he will stop at a cambio before reaching Paramaribo so you can change money and pay him. Immigration is at either end, next to the ferry terminal. Have your passport stamped before getting the boat. See Transport, 1715.

Suriname listings

Hotel and guesthouse prices

LL over US$200	**L** US$151-200	**AL** US$101-150
A US$66-100	**B** US$46-65	**C** US$31-45
D US$21-30	**E** US$12-20	**F** US$7-11
G US$6 and under		

Restaurant prices

YYY over US$12	YY US$7-12	Y under US$6

Sleeping

Paramaribo *p1706, map p1706*

Service charge at hotels is 5-10%. New, expensive hotels are opening, eg **Best Western Elegance**, Frederick Derbystraat 99-100, T420007, www.bestwestern.com, and **Courtyard Paramaribo** (Marriott), Anton Dragtenweg 52-54, T560000, www.marriott.com. Beware: many cheap hotels not listed are 'hot pillow' establishments. The Suriname Museum in Zorg-en-Hoop now has a good guest house; book in advance.

L-AL Krasnapolsky, Domineestraat 39, T475050, www.krasnapolsky.sr. A/c, central, travel agency, shopping centre, exhibition hall in lobby, good breakfast and buffet, *Atrium* restaurant for local and international cuisine (mid-range), *Rumours Grand Café* (with jazz jam sessions on Tue and Fri), poolside bar, business centre with internet and conference facilities, takes Amex, swimming pool.

L-AL Queen's Hotel and Casino, Kleine Waterstraat 15, T474969, queenshotel@parbo.net. Including breakfast, service charge and tax. A/c, TV with local and international channels, swimming pool, minibar, restaurant terrace, free entrance for hotel guests to *Starzz* disco.

L-AL Spanhoek, Domineestraat 2-4, T477888, www.spanhoekhotel.com. Delightful boutique hotel, funky, trendy décor, lovely bathrooms, continental breakfast with Surinamese delicacies.

L-AL Torarica, Mr Rietbergplein, T471500, www.torarica.com. One of the best in town, very pleasant, book ahead, swimming pool and other sports facilities, sauna, casino, tropical gardens, a/c, central, 3 expensive restaurants (*Plantation Room*, European; *The Edge*, with live entertainment; good poolside buffet on Fri evening), superb breakfast, business centre with internet and conference facilities. Its sister hotel, the **AL Royal Torarica**, Rietbergplein, T471500. More for business than leisure, but comfortable rooms, river view, pool and other sports facilities, lobby restaurant. Has subsidiary *Tangelo Bar and Terrace*, at Mr Rietbergplein 1.

AL-A Residence Inn, Anton Dragtenweg 7, T472387, www.resinn.com. TV, minibar, laundry, including breakfast, credit cards accepted, in a residential area, pool, tennis court, a/c bar and *Atlantis* restaurant, European and Surinamese food (mid-range), airport transfer US$10.

A Eco-Resort Inn, Cornelis Jongbawstraat 16, PO Box 2998, T425522, www.ecoresortinn.com. Use of *Torarica* facilities, good atmosphere and value, restaurant (mid-range), bar, Ms Maureen Libanon is very helpful, business centre, with internet and fax.

A Zeelandia Suites, Kleine Waterstraat 1a, T424631, www.zeelandiasuites.com. Smart, business-style suites with all mod cons next to a lively bar and restaurant area.

A-B De Luifel, Gondastraat 13 (about 15 mins from centre), T439933, info@de-luifel.com. A/c, warm water, cable TV, mid-priced European restaurant, special 'business-to-business' deal: 1 night with breakfast, laundry, airport transfer, car hire and taxes included, Amex accepted.

B Guest House Albergo Alberga, Lim A Po Straat 13, T520050, www.guesthousealbergoalberga.com. Central, in a 19th-century house, very pleasant, terrace and TV area, spotless rooms, a/c or fan (**C**), breakfast extra, pool, excellent value, book in advance. Recommended.

B Guesthouse Amice, Gravenberchstraat 5 (10 mins from centre), T434289, www.guesthouse-amice.sr. Quiet area, room with balcony more expensive, a/c, comfortable, internet, breakfast, airport transfer and tours available.

B Guesthouse Centre, Sommelsdijckstraat 4, T426310, www.guesthousecentre.com. A/c, TV, new, good value.

B Guesthouse Kolibrie, Jessurunstraat 9, T891 9051, www.guesthouse-kolibrie.com. Small, 3 rooms and 4 apartments with kitchen facilities, hot water, shared bath cheaper, a/c, with breakfast, pool, parking, airport transfer US$13.50. Recommended.

B Savoie, Johannes Mungrastraat 25, T432495, www.savoie-hotelapartments.com. Breakfast included, a/c, internet.

B Shereday, Cornelis Prinsstraat 87, T434564, F463844, 5 km from centre. Exercise floor, swimming pool, restaurant/bar (mid-range).

C Guesthouse Sabana, Kleine Waterstraat 7, T424158, F310022, opposite *Torarica*. A/c, safe, helpful.

C-D Guesthouse Kiwi, Mahonylaan 88a, T410744, http://guesthousekiwi.com. Rooms with a/c, TV and bath, or fan and shared bath, breakfast included.

D Guesthouse 24, Jessurunstraat 24, T420751. Simple but well-maintained rooms, bar, buffet breakfast, pleasant, "backpackers' paradise".

E Fanna, Prinsessestraat 31, T476789. From a/c with bath to basic, breakfast extra, safe, family run, English spoken.

Inland from Paramaribo *p1708*

LL De Plantage, Km 23.5 on the east-west trail at Tamanredjo, Commewijne, 40 mins from Paramaribo, T356567, www.deplantagecommewijne.com. Price is for 2-night stay. Lovely chalets for 2-4 on an old cocoa plantation, pool, restaurant, jungle walks and observation tower, bicycles for rent.

AL Overbridge River Resort, 1 hr south of the capital, via Paranam (30 km), then 9.5 km to Powerline mast 20-21, then 7.5 km to resort, or 60 km by boat down Suriname River. Reservations, Oude Charlesburgweg 47, Paramaribo, T422565, www.overbridge.net. Cabins by the river, price includes breakfast, weekend and other packages available.

B-C Hendrison Bungalows, Bersaba, contact address Andesietstraat 4, Paramaribo T/F457391, www.hendrison.com. Fully furnished cabins sleeping up 13. Other tours offered with Suriname Tour Explorer.

B Residence Inn, R P Bharosstraat 84, Nieuw Nickerie, PO Box 4330, T210950/1, www.resinn.com. Best in town, prices higher at weekend, central, a/c, bath, hot water, TV, business centre with email, internet and fax (national only - all extra), laundry, good restaurants (*De Palm* and *Café de Tropen*, 🍴), bar.

C pp **Hotel Frederiksdorp**, T305003, www.frederiksdorp.com. In an old coffee plantation, apartments, bar, restaurant, museum, conference facilities and email.

D Ameerali, Maynardstraat 32-36, Nieuw Nickerie, T231212, F31066. A/c, good, restaurant (🍴) and bar.

E Luxor, Gouverneurstraat, T231365, Nieuw Nickerie. Renovated, mirror-glass frontage.

F Tropical, Gouverneurstraat 114, Nieuw Nickerie, T231796. Mostly short stay, noisy bar downstairs.

Border with Guyana *p1710*

C Dubois, contact Eldoradolaan 22, Paramaribo T476904/2. Guesthouse near the Blanche Marie Falls, 320 km from Paramaribo on the Apura road.

Eating

Paramaribo *p1706, map p1706*

Meat and noodles from stalls in the market are very cheap. There are some good restaurants, mainly Indonesian and Chinese. Blauwgrond is the area for typical, cheap, Indonesian food, served in *warungs* (Indonesian for restaurants).

Indonesian

Try a *rijsttafel* in a restaurant such as **Sarinah** (open-air dining), Verlengde Gemenelandsweg 187. Javanese foodstalls on Waterkant are excellent and varied, lit at night by candles. Try *bami* (spicy noodles) and *petjil* (vegetables), recommended on Sun when the area is busiest. In restaurants a dish to try is *gadogado*, an Indonesian vegetable and peanut concoction.

Bali, Ma Retraiteweg 3, T422325. Very good food, service and atmosphere, check bill.

Jawa, Kasabaholoweg 7. Famous restaurant.

Chinese

Chi Min, Cornelis Jongbawstraat 83. For well-prepared Chinese food. Recommended.

Dumpling #1, Dr JF Nassylaan 12, T477904. Open 1800-2300 daily, 0930-1500 Tue-Sat, 0800-1300 Sun. Simple, well-prepared Chinese dumplings and other such dishes. Generous portions, popular with children.

Others

Spice Quest, Dr Nassylaan 107, T520747. Open 1100-1500, 1800-2300, closed Mon, same management as Dumpling #1. Creative menu, open-air and indoor seating, Japanese style setting. Recommended.

Café De Punt, Kleine Waterstraat 17. Café opposite *Toraricas*.

DOK 204, Anton Dragenweg 204, T311461. Surinamese dishes in an intimate restaurant decorated with a nautical theme.

Garden of Eden, Virolastraat via Johannes Mungrastraat. Attractive garden area and lounge bar/restaurant serving Thai food.

Mambo, opposite *Torarica*, next to Sabana Guesthouse. Local and international cuisine.

Martin's House of Indian Food, Hajaraystraat 19, T473413. Good value and tasty Indian food with friendly service and covered outside dining.

'T Lekkerbekje, Sommelsdijckstraat (near Guesthouse Centre). Specializes in fish.

'T VAT', opposite *Torarica*. A smart little square with lots of little bars and restaurants, popular after work for early evening meeting and drinking.

Zanzibar, Sommelsdijkstraat 1, near Hotel Torarica, T471848. Surinamese and international cuisine, entertainment, Tue-Sun 2000 till late.

Roopram Rotishop, Zwartenhovenbrugstraat 23, T478816. Rotis and accompanied fillings in an a/c fast-food style dining room, generous portions, *roti aard* particularly good.

Mix Food, Zeelandiaweg 1. Good location, view of river and close to Fort Zeelandia. Surinamese main dishes and snacks and sandwiches.

Pannekoek en Poffertjes Café, Sommelsdijckstraat 11, T422914. Specializes in 200 different sorts of pancakes. Open Thu, Sun 1000-2300, Fri-Sat 1000-0100.

Power Smoothie, Zwartenhovenbrugstraat and Wilhelminastraat. Healthy fast food.

Roti Joose, Zwartenhovenbrugstraat 9. Well-known roti shop in centre of town.

Uncle Ray at Waterkant by the Javanese *warungs*, opposite Central Bank of Suriname. Local Creole food.

Bars and clubs

Paramaribo *p1706, map p1706*

All are liveliest Thu-Sat.

Ballrom Energy, L'Hermitageweg 25, T497534. Younger crowd.

Broki, Waterkant next to the Ferry Docks. Hammock bar, good food and atmosphere.

Lindeboom, Wilhelminastraat 8 (near Torarica). Popular spot, live entertainment, Sun-Thu 1600-0100, Fri-Sat 1600-0300.

El Molina, J A Pengelstraat, T478485. Fri-Sat opens 2300. Cosy disco, lots of soul music/golden oldies.

Millennium, Petrus Dondersstraat 2, Rainville suburb. Popular with all ages but mostly the over-30s; **Grill** restaurant inside.

Rumors Grand Café, in the lobby of **Hotel Krasnapolsky**, T475050. Every Fri live entertainment (jamming) with "Time Out".

Starzz Disco, Kleine Waterstraat 5-7, T474993. Fri-Sat 2300.

The Jungle, Wilhelminastraat 60-62. For all ages.

Touché, Waaldijk/Dr Sophie Redmondstraat 60. Fri-Sat only 2300, small restaurant, the best disco.

Uptown Café, upstairs at Spanhoek Passage, T406181. Special entertainment programme every Fri-Sat.

Entertainment

Paramaribo *p1706, map p1706*

There are many **casinos** in the city, including at major hotels.

Shopping

Paramaribo *p1706, map p1706*

Arts and crafts Amerindian and Maroon carvings are better value at workshops on Nieuwe Domineestraat and Neumanpad. Many jewellers in the centre sell at reasonable prices. Local ceramics are sold on the road between the airport and Paranam, but are rather brittle. Old Dutch bottles are sold. **Arts & Crafts**, Kersten Shopping Mall. Amerindian goods, batik prints, basketwork and drums. **Cultuurwinkel**, Anton de Komstraat. Bosneger carvings, also available at *Hotel Torarica*.

Bookshops Second-hand books, English and Dutch, are bought and sold in the market. Maps are hard to find, but try Vaco.

The kiosk in Krasnapolsky Hotel sells books. **Boekhandel Univers NV**, Henck Aaronstraat 61. Recommended for nature, linguistic and scholarly books on Suriname. **Hoeksteen**, Henck Aaronstraat 17. **Kersten**, Domineestraat. One of 2 main bookshops in the city, selling English-language books. **Vaco**, opposite Krasnapolsky. The other main bookshop, also selling English books.

Music The following sell international and local music on CD (the latter is heavily influenced by Caribbean styles): **Beat Street** in Steenbakkerijstraat, near Krasnapolsky Hotel. **Boom Box**, Domineestraat, opposite Krasnapolsky Hotel. **Disco Amigo**, Wagenwegstraat, opposite Theater Star.

Shopping centres **Hermitage Shopping Mall**, Vieruurbloem Straat, 5 mins in taxi south of centre. The only place open until 2100, with chemists, money exchange, top quality boutiques, coffee shops and music stores. Also **Maretraite Mall** on Topaas Straat, north of the city.

Supermarkets Many, well stocked. **Choi's**, Johannes Mungrastraat, some way from centre. Excellent selections of Dutch and othe European goods, also Rossignol Deli in same complex. Another branch at the corner of Thurkowweg and Tweekinderenweg. **Tulip** supermarket on Tourtonnelaan sells many North American and European products.

Activities and tours

Paramaribo *p1706, map p1706*

If intending to take a tour to the jungle and either Amerindian or Maroon villages, check how much time is spent in the jungle itself and on the conditions in the villages. One such trip is to Palumeu, an Amerindian village (Trio, Wajana and Akurio peoples) due south of Paramaribo, not far from the Brazilian border. 3- or 4-night packages starting Mon or Fri include flights, food, accommodation, jungle hikes and boat trips. Book through **METS** (see below).

Access Suriname Travel, Prinsessestraat 37, T424533, www.surinametravel.com. Sells all major tours in Suriname and can supply general travel information on the country, manager Syrano Zalman is helpful.

Anaula Nature Resort, Wagenwegstraat 55, Paramaribo, T410700, www.anaulanature resort.com. A comfortable resort near the Ferulassi Falls about an hour's boat trip from Atjonie village, 4½ hours' drive from Paramaribo (or reached by air). It has lodges for 2-5 people, cold water, restaurant and bar, swimming pool; activities include forest and Maroon village excursions; 3, 4 and 5-day packages US$365-634 pp, all inclusive.

Arinze Tours, Wagenwegstraat 15, T425960, www.arinzetours.com. Tours to Maroon villages of Santigron, manager George Lazo.

Captain Moen's Dolphin Tours, bookable through METS, see below. Cruises to see brackish water or Guiana dolphin, the profosu (*Sotalia Guianensis*), daytime on the Commewijne river and to the beach at Braamspunt, 0900-1300, US$48, and sunset from Leonsberg to the Johannes Margareta plantation, 1615-1915, US$34. Both include refreshments and snacks, lifejackets on board.

Cardy Adventures and Bike Rental, Cornelis Jongbawstraat 31 (near Eco Resort), T422518, www.cardyadventures.com. Bike rental (bike rental@cardyadventures.com) and standard and adventure tours throughout the country, English spoken, very helpful, efficient, excellent food. Open Mon-Fri 0800-1600, Sat 0800-1300.

Danpaati Eco Lodges, Anniestraat 14 , T471113, www.danpaati.net. Danpaati River Lodge in Upper Suriname (Boven Suriname) offers 3 and 4 day packages (US$532-640 pp), or nightly rates of US$100 in cabins on Danpaati island, 345 km south of Paramaribo, excursions to the forest, on the river and to villages, has an associated health care project.

Ma-Ye-Du, Matoeliestraat 22, T410348, www.mayedusuriname.com. Tours to Maroon villages in Marowijne River.

METS Travel and Tours (Movement for Eco-Tourism in Suriname), Dr JF Nassylaan 2, Paramaribo, T422332, www.suriname vacations.com. Open Mon-Fri 0800-1600. Runs a variety of tours and is involved with various community projects. Several of their trips to the interior are detailed in the above. They also offer city and gastronomy tours. Can be booked through any **Surinam Airways** outside Suriname.
Morinda Tours, Kerkplein 1, T422986, www.morindatours.net. Nature, cultural and other tours from 1 to 4 days.
Stinasu is the Foundation for Nature Preservation in Suriname, Cornelis Jongbawstraat 14, T476597, PO Box 12252, Paramaribo, www.stinasu.sr. It offers reasonably priced accommodation and provides tour guides on the extensive nature reserves throughout the country. One can see 'true wilderness and wildlife' with them.
Suriname Experience, Chopinstraat 27, Ma Retraite 3, Paramaribo North, T463083, 865 6514 (mob). Very knowledgeable agency about Suriname.
Suriname Safari Tours, Dr S S Kaffiludistraat 27, T400925, safaritours@sr.net. Tours to the interior.
Waldo's Travel Service, Heerenstraat 8, T425428, www.waldostravel.sr. For all tours within Suriname.
Wilderness Explorers, see page 1698 (www.wilderness-explorers.com) offer a wide range of tours to Suriname, Guyana and French Guyana. They have a UK office T020-8417 1585 for advice and a list of UK operators who sell the three Guianas.

Cycling

Cardy Adventures and Bike Rental, see above.
Fietsen in Suriname, Grote Combeweg 13a, T520781, www.fietseninsuriname.com. Good quality bikes for rent. Tours with knowledgeable guides, good value, bike repair. Recommended.
Koen's Verhuur Bedrijf, Van Sommelsdijckstraat 6, T08-876106, open Mon-Sat 1000-1700, also rents scooters.

West of Paramaribo: Nieuw Nickerie *p1710*
Manoetje Tours, Crownstraat 11, Nieuw-Nickerie, T230048 (Hans Overeem). Boat tours to, among other places, Apura, Orealla, Corantijn.

Transport

Paramaribo *p1706, map p1706*
Air **Johan Pengel International Airport** is 47 km south of Paramaribo. Minibus to town costs US$11 (eg **De Paarl**, T403610, or **Buscovery/ Le Grand Baldew**, who have a booth in the arrival hall, Tourtonnelaan 59, T520966, www.legrand baldew.com/www.buscoverytours.com); bus costs US$11 with **Ashruf** taxi company, T454451 (it makes many stops), taxi proper costs US$30-35, but negotiate. Hotels **Krasnapolsky**, **Torarica**, **Eco Resort Inn** and **Residence Inn** offer free transfers to and from the international airport for guests with room reservation. There is a guesthouse near the airport. Internal flights leave from Zorg en Hoop airfield in a suburb of Paramaribo (minibus 8 or 9 from Steenbakkerijstraat). See Getting there and Getting around in Planning your trip, for airline offices.
Bus To **Nickerie** from Dr Sophie Redmondstraat, near **Hotel Ambassador**, minibuses leave when full between 0500 and 1000, US$5, 3 hrs. There are also buses after 1200, but the price then depends on the driver, 4-5 hrs, extra for large bag. (Taxis from the same area are slightly faster.) Verify fares in advance and beware overcharging.
Minibus taxis to **Albina** US$7.40, 2-3 hrs from Paramaribo cross the new bridge; there is also a bus from the station near the ferry services in Paramaribo at 0830, return 1300, US$1.65 (take an APB or PBA bus, which has a plainclothes policeman on board). **Taxis** are available, but dishonest (usually). There are irregular bus services to other towns. For full details ask drivers or enquire at the tourist office. There is much jostling in the queues and pure mayhem when boarding vehicles. They are all minivans and have no luggage space. Try to put bags under your seat or you will have to hold it in your lap.

Direct **minibuses** to **Georgetown** via South Drain (fare does not include ferry crossing), US$15-22, pick up and drop off at hotels: **Bobby's**, T498583 (very cramped); **Lambada Bus Service**, Keizerstraat 162. T411 073, and **Bin Laden**, T0-210944/0-8809271 (mob). **Buscovery/Le Grand Baldew** (address above), organizes 3 and 4-day trips to Georgetown and Cayenne respectively, US$810 each.

West of Paramaribo: Nieuw Nickerie *p1710*

Bus For services, see under Paramaribo. The bus station is next to the market on G G Maynardstraat.
Boat Ferry to Moleson Creek (for Springlands): from South Drain to Moleson/Crabwood Creek (Guyana), ferry at 1100 only, US$10, cars US$15, pick ups US$20. T472447 to check if ferry is running on holidays. Taxi bus from Nickerie market to South Drain at 0730, but can pick you up from your hotel. Bus Paramaribo-South Drain: US$5.55. See under Paramaribo, for companies.

Border with Guyane *p1711*

Boat Pirogues take people across the river to **St-Laurent du Maroni** for US$3.50-4.75, in euros. The car ferry charges US$3.50 for foot passengers, US$25-30 per car, payable only in euros. If you don't want to take a shared minibus taxi (about US$12 pp) or a private taxi (US$50) from Paramaribo, ask to join a Stinasu tour to Galibi to get to Albina. Albina-Paramaribo: a scrum meets the boats from Guyane for the minibus taxis, 2-3 hrs. A bus leaves at 1300, US$1.65.

Directory

Paramaribo *p1706, map p1706*

Airline offices **Surinam Airways**, Dr Sophie Redmondstraat 219, T432700, www.slm.firm.sr (to/from Amsterdam, joint operation with **KLM**, Hofstraat 1, T411811, Miami via Aruba, and Caribbean). **Blue Wing Airlines**, Zorg en Hoop Airport (Doekhieweg 3), T43439, www.bluewing airlines.com (fly from Suriname to Guyana on Mon US$99 one way, US$167 return excluding taxes, as well as to other destinations in Suriname). **Caribbean Airlines**, Wagenwegstraat 36, T520034 (to/from Port of Spain, www.caribbean-airlines.com). **Gum Air**, Doekhieweg 03, Zorg en Hoop Airport, T498760, www.gumair.com (Gum Air and **Trans Guyana** fly Paramaribo-Guyana Mon, Weds, Fri, US$99 one way, US$190 return, excluding taxes). **Meta**, Mahonylaan 50, T473162, www.voemeta .com (Brazil via Georgetown, schedules vary all the time). For **Air France** (flights between Cayenne and Europe), T473838. **Banks** **Finabank**, Dr Sophie Redmondstraat 61, opposite Ambassador Casino. **Hakrinbank**, Dr Sophie Redmondstraat 11-13, 0700-1400. **RBTT Bank**, Kerkplein 1, www.rbtt.com. Cash on Visa and Mastercard. ATMs issue Suriname dollars, foreign exchange desk inside bank. **De Surinaamsche Bank**, Henck Aaronstraat 26-30, www.dsbbank.sr. Cash on Visa and Mastercard. **Surinaamse Postspaar Bank**, Heiligenweg near bus station. **Volks Crediet Bank**, Waterkant 104. **Landbouwbank**, Lim A Postraat 28-30, T475945. All banks except Finabank are closed on Sat. Amex agent is C Kersten and Co, NV, in Kersten Travel building opposite Hotel Krasnapolsky, T477148. Cambios for exchange, open evenings and on Sat: **De Vries**, Waterkant 92-94; **Dallex**, Keizerstraat 8; **Multitrack Money Exchange**, Mr Rietbergplein, opposite Torarica Hotel; **Surichange**, Dr Sophie Redmondstraat 71, **Yokohama Drive Through**, Saramaccastraat (open Sun), **Surora Drive Through**, Henck Aaronstraat opposite Lands Hospitaal.
Car hire **Avis**, Kristalstraat 1, T551158, www.avis.com; **Hertz at Real Car**, Van 't Hogerhuysstraat 19,T402833, ckcmotor@sr.net; **SPAC**, Verl Gemenelandsweg 139A, T490877, www.spac .cq-link.sr. From US$30 per day, hotel delivery, drivers available. **U-Drive**, T490803, **Wheelz**, HD Benjaminstraat 20, T442929, 887 9366 (mob) or 8802361 after 1600 and at weekends, killit@sr.net. Mastercard accepted, US$35-110 daily (tax not included). Other agencies include: **City Taxi**, **Purperhart**, **Kariem**, **Intercar**. **Embassies and consulates** Brazil, Maratakkastraat 2, T400200, brasaemb1@sr.net. **British Honorary Consul**, c/o VSH United Buildings, PO Box 1300, Van't Hogerhuysstraat 9-11, T472870, britishconsulate@vshunited.com. **Canadian Honarary Consul**, Wagen-wegstraat 50B, 1st floor, T424527, cantim@sr.net. **France**, 5-7 Henck Arronstraat, T475222, www.ambafrance-sr.org. **Guyana**, Henck Aaronstraat 82, T477895, guyembassy@sr.net. **Netherlands**, van Roseveltkade 5, T477211, nlgovprm@sr.net. **USA**, Dr Sophie Redmondstraat 129, T472900, http://suriname.usembassy.gov. **Venezuela**, Henck Aaronstraat 23-25, T475401, resvensu@sr.net. **Internet** All **Telesur Dienstencentrum** offices offer email (about US$2 per hour), fax (send and receive), local and international phones and computer services. Eg **Paramaribo-West**, Zonnebloemstraat 50, T494555; **Paramaribo- Noord**, Hoek Jozel Israelstraat/ Kristalstraat, T550086; **Paramaribo-Zuid** (LATOUR), Latoruweg 57, T480093. **The Browser Internet Café**, Hoek Wilhelmina/

HJ De Vriesstraat (opposite Pizza Hut), Paramaribo, T422977. Phone cards for cheap international calls also available in newsagents, shops and hotels in Paramaribo, a far better deal than Telesur cards. Buy them at **Telesur**, Heiligenweg 1, Paramaribo (near the fountain, downtown) and its branches, or in supermarkets nationwide, T474242, www.sr.net.

West of Paramaribo: Nieuw Nickerie *p1710*
Banks There are 5 banks on the park, R P Bharosstraat with Landingstraat, and at the corner of Gouverneurstraat and Oost-Kanaalstraat. **Finabank** is in the Residence Inn Nickerie building. **Internet** At **Surtel**. Also **Telesur Dienstencentrum**, Oostkanaalstraat 3, T0-231391. **Post offices and telephones** Offices are on Oost-Kanaalstraat, between Gouverneurstraat and R P Bharosstraat. **Note** If phoning within town, omit 0 from prefix.

Guyane

Planning your trip

Where to go

Guyane is an Overseas Department of France, upon which it is heavily dependent. The capital, Cayenne, is on a peninsula at the mouth of the river of the same name. Like its neighbours, Guyane has a populated coastal strip and much of the country remains sparsely populated and underdeveloped despite French aid. The department is known internationally for its space station at Kourou, home to the European Ariane space programme, where economic activity and investment is concentrated. The site has been used to launch over half the world's commercial satellites and employs about 1,500 personnel, with 7,000 related jobs. Tourism is slowly being developed and is increasing, as in all the Guianas, with adventure trips into the forests making up for the lack of good beaches. Almost all visitors are from France and Belgium. Over 10,000 tourists arrive annually, but their numbers are dwarfed by the 60,000 other visitors, businessmen and those who work in the space programme. An unusual attraction is the remains of the former penal colony, notably the Iles du Salut, made famous by Henri Charrière's book *Papillon*.

When to go

The best months to visit are between August-November. The climate is tropical with heavy rainfall. Average temperature at sea level is fairly constant at 27°C. There is often a cool ocean breeze. Night and day temperatures vary more in the highlands. The rainy season is November-July, sometimes with a dry period in February and March. The great rains begin in May.

Getting around

Air Internal air services are by **Air Guyane** (see Airline offices, Cayenne). These flights are always heavily booked, so be prepared to wait, or phone. There are daily connections to Maripasoula and Saül. Baggage allowance 10 kg. There are also helicopter companies with domestic services.

Road There are no railways, and about 1,000 km of road. It is now possible to travel overland to Cayenne from Suriname and onwards to Macapá in Brazil. The latter takes about 24 hours from Cayenne with half a day's waiting in St-Georges de l'Oyapock for the Brazilian bus to leave. The roads are much improved. Combis (minivans) ply the coastal roads between St-Laurent, Cayenne and St-Georges de l'Oyapock. Transport is expensive, around US$2 per 10 km. **Hitchhiking** is reported to be easy and widespread.

Driving in Guyane

Roads The main road, narrow, but now paved, runs for 270 km from Pointe Macouris, on the roadstead of Cayenne, to Mana and St-Laurent. It also runs to Régina and St-Georges de l'Oyapock on the Brazilian border.
Documents There are no formalities for bringing a private car across the Guyane-Suriname border, but you must ensure that your insurance is valid.
Car hire A convenient way to get around. There are 14 agencies in Cayenne; those at the airport open only for flight arrivals. **Avis, Europcar, Hertz** and **Sixt** have offices. A local agency is **Jasmin**, T308490. All types of car available, from economy to luxury to pick-ups and jeeps. Cheapest rates are about €30/US$45 a day, km extra, €285/US$420 per week including km, insurance extra. Check insurance details carefully; the excess is very high.
Motorcycle hire, also a good way to get around, at Ave Pasteur and Dr Gippet, from US$30-US$35 per day.
Fuel Gasoline/petrol costs about €1.55/US$1.95 per litre.

Boat 1-3 ton boats which can be hauled over the rapids are used by the gold-seekers, the forest workers, and the rosewood establishments. Ferries are free. Trips by motor-canoe (*pirogue*) up-river from Cayenne into the jungle can be arranged.

Sleeping → *See page 38 for our hotel grade price guide.*
There are few hotels under our **A** bracket and almost no restaurants under the ††† bracket. Accommodation in Guyane is more expensive than Paris, but food is better value. The Comité du Tourisme de la Guyane (see Tourist information, below) has addresses of furnished apartments for rent (*Locations Clévacances*) and *Gîtes*, which are categorized as *Gîtes d'Amazonie*, with accommodation in hammocks or *carbets* (imitation Amerindian huts), *Carbets d'Hôtes*, which include breakfast, and *Gîtes Panda Tropiques Label*, which are approved by the WWF.

Essentials A-Z

Electricity
220 volts. Plugs are the same as mainland Europe.

Embassies and consulates
A full list of France's overseas representation can be found at www.mfe.org

Festivals and events
Public holidays These are the same as in Metropolitan France, with the addition of **Slavery Day**, 10 June. **Carnaval** (Feb or Mar). Guyane's Carnaval is joyous and interesting. It is principally a Créole event, but with some participation by all the different cultural groups in the department (best known are the contributions of the Brazilian and Haitian communities). Celebrations begin in Jan, with festivities every weekend, and culminate in colourful parades, music, and dance during the 4 days preceding Ash Wed. Each day has its own motif and the costumes are very elaborate. On Sat night, a dance called *Chez Nana – Au Soleil Levant* is held, for which the women disguise themselves beyond recognition as *Touloulous*, and ask the men to dance. They are not allowed to refuse. On Sun there are parades in downtown Cayenne. Lundi Gras (Fat Mon) is the day to ridicule marriage, with mock wedding parties featuring men as brides and women as grooms. *Vaval*, the devil and soul of Carnaval, appears on Mardi Gras (Fat Tue) with dancers sporting red costumes, horns, tails, pitch-forks, etc. He is burnt that night (in the form of a straw doll) on a bonfire in the Place des Palmistes. Ash Wed is a time of sorrow, with participants dressed in black and white.

Money → *US$1 = €0.74 (Apr 2010).*
The currency is the euro. Take euros with you; many banks do not offer exchange facilities, but

ATMs are common. Good rates can be obtained by using Visa or MasterCard (less common) to withdraw cash from any bank in Cayenne, Kourou and St-Laurent du Maroni. It is possible to pay for most hotels and restaurants with a Visa or MasterCard. American Express, Eurocard and Carte Bleue cards are also accepted.

Opening hours

They vary widely between different offices, shops and even between different branches of the same bank. There seem to be different business hrs for every day, but they are usually posted. Most shops and offices close for a few hrs around midday.

Tax

VAT 19.6%.

Telephone → *Country code +594.*

Ringing: equal tones with long pauses.
Engaged: equal tones with equal pauses.

Time

GMT -3.

Tourist information

The French Government tourist offices can usually provide leaflets on Guyane; also **Comité du Tourisme de la Guyane** 1 rue Clapeyron, 75008 Paris, T33-1-4294 1516, guyanaparis@tourisme-guyane.com. In Guyane: **Comité du Tourisme de la Guyane** 12 rue Lallouette, BP 801, 97300 Cayenne, T05-94-296500, www.tourisme-guyane.com. See also www.cr-guyane.fr.

Note The Amerindian villages in the Haut-Maroni and Haut-Oyapock areas may only be visited with permission from the Préfecture in Cayenne *before* arrival in Guyane.

Visas and immigration

Passports are not required by nationals of France and most French-speaking African countries carrying identity cards. For EU visitors, documents are the same as for Metropolitan France (that is no visa, no exit ticket required – check with a consulate in advance). EU passports must be stamped; be sure to visit immigration if arriving from Suriname or Brazil, it is easy to miss. No visa required for most nationalities (except for those of Guyana, Suriname, some Eastern European countries - not Croatia, and Asian – not Japan – and other African countries) for a stay of up to 3 months, but an exit ticket out of the country is essential (a ticket out of one of the other Guianas is not sufficient); a deposit is required otherwise. If you stay more than 3 months, income tax clearance is required before leaving the country. A visa costs 60 euros, or equivalent (US$79).

Weights and measures

Metric.

Cayenne → *Population: 52,000-60,000 (est). Colour map 2, B6.*

The capital and the chief port of Guyane is on the island of Cayenne at the mouth of the Cayenne River. Founded by French traders in 16th-century, but taking its name from an Amerindian prince, Cayenne remained relatively isolated until after the Second World War when Guyane became part of metropolitan France and Rochambeau airport was constructed.

Ins and outs

Getting there Cayenne is 645 km from Georgetown (Guyana) and 420 km from Paramaribo (Suriname) by sea. ▸▸ *See also Transport, page 1726.*

Tourist offices **Comité du Tourisme de la Guyane** ⓘ *12 rue Lallouette, BP 801, 97300 Cayenne, T296500, www.tourisme-guyane.com, 0800-1200, 1500-1800*, is helpful and has lots of brochures, but very little in English.

Sights

There is an interesting museum, the **Musée Départemental Franconie** ⓘ *1 rue de Rémire, near the Place de Palmistes, T295913, Mon and Wed 0800-1300, Tue and Fri 1500-1800, Thu 1030-1330,*

Sat 0830-1200, US$2.25. Its exhibits include pickled snakes and the trunk of the 'late beloved twin-trunked palm' of the Place de Palmistes. There is a good entomological collection and excellent paintings of convict life. Next door is the municipal library. **L'Orstom** (scientific research institute) ⓘ *Route de Montabo, Mon and Fri 0700-1330, 1500-1800, Tue-Thu 0700-1300*, with a research library and permanent exhibits on Guyane's ecosystems and archaeological finds. **Musée des Cultures Guyanaises** ⓘ *78 rue Mme Payé, T314172, mcg87@wanadoo.fr, Mon, Tue 0800-1245, 1500-1745, Wed 0800-1245, Thu, Fri 0800-1215, 1500-1745, Sat 0800-1145, US$3*, has a small collection of crafts from tribal communities. Also worth a visit is **La Crique**, the colourful but dangerous area around the Canal Laussat (built by Malouet in 1777); the Jesuit-built residence (circa 1890) of the Prefect (**L'Hôtel-de-Ville**) in the Place de Grenoble; the **Place des Amandiers** (also known as the **Place Auguste-Horth**) by the sea; the Place des Palmistes, with assorted palms; a pool and five cinemas. The **market** on Monday, Wednesday, Friday and Saturday mornings has a great Caribbean flavour, but is expensive. There are bathing beaches (water rather muddy) around the island, the best is Montjoly, but watch out for sharks. Minibuses run from the terminal to Rémire-Montjoly for beaches. They leave when full; check when the last one returns. There is a walking trail called **Rorota** which follows the coastline and can be reached from Montjoly or the Gosselin beaches. Another trail, **Habitation Vidal** in Rémire, passes through former sugar cane plantations and ends at the remains of 19th-century sugar mills.

Some 43 km southwest of Cayenne is **Montsinéry**, with a zoo featuring Amazonian flora and fauna, an orchid and a walking trail, Bagne des Annamites, through remains of a camp where prisoners from Indochina were interned in the 1930s.

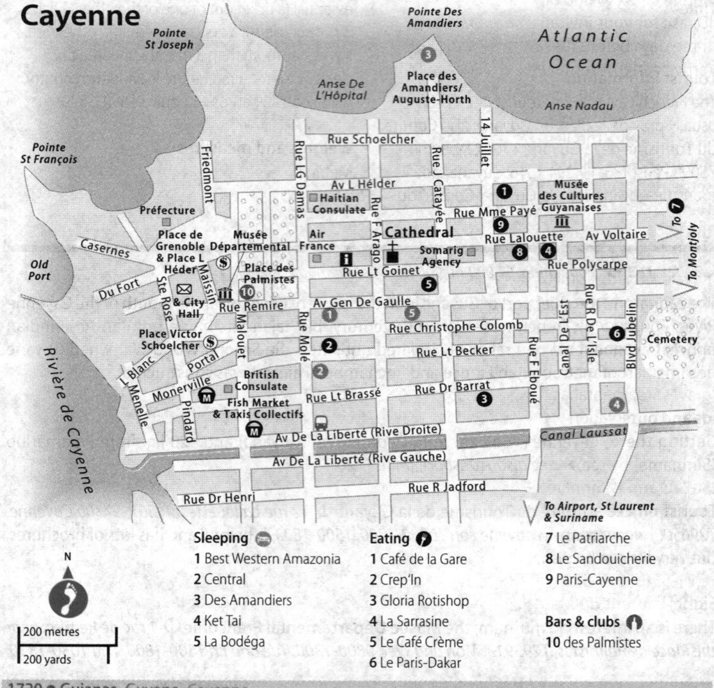

Outside Cayenne

The European space centre at Kourou is one of the main attractions, especially when a rocket is being launched. In stark contrast are the abandoned penal settlements. Beyond is largely unexplored jungle. Also in this section are the routes to Suriname and Brazil.

West to Suriname

Kourou (*Population: 20,000, 56 km west of Cayenne*) This is where the main French space centre (Centre Spatial Guyanais), used for the European Space Agency's Ariane programme, is located. It will soon also be used by the Russians to launch Soyuz. It is referred to by the Guyanais as 'white city' because of the number of French families living there. Tourist attractions include bathing, fishing, sporting and a variety of organized excursions. For **tourist information** T329833, Mon, Tue, Thu 0800-1330, 1500-1800, Wed, Fri 0800-1400.

The **space centre** occupies an area of about 750 sq km along 50 km of coast, bisected by the Kourou River. **Public guided tours** are given Monday to Thursday at 0815 and 1315 (Friday 0815 only). Tours last 3½ hours, but are only in French; under eights are not admitted. Advance reservations can be made but are not necessary on a weekday, T326123, F321745, visites.csg@wanadoo.fr, Monday to Friday 0800-1200. No tours during a launch or on the days before or after. The **Musée de l'Espace** ⓘ *T335384, Mon-Fri 0800-1800, Sat 1400-1800, US$9 (5.70 with reservation for a tour), no public transport, take a taxi or hitch*, can be visited without reservation. To watch a launch you must write to CNES at Centre Spatial Guyanais, Relations Publiques, BP 726, 97387 Kourou Cedex, T334200, F334719, csg-accueil@cnes.fr saying you want to attend; phone or fax to find out when launches take place, or www.cnes-csg.fr. Supply full names and ID; ask for your invitation from Centre d'acceuil du CSG. Invitations must be collected two to three days before the launch; if you hear nothing, it's probably full, but you can try wait-listing (arrive early). Alternatively, you can watch the launch for free, from 10 km, at Montagne Carapa at Pariacabo. Also see www.esa.int/ education and www.arianespace.com.

Iles du Salut The Iles du Salut (many visitors at weekends), opposite Kourou, include the Ile Royale, the Ile Saint-Joseph, and the Ile du Diable. They were the scene of the notorious convict settlement built in 1852; the last prisoners left in 1953. One of their most famous residents was Henri Charrière, who made a miraculous escape to Venezuela. He later recounted the horrors of the penal colony and his hair-raising escape attempts in his book *Papillon* (some say Charrière's book is a compilation of prisoners' stories). There is a museum in the Commander's House on Ile Royale; brochures for sale. The Ile du Diable (Devil's Island), a rocky islet almost inaccessible from the sea, was where political prisoners, including Alfred Dreyfus, were held (access to this island is strictly forbidden). You can see monkeys, agoutis, turtles, hummingbirds and macaws, and there are many coconut palms. Paintings of prison life, by François Lagrange (the inspiration for Dustin Hoffman's character in the film *Papillon*) are on show in the tiny church. Visit the children's graveyard, mental asylum and death cells. These are not always open, but the church is open daily. Conservation work is underway. Three guided tours in French are given weekly.

Sinnamary and St-Laurent du Maroni Between Kourou and Iracoubo, on the road west to St-Laurent, is **Sinnamary** (116 km from Cayenne), a pleasant town where Galibi Indians at a mission make artificial flowers, for sale to tourists. Carvings and jewellery are on sale here. For **tourist information** T346883. There are three- to five-day excursions up the Sinnamary River. Scarlet ibis can be seen in numbers on the Sinnamary estuary at Iracoubo. (Tours with agencies €21-65/US$29-88.)

St-Laurent du Maroni (*Population: 25,000*), formerly a penal transportation camp, is now a quiet colonial town 250 km from Cayenne on the river Maroni, bordering Suriname. It can be visited as a day tour from Cayenne if you hire a car, but note that everything closes for a long siesta. The old Camp de Transportation (the original penal centre) can be wandered round at will, but a guide is needed to enter the cells (an absolute must if visiting the country). **Guided tours** of Les Bagnes (prison camps) Monday-Saturday 0800, 0930, 1100, 1500, 1630, Sunday and holidays 0930,1100, chilling, buy tickets from tourist office here, €5/US$6.60. See also www.bagne-st-jean.com on the **Camp de la Relégation** at St-Jean du Maroni. Tourist office: **Office du Tourisme** ⓘ *1 esplanade Laurent Baudin, 97393 St-Laurent du Maroni, T342398, www.97320.com. Mon-Fri 0730-1800, Sat 0730-1245, 1445-1745, Sun 0900-1100 (1500 Jul and 1630 Aug*; has leaflet with self-guided walking tour.

Border with Suriname Make sure you obtain proper entry stamps from immigration, not the police, to avoid problems when leaving. Customs and immigration, 2 km south of the centre, close at 1900. There are aggressive touts on the St-Laurent and Albina piers. It is best to change money in the Village Chinois in St-Laurent (dangerous area); although rates are lower than in Paramaribo, it is illegal to change money in Albina. Beware theft at St-Laurent's black market.

Around St-Laurent About 3 km from St-Laurent, along the Paul Isnard road, is Saint-Maurice, where the rum distillery of the same name can be visited, Monday to Friday 0730-1130. At Km 70 on the same dirt road is access to **Voltaire Falls**, 1½ hours walk from the road 7 km south of St-Laurent on the road to St-Jean du Maroni is the Amerindian village of **Terre Rouge**; canoes can be hired for day trips up the Maroni River (see Maripasoula below).

Some 40 km north of St-Laurent du Maroni is **Mana**, a delightful town with rustic architecture near the coast (**Syndicat d'Initiatif**, T348304). 20 km west of Mana following the river along a single track access road is **Les Hattes**, or Yalimapo, an Amerindian village. About 4 km further on is Les Hattes beach where leatherback turtles lay their eggs at night; season April to August with May/June peak. No public transport to Les Hattes and its beach, but hitching possible at weekends; take food and water and mosquito repellent. The freshwater of the Maroni and Mana rivers makes sea bathing pleasant. It is very quiet during the week.

Aouara, or Awala, an Amerindian village with hammock places, is 16 km west of Les Hattes. It also has a beach where leatherback turtles lay their eggs; they take about three hours over it. Take mosquito nets, hammock and insect repellent.

There are daily flights from Cayenne to **Maripasoula**; details in Air transport, page 1717, local office T372141. It is up the Maroni from St-Laurent (2-4 day journey up river in *pirogue*). There may be freight canoes that take passengers (E40/US$53) or private boats (€180/US$235), which leave from St-Laurent; 5-6 day tours, other options with **Takari Tour** or other Cayenne operators.

South to Brazil

About 28 km southeast of Cayenne is the small town of **Roura**, which has an interesting church. An excursion may be made to the Fourgassier Falls several kilometres away (*L'Auberge des Cascades*, excellent restaurant). From Cayenne the road crosses a new bridge over the Comte River. Excursions can be arranged along the Comte River. Nearby is Dacca, a Laotian village, which has *La Crique Gabrielle*, T/F280104, a restaurant which also has rooms. For information about the area contact the **Roura tourist office**, T270827.

From Roura a paved road, RD06, runs southeast towards the village of **Kaw**, on an island amid swamps which are home to much rare wildlife including caimans. The village is reached from where the Roura road ends at the river at Approuague. Basic rooms available; take insect repellent.

At Km 53 on another road southeast to Régina is the turn-off to **Cacao** (a further 13 km), a small, quiet village, where Hmong refugees from Laos are settled; they are farmers and produce fine traditional handicrafts. The Sunday morning market has local produce, Laotian food and embroidery. Canoe/kayak rental behind *Degrad Cacao* restaurant, US$2.50 per hour, good wildlife trips upriver. Halfway along the side road is *Belle Vue* restaurant, open weekends, with superb view over the tropical forest. Ask the Comité du Tourisme de la Guyane for *gîtes* in the area.

Southwest of Kaw on the river Approuague is **Régina**, linked with Cayenne by a paved road. A good trip is on the river to Athanase with G Frétigne, T304551. A paved road runs from Régina to St-Georges de l'Oyapock (difficult in the rainy season).

Saül This remote gold-mining settlement in the 'massif central' is the geographical centre of Guyane. The main attractions are for the nature-loving tourist. Beautiful undisturbed tropical forests are accessible by a very well-maintained system of 90 km of marked trails, including several circular routes. There is running water and electricity; tourist office T374500, in the town hall. Another fascinating overland route goes from Roura (see above) up the Comte River to Belizon, followed by a 14-16-day trek through the jungle to Saül, visiting many villages en route, guide recommended. Meals from *Restaurant Pinot*. Two markets sell food.

Border with Brazil St-Georges de l'Oyapock, with its small detachment of the French Foreign Legion who parade on Bastille Day, is 15 minutes down river from Oiapoque in Brazil, €5/US$6.60 per person by motorized canoe, bargain for a return fare. The tourist office is in the library to the left of the town hall, T370454. There are bars, restaurants, supermarkets with French specialities, a post office and public telephones which take phonecards. Thierry Beltran, Rue Henri Sulny, T370259, offers guided river and forest tours. A pleasant day trip is to the **Saut Maripa** rapids (not very impressive with high water), located about 30 minutes upstream along the Oyapock River, past the Brazilian towns of Oiapoque and Clevelândia do Norte. Hire a motorized *pirogue* (canoe) to take you to a landing downstream from the rapids. Then walk along the trolley track (used to move heavy goods around the rapids) for 20 minutes to the rundown huts by the rapids (popular and noisy at weekends). There are more rapids further upstream on the way to Camopi.

Immigration, for entry/exit stamps: look for PAF (Police Federal), set away from the river about 10 minutes walk behind the Mairie; fork left at 'Farewell Greeting' sign from town. Open daily 0700-1200, 1500-1800 (often not open after early morning on Sunday, so try police at the airport); French, Portuguese and English spoken. One of the Livre Service supermarkets and *Hotel Chez Modestine* will sometimes change dollars cash into euros at poor rates; if entering the country here, change money before arriving in St-Georges. Brazilian currency is accepted in shops at poor rates.

Guyane listings

Hotel and guesthouse prices

LL over US$200 **L** US$151-200 **AL** US$101-150
A US$66-100 **B** US$46-65 **C** US$31-45
D US$21-30 **E** US$12-20 **F** US$7-11
G US$6 and under

Restaurant prices

TTT over US$12 TT US$7-12 T under US$6

Sleeping

Cayenne *p1719, map p1720*

Most hotels are in the centre. A few of the better ones are in the suburb of Monjoly, next to a coarse sand beach and muddy sea, but the best district in Cayenne nonetheless. Hotels rarely add tax and service to their bill, but stick to prices posted out- side or at the desk. B&B accommodation (gîte) is available for about €60/US$90 a night (breakfast included) – contact the tourist office for details.

L-A Novotel, Route de Montabo, Chemin St. Hilaire, T303888, www.accor-hotels.com. Beach-side hotel 3 km from the centre set in a tropical garden, pool, 2 tennis courts and a respectable French and Creole restaurant. Car hire available.

AL Best Western Amazonia, 28 Av Gen de Gaulle,T288300, www.bestwestern.com. A/c, luggage stored, pool, central location, good buffet breakfast extra.

A Hotel des Amandiers, Place Auguste- Horth, T313875. Pleasant, tranquil and breezy location next to a park on a little peninsula at the north end of town, a/c rooms, popular restaurant with varied menu and good service.

A Central Hotel, corner rue Molé and rue Becker, T256565, www.centralhotel-cayenne.fr. Good location, 100m from the Place de Palmistes, a/c rooms. Special prices for groups and business travellers. Book in advance through the net.
B La Bodéga, 42 Av Gen de Gaulle, T302513, karlb@wanadoo.fr. A variety of rooms with a/c or fan, above lively café/bar, music, tours arranged.
B Ket-Tai, Av de la Liberté corner Blvd Jubelin, T289777, g.chang@wanadoo.fr. The best cheapie in town, bottom end of this range, simple a/c rooms, en suites, look at a few before deciding. Chinese restaurant.

Around Rémire-Montjoly

A Motel du Lac, Chemin Poupon, Route de Montjoly, T380800, moteldulac@opensurf.net. In a protected area, very peaceful, garden, convenient for the airport, pool, bar, restaurant.

Near Matoury and the airport

B pp **La Chaumiere**, Chemin de la Chaumière (off the road to Kourou), 97351 Matoury, T255701, georgesrobaix@orange.fr . Set in gardens, thatched huts, restaurant, pool, at bottom end of this price band, good value, but cabs to town push up cost.

Apartment rentals

A good option, but what's on offer changes often. Best to reserve through the tourist office who publish a brochure, *Locations de Vacances*, with full details and pictures. Contact them in advance through the website, in French if possible.

Kourou *p1721*

Hotel rooms and rates are at a premium when there's an Ariane rocket launch (1 a month).
L Mercure Kourou Ariatel, Av de St-Exupéry, Lac Bois Diable, T328900, www.accor-hotels.com. Overlooking a lake, 9 hole golf course nearby and pool. See Eating, below.
AL Mercure Atlantis, near Lac Bois Diable, T321300, hotel.atlantis@laposte.net. A/c, modern, pool, best value for business visitors.
A Hôtel des Roches, Pointe des Roches, T320066, www.hoteldesroches.com. Fair, a/c, includes breakfast, pool with bar, beach, Le Paradisier restaurant, cybercafé and Wi-Fi.
B pp **Le Ballahou**, 2-3 rue Amet Martial, T220022, ballahou@wanadoo.fr. Small apart-hotel, some rooms with cooking facilities, a/c, TV, modern. Book ahead, reception open 1200-1400, 1800-2000.

Camping

At Km 17.5 south of Kourou on the Saramaca road is **Les Maripas**, tourist camp, T325548, F323660. River and overland excursions, **E** for tent.

Iles du Salut *p1721*

A Auberge Iles du Salut, on Ile Royale (postal address BP 324, 97378 Kourou, T321100, sothis2@wanadoo.fr). Price is for single room. 60-bed hotel (**AL** full board), hammock space (US$30 pp); former guard's bungalow, main meals (excellent), breakfast US$12; pricey gift shop (especially when cruise ship is in), good English guidebook for sale.

Sinnamary *p1721*

AL Hôtel du Fleuve, 11 rue Léon Mine, T345400, www.hoteldufleuve.com. Gardens, restaurant, internet access, pool, one of the grandest hotels west of Cayenne.

St-Laurent du Maroni *p1721*

AL-B La Tentiaire, 12 Av Franklin Roosevelt, T342600, latentiaire@wanadoo.fr. A/c, the best, breakfast extra, phone, pool, secure parking.
A Le Relais des 3 Lacs, 19-21 Domaine du Lac Bleu, T340505, www.relaisdes3lacs.com. A/c, cheaper with fan, shuttle to town centre, restaurant, gardens, pool.
B Chez Julienne, rue Gaston Monnerville, 200 m past Texaco station, T341153. A/c, TV, a/c, shower, good value.
B pp **Star**, 26 rue Thiers, T341084. A/c, pool.

Around St-Laurent *p1722*

Voltaire Falls

A pp **Auberge des Chutes Voltaires**, T00870-762 945774 (1900-2100), http://aubergechutes voltaire.com. Also hammock space US$16-26 (more with mosquito net), meals extra.

Mana

Gîte Angoulême, Mme Maryse Buira, PK 206/207 RN1 Saut Sabbat, T346490, or 00874-762 945782. Beside the river Mana, hammock space US$7.15, gîte **L** for weekend, breakfast US$5.

Les Hattes

Gîtes, all **D**: **Chez Jeanne**, T342982; **Chez Judith et Denis**, T342438; Pointe les Hattes, **Chez Rita**, T344914; and others.

South to Brazil *p1722*

Roura

D Auberge du Camp Caïman, RD06 29 km from Roura, T307277. Tourist camp (**G** hang hammock), tours arranged to watch caiman in the swamps.

D Auberge des Orpailleurs, 9 km after the Cacao turnoff on the road from Cayenne to Régina, on the banks of the Orapu River, T270622, reservations@aubergedesorpailleurs.com. 6 rooms and also hammocks. Canoes, trails and butterfly and moth collecting. Restaurant, closed Sun nights and Mon.

Régina

D Albergue de l'Approuague, Lieu-dit Corossony, 97390 Régina, T370802. Price is for hammock space, cheaper with own hammock, also rooms **C**, meals expensive, great views of the forest.

Border with Brazil: St-Georges de l'Oyapock *p1723*

Accommodation is far cheaper on the Brazilian side.

B Caz Cale, rue E Elfort, 1st back from riverfront, just east of the main square, T/F370054. A/c, price for single room, cheaper with fan.

B Chez Modestine, on the main square, T370013. A/c or fan, price for single room, restaurant.

C Tamarin, rue Joseph Léandre, on the riverfront near the main square, T370884. With bath, fan, bar and restaurant.

Eating

Cayenne *p1719, map p1720*

There are very few decent French *patisseries* and *boulangeries*. Many restaurants close on Sun. There are many small Chinese restaurants serving the same fare: noodles, rice, soups etc.

TTT Cric-Crac at *Motel Beauregard*, Rémire-Montjoly, T354100. Créole cooking, lovely atmosphere.

TTT La Baie des Iles, Km 10 Route des Plages, Rémire-Montjoly, T386020. On the beach, good value seafood, 1000-midnight, closed Mon evening and Tue. Recommended.

TTT La Sarrasine, 55 rue Lt Goinet, T317238. Good fish, salads, crêpes and quiches in an intimate little dining room. Good wine list and attentive service. At the bottom end of the price range.

TTT Le Kaz Kreol, 35 Av D'Estrées, T390697. Creole cooking served by waitresses in costume, delights include stuffed cassava, agouti stew and sauerkraut of papaya.

TTT Le Paris-Dakar, 103 rue Lt. Becker, T305517. Closed Sun, Mon lunch. African cooking from Zaire, Senegal, Benin and the Ivory Coast, like tropical fish on pureed aubergine, excellent vegetarian platter.

TTT Le Patriarche, rues Voltaire at Samuel Lubin, T317644. Excellent classical French and Creole cooking, one of the best in Guyane and very good value for this country. Reserve in advance.

TTT Paris-Cayenne, 59 rue de Lallouette, T317617. French cooking with tropical twist, nice decor.

TTT-TT Le Café Crème, 42 rue Justin Catayée, T281256. Pastries, superior sandwiches, juices, breakfasts and excellent coffee.

TTT-TT Café de la Gare, 42 rue Léopold Hélder, T290802. Great little restaurant with club playing classy live music every Thu and weekend. Good atmosphere, 20-40 something crowd.

TTT-TT Crep'In, 5 rue Lt Becker, T302806. Street stall and little café with sweet and savoury crêpes, breakfast specials, and a range of fresh fruit juices and sandwiches.

TTT-TT Marveen Snack Bar, rue Christophe Colomb, near Canal de L'Est. Food and staff pleasant, the patrons are very helpful (the elder of the 2 is a pilot for the Guyane Flying Club).

TT Gloria Rotishop, 14 rue Dr Barrat, T251643. Surinamese style rotis with excellent fillings and West Indian and Indian breads. English speaking.

TT Le Sandouicherie, rue Félix Eboué at Lt Goinet, T289170. French bread sandwiches, snacks, juices and breakfasts, a/c.

Snacks

Vans around Place des Palmistes in evenings sell cheap, filling sandwiches. Along the Canal Laussant there are Javanese snack bars: try *bami* (spicy noodles) or *saté* (barbecued meat in a spicy peanut sauce). Also along the canal are small, cheap Créole restaurants, not very clean.

Kourou *p1721*

🍴🍴🍴 **Le Bistrot du Lac**, Hotel Mercure Ariatel, T328900. Named chef, Dominique Pirou, has one of the best tables in Guyane, serving French Creole dishes like Grouper in wild mushroom sauce and Tiger prawns in citrus. The hotel's **Le Ti-Gourmet** (🍴🍴🍴-🍴🍴) serves up-market snacks.

🍴🍴🍴-🍴🍴 **Le P'tit Café**, 11 Place Monnerville, T228168. A good value set lunch and a respectable à la carte menu.

🍴🍴 **Le Karting**, Zone Portuaire de Pariacabo (at the entrance to Kourou), T320539 (closed Sat-Sun). Excellent lunch set meal with a big choice of starters and mains. Evening BBQ Tue and Fri.

🍴 Cheap Chinese (also takeaway), eg: **Le Chinatown**, rue Duchesne, T321769. Recommended. Many vans sell sandwiches filled with Créole food. **L'Hydromel**, rue Raymond Cresson. Good pancakes. **Le Glacier des 2 Lacs**, 68 Ave des 2 Lacs. Ice cream, cakes, teas, very good.

St-Laurent du Maroni *p1721*

🍴🍴🍴 **La Goelette**, Balaté Plage, 2.5 km from St-Laurent, T342897. In a converted fishing boat on the river, serving fish and game. Nice atmosphere in the evenings. Closed Sun evening and Mon.

🍴🍴🍴 **T Pic Kreol**, corner of rues Tourtet and Thiers (next to Star Hotel), T340983. Excellent restaurant/ bar, créole menu, popular for lunch, good service.

🍴🍴 **Le Mambari**, 7 rue Rousseau, T343590. Pizzas and light French food served in a large, upmarket *palapa*. Open until late.

🍴 Many cheap Chinese restaurants.

Bars and clubs

Cayenne *p1719, map p1720*

Acropolys, Route de Cabassou, 3 km from town, T319781. Club music, Wed-Sat, huge dance floor.

Bar des Palmistes, Place des Palmistes. Good spot for cocktails and people watching, opposite the Place des Palmistes.

Kourou *p1721*

Clibertown, rue Guynemer, T323665; at the entrance to Kourou overlooking the lake. The most popular in town by far.

Shopping

Cayenne *p1719, map p1720*

Bookshops Librairie AJC, 31 Blvd Jubelin, has an excellent stock of books and maps on Guyane (in French). There is a branch in *Drugstore des Palmistes*, Place des Palmistes.

Activities and tours

Cayenne *p1719, map p1720*

Look under Rechercher les professionnels on www.tourisme-guyane.com for listings of local tour operators. Tours to the interior cost about US$180-240 pp per day. Pick-ups from the airport and accommodation in Cayenne for a night or 2 are usually part of the package. Full details on the company websites, some in English.

JAL Voyages, 26 Av Gen de Gaulle, T316820, www.jal-voyages.com. Range of tours on the Mahury, Mana, Approuague rivers, on a house-boat on the Kaw marshes (US$85, very good accommodation, food and birdwatching) and Devil's Island, little English spoken. Recommended.

Takari-Tour-Espace-Amazonie, 8 rue du Capitaine Bernard, BP 051397332, T311960, takari.tour@wanadoo.fr. Highly recommended for inland tours.

Thomas Cook, 2 Place du Marché, T255636, tcookguyane@orange.fr . Flights, changes Thomas Cook TCs, English spoken.

Kourou *p1721*

Guyanespace Voyages, A Hector Berlioz, T223101, www.guyanespace.com.

St-Laurent du Maroni *p1721*

Ouest Guyane, 10 rue Féliz Eboué, T344444, ouestguyane@wanadoo.fr.

Youkaliba (Maroni) Expeditions, 3 rue Simon, T341645/312398. For canoe trips up the Maroni River. For example 1-night trip to Apatou, US$140.

Transport

Cayenne *p1719, map p1720*

Air Cayenne-Rochambeau Airport (T353882/89) 16 km from Cayenne, 20 mins by taxi, and 67 km from Kourou (US$60-80). Cambio changes US$ and Brazilian reais, Cirrus and Visa Plus ATMs for withdrawing Euros. Only taxis (US$25 day, US$30 night, you can bargain or share).

Cheapest route to town is taxi to Matoury US$10, then bus to centre US$2. Cheapest return to airport is by collective taxi from corner of Av de la Liberté and rue Malouet to Matoury (10 km) for US$2.40, then hitch or walk.
Bus Terminal at corner of rue Molé and Av de la Liberté. Regular services run by **SMTC**, Place du Marché, T302100, Mon-Fri 0800-1200, 1500-1700. Minibuses to St-Laurent du Maroni leave when full from the terminal (up to 4 hrs' wait), 0400-1200, 2½ hrs, US$42-48. **Mana** Mon and Thu only. **Kaw**, Wed. **Régina** US$25, and **St-Georges del' Oyapock** US$72, 3 hrs, 4 daily. Get to the bus stop at 0700 to get a seat. Be careful in this area – many drug addicts; take a cab to the bus stop. **Shared taxis** (collectifs) From the *gare routière* by the Canal Laussat early morning (Kourou US$12, St Laurent US$52). Other taxis at the stand on Place des Palmistes, corner of Av Gen de Gaulle and Molé.

Kourou *p1721*
Taxi US$10, Lopez T320560, Gilles TT320307, Kourou T321444.
Bus To **Cayenne**, leaves Shell service station, corner Av de France, Av Vermont Polycarpe.
Share taxis To Cayenne 0600, 0630, 0700, 1330, US$12. Taxi to Cayenne or airport, US$60 (US$85 at night). To St-Laurent du Maroni US$27 by *taxi collectif* (irregular) or minibus from Shell station.

Iles du Salut *p1721*
Boat La Hulotte boat from Kourou's fishing jetty at 1 rue Baudelaire, US$53 return (under 12s half price), 0800-0830 daily to Ile Royale and Ile Saint-Joseph, returns at 1600, 1-1½ hrs each way (book in advance, T323381, lahulotte@terresdeguyane.fr). Catamarans (28 seats) sail to the islands: **Royal Ti'Punch** (T320995) from the fishing jetty, and **Tropic Alizés** (T251010) from Pointe des Roches Sailing Club. **Sa Sotel** (T320995) sails from Kourou port to Ile Royale only, US$47. Book in advance in Jul and Aug. Tickets may be obtained direct or from agencies in Cayenne or Kourou. Some offer transport from Cayenne, US$20 extra. Getting back to Cayenne late in the afternoon after the boat docks may be a problem if you don't have transport arranged. No sailings between Ile Royale and Ile du Diable.

St-Laurent du Maroni *p1721*
Minibuses To Cayenne meet the ferry from Suriname, leaving when full from rue du Port, 3 hrs (not until 1830/1900), US$48. Ask the minibus to pick up your luggage from your hotel.
Shared taxis To Cayenne, 8 people, US$52 pp, 3½ hrs. Bus to Cayenne 0600, same price.
Freight pirogues Sometimes take passengers inland along the Maroni River, but they can be dangerous as they tend to be overladen, often with dubious captains. Better to fly to Maripasoula and return on a pirogue as they are empty going down river. Alternatively, groups can hire a *pirogue* for about US$200 a day.

Border with Suriname *p1722*
Boat Vehicle and passenger ferry to Albina Mon, Thu, 0700, 0900, 1400, 1600, Tue, Wed, Sat 0700, 0900, Sun, 1530, 1600, 30 mins. Passengers US$6 one way, car US$25-30 one way, payable only in euros. Speedboats US$3.60-US$4.75.
Minibuses and **taxis** Transport to/from Paramaribo meets the Albina ferry.

South to Brazil: Cacao *p1722*
Minibus From **Cayenne**, Mon 1200; Fri 1800, return Mon 0730, Fri 1400.

Saül *p1723*
Air Service with **Air Guyane** from Cayenne or via Maripasoula (see above; T309111). Try airport even if flight full. By *pirogue* from Mana up Mana River, 9-12 days, then 1 day's walk to Saül, or from St- Laurent via Maripasoula along Moroni and Inini rivers, 15 days and 1 day's walk to Saül, expensive.

St-Georges de l'Oyapock *p1723*
Air Flying and minibus, are the only options. For **Air Guyane** flights to Cayenne see Essentials. **Air Guyane** office at airport open 0700-0730, 1400- 1430 check in, 0800-1100 reservations, T/F370360. Flights fully booked days in advance; you must check in at stated times. Extra flights sometimes added. Police check that people boarding flights who have arrived from Brazil have their entry stamp; also thorough baggage search.

Minibuses To **Cayenne**, US$72, 3 hrs; US$20 on unpaved road to Régina, then US$25 to Cayenne. Taxi to Cayenne, US$72. Buses to **Macapá** leave late afternoon, 10 hrs: book when you arrive in Oiapoque (Brazilian side). Road ok.

Directory

Cayenne *p1719, map p1720*

Airline offices Air Caraïbes, Centre Commercial de Katoury, T293636, flies to Paris, Pointe-à-Pitre, Fort-de-France, Port-au-Prince, Havana, Saint-Martin, Belém (Brazil) and Dominican Republic. **Air France**, 17-19 rue Lalouette, BP 33, Cayenne, T296260. **Air Guyane**, T350300, or Rochambeau airport, T293630, www.airguyane.com. **Blue Wing Airlines**, Atlas Voyages, 15 rue Louis Blanc, T293003, atlas. voyages.guy@wanadoo.fr. **TAF**, T307000, French and Portuguese spoken, flights Cayenne-Macapá- Belém-Fortaleza twice weekly. Book at least a week ahead, www.voetaf.com.br. **Banks** Most banks have ATMs for cash withdrawals on Visa, sometimes MasterCard, never Amex. The Post Office exchanges cash and TCs at good rates, but complicated and time-consuming. Exchange facility at the airport. Central pharmacy may help when banks are closed. Almost impossible to change dollars outside Cayenne or Kourou. **Banque Nationale de Paris-Guyane (BNPG)**, 2 Place Schoelcher; no exchange facilities on Sat. **Banque Française Commerciale (BFC)**, 8 Place des Palmistes (best bank exchange rates). **Crédit Mutuel**, 13 rue Léon Damas, Visa/Plus and Cirrus/ MasterCard ATM. **Cambio Caraïbe**, Av Gen de Gaulle near Catayée (best rates for US$). **Guyane Change**, Av Gen de Gaulle near rue F Eboué. **Embassies and consulates** British (Honorary), Mr Nouh-Chaia, 16 Ave Monnerville (BP 664, Cayenne 97300), T311034, F304094. **Brazilian**, 444 chemin St Antoine, T296010. **Dutch** (Honorary), 470, Rue des Musendas Ames Claires, 97354 Montjoly, T0694-237756, consulat-pays-bas@ wanadoo.fr. **Suriname**, 3 Ave L Héder, T282160, cg.sme.cay@wanadoo.fr, Mon-Fri 0900-1200. English spoken, visa takes 2 hrs, proof of travel out of Venezuela or Guyana. For US and Canada, apply to embassies in Paramaribo. **Internet** Cybercafé des **Palmistes**, 1 Av Gen de Gaulle, US$15 per hr. **Post offices** Route de Baduel, 2 km out from town (US$2.25 by taxi or 20 mins on foot), busy. Poste Restante letters kept for 2 weeks.

Kourou *p1721*

Banks Several in town, including **Banque National de Paris Guyane**, near the Mairie. **Post offices** Ave des Frères Kennedy.

St-Laurent du Maroni *p1721*

Banks BFC, 11 Av Félix Eboué, open Tue-Fri, Sat morning. **Cambio COP**, 19 rue Montravel, near BNP, T343823, changes euros, Suriname and US$.

Falkland Islands/Islas Malvinas

Contents

1730 Planning your trip

1735 Stanley and around

1744 Beyond the Falklands
1744 South Georgia
1744 Antarctica

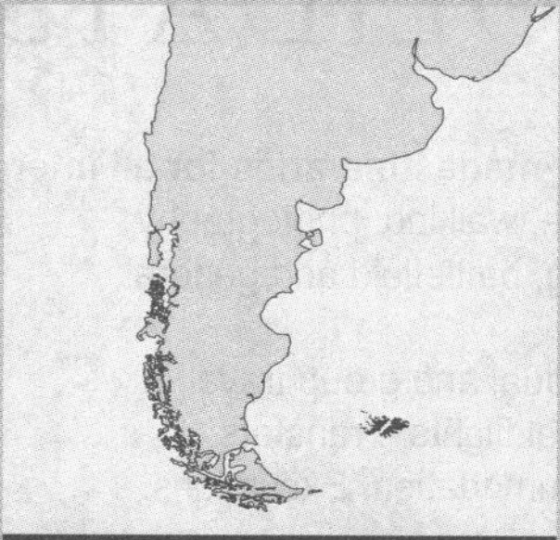

At a glance

Time required 1-2 weeks.

Best time Oct-Apr.

When not to go Outside wildlife breeding seasons.

Planning your trip

Where to go

These remote South Atlantic outposts, where there are more penguins than people, are the only part of South America where the British monarch's head appears on the stamps. Windswept they may be, but the islands are a haven for wildlife and a paradise for those who wish to see it: albatross nest in the tussac grass, sea lions breed on the beaches and dolphins cruise off the coast. About 640 km (400 miles) east of the South American mainland, the Falklands Islands/Islas Malvinas are made up of two large islands and over 748 smaller ones. The islands' remoteness adds to the charm of being able to see elephant seals, dolphins, whales, albatross, cormorants, geese and, above all, penguins at close range. Based on 2005/2006 census figures from Falklands Conservation, there are 385,824 breeding pairs of five species of penguin (king, magellanic, gentoo, rockhopper, macaroni) in the Islands. This constitutes 156 penguins per person (the Islands' human population in the 2006 census was 2,478). The capital, Stanley, is a small, modern town, with reminders of its seafaring past in the hulks of sailing ships in the Harbour. To visit the camp, as the land outside Stanley is known, 4WD vehicles make tours and you can fly to farming and island outposts for warm hospitality, huge skies and unparalleled nature watching.

In accordance with the practice suggested by the UN, we are calling the islands by both their English and Spanish names.

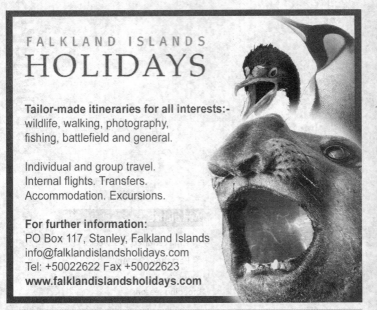

When to go

Best months to visit are October to April; some places to stay are only open in these months. This is the best time for most wildlife watching, too; see below. The islands are in the same latitude south as London is north. The climate is cool and oceanic, dominated by persistent westerly winds which average 16 knots. Long periods of calm are rare except in winter. Though not always inclement, weather is very changeable but temperatures vary relatively little. At Stanley, the capital, the mean temperature in summer (January/February) is 15.4°C, but temperatures frequently exceed this on the islands. In winter (June/July/August) 4.9°C. Stanley's annual rainfall of about 600 mm is slightly higher than London's. In the drier camp, outside Stanley, summer drought sometimes threatens local water supplies. A dusting of snow may occur at any time of the year. Always wear water and windproof clothing; wear good boots and a peaked hat to protect the eyes from rain or hail. Sunblock is essential.

Best time for wildlife For wildlife enthusiasts, especially ornithologists, the Islands are an exceptional destination. King and gentoo penguins are present the year round. Rockhoppers are on land October to May, magellanic penguins September to April. The black-browed albatross breeding season is September to May. Elephant seals are ashore September-December; adults haul out late January/early February to moult for 25 days. Sea lions can be seen December-March. Sei whales usually arrive in Falkland waters in January/February and remain till May/June. Other whale species may be seen in the same period, but not usually close to shore. Orcas are best seen on Sea Lion Island when sea lion pups are going to sea. Commerson's and Peale's dolphins are present the year round, but the former are less evident in winter. The most common birds are upland geese; other frequently-seen geese are kelp and ruddy-headed. The flightless steamer duck (logger duck) can be seen in many places, as can Falkland skuas, southern giant petrels, Patagonian crested duck, speckled teal, grebes, shags, gulls and shorebirds such as magellanic and blackish oystercatchers. The rarest bird of prey in the world, the striated caracara (Johnny Rook) can easily be seen in several places (Sea Lion, Carcass, Weddell). Smaller birds that are easy to see include the striking long-tailed meadowlark, dark-faced ground tyrant, Falkland thrush and pipit. In islands unaffected by introduced predators you'll see the friendly tussacbird and the rarer Cobb's wren. There are many other common bird species and, for botanists, plants of interest. For wildlife calendar, booklists, checklists and reports: **Falklands Conservation** ⓘ *Jubilee Villas, corner of Philomel St and Ross Rd (access from Philomel St), Stanley, T22247 (1 Princes Av, Finchley, London N3 2DA), www.falklands conservation.com, Mon-Fri 0800-1200, 1300-1630*, also sells clothing, badges and books.

Getting there

Air Flights from Santiago to Mount Pleasant, via Punta Arenas with **LAN** (www.lan.com) leave every Saturday and, once a month, stop at Río Gallegos in Argentina on both the outward and return flight. March 2009 fares: return from Santiago £710, Punta Arenas £430. Fares include Chilean airport taxes, but exclude Falklands embarkation tax: see Tax, page 1733. Passengers should confirm flights 24 hours before departure. For more information on LAN flights, see the website (tickets may be bought online), or contact **International Tours and Travel Ltd** ⓘ *1 Dean St, Stanley, FIQQ 1ZZ, T+500-22041, jf.itt@horizon.co.fk or visit www.falklandstravel.com.*

The UK Ministry of Defence operates an airbridge to the Falkland Islands twice a week (at the time of writing). They depart from RAF Brize Norton, Oxfordshire, and take about 20 hours including a refuelling stop in Ascension Island at the half way point (passengers can stop over if they wish). Fares: £2,222 return, group rates £1,999 for six or more; premium economy return: £3,850. Falkland Islands residents and contract workers receive a discount. The £22 exit tax is included in MoD flights. Confirm luggage allowance in advance and confirm the flight itself 24 hours before departure. For the latest MoD schedules and prices, contact the **Falkland Islands Company Travel Department** ⓘ *T27633, fic.travel@horizon.co.fk*, or the **Falkland Islands Government Office** in London ⓘ *T020-7222 2542, travel@falklands.gov.fk.*

Airport information Mount Pleasant airport is 35 miles from Stanley. **Falkland Islands Tours and Travel** ⓘ *Lookout Industrial Estate, Stanley, T21775, fitt@horizon.co.fk*, and **Penguin Travel** ⓘ *Crozier Place, Stanley, T27630, www.penguintravel-falklands.com* transport passengers and luggage to and from the capital for £15 single. Departing passengers should make reservations. See also Taxis, page 1743. ▸▸ *For airport departure tax, see Tax, page 1733.*

Boat Cruise ships en-route to/from South America, South Georgia and the Antarctic are also a popular way to visit the Islands. Vessels typically visit between October and April each year. Passengers usually land for tours of Stanley and nearby sites, pub lunch, farmhouse tea, and call at outlying islands, such as Saunders, Carcass, West Point, New and Sea Lion Islands. Further details of companies that include the Falklands/Malvinas in their itineraries can be found on www.visitorfalklands.com and at www.iaato.org. Alternatively you can contact local port agents **Sulivan Shipping** ⓘ *T22626, sulivantravel@horizon.co.fk* and **Penguin Travel (Falkland Islands Company)** ⓘ *T27630, ficagents@horizon.co.fk*.

Length of stay As flights from Chile only go once a week, stays in multiples of seven days are the only option. In one week you can see Stanley and a couple of nearby attractions, plus a bit of West Falkland or one or two islands, but the inter-island flight schedules will determine how much time you can stay on the outer islands. In two weeks you can see much more of East and West Falkland and several outer islands. The airbridge from the UK offers more flexibility. Cruise ship passengers do not disembark for more than a few hours.

Getting around

The only paved roads are in Stanley. Outside Stanley, the major road to the airport at **Mount Pleasant** is part paved, but requires great care. Other roads are single track, of consolidated earth and stone. None should be driven at speed; look out for sheep or cattle, cattle grids and sudden hills, bends and junctions. On East and West Falkland, roads connect most of the settlements. Elsewhere, tracks require 4WD or quad bikes. Off-road driving in the boggy terrain is a skill not easily learned by short-term visitors and is not permitted by any car-hire company. The Jetty Visitor Centre and the Museum and National Trust (see Sights, below) stock a range of maps, 1:50,000 map (£4), A3 road maps (£3.50). ▸▸ *See also Transport, page 1742.*

Note Over 30,000 landmines were laid by Argentine forces during the 1982 Conflict, of which 20,000 are still on the ground. Of the 117 landmine fields across the Falklands, 75% are located around Stanley. The fields are fenced, mapped and clearly marked and no civilian injuries or casualties have ever occurred. Should you spot anything unusual, make a note of its location and contact the Bomb Disposal Unit, T22229 or 22229, or the police on 999. Please note, it is illegal to enter any area designated as minefield, or to remove minefield signage.

Sleeping and eating

Pre-booked accommodation is obligatory before being allowed entry. Advance reservation when travelling around is essential. Almost all places to stay in Stanley and on the islands have comfortable rooms, power showers, towels, heating, honesty bars (where they have a bar) and, when not self catering, good local food. For self-catering you can get supplies, including ready-prepared meals, in Stanley. Stores in Port Howard and Fox Bay on West Falkland open only at specified times, usually 3 days a week. See www.visitorfalklands.com.

On the outer islands bear in mind that the wildlife you will see is inextricably linked with where you stay because there is no choice of lodging. Fortunately this is not a hardship.

Essentials A-Z

Accident and emergency

The emergency telephone number is T999. **Stanley Police Station** T28100. **Hospital Reception** T28000.

Activities

Fishing for trout and mullet (South Atlantic cod) is superb. The main rivers are the Chartres and Warrah on West Falkland, and the San Carlos on East Falkland. The season for trout is officially 1 Sep to 30 Apr, but two distinct runs: Sep-mid Nov and Mar/Apr. A licence is not required for rod and line fishing; catch and release is encouraged. Mullet may be caught at any time. Falkland Islands zebra trout are protected and must never be caught. Most land is privately owned, including rivers and streams, always get permission from the owner, some of whom charge a fee (eg £10 on the San Carlos). Ask travel agents about regulations for specific areas and changes to daily bag limits.

Golf: Stanley's 18-hole course costs £5 a round; no club rental so you need to find clubs to borrow. The course at Clippy Hill, Port Howard is in poor shape, but just playable. For this, hiking and touring options, see Stanley Tour operators.

Electricity

220/240 volts at 50 cycles. Rectangular, 3-blade plug as in the UK.

Festivals and events

Public holidays

1 Jan (New Year's Day), **Good Friday** (Easter), **21 Apr** (Queen's birthday), **14 Jun** (Liberation Day), **1st Mon in Oct** (Peat Cutting Monday), **8 Dec** (Battle Day). The main social event is the Christmas period, **24 Dec** (Christmas Eve), **25 Dec** (Christmas Day), **26 Dec** (Boxing Day and start of Stanley sports meeting), to 2-4 Jan. Everything closes except places to stay and eat and food shops/supermarkets.

Internet

Public internet access is limited. **Cable and Wireless** (Ross Rd), who have the monopoly, give access, as do the **Jetty Visitor Centre** (Ross Rd), Hillside (Stanley) and a few hotels and guest houses in Stanley. Internet costs £1 for 10 mins. In 2010 there were about 11 WiFi hotspots and broadband coverage was available in the islands. If going to the camp, it's best to ask in advance if internet access is important to you. Purchase a 1141 card to use WiFi (see Telephone, below).

Money → *US$1 = £0.67; €1 = £0.89 (May 2009).*

The Falklands pound (£) is on a par with sterling. Local notes and coins. UK notes and coins are also legal tender. Falklands pounds cannot be used outside the islands. Currency from Ascension Island, where the airbridge stops, is not accepted. Foreign currency (including US dollars and euros) and traveller's cheques (TCs) can be changed at the **Standard Chartered Bank**, Ross Rd, Stanley. All establishments accept pounds sterling, some also accept US dollars and euros (check when booking). Credit cards and TCs are only accepted by a handful of operators. Visitors are advised to take cash where possible, or discuss alternative payment methods with operators prior to arrival. There are no ATMs on the Islands.

Opening hours

Office hours, including government departments: Mon-Fri 0800-1200, 1300-1630 (the 1200-1300 lunch hour in Stanley is religiously observed). Banking hours: 0830-1500.

Post

There is direct and dependable air mail service from the UK. Heavy parcels come by sea from the UK every month. A weekly DHL service is operated via **Falkland Islands Chamber of Commerce** ⓘ *PO Box 378, Stanley, T22264, commerce@horizon.co.fk*. Inter-island mail service is carried out by FIGAS, Falkland Island Government Air Service.

Tax

Airport tax Departing passengers by air on **LAN** pay an embarkation tax of £22, payable in Falklands pounds, sterling or dollars (there are no exchange facilities or ATM at Mount Pleasant).

Telephone → *International phone code = +500.*

Cable and Wireless, Ross Rd, Stanley, open Mon-Fri 0800-1630, is the telecommunications provider. The islands' telephone system has direct dialling worldwide. Cable and Wireless has roaming agreements with some UK mobile phone networks (T Mobile, Vodafone and Virgin). International SMS is also available to most countries using GSM mobile phone services. Those not covered with the above networks can purchase a local SIM card from Cable and Wireless or at the West Store Entertainment Centre for £25, including £20 credit, valid 210 days. There is no signal on the extremities of East Falkland, nor on West Falkland. Handsets will generally need to be network unlocked to accept the local SIM card. Phones cannot be rented, but cheap Nokias are on sale. Mobile help line T131. Phone cards for international calls and WiFi access (1141 cards) cost from £5-20 at Cable and Wireless, Kelper Stores, the Jetty Centre; calls to UK £1 per min, to rest of world £1.10.

Time
GMT -4 in winter (May-Aug), -3 in summer. Some people use 'Camp time' (as opposed to 'Stanley time'), which does not use daylight saving.

Tourist information
The **Falkland Islands Tourist Board** ⓘ *PO Box 618, Stanley, F1QQ 1ZZ, T271019/22215*, runs the **Jetty Visitor Centre**, ⓘ *at the head of the Public Jetty, Ross Rd, Stanley, T22281, open daily during summer, www.visitorfalklands.com*. This has information on accommodation, tours, transport and activities, and offers internet, postal service and public telephones and access cards. It has a free visitor guide in English, French, Spanish and German. It sells local books, DVDs, crafts, stamps, first day covers and postcards. The **Falkland Islands Government London Office** (**FIGO**) ⓘ *Falkland House, 14 Broadway, Westminster, London SW1H 0BH, T020-7222 2542, www.falklands.gov.fk*, will answer enquiries.

Useful websites
www.falklandislands.com and www.visitorfalklands.com Falkland Islands Tourist Board site.
www.falklandnews.com Falkland Islands News Network.
http://en.mercopress.com/ Merco Press, South Atlantic's News Agency.
www.penguin-news.com *Penguin News* weekly newspaper.

Visas and immigration
All travellers must have full, current passports to visit the Islands. Citizens of Britain, North America, Mercosur, Chile, and most Commonwealth countries and the EU are permitted to visit the islands without a visa, as are holders of UN and International Committee of the Red Cross passports. Other nationals should apply for a visa from the Travel Coordinator at **Falkland House** in London (see above), the Immigration Department in Stanley (see Useful addresses, page 1743), or a British Embassy or Consulate. Visas cost £20. All visitors require a visitor permit, provided for the length of time you need on arrival. You must have a return ticket and sign a declaration that you have accommodation, sufficient funds to cover the cost of your stay and evidence of medical insurance (including cover for aero-medical evacuation). Work permits are not available. Do not stay beyond the valid period of your permit or visa without applying to the Immigration Office for an extension.

Weights and measures
Metric. On East Falkland miles are used; on West Falkland kilometres.

Stanley and around

→ *Colour map 9, inset. Population: 2,478.*

The capital, Stanley, on East Falkland, is the major population centre. Its residents live mostly in houses painted white, many of which have brightly-coloured corrugated iron roofs. Surrounded by rolling moorland, Stanley fronts the enclosed Harbour. The outer harbour of Port William is larger but less protected.

Sights

The **Museum** ⓘ *Britannia House, Ross Rd West, T27428, Mon-Fri 0930-1200, 1330-1600 (in summer, no lunch break), Sat and Sun 1400-1600, £3, www.falklands-museum.com*, merits a visit. The manager is Mrs Leona Roberts. The ticket includes a visit to Cartmell Cottage, one of the original pioneer houses on Pioneer Row, whose interior reflects life in the late 19th century and the 1940s. From the Museum, you can walk the length of the harbour front, from the wreck of the *Jhelum* (built in 1839 for the East India Company, now beginning to collapse) in the west, to the iron-built *Lady Elizabeth* at the far eastern end of the harbour (228 ft, with three masts still standing). A Maritime History Trail along the front has interpretive panels; a book describing the Stanley wrecks is sold at the museum. On the way you will pass Government House, the Anglican Cathedral (most southerly in the world, built in 1892) with a whalebone arch outside, several monuments commemorating the naval battle of 1914, the Royal Marines and the 1982 liberation. Among the latter are the Memorial Wood, off Ross Rd East, where every tree is named for a British and Falkland casuality. Where Ross Road East turns inland, you can carry on east along the coastal path, past the FIPASS floating harbour and around the head of the bay to *Lady Elizabeth*. At low tide you can walk out to her. Follow the bay round and eventually you will come to **Gypsy Cove**, 4 miles, two hours walk each way from centre (10 minutes by car). It features a colony of magellanic penguins, black-crowned night herons and other shorebirds. Occasionally visitors can also spot orca, elephant seals, variable hawks and sea lions. Observe minefield fences which prevent close inspection of the penguins (Yorke Bay, where the Argentine forces landed in 1982, is off limits).

The public library, T27147, in the Community School, has a good selection of books on travel and flora/fauna. During the December holidays, the sports meeting at the race course attracts visitors from all over the Islands. The equally popular West and East Falkland sports, at the end of the shearing season in February/March rotate among the settlements.

Outside Stanley

Cape Pembroke lighthouse sits on the end of Cape Pembroke Peninsula and is open to the general public (an access key is available from the Museum for a £5 charge). The Cape itself offers great day walking, with plenty of wildlife watching: dolphins, whales and numerous bird species. There is also an impressive memorial to the crew of the *Atlantic Conveyor*, a supply ship sunk by Argentine forces during the 1982 Conflict.

Sparrow Cove, **Kidney Cove**, and adjacent areas, only a short distance from Stanley by boat, are good areas to see four species of penguin and other wildlife. Tours are the only way to get there.

East Falkland

On **Long Island**, 20 miles from Stanley, is a 22,000-acre sheep farm belonging to a 6th generation Falkland Island family, whose traditional way of life, with a dairy and using sheep dogs and island-bred horses to gather sheep, is popular with cruise passengers and day trippers. There are excellent hikes along the beach and shore of Berkeley Sound, with rockhopper, gentoo and magellanic penguins.

Volunteer Point, on the peninsula north of Berkeley Sound, is a wildlife sanctuary ⓘ *entry £15, included in tour price, £7.50 for each extra day; open 1 Nov to Apr. Good toilets at the site. In* *recent years the wardens have offered lodging for 4 people sharing, £35 with three meals, camping £10 for first night, £5 thereafter, Nov-Apr, ask in advance: T55200, drp@ horizon.co.fk. On cruise ship days many vehicles go in convoy to Volunteer Point*. It contains the only substantial nesting colony of king penguins outside of South Georgia (the most accessible site in the world). Gentoo and magellanic penguins, geese and other birds can be photographed easily, but keep a respectful distance. Sea lions and dolphins may be seen from the beautiful beach. It is on a private farm approximately 2½ hours drive from Stanley: 1 hour to Johnson's Harbour on a good road (37 miles), then 1½ hours over the camp (12 miles, no permanent track). Visits are arranged with local guides who know the route and understand local conditions.

Bertha's Beach, a 10-minute drive from Mount Pleasant Military Complex, is popular for its beautiful white sand beach with abundant bird life. Dolphins often come close to shore as they hunt in the shallows. To get through the locked gate to the beach, ask for the key from the farm manager at Fitzroy (T32384).

Beyond Mount Pleasant, the road divides, one branch turning north to San Carlos (see below), the other going to **Darwin** (1½-2 hours from Stanley), a little community with the skeletal remains of the *Vicar of Bray* (last survivor of the California Gold Rush fleet). Another old iron ship, the *Garland*, can de seen up the bay. Just before Darwin is the Argentine cemetery for those killed in the 1982 conflict, and just beyond, the larger settlement of **Goose Green**. The *Galley Café* is usually open 0900- 2100; contact Trudi Lee (T32228) about self- catering in a 3-bedroom house, open all year £15 per person. From Goose Green a road runs to the ferry dock for West Falkland at New Haven (35 minutes). Apart from a gentoo colony, there is nothing at the ramp. **North Arm** is one of four settlements in the flat expanses of Lafonia, a three-hour drive from Stanley. Bull Point is the most southerly point of East Falkland; its wildlife includes 32 species of birds. Also

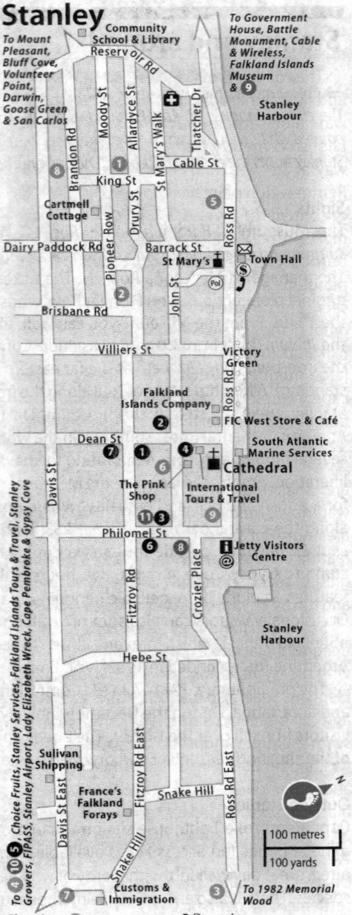

Sleeping

1 Bennett House B&B
2 Kay's B&B
3 Lafone Guest House
4 Lookout Lodge
5 Malvina House
6 Millers
7 Shorty's Motel & Diner
8 Sue Binnie's
9 Waterfront B&B

Eating

1 Bread Shop
2 Deano's
3 Falklands Brasserie
4 Jacs
5 Lighthouse Seaman's Centre
6 Michelle's Café
7 Woodbine Takeaway

Bars & clubs

8 Globe
9 Stanley Arms
10 The Narrows
11 Victory

near North Arm are Tweeds Valley, 53 species of flora and fauna, and Fanny Cove, with some great rock formations. These locations can only be reached off-road so a tour guide is necessary.

The road to **San Carlos** is hilly, with lovely views of higher mountains inland and the bays and inlets of Falkland Sound to the west. San Carlos (2 hours from Stanley) is a picturesque waterside settlement and an excellent base for explorating upper East Falkland. Here is the English cemetery from the 1982 conflict and a museum covering the conflict and the local way of life. See **Kingsford Valley Farm** below for lodging. Nearby is the ruin of the Ajax Bay Refrigeration plant, used as the British forces base in 1982. Tours from Kingsford Valley Farm, or contact the owners, Gerald and Doreen Dixon, Wreck Point, T31115. The new road network makes it possible to head north to Port San Carlos, Elephant Beach Farm (see Sleeping for both) and Cape Dolphin. At **Elephant Beach Farm**, a 1½-hour drive from Stanley, gentoo penguins and many other bird species, sea lions, Commerson's and Peale's dolphins can be seen. The private property offers fishing for Falkland mullet in the tidal lagoon, and fossicking among the whale skeletons on the coast. **Cape Dolphin**, at the northernmost tip of East Falkland, includes three species of penguin, storm petrels, sea lions, the occasional whale and large numbers of ducks and birds on Swan Pond. Allow a full day to make the most of the cape; camping is also possible by prior arrangement. You can return to Stanley on the North Camp road via Teal Inlet and Estancia.

Outer islands **Bleaker Island**, hardly bleak, has a wonderful coastline with white sandy beaches and sheltered coves. Bird species include rockhoppers, magellanic and gentoo penguins, waterfowl, ruddy-headed geese, Falkland skuas and an impressive Imperial Shag colony. The area north of the settlement was declared a National Nature Reserve in 1999. One of the key features of the island is Big Pond, where you can spot Chiloe wigeon, silvery and white-tufted grebes, speckled and silver teal and occasionally the rare flying steamer duck. The island is owned and run by Phyll and Mike Rendell ⓣ *T21355, mrendell@horizon.co.fk*; see Cobb's Cotage, below.

Sea Lion Island in the southeast, 35 minutes' flight from Stanley, is a wildlife sanctuary, a delightful place to explore and relax. The lodge (see Sleeping), open in the austral summer, is within easy reach of the wildlife. Many Southern Sea Lions breed on the beaches; Southern Elephant Seals also breed here. Up to three pods of orca whales are resident around the island and can be seen cruising the shore in search of elephant seal and sea lion pups risking their first swim (summer months). The island also has magnificent bird life: gentoo, magellanic and rockhopper penguins, giant petrels (known locally as stinkers), imperial shag, flightless steamer and other ducks, black- crowned night herons, tussacbird, oystercatcher (magellanic and blackish) and striated caracara. Also on the island is the HMS *Sheffield* memorial.

West Falkland

On West Falkland, there live fewer than 100 adults. **Port Howard** is one of the principle settlements, a neat, picturesque place, and the largest privately owned farm in the Islands with approximately 42,000 sheep and 1,000 cattle running across 200,000 acres. The original settlement is 3½ km south and Bold Cove is the site of the first British landing by Captain John Strong in 1690. It's an excellent base to explore West Falkland (see Port Howard Lodge, below). Activities include trout fishing; 4WD tours to wildlife and flora, 1982 war relics, fossil beds; hiking to Mount Maria.

About an hour west of Port Howard a road branches northwest to **Hill Cove** settlement, another 30 minutes drive. You can visit the largest forest in the Falklands (an experiment in shelter planting), or make an appointment to see the boutique skin tannery run by Henry Boughton. Further west is **Crooked Inlet** farm at Roy Cove. Joy and Danny Donnelly run the sheep farm and still use horses for sheep work (see Sleeping). The settlement is very photogenic, particularly in late spring when the yellow gorse blooms; commanding views over King George Bay to Rabbit, Hammock and Middle Islands.

In the centre of West Falkland is **Little Chartres Farm** (see Sleeping, below), which is an ideal base for trips to all points and for trout fishing. West is a beautiful road to Dunnose Head and Shallow Harbour, passing the Narrows and Town Point nature reserves. To the south is Fox Bay, the largest settlement; half is government-owned, half, Fox Bay West, is private. The road passes Hawksnest Ponds, where swans may be seen, in a region of 2,000 lakes and ponds. **Port Stephens** is a spectacular piece of country at the southwestern tip of West Falkland. Accessible by road and air, the area has rugged headlands, home to rockhopper and gentoo penguins, as well as many unusual geological formations at Indian Village and breathtaking coastal scenery. (See Sleeping, below.)

Outer islands **Pebble Island** is the third largest offshore island and is thought to be named after the unusual pebbles found on its beaches. Pebble is home to more than 40 species including gentoo, rockhopper, macaroni and magellanic penguins, imperial shag, waterfowl, and black-necked swans. Sea lions can also be found on the coast. The eastern half of Pebble Island contains large ponds and wetlands with many waterfowl and wading birds. See Sleeping, below.

Saunders Island, besides a representative sample of wildlife, contains the ruins of the 18th century British outpost at Port Egmont. There is a small group of king penguins at the Neck, a three-hour walk, 45 minutes by Land Rover from the settlement. Gentoo, magellanic, rockhoppers, imperial shag and black-browed albatross can also be seen here, as well as dolphins wave surfing and whales spouting. A further 1½-2 hours' walk goes to the point where elephant seals can be seen. At the Rookery, on the north coast, you can see rockhoppers, imperial shag and black-browed albatross. Another good place is the bay just north of the Settlement with many gentoo and magellanic penguins. There are many other wildlife sites on this large island.

Carcass Island, taking it's name from HMS Carcass which visited in the late 18th century, is west of Saunders. One of the most spectacular and attractive islands for wildlife and scenery, species include striated caracara, gentoo and magellanic penguins, gulls, geese and elephant seals. The island also has great examples of tussac grass. The island is cat, rat and mice free, allowing small bird species such as Cobb's wren to flourish. A recommended trip from Carcass is

Falkland Islands/Islas Malvinas

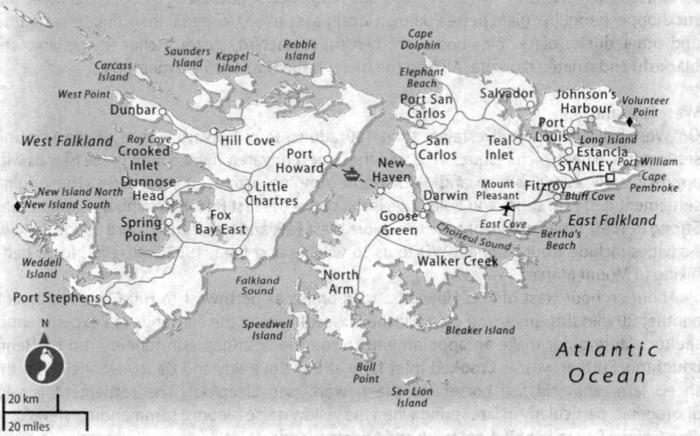

on Michael Clark's boat, *Condor*, to West Point Island, to see a large colony of black-browed albatross and rockhoppers. Dolphins may be seen on the way. Crossing is about an hour each way, £231 for the boat.

Weddell Island, in the southwest, named after explorer James Weddell, is the third largest island of the archipelago, a little bigger than Malta but with only two residents (and then only October to March). It has self-catering accommodation, an interesting history and, despite what some books suggest, plenty of wildlife. This includes magellanic and gentoo rookeries, sea lions in the tussac grass, imperial shags, shore birds, geese and introduced species such as Patagonian grey fox and nine reindeer. In the surrounding waters are albatross, Peale's and Commerson's dolphins. Good hikes straight out of the settlement.

New Island South, at the extreme west edge of the archipelago, is a nature reserve owned by the New Island Conservation Trust (www.newislandtrust.com). The aim of the project, begun in 1973 by Ian Strange, is to ensure that the island operates as a reserve in perpetuity. There is a fully equipped field station in the settlement for scientific studies. The recently refurbished Captain Charles Barnard Memorial Museum and Visitor Centre is visited by passengers on cruise vessels. Contact can be made through the Trust's website. New Island North owned by Tony Chater, has a small sheep farm.

Stanley and around listings

Hotel and guesthouse prices

LL over US$200	**L** US$151-200	**AL** US$101-150
A US$66-100	**B** US$46-65	**C** US$31-45
D US$21-30	**E** US$12-20	**F** US$7-11
G US$6 and under		

Sleeping

Stanley *p1735, map p1736*

L Malvina House, 3 Ross Rd, T21355, malvina@horizon.co.fk. Very good, spacious executive and standard rooms, full board available, power showers, hot drinks, central heating, TV, nice restaurant (open to all daily except Sun evening - guests only), bar, sauna/jacuzzi, laundry, Wi-Fi broadband for guests, recently enlarged.

AL pp **Waterfront B&B**, 36 Ross Rd, T21462, thewaterfronthotel@cwimail.fk. Comfortable rooms, most en suite, TV, modern facilities, welcoming, internet and Wi-Fi, exercise machine with great view, offers tea, coffee, cakes and Falklands smoko, very helpful, associated with Falklands Brasserie.

AL-A pp **Lafone Guest House**, T22891, arlette@horizon.co.fk. Owned and run by Arlette Betts, luxury B&B, good harbour views, evening meals on request, very good food.

AL-A Millers Hotel, John St, Bruce Miller, T21572, www.millershotel.co.fk. Central, en-suite rooms, full board available. Also has a bar. Renovated in 2009.

B pp **Bennett House B&B**, 14 Allardyce St, T21191, celiastewart@horizon.co.fk. Owned and run by Celia Stewart. Central, excellent home baking and breakfast, 3 rooms, 2 en suite, good views, welcoming. Camping £10 pp per night.

B pp **Shorty's Motel**, Snake Hill, T22861, marleneshort@horizon.co.fk. All rooms en suite, laundry, internet, next to **Shorty's Diner**.

C pp **Kay's B&B**, 14 Drury St, T/F21071, kay@horizon.co.fk. Excellent value and rightly popular, shared bath, dinner, lunch and packed lunch available £8, good food. Camping £5 per tent per night, £4 for breakfast and shower in house for campers.

C pp **Lookout Lodge**, Keil Canal Rd, contact Caroline Cotter, T22834, lookoutlodge@cwimail.fk. Bunkhouse-style accommodation, single rooms, shared facilities. Price is bed only, add £5 for breakfast, £10 for full board.

C pp **Sue Binnie's**, Brandon Rd, T21051. Central B&B with 1 double room, shared bath, Spanish spoken.

East Falkland *p1735*

L-AL pp **Sea Lion Lodge**, Sea Lion Island, T32004, sealion_lodge @horizon.co.fk or www.sealion island.com. Open 1 Sep-31 Mar, high season prices Nov-end Feb, full board, some single rooms with shared bath, purpose-built, picture windows, comfortable, central heating, good bathrooms, good home cooking, packed lunches available for when you wish to go wildlife-watching, orientation tours, internet.

A pp **Race Point Farm**, Port San Carlos, John and Michelle Jones, T41012, jhjones@horizon.co.fk. Full board or B&B at the Big House, TV, DVD, laundry facilities, internet and telephone; also comfortable, child-friendly self catering £20 pp, meals available on request. Gentoo rookeries, magellanic and rockhopper penguins at Fanning Head and Rookery Sands Beach. Good walks and excellent trout fishing on the San Carlos river. Guided 4WD tours available, also horse riding and quad biking.

AL-A Darwin Lodge, Sheena and Gabs Ross, T31313, sheena51466@hotmail.co.uk. Price is for full board; cheaper B&B available. Comfortable accommodation, some rooms with jacuzzi, suitable for families, living room, conservatory, good walking in the area, tours can be arranged.

C pp **Elephant Beach Farm**, contact Ben Berntsen, T41020. Self catering cottage sleeps up to 8, traditional Falkland Island meals by request. DVD, video, games etc, gas stove only for cooking. Tours of north coastline. Open all year.

C pp **Kingsford Valley Farm**, San Carlos settlement, East Falkland, T/F32233, kvf@horizon.co.fk. On a working farm owned and run by kind hosts Terence and Sheila McPhee. 2 comfortable self-catering cottages, one with 2-bedrooms, the other with 3, both include cots, children very welcome. Central heating, 24-hr power, TV, video, CD, enclosed gardens, meals on request, close to trout fishing, San Carlos cemetery and museum. Terence McPhee offers wildlife and general tours on East Falkland.

Cobbs Cottage, Bleaker Island, T21084 (Stanley), T32491 (Bleaker Island), mrendell@horizon.co.fk. 30-min flight south from Stanley, finished to a high standard throughout. Good wildlife.

North Arm: 4 houses have self catering, fully-equipped, sleeping 5-10 people, £10 per person a night. The farm has a small shop for everyday items and frozen food, but take your own supplies. En route to Bull Point are 4 houses for rent, basic self catering with peat stove and diesel generator. Take sleeping bags/bedding, towels and food. A taste of old-style Falkland life. Contact Ian and Eileen Jaffray, T32080.

West Falkland *p1737*

AL Pebble Island Lodge, Pebble Island, T41093, pebblelodge@horizon.co.fk. This well-appointed lodge is run by Jacqui Jennings and Alan White. En suite rooms, central heating, full board, lounge, TV and DVD, phone and internet and island tours.

AL pp **Port Howard Lodge**, Port Howard, West Falkland, T42187, porthowardlodge@horizon.co.fk. Sue Lowe and Wayne Brewer. Prices seasonal, full board, all rooms en suite, central heating, honesty bar, excellent food. Wayne takes Land Rover tours (£30 for general interest) and will drive to first class trout fishing spots, rod hire. Has a small war museum, and the chance to see the workings of a traditional large sheep station.

A Port Howard Farm Cottages, Myles and Karen Lee, T42181, phfarm@horizon.co.fk. Three houses at Port Howard, good starting point for touring West Falkland, cosy, good views, price is for self-catering.

A-B pp **Saunders Island**, Suzan and David Pole-Evans, T41298, davidpe@horizon.co.fk. At the settlement are 2 self-catering cottages, for 10 and 6, **B** pp per night. Self- catering Portakabin sleeping 8 at the Neck, with 24-hr power, heating, cooker (**A** pp, transport £50). Self catering Rookery Inn, within walking distance of the Rookery, is modern, sleeps 4, 24-hr power, kitchen/diner, shower room, heating (**A** pp, transport £20). Towels provided in all lodgings. A shop at the settlement sells supplies. Near the Rookery cottage is a backpackers' Portakabin for 2, bunks, cooker, long-drop toilet. Camping £10 pp per night.

Carcass Island, T41106, lorraine@horizon.co.fk. Owned and run by Rob and Lorraine McGill. Rooms are in the main farmhouse, full board, excellent food, honesty bar, lounge with TV and DVDs, gardens, open summer only. Tours to sites on the island, perfect combination of hospitality and wildlife.

Crooked Inlet Farm, Roy Cove, Danny and Joy Donnelly, T41102, j.d.donnelly@horizon.co.fk. A comfortable self- catering property. Also trout fishing, riding Falklands' style or guided 4WD tours of the area.

A pp **Little Chartres Farm**, West Falkland, F1ZZ 1QQ, T42215, www.littlechartres.horizon.co.fk. Operated by Lesley and Jim Woodward, who are very accommodating, 2 comfortable rooms with bath between, plus one smaller room, self-catering only. Excellent trout fishing, hiking, wildlife watching and tours available. They also have Top Dip Shanty (**D** pp) right on the Chartres estuary for more rustic lodging, self-catering, fuel and water provided.

C pp **Port Stephens**, T42307, par@horizon.co.fk. Self catering accommodation in 2-bedroom house, with kitchen/diner, central heating, DVDs, in the settlement, a great base to explore the region, very helpful hosts, Peter and Ann Robertson, who run the farm here.

Shallow Bay Self Catering 25 mins from Hill Cove settlement, contact Paul and Dae Peck, T41007, 55035 (mob), psb@horizon.co.fk or daepeck@horizon. Accommodation in the original stone home. Meals available on request.

Weddell Island, T42398, m.j.beaton@horizon.co.fk. Self-catering cottage can sleep up to 10, £132 for house, well-equipped with kitchen and microwave, washing machine, central heating, DVD, free wildlife tour if you stay 2 nights, lovely setting on an inlet. Open Oct-Mar.

West Lagoons, Shelley and Peter Nightingale, adjacent Hill Cove settlement, West Falkland, T/F41194, sptk@horizon.co.fk. Full-board accommodation on a sheep farm.

Eating

Stanley *p1735, map p1736*

Most places are casual; for fine dining, **Malvina House** and **Falklands Brasserie**. At Sun lunchtime the pubs do food, but in the evening **The Narrows**, **Shorty's Diner** and **Stanley Arms** are open. Besides local lamb, beef and fish (kingclip, toothfish, squid), try diddle-dee berry jam and, in the autumn, tea-berry buns.

The Bread Shop, corner Dean St and Fitzroy Rd. Open Mon-Sat. Wide range of breads, sandwiches, snacks, all freshly baked.

Falklands Brasserie, Philomel St, central, near Public Jetty, T21159, brasserie@horizon.co.fk. Excellent innovative cooking with local produce (seafood, meat, varied styles), opening times vary, usually closed Sun, lunchtime menu is much cheaper than evening à la carte (TTT), popular, must reserve. Recommended.

Jacs, John St, T21143, knipe@horizon.co.fk. Small, pleasant café with home-made cakes and sandwiches, great value. Mon-Sat 0900-1600 except Wed 0900-1400.

Lighthouse Seamans' Centre, over the bridge next to FIPASS ('The Seaman's Mission'). Tea/coffee, snacks, home baking, lunches, open all day for seamen, 1000-1600 for general public, Sun 1200-1600. Internet and WiFi hotspot.

Michelle's Café, Philomel St. Open Mon-Thu 0800-1600, Fri 0800-0030, Sat 1030-0030, home baking a speciality, all food cooked to order, eat in, take-away or delivery.

The Narrows Bar, 39 Ross Rd East at Kelper Stores, T22272. Daily specials, good pub food, open daily 1200-1330, 1800-2000, Sun carvery 1200-1330, book in advance. Has WiFi hotspot and internet centre, sells phone and WiFi cards.

Shorty's, Snake Hill. Good fast food, lots of choice, eat in or take away, good value. Open 6 days (seasonal), Mon-Fri 0900-2030, Sat-Sun till 2000.

Stanley Arms Bar, 1 John Biscoe Rd, T22259. Good pub food, daily specials.

Victory Bar, 1A Philomel St, T21199. Daily for specials, lunch, traditional English pub food, children welcome; evening meals Mon, Tue and Thu 1600-2030.

West Store Café, FIC West Store, Ross Rd. Choice of coffees and other hot drnks, freshly-made sandwiches, panini, pastries and cakes, closed Sun.

Woodbine Takeaway, 29 Fitzroy Rd, T21102. Fish and chips and pizza. Closed Sun and Mon.

Bars and clubs

Stanley *p1735, map p1736*

The pubs include: **Beagle Bar**, at Malvina House Hotel, **Deano's Bar**, 40 John St, T21296, bar snacks, **Narrows Bar**, see above, **Stanley Arms**, see above, **The Globe**, Philomel St, near the public jetty, open daily, bar menu, different entertainment every night; **The Trough**, Airport Rd, BYO, check Penguin News for opening dates (usually Sat night), live music and funky chill-out lounge, and **The Victory**, see above.

Shopping

Stanley *p1735, map p1736*

In Stanley there are a number of gift shops, **Capstan Gift Shop**, opposite West Store, wide selection, including books. **Harbour View**, Ross Rd. **The Pink Shop**, John St, for arts and crafts, books, pictures. **The Pod**, next to the Jetty Visitors Centre. Others include wool shops.

For groceries: **FIC West Store** (Ross Rd), Mon-Fri 0830-2000, Sat 0900-1800, Sun 0900-1700, also has an entertainment centre, **Kelper Family Stores** (39 Ross Rd East, 3 other locations), Mon-Fri 0730-2100, Sat-Sun 0900-2100, **Choice Fruits** (Industrial Lookout Estate), **Stanley Growers Garden Centre** (Stanley Airport Rd), **Seafish Chandlery and Supermarket** (Stanley Airport Rd), **Stanley Co-op** (Davis St), **Falklands Supplies** (Hebe St), **Stanley Services** (Stanley Airport Rd).

▲ Activities and tours

Stanley *p1735, map p1736*

Tour operators

See www.visitorfalklands.com for details of overseas operators.

Beauchene Fishing Company Ltd, T22260, 55830 (mob), Cheryl@beauchenefishing.co.fk. Sight-seeing tours, excursions, evening cruises and day charters out of Stanley on the *B-Mar* launch are all available.

Falkland Islands Company-Flights, T27633, fic.travel@horizon.co.fk. Local booking agent for the MoD charter flight via Brize Norton, UK.

Falkland Island Holidays (division of **Stanley Services**), Bypass Rd, Stanley, T22622, www.falklandislandsholidays.com. Offer inbound tourist services, FIGAS flights, overland 4WD excursions from Stanley to various sights, bookings for lodgings and for fishing, riding and vehicle hire.

Golden Fleece Expedition Cruises, contact: Jerome Poncet, T42326, golden.fleece@horizon.co.fk. Specializes in film-work, scientific surveys or tourism around the Falklands, South Georgia or Antarctica.

International Tours and Travel Ltd, 1 Dean St, PO Box 408, Stanley, T22041, www.falklandislands.travel. Handle inbound tourist bookings, book FIGAS flights, arrange tours etc and are the Falkland Island agents for **LAN**. Recommended.

Penguin Travel, Crozier Place, T27630, www.penguintravel-falklands.com. Wildlife tours on foot, or by 4WD, Stanley tours, battlesite tours.

South Atlantic Marine Services, Carol and Dave Eynon, PO Box 140, Stanley, T21145, dceynon@horizon.co.fk. Overland tours, boat trips, safaris and have a dive centre with deck recompression chamber (PADI courses).

Guided tours

Comprehensive list at www.visitorfalklands.com.

Adventure Falklands, PO Box 223, T21383, pwatts@horizon.co.fk. Patrick Watts offers tours of battlefield and other historical sights, ornithological trips and more. Highly recommended.

Cross Country Expeditions, T21494, scm@horizon.co.fk. Wildlife and fishing tours, airport transfers and lodging with Sam Miller.

Discovery Falklands, T21027, T51027 (mob), discovery@horizon.co.fk. Tony Smith specializes in battlefield tours, wildlife, general interest, historical, also provides logistical support and guidance for visiting TV Crews and media personnel. Highly recommended.

Falkland Frontiers, T51561, falklandfrontiers @horizon.co.fk. Neil Rowlands offers overland and boat tours, also fishing guide.
France's Falkland Forays, 7 Snake Hill, T21624, france@horizon.co.fk. Graham France's city, golf, penguin watching and historical tours.
Kidney Cove Safari Tours, T31001, allowe@ horizon.co.fk. Adrian and Lisa Lowe, offer overland 4WD tours to see 4 species of penguins at Kidney Cove, close to Stanley.

Transport

Falkland Islands/Islas Malvinas

Air The **Falkland Islands Government Air Service** (FIGAS, T27219, reservations@ figas.gov.fk) flies to farm settlements and settled outer islands on a shuttle service that varies daily accoding to demand. To book a seat, contact FIGAS with as much notice as possible; daily schedules are announced the previous afternoon on local radio and by fax and telephone. One-way airfares in 2009 cost between £30 and £120, depending on distance (Visa and MasterCard accepted); luggage limit 20 kg. Services daily Oct-end Mar, 6 days a week otherwise; no flights on 1 Jan, Good Friday, 21 Apr, 14 Jun, 25 Dec. Services and fares are continually under review. FIGAS tickets are also available from **Stanley Services Travel** and **International Tours and Travel Ltd**, see Activities and tours, above. Flights leave from Stanley Airport, 3 miles east of town on the Cape Pembroke peninsula, 10-15 mins by car.
Car hire **East 2 West Hire**, T41194, mpmwl@ cwimail.fk. Rents Mitsubishi Pajeros, allows vehicles on the ferry between East and West Falklands (see below). **Falklands Islands Company**, Travel Services, West Store, Stanley, T27678, fic.auto@horizon.co.fk. Contact Stephen Luxton. Rents Land Rover Defender, Discovery and Freelander. **Stanley Services Ltd**, Travel Division, Airport Rd, Stanley, T22622, info@ falklandislandsholidays.com. Rents Mitsubishi Pajeros. Rented vehicles may not be taken off road. On West Falkland Port Howard Farm may rent a vehicle if one is spare.
Ferry A drive-on, drive-off ferry sails between New Haven (East) and Port Howard (West) Mon, Wed, Fri one week, Fri, Sun the next, up to twice a day depending on bookings.For schedules T22300, www.workboat.co.fk. If the wind is wrong it will not sail. Cars £50, foot passengers £10.

Taxis Fares within Stanley, £3, to Stanley airport £6. **Bonner's Taxis**, T51126, abonner@ horizon.co.fk, for transport in Stanley, to Mount Pleasant airport and tours. Also in Stanley, **Town Taxis**, T52900.

Directory

Stanley *p1735, map p1736*
Internet See Internet, page 1733. **Medical services** Hospitals: Stanley has an excellent hospital, King Edward Memorial Hospital (KEMH), dental service included. T28000.
Post offices On Ross Road, open Mon-Fri 0800-1630. **Philatelic Bureau** (they sell stamps from South Georgia and the Antarctic Territories), T27180, www.falklands.gov. fk/pb.
Telephone See **Cable and Wireless**, page 1733. Directory enquiries T181. Operator Services T20800. **Useful addresses** **Immigration:** Customs and Immigration Department, 3 H Jones Rd, Stanley, T27340, admin@customs.gov.fk.

Beyond the Falklands

South Georgia

South Georgia, in latitude 54.5° south and longitude 36-38° west, has an area of 3,755 sq km, but no permanent residents. There are two British Antarctic Survey stations, King Edward Point and Bird Island, and a marine officer at the former is the government's representative and has responsibility for local administration. His duties include those of Harbour Master, Customs and Immigration Officer, Fisheries Officer and Postmaster. Visitors normally arrive by cruise ship from Ushuaia, Punta Arenas or Stanley. Some also come by chartered yachts. Intending visitors, who are not part of tour groups, must submit a request through the **Commissioner** ⓘ *Government House, Stanley, Falkland Islands, South Atlantic, T500-28200, gov.house@horizon.co.fk*. There is a landing fee of £100.

South Georgia is a largely chain of high (almost 3000 m), snow-covered glaciated mountains. At King Edward Point, near sea level, snow falls on an average of nearly 200 days annually, but the coastal area is free from snow and partially covered by vegetation in summer. This is the port of entry and is 1 km from Grytviken. Wildlife consists of most of the same species found in the Falkland Islands/Islas Malvinas, but in much larger numbers, especially penguins, albatross, and seals. Reindeer, introduced by Norwegian whalers in 1909, have flourished. Other points of interest are the abandoned whaling stations (although asbestos and other hazard restrict access), the little white whalers' church, and several shipwrecks. The explorer, Sir Ernest Shackleton, lies in the whalers' cemetery at Grytviken. A South Georgia Museum has been established there ⓘ *T+870-382-359035, www.sght.org/museum.htm*, where the whaling station is now rearranged as a display featuring amazing steam industrial archaeology. Inside is a display of artifacts, photographs and other items about the old Antarctic whaling and sealing industry with descriptions the history of the island, including events of 1982, and its wildlife. The island issues distinctive stamps, which are sold by the Post Office and museum. There is a South Georgia website: www.sgisland.org, and a South Georgia Association. The **South Sandwich Islands**, some 500 km southeast of South Georgia, are uninhabited but administered by the same government as South Georgia. Although very rarely visited they are a spectacular chain of 11 volcanoes, several of which are active.

The Antarctic

Antarctica, the fifth largest continent, is 99.8% covered with perpetual ice. Although inaccessible, the number of tourists now exceeds the number of people on government research programmes. It is known for its extraordinary scenery, wildlife, scientific stations, and historic sites. The weather can be spectacularly severe, thus visits are confined to the brief summer. Presently 25 countries operate 60 scientific stations (45 remain open during winter). A winter population of about 1,200 lives in a continent larger than Europe. The Antarctic Heritage Trust which has headquarters in New Zealand and Britain, and some other organizations maintain several historic huts where organized groups are admitted. Many current research stations allow visitors a stay of a couple of hours on an organized tour. Of the historic huts, the one at **Port Lockroy**, established in 1944 and now a museum, has become the most-visited site. The historic huts used by Scott, Shackleton, Mawson, and Borchgrevink during the 'heroic age' of exploration are on the Australian and New Zealand side of Antarctica thus very distant from South America.

Information there are many of specialist and general books about Antarctica, but the current best single source of information remains *Antarctica: great stories from the frozen continent* by Reader's Digest (first published Sydney 1985, with several later editions). General information including links to other sites can be found at **Scott Polar Research Institute** site, www.spri.cam.ac.uk. Also useful is the website of **International Association of Antarctica Tour Operators, IAATO** (see below). Most national operators also have sites dedicated to their work but often with much more information. The **Committee of Managers of National Antarctic Programmes**, in Hobart, is the best source for these details: www.comnap.aq.

Governance of Antarctica is principally through the Antarctic Treaty (1959) signed by all countries operating there (48 countries were parties to the Treaty in 2010, these represent over 80% of the Earth's population). Most visitors will be affected by several provisions of the Treaty, in particular those of the Environmental Protocol of 1991. These provisions are aimed at the protection of wildlife (do not remove or harmfully interfere with animals or plants), respecting protected areas and scientific research, alerting visitors to the need to be safe and prepared for severe changeable weather and keeping the environment pristine. Full details from www.iaato.org/docs/visitor_guidelines.pdf. Seven countries have claims over parts of Antarctica and three of these overlap (Antártida Argentina, British Antarctic Territory, and Territorio Chileno Antártico); the Treaty has neutralized these with provision of free access to citizens of contracting states. Some display of sovereignty is legitimate and many stations operate a Post Office where philatelic items and various souvenirs are sold.

The region south of South America is the most accessible part of the Antarctic, therefore over half the scientific stations are there or on adjacent islands. Coincidentally it is one of the most spectacular areas with many mountains, glaciers and fjords closely approachable by sea. Three ports are used: Stanley, Punta Arenas and Ushuaia, the last is the major base for yachts. The South Shetland Islands and Antarctic Peninsula are most frequently visited, but ships also reach the South Orkney Islands and many call at South Georgia at the beginning or end of a voyage. Most vessels are booked well in advance by luxury class passengers sometimes late opportunistic vacancies may be secured by local agencies. Ships carrying 45-280 tourists land passengers at several sites during about a fortnight's voyage. Some much larger vessels also visit; these generally do not land passengers but merely cruise around the coasts. During the 2008-2009 austral summer about 38,000 visitors arrived in Antarctica, of whom 27,200 landed on the continent.

Voyages from South America and the Falkland Islands/Islas Malvinas involve at least two days each way, crossing the Drake Passage where sea conditions may be very uncomfortable. No guarantee of landings, views or wildlife is possible and delays due to storms are not exceptional. Conversely, on a brilliant day, some of the most spectacular sights and wildlife anywhere can be seen. Visitors should be prepared for adverse conditions with warm clothing,

windproofs and waterproofs, and boots for wet landings. Weather and state of the sea can change quickly without warning.

The International Association of Antarctica Tour Operators ⓘ *11 South Angell St, Box 302, Providence, RI 02906; T+1-401-272 2152, www.iaato.org*, represents the majority of companies and can provide details of most offering Antarctic voyages. Many vessels have a principal contractor and a number of other companies bring smaller groups, thus it is advantageous to contact the principal. Antarctic Logistics and Expeditions (ALE) ⓘ *79 West 4510 South, Suite 2, Salt Lake City, UT 84107, USA, T+1-801-266 4876, www.antarctic-logistics.com*, provides flights to Antarctica from Punta Arenas where there is a local office ⓘ *Arauco 935, Punta Arenas, Chile, T+56-61-247735, chile@antarctic-logistics.com, Oct-Jan*. Wheeled aircraft fly as far as a summer camp at Patriot Hills (80° 19S, 81° 20W), the only land-based tourist facility, whence ski-aircraft proceed to the South Pole, vicinity of Vinson Massif (4,892 m, Antarctica's highest peak), and elsewhere. Some flights also go from Punta Arenas and Cape Town. 'Flightseeing' is made by Qantas from Australia aboard aircraft which do not land but spend about 4 hours over the continent (and about the same getting there and back).

Some private yachts carry passengers; enquire at Ushuaia, or the other ports listed. Travelling with the Argentine, Chilean, French or Russian supply ships may sometimes be arranged at departure ports. These are much cheaper than cruise ships but have limited itineraries as their principal object is to supply stations.

Background

Contents

1748 **Pre-independence history**

1754 **Post-independence history**

1779 **Government**

1781 **People**

1786 **Land and environment**

1794 **Culture**

Footprint features

1753 The Jesuits
1759 The Bandeirantes
1775 Chávez and Boliviarian Revolution
1796 Argentina, Chile and Uruguay: the essential CDs
1798 The South American Caribbean: the essential CDs
1803 Essential Brazilian CDs and websites
1805 Highlights of South America Literature
1807 Cinematic highlights in South America

Pre-independence history

Earliest settlement

It is generally accepted that the earliest settlers in South America were related to people who had crossed the Bering Straits from Asia and drifted through the Americas from about 50,000 BC. Alternative theories of early migrations from across the Pacific and Atlantic have been rife since Thor Heyerdahl's raft expeditions in 1947 and 1969-1970. The earliest evidence of human presence has been found at various sites: in the Central Andes (with a radiocarbon date between 12000 and 9000 BC), northern Venezuela (11000 BC), southeast Brazil, south-central Chile and Argentine Patagonia (from at least 10000 BC). After the Pleistocene Ice Age, 8000-7000 BC, rising sea levels and climatic changes introduced new conditions as many mammal species became extinct and coastlands were drowned. A wide range of crops was brought into cultivation and camelids and guinea pigs were domesticated. It seems that people lived nomadically in small groups, mainly hunting and gathering but also cultivating some plants seasonally, until villages with effective agriculture began to appear, it was orignally thought, between 2500-1500 BC. The earliest ceramic-making in the western hemisphere was thought to have come from what is now Colombia and Ecuador, around 4000 BC, but fragments of painted pottery were found near Santarém, Brazil, in 1991 with dates of 6000-5000 BC.

The coast of central Peru was where settled life began to develop most rapidly. The abundant wealth of marine life produced by the Humboldt Current, especially north of today's Lima, boosted population growth and a shift from nomadic to settled farming in this area. The introduction of sophisticated irrigation systems encouraged higher productivity and population growth, leading to organized group labour which could be devoted to building and making textiles from cotton. Evidence from Caral, Aspero and other sites in the Huaura, Supe, Pativilca and Fortaleza river valleys prove that this process happened much earlier than previously imagined. Caral dates from 2627 BC (other sites have older dates) and is a monumental construction. It flourished for some 500 years and appears to have been a city with primarily a religious, rather than a warlike purpose. The archaeological finds point to Caral and neighbouring sites predating the development of pottery in this region, but artefacts show cultural links with other communities, even as far as the Amazon. In the central Andes near Huánuco, also in what is now Peru, more advanced architecture was being built at Kotosh. There is evidence of a pre-ceramic culture here, too, but some of the earliest pottery from the site's later phases was found, showing signs of influence from southern Ecuador and the tropical lowlands. Radiocarbon dates of some Kotosh remains are from 1850 BC and Japanese archaeological excavations there in the 1960s revealed a temple with ornamental niches and friezes.

Andean and Pacific coastal civilizations

Chavín and Sechín For the next 1,000 years or so up to c900 BC, communities grew and spread inland from the north coast and south along the north highlands. Farmers still lived in simple adobe or rough stone houses but built increasingly large and complex ceremonial centres. As farming became more productive and pottery more advanced, commerce grew and states began to develop throughout central and north-central Peru, with the associated signs of social structure and hierarchies.

Around 900 BC a new era was marked by the rise of two important centres; Chavín de Huántar in the central Andes and Sechín Alto, inland from Casma on the north coast, both now in Peru. The chief importance of Chavín de Huántar was not so much in its highly advanced architecture as in the influence of its cult, coupled with the artistic style of its ceramics and other artefacts. The founders of Chavín may have originated in the tropical lowlands, as some of its carved monoliths show representations of monkeys and felines.

The Chavín cult This was paralleled by the great advances made in this period in textile production and in some of the earliest examples of metallurgy. The origins of metallurgy have been attributed to some gold, silver and copper ornaments found in graves in Chongoyape, near Chiclayo, which show Chavín-style features. But earlier evidence has been discovered at Kuntur Wasi (some 120 km east of the coast at Pacasmayo) where 4,000-year old gold has been found, and in the Andahuaylas region, dating from 1800-900 BC. The religious symbolism of gold and other precious metals and stones is thought to have been an inspiration behind some of the beautiful artefacts found in the central Andean area.

The cultural brilliance of Chavín de Huántar was complemented by its contemporary, Sechín, with which may have combined forces, Sechín being the military power that spread the cultural word of Chavín. The Chavín hegemony broke up around 500 BC, soon after which the Nazca culture began to bloom in southern Peru. This period, up to about AD 500, was a time of great social and cultural development. Sizable towns of 5-10,000 inhabitants grew on the south coast, populated by artisans, merchants and government and religious officials.

Paracas-Nazca Nazca origins are traced back to about the second century BC, to the Paracas Cavernas and Necropolis, on the coast in the national park near Pisco in Peru. The extreme dryness of the desert here has preserved remarkably the textiles and ceramics in the mummies' tombs excavated. The technical quality and stylistic variety in weaving and pottery rank them among the world's best, and many of the finest examples can be seen in the museums of Lima. The famous Nazca Lines are a feature of the region. Straight lines, abstract designs and outlines of animals are scratched in the dark desert surface forming a lighter contrast that can be seen clearly from the air. There are many theories of how and why the lines were made but no definitive explanation has yet been able to establish their place in South American history. There are similarities between the style of some of the line patterns and that of the pottery and textiles of the same period. Alpaca hair found in Nazca textiles, however, indicates that there must have been strong trade links with highland people.

Moche culture Nazca's contemporaries on the north coast were the militaristic Moche who, from about AD 100-800, built up an empire whose traces stretch from Piura in the north to Huarmey, in the south. The Moche built their capital outside present day Trujillo. The huge pyramid temples of the Huaca del Sol and Huaca de la Luna mark the remains of this city. Moche roads and system of way stations are thought to have been an early inspiration for the Inca network. The Moche increased the coastal population with intensive irrigation projects. Skilful engineering works were carried out, such as the La Cumbre canal, still in use today, and the Ascope aqueduct, both on the Chicama River. The Moche's greatest achievement, however, was its artistic genius. Exquisite ornaments in gold, silver and precious stones were made by its craftsmen. Moche pottery progressed through five stylistic periods, most notable for the stunningly lifelike portrait vases. A wide variety of everyday scenes were created in naturalistic ceramics, telling us more about Moche life than is known about other earlier cultures. Spectacular Moche tombs, discovered at Sipán since 1987, have included semi-precious stones brought from Chile and Argentina, and seashells from Ecuador. The Moche were great navigators.

The cause of the collapse of the Moche Empire around AD 600-700 is unknown, but it may have been started by a 30-year drought at the end of the sixth century, followed by one of the periodic El Niño flash floods (identified by meteorologists from ice thickness in the Andes) and finished by the encroaching forces of the Huari Empire. The decline of the Moche signalled a general tipping of the balance of power in Peru from the north coast to the south sierra.

Huari-Tiwanaku The ascendant Huari-Tiwanaku movement, from AD 600-1000, combined the religious cult of the Tiwanaku site in the Titicaca basin, with the military dynamism of the Huari, based in the central highlands. The two cultures developed independently but they are generally thought to have merged compatibly. Up until their own demise around AD 1440, the Huari-Tiwanaku had spread their empire and influence across much of south Peru, north Bolivia and Argentina. They made considerable gains in art and technology, building roads, terraces and irrigation canals across the country. The Huari-Tiwanaku ran their empire with efficient labour and administrative systems that were later adopted by the Incas. Labour tribute for state projects practised by the Moche were further developed. But the empire could not contain regional kingdoms who began to fight for land and power. As control broke down, rivalry and coalitions emerged, the system collapsed and the scene was set for the rise of the Incas.

Chachapoyas and Chimú cultures After the decline of the Huari Empire, the unity that had been imposed on the Andes was broken. A new stage of autonomous regional or local political organizations began. Among the cultures corresponding to this period were the Chachapoyas in northern highlands and the Chimú. The Chachapoyas people were not so much an empire as a loose-knit 'confederation of ethnic groups with no recognized capital' (Morgan Davis 'Chachapoyas: The Cloud People', Ontario, 1988). But the culture did develop into an advanced society with great skill in road and monument building. Their fortress at Kuélap was known as the most impregnable in the Peruvian Andes. The Chimú culture had two centres. To the north was Lambayeque, near Chiclayo, while to the south, in the Moche valley near present-day Trujillo, was the great adobe walled city of Chan Chán. Covering 20 sq km, this was the largest pre-Hispanic Peruvian city. Chimú has been classified as a despotic state that based its power on wars of conquest. Rigid social stratification existed and power rested in the hands of the great lord *Siquic* and the lord *Alaec*. These lords were followed in social scale by a group of urban couriers who enjoyed a certain degree of economic power. At the bottom were the peasants and slaves. In 1450, the Chimú kingdom was conquered by the Inca Túpac Yupanqui, the son and heir of the Inca ruler Pachacuti Inca Yupanqui.

Cultures of the northern Andes What is today Ecuador was a densely populated region with a variety of peoples. One of the most important of these was the **Valdivia culture** (3500-1500 BC) on the coast, from which remains of buildings and earthenware figures have been found. A rich mosaic of cultures developed in the period 500 BC to AD 500, after which integration of groups occurred. In the mid-15th century, the relentless expansion of the Inca empire reached Ecuador. The **Cañaris** resisted until 1470 and the Quitu/Caras were defeated in 1492. Further north, most of the peoples who occupied Colombia were primitive hunters or nomad agriculturists, but one part of the country, the high basins of the Eastern Cordillera, was densely occupied by **Chibcha Indians** who had become sedentary farmers. Their staple foods were maize and the potato, and they had no domestic animal save the dog; the use they could make of the land was therefore limited. Other cultures present in Colombia in the pre-Columbian era were the **Tayrona, Quimbaya, Sinú** and **Calima**. Exhibits of theirs and the Chibcha (Muisca) Indians' goldwork can be seen at the Gold Museum in Bogotá and other cities.

Southern Andes Although there was some influence in southern Bolivia, northern Chile and northern Argentina from cultures such as Tiwanaku, most of the southern Andes was an area of autonomous peoples, probably living in fortified settlements by the time the Incas arrived in the mid-15th century. The conquerors from Peru moved south to the Río Maule in Chile where they encountered the fierce **Mapuches** (Araucanians) who halted their advance. Archaeological evidence from the Amazon basin and Brazil is more scanty than from the Andes or Pacific because the materials used for house building, clothing and decoration were perishable and did not survive the warm, humid conditions of the jungle. Ceramics have been found on Marajó island at the mouth of the Amazon while on the coast much evidence comes from huge shell mounds, called *sambaquis*. Theories about structured societies and their large populations are being revised as aerial photography and forest clearance in the Upper Amazon and Xingu regions of Brazil reveal huge interconnected earthworks, canals, roads and other indicators of city-building . The Incas made few inroads into the Amazon so it was the arrival of the Portuguese in 1500 which initiated the greatest change on the Atlantic side of the continent.

The Inca Dynasty

The origins of the Inca Dynasty are shrouded in mythology and shaky evidence. The best known story reported by the Spanish chroniclers talks about Manco Cápac and his sister rising out of Lake Titicaca, created by the sun as divine founders of a chosen race. This was in approximately AD 1200. Over the next 300 years the small tribe grew to supremacy as leaders of the largest empire ever known in the Americas, divided into the four quarters of Tawantinsuyo, all radiating out from Cuzco: Chinchaysuyo, north and northwest; Cuntisuyo, south and west; Collasuyo, south and east; Antisuyo, east.

At its peak, just before the Spanish Conquest, the Inca Empire stretched from the Río Maule in central Chile, north to the present Ecuador-Colombia border, contained most of Ecuador, Peru, west Bolivia, north Chile and northwest Argentina. The area was roughly equivalent to France, Belgium, Holland, Luxembourg, Italy and Switzerland combined, 980,000 sq km. For a brief description of **Inca Society**, see under Cuzco. The first Inca ruler, Manco Cápac, moved to the fertile Cuzco region, and established Cuzco as his capital. Successive generations of rulers were fully occupied with local conquests of rivals, such as the Colla and Lupaca to the south, and the Chanca to the northwest. At the end of Inca Viracocha's reign the hated Chanca were finally defeated, largely thanks to the heroism of one of his sons, Pachacuti Inca Yupanqui, who was subsequently crowned as the new ruler.

From the start of Pachacuti's own reign in 1438, imperial expansion grew in earnest. With the help of his son and heir, Topa Inca, territory was conquered from the Titicaca basin south into Chile, and all the north and central coast down to the Lurin Valley. In 1460-71, the Incas also laid siege to the Chimú. Typical of the Inca method of government, some of the Chimú skills were assimilated into their own political and administrative system, and some Chimú nobles were even given positions in Cuzco.

Perhaps the pivotal event in Inca history came in 1527 with the death of the ruler, Huayna Cápac. Civil war broke out in the confusion over his rightful successor. One of his legitimate sons, Huáscar, ruled the southern part of the empire from Cuzco. Atahualpa, Huáscar's half-brother, governed Quito, the capital of Chinchaysuyo. In 1532, soon after Atahualpa had won the civil war, Francisco Pizarro arrived in Tumbes with 167 *conquistadores*, a third of them on horseback. Atahualpa's army was marching south, probably for the first time, when he clashed with Pizarro at Cajamarca. **Francisco Pizarro**'s only chance against the formidable imperial army he encountered at Cajamarca was a bold stroke. He drew Atahualpa into an ambush, slaughtered his guards and many of his troops, promised him liberty if a certain room were filled with treasure, and finally killed him on the pretext that an Inca army was on its way to free him. Pushing on to Cuzco, he was at first hailed as the executioner of a traitor: Atahualpa had ordered the death of Huáscar in 1533, while himself captive of Pizarro, and his victorious generals were bringing the defeated Huáscar to see his half-brother. Panic followed when the *conquistadores* set about sacking the city, and they fought off with difficulty an attempt by Manco Inca to recapture Cuzco in 1536.

The Spanish conquest

Pizarro's arrival in Peru had been preceded by Columbus' landfall on the Paria Peninsula (Venezuela) on 5 August 1498 and Spanish reconaissance of the Pacific coast in 1522. Permanent Spanish settlement was established at Santa Marta (Colombia) in 1525 and Cartagena was founded in 1533. Gonzalo Jiménez de Quesada conquered the Chibcha kingdom and founded Bogotá in 1538. Pizarro's lieutenant, Sebastián de Belalcázar, was sent north through Ecuador; he captured Quito with Diego de Almagro in 1534. Gonzalo Pizarro,

Francisco's brother, took over control of Quito in 1538 and, during his exploration of the Amazon lowlands, he sent Francisco de Orellana to prospect downriver. Orellana did not return, but drifted down the Amazon, finally reaching the river's mouth in 1542, the first European to cross the continent in this way. Belalcázar pushed north, founding Pasto, Cali and Popayán (Colombia) in 1536, arriving in Bogotá in 1538. Meanwhile, wishing to secure his communications with Spain, Pizarro founded Lima, near the ocean, as his capital in 1535. The same year Diego de Almagro set out to conquer Chile. Unsuccessful, he returned to Peru, quarrelled with Pizarro, and in 1538 fought a pitched battle with Pizarro's men at the Salt Pits, near Cuzco. He was defeated and put to death. Pizarro, who had not been at the battle, was assassinated in his palace in Lima by Almagro's son three years later. In 1541, Pedro de Valdivia founded Santiago de Chile after a renewed attempt to conquer Chile. Like the Incas before them, the Spaniards were unable to master the Mapuches; Valdivia was killed in 1553 and a defensive barrier along the Río Biobío had to be built in order to protect the colony.

Since 1516 European seafarers had visited the Río de la Plata, first Juan de Solís, then Sebastian Cabot and his rival Diego García in 1527. An expedition led by Pedro de Mendoza founded Buenos Aires in 1536, but it was abandoned in 1541. Mendoza sent Juan de Ayolas up the Río Paraná to reach Peru from the east. It is not known for certain what happened to Ayolas, but his lieutenant Domingo Martínez de Irala founded Asunción on the Paraguay in 1537. This was the base from which the Spaniards relaunched their conquest of the Río de la Plata and Buenos Aires was refounded in 1580.

Treasure hunt As Spanish colonization built itself around new cities, the *conquistadores* set about finding the wealth which had lured them to South America in the first place. The great prize came in 1545 when the hill of silver at Potosí (Bolivia) was discovered. Other mining centres grew up and the trade routes to supply them and carry out the riches were established. The Spanish crown soon imposed political and administrative jurisdiction over its new empire, replacing the power of the *conquistadores* with that of governors and bureaucrats.The Viceroyalty of Peru became the major outlet for the wealth of the Americas, but each succeeding representative of the Kingdom of Spain was faced with the twofold threat of subduing the Inca successor state of Vilcabamba, north of Cuzco, and unifying the fierce Spanish factions. Francisco de Toledo (appointed 1568) solved both problems during his 14 years in office: Vilcabamba was crushed in 1572 and the last reigning Inca, Túpac Amaru, put to death. For the next 200 years the Viceroys closely followed Toledo's system, if not his methods. The Major Government – the Viceroy, the *Audiencia* (High Court), and *corregidores* (administrators) – ruled through the Minor Government – Indian chiefs put in charge of large groups of natives: a rough approximation to the original Inca system.

Towards independence

The Indians of Peru rose in 1780, under the leadership of an Inca noble who called himself Túpac Amaru II. He and many of his lieutenants were captured and put to death under torture at Cuzco. Another Indian leader in revolt suffered the same fate in 1814, but this last flare-up had the sympathy of many of the locally born Spanish, who resented their status: inferior to the Spaniards born in Spain, the refusal to give them any but the lowest offices, the high taxation imposed by the home government, and the severe restrictions upon trade with any country but Spain. This was a complaint common to all parts of the Spanish empire and it fostered a twin-pronged independence movement. Given impetus by Napoleon's invasion of Spain in 1808, Simón Bolívar, El Libertador, led a revolution in the north and José de San Martín, with his Army of the Andes, led an uprising through Argentina and Chile. Both converged on Peru.

Bolívar, born in Venezuela in 1783, was involved in the early struggle to free the region from Spanish rule. In 1811 Venezuela declared itself an independent republic, only to be defeated by Spain in 1812. Bolívar led a new revolt in 1813, which was crushed in 1815. He went into exile in Jamaica and Haiti, to return in 1816 with a new army which, in a bold move, he led over the

The Jesuits

Between 1609, when they built their first *reducción* or mission in the region of Guaíra in present day Brazil, and 1767, when they were expelled from Spanish America, the Jesuits founded about 50 missions around the upper reaches of the Ríos Paraná, Paraguay and Uruguay. In 1627, the northern missions around Guaíra were attacked by slave-hunting Bandeirantes from São Paulo, forcing them to flee southwards. Some 10,000 converts, led by their priests, floated 700 rafts down the Río Parapanema into the Paraná, only to find their route blocked by the Guaíra Falls. Pushing on for eight days through dense forest, they built new boats below the Falls and continued their journey to reestablish their missions 725 km from their original homes.

Efficiently organized and strictly laid out, the missions prospered, growing indigenous and European crops and herding cattle. Their success and economic power attracted many enemies, from the Spanish crown to local landowners. When, in 1750, Spain and Portugal settled their South American border dispute, seven missions were placed under Portuguese control. This the Jesuits resisted with arms, fuelling further the suspicion of the order's excessive power. Under highest secrecy, King Carlos III sent instructions to South America in 1767 to expel the Jesuits. 2,000 were shipped to Italy, their property was auctioned and their schools and colleges were taken over by the Franciscans and Dominicans. By the early 19th century, many of the missions had fallen into disrepair.

Only four missions show signs of their former splendour: San Ignacio Miní in Argentina; Jesús and Trinidad in Paraguay; and São Miguel in Brazil.

Andes from Venezuela to liberate Nueva Granada (as Colombia was called) at the Battle of Boyacá in 1819. He proclaimed a new republic, Gran Colombia, taking in Colombia, Venezuela and Ecuador. Venezuela was freed at the Battle of Carabobo in 1821.

San Martín's Argentine troops, convoyed from Chile under the protection of the English admiral, Lord Cochrane, landed in southern Peru on 7 September 1820. San Martín proclaimed Peruvian independence at Lima on 28 July 1821, though most of the country was still in the hands of the Viceroy, José de La Serna. Bolívar sent Antonio José de Sucre to Ecuador where, on 24 May 1822, he gained a victory over La Serna at Pichincha. San Martín, after a meeting with Bolívar at Guayaquil, left for Argentina and a self-imposed exile in France, while Bolívar and Sucre completed the conquest of Peru by defeating La Serna at the battle of Junín (6 August 1824) and the decisive battle of Ayacucho (9 December 1824). For over a year there was a last stand in the Real Felipe fortress at Callao by the Spanish troops under General Rodil before they capitulated on 22 January 1826. Bolívar was invited to stay in Peru, but in 1826 he left for Colombia where he tried to hold Gran Colombia together as a single state. He failed as internal divisions and political ambitions pulled the three new republics apart. While heading for exile, Bolívar died in 1830.

Brazil: from colony to independence

The Portuguese, Pedro Álvares Cabral, landed in Brazil on 22 April, 1500. He left after a week, shortly followed by Amérigo Vespucci who had been sent to explore further. The first system of government adopted by the Portuguese was a Capitania, a kind of feudal principality – there were 13 of them, but these were replaced in 1572 by a Viceroyalty. In the same year it was decided to divide the colony into two, north and south, with capitals at Salvador and Rio; it was not until 1763 that Rio became the sole capital.

Three centuries under the paternal eye of Portugal had ill-prepared the colonists for independent existence, except for the experience of Dutch invasion (1624 in Salvador, and 1630-1654 in Recife). The colonists ejected the Dutch from Brazil with little help from Portugal, and Brazilians date the birth of their national sentiment from these events. Growing resentment against Portuguese government and trade intervention led to the **Inconfidência**, the first revolution, masterminded by **Tiradentes** with 11 other citizens of Minas Gerais. They were unsuccessful (Tiradentes was executed), but when France invaded Portugal in 1807, King João VI was shipped to safety in Brazil, escorted by the British navy. Rio was temporarily declared the capital of the Portuguese Empire. The British, as a price for their assistance in the Portuguese war, forced the opening of Brazil's ports to non-Portuguese trade. King João VI returned to the mother country in 1821, leaving his son, the young Pedro, as Regent. Pedro refused to return control of Brazil to the Portuguese Côrtes (parliament), and on 13 May 1822, by popular request, he agreed to stay and assumed the title of 'Perpetual Defender and Protector of Brazil'. On 7 September he declared Brazil's independence with the cry 'Independence or Death' by the Rio Ipiranga; on 12 October he was proclaimed the constitutional emperor of Brazil, and on 1 December he was crowned in Rio.

Post-independence history

Argentina

Independence from Spain

In 1778, Spain finally permitted Buenos Aires to conduct overseas trade. Before that it was controlled by the Viceroy in Lima and was merely a military outpost for Spain to confront the Portuguese settlement at Colonia, across the estuary. Its population then was only 24,203 and its main activity was smuggling. Following Spain's alliance with Napoleon, Britain attacked Buenos Aires in 1806 and again in 1807. The defeat of these attacks, known as the Reconquista, greatly increased the confidence of the *porteños* (the name given to those born in Buenos Aires) to deal with all comers, including the mother-country. On 25 May 1810, the *cabildo* of Buenos Aires deposed the viceroy and announced that it was now governing on behalf of King Ferdinand VII, then a captive of Napoleon. Six years later, in July 1816, when Buenos Aires was threatened by invasion from Peru and blockaded by a Spanish fleet in the Río de la Plata, a national congress held at Tucumán declared independence. The declaration was given reality by José de San Martín, who marched an Argentine army across the Andes to free Chile and embarked his forces for Peru, where he captured Lima, the first step in the liberation of Peru.

The formation of the republic

When San Martín returned home, it was to find the country rent by conflict between the central government and the provinces. On the one hand stood the Unitarist party, bent on central control; on the other the Federalist party, insisting on local autonomy. The latter had for members the great *caudillos* (the large landowners backed by the *gauchos*) suspicious of the cities. One of their leaders, Juan Manuel de Rosas, took control in 1829. During his second term as Governor of Buenos Aires he asked for and was given extraordinary powers. The result was a 17-year reign of terror which became an international scandal. When he began a blockade of Asunción in 1845, Britain and France promptly countered with a three-year blockade of Buenos Aires. In 1851 Justo José de Urquiza, Governor of Entre Ríos, one of his old henchmen, organized a triple alliance of Brazil, Uruguay, and the Argentine opposition to overthrow him. He was defeated in 1852 at Caseros, a few kilometres from Buenos Aires, and fled to England. Rosas had started his career as a Federalist; once in power he was a Unitarist. His downfall meant the triumph of federalism. In 1853 a federal system was finally incorporated in the constitution, but Buenos Aires refused to join the new federation until the city, led by Bartolomé Mitre, was finally defeated by the federal forces in 1880. Buenos Aires was consequently made into a special federal territory. The conquest at about the same time of all the Indian tribes of the pampas and the south by a young colonel, Julio A Roca, was to make possible the final supremacy of Buenos Aires over all rivals.

20th century

From 1916 to 1930 the Unión Cívica Radical (founded in 1890) held power, under the leadership of Hipólito Yrigoyen and Marcelo T de Alvear, but lost it to the 1930 military uprising. Though seriously affected by the 1930s world depression, Argentina's rich soil and educated population had made it one of the world's 10 wealthiest countries, but this wealth was unevenly distributed, and political methods used by the conservatives and their military associates in the 1930s denied the middle and working classes any effective share in their own country's wealth and government.

Peronism and its legacy

A series of military coups in 1943-44 led to the rise of Col Juan Domingo Perón, basing his power on an alliance between the army and labour; his contacts with labour were greatly assisted by his charismatic wife Eva (since commemorated in the rock-opera and film *Evita*). In 1946 Perón was elected President. His government is chiefly remembered by many Argentines for improving the living conditions of the workers. Especially in its early years the government was strongly nationalistic, but also intolerant of opposition parties and independent newspapers. Although Perón was re-elected in 1951, his government soon ran into trouble: economic problems led to the introduction of a wage freeze, upsetting the labour unions, which were the heart of Peronist support; the death of Evita in 1952 was another blow. In September 1955 a military coup unseated Perón, who went into exile. Perón's legacy dominated the period 1955-1973: society was bitterly divided between Peronists and anti-Peronists; the economy struggled; the armed forces, constantly involved in politics, were also divided. In a climate of tension and guerrilla-inspired violence, the military bowed out in 1973. Elections were won by the Peronist candidate, Hector Campora. Perón returned from exile in Madrid to resume as President in October 1973, but died on 1 July 1974, leaving the Presidency to his widow, Vice-President María Estela Martínez de Perón (his third wife). The subsequent chaotic political situation, including guerrilla warfare, led to her deposition by a military junta, led by Gen Jorge Videla in March 1976.

The Dirty War and after

Under the military, guerrilla warfare and the other features of dissidence were repressed with great brutality: about 9,000 people (although human rights organizations believe the total is at least double this) disappeared without trace during the so-called 'dirty war'. Confidence in the military ebbed when their economic policies began to go sour in 1980. In 1982-83 pressure for a democratic restoration grew particularly after the Falklands (Islas Malvinas) War with Great Britain in 1982, when Argentina invaded the South Atlantic islands run by the British, in an attempt to reclaim them. General elections on 30 October 1983 were won by the Unión Cívica Radical (UCR), with Dr Raúl Alfonsín as president. During 1985 Generals Videla, Viola and Galtieri were sentenced to long terms of imprisonment for their parts in the 'dirty war'.

The Menem years

When Alfonsín was defeated by Dr Carlos Saúl Menem of the Partido Justicialista (Peronists) in May 1989, Alfonsín stepped down early because of economic instability. Strained relations between the Peronist Government and the military led to several rebellions, which President Menem attempted to appease by pardoning the imprisoned Generals. His popularity among civilians declined, but in 1991-92 the Economy Minister Domingo Cavallo succeeded in restoring confidence in the economy and government. The key was a Convertibility Law, passed in 1991, fixing the peso against the US dollar, and permitting the Central Bank to print local currency only when backed by gold or hard currency. This achieved price stability; the annual average growth of consumer prices fell from 3,080% in 1989 to 3.9% in 1994 and remained in single figures until 2001. Having succeeded in changing the constitution to permit the re-election of the president for a second term of four years, Menem was returned to office in 1995 by an electorate favouring stability. But his renewed popularity was short lived: unemployment remained high and corruption unrestrained. Menem failed to force another constitutional change to allow him to stand for a third term, but his rivalry with Peronist candidate, Eduardo Duhalde, was one of the factors behind the victory of Fernando de la Rúa of Alianza.

The 2001-2002 crisis De la Rúa pledged to reduce joblessness, provide better healthcare and end corruption, but within a year was facing scandals and a series of economic crises. The peso became increasingly overvalued, but the government refused to modify the Convertibility Law. By the end of 2001, the country was in deep recession, unemployment was 20% and the government had practically run out of money to service its US$132 billion debt. As faith in the banking system and the government nosedived, Argentines started to take back their savings from banks; on 30 November 2001 alone, US$2 billion were withdrawn. The government imposed a US$250 weekly limit on cash withdrawals, leading to rioting, looting and 27 deaths, which eventually forced de la Rúa out of office. Three subsequent presidents resigned. On 2 January 2002, Eduardo Duhalde was sworn in as Argentina's fifth president in two weeks. The mammoth task of dragging the economy out of recession and restoring confidence could not be achieved before elections in April 2003, although positive steps were taken. The devaluation of the peso in 2002, which saw the real value of Argentines' savings plummet, did return the trade balance to surplus. Agriculture and tourism saw dramatic improvements and there was a slight fall in joblessness. Nevertheless, over half the population was living in poverty, desperate for work and food, many surviving thanks to barter clubs. Instead of a display of unity in the crisis, however, the Peronist party pulled itself apart prior to the elections, with the governor of Santa Cruz, Néstor Kirchner, running against ex-president Menem. Facing heavy defeat in the run-off, Menem pulled out of the race at the last moment, giving Kirchner the presidency but with the electoral support of just 22%.

Economic recovery and the Kirchner dynasty

By October 2005, Kirchner had gained sufficient popular support to win a substantial majority in mid-term congressional elections. At the same time, the economy recovered from a decline of 11% in 2002 to growth of over 8% between 2003 and 2007. Stresses remained, however. Inflation, cut from 26% in 2002 to below 5% in 2004, increased again to around 7.5% in 2008-2009. While unemployment had been reduced by late 2006 to under 10%, poverty and uneven distribution of wealth remained. In presidential elections in October 2007, Kirchner decided not to run again but his wife, Cristina Fernández de Kirchner, was nominated as a candidate. Her landslide victory, as Argentina's first elected female head of state, may have indicated a desire for continuity among the electorate, but her first years in office were confrontational. An increase in taxes on agricultural exports, in order to redistribute income from high soya, wheat and corn prices, led to strikes and blockades which caused food shortages, adding to problems of energy shortages and general price rises. With Congress evenly split on the vote to increase the export taxes in July 2008, Vice-President Julio Cobos voted against, setting him on a collision course with the Kirchners. While the defeat of the tax rise eased tensions, the agriculture sector was next faced with a severe fall in prices with the onset of the global economic crash of late 2008, followed by a catastrophic drought. The unpopularity of Kirchner's non-conciliatory approach was fully demonstrated in mid-term elections in June 2009 when her party lost its majorities in both houses of Congress. Her husband, Néstor, even failed to win election to Congress in Buenos Aires state. Presidential elections are due to be held in October 2011.

Bolivia

Coups, mines and wars

Bolivian politics have been the most turbulent in Latin America. Although in the 19th century the army was very small, officers were key figures in power-struggles, often backing different factions of the landowning elite. Between 1840 and 1849 there were 65 attempted *coups d'état*. The longest lasting government of the 19th century was that of Andrés Santa Cruz (1829-1839), but when he tried to unite Bolivia with Peru in 1836, Chile and Argentina intervened to overthrow him. After the War of the Pacific (1879-1883) there was greater stability, but opposition to the political dominance of the city of Sucre culminated in a revolt in 1899 led by business groups from La Paz and the tin-mining areas, as a result of which La Paz became the centre of government.

The Bolivian economy depended on tin exports during the 20th century. Railway construction and the demand for tin in Europe and the USA (particularly in wartime) led to a mining boom after 1900. By the 1920s the industry was dominated by three entrepreneurs, Simón Patiño, Mauricio Hochschild and the Aramayo family, who greatly influenced national politics. The importance of mining and the harsh conditions in the isolated mining camps of the Altiplano led to the rise of a militant miners movement.

Since independence Bolivia has suffered continual losses of territory, partly because of communications difficulties and the central government's inability to control distant provinces. The dispute between Chile and Peru over the nitrate-rich Atacama desert in 1879 soon dragged in Bolivia, which had signed a secret alliance with Peru in 1873. Following its rapid defeat in the War of the Pacific Bolivia lost her coastal provinces. As compensation Chile later agreed to build the railway between Arica and La Paz. When Brazil annexed the rich Acre Territory in 1903, Bolivia was compensated by another railway, but this Madeira-Mamoré line never reached its destination, Riberalta, and proved of little use; it was closed in 1972. There was not even an unbuilt railway to compensate Bolivia for its next loss. A long-running dispute with Paraguay over the Chaco erupted into war in 1932. Defeat in the so-called Chaco War (1932-1935) resulted in the loss of three quarters of the Chaco (see page 1767).

Modern Bolivia

The Chaco War was a turning point in Bolivian history, increasing the political influence of the army which in 1936 seized power for the first time since the War of the Pacific. Defeat bred nationalist resentment among junior army officers who had served in the Chaco and also led to the creation of a nationalist party, the Movimiento Nacionalista Revolucionario (MNR) led by Víctor Paz Estenssoro. Their anger was directed against the mine owners and the leaders who had controlled Bolivian politics. Between 1936 and 1946 a series of unstable military governments followed. This decade witnessed the apparent suicide in 1939 of one president (Germán Busch) and the public hanging in 1946 of another (Gualberto Villarroel). After a period of civilian government, the 1951 elections were won by the MNR but a coup prevented the party from taking office.

The 1952 revolution In April 1952 the military government was overthrown by a popular revolution in which armed miners and peasants played a major role. Paz Estenssoro became president and his MNR government nationalized the mines, introduced universal suffrage and began the break-up and redistribution of large estates. The economy, however, deteriorated, partly because of the hostility of the US government. Paz's successor, Hernán Siles Zuazo (president from 1956 to 1964), a hero of the 1952 revolution, was forced to take unpopular measures to stabilize the economy. Paz was re-elected president in 1960 and 1964, but shortly afterwards in November 1964 he was overthrown by his vice president, Gral René Barrientos, who relied on the support of the army and the peasants to defeat the miners.

Military rule in the 1970s The death of Barrientos in an air crash in 1969 was followed by three brief military governments. The third, led by Gral Torres, pursued left-wing policies which alarmed many army officers and business leaders. In August 1971 Torres was overthrown by Hugo Banzer, a right-wing colonel who outlawed political parties and trade unions. After Banzer was forced to call elections in 1978, a series of short-lived military governments overruled elections in 1978 and 1979 giving victories to Siles Zuazo. One of these, led by Gral García Meza (1980-1981) was notable for its brutal treatment of opponents and its links to the cocaine trade, which led to its isolation by the international community.

Return to democracy In August 1982 the military returned to barracks and Dr Siles Zuazo assumed the Presidency in a leftist coalition government with support from the communists and trade unions. Under this regime inflation spiralled out of control. The elections of 1985 were won again by Víctor Paz Estenssoro, who imposed a rigorous programme to stabilize the economy. In the elections of 1989, Gonzalo Sánchez de Lozada of the MNR (chief architect of the stabilization programme) failed to win enough votes to prevent Congress choosing Jaime Paz Zamora of the Movimiento de la Izquierda Revolucionaria (MIR), who came third in the elections, as president in August 1989. Paz had made an unlikely alliance with the former military dictator, Hugo Banzer (Acción Democrática Nacionalista).

Although Gonzalo Sánchez de Lozada just failed to gain the required 51% majority to win the presidency in the 1993 elections, the other candidates recognized his victory. The main element in his policies was the capitalization of state assets, in which investors agreed to inject fresh capital into a chosen state-owned company in return for a 50% controlling stake. The other 50% of the shares were distributed to all Bolivians over 18 via a private pension fund scheme. As the programme gained pace, so did opposition to it. In the elections of 1 June 1997, Banzer and the ADN secured 22% of the vote and ADN became the dominant party in a new coalition. After two years of economic austerity, hardship in rural areas, together with unemployment and anger at a US-backed coca eradication programme and a plan to raise water rates led to violent protests and road blocks in many parts of the country. President Banzer was forced to resign in August 2001 because of cancer and his replacement, Vice-President Jorge Quiroga, served the final year of Banzer's term before new elections were held, in which a coalition led by Sánchez de Lozada won an extremely narrow victory. The runner-up was Evo Morales, leader of the coca growers, who campaigned for a restoration of traditional coca production and an end to free market reforms.

Turbulence and the rise of Evo Morales From the outset, Sánchez de Lozada faced economic crisis. Mass demonstrations turned into riots over tax increases and the president was forced to flee the presidential palace in an ambulance. A week later, the cabinet resigned, tax hikes were cancelled, police were awarded a pay rise and Sánchez de Lozada vowed to forego his salary. Subsequent protests over the sale of Bolivian gas to the US became a national uprising and weeks of violent street demonstrations led to Sánchez de Lozada's resignation on 17 October 2003. Vice president Carlos Mesa became president, but survived only until June 2005, when new elections were called. Evo Morales of Movimiento al Socialismo (MAS), self-styled "United States' worst nightmare", managed to beat ex-president Quiroga by a clear majority on 18 December 2005.

Morales' rise to power was precipitated by the continued opposition to gas exports, mass protests by the inhabitants of El Alto calling for a more equal society and his support for coca growers. Morales soon announced elections to a new constituent assembly and, in May 2006, sent troops into the gas fields. This latter move provoked foreign hydrocarbon companies to renogotiate their contracts with Bolivia, but progress in the constituent assembly was nothing like as speedy. The Constituent Assembly only approved a new socially oriented constitution in November 2007, but the process was marred by both procedural irregularities and violence, including opposition riots in Sucre, where the session was being held. In 2008, opponents of the Morales government in northern and eastern lowland departments (Santa Cruz, Beni, Pando

The Bandeirantes

Reviled by some for their appalling treatment of the indigenous population, revered by others for their determination and willingness to withstand severe hardship in the pursuit of goals, the bandeirantes are an indispensible element in the formation of Brazil.

The Portuguese knew that South America held great riches; their Spanish rivals were shipping vast quantities back to Europe from Peru. Legends proliferated of mountains of precious stones, golden lakes and other marvels, also of terrifying places, all in the mysterious interior. Regardless of the number of expeditions sent into the sertão which returned empty-handed, or failed to return at all, there was always the promise of silver, emeralds or other jewels to lure the adventurous beyond the coast.

The one thing that Brazil had in abundance was the indigenous population. Throughout the colony there was a demand for slaves to work the plantations and farms, especially in the early 17th century when Portugal temporarily lost its African possession of Angola.

The men who settled in São Paulo proved themselves expert enslavers. Without official sanction, and certainly not blessed by the Jesuits, these adventurers formed themselves into expeditions which would set out often for years at a time, to capture slaves for the internal market. The indigenous Guaraní who had been organized into reducciones by the Jesuits around the Río Paraguay were the top prize and there developed an intense rivalry between the bandeirantes and the Jesuits. The priests regarded the Paulistas as murderous and inhumane; the slavers felt they had some justification in attacking the missions because they were in Spanish territory and, in the 17th century, the entire western boundary of Brazil was in dispute.

This was one side of the coin. The other was that the bandeirantes were incredibly resourceful, trekking for thousands of kilometres, withstanding great hardships, travelling light, inspired not just by the desire to get rich, but also by a fierce patriotism. To uncover the sertão's riches, they demystified it, trekking into Minas Gerais, Goiás and Mato Grosso looking for precious metals. Through their efforts, the Minas Gerais gold rush began. In the bandeirantes' footsteps came settlers and cattle herders who took over the lands emptied of people. Although the indigenous population were exploited as labour and became a source of income for the Paulistas, they also intermarried with the Europeans, hastening the miscegenation process that became so evident throughout Brazil.

and Tarija) pressed their case for autonomy and, in the face of these apparently irreconcilable positions, the Senate called another nationwide referendum. The mandate of the president was ratified by a 67% majority and the most important opposition departmental governors were also ratified. A subsequent referendum approved the new constitution by a 61% majority, but predictably voters in the eastern states rejected it, perpetuating Bolivia's profound divisions. With this seemingly endless political tug-of-war as a backdrop, the day-to-day concerns of most Bolivians revolved around sudden increases in the cost of basic foods, blamed by the government on business leaders seeking to destabilize the current administration, and blamed by the opposition on government economic mismanagement. In presidential and congressional elections in December 2009, however, a greater unity emerged as Morales increased his majority to 63% of the vote (the first Bolivian president to be democratically reelected) and his MAS party won outright majorities in both houses of the legislature, giving Morales a clear mandate to proceed with his substantial reforms.

Brazil

Imperial Brazil

Dom Pedro the First had the misfortune to be faced by a secession movement in the north, to lose the Banda Oriental (today Uruguay) and to get too involved in his complicated love life. Finally, he abdicated as the result of a military revolt in 1831, leaving his five-year-old son, Dom Pedro the Second, in the hands of a regent, as ruler. On 23 July 1840, the lad, though only 15, was proclaimed of age. Dom Pedro the Second, a strong liberal at heart, promoted education, increased communications, developed agriculture, stamped on corruption and encouraged immigration from Europe. Under his rule the war with the dictator López of Paraguay ended in Brazilian victory. Finally, he declared that he would rather lose his crown than allow slavery to continue, and on 13 May 1888, it was finally abolished by his daughter, Princess Isabel, who was acting as Regent during his temporary absence.

There is little doubt that it was this measure that cost him his throne. Many plantation owners, who had been given no compensation, turned against the Emperor; they were supported by elements in the army and navy, who felt that the Emperor had not given due heed to their interests since the Paraguayan War. On 15 November 1889, the Republic was proclaimed and the Emperor sailed for Europe. Two years later he died in a second-rate hotel in Paris, after steadfastly refusing a pension from the conscience-stricken revolutionaries. At the time of the first centenary of independence in 1922 the imperial family was allowed to return to Brazil, and the body of Dom Pedro was brought back and buried in the cathedral at Petrópolis.

From Republic to dictatorship

The history of the 'Old Republic' (1889-1930), apart from the first 10 years which saw several monarchist rebellions, was comparatively uneventful, a time of expansion and increasing prosperity. Brazil declared war on Germany during both wars and Brazilian troops fought in the Italian campaign in 1944-1945. In 1930 a revolution headed by Getúlio Vargas, Governor of Rio Grande do Sul, who was to become known as 'the Father of the Poor', deposed President Wáshington Luís. Vargas assumed executive power first as provisional president and then as dictator. He was forced to resign in October 1945. In 1946 a liberal republic was restored and the following 18 years saw considerable economic development and social advance.

An increase in government instability and corruption prompted the military to intervene in civil affairs. From March 1964 until March 1985, the military governed Brazil using political repression and torture, yet achieving great economic success (up to 1980). Between 1964 and 1974 average growth was 10% a year, but the divide between rich and poor widened. Labour leaders were oppressed, dissenters were jailed and *favelas* mushroomed. Political reform did not occur until 1980 and free elections were not held until 1989.

Return to democracy

In January 1985 a civilian, Tancredo Neves, representing a broad opposition to the military régime, was elected President by the electoral college introduced under the military's 1967 constitution. He was unable, because of illness, to take office: the vice-president elect, Sr José Sarney, was sworn in as acting President in March 1985, and in April became President on Sr Neves' death. After complete revision by a Constituent Assembly in 1987-1988, Brazil's new constitution of 1988 permitted direct presidential elections in November 1989. These were won by Fernando Collor de Melo, of the small Partido da Reconstrução Nacional, who narrowly defeated Luis Inácio da Silva (Lula), of the Workers Party (PT). Just over half-way through his five-year term, Collor was suspended from office after a landslide congressional vote to impeach him over his involvement in corruption. He avoided impeachment by resigning on 29 December 1992. Vice-president Itamar Franco took over, but had scant success in tackling poverty and inflation until the introduction of an anti-inflation package which introduced the real as the new currency.

The *real* plan and after

The success of the *real* plan was the main reason for its architect, finance minister Fernando Henrique Cardoso, defeating Lula in the presidential elections of October 1994. Throughout 1997 and 1998, the financial crisis in Asia threatened Brazil's currency and economic stability. Cardoso was therefore obliged to introduce policies which, at the cost of slowing down economic growth, would prevent an upsurge in inflation and a devaluation of the currency. Concurrently, social imbalances such as unemployment, crime, prison conditions, land reform and the violence associated with landlessness persisted. These issues notwithstanding, Cardoso again defeated Lula in presidential elections in October 1998. As the new administration battled to enforce greater budgetary discipline, the economy finally succumbed to internal and external pressures in early 1999. Brazil's decision in mid-January to devalue the real by 9% sent shockwaves through world financial markets as it implied that an IMF rescue package of November 1998 had failed. As capital continued to leave the country, the Government was soon forced to let the real float freely. In March 1999 the IMF resumed lending to Brazil, with support from the USA, and as early as May 1999 the economy showed signs of having confounded all the worst expectations.

Lula, fourth time lucky The recession had lowered Cardoso's popularity and thus his influence over his coalition partners. At last the door was open for Lula, who in 2002 won the presidency in the run-off vote against José Serra. Contrary to forecasts that he would lead Brazil down a left-wing path unacceptable to many outside agencies and governments, his first months in power met with approval at home and abroad. Although passionately committed to social reform, Lula did not abandon orthodox economic policies. This pragmatism has been slow to bring the benefits for which poor and dispossessed Brazilians were hoping.

The Workers Party's self-proclaimed uncorruptibility was dealt a severe blow when a number of voting and bribery scandals emerged in 2005. Many heads rolled in revelations of the scope of the *mensalão* (vote-buying) scandal. Lula himself did not escape untainted but in the October 2006 presidential elections he defeated Geraldo Alckmin of the Partido da Social Democracia Brasileira (PSDB). By 2008 Lula was presiding over a booming economy, with strong export and energy sectors, healthy consumer spending and significant investment in infrastructure projects, such as roads and hydroelectric dams. This confidence helped Brazil weather the global credit crunch better than others and President Lula continued his project of consolidating Brazil's ever strengthening position in global markets and on the political stage. Presidential and congressioal elections were to be held in October 2010. The PT's candidate (at press date) was Dilma Rousseff and her main rival was José Serra of the PSDB.

Chile

Independence

In 1810 a group of Chilean patriots, including Bernardo O'Higgins – the illegitimate son of a Sligo-born Viceroy of Peru, Ambrosio O'Higgins, and a Chilean mother – revolted against Spain. This revolt led to seven years of war against the occupying troops of Spain – Lord Cochrane was in charge of the insurrectionist navy – and in 1817 Gen José de San Martín crossed the Andes with an army from Argentina and helped to gain a decisive victory. O'Higgins became the first head of state, but his liberal policies offended the dominant landed aristocracy, leading to his downfall in 1823. A period of anarchy followed, but in 1830 conservative forces led by Diego Portales restored order and introduced the authoritarian constitution of 1833. Under this charter, for almost a century, the country was ruled by a small oligarchy of landowners.

The War of the Pacific

During the 1870s disputes arose with Boliva and Peru over the northern deserts, which were rich in nitrates. Although most of the nitrates lay in Bolivia and Peru, much of the mining was carried out by Anglo-Chilean companies. In the ensuing War of the Pacific (1879-1883), Chile defeated its neighbours, gaining the Bolivian coastal region as well as the Peruvian provinces of Tarapacá and Arica. For the next 40 years it drew great wealth from the nitrate fields. In the south settlers began pushing across the Río Biobío in the 1860s, encouraged by government settlement schemes and helped by technological developments including repeating rifles, telegraph, railways and barbed wire. At the end of the War of the Pacific the large Chilean army was sent to subdue the Mapuches who were confined to ever-diminishing tribal lands. The territory was then settled by immigrants – particularly Germans – and by former peasants who had fought in the north.

The 20th century

The rule of the Right was challenged by the liberal regime of President Arturo Alessandri in 1920. Acute economic distress in 1924, linked to the replacement of Chilean nitrates with artificial fertilizers produced more cheaply in Europe, led to army intervention and some reforms were achieved. The inequalities in Chilean society grew sharper, despite the maintenance of political democracy, and gave rise to powerful socialist and communist parties. President Eduardo Frei's policy of 'revolution in freedom' (1964-1970) was the first concerted attempt at overall radical reform, but it raised hopes it could not satisfy. In 1970 a marxist coalition assumed office under Dr Salvador Allende; the frantic pace of change under his regime polarized the country into Left- and Right-wing camps. Increasing social and economic chaos formed the background for Allende's deposition by the army; he died on 11 September 1973. Chile was then ruled by a military president, Gen Augusto Pinochet Ugarte, and a four-man junta with absolute powers. In its early years particularly, the regime suppressed internal opposition by widely condemned methods. Despite economic prosperity and efforts to make the regime more popular, Pinochet's bid for a further eight years as president after 1989 was rejected by the electorate in a plebiscite in 1988.

Post-Pinochet

As a result, presidential and congressional elections were held in 1989. A Christian Democrat, Patricio Aylwin Azócar was elected President and took office in March 1990 in a peaceful transfer of power. While Aylwin's coalition held the Chamber of Deputies, the Senate majority was controlled by eight Pinochet appointees and Gen Pinochet himself as Army Commander, who could block constitutional reform. The new Congress set about revising many of the military's laws on civil liberties and the economy. In 1991 the National Commission for Truth and Reconciliation published a report with details of those who were killed under the military regime, but opposition by the armed forces prevented mass human rights trials. In December 1993 presidential elections were won by the Christian Democrat Eduardo Frei, son of the earlier president, but in Congress his party failed to achieve the required two-thirds majority to replace heads of the armed forces and end the system of designated senators. Oblivious to public sentiment, the military's position in the senate was strengthened when General Pinochet as former president, took up an ex-officio senate seat. His presence, and therefore parliamentary immunity from prosecution for alleged crimes during his dictatorship, was offensive to parliamentarians who had suffered during his regime.

In October 1998, Pinochet's position came under threat from an unforeseen quarter when a Spanish magistrate filed for his extradition from London, where he was on a private visit, to face charges of torture against Spanish and Chilean citizens between 1973 and 1990. He was detained while the British judiciary deliberated and in March 1999 the Law Lords concluded that Pinochet should stand trial for criminal acts committed after 1988, the year Britain signed the international torture convention. Although Home Secretary Jack Straw authorized the extradition, continuous legal disputes culminated in a health report which claimed that Pinochet was too ill to stand trial. On this evidence the Home Secretary was "minded" to allow

Pinochet to return to Chile, which he did in January 2000. After arriving in Santiago apparently fully fit, Pinochet's health did decline, as did his seemingly untouchable status. Implications of his involvement in the torture and killings of the 1970s and 1980s began to surface and in June 2000 an appeals court stripped Pinochet of his immunity from trial.

Partly as a result of the Pinochet affair, but also because of economic recession, President Frei's standing suffered a sharp decline in 1999. The Concertación elected socialist Ricardo Lagos to be its December 1999 presidential candidate and he beat Joaquín Lavín only by the slimmest of majorities, thus becoming Chile's first socialist president since Salvador Allende. Despite positive economic results during his term, the main focus remained the legacy of Pinochet, whose position and image continued to be eroded. Admissions by former military personnel that, under orders from above, they had committed human rights abuses in the 1970s and 1980s, a protracted process of indictments and investigations ensured that Pinochet's past remained in the spotlight up to and even beyond his death on 10 December 2006.

In the December 2005 presidential election, Michelle Bachelet, who had survived torture while a political prisoner during the Pinochet regime, was elected and the Concertación coalition won majorities in both houses of congress. Concertación's supremacy could not prevent an upsurge in unrest, starting in 2006 with strikes by secondary school students, copper workers and, in 2008, government workers demanding better pay, and demonstrations against potentially environmentally damaging mining and energy projects. Bachelet's response to these disturbances and the chaotic introduction of the new Transantiago transport system did not initially restore confidence and her popularity ratings fell. In early 2009 ex-president Eduardo Frei was chosen as Concertación's candidate for the December 2009 elections, but his main opponent, the centre-right Sebastián Piñera, ended the coalition's hold on power. One of Piñera's first challenges was to deal with reconstruction after the massive earthquake of February 2010.

Colombia

Colombia's divided society

After the collapse of Simón Bolívar's Republic of Gran Colombia in 1829/30, what is now known as Colombia was called Nueva Granada until 1863. Almost from its inception the new country became the scene of strife between the centralizing pro-clerical Conservatives and the federalizing anti-clerical Liberals. From 1849 the Liberals were dominant during the next 30 years of insurrections and civil wars. In 1885 the Conservatives imposed a highly centralized constitution, unmodified for over 100 years. A Liberal revolt in 1899 turned into civil war, 'the War of the Thousand Days'. The Liberals were finally defeated in 1902 after 100,000 people had died. It was in 1903 that Panama declared its independence from Colombia, following US pressure.

After 40 years of comparative peace, the strife between Conservatives and Liberals was reignited in a little-publicized but dreadfully bloody civil war known as *La Violencia* from 1948 to 1957 (some 300,000 people were killed). This was ended by a unique political truce, decided by plebiscite in 1957 under which the two political parties supported a single presidential candidate, divided all political offices equally between them, and thus maintained political stability for 16 years. The agreement was ended in 1978. Belisario Betancur, the Conservative president from 1982-1986, offered a general amnesty to guerrilla movements in an attempt to end violence in the country. Following an initial acceptance of the offer, only one of the four main guerrilla groups, the FARC, upheld the truce in 1985-1987. In May 1986, when the Liberal candidate, Sr Virgilio Barco, won the presidential elections, FARC's newly formed political party, the Unión Patriótica (UP), won 10 seats in congress; the Liberal party took the majority. Right-wing groups refused to accept the UP and by the beginning of 1990, 1,040 party members had been killed in five years. During the campaign for the 1990 presidential both the Liberal Party and the UP presidential candidates, Luis Carlos Galán and Bernardo Jaramillo, were assassinated.

The narcotics trade

In Medellín and Cali, two cartels transformed Colombia's drugs industry into a major force in worldwide business and crime. Their methods were very different: Medellín being ostentatious and violent, Cali much more low-key. In 1986, President Barco instigated an international effort to bring them to justice, but opposition to extradition of suspects to the USA stymied progress. Pablo Escobar, the alleged leader of the Medillín drugs cartel, who had surrendered under secret terms in 1991, escaped from custody in July 1992. Despite a multi-million dollar reward offered for his recapture and renewed conditional offers of surrender, he remained at large until he was killed in December 1993.

Modern Colombia

Having won the presidential elections held on 27 May, 1990, César Gaviria Trujillo (Liberal), who took up the candidacy of the murdered Luis Carlos Galán, appointed a coalition government made up of Liberals from rival factions, Conservatives and the M-19 (Movimiento 19 de Abril).

The Gaviria government was unable to stem violence, whether perpetrated by drug traffickers, guerrillas or common criminals. Not surprisingly, this was one of the issues in the 1994 election campaign, in which Ernesto Samper (Liberal) defeated Andrés Pastrana (Conservative). The main thrust of Samper's programme was that Colombia's current economic strength should provide resources to tackle the social deprivation which causes drug use and insurgency. Most impetus was lost during 1995-1997, however, in the wake of revelations that Samper's election campaign had received about US$6 million from the Cali cartel. The debate over Samper's awareness of the funding lasted until June 1996, almost overshadowing the capture or surrender of most of the leading Cali drug lords.

In 1998, congressional and presidential elections were relatively peaceful and a welcome boost to confidence was given when the US withdrew its 'decertification' restrictions (in effect recognizing that Colombia was making progress against drug-trafficking, thus allowing US aid in). The new president, Andrés Pastrana, immediately devoted his efforts to bringing the guerrillas to the negotiating table. A stop-go process began with FARC in late 1998 and the insurgents were conceded a large demilitarized zone, based on San Vicente de Caguán in Caquetá. Not everyone was in favour of Pastrana's approach, especially since FARC violence and extortion did not cease. ELN, meanwhile, angry at being excluded from talks, stepped up its campaign, demanding similar treatment. Paramilitary groups, too, showed no signs of ending their activities. Pastrana also sought international aid for his Plan Colombia, aimed at combatting the drugs trade. The US$1.6 billion package, approved by the US Congress in May 2000, was to cover mainly military and anti-narcotics equipment, with the remainder destined for crop substitution and other sustainable agriculture projects. Attempts to reduce the net area under drugs cultivation were not successful and, with both left-wing guerrillas and right-wing paramilitaries involved in the narcotics trade, the two fronts of fighting terrorism and drugs became increasingly entangled.

Negotiations with the guerrilla groups continued unsuccessfully into 2002, but the terror campaigns of FARC and ELN increased the government's frustration and, with an eye on the approaching May 2002 elections, Pastrana abandoned his peace initative and sent in the Army. Strategic points in the demilitarized zone were quickly taken but the guerrillas melted away into the forests and countryside and the disruption and kidnapping continued.

Uribe vs FARC The frontrunners for the 2002 presidential elections were both Liberals: Horacio Serpa was the official party candidate, while Alvaro Uribe Vélez left the Liberals to run under his own movement, Colombia First. The main thrust of Uribe's campaign was that the time had come to stop pandering to the left-wing guerrillas and to use a firm hand to restore order and security. This struck a chord with many Colombians, not just those who supported Pastrana's later hard line, but also the illegal, right-wing paramilitary groups who are waging their own war against FARC and ELN. Consequently, Uribe won with over 50% of the vote in the first round. Despite (or maybe because of) Uribe's anti-guerrilla policies, and despite a decline in support for insurgents following numerous atrocities, violence continued, prompting a tough new anti-terrorism law. At the same time, and in the face of criticism, Uribe began peace talks with the AUC (United Self Defence Forces of Colombia), the paramilitary group implacably opposed to FARC and ELN and accused of some of the worst human rights abuses. In mid-2004, the AUC eventually agreed to disarm. Uribe then launched Plan Patriota, a huge military offensive against FARC in southern Colombia. The strength of FARC's response to the Plan continued right up to national elections in 2006, but, having altered the constitution to permit a second presidential term, Uribe won the May 2006 elections with a 62% majority. In March 2006 his supporters won most seats in the senate and chamber of deputies.

In 2007, revelations about the complicity between elected politicians and paramilitary groups led to the arrest of 20 allies of President Uribe, including congressmen and business leaders. Whether the President himself knew of these dealings was not revealed. 2006's election results not only demonstrated that public support for the hard-line approach had not dwindled, but also reassured foreign investors who were keen to support Colombia and its economy. Nevertheless, with many Colombians displaced, bereft of land and affected by violence, the country's internal conflict seemed as intractable as ever until Uribe invited President Chávez of Venezuela to mediate with FARC over the release of hostages. After several months of difficult negotiations, six hostages were finally set free in early 2008. Chávez's involvement was not problem-free. Uribe dismissed him from the process at one point and when, in March 2008, the Colombian army attacked a FARC base in Ecuador, killing among others the group's head of communications, Raúl Reyes, captured computers were alleged to prove that Venezuela was funding FARC. The raid caused fierce denunciations of Colombia by Venezuela and Ecuador, but a crisis was averted at a Latin American summit in the Dominican Republic. FARC then suffered further setbacks in March when commander Iván Ríos was murdered by his own head of security and, of deeper significance, its long-term leader Manuel Marulanda died of a heart attack. Pressure, including from Chávez, turned on FARC and its new head, Alfonso Cano, to release over 700 hostages. FARC's position was weakened even more in July 2008 when Senator Ingrid Betancourt, who had been kidnapped in 2002, was dramatically rescued with 14 other hostages, three of them US citizens. Rather than capitulate, FARC worked to regain lost ground, continuing violent actions and announcing in December 2009 a merger with ELN. Uribe meanwhile remained on the offensive, but was unable to secure a constitutional amendment to stand for a third term in May 2010 elections. Should any of his allies win that poll, his policies would more than likely continue.

Ecuador

After independence

Ecuador decided on complete independence from the Gran Colombia confederation in August 1830, under the presidency of Juan Flores.The country's 19th century history was a continuous struggle between pro-Church conservatives and anti-Church (but nonetheless devoutly Catholic) liberals. There were also long periods of military rule from 1895, when the liberal Gen Eloy Alfaro took power. During the late 1940s and the 1950s there was a prolonged period of prosperity (through bananas, largely) and constitutional rule, but the more typical pattern of alternating civilian and military governments was resumed in the 1960s and 1970s. Apart from the liberal- conservative struggles, there has been long-lasting rivalry between Quito and the Sierra on one hand and Guayaquil and the Costa on the other.

Return to democracy

Following seven years of military rule, the first presidential elections under a new constitution were held in 1979. The ensuing decades of democracy saw an oscillation of power between parties of the centre-right and centre-left. Governments of both political tendencies towed the international economic line and attempted to introduce neoliberal reforms. These measures were opposed by the country's labour organizations and by the indigenous movement, which gained considerable political power. Against a backdrop of this tug-of-war, disenchantment with the political process grew apace with bureaucratic corruption and the nation's economic woes. In 1996 the frustrated electorate swept a flamboyant populist named Abdalá Bucaram to power. His erratic administration lasted less than six months.

A succession of presidents Following an interim government and the drafting of the country's 18th constitution, Ecuador elected Jamil Mahuad, a former mayor of Quito, to the presidency in 1998. Mahuad began his term by signing a peace treaty to end the decades-old and very emotional border dispute with Peru. This early success was his last, as a series of fraudulent bank failures sent the country into an economic and political tailspin. A freeze on bank accounts failed to stop landslide devaluation of the Sucre (Ecuador's currency since 1883) and Mahuad decreed the adoption of the US Dollar in a desperate bid for stability. Less than a month later, on 21 January 2000, he was forced out of office by Ecuador's indigenous people and disgruntled members of the armed forces. The first overt military coup in South America in over two decades, it lasted barely three hours before power was handed to vice-president Gustavo Noboa. Significantly, all of the foregoing years of social unrest were never accompanied by serious bloodshed.

Noboa, a political outsider and academic, stepped into Mahuad's shoes with remarkable aplomb. With assistance from the USA and the International Monetary Fund, his government managed to flesh out and implement the dollarization scheme, thus achieving a measure of economic stability at the cost of deepening poverty. Social unrest diminished, and Ecuadoreans instead attempted to bring about change through the ballot box. In November 2002, Colonel Lucio Gutiérrez, leader of the January 2000 *coup*, was elected president by a comfortable majority. He had run on a populist platform in alliance with the indigenous movement and labour unions, but began to change his stripes soon after taking office. His administration was lacklustre and only constantly shifting allegiances and high petroleum revenues managed to keep him in power. In late 2004, the dismissal of all the supreme court judges by unconstitutional means – and tear gas – drew local and international criticism. Popular opposition in Quito grew, with peaceful, well-attended protests. The president's response, using heavy-handed police repression, led to mass demonstrations which swept Gutiérrez from office in April 2005. Vice-president Alfredo Palacio replaced him, but lacking a political party base, he found government no easy ride, having to face persistent strikes, especially in the Amazon region where protestors blocked oil pipelines to demand roads and other infrastructure projects promised by Gutiérrez. General elections, brought forward to November 2006, were won by Rafael Correa, leader of the Alianza País (AP) movement. He immediately called a national referendum to convene a constituent assembly to redraw the constitution and, the new president hoped, shift the nation's foundations toward the political left, echoing processes already taking place in Venezuela and Bolivia. 80% of voters approved Correa's plans when the referendum was held in April 2007. The Constituent Assembly was elected in September 2007, with an ample majority of pro-government members. The assembly started working in November and a referendum gave the new constitution popular approval in September 2008. With re-election of the president now permitted, new elections were held in April 2009 and Correa won comfortably.

Paraguay

Independence and dictatorship

The disturbances in Buenos Aires in 1810-16, which led to independence from Spain, enabled Creole leaders in Asunción to throw off the rule of Buenos Aires as well as Madrid. The new republic was, however, subject to pressure from both Argentina, which blocked Paraguayan trade on the Río de la Plata, and Brazil. Following independence Paraguay was ruled by a series of dictators, the first of whom, Dr Gaspar Rodríguez de Francia (1814-1840), known as 'El Supremo', imposed a policy of isolation and self-sufficiency. The opening of the Río de la Plata after the fall of the Argentine dictator Rosas enabled de Francia's successor, Carlos Antonio López (1840-1862) to import modern technology: in 1856 a railway line between Asunción and Villarrica was begun; an iron foundry and telegraph system were also developed. Carlos López was succeeded by his son, Francisco Solano López (López II), who saw himself as the Napoleon of South America. Believing Paraguay to be threatened by Brazil and Argentina, Solano López declared war on Brazil in 1865. When Argentina refused permission to send troops through Misiones to attack Brazil, López declared war on Argentina. With Uruguay supporting Brazil and Argentina, the ensuing War of the Triple Alliance was disastrous for the Paraguayan forces, who held on against overwhelming odds until the death of López at the Battle of Cerro Corá on 1 March 1870. Of a pre-war population of 400,000, only 220,000 survived the war, 28,000 of them males, mostly either very young or very old. In the peace settlement Paraguay lost territory to Brazil and Argentina, although rivalry between these neighbours prevented a worse fate.

After the war, Paraguay experienced political instability as civilian factions competed for power, often appealing to the army officers for support. Although there were few policy differences between the two political parties (the National Republican Association, known as Colorados from its red banner, and the Liberal party, who adopted the colour blue), rivalry was intense. Elections were held regularly, but whichever party was in government invariably intervened to fix the result and the opposition rarely participated.

The Chaco War

While Paraguayan leaders were absorbed with domestic disputes, Bolivia began occupying disputed parts of the Chaco in an attempt to gain access to the sea via the Río Paraguay. Although Bolivian moves started in the late 19th century, the dispute was given new intensity by the discovery of oil in the 1920s. In the four-year Chaco War (1932-1935) 56,000 Bolivians and 36,000 Paraguayans were killed. Despite general expectations, outnumbered Paraguayan troops under Mariscal José Félix Estigarribia pushed the Bolivian army out of most of the Chaco.

Victory in war only increased dissatisfaction in the army with the policies of pre-war governments. In February 1936 nationalist officers seized power and appointed the war hero, Colonel Rafael Franco as President. Although Franco was overthrown in a counter-coup in 1937, the so-called 'February Revolution' began major changes in Paraguay including the first serious attempt at land reform and legal recognition of the small labour movement. Between 1939 and 1954 Paraguayan politics were even more turbulent, as rival civilian factions and army officers vied for power. In 1946 civil war shook the country as army units based in Concepción fought to overthrow President Morínigo.

The Stroessner years

A military coup in May 1954 led to General Alfredo Stroessner becoming President. Stroessner retained power for 34 years, the most durable dictator in Paraguayan history and one of the longest in power in Latin America. His rule was based on control over the army and the Colorado party, both of which were purged of opponents. While a network of spies informed on dissidents, party membership was made compulsory for most official posts including teachers and doctors. In fraudulent elections Stroessner was re-elected eight times. Paraguay, and in particular the outlaw town of Puerto Presidente Stroessner (now Ciudad del Este), became a centre for smuggling, gambling and drug-running, much of it controlled by Stroessner's supporters. Meanwhile the government spent large amounts of money on transportation and infrastructure projects, including the giant hydroelectric dam at Itaipú. Although these projects brought employment, the completion of Itaipú in 1982 coincided with recession in Brazil and

Argentina on whose economies Paraguay was heavily dependent. Meanwhile rivalry intensified within the regime over the succession, with Stroessner favouring his son, Gustavo. Opposition focussed around General Andrés Rodríguez, who was married to Stroessner's daughter. When Stroessner tried to force Rodríguez to retire, troops loyal to Rodríguez overthrew the 75-year old Stroessner, who left to live in Brazil where he died in exile in 2006.

Liberalization

Rodríguez, who became provisional president, easily won multi-party elections in May 1989. The commitment to greater democracy permitted opponents who had previously boycotted, or been banned from elections, to gain an unprecedented number of seats in the legislative elections of the same date. Despite considerable scepticism over General Rodríguez's intentions, political liberalization became a reality. The presidential and congressional elections that he promised were held on 9 May 1993. The presidency was won by Juan Carlos Wasmosy of the Colorado Party and Domingo Laíno of the Authentic Radical Liberal Party came second.

The government's commitment to market reforms, privatization and economic integration with Argentina and Brazil within Mercosur inspired protests from all quarters. 1994 saw the first general strike in 35 years. There were also demands for land reform and increased social services. A worsening of relations between the military and the legislature led to a critical few days in April 1996. Army commander General Lino Oviedo was dismissed for threatening a coup; Wasmosy offered him the defence ministry but then withdrew the offer after massive public protest. Oviedo was later arrested on charges of insurrection, but to the dismay of the Colorado leadership, he was chosen as the party's candidate for the May 1998 presidential elections. This intensified the feud between Oviedo and Wasmosy, who eventually succeeded in having Oviedo jailed by a military tribunal for 10 years for the 1996 coup attempt. A compromise ticket of Raúl Cubas Grau (Oviedo's former running mate) and Luis María Argaña (Colorado party president and opponent of Wasmosy) won the election. Within a week of taking office in August 1998, Cubas released Oviedo from prison, despite a Supreme Court ruling that Oviedo should serve out his sentence. Matters came to a head when Vice President Argaña was shot in March 1999, just before the Senate was to vote on impeachment of Cubas. Intense diplomatic efforts, led by Paraguay's Mercosur partners, resulted in Cubas' resignation on 29 March. He was replaced by Luis González Macchi, the president of Congress. Cubas went into exile in Brazil, and Oviedo in Argentina, from where he escaped in December 1999. His military supporters staged an unsuccessful coup in May 2000 and the following month Oviedo was arrested in Brazil. The González Macchi administration, meanwhile, was facing economic recession, strikes and social discontent. The economic downturn and its repercussions worsened through 2002 as a result of Argentina's financial crisis. In February 2003, González Macchi himself was discredited by allegations of the misuse of state funds, fraud and the torture of leftwing militants (he was imprisoned for illegal enrichment in 2006). Nevertheless, in subsequent elections in April 2003, voters backed the Colorado Party and its candidate, Nicanor Duarte Frutos.

The end of Colorado rule That nothing really changed under Duarte, certainly no improvement in the living conditions of the poor majority despite record incomes from soya exports, was one of the main causes of the demise of the Colorado presidency. In 2006, Fernando Lugo, the former bishop of San Pedro diocese, left the priesthood to enter politics and soon emerged as an independent, left-leaning leader of those seeking change. He contested the April 2008 elections as a member of the coalition Patriotic Alliance for Change party, with land reform and renegotiation of the treaty with Brazil defining sales of electricity from Itaipú as principal policies. Lugo easily defeated Colorado candidate Blanca Ovelar and Lino Oviedo (who had been released from prison in 2007), but had no political party to back him in congress. The Colorado party had won most seats in both houses. Lugo's inauguration was the first in Paraguay's history in which a ruling party peacefully ceded power to an elected president from an opposition party. Early in

2009, political developments were overshadowed by claims that Lugo had fathered sons with three different women. He did acknowledge one, but the allegations lost him much prestige. By 2010 the activities of a small insurgent group, **Ejército del Pueblo Paraguayo** (EPP), forced Lugo to suspend constitutional rights in parts of the country. The left-wing EPP was involved mostly in kidnapping wealthy farmers, but also occasional acts of violence, and its presence challenged Lugo's lacklustre performance over modernisation of the security and justice systems.

Peru

After independence

Important events following the ejection of the Spaniards were a temporary confederation between Peru and Bolivia in the 1830s; the Peruvian-Spanish War (1866); and the War of the Pacific (1879-1883), in which Peru and Bolivia were defeated by Chile and Peru lost its southern territory. The 19th and early 20th centuries were dominated by the traditional elites, with landowners holding great power over their workers. Political parties were slow to develop until the 1920s, when socialist thinkers Juan Carlos Mariátegui and Víctor Raúl Haya de la Torre began to call for change. Haya de la Torre formed the Alianza Popular Revolucionaria Americana (APRA), but in the 1930s and 40s he and his party were under threat from the military and the elilte.

To the Shining Path

A reformist military Junta took over control of the country in October 1968. Under its first leader, Gen Juan Velasco Alvarado, the Junta instituted a series of measures to raise the personal status and standard of living of the workers and the rural Indians, by land reform, worker participation in industrial management and ownership, and nationalization of basic industries, exhibiting an ideology perhaps best described as 'military socialism'. In view of his failing health Gen Velasco was replaced in 1975 by Gen Francisco Morales Bermúdez and policy (because of a mounting economic crisis and the consequent need to seek financial aid from abroad) swung to the Right. Presidential and congressional elections were held on 18 May 1980, and Fernando Belaúnde Terry was elected President for the second time. His term was marked by growing economic problems and the appearance of the Maoist terrorist movement Sendero Luminoso (Shining Path).

Initially conceived in the University of Ayacucho, the movement gained most support for its goal of overthrowing the whole system of Lima-based government from highland Indians and migrants to urban shanty towns. The activities of Sendero Luminoso and another terrorist group, Túpac Amaru (MRTA), frequently disrupted transport and electricity supplies, although their strategies had to be reconsidered after the arrest of both their leaders in 1992. Víctor Polay of MRTA was arrested in June and Abimael Guzmán of Sendero Luminoso was captured in September; he was sentenced to life imprisonment (although the sentence had to be reviewed in 2003 under legal reforms). Although Sendero did not capitulate, many of its members in 1994-1995 took advantage of the Law of Repentance, which guaranteed lighter sentences in return for surrender, and freedom in exchange for valuable information. Meanwhile, Túpac Amaru was thought to have ceased operations (see below).

The Fujimori years

The April 1985 elections were won by the APRA party leader Alán García Pérez. During his populist, left-wing presidency disastrous economic policies caused increasing poverty and civil instability. In presidential elections held over two rounds in 1990, Alberto Fujimori of the Cambio 90 movement defeated the novelist Mario Vargas Llosa, who belonged to the Fredemo (Democratic Front) coalition. Fujimori, without an established political network behind him, failed to win a majority in either the senate or the lower house. Lack of congressional support was one of the reasons behind the dissolution of congress and the suspension of the constitution on 5 April

1992. With massive popular support, President Fujimori declared that he needed a freer hand to introduce free-market reforms, combat terrorism and drug trafficking, and root out corruption.

Elections to a new, 80-member Democratic Constituent Congress (CCD) in November 1992 and municipal elections in February 1993 showed that voters still had scant regard for mainstream political groups. A new constitution drawn up by the CCD was approved by a narrow majority of the electorate in October 1993. Among the new articles were the immediate re-election of the president (previously prohibited for one presidential term) and, as expected, Fujimori stood for re-election on 9 April 1995. He beat his independent opponent, the former UN General Secretary, Javier Pérez de Cuéllar, by a resounding margin. The coalition that supported him also won a majority in Congress.

The government's success in most economic areas did not accelerate the distribution of foreign funds for social projects. Furthermore, rising unemployment and the austerity imposed by economic policy continued to cause hardship for many. Dramatic events on 17 December 1996 thrust several of these issues into sharper focus. 14 Túpac Amaru terrorist infiltrated a reception at the Japanese Embassy in Lima, taking 490 hostages and demanding the release of their imprisoned colleagues and new measures to raise living standards. Most of the hostages were released and negotiations were pursued during a stalemate that lasted until 22 April 1997. The president took sole responsibility for the successful, but risky assault which freed all the hostages (one died of heart failure) and killed all the terrorists. By not yielding to Túpac Amaru, Fujimori regained much popularity. But this masked the fact that no concrete steps had been taken to ease poverty. It also deflected attention from Fujimori's plans to stand for a third term following his unpopular manipulation of the law to persuade Congress that the new constitution did not apply to his first period in office. Until the last month of campaigning for the 2000 presidential elections, Fujimori had a clear lead over his main rivals. His opponents insisted that Fujimori should not stand and local and international observers voiced increasing concern over the state domination of the media. Meanwhile, the popularity of Alejandro Toledo, a centrist and former World Bank official of humble origins, surged to such an extent that he and Fujimori were neck-and neck in the first poll. Toledo and his supporters claimed that Fujimori's slim majority was the result of fraud, a view echoed in the pressure put on the president, by the US government among others, to allow a second ballot. The run-off election, on 28 May 2000, was also contentious since foreign observers, including the Organization of American States (OAS), said the electoral system was unprepared and flawed, proposing a postponement. The authorities refused to delay. Toledo boycotted the election and Fujimori was returned unopposed, but with minimal approval. Having won, he proposed to "strengthen democracy".

This pledge proved to be worthless following the airing of a secretly shot video on 14 September 2000 of Fujimori's close aide and head of the National Intelligence Service (SIN), Vladimiro Montesinos, handing US$15,000 to a congressman, Alberto Kouri, to persuade him to switch allegiances to Fujimori's coalition. Fujimori's demise was swift. His initial reaction was to close down SIN and announce new elections, eventually set for 8 April 2001, at which he would not stand. Montesinos, denied asylum in Panama, was hunted down in Peru, Fujimori personally taking charge of the search. While Montesinos evaded capture, investigators discovered that hundreds of senior figures were under his sway and that he held millions of dollars in Swiss, Cayman Islands and other bank accounts. As the search continued, Fujimori, on an official visit to Japan, sent congress an email announcing his resignation. Congress rejected this, firing him on charges of being "morally unfit" to govern. An interim president, Valentín Paniagua, was sworn in, with ex-UN Secretary General Javier Pérez de Cuéllar as Prime Minister, and the government set about uncovering the depth of corruption associated with Montesinos and Fujimori. From 2002 onwards, Montesinos was involved in a series trials and was convicted of a number of crimes. In 2004, prosecutors also sought to charge exiled Fujimori with authorizing deaths squads at Barrios Altos (1991) and La Cantuta (1992) in which 25 people died. This followed the Truth and Reconciliation Committee's report (2003) into the civil war of the 1980s-1990s, which stated that over 69,000 Peruvians had been killed. Declaring from exile in Japan that he would be exonerated and stand for the presidency in 2006, Fujimori flew to Chile in November 2005, but the Chilean authorities jailed him for seven months and then held him on parole until an extradition request was finally approved in September 2007. In December that year the first of several trials began, Fujimori being charged with, but strenuously denying, the Barrios Altos and La Cantuta murders, kidnapping and corruption. He was found guilty of human rights abuses in 2009 and sentenced to 25 years in prison. As further convictions followed, he vowed to appeal and support for him was likely to continue as his daughter, Keiko, planned to stand for the presidency in 2011.

After Fujimori

In the run-up to the 2001 presidential ballot, the front-runner was Alejandro Toledo, with ex-President Alan García as his main opponent. After winning a run-off vote, Toledo pledged to heal the wounds that had opened in Peru since his first electoral battle with the disgraced Fujimori, but his presidency was marked by slow progress on both the political and economic fronts. With the poverty levels still high, few jobs created and a variety of scandals, Toledo's popularity plummeted. Major confrontations and damaging strikes ensued, and charges of corruption were laid at his own door.

The April 2006 elections were contested by Alán García, the conservative Lourdes Flores and Ollanta Humala, a former military officer and unsuccessful coup leader who claimed support from Venezuela's Hugo Chávez and Evo Morales of Bolivia. García and Humala won through to the second round, which García won, in part because many were suspicious of Chávez's interference in Peruvian affairs. García was anxious to overcome his past record as president and pledged to rein in public spending and not squander the benefits of an economy growing consistently since 2005. García's free-market policies were judged to have failed to address the inequality of income distribution and major demonstrations were held through 2007 and 2008. Even worse events occurred in mid-2009 when indigenous protestors from near Bagua Grande (Amazonas) clashed with police over oil-drilling rights on their land. Many feared that Peru's mineral exploration policies would put areas of the Peuvian Amazon under threat of deforestation and the fact that this protest led to over 50 deaths and claims of human rights abuse highlighted the extreme sensitivity of the issue.

Uruguay

Struggle for independence

In 1808 Montevideo declared its independence from Buenos Aires. In 1811, the Brazilians attacked from the north, but the local patriot, José Gervasio Artigas, rose in arms against them. In the early stages he had some of the Argentine provinces for allies, but soon declared the independence of Uruguay from both Brazil and Argentina. Buenos Aires invaded again in 1812 and was able to enter Montevideo in June 1814. In January the following year the Orientales (Uruguayans) defeated the Argentines at Guayabos and regained Montevideo. The Portuguese then occupied all territory south of the Río Negro except Montevideo and Colonia. The struggle continued from 1814 to 1820, but Artigas had to flee to Paraguay when Brazil took Montevideo in 1820. In 1825 General Juan Lavalleja, at the head of 33 patriots (the Treinta y Tres Orientales), crossed the river and returned to Uruguay, with Argentine aid, to harass the invaders. After the defeat of the Brazilians at Ituzaingó on 20 February 1827, Britain intervened, both Argentina and Brazil relinquished their claims on the country, and independence was finally achieved in 1828.

19th-century upheavals

The early history of the republic was marked by a civil war (known as the Guerra Grande) which began as a conflict between two rival leaders, José Fructuoso Rivera with his Colorados and

Manuel Oribe with his Blancos; these are still two of the three main parties today. Oribe was helped by the Argentine dictator, Juan Manuel de Rosas, but was overthrown in 1838. Blanco forces, backed by Rosas, beseiged Montevideo between 1843 and 1851. Although Rosas fell from power in 1852, the contest between Colorados and Blancos continued. A Colorado, General Venancio Flores, helped by Argentina, became president and, in 1865, Uruguay was dragged into the war of the Triple Alliance against the Paraguayan dictator, López. Flores was assassinated in 1868 three days after his term as president ended.

Batlle y Ordoñez

The country, wracked by civil war, dictatorship and intrigue, only emerged from its long political turmoil in 1903, when another Colorado, a great but controversial man, José Batlle y Ordóñez was elected president. During Batlle y Ordóñez' two terms as president, 1903-1907 and 1911-1915, Uruguay became within a short space of time the only 'welfare state' in Latin America. Its workers' charter provides free medical service, old age and service pensions and unemployment pay. Education is free and compulsory, capital punishment abolished, and the church disestablished.

Guerrillas and military rule

As the country's former prosperity has ebbed away since the 1960s, the welfare state has become increasingly fictitious. The military promised to reduce bureaucracy and spend more on the poor and development after the turmoil of 1968-1973, the period in which the Tupamaros urban guerrilla movement was most active. In practice the military, which effectively wiped out the Tupamaros by 1972, expanded state spending by raising military and security programmes. Real wages fell to less than half their 1968 level and only the very wealthy benefited from the military regime's attempted neo-liberal economic policies. Less than 10% of the unemployed received social security payments. Montevideo began to sprout shanty towns, once unheard of in this corner of the hemisphere. Nevertheless, the country's middle class remains very large, if impoverished, and the return to democracy in 1985 raised hopes that the deterioration in the social structure would be halted. Almost 10% of the population emigrated for economic or political reasons during the 1960s and 1970s: the unemployed continue to leave, but the political and artistic exiles have returned.

Allying himself with the Armed Forces in 1973, the elected president, Juan M Bordaberry, dissolved Congress and stayed on to rule as the military's figurehead until 1976. Scheduled elections were cancelled in that year, and a further wave of political and trade union repression instituted. Unable to convince the population to vote for a new authoritarian constitution in 1980, the military became increasingly anxious to hand back power to conservative politicians.

Return to democracy

In August 1984 agreement was reached finally on the legalization of most of the banned leftist parties and elections were held in November. Under the moderate government of Julio María Sanguinetti (of the Colorado party) the process of national reconstruction and political reconciliation began with a widespread political amnesty. The moderate conservative Partido Nacional (Blancos) won November 1989 presidential and congressional elections and Luis Alberto Lacalle became president. There was considerable opposition to plans for wage restraint, spending cuts, social reforms and privatization. As a result, his Blanco Party lost the November 1994 elections: Colorado ex-president Sanguinetti was again victorious over the Blancos and the Frente Amplio, a broad left front. Each party won about a third of the seats in Congress. Soon after taking office in March 1995, President Sanguinetti managed to forge an alliance with the Blancos to introduce economic restructuring and steps towards implementing much needed social security reforms. While the coalition worked together to reduce the influence of the public sector, the Frente Amplio gained support for its aim of maintaining the welfare state. In December 1996 a referendum approved constitutional reforms and the first elections under a new system (end-1999) were won by Jorge Batlle of the Colorados, who narrowly defeated Tabaré Vázquez of the Frente Amplio, the party with the largest number of seats in congress.

After his predecessor had implemented essential reforms of the social security system, Batlle planned to bring new impetus to the economy through diversification away from wool and beef and opening new export markets. Unfortunately, the recession that began in 1999 persisted, exacerbated by severe drought affecting domestic agriculture. Argentina's economic meltdown in 2001 ended any hope of improvement. In 2002 gdp fell by 20%, according to some estimates, unemployment stood at 20% of the workforce and the banking sector was in crisis. Financial collapse was averted in August 2002 only through an emergency loan of US$1.5 billion from the US. In this climate the ruling Colorado party lost to the Frente Amplio and its presidential candidate, Tabaré Vázquez, in the 31 October 2004 elections. Vázquez made his immediate priority the alleviation of poverty and this aim was bolstered by a strong economy, fuelled mainly by increased exports. High levels of investment in agro-industry, mining, communications and tourism helped to maintain economic growth, dampening the effects of the 2008 global economic crisis. Presidential and legislative elections were held in October 2009. The contenders were former president Lacalle of the Partido Nacional and José (Pepe) Mujica Cordano, once a Tupamaro guerrilla, now member of the Movimiento de Participación Popular. He beat his fellow Frente Amplio colleague, Danilo Astori, to the candidacy and won the elections with a 53% majority, thus continuing the leftward trend in government in South America. He vowed to continue many of Vázquez' policies.

Venezuela

After Independence

Despite being at the heart of Simón Bolívar's cherished Gran Colombia (together with Ecuador, Colombia and Panama), Venezuela under General Páez became an independent nation in 1830, before Bolívar's death. Páez was either president, or the power behind the presidency from 1831 to 1848, a time of stability and economic progress. In the second half of the 19th century, though, the rise of the Liberal Party in opposition to the ruling Conservatives led to conflicts and social upheaval. In 1870 a Liberal politician-general, Antonio Guzmán Blanco, came to power. Even though his term was peaceful, it marked the entry of the army into Venezuelan politics, a role which it did not relinquish for almost a century.

20th century

In the first half of the century presidents of note were Juan Vicente Gómez (1909-1935), a brutal but efficient dictator, and Isaías Medina Angarita, who introduced the oil laws. There was much material progress under the six-year dictatorship of Gen Marcos Pérez Jiménez (1952-1958), but his Gómez-like methods led to his overthrow in January 1958. A stable democracy has been created since, with presidential elections every five years. Carlos Andrés Pérez of the centre-left Democratic Action party (AD) took office in 1974, presiding over a period of rapid development following the first great oil-price rise, and was succeeded in 1979 by Luis Herrera Campins of the Christian Democratic party, Copei. Jaime Lusinchi of Democratic Action was elected president in 1983, to be followed by Carlos Andrés Pérez, who began his second term in 1989.

1990s: instability and economic crisis

Pérez' second term was marked by protests against economic adjustment and growing levels of poverty. In 1992 there were two unsuccessful coup attempts by military officers, including Colonel Hugo Chávez Frías, who became president by legitimate means in 1999. Among reforms designed to root out corruption, the Supreme Court and Central Bank were given greater independence. Both bodies were instrumental in the decision that Pérez himself be tried on corruption charges in 1993. The president was suspended from office, arrested and, after two years of house arrest, was found guilty in May 1996. An interim president, Senator Ramón José Velázquez, took office until the presidential elections of December 1993, in which Rafael Caldera, standing as an independent, was re-elected to office (as a member of Copei, he was president 1969-1974). Many of his aims, such as improvement in social conditions, tax reform and the control of inflation, had to be postponed, even reversed, in favour of solving an economic and financial crisis which began in 1994. This helped him to conclude an agreement with the IMF, but caused public protest at declining salaries and deteriorating public services.

Chávez' Bolivarian revolution

Presidential elections in December 1998 were won by Hugo Chávez, by an overwhelming majority. On taking office in February 1999, Chávez called for a complete overhaul of Venezuela's political system in order to root out corruption and inefficiency. He obtained special powers from Congress to reduce the budget deficit and diversify the economy away from oil. These were first steps towards his aim of eradicating poverty and restoring real incomes, which had fallen by two thirds in 15 years. He set up a constituent assembly which drew up a new constitution and 70% of the electorate approved it in a plebiscite in December 1999. New elections, scheduled for May 2000 but postponed until end-July as the electoral commission failed to make the necessary preparations, were won comfortably by Chávez. Opposition parties did, however, increase their share of seats in Congress as the middle and upper classes supported Chávez' main challenger, Francisco Arias Calderón, while the president held on to his heartland in the poverty-stricken slums.

The 2002 coup Through 2001 and into 2002 Chávez succeeded in antagonizing dissident military officers, the business sector, the Roman Catholic Church and the press. The middle classes, office workers and trades unionists blamed him for mismanaging the economy. Pro- and anti-Chávez street demonstrations became a regular event in Caracas. When Chávez tried to reform PDVSA, the state oil company, replacing executives with his own allies, the value of the bolívar slumped against the dollar and oil workers went on strike. This led to a 48-hour general strike in early April and, during the protests, 16 people were killed. On 12 April it was announced that Chávez had been replaced as president after being arrested by the military high command. His successor was businessman Pedro Carmona, who dissolved Congress and cancelled the constitution, only to resign a day later in the face of pro-Chávez demonstrations equally as strong as those that had ousted the president. On 14 April, Chávez was restored to office, but society remained deeply polarised. The opposition coalition, made up of the business sector, the main trades union and the private media, kept up its pressure on Chávez. Calls for early elections were backed by the US, but the government insisted that the first poll to be held would a mid-term referendum in August 2003, as required by the constitution if sufficient voters requested it.

By end-2002, the political situation had deteriorated to such a degree that a general strike call was met with massive support. It lasted two months and cost Venezuela some US$6 billion as the oil industry was paralized, the banking sector shut down and the bolívar plummeted to record lows against the dollar. Chávez stood firm, the strike eventually ended, but the demand for a mid-term referendum did not evaporate. This was eventually held and Chávez won comfortably. Subsequent opinion polls showed that the majority of Venezuelans supported the changes Chávez instituted in political participation, economic benefits for the poor and social reform, despite the fierce debates within and outside Venezuela over the true meaning of Bolivarian democracy. Consequently, there was little danger of Chávez losing the presidential elections of December 2006.

In early 2008 Chávez brought in a new economic team to tackle, among other problems, rapidly rising inflation, stimulated largely by oil profits being pumped into the economy for infrastructure projects and food subsidies. In late 2008 and into 2009, international oil prices fell in

Chávez and Boliviarian Revolution

Love him or hate him, the charismatic leader of Venezuela is undoubtedly the most high-profile Latin American politician of the 21st century. Outspoken critic of globalization and neoliberalism he tirelessly promotes Latin American unity and democratic socialism. Under his leadership, Venezuela pulled out of the World Bank and IMF (after paying off its debts) and key industries have been nationalized. Critics at home and abroad call him populist, even a tyrant. Supporters stress that his rule is fully democratic, with almost every important change decided by referendum.

Under Chávez, Venezuela has allied itself not only with Latin American nations sympathetic to his vision of the Bolivarian Alternative for the Americas (integration based on social welfare and equity rather than trade liberalization), for example Cuba, Bolivia, Ecuador, Argentina and Nicaragua, but also with Iran, China and Russia. His model of 21st-century socialism includes the removal of Latin America from the US sphere of influence and wresting power for the unrepresented people from the hands of the oligarchies that have controlled the region. The main methods included the supply of cheap oil, transcontinental infrastructure projects and forging ties with indigenous movements and opposition parties in other countries. At the other extreme, relations with the US were bitterly strained during the George W Bush presidency (but not so badly as to affect sales of Venezuelan oil), with Chávez unceasingly vocal in his disgust at US foreign policy. His reaction to the election of President Barack Obama was less strident, but at the Summit of the Americas in Trinidad and Tobago (April 2009), the two men greeted each other cordially and Chávez announced that he wished to restore diplomatic relations, severed in September 2008.

On the social front, the Chávez government promotes alternative models of economic development, combating poverty, malnutrition, illiteracy and disease. Subsidized food stores, well-equipped hospitals and schools are being established. There is a model housing scheme for low-income families and the government has returned land to indigenous groups. Several schemes have captured the global imagination, notably El Sistema (youth orchestras that promote classical music under the slogan 'Play and Fight!'). Started in 1975 by José Antonio Abreu, this has flourished in the Chávez era with young Venezuelans gaining international recognition. Venezuela claimed to have eradicated illiteracy in 2005, having adopted the Cuban 'Yo sí puedo' (Yes, I can) teaching method. Then there are the 'bibliomulas' (donkey libraries), which take laptops and projectors to Andean communities to aid learning.

Nevertheless, the country is hopelessly divided. The privately owned media is determined to discredit the Bolivarian Revolution. While many programmes are helping a majority of Venezuelans, the government is accused of not listening to grievances. Corruption is endemic: according to Transparency International, in 2008 Venezuela ranked 158 (out of 180 countries), second only to Haiti in Latin America. While Chávez himself seems to be untainted, many lower-ranking officials are not. Police brutality and corruption are common and statistical analyses show that Venezuela has one of the highest crime rates (including homicide) in the world.

line with the global recession, but Venezuela claimed to have sufficient reserves to weather this for the time being. If the price of oil stayed depressed, a number of additional factors might force the government to look at devaluing the fixed exchange rate, cutting public spending, or raising taxes. These factors included inflation staying at its 2008 level of over 30%, low foreign investment in response to an aggressive programme of nationalization, a growing fiscal deficit and balance of payments problems caused by imports of consumer products outweighing the revenue from oil.

In December 2007, Chávez accepted defeat in a referendum to reform the constitution (among the measures was an end to time limits in office for elected officials). Rather than indicate an increasingly coherent opposition to his Bolivarian project, it suggested that many of his core supporters decided not to vote because of disillusion over food shortages, high crime levels and the slow pace of change for certain sectors of society. A similar referendum in February 2009 gave Chávez victory and opened the way for him to stand for reelection in 2012. But his popularity continued to fluctuate, particulary in early 2010 when the handling of water and electricity shortages caused confusion and hardship. In an effort to increase oil revenues and restrict non-essential imports, the bolívar was devalued to a two-tier official exchange rate in January 2010.

Guyana

The country was first partially settled between 1616 and 1621 by the Dutch West India Company, who erected a fort and depot at Fort Kyk-over-al (County of Essequibo). The first English attempt at settlement was made by Captain Leigh on the Oiapoque River (now French Guyane) in 1604, but he failed to establish a permanent settlement. Lord Willoughby, founded a settlement in 1663 at Suriname, which was captured by the Dutch in 1667 and ceded to them at the Peace of Breda in exchange for New York. The Dutch held the three colonies till 1796 when they were captured by a British fleet. The territory was restored to the Dutch in 1802, but in the following year was retaken by Great Britain, which finally gained it in 1814, when the counties of Essequibo, Berbice and Demerara were merged to form British Guiana.

During the 17th century the Dutch and English settlers established posts upriver, in the hills, mostly as trading points with the Amerindian natives. Plantations were laid out and worked by African slaves. Poor soil defeated this venture, and the settlers retreated with their slaves to the coastal area in mid-18th century: the old plantation sites can still be detected from the air. Coffee and cotton were the main crops until the late 18th century, but sugar had become the dominant crop by 1820. In 1834 slavery was abolished. Many slaves became small landholders, and settlers had to find another source of labour: indentured workers from India, a few Chinese, and some Portuguese labourers. At the end of their indentures many settled in Guyana.

The end of the colonial period was politically turbulent, with rioting between the mainly Indo-Guyanese People's Progressive Party (PPP), led by Dr Cheddi Jagan, and the mainly Afro-Guyanese People's National Congress (PNC), under Mr Forbes Burnham. The PNC, favoured over the PPP by the colonial authorities, formed a government in 1964 and retained office until 1992. Guyana is one of the few countries in the Caribbean where political parties have used race as an election issue. As a result, tension between the ethnic groups has manifested itself mainly at election time.

On 26 May 1966 Guyana gained independence, and on 23 February 1970 it became a co-operative republic within the Commonwealth, adopting a new constitution. The next constitution of 1980 declared Guyana to be in transition from capitalism to socialism and relations with the USSR and Eastern Europe were fostered. Following the death of President Forbes Burnham in August 1985, Desmond Hoyte became president, since when relations with the United States improved.

Regular elections to the National Assembly and to the presidency since independence were widely criticized as fraudulent. In October 1992 national assembly and presidential elections, declared free and fair by international observers, the PPP/Civic party, led by Dr Jagan, won power after 28 years in opposition. The installation of a government by democratic means was greeted with optimism. Foreign investors began to study Guyana's potential and an economic recovery programme, part of an IMF Enhanced Structural Adjustment Facility, stimulated several years of positive gdp growth, but also seriously eroded workers' real income and hit the middle classes very hard.

In March 1997, President Jagan died after a heart attack. In new elections on 15 December 1997, the PPP/Civic alliance was re-elected with Jagan's widow, Janet, as president. Desmond

Hoyte and the PNC disputed the results and a brief period of violent demonstrations was ended by mediation from Caricom, the Caribbean Common Market. Even though the PPP/Civic was sworn in to office on 24 December 1997, agreeing to review the constitution and hold new elections within three years, Hoyte refused to recognize Jagan as president. In August 1999 President Jagan resigned because of ill health and Minister of Finance, Bharrat Jagdeo was appointed in her place. In subsequent elections in March 2001 the PPP/Civic alliance and Jagdeo were returned to office. After the death of Desmond Hoyte in December 2002, Robert Corbin, the new leader of the PNC/Reform agreed terms with Jagdeo for "constructive engagement", which included an end to the PNC/R's boycott of the National Assembly. Further elections on 28 August 2006 returned Jagdeo and the PPP/Civic to power, but this time without the inter-party violence that had marred previous polls. This, plus the good showing of the new Alliance for Change (AFC), which campaigned on a non-racial platform, raised hopes for better relations within Guyana's racially divided society. President Jagdeo has been in the vanguard of efforts to reduce net global deforestation, with an Avoided Deforestation initiative aimed at setting Guyana's rainforest under long-term protection in return for international compensation and support for sustainable development.

Suriname

Although Amsterdam merchants had been trading with the 'wild coast' of Guiana as early as 1613 (the name Parmurbo-Paramaribo was already known) it was not until 1630 that 60 English settlers came to Suriname under Captain Marshall and planted tobacco. The real founder of the colony was Lord Willoughby of Parham, governor of Barbados, who sent an expedition to Suriname in 1651 under Anthony Rowse to find a suitable place for settlement. Willoughbyland became an agricultural colony with 500 little sugar plantations, 1,000 white inhabitants and 2,000 African slaves. Jews from Holland and Italy joined them, as well as Dutch Jews ejected from Brazil after 1654. On 27 February 1667, Admiral Crynssen conquered the colony for the states of Zeeland and Willoughbyfort became the present Fort Zeelandia. By the Peace of Breda, 31 July 1667, it was agreed that Suriname should remain with the Netherlands, while Nieuw-Amsterdam (New York) should be given to England. The colony was conquered by the British in 1799, only to be restored to the Netherlands with the Treaty of Paris in 1814. Slavery was forbidden in 1818 and formally abolished in 1863. Indentured labour from China and Indonesia (Java) took its place.

On 25 November 1975, the country became an independent republic, which signed a treaty with the Netherlands for an economic aid programme worth US$1.5 billion until 1985. A military coup on 25 February 1980 overthrew the elected government. The military leader, Sergeant Desi Bouterse, and his associates came under pressure from the Dutch and the USA as a result of dictatorial tendencies. After the execution of 15 opposition leaders at Fort Zeelandia on 8 December 1982, the Netherlands broke off relations and suspended its aid programme, although bridging finance was restored in 1988.

The ban on political parties was lifted in late 1985 and a new constitution was drafted. In 1986 guerrilla rebels (the Jungle Commando), led by a former bodyguard of the promoted Lieutenant-Colonel Bouterse, Ronny Brunswijk, mounted a campaign to overthrow the government, disrupting both plans for political change and the economy. Nevertheless, elections for the National Assembly were held in November 1987. A three-party coalition (the Front for Democracy and Development) gained a landslide victory over the military, but conflicts between Assembly President Ramsewak Shankar and Bouterse led to the deposition of the government in a bloodless coup on 24 December 1990 (the 'telephone coup'). A military-backed government under the presidency of Johan Kraag was installed and elections for a new national assembly were held on 25 May 1991. The New Front of three traditional parties and the Surinamese Labour Party (SPA) won most Assembly seats and Ronald Venetiaan was elected president on 6 September 1991. Meetings between Suriname and the Netherlands ministers after the 1991 elections led to the renewal of aid in 1992. In August 1992, a peace treaty was signed between the government and the Jungle Commando.

It was only after the 1990 coup and a 25% fall in the price of alumina in 1991 that pressing economic issues such as unifying the complex system of exchange rates and cutting the huge budget deficit began to be addressed. In 1992 a Structural Adjustment Programme (SAP) was drawn up as a forerunner to a 1994-1998 Multi-Year Development Programme. A unified floating rate was introduced in 1994, but apart from that the New Front Government failed to reap any benefit from the SAP. New Front's popularity slumped as its handling of the economy foundered and corruption scandals undermined its claim to introduce 'clean politics'. Because of wide ideological differences, the opposition parties presented no concerted campaign against the New Front until the 23 May 1996 general election. Until then, much greater impetus was given to popular discontent by the economic decline, which reached catastrophic proportions by 1995. Although the New Front won a small majority in the National Assembly, Venetiaan did not hold enough seats to become president. Several parties defected to the NDP with the result that, in September 1996, the United Peoples Assembly elected by secret ballot Jules Wijdenbosch as president. Wijdenbosch, who had been a vice-president during Bouterse's regime, formed a coalition government of his own NDP and five other parties. Bouterse, for whom the special post of Councillor of State had been created in 1997, was dismissed by Wijdenbosch in April 1999 for failing to 'contribute to a healthy political climate'. At the same time Bouterse was tried *in absentia* in the Netherlands on suspicion of drug trafficking; he was convicted in July and is still sought there. Since January 2008, proceedings against him and 24 others have moved slowly in Paramaribo for the 1982 murders mentioned above.

Protests and strikes at the government's handling of the economy erupted in 1998-1999 and Wijdenbosch's position became precarious following the collapse of his coalition. He was forced to bring forward elections from 2001 to 25 May 2000 and was humiliated by the electorate, gaining a mere 9% of the vote. The New Front coalition led by ex-president Ronald Venetiaan won 47%. Venetiaan's most urgent priority was to stabilize the economy, which, by 2000 and with Dutch aid terminated, had fallen back into recession. From 2001, there were renewed signs of improvement, but the outlook remained grim for over 60% of the population estimated by the United Nations to be living in poverty. In January 2004, Suriname abandoned its currency, the guilder, in favour of the Suriname dollar, introduced at a rate of 2.8 to the US dollar. Exchange rates were also simplified with the aim of strengthening the currency and bringing confidence back to the economy. In general elections in May 2005, the outgoing New Front coalition won 23 seats, 10 fewer than previously. Bouterse's NDP won 15 seats, becoming the largest political party in the country. A new party, A-Combination (AC), won 5 seats, the People's Alliance for Progress (VVV) of former president Jules Wijdenbosch secured 5 seats and Alternative-1 (A-1) won 3. In August a special session of the People's Assembly reelected Venetiaan as president (next elections were due on 25 May 2010). The economy remained relatively bouyant into 2008. Alumina, for example, enjoyed record prices in July 2008, but the onset of the world economic crisis sent prices crashing and the Suriname Aluminum Company (Suralco) was forced to reduce production by 40% in May 2009. Other sectors fared less badly and the outlook for 2010 was for improvements in the trade balance and economic growth, but public spending was expected to be high in the run-up to elections.

Guyane

Several French and Dutch expeditions attempted to settle along the coast in the early 17th century, but were driven off by the native population. The French finally established a settlement at Sinnamary in the early 1660s but this was destroyed by the Dutch in 1665 and seized by the British two years later. Under the Treaty of Breda, 1667, Guyane was returned to France. Apart from a brief occupation by the Dutch in 1676, it remained in French hands until 1809 when a combined Anglo-Portuguese naval force captured the colony and handed it over to the Portuguese (Brazilians). Though the land was restored to France by the Treaty of Paris in 1814, the Portuguese remained until 1817. Gold was discovered in 1853, and disputes arose about the frontiers of the colony with Suriname and Brazil. These were settled by arbitration in 1891, 1899, and 1915. By the law of 19 March 1946, the Colony of Cayenne, or Guyane Française, became the Department of Guyane, with the same laws, regulations, and administration as a department in metropolitan France. The seat of the Prefect and of the principal courts is at Cayenne. The colony was used as a prison for French convicts with camps scattered throughout the country; Saint-Laurent was the port of entry. After serving prison terms convicts spent an equal number of years in exile and were usually unable to earn their return passage to France. Majority opinion seems to be in favour of greater autonomy and there has been some civil unrest caused by a minority calling for change in the relationship with Metropolitan France. The French government has made no move to alter the department's status. Despite heavy dependence economically on France, unemployment is a serious problem. A second problem is illegal immigration, especially by gold prospectors. The loss of Guyane's largely untouched rainforest to illicit mining is currently small, but potentially significant.

Government

Argentina (La República Argentina)

The form of government is a representative, republican federal system. The president is elected for four years and may stand for reelection once. Of the two legislative houses, the Senate has 72 seats, and the Chamber of Deputies 257. By the 1853 Constitution (amended most recently in 1994) the country is divided into a Federal Capital (the city of Buenos Aires) and 23 Provinces. Each Province has its own Governor, Senate and Chamber of Deputies. The municipal government of the Federal Capital is exercised by a Mayor who is directly elected.

Bolivia (Estado Plurinacional de Bolivia)

The Constitution of 2008 vests executive power in the President, who can stand for immediate re-election. The presidential term is five years. The rights of 36 indigenous groups are enshrined in the constitution, including the recognition of indigenous systems of justice. Congress (Asamblea Legislativa Plurinacional) consists of two chambers: the Senate, with 36 seats, and the Chamber of Deputies, with 130 seats. There are nine departments; each is controlled by a Prefecto appointed by the President. **Note** Sucre is the legal capital, La Paz is the seat of government.

Brazil (República Federativa do Brasil)

The 1988 constitution provides for an executive president elected by direct popular vote, balanced by a bicameral legislature (81 seats in the Federal Senate, 513 seats in the Chamber of Deputies) and an independent judiciary. Presidential elections are held every four years, with a second round one month after the first if no candidate wins an outright majority. The president may stand for reelection once. Congressional elections are held every four years, the deputies being chosen by proportional representation. The country is divided into 26 states and one federal district (Brasília).

Chile (República de Chile)

The March 1981 constitution was last amended in 2005. It provides for a four year non-renewable term for the President of the Republic, a bicameral Congress of a 120-seat Chamber of Deputies and a 38-seat Senate and an independent judiciary and central bank. The country is divided into 15 regions.

Colombia (República de Colombia)

The 1886 Constitution was reformed by a Constituent Assembly in 1991. The Senate has 102 members, and the Chamber of Representatives has 166. The President is elected by direct vote for a term of four years and may stand for a second term. Administratively the country is divided into 32 Departments and the Capital District of Bogotá.

Ecuador (República del Ecuador)
The Constitution dates from 2008. There are 24 provinces, including the Galápagos Islands. The president and vice-president are elected for a 4 year term and can be re-elected for a second term (once only). The parliament, Asamblea Nacional, is also elected for 4 years; it currently has 124 seats. The number of *asamblistas* will vary according to the size of the population.

Paraguay (República del Paraguay)
The current Constitution was adopted in 1992. The country has 17 departments, with Asunción, the capital, as a separate entity. Executive power rests with the president, elected for five years. There is a two-chamber Congress (Senate 45 seats, Chamber of Deputies 80).

Peru (República del Perú)
Under the constitution of December 1993, there is a single chamber, 120-seat congress. Men and women over 18 are eligible to vote; registration and voting is compulsory until the age of 70. The President, to whom is entrusted the Executive Power, is elected for five years. The country is divided into 25 regions, plus the province of Lima.

Uruguay (República Oriental del Uruguay)
The current Constitution dates from 1966, last revised 1997. Uruguay is a republic with a bicameral legislature: a Senate with 30 seats and a Chamber of Representatives with 99 seats. The president, who is head of state and of the government, holds office for five years. The country is divided into 19 departments.

Venezuela (República Bolivariana de Venezuela)
Under the Constitution of 1999, the president holds office for six years and may stand for immediate reelection. There are 23 states, a Capital District and federal dependencies of 72 islands. There is one legislative house, a chamber of deputies with 167 members who are elected every five years, with three seats reserved for indigenous peoples.

Guyana (Co-operative Republic of Guyana)
Under the 1980 constitution, a Prime Minister and cabinet are responsible to the National Assembly, which has 65 members, elected for a maximum term of five years, with not more than 4 non-elected non-voting ministers and 2 non-elected non-voting parliamentary secretaries appointed by the president. The president is Head of State. Elections must be held every five years. The country is divided into 10 administrative regions.

Suriname (Republiek Suriname)
The constitution dates from 1987. There is one legislative house, the National Assembly, which has 51 members, elected every five years. The President is head of state and of government and is elected by the National Assembly for a five-year term. Suriname is divided into 10 districts, of which the capital is one.

Guyane (République française)
The head of state is the president of France; the local heads of government are Le Préfet (the Prefect), for France, and the presidents of the local General and Regional Councils. The General Council (19 members) and the Regional Council (31 members) are the two legislative houses. Guyane sends a representative to the French Senate and two deputies to the National Assembly in Paris. The country is divided into two *arrondissements*, Cayenne and St-Laurent-du-Maroni, with 22 *communes*.

People

Argentina → *Population in 2009 was 40.9 million. Population growth 1.05%; infant mortality rate 11.4 per 1,000 live births; literacy rate 97.2%; GDP per capita US$13,800 (2009).*

In the Federal Capital and Province of Buenos Aires, where about 45% of the population lives, the people are almost exclusively of European origin. In the far northern provinces, colonized from neighbouring countries, at least half the people are *mestizos* (people of mixed Spanish and indigenous origin) though they form about 15% of the population of the whole country. It is estimated that 12.8% are foreign born and generally of European origin, though there are also important communities of Syrians, Lebanese, Armenians, Japanese and Koreans. Not surprisingly, the traditional image of the Argentine is that of the *gaucho*; *gauchismo* has been a powerful influence in literature, sociology and folklore, and is celebrated each year in the week before the 'Day of Tradition', 10 November.

In the highlands of the northwest, in the Chaco, Misiones and in the southwest, there are still some **indigenous groups**. The total of the Indian population is unknown; estimates vary from 300,000 to 500,000. The pampas Indians were virtually exterminated in the 19th century; the Indians of Tierra del Fuego are extinct. Surviving peoples include the Wichi and others in Salta and Jujuy provinces (see page 156), various Chaco Indians (see page 185) and tribes related to the Mapuche and Tehuelche nations in the southwest.

Bolivia → *Population in 2009 was 9.78 million. Population growth was 1.77%; infant mortality rate 44.66 per 1,000 live births; literacy rate 86.7%; GDP per capita US$4,600 (2009).*

Of the total population, some two thirds are Indians, the remainder being *mestizos*, Europeans and others. The racial composition varies from place to place: Indian around Lake Titicaca; more than half Indian in La Paz; three-quarters *mestizo* or European in the Yungas, Cochabamba, Santa Cruz and Tarija, the most European of all. There are also about 17,000 blacks, descendents of slaves brought from Peru and Buenos Aires in 16th century, who now live in the Yungas. Since the 1980s, regional tensions between the 'collas' (*altiplano* dwellers) and the 'cambas' (lowlanders) have become more marked. Under 40% of children of school age attend school even though it is theoretically compulsory between 7 and 14.

The most obdurate of Bolivian problems has always been that the main mass of population is, from a strictly economic viewpoint, in the wrong place, the poor Altiplano and not the potentially rich Oriente; and that the Indians live largely outside the monetary system on a self-sufficient basis. Since the land reform of 1952 isolated communities continue the old life but in the agricultural area around Lake Titicaca, the valleys of Cochabamba, the Yungas and the irrigated areas of the south, most peasants now own their land, however small the plot may be. Migration to the warmer and more fertile lands of the east region has been officially encouraged. At the same time roads are now integrating the food-producing eastern zones with the bulk of the population living in the towns of the Altiplano or the west-facing slopes of the Eastern Cordillera.

The **highland Indians** are composed of two groups: those in La Paz and in the north of the Altiplano who speak the guttural Aymara (an estimated one million), and those elsewhere, who speak Quechua (three million – this includes the Indians in the northern Apolobamba region). Outside the big cities many of them speak no Spanish. In the lowlands are some 150,000 people in 30 groups, including the Ayoreo, Chiquitano, Chiriguano, Garavo, Chimane and Mojo. The **lowland Indians** are, in the main, Guaraní. About 70% of Bolivians are Aymara, Quechua or Tupi-Guaraní speakers. The first two are regarded as national languages, but were not, until very recently, taught in schools.

Brazil → *Population in 2009 was 198.74 million. Population growth was 1.12%; infant mortality rate 22.58 per 1,000 live births; literacy rate 88.6%; GDP per capita US$10,200 (2009).*

At first the Portuguese colony grew slowly. From 1580 to 1640 the population was only about 50,000 apart from the million or so indigenous Indians. In 1700 there were some 750,000 non-indigenous people in Brazil. Early in the 19th century Humboldt computed there were about 920,000 whites, 1,960,000 Africans, and 1,120,000 Indians and *mestiços*: after three centuries of occupation a total of only four million, and over twice as many Africans as there were whites.

Modern immigration did not begin effectively until after 1850. Of the 4.6 million immigrants from Europe between 1884-1954, 32% were Italians, 30% Portuguese, 14% Spanish, 4% German. Since 1954 immigrants have averaged 50,000 a year. There are some one million Japanese-descended Brazilians. Today the whites and near-whites are about 54% of the population, people of mixed race about 40% and Afro Brazilians 5%; the rest are Asians.

The whites predominate in the south, which received the largest flood of European immigrants. Most of the German immigrants settled in the three southern states: Santa Catarina, Rio Grande do Sul, and Paraná. The Germans (and the Italians and Poles and other Slavs who followed them) did not in the main go as wage earners on the big estates, but as cultivators of their own small farms.

The arid wastes of the Sertão remain largely uncultivated. Its inhabitants are people of mixed Portuguese and Indian origin (*mestiço*); most live off the 'slash and burn' method of cultivation, which involves cutting down and burning the brushwood for a small patch of ground which is cultivated for a few years and then allowed to grow back.

Brazilian culture is rich in African influences. Those interested in the development of Afro-Brazilian music, dance, religion, arts and cuisine will find the whole country north of São Paulo fascinating; the cities of Bahia and São Luís retain the greatest African influences. Though there is no legal discrimination against black people, the economic and educational disparity – by default rather than intent of the Government – is such that successful Afro Brazilians are active almost exclusively in the worlds of sport, entertainment and arts.

Rural and urban population The population has historically been heavily concentrated along the coastal strip where the original Portuguese settlers exploited the agricultural wealth, and further inland in the states of Minas Gerais and São Paulo where more recent development has followed the original search for gold, precious stones and slaves. Much of the interior of Pará, Amazonas, Goiás and the Mato Grosso has densities of one person per sq km or less. Internal migration has brought to the cities problems of unemployment, housing shortage, and extreme pressure on services; shanty towns – or *favelas, mocambos, alagados*, according to the region – are an integral part of the urban landscape. But while the northeast, because of its poverty, has lost many workers to the industries of the southeast, many rural workers from southern Brazil have moved north, drawn by the rapid development of Amazônia, creating unprecedented pressures on the environment.

Indigenous peoples It is estimated that, when the Portuguese arrived in Brazil, there were between three and five million Indians living in the area. Today there are only about 350,000. Tribal groups number 210; each has a unique dialect, but most languages belong to four main linguistic families, Tupi-Guarani, Ge, Carib and Arawak. A few tribes remain uncontacted, others are exclusively nomadic, others are semi-nomadic hunter-gatherers and farmers, while some are settled groups in close contact with non-Indian society. The struggle of groups such as the Yanomami to have their land demarcated in order to secure title is well-documented. The goal of the Statute of the Indian (Law 6.001/73), for demarcation of all Indian land by 1978, is largely unmet. It was feared that a new law introduced in January 1996 would slow the process even more. Funai, the National Foundation for the Support of the Indian, a part of the Interior Ministry, is charged with representing the Indians' interests, but lacks resources and support. There is no nationwide, representative body for indigenous people. Most of Brazil's indigenous people live in the Amazon region; they are affected by deforestation, encroachment from colonizers, small- and large-scale mining, and the construction of hydroelectric dams. Besides the Yanomami, other groups include the Xavante, Tukano, Kreen-Akrore, Kaiapó, Arawete and Arara.

Chile ➔ *Population of Chile in 2009 was 16.60 million. Population growth was 0.88%; infant mortality rate 7.71 per 1,000 live births; literacy rate 95.7%; GDP per capita US$14,700 (2009).*
There is less racial diversity in Chile than in most Latin American countries. Over 90% of the population is *mestizo*. There has been much less immigration than in Argentina and Brazil. The German, French, Spanish, Italian and Swiss immigrants came mostly after 1846 as small farmers in the forest zone south of the Biobío. Between 1880 and 1900 gold-seeking Serbs and Croats settled in the far south, and the British took up sheep farming and commerce in the same region. The influence throughout Chile of the immigrants is out of proportion to their numbers: their signature on the land is seen, for instance, in the German appearance of Valdivia, Puerto Montt, Puerto Varas, Frutillar and Osorno.

The population is far from evenly distributed: Middle Chile (from Copiapó to Concepción), 18% of the country's area, contains 77% of the total population. The Metropolitan Region of Santiago contains, about 39% of the whole population. Many Chileans live in slum areas called *callampas* (mushrooms), or *tomas* on the outskirts of Santiago and around the factories.

There is disagreement over the number of **indigenous people** in Chile. The Mapuche nation, 95% of whom live in forest land around Temuco, between the Biobío and Toltén rivers, is put at one million by Survival International, but much less by others, including official, statistics. There are also 15,000-20,000 Aymara in the northern Chilean Andes and 2,000 Rapa Nui on Easter Island. A political party, the Party for Land and Identity, unites many Indian groupings, and legislation is proposed to restore indigenous people's rights.

Colombia ➔ *Population in 2009 was 45.64 million. Population growth was 1.38%; infant mortality rate 18.9 per 1,000 live births; literacy rate 90.4%; GDP per capita US$9,200 (2009).*
The regions vary in their racial make-up: Antioquia and Caldas are largely of European descent, Pasto is Indian, the Cauca Valley and the rural area near the Caribbean are African or *mulato*. However, continual population migrations are evening out the differences. The birth and death rates vary greatly from one area to the other, but in general infant mortality is high. Hospitals and clinics are few in relation to the population. Education is free, and since 1927 theoretically compulsory, but many children, especially in rural areas, do not attend. There are high standards of secondary and university education, when it is available.

An estimated 400,000 **tribal peoples**, from 60 ethnic groups, live in Colombia. Groups include the Wayuú (in the Guajira), the Kogi and Arhauco (Sierra Nevada de Santa Marta), Amazonian indians such as the Witoto, the nomadic Nukak and the Ticuna, Andean indians and groups of the Llanos and in the Pacific Coast rain forest. The diversity and importance of indigenous peoples was recognized in the 1991 constitutional reforms when indians were granted the right to two senate seats; the National Colombian Indian Organization (ONIC) won a third seat in the October 1991 ballot. State recognition and the right to bilingual education has not, however, solved major problems of land rights, training and education, and justice.

Ecuador ➔ *Population in 2009 was 14.57 million. Population growth was 1.50%; infant mortality rate 20.9 per 1,000 live births; literacy rate 91%; GDP per capita US$7,400 (2009).*
Roughly 50% of Ecuador's people live in the coastal region west of the Andes, 45% in the Andean Sierra and 5% in Oriente. Migration is occurring from the rural zones of both the coast and the highlands to the towns and cities, particularly Guayaquil and Quito, and agricultural colonization from other parts of the country is taking place in the Oriente. There has also been an important flux of mostly illegal migrants out of Ecuador, seeking opportunities in the USA and Spain. Meanwhile, Colombian refugees and migrants are becoming an important segment of Ecuador's population. The national average population density is the highest in South America.

There are 2-3 million Quichua-speaking **highland Indians** and about 70,000 **lowland Indians**. The following indigenous groups maintain their distinct cultural identity: in the Oriente, Siona, Secoya, Cofán, Huaorani, Zápara, Quichua, Shiwiar, Achuar and Shuar; in the Sierra, Otavalo, Salasaca, Puruhá, Cañari and Saraguro; on the coast, Chachi (Cayapa), Tsáchila (Colorado), Awa (Cuaiquer) and Epera. Many Amazonian Indian communities are fighting for land rights in the face of oil exploration and colonization.

Paraguay → *Population in 2009 was 6.99 million. Population growth was 2.36%; infant mortality rate 24.68 per 1,000 live births; literacy rate 94.0%; GDP per capita US$4,100 (2009).*
Since Spanish influence was less than in many other parts of South America, most people are bilingual, speaking both Spanish and Guaraní. Outside Asunción, most people speak Guaraní by preference. There is a Guaraní theatre, it is taught in private schools, and books and periodicals are published in that tongue, which has official status as the second national language. According to the 2002 census, the **indigenous population** is about 87,000, under 2% of the total population. There are 20 distinct ethnic groups with five different languages, among which Guaraní predominates. The 1981 Law of Native Communities in theory guarantees Indian rights to ownership of their traditional lands and the maintenance of their culture. See www.tierraviva.org.py.

Peru → *Population in 2009 was 29.55 million. Population growth was 1.23%; infant mortality rate 28.62 per 1,000 live births; literacy rate 92.9%; GDP per capita US$8,600 (2009).*
Peruvian society is a mixture of native Andean peoples, Afro-Peruvians, Spanish, immigrant Chinese, Japanese, Italians, Germans and, to a lesser extent, indigenous Amazon tribes. The first immigrants were the Spaniards who followed Pizarro's expeditionary force. Their effect, demographically, politically and culturally, has been enormous. Peru's black community is based on the coast, mainly in Chincha, south of Lima, and also in some working-class districts of the capital. Their forefathers were originally imported into Peru in the 16th century as slaves to work on the sugar and cotton plantations on the coast. Large numbers of poor Chinese labourers were brought to Peru in the mid-19th century to work in virtual slavery on the guano reserves on the Pacific coast and to build the railroads in the central Andes. The Japanese community, now numbering some 100,000, established itself in the first half of the 20th century. Like most of Latin America, Peru received many emigrés from Europe seeking land and opportunities in the late 19th century. The country's wealth and political power remains concentrated in the hands of this small and exclusive class of whites, which also consists of the descendants of the first Spanish families.

The **indigenous population** is put at about three million Quechua and Aymara Indians in the Andean region and 200,000-250,000 Amazonian Indians from 40-50 ethnic groups. In the Andes, there are 5,000 Indian communities but few densely populated settlements. Their literacy rate is the lowest of any comparable group in South America and their diet is 50% below acceptable levels. About two million Indians speak no Spanish, their main tongue being Quechua; they are largely outside the money economy. Many Indian groups are under threat from colonization, development and road-building projects.

Uruguay → *Population in 2009 was 3.49 million. Population growth was 0.47%; infant mortality rate 11.32 per 1,000 live births; literacy rate 98%; GDP per capita US$12,700 (2009).*
Uruguayans are virtually all European, mostly of Spanish and Italian stock. A small percentage in parts of Montevideo and near the Brazilian border are of mixed African and European descent. Less than 10% are mestizos. There was little Spanish settlement in the early years and, for a long time, the area was inhabited mainly by groups of nomadic *gauchos* who trailed after the herds of cattle killing them for food and selling their hides only. Organized commerce began with the arrival of cattle buyers from Buenos Aires who found it profitable to hire herdsmen to look after

cattle in defined areas around their headquarters. By about 1800 most of the land had been parcelled out into large *estancias*. The only commercial farming was around Montevideo, where small *chacras* grew vegetables, wheat and maize for the near-by town. Only after 1828 did immigration begin on any scale. Montevideo was then a small town of 20,000 inhabitants. Between 1836 and 1926 about 648,000 immigrants arrived in Uruguay, mostly from Italy and Spain, some into the towns, some to grow crops and vegetables round Montevideo. The native Uruguayans remained pastoralists, leaving commercial farming to the immigrants. More recent immigrants, however, Jewish, Armenian, Lebanese and others have chosen to enter the retail trades, textiles and leather production rather than farming.

Venezuela → *Population was 26.8 million in 2009. Population growth was 1.51%; infant mortality rate 21.54 per 1,000 live births; literacy rate 93%; GDP per capita US$13,100 (2009).*
A large number are of mixed Spanish and Indian origin. There are some pure Africans and a strong element of African descent along the coast, particularly at the ports. The arrival of 800,000 European immigrants, mostly in the 1950s, greatly modified the racial make-up in Venezuela. Despite its wealth, Venezuela still faces serious social problems. Many rural dwellers have drifted to the cities; one result of this exodus is that Venezuelan farmers do not provide all the food the nation needs and imports of foodstuffs are necessary, even for items such as beans and rice. A very small proportion of the population (150,000) is **Indian**. Among the best-known are the Yanomami, who live in Amazonas, and the Bari in the Sierra de Perijá (on the northwest border with Colombia). An Indian Reserve gives the Bari effective control of their own land, but this has not prevented infringement from mining, plantation or settlers. Other groups do not have title to their territory. These groups include the Wayuu (in the Guajira), the Panare and the Piaroa.

Guyana → *Population in 2009 was 752,940. Population growth was 0.63%; infant mortality rate 39.11 per 1,000 live births; literacy rate 98.8%; GDP per capita US$3,800 (2009).*
Until the 1920s there was little natural increase in population, but the eradication of malaria and other diseases has since led to rapid expansion, particularly among the East Indians (Asian). The 2002 census showed the following ethnic distribution: East Indian 43.4%; black 30.2%; mixed 16.7%; Amerindian 9.2%; Chinese 0.2%; Portuguese 0.2%; white 0.1%. Descendants of the original **Amerindian inhabitants** are divided into nine ethnic groups, including the Akawaio, Makuxi and Pemon. Some have lost their isolation and moved to the urban areas, others keenly maintain aspects of their traditional culture and identity.

Suriname → *Population in 2009 was 481,267. Population growth was 1.10%; infant mortality rate 18.81 per 1,000 live births; literacy rate 89.6%; GDP per capita US$9,000 (2009).*
The estimated make-up of the population is: **Indo-Pakistanis** (known locally as Hindustanis), 37%; **Creoles** (European-African and other descent), 31%; **Javanese**, 15%; **Bush Negroes**, called 'Maroons' locally (retribalized descendants of slaves who escaped in the 17th century, living on the upper Saramacca, Suriname and Marowijne rivers), 10%; **Europeans**, **Chinese** and others, 5%; **Amerindians**, 2%. About 90% of the existing population live in or around Paramaribo or in the coastal towns; the remainder, mostly Carib and Arawak Indians and Maroons, are widely scattered.The Asian people originally entered the country as contracted estate labourers, and settled in agriculture or commerce after completion of their term. They dominate the countryside, whereas Paramaribo is racially very mixed. Although some degree of racial tension exists between all the different groups, Creole-Hindustani rivalry is not as fundamental an issue as in Guyana, for example. Many Surinamese, of all backgrounds, pride themselves on their ability to get along with each other in such a heterogeneous country.

Guyane → *According to the French government, total population in 2008 was 216,000. Population growth 1999-2006 as 3.8%, 2006-2007 3.5% (infant mortality rate, according to the UN, is 14 per 1,000 live births). GDP per capita (not PPP) 10,550 (2005).*
There are widely divergent estimates for the ethnic composition of the population. Calculations vary according to the number included of illegal immigrants, attracted by social benefits and the high living standards. By some measures, over 40% of the population are Créoles, with correspondingly low figures for Europeans, Asians and Brazilians (around 17% in total). Other estimates put the Créole proportion at 36%, with Haitians 26%, Europeans 10% (of whom about 95% are from France), Brazilians 8%, Asians 4.7% (3.2% from Hong Kong, 1.5% from Laos), about 4% from Suriname and 2.5% from Guyana. The **Amerindian population** is put at 3.6% (over 4% by some estimates). The main groups are Kali'na/Galibi (1,700), Arawak (400), Wayanas (600), Palikurs (500), Wayampis-Oyampis (600) and Emerillons (300). There are also bush negroes (Alaku, Paramaca, Saramaca, Djuka), who live mostly in the Maroni area, and others (Dominicans, St Lucians, etc) at 0.7%.

Note Statistics, unless indicated otherwise, are taken from *The CIA World Factbook*, 2009 estimates. GDP per capita is measured at purchasing power parity (PPP).

Land and environment

The dominant feature of South America's geography is the Andes mountain range which defines the western, Pacific, side of the continent from 12°N to 56°S, with tablelands and older mountains stretching east to the Atlantic Ocean. The highest peaks of the Andes have no rivals outside the Himalaya. Dominant to the east are the vast river basins of the Orinoco, the Paraná and above all the Amazon. At least part of every country (except Uruguay) is in the tropics, though the southernmost tips of Chile and Argentina are close to Antarctica. No wonder the variety of scenery, climate and vegetation is immense.

The Andean countries

Colombia → *Land area: 1,242,568 sq km.*
Four ranges of the Andes (*cordilleras*) run from north to south. Between the ranges run deep longitudinal valleys. Roughly half of Colombia consists of these deep north-south valleys of the Andes and the coastal fringes along the Pacific and Caribbean shorelines. The remaining 620,000 sq km east of the Andes consists of the hot plains (*llanos*) to the north, running down to the Orinoco River, and the Amazon forests to the south. Near the foot of the Andes, the *llanos* are used for cattle ranching, but beyond is jungle. Except for the northwest corner where oil has been found, islands of settlement are connected with the rest of the country only by air and river; the few roads are impassable most of the year. Almost all Colombians live in the western 50% of the country.

The **cordilleras**, the main Andes ranges, run northwards for 800 km from the borders of Ecuador to the Caribbean lowlands. A few peaks in the Western Cordillera are over 4,000 m but none reaches the snowline. The Central Cordillera, 50-65 km wide, is much higher; several of its peaks, snow clad, rise above 5,000 m and its highest, the volcano cone of Huila, is 5,750 m. The Eastern Cordillera extends north across the border into Venezuela (see below), and includes the spectacular Cucuy ranges. Apart from the peaks (a few are active volcanoes), there are large areas of high undulating plateaux, cold, treeless and inhospitable, dissected by deep river gorges. They have interesting flora and fauna and many of these regions are protected as national parks. In a high basin of the Eastern Cordillera, 160 km east of the Río Magdalena, the

Spaniards in 1538 founded the city of Bogotá at 2,560 m, now the national capital. The great rural activity here is the growing of food: cattle, wheat, barley, maize and potatoes. The **valleys** between the Cordilleras are deep and dominated by the Magdalena and Cauca Rivers. The upper sections are filled with volcanic ash and are very fertile. With the tropical range of temperature and rainfall, this is very productive land. Coffee dominates but almost every known tropical fruit and vegetable grows here. In the upper parts of the valleys, the climate is more temperate, with another wide range of crops. There is cattle production everywhere; sugar, cotton, rice and tobacco are common.

The **Caribbean lowlands** include three centres of population, Cartagena, Barranquilla and Santa Marta, behind which lies a great lowland, the floodplain of the Magdalena, Cauca and their tributaries. During the dry season from October to March great herds of cattle are grazed there, but for the rest of the year much of it is a network of swamps and lagoons with very little land that can be cultivated except for a few ranges of low hills near the coast. The **northeast** includes one more mountain group in Colombia, the Sierra Nevada de Santa Marta, standing isolated from the other ranges on the shores of the Caribbean. This is the highest range of all: its snow-capped peaks rise to 5,800 m within 50 km of the coast. Further northeast, is La Guajira, a strange region of semi-desert, salt-pans, flamingos and unusual micro-climates. The **Pacific coast** stretches for 1,300 km. Along the coast north of Buenaventura runs the Serranía de Baudó, the shortest of the Cordilleras, thickly forested. East of it is a low trough before the land rises to the slopes of the Western Cordillera. The trough is drained southwards into the Pacific by the Río San Juan, and northwards into the Caribbean by the Río Atrato, both are partly navigable. The climate is hot and torrential rain falls daily. The inhabitants are mostly black. The 320 km south of the port of Buenaventura to the border with Ecuador is a wide, marshy, and sparsely inhabited coastal lowland.

Ecuador → *Land area: 272, 045 sq km.*

The Andes, running from north to south, form a mountainous backbone to the country. There are two main ranges, the Central Cordillera and the Western Cordillera, separated by a 400-km long Central Valley, whose rims are about 50 km apart. The rims are joined together, like the two sides of a ladder, by hilly rungs, and between each pair of rungs lies an intermont basin with a dense cluster of population. These basins are drained by rivers which cut through the rims to run either west to the Pacific or east to join the Amazon. Both rims of the Central Valley are lined with the cones of more than 50 volcanoes. Several of them have long been extinct, for example, Chimborazo, the highest (6,310 m). At least eight, however, are still active including Cotopaxi (5,897 m), which had several violent eruptions in the 19th century; Pichincha (4,794 m), which re-entered activity in 1998 and expelled a spectacular mushroom cloud in October 1999; Sangay (5,230 m), one of the world's most active volcanoes, continuously emitting fumes and ash; Tungurahua (5,016 m), active since 1999; and Reventador (3,562 m), which has erupted several times since 2002. Earthquakes too are common.

The **sierra**, as the central trough of the Andes in known, is home to about 47% of the people of Ecuador, the majority of whom are indigenous. Some of the land is still held in large private estates worked by the Indians, but a growing proportion is now made up of small family farms or is held by native communities, run as cooperatives. Some communities live at subsistence level, others have developed good markets for products using traditional skills in embroidery, pottery, jewellery, knitting, weaving, and carving. The **costa** is mostly lowland at an altitude of less than 300 m, apart from a belt of hilly land which runs northwest from Guayaquil to the coast, where it turns north and runs parallel to the shore to Esmeraldas. In the extreme north there is a typical tropical rain forest, severely endangered by uncontrolled logging. The forests thin out in the more southern lowlands and give way to tropical dry forest. The main agricultural exports come from the lowlands to the southeast and north of Guayaquil. The heavy rains, high temperature and humidity suit the growth of tropical crops. Bananas and mango are grown here while rice is farmed on the natural levees of this flood plain. The main crop comes from the alluvial fans at the foot of the mountains rising out of the plain. Coffee is grown on the higher ground. Shrimp farming was typical of the coast until this was damaged by disease in 1999. The Guayas lowland is also a great cattle-fattening area in the dry season. South of Guayaquil the rainfall is progressively less, mangroves disappear and by the border with Peru, it is semi-arid.

The **Oriente** is east of the Central Cordillera where the forest-clad mountains fall sharply to a chain of foothills (the Eastern Cordillera) and then the jungle through which meander the tributaries of the Amazon. This east lowland region makes up 36% of Ecuador's total territory, but is only sparsely populated by indigenous and agricultural colonists from the highlands. In total, the region has only 5% of the national population, but colonization is now proceeding rapidly owing to population pressure and in the wake of an oil boom in the northern Oriente. There is gold and other minerals in the south. The **Galápagos** are about 1,000 km west of Ecuador, on the Equator, and are not structuraly connected to the mainland. They mark the junction between two tectonic plates on the Pacific floor where basalt has escaped to form massive volcanoes, only the tips of which are above sea level. Several of the islands have volcanic activity today. Their isolation from any other land has led to the evolution of their unique flora and fauna.

Peru ➔ *Land area: 1,285,216 sq km.*

The whole of Peru's west seaboard with the Pacific is desert on which rain seldom falls. From this coastal shelf the Andes rise to a high Sierra which is studded with groups of soaring mountains and gouged with deep canyons. The highland slopes more gradually east and is deeply forested and ravined. Eastward from these mountains lie the vast jungle lands of the Amazon basin.

The **Highlands** (or Sierra), at an average altitude of 3,000 m, cover 26% of the country and contain about 50% of the people, mostly Indian, an excessive density on such poor land. Here, high-level land of gentle slopes is surrounded by towering ranges of high peaks including the most spectacular range of the continent, the Cordillera Blanca. This has several ice peaks over 6,000 m; the highest, Huascarán, is 6,768 m and is a mecca for mountaineers. There are many volcanoes in the south. The north and east highlands are heavily forested up to a limit of 3,350 m: the grasslands are between the forest line and the snowline, which rises from 5,000 m in the latitude of Lima to 5,800 m in the south. Most of the Sierra is covered with grasses and shrubs, with Puna vegetation (bunch grass mixed with low, hairy-leaved plants) from north of Huaraz to the south. Here the indigenous graze llamas, alpacas and sheep providing meat, clothing, transport and even fuel from the animals' dung. Some potatoes and cereals (*quinua*, *kiwicha* and *kañiwa*) are grown at altitude, but the valley basins contain the best land for arable farming. Most of the rivers which rise in these mountains flow east to the Amazon and cut through the plateau in canyons, sometimes 1,500 m deep, in which the climate is tropical. A few go west to the Pacific including the Colca and Cotahuasi in the south, which have created canyons over 3,000 m deep.

The **coast**, a narrow ribbon of desert 2,250 km long, takes up 11% of the country and holds about 45% of the population. It is the economic heart of Peru, consuming most of the imports and supplying half of the exports. When irrigated, the river valleys are extremely fertile, creating oases which grow cotton throughout the country, sugar cane, rice and export crops such as asparagus in the north, grapes, fruit and olives in the south. At the same time, the coastal current teems with fish and Peru has in the past had the largest catch in the world. The **jungle** covers the forested eastern half of the Andes and the tropical forest beyond, altogether 62% of the country's area, but with only about 5% of the population who are crowded on the river banks in the cultivable land – a tiny part of the area. The few roads have to cope with dense forest, deep valleys, and sharp eastern slopes ranging from 2,150 m in the north to 5,800 m east of Lake Titicaca. Rivers are the main highways, though navigation is hazardous. The economic potential of the area includes reserves of timber, excellent land for rubber, jute, rice, tropical fruits and coffee and the breeding of cattle. The vast majority of Peru's oil and gas reserves are also east of the Andes.

Bolivia → *Land area: 1,098,581 sq km.*

A harsh, strange land, with a dreary grey solitude except for the bursts of green after rain, Bolivia is the only South American country with no coastline or navigable river to the sea. It is dominated by the Andes and has five distinct geographical areas. The **Andes** are at their widest in Bolivia, a maximum of 650 km. The Western Cordillera, which separates Bolivia from Chile, has high peaks of 5,800 m-6,500 m and a number of active volcanoes along its crest. The Eastern Cordillera also rises to giant massifs, with several peaks over 6,000 m in the Cordillera Real section to the north. The far sides of the Cordillera Real fall away very sharply to the northeast, towards the Amazon basin. The air is unbelievably clear – the whole landscape is a bowl of luminous light.

The **Altiplano** lies between the Cordilleras, a bleak, treeless, windswept plateau, much of it 4,000 m above sea-level. Its surface is by no means flat, and the Western Cordillera sends spurs dividing it into basins. The more fertile northern part has more inhabitants; the southern part is parched desert and almost unoccupied, save for a mining town here and there. Nearly 70% of the population lives on it; over half of the people in towns. **Lake Titicaca**, at the northern end of the Altiplano, is an inland sea of 8,965 sq km at 3,810 m, the highest navigable water in the world. Its depth, up to 280 m in some places, keeps the lake at an even all-year-round temperature of 10° C. This modifies the extremes of winter and night temperatures on the surrounding land, which supports a large Aymara indigenous population, tilling the fields and the hill terraces, growing potatoes and cereals, tending their sheep, alpaca and llamas, and using the resources of the lake. The **Yungas** and the **Puna** are to the east of the Altiplano. The heavily forested northeastern slopes of the Cordillera Real are deeply indented by the fertile valleys of the Yungas, drained into the Amazon lowlands by the Río Beni and its tributaries, where cacao, coffee, sugar, coca and tropical fruits are grown. Further south, from a point just north of Cochabamba, the Eastern Cordillera rises abruptly in sharp escarpments from the Altiplano and then flattens out to an easy slope east to the plains: an area known as the Puna. The streams which flow across the Puna cut increasingly deep incisions as they gather volume until the Puna is eroded to little more than a high remnant between the river valleys. In these valleys a variety of grain crops and fruits is grown.

The **tropical lowlands** stretch from the foothills of the Eastern Cordillera to the borders with Brazil, Paraguay and Argentina. They take up 70% of the total area of Bolivia, but contain only about 20% of its population. In the north and east the Oriente has dense tropical forest. Open plains covered with rough pasture, swamp and scrub occupy the centre. Before the expulsion of the Jesuits in 1767 this was a populous land of plenty; for 150 years Jesuit missionaries had controlled the area and guided it into a prosperous security. Decline followed but in recent years better times have returned. Meat is now shipped from Trinidad, capital of Beni Department, and from airstrips in the area, to the urban centres of La Paz, Oruro, and Cochabamba. Further south, the forests and plains beyond the Eastern Cordillera sweep down towards the Río Pilcomayo, which drains into the Río de la Plata, getting progressively less rain and merging into a comparatively dry land of scrub forest and arid savanna. The main city of this area is Santa Cruz de la Sierra, founded in the 16th century, now the second city of Bolivia and a large agricultural centre.

The Southern Cone

Chile → *Land area: 756, 626 sq km.*

Chile is a ribbon of land lying between the Andes and the Pacific. The Andes and a coastal range of highland take up from a third to a half of its width. There are wide variations of soil and vast differences of climate; these profoundly affect the density of population. Down virtually the whole length, between the Andes and the coastal ranges, is a longitudinal depression. For 1,050 km south of the capital Santiago this is a great valley stretching as far as Puerto Montt.

South of Puerto Montt the sea has broken through the coastal range and drowned the valley, and there is a bewildering assortment of archipelagos and channels. The Andes, with many snow-capped peaks over 6,000 m, culminate near Santiago with several of almost 7,000 m. They diminish in height from Santiago southwards, but throughout the range are spectacular volcanoes right down to the southern seas, where the Strait of Magellan gives access to the Atlantic. Associated with the mountains are geological faults and earthquakes are common.

From north to south the country falls into five contrasted zones: The first 1,250 km from the Peruvian frontier to Copiapó is a rainless desert of hills and plains devoid of vegetation. Here lie nitrate deposits and several copper mines. There is almost no rain, just occasional mists. From Copiapó to Illapel (600 km) is semi-desert; there is a slight winter rainfall, but great tracts of land are without vegetation most of the year. Valley bottoms are cultivated under irrigation. From Illapel to Concepción is Chile's heartland, where the vast majority of its people live. Here there is abundant rainfall in the winter, but the summers are perfectly dry. Great farms and vineyards cover the country, which is exceptionally beautiful. The fourth zone, between Concepción and Puerto Montt, is a country of lakes and rivers, with heavy rainfall through much of the year. Cleared and cultivated land alternates with mountains and primeval forests.The fifth zone, from Puerto Montt to Cape Horn, stretches for 1,600 km. This is archipelagic Chile, a sparsely populated region of wild forests and mountains, glaciers, islands and channels. Rainfall is torrential, and the climate cold. South of Puerto Montt, the Camino Austral provides almost unbroken road access for more than 1,000 km. Chilean Patagonia is in the extreme south of this zone. A subdivision of the fifth zone is Atlantic Chile – that part which lies along the Magellan Strait to the east of the Andes, including the Chilean part of Tierra del Fuego island. There is a cluster of population here raising sheep and mining coal. Large offshore oilfields have been discovered in the far south.

Argentina ➔ *Land area: 2, 780, 092 sq km.*

Argentina occupies most of the southern cone of the continent. There are four main physical areas: the Andes, the north and Mesopotamia, the Pampas, and Patagonia. Much of the country is comparatively flat which made modern communications easy. The **Andes** run the full length of Argentina, low and deeply glaciated in the Patagonian south, high and dry in the prolongation in northwest Argentina adjoining the Bolivian Altiplano. Though of modest height, Cerro Fitzroy and other peaks on the fringes of the Patagonia icecap are amongst the most dramatic on the continent, while many peaks in the north are over 6,000 m, including Aconcagua, the highest outside the Himalayas. To the east, in the shadow of the Andes, it is dry. Oases strung along the eastern foot of the Andes from Jujuy to San Rafael, including Tucumán and Mendoza, were the first places to be colonized by the Spaniards. Further south is the beautiful Lake District, with Bariloche at its heart. The mountain ridges and the many lakes created by the glaciers are now withdrawing under the impact of global warming. The **north** and **Mesopotamia** contains the vast plains of the Chaco and the floodplain lying between the rivers Paraná and Uruguay. Rice growing and ranching are widespread. The Province of Misiones in the northeast lies on the great Paraná plateau while the northwest Chaco has some of the highest temperatures in the continent.

The **Pampas** make up the heart of the country. These vast, rich plains lie south of the Chaco, and east of the Andes down to the Río Colorado. Buenos Aires lies on the northeast corner of the Pampas and is the only part of the country which has a dense population – about 40% of Argentines live in and around the capital. The Pampas stretch for hundreds of kilometres in almost unrelieved flatness, but get progressively wetter going east. Cattle and cereal growing dominate. **Patagonia** lies south of the Río Colorado – a land of arid, wind-swept plateaux cut across by ravines. In the deep south the wind is wilder and more continuous. There is no real summer, but the winters are rarely severe.

Uruguay ➔ *Land area: 406,752 sq km.*
Unlike all other South American countries, Uruguay is compact (it's the smallest Hispanic country in South America), accessible and homogeneous. The **coast** along the Atlantic consists of bays, beaches and off-shore islands, lagoons and bars, the sand brought by currents north from the River Plate. Behind is a narrow plain which fringes most of the coast (but not near Montevideo). Behind is a line of mainly wooded hills (called *cuchillas*), the whole area extensively farmed with grain and cattle *estancias.* **Central Uruguay** up to the Brazilian border is pleasant, rolling country dissected by the Río Negro which rises in Brazil and on which a number of dams have been built. North of the river is agricultural and pasture country dominated by sheep. Near Minas there are stone quarries and other mining activity. **western Uruguay** is dominated by the River Plate from Montevideo round to Colonia, then north up the Río Uruguay which provides the frontier with Argentina. It consists of an alluvial flood plain stretching north to Fray Bentos where the first road crossing can be made. Thereafter, the general character of the land is undulating, with little forest except on the banks of its rivers and streams. The long grass slopes rise gently to far-off hills, but none of these is higher than 600 m. Five rivers flow westwards across the country to drain into the Río Uruguay, including the Río Negro. Cattle and wheat are the main traditional products.

Paraguay ➔ *Land area: 406, 752 sq km.*
Paraguay is landlocked, divided into two distinct regions by the Río Paraguay. Eastern Paraguay combines habitats characteristic of three ecoregions: *cerrado* (a mosaic of dry forest and savanna habitats) in the north, humid Atlantic forest in the east, and natural grasslands and marshes in the south. West of the river lies the vast expanse of the Chaco, comprised of seasonally flooded palm-savannas in the south-east, semi-arid thorn scrub-forest to the west, and in the north, the Pantanal, part of the world's largest wetland. The Río Paraná forms part of the eastern and southern boundaries of the country but the rivers are so difficult to navigate that communication with Buenos Aires, 1,450 km from Asunción, has been mainly on land.

Eastern Paraguay is the 40% of the country east of the Río Paraguay, a rich land of rolling hills in which the vast majority of the population live. An escarpment runs north from the Río Alto Paraná, west of Encarnación, to the Brazilian border. East of this escarpment the Paraná Plateau extends across neighbouring parts of Argentina and Brazil. The Plateau, which is crossed by the Río Paraná, ranges from 300-600 m in height, was originally forest and enjoys relatively high levels of rainfall. West and south of the escarpment and stretching to the Río Paraguay lies a fertile plain with wooded hills, drained by several tributaries of the Río Paraná. Most of the population of Paraguay lives in these hilly lands, stretching southeast from the capital, to Encarnación. The area produces timber, cotton, hides and semi-tropical products. Closer to the rivers, much of the plain is flooded once a year; it is wet savanna, treeless, but covered with coarse grasses. The **Chaco**, about 60% of the country's area, is a flat, infertile plain stretching north along the west bank of the Río Paraguay. The marshy, largely unnavigable Río Pilcomayo, flowing southeast across the Chaco to join the Río Paraguay near Asunción, forms the frontier with Argentina. The landscape is dominated by the alluvial material brought down in the past by rivers from the Andes. As the rainfall diminishes westwards, the land can support little more than scrub and cacti. The arrival of the Mennonites in the 1930s in the Chaco brought some intense production of fruit and other crops.

Brazil and the north

Brazil ➔ *Land area: 8,547,404 sq km.*
Brazil is one of the largest countries of the world. It stretches over 4,300 km across the continent but is one of the few in South America that does not reach the Andes. The two great river basins, the Amazon and the River Plate, account for about three-fifths of Brazil's area.

The **Amazon Basin**, in northern and western Brazil, takes up more than a third of the whole country. The basin borders the Andes and funnels narrowly to the Atlantic, recalling the geological period, before the uplift of the Andes, when the Amazon flowed into the Pacific Ocean. Most of the drained area has an elevation of less than 250 m. The rainfall is heavy: some few places receive 3,750-5,000 mm a year, though over most of the area it is no more than from 1,500 to 2,500 mm. This heavy rain comes from the daily cycle of intense evaporation plus the saturated air brought by winds from the northeast and southeast, losing their moisture as they approach the Andes. Much of the basin suffers from annual floods. The region was covered by tropical forest, with little undergrowth except along the watercourses; it is now being rapidly cut down. The climate is hot and humidity high all year. The **Brazilian Highlands** lying southeast of the Amazon and northeast of the River Plate Basin form a tableland of from 300 to 900 m high, but here and there, mostly in southeast Brazil, mountain ranges rise from it. The highest temperature recorded was 42°C, in the dry northeastern states. The highest peak in southern Brazil, the Pico da Bandeira, northeast of Rio, is 2,898 m. The **Great Escarpment** is where the Brazilian Highlands cascade sharply down to the Atlantic, leaving a narrow coastal strip which is the economic heartland of the country. It runs from south of Salvador as far as Porto Alegre and in only a few places is this Escarpment breached by deeply cut river beds, for example those of the Rio Doce and the Rio Paraíba. Along most of its course, the Great Escarpment falls to the sea in parallel steps, each step separated by the trough of a valley. The few rivers rising on the Escarpment, which flow direct into the Atlantic are not navigable. Most of the rivers flow west, deep into the interior. Those in southern Brazil rise almost within sight of the sea, but run westward through the vast interior to join the Paraná, often with falls as they leave the Escarpment, including the spectacular Iguaçú. In the central area the Escarpment rivers run away from the sea to join the São Francisco river, which flows northwards parallel to the coast for 2,900 km, to tumble over the Paulo Afonso Falls on its eastward course to the Atlantic.

The **River Plate Basin**, in the southern part of Brazil, has a more varied surface and is less heavily forested than the Amazon Basin. The land is higher and the climate a little cooler. The **Guiana Highlands**, north of the Amazon, are ancient rock structures, some of the world's oldest. The area is part forest, part hot desert. Slopes facing northeast trade winds get heavy rainfall, but south it is drier. Brazil's highest peak, Pico da Neblina, 3,014 m, is on the Venezuelan border.

Guyane → *Land area: 83,900-86, 504 sq km (estimate).*
Guyane has its eastern frontier with Brazil formed partly by the river Oiapoque (Oyapock in French) and its southern, also with Brazil, formed by the Tumuc-Humac mountains (the only range of importance). The western frontier with Suriname is along the river Maroni-Litani. To the north is the Atlantic coastline of 320 km. The land rises gradually from a coastal strip some 15-40 km wide to the higher slopes and plains or savannahs, about 80 km inland. Forests cover the hills and valleys of the interior, and the territory is well watered, for over 20 rivers run to the Atlantic.

Suriname → *Land area: 163,820 sq km. (A large area in the southwest is in dispute with Guyana. There is a less serious border dispute with Guyane in the southeast.)*
Like its neighbours, Suriname has a coastline on the Atlantic to the north. The principal rivers are the Marowijne in the east, the Corantijn in the west, and the Suriname, Commewijne (with its tributary, the Cottica), Coppename, Saramacca and Nickerie. The country is divided into topographically quite diverse natural regions: the northern lowlands, 25 km wide in the east and 80 km wide in the west, have clay soil covered with swamps. There follows a region, 5-6 km wide, of a loamy and very white sandy soil, then an undulating region, about 30 km wide. It is mainly savanna, mostly covered with quartz sand, and overgrown with grass and shrubs. South of this lies the interior highland, almost entirely overgrown with dense tropical forest, intersected by streams. At the southern boundary with Brazil there are savannas.

Guyana → *Land area: 215,083 sq km.*
Guyana has an area of 215,083 sq km, nearly the size of Britain, but only about 2.5% is cultivated. About 90% of the population lives on the narrow coastal plain, either in Georgetown, the capital, or in villages along the main road running from Charity in the west to the Suriname border. The rivers give some access to the interior beyond which are the jungles and highlands towards the border with Brazil.

The **coastal plain** is mostly below sea level. Large wooden houses stand on stilts above ground level. A sea wall keeps out the Atlantic and the fertile clay soil is drained by a system of dykes; sluice gates, *kokers* are opened to let out water at low tide. Separate channels irrigate fields in dry weather. Most of the western third of the coastal plain is undrained and uninhabited. Four **major rivers** cross the coastal plain, from west to east they are the Essequibo, the Demerara, the Berbice, and the Corentyne. Only the Demerara is crossed by bridges. Elsewhere ferries must be used. At the mouth of the Essequibo River, 34 km wide, are islands the size of Barbados. The lower reaches of these rivers are navigable; but waterfalls and rapids prevent them being used by large boats to reach the interior. (The area west of the Essequibo River, about 70% of the national territory, is claimed by Venezuela.) The **jungles** and the **highlands** inland from the coastal plain, are thick rain forest, although in the east there is a large area of grassland. Towards Venezuela the rain forest rises in a series of steep escarpments, with spectacular waterfalls, the highest and best known of which are the Kaieteur Falls on the Potaro River. In the southwest is the Rupununi Savanna, an area of grassland more easily reached from Brazil than from Georgetown.

Venezuela → *Land area: 912, 050 sq km.*
Venezuela has 2,800 km of coastline on the Caribbean Sea and many islands. The Andes run up north-eastwards from Colombia, along the coast eastwards past Caracas, ending up as the north coast of the Caribbean island of Trinidad. In the northwest corner is the Maracaibo basin. South of the Andean spine is the vast plain of the Orinoco which reaches the sea near the Guyana border and to the southeast of that are the ancient rocks known as the Guayana Highlands.

The **Andes** are highest near the Colombian border where they are known as the Sierra Nevada de Mérida. Beyond they broaden out into the Segovia Highlands north of Barquisimeto, and then turn east in parallel ridges along the coast to form the Central Highlands, dipping into the Caribbean Sea only to rise again into the North Eastern Highlands of the peninsulas of Araya and Paria. This region has an agreeable climate and is well populated with most of the main towns. The **Maracaibo Lowlands** are around the fresh water lake of Maracaibo, the largest lake in South America, is 12,800 sq km. Considerable rainfall feeds the lake and many rivers flow through thick forest to create swamps on its southern shore. The area is dominated by the oil producing fields on both sides of the lake and beneath its surface. To the west, the Sierra de Perijá forms the boundary with Colombia and outside the lake to the east is the most northerly point of the country the peninsular of Paraguaná, virtually desert.

The **Llanos**, as the Orinoco plains are called, cover about one third of the country. They are almost flat and are a vast cattle range. The Orinoco river itself is part of Latin America's third largest river system. Many significant rivers flow from the Andes and Guayana Highlands to join the Orinoco, whose delta is made up of innumerable channels and thousands of forest-covered islands. The **Guayana Highlands**, which take up almost half the country, are south of the Orinoco. This is an area of ancient crystalline rocks that extend along the top of the continent towards the mouth of the Amazon and form the northern part of Brazil. In Venezuela they are noted for huge, precipitous granite blocks known as *tepuys*, many of which have their own unique flora, and create many high waterfalls including the Angel Falls, the world's highest.

Culture

Music in South America

From buses and street buskers to bars and beaches, travel in South America comes with an almost constant and richly varied soundtrack. But just as anywhere, the music to which travellers are initially exposed tends to be the most commercial and least interesting. It's well worth spending a little time exploring further. Some of your most memorable times will be on musical nights out: learning tango steps in Buenos Aires, salsa in Medellín or *forró* on a Brazilian beach; hearing live music played by an Andean quartet in a *peña* in La Paz or Cuzco, or a symphony orchestra playing Villa-Lobos in one of São Paulo's concert halls.

South America's music falls into three broad categories; all of which are as distinct from each other as they are from music from the rest of the world. First there is the music of Spanish America, from Cuban and Spanish Caribbean-influenced Venezuela and Colombia to the indigenous melodies and rhythms of the Andean countries and the political folk music and tango of Chile, Argentina, Paraguay and Uruguay. Then there is the music of Brazil, a musical continent in its own right, whose panoply of styles and rhythms is perhaps the richest of any single country on the planet. Finally there's the music of the Guianas, whose *calypso* and *kaseko* offers a tiny Caribbean coda to a vast Latin musical manuscript.

Tango and the protest song: Argentina, Chile and Uruguay

Musically **Argentina** is forever associated with tango: an exuberant musical style and dramatic, entwined close dance which has so much become the passionate step of choice in Hollywood films, that it is in danger of becoming a cliché, even in its home city. But beyond the Buenos Aires tourist shows and in the more resolutely Argentine bars and clubs, tango remains mesmerising. Its musical origins lie in the *milonga*, an African-infused rhythm and dance popular in Argentina's small slave communities in the 19th century which later developed as a dance in its own right. According to Argentines, the fusion of *milonga* rhythms with European and Cuban styles in the overcrowded tenements and bordellos around the Buenos Aires docks in the late 19th century gave birth to tango, its name originally associated with a place where freed African slaves and impoverished Europeans would gather to dance.

Initially tango was probably played on guitar and fiddle. But as it grew in popularity it met with a new instrument, a button accordion or 'bandonion', developed in Germany by Heinrich Band and probably taken to Buenos Aires by Bavarian immigrants. By the late 19th century, a 142-note version with 71 buttons called the *bandoneón* was being played in a new, exuberant percussive style with chops on chords intertwining with more lyrical solo passages, far removed from its Protestant origins, but perfect for tango. Bandoneón-powered tango swept through blue-collar Buenos Aires in the early 20th century, where it was discovered by the young Buenos Aires elite. They in turn introduced the music to Belle Epoque Paris, where it became a fashion craze in 1913. From there it spread to the rest of Europe and thence to the United States, where it was introduced to the Hollywood screen by Fred Astaire and Ginger Rogers in the 1939 film *The Story of Vernon and Irene Castle* .

Meanwhile in Buenos Aires the tango had evolved in altogether different directions, where a French-born Porteño street urchin turned bordello singer called Charles Romauld Gardés (**Carlos Gardel**) re-invented tango - see also under Uruguay, below. Before Gardel tango was instrumental, but the singer introduced poetic lyrics, sung in a rich baritone infused with wistful Gallic melancholy. His first recording in 1917 was an instant hit with all social classes and his rakish good looks, trademark fedora hat, sharp suits and faux-Rudolph Valentino stage make-up made him one of Argentina's first pin-ups. Gardel died in a plane crash over Colombia in 1935, but he left an extensive back catalogue of tango standards, a burgeoning golden era (with new stars like Osvaldo Pugliese, Aníbal Troilo, Tita Merello, Alberto Castillo and Roberto Goyeneche) and a 14 year-old protégé, **Astor Piazzolla**.

If Gardel took tango from the underground to the mainstream, Piazzolla took it from the mainstream to the intelligentsia; creating the *nuevo tango*, a fusion of tango, jazz harmony and classical lyricism born of his exposure to international styles in pre-War New York where he lived with his parents as a teenager. On his return to Buenos Aires Piazzolla joined **Aníbal Troilo**'s tango orchestra in the 1940s. Through the 1950s and 1960s he perfected his classical composition with Nadia Boulanger in Paris, incorporated his *bandoneón* into jazz-tango octets and composed symphonic pieces rooted in tango. Not until the 1980s did his new tango quintet achieve worldwide recognition and inspire a renaissance in danced tango. Post-Piazzolla, tango is a diverse, international genre, incorporating traditional sung and instrumental tango but stretching into classical and jazz-tango and recently the tango rock and electronica of bands like the **Bajofondo**, the **Gotan Project**, **Kantango** and **Tanghetto**. Danced tango is booming, with Buenos Aires celebrating three important festivals: the Tango Championship, the Tango World Cup and the Tango Festival.

Argentine music is not of course limited to tango. Argentina's borders with Uruguay and Brazil have produced music inspired by the African-infused cultures of those countries and there has been much cross-over from other South American countries. They include *chacarera*, a popular dance in the northwest, *chamamé*, its counterpart in the north east, and *zamba*, a slow dance in waltz time played on guitar and *bombo legüero* drum. Once considered Argentina's national dance, the *zamba* is now known to have originated in the creole region of Peru.

Chile and the *nueva canción* Popular music shows an even stronger cross-over, mostly notably in the *nueva canción*, a politically aware rootsy folk music genre sung by charismatic performers and inspired by the Cuban *nueva trova*. The movement probably began in Chile in the late 1950s and early 1960s, where a group of middle-class, intellectual artists which included **Violeta Parra** began to fuse traditional Andean and creole musical forms (notably the *cueca*) with folk music. Parra and her children Angel and Isabel, were among the first middle-class musicians to 'rediscover' the armadillo-shell mandolin (*charango*) and the bamboo Inca flute (*quena*). Violeta Parra composed what later became one of the *nueva canción* anthems, *Gracias a la vida*. By the late 1960s their songs had become politically motivated and the musical textures increasingly Andean. And their work inspired groups like **Inti-Illimani** and **Quilapayún**, who used pre-Columbian rhythms and instruments, juxtaposing them with European melodies and contemporary lyrics. They sang of solidarity among Latin American peoples and demanded social justice, in particular for the oppressed native majority.

In Santiago in 1965 Angel and Isabel Parra opened what would become the crucible for nueva canción, the **Peña de los Parra**. One of the regulars at the club was a radical young poet and songwriter, **Victor Jara**, whose witty, subversive songs, which poked fun at conservative Chilean society and satirised government, earned him a loyal following. The Parras, Jara and the other artists became closely involved with **Salvador Allende's** Popular Unity government. After it came to power in 1970 Allende appeared on a giant stage in the centre of Santiago surrounded by *nuevo cancioneros* under a banner proclaiming 'No hay revolución sin canciones' (There is no revolution without songs). Three years later Allende was dead and many of the *nuevo cancioneros* were tortured and murdered by the Pinochet régime. Victor Jara's body was found in a pile of unidentified bodies in a Santiago mortuary, his hands and wrists smashed and his torso shredded by machine gun bullets. *Nueva canción* and even Andean traditional music were banned until Pinochet's fall.

In Argentina **Atahualpa Yupanqui** was perhaps the most important early figure in the *nueva canción* movement. Born Héctor Chavero in 1908, he changed his name in honour of the last Inca Emperor and in homage to the Andean people after undertaking a musicological journey

Argentina, Chile and Uruguay: the essential CDs

Astor Piazzolla, *Maestro and Revolutionary*. An excellent two-volume compilation covering a sweep of the great composer and bandoneón player's work.
Victor Jara, *Antología Musical*. A re-mastered collection of many of Jara's greatest songs.
Mercedes Sosa, *30 Años*. The best of the numerous collections with many of her classics.
Soda Stereo, *Canción Animal*. Their sixth and most successful, multi-platinum album, showcasing their trademark Hispanic Indie rock with Edge-influenced rhythm guitar.

throughout the continent between the World Wars. His song *¡Basta Ya! (que el yanqui mande)* (That's enough! Of taking orders from the Yanquees) made him one of the movement's first exiles and ironically Yupanqui later found his most appreciative audience in Europe, especially France where he was made un Chevalier dans l'ordre des Arts et des Lettre (Knight of the Order of Arts and Letters) in 1986.

The other giant figure in Argentine *nueva canción* was **Mercedes Sosa**, who had one of the most beautiful, resonant voices in 20th century popular music. Like Yupanqui she had been involved in the movement from the outset, unveiling the *nuevo canciónero* manifesto in 1962: to revive old pre-Columbian musical forms and sing about rural poverty, injustice and the beauty of native Latin America. Her renditions of songs by artists like Violeta Parra earned her the enmity of the military junta in the 1960s and 1970s. And after singing *Cuando Tenga la Tierra* (a song which championed all those who fight against oppressive landowners) she was arrested and forced into exile in Europe. She returned to Argentina after the dictatorship was weakened by the Falklands/Malvinas conflict. In the Uruguayan *canto popular* movement, artists like **Los Olimareños**, **Daniel Viglieti** and **Alfredo Zitarrosa** were similarly critical of the existing order in the 1960s and 1970s. Like their Chilean and Argentine counterparts, several were persecuted or forced into exile.

While *nueva canción* has all but disappeared, Argentine rock, or *rock nacional*, has bloomed since the fall of the military junta. It began in the 1960s, inspired strongly by British Merseybeat and the Rolling Stones, who were Latinised by Uruguayan group **Los Shakers** who arrived in Buenos Aires, complete with pudding bowl haircuts in 1965. British rock continued to be influential through the late 1960s and into the 1970s, though it increasingly incorporated national styles. Important figures include **Los Gatos**, whose 1967 *La Balsa* established a melodic national pop style, the inventive maverick **Charly García** and his groups (which included **Sui Generis** and **Serú Girán**), who fused this melodic style with psychedelia and established national rock firmly with the Porteño middle classes.

Until the collapse of the military dictatorship Argentinean rock was largely limited to Argentina. But in the 1980s, Argentine rock became popular throughout Latin America through bands like the irrepressibly funky, brass-driven **Fabulosos Cadillacs** and **Soda Stereo**, one of the biggest selling Spanish language bands of all time. National rock is now the most popular music with young Argentines, far more so than tango. Bands of the moment to look out for include: **Los Piojos, Babasónicos, La Renga, Las Pelotas, Divididos, Attaque 77, Intoxicados**, and **Bersuit**.

Uruguay has long been a cultural bridge between Brazil and Argentina and generally shares its musical heritage with both (not that many Uruguayans would agree). They complain that they are treated merely as an addendum to their giant neighbours, while in fact it was they who invented tango, and who have been hosting one of the liveliest carnivals on the continent for at least as long as Rio. The Uruguayan tango narrative is similar to Argentina's; their story merely replaces Buenos

Aires' poor Africanised quarters as the setting for tango's fomentation with Montevideo's. Carlos Gardel, say Uruguayans was born in Tacuarembó in Uruguay's cattle country, and not Paris. There's even a museum to him in that town. And while both claims are disputed by Porteños across the water, there is no question that a number of tango's biggest names are Uruguayan: **Gerardo Matos Rodríguez** who wrote many of the genres most famous standards including *La Cumparsita*; Fifties crooner **Julio Sosa** and his contemporary, the orchestra maestro and virtuoso violinst **Francisco Canaro**; bandoneón virtuoso **Marino Rivero** and singer **Elsa Morán**.

In the 18th century, half of Uruguay's population was made-up of mostly Bantu-speaking African slaves, from a similar cultural background to those transported to Brazil. And while African culture was more brutally and successfully suppressed by the Spanish than by the Portuguese, it left its rhythms and rituals which can still be seen today. *Murga* is a kind of musical theatre backed by a rhythm similar to maracatu, with extemporaneous poetry recalling the Brazilian *repentistas* and costumes inspired by a pre-Lenten festival in Cadiz. *Candombe* drum and dance troupes (who recall those of Salvador or Cuba), play in Montevideo most weekends and both *murga* and *candombe* play in huge parades during Carnival. In the 1960s *candombe* was incorporated into Uruguayan mainstream music, from chart pop to folk, rock and jazz. A tradition which continued in the music of artists like **Hugo Fattorusso** and **Jorge Drexler** and in Uruguayan rock, which is as popular as Argentine and a good deal older. As said above, it was Uruguay's Los Shakers who brought rock to Argentina. The annual rock festival in Durazno attracts hundreds of thousands, to hear a string of cult bands who include **La Vela Puerca**, **No Te Va Gustar**, **La Trampa** and **Buitres**.

The South American Caribbean: Colombia, Venezuela and the Guianas

While Venezuela and Colombia are famously at odds, musically they share much in common, both in their folk traditions and in their national obsessions with **salsa**, a style born from Cuban rhythms in the back streets of New York but kidnapped by these two nations who have made it their own. Venezuela gave the world **Oscar d'León**, a former motor mechanic from Caracas with an irrepressible smile who made his name dancing and playing upright bass with Cuban-influenced *son* band, **La Dimensión Latina** in the 1970s. He has since become one of the biggest salsa acts in the world, with a host of imitators. **Caracas**'s clubs and bars are filled with imitation Oscar d'León big bands and singers.

Colombia's most famous musical export is **Shakira**, whose good looks and high-octane salsa pop (infused with Arabic rhythms drawn from her Lebanese heritage) have made her one of the Hispanic world's most successful recording artists. She was born in Barranquilla and her sound is typical of Western and coastal Colombia. Cities like Cali, Medellín, Cartagena and Barranquilla pulsate to a fusion of contemporary Hispanic rhythms; but mostly to salsa. Much to the chagrin of Caracas, Colombia's third largest city, **Cali** declares itself the world salsa capital and has re-christened its annual, week-long July festival **La Feria de la Salsa**, the largest and loudest salsa celebration on the planet. Colombian salsa singers who often play in Cali include **Grupo Niche** and **Joe Arroyo**, the inventor of *música tropical*, a peculiarly Colombian fusion of salsa and other musical ingredients. Moreover, the city has re-invented salsa dancing; its style, possibly the most respected on the world salsa circuit, has complex, fast and furious steps and swings.

Colombians claim that salsa's roots lie in their national rhythm, *cumbia*, as much as Cuban *son* or *mambo*, or Dominican *merengue*. Indeed most visitors to Colombia will find it hard to distinguish between contemporary *cumbia* and *salsa*; both of which are powered by shuffling kit drums, congas and bass, peppered with brass and garnished with lightly syncopated piano. Traditional *cumbia* is quite different; and seeing it played and danced in a little bar in Cartagena or by a drum choir in Bogotá is a magical experience. Cumbia grew from the miscegenation of enslaved Africans and local indigenous people. Like other such styles(candombe in Uruguay or samba de roda in Brazil), it traditionally consists of no more than percussion, *flauto de millo* and

The South American Caribbean: the essential CDs

Oscar d'León, *The Millennium Collection*. A representative selection of his greatest hits.
Grupo Niche, *Los Clásicos*. The salsa groups early greatest hits.
Alejo Durán, *15 Exitos de Antología*. One of the few CDs available on the international market.
Juan Vicente Torrealba, *Concierto en la Llanura*. One of Torrealba's grand llanera compositions.
Yakki Famirie, *Gowtu*. Irrepressibly dancey kaseko music from a Suriname and Holland-based band.

gaita flutes and vocals. It is danced in a series of distinctive short, scraped steps which reputedly hark back to a time when Africans were forced to dance in leg irons.

In the 1980s a rural, accordion-driven form of cumbia called **vallenato** emerged in the north-eastern municipality of **Valledupar** and swept across Colombia. It was born from a far older style whose origins are shrouded in mystery. A Valledupar urban myth claims that vallenato was invented by a mythical figure called **Francisco el Hombre** who, like Robert Johnson, learnt his skill from the devil after being challenged to a musical duel on a dusty road in Alta Guajira. Modern vallenato's sweet ballads seem to belie any demonic origins. But an exploration of the genre's back catalogue reveals artists like the late great **Alejo Durán**, whose rootsy renditions of songs like *Fidelina* and *Altos del Rosario* have much of the Robert Johnson to them. A **Vallenato festival** is held in Durán's honour every April or May in Valledupar, offering the chance to hear some of the best traditional artists in the genre. These include the Hendrix of the genre, **Alfredo Gutiérrez**, who plays the accordion with his toes.

If **Venezuela** has a national music it is **llanera**, sung by cowboy troubadours from the sweeping grasslands, accompanied by harp, guitar and percussion. In its most refined form, as played by the likes of stetson-clad septuagenarian **Juan Vicente Torrealba**, llanera sounds like a fusion between calypso, easy listening and classical music, whilst mainstream, popular llanera's syrupy songs are closer to Mexican mariachi music. There's llanera in Colombia too, together with a broad diversity of other national musical styles. These include an alluring, seductive fusion of Caribbean, East African and Latin rhythms called *champeta* which is popular in Colombia. In the villages of the Sabana de Bolívar you'll hear lively *porro* brass bands. And in some of the southern mountain towns and in neighbouring Ecuador, there are groups of *bambuco* musicians who play *música del interior*, which is akin to the Andean music of Peru and Bolivia.

The Guianas have some of the most interesting and unexpected ethnic mixes in South America: Caribbean and East Indian, Amerindian, Dutch and Javanese, West African, Hmong, French, British, and Garifuna. While the music is strongly influenced by the Caribbean, particularly Jamaica (through **reggae** and **dub**) and Trinidad (through **calypso** and **soca**), Guianan music reflects this diversity. In Georgetown you'll hear Jamaican Reggae alongside **Bollywood film music** and South Asian Guianese music from the likes of Berbice-born **Terry Gajraj**, whose spicey mix of soca, reggae and Indian singing is known as **Chutney** music. And you'll hear **shanto**, Trinidad calypso with a Guyanese spin and mischievous lyrics, and local pop, reggae and soca from a diverse roll call of musicians from established names like **Eddy Grant** (who had big international hits with *Baby Come Back* and *I Don't Want to Dance*) and new faces like **Fojo**.

In Cayenne and Paramaribo there's energetic French Antillean **zouk** which swept out of Guadaloupe and across France in the 1990s, and **kaseko**, one of the most exciting sounds on the continent, a swirling, fast-paced fusion of African and Caribbean music played by the likes of **Yakki Famirie**, with a called vocal and choral response sung in *papamiento* Creole or Dutch over frenetic percussion. It is impossible to keep still to. And then there's Caribbean carnival music. Cayenne prides itself on having one of the best Caribbean carnivals outside Trinidad.

The pipes of the Andes: Peru, Bolivia and Ecuador
For many, the sprightly pan-pipe and *charango* mandolin music of the Andes, played by a troupe dressed in woven ponchos is synonymous with pre-Columbian South America. Yet while bamboo pipes or *siku*, and split-reed *quena* flutes have been used to make music in the Andes (together with conches and various percussion instruments) for thousands of years, contemporary Andean music is in reality a recent invention, born of a meeting between the indigenous past and the *nueva canción* movement in the late 1950s and early 1960s.

Marching bands of pan pipes swapping notes and melodic lines, accompanied by drum troupes and singers delighted the conquistadores. And the music of the Incas and their contemporaries thrives today in remote communities from southern Colombia to Bolivia, where it is played, as it probably always was, at rituals and key community events. Singing styles, melodies and modes vary from village to village, as do the instruments used, with the more traditional villages only playing percussion and woodwind. Were it not for the rise of left-wing politics in the 1950s Andean music would probably only have trickled out onto the world stage. But as discontent with dictatorship and the ruling élite grew after the Second World War and the Cuban revolution, so South American intellectuals looked to solidarity with the people. And with this came a rediscovery of their artistic and musical traditions (see *nueva canción* above). After the quiet Bolivian revolution of 1952, which saw a left-wing government sweep to power, indigenous Bolivians were afforded the greatest respect they had had since the Spanish conquest. They were granted suffrage, land was re-distributed and the new administration created a governmental department of folklore, one of whose functions was the organization of traditional music festivals. This climate and the influence of Argentine and Chilean groups like **Urubamba** (who formed in 1956 and introduced *El Cóndor Pasa* to Paul Simon) and **Quilapayún** (formed by a group of intellectuals at the Universidad de Chile), inspired a contemporaneous renaissance in Andean music in La Paz. In 1965 a singer and percussionist called Edgar 'Yayo' Joffré formed **Los Jairas**, a quartet who would provide the model for Andean music for the next 50 years.

Los Jairas were arguably the first world-music band, made up of enthusiastic middle-class intellectuals, traditional Andean musicians, a virtuoso classical guitarist called **Alfredo Domínguez** and Domínguez's musical sparring partner, the French-Swiss flute player **Gilbert Favre** (simply called 'El Gringo' by the Bolivian public). Favre was the former lover of the Chilean *nueva canciónera* Violeta Parra and one of the great unsung heroes of international musical co-operation. Los Jairas found a regular haunt in the **Peña Naira** in La Paz, where they re-invented Andean music and became a national sensation. Joffré's melodies and lyrics were imbued with wistful almost operatic melancholy and were accompanied by Ernesto Cavour's flamenco-tinged *charango* and Favre's lilting *quena* flute. All that was missing were the pan-pipes.

These were added by numerous Los Jairas imitators from La Paz to Quito. The most successful were **Los K'jarkas**, a Cochabamba-based trio of brothers with their own music school who penned what has since become the perennial *peña* encore, *Llorando se fue*. K'jarkas both consolidated and built-upon Los Jairas' Andean musical model. They retained the melancholic melodies and musical evocations of glorious pastoral landscapes, adding traditional costume, a stylised logo borrowing motifs from the carvings at Tiwanaku and a few up-tempo numbers drawing on Andean dance rhythms like the *huayno* and the *saya*. Los K'jarkas' fame spread throughout the Andean world, spawning a mini-musical revolution among the Quichua people of Ecuador whose *cachullapi* and *yumbo* dances are an interesting fusion of marching band, modern Andean and traditional Inca music.

In a *peña* in La Paz and Cuzco today what you'll hear is little more than a footnote to Los Jairas and Los K'jarkas, but music in Peru, Ecuador and Bolivia has diversified. Singers like **Emma Junaro** have taken the Andean sound and the *nueva canción* to produce a new, politically sensitive singer-songwriter genre known as **canto nuevo**. Singers like **Susana Baca** have brought the music of **Nicomedes Santa Cruz** and the musicians of African Peru to the attention of the world, through a series of stunning albums and mesmerising shows, and in the shanty towns of Lima and the lowlands of eastern Peru and Ecuador Amazonian **chicha** music has established itself as the new vernacular sound of the poor urban majority.

Brazil

Brazil is the musical capital of South America and one of the world's great musical nations, with more unique home-grown styles, breadth and diversity than the rest of the continent put together. And it's a musical continent apart: cross-overs between Brazil and Spanish America are almost non-existent and you'll struggle to find a Brazilian who's even heard of salsa, Shakira or who could name a single tango musician. Nor will you hear much *bossa nova*, that soft, lilting style sung by a breathy woman from an eternal summer and which is forever associated with Brazil abroad. It's a style which belongs to the late 1950s and which is heard mostly in tourist bars nowadays. Instead Brazilians dance to or play a bewildering array of contemporary musical styles which are unique to their country but which seldom escape its borders. Many are regional, as follows.

Rio: samba, funk and bossa nova If you've heard one Brazilian tune it's likely to be either the joyful chorus of *Mas que Nada* or a lift music version of *The Girl from Ipanema*. Both songs come from Rio de Janeiro and a time before men had walked on the moon. *Mas que Nada* is a **samba**, the country's most ubiquitous and enduring music style and the sound of Rio carnival. Samba was born in the poor, black district of Gamboa in the early 20th century and it comes in many forms, from the big drum troupes whose chorus of *tambores* and giant *surdo* bass drums can fill a stadium, to quieter, acoustic sung samba. But it is invariably best heard live and preferably in Rio de Janeiro itself. Despite its age samba lives on and remains very popular with young Brazilians – particularly as **samba soul** and **samba funk** (also known as Rio Samba, whose most famous exponents are **Jorge Ben** and **Seu Jorge**) and in its close-danced beach and barbecue form, **pagode**. Both samba and pagode are also dance styles, characterised by fast feet and leg movements and stiff hips and upper body. They are incredibly tricky to master.

For the first half of its life samba was working class, poor and black. But in the 1950s its rhythms were adopted by a group of young, white middle class boys from Ipanema and Copacabana. Musicians like the conservatory trained **Antônio Carlos (Tom) Jobim**, the poet and diplomat **Vinícius de Moraes** and Bahian émigré **João Gilberto** began to play a kind of samba on the acoustic guitar or piano. And they accompanied it with witty lyrics and more complex chord progressions drawn from French impressionist composers and a jazzier Brazilian musical style called **choro** (which is still popular today). Few of these new samba singers could sing and their breathy almost spoken vocal style became a trademark of the their sound, which was christened the new wave or **A Bossa Nova**. Bossa Nova became internationally famous when was adopted by a series of US 'cool jazz' musicians in the 1960s. The foremost of these was the saxophonist **Stan Getz** who in 1964 released one of the best-selling jazz albums of all time, *Getz/Gilberto*, with João Gilberto. It included a single version of Tom Jobim and Vinícius de Moraes' 'The Girl from Ipanema' (with English lyrics vastly inferior to Vinícius's). This rocketed into the Billboard chart and João's wife, **Astrud Gilberto**, who sang the song, was propelled to stardom. Her success defined and continues to define the Brazilian vocal style – light, happy and invariably female - in the minds of foreigners. It also stimulated an exodus of musicians from Brazil which included a Carioca session pianist called **Sergio Mendes**. He repeated Astrud's success with a popular samba song by Jorge Ben, *Mas Que Nada*. Bossa largely died in Brazil in the 1970s and it can be hard to hear it beyond the tourist bars. But it lived on in the USA as jazz-bossa and hotel lobby music and was resurrected in Europe in the new millennium with **Bebel Gilberto**'s club-chill out room re-recordings of her father João's music. Her sound is slowly beginning to filter back to Brazil's club and cocktail bar scene today.

Bahia: Tropicália and the rhythms and rituals of Africa Brazil's other great musical capital city is Salvador. From the late 1960s to the 1980s, this most African of Brazilian cities produced some of Brazil's most creative and exciting musicians. Choro, samba and bossa nova were all acoustically driven. When the Beatles and Hendrix rose to global stardom in the 1960s and Dylan picked up an electric guitar, there was something of a revolution in Brazil. Conservatives wanted to keep the country's music 'authentic' and unpolluted by foreign influences. Liberals, spearheaded by a group of avante garde musicians from Bahia led by **Tom Zé**, **Gilberto Gil** and **Caetano Veloso** and a São Paulo trio called **Os Mutantes**, embraced electric instruments and psychotropic drugs and took Brazilian music in a new electric direction. This was christened **Tropicália** or Tropicalismo after a fusion of the words psychedelia and Tropical. The seeds of Tropicália blew from Bahia over the whole of Brazil to produce fusions of rock, soul, funk and Brazilian rhythms. Collectively these came to be known as **MPB**, Música Popular Brasileira.

Acoustic music lived on in Bahia after Tropicália. The late 1970s saw the emergence of a string of heavily percussive bands focused around drum troupes and called **blocos afros**. These were cultural organizations associated with Salvador carnival and rooted in the ritual music of the African Brazilian spirit religion of **candomblé**, traditional **samba de roda** , sung in a ring of people and accompanied only by percussion, and the martial art dance of **capoeira**. Bands like **Olodum, Ilê Aiyê** and **Carlinhos Brown's Timbalada** promoted African-Brazilian issues and solidarity through their music. Seeing them up close in the streets of Salvador with dozens of drummers playing together in perfect syncopated unison is an incredibly powerful experience. But even the drums of the *blocos afros* are being drowned out by Bahia's most popular music, **axé**, which sounds a little like salsa sexed-up, fused with rock and roll and overdosing on speed. It is energetic but shallow, with slushy lyrics and little sophistication. It's also relentlessly commercial and is sweeping through the carnivals and clubs of the North East leaving musical variety and the more traditional musical styles in its wake. Thankfully Bahia's better music is undergoing a mini-Renaissance spurred on by the opening of Carlinhos Brown's **Centro de Música Negra** in Salvador's lower city and the arrival of exciting new acts like samba singer **Mariene de Castro** and African-influenced singer-songwriter **Tiganá Santana**.

Recife and São Luís: back to Africa and into the Mangroove For the time being Salvador's crown as the musical capital of the North East has passed to **Recife**, the new centre of African-Brazilian music, where the spirit of Tropicália lives on as **Mangue Beat**, and **São Luís** on the frontier of the Amazon. Going out for a Saturday night in the colonial centre of São Luís is unforgettable. Great groups of people gather together in impromptu bands to play the local equivalent of samba, **cacuriá**. Women dance, swing and swirl together in long flowing dresses and everyone is sucked into the throng. The city is at its liveliest during the **Bumba meu Boi** festivals, which have their own costumed dances. It also preserves a strong connection to the Caribbean through reggae, which is played live in many of the small bars in the city centre.

Recife is more avant garde and intellectual. The city has been producing great musicians for decades, including cult 70s and 80s singers **Alceu Valença** and **Lenine**, both of whom play superb shows at carnival. At weekends the smoky bars of the old city centre vibrate to the guitars, drums, desert fiddles and electrified accordions of dozens of experimental bands and singers, whose sound is a fusion of the traditional**maracatu** rhythms of African Pernambuco, folk sounds from the arid backlands and international rock influences from bands like Nick Cave and the Bad Seeds and Radiohead. Out of this diversity and desire to rediscover Pernambuco's African and rural-poor heritage emerged the scene known as **Mangue Beat** (or Mangue Bit) in the 1990s. It was led by the charismatic singer **Chico Science** and his band **Nação Zumbi**, Fred

Zeroquatro lead singer of another group **Mundo Livre** and rootsier **Mestre Ambrósio**. Chico died in a car crash in 1997 but Mundo Livre and Mestre Ambrósio's lead singer Siba, can be heard around Carnaval time. Their legacy and spirit live on in bands like **Mombojó** and **Cabruêra** from Paraíba who fuse mangue beat with experimental rock and hip hop.

The North East and the back-land barn dance jig The rest of North Eastern Brazil is dominated by **forró**, a kind of punchy jig originally driven by triangle, accordion and a deep bass drum, but now usually played by a full band. Popular wisdom says that the name derives from a Brazilianized pronunciation of the 'For All' dances thrown for railway workers by their British bosses in the early 20th Century. But the dance is probably far older and the name probably comes from an abbreviation of *forrobodó*, meaning dragged feet. Forró is party music. And the biggest parties of all are the **Festas Juninas** in the Sertão backlands in Caruaru, Pernambuco and Campina Grande in June when hundreds of thousands gather to dance at break net speed, yet so close that they are literally entwined. You can do the same at any time of year though in the beach bars in Maceió, Fortaleza and half a dozen other little resorts. But get a Brazilian to show you the dance steps first or you'll feel like a rugby player dancing ballet. In the last decade, perhaps inspired by Mangue Beat a number of acts have taken forró and the rhythms of the Sertão in more experimental directions. **Dona Zefinha** from Ceará mix theatre, roots music and dance in a spectacular show and **Dorivã** from Tocantins draws on North Eastern roots music to craft beautifully composed and played CDs. These and a further array of mesmerising acts can be heard at the **Mês da Música** in Fortaleza in November. The tiny states of Alagoas and Sergipe, sandwiched between Bahia and Pernambuco, have an illustrious musical heritage too, producing great names like **Hermeto Pascoal**, Brazil's Mingus, and the soul singer **Djavan**.

The Amazon: surf guitar and carimbó rock There's only one place in the Amazon for music, Belém. The city pounds to a springy West African meets the Caribbean rhythm of **carimbó** and twangs to the psychedelic sixties Dick Dale surf twang of **guitarrada**. A night out on the town is unforgettable. DJs housed in giant space-pod sets as large as a truck and covered in shimmering flashing lights play pounding **techno-guitarrada** to warehouse-sized crowds of revellers. Psychedelic carimbá-rap bands like **Coletivo Rádio Cipó** (made-up of twenty year olds and fronted by seventy year old rockers in dark glasses and satin suits) play in sweaty clubs on the riverside, sharing a stage with surf guitar bands like **La Pupuña** or red hot power metal samba bands like **Madame Saatan**, fronted by a wispy woman with dreadlocks and a tapestry of tatoos. There's really nowhere like it anywhere, even in Brazil. Come here for the **Círio festival** celebrations if you can.

Minas Gerais: Milton Nascimento and metal from the mines The state of Minas is Brazil's lyrical, reflective heart. Many of the country's finest poets and writers grew up in its pretty villages. The Minas sound is usually associated with **Milton Nascimento** and his band, the **Clube da Esquina**. Clube da Esquina formed as a loose association of like-minded musicians in 1970s Belo Horizonte and together they forged a new Brazilian musical style whose influence has spread far beyond their country. Herbie Hancock, Wayne Shorter and Stevie Wonder are admirers of Nascimento and the French modern jazz and classical composer Lionel Belmondo has called him as important a composer as Ravel. Unlike much Brazilian music the Clube da Esquina sound is textural and melodic rather than rhythmic and dancey. Milton's golden baritone or searing falsetto, telling stories of Minas Gerais, of Brazil and their marginalised and innocent, soars above a rich, pastoral landscape of sound which melds the chants of Africa, indigenous Brazil and the Catholic church, children's voices, gentle acoustic guitar, the orchestra, a distant organ or drum, a ringing bell tower. Although his legacy lives on in a hundred singer songwriters who play in the bars and theatres of Belo Horizonte, Minas continues to produce some of Brazil's most individual voices. The all-instrumental band **Uakti** build their own unique percussion instruments and play a kind of mesmerising minimalist trance on them, collaborating with composers like Philip Glass.

Essential Brazilian CDs and websites

http://redebma.ning.com/ the online bible for all things Brazilian music.
Samba: Bezerra da Silva, O Partido Alto da Samba
Bossa Nova: Elis Regina and Tom Jobim, Elis e Tom
Rio Funk: Seu Jorge, América Brasil
Tropicália: Various Artists, Tropicália Panis e Circenses; Caetano Veloso, Bicho Gilberto Gil, Realce
Blocos Afros: Olodum, 20 Anos; Carlinhos Brown, Alfagamabetizado
Bahian Samba: Mariene de Castro, Abre Caminho
Cacuriá: Dona Teté, O Divino Cacuriá de Dona Teté
Mangue Beat: Nação Zumbi, Afrociberdelia; Mundo Livre s/a, Bit; Siba, Fuloresta de Samba
Forró: Sivuca, Cabelo do Milho
Guitarrada/guitarrada rock: Pio Lobato, Technoguitarrada, La Pupuña, All right penoso
Belém Rock/Metal: Coletivo Rádio Cipó, Formigando na Calçada do Brasil; Madam Saatan, Madam Saatan
Clube da Esquina: Milton Nascimento, Clube da Esquina and Clube da Esquina II
Gaúcho music: Gilberto Monteiro, De Lua & Sol
Avant Garde: Itamar Assumpção, Preto Bras; Karnak, Karnak; Max de Castro, Max de Castro (2005)
Club: DJ Patife, Cool Steps

Erika Machado sings beautiful, catchy pop with quirky, witty lyrics, **Proa** play new wave indie electronica, and Brazil's most commercially successful band, **Sepultura**, play some of the world's most driving, exciting virtuoso death metal.

The Centre West: Rock and Rodeo crooning Brazil's Centre-West states of Goiás, the Mato Grossos and the Federal District of Brasília are dominated by Brazilian rock and Brazilian country music or **sertanejo**. Brazilian rock began with Tropicália and a maverick Bahian occult anarchist and political subversive called **Raul Seixas**. But it really took off in the 1980s when British new wave records were smuggled into Brasília in the diplomatic bag, finding their way into the hands of an introspective young bass player, **Renato Russo**. In 1982 Russo formed **Legião Urbana**, a Brazilian new-wave rock band whose combination of eighties rhythms and sarcastic lyrics struck a chord with Brazilian university students the country over. Imitators included bands like Cariocas **Barão Vermelho, Kid Abelha,Os Paralamas do Successo** (founded by friends of Russo's) and Paulistanos **Os Titãs**. In the late 1980s and 1990s, after the collapse of the dictatorship, Brazilian rock exploded producing myriad bands many of whom remain huge in Brazil today. They include Mineiro reggae rockers **Skank**, funk-rockers **Jota Quest** and indie rocker **Megarex**.

Together with pumped-up Bahian axê pop sung by the likes of **Ivete Sangalo, sertanejo** is the biggest music in Brazil. It's pretty cheesy stuff: Male duos with mullet hair cuts, usually dressed in checked shirts and Stetsons sing romantic power ballads about 'grande amor'. Videos are often intercut with shots of prize bulls and rodeos. Gigs by the likes of **Bruno & Marrone** and **Victor & Leo** are attended by tens of thousands.

The South: MPB and gaúcho music The German, Azorean and Italian immigrants who colonised the far south of Brazil were christened *gaúchos* by the Tupi indigenous people. The word translates as 'the people who sing sadly', and gaúchos have produced some of Brazil's finest MPB singers and musicians in general. They include **Elis Regina**, a tragic character with a magnificent voice that could be both sweet and tender and astonishingly powerful. She rose to fame in the late 1960s with what are now classic recordings of songs by composers like João Bosco and Milton Nascimento. Two of Brazil's finest contemporary musicians, guitarist **Yamandu Costa** and band leader **Artur Faria**, are both from the far south as are a swathe of cult rock bands and avante garde singers like **Jupiter Maça**. Regional *gaúcho* music or *música nativista* strongly features the guitar and the bandoneón and often incorporates rhythms and cadences which have much in common with nearby Uruguay and Argentina including *chamamé*, *milonga* and *tango*. Astor Piazzolla himself is said to have admired the skill of *bandoneón* player **Gilberto Monteiro**. He often plays at regional festivals like the **Canto Sem Fronteira** on the Uruguayan border at Bagé which usually takes place in November (www.cantosemfronteira.com).

São Paulo: the avant garde Everything from all over the Brazilian musical continent comes together in São Paulo. It is where the talent gravitates in search of money. On any night anywhere you can hear a bizarre *carimbó* metal act from Belém, Recife Mangue Beat, an off the wall Mineiro songwriter, cowboy ballads from Goiás or some old school samba. Yet the city has its own sound too, a kind of avant garde art rock samba formulated by one of Brazil's great unsung musical geniuses, **Itamar Assumpção**. Itamar, a supremely odd, witty, musical and lyrical voice, gathered a group of immensely talented musicians around him in the 1980s and performed strings of famously bizarre, theatrical shows. His work inspired numerous other mavericks like baroque music hall samba rockers, **Karnak** and the electronica pioneer **Max de Castro**. Together their sound became known as *vanguarda*. Many other Paulistano artists dip their feet in vanguarda: ace producer **Beto Villares** and Latin Grammy winner **CéU** fuse vanguarda with other Brazilian and international styles, **Renato Goda** with English new wave and cabaret. São Paulo also has the country's liveliest club seen which has produced many of Brazil's internationally famous DJs, notably **Patife** and **Marky**, both of whom have a predilection for drum 'n bass.

South American Literature

Early literary efforts in South America can be said to have focused primarily on chronicling the conquest and the subsequent colonisation of the Americas. It was only at the start of the independence struggles in the late 18th and early 19th centuries, as well as during the period of nation building immediately following, that South American literature starting coming into its own.

Whereas Brazil enjoyed a relatively stable transition to independence, Spanish America experienced turbulent years and long periods of social unrest, something that is reflected in the writing of the time. Literary output of the era is also characterized by a search for a true American identity, a current that runs through much of the continent's writing after independence from Spain was achieved in the 19th century. Political struggles and agendas have strongly influenced South American writing from the very beginning, with politics and literature seemingly going hand in hand across the continent, perhaps more so here than anywhere else in the world. Many literary figures have run for, even served as, presidents of their countries, or have heldg other government posts. Men of letters were frequently taking a distinctly political stance, playing active roles in influencing the course of their countries.

In many parts of the continent, essays, novels, short stories, poems and theatrical works often remain more than just lighthearted entertainment, containing political and social messages. Originally South American writers were mostly influenced by Spain and Portugal, but these were later surpassed by France and many in the "New World" were inspired by the ideas behind the French, and later the American, Revolutions. Writers who made their mark during the independence struggles and post-independence include Venezuelan **Andrés Bello** and Argentine **Domingo Faustino Sarmiento**, who published *Facundo: Civilisation and Barbarism* in 1845 (see below). He also went on to serve as president of Argentina 1868-74.

The first major poet hailing from South America was Ecuadorean **José Joaquín de Olmedo**, whose most famous poem, *La Victoria de Junín* (1825), celebrates Simón Bolívar's victory at Junín. More nation building and political messages were written into **José Marmol**'s *Amalia* (1851-1855), neatly disguising his anti-Rosas sentiments (the Argentine dictator of the time) in a romantic novel. Also from Argentina, **José Hernández** wrote the nation's best known long

Highlights of South America Literature

See also accompanying text
The poems of Chilean Nobel Laureate (1971) Pablo Neruda.
Julio Cortázar, *Hopscotch* (1963), can be read in two ways, as a straight narrative, or jumping about all 155 chapters, an unclassifiable novel ideal for a long trip.
Jorge Amado, *Dona Flor and Her Two Husbands* (1966). Set in Salvador, Brazil, this tale follows a woman's search for happiness.
Books by Gabriel García Márquez, particularly *One Hundred Years of Solitude* (1967). This seminal magical realist novel set in fictitious Macondo is Colombian García Márquez' best known novel, translated into 27 languages.
Manuel Puig, *Kiss of the Spider Woman* (1976). A homosexual and a terrorist bond in prison. Also made into a film in 1985 starring William Hurt and Raúl Julia.
Books by Peruvian Mario Vargas Llosa, particularly *Aunt Julia and the Scriptwriter* (1977), *The War of the End of the World* (1984) and *Who Killed Palomino Molero?* (1986).
Clarice Lispector, *The Hour of the Star* by (1977). This novel depicts the life of a countryside girl living in the slums of Rio de Janeiro.
Books by Isabel Allende, particularly *The House of the Spirits* (1982). Chilean Allende's best-selling debut novel, spanning four generations and the turbulent times they are living through.
Ernesto "Che" Guevara, *The Motorcycle Diaries* (first published in 1993). Che Guevara's diaries from his epic motorcycle journey through Latin America as a 23-year old medical student.

narrative poem *El Gaucho Martín Fierro* in two parts (1872, 1879), recapturing and idealising the pampas gaucho, turning this poem into something of a national epic. Another of the best loved works of 19th century South American fiction was penned by a Colombian, the novel *María* (1867), by **Jorge Isaacs**.

Early women writers might seem few and far between, but one example is Peru's **Clorinda Matto de Turner**, whose novel *Aves sin nido* (Birds without a nest) was published in 1889. The book is one of the few early works to deal with the indigenous population of the region and a precursor to the so-called *indigenista* movement, which flourished during the first half of the 20th century and included writers such as **José Carlos Mariátegui**, also Peruvian, and Ecuadorean **Jorge Icaza**. The latter penned *Huasipungo* (The Villager - 1934), one of the movement's best known works, dealing with the exploitation of Ecuador's indigenous population.

Although novelists can be said to have had great impact on cultural and political life, essayists have also very much influenced the course of South American society. Uruguayan **José Enrique Rodó** published his lengthy essay *Ariel* in 1900 and this work, contrasting the values of ancient Rome and Greece with the rising power of the United States, remained influential throughout the continent in the 1910s and 20s. The struggles of liberalism versus conservativism, city versus countryside, civilisation versus barbarism is present in much of South American literature in general. One particularly popular example is Venezuelan **Rómulo Gallegos**' *Doña Bárbara* (1929), where the author even chooses to name the protagonist "bárbara", in reference to barbarism. Gallegos was another man of letters who went on to become the president of his country in 1947.

The 20th century saw the rise of modernism, and then post-modernism, with writers and poets such as Argentine **Jorge Luis Borges**, Chilean **Pablo Neruda** and Peruvian **César Vallejo** coming to the fore and reaching worldwide renown. Neruda received the Noble Prize for Literature in 1971. In the late 1940s and early 50s magical realist writing started to appear on the scene, a genre that has since become the hallmark of some of the contemporary South American greats such as **Gabriel García Márquez** of Colombia and **Isabel Allende**, born in Peru to Chilean parents. Some of the many writers emerging and establishing themselves during this era were **Juan Carlos Onetti** of Uruguay, **João Guimarães** and **Clarice Lispector** of Brazil.

The 1960s and 70s also saw the rise of authors such as Argentine **Julio Cortázar**, Peru's **Mario Vargas Llosa** (who incidentally also ran for president in 1990), **Augusto Roa Bastos** of Paraguay and **Manuel Puig** also of Argentina. The years of repression that swept through large parts of the continent in the 1960s, 70s and early 80s had tremendous impact on the literary output, with writers forced into exile or even silenced forever. Those who chose to stay had endeavour to find different ways of using language as a means of saying the unsayable.

Although it can be difficult to find examples of early South American women writers, many prominent female authors have emerged in the last century. One of the most intellectually influential writers of the 20th century was the Argentine **Victoria Ocampo**, who founded literary journal *Sur* and wrote a number of literary works herself. Her sister **Silvina** was also a writer and poet. The first and only South American woman to receive the Nobel Prize for Literature was Chilean **Gabriela Mistral** in 1945. Other excellent women writers not already mentioned include **Marta Traba, Luisa Valenzuela, Cristina Peri Rossi** and **Alejandra Pizarnik**.

South American Cinema

Cinema in South America began and became popular surprisingly early, with moving images having arrived in both Argentina and Brazil by 1896, so it's no coincidence that these two nations have come to lead the way in terms of cinematic production across South America. The first genre to take root and become popular was the documentary, but soon many of the early efforts became highly influenced by Hollywood. There was, however, also space for more home-spun films, focusing on 'el barrio', local issues and concerns. Incidentally the world's first animated film, *El Apóstol*, was made in Argentina in 1917. Argentina captured the hearts of national and Latin American audiences generally, through the magic of tango, with singer Carlos Gardel (see above), starring in many films such as *Cuesta Abajo* and *El día que me quieras*. In neighbouring Brazil, the *chanchada*, a type of musical comedy, was the preferred vehicle of expression. In both cases music, song and dance were key elements of the earlier film efforts, often with a hearty sprinkling of melodrama.

By the 1940s and 50s cinema in South America generally, began to change - or rather, come of age - and the 1960s could be considered the start of a new cinematic era in the region. This was a decade of great socio-political changes and upheaval, inspiring lively debate, creativity and greater cultural output, with Brazil leading the way with **Cinema Novo** (New Cinema). The focus of films started veering towards the more realist, and some would argue, more grim and there was greater exploration of topics such as poverty and social ills, as well as sexuality and sensuality, with many directors taking their inspiration from literary works. State repression under the dictatorships in many South American nations in the 1970s and 80s hampered cinematic production and, indeed, the topics that could be dealt with, for a number of years, but the last few decades have seen South American cinema recover and continue to evolve with new directors reaching an international audience.

Arts and crafts

South American Art

Art and sculpture have not reached the same international success and breadth of expression enjoyed by South American literature and cinema, with far fewer artists or sculptors reaching worldwide renown. There are, however, a few notable exceptions from different eras, eg 19th-century realist painter **Juan Manuel Blanes** of Uruguay and Colombian painter and sculptor **Fernando Botero**, currently residing in Europe.

Indigenous cultures such as the Incas of the Andean countries had their own art forms, many of which would now be considered handicrafts, or *artesanías* (see below). Early South American

Cinematic highlights in South America:

1934 *Cuesta Abajo* (Downward Slope) (Louis Gasnier). Tango singer Carlos Gardel sings his heart out in one of his most popular films.
1946 *Notorious* (Alfred Hitchcock). Cary Grant and Ingrid Bergman chase neo-Nazis in Brazil.
1959 *Orfeu Negro* (Black Orpheus) (Marcel Camus). Orpheus and Eurydice mixed with the Rio Carnival.
1966-68 *La Hora de los Hornos* (The Hour of the Furnaces) (Fernando Solanas). A four-hour long Argentine documentary with a strong political message.
1969 *Butch Cassidy and the Sundance Kid* (Roy Hill). Set in Patagonia and Bolivia, this film follows the last few years of the outlaws, starring Paul Newman and Robert Redford.
1972 *Aguirre, Wrath of God* (Werner Herzog). The tale of Spanish conquistador Lope de Aguirre and his journey up the Amazon.
1982 *Fitzcarraldo* (Werner Herzog). The story of building an opera house in the Peruvian Amazonian jungle.
1983 *Romancing the Stone* (Robert Zemickis). Michael Douglas and Kathleen Turner go emerald-hunting in Colombia.
1984 *Camila* (Maria Luisa Bemberg). The story of a woman's love for a Catholic priest, leading to her execution, set in 19th century Argentina.
1985 *Kiss of the Spider Woman* (Hector Babenco). This prison cell dialogue between a homosexual and a terrorist is based on Argentine Manuel Puig's novel of the same name.
1986 *The Mission* (Roland Joffé). Robert de Niro and Jeremy Irons portray two Jesuit priests in the Missions in Argentina and Paraguay at the time of the Jesuit expulsion.
1986 *La Historia Oficial* (The Official Version) (Luis Puenzo). The first Argentine film to win an Oscar, set during the Dirty War.
1992 *Alive* (Frank Marshall). Members of the Uruguayan rugby team survive a plane crash in the Andes.
1993 *The House of the Spirits* (Bille August). Film adaptation of Isabel Allende's family epic.
1994 *Death and the Maiden* (Roman Polanski). Based on Ariel Dorfman's play, a woman (Sigourney Weaver) aims to take revenge on her torturer (Ben Kingsley).
1998 *Central do Brasil* (Central Station) (Walter Salles). A young boy's search for his father in Brazil.
2001 *Nine Queens* (Fabian Bielinsky). Argentine thriller set in Buenos Aires over 24 hours.
2003 *Cidade de Deus* (City of God) (Fernando Meirelles). A compelling, violent drama of the Rio favelas, with a great soundtrack.
2004 *The Motorcycle Diaries* (Walter Salles). The story of Ernesto 'Che' Guevara and his friend Alberto Granada's epic journey around South America in 1952.
2004 *María Llena de Gracia* (Maria Full of Grace) (Joshua Martson). Depicts 17-year old Maria's life from small-town Colombia to international drug-trafficking.
2008 *Linha de Passe* (Walter Salles). Football-obsession and poverty in São Paolo.

art was highly influenced by European styles and much of the artistic output was religious in nature. Among the first to arrive and work with the native population were priests and friars, often using skilled indigenous artisans for the construction and decoration of new churches. Religious paintings and church ornamentation are among the best preserved works of art in the Americas, many made by unnamed local artists working with the religious communities established shortly after the conquest. Arrivals from Europe also brought renaissance, baroque and rococo influences. The colonial period was characterized by a blending of indigenous and European traditions, with African influences added to the styles at a later date. One of the best, and also earliest, schools of painting in South America was the **Cuzco School** in Peru, where most of the painters were indigenous or mestizo.

It was mostly the newly arrived Europeans who were mixing the styles and influences, while many of the native communities did their utmost to keep their traditions intact. After independence from Spain and Portugal, a much greater exchange began, with Europeans coming over to South America to teach, while in turn many South Americans visited Europe, returning with new skills, techniques and knowledge. As with literary output, art and artistic expression have been strongly influenced by the politics of the region. Independence movements, in particular, fuelled a continent-wide reassessment of what it meant to be "American" and there was a widespread search for identity away from the colonial powers that played a key part in all forms of culture of the time. Despite this, many artists, art historians and scholars continued to be educated abroad, more often than not in Europe, thus continuing European influence over South American art in the centuries that have followed independence.

Muralism is mostly associated with the Mexican greats of Diego Rivera, David Alfaro Siqueiros and José Clemente Orozco, but there were also muralists working further south. Among the best known are Chilean **José Venturelli** and two Colombians, **Pedro Nel Gómez** and **Santiago Martínez Delgado**.

Popular Handicrafts in South America

South America has an abundance of different traditional handicrafts that have developed over time and although there are regional variations, many have flourished right across the continent. The distinctive crafts often show a mixture of indigenous, European and later also African influences.

Textiles and Weaving have been of utmost importance throughout South America from an economic, as well as a social and spiritual-religious perspective. The materials used in producing textiles have included fibres from trees, plants and shrubs, hemp, hides, bird feathers, human hair, horsehair and cotton, as well as the wool from llamas, alpacas, vicuñas and sheep. Traditional weaving goes a long way back, with cultures such as the Incas inheriting 3,000 years of weaving skills. These skills were to be exploited in colonial times, in large-scale *mitas*, textile workshops, and the Spaniards were soon exporting cloth to Europe. For the native population, however, textiles, apart from their utilitarian functions, were also used for rituals and ceremonies. These items often had intricate designs and patterns, such as those of the Aymara people of the islands of Lake Titicaca, who have carried on their traditions to this day. Different communities wear different traditional outfits, some introduced by the conquistadores, some of more ancient origin. You can often tell by what a person is wearing where they are from and what indigenous culture they belong to, although these days Western dress is increasingly popular. The use of materials, designs and motifs varies widely, with llama, alpaca, vicuña or sheep's wool mostly used in the Andean countries and the Southern Cone, the latter sometimes using hides in weaving. Knitting is also particularly popular in the colder climes of the Andes. The one area where textiles and weaving have far less importance is the Amazon and the Guianas, with their tropical climate. Otherwise there are many areas that are rich in weaving, knitting and embroidery traditions, making everything from tapestries and decorative blankets, to every item of clothing imaginable.

Jewellery and Metalwork These are also traditions with several thousand years of history. Copper, gold and platinum were all mined before the arrival of the Spaniards and although many of the objects of the early civilizations were functional in nature, intricately ornate jewellery and ceremonial knives have been found at archaeological sites, particularly in Peru. Precious and semi-precious stones were often used in ceremonial costumes and at burials, since metal objects on their own were not considered of worth. The conquistadores were amazed by the wealth they saw and this seemingly endless thirst for gold and silver led to some of the most appalling exploitations of the local population. Although much was plundered and sent to Europe, one of the world's best gold museums, Museo de Oro, displaying pieces from the third century BC until the 16th century, can be found in Bogotá. Ironwork was introduced to South America after the conquest and many skilled Spaniards and Italians, in particular, arrived to develop new metalworking techniques. Silverwork came to be strongly associated with the gaucho culture across Uruguay, parts of northern Argentina and southern Brazil and many riding accessories are forged from silver, along with the obligatory máte gourd with silver inlays. After the introduction of silver coins in the 18th century, the Mapuche of southern Chile became very well-known for their skills as silversmiths. The longstanding traditions of jewellery-making are carried on across the continent with many modern day artisans using precious and semi-precious stones together with metals in their designs. Inspired by old, traditional, native methods they are blending modern and ancient to create new and different motifs.

Basketry and Fibre Crafts Basketry, hat-making and bag-making are very common across the vast area of the Amazon, where the raw materials are abundant. Woven bags are household items in many parts of the continent and shopping bags are as likely to be made from natural materials, as they are from plastic. Hats, fans, mats and boxes are also common items found in many South American homes. Reeds, palm fibre, bamboo, horsehair, maguey and cane are just some of the many different materials used. Similarly to other crafts that developed, the objects were originally of a purely utilitarian nature and many still are. In Huanchaco in northern Peru, as well as on Lake Titicaca, the communities use reeds to make boats for fishing and transportation. In Colombia and Venezuela, plant fibre is used for the walls and roofs of houses, as well as in hammock-making. One of the most famous South American items produced is the Panama hat, thus named as it was shipped from Panama to Europe, although actually made in Ecuador and also southern Colombia. Its original home is the Ecuadorean village of Jipijapa, a name now sometimes used for both the fibres and the hats themselves. The southern Colombian state of Nariño became a centre for basketry and fibre crafts early on and today Boyacá, further north is particularly well-known for its fine baskets. Another area for both basket- and hammock-making is El Chaco of Paraguay and in Brazil basketry is mostly found up in the northeast of the country around the states of Bahia, Pernambuco and Paraíba.

Pottery Pottery is perhaps the oldest craft in South America with extensive ceramic archaeological findings in, for example, Nazca (Peru). Pre-Columbian pottery often carried religious or magical symbolism and although many objects were functional in nature, others carried highly spiritual significance. The Nazca, Moche and Inca cultures all used such ceramic objects and the pre-Hispanic techniques survive and remain in use. Communities often mix ancient and modern pottery production processes. So-called blackware is one example of traditional, rural pottery that can be found in different parts of the continent from as far south as Chillán in Chile to Tolima in Colombia. Terracotta ware is another popular version in many parts. Black pottery can be found in Cafayate in Argentina and the skilled artisans of Paraguay mix ceramic tiles with woodcarving.

Other Popular Crafts The art of making wind musical instruments and drums goes back to pre-Columbian times, while the Spaniards introduced stringed instruments to the continent. Materials used include ceramic, wood and gourds, as well as bamboo, particularly for the wind instruments.

Large parts of South America are forested and woodcrafts are widespread. The woods used differ from area to area; in the Amazon and along the Pacific Colombian coast wooden materials include laurel, mahogany and cedar; nogal, naranjilla and increasingly also eucalyptus are used in the Andean Highlands, while pine is popular in southern Chile and Argentina. Originally wood was used for everything from the very practical such as bows and arrows, to ceremonial, ritualistic objects such as masks. These ceremonial and festive traditions live on in many parts and wooden masks are still made and used in local fiestas. Wooden healing sticks, made by the

Cholo people of Colombia, are another example of wooden objects used in ritual. During the colonial period woodcarving became popular, in particular when decorating churches. While Peru and Chile make beautiful wooden furniture, San Antonio de Ibarra in Ecuador is a well-known centre for woodcarving. Religious figurines, influenced by the Jesuits, hail from Paraguay, northern Argentina and southern Brazil. Many of the wooden objects are beautifully dyed with resin or painted in bright colours.

Other popular crafts include gourd-making, especially in Uruguay, retablo-making and gourd-carving from Peru and bread dough craft from Ecuador, lace from Pernambuco in Brazil and beadwork from Colombia.

Footnotes

Contents

1812 Index

1821 Advertisers' index

1822 About the author

1822 Acknowledgements

1823 Travellers' letters

1824 Credits

A
Abancay 1479
Abra Pampa 171
Acandí 952
accommodation
Argentina 62
Brazil 393
Chile 691
Colombia 890
Ecuador 1032
Guyana 1681
Guyane 1718
Paraguay 1214
Peru 1259
Suriname 1702
Uruguay 1515
Venezuela 1564
Aceguá 524
Achao 826
Acobamba 1481
Aconcagua 136
Adícora 1598
Agua Blanca 1154
Aguas Blancas 173
Aguas Calientes 1456
Aguas Dulces 1548
Aguaytía 1487
Alausí 1114
Albina 1711
Alcântara 606
Almofala 604
Alter do Chão 626
Alto Nangartiza 1184
Amaicha del Valle 151
Amantaní 1413
Ambato 1102
Anchieta 491
Anco 1472
Ancoraimes 303
Ancud 826
Andahuaylas 1479
Andahuaylillas 1445
Angel Falls 1660
Angol 784
Angra dos Reis 443
Annai 1690
Antarctica 1744
Anticura 808
Antofagasta 750, **751**
Antonina 504
Apartaderos 1619
Apolobamba 305
Apura 1710
Aquidaban 669
Aquiraz 602
Aquitania 927
Aracaju 581
Aracataca 959
Aracati 602
Aragua Coast 1589
Araya Peninsula 1640
Arboletes 952
Archidona 1181
Aregua 1231
Arequipa 1382, **1383**, **1384**
Arica 769, **770**
Ariquemes 646
Ariri 471
Armenia 993
Armero 990
Arraial da Ajuda 554
Arrecifes 960
Artigas 1538
Assis Brasil 647
Asunción 1217, **1218**
Atacames 1168
Atalaya 1501
Auyán 1661
Ayacucho 1474, **1475**
Ayaviri 1415
B
Baeza 1175
Bagua Grande 1368
Bahia 532
Bahía Blanca 109
Bahía de Caráquez 1160
Bahía Murta 846
Bahía Solano 986
Baixio 562
Ballestas Islands 1371
Balmaceda 839
Baños 1104, **1105**
Baños del Inca 1122
Barão de Melgaço 679
Barichara 930
Bariloche 206, **207**, **208**
Barinas 1626
Barquisimeto 1605
Barra 537
Barra da Lagoa 508
Barra da Tijuca 413
Barra de Santo Antônio 580
Barra de Valizas 1547
Barra do Quaraí 524
Barrancas (Col) 967
Barrancas (Ven) 1665
Barranco 1275
Barranquilla 956
Barreal 140
Barreirinhas 605
Barretos 470
Bartica 1688
Belém 617, **618**
Belén 145
Bella Vista 364
Belo Horizonte 473, **474**, **476**
Bento Gonçalves 522
Berlín 931
Bermejo 346
Bertioga 469
Biribiri 495
Blanquillo 1501
Blumenau 509
Boa Vista 641
Boca Grande 1018
Boca Manu 1501
Boconó 1607
Bogotá 898, **900**, **902**
Bolívar 1085
Bonfim 642
Bonito 669
Borbón 1169
Bosque Protector Mindo-Nambillo 1069
Boyuibe 375
BR-364 646
Braamspunt 1708
Brasiléia 647
Brasília 651, **652**
Bucaramanga 930
Buenaventura 1003
Buenos Aires 67, **70**, **68**, **74**, **76**
Búzios 436
C
Caacupé 1231
Cabanaconde 1395
Cabedelo 584
Cabo 568
Cabo Blanco 1343
Cabo de Vela 967
Cabo Frio 436
Cabo Polonio 1547
Cabruta 1656
Cabure 1598
Cacao 1722
Cáceres 679
Cachi 156
Cachoeira 549
Cachora 1463
Caeté 479
Cafayate 155
Cajamarca 1351, **1351**
Cajatambo 1316
Calacalí 1068
Calama 755
Calca 1447
Caldera 746
Calderón 1074
Calera de Las Huérfanas 1535
Caleta Olivia 236
Caleta Tortel 847
Cali 998, **999**
Calingasta 140
Camarones 233
Camboriú 509
Camiña 766
camping 39
Campo Grande 668, **668**
Canaima 1660
Cananéia 471
Cañar 1122
Cañaveral 960
Canela 521
Cañete 784
Cañete valley 1370
Canoa Quebrada 602
Cañon del Pato 1318
Capão 550
Capão da Canoa 517
Capiatá 1231
Capilla del Monte 122
Capitán Badó 1232
Capitanejo 928
Capurganá 952
Carabuco 303
Caracaraí 641
Caracas 1570, **1570**, **1572**, **1574**
Caraíva 555

Caral 1317
Caranavi 312
Carapeguá 1238
Caravelas 555
Caraz 1310
Carhuaz 1311
Caripe 1640
Carlos Pellegrini 181
Carmelo 1534
Carmen de Patagones 225
carnet de passages 37
Carnival in Bahia 544
Carrasco National Park 352
Cartagena 938, **940**
Cartago 994
Caruaru 576
Carúpano 1640
Casabindo 171
Cascavel 602
Casma 1317
Caspana 756
Cassino 523
Castillos 1548
Castro 828
Cata 1589
Catac 1308
Catacaos 1340
Catacocha 1132
Catamarca 144
Catamarca Province 144
Catamayo 1132
Catatumbo 1614
Cauca Valley 998
Caxias do Sul 522
Cayambe 1074
Cayenne 1719, **1720**
Ceará 594
Celendín 1357
Cerro Castillo 840,861
Cerro Colorado (Arg) 122
Cerro Colorado (Uru) 1556
Cerro Corá 1244
Cerro de Pasco 1482
Cerro Perico 1629
Cerro Pintado 1629
Chacalluta-Tacna 771
Chacas 1309
Chachani 1386
Chachapoyas 1358, **1359**
Chachimbiro 1085
Chaco (Arg) 185
Chaco (Par) 1247
Chaitén 835
Chala 1378
Chalalán 358
Chalhuanca 1378
Chan Chán 1324
Chanaballita 755
Chañaral 746
Chanchamayo 1481
Chapada dos Guimarães 680
Chapada dos Veadeiros 660
Chaparrí 1334
Charaña 285
Charazani 305
Charity 1687
Chavín de Huantar 1308
Chichiriviche 1594
Chiclayo 1331, **1332**
Chile Chico 847
Chilean Pacific Islands 876
Chilecito 144
Chillán 780
Chiloé 825, **827**
Chimborazo 1113
Chimbote 1318
Chinchero 1448
Chipana-Río Loa 755
Chiquián 1315
Chiquinquirá 924
Chiuchín 1317
Chivacoa 1605
Chivay 1394
Chocó 985
Cholila 216
Chololó 1238
Chonchi 828
Choquequirao 1463
Chordeleg 1122
Choro 286
Choroní 1589
Choshuenco 798
Chosica 1464
Chúa 301
Chugchilán 1099
Chuí 523
Chulumani 313
Chungará 771
Chuquicamata 755
Churín 1317
Chuy 1549
Cidreira 518
Ciénaga 959
Ciudad Bolívar 1655, **1656**
Ciudad de Dios 1350
Ciudad del Este 1233, **1233**
Ciudad Guayana 1664
Ciudad Perdida 961
climate
  Argentina 58
  Bolivia 270
climate
  Brazil 390
  Chile 688
  Colombia 888
  Ecuador 1030
  Falkland Islands 1731
  Guyana 1680
  Guyane 1717
  Paraguay 1213
  Peru 1256
  Suriname 1702
  Uruguay 1514
  Venezuela 1562
Clorinda 186
Cobija 362
Coca 1180
Cochabamba 348, **349**
Cochamó 814
Cochrane 847
Coconuco 1012
Cocora 993
Coctaca 171
Colakreek 1708
Colca Canyon 1394
Colchane 766
Colchani 322
Colón 177
Colonia del Sacramento 1533, **1532**
Colonia Independencia 1233
Colonia Sarmiento 236
Colonia Suiza 1533
Colonia Tovar 1586
Colonia Volendam 1243
Colonias Valdense 1533
Comodoro Rivadavia 235
Comunidad Capirona 1188
Coñaripe 797
Conceição da Barra 491
Concepción (Bol) 380
Concepción (Chi) 783
Concepción (Par) 1244
Concepción (Per) 1465
Concepción del Uruguay 176
Conchi 755
Concón 733
Concordia 178
Conde 562
Confluencia 204
Congonhas 482
Conococha 1297
Constitución 779
Contulmo 784
Copacabana (Bol) 301, **302**
Copacabana (Bra) 411, **408**
Copiapó 745
Coquimbo 737
Cordilleras Huayhuash 1297
Córdoba 116, **117**
Corire 1399
Coro 1597, **1597**
Coroa Vermelha 554
Coroico 312
Coronel Oviedo 1232
Corral 806
Corrientes 181
Corriverton 1685
Corumbá 675
Cosquín 121
Cotacachi 1083
Cotahuasi 1399
Cotahuasi Canyon 1399
Coveñas 951
Coyhaique 838, **838**
Coyhaique Alto 839
Coyoctor 1122
credit cards 46
Crucita 1160
Cuchi Corral 121
Cúcuta 932, **932**
Cuenca 1119, **1120**
Cuestecita 967
Cueva de los Guácharos 1011
Cueva del Guácharo 1640
Cuevas de las Manos 242
Cuiabá 678, **678**
Cumaná 1637, **1638**

Cumaral 918
Curacautín 788
Curicó 778
Curimagua 1598
Curitiba 497, **498**
Curvelo 494
Cusco 1419, **1422**, **1427**
cycling 36

D

Dalcahue 826
Darién 1003
Darién Gap 952
Darwin, Charles 1190
Desaguadero 1417
Desaguadero 303
Diamantina 494
diving 23
Dolavon 232
driving
  Argentina 60
  Bolivia 273
  Brazil 392
  Ecuador 1031
  Chile 690
  Colombia 889
  Guyana 1681
  Guyane 1718
  Paraguay 1214
  Peru 1259
  Suriname 1703
  Uruguay 1515
  Venezuela 1564
drugs 47
Durazno 1556

E

Easter Island 877
eating 39
ecotourism 28
Ekeko 283
El Altar 1114
El Angel 1085
El Bolsón 216
El Brujo 1324
El Burro 1629
El Calafate 245, **246**
El Cisne 1132
El Cocuy 928
El Colorado 720
El Dorado 922,1668
El Fraile 839
El Hatillo 1576
El Maitén 846
El Misti 1386
El Moján 1602
El Morro 1617
El Palmar National Park 177
El Para 1181
El Pauji 1671
El Peñol 983
El Playón 1589
El Progreso 1196
El Retiro 983
El Rey National Park 152
El Rodeo 144
El Tambo 1125
El Tatio 759
El Valle 986
El Yaque 1648
Emas National Park 660
embassies and consulates
  Argentina 64
  Bolivia 274
  Brazil 395
  Chile 693
  Colombia 892
  Ecuador 1033
  Peru 1261
  Uruguay 1516
  Venezuela 1566
Embu 459
Encarnación 1239, **1240**
Ensenada 813
Entre Lagos 807
Escoma 303
Esmeraldas 1168
esperanza de El Tingo 1099
Espírito Santo 490
Esquel 216
Estância 582

F

Facatativá 918
Fachinal 847
Falkland Islands/Islas Malvinas 1729
Farellones 719
Faro José Ignacio 1547
Farol 510
Farroupilha 522
Fernando de Noronha 576
Ferreñafe 1334
Fiambalá 145
Fiesta de la Virgen de Urkupiña 355
Filadelfia 1249
Florencia 1011
Florianópolis 507, **508**
food and drink 39
  Argentina 63
  Bolivia 273
  Brazil 394
  Colombia 891
  Chile 692
  Ecuador 1032
  Guyana 1681
  Paraguay 1214
  Suriname 1703
  Uruguay 1515
  Venezuela 1565
Formosa 186
Fortaleza 594, **596**
Foz do Iguaçu 528, **527**
Francisqui 1653
Fray Bentos 1536
Frutillar 812
Fuerte Bulnes 854
Fundación 960
Futaleufú 836

G

Gaiman 232
Galápagos Islands 1190
Galerazamba 944
Garibáldi 522
Garzón 1011
Genipabu 589
Georgetown 1684, **1686**
Girardot 917
Girón 931
Gobernador Costa 218
Gocta waterfall 1364
Goiânia 658
Goiás 658
Goiás Velho 659
Gonzanamá 1132
Goose Green 1736
Gorgona Island 1004
government
  Argentina 1779
  Bolivia 1779
  Brazil 1779
  Chile 1779
  Colombia 1779
  Ecuador 1780
  Guyane 1780
  Paraguay 1780
  Peru 1780
  Suriname 1780
  Uruguay 1780
  Venezuela 1780
  Chile 1779
  Guyana 1780
Gramado 521
Guaduas 918
Guaíra 531
Guajará Mirim 646
Guajira Peninsula 967
Gualaceo 1122
Gualaquiza 1184
Gualeguaychú 176
Guamote 1114
Guanare 1626
Guanay 313
Guane 930
Guanillos 755
Guanta 1635
Guaranda 1113
Guarapari 491
Guarujá 469
Guasipati 1668
Guatapé 983
Guatavita 921
Guatavita Nueva 921
Guayaquil 1139, **1142**, **1140**
Guayaramerín 361
Güicán 928
Güiria 1641

H

Henri Pittier National Park 1589
Hernandarias 1234
Higuera 373
Higuerote 1631
history
  Argentina 1754
  Bolivia 1757
  Brazil 1760
  Chile 1761
  Colombia 1763
  Ecuador 1765
  Guyana 1776
  Guyane 1778
  Paraguay 1766
  Peru 1769
  Suriname 1777
  Uruguay 1771
  Venezuela 1773
Hito Cajón 760
Hohenau 1241
Holidays & festivals
  Argentina 64
  Bolivia 274
  Brazil 395
  Chile 693
  Colombia 893
  Ecuador 1033
  Guyana 1682

Guyane 1718
Paraguay 1215
Peru 1261
Suriname 1703
Uruguay 1516
Venezuela 1566
Honda 918
Horcón 733
Hornopirén 834
horse riding 24
Hotel Humboldt 1585
Huaca de la Luna 1321
Huacachina 1372
Hualahoyo 1468
Hualhuas 1468
Huallanca 1318
Huamachuco 1350
Huancacalle 1462
Huancas 1358
Huancavelica 1472
Huancayo 1466, **1467**
Huanchaco 1325
Huánuco 1482
Huaquillas 1150
Huara 766
Huaraz 1297, **1299**, **1300**
Huari 1309
Huatajata 301
Huaura Valley 1317
Humahuaca 171
Humberstone 764

I

Ibagué 994
Ibarra 1084
Iberá 180
Iberá Marshes 180
Ibibobo 375
Iboribó 1670
Ica 1371
Icho Cruz 122
ICMBio 397
Igarassu 575
Iguape 470
Iguazú Falls 191, **192**
Iles du Salut 1721
Ilha de Santa Catarina 507
Ilha do Marajó 619
Ilha do Mel 504
Ilha Grande 443
Ilhéus 553
Illampu 304
Imbassaí 562
Iñapari 1502
Inca Trail 1454
Inca Trail to Ingapirca 1122
Ingapirca 1122
internet 43
Inti Wara Yassi 352
Ipiales 1019
Iquitos 1492, **1493**
Iriri 491
Irupana 313
Iruya 171
Ischigualasto Provincial Park 140
Isinliví 1099
Isla de Coche 1647
Isla de Cubagua 1647
Isla de la Luna 303
Isla de Margarita 1645, **1646**
Isla del Sol 302
Isla Magdalena 854
Isla Mancera 806
Isla Martín García 100
Isla Navarino 872
Isla Negra 733
Isla Tenglo 819
Islas Los Roques 1653
Isluga 766
Itá 1237
Itacaré 553
Itacuruçá 442
Itahuania 1501
Itaipú 1234
Itaipu Dam 528
Itanhaém 470
Itaparica 539
Itauguá 1230
Itaúnas 491
Iturbe 171
Iwokrama 1690
Iza 927
Izcuchaca 1468

J

Jaén 1368
Jaguarão 524
Jaguaribe 539
Jají 1619
Jalapão 664
Jama 170
Jama Pass 169
Jardín 984
Jauja 1465
Jericó 984
Jericoacoara 604
Jesús 1240
Jesús María 122
Ji Paraná 646
Jijoca de Jericoacoara 604
Jipijapa 1155
João Pesso 584
Jodensavanne 1708
Joinville 510
Juan C Falcón National Park 1598
Juan Fernández Islands 876
Juan Griego 1648
Juan López 751
Juanchaco 1004
Judibana 1598
Jujuy 167
Juli 1407
Juliaca 1415
Junín 1482
Junín de los Andes 199

K

Kaieteur Falls 1688
Kaieteur National Park 1688
Kalahuta 301
Kamarata 1661
Kamoirán 1670
Kapawi Ecological Reserve 1186
Kavác 1661
Kavanayén 1669
Km 88 1668
Kourou 1721
Kuelap 1358
Kuntur Wasi 1353
Kyk-over-al 1688

L

La Arena 834
La Asunción 1647
La Azulita 1619
La Balsa 1368
La Barra 1547
La Boquilla 944
La Calera 1394
La Campana National Park 733
La Cumbre 121
La Cumbrecita 123
La Diablada festival 318
La Esperanza 1084
La Falda 121
La Florida, Quito 1045
La Guaira 1586
La Herradura 737
La Junta 837
La Merced 1481
La Mucuy 1618
La Oroya 1465
La Paloma 1547
La Paz (Bol) 277, **280**, **282**
La Pedrera 1547
La Plata (Arg) 103
La Plata (Col) 1011
La Portada 750
La Quiaca 172
La Quinua 1476
La Rioja 143
La Serena 737, **738**
La Tirana 765
La Toma 1132
La Unión 1482
Ladrilleros 1004
Lago Agrio 1176
Lago Calafquén 797
Lago Chungará 772
Lago de Janauri 632
Lago General Carrera 846
Lago Llanquihue 812
Lago Poopó 316
Lago Puyehue 807
Lago Ypacaraí 1231
Lagoinha 604
Lagos Fluminenses 435
Laguna 510
Laguna Colorada 323
Laguna Cuicocha 1083
Laguna de los Cóndores 1357
Laguna de los Pozuelos 171
Lagunas 1490
Lagunilla 1371
Lagunillas 720,1619
Lake District (Chi) 787
Lake Huiñamarca 301
Lake Titicaca (Bol) 301
Lake Titicaca (Per) 1413
Lambayeque 1333
Lampa 1415
Lamud 1359
language 44
Lanín National Park 199
Laquipampa 1335
Laraquete 783
Largo do Pelourinho 535
Las Cuevas 137

Las Grutas 225
Las Leñas 133
Las Lomas de Arena del Palmar 368
Las Pailas 156
Las Peñas 1168
Lasana 755
Lasso 1093
Latacunga 1093, **1093**
Leblon 412
Legado de Piratas 971
Lelydorp 1708
Lençóis 549
Leonsberg 1708
Lérida 990
Les Hattes 1722
Lethem 1689
Leticia 1022
Levanto 1358
Leymebamba 1357
Liberdade 456
Libertador Gen San Martín 172
Lican-Ray 797
Lima 1266, **1268**, **1270**, **1274**
Limones 1168
Linden 1689
Linhares 491
Llacanora 1352
Llachón 1407
Llano del Hato 1619
Llao Llao 207
Llapay 1370
Loja 1130
Loma Plata 1249
Loreto 188
Los Andes 720
Los Angeles 784
Los Antiguos 243
Los Libertadores 720
Los Molles 133
Los Penitentes 135
Lota 783
Luepa 1669
Luicho 1399
Luján 102
Luque 1220

M

Mabaruma 1687
Macapá 620
Macará 1132
Macas 1183
Maceió 580
Machachi 1091
Machala 1149
Machalilla 1159
Machu Picchu 1454
Macuro 1641
Madeira-Mamoré Railway 645
Madidi National Park 357
Magangué 951
Magdalena 364
Maicao 968
Maimará 170
Mairana 374
Maitencillo 733
Majorländia 602
Malagana 951
Malargüe 133
Maldonado 1546
Malpelo, Isla 1004
Mana 1722
Manantiales 1547
Manaure 967
Manaus 628, **629**
Máncora 1343
Mangaratiba 442
Manglaralto 1153
Mangue Seco 562
Manhumirim 489
Manizales 988
Manta 1160
Mantecal 1627
Manu Biosphere Reserve 1500
maps 38
Mar del Plata 108
Maracaibo 1601
Maracay 1588
Marajó 619
Maranhão 604
Marataízes 491
Marcahuasi 1464
Marechal Deodoro 580
Maresias 469
Mariana 481
Maripa 1657
Maripasoula 1722
Mariscal Estigarribia 1250
Mariscal Sucre 1085
Marsella 992
Marshall Falls 1688
Mascarilla 1085
Maturín 1640
Maullin 819
Mayocc 1472
Mbaracayú Forest Reserve 1232
Mbutuy 1232
Medellín 976, **977**, **978**
Mejillones 752
Melo 1556
Mendoza 126, **127**
Mendoza 1359
Mercedes (Arg) 180
Mercedes (Uru) 1535
Mérida 1609, **1610**
Mesa de los Indios 1619
Milo Verde 495
Mina Clavero 123
Minas Gerais 473
Minca 961
Mindo 1069
Miraflores
Miraflores 1273
Miramar 109
Miranda 670
Misahuallí 1182
Mitad del Mundo 1045
Mocha 1102
Mochima 1635
Moengo 1710
Mompós 951
money
  Argentina 64
  Bolivia 275
  Brazil 396
  Chile 693
  Colombia 893
  Ecuador 1033
  Falkland Islands 1733
  Guyana 1682
  Guyane 1718
  Paraguay 1215
  Peru 1261
  Suriname 1704
  Uruguay 1517
  Venezuela 1566
Monguí 928
Monsefú 1332
Montañita 1153
Monte Alegre 626
Monte Avila 1585
Monte Caseros 178
Monte Grande 739
Montecristi 1155
Montenegro 993
Montería 952
Montevideo 1518, **1520**
Montsinéry 1720
Moquegua 1400
Morawhanna 1687
Morretes 503
Morro de São Paulo 553
Morrocoy National Park 1594
Mórrope 1333
Mostardas 523
motorcycling 36
Mount Roraima 1675,1688
mountain biking 25
Moyobamba 1364
Mucuchíes 1618
Musichi 967

N

Nahuel Huapi National Park 203
Namballe 1368
Nanegalito 1069
Nasca 1376, **1376**
Nasca Lines 1377
Natal 587
National Vicuña Reserve 1394
Necochea 109
Neiva 1013
Neu-Halbstadt 1250
Neuland 1250
Neuquén 197
New Amsterdam 1685
Niebla 806
Nieuw-Amsterdam 1708
Nieuw-Nickerie 1710
Niquitao 1607
Niterói 435
Nova 522
Nueva Germania 1232
Nuevo Rocafuerte 1177
Nuquí 986

O

O Aleijadinho 480
Óbidos 626
Ocongate 1445
Ocucaje 1372
Ocumare de la Costa 1589
Oiapoque 620
Old Patagonian Express 217
Olinda 574, **574**
Ollagüe 756
Ollantaytambo 1449
Olleros 1308

Olmedo 1168
Olmos 1335
Olón 1154
Omaere 1183
Oncol 806
Orán 173
Orinoco Delta 1664
Oruro 315, **317**
Osório 517
Osorno 807
Otavalo 1077, **1078**
Otway Sound 854
Ouro Preto 480
Ovalle 736

P

Pacasmayo 1350
Pachacámac 1276
Pachacuti Inca Yupanqui 1420
Pailón del Diablo, El 1106
Paipa 927
Paita 1340
Pakaraima Mountains 1688
Palena 837
Palmas 665
Pampa Linda 215
Pampatar 1647
Pamplona 931
Panguipulli 797
Pantanal 665
Pântano do Sul 509
Papallacta 1067
Papudo 733
Paracas 1371
Paracuru 604
paragliding 25
Paraguaná 1598
Paraguarí 1238
Paráiba 584
Paraitepuí 1675
Paramaribo 1706, **1706**
Paramonga 1317
Paraná (Arg) 180
Paraná (Bra) 497
Paranaguá 503,504
Paranapiaçaba 459
Paraty 443
Paria Peninsula 1641
Parika 1687
Parinacota 772
Parintins 626
Pariti 301
Parnaíba 604
Parque Arqueológioco Tierradentro 1007
Parque Ecológico Río Blanco 988
Parque Manantial 1241
Parque Nacional Amacayacu 1023
Parque Nacional Amboró 374
Parque Nacional Bernardo O'Higgins 861
Parque Nacional Cajas 1123
Parque Nacional Calilegua 172
Parque Nacional Canaima 1661, **1661**
Parque Nacional Caparaó 482
Parque Nacional Chaco 186
Parque Nacional Chiloé 828
Parque Nacional Conguillio 788
Parque Nacional Cotopaxi 1092
Parque Nacional de Aparados da Serra 522
Parque Nacional de Sete Cidades 612
Parque Nacional Ensenada de Utría 986
Parque Nacional Henri Pittier 1588, **1588**
Parque Nacional Iguazú 192
Parque Nacional Itatiaia 442
Parque Nacional Laguna de Tacarigua 1631
Parque Nacional Laguna San Rafael 849
Parque Nacional Lauca 772
Parque Nacional Lençóis 604
Parque Nacional Los Alerces 217
Parque Nacional Los Glaciares 245
Parque Nacional Marumbi 503
Parque Nacional
Mburucuyá 181
Parque Nacional Mochima 1633,1635
Parque Nacional Monte Balmaceda 861
Parque Nacional Nahuelbuta 784
Parque Nacional Noel Kempff Mercado 381
Parque Nacional Pan de Azúcar 746
Parque Nacional Puracé 1010
Parque Nacional Puyehue 807
Parque Nacional Quebrada del Condorito 122
Parque Nacional Sajama 316
Parque Nacional Sangay 1183
Parque Nacional Sierra Nevada 1617
Parque Nacional Tayrona 960
Parque Nacional Tijuca 413
Parque Nacional Torotoro 351
Parque Nacional Torres del Paine 865, **867**
Parque Nacional Vicente Pérez Rosales 813
Parque Provincial Copahue-Caviahue 198
Parque Pumalin 834
Parque Tobogán de la Selva 1629
Paso Agua Negra 740
Paso Carrirriñe 797
Paso Casas Viejas 861
Paso de Icalma 791
Paso de Jama 760
Paso de los Toros 1556
Paso Hua-Hum 798
Paso Pehuenche 780
Paso Pérez Rosales 813
Paso Pino Hachado 791
Paso Puyehue 808
Paso San Francisco 746
Paso Sico 760
Passo Fundo 522
Pasto 1017
Patagonia 224
Patanemo 1593
Paucartambo 1445
Paute 1122
Paysandú 1536, **1537**
Pedernales 1161
Pedro González 1648
Pedro Juan Caballero 1244
Pedro Ruíz 1364
Pelechuco 305
Pelotas 523
Penedo 442,581
Península Valdés 228
Pereira 991
Peribeca 1620
Perito Moreno 242
Perito Moreno National Park 242
Pernambuco 564
Peruíbe 470
Petrohué 813
Petrópolis 436, **437**
Peulla 813
Pico El Aguila 1607
Pico Espejo 1617
Pico Naiguatá 1585
Pico Oriental 1585
Piedecuesta 931
Piedrabuena 236
Pikin Poika 1708
Pilaló 1099
Pilcopata 1501
Píllaro 1102
Pilón Lajas 358
Pimentel 1333
Pinamar 107
Piñán lakes 1084
Piñango 1607
Piñas 1149
Pinchollo 1395
Pirangi do Norte 588,592
Pirenópolis 659
Piriápolis 1545
Piribebuy 1232
Piripiri 613
Pisac 1446
Pisagua 766
Pisco 1370
Pisco Elqui 740
Piscobamba 1309
Pisimbalá 1007
Pissis 145
Pitalito 1011

Piúma 491
Piura 1339, **1339**
planning your trip 21
Playa Colorada 1635
Playa El Agua 1648
Playa El Aguila 755
Playa Escondida 1167
Playa Peruana 755
Playas 1152
Pocitos 172
Pomabamba 1309
Pomaire 719
Pomerode 509
Ponta de Pedras 619
Ponta Negra 588, **588**
Ponta Porã 670
Popayán 1006, **1006**
Porlamar 1647
Portezuelo 1545
Portillo 720
Porto Alegre 515, **516**
Porto Belo 509
Porto Seguro 554
Porto Velho 645
Porto Xavier 523
Portoviejo 1155
Porvenir 871
Posadas 188
post 46
Potosí 332, **333**
Potrerillos 135
Powaka 1708
Pozo Almonte 764
Pozo Colorado 1248
Praia do Forte 562
Praia do Rosa 510
Praia Iguape 602
Prainha 602
Presidente Figueiredo 631
Providencia 972
Pucallpa 1487
Pucón 795
Pueblito 960
Puelo 814
Puente del Inca 135
Puerto Acosta 1417
Puerto Acosta 303
Puerto Aisén 839
Puerto Ayacucho 1629
Puerto Ayora 1195
Puerto Baquerizo Moreno 1196
Puerto Bermúdez 1481
Puerto Bertrand 847
Puerto Bolívar 1149
Puerto Cabello 1593
Puerto Cayo 1155
Puerto Chacabuco 839
Puerto Chicama 1325
Puerto Cisnes 837
Puerto Colombia (Col) 956
Puerto Colombia (Ven) 1589
Puerto Córdenas 836
Puerto Deseado 236
Puerto Eten 1333
Puerto Fuy 798
Puerto Guadal 847
Puerto Huacho 1317
Puerto Ibáñez 839
Puerto Iguazú 193, **195**
Puerto La Cruz 1632, **1632**
Puerto López 1154, **1154**
Puerto Madryn 226, **227**
Puerto Maldonado 1501
Puerto Montt 819, **820**
Puerto Nariño 1023
Puerto Natales 859, **860**
Puerto Octay 812
Puerto Ordaz 1664
Puerto Páez 1629
Puerto Palma (Colombia) 1170
Puerto Pérez 301
Puerto Pirehueico 798
Puerto Portovelo 1161
Puerto Río Tranquilo 846
Puerto San Julián 236
Puerto Suárez 382
Puerto Varas 812
Puerto Villarroel 364
Puerto Williams 872
Pujilí 1098
Pululahua 1068
Puna West of Catamarca 145
Puno 1405, **1406**
Punta Arenas 852, **853**
Punta Ballena 1546
Punta Carnero 1153
Punta Charapotó 1160
Punta de Piedra 1652
Punta del Diablo 1548
Punta del Este 1546, **1546**
Punta Delgada 254
Punta Rosa 107
Punta Sal Grande 1343
Punta Tombo 233
Punto Fijo 1598
Puquio 1378
Puracé 1010
Purmamarca 170
Puruchuco 1276
Putre 772
Putumayo 1019
Puyango 1149
Puyo 1183
Puyuguapi 837

Q

Quaraí 524
Quebrada de Humahuaca 170
Quebrada de las Conchas 156
Quechualla 1399
Quellón 829
Quemchi 826
Quetena Chico 324
Quibdó 986
Quíbor 1605
Quichuas 1472
Quijarro 382
Quillacolla 351
Quillagua 754
Quilmes 152
Quilotoa 1099
Quincemil 1500
Quinchamalí 780
Quinchao 826
Quintero 733
Quito 1036 **1037, 1040, 1042**

R

Ralún 813
Rancagua 778
Rapa Nui 877
Raqchi 1445
Ráquira 924
Raura 1297
Recife
Recife 564, **565, 567, 569**
Recôncavo 549
Refugio de Vida Silvestre La Aurora del Palmar 177
Régina 1723
Reserva de la Biósfera del Chaco 1248
Reserva Eduardo Avaroa 322
Reserva El Para 1181
Reserva Nacional Nalcas Malalcahuello 788
Resistencia 185
responsible tourism 28
Riberalta 361
Río Blanco 720
Rio Branco (Bra) 646
Río Branco (Uru) 1556
Río Caribe 1641
Rio da Prata 669
Rio de Janeiro 399, **401, 406, 410**
Río Gallegos 239, **239**
Río Grande (Arg) 255
Rio Grande (Bra) 523
Rio Grande do Sul 515
Río Mayo 242
Río Negro 834
Río Pilcomayo National Park 186
Río Turbio 248
Río Villegas 215
Riobamba 1111, **1112**
Riohacha 966
Rionegro 983
Riosucio 984
Rivera 1557
Rondônia 645
Rosario 179
Rosario de la Frontera 152
Rumichaca 1474
Rumipamba 1045
Rurrenabaque 357,358
Ruta 40 242

S

Sabará 479
Sacred Valley 1446
safety
  general 47
  Bolivia 278
  Brazil 396
  Chile 694
  Colombia 894
  Ecuador 1034
  Paraguay 1215
  Peru 1263
  Suriname 1704
  Uruguay 1517
  Venezuela 1567

Sajama 316
Salango 1154
Salar de Atacama 760
Salar de Uyuni 322
Salento 992
Salinas 1152
Salta 159, **160**
Salto 1537
Salto del Guaíra 1232
Salto El Laja 784
Salvador 532
Samaipata 372, **373**
Same 1167
San Agustín 1012
San Agustín de Cajas 1468
San Agustín del Valle Fértil 140
San Andrés 971, **971**
San Antonio (Chi) 733
San Antonio (Ven) 1621
San Antonio de Areco 102
San Antonio de Ibarra 1084
San Antonio de los Cobres 161
San Antonio Oeste 225
San Bernardino 1231
San Borja 357
San Cipriano 1003
San Clemente 1160
San Clemente del Tuyú 107
San Cristóbal (Bolivia) 322
San Cristóbal 1620
San Félix 1664
San Fernando 778
San Fernando de Apure 1626
San Francisco de Yuruaní 1675
San Gabriel 1085
San Gil 930
San Gregorio de Polanco 1556
San Ignacio 1368
San Ignacio de Moxos 364
San Ignacio de Velasco 380
San Ignacio de Yuruaní 1670
San Ignacio Guazú 1239
San Ignacio Miní 188
San Isidro 1668
San Jacinto (Col) 951
San Jacinto (Ecu) 1160
San Javier 379
San Javier, Misiones 191
San Jerónimo 1468
San José de Chiquitos 381
San José de Jachal 140
San Juan 139, **139**
San Juan de Manapiare 1630
San Lázaro 339
San Lorenzo (Bol) 345
San Lorenzo (Ecu) 1169
San Lorenzo 1220
San Luis 1309
San Marcos (Chi) 755
San Marcos (Per) 1309
San Martín de los Andes 200
San Matías 382
San Miguel 1169
San Miguel del Bala 358
San Miguel Falls 1106
San Pablo 1181
San Pablo del Lago 1079
San Pedro 1468
San Pedro de Atacama 758, **759**
San Pedro de Casta 1464
San Rafael 133
San Rafael de Mucuchíes 1618
San Ramón 1481
San Sebastián 872
San Vicente (Bol) 328
San Vicente (Ecu) 1161
Sanaré 1605
Sandoná 1018
Santa Ana 188
Santa Bárbara (Bra) 488
Santa Bárbara (Col) 984
Santa Catarina 507
Santa Cruz Cabrália 554
Santa Cruz de la Sierra 366, **367**
Santa Elena de Uairén 1670, **1669**
Santa Fe 180
Santa Fé de Antioquia 983
Santa María (Arg) 152
Santa María (Par) 1239
Santa María (Per) 1458
Santa María 1169
Santa Marta 958, **959**
Santa Rosa (Par) 1239
Santa Rosa (Per) 1333
Santa Rosa de Cabal 992
Santa Teresa (Bra) 406
Santa Teresa (Per) 1458
Santa Teresa National Park 1548
Santana do Livramento 524
Santarém 626
Santiago 696, **696**, **697**, **698**, **700**, **702**
Santiago del Estero 149
Santigron 1708
Santo Domingo 1607
Santo Domingo de los Colorados 1162
Santos 468
São Cristóvão 581
São Félix 549
São Francisco do Sul 510
São Gonçalo do Rio das Pedras 495
São Gonçalo do Rio Preto 495
São João del Rei 483
São Joaquim 511
São José do Norte 523
São Lourenço do Sul 523
São Luis 605, **605**
São Miguel das Missões 522
São Paulo 451, **452**, **454**, **457**
São Pedro de Aldeia 436
São Sebastião 469
São Tomé das Letras 484
Sapecho 357
Sapzurro
Saquarema 435
Saquisilí 1099
Saraguro 1130
Sarmiento 236
Saül 1723
Saywite 1463
Sechín 1317
Serro 495
Shell 1183
shopping 40
Sicán 1335
Sico 161
Sierra de la Ventana 110
Sierra de San Luis 1598
Sierra Nevada de Mérida 1609
Sierra Nevada de Santa Marta 961
Sigchos 1099
Sígsig 1123
Sihuas 1309
Silvia 1007
Sinamaica 1602
Sinnamary 1721
Sinsacate 122
Sipán 1333
Sítio do Conde 562
sleeping, see under accommodation
Socorro 930
Sogamoso 927
Soledad 956
Sorata 303, **304**
Soure 620
South American Explorer's club 52
South Georgia 1744
sport 23
Stanley 1735, **1736**
St-Georges de l'Oyapock 1723
St-Laurent du Maroni 1721
Súa 1167
Subaúma 562
Sucre 338, **339**
Sullana 1342
Superagüi National Park 505
Supía 984
Surama 1690
surfing 26
Suriqui 301
Surire 772
Susques 170
sustainable tourism 28

T

Tabatinga 640
Tabay 1618
Tacna 1401, **1401**
Tacuarembó 1557

Tafí del Valle 150
Taganga 960
Takesi Trail 285
Talampaya National Park 141
Talara 1342
Talca 779
Talcahuano 783
Taltal 746
Tandil 103
Tantauco 829
Tapay 1395
Taquile 1413
Tarabuco 340
Tarapaya 335
Tarapoto 1365
Tarija 345
Tarma 1481
Tarqui 1160
Tastil 161
Tavares 523
telephone 48
Temuco 787, **790**
Tena 1181, **1182**
Teresina 612
Termas de Pangui 797
Termas de Reyes 168
Termas de Río Hondo 149
Termas de San Luis 797
Terre Rouge 1722
The Lake District (Arg) 197
The Sacred Valley (Per) **1448**
Tibau do Sul 588
Tierra del Fuego 254, 260, 871
Tierradentro 1007
Tigre 100
Tigua 1098
Tilcara 170
Timaná 1011
Tingo (Amazonas) 1358
Tingo (Arequipa) 1385
Tingo María 1486
Tinogasta 145
Tiradentes 483
Tiwanaku 284
Tobati 1231
Tocantins 664
Toconao 759
Toconce 756
Tolhuin 255
Tolú 951
Tópaga 928
Tornquist 110
Toro Muerto 1399
Totness 1710
tourist information
  Argentina 65
  Bolivia 276
  Brazil 397
  Chile 694
  Colombia 895
  Ecuador 1034
  Guyane 1719
  Paraguay 1216
  Peru 1264
  Uruguay 1517
  Venezuela 1568
Train to the Clouds 161
Trancoso 554
Transoceánica 1499
transport
  Argentina 61
  Bolivia 271, 272, 273
  Brazil 391, 392
  Chile 689, 691
  Colombia 889
  Ecuador 1030
  Paraguay 1213
  Uruguay 1515
  Venezuela 1563
Treinta y Tres 1556
Trelew 232, **233**
Tren a las Nubes 161
Trindade **444**
Trinidad (Bol) 364
Trinidad (Par) 1240
Trujillo (Per) 1320, **1322**
Trujillo (Ven) 1607
Tucacas 1594
Tucumán 150, **151**
Tucumé 1334
Tucupita 1664
Tulcán 1086
Tulipe 1069
Tumaco 1018
Tumbes 1343, **1344**
Tumeremo 1668
Tunari National Park 350
Tunja 921
Tupiza 328
Túquerres 1018
Turbaco 951
Turbo 952
Tutóia 604

U

Uaimiri Atroari Indian Reserve 641
Ubatuba 470
Ubu 491
Unduavi 312
Urcos 1445
Urcuquí 1084
Uribia 967
Uros 1413
Urubamba 1447
Urubici 511
Ushuaia 257, **258**
Uspallata 135
Uyuni 322, **323**

V

Valdivia (Chi) 805, **807**
Valdivia (Ecu) 1153
Valença 552
Valencia 1593
Valera 1607
Valle de la Luna 284
Valle de Lares 1447
Valle Nevado 720
Vallecito 140
Vallecitos 135
Valledupar 967
Vallegrande 373,378
Vallenar 745
Valles Calchaquíes 156
Valparaíso 722, **724**, **726**
vehicle documents 37
Viedma 225
Vila do Abraão 443
Vila Velha 499
Vilcabamba (Ecu) 1136, **1136**
Vilcabamba (Per) 1462
Vilcabamba Vieja 1462
Vilches 779
Villa Albina 351
Villa Alpina 123
Villa Carlos Paz 121
Villa Cerro Castillo 840
Villa de Leiva 922, **923**
Villa Dorotea 861
Villa El Chocón 197
Villa Florida 1238
Villa General Belgrano 123
Villa Gesell 107
Villa La Angostura 204
Villa Mitre 108
Villa O'Higgins 848
Villa Rosario 932
Villa Traful 203
Villa Tunari 352
Villa Unión 144
Villamontes 375
Villarrica 794,1233
Villavicencio 918
Villazón 329
Viña del Mar 731, **732**
Vinchina 144
Visviri 771
Vitória 490
Volcán Cayambe 1074
Volcán Osorno 813
Volcan Sumaco 1176
Voltaire Falls 1722
Volunteer Point 1735

W

Wageningen 1710
Waraira Repano 1585
Washabo 1710
West View 972

X

Xapuri 647

Y

Yacambú 1605
Yacuiba 375
Yaguarón 1237
Yanama 1309
Yanque 1394
Yare 1586
Yarinacocha 1487
Yatasto 152
Yauyos 1370
Yavi 172
Ybycuí 1238
youth hostels 39
Yucay 1447
Yucumo 357
Yumina 1386
Yunga Cruz 286
Yungas 312
Yungay 1311
Yunguyo 1417
Yurimaguas 1490

Z

Zamora 1131
Zapala 198
Zapallar 733
Zapiga 766
Zaruma 1149
Zipaquirá 917
Zumba 1137
Zumbahua 1099
Zumbi 1184

Advertisers' index

Academia Buenos Aires, Argentina 43
Academia de Español Quito, Ecuador 1065
AISL, Argentina 98
All about EQ, Ecuador 1082
Amauta Spanish School, Argentina 98
Amazon Antonio Jungle Tours, Brazil 637
Amazon River Expeditions, Peru 1495
Amazon Trails Peru, Peru 1508
Andean Kingdom, Peru 1304
Andean Travel Company, Ecuador 1029
Andes Explorer, Ecuador 1204
Andina Travel, Peru 1437
Antarctic Dream/Expeditions, Chile 714
Apart Hotel Santa Magdalena, Chile 708
Bala Tours, Bolivia 360
Bellavista Hostel, Chile 706
Casa Viena Villa de Leyva, Colombia 925
Casa Viena, Colombia 945
CEDEI (Centro de Estudios Interamericos), Ecuador 1129
Chimu Adventures, Peru 49
Climbing Tours, Ecuador 1057
Creter Tours, Ecuador 1207
Crillon Tours, Bolivia 309
Cross Keys, Cuzco 1433
Cusco Adventure Team, Peru 1440
Destino Nomada, Colombia 907
Dreamer Hostel, Colombia 963
El Misti (Botafogo), Brazil 415
Enchanted Expeditions, Ecuador 1204
Estancia Los Potreros, Argentina 119
Falkland Islands Holidays, Falkland Islands 1730
Favela Tour, Brazil 429
G House, Ecuador 1047
Galacruises Expeditions, Ecuador 1203
Galapagos Classic Cruises, UK 49
Galápagos Holidays, Canada 1192
Galasam, Ecuador 1206
GALEXTUR - Hotel Silberstein, Ecuador 1058
Geko Hostel, Brazil 446
Gloria Tours, Bolivia 271
Gravity Bolivia, Bolivia 295
Guyra Paraguay, Paraguay 1213
Hacienda Los Andes, Chile 741
Hacienda Santa Ana, Ecuador 1095
HI Travel, Argentina 91
Hitchhikers B&B Backpackers Hostel, Peru 1280
Hostal Rio Amazonas, Chile 705
Hostel Suites Mendoza, Argentina 129
Hosteria Pantavi, Ecuador 1088
Hotel & Mirador Los Apus, Peru 1426
Hotel Antumalal, Chile 799
Hotel Gloria Copacabana, Bolivia 306
Hotel Rasario Lago Titicaca, Bolivia 306
Hotel Rosario La Paz, Bolivia 288
Hotel Rumi Punku, Peru 1428
Hotel Sierra Madre & Restaurant, Ecuador 1048
Hotel Westfalenhaus, Paraguay 1222
IMBEX Rent a car, Bolivia 298
InkaNatura, Peru 1507
Instituto Exclusivo, Bolivia 279
International Tours & Travel Ltd, Falkland Islands 1745
International Tours and Travel, Falkland Islands 1742
Julio Verne Travel, Ecuador 1117
Kilca Hostel, Argentina 81
Kori Simi, Bolivia 271
La Chimba Hostel, Chile 707
Last Frontiers, UK 50
Latin American Travel Association, UK 33
Lipiko Tours, Bolivia 296
Madson's Private Tours, Brazil 428
Mallku Expeditions, Ecuador 1206
Manu Expeditions, Peru 1508
Misti Chill Hostel, Brazil 447
Natoura Travel, Venezuela 1563
Naugala Yacht Services, Ecuador 1207
Oasis Overland, UK 32
Pachamama by Bus, Chile 689
Pantiacolla Tours SR, Peru 1509
Peru World Travel Tour Agency, Peru 1290
Pousada Hibiscus Beach, Brazil 439
Real Nature Travel Company, Ecuador 1188
Reserva Natural Aldea Luna, Argentina 167
Restaurant Vienna, Bolivia 291
Rio Flat Rental, Brazil 418
Rio Samba Dancer, Brazil 428
Safari Tours, Ecuador 1059
Sailing Koala, Colombia 949
Say Hueque, Argentina 61
Select Latin America, UK 1191
Select Latin America, UK 51
South America Adventure Travel, Argentina 50
South American Explores, Peru 52
Surtrek, Ecuador 1036,1183,1193
Tangol, Argentina 59
Terrasenses, Ecuador 1028
Tierra de Feugo, Ecuador 1060
Tours Unlimited, Ecuador 1060
Tributrek/Hostal Tiana, Ecuador 1097
Turisbus, Bolivia 272
Wilderness Explorers, Guyana 1683,1698
Zenith Travel, Ecuador 1205,1455

About the author

One of the first assignments **Ben Box** took as a freelance writer in 1980 was subediting work on the *South American Handbook*. The plan then was to write about contemporary Iberian and Latin American affairs, but in no time at all the lands south of the Rio Grande took over, inspiring journeys to all corners of the subcontinent. Ben has contributed to newspapers, magazines and learned tomes, usually on the subject of travel, and became editor of the *South American Handbook* in 1989. He has also been involved in Footprint's Handbooks on *Central America & Mexico, Caribbean Islands, Brazil, Peru, Peru, Bolivia and Ecuador* and *Cuzco & the Inca Heartland*. Having a doctorate in Spanish and Portuguese studies from London University, Ben maintains a strong interest in Latin American literature. In the British summer he plays cricket for his local village side and year round he attempts to achieve some level of self-sufficiency in fruit and veg in a rather unruly country garden in Suffolk.

Acknowledgements

For their assistance with the 2010 edition, the author wishes to thank all at Footprint, especially Alan, Emma, Kev, Ren and Liz.

In late 2009, the author visited Peru. He and Sarah Cameron are most grateful to the following for their assistance and hospitality: in Lima, Ana Cecilia Vidal (Hoteles Libertador); Claudia Miranda and Fiorella Llanos Pretell (Sonesta); Rodrigo Custodio (InkaNatura), also Daniel; Siduith Ferrer and Rick Vecchio of Fertur; Mónica Moreno (La Posada del Parque); Judy Kamiche; Raúl Meza; Miles Buesst; Carolina Morillas (Cóndor Travel); Alessandro Fassio, Josué Maguiña and Nataly Rodríguez (Il Tucano Perú), Rafael Tapia (PromPerú). In Cajamarca, Pim Heijster. In Celendín: Susan van der Wielen and Vilzeth. In Chiclayo: Patricia Vargas (InkaNatura), Las Musas, La Casa de la Luna, Gran Hotel Chiclayo, Luis Ocas and Ever Reyes; Cecilia Kamiche (Mórrope); Andrea Martin of Rancho Santana (Pacora); Rosana Correa (Los Horcones, Túcume); Doña Piedad y Don Aldo (Hostería San Roque, Lambayeque). In Trujillo: Walter Eberhart (also in Cajamarca) and Friedy Eberhart; Clara Bravo. In Santiago de Viñac: Enrique Umbert of Mountain Lodges of Peru and Elisabeth Leitner-Rauchdobler.

For invaluable updating assistance on the individual chapters, we are most grateful to: **Argentina**: Andre Vltchek; Federico Kirbus; Lucy Cousins (author of Footprint's Argentina Handbook). **Bolivia**: Robert and Daisy Kunstaetter (authors of Footprint's Bolivia Handbook), who wish to thank Paulina Bascón, Lena Labryga, Alistair Matthew, Bastian Müller and Estefanía Sandoval; Geoffrey Groesbeck. **Brazil**: Alex Robinson (author of Footprint's Brazil Handbook). **Chile**: Andre Vltchek; Janak Jani (author of Footprint's Chile Handbook); Nicholas La Penna (Chaitén); James Grant Peterkin (British Honorary Consul, Hanga Roa); Nelson Oyarzo (Sernatur, Concepción). **Colombia**: Anna Maria Espsäter; Richard McColl (Mompós); Charlie Devereux (author of Footprint's Colombia Handbook). **Ecuador**: Robert and Daisy Kunstaetter (authors of Footprint's Ecuador and the Galápagos Handbook) who would like to thank Jeaneth Barrionuevo, Jean Brown, Katrien de Jong, Michael Resch, Iván Suárez and Popkje van der Ploeg. **Paraguay**: Richard Elsam. **Peru**: Robert and Daisy Kunstaetter, who would like to thank: Carlos and Rosario Burga, Chachapoyas, Robert Dover, Chachapoyas, Silvia Miranda V and Rocío Sánchez C, PromPerú Chachapoyas, and Nancy Ramos, Oficina Municipal de Turismo, Moyabamba. Heather MacBrayne, Aaron Zarate, and the staff of South American Explorers, Lima; Walter Eberhart; Paul Cripps and Carol Thomas; Mariella Bernasconi, Alberto Miori and Zoe Gillett; Alberto Cafferata (Caraz); and Analía Sarfati (Iquitos). **Uruguay**: Clemmy Manzo and Ed Stocker. **Venezuela**: Rachel Jones and Charlie Devereux. **Guyana**: Tony Thorne, Teri O'Brien and Luke Johnson (Wilderness Explorers, Georgetown). **Suriname**: Claire Antell and Tony Thorne (LATA and Wilderness Explorers). **Falkland Islands**: Louise Taylor (FITB). For help with proof-reading and web checking, the author would like to thank Lizzi Williams.

Travellers' letters

Travellers whose emails and letters have been used this year (in part or in full): Evan Abramson (Bol); Adrian and Tony (Arg); Andre (Arg); Amélie and Benoit, France (Per); Ard (Uru); William and Lia van den Berg (Chi); Lisa Bjerre (Bol); Kath Blakemore (Bol); Sonja Bleeker (Per); Andreas Bodio (Per); Robert Jan de Boer (Bol, Col); Yolanda Bogli (Ecu); Matias Bradbury, UK (Ecu, Per); Josh Brand (Per); Jeremy and Jeanette Brock (Bol); Ines and Bjoern Bundschuh, Germany (Arg, Bol, Chi, Col, Ecu, Per); Isabelle Calor (Per); Ian Cameron (Ecu); Adam Carroll (Chi); Julio Cezar Chaves (Per); Charlie Chen (Col); Joachim Cheutin (Per); Karin Chung, Hong Kong (Arg, Bra, Chi, Col, Uru, Ven); Albert Clusella, Spain (Chi); Eefje Cuijpers (Ecu); John Davies (Per); Brian DeBruine, USA (Per); Philip Dench (Ecu); Dewi (Arg); Christine Derouet (Per); Jan Dick, Netherlands (Per); Fleur van Dijk, Netherlands (Per); Doris and Juerg (Bol); Tim Doyle (Bol); Ben Draper (Per); Heather Drew (Chi); Claire Dubarbier (Arg, Chi, Ecu); Michael Haeberli (Bol); Esther and Hector (Per); Francine Favalier (Per); Chloe Feron (Per); Pascal Ferrat (Bol); Stephan Frei (Bol); Christoph Freundl (Ecu); Rubén Gabe (Per); Liesbeth Geuvens (Bol); Marta Giovannoni, Brazil (Bra); John Grimes, USA (Per); Claudia Haensch (Per); Matt Halla (Bra); Daphne Hameeteman (Arg); Trine Hansen (Per); Richard Hartmann, Germany (Per); Nina Hauser (Col, Ecu); Fernanda Hermenegildo (Per); Ben Hill, Australia (Col); Roberto, Betty y Carlos Alberto Hodges (Per); Jens and Daniela Hohmann, Germany (Chi, Bol, Col, Ecu, Per); Ruth and Hans Houben (Ecu); Patricia Hunt (Ecu); Jay (Chi); Ivonne Jeanneau, USA (Per); Andrea L Johnson, USA (Per); Josh Johnson (Ecu); Annemarie Jong (Per); Matthieu Kamerman, The Netherlands (Bol, Bra, Chi, Col, Ven); Karlyn (Per); Barbara Keller (Bol); Mara-Feen Kemlein (Bol, Per); Todd Kennedy (Per); Benjamin Kickhöfer (Ecu); Konrad Klatt (Bol); Thomas Kugler (Chi); Charles Largin (Ecu); Gina Lazaro (Per); Mun Yi Leong (Bra); John Lewis, UK (Bra); Jan Luedeke (Bol); Peter and Patricia McCarthy, Australia (Arg, Bra, Chi) ; Dorien Meijerink (Bol); Marcus and Elizabeth (Arg); Domingo Marchi (Per); Navinya Masters (Per); Michelangelo Mazzeo, Italy (Col) ; Andre Meyer (Per); Tim Meyer, Germany (Chi, Uru); Michelle (Ecu); Trudie Mitchell (Chi); Victoria Mitchell (Per); Ron and Judy Morrison (Bol); Deirdre Murphy, Ireland, and Sébastien Mathey, France (Arg, Bol, Bra, Chi, Col, Ven) ; Nik and Abby Nelberg, UK (Col); Marcos Neumann (Ecu); Niki Niens (Per); Levi Nietvelt (Per); Karl Nordlander, Sweden (Uru); Franz Palkowitsch (Per); Leonie Palmer (Bol); Tiziana Pederzani (Per); Patricia Powers and Edward Slimak, USA (Per); Dave Procter, Colombia (Col); Hans Erik Rasmussen (Per); Abder Rezak (Per); Rick (Ecu); Carole and Marcel Rieben, Switzerland (Chi); Camila Rodriguez (Per); Raúl Rodríguez, Colombia (Col); Emma Rogers (Per); Lorenzo Armando Rojas (Per); Barbara Rozalska (Ecu); Sandra (Arg); Andreas Sarno, Switzerland (Chi); Charlotte Savelkoul (Col); Nicole Schubert and Werner (Ecu); Paul Scotchmer, UK (Arg); Graciela Sendra (Per); George Shanks (Arg); Anita Seifert (Per); Susanne Sleegers (Per); Jenelle Stafford (Per); Alfred Steinacher (Bol); Steven (Col); Paul Taylor (Per); Ursula Theisen, Germany (Col); Anders Thomsen (Bol); Monica Ueltschi (Bol); Enzo Andres Urbina (Per); Rolf Vaardal, Norway (Per); Saskia Vandeputte (Bol); Dineke Veerman (Per); Carmen Walker (Bol); Angelique and Chris Williams, Germany (Col); Jan Willms, Germany (Arg); Naoko Yamabe (Col); Anda Zalaiskalns (Ecu); Augusto Zanardi (Per); Moises Alejandro Zapata Herrera (Per).

We should also like to thank all those travellers who have written to Footprint's Handbooks on Chile and Ecuador.

Specialist contributors: Alex Robinson for Music; Anna Maria Espsäter for Literature, Cinema, Arts and Crafts and LBGT tourism; Peter Pollard for Land and environment; Ashley Rawlings for Motorcycling; Hallam Murray for Cycling; Hilary Bradt for Hiking and trekking; Richard Robinson for World wide radio information.

Credits

Footprint credits

Editor: Alan Murphy
Production and layout: Emma Bryers
Map editors: Robert Kunstaetter, Kevin Feeney
Colour section: Kevin Feeney

Managing Director: Andy Riddle
Commercial Director: Patrick Dawson
Publisher: Alan Murphy
Publishing Managers: Felicity Laughton, Jo Williams, Jen Haddington
Digital Editor: Alice Little
Cover design: Pepi Bluck
Marketing: Liz Harper
Advertising: Renu Sibal
Finance and administration: Elizabeth Taylor

Photography credits

Front cover: Danita Delimont Stock, Kayapo (awl-images.com)
Back cover: Lago llanquihue, Chile (Prisma/Superstock)

Manufactured in India by Nutech
Pulp from sustainable forests

Every effort has been made to ensure that the facts in this guidebook are accurate. However, travellers should still obtain advice from consulates, airlines etc about travel and visa requirements before travelling. The authors and publishers cannot accept responsibility for any loss, injury or inconvenience however caused.

Publishing information

Footprint South American Handbook
87th edition

ISBN: 978 1 907263 05 7
CIP DATA: A catalogue record for this book is available from the British Library

Published by Footprint
6 Riverside Court
Lower Bristol Road
Bath BA2 3DZ, UK
T +44 (0)1225 469141
F +44 (0)1225 469461
www.footprinttravelguides.com

Distributed in the USA by Globe Pequot Press, Guilford, Connecticut

Colour section photography credits

P1: Machu Picchu (Shutterstock/Teo Dominguez). P2: Market, Peru (Shutterstock/Neal Cousland). P6 top: Tango, Buenos Aires (South American Pictures/Mike Harding). P6 mid left: Kaieteuer Falls (SAP/Tony Morrison). P6 mid right: Salvador de Bahia (Shutterstock/Vinicius Tupinamba). P6 bottom: Angel Falls (age fotostock/Superstock). P7 top: Pantanal (Naturepl/Staffan Widstrand). P7 bottom: Torres del Paine (Shutterstock/Lai Quoc Anh). P8: Lake Titicaca (Shutterstock/Rakhno A). P9 top left: Cartagena (SAP/Mike Harding). P9 top right: Salar de Uyuni Botond (Shutterstock/Horváth). P9 bottom left: Lake District, Chile (Alamy/Aaron Beck). P9 mid right: Cuzco (SAP/Kathy Jarvis). P9 bottom right: Cotopaxi (Naturepl/Pete Oxford). P10: Perito Moreno (Shutterstock/javarman). P12 left: Manu NP, Toucan (SAP/Tony Morrison). P12 right: Jaguar (Naturepl/Staffan Widstrand). P13 top left: Iguana, Galapagos (Shutterstock/nouseforname). P13 top right: Emas NP, giantAnteater (All Canada Photos/Superstock). P13 bottom left: Noel Kempff Mercado (Naturepl/Pete Oxford). P13 bottom right: Southern Right Whale (Naturepl/Pete Oxford). P14 left: Rio Carnival (Hemis fr/Superstock). P14 right: Dia de la Tradicion (SAP/Frank Nowikowski). P15: Oruro Carnival (SAP/Tony Morrison). P16: Ouro Preto (Shutterstock/ostill).

Footprint Mini Atlas
South America

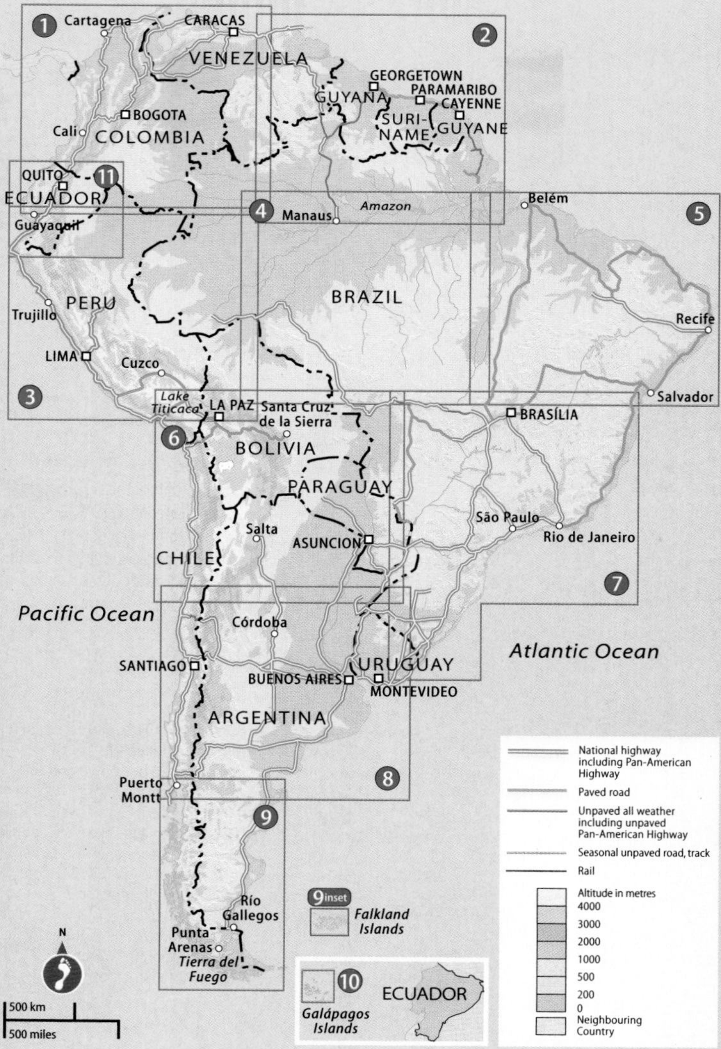

Map 1

Caribbean Sea
Pacific Ocean
PANAMA
ECUADOR
A
B
C
1
2
3
N
100 km
100 miles
PN Tayrona
Santa Marta
Palomino
Barranquilla
Ciudad Perdida
PNN Sierra Nevada
SFF Ciénaga Grande de Santa Marta
Aracataca
Baranoa
Fundación
Cartagena
Sabanalarga
Valledupar
Islas del Rosario
Turbaco
Malagana
San Jacinto
Bosconia
Islas de San Bernardo
Ovejas
Tolú
Coveñas
Magangué
Mompós
Sincelejo
Curumaní
Cauca
El Banco
Magdalena
Montería
Capurganá
Acandí
Golfo de Urabá
Turbo
Caucasia
PNN Los Katios
San Alberto
Chigorodó
PNN Paramillo
Travesía
Bucaramanga
Barrancabermeja
Atrato
Dabeiba
Santa Fé de Antioquia
Girón
Jurado
San Gil
Barichara
PNN Las Orquideas
Puerto Berrio
Socorro
Medellín
Rionegro
Puerto Boyacá
Barbosa
Bahía Solano
Duitama
Sta Bárbara
Paipa
El Valle
Bolívar
PNN de Utría
Quibdó
Chiquinquirá
Villa de Leiva
Tunja
Nuqui
Riosucio
Honda
Mariquita
Zipaquirá
Istmina
Tadó
Manizales
Armero
Villeta
Nemocón
Pereira
PNN Los Nevados
Facatativá
PNN Chingaza
Cartago
Salento
BOGOTÁ
Armenia
Girardot
Puerto López
Ibagué
Villavicencio
PNN Sumapaz
Juanchaco
Buenaventura
Buga
Natagaima
Palmira
Cali
PNN Nevado del Huila
PNN Serranía de la Macarena
Neiva
Gorgona Island
Santander
Tierradentro
Silvia
Inzá
PNN Tinigua
Popayán
La Plata
Guacamayas
Guapí
Puracé
PNN Sanquianga
Garzón
San Vicente del Caguán
PNN de Puracé
Altamira
San Agustín
Pitalito
Florencia
El Doncello
Tumaco
Barbacoas
La Montañita
Belén
Morelia
Junín
SFF Galeras
PNN Chiribiquete
San Lorenzo
La Tola
Pasto
Mocoa
Esmeraldas
Atacames
Ipiales
Lita
Tulcán
Viche
San Miguel
Puerto Asis
PNN La Paya
Muisne
Rosa Zárate (Quinindé)
Apuela
Barra
Otavalo
Cojimíes
Cayambe
Lago Agrio
Santo Domingo
Pedernales
QUITO
San Isidro
El Chaco
Coca (Puerto Francisco de Orellana)
Canoa
El Carmen
Baeza
Bahía de Caráquez
Cosanga
Zumbahua
Latacunga
Manta
Quevedo
Tena
Puerto Misahuallí
Putumayo
Portoviejo
El Corázon
Ambato
Baños
Curaray
Puerto López
Jipijapa
Puyo
Puesto Arturo
Guaranda
Riobamba
Montalvo
Manglaralto
Daule
Guamote
Marsella

Puerto Bolívar
Cabo de la Vela
Península de la Guajira
PN Macuira
Peninsula Paraguaná
Adícora
Manaure
Uribia
Riohacha
Punta Fijo
Punta Cardón
PN Médanos de Coro
Los Roques
Maicao
Paraguaipoa
Coro
Agüide
Isla de Margarita
PN Sierra San Luis
Sinamaica
Chichiriviche
El Moján
R Faun Los Olivitos
PN Morrocoy
Fonseca
PN Cueva de la Quebrada de El Torro
Tucacas
Puerto Colombia
La Guaira
Los Caracas
Araya
Cum
Maracaibo
Yumare
PN El Avila
Higuerote
PN Mochima
Serranía de Perijá
San Felipe
Puerto Cabello
Maracay
CARACAS
El Guapo
Puerto La Cruz
Cabimas
Barcelona
Carora
Barquisimeto
Ciudad Ojeda
Valencia
L de Valencia
Los Teques
PN Guatopo
Machiques
San Juan de los Morros
Camatagua
A
Uric
San Carlos
San José de Guaribe
Onote
Lago de Maracaibo
Anaco
Valera
Trujillo
Zazara
PN Ciénagas de Catatumbo
Tucupido
El Chaparro
San Carlos
Boconó
Embalse del Guárico
Encontrados
Niquitao
Guanare
El Baúl
Calabozo
El Socorro
El Tigre
Apartaderos
Santo Domingo
PN Sierra La Culata
Boconoito
La Azulita
Mérida
R Fauna Chiriguare
PNN Aguaro-Guariquito
Espino
Mo
El Vigía
Barinas
Zuata
Boca del Pao
La Fría
Tovar
PN Sierra Nevada
Libertad
Bruzual
San Fernando de Apure
Cazorla
La Grita
Caicara de Orinoco
Mapire
Cúcuta
San Cristóbal
Mantecal
Puruey
San Antonio
Abejales
La Ye
El Yagui
Maripa
Santo Domingo
Pamplona
Guasdualito
PN Tamá
VENEZUELA
Arauca
Serranía de la Cerbatana
Málaga
PN Cinaruco-Capanaparo
Guicán
Puerto Páez
PN Sierra Nevada de Cocuy
Tame
El Cocuy
El Burro
Puerto Carreño
Sogamoso
Puerto Ayacucho
Lago de Tota
Pore
PNN El Tuparro
Trinidad
San Juan de Manapiare
Yopal
B
Autana-tepuy
Puerto Gaitán
COLOMBIA
Serra Parima
San José del Guaviare
RNN Puinawai
Calamar
PN Serrania de la Neblina
PNN Chiribiquete
RF do Rio Negro
AI Içana Xié
AI Iauaretê
PN do Pico da Neblima
2
C
AI Pari Cachoeira
AI Alto Rio Negro
PNN Cahuinarí
3
4
5
6
Pucaurco

Map 2

Isla de Margarita
La Asunción
Porlamar
Carúpano
PN Paría
Güiria
Port of Spain
TRINIDAD
Golfo de Paría
Araya
Cumaná
PN Mochima
Higuerote
El Guapo
Puerto La Cruz
Cariaco
El Pilar
Caripe
PN El Guácharo
PN Turuépano
Barcelona
PN Guatopo
San José de Guaribe
Onote
Urica
Maturín
Manamo
Pedernales
Tucupita
PN Mariusa
Zazara
Anaco
Aguasay
Tucipido
El Chapparo
Temblador
Tucupita
El Socorro
El Tigre
Morichal
Delta Amacuro
Delta del Orinoco
Los Barrancos
Barrancas
Los Castillos
Morón
Orinoco
San Félix (Ciudad Guyana)
Puerto Ordaz
Sna de Imataca
El Palmar
Shell Beach
Mabaruma
Port Kaituma
Zuata
Boca del Pao
Ciudad Bolívar
Villa Lola
El Miamo
Bochinche
Caicara de Orinoco
Mapire
Puruey
Embalse de Guri
Guasipati
El Callao
Matthews Ridge
Charity
Ciudad Piar
El Manteco
Tumeremo
Maripa
Mercedes
Kauramembu Mtns
La Paragua
San Martín
Wakenaam I
Leguan I
El Dorado
GEORGETOWN
Taraipa
Canaima
San Isidro (Km 88)
Oko Mtns
Bartica
Mazaruni
San Salvador de Paúl
Angel Falls
Auyán Tepuy (2560m)
Essequibo
Linden
Kamoirán
PN Canaima
San Francisco de Yuruaní
Mt Roraima (2810m)
Pakaraima Mtns
Río Caroní
San Juan de Manapiare
San Ignacio de Yuruaní
Kaieteur Falls
Mahdia
VENEZUELA
La Gran Sabana
GUYANA
Santa Elena de Uairén
Iwokrama
Sierra de Pacaraima
Bonfim
Lethem
Serra Parima
Kakanu Mtns
Alto Alegre
Boa Vista
Caracaraí
PN Serrania de la Neblina
Serra Acaraí
Parque Indígena Yanomami
Novo Paraiso
São Luís
PN do Pico da Neblima
Rio Branco
1
Al Waimiri Atroari
Represa de Balbina
PN do Jaú
Presidente Figueiredo
Negro
EE de Anavilhanas
Rio Preto da Eva
EE Mamiraua
L Canaçari
Manaus
Itacoatiara
Manacapuru
Careiro da Várzea
A
B
C
1
2
3

Atlantic Ocean
N
100 km
100 miles
A
B
C
New Amsterdam
Fort Nassau
Nieuw Nickerie
Corriverton
Nat Res Coppename Monding
PARAMARIB
Paranam
Nat Res Wia-Wia
NR Galibi
Aouara
Mana
Albina
St-Laurent
Iracouba
Sinnamary
Iles du Salut
NR Brinckheuvel
Brokopondo
Nat Park Brownsweg
Paul Isnard
Kourou
Montsinéry
CAYENNE
Roura
Prof Dr Ir W J van Blommesteinmeer
oekornstig stuwmeer
Cacao
Kaw
Central Suriname Nature Reserve
Régina
PN de Cabo Orange
SURINAME
Cottica
Maripasoula
St-Georges de l'Oyapock
Oiapoque
Saül
GUYANE
Al Uaçá
Corantijn
Mont St-Marcel
Calçoene
Lourenço
Serra de Tumucumaque
EE de Maracá-Japioca
Amapá
Parque Indígena Tumucumaque
Al Waiãpi
Al Uaçá
Araguari
Porto Grande
Abacate
Ilha Caviana
Macapá
Arquipélago Jurupari
I Queimada
Ilha Mexicana
BRAZIL
Paru
4
5
RB do Rio Trombetas
Monte Dorado
Ilha Grande de Gurupá
I Mututi
Ilha de Marajó
Sour
Almeirim
Amazonas
EE do Marajó
Ponta de Pedras
Abaetetub
I Sirituba
Prainha
Monte Alegre
Oeiras do Pará
Abaetetuba-Miri
Alter do Chão
Santarém
Pacoval
Belterra
Xingu
Vitória
Altamira
Favânia
apajós
4
5
6

Map 3

Quevedo
Portoviejo
Jipijapa
Pedro Carbo
Manglaralto
Daule
Salinas
Santa Rosa
Guayaquil
Guaranda
Riobamba
Cajabamba
Guamote
Palmira
Alausí
Ingapirca
Azogues
Naranjal
Puerto Misahuallí
Curaray
Puyo
ECUADOR
Montalvo
Macas
Punta Arenas
Balao
Isla Puná
Cuenca
Indanza
Machala
Pasaje
Gualaquiza
Huaquillas
Arenillas
Saraguro
Tumbes
Catamayo
Loja
Bocapán
Celica
Zamora
Cañaveral
Máncora
Macará
Cariamanga
El Alto
La Tina
Atascadero
Ayabaca
Talara
Espíndola
Vilcabamba
Vichayal
Las Lomas
Frías
Sullana
Colán
Paita
Piura
Chulucanas
Canchaque
San Ignacio
Vice
Sechura
Desert of Sechura
Bayovar
Reventazón
Cascajal
Jaén
Pucará
Olmos
Motupe
Jayanca
Mórrope
Ferreñafe
Jeque
Chiclayo
Laguna
Pacasmayo
Puerto Chicama
Huamachuco
Huanchaco
Trujillo
El Carmelo
Chimbote
Pacific Ocean
Casma
Culebras
Huarmey
Patívilca
Barranca
Supe
Huacho
Chancay
Ancón
LIMA
Santa María del Mar
San Antonio
Asia
Cañete
Chincha Alta
Pisco
Paracas
Huacachina
Ica
Santiago
Santa Cruz
Lomitas
Changuillo
Monte Grande
Nazca Lines
Nazca
San Nicolás
San Juan
Lomas
Acarí
Jaquí
Yauca
Curaray
Copal Urco
Marsella
Nuevo Andoas
Andoas
Leoncia Prado
Intuto
Trompeteros
Pastaza
Morona
PERU
Concordia
Miraflores
Marañon
Parinari
Yanayacu
Requena
Cenepa
Borja
Saramerıza
Puerto Delfus
Barranca
Puerto Amelia
Bretaña
Lagunas
Santa Cruz
Iberia
Nazareth
Aramango
Jeberos
Santa Isabel
Bellavista
Florida
Moyobamba
Balsapuerto
Yurimaguas
Santa Elena
Lisboa
Pedro Ruiz
Rioja
Papa Playa
Chachapoyas
Molinopampa
Tabalosas
2 de Mayo
San Andrés
Lamas
Humibayoc
Cutervo
Tingo
Mendoza
Tarapoto
Santa Catallina
Palmira
Chota
Sisa
Buenos Aires
Orellana
Leymebamba
Saposoa
Shamboyacu
Santa Cruz
Celendín
Balsas
Huallabamba
Juanjuí
Pampas de Sacramento
Contamaná
Cajamarca
Biabo
Chepén
San Marcos
Campanilla
Chilete
Cajabamba
Ascope
Huamachuco
Chugay
Parcoy
Otusco
Tocache Nuevo
Pucallpa
Mollepata
Uchiza
Tayabamba
Masisea
Huandoval
Sihuas
San Alejandro
Ganzo Azúl
Santo
Chuquicara
Huacrachuco
Aguaytía
Aucayacu
Pachitea
Huallanca
Yanama
Llamellín
Caraz
Yungay
Carhuaz
Cordillera Blanca
Huari
Monzón
Tingo María
Las Palmas
Huaraz
Chavín de Huantar
Chaglia
Yaután
Catac
La Unión
Pozuzo
Puerto Bermúdez
Huayán
Yarumayo
Huánuco
Ambo
Palcazú
Marca
Chiquián
Cajatambo
Yanahuanca
Cerro de Pasco
Oxapampa
Villa Rica
Cochos
Oyón
Churín
Paucartambo
Puerto Prado
Ulcumayo
La Merced
Sayán
Junín
San Ramón
Satipo
Canta
La Oroya
Tarma
Mazamari
Mariposa
Chacapalpa
Matucana
Jauja
Concepción
Huancayo
Langa
Tomás
Pampas
Huampará
Yauyos
Vilca
Mayocc
Huancavelica
Huanta
Aurahua
Lircay
Pacarán
Ayacucho
Santa Inés
Chiara
Vilcanchos
Huancano
Laramarca
Grande
Laramate
Lucanas
A
B
C
1
2
3
N
100 km
100 miles

COLOMBIA
Puerto Arturo
Flor de Agosta
Putumayo
Pucaurco
Vidal
1
PNN Amacayacu
Francisco de Orellana
Pebas
Napo
Amazonas
Indiana
Iquitos
Puerto Nariño
Caballococha
Leticia
Tabatinga
Desengaño
Bosmediano
Benjamin Constant
Nauta
Yavari
Bagazán
A
BRAZIL
Lábrea
Japim
Cruzeiro do Sul
Feijó
Abujao
4
Boca de Acre
B
Abunã
Esperanza
Rio Branco
Taquaras
Curanja
Xapuri
Guajará-Mirim
Guayaramerín
Assis Brasil
Brasiléia
Riberalta
Puerto Varadero
Iñapari
Puerto Rico
Atalaya
Ucayali
Cobija
Tambo
Sepahua
Iberia
Conquista
Las Piedras
El Chorro
Manu
Manu Biosphere Reserve
Camisea
Boca Manu
Puerto Rico
Madre de Dios
Planchón
Chivé
Yavero
Itahuania
Laberinto
Puerto Heath
Puerto Pardo
BOLIVIA
Pichari
Inambari
Puerto Maldonado
Shintuya
Inambiri
Ayna
Echarate
Quillabamba
Ocobamba
Pilcopata
Mazuko
RN Tambopata
Chaullay
PN Bahuaja-Sonene
Machu Picchu
Urubamba
Quincemil
Ollantaytambo
Paucartambo
Astillero
C
Yucay
Pisac
Lanlacuni Bajo
Abancay
Limatambo
Cuzco
Ixiamas
JA Palacios
Santa Ana de Yacuma
Andahuaylas
Tambobamba
Ayapata
Cusipata
Limbani
Santa Rosa
Querobamba
Raqchi
Sandia
Puerto Salinas
6
Sicuani
Crucero
Reyes
Apurimac
Progreso
Santa Rosa
Ananea
Queara
Rurrenabaque
Challa
Yauri
Azángaro
Apolo
San Borja
Trinidad
PERU
Aten
Yucumo
Puquio
Ayaviri
Putina
San Ignacio de Moxos
Cotahuasi
Cailloma
Condoroma
Mapiri
Coracora
Moho
Consata
Pullo
Orcopampa
Guanay
Escoma
Calhua
Juliaca
Lake Titicaca
Carabuco
Chivay
Alcoche
Caranavi
Colca Canyon
Sorata
Chaparra
4
Imata
5
Puno
Chuquibamba
Ilave
Achachi
6
Iquipi
Lluta
Pati
Juli
Huarina
Corire

Map 4

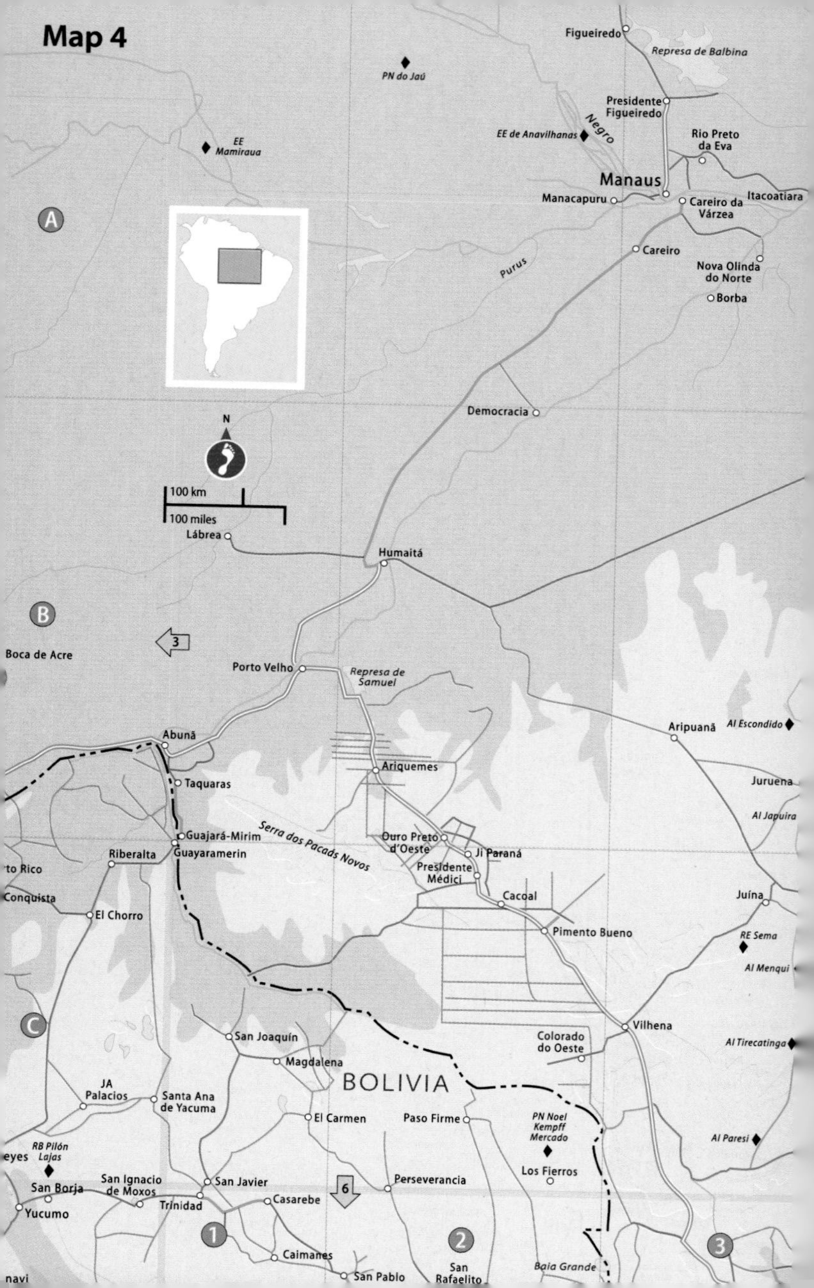

Figueiredo
Represa de Balbina
PN do Jaú
Presidente Figueiredo
Negro
EE de Anavilhanas
Rio Preto da Eva
EE Mamiraua
Manaus
Manacapuru
Careiro da Várzea
Itacoatiara
A
Careiro
Purus
Nova Olinda do Norte
Borba
Democracia
N
100 km
100 miles
Lábrea
Humaitá
B
3
Boca de Acre
Porto Velho
Represa de Samuel
Abunã
Aripuanã
Al Escondido
Ariquemes
Taquaras
Juruena
Al Japuira
Serra dos Pacaás Novos
Guajará-Mirim
Ouro Preto d'Oeste
Ji Paraná
Guayaramerin
Riberalta
rto Rico
Presidente Médici
Conquista
Cacoal
Juína
El Chorro
Pimento Bueno
RE Sema
Al Menqui
C
Vilhena
Colorado do Oeste
Al Tirecatinga
San Joaquín
Magdalena
BOLIVIA
JA Palacios
Santa Ana de Yacuma
El Carmen
Paso Firme
PN Noel Kempff Mercado
Al Paresi
RB Pilón Lajas
eyes
San Ignacio de Moxos
San Javier
Los Fierros
San Borja
Perseverancia
6
Trinidad
Casarebe
Yucumo
1
2
3
Caimanes
San Rafaelito
Baia Grande
San Pablo
navi

Monte Dorado
RB do Rio Trombetas
Ilha Grande de Gurupá
Ilha de Marajó
EE do Marajó
Almeirim
Amazonas
Prainha
Óbidos
Monte Alegre
Alter do-Chão
Santarém
Belterra
Pacoval
Canaçari
Tapajós
2
Vitória
Altamira
Favânia
A
Caima
Itaituba
Rurópolis Presidente Médici
5
Goiar
Represa de Tucuru
RI Paracanã
Jamanxim
Mara
Curuá
Tucumá
Xinguara
Araguaia
Juruena
B
BRAZIL
Conceição do Araguaia
Bandeirantes
São Manuel
Parnaita
Alta Floresta
Guarantã do Norte
Mi
Peixoto de Azevedo
AI Capoto
PN do Araguaia
AI Jarina
AI Apaica
Santa Teresinha
AI Rikbaktsa
Juará
Ilha do Bananal
Fatima
Catua
São Félix do Araguaia
Sinop
Parque Indígena do Xingu
Gurupi
PI do Araguaia
AI Irantxé
Alvorada
C
Araguaçu
São Miguel do Araguaia
Puiva
AI Batovi
Novo Crixás
Mundo Novo
Sacuriuiná
Arenópolis
AI Bakairi
RI Parabubure
RI Areões
Niquela
Crixás
7
Mozorlândia
Mozorlândia
PN da Chapada dos Guimarães
Planalto do Mato Grosso
RI São Marcos
6
4
Jangada
5
Colonel Ponce
Várzea Grande
Cuiabá
Primavera
Dois Irmãos
São Vicente
Alto
Barra do
Jaragúa

Map 5

I Queimada
Ilha Grande de Gurupá
I Mututi
Ilha do Marajó
EE do Marajó
Soure
Baía de Marajó
Curuça
Salinópolis
Ponta de Pedras
Belém
Castanhal
Bragança
Capanema
Viseu
Carutapera
Abaetetuba
I Sirituba
Oeiras do Para
Acará
Abaetetuba-Miri
Concórdia do Pará
Irituia
Turiaçu
Cururupu
Xingu
Vitória
Favânia
A
Tomé-Açu
Gurupí
Sta Helena
Alcântara
São Luís
Humberto do Campos
Baía de São Marcos
Baía de São José
Icatu
PN do Lençóis Maranhenses
Paragominas
Goianésia
AI Rio Pindaré
Pindaré
Urbano Santos
Represa de Tucuruí
Santa Luzía
Miranda do Norte
Chapadinha
RI Paracand
Bacabal
Timbiras
Açailândia
Arame
Pedreiras
Peritoró
Marabá
Imperatriz
Presidente Dutra
Caxias
Barro do Corda
4
Araguaia
Sa das Alpercatas
Colinas
Tucuma
Estreito
Pastos Bons
Xinguara
B
Araguaína
Carolina
Riachão
Represal de Boa Esperança
Floriano
Balsas
Uruçuí
Conceição do Araguaia
Bertolínia
Itaueira
AI Kraós
Flores do Piauí
Guaraí
Elisau Martins
Canto do Buriti
BRAZIL
Miranorte
RI Xerentes
Cristino Castro
PN Serra da Capivara
Miracema do Tocantins
São Raimundo Nonato
PN do Araguaia
Santa Teresinha
Gilbués
Palmas
Porto Nacional
Fatimá
Ilha do Bananal
São Félix do Araguaia
Barragem de Sobradinho
Santa Rita de Cássia
Ibiraba
Gurupi
Dianópolis
Barra
Xique-Xique
Espigão Mestre
Peixe
Boqueirão
PI do Araguaia
Conceição do Tocantins
Mimosa d'Oeste
C
Capixaba
Alvorada
Taipas
Paranã
Taguatinga
Barreiras
Pirajaba
Ibotirama
Araguaçu
Arriais
Brotas
Roda Velha
São Miguel do Araguaia
Campos Belos
Brejolândia
Mundo Novo
São Francisco
Santana
Teresina de Goiás
Nova Roma
São Domingos
Correntina
Bom Jesus da Lapa
PN Chapada dos Veadeiros
Santa Maria da Vitória
Crixás
1
Niquelândia
Posse
2
Coribe
3
Mozorlândia
7
Mambai
Dois
Caetité

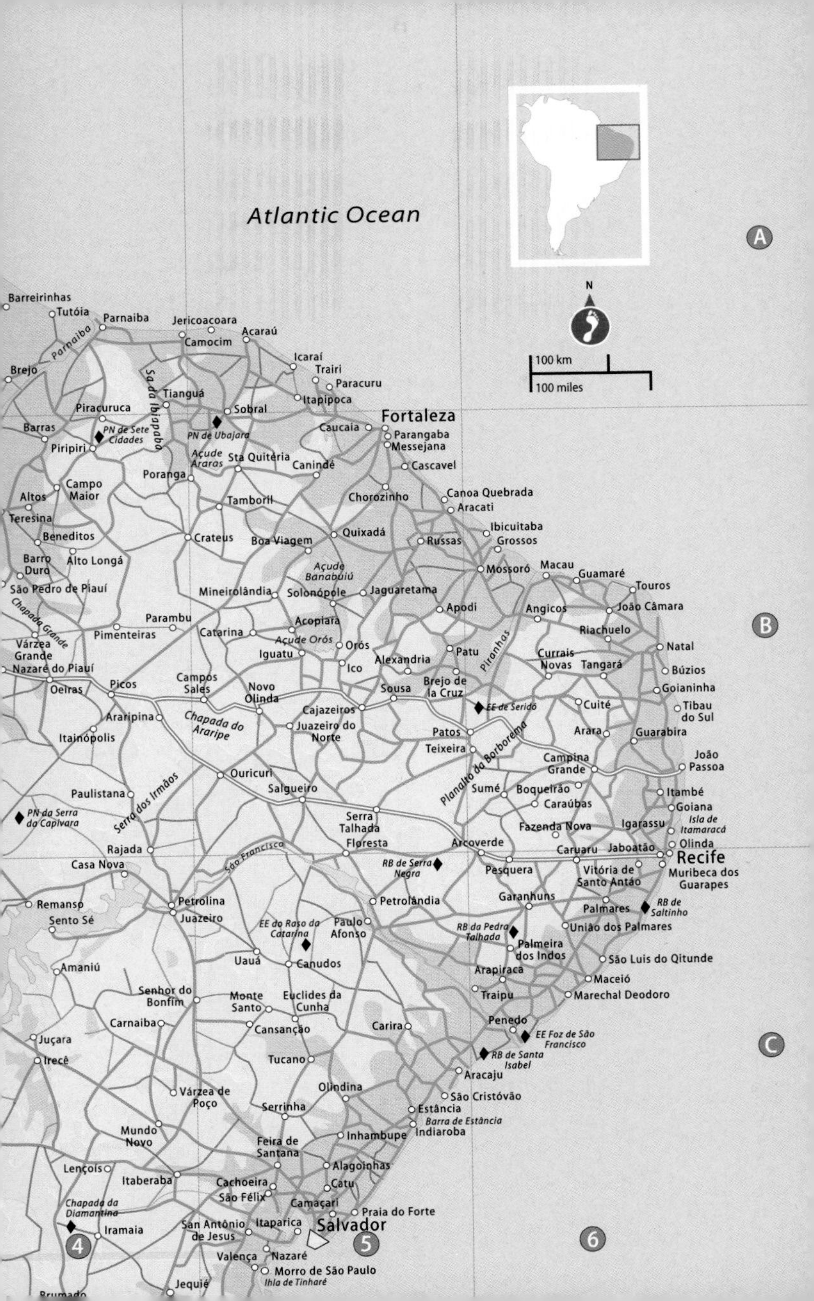
Atlantic Ocean
A
B
C
N
100 km
100 miles
Barreirinhas
Tutóia
Parnaiba
Parnaiba
Jericoacoara
Acaraú
Camocim
Icaraí
Trairi
Paracuru
Itapipoca
Brejo
Sa da Ibiapaba
Tianguá
Sobral
Piracuruca
PN de Ubajara
Fortaleza
Caucaia
Parangaba
Messejana
Barras
PN de Sete Cidades
Piripiri
Açude Araras
Sta Quitéria
Canindé
Cascavel
Poranga
Campo Maior
Altos
Tamboril
Chorozinho
Canoa Quebrada
Aracati
Teresina
Ibicuitaba
Grossos
Beneditos
Crateus
Boa Viagem
Quixadá
Russas
Barro Duro
Alto Longá
Açude Banabuiú
Mossoró
Macau
Guamaré
Touros
São Pedro de Piauí
Mineirolândia
Solonópole
Jaguaretama
Apodi
Angicos
João Câmara
Chapada Grande
Parambu
Acopiara
Riachuelo
Várzea Grande
Pimenteiras
Catarina
Açude Orós
Orós
Patu
Natal
Iguatu
Alexandria
Piranhas
Currais Novas
Tangará
Nazaré do Piauí
Ico
Búzios
Oeiras
Picos
Campos Sales
Novo Olinda
Sousa
Brejo de la Cruz
Goianinha
Cuité
Tibau do Sul
Araripina
Chapada do Araripe
Cajazeiros
EE de Seridó
Juazeiro do Norte
Patos
Arara
Guarabira
Itainópolis
Teixeira
Planalto da Borborema
Campina Grande
João Passoa
Ouricuri
Serra dos Irmãos
Salgueiro
Sumé
Boqueirão
Itambé
Paulistana
Caraúbas
Goiana
PN da Serra da Capivara
Serra Talhada
Fazenda Nova
Igarassu
Isla de Itamaracá
Floresta
Olinda
Rajada
Arcoverde
Caruaru
Jaboatão
Recife
São Francisco
Casa Nova
RB de Serra Negra
Pesquera
Vitória de Santo Antão
Muribeca dos Guarapes
Petrolina
Petrolândia
Garanhuns
Remanso
RB de Saltinho
Palmares
Juazeiro
Sento Sé
EE do Raso da Catarina
Paulo Afonso
RB da Pedra Talhada
União dos Palmares
Palmeira dos Indos
Uauá
Canudos
São Luis do Qitunde
Amaniú
Arapiraca
Maceió
Senhor do Bonfim
Monte Santo
Euclides da Cunha
Traipu
Marechal Deodoro
Carnaiba
Cansanção
Carira
Penedo
Juçara
EE Foz de São Francisco
Irecê
Tucano
RB de Santa Isabel
Aracaju
Várzea de Poço
Olindina
São Cristóvão
Serrinha
Estância
Barra de Estância
Mundo Novo
Indiaroba
Inhambupe
Feira de Santana
Lençóis
Alagoinhas
Itaberaba
Cachoeira
Catu
São Félix
Camaçari
Chapada da Diamantina
Praia do Forte
San Antônio de Jesus
Itaparica
Salvador
Iramaia
4
5
6
Valença
Nazaré
Morro de São Paulo
Ihla de Tinharé
Jequié
Brumado

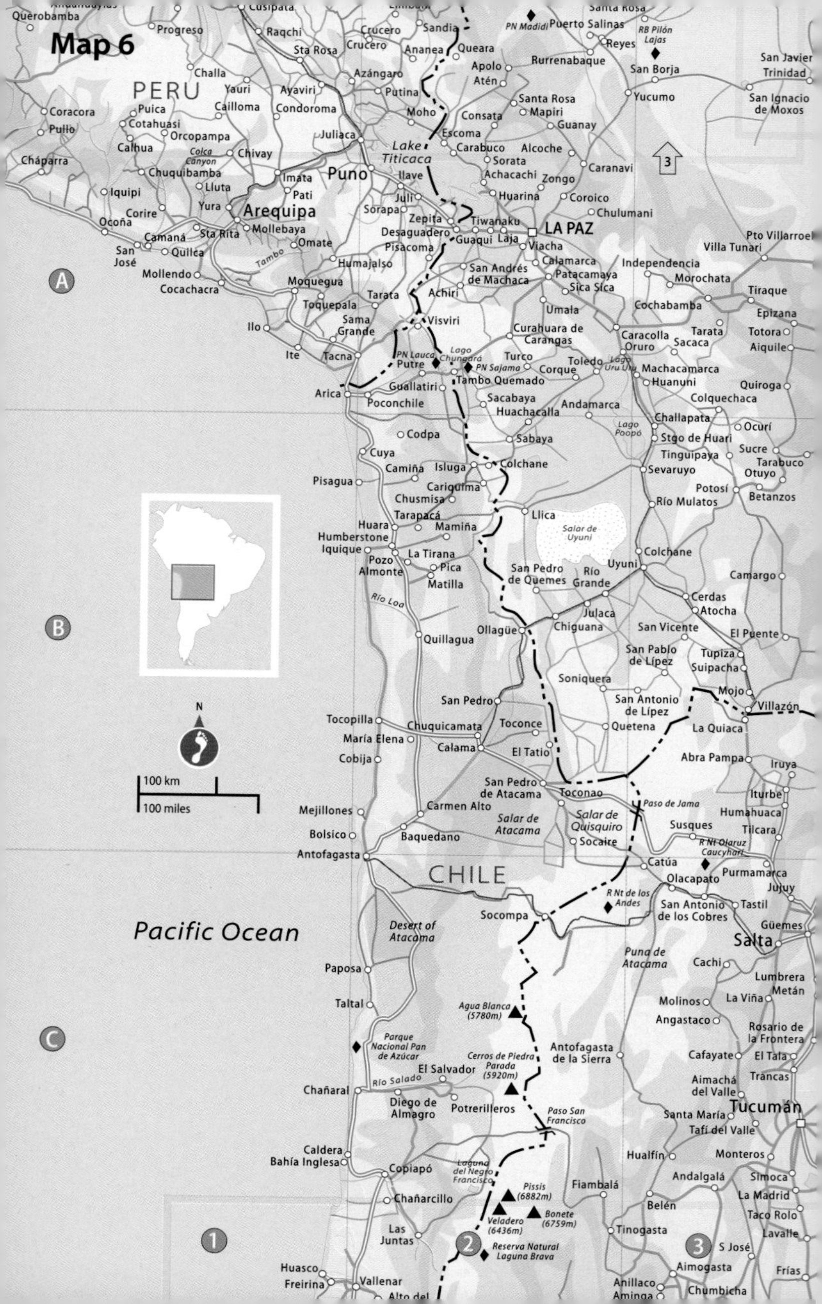
Map 6
PERU
CHILE
Pacific Ocean
LA PAZ
Arequipa
Puno
Lake Titicaca
Querobamba
Progreso
Cusipata
Raqchi
Sta Rosa
Crucero
Sandia
Ananea
Queara
PN Madidi
Puerto Salinas
Reyes
RB Pilón Lajas
Rurrenabaque
San Borja
San Javier
Trinidad
San Ignacio de Moxos
Yucumo
Challa
Yauri
Ayaviri
Azángaro
Putina
Apolo
Atén
Santa Rosa
Mapiri
Guanay
Consata
Moho
Escoma
Carabuco
Alcoche
Sorata
Caranavi
Achacachi
Zongo
Huarina
Coroico
Chulumani
Coracora
Pullo
Puica
Cotahuasi
Cailloma
Condoroma
Orcopampa
Calhua
Colca Canyon
Chivay
Juliaca
Cháparra
Chuquibamba
Imata
Ilave
Iquipi
Lluta
Pati
Juli
Yura
Corire
Sorapa
Zepita
Tiwanaku
Ocoña
Camaná
Sta Rita
Mollebaya
Desaguadero
Guaqui
Laja
Viacha
San José
Quilca
Omate
Pisacoma
Tambo
Humajalso
Mollendo
Cocachacra
Moquegua
Toquepala
Tarata
Achiri
San Andrés de Machaca
Calamarca
Patacamaya
Sica Sica
Independencia
Morochata
Villa Tunari
Pto Villarroel
Tiraque
Cochabamba
Epizana
Totora
Aiquile
Umala
Curahuara de Carangas
Caracolla
Oruro
Tarata
Sacaca
Ilo
Ite
Tacna
Sama Grande
Visviri
PN Lauca
Putre
Lago Chungará
PN Sajama
Turco
Toledo
Lago Uru Uru
Machacamarca
Huanuni
Quiroga
Corque
Tambo Quemado
Arica
Guallatiri
Poconchile
Sacabaya
Huachacalla
Andamarca
Colquechaca
Lago Poopó
Challapata
Ocurí
Stgo de Huari
Sucre
Tinguipaya
Tarabuco
Otuyo
Codpa
Sabaya
Cuya
Camiña
Isluga
Colchane
Sevaruyo
Pisagua
Cariquima
Chusmisa
Potosí
Betanzos
Río Mulatos
Tarapacá
Llica
Salar de Uyuni
Huara
Mamiña
Humberstone
Iquique
La Tirana
Pozo Almonte
Pica
Matilla
Colchane
Uyuni
San Pedro de Quemes
Río Grande
Camargo
Río Loa
Cerdas
Atocha
Julaca
Chiguana
San Vicente
Ollagüe
Quillagua
El Puente
San Pablo de Lípez
Tupiza
Suipacha
Soniquera
Mojo
San Antonio de Lípez
Villazón
San Pedro
Tocopilla
Chuquicamata
Toconce
Quetena
La Quiaca
María Elena
Calama
El Tatio
Cobija
Abra Pampa
Iruya
N
100 km
100 miles
San Pedro de Atacama
Toconao
Paso de Jama
Iturbe
Mejillones
Carmen Alto
Salar de Atacama
Salar de Quisquiro
Humahuaca
Bolsico
Baquedano
Susques
Tilcara
Socaire
R Nt Olaruz Caucyhari
Antofagasta
Catúa
Purmamarca
Olacapato
Jujuy
R Nt de los Andes
San Antonio de los Cobres
Tastil
Socompa
Güemes
Desert of Atacama
Salta
Puna de Atacama
Paposa
Cachi
Lumbrera
Metán
Molinos
La Viña
Taltal
Agua Blanca (5780m)
Angastaco
Rosario de la Frontera
Parque Nacional Pan de Azúcar
Antofagasta de la Sierra
Cafayate
El Tala
Cerros de Piedra Parada (5920m)
El Salvador
Aimachá del Valle
Trancas
Chañaral
Río Salado
Tucumán
Diego de Almagro
Potrerilleros
Paso San Francisco
Santa María
Tafí del Valle
Caldera
Bahía Inglesa
Hualfín
Monteros
Copiapó
Laguna del Negro Francisco
Andalgalá
Simoca
Pissis (6882m)
Fiambalá
La Madrid
Chañarcillo
Belén
Veladero (6436m)
Bonete (6759m)
Taco Rolo
Las Juntas
Tinogasta
Lavalle
Reserva Natural Laguna Brava
S José
Huasco
Aimogasta
Freirina
Vallenar
Frías
Anillaco
Aminga
Chumbicha
Alto del
A
B
C
1
2
3

BRAZIL
BOLIVIA
PARAGUAY
ARGENTINA
PN Noel Kempff Mercado
Sacuriuiná
Arenópolis
Al Umutuni
Perseverancia
Casarebe
Jangada
Várzea Grande
Cuiabá
4
Baia Grande
Caimanes
San Pablo
San Rafaelito
Carmen del Ruiz
EE Sa de Araras
São Vicente
Concepción
Santa Rosa de la Roca
Espíritu
Cáceres
Barao de Melgaço
San Ignacio de Velasco
Santa Ana de Velasco
San Vicente
San Matías
Poconé
Al Gomes Carneiro
San Ramón
San Miguel
San Rafael
A
L Orión (Providential)
Gral Saavedra
Montero
Porto Jofre
PN Amboró
Santa Cruz de la Sierra
Pozo del Tigre
L Uberaba
San José de Chiquitos
PN do Pantanal Matogrossense
L Gaiba
San Isidro
Mairana
Santo Corazón
7
Samaipata
Santiago de Chiquitos
B de Castelo
Roboré
Pantanal
Pantanal
Carmen Rivero
Matogrossense
Matogrossense
Abapó
PN Kaa-Iya
Puerto Suárez
Rio Verde
Corumbá
Quijarro
Padilla
Ipita
Lagunillas
Monteagudo
El Villar
Charagua
Mayor Pablo Lagerenza
PN Defensores del Chaco
Miranda
Camiri
Aquidauana
Bodoquedano
Bahía Negra
Boyuibe
Cuevo
Gral Eugenio A Garay
Villazón
FN Madrejón
Bonito
Nioaque
Machareti
PN Tte Agripino Enciso
B
Fuerte Olimpo
Porto Murtinho
Villamontes
Jardim
Tarija
Ibibobo
Fortín Infante Rivarola
Cabeceira do Apá
Itaum
Yacuiba
Vallemí
Bella Vista
Pocitos
Mariscal Estigarribia
Filadelfia
Loma Plata
PN Serranías San Luis
PN del Cerro Corá
Bermejo
Aguas Blancas
Neuland
Orán
Yby Yaú
Gral Ballivián
Río Verde
Horqueta
Pozo Colorado
Concepción
PN Calilegua
Pirahú
Puerto Antequera
Libertador
Pilcomayo
Ygatimi
Paraguay
San Pedro
Mbaracayú Forest Reserve
Rosario
Benjamin Aceval
San Estanislao
Tacuara
Curuguaty
Espinillo
Remanso
Mbutuy
ASUNCION
San Lorenzo
Coronel Oviedo
Clorinda
Ibarreta
Paraguarí
Colonia Independencia
Paraguay
Villarrica
Monte Quemedo
Ybicuí
Ybicuí NP
Caapucú
Villa Florida
Caazapá
La Fragua
Pampa de los Guanacos
Formosa
C
San Juan Bautista
Nva Esperanza
Eldorado
Va Escola
Santa Rosa
Jesús
Santos Lugares
Campo Gallo
Sachaya
Avia Terai
PN Chaco
Pilar
San Ignacio Guazú
Coronel Bogado
Tintina
Roque Sáenz Peña
Paso de Patria
Laureles
Encarnación
Pozo Hondo
Bandera Bajada
Resistencia
Ayolas
San Cosme y Damián
Posadas
Corrientes
Gramilla
Otumpa
Termas de Río Hondo
Quimilí
Esteros de Iberá
Santiago del Estero
Sta Sylvana
Empedrado
8
Azara
San Miguel
Tobas
Garruchos
São Luís Gonzaga
Carlos Pellegrini
Villa San Martín
4
Tres Pozos
5
Saladas
6
Añatuya
Los Juríes
Las Toscas
Bella Vista
Santo Tomé
São Borja
San Vicente
Bandera
Pozo Borrada

Map 7
Al Umutuni
Colonel Ponce
Planalto do Mato Grosso
RI São Marcos
4
Mozorlândia
Dois Irmãos
PN de Brasília
Cuiabá
Várzea Grande
São Vicente
Primavera
Alto Coité
EE Sa de Araras
Barra do Garças
Goiás Velho
Jaraguá
Brazlândia
Pirenópolis
BRASÍLIA
Taguatinga
Gama
Barão de Melgaço
Guiratinga
Poconé
Al Gomes Carneiro
Rondonópolis
Diamantino
Iporá
Anápolis
6
Alto Garças
Goiânia
Porto Jofre
A
Sonoro
Itiquira
Sa das Divisões
Paraúna
Indiara
Edéia
Mineiros
Jataí
Pontalina
Caldas Novas
Placa dos Mineiros
PN das Emas
Rio Verde
São Domingos
Coxim
Serranópolis
Aparecida do Rio Doce
Corumbaíba
Pantanal Matogrossense
Itumbiara
Barr Itumbiara
Catalão
Rio Verde de Mato Grosso
Caçu
Barragem de S Simão
Rep de Emborcação
Paraiso
Aporé
Ituiutaba
Raimundo
Uberlândia
Camapuã
Capim Verde
Paranaiba
BRAZIL
Miranda
Grande
Barragem Agua Vermelha
odoquedano
Aquidauana
Campo Grande
Aparecida do Taboado
Uberuba
Jales
Fernandópolis
Água Clara
Votuporanga
Bonito
Nioaque
Serra de Maracajú
Três Lagoas
Castilho
Major Prado
Nhandeara
Barretos
Franca
Jardim
Tietê
S José do Rio Preto
B
Maracajú
Novo Alvorada
Sta Rita do Pardo
Panorama
Araçatuba
Ribeirão Preto
Cabeceira do Apá
Casa Verde
Bataguassu
Penápolis
Represa Promissão
Cajuru
Itaum
Dourados
Lins
Matão
Bella Vista
PN del Cerro Corá
Ivinhema
Presidente Prudente
Tupã
Iacanga
Araraquara
Ponta Porã
Pedro Juan Caballero
Caarapã
Marília
Gália
Bauru
San Carlos
rbay Yaú
Paranapanema
Sto Ignacio
Jaú
Ubirajara
Rio Claro
rqueta
Amambai
Paraná
Bela Vista do Paraíso
Rep Capivari
Limeira
Ourinhos
Piracicaba
Puerto ntequera
Londrina
Botucatí
Americana
Campinas
Maringá
Avaré
Ygatimi
Eldorado
Umuarema
Santo Antônio da Platina
Pirajú
Res Armando
San Pedro
Mbaracayú Forest Reserve
Salto del Guaíra
Campo Mourão
Represa de Xavantes
Itapetininga
Rosario
Guaíra
Palotina
Termas de Jurema
Alecrim
Itapeva
Capão Bonito
Sorocaba
San tanislao
Tacuara
Curuguaty
Campina
Iretama
Serra Geral
Jaguariaíva
Represa de Itaipu
Toledo
Pedro Barras
Mbutuy
Cascavel
Pitanga
Piraí do Sul
Registro
Peruíbe
Iguape
Colonia Independencia
Medianeira
Catanduvas
Tunas
uarí
Cananéia
Foz do Iguaçu
Ciudad del Este
Laranjeiras do Sol
Guarabuava
Ponta Grossa
Iguaçu
Vila Velha
llarrica
Irati
PN Marumbi
Guaraqueçaba
Ybicuí NP
Puerto Iguazú
Represa de Salto Santiago
Curitiba
PN de Superagüi
Morretes
Paranaguá
Villa Florida
Caazapá
Warida
Represa de Foz Arela
Pato Branco
Areia Branca
Eldorado
União de Vitória
Guaratuba
C
S Botodo do Sol
Santa Rosa
Obligado
San Pedro
Campo Eré
Horizonte
Papanduva
Joinville
Jesús
Hohenau
Bom Jesus
Jaragua do Sol
São Francisco do Sul
Trinidad
Bella Vista
San Ignacio
Santa Cecilia
Moconá
Chapecó
San Cosme y Damián
Encarnación
Oberá
Blumenau
Posadas
El Soberbio
Curitibanos
San Javier
Exerim
Tupitanga
Rio do Sul
Camboriú
Barragem Passo Fundo
Azara
Porto Xavier
Florianópolis
Ilha de Santa Catarina
Garruchos
8
Passo Fundo
Lages
São Luís Gonzaga
Santo Ângelo
La Vermelha
Sta Rosa de Lima
to Tomé
Cruz Alta
PN São Joaquim
São Joaquim
São Lourenço das Missões
São Miguel das Missões
Vacaria
Tubarão
Laguna
Encruzilhada
1
Soledade
2
3
Mariana Pinto
Caxias do Sul
apeyú
Manuel Viana
Santa Maria
Candelaria

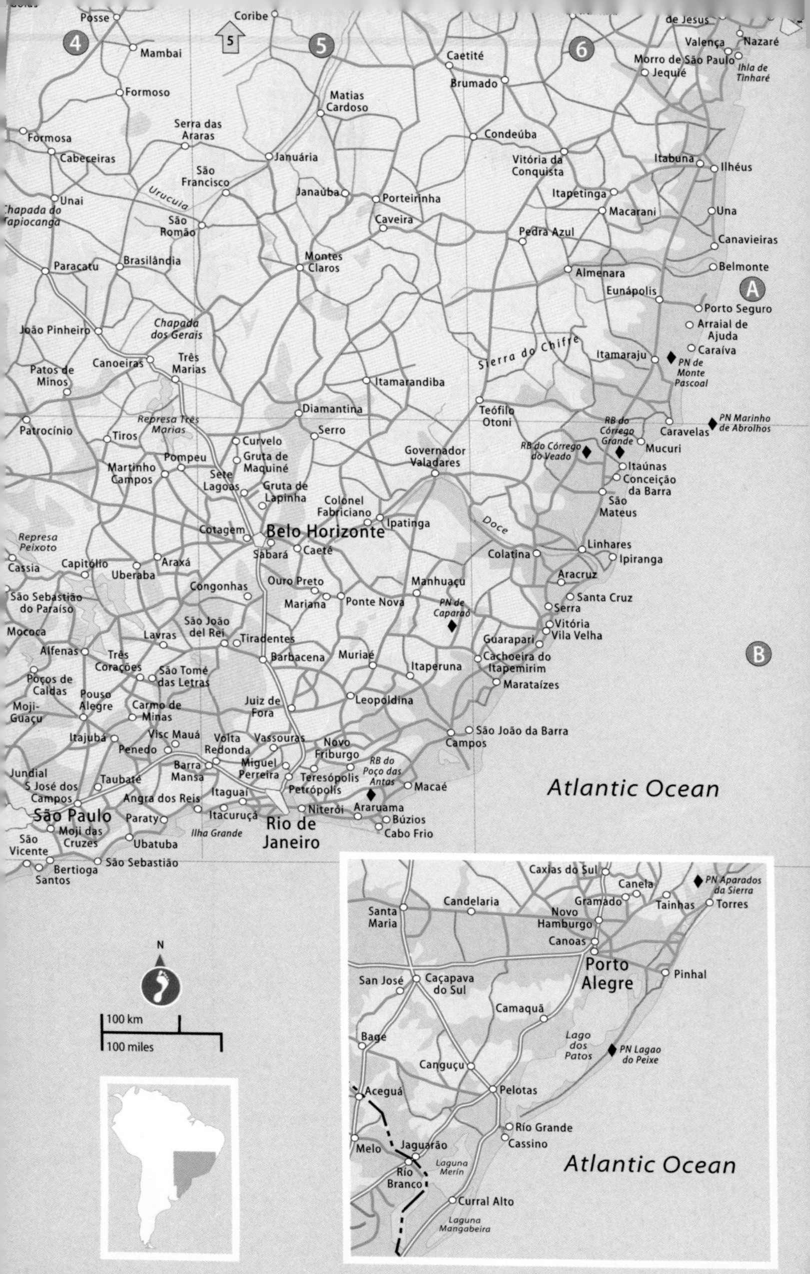
Posse
Coribe
5
de Jesus
4
5
6
Mambai
Valença
Nazaré
Morro de São Paulo
Caetité
Jequié
Ihla de Tinharé
Brumado
Formoso
Matias Cardoso
Serra das Araras
Condeúba
Formosa
Cabeceiras
Januária
Vitória da Conquista
Itabuna
Ilhéus
São Francisco
Urucuia
Janaúba
Porteirinha
Itapetinga
Unai
Macarani
Una
Chapada do Tapiocanga
São Romão
Caveira
Pedra Azul
Canavieiras
Montes Claros
Paracatu
Brasilândia
Almenara
Belmonte
A
Eunápolis
Porto Seguro
João Pinheiro
Chapada dos Gerais
Arraial de Ajuda
Caraíva
Sierra do Chifre
Itamaraju
PN de Monte Pascoal
Canoeiras
Três Marias
Patos de Minos
Itamarandiba
Diamantina
Teófilo Otoni
Represa Três Marias
RB do Córrego Grande
PN Marinho de Abrolhos
Patrocínio
Caravelas
Tiros
Serro
RB do Córrego do Veado
Mucuri
Curvelo
Governador Valadares
Pompeu
Gruta de Maquiné
Martinho Campos
Itaúnas
Sete Lagoas
Conceição da Barra
Gruta de Lapinha
São Mateus
Colonel Fabriciano
Ipatinga
Doce
Represa Peixoto
Cotagem
Belo Horizonte
Linhares
Cassia
Capitólio
Araxá
Sabará
Caeté
Colatina
Ipiranga
Uberaba
Aracruz
Congonhas
Ouro Preto
Manhuaçu
São Sebastião do Paraíso
Santa Cruz
Mariana
Ponte Nova
PN de Caparaó
Serra
São João del Rei
Vitória
Mococa
Vila Velha
Lavras
Tiradentes
Guarapari
Alfenas
Três Corações
Muriaé
Barbacena
Cachoeira do Itapemirim
Itaperuna
B
São Tomé das Letras
Poços de Caldas
Marataízes
Pouso Alegre
Leopoldina
Juiz de Fora
Moji-Guaçu
Carmo de Minas
São João da Barra
Campos
Itajubá
Visc Mauá
Volta Redonda
Vassouras
Novo Friburgo
Penedo
RB do Poço das Antas
Barra Mansa
Miguel Perreira
Jundial
Teresópolis
Macaé
Taubaté
S José dos Campos
Petrópolis
Atlantic Ocean
Itaguaí
Angra dos Reis
Araruama
São Paulo
Itacuruçá
Niterói
Búzios
Paraty
Rio de Janeiro
Moji das Cruzes
Ilha Grande
Cabo Frio
São Vicente
Ubatuba
Bertioga
São Sebastião
Santos
N
100 km
100 miles
Caxias do Sul
Canela
PN Aparados da Sierra
Gramado
Santa Maria
Candelaria
Novo Hamburgo
Tainhas
Torres
Canoas
Porto Alegre
San José
Caçapava do Sul
Pinhal
Camaquã
Lago dos Patos
Bagé
PN Lagao do Peixe
Canguçu
Aceguá
Pelotas
Río Grande
Cassino
Melo
Jaguarão
Río Branco
Laguna Merín
Atlantic Ocean
Curral Alto
Laguna Mangabeira

Map 8

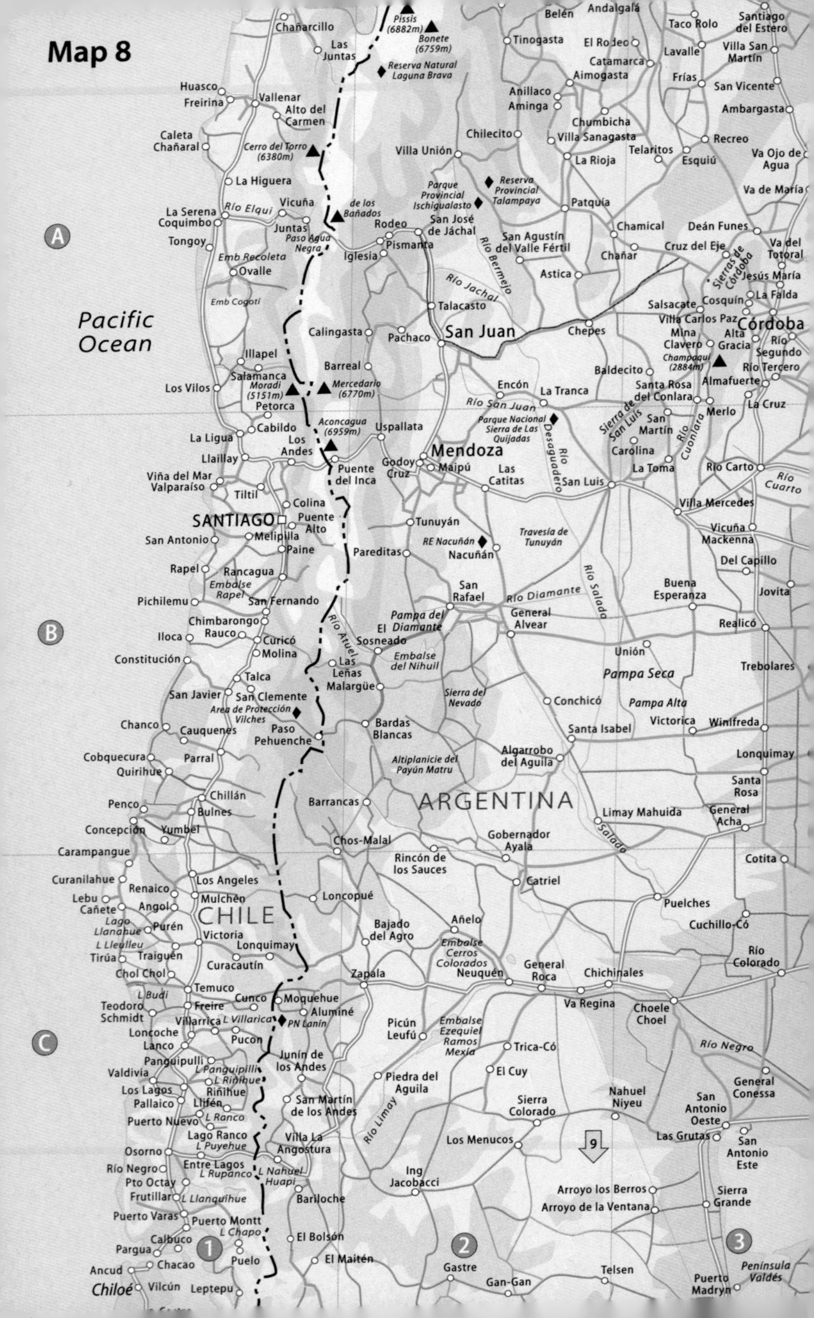

Pissis (6882m)
Bonete (6759m)
Belén
Andalgalá
Taco Rolo
Santiago del Estero
Chañarcillo
Las Juntas
Tinogasta
El Rodeo
Lavalle
Villa San Martín
Reserva Natural Laguna Brava
Catamarca
Aimogasta
Frías
San Vicente
Huasco
Freirina
Vallenar
Alto del Carmen
Anillaco
Aminga
Ambargasta
Chumbicha
Caleta Chañaral
Cerro del Torro (6380m)
Chilecito
Villa Sanagasta
Recreo
Villa Unión
Telaritos
Esquiú
Va Ojo de Agua
La Rioja
La Higuera
Reserva Provincial Talampaya
Parque Provincial Ischigualasto
Va de María
Patquía
La Serena
Coquimbo
Río Elqui
Vicuña
de los Bañados
Juntas
Rodeo
San José de Jáchal
Chamical
Deán Funes
Tongoy
Paso Agua Negra
Pismanta
San Agustín del Valle Fértil
Cruz del Eje
Va del Totoral
Iglesia
Chañar
Emb Recoleta
Río Bermejo
Sierras de Córdoba
Ovalle
Astica
Jesús María
Río Jachal
La Falda
Emb Cogotí
Talacasto
Salsacate
Cosquín
Pacific Ocean
Villa Carlos Paz
Córdoba
Calingasta
Pachaco
San Juan
Chepes
Mina Clavero
Alta Gracia
Río Segundo
Illapel
Champaquí (2884m)
Barreal
Baldecito
Río Tercero
Salamanca
Moradi (5151m)
Mercedario (6770m)
Encón
Santa Rosa del Conlara
Almafuerte
Los Vilos
La Tranca
La Cruz
Petorca
Río San Juan
Sierra de San Luis
Merlo
Aconcagua (6959m)
Parque Nacional Sierra de Las Quijadas
San Martín
Río Cuonlara
Cabildo
Uspallata
La Ligua
Los Andes
Mendoza
Río Desaguadero
Carolina
Llaillay
Godoy Cruz
Puente del Inca
Maipú
La Toma
Río Carto
Viña del Mar
Las Catitas
Río Cuarto
Valparaíso
San Luis
Tiltil
Colina
Villa Mercedes
SANTIAGO
Puente Alto
Tunuyán
Vicuña Mackenna
San Antonio
Melipilla
Travesía de Tunuyán
Paine
RE Nacuñán
Nacuñán
Pareditas
Del Capillo
Rapel
Rancagua
Río Salado
Embalse Rapel
Buena Esperanza
Jovita
San Rafael
Río Diamante
Pichilemu
San Fernando
Pampa del Diamante
General Alvear
Chimbarongo
Realicó
Río Atuel
El Sosneado
Iloca
Rauco
Curicó
Unión
Molina
Embalse del Nihuil
Constitución
Las Leñas
Trebolares
Talca
Pampa Seca
Malargüe
San Javier
San Clemente
Sierra del Nevado
Conchicó
Pampa Alta
Área de Protección Vilches
Victorica
Winifreda
Chanco
Bardas Blancas
Cauquenes
Paso Pehuenche
Santa Isabel
Cobquecura
Parral
Algarrobo del Aguila
Lonquimay
Quirihue
Altiplanicie del Payún Matru
Santa Rosa
Chillán
ARGENTINA
Penco
Barrancas
Bulnes
Limay Mahuida
General Acha
Concepción
Yumbel
Salado
Chos-Malal
Gobernador Ayala
Carampangue
Rincón de los Sauces
Cotita
Curanilahue
Los Angeles
Renaico
Catriel
Lebu
Mulchén
Loncopué
Puelches
Cañete
Angol
CHILE
Lago Llanahue
Purén
Añelo
Cuchillo-Có
Victoria
Bajado del Agro
L Lleulleu
Lonquimay
Embalse Cerros Colorados
Río Colorado
Tirúa
Traiguén
Curacautín
Chol Chol
Zapala
Neuquén
General Roca
Chichinales
Temuco
L Budi
Cunco
Moquehue
Va Regina
Choele Choel
Teodoro Schmidt
Freire
Aluminé
Villarrica
L Villarica
PN Lanín
Picún Leufú
Embalse Ezequiel Ramos Mexia
Loncoche
Pucon
Río Negro
Lanco
Junín de los Andes
Trica-Có
Panguipulli
L Panguipilli
Valdivia
El Cuy
L Riñihue
Riñihue
Piedra del Aguila
General Conessa
Los Lagos
Pallaico
Llifén
San Martín de los Andes
Sierra Colorado
Nahuel Niyeu
San Antonio Oeste
L Ranco
Puerto Nuevo
Río Limay
Lago Ranco
Villa La Angostura
Los Menucos
9
Las Grutas
San Antonio Este
L Puyehue
Osorno
Entre Lagos
Río Negro
L Rupanco
L Nahuel Huapi
Ing Jacobacci
Pto Octay
Arroyo los Berros
Frutillar
L Llanquihue
Bariloche
Sierra Grande
Arroyo de la Ventana
Puerto Varas
Puerto Montt
L Chapo
Calbuco
El Bolsón
Pargua
1
2
3
Chacao
Puelo
El Maitén
Ancud
Gastre
Telsen
Península Valdés
Chiloé
Vilcún
Leptepu
Gan-Gan
Puerto Madryn
A
B
C

BRAZIL
URUGUAY
BUENOS AIRES
MONTEVIDEO
Rosario
Atlantic Ocean
Sta Sylvana
Empedrado
San Miguel
Esteros de Iberá
Azara
Porto Xavier
Tobas
Tres Pozos
Añatuya
Los Juríes
Las Toscas
Saladas
Garruchos
Santo Ângelo
Bella Vista
Carlos Pellegrini
Santo Tomé
São Luís Gonzaga
São Lourenço das Missões
Bandera
Pozo Borrada
São Borja
Encruzilhada
São Miguel das Missões
Cruz Alta
Tostado
Reconquista
Mercedes
Itaquí
Goya
Yapeyú
Mariana Pinto
Manuel Viana
Sol de Julio
Vera
Paso de los Libres
Curuzú
Uruguaiana
Santa Maria
Ceres
Barra do Quaraí
Alegrete
Monte Caseros
Río Quaraí
Rosario do Sul
Arufo
Río Dulce
Bella Unión
Artigas
Laguna Mar Chiquita
Suardi
San Javier
Santana do Livramento
San José
Caçapava do Sul
Miramar
La Paz
Termas del Arapey
Balnearia
Rafaela
Río Paraná
Rivera
El Tío
Concordia
Salto
Bagé
Santa Fe
Paraná
San Salvador
Termas de Daymán
Tacuarembó
Minas de Corrales
Canguçu
Vialle
Villaguay
PN El Palmar
Termas de Guaviyú
Tambores
Aceguá
Diamante
Parque Nacional Diamante
Colón
Paysandú
Curtina
Ansina
Villa María
Guichón
Las Toscas
Concepción del Uruguay
Paso de los Toros
Melo
Victoria
Rincón del Bonete (Lago Artificial)
Jaguarão
Bell Ville
San Lorenzo
Río Uruguay
Tres Bocas
Quebrada de los Cuervos
Río Branco
Laguna Merín
Gualeguaychú
Río Negro
Cerro Chato
Río Cuarto
Gualeguay
Fray Bentos
Mercedes
Carlos Reyes
Sarandí del Yí
Treinta y Tres
Villa Constitucíon
S Nicolás
Curral Alto
Soriano
Durazno
José R Varela
Río Paraná
Ibicuy
Dolores
Palmitas
Laguna Mangabeira
Sarandí Grande
Venado Tuerto
San Pedro
Reserva Natural Otamendi
Nueva Palmira
Cerro Colorado
Pirajá
Lascano
Chuí
Chuy
Cardona
Pergamino
Carmelo
Velásquez
Laboulaye
Zárate
Rosario
Florida
Aiguá
San Antonio de Areco
Minas
Castillo
Rufino
Junín
Colonia del Sacramento
Libertad
Sta Rosa
Mercedes
Solís
La Paloma
Atlántida
Piriápolis
Gral Villegás
Lincoln
Río de la Plata
San Carlos
Maldonado
Punta del Este
La Plata
Pampa Húmeda
Quiroga
Rivadavia
San Miguel del Monte
Saladillo
Chascomús
Trenque Lauquén
Las Flores
Manuel Cobó
Bahía
S Carlos de Bolívar
Tres Lomas
Dolores
San Clemente de Tuyú
Azul
Olavarria
Gral Madariaga
Guaminí
Ayacucho
Carhúe
Chillar
Pinamar
Las Armas
Ostende
Laprida
Tandil
Villa Gesell
Pique
Sa de Cura Malal
Sierras del Tandil
Parque Provincial Ernesto Tornquist
Reserva Provincial Laguna de los Padres
Tornquist
Mar del Plata
Tres Arroyos
Miramar
Necochea
Bahía Blanca
Coronel Dorrego
Claromecó
Isla Trinidad
Río Colorado
Pedro Luro
Villalonga
Cubanea
Carmen de Patagones
Viedma
Balneario El Cóndor
N
100 km
100 miles
6
7
A
B
C
4
5
6

Map 9

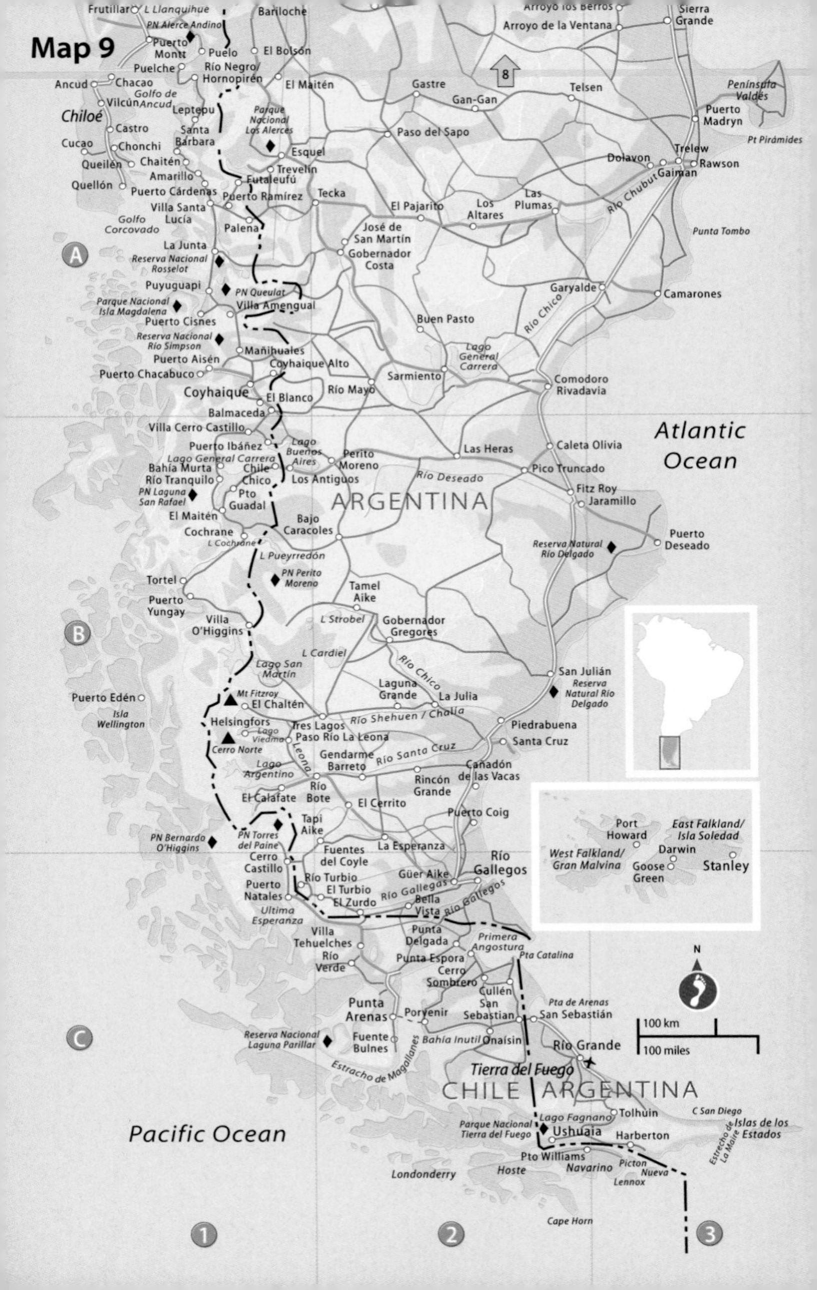

Frutillar
L Llanquihue
Bariloche
Arroyo los Berros
Sierra Grande
Arroyo de la Ventana
PN Alerce Andino
Puerto Montt
Puelo
El Bolsón
8
Puelche
Río Negro/ Hornopirén
Ancud
Chacao
Golfo de Ancud
El Maitén
Gastre
Telsen
Península Valdés
Vilcún
Chiloé
Leptepu
Parque Nacional Los Alerces
Gan-Gan
Puerto Madryn
Castro
Santa Bárbara
Paso del Sapo
Cucao
Chonchi
Esquel
Pt Pirámides
Queilén
Chaitén
Trevelín
Trelew
Dolavon
Rawson
Amarillo
Futaleufú
Gaiman
Quellón
Puerto Cárdenas
Puerto Ramírez
Tecka
Las Plumas
Río Chubut
Villa Santa Lucía
El Pajarito
Los Altares
Golfo Corcovado
Palena
José de San Martín
Punta Tombo
La Junta
Gobernador Costa
A
Reserva Nacional Rosselot
Garyalde
Puyuguapi
PN Queulat
Camarones
Parque Nacional Isla Magdalena
Villa Amengual
Río Chico
Puerto Cisnes
Buen Pasto
Reserva Nacional Río Simpson
Lago General Carrera
Puerto Aisén
Mañihuales
Puerto Chacabuco
Coyhaique Alto
Sarmiento
Comodoro Rivadavia
Coyhaique
Río Mayo
El Blanco
Balmaceda
Atlantic Ocean
Villa Cerro Castillo
Puerto Ibáñez
Lago Buenos Aires
Perito Moreno
Las Heras
Caleta Olivia
Lago General Carrera
Bahía Murta
Chile Chico
Río Deseado
Pico Truncado
Río Tranquilo
Los Antiguos
PN Laguna San Rafael
Pto Guadal
ARGENTINA
Fitz Roy
Jaramillo
El Maitén
Bajo Caracoles
Cochrane
Puerto Deseado
L Cochrane
Reserva Natural Río Delgado
L Pueyrredón
Tortel
PN Perito Moreno
Tamel Aike
Puerto Yungay
B
Villa O'Higgins
L Strobel
Gobernador Gregores
L Cardiel
Río Chico
Lago San Martín
San Julián
Reserva Natural Río Delgado
Mt Fitzroy
Laguna Grande
La Julia
Puerto Edén
El Chaltén
Isla Wellington
Helsingfors
Río Shehuen / Chalía
Lago Viedma
Tres Lagos
Piedrabuena
Paso Río La Leona
Santa Cruz
Cerro Norte
Leona
Gendarme Barreto
Río Santa Cruz
Lago Argentino
Cañadón de las Vacas
Rincón Grande
Río Bote
El Calafate
El Cerrito
Puerto Coig
Tapi Aike
PN Bernardo O'Higgins
PN Torres del Paine
Port Howard
East Falkland/ Isla Soledad
La Esperanza
Fuentes del Coyle
Río Gallegos
Darwin
West Falkland/ Gran Malvina
Goose Green
Stanley
Cerro Castillo
Río Turbio
Güer Aike
Puerto Natales
El Turbio
Río Gallegos
El Zurdo
Bella Vista
Río Gallegos
Ultima Esperanza
Villa Tehuelches
Punta Delgada
Primera Angostura
Pta Catalina
N
Río Verde
Punta Espora
Cerro Sombrero
Cullén
San Sebastian
Pta de Arenas
San Sebastián
Punta Arenas
Porvenir
100 km
100 miles
C
Reserva Nacional Laguna Parillar
Fuente Bulnes
Bahía Inutil
Onaísin
Río Grande
Estracho de Magallanes
Tierra del Fuego
CHILE
ARGENTINA
Tolhuin
C San Diego
Lago Fagnano
Parque Nacional Tierra del Fuego
Ushuaia
Islas de los Estados
Estrecho de La Maire
Pacific Ocean
Harberton
Pto Williams
Picton
Londonderry
Hoste
Navarino
Nueva
Lennox
Cape Horn
1
2
3

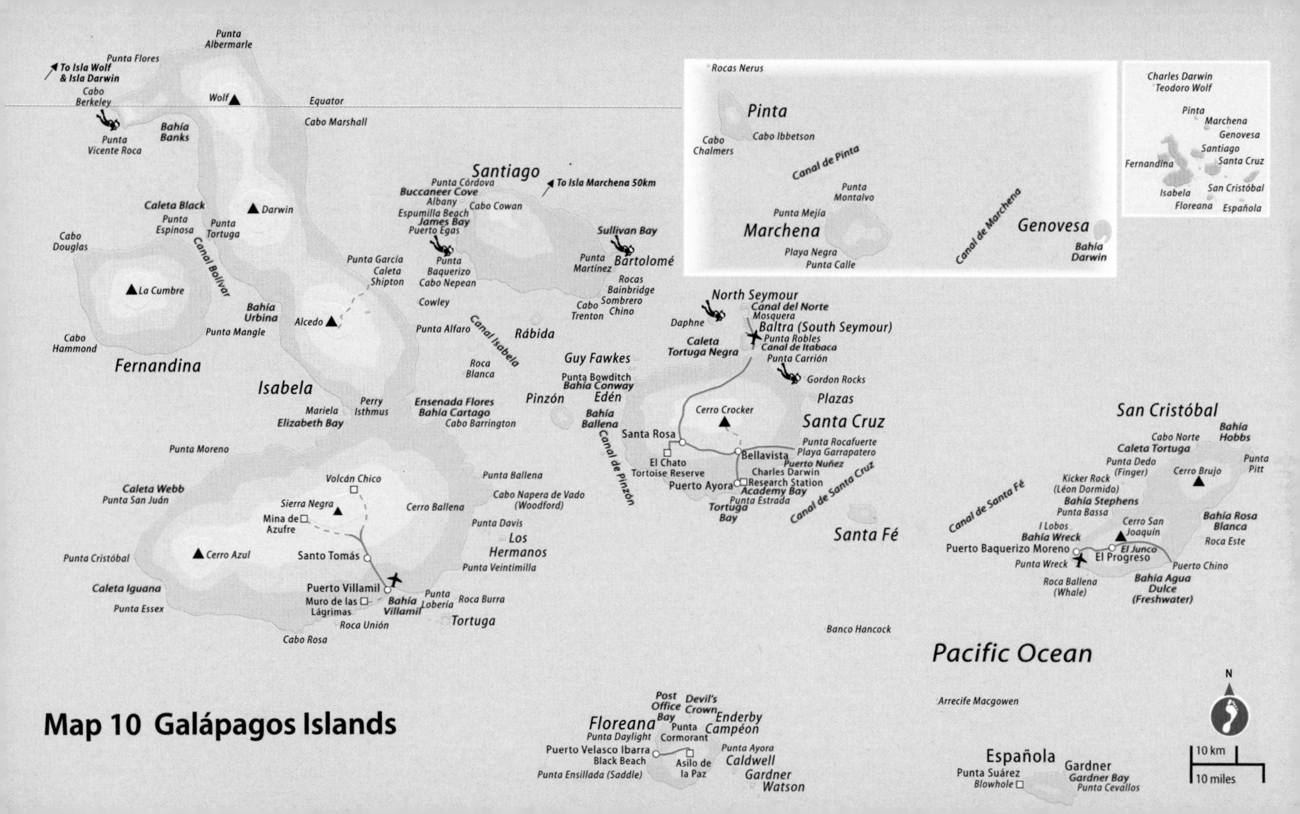

Map 10 Galápagos Islands

Map 11 Ecuador

COLOMBIA
A
Lita
Maldonado
CARCHI
Trufiño
Reserva Ecologica El Angel
Julio
Tulcán
La Libertad
Andrade
Cotacachi (4939m)
El Angel
San Gabriel
Mira
La Paz
El Juncal
Bolívar
IMBABURA
La Bonita
Urcuquí
Quiroga
Ibarra
Pimampiro
San Antonio de Ibarra
Puerto Libre
Gral Farfán
Otavalo
Cotacachi
Caricocha
Lago Agrio
Pto El Carmen de Putumayo
Lumbaquí
El Dorado de Cascales
San Antonio de Pichincha
Cayambe
El Reventador
Guayllabamba
Tarapoa
Calderón
Coca
San Sebastián de Coca
Shushifindi
R Faun Cuyobeno
Güeppi
QUITO
La Joya de los Sachas
Aguarico
Cuyobeno
Alangasí
El Chaco
Píntag
Papallacta
Pan de Azucár
Limoncocha
Pañacocha
Borja
Coca (Pto Francisco de Orellana)
Baeza
Pompeya
Napo
Zancudo
Vol Sumaco
Cosanga
Loreto
Napo
Tiputini
Cotopaxi NP
Wawa Sumaco
Tiputini
Vol Cotopaxi (5897m)
Cord Galeras
Area Nacional de Recreación El Boliche
Narupa
Chontapunta
ORELLANA
Nuevo Rocafuerte
NAPO
Yasuní NP
Archidona
Tena
Pano
Puerto Napo
Puerto Misahuallí
Shiripuno
Nashino
Arajuno
Tihuano
Curaray
Cononaco
State
Baños
Mera
Shell
Vol Tungurahua (5016m)
Puyo
Villano
Canelos
Veracruz
PASTAZA
Pavacachi
Curaray
El Altar (5319m)
Palora
Sarayacu
Conambo
Bobonaza
Pintuyaco
B
Chuitayo
Sangay NP
Conambo
Vol Sangay (5230m)
9 de Otubre
MORONA SANTIAGO
Macas
Taisha
Río Corrientes
Sucúa
Méndez
Limón (General El Plaza Gutiérrez)
Yaupi
Morona
Santiago
Cueva de los Tayos
PERU
C
N
50 km
50 miles
4
5
6

Driving distances

Cartagena – Medellín	652
Medellín – Bogotá	440
Bogotá – Ipiales	948
Ipiales/Tulcán – Quito	240
Quito – Guayaquil	420
Guayaquil – Tumbes	280
Tumbes – Lima	1320
Lima - Arequipa	1011
Lima – Cuzco	1105
Arequipa – Cuzco	521
Cuzco - La Paz	651
Lima – Arica	1348
La Paz – Arica	503
Arica – Santiago	2062
Santiago – Puerto Montt	1016
Santiago - Buenos Aires	1129
Buenos Aires – Ushuaia	3070
Buenos Aires - Asunción	1325
Asunción – Foz do Iguaçu	350
Buenos Aires – Montevideo	577
Montevideo - Porto Alegre	867
Porto Alegre - São Paulo	1123
Foz do Iguaçu - São Paulo	1045
São Paulo – Rio de Janeiro	429
Rio de Janeiro – Salvador	1726
Salvador – Belém	2149
Caracas – Manaus	2399
Caracas – Bogotá	1528

Driving distances in kms 1km = 0.62 miles

Map symbols

- Capital city
- Other city, town
- International border
- Regional border
- Customs
- Contours (approx)
- Mountain, volcano
- Mountain pass
- Escarpment
- Glacier
- Salt flat
- Rocks
- Seasonal marshland
- Beach, sandbank
- Waterfall
- Reef
- Motorway
- Main road
- Minor road
- Track
- Footpath
- Railway
- Railway with station
- Airport
- Bus station
- Metro station
- Cable car
- Funicular
- Ferry
- Pedestrianized street
- Tunnel
- One way-street
- Steps
- Bridge
- Fortified wall
- Park, garden, stadium
- Sleeping
- Eating
- Bars & clubs
- Building
- Sight
- Cathedral, church
- Chinese temple
- Hindu temple
- Meru
- Mosque
- Stupa
- Synagogue
- Tourist office
- Museum
- Post office
- Police
- Bank
- Internet
- Telephone
- Market
- Medical services
- Parking
- Petrol
- Golf
- Archaeological site
- National park, wildlife reserve
- Viewing point
- Campsite
- Refuge, lodge
- Castle, fort
- Diving
- Deciduous, coniferous, palm trees
- Mangrove
- Hide
- Vineyard, winery
- Distillery
- Shipwreck
- Historic battlefield
- Related map

Index

A

8 B1 Aconcagua
11 B3 Alausí
5 A3 Alcântara
8 A3 Alta Gracia
11 B3 Ambato
9 A1 Ancud
2 B1 Angel Falls
8 C1 Angol
7 B4 Angra dos Reis
6 C2 Antofagasta
5 C5 Aracaju
11 B4 Archidona
6 A1 Arequipa
6 A1 Arica
1 B2 Armenia
7 A6 Arraial da Ajuda
8 A6 Artigas
6 C6 Asunción
11 A2 Atacames
3 C3 Ayacucho

B

8 C4 Bahía Blanca
11 B2 Bahía de Carzáquez
11 B4 Baños
7 A1 Barão de Malgaço
2 A1 Barcelona
1 B4 Barichara
8 C1 Bariloche
1 A5 Barinas
1 A5 Barquisimeto
2 A2 Barrancas
1 A3 Barranquilla
5 A1 Belém
6 C3 Belén
7 B5 Belo Horizonte
3 A5 Benjamin Constant
7 C3 Blumenau
2 B2 Boa Vista
1 B3 Bogotá
6 B6 Bonito
7 A3 Brasília
1 B4 Bucaramanga
1 B2 Buenaventura
8 B5 Buenos Aires
7 B5 Búzios

C

6 C6 Caacupé
7 B5 Cabo Frio
6 A6 Cáceres
6 C3 Cachi
7 B5 Caeté
6 C3 Cafayate
3 B2 Cajamarca
6 B2 Calama
6 C2 Caldera
1 B2 Cali
7 C3 Camboriú
7 1 Campo Grande
2 B1 Canaima
7 C3 Cananéia
8 C1 Cañete
5 B5 Canoa Quebrada
1 A6 Caracas
6 A2 Caranavi
7 A6 Caravelas
3 B2 Caraz
3 B2 Carhuaz
8 C4 Carmen de Patagones
1 A2 Cartagena
1 B2 Cartago
5 C6 Caruaru
2 A1 Carúpano
3 B2 Casma and Sechín
9 A1 Castro
8 A2 Catamarca
7 inset Caxias do Sul
11 A4 Cayambe
2 B6 Cayenne
3 B2 Celendín
3 B2 Chachapoyas
9 A1 Chaitén
6 C2 Chañaral
7 A1 Chapada dos Guimarães
3 B1 Chiclayo
8 A2 Chilecito
8 B1 Chillán
9 A1 Chiloé
3 B2 Chimbote
1 B3 Chiquinquirá
9 A1 Chonchi
9 A3 Chubut Valley
6 A2 Chulumani
6 B2 Chuquicamata
7 inset Chuy
1 C5 Cidade de Goiás
2 A1 Ciudad Bolívar
7 C1 Ciudad del Este
2 A2 Ciudad Guayana
1 A3 Ciudad Perdida
6 C6 Clorinda
3 B5 Cobija
11 A5 Coca
6 A3 Cochabamba
8 A5 Colón
8 B5 Colonia del Sacramento
9 A2 Comodoro Rivadavia
6 B6 Concepcián
8 B1 Concepción
8 B5 Concepción del Uruguay
8 A5 Concordia
7 B5 Congonhas
6 A2 Copacabana
6 C2 Copiapó
6 C2 Copiapó
8 A1 Coquimbo
8 A3 Córdoba
1 A5 Coro
6 A3 Coroico
6 C6 Coronel Oviedo
6 C6 Corrientes
9 A1 Coyhaique
11 B2 Crucita
1 B4 Cúcuta
11 C3 Cuenca
7 A1 Cuiabá
2 A1 Cumaná
8 B1 Curicó
7 C2 Curitiba
3 C4 Cuzco

D

5 A3 Delta do Parnaíba
7 A5 Diamantina
8 B6 Durazno

E

8 C1 El Bolsón
9 B1 El Calafate
2 B2 El Dorado
6 C6 Encarnación
11 A2 Esmeraldas
9 A1 Esquel
5 C5 Estância

F

9 inset Falkland Islands/ Las Malvinas
6 B5 Filadelfia
5 B5 Florianópolis
6 C6 Formosa
5 B5 Fortaleza
8 B5 Fray Bentos
8 C1 Frutillar Bajo

G

9 A3 Gaiman
11 Galápagos Islands
2 B3 Georgetown
4 A1 Goiânia
1 B1 Gorgona Island
4 B1 Guajará Mirim
8 B5 Gualeguaychú
1 B5 Guanare
11 B3 Guaranda
7 B6 Guarapari
1 B4 Guatavita
11 B2 Guayaquil
4 C1 Guayarmerín
2 A2 Güiria

H

3 B2 Huamachuco
3 C3 Huancavelica
3 C3 Huancayo
3 B3 Huánuco
11 C2 Huaquillas
3 B2 Huaraz
6 B3 Humahuaca

I

1 B2 Ibagué
11 A4 Ibarra
3 C3 Ica and Huacachina
5 B6 Igarassu
7 C3 Iguape
7 C1 Iguazú Falls
7 C3 Ilha de Santa Catarina
7 C3 Ilha do Cardoso
5 A1 Ilha do Marajó
7 B5 Ilha Grande
7 A6 Ilhéus
11 B3 Ingapirca
1 C2 Ipiales
6 B2 Iquique
3 A4 Iquitos
6 B3 Iruya
8 A2 Ischigualasto park
2 A1 Isla de Margarita
7 B6 Itaúnas

J

3 B2 Jaén
8 A3 Jesús María
5 B6 João Pessoa
6 C4 Jujuy
6 A2 Juliaca
8 B4 Junín de los Ades

L

8 B6 La Paloma
6 A2 La Paz
8 B5 La PLata
6 B3 La Quiaca
8 A2 La Rioja
8 A1 La Serena
11 A5 Lago Agrio
8 C1 Lago Calafquén
8 C1 Lago Panguipulli
8 C1 Lago Puyehue
7 C3 Laguna
11 B3 Lasso
11 B3 Latacunga
5 C4 Lençois
3 A5 Leticia
3 C2 Lima
11 C3 Loja
8 C1 Los Angeles
1 A6 Los Roques

M

2 C6 Macapá
10 B4 Macas
5 C6 Maceió
11 A3 Machachi
11 C2 Machala
3 C4 Machu Picchu
1 A4 Maicao
8 B2 Malargüe
8 B6 Maldonado
4 A3 Manaus
11 B2 Manglaralto
1 B2 Manizales
11 B2 Manta
8 C5 Mar del PLata
1 A4 Maracaibo
1 A6 Maracay
7 B5 Mariana
2 A1 Maripa
6 B5 Mariscal Estigarribia
2 A1 Maturín
1 B2 Medellín
8 B2 Mendoza
8 B5 Mercedes
1 A4 Mérida
8 A3 Mina Clavero
8 B6 Minas
8 C5 Miramar
11 B4 Misahuallí
1 A3 Mompós
1 A6 Monte Avila
8 B6 Montevideo
6 A1 Moquegua
7 C3 Morretes
3 B2 Moyobamba

N

2 B6 Natal
3 C3 Nazca Town
8 C5 Necochea
8 C2 Neuquén
7 B5 Niterói

O

5 B6 Olinda
6 B2 Ollagüe
3 C4 Ollantaytambo
6 A2 Oruro
8 C1 Osorno
11 A4 Otavalo
7 B5 Ouro Preto
8 A1 Ovalle

P

3 A2 Pacasmayo
5 C1 Palmas
1 B4 Pamplona
1 A5 Paraguaná
6 C6 Paraguarí
2 B5 Paramaribo
8 A5 Paraná
7 C3 Paranaguá
7 B4 Paraty
5 A4 Parnaiba
7 C2 PN Vila Velha
6 C3 PN Calilegua
11 B4 PN Cotopaxi
7 inset PN de Aparados da Serra
5 C4 PN de Chapada Diamantina
7 A6 PN de Monte Pascoal
5 B4 PN de Sete Cidades
7 C1 PN Foz do Iguaçu
5 A3 PN Lençóis Maranhenses
9 A1 PN Los Alerces
1 A5 PN Morrocoy
9 B1 PN Torres del Paine
9 A1 Paso Futaleufú
8 A5 Paysandú
10 A2 Pedernales
7 B1 Pedro Juan Caballero
5 C6 Penedo
1 B3 Pereira
9 B2 Perito Moreno
7 B5 Petrópolis
1 C5 Pirenópolis
8 B6 Piriápolis
3 C4 Pisac
3 C3 Pisco
3 A1 Piura
11 B1 Playas
1 C2 Popayán
7 inset Porto Alegre
7 A6 Porto Seguro
4 B1 Porto Velho
11 B2 Portoviejo
9 C2 Porvenir
6 B3 Potosí
8 A1 Potrerillos
3 B3 Pucallpa
8 C1 Pucón
8 B2 Puente del Inca
9 A1 Puerto Aisén
1 B6 Puerto Ayacucho
1 A5 Puerto Cabello
9 A1 Puerto Chacabuco
1 A6 Puerto Columbia
9 B3 Puerto Deseado
7 C1 Puerto Iguazú
2 A1 Puerto La Cruz
11 B2 Puerto López
9 A3 Puerto Madryn
3 C5 Puerto Maldonado
8 C1 Puerto Montt
8 C1 Puerto Octay
9 B2 Puerto San Julián
6 B6 Puerto Suárez
8 C1 Puerto Varas
9 C2 Puerto Williams
6 A2 Puno
9 C2 Punta Arenas
8 B6 Punta del Este
11 B4 Puyo

Q

9 A1 Quellón
1 B2 Quibdó
6 B6 Quijarro
11 A4 Quito

R

8 B1 Rancagua
5 B6 Recife
6 C6 Resistencia
3 B6 Riberalta
3 B6 Rio Branco
4 C3 Rio de Janeiro
9 C2 Río Gallegos
9 C2 Río Grande
9 C2 Río Turbio
11 B3 Riobamba
1 A4 Riohacha
8 B5 Rosario

S

7 B5 Sabará
11 B1 Salinas

6 C3 Salta
8 A5 Salto
5 C5 Salvador de Bahia
6 A4 Samaipata
1 C2 San Agustín
8 B5 San Antonio de Areco
1 B4 San Cristóbal
1 A6 San Fernando de Apure
1 B4 San Gil
7 C1 San Ignacio Miní
6 B5 San José de Chiquitos
8 A2 San Juan
11 A2 San Lorenzo
8 C1 San Martín de los Andes
6 B2 San Pedro de Atacama
8 B2 San Rafael
6 A4 Santa Cruz
2 B2 Santa Elena de Uairén
8 A4 Santa Fe
1 B2 Santa Fé de Antioquia
1 A3 Santa Marta
4 A5 Santarém
8 B1 Santiago
6 C4 Santiago del Estero
11 A3 Santo Domingo de los Colorados
7 C4 Santos
7 C3 São Francisco do Sul
7 B5 São João del Rei
7 C2 São Joaquim
5 A3 São Luís
7 B4 São Paulo
7 B4 São Sebastião
7 B4 São Tome das Letras
11 C3 Saraguro
9 A2 Sarmiento
3 B2 Sechín
7 B5 Serro
1 C2 Silvia
1 B4 Socorro
1 B4 Sogamoso
6 A2 Sorata
5 A1 Soure
9 inset Stanley
6 B3 Sucre
11 B4 Sucúa

T

6 A1 Tacna
8 B6 Tacuarembo
8 A2 Talampaya park
8 B1 Talca
6 C2 Taltal
6 B4 Tarabuco
3 B2 Tarapoto
6 B4 Tarija
3 C3 Tarma
8 C1 Temuco
11 B4 Tena
5 B3 Teresina
9 C3 Tierra del Fuego
1 C2 Tierradentro
6 C3 Tilcara
3 B2 Tingo
6 B2 Tocopilla
9 C2 Tolhuin
7 inset Torres
9 A1 Trevelin
9 A3 Trewlew
6 A3 Trinidad
1 A5 Trujillo
3 B2 Trujillo
1 A5 Tucacas
6 C4 Tucumán
2 A2 Tucupita
11 A4 Tulcán
1 C2 Tumaco
3 A1 Tumbes
2 A2 Tumeremo
1 B4 Tunja
6 B3 Tupiza
1 A2 Turbo

U

7 B4 Ubatuba
9 C2 Ushuaia
8 A1 Uspallata
6 B3 Uyuni

V

8 C1 Valdivia
7 A6 Valença
1 A5 Valencia
1 A5 Valera
1 A4 Valledupar
8 A1 Vallenar
8 B1 Valparaíso
8 C4 Viedma
11 C3 Vilcabamba
1 B4 Villa de Leiva
8 C1 Villa La Angostura
6 B4 Villamontes
6 C6 Villarrica
8 C1 Villarrica
8 B1 Viña del Mar
7 B6 Vitória

Y

6 B4 Yacuiba
6 B3 Yavi
3 B2 Yungay
10 A3 Yunguilla

Z

8 C2 Zapala
11 C3 Zaruma
1 B3 Zipaquirá

PATAGONIA - CHILE
the pleasure of dicovering the end of the world
www.patagonia-connection.com • tel.: 56 - 67 - 325103
puyuhuapi
lodge & spa
A Secret south of Silence

IBL
International Bureau of Language
Spanish School
Buenos Aires Argentina
• Intensive Spanish Courses in Buenos Aires, Argentina
• Group and one-to-one lessons
• Specially designed materials for each levels
• Extra curricular activities
www.ibl.com.ar
info@ibl.com.ar
165, Florida street 3rd. floor
Buenos Aires, Argentina
in Buenos Aires